Penguin Books

THE PENGUIN C...
RECORDE...

Edward ...
forty year...
Cardus as ...
ly to the rec... end of
1960 he joine... ...ophone, specializing in opera... ...sues. He was a regular
broadcaster on ... records for the BBC, not just
on Radios 3 and ... but also on the BBC World Service, latterly with his weekly programme, *The Greenfield Collection*.
In 1958 he published a monograph on the operas of Puccini.
More recently he has written studies on the recorded work
of Joan Sutherland and André Previn. He has been a regular juror on International Record awards and has appeared
with such artists as Dame Elisabeth Schwarzkopf, Dame
Joan Sutherland and Sir Georg Solti in public interviews. In
October 1993 he was given a *Gramophone* Award for Special
Achievement and in June 1994 he received the OBE for
services to music and journalism.

Robert Layton studied at Oxford with Edmund Rubbra
for composition and with Egon Wellesz for the history of
music. He spent two years in Sweden at the universities of
Uppsala and Stockholm. He joined the BBC Music Division
in 1959 and was responsible for Music Talks, including
such programmes as *Interpretations on Record*. He contributed 'A Quarterly Retrospect' to *Gramophone* magazine for
thirty-four years and writes for the *BBC Music Magazine*,
International Record Review and other journals. His books
include studies of the Swedish composer Berwald and of
the Finnish Sibelius, as well as a monograph on the Dvořák
symphonies and concertos for the *BBC Music Guides*, of
which he was General Editor for many years. His prize-
winning translation of Erik Tawaststjerna's definitive five-
volume study of Sibelius was completed in 1998. In 1987 he
was awarded the Sibelius Medal and in the following year
he was made a Knight of the Order of the White Rose of
Finland for his services to Finnish Music. His other books
include *Grieg: An Illustrated Life*, and he has edited the *Guide
to the Symphony* and the *Guide to the Concerto* (OUP). In
2001, at a ceremony to mark the Swedish presidency of the
European Union, he was made a Knight of the Royal Order
of the Polar Star.

Ivan March is a former professional musician. He studied at Trinity College of Music, London, and at the Royal
Manchester College. After service in the Central Band of
the RAF, he played the horn professionally for the BBC and
travelled with the Carl Rosa and D'Oyly Carte opera companies. He is a well-known lecturer, journalist and personality
in the world of recorded music, and acts as a consultant to
Squires Gate Music Ltd, a UK mail-order source for classical CDs (www.lprl.demon.co.uk). As a journalist he has contributed to a number of record-reviewing magazines, but
now he reviews solely for *Gramophone*.

THE PENGUIN GUIDE TO
RECORDED CLASSICAL MUSIC

Edward Greenfield, until his retirement in 1993, was for forty years on the staff of the Guardian, succeeding Neville Cardus as Music Critic in 1975. He still contributes regularly to the record column he founded in 1954. At the end of 1990 he joined the reviewing panel of Gramophone, specializing in operatic and orchestral issues. He was a regular broadcaster on music and records for the BBC, not just on Radios 3 and 4 but also on the BBC World Service, latterly with his weekly programme, The Greenfield Collection. In 1958 he published a monograph on the operas of Puccini. More recently he has written studies on the recorded work of Joan Sutherland and André Previn. He has been a regular juror on international Record awards and has appeared with such artists as Dame Elisabeth Schwarzkopf, Dame Joan Sutherland and Sir Georg Solti in public interviews. In October 1993 he was given a Gramophone Award for Special Achievement, and in June 1994 he received the OBE for services to music and journalism.

Robert Layton studied at Oxford with Edmund Rubbra for composition and with Egon Wellesz for the history of music. He spent two years in Sweden at the universities of Uppsala and Stockholm. He joined the BBC Music Division in 1959 and was responsible for Music Talks, including such programmes as Interpretations on Record. He contributed A Quarterly Retrospect to Gramophone magazine for thirty-four years and writes for the BBC Music Magazine, International Record Review and other journals. His books include studies of the Swedish composer Berwald and of the Finnish Sibelius, as well as a monograph on the Dvořák symphonies and concertos for the BBC Music Guides, of which he was General Editor for many years. His prize-winning translation of Erik Tawaststjerna's definitive five-volume study of Sibelius was completed in 1996. In 1987 he was awarded the Sibelius Medal and in the following year he was made a Knight of the Order of the White Rose of Finland for his services to Finnish Music. His other books include Grieg: An Illustrated Life; and he has edited the Guide to the Symphony and the Guide to the Concerto (OUP). In 2001, at a ceremony to mark the Swedish presidency of the European Union, he was made a Knight of the Royal Order of the Polar Star.

Ivan March is a former professional musician. He studied at Trinity College of Music, London, and at the Royal Manchester College. After service in the Central Band of the RAF, he played the horn professionally for the BBC and travelled with the Carl Rosa and D'Oyly Carte opera companies. He is a well-known lecturer, journalist and personality in the world of recorded music, and acts as a consultant to Squires Gate Music Ltd, a UK mail-order source for classical CDs (www.lpmfdemon.co.uk). As a journalist he has contributed to a number of record-reviewing magazines, but now he reviews solely for Gramophone.

THE PENGUIN GUIDE
TO RECORDED
CLASSICAL MUSIC
2010

The Key Classical Recordings
on CD, DVD and SACD

IVAN MARCH,

EDWARD GREENFIELD,

ROBERT LAYTON AND

PAUL CZAJKOWSKI

Edited by Ivan March
Assistant Editor: Alan Livesey

PENGUIN BOOKS

PENGUIN BOOKS

Published by the Penguin Group

Penguin Books Ltd, 80 Strand, London wc2r orl, England

Penguin Group (USA) Inc., 375 Hudson Street, New York, New York 10014, USA

Penguin Group (Canada), 90 Eglinton Avenue East, Suite 700, Toronto, Ontario, Canada m4p 2y3
(a division of Pearson Penguin Canada Inc.)

Penguin Ireland, 25 St Stephen's Green, Dublin 2, Ireland
(a division of Penguin Books Ltd)

Penguin Group (Australia), 250 Camberwell Road, Camberwell, Victoria 3124, Australia
(a division of Pearson Australia Group Pty Ltd)

Penguin Books India Pvt Ltd, 11 Community Centre, Panchsheel Park, New Delhi – 110 017, India

Penguin Group (NZ), 67 Apollo Drive, Rosedale, North Shore 0632, New Zealand
(a division of Pearson New Zealand Ltd)

Penguin Books (South Africa) (Pty) Ltd, 24 Sturdee Avenue, Rosebank, Johannesburg 2196, South Africa

Penguin Books Ltd, Registered Offices: 80 Strand, London wc2r orl, England

www.penguin.com

First published 2009
1

Set in 7.6/9.6 FF Nexus Serif and FF Nexus Sans
Typeset by IDM, France and Andrew Barker Information Design
Printed in Finland by WS Bookwell

ISBN: 978–0–141–04162–9

CONTENTS

CONTENTS

THE HISTORY OF THE *PENGUIN GUIDE*

The *Penguin Guide* was a direct descendant of the hardback *Stereo Record Guide*. This first appeared in 1960, compiled and edited by Ivan March, with contributors Edward Greenfield and Denis Stevens offering enthusiastic collaboration. It was published as a hardback by the Long Playing Record Library Ltd, and eight more volumes appeared in the following decade. During this period Denis Stevens moved to the USA, and Robert Layton joined the reviewing team in his place.

In the mid-1970s the whole project was taken over by Penguin Books, and the contents of the hardback series was amalgamated and updated in 1975 to become the first *Penguin Stereo Record Guide* of 1,114 pages, covering stereo LPs, a few short-lived quadraphonic issues (some of which are now reappearing as surround sound SACDs), and surveying between four and five thousand recordings. The book was so successful that it was immediately reprinted, and was soon appearing in revised form on an annual basis. But it was the appearance of the compact disc in the 1980s that was to create a profound expansion of the recorded repertoire. The superiority of the CD as a music carrier was quickly established, and in 1990 our survey was retitled the *Penguin Guide to Compact Discs*. Surround sound SACDs and video DVDs were added in 2003/4; the latter becoming of increasing importance, so our title has now changed to an all-embracing *Penguin Guide to Recorded Classical Music*.

Since then, CD manufacturing costs have dropped and so have the prices of the discs in the shops, with most manufacturers now offering reissues at the budget price pioneered by that most enterprising of bargain labels, Naxos. Indeed the larger, super-budget collections now being published by the major labels bring some of the best value in recorded music ever offered to the collector.

IVAN MARCH

THE *PENGUIN GUIDE* RECORDINGS OF THE YEAR

PIZZETTI

Assassinio nella cattedrale (complete; DVD version)

✺ **** Decca **DVD** 0743253. Raimundi, Cordella, Valleggi, De Gobbi, Fabbian, Marrocu, Zarmella, Soloists & Ch. of the Conservatorio Piccinni di Bari, O Sinf. della Provincia di Bari, Morandi

The discovery of the year. This opera has nobility, dramatic coherence and great inventiveness. ROBERT LAYTON

PUCCINI

La Bohème (complete; CD version)

✺ **** DG 477 6600 (2). Netrebko, Villazón, Cabell, Daniel, Children's Ch. & Bavarian R. Ch. & SO, Bertrand De Billy

Starring **Netrebko** and **Villazón** in the key roles of Mimi and Rodolfo, with a splendid supporting cast and a fine contribution from the chorus, admirably conducted by **Bertrand De Billy**, this new DG recording is surely the *La Bohème* for our time. IVAN MARCH

TCHAIKOVSKY

The Nutcracker (ballet: complete; CD version); *Suites Nos. 3 in G; 4 in G (Mozartiana)*

✺ **** Australian Decca Eloquence 480 0557 (2). SRO, Ansermet

Ansermet's classic 1950s complete stereo *Nutcracker* glows with magic as well as character. My 'disc of the year' accolade is for this recording in particular, and Australian Decca in general, who have been indefatigable in their quest to restore so much of this company's legacy into circulation. PAUL CZAJKOWSKI

WAGNER

The Mastersingers of Nuremberg (complete; CD version; in English)

✺ **** Chan. 3148 (4). Remedos, Curphy, Hammond-Stroud, Bainley, Dempsey, Mangin, Sadler's Wells Ch & Orch, Goodall

This recording of *The Mastersingers* in English, made by the BBC at Sadler's Wells in February 1968, marks an iconic moment in the history of opera in England. The recording captures the atmosphere of the performance thrillingly, a credit to the original engineers, as well as to those making this transfer. EDWARD GREENFIELD

PREFACE TO THE 2010 EDITION

With the continued and continuing expansion of repertoire in our current compact edition, even though over 9,400 CD reviews are included, our coverage concentrates primarily on the cream of currently available recordings. So we have expanded our evaluations in two ways. First to include a four-star category of exceptional issues (or reissues); and also to indicate the key primary choices by using a key symbol ⊕→ in listing the very finest versions of each work in such a way as to catch the eye. As a new feature this year, each of the four contributors has chosen a personal Recording of the Year.

SURROUND SOUND SACDS

Genuine surround sound SACDs require a proper SACD playing deck, a second stereo amplifier, and a pair of rear speakers. These need not be large and intrusive as they are intended to supply just the hall ambience and the sense of being in the hall itself. There is no doubt that the three-dimensional effect that surround sound SACD reproduction can bring is uncannily realistic, and feeling of 'being there' enhances the musical communication between the performers and listeners. However, it takes a little time and skill to balance the rear speakers so that while the ear is subtly aware of the ambient effect, the sound image itself essentially comes from the front.

DVDS

The medium of DVD is in many ways proving most exciting of all, and the number available is expanding fast. There are already 825 DVDs listed and reviewed in the present volume.

While in the world of ballet the visual gain is obvious, in the field of opera the swift expansion of repertoire now available is proving every bit as exciting. Filmed opera CDs (with excellent stereo sound), dating back over several decades, are now flooding out and there are plenty of outstanding examples to choose from, many of them with fine traditional productions and starry casts. These DVDs can be enormously enjoyable for domestic viewing, with the stereo speakers placed either side of the TV set giving splendidly vivid reproduction, and with the choice left to the viewer of whether or not to follow the action with subtitles. We hope that this new market place for filmed opera may in the future help to prevent the worst idiosyncrasies of self-regarding producers in the opera house, who can totally ruin a superb performance with outrageous sets and costumes, and by trying to impose in the production their own subjective interpretative realization, quite foreign to the composer's original intentions.

HISTORICAL REISSUES

Many historical recordings, deriving from LPs as well as 78s, are now out of copyright in the UK, although not in the USA. These are usually reissued by enterprising smaller labels like Testament, Dutton and Regis, while on Naxos there is a whole series of Mark Obert-Thorn's superb transfers of early (mostly EMI) recordings which often seem as technically impressive as the mono originals. In the case of reissued opera sets, sometimes bonus items are included. These can either offer miscellaneous historical recordings by the same artists in the opera cast; or alternatively, celebrated earlier performances of excerpts from the same opera, by other famous singers from the past.

PORTRAIT COLLECTIONS

One of the features of reissues from the major companies during the past two years has been the emergence of a series of 'Portrait' collections (on CD or DVD) of major recording artists, usually in boxed form with accompanying biographical booklets, while there are also some smaller collections on just a single CD or pair of CDs. They are often remarkably comprehensive, and in consequence take up a great deal of space to list and review. We included a small collection in our 2009 edition, but they are being held back from our current volume to be included much more comprehensively in our 2011 edition.

FOREWORD TO THE 2010 EDITION

In most respects our 2010 Edition is a watershed for re-corded music in its two main formats, covering approximately 9,400 CDs and a very impressive number of DVDs. Mike Dutton, a key figure in the transfer to CD of older 78rpm recordings, tells us that the interest of the younger generation of collectors in historical recordings has recently waned, but the expanding Dutton and Chandos catalogues of newly recorded twentieth-century British music (for instance) demonstrates the continuing keen interest in the first modern recordings of hitherto unavailable repertoire.

As it stands, our coverage of the broad range of classical music written over the last six centuries is remarkable, introducing very many outstanding great works that are never, or very rarely, heard in the concert hall, recital room or opera house. Some artists, hitherto very famous, have all but fallen by the wayside (one thinks of Toscanini and Klemperer, who no longer dominate the catalogues as they once did). But the reputations of others are secure, and in the field of instrumental and vocal music new performers of distinction are appearing all the time, and the standard is often very high indeed. Undoubtedly certain names in all fields stand out, but considering the sheer number and variety of our reviews, we feel it is useful to draw readers' attention to some that hold their places firmly in the pantheon of recorded performances.

CONDUCTORS

Ernest Ansermet

The key figure in Decca's orchestral recording in the 1950s – the earliest days of the LP – was undoubtedly Ernest Ansermet (1883–1969), who in 1915 established his reputation as principal conductor of Diaghilev's Ballets Russes and consequently made friends with Ravel, Debussy and, most importantly, Stravinsky. In 1918 Ansermet formed L'Orchestre de la Suisse Romande in Geneva, primarily for recording purposes, and he conducted it continuously until his retirement in 1966. His 1949 record of *Petrushka* for Decca did more than any other LP to establish the new medium as the natural successor to the 78rpm shellac disc.

The Swiss conductor went on to embrace stereo in the 1960s, and although in later years his orchestra lost some of the refinement of ensemble and intonation which had originally made its playing so sharply succinct, he continued to enrich the recorded repertory throughout his career. Most of Ansermet's records have been absent from the catalogue for some years, but now, through the enterprise of Australian Decca, many of them are available again and can be readily obtained through the website listed below. Those so far not reissued will reappear in due course.

Ansermet's approach to the German classics was alive but scrupulously straightforward. He warmed to Bach, and his vigorously direct approach to the four symphonies of Brahms had a clear-sighted overall grip. He was sympathetic to the flamboyant Liszt of the *Tone poems* and *Faust Symphony*, and equally impressive in the symphonies of Prokofiev, especially the *First* and *Fifth*. But it is in exotic, oriental-influenced Russian music and French repertoire that Ansermet was at his finest, revelling in the orchestral colour and detail.

Balakirev's *Tamara*; Borodin's *In the Steppes of Central Asia; Symphonies 2 and 3*, and *Prince Igor Overture*; Glazunov's *The Seasons* ballet, *Stenka Razin* and the *Concert Waltzes*; Glinka's *Jota Argonesa, Kamarinskaya, A Life for the Tsar Overture* and the *Valse-Fantaisie*; and Liadov's Russian orchestral miniatures all emerge freshly. More memorable still is the Rimsky-Korsakov repertory, *Capriccio espagnole*, the engaging *Christmas Eve Suite, May Night Overture*, the *Snow Maiden* and *Tale of Tsar Saltan Suites*, while in *Scheherazade* (heard in a rare 1955 Paris Conservatoire recording) he and his orchestra are at their most vivid.

The extensive Ravel discography centres on the earlier mono recordings that offer more refined orchestral playing than the later stereo versions. Besides the usual orchestral works (including the *Alborada, Piano concertos, Ma Mère l'Oye, Le Tombeau de Couperin* and *Daphnis et Chloé*) the pioneering recordings of *L'enfant et les Sortileges, L'Heure Espagnole* and the song cycles are also featured

But it is in the ballet music of Tchaikovsky that Ansermet is outstanding. His complete 1958 *Nutcracker Ballet* was an early Decca stereo demonstration recording, and even today the performance is one of the very best in the catalogue. It comes coupled with the comparatively rare *Third* and *Fourth (Mozartiana) Suites*. The complete *Sleeping Beauty*, recorded in the following year, is not quite as fine, but still very impressive – dramatic and sparkling. *Swan Lake* is abridged but still brilliantly played, and the two-disc set makes room for an enjoyable *Rococo Variations* and a *Pathétique Symphony* which has an emotional austerity like no other version!

Herbert von Karajan

In 1989 Herbert von Karajan, undoubtedly the greatest conductor of our era – perhaps of any era – made his exodus, having created in the Berlin Philharmonic an unforgettably great orchestra, and recorded swathes of the classical repertoire with unique distinction. Much of it is listed in our pages but in the present volume we have a number of fine, newly issued DVDs to show just how Karajan recreated music. In particular an electrifying rehearsal and performance (with a lesser orchestra, the VPO) of Schumann's *Fourth Symphony* is a real collector's item.

Other DVD examples of his supreme interpretative skills include Berlin Philharmonic performances of a complete set of the Beethoven *Symphonies* (1982/4), the *First* and *Second Symphonies* of Brahms (1986/7 – all on Sony), and Dvořák's *Symphonies 8* and *9* (the *New World*) at concerts recorded with the VPO in the Grossesaal of the Musikverein in 1985. Karajan's most celebrated BPO Strauss recordings are also available in sight and sound, *An Alpine Symphony*, *Also sprach Zarathustra*, *Death and transfiguration*, *Don Quixote*, *Ein Heldenleben*, *Metamorphosen* and the *Sinfonia domestica*, and Tchaikovsky's *Fourth* and *Fifth Symphonies* (1984), of which he was a special master. Two years before his death he rerecorded his famous coupling of Debussy's *Prélude à l'après-midi d'un faune* and *La Mer*, plus Ravel's *Second Daphnis et Chloé Suite* (again on Sony).

Leonard Bernstein

Across the Atlantic the answer to Karajan was the supreme American musician and composer Leonard Bernstein, a genius who dominated not only the concert hall but also musical theatre with his unique stage works, *Candide* and *West Side Story*. As a recording artist he often suffered from the sometimes poorly balanced, too forward, top-heavy sound provided by CBS, but later he recorded his mainline repertoire for DG with enhanced results. Fortunately, towards the end of his life he chose to re-record some of his key repertoire on DVD and at last the sound became worthy of his music-making. Moreover the thrilling effect of watching him conduct from the front – the way he communicates with his players conveying his sheer joy in the music – is unforgettable. The video recordings currently available which demonstrate this again and again are among the most memorable of all orchestral DVDs. Bernstein is uniquely idiomatic in American music, and his DG coupling of Gershwin's *American in Paris* and *Rhapsody in Blue* (in which he takes the solo role brilliantly) and Ives's folksy *Second Symphony* and *The Unanswered Question*, is unforgettable. Bernstein also had a special feeling for the four Schumann *Symphonies* (especially the *Second*) and to have all four of them gloriously played by the Vienna Philharmonic is a treasure indeed. His rehearsal and performance of Shostakovich's *First Symphony* is almost as revealing as Karajan's similar DVD of Schumann's *Fourth*. But it is in his Tchaikovsky collection that he is at his most inspirational, with a thrillingly direct account of the *Fourth Symphony* from the New York Philharmonic and an even freer, more passionate account of the *Fifth* in Boston, where the string playing climax is almost overwhelming, while the DVD closes with a glorious account of the *Andante cantabile* returning to New York.

Vernon Handley and Richard Hickox

In 1980 we lost two great British conductors, first Vernon Handley, then, suddenly and unexpectedly, Richard Hickox. Handley had inherited the mantle of English music directly from his mentor, Sir Adrian Boult, and left us almost unsurpassed recordings of the symphonies of Elgar, Bax, E. J.

Moeran and Vaughan Williams. Other British composers he covered in depth were Stanford and Granville Bantock, including, not too long before he left us, *Omar Khayyám*. His last recording for Chandos was appropriately of Bax tone poems, including *The Garden of Fand*, *In the Faery Hills*, plus the *Sinfonietta*.

Hickox's repertoire also included the symphonies of Elgar, also Tippett, and he was perhaps even more searching in performing those of Vaughan Williams. Among his other achievements in English music was to record the complete orchestral music of Frank Bridge, a great deal of Britten, the symphonies of Rubbra, the orchestral works of Kenneth Leighton plus a comprehensive discography of the music of Lennox and Michael Berkeley, and a representative collection of Dyson. Turning to German repertoire, he also recorded the complete *Masses* of Haydn and Hummel.

Much of this was for Chandos, so he will be sadly missed by that company and indeed sadly missed by us all. His last recording was of Holst ballet music including *The Perfect Fool*, *The Lure* and two choral ballets, *The Golden Goose* and *The Morning of the Year*, with the appropriately named Joyful Company of Singers and BBC National Orchestra of Wales (CHSA 5069). The CD arrived too late to be included among our reviews, so can be welcomed here with doubled enthusiasm.

Vasily Petrenko and Gianandrea Noseda

Looking to the future, one cannot miss the name of Vasily Petrenko, who was recently appointed musical director of the Royal Liverpool Philharmonic Orchestra, and is already creating an extraordinary transformation in the quality of their playing. He can be heard at his finest in his new Naxos recording of Tchaikovsky's *Manfred Symphony*, a true masterpiece in which any flaws seem to evaporate under his exciting baton.

The Italian conductor Gianandrea Noseda is based not far away in Manchester, as conductor of the BBC Philharmonic Orchestra. He has already begun to record for Chandos, with the symphonic poems of Liszt, beautifully played and full of atmosphere, while his latest disc is a sparkling collection of the overtures and intermezzi of Wolf-Ferrari. This is another name to watch out for.

NEW KEYBOARD RECORDINGS OF SPECIAL INTEREST

The stimulating pioneering DVD of Bach's *Goldberg Variations* is introduced and expertly played by a young and sensitive Italian keyboard player new to our pages, Andrea Bacchetti. He specializes in baroque repertoire and made his debut at the age of eleven with Scimone's I Solisiti Veneti. He has made freshly appealing recordings of Bach's *English Suites*, and *Sonatas* by Cherubini and Galuppi all well worth investigating.

Bach's lautenwerk (lute-harpsichords) have not survived, and the instrument is now obsolete. So the single manual copy, ingeniously built by Keith Hill in Manchester,

Michigan, had to be reconstructed from drawings. Elizabeth Farr shows just how individual and effective it is in a contrasting collection of pieces. The range of Bach keyboard music played on the piano is also expanding, highlighted now by Perahia's recordings of three of the *Partitas*, and two new complete sets of the *Well-Tempered Clavier* by Jill Crossland and Angela Hewitt, which are equally stimulating. (A feminine touch in Bach is rather special, as Dame Myra Hess once showed us).

Also standing out is Paul Lewis's complete coverage of the Beethoven *Piano Sonatas*, issued in four separate groupings on Harmonia Mundi. Together with Kovacevich's re-recording of the *Diabelli Variations* (on Onyx) these CDs dominate the new Beethoven piano repertoire.

More than any other pianist, John Browning has been associated with the piano music of Samuel Barber, and Nimbus have now reissued his complete survey, including the celebrated *Sonata* written for Horowitz. Similarly Philips have restored to the catalogue Zoltan Kocsis's eight-disc survey of Bartók's piano music, which remains the classic set for the foreseeable future. On Nimbus, Martin Jones demonstrates the considerable interest of Czerny's piano sonatas, with their strong Beethovenian influence, and BIS have reissued all Haydn's piano sonatas and much else besides, admirably played and recorded by Ronald Brautigan, with the fifteen CDs offered for the price of three.

Also worth exploring is Hyperion's two-disc survey of Nielsen's complete piano music by Martin Roscoe, while on Naxos Victor Sangiorgio covers all Stravinsky piano repertoire on a single CD.

Turning to the harpsichord, Martha Folts provides an admirable survey of the keyboard music of the highly influential Frescobaldi, whose music demands a free, improvisatory style of which she is obviously a master. And Glen Wilson provides an equally diverting companion collection of the harpsichord music of Sweelinck.

A surprising new technology from BIS enables Jacob Lindberg, a superb lutenist, to play the complete solo and orpharion music of John Dowland *on a single SACD* (four-and-a-quarter hours of music!); and yet one can pick out any one of the 92 items instantaneously. Another interesting new recording process is the BluRay system, for which you need a special playing deck. However BluRay recordings reproduced through a normal SACD/DVD system are still enhanced. An example, discussed in our pages, combines music for piano duo by Grieg and Mozart where the piano quality is strikingly crisp and clean.

CHAMBER AND INSTRUMENTAL MUSIC

Pride of place in this category must go the collected edition of all Beethoven's music for *Piano Trio* by the Haydn Trio Eisenstadt, from the Phoenix Edition, while on Warner Classics, the Endellion Quartet celebrate their 30th anniversary with a collected edition of the complete Beethoven *String Quartets* and *Quintets* played with great inner depth and imagination.

As part of the Haydn bicentenary, Naxos have re-issued their excellent Kodály recordings of Haydn's *String Quartets* absolutely complete, including the six Op. 2 *Cassations*, the six Op. 3 *Quartets* (almost certainly written by Hoffstetter), and the *Seven Last Words* in its string quartet transcription by the composer. The set is excellent value, with first class documentation and comes in a handsome box.

The celebration of the centenary of Messiaen's birth has brought major boxed sets of reissues from all the major labels of (mostly) chamber instrumental and vocal music, among which the fourteen-disc budget set from EMI stands out as the most comprehensive. However the new BIS recording of all the complete organ music by Hans-Ola Ericsson is especially enticing, when the seven discs are offered for the price of three.

VOCAL MUSIC

Masaaki Suzuki's distinguished complete coverage of the Bach cantatas with the Japanese Bach Collegium has now reached well over forty volumes. Gardener's competing series with the Monteverdi Choir is about halfway through. Both have very considerable merits, but we are inclined to prefer the Japanese series, not least for its soloists, but also because of the remarkable quality of the BIS recordings.

Sir Colin Davis's inspired Philips version of the Berlioz *Requiem*, made in Westminster Cathedral, dates from the beginning of the 1970s, but only now is its potential being fully realized. Originally recorded in quadraphony it has now been reissued in Pentatone SACD in four-speaker surround sound. The spectacular results in the *Dies irae* – especially the *Tuba mirum* – outshines all subsequent recordings.

Mark Elder's new Hallé recording of Elgar's *Dream of Gerontius*, recorded in the splendid acoustics of the Bridgewater Hall, is also given demonstration sound, and offers magnificent singing from soloists and chorus alike. This is now a first choice for Elgar's masterpiece, alongside Andrew Davis's outstanding DVD version.

Harry Christophers directs The Sixteeen in a lively new set of Handel's *Coronation Anthems* on the Coro label (supported by a neat programme of Handelian lollipops), while on Decca Christopher Hogwood directs the New College Oxford Choir – with Emma Kirkby leading the excellent soloists – in a memorable DVD of Haydn's *Creation* sung in English.

Also not to be missed is an exhilarating collection of the choral music of William Mathias, including the *Te Deum* and *Missa brevis*, gloriously sung by the Choir of Wells Cathedral under Matthew Owens, while Naxos offers Tavener's inspired *Christmas Sequence: Ex Maria Virgine* from the Choir of Clare College, Cambridge under their new conductor, Timothy Brown. Finally Sir Colin Davis's new LSO Live recording of Tippett's *A Child of our Time* is totally compelling, especially for the superb choral contribution.

OPERA ON DVD

The expansion of DVD opera over the last two years has been one of the great bonuses of the recording scene, with key filmed recordings from the past vying with the latest issues One of the earliest, Zeffirelli's 1978 live performance of *Carmen* (on TDK) brings Eleana Obraztsova and Domingo ideally cast as Carmen and Don José, but this performance is also highlighted by a ravishing performance by Isobel Buchanan as Michaela.

Decca have finally reissued the 1969 BBC recording of *Peter Grimes*, filmed at the Maltings under the composer's auspices, with Peter Pears unsurpassed in the name role, supported by a first-rate cast which eclipses all later versions.

It is Natalie Dessay who vivaciously dominates the Covent Garden *Fille du régiment* alongside the opera's hero, Tonio, superbly sung by Juan Diego Flórez, with his nine top Cs thrown off with great panache. He also collaborates with Anna Netrebko in an equally memorable DG account of Massenet's *Manon*.

The San Carlo *Cavalleria rusticana* on DK is a true verismo performance, dominated by Ildikó Komlósi's rich-voiced Santuzza and filmed against a spectacular castellated open-air backdrop near Naples. The *Easter Hymn* is thrilling.

Turning to Mozart, one expresses much pleasure in the splendidly directed, beautifully set and costumed Medici Arts 1996 Vienna State Opera *Così fan tutte* with Barbara Frittoli, Angelika Kirchschlager (a delightful pair of sisters), and Monica Bacelli and Alessandro Corbelli a suitably conniving Despina and Don Alfonso. This is well matched by David McVicar's elegantly sparkling new-style *Le nozze di Figaro*, admirably conducted by Pappano with Erwin Schrott (a handsome Figaro), Miah Perssom (a delightful Susanna), Gerald Finlay (a disgruntled Count) and Dorothea Röschmann a dignified, rich-voiced Countess.

At last we see on DVD the extraordinary realistic sets built for Zeffirelli's Metropolitan Opera *La Bohème*, which have already been used for over 300 performances. Visitors walking in the 'Paris' street in Act II have felt they were in Paris itself! With Gheorghiu as Mimi and Ramón Vargas an equally ardent Rodolfo this is one of the most satisfying of all video *Bohèmes* (and the same pair of singers are hardly less successful starring in the Arthaus *La Traviata*).

The Warner NVC Arts *Madama Butterfly* from Verona brings an unforgettably moving portrayal of its tragic heroine from Raima Raibaivanska, while the companion *Turandot* brings breathtaking spectacle in the big scenes, with the title role taken commandingly by the Bulgarian soprano Ghena Dimitrova. Nicola Martinucci's *Nessun dorma* doesn't disappoint either.

A Warner DVD bargain box offers a sparkling triptych of early Glyndebourne productions of Rossini's *La Cenerentola*, *Le Comte d'Ory* and *Il Barbiere di Seviglia*, the latter standing out in its humour and splendidly unsurpassed singing.

Moving on to Richard Strauss, one meets an ideal *Arabella* in Renée Fleming, beautiful, with a natural freshness of characterization, and this Decca DVD is most attractively cast, including her 'Mr Right' (Morten Frank Larsen). Similarly the Warner NVC *Intermezzo*, also from Glyndebourne, is near perfection, especially as it is performed in Andrew Porter's brilliant English translation, and uses John Cox's 1920s sets and costumes. Felicity Lott is a ravishing Christine and John Pringle perfectly chosen as her husband.

Turning to Verdi one also finds Sherrill Milnes's *Simon Boccanegra* totally memorable, and this well-cast Met production conducted by James Levine is another good demonstration of what 'Live from the Met' usually brings.

Sir Colin Davis's 1978 *Tannhäuser* was the first time a production had been filmed complete at Bayreuth, and the performers are obviously aware that the performance is special. Spas Wemkoff is very fine in the title role, Gwyneth Jones is a rich-voiced Elisabeth, and Bernd Weild a first class Wolfram. Barenboim's 1995 *Tristan* is even more successful, even though the performance isn't live. Siegfried Jerusalem and Waltraus Meier are both at their finest, and Matthias Hölle's King Mark is memorably resonant. The Bayreuth Festival Orchestra again provide a powerful backcloth under Barenboim's intensely committed baton.

DOWNLOADING

For some classical CD collectors, the word 'download' may provoke a blank stare or even a feeling of queasiness which new technology often generates. Both these responses are understandable but two things are certain about downloads: (i) they are here to stay and (ii) there is nothing to fear from them.

First of all, what is a 'download'? It is simply a way of 'downloading' music directly from the internet onto your computer where it can then either be transferred to a CD, played on an iPod (or other various MP3 players), or simply played on your computer. And you don't have to download the entire contents of a CD, only the tracks you want. But more of this below.

Will downloads take over from CDs? While there has been an explosion of growth in this new way of acquiring music (especially in the pop-music world), it has not yet resulted in a comparable reduction of CD sales. Collectors regard the CD, as they did the LP, as more than just a medium to play music. The artwork, sleeve notes, presentation, etc., are all part of the CD 'experience'.

Whether or not the teenagers of today, who download music as a matter of course, will regard these things with the same importance remains to be seen, but the basic urge to buy something which you can physically hold, touch and feel is unlikely to go away. On a practical level, opera libretti, texts and translations, etc., are a key area where CDs can score over downloads: the idea of following texts on a computer is impractical and undesirable. And, just like book lovers, record collectors like to have their recorded music on shelves around them.

The sound quality is another area where hi-fi enthusiasts are suspicious of downloads. While it is true that the sound quality of most downloads is not quite of the same quality as the equivalent CD, the difference is relatively minimal, and when played through computers, MP3 players, iPods, headphones or car stereos, this is perhaps not of the greatest importance.

On top quality hi-fi equipment sound is very important and this is being addressed by the record industry. High-quality downloads are becoming available with full CD sound quality. For the technically minded, CDs are coded to play back at 16-bit/96 kHz and this will be the standard of these new downloads.

Even more impressive will be the availability of an 'ultra' hi-fi audio quality download – in theory better than CD sound – which may well be available from some companies during the lifetime of this book. These downloads will be using impressive 24-bit technology, which is the level at which many new recordings are made. This will be the format to convert and excite the hi-fi enthusiasts to this new medium.

One great advantage downloads offer is the sheer quantity of music which is being made available. Chandos Records, an independent label, has fully embraced this technology and offers a range of features. They have made their entire catalogue of deleted recordings available to download in their website, *TheClassicalShop.net*, so never again will the dreaded word 'deleted' strike the same horror as it once did. Most of Chandos's new recordings are being released as both a download and CD, with much of their current CD catalogue also available to download – a huge bonus in an age where shops can only offer a fraction of what is available.

Cost is a key factor of downloads compared with CDs, where a download is usually only about a third of the price of the equivalent CD. Chandos charges from around 40p per five minutes of music, and around £5 per for a download of a complete full-price CD (their new releases cost only a little more). Chandos's CD-quality downloads (using the 'lossless' system) are charged at a slightly higher prices, but capped at around £10 per CD.

One joy of downloads is the ability to pick and choose which track you want to buy: the times when one only wants to buy the rare fill-up or coupling on a CD is a frequent area of annoyance to collectors. Often on a compilation CD, one may only really want one or two tracks, and these can be bought independently from the rest of the CD. The cheapness of downloads may encourage one to explore, as well as duplicating favourite repertoire without adding to storage problems. Most sites offer a free one-minute sample of each track – a terrific encouragement to expand one's repertoire knowledge. In this way downloads offer the chance to experiment with new music.

Computers often – and justifiably – rate as one of the top causes of frustration in modern life. But they are getting more reliable and easier to use. As long as you have a broadband connection, downloading is a relatively easy procedure as the on-screen instructions are pretty obvious. The download time can be a bit time-consuming but this is getting a faster procedure as time goes on with broadband connections getting better all the time. Almost certainly within in a comparatively short space of time it will be a matter of seconds to download a complete opera, through we are not quite there yet.

While downloads have not been reviewed as a separate entity in the *Guide*, many of the recordings discussed will be available to download (a quick check on the relevant company's website will tell you if it is or not). Dedicated download sites, such as iTunes, are an obvious place to start, but many record companies offer their own download facility. Chandos Records download site, *TheClassicalShop.net*, one of the best and easiest sites to use, offers not only their own recordings, but a host of other labels, including LSO Live, Pristine, Avie, CRD, Nimbus, STG, Coro, Signum, Toccata and many others. *TheClassicalShop.net* now also offers flac files (free lossless audio codes) which are, in effect, lossless files (i.e. as good as the original) but have the advantage in that they can be compressed without loss of quality; therefore they take up far less room and speed up file transfer. The EMI catalogue also offers extensive download facilities.

To sum up, downloads are worth exploring and they are a complimentary and often very useful medium for recorded music. Many collectors remain loyal to the CD yet also happily explore the world of downloads. It will be interesting to see what effect they have on current teenagers, but one optimistic view is that it will encourage them to explore an ever greater range of music. Chandos claims that many of their download customers are exploring classical music for the first time. As for the effect downloads will have on the *Penguin Guide*, the view of the authors is that the performances remain the same on whatever format they are presented (noting the above remarks on the sound quality).

IVAN MARCH

INTRODUCTION

As in previous editions, the object of *The Penguin Guide to Recorded Classical Music* is to give the serious collector a continuing survey of the finest recordings of classical music on CD, irrespective of price, but also to evaluate the quality of the compatible SACDs, and video DVDs. As most recordings are issued almost simultaneously on both sides of the Atlantic and use identical international catalogue numbers, the *Guide* should be found to be equally useful in the UK and the USA, as it will in Australia, Canada and New Zealand, India, South Africa and Japan. The internationalization of repertoire and numbers now applies to almost all CDs issued by the major international companies and also by the smaller ones. Many European labels are imported in their original formats, both into Britain and the USA. Those CDs that are only available in England can be easily obtained by overseas collectors via the web address given on page xv

We feel that it is a strength of our basic style to let our own conveyed pleasure and admiration (or otherwise) for the merits of an individual recording come over directly to the reader, even if this produces a certain ambivalence in the matter of such a final choice. Where there is disagreement between us (and this rarely happens), readers will find an indication of our different reactions in the text.

We have considered (and rejected) the use of initials against individual reviews, since this is essentially a team project. The occasions for disagreement generally concern matters of aesthetics – in the manner of recording balance for instance, where a contrived effect may trouble some ears more than others, or in the matter of style, where the difference between robustness and refinement of approach appeals differently to listening sensibilities rather than involving a question of artistic integrity. But over the years our views seem to have grown closer together rather than having diverged; perhaps we are getting mellower, but we are seldom ready to offer strong disagreement following the enthusiastic reception by one of the team of a controversial recording, providing the results are creatively stimulating.

As playing standards have advanced, our perceptions of the advantages and disadvantages of performances of early music on original (as against modern) instruments seem almost irrelevant. It is the quality of the performance itself which counts, and so expert is the performer's control of period instruments today, while modern instrument performances have often been so influenced by period instrument styles, that sometimes one is hardly aware of the difference, especially in orchestral music.

EVALUATION

Most major recordings issued today are of a high technical standard and offer performances of a quality at least as high as is experienced in the concert hall. In adopting a star system for the evaluation of records, we have decided to make use of from one to four stars. Brackets around one or more of the stars indicate some reservations about a recording's rating, and readers are advised to refer to the text. Brackets around all the stars usually indicate a basic qualification: for instance, a mono recording of a performance of artistic interest, where some allowances may have to be made for the sound quality even though the recording may have been digitally remastered.

Our evaluation system may be summarized as follows:

**** A really exceptional issue on every count

*** An outstanding performance and recording of the calibre we now take for granted

** A good performance and recording of today's normal high standard

* A fair or somewhat routine performance, reasonably well performed or recorded

(N) A recording new to the present volume

⊶ Key recordings – top recommendations – are indicated by a key symbol next to the star rating

Our evaluation is normally applied to the record as a whole, unless there are two main works or groups of works, and by different composers. In this case, each is dealt with separately in its appropriate place.

ROSETTES

To certain special records we have awarded a Rosette: ✿.

Unlike our general evaluations, in which we have tried to be consistent, a Rosette is a quite arbitrary compliment by a member of the reviewing team to a recorded performance which, he finds, shows special illumination, magic, a spiritual quality, or even outstanding production values, that place it in a very special class. Occasionally a Rosette has been awarded for an issue that seems to us to offer extraordinary value for money, but that presupposes that the performance or performances are outstanding too. The choice is essentially a personal one (although often it represents a shared view) and in some cases it is applied to an issue where certain reservations must also be mentioned in the text of the review. The Rosette symbol is placed before the usual evaluation and the record number. It is quite small – we do not mean to imply an Academy Award, but a personal token of appreciation for something uniquely valuable. We hope that, once the reader has discovered and perhaps acquired a 'Rosetted' CD, its special qualities will soon become apparent. There are, of course, more of them now, for our survey has become a distillation of the excellence of CDs issued and reissued over a considerable time span.

DIGITAL RECORDINGS

Nearly all new compact discs are recorded digitally, but many digitally remastered, reissued analogue recordings are now available, and we think it important to include a clear indication of the difference:

All listed CDs are digital *unless* the inclusion of (ADD) in the titling indicates Analogue-to-Digital remastering, while of course the term mono is self-explanatory.

The indication ADD/DDD or DDD/ADD applies to a compilation where recordings come from mixed sources.

LISTINGS AND PRICE RANGES

Our listing of each recording assumes that it is in the premium-price category, unless it indicates otherwise, as follows:

(M) Medium-priced label

(B) Bargain-priced label

(BB) Super-bargain-priced label

See below for differences in price structures in the UK and the USA.

LAYOUT OF TEXT

We have aimed to make our style as simple as possible. So, immediately after the evaluation and before the catalogue number, the record make is given, sometimes in abbreviated form. In the case of a set of two or more CDs, the number of units involved is given in brackets after the catalogue number.

(N) placed before the catalogue number means that the recording is new to the present volume.

EMI and Virgin have now abandoned the use of alphabetical prefixes, and it is no longer possible to determine the price range from the catalogue listing itself, although budget Encore CDs are often marked, as are the two-for-the-price-of-one Gemini reissues.

We have taken care to check catalogue information as far as is possible, but as all the editorial work has been done in England there is always the possibility of error; American readers are therefore invited, when ordering records locally, to take the precaution of giving their dealer the fullest information about the music and recordings they want.

The indications (M), (B) and (BB) immediately before the starring of a disc refer primarily to the British CD, as pricing systems are not always identical on both sides of the Atlantic. When CDs are imported by specialist distributors into the USA, this again usually involves a price difference.

When mid-priced CDs on the smaller labels are imported into the USA, they often move up to the premium-price range.

ABBREVIATIONS

To save space we have adopted a number of standard abbreviations in listing record companies, orchestras and performing groups (a list is provided below), and the titles of works are often shortened, especially where they are listed several times. Artists' forenames are often omitted if they are not absolutely necessary for identification purposes. Also, we have not usually listed the contents of operatic highlights and collections.

We have followed common practice in the use of the original language for titles where it seems sensible. In most cases, English is used for orchestral and instrumental music, and the original language for vocal music and opera. There are exceptions, however; for instance, the Johann Strauss discography uses the German language in the interests of consistency.

ORDER OF MUSIC

The order of music under each composer's name broadly follows the following system: orchestral music, including concertos and symphonies; chamber music; solo instrumental music (in some cases with keyboard and organ music separated); vocal and choral music; opera; vocal collections; miscellaneous collections. Within each group our listing follows an alphabetical sequence, and couplings within a single composer's output are *usually* discussed together instead of separately with cross-references. Occasionally (and inevitably because of this alphabetical approach), different recordings of a given work can become separated when a record is listed and discussed under the first work of its alphabetical sequence. The editor feels that alphabetical consistency is essential if the reader is to learn to find his or her way about.

CATALOGUE NUMBERS

Enormous care has gone into the checking of CD catalogue numbers and contents to ensure that all details are correct, but the major companies are at present totally reorganizing their catalogues to make them more attractive and more competitive. EMI have brought out a huge number of reissues (usually at lower prices), There are many reissues too from Universal – Decca, DG and Philips – while the new catalogues from the UK and USA of the combined labels of Sony and RCA have caused us insoluble problems in determining which CDs are currently available and which catalogue numbers now are correct each side of the Atlantic. So the editor and publishers cannot be held responsible for any mistakes that may have crept in despite all our zealous checking. When ordering CDs, readers are urged to provide their source with full details of the music and performers, as well as the catalogue number.

DELETIONS

Compact discs regularly succumb to the deletion axe, and many highly praised CDs are likely to disappear during the lifetime of this book. But most really important and desirable recordings are eventually reissued, usually costing less! As for the others, we can only suggest to readers that if a recording we have enthused about appears to be deleted, keep your eyes on the lists of reissues for it will surely reappear before too long, unless it contains repertoire which has little public support.

ACKNOWLEDGEMENTS

Our thanks are due to our Penguin copy-editor Ruth Stimson, who has proved invaluable; also to Roger Wells for his help copy-editing part of the new material during the final assembly of all the listings and reviews for this book. Grateful thanks must also go to Kathleen March, who frequently discovers musical errors, and Alan Livesey, who as Assistant Editor proofreads the copy meticulously throughout at great speed, and manages to uncover still existing mistakes that occurred earlier in the assembly of the book's text! Grateful thanks also go to all those readers who write to us to point out factual errors and to remind us of important recordings which have escaped our notice.

THE AMERICAN SCENE

CDs are much less expensive in the USA than they are in Great Britain and because of this (so we are told), many bargain recordings available in England are not brought into the USA by their manufacturers. What this means is that while almost any recording mentioned in these pages will be available in the USA, sometimes it will cost more than the buyer might reasonably expect.

Two-CD sets, where available, are often priced at two discs for the cost of one premium-priced CD in both countries. However many excellent lower-priced discs are not issued in the USA. Where a recording is of extra special interest American collectors can obtain it readily by mail order from England, through the website address given. However it will inevitably cost more than it would domestically.

PRICE DIFFERENCES IN THE UK AND USA

Retail prices are not fixed in either country, and various stores may offer even better deals at times, so our price structure must be taken as a guideline only. This particularly applies to the line between bargain and super-bargain CDs. Premium-priced CDs cost on average approximately the same number of dollars in the USA as they do pounds in the UK.

OTHER COMPARABLE PRICES IN THE UK AND USA

Here are comparative details of the other price-ranges (note that sets are multiples of the prices quoted, and Naxos CDs are now in the lower mid-price range):

MID-PRICED SERIES (as indicated by Ⓜ in text)
UK: £10.99; often £9–£10
USA: Under $10; usually under $12

BARGAIN-PRICED SERIES (as indicated by Ⓑ in text)
UK: £5.50–£7
USA: Under $8

SUPER-BARGAIN-PRICED BUDGET SERIES (as indicated by ⓑⓑ in text)
UK: CDs: £5–£6
USA: CDs: $5–$6

THE AUSTRALIAN SCENE

We have fortunate in obtaining for review many recordings from the Australian branch of Universal Classics (responsible for the three key labels, Decca, DG and Philips), which have been making a series of local issues of Decca, DG and Philips repertoire of considerable interest, mostly not otherwise available. These are bargain issues in Australia, but because of import costs may prove more expensive in the UK and USA. All these Universal Australian CDs can easily be purchased via the Australian website: www.buywell.com.

AN INTERNATIONAL MAIL-ORDER SOURCE FOR RECORDINGS IN THE UK

Readers are urged to support a local dealer if he is prepared and able to give a proper service, and to remember that obtaining many CDs involves expertise and perseverance. However, in recent years many specialist sources have disappeared and for that reason, if any difficulty is experienced in obtaining the CDs you want, we suggest the following mail-order alternative, which offers competitive discounts in the UK but also operates worldwide. Through this service, advice on a choice of recordings from the Editor of *The Penguin Guide to Recorded Classical Music* is always readily available to mail-order customers:

Squires Gate Music Centre Ltd (PG Dept)
615 Lytham Road
Squires Gate
Blackpool
Lancashire FY4 1RG
UK

Tel/Fax: (+44) (0)1253 405599
website address: www.lprl.demon.co.uk
email address: sales@lprl.demon.co.uk

This organization can supply any recording available in Britain and patiently extends compact disc orders until they finally come to hand. A full guarantee of safe delivery is made on any order undertaken. Please write or fax for further details, or make a trial credit-card order by fax, email or telephone.

Squires Gate also offers a try-before-you-buy weekly loan service (within the UK only) so that customers can try out recordings at home for a small charge, without any obligation to purchase. If a recording is subsequently purchased, it will be discounted and the trial charge waived. Full details sent on request.

Squires Gate Music Centre also offers a simple bi-monthly or three-monthly mailing, listing a hand-picked selection of current new and reissued CDs, chosen by the Editor of the *Penguin Guide*, Ivan March. Customers of Squires Gate Music Centre Ltd, both domestic and overseas, can receive the bulletin as available, and it is sent automatically with their purchases.

ABBREVIATIONS

AAM Academy of Ancient Music
Ac. Academy, Academic
Amb. S. Ambrosian Singers
Ara. Arabesque
arr. arranged, arrangement
ASMF Academy of St Martin-in-the-Fields
(B) bargain-priced CD
(BB) super-bargain-priced CD
Bar. Baroque
Bav. Bavarian
BBC British Broadcasting Corporation
BPO Berlin Philharmonic Orchestra
BRT Belgian Radio & Television (Brussels)
Cal. Calliope
Cap. Capriccio
CBSO City of Birmingham Symphony Orchestra
CfP Classics for Pleasure
Ch. Choir; Chorale; Chorus
Chan. Chandos
CO Chamber Orchestra
COE Chamber Orchestra of Europe
Col. Mus. Ant. Musica Antiqua, Cologne
Coll. Collegium
Coll. Aur. Collegium Aureum
Coll. Voc. Collegium Vocale
Concg. O Royal Concertgebouw Orchestra of Amsterdam
cond. conductor, conducted
Cons. Consort
DG Deutsche Grammophon
DHM Deutsche Harmonia Mundi
Dig. digital recording
E. England, English
E. Bar. Sol. English Baroque Soloists
ECCO European Community Chamber Orchestra
ECO English Chamber Orchestra

ENO English National Opera Company
Ens. Ensemble
ESO English Symphony Orchestra
Fr. French
GO Gewandhaus Orchestra
Häns. Hänssler
HM Harmonia Mundi
Hung. Hungaroton
Hyp. Hyperion
IMS Import Music Service (Polygram – UK only)
⌥ key recording
L. London
LA Los Angeles
LCO London Chamber Orchestra
LCP London Classical Players
LMP London Mozart Players
LOP Lamoureux Orchestra of Paris
LPO London Philharmonic Orchestra
LSO London Symphony Orchestra
(M) mid-priced CD
Mer. Meridian
Met. Metropolitan
min. minor
MoC Ministry of Culture
movt movement
(N) new review for this Edition
N. North, Northern
nar. narrated
Nat. National
Nim. Nimbus
NY New York
O Orchestra, Orchestre
OAE Orchestra of the Age of Enlightenment
O-L Oiseau-Lyre
Op. Opera (in performance listings); opus (in music titles)
orch. orchestrated
ORR Orchestre Révolutionnaire et Romantique

ORTF L'Orchestre de la radio et télévision française
Ph. Philips
Phd. Philadelphia
Philh. Philharmonia
PO Philharmonic Orchestra
Qt Quartet
R. Radio
Ref. Référence
RLPO Royal Liverpool Philharmonic Orchestra
ROHCG Royal Opera House, Covent Garden
✿ Rosette
RPO Royal Philharmonic Orchestra
RSNO Royal Scottish National Orchestra
RSO Radio Symphony Orchestra
RTE Radio Television Eireann
S. South
SCO Scottish Chamber Orchestra
Sinf. Sinfonietta
SIS Special Import Service (EMI – UK only)
SNO Scottish National Orchestra
SO Symphony Orchestra
Soc. Society
Sol. Ven. I Solisti Veneti
SRO Suisse Romande Orchestra
Sup. Supraphon
trans. transcription, transcribed
V. Vienna
V/D Video Director
Van. Vanguard
VCM Vienna Concentus Musicus
VPO Vienna Philharmonic Orchestra
VSO Vienna Symphony Orchestra
W. West
WNO Welsh National Opera Company

ADAM, Adolphe (1803–56)

Giselle (ballet; complete. Choreography: Jean Coralli & Jules Perrot, revised Marius Petipa; DVD versions)

🎧➡ *** Warner **DVD** 0630 19397-2. Mezentseva, Zaklinsky, Selyutsky, Terekhova, Kirov Ballet, Leningrad Op. & Ballet Theatre O, Fedotov (Producer: Oleg Vinogradov, V/D: Preben Montell)

Ⓝ **** Opus Arte **DVD** OA 0993 D. Cojocaru, Kobborg, Harvey, Nuñez, Soloists and Corps of the Royal Ballet, ROHCG, Gruzin, (Prod and additional choreography, Sir Peter Wright)

Ⓝ **** TDK **DVD** DVWWW-BLGISP. Pujol, Le Riche, Gillet, Romoli. Paris Nat Opéra Ballet, Connelly (Producer: Toni Hajal, V/D: François Roussillion)

The Kirov casting has no weakness. **Galina Mezentseva** is the epitome of balletic grace in the title-role – and brings more ravishing dancing from Myrtha, Queen of the Wilis (**Tatyana Terekhova**), and the dazzling corps de ballet. **Konstantin Zaklinsky** as Albrecht and **Gennadi Selyutsky** as Hilarion are hardly less impressive, and the solo dances and pas de deux in Act II are memorable. The orchestra plays with warmth, finesse and robust vitality under **Viktor Fedotov** and is richly and vibrantly recorded. The camera is almost always where you want it to be. Costumes and scenery are gloriously traditional.

Giselle has been extraordinarily successful on DVD and it is virtually impossible to make a first choice: any of the three versions will give great pleasure and satisfaction. The most recent of the recordings comes from a BBC transmission of January 2006. It is marvellously danced with the Romanian ballerina **Alina Cojocaru** in the title role and the Danish virtuoso **Johan Kobborg** as Albrecht. They are a touching pair and the remaining roles are no less brilliant and as strongly characterised. A compelling performance on all counts with excellent playing from the **Covent Garden Orchestra** under **Boris Gruzin** and expert camera work from the BBC team.

The performance recorded live in Paris is also magnificent in every way, with attractively traditional sets and costumes. All three principals are superb, **Laetitia Pujol** an infinitely touching Giselle, perfectly matched by **Nicola Le Riche's** Albrecht, particularly in the powerful climax of Act II where **Marie-Agnes Gillet** is an admirable imperious Myrtha. But what makes the performance so visually captivating is the grace and extraordinary precision of the Corps de Ballet whose movements flow perfectly with the music, so vividly played by the **Opéra National Orchestra** under **Paul Connelly** bringing a visual and musical spectacle of a high order.

Giselle (ballet; complete; CD versions)

Ⓑ *** Double Decca 452 185-2 (2). ROHCG O, Bonynge

ⒷⒷ *** Naxos 8.550755/6. Slovak RSO, Mogrelia

Andrew Mogrelia's complete recording uses the normal performing edition. The orchestral playing has grace, elegance

and plenty of life: the brass are not ashamed of the melodrama. The recording is resonantly full and warm in ambience, yet well detailed.

Bonynge's performance on Decca restores Adam's original, but is that bit more strongly characterized, while the Decca sound has a slightly sharper and brighter profile. That remains first choice (at Double Decca price) but the Naxos set costs slightly less.

Karajan's Vienna recording is lovingly played, with the suave blandishments of the Karajan baton guiding the famous orchestra to produce a reading of beauty and elegance. The glowing Decca recording is first rate. (Decca 475 7507)

ADAMS, John (born 1947)

Berceuse élégiaque; Shaker Loops; Short Ride in a Fast Machine; (i)*The Wound Dresser*

🎧➡ ⒷⒷ *** Naxos 8.559031. Bournemouth SO, Marin Alsop; (i) with N. Gunn

If you are seeking an introduction to the music of John Adams, you cannot better this splendidly played anthology from **Marin Alsop** and the **Bournemouth Symphony Orchestra**, vividly recorded within an ideal acoustic. The whizzing *Short Ride in a Fast Machine* immediately has hit potential while the moving lament of the Walt Whitman civil war *Wound Dresser* shows just how naturally Adams writes for the voice. It is finely sung by Nathan Gunn against the simplest orchestral backcloth, with strings dominating. But the highlight of the disc is Adams's early (1978) masterpiece, heard here in a 1983 revision, *Shaker Loops*. This is now by far its finest performance on disc, with the climax of the third-movement 'Loops and Verses' quite riveting.

(i) *The Chairman Dances;* (ii) *Grand Pianola Music;* (iii) *Shaker Loops;* (i) *Short Ride in a Fast Machine*

Ⓝ 🎧➡ Ⓑ **** EMI 2 06627-2 (i) CBSO, Rattle; (ii) Ransom Wilson, NY Soloists; (iii) LCO, Warren-Green

Another excellent anthology which will be hard to beat. **Rattle** ensures that *The Chairman Dances* his foxtrot with unabated energy, matched by the *Short Ride in a Fast Machine*. The *Grand Pianola Music* has exhilarating hit potential and *Shaker Loops* was the work which first alerted us to the originality and intensity of Adams's earlier music. Splendid performances and excellent recording throughout.

(i) *The Chairman Dances;* (ii; iii) *Chamber Symphony;* (i) *Christian Zeal and Activity; Common Tones in Simple Time;* (iv; v; vi) *Violin Concerto;* (vii; vi) *El Dorado;* (viii; iii; ix) *Eros Piano;* (viii; iii) *Fearful Symmetries;* (i) *2 Fanfares for Orchestra: Tromba lontana; Short Ride in a Fast Machine;* (ii; iii; x) *Gnarly Buttons;* (ii; iii) *Grand Pianola Music;* (i) *Harmonielehre;* (xi) *Hoodoo Zephyr;* (vii; vi) *Lollapalooza;* (viii; iii) *Shaker Loops;* (vii; vi) *Slonimsky's Earbox.* Instrumental music: (xii) *John's Book of Alleged Dances.* Vocal music: (xiii)

Harmonium; (xiv; viii; iii) *The Wound Dresser;* **(xv; viii; iii) arr. of** *5 Songs* **by Charles Ives. Opera: (xvi; vi)** *The Death of Klinghoffer:* **highlights. (xvii; iii)** *I Was Looking at the Ceiling and Then I Saw the Sky;* **(xviii)** *Nixon in China:* **excerpts**

Ⓜ *** None. 7559 79453-2 (10). (i) San Francisco SO, De Waart; (ii) L. Sinf.; (iii) composer; (iv) Kremer; (v) LSO; (vi) Nagano; (vii) Hallé O; (viii) O of St Luke's; (ix) with Crossley; (x) with Collins; (xi) composer (synthesizer); (xii) Kronos Qt; (xiii) San Francisco Ch. & SO; (xiv) with Sylvan; (xv) with Upshaw; (xvi) Lyon Opéra Ch. & O; (xvii) instrumental ens.; (xviii) Ch. & O of St Luke's, De Waart

This impressive 10-CD box, with many of the performances directed by the composer himself (who is an excellent and persuasive advocate), gives an impressive survey.

The set is extensively documented and handsomely packaged, but the lack of track information with each individual disc and the complicated layout of the booklet mean that they are not easy to use together.

Violin Concerto

ⒷⒷ *** Naxos 8.559302. Hanslip, RPO, Slatkin (with WAXMAN: *Tristan Fantasia,* etc.) – CORIGLIANO: *Red Violin: Chaconne* ***

The *Violin Concerto* is an enigmatic work, with a not too easily penetrable opening movement, in which **Chloë Hanslip** is much more successful than Kremer in his Nonesuch version. She also catches the calm serenity which informs much of the Chaconne slow movement and is superb in the dazzling finale which has made the work popular. The Corigliano coupling is appropriate, but the Waxman transcriptions of Wagner (turned into a film-style piano concerto, with soloist **Charles Owen**) and the much abbreviated *First Romanian Rhapsody* of Enescu are curious, if enjoyable, encores. Vivid Abbey Road recording,

Harmonielehre; *The Chairman Dances;* **(i)** *Two Fanfares: Tromba lontana; Short Ride in a Fast Machine*

🔊 Ⓜ *** EMI 5 03403-2. CBSO, Rattle; (i) with Warren

Harmonielehre is an extraordinary, large-scale (39-minute) work in three parts. *The Chairman Dances* his foxtrot for a full 13 minutes, with unabated energy. The *Two Fanfares* pay their respects to Ives as well as to Copland, while the *Short* (exhilarating) *Ride in a Fast Machine* having an agreeably unstoppable momentum. The performances bring the most persuasive advocacy, and the excellent recording is clear, vivid and spacious.

Naive and Sentimental Music; *Mother of Man; Chain to the Rhythm*

*** None. 7550 79636-2. LAPO, Salonen

John Adams suggested that *Naive and Sentimental Music* (1998–9) is the most ambitious of his works outside his operas, although at that time *El Niño* had not yet been written. The music's peregrinations have infinite variety, and the closing section is very powerful. In *Chain to the Rhythm*

Adams returns to his familiar hypnotic dallying with 'small fragments of rhythmic cells' to form a toccata-like moto perpetuo, finally producing a great surge of energy. A considerable array of percussion is used to enhance the delicacy of texture *en route* to the thundering climax, where the bass drum underlines the coda. Performance and recording are first rate.

Shaker Loops

🔊 Ⓑ *** Virgin 3 63308-2. LCO, Warren-Green – GLASS: *Company,* etc.; REICH: *8 Lines;* HEATH: *Frontier* ***

The outstanding performance by **Christopher Warren-Green** and his London Concert Orchestra is full of imaginative intensity and it received the composer's imprimatur. Outstandingly vivid recording.

CHAMBER & PIANO MUSIC

(i) *Road Movies* **(for Violin & Piano); (ii; iii)** *Hallelujah Junction* **(for 2 pianos). Solo Piano Music: (ii)** *American Berserk; China Gates;* **(iii)** *Phrygian Gates*

*** None. 7559 79699-2. (i) Josefowicz & Novacek; (ii) Hodges; (iii) Hind

Hallelujah Junction was inspired by a small truck stop in the High Sierras on the border of California, an isolated place where Adams keeps a cabin. He described it as an '18-minute tableau', and in its variety and colour it represents his minimalist style at its most imaginative. It is only in the three movements of *Road Movies* that his lyrical vein, so important in his later music, begins to emerge.

Apart from including an extra work, the very well-recorded Nonesuch collection is a clear first choice. The performance of *Road Movies* is more vibrant and colloquial in the hands of **Leila Josefowicz** and **John Novacek**, with the final 40% *Swing* really taking off. Moreover, both the pianists on the Nonesuch disc have a real feeling for the Adams rhythmic patterns and syncopated percussive accents. The composer himself provides indispensable back-up notes about all the music.

CHORAL MUSIC

On the Transmigration of Souls

*** None. 7559 79816-2. NY Choral Artists, Brooklyn Youth Ch., P. Smith (trumpet), soloists, NYPO, Maazel

In remembering 9/11, Adams has described the piece as 'a memory space'. Against a shimmering orchestral and choral backcloth is heard a second textural layer of street sounds, muttered phrases from missing persons, their relatives and loved ones, the reading of victims' names by friends and family members. The great 'Why' is created by the quotation of haunting fragments of Ives's *Unanswered Question,* but the choral climax is on the words '*Love*' and '*Light*'. The recording laminates the music and sounds with complete success – a remarkable achievement from all concerned.

OPERA

Doctor Atomic (DVD Version)

(N) *** Opus Arte **DVD** OA0998D Finley, Rivera, Owens, Fink, Netherlands Op. Ch., & PO, Renes.

John Adams appears to be the one single composer alive today who can write operas (usually based on current events) that audiences want to attend. He can write modern yet singable vocal lines, even if passages of his vocal dialogue are not always very melodic. Even so, with spectacular orchestral and choral writing, the result is very compelling. The problem about this DVD was that is was made too soon. We saw the London production which followed this, and cuts were made, and more will be needed, especially in the second Act, for at well over three hours the opera is too long. **Gerald Finley** dominates the action as J. Robert Oppenheimer, who "invented" the atomic bomb, (and **Jessica Rivera** is sympathetic as his wife), but **Eric Owens** as General Groves (representing the military) makes a perfect foil for him in the second act, when great tension is created as everyone on the stage is waiting as the world's very first atomic explosion is about to happen. When it does, the curtain falls.

El Niño (complete)

*** Arthaus **DVD** 100 220 (CD version on None. 79634-2 (2)). Hunt Lieberson, Upshaw, White, Theatre of Voices, L. Voices, Berlin Deutsches SO, Nagano (Director: Peter Sellars, V/D: Peter Sellars)

El Niño is essentially a staged oratorio telling the story of the Annunciation and birth of Christ, the journey to Bethlehem, the visit of the Three Kings, Herod's slaughter of the firstborn and the prudent departure of Joseph, Mary and Jesus. The opera staging places the principal singers, chorus and semi-chorus (comprising three counter-tenors) on a plinth below a huge screen on which is projected a two-hour film (made by Peter Sellars and Yreina Cervántez).

It has to be said that much of the visual imagery (apart from the main events of the story) is confusing, even superfluous, and does not bear repeated viewing; but the three principals all sing with moving eloquence and are always worth watching. So there is a good case for the audio version, which includes full texts, as against the video's surtitles. Whether on CD or DVD, the recording is impressively spacious and clear.

The Death of Klinghoffer (complete; DVD version)

*** Decca **DVD** 074 189-9. Sylvan, Maltman, Howard, Randle, Boutros, Melrose, Marwa, Bickley, Blaze, L. Symphony Ch., LSO, composer (V/D: Penny Woolcock)

John Adams's second opera graphically tells the story of the hijacking of the Italian cruise liner, *Achille Lauro*, by Palestinian terrorists in 1985. The orchestral commentary underpins the narrative throughout and creates a powerfully sustained tension, which leads to a great climax at the actual death scene, followed by the poignant 'Gymnopédie', when the body is thrown overboard and sinks into the ocean. The opera closes with a choral epilogue and the tragic final scene when the Captain (**Christopher Maltman**) has to tell Marilyn

Klinghoffer (**Yvonne Howard**) of her husband's death, and she recalls their life together. The performance is in every way outstanding, and even though not all the solo singing is of the highest calibre, the dramatic commitment of the cast, the fine choral singing and superb playing of the LSO are unforgettable when so vividly recorded.

I was looking at the ceiling and then I saw the sky (Song Play)

(✿) (BB) *** Naxos 8.669003/4. Mühlpointner, Trotman, Neisser, Friedrich, De Haas, Gardell, Jonas Holst, Freiburg Young Op. Co., Band of Holst Sinf., Simon

This Naxos recording of John Adams's 'song play', set to a remarkably imaginative libretto by June Jordan, is a complete revelation, showing it to be an undoubted masterpiece, an intriguing amalgam of opera and musical, drawing on all kinds of sources, but in the main extending the style of musical pioneered by Bernstein. It is a true crossover work, and its basic parlando style, laced with set pieces, is all Adams's own. The work is inspired by the 1994 Californian earthquake. The piece centres on seven everyday characters, all young people from Los Angeles, of varying social and ethnic backgrounds and Adams's set numbers bring outstanding lyrical inspirations.

Nixon in China (complete)

(M) *** None. 7559 79177-2 (3). Sylvan, Craney, Maddalena, St Luke's Ch. & O, De Waart

It seemed an extraordinary idea to create an opera out of President Richard Nixon's greatest political gamble (which actually paid off): his 1972 visit to China to establish a friendly relationship with the Communist regime and its leader, Chou En-lai; but those who saw the ENO production will have discovered how grippingly it works in the theatre. Adams's special brand of minimalism works magnetically, and the music itself has a lyrical melodic flow absent from most post-Britten operas. The choral music is especially telling, and Chou's banquet speech/aria is memorable, as is his wife's stirring soliloquy. The singing is generally excellent, as is the recording. A full translation is included.

ADÈS, Thomas (born 1971)

Asyla (complete)

*** EMI **DVD** 4 90326-9 (2). BPO, Rattle (V/D: Bob Coles) – MAHLER: *Symphony 5* ***

Thomas Adès's brilliant orchestral piece, with its exotic use of a vast range of percussion instruments, was **Simon Rattle's** choice of work to complete his inaugural programme as the new music director of the **Berlin Philharmonic** in November 2002.

(i–ii) Asyla, Op. 17; (i; iii) … But All Shall be Well, Op. 10; (iii–iv) Chamber Symphony for 15 Players, Op. 2; (iii–v) Concerto conciso for Piano & Chamber Orchestra, Op. 18; (i; iii) These Premises are Alarmed, Op. 18

— Ⓜ *** EMI 5 03403-2. (i) CBSO; (ii) cond. Rattle; (iii) cond. composer; (iv) Birmingham Contemporary Music Group; (v) with composer (piano)

The *Chamber Symphony* is extraordinarily intricate in its rhythmic ideas, developing ear-tickling colouristic patterns. The *Concerto conciso* has the solo piano well integrated into the instrumental group, where rhythms are free and jazzy, but it brings a calm central chaconne before the closing 'Brawl'. *These Premises are Alarmed* is a brief, witty apoplexy, designed as a brilliant orchestral showpiece for the Hallé Orchestra. Balance is restored in ... *But All Shall be Well*, the title coming from 'Little Gidding', the last of T. S. Eliot's *Four Quartets*. Remarkable music, splendidly played and most vividly and atmospherically recorded.

Piano Quintet

Ⓜ *** EMI 5 03404-2. Composer, Arditti Qt – SCHUBERT: *Trout Quintet* ***

Adès's work, while still cast in a sonata-form structure, presses it to the limits of avant-garde extravagance. The **Arditti** performance with the composer at the piano was made at The Maltings and has splendid definition and atmosphere.

AHO, Kalevi (born 1949)

Clarinet Concerto

*** BIS **SACD** 1463 Fröst, Lahti SO, Vänskä – NIELSEN: *Clarinet Concerto* ***

Aho's *Clarinet Concerto* is an ambitious five-movement work covering the widest range of mood, from the unpredictable opening *Tempestuo* (with a lyrical middle section) through a virtuoso solo cadenza, to an even wilder central *Vivace*, where the time-signature changes with almost every bar. Then comes a haunting *Adagio mesto*, followed by an Epilogue marked *Misterioso*, with the soloist finally making a slow diminuendo into silence. Fröst's performance is both dazzling and sensitive and **Osmo Vänskä** and his orchestra provide splendid support. The BIS recording is very fine.

(i) Violin Concerto; Hiljaisuus (Silence). Symphony 1

*** BIS CD 396. (i) Gräsbeck; Lahti SO, Vänskä

Aho's *First Symphony* betokens an impressive musical personality at work. *Silence* is an imaginative piece. It is related to (and was conceived as an introduction to) the post-expressionist and more 'radical' and trendy *Violin Concerto*; it is a work of considerable resource and imaginative intensity. Good performances and recording.

Symphonies 2; 7 (Insect Symphony)

*** BIS CD 936. Lahti SO, Vänskä

The *Second Symphony* is a powerfully conceived and cogently argued work in one movement, predominantly fugal in texture, indebted to the world of Shostakovich and Bartók. The *Seventh Symphony* derives its material from an opera, *Insect Life* (based on a play by Karel Čapek). Aho decided to refash-

ion its ideas in symphonic form. Each of the six movements is programmatic, with titles like *Fox-Trot and Tango of the Butterflies*, *The Dung Beetles* and so on. It is more of a symphonic suite than a symphony but is scored imaginatively and with flair. Impeccable performances and extremely fine recording.

(i) Symphony 11 (for 6 Percussionists & Orchestra). Symphonic Dances (Hommage à Uuno Klami)

— *** BIS CD 1336. Lahti SO, Vänskä, (i) with Kroumata Percussion Ens.

The *Symphonic Dances* derive from a completion Aho made of the ballet *Whirls* by Uuno Klami, whose inspiration, like so much Finnish music, derives from the *Kalevala*, the last act of which the composer left unfinished. Like many of its predecessors, the *Eleventh Symphony* includes an important role for a solo instrument or instruments – in this case a battery of percussion performed expertly by the six members of the **Kroumata Ensemble**. This is a vital work, which is given state-of-the-art recording by the BIS team and some pretty state-of-the-art playing by Osmo Vänskä and his Lahti musicians.

ALAIN, Jehan (1911–40)

ORGAN MUSIC

Aria; Chorales; 3 Danses; Danses; Deuxième fantaisie; Intermezzo; Le Jardin suspendu; Litanies; Petite pièce; Préludes; Prélude et fugue; Suite; Variations sur un thème de Jannequin; Variations sur l'hymne Lucis Creator

— ⒷⒷ *** Naxos 8.553632/3. Lebrun (Cavaillé-Coll organ of the Church of Saint-Antoine des Quinze-Vingts, Paris)

Aria; 3 Danses; 2 Danses à Agni Yavishta; Le Jardin suspendu; Litanies

— *** Chan. 10315. Whitehead (organ of Saint-Étienne Cathedral, Auxerre, France) – DURUFLÉ: *Prélude et fugue*, etc. ***

Eric Lebrun is completely attuned to Alain's sound-world and his Cavaillé-Coll organ is ideal. These Naxos performances are thoroughly recommendable and at the price make a real bargain.

Alternatively, this splendidly played Chandos recital can serve as an introduction to this highly original composer, alongside the excellent Naxos discs.

Sarabande for Organ, String Quintet & Timpani (adapted from Deuils by M.-C. Alain)

ⒷⒷ *** Warner Apex 2564 61912-2. Marie-Claire Alain, Bamberg SO (members), Kantorow – DURUFLÉ: *3 Dances* etc.; POULENC: *Organ Concerto* ***

Deuils is the second of the 3 *Danses*, and is scored for a five-part string texture, organ and timpani. Calling it *Sarabande*,

Marie-Claire Alain has 'restituted and adapted' the sketch for performance. It sounds remarkably different from the organ version, the effect noble and graceful, radiantly translucent and certainly beautiful. The performance here could hardly be bettered, and this collection as a whole is very rewarding and excellently recorded.

Prière pour nous autres charnels

*** Chan. 9504. Hill, Davies, BBC PO, Y.-P. Tortelier – DUTILLEUX: *Violin Concerto*, etc. ***

Jehan Alain composed this short but beautiful setting of a prayer by Péguy for two soloists and organ; it is a moving piece, modal yet rich in its musical language, and it makes an admirable makeweight to the Dutilleux works.

ALBÉNIZ, Isaac (1860–1909)

Concierto fantástico; Rapsodia española (both for piano & orchestra)

(BB) *** Warner Apex 8573 89223-2. Heisser, Lausanne CO, López-Cobos – FALLA: *Nights in the Gardens of Spain*; TURINA: *Rapsodia sinfónica* ***

Both the *Concierto fantástico* and the *Rapsodia española* (the latter colourfully orchestrated by Georges Enescu) are given sparkling, idiomatic performances by **Jean-François Heisser** and the excellent **Lausanne Chamber Orchestra** under **López-Cobos**. The *Rapsodia* swaggers along at its close, not unlike Chabrier's *España*. The recording is excellent, and so are the couplings. Thoroughly recommended.

(i; ii) Piano Concerto 1 (Concierto fantástico), Op. 78; (iii) Catalonia; (iv) Iberia Suite (orch. Arbós); Navarra

(N) (BB) *** Regis RRC 1298. Bátiz with (i) RPO; (ii) Ciccolini; (iii) Mexico City PO; (iv) LSO.

Albéniz's *Piano Concerto* is an early work dating from 1887 and, though neither very characteristic nor very Spanish, it possesses a certain charm. The performance here is persuasive and it is well recorded. The other works offer more red-blooded Spanishry, with plenty of colourful tunes, all brightly played and well recorded. The short but frothy *Catalonia* is especially vivid and lively.

Iberia (suite; orch. Arbós)

*** Chan. 8904. Philh. O, Y.-P. Tortelier – FALLA: *Three-cornered Hat* ***

In Arbós's brilliant scoring of Albéniz's piano pieces the Philharmonia's response brings glowing woodwind colours and seductive string-phrasing, well projected by the warmly resonant recording. A clear first choice.

Rapsodia española (arr. Halffter)

(B) *** Decca 448 243-2. De Larrocha, LPO, Frühbeck de Burgos – RODRIGO: *Concierto de Aranjuez*, etc.; TURINA: *Rapsodia sinfónica* ***

*** Australian Decca Eloquence 476 2971. De Larrocha, LPO, Frühbeck de Burgos – MONTSALVATGE: *Concerto breve*;

SURINACH: *Piano Concerto*; TURINA: *Rapsodia sinfónica* ***

Alicia de Larrocha's performance is both evocative and dazzling, and she is given splendid support by **Frühbeck de Burgos** and brilliant Decca sound. This comes either coupled with Rodrigo and Turina or as part of an enterprising collection of Spanishry from Australian Decca, including two rare concertos.

GUITAR MUSIC

Cantos de España: Córdoba, Op. 232/4; Mallorca (Barcarola), Op. 202. Suite española: Cataluña; Granada; Sevilla; Cádiz, Op. 47/1–4

✇ ✿ (BB) **** RCA 74321 68016-2. Bream – GRANADOS: *Collection* (with MALATS: *Serenata*; PUJOL: *Tango español*; *Guajira*) *** ✿

Julian Bream is in superb form in this splendid recital, vividly recorded in the pleasingly warm acoustic of Wardour Chapel, near his home in Wiltshire. The playing itself has wonderfully communicative rhythmic feeling and great subtlety of colour, and its spontaneity increases the impression that one is experiencing a 'live' recital. The performance of the haunting *Córdoba*, which ends the group, is unforgettable.

Suite española 1, Op. 47, excerpts: Granada; Sevilla; Astorias

(BB) *** CFP 5 75140-2. Byzantine (with GRANADOS: *Andaluza* (Playera), Op. 37/5; TÁRREGA: *Memories of the Alhambra* (Ghiglia); MYERS: *The Deer Hunter: Cavatina*; (Manuel Barrueco & Steve Morse)) – RODRIGO: *Concierto de Aranjuez* etc. ***

Julian Byzantine plays magnetically in the three evocations of famous Spanish cities, and he is especially seductive in his sultry portrayal of *Granada*. Oscar Ghiglia is rather less enticing in the famous Tárrega *Recuerdos*.

PIANO MUSIC

Azulejos; Espagne; Navarra; Recuerdos de viaje; La Vega

(N) (BB) *** Naxos 8.570553 González

6 Danzas españolas, Op. 37; 6 Mazurkas de salón, Op.66; 6 Pequeños valses

(N) (BB) *** Naxos 8.572196 González

Guillermo González, besides being a fine pianist, is a leading authority on the composer and his performances of these genre pieces are attractively stylish and spontaneous. He is well recorded too, and he shows here that the *Mazurkas* and *Valses* are every bit as characterful as the *Danzas españolas*.

Cantos de España; Suite española

(B) *** Double Decca ADD/DDD 433 923-2 (2). De Larrocha – GRANADOS: *Allegro de concierto*, etc. ***

This makes a most rewarding bonus for the coupled Granados collection, and **Alicia de Larrocha's** playing is imbued with many subtle changes of colour and has a refreshing vitality.

Iberia (complete); Alhambra (Suite) excerpts: Navarra; 6 Hojas de Album, Op. 165; Tango; Suite española, Op. 47

Ⓑ Ⓑ *** Nim. NI 5595/8. Martin Jones – GRANADOS: *Allegro de concierto; Goyescas*, etc. ***

Iberia (complete); Azulejos; Navarra

Ⓜ *** EMI (ADD) 3 61514-2 (2). De Larrocha – GRANADOS: *Goyescas* ***

Iberia (complete); España (Souvenirs); Navarra; La vega; Yvonne en visite!

*** Hyp. CDA 67476/7. Hamelin

Iberia (complete); Navarra; Suite española

Ⓝ ❀ Ⓜ *** Decca 478 6388-2 (2). De Larrocha

Iberia (complete); Navarra

Ⓑ *** Double Decca (ADD) 448 191-2 (2). De Larrocha – GRANADOS: *Goyescas* *** ❀

Marc-André Hamelin is highly sensitive to the subtle nuances of Albéniz's evocative piano-writing and his gentle, sensuous inflexions are consistently seductive, from the opening *Evocación* of Book I onwards. Among modern versions this Hyperion set must now take pride of place alongside de Larrocha, who has special insights of her own to offer.

On her digital Decca version, **Alicia de Larrocha** brings an altogether beguiling charm and character to these rewarding miniature tone-poems and makes light of their sometimes fiendish technical difficulties. The recording is among the most successful of piano sounds Decca has achieved.

Martin Jones penetrates the ethos of these pieces with a natural feeling for their Spanish atmosphere, and he has sufficient and justified confidence in his own special insights to offer an individual reading with pianism that is brilliantly coloured, rhythmically charismatic and often quite magical in its gentle evocation. The recording is wholly natural, the ambience warm but not too resonant.

Alicia de Larrocha's earliest (1962) stereo recording of Albéniz's great piano suite now is far tougher, more daring, more fiery and, if anything, even more warmly expressive than she was later. The sound is not as fine as on her Decca recordings, but this is a worthy inclusion for EMI's 'Great Recordings of the Century'.

Alicia de Larrocha's second analogue set of *Iberia* was made in 1972. The piano recording is excellent in its realism, and the Double Decca reissue coupled with Granados's *Goyescas* makes a formidable bargain, for – on both artistic and technical merits – *Iberia* loses little ground to her later, digital set, which has rather more subtlety.

OPERA

Henry Clifford (complete)

**(*) Decca 473 937-2 (2). Machado, Marc, Alvarez, Henschel, Martinez, Madrid Ch. & SO, Eusebio

Albéniz's first large-scale opera was premièred in 1895 at the Gran Teatro del Liceo in Barcelona. The performance overall is more than acceptable, although with one major flaw in that the eponymous hero, sung by **Aquiles Machado**, is distinctly underpowered, producing some quite disagreeable top notes. **Alessandra Marc** as his mother, Lady Clifford, is far more commanding and secure, with just the right timbre for the part. **Carlos Alvarez's** dark baritone is ideally suited to Sir John St John, and **Jane Henschel** as his wife is in good voice throughout. **Ana Maria Martinez** is excellent, producing a rich, warm voice for the heroine, Ann. The choruses are especially lively and invigorating. **José de Eusebio** proves a highly sympathetic conductor, and his excellent Madrid orchestra brings out all the colour of the score and Decca's sound is flattering too, warmly atmospheric, well balanced and vivid.

Merlin (complete, DVD version)

(*) BBC Opus Arte **DVD OA0888D (2). Wilson-Johnson, Marton, Skelton, Vaness, Odena, Sierra, Madrid Ch. and SO, José de Eusebio

The BBC version is very rewarding, thanks to a passionate performance under **José de Eusebio**, spectacularly well recorded.

ALBINONI, Tomaso (1671–1751)

Adagio in G min. for Organ & Strings (arr. Giazotto)

Ⓜ *** DG (ADD) 449 724-2. BPO, Karajan – RESPIGHI: *Ancient Airs*, etc. ***

Karajan's view is stately and measured, and the Berlin Philharmonic strings respond with dignity and sumptuous tone. The anachronism of Giazotto's arrangement is obviously relished.

12 Concerti a cinque, Op. 7; 12 Concerti a cinque, Op. 9; Sinfonia

*** Chan. 0602; 0579; 0610. Robson, Latham, Coll. Mus. 90, Standage

Ⓑ Ⓑ *** Naxos 8.553002; 8.553035; 8.550739. Camden, Girdwood, Alty, L. Virtuosi, Georgiadis

Ⓑ Ⓑ *** Regis RRC 1095. *Op. 7/3, 6, 9 & 12; Op. 9/2, 5, 8 & 11* Francis, L. Harpsichord Ens.

Anthony Robson plays all eight solo concertos from Opp. 7 and 9 using a period oboe. His tone is most appealing and his phrasing and musicianship are second to none. **Simon Standage** provides alert accompaniments, also using original instruments, and creates bright, athletic string-timbres. **Catherine Latham** joins him to complete the **Collegium Musicum** sets of Opp. 7 and 9, including the works for strings. The artistic results are very lively and refreshing, although the balance is rather close.

The **London Virtuosi** use modern instruments, but their playing is fresh and refined and the digital recording is natural and beautifully balanced. On the first disc Camden's excellent colleague is **Julia Girdwood**, but for the two other collections **Alison Alty** takes over, and the partnership seems even more felicitous, with the two instruments blended quite perfectly. Also included is a *Sinfonia* arranged by Camden as a *Sinfonia concertante*. This series can be strongly recommended on all counts.

Those looking for a selection of *Oboe Concertos* from both Op. 7 and Op. 9 will find that **Sarah Francis** is an immensely stylish and gifted soloist. She is accompanied with warmth and grace, and the recording is first class. As a budget-priced Regis reissue this is very attractive indeed.

12 Concerti, Op. 10

☮— (BB) *** Warner Apex 2564 61136-2 (1–6); 2564 61256-2 (7–12). Carmignola, Toso, Sol. Ven., Scimone

Four of the Op. 10 set are violin concertos (Nos. 6, 8, 10 and 12) and three are *concerti grossi* with a small concertino group (Nos. 2, 3 and 4), while the remainder are without soloists and have non-fugal last movements. They radiate simple vitality, a love of life and a youthful exuberance that belies the composer's age. The playing is warm and musical, and the recording is made in an ample acoustic.

CHAMBER MUSIC

6 Sonate da chiesa, Op. 4; Trattenimenti armonici per camera, Op. 6

(B) *** Hyp. 2x1 Dyad CDD 22048 (2). Locatelli Trio

Albinoni's lyrically appealing '*Church*' Sonatas are here contrasted with the plainer and more secular (but no less rewarding) *Trattenimenti*, which translates as 'Entertainments'. The performances on original instruments are of high quality, as is the recording, and this set is even more attractive at its new lower price.

Trio Sonatas, Op. 1/1–12

*** CPO 999 770-2. Parnassi Musici

Albinoni's *Trio Sonatas*, Op. 1, are important not only musically – they make delightful listening – but also historically. For although the four-movement *sonata da chiesa* format (slow–fast–slow–fast) was established by Corelli in the 1680s, it appeared exclusively in Albinoni's Op. 1, with six of these *Trio Sonatas* in the major and six in the minor keys. But Albinoni's variety of invention is inexhaustible, with the opening movements of the last two *Sonatas* especially striking. The period-instrument performances here are first class in every way and they are excellently recorded.

ALFANO, Franco (1875–1954)

Cyrano de Bergerac (opera; complete)

*** DG DVD 476 739-6. Alagna, Manfrino, Troxell, Rivenq, Barrard, O Nat. de Montpellier, Guidarini (Producers: David and Frédérico Alagna)

Alfano, best known for completing Puccini's unfinished opera, *Turandot*, was also a successful opera composer in his own right, and this adaptation of Edmond Rostand's play is here presented by the Opéra National de Montpellier in a lavish, realistic production by David and Frédérico Alagna, with sets designed by themselves. With **Roberto Alagna** impressively taking the title-role, acting convincingly, the performance under **Marco Guidarini** works well. **Natalie Manfrino** is a bright-toned Roxane, casually dismissing the love-lorn Christian when he proves an incoherent rather than a poetic lover. The handsome **Richard Troxell** is well cast in that second tenor role, lighter and well contrasted with Alagna; and the others make an excellent team. The one notable shortcoming is that Alfano, unlike Puccini, is not a natural melodist, and in such a romantic piece one craves the sort of impact that Puccini was able to achieve by launching a great melody.

ALFVÉN, Hugo (1872–1960)

A Country Tale (En Bygdesaga): Suite, Op. 53; Elégie; Synnove of Solbakken, Op. 50: Suite

(BB) *** Naxos 8.557828. Norrköping SO, Willén

The two film-score suites date from the 1930s and '40s and are full of charm and easy melodic invention. Both are imbued with folk-like tunes which add bucolic piquancy. *Elégie* is the longest piece here; it is Alfvén's homage to the Swedish composer Johan Gustav Emil Sjögren. Sympathetic performances and decent recording.

A Legend of the Skerries, Op. 20; Swedish Rhapsodies 1 (Midsummer Vigil), Op. 19; 2 (Uppsala Rhapsody), Op. 24; 3 (Dala Rhapsody), Op. 47; King Gustav II Adolf, Op. 49: Adagio

☮— *** Chan. 9313. Iceland SO, Sakari

Midsummer Vigil, Alfvén's masterpiece, is quintessential Sweden, and so too is the affecting *Elegy* from the incidental music to Ludwig Nordström's play about *Gustav II Adolf*. **Petri Sakari** produces musically satisfying results, and this useful anthology can be warmly recommended. The Chandos sound is excellent.

Symphonies: 1 in F min., Op. 7; Revelation Cantata: Andante religioso; Drapa; Uppsala Rhapsody (BIS CD 395). 2 in D, Op. 11; Swedish Rhapsody 1 (BIS CD 385). 3 in E, Op. 23; The Prodigal Son: Suite; Swedish Rhapsody 3 (BIS CD 455). (i) 4 in C min., Op. 39; Legend of the Skerries, Op. 20 (BIS CD 505). 5 in A min., Op. 54; The Mountain King (Suite), Op. 37; King Gustav II Adolf, Op. 49: Adagio (BIS CD 585)

☮— (M) *** BIS CD 1478/80 (5). Stockholm PO, Järvi; (i) with Högman, Ahnsjö

The five symphonies are all individually available at full price (with fill-ups) or economically in a mid-priced box (five discs for the price of three).

Järvi's versions are superior both artistically and technically and leave the listener persuaded as to their merits. The *Uppsala Rhapsody* is based on student songs, but it is pretty thin stuff and the *Andante religioso* is rather let down by its sugary closing pages. *Drapa* opens with some fanfares, full of sequential clichés and with a certain naïve pomp and splendour that verges on bombast. Järvi gives a delightful performance of the popular *Midsummer Vigil*. *The Mountain King* is an inventive and attractive score; and both works, as well as the touching *Elegy* from the music to *Gustav II Adolf*, could hardly be presented more persuasively. The engineering is absolutely first class.

Symphony 2; The Prodigal Son (ballet)

(BB) *** Naxos 8.555072. Nat. SO of Ireland, Willén

Symphony 3; Legend of the Skerries, Op. 20; Swedish Rhapsody 3 (Dala Rhapsody), Op. 47

(BB) **(*) Naxos 8.553729. RSNO, Willén

Symphony 4 (From the Outermost Skerries), Op. 39; Festival Overture

(BB) **(*) Naxos 8.557284. Halla, Valdimarsson, Iceland SO, Willén

The sensitive, well-prepared performances under **Niklas Willén** also serve these symphonies well.

The *Fourth* is perhaps Alfvén's most ambitious and in many ways most imaginative symphony, and Alfvén takes a leaf out of Nielsen's book by incorporating two wordless voices into the score in the manner of the *Sinfonia espansiva*. The Naxos version from Iceland is well played and is highly competitive, without necessarily being a first choice, unless the Naxos coupling is preferred.

Choral music: Collection of Part-songs

*** BIS CD 633. Ahnsjö, Alin, Orphei Drängar Ch., Sund

Some of the part-songs Alfvén composed for the Orphei Drängar (Sons of Orpheus) are collected here and are sung to the highest standards of tonal virtuosity. Recommended with enthusiasm.

ALKAN, Charles-Valentin
(1813–88)

Cello Sonata in E, Op. 47

(N) *** Hyp. CDA 67624. Gerhardt, Osborne – CHOPIN: *Cello Sonata* ***

Alkan's **Cello Sonata** is an instantly appealing work, both for its spontaneity and melodic freshness. There are enough quirky moments in the score to make us realize that this is the work of Alkan. The *Adagio* is irony-free and is a movement of much beauty and the finale is a dashing *Saltarella*. It is all most enjoyable, with superlative performances from **Alban Gerhardt** and **Steven Osborne**, who surmount the work's hair-raising technical problems with seeming ease. Excellent sound.

PIANO MUSIC

Concerto for Solo Piano, Op. 39/8–10; Troisième Recueil de chants, Op. 65

(B) **** Hyp. CDA 67569. Hamelin

12 Etudes in the Minor Keys: Symphony for Piano, Op. 39/4–7; Alleluia, Op. 25; Salut, cendre du pauvre! Op. 45; Super flumina Babylonis, Op. 52; Souvenirs: 3 Morceaux dans le genre pathétique, Op. 15

(B) *** Hyp. CDA 67218. Hamelin

Grande sonate (Les Quatre Ages); Barcarolle; Le Festin d'Esope; Sonatine, Op. 61

(B) *** Hyp. CDA 66794. Hamelin

Marc-André Hamelin continues his remarkable traversal of Alkan's work with the *Concerto for Solo Piano*, a gigantic score, the first movement of which alone takes just under half an hour.

The *Symphony for Piano* comprises four movements (Nos. 4–7) from the *Douze études*. The *Symphony* and the other pieces on Hyperion must sound effortless, just as a great dancer must seem weightless, and Marc-André Hamelin makes light of their many difficulties. Superb playing and very good recording – and noteworthy not only for its virtuosity but for its refined music-making.

Alkan's *Grande sonate* over its four massive movements represents the hero at various ages, with the second, *Quasi-Faust*, the key one. The *Sonatine*, the most approachable of Alkan's major works, is done just as dazzlingly, with the hauntingly poetic *Barcarolle* and the swaggering *Festin d'Esope* as valuable makeweights.

Esquisses, Op. 63

(BB) *** Naxos 8.555496. Martin

Alkan's *Esquisses*, 49 little miniatures are expertly crafted, and full of imaginative and original touches. **Laurent Martin** is an excellent player who understands this music inside out and is generally well served by the recorded sound.

12 Etudes in the Minor Keys, Op. 39; Le Festin d'Esope, Op. 39/12; Scherzo diabolico, Op. 39/3

(BB) *** Naxos 8.555495. Ringeissen

Bernard Ringeissen gives a very brilliant account of the *Etudes*. The 1990 Naxos recording is very faithful, and at this bargain-basement price the attractions of the set are further enhanced by *Le Festin d'Esope*, also very impressive here.

Etudes in the Minor Keys, Op. 39/4–11; Esquisses, Op. 63; Gigue, Op. 24; March, Op. 37/1; Nocturne 1, Op. 22; Petit conte; 3 Petites fantaisies, Op. 41; Préludes, Op. 31/11–13, 15 & 16; Le Tambour bat aux champs, Op. 50/2; Toccatina, Op. 75

(BB) *** EMI Gemini (ADD/DDD) 5 85484-2 (2). Ronald Smith

A fine collection from **Ronald Smith's** impressive and distinguished survey of Alkan's often quite astonishing piano music.

ALLEGRI, Gregorio (1582–1652)

Miserere

- ⊕ (M) *** Gimell (ADD) GIMSE 401. Tallis Scholars, Phillips – MUNDY: *Vox patris caelestis*; PALESTRINA: *Missa Papae Marcelli* ***
- ⊕ (M) *** Decca (ADD) 466 373-2. King's College Ch., Willcocks – PALESTRINA: *Collection* ***

Mozart was so impressed by Allegri's *Miserere* when he heard it in the Sistine Chapel (which originally claimed exclusive rights to its performance) he wrote the music out from memory so that it could be performed elsewhere. With its soaring treble solo celestially sung by **Alison Stamp**, this performance by the **Tallis Scholars** holds its place at the top of the list and is now most welcome as a mid-priced celebration of the group's 25th anniversary. The famous 1963 King's performance, with its equally arresting treble solo so beautifully and securely sung by **Roy Goodman**, is also reissued, coupled with Palestrina at mid-price.

ALWYN, William (1905–85)

Aphrodite in Aulis (Eclogue for small orchestra after George Moore); (i) Concerto for Oboe, Harp & Strings; Elizabethan Dances; Festival March; The Innumerable Dance: An English Overture; The Magic Island (Symphonic Prelude)

(BB) *** Naxos 8.570144. (i) Small, Hudson; RLPO, Lloyd-Jones

The novelty here is *Aphrodite in Aulis*, an exquisite miniature creating a delicate vision of its mythological Greek namesake. But there are equally dainty textures in the engaging flimsy *Waltz* (*languidamente*) of the *Elizabethan Suite*. **Jonathan Small** also finds intricate delicacy and charm in the pastorale filigree of the *Oboe Concerto*, improvisational in feeling, with a wide variety of mood and tempo in its two movements. **Eleanor Hudson's** contribution on the harp is much lower in profile. In short, these are all highly responsive performances, beautifully played by the Liverpool orchestra, and very well recorded.

Concerto for Flute & 8 Winds; Divertimento; Flute Sonata; French Suite; Naiades, fantasy (Sonata for flute & harp); Trio for Flute, Cello & Piano

⊕ (M) *** Dutton CDLX 7176. Davies, Nash Ens.

The rare *French Suite* is an especially delightful novelty, delicate and piquant and utterly captivating. Written in 1980, the *Flute Concerto*, with its lively inner movement and shifting textures, is consistently entertaining, raising a smile or two along the way. Both *Naiades* and the *Trio* offer much beauty, and the *Divertimento* for solo flute – a real *tour de force* – does a good job of entertaining the listener for almost 14 minutes. The performances and recording cannot be faulted and the soloist, **Philippa Davies**, deserves special praise.

Piano Concertos 1–2

(N) *** Chan. 9935 Shelley, LSO Hickox

The two piano concertos now come coupled together with the *Elizabethan Dances* and *Overture to a Masque* to fill out the disc generously. **Howard Shelley** is a splendid soloist.

4 Elizabethan Dances (from the set of 6); Derby Day Overture; Festival March; The Magic Island (symphonic prelude); Sinfonietta for Strings

⊕ **** Lyrita (ADD) SRCD 229 [id.]. LPO, composer

An exceptionally attractive compilation and one of the composer's most successful records. Alwyn's *Elizabethan Dances* are extrovert and tuneful in the Malcolm Arnold tradition (if not quite so ebullient in orchestration). Alwyn is no less successful in *Derby Day* with its pithily rhythmic main theme, and he is both poetic and romantically expansive in the Shakespearean evocation of *The Magic Island*. But the most important work here is the *Sinfonietta for Strings*. The Lyrita recordings were made between 1972 and 1979 and show the usual engineering flair which distinguishes all issues on this label.

Film scores, Vol. 1

*** Chan. 9243. LSO, Hickox

Film Scores, Vol. 2

*** Chan. 9959. BBC PO, Gamba; (i) with Bullock, Canzonetta

Film Scores, Vol. 3

*** Chan. 10349. BBC PO, Gamba

Unfortunately, all Alwyn's major film-scores were inadvertently destroyed at Pinewood Studios, and Christopher Palmer has had to return to the composer's sketches for these recordings. The result in Vol. 1 is impressive. *Odd Man Out* (about the IRA) has the most compellingly poignant music, but the lightweight *History of Mr Polly* is charming and *The Fallen Idol* sophisticated in its delineation of action and character.

Philip Lane's reconstructions from the original soundtracks in Vol. 2 are also most welcome. In *Take My Life* Alwyn composed a pastiche aria for the operatic heroine and wrote a second for *Svengali*, both impressively sung by **Susan Bullock**. But the highlight here is the delightful suite compiled from the film of Arnold Bennett's *The Card*, with Alec Guinness as the whimsical hero. Both *In Search of the Castaways* and (especially) *Desert Victory* inspired Alwyn to some of his most atmospheric writing.

Vol. 3 of Chandos's Alwyn film music series brings some particularly delicate writing (and playing) in *The Magic Box*, and the jolly and robust numbers, such as the *March* from *The Way Ahead*, or the *Waltz* from *The Cure for Love*, come off well too. There is plenty of colour and variety on this CD, with the music from *The Penn of Pennsylvania* and *The Running Man* forming entertaining suites. Excellent sound and performances throughout this series.

(i) *Lyra Angelica (Harp Concerto). Symphonies 2; 5 (Hydriotaphia)*

⊕ (BB) **** Naxos 8.557647. RLPO, Lloyd-Jones; (i) with Suzanne Willison

The *Lyra Angelica* is a haunting and lyrical piece to which collectors will want to return. The *Second Symphony* (1953) is in two movements and is a well-argued piece with a real sense of the symphonic. The powerful single-movement *Fifth* (1973) takes its inspiration from Sir Thomas Browne's 'Urn Burial' or *Hydriotaphia – a Discourse of the Sepulchral Urns lately found in Norfolk!* A strong piece, which is well served by **David Lloyd-Jones** and his orchestra, as well as by the Naxos recording team. This is a good record to start with for those beginning to explore the music of this highly rewarding composer.

Symphonies 1–5; Sinfonietta for Strings

*** Chan. 9429 (3). LSO, Hickox

William Alwyn's five symphonies plus the expansive *Sinfonietta for Strings* are given outstanding performances from the **LSO** under **Hickox** to match the composer's own in natural understanding. The Chandos recordings are consistently up to the high standard of the house, and this set can be commended without reservation.

Symphonies 1 & 2

(M) (***) Dutton mono CDSJB 1029. BBC SO, Barbirolli

The *First Symphony* was premièred by **Barbirolli** and the Hallé Orchestra at the 1950 Cheltenham Festival, and Sir John also gave the première of the *Second*, in Manchester in 1953. Even if you have Alwyn's own recordings on Lyrita or either of the modern versions, this disc is an invaluable and authoritative document, and Dutton Laboratories get very good mono sound.

Symphonies 1 & 3

(N) (BB) *** Naxos 8.557648. RLPO, Lloyd-Jones

Alwyn's own recordings have a natural authority and possess vivid sound. But the 2004 Naxos recording made by the Andrew Walton – Mike Clements team is hardly less competitive and serves to bring these splendid performances under **David Lloyd-Jones** wonderfully alive. No one investing in these rewarding performances will be disappointed.

Symphonies 1; 4

*** Lyrita SRCD 227. LPO, composer

Symphonies 2–3; 5 (Hydriotaphia)

⊕ *** Lyrita SRCD 228. LPO, composer

The first of Alwyn's symphonies dates from 1950 and is a work of considerable power and maturity. The *Second Symphony* is a powerfully inventive work that also shows an original cast of mind. The *Third Symphony* is a well-argued and imaginative score, richly coloured and at times even reminiscent of Bax. All these works reward the listener, and the composer's performances could hardly be more author-

itative. The sound is full and naturally balanced, with fine presence and clarity.

Symphony 4; Sinfonietta for strings

(BB) *** Naxos 8.557649. RLPO, Lloyd-Jones

On Naxos a worthy addition to **David Lloyd-Jones's** survey of the Alwyn symphonies, and those who have collected the companion issues need not hesitate. The *Sinfonietta* is a particularly fine work.

CHAMBER MUSIC

(i) *Ballade for Viola & Piano;* (ii) *Chaconne for Tom, for Treble Recorder & Piano;* (iii) *Rhapsody for Piano Quartet;* (iv) *Sonata Impromptu for Violin & Viola;* (v) *3 Winter Poems for String Quartet;* (vi) *2 Songs for Voice, Violin & Piano;* (vii) *Three Blakemore Songs*

(BB) **(*) Naxos 8.570340. (i; iii; iv) Chase; (i; iii, vi) Ball; (ii; vii) Turner; (ii) Burnside; (iii; iv; vi–vii) Mitchell; (iii) Wilding; (v) Bridge Qt; (vi–vii) Huw Williams

The works here span Alwyn's composing career from the *Two Songs* of 1931 (in which **Huw Williams** sings sympathetically but with a rather intrusive vibrato) to the engaging little *Chaconne* variations on 'Happy Birthday' *for Tom* (Pitfield), written in 1982. However, the duet works here are the most appealing – for viola and piano and for violin and viola (both beautifully played). The *Rhapsody* (1939) is a most effectively constructed miniature and the atmospheric *Winter Poems* are certainly bleakly wintry. Performances are most sympathetic and the recording is well balanced.

Concerto for Flute & Wind; Music for 3 Players; Naiades Fantasy; Suite for Oboe & Harp; Trio for Flute, Cello & Piano

*** Chan. 9152. Haffner Wind Ens. of L., Daniel, with Jones, Drake

Alwyn's *Concerto for Flute and Eight Wind Instruments* is richly textured, yet the consistent inner movement fascinates the ear. The charmingly pastoral *Suite for Oboe and Harp* is most delectably played by **Nicholas Daniel** (oboe) and **Ieuan Jones** (harp). The *Naiades Fantasy for Flute and Harp* is a chimerical piece in six movements. The final work is an equally attractive two-movement *Trio*. The **Haffner Wind Ensemble** are very impressive, both individually as solo personalities and as a team. The recording is admirably balanced and very realistic.

Crépuscule for Harp; Divertimento for Flute; Clarinet Sonata; Flute Sonata; Oboe Sonata; Sonata Impromptu for Violin & Viola

*** Chan. 9197. Haffner Wind Ens. of L. (members), Daniel; Drake

The *Oboe Sonata* is an inspired work; the *Clarinet Sonata* is a fantasy piece. By contrast the solo *Divertimento* for flute (the responsive **Kate Hill**) is neoclassical. The *Crépuscule* for solo harp (**Ieuan Jones**) is a quiet evocation of a cold, clear and frosty Christmas Eve. The *Sonata for Flute and Piano* and the

Sonata Impromptu for Violin and Viola are no less striking. The recording is very real.

String Quartets 1; 2 (Spring Waters); 3; Novelette

(N) (BB) *** Naxos 8.570560. Maggini Qt

The *First Quartet* comes from the 1950s, a vintage period for the composer which saw the appearance of the *Second* and *Third* symphonies. Its two successors, the darker *Second Quartet* of 1975 which takes inspiration from Turgenev, and the richly inventive two-movement *Third* from the last year of his life, reward study. The **Maggini** play all three with total commitment and mastery, and as a bonne bouche offer the appealing *Novelette* written just before the Second World War.

The excellent Chandos alternative recordings by the **Quartet of London** involve two separate CDs (Chan. 8219 and 8440) but also include the *Rhapsody for Piano Quartet* and *String Trio*.

PIANO MUSIC

April Morn; Cricketty Mill; Fancy Free; Fantasy Waltzes; Green Hills; Harvest Home; Haze of Noon; Prelude and Fugue formed on an Indian Scale; Sonata alla toccata

(BB) *** Naxos 8.570359. Wass

Ashley Wass proves no less persuasive an advocate of Alwyn's piano music than he has been of Arnold Bax. The recording, made at Potton Hall in Sussex, is exemplary in every way.

Fantasy-Waltzes; Green Hills; Movements; Night Thoughts; Sonata alla toccata

*** Chan. 9825. Milford

Julian Milford plays the engaging *Fantasy-Waltzes* quite persuasively, his rubato particularly felicitous. He is given state-of-the-art recording. The *Sonata alla toccata*, too, is a most attractive work, with a single theme permeating all three movements, while the *Devil's Reel* of the finale is in essence another formidable toccata laced with angular syncopations. After this the nostalgic *Night Thoughts* and the memorably tranquil *Green Hills* come as balm.

OPERA

Miss Julie (complete)

*** Lyrita SRCD 2218 (2). Gomez, Luxon, D. Jones, Mitchinson, Philh. O, Tausky

Alwyn's operatic gestures are big and, though the melodies hardly match Puccini's, the score is rich and confident, passionately performed by the **Philharmonia** under **Tausky's** direction. **Jill Gomez** sings ravishingly as Miss Julie and **Benjamin Luxon** gives a most convincing characterization of the manservant lover, with roughness a part of the mixture. **Della Jones's** mezzo is not contrasted enough with the heroine's soprano, but she sings warmly, and it is good to have as powerful a tenor as **John Mitchinson** in the incidental role of Ulrik. The 1983 Lyrita recording is well up to standard, beautifully clear as well as full, and it projects the narrative evocatively and involvingly.

ANDERSON, Leroy (1908–75)

Belle of the Ball; The Bluebells of Scotland; Blue Tango; Chicken Reel; China Doll; Fiddle-Faddle; The First Day of Spring; The Girl in Satin; Horse and Buggy; Jazz Legato; Jazz Pizzicato; Phantom Regiment; Plink Plank Plunk; Promenade; Saraband; Serenata; Sleigh Ride; Song of the Bells; Song of Jupiter; The Syncopated Clock; Summer Skies; The Typewriter; The Waltzing Cat

(M) **** Mercury **SACD** (ADD) 475 6942. Eastman-Rochester Pops O, Fennell

The bulk of these classic recordings were made in two sessions, in 1958 and 1964 respectively, with a couple of items dating from 1956, yet the sound is full and vivid throughout. The performances are superb, with a witty precision which is very attractive and, of course, an endless succession of rollickingly good tunes. In every way this CD is thoroughly recommendable.

(i) Piano Concerto in C. Arietta; Balladette; Belle of the Ball; Blue Tango; Bugler's Holiday; Chicken Reel; China Doll; Clarinet Candy; The Classical Jukebox; The Captains and the Kings; Fiddle-Faddle; The First Day of Spring; The Golden Years; Governor of Bradford March

(BB) *** Naxos 8.559313. BBC Concert O, Slatkin, (i) with Biegel

The *Piano Concerto* dates from 1953 and is a thoroughly tuneful and entertaining work, not much more 'serious' than the pieces which make up the rest of this CD. Beginning with the vivacious *Bugler's Holiday*, this collection includes many of his popular hits, such as *Blue Tango*, as well as some lesser-known pieces, like the nostalgic *The Golden Years*. The *Classical Jukebox* simulates a 'stuck groove' in the middle of the piece, which raises a smile. The performances are excellent, as is the sound, though it lacks the sharp vividness of the classic Mercury recording.

ANTILL, John (1904–86)

An Outback Overture; Corroboree (complete ballet)

(N) (BB) *** Naxos 8.570241 New Zealand SO, Judd

The *Outback Overture* is exuberant, brilliantly scored and just the right length to act as a sparkling concert prelude. The 41-minute ballet, *Corroboree* draws on music the composer absorbed while attending an Aboriginal ritual ceremony in 1913. The music is exotically and sometimes daringly orchestrated, and ebulliently full of primitive energy. Its strongly rhythmic character brings passages which have much in common with *The Rite of Spring* (of which Antill has denied any previous knowledge). Both performances here certainly do the music full justice and the Naxos recording is spectacular.

ARENSKY, Anton (1861–1906)

Piano Concerto in F min., Op. 2; Fantasia on Russian Folksongs

*** Hyp. CDA 66624. Coombs, BBC Scottish SO, Maksymiuk – BORTKIEWICZ: Concerto ***

Arensky's *Piano Concerto in F minor* is an endearing piece, highly Chopinesque in feeling and with some very appealing ideas. **Stephen Coombs** is an artist of great sensitivity and effortless virtuosity, and he makes out the best possible case for both the *Concerto* and the much shorter *Fantasia on Russian Folksongs*. Good orchestral support and recording.

(i) Piano Concerto in F min., Op. 2; Fantasia on Russian Folksongs. To the Memory of Suvorov; Symphonic Scherzo

(N) (BB) *** Naxos 8.570 528 (i) Scherbakov; Russian PO, Yablonsky

Not surprisingly the performances on Naxos are very Russian in feeling, and after a bold opening, both orchestra and the excellent soloist make the very most of the concerto's memorable secondary theme. The *Fantasia on Russian Folksongs* is hardly less idiomatic, and again shows the pianist, **Konstantin Scherbakov**, in brilliant form. There are attractive couplings too, the commemorative march celebrates *General Suvorov* with plenty of fanfare, yet has a contrasting, folksy centrepiece, and the lively *Orchestral Scherzo* shows the composer's orchestral palette vividly. A most enjoyable collection.

Violin Concerto in A min., Op. 54

*** Chan. 9528. Trostiansky, I Musici de Montréal, Turovsky – GLAZUNOV: Concerto ballata, etc. ***

(N) *** Hyp. CDA 67642. Gringolts, BBC Scottish SO, Volkov – TANEYEV: Suite de concert, Op. 28 ***

The *Violin Concerto in A minor* is a delightful piece that deserves to be every bit as popular as, say, the Glazunov. On Chandos the concerto is beautifully played by **Alexander Trostiansky**. He has refinement, musicianship and impeccable taste. He is perhaps balanced rather too reticently, but the case for this concerto is made very persuasively by orchestra and engineers alike.

The concerto's second theme is an adorable idea that is both touching and difficult to dislodge from one's memory. **Ilya Gringolts** plays it with disarming elegance and warmth, yet elsewhere he offers effortless brilliance and is expertly and sensitively partnered by **Ilan Volkov** and the **BBC Scottish Orchestra**. The balance between soloist and orchestra is truthful and most musically judged. If you fancy the attractive Taneyev coupling this can be strongly recommended.

Suites: 1 in G min., Op. 7; 2 (Silhouettes), Op. 23; 3 (Variations in C), Op. 33

(BB) **(*) Naxos 8.553768. Moscow SO, Yablonsky.

What a good idea to put Arensky's attractive orchestral *Suites* on a single CD. *Suite 1 in G minor* opens with a Russian theme with variations, and *Suite 2, Silhouettes*, the best known, is a suite of character studies. *Suite 3* is another set of brightly coloured variations. The performances are good and enthusiastic, if not always refined, and while it all emerges quite vividly the (1995) sound lacks the richness and depth of the best recordings. A highly enjoyable disc, nevertheless.

Symphony 1 in B min., Op. 4; (i) Fantasia on Themes by I. T. Ryabinin, Op. 48 (for piano & orchestra); Variations on a Theme by Tchaikovsky, Op. 35a; (i; ii) Cantata on the 10th Anniversary of the Coronation, Op. 26; 3 Vocal Quartets with Cello Accompaniment. Op. 57

*** Chan. 10086. Russian State SO, Polyansky; with (i) Tatiana Polyanskaya; (ii) Sharova, Baturkin, Russian State Symphonic Cappella

Symphony 2 in A, Op. 22; Intermezzo, Op. 13; Overture: A Dream on the Volga, Op. 16; Suite 3; Nal and Damayanti (opera): Introduction, Op. 47

*** Chan. 10024. BBC PO, Sinaisky

The fluent and inventive *First Symphony* comes from 1883, when Arensky was in his early twenties, and it is a work of not only astonishing promise but very considerable fulfilment. The *Second Symphony* of 1889 is harmonically the more adventurous of the two as well as being tauter: the four movements are rolled into one. None of the above rarities is of much musical substance, though the *Three Vocal Quartets* with cello, which came late in his creative career, could well be the only music ever written for four-part choir and cello! All the performances are very persuasive and very well recorded.

CHAMBER MUSIC

Piano Trio 1 in D min., Op. 32

(M) *** CRD (ADD) 3409. Brown, Nash Ens. – RIMSKY-KORSAKOV: Quintet ***

*** Chan. 8477. Borodin Trio – GLINKA: Trio ***

Arensky's *D minor Piano Trio* is delightful. The account by members of the **Nash Ensemble** is first class in every way, capturing the Slav melancholy of the *Elegia*, while in the delightful *Scherzo* **Ian Brown** is both delicate and nimble-fingered. The warm, resonant (1982) analogue recording has transferred naturally to CD.

The **Borodins**, too, give a lively and full-blooded account of the *Trio*. The *Scherzo* comes off well, and the whole does justice to the Borodins' genial playing.

String Quartet 2 in A min., Op. 35

*** Hyp. CDA 66648. Raphael Ens. – TCHAIKOVSKY: Souvenir de Florence ***

The *A minor Quartet* is unusual in being for only one violin and two cellos. The second movement is a set of variations on Tchaikovsky's *Legend* from the *Children's Songs*, Op. 54. It is marvellously played by members of the **Raphael**

Ensemble, though the recording is a bit close, placing the listener in the front row of the hall.

ARIOSTI, Attilo (1666–1729)

Recueil de Pièces pour la Viola d'amore: Sonatas 15-21; (i) Cantata: Pur alfin gentil viola

Ⓝ *** BIS CD 1675 Georgi, Harris, Brinkmann; (i) Emma Kirkby

Attilo Ariosti was born in Bologna and died in London, a celebrated player of the viola d'amore, and he left as his legacy the largest single set of baroque works for his instrument. They are available on three BIS discs – the others are BISCD 1535 and 1555 – and those enjoying the present selection will want to explore further. The works are certainly agreeably inventive and the writing offers a stimulating interplay between the excellent violist, **Thomas Georgi** and **Mime Brinkmann** (cello) who leads the continuo (with **Lucy Harris** archlute and baroque guitar). Recording and balance are excellent and, as a postlude, they are joined by the ever fresh-voiced **Emma Kirkby** in a ten-minute cantata, whose text acts as a tribute to the instrument, comparing it (favourably) with the 'arrogant' rose and 'gentle' violet.

ARNE, Thomas (1710–78)

Keyboard Concertos (played as listed): Harpsichord Concertos: in C; in G min.; Organ Concertos: in B flat; in G; Piano Concertos: in A; in B flat

Ⓑ *** Hyp. Helios CDH 55251. Nicholson, Parley of Instruments, Holman

The six keyboard concertos of Arne date from different periods in his career and have a wide variety of movement-structures. Holman varies the solo instrument according to the character of each work: as a sampler, try the delectable *No. 3 in A*, given here on a gentle-toned fortepiano. Exhilarating performances, the instrumental balances perfectly managed, achieving clarity without exaggeration.

8 Overtures (1751); Overtures: Alfred; Thomas and Sally

🎧 *** Chan. 0722. Coll. Mus. 90, Standage

Thomas Arne, the composer of *Rule Britannia*, was a highly active composer of the theatre, in part due to his Catholic religion, which precluded him from posts in the church. He has a flair for writing simple, attractive melody, and his set of *Eight Overtures*, published in 1751, was an attempt to broaden his appeal through a series of publications. The invention is tuneful and elegant; though cosmopolitan in style, they have a certain 18th-century English pastoral spirit which is very pleasing. The two theatre overtures make for equally enjoyable listening, with the *Scottish Gavotte* of *Thomas and Sally* adding a dash of 'local' colour. Very stylish and alert playing from **Simon Standage** and **Collegium Musicum 90**, and the sound is vivid and full.

STAGE WORKS

Artaxerxes (complete)

*** Hyp. CDA 67051/2. Robson, Bott, Partridge, Spence, Edgar-Wilson, Hyde, Parley of Instruments, Goodman

This sparkling, lively performance impressively explains why Arne's opera was such a success when it was first produced at Covent Garden. **Catherine Bott** gives a masterly performance, with the counter-tenor **Christopher Robson** also impressive in the castrato title-role, and with **Ian Partridge** pure-toned and incisive in the role of the villain, Artabanes, even if his sweet tenor hardly conveys evil. With the mezzo-soprano **Patricia Spence** taking the castrato role of Arbaces, the others are first rate too. On two very well-filled CDs, the set owes much of its success to the inspired direction of **Roy Goodman**.

ARNELL, Richard (1917–2009)

(i) Piano Concerto, Op. 44. Symphony 2

🎧 Ⓜ *** Dutton CDLX 7184. RSNO, Yates; (i) with Norris

Arnell enjoyed a successful and productive career both in the United States and for some years after his return to England. Both concerto and symphony are rewarding and ambitious pieces, over 30 minutes each, and full of that sense of onward movement which defines the genuine symphonist.

Concerto Lirico for Violin and Orchestra; Violin Concerto in One Movement, Op. 9

Ⓝ Ⓜ *** Dutton CDLX 7221. McAslan, RSNO, Yates – CREITH: *Violin Concerto in G min* ***; PITFIELD: *Concerto Lirico* **

Arnell's *Violin Concerto* of 1940 is the most 'challenging' in this highly attractive collection of rare British Violin Concertos. Written in one movement, with clearly defined sections, Lewis Foremen (in his excellent sleeve note) accurately describes the soloists's outpourings as 'bittersweet'. There is plenty of contrast between lively and broody writing and if it doesn't possess the 'feel-good' factor of its companion pieces (it perhaps reflects the time it was written, at the beginning of WWII), it makes a very satisfying listening experience. Excellent performance and recording.

Lord Byron – a symphonic portrait, Op. 67

Ⓜ *** Dutton CDLX 7195. RSNO, Yates – DUNHILL: *Symphony* **(*)

Richard Arnell's six-movement portrait of Byron was commissioned by Sir Thomas Beecham, who had championed and recorded the ballet, *Punch and the Fool*, which he premièred at the Festival Hall with the RPO in 1952. It is an eventful score and full of dramatic incident and character, and well worth searching out. Very good playing from **Scottish Orchestra** and a vivid, well-balanced recording.

Symphonies 1, Op. 31; 6, Op. 171 (The Anvil); Sinfonia quasi variazioni, Op. 13

Ⓝ Ⓜ *** Dutton CDLX7127. RSNO, Yates

Dutton's championship of Richard Arnell is a cause for celebration. *The First Symphony* (1943) comes from his productive American period and was premièred in New York by Beecham, who also programmed the earlier *Sinfonia quasi variaziozoni* of 1941. The *Symphony* is an inventive resourceful piece which should by rights have been a popular repertoire work. Half a century separates it from the *Sixth* (1994), a concentrated and powerful utterance whose anvil is probably best tamed by nervous listeners. It is all thoroughly compelling stuff, expertly played and recorded.

Symphony 3, Op. 40; The New Age, Overture, Op. 2

Ⓜ *** Dutton CDLX 7161. RSNO, Yates

The *Third Symphony* has a lot going for it: a real sense of momentum strong musical ideas and an impressive mastery of the orchestra. Despite its length and the occasional moment of bombast, it holds the listener with its natural exuberance and life-affirming qualities. The **Scottish orchestra** plays with enthusiasm and is vividly recorded.

Symphonies 4, Op. 52; 5, Op. 77

Ⓜ *** Dutton CDLX 7194. RSNO, Yates

The concentrated *Fourth* and the more expansive *Fifth* (the latter centrally combining slow movement and Scherzo) are both further examples of Arnell's symphonic skill, and the slow movement of the *Fourth* in particular is expressive and full of passionate feeling. Splendidly committed and very well-played Scottish performances, directed with real communicative zeal by **Martin Yates**, and with vivid recording in Glasgow's somewhat intractable Henry Wood Hall.

Cello Suite; Music for Harp, Op. 72a; Piano Trio, Op. 47; String Quintet, Op. 60; Trio for Flute, Cello & Piano, Op. 168

⊖┐ Ⓜ *** Dutton CDLX 7122. Locrian Ens. (members)

The powerful *Piano Trio* of 1946 Arnell himself called 'the most compelling of my chamber works', while the compact two-movement *Trio for Flute, Cello and Piano* of 1991 is more quirky in its argument and the *Music for Harp* of 1961 brings another unusual line-up of instruments. In many ways the tautest of the works here is the four-movement *String Quintet* of 1950, with three relatively brief movements leading to a multi-sectioned *Fantasia*. The **Locrian** performances throughout are most sympathetic.

ARNOLD, Malcolm (1921–2006)

'Toward the Unknown Region': Malcolm Arnold – A Story of Survival

*** Isolde Films **DVD** ISO 001. Includes performances from Bream, Galway, Lloyd Webber, RTE NSO/Houlihan (V/D: Tony Palmer)

Tony Palmer adds to his store of deeply revelatory profiles of composers this moving portrait of Malcolm Arnold at 80. With most of Arnold's own contributions drawn from interviews given earlier in his life, the film follows his career from boyhood in Northampton, through his time as principal trumpet in the LPO – 'it inspired me to compose myself' – and on to his work, writing film music, with the nine symphonies used as cornerstones, plus contributions from such artists as Julian Bream, James Galway and Julian Lloyd Webber, for whom he has written works. The film, originally shown in two parts on Melvyn Bragg's *South Bank Show*, is here given in its full form with over half an hour of important extra material.

Anniversary Overture; Beckus the Dandipratt (Comedy Overture), Op. 5; The Fair Field, Op. 110; A Flourish for Orchestra, Op. 112; A Grand Grand Festival Overture, Op. 57; Peterloo Overture, Op. 97; Robert Kett Overture, Op. 41; The Smoke, Op. 21; A Sussex Overture, Op. 31; Tam O'Shanter Overture, Op. 51

⊖┐ **** Chan. 10293. BBC PO, Gamba

Beckus the Dandipratt came first in 1943, a characterization hailed as a cross between *Till* and *Scapino*, but possibly more of an uninhibited self-portrait. *Tam O'Shanter* is another flamboyant portrayal, with a spectacular orchestral realization of bagpipes at its witty climax. *A Grand Grand Festival Overture* came a year later. The scoring included four vacuum cleaners and a floor polisher. On the night they were despatched by the rifles of a firing squad! But this is far more than an occasional piece, not least because it has a really good tune. The noisily dramatic *Peterloo* also has one. But then so have all the other works here. They are marvellously played, with a truly Arnoldian infectious exhilaration, and the Chandos recording is spectacularly worthy, thrillingly in the demonstration bracket.

Beckus the Dandipratt Overture; (i–ii) Concerto for Piano Duet & Strings, Op. 32; Double Piano Concerto (3 hands); (i) Fantasy on a Theme of John Field, Op. 116

⊖┐ ⒷⒷ **** Naxos 8.570531. Ulster O, Heikkilä, with (i) Dyson, (ii) K. Sargent

The longest of the concertante works is the *Fantasy* on a theme of one of John Field's *Nocturnes*. This is in effect a set of variations, which for the most part are dark; but, as a totally contrasted conclusion, the piece ends with a Rachmaninov-like passages of lyricism. The *Concerto for Piano Duet and Strings* brings busy and brilliant passagework for the soloists in the first movement, a still and intense Passacaglia slow movement and a relentlessly high-spirited finale. The *Concerto for Two Pianos* (3 hands) portrays a generally lighter side of the composer, ending with a delightful rumba, full of cross-rhythms. **Phillip Dyson** and **Kevin Sargent** are brilliant and alert piano soloists, with the young Finnish conductor **Esa Heikkilä** drawing dazzling playing from the **Ulster Orchestra**, vividly recorded, not least in *Beckus*.

Beckus the Dandipratt Overture; Flourish for a 21st Birthday; The Inn of the Sixth Happiness: Suite; Philharmonic Concerto; Symphony 6

⊖┐ Ⓜ *** LPO 0013. LPO, Handley

The *Sixth Symphony* and the *Philharmonic Concerto* express more darkly personal, more introverted feelings, the symphony, written in Cornwall in 1967, enigmatic and troubled, and the rondo finale, for all its surface exuberance, never quite shaking off the work's disconsolate atmosphere. The *Philharmonic Concerto*, written in 1976 for the orchestra's USA tour in the bicentenary year, celebrates the American War of Independence without glory, with an elegiac central *Andantino* (very beautifully played here) leading to an energetic *Chacony* finale. But it is the suite from the film score for *The Inn of the Sixth Happiness* that shows his rich melodic inspiration, while in the *Happy Ending* finale we meet Arnold's infectious wit in his interpolation of the folksong *This old man* with its bouncing 'paddiwack' rhythm. These live performances are very committed indeed, and **Handley's** skill in sustaining atmosphere and holding elusive structures together is heard at its finest. Excellently balanced sound.

Clarinet Concertos 1–2; Divertimento for Flute, Oboe & Clarinet, Op. 37; Fantasy for B flat Clarinet, Op. 87; Sonatina, Op. 29; 3 Shanties for Wind Quintet

*** ASV CDDCA 922. Johnson, Martin, Kelly, Briggs, Cohen, Martineau; ECO, Bolton

Clarinet Concertos 1, Op. 20; 2, Op. 115; Scherzetto

(BB) *** Hyp. Helios CDH 55060. King, ECO, Wordsworth – BRITTEN: *Clarinet Concerto Movement*; MACONCHY: *Concertinos* ***

With the characterful **Emma Johnson** as the central figure in all six works, this makes a delightful collection of what is labelled as Arnold's 'Complete Works for Clarinet'. Above all, these performances bring out the fun in Arnold's music, his bluff sense of humour set alongside a vein of warm lyricism matched by few of his contemporaries.

   Thea King's collection makes an exceptionally attractive disc, beautifully recorded and superbly performed. The *Scherzetto* is a delightfully jaunty piece adapted by Christopher Palmer from Arnold's music for the film *You Know What Sailors Are*.

(i; ii) Double Piano Concerto (three hands); (iii) English Dances 3 & 5; Symphonies (iv) 1; (v) 2, (i) 5. Overtures: (v) Beckus the Dandipratt; (i) Peterloo; (iii) Tam O'Shanter

⌐ ✵ (M) **** EMI (mono/stereo) 382146-2 (2). (i) CBSO; (ii) Sellick, Smith; (iii) Philh. O; (iv) Bournemouth SO; (v) RPO; all cond. composer

Sir Malcolm Arnold was the most persuasive conductor of his own works, finding an emotional depth and intensity rarely matched by even his finest interpreters. Listen to the glorious melody which opens the slow movement of the *Symphony 5*, arguably his finest, and the warmth and natural expressiveness have one gulping; similarly with the *pianissimo* reprise of the melody in the closing pages of the finale, before the downbeat fades away. That is just one of the treasures in this superb compilation, which brings together all

the recordings Arnold made for EMI, as well as a great rarity, the vivid account of his *Symphony 2*, which he recorded with the vintage RPO in 1955 for Philips. No Arnold collection captures his special magic quite so compellingly as this.

Guitar Concerto; Serenade for Guitar & Strings

*** Chan. 9963. Ogden, N. Sinf., Hickox – BERKELEY: *Guitar Concerto*; WALTON: *5 Bagatelles* ***

Craig Ogden is a consummate soloist in the concerto and he is beautifully recorded. The charming, lyrical *Serenade for Guitar and Strings* which comes as supplement was written by Arnold a couple of years earlier. An excellent alternative to Julian Bream's recordings, especially if the Berkeley and Walton couplings are preferred.

Horn Concerto 2, Op. 58

⌐ *** Lyrita SRCD 316. Pyatt, LPO, Braithwaite – BOWEN; GIBBS; JACOB: *Horn Concertos*; VINTER: *Hunter's Moon* ***

Like so many works for this instrument, Arnold's masterly *Second Concerto* was written for Dennis Brain (in 1956). Although its bravura is demanding, its core is lyrical. **David Pyatt** naturally takes on Brain's mantle and gives a superbly effortless performance, catching the work's many mood changes; and he is admirably accompanied by **Braithwaite** and the **LPO**. Exuberant.

4 Cornish Dances, Op. 91; 8 English Dances, Set 1, Op. 27; Set 2, Op. 33; 4 Irish Dances, Op. 126; 4 Scottish Dances, Op. 59; 4 Welsh Dances, Op. 138

⌐ (BB) **** Naxos 8.553526. Queensland SO, Penny

The advantage this Naxos disc enjoys – to say nothing of its price – is the inclusion of the four *Welsh Dances*, the last to be written and closer in mood to the *Cornish* and *Irish Dances* than to the cheerful ebullience of the masterly *English Dances* of 1950–1. These performances have the composer's imprimatur (he was present at the recording sessions) and can be cordially recommended. The Naxos sound might be thought a shade over-resonant, but it does not lack brilliance.

Film music, Vol. 1

⌐ *** Chan. 9100. LSO, Hickox

Malcolm Arnold wrote over 100 film scores, and it was the music for *The Bridge on the River Kwai* which (as the composer has acknowledged) put his name before the wider public. All this music is superbly played by **Hickox** and the **LSO** (who obviously relish the often virtuoso instrumental scoring), and the recording is as lavish as anyone could wish – very much in the Chandos demonstration bracket.

Film music, Vol. 2

*** Chan. 9851. BBC PO, Gamba, with (i) Dyson; (ii) Bradbury

In Vol. 2 the suite arranged by Philip Lane from *David Copperfield* opens with a typical melodic sweep, followed by a whimsical *moto perpetuo* representing the Micawbers. The *Overture* from *The Roots of Heaven* has a lilting waltz tune and *The Belles of St Trinian's* (the composer's favourite film) an audacious sparkle. Arnold's jaunty samba from *The Captain's Paradise*, in which Alec Guinness starred in the bigamous title-role, makes a splendid finale. **Rumon Gamba** and the excellent **BBC Philharmonic** provide plenty of infectious zest and a sometimes bitter-sweet lyricism, and the recording is of top Chandos quality. If you enjoy film music, it doesn't come any better than this.

Sinfonietta 1, Op. 9

🎶 *** Lyrita (ADD) SRCD 257. LSO Braithwaite – LENNOX
BERKELEY; BRITTEN: *Sinfoniettas*; RAWSTHORNE; TIPPETT:
Divertimentos ***

In his time the *Sinfonietta* was one of Malcolm Arnold's most popular and frequently heard works. Now it is hardly ever played. Yet, its textures are clean and the melodic invention is fertile and gracefully written for the instruments. Lively playing from the **LSO**, fine recording and first-rate couplings make this disc very desirable.

Symphonies 1–9

🎶 (BB) *** Naxos 8.505178 (5). Nat. SO of Ireland, Penny (with
conversation between composer and conductor)

Andrew Penny's complete set of the Arnold *Symphonies* is a very considerable achievement. The five discs are reviewed separately below, but are here gathered together with admirable documentation, including a biography of the composer. Self-recommending.

Symphonies 1, Op. 22; 2, Op. 40

*** Chan. 9335. LSO, Hickox

(BB) **(*) Naxos 8.553406. Nat. SO of Ireland, Penny

Richard Hickox takes naturally to the Malcolm Arnold idiom and he is particularly impressive in the two slow movements, which are full of atmosphere, vividly coloured and strongly felt and the **LSO** response is powerful and thoroughly committed throughout.

    Andrew Penny in his Naxos version matches Hickox closely, but the **National Orchestra of Ireland** cannot command the richness of sonority of the LSO, and in the poignant *Lento* of the *Second*, with its plangent funeral march, Hickox's more spacious tempo is profoundly moving. Yet the slow movement of the *Second Symphony* communicates strongly in the Dublin performance. The Naxos recording is excellent, but the Chandos is in the demonstration bracket.

Symphonies 3, Op. 63; 4, Op. 71

*** Chan. 9290. LSO, Hickox

(BB) *** Naxos 8.553739. Nat. SO of Ireland, Penny

Arnold's *Third Symphony* is notable for the long, expressively austere string-melody in the opening movement and the desolation of its *Lento* slow movement, both played with great expressive intensity under **Richard Hickox**. The first movement of the *Fourth Symphony* is dominated by one of those entirely winning, Arnoldian lyrical tunes, even though there is jagged dissonance in the central episode. Hickox

has the work's full measure, and the Chandos recording is superb, full of colour and atmosphere.

    Andrew Penny and his Dublin orchestra also give finely played and spontaneous performances that can readily stand alongside the full-price competition, and this Naxos record understandably has the composer's imprimatur. The recording, if not as rich as the Chandos, is of high quality.

Symphonies 5, Op. 74; 6, Op. 95

*** Chan. 9385. LSO, Hickox

(BB) *** Naxos 8.552000. Nat. SO of Ireland, Penny

Arnold's *Fifth Symphony* is a consciously elegiac work, written in memory of friends who died young and the first movement brings moments of valedictory evocation in **Hickox's** hands. The disconsolate *Sixth Symphony* is a good deal less comfortable than the *Fifth*, but Hickox handles the powerfully menacing climax of the *Lento* quite superbly, which then suddenly evaporates with the arrival of the joyous, syncopated brass fanfares of the *rondo* finale. In both symphonies the committed response of the **LSO**, together with the richly expansive Chandos recording, increases the weight and power of the readings.

    Andrew Penny draws fine, concentrated playing from the **National Symphony Orchestra of Ireland**, with brass and percussion in particular brilliantly caught. As a bargain version this wins the highest recommendation.

Symphonies 7, Op. 113; 8, Op. 124

(BB) *** Naxos 8.552001. Irish Nat. SO, Penny

Andrew Penny and the **Irish National Symphony Orchestra** crown their fine cycle of the nine Arnold symphonies for Naxos with these two most troubled and challenging works, reflecting the darkest period of the composer's life. The darkness is relieved by the wealth of thematic material, demonstrating the vitality of the composer's imagination through his worst trials.

Symphony 9, Op. 128

(BB) *** Naxos 8.553540. Nat. SO of Ireland, Penny

This superb first Naxos recording confirms the *Ninth Symphony* as a fitting culmination to Arnold's symphonic series. The baldness of the arguments, with two-part writing the general rule, consistently speaks in a true Arnoldian accent, culminating in the long slow finale, almost as long as the other three movements together, registering a mood of tragedy and disillusion. As to **Penny's** performance, this is not just concentrated and consistently committed but warmly resonant, with the Dublin strings sounding glorious and the woodwind and brass consistently brilliant.

CHAMBER MUSIC

Complete Music for Brass: Brass Quintets 1–2; Fanfare for Louis; Fantasy for Horn; Fantasy for Trombone; Fantasy for B flat Trumpet; Fantasy for Tuba; Little Suites 1–3; Symphony for Brass, Op. 123

🎶 **** Nim. NI 5804. Fine Arts Brass, Roberts

Arnold was an admirer of the **Fine Arts Brass Ensemble** and composed the *Second Brass Quintet* especially for them. His writing for brass has enormous flair and his ready melodic felicity (and wit) illuminates every piece. While the *Symphony* is the major work here, the *First Brass Quintet* of 1961, with its central *Chaconne*, and the three *Little Suites* consistently show the quality of his invention, as do the solo *Fantasies*. The performances here are superb, wonderfully proficient and spontaneous, and the richly blended, sonorous recording is very much in the demonstration bracket.

Divertimento, Op 35; Dream City; Duo; Divertimento, Op. 135; Fantasia, Op. 87; Fantasy; Grand Fantasy; Hobson's Choice: Overture and Shoe Ballet; Suite Bourgeoise; 3 Shanties, Op. 4; Wind Quintet, Op. 2; You Know What Sailors Are: Scherzetto

(BB) *** Naxos 8 570294. East Winds

Sir Malcolm Arnold has always been an enthusiastic composer of wind music. **East Winds**, made up of talented young wind-players, here give brilliant performances which consistently bring out the wit of the writing.

String Quartets 1, Op. 23; 2, Op. 118; Phantasy for String Quartet (Vita Abundans)

🎵 (BB) *** Naxos 8.557762. Maggini Qt

Sir Malcolm Arnold's two *String Quartets* date from very different periods in his career, one early, written in 1949, the other later, written in 1975 at a period when his life had fallen apart and he was suffering serious tensions. The **Maggini Quartet** here add to their superb series of British quartets for Naxos with a disc that makes one marvel that these fine works are not far better known. Even in the very early *Phantasy*, which comes as a very welcome bonus, a piece written when he was still in his teens, he was using the medium with a confidence and originality which rightly won him a prize in the Cobbett competition, for which it was entered in 1941.

PIANO MUSIC

Piano Sonata in B min.; 2 Pieces: Prelude; Romance; Variations on a Ukrainian Folksong

*** Somm SOMMCD 062. Bebbington – LAMBERT: *Piano Sonata, etc.* ***

Arnold's very considerable *Piano Sonata* has a first movement of serious purpose, plus characteristic moments of quirkiness, but he lets his hair down just a little in the closing *Alla marcia*. The *Two Pieces* (a birthday present for the composer's mother) are modest in scale but gently memorable, both serene and quite lovely; the *Ukrainian Variations* (on a rather endearing theme) explore the more percussive possibilities of the keyboard, but with plenty of lyrical contrast. **Mark Bebbington** is splendidly at home in this music (as he is in the equally rewarding Lambert couplings) and the recording is very real and present.

ARRIAGA, Juan (1806–26)

Symphony in D; Overture: Los esclavos felices

*** Hyp. CDA 66800. SCO, Mackerras – VOŘÍŠEK: *Symphony in D* ***

(BB) **(*) Naxos 8.557207. Algarve O, Álvaro Cassuto – (with Concert of music by CARVALHO; MOREIRA; PORTUGAL; SEIXAS **(*))

The *Overture* is a real charmer, almost Schubertian, but also very much in the style of Rossini, complete with crescendo. The *Symphony* could scarcely be played with more character than it is under **Mackerras**, and the somewhat resonant but very well-balanced Hyperion recording does not cloud detail. Highly recommended.

The Naxos performances, recorded in Faro, convey the sunny high spirits of the pieces and also bring four other rarities that few readers are unlikely to know. Good playing and recording.

String Quartets 1 in D min.; 2 in A; 3 in E flat

🎵 *** HM HMI 1987038. Cuerteto Casals

(BB) *** Naxos 8.557628. Camerata Boccherini

*** MDG 603 0236-2. Voces Qt

Arriaga died when he was only nineteen, and these quartets were published when he was 17 and have an astonishing assurance and miraculous purity of invention. They are within the tradition of the Mozart quartets and Beethoven's Op. 18, but they also have a Schubertian feel to them.

These new performances by the **Cuerteto Casals**, recorded in 2003, use modern instruments, yet they show a background understanding of period-instrument practice without creating abrasiveness or linear distortion. Their ensemble is impeccable and their group personality striking. Excellent, truthfully balanced recording.

The **Camerata Boccherini** are also thoroughly in sympathy with these delightful quartets and they play them on original instruments with vivacity, but never losing their elegance or expressive warmth. This version is thoroughly recommendable in its own right, especially at Naxos price.

The Romanian **Voces Quartet** is also completely at home in this engaging music and gives warmly refined, polished performances of all three works, full of elegance and spirit. The recording is warm and naturally balanced in an attractively warm acoustic.

AUBER, Daniel (1782–1871)

OPERA

Fra Diavolo (complete; in Italian)

**(*) Fonit 3984 27266-2 (2). Serra, Dupuy, Raffanti, Portella, Cambridge University Chamber Ch., Martina Franca Festival O, Zedda

Alberto Zedda in this live festival performance offers the first recording of the Italian version, with all the material preserved and with accompanied recitatives by Auber in place of dialogue. The result is dramatically more convincing. In the title-role **Dano Raffanti** characterizes well, using a ringing tenor with flair and only occasional coarseness, relishing the challenge of the big arias. **Luciana Serra** has a touch of acid at the top of the voice, but this is a bright, agile soprano who brings out the charm in the role of the country-girl, Zerlina. **Nelson Portella** and **Martine Dupuy**, clear and firm, are well contrasted as the English Milord and Lady Pamela. An Italian libretto is provided but no translation.

La Muette de Porcici

(B) *** EMI 5 75257-2 (2). Kraus, Anderson, Aler, Lafont, Munier, Jean Laforge Choral Ens., Monte Carlo PO, Fulton

Auber's opera was notorious for sparking off a rebellion in Brussels that led to Belgium's separation from the oppressive Dutch. The writing has several striking melodic ideas, lively ensembles and choruses (some anticipating Gilbert and Sullivan) and a magnificent aria for the hero. Strongly cast and vigorously conducted by **Thomas Fulton**, it makes an attractive set, with lively, theatrical sound, even though it lacks a little in richness. No texts are provided, but the set is inexpensive.

AURIC, Georges (1899–1983)

L'Eventail de Jeanne (complete ballet, including music by Delannoy, Ferroud, Ibert, Milhaud, Poulenc, Ravel, Roland-Manuel, Roussel, Florent Schmitt). Les Mariés de la Tour Eiffel (complete ballet, including music by Honegger, Milhaud, Poulenc, Tailleferre)

❀ (M) *** Chan. 10290. Philh. O, Simon

A carefree spirit and captivating wit run through both these composite works; in fact these pieces are full of imagination and fun. **Geoffrey Simon** and the **Philharmonia Orchestra** give a very good account of themselves and the Chandos recording is little short of spectacular. This unique recording is even more welcome at mid-price.

Film scores

⊶ *** Chan. 8774. BBC PO, Gamba

It is remarkable that a French composer should have provided the film scores for some of the most famous Ealing comedies, so British in every other respect. But Auric's delicacy of orchestral touch and his feeling for atmosphere (together with his easy melodic gift) made him a perfect choice after his first flamboyant venture with Rank's *Caesar and Cleopatra*. From the witty railway music of *The Titfield Thunderbolt* and the distinct menace of *Dead of Night*, Auric moved easily to the buoyantly spirited *Passport to Pimlico*. But it was *Moulin Rouge* that gave Auric his popular hit, with a charming Parisian waltz song (delicately sung here by **Mary Carewe**) that was understandably to be a remarkable commercial success. Most of the excerpts are short vignettes but they make enjoyable listening when so well played and recorded.

La Belle et la Bête (complete film score)

(BB) *** Naxos 8.557707. Axios Ch., Moscow SO, Adriano

Auric's style was always distinctive and unfailingly inventive. Many consider his score to Cocteau's *La Belle et la Bête* (1945) his finest achievement; indeed its 60 minutes are full of colour and clever invention, with the large orchestra (with chorus) used with great imagination throughout.

AVISON, Charles (1709–70)

12 Concerti grossi after Geminiani's Violin Sonatas, Op. 1

⊶ (M) **** Divine Art dda 21210 (2). Avison Ens., Beznosiuk

Geminiani's *Violin Sonatas* show him at his finest and consistently inspired. Avison arranged only eleven of the twelve sonatas, so **Pavlo Beznosiuk** has himself completed the set. The period-instrument performances by the excellent **Avison Ensemble** are full of life and richly expressive, yet always freshly stylish. The recording is first class.

12 Concertos, Op. 6

(BB) *** Naxos 8.557553/54. Avison Ens., Beznosiuk

Avison's ability to pattern his works on the music of others stood him in good stead throughout his career. While he was a fine musical craftsman, his own creative powers seem to be more limited. His concertos are skilfully fashioned, have plenty of vitality and show perceptive use of dynamic contrast; but the music itself, finely wrought as it is, displays no special melodic individuality or any unconventional features. Played as vibrantly and freshly as it is here, on period instruments by this expert ensemble from Avison's own city, and led by the excellent violinist **Pavlo Beznosiuk**, one cannot help but respond to the vitality of the writing, even if these concertos are not in the same league as the similar works of Corelli or Handel.

12 Concerti grossi after Scarlatti

(N) (M) *** divine art dda 1213 (2) Avison Ens., Beznosiuk

**(*) Alpha 031. Café Zimmermann (3, 5–6, 9, 11 & 12)

**(*) Hyp. Dyad CDD 22060 (2). Brandenburg Cons., Goodman

Pavlo Beznosiuk and the **Avison Ensemble** offer thoroughly recommendable versions of these expert transcriptions of popular Scarlatti sonatas. These are performances of style and flair and also score with the warmth of the recorded sound to make a first choice for these attractive works.

The period instrument group **Café Zimmermann**, with **Pablo Valetti** expertly leading the concertino, play with great energy and zest, and in slow movements with delicacy of lyrical feeling. These performances are distinctly preferable to those from Roy Goodman and, by not offering a complete set, are placed on a single disc. Even so, the fairly close balance brings a certain 'scratchiness' on tuttis, which is not altogether mitigated by the basically warm ambience.

Roy Goodman's version has plenty of vitality. Fast movements fizz spiritedly, but the linear style of the slower movements, though not lacking expressive feeling, is altogether less smooth, and these performances are essentially for those who are totally converted to the authentic movement. The recording is excellent.

6 Sonatas for 2 Violins & a Bass, Op. 1; 6 Sonatas for Harpsichord with Accompaniments for 2 Violins and a Cello, Op. 8

(N) (M) **** divine art dda 21214 (2) Avison Ens. (members)

Here is a double example of Charles Avison's instrumental enterprise and diversity of invention, both very appealing indeed. The Corelli-inspired *Trio Sonatas de chiesa* are, all but one, based in the minor key. They usually open with a stately slow movement, then comes a vibrant fugal section, followed by another lyrical movement, before the lively finale. The featured organ continuo adds warm sonority to the textures and *Nos.* 1 and 4 stand out by their use of the Dorian mode. The *Harpsichord Sonatas* are different again, very like minia- ture concertos with the keyboard instrument dominating, and the writing often boldly rhythmic – catchily so. They are innovative and most entertaining, especially when played with such infectious vitality. In both sets the music could not be more persuasively played and the recording is very real and present.

BACH, Carl Philipp Emanuel
(1714–88)

Cello Concertos: in A min., Wq.170; in B flat, Wq.171; in A, Wq.172

⊕— 🌣 *** BIS CD 807. Suzuki, Bach Coll., Japan

⊕— (BB) *** Virgin 2×1 5 61794-2 (2). (with Hamburg Sinfonias, Wq.183/1⁄4; Sinfonia in B min., Wq.182/5) OAE, Leonhardt; with Bylsma

(i) Cello Concerto in A, Wq.172. Hamburg Sinfonias, Wq.181/1 & 4; Wq.183/1–4

⊕— *** HM HMU 807 403. E. Concert, Manze; (i) with McGillivray

Hidemi Suzuki creates a dashing flow of energy in the or- chestral ritornellos of outer movements, and the **Bach Collegium** play with great zest and commitment. In slow movements Suzuki's eloquent phrasing, warmth of feeling and breadth of tone are totally compelling, a cello line of heart-stopping intensity. The recording is splendid.

Bylsma's expressive intensity communicates strongly without ever taking the music outside its boundaries of sen- sibility, and these artists convey their commitment to this music persuasively. The *Hamburg Sinfonias* (for woodwind and strings) are striking works, notable for their refreshing originality. **Gustav Leonhardt's** account of this second set is the one to have if you want them on period instruments.

Alison McGillivray's nimble account of the *Cello Concerto* makes a fine centrepiece for the programme, and although her tone is a little dry the sombre eloquence of the *Largo* is

affectingly caught. But it is the collection of *Hamburg Sinfonias* from **Andrew Manze** and the **English Concert** which is special here. It is the most stimulating in the cata- logue.

(i) Flute Concertos: in D min., Wq.22; in A min., Wq.166; in B flat, Wq.167; in A, Wq.168; in G, Wq.169. Sonata for Solo Flute, Wq.132

⊕— 🌣 (BB) *** Naxos 8.555715/6. Gallois; (i) Toronto Camerata, Mallon

Patrick Gallois is a masterly flautist, and he gives a superb set of performances of these fine concertos written for the court of Frederick the Great and arranged by the composer from works originally featuring the harpsichord as soloist. There is much sparkling vivacity in the *allegros*, and the ex- pressive range of the slow movements, sometimes quite dark in feeling, is fully captured by both soloist and the excellent **Toronto Camerata** under **Kevin Mallon**.

Harpsichord Concertos 1–3 (BIS CD 707); 4, 7 & 12 (BIS CD 708); 5 & 35; 2 Sonatinas (BIS CD 868); 6, 8 & 18 (BIS CD 767); 9, 13 & 17 (BIS CD 768); 11, 14 & 19 (BIS CD 785); 15, 25 & 32 (BIS CD 786); 20 & 38; Sonatina (BIS CD 1127); 16 & 36; Sonatina (BIS CD 914); 21 & 27; Sonatina (BIS CD 1587); 22; 2 Sonatinas (BIS CD 1307); 23 & 39; Pieces; Sonatina; 2 Sonatas (BIS CD 1422); 24, 28 & 29 (BIS CD 857); 26 & 40; Sonatina (BIS CD 187); 30, 33 & 34 (BIS CD 867)

**(*) BIS (as above). Spányi (harpsichord, fortepiano, or tangent piano)

Miklós Spányi is now more than halfway in his ongoing sur- vey of Bach's 52 harpsichord concertos, and they are generally more successful than his accounts of the sonatas in having greater spontaneity and animation, and often a degree of el- egance and delicacy in slow movements. The earlier works use a period-instrument string group (6211) which is proba- bly larger than the ensemble the composer would have ex- pected, and the resonance of the recording militates against a really intimate effect in the tuttis of outer movements, al- though slow movements make an effective contrast. The later concertos and the more modest concertante keyboard sonatinas (the latter designed to be suitable for amateur as well as professional performance) include wind instruments.

Harpsichord Concertos: in E, Wq.14; in G, Wq.43

⊕— (M) *** CRD (ADD) 3311. Pinnock, E. Concert – J. C. BACH (arr. MOZART): *Harpsichord Concerto* ***

The *E major Harpsichord Concerto* is one of the most ambitious that C. P. E. Bach left us. **Trevor Pinnock** and his **English Concert** (using original instruments) give admirable per- formances, nicely balancing the claims of modern ears and total authenticity. First-rate recording and a fascinating cou- pling.

Berlin Sinfonias: in C; in F, Wq.174/5; in E min.; in E flat, Wq.178/9; in F, Wq.181

*** Cap. 10 103. C. P. E. Bach CO, Haenchen

The playing of **Haenchen's** excellent C. P. E. Bach group is alert and vigorous, with airy textures and attractively sprung rhythms. Modern instruments are used in the best possible way. Excellent sound.

6 Hamburg Sinfonias, Wq.182/1–6

🎵~ ⒝⒝ *** Naxos 8.553285. Capella Istropolitana, Benda

🎵~ Ⓜ *** DG 4775000. E. Concert, Pinnock

The six *Hamburg String Sinfonias* are particularly striking in their unexpected twists of imagination, and they contain some of his most inspired and original ideas. Using modern instruments at higher modern pitch, **Benda** directs light, well-sprung accounts, with extra light and shade. The excellent sound is full and open, as well as immediate.

The performing style of the **English Concert** concentrates on a concern for 18th-century poise and elegance. This disc in its LP format won the *Gramophone* Early Music Award in 1980, and the excellent recording sounds splendidly fresh and clear in its remastered format.

4 Hamburg Sinfonias, Wq.183/1–4

⒝⒝ **(*) Naxos 8.553289. Salzburg CO, Lee – W. F. BACH: *Sinfonia in F***(*)

The Naxos Salzburg versions are freshly played, the results spick and span, with polished playing from strings and woodwind alike. Obviously **Yoon K. Lee** knows about period-performance styles and, though modern instruments are used here, textures are clear and clean.

CHAMBER AND INSTRUMENTAL MUSIC

Duo for 2 Clarinets (Adagio & Allegro), H.636; 6 Sonatas for Pianoforte, Clarinet & Bassoon, H.516–21; Flute Sonatas (for flute and harpsichord): in E, H.506; in C, H.573; Oboe Sonata (for oboe & continuo) in G min., H.549; Pastorale for Oboe, Bassoon & Continuo

Ⓜ *** CPO 999 508-2. Fiati con Tasto, Cologne

This delightfully diverse cross-section of Carl Philipp Emanuel's chamber music for wind instruments could hardly be bettered as a source of exploration. The use of period instruments is expert, and the felicitous interplay at times anticipates Mozart. The recording is very natural and gives a vivid projection to one and all.

11 Flute Sonatas (for flute & continuo), Wq.123–31; 133–4; Sonata for Solo Flute in A min., Wq.132

*** MDG L 3284/5 (2). Hünteler, Bylsma, Ogg

There is nothing watery about the coolly beautiful timbre that **Hünteler** achieves on his transverse flute, and he proves a masterly exponent of this rewarding repertoire and obviously enjoys an excellent rapport with his continuo partners, **Anner Bylsma** and **Jacques Ogg**. The MDG recording is exemplary.

Quartet in D for Flute, Viola, Cello & Fortepiano, Wq.94; Solo Flute Sonata in A min., Wq.132; Sonata in G min. for Viola da gamba & Harpsichord, Wq.88: Larghetto. Trio Sonatas: in C for Flute, Violin & Continuo, Wq.147; in C min. for 2 Violins & Continuo (Sanguineus & Melancholicus), Wq.161

🎵~ ✿ *** Channel CCS 11197. Florilegium

A wholly delightful collection. **Ashley Solomon's** exquisite flute-playing dominates the *D major Quartet*, and the balance with **Neal Peres da Costa's** delicate fortepiano is quite perfect, registering subtle nuances of dynamic contrast before Bach's highly imaginative dialogue between Sanguine and Melancholy brings quixotic changes of mood and tempo. The recording balance could hardly be bettered.

Sinfonia a tre voci in D; 12 Variations on 'La Folia', Wq.118/9; Trio Sonatas: in B flat, Wq.158; in C min. (Sanguineus & Melancholicus), Wq.161/1; Viola da gamba Sonata in D, Wq.137

⒝⒝ *** Hyp. Helios CDH 55232. Purcell Qt

The *Variations on 'La Folia'* are fresh and inventive, particularly in **Robert Woolley's** hands, but the remaining pieces are hardly less rewarding. The Hyperion recording is well balanced, faithful and present.

KEYBOARD MUSIC

Alla Polacca, Wq.116/8; Fantasia in G min., Wq.117/13; 2 Menuets, Wq.116/5 & 7; Romance with 12 Variations in G, Wq.118/6; 3 Sonatas, Wq.65/43, 44 & 46

Ⓝ *** BIS CD 1492 Miklós Spányi (tangent piano)

Miklós Spányi is recording all C.P.E. Bach's keyboard music for BIS, and we have discussed his many previous issues in earlier volumes with mixed feelings, because of his sometimes eccentric rhythmic twists in the melodic lines. His recent issue of the *6 Württemberg Sonatas*, Wq.49 (BIS 1423/4) is dramatically impressive and has been generally well received, although our reservations remain. But this latest collection, played on a characterful tangent piano can be welcomed with enthusiasm, and not least because the selection includes a splendidly inventive set of variations, besides three of his most impressive sonatas. The recording is excellent.

Keyboard Sonatas: in F sharp min., Wq.52/4; in E min., Wq.59/1; in D, Wq.61/2; in G, Wq.62/19; in G min., Wq.65/17; in C min., Wq.65/31; Andante contenerezza; Rondos: in A, Wq.58/1; in C min., Wq.59/4; in D min., Wq.61/4

🎵~ ✿ **** DG 459 614-2. Pletnev

Altogether remarkable playing, even by **Pletnev's** exalted standards. He finds both the wit and depth of this music, and the resource of keyboard colour and refinement of articulation are pretty awesome. And what interesting music it is! He receives very natural recorded sound from the DG team.

Keyboard Sonatas: in B flat, Wq.62/16; in G, Wq.65/22; in E min., Wq.65/30; in A, Wq.65/37; in G, Wq.65/48; in A, Wq.70/1; Rondo in E flat, Wq.61/1

☞ (BB) *** Naxos 8.553640. Chaplin (piano)

François Chaplin plays these works freshly and confidently on the modern piano. The result demonstrates how forward-looking these sonatas are, especially the appealingly expressive slow movements of the later works. The closing *Rondo* of 1786 is particularly successful in using the piano's fuller sonority.

VOCAL MUSIC

Cantatas for Pastor Joh Jacobs Schäffer, H. 821; Pastor Joh Christoph Froderoci. Choruses: Amen! Lob und Preis und Stärke; Leite mich nach deinem Willen; Mein Heiland, meine Zuversicht

*** CPO 777 108-2. Himlische Cantorey, Les Amis de Philippe, Rémy

Much of the lively and often striking invention we know from C. P. E. Bach's orchestral music is to be found in these occasional festive pieces, written for a variety of reasons. The two large cantatas (written in 1775 and 1785 respectively) contain some splendid arias, and the *Choruses* are all enjoyable, with the orchestra (using plenty of timpani) always colourful and effective. The recordings and performances are vivid and fresh, the CPO booklet copious. Texts and translations provided.

Easter Cantata, Wq.243; (Christmas Cantata), Wq.249; Heilig, Wq.217; Klopstocks Morgengesang am Schöpfungsfeste, Wq.239

*** Cap. 10 208. Schlick, Lins, Prégardien, Elliott, Varcoe, Schwarz, Rheinische Kantorei, Kleine Konzert, Max

Klopstocks Morgengesang am Schöpfungsfeste ('Klopstock's morning song on the celebration of creation') is a work of many beauties and is well performed by these artists. *Anbetung dem Erbarmer* ('Worship of the merciful') is another late work, full of modulatory surprises. *Auf schicke dich recht feierlich* ('Up, be reconciled') and *Heilig* ('Holy') (1779) are Christmas works. A record of unusual interest, very well performed and naturally recorded.

Die Auferstehung und Himmelfahrt Jesu (The Resurrection and Ascension of Jesus)

(*) EuroArts DVD 2054039. Karthäuser, Hardt, Christoph & Stephan Genz, Ex Tempore, La Petite Bande, Kuijken – J. S. BACH: *Cantata 11 (Ascension)* *

*** Hyp. CDA 67364. Schwabe, Christoph Genz, Stephan Genz, Ex Tempore, La Petite Bande, Kuijken

Carl Philipp Emanuel Bach wrote three superb oratorios, of which this is the last and, as he thought himself, the finest, given a masterly performance here under **Sigiswald Kuijken**. All three of the soloists sing with clear, fresh tone, the tenor of **Christoph Genz** nicely related to the baritone of **Stephan Genz**, while the choir, **Ex Tempore**, brings bite and clarity to the dramatic choruses, with each half ending on an elaborate fugue. Although the timpanist makes a dramatically visual contribution to the tenor recitative, *Judäa zittert!*, for the most part this is a more lyrical, less dramatic account than the earlier, Hyperion recording, which has greater range and bite. The cameraman explores the church as well as offering every angle of the performers, including a bird's-eye-distance shot. However, this is still musically very enjoyable, and the coupling of Johann Sebastian's *Ascension Cantata* is superbly done.

BACH, Johann Christian (1735–82)

Bassoon Concerto in B flat and E flat; Flute Concerto in D & G; Oboe Concerto 1–2 in F

*** CPO 999 346 & 999 347. Ward, Brown, Robson, Hanover Band, Halstead

These early concertos had an obvious influence on Mozart's wind concertos, and if you enjoy the Mozart works you will surely enjoy these by J. C. Bach. The six concertos are played with much felicity by **Jeremy Ward**, **Rachel Brown** and **Anthony Robson** respectively, and **Halstead's** accompaniments are a model of elegance. The recording is full and natural. Most enjoyable.

Harpsichord or Clavier Concertos (complete)

(B) *** CPO 999 930-2 (6). Halstead, Hanover Band

Bach's early Berlin concertos (from the 1750s) in these splendid performances from **Anthony Halstead**, directing the **Hanover Band** from the keyboard, are appealingly fluent, full of flair and vitality. Slow movements are deeply expressive and outer movements bustle vigorously. **Halstead** has recorded Op. 7 in chamber form with just an accompanying string trio. His solo playing is very persuasive and the result is delightfully intimate. Bach's Op. 13 appeared in 1777 and shows him still developing in ideas and orchestration. Op. 14 is more ambitious, although it may have been written earlier. Halstead uses a Broadwood pianoforte and accompanies himself brightly and gracefully.

Harpsichord Concerto in D (arr. by Mozart as K.107/1)

(M) *** CRD (ADD) 3311. Pinnock, E. Concert – C. P. E. BACH: *Harpsichord Concertos* ***

It seemed more sensible to list this work here as it tends to get lost in the Mozartian discography. In the early 1770s the teenage Mozart turned three sonatas by J. C. Bach into keyboard concertos, adding accompaniments and ritornellos as well as cadenzas. The first of the group makes an excellent coupling for the two fine C. P. E. Bach concertos.

Sinfonias concertantes (complete); Cadenza in C for Oboe, Violin, Viola & Orchestra; Fortepiano Concerto in G

**(*) CPO 777 292-2 (6). Hanover Band, Halstead

Johann Christian Bach might well be regarded as the true father of the sinfonia concertante, for (among others, including Karl Stamitz) he wrote over a dozen of them for various solo instruments, and they are of a consistently higher musical quality than those of most of his contemporaries. Throughout, the performances have warmth and proper finish and refinement; the balance and recording are excellent and the effect is undoubtedly authentic.

Complete Sinfonias

6 Sinfonias, Op. 3; 6 Sinfonias, Op. 6; 3 Sinfonias, Op. 8; Sinfonias: in C (Venier 46) (2 versions); in F (manuscript); Sinfonias, Op. 9/1–2 (standard and original versions); Op. 9/3; Sinfonia in E flat with Clarinets; 6 Sinfonias, Op. 18

(M) *** CPO 999 896 (5). Hanover Band, Halstead

J. C. Bach's *sinfonias* shared the same three-part format as the Italian opera overture, and at that time the descriptive titles were interchangeable. Indeed, as we shall discover in Opp. 9 and 18, Bach borrowed overtures from his own operas to include in his published sets. The works were initially intended for his London concerts and this is the first complete coverage on period instruments, and very impressive it is.

Sinfonias, Op. 9/1–4; Sinfonia concertante in A for Violin & Cello; Sinfonia concertante in E flat, for 2 Violins, Oboe & Orchestra

(BB) **(*) Naxos 8.553085. Camerata Budapest, Gmür

This disc is of interest, not so much for the symphonies as for the two *Sinfonias concertantes*, which are beautifully played, with stylish and appealing contributions from the soloists, all drawn from the orchestra. The solo writing in the *A major Sinfonia concertante* is quite elaborate, and in the *Andante* of the *E flat* work there is a surprise when the two solo violins introduce Gluck's *Che farò senza Euridice*, which is then taken up by the oboe. The second of the Op. 9 symphonies has a real lollipop *Andante con sordini*, presented over a pizzicato accompaniment. The balance is excellent.

6 Sinfonias (Grand Overtures), Op. 18

(BB) **(*) Naxos 8.553367. Failoni O, Gmür

Hanspeter Gmür and the **Failoni Orchestra** give warm and graceful accounts of Op. 18. The spirited allegros are slightly cushioned by the resonance, but slow movements are phrased very musically (particularly the lovely, almost Handelian melody of Op. 18/2, which also has a fine oboe solo from Laszló Párkányi).

CHAMBER MUSIC

6 Symphonies for Wind Sextet (1782)

*** MDG 301 0434-2. Consortium Classicum

There is already a recommended recording of these *Symphonies for Wind Sextet*, by the London Wind Soloists under Jack Brymer (Testament (ADD) SBT 1345). But good though that is, this new set from the **Consortium Classicum**, equally well played and beautifully recorded, has more

warmth and charm, and a certain bucolic flavour from the horns, that make it even more enjoyable. A clear first choice, though not to be played all the way through at a single sitting.

KEYBOARD MUSIC

Solo Keyboard Music

Harpsichord Sonatas: in E & C min., Op. 5/5–6; in C min.; E flat & A, Op. 17/2–3 & 5

(M) *** CRD (ADD) 3453. Black (harpsichord)

Virginia Black plays a modern copy of a Goujon harpsichord, c. 1740, and she is beautifully recorded, the sound clear and robust, with the instrument given a vivid presence (yet not aggressively close) against a warm backgound ambience. A most attractive disc.

6 Keyboard Sonatas, Op. 17

(BB) *** Naxos 8.570361. Nosè (piano)

Johann Christian's Op. 17 *Keyboard Sonatas* date from the 1770s. They are most engaging works in two or three movements and obviously they had a profound influence on the young Mozart. They are played very stylishly on a modern piano by **Alberto Nosè**, and are very well recorded.

VOCAL MUSIC

(i) Laudate pueri Dominum (Vesper psalm); (ii) Salve regina (antiphon); (iii) Si nocte tenebrosa (motet)

*** CPO 999 718-2. (i) Kirkby; (ii) Schäfer; Orfeo Bar. O, Gaigg

Johann Christian's church music was all composed to Latin texts. The lyrical melodic flow has an unmistakable operatic feel to its line and the *Laudate pueri Dominum* is very reminiscent of Mozart in the opera house. **Emma Kirkby** sings the extended *Salve regina* very beautifully, and she navigates brilliantly the sparkling bravura of the second section, *Ad te clamatus*, before the melting *Ad te suspiramus*. The solo motet, *Si nocte tenebrosa*, is splendidly caught by the pleasing tenor voice of **Markus Schäfer**. **Michi Gaigg's** accompaniments are stylish and very well played, and the recording is first class.

BACH, Johann Sebastian
(1685–1750)

The Art of Fugue, BWV 1080

**(*) Naïve OP30191. Concerto Italiano, Alessandrini

The Art of Fugue; A Musical Offering, BWV 1079

(B) *** Ph. (ADD) Duo 442 556-2 (2). ASMF, Marriner

(B) **(*) Double Decca (ADD) 467 267-2 (2). Stuttgart CO, Münchinger

Sir Neville Marriner in the edition he prepared with Andrew Davis has varied the textures most intelligently, giving a fair proportion of the fugues and canons to keyboard instruments, organ as well as harpsichord, and the 1974 recording is admairably refined. Similarly, in the *Musical Offering* Marriner uses his own edition and instrumentation: strings with three solo violins, solo viola and a solo cello; flute, organ and harpsichord. The performances here are of high quality, though some of the playing is a trifle bland.

Rinaldo Alessandrini's approach to *The Art of Fugue* is to seek out its underlying expressive and colouristic possibilities. So, after opening with strings, he scores each of the *contrapuncti* for different groups of wind and/or stringed instruments, allotting only the four canons to the harpsichord. The result has distinctive aural appeal. Alessandrini's solution may not be conventional but the playing (on baroque instruments) is full of life and easy to enjoy. The recording is clear, within a pleasing ambience.

Münchinger's Stuttgart performance allots the fugues to the strings and the canons to the solo woodwind, varied with solo strings. After the incomplete quadruple fugue, Münchinger rounds off the work with the chorale prelude, *Wenn wir in höchsten Nöten sein*, BWV 668a, in principle quite wrong but moving in practice. *The Musical Offering*, although somewhat more relaxed, also brings playing of genuine breadth and eloquence. The recordings were made a decade apart (in the mid-1960s and 1970s) but are of vintage quality, with warmth and excellent presence and detail.

Brandenburg Concertos 1–6, BWV 1046–51 (DVD versions)

🌢 ❋ Ⓜ ******** EuroArts Invitation DVD 2050316. Freiburg Bar. O, von der Göltz

Ⓝ *(*) Medici Arts DVD 2056738. O Mozart, Giuliano Carmignola, Abbado

It is remarkable that so early in the DVD era we should have such an outstanding set of period-instrument performances of the *Brandenburgs*, appropriately recorded at Castle Cöthen. The castle's Spiegesaal has been magnificently restored and makes a visually entrancing backcloth for the recordings. The spacious room seems also to have an ideal acoustic for a chamber group.

The **Freiburgers** play their period instruments with great finesse and warmth. Inner detail is clear, there is no edginess on the strings or linear distortions in the expressively played slow movements. The choice of tempi seems near ideal and **Gottfried von der Göltz**, who directs proceedings almost impassively but with obvious commitment, plays with an easy virtuosity which is engrossing to watch.

Abbado himself assembled the **Orchestra Mozart** in 2004, but their DVD debut is very disappointing. They play against the splendid backcloth of the Teatro Municipale Romolo, Reggio Emilia, and the performance is musically sensitive and strikingly polished. Yet Abbado hardly moves a finger and the effect is curiously dull and inert. Excellent recording, but this is a non-starter.

Brandenburg Concertos 1–6, BWV 1046–51 (CD versions)

🌢 ******** Avie AV 2119 (2). European Brandenburg Ens., Pinnock

🌢 ******** Naïve OP 30412 (2). Concerto Italiano, Alessandrini (with *Sinfonia* from *Cantata*, BWV 174, and DVD by Phillippe Béziat on the making of the recording)

🌢 Ⓜ ******* Warner Elatus 2564 61773-2 (2). Il Giardino Armonico, Antonini

🌢 DG ******* 471 720-2 (1–3, with *Oboe d'amore Concerto, BWV 1055; Double Concerto for Violin & Harpsichord, BWV 1060*); 474 220-2 (4–6, with *Triple Concerto, BWV 1044*). E. Concert, Pinnock

🌢 Ⓑ ******* Hyp. Dyad CDD 22001 (2). Brandenburg Consort, Goodman

The arrival on Avie of a completely new recording from **Trevor Pinnock** suggests that there can be no question of a clear first choice for the Brandenburgs, although for DVD collectors the glorious **Freiburg Baroque Orchestra** version on Euro Arts is unsurpassed and perhaps unsurpassable. But on CD the splendid period-instrument versions by **Alessandrini's Concerto Italiano** and **Il Giardino Armonico** are particularly stimulating, standing alongside the pioneering versions of **Pinnock** and **Goodman**.

However, **Pinnock** has rethought his whole approach in 'revisiting' this ever renewable music, and on his latest Avie recording, although using an authentic ensemble, he is 'eager to cut through any narrow perceptions of period style'. He all but turns back the clock in the approach to tempo and manners with the **European Brandenburgers** in inviting players from different countries and different generations 'to join my new voyage of discovery'. The ensemble (using up to 16 musicians), with Pinnock leading from the harpsichord, convened in December 2006 to celebrate his sixtieth birthday. The recording, with a glowing ambience, is full and remarkably real and transparent.

Alessandrini and his **Concerto Italiano** seldom disappoint. Tempi throughout seem unerringly right and the solo playing on period instruments is rich in baroque colour. The strings are bright and resilient without abrasiveness and the recording, made in March 2005 in the Rome Palazzo Farnese, has a most attractive ambience. A DVD on the making of the recording is included as a bonus, including interesting information about the music and the early instruments involved.

The exhilarating set from the Milanese period-instrument group, **Il Giardino Armonico**, directed by Giovanni Antonini, is also among the finest. Tempi seem perfectly judged, buoyantly brisk but never exaggeratedly so. The playing is alive and joyful; slow movements have expressive warmth and serenity. The wind and brass soloists are first rate, the recorder, flute and oboe sounds are equally characterful, and the strings are bright and clean and without edge; the recording is both warm and freshly transparent so that one can hear the harpsichord coming through quite naturally. A splendid achievement.

Pinnock's *Brandenburgs* from the beginning of the 1980s represent the peak of his early achievement as an advocate of authentic performance, with sounds that are clear and refreshing but not too abrasive. Soloists are outstanding, and they are equally persuasive in the concertante works transcribed from better-known originals.

However, **Roy Goodman's** excellent Hyperion set of the *Brandenburgs* is on a Dyad, with two discs offered for the price of one. The stylish, lively playing is another attractive example of authenticity, lacking something in polish but none in spirit, with the last three concertos especially fresh. Characterization is strong, and slow movements are often appealingly expressive. Tempi of outer movements are very brisk but often bring the lightest rhythmic touch. Very good sound.

Brandenburg Concertos 1–6; (i) Flute Concerto in G min. (Keyboard Concerto in G min., BWV 1056, arr. Réty). Musical Offering, BWV 1079: Trio Sonata in C min.

(BB) *** Naxos 8.557755/6 (2). Swiss Baroque Soloists, Gabetta;
    (i) with Réty

The virtuoso players of the **Swiss Baroque Soloists**, founded and directed by the Argentinian violinist, **Andres Gabetta**, fearlessly tackle even the most challenging passages, with the recording admirably clear on detail in such movements as the opening of the *Fifth Concerto* with the harpsichordist **Giorgio Paranuzzi** articulating clearly in the virtuoso cadenza. In the *Sixth Concerto* the violas are admirably tuned, with the performance of the slow movement establishing it as one of Bach's most beautiful.

(i) Brandenburg Concertos 1–6; (ii) Violin Concertos 1–2; Double Violin Concerto; Double Concerto for Violin & Oboe; (iii) Goldberg Variations; (iv) Organ masterpieces, including Toccata & Fugue in D min.

(B) *** Decca (ADD/DDD) 475 8058 (5). (i) ASMF, Marriner;
    (ii) Grumiaux; Krebbers; Holliger & O; (iii) Schiff (piano);
    (iv) Carlo Curley

The first of a Decca composer series, 'Ultimate Bach' is highly recommendable, offering as it does **Marriner's** splendid 1980 set of the *Brandenburgs*, and **Grumiaux's** indispensable recordings of the *Violin Concertos*, alongside **András Schiff's** admirable *Goldberg Variations* (all praised above and below). **Carlo Curley's** flamboyant performances of key organ works, played on a magnificent Philadelphia organ, make an arresting bonus. In his account of a chorale from Cantata 219, '*Awake thou wintry earth*', even the dead surely could not remain asleep!

Brandenburg Concertos 1–6; Orchestral Suites 1–4

(N) (M) (***) EMI mono 2 12699-2 (3) Busch Chamber Players,
    Adolf Busch

The **Busch** performances come from 1935/6 and now re-emerge on CD among EMI's Great Recordings of the Century and serve as a reminder that these 'inauthentic' years have something to teach us. For all the period limitations, string portamenti, sweet-toned vibrato, piano continuo and so on, these readings have a radiance and a joy in music-making that completely transcend their sonic limitations, which are remarkably few, given the provenance. There is a naturalness of musical expression, never more telling than in **Marcel Moyse's** contribution to the *B minor Suite*, and a richness of feeling on the part of all concerned that make this a special document.

Brandenburg Concertos 1–6; (i) Violin Concerto in E, BWV 1042; (i;ii) Double Violin Concerto in D min., BWV 1043

(N) (BB) **(*) EMI Gemini 2 17617-2 (2) (i) Menuhin; (ii) Ferras;
    Bath Fest. O, Menuhin

Menuhin's 1959 set of the *Brandenburgs* still sound well: the recording is not always absolutely refined, but has not lost its bloom. These are modern instrument performances, but rarely have the rhythms been sprung more joyfully, and tempi are uncontroversially apt. The soloists are outstanding and there is a spontaneity here that is consistently satisfying. The *Violin concertos* were made the following year. Menuhin's solo playing gives much pleasure, with its balance of humanity and classical sympathy. **Ferras** matches his timbre to Menuhin's perfectly in the *Double Concerto*. However here the accompaniments fall slightly short, with outer movements not as rhythmically resilient as in the *Brandenburgs*.

Complete solo and multiple concertos

(i) Harpsichord Concertos 1 in D min.; 2 in E; 3 in D; 4 in A; 5 in F min.; 6 in F; 7 in G min., BWV 1052–8; (ii) Double Harpsichord Concertos: 1 in C min.; 2 in C; 3 in C min., BWV 1060–2; (i–iii) Triple Harpsichord Concertos 1 in D min.; 2 in C, BWV 1063–4; (i–iv) Quadruple Harpsichord Concerto in A min., BWV 1065; (i; v–vi) Triple Concerto for Flute, Violin & Harpsichord, BWV 1044; (vi–vii) Double Concerto for Oboe & Violin in C min., BWV 1060; (vii) Oboe d'amore Concerto in A, BWV 1055; (vi) Violin Concertos 1 in A min.; 2 in E; (vi; viii) Double Violin Concerto in D min., BWV 1041–3

(B) *** DG (ADD/DDD) 463 725-2 (5). E. Concert, Pinnock,
    with (i) Pinnock; (ii) Gilbert; (iii) Mortensen; (iv) Kraemer;
    (v) Beznosiuk; (vi) Standage; (vii) Reichenberg; (viii) Wilcock

Pinnock's performances of the Bach *Harpsichord Concertos* first appeared in 1981 and have dominated the catalogue ever since. In the solo concertos he plays with real panache, his scholarship tempered with excellent musicianship. Pacing is brisk but, to today's ears, used to period performances, the effect is convincing when the playing is so spontaneous, and the analogue sound is bright and clear.

The transcribed concertos for flute, violin and harpsichord, for oboe and violin, and for oboe d'amore are equally persuasive, both vigorous and warm, with consistently resilient rhythms, while the violin concertos are equally welcome. Rhythms are again crisp and lifted at nicely chosen speeds – not too fast for slow movements – and the solo playing here, led by **Simon Standage**, is very stylish.

Harpsichord Concertos 1–8, BWV 1052/1059

(N) (B) **(*) Virgin 2x1 5 22001-2 (2) van Asperen, Melante
    Amsterdam

Bob van Asperen favours an accompaniment with one instrument to each part, basically using a string quartet, with a double bass added in BWV 1052, a pair of recorders in BWV 1057, and one has an intimate sense of chamber music-making. Van Asperen's solo contribution is consistently nimble and has an appealing graceful delicacy, and for the most part the accompaniments from the **Melante Amsterdam** are lightly etched in, even if sometimes in slow movements the bass seems a little heavy. However overall one feels a certain paleness about these performances, even if they have no lack of character or style. The recording balance is excellent.

Harpsichord Concertos 1–7

*** HM HMU 907283-84 (2). With *Triple Concerto for Flute, Violin & Harpsichord*, Egarr; (i) with Brown, Manze; AAM, cond. Manze

The performances from **Richard Egarr** with the **Academy of Ancient Music** are more intimate, the authentic harpsichord image quite small. But what makes these performances so memorable are the slow movements, which often have a poignant expressive dolour which is very affecting. There is an improvisational quality here in both the solo playing and accompaniments which is very distinctive.

Harpsichord Concertos 1, BWV 1052; 2, BWV 1053; 4, BWV 1055; 5, BWV 1056

Ⓝ ** Decca O/L 475 9355 Dantone, Accademia Bizantina

Ottavio Dantone is a stylish soloist, but the textures created by his accompanying string group, with one instrument to a part, are at times even more meagre than those offered by Melante Amsterdam for van Asperen. The **Accademia Bizantina** play with vigour and sensibility, and the balance with the small harpsichord is well managed, but this disc is essentially for purists.

Harpsichord Concertos 1, BWV 1052; 4, BWV 1055; 5, BWV 1056; & 7, BWV1058

Ⓝ *** Virgin 213064-2 Fray, Deutsche CO, Bremen

David Fray plays nimbly and sensitively (his account of the *Adagio* from the *F minor Concerto* is memorable). The accompanying string group of 21 players from Bremen, which he directs from the keyboard, provides accompaniments which are vigorous and refined, and the effect is pleasingly transparent while not lacking warmth and body. Most enjoyable.

Clavier Concertos 1–7

🎵 ⚙ **** Sony 696998924529 (1, 2 & 4); 69698969025 (3, 5–7). Perahia, ASMF

🎵 ⒷⒷ *** Naxos 8.550422 (1–3); 8.550423 (4–7). Chang (piano), Camerata Cassovia, Stankovsky

Clavier Concertos 1–7; Brandenburg Concerto 5; (i) Triple Concerto in A min., BWV 1044

🎵 *** Hyp. CDA 67307 (*Concertos 1 & 7; Brandenburg & Triple Concerto*); CDA 67308 (*Concertos 2–6*). Hewitt (piano), Australian CO, Tognetti; (i) with A. Mitchell

Murray Perahia's set of the Bach solo keyboard concertos sweeps the board. The performances are totally pianistic, with Perahia's lightness of rhythmic touch in *allegros* and deliciously crisp ornamentation communicating an exhilarating yet intimate sense of joy. Slow movements are warmly expressive, helped by the elegant fullness of the Academy strings. Beautifully balanced recording too. In short, the effect here is to put aside any consideration of period 'authenticity' and instead give this wonderfully life-enhancing music an ageless universality.

Hae-won Chang is a highly sympathetic Bach exponent, playing flexibly yet with strong rhythmic feeling, decorating nimbly and not fussily. **Robert Stankovsky** directs freshly resilient accompaniments; and both artists understand the need for a subtle gradation of light and shade. The digital recording, made in the House of Arts, Košice, is first class, with the piano balanced not too far forward. A fine superbargain alternative.

Angela Hewitt provides refreshingly lightweight performances, both texturally and in their style. Her playing is nimble, crisply articulated and small-scale, and she is perfectly balanced with the accompanying group. It was appropriate to include also the *Fifth Brandenburg Concerto*, and here the *affetuoso* marking for the slow movement is also applied to the central *Adagio* of the *Triple Concerto* (marked *dolce*) which brings a precise delicacy of articulation which is just as engaging. Throughout, the recording is most natural.

(i) Clavier Concerto 1 D min., BWV1052. Partita 2 for violin, BWV 1004: Chaconne (arr. Busoni.); Partita 3 for Violin, BWV 1006: Prelude in E (arr. Rachmaninov). Preludes and fugues from the Well-tempered Clavier: Book 1: 2 & 4; Book 2: 6, 9 & 20 Prelude & Fugue in A minor, BWV 543 (arr. Liszt)

Ⓝ *** DG 477 7978 Hélène Grimaud with (i) Die Deutsche Kammerphilharmonie, Bremen

Hélène Grimaud possesses a fine technique and above all a keen musical intelligence. Her playing compels the listener and gives consistent pleasure. The DG recording has naturalness and presence: we were puzzled to see the orchestral sound in the concerto described as claustrophobic by one critic, though the texture could do with greater transparency.

Oboe Concerto in F (after BWV 1053); Oboe d'amore Concerto in A (after BWV 1055)

ⒷⒷ *** Hyp. Helios CDH 55269. Goodwin, King's Consort, King – TELEMANN: *Oboe Concerto in D min.; Oboe d'amore Concerto in G* (***)

Paul Goodwin's performances are delightful and he is most ably accompanied by the *King's Consort*. The Hyperion recording too is first class; so if you want a single budget disc combining concertos of Bach and Telemann, this will serve admirably.

Oboe Concertos: in F (after BWV 1053); in C (after BWV 1055); in G min. (after BWV 1056 & BWV 156)

ⒷⒷ *** EMI Gemini (ADD) 3 50905-2 (2). De Vries, I Solisti di Zagreb – TELEMANN; VIVALDI: *Oboe Concertos* ***

All three of Bach's memorable slow movements are played very beautifully by **Han de Vries**; indeed, the *Siciliano* of BWV 1053 is exquisite, and is made to sound as if written for the oboe. **I Solisti di Zagreb** provide most stylish accompaniments, and the recording is excellent (with the soloist fairly well forward). Altogether a delectable bargain anthology.

Oboe d'amore Concertos: in D, BWV 1053; in A, BWV 1055; Oboe Concertos: in G min., BWV 1056; in D min., BWV 1059; Double Concerto in C min. for Oboe & Violin, BWV 1060

(BB) **** Naxos 8.554602. Hommel, Cologne CO, Müller-Brühl

Christian Hommel's outstanding performances of concertos for oboe and oboe d'amore, all of them reconstructions of other works, are lively and sensitive; the recording, with the soloist balanced well in front, is excellent. A most enjoyable disc.

Concerto for Oboe d'amore in A, BWV 1055; Double Concerto for Oboe & Violin, BWV 1060; Triple Concerto for Flute, Violin & Harpsichord, BWV 1044

(N) (M) **(*) DG 477 7429 Beznosiuk, Standage, Reichenberg, Pinnock, E. Concert

These reissued recordings date from 1984. The soloists use baroque instruments and there is a suitable matching harpsichord timbre. All the artists play with genuine warmth and plenty of vitality too. Tempi are well judged and there is no want of style. However there would easily have been room for a fourth concerto.

(i) Violin Concertos 1–2; (ii) Double Violin Concerto, BWV 1041–3; (iii) Double Concerto for Violin and Oboe, BWV 1060

☐––☐ ✿ (M) **** Ph. (ADD) 420 700-2. Grumiaux, with (ii) Krebbers, (iii) Holliger; (i–ii) Les Solistes Romandes, Gerecz; (iii) New Philh. O, de Waart

(B) *** Nim. NI 1735 (3). Shumsky, Scottish CO; with (ii) Tunnell; (iii) Miller – MOZART: *Concertos 4 & 5*; YSAŸE: *Sonatas* ***

(N) ** Decca 478 0650 Julia Fischer, ASMF, with (i) Sitkovetsky; (ii) Rubtsov

Arthur Grumiaux is joined in the *Double Concerto* by **Hermann Krebbers**. The result is an outstanding success. The way Grumiaux responds to the challenge of working with another great artist comes over equally clearly in the concerto with oboe, reconstructed from the *Double Harpsichord Concerto in C minor*. Grumiaux's performances of the two solo concertos are equally satisfying.

One has only to sample the simple beauty of **Shumsky's** playing in the *Andante* of the *A minor Violin Concerto* to be won over to his dedicated Bach style, which is not quite as pure as Grumiaux's but is seductive in its simplicity of line and tonal beauty. **John Tunnell** makes highly musical exchanges with him in the *Double Violin Concerto*, and **Robin Miller** is a no less appealing partner in the work for violin and oboe.

Julia Fischer's first recording, after her move to Decca, proves somewhat disappointing. She takes the solo lead impressively enough, and directs the Academy briskly. They play with characteristic finesse and style. As the soloist she is at her finest in her all-but ethereal account of the *Adagio* of the *E major Concerto*, but when she is joined by **Alexander Sikovetsky** in the slow movement of the *Double Violin Concerto*, the result is disappointingly unmemorable. The oboist, **Andrey Rubtsov**, too, could be more inspiring in the *Adagio* of BWV 1060.

(i) Violin Concertos 1–2; (ii) Double Violin Concerto; (iii) Orchestral Suite 4

(B) **(*) DG 449 844-2. (i-ii) D. Oistrakh, RPO, Goossens; (ii) with I. Oistrakh; (iii) Munich Bach O, Richter

David Oistrakh's playing is peerless and can be ranked alongside the Grumiaux versions. In the *Double Concerto* father and son are suitably contrasted in timbre, and the performance of the great slow movement is Elysian. The 1961 recording hardly sounds dated. **Richter's** account of the *Fourth Orchestral Suite* is rhythmically unstylish in the matter of double-dotting but is otherwise alert – less heavy than we had remembered.

(i) Violin Concertos 1–2; (i; ii) Double Violin Concerto. (Unaccompanied) Violin Sonata 1

*** Avie AV 0007. L. St John; (i) New York Bach Ens.; (ii) with S. St John

Lara St John is a first-rate Bach violinist, her playing lithe and full of communicative intensity. Allegros are exhilaratingly fresh, favouring fleet tempi; indeed, some will feel that the outer movements of the *Double Concerto* are too brisk. Yet they set off the simplicity of approach to the beautiful slow movement in which **Scott St John** is an admirable partner. With buoyant, polished accompaniments, this collection is very enjoyable indeed, especially as the unaccompanied *G minor Sonata* is equally rewarding, and the recording throughout real and vivid.

(i–iii) Violin Concertos 1–2; (i; ii; iv) Double Violin Concerto

✿ (M) (***) EMI mono 3 91963-2. *Partita 2: Chaconne*; (i) Menuhin; (ii) O Symphonique de Paris; (iii) cond. Enescu; (iv) with Enescu (violin), cond. Monteux

(N) (BB) (****) Naxos mono 8.111288 Heifetz , LAPO, Wallenstein or RCA Victor CO, Waxman – MOZART: *Violin Concerto 5* (***)

Menuhin's 78-r.p.m. recording of the *Double Concerto*, with **Georges Enescu** his partner (and teacher) and **Monteux** conducting, is legendary for its rapport and simple expressive beauty. It was recorded in Paris in 1932, the same year that Menuhin recorded the Elgar in London. The two solo concertos – with Enescu on the rostrum – followed in 1933 and 1936. They are hardly less remarkable, with a wonderful purity of line and natural expressive feeling. The famous *Partita* is hardly less impressive (see below). In the concertos, the orchestral string-sound is dry, the violins unflattered, but this expert remastering for EMI by Andrew Walter makes the very most of the original 78s.

Heifetz, recorded in 1946, plays with wonderfully pure tone and Elysian phrasing (including the second violin part to the *Double Concerto*). He is well accompanied, especially by Waxman and Mark Obert-Thorn's transfers are remarkably clear and true. The Mozart coupling is pretty good too, and this disc is indispensable.

(i) Double Violin Concerto; (ii) (Unaccompanied) Cello Suite 1 in C: Bourrée I & II

(*) EMI **DVD** 490449-9. (i) D. Oistrakh, Y. Menuhin, RTF CO, Capdevielle; (ii) Rostropovich – MOZART: *Sinfonia concertante*; BRAHMS: *Double Concerto* **(*)**

The *Double Concerto in D minor* was recorded at the Salle Pleyel in October 1958. The two great soloists first played this together at the 1947 'Prague Spring', and their Paris account affords an admirable opportunity for contrasting the golden tone of the one with the (on this occasion) seraphic playing of the other. Of course the sound calls for some tolerance, but this film is a rarity and is to be treasured. **Rostropovich**, playing with enormous intensity the *Bourrées* from the *Third Suite for Solo Cello*, recorded in December 1962, is a welcome bonus.

Double Violin Concerto in D min., BWV 1043

(M) *** RCA **SACD** (ADD) 88697 04605-2. Heifetz, Friedman, London New SO, Sargent – BRAHMS: *Double Concerto*; MOZART: *Sinfonia concertante, K.364* ***

It is good to have **Heifetz's** 1961 stereo recording of the *Double Concerto* as a worthy successor to Menuhin's two versions. **Sargent's** tempi in the outer movements are brisk but are none the worse for that, and the Elysian dialogue of the slow movement, with Heifetz's pupil **Erick Friedman** a natural partner, is hardly less inspired and much better recorded. Indeed the new SACD transfer gives much greater body to the sound.

A Musical Offering, BWV 1079 – see also above, under Art of Fugue, and below under Chamber Music

(BB) **(*)** Naxos 8.553286. Capella Istropolitana, Benda

Christian Benda uses a small chamber orchestra. Strings alone, with a minimum of vibrato, play the framing *Ricercars*. The first group of canons add in flute, oboe and bassoon; in the second group, the stringed instruments predominate. A harpsichord joins in the first, and the cor anglais and bassoon dolorously share the last (common) solution of the four offered alternative proposals for solving Bach's so-called 'puzzle canon'. The recording is excellent, clear yet with a pleasing bloom, and the result, if a little didactic at times, is undoubtedly fresh.

Orchestral Suites 1–4, BWV 1066–9

(**) ** Telarc CD 80619. Boston Bar., Pearlman

(**) ** BIS **SACD** 1431 (Surround Sound/Compatible) (2). Japan Bach Coll., Suzuki

A splendid period-instrument recording of the *Orchestral Suites* from the excellent **Boston Baroque** under **Martin Pearlman**. All four fit on to a single CD, yet speeds are well judged and lively but not pressed too hard (with stylish flute-playing from **Christopher Krueger**) making a sprightly end to the programme. They are given first-class Telarc recording.

Like Pearlman in Boston before him, **Suzuki** alters the order of the *Suites*, only he elects to begin with the favourite *Third Suite in D*. The second (included at no extra cost) is reserved for the *Fourth Suite*. Above all, these are exhilarating performances, for some of **Suzuki's** tempi are very fast, especially in the allegros of the *Overtures*. But the famous *Air* of the *Third Suite* could not be more restrained and noble in feeling. The recording is spectacularly realistic, especially in surround sound, which adds attractively to the ambient effect and gives a remarkable feeling of presence.

Orchestral Suites 2–3; Sinfonias to Cantatas 12 & 31. Cantatas (i–iii) 45; (ii–vi) 67; (ii; v; vi) 101 (excerpts); (i–iii) 105; (ii–vi) 130

(N) **(*)** Australian Decca Eloquence (ADD) 480 0027 (2) OSR, Ansermet with (i) Giebel; Partridge; (ii) Watts; (iii) Krause; (iv) Krenn; (v) Amelingl (vi) Choeur Pro Arte de Lausanne

Ansermet's surprisingly warm-hearted way with Bach, offers much to enjoy in this two-disc survey of his complete recordings of this repertoire for Decca. The richness of the strings in the orchestral suites does not swamp the contrapuntal writing, and the allegros of the *Overtures* of the *Suites* 2 & 3 are lively and well articulated. The playing is really rather good (**André Pepin** is the stylish soloist in the famous *Badinerie* of *Suite No. 2*). However, the cantatas are perhaps the best thing here, largely on account of the superb quality of the singers – **Elly Ameling**, **Helen Watts**, **Werner Krenn**, **Tom Krause** and **Ian Partridge**, to name some of them. The opening of BWV 130, *Herr Gott, dich loben wir* is lusty and has a real sense of purpose, and in the baritone aria (the superb Tom Krause) *Der alte Drache brennt vor Neid*, the vivid timpani and brass are very tellingly recorded. André Pepin makes another stylish appearance in this cantata. *Cantatas Nos. 45, 67, 105* and excerpts from 101 are included (all music with much beauty), along with the *Sinfonias* to *Nos. 12 & 31* (an especially bright, vigorous piece). The 1960s sound is beautifully warm and rich throughout and, as always in these Australian Eloquence releases, real care has been taken over the quality of the transfers.

CHAMBER & INSTRUMENTAL MUSIC

The Art of Fugue, BWV 1080

(**) * Hyp. CDA 67138. Delmé Qt

As the tessitura lies too low to perform *The Art of Fugue* in D minor, Simpson has transposed the whole sequence into G minor. Incidentally, he includes Tovey's completion of *Contrapunctus XIV*, although the listener can play it without the conjectural ending if preferred. The **Delmé Quartet**, who have recorded ten of Simpson's own quartets, play with great dedication. Excellent recording. This outclasses other string quartet versions.

(Unaccompanied) *Cello Suites 1–6, BWV 1007–12* (DVD Versions)

🔓 ❁ **** EMI **DVD** DVA 5 99159 9. Rostropovich

🔓 ❁ *** Arthaus **DVD** & CD 101419 (4). Wen-Sinn Yang (V/D: Ruth Käch)

Rostropovich was filmed recording the six Bach *Cello Suites* in 1991 in the Basilique Sainte-Madeleine, Vézelay, Yonne, France, a venue he chose for the comparative severity of its interior architecture, which, he felt, created the right back-cloth for the music. He introduces the whole project by telling us about his own approach to the interpretation of these masterpieces, with which he has lived all his life. Of course, one can choose to hear the music without the commentaries. The performances hardly need recommendation from us: they are totally compelling and are truthfully recorded.

Like Rostropovich, the Burmese cellist **Wen-Sinn Yang** has carefully chosen the venue for his recording, in this case the intimate atmosphere of the small Romanesque Church of St Servatius, high up in the Bavarian Alps, and its warm acoustic proves perfect for his recording. Also like Rostropovich, Yang introduces and concludes each of the six *Suites* (in German, but with surtitles) with his own perceptive comments on Bach and his music, its performance, colouring and expressive feeling. These comments are of course optional, but in any case excellent CD recordings of all six works are included as a bonus for alternative performance to the visual versions. So one has the best of both worlds. Yang's performances are superb, obviously deeply felt and full of subtlety in their phrasing, both in their control of light and shade as well as in their bowing.

(Unaccompanied) *Cello Suites 1–6, BWV 1007–12*

🔓 ❁ Ⓜ **** EMI 5 18158-2 (2). Rostropovich

🔓 **** Virgin 5 45650-2. Truls Mørk

🔓 **** Hyp. CDA 67541/2 (2). Steven Isserlis (with alternative versions of Prelude from Suite 1 & The Song of the Birds)

Ⓝ Ⓑ *** CfP 2 28358-2 (2) Tortelier

Rostropovich verbally characterizes each one of the series: 'No. 1, lightness; No. 2, sorrow and intensity; No. 3, brilliance; No. 4, majesty and opacity; No. 5, darkness; and No. 6, sunlight'. True to his word, more than usual he draws distinctions between each, also reflecting the point that the structure of each suite grows in complexity. The results are both moving and strong, with the sound of the cello, as recorded in a warm acoustic, full and powerful, making one hear the music afresh, with *pianissimo* repeats magically achieved.

Not only does the Norwegian cellist **Truls Mørk** possess a fine sense of line and a wonderfully rich and expressive tone, but he has imagination too, and a feeling for character. In short, fine fingers at the service of a fine mind. Readers will find these as musically satisfying as any rival accounts now before the public, and we are inclined to rank this newcomer second to none.

Like Rostropovich, **Steven Isserlis** characterizes each of the six *Cello Suites* very personally, although for him they are 'Mystery Suites' linked to the life of Jesus. He suggests his own subtitles: 1 (Joyful Mystery: The Nativity); 2 (Sorrowful Mystery: The Agony in the Garden); 3 (Glorious Mystery: The Descent of the Holy Spirit); 4 (Joyful Mystery: The Procession in the Temple); 5 (Sorrowful Mystery; The Crucifixion); 6 (Glorious Mystery: The Resurrection). Yet although the playing is permeated with deep inner feeling, there is no sense of overflowing intensity, simply a spontaneous flow of music: this is simply great cello playing. The recording is very real and natural and this set understandably won the 2007 *Gramophone* Instrumental Award.

Heinrich Schiff is straighter but no less concentrated in feeling. Strong and positive, producing a consistent flow of beautiful tone at whatever dynamic level, he here establishes his individual artistry very clearly, his rhythmic pointing a delight. He is treated to an excellent recording, with the cello given fine bloom against a warm but intimate acoustic. This is now an outstanding bargain as a double. (EMI Gemini 5 86534-2)

Playing on a Stradivarius cello of 1693, **Maria Kliegel** gives deeply satisfying performances of these formidable works. With her flawless intonation and well-judged choice of tempi, her intense concentration and direct approach have one enjoying the music without distraction from personal mannerism, with the dark intensity of the *Sarabandes* consistently brought out. She is beautifully recorded in Budapest. (Naxos 8 557280/81)

Fournier's richly phrased and warm-toned performances carry an impressive musical conviction. He can be profound and he can lift rhythms infectiously in dance movements, but above all he conveys the feeling that this is music to be enjoyed. This recording has been remastered splendidly and now has even greater presence and realism. (DG 477 6724)

Recorded in the reverberant acoustic of the Temple Church in London, **Tortelier's** 1983 performances present clear contrasts with his set of twenty years earlier. His approach remains broadly romantic, but this time the rhythms are steadier, the command greater, and the preludes of each suite strongly characterised to ensnare the attention even in simple chattering passagework. Some will prefer a drier acoustic than this, but the digital sound is very truthful.

Flute Sonatas 1–6, BWV 1030–5

🔓 ⒷⒷ **** ASV Resonance CD RSN 3008. Bennett, Malcolm (harpsichord), M. Evans

Flute Sonatas 1–6; in G min., BWV 1020

**** Glossa GCD 920807 (2). *Sonata in C min.* (from BWV 1079); Hazelzet, Ogg (harpsichord & fortepiano), ter Linden (cello)

Flute Sonatas 1–6; in G min.; Partita in A min., BWV 1013

Ⓜ *** CRD (ADD) 3314/5 (2). Preston, Pinnock, Savall

Flute Sonatas 1–6, BWV 1030–5; in G min; Partita in A min., BWV 1013

(N)******** Nimbus NI 5829/30 Schmeiser, Müller, Rainer (with Partita in C minor, BWV 997)

William Bennett uses a modern flute, and in the first three sonatas he and **George Malcolm** manage without the nicety of using a viola da gamba in the continuo. In *Sonatas Nos. 4–6* the two players are joined by **Michael Evans**, and the bass is subtly but tangibly reinforced and filled out, though the balance remains just as impressive. The playing, as might be expected of these artists, has superb character: it is strong in personality yet does not lack finesse. Bennett himself has made the reconstruction of the first movement of BWV 1032.

Hansgeorg Schmeiser plays the two solo *Partitas* with much felicity, and his flute dominates the six sonatas too, partly because the Nimbus recording is comparatively resonant. Even so the ensemble is well integrated and well balanced, yet with clear detail. The *C minor Partita*, BWV 997 is probably authentic and makes an additional bonus, so this excellent new set now goes to the top of the list of recommendations, even if the ASV Resonance disc still remains a tempting best buy.

William Hazelzet plays with a gentle authority and sensitivity and a delicacy of articulation that are altogether most persuasive. He uses two different period instruments, with a subtle difference of colour. **Jacques Ogg**, his sympathetic partner, uses a modern harpsichord based on models of Couchet, Blanchet and Taskin for the majority of the sonatas, but an attractively bright but shallow fortepiano after Silbermann for BWV 1031, 1035 and 1079. **Jaap ter Linden** adds the cello continuo on BWV 1021 and 1033–5. The balance is expertly judged and, with excellent documentation, this must now take pride of place among period performances of this repertoire.

Using an authentic one-key instrument, **Stephen Preston** plays with a rare delicacy. Throughout, the continuo playing, led by **Trevor Pinnock**, is of the highest standard and this is an excellent alternative mid-price choice. This set now comes handsomely repackaged in a box.

Music for lute-harpsichord

Suites 1–2, BWV 996; 7 Prelude, Fugue and Allegro in E flat, BWV 998; Prelude in C min., BWV 999; Fugue in G min., BWV 100; Sarabanda con partite, BWV 990; Suite in E, BWV 1006a (transcription of BWV 1006); Sonata in D min., BWV 964 (transcription of BWV 1003)

(N) (BB) ******* Naxos 8.570470/1 (2) Elizabeth Farr (Lauten Werk)

Bach's effects as listed in his posthumous estate included a pair of Lautenwerk (lute-harpsichords). But they were not saved and the instrument is now obsolete. We know that it had one, two or three keyboards, used gut strings plucked simultaneously by several jacks and quills, and reputedly possessed an uncannily effective lute stop. So the present single-manual instrument, ingeniously built by Keith Hill in Manchester, Michigan had to be reconstructed conjecturally from drawings. The result is very impressive, the sound rather like a large-scale harpsichord only with a distinct impression of sonorous plucking, with the warm acoustic giving the sound plenty of colour.

Elizabeth Farr has obviously achieved complete mastery of this instrument and all these works project impressively and have pleasing life and spontaneity. We know the *Suites* in their guitar versions, but the *Sarabanda con partite* is especially worth having. All the music is vintage Bach and this unusual and intriguing presentation can be cordially recommended.

Lute Suites (arranged for guitar) 1–4, BWV 995–7; 1006a

⊶ (M) ******* Sony 696998 996427. Williams (guitar)

⊶ (B) ******* Oehms OC 202. Fernández (guitar)

John Williams shows a natural response to Bach, and his performances of the four *Lute Suites* are among his finest records. The flair of his playing, with its rhythmic vitality and sense of colour, is always telling.

Eduardo Fernández now joins Williams in offering all four *Lute Suites* on a single disc – and very fine they are too. His flexible rubato in the *Sarabandes* has a thoughtful intensity that is very telling, yet he plays the livelier dances with spirit. His technique has an easy facility, and this is first-class Bach playing in every sense, while the recording cannot be faulted. A most enjoyable disc, and at budget price too.

Oboe Sonatas: in G min., BWV 1020 & BWV 1030b; in E flat, BWV 1031; in C, BWV 1033. (Organ) Trio Sonata in C, BWV 529; Well-Tempered Clavier Book II; Prelude & Fugue in C min., BWV 871

*** Signum SIGCD 034. Hennessy, Parle (harpsichord)

Never mind that these works were not conceived by Bach with the oboe in mind; they sound quite delightful on **Gail Hennessy's** baroque instrument. Her tone is as pleasing as her playing is stylish; whether in the *Siciliana* of BWV 1031 or the searching *Adagio* of BWV 1033, she provides expressive playing of a high order. She has a fine partner in **Nicholas Parle**.

Viola da gamba Sonatas 1–3, BWV 1027–9

⊶ (M) ******* Alia Vox AV 9812 (with Sonata in C, BWV 529). Savall, Koopman

(i) Viola da gamba Sonatas 1–3. Preludes & Fugues: in D, BWV 850; in G, BWV 860; in G min., BWV 861

*** Signum SIGCD 024. (i) Crum (viola da gamba); Cummings (harpsichord)

Jordi Savall and **Ton Koopman's** new set completely supersedes their earlier performance on Virgin. There is a depth of expressive feeling here combined with an intimate rapport between the two players that gives an effect of eavesdropping on live music-making of the highest calibre. The recording is resonant but full, firm and cleanly focused. A clear first choice.

A fine alternative set comes from **Alison Crum** and **Laurence Cummings**. Here the harpsichord is very much in the picture, boldly played, with plenty of life and vigour, by Cummings. But Crum's firmly focused gamba is never eclipsed. Moreover, Cummings offers sparkling performances of three keyboard *Preludes and Fugues* as a bonus.

Viola da gamba Sonatas 1–3, BWV 1027–9 (cello versions)

*** Orfeo C693071A. Müller-Schott (cello), Hewitt (piano) (with C. P. E. BACH: Viola da gamba Sonata, H.559 ***)

To play these sonatas on cello and piano is to create a wholly different sound-world. The result, as with Angela Hewitt's keyboard recordings of Bach, is very stimulating indeed. Many will be convinced by these splendidly alive performances, which bring the three sonatas vividly to life. But we still have a soft spot for Jordi Savall's fine versions of the original works. The C. P. E. Bach coupling makes a pleasing bonus.

Viola da gamba Sonatas 1–3 (arr. for Viola); Sonatas: in G min. (arr. from BWV 1020); in F (arr. from BWV 1022)

(M) *** Praga 350 016. Suk (viola), Ruičová (harpsichord)

Josef Suk follows the example of Lionel Tertis and Kim Kashkashian in recording Bach's *Viola da gamba Sonatas* very successfully on a period viola. His timbre has plenty of edge and character and, with his sympathetic partner, the result is very stimulating indeed, as it is in the transcriptions of BWV 1020 (originally for flute) and BWV 1022 (originally for the violin). Excellently balanced recording.

Violin Sonatas and Partitas

(Unaccompanied) Violin Sonatas 1–3, BWV 1001, 1003 & 1005; Violin Partitas 1–3, BWV 1002, 1004 & 1006

⏺─ ❀ (M) **** EMI 4 76808-2 [4 76811-2] (2). Perlman

⏺─ (M) **** DG (ADD) 457 701-2 (2). Milstein

(M) *** Ph. (ADD) 438 736-2 (2) Grumiaux

(N) (BB) *** Naxos 8.570277/8 Kaler

(N) (B) (***) IDIS mono 6535-36 Heifetz

Perlman's inspired survey, dating from 1986/7, has long been a top recommendation for the solo *Sonatas* and *Partitas*. Here he triumphantly demonstrates his insight in bringing out the deepest qualities of these six searching masterpieces, and this reissue is fully worthy of being included among EMI's 'Great Recordings of the Century'.

Milstein's set from the mid-1970s remains among the most satisfying of all versions. Every phrase is beautifully shaped, there is a highly developed feeling for line, and these performances have an aristocratic poise and a classical finesse which are very satisfying.

Arthur Grumiaux's fine performances were recorded in Berlin in 1960/1. Now they return at mid-price and with the recording remastered. The venue offers a pleasingly warm background ambience against which the violin is forward, recorded in strong profile with complete realism, and with no microphonic exaggeration of the upper partials.

Ilya Kaler's Bach survey does not disappoint. His timbre is full, yet without romantic overtones, his sometimes dazzling virtuosity is put completely at Bach's service and his lyrical style is refreshingly free from idiosyncrasy, yet alive in every bar. The *Chaconne* of BWV 1004 is impressively structured, but the dance movements are also very appealing. The Naxos recording is remarkably live and real: he might be standing out there beyond the speakers.

Heifetz is in a class of his own and his compelling accounts of the solo Bach canon set standards that in terms of technical execution have never been surpassed. This is playing of consummate artistry and tremendous personality. We would not want to be without Grumiaux or Milstein in this repertoire but Heifetz is still immaculate.

Julia Fischer plays with immaculate purity and clarity, bringing out the separate strands in the *Fugues* of the sonatas, and never forcing her tone. Though her tone is refined rather than weighty, she plays the great *Chaconne* of the *D minor Partita* with power and concentration, with big contrasts between sections. Her set includes an additional DVD-compatible track, containing an artist interview and session impression. (Pentatone **SACD** PTC J 186 072)

Violin Sonatas (for violin & harpsichord) 1–6, BWV 1014–19

(BB) *** Naxos 8.554614 (1–4); 8.554783 (5–6 & alternative movements for BWV 1019). Van Dael, Van Asperen

(N) **(*) Sony 8697112432 (2) Zimmermann, Pace (piano)

Violin Sonatas 1–6; BWV 1019a; Sonatas for Violin & Continuo, BWV 1020–24

⏺─ ❀ (B) **** Ph. (ADD) Duo 454 011-2 (2). Grumiaux, Jaccottet, Mermoud (in BWV 1021 & 1023)

The Bach *Sonatas for Violin and Harpsichord* and for *Violin and Continuo* are marvellously played, with all the beauty of tone and line for which **Grumiaux** is renowned; they have great vitality, too. His admirable partner is **Christiane Jaccottet**, and in BWV 1021 and 1023 **Philippe Mermoud** (cello) joins the continuo. There is endless treasure to be discovered here, particularly when the music-making is so serenely communicative.

A fine new period-instrument version from **Van Dael** and **Van Asperen** on Naxos goes to the top of the list. It is beautifully played and recorded, and the violinist has a positive relationship with her distinguished keyboard partner. The set gives very great pleasure and satisfaction and includes four alternative movements for BWV 1019.

Zimmermann plays these sonatas beautifully. But he made a mistake in choosing a piano partnership (with **Enrico Pace**). Even though in many ways these works are enjoyable listening, and slow movements are pleasingly expressive using the modern instrument, the many keyboard running passages in outer movements make a far more convincing effect on the harpsichord.

KEYBOARD MUSIC

Bach Performances on the Piano by Angela Hewitt Including: *Chromatic Fantasia & Fugue, BWV 903; Italian Concerto, BWV 971; Partita 4 in D, BWV 828*

⊕— **** Hyp. **DVD** DVDA 68001 (with Daniel Müller-Schott, cello) (Director: Uli Aumüller)

This is a self-recommending DVD in which **Angela Hewitt** first explains why she is drawn to play Bach on the modern piano and then gives an illustrated, all-embracing six-part lecture on *Essentials* (Phrasing; Singing Tone, etc.); *Interpretation* (Tempo, Dynamics, etc.); *The Dance in Bach*; *Learning a Fugue*; *Ornamentation*; and *Practical Advice*. She is then seen and heard playing the live recital above which is very rewarding in itself. The recorded quality is excellent and so is the camerawork, except for one repeated shot where she is reflected in the keyboard lid! She is a communicative artist and this comes over impressively on this DVD.

The Art of Fugue

ⒷⒷ *** Naxos 8.557796. Guillot (harpsichord)

*** Häns. CD 92.134 (2). Hill (harpsichord)

The Naxos harpsichord version from **Sébastien Guillot** is in every way attractive. His instrument, by Jonte Knüf of Helsinki (after German models), is most pleasingly recorded and Guillot presents Bach's masterly survey simply but not didactically: the result is very satisfying. Moreover the Naxos documentation by Pierre Bachmann and Keith Anderson is excellent. Why pay more?

   Robert Hill lays out Bach's fugal progression in front of the listener with admirable clarity and concern for the contrapuntal detail, and he varies tempi with excellent judgement to keep the music continually alive. In the *Duet Fugue* he is joined by **Michael Behringer**. As an appendix he offers four contrapuncti and the *Augmented Canon in Contrary Motion* from Bach's early draft (BWV 1080a). The harpsichord itself has a fine, strong personality and is recorded in a warm acoustic which yet never blurs the interplay of the part-writing.

The Art of Fugue, BWV 1080; Canons 1–4; Chromatic Fantasia and Fugue, BWV 903; Fantasia in A min., BWV 922; etc.

*** Lyrichord LEMS 8048 (2). Troeger (clavichord)

There is no reason why *The Art of Fugue* should not be played on the clavichord, and **Richard Troeger** here offers its début on this relatively intimate instrument. It works well, and he provides enough variety of tempi and colour to keep the listener's attention. Moreover, he has decided to complete the final fugue himself, very simply and logically, in a passage of 40 bars, which is perhaps better than being left hanging in mid-air! He adds the four *Canons* at the beginning of the second disc and follows with brilliant performances of the *Chromatic Fantasia and Fugue* and *A minor Fantasia*, used to frame his transcription of the *Violin Partita*, all of which sound very different from harpsichord or piano perform-

ances, and engagingly so. The recording is truthful and the discs come with excellent documentation.

Capriccio on the Departure of a Beloved Brother, BWV 992; Fantasias, BWV 906 & 919; Goldberg Variations, BWV 988; 2-Part Inventions and 3-Part Inventions etc.; The Well-Tempered Clavier, Books I & II, BWV 846–93

Ⓑ (***) RCA mono 82876 67891-2 (7). Wanda Landowska (harpsichord)

Wanda Landowska (in 1933) not only discovered and reintroduced Bach's complete *Goldberg Variations* to the European musical public, but soon afterwards she made its first recording. These are later recordings, made between 1945 and 1959. She favours a large, two-manual Pleyel harpsichord built especially for her, and at times she gives it a grand presence, but for the most part her playing is quite contained and is often expressive. At other times her virtuosity is very compelling. She is not only convincing but she leads the ear forward most spontaneously. *The Well-Tempered Clavier* was recorded over a period (between 1949 and 1954) and still sounds marvellous. Her playing has a colour, vitality, authority and grandeur that make it difficult for one to stop listening, and the CD transfers are very well managed.

Concertos (for solo harpsichord) after Vivaldi Violin Concertos: 1 (after Op.3/9); 2 (after Op. 7/2); 4 (after Op.4/6); 5 (after Op. 3/12); 7 (after Op.3/3), 9 (after Op. 4/1), BWV 972-3, 975-6, 978 & 980; Italian Concerto, BWV 971

Ⓝ ⒷⒷ **** Warner Apex 2564 69325-4 Olivier Baumont (harpsichord)

We are used to hearing Bach's Vivaldi transcriptions on the organ, but they were intended for either a harpsichord or possibly an organ without pedals. In **Olivier Baumont's** hands they sound splendid on the harpsichord, full of vitality and vividly coloured. Baumont plays a modern French copy of a German harpsichord 'from the school of Silbermann' of 1735 and it has a particularly effective range of dynamic. He produces some splendidly dramatic staccato effects in the slow movement of *Op.4/6*. The *Italian Concerto* is offered as an encore and how eloquently Baumont plays the slow movement. This collection is very enjoyable indeed.

Chromatic Fantasia and Fugue in D min., BWV 903; Chorale Preludes, BWV 639; BWV 659 (both arr. Busoni); Fantasia in A min., BWV 922; Fantasia & Fugue in A min., BWV 922; Italian Concerto

⊕— Ⓜ *** Ph. (ADD) 475 7760. Brendel (piano)

Brendel's fine Bach recital originally appeared in 1978. The performances are of the old school, with no attempt made to strive after harpsichord effects and with every piece creating a sound-world of its own. The *Italian Concerto* is particularly imposing, with a finely sustained sense of line and beautifully articulated rhythm. The original analogue recording was in every way truthful, and it sounds admirably present in this new CD remastering for Universal's extended series of Originals.

Chromatic Fantasia & Fugue; 4 Duets, BWV 802–5; Italian Concerto; Goldberg Variations; Partitas 1–6; in B min., BWV 831

🔑 ☀ (B) **** Decca 475 7079 (4). Rousset (harpsichord)

Christophe Rousset's playing combines the selfless authority and scholarly dedication of such artists as Leonhardt and Gilbert with the flair of younger players. He plays a 1751 Hemsch, which is superbly recorded within a generous but not too resonant acoustic, so that the harpsichord is very real and apparent. On their original issue we placed the *Goldberg Variations* and the *Partitas* at the top of the list, and the playing has great freshness and spontaneity. The *Partitas*, too, have complete naturalness and are obviously, like the *Goldberg*, the product of a vital imagination.

Chromatic Fantasia and Fugue; English Suite 2; French Suite 5; Italian Concerto; Partita 4 in D; 15 2-Part Inventions, BWV 772/786; The Well-Tempered Clavier, Book 1: Preludes and Fugues 1–2, 5–6, 14 & 17; Book 2: Preludes and Fugues 1, 3, 7, 12 & 24

🔑 (B) *** Decca 475 193-2 (2). András Schiff

This compilation of **András Schiff's** Bach recordings makes an ideal introduction to his way with this composer: the playing has freshness and individuality, and his sparkling ornamentation is always winning. The *Preludes and Fugues* are translated into pianistic terms, rarely if ever imitating the harpsichord, yet one is soon won over. Try the *Gavotte* in the *Fifth Suite* for rhythmic lift or the slow movement of the *Italian Concerto* to experience his sustained line at its most beautiful. Superb recordings, and inexpensive to buy.

4 Duets, BWV 802–5; English Suite 6 in D min., BWV 811; Italian Concerto, BWV 971; Toccata in C min., BWV 911

*** Australian DG Eloquence 442 9446. Hewitt (piano)

This was **Angela Hewitt's** début recording, following her winning the 1985 International Bach Competition in Toronto. It is a splendid vindication of the wisdom of the judges' decision. In both the *Italian Concerto* and the *English Suite* her playing is enormously alive and stimulating. Textures are clean, with every strand in perfect focus and every phrase clearly articulated. She plays with vital imaginative resource, totally free from idiosyncrasy and affectation. These are exhilarating performances. The piano is beautifully captured on this recording, and thanks must be given to Australian Universal Records for restoring it to circulation.

English Suites 1–6, BWV 806–11

(N) 🔑 **** Sony 88697310502 (2) Perahia (piano)

🔑 **** Hyp. **SACD:** SACDA 67451/2; CD: CDA 67451/2. Hewitt (piano)

(N) *** Italian Universal Decca 476 3127 (2) Andrea Bacchetti (Piano)

The two discs of **Murray Perahia's** *English Suites* (recorded separately, a year apart) now come together, to make a clear primary recommendation, although both Angela Hewitt and Bacchetti are strong competitors. But in Perahia's hands the forward flow is a living thing in itself, and the listener is always made conscious of the richness of the underlying harmony, especially in the *Sarabandes* which are played very beautifully indeed. The lighter dance movements have a refreshing lightness of articulation, with the decoration made to seem integral. The recording is excellent.

The opening *Preludes* (which **Angela Hewitt** relishes) show Bach at his most imaginative and exploratory. But it is in the *Sarabandes* that she finds a depth of feeling and richness of colour that is possible only on the piano, while the exuberant closing *Gigues* (sample that for No. 4) are sparklingly buoyant and spirited. The recording on CD is first class; we see no reason to prefer the SACD.

The Italian pianist, **Andrea Bacchetti** is a comparatively new name to us but he has already given us an outstanding DVD of the *Goldberg Variations*, and is a very impressive exponent of this repertoire. His set of the *Italian Suites* is very appealing, and can be spoken of alongside that of Perahia. His lyrical flow is most winning, his range of dynamic beautifully modulated, and the dance movements, neatly articulated, are full of character. He plays a Faziola piano, perfectly suited to the music, and is recorded with perfect realism and naturalness in the Fazioli Concert Hall, Sacile.

English Suites 1–6; French Suites 1–6

(BB) *** Warner Apex (ADD) 0927 40808–2 (1–2); 09027 40814–2 (3–4); 09027 40813–2 (5–6) (available separately). Curtis (harpsichord)

Anyone wanting both the *English* and *French Suites* together at a modest cost, played on a fine period harpsichord, will find **Alan Curtis's** Teldec set excellent value. Curtis uses a harpsichord made by Christian Zell of Hamburg in 1928. The sound is resonant, but pleasingly so, and the full-bodied character of the sound suits Curtis's lively, comparatively robust approach. His playing is both thoughtful and spontaneous.

English Suites 1–6; Partitas 1–6

(BB) *** Virgin 5 62379-2 (4). Leonhardt (harpsichord)

Leonhardt's playing here has a flair and vitality that one does not always associate with him. His set now comes coupled with the six *Partitas*. In terms of sheer sound these are among the most satisfactory versions available, and in terms of style they combine elegance, spontaneity and authority. In many respects this too is musically among the most satisfying of current harpsichord sets, save for the fact that Leonhardt observes no repeats.

English Suite 2 in A min.; Prelude in G, BWV 902

(**(*)) BBC Legends mono BBCL 4201-2. Hess – HAYDN: *Sonata 62 in G min.* (**); SCHUMANN: *Carnaval* (***)

Dame Myra Hess's gift for making contrapuntal lines sing lyrically is wonderfully illustrated in these BBC recordings, made in 1956, with textures beautifully clarified. Her incisiveness in fast music is also most persuasive. A good coupling with her Schumann party-piece and her very last recording of Haydn, in acceptable mono sound.

French Suites 1–6, BWV 812–17

♫ **** Ambroisie AMB 9942 (2). Rousset (harpsichord)

♫ **** Nim. NI 5744/5. Roberts (piano)

The comparison between the performances by the extrovert **Christophe Rousset** (handsomely packaged) and the comparatively laid-back **Bernard Roberts** is a fascinating one. Rousset chooses a large-scale Ruckers, restored in 1787. He plays the dance movements with real gusto – they are usually faster than with Roberts, who is by no means lacking in impetus, yet the tempi of the *Allemandes* and *Sarabandes* are slightly more relaxed in Rousset's hands. That is not to say that Roberts is not wonderfully cool; his slow movements are sensitive and gentle, and you have only to try the famous *Gavotte* in the *Fifth Suite* to revel in his spirited elegance. Both are spendidly recorded, so if you like exuberance (and a harpsichord) go for Rousset; if you have already discovered the natural grace and refinement which Roberts brings to Bach on the piano, without any loss of underlying vitality, he is your man.

French Suites 1–6 (including 3 additional movements); 18 Little Preludes, BWV 924–8; 930; 933–43; 999; Prelude & Fugue in A min., BWV 894; Sonata in D min., BWV 964

♫ *** Hyp. CDA 67121/2. Hewitt (piano)

French Suites 1–6; Italian Concerto; Partita in B min., BWV 831

*** Decca 433 313–2 (2). Schiff (piano)

French Suites 1–6; Suites in A min., BWV 818a; in E flat, BWV 819a

(B) *** Double Decca 466 736–2 (2). Hogwood (harpsichord) (with *Allemande*, BWV 819a)

Hogwood coaxes superb sounds from his pair of harpsichords: his playing is expressive, and the relentless sense of onward momentum that disfigures so many harpsichordists is pleasingly absent. These performances have both style and character and can be recommended with some enthusiasm.

Angela Hewitt's playing is informed by an intelligence and musicianship that are refreshing. Whether in the *Preludes*, written for Wilhelm Friedemann, or the suites themselves, she displays an imaginative vitality of a high order. The recorded sound is very natural.

András Schiff gives highly rewarding performances of just Nos. 1–6, his expressive style entirely without personal indulgence, his freedom in slow movements seemingly improvisatory and spontaneous, and his faster dance-movements an unqualified delight. The *Partita in B minor* is slightly more severe in style than the rest of the programme. As with the rest of his series, the Decca recording is appealingly realistic and an ideal acoustic has been chosen.

French Suite 4 in E flat, BWV 815; Ricercare a 3

*** Orfeo C612031. Nikolaieva (with SHOSTAKOVICH: *4 Preludes and fugues, Op. 87*) – BEETHOVEN: *Piano Sonatas 25 & 32* ***

An Austrian Radio recording from the 1987 Salzburg Festival by **Tatiana Nikolaieva**, for whom Shostakovich wrote his *Preludes and fugues*, Op. 87. Listening to this, one realizes why this Bach playing made so strong an impression. Nikolaieva was a great pianist and her appearances in the West were far too few.

Goldberg Variations, BWV988 (DVD Version)

(N) *** Arthaus Musik **DVD** (plus CD) 101 447 Bacchetti

Andrea Bacchetti performs the *Goldberg Variations* in the handsome Villa Trissino Marzotto, Trissino, Vincenza in 2006 and offers a ten-minute introduction to them, albeit not particularly revealing, as well as much more perceptive notes. The performance itself is satisfyingly musical, with fine tonal shading and an effortless technique. Very good camera work which never detracts attention from the music. The set also includes a CD of another, later performance recorded at the Teatro Chiabrera, Savona in 2007. Very recommendable.

Goldberg Variations, BWV 988 (CD Versions)

♫ **** Hyp. CDA 67305. Hewitt (piano)

♫ ✹ **** VAI (ADD) VAIA 1029. Tureck (piano)

♫ **** Sony 696998924321. Perahia (piano)

♫ (M) *** Decca 475 7508. A. Schiff (piano)

(N) (M) *** EMI 2 19578-2 Lim (with *chaconne*, arr. Busoni)

(M) ** Sony mono 074645259420 (1955 recording). Gould (piano)

(BB) (**(*)) Naxos 8.111247. Gould (piano) (with *Partita 5 in G*)

Angela Hewitt's performance is totally pianistic, involving the widest range of dynamic contrast, variety of touch and colour. It is imbued with what she calls 'the joyous tone that is characteristic of so much of this work'. She rightly regards the 'black pearl' Variation 25 as 'the greatest of all' and fully reveals its gentle, celestial beauty. After the bold *Quodlibet*, the return of the *Aria* on a magical half-tone reminds one of Tureck – and there can be no higher praise. The Hyperion recording is first class in every way.

Rosalyn Tureck's recording is very special indeed – there is no other record of Bach played on the piano quite as compelling as this, and for I. M. it would be a desert island disc.

Murray Perahia's set is even more personalized than Rosalyn Tureck's VAI version, essentially thoughtful and intimate, often introvert, even ruminative, but with moments of high drama. Some might prefer a more direct, less individualized approach, but Perahia's involvement and dedication are present in every bar of Bach's music, with continual contrasts of pianistic colour and dynamic, yet always with superbly clean articulation. The piano recording is wonderfully true and natural.

It is good to see **András Schiff's** earlier, Decca piano recording returning in the same Universal series of Originals. It can receive enthusiatic advocacy, and in some respects is preferable to his later, premium-priced version on ECM, for the Decca digital recording is excellent in every way, clean and realistic, so that the part-writing emerges with splendid definition and subtlety. Schiff does not play as if he is performing a holy ritual, but with a keen sense of enjoyment of the piano's colour and sonority.

Dong Hyek Lim made a strong impression with his début recital last year and enhances it with this thoughtful and imaginative reading of the *Goldberg*. He has a masterly technique and a fine musical head. The Busoni arrangement of the *D minor Chaconne* is also rather special.

Gould's famous (1955) mono recording enjoyed cult status in its day, and its return will occasion rejoicing among his admirers. He observes no repeats and in terms of sheer keyboard wizardry commands admiration, even if you do not respond to the results. There is too much that is wilful and eccentric for this to be a straightforward recommendation, but it is a remarkable performance nevertheless.

However, Naxos have had the even better idea of coupling the 1955 *Goldberg* set with a stimulating broadcast performance of the *G major Partita* – a favourite work of Gould's – dating from the year before. Both transfers are first class. It is also available on Sony in surround sound.

Goldberg Variations (arr. for harp by Catrin Finch)

(N)(***) 477 8097 Finch (harp)

Catrin Finch is a very musical harpist and she opens the *Goldberg Aria* gently and seriously and elsewhere shows she is not intent on display. But at times there is an element of deliberation and the resonant sound seems to add a glow of romanticism to the music-making which is all but anachronistic. However this dedicated performance may make new friends for the work.

Goldberg Variations, BWV 988; Chorale: Jesu, joy of man's desiring, BWV 147; Partita 5 in G, BWV 829

*** BBC BBCL 4228-2. Nikolayeva

Nikolayeva's performance came from a (1986) BBC Lunchtime Concert in St John's, Smith Square, and formed part of a Russian season which also included Mikhail Pletnev's London début. The legendary Tatiana Nikolayeva was the dedicatee of the Shostakovich *Preludes and Fugues* which were inspired by her Bach performances in Dresden. Magisterial and compelling Bach, and masterly in every way.

(i) Goldberg Variations; (ii) Chorale Preludes BWV 599 & 639 (arr. Busoni); Jesu, joy of man's desiring; Partita 1 in B flat; Siciliana (arr. Kempff)

(BB)(***) Regis mono RRC 1264. (i) Gould; (ii) Lipatti

Goldberg Variations; Italian Concerto; Partitas 1–6, & in B min. (French Overture), BWV 825–31

🎵 (M) *** DG (ADD/DDD) Trio 474 337-2 (3). Pinnock (harpsichord)

Trevor Pinnock uses four different harpsichords here. The playing is vital and intelligent, with alert, finely articulated rhythm. In the *Partitas* he conveys a sense of pleasure that is infectious, and he has great spirit and panache throughout. The recording is eminently truthful and vivid, a bit close in the *B minor Partita*, which nevertheless still conveys plenty of expressive feeling.

Regis have had the bright idea of coupling **Glenn Gould's** famous 1955 recording of the *Goldberg Variations* (out of copyright in the UK) with **Lipatti's** legendary Bach recordings made five years earlier. The transfers are faithful and this makes an excellent bargain.

15 2-Part Inventions, BWV 772–86; 15 3-Part Inventions, BWV 787–801

🎵 **** BIS CD 1009. Suzuki (harpsichord)

🎵 *** Cap. 10 210 (with 6 Little Preludes, BWV 933–8). Koopman (harpsichord)

🎵 **(*) Sony 82876 787662. Gould (piano)

Masaaki Suzuki plays with perception and skill. These *Inventions* can sound dry, but not in his hands. His response is naturally spontaneous, fresh and alive, never didactic and rigid. Suzuki is one of the finest Bach exponents of our time and he is truthfully recorded.

Ton Koopman scores over rivals in offering the *Six Little Preludes* in addition to the two sets of *Inventions*, and he plays with spontaneity and sparkle.

The *Inventions* are admirably suited to **Glenn Gould's** clear, didactic style, and they are among his most impressive Bach recordings. As he pairs each of these *Two-* and *Three-Part* works (each in identical keys) listeners are always conscious that they are in the presence of a penetrating musical mind: the clarity of the individual strands is remarkable. As usual, the ear cannot fail to be exasperated by the vocalizations. One longs for vocal silence. The current reissue includes extra takes, some unedited.

Partitas 1–6, BWV 825–30

🎵 **** BIS CD 1313/4 (2). Suzuki (harpsichord)

🎵 ❀ (B) **** Nim. 5673/4. Roberts (piano)

🎵 **** None. 7559 79698-2 (1, 3 & 6); 7559 79483-2 (2, 4 & 5). Goode (piano)

🎵 *** Häns. CD 92.115 (2). Pinnock (harpsichord)

🎵 *** Hyp. CDA 67191/2. Hewitt (piano)

Masaaki Suzuki plays a modern Dutch copy of an enlarged two-manual Rückers, which is forwardly recorded and has a strong personality. If you like a bold harpsichord sound, this very realistic BIS disc should provide great satisfaction, for Suzuki's Bach perceptions are fully revealed here and he plays thoughtfully, commandingly and spontaneously.

However, the *Partitas* are heard more often today on the piano, and the splendid set from **Bernard Roberts** shows why. His clear, clean articulation is a constant joy, and the dance movements are delightfully played. Throughout, Roberts's playing reveals new aspects of these many-faceted works, at times light-hearted but with an underlying profundity that is fully realized here. The Nimbus recording is first class in every way, beautifully focused, with just the right degree of resonance in an ideal acoustic.

Not surprisingly, **Richard Goode's** Nonesuch set on the piano is equally stylish and appealing. The clean articulation and crisp, well-lifted rhythms (sample the *Gavotta* and *Gigue* of the final *Partita in E minor*) are as arresting as the pianistic use of light and shade. With piano tone that is clear but never too dry, this is very stimulating.

Trevor Pinnock has recorded the six *Partitas* before for DG, but this new set is even finer. He uses a superb American copy of a Hemsch made by David Way in Stonington, Connecticut (with a particularly effective mute stop). As before, he plays these works with a keen sense of enjoyment and projects the music with enormous panache. The harpsichord is superbly recorded and given fine presence in a spaciously resonant acoustic.

Angela Hewitt's performances are fluent, deeply musical and, while expressively flexible, not personally wayward in the *Sarabandes*, which she still plays very sensitively. The Hyperion recording is first class.

Partitas 2 in C min.; 3 in A min.; 4 in D, BWV 826/8

(N) **** Sony/BMG 88697226952 Perahia (piano)

Murray Perahia is again in his element here. Bach keyboard playing does not come any finer than this. A disc of true distinction most truthfully recorded.

Partita 4, BWV828

(N) **** Onyx 4035. Kovacevich – BEETHOVEN: *Diabelli Variations, Op. 120* ****

Stephen Kovacevich's magisterial set of the *Diabelli Variations* comes with a Bach *Partita*, a reminder that he was the pupil of Dame Myra Hess whose Bach playing was legendary in the post-war years. He plays with an impressive and natural eloquence that gives enormous musical satisfaction.

7 Toccatas; BWV 910–16

⌀ *** Hyp. CDA 67310. Hewitt (piano)

Hewitt always holds Bach's disparate motivations convincingly together, as in the *G minor* which, as she comments, can be made to sound uniquely varied and buoyant on the piano, especially the bouncing closing fugue. And how engaging is her sparkling articulation of the first section of the *D major Toccata*, with which she ends her programme. We have no hesitation in declaring this the most stimulating and rewarding CD of these complex and episodic works on any instrument, consistently showing Bach's youthful explorations at their most stimulating. The recording is excellent.

Toccatas 1–7; Partita 7 in B min. (Overture in the French Style), BWV 831

(M) ** Sony (ADD) SM2K 52612 (2). Gould (piano)

Glenn Gould's *Toccatas* were recorded in the mid- to late 1970s and combine the most fastidious and remarkable pianism with some characteristically impulsive, not to say wilful, touches. Though the playing is of the highest distinction, the piano tone is not, and the wearisome vocalization, on which this artist seems to insist, somewhat dampens one's enthusiasm.

The Well-Tempered Clavier (48 Preludes & Fugues), BWV 846–93

(*) EuroArts **DVD 2050309 (2). Gavrilov (*Book I/1–12*); MacGregor (*13–24*); Demidenko (*Book II/1–12*); Hewitt (*13–14*)

The idea of filming and recording *The Well-Tempered Clavier* with four different pianists in four different venues is a novel one, and it certainly offers a variety of interpretative manners, none more controversial than **Andrei Gavrilov's** opening approach, which is both highly individual and wilful, yet obviously deeply considered. Altogether stimulating, but a very personal view. **Joanna MacGregor** then creates a complete contrast following her Russian colleague. There is both momentum and character in her playing, which is attractively crisp and clean in the major keys. **Nikolai Demidenko's** way is even more bold and direct, his pacing often brisk but never seeming pressed too hard, and there is never a hint of the romantic dallying which Gavrilov indulges in. Simplicity is **Angela Hewitt's** hallmark, with well-judged tempi and unexaggerated use of light and shade so that rhythms are precise, the contrapuntal interplay always clear. Throughout, the music is allowed to unfold naturally and sometimes quite intimately. The visual presentation is far from plain and the cameras are constantly moving, especially in the angle of approach to the pianist's hands. The palaces at Barcelona and Venice, where MacGregor and Demidenko play, are fully explored and the glory of the interiors at the Wartburg, Eisenach, are realized during Hewitt's final group. The recorded sound is excellent.

The Well-Tempered Clavier (48 Preludes & Fugues), BWV 846–93 (complete)

⌀ (M) **** BBC (ADD) BBCL 4109-2 (2) (*Book I*); BBCL 4116-3 (3) (*Book II*). Tureck (piano)

⌀ **** Decca 475 6832 (3). Ashkenazy (piano)

**** BIS CD 813/4 (Book 1); BIS CD 1513/4 (Book 2) Masaaki Suzuki (harpsichord)

(M) ⌀ **** Hyp. CDA 66741/4 (4) Angela Hewitt (piano)

(N) **** Signum SIGCD 136 (4); or SIGCD 113 (Book I); SIGCD 123 (Book II) Jill Crossland (piano)

⌀ (B) *** Hyp. CDS 44291/4. Hewitt (piano)

⌀ (B) *** Nim. NI 5608/11 (4). Roberts (piano)

(N) (M) *** Decca 478 0391 (4) Schiff (piano)

(M) (***) EMI mono 3 91958-2 (3); or (BB) (***) Naxos mono 8.110651/2 (*Book I*); 8.110653/4 (*Book II*). Edwin Fischer (piano)

In the autumn of 1975, when she was at her artistic peak, the BBC invited **Rosalyn Tureck** into the studio to re-record the entire '48' in groups, and the project was completed in November 1976. Because of her innate understanding of Bach, the result, for all its remarkable variety of mood, remains essentially pure in a classical sense and immensely satisfying, a miraculous blend of scholarship and personal insight and feeling. As can be seen, because of Tureck's often measured tempi, *Book II* extends over three CDs (the third playing for only 40 minutes, but including a 6-minute bonus – a brief conversation between Tureck and Michael Oliver). Throughout, the BBC recording is excellent, and the two Books are available separately.

Ashkenazy returned to the studio (or, rather, to Potton Hall, Suffolk) on two occasions in 2004 and once in 2005, to record Bach's *Well-Tempered Clavier*. The result is an extraordinary *tour de force* in the variety of its pianism. Ashkenazy obviously prepared well and he thought deeply about every prelude and every fugue as an individual entity, and he also considered the way each pair links and brings a potential for contrast. While the consistent spontaneity of his playing often brings an improvisatory feeling in the *Preludes*, he is very economical in the matter of ornamentation, obviously preferring to leave well alone, rather than to over-embellish.

Suzuki lays claim to being first choice for a harpsichord version of the '48'. His two-manual instrument (by Willem Kroesbergen of Utrecht after an enlarged Rückers) has a fine personality and is splendidly recorded. His pacing is admirably judged, his flexibility never sounds mannered and he brings Bach's great keyboard odyssey fully to life at every turn. A most satisfying achievement. The recording is in the demonstration bracket.

During 2007 and 2008 **Angel Hewitt** undertook a world tour playing the *Well-Tempered Clavier* in 58 cities in 21 countries. Then during September 2008 she recorded the complete work for the second time in the famous Jesus-Christus Kirche, Berlin, with the producer Ludger Böckenhoff providing a superbly real piano image and with little editing needed. The result is something of a triumph, for the performance as recorded has the ongoing spontaneity of a live performance. As before she uses all the resources of the modern piano. Her range of timbre is wide and her wide control of dynamic is ever subtle. Every bar is imaginatively alive with a pervading freshness, and many details are even more searching than before. She holds the listener firmly in her grip, and her expressiveness (as in her previous version) is never self-aware, not does it obscure the clarity of the part-writing. Truly an inspirational set of the highest calibre.

Jill Crossland is new to this repertoire but plays it with distinction and individuality. She opens the *C major Prelude* of Book I very gently but builds firmly to a considerable climax. Yet her delicate approach returns quite often during her survey – as in both the *E flat* and *A flat major Preludes*, which are very touching. Indeed her playing brings much felicity of articulation which constantly pleases the ear. As Book II soon demonstrates, she can also be bold and strong and the result is a refreshing variety of expression with the ongoing musical flow always secure. Altogether this per-

formance ranks with the finest previous versions, a remarkable achievement, and Signum have given her very truthful recording and the opportunity to buy the set complete of a Book at a time.

In her earlier recording (CDS 44291/4) **Angela Hewitt** used all the resources of the modern piano to turn these preludes and fugues into ongoing concert music of great variety and interest. Her range of timbre and dynamic is wide, her articulation can be bold, lightweight or gently searching (as, for instance, in BWV 849). But every bar is imaginatively alive and her thoughtful expressiveness is never self-aware, nor does it obscure the clarity of the part-writing.

Bernard Roberts's Nimbus survey is full of individual touches and insights. That goes with the deepest concentration, bringing out the full power as well as the beauty, with counterpoint consistently clarified. To confirm the recommendation, the four discs come as a bargain offer, and this is the version, superbly recorded, which for many will be a first choice. He is very truthfully recorded, and his set has the added advantage of economy, in being complete.

Schiff often takes a very individual view of particular preludes and fugues, but his unexpected readings regularly win one over before the end. Consistently he translates the music into pianistic terms, and his voyage of discovery is increasingly compelling as he makes his way through this supreme keyboard collection. Not now a first choice, perhaps, but a very stimulating one, with first-rate sound.

Edwin Fischer's set was the first ever '48' to be put on shellac 78s, being recorded in 1933–6. Fischer produced a quality of sound and a sense of line that are an unfailing source of musical nourishment. The EMI transfers (by Andrew Walter) for EMI's 'Great Recordings of the Century' are first class and the set is economically laid out on three mid-priced CDs, each accommodating close on 80 minutes. The Naxos transfers are also very impressive, the piano sound full and pleasing. However, Naxos has issued each Book on a pair of super-bargain discs, so the saving in cost is less than it might have been. The mastery and subtlety of Fischer's Bach playing needs no restating, for it has never been surpassed.

Glenn Gould's very opening *Prelude* of Book I is an instance of his staccato style, and the clarity of his playing is matched by his charisma. There are undoubtedly many imaginative if obdurate touches, and his often curious choice of tempi – sometimes rattlingly fast, sometimes slow and pensive – is wilfully personal, favouring rallentandos at the end of each prelude or fugue. Certainly this is a fascinating set and it has never sounded better. But the vocalise also remains, to interfere with one's concentration. For this repertoire on the piano, Tureck or Hewitt are safer recommendations. (Sony 5179702)

KEYBOARD RECITAL COLLECTIONS

Rosalyn Tureck recitals

'Bach and Tureck at Home' (a birthday offering): (i) *Adagio in G, BWV 968; Aria & 10 Variations in the Italian Style, BWV 989; Capriccio on the Departure* *of a Beloved Brother, BWV 992; Chromatic Fantasia & Fugue, BWV 903; Fantasia, Adagio & Fugue in D, BWV 912; The Well-Tempered Clavier, Book I: Prelude & Fugue in B flat, BWV 866. (ii) English Suite 3 in G min., BWV 808; Italian Concerto; Sonata in D min., BWV 964 (trans. from Unaccompanied Violin Sonata 2 in A min., BWV 1003); Well-Tempered Clavier, Book I: Preludes & Fugues: in C min.; in C, BWV 847–8; Book II: Preludes & Fugues: in C sharp, BWV 872; in G, BWV 884. (iii) Goldberg Variations; (iv) Partitas 1 in B flat; 2 in C min.; 6 in E min.*

⊕ 🏵 **** VAI (i) VAIA 1041; (ii) VAIA 1051; (iii) VAIA 1029; (iv) VAIA 1040 (available separately). Tureck (piano)

Rosalyn Tureck's Bach playing is legendary, and the performances here show that her keyboard command and fluent sense of Bach style are as remarkable as ever. Tureck uses a wide dynamic and expressive range with consummate artistry, her decoration always adds to the musical effect and she makes us feel that Bach's keyboard music could be played in no other way than this – the hallmark of a great artist.

Other keyboard collections

Capriccio in E in Honour of Johann Christoph Bach, BWV 993; Capriccio on the Departure of a Beloved Brother, BWV 992; Chromatic Fantasia & Fugue, BWV 903; Fantasia & Fugues: in A min., BWV 944; in C min., BWV 906; Fantasias: in A min., BWV 922; in G min., BWV 917; Fantasia on a Rondeau in C min., BWV 918; Prelude in C min., BWV 921; Fantasia & Fugue in A min., BWV 944; Fugue in A on a Theme of Albinoni, BWV 950; Prelude & Fugue on a Theme by Albinoni, BWV 923/951

*** BIS CD 1037. Suzuki (harpsichord)

Masaaki Suzuki opens with a dazzlingly bravura account of the *Chromatic Fantasia*, and is equally impressive later in his brilliant articulation of the Albinoni *Prelude* and the engaging *C minor Prelude*, BWV 921 (which is marked *Harpeggiando – Prestissimo*). Yet the fugues are given aptly judged tempi, never rushed. The rest of this varied programme is played with comparable flair and all of it is very well recorded. In short, this is a very winning and often exciting collection, and if you are looking for keyboard virtuosity you won't be disappointed here.

Aria variata in A min., BWV 989; Chromatic Fantasia & Fugue, BWV 903; Fantasia & Fugue in A min., BWV 904; Prelude & Fugue in A min., BWV 894; Partita in B min. (Overture in the French Style), BWV 831

⊕ **** Naxos 8.570291. Jandó (piano)

This is not only one of **Jenö Jandó's** finest records, it is one of the finest available recitals of Bach's shorter keyboard pieces on the piano. Jandó's opening of the *Chromatic Fantasia* is dazzling in its flair and crisp virtuosity, and the following *Aria variata* with its ten variations is ear-tweaking

in its diversity. The two works with fugues are spacious and splendidly articulated, and the *Overture in the French Style* completes a most satisfying disc, very well recorded.

Capriccio in E, BWV 993; Capriccio on the Departure of a Beloved Brother, BWV 992; 4 Duets, BWV 802–5; Italian Concerto; Partita in B min., BWV 831

⊕ **** Hyp. CDA 67306. Hewitt (piano)

Angela Hewitt's striking sense of keyboard colour is shown in the *'Departure' Capriccio*, especially the *Adagissimo*, and, together with an imaginatively wide variety of touch, makes the four *Duets* (so called on account of their two-part counterpoint) unusually diverse, like a suite. As for the famous *B minor Partita* (or *French Overture*), the sparklingly rhythmic dance-movements make a perfect setting for the lovely central *Sarabande*. Hewitt is recorded most naturally and provides her own excellent notes.

English Suite 2 in A min., BWV 807; Partita 2 in C min., BWV 826; Toccata in C min., BWV 911

Ⓜ *** DG (ADD) 463 604-2. Argerich (piano)

Martha Argerich's playing provides a genuinely musical experience: alive, keenly rhythmic, but also wonderfully flexible and rich in colour. There is an intellectual musical vitality here that is refreshing. She is very well recorded indeed, even if the measure (50 minutes) is not especially generous.

Chromatic Fantasia and Fugue in D min., BWV 903; Prelude, Fugue and Allegro in E flat, BWV 998; 4 Toccatas, BWV 911/14

Ⓝ (***) Lyrichord mono LEMS 8062 Fernando Valenti (harpsichord)

Here is a fascinating reminder of the early 1950s when Bach harpsichord recitals on LP were rare indeed. **Fernando Valenti** made many recordings for the Westminster label, including over 300 Scarlatti sonatas. His performances were famous for their dazzling virtuosity, immediately demonstrated here in the super-brilliant account of Bach's *Chromatic Fantasia*. The four *Toccatas* show the range and spontaneity of his style and his readiness also to play gently. The instrument in use is not documented, but it sounds like a copy of a large-scale Two-manuel Rückers, offering a full range of dynamic and colour. A fascinating disc. The mono recording is admirable clear.

ORGAN MUSIC

Peter Hurford Complete Decca Series

Ⓑ *** Decca (ADD/DDD) 444 410-2 (17). Hurford (organs of Ratzeburg Cathedral, Germany; Church of Our Lady of Sorrows, Toronto, Canada; New College Chapel, Oxford; Knox Grammar School Chapel, Sydney, Australia; Eton College, Windsor; Stiftskirche, Melk, Austria; Augustinerkirche, Vienna, Austria; All Souls Unitarian Church, Washington, DC, USA; Domkirche, St Pölten, Austria; St Catharine's College Chapel, Cambridge)

It was Peter Hurford's achievement to influence a complete change in approach to this repertoire, moving away from an enduring and essentially pedagogic, German tradition (shown at its best by organists like Helmut Walcha on DG Archiv). Vigour and energy are the keynotes of Hurford's approach to the large-scale works and, without losing their majesty, he never lets the fugal momentum get bogged down by the music's weight and scale. We hear Bach's organ writing with new ears, its human vitality revealed alongside its extraordinary architecture. The set is supported with very good notes by Clifford Bartlett which are both scholarly and readable; full specifications of all the organs used are included. The recordings are splendidly transferred to CD, and while newer digital surveys are now appearing, this set of 17 bargain-price CDs remains a cornerstone among available recordings of this repertoire. Apart from the selection below, the discs unfortunately are not available separately.

Chorale Preludes, BWV 727, 729–30, 734, 659, 645 & 694; Fantasias: BWV 562, 572; Preludes & Fugues: BWV 537 & 542; Passacaglia & Fugue, BWV 582; Preludes & Fugues, BWV 543, 532 & (St Anne) BWV 552; Toccata, Adagio & Fugue, BWV 564; Toccatas & Fugues: in D min. (Dorian), BWV 538; BWV 565

🎧 (B) *** Double Decca (ADD) 443 485-2 (2). Hurford (various organs)

A generous 146-minute collection of major Bach organ works, taken from **Peter Hurford's** complete survey (see above), brings two separate recitals, each framed by major concert pieces, with the beautifully played chorales used in between the large-scale pieces to add contrast.

Marie-Claire Alain Complete Erato Series

(BB) *** Warner 4509 96358-2 (14). Alain (various organs)

Marie-Claire Alain's integral survey, made for Erato during the early 1990s, is again available, in a box of 14 CDs at budget price. Throughout, she plays to excellent effect on some splendid instruments; but competition is strong, and for most collectors a choice from among the separate issues would seem more sensible. Each volume (usually) centres on a group of *Chorale Preludes*, framing them with weightier (often very substantially textured) *Preludes* or *Toccatas* and *Fugues*.

Simon Preston DG Series (Complete Organ Works)

(B) *** DG 469 420-2 (14). Preston (various organs)

Simon Preston's survey was recorded over more than a decade from 1987 onwards, beginning with the solo *Concertos*, which set the standard for the entire series. These performances are first class in every way, and the recording of the Lübeck organ admirably clear, yet with an attractively resonant ambience. Preston revels in the extrovert brilliance of the early Weimar *Preludes and Fugues* (and indeed also the *'Dorian' Toccata*) with their elaborately virtuoso use of the pedals, but relishes also the more mature, tightly structured works, which he plays with genuine panache. Another highlight of the series is the (1993) set of *Trio Sonatas*.

Some of the repertoire has been issued on separate

recital discs, including a few works not included here, such as the *8 Little Preludes and Fugues*, which are wrongly attributed to Bach. But apart from these omissions the whole series now appears in a DG bargain box, with the various genres sensibly grouped together. The performances are consistently alive and distinguished, and the choice of organs ear-ticklingly perceptive. Good notes, although the analysis of the music itself is general rather than detailed.

Ton Koopman Novalis Series

Disc 1: (i) Chorale Prelude: Liebster Jesu, wir sind hier, BWV 730/1; Fantasias: in C min., BWV 562; in G, BWV 572; Passacaglia & Fugue in C min., BWV 582; Preludes & Fugues, BWV 532, 543; Toccata, Adagio & Fugue in C, BWV 564; Toccata, BWV 538 (Dorian)

Disc 2: (ii) Chorale Preludes, BWV 639, 659; Schübler Chorale: Wachet auf, BWV 645. Fantasia (Prelude) & Fugue in G min., BWV 542; Partita: O Gott, du frommer Gott, BWV 767; Prelude & Fugue (St Anne), BWV 552; Toccata & Fugue in D min., BWV 565

🎧 (B) *** Regis RRC 2042 (2). Koopman, (i) Dreifaltigkeits organ, Ottobeuren, Christian Müller organ, Leeuwarden, or Garrels organ, Grote Kerk, Maassluis; (ii) Christian Müller organ, Waalse Kerk, Amsterdam

This two-CD set brings together two outstanding recitals drawn from a series for Novalis, using various Dutch organs. **Ton Koopman's** playing is superb throughout, always using organs admirably suited to Bach's music and all splendidly recorded. The first disc has been put together by Regis to include key items from several individual compilations and to demonstrate three different organs. All three organs are superbly caught by the Novalis engineers. The second disc brings a complete recital (originally issued on 150 005-2). The Waalse Kerk organ is itself a co-star of this programme, producing magnificent, unclouded sonorities in the spacious tapestry of the *St Anne Prelude and Fugue*, and a wide palette of colour. For the most popular of all Bach's organ pieces Ton Koopman then changes to a more flamboyant style, which he establishes immediately by decorating the opening flourishes so that they become almost a series of trills. The recording is in the demonstration bracket, the microphones in the right place for a proper illusion of reality.

Other organ music

The Art of Fugue, BWV 1080

*** BIS CD 1034. Fagius (organ of Garnisons Kirke, Copenhagen)

The approach of the Swedish organist **Hans Fagius** is refreshingly straightforward and unaffected. Here he plays a Danish organ, a reconstruction from 1995 of an instrument made in 1724 by Lambert Daniel Kastens, a pupil of Arp Schnitger. He has the advantage of a first-class recording, as one would expect from this label and the producer-engineer

Ingo Petry. This version has a lot going for it, quite apart from the sound, and those who like their Bach plain and unadorned will find it well worth considering.

The Art of Fugue, BWV 1080; Prelude & Fugue in C, BWV 547; Toccata, Adagio & Fugue in C, BWV 554; Toccata & Fugue in D min., BWV 565; Trio Sonatas, BWV 525 & 530

Ⓜ *** DG (ADD) 477 6508 (2). Walcha (St Laurenskerk organ, Alkmaar)

Helmut Walcha's *Art of Fugue* was DG's very first stereo recording, recorded in 1955. He had previously made a series of mono recordings of Bach's organ music and was to go on to make, between 1959 and 1971, a distinguished but incomplete stereo series (now on a dozen CDs: 463 712-2). In his account of *The Art of Fugue* the registration is admirably varied, yet with the contrasts of register and timbre heightened by the spatial effects of the stereo. The *D major Toccata and Fugue* certainly does not lack bravura; and typical of Walcha's playing at its most monumental is the gigantic triptych of the *Toccata, Adagio and Fugue*, a rigorous test of any organist's technique and a work which he comes through with flying colours.

Concertos (for solo organ) 1–5; 6 in E flat (arr. of concerto by an unnamed composer), BWV 592–7; Trio in C min. (after FASCH), BWV 585; Trio in G (after TELEMANN), BWV 586; Aria in F (from COUPERIN: Les Nations), BWV 587

ⒷⒷ *** Naxos 8.550936. Rübsam (Flenthrop organ of St Mark's Cathedral, Seattle, Washington)

Wolfgang Rübsam's recital for Naxos is strikingly successful. Moreover it is very comprehensive in including the rarely played 'anonymous' concerto transcription, BWV 597. This is a most engaging piece, particularly the jaunty closing section, and it is nicely registered, as are the other individual movements here, by Couperin, Fasch and Telemann. Rübsam's tempi for allegros remain buoyant throughout and the playing is always seemingly spontaneous. The recording is in the demonstration class.

18 Leipzig Chorale Preludes, BWV 651–68; Fantasia in G, BWV 572; Prelude & Fugue in B min., BWV 544; Toccata & Fugue in F, BWV 540; Trio Sonata 4 in E min., BWV 528

Ⓜ *** Priory PRCD 800AB (2). Weir (Gerald Woehl Bach organ of Thomaskirche, Leipzig)

The new Gerald Woehl organ has 61 stops and a magnificent range of colour which **Gillian Weir** exploits to the full (many of her registrations are captivating; others show the organ's dramatic power), and she is very gentle in the final sublime chorale, *Vol deinem Thron tret ich hiermet*, the first part of which Bach supposedly dictated from his deathbed. She then goes on to play a selection of miscellaneous works to display the organ's full range, from the brilliant filigree of the Arnstadt *Fantasia in G minor* and the charm of the *Trio Sonata* to the full power of BWV 540 and 544. The recording is first class, completely worthy of the occasion, and the documentation excellent.

Orgelbüchlein: 19 Chorale Preludes for Advent, Christmas, New Year and the Purification, BWV 599–617; Fantasia in C, BWV 570; Fugue on a Theme of Corelli, BWV 579; Preludes & Fugues, BWV 531 & 534; Prelude in G, BWV 568

ⒷⒷ *** Naxos 8.553031. Rübsam (Flenthrop organ of Duke Chapel, Duke University, Durham, North Carolina)

Orgelbüchlein: 27 Chorale Preludes for Passiontide; Easter; Pentecost; and expressing Faith, BWV 618–44; Fantasia in C, BWV 570; Fugue in B min., BWV 579; Preludes & Fugues, BWV 531 & 534; Prelude in G, BWV 568

ⒷⒷ *** Naxos 8.553032. Rübsam (Flenthrop organ of Duke Chapel, Duke University, Durham, North Carolina)

Rübsam finds great variety for his presentation of each chorale. The Christmas section is preceded by the flamboyant and joyous *Prelude and Fugue in C*, with its resounding pedals, and the first recital is rounded off with a characteristically spacious account of the imposing *F minor Prelude and Fugue*, BWV 534. The *Easter Chorales* are more robust, while the four *Pentecost Chorales* are touchingly contemplative. There is infinite variety of mood and colour in the last group, opening with a piece symbolizing the Ten Commandments and showing Bach reflecting on various aspects of the Christian faith. The introduction of the closing *Prelude and Fugue in D minor*, BWV 539, is grave and dignified, but the fugue itself is optimistic and vital, ending the concert satisfyingly. The Duke University Chapel organ is a magnificent instrument, and the recording is superb throughout.

Chorale Preludes: Ach bleib' bei uns, BWV 649; Liebster Jesu, BWV 731; O Mensch, bewein, BWV 622; Wachet auf, BWV 645; Fantasia in G, BWV 572; Fugue in E flat (St Anne), BWV 552; Prelude and Fugue in C, BWV 545; Sinfonia (arr. Rawsthorne) from Cantata 29; Toccatas & Fugues in D min. (Dorian), BWV 538; & BWV 565

ⒷⒷ **(*) Regis RRC 1248. Rawsthorne (Willis Organ of Liverpool Anglican Cathedral)

Those who like their Bach on a really big organ, with a distinctly non-baroque flavour, will find that **Noel Rawsthorne's** performances have plenty of vigour, and they are effectively registered too, especially the better-known chorale preludes. The larger works have the right balance of momentum and controlled tension, and inner detail is only slightly blurred. With the wider reverberation period of Liverpool Cathedral, as sheer sound this is undoubtedly thrilling (especially the climax of the *St Anne Fugue*, which the *Gramophone* review commented on with great enthusiasm).

Chorale Preludes: Alle Menschen müssen sterben, BWV 643; Vater ünser im Himmelreich, BWV 737; Fantasia & Fugue in G min., BWV 542; Passacaglia

& Fugue in C min., BWV 582; Toccata in F, BWV 540

Ⓜ **(*) Telarc CD 80049. Murray (Great organ at Methuen Memorial Music Hall, Massachusetts)

The Methuen organ is a famous instrument and the Telarc engineers catch its wide panoply of sound very impressively, if without crystal-clear detail. The most impressive performance here is the *Passacaglia and Fugue in C minor*, well judged and powerful with an effectively wide dynamic range. **Michael Murray's** approach to the *Fantasia and Fugue* and *Toccata* is traditional and rather measured. The chorale preludes are given serene and (it must be admitted) slightly static performances, but the sense of repose of *Alle Menschen müssen sterben* which ends the recital is enhanced by the clean focus, although the background is not quite silent, for the organ contributes its own characteristic sound as the air goes through the pipes.

VOCAL MUSIC

Complete Cantatas: Harnoncourt/Leonhardt Teldec Series

Cantatas 1–14; 16–52; 54–69; 69a; 70–117; 119–40; 143–59; 161–88; 192; 194–9 (complete)

ⒷⒷ **(*) Warner (ADD/DDD) 2564 699 43-7 (60). Treble soloists from V. Boys' & Regensburg Choirs, Esswood, Equiluz, Van Altena, Van Egmond, Hampson, Nimsgern, Van der Meer, Jacobs, Iconomou, Holl, Immler, King's College, Cambridge, Ch., V. Boys' Ch., Tölz Boys' Ch., Ch. Viennensis, Ghent Coll. Voc., VCM, Harnoncourt; Leonhardt Cons., Leonhardt

This pioneering project, a recording of most – but not all – of Bach's sacred cantatas, is offered as a 60-CD box at bargain price.

The recordings got off to a very good start but, later in the project, various flaws of intonation, and sometimes a feeling that the ensemble would have benefited from more rehearsal, plus occasionally sluggish direction, slightly undermined the overall excellence. However, the authentic character of the performances is in no doubt. Boys replace women not only in the choruses but also as soloists (which brings occasional minor lapses of security), and the size of the forces is confined to what we know Bach himself would have expected. The simplicity of the approach brings its own merits, for the imperfect yet otherworldly quality of some of the treble soloists refreshingly focuses the listener's attention on the music itself. Less appealing is the quality of the violins, which eschew vibrato and, it would sometimes seem, any kind of timbre! Generally speaking, there is a certain want of rhythmic freedom and some expressive caution. Rhythmic accents are underlined with some regularity and the grandeur of Bach's inspiration is at times lost to view. Nevertheless there is much glorious music here which, to do justice to **Harnoncourt** and **Leonhardt**, usually emerges freshly to give the listener much musical nourishment. The CD transfers are first class. The acoustic is usually not too dry – and not too ecclesiastical either – and the projection is

realistic. The set now comes at budget price with each CD in an individual slipcase, with two 300-page booklets containing full texts and translations.

Complete Cantatas: Koopman Series with Amsterdam Baroque Chorus & Orchestra on Challenge Classics

Volumes 1–22

Ⓜ *** Chall CC 72201/722022 (67) Soloists including Schlick, Wessel, De Mey, Mertens, Prégardien, Stam, Holton, Bongers, Von Magnus, De Groot, Agnew, Türk, Stam, Chance, Rubens, Dürmüller, Gilchrist, Barosz, Stutzmann, Amsterdam Bar. Ch. & Orchestra

Koopman favours an intimate approach to choruses – namely one voice to a part – which seems to rob this repertory of some of its sheer majesty and breadth. He opts for female soloists rather than boys, as would have been the case in Bach's day, and he favours mixed rather than solely male choirs. For many this will be a plus point – and it is good news for fans of **Barbara Schlick**. Moreover, he goes for slightly higher than normal pitch – a semitone above present-day pitch, which, as Christoph Wolff's notes point out, is what Bach used in Mühlhausen and Weimar, brightening the sonority quite a lot. The singing in virtually all the cantatas is pretty impressive and the instrumental playing is of a high order of accomplishment. Moreover, Koopman offers the collector variants and alternative versions, which will again be an undoubted plus. For the most part the singing here is of a high order of accomplishment – in particular **Andreas Scholl** and **Elisabeth von Magnus** – and the instrumental playing is certainly finished, though here it is by no means always as fresh or secure as on the Japanese series now under way from BIS.

Taken as a whole, Koopman's cycle is an impressive achievement which will give much pleasure. If the solo singing is sometimes variable, the choral and orchestral contributions (with very sensitive solo obbligati) make a bedrock on which the whole project rests. Koopman's directing vitality keeps the music spontaneously alive, with no sense of over-refinement or scholarly rectitude; the recording is first class, and the documentation could hardly be more informative. In short this is a most enjoyable and rewarding series that will give much satisfaction.

The CDs are packaged in 22 separate volumes with 3 discs and a cross section of cantatas to each volume. No doubt the set will come out as a boxed set in the lifetime of this book.

Complete Cantatas: BIS Masaaki Suzuki Series with Japan Bach Collegium

Cantatas 1; 126; 127 (● ➡ ✺ ** BIS SACD 1551; with Sampson, Blaze, Türk, Kooy)**

Cantatas 2; 3; 38; 135 (● ➡ ** BIS SACD 1461; with Mields, Berlin, Türk, Kooy)**

Cantatas 4; 150; 196 (** BIS CD 751; with Kuriso, Tachikawa, Katano, Kooy)**

Cantatas 5; 80; 115 (**** BIS CD 1421; with Rydén, Bertin, Türk, Kooy)

Cantatas 6; 42; 103; 108 (**** BIS SACD 1611; with Nonoshita, Blaze, Gilchrist, Wörner)

Cantatas 7; 20; 94 (**** BIS CD 1321; with Nonoshita, Blaze, Kobow, Kooy)

Cantatas 8; 33; 113 (**** BIS CD 1351; with Nonoshita, Blaze, Türk, Kooy)

Cantatas 10; 93; 107; 178 (**** BIS CD 1331; with Nonoshita, M. White, Sakurada, Kooy)

Cantata 11 (Ascension); Easter Oratorio, BWV 249 (⌕ **** BIS SACD 1561; with Nonoshita, Van Goethem, Kobow, Uramo)

Cantatas 12; 54; 162; 182 (**** BIS CD 791; with Kuriso, Mera, Sakurada, Kooy)

Cantatas 13; 16; 32 (Concerto in Dialogo); 9; 72 (**** BIS SACD 1722; with Nicholls, Blaze, Türk, Kooji)

Cantatas 18; 152; 155; 161; 163 (**** BIS CD 841; with Midori Suzuki, Schmithüsen, Mera, Sakurada, Kooy)

Cantatas 21 (with 3 alternative movements); 31 (**** BIS CD 851; with Frimmer, Türk, Kooy)

Cantatas 21; 147 (⌕ **** BIS CD 1031; with Nonoshita, Blaze, Türk, Kooy, Concerto Palatino (BWV 21))

Cantatas 22–3; 75 (**** BIS CD 901; with M. Suzuki, Mera, Türk, Kooy)

Cantatas 24; 76; 167 (**** BIS CD 931; with M. Suzuki, Blaze, Türk, Urano)

Cantatas 25; 50; 64; 69a; 77 (**** BIS CD 1041; with Nonoshita, Blaze, Sollek-Avella, Türk, Sakurada, Kooy, Concerto Palatino (BWV 25 & 64))

Cantatas 25; 68; 85; 175; 183 (BIS SACD 1641; with Sampson, Blaze, Türk, Kooy)

Cantatas 35; 169; 170; Aria, BWV 200 (**** BIS SACD 1621; with Blaze)

Cantatas 37; 86; 104; 166 (*** BIS CD 1261; with Nonoshita, Blaze, Sakurada, MacLeod)

Cantatas 40; 60; 70; 90 (**** BIS CD 1111; with Nonoshita, Blaze, Türk, Kooy)

Cantatas 41; 92; 130 (⌕ **** BIS SACD 1541; with Nonoshita, Blaze, Kobow, Wörner)

Cantatas 44; 59; 173; 184 (**** BIS CD 1271; with Nonoshita, Hatano, Türk, Kooy)

Cantatas 46; 95; 136; 138 (**** BIS CD 991; with M. Suzuki, Wessel, Sakurada, Kooy)

Cantatas 48; 89; 109; 148 (**** BIS CD 1081; with M. Suzuki, Blaze, Türk, Urano)

Cantata 51; Cantata 210: Aria: Spielt, ihr besellen Lieder. Aria: Alles mit Gott und nichts ohn' ihn, BWV 1127 (✿ **** BIS SACD 1471. with Sampson, Bach Collegium, Japan, Masaaki Suzuki)

Cantatas (i) 52; (ii) 55; (iii) 58; (iv) 82 (**** BIS SACD 1631; with (i) Sampson; (ii) Türk; (iii) Sampson, Kooy; (iv) Kooy)

Cantatas 61; 63; 132; 172 (**** BIS CD 881; with Schmithüsen, Mera, Sakurada, Kooy)

Cantatas 65; 81; 83; 190 (**** BIS CD 1311; with Blaze, Gilchrist, Kooy)

Cantatas 66; 67; 134 (**** BIS CD 1251; with Blaze, Sakurada, Kooy)

Cantatas 71; 106; 131 (**** BIS CD 781; with M. Suzuki, Yanagisawa, Mera, Türk, Kooy)

Cantatas 73; 144; 153; 154; 181 (**** BIS CD 1221; with Nonoshita, Blaze, Türk, Kooy)

Cantatas 74; 87; 128; 176 (**** BIS SACD 1571; with Nonoshita, Blaze, Sakurada, Kooy)

Cantatas 78; 99; 114 (**** BIS CD 1361; with Nonoshita, Taylor, Sakurada, Kooy)

Cantatas 79; 137; 164; 178 (BIS SACD 1671 with Nonoshita, Blaze, Sakurada, Kooy)

Cantatas 91; 101; 121; 133 (⌕ **** BIS SACD 1481; with Nonoshita, Blaze, Türk, Kooy)

Cantatas 96; 122; 180 (**** BIS CD 1401; with Nonoshita, Kenworthy-Brown, Sakurada, Kooy)

Cantatas 105; 179; 186 (⌕ Ⓜ **** BIS CD 951; with Persson, Blaze, Sakurada, Kooy)

Cantatas 111; 123; 124; 125 (⌕ **** BIS SACD 1501; with Nonoshita, Blaze, Weller, Kooy)

Cantatas 119; 194 (**** BIS CD 1131; with Hida,

Nonoshita, Sollek-Avella, Sakurada, Kupfer, Kooy)

Cantatas (i) 163; (ii) 165; (iii) 185; (iv) 199 (**** BIS CD 801; with (i–ii) Yanagisawa; (i–iii) Tachikawa, Sakurada, Schreckenberger; (iii–iv) M. Suzuki)

The variety of recordings of the Bach Cantatas is remarkable, but (although Koopman's Amsterdam set probably comes a close second), undoubtedly Suzuki's series with the Japan Bach Collegium is in a very special class. Each new volume seems to surpass its predecessor and offers performances of total conviction and consummate artistry. These performances radiate freshness, and their vitality is matched by a wonderfully present recorded sound which, in the later volumes, with the addition of the surround effect of SACD, is very realistic indeed, giving one the feeling that one is in the auditorium where the performances are taking place. With Carolyn Sampson, Robin Blaze and Yukari Nonoshita among others joining the soloists in recent volumes, the quality of the solo singing, and indeed of the instrumental obbligati, seems unsurpassable.

Suzuki uses a higher pitch (A = 465) with its concomitant brighter sound, and he also favours female voices. The strings are clean yet have bloom, and the sense of inhibition – of excessive awareness of the constraints of period performance that sometimes mars the Harnoncourt/Leonhardt set – is refreshingly absent here. This set, which comes with each disc fully documented and with texts and translations included, is now occupying a key position in the Bach discography and if one needs to choose from the various cycles currently available, the BIS set would be an obvious first choice. It is now impossible to discuss each CD individually. As each recording appears, the sheer quality of this achievement continues to prove a source of admiration and satisfaction. Masaaki Suzuki is proceeding chronologically. Although the excellence of rival surveys is not in doubt, this Japanese survey is the strongest and most consistent, and the BIS recordings are altogether exemplary.

Cantatas 210 (Wedding); 211 (Coffee)

🎵 *** BIS CD 1411; with Sampson, Sakurada, Schreckenberger

While the series of church cantatas continues, Suzuki and his team here inaugurate a separate collection of the secular cantatas, including two of the most famous. Carolyn Sampson is the star of both, singing with style and much aplomb in the Coffee Cantata, where Stephan Schreckenberger characterizes equally strongly as her father. Perhaps the bold humour of this work suits Suzuki less well than its companion wedding celebration, which is most beautifully sung and is very successful on all counts.

Cantatas: Gardiner DG Archiv Series with Monteverdi Choir and English Baroque Soloists

Cantatas 113; 179; 199 (🎵 *** Opus Arte DVD OA 0816D; with Kožená, Towers, Padmore, Loges)

Cantatas for Easter 6; 66 (*** DG 463 580-2; with soloists)

Cantatas for Ascension Day 11; 37; 43; 128 (*** DG 463 583-2; with Argenta, Blaze, Rolfe Johnson, Genz, Varcoe, Hagen)

Cantatas for Whitsun 34; 59; 74; 172 (*** DG 463 584-2; with soloists)

Cantatas for Advent 36; 61; 62 (*** DG 463 588-2; with Argenta, Lang, Rolfe Johnson, Bär)

Cantatas for Christmas 63; 64; 121; 133 (*** DG 463 589-2; with soloists)

Cantatas for 3rd Sunday after Epiphany 72; 73; 111; 156 (DG 463 582-2; with soloists)

Cantatas for Feast of the Purification of Mary 82; 83; 125; 200 (*** DG 463 585-2; with Tyson, Agnew, Harvey)

Cantatas for 9th Sunday after Trinity 94; 105; 168 (*** DG 463 590-2; with soloists)

Cantatas 106; 118; 198 (*** DG 463 581-2; with Argenta, Chance, Rolfe Johnson, Varcoe)

Cantatas for 11th Sunday after Trinity 113; 179; 199 (*** DG 463 591-2; with soloists)

Cantatas 140; 147 (🎵 Ⓜ *** DG 463 587-2; with Holton, Chance, Rolfe Johnson, Varcoe)

During the 250th anniversary of Bach's death in 2000 John Eliot Gardiner embarked on an ambitious project to perform all the cantatas on the appropriate days of the liturgical year in a variety of English and European venues. Deutsche Grammophon had planned to record the whole series, but the costs involved, the emergence of rival versions at budget price and the magnificent BIS series from Japan prompted them to reconsider the viability of the project.

The DVD offers not just three complete Bach cantatas but an hour-long feature film. The cantatas are very well chosen; the outer ones from 1723 and 1724 respectively are from Bach's Leipzig period, the central one (for solo soprano) dates from 1714 when Bach was in Weimar. Gardiner characteristically relies on fresh young voices, with the Monteverdi Choir typically bright and incisive, matched by the four soloists. The tenor, Mark Padmore, is excellent; the counter-tenor, William Towers, and the young German baritone, Stephan Loges, are consistently firm and clear. But it is the Czech soprano, Magdalena Kožená, who wins first honours with her superb singing in the solo cantata, Mein Herz schwimmt im Blut. Aptly, she also appears in the St David's sequence in the feature film, one of the 11 venues visited.

The eventual outcome was the release of the CDs listed above. Some are live performances and two are reissues. It goes without saying that in the course of these beautifully recorded performances there is much to refresh the spirit alongside much that has spirit rather than a sense of the spiritual. Gardiner is marvellously alive to the texture and is dedicated and enthusiastic, but he can also be unyielding and lacking in breadth and majesty. Despite such reservations and the fact that Suzuki's series with the Bach Collegium of Japan is even more rewarding, Gardiner's performances are undoubtedly of a consistently high calibre. Both the documentation and presentation are of the usual fine Archiv standard. The recordings are immediate and well balanced.

Soli Deo Gloria Gardiner Series

Cantatas 1, 22–3, 54, 127, 129 & 182 (Ⓜ) *** Soli Deo Gloria SGD 118 (2) with Holton, Hartelius, Schubert, Stutzman, Gilchrist, Oxley, Harvey, Trinity College Cambridge Ch.)

Cantatas 5; 48; 56; 79; 80; 90; 192 (Ⓜ) **(*) Soli Deo Gloria SDG 110 (2); with Lunn, Towers, Gilchrist, Harvey)

Cantatas 16; 41; 58; 143; 153; 171 (Ⓜ) *** Soli Deo Gloria SDG 150 (2) with Holton, Ballard, Humphries, Gilchrist, Harvey, Bruce-Payne

Cantatas: 17; 19; 25; 50; 78; 130; 149 (Ⓜ) **(*) Soli Deo Gloria SDG 124 (2); with Hartelius, Tyson, Roberts, Gilchrist, Harvey)

Cantatas 18; 84; 92; 126; 144; 181 (Ⓜ) *** Soli Deo Gloria SDG 153 (2); with Keith, Gruffydd Jones, Tyson, Gilchrist, Persson, Brummelstroete, Oxley, Brown)

Cantatas (i) 24; (ii) 71; 88; 93; 131; (i) 177; 185 (Ⓜ) *** Soli Deo Gloria SDG 141; with (i) Kožená, Stutzmann, Agnew, Teste; (ii) Lunn, Towers, Van Rensburg, Harvey)

Cantatas 40; 91; 110; 121 (Ⓜ) **(*) Soli Deo Gloria SDG 113 (2); with Lunn, Fuge, Towers, Tyson, Gilchrist, Harvey)

Cantatas (i) 42; 67; (ii) 85; 104; 112; (i) 150; 158 (Ⓜ) *** Soli Deo Gloria SDG 131; with (i) Keith, Taylor, Daniels, Varcoe; (ii) Fuge, Towers, Meyn, Varcoe)

Cantatas 45; 46; 101; 102; 136; 178 (Ⓜ) *** Soli Deo Gloria SDG 147; with Tyson; Genz; Sherratt; Lunn; Taylor; Schwarz)

Cantatas 54; 71; 78; 151; 155; 159; 182; 190; Aria: Alles mit Got und nichts ohn'ihn, BWV 1127 (Ⓜ) **(*) Soli Deo Gloria SDG 113 (2); with Hartelius, Keith, Lunn, Manahan Thomas, Stutzmann, Tyson, Gilchrist, Harvey)

Cantatas (i) 129; 165; (ii) 175; (i) 176; (ii) 184; (i) 194 (Ⓜ) *** Soli Deo Gloria SDG 138; with (i) Holton,

Taylor, Agnew, Harvey; (ii) Larsson, Stutzmann, Genz, Loges)

When DG decided they could no longer sustain **John Eliot Gardiner's** ongoing pilgrimage to record all of Bach's cantatas in various venues, he bravely decided to set up his own label and underwrite the project himself and the project has proved successful on all counts. Performances are of a high standard, especially with regard to the soloists, and while ensemble cannot be as immaculate as it would be in the studios, the extra vividness of 'live communication' more than compensates.

The discs are being issued in handsomely produced double-packs, each like a book with notes, texts and translations bound into the leaves, although the reason for the choice of the picture which illuminates the front of each pack is elusive. The venues include Tewkesbury Abbey, St Magnus Cathedral, Kirkwall, and the Bach-Kirche in Arnstadt, and in all the concerts here the usual high standard of performance and recording are maintained. However, we have to comment that **Gardiner's** performances, fresh and clearheaded as they are, and often imbued with considerable intensity, do not quite match those of Suzuki in concentration, warmth and ultimate polish; nor are the recordings as seductive as the glorious SACD surround sound which BIS provide for the Japan Bach Collegium.

Cantatas: New Chandos Purcell Quartet Series

Early Cantatas, Volume 1: Cantatas 4; 106; 131; 196

*** Chan. 0715. Kirkby, Chance, Daniels, Harvey, Augmented Purcell Qt

Early Cantatas, Volume 2: Cantatas 12; 18; 61; 161

**** Chan. 0742. Kirkby, Chance, Daniels, Harvey, Augmented Purcell Qt

Early Cantatas, Volume 3: Cantatas 21; 172; 182

*** Chan. 0752 (2). Kirkby, Chance, Daniels, Harvey, Augmented Purcell Qt

These Chandos discs are the first in a new survey of the Bach cantatas, using period instruments and creating a chamber scale of considerable intimacy. The first-rate soloists join together here to act as the chorus. No quarrels with the performances at all – they have a great sense of style – or with the excellent recordings, but obviously this is not for those who require a greater amplitude of sonority in this repertoire. Although the **Purcell Quartet** is listed as the accompanying group, it is augmented by other players, and there are some memorable obbligato contributions, showing just how effective small-scale performances can be.

Other cantata groupings

Cantata 11 (Ascension)

*** EuroArts **DVD** 2054039. Karthäuser, Hardt, Einhorn, Van de Crabben, La Petite Bande, Kuijken (V/D: Michael Beyer) – C. P. E. BACH: *Die Auferstehung und Himmelfahrt Jesu* **(*)

It was a happy idea to combine a performance of Bach's *Ascension Cantata, Lobett Got* with his son's *Ascension Oratorio*, although the juxtaposition shows that while the latter is a fine work, Johann Sebastian's cantata is a supreme masterpiece. It is splendidly sung here, with excellent soloists and a first-class period-instrumental group, all working together as a team. The result is very enjoyable indeed, and beautifully recorded.

Cantatas 49, 57 & 152

**(*) DG 477 6591. Quasthoff, Röschmann, Berlin RIAS Chamber Ch. & Berlin Bar. Sol., Kussmaul

The glory of this triptych is the wonderfully refined and richly coloured accompaniments from **Kussmaul** and the **Berlin Baroque Soloists**, but the disc does not quite repeat the success of its predecessor, below. In these *Dialogue Cantatas* **Thomas Quasthoff** is as impressive as ever, but **Dorothea Röschmann**, although she sings confidently and phrases eloquently, at times has quavery tone production which not all will take to.

Cantatas 51; 82a; 199

(N) **** Virgin 235004-2 Dessay, Le Concert d'Astrée, Haim

Natalie Dessay's dramatic experience adds to the projection of singing that is also movingly pure in line, especially in the ravishing account of *Ich habe genug* with its gentle flute obbligato. But the opening of *Jauchzet Got*, with its sparklingly joyful trumpet contributions is equally telling, with Dessay's exuberant vocal virtuosity always at the service of the composer. The disc concludes with *Mein Herze schwimmt im Blut*, with its theme of the repentant sinner joyfully accepting God's forgiveness, which is perhaps most emotionally demanding of all. Dessay's response is very moving in its simplicity and vocal beauty. Its pair of oboe solos bring the most sensitive playing from **Patrick Beaugirade**, as do **Alexis Kossenko's** lovely flute decorations of *Ich habe genug*, and the orchestral playing is wonderfully warm and refined throughout the disc. It is handsomely packaged, and comes with a 52-minute bonus DVD made at the recording sessions.

Cantatas 54; 169; 170

(B) *** Hyp. Helios CDH 55312. Bowman, King's Consort, King

James Bowman is on impressive form and his admirers need not hesitate here. The present disc is very desirable and the **King's Consort** under **Robert King** give excellent support. Good recorded sound.

Cantatas 56; 82; 158

**** DG Surround Sound **SACD** 477532-6; CD 474505-2. Quasthoff, Berlin Bar. Sol., Kussmaul

Here is another of the most beautiful Bach cantata records in the catalogue. **Thomas Quasthoff** has the warmest bass-baritone voice you could possibly imagine, and his performance of the famous *Ich habe genug* is second to none (even remembering the many famous past recordings). His phrasing is wonderfully musical, and **Rainer Kussmaul** and his

Berlin Baroque Soloists, playing modern instruments with authentic manners, accompany him with comparable warmth and style. The splendid oboe soloist is Albrecht Mayer. The recording is splendid, but if you have four-channel SACD facilities with back speakers, the added realism with a feeling of sitting within the ambience of the Berlin Dahlem Jesus-Christus-Kirche is uncannily real, and it brings an added depth to the voice as well as spaciousness to the accompaniment.

Cantatas 63; 91; 121 & 133. Magnificat in E flat, BWV 243a

**** HMC 90 1781/2. Mields, Sampson, Danz, Padmore, Kooy, Noack, Ghent Coll. Voc., Herreweghe

A splendid compilation of Christmas cantatas from 1723/4, plus the glorious original version of the *Magnificat*, which was also intended for Christmas Day. *Cantata 63, Christen, äztet diesen Tag*, is equally jubilant and celebratory, richly scored for brass; and the other cantatas offer considerable variety of mood, reflecting Bach's remarkably varied musical response to this special time in the Christian calendar. Apart from fine choral singing, the soloists are memorable, especially **Carolyn Sampson**, surely an ideal Bach soprano, **Ingeborg Danz** and **Mark Padmore**.

Cantata 82: Ich habe genug

(M)(****) EMI mono 5 62807-2. Hotter, Philh. O, Bernard — BRAHMS: *Lieder* ***

One of the greatest cantata performances ever. Glorious singing from **Hans Hotter** and wonderfully stylish accompanying from **Anthony Bernard** and the **Philharmonia**. This 1950 mono recording was never reissued on LP and it sounds vividly present in its current remastering. Moreover, EMI have found some extra Brahms songs to add to the coupling.

Cantatas (i) 82; (i–iii) 159; (ii) 170

(B) **** Australian Decca Eloquence (ADD) 476 2684. ASMF, Marriner; with (i) Shirley-Quirk; (ii) J. Baker; (iii) Tear

Classic accounts of three cantatas, including *Seher, wir geh'n gen Jerusalem* (159), one of Bach's most inspired works. Particularly glorious is the meditation *Es ist vollbracht* ('It is finished'), with its poignant oboe obbligato (played by Rachel Lord). Both **Dame Janet Baker** and **John Shirley-Quirk** are in marvellous voice, as they are in Nos. 82 and 170 – hardly less inspired works and performances. Indeed, this collection of cantatas is among the finest in the catalogue and is well worth seeking out. The mid-1960s recordings are of Decca's best vintage quality.

(i) Cantatas 82; 199; (ii) Double Concerto for Oboe & Violin, BWV 1060

**** Priory/Carus 83 302. (i) Kirkby; (ii) Arften, Von der Golz; Freiburg Bar. Ens., Golz

Emma Kirkby's outstandingly fine account of *Ich habe genug* virtually ranks alongside the highly praised baritone versions of Hans Hotter and John Shirley-Quirk and this is claimed to be the first recording of the present E minor version. What is remarkable about the coupling, *Mein Herz schwimmt im Blut*, is not only the lyrical beauty of the arias, but the way this great baroque soprano invests the recitatives with comparable feeling. Here the obbligato is for oboe, and **Katherina Arften** is most sensitive in this role while, as a refreshing interlude, she joins the leader and conductor **Von der Golz** in the engaging *Double Concerto, BWV 1060*. The accompaniments could hardly be bettered, and the recording ambience and balance are just about perfect.

Cantatas 199; 202. Arias from Cantatas 68; 208

*** Testament (ADD) SBT 1178. Schwarzkopf, Philh. O, Dart –
    MOZART: *Ch'io mi scordi di te?* (***)

Testament have here gathered together **Schwarzkopf** recordings made in 1955–8 that for various reasons were never published. It is especially fascinating to compare the two versions (in German) of 'Sheep may safely graze', recorded a year apart in 1957 and 1958 – the second one far more dramatic in the recitative, and generally more freely expressive. The poised Schwarzkopf predominates, but the vehement Schwarzkopf also repeatedly comes through vividly, directly reflecting the singer's strong, positive character. Excellent transfers.

Cantatas 199; 202; 209

(BB) *** Naxos 8.550431. Wagner, Capella Istropolitana, Brembeck

Mein Herz schwimmt im Blut (BWV 199) comes from Bach's Weimar years, and **Friederike Wagner** proves both sympathetic and lively; and both *Weichet nur, betrübte Schatten*, popularly known as the 'Wedding Cantata', and 209, *Non sà che sia dolore*, are given thoroughly enjoyable performances. Not for devotees of authentic-performance practice, but enjoyable for those who prefer a more traditional approach. Decent recording too.

Cantatas 202; 210 (Wedding Cantatas). Cantata 82 (excerpt): Ich habe genug. Arias (attrib.): Bist du bei mir (BWV 508, probably by Gottfried Stölzel); Gedenke doch, mein Geist (BWV 509, Anon.)

⊝– **** Decca 455 972-2. Kirkby, AAM, Hogwood

This is among the most delightful of all the records of Bach's solo secular cantatas. **Emma Kirkby**, in her freshest voice, is ideally cast – as the lovely opening aria, *Weichet nur*, from the more famous of the two *Wedding Cantatas*, immediately shows. Her singing is no less ravishing in *Schlummert ein* from BWV 82, *Schweigt, ihr Flöten* ('Hush, you flutes' – Bach here isn't meaning to be taken seriously) from BWV 210, or the most famous 'Bach aria' which is not written by Bach, *Bist du bei mir*. The accompaniments from **Hogwood** and his **Academy of Ancient Music** could not have a lighter touch or more finesse, and the obbligato playing (of which there is a great deal) could not be more sensitive or more fluent.

Cantatas 208 (Hunting); 212 (Peasant)

(N) (M) *** Warner 2564 69259-2 Blasi, Holl, Kenny, Equiluz, Arnold Schoenberg Ch., VCM, Harnoncourt

Harnoncourt topped off his complete recording of Bach's church cantatas with admirably ebullient accounts of a pair of secular cantatas, celebrating the name-days of two local dignitaries. The solo contributions in both works are splendid, and **Blasi** and the robust **Robert Holl** both enjoy themselves hugely in the boisterous *Peasant Cantata*. A typical eulogy from the soprano is introduced by a quotation of the famous *La Folia*, and the musical interest of this remarkably inspired cantata (considering its ragbag of a text) is Bach's use of various old melodies familiar to his audience. The exuberance of the performance carries over to Harnoncourt's accompaniments – no scholarly rectitude here – and the recording is first rate.

Cantatas 211 (Coffee Cantata); 212 (Peasant Cantata)

*** O-L 417 621-2. Kirkby, Covey-Crump, Thomas, AAM, Hogwood

Emma Kirkby is particularly appealing in the *Coffee Cantata* and her father is admirably portrayed by **David Thomas**. **Hogwood** opts for single strings, and some may find they sound thin; however, there is a corresponding gain in lightness and intimacy. The recording is altogether first class.

Major choral works

Christmas Oratorio, BWV 248; Mass in B min., BWV 232; St John Passion, BWV 245; St Matthew Passion, BWV 244

⊝– (B) *** DG 469 769-2 (9). Soloists, Monteverdi Ch., E. Bar. Sol., Gardiner

All these performances are among our primary choices for these works, and this bargain box in DG's Collectors' Edition cannot be too highly recommended. The documentation is excellent, although no translations are included.

Christmas Oratorio, BWV 248

⊝– *** DG 423 232-2 (2). Rolfe Johnson, Argenta, von Otter, Blochwitz, Bär, Monteverdi Ch., E. Bar. Sol., Gardiner

⊝– *** BIS CD 941/2. Frimmer, Mera, Türk, Kooy, Bach Coll., Japan, Suzuki

(N) (BB) *** EMI Gemini (ADD) 5 69503-2 (2) Ameling, J. Baker, Tear, Fischer-Dieskau, King's College Cambridge Ch., ASMF, Ledger

The freshness of the singing and playing in the DG CD set is a constant pleasure. Far more than usual, one registers the joyfulness of the work, from the trumpets and timpani at the start onwards. **Anthony Rolfe Johnson** makes a pointful and expressive Evangelist, and also outstanding is **Anne Sofie von Otter** with her natural gravity and exceptionally beautiful mezzo. Beauty of tone consistently marks the singing of **Nancy Argenta**, **Hans-Peter Blochwitz** and **Olaf Bär**. The sound is full and atmospheric.

As in his recordings of the Bach cantatas, **Masaaki Suzuki** directs an exceptionally fresh and alert reading of the *Christmas Oratorio*, bringing out the joy of Bach's inspiration, with outstandingly crisp singing from the chorus. Speeds are often fast, but in the beautiful cradle-song, *Schlafe mein Liebster*, relaxed pacing allows full expressiveness, here with **Yoshikazu Mera** as a characterful male alto soloist. Mera in florid writing does not always avoid the intrusive 'h', but that is one of the few blemishes in the solo singing, with **Gerd Türk** a fine Evangelist and **Peter Kooy** a firmly focused bass. Warm, atmospheric sound, though with the choir behind the instruments in the main choruses. This makes a fine alternative to the Gardiner version.

It was **Ledger** who played the harpsichord continuo in many of Benjamin Britten's performances of this work, and some of Britten's imagination comes through here, helped by four outstanding and stylish soloists. The King's College acoustic gives a warm background to the nicely scaled performance of choir and orchestra; the timpani at the very start sound spectacularly impressive.

Easter Oratorio, BWV 249; Cantata 66: Erfreut euch, ihr Herzen

⊖━ *** HM HMC 901513. Schlick, Wessel, Taylor, Kooy, Coll. Voc., Herreweghe

Bach's *Easter Oratorio* derives from a secular cantata, more than once revised. It opens with a joyful *Sinfonia* and an *Adagio* with oboe solo (very well played in the **Herreweghe** account), followed by a lively chorus ('Come hasten, come running, ye swift feet') with trumpets, but then it depends very much on the soloists, who blend beautifully together in their introductory recitativo before taking their individual roles with distinction – as Mary Magdalene, Peter and John respectively. The chorus and trumpets then return to end the work joyfully. The apt coupling of the *Easter Cantata*, BWV 66, with its lovely closing *Alleluja* completes a disc which is fresh and vivid and will be hard to surpass.

Easter Oratorio, BWV 249; Magnificat, BWV 243

**(*) DG 477 6359. Gabrieli Consort & Players, McCreesh

Using five solo voices in the choruses and choosing Bach's less spectacular version of the Magnificat, with flutes tellingly added to the scoring, **Paul McCreesh's** authenticity brings above all a dedicated approach, so that the opening *Sinfonia* in the oratorio and the opening chorus in the *Magnificat* are colourful but less than overwhelming. However, the performances are made both distinctive and appealing by the lovely solo singing from **Kimberly McCord** and **Julia Gooding** (sopranos), **Robin Blaze** (alto) and **Paul Agnew** (tenor), especially in the *Magnificat*. The recording is suitably refined and clear.

Magnificat in E flat, BWV 243a; Cantata 10: Meine Seele erhebt den Herren

*** EuroArts DVD 2053419. York, Bartosz, Dürmüller, Mertens, Amsterdam Bar. Ch. & O, Koopman – KUHNAU: *Magnificat*

Koopman chooses the earlier, E flat major version of the *Magnificat*, and it makes a magnificent début on DVD, recorded at St Thomas's Church, Leipzig, where, like its Kuhnau coupling, it was first heard. The performance is

thrilling, with its bolder E flat major trumpets and splendidly incisive choral contribution. The soloists too are first class, both individually and as a team. Like Suzuki, Koopman offers the Kuhnau setting and includes also a fine performance of the cantata *Meine Seele erherbt den Herren*, which has associations with the more ambitious work. The camera is used sensibly and follows the music from soloists to chorus to instrumentalists. The cantata too is very successful in all respects.

(i) Magnificat in D; (ii) Violin Concerto 2

*** Sony **DVD** SVD 45983. BPO, Karajan; with (i) Blegen, Mollinari, Araiza, Holl, Berlin RIAS Chamber Ch.; (ii) Mutter (Director: Humphrey Burton)

There are few better examples on DVD than this of a conductor's magnetism being almost tangible. It is apparent during **Anne-Sophie Mutter's** fine performance of the *Violin Concerto*, although she is given the limelight; but in the *Magnificat* one can feel the whole orchestra, chorus and soloists responding to the conductor, while **Karajan's** actual movements are minimal, his face all but impassive. This is gloriously old-fashioned Bach with a large orchestra, and when the camera dwells on the blazing trumpets, one feels almost able to reach out and touch them. It is a thrilling performance, richly and vividly recorded, and one feels right in the middle of it.

Magnificat in D, BWV 243

⊖━ **** Telarc **SACD** 60651. Tamara Matthews, Deanne Meek, Mary Phillips, Boston Baroque, Pearlman – VIVALDI: *Gloria* ***

⊖━ Ⓜ *** Virgin 3 63299-2. De Reyghere, Jacobs, Prégardien, Lika, Netherlands Chamber Ch., La Petite Bande, Kuijken

⊖━ *** Chan. 0518. Kirkby, Bonner, Chance, Ainsley, Varcoe, Coll. Mus. 90, Hickox – VIVALDI: *Gloria* ***

Ⓝ Ⓑ *** EMI Encore 2 08125-2 Hendricks, Murray, Rigby, Hellman, Hynninen, ASMF, Marriner – VIVALDI: *Gloria* ***

The opening of the new Telarc (Surround Sound) SACD from **Martin Pearlman's Boston Baroque** is immediately arresting. If one gets the balance of the back speakers just right, the sense of presence in the warm hall acoustic is very real. All the soloists are excellent, and they blend beautifully when they sing together in the *Et misericordia* and *Suscepit Israel*. The choral singing is committedly expressive and, if not always precise in the runs, this is partly the effect of the warm acoustic which prevents absolute sharpness of focus. But the overall impression is wholly natural and Pearlman's tempi are aptly vivacious. The Vivaldi coupling is comparably successful.

Splendidly framed by the vigorous opening and closing choruses with their resplendent trumpets, **Kuijken's** reissued version of the *Magnificat* from 1988, performed by the excellent **Netherlanders** and **La Petite Bande**, makes a strong mid-priced recommendation. There are some first-class contributions from **Greta de Reyghere** and **Christoph**

Prégardien with lovely singing from the soprano and a finely matched oboe obbligato in the aria *Quia respexit*. There are moments of vulnerable intonation from the oboe, but this is a small blemish. The choral singing is warmly expressive (especially in *Suscepit Israel*) and as lightly articulated as you could wish. The coupling is one of Bach's most expansive and celebrated Weimar cantatas, *Ich hatte viel Bekümmernis*, which again gives the soprano and tenor plenty of opportunities for espressivo, individually and as a duo, after which the trumpets return for the intricate closing chorus of praise. Above all there is a sense of breadth and majesty fully worthy of Bach. A highly recommendable disc in every respect.

Both **Richard Hickox** and **Pearlman** couple the *Magnificat* with the popular D major *Gloria*, RV 589, of Vivaldi, and for collectors seeking this coupling the clear choice is between period and modern instruments. Those who like the former will gravitate towards Hickox, who directs a most musical account and has the benefit of such fine singers as **Emma Kirkby**, **Michael Chance** and **Stephen Varcoe**, and good Chandos recording.

Marriner's performance with the **Academy** is well paced and executed with precision and fine musical intelligence. No quarrels with the soloists either, or with the splendidly warm and present recording. This can be recommended with confidence.

Markus Passion (1731) (reconstructed Koopman)

*** Chall. **DVD** CCDVD 72141. Prégardien, Kooy, York, Landauer, Agnew, Mertens, Amsterdam Bar. Ch. & O, Koopman

The *St Mark Passion* is lost, and for many years scholars have been conjecturing as to whether its music had found its way into other Bach works. **Ton Koopman** has started afresh, drawing on Bach's music written before Easter 1731 and composing his own recitatives to the text by Christian Friederick Henrici, alias Picander, with the soloists participating in the words of the arias. The result is a triumphant success: a modest work, setting the Passion story with an appealing simplicity, but one which is very convincing in the present splendid performance. Indeed, it is difficult to imagine it being bettered, with superb soloists and **Christoph Prégardien** as Evangelist telling the story and **Peter Kooy** as Christ. There are only a limited number of arias but they are finely sung by the starry cast, and the chorus is as dedicated as it is excellent. The performance has all the virtues of a live performance, and the recording and camerawork against the beautiful backcloth of the Chiesa di San Simpliciano, Milan, is well handled. A most rewarding and repeatable experience.

(i) Masses (Missae breves): in F, BWV 233; in G, BWV 236. Trio Sonata in C, transposed to D, BWV 529

●—*** Chan. 0653. (i) Argenta, Chance, Padmore, Harvey, instrumental soloists; Purcell Qt

Masses (Missae breves): in A, BWV 234; in G min., BWV 235

●—*** Chan. 0642. Gritton, Blaze, Padmore, Harvey, Purcell Qt

There have been various good modern-instrument performances of these so-called short or Lutheran Masses over the years, but the authentic period-instrument performances on Chandos must now take pride of place. Although the soloists provide the one-voice-to-a-part chorus, their voices blend so richly together that one is not conscious of any lack of body or contrast: indeed the effect is glorious, while in the F major work the vigorous trumpeting horns add to the joyfulness of the *Gloria* and *Cum Sancto Spiritu*. The solo singing is splendid, and the overall balance quite excellent. The first disc uses a *Trio Sonata* to act as a kind of extended opening sinfonia, and very effectively too. This is the CD to try first, and you will surely want the other one also.

Masses (Missae breves), BWV 232: Sanctus (only); 233; 234; 235; 236; Gloria in excelsis Deo (from Cantata 191); Magnificat, BWV 243

Ⓝ *** Challenge CC 72188 (2) Soloists, Amsterdam Bar. Ch. & O, Koopman

Following on after his set of the Cantatas, **Koopman** turns his attention to the *Missae breves*, with comparably impressive results. There are generally first class solo contributions (especially in the *Gloria in excelsis Deo*) and the **Amsterdam Chorus** and **Baroque Orchestra** are well up to form. Recommended especially to those not favouring one instrument to a part performances as are offered on Chandos.

Mass in B min., BWV 232 (DVD Version)

●—*** Virgin **DVD** 00946 370636-9. Ziesak, DiDonato, Taylor, Agnew, Henschel, Maîtrise Notre-Dame de Paris, O Ens. de Paris, Nelson (Director: Olivier Simonnet)

John Nelson gives the *Mass in B minor* a splendid DVD debut with a wholly invigorating and deeply expressive performance. He has excellent soloists, both individually (**Daniel Taylor's** *Agnus Dei* is memorable) and singing together (the *Domine Deus* another highlight). The soprano **Ruth Ziesak** sings radiantly and her duet with **Joyce DiDonato** in the *Kyrie* is an early highlight. The choral group have the men outnumbered by the women, and this affects the balance at times; but the singing in the *Gloria*, *Sanctus*, and especially the *Osanna* is thrilling. Nelson's tempi are admirably chosen and the performance moves forward spontaneously to its satisfying closing *Donna nobis pacem*. The authentic-sized orchestra plays modern French instruments. The cameras make the most of the interior, yet perceptively concentrate on the performers. In short, Olivier Simonnet's film is fully worthy of the music-making.

Mass in B min., BWV 232 (CD versions)

●—**** DG 415 514-2 (2). Argenta, Dawson, Fairfield, Knibbs, Kwella, Hall, Nichols, Chance, Collin, Stafford, Evans, Milner, Murgatroyd, Lloyd-Morgan, Varcoe, Monteverdi Ch., E. Bar. Sol., Gardiner

🎵 *** BIS **SACD** 1701/2. Sampson, Nicholls, Blaze, Türk, Kooy, Japan Bach Collegium, Suzuki

🎵 *** BBC (ADD) BBCL 4062-2 (2). Hill, J. Baker, Pears, Shirley-Quirk, New Philh. Ch. and O, Giulini

🎵 (M) *** Hyp. Dyad CDD 22051 (2). Ritter, Mrasek, Schloderer, Fraas, Rolfe Johnson, George, Tölz Boys' Ch., King's Cons. Ch., King's Cons., King

🎵 (M) *** EMI 2 28507-2 (2). Donath, Fassbaender, Ahnsjö, Hermann, Holl, Bav. R. Ch. & O, Jochum

John Eliot Gardiner gives a magnificent account of the *B minor Mass*, one which attempts to keep within an authentic scale but which also triumphantly encompasses the work's grandeur. Gardiner masterfully conveys the majesty (with bells and censer-swinging evoked) simultaneously with a crisply resilient rhythmic pulse. The choral tone is luminous and powerfully projected. The regular solo numbers are taken by choir members making a cohesive whole. The recording is warmly atmospheric but not cloudy.

Masaaki Suzuki's performance is gloriously recorded in the BIS surround sound we now take for granted in his fine Bach series. The opening *Kyrie* sets the warmly relaxed style of the performance, with the *Gloria*, *Cum Sancto Spiritu* and *Sanctus* contrastingly exuberant and the closing *Dona nobis pacem* richly dignified. The choral singing is characteristically fine, and **Carolyn Sampson** and **Robin Blaze's** contributions stand out: *Qui sedes* and *Agnus Dei* are very moving. Instrumental obbligati are also memorable. This account may not be as extrovert and vital as with Gardiner, but in his warmer, more restrained way Suzuki is just as persuasive.

In the echoing acoustic of St Paul's Cathedral – remarkably well-tamed by the BBC engineers – **Giulini** conducts a spacious, dedicated reading with a superb quartet of soloists, notably **Dame Janet Baker**, whose contributions shine out with heart-warming fervour. **Peter Pears**, then 62, is in fine, clear voice, as is the bass, **John Shirley-Quirk**, with the soprano, **Jenny Hill**, fresh and bright. The chorus is not so clearly focused as the soloists, particularly in the meditative numbers, yet in vigorous sections and in the great censer-swinging rhythms of the *Sanctus* the weight and bite of the singing come over thrillingly. Giulini adopts speeds on the broad side even for a traditional, large-scale performance, but soloists and chorus alike sustain them superbly, as do the orchestra. As an illuminating supplement an interview with Giulini by John Amis is included at the end.

With the distinctive continental tone of the **Tölzer Boys**, very different from their English counterparts, **Robert King's** vigorous and alert reading has extra freshness, with 24 boys set brightly against 12 of the **King's Consort** tenors and basses. The individual finesse of the boy singers is impressively demonstrated in the solos. This is a reading which consistently brings out the joy of Bach's inspiration, not least in the great celestial outbursts of the *Sanctus* and the final *Dona nobis pacem*. Warm, atmospheric recording.

Jochum's memorable, dedicated (1980) performance, marked by resilient rhythms, remains among the most completely satisfying versions even today. The choral singing –

by far the most important element in this work – is superb and, though the soloists are variably balanced, they make a fine, clear-voiced team to leave Bach's inspired music resonating in the listener's memory. The digital recording is admirably spacious and clear. Documentation is just about adequate, but with no text.

Motets: *Singet dem Herrn ein Neues Lied; Der Geist hilft unsrer Schwachheit; Jesu, meine Freude; Der Gerechte Kommt um Fürchte dich nicht; Komm, Jesu, Komm; Lobet den Herrn; Sei Lob und Preis mit Ehren, BWV 225–31*

🎵 (M) *** Teldec 0630 17430-2. Stockholm Bach Ch., VCM, Harnoncourt

The Teldec recording is very successful indeed, beautifully fresh and clear, the acoustic attractively resonant without clouding detail, and the accompanying instrumental group giving discreet yet telling support. The vigour and joy of the singing come over splendidly. This is one of **Harnoncourt's** most impressive Bach records, while the **Stockholm chorus** show stamina as well as sympathy. At mid-price this must now be the prime recommendation for these six works.

St John Passion, BWV 245 (DVD versions)

🎵 (M) *** EuroArts Invitation **DVD** 2050396. Türk, Midori Suzuki, Blaze, Urano, MacLeod, Japan Bach Coll., Masaaki Suzuki (includes interview with conductor)

🎵 *** DG **DVD** 073 4291. Equiluz, Holl, Soprano & Alto Soloists of Vienna Boys' Ch., Moser, Scharinger, Tölz Boys' Ch., VCM, Harnoncourt (Director: Humphrey Burton)

Recorded in Suntory Hall, Tokyo, on 28 July 2000 – the day marking the 250th anniversary of Bach's death – this is an outstanding version on DVD of the *St John Passion*, a tribute to the work of **Masaaki Suzuki** in Japan. The interpretation remains very similar to Suzuki's earlier CD account on BIS, with fresh, light textures and generally brisk speeds which yet allow for depth of feeling, and the sense of occasion is irresistible. Only **Gerd Türk** as the Evangelist is presented as a soloist in front of the choir, giving an achingly beautiful performance, with his profound involvement all the more evident when seen as well as heard. Türk also sings the tenor arias, and the other soloists, all first rate, also have double roles, singing in the sixteen-strong choir (4–4–4–4) before stepping forward when needed as soloists: **Stephan MacLeod** singing Christus as well as the bass arias, **Chiyuki Urano** singing Pilate and other incidental solos, **Robin Blaze** a superb alto soloist and the ravishing **Midori Suzuki** in the two soprano arias.

Harnoncourt has successfully recorded the *St John Passion* three times, first in 1971 with similar forces to this 1985 DG set, and more recently in 1993 when he opted for the mixed voices of the Schoenberg Choir and a fine team of soloists. But this DVD version continued his earlier pattern with all-male forces and boy trebles in the choir as well as singing the soprano and alto arias. The result is very successful indeed, authentic in every respect, and the visual and acoustic ambience of Graz Cathedral adds much to the projection of what is an outstandingly vibrant account, second to none. The two soloists from the **Vienna Boys' Choir** are extraordinarily assured, the singing of the alto especially fine. But what sets the seal on the power of the performance is **Kurt Equiluz's** vividly inspired narrative as the Evangelist, answered eloquently by **Robert Holl** as a richly resonant Jesus. The choral contribution is a pleasure to watch, when the boys are so obviously committed and involved, and the period instrumental support of the **Vienna Concentus Musicus** is splendid, tempi are admirably flexible (the chorales especially moving) and Harnoncourt himself electrifyingly dominates the proceedings. Humphrey Burton's visual direction uses the church interior very tellingly, although concentrating mainly on the performers. The sound is excellent and surtitles are available.

St John Passion (CD versions)

🔾 ⓑⓑ *** Naxos 8.557296/7 (2). Gilchrist, Bernays, Dougan, Littlewood, Bowman, Beale, Baldy, New College, Oxford, Ch., Coll. Novum, Higginbottom

🔾 *** DG 419 324-2 (2). Rolfe Johnson, Varcoe, Hauptmann & soloists, Monteverdi Ch., E. Bar. Sol., Gardiner

🔾 *** BIS CD 921/22. Schmithüsen, Mera, Türk, Sakurada, Hida, Urano, Kooy, Bach Coll., Japan, Suzuki

The Naxos CD version of the *St John Passion*, with the choir of **New College, Oxford**, at budget price, offers an outstanding period performance which can stand comparison with any in the catalogue. Only male voices are used, with the soprano arias sung by a boy treble. The choir itself is fresh and bright, singing incisively, with the crowd choruses vividly adding to the drama, helped by the natural balance. **Higginbottom's** speeds on the fast side follow period practice, except in relatively broad chorales. **James Gilchrist** is a superb Evangelist, fluent and expressive, and the main quartet of soloists makes a sensitive team, including the confidently firm-toned treble, **Joe Littlewood**, and the veteran counter-tenor, **James Bowman**, still in fine voice. The wind instruments of the **Collegium Novum** have a sharp edge, which brings out the agony implied in the accompaniment to the opening chorus, while the darkness of instrumentation in the great alto aria, *Es ist vollbracht*, adds to the poignancy of Bowman's singing.

    Gardiner conducts an exhilarating performance. Speeds are regularly on the fast side but, characteristically, he consistently keeps a spring in the rhythm. Chorales are treated in contrasted ways, which may not please the more severe authenticists; but, as with so much of Gardiner's work, here is a performance using authentic scale and period instruments which speaks in the most vivid way to anyone prepared to listen, not just to the specialist. Soloists – regular contributors to Gardiner's team – are all first rate. Warm and atmospheric, yet clear and detailed recording.

    Suzuki directs an urgently refreshing reading of the *St John Passion* on BIS, with fine singing from the chorus giving dramatic impact to the 'turba' choruses. The big choruses at the beginning and end are beautifully sung too, though here

the voices are set back behind the orchestra and are rather lightweight. Suzuki's feeling for the natural timing of numbers – generally on the fast side in the modern period manner – is impeccable, and the soloists make an excellent team, with **Gerd Türk** an outstanding Evangelist, light and clear. There is additionally a reduced price boxed set combining Suzuki's outstanding performances of the *St John* and *St Matthew Passions* (BIS CD 1342/4).

St John Passion (in English)

✿ ⓑ *** Double Decca (ADD) 443 859-2 (2). Pears, Harper, Hodgson, Tear, Howell, Shirley-Quirk, Wandsworth School Boys' Ch., ECO, Britten

Britten characteristically refuses to follow any set tradition, whether baroque, Victorian or whatever, and, with greater extremes of tempo than is common (often strikingly fast), the result makes one listen afresh. The soloists are all excellent, **Heather Harper** radiant, and the Wandsworth School Boys' Choir reinforces the freshness of the interpretation. A superb bargain.

St Matthew Passion, BWV 244 (DVD version)

🔾 *** Chall. **DVD** CCDCD 72233 (2). Dürmüller, Abele, Samuelis, Bartosz, Agnew, Mertens, Breda Sacraments Church Boys' Ch., Amsterdam Bar. Ch. & O, Koopman

Having completed his cycle of cantatas, in 2005 **Koopman** turned to the *St Matthew Passion*, which he recorded live at St Joriskerk, Amersfoort, using the tenor and bass soloists from his cantata series – **Paul Agnew** and **Klaus Mertens**, who make distinguished contributions, although Mertens is comparatively light-voiced. **Jörg Dürmüller** (the Evangelist) is first class in every way. He tells the tragic story sympathetically and often dramatically, and he has a fine, rich tone, and when he makes a lyrical comment his voice is honeyed. **Ekkehard Abele** (Christ), darker but not gruff, is similarly impressive, and the crucifixion dialogues of Part II are among the most telling elements of the performance, supported by vivid choral interjections, typical of the choral singing as a whole which, when needed, is full of vitality, as for instance in *Sind Blitze sind Donner* at the end of Part I.

St Matthew Passion, BWV 244 (CD versions)

🔾 *** DG 474 200-2 (2). York, Gooding, Ko\u017een\u00e1, Bickley, Padmore, Gilchrist, Harvey, Loges, Gabrieli Players, McCreesh

🔾 *** DG 427 648-2 (3). Rolfe Johnson, Schmidt, Bonney, Monoyios, von Otter, Chance, Crook, Bär, Hauptmann, Monteverdi Ch., E. Bar. Sol., Gardiner

🔾 *** BIS CD 1000/1002 (3). Türk, Kooy, Argenta, Blaze, Sakurada, Urano, Sollek-Avella, Hagiwara, Odagawa, Bach Coll., Japan, Ch. & O, Suzuki

Though **Paul McCreesh** uses minimum forces for Bach's masterpiece, with one voice per part, the result has the sharpest dramatic impact, thanks not only to the incisiveness of the performance but also to the vivid immediacy of the recorded sound, with words exceptionally clear. The great opening chorus sets the pattern. The speed is far faster than usual, with the compound time conveying jollity. **Mark Padmore** as the Evangelist is fresh and fluent throughout, also taking on the tenor arias with his light, heady tone. Though **Peter Harvey**, more a baritone than a bass, has his moments of grittiness, as in the bass aria, *Gerne will ich*, with its low tessitura, he makes a suitably grave Jesus in the recitatives. **Deborah York** as first soprano and **Magdalena Kožená** as alto, both solo and choral, are excellent with clear, firm voices. As for the supreme alto aria, *Erbarme dich mein Gott*, with its baroque violin obbligato, Kožená in an intimate atmosphere conveys the ecstatic devotion of resting on God's mercy. In the closing numbers the mood is made to grow lighter, with the reservation that the final chorus with such small forces makes for a downbeat close, hardly weighty enough.

Gardiner's version of the *St Matthew Passion*, the culminating issue in his Bach choral series for DG Archiv, brings an intense, dramatic reading which now makes a fine alternative choice, not just for period-performance devotees but for anyone not firmly set against the new authenticity. The result is an invigorating, intense telling of the story, with Gardiner favouring high dynamic contrasts and generally fast speeds, which are still geared to the weighty purpose of the whole work. He and his performers were recorded in what proved an ideal venue, The Maltings at Snape, where the warm acoustic gives body and allows clarity to period textures.

Masaaki Suzuki provides a fresh and beautifully sung reading of the most challenging of all Bach choral works with a first-rate team of soloists led by the free-toned **Gerd Türk** as the Evangelist, and with **Nancy Argenta** outstanding among the others. If the result is a little short on devotional intensity in the culminating sections of this work, that is partly the result of the rather close-up recording, with solo voices and orchestra not always cleanly separated. More seriously, the double choir in the great double-choruses at the beginning and end is more backwardly balanced than elsewhere, set behind the orchestra, so that the dramatic impact is lessened. Nevertheless, this remains a powerful achievement.

Koopman's fine performance is mirrored by its DVD equivalent and is discussed above. It would not be a first choice on CD, as undoubtedly the visual element adds much to its impact on the listener.

While it certainly will not appeal to the authentic lobby, **Klemperer's** 1962 Philharmonia recording of the *St Matthew Passion* represents one of his greatest achievements on record, an act of devotion of such intensity that points of style and interpretation seem insignificant. The whole cast clearly shared Klemperer's own intense feelings, and one can only sit back and share them too, whatever one's preconceptions. (EMI 5 67538-2 [67542-2])

St Matthew Passion (in English)

Ⓑ (**(*)) Dutton mono 2CDAX 2005 (3). Greene, Suddaby, Ferrier, Cummings, Bach Ch., Jacques O, Jacques – PERGOLESI: *Stabat Mater* (**)

In 1947–8 Decca recorded the *St Matthew Passion*, based on the annual performances conducted by **Dr Reginald Jacques**, and that is what Michael Dutton has here transferred immaculately to CD, with the bonus of the 1946 Decca recording of the Pergolesi *Stabat Mater*, also with **Ferrier** as soloist. The Bach is very much a performance of its time. Only the 'turba' choruses commenting on the action are brisk in the way one would now expect. **Eric Greene** is the noble Evangelist and the sweet-toned **Elsie Suddaby** shines out in the soprano arias, but it is Ferrier who instantly on each entry conveys quite a different degree of intensity from the rest, immediately magnetic. Having an English text is well justified, when the words are so clear.

Vocal collections

Arias: *Bist du bei mir; Cantata 202: Weichet nur, betrübte Schatten. Cantata 209: Ricetti gramezza. St Matthew Passion: Blute nur; Ich will dir mein Herze schenken*

**(*) Delos D/CD 3026. Augér, Mostly Mozart O, Schwarz – HANDEL: *Arias* **(*)

Arleen Augér's pure, sweet soprano, effortlessly controlled, makes for bright performances of these Bach arias and songs, very recommendable for admirers of this delightful singer, well coupled with Handel arias.

Arias from: *Cantatas BWV 32; 151; 202 (Wedding); St Matthew Passion*

Ⓑ *** EMI 3 68255-2. Yu, Prague Philh., Sato – MOZART: *Arias* ***

The Korean-American soprano, **Hyunah Yu**, with her firm, creamy voice is just as stylish in Bach as she is in the Mozart arias which provide the coupling on this excellent issue in EMI's Debut series. There is a natural intensity in her singing, backed by a fine technique, readily surmounting any technical difficulties. On this showing Yu is going to make an important career.

Arias: *Mass in B min.: Agnus Dei; Qui sedes. St John Passion: All is fulfilled. St Matthew Passion: Grief for sin*

Ⓜ (***) Decca mono 4756411. Ferrier, LPO, Boult – HANDEL: *Arias* (***) ✿

On 7 and 8 October 1952 **Kathleen Ferrier** made her last and perhaps greatest record in London's Kingsway Hall, coupling four arias each by Bach and Handel. The combined skill of John Culshaw and Kenneth Wilkinson ensured a recording of the utmost fidelity by the standards of that time. Now it re-emerges with extraordinary naturalness and presence.

Orchestral transcriptions and arrangements

Conductors' transcriptions: *Aria: Bist du bei mir? (Klemperer); Chorales: Ein feste Burg (Damrosch); Herzlich tut mich verlangen (Leinsdorf); Ich ruf' zu dir, Herr Jesu Christ (Gui); Jesu, Joy of Man's Desiring (Ormandy); Sheep may safely graze*

(Barbirolli); *Fantasia & Fugue in G min., BWV 542* (Mitropoulos); *Suite 3: Air* (Sargent); *Suite 6* (Sir Henry Wood); *Toccata & Fugue in D min., BWV 565* (Skrowaczewski)

**** Chan. **SACD** CHSA 5030. BBC SO, Slatkin

What this collection confirms yet again is that Stokowski's orchestral transcriptions, however flamboyant, are almost unique in catching the innate spirit of Bach's music. Mitropoulos's spectacular scoring of the *Fantasia and Fugue in G minor* combines panache with individuality. Klemperer's restrained scoring of the lovely *Bist du bei mir* for strings alone is wonderfully luminous as played here, where Sargent's string version of *Jesu, Joy of Man's Desiring* curiously omits Bach's oboe obbligato, and both this and his semi-luscious treatment of what he calls the *Air on a G String* are somewhat bland. The six-movement Suite arranged by Sir Henry Wood is unexpectedly diverse and enjoyable. The programme opens with Skrowaczewski's spectacular alternative transcription of the famous *D minor Toccata and Fugue*, owing much to Stokowski, especially in the use of the horns; although the effect is essentially brasher, especially in its use of percussion. Very fine playing throughout from the **BBC Symphony Orchestra**, and superbly spacious, demonstration-worthy sound from Chandos.

Chaconne from solo *Violin Partita 2, BWV 1004* (orch. Raff); *Chorales: O Mensch, bewein' dein' Sünde gross* (orch. Reger); *Wachet auf* (orch. Bantock); *Fantasia & Fugue in C min., BWV 537* (orch. Elgar); *Fugue à la gigue in G* (orch. Holst); *'Giant Fugue' (Wir glauben all' an einen Gott)* (orch. Vaughan Williams & Foster); *Passacaglia & Fugue in C min.* (orch. Respighi); *Preludes & Fugues: in C* (orch. Honegger); *in E flat (St Anne)* (orch. Schoenberg)

**** Chan. 9835. BBC PO, Slatkin

Flying boldly in the face of period performance, these transcriptions by nine celebrated composers, including Respighi, Elgar, Holst, Vaughan Williams, Schoenberg and Raff, bring out the grandeur of Bach's vision in his organ music. That is greatly helped by the sumptuous Chandos sound and the magnificent playing of the **BBC Philharmonic** under **Leonard Slatkin**. Respighi is weightily dramatic in the *Passacaglia and Fugue in C minor*, and so is Schoenberg in the *St Anne Prelude and Fugue*, while Honegger even uses a saxophone in the *Prelude and Fugue in C*. Most imaginative of all is the *Fantasia and Fugue in C minor*, with Elgar glorying in percussion and harp.

Arrangements: Bach–Stokowski

Orchestral Suite 3, BWV 578. Fugue in G min., BWV 578; Passacaglia and Fugue, BWV 582; Excerpts from Cantatas: Chorales: *Nun komm, der Heiden Heiland; Komm süsser Tod, BWV 478; Wir glauben all'an einen Gott, BWV 437;* Aria: *Schafe können sichter weiden.* Easter Oratorio: *Kommt, eilet und laufer.* St John Passion: *Es ist vollbracht!*

(N) (BB) ***Naxos 8.557883 Bournemouth SO, Serebrier (with: HANDEL: *Messiah: Pastoral Symphony;* PURCELL: *Dido and Aeneas: When I am laid in earth;* STOKOWSKI: 2 Ancient Liturgical Melodies)

Harpsichord Concerto in F minor, BWV 1056: Largo (Arioso). Chorales: Ich ruf' zu dir, Herr Jesu Christ, BWV 639; Ein Feste Burg; Mein Jesu! was vor Seelenweh, BWV 487; Jesu, Joy of Man's Desiring, BWV 147; (Organ): *Schübler Chorale: Wachet auf, BWV 645 Adagio in C major, BWV 564 Toccata and Fugue in D minor, BWV 565. Violin Sonata in C minor, BWV 1017: Siciliano. The Well-Tempered Clavier, Book I: Fugue 2 in C minor, BWV 847; Prelude 24 in B minor, BWV 869*

(N) (BB) *** Naxos 8.557050. Bournemouth SO, Serebrier. (with: PALESTRINA: *Adoramus te Christe;* BYRD: *Pavane and Gigue;* CLARKE: *Trumpet Voluntary;* BOCCHERINI: *Minuet;* MATTHESON: *Suite 5 in C minor for Harpsichord: Air;* HOFFSTETTER: *String Quartet in F major (attrib HAYDN as Op. 3/5: Serenade (Andante cantabile))*

José Serebrier's first disc of Stokowski's sumptuous Bach transcriptions is outstanding in every way, not just for the performances but for the spectacular recording, never more telling than in the powerful account of the *C minor Passacaglia and Fugue*. Yet the sprightly contrasting *G major Fugue* is also one of the highlights of the programme. In the *Air* from the *Third Orchestral Suite* and the *Chorales* Serebrier (as a former pupil of Stokowski) follows the maestro's romantic style with portamento slides in string phrasing, and this is carried through to the warmly appealing account of Purcell's *Dido's Lament*, one of the pieces by other composers included here.

The second instalment begins with the popular *D minor Toccata and Fugue*, and the recording brings out to the full, as never before, the subtlety of Stokowski's orchestrations with their brilliant terracing of texture, with colourings which designedly echo the sound of the organ: its impact is magnificent, here more than ever. The other pieces here include other popular favourites such as the *Wachet auf Chorale Prelude*, *Eine feste Burg* and *Jesu Joy of Man's Desiring*, all sumptuously presented with the strings in particular made to sound glorious.

The extra items are all valuable in their way. Popular favourites include Boccherini's *Minuet* (with the central section wonderfully elegant), and the collection ends with a Bach piece that Stokowski himself often used as an encore, the *Fugue* from No. 2 of Bach's *48*, with each section arriving one after the other.

Chorale Preludes: Ein feste Burg ist unser Gott; Komm, süsser Tod; Mein Jesu, was vor Seelenweh. Christmas Oratorio: Sinfonia. English Suite 2 in A min., BWV 807: Bourrée. Fugue in G min., BWV 578 (Little Fugue); Orchestral Suite 3 in D, BWV 1068: Air on the G String. Passacaglia & Fugue in C min., BWV 582; Toccata & Fugue in D min., BWV

565; Violin Partita 1 in B min., BWV 1002: Sarabande; 3 in E, BWV 1006: Preludio

Ⓜ *** EMI Legend CD/**DVD** (ADD) 5 57758. Symphony O, Stokowski (with DVD Bonus: DEBUSSY: *Prélude à l'après-midi d'un faune*)

A welcome return to circulation of **Stokowski's** (American Capitol) late-1950s recordings of Bach arrangements. The earliest sessions date from 1957, and if the sound, understandably, displays a degree of thinness, it is well balanced, the ambience is remarkably warm, and overall the quality is certainly impressive for its time. The *Chorale Preludes* are played with great intensity, while in the spectacular showpieces, such as the *D minor Toccata and Fugue* and the *Passacaglia*, with their generous splashes of romantic colour, plenty of electricity is generated. The bonus DVD records the 1972 film of Debussy's *Prélude à l'après-midi d'un faune*, played at the Royal Festival Hall. It is a joy to watch – deeply felt and magical.

Harpsichord Concerto in F min., BWV 1056: Arioso (Largo). Chorales: Aus tiefer Noth (De profundis), BWV 1006; Ein feste Burg; Jesu, Joy of Man's Desiring (from Cantata 147); My Soul is Athirst (from St Matthew Passsion). Wachet auf, BWV 645; Fantasia & Fugue in G min., BWV 542; Violin Partitas: 1 in B min., BWV 1002: Sarabande. 2 in D min., BWV 1004: Chaconne. 3 in E, BWV 1006: Preludio. Violin Sonata 2, BWV 1003: Andante sostenuto. Well-Tempered Clavier: Fugue in C min., BWV 847; attrib. C. P. E. BACH: *Chorale: Aus der Tiefe rufe ich*

**** Chan. 10282. BBC PO, Bamert

Matthias Bamert manages the kind of spontaneous, flexible rubato that was Stokowski's personal style and, with superb playing from the augmented **BBC Philharmonic** and marvellous Chandos recording, the result is spectacular indeed. Yet, when one turns to the richly opulent scoring of the piece which Stokowski describes as 'Arioso' (the beautiful *Largo* from the *Harpsichord Concerto in F minor*) and the equally lovely *Andante sostenuto* from BWV 1003, the music moves entirely out of Bach's era into Stokowski's own world of ripe romanticism, while *Ein feste Burg* brings flamboyant contrasts of sonorous brass and strings. Yet it is in the *Fantasia and Fugue in G minor* that we are thrilled by the most spectacular Stokowski sound. The piece is recorded here for the first time in the original scoring with the fullest possible string sections, and laced with percussion.

Toccata & Fugue in D min., BWV 565 (arr. Fox-Lafiche for unaccompanied violin)

*** EMI 5 57384-2. Vengerov – SHCHEDRIN: *Balalaika; Echo Sonata*; YSAŸE: *Solo Violin Sonatas 2, 3, 4 & 6* ***

The arrangement for unaccompanied violin by Fox-Lafiche of Bach's most popular organ piece in **Vengerov's** hands works surprisingly well, backing up the scholarly argument that, stylistically unlike any other Bach organ work (and possibly not by Bach at all), it is better suited to the violin (for

which it may have originally been written) than the organ. A welcome makeweight for the four Ysaÿe *Sonatas* and the Shchedrin pieces.

BACH, Wilhelm Friedemann
(1710–84)

Adagio & Fugue in D min., F.65; Adagio & Fugue in F min.; (i) Harpsichord Concerto in E min., F.43; Sinfonias in D, F.64; in F, F.67

*** HM HMC 901772. (i) Alpermann; Berlin Akademie für Alte Musik, Mai

This fine Harmonia Mundi disc makes an ideal introduction to the music of Bach's favourite son. It opens with the *Sinfonia in D* with its most engaging woodwind writing, particularly for the flutes in the *Andante*, and closes with the whimsical *Sinfonia in F*, which nevertheless has a gracious *Andante* and ends mellowly with a warm-hearted Minuet. The *Concerto* exudes the striking rhythmic life that characterizes this composer's music, but suffers from a recessive balance for the modest-sized chosen harpsichord. However, **Raphael Alpermann** plays its *Adagio* with appealing delicacy, and survives the rough buffeting of the orchestral tuttis in the finale. Most remarkable of all are the pair of *Adagios and Fugues*, the *F minor* arranged for strings from a keyboard piece by Mozart, who added the spacious introduction. Excellent recording thoughout, apart from the backward balance of the harpsichord.

Sinfonia in D, F.64

ⒷⒷ **(*) Naxos 8.553289. Salzburg CO, Lee – C. P. E. BACH: *Sinfonias* **(*)

Wilhelm Friedemann's three-movement *Sinfonia in D major* was intended for use as an introduction to the Whitsun cantata, *Dies ist der Tag*. The *Sinfonia* is given a lively account in Salzburg; modern instruments are used, but textures are clean and fresh and the recording is faithful and well balanced.

6 Sonatas for flute duet, F.54–9

*** MDG 311 984402. Hüteler, Schmidt-Casdorf

These works must be fun to play, especially when the two instruments chirrup together as in the first-movement *Allegro* of No. 2, dance along graciously as in the final *Gigue* of the same work, or chase each other's tails as in the *Presto* finale of No. 4. Slow movements are innocent, yet have a thoughtful melancholy. Overall, the final work in *F minor* is the most individual of the six, but all are different and this simple polyphony stands up to repeated listenings. The performances here are technically immaculate, have a pleasing, spontaneous simplicity and are beautifully recorded.

12 Polonaises, F12; Sonata in D, F3; Fantasia in A, F23

ⒷⒷ *** Naxos 8.57966. Hill (fortepiano)

Wilhelm Friedmann was the oldest (and favourite) son of Bach: the first book of the '48' was written for him. He combined rich melodic invention and originality of harmony with a highly personal expressive style and these are much in evidence in the *Polonaises*. In this admirable recording, the American scholar **Robert Hill** uses a reconstruction of a Florentine fortepiano of 1720 in the manner of Bartolomeo Cristofori. His playing has great flair and style and it makes out the strongest case for this interesting and individual master. Excellent recorded sound too.

BAERMANN, Heinrich
(1784–1847)

Adagio for Clarinet & Orchestra

*** ASV CDDCA 559. Johnson, ECO, Groves – CRUSELL: *Concerto 2* *** ✿; ROSSINI: *Introduction, Theme & Variations* *** ; WEBER: *Concertino* ***

Heinrich Baermann's rather beautiful *Adagio*, once attributed to Wagner, is offered by a celebrated clarinettist who plays the work warmly and sympathetically.

Clarinet Concertinos: in C min.; E flat; Concertstück in G min.; Sonata in D min.

*** Orfeo C065011A. Klöcker, Prague CO, Lajèík

With an unexpected drum-roll beginning the *G minor Concertstück*, which opens this disc, no one could accuse Baermann of not being entertaining in these works. Indeed, these are enjoyably unpretentious concertos, with lively, vivacious writing which fully shows off the prowess of the soloist. With three of these works in a minor key, a certain drama is evident too, but it is Baermann's catchy tunes to which one most readily responds, with the *Polacca* of the *E major Concertino* being especially enjoyable. The *Sonata in D minor* (also for clarinet and chamber orchestra), uniquely here, begins with an attractive *Adagio*, and is followed by two movements at the composer's perky best. Virtuoso performances from **Dieter Klöcker**, well supported by the **Prague Orchestra**, and all in good sound, too.

BAINES, William (1899–1922)

Coloured Leaves; Paradise Gardens; 7 Preludes; Silverpoints; Tides; Twilight Pieces

*** Lyrita (ADD) SRCD 266. Parkin – MOERAN: *Piano music* ***

William Baines came from Yorkshire and died in his early twenties. These small piano miniatures show a very considerable talent, with a refined harmonic palette and a nice melodic strain. The influence of Delius, Cyril Scott and others can be discerned, but some of these pieces deserve wider recognition and are quite powerful and individual, and often ear-catching (try *Water-Pearls* from *Silverpoints* or the *Valse* from *Coloured Leaves*). **Eric Parkin** plays persuasively and the recording is quite vivid if slightly shallow.

BAINTON, Edgar (1880–1956)

(i) Concerto fantasia (for piano and orchestra). The Golden River; 3 Pieces for Orchestra; Pavane, Idyll and Bachanal

Ⓝ **** Chan 10460 (i) Fingerhut; BBC PO, Paul Daniel

This Chandos collection makes an ideal introduction to Edgar Bainton's music. He was to become a key figure in the musical life of Newcastle-upon-Tyne, and his attractive melodic ideas and colourful command of the orchestral palette show him as a composer of some distinction. The pair of triptychs are winningly scored, the *Three Pieces* opening in the English pastoral tradition but gathering energy in the third, mirrored by more delicate *Pavane, Idyll* (with an engaging flute solo) and robust *Bacchanale*.

The *Golden River*, written as a four-movement suite, is a passionately atmospheric tone-poem, based on a short story by Ruskin, about three brothers, with the youngest defeating the machinations of the two eldest to restore the 'treasure valley' through which the river flows. But most striking of all is the tuneful five-movement *Concerto fantasia*, opening unusually in the glittering upper register of the piano but soon developing a passionately memorable theme on the strings, which is to return in the finale after a delectably witty scherzo and a slow movement Improvisation. The work ends with a peaceful Epilogue and this is a concerto which immediately tempts one to return to it, especially when it is superbly played by **Margaret Fingerhut**, while **Paul Daniel** clearly shares her enjoyment in this rewarding music, and directs the whole programme with sympathy and flair. Typically excellent Chandos sound makes this CD very recommendable.

Epithalamion; (i) An English Idyll

*** Chan. 10019. (i) Whelan; BBC PO, Brabbins – CLIFFORD: *A Kentish Suite, etc.* ***

The rhapsody, *Epithalamion*, is a brilliant fantasy Scherzo dazzlingly orchestrated, which carries you exhilaratingly along with its elaborate cross-rhythms. The *English Idyll* sets words by the critic Neville Cardus, who at the time, 1946, was also an English exile in Sydney. Atmospheric and sensuous, it vividly catches a mood of nostalgia for England, not just the countryside but central London and a West Country cathedral. **Martyn Brabbins** draws dedicated performances from the **BBC Philharmonic**, with **Paul Whelan** a sensitive baritone soloist.

Symphony 2 in D min.

*** Chan. 9757. BBC PO, Handley – CLIFFORD: *Symphony*; GOUGH: *Serenade* ***

Symphony 3 in C min.

⊶ Ⓜ *** Dutton CDLX 7185. BBC Concert O, Handley – BOUGHTON: *Symphony 1 (Oliver Cromwell)* ***

Bainton's *Second* and *Third Symphonies* are also well worth exploring, both full of good and interesting ideas. Both are impressively structured, the lyrical writing is especially enjoyable, and there is no lack of energy in the dramatic passages. Both performances and recordings are first class.

String Quartet in A

(M) *** Dutton CDLX 7163. Locrian Ens. – CLIFFORD: *String Quartet* ***

The *String Quartet* is pastoral in content, with some touches of Ravelian influence. It is well served by the **Locrian Ensemble** and the recording is exemplary.

BAIRSTOW, Edward (1874–1946)

Blessed city, heavenly Salem; Evening Services in D & G: Magnificat & Nunc dimittis. If the Lord had not helped me; Jesu, the very thought of thee; Let all mortal flesh keep silence; Lord, thou hast been our refuge; (i) 5 Poems of the spirit. Save us, O Lord

*** Hyp. CDA 67497. St John's College, Cambridge, Ch., Hill, Provost (organ); (i) Williams, Britten Sinfonia

Edward Bairstow's beautiful unaccompanied *Let all mortal flesh keep silence* keeps the composer's name before the public, but *If the Lord had not helped me* and *Blessed city, heavenly Salem* are hardly less fine and, as this superbly sung collection shows, he wrote much else of quality and general appeal. The *Five Poems of the Spirit* for solo baritone and orchestra, impressively sung here by **Roderick Williams**, are late works, dating from 1944; they show him at his most mature and make a fine climax for the concert before the touching *Save us, O Lord* (written nearly half a century earlier) ends a satisfyingly planned programme, splendidly sung and recorded in St John's itself. **Paul Provost's** organ contribution adds much to the accompanied items.

BALAKIREV, Mily (1837–1910)

(i) Piano Concerto 1. In Bohemia; King Lear Overture; Symphonies 1–2; Tamara

(M) *** Chan. 2 for 1 CHAN 241-20. (i) Shelley; BBC PO, Sinaisky

Piano Concertos 1 in F sharp min., Op. 1; 2 in E flat, Op. posth.

*** Hyp. CDA 66640. Binns, E. N. Philh. O, Lloyd-Jones – RIMSKY-KORSAKOV: *Concerto* ***

Piano Concertos 1 F sharp min., Op. 1; 2 E flat (ed. Lyapunov); Grande Fantaisie on Russian folksongs, Op. 4

(N) (BB) **(*) Naxos 8.570396. Seifetdinova, Moscow PO, Dmitri Yablonsky

(i) Piano Concerto 1; Symphony 2 in D min; Tamara

*** Chan. 9727. (i) Shelley; BBC PO, Sinaisky

The one-movement *First Piano Concerto* (*Youth*) is well served by **Malcolm Binns's** intelligent and sensitive performance. It also has the only available account of the more character-

istic *Second Concerto*. This was left incomplete and was finished after his death by Lyapunov.

Howard Shelley too is a powerful soloist in the first *Piano Concerto*, relishing the bravura writing, and though the *Second Symphony* cannot compare with the *First* in scale or memorability, Vassily Sinaisky makes a most persuasive case for it in his warm and thrustful performance. *Tamara* is played with similar panache.

The Naxos coupling of the two concertos and the *Grande Fantaisie on Russian Folksongs* comes as a useful appendage to the versions by Howard Shelley and Malcolm Binns (see above). **Anastasia Seifetdinova** is a formidable soloist who comes from the Ukraine but is now resident in the university of Hartford, Connecticut. Good sound.

Islamey (orch. Lyapunov)

🎧 *** Ph. **SACD** 470 618-2; CD 470 840-2. Kirov O, Gergiev – BORODIN: *In the Steppes of Central Asia*; RIMSKY-KORSAKOV: *Scheherazade* ***

Balakirev's virtuoso piano piece as orchestrated by Lyapunov sounds surprisingly like another section of *Scheherazade*, making it an apt and exciting coupling from **Gergiev** and the **Kirov Orchestra**, although the resonance clouds detail somewhat, especially on the SACD, where the added hall resonance is the more noticeable.

Symphony 1 in C

🎧 (***) BBC Legends mono BBCL 4084-2. BBC SO, Beecham – RIMSKY-KORSAKOV: *Le Coq d'or: Suite*; BORODIN: *Prince Igor: Polovtsian Dances* (***)

Symphony 1; Russia; Tamara (symphonic poems)

🎧 (BB) *** Regis RRC 1131. USSR State SO, Svetlanov

Svetlanov's earlier (1974) Russian recording of Balakirev's *First Symphony* brings an interpretation that has grip and tension. The wonderfully lyrical slow movement is both atmospheric and warmly relaxed, and the finale has both striking impetus and gleaming Russian woodwind colour. The recording is rich and well detailed. While **Beecham** reigns supreme in the symphony, this is still a first-rate bargain, for the two melodically attractive symphonic poems are splendidly done.

Tamara

(N) *** Australian Decca Eloquence (ADD) 480 0047. OSR, Ansermet – MUSSORGSKY: *Night on a Bare Mountain; Pictures at an Exhibition*, etc. ***

A rarity on disc. Balakirev's *Tamara*, who lures hapless men to their death with her siren calls and casts their bodies in raging waters as dawn breaks, emerges as quite a strong work here. **Ansermet** understands the melodrama of the music, and the quality of the 1954 stereo sound amazes. The 'exotic' qualities of the score are particularly enjoyable.

Islamey (Oriental Fantasy)

🎧 (BB) **** EMI Encore 5 86881-2. Gavrilov – PROKOFIEV:

Piano Concerto 1, etc.; TCHAIKOVSKY: *Piano Concerto 1*, etc. ***

Gavrilov's dazzling account of Balakirev's piano fantasy is outstandingly charismatic; it is well recorded too. It comes in harness with an equally dazzling account of Prokofiev's *First Piano Concerto*.

Piano Sonata in B flat min.

**(*) Kingdom KCLCD 2001. Fergus-Thompson – SCRIABIN: *Sonata 3*, etc. **(*)

The Balakirev is arguably the greatest Russian piano sonata of the pre-1914 era. **Gordon Fergus-Thompson** is fully equal to its considerable demands and he offers excellent playing.

BANTOCK, Granville
(1868–1946)

Caristiona; A Celtic Symphony; Cuchullan's Lament; The Cyprian Goddess (Symphony 3); Dante and Beatrice; Fifine at the Fair; Hebridean Symphony; Helena Variations; Kishmul's Galley; Omar Khayyám: Prelude & Camel Caravan; Overture to a Greek Tragedy; Pagan Symphony; Pierrot of the Minute; Processional; Sapphic Poem for Cello & Orchestra; Sappho; The Sea Reivers; Song of Songs (Prelude & extracts); Thalaba the Destroyer; The Wilderness and the Solitary Place; The Witch of Atlas

Ⓜ *** Hyp. CDS 44281/6 (6). Lloyd Webber; Bickley; Connell; Begley; RPO (with Ch.), Handley

Between 1990 and 2003 **Vernon Handley** recorded all the principal orchestral works of Bantock (although the complete *Omar Khayyám* had to wait until 2006/7 and now appears on Chandos). It was a considerable achievement revealing Bantock as a major figure in English music in the late nineteenth and early twentieth century. Handley is a dedicated advocate and the standard of performances and recordings in this box is very high indeed. If you have not already invested in this rewarding composer, Hyperion's box with the sirens visually enticing on the front cover offers a chance to respond to their allure, with a promise of many rewards from this often sumptuously scored and consistently inventive music.

The Pierrot of the Minute: Overture

Ⓜ *** Chan. 6566. Bournemouth Sinf., Del Mar – BRIDGE: *Summer*, etc.; BUTTERWORTH: *Banks of Green Willow* ***

Bantock's overture is concerned with Pierrot's dream in which he falls in love with a Moon Maiden, who tells him their love must die at dawn, but he will not listen. He wakes to realize that his dream of love lasted a mere minute. The writing is often delicate and at times Elgarian, and the 1978 recording sounds remarkably fresh.

Symphony 3 (The Cyprian Goddess); Dante and Beatrice; Helena (Variations on the Theme HFB)

*** Hyp. CDA 66810. RPO, Handley

The Cyprian Goddess echoes Strauss in its sumptuous orchestration and melodic writing, and in its refinement it has something of the elegiac tone of late Strauss. The *Helena Variations*, written in tribute to his wife, echo the freshness and variety of Elgar's newly completed *Enigma*, while *Dante and Beatrice* is a free-ranging programme work which in its warmth and dramatic contrasts recalls Tchaikovsky's *Romeo and Juliet*. Whatever the echoes, in each piece Bantock establishes his own distinctive voice, here more tautly controlled than in his expansive, middle-period works. First-rate sound.

Omar Khayyám

🎧 **** Chan. CHSA 5051 (3). Wyn-Rogers, Spence, Robinson, Menna, Williams, Price, BBC SO & Ch., Handley

Omar Khayyám is by far the most ambitious work of Granville Bantock; like many of his works, his spectacular setting of the words in Fitzgerald's translation is influenced by oriental music, both in the melodic material and by drawing on his personal impressions of the Middle East. The result is a sumptuous tapestry, with the poet communing with the beloved. The layout for six soloists, large double chorus and orchestra (with the strings divided antiphonally) is heard at its most spectacular in the 'Caravan' processional, with rich brass and percussion and tuned 'camel bells' resourcefully borrowed from an earlier performance. The performance is fully worthy of Bantock's vision; the soloists are excellent, **Toby Spence** and **Catherine Wyn-Rogers** singing with clean attack, and the others providing excellent support. Under Handley, the most sympathetic conductor, the result is exceptionally warm and idiomatic, and the Chandos recording, made in the Watford Colosseum, is fully worthy.

(i) Nebuchadnezzar; (ii) 2 Coronation Anthems; 3 Songs of Praise. Woodland Suite

*** Chan. 10439. (i) Padmore, Davids; (i–ii) BBC Ch.; BBC SO, Hickox

Nebuchadnezzar features Bantock's skilful choral writing, powerfully dramatic. In the title-role **Neal Davids** sings with dark, firm tone, strongly characterful with the excellent **Mark Padmore** providing contrast in the subsidiary role of the Herald. The two *Coronation Anthems* are both dramatic but surprisingly brief. The *Woodland Suite* displays Bantock's gift in writing for young performers, a delightfully atmospheric piece designed for schools. Altogether this is an attractive and enjoyable collection.

BARBER, Samuel (1910–81)

Adagio for Strings, Op. 11

🎧 Ⓜ **** Decca (ADD) 475 8237. ASMF, Marriner – COPLAND: *Quiet City*; COWELL: *Hymn & Fuguing Tone*; CRESTON: *Rumor*; IVES: *Symphony 3* ****

Ⓜ *** DG 477 6352-2. LAPO, Bernstein – COPLAND: *Appalachian Spring* ***; GERSHWIN: *Rhapsody in Blue* **(*)

Marriner's 1976 performance of Barber's justly famous *Adagio* is arguably still the most satisfying version available. The quality of sound on the remastered Argo recording remains very impressive indeed, and Marriner's climax is absolutely gripping. This splendid anthology is now reissued as one of Decca's 'Originals'.

In Barber, **Bernstein's** expressiveness is more restrained and elegiac, but his control of the climax – in what is substantially a live recording – is unerring. Recording somewhat close but full and clear. The original coupling with Copland's *Appalachian Spring* and Gershwin's *Rhapsody in Blue* is now reissued in Universal's 'Critics' Choice' series.

Adagio for Strings; (i) Cello Concerto, Op. 22. Medea (ballet suite) Op. 23

☋ **(BB)** *** Naxos 8.559088. (i) Warner; RSNO, Alsop

Barber's *Cello Concerto* of 1945 is more elusive than the *Violin Concerto*, but **Wendy Warner** concentrates on its sometimes wry lyricism, and she articulates with brilliant point in the gentle scherzando passage of the finale. **Marin Alsop** is a persuasive partner, relishing the often plangent orchestral backcloth and securing a splendidly committed response from the Scottish players, both here and in the often astringent score for *Medea*. The famous *Adagio for Strings* then becomes essentially an elegy, but reaches a passionate climax. Fine, vivid recording, though the massed upper strings could have more weight.

(i) Adagio for Strings; (ii) Cello Concerto; (iii; iv) Violin Concerto; (iv) Essay 1, Op. 22; (v) Agnus Dei

(N) (B) *** CfP 2 28275-2 (i) LSO, Previn; (ii) Kirshbaum, SCO, Saraste; (iii) Oliveira; (iv) Saint Louis SO, Slatkin; Winchester Cathedral Ch., Hill

Previn's LSO*Adagio for Strings*, from the 1970s, is especially fine. **Kirshbaum's** view of the *Cello Concerto* is darker and spikier than those of his direct rivals, and rather more urgent in the outer movements, yet it is played just as beautifully. **Oliveira's** excellent account of the *Violin Concerto* is included in the Gemini set below and the other items are just as successful, including the choral version of the *Adagio*.

(i) Adagio for Strings; (i; ii) Violin Concerto; (i) Essays 1–3; Medea: Medea's Dance of Vengeance, Op. 23a; Overture: School for Scandal, Op. 5; (iii; iv) Canzone for Flute & Piano, Op. 38a; (iv; v) Cello Sonata, Op. 6; (iii; v) Summer Music, Op. 31 (for wind quintet); (iv) (Piano) Excursions, Op. 20; Nocturne (Homage to John Field), Op. 33; Souvenirs, Op. 28

☋ **(B)** **** EMI Gemini 5 86561-2 (2). (i) St Louis SO, Slatkin; (ii) Oliveira; (iii) Baxtresser; (iv) Margalit; (v) Stepansky; Robinson, Drucker, Le Clair, Myers

Slatkin's accounts of the orchestral pieces are superbly played and recorded, and he includes all three of the *Essays*, which is quite rare, as well as the amusing *School for Scandal Overture*. **Elmar Oliveira's** version of the *Violin Concerto* reacts to the nostalgia of the *Andante* with a vein of bitter-sweet

yearning that is most affecting. It is a fine performance overall with a brilliantly played finale. The chamber music is especially valuable, with the performers producing the spontaneous feeling that they have lived with the music before performing it. The *Canzone for Flute and Piano* has an Elysian, soaring melody (slightly French in atmosphere) which **Jeanne Baxtresser** plays very beautifully. The *Cello Sonata* has a powerful impulse and is given the most eloquent advocacy here, while the *Excursions* have wit and elegance. The shorter pieces are all distinctive and well worth having.

(i) Adagio for Strings; (ii; iii) Violin Concerto; (iii) Essay 1; Medea's Dance of Vengeance; The School for Scandal Overture; (i; iv) Knoxville: Summer of 1915

(N) (M) *** EMI 2 06625-2 (i) LSO, Tilson Thomas; (ii) Oliveira; (iii) Saint Louis SO, Slatkin; (iv) Hendricks

Knoxville is one of the most magically evocative pieces of its kind, and it is all the more magical here for the authentically American inflexions that **Hendricks** gives it, together with glowing string tone. The celebrated *Adagio* is taken at a flowing tempo, with no self-indulgence or sentimentality. With the addition of the fine account of the *Violin Concerto* this is a radiant disc.

Adagio for Strings; Essays 1, Op. 12; 2, Op. 17; Music for a Scene from Shelley, Op. 7; Overture: The School for Scandal, Op. 5; Symphony 1, Op. 9

☋ *** Argo 436 288. Baltimore SO, Zinman

These performances are very alert and vital, particularly that of the *First Symphony*; the recording has superb presence and detail. Apart from the first two *Essays* for orchestra, **Zinman's** disc includes the more rarely heard *Music for a Scene from Shelley*, sumptuously scored and gloriously atmospheric. This adds greatly to the attractiveness of an already desirable issue, and Zinman and his excellent orchestra play the *Overture* to Sheridan's *The School for Scandal* with equal commitment.

(i) Canzonetta for Oboe & Strings. Capricorn Concerto; Fadograph of a Yestern Scene; Mutations from Bach; Vanessa: Interlude; (ii) A Hand of Bridge

☋ **(BB)** *** Naxos 8.559135. RSNO, Alsop, with (i) Stéphane Rancourt; (ii) Craigie, Winter, Wall, Williams

The neoclassical *Capricorn Concerto*, which takes its name from the house that Barber and Menotti shared, is a relative rarity, but this excellent budget version does it proud. The *Canzonetta* was left in short score on Barber's death, but this arrangement with strings is expertly done, and the piece is as moving as the very best of Barber. The *Fadograph of a Yestern Scene* is another rarity, a ruminative and reflective score with a strong vein of melancholy to sustain it. The witty ten-minute opera, *A Hand of Bridge*, which Barber wrote for Menotti's festival at Spoleto, also comes off well. Good recorded sound, too. In short this is a most pleasurable issue and repays repeated hearing.

Cello Concerto, Op. 22

*** Naïve V4961. Gastinel, CBSO, Brown – ELGAR: *Cello Concerto* ***

*** Chan. 8322. Wallfisch, ECO, Simon – SHOSTAKOVICH: *Cello Concerto 1* ***

Anne Gastinel couples this fine account of the Barber *Cello Concerto* with a noble and dignified account of the Elgar. Gastinel is a thoughtful and sensitive artist and her recording is among the very finest now available, although the Wendy Warner/Alsop version on Naxos (see above) is also highly recommendable, and for many will have a more suitable coupling.

Wallfisch gives an impressive and eloquent reading, and the elegiac slow movement is especially fine. Wallfisch is forwardly balanced, but otherwise the recording is truthful; the orchestra is vividly detailed.

(i) *Piano Concerto. Medea: Medea's Meditation and Dance of Vengeance. Die Natali; Commando March*

(BB) **(*) Naxos 8.559133. (i) Prutsman; RSNO, Alsop

Stephen Prutsman gives a powerful reading of Barber's formidable *Piano Concerto*, fully in command of the bravura writing of the outer movements and tenderly expressive in the central *Canzone*. As a bargain alternative, this is very welcome. With **Marin Alsop** a most sympathetic Barber interpreter, the *Concerto* is well supplemented by the well-known concert work drawn from the *Medea* ballet, the genial and colourful fantasia on Christmas Carols, *Die Natali*, written at the same period as the concerto in memory of Serge and Natalie Koussevitzky, and the wartime *Commando March*. Well-balanced sound, if with strings on the light side.

(i) *Piano Concerto;* (ii) *Violin Concerto. Souvenirs, Op. 28*

*** Telarc CD 80441. (i) Parker; (ii) McDuffie; Atlanta SO, Levi

Robert McDuffie is a powerful violinist with a formidable technique, if not as individual an artist as many rivals in this warmly romantic *Violin Concerto*. His reading makes an excellent coupling for **Jon Kimura Parker's** outstanding performance of the *Piano Concerto* and the suite, *Souvenirs*, in its orchestral form. The performance is rather tauter and more purposeful than the fine one which John Browning (the pianist for whom the work was written) recorded for Sony.

Violin Concerto, Op. 14

☷─ ✦ **** Onyx 4016. Ehnes, Vancouver SO, Tovey – KORNGOLD; WALTON: *Violin Concertos* *** ✦

☷─ (M) *** Decca 475 7710. Bell, Baltimore SO, Zinman – BLOCH: *Baal Shem;* WALTON: *Violin Concerto* ***

(N) (BB) *** EMI Encore 2 08124-2. Perlman, Boston SO, Ozawa – BERNSTEIN: *Serenade;* FOSS: *3 American Pieces* ***

(i) *Violin Concerto. Adagio for Strings*

(M) *** Sony 516235-2. (i) Stern; NYPO, Bernstein (with IVES: *The Unanswered Question;* COPLAND: *Fanfare for the Common Man*) – SCHUMAN: *In Praise of Shahn*, etc. ***

Barber's *Violin Concerto* grows in stature with every hearing and the young Canadian violinist **James Ehnes** proves an ardent and committed advocate, mirrored by **Bramwell Tovey's** glowing partnership, particularly in the lyrical, inspired slow movement, which has exquisite delicacy of feeling. It is an inspired coupling, as well as a generous one, having the Barber alongside two other high-romantic concertos together. Ehnes gives superb performances of all three, bringing out their full emotional thrust without vulgarity or exaggeration.

Joshua Bell's passionate playing in the Barber, full of tender poetry, is well matched by the excellent orchestra, ripely and brilliantly recorded, with the soloist well forward, but not aggressively so. This won the 1998 *Gramophone* Concerto Award and has now become one of Decca's Originals.

Isaac Stern gave the Barber *Violin Concerto* its stereo première in 1964, and his performance, which is consistently inspired, is of superlative quality. It has warmth, freshness and humanity, and the slow movement is glorious. The CBS forward balance for the orchestra is less than ideal, but the recording is otherwise very good and has been impressively remastered.

For **Perlman** the kernel of the Barber *Concerto* lies in the central slow movement: he plays with a warmth and intensity that even he has rarely matched. Weight, power and virtuoso brilliance then come together in his dazzling account of the finale

(i) *Violin Concerto. Music for a Scene from Shelley, Op. 7; Souvenirs* (ballet suite), *Op. 28; Serenade for Strings, Op. 1*

(BB) *** Naxos 8.559044. (i) Buswell; RSNO, Alsop

Marin Alsop with the **Royal Scottish National Orchestra** backs up the masterly *Violin Concerto* with the witty and delightfully parodic ballet, *Souvenirs*, and two early works, the evocative *Scene from Shelley* and a long-neglected three-movement *Serenade*, which is based on a string quartet written when Barber was nineteen and which anticipates the *Adagio for Strings*. **James Buswell** is a refined, sensitive soloist, warm without being soupy, if not quite as individual as Isaac Stern in his vintage version with Bernstein.

Essays for Orchestra 1, Op. 12; 2, Op. 17; 3, Op. 47

*** Chan. 9053. Detroit SO, Järvi – IVES: *Symphony 1* ***

In terms of both sonority and approach, **Neeme Järvi's** account of these appealing works differs from the American competitor. The strings have lightness and subtlety and are highly responsive. The recording is very natural and present, and beautifully balanced.

Essays for Orchestra 2; 3; (i) *Toccata Festiva, Op. 36.* (ii) *Knoxville: Summer of 1915, Op. 24*

(BB) *** Naxos 8.559134. RSNO, Alsop, with (i) Trotter; (ii) Gauvin

In the evocative *Knoxville: Summer of 1915*, **Karina Gauvin's** voice is so rich that the diction is not as clear as it might be, but happily the booklet provides the full text. **Alsop's** reading in both of the *Essays* highlights contrasts to bring out the feeling in both of compressed symphonic structures. The *Toccata Festiva* for organ and orchestra is an exuberant piece that brings the widest expressive range in the organ part and with the orchestra colourful too, here superbly played and recorded.

Symphonies 1; 2; Essay for Orchestra 1; Overture: The School for Scandal

⊖– 🌼 (BB) **** Naxos 8.559024. RSNO, Alsop

The two symphonies are played on Naxos with passionate commitment and deep lyrical feeling by the Scottish orchestra. The account of the complete *Second Symphony* will surely confirm the reputation of a wartime work which the composer partly withdrew in despondency after its neglect. The *First Essay for Orchestra* also generates a powerful atmosphere when played with such depth of feeling. With spectacular recording, this exciting collection is very strongly recommended.

(i) Symphony 1 (in one movement); Essays for Orchestra, 1; 2; (ii) Music for a Scene from Shelley; (i) Night Flight, Op. 19a; (ii; iii) Knoxville (Summer of 1915)

⊖– (BB) *** Regis (ADD) RRC 1139. (i) LSO; (ii) Western Australia SO; Measham; (iii) with McGurk

David Measham proves a splendid advocate of Barber's music, securing passionately committed performances of the *First Symphony* (where at times he brings out its somewhat Waltonian manner) and the powerfully romantic yet mysterious *Music from Shelley*, an inspired early work from 1933, which ought to be better known. The two *Essays for Orchestra* are also very well played, as is the haunting movement, *Night Flight*, all that the composer originally wanted to survive from the *Symphony 2*. **Molly McGurk's** ravishing account of Barber's Coplandesque setting of *Knoxville* could hardly be more warmly evocative.

Toccata Festiva, Op. 36

*** Ondine ODE 1094-5. Latry, Phd. O, Eschenbach – SAINT-SAËNS: *Symphony 3*; POULENC: *Organ Concerto* ***

Toccata Festiva was written in 1960 in response to a commission to celebrate the new organ for the Academy of Music, then the Philadelphia Orchestra's home. This live performance could hardly be bettered and the sound, though rather dry, is very full and vivid.

CHAMBER MUSIC

(i; ii) Canzone for Flute & Piano; (ii; iii) Cello Sonata; (iii; iv) Summer Music for Wind Quintet; (ii) Excursions, Op. 20; Nocturne (Homage to John Field), Souvenirs: excerpts

(N) (B) *** EMI 2 34473-2 (i) Baxtresser; (ii) Margalit; (iii) Stepansky; (iv) with Wind Qt

The *Canzone for Flute and Piano* has an Elysian, soaring melody (slightly French in atmosphere) which **Jeanne**

Baxtresser plays very beautifully. The *Cello Sonata* has a powerful impulse and is given the most eloquent advocacy here, while the *Excursions* have wit and elegance. The shorter piano pieces are all distinctive. An unusual collection, well worth seeking out.

Summer Music

*** Crystal (ADD) CD 750. Westwood Wind Quintet – CARLSSON: *Nightwings*; LIGETI: *Bagatelles*; MATHIAS: *Quintet* ***

(BB) **(*) Naxos 8.553851. Michael Thompson Wind Quintet – HINDEMITH: *Kleine Kammermusik* **(*); JANÁČEK: *Mládí* **(*); LARSSON: *Quattro tempi* **

Samuel Barber's *Summer Music* is an evocative mood-picture of summer, a gloriously warm and lyrical piece. The Crystal CD offers superbly committed and sensitive playing; a vivid, warm recording.

The **Michael Thompson Wind Quintet** offer the piece with an enterprising choice of coupling and give an expressive account. The playing is wonderfully accomplished and sensitive, but the close balance does rob it of atmosphere.

PIANO MUSIC

Ballade, Op. 46; Excursions, Op. 20; Interlude 1 (Adagio for Jeanne); Nocturne, Op. 33; Piano Sonata, Op. 26

(N) ⊖– **** Nimbus NI 2528 John Browning

Horowitz gave the première of Barber's formidable *Piano Sonata* in 1950 and his performance has never been surpassed. Van Cliburn's later stereo version was pretty masterly too. Since then **John Browning** has rather made the sonata his own. He met the composer first in 1956 and frequently visited him until he died. In 1962 he was soloist in the New York première of the *Piano Concerto* which was commissioned for him. His performance of the *Sonata* from 1993 is very impressive, the Scherzo articulated with witty delicacy, and he confidently surmounts the technical difficulties of the closing fugue, which was added to the work at Horowitz's request. It comes here as part of the composer's complete solo piano music and includes the very first recording of the haunting *Interlude* (subtitled *Adagio for Jeanne*). The *Nocturne* is subtitled 'Homage to John Field', the *Excursions* draw on jazz idioms with real flare, and the *Ballade*, the composer's last completed piano piece, is in ternary form with a stormy middle section. All this music is played with a spontaneous virtuosity and much understanding, and the 1993 recording is excellent.

Piano Sonata

⊖– *** Hyp. CDA 67469. Hamelin – IVES: *Piano Sonata 2* ***

Mark-André Hamelin makes an ideal alternative choice in coupling *Sonatas* by Barber and Ives. In Hamelin's hands the complex first movement unravels spontaneously to demonstrate both power and underlying lyricism, and he is equally at home in the catchily syncopated Scherzo and the thoughtful threnody of the slow movement. He is superbly recorded.

VOCAL MUSIC

Agnus Dei

*** Hyp. CDA 66219. Corydon Singers, Best – BERNSTEIN: *Chichester Psalms*; COPLAND: *In the Beginning*, etc. ***

Barber's *Agnus Dei* is none other than our old friend the *Adagio*, arranged for voices by the composer in 1967. **Matthew Best's** fine performance moves spaciously and expansively to an impressive climax.

Choral Music

🎧 ⁓ BB *** Naxos 8.559053. Ormond College Ch., Melbourne Orchestra, Lawrence

Apart from his vocal arrangement of the famous *Adagio*, Barber's highly original, stimulating and immediately compelling choral music is still little known. None is more telling than the dramatic *A Stopwatch and an Ordnance Map*, a setting of a poem by Stephen Spender describing the death of a soldier in the Spanish Civil War, with its atmospheric accompaniment for three kettledrums. *Reincarnations*, a strikingly contrasted trio of Celtic folk songs, is equally memorable, as is *The Virgin Martyrs* for female voices, while many of the other items are lyrically and melodically highly appealing, not least *Twelfth Night* and the serene *To be sung on water*. The collection ends with a pair of avant-garde choruses from the opera, *Antony and Cleopatra*, followed by the powerful eight-part setting of Gerard Manley Hopkins's *God's Grandeur*. The performances are very accomplished and deeply felt, and the recording is first class.

Songs (Collection)

*** Hyp. CDA 67528. Finley, Aronowitz Qt, Drake

This is an ideal collection of Barber's songs, including some of the *Hermit* songs, with the recital culminating in his setting of Matthew Arnold's *Dover Beach*. The quartet drawn from the **Aronowitz Ensemble** features in a performance which inspires **Gerald Finley** to some of the most delicate tonal shading, perfectly controlled. Interestingly, only one of the songs is a setting of an American poem, by James Agee. Otherwise the orientation is towards Britain and Ireland, bringing out Barber's natural inclination away from his American background.

BARRIOS, Agustin (1885–1944)

Humoresque; Junto a tu corazion – Vals; Mabilita; Madrigal – Gavota; Maxixa; Pepita; Sarita (Mazurka); Suite Andina; Tu y Yo (Gavota romántica); Un sueño en la floresta; Vals, Op. 8/4; Vidalita con variaciones; Vallancico de Navidad

BB *** Naxos 8.554558. Goni

Goni's ebb and flow of rubato is a natural response to the line of the music and her playing always sounds spontaneous. She is very well recorded, and the back-up documentation is first class.

Canción de la Hilandera; La catedral; Confesión; Contemplación; Invocación a mi madre; Madrecita; 4 Minuets; Oración (Piegaria); Oración para todos; La Samaritana; El sueño de la muñequita; Variations on a Theme of Tárrega

🎧 ⁓ BB *** Naxos 8.555718. Enno Voorhoost

Enno Voorhoost's playing is of the highest order. His flexing of rubato and flowing lines are totally spontaneous-sounding, and his beguilingly subtle control of dynamic brings the most disarmingly attractive results. The recording is very real and properly intimate.

BARTÓK, Béla (1881–1945)

Concerto for Orchestra

*** Australian Decca Eloquence (ADD) 467 602-2. Israel PO, Mehta – JANÁČEK: *Taras Bulba*; KODÁLY: *Concerto for Orchestra* ***

(M) **(*) DG (ADD) 477 7160. BPO, Karajan – STRAVINSKY: *Rite of Spring* **(*)

Mehta's performance lacks the last degree of bite, but its combination of brilliance and warm expressiveness is very attractive. The finale has a measure of jollity in it (what Bartók called its 'life-assertion') at a tempo that allows the strings to articulate their rushing semi-quavers clearly. The recording was in the demonstration bracket in its day, with translucent woodwind, firmly focused brass and plenty of sheen on the strings.

On DG, the **Berlin Philharmonic**, in superb form in the 1960s, gives a performance that is rich, romantic and smooth – to some ears perhaps excessively so. **Karajan** is right in treating Bartók emotionally, but the comparison with Solti on Decca immediately points the contrast between Berlin romanticism and earthy, red-blooded, Hungarian passion. Both conductors allow themselves a fair degree of rubato, but Solti's is linked with the Hungarian folksong idiom, while Karajan's moulding of phrases is essentially of the German tradition.

Concerto for Orchestra; (i) Piano Concertos 1-3; (ii) Concerto for 2 Pianos, Percussion & Orchestra; (iii) Violin Concerto 2. The Miraculous Mandarin (complete ballet). Rhapsodies (for Violin & Orchestra) 1-2; (ii) Sonata for 2 Pianos & Percussion. Excerpts from: Music for Strings, Percussion & Celesta (opening); (iv) Bluebeard's Castle: The Lake of Tears

(N) (B) ***EMI 2 15037-2 (4) CBSO, Rattle; with (i) Donohoe; (ii) Katia & Marielle Labèque (iii) Kyung-Wha Chung; (iv) von Otter & White

Rattle's live recordings of the *Concerto for Orchestra* and the studio version of *The Miraculous Mandarin* both draw on an exceptionally wide emotional and expressive range with rich and well-balanced recording. **Donohoe** then joins the **CBSO** for first class accounts of the three solo piano concertos and **Kyung-Wha Chung** gives commanding, inspired performances of the *Violin Concerto* and the *Two Rhapsodies* full of fire and imagination.

Concerto for Orchestra; Dance Suite; Divertimento; Hungarian Sketches; The Miraculous Mandarin: Suite; Music for Strings, Percussion & Celesta; Romanian Folk Dances

☞ (B) *** Double Decca 470 516-2 (2). Chicago SO, Solti

Solti's digital Bartók recordings may not quite have the searing intensity of his classic LSO accounts of the major works here, but the extra warmth of the later readings brings out the lyrical qualities to the music. The *Divertimento* is superbly done too, incisive and full-bodied, and the Hungarian and Romanian dances have all the atmosphere one could wish for. In short, this is excellent value in the Double Decca series and brings typically fine Decca sound.

Concerto for Orchestra; Hungarian Sketches; Music for Strings, Percussion & Celesta

☞ (M) **** RCA (ADD) **SACD** 82876 61390-2. Chicago SO, Reiner

Reiner's superlative account of the *Concerto for Orchestra* sounds better than ever in the new compatible-SACD version heard through two speakers. The performances of the *Music for Strings, Percussion and Celesta* and the splendid *Hungarian Sketches* also benefit from the additional presence and sumptuousness of the new transfer. Indispensable, even if you have other accounts of these scores.

Concerto for Orchestra; Dance Suite; Kossuth; The Miraculous Mandarin; 3 Village Scenes; The Wooden Prince

☞ (N) (M) **** Ph. 475 7684 (3). Budapest Festival O, Iván Fischer

The **Budapest Festival Orchestra** conducted by **Iván Fischer** add to their laurels with their outstanding account of the *Concerto for Orchestra*, also offering, as well as the *Village Scenes*, an equally compelling account of the rarely heard symphonic poem, *Kossuth*, and a modern recording was badly needed. The recording is first class, as it is in the other three works included.

Concerto for Orchestra; Miraculous Mandarin: Suite

(*) Sony 88869 7123632. Bav. RSO, Jansons – RAVEL: *Daphnis et Chloë: Suite 2* *

Concert performances from 2004 and 2007 – and very good ones, too. The **Bayerisches Rundfunkorchester** is magnificent, with particularly lush string-tone, heard to excellent effect both in the *Concerto for Orchestra* and in the Ravel; the latter, incidentally, is without chorus. There are more polished *Concerto for Orchestra* versions to be found (Reiner still sounds marvellous on RCA – see above) but **Jansons's** *Daphnis* is very seductive.

Concerto for Orchestra; Music for Strings, Percussion & Celesta

(B) *** EMI (ADD) 4 76897-2. BPO, Karajan

Karajan is right in treating Bartók emotionally, but comparison with Solti points the contrast between Berlin romanticism and earthy Hungarian passion. Karajan's moulding of phrases is essentially of the German tradition. The *Music for Strings, Percussion and Celesta* has a well-upholstered timbre, and here Karajan's essentially romantic view combines with the recording to produce a certain urbanity.

(i) Piano Concertos 1–2; (ii) 2 Portraits, Op. 5

(M) *** DG (ADD/DDD) 477 6353. (i) Pollini, Chicago SO; (ii) Mintz, LSO; Abbado

The DG issue forms a partnership between two of the most distinguished Italian musicians of the day, collaborating in performances in which virtuosity goes with a sense of spontaneity. Rhythms in fast movements are freely and infectiously sprung to bring out bluff Bartókian high spirits, rather than any brutality. The **Chicago Orchestra**, vividly recorded, is in superb form and this reissue gives a new lease of life to the 1979 analogue recording, enhanced by **Mintz's** account of the 2 *Portraits*.

Piano Concertos (i) 1; (ii) 2; (iii) 3

☞ **** DG 477 5330. (i) Zimerman, Chicago SO; (ii) Andsnes, BPO; (iii) Grimaud, LSO; all cond. Boulez

(M) *** Ph. (ADD) 475 8690. Kovacevich, LSO or BBC SO, C. Davis

☞ (M) *** Warner Elatus 0927 46735-2. Schiff, Budapest Festival O, Fischer

Krystian Zimerman gives an aristocratic and searching account of the *First Concerto* with the Chicago orchestra, made in 2001. **Leif Ove Andsnes** with the **Berlin Philharmonic** give a thrilling reading of the *Second*, arguably the most visionary of the three, which many readers will recall from BBC broadcasts. **Hélène Grimaud's** performance of the *Third* with the LSO is the most recent and can hold its own with any of the current competition. Masterly performances and clean, meticulously conducted support from all three orchestras, plus eminently fine DG recording. Arguably the most recommendable set of the concertos now before the public.

Kovacevich's direct, concentrated readings of the three *Concertos* now returns to the catalogue as one of Philips's Originals. Though No. 2 was recorded (with the **BBC Symphony Orchestra**) in 1968, and the other two in 1975, the sound is bright and clear, giving extra bite to the performances, although the effect of the original resonance remains. **Sir Colin Davis** accompanies sensitively and vigorously, with lifted folk rhythms in No. 1 sharply pressed home and the violent finale exhilarating, with its many unexpected changes of tempo expertly controlled. At mid-price this disc is still very competitive.

András Schiff's colourful, winning performances are totally idiomatic, brilliantly and warmly accompanied by the fine Budapest orchestra, bringing out point and sparkle. His depth of meditation in the slow movements matches that which he brings equally to Bach or Schubert. Now on Elatus, this is a real bargain.

(i) Piano Concertos 1–3; (ii) Violin Concertos 1–2

(N) (B) *** EMI 2 06885-2 (i) Donohoe, CBSO, Rattle; (ii) Sitovetsky, Philh. O, Pešek

Donohoe's highly successful account of the three *Piano Concertos* are here joined with **Sitkovetsky's** equally recommendable versions of the *Violin Concertos*.

(i; ii) *Piano Concertos 1–3. Violin Concertos:* (iii; iv) 1; (iii; ii) 2

⊕ (B) *** Double Decca (ADD/DDD) 473 271-2 (2). (i) Ashkenazy; (ii) LPO; (iii) Chung; (iv) Chicago SO; all cond. Solti

If, in the *Violin Concertos*, **Chung** is rather forwardly balanced, the hushed intensity of the writing, as well as the biting Hungarian flavour, is caught superbly, thanks to **Solti** as well as to the soloist, and there is no sentimental lingering. In the *Piano Concertos*, the partnership between **Ashkenazy** and **Solti** works equally well. The *Second* and *Third Concertos* spark off the kind of energy one would expect from a live performance. The *First Concerto* (digital) is even tougher, urgent and biting, and the slow movements in all three works bring a hushed inner concentration, beautifully captured in warmly refined sound. Indeed, the recording throughout, whether analogue or digital, is of vintage Decca quality.

Piano Concerto 3

(N) (M) *** EMI 2 28591-2 Argerich, Montreake SO, Dutoit – PROKOFIEV: *Piano Concertos 1 & 3*

(i) *Piano Concerto 3. Mikrokosmos Vol. 6: 140, 144, 146–9, 151, 153*

(***) Testament mono SBT 1300. Katchen, (i) SRO, Ansermet – PROKOFIEV: *Piano Concerto 3* (***)

Katchen's 1953 account of the then relatively new *Third Concerto* was the first LP version issued in Britain. Even now, half a century later, its freshness and spontaneity make its reissue welcome, particularly in so excellent a transfer. The excerpts from *Mikrokosmos* are also brilliant.

Elegant playing from **Martha Argerich**. There is a wonderful, improvisatory feel to much of it, though at times in the slow movement she caresses a phrase in a way that draws attention to her rather than the composer. Not perhaps a first recommendation then, but a very stimulating one.

(i) *Viola Concerto* (two versions: ed. Péter Bartók & ed. Tibor Serly); *Two Pictures, Op. 10*

(BB) *** Naxos 8.554183. Xiao, Budapest PO, Kovacs (with SERLY: *Rhapsody for Viola & Orchestra* ***)

Bartók's *Viola Concerto* was the uncompleted work which, soon after his death, Tibor Serly put together from sketches. Now Bartók's son Péter, with the scholar Paul Neubauer, has re-edited those sketches. Though the differences are small, this first recording of the revised version, superbly played, proves fascinating, sounding closer to the *Concerto for Orchestra*. With the rich-toned Chinese viola-player **Xiao** as soloist, that version is here presented alongside Serly's. The warmly atmospheric *Two Pictures* and a viola work by Serly make a good coupling.

(i) *Viola Concerto; Violin Concertos 1–2;* (ii) *Rhapsodies 1–2 for Violin & Orchestra;* (iii) *Duos 28, 31, 33, 36, 41, 42 for 2 Violins. Solo Violin Sonata*

⊕ (BB) *** EMI Gemini (ADD) 5 85487-2 (2). Y. Menuhin; (i) New Philh. O, Dorati; (ii) BBC SO, Boulez; (iii) Gotkovsky

Menuhin, with his strongly creative imagination, plays these concertos with characteristic nobility of feeling, and he and **Dorati** make much of the Hungarian dance-rhythms. There is an appealing, earthy, peasant manner in Menuhin's playing of the *Two Rhapsodies*, which are given an authentic tang, and rather surprisingly this is matched by **Boulez's** approach, warm, rather than clinical. The great violinist commissioned the *Solo Violin Sonata*, and this is his third recording, made at Abbey Road in 1974/5. The six individually chosen *Duos* make a bonus for what is a very attractive bargain double.

Violin Concertos 1; 2

(BB) *** Naxos 8.554321. Pauk, Polish Nat. RSO (Katowice), Wit

*** Nim. NI 5333. Hetzel, Hungarian State SO, Fischer

György Pauk plays both concertos with exemplary musicianship and is given very good support by the **Polish National Radio Orchestra** at Katowice. No one investing in this coupling need feel disappointed, and the sound has great warmth and naturalness. Though not a first choice, this offers value for money and gives musical satisfaction.

Gerhart Hetzel also plays both concertos with great feeling and understanding. These are performances of strong but unintrusive personality. Both concertos are very well recorded, with a natural, excellent balance which helps the soloist to just the right extent, and it must rank among the very best now available.

Violin Concerto 2; 2 Rhapsodies for Violin & Orchestra.

⊕ *** DG 459 639-2. Shaham, Chicago SO, Boulez

Shaham's reading of the *Second Violin Concerto* is full of flair and imagination, taut and intense, while Boulez draws superb playing from the Chicago orchestra. The hushed intensity of Shaham's playing in the slow movement has rarely been matched. The two *Rhapsodies* make an ideal coupling. Full-bodied, well-detailed sound.

(i) *Violin Concerto 2;* (ii) *Contrasts for Clarinet, Violin & Piano;* (iii) *Violin Sonata 1. Sonata for Solo Violin*

*** Naïve V4991 (2). Korcia, with (i) CBSO, Oramo; (ii) Portal; (ii; iii) Bavouzet

Laurent Korcia won much acclaim and many international prizes. This two-CD Bartók set shows his virtuosity and musicianship to excellent effect. The *Concerto* was recorded in 2004 in Symphony Hall, Birmingham, and the *Contrasts* the following year in Brussels. The *Solo Sonata* and the *First Violin Sonata* are earlier (Marseilles, 1997) but are no less accomplished and persuasive.

Dance Suite; Hungarian Pictures; (i) The Miraculous Mandarin (ballet; complete)

(BB) *** Naxos 8.557433. Bournemouth SO, Alsop, (i) with Bournemouth SO Ch.

Marin Alsop conducts powerful, colourful performances of the controversial and violent ballet, *The Miraculous Mandarin* in its full form, coupled with the *Dance Suite* of 1923, demonstrating in both the orchestra's virtuosity and the conductor's versatility. Helpfully, each of the 12 sections is separately banded. The *Dance Suite* in this performance brings together rustic vitality and orchestral refinement, a more genial reading than many, while the *Hungarian Pictures*, with Bartók's own colourful orchestrations of early piano pieces, makes a relaxed tailpiece.

Divertimento for Strings

⌐💮 **** Chan. 9816. Norwegian CO, Brown — JANÁČEK: *Idyll*, etc. **** 💮

Iona Brown gives an arrestingly vibrant account of a piece that can sound dour but here is life-enhancing. The concentration is matched with playing of virtuosity and warmth and demonstration-standard sound of great presence.

Divertimento for Strings; Music for Strings, Percussion & Celesta

*** Linn CKD 234. Scottish CO, Mackerras — KODÁLY: *Dances of Galánta* ***

In his warmth and refinement **Sir Charles Mackerras** evidently regards Bartók as a composer more expressive than brutal and the dance element is delightfully brought out in the two fast movements of the *Music for Strings, Percussion and Celesta*, with rhythms wittily pointed and the jazzy syncopations given a lift to bring fun to the finale. In the *Divertimento* that natural, easy flexibility makes for just as much of an idiomatic feeling as in the *Music for Strings, Percussion and Celesta*.

Hungarian Pictures

(M) *** Chan. 6625 [id.]. Philh. O, Järvi — ENESCU: *Romanian Rhapsodies 1–2*; WEINER: *Hungarian Folkdance Suite* ***

The *Hungarian Pictures* are superbly played here and given spectacular sound. They are aptly coupled, not only with Enescu's pair of *Romanian Rhapsodies* but also with an equally engaging suite by Leó Weiner.

Kossuth: symphonic poem; The Wooden Prince: ballet (complete)

*** Hungaroton HSACD 32502. Hungarian Nat. PO, Kocsis

Zoltán Kocsis is as authoritative an advocate of Bartók on the podium as he is at the piano. *Kossuth* is heavily indebted to the world of Strauss and Liszt and offers few glimpses of the Bartók who was soon to emerge. *The Wooden Prince* followed *Bluebeard's Castle*, occupying the composer during 1914–17 when the Stravinsky ballets and *Le Rossignol* were new music. Kocsis directs performances of real poetic feeling and his orchestra is first class. János Kárpáti's thorough

and scholarly notes are particularly informative and helpful, and the recording is excellent.

(i) The Miraculous Mandarin (complete); Hungarian Peasant Songs; Hungarian Sketches; Romanian Folk Dances; Transylvanian Dances

⌐(M) **** Ph. 454-430-2. (i) Hung. R. Ch.; Budapest Festival O, Fischer

Iván Fischer's account of *The Miraculous Mandarin* is possibly the best ever committed to disc, and certainly the best recorded. The sound is in the demonstration category, with enormous range and depth. It has vivid presence and impact, and the balance is both truthful and refined. The performance has collected golden opinions almost everywhere and has virtuosity, bite and real flair. It won the *Gramophone* Orchestral Award in 1998 and is now reissued at mid-price in Universal's Award Collection: it makes a first-class recommendation for this repertoire.

2 Portraits, Op. 5

(M) *** Australian Decca Eloquence (ADD) 476 2700. VPO, Dohnányi — STRAVINSKY: *The Firebird* **(*)

Dohnányi's Bartók style, rather more mellow than usual, is suited to the *Two Portraits*, the first of which is used also as the first movement of the *First Violin Concerto*. The 1977 recording is warm and spacious.

Portrait, Op. 5/1

💮 (BB) (***) Naxos mono 8.110973. Szigeti, Philh. O, Lambert — BLOCH: *Violin Concerto*; PROKOFIEV: *Violin Concerto 1* (***)💮

Szigeti was a stylist and one of the greatest and most individual artists of his day and there is no questioning the strength of his personality or the quality of his artistry. They are heard to admirable effect in this outstanding account of the first of the Bartók *Portraits*, which he recorded with **Constant Lambert** on one of his first post-war visits to London.

Rhapsody 1 for Cello & Orchestra

(BB) *** Warner Apex 0927 40600-2. Noras, Finnish RSO, Saraste — ELGAR: *Cello Concerto*; DVOŘÁK: *Cello Concerto* **(*)

Bartók scored only the first of his two *Rhapsodies* (originally written for violin and piano) for cello and orchestra, and very effective it is on the responsive bow of **Arto Noras**. Good though not outstanding recording, with the cello dominating the sound-picture.

CHAMBER AND INSTRUMENTAL MUSIC

(i; ii) Contrasts for Clarinet, Violin & Piano; (ii) 2 Rhapsodies; Romanian Folk Dances. (Solo) Violin Sonata

⌐(BB) *** Hyp. Helios CDH 55149. Osostowicz, with (i) M. Collins; (ii) Tomes

(i) *Contrasts. Violin Sonatas 1–2*

☐– ⑧⑧ *** Naxos 8.550749. Pauk, Jandó, (i) with Berkes

Hyperion's distinguished coupling of the Bartók *Contrasts* with the *Rhapsodies* and the *Sonata for Solo Violin* now re-emerges on the Helios budget label. All these artists are on excellent form. **Krysia Osostowicz** is as good as almost any of her rivals in the *Sonata*, and the remainder of the programme is hardly less impressive.

The Naxos collection is very highly recommendable too, particularly when these works are played by such experienced artists as **György Pauk** and his fellow Hungarian, **Jenö Jandó**. The refinement and subtlety of **Pauk's** playing here is very persuasive. In the superb account of *Contrasts*, in which **Kálmán Berkes** joins them, the balance is better than in the *Sonatas*. Outstanding value.

(i) *44 Duos. Solo Violin Sonata*

⑧⑧ *** Naxos 8.550868. Pauk, (i) with Sawa

György Pauk's impressive recording of the remarkable *Solo Sonata* of 1944 is commanding, and everywhere his pacing seems just right and his playing effortless. In the *44 Duos* **Pauk**, partnered by the Japanese violinist, **Kazuki Sawa**, offers expertly judged and splendidly characterful accounts of these pieces. The Naxos recording is very good indeed and enhances the attractions of this super-bargain issue.

Romanian Folk Dances (arr. Székely)

*** Warner 8573-85769-2. Repin, Berezovsky – R. STRAUSS: *Violin Sonata*; STRAVINSKY: *Divertimento* ***

Repin and **Berezovsky** give an exemplary account of these Székely transcriptions as a makeweight in their outstanding Strauss–Stravinsky recital. There is nothing flashy about this impeccable and relaxed music-making.

(i) *Sonata for 2 Pianos & Percussion. Suite for 2 Pianos, Op. 4b*

⑧⑧ *** Warner Apex 0927 49569-2. Heisser, Pludermacher, with (i) Cipriani, Perotin

Heisser and **Pludermacher** offer a particularly useful coupling, and it is good to see their eminently vital and intelligent reading of the *Sonata* returning to circulation, particularly as the Argerich–Kovacevich account, arguably the finest, is currently out of circulation. Heisser and Pludermacher and their two percussionists are completely at one and totally idiomatic. The attractions of the disc are considerably enhanced by the coupling, the 1941 two-piano transcription of the *Second Suite for Orchestra* of 1905–7. Decent sound and excellent value.

String Quartets 1–6

☐– ⑧⑧ *** Warner Apex 2564 62686-2. Keller Qt

☐– *** Decca 455 297-2 (2). Takács Qt

⑧⑧ *** Naxos 8.557543/44. Vermeer Qt

*** DG 463 576-2 (2). Hagen Qt

Ⓜ *** DG 477 6322. Emerson Qt

The **Keller** made their recordings of the Bartók cycle in the Salle de Musique de la Chaux-de-Fonds, where the Végh recorded their second cycle. The performances are totally idiomatic, intense yet natural, and at their new and highly competitive price are among the best you can find.

The **Takács Quartet** also bring to these masterpieces the requisite virtuosity, tonal sophistication and command of idiom. These are full-blooded accounts of enormous conviction, with that open-air quality which suggests the fragrance of the forests and lakes of Hungary. The recording is excellent, and this Decca set now takes its place near the top of the list.

The **Vermeer** are a superbly equipped quartet with first-class ensemble and attack. These are recent recordings and are certainly highly recommendable, though earlier recordings are perhaps even more idiomatic. However, the Vermeer recording has a considerable price advantage.

The **Hagen Quartet** also have all the requisite fire and virtuosity for these marvellous scores. One or two expressive emphases in the *Third Quartet* may disturb some listeners, but on the whole theirs is a set with strong claims to commend it – among which is the vivid recording. Not necessarily a first recommendation, but certainly among the finest in the catalogue.

The **Emerson Quartet** project very powerfully and, in terms of virtuosity, finesse and accuracy, outstrip most of their rivals. If at times their projection and expressive vehemence are a bit too much of a good thing, these are concentrated and brilliant performances that are very well recorded. Although not our first choice for this repertoire, this set won the 1989 *Gramophone* 'Record of the Year' award.

String Quartet 5

*** ECM 476 5779. Zehetmair Qt – HINDEMITH: *Quartet 4* ***

An excellent coupling which serves to introduce collectors of the Bartók quartets to the now grievously (and unjustly) neglected Hindemith. The **Zehetmair Quartet** give as fine a performance of the *Fifth* as it has ever received on record and they convey a freshness and passion that recalls the pioneering Hungarians.

Violin Sonatas 1–2; (Solo) Violin Sonata

☐– Ⓜ *** Virgin 5 18177-2. Tetzlaff, Andsnes

Violin Sonata 1; Sonatina (trans. André Gertler); *Rhapsody 2 for Violin & Piano; Hungarian Folksongs* (trans. Tivadar Országh); *Hungarian Folk-Tunes* (trans. Jozsef Szigeti)

☐– *** ASV CDDCA 883. Stanzeleit, Fenyö

(Solo) Violin Sonata; Violin Sonata 2; Rhapsody 1; Romanian Folk Dances

☐– *** ASV CDDCA 852. Stanzeleit, Fenyö

Christian Tetzlaff and **Leif Ove Andsnes** offer both the *Violin Sonatas* and the solo work on a single mid-priced disc and bring a commanding intensity and fine discipline to all three, and their vividly recorded accounts must rank as the finest since the Oistrakh versions with Frida Bauer (No. 1) and Richter (No. 2) in the early 1970s. In the *Solo Sonata* Tetzlaff can withstand the most exalted comparisons.

Susanne Stanzeleit and her partner, **Gusztáv Fenyö**, are completely inside the idiom. The *Violin Sonata 1* and the *Rhapsody 2* are every bit as well played and recorded as the *Solo Sonata* and the *Second Sonata* for violin and piano (1922), and the performances are as good as any you can find in the current catalogue. The recording, too, is altogether first rate.

COMPLETE PIANO MUSIC

Allegro barbaro; 14 Bagatelles, Op. 6; 3 Burlesques, Op. 8c; Dance Suite; 4 Dirges, Op. 9a; 10 Easy Pieces; 2 Elegies, Op. 8b; 7 Esquisses, Op. 9b; First Term at the Piano; For Children, Books 1–4; 3 Hungarian Folksongs from Csik; 3 Hungarian Folk Tunes; 15 Hungarian Peasant Dances; Improvisations on Hungarian Peasant Songs, Op. 20; Kossuth; March funèbre; Mikrokosmos (complete); Out of Doors; 4 Pieces; Rhapsody Op. 1 (2 versions); Romanian Christmas Carols; 2 Romanian Dances, Op. 8a; 6 Romanian Folk Tunes; 3 Rondos on Folk Tunes; Sonatina; Sonata; 3 Studies, Op. 18; Suite, Op. 14

Ⓝ 🌑 Ⓑ **** Ph. (ADD/DDD) 475 6720 (8) Kocsis

Philips have restored **Kocsis's** coverage of the complete piano music to the catalogue and it remain the classic set for the foreseeable future. Bartók playing doesn't come any better than this – nor does piano recording. Kocsis penetrates to the very centre and soul of this music more deeply than almost any rival. Scrupulously attentive to the composer's wishes, Kocsis can produce power and drama when required, but he also commands a wide-ranging palette and a marvellously controlled vitality. His playing calls to mind Bartók's own injunction that performances must be 'beautiful but true'.

Allegro barbaro; 6 Dances in Bulgarian Rhythm; 3 Hungarian Folksongs; 15 Hungarian Peasant Songs; Mikrokosmos (excerpts); 3 Rondos on Slovak Folk Tunes; Sonatina

ⒷⒷ **(*) Naxos 8.550451. Szokolay

Balázs Szokolay is a highly musical player. His performances are always vitally intelligent and perceptive, and he is acceptably recorded. This is a thoroughly recommendable recital and excellent value.

Piano Music Vol. 1: *Andante for Piano; 3 Hungarian Folksongs from Csík; 15 Hungarian Peasant Songs, Sz.71; 3 Rondos on Folk Tunes, Sz.84; 7 Sketches, Op. 9b; Sonata, Sz.80; Suite, Op. 14*

ⒷⒷ **(*) Naxos 8.554717. Jandó

Piano Music Vol. 2: *Dance Suite; Improvisations, Op. 20; Petite Suite; Romanian Christmas Carols; Romanian Folk Dances 1–6; Slovakian Dance; Sonatina*

ⒷⒷ **(*) Naxos 8.554718. Jandó

Jenö Jandó is very well served by the Naxos engineers and gives far more than just serviceable accounts of this repertoire. His playing is thoroughly idiomatic without being really special.

14 Bagatelles; 3 Hungarian Folk Songs; Out of Doors; 2 Romanian Dances, Op. 8a; Romanian Christmas Carols; Sonatina; Sonata

🎧 Ⓜ **** Ph. 464 676-2. Kocsis

This representative collection, chosen as one of Philips's '50 Great Recordings', comes from the Kocsis complete survey, and as it includes the *Sonata* and *Sonatina* and is superbly recorded, it can be highly recommended.

For Children (Books 1–4) complete; Mikrokosmos (Books 1–6) complete

Ⓜ *** Teldec (ADD) 9031 76139-2 (3). Ránki

For Children, Volumes I & II (revised version); 10 Easy Pieces; 15 Hungarian Peasant Songs. Mikrokosmos, Vol. VI: 6 Bulgarian Dances; 6 Romanian Folk Dances; Sonata; Sonatina

ⒷⒷ *** EMI Gemini (ADD) 3 50869-2 (2). Béroff

Dezsö Ránki here shows his musicianship and plays all 85 pieces with the utmost persuasion and with the art that conceals art, for the simplicity of some of these pieces is deceptive; darker currents lurk beneath their surface. He gives us the composer's original edition of 1908–9. Ránki also plays the *Mikrokosmos* with an effortless eloquence and a welcome straightforwardness. He is very clearly (if forwardly) recorded, and he is given a realistic presence.

Choice between **Michel Béroff** and **Dezsö Ránki** is simplified by the fact that Béroff records the revised score and Ránki gives us the original edition of 1908/9. Moreover, Ránki's set is coupled with the complete *Mikrokosmos*, whereas Béroff offers a number of Bartók's other major piano works. Béroff's playing has an unaffected eloquence that is touching, and the recording, made in the Salle Wagram, Paris, is very good.

Mikrokosmos (complete)

🎧 ⒷⒷ *** Naxos 8.557821/22. Jandó, Szokolay, Takács

Jenö Jandó's plain style suits the earlier *Mikrokosmos*; and he has an excellent partner in the pieces for piano duo, and those needing a vocal contribution bring eloquent contributions from the rich-voiced **Tamara Takács**. Excellent recording makes this an economical first choice, with good documentation.

OPERA

Bluebeard's Castle (DVD Version)

🎬 **** Decca **DVD** 074 3254. Sass, Kováts, LPO, Solti (Director: Miklós Szinetár)

Solti made this electrifying video recording of *Bluebeard's Castle* in 1981. His two soloists could not have been better chosen, for both the dark-timbred **Kolos Kováts** and the rich-voiced **Sylvia Sass** are totally convincing in their roles as a grim, unmoving Bluebeard and an increasingly apprehensive but determinedly wilful Judith. The sets in Miklós Szinetár's production are extraordinarily imaginative, creating an uncannily gloomy atmosphere as Duke Bluebeard and his wife make their way slowly through the dank, ill-lit passages of his castle, and always bringing a vivid surprise to the viewer as well as to Judith as each door is opened. The tension steadily increases until the seventh door reveals Judith's own destiny. With the LPO responding with great concentration, Solti's orchestral commentary is superbly controlled: the taut grip for which his conducting is celebrated is felt at its most magnetic, and the powerful closing scene is haunting. It is difficult to believe that Bartók's masterpiece could be brought to life more convincingly, the recording and camerawork are of the highest quality and, for good measure, Chris Hassall has provided the translation for the surtitles.

Bluebeard's Castle (sung in Hungarian)

(BB) *** Naxos 8.660928. Beláček, Meláth, Bournemouth SO, Alsop

Marin Alsop has made a series of impressive recordings for Naxos, of which this is one of the finest yet, with gloriously rich sound, very well focused. The big climax when Judith opens the door on to Bluebeard's vast kingdom is thrilling, a wonderfully weighty focus for the whole sequence of doors, a sequence which Alsop sustains masterfully. **Gustáv Beláček** has a Slavonic-sounding bass, firmly controlled, very apt for the role and well matched by the Judith of **Andrea Meláth**, an imaginative choice of soloist.

BATE, Stanley (1911-59)

Viola Concerto

(N) (M) *** Dutton CDLX 7216. Chase, BBC Concert O, Bell –
BELL: *Rosa Mystica*; VAUGHAN WILLIAMS: *Romance* ***

Stanley Bate studied with Vaughan Williams, R.O. Morris, Gordon Jacob and Arthur Benjamin, and then continued his musical schooling in Paris with Nadia Boulanger and in Berlin with Hindemith. He returned to London in 1949. His output includes five piano concertos and four symphonies. But his work remained little played and after his death in 1959 fell completely out of the repertoire. Hindemith, Vaughan Williams and Walton are major influences. The *Viola Concerto* was written in America during 1944– 6 and first broadcast with Emanuel Vardi and the NBC Orchestra in 1947 but never heard again until the present recording. It is a big piece, nearly forty minutes in length, warmly romantic in idiom, well laid out for the instrument and well worth investigating. Indeed it is both compelling and eloquent. **Roger Chase** is the excellent soloist and plays the Montagnana viola that once belonged to Lionel Tertis and he receives excellent orchestral support under **Stephen Bell**.

BAX, Arnold (1883–1953)

Cathaleen-ni-Hoolihan; (i) *Concertante for 3 Wind Instruments & Orchestra; London Pageant; Tamara Suite* (orch. Parlett)

*** Chan. 9879. BBC PO, Brabbins; (i) with Callow, Bradbury, Goodall

Cathaleen-ni-Hoolihan began life in 1903 in Bax's student years as the slow movement of a quartet. The score of *Tamara* was inspired by Karsavina, Diaghilev's prima ballerina. He never finished the orchestration, and the present 23-minute suite was compiled by the Bax scholar Graham Parlett. *London Pageant* comes from the Coronation year, 1937. The *Concertante for Cor Anglais, Clarinet, Bassoon and Orchestra* finds Bax at the very end of his creative life as it was being composed for the Henry Wood memorial concert in 1949. The performances are first class, persuasive in every way, and so, too, is the richly sonorous recording.

(i) *Cello Concerto*; (ii) *Violin Concerto*; (iii) *Morning Song (Maytime in Sussex)*

⊶ (M) *** Chan. X10154. (i) Wallfisch; (ii) Mordkovitch; (iii) Fingerhut; LPO, Thomson

Chandos is re-grouping its vintage Bax recordings at midprice, and Volume 1 includes two major concertante works plus the short but attractive *Morning Song*, an aubade for piano and chamber orchestra written to celebrate the twenty-first birthday of Princess Margaret. The *Cello Concerto* is marvellously played by **Raphael Wallfisch**, while **Lydia Mordkovitch** is equally committed to the *Violin Concerto*. This is full of good, easily remembered tunes, yet there is a plangent, bitter-sweet quality about many of its ideas and an easy, Mediterranean-like warmth that is very appealing. All three soloists are given splendid support by the **LPO** under **Bryden Thomson**, and the recording sets and maintains high standards for this Bax series.

Concerto for Piano (Left Hand); Symphonic Variations

(N) ⊶ (BB) **** Wass, Bournemouth SO, James Judd

Bax's *Left Hand Piano Concerto* is a real find – one of his most appealing concertane works. It has a hauntingly atmospheric central *Moderato tranquillo* with a lovely, gentle main theme and a perky marching figure with variations for its attractive diverse finale. The *Symphonic Variations* takes twice as long (46 minutes) and is in two sections combining eight linked movements. All are titled, but with no explanation given of their meaning, although the lovely third-movement *Nocturne* has touching serenity. The work is complex but full of Baxian lyricism and indeed in the opening sections reminds one a little of Rachmaninov, with full-blooded strings. The piano writing is demandingly complex, but, as **Ashley Wass** demonstrates, the bravura is very rewarding. His performances of both works are superb, and he gets admirable support from **James Judd** and the **Bournemouth Orchestra**. With a fine balance and spectacular sound this is a Bax disc not to be missed.

(i) Violin Concerto; (ii) Symphony 3

Ⓜ (***) Dutton mono CDLX 7111. (i) Kersey, BBC SO, Boult; (ii) Hallé O, Barbirolli

Barbirolli's wartime recording of Bax's *Third Symphony*, made in the winter of 1943–4 when he was rebuilding the Hallé Orchestra, has never been surpassed as an interpretation, and this Dutton version brings astonishingly full and vivid sound, heightening the power of the performance. It is good too to have another powerful performance in the *Violin Concerto*. **Eda Kersey** recorded this with **Boult** and the BBC orchestra in Bedford in 1944. The result again is astonishingly vivid, with Kersey, sadly short-lived, demonstrating her virtuosic flair and depth of feeling.

(i; ii) Eire: I, Into the Twilight; II, In the Faery Hills; III, Rose-Catha. (iii; ii) A Legend; (i; iv) On the Sea-Shore (ed. Parlett); (i; ii) The Tale the Pine Trees Knew

Ⓜ *** Chan. X10157. (i) Ulster O, (ii) Thomson; (iii) LPO; (iv) Handley

These three tone-poems form an Irish trilogy. The first two are filled with typical Baxian Celtic twilight, but the last, *Rose-Catha* (meaning 'battle-hymn') presents the composer in vigorous, extrovert mood, making an excellent contrast. Also included is *The Tale the Pine Trees Knew*, one of the better known as well as one of the most evocative of Bax's tone-poems. All are directed with total sympathy by **Bryden Thomson**. The prelude, *On the Sea-Shore*, makes a colourful and atmospheric companion in the hands of **Vernon Handley**, played and recorded with similar warmth and brilliance. A fine disc.

Film Music: (i) Oliver Twist (complete original score, prepared Graham Parlett). Malta GC, Part 2: Gay March; Quiet Interlude; Work and Play; March

☊ *** Chan. 10126. BBC PO, Gamba; (i) with James

Bax's richly detailed score for David Lean's masterly *Oliver Twist* comes from 1948, music of quality that could stand on its own apart from the visual images. Bax writes in effect a concertante piano part, originally written for (and recorded by) Harriet Cohen, but very well played here by **Paul James**.

The writing for *Malta GC* is less individual but still attractive. Only the music for the first reel is included here, but it features a notable *March* with a genuine *nobilmente* theme in the best Elgarian tradition. The performances under **Rumon Gamba** are persuasively sympathetic and spontaneous in their narrative flow and are gloriously recorded – just sample the luscious strings in the opening *Prelude* for *Oliver Twist*.

The Garden of Fand; The Happy Forest; November Woods; Summer Music; Tintagel

☊ Ⓜ **** Chan. X10156. Ulster O, Thomson

This is perhaps the most attractive so far of these reissued Chandos Bax compilations in including not only *The Garden of Fand* but also Bax's masterly Cornish evocation, *Tintagel*.

The Celtic twilight is ripely and sympathetically caught in the first three items, while *Summer Music*, dedicated to Sir Thomas Beecham and here given its first ever recording, brings an intriguing kinship with the music of Delius. The Chandos recording is superb.

The Garden of Fand; The Happy Forest; November Woods; The Tale the Pine Trees Knew; Tintagel

ⒷⒷ **(*) Naxos 8.557599. RSNO, Lloyd-Jones

A truly worthwhile collection of symphonic poems, which originally accompanied **David Lloyd-Jones's** recordings of the symphonies. The performances are warm and flexible and very well played. The slight reservation concerns the recording, which is not always as expansive in the middle frequencies as it might be, though the gentler passages in *The Garden of Fand*, *Happy Forest* and *November Woods* have attractive atmospheric lustre.

The Garden of Fand; In the Faery Hills; November Woods; Sinfonietta

☊ *** Chan. 10362. BBC PO, Handley

Vernon Handley is no less eloquent and authoritative in the tone-poems, and the **BBC Philharmonic** respond with enthusiasm. The *Sinfonietta* comes from the period of the *Third Symphony* and is vintage Bax, full of invention and colour. A superb issue, and recorded in lifelike and vivid sound.

The Garden of Fand (symphonic poem); Mediterranean; Northern Ballad 1; November Woods; Tintagel (symphonic poems)

*** Lyrita (ADD) SRCD 231. LPO, Boult

Sir Adrian Boult's recording of *The Garden of Fand* is full of poetry and almost erases memories of Beecham's magical account. *Tintagel* is no less involving and beguiling and, though not as uninhibited as Barbirolli's, is equally valid. The *Northern Ballad 1*, though less memorable than either *Fand* or *Tintagel*, is well worth having, as is *November Woods*, a lush, romantic score. *Mediterranean*, a Spanish picture post-card and almost a waltz, has an endearing touch of vulgarity uncharacteristic of its composer. Excellent sound.

Golden Eagle: incidental music; Romantic Overture; Russian Suite; (i) Saga Fragment; (ii) 4 Songs

Ⓝ *** Chan. 10159. LPO, Thomson with (i) Margaret Fingerhut; (ii) Martyn Hill

Interesting repertoire from the Baxian foothills, so to speak. The *Russian Suite* comprises orchestrations of piano pieces including *In a Vodka Shop*, which served as an interlude during the 1919 Diaghilev Season in London. Two of the *Four Songs*, date from 1910, the period of his infatuation with the Ukrainian Natalia Skarginski, and the *Saga Fragment* written for Harriet Cohen's American tour (1933) is a transcription of his single-movement *Piano Quartet* written ten years before at the time of the *First Symphony*. The *Golden Eagle* is a play by his brother, Clifford, about Mary Queen of Scots, produced in 1945. The *Romantic Overture* was written for Delius whom Bax had visited at Grez-sur-Loing in the company of Peter Warlock. Expert performances from all concerned and fine recorded sound. A disc to reward all admirers of the composer, it comes with authoritative and fascinating notes by Lewis Foreman.

The Happy Forest; Into the Twilight; 3 Northern Ballads; Nympholept; Red Autumn (orch: Graham Parlett)

(N) **** Chan. 10446. BBC PO, Handley

The 3 *Northern Ballads* ooze atmosphere, with **Handley** bringing out all the harmonic colours with incredible vividness. The ebb and flow of Bax's writing is something Handley well understood, and he superbly holds together the longest work here, *Nympholept* with marvellous intensity (and what a fine, imaginative score it is too!). *Red Autumn* is the rarity here. Graham Partlett has done a magnificent job in entering Bax's sound-world and the result is another rather good and dramatic Bax tone poem. The picturesque qualities of both *The Happy Forest* and *Into the Twilight* are magnificently captured by the Chandos engineers, and this CD is an unqualified success in every way.

On the Sea-Shore

(M) **** Chan. 10426X. Ulster O, Handley – BRIDGE: *The Sea*; BRITTEN: *Sea Interludes*; STANFORD: *Irish Rhapsody 4* ****

Bax's Prelude, *On the Sea-Shore*, makes a colourful and atmospheric companion to the masterly Bridge, Britten and Stanford pieces on the disc, played and recorded with similar warmth and brilliance.

Symphonies 1–7; Rogue's Comedy Overture; Tintagel

⊶ ✪ (M) **** Chan. 10122 (5). BBC PO, Handley (set includes free bonus CD of an interview between Vernon Handley and Andrew McGregor)

Vernon Handley's is the most satisfying survey of the cycle we have yet had, and it is difficult to imagine it being superseded. Handley holds the scores together very convincingly. His tempi are expertly judged and allow the music to unfold naturally and eloquently. The *Second* (in some ways the most imaginative of them all) comes over impressively, and the *Third* is both tauter yet freer in spirit than any of its rivals, including Barbirolli's wartime pioneering set. Perhaps in the *Fifth* and *Sixth* honours are more evenly divided between Handley and David Lloyd-Jones and the Scottish National Orchestra; both show this music in the best possible light. Listening to Handley's *Seventh*, one is forced to question earlier doubts as to its weakness, and much the same goes for the *Fourth*, even though this is incontrovertibly the weakest of the seven. The orchestral playing is highly responsive and excels in all departments, and the Chandos BBC recording produces sumptuous tonal results and it all comes at mid-price together with a rarity from the 1930s, the *Rogue's Comedy Overture*, as well as the (rightly) popular *Tintagel*.

Symphony 1; The Garden of Fand; In the Faery Hills

(BB) *** Naxos 8.553525. RSNO, Lloyd-Jones

Symphonies: (i) 1 in E flat; (ii) 7 in A flat

*** Lyrita (ADD) SRCD 232. LPO, (i) Fredman; (ii) Leppard

This first disc in the Naxos Bax series offers warmly idiomatic readings of two early symphonic poems, as well as the *First Symphony*, in recordings less weighty than in the rival Chandos versions but finely detailed. In the two symphonic poems, more specifically inspired by Irish themes, **Lloyd-Jones** draws equally warm and sympathetic performances from the **Scottish Orchestra**, bringing inner clarity to the heaviest scoring. First-rate sound, though Bryden Thomson on Chandos has even richer recording.

The Lyrita coupling is particularly generous (78 minutes) and the performances by **Myer Fredman** and **Raymond Leppard** are powerful and finely shaped and can well hold their own with the later, Chandos digital versions. The Lyrita 1970s analogue sound, too, is vivid and clear.

Symphonies (i) 2; (ii) 5

⊶ **** Lyrita (ADD) SRCD 233. LPO, (i) Fredman; (ii) Leppard

Myer Fredman has secured a first-class account of the *Second*; the **LPO** sound as if they have been playing it all their lives, and the analogue recording is in the demonstration bracket for its period (the early 1970s). The *Fifth* symphony shows Bax holding in check the purely lyrical impulse, to which he could give such generous vein, in favour of a greater degree of motivic integration, though the music has characteristic brooding intensity and a powerful atmosphere. **Raymond Leppard** gives a dedicated and indeed inspired account, the LPO are at their very best, and so too are the Lyrita engineers.

Symphony 3; The Happy Forest (symphonic poem)

(BB) *** Naxos 8.553608. RSNO, Lloyd-Jones

Symphony 5; The Tale the Pine-Trees Knew

⊶ (BB) *** Naxos 8.554509. RSNO, Lloyd-Jones

David Lloyd-Jones continues his admirable Bax series with a warmly idiomatic accounts of the *Third and Fifth Symphonies*. The playing of the **Scottish Orchestra** is clear and refined, helped by the transparency of the recording, clarifying often thick textures. From earlier in Bax's career *The Happy Forest*, described as a 'nature poem', provides a refreshing contrast in its youthful energy, tauter, less expansive. *The Tale the Pine-Trees Knew* of 1931, another northern inspiration, makes the ideal coupling. An excellent bargain.

Symphony 6; Into the Twilight; Summer Music

⊶ ✪ (BB) *** Naxos 8.557144. RSNO, Lloyd-Jones

(i) Symphony 6; (ii) Irish Landscape; Overtures: To Adventure; Rogue's Comedy; Work in Progress

*** Lyrita (ADD/DDD) SRC 296. (i) New Philh. O, Del Mar; (ii) RPO, Handley

David Lloyd-Jones's account of the magnificent *Sixth* has sweep and breadth, and the splendid Naxos recording has plenty of range, detail and presence. *Into the Twilight* (1909) is prefaced by a quotation from Yeats and its rich, luxuriant textures are fully characteristic of the mature Bax. *Summer*

Music (1921, revised 1932) was dedicated to Beecham, and it is an affecting piece for a much smaller orchestra than we associate with the composer, though the sonority he produces is characteristically sumptuous. David Lloyd-Jones secures eloquent playing from the Scottish orchestra throughout.

Del Mar's performance of the *Sixth* is committed, though a greater attention to dynamic nuance would have been welcome and the balance is too close at times. The *Irish Landscape* is much earlier, written during the First World War. Scored for strings and harp, the music includes 'a long melody of a folksong nature' and is full of yearning intensity. The three overtures are all extrovert pieces: the rambunctious *Rogue's Comedy Overture* is matched by the equally exuberant *Overture to Adventure* and the bustle of the later *Work in Progress* which whimsically even quotes briefly from Haydn's *Emperor Quartet*. Fine performances from **Handley**, and recording well up to Lyrita standard.

Symphony 7; Tintagel

(BB) **(*) Naxos 8.557145. RSNO, Lloyd-Jones

The *Seventh Symphony* comes from 1939 and one in which the creative fires seem to burn less intensely than in its two immediate predecessors. **David Lloyd-Jones** makes out a strong case for it and is as persuasive as (or more persuasive than) his predecessors on record. Despite its length (it is the longest of the seven), the score is still richly stocked. The recording's climaxes do not have the transparency of earlier issues in the series nor the strings quite the bloom. David Lloyd-Jones also gives a thoroughly committed account of *Tintagel*.

The Truth about the Russian Dancers (incidental music); From Dusk till Dawn (ballet)

(M) *** Chan. 10457x. LPO, Thomson

The *Truth about the Russian Dancers* is vintage Bax, full of characteristic writing decked out in attractive orchestral colours. *From Dusk till Dawn* has many evocative ideas with some impressionistic orchestral touches. Not top-drawer Bax, but often delightful, and very well played by the **London Philharmonic** under **Bryden Thomson**, and splendidly recorded.

Tintagel

(M) **** EMI (ADD) 3 79983-2. LSO, Barbirolli – DELIUS: *La Calinda*, etc.; IRELAND: *London Overture* ****

(N) (M) *** LPO036. LPO, Vänskä – RACHMANINOV: *Symphony 3*

Barbirolli's *Tintagel* is the finest ever recorded and is unlikely ever to be surpassed. The performance has a great romantic sweep and the full-bodied 1965 recording is superbly remastered.

Osmo Vänskä gives a first-rate account of Bax's most popular (and inspired) tone-poem recorded at a concert at London's Royal Festival Hall in December 2007. Plenty of spontaneity and vigour from the **LPO** and faithful recorded sound.

(i; ii) Winter Legends (for piano and orchestra); (i) A Hill Tune; A Mountain Mood; (i; iii) Viola Sonata

(BB) (**(*)) Dutton mono CDBP 9751. (i) Cohen; (ii) BBC SO, Raybould; (iii) Primrose

Winter Legends is a masterly and imaginative score that enshrines much of the best of Bax. The piano writing places considerable demands on **Harriet Cohen** and this performance from a live (1954) BBC studio concert has less authority than the more recent recording by Margaret Fingerhut. However, **Clarence Raybould** and the **BBC Symphony Orchestra** give sympathetic support. The two miniatures come from 1942 and the days of 78s, while the *Viola Sonata*, which she recorded with **William Primrose**, was made in 1937.

CHAMBER AND INSTRUMENTAL MUSIC

Clarinet Sonata

⌐─ *** Chan. 8683. Hilton, Swallow – BLISS: *Clarinet Quintet*; VAUGHAN WILLIAMS: *6 Studies* ***

(i) Clarinet Sonata; (ii) Elegiac Trio (for flute, viola & harp); (iii) Harp Quintet; (iv) Nonet; (v) Oboe Quintet

⌐─ *** Hyp. CDA 66807. (i; iv) Collins; (i) Brown (piano); (ii; iv) Davies; (ii–v) Chase; (ii–iv) Kanga; (iii–v) Crayford, Van Kampen; (iii; v) Juda; (iv) Wexler, McTier, Brown (cond.); (iv–v) Hulse

Bax's *Clarinet Sonata* opens most beguilingly, and **Janet Hilton's** phrasing is quite melting. Moreover the Bliss coupling is indispensable.

The Hyperion performances are of exemplary quality. The members of the **Nash Ensemble**, including **Michael Collins** in the *Clarinet Sonata* and **Gareth Hulse** in the *Oboe Quintet*, seem totally attuned to the idiom, and they play with their usual artistry and dedication. Excellent recording.

Concerto for Flute, Oboe, Harp & String Quartet; In memoriam, for Cor Anglais, Harp & String Quartet; Threnody & Scherzo for Bassoon, Harp & String Sextet; (i) Octet for Horn, Piano & String Sextet; String Quintet

*** Chan. 9602. (i) Fingerhut; ASMF Ch. Ens.

In memoriam is the earliest piece here. The *Octet* is arguably the most appealing work in this collection. However, most of this music is captivating; the performances are absolutely first class and the recording in the best traditions of the house.

Elegiac Trio; Fantasy Sonata for Harp & Viola; Harp Quintet; Sonata for Flute & Harp

(BB) *** Naxos 8.554507. Mobius

Ideal late-night listening for a balmy summer evening: a collection of Bax chamber music centred around the harp played by an accomplished group called **Mobius**.

(i) *Harp Quintet*; (ii) *Piano Quartet. String Quartet 1*

*** Chan. 8391. (i) Kanga; (ii) McCabe; English Qt

The *First String Quartet* is music with a strong and immediate appeal. The *Harp Quintet* is more fully characteristic and has some evocative writing to commend it, alongside the *Piano Quartet* with its winning lyricism, and the performances are thoroughly idiomatic and eminently well recorded.

Oboe Quintet

*** Chan. 8392. Francis, English Qt – HOLST: *Air & Variations*, etc.; MOERAN: *Fantasy Quartet*; JACOB: *Quartet* ***

Bax's *Oboe Quintet* is a confident, inventive piece. **Sarah Francis** proves a most responsive soloist, though she is balanced too close; in all other respects the recording is up to Chandos's usual high standards, and the playing of the **English Quartet** is admirable.

Piano Trio in B flat

(N) *** RTE Lyric CD 116. Ens Avalon – BERNSTEIN: *Piano Trio Op. 2* ***; BEETHOVEN: *Piano Trio, Op.70/1 (Ghost)* **(*)

The Bax Trio on this Irish disc is a rarity, a late work dating from 1946, and unlike most of this often diffuse composer's chamber works compact in its structure and sharp in its thematic material. Good performances and recording.

Rhapsodic Ballad (for solo cello)

*** Chan. 8499. Wallfisch – BRIDGE: *Cello Sonata*; DELIUS: *Cello Sonata*; WALTON: *Passacaglia* ***

The *Rhapsodic Ballad* for cello alone is a freely expressive piece, played with authority and dedication by **Raphael Wallfisch**. The recording has plenty of warmth and range.

String Quartet 1

*** Discrete 0701. Pavão Qt – ELGAR: *Quartet* ***

The *First Quartet* is an early work, composed some years before the Elgar with which it is coupled. It comes from 1910 when Bax's distinctive voice was yet to emerge. The four ladies who comprise the **Pavão** lack neither strength nor sensitivity and they give a well-thought-out and well-integrated account of the piece. Those who do not want the Naxos coupling with Bax's *Third Quartet* will find this more than serviceable.

String Quartets 1; 3 in F; String Quartet in E: Adagio ma non troppo 'Cathaleen-ni-Hoolihan'; (i) Lyrical Interlude for String Quintet

⊛– (BB) *** Naxos 8.555953. Maggini Qt, with (i) Jackson

The **Maggini Quartet's** series of British music recordings for Naxos goes from strength to strength and this *Quartet* represents Bax at his sharpest, with no meandering. The opening of the first movement sweeps the listener forward in a way that reminds one of Mendelssohn's *Octet*, despite the far more modern idiom. The *Lyrical Interlude* is a re-working Bax made in 1922 of the slow movement of his *String*

Quintet of 1908. It is a rather beautiful piece, like the *Adagio ma non troppo* from an even earlier quartet. The Magginis are masterly throughout, not just in the four substantial movements of the *Quartet* but in the two evocatively Irish-inspired movements written much earlier.

Viola Sonata; Legend; Concert Piece; (i) Trio, Op. 4

(BB) *** Naxos 8.557784. Outram, Rolton with (i) Jackson

The *Viola Sonata* comes from 1922 and the *Legend* seven years later. The other pieces are both early. All are beautifully played and very well recorded.

Violin Sonatas: 1 in E; 2 in D

*** Chan. 8845. Gruenberg, McCabe

The *Second* is the finer of these two *Sonatas* and is thematically linked with *November Woods*. Rhapsodic and impassioned, this is music full of temperament. **Erich Gruenberg** is a selfless and musicianly advocate and **John McCabe** makes an expert partner.

Violin Sonatas: 1 in F; 3

(BB) *** Naxos 8.557540. Jackson, Wass

Bax's writing for the violin is always grateful and these two artists are persuasive and eloquent interpreters. As an appendix **Laurence Jackson** and **Ashley Wass** give us the original second and third movements of the *First Sonata*, as well as the later and more personal *Third* from 1927.

Violin Sonata 2

*** Global Music Network GMN CO113. Little, Roscoe – ELGAR: *Violin Sonata* ***

Tasmin Little gives a powerful, big-scale reading of the four-movement Bax *Sonata 2*, relishing the virtuosity of the writing, with **Martin Roscoe** similarly brilliant. An excellent if unusual coupling for Tasmin Little's fine version of the Elgar, very well recorded.

Music for 2 pianos: The Devil That Tempted St Anthony; Festival Overture; Hardanger; Moy Mell; The Poisoned Fountain; Red Autumn; Sonata

(BB) *** Naxos 8.570413. Wass, Roscoe

The earliest works here are the 1909 *Festival Overture* and *Moy Mell*, a wartime piece from 1916, which is highly Celtic. *The Devil That Tempted St Anthony* was originally for one piano, as indeed was *Red Autumn*, and both are full of resource and originality. The *Sonata* comes from the same period as the *Third* and *Fourth* Symphonies and is full of their resonances. **Ashley Wass** and **Martin Roscoe** are fully inside the idiom and play with great sympathy and authority. Excellent sound too.

Piano Music (complete)

(M) *** Chan. X10132 (4). Parkin

Eric Parkin proves a sympathetic guide through this repertoire. The *Sonatas* are grievously neglected in the concert hall but are most convincingly presented here. The recording is on the resonant side, but the playing is outstandingly responsive.

A Hill Tune; Lullaby; The Maiden and the Daffodil; Mediterranean; A Mountain Mood; Pæan; The Princess's Rose Garden; 2 Russian Tone Poems; Sleepy-Head; What the Minstrel Told Us

ⒷⒷ *** Naxos 8.557769. Wass

The earliest works here are the *Two Russian Tone Poems*, the *Nocturne – May Night in the Ukraine* and *Gopak*, written in 1912. They are inventive and atmospheric, as are most of the pieces here. The annotations by Bax's biographer, Lewis Foreman, are very helpful and highly interesting. What a fine pianist this young artist is!

Piano Sonatas: 1 in F sharp min.; 2 in G; 3 in G min.; 4 in G

*** British Music Society BMS 434-444. Binns (with BRIDGE: *Sonata*; IRELAND: *Sonata*)

Bax himself was a formidable pianist and his writing for the keyboard offers plenty of challenges: the four sonatas span the period 1910–33 and **Binns** has made a deep and thorough study of them. He had worked on the *Second* with Arthur Alexander, who had given its first performance in 1919, and has researched the various editions of all four. To a certain extent they sound like short-score versions of un-written symphonies, though they are highly pianistic in layout. The set also includes sonatas by Frank Bridge, a fine work, and John Ireland (by no means as well laid out for the piano as one might expect). Binns makes all this music his own. The recording is decent rather than distinguished.

Piano Sonatas 1–4; Sonata in E flat (1919)

Ⓜ *** Oehms OC565. Endres

Michael Endres's survey of the *Sonatas* enjoys an advantage in that it includes the early *E flat Sonata*, which is the keyboard version of the *First Symphony*. It is good to see a distinguished German pianist championing Bax not only in these magnificent performances but in his equally persuasive sleeve-notes.

Piano Sonatas 1–2; Burlesque; Dream in Exile (Intermezzo); In a Vodka Shop

ⒷⒷ *** Naxos 8.557439. Wass

Piano Sonatas 3–4; Allegro quasi Andante (Very difficult throughout); Country Tune; O Dame get up and Bake your Pies; Water Music; Winter Tune

ⒷⒷ *** Naxos 8.557592. Wass

Ashley Wass plays all four works with great authority and panache and is equally sympathetic in the shorter pieces, most persuasively bringing out the freely improvisational style. Excellent recording in Potton Hall, Suffolk, and authoritative notes from Lewis Foreman to guide the listener.

VOCAL MUSIC

(i) Enchanted Summer; (ii) Fatherland; (iii) Walsingham

Ⓜ *** Chan. 10366X. Brighton Festival Ch., RPO, Handley; with (i) Williams-King; (i; ii) McWhirter; (ii; iii) Hill

Three richly romantic choral works of Bax, with *Enchanted Summer* the finest of the three, an imaginatively ambitious setting of the text of Act II of Shelley's *Prometheus Unbound*, using three soloists. The earliest is the quite brief *Fatherland*. It envisaged a strolling ballad singer (here the eloquent **Martyn Hill** in good voice). But its patriotic feeling was originally directed to Scandinavia. *Walsingham* (1926) sets a poem by Sir Walter Raleigh and it was long neglected and is every bit as much of a revelation as *Enchanted Summer*, showing Bax at his most fluently mature. But all three works here are given dedicatedly intense performances, with **Handley** at his finest, and chorus and orchestra responding to his spontaneous fervour. The Chandos recording too is magnificently full-blooded.

Songs

Ⓜ *** Dutton CDLX 7136. Partridge, Rigby, Dussek

Many of these Bax songs were inspired by his love affairs from his student days onwards, not least his culminating love for the pianist, Harriet Cohen. The opening song, *Youth*, from this sequence is a fine example, and the composer's emotions plus his prowess as a pianist led him to write the most elaborate accompaniments, here brilliantly played by **Michael Dussek**, making light of the technical difficulties. **Ian Partridge** with his heady tenor-tone is the ideal interpreter, bringing out word-meaning with fine clarity, and characterizing well in wide-ranging settings of texts ranging from Chaucer to Housman and Bax himself, as well as Yeats and other Irish poets. The mezzo-soprano, **Jean Rigby**, is similarly persuasive in the *Celtic Song Cycle*, an early work dating from 1904, in a rather simpler, more openly lyrical style.

BEACH, Amy (1867–1944)

(i) Piano Concerto, Op. 45. Symphony in E min. (Gaelic)

🎵–ⒷⒷ *** Naxos 8.559139. (i) Feinberg; Nashville SO, Schermerhorn

It is Naxos who have had the happy idea of coupling Amy Beach's attractive *Piano Concerto* with the equally diverting *Gaelic Symphony*, which was written in 1894–6 after she had been impressed with the Boston première of Dvořák's *New World Symphony* and determined to build her own symphony by drawing on four traditional Irish tunes of 'simple, rugged and unpretentious beauty'. Yet much of the invention is her own and of high quality to match the concertante work for piano. **Alan Feinberg's** performance of the latter is in the grand romantic tradition, with splendid digital bravura in the finale, balanced by warm and often passionately lyrical support from the excellent **Nashville orchestra**.

The *Symphony* receives a no less sympathetic and committed reading under **Kenneth Schermerhorn**. The recording is vivid throughout, not in the very front rank perhaps, but bright and atmospheric.

Symphony in E min. (Gaelic)

*** Chan. 8958. Detroit SO, Järvi (with BARBER: *Symphony 1*, etc. ***)

Amy Beach was largely self-taught. Her *Symphony in E minor* operates at a high level of accomplishment and has a winning charm, particularly its delightful and inventive second movement. Once heard, this haunting movement is difficult to exorcize from one's memory. A very persuasive performance by the **Detroit Orchestra** under **Neeme Järvi**, and good recorded sound.

CHAMBER MUSIC

Pastorale for Wind Quintet, Op. 151; String Quartet (in one movement), Op. 89; Violin Sonata, Op. 34; 4 Sketches for Piano: Dreaming (trans. for cello & piano)

✿ *** Chan. 10162. Ambache

The early *Violin Sonata* of 1897 is characteristically lyrical and very traditional in style. The slow movement is melodically and harmonically rich, but the confident finale establishes the work's distinction, for its secondary theme is memorable. The character of the one-movement *String Quartet* is determined by the three Alaskan folk themes on which it draws. The *Pastorale* is a charming, gentle, folksy evocation with the balmy atmosphere of a summer afternoon. The arrangement of *Dreaming*, a song without words for cello and piano, gives the cello the gently rhapsodic melodic line, but the piano remains insistent. First-class performances and recording, and worth having for the *String Quartet*, one of Beach's most memorable works.

(i) Piano Quintet; Piano Trio in A min., Op. 150; (ii) Theme & Variations for Flute & String Quartet

⊶ ✿ **** Chan. 9752. (i) Ambache; (ii) Keen; The Ambache

Amy Beach's glorious 1908 *Piano Quintet* with its passionately lyrical first movement and hauntingly beautiful *Adagio* is already available. But the Chandos version from **Diana Ambache** and her group is even richer, more passionately involving, and the coupling with two other fine chamber works is more apt. The *Theme* for the *Flute Variations* (1916) has a touching nostalgia and, with exquisite flute-playing from **Helen Keen**, this music comes over as equally deeply felt. The *Piano Trio* is a late work (1939), the opening movement delicate in the manner of Fauré. These are marvellous performances of three very highly rewarding works, superbly recorded.

Piano Trio in A min., Op. 150; String Quartet in One Movement, Op. 89; Violin Sonata in A min., Op. 34

*** Ara. Z 6747. Polk; Lark Qt

The early *Violin Sonata* (1896), which introduces this highly recommendable collection, opens most beguilingly on the bow of **Diane Pascal**, its warm lyricism pervading the first movement and the equally melodically fluent *Largo*. The performances here are first class (**Joanne Polk**, the pianist, especially worthy of mention) and so is the recording. Most enjoyable and highly recommended.

PIANO MUSIC

By the Still Waters; Far Awa'; Gavotte fantastique; A Humming Bird; 3 Morceaux caractéristiques, Op. 28; Out of the Depths; Scherzino: A Peterboro Chipmunk; Scottish Legend; Variations on Balkan Themes, Op. 60; Young Birches (Ara. Z 6693); Ballad, Op. 6; A Cradle Song of the Lonely Mother; The Fair Hills of Eire, O!; A Hermit Thrush at Eve; A Hermit Thrush at Morn; Prelude & Fugue, Op. 81; Les Rêves de Columbine: Suite française, Op. 65; Valse-caprice, Op. 4 (Ara. Z 6704); Eskimos, 4 Characteristic Pieces, Op. 64; Fantasia fugata, Op. 87; From Grandmother's Garden, Op. 97; 5 Improvisations, Op. 148; Nocturne, Op. 107; 4 Sketches, Op. 15; Tyrolean Valse-fantaisie, Op. 116. Transcription: R. STRAUSS: Serenade (Ara. Z 6721)

*** Polk

Arabesque are now exploring Amy Beach's piano music in depth and confirming the consistency of its quality. The *Variations on Balkan Themes* readily demonstrates her ability to sustain a major work. The imaginative pictorial evocations from nature are capped by the beautiful evocation of *Young Birches*, while the nocturnal *Cradle Song of the Lonely Mother* is quite haunting. Beach's ability to assimilate different styles in a single work is never better displayed than in the attractive *Four Sketches*, Op. 15, where at times Schumann, Beethoven, Mendelssohn and Liszt all look over her shoulder; while the disarming simplicity of characterization in *Eskimos* and *From Grandmother's Garden* is quite delightful. **Joanne Polk** is an understanding and persuasive advocate, capturing the music's special combination of sophistication and innocence with fine spontaneity. She is most truthfully recorded.

SONGS

Songs

**(*) BRIDGE 9182. Mason, Polk

It is good to hear the ballad, *Shena Van* (complete with Scottish rhythmic snap) from a pleasing male voice, so suitable too for a simple song like *Good Morning*. **Patrick Mason** has a vibrato, but he is particularly good at the passionate songs like *Ah Love, but a day!*, which he sings with real fervour. Once again the ear is struck throughout by the sheer quality of Beach's piano accompaniments, here relished and sparkling in the hands of **Joanne Polk**. With warm, well balanced recording, this disc has much to offer Beach aficionados.

BEETHOVEN, Ludwig van
(1770–1827)

'Beethoven 50': EMI Collector's Edition of CDs: *Piano Concertos 1–2* (Gilels, Vandernoot); *3 & 5* (Gelber, Leitner); *4* (Gilels, Ludwig); *Violin concerto* (D. Oistrakh, Cluytens); *Romances for Violin & Orchestra* (Fontanarosa); *Triple Concerto* (Oborin, D. Oistrakh, Knushevitsky, Sargent); *Choral Fantasia* (Lill, Gibson); *Overtures including Leonora 3; Symphonies 1–9* (BPO, Cluytens); *Cello Sonatas & Variations* (Tortelier, Heidsieck); *Clarinet Trio* (Boutard); *Flute Sonata & Variations* (Debost, Ivaldi; *Mandolin & Harpsichord works* (Schivittaro, Veyron-Lacroix); *Piano Trios* (Hungarian Trio); *Serenade for Flute, Violin & Viola, Op. 25; Trio for Flute, Bassoon & Piano, WoO 37* (Debost Ens.,) *Serenade for String Trio; String Trios* (Trio à cordes Français); *String Quartets 1–15 & Grosse Fuge* (Hungarian Qt); *Duo for Clarinet & Bassoon; Octet, Op. 103; Piano & Wind Quintet; Septet, Op. 20; Sextet, Op. 81b; March & Rondino for Wind, WoO 29 & 25* (all Melos Ens.); *Violin Sonatas 1–10* (Ferras, Barbizet); *Piano Sonatas 1–32* (Heidsieck); *Bagatelles; Für Elise; Variations including Diabelli & Eroica Variations* (Solchany; Cziffra; Danielle Laval); *Christ on the Mount of Olives* (Soloists, Bonn Ch. & O, Wangenheim); *Aria: Ah Perfido* (Nilsson); *Adelaide; An die ferne Geliebte; 7 Goethe Lieder; 6 Gellert Lieder* (Fischer-Dieskau, Moore or Hertha Klust); *Mass in C* (Ameling, J. Baker, Altmeyer, Rintzler); *Missa solemnis* (Harper, J. Baker, Tear, Sotin; both: New Philh. Ch., LPO, or Philh., Giulini); *Fidelio* (Dernesch, Vickers, Ridderbusch, Van Dan, Donath, Laubenthal, Deutsch Opera Ch., BPO, Karajan)

(BB) **(*) EMI 3 87739-2 (50)

Even though the cast list contains some unknown names, there are plenty of familiar ones here: **Gilels, David Oistrakh, Cluytens** (whose recordings of the symphonies will not disappoint); **Tortelier,** the **Hungarian Quartet,** and **Karajan,** while the cast lists for the two *Masses* and *Fidelio* are distinguished. Fifty-five minutes of music on each of 50 CDs at around a pound per CD must be one of the bargains of all time.

DVD Recordings

(i) *Piano Concertos 1–5. Overtures: Egmont; Leonora 2 & 3; Symphony 8*

*** Decca **DVD** 074 3214 (2). (i) Ashkenazy; LPO, Haitink (V/D: Brian Large)

These video recordings were made jointly by the BBC and Decca during the live broadcasts from the Royal Festival Hall in 1974, but the sound quality is remarkably good. The performances by a strikingly youthful **Ashkenazy** are full of spirit (he shows his individuality and really lets himself go

in the cadenzas – those for the first two concertos are his own), and his crisp virtuosity elsewhere is a joy in itself, with finales sparkling. The partnership with **Haitink** (who also provides excellent, direct accounts of the three *Overtures* and the *Eighth Symphony*) produces crisp, classical reading of the first three concertos, apt for early Beethoven, but with slow movements touchingly simple, easily lyrical, and that for No. 3 more romantic and memorably expressive. Ashkenazy is at his most poetic in the *Fourth Concerto*, although Haitink is perhaps just a little phlegmatic in the dialogue of the slow movement. In many ways the *Emperor* is finest of all, freshly inspired, not barnstorming, with a beautiful, hushed slow movement. The camerawork is straightforward, as one would expect from **Brian Large**, and he can't resist showing the moment when in *Leonora 3* Haitink is seen avidly listening to the offstage trumpet.

Piano Concertos 1–5

(N) **** Medici Arts **DVD** 3085298 (2 discs). Perahia, ASMF, Marriner

*** EuroArts **DVD** 2056778 (2). Barenboim, Staatskapelle Berlin

Murray Perahia recorded in 1988 with **Neville Marriner** and the **Academy of St Martin-in-the-Fields**. His playing is peerless and Marriner gives him vital and sensitive support. The camera gives us a lot of Perahia's facial expressions which at times seems a little intrusive. But admirers of this great pianist need not hesitate for the sound is first class.

Impressively thoughtful and finely wrought accounts from **Daniel Barenboim** and the **Staatskapelle Berlin**. Barenboim never attempts to draw attention to himself and the listener is consistently held under his spell. The performances are recorded at the Klavier-Festival Ruhr in May 2007 at the Jahrhunderthalle in Bochum, which must be one of the ugliest venues in Europe, though the audiences are wonderfully responsive and attentive and the camera direction admirable. Recommended.

(i) *Piano Concerto 1. Symphony 7; Coriolan*

**** Arthaus **DVD** 100 148. (i) Perahia; LSO, Solti (V/D: Humphrey Burton)

This is a straight recording directed by Humphrey Burton of a concert at London's Barbican Centre in 1987. The camerawork is discreet and unfussy and the sound impeccably balanced throughout. **Solti's** accounts of both the *Coriolan Overture* and the *Seventh Symphony* are very fine, and in the concerto **Murray Perahia** is unfailingly thoughtful, intelligent and imaginative. A memorable concert; and the first-rate recording will give much pleasure.

(i) *Piano Concerto 2 in B flat; (ii) Symphony 9 (choral)*

*** TDK **DVD** DV-EC10A. (i) Pletnev; (ii) Mattila, Urmana, Moser, Schulte, Swedish R. Ch., Eric Ericson Chamber Ch.; BPO, Abbado (Producer: Paul Smaczny, V/D: Bob Coles)

Pletnev's account of the *B flat Concerto* is immaculate, both artistically and technically. In short, it is wonderfully fresh and exhilarating. The *Ninth Symphony* has a fine line-up of soloists, together with the legendary **Eric Ericson Choir** and the **Swedish Radio Choir**, and is a hardly less fine performance, direct and powerful. It comes with a 20-minute documentary, with commentaries and subtitles in English.

Piano Concerto 4 in G, Op. 58

(*) EMI **DVD 492840-9. Rubinstein, LPO, Dorati (with Bonus: CHOPIN: *Polonaise in A flat (Heroic)*) – MENDELSSOHN: *Violin Concerto* **; WALTON: *Cello Concerto* ***

Rubinstein's present performance comes from a Royal Festival Hall concert by the **LPO** under **Antal Dorati**, when the great pianist was already eighty. He was a fine Beethoven interpreter, albeit slightly underrated as a Beethovenian by the wider generality of critics. Although this performance does not offer the effortless keyboard mastery of Rubinstein's youth and maturity, it is a valuable document and will be treasured by all admirers of this artist.

CD Recordings

Piano Concertos (i) 1 in C, Op. 15; (ii) 2 in B flat, Op. 19 ((***) Testament mono SBT 1219)

Piano Concertos (i) 3 in C min., Op. 37; (ii) 4 in G, Op. 58 ((***) Testament mono SBT 1220)

Piano Concerto 5 (i) (Emperor)((***) Testament mono SBT 1221. Solomon, Philh. O, (i) Menges, (ii) Cluytens)

Olympian performances from **Solomon** are restored on the Testament label in altogether exemplary sound. They have been out many times since they were made in the 1950s but have never sounded richer and fresher than they do here. Solomon's performances celebrate a dedication to musical truth and a timeless purity that place him among the keyboard giants. This is great Beethoven playing.

Piano Concertos 1; 3 (Ⓜ *** Telarc CD 80663)

Piano Concertos 2; 4 (Ⓜ *** Telarc CD 80664)

Piano Concerto 5 (Emperor) (Ⓜ *** Telarc CD 80665. Rudolf Serkin, Boston SO, Ozawa)

Serkin's cycle for Telarc dates from 1981/2, the very beginning of the digital era, yet the sound is excellent: full, warm and natural. It presents a deeply satisfying series of performances. Serkin brings those moments of total magic which are the mark of live performances from a master, here caught in the studio. Technically, the playing of the octogenarian is flawed (there is one amazing slip of finger in the C *major Concerto*); where in his late Mozart recordings for DG the lack of polish is distracting, here one consistently registers certainty and power. The accompaniments have comparable distinction – **Ozawa** has never sounded more spontaneous on record.

Piano Concertos 1–5

Ⓑ—**** Ph. 462 781-2 (3). Brendel, VPO, Rattle

Ⓜ **** DG 477 6409 (3). Pletnev, Russian Nat. O, Gansch

Piano Concertos 1–5 (Emperor)

Ⓝ *** DG **DVD** 440 073 4269 (2). Krystian Zimerman; (1 & 2) VPO, Zimerman; or (3–5) cond. Bernstein

Ⓝ ⒷⒷ ***Virgin 2x1 5 22014-2 (2) Tan (fortepiano), L. Classical Players, Norrington

Piano Concertos 1–5. Piano Sonata 23 (Appassionata), Op. 57

Ⓑ— Ⓜ **** Warner Elatus 2564 60130-2 (1–2); 2564 60433-2 (3–4); 2564 60348-2 (5 & *Piano Sonata* 23). Schiff, Dresden State O, Haitink (available separately)

(i) Piano Concertos 1–5; (ii) Triple Concerto

Ⓝ ** DG 477 7244 (3). (i) Pollini, Berlin PO; (ii) Lonquich, Gingolts, Brunello, Simón Bolívar Youth O; Abbado

(i) Piano Concertos 1–5; (ii) Choral Fantasia, Op. 80

Ⓑ *** CfP (ADD) 575 752-2 (3). Lill, SNO, Gibson

Alfred Brendel offers this new Philips set as his third and last recorded survey of the Beethoven concertos, made in Vienna with **Sir Simon Rattle**. With each concerto recorded immediately after live performances, the results have an extra spontaneity, usually at speeds marginally faster than in his previous recordings. The dynamic range is greater too, with hushed *pianissimos* more intense, and with Rattle encouraging lightness in his accompaniments. The ambience of the Musikverein casts a warm, natural glow over the proceedings and adds the necessary weight to the *Emperor*. A fine achievement. The separate issues include Concertos 1 & 4 (462 782-2), 2 & 3 (462 783-2), 5 (Emperor) plus Appassionata Sonata (468 666-2).

Pletnev's performances were recorded at the Bonn Beethovenfest in September 2006, and his playing is pretty well in a class of its own. The remaining three concertos will be appearing during the lifetime of this book. Pletnev produces a distinctively original sonority and his keyboard articulation is highly individual. These are performances of commanding stature and deep musical insight.

The original intention for **Zimerman** had been to record all five concertos with **Bernstein** but the latter's death in 1990 prevented that, and so he directed the first two concertos from the keyboard. In the last three there is a close rapport and unity of purpose between these two in many ways highly differing musical personalities; Zimerman poised and aristocratic, Bernstein a full-bodied, brilliant temperament. Their collaboration is a triumphant success, and these readings are both compelling and insightful. Zimerman's own direction from the keyboard in the earlier works also recorded in the Grossermusiksaal of the Musikverein, shows impressive grip and command, and his playing, as one might expect, is immaculate. The camera work by Klaus

König is discreet and John McClure's sound balance in *Nos. 3–5* cannot be faulted.

András Schiff with ideal, transparent support from **Haitink** and the **Dresden Staatskapelle** offers one of the most refreshing, deeply satisfying Beethoven concerto cycles of recent years. He crowns the cycle with a scintillating account of the *Emperor Concerto*, electrifying from first to last, aptly coupled with the most heroic sonata of Beethoven's middle period, the *Appassionata*. Clear, well-balanced sound to match. The discs are available separately.

Melvyn Tan's playing has a flair and poetic feeling that are rather special and this partnership with **Norrington** in the five Beethoven concertos has great spontaneity. Tan's individuality comes over unforcedly to make these readings characterful without unwanted wilfulness. The set is capped by a superb account of the *Emperor* in which Tan displays a poetic fire and brilliance all his own. The reading urgently conveys a feeling of a live performance.

The combination of **Barenboim** and **Klemperer**, recording together in 1967–8, brings endless illumination, with Klemperer's measured weight set against Barenboim's youthful spontaneity, specially compelling in slow movements. The *Choral Fantasia* too is given an inspired performance. The remastered sound is clear and full. (EMI 3 61525-2)

John Lill has never been more impressive on record than in his set of the Beethoven concertos, recorded in 1974–5. In each work he conveys spontaneity and a vein of poetry that in the studio have too often eluded him. **Gibson** and the **Scottish National Orchestra** provide strong, direct support, helped by very good analogue recording using the spacious City Hall, Glasgow. Very competitive with other versions at whatever price.

Starry as the line-up is, **Pollini's** set of the Beethoven *Piano Concertos* with **Abbado** and the **Berlin PO**, is a surprisingly disappointing set, but in this reissue DG offer the bonus of a lively account of the *Triple Concerto* with Abbado conducting the brilliant youth orchestra from Venezuela. That hardly makes the main offering recommendable, when the piano tone is woolly, the playing lacks tension and the finales are generally too fast with no wit in the pointing of rhythm.

(i) *Piano Concertos 1–5;* (ii) *Triple Concerto*

(B) *** EMI 5 00927-2 (3). Zacharias, with (i) Dresden State O, Vonk; (ii) Hoelscher, Schiff, Leipzig GO, Masur

Christian Zacharias's set, which dates from 1986 and 1989, is first class in every way and is well worth its modest cost. With consistently clean, rhythmic playing, he gives fresh, bright performances, the brightness and clarity go with concentration, to make the slow movements deeply thoughtful. The weight and body of the orchestral sound equally rebuts any feeling of excessive lightness, though **Vonk** does not quite match the Mozartian elegance of his soloist in No. 2. The *Emperor*, however, is really commanding. The performance of the *Triple Concerto* dates from two years earlier. Led by cellist **Heinrich Schiff** (a balance of responsibility suggested by Beethoven's own priorities in this work) the soloists make a characterful but finely integrated trio. Their

rhythmic flair prompts **Masur** in turn to give one of his most sparkling performances on record.

Piano Concertos (i) 1; (ii) 2–4; (i) 5 (Emperor); (iii) Cello Sonata in G min., Op. 5/2. Bagatelle in A min. (Für Elise); Rondo in C, Op. 51/1

(BB) (***) Naxos mono 8.505189 (5). Schnabel, with (i) LSO; (ii) LPO; Sargent; (iii) Piatigorsky – BRAHMS: *Piano Concertos 1–2, etc.* *(*); SCHUMANN: *Kinderszenen* (**)

Schnabel's early set has a nobility and robustness that makes one realize why audiences of the 1930s identified Schnabel with Beethoven. The playing is in every way typical: in other words, he is fully aware of the deepest musical currents. **Sargent** gives him impressive support, even though wind tuning is not always impeccable. These performances are boxed together with his less impressive accounts of the Brahms, but they are also available separately. Decent transfers.

Piano Concertos (i) 1–4; (ii) 5 (Emperor). 7 Bagatelles, Op. 33; 6 Bagatelles, Op. 126; 11 Bagatelles, Op. 119; Piano Sonatas 5 in C min., Op. 10/1; 8 (Pathétique); 17 (Tempest), Op. 31/2; 18, Op. 31/3; 28, Op. 101; 30, Op. 109; 31, Op. 110; 32, Op. 111; 33 Variations on a Waltz by Diabelli, Op. 120

❀ (B) **** Ph. (ADD) 475 6319 (6). Kovacevich, with (i) BBC SO; (ii) LSO; C. Davis

Stephen Kovacevich's Beethoven concerto recordings remain undisputed classics of the catalogue and have been benchmark recordings since their release in the early 1970s. In the first four concertos, with the **BBC Symphony Orchestra**, Kovacevich and **Colin Davis** are consistently crisp and fresh, and it is impossible not to respond to their spontaneity, no matter how may times one hears them. In the *Emperor*, with the **LSO**, Kovacevich is unsurpassed, and in its time this famous (1973) account set a model for everyone else. The sound remains excellent. This new, economical packaging also conveniently gathers together **Kovacevich's** Philips piano sonata recordings for the first time. The 1970s recording sounds consistently fresh, full and vivid. Altogether, this box reflects an outstanding achievement.

Piano Concerto 1 in C. 6 Bagatelles Op 126

(N) ** Virgin 5 03111-2. Anderszewaki, with (i) Deutsch CO, Bremen

Directing the **Deutsche Chamber Orchestra of Bremen** from the keyboard, **Piotr Anderszewski** gives a powerful performance of the *First Concerto*. Speeds and dynamic contrasts tend to be exaggerated, making the version less attractive, and the *6 Bagatelles* make a mean coupling.

Piano Concertos 1–2

(BB) *** Arte Nova 82876 82587-2. Bronfman, Tonhalle O, Zurich, Zinman

Piano Concertos 1–2; Rondo in B flat

*** Simax PSC 1181. Berezovsky, Swedish CO, Dausgaard

A worthy successor to their accounts of *Nos.* 3 and 4, **Bronfman**'s playing has great elegance and he has a close rapport with **Zinman** and his **Tonhalle** players. Very good recording, which should satisfy the most demanding listener.

Berezovsky's Beethoven has real stature: it has sparkle and zest, and both concertos are paced beautifully and are full of vitality. In terms of their pianism and interpretation they are to be recommended among the best. Very good sound, as one would expect from a record produced by Andrew Keener.

Schnabel's performances reigned supreme in the 1930s, when they first appeared, and still make for powerfully compelling listening 70 years on. Mark Obert-Thorn's transfers do justice to the vitality and beauty of sound that Schnabel commanded. (Naxos 8.110638)

Piano Concertos 1, 3 & 4

(N) (M) **(*) Telarc 805704 (2). O'Conor, LSO, Delfs

In a two-for-the-price-of-one package on Telarc, the Irish pianist **John O'Conor** offers three concertos in generally crisp and direct performances on the brisk side. The **LSO** under **Andreas Delfs** match the pianist's crispness making it a reasonable, generously priced recommendation.

Piano Concerto 2

(BB) (***) Naxos mono 8.110767. Kapell, NBC SO, Golschmann – SCHUBERT: *Waltzes*, etc.; RACHMANINOV: *Cello Sonata* (***)

We have written with enthusiasm about the **Kapell** Beethoven *B flat Concerto* in earlier editions, and its commanding authority is evident from the outset. Moreover, this newcomer is worth investigating for the sake of the Rachmaninov *Sonata*.

Piano Concertos 2–3

*** DG 477 5026. Argerich, Mahler CO, Abbado

There is an element of daring in **Martha Argerich's** inspired readings of the *Second* and *Third Concertos* which, with stylish accompaniment from the Mahler Chamber Orchestra under Abbado, makes it a winning coupling. Both have the characterful stamp of a unique artist, and one hopes that both will remain available.

Piano Concertos 2; 5 (Emperor)

(B) **(*) RCA 82876 65838-2. Rubinstein, LPO, Barenboim

Rubinstein, in the *Emperor*, plays with spontaneous inspiration in every bar, and the LPO under a relatively young **Barenboim** accompany with keen understanding. The *B flat Concerto* is not quite so arresting but is still very fine, with a beautifully poised slow movement. The piano timbre is truthful and fuller than Rubinstein often received, but the upper range of the violins is a bit fierce and lacks refinement of focus. A very worthwhile reissue, just the same.

Piano Concerto 3 in C min., Op. 37

(BB) (***) Naxos mono 8.111263. Arrau, Phd. O, Ormandy (with WEBER: *Konzertstück in F min., Op. 79; Sonata 1 in C, Op. 24* (***))

(N) (**(*)) Sony mono 88697. Gould, Berlin PO, Karajan (with SIBELIUS: *Symphony 5* **(*))

This is **Arrau** at the height of his powers. The *Third Concerto* finds Arrau's performance (in the words of the *Record Guide*) 'powerful, masculine, yet informed with a thoughtful, imaginative quality'. The *Konzertstück* is a 'live' performance and has great dash and sparkle. It remains one of the best ever records of this piece, once often encountered in the concert hall but now much neglected.

This Sony disc offers a live recording of the legendary concert in May 1957, when **Glenn Gould** appeared with **Karajan** and the **Berlin Phil**. Karajan keeps Gould, then aged 25, in order without his usual eccentricities, though the slow movement is exceptionally slow, if well sustained, and the finale is brisk and light. The limited mono sound is acceptable for a historic issue. This means that the Karajan version of Sibelius's *Fifth Symphony* makes less than its full effect; although Karajan is at his finest in a live performance and the present account is no exception.

(i) Piano Concerto 3. Coriolan Overture (with rehearsal sequence)

(BB) (***) Naxos mono 8.110804. (i) Hess; NBC SO, Toscanini (with WAGNER: *Götterdämmerung: Siegfried's Rhine Journey* (***))

On this live recording of a 1946 broadcast **Dame Myra Hess** gives a thrilling performance, one of her very finest on disc, with the outer movements crisply articulated and beautifully sprung at high speed and the slow movement warmly expressive, bringing out a rare warmth in **Toscanini** too. *Coriolan* is high-powered, dry and incisive, and the Wagner makes a welcome fill-up.

Piano Concertos 3 in C min., Op. 37; 4 in G, Op. 58

🎵 (BB) *** Arte Nova 82876 64010-2. Bronfman, Tonhalle O, Zürich, Zinman

Yefim Bronfman plays very stylishly, with exceptionally clean attack and clarity of articulation. The slow movement of No. 3 also brings high contrasts, as does the dialogue in the slow movement of No. 4. The sparkle of the finale in No. 3 is matched by the rippling wit of the playing in the finale of No. 4, while poetry marks the whole performance. A splendid coupling, the more attractive at super-bargain price, with excellent sound.

Schnabel's 1933 versions of the *Third* and *Fourth Piano Concertos* with **Malcolm Sargent** conducting the **LPO** have long been absent from the catalogues. Their return in these fine transfers is welcome: Schnabel's insights are always special, and although they do not occupy quite the same awesome pinnacle as the sonatas in Schnabel's Beethoven discography, they are still memorable. (Naxos mono 8.110639)

(i) Piano concertos 3–5 (Emperor). Piano Sonatas 24, Op. 78; 31, Op. 110

🎵 ✿ (***) Testament mono SBT2 1351 (2). Arrau; (i) with Philh. O, Klemperer

These 1957 Festival Hall performances sound as magnificent and magisterial on CD as they did in the concert hall, all those years ago. The *Fourth* is particularly fine and the *Emperor* is masterful. The two sonatas were recorded at about the same time and are, as one might expect, performances of some stature: poised, considered, cultivated. Paul Baily's transfers give a truthful and vivid sound-picture and enhance the musical experience these artists offer. Not to be missed.

Piano Concertos 3 in C min., Op. 37; 5 (Emperor) in E flat, Op. 73

(*) DG **DVD 073 4097 (2). Pollini, VPO, Boehm – MOZART:
   Piano Concertos 19 & 23; BRAHMS: *Piano Concerto 2***(*)

Both Beethoven concertos exhibit **Pollini's** cool and dedicated classicism, shorn of expressive exaggeration, characteristic of this partnership. There is considerable poetic feeling in both slow movements, but the overall impression is of majestic prose resounding. Pollini is faithful and sober in much the same way that Backhaus was in the 1950s. In the *C minor*, Christopher Nupen's camera is always where one wants it to be and the production is straightforward and unfussy, with no attempt at eye-catching visual tricks. In the *Emperor*, Franz Kebelka's direction is similarly unobtrusive and the sound-balance from the legendary Günther Hermanns is clean but full-bodied.

Piano Concerto 4 in G, Op. 58

** EMI **DVD** 492840-9. Rubinstein, LPO, Dorati (Bonus:
   CHOPIN: *Polonaise in A flat (Heroic)* ***) –
   MENDELSSOHN: *Violin Concerto, etc.* (***) ; WALTON: *Cello Concerto* (***)

*** Warner Elatus 0927 49617-2. Grimaud, NYPO, Masur –
   SCHUMANN: *Piano Concerto* ***

*** Sup. SU 3714-2. Moravec, Prague Philh. O, Bělohlávek –
   FRANCK: *Symphonic Variations* *** ; RAVEL: *Piano Concerto in G* **(*)

(**(*)) BBC mono BBCL 4111-2. Hess, LPO, Boult – MOZART:
   Piano Concerto 23, etc. (**(*))

Rubinstein is splendidly patrician, though he is not as poetic in fashioning detail as he was in his earlier LP cycle with Krips. Good orchestral playing from the **LPO** and **Dorati**, and it is good to see some of the celebrated players of the day, including Richard Adeney. Anthony Craxton directs the viewer's eyes where they need to be and the camerawork is unfussy and economical. The stirring Chopin encore also comes from the Festival Hall, from a recital given a few months later.

Hélène Grimaud rises to the occasion in both works, and in the Beethoven she has excellent support from **Masur**, who provides a spacious accompaniment for the first movement, which Grimaud opens with Kempff-like gentleness, and is poetically lyrical throughout. The interchange of the *Andante* is similarly thoughtful, and the vigorous finale brings a joyful, exhilarating conclusion. Warmly resonant recording which adds weight without clouding detail.

Thanks to the distinctive artistry of the Czech pianist, **Ivan Moravec**, with his extraordinary clarity of articulation,

as well as to the conductor, **Jiří Bělohlávek**, the result has an attractive consistency. With incisive support from Bělohlávek and the **Prague Philharmonia**, there is no lack of muscular strength either, with Moravec drawing on a wide tonal range, as he does in his deeply meditative reading of the slow movement. In the finale Bělohlávek matches his soloist in drawing comparably transparent textures.

Though **Dame Myra Hess** was among the most celebrated British pianists of her time, she recorded disappointingly little commercially, and the Beethoven marked her Prom farewell, while the Mozart *Concerto* was her very last public performance. You would never know it from the vigour of the playing. Hess may above all have been noted for the poetry of her performances – the slow movement has a rapt quality and a radiance that compel admiration. This may not be a flawless performance but, even with limited mono sound and a very close balance for the piano, it retains a winning freshness and spontaneity.

(i; ii) Piano Concerto 4 in G, Op. 58; Overtures: (iii) Coriolan; The Creatures of Prometheus; Egmont; Fidelio; King Stephen; (ii) Leonore III. Symphonies: (i) 5 in C min., Op. 67; (iv) 7 in A, Op. 92; (ii; v) 9 (Choral) in D min., Op. 125. (iii) String Quartets 14 in C sharp min., Op. 131; 16 in F, Op. 135 (arr. for string orchestra); (vi) Missa solemnis, Op. 123

Ⓜ *** DG (ADD/DDD) 477 6690 (6). Bernstein, with (i)
   Arrau; (ii) Bav. RSO; (iii) VPO; (iv) Boston SO; (v)
   Anderson, Walker, König, Rootering, various choirs,
   Dresden State O; Kirov O, LSO, NYPO, O de Paris (members); (vi) Moser, Schwarz, Kollo, Moll, Hilversum R. Ch.,
   Concg. O

The *Fourth Piano Concerto* and the *Fifth Symphony* come from a live 1976 concert in aid of Amnesty International and, along with the *Leonore III Overture*, are released on CD for the first time. The one or two indulgences in the *Piano Concerto* are nothing compared to the emotional intensity of the overall experience, and the same can be said of the compelling *Fifth Symphony* and *Leonore III Overture*. The sound is surprisingly vivid and full. The *Seventh Symphony* was recorded live at the very last concert **Bernstein** conducted with the **Boston Symphony Orchestra** at Tanglewood on 19 August 1990. He takes an extraordinarily expansive view, quite different from his previous recordings. Yet, for all the slowness of the basic speeds, he consistently conveys the joy of Beethoven's inspiration while springing rhythms with characteristic infectiousness. Again, good sound. Recorded live on the morning of Christmas Day 1989, Bernstein's *Choral* brings a performance that has something special to say, even after all the many recordings of this work, and not only because Bernstein substitutes the word '*Freiheit*', 'Freedom', for '*Freude*', 'joy', in the choral finale, something Beethoven himself might well have approved of. For many, the uniqueness of this version and the emotions it conveys make it a top choice despite obvious flaws. The lively, sympathetic performances of the overtures with the **VPO** were originally the fill-ups for Bernstein's set of the Beethoven symphonies. The *Missa Solemnis* was edited together from tapes of two live performances in 1978, and the result has a special intensity matched by few rivals. Bernstein was not the first person to record the late *Quartets* in a full string-version form. There is no doubt as to the commitment and depth of feeling that Bernstein brings to these performances (dedicated to the memory of his wife), nor are there any doubts as to the quality of the response he evokes from the VPO strings; it could not be given more eloquent advocacy than it is here. Excellently recorded, too. This set is a must for Bernstein fans.

Piano Concertos 4; 5 in E flat (Emperor)

◐⟶ ✪ Ⓜ **** EMI (ADD) 4 76828-2. Gilels, Philh. O, Ludwig

◐⟶ *** Testament SBT 1299. Richter-Haaser, Philh. O, Kertész

◐⟶ Ⓜ *** DG (ADD) 447 402-2. Kempff, BPO, Leitner

◐⟶ Ⓜ *** Decca mono/stereo 467 126-2. Curzon, VPO, Knappertsbusch

Fascinatingly, EMI have chosen **Gilels's** earlier (1957) **Philharmonia** performances with **Leopold Ludwig** rather than the later, Cleveland versions partnered by Szell, to be included among their 'Great Recordings of the Century'. About the magisterial *G major Concerto* there can be no reservations whatsoever. It is a masterly reading of striking authority and eloquence, strong and poetic, yet warm-hearted. The poetry of the dialogue in the slow movement is of the purest kind, tone control such as we rarely hear these days is finely realized, and there is a rare combination of strength and sparkle in the finale. The early stereo recording is remarkably good and is splendidly remastered.

These noble performances from **Hans Richter-Haaser** on Testament stand the test of time well and deserve the strongest recommendation. This is Beethoven playing of the first order, and we hope that Testament will bring other of Richter-Haaser's records back into circulation. The transfer does the original LPs (which we have long cherished) full justice.

In the *Fourth Concerto* **Kempff's** delicacy of fingerwork and his shading of tone-colour are unsurpassed. Though his version of the *Emperor* is not on an epic scale, Kempff's exceptionally wide range of tone and dynamic gives it power in plenty.

Curzon's *Fourth Concerto* is an Elysian performance, full of delicate lyrical feeling, the slow movement unsurpassed on record, not even by Kempff. Moreover, the 1954 mono recording, made in the Musikverein, is of outstanding quality, with warm, luminous piano-tone and a clear, transparent orchestral image, not lacking bloom. The *Emperor* is stereo, made in the Sofiensaal three years later. Again it is a refined and thoughtful reading. Yet the keen intelligence of the playing and the inner concentration working throughout the reading keep it fully alive. The **Vienna Philharmonic** plays strongly and authoritatively under **Knappertsbusch**, and the new transfer of the 1957 master has miraculously cleaned up the sound.

Piano Concerto 5 in E flat (Emperor), Op. 73

◐⟶ *** DG 477 641-7 Pletnev, Russian Nat. O, Gansch

◐⟶ Ⓜ *** BBC (ADD) BBCL 4020-2. Curzon, BBC SO, Boulez – MOZART: *Piano Concerto 26* ***

(i) Piano Concerto 5 (Emperor). Piano Sonata 28 in A, Op. 101

*** DG 477 6595. Grimaud, (i) with Dresden State O, Jurowski (with bonus DVD on the making of the recording)

Piano Concerto 5; Grosse Fuge, Op. 133

Ⓑ *** CfP 585 6162. Kovacevich, Australian CO

Strictly speaking, at 37 minutes **Pletnev's** CD offers very short measure, so we must withhold a fourth star. But there is nothing short measure about the performance, which is magisterial and commanding, full of the most remarkable pianistic colour and penetrating musicianship. One of the finest *Emperors* of recent years, this ranks among the greats.

Kovacevich's later, EMI digital version of the *Emperor*, sharper and tauter than the earlier, Philips account, now arrives on Classics for Pleasure. His version with the soloist directing from the keyboard is recognizably from the same inspired artist, though speeds are consistently faster and the manner is sharper and tauter. The piano-sound on the digital recording is brighter, if not so well balanced. The *Grosse Fuge* makes an unusual but apt coupling.

There is a fantasy-like quality in **Hélène Grimaud's** playing which is very attractive. In this, the mightiest of Beethoven's concertos, the soloist finds an often magical poetry in the piano writing . The slow movement is extraordinarily beautiful and the finale radiates joy. Again, in Op. 101, Grimaud lavishes much care on detail and it is her poetic qualities which most strike the listener, with an often haunting beauty permeating this late-Beethoven score. The bonus DVD includes a short behind-the-scenes documentary on the making of this recording, with interviews with the soloist and conductor, along with some other items. Full, rich DG sound.

The partnership of the introspective **Clifford Curzon** and the incisive **Boulez** may not seem a promising one, but in this live performance (recorded in 1971 at the Royal Festival Hall) the challenge between the two brings electrifying results. Curzon is at his most taut and incisive, while finding depths of poetry, and Boulez proves a surprisingly sympathetic interpreter of Beethoven, matching his soloist in subtle dynamic shading, while bringing home the work's dramatic power. Full, forward recording.

Horowitz was underrated as a Beethoven interpreter: his *Emperor* is wonderfully authoritative and completely devoid of ostentation or display. It is among the most classical of readings and **Reiner** is a totally like-minded partner. The coupled Rachmaninov *Third Concerto* is equally fine. Good new transfers. (Naxos mono 8.110787)

(i) Piano Concerto 5; (ii) Triple Concerto for Violin, Cello & Piano

(BB) **(*) Sony (ADD) SBK 46549. (i) Fleisher, Cleveland O, Szell; (ii) Stern, Rose, Istomin, Phd. O, Ormandy

Leon Fleisher, who worked with **Szell** with special understanding, gives a reading of the *Emperor* impressive for its dramatic vigour. **Stern**, **Rose** and **Istomin** make an inspired trio of soloists in the *Triple Concerto*, sadly marred by their close balance.

(i) *Piano Concerto 5*; (ii) *Cello Sonata in G min., Op. 5/2*

(BB) (***) Naxos mono 8.110640. Schnabel, (i) LSO, Sargent; (ii) Piatigorsky

Schnabel's *Emperor* was recorded in 1932 when he was at the height of his powers. Schnabel had met Piatigorsky in the 1920s. Alas, they made no records, and this 1934 set of the *G minor Cello Sonata* is the sole representation of Schnabel's collaboration with the great cellist. It is very distinguished indeed.

Violin Concerto in D, Op. 61 (DVD versions)

(key) *** EMI **DVD** 5 44544-9. Perlman, BPO, Barenboim (Producer: Johannes Müller) – BRAHMS: *Violin Concerto* ***

*** EMI **DVD** 490445-9. Grumiaux, O Nat. de l'ORTF, Dorati (Bonuses: BACH: *Violin Partita 2, BWV 1004: Sarabande & Chaconne*. BLOCH: *Nigun (Baal Shem)*. PAGANINI: *Caprice, Op. 1/14*) – MENDELSSOHN: *Violin Concerto* (***)

(N) ***(*) Medici Arts **DVD** 2072 518 (**Karajan Memorial Concert**) Mutter, BPO, Ozawa (with BACH: *Partita for Solo Violin 2: Sarabande*; TCHAIKOVSKY: *Symphony 6 (Pathétique)* **(*))

(*) EMI **DVD (ADD) DVB 38845690. Milstein, LPO, Boult (V/D: Brian Large) – VAUGHAN WILLIAMS: *Symphony 8* ***

(***) EMI **DVD** 492834-9. Kogan, O Nat. de l'ORTF, Louis de Froment (With recital: BACH: *Violin Partita in D min., BWV 1004: Sarabande*. HANDEL: *Violin Sonata in E, HWV 373*. DEBUSSY: *Beau soir*. SHOSTAKOVICH: *Preludes, Op. 34/10, 15, 16 & 24* (with Andrei Mytnik, piano). BRAHMS: *Hungarian Dance 17*. PAGANINI: *Cantabile*. FALLA: *Suite populaire espagnole* (with Naum Walter, piano). LECLAIR: *Sonata for 2 Violins in C, Op. 3/3* (with Elizaveta Gilels-Kogan, violin) ***)

Whether or not **Perlman's** 1992 DVD with **Barenboim** represents his finest recorded performance on record, it is very satisfying, with a particularly beautiful and serene *Larghetto* and a genial, dancing finale. The live recording at the Schauspielhaus, Berlin, is excellent, better balanced than some of his studio recordings, and the camerawork is excellently managed. If you want a recommendable DVD coupling with Brahms, this will give every satisfaction.

Grumiaux has great naturalness of eloquence – and what a good accompanist **Dorati** was. The sound is very good, though the quality of the picture is not much more than serviceable. Memorable music-making. The remaining pieces come off equally well, as you would expect from this great artist, and there is a remarkable bonus in the form of a very characterful account of the Saint-Saëns *Introduction et Rondo capriccioso* by **Ivrys Gitlis** and the young **Georges Pludemacher**, recorded at the ORTF studios in 1971 which gives much pleasure.

Anne-Sophie Mutter surpasses herself in her memorable account of the greatest of all *Violin Concertos*, with the slow movement movingly beautiful, and the finale fresh and joyful. Her accompaniment from Karajan's own orchestra is worthy of this superbly recorded memorial concert, and this is certainly a three-star and perhaps a four-star performance. The camera is rather restless, but the close-ups of the violin, and Mutter's bow and fingers, often closely observed during the performance, are visually fascinating. Her personal tribute is a Bach *Sarabande*, played simply and eloquently. However, **Ozawa's** reading of Tchaikovsky's *Pathétique*, very well played by this great orchestra, lacks the overwhelming intensity worthy of the occasion.

It is really good to watch both **Milstein** and **Boult** working together at a Royal Festival Hall concert in 1972. Milstein, as ever, is aristocratic and patrician in Beethoven, and the reading is essentially classical, with a fine but not profound slow movement – affected, alas, by some bronchial afflictions from the audience and one unexplained 'bump' in the slow movement. The documentation is non-existent and the coupling curious but welcome.

Leonid Kogan was the most natural and supremely classical of artists, and his purity of vision and undemonstrative demeanour are well captured on film. Admirers of this great player should snap this up while it is in circulation. As for the coupled recital: the Handel, Debussy and Dmitri Tsiganov's arrangements of four of Shostakovitch's Op. 34 *Preludes* for piano were recorded on a visit to the BBC studios in 1962 (the Shostakovich are particularly beguiling). The remainder come from the Paris studios of French Radio in 1968. The bonus is a *Sonata for Two Violins* by Leclair, which he recorded with his wife, Elizaveta, the sister of Emil Gilels.

Violin Concerto in D, Op. 161 (CD versions)

(key) **** Pentatone **SACD** Surround Sound PTC 5186. Grumiaux, Concg. O, C. Davis – BRUCH: *Violin Concerto 1* ***

(key) (M) *** Warner Elatus 0927 49773-2. Kremer, COE, Harnoncourt (with *Romances 1 in G; 2 in F*)

(key) (M) *** EMI (ADD) 5 62607-2. Y. Menuhin, Menuhin Festival O (with *Romance 1 in G*) – TCHAIKOVSKY: *Sérénade mélancolique* ***

(key) (M) *** EMI 5 66900-2. Perlman, Philh. O, Giulini

(key) (rosette) (M) *** DG (ADD) 447 403-2. Schneiderhan, BPO, Jochum – MOZART: *Violin Concerto 5* ***

*** EMI 7 54072-2. Kyung-Wha Chung, Concg. O, Tennstedt – BRUCH: *Violin Concerto 1* ***

*** DG 471 349-2; **SACD** (compatible) 471 633-2. Mutter, NYPO, Masur (with *Romances 1 & 2*)

(M) *** DG (ADD) 477 7165. Mutter, BPO, Karajan

Ⓜ *** EMI 5 03410-2. Kyung-Wha Chung, Concg. O,
Tennstedt – BRUCH: *Violin Concerto 1* ***

Ⓜ *** RCA (ADD) **SACD** 82876 61391-2. Heifetz, Boston SO,
Munch – BRAHMS: *Concerto* ***

Ⓜ *** RCA (ADD) 09026 68980-2. Heifetz, Boston SO,
Munch – MENDELSSOHN: *Violin Concerto* ***

Grumiaux made this glorious recording of the Beethoven
Violin Concerto for Philips in 1974 with **Sir Colin Davis**. The
balance between soloist and orchestra is perfect, the
Concertgebouw sound, full and ambient-rich, is marvellously, uncannily realistic in this new Pentatone SACD transfer, whether or not the back speakers are put to use.
Grumiaux imbues the performance with a wonderful spirit
of classical serenity, specially in the slow movement, and the
finale dances gracefully. A first choice for those with a four-
speaker set-up.

Gidon Kremer's Elatus account with **Nikolaus
Harnoncourt** and the **Chamber Orchestra of Europe** offers
one of his most commanding recordings, both polished and
full of flair, with tone ravishingly pure. The controversial
point is the cadenza in the first movement, for (like
Schneiderhan) he uses a transcription of the big cadenza
which Beethoven wrote for his piano arrangement of the
work, but with added piano as well as timpani. Kremer also
plays violin versions of the other cadenzas and flourishes
that punctuate Beethoven's piano version. One of the most
refreshing versions of the *Concerto* ever put on disc, backed
up by crisp, unsentimental readings of the two *Romances*,
and at mid-price too!

Recorded in 1971 but never issued until 2003, **Menuhin's**
version of the Beethoven *Concerto*, with the soloist directing
the Menuhin Festival Orchestra from the bow, is on balance
the finest he ever made, an inspired reading which brings
extra expressive freedom and a sense of urgency beyond
his performances with a conductor, however great, while
the silvery beauty of Menuhin's playing above the stave is
bewitching throughout. The *Romance* too is light and spontaneous-sounding, and the Tchaikovsky piece makes an attractive filler.

Perlman's outstanding first digital recording of
Beethoven's *Violin Concerto* is rightly reissued as one of EMI's
'Great Recordings of the Century'. The element of slight understatement, the refusal to adopt too romantically expressive a style, makes for a compelling strength, perfectly
matched by Giulini's thoughtful, direct accompaniment. The
beautiful slow movement has a quality of gentle rapture, almost matching Schneiderhan's sense of stillness; and the
finale, joyfully and exuberantly fast, is charged with the
fullest excitement. The digital recording is satisfyingly full
and spacious.

Wolfgang Schneiderhan's stereo version of the *Violin
Concerto* is still among the greatest recordings of this work:
the serene spiritual beauty of the slow movement has never
been surpassed on record. Schneiderhan, like Kremer, uses
cadenzas transcribed from Beethoven's piano version of
the *Concerto*. The transfer of the well-balanced 1962 recording is fresh and realistic. The Mozart coupling is apt and
generous.

Kyung-Wha Chung's EMI performance, recorded live in
the Concertgebouw, is searching and intense. Next to
Perlman, Chung is lighter, more mercurial. The element of
vulnerability adds to the emotional weight, above all in the
wistfully tender slow movement, while the outer movements
are full of flair. The recording is full and atmospheric.

In her 1979 recording, the slow basic tempi of **Anne-
Sophie Mutter's** beautiful reading on DG were her own
choice, she claims, and certainly were not forced upon her
by **Karajan**. The first two movements have rarely if ever been
more expansively presented on record, but the purity of the
solo playing and the concentration of the whole performance make the result intensely convincing.

Anne-Sophie Mutter's very distinguished second performance with Masur stands out, both for its sheer individuality and for the rapt, lyrical beauty of phrase and tone that
often brings one to catch one's breath. The playing is deeply
felt in an entirely personal way, often conveyed by moments
of magically hushed *pianissimo*, the use of the widest variety
of dynamic and great variation of vibrato, and Mutter is obviously determined to think and feel the music through
afresh.

His supreme mastery has **Heifetz** finding time for
individuality and imagination in every phrase. For some,
the comparative lack of serenity in the first movement
(though not in the *Larghetto*) may be a drawback, but the
drama of the reading is unforgettable. Heifetz's unique
timbre is marvellously captured on SACD, as is **Munch's**
conducting, with its distinctive character, notably its clarity
and crispness, and the normal CD transfer of the alternative
coupling with Brahms also has a fine sense of realism and
presence.

Other versions by **Menuhin** (Naxos 8.110996 or EMI
5669752), **Milstein** (EMI 5 67583-2), **Tetzlaff** (Arte Nova 82876
76994-2), **Shumsky** (ASV Resonance CDRSN 3032), **Nishizaki**
(Naxos 8.550149) and **Zukerman** (DG 453 142.2) are all distinctive but perhaps do not reach the top of the recommended
list.

Historical Recordings

Kreisler is at his very peak in this wonderful, poetically
rich account of the Beethoven *Concerto*, particularly the
ravishing account of the *Larghetto* which causes one to
catch one's breath (Naxos mono 8.110909). **Szigeti's** searching and magical account of the *Concerto* enjoys legendary
status. Made in 1932, when he was at the height of his
career, it has the refinement and purity for which he was
famous (8.110946). The partnership of **Heifetz** and
Toscanini in the Beethoven *Violin Concerto* is uniquely powerful and purposeful, with the purity of the violinist's playing, notably above the stave, making up for any lack of
tenderness. Heifetz's example leads Toscanini to a rare gentleness in the slow movement, while the finale is exhilarating in its rhythmic drive. The hard NBC recording is nicely
mellowed in the Naxos transfer, if with some audible hiss
(8.110936).

(i) *Violin Concerto* (ii) *Violin Sonata 9 (Kreutzer)*

Ⓝ **** DG 477 6596 Repin with (i) VPO, Muti; (ii) Argerich

(i;ii) *Violin Concerto;* (iii) *Violin Sonata 7 in C min., Op. 30/2*

Ⓝ *** Sony 88697 144422. (i) Kym; (ii) Philh. O, A Davis; (iii) Brown

There are two outstanding new versions of the Beethoven *Violin Concerto.* **Vadim Repin's** new DG recording is one of the very finest of recent years. It is a performance which is for the first decade of the twenty-first century what Schneiderhan's famous version was for the twentieth. **Muti** and the **VPO** (an accompanying team chosen by the soloist) provide a strong, ever-flexible backcloth and the result has both charisma and an inspired sensitivity. In the exquisitely measured slow movement Repin plays on a thread of tone with a magical tenderness. Then he and Muti join joyfully together in the dancing finale, which lifts and sparkles to make a satisfying conclusion. Repin plays Kreisler's cadenzas in the outer movements and makes them his own. In the brilliant coupled performance on the *Kreutzer Sonata* one senses that **Argerich** is the dominant partner in the first movement which is played with enormous dash and verve. But in the variations Repin comes into his own and again produces effortlessly beautiful phrasing, and overall this is a highly spontaneous account. The two CDs are offered for the price of one.

The young Korean violinist, **Min-Jin Kym** is another newcomer of distinction and begins her recording career with this impressive coupling of the Beethoven *Violin Concerto* and the *C minor Violin Sonata Op. 30/2.* Her pure tone and fine range of expression immediately grips the listener, and in the slow movement she plays with a natural magnetic gravity with hushed tension and finely graded pianissimos. The 6/8 finale brings nicely lifted rhythms, helped by **Sir Andrew Davis's** tense direction of the Philharmonia. The *Sonata* is equally impressive with **Ian Brown** an ideal partner. The tension, urgency and witty pointing make one wish she might record more sonatas before long. Excellent sound with clean separation.

Triple Concerto for Violin, Cello & Piano in C, Op. 56 (DVD Version)

*** TDK **DVD** DVWW-COMARG. Argerich, Renaud, Gautier Capuçon, Flanders SO, Rabinovitch-Barakovsky (V/D: Frédéric Le Clair) – PROKOFIEV: *Piano Concerto 1; Symphony 1 (Classical)*; SCHUMANN: *Violin Sonata 1* ***

(i) *Triple Concerto;* (ii) *Choral Fantasia* (DVD Version)

⊕– *** EMI **DVD** 4 92994-9; CD 5 55516-2. BPO, Barenboim, with (i) Perlman, Ma; (ii) Deutsche Staatsoper Ch.

The TDK DVD is designed as a showcase for **Martha Argerich**, but she is very much part of a team in the Beethoven *Triple Concerto* and indeed in the expressive slow movement it is the cellist **Gautier Capuçon** whose solo remains in the memory. **Alexandre Rabinovitch-Barakovsky**, his hair flying, energetically directs vital accounts of the outer movements, with a spontaneous accelerando at the very end of the work and throughout the balance between the highly responsive solo trio is all but ideal.

Recorded at concerts on consecutive days in February 1995, with **Barenboim** directing from the keyboard in both works, this makes an excellent if ungenerous coupling on EMI. These are all spontaneously imaginative artists, never more so than when recorded live. That makes both performances very compelling, with delightful interplay between the soloists in the *Triple Concerto,* led by **Yo-Yo Ma.** Barenboim's piano may be backwardly placed in the sound spectrum but one barely notices it, particularly when the orchestra is satisfyingly full-bodied. The *Choral Fantasia* depends above all on the solo pianist, and here Barenboim is in his element, not only revelling in the improvisatory quality of the opening solo but also bringing out the fun of the variations on the main theme.

Triple Concerto for Violin, Cello & Piano in C, Op. 56 (CD Versions)

⊕–Ⓜ *** EMI 5 57773-2. Argerich, Capuçon, Maisky, Svizzera-Italiana O, Rabinovitch-Barakovsky – SCHUMANN: *Piano Concerto* ***

⊕–ⒷⒷ *** EMI Gemini (ADD) 381487-2 (2). D. Oistrakh, Oborin, Knushevitsky, Philh. O, Sargent – BRAHMS: *Double Concerto;* MOZART: *Violin Concerto 3;* PROKOFIEV: *Violin Concerto 2* ***

Ⓝ (***) BBC Legends mono BBCL 42652-2. Menuhin, Gendron, H Menuhin, LSO, Kertesz – BRAHMS: *Double Concerto* (***)

This live recording of the *Triple Concerto,* like the Schumann *Piano Concerto* with which it is coupled, was made at the Lugano Festival, reflecting throughout the magnetism of **Martha Argerich.** Not that the cellist **Mischa Maisky** is any less charcterful; but Argerich's powerful presence seems to modify his customary wilfulness.

The vintage EMI recording now on Gemini features distinguished Russian soloists led by **David Oistrakh,** and it dates from the early days of stereo; yet the sound is excellent for its period, the balance one of the most successful this concerto has received even to date. **Sargent** is authoritative, and his soloists make a good team.

Though recorded in mono only at the 1964 Bath Festival in the Colston Hall, Bristol, the sound is clear and vivid, heightening the outstanding performances of all three soloists. **Menuhin** and his sister **Hephzibah** were regularly joined by **Maurice Gendron** in chamber music, which helps to make this account of the *Triple Concerto* satisfyingly cohesive, with the **LSO** under **Istvan Kertesz** in superb form. Soloists are balanced forward with Gendron's playing in the lovely slow movement warm and tender, and the finale full of rhythmic bounce. Well coupled with an equally fine account of the Brahms *Double Concerto.*

(i) *Triple Concerto.* *Piano Concerto in D* (arr. from *Violin Concerto*), Op. 61a

ⒷⒷ *** Naxos 8.554288. Jandó, (i) with Kang, Kliegel; Nicolaus Esterházy O, Drahos

(i) *Triple Concerto for Violin, Cello & Piano. Symphony 7*

⊕–¬ ⒷⒷ *** LSO Live LSO 0078. (i) Nikolitch, Hugh, Vogt; LSO, Haitink

(i) *Triple Concerto*; (ii) *Symphony 10: 1st movt* (realized & completed Cooper)

Ⓜ *** Chan. 6501. (i) Kalichstein-Laredo-Robinson Trio, ECO, Gibson; (ii) CBSO, Weller

The partnership of **Dong-Suk Kang**, **Maria Kliegel** and **Jenö Jandó** may not be familiar, but it is none the less formidable. All three are accomplished soloists. **Béla Drahos** draws clean-cut, consistently alert playing from the orchestra, more crisply detailed than in most versions. Beethoven's piano version of the *Violin Concerto* makes an apt and exceptionally generous coupling. Jenö Jandó uses his artistry to minimize any ungainliness in the piano-writing, articulating as cleanly and crisply as he does in the *Triple Concerto*.

On the LSO label an appealingly spontaneous account of the *Triple Concerto* (recorded live in the Barbican in November 2005), successfully combining a tonally light-weight trio of soloists, with **Haitink's** full-bodied orchestral backing. The slow movement brings a moving cantilena from cellist **Tim Hugh**, and in the ebullient finale **Lars Vogt** leads the high spirits with scintillating piano roulades. The coupling is even more impressive. Haitink has the full measure of the *Seventh Symphony*, and the weight of his reading gives it strength and gravitas, while still preserving the spirit of the dance in the finale which is very exciting. Good, full-bodied sound, but the Barbican acoustic is slightly damped by the close microphones. But not the performance.

(i) *Triple Concerto for Violin, Cello & Piano*; (ii) *Septet*

⊕–¬ ⒷⒷ *** Arte Nova 82876 64015-2. Shaham, Mørk; with (i) Bronfman, Tonhalle O, Zinman; (ii) Rouilly, Dangel, Reid, Jenny, Helfti

The coupling of the *Triple Concerto* and the *Septet* is unique. **Zinman** and his soloists treat it with light, clear textures and wonderfully clean articulation from all three soloists. The slow movement with its soaring cello melody is played by **Truls Mørk** with total dedication and not a hint of sentimentality. The *Septet* is played with similar blitheness, with allegros often challengingly fast, yet never rushed, and the wit of the fifth-movement Scherzo, with its galumphing horn, beautifully brought out. First-rate, cleanly focused sound.

The Creatures of Prometheus: Overture & Ballet, Op. 43

ⒷⒷ *** Hyp. Helios CDH 55196. SCO, Mackerras
ⒷⒷ *** Naxos 8.553404. Melbourne SO, Halász

Here, in fresh, vigorous performances, **Sir Charles Mackerras** and the **Scottish Chamber Orchestra** bring out not only the drama of the piece but also the colourful qualities which made Beethoven a great composer of light music. The ballet ends with the number which gave him one of his most fruitful themes, used for the finale of the *Eroica*

Symphony. Highly recommended, especially at its new Helios price.

The Naxos issue provides another bargain version. The playing is neat and fresh, with rhythms well pointed. Though the string-sound is at times a little cloudy, dramatic passages such as the military trumpets and timpani of the *Allegro con brio* (No. 8) are very well caught, bringing out the panache of the playing. In the big *Adagio* (No. 5) the important cello solo confirms the quality of the **Melbourne** players.

OVERTURES

Overtures: *The Consecration of the House; Coriolan; The Creatures of Prometheus; Egmont; Fidelio; King Stephen; Leonora 1–3; The Ruins of Athens; Zur Namensfeier*

⊕–¬ Ⓜ *** Arte Nova 82876 57831-2 (2). Zurich Tonhalle O, Zinman

David Zinman and the **Zürich Tonhalle Orchestra** here take on board the lessons of period performance in this performance of Beethoven's 11 overtures. The very first, *Prometheus*, sets the pattern with the phenomenal clarity of articulation in an exceptionally fast Allegro, and transparency of texture marks all these performances. The drama of Beethoven's writing is underlined in the sharpness of attack and high contrasts of dynamic. Helpfully, the two discs present the sequence of 11 works in an order to make a satisfying programme.

(i) Overtures: *The Consecration of the House; Coriolan; The Creatures of Prometheus; Egmont; Fidelio; King Stephen; Leonora 1–3; The Ruins of Athens; Zur Namensfeier*; (ii) *12 Contredanses, WoO 14; 12 German Dances, WoO 8; 12 Minuets, WoO 7*

Ⓑ *** Ph. (ADD) Duo 438 706-2 (2). (i) Leipzig GO, Masur; (ii) ASMF, Marriner

Masur's performances of the *Overtures* are more direct than those of Karajan, satisfying in their lack of mannerism. The Philips recording from the early 1970s is of high quality, and the remastering has enhanced its vividness and impact. To complete the second CD, **Marriner** and the **Academy** offer a splendid foil with the dance music. Even as a composer of light music, Beethoven was a master.

Romances for Cello and Orchestra 1, Op. 40; 2, Op. 50

**(*) Orfeo C080031A. Müller-Schott, Australian CO, Tognetti – HAYDN: *Cello Concertos 1 & 2* **(*)

Daniel Müller-Schott has transcribed the two Beethoven *Violin Romances* for his own instrument – and very successfully too! This is playing of some eloquence and finesse.

Romances for Violin and Orchestra 1, Op. 40; 2, Op. 50

Ⓜ *** CRD (ADD) CRD 3369. R. Thomas, Bournemouth SO – MENDELSSOHN: *Violin Concerto*; SCHUBERT: *Konzertstück* ***

The purity of **Ronald Thomas's** intonation (particularly important in the double-stopping at the start of Op. 40) makes for sensitive, clean-cut readings which, along with the Schubert *Konzertstück*, provide enjoyable if unexpected couplings for the Mendelssohn *Concerto*. The recording is first rate.

SYMPHONIES

Symphonies (DVD versions)

Symphonies 1–3 (Eroica)

⊕–¬ *** DG **DVD** 073 4101 (5.1 Surround Sound). BPO, Karajan (V/D: No. 1: Arne Arnbohm; No. 2: Hans Joachim Schulz; No. 3: Karajan)

During the analogue LP era, **Karajan** recorded the Beethoven symphonies in stereo, both in 1961/2 and again in 1977, and undoubtedly the later set was the more successful of the two. But Karajan also planned a video cycle, and this has now been issued on DVD. Nos. 1–7 were filmed in 1971; No. 5 was made a year later; but the joyous *Pastoral* dates from 1967.

The DVD accounts of the earlier symphonies are interpretatively closer to the second cycle. No. 1 is elegant enough, but the finale is already giving way to genuine Beethovenian strength and urgency, and this maturity is even more noticeable in No. 2, where the slow movment is richly and beautifully played, and the finale full of characteristic energy and impulse. The *Eroica* is splendid: the first movement presses forward strongly but does not sound rushed (especially today when we are more used to brisk pacing), and the hushed opening of the *Funeral March* brings an account which is both deeply felt and intense.

The ever-reliable Arne Arnbohm was the Video Director for the *First Symphony*, where the cameras follow the music vividly. Hans Joachim Schulz directs the cameras in the same vein in No. 2, but Karajan himself apparently takes over for the *Eroica*, where the orchestra is re-positioned, now laid out in three triangular groups, with wind and brass placed in the central triangle. The camera close-ups continue to involve the listener in the intensity of the music-making.

Symphonies 4–6 (Pastoral)

⊕–¬ **(*) DG **DVD** 073 4102 (5.1 Surround Sound). BPO, Karajan (V/D: Nos. 4 & 5: Karajan; 6: conceived and directed by Hugo Niebling)

The *Fourth* and *Fifth Symphonies* are live performances and have all the added communicative intensity that this brings. **Karajan** is now credited as having taken over the video direction himself, and the very opening of the *Fourth* is arresting, both visually and musically. The camera often places one very close to the orchestra, seeing the players almost from the conductor's own viewpoint. The *Fifth* (with exposition repeat included) is superb, with all the adrenalin and warmth for which Karajan is famous, and a thrilling finale. Alas, the *Pastoral*, beautifully played though it is, is the one blot on the set. Hugo Niebling, the Director, lays out the orchestra in serried ranks, as if on the barrack square, and

there are exaggerated lighting effects, fades, losses of focus, and so on – which is a pity, for the music-making is glorious and deserves better.

Symphonies 7–9 (Choral)

⊕–¬ *** DG **DVD** 073 4103 (5.1 Surround Sound). Janowitz, Ludwig, Thomas, Berry. Deutsche Opera, Berlin, Ch. in No. 9; BPO, Karajan (V/D: No. 8: Hans Joachim Scholz; Nos. 7 & 9: Karajan)

The *Seventh Symphony* returns the orchestral layout to the triple triangle, but the cameras again frequently take us among the players, which is very stimulating. The performance of the *Seventh* is excitingly hard-driven and rhythmically vibrant, but it mellows in the beautifully played *Allegretto*. The visual layout for the *Eighth* is more conventional, but not the performance. For **Karajan** it is no 'little' symphony. He takes the first-movement exposition repeat, and drives forward strongly. The central movements bring lighter, refined contrast, but the finale again has powerful thrust and an exciting coda.

The *Choral Symphony*, which dates from 1968, brings four superb soloists, both individually and singing splendidly as a team. Karajan opens his eyes at last, to communicate with the chorus. The performance caps the cycle thrillingly and exudes all the vitality of live music-making, even though recorded in the studio. The layout, with a huge chorus who sing with great involvement and zest, is visually gripping. The sound throughout is excellent, brilliant, wide-ranging and full-bodied, and the chorus has plenty of bite. Even with the flawed production of the *Pastoral Symphony* this set is wonderfully stimulating.

Symphonies 1–8 (i) 9

Ⓜ **** Sony **DVD** 88697195439. Berlin PO, Karajan with (i) Soloists, Vienna Singverein

This set comes from 1982–4, only a few years after his third cycle which appeared in 1977 (in a very handsomely presented boxed set). The performances are inspiring and among the finest Beethoven this great conductor has given us. However documentation and presentation is distinctly on the sketchy side: neither the booklets nor the disc themselves identify the soloists in the finale of the *Ninth*. Nevertheless, a strong recommendation.

Symphony 9 (Choral)

Ⓝ ⊕–¬ **** EuroArts **DVD** 2072408 Tomowa-Sintow, Baltsa, Kollo, Van Dam, Deutsch Opera Ch., BPO, Karajan (V/D Humphrey Burton)

Recorded live on New Year's Eve 1977, a decade before he died, **Karajan's** thrilling account of the *Choral Symphony* in many ways caps his previous versions. It has a superb solo quartet and the tremendously vivid choral response is matched by the **Berlin Philharmonic** playing with great and consistent intensity, yet with a moving warmth in the *Adagio*. The closing pages are overwhelming. Throughout one watches Karajan, eyes closed, and using a minimum of gesture, completely in control at every moment and obviously totally dedicated to Beethoven's masterpiece. The sound is extremely vivid and Humphrey Burton's video direction is admirably poised between showing the orchestra and conductor, together and in alternation.

Symphonies 1 in C, Op. 21; 6 in F (Pastoral), Op. 68; 8 in F, Op. 93

*** EuroArts **DVD** DV BPAB 168. BPO, Abbado (V/D: Bob Coles)

Symphonies 2 in D, Op. 36; 5 in C min., Op. 67

*** EuroArts **DVD** DV BPAB 25. BPO, Abbado (V/D: Bob Coles)

These two DVDs offer **Abbado's** live recordings made in February 2001 in the Santa Cecilia Academy in Rome, exhilarating performances rapturously received by the Italian audience. Interpretatively, they very much follow the pattern set by Abbado in the complete cycle he recorded for DG in Berlin in 1999, using the new edition of Jonathan del Mar, with an extra repeat in the Scherzo of No. 5, for example. Abbado again opts for a performance-style that takes some note of period practice, lighter and more resilient than before, with sharp, clean attack. That particularly applies to slow movements, which flow easily, though he tends to avoid the extreme speeds in fast movements suggested by some of Beethoven's metronome markings. One facility offered in all the symphonies except No.2 is an alternative camera-angle. The first option varies the shots of the conductor with those of different instruments, whereas the second option concentrates the whole time on the conductor. There is a marked discrepancy between the running time of each DVD, with Nos. 1, 6 and 8 lasting almost half an hour longer than Nos. 2 and 5.

Symphonies (CD versions)

Symphonies 1–9

✹ (B)(***) EMI (mono) 5 15863-2 (5). Philh. O, Karajan (with Schwarzkopf, Höffgen, Haefliger, Edelmann & Vienna Gesellschaft Ch. der Musikfreunde in No. 9)

⊶ (M) *** EMI 3 75812-2 (5). VPO, Rattle (with Bonney, Remmert, Streit, Hanson & CBSO Ch. in 9)

(M) *** Hyp. CDS 44301/5 (5). SCO, Mackerras (with Watson, Wyn-Rogers, Skelton, Roth, Edinburgh Festival Philh. O & Ch. in No. 9).

⊶ (BB) *** Arte Nova 74321 65410-2 (5). Zurich Tonhalle O, Zinman (with Ziesak, Remmert, Davislim, Roth, Swiss Chamber Ch. in 9)

⊶ (B) *** CfP 575 7512 (5). RLPO, Mackerras (with Rodgers, D. Jones, Bronder, Terfel, RLPO Ch. in 9)

⊶ (B) *** DG (ADD) 474 924-2 (5). VPO, Bernstein (with Jones, Schwarz, Kollo, Moll, V. State Op Ch. in 9)

(N) (M) *** DG 477 5864 (5), BPO, Abbado (with Nattila, Urmana, Moser, Quastoff, Swedish R Ch. & Eric Robinson Chamber Ch. in 9)

⊶ *** DG 439 900-2 (5). ORR, Gardiner (with Orgonasova, von Otter, Rolfe Johnson, Cachemaille, Monteverdi Ch. in 9)

(i) Symphonies 1–9; Overtures: Consecration of the House; Coriolan; Creatures of Prometheus; Egmont; Fidelio; King Stephen; Leonora 2; The Ruins of Athens; (ii) Missa solemnis

(BB) **(*) Nim NI 1760 (7). Hanover Band, (i) cond. Goodman or Huggett (with Harrhy, Bailey, Murgatroyd, George, Oslo Cathedral Ch. in 9); (ii) Hirsti, Watkinson, Murgatroyd, George, Oslo Cathedral Ch., cond. Kvam

Symphonies 1–9; Overtures: Coriolan; Creatures of Prometheus; Egmont; Fidelio; Leonora 3; Ruins of Athens

⊶ (B) *** DG (ADD) 463 088-2 (5) (or **SACD** 474 600-2 (6) with rehearsal of no.9) BPO, Karajan (with Janowitz, Rossel-Majdan, Kmentt, Berry in No. 9)

(N) (B) *** DG (ADD) 429 089-2 BPO, Karajan (with Tomowa-Sintow, Baltsa, Schreier, V. Singverein, Van Dam in No. 9)

(N) (BB) ** Zig-Zag Territories ZZT080402/6 (5) (without *Fidelio*; *Leonora* 3 but with *Turkish March*) Anima Eterna, Jos van Immersel (with Kaapola, Kielland, Schäfer, Bauer in No. 9)

Symphonies 1–9; Overture Coriolan

⊶ (BB) *** Warner Apex 2564 60457-2 (5). Sinfonia Varsovia, Y. Menuhin (with Glennon, Schaechter, Janutas, Schollum, Lithuania Kaunas State Ch. in 9)

Symphonies 1–9; Overtures: Coriolan; Egmont; Leonora 3

(B) **(*) Decca (ADD) 475 9090 (6). Chicago SO, Solti (with Lorengar, Minton, Burrows, Talvela, Chicago Ch. in No. 9)

Karajan's mono set is placed first in our listings, not because it is an obvious 'best buy' – although it is both distinguished and rewarding – but because it has a very special place in the catalogue. Recorded between 1952 and 1955 with the **Philharmonia Orchestra** at their peak, it was the first time Karajan delivered all the Beethoven symphonies. Though the recordings are in mono only, the separation of the new EMI transfers is remarkable, with excellent clarity and definition and no loss of body and weight, partly a tribute to the acoustics of the Kingsway Hall. The approach finds Karajan at his freshest, in no way self-conscious (as he came to be later) and above all conveying the joy of the music-making. Speeds are admirably chosen, the playing generally crisp and resilient, with a wide dynamic range obtained throughout. The *Ninth* is different from all the rest in being recorded not in London but in Vienna, with the Philharmonia joined by the *Gesellschaft der Musicfreunde*. It is a powerful reading, with the two contrasted themes of the slow movement taken at very different speeds. The finale benefits not only from the fine singing of the chorus, but from an outstanding team of soloists, led by **Elisabeth Schwarzkopf**.

Of **Karajan's** later stereo recordings the 1961/62 set (DG 463 088-2 but also now available in a new hybrid **SACD** transfer) is most compelling, combining high polish with a biting sense of urgency and spontaneity. There is one major disappointment, the over-taut reading of the *Pastoral*, which in addition omits a vital repeat in the Scherzo. Otherwise these are incandescent performances, superbly played and with excellent sound. On five CDs at bargain price, this set should be a cornerstone of any collection.

In **Karajan's** 1977 recordings the character of the first two symphonies has genuine Beethovenian strength and urgency. The *Eroica*, however, presents the one major disappointment, at least in the outer movements: faster than before, though the *Funeral March* remains very measured and direct. To compensate the first movement of the *Pastoral* now has elegance and joyfulness at a tempo barely any slower than before, while the other movements, too, avoid the tense manner. Otherwise the middle symphonies remain very much as they were. Most important of all the *Ninth* is given a superlative performance, with the slow movement warmer and an extra toughness and intensity in outer movements. In the finale the singing of **Peter Schreier** and **Van Dam** stands out within a fine quartet.

Sir Simon Rattle's Beethoven cycle is not the first to be recorded in concert, but the quality of immediacy and spontaneous expression is something that marks it out more than most of its rivals.

With Rattle's approach reflecting his experience with period performers, textures are clarified and string-tone is thinned down with reduced vibrato, but the string sound still has VPO sweetness. In the heat of the moment Rattle allows himself an element of freedom, and generally his approach is more warmly expressive than that of other performances with modern instruments which have taken note of period practice. Overall, Rattle regularly conveys exuberance, not least in the finales, notably in the *Fifth*. In the finale of the *Ninth* he scores palpably with one of the finest quartets of soloists assembled for many years, and the decision to bring over the **CBSO chorus** is triumphantly justified, with incandescent choral sound. Though Rattle adopts the new Bärenreiter editions of Jonathan del Mar, he does not include the extra repeat of the Scherzo section in the third movement of No. 5 but leaves the structure as we have long known it. The five discs come at mid-price in a lavish presentation package, complete with hardback booklet.

Mackerras's Hyperion set was also recorded live and it gains in vitality from that. The approach is very much influenced by the lessons Mackerras has learned from conducting period performances, with textures light and clear and speeds which tend to be fast, at times challengingly fast. The players respond superbly, and the clarity of even the most rapid semiquaver passagework is astonishing. The timpani too is prominently presented, clean and dry, as in period performances. When it comes to the *Ninth*, Mackerras understandably opts for a full orchestra rather than a chamber band, with the first movement strong and incisive, and the second subject of the slow movement flowing much faster than usual. The choral finale is impressively done with fine chorus-work and strong soloists. Although Mackerras's

CfP survey remains fully competitive (and the discs are available separately), the newer performances are marginally even finer.

David Zinman too, has learnt from the example of period performance and has consistently presented performances of all the symphonies, early and late, which have a transparency not usually achieved with modern instruments, helped by the clear, fresh acoustic of the Zurich hall. There is an important advantage too that this was the first modern-instrument cycle to use the new edition prepared by Jonathan Del Mar, with important modifications in the text. Zinman also allows a degree of ornamentation beyond convention. What matters above all is that not only are the performances electrifying, with the players responding to the challenge of fast speeds in observance of Beethoven's metronome markings, but there is also refinement and tenderness in slow movements, even in the face of fast-flowing tempi. The sound is vivid and beautifully balanced, making this a front-runner among recommendations for cycles using modern instruments.

Sir Charles Mackerras's CfP Beethoven cycle is also among the most recommendable of all at any price, beautifully recorded and interpretatively refreshing, in a refined way steering a satisfying mid-course between traditional and period performance. So the brass have a satisfying braying roundness and the timpani echo period practice, not only in the sharp attack with hard sticks but also in their prominent balance, as in the finale of No. 5. Speeds are on the fast side, but it is a measure of Mackerras's mastery that rhythms are always beautifully sprung without any hint of breathlessness and with consistently refined detail.

Bernstein's late-1970s cycle is dramatic, perceptive, rich in emotion but never sentimental, and it has a natural spontaneous quality that stems in part from his technique of recording. As in other Bernstein/DG recordings of this period, the maestro opted to have live performances recorded and then (with some tidying of detail) edited together. Those who know the thrilling account of the first movement of the *Eroica* in his earlier, New York cycle may be disappointed that the voltage here is lower, but with Bernstein's electricity matched against the traditional warmth of Viennese playing, the results are consistently persuasive. It culminates in a superb account of the *Ninth*, with a fast, tense first movement, a resilient Scherzo, a hushed, expansive reading of the *Adagio* and a dramatic account of the finale. Balances are not always perfect, with microphones placed in order to eliminate audience noise, but the results are generally undistracting, and the CD transfers are very good.

DG have now issued **Abbado's** complete 2001 live recording of his Rome Beethoven cycle (partly available on DVD – see above) to which the re-edited version of his earlier recording of the *Choral Symphony*, made in Berlin, has been added. The conductor himself feels that for this cycle his 'interpretative vision matured, becoming more natural and shared', so this set now replaces the earlier 2000 cycle as representing the conductor's final views on these works.

Menuhin's set represents the refreshing response of a great interpretative musician who remained perennially young to the very end of his musical life. Though the applause that greets the opening of some of the symphonies is irritating (though it is now edited out on the CD containing *Coriolan* and Nos. 4 and 8), the tensions of live performance regularly bring magical results, as in the dedicated, ecstatic performance of the great *Adagio* of the *Ninth*.

Gardiner's cycle makes a clear first choice for those wanting period versions. These are exhilarating versions which have bite and imagination and a sense of spontaneity. Like others, Gardiner observes Beethoven's own fast metronome markings, but allows himself expansion in the slow movements of the *Eroica* and the *Ninth*. With Jonathan del Mar a scholarly helper, his amendment of the marking for the Turkish March in the finale of the *Ninth* is twice as brisk as Norrington's and leads logically into the fugue. The set comes in full, luminous sound, complete on only five discs, with a sixth containing an illustrated talk by Gardiner in three languages.

Solti's first cycle with his own **Chicago orchestra** has a firm centrality to it, following the outstandingly successful version of the *Ninth* with which he started the series. The performance of the *Eroica* has comparable qualities, with expansive, steady tempi and a dedicated, hushed account of the slow movement. The CD transfers give an admirable consistency, with plenty of weight in the bass balancing the bright top register. At bargain price, Solti admirers should not miss this set, particularly as these performances are more satisfying than those in the later, digital series. The reissue comes with a bonus CD including Solti in conversation with William Mann.

By unearthing a live recording of No. 2, made in the Royal Albert Hall in 1948, and borrowing a radio recording of No. 8 made in Stockholm, EMI has put together a complete **Furtwängler** cycle – and very impressive it is interpretatively. The sound of those two ad hoc recordings may be rough, with heavy background noise, but the performances are electrifying. No. 9 comes in the dedicated performance given at Bayreuth in 1951, but the others are EMI's studio versions, not always as inspired as **Furtwängler's** live performances but still magnetic and, with well-balanced mono sound, well transferred. (EMI 567496-2)

The small-scale Belgian period instrument set from **Jos van Immersel** and **Anima Eterna**, with its string timbre slightly meagre and without vibrato, can hardly match the competition from other more distinguished authentic sets, but it has spontaneity and stimulation, and makes points of its own, notably the use of Viennese period instruments in the orchestra of two dozen players (more in the *Choral Symphony* – not one of the more memorable performances). The highlight is undoubtedly the *Eroica*, with the *Seventh* not far behind; and the early symphonies certainly have plenty of life, as do the overtures, all played with plenty of vitality.

Symphonies 1–9. Overtures: Fidelio; Leonore 1–3

Ⓜ *** Ph. (ADD) 475 8147 (6). Concg. O, Jochum (with Rebmann, Reynolds, Ridder, Feldhoff, Netherlands R. Ch. in 9)

Eugen Jochum recorded his earlier Beethoven symphony cycle with the **Concertgebouw Orchestra** in the late 1960s, the period when he also recorded with the same orchestra

what has claims to be the most dedicated version of the *Missa Solemnis* ever. There is something of the same dedication in these symphony recordings, notably in the hushed tension in such movements as the *Funeral March* of the *Eroica*, given a spacious reading, powerful in the fugatos. Jochum as an admirer of Furtwängler conveys many similar qualities, but without the idiosyncratic approach to tempo. Fast movements are crisp and incisive, with rhythms well lifted and offbeat accents sharply attacked, helped by the superb Concertgebouw ensemble. The spacious, intense account of the *Ninth* makes an apt culmination to a memorable cycle. The sound is still full-bodied and clear, with ample detail, as it is in the four overtures Beethoven wrote for his opera *Fidelio*. An outstanding bargain box in Philips's 'Original Masters' series.

Symphonies. (i) 1; (ii) 2. Overtures: (i) The Creatures of Prometheus; (iii) Fidelio; (ii) Leonore 2; The Ruins of Athens (ⓑⓑ (***) Naxos mono 8.110854)

Symphonies. (i) 3 (Eroica); (ii) 4 (ⓑⓑ (***) Naxos mono 8.110856)

(i) Symphony 5; (ii) Piano Sonata 29 ((Hammerklavier) arr. Weingartner); (i) Overture: The Creatures of Prometheus (ⓑⓑ (***) Naxos mono 8.110913)

Symphonies. (i) 5; (ii) 6 (Pastoral). (iii) 11 Viennese Dances, WoO 17 (ⓑⓑ (***) Naxos mono 8.110861)

(i) Symphonies 7; 8. Egmont: Overture; (ii) Clärchens Tod; Entr'acte 2 (ⓑⓑ **(*) Naxos mono 8.110862)

(i) Symphony 9 in D min. (Choral); (ii) Overture: Consecration of the House (ⓑⓑ (***) Naxos mono 8.110863. LSO, LPO, RPO, British SO, (i) Helletsgruber, Anday, Maikl, Mayr, V. State Op. Ch., VPO; (ii) LPO; Weingartner)

Weingartner's accounts of the symphonies are free of the opulence and weight that characterized some of his contemporaries (including the often glorious Furtwängler). They have a sinewy classicism, and for many collectors they stood for the voice of Beethoven in much the same way as did Schnabel in the late *Sonatas* or the Busch Quartet in the late *Quartets*. The sound is generally more than just acceptable. For many older collectors Weingartner's 1936 account was the *Eroica*, speaking with an altogether special authority.

Weingartner recorded the *Fifth Symphony* no fewer than four times, and this third version, made in London in 1932 with an ad hoc orchestra, is distinguished by sobriety and freedom from any self-regard. His *Pastoral* from 1927 is totally unaffected and sounds strikingly good in this transfer, as do the delightful *Viennese Dances* made with the LPO in 1938. Weingartner's follow-up 1933 version of the *Fifth Symphony* with the **LPO** was his fourth and most satisfying. But not even Weingartner can make out a totally convincing case for the *Hammerklavier* being transcribed for the orchestra. Apart from the *Eroica* and his magisterial *Ninth*, the

Seventh and *Eighth* are the most commanding of Weingartner's Beethoven cycle. The *Seventh* is completely classical in approach, without the (very slightly overdriven) intensity of the contemporaneous Toscanini version, while the *Eighth* has a mercurial quality that is quite special. The sound is better than we have had in any previous transfer of the *Eighth*.

Symphonies 1; 2; (Eroica); 3 (Eroica); & 8

(N) (BB) *** EMI Gemini 2 17635-2 (2) Concg. O, Sawallisch

Symphonies 4; 5; 6; (Pastoral); 7

(N) (BB) **(*) EMI Gemini 5 17659-2 (2) Concg. O, Sawallisch

The first of these two **Sawallisch** Gemini reissues is the one to go for. The orchestral playing is of a very high standard throughout and Sawallisch has a fine sense of proportion. The *First Symphony* immediately sounds fresh and vibrant; the *Second* and *Eighth* receive lovely, alert accounts that give much pleasure, and textures are clean and transparent. The *Eroica* receives a performance of some stature and has great breadth and dignity; the orchestral playing is a joy in itself.

The mellow acoustic of the Concertgebouw Hall must, however, have encouraged Sawallisch into middle-aged spread for the first movement of the *Fifth Symphony*, but blazing brass introduce an altogether more electrifying view of the finale. A relaxed view of the *Pastoral* is altogether more sympathetic, but the sound is not ideally clear. The *Seventh* is fully acceptable, but not memorable.

Symphonies 1–5; 7; (i) 9 (Choral); Missa solemnis

(M) (***) Testament mono/stereo SBT 1284 (1 & 7); SBT 1285 (2 & *Overtures: Coriolan, Egmont, Leonora 3*); SBT 1286 (4 & 5); SBT2 1283 (2) (3 (*Eroica*) & *Missa solemnis*); SBT 1287 (9 (*Choral*)). Gurzenich O, Wand; (i) with Kirschstein, Deroubaix, Schreier, Morbach, Gurzenich Ch.

These recordings, made between 1955 and 1986, demonstrate **Wand's** Beethoven interpretations from earlier in his career. The **Gurzenich Orchestra**, with which he made the recordings in Cologne, was the orchestra of the Cologne Opera when performing in concert. The comparisons with Wand's outstanding Beethoven cycle for RCA/BMG reveal that the interpretations themselves are remarkably similar. If the ensemble of the Gurzenich Orchestra is not always quite as crisp as that of the Hamburg players there is an extra freshness and spontaneity, helped by the bright forward sound, more sharply focused than on RCA, whether in the earlier mono recordings (*Symphonies 1, 2, 3, 4* and *9*) or the later ones in stereo.

The two-disc package of the *Missa solemnis* and the *Eroica Symphony* is the pick of the series. The *Eroica* is more urgent here than it is in Wand's later recordings, with a dedicated reading of the Funeral March as centrepiece. Finer still is the *Missa solemnis*, conveying the impression not of a studio recording but of a great occasion. With high dynamic contrasts Wand is bold, strong and dramatic, incandescent in the culmination of the *Dona nobis pacem* with its spine-tingling military incursions. The chorus, despite rather backward placing, sings with admirable freshness, and among

the soloists the soprano and tenor (the young **Peter Schreier**) stand out.

Symphonies 1–2

𝄞 **** Pentatone Surround Sound SACD PTC 5186 118. ASMF, Marriner

𝄞 (BB) *** Arte Nova 74321 63645-2. Zürich Tonhalle O, Zinman

*** Simax PSC 1179. Swedish CO, Dausgaard (with *Ritterballet, WoO 1*)

Marriner's 1970 recordings were originally made in quadraphonic sound of amazingly realistic quality, with the ambience warmly captured, notably the natural strings. Here they are reissued for the first time as they were meant to be heard, although the disc also reproduces admirably on a normal CD system. Marriner presents the first two symphonies authentically on a Mozart-sized orchestra. The result is lithe and fresh, with plenty of character but few if any quirks and mannerisms, and the dramatic contrasts are now the more powerful. Yet the proper scale is most realistically captured and in many ways this coupling has never been surpassed.

Using the Bärenreiter scores newly edited by Jonathan del Mar, **David Zinman** conducts electrifying performances of the first two symphonies, with a rather smaller band of strings than in later works. With textures transparent and rhythms crisply sprung at generally fast speeds, the results consistently reflect the influence of period performance. For the *Andantes* in both symphonies there is a hushed dedication.

Dausgaard's Simax coupling offers engagingly fresh performances, stylish and elegant, and with plenty of spontaneous excitement in the outer movements. They combine the vigour of period performance with the richness of a modern orchestra. The early but delightful ballet music is a bonus, and the sound is superb.

Symphonies 1 in C; 3 in E flat (Eroica)

𝄞 (B) *** CfP 575 9842. RLPO, Mackerras

With **Mackerras**, the *First* is fresh and alert in a Haydnesque way, while the *Eroica* has ample power, with heightened dynamic contrasts and with the flowing speed for the Funeral March still conveying dedication. First-rate recording.

The one irritant to **Menuhin's** performances on Apex is the welcoming applause that comes before the music begins and at the close of No. 1, but not before the opening of No. 3. This is intrusive without the visual element. Otherwise these highly musical performances, strong, but on a convincing chamber scale, are among the most satisfying available, with a dedicated reading of the *Eroica* Funeral March. Warm, well-balanced recording. (Warner Apex 2564 60452-2)

Symphonies 1; 5

𝄞 (B) *** LSO LSO0590. LSO, Haitink

Haitink's Beethoven cycle with the **LSO** was recorded at live concerts in 2005–6 at the Barbican, London. This CD begins with a fast and exciting version of the *Fifth Symphony*, with biting urgency and dramatic timpani thwacks. The slow movement flows at a fair pace but is beautifully moulded and phrased. The finale is as bracing and exhilarating as one could wish for, and the sound is immediate and warm. The *First* receives a crisply elegant performance, with Haitink making the most of the woodwind detail. The *Menuetto* here looks forward to the Beethovenian Scherzo in its high-spirited drama. The finale is fast without sounding rushed, and is always beautifully phrased. As in the *Fifth Symphony*, the audience is very quiet and the sound full and vivid.

(i) Symphonies 1 in C, Op. 21; 8 in F, Op. 93; (ii) Grosse Fuge, Op. 133

(N) **(*) Testament mono SBT1405. Klemperer, with (i) Philh., (ii) NPO

The two symphonies come from **Klemperer's** 1963 Beethoven cycle and the *Grosse Fuge* from a Festival Hall concert given three years later after the orchestra had broken with its founder Walter Legge and reformed itself as a self-governing body. The BBC mono recordings are excellently balanced and though the *Eighth Symphony* does not have the lightness of touch of, say, Karajan, it is not as ponderous as Klemperer's Beethoven was to become towards the end of his life. The *Grosse Fuge* is titanic.

Symphony 2 in D, Op. 36

(M) (***) BBC mono BBCL 4099-2. RPO, Beecham – BRAHMS: *Symphony 2* (***)

The *Second Symphony* was the work of Beethoven that **Beecham** most enjoyed, and he gives an electrifying performance, recorded in 1956 with clear, well-balanced mono sound. The reading is typical of Beecham, if anything even more magnetic than his EMI studio recording, fiery in the outer movements and warmly persuasive in the *Larghetto* slow movement, affectionately moulded at a steady speed.

Symphonies 2; 6 in F (Pastoral)

&— (B) *** LSO LSO0082. LSO, Haitink

(BB) *** Warner Apex 2564 60453-2. Sinfonia Varsovia, Y. Menuhin

Haitink's *Pastoral* is a fresh, bracing performance of tremendous vitality as well as warmth. With generally fast speeds, any feeling of being rushed is suppressed by the beautiful quality of the playing, with the **LSO** on fine form, and Haitink coaxing exquisite phrasing from the strings especially. The second movement, *Scene by the Brook*, is simply gorgeous. In the *Second Symphony*, the dramatic qualities are well brought out, again with fast tempi in the outer movements, sharply pointed rhythmically. The slow movement is beautifully moulded. The closely miked 'live' sound throughout this CD is excellent, bringing out much detail in its warmth.

After the opening applause, **Menuhin's** reading of the *Second Symphony* is weighty and mature-sounding, the first movement lacking a little in bite but not in buoyancy. The *Larghetto* is nobly phrased, the finale vigorous and high-spirited. Alongside the *Choral Symphony*, Menuhin's performance of the *Pastoral Symphony* (which opens without applause)

crowns his cycle in its sheer lyrical beauty. The chamber scale and the combination of warmth and lightness of touch bring a joyous momentum. The storm bursts in dramatically, and the heartfelt *Shepherds' Thanksgiving* brings a lyrical apotheosis. Satisfyingly full sound, with a natural brilliance.

Symphonies 2; 7 in A, Op.92

(N) **(*) BIS **SACD** 1816. Minnesota O, Vänskä

Osma Vänskä's account of the *Second Symphony* is crisp and precise, lacking a little poetry, but always thrusting, with speed on the fast side, whether in the powerful first movement or in the flowing account of the slow movement. In the first movement of No. 7 Vänskä brings out the rustic quality in the dotted rhythms in compound time. The second movement Allegretto is on the slow side though nicely flowing, but the last two movements are brisk and exciting. Very sound, but not a first choice.

Symphonies 2; 7, (i; ii) Mass in C, Op. 86; (ii) The Ruins of Athens (incidental music; excerpts), Op. 113

(BB) **(*) EMI Gemini (ADD) 5 86504-2 (2). RPO, Beecham, with (i) Vyvyan, Sinclair, Lewis, Nowakowski; (ii) Beecham Ch. Soc.

In both symphonies **Beecham's** pacing is highly personal, yet has plenty of Beecham elegance. The *Allegro con brio* of the first movement of the *Second* is extreme, exhilaratingly fast to challenge the RPO players at their peak; while the last two movements are both taken easily and and wittily. It is a strong, individual performance. Beecham's *Seventh* is comparably brisk; yet the result is exhilarating. The digital transfer of the 1956/7 recording of the *Second Symphony* brings some stridency in the violins, and the analogue hiss is relatively high, but the 1958 sound of the *Seventh* is much more successful, the sound full and well balanced.

On the companion disc, the *C major Mass* is a vintage performance, passionately committed. With a first-rate team of soloists and excellent choral singing, Beecham is still a front-runner among modern-instrument performances of this work. The transfer of the 1958 recording is vivid and lively, with clear choral sound. The fill-up of incidental music is equally vibrant, with Beecham roaring through the *Chorus of Dervishes* (finely sung by the Beecham Choral Society), whiskers obviously bristling, these are all memorable performances by a great conductor in his prime, and we must be grateful they were recorded in stereo.

Symphonies 2; 8

&— (B) *** CfP 575 9852. RLPO, Mackerras

Mackerras rounded off his outstanding Beethoven cycle with performances of these two even-numbered works which bring out the dramatic bite in performances at once refined and full of sharp contrasts, with exhilarating results.

Symphony 3; 12 Contredanse; Prometheus Ballet Music: finale

(N) *** HM HMU Helsingborg SO, Manze

Symphony 3 in E flat; Overtures: Leonora 1–2

Ⓜ (***) EMI mono 5 67740-2. Philh. O, Klemperer

Symphony 3 (Eroica); Leonore Overture 2

⊶ Ⓑ *** LSO LSO0080. LSO, Haitink

Symphony 3; Overture: Leonora 3

⊶ (**(*)) Testament (mono) SBT 2242 (2). Royal Danish O, Klemperer – BRAHMS: Symphony 4; MOZART: Symphony 29 (**(*))

The exceptional clarity of Haitink's Eroica is due in part to the close microphones, which bring out amazing detail, as well as minimizing any audience noise from this live recording. There is a tremendous forward impulse to the music-making here, so that the first movement's (almost) 18 minutes don't seem at all too long. The Marcia funèbre is done very convincingly, its steady tempo creating an impressive, cumulative effect. The Scherzo is full of life and energy, with the horns in the Trio especially enjoyable. The finale is hugely satisfying in terms of tempi and overall effect, with the drama, as well as the joy, fully brought out. The Leonore Overture 2 is played dramatically, with its splendidly controlled, atmospheric opening. Warm, vivid sound throughout.

Imaginatively, Andrew Manze's version of the Eroica comes coupled with three other Beethoven works using the Prometheus theme which is the subject of the Variations in the Eroica finale. As one would expect of this conductor, the approach has much in common with period practice with clean textures and limited vibrato in the strings. With a big dynamic range the Funeral March is both powerful and relatively measured. The scherzo is jolly in its bouncing rhythms and the finale is clean and direct. Excellent sound.

Recorded in April 1957 on Klemperer's last visit to conduct the Royal Danish Orchestra in Copenhagen, the version of the Eroica on Testament is even more magnetic than either of his studio recordings with the Philharmonia, fine as they are. The Third Leonora Overture, like the Brahms and Mozart symphonies, derives from a concert Klemperer conducted in January 1954, and though the slow introduction brings some rough ensemble and the recording is rougher too, the weight and intensity of the performance come over strongly, with the main Allegro fiercely dramatic.

The 1954 recording of the Leonora Overtures 1 and 2 and the 1955 mono version of the Eroica were among the first recordings Klemperer made with the Philharmonia Orchestra, and their success immediately revealed his full strength. This Eroica is one of his supreme achievements, with speeds generally more urgent than in his 1961 stereo version.

Symphonies 3; 4

⊶ Ⓜ *** DG (ADD) 477 7157. BPO, Karajan

⊶ (BB) *** Arte Nova 74321 59214-2. Zürich Tonhalle O, Zinman

Ⓝ **(*) Sony 886971 92522 (2). Basel CO, Antonini

Karajan's 1962 Eroica is among his finest Beethoven recordings, refreshing and urgent, without the hint of excessive tension which makes the first movement of the 1977 performance slightly controversial. The refinement of detail never gets in the way of the dramatic urgency, and this is an outstandingly safe central recommendation, with the Berlin Philharmonic on top form. His reading of the Fourth is equally splendid with the dynamic contrasts heavily underlined in the outer movements. In the slow movement there is a lyrical feel to the playing that suggests Schubert. The remastering means that the recording still sounds excellent.

David Zinman and the Tonhalle Orchestra give outstanding performances of both symphonies. The string and wind articulation in both symphonies is phenomenally crisp and clear so that there is no feeling of excessive haste. In the Eroica, even with the exposition repeat observed, the first movement lasts barely 15 minutes, and the Funeral March at a flowing speed still conveys darkly tragic intensity, not least at the close. First-rate recording, with ample bloom on the sound.

With his chamber forces Antonini opts for a very fast speed, generally crisp and well-pointed. This works well in the Eroica, with its fine slow movement offering real contrast. In No. 4 he is less clear in his articulation than most rivals, with the rushed finale sounding fierce and the interpretation offers less lyrical contrast.

Symphonies 3 (Eroica); 6 (Pastoral); 8; Overtures: Coriolan; Creatures of Prometheus; Egmont; Fidelio

⊶ (BB) *** EMI Gemini 3 71462-2 (2). LPO, Tennstedt

Tennstedt's outstanding and unerringly paced account of the Eroica derives from a 1991 performance in the Festival Hall, and it has the true hallmark of a live occasion, natural spontaneity and gripping tension throughout. The recording is remarkably spacious and full, and this is one of the really memorable Eroicas on disc. Nos. 6 and 8 plus the Overtures were recorded at Abbey Road between 1984 and 1986. The fresh, alert yet imaginative performance of the Pastoral brings a warmly moulded Andante, a dramatic account of the Storm and a radiant reading of the finale, with beautiful string-playing from the LPO. The Eighth is given an equally enjoyable reading, in which the second-movement Allegretto at a fast speed is made into a Scherzo, while the Minuet is spaciously lyrical. Altogether an unmissable set for Tennstedt's admirers, and a splendid general recommendation.

Symphonies 3 (Eroica); 8

*** Sony SACD 88697 00655-2. Deutsche Kammerphilharmonie, Bremen, Paavo Järvi

Järvi's is by no means a conventional view of the Eroica, but it is a very enjoyable one, taking a fresh look at a familiar work. He plays the first movement very fast, and it skips along all but light-heartedly (exposition repeat included) and he takes the listener along with him irresistibly. Then the Funeral March makes a striking contrast, sombre and intense. But the Minuet prepares the way for the finale which again overflows with high spirits. The Eighth is weightier, but the pacing is nicely judged, though the *Allegretto* is a genuine scherzando and makes a happy, bouncing contrast. The playing throughout is of the highest quality and the surround sound recording very impressive indeed (with or without the rear speakers).

Symphony 4 B flat, Op. 60

(N) *** Testament STB1430. BPO, Karajan – STRAUSS: *Ein Heldenleben, Op. 40* ****

Symphony 4

*** Orfeo (ADD) C 522 991 B. VPO, Boehm – MAHLER: *Lieder eines fahrenden Gesellen;* SCHUMANN: *Symphony 4* ***

Symphonies 4 in B flat; 5 in C min.; Egmont Overture

(***) Testament mono SBT1407. Philh. O, Klemperer

A masterly **Karajan** *Fourth* recorded at the Royal Festival Hall when the **Berlin Philharmonic** came to London in April 1985. The performance unfolds with an imposing fluency and logic, and can only be described in superlatives: the Testament sound is similarly impressive. The *Heldenleben* in the second half of the concert is terrific.

These **Klemperer** performances come from the celebrated 1957 cycle which received such critical and public acclaim. The late Mosco Carner wrote that 'there were many moments in the *Fifth* where I thought I was hearing the symphony for the first time'. There were many revelatory qualities about this cycle that did not always distinguish later ones. Classic accounts, in very decent sound, which are self-recommending.

This Orfeo issue vividly portrays the mastery of **Karl Boehm** in varied repertoire, electrifying from first to last. His account of No. 4 is bitingly intense in the fast movements, with sharply rhythmic attack, and tender and sweet in the spacious slow movement.

Symphonies 4; 6 (pastoral)

🎵 (B) *** CfP 575 9862. RLPO, Mackerras

Mackerras adopts consistently fast speeds in both symphonies, except in the slow introduction to No. 4. Crisp, light articulation allows for superb definition from the strings, and **Mackerras's** subtle rubato ensures that the opening of the *Pastoral* avoids any feeling of rigidity. With hard sticks used by the timpanist, the *Storm* has rarely sounded so thrilling, resolving on an ecstatic, glowing finale.

Symphonies 4 & 7

(N) *** RCA 88697129 332. Bremen Deutsche CO, Paavo Järvi

With his chamber orchestra based in Bremen **Paavo Järvi** takes advantage of limited string forces to favour very fast speeds with clean, crisp, well-pointed rhythms, so that only in the finale does the speed makes it sound breathless. Similarly in the first movement of No. 7 the fast speed for the first movement still allows a delightful lilt to develop in the compound time of the main *Allegro*. The *Allegretto* flows very freely, and no one could mistake this for an *Andante*,

while the remaining movements are similarly fast with crisp pointing.

Symphonies 4; 8

🎵 (B) *** LSO 0087. LSO, Haitink

This coupling of Nos. 4 and 8 continues **Bernard Haitink's** Beethoven cycle on LSO Live. These are traditional readings which, with their generally brisk speeds, are exceptionally powerful. No one would ever dismiss either work in these performances as in any way lacking in Beethovenian bite. After the refined strings of the slow movement the Scherzo and finale of No. 4 are exceptionally tough in the sharpness of their syncopated rhythms, yet the clarity of the running quavers in the finale add a delightful sparkle. The *Eighth* has similar power which Haitink builds up wonderfully thrustfully to the climactic recapitulation in the first movement. The second movement is deliciously sprung, and the third-movement Minuet flows easily, leading to an account of the finale with the right element of wildness. Altogether a fine culmination for an outstanding cycle, made the more attractive by its bargain price.

Symphonies 4; 8; Coriolan Overture

🎵 (BB) *** Warner Apex 2564 60454-2. Sinfonia Varsovia, Y. Menuhin

On the reissued Apex CD the opening applause has been edited, and the opening of the *Fourth Symphony* is immediately full of tension, the Allegro joyful and vigorous without being over-driven, and the rapt *Adagio* played most beautifully. The opening movement of the *Eighth* brings more joyous spirits and a most elegant second subject. This elegance also pervades the *Allegretto*, but here **Menuhin's** pacing is rather too relaxed and there is a lack of rhythmic uplift. However, all is forgiven when the finale erupts with buoyant energy. Again very fine playing, with the widest dynamic range, adds much to the character of the performances, and the spacious yet clear sound-picture is very satisfying.

Symphony 5 (DVD versions)

🎵 **** EMI DVD DVA 492843-9. LPO, Stokowski – SCHUBERT: *Symphony 8 (Unfinished)* ****🌑 (with LSO: DEBUSSY: *Prélude à l'après midi d'un faune;* WAGNER: *Die Meistersinger: Overture* ***; Bonus: DUKAS: *L'Apprenti Sorcier;* Monteux **)

🎵 **** EuroArts DVD 2072118 (with rehearsal of 2nd movt). BPO, Karajan – SCHUMANN: *Symphony 4* (with rehearsal) ****🌑

Symphony 5 (Part of The Ramallah Concert) DVD Version (with 'Knowledge is the Beginning' (Documentary))

(N) *** Warner DVD 2564 62792-2 (2) West-Eastern Divan O, Barenboim (including: MOZART: *Sinfonia concertante in E flat, K.297b;* ELGAR: *Enigma Variations: Nimrod*)

Stokowski's EMI DVD of Beethoven's *Fifth* is part of one of the very finest of all orchestral concert DVDs and offers an electrifying performance, coupled with a superb Schubert *Unfinished*, with the **LPO** in peerless form. In the slow movement the glorious tonal richness of the cellos is unforgettable, while the double basses come into their own in the Scherzo (after an unfortunate but momentary slip from the horns). These are both great performances, caught on the wing with all the advantages of live music-making, and the wide-ranging recording, made in the attractive ambience of Croydon's Fairfield Halls, is worthy of them, as indeed is the visually appealing colour photography. The expansive Wagner overture and beautifully played Debussy *Prélude*, both featuring the **LSO** in the London Festival Hall, are fine performances too, but without quite the total memorability of the two main works. As a bonus, the dapper **Pierre Monteux** directs a lively *L'Apprenti Sorcier*, with a perfectly judged basic tempo, although here the black-and-white photography and compressed sound are a drawback. But this remains an indispensable DVD, both for Stokowskians and Beethovenians. One soon becomes totally caught up in the communicated tension of the music-making: it really is very like being in the hall itself.

This EuroArts DVD (from 1966) is apparently the only available film of **Karajan** in rehearsal. In this instance, the exercise is part of his master class for one of his students and concerns the second movement only. One feels sorry for the student, for he is very much upstaged by his mentor, who at one point shows him the subtleties he has missed in the playing of the musicians he is directing. This is illuminating but not as enthralling as the hour-long rehearsal for Schumann's *Fourth Symphony* which acts as coupling. However, the complete performance of Beethoven's *Fifth* which follows is visually and musically electrifying in its visceral intensity.

Barenboim's electrifying performances of the *Fifth Symphony* and Mozart *Sinfonia concertante*, bringing together young Arab and Israeli musicians, is reviewed below in its CD format. Together with an extraordinarily vivid DVD of the concert itself, held in Ramallah on the occupied West Bank, comes a documentary exploring the problems of getting the players from two different cultures safely to the concert hall and home again afterwards. It also features interviews with the orchestral players, Barenboim, the Palestinian co-founder, Edward Said, plus a film of a visit to Buchenwald. But it is the music-making itself that captures the imagination, with Elgar's *Nimrod* also creating a 'gulp-in-the-throat' element in the performance.

Symphony 5 (CD versions)

🔊 **** Warner 2564 621791-2. West-Eastern Divan O, Barenboim (with ELGAR: *Nimrod*) – MOZART: *Sinfonia concertante*, *K.297b* ***

Recorded in Ramallah in August 2005, **Barenboim** conducts an electrifying performance of Beethoven's *Fifth* with his brilliantly talented young musicians, Arab and Israeli. Characteristically, he takes an emphatic view of the opening 'Fate knocking on the door' motif, but then launches into the first movement at exhilaratingly high speed. The mystery of the Scherzo (in which the strings play with wonderfully

clean articulation in the Trio) leads then to the bold and thrustful account of the finale. Barenboim makes a moving speech afterwards (in English) and rounds the concert off with Elgar's *Nimrod*, an account joyful rather than valedictory in its nobility at a steady speed, wonderfully warm. That such magnetic, finely detailed performances have stemmed from a single live event makes them all the more remarkable.

Symphony 5 in C min., Op. 67

🅱🅱 (**(*)) Naxos mono 8.110879. BPO, Furtwängler – WAGNER: *Parsifal: Prelude & Good Friday Music* (***); FURTWÄNGLER: *Symphonic Concerto: Andante* (**(*))

John Ardoin speaks of **Furtwängler's** 1937 *Fifth Symphony* as 'a performance of the greatest brilliance and clarity, with incisive attacks, fewer extremes of dynamics and tempo and, despite its fire and fury, more classically controlled than the earlier Polydor or the second EMI version of 1954'. These Obert-Thorn transfers were previously available in England on the Biddulph label and are of high quality.

Symphony 5; (i) Egmont: Overture & Incidental Music, Op. 84 (complete)

🅱🅱 *** Warner Apex 8573 89078-2. NYPO, Masur; (i) with McNair, Quadflieg (narr.)

Masur's rugged **NYPO** account of the *Fifth Symphony* is immensely powerful, compelling from the first bar to the last. The reading is given even greater weight by Masur's observing the repeat both of the Scherzo and of the finale's exposition. As if that were not enough, he also provides the finest account of the complete *Egmont* incidental music in the catalogue, opening with a thrillingly positive account of the *Overture*, and **Sylvia McNair** is a highly responsive and rich-voiced soloist. Will Quadflieg speaks his melodrama with dignity (separately banded, in German, untranslated in the notes) before the trumpets anticipate the final exultant paean of victory. The full-bodied sound is ideal for both works, with warm string-tone as well as a vivid overall brilliance and projection.

Symphony 5; Egmont Overture

🔊 ✿ (B) (***) Dutton mono CDBP 9784. BPO, Nikisch (with WEBER: *Overtures: Der Freischütz; Oberon.* MOZART: *Overture: Nozze di Figaro*; LISZT: *Hungarian Rhapsody* 1; all LSO)

This is a key record if ever there was one – the very first complete recording of a Beethoven symphony and arguably the first complete recording of *any* symphony. Played by the **Berlin Philharmonic Orchestra** under **Arthur Nikisch**, it gives the listener a real frisson, listening to a record made nearly a century ago, for it was recorded on 10 November 1913! What is astonishing is that, once the ear has adapted to the cavernous sound quality – recorded acoustically through a horn – one can really listen to and enjoy the performance as a fine interpretation, and from a great conductor who, even in the recording studio directs the music flexibly and spontaneously. Also included are impressive versions of the *Egmont Overture* and two Weber overtures, both featuring the horns which take so well to the acoustic process. But the technical highlight of the disc is the Liszt *Hungarian Rhapsody* 1, recorded six months before the symphony, a virtuoso performance from the **LSO**, in which the orchestral sound has amazingly vivid detail. Of course, all this is thanks to Mike Dutton's miraculous transfers which, apart from freeing up the sound, have removed virtually all the background noise.

Symphonies 5; 6 (pastoral)

*** Arte Nova 74321 49695-2. Zürich Tonhalle D., Zinman

David Zinman conducts the **Tonhalle Orchestra** in unusually direct and incisive readings. The use of Jonathan del Mar's Bärenreiter edition in No. 5 brings a full repeat of the Scherzo and Trio. If in No. 5 Zinman's approach works extremely well, the *Pastoral* is more problematical. The opening allegro, at a brisk speed, has plenty of energy but not much warmth. The slow movement by contrast is spaciously done, and the *Storm* is biting rather than atmospheric, with the finale plain, strong and intense, rather than warmly persuasive. The sound is fresh and clean, perhaps a little lacking in weight, although this suits the performances.

Symphonies 5; 7

⊶ 🌣 Ⓜ *** DG (ADD) **SACD** 471 630-2; CD 447 400-2. VPO, C. Kleiber

⊶ ⒃ (***) Naxos mono 8.111 248. Philh. O, Klemperer

⊶ Ⓜ (***) EMI mono/stereo (ADD) 5 67851-2 [576852]. Philh. O, Klemperer

⊶ Ⓑ *** CfP 572 849-2. RLPO, Mackerras

In **Carlos Kleiber's** hands the first movement of the *Fifth* is electrifying but still has a hushed intensity. The slow movement is tender and delicate, with dynamic contrasts underlined but not exaggerated. In the Scherzo, the horns (like the rest of the VPO) are in superb form; the finale then emerges into pure daylight. In Kleiber's *Seventh*, symphonic argument never yields to the charm of the dance. Incisively dramatic, his approach relies on sharp dynamic contrasts and thrustful rhythms. A controversial point is that Kleiber, like his father, maintains the pizzicato for the strings on the final phrase of the *Allegretto*, a curious effect. The latest digital remastering has again greatly improved the sound, especially on SACD.

Klemperer's EMI performances are now coupled together as one of EMI's 'Great Recordings of the Century'. Both works have a clarity, immediacy and fidelity of balance that enhance electrifying readings, revealing Klemperer at his best. The *Fifth* is mono only, the *Seventh* stereo.

Unless you insist on stereo for the *Seventh Symphony*, Mark Obert-Thorn's Naxos transfers (using the mono masters for both works) all but upstage the EMI versions, the sound vividly bold and fresh, certainly not sounding dated. The performances are among **Klemperer's** very finest.

Sir Charles Mackerras and the **Royal Liverpool Philharmonic** also give revelatory performances of both

the *Fifth* and *Seventh*. Tempi are on the fast side in all four movements but, thanks to rhythmic control, they never sound hectic. The superb recording is both weighty and atmospheric.

After the inevitable opening applause, **Menuhin** opens the *Fifth* unselfconsciously, if not very sharply, immediately setting a brisk tempo for the *Allegro*, which is played comparatively lightly. The *Andante*, too, begins with a sense of delicate lyricism, and it is in the finale that the performance explodes into joyful illumination. The *Allegro* certainly dances along in the first movement of the *Seventh*, but here the pacing is relatively steady. The *Allegretto* is deeply eloquent and, as in the *Fifth*, it is the finale that carries the work to its exhilarating yet weighty conclusion. (Warner Apex 2564 60455-2)

Symphonies 5; 8; Fidelio: Overture

Ⓜ *** DG (ADD) 419 051-2. BPO, Karajan

Karajan's 1977 version of the *Fifth* (419 051-2) is magnificent in every way, tough and urgently incisive, with fast tempi bringing weight as well as excitement. The coupling is an electrically intense performance of the *Eighth*, plus the *Fidelio Overture*.

Symphony 6 (Pastoral)

⊶ Ⓜ *** DG (ADD) 447 433-2. VPO, Boehm – SCHUBERT: *Symphony 5* ***

⒃ (***) Naxos mono 8.110877. BBC SO, Toscanini (with MOZART: *Die Zauberflöte: Overture*; ROSSINI: *La Scala di seta: Overture*; WEBER (arr. BERLIOZ): *Invitation to the Dance*; BRAHMS: *Tragic Overture*)

Ⓜ (***) Cala mono CACD 0545. NBC SO, Stokowski (with Talk: 'Sounds of Nature') – LISZT: *Hungarian Rhapsodies 1–3* (***)

**(*) Testament SBT2 1217 (2) (with rehearsal). BPO, Klemperer – with BACH: *Suite 3 in D*; MOZART: *Symphony 29* **(*)

Symphony 6; Overtures: Coriolan; The Creatures of Prometheus; (i) Egmont: Overture; Incidental Music: Die Trommel gerühret; Freudvoll und leidvoll; Klärchens Tod, Op. 84

⊶ Ⓜ **** EMI (ADD) 5 67965-2. Philh. O, Klemperer; (i) with Nilsson

Symphony 6 (Pastoral); Overtures: Coriolan; Fidelio; Leonora 2

Ⓝ Ⓑ *** Warner Maestro2564 69367-0 COE, Harnoncourt

(i) Symphony 6 (Pastoral); Overtures: Creatures of Prometheus; (ii) Coriolan; (iii) Fidelio; (i) Leonora 3

For its reissue as one of EMI's 'Great Recordings of the Century' **Klemperer's** outstanding account of the *Pastoral* has its previous couplings restored, with the *Coriolan Overture* thrown in for good measure. The extra items act as a prelude to the symphony, with **Birgit Nilsson** in her prime in the *Egmont* music, effectively cast in the two simple songs, the first made to sound almost Mahlerian. The recordings have been newly remastered, and the 1957 Kingsway Hall recording now sounds astonishingly vivid, less confined.

Boehm's 1971 version of the *Pastoral* is as fine as any, a beautiful, unforced reading, one of the best-played and (in its day) one of the best-recorded. It still sounds fresh in its current reissue in DG's 'Originals' series with a Schubert coupling.

There is nothing over-tense about **Harnoncourt's** *Pastoral* with the brook flowing freely and perhaps bubbling a little over the stream bed. A most enjoyable performance and the *Overtures*, recorded live, have plenty of character too, *Coriolan* powerful in tragic atmosphere, and *Fidelio* and *Leonora 2* (with an impressive trumpet solo) not rushed but with plenty of impetus and exciting codas. Excellent sound too.

The famous **Toscanini/BBC** performance has often been reissued, and the present compilation and transfer can hold its own with the best. A useful reminder that the *Pastoral* with the BBC Symphony Orchestra, with its extra dimension of humanity, more than deserves its classic status.

Though **Leopold Stokowski's** 1954 version of the *Pastoral Symphony* is among the slowest ever, the performance is magnetic, thanks to the conductor's concentration. Not only that, he draws from what till then was regarded as Toscanini's orchestra not only a reading totally contrasted with that of the Italian maestro, but one in which the sound is totally different too: warm, with a bloom on each instrument. One oddity is that the disc, following the original issue, also contains a brief talk by Stokowski on 'Beethoven and the Sounds of Nature', set against the natural sounds – birdsong, a brook and a storm – not in itself of great interest; but it is good to hear the conductor's distinctive voice.

When in May 1964 **Otto Klemperer**, aged 79, returned to Berlin to conduct the **Berlin Philharmonic** after a gap of over 40 years, the climax of the occasion, rapturously received, came with Beethoven's *Pastoral Symphony*. As the 45-minute rehearsal sequence on the first disc demonstrates, Klemperer was intent on getting the orchestra to produce a distinctive Klemperer sound, making his version fresher, encouraging each soloist to play out individually. The result is fresh and dedicated, rustic and refined. The rehearsal sequence is spoken in German, but the booklet provides a helpful summary in English.

Symphonies 6 (Pastoral); 8

⊕ (BB) *** EMI Encore 5 08993 2. LPO, Tennstedt

Tennstedt's fresh, alert and imaginative 1986 performance of the *Pastoral* comes with an equally enjoyable reading of the *Eighth* in which the second-movement *Allegretto* at a fast speed is made into a Scherzo while the Minuet is spaciously treated. In the *Pastoral*, the slow movement brings a finely moulded performance, a dramatic account of the *Storm* and a radiant reading of the finale. Well-balanced Abbey Road recording, bright and fresh. A bargain.

Symphony 7 in A, Op. 92 – see also under *Missa solemnis*, below and *Triple Concerto* above

⊕ 🏵 (M) *** Orfeo **SACD** (Surround Sound Compatible) C 700 051B. Bav. State Op. O, Carlos Kleiber

Symphony 7

(N) **(*) Channel Classics CCS SA 25207. Budapest Fest O, Fischer. (With: WEBER: *Clarinet Concerto 1: Adagio* (soloist Akos Acs); ROSSINI: *Italiana in Algeri Overture*; WILMS: *Symphony 4: Rondo* (**))

This is the real thing! **Carlos Kleiber's** (1982) live recording of the *Seventh*, made in Munich with the **Bavarian State Orchestra**, that is if anything even more electrifying than his *Fifth*. The Bavarian orchestra play as if their very lives depended on it: the first movement is riveting enough, with a thrilling coda. But the tension is maintained through the finely graduated and ideally paced *Allegretto*, with richly expresssive string-playing. The Scherzo is dazzling, but the finale, taken *Allegro molto* (rather than *con brio*), carries all before it, generating enormous energy and thrust, and the coda is built to a height of tension not even matched by Toscanini. Yet overall this is a performance that, for all its excitement, has an underlying depth of feeling. The sound has a superbly resonant hall acoustic, and the orchestra is naturally balanced within that ambience; on SACD playback, with the back speakers properly balanced, the feeling of sitting in the hall is uncanny.

Though **Ivan Fischer** directs his splendid **Festival Orchestra** in an outstanding version of the *Seventh Symphony*, crisply pointed at well-chosen speeds, the odd coupling of fragments makes the disc uncompetitive. The fill-ups have been chosen as representing the sort of music that might have been played when Beethoven's *Seventh* was new.

Symphonies 7; 8

⊕ *** DG 471 490-2. BPO, Abbado

⊕ (BB) **(*) Arte Nova 74321 56341-2. Zürich Tonhalle O, Zinman

Abbado's coupling of Nos. 7 and 8 is more impressive even than his highly praised earlier coupling with the VPO (currently withdrawn). Dynamic contrasts are heightened, and the description 'Little One' of No. 8 is again in no way apt, when the outer movements are so dramatic and the middle two winningly direct, avoiding mere charm while maintaining refinement. Only in the hectic tempo for the finale is there a reservation, when the recording, well balanced in the Philharmonie, obscures the rapid semiquaver articulation. But this remains an outstanding disc.

Zinman's coupling of Nos. 7 and 8 has similar qualities to his earlier, less recommendable coupling of Nos. 5 and 6. That works very well in No. 7, with speeds on the brisk side, which still have rhythmic resilience, notably in the *Allegretto*. In No. 8 Zinman, like Toscanini, takes a rather fierce view of this most compact of the symphonies, with a clipped manner and a fast speed in the first movement and with little or no charm in the middle movements. With clean, crisp ensemble and vivid recording, the power of the piece is reinforced.

Symphonies 8; (i) 9 (Choral) (with rehearsal of the 9th)

Ⓝ *** DG 477 7568 (2) BPO, Karajan; (i) with Janowitz, Rossel-Majdan, Kmentt, Berry, V. Singverein

When recording his 1962 cycle **Karajan**, in a concentrated series of sessions, kept till the end the biggest challenge of all – the *Ninth*, and one senses that feeling of a challenge accepted in triumph throughout this incandescent performance. Though the great *Adagio* has received more intense readings, the hush of *pianissimo* has never been recorded with greater purity than here, and the electricity of the finale has all the tension of Karajan at his most inspired. The recording still sounds very well, and the sharply dramatic account of the *Eighth* makes an excellent coupling, together with part of the rehearsal of No. 9.

Symphony 9 in D min. (Choral), Op. 125 (DVD version)

*** Euroarts **DVD** 2072038. Anderson, Walker, König, Rootering, Bav. R. Ch., Berlin R. Ch., Dresden Philharmonic Children's Ch., Bav. RSO, Kirov O, LSO, O. de Paris, NYPO, Bernstein

Even **Leonard Bernstein** rarely made a recording quite as historic as this, here vividly presented in a television relay seen in 20 countries. At Christmas 1989, just after the Berlin Wall came down, Bernstein devised this unique performance of Beethoven's *Ninth* in celebration, drawing not just on the **Bavarian RSO** but on members of orchestras from Russia, Britain, France and the USA, as well as choirs from East and West Germany. Reflecting what had just happened he replaced the word '*Freude*', 'Joy', in the Schiller ode set in the choral finale with the word '*Freiheit*', 'Freedom', a sentiment which Bernstein thought was originally in Beethoven's mind. The result is a performance of unique tensions, with speeds broader than have become the rule latterly, and with the great *Adagio* as slow as on any version, wonderfully sustained. The finale, with four excellent soloists, crowns the occasion, received rapturously by the newly united citizens of East and West Germany.

(i) *Symphony 9 (Choral). Overture Leonora 3* (DVD Version)

Ⓝ *** Medici Arts **DVD** 2055528 Denoke, Fritz, Meier, Pape, Deutsche State Opera Ch., West-Eastern Divan O, Barenboim

Barenboim and his **West–Eastern Divan Orchestra** followed their 2005 Ramallah Concert by going to Berlin in August 2006 to record the *Choral Symphony* live in the Philharmonie. It was certainly an occasion, with Barenboim and his players creating consistent tension throughout, notably so at the bravura close of *Leonora 3* and the thrilling final section of the *Ninth*. The four soloists made an excellent team, and were especially fine in their lyrical quartet, topped by the soprano, **Angela Denoke**, not long before the exciting acceleration to the work's close. The chorus were predictably first rate. Barenboim's reading was above all spacious, warmly humane in the *Adagio*, yet the incisiveness of the playing elsewhere prevented any slackness and he created remarkable pianissimo openings to the first and slow movements. Altogether a memorable concert well covered by the cameras, but not quite as electrifying as their earlier account of the *Fifth Symphony*.

Symphony 9 in D min. (Choral) (CD versions)

🔑 Ⓑ *** CfP 575 9882. Rodgers, D. Jones, Bronder, Terfel, RLPO Ch. & O, Mackerras

Ⓝ Ⓜ *** LPO LPO 0026. Popp, Murray, Rolfe Johnson, Pape, LPO Ch., LPO, Tennstedt

🔑 ⒷⒷ *** Arte Nova 74321 65411-2. Ziesak, Remmert, Davislim, Roth, Swiss Chamber Ch., Zürich Tonhalle O, Zinman

🔑 Ⓑ *** LSO LSO0092. Robinson, Cargill, Master, Finley, LSO Ch., LSO, Haitink

*** BIS **SACD** 1616. N. Davies, Juntunen, Karneus, Norman, Minnesota Chorale & O, Vänskä

Mackerras conducts the **Royal Liverpool Philharmonic** in an inspired account of the *Ninth*, one which has learnt from the lessons of period performance, and, like period specialists, Sir Charles has taken careful note of Beethoven's controversial metronome markings. The recording is outstanding, warm yet transparent and with plenty of body; and the singing in the finale is fine, even if the tenor, Peter Bronder, is on the strenuous side.

Klaus Tennstedt never recorded the Beethoven *Ninth* commercially which makes this outstanding version, recorded live in October 1992 at the Royal Festival Hall, especially welcome. Terminally ill as he was, a fact widely known, made each of his last concerts into an event, which added to tensions. This concert marked the 60th anniversary of the orchestra's founding, and stands comparison with any rival version in the thrusting intensity of the performance, brisk in the first movement with timpani prominent, lilting in the scherzo (though with no repeats observed), radiant in the slow movement, with the **LPO** strings at their most mellifluous and violent at the start of the choral finale, leading to an exceptionally intense and well-coordinated sequence of sections, with outstanding soloists and chorus. The sound, though on the dry side has vivid separation.

David Zinman, too, crowns his Beethoven cycle with a magnificent account of the *Ninth*, using the new Bärenreiter Edition, opting for the fast speeds which have latterly come to be thought authentic, always giving the music the deeper qualities needed and with a sense of hushed dedication in the slow movement, even when taken at a flowing speed. The finale crowns his performance, with the chamber chorus not only fresh and dramatic but deeply dedicated too in the prayerful sections. The soloists are an excellent team of young-sounding singers, and the sound is full and well balanced. On a separate track the last half of the finale is given in an alternative version, with a pause included towards the end, representing Beethoven's first thoughts, later amended.

Haitink tops his LSO Live Beethoven cycle with a superb performance of the *Ninth Symphony* which from the word go is full of conviction. Choice of tempi is admirable in conveying the drama and epic scope of this work in an unforced yet lively way. The Scherzo is exceptionally well characterized with its sharply pointed rhythms and timpani strokes, and it contrasts superbly with the strikingly beautiful slow movement which follows, with radiant playing from the **LSO**. With an excellent team of soloists and the **London Symphony Chorus** on magnificent form, the finale is superb, with Haitink's tempi, as usual, providing a dramatically cumulative effect. The sound for this live performance is amazingly good, considering it was recorded in the hardly ideal Barbican acoustic.

Osmo Vänskä's first movement is incisive and sharp, with textures clean and transparent, while the Scherzo is similarly fast and transparent. The great slow movement is hushed and meditative, with a clear distinction made between the two interweaving variation themes, and with clean attack on the climactic fanfare passages. The choral finale brings more clean and incisive singing from the excellent chorus and soloists, building up powerfully to give the impression of a live occasion. First-rate surround sound – the finest this symphony has received on CD with the chorus particularly clear.

The previously unpublished live recording of **Klemperer** conducting Beethoven's *Ninth* on Testament is magnetic from beginning to end. The occasion at the Royal Festival Hall in November 1957 was the very first concert of the newly founded **Philharmonia Chorus** – the culmination of Klemperer's first Beethoven symphony cycle in London. He followed that up immediately by recording the *Ninth* in the studio with exactly the same forces; but in all four movements this live performance has an extra bite and intensity at marginally faster speeds. In every way it is preferable to the published EMI studio recording, when even the sound is both warmer and kinder to the voices. (Testament SBT 1177)

Of the three stereo recordings **Karajan** has made of the *Ninth*, his 1976 account (477 6325) is the most inspired, above all in the *Adagio*, where he conveys spiritual intensity at a slower tempo than before. In the finale, the concluding eruption has an animal excitement rarely heard from this highly controlled conductor. The soloists make an excellent team. The sound has fine projection and drama. This 1976 Karajan recording, newly remastered, is also available in a two-CD set (see above) together with the *Fifth* and *Sixth Symphonies*.

Though the opening applause is distracting and the first movement is less biting than the rest, the *Choral Symphony* brings a fitting culmination to **Menuhin's** cycle, thanks also to the fresh, clear singing of the Lithuanian choir and a young, rather lightweight quartet of soloists. Following the Gardiner thesis, the drum-and-fife sequence in the finale of No. 9 is taken very fast, like a French military march. But with a deeply felt slow movement, this must be counted among the very finest of performances on modern instruments at bargain price. (Warner Apex 2564 60456-2)

With **Gardiner** there is no mystery in the tremolos at the start of the *Ninth*, but the movement at its brisk speed builds up inexorably. The slow movement is far faster than usual but still conveys repose. The finale is urgent and dramatic, and the quartet of fresh-voiced soloists is exceptionally strong. An exuberant conclusion confirms this as a clear first choice among period versions. (DG 447 074-2)

As bitingly dramatic as Toscanini in the first movement and electrically intense throughout, **Szell** directs a magnetic account of the *Ninth* which demonstrates the glories of the **Cleveland Orchestra**. The chorus sings with similar knife-edged ensemble, set behind the orchestra. The performance of the *Fidelio Overture* is electrifying. (Sony 696998995925)

It is thrilling to have such a splendid new transfer of **Furtwängler's** historic recording, made at the reopening of the Festspielhaus in Bayreuth in 1951. The chorus may not be ideally focused in the background, and the audience noises are the more apparent on CD, but the extra clarity and freshness impressively enhance a reading without parallel. The spacious, lovingly moulded account of the slow movement is among Furtwängler's finest achievements on record and, with an excellent quartet of soloists, the finale crowns a performance fully worthy of reissue among EMI's 'Great Recordings of the Century'. (5 66901-2 [566953-2])

Recorded at the Edinburgh Festival on 19 August 1956, **Beecham's** account of the *Ninth* suffers inevitably from the dry acoustic of the Usher Hall and the limited mono sound. Beecham takes a relatively direct view of the first two movements, getting a shade faster in the first, with god contrasts in the *Scherzo*, with the Trio unusually light. The *Adagio* sections of the slow movement are very slow, but well-sustained, with a warmly expressive, well contrasted Andante at a flexible tempo, with beautifully shaded dynamics and the fanfare passages crisply dramatic. The finale benefits from having first-rate chorus and soloists, even if **Sylvia Fisher** is rather squally at times. The movement builds to a thrilling climax, though here as elsewhere ensemble is not as crisp as it might have been in a studio performance. Nonetheless, well worth hearing (BBCL 4209).

Wellington's Victory (Battle Symphony), *Op. 91*

✿ Ⓜ *** Mercury (ADD) 475 8508. Cannon & musket fire directed by Gerard C. Stowe, LSO, Dorati (with separate descriptive commentary by Deems Taylor) –
TCHAIKOVSKY: *1812*, etc. *** ✿

This most famous of all Mercury records was one of the most successful classical LPs of all time, selling some two million copies in the analogue era. Remastered for CD, it sounds even more spectacular than it ever did in its vinyl format, vividly catching Beethoven's musical picture of armies clashing. The presentation, with excellent documentation, now comes as one of Philips's 'Originals'.

CHAMBER MUSIC

Cello Sonatas 1–2, Op. 5/1–2; (i) 3, Op. 69; 4–5, Op. 102/1–2

(***) EMI **DVD** mono 492848-9. Rostropovich, Richter (Bonus: MENDELSSOHN: *Variations sérieuses* (for piano) (***))

The **Rostropovich/Richter** DVD was recorded at the Edinburgh Festival in 1964 at a mammoth Usher Hall recital, which, incidentally, began at midnight! Now we can see as well as hear the extraordinary rapport between the two and the intensity of their expressive dialogue. Both artists were in their prime, and Richter never subsequently played these sonatas again. The camerawork is a model of discretion and there is a splendid bonus in the form of a studio recording of the Mendelssohn *Variations sérieuses*, which Richter made in the late 1950s in Moscow. Here the camerawork is pretty austere (we stay on one angle for a long time) but none the worse for that. In any event, his playing is quite electrifying.

Cello Sonatas 1–5; 7 Variations on 'Bei Männern, welche Liebe fühlen', WoO 46; 12 Variations on 'Ein Mädchen oder Weibchen', Op. 66 (both from Mozart's Die Zauberflöte); 12 Variations on Handel's 'See the conqu'ring hero comes' (from Judas Maccabaeus), WoO45

🎵 **** Ph. 475 379-2 (2). Adrian & Alfred Brendel

This new set of Beethoven's *Cello Sonatas* (and *Variations*) is among the finest ever on disc and is now a clear first choice. Not only is **Adrian Brendel** a marvellous artist in his own right, with a clean, pure tone and naturally musical phrasing, but he also inspires his father to spontaneously imaginative playing of the kind that has sometimes eluded him in the recording studio. There are countless details in **Alfred Brendel's** playing that reveal how thoughtful is his approach to the piano part, which his son matches at every turn. The recording is out of Philips's top drawer, admirably truthful and naturally balanced.

(i) Cello Sonatas 1–5; (ii) 7 Variations on 'Bei Männern'; 12 Variations on 'Ein Mädchen'; 12 Variations on 'See the conqu'ring hero comes', WoO 45

🎵 (B) **** Ph. (ADD) Duo 442 565-2 (2). (i) Rostropovich, Richter; (ii) Gendron, Françaix

🎵 (B) *** DG (ADD) 477 6266 (2). Fournier, Gulda

Made in the early 1960s, the Philips performances by **Mstislav Rostropovich** and **Sviatoslav Richter**, two of the instrumental giants of the day, have also withstood the test of time astonishingly well and sound remarkably fresh in this transfer. The performances of the *Variations* by **Maurice Gendron** and **Jean Françaix** have an engagingly light touch and are beautifully recorded.

The masterly performances of **Fournier** and **Gulda** date from 1959, but in the CD transfer the realism is remarkable enough to convince you, with closed eyes, that the bow is really touching the strings only a few feet away, and the piano sounds equally real and beautifully balanced with the cello. Fournier's playing is glorious throughout, with the great *D major Sonata* (5) given a wonderfully rounded performance in which Gulda is more than a mere partner. In the hands of these artists the *Variations* also assume a

much greater significance than one might have supposed possible.

The **Harrell–Ashkenazy** mid-1980s performances are very fine too: they are unfailingly sensitive and alert, well thought out and yet seemingly spontaneous, with superb digital recording. The inclusion in this Double Decca issue of the *Horn Sonata*, equally recommendable (from 1974), makes this particularly attractive for those who regard sound-quality to be of importance. (Decca 466 733-2)

The set of performances by **Jacqueline du Pré** with **Daniel Barenboim** was recorded live for the BBC during the Edinburgh Festival of 1970. The playing may not have the final polish of a studio-made version, but the concentration and intensity of the playing are wonderfully caught. (EMI Gemini 5 86242-2)

Fournier and **Kempff** also recorded their cycle of the sonatas at live festival performances. These fine artists were inspired by the occasion to produce unexaggeratedly expressive playing and to give performances which are marked by their light, clear textures and rippling scale-work, even in the slow introductions, taken relatively fast. In this remastering as a DG Double, the sound is beautifully clear. (453 013-2)

Clarinet Trio in B flat, Op. 11

(BB) *** EMI Encore 3 55674-2. de Peyer, du Pré, Barenboim – BRAHMS: *Clarinet Sonatas 1–2* ***

Beethoven's delightful *Clarinet Trio* is most beautifully played by this finely balanced trio, with **Jacqueline du Pré** coming into her own in her gently played solo in the slow movement. The 1970 Abbey Road recording is fresh and clear, with an attractive ambience. The coupling with Brahms is surely ideal. A real bargain.

(i) Clarinet Trio, Op. 11; (ii) Septet, Op. 20

(N) 🎵 (B) **** Virgin 50999 522126 2 8 (i) Collins, Iona Brown, van Kampen; (ii) Nash Ens

A wholly delightful coupling, recorded in 1989, which has hitherto eluded us, of two of Beethoven's most engaging early chamber works. With **Michael Collins** in the lead, and with fine support from **Iona Brown** and **Christopher van Kampen**, the *Clarinet Trio* is wonderfully spirited and infectious, and the *Septet* is hardly less winning, with all six movements as fresh as new paint. The *Theme and Variations*, *Scherzo* and vivacious finale are particularly delectable in the latter work and both slow movements are memorable. The recording is absolutely first class, and this is truly a key recording in the Beethoven discography.

Clarinet Trio, Op. 11; Serenade for Flute, Violin & Viola, Op. 25; Piano and Wind Quintet, Op. 16

*** Hyp. CDA 67526. Gaudier Ens.

Ideal chamber music-making from this distinguished group, with particularly enjoyable playing from their pianist, **Susan Tomes**. The collection is generous, and those wanting these attractive pieces need not hesitate. The recording quality, as one would expect from Simon Eadon and Andrew Keener, is very natural and lifelike.

Horn Sonata in F, Op. 17

⊕ (BB) *** Naxos 8.557471. Tomboeck, Inui – BRAHMS: *Horn Trio*; SCHUBERT: *Auf dem Strom*; SCHUMANN: *Adagio and Allegro in A flat* ***

*** HM HMC 90 9250. Müller, Torbianelli – DANZI; RIES: *Horn Sonatas* ***

The distinctively fruity sound of the Vienna horn is wonderfully caught on the superb Naxos disc with its programme perfectly designed to show off the instrument. **Wolfgang Tomboeck** has been first horn in the Vienna Philharmonic since 1980, and here in all four works he demonstrates what a fine artist he is. The Beethoven *Horn Sonata* brings a stylish performance, crisp in attack, yet warm too, with the brief central *Adagio* given the gravity of a funeral march before the sparkling finale. The piano sound is relatively lightweight, which **Madoka Inui** with her clean articulation turns to advantage in suggesting the sound of a fortepiano.

As **Thomas Müller** shows here, Beethoven's very classical *Horn Sonata* gains much character from a period instrument with stopped notes. How striking is the opening theme of the first movement (after the bold fanfare) played on the hand horn used here, with the stopped note undisguised at the end of the first phrase. **Eduardo Torbianelli's** fortepiano, too, makes a naturally supportive partnership. Müller plays with great spirit, and then in the brief *Poco Adagio* he achieves a wan, gentle melancholy, so that the joy of the finale is the more infectious. (Again the ear soon notices the stopped notes.) This is coupled with two other sonatas, and that by Danzi pays its respects to the Beethoven model.

Piano Trios 1–12 (complete); Septet, Op. 20 (arr. for Piano Trio)

(N) ⊕ *** Phoenix Edition 122 (4). Haydn Trio Eisenstadt

Pride of place in this collection must go to the collected edition of all of Beethoven's music for *Piano Trio* from the **Haydn Trio Eisenstadt**. It is particularly valuable to have not just the six regular trios with opus numbers and the different variations and the shorter works without opus numbers, but such a rarity as Beethoven's own arrangement of his popular *Septet Op. 20*. That last is remarkably successful (even though it lacks the tonal variety of the original), particularly when it is played here with such sparkle by the Haydn Trio Eisenstadt.

Witty pointing of rhythm marks all the playing of this fine Austrian Trio, though some may find the balance favouring the piano emphasizes the way that the pianist, **Harald Kosik** is plainly the leader of the ensemble. But sparkle marks all the performances, as in both the *Scherzo* and the Finale of the *Archduke Trio*, the greatest work of the cycle, even if the *Ghost Trio* is a close rival. One omission is the piano trio transcription of the second symphony, though that would have been a much more questionable choice than the arrangement of the Septet.

Piano Trios: 1–3, Op. 1/1–3; 7 (Archduke); 9 (Allegretto in E flat), WoO39; 10 (Variations in E flat), Op. 44; 12 (Allegretto in E flat), Hess 48

(BB) *** EMI (ADD) Gemini 3 50798-2 (2). Barenboim, Zukerman, du Pré

(i) Piano Trios: 4 in D (Ghost); 5 in E flat, Op. 70/1–2; 8 in E flat, WoO38; 11 (Variations on 'Ich bin der Schneider Kakadu'), Op. 121a; (ii) Cello Sonatas 3 in A, Op. 69; 5 in D, Op. 102/2

(BB) *** EMI (ADD) Gemini 3 50807-2 (2). (i) Barenboim, Zukerman, du Pré; (ii) du Pré, Kovacevich

The 1970 **Barenboim/Zukerman/du Pré** set is economically fitted here on to a pair of super-bargain Gemini Doubles, together with the two *Cello Sonatas* **Barenboim** and **du Pré** recorded earlier, in 1966, music-making of rare concentration, spontaneity and warmth. Any tendency to self-indulgence plus a certain leaning towards romantic expressiveness, is counterbalanced by their urgency and intensity, and the *Innigkeit* of some of the slow movments, especially in the *Ghost Trio*, Opus 70, No. 1, has the depth of really mature artistry, extraordinary in the work of musicians so young at the time of the recordings. The excellent analogue recording has been newly remastered on CD, and the players are given a natural presence, with plenty of depth to the sound and a convincing hall ambience.

The alternative EMI recordings of the *Cello Sonatas* come from the year after Jacqueline had made her definitive recording of the Elgar *Cello Concerto*. Du Pré's tone ranges from full-blooded *fortissimo* to the mere whisper of a half-tone, and these artists allow the most free range of expressive rubato. With excellent recording, well transferred, these performances make a welcome return to the catalogue, sounding crisp and present on CD, without loss of body and warmth.

Piano Trios 1 in E flat, Op. 1/1; 2 in G, Op. 1/2; 3 in E flat, WoO 38 (⊕ *** Hyp. CDA 67393)

Piano Trios: 3, Op. 1/3; 4 in B flat, Op. 11; 10 (Variations in E flat), Op. 44. Theme & Variations on 'Pria ch'io l'impegno' from Weigl's 'L'amor marinaro' (⊕ *** Hyp. CDA 67466)

Piano Trios 5 (Ghost) in D, Op. 70/1; 6 in E flat, Op. 70/2; Allegretto in B flat, WoO 39 (⊕ *** Hyp. CDA 67327)

Piano Trios 7 in B flat (Archduke), Op. 97; 12 (Allegretto in E flat, Hess 48); Variations on 'Ich bin der Schneider Kakadu', Op. 121a (⊕ *** Hyp. CDA 67369)

The performances by the **Florestan Trio** bring an admirable lightness of touch and inner vitality throughout. The playing of **Susan Tomes** is particularly felicitous, and the Hyperion recording does it full justice. The account of the two Op. 70 trios is outstanding in every way. The playing is quite gripping and masterly, and the sound is very vivid and well balanced. Their commanding, dramatically conceived account of the *Archduke* is no less superb. The variations make a neat encore, and the set as a whole can be strongly recommended as a key recommendation in this repertoire.

Piano Trios 1–2, Op. 1/1–2 (*** MDG 303 1051-2. Trio Parnassus)

Piano Trios 3, Op. 1/3; 10 (14 Variations in E flat), Op. 44; 11 (Variations on 'Ich bin der Schneider Kakadu'), Op. 121a (*** MDG 303 1052-2)

Piano Trios 5 (Ghost); 6, Op. 70/1–2 (*** MDG 303 1053-2)

The **Trio Parnassus** use modern instruments, but their spiritedly vibrant style, with bold accents, is every bit a match for their competitors. It is balanced by a warm legato from the excellent pianist (**Chia Chou**) in slow movements, and the finale of Op. 1/2 has exhilarating dynamism. The recording is vividly realistic. The remaining trios, plus the *Kakadu* and Op. 44 *Variations*, are hardly less satisfying. Indeed, they can be thought of as among the best of the recent versions of these pieces. The playing is unfailingly musical, and the recordings are fresh and vivid.

Piano Trio 3, Op 1/3

(N) **(*) DUX 0626. Trio Cracovia – BRAHMS: *Piano Trio Op. 101* **(*); RACHMANINOV: *Piano Trio in G min, (Elégiaque)* **(*)

The disc from the **Trio Cracovia** brings together two well-known works alongside Beethoven's *Trio Op. 1/3*. It is a slight disappointment that these performances suffer from the relative weakness of the solo cello, though they still might be considered by those who fancy the coupling.

Piano Trios 4, Op. 11; 5 (Ghost); 7 (Archduke)

(M) *** Ph. (ADD) 464 683-2. Beaux Arts Trio

From the **Beaux Arts Trio** the *Archduke* is a particularly successful transfer, with an attractive bloom on the sound, yet detail is clear. This performance has more spontaneity than their later version and the overall feeling is of lightness and grace. The Op. 11 *Trio* is usually heard in its clarinet version. The Beaux Arts players are again on excellent form here and they project the drama and intensity of the *Ghost Trio* to brilliant effect.

Piano Trio 5 (Ghost), Op.70/1

(N) **(*) RTE Lyric CD 116. Ens Avalon – BAX: *Piano Trio in B flat*; BERNSTEIN: *Piano Trio Op. 2* **(*)

The *Ghost Trio* is offered in a competitive version from the **Ensemble Avalon**, an Irish group with members drawn from both north and south of Ireland. One criticism is that the violin and cello play with rather excessive portamento, though it remains an enjoyable performance.

Piano Trios 5 (Ghost); 6; 7 (Archduke); 8 in E flat, WoO 38; 10 (Variations in E flat), Op. 44; 12 (Allegretto in E flat), Hess 48

(BB) *** EMI Gemini (DDD/ADD) 5 85496-2 (2). Ashkenazy, Perlman, Harrell

This generous bargain-priced EMI Gemini compilation (which includes both the *Archduke* and *Ghost Trios*) is drawn from the complete set by these artists, which was made over a period of five years between 1979 and 1984. The playing is unfailingly perceptive and full of those musical insights that make one want to return to the set. The recording is a shade dry but very present and realistic.

Piano & Wind Quintet in E flat, Op. 16

*** BIS CD 1552. Hough, BPO Wind Quintet – MOZART: *Piano & Wind Quintet; Adagio & Rondo* ***

*** CBC MCVD 1137. Kuerti, Campbell, Mason, Sommerville, McKay – MOZART; WITT: *Quintets* ***

(***) Testament mono SBT 1091. Gieseking, Philh. Wind Ens. – MOZART: *Quintet, etc.* (***)

Stephen Hough joins members of the **Berlin Philharmonic Wind Ensemble** to give a totally captivating account of this light-hearted work. They open fairly robustly, but soon take off into the allegro, and in the *Andante* Hough creates an expressive cantabile, subtly varied in dynamic, to contrast with the sparkling finale. First-class sound makes this a first choice for this attractive coupling.

A totally winning performance too from this group of leading Canadian wind soloists, appropriately led by the Viennese-born pianist **Anton Kuerti**. They play together with total rapport and their performance has great freshness and all the spontaneity of live music-making. The finale is particularly infectious. The recording has great vividness and realism – indeed, it is in the demonstration bracket.

Ideal chamber music-making in this version by **Walter Gieseking** and members of the **Philharmonia Wind** (Dennis Brain, Sidney Sutcliffe, Bernard Walton and Cecil James). Recorded in 1955, it has few rivals in tonal blend and perfection of balance and ensemble. The mono sound comes up wonderfully fresh in this Testament transfer.

Septet in E flat, Op. 20; Octet for Wind in E flat, Op. 103

(BB) *** EMI Gemini (ADD) 3 50864-2 (2). Melos Ens. of London – MENDELSSOHN: *Octet* **; SCHUBERT: *Octet* ***

(i) Septet, Op. 20; (ii) Wind Sextet in E flat, Op. 81b

(BB) *** Helios CDH 55189. Gaudier Ens.

The young members of the **Gaudier Ensemble** give an exuberant performance, bringing the *Septet* home as one of the young Beethoven's most joyfully carefree inspirations. The rarer *Sextet* for two horns and string quartet makes a generous coupling. Excellent sound, with the wind well forward. A superb bargain.

The **Melos Ensemble** give a reading of the *Septet* that brims with life and energy, wonderfully idiomatic and spontaneous-sounding, and much the same comments apply to the companion work for wind instruments.

An enchanting version of the evergreen *Septet* from the **Vienna Octet**: it oozes Viennese charm but is without any cloying sentimentality. The 1956 recording is astonishingly warm and vivid (a tribute to whoever made this transfer, as well as to the original Decca engineers). Delightful Spohr coupling, too. (Testament SBT 1261)

Serenade in D for Flute, Violin and Viola, Op. 25

*** Avie AV 2108. Lisa & Pavlo Beznosiuk, Dunn – MOZART: *Flute Quartets* ***

The light and charming combination of flute, violin and viola inspired the youthful Beethoven to write in an unexpectedly carefree and undemanding way. The sequence of tuneful, unpretentious movements reminds one of Mozart's own music for flute, so the couplings on this Avie CD are entirely apt. The stylish, light-textured period-instrument performances from the **Beznosiuk** group are admirable and are beautifully recorded.

STRING QUARTETS

String Quartets (DVD versions)

String Quartets: 1, 3 & 4, Op. 18/1, 3 & 4; 10 (Harp), Op. 74; 13, Op. 130; 14, Op. 131

*** EMI **DVD** 3 38567-9 (2). Alban Berg Qt

String Quartets: 2, Op. 18/2; 7 (Rasumovsky), Op. 59/1; 11, Op. 95; 12, Op. 127; 15, Op. 132

*** EMI **DVD** 3 38580-9 (2). Alban Berg Qt

String Quartets: 5–6, Op. 18/5–6; 8–9 (Rasumovsky), Op. 59/2–3; 16, Op. 135; Grosse Fuge, Op. 133

*** EMI **DVD** 3 38592-9 (2). Alban Berg Qt

Anyone who has ever felt that the **Alban Berg Quartet's** performances of Beethoven are too rigid or lack warmth should watch these fascinating DVDs. These are performances that bring out the many varied aspects of Beethoven, the joy of the early quartets and the power of the middle-period works, as well as the depth and weight of the last-period works. Where too often on disc this quartet has seemed to slide over the profundities, here they give rapt, dedicated performances, with hushed intensity a necessary element, and fine shading of dynamic as evident as the brilliance and precision of the ensemble. Some may find their dynamics exaggerated and the *pianissimos* do occasionally strike one as a little self-conscious. But there is far more to admire than to cavil at, and the cycle offers much musical satisfaction. Watching and listening to them, for the most part this is music-making on such a high level of accomplishment that criticism is muted. Visually, the direction is impeccable, completely unobtrusive and musical.

String Quartets (CD versions)

String Quartets 1–16; Grosse Fugue; String Quintets & Fragments

(N) ⊕─ **** Warner 2564 6947 1-3 (10). Endellion Qt

This collected edition of Beethoven's quartets and string quintets, celebrating the **Endellion Quartet's** 30th anniversary, includes not just the regular Beethoven *String Quartets*

but variants as well as the *String Quintets* and *Fragments*. The first version of *Opus 18 No. 1* for example, is markedly different from the text we know. It is fascinating here to have both versions on the first of the ten discs, with Misha Donat's authoritative notes analysing the principal differences. *Opus 59 No. 2* draws from the Endellions the most refined, dedicated playing in the slow movement, one of Beethoven's most visionary, on a par with the late Quartets. It is also good to have Beethoven's own neat arrangement of the *Piano Sonata, Opus 14 No. 1*. As for the fragments, none is specially valuable, but they are all worth hearing, as are the *String Quintets Opp. 4 & 29* as well as two *Fugues* for string quintet.

At every point the Endellions demonstrate their extra maturity, and so they do in the remaining quartets, including the late masterpieces, in which they make impeccable choices over tempos, and consistently play with inner depth and dedication, bringing out the visionary qualities, not least in daring to employ the widest dynamic range, with whispered *pianissimos* as intense as the biting *fortissimos*. The recordings are a model of balance and refinement.

String Quartets 1–16; Grosse Fuge, Op. 133

⊕─ (M) *** Valois (ADD) V 4400 (8). Végh Qt

⊕─ (B) *** Ph. (ADD) 454 062-2 (10). Italian Qt

For long a first choice, the **Végh** performances, recorded in the mid-1970s, have rightly been acclaimed for their expressive depth. That intonation is not always immaculate matters little in relation to the wisdom and experience conveyed. There is no cultivation of surface polish, though there is both elegance and finesse. The CD transfers have a far cleaner image than the original LPs. The eight discs are not now available separately.

The **Italian** performances, superbly stylish, are now offered in a bargain box of unbeatable value. The Végh versions, in some ways even finer, are at mid-price, but on eight discs instead of ten, so the difference in cost is relatively marginal. The latest Philips remastering is most impressive, with the sound much smoother than before and very naturally balanced. In the *Rasumovsky Quartets* in particular, their tempi are perfectly judged and every phrase is sensitively shaped, while the late quartets receive satisfyingly thoughtful and searching interpretations.

The great merit in the earlier **Lindsay** recordings of Beethoven lies in the natural expressiveness of their playing, most strikingly in slow movements, which brings a hushed inner quality too rarely caught on record. The sense of spontaneity necessarily brings the obverse quality: these performances are not as precise as those in the finest rival sets; but there are few Beethoven quartet recordings that so convincingly bring out the humanity of the writing, its power to communicate. They regularly find tempi that feel completely right, conveying both the letter and the spirit of the music in rich, strong characterization. These are among the very finest versions to have been made in recent years and, at budget price, are excellent value. (ASV Resonance RSB801)

The **Alban Berg Quartet's** earlier performances are characterized by assured and alert playing, a finely blended tone and excellent attack; they generally favour brisk tempi in the first movements, which they dispatch with exemplary polish and accuracy of intonation. Occasionally a tendency to exaggerate dynamic extremes (Op. 59/3, for example) is evident and sounds self-conscious, but by any standards this is superb quartet playing. Other versions have displayed greater depth of feeling in this repertoire – including their own live performance cycle on the same label – but this well-packaged, beautifully recorded set (from 1978–83) at bargain price is well worth considering. (EMI 5 73606-2)

The **Amadeus Quartet** are at their very best in the Op. 18 *Quartets*, where their mastery and polish are heard to excellent advantage. The smooth and beautifully balanced DG recording from the early 1960s disguises its age. In the middle-period and late quartets, their richly blended tone and refinement of balance are always in evidence and are caught equally well by the DG engineers, but their playing does not always penetrate very far beneath the surface, particularly in the late quartets. The set is now offered at bargain price in DG's Collector's Edition and is well documented. (DG 463143-2)

String Quartets 1–6, Op. 18/1–6; Op. 14/1 (arr. Beethoven); (i) *String Quintet*

 ☞ *** ASV CDDCA 1111 (1–3); CDDCA 1112 (4–5 & Op. 14); CDDCA 1113 (6 & Quintet). Lindsay Qt; (i) with L. Williams

The **Lindsay Quartet** set out on a new recorded cycle of the Beethoven string quartets after an interval of almost 20 years. Already in the Op. 18 *Quartets* the trends are clear, all encouraging. Consistently throughout these performances, speeds are a fraction faster than before, in Scherzos often markedly so, with interpretations tauter and more positive, as well as more spontaneous sounding. In the two key *Adagios* which point forward to the visionary qualities of the late quartets – the D minor slow movement of No. 1 in F and the deeply mysterious *Adagio, La Malinconia*, at the start of the finale of No. 6 – the speeds, as in the rest, are a fraction more flowing than before, but the hushed intensity is even greater, with no hint of heaviness inappropriate to these early works.

String Quartets 1–6, Op. 18/1–6

Ⓝ ☞ **** HM HMU 90 7436/7 Tokyo Qt.

*** Decca 470 848-2 (2). Takács Qt

Fine as their competitors are, the new set of *Opus 18* by the **Tokyo Quartet** is finer still. Tempi are consistently apt, internal balance and phrasing cannot be faulted, and the overall combination of freshness and spontaneity is irresistible.

The **Takács Quartet** in their ongoing Beethoven cycle maintain the high standards they have achieved in earlier releases, their command of nuance, sensitive phrasing and musical architecture. Their sound musical intelligence and freshness of approach are always in evidence, and they are given splendid recorded sound.

The **Talich** have great directness of approach and a simplicity of manner which is disarming. They are recorded clearly, if somewhat dryly. It has to be said that this set won

a Grand Prix du Disque and a Diapason d'Or. Excellent value. (Calliope CAL 3633/4)

String Quartets 1–6, Op. 18/1–6

*** Chan. 10381 (3). Borodin Qt

String Quartets 11, Op. 95; 14, Op. 131, Grosse Fuge, Op. 133

*** Chan. 10268. Borodin Qt

Although the **Borodins** included Op. 95 in one of their first concerts, they have never essayed a complete Beethoven cycle before now. Theirs is as deeply felt as any; their survey can be recommended alongside the very finest of recent years, such as the Takács. Recorded in the Grand Hall of the Moscow Conservatory, the sound is satisfyingly warm and present. Most distinguished performances.

String Quartets 1 in F, Op. 18/1; 11 in F min., Op. 95; 16 in F, Op. 135; Satz (Allegretto) in B min., WoO

*** Warner 2564 62161-2. Endellion Qt

String Quartets 3 in D, Op. 18/3; 15 in A min., Op. 132

*** Warner 2564 62196-2. Endellion Qt

The **Endellion Quartet** is the latest ensemble to embark on a complete cycle, based on the new Henle edition. This newcomer, as Jonathan del Mar observes in a note, embodies some newer discoveries, based on the original first edition parts and a set of the parts in manuscript which came to light in the 1980s with some corrections in Beethoven's hand. The autograph manuscript of Opus 132 survives in the Staatsbibliothek zu Berlin, and the 2002 edition includes a number of corrections, two actually affecting the melodic line. The Endellions are, as always, selfless interpreters, unconcerned with anything other than presenting the music as expertly and imaginatively as possible. They are recorded in the excellent acoustic of Potton Hall, Ipswich, and are truthfully balanced by Tony Faulkner.

String Quartets 1, Op. 18/1; 11, Op. 95; 16, Op. 135

✿ ⒷⒷ **** Dutton mono CDBP 9765. Busch Qt

The **Busch** recordings come from 1932–3 and were made at the then new Abbey Road Studios. To say that they have never been equalled – let alone surpassed – is no exaggeration and no serious collector of these great works should be without the Busch. Dutton makes them sound better than ever.

String Quartets 4 in C min., Op. 18/4; 7 in F (Rasumovsky), Op. 59/1; 14 in C sharp min. 131 (DVD Versions)

Ⓝ **(*) Medici DVD 2072348. Juilliard Qt

Polished and committed playing of a quartet drawn from each period of Beethoven's life. The performances were recorded and filmed in 1975 at a particularly beautiful venue, the Bibliotheksaal, Polling in Bavaria. Although the camera work, directed by Hugo Käch is admirably discreet the colours are a little faded and the focus wanting in sharpness.

String Quartets Nos. 4, Op. 18; 8, Op. 59/2 (Razumovsky No.2)

(N) **(*) Virgin 00946 3802 6822. Artemis Qt

Polished as the playing of the **Artemis** is, in Op. 59/2, they are relatively earthbound, and they cannot match, for instance, the Endellions in Op. 18/4.

String Quartets 7–9 (Rasumovsky), Op. 59/1–3; 10 in E flat (Harp), Op. 74

🎵 *** Decca 470 847-2 (2). Takács Qt

These are sober and perceptive readings, which make one think anew about this great music. The slow movement of the E minor, Op. 59, No. 2, taken more slowly than usual, is searching, and generally they find the right tempi to enable the music to speak effortlessly. Technically impeccable playing, well thought through and scrupulously attentive to detail (with all repeats made), this is a set to rank alongside the very best, and the recording is of Decca's finest quality.

String Quartets 7–9 (Rasumovsky), Op. 59/1–3; 10 (Harp), Op. 74; 11, Op. 95

(M) *** Ph. (ADD) 475 8503 (3). Italian Qt

The remastered **Italian** set (now on Originals) still sounds well: there is only a slight thinness on top to betray their age (the early 1970s), with no lack of body and warmth. Superb playing is marked by purity of intonation, perfectly blended tone and immaculate attack and ensemble. With tempi that are perfectly judged and every phrase sensitively shaped, these performances remain a strong recommendation at mid price.

String Quartets 7 in F (Rasumovsky); 11, Op. 95 (Naxos 8.554181); String Quartets 8, Op. 59/2; 10 (Harp), Op. 74 (Naxos 8.550562); String Quartets 9, Op. 59/3; 12, Op. 127 (Naxos 8.550563); String Quartet 13, Op. 130; Grosse Fuge (Naxos 8.556593); String Quartets 14, Op. 131; 16, Op. 135 (Naxos 8.556594); String Quartets 15, Op. 132; in F (arr. of Piano sonata, Op. 14/1) (Naxos 8.556592)

(BB) *** Kodály Qt

The **Kodály** have the benefit of very good recorded sound, with a particularly good balance, and the actual playing is very fine, with judiciously chosen tempi and expertly moulded phrasing. Both the Rasumovsky Quartets here are very good indeed: thoughtful, decently paced and thoroughly musical accounts, which will give satisfaction. No one getting any of these discs is likely to be disappointed, although they are not a first choice in the bargain range.

String Quartets 8 (Rasumovsky); 10 (Harp)

🎵 *** ASV CDDCA 1115. Lindsay Qt

This fifth disc in the new **Lindsay** series follows the pattern of earlier issues in the extra sharpness of the characterization as well as the extra warmth, compared with the fine performances in their earlier Beethoven cycle for ASV. So in the Rasumovsky No. 2 the three fast movements are all noticeably faster and sharper than before, while the sublime Molto adagio has an inner hush beyond what was conveyed in the earlier version. The contrast in the Harp Quartet is different in that the first two movements are this time lighter in mood, and the Adagio treated songfully at a markedly more flowing speed. Ensemble is not always as immaculate as it was before, but the vital qualities easily outweigh any reservations. Excellent sound.

String Quartets 8; 10–16; Grosse Fuge

*** Chan. 10191 (8 & 10); Chan. 10269 (11, 14 & Grosse Fuge); Chan. 10292 (12–13); Chan. 10304 (15–16). Borodin Qt (available separately)

The **Borodin Quartet's** Beethoven cycle has magisterial authority. They shape each movement with exemplary feeling and there is a pleasing naturalness of phrasing. They bring us closer to the soul of this music than do many rivals and they are accorded first-rate sound. These accounts can rank along with the finest.

String Quartets 9 in C, Op. 59/3 (Rasumovsky); 14 in C sharp min., Op. 131

(B) (***) Dutton CDBP 9773. Busch Qt

Whichever versions of these quartets you may have, these accounts from the 1930s are mandatory listening. Neither Op. 59, No. 3 nor the C sharp minor quartet, Op. 131, has ever been played better; the **Busch** bring a depth to their music-making which has never been surpassed and Dutton lets us hear them in better sound than ever before.

String Quartets 11, Op. 95; 12 in E flat, Op. 127

🎵 **** ASV CD DCA 1116. Lindsay Qt

In their sixth disc the **Lindsays** launch into their biggest challenge yet with the first of the last-period quartets, the Op. 127 Quartet. The big contrast in this new version is that the heavenly slow movement flows much more freely than it did before, conveying an even deeper concentration, with subtler shading and sharper contrasts. Also, the more refined recording brings cleaner textures in a reading that is more detailed and sharply characterized throughout. In the Op. 95 Quartet, more compact than any, the Lindsay's speeds in all four movements are faster than before, giving an extra bite to the arguments, recognizing this as a halfway house towards the quirky sublimity of the last-period work.

String Quartets 11–16; Grosse Fuge

🎵 *** Decca 470 849-2 (3). Takács Qt

The **Takács** have the advantage of working with the new Henle edition by Ernst-Günter Heinemann and Rainer Cadenbach, and their leader Edward Dusinberre's sleeve-note draws attention to some of the detailed differences. But apart from the letter of the score, it is the spirit they project. The Decca recording, made at St George's, Bristol, is first class.

String Quartets 12–16; Grosse Fuge, Op. 133

(M) (***) EMI mono 5 09655-2 (3). Busch Qt

*** EMI 5 86405-2 Alban Berg Qt

Ⓜ *** Ph. (ADD) 475 8685 (3). Italian Qt

An indispensable set: the **Busch** are to the *Beethoven Quartets* what Schnabel is to the piano sonatas. The musical insight of these players, their wisdom, humanity and total absorption in Beethoven's art have never been surpassed and only occasionally matched. These performances are so superb that, despite their sonic limitations, it is possible to recommend them to young, non-specialist collectors. There are portamenti at times that were in general currency in the 1930s but which are unfashionable now, but few will find them irksome. No. 11 dates from 1932, 12 and 14 from 1936, and 16 from 1933, all produced by Fred Gaisberg at Abbey Road. Nos. 13 and the *Grosse Fuge* were recorded by Sony in New York in 1941: the sound is mellower, but less sharply defined. The present transfers were made at Abbey Road by Andrew Walter in 2008 and are very truthful, if not as impressive as Dutton's (see above). However, the set rightly takes its place among EMI's 'Great Recordings of the Century'.

On balance, these **Alban Berg** performances, seeking to ensure the greater intensity and spontaneity generated by the presence of an audience, are freer and more vital than those on the earlier set, but the differences are small.

The merits of the **Italian Quartet's** performances are very considerable. The remastered sound is very satisfying.

The renowned (1957) **Hollywood** set is one of the classic sets. Technically, the Hollywood players are superior and their virtuosity in the *Grosse Fuge* has to be heard to be believed. But there is no playing to the gallery at any time: this is Beethoven perfectly played without any thought of display. The recordings are mono but have plenty of presence. (Testament SBT 3082)

String Quartet 13, Op. 130; Grosse Fuge, Op. 133

🎵 **** ASV CDDCA 1117. Lindsay Qt

The **Lindsays** play not just as if they have lived a whole lifetime in the presence of Op. 130 but as if they are discovering it for the first time. The opening movement is perfectly paced – the *Adagio* opening having all the space that it needs – and the *Allegro* unfolding at the *tempo giusto*. Indeed this is a performance that soon has you forgetting the players and concentrating on the score. They speak with a naturalness and understanding that makes for a totally satisfying musical experience. Here the Lindsays repeat the *Cavatina*, each time subtly modified, so that the listener can proceed either with that and the *Grosse Fuge* (Tracks 1–6) or with Beethoven's second thoughts (Tracks 1–4, 7 & 8) with the appropriate musical preparation, another performance of the *Cavatina*. The *Grosse Fuge* is given a shattering performance, crisper and more urgent than before, easily lyrical before the regular finale, an ultimate demonstration of the players' responsiveness.

String Quintets: in E flat Op. 4; C, Op. 29

Ⓝ 🎵 **** Hyp. CDA67683. Nash Ens

The **Nash Ensemble**, with a distinguished line-up of players, here give flawless, superbly disciplined performances of Beethoven's two *String Quintets*. *Opus 4* is a transcription and rewriting by the composer himself of the *Wind Octet* that he wrote in emulation of Mozart's great examples of *Harmoniemusik*, the *Wind Octets in E flat* and *C minor*. *Opus 29* on the other hand is Beethoven's first completely original exploitation of the String Quintet genre. It is fascinating to find how in his string rewriting of wind music, Beethoven took the opportunity to develop and expand his arguments, as Richard Wigmore explains in his excellent note with the disc. Key-modulations are much more adventurous, and textures lightened compared with the wind original, making this by far the finer work. The Nash players by their careful balancing, helped by the transparent recording, bring out the inner lines with admirable clarity and with clean separation. First-rate sound and immaculate performances.

String Trios 1 in E flat, Op. 3; 2 in G; 3 in D; 4 in C min., Op. 9/1–3; Serenade in D, Op. 8

Ⓑ *** DG Double (ADD) 459 466-2 (2). Italian String Trio

String Trios: 1, Op. 3; 2-4 Op. 9/1–3; Serenade, Op. 8

Ⓝ Ⓜ *** DG 477 7430 (2) Mutter, Giuranna, Rostropovich

String Trio 1; Serenade in D, Op. 8

*** Hyp. CDA 67253. Leopold String Trio

String Trios 2–4

*** Hyp. CDA 67254. Leopold String Trio

The young Beethoven, in preparation for writing string quartets, composed the three Op. 9 *String Trios* in 1798. They have a winning originality, each well contrasted with the others. The delightful seven-movement *Serenade* was published in 1797. The performances by the prize-winning **Leopold Trio** are particularly alive and fresh, and the Hyperion recording is remarkably real and vivid.

The **Italian** performances are immaculately played, full of vitality and vivid in sound, and choice is a matter of taste: both are equally valid interpretations.

DG have reissued their 1989 two-disc package of the *String Trios* from **Anne-Sophie Mutter**, **Bruno Giuranna** and **Rostropovich** and it goes without saying that they are splendidly played. They deserve a three-star recommendation – but if pressed to a choice, the less glamorous but highly accomplished performances by the Leopold Trio on Hyperion are to be preferred. The sound in the DG set is rather forward and dry: the Hyperion quality is far more natural, and though their playing is less high-powered, it better conveys the spirit of chamber music-making in domestic surroundings.

VIOLIN SONATAS

Violin Sonatas 1–10 (complete); 'A Life with Beethoven' (documentary by Reiner Moritz)

**(*) DG DVD 073 014-2 (2). Mutter, Orkis

Violin Sonatas 5 in F, Op. 24 (Spring); 9 in A, Op. 49 (Kreutzer). 'A Life with Beethoven' (documentary by Reiner Moritz)

** DG DVD 073 004-9 (2). Mutter, Orkis

Violin Sonatas 5 (Spring); 9 (Kreutzer)

(*) DG **SACD** (compatible) 471 641-2. Mutter, Orkis (from above)

This hour-long documentary follows **Anne-Sophie Mutter** and **Lambert Orkis** during their year spent preparing and touring the Beethoven sonata cycle. The performances were recorded at the Théâtre des Champs Elysées in 1999. To follow them over an extended period yields useful insights, though the playing, particularly that of the distinguished violinist, will strike some as being at times just a little self-regarding. However, the complete set yields considerable rewards and is probably a better investment than the single disc. Good, straightforward camerawork and excellent sound. Subtitles for the English-language documentary are also available in German and French.

The two performances are also available on a very successfully transferred compatible SACD, which readily conveys the sense of 'live' music-making. The variations and finale of the *Kreutzer* are particularly spontaneous sounding.

Violin Sonatas 1–10

⌗⌁ *** DG 471 495-2 (3). Dumay, Pires

⌗⌁ Ⓜ *** Decca 421 453-2 (4). Perlman, Ashkenazy

Ⓜ (***) Decca mono 475 8460 (3). Grumiaux, Haskil

The set by **Augustin Dumay** and **Maria João Pires** is another of the finest recent surveys. These two artists have a special rapport and play as if they were controlled by one mind. Pires's sense of keyboard colour and pianistic control are to be relished, and the violinist is both thoughtful and individual. He does take some liberties of phrasing, and some may be worried by the odd moment of self-consciousness. But these are intelligently conceived accounts that sound beautiful and are very vividly and naturally recorded. They are elegantly and economically packaged.

Perlman and **Ashkenazy's** performances offer a blend of classical purity and spontaneous vitality that is hard to resist; moreover, the realism and presence of the recording in its CD format are very striking.

The 1962 versions by **David Oistrakh** and **Lev Oborin** are also performances to treasure. There is a relaxed joy in the music-making, an almost effortless lyricism and an infectious sparkle. Some might feel a lack of inner tension, and the recording is rather wider in separation than we favour nowadays, but it is a beautiful sound in every other respect. (Ph. 468 406-2)

The combination of **Schneiderhan's** refinement and classical sense of poise with **Kempff's** concentration and clarity makes these 1953 performances highly competitive, even compared with Kempff's later set with Menuhin. One has only to sample the *Spring* or *Kreutzer Sonatas* to discover the calibre of this partnership, spontaneous, dramatic and full of insights, while Kempff's opening of the slow movement of the *C minor Sonata*, Op. 30/2, is unforgettable, and his partner joins him in comparable rapt concentration. The mono recording obviously does not separate violin and piano as clearly as in the stereo set, but the internal balance could hardly be bettered. (DG 463 605-2)

Arthur Grumiaux and **Clara Haskil** made their celebrated recordings in 1956–7 and these versions sound remarkably well for their age. The performances are wonderfully civilized and aristocratic, and no one investing in them will regret it. They accommodate all ten *Sonatas* on three CDs at mid-price in an attractive box. Recommended.

Violin Sonatas 1–3, Op. 12/1–3 (Naxos 8.550284); Violin Sonatas 4, Op. 23; 10, Op. 96; 12 Variations on Mozart's 'Se vuol ballare', WoO 40 (Naxos 8.550285); Violin Sonatas 5 (Spring); 9 (Kreutzer) (Naxos 8.550283); Violin Sonatas 6–8, Op. 30/1–3 (Naxos 8.550286)

ⒷⒷ *** Nishizaki, Jandó

Naxos offer a winning combination here, in performances wonderfully fresh and alive. **Takako Nishizaki's** timbre, though not large, is admirably suited to Beethoven and she is in complete rapport with **Jandó**, who is in excellent form. The recording is most naturally balanced and the acoustic is spacious without clouding the focus.

Violin Sonatas: 1; 7; 10

⌗⌁ *** ASV Gold GLD 4024. Cropper, Roscoe

Peter Cropper, leader and founder of the Lindsay Quartet, and **Martin Roscoe** embark on what promises to be a complete cycle of the *Sonatas* and, if the rest are as good as the present issue, one that promises to hold its own with the very best now before the public, and one which looks set to become a top recommendation among modern recordings. There is a naturalness about this playing that gives delight. All in all, a superb partnership, given vividly present recording.

Violin Sonatas 5 in F, Op. 24 (Spring); 6 in A, Op. 30/1; 7 in C min., Op. 30/2

Ⓝ ⒷⒷ (**) Naxos mono 8.111252. Fuchs, Balsam

Joseph Fuchs's set with **Artur Balsam** of the Beethoven sonatas on the Brunswick label was the first to appear on LP. They are refreshingly sane performances, free from any kind of exaggeration, but with no want of personality. The sound – a little on the dry side perhaps – comes up well. The authors of *The Record Guide* found 'this bright, bold playing most attractive and nowhere more so than in the first movement of the *Kreutzer* which sweeps forward with superlative panache'. Yet ultimately they were disappointed by the absence of a thoughtful quality particularly in the slow movements. Nevertheless these are eminently serviceable readings.

Violin Sonatas 5 (Spring); 9 (Kreutzer)

⌗⌁ Ⓜ *** Decca 475 7509. Perlman, Ashkenazy

On Decca, an obvious candidate for the Originals label. The dynamism is there but never becomes too extrovert, and the music unfolds naturally and spontaneously. The recording quality is excellent: the disc has been remastered for this reissue.

Violin Sonata 9 in A (Kreutzer), Op. 47

*** EMI 5 56815-2. Perlman, Argerich – FRANCK: *Violin Sonata* ***

Perlman and **Argerich**, both big musical personalities, strike sparks off each other in this vividly characterful reading of the *Kreutzer*, recorded live. Ensemble is not always immaculate, and audience noises intrude, but this playing could not be more vital, with the first movement fiery and dramatic, the slow movement warmly expressive, and the finale sparkily volatile. The recording, not as immediate as most of Perlman's studio recordings, gives a better idea than usual of his full range of dynamic and tone. Well coupled with a comparable reading of the Franck.

Wind Music

Chamber Music for Wind (complete)

(M) **(*) CPO 999 658-2 (4). Consortium Classicum

The **Consortium Classicum** are a highly musical and eminently stylish group, and anyone wanting all Beethoven's important music for wind ensemble will find the CPO recordings well balanced and pleasing. However, few will want to repeat the 38-minute selection (*Harmoniemusik*) from *Fidelio* very often and, four key works are available together on ASV in rather more characterful performances (see below): their superiority is most apparent in their more imaginative response to slow movements.

(Wind) Octet in E flat, Op. 103; Quintet in E flat for Oboe, 3 Horns & Bassoon; Rondino in E flat for Wind Octet, WoO 25; Sextet in E flat, Op. 71

⊕— (BB) **** ASV CDCOE 807. Wind Soloists of COE

The wind soloists of the **Chamber Orchestra of Europe** give strong and stylish performances of this collection of Beethoven's wind music, marked by some outstanding solo work, notably from the first oboe, **Douglas Boyd**. They are recorded in warm but clear sound, with good presence, and this is a real bargain.

Wind Ensemble transcriptions: Overtures: Egmont (arr. Starke); Fidelio & March (arr. Sedlak). Pathétique Sonata (arr. Anon); Symphony No.1 (arr. Schmitt). Piano & Wind Quintet, Op. 16: Andante cantabile (arr. Triebensee)

(N) *** Somm SOMMCD 070. Albion Ens

The **Albion Ensemble** give brilliant performances of this collection of Beethoven wind arrangements, guaranteed to delight lovers of wind music. The first point that strikes one is the clarity of definition brought by wind arrangements. The *Egmont Overture* ends with a spectacular fanfare display in the final, while the arrangement of the *First Symphony* encourages speeds rather faster than one expects with the full orchestral version, at least in outer movements. The sharp syncopations in the *Scherzo* are particularly effective, as they

are in the exuberant finale. The arrangement of the *Fidelio Overture* brings a transposition of key, and a judicious cut is made for the ease of execution. The arrangement of the slow movement of the *Piano and Wind Quintet, Opus 16*, has the piano part incorporated in the wind textures. In some ways the most successful of all these arrangements is the one of the *Pathétique Sonata*, bringing out the high romanticism of the opening. In the lovely slow movement a horn takes the first statement of the main melody, while the central contrasting section is lightened, compared with the piano original, and the finale again emphasises the sharpness of attack encouraged in wind arrangements. The disc has been jointly sponsored by the Birmingham Conservatoire, and the Royal Northern College of Music in Manchester.

PIANO MUSIC

Piano Sonatas 1–32 (DVD version)

(N) *** EMI **DVD** 3 68993-9 (6). Barenboim. (Dir. Andy Sommer). Bonus: 6 Master Classes (Director Allan Miller) With Ashkar, Bax, Biss, Kadouch. Lang Lang, Wosner

Barenboim's new survey of the complete canon was recorded over eight concerts during late May and early June 2005 at the Staatsoper Unter den Linden, Berlin, and they are unfailingly impressive and searching. Start one of these concerts and you will be held spellbound. They are supplemented by six master classes which underline the fact that not only are his fingers magnificent but there is a mind of vision and imagination to guide them. We doubt whether any Beethovenian would fail to learn from them or the recitals themselves. The concerts are directed by Andy Sommer and the classes by Allan Miller and both find the ideal placing for the cameras. Excellent sound, too.

Piano Sonatas 1–32 (complete CD versions)

⊕— *** Nonesuch 7559 79328-2 (10). Goode

⊕— ✿ (B)(***) DG mono 447 966-2 (7). Kempff

⊕— (BB) **** EMI 5 72912-2 (10). Barenboim

(N) (B) *** DG 477 7958 (8). Kempff

Piano Sonatas 1–32; Bagatelles, Opp. 119 & 125

⊕— ✿ (B) **** EMI 5 62700-2 (9). Kovacevich

Stephen Kovacevich recorded his Beethoven cycle for EMI between 1992 and 2003 with consistent success, capping the series with an extraordinarily powerful and imaginative account of the *Hammerklavier*. The individual CDs have been highly praised by us. However, some of them have been withdrawn, so the arrival of the complete set at bargain price is doubly welcome. EMI's recording is of consistently high quality, and this cycle must now be counted a first choice, alongside those by Goode, Kempff, Paul Lewis, and (of course) the pioneering Schnabel readings.

It is not just the power of **Goode's** playing that singles him out, but also the beauty, when he has such subtle control over a formidably wide tonal and dynamic range. Even at its weightiest, the sound is never clangorous. Particularly in the early sonatas, Goode brings out the wit and parody, while slow movements regularly draw sensuously velvety legato. Helped by unusually full and clear recording, with no haze of reverberation, the clarity of his articulation is breathtaking, as in the running semiquavers of the finale of the *Appassionata Sonata*. Above all, Goode has a natural gravity which compels attention. One has to go back to the pre-digital era to find a Beethoven cycle of comparable command and intensity.

It is good to have **Kempff's** second recording (in stereo and dating from 1964/5) back in the catalogue – performances which alongside those of the earlier mono set still represent a yardstick by which all others are judged. Kempff's shading of pianistic colour is so imaginative that the ear readily accommodates any slight dryness in the upper range. The interpretations have a commanding stature, yet Kempff brings his own individuality to every bar and a clarity and sparkle that make you want to go on listening.

Those who have cherished **Kempff's** later, stereo cycle for its magical spontaneity will find this quality conveyed even more intensely in his mono set, recorded between 1951 and 1956. The interpretations are the more personal, the more individual, at times the more wilful; but for any listener who responds to Kempff's visionary concentration, this is a magical series.

Barenboim's earlier set of the Beethoven *Sonatas*, recorded for EMI when he was in his late twenties, remains one of his very finest achievements on record. The readings often involve extreme tempi, both fast and slow, but the spontaneous style is unfailingly compelling. At times Barenboim's way is mercurial, with an element of fantasy. But overall this is a keenly thoughtful musician living through Beethoven's great piano cycle with an individuality that puts him in the line of the master pianists. The admirably balanced recordings were made at Abbey Road between 1967 and 1970, and the remastered quality brings a most believably natural piano-image.

Bernard Roberts's cycle – his second for Nimbus – can be warmly recommended, the more so when it too comes at super-bargain price. These are dedicated, undistracting readings which consistently reflect Roberts's mastery as a chamber-music pianist, intent on presenting the composer's arguments as clearly as possible, not drawing attention to himself. Always spontaneous-sounding, the digital sound is full-bodied, with the piano set in a helpful, quite intimate acoustic. (Nimbus NI 1774)

Spontaneity and electricity, extremes of expression in dynamic, tempo and phrasing, as well as mood, mark **Daniel Barenboim's** DG cycle, as they did his much earlier one for EMI, though that means he has a tendency at times to rush his fences, particularly in the early sonatas. All three movements of the *Waldstein* are more lyrical this time, and that applies to the late sonatas too, not just in slow movements but equally strikingly in the great fugal movements, where inner parts are brought out more clearly and warmly. The sound is full and spacious, more consistent than before. The CD transfers, on one disc fewer than

Barenboim's EMI set, are of consistently high quality. (DG 463 127-2)

Piano Sonatas 1–4; 12-13; 14 (Moonlight); 22; 23 (Appassionata)

(N) **** HM HMC 90 906.8. Paul Lewis

Piano Sonatas 5–7; 15; 19; 20; 26 (Les Adieux); 30–2

(N) **** HM HMC 901 909.11. Paul Lewis

Piano Sonatas 8 (Pathétique); 9–11; 21 (Waldstein); 24–5; 27; 28; 29 (Hammerklavier)

**** HM HMC 901903.5

Piano Sonatas 16–18

****HM HMC 901 902. Paul Lewis

At once thoughtful and incisive, but with underlying inspiration, **Paul Lewis** is one of the most magnetic personalities of our generation, here rising masterfully to the challenge of these great sonatas. He began with fine accounts of the three *Opus 31 Sonatas* and his second chosen group culminated in the most challenging of them all, the epic *Hammerklavier*, which is given a taut structural coherence, matching even the greatest accounts of earlier generations. The *Waldstein* and *Pathétique* have a freshness, strength and lyrical appeal that makes them stand out among the early and middle-period works, and some of the other most popular works, including the *Moonlight* and *Appassionata* are equally revelatory. The last three sonatas now stand among the finest in the catalogue, and throughout the series there is not a suspicion of routine. Lewis's playing, with each movement perfectly paced and textures wonderfully clarified, even when he opts for unusually fast speeds, still involves no lack of weight. Excellent sound throughout places this set among the very finest modern surveys of these demanding works.

Piano Sonatas 1–3, Op. 21/1–3 (Naxos mono 8.110693); Piano Sonatas 4, Op. 7; 5–6, Op. 10/1–2; 19–20, Op. 49/1–2 (Naxos mono 8.110694); Piano Sonatas 7, Op. 10/3; 8 (Pathétique); 9–10, Op. 14/1–2 (Naxos mono 8.110695); Piano Sonatas 11 in B flat, Op. 22; 12 in A flat, Op. 26; 13 in E flat, Op. 27/1 (Naxos mono 8.110756); Piano Sonatas 14 in C sharp min. (Moonlight; 15 in D (Pastoral; 16 in G, Op. 31/1) (Naxos mono 8.110759); Piano Sonatas 17 in D min. (Tempest; 18 in E flat, Op. 31/3; 21 in C (Waldstein) (Naxos mono 8.110760)

(BB) (***) Schnabel

Schnabel brought to this great repertoire a rare depth and vision. There are pianistic inelegances (rushed triplets, etc.), sometimes extreme tempi and a bad-tempered quality that sound totally Beethoven; but the concentration, wisdom and insights (particularly of the late sonatas) remain in a class of their own. There is no question as to the superiority of Mark Obert-Thorn's transfers in comparison with the previous EMI issues: they are more present and vivid, and have much greater body. They also have the advantage of being available singly, so that those who want the greatest performances, such as the *Waldstein*, and the Opp. 110 and 111, can get them without having necessarily to bother with the earlier ones or the very approximate *Hammerklavier*. (This is no match for Solomon's classical and articulate account or his *C major*, Op. 2/3, for example, now on Testament.) But the best are beyond price and they have never sounded better. They come closer to Beethoven than has almost any other musician since, and in these excellent transfers remain an indispensable part of any self-respecting collection.

Piano Sonatas 1, Op. 2/1; 3, Op. 2/3; 32, Op. 111 (Testament mono SBT 1188); *Piano Sonatas 7, Op. 10/3; 8 (Pathétique); 13; 14 (Moonlight), Op. 27/1–2* (Testament mono SBT 1189); *Piano Sonatas 17; 18, Op. 31/2–3; 21 (Waldstein); 22, Op. 54* (Testament mono SBT 1190); *Piano Sonatas 23 (Appassionata); 28, Op. 101; 30 & 31, Opp. 109–110* (Testament mono SBT 1192); *Piano Sonatas 26 (Les Adieux); 27, Op. 90; 29 (Hammerklavier)* (Testament mono SBT 1191)

❀ (***) Solomon

This five-CD set provides a welcome reminder of **Solomon's** artistry and stature. Alas, it was never completed, as his stroke in 1956 brought his career prematurely to an end. All these discs are available separately, and no one who cares about Beethoven and great piano-playing should lose this opportunity of acquiring them. Solomon was the least assertive of musicians yet the most deeply satisfying, and his interpretations never obscure Beethoven's intentions. His approach has a unique gravity, an Olympian serenity and an unforced naturalness. These transfers have never sounded better, surpassing in every respect the earlier, EMI Références issues.

Piano Sonatas 1–3, Op. 2

**(*) DG 477 6594. Pollini

Impressive pianism from this great Italian artist, but there is a want of spontaneity that somewhat diminishes its appeal. Wonderfully 'present' piano sound, recorded in the Herkulessaal in Munich.

Piano Sonatas 1–3; 5–7; 16–18; 11; 13; 14 (Moonlight); 16; 17 (Tempest); 18–20; 21 (Waldstein); 23 (Appassionata); 25; 26 (Les Adieux)

(BB) *** Virgin 5 62368-2 (5). Tan (fortepiano)

Melvyn Tan began his survey of Beethoven's sonatas using the fortepiano in 1990, continuing in 1991 and 1992; but it was never completed, presumably because of lack of demand, certainly not because of any lack of artistry. Tan has a strong musical personality and in the named middle-period sonatas attacks his instrument with tremendous spirit and flair; every phrase lives, and he is not afraid to present the widest dynamic range. There is consummate artistry and real temperament and fire. Nor is there any want of poetic feeling. In the earlier sonatas he plays with brilliance and sensitivity in equal measure. He uses a copy by Derek Adlam of a Streicher (1814), an instrument for which Beethoven himself expressed a strong preference. The EMI recording is excellent.

Piano Sonatas 1 in F min.; 2 in A; 3 in C, Op. 2/1–3

*** Chan. 9212. Lortie

(BB) **(*) Naxos 8.550150. Jandó

Louis Lortie has the benefit of an immediate and truthful recording, greatly enhancing his playing. He brings his usual refined musical intelligence to all three of the Op. 2 *Sonatas*, giving ample evidence of his instinctive musicianship and artistry.

Jenö Jandó's complete recording of the Beethoven *Piano Sonatas* is also available in two flimsy slip-cases, each comprising five CDs (8.505002 and 8.505003). This first CD (actually Volume 3) establishes Jandó's credentials as a strong, unidiosyncratic Beethovenian. The piano sound is full and bold.

Piano Sonatas 2–3, Op. 2/2 & 3; 4, Op. 7; 5–7, Op. 10/1–3; 8 (Pathétique); 10, Op. 14/2; 11, Op. 22; 12, Op. 26; 13; 14 (Moonlight), Op. 27/1–2; 15 (Pastoral); 16–18, Op. 31/1–3; 19–20, Op. 49/1–2; 21 (Waldstein); 23 (Appassionata); 25, Op. 79; 26 (Les Adieux); 27, Op. 90; 28, Op. 101; 29 (Hammerklavier); 30, Op. 109; 31, Op. 110; 2 Electoral Sonatas, WoO 47/1–2. Eroica Variations & Fugue, Op. 35

🔑 ❀ (B) **** DG (ADD/DDD) 477 6360 (9). Gilels

Gilels's survey of the Beethoven *Sonatas*, made between 1972 and 1985, was left unfinished at his death, although he did include a masterly account of the *Eroica Variations* and the two so-called 'Electoral Sonatas'. Throughout, he manages to make one believe that his is exactly the *tempo giusto*, even when one feels tempted to question the very deliberate speed he adopts, for instance in the slow movement of the *C minor*, Op. 10, No. 1, or his strange reserve at the opening movement of *E flat Sonata*, Op. 27, No. 1. Among the named sonatas the *Appassionata* has been hailed by us as being among the finest ever made, and much the same must be said of the *Waldstein*; it has a technical perfection denied even to Schnabel, and though in the slow movement the latter found special depths, Gilels is hardly less searching and profound. If the *Pathétique* does not quite rank among his very best, such are the strengths of his playing that the reading still leaves a profound impression. Gilels's *Hammerklavier* is a performance of supreme integrity: Olympian, titanic, subtle, imperious, one of the finest accounts ever recorded. However, as in some other performances here (the *Pathétique* for instance) the digital recording is very close and bright, harder than usual. In the earlier analogue recordings the piano is usually much less closely observed. *No. 31 in A flat* is also given a performance of real stature. Even when Gilels storms the greatest heights in the closing fugue, no *fortissimo* ever sounds percussive or strained. Such is his magic that doubts are silenced. Altogether this set is a unique achievement and well worth its modest cost, even if the documentation is meagre.

Piano Sonatas 3 in C, Op. 2/3; 4 in E flat, Op. 7; 27 in E min., Op. 90

▣— →⃝ **(BB)** **** Regis (ADD) RRC 1185. S. Richter

A superb disc which, at Regis price, ought to be in every collection, if only for the inspired and very beautful account of the rapt slow movement of Op. 2/3 and the rippling finale of Op. 90, which all but smiles. But all three performances are masterly in their control of structure and intensity, and none sounds either early or immature, just great Beethoven.

Piano Sonatas 3; 29 (Hammerklavier); 6 Bagatelles, Op. 126

▣—⃝ **(M)** (***) BBC (ADD) BBCL 4052-2. S. Richter

Sviatoslav Richter's opening of the *Hammerklavier* explodes like some galactic force, and the intensity and fire of the performance carries all before it. There is tremendous spontaneity as well as a magnificence about it. Unusually for Richter, he does not repeat the exposition in the first movement of Op. 2, No. 3. Both this piece and the *Bagatelles* complete a memorable musical occasion, which fortunately escaped oblivion in the BBC Archives. Very acceptable sound.

Piano Sonatas 3 in C, Op. 2/3; 32 in C min., Op. 111

*** Opus Arte **DVD** OA 0939D. Michelangeli – GALUPPI; SCARLATTI: *Sonatas* ***

These magisterial performances come from the Archives of RAI (Italian Radio-TV) and derive from a 1962 recital given in Turin. The playing is of the utmost elegance and refinement, and there is a cool poise that is totally appropriate to the early *C major Sonata* but less so to Op. 111. Marvellous pianism in terms of range and colour, and something to wonder at rather than to be involved by. Unobtrusive camerawork. Though the black-and-white image is not always sharp in focus, **Michelangeli** is totally compelling.

Piano Sonatas 4; 13 in E flat, Op. 27/1; 19–20, Op. 49/1–2; 22 in F, Op. 54

(BB) **(*) Naxos 8.550167. Jandó

The performances of both the *E flat Sonata*, Op. 7, and the *Sonata quasi una fantasia*, Op. 27/1, in which **Jandó** is totally responsive to Beethoven's wide expressive range, show the excellence of this series, and the three shorter works are also freshly presented.

Piano Sonatas 5–7, Op. 10/1–3; 8 (Pathétique)

**(*) DG 474 810-2. Pollini

These accounts of the Op. 10 set and the *Pathétique* offer the superb pianism and intelligence which **Pollini's** admirers rightly treasure. But, as with other recent Beethoven from this artist, they remain for us curiously uninvolving. Excellent sound.

Piano Sonata 7; Eroica Variations

(N) **(*) BBC Legends mono BBCL 4250-2. Gilels (with SCRIABIN: *Etudes*; RAVEL: *Jeux d'eau, Alborada del gracioso*)

This recital by **Emil Gilels**, recorded live by the BBC from Cheltenham in October 1950, gives a wider view of this great Soviet pianist than most of his commercial recordings, with the quirkiness of the finale of the Beethoven and the wit of Ravel's *Alborada del gracioso* deliciously brought out. Good broadcast sound.

Piano Sonatas 8 (Pathétique); 14 (Moonlight); 15 (Pastoral); 17 (Tempest); 21 (Waldstein); 23 (Appassionata); 26 (Les Adieux)

(B) *** Ph. (ADD) Duo 438 730-2 (2). Brendel

(B) *** Double Decca (ADD) 452 952-2 (2). Ashkenazy

All the performances here are taken from **Brendel's** analogue cycle for Philips; they are impressive and the recording is consistently excellent. The *Tempest*, Op. 31/2, is finely conceived and thoroughly compelling, and the central movements of the *Pastoral* resonate in the memory. Outstanding too is Brendel's account of the *Waldstein*.

The comparable Decca collection of named sonatas shows **Ashkenazy** consistently as a penetrating and individual Beethovenian. The *Moonlight* is poetic and unforced, and he brings concentration together with spontaneity of feeling to the *Tempest*, with an impressive command of keyboard colour. Taking a broadly lyrical view, the *Waldstein* is splendidly structured, and the *Appassionata* is superb. The very good analogue recordings are excellently transferred to CD.

Piano Sonatas 8 (Pathétique); 14 (Moonlight); 15 (Pastoral); 17 (Tempest); 21 (Waldstein); 23 (Appassionata); 26 (Les Adieux); 29 (Hammerklavier): 31, Op. 110; 32, Op. 111

(N) **(B)** **** EMI 2 15314-2 (3) Kovacevich

A self-recommending collection taken from **Kovacevich's** cycle. Returning to these performances one is all but surprised how compelling is the experience they provide. Playing of stature, excellent EMI recording, remarkable value.

Piano Sonatas 8 (Pathétique); 14 (Moonlight); 23 (Appassionata)

(BB) **(*) Naxos 8.550045. Jandó

Jandó's clean, direct style and natural spontaneity are particularly admirable in the slow movements of the *Pathétique* and *Appassionata*, warmly lyrical in feeling, yet not a whit sentimental. Only in the coda of the finale of the *Appassionata* does one feel a loss of poise, when the closing *presto* becomes *prestissimo* and the exuberance of the music-making nearly gets out of control.

Piano Sonatas 8 (Pathétique); 14 (Moonlight); 23 (Appassionata); 26 (Les Adieux)

▣—❀ **(M)** **** RCA (ADD) **SACD** 82876 71619-2. Rubinstein

(M) **(*) Sony (ADD) 5174812. Serkin

Artur Rubinstein had never recorded the *Moonlight* previously, and he brings to it a combination of freshness and maturity to make it stand out even among many fine recorded versions, with an improvisatory feel to the opening movement which is unforgettable and which also extends to the performance of *Les Adieux*, which is hardly less magical. The *Pathétique* has a youthful urgency in the outer movements, and the simplicity of the *Adagio cantabile* brings a wonderfully sustained sense of spiritual peace, while the impulsive surge of feeling in the *Appassionata* is equally compelling. The recordings, made in the Manhattan Center in New York City in 1962 and 1963, have been superbly remastered by John Newton from the original three-track source, and this compatible SACD brings a remarkable sense of realism and presence, and is firmer in the bass than on LP.

Rudolf Serkin's aristocratic approach is immediately apparent at the opening of the *Moonlight Sonata*, and in the *Allegro* he is as incisive and dramatic as ever. As with all master pianists, one finds many points of insight emerging as well as one or two points of personal mannerism. The studio recording dates from December 1962 and the *Les Adieux Sonata*, added for the present reissue, was recorded in Carnegie Hall exactly 15 years later. The present transfers are firmer and more real than in the original LP incarnations, although, surprisingly, the effect is drier in the concert hall than in the studio.

Piano Sonatas 8 (Pathétique); 15 (Pastoral); 27 in E min, Op. 90; 30 in E, Op. 109

*** EMI 3 94422-2. Biss

Jonathan Biss's début CD of the *Appassionata* and Schumann's *Davidsbündlertänze* was very impressive. This newcomer is hardly less successful. The young American pianist is a serious artist, with intelligence and fine musicianship to commend him.

Piano Sonatas 8 (Pathétique); 19; 20 (Hammerklavier)

🎵 *** Naïve V 3023. Guy

Of the many rival versions of the *Hammerklavier*, this one from **François-Frédéric Guy** was chosen as the finest of all on BBC Radio 3's *Record Review*, a well-deserved tribute. The intensity of the playing is formidable, with speeds very well chosen and maintained, and with textures clarified. The *Pathétique Sonata* and the tiny *G minor*, Op. 49/2, make a welcome and generous supplement.

Piano sonatas 8 in C min. (Pathétique); 23 (Appassionata); 31 in A flat, Op. 110

🎵 ✦ (M) *** DG (DDD/ADD) 476 2194. Gilels

If the *Pathétique* does not rank among **Emil Gilels's** very finest Beethoven performances on record, such are the strengths of his playing that the reading still leaves a profound impression. The account of the *Appassionata* has previously been hailed by us as among the finest ever made, and the 1973 analogue recording is both full and believably present. Op. 110 is given a performance of real stature. Even when Gilels storms the greatest heights in the closing fugue, no *fortissimo* ever sounds percussive or strained. The *Pathétique* and Op. 110 are truthful digital recordings, both made in the Berlin Jesus-Christus-Kirche; the *Pathétique*, made in 1980,

has the microphones a bit close, but in No. 31 (dating from five years later) the balance is better judged. An outstanding bargain, all the same.

Piano Sonatas 9–10, Op. 14/1–2

(M) (***) BBC mono BBCL 4126-2. Sviatoslav Richter (with CHOPIN: *Etude in F sharp min., Op. 10/4*) – SCHUBERT: *Wanderer Fantasy* (***); SCHUMANN: *Abegg Variations, Op. 1; Faschingsschwank aus Wien* (**)

The two Op. 14 *Sonatas* come from a festival recital in February 1963, two years after **Richter's** first concert appearances in the West (he had already recorded them commercially for Philips). His very deliberate pace for the *Allegretto* movement of the *E major* lends it a reflective, almost melancholy character, which is unusual, but (as always with this great artist) his readings are the product of much thought. The mono sound is perfectly acceptable.

Piano Sonatas 9–10; 24, Op. 78; 27, Op. 90; 28, Op. 101

(BB) *** Naxos 8.550162. Jandó

Opp. 90 and 101 show this artist at full stretch. These are demanding works and **Jandó** does not fall short, particularly in the eloquent slow movements. The piano-sound is most believable.

Piano Sonatas 10, Op. 14/2; 19–20, Op. 49/1–2

(M) *** Ph. (ADD) 464 710-2 (2). S. Richter – LISZT: *Piano Concertos 1–2* ***

These three sonatas (sonatinas in all but name) are among those works that most budding amateur pianists have tried to play. **Richter** presents them with disarming ease and simplicity, and with the utmost eloquence. He is beautifully recorded (in 1963), but this was a curious coupling for his famous versions of the Liszt *Concertos* with Kondrashin, dating from two years earlier, which also had a London venue.

Piano Sonatas 11–12; 19–20

*** Chan. 9755. Lortie

Performances of vital and unfailing intelligence which make one think afresh about the music itself. What we have heard so far of **Louis Lortie's** Beethoven odyssey makes one feel that it is worth placing alongside Stephen Kovacevich's sonata cycle on EMI; it is certainly not inferior to it. The Chandos recording is state of the art and wonderfully natural. A most distinguished issue.

Piano Sonatas 11, Op. 22; 29 (Hammerklavier)

(BB) **(*) Naxos 8.550234. Jandó

Piano Sonatas 12, Op. 26; 16 & 18, Op. 31/1 & 3

(BB) **(*) Naxos 8.550166. Jandó

Jandó's trio of middle-period sonatas can be recommended with few reservations. No. 18 is a considerable success, and there is much to stimulate the listener's interest here. Excellent sound. From its very opening bars, the *Hammerklavier* is commanding; there is rapt concentration in the slow movement, and the closing fugue runs its course with a powerful inevitability. Again, most realistic recording.

Piano Sonatas 14 (Moonlight); 21 (Waldstein); 23 (Appassionata)

(B) *** Virgin 3 63280-2. Pletnev

(M) **(*) Sony (ADD) 827969274422. Horowitz (with *Sonata 8 Pathétique* excerpts: 1st and 2nd movements only)

Some will find the **Pletnev** *Moonlight* rather mannered, but he has the capacity to make you listen intently, and he finds the right depths in the slow movement and finale of the *Waldstein*. The account of the *Appassionata* is masterly. The engineering is immaculate. A fine bargain reissue.

In his 1972 Sony/CBS recording of the *Moonlight Sonata*, **Horowitz** takes the first movement faster than he did on his earlier 1956 RCA account and the result is undoubtedly less poetic. The other works on the Sony disc are much more successful, with the finale of the *Waldstein* magically introduced and the *Appassionata* very powerful. This extends to the bonus of the 1963 excerpts from the *Pathétique Sonata*, which are equally impressive. No explanation is given for the omission of the finale.

Piano Sonatas 15–18; 30–2

(M) (**) Sony mono 874645263823 (3). Gould

'Wilful yet charismatic' is a phrase to which many have recourse whenever **Glenn Gould's** name is mentioned. There are no doubts as to his pianism or control or the quality of his musicianship; but his late Beethoven, for all its intelligence, is quirky and marred by his vocal contributions. It can be recommended only to his admirers.

Piano Sonatas: 15 (Pastoral); (Kurfürstensonaten) in E flat, F min., D, WoO 47/1–3; in C (incomplete), WoO 51; Sonatinas: in G, F, Anh. 5/1–2

(BB) **(*) Naxos 8.550255. Jandó

Jenö Jandó's playing is fresh, clean and intelligent and, if the two *Sonatinas* are not authentic, they make agreeable listening here. The *Pastoral Sonata* is admirably done.

Piano Sonatas 16–17 (Tempest); 18, Op. 31/1–3

⊕┐ *** Chan. 9842. Lortie

Louis Lortie's ongoing Beethoven sonata cycle is second only to Stephen Kovacevich's magisterial cycle on EMI, and in some instances (thanks to the quality of the Snape recording) it is every bit as fine. Lortie's playing is tremendously alive and vibrant, and the vivid nature of the sound makes for supremely satisfying listening.

Piano Sonata 17 (Tempest)

⊕┐ ✿ (BB) *** EMI (ADD) Gemini 5 86543-2 (2). Sviatoslav Richter – HANDEL: *Suites 9–16* *** ✿

Richter makes the most of possibilities of contrast. He plays the opening extremely slowly and then, when the *Allegro* comes, he takes it unusually fast. Far from being odd, this effect is breathtaking. Excellent Abbey Road sound, and a bargain price.

Piano Sonatas 17 (Tempest); 21 (Waldstein); 26 (Les Adieux)

(BB) **(*) Naxos 8.550054. Jandó

Jenö Jandó offers here three famous named sonatas, and very enjoyable they are in their direct manner.

Piano Sonatas 17 in D (Tempest), Op. 31/2; 31 in A flat, Op. 110

(*) EuroArts Callico Classics CCCR 101. Jill Crossland – MOZART: *Sonata in F* *

Jill Crossland is a new name to be reckoned with. A highly individual player, thoughtful yet compelling, she has the gift of spontaneity in the recording studio to carry the personal insights of her interpretations, as at a live performance. Her account of the *Adagio* of the 'Tempest' *Sonata* is wonderfully lyrical, and the delicacy of the finale equally persuasive. The following performance of Opus 110 is undoubtedly very wayward, but her strength of commitment is always convincing. She is very well recorded.

Piano Sonatas 21–5; 27; 30–2

(M) (***) EMI mono 5 62880-2 (2). Schnabel

Piano Sonatas 22–26

(BB) (***) Naxos mono 8.110761. Schnabel

These classic accounts have rarely been out of the catalogue. Keith Hardwick's 1991 transfers of the eight-CD EMI Références set have been replaced by new ones by Andrew Walter which have considerably more freshness, smoothness and transparency. There are some marvellous things, including a magnificent *Waldstein* and the final Opp. 109–111, which have arguably never been surpassed since they were made in 1932. The Naxos transfers are hardly less fine.

Piano Sonatas 25; 32

*** Orfeo C 612031. Nikolaieva (with SHOSTAKOVICH: 4 *Preludes & Fugues, Op. 87*) – BACH: *French Suite 4*, etc. ***

An Austrian Radio recording by **Tatiana Nikolaieva**, for whom Shostakovich wrote his *Preludes and Fugues*, Op. 87. Nikolaieva was a great pianist and her musical insights matched her technical mastery. A searching performance of Op. 111 and a bonus of four Shostakovich *Preludes and Fugues*.

Piano Sonatas 26 (Les Adieux); 29 (Hammerklavier); Bagatelles, Op. 119

(B) **** EMI 2 28515-2. Kovacevich

Stephen Kovacevich opens the *Hammerklavier*, like Schnabel, with an urgent, impatient forward momentum, as if to show Beethoven's ideas straining at the leash and attempting to transcend the constraints of the medium. The slow movement has a depth and imagination that only the greatest interpretations can rival. This is arguably the finest *Hammerklavier* since Gilels and it has the advantage of excellent recorded sound. The *Bagatelles*, Op. 119, and the *Les Adieux Sonata* are worthy companions.

Piano Sonatas 27–8; 29 (Hammerklavier)

(BB) **(*) Regis (ADD) RRC 1205. Brendel

(BB) (***) Naxos mono 8.110762. Schnabel

Brendel's early Vox/Turnabout recordings make for another enterprising budget reissue on Regis. Brendel's first movement of Op. 101 is disappointingly underplayed, but there is much more *Innigkeit* in the wayward and elusive opening movement of Op. 90, and a smoothly flowing reading of the haunting second movement. The *Hammerklavier* is another matter. The concentration and sense of drama in the first movement are most striking, and only the comparatively un-hushed reading of the slow movement – taken on the fast side – mars the interpretation.

The Naxos transfers of **Schnabel's** recordings are of a very high standard. Comparing Mark Obert-Thorn's transfer of the *E minor Sonata*, Op. 90, with Andrew Walter's is instructive. Walter favours a rather forward sound and a much higher level, while the Naxos is relatively recessed and in some ways does greater justice to the tonal subtlety of Schnabel's playing. The *Hammerklavier*, not included in the EMI set, is perhaps the least technically successful of Schnabel's Sonata Society records, though there are wonderful insights in the slow movement.

Piano Sonatas 27, Op. 90; 28, Op. 101; 29 (Hammerklavier); 30, Op. 109; 31, Op. 110; 32, Op. 111

●–• ✹ (B) *** DG Double (ADD) 453 010-2 (2). Kempff

●–• (B) *** Ph. (ADD) Duo 438 374-2 (2). Brendel

Kempff has never been more inspirationally revealing than in these performances of the last six Beethoven sonatas. These are all great performances, and the remastered recordings have been enhanced to an extraordinary degree, to give an uncannily realistic piano-image, helped by the immediacy of Kempff's communication.

Brendel's set is among the most distinguished Beethoven playing of the analogue era. The recordings, made in the 1970s, are most realistic and satisfying in the CD transfers. The documentation too is first rate.

Piano Sonata 28 in A, Op. 101; (i) String Quartet 12 in E flat, Op. 127 (trans. Marrion)

**(*) Sony SK93043. Perahia, (i) with ASMF

Perahia's reading of Op. 101 does not fall short of the highest expectations. Indeed it is one of his most perfect recordings, immaculate in delivery and flawless in musical judgement. He leaves you feeling that there is no other way of playing this work. However, the coupling is more controversial, even though there are precedents. Decent playing, though intonation in the Trio of the Scherzo is problematic on occasion. But Op. 101 is exceptional.

Piano Sonatas 28, Op. 101; 29 (Hammerklavier)

●–• (M) **** DG (ADD) 463 639-2. Gilels

Gilels is at his most inspired in both sonatas, playing with the sort of rapt concentration that makes one forget that

these are not live performances. His *Hammerklavier* is a reading of supreme integrity. Olympian, subtle, imperious, one of the finest ever recorded. However, allowances have to be made for the digital recording, which is close and bright and harder than is ideal. The more elusive Op. 101 is also given a superb reading, with a deeply expressive first movement and *Adagio* before the contrapuntal finale. Here the analogue recording of a decade earlier is first rate and very well transferred.

Piano Sonatas 28–9 (Hammerklavier); 30–2

(B) *** Ph. Duo (ADD) 468 912-2 (2). Arrau

(M) **(*) DG 449 740-2 (2). Pollini

Claudio Arrau's famous *Hammerklavier* is particularly impressive, one of the triumphs of the cycle (Richard Osborne called it 'a torrential performance in full Niagaran spate'). Its middle movement is particularly searching. As always, the Arrau sonority is sumptuous, and the Philips recording still sounds pretty magnificent.

Pollini's recordings of the late sonatas, which won the 1977 *Gramophone* critics' award for instrumental music, contain playing of the highest mastery. The remastering for reissue as a DG 'Original' has brought no marked improvement, but the two discs are now packaged like a DG Double and are offered at a special price.

Piano Sonata 28 in A, Op. 101

(M) *** Wigmore Hall Live WHL018. Cooper (with DEBUSSY: *La terrasse des audiences du clair de Lune*; MOZART: *Sonata in A min., K.310*) – RAVEL: *Miroirs etc.* ***

It is puzzling that **Imogen Cooper** has been so neglected by the record companies, and so it is all the more gratifying to have this Wigmore recital from February 2007. Her account of the *A major Sonata*, Op. 101, is expertly paced and beautifully shaped; in short, it is one of the finest currently before the public, and the remainder of the programme is hardly less impressive. (Some may find her rubato in the slow movement of the Mozart a little excessive.) This issue offers some very distinguished and satisfying music-making. Good sound, too.

Piano Sonata 29 (Hammerklavier); Bagatelles, Op. 126/2 & 3

*** EMI **DVD** 4 901239. Alfred Brendel (with SCHUBERT: *Wanderer Fantasy*; Julius Katchen)

Brendel's DVD, in black and white, was made in Paris in February 1970 and offers a rare opportunity to see as well as hear him. He puts the listener immediately under his spell and proves (as ever) a dedicated and faithful guide. The bonus is a rare telerecording from ORTF of Julius Katchen playing the *Wanderer Fantasy* in the last months before his death.

Piano Sonatas 29 (Hammerklavier) Op. 106; 30 in E, Op. 109; 31 in A flat, Op. 101; 32 in C min., Op. 111; 6 Bagatelles, Op. 126

●–• ✹ (BB) *** EMI Gemini (ADD) 5 85499-2 (2). Eschenbach

Christoph Eschenbach recorded the *Hammerklavier Sonata* in 1979 for EMI at the Abbey Road Studios along with Opp. 109, 110 and 111 and the *Six Bagatelles*, Op. 126. The Op. 111 is among the most concentrated, powerfully conceived and sensitive realizations of the score currently before the public, and the *Hammerklavier* is no less magisterial and commanding. Listening to Beethoven playing of this quality is a wonderfully satisfying experience. These are readings of great musical insight that have the strengths of a master pianist combined with the wisdom of a great musician. The recorded sound is very present and lifelike.

Piano Sonatas 30 in E flat, Op. 109; 31 in A flat, Op. 110; 32 in C min., Op. 111

*** Ph. 446 701-2. Brendel

Brendel's performances are searching and concentrated. They draw one into Beethoven's world immediately, with an eloquence that is all the more potent for being selfless. The recordings, made at the Henry Wood Hall and at The Maltings, Snape, are excellent, real and full of presence.

The last three sonatas of Beethoven, offered in Naxos's Volume 4, are very imposing indeed in **Jandó's** hands. There is serenity and gravitas in these readings and a powerful control of structure. (Naxos 8.550151)

Piano Sonatas 31, Op. 110; 32, Op. 111; Bagatelles, Op. 126/5 & 6

*** EMI **DVD** 3 314949-2. Stephen Kovacevich

Beethoven's last two piano sonatas have inspired **Stephen Kovacevich** for many years to some of the most dedicated pianism imaginable. Here, in a DVD recorded in August 2004 at La Roque d'Antheron, one can visually witness the depth of his concentration, adding to the intensity of the experience. These are not just thoughtful readings but powerful ones, notably in the first movement of Opus 111. Some may find the camerawork distracting when, quite frequently, the pianist's hands are made to fill the whole screen, but that is a minor distraction.

Miscellaneous piano music

Allegretto in C min., WoO 53; Allegretto, WoO 61; Allegretto quasi andante, WoO 61; Bagatelles, WoO 52 & 56; in B flat, WoO 60; in C; 2 Bagatelles; Für Elise, WoO 59; 12 German Dances, WoO 8; 7 Ländler, WoO 11; 6 Ländler, WoO 15; Minuet in C; 6 Minuets, WoO 10

(BB) **(*) Naxos 8.553795. Jandó

Allegretto in C min., H.69; Bagatelle in C (Lustig-Traurig), WoO 54; Fantasia, Op. 77; 12 German Dances, WoO 13; 7 Contredanses, WoO 14; 6 Ecossaises, WoO 83; Fugue in C, H.64; Minuet in E flat, WoO 82; Polonaise in C, Op. 89; 2 Preludes, Op. 39; Prelude in F min., WoO 55; (Concerto) Rondo in C, WoO 48; (Concerto) Finale in C, H.65

(BB) **(*) Naxos 8.553798. Jandó

It is always a joy to witness Beethoven relaxing. These collections of shorter piano pieces may offer no great music, but they have a freshness and vitality that is an endless delight. **Jenö Jandó** is at his finest in the two *C minor Allegrettos* and the *C major Rondo*. He opens the second disc with an appropriately impulsive and enjoyable account of the Op. 77 *Fantasia*. Elsewhere his clear, direct manner certainly evokes the spirit of Beethoven. The set of six *Ecossaises* (in essence, contredanses, and little to do with Scotland) are rhythmically very jolly and emerge as an exhilarating offering. The two *Preludes*, Op. 39, modulating through all the major keys in turn, have their fascination too. With playing fresh and clear, this is for the most part a delightful supplement to Jandó's cycle of Beethoven sonatas for Naxos.

Andante favori, WoO 57; 2 German Dances, Hess 67; 12 Minuets, WoO 7; Rondo in A, WoO 49; 2 Rondos, Op. 51/1 & 2; Rondo a capriccio in G, Op. 129

(BB) *** Naxos 8.553799. Jandó

With such lightweight items as the two *German Dances* and the *Twelve Minuets* **Jandó's** fresh, alert manner unobtrusively enhances their charms alongside equally winning performances of the headlong *Rage over a Lost Penny* and the substantial set of variations, *Andante favori*, that Beethoven originally intended as a middle movement for the *Waldstein Sonata*. Excellent sound.

Andante favori, WoO 57; Bagatelles, Opp. 33, 119; WoO 52; C, WoO 56; 6 Minuets, WoO 10; Rondos: 1, 2, Op. 51; WoO 48; WoO 49; 6 Variations on an Original Theme, Op. 34; 9 Variations on a March by Dressler, WoO 63; Variations on a Swiss Song, WoO 64; 24 Variations on Righini's 'Venni Amore', WoO 65; 12 Variations on Haibel's 'Menuet à la Viganò'; 6 Variations on Paisiello's 'Nel cor più non mi sento', WoO 70

⊕—*** DG 457 493-2 (2). Pletnev

These performances are articulated with characteristic mastery and clarity, with no nuance of phrasing or dynamic left unobserved. **Pletnev** always makes an individual sound and brings his own special insights to bear on this repertoire. The sound is very clean and well focused.

7 Bagatelles, Op. 33; 11 Bagatelles, Op. 119; 6 Bagatelles, Op. 126

(BB) **(*) Naxos 8.550474. Jenö Jandó

Bagatelles, Opp. 33; 119; 126; WoO 52 & 56

*** Chan. 9201. John Lill

John Lill characteristically takes a serious view of these miniatures, bringing out their relationship to some of the full masterpieces.

Jandó plays with a crisply rhythmic style, almost at times as if he were thinking of a fortepiano. Then, in the later works, he finds more depth of tone and is thoughtful as well as flamboyant. He is given an excellent, modern, digital recording.

*7 Bagatelles, Op. 33; 6 Bagatelles, Op. 126; 6
Variations in F, Op. 34; 15 Variations with Fugue in
E flat (Eroica), Op. 35; 32 Variations on an Original
Theme in C min., WoO 80*

(M) **(*) Sony (ADD) SM2K 52646 (2). Gould

*6 Bagatelles, Op. 126; Polonaise in C, Op. 89;
Variations & Fugue on a Theme from 'Prometheus'
(Eroica Variations), Op. 35*

*** Nim. NIM 5017. Roberts

Bernard Roberts gives a characteristically fresh and forthright reading of the *Eroica Variations*, recorded in exceptionally vivid sound. He may not have quite the flair of
Brendel, but the crispness and clarity of his playing are
most refreshing. The shorter pieces bring performances
even more intense, with the *Bagatelles* – for all their brevity
– given last-period intensity.

Glenn Gould's *Bagatelles* and *Variations* are better and
less quirky than his Beethoven piano sonatas, which are not
competitive. Gould fanatics can invest in them; others who
are not converted can be assured that any eccentricity is positive and thought-provoking. Not a first choice but deserving
of a place in the catalogue.

*Bagatelles, Op. 33; in A min. (Für Elise), WoO 59;
Fantasia in G min., Op. 77; Minuet in E flat, WoO
82; Rondo in A, WoO 49; 6 Variations on an
Original Theme in F, Op. 34; 15 Variations & Fugue
on a Theme from Prometheus (Eroica), Op. 35*

(BB)(***) Naxos mono 8.110764. Schnabel

These pieces are played by **Schnabel** with a refreshing simplicity: the way he presents the *Original Theme* of Op. 34 is
extraordinarily apt, and there is a remarkable amalgam of
drama and classicism in the *Eroica Variations* that is totally
compelling. Mark Obert-Thorn's transfers of the 1937–8
Abbey Road recordings are as satisfying as ever.

*Bagatelles, Op. 126; Rondo a capriccio, Op. 129; 33
Variations on a Waltz by Diabelli*

🌑 (BB)(***) Naxos mono 8.110765. Schnabel

Schnabel's account of the *Diabelli Variations* was made in the
1930s. It has never been surpassed, although there have been
readings which have come some of the way close to approaching it (Horszowski, Kovacevich, Brendel and, more
recently, Piotr Anderszewski). But there is a special authority
and wisdom here, and this set should be in every collector's
library.

*6 Variations, Op. 34; 6 Variations on 'Nel cor più
non mi sento', WoO 70; 15 Variations & Fugue on a
Theme from 'Prometheus' (Eroica Variations), Op.
35; 32 Variations, WoO 80*

(BB) **(*) Naxos 8.550676. Jandó

*6 Variations, Op. 34; 15 Variations & Fugue on a
Theme from 'Prometheus' (Eroica Variations), Op.
35; 2 Rondos, Op. 51; Bagatelle: Für Elise, WoO 59*

🎧 *** Chan. 8616. Lortie

Louis Lortie's readings have both grandeur and authority.
This account of the *Eroica Variations* belongs in exalted company and can be recommended alongside such magisterial
accounts as that of Gilels.

Jenö Jandó essays the same strong, direct style in his performances of the two major sets of variations as he does in
the sonatas. Occasionally his forceful manner in Op. 35 and
the *C minor Variations* reaches the point of brusqueness, but
no one could deny the strength of his playing. His approach
is appropriately lighter in Op. 34. Excellent recording, clear
and vivid.

33 Variations on a Waltz by Diabelli, Op. 120

(N) 🎧 **** Onyx 4035. Kovacevich – BACH: *Partita 4,
BWV828* ****

🎧 (B) **** Virgin 5 03406-2. Anderszewski

Stephen Kovacevich first recorded the *Diabelli Variations* in
1968 and his version (available on Philips 475 7556) long
reigned supreme. Forty years and much experience (including recording the thirty-two sonatas and the concertos) separate it from this newcomer. Nothing this artist does is less
than compelling and this masterly newcomer enriches his
discography with its sweep and control, and depth of feeling.
This is balm for the soul.

Piotr Anderszewski's Wigmore performance of the
Diabelli excited rave reviews and this searching and finely
recorded account is also outstanding, most thoughtful and
impressively played.

On Philips **Alfred Brendel**, here working in the studio,
captures the music's dynamism, the sense of an irresistible
force building up this immense structure, section by section.
It would be hard to imagine a more dramatic reading,
sparked off by the cheeky wit of Brendel's treatment of the
Diabelli theme itself. The whirlwind power of the whole performance is irresistible, and the piano-sound is full and immediate. (Ph. 426 232-2)

*33 Variations on a Waltz by Diabelli, Op. 120; 32
Variations on an Original Theme in C min., WoO
80*

🎧 (BB) *** ASV Resonance CD RSN 3058. Frith

Benjamin Frith brings out both the rhythmic urgency and
power of the *Diabelli Variations*, playing with a consistent
sense of spontaneity, persuasively leading on from one
variation to the next and bringing magnetic intensity to
the meditative variations. He then takes the great fugue
just before the end of the work at a sensible speed that allows him to spring the rhythms and shape it effectively,
rounding off the work with a crisply pointed account of
the final Minuet which keeps in mind its dance origin. He
follows with a masterly account of the 32 *Variations in C
minor*, in which flamboyant virtuosity and poetry are well
contrasted. Good, bright piano-sound, set in a helpfully
warm acoustic.

VOCAL MUSIC

Adelaide; An die ferne Geliebte, Op. 98; An die Geliebte; An die Hoffnung; Aus Goethes Faust; Klage; Der Liebende; Das Liedchen von der Ruhe; 6 Lieder aus Gellert; Mailied; Neue Liebe, neues Leben; Sehnsucht; Wonne der Wehmut

*** Hyp. CDA 67055. Genz, Vignoles

The German baritone **Stephan Genz** not only has a voice of warm, velvety beauty, but he already shows a rare depth of understanding. In the very first song here, *An die Hoffnung* ('To Hope') – Beethoven's response to suffering – he sings with rapt concentration, using the widest range of expression, while songs like *Adelaide* bring out his honeyed tone, allied to flawless legato. That contrasts with the youthful energy of the brisk songs and the biting irony of Goethe's *Song of the Flea*, taken very fast. A disc to have one reassessing Beethoven as songwriter, with the mould-breaking cycle, *An die ferne Geliebte*, as a fine climax.

Adelaide; Der Kuss; Resignation; Zärtliche Liebe

(M) *** DG (ADD) 449 747-2. Wunderlich, Giesen – SCHUBERT: *Lieder*; SCHUMANN: *Dichterliebe* ***

Wunderlich was 35 when he recorded these songs, and the unique bloom of the lovely voice is beautifully caught. Though the accompanist is too metrical at times, the freshness of Wunderlich's singing makes one grieve again over his untimely death.

Ah, perfido, Op. 65; Fidelio: Abscheulicher!

(N) (BB) (***) Naxos mono 8 111287. Schwarzkopf, Philh. O, Karajan – SCHUBERT: *Lieder* (***)

Schwarzkopf's celebrated performances with **Karajan** date from 1954 and make a fine bonus for her early Schubert recital with Edwin Fischer.

(i–iv) Cantata on the Death of Emperor Joseph II, WoO 87; (ii–v) Cantata on the Accession of Emperor Leopold II, WoO 88. Meeresstille und glückliche Fahrt, Op. 112; (ii) Opferlied

⊕— ✸ *** Hyp. CDA 66880. (i) Watson; (ii) Rigby; (iii) Mark Ainsley; (iv) van Dam; (v) Howarth; Corydon Singers & O, Best

Arguably Beethoven's first major masterpiece, WoO 87 was one of the few early, unpublished works of which he approved: when he came to write *Fidelio* he used the soaring theme from the first of the cantata's soprano arias for Leonore's sublime moment in the finale, *O Gott! Welch ein Augenblick*. The aria is sung radiantly here by **Janice Watson**. Relishing the tragic C minor power of the choruses, **Matthew Best** conducts a superb performance, incisive and deeply moving, with excellent soloists as well as a fine chorus. The second cantata, much shorter, written soon afterwards, brings anticipations of the *Fifth Symphony* and of the choral finale of the *Ninth*, while the two shorter pieces – with **Jean Rigby** as soloist in the *Opferlied* – make a generous fill-up, equally well performed. The atmospheric recording combines weight and transparency.

(i) Cantata on the Death of Joseph II; (ii) Mass in C Op. 86

(N) *** Accord 480 0793. Radio Lettone Ch, Montpellier National Orch, Friedmann Layer with (i) Ptasseek, Davidchuka, Soulis, Antoun, Burmester; (ii) Komocar, Gubish, Salens, Wilde

On this Accord disc the **Lettone Radio Choir** give a fresh, incisive performance, the more compelling for being recorded live, and the soprano, **Cornelia Ptasseek**, brings out the 'gulp' quality in the great sublime theme in its build-up in triple time. The *Mass* is fully the equal of Haydn's late Masses. The performance under Friedmann Layer has the same positive qualities as the Cantata under the same conductor, and though the mezzo falls short of the other soloists, the singing of choir and soloists alike is excellent. The live recordings are generally first-rate, even if the inclusion of applause at the end of each work tends to be intrusive. An exceptionally generous coupling at almost exactly 80 minutes. A credit to Accord, a French subsidiary of Universal.

Che fa il mio bene? (2 versions); Dimmi, ben mio; Ecco quel fiero istante!; In questa tomba oscura; La partenza; T'intendo, si, mio cor

*** Decca 440 297-2. Bartoli, A. Schiff – HAYDN: *Arianna a Naxos*; MOZART: *Ridente la calma*; SCHUBERT: *Da quel sembiante appresi*, etc. ***

These rare Italian songs come as part of a recital which has an outstanding account of Haydn's *Arianna a Naxos* as its highlight. *La partenza* has a winningly ingenuous simplicity and the *Ariettas* (including two completely contrasting settings of *Che fa il mio bene?*) are also full of charm.

Mass in C, Op. 86; Cantatas: Elegischer Gesang, Op. 118; Meeresstille und glückliche Fahrt, Op. 112

⊕— *** Chan. 0703. Evans, Stephen, Padmore, Varcoe, Coll. Mus. 90, Hickox

(i) Mass in C, Op. 86; Meeresstille und glückliche Fahrt (Calm Sea and a Prosperous Voyage), Op. 112

⊕— *** DG 435 391-2. Margiono, Robbin, Kendall, Miles, Monteverdi Ch., ORR, Gardiner

Beethoven's *Mass* was initially a failure. Yet **Hickox** consistently brings out the joy of the inspiration, with excellent soloists and a fresh-toned choir, and directs similarly concentrated readings of two brief choral works of 1814, the fine Goethe setting, *Meeresstille und glückliche Fahrt*, and the simple but deeply felt *Elegiac Song* (not offered by Gardiner), which come as welcome couplings.

In this long-underrated masterpiece, **Gardiner** gives just as refreshing a performance as his earlier, prize-winning account of the *Missa solemnis*. Aptly clear-toned soloists match the freshness of the **Monteverdi Choir**. As an imaginatively chosen coupling Gardiner offers the dramatic soprano scena, *Ah! perfido*, with **Charlotte Margiono** as soloist, and the brief choral cantata, *Meeresstille und glückliche Fahrt*.

Mass in C; Fidelio: Prisoners' Chorus

(N) (M) LSO Live SACD LSO 0594. Matthews, Mingardo, Ainslie, Miles, LSO Ch & O, Colin Davis

The LSO Live performance is more vigorous and intense, less heavy, than Davis's previous version. The singing of the **LSO Chorus** is incandescent from beginning to end, with high dynamic contrasts, so that the *fortissimos* hit the ear thrillingly, and the engineers have here managed to get a good clear and open sound in the notoriously difficult Barbican acoustic. The *Gloria* opens with exhilarating attack, and so does the *Credo*, with dramatic contrasts for such intimate passages as the *Et incarnatus est* (with its clarinet solo) and with the *Et resurrexit* introduced not by the full chorus but by the bass, **Alistair Miles** in glorious voice. The soloists make a first-rate team, with the soprano, **Sally Matthews** and the mezzo, **Sarah Mingardo** both excellent, and though the tenor, **John Mark Ainslie**, is not as sweet-toned as once he was, he sings sensitively with clean focus.

(i) Mass in C, Op. 86; (ii) Missa solemnis in D, Op. 123

(N) (BB) ** EMI Gemini (ADD) 5 17664-2 (2) New Philh. Ch., with (i) Harper, (i; ii) Janet Baker, Tear, Sotin; (ii) Ameling, Altmeyer, Rintzler; (i) New Phil. O; (ii) LPO, Giulini 1971, 1976

Giulini recorded Beethoven's two masses six years apart, in 1971 and 1976. The performance of the C major work is by far the finer of the two, inspired, polished and intense, with a fine quartet of soloists and a superb choir. Alas, while the recording of the *Missa solemnis* is comparably vivid, the performance rarely conveys and kind of hushed tension, and the ensemble of the chorus is far from perfect. There are excellent soloists but they are very closely balanced.

Missa solemnis in D, Op. 123 (DVD Version)

⊕→ *** DG DVD 073 4391. Tomowa-Sintow, Baldani, Tappy, van Dam, Vienna Singverein, BPO, Karajan

Karajan first conducted the *Missa solemnis* in 1937 and he returned to the score many times throughout his life. He also recorded it on four occasions. The present performance comes from the Salzburg Easter Festival of 1979 and was televised by Österreichesrundfunk that year; their transmission forms the basis of this DVD. It is good to see as well as hear Karajan in this mighty score for, along with Klemperer, he was probably its greatest modern interpreter. His soloists, especially Tomowa-Sintow and José van Dam, are in imposing form and the **Wiener Singverein** and the **Berlin Philharmonic** magnificent. No other partnership has ever produced so extraordinary a tonal refinement or range of colour. Self-recommending.

Missa solemnis in D, Op. 123 (CD Versions)

⊕→ *** DG 429 779-2. Margiono, Robbin, Kendall, Miles, Monteverdi Ch., E. Bar. Sol., Gardiner

⊕→ (***) Testament mono SBT 1408. Söderström, Höffgen, Haefliger, Frick, Philh. Ch. & O, Klemperer

⊕→ *** HM HMC 901557. Mannion, Remmert, Taylor, Hauptmann, La Chapelle Royale Coll. Voc., O des Champs Elysées, Herreweghe

(M) (***) Medici Arts (mono) MMO 15-2. Kupper, S. Wagner, Schock, Greindl, N. German R. Ch., Cologne R. Ch. & RSO, Klemperer

Gardiner's inspired reading matches even the greatest of traditional performances on record in dramatic weight and spiritual depth, while bringing out the white heat of Beethoven's inspiration with new intensity. Though the performers are fewer in number than in traditional accounts, the **Monteverdi Choir** sings with bright, luminous tone, and the four soloists are excellent. The recording is vivid too. Even those who normally resist period performance will find this compelling.

In this radio recording from Cologne in 1955, **Klemperer**, with excellent forces, conducts an intensely dramatic reading. In every way this is preferable to the studio recording he made with Philharmonia forces, except that it is made in mono. There is no suspicion of the excessive heaviness which later afflicted Klemperer's Beethoven.

Klemperer's legendary 1963 broadcast of the *Missa solemnis* with a distinguished line-up of soloists and the magnificent **Philharmonia** forces does not disappoint memories, and it is good to have it in such miraculously restored sound.

OPERA

Fidelio (complete; DVD versions)

⊕→ **** DG DVD 940 073 4159. Janowitz, Popp, Kollo, Sotin, Jungwirth, Dallapozza, V. State Op. Ch & O, Bernstein

(N) *** DG DVD 073 4438 Gwyneth Jones, Talvela, Greindl, Miljakovic, Greindl, Ch. & O of Berlin Deusche Oper, Boehm V/D Ernst Wild

⊕→ *** Arthaus DVD 101 099. Söderström, De Ridder, Gale, Appelgren, Allman, Glyndebourne Festival Ch, LPO, Haitink (Director: Peter Hall; V/D: Dave Heather)

In a production by Otto Schenk and with sets by Gunther Schneider-Siemssen, **Bernstein** conducts a classic account of *Fidelio* with an outstanding cast. This live recording, made in January 1978, anticipated the studio recording made for DG a month later with an almost identical cast. The great finale of Act II in particular conveys a rare dedication, with Bernstein conducting 'as though in a trance', as one commentator put it. **Gundula Janowitz** sings gloriously as Leonore, with **Lucia Popp** radiant as Marzelline. All the male soloists are firm and clear, each of them at their peak, not least **René Kollo** as Florestan and **Hans Sotin** as Pizarro. The sound is on the dry side, but the magnetism of the performance quickly makes one overlook that.

It is a joy to see **Karl Boehm** (rarely caught on video) directing the Overture of **Fidelio** with great spirit, before he and the orchestra are observed no more, for Ernst Wild's 1970 film takes us straight into the opera's opening scene, photographed as in a normal movie, with close-ups (sometimes superimposed in duets and trios) and the big scenes widely spatial. The sets, too, are totally realistic, with the domestic scene in the living room of Rocco's quarters contrasted with the fortress courtyard where the prisoners encounter daylight and spring, and finally the dark, subterranean dungeon where Florestan is incarcerated. During the opening scene, subtitles give a simple synopsis of the background to the story. With a splendidly assembled cast, without a vocal flaw, this realization of Beethoven's great score could not be more accessible or rewarding. **Gwyneth Jones** looks the part of Fidelio and sings gloriously as Leonora, and is matched by her companions; **Josef Greindl's** resonant Rocco is splendidly characterized, and his daughter, Marzelline has an unexaggerated charm. **Gustav Neidlinger** makes an effectively villainous governor. Boehm conducts with consistent vitality and the recording is full-blooded if a little over-bright at times.

It is good to have as consummate an actress as **Elisabeth Söderström** as Leonore in this vintage Glyndebourne account of *Fidelio*, recorded in 1979. That was well before the new opera house was built there; in the old, small auditorium there is no question of Söderström's pure soprano being overwhelmed, even if the dry acoustic is not a help. **Bernard Haitink** conducts a powerful performance, with **Kurt Appelgren** a superb Rocco, **Elizabeth Gale** a sweet Marzelline, and **Anton de Ridder** an unstrained Florestan. Though **Robert Allman** is a rather gritty-toned Pizarro, that goes well with the character. John Busy's sets for Peter Hall's production vividly capture the atmosphere of the Napoleonic period, including the domestic scenes at the start.

Fidelio (complete; CD versions)

⊕— 🌑 (***) Testament mono SBT 2 1328 (2). Jurinac, Vickers, Frick, Hotter, Morison, Dobson, ROHCG Ch. & O, Klemperer

⊕— 🌑 Ⓜ **** EMI (ADD) 5 67364-2 (2). Ludwig, Vickers, Frick, Berry, Crass, Philh. Ch. & O, Klemperer (with *Overture: Leonora 3*)

Ⓜ *** DG 474 420-2 (2). Janowitz, Kollo, Jungwirth, Sotin, Popp, Dallapozza, Fischer-Dieskau, V. State Op. Ch., VPO, Bernstein

ⒷⒷ *** LSO Live LSO 0593 (2). Brewer, MacMaster, Sigmundsson, Matthews, Uusitalo, Kennedy, L. Symphony Ch., LSO, C. Davis

ⒷⒷ *** Naxos 8.660070/71. Nielsen, Winbergh, Moll, Titus, Lienbacher, Pecoraro, Hungarian R. Ch., Nicolaus Esterházy Sinfonia, Halász

The superb BBC recording of the first **Klemperer** performance at Covent Garden in February 1961 in many ways even outshines his classic studio recording, so that the drama of the piece comes over the more vividly, with speeds generally a degree faster than in the studio, and though his decision to include the *Leonore 3* overture in the once-traditional place just before the finale is controversial, the performance of it is hair-raisingly exciting, leaving one agog to hear the sublime sequence of the finale. **Vickers** and **Frick** are if anything even more magnetic than in the studio recording, and the

rest of the cast includes at least one singer who totally outshines her studio counterpart, **Elsie Morison**, whose enchanting portrait of Marzelline makes her EMI rival seem characterless. The casting of the great Wagnerian, **Hans Hotter**, as Pizarro brings impressive weight to the role, making this arch-villain far more of a threat than he is with the excellent but relatively lightweight Walter Berry on EMI. **John Dobson** makes a warmly engaging Jaquino, and **Forbes Robinson** is a noble Don Fernando; but it is **Sena Jurinac** singing Leonore for the very first time who sets the seal on the whole performance. She may not have quite the same weight as Ludwig on the studio set, but her projection is superb in singing which combines both brightness and warmth, both noble defiance and womanly compassion. In the excellent Testament transfer the radio sound is astonishingly vivid, with the voices cleanly balanced even when the singers move around on stage.

Klemperer's great studio set of *Fidelio*, now rightly reissued as one of EMI's 'Great Recordings of the Century', has been freshly remastered by Allan Ramsay. For some reason, the *Overture*, though full-bodied, lacks absolute sharpness of focus; but, once the singers enter, the quality of the splendid (1962) Kingsway Hall recording is very apparent, with the voices beautifully caught in relation to the orchestra, all within a glowing ambience. The result is a triumph to match the unique incandescence and spiritual strength of the performance, superbly cast, which leads to a final scene in which the parallel with the finale of the *Choral Symphony* is underlined. The documentation, including a full translation, is in every way excellent. The *Overture, Leonore 3* has been added as a postlude, an outstanding performance excellently transferred.

Bernstein's highly dramatic *Fidelio* brings some splendid singing from a consistently fine cast, with **Lucia Popp** a delightful Marzelline, **Janowitz** an outstanding Leonore and **Kollo** an equally strong Florestan. This now re-emerges as one of DG's 'Originals'.

Recorded at concerts in the Barbican in May 2006, **Sir Colin Davis's** version is crisp and dramatic, dedicated in such numbers as the great canon *Quartet* of Act I, and rising to a thrilling climax in Act II. **Christine Brewer** is the superb Leonore, if anything even stronger and warmer than she is in the Chandos version in English. Her *Abscheulicher* brings out all her masterly qualities to the full, thanks to her big, firm, creamy voice, perfectly controlled, whether in the spacious legato of the main section or in the florid passages of the final cabaletta, which she shades expressively. The rest of the cast sings strongly too, with **John MacMaster** a clear, bold Florestan, **Juha Uusitalo** a Pizarro more lyrical than usual, and **Kristinn Sigmundsson** a finely controlled Rocco, baritonal but not as old-sounding as he might be. **Sally Matthews** as Marzelline and **Andrew Kennedy** as Jaquino make a charming pair of lovers, and though the Barbican sound is on the dry side, the clarity of textures brings compensation, with ample weight in the sublime concluding scene.

The Naxos *Fidelio* from Budapest offers a first-rate modern cast incisively directed by **Michael Halász**, and very well recorded. **Inga Nielsen** is an outstanding Leonore, with every note sharply focused, using the widest tonal and dynamic range from bright *fortissimo* to velvety half-tone. Few singers on disc in recent years begin to rival her account of the *Abscheulicher*, ranging from venomous anger to radiant tenderness. **Gösta Winbergh** makes a formidable Florestan, with **Alan Titus** a firm, sinister Pizarro and **Kurt Moll** a splendid Rocco. Only the Don Fernando falls short, with a voice too woolly to focus cleanly. Even making no allowance for price, this version is among the very finest to have arrived in years, gaining in clarity and incisiveness from the relatively small scale.

Rattle's Berlin recording was made at a concert performance in the Philharmonie soon after he had conducted staged performances at the Salzburg Easter Festival. Yet, with a flawed cast, the result is one of the rare failures of his discography – a comfortable run-through rather than a genuinely dramatic experience. Even the *Canon Quartet* in Act I lacks tension, with none of the rapt mystery it should have. Only at the end of Act II does the performance acquire something of the bite one expects, and even then the opening of the finale is brisk to the point of sounding perfunctory. (EMI Gemini 2 17630-2).

Fidelio (sung in English; CD Version)

Ⓜ *** Chan. 3123 (2). Brewer, Lloyd, Evans, Hunka, Purves, Margison, Philh. Ch. & O, Parry

It is a measure of **David Parry's** achievement as an opera conductor (not least in Peter Moores's Opera in English series) that, facing the challenge of directing Beethoven's *Fidelio*, he offers so strong and cohesive a reading. Parry is helped not only by outstandingly vivid recording, among the finest ever to come from Chandos, but an exceptionally consistent cast, with no weak link in it. It is good to have so distinguished a soprano as **Christine Brewer** as Leonore, at once heroic but intensely human and warm, brilliant in the demanding *Abscheulicher*. She is well matched by the Florestan of **Richard Margison**, who sings his long opening aria in Act II with unusual subtlety, starting on the gentlest *pianissimo*, always vocalizing lyrically and never barking in heldentenor style, suggesting a fresh, youthful hero. **Rebecca Evans**, sweet and radiant, is outstanding as Marzelline, opposite the light, clear Jaquino of **Peter Wedd**, with the veteran, **Robert Lloyd**, as a characterful Rocco. Like the Florestan, the Pizarro of **Pavlo Hunka** sounds relatively youthful, again a singer who vocalizes well instead of barking, and **Christopher Purves** too as the governor, Don Fernando, sounds youthfully firm. A fresh, convincing reading that offers well-produced dialogue in English.

BELL, William Henry (1873–1946)

Viola Concerto (Rosa Mystica)

Ⓝ Ⓜ *** Dutton CDLX 7216. Chase, BBC Concert O, Bell – STANLEY BATE: *Viola Concerto*; VAUGHAN WILLIAMS: *Romance* ***

William Henry Bell was born in St Albans and spent the first thirty-nine years of his life there or in London. He studied

with Stanford and Frederick Corder and made a name for himself as a composer with his Walt Whitman symphony of 1902. In 1912 Bell was appointed Director of Music in Capetown and his creative career flourished: there are five settings of Japanese No plays, and much orchestral music including five symphonies. The *Viola Concerto* comes from 1916 and though wanting a strongly distinctive personality (it is not as individual as the Stanley Bate coupling), it is meditative and thoughtful. Lewis Foreman's authoritative note is supplemented by a personal reminiscence by John Joubert who grew up in South Africa. The Vaughan Williams *Romance* makes an appealing makeweight.

BELLINI, Vincenzo (1801–35)

OPERA

Beatrice di Tenda (complete; DVD version)

*(**) TDK **DVD** DV OPBDT (2). Gruberová, Volle, Kaluza, Hernández, Zurich Op. Ch. & O, Viotti (V/D: Yves Andreé Hubert)

Recorded in December 2001, the TDK DVD version offers an updated production from Zurich Opera House, with modern dress and geometric sets with stairs and handrails as though on an ocean liner. The performance – after Beatrice's delayed entry into the story – revolves round the fine performance of **Edita Gruberová** in the title-role, bright and agile, if occasionally edgy as recorded. **Raul Hernández** sings stylishly as the hero, Orombello, and the mezzo, **Stefania Kaluza**, is strongly cast as Agnese, with Marcello Viotti the purposeful conductor. The opera alone (144 minutes) might have been squeezed on to a single disc, but with a 26-minute interview (in French) with the conductor also included, the set spreads to a second disc.

Beatrice di Tenda (complete; CD version); Arias: Norma: Casta diva. I puritani: Son vergin vezzosa; Oh rendetemi la speme. La sonnambula: Ah, non credea mirarti

⊖ Ⓜ *** Decca (ADD) 433 706-2 (3). Sutherland, Pavarotti, Opthof, Veasey, Ward, Amb. Op. Ch., LSO, Bonynge

Dame Joan Sutherland had made *Beatrice di Tenda* her own when this recording was made in 1966, a dazzling example of her art with **Bonynge**, a natural Bellini conductor. The supporting cast could hardly be better, with **Pavarotti** highly responsive. The recording, of Decca's best vintage, has been transferred to CD with vivid atmosphere and colour. Four famous arias are provided as a filler: one from Sutherland's 1964 *Norma*, two from her 1963 *I puritani* and one from the 1962 *La sonnambula*.

I Capuleti ed i Montecchi (DVD version)

(*) Dynamic **DVD 33504. Ciofi, Polito, Formaggia, Sacchi, Amodio, Italian International O, Acocella (V/D: Marco Scalti)

Luciano Acocella's performance was recorded live at the Martina Franca Festival in the summer of 2005. It is a contemporary-dress production – which we tend to resist – with machine- and hand-guns instead of swords. But the Ducal Palace makes an attractive backcloth, so if you can swallow the director's unwillingness to mount a traditional in-period production you will find the attractively young **Patrizia Ciofi** as Giulietta and **Clara Polito** (mezzo) as Romeo make an ardent pair of lovers. Friar Laurence, a tenor role, is impressively sung by **Nicola Amodio**. On DVD this is only a stopgap, but it is an enjoyable one from a vocal point of view, and the chorus does not let the side down.

I Capuleti ed i Montecchi (CD versions)

🎬 *** Teldec 3984 21472-2 (2). Larmore, Hong, Groves, Aceto, Lloyd, SCO, Runnicles

(M) **(*) EMI 5 09144-2 (2). Baltsa, Gruberová, Raffanti, Howell, Tomlinson, ROHCG Ch. & O, Muti

Donald Runnicles offers a fresh and sympathetic reading of Bellini's 'Romeo and Juliet' opera with an outstanding cast. **Jennifer Larmore** is warm, fresh and firm as Romeo, youthfully ardent. Most remarkable of all is the Korean soprano **Hei-Kyung Hong** as Juliet, at once pure and warm of tone and passionate of expression, equally bringing out the youthfulness of the heroine. As Tebaldo, **Paul Groves** is clear and stylish, even though the tone is not Italianate, and **Robert Lloyd** is a commanding Lorenzo. Though the competition is strong, the Teldec set scores both in its casting and in its fullness of sound.

Muti's set was recorded live at Covent Garden in March 1984, the sound is hard and close. **Agnes Baltsa** makes a passionately expressive Romeo and **Edita Gruberová** a Juliet who is not just brilliant in coloratura but also sweet and tender. Muti's conducting is masterly, especially striking at the end of Act I, when the five principals sing a hushed quintet. With excellent contributions from the refined tenor **Dano Raffanti** (as Tebaldo), **Gwynne Howell** and **John Tomlinson**, it is a performance to blow the cobwebs off this once-neglected opera.

In the earlier EMI studio recording, made at Abbey Road in 1975, **Janet Baker** responds richly to the unfailing lyricism of Bellini's writing. **Beverly Sills** has her moments of shrillness, but the rest of the singing is very commendable, and the conducting of **Giuseppe Patanè** is beautifully sprung and the recording is atmospheric. No libretto with translation or synopsis is provided, but the former is available on the EMI Classics Website (www.musicfromemi.com). (EMI Gemini 5 86055-2)

Norma (complete; DVD versions)

🎬 *** DG DVD 073 4219 (2). Gruberová, Ganassi, Todorovich, Scandiuzzi, Bav. State Op. Ch. & O, Haider (Director: Jürgen Rose; V/D: Brian Large)

🎬 *** Arthaus DVD 100 180. Sutherland, Elkins, Stevens, Grant, Opera Australia Ch., Sydney Elizabethan O, Bonynge (V/D: Sandro Sequi)

Edita Gruberová is a superb Norma. At her peak, her glorious singing is matched by fine acting, a totally convincing performance of the tragic heroine forced to choose between her lover and children, and her key religious role. **Sonia Ganassi** makes a fine, touching partner as Adalgisa. Their great central duet scene is memorably beautiful. **Zoran Todorovich** is a strong Pollione, with a bold, ringing tenor voice, and **Roberto Scandiuzzi** is an impressive Oroveso, and his contribution to the final scene is very moving. **Friedrich Haider** conducts his excellent chorus and orchestra with understanding and real flair. Altogether, this is very impressive indeed, and the sets and costumes are simple and effective. Choice between this and the Sutherland Australian set is not an easy one, for both have much to offer. But while Sutherland is at her finest, she does not have a Pollione to match Todorovich, and this Bavarian production is admirably directed.

Recorded live at the Sydney Opera House in 1978, this Australian Opera production by Sandro Sequi is chiefly valuable for presenting **Dame Joan Sutherland** in one of her most important roles when she was still at the peak of her powers. *Casta diva* finds Dame Joan in glorious voice, at once powerful, creamily beautiful and wonderfully secure. With sets by Fiorella Mariani it is a traditional production, springing no surprises, encouraging the diva to relax in the role, never more so than in her big duet with Adalgisa, *Mira o Norma*, ending in a dazzling account of the cabaletta, where **Margreta Elkins** equally sparkles, and **Richard Bonynge** draws light, crisply sprung playing from the orchestra. Less satisfying is the singing of **Ronald Stevens** as Pollione, powerful and heroic, but rather too coarse for Bellinian cantilena. **Clifford Grant** by contrast could hardly be more cleanly focused as Oroveso. The sound is a little dry, not as full-bodied as in the finest, fully digital recordings, but the sharpness of attack heightens the dramatic thrust of Bonynge's conducting.

Norma (complete; CD versions)

🎬 (M) *** Decca (ADD) 475 7902 (3). Sutherland, Horne, Alexander, Cross, Minton, Ward, L. Symphony Ch. & O, Bonynge

🎬 (M) (***) EMI mono 5 62668-2 (3). Callas, Picchi, Stignani, Vaghi, ROHCG Ch. & O, Gui

(M) (***) EMI mono 5 62638-2 [562642-2] (3). Callas, Stignani, Filippeschi, Rossi-Lemeni, La Scala, Milan, Ch. and O, Serafin

**(*) Decca 414 476-2 (3). Sutherland, Pavarotti, Caballé, Ramey, Welsh Nat. Op. Ch. & O, Bonynge

(M) **(*) EMI (ADD) CMS5 66428-2 (3). Callas, Corelli, Ludwig, Zaccharia, Ch. & O of La Scala, Milan, Serafin

In her first, mid-1960s recording of *Norma*, **Sutherland** was joined by an Adalgisa in **Marilyn Horne** whose control of florid singing is just as remarkable as Sutherland's own. The other soloists are very good indeed. A most compelling performance, helped by the conducting of **Richard Bonynge**; and the Walthamstow recording is vivid but also atmospheric in its CD format. This set has now been reissued at mid-price as part of Decca's 'Classic Opera Collection', which carries full text and translation.

Recorded live at Covent Garden, the 1952 account of *Norma* presents **Callas** at her very peak, with **Ebe Stignani**, ideally cast as Adalgisa, a splendid foil. More than her studio recordings of the role, this finds Callas in perfect voice, with none of the flaws that developed later in her career, notably unsteadiness under pressure. Callas's top notes are immaculate, and her coloratura agile, but it is the weight of emotion conveyed that makes this performance unique. As Pollione, the tenor **Mirto Picchi** cannot match the women in the cast, but at least he sings with firmer, less strained tone than Mario Filippeschi in Callas's first studio recording of *Norma*, made for EMI in 1954.

In **Callas's** later mono set, the recording is opened out impressively in the new transfer, and the sense of presence gives wonderful intensity to one of the diva's most powerful performances. Balance of soloists is close but Callas justifies everything, even the cuts. The veteran, **Ebe Stignani**, as Adalgisa is a characterful partner in the sisters' duets, but **Filippeschi** is disappointingly thin-toned and strained, and **Rossi-Lemeni** is gruff. This is now one of EMI's 'Great Recordings of the Century'.

Though **Dame Joan Sutherland** was 58 when her second *Norma* recording was made, her singing is still impressive, but **Pavarotti** is in some ways the set's greatest strength, easily expressive as Pollione. **Caballé** as Adalgisa seems determined to outdo Sutherland in cooing self-indulgently. Full, brilliant, well-balanced recording of the complete score.

By the time **Callas** came to record her 1960 stereo version, the tendency to hardness and unsteadiness in the voice above the stave, always apparent, had grown serious; but the interpretation was as sharply illuminating as ever, a unique assumption, helped by **Christa Ludwig** as Adalgisa, while **Corelli** sings heroically. **Serafin** as ever is the most persuasive of Bellini conductors.

(i) *Norma* (complete). Excerpts: (ii) *Ite sul colle, o Druidi; Ah! Del Tebro al giogo indegno*; (iii) *Merco all'altar di Venere . . . Me protegge!*; (iv) *Sedioze voci . . . Casta diva . . . Ah! bello a me ritorna; Mira, o Norma*; (v) *Sgombra è la sacra selva*; (vi) *Deh! Non voleri vittime*

🔊 (BB) (***) Naxos mono 8.110325/7. (i) Callas, Stignani, Filippeschi, Rossi-Lemeni, La Scala, Milan, Ch. & O, Serafin; (ii) Pinza, Met. Op. Ch.; (iii) Merli; (iv) Ponselle; (v) Minghini-Cattaneo; (vi) Cigna, Pasero, Breviario

Mark Obert-Thorn's impressive new transfer has been made from the best portions of two 1950s-era British LP pressings, and he has taken the opportunity to add earlier, historical recordings (made between 1927 and 1937), among which the **Pinza** and **Ponselle** items obviously stand out, but the final excerpt (*Deh! Non voleri vittime*) includes some superb singing from **Gina Cigna**.

Il pirata (complete)

(M) (**(*)) EMI mono 5 66432-2 (2). Callas, Ego, Ferraro,

Peterson, Watson, Sarfaty, American Op. Soc. Ch. & O, Rescigno

Though Callas herself shows signs of vocal deterioration, with top notes often raw and uneven, hers is a fire-eating performance, totally distinctive, instantly magnetic from the moment she utters her first word, '*Sorgete*', in Act I. The rest of the cast is indifferent, with **Constantine Ego** strenuous in the tenor role of Ernesto. The second disc offers an alternative recording of the final scene, made in Amsterdam six months later, with **Rescigno** conducting the **Concertgebouw Orchestra** and with Callas in smoother vocal form, helped by less raw recording.

I Puritani (DVD Version)

*** DG DVD 073 4421 (2). Netrebko, Cutler, Vassallo, Relyea, NY Met. Opera Ballet, Ch. & O, Summers (Director: Sandro Sequi; V/D: Gary Henderson)

At last a worthy DVD of *I Puritani*, recorded live at the Met. in 2007, a traditional production but an imaginative one. It is very much dominated by the superb portrayal of Elvira by **Anna Netrebko**, who sings superbly throughout and acts as a convincingly unhinged heroine, to make the Mad Scene visually as well as vocally a dramatic highlight. She is well matched by **Eric Cutler's** Arturo and the celebrated quartet of singers needed for this opera is completed by **Franco Vassallo** as Riccardo and **John Relyea's** resonant Giorgio. **Patrick Summers** directs the score with conviction, and with attractive sets and costumes it is no wonder that the return of this vintage production brought rave reviews all round. The camerawork is excellent and so is the recording. As a bonus, we go backstage with Renée Fleming talking to Netrebko. A strong recommendation.

I Puritani (complete; CD versions)

🔊 **** Decca (ADD) 417 588-2 (3). Sutherland, Pavarotti, Ghiaurov, Luccardi, Caminada, Cappuccilli, ROHCG Ch. & O, Bonynge

🔊 (***) EMI mono 5 56275-2 (2). Callas, Di Stefano, Panerai, Rossi-Lemeni, La Scala, Milan, Ch. & O, Serafin

Whereas her earlier set was recorded when **Sutherland** had adopted a soft-grained style, with consonants largely eliminated, her singing brings fresh, bright singing, rich and agile. **Pavarotti** emerges as a Bellini stylist, with **Ghiaurov** and **Cappuccilli** making up an impressive cast, but with **Anita Caminada** disappointing as Enrichetta. Vivid, atmospheric recording.

In 1953, when she made this recording, **Callas's** voice was already hard on top and with some unsteadiness, but her portrayal is uniquely compelling. None of the other soloists is ideal, though most of the singing is acceptable. The mono sound is now opened up and the solo voices project well. Like other EMI/Callas recordings, this has been handsomely redocumented. Highlights are available on 5 66665-2.

La sonnambula (complete; CD versions)

🔊 *** Decca 417 424-2 (2). Sutherland, Pavarotti, D. Jones, Ghiaurov, L. Op. Ch., Nat. PO, Bonynge

🎵 Ⓑ ******* Naxos 8.660042/3. D'Artegna, Papadjiakou, Orgonasova, Giménez, Dilbèr, De Vries, Micu, Netherlands R. Ch. and CO, Zedda

🎵 Ⓜ **(***)** EMI mono 5 62672-2 (2). Callas, Monti, Cossotto, Zaccaria, Ratti, La Scala, Milan, Ch. and O, Votto

Ⓝ 🎵 ⒷⒷ **(***)** Naxos mono 111284/5 Callas, Monti, Cossotto, Zaccaria, Ratti, La Scala Milan Ch. & O, Votto (with CHERUBINI: *Medea: Dei tuoi figli*; SPONTINI: *La Vestale: Tu che invoco; O Nume, tutelary; Caro oggetto*)

Ⓝ ****** Decca 478 1082. Bartoli, Flórez, d'Arcangelo, Zurich Op House Ch, orch La Scintilla, De Marchi

**(*) Virgin 3 95138-2 (2). Dessay, Meli, Columbara, Mingardo, Lyon Op. Ch. & O, Pidò

Sutherland's singing in her later version is even more affecting and more stylish than before, generally purer and more forthright, if with diction still clouded at times. The challenge of singing opposite **Pavarotti** adds to the bite of the performance, crisply and resiliently controlled by **Bonynge**.

The Naxos issue offers the finest version of the opera at any price since Joan Sutherland's. **Luba Orgonasova** is an expressive and characterful heroine, agile and pointed in her phrasing of coloratura, deeply affecting in the tender legato of *Ah non credea mirarti*, with tone delicately varied. **Raul Giménez** is equally stylish as Elvino, the rich landowner, using his light Rossinian tenor most sensitively, with **Alberto Zedda**, scholar as well as conductor, pointing the accompaniment lightly. The other principals are not quite on this level but they make an excellent team. As usual with Naxos opera issues, there is a libretto in Italian but only a detailed summary of the plot in English.

Substantially cut, the **Callas** version was recorded in mono in 1957, yet it gives a vivid picture of the diva at the peak of her powers. **Nicola Monti** makes a strong rather than a subtle contribution, but he blends well with Callas in the duets; and **Fiorenza Cossotto** is a good Teresa. Again, the remastered recording for the Callas Edition shows considerable improvement.

Mark Obert-Thorn's faithful remastering for Naxos is transferred from a first edition British LP pressing as are the Cherubini and Spontini arias included as a supplement. The set comes with an acceptable cued synopsis.

Natalie Dessay proves a formidable heroine in this demanding opera with her pure, precise soprano, ideally agile, adding extra decorations for the Cabaletta repeats. **Carlo Columbara**, not nearly so characterful, is still a clear-voiced hero, and **Evelino Pidò** draws sympathetic singing and playing from the **Lyon Choir** and **Orchestra**. First-rate sound.

In **Sutherland's** earlier version, her use of *portamento* is often excessive, but the freshness of the voice is a delight, **Bonynge's** direction is outstanding, and the casting is first rate too, with **Nicola Monti** a Bellini tenor. Both **Sylvia Stahlman** as Lisa and **Margreta Elkins** as Teresa sing beautifully and with keen accuracy. Even **Fernando Corena's** rather coarse, *buffo*-style Rodolfo has an attractive vitality. The recording has come up vividly on CD. (Decca 448 966-3)

It was bold of Decca to bring out a version of Bellini's opera that in two ways breaks new ground, the first using a mezzo instead of a high coloratura soprano, echoing to example of Malibran, and using a period orchestra. Admirable as that initiative is, the result is overall disappointing, lacking sparkle, with the rapid vibrato in **Bartoli's** voice and the flicker in **Juan Diego Flórez's** tending to be obtrusive, though the baritone **Ildebrando d'Arcangelo** is excellent.

La Straniera

Ⓝ ******* Opera Rara ORC38 (2). Ciofi, Schmunck, Shkosa, Mitchell Choir, LPO, Parry

Written in 1829 when Bellini was 27, *La Straniera* ('The Stranger') comes after *Il Pirata*, and points forward very clearly to the three masterpieces, *Sonnambula, Norma* and *I Puritani*. The very opening brings a brief, lively prelude leading in to a warmly attractive chorus without any delay. The story is typically involved, centring around the identity of the mysterious woman, who roams through the Brittany countryside, wearing a heavy veil. The peasants think she must be a witch, but she is in fact Alaide, the exiled wife of the King of France. There are misunderstandings on every side, involving also the local Count, Arturo and Alaide's disguised brother, Veldeburgo. The confusion leads to violence and a tragic end, when Alaide is falsely accused of murder.

It is no more confusing than many opera plots of the period, and what matters is the quality of the melodic writing, which inspires some excellent singing from this strong cast, led by the fresh-voiced soprano, **Patrizia Ciofi**, opposite **Dario Schmunck** in the principal tenor role of Arturo. The recording is excellent, clear and well-balanced, and like so many Opera Rara sets it offers an important rarity that stands as a key work in the composer's development.

BENJAMIN, Arthur (1893–1960)

(i) Cotillion, A Suite of Dance Tunes; (ii) North American Square Dance Suite; (iii) Overture to an Italian Comedy; (ii) Symphony

*** Lyrita (ADD/DDD) SRCD 314. (i) LSO, Braithwaite; (ii) LPO, Wordsworth; (iii) RPO, Fredman

Arthur Benjamin was gifted with much natural facility and his *Overture to an Italian Comedy* is as gay and vivacious as anyone could wish, and it is delightfully scored. At its best, his invention approached real distinction. However, *Cotillion*, an arrangement of melodies found in 'The Dancing Master' by W. Pearson and John Young in London in 1719, and scored for a fairly large orchestra, hardly seems worth putting on record. The *North American Square Dances* (originally fiddle music) are more agreeably inventive and pleasingly scored, but much of the music is lyrical – one would have expected more catchily lively dances. The *Symphony* was written when the composer was 51, suffering from what Benjamin called 'that awful Brahms influence' – the feeling that it was 'impertinent' to compose a symphony before reaching middle age. Yet it is a spectacular work of great confidence. **Barry Wordsworth** and the **LPO** play the work with great energy and commitment, and the digital recording is both brilliant and vividly expansive.

(i) *Cello Sonatina*; (ii) *Viola Sonata*; (iii) *Violin Sonatina*; *3 Pieces for Violin & Piano*; *Jamaican Rumba*; (iv) *Le Tombeau de Ravel* (for clarinet and piano)

*** Tall Poppies TP 134. Tall Poppies Ensemble: Munro, with (i) Pereira; (ii) Van Stralen; (iii) Harding; (iv) Jenkin

Although opening with a lilting account of the *Jamaican Rumba* in the 1944 arrangement for violin and piano, dedicated to and played by Heifetz, the earliest music here is also for violin and piano, a set of *Three Pieces*. A lively *Humoresque* and *Carnavalesque* (with a curious tolling-bell introduction) frame a ghostly *Arabesque*. The *Violin Sonatina* followed in 1924. The *Cello Sonatina* of 1938 is perhaps the most warmly lyrical of Benjamin's string duos, easily melodic but with a highly rhythmic closing *March*. The *Viola Sonata*, written in 1942 for William Primrose, is a particularly fine work, combining a haunting *Elegy* with a nostalgic *Waltz*, and ending with a boldly virtuosic *Toccata*. But especially beguiling is the *Tombeau de Ravel*, written for Gervase de Peyer.

All the performances here are of high quality and show a composer of great resource who always captures and holds the listener's ear. The recording is excellent.

Pastoral Fantasy (for string quartet); *5 Spirituals* (for cello & piano); *Viola Sonata*; *3 Violin Pieces*; *A Tune & Variations for Little People*; *Violin Sonatina*.

Ⓜ ******* Dutton CDLX 7110. Locrian Ens.

This excellent Dutton collection duplicates the *Viola Sonata* and *Violin Sonatina*, and the *Three Pieces* also offered on the Tall Poppies disc above, with the performances here if anything more persuasive, no less passionate and often with appealing touches of fantasy. These artists are completely inside all this music and have the advantage of the warm acoustic of The Maltings, Snape. The *Five Spirituals* are delightful vignettes which ought to be in the regular cello repertoire, while the *Pastoral Fantasy* is in the best tradition of English pastoralism. The *Tune* on which he bases his *Variations for Little People* is also very beguiling. This disc has a price advantage over its equally admirable Tall Poppies competitor, but both collections are well worth investigating.

PIANO MUSIC

Brumas Tunes; *Chinoiserie*; *Elegiac Mazurka*; *Fantasies I–II*; *Haunted House*; *Jamaican Rumba*; *Let's Go Hiking*; *3 New Fantasies*; *Odds and Ends I–II*; *Pastorale, Arioso & Finale*; *Romance-impromptu*; *Saxophone Blues*; *Scherzino*; *Siciliana*; *Suite*

*** Tall Poppies TP 105. Munro

Australian born, Arthur Benjamin's *Jamaican Rumba* was the result of a professional examination visit to England in 1938, and it soon became a worldwide hit. He did not repeat that success, yet his other genre pieces here are full of attractive

ideas and comparably catchy rhythmic invention, at times cool in the jazz sense of the word (*Saxophone Blues*), at others (the *Odds and Ends* or the *Fantasies*, for instance) offering writing of charming but indelible simplicity. Throughout, **Ian Munro** plays with great style and elegance and with obvious affection. This is a wholly delightful recital, with never a dull moment throughout its 78 minutes. The recording is admirably natural. (If you find it difficult to obtain this CD, you can order it direct from Tall Poppies, PO Box 373, Glebe, NSW 2037, Australia.)

BENNETT, Richard Rodney
(born 1936)

(i) *Piano Concerto*; (ii) *Commedia IV* (for 2 trumpets, horn, trombone & tuba); (iii) *Capriccio for Piano Duet*; (iv) *5 Studies for Piano*

*** Lyrita (ADD) SRCD 275. (i) Kovacevich, LSO, Gibson; (ii) Philip Jones Brass Ens.; (iii) Thea Musgrave; (iii; iv) composer

Richard Rodney Bennett wrote his *Piano Concerto*, a work involving complex, endlessly fluttering fragments, especially with **Stephen Kovacevich** in mind. The *Commedia IV* for brass quintet is also one the composer's most strikingly memorable works. Six ensemble passages for the full ensemble frame five groups of solos, duets, and trios, with a central solo for horn. The music is virtuosic but it has a central gravity and ends very positively. It is marvellously played here by the **Philip Jones Brass Ensemble** and makes highly stimulating listening. The works for piano show Bennett at his most unpredictable, especially in their rhythmic punctuation. The performances here could not be more authoritative, and the recording is excellent.

BERG, Alban (1885–1935)

Documentary: *The Secret Life of Alban Berg* (narrated by Kristine Ciesinski): (i) *Violin Concerto*

*** Arthaus DVD 102 117. Kremer, Bav. Rad. SO Colin Davis

The documentary is most valuable and includes contributions from such authorities as the American composer and Berg scholar, George Perle and the British Berg authority, Douglas Jarman – and also Louis Krasner who gave the very first performance of the concerto in 1936. The film reveals that all is not what it seemed in Berg's marriage and that his wife took little real interest in his compositions until the 1960s (not even attending their first performances) and talks frankly about his personal life. **Kristine Ciesinski** narrates and also sings excerpts from *Wozzeck* and *Lulu* with the **BBC Symphony Orchestra** under **Elgar Howarth**. The performance of the *Concerto*, recorded during **Sir Colin's** tenure in Munich, is very leisurely indeed though **Kremer** is appropriately neurasthenic and inward-looking. A fascinating programme.

(i; ii) *Chamber Concerto for Piano, Violin & 13 Wind*; (iii) *Violin Concerto* (*To the Memory of an*

Angel); (iv) *Lyric Suite: 3 Pieces; 3 Pieces for Orchestra, Op. 6*; (v; vi) *Adagio* from *Chamber Concerto* (arr. for Violin, Clarinet & Piano); (vii) *Lyric Suite for String Quartet*; (vi) *4 Pieces for Clarinet and Piano*; (vii) *String Quartet, Op. 3*; (i) *Piano Sonata, Op. 1*; (viii; iv) *Altenberg Lieder, Op. 4*; (ix) *7 Early Songs* (versions with (x) piano; (iv) orchestra); (xi) *4 Lieder, Op. 2*; (xii) *Lieder: An Leukon; Schlieffe mir die Augen beide* (2 settings); (ix; iv) *Der Wein* (concert aria); (viii; iv) *Lulu: Suite* (symphonic pieces); (xiii) *Lulu* (opera; complete); (xiv) *Wozzeck* (complete); (xv) **Transcription of** JOHANN STRAUSS JR: *Waltz: Wein, Weib und Gesang*

(B) *** DG (ADD/DDD) 474 657-2 (8). (i) Barenboim; (ii) Zukerman, Ens. InterContemporain, Boulez; (iii) Mutter, Chicago SO, Levine; (iv) VPO, Abbado; (v) Kremer, (vi) Meyer, Maisenberg; (vii) LaSalle Qt; (viii) Banse; (ix) von Otter; (x) Forsberg; (xi) Fischer-Dieskau, Reimann; (xii) Marshall, Parsons; (xiii) Stratas, Minton, Schwarz, Mazura, Blankenheim, Riegel, Tear, Paris Op. O, Boulez; (xiv) Grundheber, Behrens, Haugland, Langridge, Zednik; (xv) Boston Symphony Chamber Players

An impressive and inexpensive collection that should satisfy the most demanding Berg enthusiast. Nearly all these recordings are three star and most are still currently available separately and are praised below, including the *Chamber Concerto*, *Violin Concerto*, *Three Pieces for Orchestra*, *Lulu Symphonic Suite*, the *Seven Early Songs* and **Boulez's** pioneering recording of *Lulu*. **Abbado's** *Wozzeck*, recorded live, has the inevitable drawback of intrusive stage noises and backwardly balanced singers, but is still very compelling.

Among the other recordings, the **LaSalle Quartet** provide the most persuasive advocacy in the Op. 3 *String Quartet* and *Lyric Suite* arrangement and are vividly recorded. **Sabine Meyer's** contribution to the works including clarinet is hardly less impressive, and **Barenboim**, if not quite a match for **Pollini**, gives a concentrated account of the *Piano Sonata*.

Juliane Banse sings expressively and lyrically in the *Altenberg Lieder*, atmospherically accompanied by the **VPO** and **Abbado**; though some Bergians may prefer tougher, edgier performances, few will resist such a warmly musical response. The contribution of the rich-toned **Margaret Marshall** and **Geoffrey Parsons** is hardly less impressive. **Fischer-Dieskau** with highly sensitive accompaniment from **Aribert Reimann** is equally communicative in the early Op. 2 *Songs*, and the **Boston Chamber Players** provide an unexpected bonus in Berg's arrangement of a familiar waltz by Johann Strauss. The documentation is generally very good and includes synopses for the operas but no translations.

(i) *Chamber Concerto*; (ii) *Violin Concerto* (*To the Memory of an Angel*)

(M) *** Warner Elatus 0927 46737-2. Dresden State O, Sinopoli, with (i) Lucchesini; (ii) Watanabe

It would be hard to imagine more romantic readings of Berg's principal orchestral works than those under **Giuseppe Sinopoli**. The atonal arguments of Berg have never been pre-sented more sinuously, cocooning the ear, helped by sumptuous playing and recording. The violinist, **Reiko Watanabe**, is totally in sympathy with this approach, using the widest range of expression, tone and dynamic, with the music at the start seeming to emerge out of mists. Romantic readings of the *Violin Concerto* are common enough, but with the pianist, **Andrea Lucchesini** as a perfectly matched partner for Watanabe, the *Chamber Concerto*, which can seem one of Berg's more cerebral works, is just as seductive.

Violin Concerto

*** Warner 2564 60291-2. Hope, BBC SO, Watkins – BRITTEN: *Violin Concerto* ***

(M) *** DG 447 445-2. Perlman, Boston SO, Ozawa (with RAVEL: *Tzigane*; STRAVINSKY: *Concerto* ***)

*** DG 437 093-2. Mutter, Chicago SO, Levine – RIHM: *Gesungene Zeit*, etc. ***

(BB) *** Warner Apex 0927 40812-2. Zehetmair, Philh. O, Holliger – HARTMANN: *Concerto funèbre*; JANÁČEK: *Concerto* ***

It was **Daniel Hope** who, a year before publication, gave the first performance of the corrected version of the *Violin Concerto* in Manchester; here, in a warm and purposeful performance, he is the soloist in the first recording of it. He sustains spacious speeds with no sense of self-consciousness, intense and concentrated from first to last, subtly varying his vibrato to heighten emotion, notably in the hushed and tender resolution on the Bach chorale theme, *Es ist genug*. The cellist **Paul Watkins** proves himself a fine conductor, drawing warmly intense playing from the **BBC Symphony Orchestra**, helped by full, immediate recording with impressively weighty brass.

Perlman's performance is above all commanding. The **Boston Orchestra** accompanies superbly and, though the balance favours the soloist, the recording is excellent. The current transfer shows the Boston acoustic at its most seductive.

Anne-Sophie Mutter begins the *Concerto* with a *pianissimo* of much delicacy. She proceeds to give an intensely passionate reading, both freely expressive and intensely purposeful, with **James Levine** and the **Chicago orchestra** matching her in subtle shading. As an imaginative coupling, Mutter offers a concerto written for her by the forty-year-old German composer, Wolfgang Rihm.

On the inexpensive Apex disc **Zehetmair** plays with great sensitivity and a natural eloquence, and many will prefer this to Mutter on DG. That has tremendous brilliance and panache but Zehetmair's less sensational reading brings one closer to the heart of this poignant music. Moreover, apart from the price advantage, he offers more interesting couplings. The recording, made at The Maltings, Snape, is of exemplary clarity and has great presence, making this triptych a very real bargain.

Violin Concerto. Lyric Suite: 3 Pieces; 3 Pieces for Orchestra, Op. 6

(BB) *** Naxos 8.554755. Netherlands RSO, Klas, (i) with Hirsch

This Naxos issue brings together clear, positive versions of three key works by Berg, with the recordings, made in the Hilversum concert hall under the Estonian conductor **Eri Klas**, presenting each work in close focus. **Rebecca Hirsch** is an outstanding young violinist who has concentrated on twentieth-century music, and here she combines clean, precise attack with natural tonal warmth. The balance is securely held between weight of emotion and fresh modernity.

(i) Violin Concerto; (ii) Lulu Suite; (iii) 3 Orchestral Pieces, Op. 6; (iv) 4 Pieces for Clarinet and Piano; (v) Lyric Suite; (vi) Piano Sonata, Op. 1; (vii) 7-Frühe Lieder; (viii) Wozzeck: Act III: Interlude

⊛── (**BB**) EMI Gemini 3 81771-2 (2). (i) Zimmermann, Stuttgart RSO; (ii) CBSO, Rattle, with Augér; (iii) Bamberg SO; (iii; viii) Metzmacher; (iv) Meyer, Vogt; (v) Alban Berg Qt; (vi) Donohoe; (vii) Sine Bundgaard, Danish R. O, Pintscher; (viii) Hamburg Philharmonic State O

These are all key performances of Berg's major works, recorded between 1987 and 2004. The cast list is very impressive, and the recordings of uniformly high quality. **Zimmermann's** account of the *Violin Concerto* is very competitive. If you can take this much Berg, the set is a real bargain. If you want just a sampler, the set's highlight is **Rattle's** superb account of the *Lulu Suite*, with **Arleen Augér**, which is available separately, coupled with Schoenberg and Webern – see below.

(i) Violin Concerto. Passacaglia (realized by Borries & Venzago); Lulu: Symphonic Pieces. Piano Sonata, Op. 1 (orch. Verbey); 3 Pieces, Op. 6; Wozzeck: 3 Fragments. Der Wein (sung in (ii) French & (iii) German). Transcription of JOHAN STRAUSS II: Wein, Weib und Gesang!

(**N**) (**M**) **** Chan. (**SACD**) CHSA 5074 (2). Gothenburg SO, Venzago with (i) Keulen; (ii) Murray; (iii) McGreevy

An outstanding new collection of the key works of Berg, spanning the creative career of the composer, with a few novelties thrown in too. These include Theo Verbey's superb orchestration of Berg's solo *Piano Sonata*, which transforms the piece into virtually a new work. In the *Passacaglia* fragment (1913), each variation builds on the former one rather than on the original theme, and the result is an intense piece of orchestral writing, put together from sketch by the composer by Christan von Venzago. The concert aria, *Der Wein* ('The Wine') is heard here in two performances, one in the usual German, by **Geraldine McGreevy**, and the other in French, by the tenor **Robert Murray**. The latter, in Baudelaire's original French, is markedly sweeter in tone. The main orchestral works come off extremely well here: both the soloist and the conductor bring out all the colours which make up the *Violin Concerto*, and the orchestral suites from *Wozzeck* and *Lulu* have both intensity and atmosphere. The *Three Pieces, Op. 6* have more warmth here than usual, though the finale has a fine sense of impending doom. The disc ends with Berg's enjoyable arrangement of Strauss's *Wein, Weib und Gesang!* Throughout, these performances benefit from superb Chandos SACD sound, and excellent

playing from the **Gothenburg Orchestra**. The two new CDs are offered for the price of one.

Lyric Suite: 3 Pieces; (i) 5 Altenberglieder, Op. 4

⊛── (**M**) *** Warner Elatus 0927 49009-2. Dresden State O, Sinopoli, (i) with Marc

(**BB**) *** Arte Nova 74321 27768-2. (i) Orsanic; SW German RSO, Gielen – ZEMLINSKY: *Lyric Symphony* ***

The three movements from his *Lyric Suite* make an ideal coupling for the Zemlinsky *Lyric Symphony*, the work which Berg quotes and which prompted his title. They are beautifully played and recorded here, as are the five settings of Altenberg poems, crisp and compact yet full of emotion, here sung superbly with fresh tone and clean attack by the soprano, **Vlatka Orsanic**. First-rate recording. A pity the documentation does not match the musical excellence.

The Elatus disc is taken from live recordings made at the Saxon State Opera in Dresden in 1997–8, and if anything is even warmer. It offers the very generous coupling of the three-movement orchestral version of the *Lyric Suite* plus the two orchestral works based on Berg's two operas. In those the atmospheric warmth of the playing and conducting is enhanced by the expressive singing of **Alessandra Marc**, making one wish that these same performers had recorded the complete operas. With late-nineties recording, excellent value.

3 Pieces for Orchestra, Op. 6; (i) 5 Orchestral Songs, Op. 4; Lulu: Symphonic Suite

(**M**) *** DG (ADD) 449 714-2. (i) M. Price; LSO, Abbado

Abbado makes it clear above all how beautiful Berg's writing is, not just in the *Lulu* excerpts but in the early Op. 4 *Songs* and the Op. 6 *Orchestral Pieces*.

Lyric Suite (String Quartet version)

*** Testament SBT 1374; Juilliard Qt – CARTER: *Quartet 2*; SCHUMAN: *Quartet 3* ***

(**B**) *** None. 7559 79696-2. Upshaw, Kronos Qt

Recorded in 1959, this is as fine an account of the *Lyric Suite* as you can ever hope to hear; indeed, a first recommendation. The **Juilliard** took the piece into their repertoire at an early stage and play it with consistent fervour and deep understanding. Excellent recorded sound, too.

The Nonesuch disc offers a *Lyric Suite* with a difference and so has a special claim on the collector's allegiance. The work originally included a setting of lines from Baudelaire's *Fleurs du mal*. George Perle has reconstructed the original version of the finale and this is its first recording, very eloquently sung by **Dawn Upshaw**. The **Kronos** play with a certain robust intensity and fire (nothing in the least mellifluous here), and they are decently recorded. Since this disc contains only 27 minutes of music, it comes at bargain price.

Lyric Suite for String Quartet; String Quartet, Op. 3

*** MDG 307 0996-2. Leipzig Qt (with WEBERN: *3 Pieces* ***)

The **Leipzig Quartet's** performances were coolly received in some quarters but have much warmth and generosity of spirit to commend them. They offer the Webern 3 *Pieces* (which take two minutes) as a bonus. (**Christiane Oelze** is the singer in the second.)

Piano Sonata, Op. 1

8—*** Ph. 468 033-2. Uchida – SCHOENBERG: *Piano Concerto, etc.*; WEBERN: *Variations*

8— (BB) *** Naxos 8.553870. Hill – SCHOENBERG: *Piano Pieces, etc.*; WEBERN: *Variations* ***

In the Berg *Piano Sonata*, Op. 1, as in the remainder of her programme devoted to the Second Viennese School, **Uchida** is very persuasive indeed. The main work on the disc, Schoenberg's *Piano Concerto*, receives one of its most successful readings on record.

Peter Hill's account of the Berg *Sonata* on Naxos has more than just its bargain price to commend it. He is a pianist of proven intelligence and sensitivity and is decently recorded. It comes with the Schoenberg piano music, played with no less expertise and authority.

7 Early Songs

*** DG 437 515-2. von Otter, Forsberg – KORNGOLD; STRAUSS: *Lieder* ***

*** Decca 466 720-2. Bonney, Concg. O, Chailly – MAHLER: *Symphony 4* **(*)

In the *Seven Early Songs* of Berg, **Anne Sofie von Otter** and **Bengt Forsberg** offer inspired playing and singing, drawing out the intensity of emotion to the full without exaggeration or sentimentality. Along with Strauss and Korngold songs, a fascinating programme, magnetically performed.

Barbara Bonney also sounds spontaneous and warm in the *Seven Early Songs*, which come as a coupling for Mahler's *Fourth Symphony*, and **Chailly** and the orchestra too sound a degree more involved than in the Mahler.

Lulu (with orchestration of Act III completed by Friedrich Cerha)

(M) *** EMI 5 09400-2 (3). Wise, Fassbaender, Straka, Clark, Schöne, Clarey, O Nat. de France, Tate

*** Chan. 9540 (3). Haupman, Jaffe, Straka, Juan, Danish Nat. RSO, Schirmer

Jeffrey Tate's live recording of the full three-Act version provides a welcome alternative to the Chandos version. Tate's reading is more flexible, more volatile than Schirmer's even if there are stage noises, and some minor flaws of ensemble. On casting, Tate's set is marginally preferable, with **Patricia Wise** sensuous in the title-role and with **Brigitte Fassbaender** incomparable as the predatory Countess Geschwitz, spontaneously expressive for Tate. **Graham Clark** is excellent too and **Peter Straka** is again a fine Alwa. At its new price this is very recommendable (with a good synopsis).

Recorded at a series of live performances, the Chandos version is strongly and purposefully conducted by **Ulf Schirmer**. **Constance Haupman** makes Lulu a girlish, vulnerable figure, as well as thrusting and selfish. Her singing is commendably precise, even if under pressure the tone

grows shrill. As Dr Schön, **Monte Jaffe** relies too heavily on unpitched sing-speech, but his is a vividly characterful performance too; and among the others **Peter Straka** makes a fresh, clear Alwa and **Julia Juan** a touchingly mature Geschwitz.

Lulu (in English)

(M) **(*) Chan. 3130 (3). Saffer, Parry, Kale, Hayward, Graham-Hall, Howell, ENO Ch. & O, Daniel

Paul Daniel (using his own English translation) conducts an exceptionally persuasive account, more than is usual bringing out the work's lyricism alongside the lilt of the many dance-passages. The element of cabaret and circus is after all behind much of Berg's writing, but this is also a performance which underlines the stylized structure that Berg ingeniously developed – sonata, variations, rondo, etc. In the title-role **Lisa Saffer** with her bright, fresh soprano is most convincing through all the sinister developments in this often repellent story, well supported by a strong team of incidental characters, of whom the most striking are **Gwynne Howell** as Schigolch and **Susan Parry** as Geschwitz. Saffer sings strongly and movingly, even though this is a role which has prompted even more characterful readings from others.

Wozzeck (complete; DVD versions)

8—*** Arthaus DVD 101 277. Blankenheim, Janowitz, Cassilly, Unger, Sotin, Moll, Grundheber, Hamburg State Op. Ch. & O, Maderna (V/D: Jurgen Hess)

(M) *** Warner DVD 2564 69742-2. Grundheber, W. Meier, M. Baker, Wottrich, Clark, von Kannen, German Opera, Berlin, Ch., Berlin State O, Barenboim (Director: Patrice Chéreau; Video Editor: Jean-Claude Piroué)

It is rare that a performance of Berg's 12-note masterpiece is as well sung as on this studio recording, made with **Hamburg State Opera** forces in 1970. You hear every note of this difficult, atonal score on pitch with minimal use of sing-speech, which adds to the musical delights of **Bruno Maderna's** powerful reading. **Toni Blankenheim** is outstanding in the title-role, poignantly conveying the suffering of the central character, while **Gerhard Unger** is brilliant as the domineering Captain, well contrasted with **Richard Cassilly** in the other leading tenor role of the Drum major. **Gundula Janowitz**, with her sweetly pure soprano, sings beautifully as Marie, but also gives the necessary edge to the character, and **Hans Sotin** is strong and sinister as the Doctor. The miming of the singers to the studio recording is not always perfectly coordinated, but the musical precision is a great benefit, and the settings, with many scenes shot out of doors, are aptly atmospheric. The recorded sound is on the dry side, but that too adds to the precision. An excellent version of a difficult opera.

Already available on CD (see below), **Barenboim's** performance gains much from a visual presentation, even if Richard Peduzzi's sets are bare and unatmospheric. But Patrice Chéreau's direction is powerful, to match Barenboim's warmly committed contribution. As on disc, Franz Grundheber is strong in the title-role, and the only disappointment is **Waltraud Meier's** lack of vocal bloom in the part of Marie. But with excellent video direction, this performance projects powerfully and can be recommended as a fine (but less atmospheric) alternative to the Arthaus version.

Wozzeck (complete; CD versions)

 (BB) *** Naxos 8.660076/7. Falkman, Dalayman, Qvale, Wahlund, Stregard, Stockholm Royal Op. Ch. & O, Segerstam

(M) *** EMI 5 56865-2 (2). Skovhus, Denoke, Olsen, Merritt, Blinkhof, Sacher, Hamburg State Op. Ch. & State PO, Metzmacher

**(*) Teldec 0630 14108-2 (2). Grundheber, Meier, Baker, Wottrich, Clark, von Kannen, German Opera, Berlin, Ch. & Children's Ch., Berlin State O, Barenboim

Segerstam proves a strong, thrusting interpreter, tautly holding the drama together, with the impact heightened by the vividness of the live recording. Though the *Sprechstimme* ('sing-speech') is sometimes free – again not surprisingly – the great merit of all the singers is their musicality, with the Captain and the Doctor less caricatured than usual, and with a firm, central account of the title-role from **Carl Johan Falkman**. **Katarina Dalayman** is also superb as Marie, singing with character as well as beauty. A detailed synopsis is provided in the booklet and a complete libretto in German but no translation. An excellent issue which, at the Naxos price, should tempt collectors to experiment with a challenging work that in a performance like this is deeply moving.

Ingo Metzmacher's live recording for EMI was made at the Hamburg State Opera, with Metzmacher drawing powerful, clean-textured playing from his orchestra, firmly establishing this as a high romantic work, whatever its modernist credentials. The casting is strong too, with **Bo Skovhus** singing with clean focus in the title-role, and with Marie superbly sung by **Angela Denoke**, sensuous on the one hand, tenderly affecting on the other. Otherwise, the production on a bare stage seems to have encouraged each character to overact, Skovhus included, even while the results are exceptionally vivid, with the sense of a live performance consistently adding to the dramatic impact.

Barenboim's Teldec version of *Wozzeck* was recorded live at the Deutsche Staatsoper in Berlin in 1994. With **Grundheber** even finer than under Abbado, Barenboim leads a warmly expressive performance. The cast is an outstanding one, with such characterful singers as **Graham Clark** (Captain) in incidental roles. Less successful is **Waltraud Meier** as Marie, with an uneven, grainy quality in the voice.

Wozzeck (in English)

(M) **(*) Chan. 3094 (2). Shore, Woodrow, Kale, Bayley, Barstow, Rigby, Geoffrey Mitchell Ch., Philh. O, Daniel

In **Paul Daniel's** account of *Wozzeck* the drama is intensified, even if the sinister element in this story of neurosis is minimized. **Andrew Shore** is strongly cast in the title-role, even if the firm clarity of his singing equally underplays the neurosis. He is strong and positive rather than mad-sounding, at least until the final scenes of Marie's murder and his own

suicide. There the atmospheric recording vividly captures the sinister ambience of this disturbing opera. The extremes of expression and dynamic in the scenes with Marie are also very well caught. **Dame Josephine Barstow** sounds too mature for the role, not quite steady enough, even though dramatically she gives a vivid portrayal, with **Jean Rigby** a fine foil as Margret. The grotesques among the male characters are all very well portrayed, their characterization the more vivid thanks to the clarity of words.

BERKELEY, Lennox (1903–89)

Guitar Concerto

*** Chan. 9963. Ogden, N. Sinf., Hickox – ARNOLD: *Guitar Concerto*; WALTON: *5 Bagatelles* ***

The Berkeley *Concerto*, one of his last works, begins atmospherically with a duet for two unaccompanied horns, relaxed in its mood, gaining in this performance under **Richard Hickox** from relatively urgent speeds. It leads via a mysterious slow movement to a finale which starts with a sly quotation from Rodrigo's *Concierto de Aranjuez*. **Craig Ogden** gives a commanding performance.

(i) Piano Concerto in B flat, Op. 29; (ii) Double Piano Concerto, Op. 30

*** Lyrita SRCD 250. (i) Davis Wilde, New Philh. O, Braithwaite; (ii) Garth Beckett, Boyd McDonald, LPO, Del Mar

The *Piano Concerto* was written in the immediate wake of the Second World War and is traditional in layout, but every bit as rewarding as the symphonies. The *Double Concerto*, no less finely wrought and enjoyable, comes from 1948. The orchestral playing and the contributions of all three soloists deserve the warmest plaudits and the analogue recording maintains the high standards of the Lyrita series. But the new Chandos version is even finer – see below.

Divertimento in B flat, Op. 18; Partita for Chamber Orchestra, Op. 66; Serenade for Strings, Op. 12; (i) Sinfonia concertante for Oboe & Chamber Orchestra, Op. 84: Canzonetta (only). Symphony 3 in 1 Movement, Op. 74; Mont Juic (with Britten), Op. 9

 *** Lyrita (ADD) SRCD 226 [id.]. LPO, composer; (i) with Winfield

The *Divertimento* is enchanting, with its four stylish and highly inventive movements, while the *String Serenade*, similarly in four sections, is hardly less attractive and brings a beautiful *Lento* closing movement. In its rather weightier tone of voice the *Partita* belies that it was written originally with a youth orchestra in mind, while the fourth movement from the *Sinfonia concertante* makes a splendid interlude before the closing *Symphony 3*. This is a concise, one-movement work, slightly more austere in its lyricism, but with a popular element entering the finale. The recording from the early 1970s, is first class, and the CD transfers only improve the sense of presence and realism. The programme opens with the charmingly spontaneous *Mont Juic Suite* which Berkeley wrote in collaboration with Benjamin Britten, two movements each (Berkeley contributing the opening pair), and the work was later published jointly as Berkeley's Op. 9 and Britten's Op. 12.

Double Piano Concerto

🔑 *** Chan. 10408. Stott, Shelley, BBC Nat. O of Wales, Hickox – MICHAEL BERKELEY: *Concerto for Orchestra*, etc. ***

Written in 1948 for the husband-and-wife team of Cyril Smith and Phyllis Sellick, Lennox Berkeley's *Double Piano Concerto* adopts a layout similar to that of Beethoven's last *Piano Sonata*, Opus 111, with a compact first movement leading to an extended set of variations. The piano writing is unusual too in employing the two pianos as a unit, and only rarely in contrast. The result, warmly recorded, is a strong and attractive work, here beautifully performed by **Kathryn Stott** and **Howard Shelley** with **Richard Hickox** providing excellent support.

The Judgement of Paris (ballet)

Ⓜ *** Dutton CDLX 7149. Royal Ballet Sinfonia, Wordsworth – LAMBERT: *Apparitions*; LANCHBERY: *Tales of Beatrix Potter* ***

Sir Lennox Berkeley's *Judgement of Paris* is genuine ballet music and winningly scored, even if the melodic invention is unmemorable. It is splendidly played by the Royal Ballet Sinfonia under Barry Wordsworth, and the recording is first class in every way.

(i) *Sinfonia concertante, Op. 84; Symphony 3*

*** Chan. 10022. BBC Nat. O of Wales, Hickox, with (i) Daniel – MICHAEL BERKELEY: *Oboe Concerto*, etc. ***

In Lennox Berkeley's *Sinfonia concertante* the first two of the five movements are linked by using the same material, while the third and fourth, *Aria* and *Canzonetta*, bring a relaxation before the vigorous finale, with a cadenza in the middle and a thoughtful passage before the strongly rhythmic coda. *Symphony 3*, written in 1968–9, is in a single movement divided into three sections. It represents his late style at its most striking, dark and compressed in the first section, with rapidly contrasting motifs, before a brief, slow, central section leads to a rather more extrovert finale with galloping 6/8 rhythms and a brassy conclusion, all brilliantly caught in the full-ranging Chandos recording.

Sinfonietta, Op. 34

*** Lyrita (ADD) SRCD 257. ECO, Del Mar – ARNOLD; MICHAEL BERKELEY; BRITTEN: *Sinfoniettas*; RAWSTHORNE; TIPPETT: *Divertimentos* ***

Berkeley's *Sinfonietta* is a delightful example of his genius for miniature. Perfectly crafted, it says much in the shortest possible span, lightly but with no feeling of triviality. It is beautifully performed and recorded.

Symphony 1; Serenade for Strings

🔑 *** Chan. 9981. BBC Nat. O of Wales, Hickox – MICHAEL BERKELEY: *Horn Concerto; Coronach* ***

The *First Symphony* is one of Lennox Berkeley's most luminous and captivating scores – and very good it is too. It is a fresh and beautifully written work, prompting a strong, committed performance from the **BBC National Orchestra of Wales** under **Richard Hickox** which has been superbly recorded. The *Serenade for Strings* is a delightful piece, carefree until the final *Lento*, where, reflectively, Berkeley touches deeper emotions. In **Hickox's** hands it comes off splendidly. The **BBC National Orchestra of Wales** again play with zest and sensitivity, and the recording is extremely vivid and present. Recommended with enthusiasm.

Symphonies (i) *1, Op. 16*; (ii) *2, Op. 51*

*** Lyrita (ADD) SRCD 249. LPO, (i) Del Mar; (ii) Braithwaite

The *First Symphony* is distinctly individual and memorable. The *Second Symphony* is also a work of a sophisticated and cultivated musical mind; textures are clean and the ideas are beautifully laid out. This is civilized music, and its originality is all the more rewarding for the restrained expressive means. The warmly sympathtic playing of the **LPO** under **Norman Del Mar** and **Nicholas Braithwaite** is of the highest quality and the analogue Lyrita recording has impeccable depth and realism.

Symphony 4

*** Chan. 10080. BBC Nat. O of Wales, Hickox – MICHAEL BERKELEY: *Cello Concerto*, etc. ***

Lennox Berkeley's *Fourth Symphony* of 1977/8, one of his most ambitious works, is a remarkable piece for a composer in his mid-seventies, starting disconcertingly in darkness but with the slow introduction leading to an energetic first-movement *Allegro*, followed by a strongly contrasted set of variations and a sharply rhythmic finale, all colourfully orchestrated. **Richard Hickox** and the **BBC National Orchestra of Wales** are powerful advocates, brilliantly recorded. The *Symphony* makes a fine coupling for the two major works by the composer's son, Michael.

CHAMBER MUSIC

Concertino, Op. 49; Duo for Cello & Piano, Op. 81/1; Elegy for Violin & Piano, Op. 35/2; Introduction & Allegro for Solo Violin, Op. 24; Oboe Quartet, Op. 70; Petite suite for Oboe & Piano; Sextet, Op. 47; Toccata for Violin & Piano, Op. 33/3

Ⓜ *** Dutton CDLX 7100. Endymion Ens.

Lennox Berkeley's elegantly fashioned music is fastidiously crafted and musically rewarding, unpretentious, urbane and charming. The **Endymion Ensemble** do it proud, and so does the natural and well-balanced recording.

(i) *Diversions* (for oboe, clarinet, bassoon, horn, piano & string trio), *Op. 61; Oboe Quartet; Sextet* (for clarinet, horn & string quartet), *Op. 47*; (ii) Piano Duet: *Palm Court Waltz, Op. 81/2. Sonatina, Op. 39*

🔑 Ⓑ *** Hyp. Helios CDH 55135. (i) Nash Ens.; (ii) I. Brown; Stott

Diversions is particularly diverting. Both the slow movement and finale are unostentatious essays in counterpoint, yet in addition they manage to be (respectively) lyrically appealing and attractively jaunty. The *Sextet* for clarinet, horn and strings brings an aurally fascinating linear interplay between the wind and string lines. The *Oboe Quartet* is a good deal more than just the usual pastoral excursion. The slow movement comes last, at first hauntingly sad and mysterious, growing more animated, then returning to the mood of the opening, with each instrument dropping out in turn, leaving the cello alone at the close. The *Palm Court Waltz* for piano duet has a disarming insouciance, and it goes well with the elegant *Sonatina*. Of the soloists, the oboist, **Gareth Hulse**, and the clarinettist, **Michael Collins**, deserve special mention; the recording, although a shade resonant in the two piano works, is very good, with woodwind balanced a little forward from the strings.

4 Pièces pour la guitare, Op. post.; Sonatina, Op. 1; Theme and Variations, Op. 77

*** Chan. 10261. Craig Ogden – MICHAEL BERKELEY: *Impromptu; Lament*, etc. ***

It was the artistry of Julian Bream that inspired Lennox and Michael Berkeley to compose these works for the guitar. They both find an extraordinarily idiomatic style, so that the *Quatre Pièces*, dedicated to Segovia, sound like anglicized Spanish music, yet they are wholly individual. The invention is consistently ear-catching, as it is in the *Sonatina* (written for Bream), which has a musing slow movement that brings just a faint hint of Rodrigo before the equally appealing and vibrant rondo finale. Finest of all is the *Theme and Variations*, which explores the widest range of guitar figurations and musical divisions, before the haunting closing epilogue, which returns to the mood of the opening. **Craig Ogden** plays all this music superbly, sustaining great concentration, so that one has a continuing sense of a live performance, borne out by the totally realistic recording. If you enjoy the guitar, this disc is on no account to be missed.

(i) Sextet for Clarinet, Horn, & String Quartet, Op. 47; (ii) Violin Sonatina, Op. 17

*** Lyrita (ADD) SRCD 256. (i) Brymer, Civil, Bean, Routh, Wellington, Croxford; (ii) Bean, Parkhouse – A. BUSH: *Concert Studies*, etc. **(*); RAWSTHORNE: *Clarinet Qt*

Lennox Berkeley recorded his *Sonatina* with Frederick Grinke in the early days of LP, and this new version reinforces the pleasing impression it made. Like the *Sextet* (with its star-studded group of performers) it is inventive, refined and polished, and it could hardly be more persuasively played than it is here.

String Quartets 1, Op. 6; 2, Op. 15; 3, Op. 76

(BB) *** Naxos 8.570415. Maggini Qt

The *First Quartet* comes from 1935 and shows a debt to Stravinsky and Bartók, as well as the composer's strong Gallic sympathies. The *Second* too has a certain astringency, as does the *Third*, composed in 1970, written in the immediate wake of the *Third Symphony* and notable for an ethereal slow movement, bringing an intense, emotional climax, resolved in the sharply rhythmic finale. The **Maggini** play these rewarding scores with great dedication: the contribution of Lorraine McAslan as leader is particularly impressive, especially in the lyrical slow movement of No. 1. The recording, made at Potton Hall, Suffolk, has clarity and presence.

PIANO MUSIC

Concert Study in E flat, Op. 48/2; Improvisation on a Theme of Falla; Paysage, Mazurka, Op. 32/1; 3 Pieces, Op. 2; 6 Preludes, Op. 23; Scherzo, Op. 32/2; Sonata

*** Chan. 10247. Fingerhut (with MICHAEL BERKELEY: *Strange Meeting* ***)

Lennox Berkeley wrote for the piano with exceptional fluency and natural feeling. **Margaret Fingerhut**, vividly recorded, has both eloquence and authority. This is a fine survey of rewarding repertoire, as well played as it is recorded. Piano sound does not come much better than this. As part of the series devoted to both father and son, Michael is represented by an early piece from the early 1970s, *Strange Meeting*, inspired by the poem by Wilfred Owen which his godfather, Benjamin Britten, had used a decade earlier in his *War Requiem*.

(i) Music for Piano 4 Hands: Sonatina, Op. 39; Theme & Variations, Op. 73; Palm Court Waltz, Op. 81/2. Solo piano music: 6 Preludes, Op. 23; 5 Short Pieces, Op. 4; Sonata, Op. 20

*** British Music Society BMS 416CD. Terroni, (i) with Beedle

A generous selection of the cultivated and tuneful piano music of Lennox Berkeley: the fine *Sonata* with its sensuously coloured *Adagio*, the often witty *Preludes* and the five charming *Short Pieces*, which often have a whiff of Poulenc, the *Sonatina* with another elegantly individual slow movement, and the more complex *Theme and Variations*. **Raphael Terroni** is an accomplished and sympathetic exponent, with **Norman Beedle** an admirable partner in the *Music for Piano Four Hands*. The piano recording is most natural. The CD is available direct from the British Music Society, 7 Tudor Gardens, Upminster, Essex.

OPERA

A Dinner Engagement (complete)

*** Chan. 10219. Williams, Kenny, Rigby, Collins, City of L. Sinfonia, Hickox

Richard Hickox conducts a performance of Lennox's most popular opera which, with an excellent cast, brings out the light-hearted fun in this comedy of manners. It tells of a diplomat and his wife, the Earl and Countess of Dunmow, who, fallen on hard times, have royal guests, the Grand Duchess and her son, Prince Philip, from Monteblanco, where the Earl was ambassador. The comedy lies in the hosts' embarrassment when, with only the help of a comic char (a stock 1950s figure), their efforts at self-catering go wildly wrong. All comes well in the end, with the Dunmow daughter, Susan, falling in the arms of the Prince. As a comedy it may be dated, but on disc Berkeley's light and lyrical score works well, with excellent singing all round, including **Roderick Williams** and **Yvonne Kenny** as the Earl and Countess, **Claire Rutter** as Susan and **Robin Leggate** as Philip, with the resonant **Anne Collins** as a characterful Grand Duchess.

Ruth (complete)

*** Chan. 10301. Rigby, Tucker, Kenny, Rutter, Williams, Joyful Company of Singers, City of L. Sinfonia, Hickox

The story of Ruth and her loyalty to her mother-in-law, Naomi, is among the most touching in the Bible, and Lennox Berkeley, helped by a libretto by Eric Crozier, builds it into a moving opera in three scenes lasting 80 minutes. After a brief prelude, the opening scene brings a warmly expressive trio, with Ruth and Naomi joined by the other daughter-in-law, Orpah. When Orpah opts to return to the land of Moab, Ruth pledges her loyalty to Naomi in the memorable solo, *Whither thou goest, I will go*, leading on to a duet and an atmospheric chorus to round the scene off. The role of Boaz is taken by a tenor, the farmer who, against the hostility of the villagers, supports the right of Ruth, a Moabite, to glean in his fields with the others. The happy ending comes when Boaz declares his love for Ruth, leading on to the founding of the House of David. **Richard Hickox**, drawing excellent singing and playing from chorus and orchestra, as well as from the first-rate team of soloists, paces the three scenes most persuasively, bringing out dramatic contrasts in what might have been too gentle a sequence. Warm, clear sound.

BERKELEY, Michael (born 1948)

(i) Cello Concerto. The Garden of Earthly Delights

*** Chan. 10080. BBC Nat. O of Wales, Hickox (i) with Gerhardt – LENNOX BERKELEY: *Symphony 4* ***

Dating from 1998, *The Garden of Earthly Delights* is a formidable piece for a huge orchestra, including quadruple woodwind and a wide-ranging percussion section, complete with 'lion-roar'. Berkeley uses these forces with a winning exuberance in some of the strongest, most colourful music he has ever written. **Richard Hickox** inspires the BBC National Orchestra of Wales to a brilliant performance, vividly recorded.

The *Cello Concerto* makes the cello soloist very much the centre, with a series of cadenzas, often meditative, punctuated by orchestral passages which emerge almost as interludes rather than the main meat. Well supported by Hickox and the orchestra, **Alan Gerhardt's** performance is both brilliant and dedicated.

(i) Horn Concerto (for horn and string orchestra). Coronach (for strings)

*** Chan. 9981. BBC Nat. O of Wales, Hickox; (i) with Pyatt – LENNOX BERKELEY: *Symphony 1; Serenade* ***

Coronach is a lament for string orchestra which explores the 'complex emotions of grief; the rage and anger as well as the sadness'. It builds up powerfully in the manner of a funeral dirge, with a quotation from the Scottish ballad, 'The Bonny Earl of Moray'. The *Horn Concerto* in two movements is more powerful still. Written in 1984, it represents a new departure for the composer in its often gritty, uncompromising tone. Yet it makes an immediate emotional impact, with the naggingly energetic first movement giving way to a deeply thoughtful and spacious slow movement. **David Pyatt** is the superb soloist, magnetically bringing out the logic of each development, with **Hickox** and the orchestra equally powerful in support. Full, brilliant sound.

(i) Oboe Concerto. Secret Garden

🎧 *** Chan. 10022. BBC Nat. O of Wales, Hickox with (i) Daniel – LENNOX BERKELEY: *Sinfonia Concertante*, etc. ***

Next to Lennox Berkeley's *Sinfonia concertante*, a late work, Michael Berkeley's early *Concerto for Oboe and Strings* of 1976–7 seems all the more warmly conservative, with two substantial slow movements framing a relatively brief central Scherzo. One notes the writing for the strings is often sensuous, not least in the finale, entitled *Elegy in memoriam Benjamin Britten*. The disc is rounded off impressively with the *Secret Garden* of 1997, in which stuttering brass fanfares at the start create what the composer describes as a wall of sound. The coda brings a warm echo of the great horn theme in Sibelius's *Fifth Symphony*, reflecting the love of both Berkeleys for that work. As on the companion disc, **Richard Hickox** and the **BBC National Orchestra of Wales** give powerfully committed performances, warmly and fully recorded.

Concerto for Orchestra (Seascapes); Gregorian Variations

*** Chan. 10408. BBC Nat. O of Wales, Hickox – LENNOX BERKELEY: *Double Piano Concerto* ***

Michael Berkeley's *Gregorian Variations*, using a chant-like theme, contrast lyricism (notably in a beautiful cor anglais solo) with syncopated, jazzy rhythms. The orchestration is colourful too, with timpani and bells. 'Seascape' belies its title in offering an abrasive style, hardly at all atmospheric, but it is well constructed, beautifully recorded and very well performed by **Richard Hickox** and the Welsh orchestra.

Guitar music: Impromptu; Lament; Sonata in One Movement; Worry Beads

🎧 *** Chan. 10261. Craig Ogden – LENNOX BERKELEY: *4 Pièces pour la guitare*, etc. ***

The haunting *Lament* and the intriguing *Worry Beads* (with a main theme that mirrors a more famous piece by another composer) are followed by a one-movement *Sonata*, improvisatory in feeling, written for Julian Bream; the final encore is an *Impromptu*, a fiftieth birthday present for Bream. **Craig Ogden** plays all this music with total spontaneity, and he is superbly recorded.

Jane Eyre (complete opera)

*** Chan. 9983. Marsh, Wyn, Mills, Bauer-Jones, Slater, Music Theatre Wales Ens., Rafferty

Michael Berkeley took on the formidable challenge of adapting Charlotte Brontë's long novel as a compact opera just over 70 minutes long. With a libretto by David Malouf, he has devised a surreal, dream-like sequence that, instead of telling the full story direct, sketches in its outlines with time treated kaleidoscopically, whether in selective moments, flashbacks or offstage voices from the past. Setting the sinister scene, the writing is lyrical in free arioso, with clear tunes emerging. When, for example, Adele, Rochester's ward, refers to the mad scene from *Lucia di Lammermoor*, the main melody from Donizetti's opera is quoted. **Michael Rafferty** conducts the **Music Theatre Wales** in a compelling performance, with **Natasha Marsh** as Jane and **Andrew Slater** as Rochester singing strongly in the principal roles, and **Ffiur Wyn** bright and girlish as Adele.

BERLIOZ, Hector (1803–69)

COMPLETE ORCHESTRAL WORKS

(i) *Grande symphonie funèbre et triomphale, Op. 15*; (i–ii) *Harold in Italy, Op. 16*; (i; iii) *Lélio, Op. 14b*; *Overtures:* (i) *Béatrice et Bénédict*; (iv) *Benvenuto Cellini*; (i) *Le Carnaval romain, Op. 9*; *Le Corsaire, Op. 21*; *Les Francs-juges, Op. 3*; *Le Roi Lear, Op. 4*; *Waverley, Op. 1*; (v) *Rêverie et caprice (for violin & orchestra), Op. 8*; (vi–vii) *Symphonie fantastique, Op. 14*; (i; vii) *Tristia, Op. 18 (excerpt): Marche funèbre pour la dernière scène d'Hamlet*; (i) *La Damnation de Faust, Op. 24 (excerpts): Menuet des follets; Marche hongroise*; (i; viii) *Romeo and Juliet, Op. 17*; (i) *Les Troyens à Carthage, Part II, Prélude, Act III*; (ix) *Les Troyens, Act IV: Royal Hunt and Storm; Marche pour l'entrée de la reine; Ballet Music*

(B) *** Ph. 456 143-2 (6). (i) LSO; (ii) with Imai; (iii) with Carreras, Allen, Constable (piano), Jowitt (clarinet), Scheffel-Stein (harp); (iv) BBC SO; (v) Grumiaux, New Philh. O, De Waart; (vi) Concg. O; (vii) with Alldis Ch.; (viii) with Kern, Shirley-Quirk, Tear, L. Symphony Ch.; (ix) ROHCG O; all (except *Op. 8*) cond. C. Davis

This bargain-priced collection of **Sir Colin Davis's** Berlioz recordings is self-recommending.

(i) *Grande symphonie funèbre et triomphale*; (ii) *Overtures: Benvenuto Cellini; Le Carnaval romain; Le Corsaire; Les Francs-juges*; (iii) *Les Troyens: Royal Hunt and Storm; Ballet Music; Trojan March*; (iv) *La Mort de Cléopâtre*

(BB) *** Warner Apex 2564 62183-2 (2). (i) Chorale Populaire de Paris, Musiques des Gardiens de la Paix, Dondeyne; (ii) Strasbourg PO, Lombard; (iii; iv) Nouvel PO de Strasbourg, Amy; (iv) with Denize

Désiré Dondeyne's 1958 performance of the *Grande symphonie funèbre et triomphale*, spaciously recorded in Notre

Dame, is exciting and convincing in a specially French way. The central movement has a very French trombone solo which some non-Gallic listeners may not take to, but overall this is impressive. The sound has plenty of spectacle and bite. **Nadine Denize** is equally at home in *La Mort de Cléopâtre*, which combines dramatic flair with a moving closing section. The four key overtures, recorded digitally two decades later, are also very well played, and the programme ends with excerpts from *Les Troyens*, the *Royal Hunt and Storm*, without chorus but still impressive. Excellent recording throughout, but the documentation is totally inadequate, with no texts.

(i; ii) *Harold in Italy. Overtures:* (ii) *Le Corsaire*; (iii) *King Lear*; (ii) *Les Troyens: Trojan March*

(**(*)) BBC mono BBCL 4065-2. (i) Riddle; (ii) RPO; (iii) BBC SO; Beecham

(i) *Harold in Italy. Les Troyens: Ballet Music*

⊶ (BB) *** LSO Live LSO 0040. (i) Zimmermann; LSO, C Davis

Sir Colin Davis demonstrates his supreme mastery as a Berlioz interpreter in a version of *Harold in Italy* recorded live, even tauter and more dramatic than his earlier ones made in the studio, with speeds consistently faster, notably in the first movement. One other benefit of the recording is that the soloist, the magnificent **Tabea Zimmermann**, is balanced as part of the orchestra instead of being spotlit. The *Ballet Music*, taken from Davis's prize-winning LSO Live version of *Les Troyens*, makes a warmly atmospheric bonus. The disc comes at super-budget price, complete with authoritative notes by David Cairns, and now becomes a primary recommendation.

The radio recordings of **Beecham** in full flight are most welcome. All these items confirm how Beecham in live performances of Berlioz conveyed a red-blooded manic intensity, to match the composer's revolutionary wildness, making almost any rival seem cool. The *Corsaire Overture* has a fierceness and thrust entirely apt to the Byronic subject, culminating in a swaggering climax that verges on the frenetic. *Harold in Italy*, recorded in 1956 with the dynamic range compressed so as to magnify *pianissimos*, is valuable for having as soloist Beecham's chosen leader of the RPO violas, **Frederick Riddle**. The *Trojan March* makes a swaggering encore, an electrifying performance from the historic opening concert of the Colston Hall in Bristol in 1951.

(i) *Harold in Italy. Symphonie fantastique* (DVD versions)

⊶ *** Bel Air DVD BAC 016. O de Paris, Eschenbach, (i) with Zimmermann (V/D: Andy Sommer)

In his excellent note Professor Kern Holoman calls the *Symphonie fantastique* 'probably the most extraordinary first symphony ever composed' and in a great performance one is almost tempted to say the most extraordinarily original symphony ever. **Christoph Eschenbach** secures a first-class response from the superb **Orchestre de Paris**. *Harold in Italy*, inspired by Berlioz's time in Italy and by the playing of Paganini, who commissioned the piece for his Stradivarius viola, was the winner of the Prix de Rome. It is another work of remarkable vision and originality, which Eschenbach and his distinguished soloist play marvellously. The recording was made in 2001 at the Salle Gavaux, Paris.

Overtures: *Béatrice et Bénédict; Benvenuto Cellini; Le Carnaval romain; Le Corsaire; Les Francs-juges; Le Roi Lear; Waverley*

🗝 ✿ Ⓜ **** RCA 82876 65839-2. Dresden State O, C. Davis

Mercurial, full of vitality and poetic feeling, wonderfully light in articulation, and superbly played and recorded. This RCA disc completely supersedes **Sir Colin's** recordings on Philips in every way. A glorious issue, outstanding in every way, and now the best Berlioz overtures disc in the catalogue.

Symphonie fantastique, Op. 14 (DVD Version)

Ⓝ *** Medici Arts **DVD** 2020 0098 BPO, Jansons (with HAYDN: *Symphony 94 (Surprise)*; MOZART: *Flute Concerto 2 in D, K.314* (with Emmanuel Pahud))

Jansons's interpretation is of the kind that dashes off passionately at the very opening, but otherwise the performance is well paced and finely controlled. The slow movement brings glorious **Berlin Philharmonic** playing, and the finale unleashes plenty of spectacle and excitement. One of the advantages of DVD is that the camera reveals, with close-ups, the way Berlioz's extraordinarily imaginative orchestration achieves the colouristic effects with which the work abounds. The modern-instrument account of the Haydn *Surprise Symphony* is amply textured, but elegantly turned and warm-hearted. **Emmanuel Pahud** is the prince of flautists, and his contribution to the Mozart *Flute Concerto* is completely captivating, even including a neat little cadenza just before the close. Excellent recording throughout.

Symphonie fantastique, Op. 14 (CD versions)

**** Pentatone Surround Sound **SACD** PTC 5186. Concg. O, C. Davis

🗝 Ⓜ *** BBC (ADD) BBCL 4018-2. New Philh. O, Stokowski (with conversation with Deryck Cooke) – SCRIABIN: *Poème de l'extase* ***

🗝 **** BBC BBCL 4163-2. Leningrad PO, Rozhdestvensky – TCHAIKOVSKY: *Francesca da Rimini* ***

(i) Symphonie fantastique; Overture: Le Corsaire; (ii) Les Troyens: March troyenne; (iii) Royal Hunt and Storm

🗝 ✿ Ⓜ *** EMI 5 67971-2. (i) O Nat. de France; (ii) RPO; (iii) with Beecham Ch. Soc., Beecham

Beecham's account still enjoys classic status and has a demonic intensity that is immediately compelling and holds the listener on the seat-edge until the work's electrifying close. In this extraordinary new transfer, in which every de-

tail is crystal clear, the strings have an especially rich sheen and the brass a sonority and depth more telling than on any previous incarnation of the 1959 recording. Even the tolling bells of the finale deserve a credit for their remarkable tangibility, while the warm acoustic of the Salle Wagram, Paris, frames a concert-hall balance of remarkable realism. This is an indispensable record, made the more so for a tinglingly atmospheric account of the *Royal Hunt and Storm* (with chorus) and the classic account of the *Corsaire Overture*. Ian Jones, the remastering engineer, deserves to share the honours.

In 1974 **Sir Colin Davis** chose the *Symphonie fantastique* for his first recording with the Amsterdam **Royal Concertgebouw Orchestra**. The interpretation is very similar to his earlier account with the LSO, only the performance has even more energy, life and colour. The slow movement too is more atmospheric than before, and it sounds richly beautiful. Even on CD the recording is outstanding but, by returning to the original quadraphonic master tapes, a more spectacularly realistic sound has been achieved for those with a four-channel reproducer. The results place the Pentatone disc alongside Beecham as a primary recommendation.

A really high-voltage performance from **Stokowski** and the **New Philharmonia Orchestra** of the *Symphonie fantastique*, recorded in 1968. The great conductor was eighty-six and in astonishing form. Though this would not be a first choice, every bar is stamped with personality. There are characteristic expressive exaggerations, but everything rings true and has conviction. The sound is acceptable, though not all the strands in the texture are ideally balanced. This comes in tandem with an outstanding performance of *Le poème de l'extase* and a conversation between the great conductor and Deryck Cooke.

The high-powered (1971) Prom performance from **Rozhdestvensky** and the **Leningrad Philharmonic** demonstrates the orchestra's superlative quality at the time, astonishing British listeners. There is an element of wildness in the reading, perfectly suited to the work, encouraged no doubt by the live occasion, and the stereo recording, good for its period, brings the drama of that out to the full, even if again inner detail is not always ideally clear. The thrill of a great Prom event is vividly caught, not least in the eruption of cheering at the end. The 1960 account of *Francesca da Rimini* makes an equally compelling coupling.

Gardiner with his **Orchestre Révolutionnaire et Romantique** uses the extra sharpness of focus to add to the dramatic bite. In his electrifying, warmly expressive performance, heightening Berlioz's wild syncopations, he is second to none in conveying the astonishing modernity of music written within three years of Beethoven's death. (Ph. 434 402-2)

Symphonie fantastique, Op. 14; (ii) Lélio, Op. 14b

Ⓝ ⓑⓑ *** EMI Gemini (ADD) O. Nat. de l'ORTF; (ii) with Soloists, French R Ch, Martinon

Berlioz provided **Lélio** as a sequel to the *Symphonie fantastique* and **Martinon** conveniently offers the works paired together at bargain price. His account of the *Symphonie* is uniquely seductive, for though he is brilliant he never presses on too frenetically. The finale, with its tolling bells of doom, has a flamboyance and power to match any available, and the 1973 sound remains remarkably vivid. Lélio quotes the *idée fixe* from the *Symphonie*, which helps the listener to feel at home.

CHORAL WORKS

Le Ballet des ombres, Op. 2; Chanson à boire, Op. 2/5; Chant de chemin de fer, Op. 19/3; Chant guerrier, Op. 2/3; Chante sacré, Op. 2/6 (versions I & II); Le Cinq Mai; Hymne pour la consécration du nouveau tabernacle; Marche funèbre pour la dernière scène d'Hamlet; La Mort d'Orphée; La Mort d'Ophélie; Sara la baigneuse, Op. 11; Scène héroïque (La Révolution grecque); Tantum ergo sacramentum; Tristia, Op. 18; Veni Creator Spiritus

**(*) EMI 5 57499-2 (2). Villazón, Naouri, Riveno, Les Eléments Ch., Capitole Toulouse O, Plasson

La Révolution grecque, written in 1825–33 and described as a *scène héroïque*, harks back to the music of a generation earlier, inspired by the French Revolution, a rousing piece in four sections for two basses, chorus and orchestra. *Le Cinq Mai*, written to commemorate the death of Napoleon, is equally rare, part of a planned major work to celebrate the defeated Emperor, which Berlioz abandoned. The Op. 2 pieces are taken from a collection of settings of poems by the poet Thomas Moore (in translations by Thomas Gounet), usually given the collective title *Irlande*. Most of the Op. 2 pieces are simple songs, but **Plasson** has here extracted the choral items, which, like the songs, have piano accompaniment. One of the weirdest pieces here is the ronde nocturne, *Ballet des ombres*, and one of the liveliest the *Chants des chemins de fer*, celebrating the opening of the railway line from Paris to Lille in 1846. The lovely Hugo setting, *Sara la baigneuse*, the three movements labelled *Tristia*, *Méditation religieuse* and *La Mort d'Ophélie* and the *Hamlet Funeral March*, are all relatively well known, here given warmly idiomatic performances, but curiously two of the later choral works, both settings of Latin for female chorus, *Veni creator spiritus*, *a cappella*, and *Tantum ergo*, with harmonium accompaniment, are the least typical. Good, warm sound for most items, though the piano in the Op. 2 songs is shallow and clangy.

VOCAL MUSIC

Cantatas: (i) Herminie; (ii) La Mort de Cléopâtre; (iii) La Mort d'Orphée; La Mort de Sardanapale

(BB) **(*) Naxos 8.555810. Ch. Régional Nord, O Nat. de Lille, Régional Nord, Pas-de-Calais, Casadesus; with (i) Lagrange; (ii) Uria-Monzon; (iii) Vallejo

La Mort de Sardanapale, though ironically only a fragment has survived, that fragment is markedly less original than any of the earlier works, even if it is well worth hearing for the hints of Berlioz themes to come. *Herminie*, based on Tasso's *Jerusalem Liberated*, strikingly uses as a central theme the motif that soon after became the *idée fixe* of the *Symphonie fantastique*, while *La Mort de Cléopâtre* even more clearly an-

ticipates the operatic tone of voice that reached its culmination in *Les Troyens*. Even the earliest cantata, *La Mort d'Orphée*, with tenor and a chorus of raging bacchantes, brings a memorable close, though the soloist, **Daniel Galvez Vallejo**, is coarser than either the excellent soprano, **Michèle Lagrange**, in *Herminie* or the mezzo, **Beatrice Uria-Monzon**, in *Cléopâtre*, with the **Lille Orchestra** under **Jean-Claude Casadesus** warm and refined.

La Damnation de Faust (complete; DVD version)

*** Arthaus DVD 102 023. von Otter, Lewis, van Dam, Rose, Chicago SO Ch. & O, Solti

Recorded at the Proms at the Royal Albert Hall in 1989, with Chicago forces imported en masse, **Sir Georg Solti's** brilliant version is excellent in every way. The performance is not as fierce as this conductor could be in this music, but it is wonderfully dramatic, with the Prom audience cheering the visitors on. Margaret Hillis's **Chicago Symphony Chorus** matches the orchestra in brilliance and responsiveness, and the trio of soloists makes an ideal team. **Keith Lewis** as Faust is fresh and unstrained, while **José van Dam** is a superb Mephistopheles, tender and seductive as well as flamboyant, and **Anne Sofie von Otter**, handsome in royal blue, sings flawlessly as Marguerite, at her most tender in the *Roi de Thule* aria. Rodney Greenberg's video direction effectively brings out the atmospheric qualities of the Royal Albert Hall.

La Damnation de Faust (complete; CD version)

&—(BB) *** LSO Live LSO 0008 (2). Sabbatini, Shkosa, Pertusi, Wilson-Johnson, L. Symphony Ch., LSO, C. Davis

Sir Colin Davis's new version at super-bargain price offers a performance and sound which, even more than in his classic 1973 recording for Philips, Davis involves you in the painful quandary obsessing Faust, never letting tension slip for a moment. This time the playing of the **LSO** is even more refined, with rhythms even more lightly sprung, as in the witty treatment of Mephistopheles's *Flea song*, characterfully sung by Michele Pertusi, weighty yet agile. As Faust, **Giuseppe Sabbatini** is more overtly emotional than any rival, Italianate in his expressiveness helped by his radiant tonal range down to a perfectly controlled head-voice. The Albanian soprano **Enkelejda Shkosa** is a warm, vibrant Marguerite, with a flicker in the voice giving a hint of the heroine's vulnerability. Not just the **LSO** but the **London Symphony Chorus** too are in searing form, and the recording brings out the detail of Berlioz's orchestration with ideal transparency. The complete text is provided in the booklet, along with David Cairns's authoritative notes, if in microscopic print.

L'Enfance du Christ, Op. 25

&—(N)(M) *** Hyp. Dyad CDD 22667 (2) / CDA 66991/2. Rigby, Miles, Finley, Aler, Howell, Corydon Singers & O, Best

(B) **(*) LSO Live SACD LSO 0606 (2). Beuron, Cargill, Dazeley, Matthew & Peter Rose, Tenebrae Ch., LSO, C. Davis

(M) **(*) HM HMX 2971632.33. Gens, Agnew, Lallouette, Naouri, La Chappelle Royal, Coll. Voc., O de Champs-Élysées, Herreweghe

This atmospheric oratorio for Christmas, so different from almost any other Berlioz work, has been lucky on disc, vividly recorded in beautifully balanced digital sound, immediate yet warm. **Matthew Best's** version offers a keenly dramatic view. So **Alastair Miles** conveys pure evil in Herod's monologue at the start and, with words exceptionally clear, Joseph's pleas for shelter are movingly urgent. **Jean Rigby** is a fresh, young-sounding Mary, with **Gerald Finley** warm and expressive as Joseph. **John Aler** is a powerful Reciter and **Gwynne Howell** a strong, benevolent-sounding Father of the family. This makes an ideal choice for those who want an intimate view and a superb modern recording.

This is the third recording of *L'Enfance du Christ* that **Sir Colin Davis** has made, and the line-up of soloists is not so starry this time. The result is bitingly dramatic (although the famous *Shepherds' Chorus* is lyrically beautiful), gaining from being recorded live, with vigour the keynote. Like the soloists, the choir sings with clean, clear voices; but, gripping though this is, the work's atmospheric side emerges less tellingly.

Herreweghe has the advantage of a French-singing cast, except for **Paul Agnew**, whose pronunciation is as impeccable as his vocal contribution. It is an attractively warm performance, un-idiosyncratic in choice of tempi and, because it is a live recording, spontaneous in feeling. Not quite a first choice perhaps, but in its attractive new livery, admirably documented, with full texts and translation included, most attractive at mid-price.

Mélodies: *Aubade; La Belle Voyageuse; La Captive; Le Chasseur danois; Le Jeune Pâtre breton; La Mort d'Ophélie; Les Nuits d'été; Zaïde*

(BB) *** Warner Apex 0927 49583-2. Montague, Robbin, Fournier, Crook, Cachemaille, Lyon Op. O, Gardiner

Like Davis before him, **John Eliot Gardiner** here divides the six keenly atmospheric songs of *Les Nuits d'été* between four singers, in some ways an ideal solution when his choice of singers is inspired and the presiding genius of the conductor makes this a memorable Berlioz bargain disc. In *Les Nuits d'été* **Catherine Robbin**, with clear echoes of Dame Janet Baker, gives a rich and moving account of *Le Spectre de la rose* (as she does also of the final item from among the miscellaneous orchestral songs, *La Mort d'Ophélie*), and **Diana Montague** is full and bright in her two songs, coping splendidly with Gardiner's very fast speed for the final *L'Île inconnue*, which brings a delightful pay-off. **Pierre Cachemaille** gives a thrilling bite to *Sur les lagunes*, and **Howard Crook**, with his rather thin, reedy tenor, is well suited to *Au cimetière* but is even more striking in the extraordinary *Aubade*, the rarest of the miscellaneous songs, with its accompaniment of two cornets and four horns. The **Lyon Opéra Orchestra** is helpfully recorded, not in the dry acoustic of the opera house, but atmospherically in a Lyon church. Altogether this Apex reissue is an outstanding bargain.

Mélodies: *'Chant d'amour': La Mort d'Ophélie; Zaïde*

*** Decca 452 667-2. Bartoli, Chung – BIZET; DELIBES; RAVEL: *Mélodies* ***

Cecilia Bartoli's collection of French songs is one of the most ravishing of her records yet, and these Berlioz items are among the highlights. **Myung-Whun Chung's** contribution is both imaginative and supportive.

Messe solennelle; Resurrexit (revised version)

(M) *** Ph. 464 688-2. D. Brown, Viala, Cachemaille, Monteverdi Ch., ORR, Gardiner

This massive work, completed in 1824, is uneven, but the glow of inspiration shines out over any shortcomings. **Gardiner** conducts with characteristic flair and a sense of drama, bringing brilliant singing from the **Monteverdi Choir**, though the choral sound is backwardly balanced. A second, modified and slightly expanded version of the violent *Resurrexit* is included as a supplement, a revised version that Berlioz himself acknowledged.

Les Nuits d'été (song-cycle)

🎧 (M) *** Decca 475 7712. Crespin, SRO, Ansermet (with Recital of French Songs ****) – RAVEL: *Shéhérazade* ****❀

(***) Testament mono SBT 3203 (3). de los Angeles, Boston SO, Munch – DEBUSSY: *La Demoiselle élue*; MASSENET: *Manon* (***)

With **Crespin's** richness of tone, and with **Ansermet** at his finest, accompanying brilliantly, this glowing performance is truly legendary and fully worthy of a place among Universal's 'Originals'. Moreover, the Ravel coupling is even more inspired, and the superb new transfers enhance the listener's pleasure further.

Victoria de los Angeles's RCA recording of *Les Nuits d'été*, like Debussy's *La Demoiselle élue*, both dating from 1955, makes a splendid, generous bonus to the classic Monteux version of Massenet's *Manon*, recorded in Paris, also in 1955 and the charm of the lovely voice is still a delight.

Requiem (Grande Messe des Morts, Op. 5; DVD version)

🎧 **** Arthaus Musik **DVD** 102 027. Keith Lewis, Bav. R. Symphony Ch. and O, C. Davis (V/D: Klaus Lindemann)

The spectacular setting of Regensburg Cathedral adds greatly to the impact of **Sir Colin Davis's** inspired performance of the Berlioz *Requiem*. With orchestra and chorus set at the far end, like an elaborate altarpiece, there is less spread of sound than in a broader church or concert hall, but the clarity of detail is remarkable, no doubt a tribute to the engineers as well. Davis as ever gives a dedicated performance, rising brilliantly to the relatively few moments of Berliozian drama, as in the *Tuba mirum*, with its array of brass and timpani, but bringing out the fundamentally devotional quality of the work. That stamp of dedication is sealed when, at the very end of the final *Agnus Dei*, Davis remains standing impassively, and one hears the distant boom of the bells from outside. Chorus and orchestra are superb, at once warm and incisive, responding to Davis's every gesture, as he leads them through a work they are unlikely to know well. Unison passages for whichever section emerge with exceptional purity. In the *Sanctus* **Keith Lewis**, at his peak, gives an ideal performance as soloist, totally unstrained. The DVD gives one the option of having the Latin text on the screen as though on a gauze over the main picture.

Requiem Mass, Op. 5 (CD Version)

(N) 🎵── ******** Pentatone **SACD** Surround Sound PTC 5186 (2) Dowd, Wandsworth School Boys' Ch., LSO Ch., LSO, C. Davis

🎵── ******* Telarc **SACD** 60627; CD 806276. Lopardo, Atlanta Ch. & O, Spano

🎵── (M) ******* RCA **SACD** 82876 66373-2 (2). Simoneau, New England Conservatory Ch., Brass Bands, Boston SO, Munch

(***) BBC mono BBCL 4011-2. Lewis, RPO Ch., RPO, Beecham

Sir Colin Davis's inspired Philips recording of the Berlioz *Requiem*, made in Westminster Cathedral, dates from the very beginning of the 1970s, yet only now is its sonic potential being fully realized. Recorded in quadraphony, the performance is made available by Pentatone for the first time in four-speaker surround sound. The result, especially in the *Dies irae – Tuba mirum* outshines all other versions in amplitude and spectacle. The large-scale brass and drum climaxes are quite astonishing, and the choral *fortissimos* are glorious, helped by the fresh cutting edge of the **Wandsworth School Boys' Choir**. It was Davis's idea, not Berlioz's to have boys' voices, but the result is a triumph. The **LSO** provides finely incisive accompaniment and this reissue is now a clear first choice for Berlioz's masterpiece.

This new Telarc version of the Berlioz *Requiem* also brings the recorded sound of current demonstration quality, spectacular in capturing extremes of dynamic and tonal weight, outshining the previous Telarc version under Robert Shaw. The spectacular sound goes with a reading under the present Atlanta music-director, **Robert Spano**, which confirms that the chorus and orchestra are still in superb form, with Norman Mackenzie as chorus-master carrying on the tradition so brilliantly established by Shaw. That Spano's speeds are marginally more flowing than in most rival versions means that the whole work has been fitted on a single CD, a palpable advantage. The excellent tenor soloist in the *Sanctus*, **Frank Lopardo**, is set at a distance, almost off-stage, a heavenly voice heard from afar.

Munch's Boston version was recorded as early as 1959, yet in some ways it has still not been surpassed, although technically of course the new Telarc version is even more breathtaking. But it was an astonishing technical achievement for its time, and its full glories have not been realized on record until now. The four brass groups make a superbly bold effect within the resonant Boston acoustics and the big climaxes of the *Dies irae* and *Tuba mirum* are thrilling. Munch's overall direction has a fine lyrical flow; he brings powerful expressive feeling to the *Lacrymosa*, where the cho-

rus is at its finest. The deep trombone effects come off splendidly in the *Hostias* and the *Sanctus* – where **Leopold Simoneau**, with headily beautiful tone, does full justice to the tenor solo – is particularly moving. All in all, this is a most distinguished set.

Though Beecham's live recording, made at the Royal Albert Hall in December 1959, comes in mono only, the BBC sound is warm and full. The weight and intensity of the performance and the sense of a great occasion are caught vividly, not least in the great outburst of brass bands, widely separated, in the *Tuba mirum*. Although the professional choir takes a little time to settle down, the Beecham magic gets to work quickly, to make this one of the most compelling performances on disc. The tenor, **Richard Lewis**, is in superb form in the *Sanctus*, his voice given a halo of reverberation. A most cherishable historic issue.

DG have reissued **Munch's** 1968 Bavarian set as one of their 'Originals' but the choice is hardly appropriate for it is much less successful than his later Boston version. The playing of the **Bavarian Radio Symphony Orchestra** cannot match that of the Boston Symphony and though the **Bavarian Radio Chorus** sings with professional precision, the result is not massive enough. The recording quality, though cleaner than the American one, has less atmosphere (DG 477 761-2).

Roméo et Juliette, Op. 17 (DVD versions)

🎵── ******* Arthaus **DVD** 102 017. Schwarz, Langridge, Meven, Bav. R. Ch. & SO, C. Davis (V/D: Klaus Lindemann)

Sir Colin Davis is without peer as a Berlioz interpreter and it is good to have this fine (and often inspired) account of the master's dramatic symphony on DVD. Recorded fairly early in his days in Munich with the **Bayerischer Rundfunk Orchestra**, it has great fire and dramatic intensity – as well as the sensibility and poetic feeling we associate with him. Quite apart from the virtuosity of this wonderful orchestra, listeners will be riveted by the singing of the three soloists: **Hanna Schwarz**, whom we associate mainly with Wagner, the impeccable **Philip Langridge** and the splendid, dark-toned **Peter Meven**, who, alas, died in 2003. The video direction of Klaus Lindemann could hardly be bettered. A thrilling performance.

Roméo et Juliette, Op. 17; Les Nuits d'été

(BB) ******* LSO Live 0003CD (2). Barcellona, Tarver, Anastassov, L. Symphony Ch., LSO, C. Davis

(i) Roméo et Juliette; (ii) Les Nuits d'été

(N) (BB) ****** EMI Gemini 2 17640-2 (2) (i) Norman, Aler, Estes, Westminster Ch., Phd. O, Muti; (ii) J. Baker, New Philh. O, Barbirolli

(i) Roméo et Juliette; (ii) Overtures: Béatrice et Bénédict; Le Corsaire; Les Francs-juges; Le Roi Lear; Waverley

🎵── ✹ (B) ******* Ph. Duo (DDD/ADD) 470 543-2 (2). (i) Borodina, Moser, Miles, Bav. R. Ch., VPO; (ii) LSO; all cond. C. Davis

Sir **Colin Davis's** (1993) recording of *Roméo et Juliette* has the advantage of very fine soloists, and **Olga Borodina** has the full measure of the Berlioz style. **Thomas Moser** is no less ardent and idiomatic, and **Alastair Miles** is a more than acceptable Friar Laurence. Apart from its all-round artistic excellence, this scores over all-comers in sheer quality of sound, which reproduces the whole range of Berlioz's luminous orchestration in all its subtle colourings with remarkable detail and naturalness. The five superbly played and recorded overtures (dating from 1965, except *Béatrice*, which dates from 1977) make this an exceptional bargain on the Philips Duo series, though, sadly, no texts are included.

Davis's live Barbican recording may not match in opulence the 1993 recording with the Vienna Philharmonic, for the Barbican acoustic (as recorded) is drier. Yet the refinement of the sound, with orchestra and chorus set at a slight distance, brings *pianissimos* of breathtaking delicacy, focused in fine detail. The three young soloists are first rate, characterizing strongly. The Italian **Daniela Barcellona** controls her vibrant mezzo well in the strophes, and the American tenor, **Kenneth Tarver**, sings his *Scherzetto* with fluency and sparkle, while the tangily Slavonic timbre of the Bulgarian bass, **Orlin Anastassov**, stands out well in the Friar Laurence episodes.

Despite the impressive line-up of soloists, **Muti's** version of *Roméo et Juliette* is disappointing. This is partly a question of recording, relatively thick and ill-focused, but also a matter of interpretation, less idiomatic and fanciful, whatever the brilliance of the **Philadelphia** playing. It is good to hear **Jessye Norman** in the lovely *Strophes*, but the weight of voice and personality hardly match the incidental quality of that sequence. **Dame Janet's** superb version of *Les Nuits d'été* badly needs a new coupling.

Te Deum, Op. 22

🎵 *** Profil Medien PH 6039. Stuart, Schone (organ), Dresden Philharmonic Children's Ch., Dresden State Opera Ch. & Children's Ch., Dresden Symphony Ch., Dresden Singakademie, Dresden State O, Colin Davis (with MOZART: *Kyrie, K.341/K.368a* ***)

🎵 Ⓑ *** Virgin 5 03 4072. Alagna, O de Paris, Nelson; Alain

*** DG 410 696-2. Araiza, L. Symphony Ch., LPO Ch., Woburn Singers, Boys' Ch., European Community Youth O, Abbado

Berlioz is credited with assembling no fewer than 900 performers for the first performance of his *Te Deum* in Paris in 1855. This live performance from a concert celebrating the Dresden Staatskapelle's 250th anniversary cannot match that scale at 400 performers, but by today's standards that is an enormous body, which in this radio recording is thrillingly caught. **Davis's** 1969 recording with LSO forces for Philips remains impressive, but the sheer weight of sound on the new version is very much in its favour, particularly when the live occasion adds electricity to its impact. **Neil Stuart** this time is an impressive tenor soloist, firm and steady, with crystal-clear diction. In the same concert, Davis conducted music by his other favourite composer, Mozart, the *Kyrie in*

D minor, K.341, included here as a supplement; but what will be disconcerting to many listeners today is that he treats it almost as though it is by Berlioz, with all idea of an apt eighteenth-century scale abandoned in a massive celebration.

John Nelson not only has a full, brilliant sound, with the complex textures well terraced, it offers two extra instrumental movements that Berlioz suggested should be included for performances celebrating victory, both with military overtones – a Prelude using one of the work's main themes in fugato and a rather corny 'March for the Presentation of the Colours'. It is good too to have **Roberto Alagna** as an imaginative soloist in the prayer, *Te ergo quaesumus*, and **Marie-Claire Alain** warmly idiomatic on the organ of the Madeleine, Paris.

The DG recording of the *Te Deum* from **Abbado** is very impressive. The sound is wide-ranging, with striking dynamic contrasts: Abbado brings great tonal refinement and dignity to this performance, and the spacious sound helps. **Francisco Araiza** is the fine soloist, but the Davis version is first choice.

OPERA

Complete operas

Benvenuto Cellini (original version)

*** Virgin 5 45706-2 (3). Kunde, Ciofi, Di Donato, Lapointe, Naouri, Delaigue, R. France Ch., & O Nat. de France, Nelson

John Nelson has now recorded the original text, after concert performances in Paris. As the Berlioz scholar, David Cairns, says, this original score 'is Berlioz at his most recklessly inspired', and Nelson's fine performance brings that out, if anything more warmly expressive than Davis's. With one reservation, the cast is first rate, with **Laurent Naouri** singing characterfully in the equivocal role of Balducci, Treasurer to the Pope, and **Patricia Ciofi** fresh and pure as his daughter, Teresa, both given important extra material. In the title-role **Gregory Kunde** has a satisfyingly heroic tenor, but too often finds problems in tackling his top notes cleanly. A fine set, unmissable for anyone interested in the composer.

Les Troyens, Parts I & II (complete)

Les Troyens (complete; DVD versions)

**** DG **DVD** 073 4310 (2). Troyanos, Norman, Domingo, Monk, Plishka, NY Met. Op. Ch., O & Ballet, Levine (Director: Fabrizio Melano; V/D: Brian Large)

*** Opus Arte **DVD** OA 0900D (3). Graham, Antonacci, Pokupic, Kunde, Tezier, Monteverdi Ch., ORR, Gardiner (Director: Yannis Kokkos; V/D: Peter Maniura)

Recorded at the Met. in 1983, this very fine account of Berlioz's epic opera, *Les Troyens*, features the most starry cast of soloists, all at their peak, and is strongly directed by **James Levine**. **Jessye Norman** is magnetic in the Fall of Troy, commanding in her prediction of doom. **Plácido Domingo** is at his most heroic in both halves of the massive narrative, as Aeneas both in Troy and in Carthage. As Dido, **Tatiana**

Troyanos is touching and tender, more vulnerable by far than as Cassandra in the first opera. The staging is nicely stylized, with grandly traditional costumes and unobtrusive hangings in the set. The recorded sound is remarkably good, and Brian Large's video direction is characteristically well managed. This version is very rewarding on all counts and it makes an obvious principal recommendation for the foreseeable future.

In October 2003 **John Eliot Gardiner** with his **Monteverdi Choir** and the **Orchestre Révolutionnaire et Romantique** had a great success when they visited Paris to give Berlioz's epic opera in the relatively intimate Théâtre du Châtelet but, as the video shows, the stage production by Yannis Kokkos neatly achieves clarity and directness in the complex plot with an economical but effective staging. The first two Acts, covering the fall of Troy, have the darkest of settings, with costumes of unrelieved black, with an angled mirror giving one views from above as well as laterally. The performance gains from the fine singing in the central role of Cassandra of **Anna Caterina Antonacci**, then coming to the fore as a star of the future. **Ludovic Tezier** is also excellent as her lover, Chorebus, and the final chorus of Trojan women, led by Cassandra, brings a thrilling climax.

In Act III, 'The Trojans in Carthage', the set brings a complete contrast, light and airy and with bright colours. Again simplicity is the keynote, with spaciousness rather than crowded scenes; and again, surprisingly, it works well, with the story clarified. What is slightly disappointing is that the great love duet between Aeneas and Dido uses a set without any hint of foliage or any atmospheric background; but the singing of **Susan Graham** as well as of **Gregory Kunde** as Aeneas is first rate. What is remarkable in an age of wobblers is that Gardiner has gathered a whole team of singers, most of them native French-speakers, with exceptionally well-focused voices. The final Act, of Aeneas's departure and Dido's death, brings a return of the angled mirror, with Aeneas's fleet represented by model ships floating in the air. Fine as Graham's singing is, it does not have quite the weight of emotions of a Janet Baker, yet it still makes a moving impact. Altogether a preferable video presentation, with its period instruments and excellent cast, to the Salzburg Festival DVD of the opera on Arthaus.

Les Troyens, Parts I & II (complete; CD versions)

☛ ✿ (BB) **** LSO Live 0010CD (4). Heppner, DeYoung, Lang, Mingardo, Mattei, Milling, L. Symphony Ch., LSO, C. Davis

*** Decca 443 693-2 (4). Lakes, Pollet, Voigt, Montreal Ch. & SO, Dutoit

Recorded live at performances (and rehearsals) in the Barbican in London, **Sir Colin Davis's** second recording of this epic opera magnificently crowns his whole career as a Berlioz interpreter on record, generally outshining even his pioneer version of 30 years earlier. The first wonder is that the sound of chorus and orchestra is even fuller, more spacious and certainly brighter and clearer than on the earlier, Philips recording, or even the opulent digital recording given to Charles Dutoit in his Montreal set for Decca. Davis

is marginally faster in all five Acts, a degree more thrustful, with the excitement of a live occasion consistently adding extra intensity. The casting too is marginally even finer than before. **Petra Lang**, a last-minute substitute as Cassandra, is superb: firm, rich and intense, investing every phrase with emotional power, instantly establishing her dominance in the very first scene. Opposite her, **Peter Mattei** makes a powerful Chorebus. Both in The Fall of Troy and The Trojans at Carthage **Ben Heppner** excels himself, not just heroic with his unstrained Heldentenor, but finding a degree of refinement in the love duet of Act III that few rivals can match, let alone on disc. **Michelle DeYoung** may not be quite so rich and firm a Dido as Josephine Veasey on Davis's earlier set, but the vibrancy of her mezzo is warmly caught by the microphones, and her death monologue is the more moving for the vulnerability she conveys. The rest make an excellent team without any significant shortcoming. Though the set comes on four discs at super-budget price, full libretto and notes are provided, printed in very small type.

The Trojans: Royal Hunt and Storm

(**(*)) BBC mono BBCL 4113. RPO, Beecham, with BBC Ch. – CHABRIER: *España; Gwendoline Overture;* DEBUSSY: *L'Enfant prodigue: Cortège et air de danse;* DELIUS: *Brigg Fair;* MASSENET: *La Vierge: Le Dernier sommeil de la vierge;* SAINT-SAËNS: *Le Rouet d'Omphale* (with MOZART: *Divertimento in D, K.131:* excerpts (**(*))

Beecham brought an almost unique gusto and excitement to the *Royal Hunt and Storm,* heard here with choral interjections, and it is a pity that the BBC recording has not more brilliance and range. Even so, the storm thunder is pretty impressive and the poetic close memorably atmospheric.

BERNERS, Lord (1883–1950)

Film Music from: (i) Champagne Charlie. The Halfway House; Nicholas Nickleby

(N) *** Chan. 10459. BBC Concert O, Gamba with (i) Carewe – LAMBERT: *Anna Karenina; Merchant Seamen* ***

Three classic Lord Berners scores here: the effervescence of *Champagne Charlie,* with its marvellous mock music-hall song, *Come On Algernon* (though not quite effacing memories of the film version) is well brought out here, as is the Dickensian atmosphere of *Nicholas Nickleby* (Lord Berners contrived a massive fanfare when the credits read, MUSIC BY LORD BERNERS). Some excellent tunes are found in both scores and the creepy atmosphere of *The Halfway House* is well-conveyed too. The *Séance Waltz* is particularly haunting. A splendidly entertaining addition to Chandos's film music series, with superb performances and sound.

The Triumph of Neptune (ballet): extended suite; Fantaisie espagnole; Fugue in C min.; 3 Morceaux; Nicholas Nickleby (film music)

*** Olympia OCD 662. RLPO, Wordsworth

Barry Wordsworth captures the character of this music remarkably well. Moreover, the *Trois morceaux* and the *Fantaisie* *espagnole* are new to the catalogue. They are Gallic in inspiration and are attractively imaginative. The recording is good without being in the demonstration class; detail is well defined and there is plenty of body. Originally issued on EMI, this rather surprisingly reappears on the Olympia label and is very welcome.

BERNSTEIN, Leonard
(1918–90)

(i) *Candide: Overture;* (ii) *Concerto for Orchestra (Jubilee Games); Divertimento;* (iii) *Dybbuk (ballet): Suites 1–2.* (ii) *Facsimile (Choreographic Essay); Fancy Free (ballet);* (ii; iv) *Halil (Nocturne) for Flute, Strings & Percussion;* (ii; v) *3 Meditations from Mass* (for cello & orchestra); (ii) *A Musical Toast; On the Town: 3 Dance Episodes. On the Waterfront: Symphonic Suite.* (vi) *Prelude, Fugue & Riffs* (for clarinet & jazz ensemble); (ii; vii) *Serenade after Plato's Symposium.* (ii) *Slava; Symphonies* (viii; ii) *1 (Jeremiah);* (ix; ii) *2 (Age of Anxiety);* (x; xi; ii) *3 (Kaddish: revised version);* (x; ii) *Chichester Psalms;* (xii) *Songfest;* (i) *West Side Story: Symphonic Dances*

Ⓑ *** DG (DDD/ADD) 469 829-2 (7). (i) LAPO; (ii) Israel PO; (iii) NYPO; (iv) Rampal; (v) Rostropovich; (vi) Schmidl, VPO (members); (vii) Kremer; (viii) Ludwig; (ix) Foss; (x) V. Jeunesse Ch.; V. Boys' Ch. (xi) Caballé, Wager; (xii) Soloists, Nat. SO

A self-recommending set in DG's Collector's Edition. A reminder of the composer's supreme theatrical talent comes with the *Candide Overture,* the excerpts from *On the Town* and the *West Side Story Symphonic Dances.* It may be that posterity will decide that his symphonies are too uneven in inspiration to be among the finest to have emerged from the USA in the twentieth century, but no one can doubt the composer's imaginative flair and ready flow of catchy, memorable ideas. Among the other works, the *Serenade after Plato's Symposium* and the *Chichester Psalms* are undoubted masterpieces. As can be seen below, Bernstein recorded much of his music earlier with the **New York Philharmonic**, and those initial accounts have a unique flair and vitality. But if the **Israel Philharmonic** is not as virtuosic as the NYPO, they respond to the composer committedly and persuasively, and the DG sound is generally fuller and better balanced than the vividly up-front CBS/Sony recordings. There is much to stimulate the listener here, and with good back-up documentation this box is fully worth its modest cost.

(i) *Candide Overture; Facsimile;* (i; ii) *On the Town: 3 Dance Episodes;* (iii) *Prelude, Fugue & Riffs;* (iv) *Symphonic Dances from West Side Story;* (v) *Mass: A Simple Song; 1600 Pennsylvania Ave: Scena*

Ⓝ Ⓑ *** EMI 2 06626-2 (i) Saint Louis SO, Slatkin; (ii) with Barbara Lieberman; (iii) L. Sinf., Rattle; (iv) CBSO, Jarvi; (v) Hubbard, O of St Lukes, Russell Davies

Though **Slatkin** cannot quite match Bernstein himself in the flair he brings to his jazzier inspirations, this EMI bar-

gain collection is very attractive. Slatkin directs a beautiful, refined reading of the extended choreographic essay, *Facsimile,* while in the *West Side Story Dances* Järvi relishes the romantic melodies.

Divertimento for Orchestra; (i) *Facsimile (choreographic essay);* (ii) *Prelude, Fugue & Riffs. West Side Story: symphonic dances (original version)*

Ⓑ *** Virgin 3 63301-2. CBSO, Järvi, with (i) Marshall; (ii) Meyer

Järvi and the **CBSO** clearly enjoy themselves, especially in the elegantly polished and very spirited account of the *Divertimento.* There is some beautiful woodwind-playing in *Facsimile* and, not surprisingly, **Wayne Marshall's** contribution is glitteringly idiomatic. The same could be said for **Sabine Meyer** in the very jazzy account of the *Prelude, Fugue and Riffs,* while in the *West Side Story Dances* Järvi relishes the romantic melodies, which are exquisitely played, and finds plenty of rhythmic venom for the *Rumble.*

Divertimento for Orchestra; Facsimile: Choreographic Essay for Orchestra; (i) *Serenade for Solo Violin, Strings, Harp & Percussion*

ⒷⒷ **(*) Naxos 8.559245. Bournemouth SO, Alsop; (i) Quint, Bournemouth SO (members)

The *Serenade* for solo violin and strings is one of the deepest, most ambitious works that Bernstein ever wrote. **Philippe Quint** gives a thoughtful, refined reading of a work inspired by the idea of mirroring Plato's *Symposium.* He is well supported by **Marin Alsop** and the **Bournemouth orchestra.** *Facsimile* is a ballet score on the theme of postwar life and the vain attempt to fill a spiritual vacuum, which results in a grim score with little evidence of Bernstein's lyrical gifts; it is most effective in the fast music, which distantly echoes *West Side Story.* The *Divertimento,* written for the Boston Symphony Orchestra, is an occasional piece that has its moments of fun, but which fails to make its full mark in this performance, refined as it is. Excellent sound.

(i) *Divertimento;* (ii; iii) *Serenade after Plato's Symposium;* (ii; iv) *Symphony 2 (The Age of Anxiety)* (DVD Versions)

Ⓝ ⌐ **** DG DVD 073 4514. (i) VPO; (ii) LSO; (iii) Kremer; (vi) Zimerman

This is truly a key recording in the Bernstein discography. The performances are full of joyful, spontaneous life. **Bernstein** clearly revels in the *Divertimento,* all but jigging to the infectious dance movements, and elsewhere he creates and sustains great tension, never more so than in the final climax of the *Symphony.* **Gidon Kremer** too has all the nervous intensity and vibrant energy to do justice to the inspired *Serenade,* and **Zimerman** proves a brilliant and understanding soloist in *The Age of Anxiety,* finding, like the composer himself, a natural idiomatic feeling for the jazz element in the *Masque* of Part II, yet rising to the work's visionary *Epilogue.* The orchestral playing, infected by the composer, is superb, and splendidly recorded and photographed, under Humphrey Burton's direction. Bernstein himself introduces the *Serenade* and *Symphony* and the bonus is a documentary 'Teachers and Teaching' in which he reminiscences and rehearses. An indispensable issue.

Dybbuk; Fancy Free (complete ballets)

(BB) *** Naxos 8.559280. Burke, Nashville SO, Mogrelia

Dybbuk, written to celebrate the 25th anniversary of the State of Israel, is one of Bernstein's darkest scores. Over 45 minutes in length, it tells the creepy story of a sinister ghost, with the battle between good and evil represented respectively (and very aptly) by tonality and atonality. It is well coupled with another ballet written for Jerome Robbins 30 years earlier, including **Abby Burke**, the jazz-influenced vocalist. It is a work involving three sailors and anticipates the musical *On the Town* and is one of Bernstein's most colourful scores with its sharp syncopations well realized here.

(i) Facsimile; (ii) On the Town; (iii) Jeremiah Symphony

(BB) (***) Dutton mono CDBP 9758. (i) RCA Victor SO; (ii) On the Town O; (iii) Merriman, St Louis SO; composer – RAVEL: *Piano Concerto in G* (***)

Bernstein made brilliant stereo recordings of these three pieces, but these accounts from the 1940s have enormous zest and freshness, and they are every bit as treasurable as the later, LP versions he made. Dutton draws very lively and lifelike sounds from the 78-r.p.m. grooves. The disc also brings his 1946 recording of the Ravel *G major Concerto* with the then newly formed Philharmonia Orchestra.

Serenade after Plato's 'Symposium'

(B) *** EMI 2 08124-2. Perlman, Boston SO, Ozawa – BARBER: *Violin Concerto*; FOSS: *3 American Pieces* ***

Perlman may initially seem almost too confident in the *Serenade*, missing an element of fantasy. Yet he brings home tellingly how each movement leads thematically out of the preceding one, until the final movement, much the longest, with its references back to the beginning. He also makes it seem a warmer piece, thanks to his range of rich tone-colours, set against the richness of the Boston string-sound.

Symphonies 1 (Jeremiah); 2 (The Age of Anxiety); (i) Chichester Psalms

⊶ (M) *** DG (ADD) 457 757-2. Israel PO, composer, (i) with soloists from V. Boys' Ch.

The *Jeremiah Symphony* dates from Bernstein's early twenties and ends with a moving passage from *Lamentations* for the mezzo soloist (on DG, **Christa Ludwig**). As its title suggests, the *Second Symphony* was inspired by the poem of W. H. Auden, though no words are set to music in this purely orchestral work. The *Chichester Psalms* is one of the most attractive choral works written in the twentieth century: its jazzy passages are immediately appealing, as is the intrinsic beauty of the reflective sequences. These live performances

with the **Israel Philharmonic** are not quite as polished or forceful as those **Bernstein** recorded earlier in New York, but the warmth of his writing is fully conveyed in these excellent recordings. With a playing time of just under 80 minutes, this DG 'Originals' CD is exceptionally good value.

(i) Symphony 3 (Kaddish); (ii) Chichester Psalms

(M) *** Warner Elatus 092746722-2. (i) Mattila, Menuhin; (ii) Mills; French R. Ch. & PO, Sado

Menuhin, with his thoughtful, measured tones, is the opposite of most narrators in the *Kaddish Symphony*, but the emotion is conveyed just as intensely. **Karita Mattila** is a radiant soprano soloist and the choir sings brilliantly, but at relatively measured speeds this does not have the dramatic bite of Bernstein's own recordings, though the sound here is fuller and clearer. In the *Chichester Psalms* the choir and orchestra seem more at home in Bernstein's jazzy syncopations, giving a dazzling performance, vividly recorded, with **Joseph Mills** from the New College, Oxford choir a fine treble soloist.

CHAMBER MUSIC

Clarinet Sonata

(N) ⊶ (BB) **** Naxos 8.572240 Johnson, Lenehan – COPLAND: *Clarinet Sonata; Romance*; DANKWORTH: *Suite for Emma; Picture of Jeannie* ****

Bernstein's *Clarinet Sonata* (1942) is an early work, yet surprisingly characteristic in its melodic flair. In two movements, the first is ruminative, marked *Grazioso*, the second begins with a cool *Andantino*, then moves into a joyous burst of jazzy 5/8, 6/8 and 7/8 rhythmic drive, ending suddenly. It is here given an inspired account by **Emma Johnson** and **John Lenehan**, who are totally at home in the idiom, and vividly recorded. The couplings of music by Copland and Dankworth are equally rewarding.

Piano Trio Op. 2

(N) *** RTE Lyric CD 116. Ens Avalon – BAX: *Piano Trio* ***; BEETHOVEN: *Piano Trio, Op.70/1 (Ghost)* **(*)

The *Piano Trio* is another attractive rarity, an early work written when Bernstein was only nineteen and still dabbling with atonality. It remained unpublished in the composer's lifetime, an even more compact work than the Bax Trio, and it certainly deserves an airing also.

VOCAL MUSIC

Chichester Psalms (reduced score)

*** Hyp. CDA 66219. Martelli, Corydon Singers, Masters, Kettel, Trotter; Best – BARBER: *Agnus Dei*; COPLAND: *In the Beginning*, etc. ***

Martin Best uses the composer's reduced orchestration. The treble soloist's chaste contribution is persuasive and the choir scales down its *pianissimos* to accommodate him. Excellent, atmospheric sound, set in a church acoustic.

Mass (for the death of President Kennedy)

Ⓝ *** Chan. **SACD** CHSA 5070 (2). Scarlata, Company of Music, Tolzer Boys Choir, Sine Nomine Ch, Tonkunstler Orch, Krystian Järvi

Ⓜ **(*) Sony (ADD) SM2K 63089 (2). Titus (celebrant), Scribner Ch., Berkshire Boys' Ch., Rock Band & O, composer

Described as 'Theatre Piece for Singers, Players and Dancers', Bernstein's Mass was written to celebrate the election of John F. Kennedy as the first Catholic President of the United States. Taking his cue from the then recently completed War Requiem of Benjamin Britten with its interleaving of Wilfred Owen poems with the liturgy of the Requiem, Bernstein similarly interleaves various texts with the liturgy of the Mass. He does more than that in ranging very wide in the styles of the various elements in the music, from simple songs, to jazz and black music, with one section of the Credo prompting an ensemble number that could well have come from West Side Story.

The result is alarmingly disparate, but Bernstein cleverly draws the ends together by the use of motifs that are transformed from number to number – one brings in the words Lauda Laude. The Celebrant in the role of Priest is a high baritone superbly sung with no sense of strain by **Randall Scarlata**. This new version stands in direct competition with Bernstein's own original recording, but gains enormously in the impact of the spectacular surround sound, very helpful in this work. Massed choruses and orchestra are all excellent, powerfully marshalled by the youngest of the **Järvi** family of conductors, **Krystian**. A formidable and compelling issue.

The composer's own performance remains uniquely persuasive and the Sony (originally CBS) recording is both vividly present and has a convincing ambience.

Songs: La bonne cuisine (French and English versions); I hate music (cycle); 2 Love Songs; Piccola serenata; Silhouette; So pretty; Mass: A simple song; I go on. Candide: It must be so; Candide's lament. 1600 Pennsylvania Ave: Take care of this house. Peter Pan: My house; Peter Pan; Who am I; Never-Never Land

*** Etcetera KTC 1037. Alexander, Crone

A delightful collection, consistently bearing witness to Bernstein's flair for a snappy idea as well as his tunefulness. **Roberta Alexander's** rich, warm voice and winning personality are well supported by **Tan Crone** at the piano. The recording is lifelike and undistracting.

STAGE WORKS

Candide (final, revised version)

⊶ ✿ Ⓑ *** DG Double 474 472-2 (2). Hadley, Anderson, Green, Ludwig, Gedda, D. Jones, Ollmann, L. Symphony Ch., LSO, composer

(i) Candide (final, revised version); (ii) West Side Story: complete recording

⊶ ✿ Ⓜ *** DG 447 958-2 (3). (i) Hadley, Anderson, Green, Ludwig, Gedda, D. Jones, Ollmann, L. Symphony Ch., LSO; (ii) Te Kanawa, Carreras, Troyanos, Horne, Ollmann, Ch. and O; composer

The composer's complete recordings of Candide and West Side Story have been coupled together on three mid-priced discs for those who have not already acquired one or the other of these inspired scores. Candide is a triumph, both in the studio recording (which **Bernstein** made immediately after concert performances in London) and in the video recording of the actual concert at the Barbican, bringing out not just the vigour, the wit and the tunefulness of the piece more than ever before, but also an extra emotional intensity. There is no weak link in the cast. **Jerry Hadley** is touchingly characterful as Candide, and **June Anderson** as Cunegonde is not only brilliant in coloratura but also warmly dramatic. It was an inspired choice to have **Christa Ludwig** as the Old Woman, and equally original to choose **Adolph Green** for the dual roles of Dr Pangloss and Martin. **Nicolai Gedda** also proves a winner in his series of cameo roles, and the full, incisive singing of the **London Symphony Chorus** adds to the weight of the performance without inflation.

Bernstein's recording of the complete score of West Side Story takes a frankly operatic approach in its casting, but the result is highly successful, for the great vocal melodies are worthy of voices of the highest calibre. **Tatiana Troyanos**, herself brought up on the West Side, spans the stylistic dichotomy to perfection in a superb portrayal of Anita. The clever production makes the best of both musical worlds, with Bernstein's son and daughter speaking the dialogue most affectingly. Bernstein conducts a superb instrumental group of musicians 'from on and off Broadway', and they are recorded with a bite and immediacy that is captivating. The power of the music is greatly enhanced by the spectacularly wide dynamic range of the recording.

Trouble in Tahiti

*** Opus Arte **DVD** OA 0838 D. Novacek, Daymond, Randle, Stafford-Allen, Hegarty, Gibbon, City of London Sinfonia, Daniel (V/D: Tom Cairns)

Directed for video by Tom Cairns, this DVD offers a lively revival of Bernstein's brilliant one-acter of 1952, a work that neatly spans the gap between opera and Broadway musical. In seven scenes introduced by a Prologue it focuses on a couple, Sam and Dinah, whose marriage is under strain in the artificial atmosphere of suburban America in the 1950s, as symbolized by their 'little white house'. From the Prologue onwards their problems are commented on by a vocal trio, often singing in jazzy close harmony. In the staging, period clips heighten the atmosphere of such scenes as the Psychiatrist's Office, where Dinah is having a consultation. **Karl Daymond** and **Stephanie Novacek** make an attractive couple, with their monologues and duets set against sharply rhythmic contributions from the vocal trio, helped by idiomatic playing from the **City of London Sinfonia** under **Paul Daniel**. Daniel is the principal contributor to a useful introduction, and Humphrey Burton, Bernstein's official biographer, offers a 20-minute personal portrait of the composer as a supplement for the 40-minute opera.

West Side Story: The Making of the Recording

*** DG DVD 073 4054. Te Kanawa, Carreras, Troyanos, Ollmann, Bernstein (V/D: Chris Swann)

With narration from **Bernstein** himself, this classic feature film about the making of the controversial opera-style recording of West Side Story gives a vivid portrait of the composer at work. His unique combination of toughness, warmth, shining charisma and overwhelming genius is vividly conveyed. There is no false modesty in his approach to a work which he had written over 30 years before but never previously conducted. For the first time he had studied it in depth, and was surprised and gratified that it is 'so funky'. He goes on to explain that although it had been tiring listening to play-backs, the experience of recording it 'made me feel very young. It sounds as though I wrote it yesterday.'

West Side Story (complete)

⊕ *** DG 457 199-2. Te Kanawa, Carreras, Troyanos, Horne, Ollman, Ch. & O, composer

The composer's own recording of West Side Story is now available on one CD; the alternative choice combines it with Candide at mid-price on three CDs.

Wonderful Town

⊕ Ⓜ *** EMI 5 556753-2. Criswell, McDonald, Hampson, Barrett, Gilfry, L. Voices, Birmingham Contemporary Music Group, Rattle

Wonderful Town was one of Leonard Bernstein's earliest successes, but unfairly it has tended to be eclipsed by the later success of West Side Story. Here, in a fizzing performance, starrily cast, **Rattle** rights the balance in a performance at once vigorously idiomatic and also refined in the many lyrical moments. The two characterful sisters finding their feet in the big city are brilliantly played here by **Kim Criswell** and **Audra McDonald**, not just charismatic as actresses, but singing superbly. **Thomas Hampson** as Robert just as commandingly bestrides the conflicting problem of Broadway and the classical tradition, and **Brent Barrett** in the secondary role of Wreck delightfully brings in the cabaret tradition. Such numbers as 'Ohio', 'A little bit in love', 'Conversation piece' and 'Wrong note rag', rounded off with the big tune of 'It's love', can be appreciated for their full musical quality, with Rattle and his talented Birmingham group relishing the jazzy idiom. Bright, forward sound to match, and a helpful booklet which gives the full text.

BERWALD, Franz (1796–1868)

Allvarliga och muntra infall; Bajadärfesten; (i) Piano Concerto; (ii) Violin Concerto. Overtures: Drottningen av Golconda; Estrella de Soria; Play of the Elves; Racing; Reminiscences from the

Norwegian Mountains. Symphonies 1–4; Symphony in E flat

Ⓑ **(*) EMI (ADD) 5 00920-2 (3). (i) Migdal; (ii) Tellefsen; RPO, Björlin

All these performances date from 1976. The Piano Concerto is a strange piece. There are some beautiful ideas, including the Chopinesque second group, and they are heard to splendid advantage in **Marian Midgal's** poetic and imaginative reading. The Violin Concerto is an early work, written in the shadow of Spohr and Weber. A beautiful and elegant performance from **Arve Tellefsen** and the **RPO**. The shorter pieces are also delightful: the two tone-poems are vintage Berwald. In the symphonies the orchestral playing under **Ulf Björlin** is a little deficient in vitality; other versions are more vital and alert, but this set is worth exploring at its very reasonable cost, and the EMI engineers have provided very good recording, clear and quite full blooded.

(i) Konzertstück for Bassoon & Orchestra. Drottningen av Golconda: Overture; Reminiscences of the Norwegian Mountains (Erinnerung an die norwegischen Alpen); Play of the Elves; Racing (Wettlauf); Serious and Joyful Fancies (Ernst und heitere Grillen)

ⒷⒷ *** Naxos 8.555370. Gävle SO, Sakari; (i) with Håkansson

The Overture to Drottningen av Golconda ('The Queen of Golconda') is one of the Swedish master's most delightful and engaging pieces and deserves the widest currency. The performances under Petri Sakari are eminently lively and musical, Wettlauf and Play of the Elves are particularly enjoyable. Least original is the Konzertstück for Bassoon (excellently played though it is by **Patrik Håkansson**), which is much indebted to Spohr; but there is nothing to preclude a strong recommendation.

Symphony 1; Overtures: The Queen of Golconda; Estrella de Soria. Tone-poems: Festival of the Bayadères; Play of the Elves; Reminiscences from the Norwegian Mountains

*** Bluebell (ADD) ABCD 047. Swedish RSO, Ehrling

The Sinfonie sérieuse was recorded in 1970 and is arguably the finest account of the work ever recorded (including Ehrling's later, BIS version). It is beautifully played and unerringly paced. The overtures and tone-poems were recorded in 1966. Excellent performances, vital and imaginative. Very well recorded, too.

Symphonies 1–4; (i) Konzertstück for Bassoon & Orchestra

⊕ *** BIS CD 795/6. (i) Davidsson; Malmö SO, Ehrling

As his earlier recordings of Berwald demonstrate, **Sixten Ehrling** has a natural feeling for the classic Swedish symphonist. Tempi are all well judged and there is an admirable lightness of touch. There is plenty of breadth in the Sinfonie sérieuse and no want of sparkle in the E flat Symphony. The Konzertstück was composed in 1827 (the year before the Septet). This could well be regarded as a first choice in this repertoire.

Symphonies 1 (Sérieuse); 2 (Capricieuse); Memory of the Norwegian Alps

*** Chan. 10303. Danish Nat. RSO, Dausgaard

Symphonies 3 (Singulière); 4 in E flat; Play of the Elves

*** Chan. 9921. Danish Nat. RSO, Dausgaard

The sheer excellence of the **Danish orchestra's** playing of these sparkling and original pieces under Dausguard is not in question, nor is the quality of the sound. A strong recommendation. However, first choice for a complete set of the four symphonies rests with Sixten Ehrling on BIS 795/6.

CHAMBER MUSIC

Duos: in B flat for Cello & Piano; in D for Violin & Piano; Duo Concertante in A min. for 2 Violins; Concertino in A min. for Violin & Piano: fragment; Fantasy on 2 Swedish Folk Melodies

(BB) *** Naxos 8.554286. Rondin; Lundin; Ringborg, Bergström

The *Duo for Cello and Piano* (1857), played persuasively by **Mats Rondin** and **Bengt-Ake Lundin**, alludes to material from the *A minor Quartet*. In both the *Duo* and the *Quartet* the piano is hyperactive, as it tends to be in the roughly contemporaneous *Piano Quintets*. The *Duo Concertante* is quite inventive and well written, although it is nowhere as individual as the *G minor Quartet* (1818). The playing throughout is accomplished, although Lundin dominates in the *Duos* because of the recording balance. The sleeve and cover state incorrectly that the *Duo in D major* is in D minor, but this issue is well worth exploring.

Duo in D for Violin & Piano; Grand Septet in B flat; Piano Quintet 1 in C min.; Piano & Wind Quintet in E flat; Piano Trios 2 in F min.; 4 in C

(M) **(*) Hyp. Dyad CDD 22053 (2). Tomes, Gaudier Ens.

Hyperion have put together their two separate discs of Berwald's chamber music as a Dyad. The performances are nearly all first class. If the recording balance is not always ideal, the *Piano Quintet* (1853) comes off marvellously and, with **Susan Tomes** participating, there is much elsewhere to delight the ear, even if in the *Duo* **Marieke Blankestijn's** violin timbre sounds too pale and reticent; in this work **Susan Tomes** plays with great flair and finesse.

Grand Septet in B flat

(M) *** CRD 3344. Nash Ens. – HUMMEL: *Septet* ***

Berwald's only *Septet* is an imaginative work which deserves a secure place in the repertoire instead of on its periphery. It is very well played by the **Nash Ensemble**, and is finely recorded.

String Quartet 1 in G min.

(M) *** CRD (ADD) 3361. Chilingirian Qt – WIKMANSON: *Quartet 2* ***

The *G minor Quartet* is a remarkably assured piece, and the first movement is full of audacious modulations, with themes both characterful and appealing. The **Chilingirian** players give a well-shaped and sensitive account of it. They are truthfully recorded, and the coupling – another Swedish quartet – enhances the attractions of this issue. Strongly recommended.

String Quartets 1; 2 in A min.; 3 in E flat

*** BIS CD 759. Yggdrasil Qt

First-rate performances by this young Swedish ensemble of their great compatriot's output in this medium. They are both original and rewarding. This gifted ensemble play them very well indeed and are splendidly recorded. Anyone who enjoys the Mendelssohn or Schumann *Quartets* should not delay in investigating this music.

BIBER, Heinrich (1644–1704)

(i) Ballettae a 4 Violettas, 1–7; Battaglia in D; Peasants' Churchgoing Sonata in B flat a 6; Sonata Sancti Polycarpi a 9 (for 8 trumpets & bass); Sonatas 1–2 a 8 for 2 Clarini, 6 violae; 3–4 a 5 Violae; Sonata a 7 for 6 Trumpets, Taburin & Organ; (ii) Requiem in F min.; (iii) In festo trium regium, muttetum Natale (Epiphany Cantata) à 6; Laetatus sum à 7

🎵 (BB) *** Warner Apex 2564 62031-2. (i) V. Concentus Musicus, Harnoncourt; (ii; iii) with Equiluz, von Egmond, Villesech, Soloists of Vienna Boy's Ch.; Ch. Viennensis; (ii) cond. Gillesberger

This is a good, varied and inexpensive introduction to Biber's music. The *Battle* sequence itself has some hair-raising instrumental effects, including barbaric pizzicati representing the cannon. The picture of 'the dissolute company' brings a half-minute of well-organized instrumental cacophony. In the *March* there is a bizarre drum-and-fife imitation by violin and double-bass. The *Polycarp Sonata*, using eight trumpets, makes a thrilling sound. The piece closes with a *Lament of the Wounded Musketeers*. The *Sonatas* for strings and clarini (and notably the *Peasants' Churchgoing*) show lyrical effects as well as dramatic ones. The performances have great character – **Nikolaus Harnoncourt** was always good at explosive accents – and are very well recorded. The *Requiem* has since been recorded with even greater success. The present version tends to lack some consistency of musical purpose, but still has fine moments. The two *Cantatas* contain music that is both beautiful and striking and are well sung, and the sound is excellent.

Battaglia à 10; (i) Requiem à 15 in A

🎵 *** Alia Vox AV 9825. (i) Soloists; La Capella Reial de Catalunya, Concert de Nations, Savall

Jordi Savall's *Battaglia* opens with a dance-like vigour and has more musical light and shade. The closing *Lament* is gently touching. The *Requiem* is recorded – like the *Missa Bruxellensis* below – in Salzburg Cathedral, which Savall accommodates in a spacious performance that moves forward strongly – in every way a superbly eloquent account with splendid soloists. The elaborate and sumptuous documentation even includes a reproduction of the cathedral interior showing where the various vocal *soli in concerto*, the antiphonal brass and the string group were placed for the recording. The overall balance is amazingly successful, the separation is natural, but all is bathed in the richly resonant cathedral ambience. This is a magnificent disc in every way and almost certainly first choice for the *Requiem*, although other fine versions are mentioned below.

(12 Sonatae) Fidicinium sacro-profanum; Balletti lamentabili; (i) Passacaglia for Solo Violin; (ii–iii) Laetatus sum; (iii) Nisi Dominus; (ii) Serenada (der Nachtwächer)

*** Chan. 0605 (2). (i) Mackintosh; (ii) Harvey; (iii) Wistreich; Augmented Purcell Qt

The *Fidicinium sacro-profanum* (1682) are characteristically inventive works, varying between three and eight linked sections of considerable variety (rhythmic as well as melodic) and interest, very much the precursor of the concerto grosso. They are presented here with great freshness and give consistent pleasure. To add contrast, the **Purcell Quartet** intersperse them with other key works: the solo *Nisi Dominus* (**Richard Wistreich** in excellent form) and the dramatic duet setting of *Laetatus sum*, which is equally stimulating. Later, **Peter Harvey** returns as the Nightwatchman, singing against a winning pizzicato accompaniment. The famous *Battle* evocation is as impressive here as in any competing version. The second disc opens with the *Balletti lamentabili*, in which a haunting *Sonata* and a delicate closing *Lamenti* frame an *Allemande*, *Sarabande*, *Gavotte* and *Gigue*, all of which, for all their dance rhythms, maintain a mood of gentle melancholy. The programme ends with Biber's masterly *Passacaglia for Solo Violin*, which undoubtedly anticipates Bach's unaccompanied violin music. It is played superbly by **Catherine Mackintosh**. A splendid set, among the Purcell Quartet's finest achievements. The recording is very real indeed.

Harmonia artificiosa-ariosa (7 Partitas), 1–3 & 5 for 2 Scordatura Violins & Continuo; 4 for Scordatura Violin, Viola di braccio & Continuo; 6 for 2 Violins & Continuo; 7 for 2 Violas d'amore & Continuo (complete)

*** Astrée E 8572. Rare Fruits Council

This complete recordings of Biber's masterly *Harmonia artificiosa-ariosa* shows us the amazing range of these seven partitas (or suites) which were published posthumously in 1712. The curiously named **Rare Fruits Council** play with great energy and virtuosity and effectively use an organ to add colour and weight to the texture. They are balanced rather forwardly, which reduces the dynamic range somewhat, but some of the solo passages have striking delicacy, and the chaconne-like variations of the closing *Seventh Partita* are very powerfully integrated. In short, you cannot go wrong with this recording. Auvidis manages to squeeze all seven partitas on to a single CD.

Harmonia artificiosa-ariosa: Partitas III & V. Rosenkranz Sonata 10; Passacaglia 16 for Solo Violin; Sonata VI; Sonata representativa (for violin & continuo)

*** BIS CD 608. Lindal, Ens. Saga

Biber's melancholy *Passacaglia* for solo violin is totally memorable. But the hit of the programme is the *Sonata representativa* with its bird evocations – they are more than just imitations – including the nightingale, thrush, cuckoo (a most striking approach) and cockerel. **Maria Lindal** is a splendid soloist and the style of the playing here is vibrantly authentic: the ear quickly adjusts to the plangent (but in no way anaemic) timbres which suit this repertoire admirably.

Mensa sonora (Instrumental Taffel-Music) (Parts 1–6)

⊕ *** Chan. 0748. (augmented) Purcell Qt

Completed in 1680, the six chamber sonatas which make up Biber's *Mensa sonora* were subtitled 'Instrumental table-music with fresh-sounding violins'. Each has the usual mixture of baroque movements, including Allamanda, Courante, Sarabanda and Gigue, and sometimes a Balletto or Ciacona. They are lightweight but inventive and are readily appealing. The **Purcell Quartett** is augmented by **Jane Rogers** (viola); their performances are spirited and polished, and certainly fresh-sounding; this is much more enjoyable than the alternative version from the **Musica Antiqua Köln** on DG (477 5001), where the closely observed strings have a buzzy abrasiveness. The Chandos recording is beautifully balanced.

Mystery (Rosenkranz) Violin Sonatas (complete)

⊕ *** HM HMU 907321.22 (2). Manze, Egarr (with McGillivray in Sonata XII)

❀ (BB) *** Virgin 5 62062-2 (2). Holloway, Moroney, Tragicomedia

*** ASV Gaudeamus CDGAU 350 (1–9); CDGAU 351 (10–16). Huggett, Sonnerie

Biber's set of *Mystery* (or *Rosary*) Sonatas for violin and continuo tells the Christian story in instrumental terms. There are 15 Sonatas divided into three groups: *The Five Joyful Mysteries* (The Annunciation; Visitation; Nativity; Presentation of the Infant Jesus; and the Twelve-year-old Jesus in the Temple); *The Five Sorrowful Mysteries* (Christ on the Mount of Olives; the Scourging at the Pillar; Crowning with Thorns; Carrying of the Cross; and the Crucifixion) and *The Five Glorious Mysteries* (The Resurrection; Ascension; Descent of the Holy Ghost; Assumption of the Virgin; and Coronation of the Virgin). The work ends with an expressively powerful extended slow *Passacaglia* which becomes steadily more complex.

Needless to say, **Andrew Manze's** playing is of the highest quality. He is a master of this repertoire, and his timbre is strikingly full, his lyrical phrasing highly responsive, his use of scordatura has plenty of edge, and his supreme virtuosity is ever apparent, without exaggeration. He also opts for a comparatively simple backcloth for the solo violin. He could not have chosen a more distinguished accompanist than **Richard Egarr**, who provides a chamber organ continuo in nine of the sonatas, and uses a harpsichord in the remaining three. **Alison McGillivray** (cello) joins them in Sonata XII (*The Ascension*) to lead the way up to heaven and add to the sonority. The effect here is less dramatic than in the Virgin set, much plainer than in the Gaudeamus, but even more emotionally telling in its relatively austere presentation, and his restrained and dedicated account of the final *Passacaglia* makes a very moving apotheosis at the close of Part II. The recording is finely balanced, and this set is made the more attractive by an appendix, including Andrew Manze's spoken explanation of what scordatura means, with plenty of examples.

John Holloway's strong instrumental personality is very telling. **Davitt Moroney** (chamber organ or harpsichord) and **Tragicomedia** provide an imaginative continuo, using viola da gamba, lute, harp and a regal for the Crowning with Thorns. The recording gives a most vivid presence to the soloist.

Monica Huggett is also very persuasive in these wonderful sonatas and, besides vigorous bravura and characteristic sensitivity, she brings a sense of fantasy to her solo playing which is particularly appealing. Moreover, the sounds made by **Sonnerie** are aurally captivating, with **Matthew Halls's** organ continuo adding a rich background of colour to underpin the rest of the continuo. The recording balance is close, but the overall effect is most vivid within a pleasing acoustic. One drawback, however, is that there are only 12 separating bands, one for each sonata, with no cues for individual movements. However, this makes a genuine alternative to the Harmonia Mundi set.

12 Sonatae tam Aris, quam Aulis servientes

*** Astrée E 8630. Rare Fruits Council, Kraemer

*** Chan. 0591. Bennett, Laird, McGillivray, Cronin, Purcell Qt

Biber's *Sonatae tam Aris, quam Aulis servientes* are among his most immediately attractive works, their direct appeal comparable with the Bach *Brandenburgs*. They combine appealing expressive elements and great rhythmic vitality. The robustly extrovert recording from the **Rare Fruits Council** is full of character, vividly colourful and alive. In about half the *Sonatas* (Nos. 1, 4, 7, 10 and 12) the authentic string group of seven players plus continuo is joined by one or two trumpets, and here the effect is quite spectacular. The works for strings alone, however, are splendidly full-bodied and colourful (helped by the liberal use of organ in the continuo). The energy and expressive vigour of the music-making here bubbles over. Highly recommended.

The Chandos complete set from the augmented **Purcell Quartet** is also excellent in every way, full of life and imaginative detail. The sound is first class, but the Rare Fruits Council remains first choice.

Unam Ceylum: Violin Sonatas 3, 4, 6, 7; in A & in E (unpublished)

*** ECM 472 084-2. Holloway, Assenbaum, Mortensen

Biber is presented here as the Paganini of his time. The writing, always entertaining, is both dazzling and tuneful and includes, besides the occasional *Gigue* and *Gavotte*, plenty of examples of his inventive writing in variation, passacaglia and chaconne styles. John Holloway presents the sonatas with great panache and obvious pleaure in their technical intricacies, while the continuo is admirably realized by **Aloysia Assenbaum** (organ) and **Lars Mortensen** (harpsichord). The recording is truthful – forwardly balanced in a warm acoustic.

8 Violin Sonatas (for violin & continuo) (1681); Sonata pastorella; Sonata representativa in A (for solo violin); Passacaglia for Solo Violin; Passacaglia for Lute

*** HM HMX 2907344/45 (2). Romanesca (Manze, North, Toll)

Andrew Manze conveys to the full the tension that always springs from strong performances of technically demanding music, yet at the same time he retains an essentially expressive style, also featuring the improvisatory feeling in the writing, to say nothing of its sublimely volatile unpredictability. The recording has a fine, spacious acoustic, and only those who find the abrasiveness of authentic fiddling aurally difficult should stay away from this highly stimulating pair of discs.

Violin Sonatas 2, 3, 5, 7 (1681); Passacaglia for Solo Violin; (i) Nisi Dominus for Violin, Bass Voice & Continuo

*** Gaudeamus CDGAU 203. Huggett, Sonnerie; (i) with Guthrie

Violin Sonatas (with continuo, 1681), 3–4; 6–8; 81 in A; 84 in E (unpublished)

*** ECM 472 084-2. Holloway, Assenbaum, Mortensen

Monica Huggett's period-instrument timbre and style of attack are no less gutsy and vibrant than those of Andrew Manze, with plenty of vibrant edge on the phrasing. But this is superbly alive playing and the unaccompanied solo flourishes of the *Second Sonata in D minor* surely anticipate Bach, as the unaccompanied *Passacaglia* reminds one initially of his famous *Chaconne*. The Psalm setting, so resonantly, dramatically and touchingly sung by **Thomas Guthrie**, recalls Monteverdi. Here the violin figurations are clearly as important as the vocal line, and the continuo, using organ as well as theorbo, gives fine support. Excellent, vividly forward recording.

Holloway's performances have great flair. He creates a beautiful timbre on his Hoog copy of a 1649 Amati violin, and he obviously revels in the music's ready fund of melody. The continuo backing is very supportive and ideally balanced and recorded.

VOCAL MUSIC

Litaniæ de Sancto Josepho; Sonatas: Fidicinium sacro-profanum; Sancti Polycarpi

⌕— Ⓑ *** HM HMA 1951667. Soloists, Cantus Köln, Concerto Palatino, Junghänel – MUFFAT: *Missa in labore requies* ***

This is a particularly recommendable coupling in its combination of the music of Biber and his lesser-known, but equally enterprising contemporary, Georg Muffat. The *Litaniæ de Sancto Josepho* was a late work, with its focal point the Feast of St Joseph which Pope Gregory XV had instituted in 1621, although Biber's music dates from the 1690s. It is characteristically spectacular, indeed one of the composer's most ambitious settings. The vocal and instrumental forces here do it full justice. The introductory *Sonata Sancti Polycarpi* (instrumental and drums) was used to accompany the exit of the Archbishop. (The other *Sonata* is interpolated in the Muffat *Mass*.) With **Maria Cristina Kehr** leading a fine group of soloists and some spectacular brass playing, this performance, recorded in the resonant Chapel of Melk Abbey, is very satisfying indeed. Highly recommended.

Mass in B flat a 6; Requiem in F min.

*** DG 474 7142. Hemington, Holton, Auchinloss, Grant, Pott, Gabrieli Consort & Players, McCreesh (with MUFFAT: *Ciacona*; SCHMELZER: *Sonatas II & XIII*; MEGERLE: *Peccator et consolator a 2*; ANON.: *Praeludium; Praeludium legatura*; LASSUS: *Ave verum corpus a 6; Media vita in morte sumus a 6*)

Paul McCreesh offers a chance to enjoy and compare the relatively small-scale *Mass for Six Voices and Continuo* with the more familiar and more spectacular *F minor Requiem* which was probably written for performance in Salzburg Cathedral and which is here performed with a string ensemble and the chorus reinforced with trombones in the generous acoustic of Tonbridge School Chapel in Kent. Biber's *Mass* setting is here introduced by a *Ciacona* by Muffat and interspersed with other contemporary music to form a quasi-liturgical sequence in which the *Ave verum* and (closing) *Media vita* of Lassus stand out for their serene beauty. Characteristically McCreesh directs the proceedings with great vitality: the *Gloria* and *Credo* of the *Mass*, sung with resplendent vigour, really move along, and the *Requiem* too is never left to languish. The choral singing is splendid, and the **Gabrieli Consort** and brass players add a fine backing sonority. One of the highlights of the recording is the *Offertory* in the *Mass*, a setting of *Peccator et consolator* for two soprano voices, beautifully sung by **Susan Hemington** and **Ruth Holton**, in which the second voice is placed distantly to achieve an echo effect. If you acquire this superbly recorded disc, this is the excerpt you will be playing to your friends as an unforgettable sampler.

Missa Bruxellensis

⌕— ✿ **** Alia Vox AV 9808. Soloists, La Capella Reial de Catalunya, Concert des Nations, Savall

This gloriously festive *Missa Bruxellensis* – a late (perhaps final) work, dating from 1700 – is scored for two eight-voice choirs, groups of wind, strings, trumpets, horns and trombones, and a bass continuo of organs and bassoons. The disposition of the soloists, choristers and instruments in the stalls, around the transept and in the cathedral choir was designed to add to the sense of spectacle, and the music is fully worthy of its ambitious layout. Its imaginative diversity, with continual contrasts between tutti and soli of great expressive power, shows the composer working at full stretch. The *Kyrie* opens in great splendour with the two antiphonal choirs and festive trumpets (*cornets à bouquin*). The closing *Agnus Dei* has the soloists singing radiantly but with piercing dissonance from Biber's extraordinary sustained suspensions, with the full forces then entering for the closing *Amen*. The performance here, superlatively recorded in the echoing – but never blurring – acoustics of Salzburg Cathedral, recreates the work's première and is truly inspired. This marvellous disc cannot be recommended too highly.

Missa Christi Resurgens

*** Kleos **SACD** Compatible Surround Sound KL 5135. Soloists, NY Coll., Parrott

Andrew Parrott and his excellent **New York Collegium** here première on CD the lyrically exultant *Missa Christi Resurgens* from around 1673. It is written for the usual double choir, groups of soloists, cornets, sackbuts and strings, and two trumpets stationed across the transept from the other musicians. The performance places the Mass in the context of contemporary Salzburg performance, interspersing appropriate chant and instrumental interludes, mainly string pieces, taken from Biber's own works. The *Sanctus* interchanges voices and brass and the *Benedictus* brings a duet between alto soloist and principal violin. Organ voluntaries (by Alessandro Poglietti) frame the beautiful *Agnus Dei*, and the performance ends with an evocation of the Resurrection by using one of Biber's own *Mystery Sonatas*. In this way the New York performance imaginatively and authentically brings together a great variety of music, and the playing and singing could hardly be more persuasive.

Missa Salisburgensis

⌕— **** DG 457 611-2. Gabrieli Cons. & Players, Col. Mus. Ant., McCreesh; Goebel

Paul McCreesh in partnership with **Reinhard Goebel** turns to one of the grandest of all ecclesiastical events, when in Salzburg Cathedral in 1682 they celebrated the 1,100th anniversary of Salzburg as a centre of Christianity. Though the score survived, there is no specific mention of the composer – all was created for the glory of God alone – but shrewd detective work, described in the note, clearly points to Heinrich Biber, who was soon to be appointed Kapellmeister to the archbishop. The blaze of sound on the disc is magnificent, with widely spaced antiphonal groups, choirs and instrumentalists, thrillingly capturing massive contrasts of sound.

BINGE, Ronald (1910–79)

(i) *Elizabethan Serenade*; (ii; iii) *Saxophone Concerto*; (iii) *Saturday Symphony*; (iv) *At the End of* the Day; Autumn Dream; Butterflies; Candles on the Table; Farewell Waltz; Fugal Fun; Give Me a Ring; Homeward; Inamorata; I Like Your Smile; I Sent You Roses; The Last of the Clan; The Look in Your Eyes; Man in a Hurry; Miss Melanie; The Moon Looks Down; Morning Light; Perhaps I'm Young; Sailing By; A Scottish Rhapsody; The Sound of Music is Everywhere; A Star is Born; Tango Corto; There's a Light in Your Eyes; Under the Sun; Waiting for Moonlight; The Watermill; What Do You Know?; When You are Young

Ⓜ *** ASV (ADD) CDWLZ 245 (2). (i) Nat. PO, Gerhardt; O, Heller; (ii) Voss; (iii) S German R. O, composer; (iv) Walter Heller & his O; O Raphael, Hotter; or Dreamland O

Ronald Binge's most famous pieces must be the *Elizabethan Serenade* (which rightly opens disc 1), *Sailing By*, which was played at the closing of BBC Radio 4, accompanying the Shipping Forecast, from 1973, or the delightful watercolour portrait of *The Water Mill*. As this CD shows, his fund of melody was unquenchable and, with his deftness of orchestration, it resulted in some first-class light classical music of the type that blossomed in the 1950s and 1960s. The *Saxophone Concerto* and *Saturday Symphony* (conducted here by the composer) are much longer than his usual short character-pieces, though they are just as enjoyable. The recordings (mainly from the 1960s) are taken from a variety of sources but mostly feature **Walter Heller and his Orchestra**. Recommended to all lovers of good tunes. The recordings range from very good to thoroughly acceptable, and it is fascinating to note that the performers of four of the pieces are unknown.

BINGHAM, Judith (born 1952)

Choral music: (i) *Irish Tenebrae* (cantata); *Beneath these Alien Stars*; *Ghost Towns of the American West*; *Gleams of a Remoter World*; *The Shepheardes Calendar*; *Unpredictable but Providential*; *Water Lilies*

Ⓝ *** Signum SIGCD 144 BBC Singers, Hill; (i) with Robinson, Osostowicz, Farrington (organ), Benjafield & Brannick (percussion)

Judith Bingham has been a member of the BBC Singers for over a decade and their Associate Composer for nearly five years. Her best-known work here is the engaging three-part *Shepheardes Calendar*, her most ambitious and individual is the *Irish Tenebrae*, a cantata of much diversity for soloists and chorus with organ, violin obbligato and percussion. The reader will surely be tempted by the titles of the other works and will not be disappointed by their imaginative settings including two poems *Ghost Towns of the American West* and *Beneath these Alien Stars* by the Mormon writer, Vesta Crawford. Performances throughout could not be more expert or persuasive. A disc for those who like to explore contemporary music which really communicates.

BIRTWISTLE, Harrison
(born 1934)

Carmen Arcadiae mechanicae perpetuum; Secret Theatre; Silbury Air

*** Etcetera KTC 1052. L. Sinf., Howarth

Silbury Air is one of Birtwistle's 'musical landscapes', bringing ever-changing views and perspectives on the musical material and an increasing drawing-out of melody. With melody discarded, *Carmen Arcadiae mechanicae perpetuum* (*The Perpetual Song of Mechanical Arcady*) superimposes different musical mechanisms to bring a rhythmic kaleidoscope of textures and patterns. The title of *Secret Theatre* is taken from a poem by Robert Graves which refers to 'an unforeseen and fiery entertainment', and there is no doubting the distinctive originality of the writing, utterly typical of the composer. **Howarth** and the **Sinfonietta** could hardly be more convincing advocates, recorded in vivid, immediate sound.

VOCAL MUSIC

An Interrupted Endless Melody; Duets for Storab; Entr'actes & Fragments; 9 Settings of Niedecker; The Woman & the Hare

*** Black Box BBM 1046. McFadden, Watson, Nash Ens., Brabbins

This collection of Birtwistle chamber works spans his whole career, from *The Entr'actes* and *Sappho Fragments* of 1962-4, his uncompromising style already established along with his love of a ritualistic structure, to the Harsent setting of 1999. In response to the verses, the music evokes the wildness of nature and of man himself in a sequence of fragments that characteristically still holds firmly together, thanks also to the performers here, including the soprano **Claron McFadden** and the reciter, **Julia Watson**. The Niedecker settings were again built on brief evocative images, while the *Duets for Storab* (1983) take their inspiration from a legendary Neolithic king and comprise duets for two unaccompanied flutes with echoes of Stravinsky. *An Interrupted Endless Melody* was written in 1991-4 in memory of the oboist, Janet Craxton, with a single melody varied by strongly contrasted accompaniments on the piano. A fascinating collection, vividly recorded.

Pulse Shadows

*** Warner 3984 268672-2. McFadden, Arditti Qt, Nash Ens., De Leeuw

This sequence of laments, inspired by the cryptic verses of the poet, Paul Celan, is one of the most moving of Birtwistle's later works. In it he interleaves two works that had a separate genesis – his nine settings of Celan and the nine pieces for string quartet – making a two-tier sequence of over an hour which, among much else, enshrines the composer's response to the Holocaust. In this version the English translations of Paul Hamburger are used for all the poems except one, *Todtnauberg*, which is recited in English while the song is sung in German. The eighteen sections, most of them brief, far from seeming fragmentary, hang together in a kaleidoscope of sharp inspiration, superbly realized here by all the performers, not least the soprano, **Claron McFadden**, totally unfazed by the cragginess of the writing and helped by the vividly immediate sound.

OPERA

The Mask of Orpheus (complete)

🎵 (M) *** NMC D 050 (3). Garrison, Bronder, Rigby, Owens, Opie, Ebrahim, BBC Singers & O, A. Davis

Birtwistle's *The Mask of Orpheus* is one of the most challenging operas ever written. With **Andrew Davis** controlling his massed forces masterfully, helped by **Martyn Brabbins** as assistant conductor, the intense originality of a score dotted with havens of sheer beauty is never in doubt. Central to its success is the thrilling performance of the American tenor, **Jon Garrison**, as Orpheus the man, well supported by **Peter Bronder** as Orpheus the myth. **Jean Rigby** and **Anne-Marie Owens**, less prominent in the story, similarly take on the divided and superimposed role of the heroine, Eurydice woman and myth. The recorded sound is superb, vivid in conveying the different musical layers, electronic as well as instrumental and vocal. The documentation is very full. It is good that NMC have issued this important set as 'three discs for the price of two'.

The Minotaur (DVD version)

(N) *** Opus Arte **DVD** OA1000D. Tomlinson, Reuter, Rice, Watts, Langridge, Echalaz, O & Ch, of ROHCG, Pappano (Dir: Stephen Langridge)

This, Birtwistle's eighth opera, like his earlier commission from Covent Garden, *Gawain*, has a libretto by David Harsent, using a language nicely balanced between poetry and the vernacular, while Birtwisle's idiom, always abrasive, has developed here a more lyrical strain. As in previous operas Birtwistle is not only preoccupied with Greek myth but with central characters who are anti-heroes.

In *The Minotaur* the piece rises to a superb final climax, when Theseus has killed the Minotaur (in this incarnation with a bull's head and a human body), the monster is finally allowed to speak, so that the concluding monologue as he is dying echoes directly the Death of Boris in Mussorgsky's *Boris Godunov*, a likeness that Birtwistle intends. With typical ingenuity Birtwistle has created a lyrical thread passed from instrument to instrument symbolizing the thread that Ariadne gives to Theseus to lead him back through the Minotaur's maze.

The impact of the opera is greatly heightened not just by the casting but by the staging by Stephen Langridge at the Royal Opera House Covent Garden, very well filled on this DVD, with simple yet vividly atmospheric designs by Alison Chitty. The role of The Minotaur as a sort of Jekyll and Hyde figure was expressly designed for **John Tomlinson**, the famed Wotan from *Bayreuth* and centrally cast too in Birtwistle's earlier *Gawain*. His voice may no longer be as steady as it was, but his singing could not be more moving.

There are no reservations whatever about **Christine Rice** as Ariadne, superb in every way, and other fine contributions come from the bass-baritone **Johan Reuter** as Theseus and **Philip Langridge** as the Oracle, while **Antonio Pappano**, Music Director at Covent Garden, excels himself conducting an electrifying performance with orchestra and chorus finely coordinated.

Punch and Judy (opera; complete)

*** NMCD 138 (2). Roberts, DeGaetani, Bryn-Julson, Langridge, Wilson-Johnson, Tomlinson, L. Sinf., Atherton

Punch and Judy is a brutal, ritualistic piece. It may not make easy listening, but nor is it easy to forget: behind the aggressiveness, Birtwistle's writing has a way of touching an emotional chord, just as Stravinsky's so often does. **Stephen Roberts** is outstanding as Punch, and among the others there is not a single weak link. **David Atherton**, conductor from the first performances, excels himself. The clear, vivid recording, originally made by Decca for their enterprising LP Headline series, has been licensed by NMC.

BIZET, Georges (1838–75)

L'Arlésienne (complete incidental music; ed. Riffault)

🎵 (M) *** EMI 3 55671-2. Orféon Donostiarra, Toulouse Capitole O, Plasson

The score of the complete incidental music that **Michel Plasson** and his excellent French forces have recorded is based on the 1872 autograph, and the singing of the **Orféon Donostiarra** is as excellent as the Toulouse orchestral playing. The less familiar music is every bit as captivating as the suites, so that the performance has great charm, and the EMI recording is very good indeed. Strongly recommended.

L'Arlésienne : Suites 1 & 2; Incidental Music: Suite 3 (compiled Minkowski); Carmen: Suite 1

🎵 ❁ **** Naïve V 5130. Lyon Nat. Opéra Ch., Musiciens du Louvre, Minkowski

Minkowski's new disc stands alone, and in front of its competitors, in including a considerable amount of extra music from *L'Arlésienne*. Fitting neatly between the familiar *Suites 1* and *2* is a third, including extended excerpts from the original score, with the chorus adding much beauty to the *Pastorale*, the second Act *Tableau*, and extra vividness to the *Farandole*. The whole compilation is a delight, not least because of the refreshingly polished orchestral playing (with a really authentic French colouring). Minkowski's choice of tempi and crisp pointing of the woodwind are particularly telling – notably in the first *Entr'acte* from *Carmen* and the vivacious *Minuet* which follows. The *Farandole*, too, is given a splendid lift by Minkowski's rhythmic double dotting, while the flute solos in all three suites (plus the siciliano for a pair of flutes in tableau 4 of Act III of the latter) are delectably delicate. The famous *L'Arlésienne Adagietto*, played *Andante quasi Adagio*, as Bizet wanted, is very moving (and it touchingly returns before the final reprise of the exuberant *Farandole*, heard first with men's voices, and then excitingly with full choir. The choral singing and the playing of **Les Musiciens du Louvre** are very sensitive indeed, while the recording is first class. Moreover, the packaging, in book-format, is a pleasure in itself. The three-language documentation (including texts and translations) is interspersed with reproductions of famous French paintings by Van Gogh, Gauguin and others, increasing the pleasure of using the handsomely bound booklet which holds the disc. This is now a definitive first choice for those wanting a CD combining excerpts from *Carmen* and *L'Arlésienne*, unless the second suite from *Carmen* is essential.

L'Arlésienne (incidental music), Op. 23 (complete); Jeux d'enfants, Op. 22; Marche funèbre; Overture in A; Patrie Overture, Op. 19; Les 4 Coins; Roma Suite 3; Symphony in C; Carmen: Suite 1

☙ Ⓑ *** EMI 5 09414-2 (3). Orféon Donostierra, O Nat. du Capitole Toulouse, Plasson

This valuable reissue includes the complete incidental music of *L'Arlésienne*. **Plasson** also offers *Les Quatre coins* with *Jeux d'enfants*, which the composer unaccountably discarded. The other important novelty here is the delightful *Overture in A* which is contemporary with the *Symphony* and is scored equally felicitously. The *Marche funèbre* is in fact the flamboyant *Prélude* to the discarded opera, *La Coupe du roi de Thulé*. *Roma* was written over a period, some years after the *Symphony in C*. It has not the overall spontaneity of the *Symphony* and is uneven in quality, but it remains an easy piece to indulge if you are a lover of Bizet's feeling for the orchestral palette. The warmth of the opening horn chorale and the gaiety of the pleasing secondary tune are brought out enjoyably in Toulouse. The *Symphony* too is well played (with an imaginative oboe soloist) and is certainly enjoyable, if not distinctive. But there are no reservations about the *Carmen Suite*, and the recording is very good throughout, vividly coloured if not of demonstration standard.

(i) L'Arlésienne: Suites 1–2; (ii) Symphony in C

☙ Ⓜ *** EMI (ADD) 5 67231-2. (i) RPO; (ii) Fr. Nat. R. O; Beecham

L'Arlésienne: Suites 1–2. Carmen: Suite 1

Ⓑ *** DG (ADD) 477 6350. LSO, Abbado

L'Arlésienne: Suites 1–2. Carmen: Suites 1–2

☙ Ⓜ *** Decca 466 421-2. Montreal SO, Dutoit

With playing that is both elegant and vivid, and with superb, demonstration-worthy sound, **Dutoit's** polished yet affectionate coupling of the *L'Arlésienne* and *Carmen* suites makes a clear first choice.

Beecham's famous Bizet coupling now rightly reappears as one of EMI's 'Great Recordings of the Century'. His magical touch is especially illuminating in the two *L'Arlésienne* suites, and the early (1956) stereo gives the **RPO** woodwind striking luminosity yet plenty of body. The *Symphony* too sounds freshly minted. Although the playing here has slightly less finesse, its zest is in no doubt, especially in the finale, and the oboe soloist in the slow movement distinguishes himself.

Among other analogue couplings of the *L'Arlésienne* and *Carmen* suites, **Abbado's** 1981 DG recording also stands out. The orchestral playing is characteristically refined, the wind solos cultured and eloquent, especially in *L'Arlésienne*, where the pacing of the music is nicely judged.

Carmen Suite 1; Patrie Overture; Roma: Carnaval à Roma

☙ *** EMI (ADD) 3 79986-2. Fr. Nat. R. O, or RPO, Beecham
– CHABRIER: *España; Joyeuse marche; Gwendoline Overture;* FAURÉ: *Dolly;* SAINT-SAËNS: *Le rouet d'Omphale ***

No one conducts the *Carmen Prélude* with quite **Beecham's** flair, set off by an explosive cymbal crash, while in his hands the *Patrie Overture*, even though it is played by the **RPO**, is as ebulliently Gallic as *La Marseillaise*, with a degree of brashness for good measure. With its equally illustrious lollipop companions, this is another obvious choice for EMI's 'Great Recordings of the Century'.

Jeux d'enfants (Children's games), Op. 22

Ⓜ **(*) BBC (ADD) BBCL 4039-2. Philh. O, Boult – RAVEL: *Daphnis et Chloé: Suite 2;* SCHUBERT: *Symphony 8 (Unfinished);* SIBELIUS: *Symphony 7 ***(*)

Sir Adrian's Bizet is performed with elegance, sparkle and tenderness. Marvellous playing from the **Philharmonia** and a good BBC recording which lacks only the last degree of range and sparkle.

La Jolie Fille de Perth: Suite

(*) Testament SBT 1238. Fr. Nat. R. O, Cluytens – RAVEL: *Daphnis et Chloé Suites, etc.;* ROUSSEL: *Le Festin de l'araignée *

Unfussy, straightforward and fresh, even if the last ounce of polish is missing. But this CD is a must for the coupling, **Cluytens's** inspired and atmospheric account of Roussel's *Le Festin de l'araignée.*

Symphony in C

Ⓜ *** Häns. CD 93013. Stuttgart SW RSO, Prêtre – RAVEL: *Daphnis et Chloé: Suite 2; La Valse ***

Prêtre's tempo for the opening movement (exposition repeat included) is just right, with a nice rhythmic lift, and the *Adagio* brings a memorable oboe solo. The unnamed principal has an almost vocal vibrato, and he phrases exquisitely. In the very brisk *moto perpetuo* finale the strings articulate with tremendous bustling precision, yet the second theme is able to relax and lilt seductively. The Liederhalle, Stuttgart, has a most attractive acoustic and the recording, although digital, has an almost analogue ambient warmth. If you want the couplings this disc is highly recommendable.

PIANO MUSIC

Jeux d'enfants, Op. 22

(BB) **(*) EMI Gemini 5 86510-2 (2). Collard, Béroff – DEBUSSY & RAVEL: *Music for piano, 4 hands & 2 pianos*; DUKAS: *L'Apprenti Sorcier* **(*)

Jeux d'enfants is a collection of 12 engaging piano miniatures, of which Bizet scored just five for his familiar orchestral suite. While he adroitly picked the highlights, many of the other pieces are delightful too. **Jean-Philippe Collard** and **Michel Béroff** play them appealingly, with items like *Les Chevaux de bois* and *Les Quatre Coins* standing out. The digital recording, made in the Paris Salle Wagram in 1994, is not flattering, but very acceptable when the repertoire is so rare.

VOCAL

'Chant d'amour': Mélodies: *Adieux de l'hôtesse arabe; Chant d'amour; La Coccinelle; Ouvre ton cœur; Tarantelle*

*** Decca 452 667-2. Bartoli, Chung – BERLIOZ; DELIBES; RAVEL: *Mélodies* ***

These delightful Bizet songs come as part of an outstanding recital of French repertoire, readily demonstrating the versatility of **Cecilia Bartoli**, who is so sympathetically accompanied by **Myung-Whun Chung**. Both voice and piano are recorded beautifully. The collection is considered more fully in our Recitals section, below.

Te Deum

(*) Australian Decca Eloquence 476 2947. Greenberg, Winbergh, Lausanne Pro Arte Ch., Swiss R. Ch., SRO, Lopez-Cobos – POULENC: *Gloria; Stabat Mater* *

Bizet's *Te Deum* of 1858 is a product of his youth and was written while he was still at Rome. It is very much a student work, with little of the effortless mastery that distinguishes the even earlier *Symphony*, and there is much that is derivative. There are some entertaining moments in the course of its 25 minutes, along with some obviously manufactured ideas, not all of which are effective. However, with such a good performance and recording, there is enough of interest here to make it worth considering.

OPERA

Carmen (complete; DVD versions)

(N) **** TDK **DVD** DV-CLOPCAR Obraztsova, Domingo, Buchanan, Mazurok, Vienna State Op., Ch. & O, Carlos Kleiber (Stage and V/D Franco Zeffirelli)

*** DG **DVD** 073 4032. Bumbry, Vickers, Freni, Diaz, V. State Op. Ch., VPO, Karajan (Dir. & V/D: Karajan)

*** Columbia Tristar **DVD** CDR 10530. Migenes, Domingo, Raimondi, Esham, Fr. Nat. RSO and Ch., Maazel (V/D: Franco Rossi)

(N) *** Decca **DVD** 074 3312DH (Blu-ray version 074 3313) Antonacci, Kaufmann, D'Arcangelo, Amsellem, ROHCG Ch. & O, Pappano

(*) DG **DVD 073 000-9. Baltsa, Carreras, Ramey, Mitchell, Met. Op. Ch. & O, Levine (V/D: Brian Large)

Zeffirelli's 1978 live DVD recording will be hard to surpass. **Eleana Obraztsova** and **Domingo** are ideally cast as Carmen and Don José. They act very convincingly and sing gloriously (the *Flower Song* is as memorable as Carmen's hit numbers). Moreover, for once there is a totally convincing Micaëla in **Isobel Buchanan**, who also sings ravishingly. Her Act III scene and *aria* is a highlight of the opera. From the opening Prelude **Carlos Kleiber** directs with fizzing vitality and drama, yet creates a warmly sympathetic backcloth for the voices in the lyrical writing: the close of Act II is unforgettable, as, of course, is the opera's final scene. Zeffirelli's production is predictably spectacular (especially in the outer Acts) and traditional in the best possible way, and the camera follows the action admirably. The sound cannot be faulted. The set is additionally offered in a reduced price box with Giordano's *Fedora* and Verdi's *Il trovatore*, both with Domingo, *Il trovatore* conducted by Karajan (TDK Gold Edition: DV-GOLDBOX2).

Based on a lavish Salzburg Festival production, directed (like the video production) by **Karajan** himself, his film of *Carmen* was made in 1967 with the starriest of casts. Though the sound recording was made in the Sofiensaal in Vienna, the filming was done in Munich, using an expansion of Teo Otto's impressive stage sets. That involved the singers miming to their own voices, so that when the film regularly uses revealing close-ups of the soloists, the discrepancies between lips and voice become obvious. That is one of the few flaws in an exceptionally powerful production. **Grace Bumbry** as Carmen is at her most seductive, sensuous in both voice and looks, establishing herself as sultry and provocative even before she starts singing in Act I. **Jon Vickers** is equally powerful as Don José, defiant of authority from the very beginning, and though his tenor is of heroic scale, he shades it down beautifully for such an aria as the *Flower Song*, using a perfectly controlled head-voice at the end in genuinely hushed singing. **Mirella Freni** is an enchanting Micaëla, girlish and fun-loving, with **Justino Diaz** a powerful and handsome Escamillo completing a quartet of principals not just characterful but vocally firm and clear. The rest of the cast cannot be faulted either, and Karajan conducts with a combination of bite and warmth to match and even outshine his two regular CD versions. Recitatives are preferred to spoken dialogue, and the full ballet is included.

Filmed on location in the most atmospheric of sites, few operatic films add so vividly to the music as this version of *Carmen*, directed by Franco Rossi. It starts with a striking visual coup: the credits are shown with merely the murmur of a bullring crowd in the background, while a matador is seen playing with a bull. He finally brings his sword down for the kill, and Bizet's opening *Prélude* thunders out. The film is set to a recording specially made in the studio, and issued on CD by Erato. An excellent performance, under **Lorin Maazel**, on DVD it projects as sharply dramatic, with **Plácido Domingo** at his finest and **Julia Migenes** the most vibrantly characterful of Carmens. **Ruggero Raimondi** makes a noble Escamillo, and though **Faith Esham's** voice is not ideally sweet as Micaëla, it is a tender, sensitive performance. The sound is first rate, and having the singers miming to the music is not too distracting.

The newest **Covent Garden** version of *Carmen* is traditional and large-scale, although some of the background detail is overdone, including the provision of animals! **Pappano** uses his own edition of the score, but his few cuts and adjustments will only worry purists. He directs the proceedings with much élan and Bizet's delightful score emerges in vivid colouring. **Jonas Kaufmann** gives a bold, lusty portrayal of Don José matched by a similarly strong and sexy Carmen in Anna Caterina Antonacci. **Norah Amsellem's** Micaëla has pathos and charm, but not a great deal else. **Ildebrando D'Arcangelo** is a potent Escamillo. An enjoyable version overall, with 5.1 surround sound available, plus an optional Blu-ray alternative (with a different catalogue number).

DG's alternative DVD version of *Carmen* offers a grandly traditional production from the Met. in New York. It is starrily cast, with **James Levine** bringing out all the brilliance of the score, almost to a fault, when the sound is bright to the point of edginess. This 1988 production, directed for the stage by Paul Mills and imaginatively directed for television by Brian Large, has the most lavish, solidly realistic sets and costumes by John Bury, so grand that at each curtain-rise the stage picture prompts loud applause. Happily, at the time the four principals, all noted for taking their respective roles, were at their peak. **Agnes Baltsa**, who earlier sang Carmen for Karajan, is as ever a tough, defiant heroine, sultry, with rarely a smile on her face, initially sneering at the attentions of the glamorous Escamillo of **Samuel Ramey**. Her mezzo is firm and dark if hardly beautiful, with none of the vocal unevenness that developed later. Similarly, **José Carreras** as Don José is in superb voice, singing with a honeyed range of tone before his voice was affected by leukaemia. The *Flower Song* is exquisitely shaded with a perfectly controlled head-voice for the *pianissimo* high note at the end. Samuel Ramey, more noble than flamboyant or dangerous, makes a powerful Escamillo, and **Leona Mitchell** with her warm soprano is an appealing Micaëla. Though Levine's fast speeds occasionally trip up the very large chorus, they sing brilliantly, even though stage movement is on the primitive side. Though this cannot match Rossi's film of Migenes and Domingo in imagination, it makes a fine recommendation for a live performance filmed in the opera house.

Carmen (complete; CD versions)

🔊 **** EMI 5 57434-2 (3). Gheorghiu, Alagna, Hampson, Mula, Les Elements Ch., Toulouse Capitole O, Plasson

🔊 *** DG 410 088-2 (3). Baltsa, Carreras, van Dam, Ricciarelli, Barbaux, Paris Op. Ch., Schoenberg Boys' Ch., BPO, Karajan

🔊 Ⓜ **(*) EMI 5 67357-2 (3). De los Angeles, Gedda, Micheau, Blanc, French R. Ch. & O, Beecham

It is only the first of the delights of EMI's richly enjoyable set of *Carmen* with **Angela Gheorghiu** that it is restored as a grand opera, returning to the traditional version, with spoken dialogue replaced by the recitatives that Ernest Guiraud provided at the suggestion of the composer just before he died. This is a Carmen at once threatening and seductive, using a glorious range of tone, with a hearty chest register and the subtlest control of vibrato to give moments of heightened emotion extra intensity. So in the Quintet, leading up to Carmen's confession, *'Je suis amoureuse'*, her vibrancy is suddenly transformed into rich, glowing tone on that confession, a moment of rapture. This is a performance full of just such imaginative detail, and it includes as a fascinating supplement the first version of what became the *Habañera* in Act I. Gheorghiu is well matched by **Roberto Alagna** as Don José, always at his happiest singing French and, most moving as the beaten victim in Act IV. **Thomas Hampson** is a heroic, swaggering Escamillo and **Inva Mula** a touching Micaëla, idiomatically French, with **Michel Plasson** drawing crisp and incisive playing from his Toulouse team, bringing lightness to ensembles, often at speeds faster than usual.

Otherwise **Karajan's** DG set of *Carmen* makes a first choice among modern versions. In **Carreras** he has a Don José who is lyrical and generally sweet-toned. **José van Dam** is incisive and virile, the public hero-figure; which leaves **Agnes Baltsa** as a vividly compelling Carmen, tough and vibrant, yet with tenderness under the surface.

De los Angeles's portrayal of Carmen is absolutely bewitching, and when in the Quintet scene she says *Je suis amoureuse* one believes her absolutely. Naturally the other singers are not nearly as dominant as this, but they make admirable foils; **Nicolai Gedda** is pleasantly light-voiced as ever, **Janine Micheau** is a sweet Micaëla, and **Ernest Blanc** makes an attractive Escamillo. The hall acoustic makes the chorus sound very resonant but gives an attractive theatrical atmosphere to the solo voices, caught naturally and without edginess, and well balanced in relation to the orchestra. At its mid-price, this famous set reasserts its position near the top of the list of recommendations and makes a worthy addition to EMI's 'Great Recordings of the Century'. **Beecham** adds his own special touch to the orchestral interludes. The documentation cannot be faulted, including session photographs and a full translation.

Bernstein's 1973 *Carmen* was recorded at the New York Metropolitan Opera. Some of his slow tempi are very controversial, but what really matters is the authentic tingle of dramatic tension which permeates the whole entertainment. **Marilyn Horne** – occasionally coarse in expression – gives a fully satisfying reading of the heroine's role, a vivid characterization. The rest of the cast similarly works to Bernstein's consistent overall plan. It is very well transferred and comes as a Trio offered with only a cued synopsis. (DG 471 750-2)

Karajan's RCA version, made in Vienna in 1964, owes much to **Leontyne Price's** seductive, smoky-toned Carmen. **Corelli** has moments of coarseness but his is still a heroic performance. **Robert Merrill** sings with gloriously firm tone, while **Mirella Freni** is enchanting as Micaëla. With recording full of atmosphere, and attractively repackaged at mid-price, this is a very strong contender. (74321 39495-2)

Solti's Decca performance is remarkable for its new illumination of characters. **Tatiana Troyanos** is one of the subtlest Carmens on record. Escamillo too is more readily sympathetic, not just the flashy matador who steals the hero's girl, whereas Don José is revealed as weak rather than just a victim. **Troyanos's** singing is delicately seductive too, with no hint of vulgarity, while the others make up a consistent singing cast. Though the CD transfer brings out the generally excellent balances of the originally analogue recording, it exaggerates the bass, although the voices retain their fine realism and bloom. (414 489-2)

Maria Callas was ideally suited to the role of Carmen, but her complete recording is disappointing. One principal trouble is that the performance, apart from her, lacks a taut dramatic rein, with slack ensemble from singers and orchestra alike. The moment the heroine enters, the tension rises; but by Callas's standards this is a performance roughhewn, strong and characterful but lacking the full imaginative detail of her finest work. The set has been remastered and a new booklet prepared for this latest reissue. (EMI 5 56281-2)

Les Pêcheurs de perles (complete)

Ⓜ (***) EMI mono 5 65266-2 (2). Angelici, Legay, Dens, Noguera, Théâtre Nat. de l'Opéra-Comique Ch. & O, Cluytens

Unavailable since the early days of LP, this superb EMI/**Cluytens** set of 1954 offers the finest, most warmly expressive performance on disc of this delectable opera. Ironically, its nearest rival is the Philips set of the previous year under Jean Fournet, also in mono, both of them outshining later, stereo sets. **Cluytens** is an even more sensitive conductor than his Philips rival, less four-square, getting the music to flow flexibly; and his cast, idiomatically French, has no weak link. **Martha Angelici** as the heroine, Leila, is both sweet and bright, with no Gallic shrillness, and **Henry Legay** has a degree of heroic timbre in the rounded, lyric quality of his tenor, while **Michel Dens**, as in other French opera recordings of the period, proves a firm, characterful baritone. With excellent choral and orchestral work, one gets the impression of a stage experience translated to the studio. The mono transfer is a little dull on orchestral sound, but it captures voices vividly.

BLAKE, Howard (born 1938)

Clarinet Concerto

ⒷⒷ *** Hyp. Helios CDH 55068. King, ECO, composer (with LUTOSŁAWSKI: *Dance Preludes*; SEIBER: *Concertino* ***)

Howard Blake provides a comparatively slight but endearing *Clarinet Concerto*, which is played here with great sympathy by **Thea King**, who commissioned the work. At budget price this is even more attractive.

(i) Violin Concerto (Leeds). A Month in the Country (film incidental music): Suite; Sinfonietta for Brass

🎵 *** ASV CDDCA 905. (i) Edlinger; E. N. Philh., Daniel

It was the success of his music for *The Snowman* that gave Howard Blake the encouragement and the artistic breathing-space to write his beautiful and stimulating *Violin Concerto*. **Christiane Edlinger** is the soloist in what proves to be an inspired performance, caught 'on the wing'. The only snag is the excessively wide dynamic range of the recording. Blake's suite of string music written for the film *A Month in the Country* brings moments of comparable bitter-sweet, elegiac feeling. It is played most sensitively, as is the brass *Sinfonietta*, sonorous and jolly by turns. In terms of overall concert-hall realism, the recording is impressive and this record is strongly recommended.

Penillion for Violin and Piano, Op. 571; (i) Piano Quartet, Op. 179; Violin Sonata, Op. 586; Jazz Dances, Op. 520a

Ⓝ ⒷⒷ **** Naxos 8.572083 Madeleine Mitchell, Composer (piano); (i) with Rothestein, Essex, Willison

Howard Blake follows his concertos for clarinet and violin, plus an enjoyable collection of piano miniatures (ABC Classics 476 118-4) with this splendid collection of chamber music again showing his seemingly unlimited melodic flow and structural felicity. *Penillion* is an appealing inventive set of seven variations on a 'Welsh-like' theme; the *Piano Quartet* is a highly spontaneous work with a deeply reflective Lento; but the highlight of the disc is the *Violin Sonata*, with its Elysian slow movement exquisitely played by **Madeleine Mitchell** in partnership with the composer. The *Jazz Dances* are not Jazz at all, but infectiously 'pay mischievous, but affectionate homage to its rhythmic intricacies'. Altogether four splendid works very persuasively played and recorded.

PIANO MUSIC

Piano miniatures

*** ABC Classics 476 118-4. Chen

Howard Blake has a natural, easy-going melodic gift, which makes this series of unassuming piano miniatures very beguiling when they are so sympathetically played by **William Chen** and very well recorded. The simple, tuneful items like the *Ballad, Impromptu, Berceuse, Walking Song* and the film theme, *The Music Box*, may lack contemporary harmonic astringencies, yet they contrast well with the dancing staccato of the *Toccatino*, while the gentle portrait of Isabelle, written for a wedding, makes a foil for the vigorous ballet number, *Dance of the Hunters*, and the catchily syncopated *Rag* and *Jump*. Blake's famous *Snowman* tune is predictably included; perhaps the final item, *Make-Believe*, written for the animated film *Grandpa* will become a similar hit.

BLISS, Arthur (1891–1975)

(i; iii) *Adam Zero* (Ballet Suite); (iii; iv) *Christopher Columbus* (Film Score: Suite); (v) *Cello Concerto*; (iii; vi) *Concerto for 2 Pianos*; (vii) *A Colour Symphony*; (ii; iii) *Discourse for Orchestra*; (vii) *Things to Come* (Music from the film)

(B) *** EMI 5 86589-2 (2). (i) RLPO; (ii) Handley; (iii) CBSO; (iv) Marcus Dods; (v) Noras, Bournemouth SO, Berglund; (vi) Smith & Sellick; cond. Arnold; (vii) RPO, Groves

A fascinating cross-section of Bliss's orchestral and concertante music. *Adam Zero* for the most part shows his muse at its most fertile and the first movement of the *Cello Concerto* is one of the most inspired that Bliss ever wrote. The slow movement, with its rhapsodic style and elegiac atmosphere, is not sharply memorable, but the finale has splendid vigour and momentum. **Arto Noras** is the superbly eloquent soloist, and Berglund's accompaniment, pulsing with life, is little short of inspired.

The *Two-Piano Concerto* was arranged for three hands for Cyril Smith and Phyllis Sellick to play. The vigour of early Bliss makes for attractive results, with echoes of *Petrushka* and Debussy nicely worked in. Superbly played and richly recorded, it makes a delightful companion for the piano work. *A Colour Symphony* is too episodic to be truly symphonic, but it is nevertheless highly effective and is expertly scored. It comes into its own in **Groves's** sympathetic performance.

Of the two examples of Bliss's film music, it is the *March* from *Things to Come* which offers what is perhaps the single most memorable idea to come from its composer's pen. The invention shows Bliss at his finest, and once again Groves and the **RPO** are splendid advocates and the HMV engineers rise to the occasion.

(i; ii) Adam Zero (Ballet Suite); Mêlée fantasque; Hymn to Apollo; (i; ii; iii) Rout for Soprano & Orchestra; (i; iv; v) Serenade for Orchestra & Baritone; (i; vi; vii) The World is charged with the grandeur of God

*** Lyrita (ADD) SRCD 225 [id.]. (i) LSO; (ii) cond. composer; (iii) with Rae Woodland; (iv) Shirley-Quirk; (v) cond. Brian Priestman; (vi) with Amb. S.; (vii) cond. Ledger

The ballet *Adam Zero* contains some attractive moments. The *Mêlée fantasque* (well named) is even more striking, with strong Stravinskian influences but with a characteristic elegiac section at its centre. After the *Hymn to Apollo*, although the rest of the programme is primarily vocal, it is in fact the orchestral writing that one remembers most vividly, for the *Serenade* has two purely orchestral movements out of three. The second, *Idyll*, shows Bliss's lyrical impulse at its most eloquent. The orchestra is almost more important than the voice in *Rout*. The solo vocal performances throughout this CD are of high quality, and **John Shirley-Quirk**'s swashbuckling account of the gay finale of the *Serenade* must have pleased the composer greatly. The recordings date from the early 1970s and are of high quality.

Adam Zero (ballet; complete); A Colour Symphony

⊕ (BB) *** Naxos 8.553460. N. Philh. O, Lloyd-Jones

Full of striking ideas and effects to illustrate four heraldic colours, the *Colour Symphony* here receives a refined and idiomatic reading, marked by superb wind-playing. More valuable still is the first complete recording of the ballet, *Adam Zero*, in which the process of creating a ballet is pre-sented as an allegory for the ongoing life-cycle. **Lloyd-Jones** directs a dramatically paced performance, amply confirming this as one of Bliss's most inventive, strongly coordinated scores, shamefully neglected. Full, well-balanced sound.

Checkmate (ballet); Prologue; 5 Dances

⊕ (BB) *** Hyp. Helios CDH 55099. E. N. Philh. O, Lloyd-Jones – LAMBERT: *Horoscope* ***✿; WALTON: *Façade* ***

David Lloyd-Jones is a highly sympathetic advocate of Bliss's ballet suite, and he includes also the *Prologue*. The Hyperion recording, while warm enough to convey the score's lyricism, has plenty of bite in the *Red Knight's Mazurka*. This is most enjoyable, but it is the superb couplings that make this triptych both distinctive and now very desirable at Helios price.

(i) Checkmate: Suite; Hymn to Apollo; (ii) Music for Strings; (iii) Clarinet Quintet; (ii, iv) Lie strewn the white flocks

⊕ (B) *** Chan. 2-for-1 241-1 (2). (i) Ulster O, Handley; (ii) N. Sinfonia, Hickox; (iii) Hilton, Lindsay Qt; (iv) D. Jones, N. Sinfonia Ch.

The *Music for Strings* is surely the key work here, and **Hickox** directs it spontaneously and with deeply expressive feeling. **Vernon Handley** conducts with complete authority and evident enthusiasm both the *Checkmate Suite* and the less familiar *Hymn to Apollo*. In the masterly *Clarinet Quintet* (see below) **Janet Hilton** and the **Lindsays** are totally persuasive, and the recording is most naturally balanced. The *Pastoral, Lie strewn the white flocks*, is another of the composer's most memorable works and is brought vividly to life by the passionate singing of the **Northern Sinfonia Chorus**. **Della Jones** sings the *Pigeon song* touchingly, and the recording is in the demonstration bracket. On the whole, this is to be preferred to the Hyperion version (see above).

Checkmate (ballet): 5 Dances

(M) *** Chan. 6576. West Australian SO, Schönzeler – RUBBRA: *Symphony 5* ***; TIPPETT: *Little Music* **(*)

The five dances from *Checkmate* on the Chandos issue are well played under **Hans-Hubert Schönzeler** and, with its valuable Rubbra coupling, this is welcome back in the catalogue at mid-price.

(i) Cello Concerto. A Colour Symphony; (ii) The Enchantress (scena for contralto and orchestra)

(M) *** Chan. 10221X. (i) Wallfisch; (ii) Finnie; Ulster O, Handley

Raphael Wallfisch is a powerful soloist in the *Cello Concerto*. This is a reading which brings out the red-blooded warmth of the writing, with the soloist strongly supported by the **Ulster Orchestra** under **Handley**. They are equally persuasive accompanying **Linda Finnie** in the extended scena which Bliss wrote for Kathleen Ferrier nearly 20 years earlier. For this reissue Chandos have added Vernon Handley's authoritative and enthusiastic account of the *Colour Symphony* and the recording is warm and atmospheric throughout.

Piano Concerto

☛ 🏵 (***) British Music Society mono BMS 101 CDH. Mewton-Wood, Utrecht SO, Goehr – STRAVINSKY: *Concerto for Piano & Wind* (***); SHOSTAKOVICH: *Piano Concerto 1* (***)

Bliss was so impressed with **Noel Mewton-Wood's** playing of his *Concerto* that he wrote a sonata especially for him. The *Concerto* was recorded in 1952, and it is a truly prodigious performance, full of flair and with a vein of easy lyricism that invests the slow movement with magical, poetic feeling. The concert hall recording of the orchestra is two-dimensional and lacks body, but the piano is well caught, and one adjusts when Brian Crimp's remastering is clear and clean and the playing so thrillingly compulsive.

(i) Violin Concerto. A Colour Symphony

☛ *** Chan. 10380. BBC Nat. O of Wales, Hickox, (i) with Mordkovich

The music that makes the greater impact here is the *Violin Concerto*, thanks above all to the inspired interpretation of **Lydia Mordkovich**, very much at home in rare British works. Rightly, she treats the piece as a concerto in the great romantic tradition, not only powerful in the bravura passages, but tenderly affecting in the moments of pure lyricism, which are made deeply reflective. This version of the *Colour Symphony* readily matches and even outshines the earlier one on Chandos, bringing out the structural strength.

Discourse for Orchestra; Miracle in the Gorbals (complete ballet); Things to Come (complete film score, reconstructed Christopher Palmer)

(BB) **(*) Naxos 8.553698. Queensland SO, Lyndon-Gee

The Naxos issue is most valuable for offering the complete ballet-score of *Miracle in the Gorbals*, colourful and vigorous in illustrating the sordid but moving tale of murder and salvation in the slums of Glasgow. The five movements from *Things to Come* are also welcome in Christopher Palmer's reconstruction of the original opulent scoring, though it is astonishing to find the famous *March* omitted. Good, warm sound.

Film music

☛ 🏵 *** Chan. 9896. BBC PO, Gamba

It seems extraordinary that Bliss's great pioneering filmscore for *Things to Come*, some 45 minutes of music, became lost in its original form. Now, thanks to Philip Lane, we can at last hear this inspired, wonderfully orchestrated score as Bliss conceived it, with the closing *Epilogue* so full of Elgarian *nobilmente* spirit. *Caesar and Cleopatra* exists in a faded working manuscript, and again shows him in inspirational form. *War in the Air*, with its Waltonesque opening fanfare, was a splendid title and closing-credits piece of considerable panache.

The *Royal Palaces Suite* displays plenty of regality and also shows the composer at his most diverting and tuneful in the charming Waltz for *The Ballroom in Buckingham Palace* and altogether this splendid CD confirms Bliss as a composer of resource, who could write good tunes to order – at least in the early part of his career.

(i) Miracle in the Gorbals: Suite; Music for strings; (ii) Ceremonial Prelude; (i; iii) Welcome the Queen; A Song of Welcome

(M)(***) EMI mono 3 70564-2. Composer, with (i) Philh.; (ii) Simon Preston, New Philh. O; (iii) Joan Sutherland, John Cameron, BBC Ch.

All but the *Ceremonial Prelude* were recorded in 1954 and in mono. **Bliss** gets a responsive account of the *Music for Strings* from the **Philharmonia Orchestra**. *A Song of Welcome*, settings of Cecil Day Lewis for soprano, baritone, chorus and orchestra, was **Joan Sutherland's** very first recording, but for some reason the work was not issued at the time. It is a most useful addition to the Bliss discography and readers should snap it up.

CHAMBER MUSIC

Conversations; Madam Noy; (i–ii) Rhapsody; (ii) Rout. The Women of Yueh; Oboe Quintet

*** Hyp. CDA 66137. Nash Ens., with (i) Rolfe Johnson; (ii) Gale

The predominant influence in *Rout*, for soprano and chamber orchestra, and in the *Rhapsody*, with its two wordless vocal parts, is Ravel. The *Oboe Quintet* is a work of considerable quality. The music assembled here represents Bliss at his very best. A lovely disc which can be warmly recommended, and eminently well engineered, too.

Clarinet Quintet

*** Redcliffe RR 010. Cox, Redcliffe Ens. – RAWSTHORNE: *Clarinet Quartet*; ROUTH: *Clarinet Quintet* ***

(i) Clarinet Quintet. String Quartet 2

☛ (BB) **** Naxos 8.557394. Maggini Qt, (i) with Campbell

The *Clarinet Quintet* of 1932 is arguably Bliss's masterpiece, and **David Campbell** and the **Maggini Quartet** give an authoritative and searching account. Bliss dedicated his *Second Quartet* of 1950 to the Grillers, and in terms of intensity and imagination the Maggini come pretty close to them. These are totally dedicated performances, concentrated in feeling and expertly finished, which should do much to restore these pieces to their rightful place in the repertoire.

The *Quintet* is also played very beautifully by **Nicholas Cox** and members of the **Redcliffe Ensemble**, who readily catch the flowing lyricism of the opening movement and the intense valedictory feeling of the *Adagietto*, in which the composer remembers his younger brother, Kennard, killed at the Somme in 1916. The recording too, in the glowing acoustic of St George's, Brandon Hill, Bristol, is quite ideal. Moreoever the Rawsthorne coupling may be perceived by some collectors as being more appropriate than the Bliss *Quartet*.

(i; ii) *Oboe Quintet*; (ii; iii) *Piano Quartet*; (iv) *Viola Sonata*

🔑 (BB) *** Naxos 8.555931. (i) Daniel; (ii) Maggini Qt; (iii) Donohoe; (iv) Outram, Rolton

Bliss's *Piano Quartet* is brim full of attractive melody and, in the hands of **Peter Donohoe** and the **Maggini Quartet**, is quite captivating. The later (1927) *Oboe Quintet* is mainly pastoral in feeling, but with a vigorous *Vivace* finale which quotes from *Connell's Jig*. **Nicholas Daniel** is a nimble, elegant soloist and catches the work's light-hearted mood to perfection. Bliss's *Sonata* is highly demanding for both participants, both in the rhapsodic expressive lyricism of the *Andante* and in the *Furiant* Scherzo. **Martin Outram**, with **Julian Rolton** a fine partner, rises to the occasion in a highly persuasive account of another work that deserves a more frequent hearing. Excellent recording throughout, and good documentation.

String Quartets 1 in B flat; 2 in F min.

(M) (***) Dutton mono CDBP 9780. Griller Qt

The *First Quartet*, written in 1941 at the height of the war, first appeared on four Decca 78-r.p.m. discs two years later, and its successor of 1950 was among the earliest LP issues. Both are played with masterly eloquence by the **Grillers**, and their return to the catalogue in Dutton's excellent transfers is a cause for celebration.

Piano Sonata; Pieces: *Bliss (One-Step)*; *Miniature Scherzo*; *Rout Trot*; *Study*; *Suite*; *Triptych*. arr. of BACH: *Das alte Jahr vergangen ist* ('The old year has ended')

*** Chan. 8979. Fowke

The biggest work on the Chandos disc is the *Sonata*. Its neo-romantic rhetoric is less convincing than some of the earlier pieces Bliss composed, in particular the *Suite* (1925). There are some other lighter pieces, like the *The Rout Trot* and *Bliss (One-Step)*, written in the 1920s when his inspiration was at its freshest. Good performances and excellent recording, made in The Maltings, Snape.

VOCAL MUSIC

Song-cycles and other songs

*** Hyp. CDA 67188/9. McGreevy, Spence, Herford, Sturrock, Nash Ens., Brabbins

The collection spans the full extent of Bliss's composing career, from a boyhood song like the Housman setting, *'Tis time, I think, by Wenlock town*, through to two of his last works, *A Knot of Riddles* (for baritone and 11 instruments) and *Angels of the Mind*, another song-cycle for soprano and piano setting poems by Kathleen Raine, a work he wrote not on commission but simply for his own enjoyment. **Geraldine McGreevy** is the outstanding soloist in that and the other soprano items, and the others also respond sensitively to Bliss's distinctive word-setting, often helped by sharply rhythmic accompaniments. It is striking how often Bliss liked to have more than a piano in accompaniment, not just in *A Knot of Riddles* but in such an isolated song as his *Elegiac sonnet* for tenor, string quartet and piano to words by Cecil Day Lewis, written for the memorial concert commemorating the pianist, Noel Mewton-Wood. **Kathleen Sturrock** is the excellent pianist in most of the songs, with members of the **Nash Ensemble** ever stylish in the rest. First-rate recording.

Lie strewn the white flocks

*** Hyp. CDA 66175. Minty, Pierce, Holst Singers & O, Davan Wetton – BRITTEN: *Gloriana: Choral Dances*; HOLST: *Choral Hymns from Rig Veda* ***

Bliss's *Pastoral* is given a winning performance by the **Holst Singers and Orchestra**, with the choral sections (the greater part of the work) aptly modest in scale but powerful in impact. With glowing sound and very attractive works for coupling, this is an outstanding issue.

BLOCH, Ernest (1880–1959)

Baal Shem

🔑 (M) *** Decca 475 7710. Bell, Baltimore SO, Zinman – BARBER; WALTON: *Violin Concertos* ***

Bloch's own (1939) orchestrations of his three popular Hasidic pieces for violin and piano, *Baal Shem*, offers a fine, unusual makeweight for **Bell's** prize-winning disc of the Barber and Walton concertos; it won the 1998 *Gramophone* Concerto Award and now re-appears at mid-price in Universal's *Gramophone* Award Collection.

Baal Shem: Suite; *Suite hébraïque*; *Suites 1 & 2*

🔑 *** Hyp. CDA 67571. Shaham, Erez (with Pal BEN-HAÏM: *Sonata for solo violin; Improvisation and Dance, Berceuse sfaradite* ***)

A follow-up to the highly successful Shaham–Erez set of the two *Sonatas*. Like its companion, this disc offers superbly shaped and highly musical playing in vivid and lifelike sound.

(i) *Concertino for Flute and Viola*; (ii) *4 Episodes (Humoresque macabre; Obsession; Calm; Chinese)*; (iii) *Suite Modale for Flute and Strings*; (iv) *Two Poems (Hiver; Printemps)*

🔑 (BB) *** Naxos 8.570259. (i; iii) Buchman; (i) Gandelsman; (i; iii) Atlas Camerata O; (ii) Soloists of Israel PO; (iv) Slovak R. O; all cond. Atlas

A fascinating and highly rewarding collection, involving two soloists, two orchestras and, in the case of the *Four Episodes*, scored (in 1926) for a combination of string quintet, wind quintet and piano. The *Two Poems* are earlier (1905) and are appropriately titled in French, for there is an atmospheric warmth and transparency to the scoring which has influences from both Debussy and Ravel. But perhaps the highlights are the two late concertante works; the charming three-movement *Concertino for violin and viola* (1948) ends with a fugue which then gives birth to a lively polka. The

Suite Modale, with a serene ancient-and-modern flavour, was written in 1956, three years before the composer's death – an engagingly nostalgic reverie, interrupted by a bright central Gigue. The performances here are excellent, all very persuasively directed by **Dalia Atlas**; they are splendidly played and given top-quality Naxos sound. A disc not to be missed.

Violin Concerto in A min.

� **BB** (***) Naxos mono 8.110973. Szigeti, Paris Conservatoire O, Munch – BARTÓK: *Portrait*; PROKOFIEV: *Violin Concerto 1* (***)�

Szigeti's pioneering record of the Bloch *Concerto* has long been a classic of the gramophone. A wonderfully serene yet intense performance from both Szigeti and **Munch** that penetrates to the core of Bloch's masterpiece. Szigeti's nervous vibrato is heard to perfect effect here.

Violin Concerto; Baal Shem; Suite Hébraïque

BB *** Naxos 8.557757. Z. Schiff, RSNO, Serebrier

The American violinist **Zina Schiff** is a protégé of Heifetz and is very much inside the Bloch idiom, both in the *Concerto* and in the shorter pieces on this disc. Recommended; but it is amazing that after all these years Szigeti's eloquent performance still resonates in the memory.

Schelomo (Hebraic Rhapsody) for cello & orchestra

🎕 *** Virgin 5 45664-2. Truls Mørk, Fr. R. PO, Paavo Järvi – BRUCH: *Kol Nidrei*; SCHUMANN: *Cello Concerto* ***

🎕 **BB** *** Virgin 2x1 5 61490-2. Isserlis, LSO, Hickox – ELGAR: *Cello Concerto*; KABALEVSKY: *Cello Concerto 2*; R. STRAUSS: *Don Quixote*; TCHAIKOVSKY: *Andante cantabile*, etc. ***

Ⓜ *** DG 457 761-2. Fournier, BPO, Wallenstein – BRUCH: *Kol Nidrei*; LALO: *Cello Concerto*; SAINT-SAËNS: *Cello Concerto 1* ***

Truls Mørk gives a superb account of Bloch's *Schelomo*, concentrated and powerful. The solo rhapsodizings suit his freely expressive style perfectly, and **Paavo Järvi** draws from the **French Radio Philharmonic** a performance of wonderful weight and clarity. The clarity of the sound heightens the magnetic impact of the playing of both soloist and orchestra.

The dark intensity of **Isserlis's** solo playing and the sharp, dramatic focus of **Hickox** in the big, climactic orchestral tuttis are magnetic, preventing Bloch's youthful outpouring on Solomon and the Song of Songs from sounding self-indulgent. Warm, refined recording.

Fournier is a bit too closely balanced in this fervent performance, but the sound is very beautiful and he is excellently supported by the **Berlin Philharmonic** under **Wallenstein**. Apart from the balancing of the cello, the 1967 recording is excellent.

3 Nocturnes for Piano Trio

*** Simax PSC 1147. Grieg Trio – MARTIN: *Piano Trio on Irish Folktunes*; SHOSTAKOVICH: *Piano Trios* ***

The first *Nocturne* (*Andante*) finds Bloch in Hebraic-Debussy mode, while the second (*Andante quieto*) is more overtly romantic and less interesting, though the **Grieg Trio** play it with much feeling, as they do the final *Tempestuoso*. The couplings further enhance the value of this issue, arguably the best the Grieg Trio have given us.

(i) Piano Quintets 1 & 2. Night; Paysages; 2 Pièces

*** Hyp. CDA 67638. (i) Lane; Goldner Qt

The *First Quintet* is expansive and romantic, and its subsequent neglect is difficult to understand for it is a powerful and thoughtful piece with carefully fashioned ideas and imaginative invention. The *Second*, the composer's last chamber work, is concentrated with a hint of neo-classicism. The central slow movement brings a mystical air, with variations leading to a clear and direct finale with a beautiful, hushed ending. The smaller pieces, *Night* (1923) and *Paysages* ('Landscapes') and the *Deux Pièces* are all evocative in their textures and serve to make this finely paced and immaculately recorded set a most desirable issue. Strongly recommended.

String Quartets 1–4

🎕 (***) Decca mono 475 6071 (2). Griller Qt

These are clearly great performances, with any slight faults of intonation made irrelevant in the thrust of the music-making. Bloch's wonderfully rich, haunting harmonies are played by the Grillers with spine-tingling concentration, often producing sounds of otherworldly beauty, casting a powerful spell indeed. All in all, a worthy, enterprising (and unexpected) release on Decca's 'Original Masters' series, and the transfers of the relatively dry but atmospheric (1954) sound are excellent.

Violin Sonatas 1–2 (Poème mystique); Abodah; Melody; Nuit exotique

🎕 *** Hyp. CDA 67439. Hagai Shaham, Arnon Erez

Violin Sonatas 1; 2 (Poème mystique); Abodah (Yom Kippur Melody); Melody; Suite hébraïque

BB *** Naxos 8.554460. Kramer, Over

This fine Israeli duo bring appropriate fervour and mystical feeling to this repertoire, and they are vividly recorded in Hyperion's high standard. This is now a first recommendation.

In **Miriam Kramer** and **Simon Over** the sonatas also have sympathetic advocates: both artists play with exemplary taste and sensitivity, and Simon Over produces a wonderful range of colour. So, for that matter, does Kramer, who has great refinement of tone. Good recordings, with plenty of space round the aural image.

Enfantines, 5 Sketches in Sepia; In the Night; Nirvana; Piano Sonata; Visions and Prophecies

*** Chan. 9887. Fingerhut

Bloch's muse is essentially rhapsodic and improvisatory and his piano writing cries out for the colours of the orchestra, but it is difficult to imagine it better played than it is here by **Margaret Fingerhut** or more naturally recorded.

Sacred Service

Ⓜ ** Chan. 10288X. Berkman, Zemel Ch., L. Chorale & Concord Singers, LSO, Simon

Bloch's *Sacred Service* has long been neglected by the gramophone. So the reappearance of this 1978 version must be welcomed, particularly in such vivid sound. The singing is perhaps wanting in ardour and intensity, and there could be greater attention to dynamic nuances. However, it would be unfair to dwell on the shortcomings of this performance in the light of so much that is good, not least of which is the orchestral playing. The recording is spacious and well focused.

BLOW, John (1649–1708)

Anthems

🎧– Ⓜ *** Hyp. Dyad CDD 22055 (2). Winchester Cathedral Ch., Parley of Instruments, Hill

Blow's anthems are of diverse kinds. The opening *God spake sometimes in visions* is a glorious example of the grandest style of all; it was written for the Coronation of James II in 1685. Then there is the 'full and contrapuntal' anthem, of which *God is our help and strength* is a sonorous illustration. Many listeners will also be delighted to encounter a new and memorable setting of *The Lord is my Shepherd*, in which the layout is in sections, with limited polyphony and a warmly lyrical style. Other anthems are less ambitious, yet musically poignant. *O Lord I have sinned* (written for a funeral) is particularly beautiful, using a solo group intimately, with organ accompaniment. *Lord, who shall dwell in thy tabernacle?* has three obbligato recorders and combines soloists with a full chorus, like a vocal concerto grosso. The soloists from the choir sing most pleasingly individually, and (of course) beautifully together; the full choir is stirring, and the accompaniments are warm and refined. Altogether a remarkable valuable anthology. Full texts are included.

(i) Ode on the Death of Mr Henry Purcell. Fugue in G min.; Grounds: in C min.; in D min.; Sonata in A; Suite in G

**(*) Virgin 5 45342-2. (i) Lesne, Dugardin; La Canzona – PURCELL: *Songs & Duets* **(*)

Ode on the Death of Mr Henry Purcell: Mark how the lark and linnet sing. Ah, heav'n! What is't I hear?

*** Hyp. CDA 66253. Bowman, Chance, King's Consort, King – PURCELL: *Collection* ***

The *Ode on the Death of Mr Henry Purcell* is a most welcome addition to the catalogue. There are some striking chromaticisms and dissonances and some inventive and noble music. **Robert King's** spontaneous style is infectious, with the orchestral comments engagingly animated. Both performances are highly rewarding, and in the last resort couplings will dictate choice.

Venus and Adonis

Ⓑ *** HM HMX 2901684. Joshua, Finley, Blaze, Clare College Chapel Ch., OAE, Jacobs

(i)Venus and Adonis; (ii) Organ Voluntaries in D min.; A min.; G (2 versions)

Ⓜ *** Decca 4780019. (i) Bott, George, Crabtree, Gooding, King, Grant, Robson, Agnew, Westminster Abbey School Choristers, New L. Cons., Pickett; (ii) Leonhardt

Venus and Adonis has been well served on record, but **Pickett's** version has a pair of trump cards to play: **Catherine Bott's** imaginative, enticing Venus and **Michael George's** strongly characterized Adonis. The result is that this simple drama springs to life with unexpected vividness. The supporting cast is excellent, and so is the (1992) recording, and we are made to realize that this is a far finer and deeper work than hitherto suspected.

René Jacobs too conducts a lively performance. Speeds are on the brisk side, never rushed, and **Rosemary Joshua** makes a delightful Venus, bright and sweet, singing with ravishing tone in her big solo towards the end. **Gerald Finley**, clear and firm, makes a splendid Adonis, and it is good to have a counter-tenor, not a soprano, in the role of Cupid, the excellent **Robin Blaze**. Fresh, incisive singing from the **Clare College Chapel Choir**, and clear, atmospheric sound. A bargain.

BLUMER, Theodor (1881–1964)

WIND CHAMBER MUSIC

Kinderspielzeug (Children's Toys), Op. 64; Schweizer Quintett; (i) Piano Sextet (Chamber Symphony), Op. 92

*** Crystal CD 755. Moran Woodwind Quintet; (i) with Paul Barnes

(i) From the Animal Kingdom; From the Plant World, Op. 57a/b; 10 Waltzes (Hausmusik), Op. 56 (all for flute & piano); (ii) Serenade & Theme & Variations for Wind Quintet, Op. 34

*** Crystal CD 757. (i) John Bailey, Mark Clinton; (ii) Moran Woodwind Quintet

Theodor Blumer, director and principal conductor of the radio orchestras in Dresden and Leipzig, wrote delightfully for wind ensemble, and both these discs give much pleasure. The first CD is all but dominated by the *Schweizer Quintet*, which is charmingly melodic throughout and includes an inimitable set of variations on a Swiss folk tune, first heard on the horn. The **Moran Quintet** are excellent in every way, blending and taking solos with aplomb. **Paul Barnes** makes an agreeable, if not dominating, contribution to the *Sextet*.

The second disc opens with another *Theme and Variations* as part of a *Serenade* of much felicity. The following series of works for flute and piano are again highly inventive. The two *Suites* devoted to animals and plants also have some very attractive ideas, and the *Waltzes* too overflow with diversity. Again excellent performances.

BOCCHERINI, Luigi
(1743–1805)

COMPLETE CELLO CONCERTOS

Cello Concertos 1 in E flat, G.474; 2 in A, G.475; 3 in D, G.476; 5 in D, G.478 (⒝ℬ *** Naxos 8.553571)

Cello Concertos 4 in C, G.477; 6 in D, G.479; 7 in G, G.480; 8 in C, G.481 (⒝ℬ *** Naxos 8.553572. Hugh, SCO, Halstead)

Cello Concertos 9 in B flat, G.482; 10 in D, G.483; 11 in C; 12 in E flat (⒝ℬ *** Naxos 8.557589. Wallfisch, N. CO, Ward)

Cello Concertos 4 in C, G.477; 6 in D, G.479; 7 in G, G.480; 8 in C, G.481 (🔗 ⒝ℬ *** Warner Apex (ADD) 0927 49805-2. Bylsma, Concerto Amsterdam, Schröder)

Cello Concertos 7 in G (G.480); 10 in D (G.483); Sinfonias: in D min. (La casa del diavolo), Op. 12/4; in B flat, Op. 21/5 (G. 497) (❀ Ⓜ *** DHM 82876 60150-2. Bylsma, Tafelmusik, Lamon)

Naxos has an impressive new series covering Boccherini's twelve cello concertos. They are beautifully performed on modern instruments but with concern for period practice, and superbly recorded. There is dedicated playing not just from the soloist but also from the excellent **Scottish Chamber Orchestra** under **Anthony Halstead**. **Tim Hugh** offers substantial cadenzas not only in the first movements of each work but also in slow movements and finales too. Throughout, Hugh and Halstead make a stimulating partnership and all these works spring appealingly to life. Naxos then turned to **Raphael Wallfisch** and the **Northern Chamber Orchestra** under **Nicholas Ward**, with predictably stimulating results. Indeed, this is one of the finest single discs of Boccherini cello concertos in the catalogue.

Anner Bylsma on Apex is a fine player, well suited to this repertoire, while **Schröder's** accompaniments are most stylish and full of vitality. The 1965 recording is first class and the immaculate CD transfer makes the very most of the sound. Bylsma (a superb cellist) was at his peak in the *G major Concerto*. He is lucky to have **Jeanne Lamon's Tafelmusik** as his accompanying group, one of the most elegant and polished of all period-instrument ensembles. They come into their own in the pair of symphonies, playing with a Mozartian grace and zest. The recording is absolutely first class.

(i) Cello Concerto 9 in B flat (original version, revised Gendron); (ii–iii) Flute Concerto in D, Op.

27 (attrib.; now thought to be by Franz Pokorny); (iv) *Symphonies 3 in C; 5 in B flat, Op. 12/3 & 5;* (v) *Guitar Quintets 4 in D (Fandango); 9 in C (La Ritirata di Madrid);* (vi) *String Quartet in D, Op. 6/1;* (iii) *String Quintet in E, Op. 13/5: Minuet* (only)

🔗 Ⓑ *** Ph. Duo 438 377-2 (2). (i) Gendron, LOP, Casals; (ii) Gazzelloni; (iii) I Musici; (iv) New Philh. O, Leppard; (v) Pepe Romero, ASMF Chamber Ens.; (vi) Italian Qt

This most attractive anthology is well documented, and the famous *Minuet* could hardly be presented more winningly, the one digital recording here. It is also good that **Gendron's** version of the *Cello Concerto* is included, for he pioneered the return of the original version (without Grützmacher's reworking), and he plays it admirably. The *Flute Concerto* is a *galant* piece, elegantly played by **Gazzelloni**, and one can see why it was mistakenly attributed. Both *Symphonies* are full of vitality in these excellent performances under **Raymond Leppard** and are very well recorded. The **Italian Quartet's** performance of the *D major Quartet* is notable for its freshness and refinement. The charming *Guitar Quintets* are unfailingly warm and sensitive, and they are well recorded too, although there is a touch of thinness on top.

Cello Concerto in B flat (arr. Grützmacher)

Ⓜ *** EMI (ADD) 5 66896-2. du Pré, ECO, Barenboim – HAYDN: *Concertos 1–2* ***

Working for the first time in the recording studio with her husband, **Daniel Barenboim**, **Jacqueline du Pré** was inspired to some really heart-warming playing, broadly romantic in style – but then that is what Grützmacher plainly asks for, and the disc now offers two Haydn cello concertos instead of one.

28 Symphonies (complete)

Ⓜ *** CPO 999 401 (8). Deutsche Kammerakademie, Neuss, Goritzki

In this first complete survey of the Boccherini symphonies, **Johannes Goritzki's** achievement is remarkable. Himself a cellist, he shows a natural feeling for Boccherini's special combination of *galant* and classical styles, revealing the music's strengths rather than its weaknesses. The playing – on modern instruments – of the **German Chamber Academy Orchestra of Neuss** is alert, polished and warm-hearted, besides showing a nice feeling for Boccherini's delicate *Andantinos*, which are never sentimentalized. The recording is excellently balanced and has plenty of life and bloom.

Symphonies: in A, Op. 15/6, G.508; in E flat, Op. 35/5, G.513; in C min., Op. 41, G.519; in D, Op. 42, G.520

Ⓑ **(*) HM Musique d'abord HMA 1951597. Berlin Akademie für Alte Musik

Four characteristic Boccherini *Symphonies*, given bold and energetic performances by the **Berlin Akademie**. In the A major work of 1771 Boccherini writes engagingly for the flutes, but the high horns here dominate the *fortissimos*. The *C minor* has a winning *Pastorale* slow movement, sympathetically presented here, but the *D major* is the finest of the four with a memorable Minuet (with violin obbligato) and a charming, Laendler-like trio, followed by a vigorous finale full of contrasts. The playing throughout lacks neither polish nor strength, but tuttis are gruff, with powerful accents, and at times one wishes the orchestra could relax more and convey a greater sense of elegance.

Symphonies: in D; in E flat; in A; in F; in E flat; in B flat, Op. 35/1–6

**(*) Hyp. CDA 66903. L. Festival O, Pople

Symphonies: in C; in D min.; in A, Op. 37/1, 3 & 4, G.515, 517–18; in D, Op. 42, G.520

**(*) Hyp. CDA 66904. L. Festival O, Pople

Ross Pople's directing lively, characterful and polished performances with his excellent chamber orchestra. As can be seen above, these are attractive and mature works. The Hyperion sound is pleasingly fresh and open, and this is a most enjoyable pair of discs.

Symphonies: in A, Op. 35/3, G.511; in D min. (Grande), Op. 37/3, G.517; Guitar Quintet 4 in D (Fandango), G.448; String Quintet 9 in C (La Musica Notturna delle Strada di Madrid), Op. 30/6, G.324

🎵 *** Alia Vox **SACD** AVSA 9815. Lislevand, Concert des Nations (members), Savall

Anyone wanting a single Boccherini disc as a sampler, in authentic, period-instrument costume, could hardly do better than this. The performances are exceptionally vivid. **Rolf Lislevand** is an excellent guitarist, and José de Udaeta's castanets glitter appropriately in the famous *Fandango*, while in the *C major Quintet* the patrol sequence is admirably managed. The outer movements of the two symphonies are played with abrasive period-instrument vigour and gusto, but the inner movements are engagingly refined, while the SACD recording has both depth and striking presence.

CHAMBER MUSIC

Cello Quintet, Op. 37/7

*** Australian Decca Eloquence (ADD) 421 637-2. ASMF –
  MENDELSSOHN: *Octet* ***

The *Quintet* is an inspired piece and makes this disc worth getting for its own sake, though the coupled performance of Mendelssohn's *Octet* is a particularly fine one. The 1968 recording remains rich and full, and this Australian Eloquence CD has full sleeve-notes.

Cello Sonatas: in C min., G.2 (first version); in A, G.4 (first version); in G, G.5; in C, G.17; in F min.

🎵 (BB) *** Naxos 8.554324. C. & S. Benda

Boccherini could hardly be boring if he tried, and these cello sonatas (of which he wrote thirty-four!) are full of attractive invention. They could hardly be more persuasively played.

The *A major Sonata* which opens the disc is particularly enticing, warmly melodic and with fizzing display passages which **Christian Benda** handles with easy virtuosity against the simple fortepiano backing. The finale is marked *Affetuoso*, which sums up this team's approach throughout. The *F minor Sonata* was discovered as recently as 1987 and has a lovely *Cantabile siciliano* for its slow movement which is quite haunting in the hands of these players. In short this is a first-class disc, very naturally recorded.

6 Flute Quartets, Op. 19

*** Hyp. CDA 67646. Ipata, Auser Music

Boccherini described his *Flute Quintets* as 'quintetti piccolo'. The sixth work is programmatic and is subtitled *Las Parejas* ('The Couples'), referring to a Spanish horse race in which two horsemen ride side by side. Here a vigorous central gallop is framed by an *Entrada* and a more sober *Marcia*. The other five quintets have an engaging diversity of style and often bring that element of gentle melancholy which so often lies beneath the surface of the composer's music. The flautist **Carlo Ipata** is sensitively expressive and sparkling by turns, and **Auser Music** provide an engaging period-instrument partnership. The recording is well up to Hyperion's standard.

Flute Quintets (for flute, violin, viola, 2 cellos), Op. 17/1–6, G.419–24)

(BB) *** Naxos 8.553719. Magnin, Janáček Qt

The Op. 17 *Quintets* are comparatively familiar and certainly rewarding, and they are very well played and recorded here. This Naxos disc is excellent value.

Flute Quintets, Op. 55/1–6, G.431–6 (for flute & string quartet)

(M) *** CPO 999 382-2. Faust, Auryn Qt

These six *Flute* (or oboe) *Quintets* are late works, dating from 1797, and show the composer at his most felicitous and charming. No. 6 is the only work in the minor key and it ends delicately. **Michael Faust** is a first-rate flautist and his performances here are vivacious and elegant, and recorded with a vivid presence.

Guitar Quintets 1–7, G.445–51; 9 (La ritirata di Madrid), G.453

🎵 (B) *** Ph. Duo (ADD) 438 769-2 (2). P. Romero, ASMF Chamber Ens. (members)

Boccherini wrote or arranged 12 guitar quintets, but only the present eight have survived, plus another version of *4 in D (Fandango)*, G.448. Although some of the music is bland, it is nearly all agreeably tuneful in an unostentatious way, and there are some highly imaginative touches, with attractive hints of melancholy and underlying passion. These performances by **Pepe Romero** (often willing to take a relatively minor role) and members of the **ASMF Chamber Ensemble** are wholly admirable, and Philips are especially good at balancing textures of this kind in the most natural way, the guitar able to be assertive when required without overbalancing the ensemble.

Guitar Quintets 4 in D (Fandango), G.448; 5 in D, G.449; 6 in G, G.450

(BB) *** HM HCX 3957026. Savino, Artaria Qt

It is good to have performances on period instruments which create such a natural balance between the strings and the guitar. Although textures are less ample, they can also be attractively delicate, and there is no lack of warmth in the lovely *Pastorale* which forms the second movement of the most famous work (4), with its *Fandango* finale. Here there is a spirited contribution from **Peter Mund** with his castanets. Performances are stylishly intimate with recording to match. Most recommendable.

Guitar Quintets Nos. (i) 4 in D (Fandango), G.448; 9 in C (La ritirata di Madrid), G.453. String Quartet in G min., Op. 24/6 (G.194)

**(*) Virgin 5 45607-2. (i) Pinardi, Europa Galante, Biondi

The Virgin coupling of the *Fandango* and *Riterata di Madrid* Quintets is the most dramatic on record, with **Mauro Occhinieri's** castanets as spectacular in the one as the histrionic *crescendo* and *decrescendo* in the other, with the music finally fading away completely into the distance. The playing itself is immensely vigorous, with the cello line at times guttural in its intensity. The snag is the lack of charm (an important feature in Boccherini's music), entirely absent in the *Adagio* of the *G minor String Quartet*. The recording is vividly projected and it is easy to respond to the visceral power of this playing, but this is not the whole story.

Piano Quintets, Op. 56/1–2 & 5, G.407–8 & G.411; Op. 57/2–3 & 6, G.414–15 & G.418

(M) *** Astrée E3001 (2). Cohen, Mosaïques Qt

There are 12 piano quintets, and **Patrick Cohen** and the **Mosaïques Quartet** are obviously embarking – so far with great success – on a complete set. There is drama and grace and warmth of feeling, balanced by elegance, in this music; and the playing here also emphasizes its vitality. Slow movements are particularly eloquent, and the use of period instruments in no way inhibits the expressive range of the music.

String Quartets, Op. 32/1–6

(B) *** Warner Elatus (ADD) 2564 60028-2 (2). Esterházy Qt

String Quartets, Op. 32/1–2; String Quartet in A, Op. 39

(BB) *** Naxos 8.555042. Borciani Qt

String Quartets, Op. 32/3–6

(BB) *** Naxos 8.555043. Borciani Qt

The **Esterházy Quartet** set dates from 1780, about the same period as Haydn's Op. 33. They may ultimately lack the depth and vision of Haydn and Mozart, but to listen to this pioneering Elatus recording is to be amazed that music of this quality has been so long neglected. The Esterházy Quartet are led by **Jaap Schröder** and theirs is thoroughly rewarding music-making. The Quartet was beautifully

recorded in Haarlem, Holland, in 1976 and the new CD transfer of these two *Das alte Werk* discs is outstandingly natural.

The **Quartetto Borciani** offer an equally accomplished alternative on modern instruments, which have plenty of character and vitality and are always sensitive to Boccherini's gentle touches of expressive melancholy. They include Boccherini's later *A major Quartet*, Op. 39 (1787), which has a particularly touching *Grave* third movement, most affectingly played here. The Naxos recording is vivid and truthful and there are excellent notes.

String Quartets: in C; in G min.; in A, Op. 32/4–6

(BB) *** CPO 999 202-2. Nomos Qt

These are three most attractive works, of Boccherini's best quality. All three slow movements are expressively potent; the *Andantino lentarello* of the *A major* is particularly searching, and the following Minuet is hardly less striking. The **Nomos** is a first-class group, using modern instruments but in such a way as to provide textures which are fully blended and sweet while avoiding 19th-century opulence. The recording is excellent.

String Quintets: in A, Op. 10/1; in D min., Op. 18/5; in A (Della disgrazia), Op. 28/2; in A, Op. 29/4; in A, Op. 40/4; in F, Op. 41/2 (Testament mono SBT 1245)

String Quintets: in F, Op. 11/3; in C min. (Di Nina), Op. 18/1; in D min., Op. 25/1; in C min., Op. 29/2 (Testament mono SBT 1244)

String Quintets: in E, Op. 11/5; in D (L'Uccelliera), Op. 11/6; in G, Op. 25/3; in E flat, Op 31/1: Grave in D (Fandango), Op. 40/2 (Testament mono SBT 1243)

(***) Quintetto Boccherini

These mono recordings were all made in the mid-1950s by one of the finest ensembles of the day; they produce a finely balanced sound of great refinement and tonal beauty. This is most civilized music-making and much to be cherished. Very little allowance need be made for the 1950s recording, and the transfers are eminently truthful and present.

String Quintets Op. 11/5; Op. 25/1, 4 & 6

(B) *** Virgin 5 03408-2. Europa Galante

Boccherini's quintets are an unfailing delight and their sunny, gentle aspect at times masks a touching melancholy. **Europa Galante** play with great sympathy and style and round things off with the famous minuet. A most attractive issue.

String Quintets: in E, Op. 13/5, G.275; in G min., Op. 37/13, G.348; in F min., Op. 37/19, G.351

*** Hyp. CDA 67287 Vanbrugh. Qt, with Lester

It is particularly refreshing in the **Vanbrugh** performance to hear Boccherini's famous *Minuet* in context with the work's other three movements; their approach pays obvious tribute to period practice in the choice of tempo, far faster than one usually associates with this well-known 'lollipop', light and crisp. Both the other quintets here regularly rely on the characteristic Boccherini device of quickly switching between major and minor keys. Vividly recorded and with fine performances, both polished and refreshing, with **Richard Lester** a perfect partner for the prize-winning Vanbrugh Quartet, this is an outstanding disc in every way.

String Quintets: in C, Op. 28/4, (G.310); in C, Op. 42/2 (G.349); (Quintettino) in B min., Op. 42/3 (G.350); in D, Op. 43/2 (G.353)

*** Hyp. CDA 67383. Vanbrugh Qt, with Lester

Throughout the four works Boccherini's invention never fails him, and these excellent players relish all the felicities of his writing. Excellent recording.

String Quintets, Op. 39/1–3, G.337–9; String Quartet, Op. 64/2, G.249

*** MDG 603 1040-2. Frankfurt Ens. Concertante

The three *Quintets* of Op. 39, dating from 1787, are scored for a double bass in the place of second cello, which adds considerably to the body of the sound. The *String Quartet*, Op. 64/2, of 1804 was Boccherini's last composition, and he completed the first movement only. First-class performances throughout, polished and committed, and fine recording make this collection very recommendable.

VOCAL MUSIC

(i) Stabat Mater, G.532 (First Version); Concert Arias: Ah, no! son io che parlo; Care luci. Symphonies: in D min. (La Casa del Diavolo), Op. 12/4 (G.506); in C, Op. 23/3 (G.523); in A, Op. 37/4 (G.518)

🎵 (BB) *** Warner Apex 2564 61689-2 (2). (i) Gasdia; Sol. Ven., Scimone

Boccherini wrote comparatively little vocal music but his *Stabat Mater*, in its original version an extended solo setting for soprano, here gloriously sung by **Cecilia Gasdia**, must be counted among his most inspired works. The beautiful sequence of movements towards the close – *Eja mater fons amoris . . . Tui nati vulnerati . . . Virgo virginum praeclara*, sung most affectingly here – contains some exquisite music, and in the despairing closing *Quando corpus moretur*, Gasdia is very moving indeed. The music has a Mozartian purity of line, and the two concert arias which follow also take Mozart as their model. They are brilliantly sung: **Claudio Scimone** provides highly sensitive support. Then on the second disc (with his **I Solisti Veneti**) offers vital and expressive accounts of three *Symphonies*, including not only *La Casa del Diavolo*, but a most appealing concertante work in C major. This was the composer's last symphony to be published (in 1798) and has prominent obbligato parts for oboe, violin and guitar, which are most sympathetically played here.

Stabat Mater (revised 1800 version)

🎵 *** Hyp. CDA 67108. Gritton, Fox, Bickley, Agnew, Harvey, King's Consort, King – D'ASTORGA: *Stabat Mater* ***

Boccherini's ambitious revision is masterly in increasing the range and expressive power of the work. With first-class soloists, **Robert King's** performance is as moving as it is gripping in the more dramatic moments. Notable are the lovely soprano duets, so beautifully sung by **Susan Gritton** and **Sarah Fox**, contrasting with the dramatic trios with tenor, and the closing *Quando corpus morietur* (another trio) is exquisitely managed. The apt coupling, a fine setting of the same text, written nearly a century earlier by an almost unknown Spanish composer, increases the value of this disc.

BOÏELDIEU, François
(1775–1834)

Harp Concerto in 3 Tempi in C

🎵 ❀ (M) **** Decca 425 723-2. Robles, ASMF, Brown – DITTERSDORF; HANDEL: *Harp Concertos, etc.* **** ❀

Boïeldieu's *Harp Concerto* has been recorded before but never more attractively. The (originally Argo) recording is still in the demonstration class and very sweet on the ear. To make the reissue even more attractive, three beguiling sets of *Variations* have been added, including music by Handel and Beethoven and a *Theme, Variations and Rondo Pastorale* attributed to Mozart.

BOITO, Arrigo (1842–1918)

Mefistofele (complete)

(M) *** Decca 475 6666 (2). Ghiaurov, Pavarotti, Freni, Caballé, L. Op. Ch., Trinity Boys' Ch., Nat. PO, Fabritiis

Boito's *Mefistofele* is a strange and episodic work to come from the hands of the master-librettist of Verdi's *Otello* and *Falstaff*, but it has many fine moments. The early digital recording gives the brass and percussion plenty of weight – most importantly in the heavenly prologue. With the principal soloists all at their best – **Pavarotti** most seductive in *Dai campi, dai pratti*, **Freni** finely imaginative on detail, **Caballé** consistently sweet and mellifluous as Elena, **Ghiaurov** strongly characterful, if showing some signs of strain – this is a most recommendable set, though **Fabritiis** in his last recording lacks a little in energy, and the chorus is placed rather distantly. Texts and translation are included in its Classic Opera release.

BORODIN, Alexander (1833–87)

'The World of Borodin': (i) In the Steppes of Central Asia; Prince Igor: (ii) Overture; (ii–iii) Polovtsian Dances; (iv) Symphony 2 in B min.; (v) String

Quartet 2: Nocturne; (vi) Scherzo in A flat; (vii–viii) Far from the shores of your native land; (vii, ix) Prince Igor: Galitzky's Aria

⊕ Ⓜ ******** Decca (ADD) 444 389-2. (i) SRO, Ansermet; (ii) LSO, Solti; (iii) with L. Symphony Ch.; (iv) LSO, Martinon; (v) Borodin Qt; (vi) Ashkenazy; (vii) N. Ghiaurov; (viii) Z. Ghiaurov; (ix) L. Symphony Ch., LSO, Downes

'Essential Borodin': Symphonies. (i) 1 in E flat; (ii) 2 in B min.; (iii) 3 in A min.; In the Steppes of Central Asia; (iv) String Quartet 2 in B min.; (v–vi) Song: Far from the shores of your native land. Prince Igor: (vii) Overture; (vii–viii) Polovtsian Dances; (v; viii–ix) Galitzky's Aria; Konchak's Aria

Ⓑ ******* Double Decca (ADD) 455 632-2 (2). (i) RPO, Ashkenazy; (ii) LSO, Martinon; (iii) SRO, Ansermet; (iv) Borodin Qt; (v) N. Ghiaurov; (vi) Z. Ghiaurov; (vii) LSO, Solti; (viii) L. Symphony Ch.; (ix) LSO, Downes

The 'World of Borodin' is an extraordinarily successful disc. There can be few if any other collections of this kind that sum up a composer's achievement so succinctly or that make such a rewarding and enjoyable 76-minute concert. **Solti's** *Prince Igor Overture* is outstanding. The *Nocturne* follows the *Overture* so effectively that one might have thought it the composer's own plan. **Ansermet's** *In the Steppes of Central Asia* is warm and atmospheric. After **Nicolai Ghiaurov** has reminded us of the melancholy side of the Russian spirit, we come finally to **Martinon's** unsurpassed 1960 **LSO** performance of the *B minor Symphony*: the sound has remarkable presence and sparkle.

Decca have now happily expanded the programme to fit on to a Double, and in doing so they represent the composer even more comprehensively for very little extra outlay. **Ashkenazy's** reading of the *First Symphony* is less high-powered than Martinon's superb account of No. 2, but its many delights come over richly, thanks not only to the quality of the **RPO** playing but also to the warm (1992) digital recording. **Ansermet's** touch in the unfinished *Third* is most attractive, with some delightful moments from the **SRO** woodwind. What makes this extended programme especially attractive is the inclusion of the whole of the *Second String Quartet*, rather than just the slow movement. The performance by the eponymous **Borodin Quartet** is masterly in every respect. In *Prince Igor* **Ghiaurov** now adds a second role by singing Konchak's aria from Act II in addition to Galitzky's aria from Act I.

In the Steppes of Central Asia

⊕ ******* Ph. SACD 470 618-2; CD 470 840-2. Kirov O, Gergiev – BALAKIREV: *Islamey*; RIMSKY–KORSAKOV: *Scheherazade* *******

Borodin's evocative tone-poem in a concentrated performance provides a well-judged contrast with the main work, *Scheherazade*, in **Gergiev's** exciting reading. The recording's rich atmosphere is undoubtedly enhanced on the surround-sound SACD stereo version.

In the Steppes of Central Asia; Prince Igor: Polovtsian Dances

ⒷⒷ ****(*)** EMI Encore (ADD) 5 74763-2. Phil O, Cluytens – RIMSKY–KORSAKOV: *Capriccio espagnol*, etc.; MUSSORGSKY: *Night on the Bare Mountain* ****(*)**

From **Cluytens** comes a beautifully controlled performance of *In the Steppes of Central Asia* and a lively *Polovtsian Dances*, both enjoyable. The 1958 recording sounds astonishingly well, with only a touch of thinness betraying its age. Part of an attractive bargain CD of Russian show-pieces.

In the Steppes of Central Asia; Symphonies 2 & 3; Prince Igor: Overture & (i) Polovtsian Dances

Ⓝ Ⓑ ****(*)** Australian Decca Eloquence (ADD) 480 0048. SRO, Ansermet with (i) Lausanne Rad. Ch., Choeur des Jeunes, Lausanne

Ansermet's pioneering version of Borodin's *Second Symphony* dates from 1954 but sounds far more recent. It has many fine qualities. If others have found more blazing excitement in the fast movements, Ansermet's ear of inner detail makes plenty of amends and the way he shapes the work makes this a thoroughly satisfying performance. The rarer *Third Symphony* is nicely done too, but it is the sparkling *Scherzo* second movement which finds the conductor on his colourful best form. The *Prince Igor* items go well enough: the *Overture* is lively and well played, and although the percussion are well brought out in the *Polovtsian Dances*, the tension sags a little when the choir (not the best in the world) is carrying the composer's memorable theme. It does, however, end in a blaze of excitement – and again, the brilliant recording (1960) is a thing of wonder. This disc ends in a beautifully shaped (and recorded) reading of *In the Steppes of Central Asia*.

Symphonies 1–3

Ⓜ ****(*)** RCA 82876 62321-2. Nat. PO, Tjeknavorian

Tjeknavorian's performances, while lacking the last ounce of character, are polished and full of colour, and the orchestral response is on the whole lively. The RCA recordings are certainly vivid and well balanced with wide range and a warm ambience. However to have all three symphonies in modern recordings on a single disc is very attractive.

Symphony 1 in E flat

ⒷⒷ ****(*)** Warner Apex 0927 40597-2. Norwegian R. O, Rasilainen – TCHAIKOVSKY: *Symphony 2* *******

A very enjoyable and recommendable account of this delightful symphony from the **Norwegian Radio Orchestra** and their Finnish conductor is spirited, and is well enough played and recorded if you want the coupling. It certainly gives pleasure.

Symphony 2 in B min.

(***) Testament mono SBT 1048. Philh. O, Kletzki – TCHAIKOVSKY: *Manfred Symphony* **(***)**

Symphony 2 in B min.; In the Steppes of Central Asia; Prince Igor: Overture; Polovtsian March; Polovtsian Dances

⊕ (BB) *** Regis RRC 1215. RPO, Schmidt

Ole Schmidt with the **RPO** offers an outstanding bargain version of Borodin's *Second Symphony*, beautifully played and recorded in vivid, open sound, one of the finest at any price. In the first movement Schmidt evades the pitfall of adopting too slow a speed. At a nicely flowing tempo the great horn solo of the slow movement is gloriously played by the RPO's long-time principal, Jeffrey Bryant, his radiant playing matches and even outshines the finest of the past. The crisp finale is full of panache. The *Prince Igor Overture* again brings masterly horn-playing, while the *Polovtsian Dances* and *March* show off the brilliance of the RPO wind soloists.

Kletzki draws superb playing from the **Philharmonia** at a vintage period in the mid-1950s. The ravishing account of the slow movement has Dennis Brain at his peak in the big horn solo, backed by Bernard Walton on the clarinet and Sidney Sutcliffe on the oboe producing whispered pianissimos that caress the ear. The first movement is brisk and dramatic, while in the Scherzo the tonguing of the woodwind makes for phenomenal precision. As for the transfer, after a dull opening the bite and immediacy of the brass and woodwind are so vivid they give an illusion of stereo.

String Quartets 1 in A; 2 in D

*** Chan. (ADD) 9965. Borodin Qt

Borodin's *First Quartet* is one of the most lyrical quartets in the repertoire, and its familiarity prompts some music-lovers to underrate its consummate mastery of form. The **Borodins** made this classic recording in 1979, and it remains the yardstick by which all others are judged.

String Quartets 1 in A; 2 in D; (i) String Sextet in D min.

⊕ *** ASV CD DCA 1143. The Lindsays, (i) with Williams, R. Wallfisch

The **Lindsays** add to their repertory of warm, intense recordings this splendid coupling of Borodin's two *String Quartets* alongside a rarity from early in the composer's career, the *String Sextet*, composed in Heidelberg in 1860, of which only two movements survive. The Lindsays, very well recorded, give glowing, ripely expressive and finely balanced performances that confidently bring out the light and shade of the writing of both scores, as well as a more convincing reading of the *Sextet* than any other we have heard.

String Quartet 2 in D

(M) *** Classic fM 75605 57027-2. Chilingirian Qt – DVOŘÁK: *Quartet in F*; SHOSTAKOVICH: *Quartet 8* ***

(***) Testament mono SBT 1061. Hollywood Qt – GLAZUNOV: *5 Novelettes*; TCHAIKOVSKY: *String Quartet 1* (***)

On the Classic fM label the **Chilingirian Quartet** offer powerful, incisive performances of an apt and generous coupling. With Levon Chilingirian an exceptionally alert leader, rhythms in the Borodin are consistently well sprung, with no sentimentality, in a warmly expressive account of the celebrated slow movement.

Although later recordings may match the **Hollywood**

version, it is still a performance with persuasive freshness and ardour. The sound has been improved, and the addition of the Glazunov, which is new to the catalogue, enhances the disc's value. The playing time runs to one second short of 80 minutes.

Prince Igor (complete; DVD versions)

⊕ *** Ph. **DVD** 074 173-9 (2). Putilin, Gorchakova, Akimov, Aleksashkin, Vaneev, Borodina, Kirov Ballet Ch. & O, Gergiev (Producer: Paul Smaczny, V/D: Arno Cronvall)

⊕ *** Ph. **DVD** 075 099-9 (6). As above – GLINKA: *Ruslan and Ludmilla*; MUSSORGSKY: *Boris Godunov*

The Kirov production was mounted six years after the CD recording below, in 1998, with a different but equally strong cast. Both **Galina Gorchakova** and **Olga Borodina** sing the same roles (Yaroslavna and Konchakovna respectively) but the Khan Konchak is **Vladimir Vaneev** while the performance is dedicated to the memory of the Khan in the earlier set, the incomparable Bulat Minjelkiev; most of the other male roles are differently (but no less superbly) cast. The notes replicate the scholarly account in the CD set of what this edition restores. It includes passages discovered among Borodin's papers that were rejected by Rimsky-Korsakov in his superb edition, and they have been specially orchestrated for this new production by Yuri Faliek. The Gergiev production reverts to a structural outline of 1883, which proposed alternating the Russian and Polovtsian acts. This is not the place to discuss the re-ordering of the material of the opera, but its artistic interest and success are not in question.

Prince Igor (complete; CD versions)

⊕ *** Ph. 442 537-2 (3). Kit, Gorchakova, Ognovienko, Minjelkiev, Borodina, Grigorian, Kirov Ch. & O, St Petersburg, Gergiev

Gergiev's electrifying account of Borodin's epic opera reflects not only his own magnetic qualities as a conductor but also the way he has welded his principal singers as well as the chorus and orchestra into a powerful team. Acts I and II are given in reverse order from the usual, with the substantial Prologue here followed by the first Polovtsian scene and its spectacular dances. Only then do you get the scene at Prince Galitsky's court, leading up to Yaroslavna's great lament, here sung superbly by **Galina Gorchakova**. Otherwise Gergiev generally follows the well-established edition, but he has included material omitted from Borodin's copious sketches, notably an extended monologue of lament for Igor himself as a prisoner of Khan Konchak in Act III: 'Why did I not fall on the field of battle?' On the solo casting, honours are much more even. The two principal women, not just Gorchakova but **Olga Borodina** too as Konchak's daughter, Konchakovna, are both magnificent, **Ghiuselev** and **Ghiaurov**, both older-sounding but still compelling. **Gegam Grigorian** in the tenor role of Igor's son gives a lusty performance, while **Mikhail Kit** as Igor himself, though often gritty and even fluttery of tone, sings thoughtfully and intelligently, making him a fair match for his Bulgarian rival.

Prince Igor: Overture & Polovtsian Dances

⊕—↻ Ⓜ *** EMI 5 66983-2. Beecham Choral Soc., RPO, Beecham – RIMSKY-KORSAKOV: *Scheherazade* ***

Ⓜ *** Telarc CD 80039. Atlanta Ch. & SO, Shaw – STRAVINSKY: *Firebird Suite* ***

Beecham's 1957 performance of the *Polovtsian Dances* – now reissued as one of EMI's 'Great Recordings of the Century' – sweeps the board, even though it omits the percussion-led opening *Dance of the Polovtsian Maidens*. Beecham draws an almost Russian fervour from his choristers. The recorded sound is little short of astonishing in its fullness, vividness and clarity.

In the *Polovtsian Dances* the choral singing on the remarkable Telarc recording is less clearly focused in the lyrical music than at climaxes, but the **Atlanta Singers** undoubtedly rise to the occasion. The entry of the bass drum is riveting and the closing section very exciting. The vivid sound-balance is equally impressive in the *Overture*, and if the **Atlanta Orchestra** does not possess the body of string timbre to make the most of the sweeping second subject, the playing has spontaneity and vitality throughout. Most enjoyable and, as a recording, in the demonstration bracket.

The Polish conductor **Gregor Fitelberg** recorded the *Polovtsian Dances* for Decca in 1946, a fresh, colourful reading enhanced by early Decca *ffrr* recording at its most impressive, very well transferred by Dutton. It makes an attractive fill-up for the Rimsky-Korsakov items from Ansermet and Constant Lambert. (Dutton CDBP 9712)

BOTTESINI, Giovanni
(1821– 89)

Double Bass Concertino in C minor; Duo Concertante on theme from Bellini's I Puritani. Elegy in D; Passioni amorose for 2 Double Basses; Overtures: Ali Baba; Ero e Lenadro. Sinfonia: Il diavolo delle notte

Ⓝ ⑧⑧ *** Naxos 8.570398 Thomas Martin; LSO, Matthew Gibson; with Welsh; Petracchi

Gran Concerto in F sharp min.; (i) Gran Duo Concertante for Violin, Double Bass and Orchestra. Andante sostenuto for Strings; (ii) Duetto for Clarinet and Double Bass

Ⓝ ⑧⑧ **** Naxos 8.570397 Thomas Martin, ECO, Litton; with (i) Garcia; (ii) Johnson

Capriccio à la Chopin; Fantasia La Sonnambula; 2 Melodies; Introduction and Gavotte; Meditation; Rêverie Variations on a Scottish Air (Auld Robin Gray); Intro & Variations on Carnaval of Venice; (i) Arias: Ci divide l'ocean; Giovinetto innamorato; Romanza; Tutto che il mondo serra

Ⓝ ⑧⑧ *** Naxos 8.570400 Thomas Martin, Halstead; (i) with Fugelle

Giovanni Bottesini was an all-purpose musician. Although as a famous virtuoso/composer for that instrument he was nicknamed the 'Paganini of the Double Bass' and as such appeared before all the crowned heads of Europe; he was also a highly regarded conductor, and Verdi chose him to direct the first performance of *Aida* in Cairo. His expertise on the double bass is well reflected here by the superb contribution of the soloist, **Thomas Martin**, whose lyrical style is warmly appealing and whose uncanny ease in the instrument's upper register (complete with harmonics) often suggests a cello, although the instrument's lower register has plenty of resonant warmth. The enjoyable collection of short pieces with **Anthony Halstead** on piano demonstrates the kind of repertoire featured at those illustrious venues including three vocal items. But the catchy *Overtures* included on the first disc listed shows that Bottisini could orchestrate vividly. The major double bass concertos on the second CD are less melodically distinctive, the highlight being the *Duo Concertante* using themes from *I puritani*. Undoubtedly the most rewarding disc here is the collection which includes the duet works with violin or clarinet which are both most entertaining, and very well presented, while the *Andante sostenuto for Strings* makes a splendid passionate interlude. Performances are peerless; recordings first class, although in the concertos the balance of the soloist bass at lower dynamic levels could be bolder.

BOUGHTON, Rutland
(1878–1960)

Symphony 1 (Oliver Cromwell)

Ⓜ *** Dutton CDLX 7185. BBC Concert O, Handley – BAINTON: *Symphony 3* ***

Any symphony inspired by Oliver Cromwell has to be at least interesting, and so this 35-minute work, dating from 1904, proves to be. There is plenty of lusty melodrama in the late-romantic (almost swashbuckling) writing which is thoroughly entertaining, with the composer's admiration of Wagner strongly felt. Superb performances and recorded sound, and coupled to an impressive work by Edgar Bainton.

(i) Oboe Quartet 1; 3 Songs without Words (for Oboe Quartet). String Quartets: in A (On Greek Folk Songs); in F (From the Welsh Hills)

⑧⑧ *** Hyp. Helios CDH 55174. (i) Francis; Rasumovsky Qt

Nearly all this music is inspired by the countryside. The second movement of the *F major Quartet* hauntingly evokes the *Landscape from the* (Welsh) *Hilltops*. The *Oboe Quartet* has two perky movements and a third, more reflective *Andante con variazione*. **Sarah Francis**, who has already given us a fine account of Boughton's *First Oboe Concerto* (see above), is equally persuasive both here and in the three equally winning *Songs without Words*. The **Rasumovsky Quartet** gives sympathetic support throughout and, with good, clear recording, this inexpensive disc has much to offer.

Pastoral

ⓑⓑ *** Hyp. Helios CDH 55008. Francis, Rasumovsky Qt –
HARTY: 3 *Pieces*; HOWELLS: *Sonata*; RUBBRA: *Sonata* ***

Boughton's enchanting *Pastoral* for oboe and string quartet
has a disarmingly attractive, folksy pastoral melody which
haunts the memory. The performance could hardly be more
persuasive.

The Immortal Hour (opera; complete)

☞– Ⓑ **** Hyp. Dyad CDD 22040 (2). Kennedy, Dawson,
Wilson-Johnson, Davies, George Mitchell Ch., ECO,
Melville

Analysed closely, much of *The Immortal Hour* may seem like
Vaughan Williams and water; but this fine performance, conducted by a lifelong Boughton devotee, brings out the hypnotic quality which had 1920s music-lovers attending
performances many times over, entranced by its lyrical evocation of Celtic twilight. The simple tunefulness goes with a
fine feeling for atmosphere. The excellent cast of young
singers includes **Anne Dawson** as the heroine, Princess
Etain, and **Maldwyn Davies** headily beautiful in the main
tenor rendering of the *Faery song*. Warm, reverberant recording, enhanced in its CD format, and this delightful opera is
not to be missed at its new Dyad price.

BOULANGER, Lili (1893–1918)

(i) *Clairières dans le ciel* (song-cycle); (ii) Choral Music: *Hymne au soleil; Les Sirènes; Pour les funérailles d'un soldat; Renouveau; Soir sur la plaine*

ⓑⓑ **(*) Hyp. Helios CDH 55153. (i) Hill, Ball; (ii) New L.
Chamber Ch., Wood

Clairières dans le ciel is fragrantly sensuous in a particularly
French way, the introduction balmy and exotic. **Martyn Hill**
fully captures the work's essence and for the most part sings
beautifully, though his bursts of intensity bring an intrusive
vibrato. **Andrew Ball's** accompaniment, rippling and ardent,
is delightfully supportive. The short choral works each have
a soloist, *Renouveau* and *Soir sur la plaine* have three each. The
piano accompaniments serve well enough when the choral
writing is so exquisitely sumptuous in the blending of female voices, richly impressionistic. The most striking piece,
however, is a dark evocation of a soldier's funeral. The **New
London Chamber Choir** admirably catch the lavish impressionistic colouring of this highly original writing and sing
with fervour, and Andrew Ball again rises to the occasion.
Excellent recording and full texts and translations make this
a bargain.

Faust et Hélène; Psaume 24; Psaume 130: Du fond de l'abîme; D'un matin de printemps; D'un soir triste

*** Chan. 9745. Dawson, Murray, Bottone, MacKenzie,
Howard, CBSO Ch., BBC PO, Y.-P. Tortelier

Faust et Hélène has astonishing beauty and a natural eloquence. Like *Psaume 24*, *Du fond de l'abîme* and the other
music on the disc, it offers testimony to an altogether re-

markable talent. There is a distinguished team of soloists
(**Lynne Dawson** and **Bonaventura Bottone** in the cantata and
Ann Murray in one of the Psalms) and first-rate contribu-
tions from the **Birmingham chorus** and the **BBC
Philharmonic** under **Yan-Pascal Tortelier**.

Psaume 24; Psaume 130: Du fond de l'abîme; Pie Jesu

Ⓜ **(*) BBC (ADD) BBCL 4026-2. Price, Greevy, Partridge,
Carol Case, BBC Ch., BBC SO, N. Boulanger – FAURÉ:
Requiem **(*) ✿ ❀

The *Pie Jesu*, dedicated to her sister Nadia, certainly conveys
her fervour and belief in these remarkable scores, and *Du
fond de l'abîme* is a work of astonishing originality and imagination. Recorded at a live concert in the Fairfield Halls,
Croydon, the BBC engineers provide more than acceptable
sound, and the balance is skilfully done. A rather special musical document.

BOULANGER, Nadia (1887–1979)

Mademoiselle: A film by Bruno Monsaingeon

*** Ideale Audience **DVD** 5DM41

Bruno Monsaingeon has produced impressive and revealing video portraits of Richter, Oistrakh and Menuhin. This
film is about Nadia Boulanger, the most formidable teacher
of the twentieth century, with whom practically everyone
of note studied, including Aaron Copland, Walter Piston,
Lennox Berkeley, Igor Markevitch and Leonard Bernstein
to name only a handful. Much of the film is based on mas-
terclasses she gave at her home in Paris, but it was reworked
into its present form for her ninetieth birthday in 1977.
There is a moving coda printed in the booklet, in which
Bernstein describes a visit during her dying days. RL had
the privilege of recording her on a number of occasions
during his BBC career and can testify that the film brings
one closer to a remarkable presence whose spirit still casts
a strong spell.

BOULEZ, Pierre (born 1925)

Anthèmes 2; Messagesquisse; Sur Incises

*** DG 477 635-1. Ens. InterContemporain, composer

All three of these contrasted works display Boulez's fascination with colour and texture. This collection is essentially
for those who do not believe music is mainly concerned with
melody. But it won a Gramophone Contemporary Music
Award in 2001 and also a Grand Prix.

(i) . . . explosante-fixe . . . ; (ii) Notations; (iii) Structures pour deux pianos, Livre II

*** DG 477 5385. (i) Ens. InterContemporain, composer, with
Cherrier, Ophèle, Valade; (ii; iii) Aimard; (iii) Boffard

Notations demonstrates his application of serialism to the
widest range of parameters. In Book 2 of Boulez's *Structures*

for *Two Pianos* he felt tempted to exploit the special effects that the medium itself offered, echoing electronic effects at times. **Aimard** with **Florent Boffard** again proves magnetic, but it is with the main work on the disc, ... *explosante-fixe* .. ., 37 minutes long, that Boulez as composer emerges at full stretch in the colour and energy of his writing for chamber orchestra with electronic effects.

Figures-Doubles-Prismes; (i) *Pli selon pli*; (ii) *Le Soleil des eaux*; (i; ii; iii) *Le Visage nuptial*

(BB) *** Warner Apex 2564 62083-2 (2). BBC SO, Boulez, with (i) Bryn-Julson; (ii) BBC Singers; (iii) Laurence

Pli selon pli has long been accepted as a modern classic. **Phyllis Bryn-Julson** is the superb soloist, and in duet with the contralto, **Elizabeth Laurence**, she is just as persuasive in the more sumptuous sounds of *Le Visage nuptial* with the two interweaving soloists supplemented by the **BBC Singers**. The BBC Singers then take centre stage for another setting of Char, *Le Soleil des eaux*, giving a virtuoso performance in the vigorous choral writing. As a coda comes the orchestral work, *Figures-Doubles-Prismes*, by turns darkly intense and powerfully abrasive; superbly controlled in this performance under the composer, as it is in all the works. First-rate digital sound all through.

CHAMBER MUSIC

Dérive (for flute, clarinet, violin, cello, vibraphone & piano); (i) *Dialogue de l'ombre double*; (ii) *Flute Sonatine*; *Mémoriale (... explosante-fixe ... originel)* for Flute & 8 Instruments; (iii) *Piano Sonata*; (iv) *Cummings ist der Dichter*

(BB) *** Warner Apex 0927 49987-2. (i) Daimins; (ii) Cherrier; (iii) Aimard; (iv) BBC Singers; Ens. InterContemporain, composer

No one could suggest that the recklessly spiky progress of the *Sonatine for Flute* (a most assured performance) and the *Piano Sonata* are anything but intractable. But the *Dialogue de l'ombre double* (another superbly played work for clarinet in electronic duet with itself) is both imaginative and aurally fascinating, while *Dérive* and *Mémoriale* (which are not too long) are similarly exotically ear-tickling, if with no formal logic. Most strikingly original of all is the longest piece here, the weirdly atmospheric choral work, *Cummings ist der Dichter* and the result is nothing if not extraordinary.

Domaines

(B) ** HM HMA 195930. Ens. Portal, Musique Vivante, Masson

Domaines was first performed in 1968 as a work for solo clarinet, but two years later Boulez rewrote the score to include a responding concertante ensemble of 20 additional instrumentalists including percussion, divided into five groups arranged in a circle. The solo clarinet moves among them throughout the performance, yet remains a fulcrum. In the second *Mirror* half, the soloists reflect the instrumental tuttis which are now more elaborate, but the stereo here readily conveys the mobility of the soloist. Although this is a bargain

reissue, the playing time is only just over half an hour, which many will say is quite long enough!

Piano Sonatas 1–3

(BB) *** Naxos 8.553353. Biret

Those with an interest in this repertoire will be well rewarded by **Idil Biret** on Naxos; she is more than equal to their technical demands and is given good sound.

Piano Sonata 2

(M) (***) DG (ADD) (IMS) 471 359-2. Pollini – DEBUSSY: 12 *Etudes* **

In Boulez's *Second Sonata* the composer's stated intention was to 'destroy what was first-movement sonata form, to dissolve slow-movement form by means of the trope, to dissolve repetitive scherzo-form by means of variation form, and in the fourth movement to destroy fugal and canonic form'. Indeed in the finale the pianist at one point has an instruction to 'pulverize the sound'. So, if you like musical disintegration, this is the piece for you. **Pollini** truly believes in this sonata, readily demonstrated by the forceful driving momentum of his playing throughout.

BOWEN, York (1884–1961)

Horn Concerto (for Horn, String Orchestra & Timpani), Op. 58

🎧 *** Lyrita SRCD 316. Pyatt, LPO, Braithwaite – ARNOLD; GIBBS; JACOB: *Horn Concertos*; VINTER: *Hunter's Moon* ***

Like the Malcolm Arnold *Concerto*, York Bowen's attractive work was written for Dennis Brain and, again like Arnold, Bowen underpins the bravura writing with a richly melodic lyrical strain, which **David Pyatt** plays very sensitively. The spirited finale dances off perkily, again paying homage to the Strauss *First Concerto*. David Pyatt's superlative performance here is splendidly recorded, like the Arnold, in the warm acoustic of Watford Town Hall.

(i) *Piano Concerto 1, Op. 11*; (ii) *Violin Concerto, Op. 33*

(M) *** Dutton CDLX 7169. BBC Concert O, Handley, with (i) Michael Dussek; (ii) Lorraine McAslan

The *Piano Concerto* is an early work, composed when Bowen was nineteen. There are some reminiscences of Saint-Saëns and Litolff, but the piece has refreshing fluency and charm. The *Violin Concerto* failed to find a persuasive champion and soon disappeared from the repertoire until this excellent recording restored it to circulation. As an eight-year-old boy, York Bowen made his debut in a Dussek concerto, so it is appropriate that **Michael Dussek** who is descended from the composer should play it here.

Piano Concertos 2 (Concertstück), Op. 17; 3 (Fantasia), Op. 23; Symphonic Fantasia, Op. 16

(M) *** Dutton CDLX 7187. Dussek; BBC Concert O, Handley

This couples the *Second Concerto* (subtitled *Concertstück*) with the *Third* (1907) and the *Symphonic Fantasia*, which no less a conductor than Hans Richter championed with the LSO. Bowen was still in his early twenties and these pieces all have a youthful freshness and generosity of feeling. Excellent notes from Lewis Foreman enhance the appeal of these most welcome and admirably performed issues.

Piano Concertos 3 in G minor 'Fantasia', Op 23; 4 in A minor, Op 88

Ⓝ *** Hyp. CDA67659. Driver, BBC Scottish SO, Brabbins

Danny Driver is the engaging soloist in the one-movement *Third Concerto* from Dutton, and he also tackles the much later *Fourth* which the composer himself thought highly of. Indeed he regarded it as his finest work for the keyboard while Sorabji, no less, hailed it as the most important concerto written by an Englishman. Fine recorded sound makes this a most desirable acquisition.

Viola Concerto in C min., Op. 25

*** Hyp. CDA 67546. Power, BBC Scottish SO, Brabbins –
   FORSYTH: *Viola Concerto in G min.* ***

Bowen was himself a viola-player as well as a pianist and he exploits the instrument masterfully, launching powerfully in the first subject of the opening *Allegro assai*. That restless theme is quickly set against a warmly relaxed second subject. The central *Andante cantabile* brings a rich, song-like melody, exploiting the viola's lower register, leading to a jaunty finale, witty in its use of woodwind, which combines elements of scherzo and finale. Well coupled, superbly played by **Lawrence Power**, with **Martyn Brabbins** and the BBC Scottish Orchestra, and very well recorded, with the viola well forward.

Cello Sonata

*** British Music Soc. BMS 423CD. Cole, Talbot – FOULDS;
   WALKER: *Cello Sonatas* ***

Jo Cole does not produce a big tone, but she is highly sensitive to York Bowen's very English lyricism and she is at her finest in the elegiac main theme of the slow movement and in catching its passionate, rhapsodic feeling. The finale is a brilliant rondo, which brings back the principal themes from all three movements to make a powerful close, and it invites and receives a passionate response from both artists. The recording is essentially well balanced, but the piano often dominates, as much as anything because of the bold character of the piano writing.

Cello Sonata; Suite for Violin & Piano; Violin Sonata in E min.

Ⓜ *** Dutton CDLX 7120. Endymion Ens.

What these keenly intense performances consistently demonstrate is the cogency of York Bowen's writing, with strongly argued structures built on striking thematic material. So the *Violin Suite* in four movements is framed by strongly rhythmic movements in sonata form, with a flowing *Barcarolle* for slow movement and a *Humoresque* Scherzo that Kreisler himself might have written as one of his encore pieces. The later works bring no lessening of passion behind

the writing. With **Krysia Osostowicz** the outstanding violinist and **Jane Salmon** the fine cellist, these very well-recorded performances could not be better designed.

Horn Quintet; Piano Trio; Rhapsody Trio

⊟ Ⓜ *** Dutton CDLX 7115. Endymion Ens.

Three more superb chamber-works that never seem routine, particularly in outstanding performances like these. The *Horn Quintet* is a glorious piece, with **Stephen Stirling** magnificent in the central horn part, and if the main motif of the first movement reminds one of Vaughan Williams's *Fifth Symphony*, York Bowen was writing almost 20 years earlier. One looks forward to hearing much more.

String Quartets 2 in D min., Op. 41; 3 in G, Op. 46b; (i) Phantasy-Quintet for Bass Clarinet & String Quartet, Op. 93

*** British Music Society BMS 426CD. Archaeus Qt, (i) with
   Timothy Lines

The *Second Quartet in D minor* has a hauntingly melodic first movement. The *Poco lento* is unforgettably nostalgic and the busily folksy finale of contrasting brilliance, offset by more appealing lyricism. The *Third Quartet* opens with another lovely melodic contour reminding one a little of Dvořák, with the slow movement following in the same mood of intimate melancholy. The bass clarinet does not dominate the *Phantasy-Quintet*, but adds a beguiling touch of darkness to its texture, interwoven with solo interludes. Highly sympathetic performances and excellent recording ensure this CD receives a strong recommendation.

Viola Sonatas 1 in F; 2 in C min.; Phantasy for Viola & Piano, Op. 54

Ⓜ *** Dutton CDLX 7126. Boyd, Forsberg

With **James Boyd** the rich-toned soloist, this collection of Bowen's music for viola and piano is equally welcome. In the unashamedly lyrical style that brought him such early success as a composer, this is warmly approachable music. The Swedish accompanist, **Bengt Forsberg**, proves as understanding an accompanist as he is in the song repertory.

PIANO MUSIC

Ballade 2, Op. 87; Berceuse, Op. 83; Moto perpetuo from Op. 39; Preludes, Op. 102: excerpts; Romances 1, Op. 35/1; 2, Op. 45; Sonata 5 in F min., Op. 72; Toccata, Op. 155

⊟ *** Hyp. CDA 66838. Hough

Hough, always compelling on disc, not only technically brilliant but spontaneously expressive, consistently conveys his love for Bowen's music, starting with 13 of the 24 *Preludes*. He puts them in his own very effective order, bringing out the contrasted qualities of jewelled miniatures, reflecting Rachmaninov on the one hand, Ireland and Bax on the other, but with a flavour of their own. The most powerful, most ambitious work is the *Sonata 5*, with two weighty, wide-ranging movements separated by an *Andante* interlude. Vivid piano-sound and illuminating notes by Francis Pott and Hough himself.

Ballade 2; 3 Miniatures, Op. 44; 3 Pieces. Op. 20; 3 Preludes: 2 & 3; 3 Serious Dances, Op. 51; 3 Songs without words, Op. 94

(N) *** Chan. 10506. Celis

24 Preludes, Op. 102; Sonata 6 in B flat min., Op. 160; Reverie, Op. 86

*** Chan. 10277. Celis

The Dutch pianist **Joop Celis** proves an enthusiastic and highly virtuosic exponent of York Bowen and offers a valuable anthology of his solo piano music that well withstands comparison with Stephen Hough. Apart from the shorter pieces he is very impressive in the magnificent *Sixth Sonata*, and even more rewarding in the 24 *Preludes*, eclectic but with something unmistakeably English about them.

Partita, Op. 156; 10 Preludes, Op. 102; Toccata, Op. 155

(N) (M) **(*) Lyrita mono REAM 2105(2). Composer –
 REIZENSTEIN: *Sonata, Op. 19* etc

York Bowen was himself a pianist of great distinction and these performances recorded a year before his death, when he would have been seventy-four, testify to his elegance and mastery. The *Partita* was composed the year of this recording and has much of the charm he exuded as a man. It comes as a two CD set coupled with rarities by Franz Reisenstein.

BOYCE, William (1711–79)

Overtures 1–12; Concerti grossi: in B flat; B min. & E min.

(B) *** Chan. Double 6665 (2). Cantilena, Shepherd

Cantilena's performances readily convey the freshness of Boyce's inspiration, and this is one of the most recommendable of all their recordings, the more attractive for being reissued as a bargain Double. They are oddly balanced but the sound is both atmospheric and vivid and provides a refreshing musical experience.

Symphonies 1–8, Op. 2

*** DG 419 631-2. E. Concert, Pinnock

(M) *** CRD 3356. Bournemouth Sinf., Thomas

Pinnock's disc of the Boyce *Symphonies* wears its scholarship very easily and in so doing brings not only lively, resilient playing but fresh revelation in the treatment of the *vivace* movements. Nicely scaled recording, bright but atmospheric.

 Thomas's tempi are often brisk. But even against such strong competition as this, the buoyant playing of the **Bournemouth Sinfonietta** still gives much pleasure by its sheer vitality. Bright, clear sound and a price advantage.

12 Trio Sonatas (1747); Sonatas 13–15 (unpublished)

*** Hyp. CDA 67151/2. Parley of Instruments or Parley B. O, Holman

Boyce gave the English trio sonata a new lease of life at a time when the format was in danger of falling into neglect, and they are consistently inventive and a good example of baroque 'easy listening'. As an appendix, **Peter Holman** has discovered three extra sonatas (here numbered 13–15) which survive in a manuscript in the Cambridge Fitzwilliam Museum. There is evidence to suggest that these sonatas were sometimes played in orchestral form, so the Hyperion recording alternates orchestral and chamber performance, with Nos. 1, 3, 5, 7–9, 11 and 13 heard on a full string group. These period performances are vigorously alert and stylish, with slow movements refined yet warmly relished. Excellent recording without edginess.

The Secular Masque. Overtures: Birthday Ode for George III (1768); King's Ode for the New Year (1772); Ode for St Cecilia's Day

⊶ *** Gaudeamus CDGAU 176. Howarth, Kuhlmann, Daniels, Robinson, Varcoe, Thomas, New College, Oxford, Ch., Hanover Band, Lea-Cox

The Secular Masque represents Boyce at his freshest and most unbuttoned. So 'Diana's song' – which Boyce published separately – with elaborate horn parts, brims with rustic jollity and is sung radiantly here by **Judith Howarth**. 'Mars's song', *Sound the trumpet, beat the drum*, also has Boyce responding with engaging directness, vigour and colour. Each of the overtures here, including the one for the *Secular Masque*, follows a similar form in two, three or four brief movements. **Graham Lea-Cox** draws lively performances from the **Hanover Band**, the choir and his excellent team of soloists. Warm, full sound.

Solomon (serenata)

*** Hyp. CDA 66378. Mills, Crook, Parley of Instruments, Goodman

William Boyce's *Solomon* is a totally secular piece, a dialogue between She and He, with the verses freely based on the *Song of Solomon*. As this stylish and alert period performance using young, fresh-voiced soloists makes clear, it has some delightful inspirations, less influenced by Italian models than by popular English song. First-rate sound.

BRAHMS, Johannes (1833–97)

Piano Concertos. 1 in D min., Op. 15; 2 in B flat, Op. 83

⊶ *** Decca 475 7637 (2). Freire, Leipzig GO, Chailly

⊶ ✦ (M) *** Sup. SU 3865-2 (2). Ivan Moravec, Czech PO, Bělohlávek

Piano Concertos (i) 1; (ii) 2

(N) (B) (***) mono/stereo (ADD) Curzon; (i) LSO, Szell; (ii) VPO, Knappertsbusch

(i) Piano Concertos 1–2; (ii) Academic Festival Overture; Tragic Overture; Variations on a Theme of Haydn, Op. 56a

🎵 (BB) *** EMI (ADD) Gemini 4 76939-2 (2). (i) Barenboim, New Philh. O; (ii) VPO; (i; ii) Barbirolli

(i) Piano Concertos 1–2. Variations & Fugue on a Theme of Handel; Waltzes, Op. 39

🎵 (M) *** Sony Heritage (ADD) MH2K 63225 (2). Fleisher; (i) Cleveland O, Szell

(i) Piano Concertos 1–2. Fantasias, Op. 116

🎵 (M) *** DG (ADD) 447 446-2 (2). Gilels, (i) BPO, Jochum

The **Gilels** performances can still hold their own against virtually all the competition, but the two concertos are also available separately. However, the present set is offered at a reduced price and the remastered recording is quite outstanding.

Nelson Freire and **Chailly** make a superb partnership, readily combining adrenalin, power and Brahmsian lyricism. Perhaps it is the stimulus of live recording, but the unleashed energy of the opening of No. 1 reminds the listener immediately of Curzon and Szell. The **Leipzig Gewandhaus Orchestra**, while retaining its fullness of texture, sounds revitalized by Chailly, yet the poetry of the slow movements is fully revealed. The Decca recording is in the demonstration class to match the virtuosity of the solo playing, and this new pairing is very recommendable indeed.

Electrifying playing from **Ivan Moravec**, matched by **Bělohlávek's** wonderfully understanding accompaniments. Moreover, this newer set also has the advantage of first-class digital recording and a natural orchestral balance, with the piano forward and dramatically present, within the warm acoustic of the Dvořák Hall of the Rudolfinum in Prague. The recordings were made in 1988 and 1989 respectively, and so gripping and spontaneous is the playing throughout that it is difficult to believe that the music-making did not take place in front of a live audience.

Barenboim's performances with **Barbirolli** of the two *Piano Concertos* from the late 1960s (and especially the *First* with the **New Philharmonia**) are also among the most inspired ever committed to disc, and the orchestral works also show Barbirolli at his finest. Excellent recording makes this budget Gemini reissue very desirable indeed.

Leon Fleisher's two concerto recordings are both masterly examples of joint inspiration, bringing out the point that these are in many ways symphonies with piano, when **Szell's** direction is so powerful and incisive as well as warmly expressive. Not that Fleisher in any way lacks individuality, for the crisp confidence of his virtuosity has a sureness in its musical and emotional thrust that carries one magnetically on. The sound is among the best offered by CBS/Sony at that period, with the piano balanced forwardly but not aggressively so. Generously, this Heritage issue also includes solo recordings by Fleisher of the *Handel Variations* and *Waltzes*, similarly crisp and concentrated.

Stephen Hough gives keenly distinctive and deeply thoughtful readings of both Brahms concertos, so that with refined recording the transparency of textures may be disconcerting to those who insist on a fat Brahms sound. He adopts the widest range of tone and dynamic, with the recording beautifully capturing the hushed *pianissimos* in both works, not least in both slow movements. Both recordings were made in 1989 (Virgin 2x1 5 61412-2). They are also available seperately (no. 1: 5 22098-2; no. 2: 3 91366-2).

While **Curzon's** memorable account of the *First Concerto* with **Szell** has long held an honoured place in the catalogue (see below) his 1957 recording of the *Second Concerto* (surprisingly only available in mono) fell by the wayside. Yet it is a remarkable interpretation, the pianism totally commanding (and well recorded); and if the orchestral upper strings are at times very thin, the acoustic of the Sofiensaal adds an overall warmth. **Knappertsbusch's** direction is volatile but convincingly Brahmsian, and altogether this version is well worthy of reissue alongside its more celebrated companion.

(i) Piano Concertos 1–2; (ii) Piano Quartet 1 in G min., Op. 25 (arr. Schoenberg)

(N) (B) *** CfP 2 28363-2 (2) Tirimo, (i) LPO, Sanderling; (ii) CBSO, Rattle

The *Second Concerto* was **Tirimo's** début recording, made in 1972. He gives a commanding if measured account of the first movement, not always quite tidy in its occasional impulsiveness (but then neither is Richter). The second and fourth movements too have slow basic tempi, but the clarity of articulation gives a sharpness of focus to conceal that, and both are made exuberant and joyful. Similarly in the *First Concerto*, made six years later, **Sanderling** and Tirimo amply justify their straight and measured manner in the thoughtful concentration of the whole reading, with crisp, lifted rhythms in outer movements, while the slow movement has a rapt quality, holding one's attention as a live performance would. With excellent recording this is one of the best of the Classics for Pleasure reissued doubles, for **Rattle** makes quite a case for Schoenberg's transcription of the *Piano Quartet*.

(i) Piano Concerto 1. Piano Quartet 1 (orch. Schoenberg)

🎵 *** EuroArts DVD 2053659. (i) Barenboim; BPO, Rattle (Director: Bob Coles, Producer: Paul Smaczny)

The **Barenboim/Rattle** DVD of the *First Concerto*, coupled with Schoenberg's orchestration of the *First Piano Quartet*, (curiously scored minus a piano) is visually and sonically one of the most successful of all the available orchestral concert DVDs, and the *Concerto* is an overwhelming musical experience. The sound is magnificent – full, rich, resonant and vivid in its detail, as if the recording were made in a normal concert hall with perfect acoustics. It is a superb performance, with free-running adrenalin, to match Barenboim's much earlier studio partnership with Barbirolli. Indeed, it is remarkably like being present at the concert itself. The choice of Schoenberg's orchestration of the *Piano Quartet* for the second half of the concert was a curious one, yet that too is played with great conviction. But this DVD is an essential purchase for the *Concerto* alone.

Piano Concerto 1 in D min., Op. 15

**** DG 477 6021. Zimerman, BPO, Rattle

(M) ******* Decca (ADD) 466 376-2. Curzon, LSO, Szell – FRANCK: *Symphonic Variations;* LITOLFF: *Scherzo* ***

(M) ******* Warner Elatus 0927 46768-2. Grimaud, Berlin State O, Sanderling – STRAUSS: *Burleske* ***

Krystian Zimerman, **Simon Rattle** and the **Berlin Philharmonic** took their masterly account of the *D minor Concerto* into the studio the day after a concert performance. Of the latter, the *Frankfurter Allgemeine Zeitung* is quoted as saying 'Zimerman infused his piano part with that spark of individual genius which separates a merely committed and faithful interpretation from the revelation of absolute truth.' There is no doubt that this is a distinguished performance indeed, and it is very well recorded.

Clifford Curzon's 1962 recording, produced by John Culshaw in Kingsway Hall, returns to the catalogue, superbly remastered. The fierceness of attack in the upper strings, especially in the powerful opening tutti, sounds naturally focused on CD, adding a leonine power to Szell's orchestral contribution, and the piano tone is admirably natural.

Hélène Grimaud is an impressive Brahms interpreter and totally attuned to his world, while **Kurt Sanderling** is equally persuasive here. Grimaud's is a performance to reckon with and the recording has splendour and presence. No one buying this, particularly at so modest a price, is likely to be disappointed on any count.

Piano Concerto 2 in B flat, Op. 83 (DVD version)

**(*) DG DVD 073 4097. Pollini, VPO, Abbado – BEETHOVEN: *Piano Concertos 3 & 5;* MOZART: *Piano Concertos 19 & 23* **(*)

Pollini is commanding and majestic in the *B flat concerto*, recorded in May 1976 at the Musikvereinssaal, Vienna, and the **Vienna Philharmonic** give sympathetic support. By the side of the Gilels–Jochum performances, this does not seem as warm or involving. Of course it offers some superb pianism and eloquent orchestral playing but, as with the Beethoven, it exhibits cool and dedicated classicism, shorn of expressive exaggeration, characteristic of this partnership. Exemplary visual direction and predictably fine sound from Klaus Hiemann and Rainer Brock.

Piano Concerto 2 in B flat, Op. 83 (CD versions)

*** Naïve V4944. Guy, LPO, Berglund

(M) **(***)** BBC mono BBCL 4125-2. Arrau, SCO, Gibson – SCHUBERT: *3 Klavierstücke* (***)

(i) Piano Concerto 2. Piano Sonata 1, Op. 1/2

(B) ******** RCA 82876 60860-2 (2). S. Richter, (i) Chicago SO, Leinsdorf

Richter's Brahms B flat is one of the very finest performances of this great work. There is nothing self-conscious or studied here; the music is allowed to unfold naturally and with warmth and eloquence. This belongs alongside the greatest. This two-CD package also includes Richter's classic version of the early *C major Sonata*, Op. 1, an outstanding performance in every way, and both 1960 recordings sound very good indeed.

The young French pianist **François-Frédéric Guy's** account of the Brahms *B flat Concerto* is very commanding. It comes from a concert given at the Royal Festival Hall on 30 May 2003 – and can hold its own against the finest – and, having the electricity of a live occasion, is in some ways to be preferred to many rivals. **Berglund** is a supportive and sympathetic accompanist and audience noises are unobtrusive. The Festival Hall acoustic does not flatter the upper strings but, that apart, readers should find this a most rewarding issue.

Arrau could be a masterly interpreter of the Brahms concertos, often performing both at the same concert. This concert performance was given in Glasgow in 1963 and shows him in splendid form: there is a breadth, warmth and luminosity of tone that are peculiar to Arrau at his finest, and an intensity he brought to everything he did in the concert hall. The mono sound is very faithful.

The commanding **Solomon** version of the *B flat Concerto* with **Issay Dobrowen** and the **Philharmonia Orchestra** comes from 1947. There is a leonine nobility about this performance and an immediacy, spontaneity and dramatic fire that sweep all before it. The piano is not always perfect (the C above the stave is out of tune in one passage) but the pianist is! One soon forgets the sonic limitations and is swept along by the performance. (Testament SBT 1042)

Violin Concerto in D, Op. 77 (DVD version)

*** EMI DVD 5 44544-9. Perlman, BPO, Barenboim (Producer: Ursula Klein, V/D: Klaus Lindemann) – BEETHOVEN: *Violin Concerto* ***

Perlman's DVD, recorded live in 1992 at the Berlin Schauspielhaus with the **Berlin Philharmonic** under **Barenboim**, is in every way satisfying but is especially notable for the raptly beautiful performance of the *Adagio*, and is followed by a sparkling account of the finale. Barenboim is a splendid partner, and the Berlin Philharmonic are on top form; the balance is unusually good for a Perlman recording, though he certainly dominates the performance. The sound itself is excellent, and the producer has directed the changing camera angles very perceptively, not missing out the conductor. If you want a DVD of the coupling with Beethoven, this will give every satisfaction.

Violin Concerto in D, Op. 77 (DVD Version; with Documentary 'Discovering Masterpieces')

*** EuroArts DVD 2056078. Shaham, BPO, Abbado (Performance Director: Bob Coles; Documentary Director: Angelika Stielhler)

A lovely performance of the *Concerto* from **Gil Shaham**, the beautiful slow-movement oboe solo generating an exquisite response from the soloist. With **Abbado** looking very mature and generating plenty of vitality in the outer movements, he yet maintains the warmly lyrical approach of his soloist. The camerawork is sensible and the music-making comes fully alive for the listener/watcher. This can be recommended alongside Perlman. The documentary (which opens in German with subtitles) is mostly in English. It is quite visual and provides a great deal of illuminating background information about all aspects of the work and its gestation.

Violin Concerto in D, Op. 77 (CD versions)

⊕─ (B) *** Decca 475 6703 (2). Bell, Cleveland O, Dohnányi – SCHUMANN; TCHAIKOVSKY; WIENIAWSKI: Violin Concertos ***

⊕─ ✿ (M)(***) EMI mono 5 67583-2 [567584]. Milstein, Pittsburgh SO, Steinberg – BEETHOVEN: Violin Concerto (***)

⊕─ (M) *** RCA (ADD) SACD 82876 61391-2. Heifetz, Chicago SO, Reiner – BEETHOVEN: Violin Concerto ***

⊕─ (BB) *** DG Entrée 474 569-2. Mutter, BPO, Karajan – BEETHOVEN: Triple Concerto ***

*** Avie AV 2125. Zehetmair, N. Sinf. – SCHUMANN: Symphony 4 ***

*** Sony SK89649. Hahn, ASMF, Marriner – STRAVINSKY: Violin Concerto ***

(BB) (***) Dutton mono CDBP 9710. Neveu, Philh. O, Dobrowen – RAVEL: Tzigane; SUK: 4 Pieces (***)

(BB) (***) Naxos mono 8.110999. Menuhin, Lucerne Festival O, Furtwängler (with BRAHMS: Hungarian Dances, 1–3. MENDELSSOHN: Hebrides Overture; WAGNER: Siegfried Idyll (***))

Joshua Bell's commanding performance of the Brahms Violin Concerto is full of flair, demonstrating not only his love of bravura display, but also his ready gift for turning a phrase individually in a way that catches the ear, always sounding spontaneous. Full, atmospheric recording and no less outstanding couplings put this among the very finest versions. This now comes as part of a bargain-priced two-CD set which, if you want the couplings, is very recommendable indeed.

The EMI mono **Milstein–Steinberg** recording originally appeared on Capitol in Britain and was long treasured. Returning to it after many years, its stature impresses more than ever before. It is quite simply glorious: a performance of surpassing beauty, its virtuosity effortless, and with a tremendous breadth, warmth and eloquence. There is, above all, a nobility here that shines through. Milstein re-recorded it in the 1980s in Vienna with Jochum – very well, too – but this remains in a class of its own.

Like the Beethoven with which it is coupled, the SACD transfer of **Heifetz's** dazzling performance makes vivid and fresh what on LP was originally a rather harsh Chicago recording, more aggressive than the Boston sound in the Beethoven. With the CD, the excellent qualities of RCA's Chicago balance for **Reiner** come out in full, giving a fine, three-dimensional focus.

Mutter's early partnership with **Karajan** proved naturally spontaneous, and her 1981 account of the Brahms Concerto has stood the test of time. In many ways her playing combines a natural feeling with the flair and individuality of Perlman. Needless to say, Karajan's accompaniment is strong in personality and the **Berlin Philharmonic** play beautifully; the performance represents a genuine musical partnership between youthful inspiration and eager experience.

Zehetmair's is a warmly lyrical reading, which gives much pleasure. It is traditional in that he takes no liberties with tempi, but there a real Brahmsian lyricism yet no lack of individuality. The result, with a matchingly eloquent response from the **Northern Sinfonia**, places this among the most directly enjoyable versions, for the Avie recording is naturally balanced. If you want the Schumann coupling, this can certainly be recommended.

Hilary Hahn's very first entry establishes her total command, coupled with a purity and precision which make for a magnetic reading from first to last, sensitively matched by the full and incisive playing of the **Academy** under **Sir Neville Marriner**. The close balance means that Hahn is much less hushed in the slow movement, but then her urgent reading of the finale is given extra impact.

Ginette Neveu's magnificent performance now becomes one of EMI's 'Great Recordings of the Century' in its coupling with a magnetic account of the Sibelius Concerto. We are inclined to prefer the Dutton transfer of the Brahms, but that comes with music by Ravel, Suk and others, and the EMI transfer from the original 78s is very acceptable, clear and not lacking body. (4 76830-2 [4 76831-2])

Menuhin's classic 1949 account has been out many times during the last sixty years, but the present transfer by Ward Marston is arguably the finest. It comes with other 1949 recordings made in Vienna, including the poignant Siegfried Idyll.

(i) Violin Concerto; (ii) Double Concerto for Violin, Cello & Orchestra, in A min., Op. 102

(N) *** DG 477 7470. Repin, Gewandhaus O, Chailly, with (i) Mørk

**** Pentatone SACD Surround Sound PTC 5186 066. Fischer, (ii) Müller-Schott ; Netherlands PO, Kreizberg

(M) *** RCA (ADD) 82876 59410-2. Heifetz, with (i) Chicago SO, Reiner; (ii) Piatigorsky, RCA Victor SO, Wallenstein

(BB) **(*) Sony (ADD) SBK46335. Stern, (i) with Rose; Phd. O, Ormandy

Vadim Repin's Brahms Violin Concerto is spontaneously compelling, and like his account of the Beethoven concerto, admirably classical in feeling. He has first class support from **Chailly** and the **Gewandhaus Orchestra**. This comes in harness with the Double Concerto in which he is partnered by the Norwegian cellist, **Truls Mørk**, whose artistry is hardly less impressive. Like its companion, this immaculately recorded version is very impressive indeed and this DG issue is among the finest available versions of this coupling.

In the first movement of the Violin Concerto, **Fischer** takes an exceptionally expansive view, freely varying the tempo as she did in her equally outstanding version of the Tchaikovsky Violin Concerto, also for Pentatone. Fischer amply justifies her spacious and flexible speeds in the total feeling of spontaneity throughout. When it comes to the *Double Concerto*, there is a contrast of approach, with Fischer and **Müller-Schott** not nearly as expansive, though Fischer in her expressive freedom plays with an improvisatory quality that is apt for the music, and Muller-Schott matches his partner in warmth and brilliance. They choose ideal speeds for both the slow movement and the finale, relaxed and easily lyrical in the slow movement, brilliant and thrusting in the finale. Very well recorded, with excellent separation; if you have back speakers the surround sound is impressively natural.

An excellent and logical coupling of these two vintage **Heifetz** accounts for RCA's new 'Classic Library' series. The sound for both these recordings has been vastly improved in recent incarnations, and this CD certainly retains its classic status.

Stern's glorious (1959) account of the *Violin Concerto* with **Ormandy** is now given a coupling that is both generous and suitable, the mid-1960s' collaboration with **Leonard Rose** in the *Double Concerto*. The two soloists unfailingly match each other's playing, with Ormandy always an understanding accompanist. The only drawback is the characteristically forward balance of the soloists.

Double Concerto for Violin, Cello & Orchestra in A min., Op. 102

(*) EMI **DVD 490449-9. (i) D. Oistrakh, Rostropovich, Moscow PO, Kondrashin – BACH: *Double Violin Concerto*, etc.; MOZART: *Sinfonia concertante* **(*)

David Oistrakh and **Rostropovich** were recorded during the **Moscow Philharmonic's** visit to London in October 1965. It is a highly charged account which shows both artists at their most emotionally intense yet profoundly disciplined. As usual at this period, the camerawork, expertly produced by the young Brian Large, is very restrained, with a limited number of angles and the minimum of visual distraction. Of course the sound is less transparent and present than the commercial records of the period, but this DVD does convey the sense of occasion and musical excitement.

Double Concerto for Violin, Cello & Orchestra in A min. (CD Versions)

(N) (M) *** Warner Maestro 2564 69366-8 Perlman, Ma, Chicago SO, Barenboim – MENDELSSOHN: *Violin Concerto* ***

⊕ (BB) *** EMI Gemini (ADD) 381487-2 (2). D. Oistrakh, Fournier, Philh. O, Galliera – BEETHOVEN: *Triple Concerto*; MOZART: *Violin Concerto 3*; PROKOFIEV: *Violin Concerto 2* ***

⊕ (BB) (***) Naxos mono 8.110940. Heifetz, Feuermann, Phd. O, Ormandy – BRUCH: *Scottish Fantasy*; GLAZUNOV: *Violin Concerto* (***)

⊕ (M) *** RCA (ADD) **SACD** 88697 04605-2. Heifetz, Piatigorsky, RCA Victor SO, Wallenstein – J. S. BACH: *Double Violin Concerto in D min.*; MOZART: *Sinfonia concertante* ***

(N) (***) BBC Legends mono 4252-2. Menuhin, Gendron, LSO, Kertesz – BEETHOVEN: *Triple Concerto* (***)

In the live Warner recording conducted by **Barenboim**, **Perlman** in collaboration with **YoYo Ma**, is more volatile, more flexible than in his previous recording with Rostropovich and Haitink. Although in the outer movements the speeds are noticeably faster than before, Perlman and Ma are both freer, broadening more markedly in moments of repose, while the finale dances with extra lightness. Overall a very satisfying account.

The reissue as a 'Great Recording of the Century' of **David Oistrakh's** first (1959) stereo recording of the *Double Concerto* with **Fournier** has claims to be considered the most desirable of all versions, and it is joined by a splendid account of the *Tragic Overture* which opens the CD compellingly. It has been remastered and the recording is remarkably rich, yet with plenty of detail.

Recorded in December 1939 in very good sound for the period, the **Philadelphia** account of the Brahms *Double Concerto* finds **Heifetz** perfectly matched with **Emanuel Feuermann**, as near a cellist counterpart to the violin wizard as could ever be found. This is passionate as well as purposeful, if lacking a little in tenderness. The incisiveness of the playing in the most taxing bravura passages makes for exciting results. Generously coupled with Heifetz's pioneering account of the Glazunov concerto and his 1947 version of the *Scottish Fantasy*, the Naxos issue brings a first-rate transfer.

Although **Wallenstein** is not as fine an accompanist as Ormandy, he provides a sympathetic backcloth for the 1960 **Heifetz–Piatigorsky** partnership which, even if it does not quite match Heifetz's earlier version with Feuermann, is still a strong, warm-hearted account with a strikingly brilliant finale. The 1960 recording, although a bit close, has been improved out of all recognition on SACD compared to the harsh quality of the LP, and there is certainly no lack of warmth here.

Menuhin and **Gendron** are both at their peak in this fine account of the Brahms *Double Concerto* with Menuhin's intonation, as well as that of Gendron, strong and secure. Speeds are all well-chosen with the finale clean and incisive. A strong and attractive coupling vividly recorded, though only in mono.

(i) Double Concerto. Symphony 2, Op 73

(BB) **** LSO Live LSO 0043. (i) Nikolitch, Hugh; LSO, Haitink

Gordon Nikolitch and **Tim Hugh**, the soloists in **Haitink's** live **LSO** version of the *Double Concerto*, recorded at the Barbican in 2003, are taut and thrusting in the first movement, warm and flowing in the central *Andante*, and clean and incisive in the finale. The weight and warmth of the sound help to make this the finest of Haitink's Brahms series, with an equally persuasive account of the *D major Symphony*. There is no exposition repeat in the first movement, but that adds to the tautness and concentration, relaxing in an exceptionally charming account of the third movement, before a strong and steady reading of the finale, exciting yet with no headlong rush at the end.

(i) *Double Concerto in A min., Op. 102*; (ii) *Clarinet Quintet, Op. 115*

₿— **** Virgin 3 95147. (i) R. & G. Capuçon, Gustav Mahler Youth O, Myung-Whun Chung; (ii) Meyer, Capuçon Qt

Renaud and **Gautier Capuçon** are in complete accord in this impassioned and sensitive reading of Brahms's masterpiece and they receive imaginative support from **Myung-Whun Chung** and the **Gustav Mahler Youth Orchestra**. This is one of the most eloquent recent versions of the work and its attractions are enhanced by the excellence of the coupling, the pensive and autumnal *Clarinet Quintet*, marvellously played by **Paul Meyer** and the Capuçons and two colleagues. A highly satisfying disc.

Hungarian Dances 1–21 (complete)

₿— ✦ (BB) **** Naxos 8.550110; (1–2; 4–21). Budapest SO, Bogár

The **Budapest Symphony Orchestra** recording of the Brahms *Hungarian Dances* is sheer delight from beginning to end. The playing has warmth and sparkle, and the natural way in which the music unfolds brings a refreshing feeling of rhythmic freedom. **Bogár's** rubato is wholly spontaneous. The recording is warm and full yet transparent, with just the right brilliance on top. This is an outright winner among the available versions.

Hungarian Dances 1, 3, 5–6, 17–20

(M) *** DG (ADD) 447 434-2. BPO, Karajan – DVOŘÁK: *Scherzo capriccioso*, etc. **(*)

Karajan's performances have great panache and brilliance and the brightly lit (1959) recording is given added fullness in the current remastering, and the superlative orchestral playing is by turns warmly affectionate and dazzling.

Serenades 1 in D, Op. 11; 2 in A, Op. 16 – see also above

₿— ✦ *** Australian Decca Eloquence [ADD] 466 672-2. LSO, Kertész

Kertész's classic performances remain as fresh as ever. Recorded in the mid-1960s, they have an unforced spontaneity, as well as robust vigour when called for. The recording in its new transfer is full and vivid, and this remains very highly recommendable on all counts.

Serenade 1 in D, Op. 11

*** Finlandia 3984-25327-2. Royal Stockholm PO, A. Davis – STENHAMMAR: *Serenade for orchestra* *** ✦

Andrew Davis and the **Stockholm Orchestra** give a spirited account of Brahms's early masterpiece. Davis's direction is as sympathetic as the players' response. The recording is very good, even if the texture could be more transparent. However, Stenhammar's glorious *Serenade* is a logical and useful coupling, and this performance is very special.

Symphonies 1–4 (with introductions by the conductor) (DVD Version)

₿— ***(*) DG **DVD** 073 4331(2). VPO, Bernstein (Director: Humphrey Burton)

Bernstein introduces each symphony himself. He is succinct and friendly but manages to say quite a lot about each work, more about *Three* and *Four* than about the first two. All four works are played with great warmth, intensity and concentration, and of course complete spontaneity; although some may feel that in the first movement of the *Third Symphony*, marked *Allegro con brio*, Bernstein is too measured. This means that, with the exposition repeat, the movement takes nearly 16 minutes. Yet the interpretation is consistent, for tempi are broad throughout and the conclusion is especially effective at the slower tempo. The *Fourth Symphony* is spacious, but convincingly so. It opens with delectable simplicity, the *Andante* is deeply expressive in a special Bernstein way, and after the lively *Allegro giocoso* the finale has tremendous gravitas and sonority, a truly noble *Passacaglia*, with some superb brass playing. Indeed, the **Vienna Philharmonic** is on terrific form throughout. **Humphrey Burton's** video direction is as perceptive as ever, following the orchestral action but never losing sight of Bernstein, who communicates to us as well as to the orchestra.

Academic Festival Overture; Tragic Overture; Serenade 2 in A, Op. 16; Variations on a Theme of Haydn

₿— *** DG **DVD** 073 4354. VPO, Bernstein (Director: Humphrey Burton)

Symphonies 1–4 (CD Versions)

₿— (B) **** DG (ADD) Double 453 097-2 (2). BPO, Karajan

₿— (B) **(*) RCA 74321 20283-2 (2); or 74321 89102-2 (1 & 3); 74321 89101-2 (2 & 4). N. German RSO, Wand

Symphonies 1–4; Academic Festival Overture; Tragic Overture; Variations on a Theme of Haydn; (i) Alto Rhapsody

₿— (M) *** EMI (ADD) 5 62742-2 [5 627602] (3). Philh. O, Klemperer; (i) with Ludwig, Philh. Ch.

Symphonies 1–4; Academic Festival Overture; Tragic Overture; Variations on a Theme of Haydn; (i) Alto Rhapsody; Fragment from Goethe's Harz Journey in Winter; (ii) Gesang der Parzen (Song of the Fates); Nänie; Schicksalslied

₿— *** DG 435 683-2 (4). BPO, Abbado; (i) with Lipovšek, Senff Ch.; (ii) Berlin R. Ch. (also available separately with fill-ups No. 1: 431 790-2; No. 2: 427 643-2; No. 3: 429 765-2; No. 4: 435 349-2)

Symphonies 1–4; Tragic Overture; Variations on a Theme by Haydn

(***) Testament mono SBT 3167 (3). Philh. O, Toscanini

*** Telarc CD-80450 (4). SCO, Mackerras

Symphonies 1–4; Academic Festival Overture; Tragic Overture; Variations on a Theme by Haydn. (i) Alto Rhapsody; (ii) German Requiem. (i) Nänie

Ⓝ **(*) Australian Decca Eloquence (ADD) 480 0448. SRO, Ansermet with (i) Watts; (ii) SRO Choir & Lausanne Pro Art Ch

Abbado's remains the most successful of the modern, digital cycles and still makes a clear first choice, with playing at once polished and intense, glowingly recorded. The set gains from having a generous collection of imaginatively chosen couplings: the rare, brief, choral works, as well as the usual supplements in the Overtures and Variations.

Anyone wanting Karajan's readings of the four Brahms symphonies should be well satisfied with the DG Double, which offers his recordings made in the late 1970s. The current remastering makes the most of the analogue sound. The playing of the Berlin Philharmonic remains uniquely cultivated: the ensemble is finely polished yet can produce tremendous bravura at times, and there is no lack of warmth. Karajan's interpretations, with lyrical and dramatic elements finely balanced, changed little over the years. A very real bargain, hard to beat. This 1977 set also comes on three discs, including also the Tragic Overture and Variations on a theme of Haydn from 1964 (DG 477 7579), but the two-CD Double makes an obvious first choice.

Leonard Bernstein is a very visually communicative conductor: his intensity and commitment to the music project vividly. The very opening Academic Festival Overture is a joy, especially at the irresistible final climax when he can't help joining in and mouthing the words of Gaudeamus igitur with the exultant orchestra. The other works are relaxed (even the Variations) and Bernstein conveys his pleasure in the delightful lyricism of the Second Serenade. 'I was in perfectly blissful mood. I have rarely written music with such delight,' wrote Brahms to Joachim, and the Vienna Philharmonic wind players reflect that mood. The recording, made in the Musikvereinsaal, is excellent, and the cymbals at the close of the Overture cap the music splendidly.

Klemperer's 1 is unsurpassed; 2 and 3 may be a trifle austere for some tastes, but their emotional power is in no doubt. The combination of gravity and drama in 4 makes a continuing impact on almost all listeners. The Tragic Overture is done with equal strength, and the Alto Rhapsody also shows the conductor at his most masterful and, with Christa Ludwig on fine form, it is a beautifully expressive performance. The Haydn Variations is chosen to open the first disc, made in 1954, and he enters fully into the spirit of the Academic Festival Overture.

The concerts on Testament preserve the two legendary occasions in the autumn of 1952 when, in a Brahms cycle at the Royal Festival Hall, Toscanini conducted the Philharmonia Orchestra on his one visit to London after the war. The Philharmonia consistently bring a moulding of phrase and subtlety of rubato which bear out the regular Toscanini instruction to 'Sing!'. Though mono recordings made in the Royal Festival Hall are inevitably limited in range, the clarity and definition of the EMI recording quickly make one forget such limitations and the intrusive coughing. There are a couple of blips to note, which in con-

text hardly matter. The chorale on trombones just after the great horn theme in the introduction to the finale of 1 brings a series of split notes, and the finale of 4 is disturbed by firecrackers, let off by pranksters. Toscanini was completely unfazed.

Mackerras uses forces of the same size as Brahms would have had at his disposal in Meiningen. The smaller numbers remove some of the thick-textured, overweight quality that the strings can produce in Brahms, while retaining their warmth and richness. The SCO strings are often thinned out to single parts at times, and the effect is – strangely enough – enriching. The set includes the very first version of the slow movement of the First Symphony as it was originally performed at Karlsruhe and Cambridge. There are fascinating differences both in the order of the material and, at times, in the harmony. The playing is exemplary and has no lack of warmth, and the same must be said of the recording. Well worth getting.

Ansermet's Brahms is direct, straight-up-and-down, with virtually no distracting mannerisms. Indeed, this clear-sighted view of these works brings its own rewards. One is compelled by the lusty vigour as much as the sensitive pointing of detail, partly due to the recording, and partly due to Ansermet's acute sense of balance; and he never loses a grip in his readings, choosing steady tempi – never allowing the music to run away with him. Of the orchestral fill-ups, the Tragic Overture is astonishingly good – the opening on the timpani is as arresting as the performance is dramatic and intense. The Variations on a Theme by Haydn suffers from some less than exact intonation, especially from the woodwind, but the Academic Festival Overture comes off very well. Of the choral items, both Nänie and Rhapsody for Alto, Chorus and Orchestra are very good indeed. Both are sung by Helen Watts, and her sensitive account of the more famous work is excellent. The German Requiem is less successful. Here Ansermet's 'straight' approach lacks a spiritual quality, not quite made up for by the beautiful quality of the recorded sound, which throughout these four CDs is of astonishingly good quality.

Symphonies 1 in C min., 2 in D, Op. 73 (DVD versions)

Ⓝ 🎞 **** Sony DVD 88697202419. Berlin PO, Karajan

🎞 *** Arthaus DVD 101243. West German RSO, Cologne, Bychkov (V/D: Hans Hadulla)

What amazing sound Karajan draws from his wonderful orchestra! Tonally luxuriant with seamless phrasing and sheer unanimity of purpose, this partnership was peerless. Koussevitzky and Boston, Ormandy and Philadelphia were no less remarkable but even they did not have the subtlety of colour and phrasing that is encountered here. If the sonority is unique, watching Karajan mould the phrasing enhances its impact. The performances were recorded at the Philharmonie in 1986 and 87.

Bychkov never tries to make points or indulge in any interpretative idiosyncrasies. He gives us both symphonies pure and simple, shaping detail sensitively and keeping a firm grip on the flow of the music. Camerawork is unfussy and clearly directed, both in the fine and warm studio acoustic and in the intelligent documentary about the conductor that comes as a bonus.

Symphony 1 in C min., Op. 68 (DVD Version)

(N) (**(*)) EMI **DVD** 50677290. Orch Nat. de l'ORTF, Munch (with CHABRIER: *Bourrée Fantasque*; FAURÉ: *Pelléas suite*) – RAVEL: *Daphnis et Chloé Suite 2* ***

A Brahms *First* with a difference from EMI: there is no first movement! An extensive search has failed to bring to light the whole performance given in Tokyo in 1966 on a Japanese tour by the **Orchestre National de la Radio-Television Française** but the orchestra responds so wonderfully to **Munch's** inspiring and endearing direction that its appearance on DVD is to be greatly welcomed. He gets great depth of meaning and warmth from the orchestra which was on peak form at this period.

Symphony 1 in C min., Op. 68 (CD Versions)

🎜– (M) **** DG (ADD) 447 408-2. BPO, Karajan – SCHUMANN: *Symphony 1* ****

(N) *** BBC Legends BBCL 4251-2 LPO, Tennstedt – SCHUMANN: *Piano Concerto* **(*)

(N) (BB) (***) Naxos 8.111298 Concertg. O, Karajan (with BEETHOVEN: *Leonore Overture 3*; RICHARD STRAUSS: *Salome: Dance of the Seven Veils*)

Symphony 1 in C min; Academic Festival Overture; Tragic Overture

(BB) *** Naxos 8.557428. LPO, Alsop

Symphony 1; Tragic Overture; (i) Alto Rhapsody

🎜– 🌑 (M) **** EMI (ADD) 5 67029-2. Philh. O, Klemperer, (i) with Ludwig, Philh. Ch.

Klemperer's 1956–7 Kingsway Hall recording remains among the greatest performances this symphony has ever received on disc. This is Klemperer at his very finest, and his reading remains unique for its authority and power, supported by consistently superb Philharmonia playing. The sound is both clear and full-bodied. The *Alto Rhapsody* also shows him at his most masterful and **Ludwig** on fine form: it is a beautifully expressive performance.

Karajan's 1964 recording of Brahms's *First Symphony* (the conductor's third version of five seems by general consensus to be regarded as his finest. The control of tension in the first movement is masterly, the orchestral playing is of superlative quality and the result is very powerful, with the finale a fitting culmination. The remastering has restored the original, full, well-balanced, analogue sound, with plenty of weight in the bass. The coupling with Schumann's *First Symphony* makes this a very desirable record indeed.

Recorded live at the Royal Festival Hall by the BBC in May 1990, **Tennstedt's** reading of the Brahms *First Symphony* could hardly be more persuasive. He was of the school which allows a fair degree of freedom over tempo, but in this live performance speed changes are all very convincing. After the

powerful account of the first movement, the *Andante* taken at a slow speed and the third movement are warmly relaxed with radiant playing by the **LPO** strings. The performance culminates in a ripely convincing performance with glorious playing from the LPO horns. The recording is on the dry side with timpani satisfyingly prominent.

This Naxos **Concertgebouw** record documents a visit to Amsterdam by **Karajan** in September 1943 at the height of the Nazi occupation of the Netherlands. Mengelberg was still the Concertgebouw's chief conductor but Karajan's personality (his feeling for line and his lyrical intensity) comes through and leaves a strong impression. The Concertgebouw sounds very vivid for the period and the engineers get imposing results. The *Dance of the Seven Veils* comes off very well indeed in this concert, a portent of Karajan's later recording of the opera.

Marin Alsop conducts the **LPO** in a strong, thrusting performance of the *First Symphony*, very well recorded and persuasively paced. After the power of the first movement Alsop brings out the tenderness of the following *Andante* and the lyrical freedom of the third movement, before unleashing more power in the finale. Only her slowing for the two big statements of the great march theme fails to sound entirely convincing. The two overtures are just as taut and fresh. An excellent start to a projected Brahms cycle.

Symphony 2 in D, Op. 73

🎜– (M) **** Cala CACD 0531. Nat. PO, Stokowski – MENDELSSOHN: *Symphony 4* ****

(M) (***) BBC mono BBCL 4099-2. RPO, Beecham – BEETHOVEN: *Symphony 2* (***)

(***) Testament mono SBT 1015. BBC SO, Toscanini – MENDELSSOHN: *Midsummer Night's Dream*: excerpt; ROSSINI: *Semiramide: Overture* (***)

Symphony 2; Hungarian Dances 1, 3, 10, 17–21

(BB) **(*) Naxos 8.557429. LPO, Alsop

Symphony 2; (i) Alto Rhapsody

(N) *** Solo Deo Gloria SDG 703. ORR, Gardiner with (i) Stutzmann, Monteverdi Choir (with SCHUBERT: *An Schwager Kronos; Gesang der Geister über den Wassern; Gruppe aus dem Tyartarus* (all arr. BRAHMS))

Stokowski's recording of the *D major Symphony* was one of the last he made, in London in 1978. It is a performance of warmth and power and, for all his free rubato, the effect is totally spontaneous, with the symphonic structure unimpaired, first-movement exposition repeat included. The concert-hall acoustic adds richness and breadth to the sound and the reading itself grips the listener throughout; after the reprise of the second subject of the finale, the brass ring out to make a thrilling conclusion. The CD transfer is first class and, with its equally impressive Mendelssohn coupling, this is one of Stokowski's very finest later recordings.

John Eliot Gardiner, recorded live, in addition to the *Alto Rhapsody* has three Schubert items with a special relevance. The *Gesang der Geister* uses forces very similarly to the *Alto*

Rhapsody plus two motets for which Brahms did arrangements for orchestra. The **Second Symphony** comes in a powerful reading with all the attributes of a period-style account – notably little vibrato in the strings, steady speeds and a big dynamic range. Each movement is strongly characterized, with the finale leading to a thrilling coda which enters on a shattering *fortissimo*. The acoustic of the Salle Pleyel in Paris helps to intensify this impact. The *Alto Rhapsody* brings rich, creamy singing from **Natalie Stutzmann**, as does the Schubert *Gesang der Geister*. An outstanding issue, for anyone wanting period-style in Brahms – Gardiner at his most electrifying.

The radio recording of Brahms's *Second Symphony*, always a favourite work with **Beecham**, comes from an Edinburgh Festival performance given in August 1956 which has become legendary. Though the dry Usher Hall acoustic and the bronchial audience prevent it from matching in sound Beecham's stereo recording for EMI (currently withdrawn), the incandescence of the performance makes it magnetic, at once warm and impulsive in the first movement, richly expressive in the second and elegant in the third, leading to the fieriest, most biting account of the finale, with a marked *stringendo* in the coda and wild cheering from the audience before the last chord has ended. The excitement of the event is vividly caught despite the limited sound.

Toscanini's account with the **BBC Symphony Orchestra** on Testament, recorded in 1938, will come as a revelation to those who view the legendary Italian as a hard-driving, demonic maestro. Tempi are relaxed, the first movement is unhurried and the mood is sunny and smiling. There is none of the hard-driven momentum and over-drilled intensity that marked his final, NBC version. The sound calls for tolerance, but the playing is worth it.

In its glowing warmth **Marin Alsop's** Brahms *Second* makes a strong contrast with her account of the *First*. She conveys her obvious affection for the work in the way she lyricizes the lower strings, with the central movements particularly mellow. The oboe tune in the *Allegretto grazioso* is delicate (Beecham used to do it that way). But the finale brings a satisfying conclusion. The *Hungarian Dances* (in varied orchestrations) offer an attractive bonus. But there would have been room to combine this with 3.

Symphonies 2–3

᪣– ******** Pentatone Surround Sound **SACD** PTC 5186 308. Pittsburgh SO, Janowski

᪣– ******* Simax PSC 1204. Oslo PO, Jansons

᪣– (M) ******* Sony (ADD) 074646447123. Columbia SO, Walter

An outstanding coupling in every respect on Pentatone, and for those with surround sound the very fine recording is very much in the demonstration bracket. **Janowski** conducts both works with a strong yet warmly lyrical forward thrust, observing both first-movement exposition repeats, then relaxing warmly for the central movements and generating plenty of impetus in the finales, the bold recapitulation of each second subject a highlight. The playing of the **Pittsburgh Orchestra** reveals a natural feeling for Brahms

and they respond to the conductor's flexibility with impressive spontaneity. A first-class recommendation in every way.

Jansons draws incandescent playing from his **Oslo Philharmonic** in outstanding versions of both symphonies. The refinement of the playing and the subtlety of Jansons's dynamic shading go with an approach which is at once direct and refreshing, with generally steady speeds yet warmly expressive on detail. Whereas in 3 Jansons observes the exposition repeat in the first movement, in 2 he omits it, a justifiable decision when it is very much a question of proportion. These now stand among the very finest versions of both symphonies, a formidable addition to the Simax catalogue, recorded in full, well-detailed sound.

The **Bruno Walter** coupling of the *Second* and *Third Symphonies* is very recommendable indeed. Walter's performance of the *Second* is wonderfully sympathetic, with an inevitability, a rightness which makes it hard to concentrate on the interpretation as such, so cogent is the musical argument. Walter's pacing of the *Third* is admirable, and the vigour and sense of joy which imbue the opening of the first movement (exposition repeat included) dominate throughout, with the second subject eased in with wonderful naturalness.

Symphonies 2 & 4 (DVD Version)

(N) *****(*)** Medici Arts **DVD** 2072138 Boston SO, Bernstein (V/D Robert Englander)

Returning to Tanglewood in the summer of 1972 **Bernstein** had a 'particularly vivid memory of Koussevitzky' – his mentor – 'conducting Brahms' and so he made these two recordings. Both performances are warmly Brahmsian, beautifully paced and thrillingly alive. The reprise of the secondary theme in the finale of the *Second Symphony* has an unforgettable passionate warmth, and the string playing in the *Andante* of the *Fourth* is Elysian in its combination of purity and rapture. The snag is the recording. The Tanglewood acoustics do not match those of Symphony Hall, Boston and the upper strings sound relatively thin. Glorious performances nevertheless.

Symphonies 2 & 4 (CD Versions)

(N) ***(**)** Signum SIGCD 132 (2) Philh. O, Dohnányi

Dohnányi's rare coupling, although very well played, is let down by a disappointingly low-key reading of the *Second Symphony* which only fully springs to life in the surging finale. The *Fourth* is another matter, gripping in its lyrical simplicity, with a memorable closing *passacaglia*, and an excellent recording made in the Queen Elizabeth Hall.

Symphony 3 in F, Op. 90

(***) Testament mono SBT 1173. Philh. O, Cantelli – MENDELSSOHN: *Symphony 4* **(***)**

Symphony 3; Variations on a Theme by Haydn

(BB) ******* Naxos 8.557430. LPO, Alsop

Cantelli's 1955 version of Brahms's *Third*, justly famous in the mono LP era, is among the warmest, most glowing accounts ever put on disc, with **Dennis Brain's** glorious horn-playing, ripely recorded, crowning the whole incandescent performance. Sadly, in mono, it has been available only rarely in the years since 1955, making this superbly transferred reissue very welcome, particularly when the coupling is an equally unforgettable, previously unissued version of the Mendelssohn.

Marin Alsop in Brahms takes a romantic view in her expressive phrasing, well supported by the **LPO**, but then she tends to favour steady speeds, getting the best of both worlds. Indeed, tempi are perfectly chosen, with the second movement taken at a flowing *Andante*. Similar qualities extend to her fine reading of the *Haydn Variations*, well recorded, the *Symphony* in the Blackheath Concert Halls, the *Variations* in the Watford Colosseum.

Symphonies 3–4 (DVD version)

*** Arthaus Musik **DVD** 101245. West German RSO, Bychkov

Bychkov's performances have concentration, imagination and passion to commend them, along with a finely disciplined orchestral response. These are readings of some stature and can be mentioned in the same breath as the classic Karajan and Jochum sets, even if the **WDR Orchestra** is not quite in the Berlin class. The DVD also includes documentaries about Bychkov and the Cologne Orchestra.

Symphony 4 in E min., Op. 98 (DVD version)

(*) DG **DVD 073 4017. Bav. State O, Carlos Kleiber (Producer Harald Gerick) (with BEETHOVEN: *Overture Coriolan* ***) – MOZART: *Symphony 33* **(*)

Carlos Kleiber's DVD version is a performance of some distinction, even if the interpretation does not match his earlier, VPO account. In Munich in 1996, while Kleiber did not exert quite the overall grip which made his VPO CD version so memorable a decade earlier, the closing *Passacaglia* still makes an impressive and satisfying finale. The concert opens with a superbly dramatic account of Beethoven's *Coriolan Overture*; if the symphony had sustained this degree of tension, it would have been a world-beater.

Symphony 4 in E min., Op. 98 (CD versions)

☛—Ⓑ *** DG (ADD/DDD) 477 5324. VPO, Carlos Kleiber – SCHUBERT: *Symphony 8 (Unfinished)* **(*); WAGNER: *Tristan und Isolde: Act III excerpts* ***

☛— *** Simax PSC 1205. Oslo PO, Jansons – JOACHIM: *Overture: Heinrich IV* ***

*(**) BBC BBCL (ADD) 4205-2. New Philh. O, Stokowski (with KLEMPERER: *Merry Waltz*; NOVÁČEK: *Perpetuum mobile*) – RAVEL: *Rapsodie espagnole*; VAUGHAN WILLIAMS: *Tallis Fantasia* **(*)

Symphony 4 in E min.; Hungarian Dances 2; 4–9

ⒷⒷ *** Naxos 8.570233. LPO, Alsop

Carlos Kleiber's famous CD version is a performance of real stature and much strength, with the attention to detail one would expect from this great conductor. A gripping and compelling performance, at the opposite end of the scale

from Walter's coaxingly lyrical approach. DG have successfully remastered the 1981 sound, which now has more than sufficient weight in the bass and more bloom than before. The violins under pressure still sound somewhat shrill at *fortissimo*, but this adds to the edge of the performance, and there is room for the strings to expand in the *Andante*. The finale has tremendous thrust. With its generous new couplings, this carries the strongest recommendation.

Jansons with the **Oslo Philharmonic** directs a performance which underlines the contrasts between the first two movements, predominantly lyrical and reflective, and the last two, with their sharper impact. As in the rest of Jansons's Brahms series, the playing is polished and refined, the more magnetic for being recorded live. The recording beautifully captures the delicacy of the *pianissimo* playing of the strings, while offering ample warmth and power in the last two movements. The Joachim overture, *Heinrich IV*, finer than the earlier *Hamlet Overture*, makes an apt if not very generous bonus, when it was so admired by Brahms.

Recorded in vivid sound in the Blackheath Concert Hall, with vivid separation heightening the impact of **Marin Alsop's** clear and direct interpretation, this stands high among recent recordings of the *Fourth Symphony*, if not perhaps a first choice. However, the bonus *Hungarian Dances* come in new arrangements by Peter Breiner that are very successful indeed.

One only has to hear the glowing strings to know that **Stokowski's** magic is in operation in this 1974 performance. This account is thrusting yet totally unforced, and with the tension maintained throughout. The sound is more than acceptable for a live Royal Albert Hall performance. Klemperer's *Merry Waltz* is captivating (and very merry here indeed!) and the rare *Perpetuum mobile* of Nováček makes a brilliant and entertaining bonus.

(i) Variations on a Theme of Haydn; (ii) Variations & Fugue on a Theme by Handel, Op. 24 (arr. Rubbra)

*** Australian Decca Eloquence (ADD/DDD) 467 608-2. (i) VPO, Kertész; (ii) Cleveland O, Ashkenazy – DVOŘÁK: *Symphonic Variations* ***

Rubbra's orchestration of the *Handel Variations* with a vivid orchestral palette becomes ever more imaginative as it goes along; all 25 variations are a delight. **Ashkenazy's** performance is superb and the digital recording excellent. The more familiar *Haydn Variations* is warmly recorded and receives a strongly affecting performance under István Kertész.

COMPLETE CHAMBER MUSIC

(i) *Cello Sonatas 1–2*; (ii; iii) *Clarinet Trio, Op. 114*; (iv; v) *Clarinet Quintet, Op. 115*; (iv; v) *Clarinet Sonatas 1–2, Op. 120/1–2*; (vi) *Piano Quartets 1–3*; (vii; viii) *Piano Quintet, Op. 34*; (iii; ix) *Horn Trio, Op. 40*; (iii) *Piano Trios 1–3*; (viii) *String Quartets 1–3*; (x) *String Quintets 1–2*; *String Sextets 1–2*; (xi) *Viola Sonatas 1–2, Op. 120/1–2*; (xii) *Violin Sonatas 1–3*; (xiii) *F. A. E. Sonata: Scherzo*

Ⓝ ⒝⒝ *** Hyp. CDS 44331/42 (12) (i) Isserlis, Evans; (ii) Hosford; (iii) Florestan Trio; (iv) Thea King; (v) Gabrieli Qt; (v) Benson; (vi) Hamelin, Leopold String Trio; (vii) Lane; (viii) New Budapest Qt.; (ix) Stirling; (x) Rafael Ens.; (xi) Power, Crawford-Phillips; (xii) Osostowicz, Tomez; (xiii) with Crawford-Phillips (piano) instead of Tomez

Most of these performances have been praised by us over the years with the contributions of **Isserlis**, the **Florestan Trio**, the **Rafael Ensemble**, **Osostowiz** and **Tomez** standing out. A high recording standard throughout ensures that this set can be strongly recommended.

Cello Sonata 1 in E min., Op. 38

(***) Testament mono SBT 2158. Piatigorsky, Rubinstein – BEETHOVEN: *Cello Sonatas*; WEBER: *Sonata in A* (***)

Piatigorsky's patrician account of the *E minor Sonata* with **Artur Rubinstein** was recorded in Paris in the summer of 1936. It has been out of the catalogue for nearly half a century, and Testament has put matters right with this exemplary transfer.

Cello Sonatas 1 in E min., Op. 38; 2 in F, Op. 99

🎧 **** DG 410 510-2. Rostropovich, Serkin

🎧 *** Hyp. CDA 67529. Isserlis, Hough (with DVOŘÁK: *Waldesruhe; Rondo in G min.*; SUK: *Ballade in D min.; Serenade in A, Op. 3/2* (****))

🎧 *** Channel CCS 5493. Wispelwey, Komen

The partnership of the wild, inspirational Russian cellist and the veteran Brahmsian, **Serkin**, on DG is a challenging one. It proves an outstanding success, with inspiration mutually enhanced, whether in the lyricism of Op. 38 or the heroic energy of Op. 99. Good if close recording.

Steven Isserlis's impassioned yet aristocratic accounts are made in a fine partnership with **Stephen Hough**. This is natural playing, truthful and unadorned, which belongs among the finest. The two *Sonatas* are separated by some elegantly played Dvořák and Suk miniatures which are a real bonus.

The Dutch partnership, **Pieter Wispelwey** and **Paul Komen**, offers something rather different. The cellist plays a 19th-century Bohemian cello and the pianist a Viennese period-instrument: thus theirs is the only version of the sonatas to approximate to the sound Brahms himself might have heard. There is nothing anaemic or academic about their playing, and no sense of scholarly inhibition. These are full-blooded performances, vivid in feeling and passionate, at no time wanting in eloquence.

Clarinet Quintet in B min., Op. 115

🎧 *** DG 459 641-2. Shifrin, Emerson Qt – MOZART: *Clarinet Quintet* ***

🎧 ⒝⒝ *** Warner Apex 0927 44350-2. Leister, Berlin Soloists – MOZART: *Clarinet Quintet* ***

(***) Testament mono SBT 1381. B. Walton, L. Music Group – MOZART: *Clarinet Concerto* ***

(i) Clarinet Quintet; (ii) Clarinet Sonata 2

Ⓜ *** Chan. 6522. Hilton, (i) Lindsay Qt; (ii) Frankl

(i) Clarinet Quintet; (ii) Clarinet Trio in A min.

🎧 *** Hyp. CDA 66107. King, (i) Gabrieli Qt; (ii) Georgian, Benson (piano)

*** MDG 307 079-2. (i) Leister; Leipzig Qt

(i) Clarinet Quintet; (ii) String Quintet 2 in G, Op. 111

Ⓑ *** HM HMA 1951349. (i) Portal; (ii) Caussé; Melos Qt

David Shifrin's recording of the Brahms *Quintet* is outstandingly fine. He establishes a natural partnership with the **Emersons**; the outer movements, while warmly lyrical, are much more characterful and positive than in his earlier version. Yet the *Adagio* achieves a gentle, ruminative, almost improvisational quality. The recording is admirably balanced and the equally recommendable Mozart coupling has an appealing simplicity.

Thea King and the **Gabrieli Quartet** give a radiantly beautiful performance of the *Clarinet Quintet*, as fine as any put on record, expressive and spontaneous-sounding, with natural ebb and flow of tension as in a live performance. The recording of the strings is on the bright side, very vivid and real.

On Apex, **Karl Leister's** easy-going lyricism does not mean that there is not a firm overall grip on the proceedings, yet in the Elysian slow movement he seems to be tenderly and thoughtfully improvising, and his relaxed warmth is captivating. His supporting **Berlin Soloists** match his playing serenely and they are well balanced and beautifully recorded. A lovely performance, well matched by the Mozart coupling – and this CD is very inexpensive.

Leister's later performance with the **Leipzig Quartet** is second to none. The quartet and its distinguished soloist produce impressive results in what is surely Brahms's most serene utterance, and the *A minor Quartet* also receives an authoritative and musical performance. For those wanting this particular coupling, this disc can certainly be recommended.

Janet Hilton's essentially mellow performance of the *Clarinet Quintet*, with the **Lindsay Quartet** playing with pleasing warmth and refinement, has a distinct individuality. Her lilting syncopations in the third movement are delightful. Hilton's partnership with **Peter Frankl** in the *E flat Clarinet Sonata* is rather less idiosyncratic and individual; nevertheless, this performance offers considerable artistic rewards.

The warm resonance of the recording gives an almost orchestral richness of timbre to the **Melos group**, joined by **Gérard Caussé**, yet they open the *Adagio* of Op. 111 (which comes first on the disc) with an exquisite delicacy of texture and feeling. The sound in the *Clarinet Quintet* is equally beguiling and **Michel Portal** matches the strings with his gently luscious tone in the *Clarinet Quintet*, with the beautiful slow movement dreamily ruminative and the theme-and-variations finale hardly less delightful. This coupling is highly recommendable in all respects.

Bernard Walton's account of the *Quintet* is one of the most thoughtful and deeply felt in the catalogue. It emanates from a BBC studio broadcast that was repeated in the year of this artist's death and is a poignant reminder of his stature.

Clarinet Sonatas 1 in F min.; 2 in E flat, Op. 120/1–2

⊕— **** Chan. 8563. de Peyer, Pryor

⊕— (BB) *** EMI Encore 3 55674-2. de Peyer, Barenboim – BEETHOVEN: *Clarinet Trio* ***

Superb performances from **Gervase de Peyer** and **Gwenneth Pryor** on Chandos, commanding, aristocratic, warm and full of subtleties of colour and detail, but the earlier EMI versions are eminently satisfying performances which stand up well against the competition, especially at bargain price. The 1967 recordings are particularly good and the Beethoven *Clarinet Trio* is added as a splendid bonus.

Clarinet Sonatas 1–2; (i) Clarinet Trio in A min. Op. 114

*** BIS CD/**SACD** 1353. Fröst, Pöntinen, (i) with Torleif Thedéen.

The young Swedish clarinettist **Martin Fröst** in the *Trio* tends to favour speeds on the fast side so that the dramatic bite and purposeful thrust of the outer movements are enhanced. Though the cellist **Torleif Thedéen** matches the impressive tonal range of Fröst, the pianist **Roland Pöntinen** is more recessive, largely a question of the recording balance. The backward balance for the piano is even more noticeable in the two sonatas, but Fröst's dedicated playing makes the performances magnetic and the recorded sound is wonderfully lifelike and natural.

(i) Clarinet Sonatas 1–2; (ii) String Quartets 1–3

(B) *** Ph. (ADD) Duo 456 320-2 (2). (i) Pieterson, H. Menuhin; (ii) Italian Qt

The *Clarinet Sonatas* are very well played by **George Pieterson** and **Hephzibah Menuhin**, with plenty of light and shade. Vivid recording from 1980 adds to the feeling of boldness. The three *String Quartets* are marvellously played by the **Quartetto Italiano**, and the CD transfers are admirably truthful in timbre and balance.

(i) Clarinet Trio, Op. 114; (ii) Horn Trio, Op. 40

(BB) *** Warner Apex 2564 61792-2. (i) Portal; Lodeon; (i; ii) Dalberto; (ii) Del Vescovo, Amoyal

A persuasively warm performance of the *Clarinet Trio* from **Michel Portal**, whose tone is rich and succulent, **Frédéric Lodeon** and **Michel Dalberto**, recorded in a suitably resonant, Brahmsian acoustic. It is joined to an equally fine – if not even finer – account of the *Horn Trio* from the full-timbred **Pierre Del Vescovo**, a first-class horn player, and the ever-sensitive **Pierre Amoyal**. The recording, again in a warm acoustic, is even more vivid and clear. A first-class bargain, if you want both works.

(i) Clarinet Trio; (ii) Horn Trio. Piano Trios 1–3

⊕— **** Hyp. CDA 67251/2. Florestan Trio, with (i) Hosford; (ii) Stirling

(i) Clarinet Trio; (ii) Horn Trio; (iii) Piano Trios 1–4

⊕— (B) *** Ph. (ADD) Duo 438 365-2 (2). (i) Pieterson; (ii) Orval, Grumiaux, Sebök; (i; iii) Beaux Arts Trio

The **Florestan** set is among the finest since the Beaux Arts' comparable grouping, in terms of both performance and recording. There is a freshness and spontaneity that rekindles one's own enthusiasm for this music, and such is its dedication that one is left marvelling at the richness and quality of Brahms's inventive resource. The same must be said of the *Horn Trio* and the late *A minor Clarinet Trio*. The recorded sound is very natural and lifelike and brings the players into your living room.

George Pieterson is a first-rate artist and his account of the *Clarinet Trio* with members of the **Beaux Arts** group offers masterly playing from all three participants. The balance in the *Horn Trio* is perhaps the most successful on record. The fine horn player, **Francis Orval**, achieves this without any loss of personality in his playing. As for the *Piano Trios*, the performances are splendid, with strongly paced, dramatic *allegros*, consistently alert and thoughtful, and with sensitive playing in slow movements. The sound is first class. The CD transfer has brightened the top a little, but not excessively.

Horn Trio in E flat, Op. 40 (see also above)

⊕— (BB) *** Naxos 8.557471. W. Tomboeck, Inui, J. Tomboeck – BEETHOVEN: *Horn Sonata*; SCHUBERT: *Auf dem Strom*; SCHUMANN: *Adagio and Allegro in A flat* ***

(N) *** Tudor TUDOR 771 Tuckwell, Langbein, M. Jones (with BANKS: *Horn Trio*; KOECHLIN: *4 Petites Pièces* ***)

Wolfgang Tomboeck, first horn in the Vienna Philharmonic since 1980, here in all four works demonstrates what a fine artist he is, producing the ripest tones on the Vienna horn. The galloping rhythms of the second and fourth movements of the Brahms have an infectious brilliance and swagger. With Tomboeck's son, **Johannes**, playing the violin, they have a lift and energy to make some rival versions seem cool, while the *Andante* first movement is warm and relaxed, freely expressive in a very Viennese way.

Barry Tuckwell's new Tudor recording of the Brahms *Horn Trio* now replaces his earlier 1968 version with Perlman and Ashkenazy (Decca 475 8246) which, fine as it is, is let down by the poorly focused ADD transfer to CD. The new performance is equally fine, very realistically recorded and balanced in an ideal acoustic. The Banks *Trio* is a serial work of some distinction, if not melodically memorable; but it could not be better played, and the *Four Pieces* of Koechlin are quite delightful – a real find.

(i) Horn Trio in E flat; (ii) Piano Quintet in F min., Op. 34

(M) *** CRD 3489. Nash Ens. (members); (i) Lloyd; (ii) Brown

The **Nash Ensemble's** playing is refreshingly unforced, with the *Quintet* underpinned firmly by the incisive playing of the pianist, **Ian Brown**. In the *Horn Trio* **Frank Lloyd** produces an exceptionally rich tone and helps the group to give a raptly beautiful account of the *Adagio*; the galloping finale is then performed with joyful panache. Tempos are well chosen and there is great naturalness of phrasing. These players convey the sense of music-making in the home rather than the concert hall, and they have lively, faithfully recorded sound in their favour.

(i-iii) *Horn Trio in E flat; (ii-iii) Violin Sonata 1, Op. 78; (iii) 7 Fantasias, Op.116*

(N) ⌐ **** HMI HMC 90 1981 (i) van der Zwart; (ii) Faust; (iii) Melnikov

Brahms specifically requested that his *Horn Trio* be played using a natural Waldhorn without valves, and here for the first time we have an inspired performance in which **Teunis van der Zwart** uses a natural horn from Lorenz, built in 1845. The result is a triumph. It is superbly played by all concerned and the highly individual horn timbre is very telling throughout the register. This is a key performance if ever there was one, and the lovely *G major Violin Sonata* is also played with much warmth by **Isabelle Faust**. **Alexander Melnikov** is a fine partner, although the piano is rather more forwardly balanced than in the *Horn Trio* and this adds a touch of hardness to the timbre both in the *Sonata* and *Fantasias* which are also very enjoyable.

(i) *Piano Quartets 1–3. Piano Trio in A, Op. posth.*

⌐ (B) *** Ph. (ADD) Duo 454 017-2 (2). Beaux Arts Trio, (i) with Trampler

The **Beaux Arts** set of *Piano Quartets* is self-recommending at Duo price, with the *A major Piano Trio* thrown in as a bonus. Thoughtful, sensitive playing in slow movements, lively tempi in *allegros*, characteristic musicianship plus spontaneity combine to make these recordings highly recommendable throughout.

Piano Quartets 1 in G min., Op. 25; 2 in A, Op. 26; 3 C min., Op. 60

(N) (B) *** Virgin Classics 519320 (2). Renaud & Gautier Capuçon, Caussé, Angelich

The **Capuçons** enjoy the support and patronage of Martha Argerich and their set of the *Brahms Piano Quartets* with the violist **Gérard Caussé** and the pianist **Nicholas Angelich** more than rewards her judgement. These are fresh and interesting performances that hold the listener from first to last, and generate enthusiasm for this magnificent repertoire. However unlike the Beaux Arts they do not include the Op. posth. Piano trio.

Piano Quartets 1 in G min., Op. 25; 3 C min., Op. 60

(N) *** Onyx Classics ONYX4029. Nash Ens

(N) *** Marquis 81377 Xiayin Wang, Amity Players

The discs from the **Nash** and **Amity Players** are recommendable with the considerable proviso that they both omit the *Second A major Quartet*. The Nash certainly give magisterial

accounts of the other two and are accorded sound of comparable quality. Their musicianship and fine sense of colour are much in evidence. Indeed these belong among the very best versions in the catalogue.

An outstanding coupling too from the Canadian Amity Players. Their pianist, **Xiayin Wang**, although standing out in the virtuosity of the Hungarian finale of *No. 1* (and elsewhere), proves a highly musical partner, well integrated into the ensemble. Both performances have a fluent spontaneity, and an enjoyable Brahmsian impetus, but *No. 3* is particularly successful in its warmth and vividness, with a truly memorable *Andante*. Excellent recording. (The CD is available via www.marquisclassics.com).

(i) *Piano Quartet 1. 4 Ballades, Op. 10*

(M) **(*) DG (ADD) 447 407-2. Gilels, (i) with Amadeus Qt

Gilels is in impressive form, and most listeners will respond to the withdrawn delicacy of the Scherzo and the gypsy fire of the finale. The slow movement is perhaps somewhat wanting in ardour, and the **Amadeus** do not sound as committed or as fresh as their keyboard partner. The DG recording is well balanced and sounds very natural in its new transfer. Moreover, in the *Ballades* Gilels offers artistry of an order that silences criticism.

Piano Quintet in F min., Op. 34

**** Virgin Classics 3 951413-2. Andsnes, Artemis Qt – SCHUMANN: *Piano Quintet* ****

⌐ *** BBC (ADD) BBCL 4009-2 (2). Curzon, Amadeus Qt – SCHUBERT: *Trout Quintet* ***

⌐ (M) *** MDG 307 1218-2. Staier (early piano), Leipzig Qt

(BB) *** Naxos 8.550406. Jandó, Kodály Qt – SCHUMANN: *Piano Quintet* ***

A magisterial and compelling account of this great work from **Andsnes** and the **Artemis Quartet** that is unlikely to be surpassed. A very natural and vivid recording. A first recommendation.

Clifford Curzon is captured at his most spontaneously expressive in his live performance, recorded at the Royal Festival Hall in 1974. Similarly the **Amadeus Quartet** are at their most compelling. Ensemble may not be quite as polished as in a studio performance, but the warmth and power are ample compensation, and the bonus disc of Schubert's *Trout Quintet* makes a very attractive package.

The **Leipzig Quartet** has an almost unrivalled reputation in the Viennese classical repertoire, and **Andreas Staier** is unfailingly illuminating and sensitive. He plays a 1901 Steinway which is much lighter in colour and body than the modern concert grand. This version demands to be heard and, though there is no fill-up, it is competitively positioned at mid-price and deserves a strong recommendation. Natural recorded sound.

The fine Naxos account has a great deal going for it, even though it does not include the first-movement exposition repeat. The playing is boldly spontaneous and has plenty of fire and expressive feeling. The opening of the finale also has mystery; overall, with full-bodied recording and plenty of presence, this makes a strong impression. It is certainly a bargain.

(i) Piano Quintet in F min., Op. 34. String Quartets 1–3

*** DG 477 6458 (2). Emerson Qt, (i) with Fleisher

Ⓝ **(*) HM 198 7074/5 (i) Mehner; Casals Qt

We have sometimes complained that the **Emerson Quartet**, for all the precision and technical finish of their playing, sometimes seem to concentrate on virtuosity and projection rather than seeking the music's inner core. However, that is not so with their Brahms recordings. Perhaps **Leon Fleisher** has had an influence in the *Piano Quintet* for, apart from the sparkling brilliance of the Scherzo, the performance is relatively intimate. The *String Quartets* are marvellously polished, but have delicacy and deeper feeling too, with *No. 3, Op. 67*, outstandingly fine. The recording is clear and present and the set is certainly recommendable on its own terms.

The **Casals Quartet** play with an appealing combination of warmth and refinement, playing which is never heavy-handed, and this is carried through into their account of the *Piano Quintet* where they are joined by **Claudio Mehner**, who is an impressive Brahmsian. They are very well recorded. Not a first choice, perhaps, but an enjoyable one.

(i) Piano Quintet in F min., Op. 34. String Quartet 2 in A min., Op. 51/2

**** Hyp. CDA 67551. Takács Qt, (i) with Hough

We really are spoilt for choice in this repertoire: **Stephen Hough** and the **Takács** are hardly less impressive than Andsnes and the Artemis. They give a superb performance of the *Quintet*, beautifully balanced, with the piano not too far forward. The first movement is powerfully presented, with Stephen Hough playing magnetically, and with the slow movement taken steadily. Those wanting the glorious *A minor Quartet* rather than the Schumann need not hesitate, and the recorded quality is extremely fine.

Piano Trio 1, Op. 8

*** Daphne DAPHNE 1026. Trio Poseidon – HAYDN: *Piano Trio 32*; IRELAND: *Phantasie* ***

Formed in 2002, the **Trio Poseidon** make an excellent, responsive team, modifying their playing to suit the varying needs of these three very different composers. The Brahms brings warmth and passion in the playing, with no hint at all of self-indulgence and with each player responding to the others' individual phrasing. Above all, one relishes the way that Brahms in this early work (which he revised late in life) creates one superb theme after another, with the second-movement Scherzo rather like a witty dance of death and the third-movement *Adagio* played with totally sustained concentration, and the finale surging infectiously onwards.

Piano Trios 1 in B, Op. 8; 2 in C, Op. 87; 3 in C min., Op. 101; 4 in A, Op. posth.

Ⓝ Ⓑ *** Decca 478 0338 (2) Beaux Arts Trio

🔗 ⒷⒷ *** Warner Apex 2564 61259-2 (1 & 2); 2564 61690-2 (3 & 4). Trio Fontenay

🔗 Ⓑ *** Double Decca (ADD) 448 092-2 (2). Katchen, with (i–ii) Starker; (i; iii) Suk (with *Cello Sonata 2*; *F.A.E. Sonata: Scherzo*)

The digital recordings by the **Beaux Arts Trio** of the Brahms *Piano Trios* brought the group onto the Decca label, and they bring us close to the artists. The playing is always highly vital and sensitive. There is splendid, finely projected sense of line and the delicate, sensitive playing of **Menahem Pressler** is always a delight. Now the disc returns to the catalogue as one of the Originals.

Powerful, spontaneous playing with a real Brahmsian spirit, given excellent, modern recording, puts these admirable performances by the **Trio Fontenay** (now at budget price) at the top of the list.

The **Katchen/Suk/Starker** performances of the first two *Piano Trios* are warm, strong and characterful, while the tough *C minor Trio* and the epic, thrustful *Cello Sonata* bring a comparably spontaneous response. If the sound of the CD transfers is a little limited in the upper range, the ear is grateful that no artificial brightening has been applied, for it provides a real Brahmsian amplitude which is very satisfying. Highly recommended.

Piano Trio 3 in C min., Op. 101

Ⓝ **(*) DUX 0626. Trio Cracovia – BEETHOVEN: *Piano Trio Op 1/3* **(*); RACHMANINOV: *Piano Trio in G min, (Elégiaque)* **(*)

Brahms's *C minor Trio Op. 101* is the most compact of those he wrote with sharply memorable thematic material, and received a decent enough performance here, though the relative weakness of the cello is a slight drawback.

String Quartets 1 in C min.; 2 in A min., Op. 51/1–2; 3 in B flat, Op. 67 (see also under Clarinet Sonatas)

🔗 Ⓑ *** Teldec (ADD) 4509 95503-2 (2). Alban Berg Qt (with DVOŘÁK: *String Quartet 13* ***)

🔗 *** EMI 7 54829-2 (2). Alban Berg Qt

String Quartets 1–3; (i) Piano Quintet in F min., Op. 34

🔗 Ⓜ *** Hyp. Dyad CDD 22018 (2). (i) Lane; New Budapest Qt

The analogue Teldec **Alban Berg** performances were made in the mid-1970s when the quartet was on peak form, highly polished yet completely fresh in their musical responses. This set is strongly recommended and can stand alongside the best in the catalogue, even if the Dvořák coupling is not quite as fine as the Brahms.

The **New Budapest Quartet** bring warmth and spontaneity to all three scores, responding to their dramatic fervour and lyrical flow in equal measure. Their intonation is altogether impeccable and they are scrupulously attentive to Brahms's dynamic markings, with pleasing results in terms of clarity and transparency. They also offer an excellently shaped and musicianly account of the *F minor Piano Quintet*, with responsive playing from **Piers Lane**.

On EMI, the performances have all the finesse and attack one expects from the **Alban Berg Quartet**, along with impeccable technical address. The *A minor* has just the right kind of dramatic intensity and the range of colour and dynamics they produce in all three works is impressive. The EMI engineers produced well-detailed, truthful sound. These are all performances of quality and can be recommended even to those who find this ensemble at times a little too glossy.

String Quartets 1–2

*** Chan. 8562. Gabrieli Qt

(BB) *** Naxos 8.554271. Ludwig Qt

Richly recorded in an agreeably expansive ambience, the **Gabrielis** give warm, eloquent performances of both the Op. 51 *Quartets*, deeply felt and full-textured without being heavy; the *Romanze* of Op. 51, No. 1, is delightfully songful. There are both tenderness and subtlety here, and the sound is first class.

The Naxos issue is an eminently satisfactory bargain. Indeed, it provides more musical pleasure than one might find from more celebrated ensembles, and the recording has good presence and is well balanced.

String Quartet 1, Op. 51/1; (i) String Quintet 2, Op. 111

(N) (B) **(*) EMI 2 35712-2 Belcea Qt (i) with Kakushka

The approach of the **Belcea Quartet** to the Brahms *C minor Quartet* is less urgent and dramatic than many ensembles: the players' ruminations are gentler, they find both a sense of mystery and a Schubertian grace in its course, and they are consistently imaginative in their approach. In the *G minor Quintet* they are joined by **Thomas Kakushka** (their mentor) and they produce a finely shaped, well thought-out and often searching account of the piece. Not perhaps a first recommendation, for there is a touch of self-consciousness about the music-making, but both performances are individual and illuminating. Good recorded sound.

String Quartet 1, Op. 51/1; (i) String Sextet 2 in G, Op. 36

*** MDG 307 1261-2. Leipzig Qt, (i) with Rohde, Peter Bruns

This **Leipzig Quartet** playing is wonderfully civilized and musicianly, and completely free of superficial gloss. The sound that MDG give them is as faithful a recording as we have come to expect from this source.

String Quintets 1 in F, Op. 88; 2 in G, Op. 111

θ⌐ *** Hyp. CDA 66804. Raphael Ens.

θ⌐ *** MDG 307 1251-2. Leipzig Qt, Rohde

θ⌐ *** DG 453 420-2. Hagen Qt, Caussé

With the *First Quintet* opening seductively, these are fine, vital performances of both works from the **Raphael Ensemble**. Indeed, these performances are on the same level of distinction as their accounts of the *String Sextets* and, like that companion Hyperion disc, the recording is

very present indeed, which to some ears may seem a minor drawback.

The **Leipzig Quartet** and the violist **Hartmut Rohde** give warm and musicianly accounts of these masterpieces. This is music-making in the old style, selfless and totally dedicated. Our first choice in these *Quintets* has been members of the Raphael Ensemble on Hyperion, but this splendidly recorded version makes an excellent alternative.

The **Hagen Quartet** and **Gérard Caussé** also give highly enjoyable accounts of the two *Quintets*, and the DG engineers give them good recorded sound. No need to say more than that it can also rank alongside the Raphael Ensemble on Hyperion.

String Quintet 2 in G, Op. 111

*** Naim CD 010. Augmented Allegri Qt – BRUCH: *String Quintet* ***

*** Nim. NI 5488. Brandis Qt, with Dean – BRUCKNER: *String Quintet* ***

The second of the two string quintets makes the ideal coupling for the long-buried Bruch *Quintet*, which was also the product of old age. Very well played and recorded by the **Allegri**.

The **Brandis** version of the *G major Quintet* offers good value in being coupled with Bruckner's *F major Quintet*. The Brandis are a fine quartet and they give a warm and sympathetic account of this lovely work; the Nimbus recording is natural and lifelike.

String Sextets 1 in B flat, Op. 18; 2 in G, Op. 36

θ⌐ **** Hyp. CDA 66276. Raphael Ens.

**** Onyx ONYX 4019. Nash Ens.

θ⌐ *** Chan. 9151. ASMF Chamber Ens.

*** ASV GLD 4016. Williams, Watkins, Lindsay Qt

*** Cal. CAL9369. Talich Qt, with Kluson, Kânka

The *Sextets* are among Brahms's most immediately appealing chamber works. The **Raphael Ensemble** are fully responsive to all their subtleties as well as to their vitality and warmth. In short, these are superb performances; the recording is very vivid and immediate, although some ears might find it a shade too present.

The **Nash Ensemble** – with a particularly strong line-up of violas and cellos (**Lawrence Power** and **Phillip Dukes** violas, **Paul Watkins** and **Tim Hugh** cellos) – offers superb new versions, crisp and clear, beautifully coordinated, with plenty of light and shade and infectious springing of rhythms. Try the delectable third movement Scherzo of No. 1, beautifully and wittily sprung, one of the gems of Brahms's chamber music.

Eminently enjoyable accounts of these masterpieces come from the **Lindsays** with **Louise Williams** and **Paul Watkins** as second viola and cello, recorded in 2004. They make a more than acceptable alternative to the Raphael Ensemble on Hyperion and can be recommended alongside (though not in preference to) them.

The augmented **Talich** group offer eloquent performances that will give pleasure. They too can be recommended alongside the Raphael Ensemble on Hyperion, though not in preference to them.

The Chandos alternative is also highly recommendable, with both *Sextets* again accommodated on one CD without sacrificing the exposition repeats, so that at almost 78 minutes the **Academy of St Martin-in-the-Fields** offer excellent value for money. Moreover, these well-prepared and musical performances are perceptive and intelligent, and they receive finely detailed and present recording.

Viola Sonatas 1–2; Violin Sonatas 1–3; F.A.E. Sonata: Scherzo

⏁– Ⓜ *** Avie AV 2057 (2). Mintz, Golan

Ⓑ *** DG Double (ADD) 453 121-2 (2). Zukerman, Barenboim

Shlomo Mintz and **Itamar Golan** give highly spontaneous performances of all five sonatas, with Mintz obviously equally at home on violin and viola, but creating a different sound-world for each instrument. At times there is a richly ruminative quality in the *Violin Sonatas* which is very special, and slow movements are most beautifully played, by violinist and pianist alike. These performances have a natural Brahmsian warmth that is second to none. The *F.A.E. Scherzo* makes a vibrant postlude and, throughout, the recording is of the highest quality.

The **Zukerman–Barenboim** performances of the *Viola Sonatas* may be a little sweet for some tastes, but they are easy to enjoy, with the expressiveness never sounding contrived, always buoyant. In the *Violin Sonatas*, they produce songful, spontaneous-sounding performances that catch the inspiration of the moment. The sound itself is very natural, with good presence. The lively *Scherzo in C minor* from the *F.A.E. Sonata* is thrown in for good measure.

Viola Sonatas 1–2; (i) Trio in A min.

*** Hyp. CDA 67584. Power, Crawford-Phillips, (i) with Hugh

Lawrence Power is one of the most gifted players of his generation and proves a persuasive advocate in these wonderful examples of late Brahms. There is a concentration and feeling here, and readers who want these pieces in the viola rather than the clarinet version can turn to this finely balanced recording with confidence.

Violin Sonatas 1 in G, Op. 78; 2 in A, Op. 100; 3 in D min., Op. 108

⏁– ⓑⓑ **** Hyp. Helios CDH 55087. Osostowicz, Tomes

Ⓝ Ⓜ *** EMI 2 35717 Kyung-Wha Chung, Peter Frankl

⏁– Ⓜ *** EMI 5 66893-2. Perlman, Ashkenazy

Krysia Osostowicz and **Susan Tomes** give performances of such natural musicality that criticism is almost disarmed. They phrase with great spontaneity yet with apparently effortless care and artistry, and the interplay between the two partners is instinctive. The Hyperion engineers manage the sound and balance with their customary skill, and theirs is certainly to be preferred to some of the more glamorous rivals now on the market. At its new bargain

Helios price this goes straight to the top of the recommended list.

Kyung-Wha Chung and **Peter Frankl** offer all three sonatas at a very competitive price. Their performances can hold their own with the best. They were recorded in 1995 by the late lamented Christopher Raeburn, obviously after he had retired from Decca, and musically and as recorded sound they are distinguished.

Perlman and **Ashkenazy** bring out the trouble-free happiness of these lyrical inspirations, fully involved yet avoiding underlying tensions. In their sureness and flawless confidence at generally spacious speeds, these are performances which carry you along, cocooned in rich sound.

Violin Sonatas 1 in G, Op. 78; 3 in D min., Op. 108

ⓑⓑ (***) Naxos (mono) 8.119771. Yehudi & Hephzibah Menuhin – SCHUMANN: *Sonata 2* (***)

The **Menuhins** recorded the *G major Sonata* in Australia in 1940 and it radiates the serenity and happiness that the two artists were experiencing then. The *D minor* was from 1936 and was recorded in London. Spontaneous and lyrical playing that continues to astonish. Impeccable transfers and sound restoration from Ward Marston.

Violin Sonatas (i) 2; (ii) 3

Ⓜ *** Warner Elatus 2564 60661-2. Vengerov, (i) Markovich; (ii) Barenboim – ELGAR: *Violin Sonata* ***

Vengerov's partnership with **Alexander Markovich** works admirably. They both catch the *amabile* of the *A major Sonata*. Yet there is an underlying vitality, and Vengerov rises to the climaxes. The account of the *D minor Sonata* is also very fine, with **Barenboim** at the piano also freely spontaneous. Excellent recording and the coupled performance of the Elgar is passionately convincing.

PIANO MUSIC

Piano music for four hands

(i) 21 Hungarian Dances (original version); (ii) 16 Waltzes, Op. 39. Solo Piano: 4 Ballades, Op. 10; 7 Fantasias, Op. 116; 3 Intermezzi, Op. 117; 8 Pieces, Op. 76; 6 Pieces, Op. 118; 4 Pieces, Op. 119; 2 Rhapsodies, Op. 79; Sonata 3 in F min., Op. 5; 16 Waltzes, Op. 39; Variations & Fugue on a Theme by Handel, Op. 24; Variations on a Theme by Schumann, Op. 9; 16 Waltzes, Op. 39

⏁– ✦ ⓑⓑ **** Regis Vox CD5X 3612 (5). Walter Klien, with (i) Brendel; (ii) Beatriz Klien

As a Brahms pianist, **Walter Klien** is in the front rank and his recordings can be discussed in the same breath as those of Katchen and Kempff, although his style is nearer to that of the latter than the former. He has a natural sensitivity to Brahms's melodic line and in the shorter *Pieces* and *Intermezzi* his gentle touch and subtle control of nuance and colour is magical; always the pianistic textures are fresh and lacking in turgidity. The performance of the *F minor Sonata* has all the spontaneous buoyancy of youth, and this alone is worthy of the Rosette. Moreover, Klien shows he is as able to bring out the classical power of the *Handel Variations* as he is willing to evoke the romanticism of the Schumann set. For this reissue, **Alfred Brendel** joins Klien for equally fine performances of the piano-duo version of the *16 Waltzes*, and the original version for piano, four hands, of the *Hungarian Dances*, and it is unlikely that we shall have a jollier performance of the latter. Fortunately, the Vox engineers excelled themselves, for the the piano-tone is fully convincing and often very beautiful. We must be grateful to Regis for making these fine discs available again.

Hungarian Dances 1–21; 18 Liebeslieder Waltzes, Op. 52a

(BB) *** Naxos 8.553140. Matthies, Köhn

It makes a generous and very attractive coupling to have all 21 *Hungarian Dances* in their original form, coupled with the piano-duet version of the first and more popular set of *Liebeslieder Waltzes*. Crisp, clean ensemble, matched by well-focused sound.

Sonata for 2 Pianos in F min., Op. 34b; Variations on a Theme of Haydn, Op. 56b

(BB) *** Naxos 8.553654. Matthies, Köhn

What the German duo demonstrates is that the two-piano format brings formidable advantages in bite and attack, as well as some disadvantages. Speeds are sensibly chosen for the sonata, as they are in Brahms's own piano-duet version of the *Haydn Variations*, again clarified. Bright, clear sound to match.

Solo piano music

4 Ballades, Op. 10; 7 Fantasias, Op. 116; Hungarian Dances 1–10; (i) 11–21. 3 Intermezzi, Op. 117; 8 Piano Pieces, Op. 76; 6 Piano Pieces, Op. 118; 4 Piano Pieces, Op. 119; Piano Sonatas 1 in C, Op. 1; 2 in F sharp min., Op. 2; 3 in F min., Op. 5; 2 Rhapsodies, Op. 79; Variations on a Hungarian Song, Op. 21/2; Variations on a Theme by Paganini, Op. 35; Variations & Fugue on a Theme by Handel, Op. 24; Variations on a Theme by Schumann, Op. 9; Variations on an Original Theme, Op. 21/1; Waltzes, Op. 39

🎧 (B) *** Decca (ADD) stereo/mono 455 247-2 (6). Katchen, (i) with J.-P. Marty

Katchen's magisterial survey of Brahms's keyboard music was made for Decca between 1962 and 1965, save for the last three *Ballades*, which come from the 1950s and are in mono. Those wanting a comprehensive survey need look no further. Katchen is an eminently faithful and sound interpreter who brings refined musicianship and a natural authority to this repertoire; he is given the benefit of Decca recording which was excellent for its period, and remains so. The six CDs are offered at a very low price and, although they are not available separately, they still make a tremendous bargain. In addition to the three *Ballades*, the following are

mono recordings: the *Schumann Variations*, Nos. 1, 5 and 7 of the *Fantasias* and Nos. 11–21 of the *Hungarian Dances*.

4 Ballades, Op. 10

(M) *** DG (ADD/DDD) 457 762-2. Michelangeli (with SCHUBERT: *Piano Sonata in A min.* **; BEETHOVEN: *Piano Sonata 4* *)

Michelangeli produces a wonderfully blended tone and fine, mellow sonority. The *Ballades* are given a performance of the greatest distinction, without the slightly aloof quality that sometimes disturbs his readings; and the 1981 digital recording is excellent. The couplings, alas, are not in the same league.

4 Ballades, Op. 10; 2 Rhapsodies, Op. 79; Variations on a theme of Paganini, Op. 35

🎧 *** Virgin 3 32628-2. Nicholas Angelich

Nicholas Angelich seems completely attuned to this world and, whether in the virtuosity of the *Paganini Variations* or the poetic sensibility of the *Ballades*, he plays with rare authority and conviction. He has received plaudits in both the British and French press, and he deserves them, and the piano-sound is very well captured by the Virgin Classics engineer.

7 Fantasias, Op. 116

🎧 *** Ottavio OTRC 39027. Cooper – SCHUMANN: *Abegg variations*, etc. ***

Imogen Cooper's stirring account of the *Capriccio* which opens the set captures the listener immediately, and the variety of colour and mood gives enormous pleasure throughout. The gentle *Intermezzi* are most beautiful, for the recording does this memorable playing full justice. The listening experience here is as if one was present at a live recital.

Fantasias, Op. 116; 3 Intermezzi, Op. 117; 6 Pieces, Op. 118; 4 Pieces, Op. 119

(M) **(*) DG (ADD) 437 249-2. Kempff

Kempff's style in Brahms is characteristically individual: poetry emphasized rather than brilliance, subtle timbres rather than virtuosity. It follows that Kempff shines in the gentle fancies of Brahms's last period, with his magic utterly beguiling in the *Intermezzi in A minor, E major* and *E minor* from Op. 116, and especially in the lovely *E flat major Andante* of Op. 117.

7 Fantasias, Op. 116; 3 Intermezzi, Op. 117; 6 Piano Pieces, Op. 118; 4 Pieces, Op. 119

(N) *** Avie SACD AV 2136 Markus Groh

🎧 *** EMI 379 3022. Angelich

In a generous eighty-minute recital **Markus Groh**, the young prize-winning pianist from Germany offers all twenty of the late *Piano Pieces* of Op. 116 to Op. 119. He plays with a ripe Brahmsian feeling, his style, reflective, often romantically passionate, and in the gentler moments appealingly delicate.

The performances have a natural spontaneity and he is superbly recorded. The acoustic is resonant, but with the back speakers in use, one is given a real concert hall feeling to the music-making.

There are impressive sets of these searching late Brahms masterpieces from both Kempff and Lupu, but these new readings from **Nicholas Angelich** are second to none and are finer than most. He is a Brahmsian of outstanding quality. Thoughtful, beautifully rounded and natural playing which has the measure of Brahms's depths. Lifelike recording.

7 Fantasias, Op. 116; 8 Pieces, Op. 76; 2 Rhapsodies, Op. 79

(BB) *** Naxos 8.550353. Biret

Idil Biret readily captures the graceful intimacy of the *A flat* and *B flat Intermezzi*. Of the two *Rhapsodies*, the second is particularly fine, boldly spontaneous, its dark colouring caught well. The *Fantasias*, Op. 116, bring some beautifully reflective playing, notably in the three *Intermezzi* grouped together (in E major and E minor), while the framing *G minor* and *D minor Capriccios* are passionately felt, the latter ending the recital strongly. This is all impressively characterized Brahms playing, and the recording does not lack sonority.

3 Intermezzi, Op. 117; 6 Pieces, Op. 118; 4 Pieces, Op. 119; 2 Rhapsodies, Op. 79

⊶ *** Decca (ADD) 417 599-2. Lupu

Radu Lupu's late Brahms is quite outstanding in every way. There is great intensity and inwardness when these qualities are required, and a keyboard mastery that is second to none. This is undoubtedly one of the most rewarding Brahms recitals currently before the public.

3 Intermezzi, Op. 117; 2 Rhapsodies, Op. 79; Waltzes, Op. 39; Variations on a theme by Handel, Op. 24

(BB) **(*) Naxos 8.570290. Jandó

Jandó opens with the *Rhapsodies*: the first, although marked *Agitato*, seems just a shade rushed at the opening, but it soon settles down; the *Molto passionato* of the *G minor* is well judged. The lovely *Intermezzi* are sensitively done, but Jandó is at his best in the *Waltzes*, which have both sparkle and affection. The *Handel Variations* are well characterized but a little lightweight. Yet this may be partly due to the Hungarian studio acoustic; the recording is truthful and present, but one wants a slightly warmer timbre for Brahms.

Piano Sonatas 1 in C, Op. 1; 2 in F sharp min., Op. 2

⊶ (M) *** Decca 4758628 (2). S. Richter

Recorded in Mantua in February 1987, these performances show **Sviatoslav Richter** at his most commanding. He makes the most heavily chordal piano writing sound totally pianistic and there is exquisite shading of tone and flawless legato. Both slow movements are coloured most subtly and the opening of the finale of the *F sharp minor Sonata* has a wonderful improvisatory feeling. The playing throughout has

the spontaneity of live music-making and the Decca engineers have secured most realistic sound.

Piano Sonata 3; 4 Ballades, Op. 10

⊶ **** Hyp. CDA 67237. Hough

(M) *** Warner Elatus 0927 49562-2. Barenboim

(BB) **(*) Naxos 8.550352. Biret

Piano Sonata 3 in F min., Op. 5; 16 Waltzes, Op. 39

⊶ *** Ondine ODE 1044-2. Siirala

The *F minor Sonata* and the *Ballades*, Op. 10, are a young man's music. **Stephen Hough** gives us a finely conceived, naturally paced and beautifully controlled account of both pieces. The intellect and emotions, the 'classical' Brahms and youthful romanticism are well balanced. The recorded sound is very good and lifelike.

Antti Siirala's Brahms *F minor Sonata* announces the arrival of a serious artist whose musical armoury, while it has no want of bravura and virtuosity, is profoundly well equipped to deal with the artistic challenges posed by this great work. Siirala's recording is to be ranked along with the very best, and he is hardly less impressive in the Op. 39 *Waltzes*. First-class piano recording.

Barenboim's *Sonata* and *Ballades* are distinguished by an effortless technical command and excellent musical characterization and insight. Although he is not necessarily a first choice, this generally well-recorded account is certainly most impressive. Good value too.

As a pupil of Kempff, **Idil Biret** has a fine understanding of this repertoire, although her approach is more muscular than Kempff's. The fourth *Ballade* is gravely beautiful and shows her at her finest. The *Sonata* opens commandingly and its lyrical side is well balanced. These performances are full of character. Good recording, made in the Heidelberg studio.

Variations & Fugue on a Theme of Handel, Op. 24

⊶ (M) *** Warner Elatus 2564 61762-2. Schiff (piano) – HANDEL: *Keyboard Suite in B flat (HWV 434)*; REGER: *Variations & Fugue on a Theme of Bach* ***

Schiff's splendid performance is made the more attractive by being preceded by the Handel *Suite* from which Brahms draws his theme. The Reger *Variations* are also given a first-class, highly imaginative performance of wide dynamic contrasts, lyricism alternating with strength. The (excellent) recording comes from a live recital at the Concertgebouw in 1994.

ORGAN MUSIC

11 Chorale Preludes, Op. 122; Chorale Prelude & Fugue on 'O Traurigkeit, O Herzeleid'; Fugue in A flat min. (original and published versions); Preludes & Fugues: in A min.; G min.

*** Nim. NI 5262. Bowyer (organ of Odense Cathedral)

11 Chorale Preludes, Op. 122; Chorale Prelude & Fugue on 'O Traurigkeit, O Herzeleid'; Fugue in A flat min.; Preludes & Fugues: in A min.; G min.

*** CRD 3404. Danby (organ)

Kevin Bowyer has the advantage of the splendid Danish organ in Odense Cathedral, which combines a full tone and a warmly coloured palette with a clear profile. Like Nicholas Danby, Bowyer is obviously at home both in the early *Preludes and Fugues*, in which he produces considerable bravura (helped by the fresh, bright sound of the organ), and in the very late set of *Chorale Preludes*. He then closes the recital with Brahms's original manuscript forms of the two earliest pieces (which we have already heard in their published formats), the *Chorale Prelude and Fugue on 'O Traurigkeit'* and the unpolished *A flat minor Fugue*. The disc is very well documented.

    Nicholas Danby, playing the organ of the Church of the Immaculate Conception in London, gives restrained, clean-cut readings which yet have a strong profile. Choice between these two discs might well depend on preference for the type of organ used. The effect on CRD is rather more incisive but has firmness and weight of tone and certainly does not lack amplitude.

LIEDER

Lieder

*** DG 429 727-2. von Otter, Forsberg, (i) with Sparf

Anne Sofie von Otter gives these Brahms Lieder the natural freshness of folksong which so often they resemble. She phrases unerringly, holding and changing tension and mood as in a live recital, and her accompanist is strongly supportive. In the Op. 91 settings they are joined by **Nils-Erik Sparf**, who plays with admirable taste.

Lieder

▣—⑧ **** DG (ADD) Double 459 469-2 (2). Norman, Barenboim

This double CD concentrates on Brahms's 'women's songs'. **Jessye Norman's** tone is full and golden. Her imagination even matches that of Fischer-Dieskau, and no praise could be higher. Her voice is ideally suited to many of these songs, and if occasionally there is a hint of an over-studied quality this is of little consequence, considering the overall achievement. **Barenboim's** accompaniments are superb, contributing much to the success of this recital. The recording is excellent and this is a real bargain.

Alto Rhapsody, Op. 53

▣—⑧⑧ (***) Regis mono RRC 1146. Ferrier, LPO Ch. & O, Krauss – MAHLER: *Das Lied von der Erde* (**)

The *Alto Rhapsody* was one of **Kathleen Ferrier's** own favourites among her records, and well it might have been, for the spacious phrases of Brahms's setting of Goethe suited the glorious tonal beauty of her voice to perfection, and the closing section with chorus is particularly moving. The Regis

transfer is admirable, bringing out all the vocal warmth and radiance.

Alto Rhapsody

Ⓝ(***) BBC Legends mono BBCL4243-2. J. Baker, BBC Men's Ch, BBC SO, Boult – MAHLER: *Das Lied von der Erde* (***)

Janet Baker recorded the *Alto Rhapsody* with **Boult** conducting around the same period as this live performance (Royal Festival Hall 6 November 1968) with the advantage of stereo, but this BBC Broadcast gains in the extra warmth of expressiveness, and makes a splendid and generous supplement to Mahler's *Das Lied* with Baker and Mitchinson, conducted by Raymond Leppard.

(i) Alto Rhapsody. Academic Festival Overture

Ⓜ *** EMI (ADD) 5 62791-2. J. Baker, Alldis Ch., LPO, Boult – SCHUBERT: *Symphony 9* ***

Dame Janet Baker's devoted (1970) recording of the *Alto Rhapsody* with **Boult** was originally coupled with the *Second Symphony*. Now it comes equally attractively paired with Schubert. The Brahms remains meditative, even though the tempo is unlingering and the manner totally unindulgent. The warm Abbey Road recording is transferred very successfully to CD.

6 Lieder und Romanzen, Op. 93a; (i) 5 Gesänge, Op. 104; (i) 3 Quartets, Op. 64. Zigeunerlieder, Op. 103. Funeral Ode: Dem dunken Schloss dell'Heil'gen Erde, WoO 20

Ⓝ *** Hyp. CDA 67775 Consortium, Andrew-John Smith; (i) Glynn

Apart from his choral music Brahms wrote many vocal quartets, either with piano or *a cappella* for use as Hausmusik, after the style of the Schubertiades. He was, alas, not personally lucky in love, as the woman he adored and admired, Clara Schumann, was already married to his friend and mentor Robert died. So it is not surprising that most of these settings have words full of regret for what might have been, of languishing for the unattainable, and many of them touch a chord of nostalgia in the listener. The folksy *a cappella Songs and Romances* are often more philosophical, even offering practical solutions for the unrequited lover, like the girl encouraged to wash her face in rosewater to tempt her young man to kiss her. The *Zigeunerlieder* are more cheerfully extrovert, often sentimental, sometimes offering a joyful solution. *Dem dunken Schloss* (a partsong for mixed voices) makes a gentle epilogue. **Consortium** sing them all with sensitivity and ardour, with apt accompaniments, where needed by **Christopher Glyn**. Fine recording, although the piano sound is rather resonant.

Lieder Collection from Broadcasts

(***) BBC mono BBCL 4200-2. Janet Baker, Ernest Lush or Paul Hamburger

This collection of over two dozen songs was culled from broadcasts made in 1960, 1961 and 1968, when **Dame Janet** was in her absolute prime. She is well accompanied by **Paul Hamburger** and **Ernest Lush**, and every song springs to life in the most electrically communicative way. The recording may be mono but it is very faithful. A disc not to be missed by all admirers of this remarkably individual and inspirational singer.

Lieder

(***) BBC Legends mono BBCL 4100-2. J. Baker, Lush or Hamburger

It is good to have two further inspired recitals of the young **Janet Baker** singing Brahms Lieder, one made in 1961, the other in 1968. Though the artistry remains supreme in both, not just the flawless legato and natural sense of stillness and repose, with strong dramatic contrasts, the development in the voice is very clear. The tone is richer and warmer in 1968, more suited to the weightier songs in that recital, notably the culminating song, *Von ewiger Liebe*, one of Brahms's greatest, here deeply moving with the most powerful climax.

Lieder

⊖ ⊛ Ⓜ **** EMI mono 5 62807-2. Hotter, Moore – BACH: *Cantata 82: Ich habe genug* ****⊛

Glorious singing from **Hans Hotter**, wonderfully accompanied by **Gerald Moore**. A splendid transfer of the 1950 recordings – an indispensable coupling, with two extra songs included that were not on the old Références CD.

Ave Maria, Op. 12; Nänie, Op. 82; Schicksalslied, Op. 54; (i) Triumphlied, Op. 55

⊖ *** Chan. 10165. Danish Nat. Ch. & SO, Albrecht; (i) with Skovhus

It is fascinating to find Brahms banging the patriotic drum in his *Triumphlied*, written to celebrate the Prussian victory over the French in 1870 and the establishment of the German empire. **Albrecht's** performance with the **Danish National Choir and Orchestra** may be less polished than Sinopoli's DG version, but it is markedly warmer and more idiomatic, well coupled with a devotional reading of *Schicksalslied, Song of Destiny* (with a Hölderlin text) and the valedictory *Nänie*. The rare setting of *Ave Maria* for women's voices, an early work, makes a charming supplement.

Lieder

⊖ Ⓜ **** DG 474 856-2. Norman, Barenboim; (i) with Christ

Winner of the *Gramophone* Solo Vocal Award in 1983, this delightful and strongly contrasted selection from DG's Lieder Box in the Brahms Edition shows **Jessye Norman** at her finest. For the CD equivalent of an earlier digital LP, the two *Songs with Viola* have been added to make a highlight of the new recital. The task of recording a complete set of women's songs seems in this instance to have added to the warmth and sense of spontaneity of both singer and pianist in the studio, while **Wolfram Christ** makes a distinguished contribution to Op. 91. The heroic scale of *Der Schmied* is superb, as is the open simplicity of *Zigeunerlieder*, while the gentler

songs find the gloriously ample voice exquisitely scaled down. The recording is wonderfully vivid, giving the artists a tangible presence. An outstanding reissue.

Deutsche Volkslieder (42 German folksong settings)

Ⓑ *** EMI Gemini (ADD) 5 85502-2 (2). Schwarzkopf, Fischer-Dieskau, Moore

In Brahms's simple folk-settings no singers in the world can match **Schwarzkopf** and **Fischer-Dieskau** in their musical imagination and depth of understanding. **Gerald Moore** as ever is the ideal accompanist, and the recording quality is natural and vivid, with some enchanting conversation pieces between the soloists. However, no translations are included and no attempt is made to explain the meaning of each song.

German Requiem, Op. 45 (DVD versions)

⊖ ⊛ *** DG **DVD** 0734 4398. Janowitz, van Dam, V. Singverein, VPO, Karajan

(*) EMI **DVD 3 8846093. Lear, Stewart, ORTF Ch. & O Philharmonique, Richter (V/D: Andrew Leroux) – WAGNER: *Götterdämmerung; Tristan*: orchestral excerpts ***

Karajan's DVD of the Brahms *Requiem*, recorded live at the 1978 Salzburg Easter Festival, with two of his favourite solo singers, sweeps the board. He may keep his eyes closed, but his conducting is very physical, and the cameras reveal him as deeply impassioned in a work that he clearly loved greatly. His two soloists are on splendid form; **Gundula Janowitz** sings gloriously and **José van Dam** is both full-toned and boldly dramatic. Karajan's opening may be characteristically refined, but the arresting timpani in *Denn alles Fleisch, es ist wie Gras* soon shows that this is to be a performance of both fervour and fully revealed detail. The huge chorus visually creates a magnificent backcloth and their singing is increasingly rich and powerful, with the closing section very moving. Karajan himself directed the production and it is fully worthy of him at his finest.

Karl Richter's fine performance was recorded live by French Radio in 1964 and it comes in an excellent black-and-white video with good stereo sound within a warm acoustic which still retains a vivid choral edge. He opens darkly, spaciously and movingly, and soon builds a thrilling choral climax in *Denn alles Fleisch, es ist wie Gras*, and maintains a high level of tension to the end. He broadens his tempo considerably in the closing *Selig sind die Toten*, and the large French chorus (which has moments of roughness at times) sings with much feeling and even a touch of radiance from the female voices. Of the two soloists, **Thomas Stewart** sings well enough but is rather put in the shade by **Evelyn Lear's** moving contribution to *Ihr habet nun Traurigkeit*. Overall this account is worthy of Richter at his best and the cameras are unobtrusively effective.

German Requiem, Op. 45 (CD versions)

⊖ **** EMI 3 65393-2. Roschmann, Quasthoff, Berlin R. Ch., BPO, Rattle

&— ✹ *** Ph. 432 140-2. Margiono, Gilfry, Monteverdi Ch., ORR, Gardiner

&— (BB) *** Warner Apex 8573 89081-2. M. Price, Ramey, Amb. S., RPO, Previn

(N) (BB) (***) Naxos mono 8.111038. Schwarzkopf, Hotter, Wiener Sangverein, VPO, Karajan

Recorded live in October 2006, **Rattle** conducts a warm and urgent account of Brahms's *German Requiem*, bright and fresh, with brilliant recording, heightening the drama in a work which with seven generally measured movements can seem to lack contrast. One early test comes on the words, *An die Freude*, 'To joy', in the first movement, which here have a rare exuberance. Regularly the dynamic contrasts bring powerful, weighty climaxes, while the two soloists are both excellent, **Dorothea Roschmann** a pure-toned soloist and **Thomas Quasthoff** the firmly intense baritone.

Gardiner's 'revolutionary' account of the *German Requiem* brings a range of choral sound even more thrilling than in the concert hall. With period instruments and following Viennese practice of the time, speeds tend to be faster than usual, though the speed for the big fugue is surprisingly relaxed. **Charlotte Margiono** makes an ethereal soprano soloist, while **Rodney Gilfry**, despite a rapid vibrato, is aptly fresh and young-sounding. One could not ask for a more complete renovation of a masterpiece that is often made to sound stodgy and square.

It is the seeming simplicity of **Previn's** dedicated approach in his earlier, Apex recording, with radiant singing from the chorus and measured speeds held steadily, that so movingly conveys an innocence in the often square writing, both in the powerful opening choruses and in the simple, songful *Wie lieblich*. The great fugatos are then powerfully presented. Both soloists are outstanding, **Margaret Price** golden-toned, **Samuel Ramey** incisively dark. The recording, of high quality, is warmly set against a helpful church acoustic with the chorus slightly distanced.

This was the first complete recording of the *Requiem* and the first major recording that Walter Legge made after the war with **Karajan** and the **Vienna Philharmonic**. The excellence of the 1947 sound, thanks to the expertise of Legge's balance engineer, Douglas Larter, is admirably clear in this transfer. It has been absent from the catalogue for over sixty years and notwithstanding the many fine versions we have had in the intervening years including those from Karajan himself, this deserves a special place in the Brahms discography thanks to its depth and spontaneity of feeling.

German Requiem, Op. 45 (sung in English)

*** Telarc CD 80501. Chandler, Gunn, Mormon Tabernacle Ch., Utah SO, Jessop

Craig Jessop directs a dedicated reading of a new translation by Robert Shaw which for English-speaking listeners will communicate warmly, not least thanks to the extra immediacy of the words. The choir, which too often has been recorded mushily, here emerges far fresher than before, and the two soloists are both first rate. **Janice Chandler** has a warm, creamy soprano, and **Nathan Gunn** has a youthfully

clear baritone which he uses with finesse and passion. Full, warm sound, not always ideally transparent; but this remains a fully worthy tribute to Shaw.

(i) Vier ernste Gesang (4 Serious Songs), Op. 121; (ii) 2 Songs with viola, Op. 91

(BB) (***) Regis mono RRC 1153. Ferrier, (i; ii) Spurr, Gilbert – MAHLER: *Kindertotenlieder*, etc. (***)✹

This vintage **Kathleen Ferrier** record brings together a group of the great contralto's early Decca Brahms recordings from 1949–50, showing the richness of the voice and her natural expressive involvement. These recordings are also available elsewhere, notably in Decca's various Ferrier groupings, but these Regis transfers are appealingly smooth and natural, and the recording is inexpensive.

3 Gesänge, Op. 42; (i) 4 Gesänge, Op. 17; 5 Gesänge, Op. 104; (ii) 6 Quartette, Op. 112; Zigeunerlieder, Op. 109

&— ✹ *** Chan. 9806. Danish Nat. R. Ch., Parkman; with (i) Yeats, McClelland, Lind; (ii) Forsberg

The **Danish National Radio Choir** have already brought us a fine collection of motets, including the *Marienlieder* (see below). Here they turn their attention to some of the lovely unaccompanied *Gesänge*, and include also as a highlight of the concert the luscious settings of Op. 17, which have delectable harp accompaniments and obbligatos for one or two horns. *Sehnsucht*, the first of the six piano-accompanied *Quartets* which follow, has one of the composer's most seductive melodies, and the robust set of *Zigeunerlieder* which close the recital, sung with great vigour, show the composer at his most infectiously boisterous.

Liebeslieder Waltzes, Op. 52

*** BBC (ADD) BBCB 8001-2. Harper, J. Baker, Pears, Hemsley, Britten & Arrau (piano duet) – ROSSINI: *Soirées musicales*; TCHAIKOVSKY: *4 Duets* ***

Britten was allergic to the music of Brahms, but you would never know that from this magical performance of the *Liebeslieder Waltzes*. As an inspired accompanist he is joined by **Claudio Arrau** in a perfect partnership. The soloists make an outstanding and characterful team, whoopsing away throughout, with **Janet Baker** striking a deeper note in the poignant seventh waltz. Full, clear, radio sound.

Motets

Sacred motets: Ach, arme Welt, du trügest mich, Op. 110; Es ist das Heil uns kommen her, Op. 29; O Heiland reiss die Himmel auf, Op. 74

**(*) Paraclete Press GDCG 107. Dei Cantores, Patterson – MENDELSSOHN: *Motets* **(*)

Brahms's *Es ist das Heil* owes a debt to Bach in its four-part chorale followed by a five-part fugue, where the part-writing could be more sharply delineated. But the other two works have a simple eloquence which is well caught by these persuasively committed performances, beautifully recorded.

Ave Maria, Op. 12; 3 Fest- und Gedenksprüche, Op. 109; Geistliches Lied, Op. 30; 2 Motets, Op. 29; 2 Motets, Op. 74; 3 Motets, Op. 110; Psalm 13, Op. 27

(BB) *** Naxos 8.553877. St Bride's Ch., R. Jones; Morley (organ)

Throughout his composing career, from his Hamburg days onwards, Brahms was devoted to writing choral music, both religious and secular, superbly crafted. In their first recording, **Robert Jones** and the **Choir of St Bride's, Fleet Street**, give fresh, clear performances. They are beautifully scaled to give the illusion of church performance, helped by warm, atmospheric recording.

3 Fest- und Gedenksprüche, Op. 109; Marienlieder, Op. 22; 2 Motets, Op. 29; 2 Motets, Op. 74; 3 Motets, Op. 110

*** Chan. 9671. Danish Nat. R. Ch., Parkman

The programme from the **Danish Radio Choir** is made especially attractive by the inclusion of the seven *Marienlieder*, which include some of Brahms's simplest and most beautiful lyrical inspirations. They are gloriously sung by this justly famous Danish choir, who are on splendid form throughout the disc and are beautifully recorded.

(i) *Rinaldo, Op. 50*; (ii) *Alto Rhapsody. Gesang der Parzen, Op. 89*

*** Chan. 10215. (i) Stig Andersen; (ii) Larsson; Danish Nat. Ch. & SO, Albrecht

Brahms's cantata, *Rinaldo*, like operas by Handel and Gluck among others, tells of the crusader Rinaldo, ensnared by the enchantress Armida. His fellow-knights finally rescue him, persuading him to return to the cause. Brahms's setting for tenor soloist, male chorus and orchestra, with a text by Goethe, moves from the ecstasy inspired by Armida to his final mood of resolution, backed up in a stirring final chorus, written long after the rest. It is hardly a dramatic sequence but it is a moving one, here superbly realized by Danish forces under **Gerd Albrecht**. It is very well coupled with two other Goethe settings by Brahms, the radiant *Alto Rhapsody*, with **Anna Larsson** the rich-toned soloist, and the greatest and darkest of his shorter choral works, *Gesang der Parzen*, 'Song of the Fates'.

Die schöne Magelone (song-cycle)

**(*) Orfeo C490 981B. Fischer-Dieskau, S. Richter

Dietrich Fischer-Dieskau has done more than any other singer to bring this once-neglected song-cycle back into the repertory, a love-story from the age of chivalry. This version offers a live Salzburg Festival recording, made in July 1970, and though audience noises occasionally intrude, the thrust and impulse of the reading are irresistible. As a bonus come his three encores of other Brahms songs. No texts are given nor even translations of titles.

BRIAN, Havergal (1876–1972)

(i) *Violin Concerto. The Jolly Miller (Comedy Overture); Symphony 18*

(BB) ** Naxos 8.557775. (i) Bisengaliev; BBC Scottish SO, Friend

The *Violin Concerto* is a work on the most ambitious scale, obviously with an eye on the Elgar *Concerto* in the use of a large orchestra as a backcloth. It is an impressive work, and it is played with much feeling by **Marat Bisengaliev**, who is given powerful support by the **BBC Scottish Orchestra** under **Lionel Friend**. The snag is the close-miked recording, which at times brings an edge to the solo violin-timbre and makes the many passionate orchestral tuttis sound thin and over-bright. The *Concerto* is prefaced by a jolly little overture introducing the folksong, *The Miller of Dee*, and is followed by a rather good, small-scale symphony, with its three movements all based on march-like themes, ranging over a whole gamut of emotions and ending forcefully. There is very good back-up documentation.

Symphony 1 (Gothic)

🔁 (BB) *** Naxos 8.557418/9. Jenisová, Pecková, Dolžal, Mikulás, Slovak Op. Ch., Slovak Folk Ens. Ch., Lúčnica Ch., Bratislava City Ch. & Children's Ch., Youth Echo Ch., Slovak RSO & PO & Ch., Lénard

The first of the Havergal Brian symphonies here receives a passionately committed performance from Slovak forces. Despite a few incidental flaws, it conveys surging excitement from first to last, helped by a rich recording, which gives a thrilling impression of massed forces. The final *Te Deum*, alone lasting 72 minutes, brings fervent choral writing of formidable complexity, with the challenge taken up superbly by the Slovak musicians. Originally on Marco Polo, this is now a very real bargain in its Naxos reissue.

Symphony 2; Festival Fanfare

(BB) **(*) Naxos 8.570506. Moscow SO, Rowe

Havergal Brian's *Second Symphony*, scored for no fewer than sixteen horns (though only eight are used here), three sets of timpani, two pianos and organ, was written in 1930–1. The composer later distanced himself from all programmatic associations with the score, merely allowing, in a letter in 1972, that the work represents 'Man in his cosmic loneliness: ambition, loves, battles and death'. Cast in conventional four movements – though, as the composer said, 'very unorthodox inside' – one is helped through this complex score by Naxos's generous cueing points, allied to very helpful notes by Callum MacDonald. Throughout the work, one senses the composer exploring with textures, harmonies – and melody. The ostinato-Scherzo, with its hunting horns, one group after another, is particularly memorable. The finale evokes *Siegfried's Funeral March* from *Götterdämmerung*. An excellent performance, even if the orchestra lacks refinement at times, the strings struggling a bit in the demanding passages. The CD opens with the composer's single brass-only work, the short, pithy *Festival Fanfare* of 1967. Good sound throughout.

Symphony 3 in C sharp min.

(BB) **(*) Hyp. Helios CDH 55029. Ball, Jacobson, BBC SO, Friend

The *Third Symphony* began life as a concerto for piano; this perhaps explains the prominent role given to two pianos in the score. The work is full of extraordinarily imaginative and original touches, but the overall lack of rhythmic variety is a handicap. The playing of the **BBC Symphony Orchestra** under **Lionel Friend** is well prepared and dedicated, but the recording does not open out sufficiently in climaxes. Even so, this is well worth considering at Helios price.

Symphonies 4 (Psalm of Victory); 12

(BB) **(*) Naxos 8.570308. Valásková, Slovak Philharmonic Ch., Slovak Nat. Op. Ch., Echo Youth Ch., Cantus Mixed Ch., Czech Philharmonic Ch., Brno Slovak RSO, Leaper

The sheer quantity of choral voices required for Havergal Brian's *Fourth Symphony* can be can seen from the above listing, and that gives a fair indication of the scale of this work. Based on Psalm 68, a text full of apocalyptic and violent temperament with the most extreme of Old Testament passions, it was written in 1932–3 when many forces of evil were indeed gathering. There are many inventive ideas, and the work's impetus is surprisingly consistent, if the drama is a little wearing at times. The *Twelfth Symphony*, written in 1957, lasts a little over 11 minutes. Inspired by Greek tragedy, the large orchestra is terse and direct, atmospheric and richly orchestrated. The performances are very good and enthusiastic, and they convey the music well. The recording (1992, originally Marco Polo) is decent enough and, at bargain price, well worth exploring. The helpful sleeve-notes take you through the enormous *Fourth Symphony* track by track, and texts and translations are included.

Symphonies 6 (Sinfonia Tragica); 16

*** Lyrita (ADD) SRCD 295. LPO, Fredman – COOKE: *Symphony 3* ***

The opening of the *Sixteenth Symphony* (1960) is quite magical, and one is never unmindful of the presence of a stern and powerful imagination. It is the moments of stillness and tranquillity in Brian's music that leave the strongest impression. Not all the awkwardness is the product of bluntness of utterance, and rhythmically he is not fleet of foot. But both these symphonies have genuine depths, and a wholly personal vision. The *Sixth* (1948) also withstands the test of time extremely well and will repay familiarity. The performances are excellently played by the **LPO** under **Myer Fredman** and the recording has splendid clarity and body, the perspective is most musically judged, but there is no loss of vividness, presence or impact in achieving a concert-hall balance.

BRIDGE, Frank (1879–1941)

Vol. 1: *Enter Spring; Isabella; Mid of Night; 2 Poems for Orchestra* (Chan. 9950)

Vol. 2: *Dance Poem; Dance Rhapsody; 5 Entr'actes; Norse Legend; The Sea* (Chan. 10012)

Vol. 3: *Coronation March; (i) Phantasm; Sir Roger de Coverley (A Christmas Dance); Summer; There is a willow grows aslant a brook; Vignettes de danse* (Chan.10112 (with (i) Shelley))

Vol. 4: *Allegro moderato; Lament for String Orchestra; (i) Oration (Concerto elegiaco). Rebus – Overture for Orchestra; (ii) A Prayer (for chorus & orchestra)* (Chan. 10188 with (i) Gerhardt; (ii) BBC Nat. Ch. Of Wales)

Vol. 5: *2 Entr'actes; 2 Intermezzi from 'Threads'; 2 Old English Songs; Sir Roger de Coverley (A Christmas Dance); Suite for Strings; Todessehnsucht; Valse Intermezzo à cordes (arr. Hindmarsh); (i) The Hag; 2 Songs of Robert Bridges* (Chan. 10246 with (i) Williams)

Vol. 6: *Berceuse; Chant d'espérance; The Pageant of London; A Royal Night of Variety; Serenade. (i) Adoration; (ii) Berceuse; (i) Blow out, you bugles; (ii) Day after day; (i) Love went a-riding; (ii) Mantle of blue; Speak to me; (i) Thy hand in mine; Where She lies sleep* (Chan. 10310. (with (i) Langridge; (ii) Connolly))

(N) *** BBC Nat. O of Wales, Hickox

Richard Hickox's survey of Frank Bridge's orchestral music with the **BBC National Orchestra of Wales** is one of the highlights of the Chandos Catalogue. Volume 1 begins with his fresh, bracing rhapsody *Enter Spring*, dating from 1927, while his second tone poem, *Isabella* (1907), brooding and haunting, fully captures Keats's gruesome story which inspired this Lisztian tone poem. In the longest work on this volume, *Mid of Night*, Liszt is recalled again, and one has the feeling of a young composer (24) spreading his wings and exploring orchestral colour. The *Two Poems for Orchestra* (1915), the first chromatically sinuous, and the second, a lively orchestral dance, are also vividly scored.

Volume 2 includes perhaps Bridge's most celebrated piece, the tone poem *The Sea*, and it here receives a superbly briny performance. The disc opens with an exceptionally lively *Dance Rhapsody* (1908), again brilliantly orchestrated. The light, but very charming folk-tune inspired *5 Entr'actes* comes from the music Bridge wrote for a play, *The Two Hunchbacks*, while the more experimental *Dance Poem*, premiered in 1914, is harmonically and melodically more diffuse. This is followed by the short but beautiful *Norse Legend*, an evocative miniature tone poem, originally written for violin and piano in 1905, but later orchestrated (1938).

Volume 3 begins with stirring *Coronation March* of 1911 which just misses having a truly memorable big tune. *Summer* (1915) evokes a summer's day in the country while *Phantasm* finds Bridge at his most searchingly exploratory. As Paul Hindmarsh writes in the sleeve notes, 'it inhabits a spectral world of dreams and ghostly apparitions'. **Howard Shelley** is the responsive soloist. *There is a willow grows aslant a brook* is hauntingly dark and bleak as befits its Shakespearian inspiration, Gertrude's Act IV speech in *Hamlet*, in which she describes the drowning of Ophelia. The *Vignettes de dance* are orchestrations of earlier piano pieces, as is the much more famous and hugely enjoyable

Sir Roger de Coverley, which ends this disc in its full orchestral version.

Volume 4 contains perhaps Bridge's finest orchestral work, the *Oration* for cello and orchestra. **Gerhardt's** performance can stand alongside the finest earlier accounts. Rarities on this disc include the *Rebus Overture*, the composer's last completed work (1940) and, although the textures are sparer than his earlier music, the scoring is characteristically original. The *Allegro moderato* (or *Symphony*) *for String Orchestra*, completed by Anthony Pope, shows Bridge at his most deeply eloquent, as does the poignant *Lament* (1915), written for a young friend who died with her family when the *Lusitania* was sunk. *A Prayer* – an anti-war work, completed in orchestrated form in 1918, is Bridge's only setting for chorus and orchestra. Deliberately written to be performed by amateur choral societies, its relatively simple style is direct and affecting. The performance and recording here – and throughout this CD – is excellent.

The highlight of Volume 5, the *Suite for Strings* (1909) is full of delightful pastoral writing and piquant colour. Of the *Two Intermezzi from 'Threads'*, the second movement, a pastiche of a Viennese dance, is sparklingly toe-tapping. Both the *Two Old English Songs*, 'Sally in our alley' and 'Cherry ripe' are imaginatively scored, with the former in lush harmonies, and the latter turned into a virtuoso tour-de-force for strings, where the tune only emerges from the hustle and bustle towards the close. *Todessehnsucht* is an arrangement of Bach (the funeral chorale, *Komm Süsser Tod*) which is Stokowskian in its sumptuous grandeur. The nostalgic pair of *Entr'actes* are orchestrated piano works and evoke much warm nostalgia. The *Valse Intermezzo à cordes* is a stylish early student work, beautifully crafted and surprisingly memorable. **Roderick Williams** is the superb baritone in the lively setting of Robert Herrick's poem, *The Hag*, and the *Two Songs of Robert Bridges* are no less colourfully evocative.

This final volume largely comprises Bridge's orchestral songs, beginning with the stirring *Blow out, you bugles*, based on Rupert Brooke's most famous war poem. The contrasting *Berceuse* is also memorable, with again Bridge's orchestral colour very telling. **Sarah Connolly** sings it most beautifully too, as she does in all her items. *Love went-a-riding*, with its galloping accompaniment, is very enjoyable with **Langridge** the most lustily vigorous. The orchestral items here include the colourful suite *The Pageant of London* for wind orchestra, written for a pageant performed at the Crystal Palace in 1911. These are lively music vignettes of 'Ye Old England', and receive their premiere recording here in their original version. The *Berceuse, Chant d'espérance* and *Serenade* are all orchestral miniatures of much pastoral charm. The CD ends with the brief *A Royal Night of Variety*, written for the BBC in 1934, which starts robustly and ends unexpectedly quietly.

Throughout these six collections the BBC National Orchestra of Wales are on top form. They obviously enjoy the music, Hickox is persuasively idiomatic and spontaneous, and the Chandos recording is first class.

Allegro moderato for Strings; Dance Poem; Dance Rhapsody; 2 Poems (The Open Air; The Story of my Heart); Rebus Overture

*** Lyrita (ADD) SRCD 243. LPO, Braithwaite

This anthology spans Frank Bridge's creative career. The most important work here is the *Rebus Overture*, dating from 1940, spare and original in its scoring – and for that matter in substance. This was his last complete work, but in the year of his death he had also nearly finished the *Allegro moderato* (or *Symphony*) *for String Orchestra*: its inconclusive final cadence surely suggests more music to come, but the final page of the score of what exists has been reconstructed by Anthony Pope from a complete and fairly explicit sketch. These are all valuable additions to Bridge's representation on record, and it would be hard to imagine more responsive and idiomatic orchestral playing than the **LPO's** under **Nicholas Braithwaite** or more sumptuous and vivid analogue sound.

(i) *Enter Spring*; (ii) *The Sea*

Ⓜ *** BBC mono/stereo BBCB 8007-2. (i) New Phil. O; (ii) ECO, Britten – HOLST: *Fugal Concerto*, etc. BRITTEN: *The Building of the House: Overture* ***

Benjamin Britten as Frank Bridge's devoted pupil conveys a warmth and depth of understanding which transform two of Bridge's finest, most ambitious orchestral works, both evocative and intensely imaginative, giving them a focus that other interpreters do not always find. The radio recordings have been very well transferred.

Phantasm for Piano and Orchestra

Ⓜ *** Dutton CDLX 7223 Stott, RPO, Handley – IRELAND: *Piano Concerto* ****; WALTON: *Sinfonia concertante* ***

Bridge's curiously titled *Phantasm* is a large-scale piano concerto, some 26 minutes long, in a single, massive movement. **Kathryn Stott**, most sympathetically accompanied by **Vernon Handley**, and the **RPO**, proves a persuasive, committed interpreter, matching her achievement in the other two works on the disc, and especially the delightful Ireland *Piano Concerto*. Warm, generally well-balanced (originally Conifer) recording.

Oration: Concerto elegiaco (for cello & orchestra)

**** Nim. NI 5763. Wallfisch, RLPO, Dickins – ELGAR: *Cello Concerto*; HOLST: *Invocation* ***

Ⓑ *** EMI 5 05916-2. Isserlis, City of L. Sinfonia, Hickox – BRITTEN: *Cello Symphony* ***

Bridge's masterly *Oration* was written in 1929/30: its ethos is a passionate outcry against the human slaughter of the First World War, which haunted the composer. The work is written in a single movment like an arch, with seven diverse episodes, and the solo cello dominating hauntingly throughout. The work is superbly played by **Raphael Wallfisch**, movingly accompanied by the **RLPO**, sensitively directed by **Richard Dickins**. The recording is beautifully balanced, and of the highest quality. The coupled Elgar and Holst performances are no less distinctive.

Though **Isserlis** is not always as passionate as Julian Lloyd Webber on the earlier, Lyrita CD (SRCD 244), his focus is sharper, and with **Hickox** at the helm he brings out the originality of the writing all the more cleanly. It is fascinating to find some passages anticipating the more abrasive side of Britten and specifically the *Cello Symphony*, with which this is coupled.

The Sea (suite)

⊕—Ⓜ **** Chan. 10426X. Ulster O, Handley – BAX: *On the Sea-Shore*; BRITTEN: *Sea Interludes*; STANFORD: *Irish Rhapsody 4* ****

The Sea receives a brilliant and deeply sympathetic performance from **Handley** and the **Ulster Orchestra**, recorded with a fullness and vividness to make this a demonstration disc. The Stanford *Rhapsody* makes a splendid bonus for this highly desirable reissue.

Suite for String Orchestra

*** Chan. 8390. ECO, Garforth – IRELAND: *Downland Suite*, etc. ***

*** Nim. NI 5068. E. String O, Boughton – BUTTERWORTH: *Banks of Green Willow*, etc.; PARRY: *Lady Radnor's Suite* ***

Suite for String Orchestra; Summer; There is a willow grows aslant a brook

Ⓜ *** Chan. 6566. Bournemouth Sinf., Del Mar – BANTOCK: *Pierrot of the Minute*; BUTTERWORTH: *Banks of Green Willow* ***

Summer is beautifully played by the **Bournemouth Sinfonietta** under **Norman Del Mar**. The same images of nature permeate the miniature tone-poem, *There is a willow grows aslant a brook*, an inspired piece, very sensitively managed. The *Suite for String Orchestra* is equally individual. Its third movement, a *Nocturne*, is lovely. The CD transfer is excellent and one can relish its fine definition and presence.

The **ECO** also play well for **David Garforth** in the *Suite for String Orchestra*. This performance is extremely committed; it is certainly recorded excellently, with great clarity and presence.

The Nimbus collection is more generous and is certainly well chosen. Here Bridge's *Suite* again receives a lively and responsive performance, from **William Boughton** and his excellent Birmingham-based orchestra, treated to ample, sumptuously atmospheric recording, more resonant than its competitors.

CHAMBER MUSIC

Cello Sonata

*** Chan. 8499. Raphael & Peter Wallfisch – BAX: *Rhapsodic Ballad*; DELIUS: *Sonata*; WALTON: *Passacaglia* ***

It is a distinctive world that Bridge evokes in the *Cello Sonata* and one to which **Raphael Wallfisch** and his father, **Peter**, are completely attuned, and they are beautifully recorded.

Cello Sonata; Berceuse; Cradle Song; Elegie; Meditation; Melodie; Scherzo; Serenade; Spring Song

*** Simax PSC 1160. Birkeland, Anvik – BRITTEN: *Cello Sonata* ***

The Norwegian partnership of **Øystein Birkeland** and **Vebjørn Anvik** is totally inside the Bridge idiom and they give fluent and impressive accounts not only of the *Sonata* but also of the companion pieces. Sympathetic performances and excellent recorded sound.

3 Idylls for String Quartet

*** Hyp. CDA 66718. Coull Qt – ELGAR: *Quartet* **(*); WALTON: *Quartet* ***

As this superb, purposeful performance by the **Coull Quartet** shows, the *Three Idylls*, each marked by sharp changes of mood as a phantasie-form, make up a satisfying whole, a quartet in all but name. Excellent sound.

(i) Piano Quintet. 3 Idylls; String Quartet 4

Ⓝ **** Hyp. CDA 67726. (i) Lane; Goldner Qt

The *Piano Quintet* dates from 1905, but Bridge completely rewrote it in 1912. The passionate energy of the original first movement remains, but it is the memorable secondary theme that all but dominates. The broodingly enticing *Adagio* frames a sparkling scherzo and the finale reintroduces the main ideas from the first movement at its climax. It is altogether most rewarding, and with **Piers Lane** leading the **Goldner Quartet** the performance here has irresistible impetus and responds to the music's rich lyrical feeling.

The *Three Idylls*, the second of which Britten used for his celebrated *Variations*, are sheer delight, the first ravishingly delicately sensuous, and the third more animated but no less winning. They are most beautifully played here. The *Fourth Quartet* (1937), Bridge's last chamber work, is thematically and harmonically much more forward-looking, although it is not atonal. Its atmosphere has a haunted quality, with even the central *Quasi minuetto* far from conventional. The finale is pithily energetic, and one again Bridge closes with quotations from his first movement. But the work has moments of ethereal beauty that place it among the composer's most deeply felt music.

(i) Phantasie Quartet. Phantasie Trio in C min.; Piano Trio 2

⊕—ⒷⒷ *** Hyp. Helios CDH 55063. Dartington Trio, (i) with Patrick Ireland

The playing of the *Phantasie Trio* by the **Dartington Trio** is of exceptional eloquence and sensitivity. They are no less persuasive in the *Phantasie Quartet*. Their account of the visionary post-war *Piano Trio 2* of 1929 is completely inside this score. The Hyperion recording is altogether superb, in the demonstration bracket, perfectly natural and beautifully proportioned, and this is even more attractive on the bargain Helios label.

(i) Phantasie Quartet; Piano Trio 2; Miniatures for Piano Trio (Set 3); (ii) String Quartets 3 & 4

*** Lyrita (ADD) SRCD 302 (2). (i) Tunnell Trio; (ii) Allegri Qt

If the most haunting work here is the *Piano Trio 2* of 1929, the *Phantasie Quartet*, written 19 years earlier, shows more than just promise. The *Miniatures* (*Valse Russe*, *Hornpipe* and

Marche Militaire) are uncomplicated but charming. The *Third Quartet* of 1927 is a powerful piece, even showing affinities with the Second Viennese school, while the pithier, more rarefied *Fourth Quartet* equally reveals the questing spirit. All this music is beautifully played and recorded, and is well worth investigating.

Phantasie Trio in C min.; Piano Trio 2; 9 Miniatures for Piano Trio

(N) ⊕— (BB) **** Naxos 8.570792 Liebeck, Chaushian, Wass

Jack Liebeck and his colleagues, **Alexander Chaushian** and the sensitive **Ashley Wass**, provide here a genuinely inspirational collection of Frank Bridge's chamber music with a glorious performance of the visionary *Second Piano Trio* balanced by the *Phantasie Trio* and the engaging *Nine Miniatures*, lightweight and winningly varied, but never trivial. They are splendidly recorded and this inexpensive disc is the ideal way to begin an exploration of Bridge's chamber music.

String Quartets 1 (Bologna); 3

⊕— (BB) *** Naxos 8.557133. Maggini Qt

String Quartets 2 in G min.; 4; (i) Phantasie Quartet in F sharp min. (for piano, violin, viola & cello)

⊕— (BB) *** Naxos 8.557283. Maggini Qt, (i) with Roscoe

The **Maggini's** complete outstanding cycle, arguably the finest British contribution to quartet literature. The *Phantasie Quartet*, with **Martin Roscoe** joining three of the quartet members, in seven sections lasting only 12 minutes, is another striking piece in Bridge's early style. Passionate performances and vivid recording.

String Sextet in E flat

⊕— *** Kleos KL 5142. Concertante – KORNGOLD: *Sextet* ***

*** Chan. 9472. ASMF Chamber Ens. – GOOSSENS: *Concertino*, etc. ***

The splendid American string group **Concertante** are completely at home in this very appealing work of Frank Bridge, fully capturing its underlying, very English nostalgia, which appears in the secondary theme of the first movement and dominates the haunting *Adagio* (with its central Scherzo) and is felt again in the lyrical essence of the finale, which is to quote the work's opening theme at its close. The performance is warmly persuasive throughout, making this a totally memorable coupling for the similarly unfamiliar Korngold *Sextet*.

The **Academy of St Martin-in-the-Fields Chamber Ensemble** also plays with great eloquence.

Piano music (complete)

*** Continuum CCD 1016, 1018 & 1019. Jacobs

Peter Jacobs provides a complete survey of the piano music of Frank Bridge, and it proves an invaluable enterprise. The recorded sound is very good indeed: clean, well defined and present, and the acoustic lively. Calum MacDonald's excellent notes tracking Bridge's development over these years are worth a mention too.

Fairy Tale Suite; The Hour Glass; In Autumn; 3 Lyrics; Miniature Pastorals, Set I; 3 Pieces; 3 Poems

⊕— (BB) *** Naxos 8.557842. Wass

Bridge's writing has a pensive simplicity, an almost ingenuous quality which is all his own. The *Three Pieces* are from 1912, and the first, *Columbine*, is a deliciously inconsequential portrait in waltz-time, and the third, a *Romance*, is charmingly and delicately understated but the most concentrated in feeling is the central *Ecstasy*, gently simmering. **Wass's** performances are totally sympathetic throughout, he is beautifully recorded, and this programme will give much pleasure.

Piano Sonata; 3 Improvisations for the Left Hand; Lament for Catherine; Moderato; Pensées fugitives I: Andante moderato. 3 Sketches; Scherzettino

⊕— (BB) *** Naxos 8.557921. Wass

Much of this music was influenced by the composer's response to the slaughter of the First World War. The *Piano Sonata*, written between 1921 and 1924, is a formidable work, with its considerable dissonance arising from bitonal and very chromatic harmony. Reward for the listener then comes in the touchingly beautiful *Lament for Catherine* (a child drowned in the *Lusitania*). The three tellingly atmospheric *Improvisations for the Left Hand* (*At Dawn*, *A Vigil* and *A Revel*) were composed for a pianist who had lost his arm in the war. But the *Three Sketches* make a charming interlude from violence (looking back nostalgically), and the programme ends with a dazzling *Scherzettino* which **Ashley Wass** plays with delicious precision. This is a real showpiece, but he is truly at home in all this music and is admirably recorded.

BRITTEN, Benjamin (1913–76)

The Hidden Heart – A Life of Benjamin Britten and Peter Pears

(N) *** EMI **DVD** 50999 2 16571-9. (Ed. Jake Martin, Exec. Prods: Nicolas Kent, Vanessa Phillips, Producer & Director Teresa Griffiths)

This fine documentary was originally produced for Channel 4 and offers an intimate and sympathetic portrait of the composer and his friend and interpreter, Peter Pears. Those taking part include Pears' niece, and briefly, members of the Britten family, Donald Mitchell and John Evans. The programme is full of valuable documentary and archival material and concentrates on three periods of Britten's life, *Peter Grimes* from the war's end, with an engaging contribution from the original apprentice, the *War Requiem* from the 1960s and his last opera, *Death in Venice* imaginatively pictured and evoked with Robert Tear in the role of Aschenbach, and illuminating commentary by James Bowman and John Amis. It brings both the composer and Peter Pears vividly to life and affords many insights into their achievement.

A Time There Was: A portrait of the composer by Tony Palmer

*** Isolde Films Digital Classics **DVD** DC10017 (Contributions from Benjamin Britten, Janet Baker, Leonard Bernstein, Julian Bream, Heather Harper, Imogen Holst, Peter Pears, Sviatoslav Richter, the ECO, Steuart Bedford)

Tony Palmer uses the title of Britten's last and haunting orchestral suite for his indispensable survey of the composer's life. There are contributions from **Britten** himself, from **Peter Pears** and members of the Britten family, and from **Imogen Holst**, **Bernstein**, **Richter** and **Janet Baker** among many others. The archival material is invaluable and the extracts include *Peter Grimes*, *The Rape of Lucretia*, *Billy Budd* and the *Turn of the Screw*, as well as the exquisite *Nocturne*, *Sinfonia da Requiem* and the GPO film, *Night Mail*. This portrait is rounded (the assistant producer is Donald Mitchell, so it carries special authority) and sympathetic, and it brings the viewer closer to the unique qualities of Britten's genius.

An American Overture; Ballad of Heroes; The Building of the House; Canadian Carnival; (i) Diversions for Piano (left hand) & Orchestra. Occasional Overture; Praise we Great Men; Scottish Ballad; Sinfonia da Requiem; Suite on English Folk Tunes; A time there was; Young Apollo; (ii) 4 Chansons françaises

⊕─ (B) *** EMI 5 73983-2 (2). (i) Donohoe; (ii) Gomez, CBSO Ch.; CBSO, Rattle

A valuable compilation, most of it rare. It is good to have the *Diversions for Piano (left hand) and Orchestra*, with **Peter Donohoe** as soloist – amazingly, this was the first version in stereo – and the most cherishable item of all is the radiant performance by **Jill Gomez** of the four *Chansons françaises*, the remarkable and tenderly affecting settings of Hugo and Verlaine composed by the 15-year-old Britten. This fine collection is most economically priced and as such is unmissable.

An American Overture; Sinfonia da Requiem, Op. 20; Peter Grimes: 4 Sea Interludes & Passacaglia, Op. 33

(BB) **(*) Naxos 8.553107. New Zealand SO, Fredman

Myer Fredman conducts warm and purposeful performances of this group of orchestral works from early in Britten's career. Dramatic and atmospheric points are well made with the help of a warm hall acoustic and full-ranging recording. Recommendable at super-budget price.

Canadian Carnival, Op. 19; (i) Violin Concerto, Op. 15. (with LENNOX BERKELEY) Mont Juic, Op. 12

(BB) *** Naxos 8.557198 (i) McAslan; ECO, Bedford

Britten's *Violin Concerto* grows in stature with each hearing, and **Lorraine McAslan** and the **ECO** under **Steuart Bedford** give a particularly intense and sensitive account. It is a most moving account, in some ways even more searching than Mark Lubotsky's with the composer himself conducting, on

Decca. The *Canadian Carnival* is not a major piece and is much influenced by Copland. *Mont Juic*, a suite of Catalan dances, is a joint composition, the first two movements being by Lennox Berkeley, the last two by Britten. It is witty, colourful and melodious, and the Lament is poignant. Bedford gets impressive results from the ECO, and in the concerto the balance between soloist and orchestra is most realistically and musically judged. A distinguished issue in every way, and a bargain at the price.

The Building of the House: Overture, Op. 79

(M) *** BBC mono/stereo BBCB 8007-2. ECO, composer – BRIDGE: *The Sea*, etc.; HOLST: *Fugal Concerto*, etc. ***

(M) *** BBC BBCL 4140-2. New Philh. Ch. and O, Giulini – SCHUBERT: *Symphony 9*; WEBER: *Der Freischütz: Overture* ***

Written for the opening of the Maltings Concert Hall in June 1967, *The Building of the House Overture* comes in a performance **Britten** conducted only two days after the première. The excitement of the occasion is carried over, even though the choral entry is initially off-pitch. A historic supplement to Britten's revealing interpretations of Bridge and Holst, well transferred from a radio recording.

Giulini's is a dramatic rather than a polished reading, with the **New Philharmonia Chorus** brought in to sing the passages from Psalm 127 that distinguish this energetic but relatively lightweight piece.

Clarinet Concerto Movement (orch. Matthews)

(BB) *** Hyp. Helios CDH 55060. King, ECO, Wordsworth – ARNOLD: *Clarinet Concertos 1–2*; *Scherzetto*; MACONCHY: *Concertinos* ***

Benny Goodman commissioned the young Benjamin Britten to write a concerto for him. Sadly, just before Britten returned to England, Goodman suggested a delay, and the composer never even sorted out the sketches. Colin Matthews, who worked closely with Britten during his last three years, has here fathomed what Britten intended and has orchestrated the result to make a highly attractive short piece, alternately energetic and poetic, with material adroitly interchanged and percussion used most imaginatively. **Thea King**, as in the rest of the disc, plays the piece most persuasively, making one deeply regret that it was never completed.

(i) Piano Concerto; (ii) Violin Concerto, Op. 15

⊕─ (M) *** Decca (ADD) 473 715-2. (i) Richter; (ii) Lubotsky; ECO, composer

(i; ii) Piano Concerto; (ii) Johnson over Jordan: Suite; (iii) Overture: Paul Bunyan (arr. Colin Matthews)

(BB) *** Naxos 8.557197. (i) MacGregor; (ii) ECO; (iii) LSO; Bedford

Richter is almost incomparable in interpreting the *Piano Concerto*, not only the thoughtful, introspective moments but also the Liszt-like bravura passages. With its highly original sonorities the *Violin Concerto* makes a splendid vehicle for another Soviet artist of the time, **Mark Lubotsky**. Recorded in The Maltings, the playing of the ECO under the composer's direction matches the inspiration of the soloists.

Joanna MacGregor's powerful performance of Britten's *Piano Concerto* has a formidable advantage over rival versions when it includes as a supplement the slow movement from the original (1938) version of the *Concerto*, which Britten replaced with the impressive *Impromptu* when he revised the work in 1945. **Steuart Bedford** is the ever-sympathetic conductor in this and the other two works, the overture for the early opera, *Paul Bunyan*, with orchestration amplified by Colin Matthews, and the incidental music which Britten wrote in 1939 for J. B. Priestley's *Johnson over Jordan*, one of his 'time' plays. Written at high speed, the score is most enjoyable and includes one gem in the delightful dance-band parody, *The Spider and the Fly*.

Violin Concerto in D min., Op. 15

⌐*** Warner 2564 60291-2. Hope, BBC SO, Watkins – BERG: *Violin Concerto* ***

Ⓝ Ⓜ *** EMI 2 28525-2 Vengerov, LSO, Rostropovich – WALTON: *Viola Concerto*

*** Chan. 9910. Mordkovitch, BBC SO, Hickox – VEALE: *Violin Concerto* ***

(i) Violin Concerto, Op. 15; (ii) Symphony for Cello & Orchestra, Op. 68

ⒷⒷ *** Naxos 8.553882. (i) Hirsch; (ii) Hugh; BBC Scottish SO, Yuasa

(i) Violin Concerto; (ii) Serenade for Tenor, Horn & Strings, Op. 31

Ⓑ *** CfP 5 75978-2. (i) Friend; (ii) Partridge, Busch; LPO, Pritchard – TIPPETT: *Concerto for Double String Orchestra* ***

As in the Berg *Concerto*, with which his account of the Britten is coupled, **Daniel Hope** sustains broad speeds in the spacious outer movements, conveying passionate intensity without expressive exaggeration. The slow *passacaglia* of the finale is particularly moving, from Hope's ethereal first entry to the inner meditation of the closing pages, while fast music finds him playing with sharp clarity of articulation. The cellist **Paul Watkins** demonstrates his formidable powers as a conductor, drawing comparably warm, sympathetic playing from the **BBC Symphony Orchestra**, fully and brilliantly recorded.

The unexpected conjunction in English music of the young **Maxim Vengerov** and the veteran **Rostropovich** brings the most ravishing string playing, and the greatness of both works is reinforced. The sweetness of Vengerov's playing in the high-lying cantilena of the first movement is nothing short of heavenly, matched by the 'dance of death' rhythms of the exuberant central *Scherzo*. When a virtuoso so completely masters a challenge, the fun behind the demonic music is evident, and the long *Passacaglia* finale finds both soloists and conductor so concentrated that each section builds up with unstoppable momentum, while the long epilogue ends on a breathtaking 'inquieto'.

Rodney Friend proves a masterful soloist in the *Violin Concerto*, magnificently incisive and expressive. As for **Ian Partridge**, one of the most consistently stylish of recording tenors, he gives a reading, often strikingly new in its illumination, more tenderly beautiful than Peter Pears's classic reading, culminating in a heavenly performance of the final Keats sonnet setting. Excellent recording in both works and a fine Tippett coupling, giving an overall playing time of 79 minutes.

The hushed opening, which can seem just sweet and easy, here conveys mystery and expectation thanks to **Mordkovitch**, and the tautness and purposefulness of her bravura playing then keep the wayward structure together, helped by warmly responsive playing from the **BBC Symphony** under **Hickox**. The opulent Chandos recording, finely detailed, bringing out the richness of Mordkovitch's tone and the high dramatic contrasts of the orchestra, adds greatly to the impact.

Tim Hugh gives a superb reading of Britten's *Cello Symphony*, strong and purposeful, making light of the formidable technical demands and the gritty double-stopping, with lyrical moments standing out. **Rebecca Hirsch** gives a spacious reading of the *Violin Concerto*, her tone clear and fresh rather than warmly romantic. The scherzando writing of the middle movement is full of fun, and the elegiac close of the finale is made poignant by understatement. Full, clear recording, with timpani specially vivid.

(i) Double Concerto in B min. for Violin, Viola & Orchestra. 2 Portraits for Strings; Sinfonietta (version for small orchestra); (ii) Young Apollo (for piano, string quartet & strings), Op. 16

Ⓜ *** Warner Elatus 0927 46718-2. (i) Kremer, Bashmet; (ii) Lugansky; Hallé O, Nagano

This striking three-movement *Double Concerto for Violin and Viola* was left in short score with indications of orchestration, which Colin Matthews had little difficulty in completing. It is stylistically less radical than the *Sinfonietta*, warmer and more recognizably the work of Britten, with its distinctive melodies and orchestration both spare and striking. It receives a magnetic reading here from the two high-powered Russian soloists, with **Kent Nagano** and the **Hallé Orchestra**. The *Sinfonietta* comes in a version that Britten made in America, for small orchestra rather than solo instruments, and the *Two Portraits*, written when Britten was 16, offers a vigorous, purposeful picture of a friend and a reflective, melancholy one of himself, with the viola solo beautifully played by **Bashmet**. A revelatory disc.

(i) Double Concerto for Violin and Viola (ed. Colin Matthews); Variations on a Theme of Frank Bridge, Op. 10; (ii) Les Illuminations, Op. 18

Ⓝ ⌐ Ⓜ **** LPO 0037 LPO, Jurowski; with (i) Schoeman, Zemtsov; (ii) Sally Matthews

The *Double Concerto* brings inspired solo contributions from **Pieter Schoeman** and **Alexander Zemtsov** who play with great delicacy of feeling and warmth to reveal this work (in Colin Matthews's completion) among the composer's most memorable. That description certainly applies also to the *Variations*, which are given a splendidly characterized account under **Jurowski** which brings much orchestral bravura as well as a rich depth of feeling. The hat trick is completed by **Sally Matthews** in *Les Illuminations*, a work which is more often given to a male singer. Here she triumphantly demonstrates how ravishingly the cycle projects on a soprano voice, and besides creating much lyrical beauty, she is arrestingly dramatic in her invocations of 'Towns'. Excellently vivid recording throughout, which confirms this as a key Britten triptych.

(i) *Lachrymae, Op. 48a. Movement for Wind Sextet;* (ii) *Night Mail* (end sequence). *Sinfonietta; The Sword in the Stone* (concert suite for wind & percussion); (iii) *Phaedra, Op. 93*

*** Hyp. CDA 66845. (i) Chase; (ii) Hawthorne; (iii) Rigby; Nash Ens., Friend

Lachrymae, for viola with string accompaniment, is played here with the beauty intensified, thanks to the firm, true playing of **Roger Chase**. Both the *Sinfonietta* and the *Wind Sextet* movement of 1930 reflect the mature Britten style only occasionally. The concert suite for wind and percussion was drawn from music for a radio production of T. H. White's ironic Arthurian piece, *The Sword in the Stone*, and brings some delightful Wagner parodies. It is also good to have the final sequence from Britten's music for the GPO film documentary, *Night Mail*, with Auden's rattling verse spoken by **Nigel Hawthorne**. In the dramatic scena, *Phaedra*, **Jean Rigby** sings beautifully but lacks the biting intensity of Janet Baker. Excellent playing from the Nash Ensemble, and first-rate recording.

Lachrymae; Prelude & Fugue for 18-part String Orchestra; Simple Symphony; A time there was . . . (suite on English folk tunes), *Op. 90; Variations on a Theme of Frank Bridge; Young Person's Guide to the Orchestra.* (i) *Song-cycles: Les Illuminations, Op. 18; Nocturne, Op. 60;* (i; ii) *Serenade for Tenor, Horn & Strings, Op. 31. Gloriana: Courtly Dances. Peter Grimes: 4 Sea Interludes*

Ⓑ **(*) Nim. NI 1751 (3). E. String O or ESO, Boughton; with (i) Hadley; (ii) Halstead

This inexpensive bargain box will seem to many collectors an admirable way of collecting Britten's key orchestral works plus the three major song-cycles. In the latter, **Jerry Hadley** is a dramatic and involving soloist; his is not far short of an operatic approach, with the crystal-clear projection of words and histrionic power of his singing compensating for some lack of subtlety in word-colouring. *Les Illuminations* (in easily colloquial French) is strikingly fresh and spontaneous, and in the *Nocturne*, which opens magnetically and evocatively, the orchestral playing is full of tension. **Anthony Halstead's** horn contribution in the *Serenade* is hardly less impressive. **William Boughton** shows himself a fine Britten advocate throughout, and the works both for strings and for full orchestra are most sympathetically played and certainly do not lack vitality. The recording (for the most part made in the

Great Hall of Birmingham University) is outstandingly rich and resonant in a characteristic Nimbus way, while the powerful evocation of the *Peter Grimes Sea Interludes* is enhanced by the acoustic of Birmingham's Symphony Hall – one of the first recordings to be made there. Excellent value.

(i) *Lachrymae, Op. 48a. Simple Symphony, Op. 4; Suite on English Folk Tunes, Op. 90;* (ii) *Temporal Variations* (orch. C. Matthews); (iii) *A Charm of Lullabies, Op. 41* (orch. C. Matthews)

⊕–₁ Ⓑ Ⓑ *** Naxos 8.557205. N. Sinf., Bedford, with (i) Dukes; (ii) Daniel; (iii) Wyn-Rogers

Steuart Bedford brings the keenest intelligence and intuitive feeling to everything here. The anthology spans the whole of Britten's career. The *Temporal Variations* of 1936, originally for oboe and piano, are effectively scored for strings by Colin Matthews – as, for that matter is his orchestration of *A Charm of Lullabies* of 11 years later. The elegiac, valedictory *Suite on English Folk Tunes* is touching and affecting, and Bedford's is the finest reading of it in the current catalogue. All the soloists are impeccable and the disc fills an important gap in the Britten discography with real distinction, to say nothing of economy.

(i; ii) *Lachrymae;* (i) *Simple Symphony; Variations on a Theme of Frank Bridge; Young Apollo, Op. 16.* (iii) *Death in Venice: Suite* (arr. Bedford); (iv) *Peter Grimes: 4 Sea Interludes & Passacaglia*

Ⓑ *** Chan. 2-for-1 241-2 (2). (i) Montreal I Musici, Turovsky; (ii) Golani; (iii) ECO, Bedford; (iv) Ulster O, Handley

Young Apollo is particularly successful here, with vivid recording capturing the unusual textures with piano and string quartet as well as strings. **Rivka Golani** is a resonant soloist in *Lachrymae*, and the *Variations* and *Simple Symphony* have similar heft, helped by the rich, upfront recording. Representing Britten's operas, **Steuart Bedford's** *Death in Venice Suite* is well worth having, and **Handley's** *Peter Grimes* excerpts are second only to Previn's splendid EMI recording, helped by richly atmospheric digital sound of demonstration quality. This is one of the most recommendable of Chandos's two-for-one Doubles.

(i) *Matinées musicales; Soirées musicales;* (ii; iv) *Young Person's Guide to the Orchestra;* (iii; iv) *Peter Grimes: 4 Sea Interludes & Passacaglia*

Ⓜ *** Decca (ADD) 425 659-2. (i) Nat. PO, Bonynge; (ii) LSO; (iii) ROHCG O; (iv) composer

Bonynge's sparkling versions of the *Matinées* and *Soirées musicales* are here reissued, coupled with **Britten's** accounts of the *Young Person's Guide to the Orchestra* and the *Sea Interludes and Passacaglia*.

Occasional Overture; Prelude & Fugue for 18-Part String Orchestra; Variations on a Theme of Frank Bridge; Young Person's Guide to the Orchestra.

Ⓑ Ⓑ *** Naxos 8.557200. LSO or ECO, Bedford

The *Occasional Overture* is a rumbustious piece that might

almost have been written by Malcolm Arnold rather than Britten. All three performances here under **Steuart Bedford** are of the highest calibre, with superb playing from the strings of the **ECO** in the *Frank Bridge Variations* and *Prelude and Fugue*, and the **LSO** on top form in the other two works. Excellent recording too. Originally issued by Collins, this is a genuine Naxos bargain.

Prelude & Fugue for 18 Solo Strings, Op. 29; Simple Symphony Op. 4; Variations on a Theme of Frank Bridge, Op. 10

⊕— Ⓑ *** ASV Resonance CD RSN 3042. N. Sinf., Hickox

This ASV reissue is notable for an outstandingly fine account of the *Frank Bridge Variations* which stands up well alongside the composer's own version. **Hickox's** reading encompasses the widest range of emotion and style; throughout, the string playing is commitedly responsive, combining polish with eloquence, the rich sonorities resonating powerfully in the glowing ambience of All Saints Quayside Church, Newcastle. Even if in the *Simple Symphony* Hickox does not quite match the composer's rhythmic bounce in the *Playful Pizzicato*, he finds a strain of nobilmente in the *Sentimental Sarabande*. The *Prelude and Fugue* is comparably eloquent, although here the playing is marginally less assured. The 1987 recording is excellent.

The Prince of the Pagodas (Complete Ballet; choreography Kenneth Macmillan)

⊕— *** Warner **DVD** 9031-738262. Darcey Bussell, Jonathan Cope, Artists of The Royal Ballet, ROHCG O, Ashley Lawrence (V/D: Derek Bailey). Includes *Out of Line* (feature on Kenneth Macmillan by Derek Bailey)

The Prince of the Pagodas is a masterly score that repays much repetition, and both the outer Acts are wonderfully inventive. The performances of **Darcey Bussell** as Princess Rose and **Jonathan Cope** as the Prince are every bit as impressive as we remembered them, and MacMillan's choreography is, as always, distinguished by imagination and his great musicality. The DVD also includes the feature on MacMillan by Derek Bailey which is full of interest and includes excerpts from some of his other ballets, but seeing MacMillan's choreography greatly enhances the musical experience.

(i) The Prince of the Pagodas (complete ballet: CD version); (ii) Gloriana (Symphonic Suite, Op. 53a)

Ⓑ *** EMI 3 52274-2 (2). (i) L. Sinf., Knussen; (ii) Bournemouth SO, Segal

The multicoloured instrumentation of *The Prince of the Pagodas* – much influenced by Britten's visit to Bali – is caught with glorious richness in **Oliver Knussen's** complete version of the full-length ballet. The ballet is paired with a suite of music from *Gloriana* which, by concentrating on the pageant sequence remains enjoyable in its own right when the performance is warmly understanding and vividly recorded, even if the playing of the **Bournemouth Orchestra** is not quite as crisp in ensemble as in some of its finest records.

Simple Symphony, Op. 4.

⊕— ⒷⒷ *** Warner Apex 2564 61437-2. RPO, Warren-Green – BUTTERWORTH: *Banks of Green Willow*; ELGAR: *String Serenade*; HOLST: *St Paul's Suite*; VAUGHAN WILLIAMS: *Fantasia on a Theme of Tallis* ***

A truly outstanding super-bargain anthology. **Christopher Warren-Green** is an underrated conductor of English music and here he is at his most spontaneously successful. The outer movements of the *Simple Symphony* sparkle with vivacity, the *Playful Pizzicato* bounces with joy and the *Sentimental Sarabande* has never been more touchingly expressive. Excellent sound.

(i) Sinfonia da Requiem; (ii) Symphony for Cello & Orchestra, Op. 68; (iii) Cantata misericordium, Op. 69

Ⓜ *** Decca (ADD) 425 100-2. (i) New Philh. O; (ii) Rostropovich, ECO; (iii) Pears, Fischer-Dieskau, L. Symphony Ch., LSO; composer

All the performances on the Decca CD are definitive, and **Rostropovich's** account of the *Cello Symphony* in particular is commanding. The CD transfers are managed admirably.

Sinfonia da Requiem, Op. 20; Gloriana: Symphonic Suite, Op. 52a; Peter Grimes: 4 Sea Interludes & Passacaglia

ⒷⒷ *** Naxos 8.557196. LSO, Bedford

Steuart Bedford conducts strong, idiomatic performances of these works, helped by exceptionally vivid recording. The atmosphere of the *Peter Grimes Interludes* is caught superbly, and the *Sinfonia da Requiem*, treated expansively, culminates in a radiant account of the final *Requiem aeternam*.

Sinfonia da Requiem, Op. 20; Peter Grimes: 4 Sea Interludes & Passacaglia

⊕— ✺ Ⓜ **** EMI 5 62615-2. LSO, Previn – HOLST: *Egdon Heath*, etc. ***

Previn gives a passionately intense reading of the *Sinfonia da Requiem*, the most ambitious of Britten's early orchestral works, written after the death of his parents. It is warmer than the composer's own, less sharply incisive but presenting a valid alternative. So too in the *Four Sea Interludes*, with Previn springing the bouncing rhythms of the second interlude – the picture of *Sunday Morning in the Borough* – even more infectiously than the composer himself. These superb performances are presented in expansive 1970s recordings of demonstration quality. With its new Holst coupling, this is one of Previn's finest CDs, fully worthy of inclusion among EMI's 'Great Recordings of the Century'.

Sinfonietta, Op. 1

*** Lyrita (ADD) SRCD 257. ECO, Del Mar – ARNOLD; BERKELEY: *Sinfoniettas*; RAWSTHORNE; TIPPETT: *Divertimentos* ***

*** BIS CD 540. Tapiola Sinf., Vänskä – *Nocturne*, etc. ***

Britten's Opus 1 was written when he was in his teens. It has some of the composer's fingerprints, but points uncharacteristically towards central Europe. In the **ECO** version with full strings, its astringency and assurance are the more convincing, particularly in a performance as fine as this on Lyrita.

The *Sinfonietta* is also presented on BIS with rare strength and warmth to make it totally convincing. It is very well recorded and comes with an attractive collection of vocal music.

Symphony for Cello & Orchestra, Op. 68

🎵 *** Virgin 5 45356-2. Mørk, CBSO, Rattle – ELGAR: *Cello Concerto* ***

Ⓑ *** EMI 5 05916-2. Isserlis, City of L. Sinfonia, Hickox – BRIDGE: *Oration* ***

Ⓝ (*) Signum SIGCD137. Walton, Philh. O, Briger – SHOSTAKOVICH: *Cello Concerto 2* (*)

(i) Symphony for Cello & Orchestra, Op. 68. Death in Venice: suite, Op. 88 (arr. Bedford)

Ⓜ *** Chan. 10274X. (i) Wallfisch; ECO, Bedford

This is the second recording **Truls Mørk** has made of the *Cello Symphony*. He is completely attuned to the Britten sensibility, playing with ardour and vision. **Rattle** gets a superb response from the **Birmingham** players and the sound is state-of-the-art, with particularly impressive depth and naturalness of perspective.

Wallfisch and **Bedford** are purposeful, and the weight and range of the brilliant and full Chandos recording quality add to the impact, with direction even more spacious than the composer's. Steuart Bedford's encapsulation of Britten's last opera into this rich and colourful suite makes a splendid coupling.

With speeds generally a little slower, **Isserlis** is not quite as taut and electric as his rivals, partly because the recording does not present the solo instrument so cleanly. It remains a powerful, dramatic performance, highly recommendable if the Bridge coupling is preferred.

A welcome and intelligent coupling with an excellent soloist in **Jamie Walton** but let down by badly balanced recorded sound. Whether played on a simple straightforward set-up or highly sophisticated equipment, it still sounds unpleasing.

Variations & Fugue on a Theme by Frank Bridge; Young Person's Guide to the Orchestra; Peter Grimes: 4 Sea Interludes & Passacaglia

🎵 ⒷⒷ *** Warner Apex 8573 89082-2. BBC SO, A. Davis

In his admirable British music series, **Andrew Davis** gives full weight as well as brilliance to these masterpieces from early in Britten's career, making a particularly attractive triptych. The *Frank Bridge Variations*, set here against the more popular Purcell set, gain particularly from large-scale treatment, with each variation strongly characterized. Excellent recording. This is one of the outstanding bargains among the Warner Classics super-bargain Apex series.

Young Person's Guide to the Orchestra (Variations & Fugue on a Theme of Purcell), Op. 34

*** BBC Legends (ADD) BBCL4184-2. Leningrad PO, Rozhdestvensky – PROKOFIEV: *Symphony 5; Romeo and Juliet: Death of Tybalt* ***

Ⓑ *** CfP 586 1752. LPO, Sian Edwards (with DEBUSSY: *Children's Corner: 3 Pieces:* ECO Wind Ens.) – PROKOFIEV: *Peter and the Wolf* **(*); RAVEL: *Ma Mère l'Oye* ***

Ⓜ **(*) BBC (ADD) BBCL 4005-2. BBC SO, Stokowski – BEETHOVEN: *Symphony 7* *(**); FALLA: *El amor brujo* **** 🏵

Coupled with a dazzling, high-voltage account of Prokofiev's *Fifth Symphony*, **Rozhdestvensky's** *Young Person's Guide* comes from the **Leningrad Orchestra's** first visit to these shores at the 1960 Edinburgh Festival. The Britten receives a virtuosic account that still lifts the spirits and sounds extraordinarily vivid.

The underrated **Sian Edwards**, always impressive in the recording studio, does not press the earlier variations too hard, revelling in the colour of her wind soloists, yet the violins enter zestfully and the violas make a touching contrast. The brass bring fine bite and sonority, and the fugue has plenty of vitality, with the climax spectacularly expansive in the resonant acoustics of Watford Town Hall. The three pieces from *Children's Corner*, skilfully scored for wind by Graham Sheen, make a pleasing bonus, with the *Golliwog's Cake-Walk* easily the most effective.

Stokowski's 1962 Prom performance with the BBC Symphony Orchestra is quite spectacular. The whole occasion was highly charged and the quality of the orchestral response pretty breathtaking. Even if the opening is very relaxed, almost lethargic, this is a reading of outstanding personality and intensity, the sound very good for its age.

Young Person's Guide to the Orchestra (with narration)

ⒷⒷ *** Naxos 8.554170. Everage, Melbourne SO, Lanchbery – POULENC: *The Story of Babar* *** 🏵; PROKOFIEV: *Peter and the Wolf* ***

Ⓜ **(*) Decca Phase Four 444 104-2. Connery, RPO, Dorati – PROKOFIEV: *Peter and the Wolf*, etc. **(*)

Ⓑ ** CfP (ADD) 3 82230-2. Richard Baker, New Philh. O, Leppard – PROKOFIEV: *Peter and the Wolf*; RAWSTHORNE: *Practical Cats* **

Using her own enthusiastically expanded version of the original commentary, **Dame Edna Everage** is sure to draw any young possum into the world of the orchestra. Her exuberance offsets any twee moments, and the Melbourne orchestra illustrate vivid instrumental descriptions with splendidly alive and colourful playing. The Naxos recording is excellent and, with its highly enjoyable couplings, this inexpensive triptych is warmly recommendable.

Sean Connery's voice is very familiar and his easy style is attractive. His narration should go down well with young people, even if some of the points are made heavily. The orchestral playing is first rate and the vivid, forwardly balanced recording – with a Decca Phase Four source – is effective enough. The performance has plenty of colour and vitality.

Richard Baker's rather cosy narration seems to hold up the flow of the music. The orchestral playing is lively and the recording vivid, but one feels there are too many words here: this is not a version to stand constant repetition. The great interest of this reissue is the inclusion of Rawsthorne's *Practical Cats.*

Young Person's Guide to the Orchestra; Peter Grimes: 4 Sea Interludes

☷— **** Telarc CD 80660. Cincinnati SO, Paavo Järvi – ELGAR: *Enigma Variations* ****

For anyone wanting Britten's two most popular orchestral works, together with Elgar's *Enigma*, this superbly recorded Telarc disc is an obvious choice. The **Cincinnati Orchestra** are on their toes throughout, and **Järvi** produces the most vividly refined detail. In the opening *Dawn* sequence in the *Sea Interludes* he creates a magical contrast between the high violins and the deep brass sonorities, and every variation in the *Young Person's Guide* is vividly projected, against a warmly atmospheric backcloth.

CHAMBER MUSIC

Cello Sonata in C, Op. 65

*** Simax PSC 1160. Birkeland, Anvik – BRIDGE: *Cello Sonata,* etc. ***

(i) Cello Sonata in C; (Unaccompanied) Cello Suites 1, Op. 72; 2, Op. 80

☷— Ⓜ *** Decca (ADD) 421 859-2. Rostropovich; (i) with composer

The strange, five-movement *Cello Sonata* was written especially for **Rostropovich's** appearance in 1961 at the Aldeburgh Festival. Although technically it demands fantastic feats of the cellist, it is hardly a display piece. It is an excellent work to wrestle with on a record, particularly when the performance is never likely to be outshone. The recording is superb in every way.

On Simax these Norwegian artists give as sympathetic and idiomatic account of the Britten *Sonata* as any now in the catalogue. Britten and Rostropovich command a special authority, but those wanting an alternative with up-to-date recorded sound need not hesitate.

Cello Suites (Suites for Unaccompanied Cello) 1, Op. 72; 2, Op. 80; 3, Op. 87

*** Virgin 5 45399-2. Mørk

*** BIS CD 446. Torleif Thedéen

The Norwegian cellist **Truls Mørk** gives richly eloquent accounts of all three suites. He produces a magnificent sound and has a flawless technique. Even if you have the pioneering Rostropovich set or one of its successors, you will find something new here.

Torleif Thedéen has magnificent tonal warmth and elo-

quence, and he proves a masterly advocate of these *Suites*, which sound thoroughly convincing in his hands, if not quite as powerful as Rostropovich in the concertos and sonatas.

(i) Gemini Variations (for violin, flute & piano duet), Op. 73; (ii) 2 Insect Pieces (for oboe & piano); (iii) Russian Festival (for brass); (iv; v) A Birthday Hansel, Op. 92; (iv; vi–viii) Cantata academica, Op. 62; (iv; vii; ix; x) Cantata misericordium, Op. 69; (iv; xi; xii) Canticle II (Abraham and Isaac); (xiii; x) Children's Crusade, Op. 82; (iv; xii) 6 Hölderlin Fragments, Op. 61; (xiv) Poet's Echo

Ⓜ *** Decca ADD 468 811-2 (2). (i) Gábor & Zoltán Jeney; (ii) Holliger, Schiff; (iii) Philip Jones Brass, Iveson; (iv) Pears, (v) Ellis; (vi) Vyvyan, Watts, Brannigan, (vii) L. Symphony Ch., LSO, (viii) Malcolm; (ix) Fischer-Dieskau; (x) cond. Burgess; (xi) Procter; (xii) composer (piano); (xiii) Soloists, Wandsworth School Boys' Ch.; (xiv) Vishnevskaya, Rostropovich

This collection is called 'Rarities' and ranges from the *Insect Pieces* for oboe and piano of 1935 and the sonorous *Russian Funeral* of 1936 to *A Birthday Hansel* (a Burns setting celebrating the seventy-fifth birthday of the Queen Mother), completed the year before the composer's death. The *Gemini Variations* were commissioned by the Hungarian **Jeney twins**, who perform the piece here. More than anything the *Cantata academica*, written for Basle University, is an expression of joy and optimism, while in the *Cantata misericordium* (telling the story of the Good Samaritan) the composer's theme is the resolution of stress in peace and tranquillity which come from within.

The *Children's Crusade* is darker, a setting of a Brecht poem which in the most direct way, with vivid percussion effects, tells of children lost in Poland in 1939. *The Poet's Echo*, Britten's setting of Pushkin in the original Russian, was written for **Vishnevskaya** and with the help of her husband the performance is warm and highly atmospheric. The six *Hölderlin Fragments*, with **Peter Pears** responding eloquently, reflect a highly individual response to the German language and the sensitive word-painting of Hölderlin. (Surprisingly for Decca, no translations are included for either of these cycles.)

(i; ii) Lachrymae; (ii; iii; iv) Canticle 3: Still falls the rain, Op. 55; (iii; v) Our Hunting Fathers; (ii; iii) Who are these children?, Op. 84

(**(*)) BBC mono/stereo BBCB 8014-2. (i) Major; (ii) composer (piano); (iii) Pears; (iv) Brain; (v) LSO, composer

Our Hunting Fathers created something of a scandal when it was first performed, at the Norwich Festival in 1936, thanks to its anti-blood-sports theme, prompted by W. H. Auden. **Pears** is in superb voice, focused sharply in this rather dry mono BBC studio recording of 1961. In *Lachrymae*, the playing of **Britten** at the piano magnetizes the ear almost as in an improvisation, with the viola player **Margaret Major** characteristically warm in a beautifully sustained reading.

Who are these children? serves to intensify, by contrast, the darkness of the four more substantial war-inspired songs, with both **Britten** and **Pears** at their finest. It is good, too, to have this 1956 Aldeburgh Festival account of the *Canticle 3* with **Dennis Brain** as horn soloist, warm even in face of a dry acoustic. The big snag is the absence of texts – particularly serious in the case of the little-known Soutar poems.

(i) 6 Metamorphoses after Ovid; (i; ii) Phantasy Quartet (for oboe, violin, viola & cello), Op. 2; (i; iii) 2 Insect Pieces; Temporal Variations; (iii) Holiday Diary, Op. 5; Night Piece; 5 Waltzes

🎵 **(BB)** *** Hyp. Helios CDH 55154. (i) Francis; (ii) Delmé Qt (members); (iii) Dussek

Sarah Francis gives strong and distinctive characterizations not only to the six *Ovid* pieces but also to the early *Phantasy Quartet* and to the pieces for oboe and piano as well. **Michael Dussek** proves a magnetic interpreter of the solo piano music, bringing out the sparkle of the boyhood waltzes (or 'Walztes' as Britten originally called them) and the *Holiday Diary*. He then finds intense poetry and magic in the *Night Piece*.

String Quartets: in F (1928); in D (1931); 2, Op. 36

*** Chan. 9664. Sorrel Qt

String Quartets 1 in D, Op. 25; 2 in C, Op. 36; 3 Divertimenti

(BB) *** Naxos 8.553883. Maggini Qt

String Quartet 3, Op. 94; Quartettino (1930); Alla marcia (1933); Simple Symphony

(BB) *** Naxos 8.554360. Maggini Qt

String Quartets 1–3; 3 Divertimenti

🎵 **(M)** *** EMI 2 28518-2 (2). Belcea Qt

String Quartet 1 in D, Op. 25; 3 Divertimenti, Op. 36

🎵 ✿ *** Challenge CC 72106. Brodsky Qt – TCHAIKOVSKY: *String Quartet 1* *** ✿ (Available from www.challengeclassics.com)

String Quartets 2 in C, Op. 36; 3, Op. 94

🎵 *** Challenge CC 72099. Brodsky Qt

In a compact two-disc package, the **Belcea Quartet** offer outstanding performances of all Britten's works for string quartet published in the composer's lifetime: the three numbered *Quartets* plus the brightly inventive *Divertimenti* of 1936, assembled from pieces written earlier. With the help of warm, full recorded sound, these are performances which from first to last bring out the originality of the timbres which Britten created in all the numbered *Quartets*.

The spontaneity of the playing of the **Brodsky Quartet** immediately grips the listener, with the gleamingly luminous opening of the *D major Quartet* bringing a raptly concentrated pianissimo, and this degree of intensity pervades the whole set of performances. The *Three Divertimenti* of 1936 are equally vividly characterized, the flimsy central *Waltz* delectably slight and transparent and full of charm. The recording could hardly be more real and present.

The **Maggini** give clean, direct performances of the first two numbered quartets, not as intense as some but fresh and thoughtful, well coupled with the three colourful *Divertimenti* of 1936. The Maggini's second CD is even finer than their first. They give a strongly characterized reading of Op. 94. The *Poco adagio* of the *Quartettino* is particularly searching, while the account of the *Simple Symphony* (which opens the programme) is as sprightly and sparkling as you could wish. First-class recording.

This première recording by the **Sorrel Quartet** of the *F major* work of 1928, his first written under the tutelage of Frank Bridge, is strong and confident, with hints of later Britten. The *D major Quartet* of 1931 was revised by the composer himself not long before he died. Warmly performed, they make a fine coupling for the magnificent *Second Quartet*, here made to start waywardly, leading to a passionate, concentrated reading, helped by wide-ranging sound.

String Quartet 2 in C, Op. 36

*** Testament **DVD** SBDVD1001. Amadeus Qt – SCHUBERT: *Piano Quintet in A (Trout); Quartettsatz* ***

The **Amadeus** made the first recording of the Britten Op. 36 *Quartet* on seven 78-r.p.m. plum label sides, not long after its composition and their own formation. This performance was telerecorded in Aldeburgh by a team that included John Culshaw, previously of Decca but by then Head of Music at BBC Television. It is superbly and simply directed with totally unobtrusive camerawork and expertly balanced sound, with the legendary Jimmy Burnett in charge.

String Quartet 3, Op. 94

*** Testament **DVD** SBDVD1002. Amadeus Qt – SCHUBERT: *String Quintet in C* ***

This performance came from the week devoted to Britten and Schubert at a special autumn festival in 1977 and, like its companion issue, was recorded by the same team. The performance is every bit as authoritative as (and even more moving than) the Decca sound recording discussed above and made at much the same time.

VOCAL MUSIC

Advance Democracy; (i) A Boy Was Born, Op. 3; 5 Flower Songs, Op. 47; Sacred and Profane, Op. 91

*** Chan. 9701. Finzi Singers; (i) Lichfield Cathedral Choristers, Spicer

Advance Democracy, with its adventurous choral writing, sets the seal on a wide-ranging group of works representing Britten: both early (the nativity cantata, *A Boy Was Born*, written at the age of 19) and late (*Sacred and Profane*, dating from 1975, the year before Britten died, which poignantly sets death-obsessed medieval lyrics). The five *Flower Songs*, written in 1949, demonstrate Britten's gift for writing occasional music, pointful and elegant. Under **Paul Spicer** the **Finzi**

Singers give virtuoso performances, vividly caught in the warm and atmospheric Chandos recording.

A.M.D.G.; Chorale after an Old French Carol; 5 Flower Songs; Hymn to the Virgin; Sacred and Profane, Op. 91; Gloriana: Choral Dances

*** Hyp. CDA 67140. Polyphony, Layton

Under **Stephen Layton** the brilliant group, **Polyphony**, give superb performances of a wide range of Britten's unaccompanied choral music, from the *Hymn to the Virgin*, written in 1930 when the teenage composer was confined to the school sickbay, to *Sacred and Profane*, one of his last works, settings of medieval texts both religious and secular, from the delicate *Flower Songs* to the often lusty dances from the Elizabethan opera, *Gloriana*, incisively done. *A.M.D.G.*, sensitive settings of poems by Gerard Manley Hopkins was written in 1939 when Britten was in the United States. Finely balanced sound to match the refined beauty of the performances.

Antiphon; Festival Te Deum; Hymn to St Cecilia; A Hymn of St Columba; Hymn to St Peter; Hymn to the Virgin; Jubilate Deo; Missa brevis; Rejoice in the Lamb; Te Deum in C. (Organ) Prelude & Fugue on a Theme of Vittoria

🔓 (BB) **** Naxos 8.554791. St John's College Ch., Robinson

This collection of 11 choral works may omit the much-recorded *Ceremony of Carols* but as a result it gives a wider view of Britten's achievement in this area, with Barry Holden's excellent notes relating each work to the composer's career and personal associations. The biting attack of these young singers is enhanced by refined recording which thrillingly brings out the wide dynamic contrasts. The *Prelude and Fugue* for organ with its elaborate counterpoint is also brilliantly done. The booklet includes full texts.

A Boy Was Born; Christ's Nativity; Hymn to the Virgin; Jubilate in C; Shepherd's Carol; Te Deum in C

*** Hyp. CDA 66825. Gritton, Wyn-Rogers, Holst Singers, St Paul's Cathedral Choristers, Layton; Goode (organ)

Here is a disc to illustrate Britten's special fascination with the Christmas story, including *Christ's Nativity*. The writing has many bold and original touches typical of the mature composer, not least in the opening cries of *Awake!* **Stephen Layton** conducts a finely controlled performance, full of sharp dynamic and rhythmic contrasts. Despite speeds slower than usual, the performance of the cantata *A Boy Was Born*, of 1934, has similar merits, with the *Jubilate* and *Te Deum* made the more vigorous by the organ accompaniment of **David Goode**. Atmospheric, spacious choral sound.

A Boy Was Born; Festival Te Deum, Op. 32; Rejoice in the Lamb, Op. 30; A Wedding Anthem, Op. 46

(BB) *** Hyp. Helios CDH 55307. Corydon Singers, Westminster Cathedral Ch., Best; Trotter (organ)

All the works included here are sharply inspired. The refinement and tonal range of the choirs could hardly be more impressive, and the recording is refined and atmospheric to match.

Canticles 1–5

(BB) *** Hyp. Helios 55244. Rolfe Johnson, Chance, Opie, Vignoles, Williams, Thompson – PURCELL, arr. BRITTEN: *An Evening Hymn*, etc. ***

(M) *** Decca (ADD) 425 716-2. Pears, Hahessy, Bowman, Shirley-Quirk, Tuckwell, Ellis, composer

*** Virgin 5 45525-2. Bostridge, Daniels, Maltman, Drake, with Brown, Brewer (with 8 *Folksongs*, arr. Britten)

The Decca CD brings together on a single record all five of the miniature cantatas to which Britten gave the title 'Canticle', plus the *Birthday Hansel*, written in honour of the seventy-fifth birthday of Queen Elizabeth the Queen Mother, and a Purcell song-arrangement. A beautiful collection as well as a historical document, with recording that still sounds well.

The Hyperion versions make an excellent modern alternative. **Rolfe Johnson's** tenor is sweeter even than Pears's, most of all in the fifth of the *Canticles*, *The Death of St Narcissus*, written with harp accompaniment at the very end of Britten's life. Like the fourth, *The Journey of the Magi*, it sets a T. S. Eliot poem. The three Purcell realizations are shared among the soloists, one apiece, all representing Purcell at his most beautiful and intense.

Ian Bostridge's heady tenor is also ideally suited to the inflexions of Britten's music, and he gives colourful, vigorously dramatic readings of pieces that can seem wayward, helped by inspired accompaniment from **Julius Drake**. He is joined by the counter-tenor, **David Daniels** and **Christopher Maltman** and the *Fifth Canticle*, with harp accompaniment, brings ear-tweaking textures. The seven folksong arrangements, including the most popular ones, are shared among the three singers. Excellent recording.

Canticle 1; Four Folksong arrangements: 7 Sonnets of Michelangelo, Op. 22; Winter Words, Op. 52

(BB) *** Hyp. CDH 55067. Rolfe Johnson, Johnson

In this 1985 recording, the *Michelangelo Sonnets* have a freshness and exuberance apt for that earliest of the song-cycles with piano, and the folksongs are deliciously pointed, notably *Little Sir William*. Even more valuable is the Hardy song-cycle, *Winter Words*, which contains some of the most striking and atmospheric of all Britten's songs, exactly evoking the world of Hardy. **Graham Johnson** proves an ideal accompanist. Refined, well-balanced sound.

(i) A Ceremony of Carols. (ii) Deus in adjutorium meum; Hymn of St Columba; Hymn to the Virgin; Jubilate Deo in E flat; Missa brevis, Op. 63

🔓 **** Hyp. CDA 66220. Westminster Cathedral Ch., Hill; (i) with S. Williams; (ii) J. O'Donnell (organ)

Particularly impressive here is the boys' singing in the *Ceremony of Carols*, where the ensemble is superb, the solo work amazingly mature and the range of tonal colouring a delight. Along with the other, rarer pieces, this is an outstanding collection, beautifully and atmospherically recorded.

(i; ii) A Ceremony of Carols; (i; iii) Friday Afternoons, Op. 7; Francie; King Herod and the cock; The oxen; (i) Sweet was the song; (iv) Song: The birds; (iv; v; iii) 3 2-part Settings of Walter de la Mare: The Ride-by-nights; The Rainbow; The Ship of Rio. A Wealden Trio

(BB) *** Naxos 8.553183. (i) New L. Children's Ch., Corp; (ii) Kanga; (iii) Wells; (iv) Hopper; (v) Attree; Kenyon

Ronald Corp directs bright, refreshing performances of a delightful collection of Britten choral pieces written for children's voices. The **New London Children's Choir** is relatively large and is recorded against a lively hall acoustic, but there is no lack of impact, and the tenderness of expression as well as the liveliness is consistently refreshing.

(i) A Ceremony of Carols. Hymn to the Virgin; Shepherd's Carol

*** Regent REGCD 243. (i) Christ Church College, Cambridge, Ch., Rowland – LEIGHTON: Carols ***

Christ Church College Choir, directed by **David Rowland**, give a vivid but warm-hearted account of Britten's cycle and the two equally appealing companion works with first-rate contributions from the unnamed treble soloists. **Laurence Pope's** contribution is also most sensitive, especially in the *Interlude*. The ambience of the chapel casts a warm glow over the recording, rather negating any earthy quality in the performance. But of its kind this is first class, as are the Leighton couplings.

(i) A Ceremony of Carols; (ii) St Nicholas

(M) *** EMI (ADD) 5 65112-2. King's College Ch., Willcocks; with (i) Ellis; (ii) Tear, Russell, Cambridge Girls' Ch.

In *St Nicholas*, though the balance of the solo voices – the Saint as a boy and a man respectively – is rather too close, the performance is vivid and dramatic, with particularly fine contributions from the trebles of the choir, belying the old idea that their style was too pure to be adapted to rugged modern works. A delightful coupling.

(i) 4 Chansons françaises; (ii) Our Hunting Fathers; (iii) Serenade for Tenor, Horn and Strings

(BB) *** Naxos 8.557206. (i) Lott; (ii) Bryn-Julson; (iii) Langridge; ECO, Bedford

In the anti-blood-sports cantata, *Our Hunting Fathers*, **Phyllis Bryn-Julson** is refreshingly fluent and agile, and if in the even earlier cycle, *4 Chansons françaises*, **Felicity Lott** could be warmer, the characterful, heady-toned **Philip Langridge** is superb in the *Serenade* (horn soloist **Frank Lloyd**). Bright, forward sound.

Coal Face; The King's Stamp; Men behind the Meters; Negroes; Night Mail; Peace of Britain; The Tocher (Rossini suite); Telegrams; The Way to the

Sea; When you're feeling like expressing your affection

*** NMC D112. Beale (nar.), Carewe, Birmingham Contemporary Music Group; CBSO Ch.; King Edward's School, Birmingham, Ch., Brabbins

This collects the ingenious scores Britten composed in 1935–6 for various film projects, not all of which were carried through. He was unfailingly inventive, not only in the famous score for *Night Mail* but in almost all the music he wrote for John Grierson at the GPO Film Unit. A very rewarding issue.

Curlew River (1st parable for church performance)

(M) *** Decca (ADD) 421 858-2. Pears, Shirley-Quirk, Blackburn, soloists, Instrumental Ens., composer and Tunnard

In Britten's own version, which has its own special character, **Harold Blackburn** plays the Abbot of the monastery who introduces the drama, while **John Shirley-Quirk** plays the ferryman who takes people over the Curlew River and **Peter Pears** sings the part of the madwoman who, distracted, searches fruitlessly for her abducted child. The recording is outstanding even by Decca standards.

Folksong Arrangements: Volumes 1–7 (complete)

(B) *** Hyp. Dyad CDD 22042 (2). Anderson, Nathan, MacDougall; Martineau, Lewis, Ogden

Now reissued as a Dyad Double, this is a delightfully varied set, conveniently bringing together the seven volumes of folksong settings, five with piano accompaniment, and one each with guitar and harp. **Jamie MacDougall**, youthfully fresh and clear, has the majority of the songs, and though he may not be as characterful as Peter Pears, for whom they were written, his directness and clear diction are just as winning, undaunted as he is by singing not just in French but in Welsh for two of the songs in the volume with harp. **Lorna Anderson**, also fresh and clear, provides contrast in six of the seven volumes, with the second soprano, **Regina Nathan**, warmer in tone, singing all nine of the Irish songs in the final volume. Much of the success of the collection, certainly its variety, is owed to **Malcolm Martineau**, who relishes the sharp originality of Britten's piano-writing, making one regret that he wrote so few solo piano pieces. **Bryn Lewis** on the harp and **Craig Ogden** on the guitar are equally idiomatic. First-rate sound. Full texts are given in the notes.

Folk Song Arrangements (complete)

(BB) *** Naxos 8.557220/21 (Vols 1–5). Lott, Langridge, Johnson (piano); Bonell (guitar); van Kampen (cello)

(i; ii) 8 Folk Song Arrangements for High Voice and Harp; Choral Folk Songs. (i; v) 14 Folksongs with Orchestra (5 French & 9 English)

(BB) *** Naxos 8.557222. (i) Langridge, (ii) Ellis; (iii) Feaviour, J. Harris, Kirk, Joly, BBC Singers; (iv) Wenhaston Boys' Ch., Barnet; Norris (piano); (v) T. Allen, N. Sinfonia, Bedford

In this Naxos reissue, the first two CDs are together in a single jewel-case, and the third comes separately. The important extras are 10 unpublished settings, as well as 14 orchestral arrangements. With **Philip Langridge**, **Felicity Lott** and **Thomas Allen** more positively characterful than their opposite numbers on Hyperion, and with **Graham Johnson** grippingly imaginative at the piano, one appreciates far more here that Britten's folksongs were not simple settings but original art songs. Tantalizingly, no one has yet identified the words for one tenderly beautiful song, superbly performed here on the cello by **Christopher van Kampen**.

(i) *The Golden Vanity*; (ii) *Noye's Fludde*

☞ (M) *** Decca (ADD) 436 397-2. (i) Wandsworth School Boys' Ch., Burgess, composer (piano); (ii) Brannigan, Rex, Anthony, East Suffolk Children's Ch. & O, E. Op. Group O, Del Mar

The **Wandsworth Boys** are completely at home in *The Golden Vanity* and sing with pleasing freshness. The coupling was recorded during the 1961 Aldeburgh Festival, and not only the professional choristers but the children too have the time of their lives to the greater glory of God. All the effects have been captured miraculously here, most strikingly the entry into the Ark, while a bugle band blares out fanfares, with the stereo readily catching the sense of occasion and particularly the sound of *Eternal Father* rising above the storm at the climax of *Noye's Fludde*.

6 Hölderlin-Fragmente; *Um Mitternacht*; *Who are these children?*

*** Hyp. CDA 67459. Padmore, Vignoles – FINZI: *A Young Man's Exhortation*; TIPPETT: *Boyhood's End* ***

Mark Padmore, brilliantly accompanied by **Roger Vignoles**, here couples four cycles, all undeservedly neglected, on the theme of youth and friendship. In the ease of his fine control of the two Britten works, he even outshines the example of Peter Pears, for whom they were all written. Written in 1969, late in his career, Britten's cycle, *Who are these children?*, sets 12 brief poems by William Soutar, most of them in the Scots dialect, while the *Six Hölderlin Fragments* bring Britten's only essay in setting German verse, supplemented here by his setting of Goethe's *Um Mitternacht*, discovered only after his death.

The Holy Sonnets of John Donne, Op. 35; *Harmonia sacra* (realizations of Pelham Humfrey): *Hymn to God the Father*; *Lord I have sinned* (realization of William Croft): *A Hymn on Divine Musick*. The Way to the Tomb (incidental music for Ronald Duncan's masque): *Evening*; *Morning*; *Night*. W. H. Auden settings: *Fish in the unruffled lakes*; *Night covers up the rigid land*; *To lie flat on the back with the knees flexed*. Songs: *Birthday song for Erwin*; *Cradle song for Eleanor*; *If thou wilt ease thine heart*; *Not even summer yet*; *The Red Cockatoo*; *Um Mitternacht*; *When you're feeling like expressing your affection*; *Wild with passion*

✹ *** Hyp. CDA 66823. Bostridge, Johnson

In the Donne *Sonnet* cycle, written when the composer returned in deep shock after playing at the death camp of Belsen at the end of the war, **Bostridge** makes one concentrate afresh on Britten's powerful response to Donne's grittily uncompromising poems. His voice may be lighter than that of Pears, but in its lyrical beauty it can encompass a wider range of tone and dynamic. The disc also offers inspired performances of 18 of the Britten songs which earlier fell by the wayside: the four Auden settings, which include a provocatively sexual one, a dreamily atmospheric setting of *Fish in the unruffled lakes* and a jolly cabaret song.

The Holy Sonnets of John Donne, Op. 35; *7 Sonnets of Michelangelo*, Op. 22; *Winter Words*, Op. 52; *The Children and Sir Nameless*; *If it's ever Spring again*

(BB) *** Naxos 8.557201. Langridge, Bedford

With **Steuart Bedford**, Britten's long-term collaborator, as accompanist, this reading of the Donne sonnet-cycle is marked by high contrasts of dynamic and tone, so that one hears echoes of Peter Grimes's music. In the other two cycles **Langridge** is just as expressive but is generally lighter in manner, certainly more than Pears in his recordings. Valuably, Langridge adds two more Hardy settings, originally intended for *Winter Words* but that neither fit the main pattern nor quite match the rest in imagination.

(i; ii) *Nocturne*, Op. 60; (iii; iv) *Les Illuminations*, Op. 18; (i; iv; v) *Serenade for Tenor, Horn and Strings*, Op. 32

☞ ✹ **** EMI 5 58049-2. Bostridge, BPO, Rattle, with Radek Baborak (horn)

☞ (M) **** Decca (ADD) 436 395-2. Pears; (i) ECO; (ii) wind soloists; (ii–iii) LSO strings, composer; (iii) with Tuckwell

(B) *** CfP 575 5632. Mark Ainsley, with (i) Britten Sinf. wind soloists; (ii) Pyatt; Britten Sinf. Strings; Cleobury

(B) *** EMI (DDD/ADD) 3 52286-2. (i) Tear; (ii) ECO, Tate; (iii) Harper; (iv) N. Sinfonia, Marriner; (v) with Civil

(***) Australian Decca Eloquence (mono/stereo) 476 8470. Pears; (i) LSO (members), composer; (ii) New SO, Goossens, (iii) with Brain

Ian Bostridge proves an ideal interpreter of Britten's three often taxing orchestral song-cycles, and here his light, clear tenor makes him an excellent successor to Peter Pears, for whom they were all written. **Rattle** and the **Berlin Philharmonic** are persuaded to give totally committed performances of music outside their usual repertoire. With **Radek Baborak** playing the horn obbligato with wonderful sophistication in the *Serenade*, the clarity in each of these masterly works is enhanced, with Bostridge's tone at its purest in whatever register. The Tennyson setting of the *Hymn to Diana* is light, fast and agile, and Bostridge's word-pointing is masterly throughout, matching the example of Peter Pears. The outstanding section of the *Nocturne* is the Wordsworth setting of *The Prelude*, describing the French Revolution, ending on the words 'Sleep no more', with the timpani obbligato adding bite. Full texts are included.

With dedicated accompaniments under the composer's direction, these classic **Pears** versions of *Les Illuminations* and the *Serenade* (with its horn obbligato superbly played by **Barry Tuckwell**) make a perfect coupling, with the *Nocturne* from 1960 making an ideal addition on CD. Pears, as always, is the ideal interpreter, the composer a most efficient conductor, and the fiendishly difficult obbligato parts are played superbly. The recording is brilliant and clear, with just the right degree of atmosphere, although the transfer of *Les Illuminations* is brighter than the other two works.

The ideal triptych of Britten's three great orchestral song-cycles finds **John Mark Ainsley** echoing the example of the inspirer, Peter Pears, in the shading and moulding of each phrase, above all in the *Serenade*, where the brilliant horn-playing of **David Pyatt** provides an extra reason for recommending the CfP disc. Mark Ainsley's range of expression is wide, and under pressure the voice grows a little rough, as in the final Shakespeare setting of the *Nocturne*. But that is contrasted with an exceptionally beautiful use of the head-voice, with total freedom in the upper register, as in the *Lyke-Wake Dirge* from the *Serenade*. Warm, immediate recording.

Les Illuminations is headily beautiful with glorious tone from **Heather Harper**. The couplings both feature **Robert Tear**, a singer very much in the Aldeburgh tradition created by Peter Pears. Tear yet gives a new and positive slant to each of the lovely songs in the *Serenade*, with the Jonson *Hymne to Diana* given extra jollity, thanks partly to the brilliant galumphing of **Alan Civil** on the horn. In the *Nocturne*, Britten's wide-ranging cycle on the subject of night and sleep, Tear proves a true successor to Pears, and the intricate instrumental parts are splendidly managed by members of the **ECO** under the ever-versatile **Jeffrey Tate**.

The Australian Decca CD contains the first release of the 1953 recording of the *Serenade for Tenor, Horn and Strings* and *Les Illuminations*, conducted by **Goossens**. Dennis Brain's horn playing is magical, almost ethereal in its beautiful timbre, with **Peter Pears** superb in both these works, fresher than in the famous stereo versions under the direction of the composer. Goossens's conducting cannot be faulted – it is highly sensitive and strikingly alert – and the Decca sound is exceptionally good for its period; these performances are full of atmosphere. The composer directs the *Nocturne* in stereo.

Nocturne, Op. 60

Ⓜ **(*) BBC (ADD) BBCB 8013-2. Pears, ECO, Britten –
SHOSTAKOVICH: *Symphony 14* **(*)

Nocturne; Now sleeps the crimson petal; Serenade, Op. 31 (both for tenor, horn & strings)

*** BIS CD 540. Prégardien, Lanzky-Otto, Tapiola Sinf., Vänskä – *Sinfonietta* ***

This vivid live broadcast performance contrasts well with Britten and Pears's studio recording for Decca (see above). **Peter Pears** here sounds warmer and sweeter, more closely balanced than in the Decca recording, adding to the impact of such a song as the Wordsworth with its terrifying timpani solo, superbly played by **James Blades**. Sadly, no texts are included.

Osmo Vänskä brings together not only the two best-loved orchestral song-cycles but also the supplementary Tennyson setting intended for the *Serenade* and the elusive work, the *Sinfonietta*, which Britten honoured as his Opus 1. **Christophe Prégardien** has an ideally light and sweet tenor which, even in the high tessitura of the *Lyke-Wake Dirge* from the *Serenade*, shows no strain whatever. Though one detects that he is not English, that is a tribute to his articulation, and he is totally in tune with the idiom. Excellent, spacious sound, if with the tenor soloist slightly backward.

(i) Noye's Fludde, Op. 59. A Ceremony of Carols, Op. 28

☌ *** Somm SOMMCD 212. (i) Wyn-Rogers, Luxon, Wilson-Johnson; Finchley Children's Music Group, Wilks

Noye's Fludde is here delightfully fresh and energetic, capturing the atmosphere of a live performance very well, with its processions of birds and animals and the off-stage Voice of God. With **Benjamin Luxon** providing a sonorous Voice of God, **David Wilson-Johnson** a characterful Noye and **Catherine Wyn-Rogers** a fruity Mrs Noye, all the other roles are performed sharply and incisively by members of the group. *A Ceremony of Carols*, given with comparable freshness and confidence, makes an ideal coupling, also well recorded.

On This Island; Folksong arrangement: The Salley Gardens

Ⓜ *** BBC (ADD) BBCB 8015-2. Pears, composer –
SCHUBERT: *7 songs*; WOLF: *7 Mörike Lieder* *** (with ARNE: *Come away death; Under the greenwood tree*; QUILTER: *O mistress mine*; TIPPETT: *Come unto these yellow sands*; WARLOCK: *Take, O take those lips away* ***)

Britten's early song-cycle, set to poems by his friend W. H. Auden, is especially valuable, as he did not otherwise record it, and typically it brings a bitingly dramatic reading. Inspired performances of the Lieder by Schubert and Wolf, as well as the sharply contrasted Shakespeare settings by a wide range of British composers.

Our Hunting Fathers, Op. 8

ⓑⓑ *** LPO LPO 0002. Harper, LPO, Haitink – ELGAR: *Enigma Variations*, etc. ***

Heather Harper in this live (1979) recording, made during the Proms at the Royal Albert Hall, is at her peak, commandingly impressive even in the tricky song, *Rats Away*. Well coupled with noble accounts of the two Elgar works.

Purcell realizations: Orpheus Britannicus: The knotting song; 7 Songs (1947); 6 Songs (1948); O Solitude; 5 Songs (1960); Celemene; 6 Duets (1961). Harmonia sacra: The Blessed Virgin's expostulation; The Queen's Epicedium; Saul and the Witch of Endor; 3 Divine Hymns (1947); 2 Divine Hymns & Alleluia (1960). Miscellaneous songs (1971): Dulcibella; When Myra sings

*** Hyp. CDA 67061/2 (2). Lott, Gritton, S. Walker, Bowman, Mark Ainsley, Bostridge, Rolfe Johnson, Jackson, Keenlyside; Johnson

With an outstanding team of soloists and with **Graham Johnson** as the inspired pianist, this collection stands as a monument to the devotion of one English master to another. The first disc, drawn from the *Orpheus Britannicus* collection, includes songs like *Fairest isle*, better known in the context of *King Arthur* or other entertainments. The second, from *Harmonia sacra*, has darker, weightier and more extended items, notably the magnificent scena, *Saul and the Witch of Endor*, involving three singers and with side-slipping chromatics as daring as any Purcell ever imagined. The tenor **Ian Bostridge** displays high mastery and **Simon Keenlyside** sings magnificently in the dark, bass items like *Job's curse* and the late *Let the dreadful engines*. Excellent, well-balanced sound.

(i) *The Rescue of Penelope*; (ii) *Phaedra*

(M) *** Warner Elatus 0927 49010-2. (i) Hagley, Wyn-Rogers, Mark Ainsley, Dazeley, Baker (narrator); (ii) Hunt; Hallé O, Nagano

Drawn from the complete score, *The Rescue of Penelope* is compressed into a 36-minute cantata. The most important role is that of the narrator, here masterfully taken by **Dame Janet Baker** to bring the story vividly to life despite the stylized classical language. The commentaries, beautifully sung, regularly add to the atmospheric beauty of the piece. **Lorraine Hunt's** performance of *Phaedra*, Britten's last vocal work, characteristically spare, may not quite match that of the dedicatee, Dame Janet, in conveying the heroine's agony, but the portrait of a deranged woman is chillingly powerful, with singing comparably beautiful and intense.

Saint Nicolas, Op. 42

(M) (***) Decca Heritage mono 475 6156. Pears, Hemmings, Girls' Ch. of Sir John Leman School, Boys' Ch. of Ipswich School Preparatory Dept, Aldeburgh Festival Ch. & O, composer

St Nicolas; Hymn to St Cecilia

*** Hyp. CDA 66333. Rolfe Johnson, Corydon Singers, St George's Chapel, Windsor, Ch., Girls of Warwick University Chamber Ch., Ch. of Christ Church, Southgate, Sevenoaks School, Tonbridge School, Penshurst Ch. Soc., Occasional Ch., Edwards, Alley, Scott, ECO, Best

With rare exceptions, Britten's first recordings of his own works have a freshness and vigour unsurpassed since. *Saint Nicolas* was recorded in 1955 and possesses both those qualities, as well as atmosphere in abundance, all sounding uncannily vivid in this Decca Heritage transfer. While the use of the original cover is a big plus point, the minuscule facsimile of the LP notes is not.

For the first time in a recording, the congregational hymns are included in **Matthew Best's** fresh and atmospheric account of *St Nicolas*, adding greatly to the emotional impact of the whole cantata. Though the chorus is slightly distanced, the contrasts of timbre are caught well, with the waltz-setting of *The birth of Nicolas* and its bath-tub sequence delightfully sung by boy-trebles alone. The *Hymn to St Cecilia* is also beautifully sung, with gentle pointing of the jazzy syncopations in crisp, agile ensemble and with sweet matching among the voices.

(i) *Spring Symphony*, Op. 44. *Peter Grimes*: 4 Sea Interludes

(M) **** EMI (ADD) 7 64736-2. (i) Armstrong, J. Baker, Tear, St Clement Dane's School Boys' Ch., L. Symphony Ch.; LSO, Previn

Previn makes this above all a work of exultation, a genuine celebration of spring; but here, more than in Britten's recording, the kernel of what the work has to say comes out in the longest of the solo settings, using Auden's poem, *Out on the lawn I lie in bed*. With **Janet Baker** as soloist it rises above the lazily atmospheric mood of the opening to evoke the threat of war and darkness. The *Four Sea Interludes*, which make a generous bonus, are presented in their concert form, with tailored endings.

(i) *Tit for Tat*; (ii) *Folksong arrangements: Bird scarer's song; Bonny at morn; David of the White Rock; Lemady; Lord! I married me a wife!; She's like the swallow*

*** Mer. CDE 84119. Shirley-Quirk; (i) Ledger; (ii) Ellis – *6 Metamorphoses*, etc. ***

John Shirley-Quirk is unrivalled in the sharp yet subtle way he brings out the irony in these boyhood settings of De la Mare poems. It is also good to have him singing the six late folk-settings with harp accompaniment, here played by **Osian Ellis**, for whom they were originally written.

War Requiem, Op. 66

(M) **** Decca (ADD) 475 7511 (2). Vishnevskaya, Pears, Fischer-Dieskau, Bach Ch., L. Symphoy Ch., LSO, composer

*** LPO 0010 (2). Brewer, Griffey, Finley, Tiffin Boys' Ch., Chamber O, Creed, LPO, Masur

(M) *** BBC (ADD) BBCL 4046-2. Woytowicz, Pears, Wilbrink, Wandsworth School Boys' Ch., Melos Ens., New Philh. Ch. O, Giulini

(i) *War Requiem*; (ii) *Ballad of Heroes*, Op. 14; *Sinfonia da Requiem*, Op. 20

**** Chan. SACD CHSA 5007 (2); CD: Chan. 8983/4. (i) Harper, Langridge, Shirley-Quirk; (ii) Hill; St Paul's Cathedral Choristers, L. Symphony Ch., LSO & CO, Hickox

Britten's own 1963 recording of the *War Requiem* comes near to the ideal and it has been splendidly remastered for this first reissue at mid-price, to take an honoured place among Universal's new series of Originals (which now include Decca and Philips recordings alongside the present DG list). Full documentation is included.

Richard Hickox's Chandos version rivals even the composer's own definitive account in its passion and perception. Hickox thrusts home the big dramatic moments with unrivalled force, helped by the weight of the Chandos sound. The boys' chorus from St Paul's Cathedral is exceptionally fresh. **Heather Harper** is as golden-toned as she was at the very first Coventry performance, fearless in attack. **Philip Langridge** and **John Shirley-Quirk** bring many subtleties to their interpretations. Adding to the attractiveness of the set come two substantial choral works, also in outstanding performances. The recording is now also available on Compatible SACD with multi-channel surround sound.

Masur's version of the *War Requiem* has arguably the finest trio of soloists since the original performance under the composer. **Christine Brewer**, **Gerald Finley**, and **Anthony Dean Griffey** are all superb in their clean focus, pure and clear of tone, and the chorus is incisive throughout. The recording too is exceptionally vivid for one made in the Royal Festival Hall, with powerful timpani and ample weight. The final Owen setting, *Strange meeting*, ends most movingly with Finley singing the line 'I am the enemy, you killed my friend' bringing a big climax. Masur did not seem the most likely choice to direct a recording of this work, yet in the event he rivals all those who have gone before him.

Recorded live by the BBC in 1969, this thrilling BBC account of the *War Requiem* finds **Giulini** as the principal conductor bringing the sort of biting, even wild intensity and deep dedication to Britten's score that marked his readings of the Verdi *Requiem*. The spacious Albert Hall acoustic enhances the electric atmosphere, while **Britten** himself conducts the **Melos Ensemble** just as dramatically in the Wilfred Owen settings. **Peter Pears** as tenor soloist is matched by the fresh, clear Dutch baritone, **Hans Wilbrink**, while **Stefania Woytowicz** is the bright, incisive soprano, alongside the **New Philharmonia Chorus** at its most brilliant. A bargain squeezed on to a single disc at rather more than mid-price.

OPERA

(i) *Albert Herring*; (ii) *Billy Budd*; (iii) *Owen Wingrave*; (iv) *Peter Grimes*

(B) *** Decca 475 6020 (8). (i; iv) Pears; (i; iii) ECO; (ii) Glossop, Amb. Op. Ch., LSO; (iii) Luxon; (iv) ROHCG Ch. & O; all cond. composer

An indispensable set, an obvious basis for any collection, large or small, offering the composer's definitive performances, admirably recorded between 1959 and 1971, and since unsurpassed. The documentation is sparse but adequate, including cued synopses.

Albert Herring (DVD version)

🎬 **** Warner **DVD** 5046 78790-2. Graham-Hall, Kerns, Johnson, Palmer, Hammond-Stroud, Van Allan, Gale, Oliver, Opie, Rigby, Glyndebourne Ch., LPO, Haitink (V/D: Peter Hall)

If all opera DVDs were as successful as this 1985 Glyndebourne production of *Albert Herring*, a DVD guide would hardly be necessary. John Gunter's sets are imaginatively, charmingly real, and the casting could hardly be improved on. **John Graham-Hall** in the title-role is splendidly offset by **Patricia Kerns's** portrayal of his dominating mother, **Patricia Johnson's** pompous but believable Lady Billows almost but not quite an amusing caricature, and

Felicity Palmer a whimsically idiosyncratic Florence Pike. The rest of the cast sing splendidly and take their roles as to the manner born, and the whole show is conducted marvellously by **Bernard Haitink**. Moreover Peter Hall's direction is unerringly prescient. Excellent sound too.

Albert Herring (complete; CD versions)

🎬 *** Chan. 10036 (2). Gilchrist, Stephen, Williams, Bullock, Burgess, Opie, Tear, City of L. Sinfonia, Hickox

(BB) *** Naxos 8.660107/08 (2). Gillett, Taylor, Finley, Barstow, Palmer, Savidge, Kale, N. Sinfonia, Bedford

(N) 🎬 (****) Nimbus NI 5824/6 (3). Pears, Cross, Parr, Kraus, Ashton, Evans, Lawson, English Opera Group, composer

**(*) Decca (ADD) 421 849-2 (2). Pears, Fisher, Noble, Brannigan, Cantelo, ECO, Ward, composer

Richard Hickox more than any rival brings out the fun of Britten's comic chamber opera, lifting rhythms in an infectious way. The result is warm and welcoming, helped by a full, rich Chandos recording. In the title-role of the hapless Albert, **James Gilchrist** is outstanding, with a tenor light enough to sound wimpish in the first half of the opera, and then to convey the anger of the character in the monologue that marks his change of heart at the end of Act II. **Pamela Helen Stephen** as Nancy and **Roderick Williams** as Sid, the two lovers, are also the more convincing for having relatively light voices, and the line-up of village characters, all of them larger than life, is taken by an excellent team, even if **Susan Bullock** as Lady Billows sounds rather young for such a battle-axe of a woman.

On Naxos, **Christopher Gillett** in the title-role has a clear, youthful-sounding tenor. As Lady Billows, **Josephine Barstow**, with rasp in the voice, is every bit as formidable as Sylvia Fisher was before, and **Felicity Palmer** is wonderfully characterful as her prim housekeeper, Florence Pike. What seals the set's success is the way that in the ensembles **Bedford** secures such crispness, wittily lifting rhythms, making the music swagger. At the Naxos reissue price this is a phenomenal bargain and, like full-price sets, this one includes a full libretto.

This lively Nimbus performance of *Albert Herring* cuts through any sonic limitation of this 1949 broadcast, conducted by the composer at the Theatre Royal, Copenhagen on 15 September 1949. Indeed, it surpasses the composer's studio Decca recording in sparkle and life made in the 1960s, with this cast largely comprising members of the first performance of this work. **Pears** here seems ideally suited as the gormless Albert Herring, but the entire cast is pretty flawless (**Otakar Kraus** as Mr Gedge, the vicar, is a delight), and the excellence of the performance is reflected in the (unobtrusive) laughter from the audience. **Britten's** electrifying conducting keeps the story rattling on with an exhilarating deftness and lightness of touch but all sharply characterized. The booklet gives a fascinating, personal history of the opera by Nigel Douglas and a complete libretto is included. At the end, the composer thanks the audience in a short but charming speech, quoting Albert's key line, 'Thank you very much', and we thank Nimbus very much for making this performance available once again. No admirer of this opera should be without this set.

Britten's own 1964 recording of the comic opera, *Albert Herring*, remains a delight. Peter Pears's portrait of the innocent Albert was caught only just before he grew too old for the role, but it is full of unique touches. Sylvia Fisher is a magnificent Lady Billows, and it is good to have such a wide range of British singers of the 1960s presented so characterfully. The recording, made in Jubilee Hall, remains astonishingly vivid.

Billy Budd (original four-act version; DVD versions)

(N) *** Decca DVD 074 3256. Pears, Glossop, Langdon, Shirley-Quirk, Bowman, Tear, Kelley, Ambrosian Op. Ch., LSO, Mackerras. (Producer: Cedric Messina; Director: Basil Coleman)

⌕ *** Arthaus DVD 100278. Allen, Langridge, Van Allan, Howlett, ENO Ch. & O, Atherton (Dir: Albery; V/D: Gavin)

This marvellous film version conducted by Mackerras dates from 1966, and immediately this black and white film starts there is a compelling intensity to this performance which is almost unsettling. Peter Pears was a definitive Edward Fairfax Vere, a role to which he is inextricably linked. With a supreme cast, including Peter Glossop as a superb Billy Budd and Michael Langdon as the sinister Claggart, the performance could hardly fail – and it doesn't. The performance crackles with intensity with superb direction and an excellent production. Mackerras secures plenty of electricity from the orchestra, with all the interjections from the brass heard crisply on the soundtrack.

Tim Albery's production of *Billy Budd* with Thomas Allen powerful in the title-role was one of the classic English National Opera presentations of the 1980s. This 1988 video version, made originally for BBC Television, with an introduction by Michael Berkeley, vividly captures the intense atmosphere. It is helped by the bare, stylized sets of Tom Cairns and Antony McDonald and by David Cunningham's clever lighting. The performance under David Atherton is outstanding, with Philip Langridge as Captain Vere, interpreting the role in a strikingly different way from Peter Pears, for whom it was written, but just as magnetically. Thomas Allen may in 1988 have seemed rather old for the role of the innocent Billy, but the power not just of his singing but of his acting too, with the voice clear and fresh, makes his performance deeply moving. Just as striking is the venomous figure of Claggart, superbly taken here with terrifying intensity by Richard Van Allan in one of his very finest recorded performances. Barrie Gavin's direction for video adds to the power of the performance with imaginative camerawork. The DVD is provided with plentiful index-points.

Billy Budd (CD version of original score)

*** Erato 3984 21631-2 (2). Hampson, Rolfe Johnson, Halfvarson, Manchester Boys' Ch., Hallé Ch. & O, Nagano

Billy Budd (revised version; complete)

⌕ *** Chan. 9826 (3 for 2). Keenlyside, Langridge,

Tomlinson, Opie, Bayley, Best, L. Symphony Ch., LSO, Hickox

*** Decca (ADD) 417 428-2 (3). Glossop, Pears, Langdon, Shirley-Quirk, Wandsworth School Boys' Ch., Amb. Op. Ch., LSO, composer (with *Holy Sonnets of John Donne; Songs & Proverbs of William Blake* ***)

Hickox's brilliant Chandos version of *Billy Budd*, with the finest cast of principals yet assembled, uses the revised two-Act score. In Philip Langridge the role of Vere has found its most thoughtful interpreter yet, so that from the start his self-searching is the key element in the whole work. Comparably magnetic is John Tomlinson's Claggart, the personification of evil, chillingly malevolent in every inflexion, oily in the face of authority. Equally, Simon Keenlyside as Billy gains over all rivals in the fresh, youthful incisiveness of the voice, movingly shaded down to a rapt half-tone for the lyrical monologue sung by Billy about to die. Helped by sound of spectacular quality.

On Erato we have a complete recording of Britten's original, four-Act version of *Billy Budd*, above all urgent and intense, more dramatic, less reflective than Britten's own recording for Decca of the revised, two-Act version. Not only that, Thomas Hampson brings to the title-role an extra beauty alongside heroic power. It also provides a thrilling fortissimo close to the original Act I, superbly achieved in Kent Nagano's powerful performance with the Hallé Orchestra and Choir. Set against the velvet-toned Hampson, Anthony Rolfe Johnson as Vere has some grit in his voice, creating a believable character at once rugged and introspective. Eric Halfvarson as the evil Claggart is not as sinister as some of his predecessors but, apart from some roughness in the upper register, it is a forceful, incisive performance, matching the urgency of Nagano's approach.

On Decca, Britten himself has an outstanding cast, with Glossop a bluff, heroic Billy and Langdon a sharply dark-toned Claggart, making these symbol-figures believable. Magnificent sound, and the many richly imaginative strokes – atmospheric as well as dramatic – are superbly managed. The extravagant layout on three CDs begins with the *John Donne Holy Sonnets* (sung by Pears) and the *Songs & Proverbs of William Blake* (sung by Fischer-Dieskau), with the Prologue and Act I of the opera beginning thereafter. They are equally ideal performances.

(i) Death in Venice; (ii) Gloriana; (iii) A Midsummer Night's Dream; (iv) Phaedra (Dramatic Cantata); (v) The Rape of Lucretia; (vi) The Turn of the Screw

(B) *** Decca (ADD/DDD) 475 6029 (10). (i) Shirley-Quirk, Bowman; (i; v; vi) Pears; (ii) Barstow, Langridge, Della Jones, Opie, Van Allan; (iii) Deller, Harwood, Terry, Shirley-Quirk, Brannigan; (iv) J. Baker; (v) Harper, Shirley-Quirk, Luxon; (vi) Vyvyan, Hemmings, Dyer, Cross; (i; iv) ECO, Bedford; (ii) Welsh Nat. Op. O, Mackerras; (iii) LSO, composer; (v–vi) ECO, composer

Decca's second bargain box of Britten's operas perhaps may not be of such universal appeal as the first, but the set remains an essential bargain investment for collectors drawn to this repertoire. As before, the documentation includes cued synopses.

Death in Venice (complete; CD versions)

🎧 *** Chan. 10280 (2). Langridge, Opie, Chance, BBC Singers, City of L. Sinf., Hickox

*** Decca (ADD) 425 669-2 (2). Pears, Shirley-Quirk, Bowman, Bowen, Leeming, E. Op. Group Ch., ECO, Bedford

Richard Hickox's superb account of *Death in Venice*, the composer's last opera, matches and in many ways even outshines the fine model of the original recording conducted by Steuart Bedford (instead of the ailing Britten himself), with Peter Pears in the central role. **Philip Langridge** proves an inspired interpreter of the role of Ashenbach, more passionate than Pears, and in his death scene he is even more poignant. Even so, he fails to convey quite the same agony of self-realization as Pears at the end of Act I on the whispered line *I love you!* Equally, **Alan Opie** makes a more robust figure than John Shirley-Quirk in the seven contrasted portraits of the tormenting figures who beset Aschenbach on his fatal trip to Venice, varying them vividly. The countertenor **Michael Chance** sings even more eerily as the Voice of Apollo, helped by distancing by the engineers, while the recording throughout is even more open and vividly atmospheric than the original Decca, fine as that is. Add to that Hickox's powerful, finely timed pacing of a work which is largely meditative, and the result is totally magnetic.

Peter Pears's searching performance in the central role of Aschenbach is set against the darkly sardonic singing of **John Shirley-Quirk** in a sequence of roles as the Dionysiac figure who draws Aschenbach to his destruction and, though **Steuart Bedford's** assured conducting lacks some of the punch that Britten would have brought, the whole presentation makes this a set to establish the work outside the opera house.

Gloriana (DVD versions)

*** Opus Arte DVD OA 0955. Barstow, Randle, Soloists, Opera North Ch., E. N. Philh. O, Daniel (film by Phyllida Lloyd)

*** Arthaus DVD 102 097. Walker, Rolfe Johnson, Rigby, Van Allan, Vaughan, Opie, ENO Ch. & O, Elder (V/D: Bailey)

Although Britten's coronation opera was not well received at Covent Garden in 1953, it came into its own when it was revived ten years later to celebrate the composer's fiftieth birthday. This 1999 production by Opera North, filmed for the BBC the following year, is a compelling and powerful one. **Josephine Barstow's** portrayal of Queen Elizabeth I could not be more magisterial and **Tom Randle's** Essex is hardly less convincing. A very strong cast with a strong sense of dramatic purpose and a first-class orchestral response under **Paul Daniel**. There is some irritating behind-the-scenes 'business' but, this apart, the performance is first class, camerawork otherwise unobtrusive and the recording vivid and well balanced. Hugely enjoyable and rewarding.

Recorded in 1984 in good, bright sound, the alternative Arthaus DVD presents a production by Colin Graham, with

sets by himself reflecting the layout of an Elizabethan theatre. With an ideal cast, led by **Sarah Walker** as Elizabeth I and **Anthony Rolfe Johnson** as Essex, both in superb form, it offers one musical jewel after another, with Britten's melodic writing at its most winning. Sarah Walker sings and acts powerfully, with her final signing of Essex's death warrant at once vehement yet regretful. Even the small roles are splendidly taken.

Gloriana: Choral Dances

*** Hyp. CDA 66175. Hill, Owen, Holst Singers & O, Davan Wetton – BLISS: *Lie strewn the white flocks;* HOLST: *Choral Hymns from the Rig Veda* ***

The composer's own choral suite, made up of unaccompanied choral dances linked by passages for solo tenor and harp, makes an excellent coupling for the equally attractive Bliss and Holst items. Excellent, atmospheric recording.

A Midsummer Night's Dream (DVD version)

🎧 *** Warner DVD 0630 16911-2. Cotrubas, Bowman, Appelgren, Buchen, Ryland Davies, Duesing, Lott, Bryson, LPO, Haitink (Producer: Peter Hall; TV Director: Dave Heather)

Recorded at Glyndebourne in 1981, the Warner DVD offers a magical production of Britten's fairy opera based on Shakespeare. The atmospheric sets of John Bury brilliantly exploit the limited space of the Glyndebourne stage in the old theatre, with forest trees manipulated by wood spirits amid mists, with moonlight adding to the mystery, and with fantastic costumes for the fairy characters. Peter Hall, as ever at Glyndebourne, is an inspired director, capturing the unique mixture of fantasy, comedy and downright farce with the surest hand, and with **Bernard Haitink** adding to the fun in his conducting, when in the final play scene with the Rude Mechanicals he brings out the parodies of Berg (in the music for Wall), Verdi (for Bottom) and Donizetti (for Flute). The cast is a vintage one, with **James Bowman** as Oberon and **Ileana Cotrubas** as Tytania unsurpassed, and with **Felicity Lott**, **Ryland Davies** and **Dale Duesing** outstanding among the lovers. **Curt Appelgren** is rightly dominant among the Rude Mechanicals as Bottom, both imposing and funny, with **Patrick Power** comic in his embarrassment as Flute. A fine memorial to traditional stage values in opera.

A Midsummer Night's Dream (complete; CD versions)

*** Decca (ADD) 425 663-2 (2). Deller, Harwood, Harper, Veasey, Watts, Shirley-Quirk, Brannigan, Downside and Emanuel School Ch., LSO, composer

ⓑ *** EMI 3 818322-8 (2). Bowman, Watson, Graham-Hall, Herford, D. Jones, Gomez, Bailey, Walker, Maxwell, Trinity Boys' Ch., City of L. Sinfonia, Hickox

Britten again proves himself an ideal interpreter of his own music and draws virtuoso playing from the **LSO**. **Peter Pears** has shifted to the straight role of Lysander. The mechanicals are admirably led by **Owen Brannigan** as Bottom; and among the lovers **Josephine Veasey** (Hermia) is outstanding.

Deller, with his magical male alto singing, is the eerily effective Oberon.

Britten's own version set standards all round that were almost impossible to surpass, yet **Richard Hickox** in his 1990 recording provides an alternative which in significant ways is preferable. With a chamber orchestra rather than the LSO, the scale is more intimate and the full EMI recording captures the sound just as vividly as John Culshaw's vintage Decca. Hickox too, with his smaller band, points jazzy syncopations more infectiously, yet only in the 'Pyramus and Thisbe' play does the comedy of the rude mechanicals come over as it did under Britten. **Donald Maxwell** sings the role of Bottom with a clear, virile directness, but he does not have the sense of fun of Owen Brannigan in the composer's set. Conversely, the two pairs of lovers on the EMI set capture more pointedly than their predecessors the element of melodramatic parody in the mismatching of partners caused by Puck's machinations. **John Graham-Hall** as Lysander and **Henry Herford** as Demetrius are both aptly fresh and young-sounding. Among the others, **Lilian Watson** makes a bright Tytania, less beautiful in tone than Elizabeth Harwood on Britten's set but more clearly an other-worldly spirit; while central to the success of Hickox's performance is the masterly characterization of Oberon by **James Bowman** (who also sings on the later, DVD version), far more telling and mysterious than Alfred Deller's original. What makes the set indispensable is that it includes a brief 90-second sequence, intensely poetic, in the scene of the lovers' awakening in Act III, where Britten's own recording observes a cut as made in the original Aldeburgh staging. The reissued set comes with a synopsis and a separate listing of items and is well worth seeking out.

Owen Wingrave; The Hidden Heart (DVD Versions)

*** Arthaus **DVD** 100 372. Finley, Hellekant, Hill, Savidge, Barstow, Dawson, Gale, Marlton, Westminster Cathedral Ch., Deutches SO, Berlin, Nagano (DVD Dir: Margaret Williams)

This television production presents the piece evocatively and convincingly in a setting updated to 1958, with khaki battledress for the soldiers, with **Gerald Finley** singing and acting superbly. The unsympathetic fiancée, Kate, also seems a more complex character than before, well taken by **Charlotte Hellekant**, and the gallery of disagreeable family-members is strongly cast too, notably **Martyn Hill** as the old, unforgiving Sir Philip Wingrave and **Josephine Barstow** as Miss Wingrave. **Peter Savidge** sings well in the role of the tutor, Spencer Coyle, the lone voice of sanity, with **Anne Dawson** as Mrs Coyle and **Hilton Marlton** as the wimpish Lechmere. Set mainly in the Wingrave country house, the result is nicely evocative, with the misty ghost scenes sufficiently creepy. With the orchestral score evidently recorded separately by the **Deutsches Symphony Orchestra of Berlin** under **Kent Nagano**, the musical results are still well coordinated.

What makes this issue especially valuable is that it also contains as an extra the moving film, *The Hidden Heart*, made for Channel 4 by Teresa Griffiths. Subtitled 'A Love Story in Three Pieces', this hour-long film gives a striking portrait of Benjamin Britten from the 1930s onwards, centring on his lifelong love for the tenor, Peter Pears. It consistently comes out that Britten and Pears were in many ways deeply conventional figures, 'like two prep-school masters' as the counter-tenor James Bowman says, with Britten even described as 'strait-laced'.

Owen Wingrave (CD Version)

(N) *** Chan. 10472 (2). Coleman-Wright. Opie, Connell, Watson, Stephen, Leggate, CLS Hickox

Owen Wingrave is nowhere near as effective dramatically as Britten's finest operas, largely the fault of the plot dependent on Owen's dilemma as a pacifist in a military family. Though the libretto gives positive roles for each character, they hardly react with each other convincingly, with barely a single sympathetic character. This new version from **Richard Hickox** and the **City of London Sinfonia** may not have the advantage of featuring the original singers chosen by the composer, but the singing is equally powerful, in some ways even stronger, notably in the casting of **James Gilchrist** as Lechmere, Owen's fellow student, a clear advantage. Otherwise the casts are evenly matched with **Peter Coleman-Wright** a strong Owen and **Alan Opie** as Spencer Coyle, Owen's teacher. **Pamela Helen Stephen** as Owen's fiancé does not have so warm a voice as the original Janet Baker, but that is more apt for a largely unsympathetic character. First-rate atmospheric sound, apt in a ghost story.

Paul Bunyan (complete; CD versions)

🔗 ✿ (M) *** Virgin VCD7 59249-2. Lawless (spoken part), Dressen, Comeaux, Nelson, Soloists, Ch. & O of Plymouth Music Series, Minnesota, Brunelle

*** Chan. 9781 (2). Gritton, Streit, Robinson, Egerton, Broadbent, White, Coleman-Wright, Graham, Royal Opera Ch. & O, Hickox

Aptly, this first recording of Britten's choral operetta comes from the state, Minnesota, where the story is set. When the principal character is a giant who can appear only as a disembodied voice, the piece works rather better on record or radio than on stage. Musically, Britten's conscious assumption of popular American mannerisms does not prevent his invention from showing characteristic originality. Well cast and recorded in clean, vivid sound, with **Philip Brunelle** a vigorous conductor, this excellent first recording deserves all the prizes it won in its original issue on Virgin Classics.

The much-admired Covent Garden production of *Paul Bunyan* was recorded live at the Sadler's Wells Theatre in 1999. Though there are intrusive stage noises, the Chandos sound vividly captures the dramatic atmosphere of this ballad opera with its witty libretto by W. H. Auden. **Hickox** directs a warmly idiomatic reading which gains over the only previous version in featuring such fine singers as **Susan Gritton** as Tiny and **Kurt Streit** as Johnny Inkslinger. The Chandos sound is more open and atmospheric than the studio recording for Virgin, which yet in many ways gains from the closeness of the voices.

Peter Grimes (DVD versions)

(N) 🎗►**** Decca DVD 074 3261. Pears, Harper, Drake, Brannigan, Bainbridge, Gomez, Tear, Ambrosian Op. Ch., LSO, Composer. (Producer: John Culshaw; V/D: Brian Large)

🎗►*** Arthaus DVD 100 382. Langridge, Cairns, Opie, Howard, Orton, ENO Ch. & O, Atherton (V/D: Barrie Gavin)

*** Warner DVD 0630 16913-2. Vickers, Harper, Bailey, ROHCG Ch. & O, C. Davis (Dir: Elijah Moshinsky; V/D: John Vernon)

(N) **(*) EMI DVD 50999 2 17414 9 4 (2). Griffey, Palmer, Racette, Grove, Michaels-Moore, Ratu Rhodes, Met Ch & Orch, Runniles (Director: John Doyle. Sets: Scott Pask. TV Director: Halvorson)

At last, the BBC's 1969 recording of Peter Grimes has been released on DVD, in excellent sound and a decent colour picture. Filmed at Snape Maltings, this performance is self-recommending. **Pears** is a superb Grimes, every bit as compelling as in his classic Decca recording, though naturally a decade or so older here. What makes this performance so compelling is the excellence of the cast in general: from the beauty of **Heather Harper's** Ellen Orford, to the superb characterizations of **Ann Robson's** Mrs Sedley – all the roles here are superbly done, and everything about the production and direction brings top quality. A classic and a must for all Britten fans.

Tim Albery's darkly intense production of Peter Grimes for ENO, updated to the interwar period, makes a powerful impression on DVD, thanks not just to the outstanding performance and production but also to Barrie Gavin's television presentation. One does not see **David Atherton** and the orchestra; instead, seascapes are shown during the important orchestral interludes. As for the principals, their singing, vivid and characterful from first to last, can hardly be faulted, with **Philip Langridge** even more moving as Grimes than on CD, thanks to his deeply involved acting, with his big solos, notably the one in his hut in Act II and the final mad monologue, bringing the most powerful climaxes. **Janice Cairns** makes a touching Ellen, clear and firm throughout, with just a touch of the stiffness of a schoolmistress adding to the effectiveness of her acting. **Alan Opie** is an ideal Balstrode, even more than usual emerging as a central figure in the action, and the individual characters from the Borough are all vividly drawn, notably the Mrs Sedley of **Susan Orton** and the Auntie of **Ann Howard**. The women's quartet in Act II is radiantly sung, and the option on DVD of having English subtitles even with an opera in English adds powerfully to the impact of the piece.

Though the composer himself disapproved, **Jon Vickers's** radical portrayal of the role of Grimes in this unforgettably powerful Covent Garden production by Elijah Moshinsky was generally acclaimed as both musically inspired and powerfully convincing. With Vickers such a solo as *What harbour shelters peace* brings a sudden transformation from an agonized mood into one of fleeting hope, and Vickers rises superbly to the challenge of the final mono-

logue, with paranoia tipped over into madness. **Heather Harper** is equally moving as Ellen Orford, unsurpassed in the role, with **Norman Bailey** powerful as Balstrode. The other characters are also colourfully portrayed, with fine singing all round. **Colin Davis**, as on his Philips audio recording, proves an inspired interpreter, taut in control as well as warmly expressive, drawing vividly atmospheric playing from the orchestra to supplement the brilliantly effective sets, minimal but wonderfully evocative in their dark picture of the Borough. Irritatingly, no cast list is given on the box, only at the very end of the film.

In this EMI DVD designed for television, the Met presents the March 2008 production of Britten's atmospheric opera. Much of the mystery of more realistic productions is missing thanks to the heavily stylized sets of Scott Pask and the neutral, anonymous costumes of Ann Hould Ward, but in the openness and simplicity they never get in the way of a fine performance, powerfully conducted by **Donald Runnicles**. In the title role **Anthony Dean Griffey** matches that power – important in so large a house as the Met – with a tenor that is confidently firm and precise, matching his fine acting as a lumbering figure. Though **Patricia Racette** as Ellen Orford starts rather shrilly, her voice warms up and focuses far better during the performance, while **Felicity Palmer** as Mrs Sedley is vividly characterful. The other roles are very well defined in this gallery of strongly defined characters, with **Anthony Michaels-Moore** as Balstrode and **Teddy Ratu Rhodes** as Ned Keene particularly powerful in their singing and acting.

Peter Grimes (CD versions)

🎗► ✹ (M) **** Decca (ADD) 475 7712 (2). Pears, C. Watson, Pease, Nilsson, Brannigan, Evans, ROHCG Ch. & O, composer

*** Chan. 9447/8 (2). Langridge, J. Watson, Opie, Connell, Harrison, Opera London, L. Symphony Ch., City of L. Sinf., Hickox

(B) *** EMI 509156-2 (2). Rolfe Johnson, Lott, Allen, Ch. & O of ROHCG, Haitink

(B) *** Ph. (ADD) Duo 462 847-2 (2). Vickers, Harper, Summers, Bainbridge, Cahill, Robinson, Allen, ROHCG Ch. & O, C. Davis

The Decca recording of Peter Grimes was one of the greatest achievements of the early analogue stereo era. Few opera recordings can claim to be so definitive, with **Peter Pears**, for whom it was written, in the name-part. While there are now two outstanding DVD versions, the Decca CD recording (newly transferred here) is so atmospheric that one hardly misses the visual effects. The reissue in Universal's Originals series now includes full documentation, including text.

The rhythmic spring which **Hickox** gives this colourful score harks back to the composer's classic set, and Chandos backs him up with an exceptionally rich recording, with bloom on the voices and full, immediate orchestral sound. The casting of **Philip Langridge** in the title-role is central to the set's success. As on stage, he is unrivalled at conveying the character's mounting hysteria, and the result is chilling. **Janice Watson** makes a most touching Ellen Orford, younger and less maternal than her rivals, but all the more tender, with the golden tones of the voice well caught. The others make a superb team, with **Alan Opie** an outstanding Balstrode and **John Connell** commanding as lawyer Swallow at the start.

On EMI, **Anthony Rolfe Johnson** brings out the inward intensity of Grimes, singing most beautifully, hardly troubled by the high tessitura. **Felicity Lott** makes a tenderly sympathetic Ellen Orford, and **Sarah Walker** is unforgettable as Mrs Sedley, the laudanum-taking gossip. **Thomas Allen** is a wise and powerful Balstrode, making the Act III duet with Ellen an emotional resolution. The **Covent Garden Chorus and Orchestra** benefit from the extra range and vividness of EMI's digital recording and this adds to the impact.

Sir Colin Davis takes a fundamentally darker, tougher view of *Peter Grimes* than the composer himself. **Jon Vickers's** powerful, heroic interpretation sheds keen new light on what arguably remains the greatest of Britten's operas. **Heather Harper** as Ellen Orford is most moving, and there are fine contributions from **Jonathan Summers** as Captain Balstrode and **Thomas Allen** as Ned Keene. The recording is full and vivid, with fine balancing. Now reissued as a Duo, this is a genuine bargain.

Peter Grimes: Four Sea Interludes

*** Atma SACD 2 2549. Montreal Met. O, Nézet-Séguin –
  DEBUSSY: *La Mer, Prélude à l'après-midi d'un faune*;
  MERCURE: *Kaléidoscope* ***

The **Metropolitan Orchestra of Montreal** may not be as well known outside Canada as the great Montreal Symphony Orchestra, but here under its Music Director, **Yannick Nézet-Séguin**, it shows what a formidable band it is, offering performances both incisive and clean-cut, with transparent textures.

Peter Grimes: 4 Sea Interludes & Passacaglia

(M) **** Chan. 8473. Ulster O, Handley – BAX: *On the Sea-shore*; BRIDGE: *The Sea*; STANFORD: *Irish Rhapsody 4* ***

Handley draws brilliant, responsive playing from the Ulster Orchestra in readings that fully capture the atmospheric beauty of the writing, helped by vivid recording of demonstration quality.

The Rape of Lucretia (complete; DVD Version)

**(*) Arthaus DVD 101 021. Rigby, Smythe, Van Allan, Opie, Owens, Pope, Rolfe Johnson, Harries, ENO, Friend (Director: Michael Simpson)

The English National Opera production from Arthaus, recorded in 1987, offers an effective presentation of an imaginative if rather bald production in modern dress by Michael Simpson. So at the start, **Kathryn Harries** and **Anthony Rolfe Johnson** as the Female and Male Choruses, both singing strongly, appear in severe grey costumes, and the set for the main action might have been devised for *Madam Butterfly* with its sliding translucent panels like Japanese shosees. At least the visual side of the production does not distract from the excellence of the singing and acting, led by **Jean Rigby**,

steady as a rock as Lucretia, darkening her tone for her response to Tarquinius's assault with a powerful chest register. Opposite her as Bianca, **Anne-Marie Owens** makes a splendid foil, while the male cast is well led by the Tarquinius of **Russell Smythe**, with **Richard Van Allan** equally positive as Collatinus. One of the few oddities is that Rolfe Johnson's narration for the actual rape is whispered, not spoken, making it less characterful.

The Rape of Lucretia (complete; CD Version)

*** Chan. 9254/5. Rigby, Robson, Pierard, Maxwell, Miles, Rozario, Gunson, City of L. Sinf., Hickox

(i) The Rape of Lucretia (complete); (ii) Phaedra, Op. 93

🎧 *** Decca (ADD) 425 666-2 (2). (i) Pears, Harper, Shirley-Quirk, J. Baker, Luxon, ECO, composer; (ii) J. Baker, ECO, Bedford

In combining on CD *The Rape of Lucretia* with *Phaedra*, Decca celebrates two outstanding performances by **Dame Janet Baker**, recorded at the peak of her career. Among other distinguished vocal contributions to the opera **Peter Pears** and **Heather Harper** stand out, while **Benjamin Luxon** makes the selfish Tarquinius into a living character. The seductive beauty of the writing – Britten then at his early peak – is caught splendidly, the melodies and tone-colours as ravishing as any he ever conceived.

Jean Rigby as Lucretia may lack the warmth and weight of Baker, but she gains from having a younger-sounding voice. Equally, the timbre of **Nigel Robson** as the Male Chorus, rather darker than Peter Pears's, adds to the dramatic bite of his characterization, virile in attack. **Catherine Pierard** as the Female Chorus has a more sensuous voice, making it a more involved commentary. Quite apart from its unique authority, Britten's Decca set (also at full price) comes with a valuable fill-up in *Phaedra*, the work he wrote for Janet Baker; but the Chandos rival gives an equally strong, in some ways more dramatic, view of a masterly opera.

The Turn of the Screw (DVD versions)

*** Opus Arte DVD OA 0907D. Milne, Padmore, Wyn Davies, Montague, Kirby Johnson, Wise, City of L. Sinfonia, Hickox (TV Director: Katie Mitchell)

**(*) Arthaus DVD 100 198. Field, Davies, Greager, Obata, Stuttgart RSO, Bedford (Dir: Michael Hampe. V/D: Claus Viller)

What Katie Mitchell has devised is a highly evocative film to go with a performance of *The Turn of the Screw*. The result is very different from a conventional staging, with the singers, for much of the time, acting out their roles without being seen singing. The performance itself is excellent, with **Richard Hickox** drawing taut playing from the **City of London Sinfonia** in support of a first-rate cast. **Lisa Milne** (as the Governess) and **Diana Montague** make an impressive duo, vocally outstanding, though the small, buxom Milne and the tall, statuesque Montague are visually the wrong way round. **Mark Padmore** is superb as Peter Quint and as the

Prologue, establishing himself as the most mellifluous of Britten tenors, while **Catrin Wyn Davies** sings with a rich mezzo as Miss Jessel. The children both sing and act beautifully, very well cast, genuinely youthfully exuberant. A distinctive version with many great qualities, most of all in presenting the full horror of the story, set against an eerie background.

The hero of this Arthaus DVD production is **Steuart Bedford**, who gets vibrant singing and playing from all concerned. **Helen Field** is a thoroughly convincing Governess and the cast is in every respect excellent, even if **Machita Obata** looks a little too mature for Flora. A good production, very atmospheric, and with generally unobtrusive video direction.

The Turn of the Screw (CD versions)

🔊 (BB) *** Naxos 8.660109/10. Langridge, Lott, Pay, Hulse, Cannan, Secunde, Aldeburgh Festival Ens., Bedford

(M) (***) Decca mono 425 672-2 (2). Pears, Vyvyan, Hemmings, Dyer, Cross, Mandikian, E. Op. Group O, composer

Bedford, who took over from Britten himself when the composer could no longer conduct his own recordings, here presents a similarly idiomatic performance with a comparable sharpness and magnetism that, thanks to the spacious recording, brings out the eerie atmosphere of the piece. The recording also allows one to appreciate the sharp originality of the instrumentation in what by any standards is the tautest of Britten's operas. The singers too have been chosen to follow the pattern set by the original performers. **Langridge** here, like Pears before him, takes the double role of narrator and Peter Quint, echoing Pears's inflexions, but putting his own stamp on the characterization. **Felicity Lott** is both powerful and vulnerable as the Governess, rising superbly to the big climaxes which, thanks to the recording quality, have a chilling impact, not least at the very end. **Sam Pay** is a fresh-voiced Miles, less knowing than David Hemmings in the Britten set, with **Eileen Hulse** bright and girlish as Flora. **Nadine Secunde** is a strong Miss Jessel, and **Phyllis Cannan** matches up to the strength of her predecessor, Joan Cross. An outstanding set.

Though the recording is in mono only, the very dryness and the sharpness of focus give an extra intensity to the composer's own incomparable reading of his most compressed opera. **Peter Pears** as Peter Quint is matched superbly by **Jennifer Vyvyan** as the Governess and by **Joan Cross** as the housekeeper, Mrs Grose. It is also fascinating to hear **David Hemmings** as a boy treble, already a confident actor. Excellent CD transfer.

Collection

'The World of Britten': (i–ii) *Simple Symphony*; (iii; ii) *Young Person's Guide to the Orchestra*; (iv–v) **Folksong arrangements**: *Early one morning; The Plough Boy*; (vi) *Hymn to the Virgin*; (iv; vii; iii; ii) *Serenade for Tenor, Horn & Strings: Nocturne.* **Excerpts from**: *Ceremony of Carols; Noye's Fludde; Spring Symphony; Billy Budd; Peter Grimes*

(M) *** (ADD) Decca 436 990-2. (i) ECO; (ii) cond. composer; (iii) LSO; (iv) Pears; (v) composer (piano); (vi) St John's College Ch., Guest; (vii) Tuckwell; & various artists

The **Britten** sampler is well worth having for the composer's own vibrant account of the *Variations on a Theme of Purcell* and the *Simple Symphony*, where the *Playful Pizzicato* emerges with wonderful rhythmic spring and resonance (in the warm Maltings acoustics). The **Pears** contributions are very enjoyable too, notably the haunting *Nocturne* from the *Serenade*, with **Barry Tuckwell** in splendid form. Excellent sound throughout, although the tuttis in the *Young Person's Guide to the Orchestra* could with advantage have had a more expansive sonority.

BROWNE, John (c. 1490)

O Maria salvatoris; O regina mundi clara; Salve regina I; Stabat iuxta; Stabat mater

(M) *** Gimell 2-CD CD-GIM 219-2 (2). Tallis Scholars, Phillips – CORN SH: *Motets*; TAVERNER, TYE: *Western Wind Mass* ***

We know very little about John Browne except that he was ahead of his time, both in the richness of sonorities he created and in the remarkable length of his melodic lines. The beauty is self-evident in these superb performances from the **Tallis Scholars**, recorded in the sumptuous acoustic of the Church of St Peter and St Paul, Salle, Norfolk. All this music is to be found in the earlier folios of the Eton Choirbook, dating from about 1490 to 1500, alongside more pieces that are lost. The richness of the soaring treble texture is immediately striking in the opening *Salve regina*, but the radiant antiphon *O Maria salvatoris*, is even more remarkable. This is the longest work and the climactic piece in this programme, written in the most lavish eight-part polyphony. It was so celebrated in its day that it was given pride of place as the opening item in the Choirbook. It is an extraordinary piece, in its time a work almost as unprecedented as Tallis's 40-part motet, *Spem in alium*, although its means are more modest.

BRUCH, Max (1838–1920)

Double Concerto in E min., for Clarinet, Viola & Orchestra, Op. 88

(B) *** Hyp. Dyad CDD 22017 (2). King, Imai, LSO, Francis (with Concert ***)

*** Sup. SU 3554-2. Peterkova, Besa, Prague Philh., Bělohlávek – MENDELSSOHN: 2 *Concert Pieces*; ROSSINI: *Introduction, Theme and Variations*, etc. ***

Bruch's *Double Concerto* is a delightful work with genuinely memorable inspiration in its first two lyrical movements and with a roistering finale making a fine contrast. Clarinet and viola are blended beautifully, with melting phrasing from **Thea King**. The recording is excellent. This is part of an excellent two-disc set, including other attractive concertante works by Mendelssohn, Crusell, Spohr and other, less familar names.

With the viola-player, **Alexander Besa**, as an inspired partner, the Czech clarinettist, **Ludmila Peterkova**, includes the *Double Concerto* in a delightfully off-beat collection of neglected clarinet music, warmly accompanied by **Jiri Bělohlávek** and the **Prague Philharmonia**. She is an artist who is not only warmly expressive, but sparkles in everything she plays.

(i) *Double Concerto in E min.*; (ii) *Romance for Violin & Orchestra*; (iii) *8 Pieces for Clarinet, Viola & Piano*

🔑 (BB) *** Warner Apex 8573 89229-2. Caussé, (i; iii) Meyer; (i; ii) Lyon Op. O, Nagano; (iii) Duchable

The performance of the *Double Concerto* from **Paul Meyer** and **Gérard Caussé** is affectionately mellow, yet does not miss the lilt of the lively finale. Caussé then goes on to give a richly romantic account of the *Romance*, another work with an endearing melodic flow. The *Eight Pieces* are full of charm, their romanticism pastel-shaded, but they are by no means insubstantial (No. 3 extends to nearly eight minutes). These highly sympathetic performances are beautifully recorded, and this Apex reissue makes a fine bargain.

Double Piano Concerto in A flat min., Op. 88a

*** Chan. 9711. Güher and Süher Pekinel, Philh. O, Marriner – MENDELSSOHN: *Double Concerto*; MOZART: *Double Concerto* ***

The Max Bruch *Double Concerto* is well worth hearing in a performance as strong, sympathetic and well recorded as the one on Chandos. With some attractive themes it makes a welcome rarity, whatever its limitations.

Violin Concertos: 1 in G min.; 2 in D min., Op. 44; 3 in D min., Op. 58; Serenade for Violin & Orchestra, Op 75; Scottish Fantasy, Op. 46

(B) *** Ph. (ADD) Duo 462 167-2 (2). Accardo, Leipzig GO, Masur

This Philips Duo gathers together Bruch's three *Violin Concertos*, plus two other major concertante works. Although no other piece quite matches the famous *G minor Concerto* in inventive concentration, the delightful *Scottish Fantasy*, with its profusion of good tunes, comes near to doing so, and the first movement of the *Second Concerto* has two soaringly lyrical themes. The *Third Concerto* brings another striking lyrical idea in the first movement and has an endearing *Adagio* and a jolly finale. The engagingly insubstantial *Serenade* was originally intended to be a fourth violin concerto. Throughout the set **Accardo's** playing is so persuasive in its restrained passion that even the less inspired moments bring pleasure. With the soloist balanced rather close, the orchestral recording is full and spacious.

Violin Concerto 1 in G min., Op. 26

🔑 ✦ **** Telarc CD 80507. McDuffie, SCO, Swensen – MENDELSSOHN: *Violin Concerto* ***

🔑 *** Sony SK87740. Midori, BPO, Jansons – MENDELSSOHN: *Concerto* ***

🔑 (M) *** EMI 5 03410-2. Chung, LPO, Tennstedt – BEETHOVEN: *Concerto* ***

(M) *** EMI (ADD) 5 66906-2. Menuhin, Philh. O, Susskind – MENDELSSOHN: *Concerto* ***

(M) *** DG 477 6349. Mintz, Chicago SO, Abbado (with KREISLER: *Caprice Viennoise; Liebesleid; Liebesfreud* with Benson, piano) – MENDELSSOHN: *Violin Concerto* **(*)

(M) *** DG 463 641-2. Mutter, BPO, Karajan – MENDELSSOHN: *Concerto* ***

*** Pentatone SACD PTC 5186. Grumiaux, Philh. O, Wallberg – BEETHOVEN: *Violin Concerto* ***

The American violinist **Robert McDuffie** opens the work gently and tenderly, with bewitching phrasing and the most beautiful tone, never pressing too hard. The hushed opening of the beautiful *Adagio* again finds a tenderness that gives a magical frisson. Throughout the concerto, the interchanges between soloist and orchestra have the natural flowing spontaneity of live music-making and the finale bounces off spiritedly, with the bold orchestral tuttis in a stimulating balance with the dancing soloist. The Telarc recording, full-blooded and with a believable perspective, is well up to the high standards of the house, and the Mendelssohn coupling is also outstandingly fine.

Midori's first entry in the Bruch is also musingly reflective, with the recording heightening contrasts between soloist and orchestra, even though the violin is placed relatively close. The panache of her performance of the first movement is followed by a rapt account of the second. The finale again benefits from bold orchestral playing, with high contrasts setting off the sparkle of the soloist. Here we have a disc that – in the face of formidable competition – remains a clear winner.

Compared with her earlier, Decca recording (see below), **Kyung-Wha Chung's** expressive rubato in her EMI version is more marked, with her freedom vividly conveying magic such as you find in her live performances, and the finale is again impulsive in its bravura. An exceptionally attractive version.

Menuhin's performance with Susskind, now reissued as one of EMI's 'Great Recordings of the Century', has long held an honoured place in the catalogue. The performance has a fine spontaneity, the work's improvisatory quality very much part of the interpretation, and there is no doubting the poetry Menuhin finds in the slow movement or the sparkle in the finale. The bright, forward sound of the 1960 recording has transferred vividly and naturally to CD.

Shlomo Mintz's compelling playing makes the listener hang on to every phrase. The vibrato is wide, but his approach is so distinctive and interesting that few listeners will resist. The **Chicago Symphony Orchestra** plays with great brilliance and enthusiasm, and **Abbado's** direction is most sympathetic. The vivid recording has transferred splendidly to CD. Mintz's version is coupled with the Mendelssohn *Concerto*, and now with three favourite Kreisler encores, beautifully played, for good measure.

In **Anne-Sophie Mutter's** hands the concerto has an air of chaste sweetness, shedding much of its ripe, sensuous quality, but retaining its romantic feeling. There is a delicacy and tenderness here which is very appealing and, although the tuttis have plenty of fire, **Karajan** sensuously scales down his accompaniment in the lyrical passages to match his soloist. The digital recording provides a natural balance and a vivid orchestral texture.

Grumiaux's version with **Wallberg** has never been counted an obvious first choice; he does not wear his heart on his sleeve as some violinists do. But it offers a refreshingly different view, warm and civilized, and Grumiaux brings all his beauty of tone and expressive technique to the music-making, with the famous slow movement totally memorable. He is very well accompanied, and the 1973 Philips recording sounds wonderfully natural in this superb Pentatone SACD transfer, whether or not ones uses the back speakers.

Jaime Laredo's budget version, fresh and delightfully direct (Regis RRC 1152) and **Nigel Kennedy's** unsentimental view (EMI 5 181173-2) are both highly individual but not first choices.

Violin Concerto 1 in G min.; Romance, Op. 85

*** Decca 465 7692. Jansen, Leipzig GO, Chailly – MENDELSSOHN: *Violin Concerto* ***

Janine Jansen here adds as an important and rare extra: Bruch's *Romance*, Op. 85, one of his many neglected concertante works. In that work, demonstrating her versatility, Jansen takes up the viola, revealing equal facility on the larger instrument. Her violin tone is distinctive, clear and bright, not at all fruity in a conventional way, encouraging her to take a light, athletic view of *allegros*, adopting daringly fast speeds in the finales of both concertos, while the slow movement is movingly tender, taken at a flowing *Andante*.

Violin Concerto 1 in G min., Op. 26; Scottish Fantasy, Op. 46

⊕—(M) **** Decca (ADD) 460 976-2. Chung, RPO, Kempe – MENDELSSOHN: *Concerto* ***

(M) *** RCA **SACD** 82876 71622-2. Heifetz, New SO of London, Sargent – VIEUXTEMPS: *Violin Concerto 5* ***

The magic of **Kyung-Wha Chung**, always a spontaneously inspired violinist, comes over beguilingly. Chung goes straight to the heart of the famous *G minor Concerto*, finding mystery and fantasy as well as more extrovert qualities. Just as strikingly in the *Scottish Fantasy* she transcends the episodic nature of the writing to give the music a genuine depth and concentration, above all in the lovely slow movement. **Kempe** and the **RPO** accompany sympathetically, well caught in a glowing recording.

Heifetz plays with supreme assurance, and the slow movement shows this fine artist in masterly form. Heifetz's panache and the subtlety of his bowing and colour also bring a striking freshness to Bruch's charming Scottish whimsy. **Sargent** accompanies sympathetically and, though the soloist is balanced much too closely, there is never any doubt that he can produce a true *pianissimo*. The new SACD transfer adds body to the sound, and the violin is vividly real.

Violin Concertos 1; 3 in D min., Op. 58

*** Warner 0927 45664-2. Hanslip, LSO, Brabbins (with – SARASATE: *Navarra* ***)

Warm and confident as she is in 1, **Hanslip** tends to underline phrasing rather heavily, where in the expansive 3 she is fresher, more imaginative and more individual. With clean attack, flawless intonation and crisp double-dotting, she gives a winningly spontaneous-sounding reading, revelling in the beauty of the violin writing and its range of expression, while **Martyn Brabbins** draws incisive playing from the **LSO**. The Sarasate showpiece – in which Hanslip is joined in duet by **Mikhail Ovrutsky** – with its jaunty Spanish dance rhythms makes a delightful supplement.

Violin Concerto 2 in D min., Op. 44

⊕—*** Delos DE 3156. Hu, Seattle SO, Schwarz – GOLDMARK: *Concerto* ***

Violin Concerto 2; Scottish Fantasy, Op. 46

**(*) EMI 7 49071-2. Perlman, Israel PO, Mehta

(i) Violin Concerto 2. Symphony 3 in E, Op. 51

*** Chan. 9738. (i) Mordkovitch; LSO, Hickox

Nai-Yan Hu is ideally balanced and well accompanied by **Schwarz** and the **Seattle** orchestra. Hu's soaring lyrical lines underline the music's warmth and consistent melodic inspiration. Though Perlman strikes a high profile in his EMI version, the sympathetic warmth of this Hu/Schwarz partnership and the concert-hall fullness of the Delos recording is preferable.

In the *Second Violin Concerto*, **Lydia Mordkovitch** gives a raptly intense reading, making the long, slow first movement (in sonata form) into a deeply reflective meditation, punctuated by virtuoso flurries, readily justifying her spacious speeds. In the *Third Symphony* **Hickox** takes an affectionate view of the work. Speeds are broad in the first three movements, markedly so in the *Adagio*, with the chorale theme spacious and dedicated, and the surging theme which opens the finale has a hint of English folksong.

In his later, Israel recording, **Perlman** may be less intimately reflective in both works than he was when he recorded this coupling with the New Philharmonia, but in the fast movements there are ample compensations in the sharp concentration from first to last.

(i) Violin Concerto 3 in D min., Op. 58. Symphony 1 in E flat, Op. 28

⊕—*** Chan. 9784. (i) Mordkovitch; LSO, Hickox

The *Third Violin Concerto* is laid out spaciously; yet Bruch characteristically allows himself plenty of lyrical lingering, which inspires **Lydia Mordkovitch** to playing of rapt intensity down to magical *pianissimos*, before the vigorous *moto perpetuo* finale. *Symphony 1*, written soon after the popular *Violin Concerto in G minor*, is also based on striking material. **Hickox** is a warmly expressive but never self-indulgent interpreter, and the Chandos recording is full and atmospheric.

(i) Double Concerto for Violin & Viola, Op. 88. Kol Nidrei, Op. 47; Romance for Viola & Orchestra, Op. 85

⊕→ *** RCA 09026 63292-2. Bashmet, LSO, Järvi; (i) with Tretyakov – WALTON: *Viola Concerto* ***

Bruch's fund of melodic invention, usually a youthful gift, stayed with him well into his seventies, as the *Double Concerto* and the *Romance* winningly demonstrate. The latter work for viola and orchestra of 1912 harks straight back to the slow movement of the *G minor Violin Concerto*. It is a radiant piece and draws a heartfelt performance from **Bashmet**, as does the well-known *Kol Nidrei*, made the more poignant with viola taking the place of cello. The *Double Concerto* brings extra sensuousness, thanks also to the pure-toned playing of **Viktor Tretyakov**, a perfect foil for the resonant Bashmet.

Kol Nidrei, Op. 47

⊕→ *** Virgin 5 45664-2. Truls Mørk, French RPO, Paavo Järvi – BLOCH: *Schelomo*; SCHUMANN: *Cello Concerto* ***

⊕→ **** EMI 5 56126-2. Chang, LSO, Rostropovich – FAURÉ: *Elégie* ***; SAINT-SAËNS: *Cello Concerto 1* ***; TCHAIKOVSKY: *Rococo Variations* *** ✿

Ⓜ *** DG (ADD) 457 761-2. Fournier, LOP, Martinon – BLOCH: *Schelomo*; LALO: *Cello Concerto*; SAINT-SAËNS: *Cello Concerto 1* ***

Ⓜ **(*) Mercury 432 001-2. Starker, LSO, Dorati – DVOŘÁK: *Concerto*; TCHAIKOVSKY: *Rococo Variations* **(*)

Like Bloch's *Schelomo*, Bruch's *Kol Nidrei* is a Jewish rhapsody, even though the composer was not Jewish himself. It suits **Mørk's** freely expressive style just as well as the Bloch, resulting in a deeply concentrated reading, with *pianissimo* playing magically refined.

Han-Na Chang catches the intense atmosphere of Bruch's Hebrew melody with a natural sensitivity, spontaneous in her dynamic contrasts; and indeed the extraordinary poise and assurance of this playing, matched by her ability to touch the listener, reminds one of the young Yehudi Menuhin. Her mentor accompanies her with great sympathy and the Abbey Road recording is beautifully balanced.

If **Fournier's** performance lacks the last degree of romantic urgency, it makes up for it in the beauty and style of the solo playing, and he is well supported by **Martinon's Lamoureux Orchestra**.

Starker's Mercury recording is transformed by the new transfer, warm and glowing. The performance may lack romantic urgency but it has a relaxed, ruminative quality which is very endearing. **Dorati** accompanies most persuasively, providing a highly sympathetic orchestral backcloth.

Scottish Fantasy (for violin & orchestra), Op. 46

⊕→ Ⓑ *** Decca (ADD) 476 7288 (2). D. Oistrakh, LSO, Horenstein – MOZART: *Sinfonia concertante*, etc. **(*); HINDEMITH: *Violin Concerto* ***

Ⓑ **** CfP 575 8022. Little, RSNO, Handley – LALO: *Symphonie espagnole* ***

ⒷⒷ (***) Naxos mono 8.110940. Heifetz, LPO, Barbirolli – BRAHMS: *Double Concerto*; GLAZUNOV: *Violin Concerto* ***

The extrovert 1962 **Oistrakh/Horenstein** performance of the *Scottish Fantasia* owes nearly as much to the conductor as to the soloist. The expansive dignity of the opening of the brass shows immediately how fine the orchestral contribution is going to be, and Oistrakh's playing throughout is ravishing, enhancing the stature of the work immeasurably.

Tasmin Little takes a ripe, robust and passionate view of both works, projecting them strongly, as she would in the concert hall. In this she is greatly helped by the fine, polished playing of the **Scottish Orchestra** under **Vernon Handley**, a most sympathetic partner. The recording is superb, with brass in particular vividly caught. Little plays the Guerriero finale absolutely complete.

Bruch's *Scottish Fantasy* was always a favourite work with **Heifetz**, and although his pioneering 1947 version cannot quite match his stereo remake with Sargent and the LSO in thoughtful intensity, the passion and brilliance of the playing are most compelling, with the songful *Adagio* section even more moving in its simpler, more flowing manner, hushed and dedicated. Generously coupled with the powerful Brahms performance and the exuberant account of the Glazunov, another first recording. Good Naxos transfers, if with audible surface hiss.

Scottish Fantasy, Op. 46; Serenade, Op. 75

ⒷⒷ **(*) Naxos 8.557395. Fedotov, Russian PO, Yablonsky

It is good to have one of Bruch's rarer concertante pieces for violin coupled with the colourful *Scottish Fantasy*. In warm, thrustful performances **Maxim Fedotov** may be a little short on the subtler qualities of mystery and tenderness, but the bravura of his playing, helped by full-blooded accompaniment from **Dmitry Yablonsky** and the **Russian Philharmonic**, makes the results compelling enough. The *Serenade*, Op. 75, dating from 1900, 20 years after the *Fantasy*, belies its lightweight title in its breadth and weight over four substantial movements.

Octet in B flat (for strings), Op. posth.

ⒷⒷ *** Naxos 8.557270. Kodály & Auer Qts – MENDELSSOHN: *Octet* ***

Bruch's ripely romantic late *Octet* (scored for 4 violins, 2 violas, cello and double bass) may not be as melodically inspired as its Mendelssohn coupling, but it has a genuine romantic sweep and has much of Mendelssohn's infectious exuberance. It is played with persuasive warmth and conviction by the combined **Kodály** and **Auer Quartets** and is a thoroughly worthwhile addition to the Bruch discography.

String Quintet in A min., Op. posth.

*** Naim CD 010. Augmented Allegri Qt – BRAHMS: *String Quintet 2* ***

Bruch's *A minor Quintet* was one of two he wrote for sheer joy at the age of eighty. It is an unashamed throwback in idiom to Beethoven and Brahms, but the freshness of ideas and argument is most winning. Like the Brahms *G major*

Quintet, with which it is ideally coupled, it is very well performed and vividly recorded.

BRUCKNER, Anton (1824–96)

Symphonies 0; 00; 1–9; Symphony 4: Volksfest finale (1878)

⊕— ⑧⑧ *** Naxos 8.501101 (11). RSNO, or Nat. SO of Ireland, Tintner

Symphonies 0; 1–9

⑧ **(*) Decca (DDD/ADD) 448 910-2 (10). Chicago SO, Solti

Symphonies 1–9 (complete)

⊕— ⑧ *** DG (ADD) 477 7580-2 (9). BPO, Karajan

⑧ *** EMI (ADD) 5 73905-2 (9). Dresden State O, Jochum

⑧ *** DG (ADD) 469 810-2 (9). BPO or Bav. RSO, Jochum

Symphonies 1–9; (i) Helgoland

⊕— ⑧⑧ **** Warner 2564 61891-2 (9). BPO, Barenboim, (i) with Berlin R. Ch., Ernst Senff Ch.

Recorded between 1990 and 1997, **Daniel Barenboim's** cycle of the Bruckner *Symphonies* is among his finest achievements with the **Berlin Philharmonic**. These are powerful, concentrated performances, with tension and impact heightened by the fact that all but two of them, 4 and 7, were recorded live in concert. They also gain in competition with direct rivals – certainly in the super-bargain category – by enjoying spectacular sound, with Barenboim's preference for extreme dynamics fully and thrillingly caught, even though the extremes may be too great for easy domestic listening for some. The cycle rises to a climax with Barenboim's masterly readings of the last two symphonies. 8 in the full Haas edition is dedicated in all four movements. 9 is equally dedicated, ending on a noble account of the finale so satisfying that one has no regrets that Bruckner failed to complete a finale. The symphonic chorus for male voices and orchestra, *Helgoland*, makes a valuable supplement as a fill-up for 1. The nine discs come in a convenient compact box with full notes in a booklet.

The reappearance of **Karajan's** magnificent cycle recorded between 1976–1978, long a yardstick by which others were measured – and at mid-price – must be warmly welcomed. We have sung the praises of these recordings loud and long, and in their new format they are outstanding value.

Jochum's DG cycle was recorded between 1958 (5) and 1967 (2), all but four (2, 3, 5 and 6) with the **Berlin Philharmonic**. No apology need be made for either the performances or the quality of the recorded sound, which wears its years lightly. One of the finest is the 1957 *Fifth*, in which Jochum brought a unique sense of mystery and atmosphere to Bruckner, and it more than compensates for the occasional freedom he permitted himself. The set now comes economically packaged and priced and well documented in

DG's Collector's Edition and can be thoroughly recommended.

Eugen Jochum's second Bruckner cycle was recorded in Dresden with the magnificent **Staatskapelle** between 1975 and 1980 in the last days of analogue recording. There is little difference in his approach here when compared to his earlier, DG set: he always favoured the Nowak editions, but the Dresden set has the richer, more opulent sound. Jochum had wisdom and nobility as well as a sense of vision, and his lifelong feeling for Bruckner's music and his grasp of its architecture shine through in every bar. At a bargain price, this is very competitive indeed.

There are few more persuasive Bruckner conductors than **Georg Tintner**, and his symphonic cycle on Naxos is uniquely complete in including not only *Die Nullte* and the '*Study Symphony*', but also the '*Volksfest*' Finale of 4. The performances are very well played by the **Royal Scottish National Orchestra**, the readings dedicated and intense, often inspired, and the recordings are full, atmospheric and clear. The Naxos Box includes admirably extensive documentation, and this set must receive the strongest recommendation, quite irrespective of its modest cost.

Solti had previously recorded the *Eighth* with the VPO for John Culshaw in the Sofiensaal as early as 1966. With the **Chicago Symphony Orchestra** he recorded the whole cycle between 1979 (6) and 1995 (5). The two early symphonies are very impressive, but the *Third* is the one failure, relatively crude and coarse. Otherwise, the *Seventh*, with refined playing, lacks tension in the outer movements, but the series culminates in an inspired account of the *Eighth* and the *Ninth*, similarly spacious, with the music given full time to breathe.

Symphony 00 in F min.; Overture in G min.

Ⓜ *** Oehms OC 208. Saarbrücken RSO, Skrowaczewski

Skrowaczewski's is a fine performance, very well recorded, making an outstanding bargain. The *Overture in G minor* from the same period makes an ideal fill-up with its mysterious slow introduction leading to a light, Mendelssohnian Allegro.

Symphony 00 in F min. (Study Symphony); String Quintet: Adagio (arr. for strings)

*** Ondine ODE 920-2. German SO, Berlin, Ashkenazy

Symphony 00 in F min. (Study Symphony); Symphony 4: Volkfest Finale (1878)

⊕— ⑧⑧ *** Naxos 8. 554432. RSNO, Tintner

With excellent playing and recording – as in the rest of the series – **Tintner** could not be more persuasive; as a welcome bonus he adds the very rare second version of the finale of the *Fourth Symphony*, which Bruckner entitled *Volksfest*, 'Festival of the People'. Strikingly different, particularly at the start, from the 1880 version of that movement, which is generally performed, it is well worth hearing in a fine performance like this, even if it hardly displaces the usual version.

Ashkenazy conducts his Berlin orchestra in a strong and

purposeful reading. His speeds are consistently fast, his manner direct but still expressive, so that he brings out the inner intensity of the fine slow movement. The lovely *Adagio* of the *String Quintet* in string orchestra format brings just as dedicated a performance, an excellent bonus. Full, warm sound. However, the Naxos version has a considerable price advantage.

Symphonies 0 in D min. (Die Nullte); 8 in C min. (1887 Nowak edition)

⊕ⓑ (BB) *** Naxos 8.554215/6. Nat. SO of Ireland, Tintner

In a moving note **Georg Tintner** passionately argues the case for Bruckner's original (1887) version of 8, fresh and spontaneous. The result is an intense, keenly concentrated reading, with total dedication in the playing, which rises to supreme heights in the long *Adagio* slow movement, where the refined *pianissimo* playing of the Irish orchestra is magically caught by the Naxos engineers. Even for those with rival versions, this makes a very necessary recommendation, particularly when the two-disc package brings so generous and revealing a coupling as the *D minor Symphony (Die Nullte)* in a very good performance. Tintner powerfully brings out the Brucknerian qualities in embryo, and again he is served very well by the Irish orchestra.

Symphony 1 in C min.

⊕ⓜ (M) *** Oehms OC 210. Saarbrücken RSO, Skrowaczewski

Skrowaczewski draws dedicated, tautly sprung playing from the **Saarbrücken** orchestra in what remains a problematic work. At speeds on the fast side, this is a fresh and urgent reading, which yet brings out the hushed intensity of the spacious second movement *Adagio*. Beautifully recorded in a helpful acoustic, it is a match for any version at whatever price.

Symphonies 1 in C min. (1866 version, revised Carragan); 3 in D min.: Adagio (1876)

(BB) *** Naxos 8.554430. RSNO, Tintner

Georg Tintner opts for the earliest version of the *Symphony* 1. The principal differences here are in the finale, which brings angular writing and orchestration that is more radical than in the revisions. Tintner in his dedicated performance, with refined playing from the Scottish orchestra, amply justifies his choice, powerfully bringing out the bald originality of the writing. The generous makeweight also offers a rare text, a version of the slow movement of *Symphony 3*, which was composed in 1876. Again the intensity and refinement of the performance sustain the expansiveness compellingly.

Symphony 2 in C min. (original, 1872 score)

⊕ⓑ (BB) *** Naxos 8.554006. Nat. SO of Ireland, Tintner

Georg Tintner here opts for the edition of the original (1872) score, presenting the work at its most expansive and with the middle two movements in reverse order from usual. The Scherzo has an extra repeat, but more important is the expansion of both the slow movement and the finale, here presented in concentrated performances that feel not a moment too long. The coda of the *Andante* brings a horn solo at the very end (substituted by Herbeck in 1876), challenging to the player, which is more strikingly beautiful than the clarinet solo with which Bruckner replaced it. Excellent, refined playing from the Irish orchestra and full, rich sound, with the brass gloriously caught.

Symphony 3 in D min. (original, 1873 version)

⊕ⓑ (BB) *** Naxos 8.553454. RSNO, Tintner

With characteristic boldness, **Georg Tintner** opts here to record the very rare first version, far more expansive than the final, revised version normally heard. Tintner holds the vast structure together masterfully; even though his speeds in the three expanded movements are daringly slow the concentration of the performance, with dynamic contrasts heightened, never falters for a moment. The slow movement too is rapt and dedicated, with *pianissimos* of breathtaking delicacy. The Scherzo is then fast and fierce, before the spacious account of the finale. Tintner in every way justifies his daring and revelatory choice of text.

Symphony 3 in D min. (1877 version)

*** Hyp. CDA 67200. BBC Scottish SO, Vänskä

The key point about **Vänskä's** version, given a brilliant and refined performance by the **BBC Scottish Symphony**, is that he uses a long-buried text for the *Adagio* slow movement, more expansive, with more quotations from Wagner included. The liner-notes clarify these points, making an excellent case for preferring this text. Vänskä effectively heightens the Wagnerian qualities of the score, while drawing a ripe, Brucknerian sound from his players, helped by full, atmospheric recording.

Symphony 3 (1890 version)

ⓜ (M) *** Oehms OC212 Saarbrücken RSO, Skrowaczewski

Skrowaczewski offers a mid-priced version of the *Third*, which in both performance and recording rivals any more expensive version. Unlike Tintner he opts for the usual text, following Bruckner's final reworking in his third version of the work. As in Skrowaczewski's other Bruckner recordings on the Oehms label, the playing of the **Saarbrücken Orchestra** is strong and intense, with opulent sound to match. So the slow movement is sweet and warm in its lyrical flow, and the finale glows with resplendent brass.

Symphonies 3 in D min. (1877 version); 8 in C min.

⊕ⓑ (BB) *** Ph. Duo 470 534-2 (2). VPO, Haitink

Haitink's is a performance of enormous breadth and majesty, and Philips give it a recording to match. The playing of the **VPO** is glorious throughout. No less enticing is the recording of the *Eighth Symphony*, with the same formidable combination of conductor and orchestra, and first-rate engineering (by the doyen of Philips engineers, Volker Strauss), and the results are outstanding. The VPO play with great fervour and warmth, and the recorded sound is sumptuous. It is still among the most satisfying versions available. In short, these two symphonies make a remarkable bargain on the Philips Duo label.

Symphony 4 in E flat (original, 1874 version)

(BB) **(*) Warner Apex 2564 61371-2. Frankfurt RSO, Inbal

Like the *Third*, there are three versions of the *Romantic Symphony*, and no one had recorded the original version before **Inbal**. The Scherzo here is a completely different and more fiery movement, and the opening of the finale is also totally different. Inbal's performance is good, with a genuine feeling for the Bruckner idiom, paying scrupulous attention to dynamic refinements. The recording is well detailed, though the climaxes almost (but not quite) reach congestion. A fascinating issue, and especially attractive at budget price.

Symphony 4 in E flat (Romantic)

⊕ **** RCA 09026 68839-2. BPO, Wand

⊕ (BB) *** Naxos 8.554128. RSNO, Tintner

(M) *** Decca (ADD) 475 8403. VPO, Boehm

Symphony 4 in E flat; Overture in G min.

(***) Testament mono/stereo SBT 1050. Philh. O, von Matačič

Günter Wand's Berlin version of the *Fourth Symphony* crowns his achievement as one of our greatest Bruckner conductors. The recording derives from a concert at the Philharmonie in Berlin and conveys a sense of occasion so often missing in the studio. Wand knows what this music is about and has the command of its architecture and space, with consistently warm textures from the **Berlin Philharmonic**. Keenly dramatic, capped by towering climaxes, it offers full, rich sound, if with *pianissimos* not quite as hushed as they might be.

There are not many versions as fine as **Georg Tintner's** on Naxos, at whatever price. With extreme *pianissimos* magically caught, full of mystery, this is an exceptionally spacious reading, deeply reflective and poetic, which brings out the Schubertian qualities in Bruckner, sweet and songful as well as dramatic. The playing of the **Royal Scottish National Orchestra** is as refined as the recording, with subtly terraced dynamics beautifully clear.

There are many who admire **Boehm's** Bruckner, and he certainly controls the lyrical flow of the fourth symphony convincingly, helped by first-rate playing from the **VPO**, and vintage Decca sound from 1973, with the advantage of the spacious acoustics of the Sofiensaal. The balance provides splendid detail and a firm sonority. Boehm's sobriety was also his strength; in every bar he gives the impression that he knows exactly where he is going and, choosing the Nowak edition, he shapes the structure compellingly.

Skrowaczewski's reading of Bruckner's most popular symphony is characteristically strong and refined, with extreme dynamic contrasts heightened by the excellent recording, so that the crescendo at the start of the finale is exceptionally powerful. Only in the third movement Scherzo does he adopt a tempo at all out of the ordinary, challenging the horns in daringly fast hunting calls, which yet are finely disciplined. (Oehms 01213)

Symphonies (i) 4 in E flat; (ii) 8 in C min.

(BB) *** EMI Gemini 3 81761-2 (i) BPO; (ii) LPO; Tennstedt

Tennstedt's *Fourth* is a reading that combines concentration and a degree of ruggedness, less moulded than with Karajan or Jochum in their very different ways. Here plainness goes with pure beauty and natural strength in the first two movements. The Scherzo is urgent, the finale resplendent. Tennstedt's plainness and beauty are again heard at their finest in his impressive account of the *Eighth*. The inwardness and hushed beauty of the great *Adagio* in particular are superbly projected in unforced concentration. Where in *4* he prefers the Haas Edition, here he is in favour of Nowak, without the additional material in the recapitulation. Fine, well-balanced recording in EMI's No. 1 studio.

Symphony 5 in B flat

⊕ (M) ✾ *** DG 469527-2. Dresden State O, Sinopoli

⊕ *** BBC (ADD) BBCL 4033-2. BBC SO, Horenstein

Sinopoli's reading is characterful and strong in a positive, even wilful way distinctively his. The **Dresden Staatskapelle** responds with playing of incandescent intensity, totally allied with the conductor in silencing any stylistic reservations. This is a live recording, and the inspiration of the moment comes over at full force. The energy of the *Scherzo* and the passion of the slow movement complete the picture of an exceptionally high-powered reading, recorded in glowing sound.

Horenstein's magisterial account of the *Fifth Symphony* with the **BBC Symphony Orchestra** has the advantage of relatively rich and vivid sound and comes from a 1971 Prom. It is an eloquent and compelling performance of a symphony which Horenstein (to the best of our knowledge) never recorded commercially.

Symphonies 5 in B flat; 7 in E (both ed. Nowak)

(N) (M) **(*) EMI 5 20943-2 LPO, Welser-Möst

The **LPO** plays well for **Welser-Möst** and in both symphonies are very responsive. *5* was recorded in the Konzerthaus, Vienna, in late May–early June 1993, before an attentive and silent audience, whose presence emerges only at the very end. Their applause is deserved. There are some potentially disruptive agogic touches, but he succeeds in persuading you that they have some logical motivation. The LPO create an impressive eloquence and radiance of texture. The *Seventh* comes from a 1991 Prom and so again enjoys a warmer ambience than most studio performances. The LPO produce a real Bruckner sound, save perhaps at the bottom end of the spectrum. Welser-Möst again shows a natural feel for Bruckner's spacious lyricism and audience noise is minimal, save at the very end, when it is anything but!

Symphony 6 in A

*** HM HMC 90 1901. Deutsches SO, Berlin, Nagano

⊕ (BB) *** LSO Live LSO 0022. LSO, C. Davis

(M) *** EMI (ADD) 5 62621-2. New Philh. O, Klemperer (with Overtures: GLUCK: *Iphigénie en Aulide*; HUMPERDINCK: *Hänsel und Gretel* **)

*** Australian Decca Eloquence (ADD) 476 2745. VPO, Stein – WEBER: *Overtures* ***

Nagano's new version with the **Deutsches Symphony Orchestra** goes fairly readily to the top of the list. It has something of the strength and directness of Klemperer's account, with the first movement spontaneously flowing and the slow movement having a powerful gravitas. The finale is comparatively episodic in its control of tempo, but it still holds together as part of an impressive overall interpretation. The recording, made in the Philharmonie, is full-bodied, well balanced and clear.

Sir Colin Davis's live recording of the *Sixth*, made in February 2002, is above all warm and purposeful. The high contrasts of the outer movements are superbly caught, with weighty resonant string-tone bringing incandescent climaxes. The weight of strings adds to the slow-paced moment of the expansive slow movement too, inexorably building up over long paragraphs, with the second subject treated *con amore*. The conductor's concentration finally brings sharp coherence to the wayward structure of the finale, with the engineers confirming their mastery over the Barbican acoustic in full-bodied sound.

Klemperer's 1964 version remains a characteristically strong and direct reading. It is disarmingly simple rather than overly expressive in the slow movement (faster than usual) but is always concentrated and strong, and the finale is held together particularly well. Splendid playing from the **New Philharmonia Orchestra**, and the Kingsway Hall recording is clear and bright, but even more full-bodied in the present remastering. The two overtures are earlier (1960) and feature the Philharmonia: *Hänsel und Gretel* is richly atmospheric, but the Gluck is heavy-going.

Horst Stein's is a nobly wrought account of the *Sixth Symphony* with the **Vienna Philharmonic**. The slow movement has genuine eloquence and gravity, and the performance of the other three is refreshingly free of eccentricity, striking the right degree of breadth and dignity. Stein brings both imagination and feeling to this score, and he is excellently recorded in vintage (1973) Decca sound.

Symphony 7 in E (original version)

(BB) ** Warner Apex 0927 40817-2. Frankfurt RSO, Inbal

For excellence of orchestral playing and vividness of recording, **Inbal's** *Seventh* is well up to the standard of his Bruckner series, using the original scores; but the performance itself, although not lacking an overall structural grip, is without the full flow of adrenalin that can make this symphony so compulsive.

Symphony 7 in E (DVD versions)

⊶ *** EMI DVD 3 101909. O Nat. de France, Jochum (with WAGNER: *Tristan and Isolde, Prelude and Liebestod*; MOZART: *Le Nozze di Figaro: Overture* (***))

*** TDK **DVD** WW COWAND8. NDR SO, Wand (V/D: Hugo Käch)

Jochum was one of the finest Brucknerians of his day and this beautifully prepared and subtly executed reading of the *Seventh Symphony* is magnificent. The **Orchestre National de France** is in responsive form and play with great sensitivity and feeling. Recorded in the Théâtre des Champs-Elysées, Paris, in 1980, along with the *Tristan Prelude and Liebestod*. As a bonus we have a black-and-white *Figaro Overture* with the **French Radio Orchestra**, well played, though not the lightest in touch. But this is easily the best Bruckner we have had yet on DVD. Unobtrusive and intelligent camerawork, and it is very compelling.

Like its companions in this series **Günter Wand** and the **NordDeutscher Rundfunk Orchester** are recorded in the excellent acoustic of the Musik- und Kongresshalle in Lübeck during the 1999 Schleswig-Holstein Festival. The performance is dedicated and completely straightforward, without a trace of ego. Hugo Käch's video direction serves us well.

Symphony 7 in E (CD versions)

⊶ **** Teldec 3984 24488-2. VPO, Harnoncourt

⊶ (B) *** EMI 4 76888-2. BPO, Karajan

⊶ (M) *** BBC (ADD) BBCL 4123-2. Philh. O, Giulini (with FALLA: *Three-Cornered Hat* (excerpts); MUSSORGSKY: *Khovanshchina: Prelude* ***)

⊶ (BB) *** Naxos 8.554269. RSNO, Tintner

Harnoncourt's outstanding performance of the *Seventh* was recorded live in the Sofiensaal and is one of his very finest records. The sound is magnificent: the Viennese strings have a radiant sheen and the brass is gloriously sonorous. The performance could hardly be more compelling. In the slow movement the cymbal crash at the climax is omitted, but even this does not spoil its impact, and in the beautiful coda Harnoncourt draws out the resemblance in the valedictory overlapping horn parts to Wagner's *Das Rheingold*. This is very highly recommendable in its own right. Harnoncourt admirers need not hesitate.

Karajan's outstanding early EMI version, recorded in the Jesus Christus Kirche in 1971, remains among the very finest. The reading shows a special feeling for the work's architecture, and the playing of the **Berlin Philharmonic** is gorgeous. The sound has striking resonance and amplitude. This EMI reading, generally preferable to his later, digital recording for DG, has a special sense of mystery.

Giulini's account with the **Philharmonia Orchestra** comes from the BBC's 1982 Prom season, a performance totally dedicated from beginning to end, so that climaxes are all the more thrilling, and the sound achieved by the BBC engineers is very fine indeed, natural in perspective and finely balanced. The Falla fill-up comes from an earlier Prom season (1963) and the *Khovanshchina Prelude* from an Edinburgh Festival concert at the Usher Hall. Strongly recommended.

Like his other Bruckner recordings for Naxos, **Tintner's** account of 7 brings a performance both subtle and refined, concentrated from first to last, often at spacious speeds. The glow of Brucknerian sound is caught beautifully, with the full nobility of the slow movement brought out. The Scherzo is not as rugged as it can be but, with sprung rhythms, the dance element is infectious. An outstanding bargain to rival any version.

Symphony 8 in C min. (DVD version)

⊶ *** TDK **DVD** DV-COWAND3. NDR SO, Wand (V/D: Barrie Gavin)

Günter Wand has great musical integrity and is a totally dedicated Brucknerian. He conveys a genuine sense of mystery, though ultimately he does not surpass the finest CD versions. The performance is very fine, however, and Barrie Gavin's camerawork places the viewer at the best vantage point. The orchestral sound is very well balanced.

Symphonies 8 in C min.; 9 in D min.; (i) Te Deum (DVD version)

**** DG **DVD** 073 4395 (2). VPO, Karajan, (i) with Tomowa-Sintow, Baltsa, Rendall. Van Dam, Wiener Singverein

The present *Eighth* with the **Vienna Philharmonic Orchestra** was recorded in St Florian, Linz, in 1979, six months or so after the celebrated DG record made in the Grosser Saal of the Philharmonie. The performance is equally exalted, though Karajan takes a more leisurely view of the slow movement and a brisker one of the finale. The *Ninth* and the *Te Deum* are recorded in the Musikverein in May 1978 and are hardly less impressive. Very good sound and discreet camerawork.

Symphony 8 in C min. (CD versions)

⊶ ✹ Ⓜ **** DG 427611-2. VPO, Karajan

Ⓑ *** EMI (ADD) 4 76901 (2). BPO, Karajan (with Overtures: WEBER: *Der Freischütz*; MENDELSSOHN: *Fingal's Cave*; WAGNER: *Der fliegende Holländer*; NICOLAI: *The Merry Wives of Windsor* ***)

*** DG 459 678-2. VPO, Boulez

Karajan's last version of the *Eighth Symphony* is with the **Vienna Philharmonic Orchestra** and is the most impressive of them all. The sheer beauty of sound and opulence of texture is awe-inspiring but never draws attention to itself: this is a performance in which beauty and truth go hand in hand. The recording is superior to either of its predecessors in terms of naturalness of detail and depth of perspective.

The new transfer of **Karajan's** early (1957) **Berlin Philharmonic** recording is also remarkably successful. The EMI sound is spacious and, if the sonorities are not quite as sumptuous as we would expect today, the strings have substance and the brass makes a thrilling impact. The performance has much in common with Karajan's later (mid-price) version for DG, and has compelling power. The slow movement is very fine indeed, conveying dark and tragic feelings, and the finale makes a real apotheosis. While Karajan's last VPO version remains special, this is very worthwhile and the Overtures are all splendidly played and recorded, with *Der fliegende Holländer* standing out.

With taut control **Pierre Boulez** directs a tough, intense reading of this most expansive of the Bruckner symphonies, one which is also warmly expressive in the great Bruckner melodies, helped by glowing playing from the **Vienna Philharmonic**. The great slow movement proceeds magnetically, in Boulez's hands a powerful symphonic structure rather than a visionary statement. The finale – using the more expansive text of the Haas Edition – is then rugged and bitingly dramatic, with Boulez's use of rubato warmly idiomatic.

Symphonies (i) 8 in C min.; (ii) 9 in D min.

*** BBC (ADD) BBCL 4017-2 (2). (i) LSO; (ii) BBC SO; Horenstein

These BBC recordings of performances at the Royal Albert Hall in 1970 reveal the genius of **Jascha Horenstein** more tellingly than almost any of his studio recordings. Though he draws out the warm expressiveness in Bruckner's lyrical writing, moulding phrases, he takes a rugged view of the overall structure, not least in his rapt account of the great *Adagio* in *Symphony 8*. Fine as the **LSO** is in that symphony with its brighter string-tone, the performance of the *Ninth* with the **BBC Symphony** brings even finer playing, strong and purposeful. Warm, atmospheric, radio sound.

Symphony 9 in D min. (DVD versions)

⊶ *** EuroArts **DVD** 2072197. VPO, Bernstein (V/D: Humphrey Burton)

⊶ *** TDK **DVD** DV-COWAND4. N. German RSO, Wand – SCHUBERT: *Symphony 8 (Unfinished)* ***

Although he had recorded Mahler symphonies with his much-loved Vienna Orchestra, Bernstein was slow to turn to Bruckner, believing that Karajan's recordings of them could hardly be surpassed. Now, some years after Bruckner's death and only a year before his own, he performed the *Ninth* at the Grosser Musikvereinsaal during a week in late February and early March, and this record is a compilation of these. A powerful document, which will make a special appeal to admirers of this remarkable partnership and this great work. Unobtrusive camerawork, which invariably places the listener-viewer where he would wish to be.

Günter Wand recorded this coupling of two unfinished symphonies at the 2001 Schleswig-Holstein Festival in Lübeck at the Musik-und-Kongreßhalle when he was 89. The present account with the **NDR Orchestra** has great majesty and a magnificent string sonority; the wind players are very fine, as indeed are the brass. Hugo Käch's camera direction is exemplary and never draws attention to itself. In all, a satisfying reading and, as always with Wand, selfless and free from idiosyncrasy.

Symphony 9 in D min. (CD versions)

⊶ ✹ Ⓜ (****) Sony 518812-2 (Stereo-mono). Columbia SO, Walter (with *Te Deum*: Yeend, Lipton, Lloyd, Harrell, Westminster Ch., NYPO, Walter)

ⒷⒷ *** Naxos 8.554268. RSNO, Tintner

*** Profil-Medien PH 4058. Stuttgart RSO, Wand

Ⓜ *** Warner Elatus 0927 46746–2. BPO, Barenboim

Bruno Walter's 1959 account of Bruckner's *Ninth Symphony* represents the peak of his achievement during his Indian summer in the CBS recording studios just before he died. His mellow, persuasive reading leads one on through the leisurely paragraphs so that the logic and coherence seem obvious where other performances can sound aimless. Some may not find the Scherzo vigorous enough to provide the fullest contrast, but the final slow movement has a nobility which suggests that after this, anything would have been an anticlimax.

For the reissue Sony have added Walter's fine (1959) Carnegie Hall mono recording of the *Te Deum*, a characteristically spacious account with a well-matched team of soloists and an excellent contribution from the **Westminster Choir**. The transfer of the very good mono recording is well managed, but the four stars are for the symphony.

Like others in his Bruckner series, **Georg Tintner's** Naxos recording of the *Ninth Symphony* is a match in every way for the finest rival versions, whatever the price. The refinement of *pianissimos* brings out the full mystery of the massive outer movements, while the delicate fantasy of the Scherzo is brilliantly touched on at high speed, with a touch of wildness. The final *Adagio* builds up in exultation: this may not have been planned as the finale, but here it becomes the most deeply satisfying conclusion. The playing of the **Royal Scottish National Orchestra** is superb, with recording at once transparent and refined, as well as weighty.

Günter Wand's Stuttgart account with the **SüdWestfunk Orchestra** is a live performance in the opulent acoustic of the Benedictine Monastery of Ottobeuren, which the Stuttgart engineers manage with real mastery; it offers a glorious, satisfying sound, rich and sonorous. This ranks high among Bruckner *Nines* both interpretatively and as sound.

Daniel Barenboim's Berlin account has depth and strength, with the advantage of superb orchestral playing, and the recorded sound has splendid body and transparency. One of the strongest of newer recommendations.

CHAMBER MUSIC

String Quintet in F

*** Nim. NI 5488. Brandis Qt, with Dean – BRAHMS: *String Quintet 2* ***

*** Australian Decca Eloquence (ADD) 476 2455. VPO Quintet, with H. Weiss – SCHMIDT: *Piano Quintet* ***

String Quintet in F; Intermezzo for String Quintet

(*) Hyp. CDA 66704. Raphael Ens. – R. STRAUSS: *Capriccio: Sextet* *

Bruckner's beautiful *Quintet* dates from 1878, immediately after the revision of the *Third* and *Fourth Symphonies*. It is music of substance and depth, and this superb account by the **Vienna Philharmonic Quintet** remains an excellent way of getting to know this fine work. The rich (1974) Decca/Sofiensaal sound – full and sweet – retains its qualities on CD.

The **Brandis** version of the *Quintet* offers a splendid coupling in Brahms's *G major Quintet*, Op. 111, and their playing

stands up well alongside the current competition. They are well recorded and have a natural feeling for the space and pacing of this piece. For those attracted by the coupling, this could well be a first choice.

The **Raphael Ensemble**, coupling their performance with the *Intermezzo in D minor* and the opening *Sextet* from Strauss's *Capriccio*, are ardently full-blooded in an eloquent account and have the benefit of rich recorded sound.

VOCAL MUSIC

Masses (i) 1 in D min.; 2 in E min.; (ii) 3 in F min.

🔊 ⚙ Ⓜ *** DG (ADD) 447 409-2 (2). (i) Mathis, Schiml, Ochman, Ridderbusch; (ii) Stader, Hellman, Haefliger, Borg; Bav. R. Ch. & O, Jochum

Bruckner composed his three *Masses* between 1864 and 1868, although all three works were revised two decades later. Each contains magnificent music. **Eugen Jochum** is surely an ideal interpreter, finding their mystery as well as their eloquence, breadth and humanity. The *Kyrie* of the *E minor* swelling out gloriously from its gentle opening is breathtaking, while the fervour of the passionate *F minor* work is extraordinarily compelling, with the intensity and drive of an inspirational live performance. Throughout all three works, the scale and drama of Bruckner's inspiration are fully conveyed, and in these newest transfers the warmly atmospheric analogue recordings from the early 1970s are given remarkable vividness and presence.

Masses 1–3; Aequalis 1 & 2; Motets: Afferentur regi virgines; Ave Maria; Christus factus est; Ecce sacerdos magnus; Inveni David; Locus iste; Os justi; Pange lingua; Tota pulchra es, Maria; Vexilla regis; Virga Jesse; Libera me. Psalm 150; Te Deum

Ⓜ *** Hyp. CDS 44071 (3). Soloists, Corydon Singers and O; ECO Wind Ens., Best; T. Trotter (organ)

It makes good sense to assemble all of the Bruckner choral music that the **Corydon Singers** and **Matthew Best** have recorded during the last few years in one three-CD set. They are very fine indeed and make a splendid modern alternative to Jochum; when eloquent and natural, Best's direction is imaginative and he achieves a wide tonal range.

Mass 2 in E min.; Mass in C

*** Chan. 9863. Kuznetzova, Golub, Russian State Symphonic Cappella, Russian State SO, Polyansky

There is something seraphic about the *E minor Mass*. It may not have the grandeur and majesty of the later symphonies, but there is a simplicity of invention and an elevation of feeling that are affecting, particularly when it is recorded so beautifully and performed with the eloquence of **Polyansky** and his Russian forces on Chandos. The early *C major Mass* is a most welcome coupling.

(i) Mass 2 in E min. Motets: Ave Maria; Christus factus est; Os justi; Locus iste; Pange lingua; Vexilla regis; Virga Jesse floruit

**** Hyp. CDA 67629. Polyphony, Layton; (i) with Britten Sinfonia

Glorious singing from **Polyphony** under **Stephen Layton**, especially in the *Credo* and *Sanctus* of the *Mass*, which in his hands have all the exultant power you could wish for, yet the work's gentler qualities are well displayed in the *Benedictus* and *Agnus Dei*. The motets are for the most part more seraphic and are beautifully sung. The music-making is projected within the richly resonant acoustics of Ely Cathedral, which surely is perfect for Bruckner, with the climaxes soaring with a moving ecclesiastical rapture.

Motets: *Afferentur regi; Ave Maria; Christus factus est; Ecce sacerdos; Iam lucis orto sidere; Inveni David; Libera me; Locus iste; Os justi; Pange lingua; Salvum fac populum tuum; Tantum ergo; Tota pulchra es; Vexilla regis; Virga Jesse*

(BB) *** Naxos 8.550956. St Bride's Church Ch., Jones

(i) Motets: *Afferentur regi; Ave Maria; Christus factus est; Ecce sacerdos; Locus iste; Os justi; Pange lingua; Tota pulchra es; Vexilla regis; Virga Jesse.* (ii) Psalm 150; Te Deum

(M) *** DG (ADD) 457 743-2 (2). (i) Bav. R. Ch.; (ii) Stader, Wagner, Haefliger, Lagger, German Op. Ch., Berlin, BPO; Jochum

This Naxos disc is the first commercial recording of the **St Bride's Church Choir**, and very impressive it is, for with crisp, clear ensemble and fresh tone from boyish-sounding sopranos they give warmly sympathetic performances of these fine Bruckner motets, an excellent selection covering most of the best known. The recording is full and vivid, set against a helpful church acoustic which does not obscure detail.

On DG, the ten motets are sung superbly and are among **Jochum's** most distinguished recordings. With excellent soloists, the performances of the two larger-scale works here have fine eloquence and admirable breadth and humanity and no lack of drama and, with some fine singing from **Maria Stader** and **Ernst Haefliger**, as well as superbly loving orchestral support from the Berliners, this has a special eloquence. The original recordings tended to be distanced; in making the sound more present and clear the remastering is undoubtedly fresher and brighter.

Requiem in D min.; Psalms 112 & 114

**(*) Hyp. CDA 66245. Rodgers, Denley, M. Davies, George, Corydon Singers, ECO, Best; T. Trotter (organ)

Matthew Best here tackles the very early setting of the *Requiem* which Bruckner wrote at the age of 25. The quality of the writing in the Psalm settings also varies; but with fine, strong performances from singers and players alike, including an excellent team of soloists, this is well worth investigating by Brucknerians. First-rate recording.

Te Deum

(M) *** EMI 2 12718-2 Pashley, Finnila, Tear, Garrard, New Philh. Ch. & O, Barenboim – MOZART: *Requiem* ***

(BB) *** Warner Apex 8573 89128-2. Spreckelsen, Ankerson, Adalbert Kraus, Moll, Bielefeld Musikverein Ch., Philh. Hung., Stephani – VERDI: *Te Deum* ***

Bruckner's *Te Deum* is an unexpected coupling for Mozart's *Requiem*, but by the dynamism which **Barenboim** injects in both works there is an unexpected link of style. The Bruckner, like the Mozart, receives a vivid, very lively performance, relying not so much on massive choral effects (the recording was done with a comparatively small choir in a smallish church) as on rhythmic energy. Barenboim's approach to Bruckner proves warmly enjoyable and this disc is an excellent choice if the coupling suits.

Another outstanding account of Bruckner's 1884 setting of the *Te Deum* from **Martin Stephani**, vibrantly direct and gripping, with an excellent team of soloists and very fine choral singing over a wide range of dynamic. Stephani is fully sympathetic to the composer's deeply felt religious feeling. The well-balanced recording provides a warm acoustic while giving the chorus bite and amplitude. Text and translation are included. A bargain.

BRUSA, Elisabetta (born 1954)

Adagio; Favole; Firelights; Requiescat; Suite grotesque; Wedding Song

(BB) **(*) Naxos 8.555267. Nat. SO of Ukraine, Mastrangelo

Elisabetta Brusa was born in Milan and studied at the Conservatoire, before moving on to participate at Dartington and Tanglewood. The glittering Scherzo, *Firelights*, is characteristic of her orchestral skill, but the expressive eloquence of the following 16-minute *Adagio* would not be out of place in almost any late 20th-century symphony, and the engagingly rhapsodic *Wedding Song* is memorable in a lustrously romantic way,

The yearning *Requiescat* for large orchestra ends with a soaring solo soprano voice adding to the passionate celebration of the coda. The *Suite grotesque* might be regarded as a sinfonietta, with its slightly weird opening Scherzo, a darkly atmospheric slow movement, and a vigorous finale that gathers together the themes of the preceding movements 'in quadruple counterpoint', to reach a very positive apotheosis.

In the *Fables* Brusa uses the same orchestral identifications as did Prokofiev in *Peter and the Wolf*, so the listener has no trouble in identifying the characters. Most imaginative are Hans Andersen's *The Real Nightingale and the Mechanical One*, and the innocently poignant portrait of *The Ugly Duckling*. Most picaresque is La Fontaine's *The Ant and the Grasshopper* (a saxophone), but *The Philosophical Fly* (Aesop) meets his end spectacularly, and Perrault's *Puss in Boots* is given a jolly royal march, with a winningly jaunty main theme. First-class performances and a splendidly vivid recording, with the only real reservation being the unflattering sound of the **Ukrainian** upper strings.

Fanfare; Florestan (orchestral portrait); Nittemero Symphony; Messidor (fantasy); La Triade (symphonic poem)

(BB) **(*) Naxos 8.555266. Nat. SO of Ukraine, Mastrangelo

Messidor is the most immediately attractive work here, an orchestral fantasy inspired by 'A Midsummer Night's Dream'. *Florestan* (1997) evokes Schumann's imaginary character. 'Rain pours down incessantly' in *La Triade* (1994), an orchestral 'curtain of water', its scenario drawn both by an Aesop fable (with a fox and snake the central characters) and by Leonardo da Vinci's description of 'The Deluge'. The *Nittemero* ('Night and Day') *Symphony* (1985–8) is scored for 14 players, and again the ear is immediately struck by the composer's vivid orchestral world. The three-movement work is cyclic, depicting the 24 hours, from midday to midday. The performances here are bold and committed and generally well recorded, except that the **Ukrainian** violins sound thin in their upper range. But this is a promising début, and worth sampling at Naxos price.

BULL, John (c. 1562–1628)

Keyboard Music: 'Dr Bull's Jewel': for Clavichord & Harpsichord

**** Lyrichord LEMS 8060. Kathryn Cok (harpsichord & virginal)

An aptly named collection, for **Kathryn Cok** really does make a jewel out of Bull's piece of that name, and she is equally imaginative in picturing *The King's Hunt*. She opens invitingly with *Bull's Goodnight*, the virtuoso divisions of *Walsingham* and the embroidery of the *In nomine* are encompassed with flair, and *Bonny Peg of Ramsey* has proper wit. This is a very attractive collection indeed, and the recording of the harpsichord is remarkably clear and present.

BUSH, Alan (1900–95)

Cello Sonata, Op. 120; 3 Contrapuntal Studies for Violin and Viola, Op. 13; Phantasy for Violin and Piano, Op. 3; Piano Quartet, Op. 5

▣—(M) *** Dutton CDLX 7130. London Piano Qt

The *Cello Sonata* was written in 1989, sixty years after the other works here, and it shows the mature composer at his finest in such a sympathetic performance as this by **David Kennedy** and **Philip Fowke**. The *Piano Quartet* (1924, revised 1929) is also highly inventive and full of character, its warm underlying lyricism ensures the music's ready communication throughout. The equally appealing *Phantasy for Violin and Piano* (1923) is similarly lavish in its melodic flow and it brings matching rhythmic freedom, while the three *Contrapuntal Studies* are as aurally enticing as they are skilfully contrived. All these performances from members of the **London Piano Quartet** are deeply felt and show how well these four fine artists identify completely with the composer. The recording too, is very lifelike, to make this a most rewarding collection.

(i; ii) Concert Piece for Cello & Piano, Op. 17; (i–iii) 3 Concert Studies for Piano Trio, Op. 31; (i; ii) 2 Easy Pieces for Cello & Piano; (ii; iii) 2 Melodies, Op. 47; Sonatina, Op. 88 (both for viola & piano); (i; ii) Summer Valley for Cello & Piano

*** Mer. CDE 84458. (i) Spooner; (ii) C. Summerhayes; (iii) A. Summerhayes

The instrumental programme on Meridian is stimulating and includes the other key work in the composer's output, the riveting *Concert Piece* for cello and piano of 1936, written prophetically as war clouds were gathering in Europe. The balm of the *Viola Sonatina* with its pastoral feeling and the lovely, very English evocation of a *Summer Valley* (both ravishingly played here) offer genuine solace. The two charming *Easy Pieces* for cello, and the pair for viola (both with piano) show Bush's disarming melodic gift.

(i) 3 Concert Studies For Piano Trio, Op. 31; (ii) (Piano) 2 Ballads of the Sea, Op. 50: The Cruel Sea Captain. Suite, Op. 54: Galliard; Air. Corentyne Kwee-Kwe, Op. 75

(*) Lyrita (ADD) SRCD 256. (i) Bean, Croxford, Parkhouse; (ii) composer – BERKELEY: *Sextet; Sonatina*; RAWSTHORNE: *Clarinet Qt* *

Alan Bush's *Concert Studies* are not quite as successful as the Berkeley and Rawsthorne couplings: their content is not wholly in harmony with their dimensions, and the composer's piano playing is not as completely assured as one would like. However, this is still well worth having.

(i) Lyric Interlude, Op. 26; Meditation on a German Song (The Trooper's Pledge), Op. 22; Le quatorze juillet: esquisse, Op. 38; Preludes & Fugues 1–2, Op. 108; Serenade and Duet, Op. 111; Song and Dance, Op. 117a. 3 Raga Melodies for Unaccompanied Violin, Op. 59

▣— *** Mer. CDE 844481. Adam Summerhayes; (i) Catherine Summerhayes

Alan Bush's splendid four-movement *Lyric Interlude* (1944) shows the composer at his most appealingly melodic. Its intensity of feeling derives from the tragic death of one of his daughters in a road accident. The *Meditation on a German Song* of 1848 perhaps expresses the composer's feelings about death even more tellingly. *Le quatorze juillet*, both jaunty and reflective, is a very French tribute to the wartime Résistance. The *Three Raga Melodies* (1961), for solo violin, although written in classic Raga styles, still have a surprisingly Western feeling. Apart from the concentration of the writing, there is little Bachian influence in the two late *Preludes and Fugues* (1986) and the connecting rhapsodic 'Interlude' emphasizes the lyricism of the composer's style. With the *Serenade and Duet*, Op. 111, and the delightful miniatures of Op. 117a Bush finally moves into a distinctly English modal style and an appealing personal simplicity of utterance. Altogether this is a first-class survey. **Adam Summerhayes** proves a committed, accomplished and understanding advocate, admirably partnered by **Catherine**, and the Meridian balance and recording cannot be faulted.

BUSH, Geoffrey (born 1920)

Symphonies (i) 1; (ii) 2 (Guildford); (iii) Music for Orchestra; (iv) Overture Yorick

*** Lyrita (ADD/DDD) SRCD 252. (i) LSO, Braithwaite; (ii) RPO, Wordsworth; (iii) LPO; (iv) Philh. O; (iii–iv) Handley

The vigorous *Yorick Overture* (1949), written in memory of the comedian Tommy Handley, opens this concert most invitingly. It has all the exuberance of a Walton overture and is an immensely jolly piece. The first of the two symphonies dates from 1954 and is a positive, three-movement structure centring on an elegiac slow movement with blues overtones, written in memory of Constant Lambert. The *Second Symphony* is outgoing, too. This is no formal exercise but a warm statement of personal feeling. *Music for Orchestra* (1967) is also designed to be played continuously. It is, in the composer's words, 'a miniature symphony', with the string parts carefully written to be playable by amateur performers, yet with plenty of opportunities for bravura offered to the wind and brass. Ample percussion and a piano add to the vividness. All the performances and recordings are outstandingly good, notably that of the *Symphony No. 2*, conducted by **Barry Wordsworth**.

Farewell, Earth's Bliss; 4 Hesperides Songs; A Menagerie; (i) A Summer Serenade

*** Chan. 8864. Varcoe, Thompson, Westminster Singers, City of L. Sinfonia, Hickox, (i) with Parkin

The delightful *Summer Serenade* of seven song-settings has long been Bush's most frequently performed work, and this first recording glowingly brings out the sharp contrasts of mood within and between the songs, with instrumentation just as felicitous as the choral writing. It is well coupled with a solo song-cycle of comparable length, *Farewell, Earth's Bliss*, with **Stephen Varcoe** the baritone soloist; four songs from Herrick's *Hesperides*, also for baritone and strings; and three for unaccompanied voices, including an insistently menacing setting of Blake's *Tyger*. The tenor **Adrian Thompson**, not ideally pure-toned, contributes to only two of the *Serenade* songs; otherwise these are near-ideal performances in warm, open sound.

BUSONI, Ferruccio (1866–1924)

Berceuse élégiaque, Op. 42; (i) Concertino for Clarinet & Small Orchestra. Geharnischte Suite; 2 Studies for Doktor Faust, Op. 51; Tanz Walzer

*** Chan. 9920. (i) Bradbury; BBC PO, Järvi

The *Geharnischte Suite* is the rarity here, and although not top-drawer Busoni, it is still rewarding and inventive. **Neeme Järvi** and the **BBC Philharmonic** produce sumptuous performances of the moving, dream-like *Berceuse élégiaque*, written on the death of the composer's mother, and the inspired *Sarabande* and *Cortège*, the *Studies for Doktor Faust*. The *Tanz Walzer* also found their way into *Doktor Faust*, where they were used to depict festivities at the Court of Parma. The BBC Philharmonic play with evident commitment, and **John**

Bradbury is the elegant and sensitive soloist in the *Concertino for Clarinet and Small Orchestra*. The sound is first class and in the best traditions of the house.

Berceuse élégiaque; 2 Studies for Doktor Faust; Turandot Suite, Op. 41

(BB) **(*) Naxos 8.555373. Hong Kong PO, Wong

The *Turandot Suite* has all the qualities of melodic appeal (its fifth movement quotes *Greensleeves*), resourceful invention and brilliant orchestral colour that should ensure its popularity. The two *Studies*, the *Sarabande* and *Cortège*, written in preparation for his opera, *Doktor Faust*, remain the composer's masterpiece, highly searching and imaginative music that can claim to be profound, as, indeed, can the *Berceuse élégiaque*. Both performances and recording are very good, and this disc serves as an admirable and inexpensive introduction to a fascinating and underrated master.

Elegien 1–7; Fantasia after Bach; Toccata; BACH: Prelude and Fugue in D, BWV532 (arr. Busoni)

(N) (BB) *** Naxos 8.570543 Wolf Harden

The *Elegies* (1907) show the subtle, visionary and inward-looking side of Busoni's personality and the *Seventh* from 1909 is the exploratory piece that Busoni was to expand after the war as *Berceuse élégiaque* for orchestra. This CD, part of Naxos's survey of Busoni's piano music, is the most important and essential buy for collectors. **Wolf Harden**, well known for his playing in the **Trio Fortenay**, is a thoughtful and perceptive exponent of this repertoire and readers should lose no time in investigating his artistry for themselves. Other Volumes include the *Tanzwalzer*, *Dance Pieces*, *Ballet Scenes* and *Indian Diary, Book I* (8.570249); and the *Opus 16 Etudes, 6 Pieces, Op. 33b* and the *Variations on Chopin's C minor Prelude* (8.555699).

Piano Concerto, Op. 39

⊕⊸ *** Hyp. CDA 67143. Hamelin, CBSO Ch., CBSO, Elder

(M) *** Telarc CD 80207. Ohlsson, Cleveland O & Ch., Dohnányi

Busoni's *Piano Concerto* is arguably the most formidable in his repertory, but in such an inspired reading as **Hamelin's** it emerges as a genuine Everest of a work. The challenge it presents has already sparked off an impressive list of recordings, but Hamelin's is the finest yet. Even before the piano enters, the opening tutti, four minutes long, establishes the rapt, glowing intensity of the performance, thanks to **Mark Elder's** dedicated conducting of the **Birmingham Orchestra**, with radiant recording to match. Above all, Hamelin and Elder bring out the warmer, more colourful qualities behind the five massive movements, the dedication of the long *Pezzo serioso* beautifully sustained.

With extra prominence given to the solo instrument, **Garrick Ohlsson's** bravura display is very exciting, and the pianist's own pleasure in virtuosity enhances his electricity and flair. However, in the choral finale the CBSO Chorus on Hyperion has more impact than the **Cleveland Orchestra Chorus**, creating a more impressive culmination.

(i) *Indianische Fantasie, Op. 44. Lustspiel Overture, Op. 38; Gesang vom Regen der Geister; Die Brautwahl: Suite*

*** Chan. 10302. (i) Goerner; BBC PO, Järvi

Starting attractively with the sparkling *Lustspiel Overture* there is much to enjoy here, not least in the two works built on 'Indian' themes, the music of Native Americans, not from the subcontinent. The *Indian Fantasy* is in effect a piano concerto in a single movement of eight contrasted sections, and **Nelson Goerner** copes brilliantly with the virtuoso writing that Busoni designed for himself. On a much smaller scale *Gesang vom Regen der Geister*, 'Song of the Spirit Dance', involves equally colourful use of similar ideas, for strings, wind and timpani. *Die Brautwahl*, 'Bridal Choice', was Busoni's first opera, based on a story by E. T. A. Hoffmann, and in this suite he puts together an atmospheric sequence of segments from it, with instruments taking over vocal lines in vivid orchestration, with an element of grotesquerie. Brilliant playing under **Järvi** and vivid recording.

Violin Sonatas 1–2; in C (1876), BN52

*** Finlandia 2564 61078-2. Lev, Raekallio

These Finlandia performances are coupled with an early sonata, written when Busoni was ten. This playing is utterly compelling and has an authenticity of feeling and dedication that is completely persuasive, and these fine players serve it to perfection. Very natural recorded sound.

SOLO PIANO MUSIC

An die Jugend: Giga bolero e variazione. Elegies: All'Italia; Berceuse; Turandots Frauengemach. Exeunt omnes; Fantasia nach J. S. Bach; Indianisches Tagebuch (Red Indian Diary), Book I; Sonatinas 2; 6 (Kammerfantasie on 'Carmen'); Toccata. Transcription of BACH: *Prelude & Fugue in D, BWV 532*

*** Chan. 9394. Tozer

This collection is thoroughly worthwhile. The Chandos disc assembles nearly 80 minutes of Busoni's piano music and makes an admirable and well-chosen introduction to it. Most pieces come off very well indeed, and often brilliantly, from the *Exeunt omnes* and the *Elegien* to the *Indianisches Tagebuch* and the attractive *Turandots Frauengemach*. This is an excellent CD, very well recorded and thoroughly recommendable.

4 Elegies; Sonatina seconda; Toccata; arr. of BACH: *Toccata & Fugue in D min., BWV 565; Chorales: Ich ruf' zu dir, Wachet auf*

*** MDG 312 0436-2. Tanski

Claudius Tanski proves a most persuasive Busoni interpreter. He plays four of the *Elegies*, Nos. 3–6. Both in Busoni's visionary pieces and in the transcriptions of the Bach, he is more than equal to the technical and imaginative challenges this music presents. Artistically this is three-star playing

Fantasia contrappuntistica; Fantasia after J. S. Bach; Toccata

**(*) Altarus (ADD) AIR-2-9074. Ogdon

Ronald Stevenson calls Busoni's remarkable *Fantasia contrappuntistica* a masterpiece and, listening to **John Ogdon's** performance, one is tempted to agree. The *Fantasia after J. S. Bach* was written a year earlier and is among Busoni's most concentrated and powerful piano works. The balance places Ogdon rather far back and, as the acoustic is somewhat reverberant, the piano sounds a little clangy.

OPERA

Doktor Faust (DVD Version)

*** Arthaus **DVD** 101 283 (2). Hampson, Groissböck, Kunde, Trattnigg, Zurich Op. Ch. & O, Jordan

A rarity in the opera house and the recording studio, and in this respect this first DVD set does not prove a major disappointment. **Fischer-Dieskau** is memorable in the title role, **Thomas Hampson** is in good voice, and particularly noteworthy is the Mephistopheles of **Gregory Kunde**, marvellously characterized and vocally no less distinguished. **Philippe Jordan** opts for the edition by Busoni's pupil, the composer Philipp Jarnach, and does justice to the mysterious sonorities, the magical atmosphere and complex invention. Jarnach did not have access to all the surviving sketch material, which did not surface in the public domain until Antony Beaumont's edition. Such is the quality of this work that, whatever the shortcomings of this version and the flaws of the production, it is still worth having.

Doktor Faust (complete)

**(*) Erato 3984 25501-2 (3). Henschel, Begley, Hollop, Jenis, Kerl, Fischer-Dieskau, Lyon Op. Ch. & O, Nagano

Kent Nagano and his **Lyon Opéra** forces fill an important gap in the catalogue with this first really complete recording of Busoni's masterpiece, using the score as completed after Busoni's death by his pupil, Philipp Jarnach. The set seeks to get the best of both worlds by also offering the extended realization of the closing scenes prepared by Anthony Beaumont with the help of newly discovered extra sketches. **Fischer-Dieskau** here recites the opening and closing superscriptions, normally omitted in stage productions. **Dietrich Henschel** may not be a searching or weighty interpreter, but the clarity and incisiveness of his singing are most impressive, leading to a noble account of the death scene, one of the passages expanded in the Beaumont version. He is well contrasted with the powerful Mephistopheles of **Kim Begley**, a tenor role that is Wagnerian in its demands. The rest of the cast is first rate, with voices well forward; but the impact of the performance is slightly blunted by the backward balance of the orchestra, distanced in a more spacious acoustic.

BUTTERWORTH, Arthur
(born 1923)

(i; ii) *Viola Concerto. Symphonies* (iii) 1; (ii) 4

(N) (M) *** Dutton stereo/mono CDLX 7212. (i) RSNO,
Butterworth with (ii) Bradley; (iii) Hallé O, Barbirolli

Arthur Butterworth's Sibelian *First Symphony* is powerfully
argued and arresting, the product of a resourceful mind.
Barbirolli gave the work its prèmiere and here he directs a
performance from the Proms in 1958. The performance has
a compelling intensity (the opening of the slow movement
is magical) which overcomes the sonic limitations of the
mono sound. The *Fourth symphony*, completed in 1986, and
composed in Yorkshire, is again Sibelian in atmosphere.
There is much beauty found in the often wind-swept writing – the slow movement is particularly haunting and atmospheric, and the finale bold and dramatic. It receives a
first-rate performance under the direction of the composer
and the Dutton sound is superb. Butterworth's *Viola concerto*
(1988–92) is another example of a contemporary composer
able to write romantically inspired music of top quality yet
without sounding contrived. The opening theme floats out
of the combination of timpani strokes and a passage for
two horns which begins the first movement and the music,
rather melancholy in nature, unfolds with imagination and
inspiration. As often with this composer, he provides a
striking slow movement, intense and beautiful, and the
finale, as the composer says, 'is another kind of *moto perpetuo*, which makes its relentless way to a violent conclusion'. Superb performances and recording. This CD also
includes a fascinating 30-minute talk by the composer
about his life and work.

Summer Music, Op. 77

(M) *** ASV CD WHL 2132. Salvage, Royal Ballet Sinfonia,
Sutherland (with Collection of Bassoon Concertos and
Concertinos ***)

Although a concertante piece, led by the soliloquizing bassoon, Arthur Butterworth's unforgettably atmospheric triptych is more like a three-part symphonic poem, organically
whole in the way of Sibelius, yet reflecting not Nordic
scenery but the North Yorkshire moors, which, as the composer tells us, 'despite the exhilaration of sun and wind on
the high hills in summertime' (tellingly evoked in the
finale), 'there ever seems to be a faint indefinable air of
lonely melancholy brooding'. This is imaginatively caught
by the soloist here; and Butterworth's subtly vivid use of
orchestral colour increases the music's evocation and intensity. The performance is altogether first class and so is
the recording. It comes within an attractive collection of
more lightweight bassoon concertos and the disc is well
worth investigating.

Symphony 1, Op. 15

🎵 *** Classico CLASSCD 274. Munich SO, Bostock – GIPPS:
Symphony 2 ***

How is it possible for a symphony of this quality to be so
neglected by the British musical establishment? It is powerful, imaginative and atmospheric. Arthur Butterworth
comes from Manchester and played in the Hallé and
Scottish National Orchestras. His *First Symphony* is a large-
scale, 40-minute work which Sir John Barbirolli premièred
in 1957. Sibelian in outlook (but none the worse for that)
and with an innate feeling for the landscape of northern
England and Scotland, it is powerfully argued and arresting
– the product of a resourceful musical mind. It resonates
in the memory, and **Douglas Bostock** and the **Munich
Orchestra** capture both its sombre mood and its stormy
climaxes; the composer had the desolate Cape Wrath in
mind in the last movement, where the music's whirlwind
energy is splendidly conveyed. The recording is excellent,
spacious and full-bodied.

MUSIC FOR BRASS

3 Impressions for Brass, Op. 36; Passacaglia on a Theme of Brahms, Op. 87; Sinfonia concertante, Op. 111; arr. for brass of BRAHMS: *Variations on a Theme of Handel, Op. 24*

*** Doyen DOYCD 130. Black Dyke Band, Childs

With the moorlands of northern England for his inspiration,
Arthur Butterworth's *Three Impressions for Brass* draws a parallel with Malcolm Arnold's nostalgic *Cornish Dances*, although moving northeast to reflect the 19th-century
industrial heritage of Northumberland. A direct association
with Brahms then brings a brilliant *Passacaglia* on (an inverted version of) the main theme of the final movement of
that composer's *Fourth Symphony*, itself a *Passacaglia*, with
Brahms's original chorale emerging thrillingly to dominate
the climax.

The confidently structured *Sinfonia concertante*, with
tenor horn and (brass) baritone as soloists, moves from a
pastoral first movement (with distinct echoes of Vaughan
Williams's *Fifth Symphony*) through a brilliant Scherzo, and a
slow movement called *Night Music*, where there are darker,
even sinister, undercurrents, and on to an excitingly ebullient closing *Rondo*.

For the final item the band offers Butterworth's brilliant
transcription for brass of Brahms's *Variations and Fugue on a
Theme of Handel*, Op. 24. The playing of the **Black Dyke Band**
is pretty marvellous throughout, and in the notes the composer expresses his own praise for the conductor of what he
calls 'these magnificent and stunning performances'. The
recording is excellent.

Piano Trios 1, Op. 73; 2, Op. 121; Viola Sonata, Op. 78

(M) *** Dutton CDLX 7164. Terroni Piano Trio (members)

The fully mature *First Piano Trio* has associations with
Sibelius's *Sixth Symphony* and is the highlight of the disc; its
confident opening movement, surging forward lyrically, and
the lighter, engaging *Allegretto* finale are used to frame a
hauntingly atmospheric central *Adagio*, translucent in texture, which the composer tells us recalls a radiant summer
evening crossing the Baltic. The *Second Trio*, much more re-

cent (2004), again has a nostalgic *Adagio* as its lyrical kernel, and an energetically driven finale suggestive of a 'cor de chasse'. The *Viola Sonata*, written in the early 1980s, brings 'a faint whiff of the Celtic twilight of Bax'. It is a comparatively robust and lively work in which the piano takes a major role, and it is the finale, marked *Lento penserosiamente*, which is more characteristic of the viola's usual darker, nostalgic role. Performances here are strong and spontaneous, persuasive in their expressive eloquence, and the recordings are first class and most realistically balanced.

BUTTERWORTH, George
(1885–1916)

The Banks of Green Willow

☛ (BB) *** Warner Apex 2564 61437-2. RPO, Warren-Green – BRITTEN: *Simple Symphony*; ELGAR: *String Serenade*; HOLST: *St Paul's Suite*; VAUGHAN WILLIAMS: *Fantasia on a Theme of Tallis* ***

*** Chan. Compatible **SACD** CHSA 5001; CD CHAN 9902. LSO, Hickox – VAUGHAN WILLIAMS: *London Symphony (Original Version)* ***

(M) *** Chan. (ADD) 6566. Bournemouth Sinf., Del Mar – BANTOCK: *The Pierrot of the Minute: overture*; BRIDGE: *Summer*, etc. ***

The Banks of Green Willow; 2 English Idylls; A Shropshire Lad (rhapsody)

*** Nim. NI 5068. E. String O, Boughton – BRIDGE: *Suite*; PARRY: *Lady Radnor's Suite* ***

The **RPO**, woodwind and strings alike, play most beautifully in **Christopher Warren-Green's** idyllic performance which brings out the music's pastoral colouring as well as its rapture. The recording is first class, and the couplings are equally recommendable.

Butterworth's idyll makes a warmly atmospheric coupling for Vaughan Williams, and it is available additionally in multi-channel sound, where it sounds even more richly atmospheric.

Boughton secures from his Birmingham-based orchestra warm and refined playing in well-paced readings. In an ample acoustic, woodwind is placed rather behind the strings.

On Chandos, **Del Mar** gives a glowingly persuasive performance, which comes as part of another highly interesting programme of English music devoted also to Butterworth's somewhat older contemporaries, Bantock and Frank Bridge. The digital transfer of a 1979 analogue recording has the benefit of even greater clarity without loss of atmosphere.

A Shropshire Lad (rhapsody)

(M) (**) Cala mono CACD 0528. NBC SO, Stokowski – ANTHEIL: *Symphony 4*; VAUGHAN WILLIAMS: *Symphony 4* (***)

Stokowski in this evocative Butterworth tone-poem draws ravishing, sensuous sounds from the **NBC Orchestra**, no-

tably the strings, unrecognizable as Toscanini's players. Sadly, the 1944 radio recording, cleanly focused and well transferred, is marred by some 'wow' on the tape.

Love Blows as the Wind (3 songs)

(M) *** EMI (ADD) 7 64731-2. Tear, CBSO, Handley – ELGAR; VAUGHAN WILLIAMS: *Songs* ***

These three charming songs (*In the year that's come and gone*, *Life in her creaking shoes*, *Coming up from Richmond*), to words by W. E. Henley, provide an excellent makeweight for a mixed bag of orchestral songs based on the first recording of Vaughan Williams's *On Wenlock Edge* in its orchestral form. The sound is clear, yet enjoyably warm and atmospheric.

BUXTEHUDE, Dietrich
(c. 1637–1707)

7 Trio Sonatas, Op. 1, BuxWV 252–8

☛ (BB) *** Naxos 8.557248. Holloway, Mortensen, Ter Linden

*** HM HMC 901746. Kraemer, Quintama, Roberts, Börner

*** Hyp. CDA 67236. Wallfisch, Tunnicliffe, Nicholson

7 Trio Sonatas, Op. 2, BuxWV 259–65

☛ (BB) *** Naxos 8.557249. Holloway, Mortensen, Ter Linden

Buxtehude was nearly sixty when he published his *Sonatas*, Op. 1 and Op. 2. Each contains seven works and together they ambitiously explore all the major and minor keys, beginning with F major and omitting only F minor and B flat minor. What is immediately striking about both Op. 1 and Op. 2 is not just the variety of invention, but the way Buxtehude heightens the contrasting vitality of his *allegros* by introducing them with *Lentos* or *Adagios* of considerable expressive intensity. With **John Holloway** a very stylish leader, the performances on Naxos are expert, fresh and alive, using period instruments brightly without edginess or unattractive linear squeezing. The group is very well balanced and the recording immediate and real.

Of the other sets of Op. 1, the Hyperion recording is rather more intimate than the Harmonia Mundi version. Much depends on the lead violin in these works, and **Manfredo Kraemer's** virtuosity and strong instrumental personality are reminiscent of Andrew Manze, although of course **Elizabeth Wallfisch** who leads the Hyperion group certainly does not lack a strong profile and she and her colleagues make an impressive team. But Kraemer is especially appealing both in the lyrical writing, and in his witty pointing of the rhythmic snaps which are a feature of the splendid *Ciaconna Vivace* which opens the *Fourth Sonata*. The volatility of tempo is a splendid example of Buxtehude's *stylus fantasticus* which so impressed Bach and which is particularly well handled by Kraemer and his colleagues. In short, both these sets of performances are first class, but to us the Harmonia Mundi disc is marginally the more appealing, and it is very well recorded. But the Naxos complete set is first choice.

KEYBOARD MUSIC

Aria: La Capricciosa (32 Variations), BuxWV 250; Aria: More Palatino (12 Variations), BuxWV 247; Courant simple in A min., BuxWV 245 (7 Variations); Preludium manualiter in G min., BuxWV 163; Suites: in C, BuxWV 226, 228, 230, 231; in D, BuxWV 232; in D min., BuxWV 233 & 234; in E min., BuxWV 235; in F BuxWV 238 ; in G min., BuxWV 242; in A, BuxWV 243. Suite in D min (ed. E. Roger)

⊕ ✹ *** Chall. CC 72240 (2). Koopman (harpsichord)

Ton Koopman's survey of Buxtehude's keyboard music is very distinguished indeed. He uses two instruments by Willem Kroebergen, preferring a copy of a Flemish two-manuel Ruckers for most of the repertoire here, but offering variety by also using an Italian copy of a single-manual instrument after Giusti. They are splendidly recorded and he plays throughout with imagination and spontaneity, always holding the listener's interest. He includes three key sets of variations, the remarkably varied *La Capricciosa*, which almost certainly proved a model for Bach's *Goldberg* set, the *Aria, More Palatino* (12 often virtuosic variations on a 17th-century folk tune), and the hardly less demanding *Courant simple*, with seven variations. But the bulk of the collection is made up of 12 *Suites* in the French style, full of attractive invention.

Aria with 2 Variations in A min., BuxWV 249; La Capricciosa (32 Variations on the Bergamasca), BuxWV 250; Chorale Partita: Auf meinen lieben Gott, BuxWV 179; Praeludia in G & G min., BuxWV 162 & 163; Suite in G min., BuxWV 241; Toccata in G, BuxWV 165

⊕ (BB) *** Naxos 8.557413. Wilson

An outstanding recital to show the full range and scope of Buxtehude's keyboard writing. The two *Praeludia* are written in the very free style known as *stylus fantasicus*. The *Suite in G minor* is particularly attractive, while the *Chorale Partita* is in a hybrid format, using the same four dance movements to characterize the variants of the chorale theme. **Wilson** plays with great flair, and in addition provides excellent back-up documentation. He uses a modern copy of a 1626 Ruckers, which is vividly if somewhat resonantly recorded; this means that one needs to set not too high a volume in the opening virtuoso *G major Toccata*.

ORGAN MUSIC

Complete Organ Music, Volume 1

*** dacapo 8.226002. Bryndorf (Elsinore Chapel organ)

Complete Organ Music, Volume 2

**(*) dacapo 8.226008. Bryndorf (organ of St Mary's Church, Elsinore)

Complete Organ Music, Volume 3

*** dacapo 8.226023. Bryndorf (organ of St Mary's Church, Helsingborg)

Complete Organ Music, Volume 4

*** dacapo 6.220514. Bryndorf (organ of German Church, Stockholm)

A collaboration between Danish Radio and dacapo, these four issues are part of a complete survey of the organ works, using different organs. The discs are authoritatively annotated with details of registration, and with music-type illustrations for the choral harmonization. **Bine Bryndorf** studied in Vienna, Boston and Paris, and collected various prizes in Bruges and Innsbruck. Listening to these vividly recorded and expertly balanced programmes leaves no doubt as to her artistry and intelligence, and the discs provide an admirable start to the series. These discs reaffirm the quality of Buxtehude's musical invention (which had a profound influence on Bach) and imagination.

Complete Organ Works, Volume I: includes 2 Chorale Fantasias; 4 Chorale Preludes; 2 Chorale Variations; Canzona in D min.; Ciaccona in G min.; Fuga in C; Preludes in A, G min., & G; Toccata in F

(N) *** Hyp. CDA 67666 Herrick (organ of Helsinger Cathedral, Denmark)

The Helsinger Cathedral organ seems to be highly suitable for Buxtehude's music and **Christopher Herrick's** new survey, of which this is the first instalment, now seems to be shaping up as first choice for this repertoire. Not surprisingly the Hyperion recording is first class.

VOCAL MUSIC

Cantatas: An filius non est Dei, BuxWV 6; Dixit Dominus Domino meo, BuxWV 17; Herr, nun läßt du deinen Deiner, BuxWV 37; Jesu dolcis memoria, BuxWV 57; Jesu, komm, mein Trost und Lachen, BuxWV 58; Lobe den Herrn, meine Seele, BuxWV 71; Das neugebor'ne Kindelein, BuxWV 13; Nichts soll uns scheiden von der Liebe Gottes, BuxWV 77; Quemadmodum desiderat cervus, BuxWV 92

*** Chan. 0723. Kirkby, Chance, Daniels, Harvey, Augmented Purcell Qt

This further selection of Buxtehude's cantatas follows on naturally from the first (Chan. 0691, see below), with its star-studded cast, individual voices which yet blend beautifully together, stylish accompaniments and a recording which is again attractively warm and intimate.

Sacred Cantatas: Cantata Domino, BuxWV 12; Herr, wenn ich nur dich hab, BuxWV 38; Ich habe Lust abzuscheiden, BuxWV 47; Ich halte es dafür, BuxWV 48; Jesu meine Freude, BuxWV 60; Salve, Jesu, Patris gnate unigenite, BuxWV 94; Jesu dulcis memoria, BuxWV 56; Mein Herz ist bereit, BuxWV 73. (Organ) Fugue in C, BuxWV 174

⊕ **** Chan. 0691. LeBlanc, Kirkby, Harvey, Purcell Qt; Woolley

A wholly admirable collection in which **Emma Kirkby**, although given prime billing, takes second place to the similarly light-timbred Canadian soprano, **Suzie LeBlanc**. Their voices match admirably in the many delightful passages of imitative part-writing that Buxtehude writes so deftly, never more so than in the lovely *Jesu dulcis memoria* and *Salve Jesu*. Harvey also has his own confidently affirmative solo cantata, *Mein Herz ist bereit*, and Suzie LeBlanc enjoys both a memorable duet cantata with the bass, *Ich halte es dafür* and a brief solo cantata, *Herr, wenn ich nur dich hab*. The **Purcell Quartet** accompany beautifully, and are usually given an introductory sonata to open the proceedings. As an interlude **Robert Woolley** plays the *C major 'Gigue' Fugue*, which provided the inspiration for Bach's *G major Fugue*, BWV 577. The recording is warm and intimate, and this collection cannot be too highly recommended.

Sacred Cantatas and Arias: *Fried und freudenreich Hinfahrt; Organ Contrapuncti I–III; Klag-Lied, BuxWV 76. Gen Himmel zu dem Vater main, BuxWV 98; Herr, wenn ich nur dich hab, BuxWV 38; O dulcis Jesu, BuxWV83; O fröliche Stunden, BuxWV84; Schaff in mir, Gott, BuxWV95; Sicut Moses exaltavit serpentem, BuxWV97; Singet dem Herrn, BuxWV98; Was mich auf dieser Welt betrübt, BuxWV105*

⊕ ⒝⒝ **** Naxos 8.557251. Kirkby, Holloway, Kraemer, Ter Linden, Mortensen

Buxtehude wrote his *Fried und freudenreich Hinfahrt* at the time of his father's death in 1674. The three *Contrapuncti* (used here effectively as interludes) were probably intended to manifest the learning of the deceased, but the *Klag-Lied* is a poignant strophic song of mourning, sung here with infinite tenderness. Yet the programme opens with the delightfully jubilant aria, *O fröliche Stunden* ('Oh Happy Hours'), which is then followed by the beautiful sacred concerto (or cantata), *O dulcis Jesu*, in which **Emma Kirkby** alternates expressive richness with a more florid, arioso style. *Was mich auf dieser Welt betrübt* is another simple aria of great charm. But the most ambitious work here is *Singet dem Herrn* (a setting of the first four verses of Psalm 98) in which the soprano voice duets delightfully with a solo violin, while the closing *Herr, wenn ich nur dich hab* is in the form of a chaconne. With **Kirkby** in freshest voice, this is a wholly enjoyable disc. But the contribution of organist **Lars Mortensen**, who also doubles on harpsichord, is hardly less musical and pleasing. Full texts and translations are included.

Sacred Cantatas: *In te, Domine, speravi, BuxWV 53; Jesu meine Freude, BuxWV 59; Jubilate Domino, BuxWV 64; Sicut Moses, BuxWV 97; Was frag'ich nach der Welt, BuxWV 104; Wenn ich, Herr Jesu, habe dich, BuxWV 107; Wir schmeckt es so lieblich und wohl, BuxWV 108*

⒝⒝ *** Naxos 8.557041. Hill, White, Graindlay, Artia Ens., Mallon

Buxtehude's sacred cantatas are in no way laden with heavy religious symbolism but are remarkably fresh. The opening

Was frag'ich nach der Welt ('What is the world to me') has a pastoral character, and the following *Jesu meine Freude* is full of joy. *Wenn ich, Herr Jesu, habe dich*, which follows the measured string *Passacaglia*, is more sombrely expressive in feeling, but *Jubilate Domino* (a solo cantata, nimbly sung here by the counter-tenor, **Matthew White**) demands considerable virtuosity. The concerted *Wie schmeckt es so lieblich und wohl* ('How lovely and good the saviour') is full of light-hearted praise. The performances here are pleasingly intimate, well sung (**Katherine Hill**, the soprano soloist in *Sicut Moses*, particularly fresh) and truthfully recorded. Full texts and translations are included, plus excellent documentation.

Membra Jesu nostri, BuxWV 75

⊕— *** BIS CD 871. Hida, Midori Suzuki, Yanagisawa, Anazawa, Mera, Sakurada, Ogasawara, Bach Coll., Japan, Masaaki Suzuki

⒝⒝ *** Naxos 8.553787. Trogu, Invernizzi, Balconi, Cecchetti, Carnovich, R. Svizzera (Lugano) Ch., Sonatori de la Gioiosa Marca, Treviso, Accademia Strumentale Italiana, Verona, Fasolis (with ROSENMULLER: *Sinfonia XI* ***)

Membra Jesu nostri, BuxWV 75; Fried und freudenreich Hinfahrt, BuxWV 76

⊕— *** Channel Classics **SACD** CCS SA 4006. Grimm, Zomer, De Groot, Tortise, Ramselaar, Netherlands Bach. Soc., van Veldhoven

The *Membra Jesu nostri* is a cycle of seven cantatas, each addressed to a different part of the body of the crucified Christ, all of a simple and dignified expressive power that movingly makes the strongest impression. Yet although each cantata is prefacd by a Bible motto, the cycle was not intended for liturgical use.

On BIS, **Suzuki's** Japanese ensemble bring a remarkably authentic feeling for period to this lovely work (Masaaki Suzuki worked with Ton Koopman for many years) and, although the recording is made in a rather reverberant acoustic environment, this does not seriously diminish the pleasure this set gives. However, unlike both its competitors, it is without a coupling.

The **Netherlands** performances under **Jos van Veldhoven** are very beautifully sung within an ideal acoustic, warmly resonant, yet with everything clearly detailed. The accompanying instrumental group which provides the sonatas and interludes is just as impressive. The disc is rounded off with another solo cantata, *Fried und freudenreiche Hinfahrt*, in which the closing *Lamentation* is beautifully sung by **Johannette Zomer**. This is a very successful collection indeed, which can hardly be praised too highly.

The performance from the **Swiss–Italian Radio** and ensembles from **Verona** and **Treviso** under **Diego Fasolis** is marginally less polished and accomplished vocally, but it has feeling and depth. They are most expertly balanced and the sound is excellent in every way. Those wanting a bargain need not hesitate.

BYRD, William (1543–1623)

The Byrd Complete Edition, Volume I: *Early Manuscript Works*

*** Gaudeamus CDGAU 170.

Cardinall's Musick are putting us in their debt by providing (in new editions by David Skinner) a complete recorded survey of the vocal music of William Byrd. Volume I commences the series with a programme of the early manuscript works, which are used to frame the three Gradualia for the Lady Mass in Advent. At a centre point in each group of motets, a recorder consort provides two contrasting instrumental pieces. Most of this music is virtually unknown: it is all sung with great conviction, richly blended and convincingly paced. The recording was made in the Fitzalan Chapel at Arundel Castle, which provides an ideal acoustic, resonant yet never blurring detail.

The Byrd Complete Edition, Volume II: Christmas Music

*** Gaudeamus CDGAU 178

Volume 2 is, if anything, even more stimulating than Volume 1, including as it does *O salutaris hostia* with its extraordinarily plangent harmonic clashes – the most musically daring work in the composer's whole output. The Propers for Christmas and the three associated Gradualia provide the central core of the recital.

The Byrd Complete Edition, Volume III

*** Gaudeamus CDGAU 179

In Volume 3, **Cardinall's Musick** turn to rare music, mainly pieces which Byrd left unpublished. Most moving of all is the culminating item, an eight-part setting of four verses from Psalm 136, reflecting the trials of a recusant Catholic in Elizabeth I's England, with the poignant message (in Latin), 'How shall we sing the Lord's song in a strange land?'

The Byrd Complete Edition, Volume IV: *Cantiones sacrae*, Book I (1575): complete

*** Gaudeamus CDGAU 197.

Byrd published the first of his three collections of *Cantiones sacrae* in conjunction with his teacher and mentor, Thomas Tallis, contributing 17 motets to this initial collection, and the performances are beautifully blended, while **Andrew Carwood's** tempi move the music on at what seems a natural pacing.

The Byrd Complete Edition, Volume V: (i) *Masses for 3, 4 & 5 Voices;* (ii) *Organ Fantasia in C & D min.; Voluntary a 3*

✱ *** Gaudeamus CDGAU 206.

Byrd's three great Masses were written for recusant private performance in English country houses. The three organ voluntaries which act as introductions and interludes are taken from *My Ladye Nevell's Booke* and are admirably played on an appropriate (modern) chest organ by **Patrick Russill**.

The Byrd Complete Edition, Volume VI: Music for Holy Week and Easter (1605 & 1607)

*** Gaudeamus CDGAU 214.

Shortly after publishing his three Masses Byrd began his comprehensive anthology of Gradualia (Mass Propers for the Church Year). The First Book was published in 1605, the Second Book in 1607; all the music in this collection comes from these two books.

The Byrd Complete Edition, Volume VII: *Cantiones sacrae* (1589) 1–8: *Propers for Lady Mass from Christmas to the Purification* (1605)

*** Gaudeamus CDGAU 224.

By the time Byrd came to publish what he described as his own first Book of his *Cantiones sacrae* in 1589, the position of practising Catholics in Protestant England had become extremely vulnerable and dangerous, and in his *Cantiones sacrae* expresses the anguish of his fellow Catholics. These beautiful motets are used to frame Byrd's first volume of Gradualia.

The Byrd Complete Edition Volume VIII: *Cantiones sacrae* (1589) 8–15: *Propers for the Feast of the Purification*

*** Gaudeamus CDGAU 309.

Volume VIII concludes the 1589 *Cantiones Sacrae*, written to be sung at domestic devotions against the background of the increasing Catholic oppression. The message of the texts is cryptic: *Vigilate* ('Keep watch, for you know not when the Lord of the House will come'), which surely has an underlying message to the faithful that deliverance might be at hand.

The Byrd Complete Edition Volume IX: *Propers for Ascension; Pentecost; Corpus Christi. Devotions to the Blessed Sacrament*

*** Gaudeamus CDGAU 332.

In 1605 and 1607 Byrd published two books of *Gradualia*, propers to punctuate the Roman Catholic Mass settings for three main festivals of the church year. As **Andrew Carwood** points out in his notes, they are mainly short, are madrigalian in character and with considerable variety of style, those for Ascension and Pentecost well laced with 'Alleluias'.

The Byrd Complete Edition Volume X: *Cantiones sacrae* (1591); *Gradualia for Lady Mass in Eastertide* (1605)

*** Hyp. CDA 67568.

For Volume X the **Cardinall's Musick** have moved to Hyperion but continue to record in the Fitzalan Chapel, Arundel Castle, while Martin Haskell remains the recording engineer, so quality is unchanged. The collection here is particularly rich in Byrd's finest settings. Among the memorable Easter *Gradualia* the Introit, *Salve sancta parens*, leads to a succession of 'Alleluias' praising the Virgin Mary, while *Domine, exaudi orationem meum inclina* has a peaceful serenity, and by contrast *Laudibus in sanctis* makes a radiantly fresh conclusion.

The Byrd Complete Edition, Volume XI:
Cantiones sacrae (1591); Gradualia (1607)

(N) *** Hyp. CDA 67653

Volume 11 continues the survey of the Cantiones sacrae of 1591 which show their composer in his more plangent writing very much involved with the problems of his fellow recusant Catholics. The seven motets included here all have great intensity of feeling, not least Haec dicit Dominus and the melancholy Circumdederunt me, although none are without hope for a more positive future. The Gradualia, of course, are more affirmative in character, for instance Tu es Petrus is very clear: 'You are Peter, and on this rock I will build my church'. As throughout the series, the documentation is excellent, and the performances, besides relishing all the many felicities of Byrd's heartfelt settings, are dedicated and often movingly beautiful. The recording too is first class.

OTHER RECORDINGS

Music for Consorts and Virginals

🎵 *** Astrée E 8611. Capriccio Stravagante, Sempé

Skip Sempé and his colleagues play every note with that authenticity of feeling which is so often missing from period performance. Sempé has poetic feeling, an astonishing keyboard flair and rare artistry. Browning has the alternative title of The leaves be green and consists of divisions on a popular song, while the Fantasia a 6 which closes the concert is a masterly compression of ideas into a fluid structure as powerful as Purcell's famous Chaconne. The sound of his Skowroneck harpsichord is vividly reproduced. One of the best CDs of its kind to have appeared in recent years, and a splendid introduction to the composer.

Music for viols

*** Lyrichord LEMS 8015. (i) Bagger; (ii) Crout; (iii) Lipnik; NY Cons. of Viols

The New York Consort of Viols play with an attractive blend of timbre, and everything they play is thoroughly alive. The harpsichordist, Louis Bagger, plays with great bravura when Ut re mi fa sol la becomes more and more florid as it proceeds. The two vocal soloists work well together, especially in the rustic dialogue song, Who made thee, Hob, forsake the plough? Tamara Crout sings with great charm in her solo numbers: with the lightest touch in the charming song about the 'murdered' pet dog, and very expressively in Rejoice unto the Lord and the touching Ye sacred muses. In every way this is a most rewarding programme, excellently balanced and recorded.

Consort, keyboard music, anthems and songs:
Fantasia for 4 viols; Fantasia 2 for 6 viols; Fantasia 3 for 6 viols; Galliard; Have mercy upon me, O God; In nomine 2 for 4 viols; In Nomine 5 for 5 viols; Pavane; (i) (Keyboard) John, come kiss me now; Pavan in A min.; Qui passe (for my Ladye Nevell). (Vocal) (ii) Christ rising again; Fair Britain Isle; In angel's weed; Rejoice unto the Lord; Susanna fair; Triumph with pleasant melody

🎵 (BB) *** Naxos 8.550604. Rose Consort, Red Byrd; (i) Roberts (harpsichord or virginals); (ii) Bonner

Here is a useful and inexpensive cross-section of Byrd's secular output that gives a good idea not only of its artistic riches but of its sheer variety. Both the ensembles recorded here, the Rose Consort of viols and Red Byrd, are in good form, and Timothy Roberts and Tessa Bonner are sensitive and expert exponents of this repertoire. The recorded sound is eminently clean and well balanced, and there is plenty of space round the aural image, which greatly enhances the undoubted attractions of a pleasant anthology.

Complete keyboard music

(M) *** Hyp. CDA 66551/7. Moroney (harpsichords, muselar virginal, organ, chamber organ, clavichord)

Davitt Moroney's impressively comprehensive Gramophone award-winning undertaking includes also the organ music played on the highly suitable Ahrend organ of L'Eglise-Musée des Augustins, Toulouse. To add maximum variety, he also uses a number of keyboard instruments based on north European 17th-century models, including a clavichord by the estimable Thomas Goff, a chamber organ by Martin Goetz and Domenic Gwynn, and harpsichords by Hubert Bédard and Reinhard von Nagel. The most fascinating of these instruments is the so-called muselar virginal (by John Philips of Berkeley after a 1650 Couchet), which has a remarkably rich timbre. This instrument is heard at its finest and most spectacular (on Disc 7) in Byrd's description of The Battel, with its introductory Marche and a Galliard for the Victorie. Quite as fascinating aurally are the five items with which Moroney closes his programme. Four different versions of the Praeludium to the Fancie from Book 12 are given, each heard on a different instrument, and he concludes with the Fantasia from Book 13, one of the composer's most complex and original pieces, presented with considerable flair. Throughout, the playing is committed, authoritative and nicely embellished, if at times a shade didactic. The recording is most realistic, though it is important not to set the volume level too high. The accompanying notes are as thorough as they are scholarly and comprehensive. The set is offered at a special price: seven discs for the cost of five.

Keyboard music: The Battell: Marche; The Trumpets; The Bells; The Carman's Whistle; Christe qui lux; Fantasia; Galliard; Galliard for the Victorie; Galliard to Johnson's Delighte; Go from my window; A Grounde; Miserere I & II; Have with yow to Walsingham; My Ladye Nevell's Grownde; O quam gloriosum est regnum; 7th Pavan; A Pavion; Praeludium to the Fancie; Ut, re, mi, fa, sol, la

*** Hyp. CDA 66558. Moroney (harpsichords, muselar virginal, organ, chamber organ, clavichord)

A well-chosen 78-minute programme from Davitt Moroney's distinguished survey, including favourite items like the hypnotic portrayal of The Bells, the jolly Carman's Whistle (on chamber organ), and The Trumpets from The Battell, to demonstrate the extraordinary sound of the muselar virginal (here sounding something like a highly amplified jew's harp!), but given a less bizarre image in the following *Galliard for the Victorie*. In complete contrast the pair of delicate *Misereres* are played on a small clavichord, so you will have to be careful with the volume control. As with the complete set, the documentation is first class.

VOCAL MUSIC

Anthems

🎵 (M) *** Coll. CSCD 507. Cambridge Singers, Rutter

John Rutter brings a composer's understanding to these readings, which have a simple, direct eloquence, the music's serene spirituality movingly caught; and the atmospheric recording is very faithful, even if detail could be sharper. The programme is divided into four groups: Anthems; then Motets: of penitence and prayer; of praise and rejoicing; and for the Church year.

Cantiones sacrae (1589 & 1591) & Gradualia (1607): Pentecost propers (excerpts)

*** HM Surround Sound **SACD** HMU 807463. Stile antico – TALLIS: *Psalm Tunes* ***

To enhance their effect, under the titles 'Heavenly harmonies' this collection intersperses Byrd's motets with Tallis's deceptively simple Psalm tunes. Beautifully sung and recorded, this is a disc which by its very variety is most stimulating. The surround sound recording really gives one the sense of being in the unnamed cathedral (or abbey) where the recording was made; but on ordinary CD equipment the quality is still most impressive.

The Great Service (with anthems)

*** Hyp. CDA 67533. Westminster Abbey Ch., O'Donnell; Quinney (organ)

*** Gimell CDGIM 011. Tallis Scholars, Phillips

Collectors wanting these famous settings for Matins and Evensong in a resonant, cathedral-type acoustic can now turn to the **Choir of Westminster Abbey**, under **James O'Donnell**, which is very well recorded on Hyperion. They have the advantage of boy trebles, a larger complement of singers who can offer greater contrast between solo and full verses, and an excellent organ contribution from **Robert Quinney**. The recording includes five extra anthems, four used in pairs to frame each service, plus two organ voluntaries, and a final anthem, *Sing Joyfully*, to end the proceedings jubilantly.

    Peter Phillips and the **Tallis Scholars** give a lucid and sensitively shaped account of Byrd's *Great Service*. Theirs is a more intimate performance than one might expect to encounter in one of the great English cathedrals; they are fewer in number and thus achieve greater clarity of texture. The recording is quite excellent: it is made in a church acoustic (the Church of St John, Hackney) and captures detail perfectly. It includes three other anthems.

Lamentations: Tenebrae for Good Friday. Mass for 4 Voices

(M) *** CRD 3499. Clerks of New College Oxford, Ch., Higginbottom – TALLIS: *Lamentations I & II*, etc. ***

Only one set of *Lamentations* by Byrd survives: the first lesson at Tenebrae on Good Friday. Deeply felt, radiant in its simplicity, Byrd's setting of Jeremiah's lament on the destruction of Jerusalem undoubtedly had a double significance for its composer, a devout Catholic, deploring the reformation of the English church. The *Mass in four parts*, written for private performance, has a similar combination of simplicity and deep feeling. The closing *Agnus Dei* is particularly intense, with the closing words '*dona nobis pacem*' ('grant us peace') given a gentle, musical emphasis. **The Clerks of New College, Oxford**, 16 in number, give admirably scaled performances, richly recorded in an ideal acoustic.

Masses for 3, 4 and 5 Voices; Ave verum corpus; Diffusa est gratia; Magnificat (Great Service); Nunc dimittis; Prevent us, O Lord; Tristitia et anxietas; Vigilate (DVD Version)

*** Gimell **DVD** GIMDP 901. Tallis Scholars, Phillips

Tudor and Renaissance music is not well represented in the DVD catalogue (understandably so, perhaps) but this, a model of its kind, may encourage others to explore early music. Some of these performances (the *Missa a 3*, and many of the remaining items) are recorded in Tewkesbury Abbey and beautifully filmed by candlelight, while the two remaining Masses were (appropriately enough, given the period) filmed in the Chapel of Merton College, Oxford. As one expects from the **Tallis Scholars**, these are expert performances, impeccable in intonation and tonal blend. In addition, there is a feature on Byrd. Time was when the BBC would have turned to a leading authority on the music of the period to present such a programme, but this 70-minute feature is fronted by Charles Hazlewood. However, many viewers respond positively to him and the feature is undoubtedly informative.

Mass for 3 Voices; Mass for 4 Voices; Mass for 5 Voices; Ave verum corpus; Diffusa est gratia; The Great Service (with anthems); Infelix ego; Ne irascaris, Domine; Prevent us, O Lord; Tristitia et anxietas; Vigilate

(M) *** Gimell CDGIM 218 (2). Tallis Scholars, Phillips

Peter Phillips is a master of this repertoire; undoubtedly these performances of the three *Masses* have more variety and great eloquence, so that when the drama is varied with a gentle mood, the contrast is the more striking. The collection has now been expanded to include an intimate, sensitively shaped account of the *Great Service* and other items also included on the DVD above. The sonority created by the **Tallis Scholars**, whether in Merton College, Oxford, Tewkesbury Abbey or St John at Hackney, is most beautiful, warm and fresh, and there is full documentation.

Mass for 4 Voices; Mass for 5 Voices; Infelix ego

(BB) *** Naxos 8.550574. Oxford Camerata, Summerly

This coupling from the **Oxford Camerata** represents one of Naxos's most enticing bargains. The full-throated singing has spontaneous ardour but no lack of repose in the music's more serene moments. **Summerly** offers the motet, *Infelix ego*, as a bonus. These readings are distinctive in a different way from those by the Tallis Scholars. The recording is outstandingly vivid.

SONGS

Consort Songs

🎵 *** Hyp. CDA 67397. Blaze, Concordia

Robin Blaze, with the natural beauty of his vocal colouring, stands out among contemporary counter-tenors as being ideal for illuminating these lovely, expressive songs of sadness, like *O dear life, when may it be* (with lute accompaniment) and the two Funeral Consort Songs for Sir Philip Sydney, *Come to me, grief, for ever*, and *O that most rare breast*, and the song of pietie, *How vain the toils that mortal man do take*. Of course there are lighter songs here too, including the jaunty *Who likes to love* (again with lute), while the opening *Rejoice unto the Lord* is full of confidence. But the gem of the collection is also one of the earliest and most extended. *My sweet little Baby* dates from that collection of 1588, and is an entirely delightful Christmas lullaby. With highly pleasing accompaniments, beautifully balanced, this is a record to treasure and draw upon, though not to play all at once.

Consort Songs

*** Globe GLO 5159. Cordier, Royal Consort – GIBBONS: *Fantasias; In nomines* ***

Although there is a pervading atmosphere of dolour, these fine Byrd songs, interspersed with *Fantasias* and *In Nomines* of Orlando Gibbons, make a highly rewarding programme when this Dutch gamba group play with such warmth, sensibility and refinement. Moreover, the counter-tenor **David Cordier** has just the right delicacy of timbre for these Elizabethan songs, which he sings with spirit and deep expressive feeling (especially Byrd's poignant elegy for the Prince of Wales and the touching *Ah, silly soul*). First-class recording.

Consort Songs: *Pavan a 6; Fantasia a 4 (for Viols)*

*** HM HMU 907383. Emma Kirkby, Fretwork

Emma Kirkby's voice is as fresh as ever and her singing is full of charm. Here she is authentically accompanied by a consort of six viols, who also provide interludes. In songs as varied as *O Lord how vain, My mistress has a little dog, The noble famous Queen* and *O that most rare breast* (not belonging to a lady, but an elegy for Sir Philip Sidney) she is equally eloquent in different ways. Unless you do not respond to the viol's sonority, this collection, nicely varied and generous (75 minutes), is self-recommending and very well recorded.

Consort Songs

*** Simax PSC 1191. McGreevy, Partridge, Phantasm

Geraldine McGreevy dominates this attractive recital, opening with the lovely *La Verginella*, and very touching in the surprisingly melancholy *Fair Britain Isle* and the poignant *Lullaby*, though perking up for *Susanna fair* and *Though Amaryllis dance in green*. **Ian Partridge** is in good voice too, although his contribution is perhaps less striking. These are all songs in which the vocal line is part of the polyphonic texture of the viol accompaniment, which **Phantasm** handle admirably, as they do their three solo consort pieces. Excellent recording with no edginess on the string timbres.

CACCINI, Giulio (1551–1618)

Le Nuove Musiche (1602): **Complete solo madrigals**

Ⓝ **(*) SOMMCD 083 La Nuova Musica, Bates (with MONTEVERDI: *Madrigals, Books 3–5*; KAPSBERGER & PHILIPS: *Harpsichord pieces*)

A well planned collection. Caccini's solo madrigals are individual and often have a touching melancholy; but to provide variety **David Bates** has interspersed them with polyphonic madrigals by Monteverdi and a pair of instrumental *Toccatas* (by Kapsberger and Frescobaldi). Although the solo singing is eloquent, it is not always of a star quality, but the group madrigals make a successful contrast. Curiously, translations are provided for only twelve of the twenty-one vocal items. But this is still worth exploring.

CAGE, John (1912–92)

Concerto for Prepared Piano & Chamber Orchestra (1950/1); The Seasons (ballet); Seventy-Four (for orchestra), Versions I & II; Suites for Toy Piano (original and orchestral version, scored by Lou Harrison)

*** ECM 465 140-2. (i) Tang (prepared piano; toy piano); American Composers' Orchestra, Russell Davies

Seventy-Four, hypnotic in atmosphere, is nevertheless remarkably static. *The Seasons* is, in the composer's own words, 'an attempt to express the traditional Indian view as quiescence (winter), creation (spring), preservation (summer), and destruction (fall)'. It is not easy to follow, but certainly has plenty of movement, and its textures are exotic. The simplistic *Suite for Toy Piano* has also been ingeniously scored by Lou Harrison and most listeners will respond to the vividly contrasting sonorities of this instrumental version, which has instant appeal. The performances here are dedicated and of the highest calibre, and the recording excellent.

Piano Sonatas (for prepared piano) 1–16 with 4 Interludes

Ⓜ *** Explore (ADD) EXP 004. Tilbury

This is among the most persuasive CDs of Cage's music yet issued, sensitively performed and very well recorded, with the peculiar sounds of Cage's prepared piano vividly caught. The sonatas follow each other in groups of four, each group separated by an interlude, but the results tend to be hallucinatory, as eastern music can be. Sympathy with Indian music, the composer has explained, lies behind this music, which he wrote in 'controlled improvisation'. It may be just a twitter, but it is an agreable twitter.

CAMILLERI, Charles
(1931–2009)

(i) Piano Concertino 4 (Summer Nights in Malta) for 2 Pianos; Il-Weghda: Intermezzo. Knights of Malta (Ballet Suite); Malta Suite; (ii) 4 Legends. Overture Classique

**** Divine Art dda 24126. Bournemouth SO, Schembri; with
(i) Micallef & Inanga; (ii) Mifsud

Malta is not a venue one first thinks of as a source of concert music, but now Charles Camilleri has certainly put it on the map, for this compilation is one of the most delectable collections of new twentieth-century music we have encountered in a long time. True it is lightweight, but it is all elegantly crafted, colourfully scored, hauntingly tuneful and memorable from beginning to end. Much of it is vividly descriptive, and the result is far more rewarding than many a more ambitious work of our time. The expressive writing for the strings is very touching, while elsewhere there is wit and high spirits in abundance. These performances from **Brian Schembri** and the excellent **Bournemouth Symphony Orchestra** could not be more stylish or persuasively spontaneous, and the vividly atmospheric recording is first rate. A CD not to be missed.

CANTELOUBE, Marie-Joseph (1879–1957)

Dans le montagne (for Violin & Piano)

*** Hyp. CDA 67427. Graffin, Devoyon – with BREVILLE: Violin
Sonata 1

It is good to have an instrumental work from Canteloube, a work of great charm. Canteloube loved the mountains and lived among them in his early years. Altogether this is as delightful and ingenuous as the more famous songs, and it is most persuasively performed here, and excellently recorded.

Songs of the Auvergne: Series 1–5 (complete)

⊕-*** Erato 0927 44656-2 (2). Upshaw, Lyon Op. O, Nagano –
EMMANUEL: Chansons bourguignonnes ***

Ⓑ *** Double Decca 444 995-2 (2). Te Kanawa, ECO, Tate –
VILLA-LOBOS: Bachianas brasileiras 5 ***

ⒷⒷ *** Naxos 8.557491 & 8.570338. Gens, O. Nat. de Lille, J.-C.
Casadesus (with 6 Chants de France; Triptych)

Dawn Upshaw sings with tenderness and character in a style less sensuous than that of Kiri Te Kanawa (notably so in the fresh, open account of the famous Baïlèro, where she uses greater variety of dynamic, with an echo effect). Her line in the lyrical numbers is often very beautiful, while in the quirkier items her manner is nearer to the more folksy idiom of Natania Davrath. She is persuasively accompanied by **Kent Nagano** and the **Lyon Opera Orchestra**, with their distinctly French colouring. What makes this Erato set particularly enticing is the inclusion of a half-dozen rather similar and no less charming arrangements of Burgundian songs by Maurice Emmanuel. Full translations are provided, if in minuscule print.

Véronique Gens gives performances that bring out the folk qualities far more than usual. Gens gives them an authentic French timbre, whether in the melismatic phrases of Baïlèro, always a favourite item, or the vigour of the two sets of Bourrées. **Jean-Claude Casadesus** conducts the excellent **Lille Orchestra** in similarly idiomatic performances, atmospherically recorded. To fill out the second disc, Gens includes six excerpts from the Chants de France, another winning collection derived from folk material, and also the Triptych, three memorable and original settings of the poems of Roger Frêne, rather in the style of Chausson. Full texts and translations make this a genuine bargain.

In **Dame Kiri Te Kanawa's** recital the warmly atmospheric Decca recording brings an often languorous opulence to the music-making. In such an atmosphere the quick songs lose a little in bite, and Baïlèro, the most famous, is taken extremely slowly. With the sound so sumptuous, this hardly registers and the result remains compelling, thanks in large measure to sympathetic accompaniment from the **ECO** under **Jeffrey Tate**. There is also a paired CD/DVD combined with a DVD filmed in the Auvergne countryside (Decca 475 6145). However, the photography is pleasing but unmemorable.

Chants d'Auvergne (excerpts)

Ⓜ *** EMI (ADD) 5 66978-2. De Los Angeles, LAP, Jacquillat

*** Auvidis V 4811. Bayo, Tenerife SO, Perez (with 5 Chants de
Pays Basques)

⊕-✿ Ⓑ *** CfP 575 1382. Gomez, RLPO, Handley – FAURÉ:
Masques et bergamasques; Pavane ***

The warmth and sweetness of **Victoria De Los Angeles's** tone when her own pioneering recordings were made (1973 and 1975) match the allure of Canteloube's settings, bringing them into the concert hall. In the lighter numbers, the Bourrées for instance, the singing combines sparkle with a natural feeling for the folk idiom, and elsewhere De Los Angeles can be ravishing with her fine-spun vocal timbre, as in La Delissádo or the gentle Lou Boussu, while Lou coucut speaks for itself.

María Bayo is a most engaging artist and has just the temperament to sing her selection of favourites idiomatically (Lo Fiolairé is deliciously done), and yet in Baïlèro and La Delaïssádo her line and timbre are ravishing. **Víctor Pablo Perez** directs the accompaniments with sultry Mediterranean warmth and real character. What makes this collection especially attractive is the bonus of five Chants de Pays Basques. Full translations are included.

Jill Gomez's selection of these popular songs makes for a memorably characterful record which, as well as bringing out the sensuous beauty of Canteloube's arrangements, reminds us, in the echoes of rustic band music, of their genuine folk base. The inclusion of the charming Fauré works makes this reissue more attractive than ever.

CAPLET, André (1878–1925)

(i) Conte fantastique: La Masque de la mort rouge. Divertissement; Les Prières; Septet; 2 Sonnets

Ⓑ *** HM Musique d'abord HMA 1951497. Coste, Piau, Deguy, Ens. Musique Oblique; (i) with Laurence Cabel (harp)

Although his idiom is strongly Debussian, André Caplet possessed fastidious craftsmanship and a refined sensibility of distinctive quality. His best-known work is the *Conte fantastique* for harp and strings, based on Edgar Allan Poe's *Masque of the Red Death*, a work strong on evocative menace. The present Harmonia Mundi version offers the more intimate chamber version of the score and makes a strong challenge to previous versions, for the accompanying programme is well chosen and serves to flesh out a portrait of Caplet himself. It is very well played and balanced, and is well worth its modest cost.

CARDOSO, Frei Manuel
(c. 1566–1650)

Lamentatio; Magnificat secundi toni

ⒷⒷ *** Naxos 8.553310. Ars Nova, Bo Holten – LÔBO: *Motets*; MAGALHAES: *Missa O Soberana luz*, etc. *** (with Concert of Portuguese polyphony ***)

Cardoso's serene, flowing polyphony with its forward-looking use of augmented chords is heard at its most striking in the *Magnificat*, while his *Lamentatio* for six voices is touchingly beautiful. Remarkably eloquent singing from this fine Danish choir and good recording in a suitably ecclesiastical acoustic. The rest of the programme is hardly less stimulating.

Requiem (Missa pro defunctis)

☛– Ⓑ **** Gimell CDGIM 205 (2). Tallis Scholars, Philips – Duarte LÔBO: *Requiem*; Alonso LÔBO: *Motets*; VICTORIA:*Requiem*, etc. ****

ⒷⒷ *** Naxos 8.550682. Oxford Schola Cantorum, Summerly – LÔBO: *Missa pro defunctis* ***

Requiem; Magnificat; Motets: Mulier quae erat; Non mortui; Nos autem gloriari; Sitivit anima mea

☛– *** Gimell (ADD) CD GIM 021. Tallis Scholars, Phillips

Cardoso's *Requiem* opens in striking and original fashion. The polyphony unfolds in long-breathed phrases of unusual length and eloquence, and both the motets, *Mulier quae erat* ('A woman, a sinner in that city') and the short *Nos autem gloriari* ('Yet should we glory'), are rich in texture and have great expressive resplendence. Cardoso's use of the augmented

chord at the opening of the *Requiem* gives his music some of its distinctive stamp. The **Tallis Scholars** sing with characteristic purity of tone and intonation, and they are splendidly recorded. A glorious issue. The new bargain-priced Double links it to music by Lôbo and Victoria which is equally desirable.

In **Summerly's** Naxos account, Cardoso's *Missa pro defunctis* is not as dramatic in its contrasts as the coupled setting of Duarte Lôbo. As with the Lôbo coupling, a solo treble makes a brief but effective introduction for each movement, a device which works very touchingly. The performance by **Oxford Schola Cantorum** is beautifully paced and the calibre of the singing itself is very impressive indeed, as is the Naxos recording.

CARISSIMI, Giacomo (1605–74)

Cantatas: Ahi, non torna; Piangete, ohimè piangete; Si dia bando, alla sperenza; Siam tre miseri piangente; Va dimanda al mio pensiero. Motets: Benedictus Deus et Pater; Exulta gaude, filia Sion; O dulcissimum Mariae nomen; Omnes gentes gaudate cum victore; Surrexit pastor bonus (with keyboard interludes by FRESCOBALDI; KAPSBERGER; ROSSI)

**(*) Signum SIGCD 040. Concerto delle Donne

All but three of the cantatas and motets here are settings for two or (mainly) three soprano voices, the remainder are solo works. There is plenty of musical variety; Carissimi's invention is unflagging and the contrapuntal interplay of the three voices is appealing when all three soloists have fine, rich voices which match well together and there are no wobblers. Each of the three soloists, **Donna Deam**, **Gill Ross** and **Elin Thomas**, has a solo work, but Donna Deam, the leader of the team, is allotted the most striking, *Piangete, ohimè, piangete*, with its melancholy semitone droops (which gives its name to the collection), while the duet cantata which follows, *Si dia bando*, is delightfully fresh. The instrumental accompaniments are stylishly managed and vocal works are interwoven by keyboard interludes, intimately played by **Alastair Ross**. Full texts and translations are included.

Damnation lamentatio; Felicitas batorum; Historia di Jephte

*** Naïve OP 30296. Franzetti, Hernandez, Halimi, Van Dyck, Dordolo, Imboden, Le Parlement de Musique, Gester (with Lelio COLISTA: *Sinfonia in D min.*) – FRESCOBALDI: *Motets & Partita* ***

A first-class programme which attempts to re-create a sacred concert in Rome in the middle of the 17th century. Carissimi's *Jephte* is comparatively well known, and it is beautifully and dramatically sung here. Excellent documentation and full texts and translations make this a very attractive compilation.

Historia di Abraham et Isaac; Historia di Ezechias (Oratorios). Mass for 8 Voices; Motets: O vulnera doloris; Salve, salve, puella

(M) *** Erato 2564 60590-2. Soloists, Lisbon Gulbenkian
Foundation Ch. & O, Corboz

The *History of Hezekiah* is a memorably concise oratorio
with superb choral writing, splendidly sung here.
Resourcefully, Carissimi sets King Hezekiah's plea for divine
mercy in the minor key, while God's music is always in the
major. The narrator's role is given to two sopranos and
then to the final chorus. The story of Abraham's willingness
to sacrifice his son at God's command makes for another
compressed but dramatic setting. The three *Mass* movements (which may not be authentic) offer rich polyphony,
with the serene *Kyrie* contrasted with the vigorous settings
of the *Gloria* and *Credo*. This is a very stimulating collection,
well sung and recorded, but it is let down by the lack of
documentation.

The Story of Jephtha; The Story of Jonah; Dai piu riposti abissi

⊕⊸ (BB) **** Naxos 8.557390. Consortium Carissimi, Zanon

The Story of Jephtha has interlacing solos, some for characters
in the story, others involving narration (Historicus) in free
arioso. Punctuating this crisp telling of the story come four
choruses in six parts, and a duet for two sopranos. They add
to the attractive variety of the piece in madrigal-like numbers, ending with the longest and most impressive. *The Story
of Jonah* follows a similar pattern, with the dialogue between
Jonah and the Sailors playing an important part, and ending
with a fine eight-part chorus for the people of Nineveh, *We
have sinned Lord*. Described as a Serenade, the third work is
equally mellifluous, involving more chordal writing. It is
here given with the top lines taken by two tenors instead of
two sopranos. The brilliant singers of **Consortium Carissimi**
– with the director, **Vittorio Zanon**, only indicated in small
print at the end of the long list of artists – give magnetic
performances, beautifully recorded. In this outstanding bargain issue full texts are given.

De Tempore interfecto Sisar; Dialogo del Gigante Golia; Diluvium Universale (Dialogo del Noe); Regina Hester (Oratorios)

*** CPO 999 983-2. Mauch, Backes, Carmignani, Jochens, van
der Kempe, Musica Fiesta., La Capella Ducalle, Wilson

This enterprising disc gathers together four contrasted oratorios, hitherto thought to have been lost. Most striking
among them are *The Dialogue of the Giant Goliath*, and the
Dialogue of Noah. In the former, **Harry van der Kempe**, from
his very opening aria, is lugubriously sinister as the deep-
voiced Goliath, and **Constanze Backes** a contrastingly fresh-
voiced David. Van der Kempe then transforms himself into
a warmly sympathetic Noah, to plead with an unrelenting
God (**Wilfried Jochens**), and it is the choral interplay which
represents the rushing winds and the downpour of rain,
until finally the future covenant is established and a peaceful
future promised. The singing here is fresh, the ornamentation impressive and the vigorous rhythmic articulation has
plenty of vigour, while the expressive music is most sympathetically sung. The recording is very good and full translations are included.

CARLSSON, Mark (born 1952)

Nightwings

*** Crystal CD 750. Westwood Wind Quintet – BARBER:
Summer Music; LIGETI: *Bagatelles;* MATHIAS: *Quintet* ***

In *Nightwings* the flute assumes the persona of a dreamer,
the taped music may be perceived as a dream-world, and the
other four instruments appear as characters in a dream. On
this evidence, however, the conception is in some respects
more interesting than the piece itself. Excellent playing and
recording.

CARMINA BURANA (c. 1300)

Carmina Burana (Songs from the Original Manuscript)

*** Decca 475 9106, Bott, George, New London Consort,
Pickett

This was the collection on which Carl Orff drew for his popular cantata. To quote **Philip Pickett**: 'In view of the lewd
and offensive nature of part of the collection, it is miraculous
that the manuscript survived at all.' The performances on
this (originally L'Oiseau-Lyre) CD, reissued in its original
livery with full notes, texts and translations, have the merit
of excellent singing from **Catherine Bott** and **Michael
George** and sensitive playing from the instrumentalists
under Pickett. The engineering is excellent and strikes a virtually ideal balance between voices and instruments. There
is a pleasing acoustic ambience.

CARPENTER, John Alden (1876–1951)

Adventures in a Perambulator; Symphonies 1–2

⊕⊸ (BB) *** Naxos 8.558065. Nat. SO of Ukraine, McLaughlin
Williams

John Alden Carpenter came from a wealthy Illinois family.
His musical training included study under Elgar and this
shows in his confident handling of the orchestra. *Adventures
in a Perambulator* (which includes encounters with *Dogs,
Dreams, The Lake, The Hurdy-Gurdy* and *The Policeman*) is
charmingly scored and pleasantly tuneful. The *First
Symphony*, a well-planned single-movement work, divided
into five linked sections, is hardly more ambitious. But again
its invention is warmly attractive and its nostalgic atmosphere holds the listener in its undemanding spell. The
Second opens more dramatically, but similarly it does not
probe any depths, seeking mainly to divert, especially the
jolly, boisterous finale. The **Ukraine Orchestra** obviously
enjoy this music and play it very well indeed. The Naxos
recording is first class and the documentation includes the
composer's own notes for *Adventures in a Perambulator*.

String Quartet; (i) Piano Quintet; (i; ii) Violin Sonata

⌐━ (BB) *** Naxos 8.559103. Vega Qt; (i) Posnak; (ii) Chen

These three immediately attractive chamber works are a splendid way of experiencing and enjoying the calibre of Carpenter's music. The early *Violin Sonata* (1912) is a delightfully spontaneous piece, sweetly lyrical but by no means slight, with striking ideas throughout all four traditional movements. The *String Quartet* of 1927 is altogether more nostalgic and chromatically searching; the *Piano Quintet* of a decade later is more extrovert. First-class performances and fine recording make this a very enjoyable programme indeed.

CARTER, Elliott (born 1908)

(i; ii) Oboe Concerto; (iii) Esprit rude; (ii) Penthode (for 5 groups of instruments); (iv; ii) A Mirror on Which to Dwell

(BB) *** Warner Apex 8573 89227-2. (i) Holliger; (ii) Ens. InterContemporain; (iii) Cherrier, Troutet; (iv) Bryn-Julson, Boulez

The *Oboe Concerto* was written for **Heinz Holliger**, who gives a superb performance of a work which is underlyingly lyrical and appealing. *Esprit rude* ('rough breathing') is an even less predictable duet for flute and clarinet, and the atmospheric *Penthode* ('concerned with the experiences of connectedness and isolation') written for five groups of four players, is no more easy to unravel.

In the song-cycle, setting poems of Elizabeth Bishop, one cannot but admire the expertise of **Phyllis Bryn-Julson**, accurately leaping from note to note against often bizarre accompaniments, and producing a remarkably expressive line of real tonal beauty. The recording is admirable, clear and well balanced. A classic and indispensable reissue.

Concerto for Orchestra; (i) Violin Concerto. 3 Occasions for Orchestra

(M) *** EMI 2 06629-2 L. Sinf., Knussen; (i) with Ole Bohn

The *Concerto for Orchestra* is inspired by a sequence of poems, *Vents* ('Winds') by St John Perse and Carter's response is to divide the orchestra into four groups with conflicting interplay between them. Needless to say **Knussen** creates a brilliant effect with members of the **London Sinfonia**. Ole Bohn commissioned the *Violin Concerto* himself and plays it with great dedication, even though it cannot be described as an immediately appealing work. The *Three Orchestral Occasions* complete a commanding triptych for those who respond to this extraordinarily unconventional composer who never makes for easy listening.

(i) Piano Concerto. Holiday Overture; Symphony 1

⌐━ (BB) **(*) Naxos 8.559151. Nashville SO, Schermerhorn; (i) with Wait

Both the *Holiday Overture* (1945) and the *Symphony 1* (1942) are fresh and open in Carter's earlier manner. The *Symphony* is rewarding, close in idiom to Copland and Piston. Its material is interesting and the feeling for form strong. The disc is worth having for this alone, particularly in this strong, understanding and well-recorded performance, culminating in a sparkling account of the finale. The *Piano Concerto* is pretty rebarbative, highly intricate rhythmically, its ideas firmly embedded in barbed wire and its spikey charms eminently resistible. In short, it is deeply unappealing. First-rate sound, if with the piano balanced rather too forwardly.

(i) Piano Concerto; Variations for Orchestra

*** New World (ADD) NW 347. (i) Ursula Oppens; Cincinnati SO, Gielen

Michael Gielen directs strong, purposeful readings, very well played, of this taxing music, clarifying the thornily complex arguments with **Ursula Oppens** a powerful soloist. The *Variations* is an inventive and fascinating work, splendidly played by the **Cincinnati** forces. The recording was made at concert performances and is excellent.

String Quartets 1 & 5

(N) (BB) *** Naxos 8.559362 Pacifica Quartet

String Quartet 2

*** Testament SBT 1374. Juilliard Qt – BERG: *Lyric Suite*; SCHUMAN: *Quartet 3* ***

The **Julliard** gave the first performance of Elliott Carter's *Second Quartet* and their recording comes from 1960. They play it superbly, but the **Pacifica Quartet** seem even more completely at home in the dynamism and high tension of this music with its fair share of tough writing and barbed wire. The *Variations* of No. 1 are a highlight. The recording too is very fine.

Piano Sonata; 90+; 2 Diversions; Matribute; Night Fantasies; 2 Thoughts about the Piano (Intermittences; Caténaires)

*** Cedile CDR 90000 108. Ursula Oppens

Ursula Oppens's collection gives us all Carter's piano music to date, centring on her breathtakingly powerful account of the *Sonata*, which the composer himself described, with considerable understatement, as 'very advanced'. It is logically structured in two movements, with the finale built on four different time signatures, and a fugue as its centrepiece. The work, overall, is one of the most remarkable of the twentieth century and Oppens's continually arresting performance is fully worthy of it. There is currently another new version by Peter Seivewright (on Divine Art dda 15052) coupled with a *Sonata* by Rózsa and the *Fourth Sonata* of MacDowell. This is also impressive, but is less taut, with a playing time eight minutes longer than the Oppens account which seems ideally paced and has great intensity.

The other works here include *90+*, built around ninety accented regular notes, *Retrouvailles* (using a motto based on the letters of the name of its dedicatee, Boulez), an interrupted sequence of *Night Fantasies*, the fragmentary fast figurations of *Matribute*, a continuous chain of notes with no chords (*Caténaires*) and the brusque 'jump-cuts' and unpredictable pauses of *Intermittences*. This is all formidable stuff, but Carter enthusiasts will not be disappointed.

CARWITHEN, Doreen
(1922–2003)

(i) Concerto for Piano & Strings. Overtures: ODTAA ('One damn thing after another'); Bishop Rock; Suffolk Suite

Ⓜ *** Chan. 10365X. (i) Shelley; LSO, Hickox

The two overtures in their vigour and atmospheric colour relate readily to Doreen Carwithen's film music, the one inspired by John Masefield's novel, *ODTAA*, the other inspired by the rock in the Atlantic that marks the last contact with the British Isles, stormy in places, gently sinister in others. The charming *Suffolk Suite* uses melodies originally written for a film on East Anglia. Much the most ambitious work is the *Concerto for Piano and Strings*, with powerful virtuoso writing for the piano set against rich-textured strings. A deeply melancholy slow movement – in which the piano is joined by solo violin – leads to a strong finale which in places echoes the Ireland *Piano Concerto*. **Howard Shelley** is the persuasive soloist, with **Richard Hickox** and the **LSO** equally convincing in their advocacy of all four works. Warm, atmospheric sound.

CASTELNUOVO-TEDESCO, Mario (1895–1968)

Guitar Concerto 1 in D, Op. 99

ⒷⒷ *** Naxos 8.550729. Kraft, N. CO, Ward – RODRIGO; VILLA-LOBOS: *Concertos* ***

On Naxos a first-class version of this slight but attractive concerto, which is well suited by the relatively intimate scale of the performance. The recording is well balanced and vivid, and the soloist, **Norbert Kraft**, has plenty of personality; and the accompaniment is fresh and polished. Typically excellent Naxos value.

Cello Sonata, Op. 50; Notturna sull'acqua, Op. 82a; Scherzino, Op. 82b; I Nottambu i (Variazione fantastiche), Op. 47; Paraphrase on Rossini's 'Largo al factotum'; Toccata, Op. 83; Valse on the Name of Gregor Piatigorsky

*** Biddulph LAW 024. Green, Moyer

Castelnuovo-Tedesco's *Cello Sonata* is a splendid work, opening with a striking main theme (marked *Arioso e sereno*) followed by a highly inventive *Aria with Variations* to act as slow movement and finale combined. The two nocturnal pieces are full of Mediterranean atmosphere. **Nancy Green** is in full sympathy with this repertoire and she plays very persuasively indeed, with excellent support from her partner, **Frederick Moyer.**

SOLO GUITAR MUSIC

Aranci in fiore, Op. 87a; Capriccio, Op. 195/18; Escarramán, Op. 177/1-5; La guarda cuydadosa, Op. 177/6; 3 Preludi mediterranei, Op. 176; Variations à

travers les siècles, Op. 71; Variations plaisantes sur un petit air populaire, Op. 95; Tarantella, Op. 87b

ⒷⒷ **(*) Naxos 8.554831. Micheli

Lorenzo Micheli refrains from duplicating the familiar Villa-Lobos or Sor repertoire and concentrates on rarities by his countryman, Castelnuovo-Tedesco. The music is slender in substance but appealing. Artistically this is first rate, as Micheli plays with assurance and elegance, but he is balanced very closely.

CASTILLON, Alexis de
(1838–73)

Piano Quartet in G min., Op. 7

ⒷⒷ *** Virgin 2x1 4 82061-2 (2). Kandinsky Qt – CHAUSSON; LEKEU; SAINT-SAËNS: *Piano Quartets* ***

Like Chausson and Lekeu, with whom he shares this two-CD set, Alexis de Castillon was a pupil of César Franck. His Op. 7 *Piano Quartet* of 1869 is an engaging piece, much indebted to Schumann. The performance, like the others in this coupling, comes from the early 1990s and is expert and well recorded.

CATALANI, Alfredo (1854–93)

La Wally (opera; complete)

⌕– Ⓜ *** Double Decca (ADD) 475 8667 or 460 744-2 (2). Tebaldi, del Monaco, Diaz, Cappuccilli, Marimpietri, Turin Lyric Ch., Monte Carlo Op. O, Fausto Cleva

The title-role of *La Wally* prompts **Renata Tebaldi** to give one of her most tenderly affecting performances on record, a glorious example of her singing late in her career. **Mario del Monaco** begins coarsely, but the heroic power and intensity of his singing are formidable, and it is good to have the young **Cappuccilli** in the baritone role of Gellner. The sound in this late-1960s recording is superbly focused and vividly real.

CAVALLI, Francesco (1602–76)

Messa Concertata; 4 Canzonas; Motets: O bone Jesu; O quam suavis et decora

ⒷⒷ *** Hyp. Helios CDH 55193. Hyde, Carwood, Seicento, Parley of Instruments, Holman

Much of Cavalli's church music was published in his *Musica Sacre* of 1656. It begins with a concerted setting of the *Messa Concertata*, and that is what **Peter Holman** has recorded here. He follows the custom at St Mark's at the time of interspersing the five movements of the Ordinary with offertory and communion motets and ensemble sonatas, sonorously but modestly scored. The Mass uses two four-part choirs of voices, with two violins, three trombones and continuo, reflecting Monteverdi's *Magnificat* setting of 1641, which tends to confirm that Cavalli was the latter's pupil. His own music, with its jolly three-bar dactylic rhythms and rich chording for voices and brass, is extrovert and vigorous, although the soprano **Philippa Hyde's** contribution to the two motets shows the depth of his touching lyrical writing. Cavalli is no carbon copy of his mentor but a fine composer in his own right. The performance, with excellently blended voices and instruments, is most appealing and is very well recorded. Full texts and translations are included.

OPERA

La Calisto (DVD version)

*** HM **DVD** HMD 9909 001/2 (2). Bayo, Lippi, Kamerer, Pushee, Winter, Visse, Oliver, Concerto Vocale, Jacobs

Unlike the classic Glyndebourne production by Peter Hall with a score prepared by Raymond Leppard, Jacobs is much more faithful to Cavalli's text, with the result that, where at Glyndebourne the love of Diana and Endimione (Endymion) was central to the action, here it is the love of Giove (Jupiter) for the nymph La Calisto which is central. So Giove, when he is wooing Calisto, appears in drag, singing falsetto; the other characters too appear comically in drag, the irrepressible **Dominique Visse** as Furia and **Alexander Oliver** as Linfea. Though the fun is extreme, it can be argued that it follows period practice, and the sets with their elaborate trapdoors and gods descending from the heavens have a 17th-century flavour. There are also echoes of the *commedia dell'arte*, with Mercury a clown and Endimione a Harlequin figure. The sets dotted with nymphs are pretty and atmospheric.

Arias and Duets from: Calisto; Didone; Egisto; Giasone; Ormindo

(BB) **(*) Naxos 8.557746. Banditelli, Frisandi, Abbandanza, Doro, Cecchetti, Mediterraneo Concento, Vartolo

Here is a well-planned and ideally documented aural window opening on to five of Cavalli's key operas, very well sung by a fine cast who are obviously at home in this repertoire. If there are no stellar names in the cast list, there was no star system in Cavalli's time, and the vocal acting here is at one with the melodramatic (and sometimes sexually explicit) story-lines. The accompaniments are most stylishly managed, and the conductor, **Sergio Vartolo**, is also to be praised for his sensitive accompaniments at the harpsichord.

Gli amori d'Apollo e di Dafne (The Loves of Apollo and Daphne)

(BB) **(*) Naxos 8. 660187/8 (2). Zeffiri, Pizzolato, Mateu, Galicia Youth SO, Zedda

This was the second of Cavalli's operas, using a libretto by Busenello, and, like Cavalli's better-known, lighter-hearted *La Calisto*, it deals with an illicit love of Jupiter, this time not for Diana but for Daphne, with Daphne finally escaping his attentions by transforming herself into a tree. This live performance brings some odd balances, but the performance is most enjoyable. At bargain price, well worth investigating.

CHABRIER, Emmanuel
(1841–94)

Bourrée fantasque; España (rhapsody); Joyeuse marche; Suite pastorale; Gwendoline: Overture. Le Roi malgré lui: Danse slave; Fête polonaise

●— *** Mercury (ADD) 434 303-2. Detroit SO, Paray – ROUSSEL: *Suite* **(*)

This finely played and idiomatically conducted Mercury collection of Chabrier's best orchestral pieces does not disappoint. **Paray's** whimsically relaxed and sparkling account of *España* gives great pleasure and his rubato in the *Fête polonaise* is equally winning. The *Suite pastorale* is a wholly delightful account, given playing that is at once warm and polished, neat and perfectly in scale, with the orchestra beautifully balanced. The *Joyeuse Marche* was recorded in Detroit's Old Orchestral Hall, the quality now enhanced on SACD. The Roussel coupling makes an excellent and imaginative bonus.

España; Gwendoline Overture

(**(*)) BBC mono BBCL 4113. RPO, Beecham (with spoken introduction) – BERLIOZ: *The Trojans: Royal Hunt and Storm*; DEBUSSY: *L'Enfant prodigue: Cortège et air de danse*; DELIUS: *Brigg Fair*; MASSENET: *La Vierge: Le Dernier Sommeil de la vierge*; SAINT-SAËNS: *Le Rouet d'Omphale* (with MOZART: *Divertimento in D, K.131: excerpts*) (**(*))

España; Habanera; Joyeuse marche; Lamento; Prélude pastorale; Suite pastorale; Le Roi malgré lui: Danse slave; Fête polonaise

(BB) **(*) Naxos 8.554248. Monte-Carlo PO, Niquet

Beecham's BBC recording of *España* comes from a 1956 live broadcast concert of '*Lollipops*', and enjoyable though it is, it does not quite match his earlier studio recording with the LPO, partly because the sound has less range and sparkle. However, it does have a spoken introduction from the conductor, and the *Gwendoline Overture*, recorded a year earlier, does not lack either charm or gusto. The excerpts from the Mozart *Divertimento* were part of the main concert and bring some predictably fine string and horn playing.

A very well-recorded programme on Naxos, played with considerable idiomatic flair if without always the very last degree of finesse (*Sous-bois*, for instance, could be more delicate in the bass).

España; Joyeuse marche; Gwendoline Overture

●— (M) (***) EMI mono 3 79986-2. LPO, RPO, Fr. Nat. RO or RPO, Beecham – BIZET: *Carmen Suite 1*; *Patrie Overture*; *Roma: Carnaval à Roma*; FAURÉ: *Dolly*; SAINT-SAËNS: *Le rouet d'Omphale* ***

All these pieces are supercharged, although the *Gwendoline Overture* has much charm, too. **Beecham's LPO** *España* is, of course, mono, yet it remains the highlight, both for its unique exuberance and for the amazingly realistic recording, produced by Walter Legge at Abbey Road in 1939.

España; Suite pastorale

*** Chan. 8852. Ulster O, Y. P. Tortelier – DUKAS: *L'Apprenti sorcier; La Péri* **(*)

Yan Pascal Tortelier and the excellent **Ulster Orchestra** give an altogether first-rate account of Chabrier's delightful *Suite pastorale*, distinguished by an appealing charm and lightness of touch. There is a spirited account of *España*, too.

PIANO MUSIC

Aubade; Ballabile; Bourrée fantasque; Caprice; Feuillet d'album; Habanera; Impromptu; 10 pièces pittoresques; Ronde champêtre

☒— **** Hyp. CDA 67515. Hewitt

This is a model collection of pieces by one of the most engaging of all 19th-century French composers, showing what sparkling inventiveness he brings to any idea. The 18 pieces here are all beautifully realized by **Hewitt**, with exquisite control of the widest tonal range and ever-persuasive control of rubato. Beautifully recorded.

Aubade; Ballabile; Caprice; Feuillet d'album; Impromptu; Pièces pittoresques; Ronde champêtre; (i) 3 Valses romantiques

(BB) *** Regis RRC 1133. Stott; (i) with Burley

For those wanting a representative bargain selection, **Kathryn Stott** provides the ideal answer. She plays this long-neglected but rewarding repertoire with intelligence, wit and elegance.

VOCAL MUSIC

Mélodies (complete); Folksong arrangements

*** Hyp. CDA 67133/4. Lott, Burden, Varcoe, Spence, Johnson, McGreevy, Polyphony, Layton

These two generously filled discs, appropriately sub-titled *'Musique adorable!'* offer a wide-ranging selection of Chabrier's songs, as well as the *Ode à la musique* (sung by **Geraldine McGreevy** with the choral group, **Polyphony**), and a curious duo for a programme-seller at the Opéra Comique and an assistant at the Bon Marché department store. That jokey piece, with each section ending in a Swiss yodelling song, demonstrates the humorous side of Chabrier. Yet many of these songs are deeply expressive, even some of those which date from 1862 when he was only 21. As always in his song recordings for Hyperion, **Graham Johnson** greatly adds to one's enjoyment, not only with his ever-sensitive playing but in his comprehensive, scholarly notes. **Felicity Lott**, Geraldine McGreevy, **William Burden** and **Toby Spence** are all in fine voice, singing stylishly.

OPERA

Briséïs (complete)

✹ *** Hyp. CDA 66803. Rodgers, Padmore, Keenlyside, Harries, George, BBC Scottish SO, Jean-Yves Ossonce

Starting with a ripely seductive sailors' chorus, few operas are as sensuous as *Briséïs*. On disc it matters little that this is a torso. The writing is not just sensuous but urgent, a warm bath of sound that is also exhilarating. Casting is near ideal, with **Joan Rodgers** in the title-role rich and distinctive, and with **Mark Padmore** as the sailor, Hylas, equally warm, producing heady, clear tenor tone. Symbolizing the forces of Christian good, **Simon Keenlyside** as the Catechist and **Kathryn Harries** as the mother of Briseis, cured through faith, both sing with character and apt resonance. Full, atmospheric sound.

CHADWICK, George (1854–1931)

Aphrodite; Angel of Death; Overtures: Euterpe; Melpomene; Thalia

(BB) *** Naxos 8.559117. Nashville SO, Schermerhorn

Although an American composer, George Chadwick still relates to the world of Brahms and Dvořák, if with an attractive transatlantic flavour in the manner of the *New World Symphony*. But these tone-poems and (symphonic) overtures, although they have engaging invention, do not always fully sustain their length. The three overtures are each named after one of the muses. *Thalia* (the muse of comedy) highlights Chadwick's particular skill at writing wittily and light-heartedly; the more substantial *Melpomene* (the muse of tragedy) was one of the composer's most often performed works during his lifetime, its opening almost *Tristanesque*, while *Euterpe* (the muse of music), is enjoyably colourful.

Symphonies 2 in B flat; 3 in F

*** Chan. 9685. Detroit SO, Järvi

Chadwick's *Second Symphony* dates from the early 1880s, though its delightful *Scherzo* was premièred two years ahead of the rest of the work. When this was first heard it had to be encored, which is hardly surprising. It has an engaging, cheeky quality and Järvi makes the very most of it. The *Third Symphony* is hardly less fresh and appealing. It breathes much the same air as Brahms, Dvořák and Svendsen; it is very compelling in so persuasive a performance as is given here by **Järvi** and his **Detroit Orchestra**. Absolutely first-class recording too.

CHAGRIN, Francis (1905–72)

Helter Skelter (Concert Overture)

**** Lyrita SRCD 318. LPO, Pritchard (with Henry PIERSON. *Macbeth*; David MORGAN: *Contrasts* ***) – ARNOLD: *Beckus the Dandipratt*; RAWSTHORNE: *Cortèges*; WARLOCK: *Serenade for Strings* ****

This delightfully whimsical overture derives from a film of the same name involving an heiress with hiccups. The film is long forgotten but the overture certainly should not be, a winning piece using memorably quirky themes in the most engaging way. It is splendidly played and recorded here.

CHARPENTIER, Gustave
(1860–1956)

Louise (gramophone version conceived and realized by the composer)

Ⓜ (***) Nim. mono NI 7829. Vallin, Thill, Pernet, Lecouvreur, Gaudel, Ch. Raugel & O, Eugène Bigot

These substantial excerpts from *Louise* were recorded in 1935 under the 75-year-old composer's supervision; they feature two ideally cast French singers as the two principals, **Ninon Vallin** enchanting in the title-role and the tenor, **Georges Thill**, heady-toned as the hero, Julien. The original eight 78-r.p.m. records are fitted neatly on to a single CD, and – in the selection of items, made by the composer himself – just the delights and none of the longueurs of this nostalgically atmospheric opera are included. The voices are caught superbly in the Nimbus transfers, but with an early electrical recording like this the orchestral sound becomes muddled. Yet even Nimbus has rarely presented voices as vividly as here.

CHARPENTIER, Marc-Antoine (1643–1704)

Les Antiennes 'O' de l'Avent, H.36–43, with Noëls pour les instruments, H.534; Canticum in nativitatem Domini nostri Jésus Christ, H.416; Pastorale sur la naissance de Notre Seigneur Jesus Christ, H.482 (HMX 2908141). Canticum in nativitatem Domini nostri Jésus Christ, H.414; Pastorale sur la naissance de notre Seigneur Jésus Christ, H.483 (HMX 2908140). Litanies de la Vierge, H.83; Missa Assumpta est Maria, H.11; Te Deum, H.146 (HMX 2908144). Méditations pour le Carême; Le Reniement de St Pierre (HMX 2908143). Les Arts Florissants (opéra et idylle en musique). (HMX 2908142)

Ⓑ *** HM (ADD) HMX 2908140/44 (5). Les Arts Florissants, Christie

These two pioneering collections from **William Christie** and his **Arts Florissants** of the music of Charpentier, made over two decades, are complementary, the Harmonia Mundi compilation being recorded between 1981 and 1989 and the Warner Classics box between 1995 and 2001. Charpentier wrote numerous works in celebration of Christmas, and he set the words of the *Canticum in nativitatem Domini* four times, only one of which (H.416) is included in both compilations.

The solemn 'O' Antiphons on the first disc listed here are so called because of their opening invocation: *O salutaris hostia, O Sapientia*, etc. Charpentier explained in his manuscript that custom demanded that *Noëls* were performed between them when they were sung on the days preceding the Nativity. The musical delights are considerable and the same high standards of performance and recording that are found here prevail throughout the box.

Christie's performance of the *Te Deum* is among the finest in the catalogue. The disc also includes the much less familiar but no less beautiful *Missa Assumpta est Maria* and the more restrained *Litanies de la Vierge*. Framed by a *Kyrie* and closing *Agnus Dei*, the seven movements each radiantly describe one of the Virgin's mystical attributes, followed by an intercessionary prayer.

The *Méditations pour le Carême* are a sequence of three-voice motets for Lent with continuo accompaniment (organ, theorbo and bass viol) that may not have quite the same imaginative or expressive resource as their coupling, but they are full of nobility and interest. *Le Reniement de St Pierre*, however, is one of Charpentier's most inspired and expressive works, and its text draws on the account in all four Gospels of St Peter's denial of Christ. The performance and recording maintain the high standards of this series.

Les Arts Florissants is a short entertainment in five scenes; the libretto tells of a conflict between the Arts, who flourish under the rule of Peace, and the forces of War, personified by Discord and the Furies. This and the little Interlude that completes the music include some very invigorating and fresh ideas, performed very pleasingly indeed. The five CDs come in a box, each in an elegantly illustrated cardboard inner, and there is an excellent booklet, including full texts and translations.

Concert for viols in 4 Parts, H.545; Il faut rire et chanter: Dispute de bergers, H.484; La Pierre Philosophale, H.501. Airs: Ah! laissez-moi rêver; Ah! qu'ils sont courts les beaux jours; Ah! qu'on est malheureux d'avoir eu des désirs; Auprès du feu l'on fait l'amour; Ayant bu du vin claire; Charmantes fleurs, naissez; En vain rivaux assidus; Fenchon, la gentille Fenchon; Non, non, je ne l'aime plus; Quoi! Je ne verrai plus; Quoi! rien ne peut vous arrêter?; Rentrez, trop indiscrets soupirs; Tristes déserts, sombre retraite. Chaconne: Sans frayeur dans ce bois (3984 25485-2) (with Daneman, Petibon, Eikenes, Agnew, Sinclair, Piolino, Le Monnier, Ewing). Canticum in nativitatem Domini, H.416; Messe de Minuit pour Noël, H.9; 4 Noëls sur les instruments (8573 85820-2) (with soloists). (i) Amor vince ogni cosa (pastoraletta); (ii) Les Plaisirs de Versailles; (iii) 3 Airs on Stanzas from 'Le Cid' (0630 14774-2) (with (i) Petibon, Lallouette; (i; ii) Daneman, Piolino; (ii) Károlyi, Duardin, Gardeil; (i; iii) Agnew). La Descente d'Orphée aux Enfers (chamber opera; complete). (0630 11913-2) (with Agnew, Daneman, Zanetti, Petibon, Károlyi, Gardeil)

Ⓑ *** Warner 2564 61758-2 (4). Les Arts Florissants, Christie

The first disc in the later, Warner Classics box, described as 'Divertissements and Airs et Concert', shows something of the range of Charpentier's instrumental and secular vocal writing. The programme is framed by a dramatic setting, the first, *La Pierre Philosophale* (1681) and all we are left with is eight minutes of charmingly scored music. Its choruses of Four Elements glorify the victory of love, while the central arias are sung by a *gnomide* celebrating her forthcoming wedding, and a Marquis (disguised as a sylph) who seeks her hand, though wishing she were taller. The union of such opposites is appropriately acclaimed by a duet of Fire and Water, and the marquis is then astonished at the metamorphosis of his bride into a voluptuous, full-sized beauty!

The centrepiece of the programme is a collection of *chansonettes* and *airs sérieux*. These are then followed by the more successful amours experienced after a glass or two of wine. The songs are made the more appealing for being interspersed with attractive movements from Charpentier's *Concert pour quatre parties de violes*. The programme ends with *Il faut rire et chanter: Dispute de Bergers*, a miniature pastoral chamber-opera. The arguments are about the winter weather, which is then banished and spring celebrated. The performance is splendidly sung and played, and the recording is full of atmosphere.

Christie's apt coupling of the beautiful *Canticum in nativitatem Domini*, H.416, and its interpolated instrumental *Noëls*, with the *Messe de Minuit pour Noël*, seems made in heaven, and the whole work is a marvellous example of simple means used to maximum musical effect.

Amor vince ogni cosa is a charming pastoral conversation-piece (with shepherds' chorus) about unrequited love. *Les plaisirs de Versailles* is a 'mini-opera' in which the characters are Music, Conversation, Le Jeu, Comus and Un Plaisir. They engage in a vociferous dialogue which is in turns lyrical, dramatic and bizarrely humorous. Finally the protagonists are reconciled and the piece ends with a happy chorus. The three ardent airs from Corneille's *Le Cid* make a passionate central interlude. Throughout, the solo singing is delightful and full of lively and charming characterization, while Charpentier's orchestration is equally diverting when Christie provides such sparkling accompaniments.

La descente d'Orphée aux enfers starts with lightweight, sparkling movements in dance rhythms, but then dramatically changes tone with the death of Euridice, a moment superbly interpreted by **Sophie Daneman**. The following lament for Orphée is just the first of his moving and expressive solos, each of them brief but intense, beautifully sung by **Paul Agnew**. They culminate in a sequence when he seeks to charm Pluton in the Underworld, finally succeeding. The work ends with the lamenting of Pluton's subjects at losing Orphée and his musical magic. The four discs come in their original jewel cases in a sleeve, and throughout there is excellent documentation, plus full texts and translations.

Motets

(B) *** HM (ADD) HMA 1951149. Concerto Vocale

Half of the motets on this record are for solo voice and the others are duets. Among the best and most moving things here are *O vos omnes* and *Amicus meus*, which are beautifully done. Another motet to note is *Magdalena lugens*, in which Mary Magdalene laments Christ's death at the foot of the Cross. Expressive singing from **Judith Nelson** and **René Jacobs**, and excellent continuo support.

Motets

*** Astrée E 8598. Les Demoiselles de Saint-Cyr, Mandrin

In the mid-1680s, Charpentier composed several works 'for Port Royal'. The music is scored for female voices only and is generally austere in style. The main work, after which the record is titled, is the *Messe pour le Port-Royal* for three soloists, chorus and organ. This is supplemented by various other pieces, psalm settings and the fine *Magnificat*, also written for the convent. This is reposeful music, predominantly meditative in character, and very persuasively performed by **Les Demoiselles de Saint-Cyr** under **Emmanuel Mandrin**, with **Michel Chapuis** providing the solo organ interludes. A rewarding issue.

Canticum in nativitatem Domini, H.393; In nativitatem Domini canticum, H.314; In nativitatem Domini canticum: Chanson, H.416; In nativitatem Domini Nostri Jesus Christi, H.414; 9 Noëls

⊕ (BB) *** Naxos 8.554514. Aradia Ens., Mallon

In this Christmas disc with a difference, the talented Canadian group, the **Aradia Ensemble**, warmly recorded, present the nine charming sets of simple variations Charpentier wrote on French Christmas carols, or *Noëls*. Standing out from the rest is the minor-key *Or nous dites Marie*, with chromatic writing like Purcell's. These instrumental pieces are set alongside a sequence of lively vocal motets on a Christmas theme, culminating in a miniature Nativity oratorio.

Canticum in nativitatem Domini, H.416; Dialogus inter angelos et pastores Judeae in nativitatem Domine, H.420; Noël: Un flambeau, Janette, Isabelle (3 versions), H.460

⊕ (BB) *** Naxos 8.557036. Smith Bessette, Stelmacovitch, Nortman, Streetman, Aradia Ens., Mallon

Here is a natural and equally beguiling follow-up to the **Aradia Ensemble's** first Naxos collection of Christmas music, including *Noëls*. The two cantatas both use the same text from St Luke, telling of the angel's dialogue with the shepherds. Each then creates a nocturnal atmosphere, followed by the shepherds' joyful 'awakening', devotion and exultation. The innocence of the pastoral scene is richly conveyed in Charpentier's simple but inspired settings. The three versions of the *Nöel* (the first for soloists and organ, the second for choir, the third instrumental) act as prelude, intermezzo and postlude in the most effective way, so that the concert makes a perfect whole. Singing, playing and recording are of high quality and so is the documentation.

Canticum in Nativitatem D. N. J. C., H.414; Pastorale sur la naissance de N. S. Jésus-Christ, H.483

⊕ (M) **** HM HMX 2971082. Les Arts Florissants, Christie

Charpentier wrote numerous works in celebration of Christmas and he set the words of the *Canticum in nativitatem Domini* four times involving recitatives for the Evangelist and an Air and chorus for the shepherds. In both works the music's charm and grace continue to win one over to this eminently resourceful composer. One thing that will immediately strike the listener is the delicacy and finesse of the scoring. This series undertaken by **William Christie** seems almost self-recommending, so high are the standards of performance and so fertile is Charpentier's imagination. The reissue is handsomely presented in silver livery and includes full texts and translations.

Canticum in nativitatem Domini Nostri Jesus Christi, H.416; Pastorale sur la naissance de notre Seigneur Jésus Christ, H.482

*** HM (ADD) HMC 905130. Les Arts Florissants Vocal & Instrumental Ens., Christie

The cantata, a finely balanced edifice in two complementary halves, is separated by an instrumental section, an eloquent evocation of the night. The little pastorale was written in the tradition of the *ballet de cour* or divertissement. This is enchanting music, elegantly played and excellently recorded.

Canticum pro pace, H.392; Josué, H.404; Mors Saülis et Jonathae, H.403; Praelium Michaelis Archangeli factum in coelo cum dracone, H.410; Quam dilecta tabernacula tua, H.167; Troisième Leçons de ténèbres du mercredi, du jeudi et du vendredi Saint, H.135/7

(BB) **(*) Warner Apex 2564 61744-2 (2). Schlick, Wessel, Prégardien, Mertens, Kooy, Zijlstra, Visse, Van Berne, Amsterdam Bar. O, Koopman

Curiously, Charpentier often wrote for double choir in a warlike ambience, and the *Canticum pro pace* (1674–6), which opens with a Prelude suggesting 'the clamour of war', probably celebrated the successful outcome of one of Louis XIV's battles with the Dutch. *Josué* and *Mors Saülis et Jonathae* are motet/oratorios based in Old Testament stories, and the latter is very theatrical, almost operatic, opening with an even more dramatic orchestral *Rumor bellicus* ('Noise of War'). The chorus (often in very lively fashion) both narrates the story and takes part in the action, making a lively contrast to the dialogues between Saul, David and the Soldier who kills the lamenting Saul at his own request. There is a memorably expressive aria for the Witch, and the closing section with David's *Air* and a choral lament is very touching. The performances here, with a first-class group of soloists who join together for the choruses, are in every way excellent, and the recording is of equal excellence. The one snag is that, while full texts and translations are included, there is only a single cue for each work, which makes finding one's way very difficult.

Canticum Zachariae: Benedictus, H.345; Mass, H.1; Te Deum, H.147

(BB) *** Naxos 8.553175. Le Concert Spirituel, Niquet

The *Canticum Zachariae* dates from 1687, and its lovely six-part *Benedictus* shows Charpentier in characteristically fluent lyrical and contrapuntal form. The four-part *Mass* – the first of the composer's eleven settings – which opens simply, extends to six voices in the *Sanctus*, with the spirited *Hosanna* extended to double choir. But it is the short *Agnus Dei*, serenely beautiful, that haunts the memory.

The *Te Deum* was the composer's last setting, written not too long before his death. If without the instrumental spectacle of his most famous setting, it is supremely confident in its variety of style, superbly written, ending exultantly. The performances here are splendid, not inflated, but in every way satisfying. The recording is excellent and there is full documentation.

Elévation; In obitum augustissimae nec non piissimae gallorum Reginae lamentum; Luctus de morte augustissimae Mariae Theresiae Galliae

&— (BB) *** Warner Apex 2564 61743-2. Degelin, Verdoodt, Smolders, Crook, Vandersteene, Widmer, Namur Chamber Ch., Musica Polyphonica, Devos

All three works here lament the death of the queen, Marie Thérèse. Clearly the event moved Charpentier deeply, and each reflects the paradox of the Christian faith in contrasting grief with joy and hope in the life hereafter. Here **Devos's** performances could hardly be bettered, bringing out all the music's drama, joy, and depth of feeling. The recordings, both made in spacious acoustics, are also first class and this Apex reissue is highly recommended.

Judicium Salomonis (The Judgement of Solomon); Motet pour une longue offrande

*** Virgin 3 59294-2. Agnew, Aruhn-Solén, Davies, Fernandes, Les Arts Florissants, Christie

Judicium Salomonis is a grand dramatic motet, one of the kind called by the French '*histoire sacrée*', dating from 1702. It is above all a happy work. The first part celebrates the peace and piety of Israel under Solomon, who appears to bless the Lord for his goodness, and the chorus echoes his praise jubilantly. Then comes a magical orchestral interlude suggesting Solomon's dream, and a duet in which he asks God for wisdom. More vigorous celebrations, and the third part brings the famous judgement (after an agitated dialogue), and the work ends in jubilation. All this shows Charpentier at his most resourceful and imaginative, especially in orchestral colour, and this is again apparent in the following motet, which is again elaborate and no less grand. The performances here, with fine soloists, eloquent choral singing and some beautiful orchestral playing is another triumph for **Christie** and his **Arts Florissants**, who are beautifully recorded.

Leçons de ténèbres for Maundy Thursday

&— (B) *** HM (ADD) HMC 901006. Jacobs, Nelson, Wieland Kuijken, Verkinderen, Christie, Concerto Vocale, Jacobs

Charpentier's melismatic setting is sung with great eloquence by **René Jacobs**. Yet one must remember that this music was written for nuns (the names of the sisters who sang them are known) and Charpentier observed that the leading soprano should possess a '*voix touchante*' rather than a '*voix brillante*'. So it is here, in the second and third lessons, with **Judith Nelson's** *dolce* leading the small female group, accompanied (as the composer suggested) by a continuo of bass viol, organ and theorbo. They are beautifully recorded and this reissue is a real bargain.

Leçons de ténèbre for Maundy Thursday & Good Friday

(N) (BB) *** Virgin 2x1 5 22021-2 (2) Piau, Mellon, Lesne, Seminario Musicale

The *Leçons de ténèbre for Maundy Thursday and Good Friday* from **Il Seminario Musicale** offer music of great variety and beauty, featuring soloists naturally attuned to this repertoire. The accompaniments are provided by a varied instrumental group, and their use is consistently imaginative and refreshing to the ear. The Psalms are sung by a smaller choral group. The effect is warm yet refined, the lyrical melancholy of much of this music is quite haunting, and the acoustic of L'Abbaye Royale de Fontevraud is ideal for the music. The reissued CDs are inexpensive and any collector attracted to this remarkable and inspired composer should consider them.

Mass for 4 Choirs & Orchestra

(BB) **(*) Warner Apex 2564 61745-2. Mellon, Poulenard, Brett, Aubin, Elwes, Laplenie, Cantoe, Gardell, Regional Ch. of N. Pas-de-Calais, Jean Bridier & Françoise Herr Vocal Ensembles, Gabrieli Ch., Grande Ecurie et la Chambre du Roy, Malgoire (with BOYVIN: *Organ Pieces* ***)

Charpentier wrote his *Mass for Four Choirs* when he returned to Paris in the early 1670s after spending three years in Italy, where he would certainly have encountered such multi-chorus antiphonal works. Though these were not part of the French tradition, he adapted them to the style of the French organ mass, interspersing organ interludes between the Propers. For the present live performance, **Jean-Claude Malgoire** has used – to great effect – organ pieces by Jacques Boyvin (1646–1707) whose characterful music is exactly contemporary with that of Charpentier. The performance here is of high quality, but the 1990 recording, made in the Abbaye of Saint-Michel en Thiérache, although providing a richly atmospheric ambience does not give clear separation between the various choral groups. Nevertheless, this is a thoroughly worthwhile disc, with Latin text included.

Messe de minuit pour Noël (Midnight Mass for Christmas Eve); Dixit Dominus; Te Deum

🔑 (BB) *** Naxos 8.557229. Aradia Ens., Mallon

Kevin Mallon and his excellent Canadian group, the **Aradia Ensemble**, give bright, clear readings of two of the most popular of Charpentier's choral works. This period performance of the *Prélude* for the *Te Deum* is very different from the one that used to introduce Eurovision programmes; it is altogether lighter and more joyful, with an exuberant display of timpani at the start and with bright trumpet flourishes throughout. In the *Christmas Mass* Mallon equally brings out the joy of the writing, giving more prominence than usual to the carols that punctuate the *Kyrie*, and springing rhythms infectiously in writing that in many sections offers a thoughtfully original setting of the liturgy. The *Dixit Dominus*, with its unexpectedly gentle minor-key introduction, makes an attractive extra item. Clear, well-balanced sound.

Miserere, H.219; Motets: *Pour la seconde fois que le Saint Sacrament vient au même reposoir, H.372; Pour le Saint Sacrement au reposoir, H.346; Motet pour une longue offrande, H.434*

(B) *** HM HMA 195 1185. Mellon, Poulenard, Ledroit, Kendall, Kooy, La Chapelle Royale, Herreweghe

All four works on the disc are powerfully expressive and beautifully performed. The recording, made in collaboration with Radio France, is most expertly balanced.

Te Deum; Grand Office des Morts (reconstructed by John S. Powell from the *Messe et Motet pour les trépassés* and the *Pose des morts*)

🔑 *** Virgin 5 45733-2. Soloists, Les Arts Florissants, Christie

William Christie and his **Arts Florissants** here give a splendid account of the *Te Deum*, heralded by a spectacular opening flourish of drums and Philidor's *Marche de timbals* as part of the *Prélude*. But it is the coupling that is the main interest here, a reconstruction of the *Grand Office des Morts* from three works which almost certainly were never performed together in the composer's lifetime. It works remarkably well, and the entry of the *Dies Irae* in the *Pose des morts* sequence is a truly dramatic moment, while the *Sanctus*, *Pie Jesu* and *Benedictus* of the *Messe pour les trépassés* make a beautiful following group, and the closing triple *Agnus Dei* is wonderfully serene. The performance, as always from this group, is spiritually intense and dedicated, made the more so by the live recording, in the Cité de la Musique, Paris, which is wonderfully atmospheric.

OPERA AND THEATRE MUSIC

Médée (complete)

✿ *** Erato 4509 96558-2 (3). Hunt, Padmore, Delétré, Zanetti, Salzmann, Les Arts Florissants, Christie

In his second recording of this rare opera, again with his group, **Les Arts Florissants**, **Christie** was glad to be able to open out the small cuts that were made before so as to fit the LP format. The success of his new interpretation is readily borne out in the finished performance, which easily surpasses the previous one in its extra brightness and vigour, with consistently crisper and more alert ensembles, often at brisker speeds, with the drama more clearly established. The casting is first rate, with **Lorraine Hunt** outstanding in the tragic title-role. Her soprano has satisfying weight and richness, as well as the purity and precision needed in such classical opera; and **Mark Padmore's** clear, high tenor copes superbly with the role of Jason, with no strain and with cleanly enunciated diction and sharp concern for word-meaning. The others follow Christie's pattern of choosing cleanly focused voices, even if the tone is occasionally gritty.

CHAUSSON, Ernest (1855–99)

Poème for Violin & Orchestra, Op. 25 (Original Version)

(M) *** Avie AV 2091. Graffin, RLPO, Handley – ELGAR: *Violin Concerto* ***

Graffin has an ideal silvery tone for this work, and his performance is richly rhapsodic, with totally idiomatic support from Handley, whose atmospheric opening sets the scene magnetically for his gentle entry. The recording, made in Philharmonic Hall, Liverpool, is warmly full-bodied and very naturally balanced, and the solo violin rides the passionate climax impressively.

Poème for Violin & Orchestra

🎧— (M) **** Decca (ADD) 460 006-2. Chung, RPO, Dutoit – DEBUSSY; FRANCK: *Violin Sonatas* **** ✿

🎧— (M) *** EMI 5 62599-2. Perlman, O de Paris, Martinon (with MASSENET: *Thaïs: Méditation:* Abbey Road Ens., Foster) – RAVEL: *Tzigane;* SAINT-SAËNS: *Introduction and Rondo capriccioso,* etc. ***

(M) **(*) DG 477 7113. Perlman, NYPO, Mehta – ELGAR: *Violin Concerto* **

Chung's performance is deeply emotional, if not as opulent as Perlman's; but, with committed accompaniment from the RPO and excellent (1977) recording, this makes an apt bonus for superb performances of the Debussy and Franck *Violin Sonatas.*

Perlman's 1975 account of Chausson's beautiful *Poème,* with the Orchestre de Paris under Martinon, is a classic account by which all newcomers are measured. A luscious account of the *Thaïs Méditation,* recorded digitally two decades later, has now been added.

Perlman's digital remake, although certainly a fine performance, is not quite its equal. Martinon displayed more subtle feeling for the atmosphere of the piece, while Perlman sounds slightly more detached on DG.

Heifetz too is recorded very closely, as if in the glare of a spotlight, and the performance is robbed of much of its subtlety. Even so, the playing itself is quite remarkable. (09026 61753-2)

Nigel Kennedy's version of the *Poème,* unusually expansive and sensuous, with ripe and powerful build-up of climaxes, comes as a welcome, if not very generous, coupling for his warmly romantic reading of the Tchaikovsky *Concerto,* recorded in similarly rich, full sound. (CfP 585 6192)

(i) Poème for Violin & Orchestra; (ii) Poème de l'amour et de la mer

*** Chan. 8952. (i) Y. P. Tortelier; (ii) Finnie; Ulster O, Tortelier – FAURÉ: *Pavane,* etc. ***

Yan Pascal Tortelier's brings consistent beauty of timbre and, what is more important, refinement of feeling. In the *Poème de l'amour et de la mer* **Linda Finnie** can hold her own with the very best; her feeling for the idiom is completely natural.

Symphony in B flat, Op. 20

🎧— **** Pentatone SACD Surround Sound PTC 5186 078. SRO, Janowski – FRANCK: *Symphony* ***

*** Universal Accord 476 8069. Liège PO, Langree – FRANCK: *Symphony* ***

Symphony in B flat; Soir de fête, Op. 32; La Tempête, Op. 18; Viviane, Op. 5

🎧— *** Chan. 9650. BBC PO, Y. P. Tortelier

Janowski gets very impressive results indeed from the **Suisse Romande Orchestra,** which offers a much weightier and more opulent string sonority here than in earlier recordings, especially for listeners who have the surround sound facility. Indeed this is now the most impressive account of this symphony available, the finest since Monteux, and is a clear first choice for this marvellous work.

Yan Pascal Tortelier and the **BBC Philharmonic** give thoroughly idiomatic and well-played accounts of all these Chausson pieces. They more than hold their own against any of the competitors and, given the excellence of the sound, may well be a first choice for collectors wanting an up-to-date recording of the *Symphony.*

Louis Langree draws a persuasive, totally idiomatic performance from his finely drilled **Belgian Orchestra,** opting for a flowing speed in the central slow movement, marked *Tres lent,* very slow, but never sounding at all rushed. The clarity and immediacy of the sound adds to the impact and, as in the Franck, Chausson's syncopated rhythms come over most persuasively.

CHAMBER MUSIC

Andante & Allegro (for clarinet and piano); Piano Trio in G min., Op. 3; Pièce for Cello & Piano, Op. 39; Poème Op. 25 (arr. for violin, string quartet & piano)

*** Hyp. CDA 67028. Neidlich, Devoyon, Hoffman, Graffin; Chilingirian Qt

The *Poème* appears here in a newly discovered arrangement by the composer. There is a complete naturalness and conviction about this performance in which **Graffin** is a wonderfully persuasive soloist. The remaining pieces, including the early *Piano Trio,* come off well and can hold their own against any rival. The rich acoustic environment enhances the appeal of these dedicated performances.

(i) Concerto for Violin, Piano & String Quartet, Op. 21; Piano Quartet, Op. 30; Piano Trio, Op. 3. String Quartet, Op. 35

*** Talent DOM 381 006/007 (2). Sharon Qt, (i) with Ouziel

The four major chamber works on this two-disc set neatly encompass the full span of Chausson's all-too-short composing career. The *Piano Trio* is a teenage work, written when Chausson was still a student. At the other end of Chausson's career, he failed to complete his *String Quartet,* and it was with the greatest difficulty that his heirs were persuaded to allow Vincent d'Indy to complete the few bars needed to round off the third of the four projected movements. The *Piano Quartet* receives a strong, warm and purposeful performance from the **Sharons**, with **Dalia Ouziel** the excellent, agile pianist. Best known of Chausson's chamber works is the so-called *Concerto* for the unusual combination of piano, violin and string quartet. This version is most persuasive, with hushed tension in the slow movement and winning agility in the finale. Dalia Ouziel at the piano plays with dazzling brilliance and clarity of articulation.

Piano Quartet in A, Op. 30

*** Aeon AECD 0540. Favre, Schumann Qt – FAURÉ: *Piano Quartet 1* ***

(BB) *** Virgin 2x1 4 82061-2 (2). Kandinsky Qt – CASTILLON; LEKEU; SAINT-SAËNS: *Piano Quartets* ***

The first thing that strikes you on the Aeon version is the bright, full sound of **Christian Favre's** piano at the start of the Chausson, and the excellent recorded sound generally adds to the brilliance and persuasiveness of these performances. The precision of ensemble adds greatly to the impact of the strongly rhythmic passages. What seals the quality of the **Schumann Quartet's** performance is their superb reading of the slow movement, marked *Très calme*. From the tender and hushed opening the players build up the argument into a towering climax. Well coupled with the Fauré, this is very recommendable.

The Chausson *Piano Quartet* is the centrepiece of this rewarding Virgin two-CD compilation, and the performance from the early 1990s is most alive and satisfying.

Piano Trio in G min., Op. 3

*** HM HMC 1951967. Trio Wanderer – RAVEL: *Piano Trio* ***

The Chausson *Trio* is rarely encountered in the recital room or, for that matter, on records. The **Trio Wanderer** give a refined and well-shaped account that does justice to this elegant and neglected piece, and they are very well recorded.

Poème (for violin and piano) Op. 25

*** New Note Quartz QTZ 2002. Liebeck, Apekisheva – PROKOFIEV; SAINT-SAËNS; YSAŸE: *Violin Sonatas* ***

Katya Apekisheva's piano introduction prepares the way for **Jack Liebeck's** entry very seductively and his playing is full of passionate feeling. There may be more subtle accounts of Chausson's *Poème* on record, but none more deeply felt or ardent. The balance places the violin vividly forward, but with this degree of passionate advocacy one is swept away, and the close of the piece is exquisitely gentle. The rest of this enterprising début programme is not less stimulating.

String Quartet in C min., Op. 35 (completed d'Indy)

*** Hyp. CDA 67097. Chilingirian Qt. – D'INDY: *String Quartet 1* ***

(BB) *** Naxos 8.553645. Quatuor Ludwig – FRANCK: *Piano Quintet* ***

This superb disc from the **Chilingirians**, sensitively played

and beautifully recorded, is a revelation. Chausson's work, completed by Vincent d'Indy after the composer's tragic death, has echoes of his teacher, Franck, touched in with point and elegance.

The **Quatuor Ludwig** also play it with conviction and aplomb. The recording is excellent.

VOCAL MUSIC

Mélodies (complete)

*** Hyp. CDA 67321/2. Lott, Murray, Trakas, Greevy, Johnson; Chilingirian Qt

These two superb, revelatory discs contain all the regularly published songs of Chausson, plus five songs drawn from manuscript sources. Beautifully performed, they come with the same kind of scholarly notes that **Johnson** provides for his Schubert and Schumann series, plotting the composer's development from his student years to his untimely death in a cycle accident. What consistently comes out far more than in Chausson's instrumental music is his gift of tunefulness, fresh and memorable. Not that they are lacking refinement in any way, and the piano accompaniments, particularly in the early songs, from the sparkling first item, *Les papillons*, are models of refinement and imagination, consistently inspiring Johnson as accompanist.

(i) Chanson perpétuelle, Op. 37; (ii) Poème de l'amour et de la mer, Op. 19; (iii) Mélodies: Le Charme; Le Colibri; La Dernière Feuille; Sérénade italienne; Les Papillons

(BB) *** Warner Apex 0927 48992-2. Norman; (i) Monte Carlo Qt; (ii) Monte Carlo PO, Jordan; (i; iii) Dalberto

Although **Jessye Norman's** account of the glorious *Poème de l'amour et de la mer* does not wholly eclipse memories of Dame Janet Baker's version, it is still very recommendable in its own right. The orchestral texture is splendidly opulent and atmospheric, and Jessye Norman makes an impressive sound throughout. Even if the playing time (45') is comparatively short, this is a real bargain at Apex price.

Poème de l'amour et de la mer, Op. 19

*** Warner 2564 61938-2. Graham, BBC SO, Yan Pascal Tortelier – DEBUSSY: *Poèmes de Charles Baudelaire*; RAVEL: *Shéhérazade* ***

Susan Graham is in her element in Chausson's lovely song cycle, phrasing with a natural sensuous charm and producing an unstrained beauty of line. She is very sensitively accompanied and beautifully recorded. But the great interest of this triptych is the Debussy coupling, re-orchestrated by John Adams.

Le roi Arthus (complete)

*** Telarc CD-80645 (3). Schroeder, Bullock, O'Neill, Le Roux, Okulitch, McIntyre, Apollo Voices, BBC SO, Botstein

Recorded in association with BBC Radio 3, the Telarc version of *Le roi Arthus*, Chausson's opera based on the Arthurian legend, brings out the sensuality of this piece which is much influenced by Wagner. Chausson aimed to transcend that influence, and with sumptuous sound and a passionate approach to the score **Leon Botstein** clearly demonstrates that this is not just a Wagnerian imitation but a work that brings out Chausson's distinctive voice. In its ripe melodic writing it is moving in a way that reminds one that Puccini too was much influenced by Wagner. The dreamy beauty of the first big love duet between Queen Guinevere (in French Genièvre) and Lancelot brings the clearest echoes of the Act II love duet from *Tristan und Isolde*, and the love-triangle, with Arthur himself the rejected husband, directly reflects the situation in Tristan.

CHERUBINI, Luigi (1760–1842)

Anacréon Overture

(***) BBC BBCL mono 4016-2 (2). BBC SO, Toscanini –
BEETHOVEN: *Missa solemnis; Symphony 7* (**(*)); MOZART: *Symphony 35 (Haffner)* (***)

Cherubini's fine *Anacréon Overture* enjoyed considerably more exposure in the 1930s and 1940s. (At the time of writing there is no modern recording at all!) **Toscanini's** account comes from 1935 and finds the **BBC Symphony Orchestra** at its most responsive and alert. For a 1930s broadcast the sound, though not the highest of fi, is really very good indeed.

Symphony in D; Overtures: Faniska; Lodoïsa; Médée

⊕→ ⒝⒝ *** Naxos 557908. Sanremo SO, Bellugi

Cherubini's music was greatly admired by Beethoven, and this fine symphony readily explains why. Its invention is consistently appealing and its structure no less impressive. The layout of the three overtures (again with attractive themes) is said to have influenced Beethoven. They once featured regularly in concert programmes but are now (like the *Symphony*) almost never performed. Fortunately the **Orchestra Sinfonica di Sanremo** is a first-class ensemble and their conductor, **Pieri Bellugi**, provides dramatic and cultured performances of all this music, very well recorded. So this disc cannot be recommended too highly.

String Quartets 1–6

⊕→ Ⓜ *** CPO 999 949-2 (3). Hausmusik

String Quartets 1 in E flat; 2 in C

⊕→ *** BIS CD 1003. David Qt

String Quartets 3 in D min.; 4 in E

*** BIS CD 1004. David Qt

Cherubini's quartets are of very high quality and it is good to have outstanding new recordings of them. Listening to them makes one realize the justice of Beethoven's admiration for the composer, for Cherubini's melodic inspiration

is often distinguished and instinctive, there is always a fine musical intelligence at work and polished craftsmanship is always in evidence.

The first four works bring an exhilarating response from this excellent BIS group, who are superb individual players yet perfectly integrated tonally. They are thoroughly at home in Cherubini's sound-world. In short these modern-instrument performances could hardly be bettered, and the recording, as one expects from this label, is in every way first class.

The performances by **Hausmusik** on period instruments are also of the very highest quality. Although textures are less ample, inner detail is wonderfully clear, there is no lack of warmth and the playing itself is highly eloquent. In short, except for those allergic to period instruments, this set leads the field, and the recording is strikingly vivid and present.

6 Keyboard Sonatas (1783)

⊕→ Ⓝ ✿ **** RCA 88697057742 Bachetti (piano)

Andrea Bacchetti has given us several outstanding new recordings in the present volume (including an impressive DVD of Bach's *Goldberg Variations*), but none is more valuable than this set of Cherubini's *Six Keyboard Sonatas*, published in 1783 but probably written earlier (perhaps 1780). They are most engaging two-movement works, with a strong flavour of early Mozart, but with gallant touches to add charm. Their invention is consistently diverse and in these captivating performances one is drawn to return to them often. They are beautifully recorded and this is a disc to be snapped up before it disappears. Highly recommended indeed.

(i) Coronation Mass in A for King Charles X; March religieuse; (ii) Solemn Mass in G for the Coronation of Louis XVIII; (iii) Requiem in C min.

⊕→ Ⓑ *** EMI Rouge et Noir 5 85258-2 (2). (i) Philh. Ch. & O; (ii) LPO Ch. & O; (iii) Amb. S., Philh. O; Muti

The *G major Mass* was finished in 1819, but meanwhile Louis XVIII had postponed his coronation a number of times, and in the end it never took place, so Cherubini's music remained unperformed and the full score was prepared for publication only recently. As is so often the case with Cherubini, the musical inspiration is not only dignified but noble – and, on occasion, inspired. **Muti** seems persuaded of its distinction and performs the work with dedication and conviction.

The *Coronation Mass for Charles X* dates from 1825 and there are signs in the *Gloria* that Cherubini was influenced by both Beethoven's *Fidelio* and the *Ninth Symphony*, and in the *Incarnatus* and *Crucifixus* by the *Missa solemnis*. But Cherubini's church music has a character of its own, beautifully crafted, with moments of real memorability, such as the closing bars of the *Kyrie*. Muti presents the music with an intensity to hide any limitations, and both chorus and orchestra respond superbly. There is an instrumental appendix in the form of a *Marche religieuse*, a very fine piece. The *C minor Requiem* was praised extravagantly by Berlioz with the claim that 'no other production of this great master can bear any comparison with it for abundance of ideas, fullness of form and sustained sublimity of style'.

Mass 2 in D min.

⊕– 🏵 *** Häns. CD 98.325. Coburn, Kallisch, Thompson, Will, Stuttgart Gächinger Kantorei & Bach Collegium, Rilling

Cherubini began composing his *D minor Mass* in 1811, but added a newly composed *Sanctus* in 1822. Thus it was contemporary with Beethoven's *Missa solemnis*, and it has much of that work's lyrical gravitas and depth. This outstanding Hänssler recording by the **Gächinger Kantorei** and **Stuttgart Bach Collegium** is fully worthy of this glorious work.

Missa Solemnis in E; Motets: Antifona sul canto fermo; Nemo Gaudeat

*** EMI 3 94316-2. Ziesak, Pizzolato, Lippert, Abdrazakov, Bav. R. Ch. & O, Muti

This latest in **Muti's** survey of the music of Cherubini is every bit as successful as previous recordings. Cherubini's music is never less than entertaining, even if it might be said that it is effect over spirituality. The fugato on '*Amen*' which ends the *Credo* is more reminiscent of the opera house than the church, but it is very exciting. Similarly, in that section a series of jabbing heartbeat strokes on the strings leading on to *Et resurrexit* is strikingly dramatic and operatic. The two *Motets* are slighter works, gentle in nature and beautifully sung, making a fine bonus. The *Mass* was recorded live but has been atmospherically and vividly captured, and the audience is very quiet.

Requiem in C min.

ⒷⒷ *** EMI Gemini 5 86239-2 (2). Ambrosian Ch., Philh. O, Muti – VERDI: *Requiem* ***

The *C minor Requiem* was called by Berlioz 'the greatest of the greatest of his [Cherubini's] works'. Muti directs a tough, incisive reading, underlining the drama. The digital recording is excellent.

CHOPIN, Frédéric (1810–49)

DG Complete Chopin Edition

Ⓑ **(*) DG (DDD/ADD) 463 047-2 (17)

To commemorate the 150th anniversary of Chopin's death in 1999, DG assembled for the first time the complete works of Chopin – even making several new recordings to fill in the gaps. There are many outstanding Chopin recordings here notably from Argerich, Pollini and Zimerman, but almost all of these are available separately. However there are several where DG might have made a better choice, the *Waltzes* and *Mazurkas*, for instance. At a bargain price and with a lavishly illustrated booklet, this is still good value, especially for those beginning a Chopin collection. These discs are no longer available separately.

Idil Biret Complete Chopin Edition

Piano Concerto 1, Op. 11; Andante spianato et Grande Polonaise brillante, Op. 22; Fantasia on Polish Airs, Op. 13

ⒷⒷ **(*) Naxos 8.550368 (with Slovak State PO, Stankovsky)

Piano Concerto 2, Op. 21; Krakowiak; Variations on Mozart's 'Là ci darem la mano'

ⒷⒷ ** Naxos 8.550369 (with Slovak State PO, Stankovsky)

Ballades 1–4; Berceuse; Cantabile; Fantaisie; Galop marquis; Largo; Marche funèbre; 3 Nouvelles études

ⒷⒷ ** Naxos 8.550508

Mazurkas, Op. posth.: in D; A flat; B flat; G; C; B flat; Rondos, Op. 1, Op. 16 & Op. 73; Rondo à la Mazurka, Op. 5; Souvenir de Paganini; Variations brillantes; (i) Variations for 4 Hands. Variations on a German Theme; Variations on Themes from 'I Puritani' of Bellini

ⒷⒷ *** Naxos 8.550367 ((i) with Martin Sauer)

Nocturnes 1–21

ⒷⒷ *** Naxos 8.550356/7 (available separately)

Polonaises 1–6; 7 (Polonaise fantaisie)

ⒷⒷ **(*) Naxos 8.550360

Polonaises 8–10, Op. 71; in G min.; B flat; A flat; G sharp min.; B flat min. (Adieu); G flat, all Op. posth.; Andante spianato et Grande Polonaise in E flat, Op. 22 (solo piano version)

ⒷⒷ **(*) Naxos 8.550361

Piano Sonatas 1, Op. 4; 2 (Funeral March); 3, Op. 58

ⒷⒷ *** Naxos 8.550363

The Turkish pianist, **Idil Biret**, has all the credentials for recording Chopin. Among others, she studied with both Cortot and Wilhelm Kempff. She has a prodigious technique and the recordings we have heard so far suggest that overall her Chopin survey is an impressive achievement. Her impetuous style and chimerical handling of phrasing and rubato are immediately obvious in the *First Concerto*, and she makes a commanding entry in the *F minor Concerto*; in the *Larghetto*, too, the solo playing brings a gently improvisatory manner, and the finale really gathers pace only at the entry of the orchestra (which is recorded rather resonantly throughout). Of the other short concertante pieces, the opening of the *Andante spianato* is very delicate and there is some scintillating playing in the following *Grande Polonaise* and *Fantasia on Polish Airs* – and a touch of heaviness, too, in the former. The introductory *Largo* of the *Mozart Variations* is a bit too dreamy and diffuse but, once the famous tune arrives, the performance springs to life. Similarly, the introduction to the charming *Krakowiak Rondo* hangs fire, but again the *Rondo* sparkles, with the rhythmic rubato nicely handled, though the orchestral tuttis could ideally be firmer.

The *Ballades* bring impetuously romantic interpretations where the rubato at times seems mannered; the *Berceuse* is tender and tractable, the *Fantaisie in F minor* begins rather deliberately but opens up excitingly later; though the playing is rather Schumannesque, it is also imaginative; the three *Nouvelles études*, too, are attractively individual.

The disc called *Rondos and Variations* (8.550367) is worth anyone's money, showing Biret's technique at its most prodigious and glittering. Much of the music here is little known and none of it second rate. The *Nocturnes* are a great success in a quite different way: the rubato simple, the playing free and often thoughtful, sometimes dark in timbre, but always spontaneous. The recording is pleasingly full in timbre. The *Polonaises* demonstrate Biret's sinewy strength: the famous *A major* is a little measured but the *A flat* is fresh and exciting and the whole set commanding, while the *Polonaise fantaisie* shows imaginative preparation yet comes off spontaneously like the others. The recital ends with a fine account of the solo piano version of the *Andante spianato* (quite lovely) and *Grande Polonaise*, which is more appealing than the concertante version.

The three *Sonatas* are fitted comfortably on to one CD and, irrespective of cost, this represents one of the finest achievements in Biret's series so far.

OTHER RECORDINGS

Concertos and concertante music

Andante spianato et Grande polonaise, Op. 22

(***) BBC mono 4031-2. Richter, LSO, Kondrashin − LISZT: *Piano Concertos 1–2*, etc. (***)

Both in the *Andante* and the *Polonaise*, **Richter** is at his most magical, not just brilliant but intensely poetic too, the more moving in a live performance. The playing has great delicacy and bravura.

Piano Concertos (i) 1; (ii) 2; (i) Krakowiak Rondo in F, Op. 14; Ballade 3 in A flat, Op. 47; Barcarolle, Op. 60; Berceuse, Op. 57; Impromptus 1–3 & Fantaisie-impromptu; 4 Mazurkas, Op. 41; Nocturnes 1–20; Polonaises 1–7; Polonaise-Fantaisie; 24 Preludes, Op. 28; Scherzos 2 in B flat, Op. 31; 3 in C sharp min., Op. 31 Sonatas 2 (Funeral March) & 3; Waltzes 1–14

Ⓑ **(*) DG stereo/mono 477 5242 (7). Askenase, with (i) Hague Residentie O, Otterloo; (ii) BPO, Lehmann (with MOZART: *Sonata 17, K.570*; LISZT: *Liebestraum 3; Valse oubliée 1*; MENDELSSOHN: *Songs without Words, Op. 19/1–2; Op. 67/4; Scherzo in E min., Op. 16/2*. SCHUBERT: *Medley of Ländler, Waltzes & Valses sentimentales* (arr. Askenase). SMETANA: *4 Polkas*)

Stefan Askenaze was DG's key Chopin recording artist in the early days of LP, and his recording career stretched for two decades, from 1951 to 1971. Many of his finest records were made during the mono era, but the quality of DG piano recording in the 1950s was of such a high standard that all these records sound very well indeed. So, while DG have chosen here his stereo recording of the *First Piano Concerto* plus the charming *Krakowiak Rondo*, they have preferred the mono version of the *Second* because of the highly sympathetic accompaniment from the **Berlin Philharmonic** under **Fritz Lehmann**. The *Waltzes* (1951), with which this survey opens, were long regarded as a gramophone classic in their Heliodor LP format.

The *Second* and *Third Sonatas* (also 1951), *24 Preludes* (1953) and *Nocturnes* (1954) are also all mono recordings, although one would hardly guess it from the quality of the sound. The *Sonatas* are outstanding, showing Askenase to be a magician among Chopin pianists. The *24 Preludes* are hardly less impressive and are played with great sympathy and insight. In the *Nocturnes* his finely graded colours and great sensitivity to dynamic are again admirably enhanced by the excellent recording.

Characteristically, there is no barnstorming in the *Polonaises* (again mono, 1951/2). As always, Askenase relies on subtlety and imagination rather than sheer volume, and, being a Pole, he seems naturally to inflect the polonaise rhythms with an infectious lift. The *Barcarolle*, *Berceuse*, *Ballade 3*, *Scherzi*, *Impromptus*, *Op. 41*, and *Mazurkas* are among his later recordings and the stereo shows him still on top form.

Piano Concerto 1 in E min., Op. 11

Ⓑ (***) Archipel mono ARPCD 0373. Rubinstein, Barbirolli − SUPPÉ: *Overtures* (***)

Rubinstein's magical 1937 (originally EMI) recording of the *E minor Concerto* is offered as an extraordinary 'bonus' for **Barbirolli's** zestful 1957 collection of Suppé *Overtures*. It is a bonus indeed, for the transfer is absolutely faithful and few apologies have to be made for the sound: if the tutti violins are a bit thin, the piano is reproduced most faithfully.

(i) Piano Concertos 1–2. Ballades 1–4; Barcarolle; Fantasia in F min.; Impromptus 1–4 (Fantaisie-impromptu); Nocturnes 1–21; Preludes 1–28; Scherzos 1–4; Waltzes 1–19.

Ⓑ **(*) Ph. (ADD) 468 391-2 (7). Arrau; (i) with LPO, Inbal

Arrau's survey was recorded over a decade in the 1970s. The two piano concertos came first and set the seal on his approach: immaculately aristocratic, but with personal touches of rubato which will not convince everybody. The *Préludes* followed in 1974, with each and every one bearing the imprint of a strong personality to which not all listeners respond. Yet these performances appear to spring from a strong inner conviction. The *Ballades*, too, are particularly impressive and, as always with the Philips recordings of this artist, there is unfailing beauty of tone. Some of the rubato Arrau adopts in the *Nocturnes* may again strike some listeners as a shade too personal, but his artistry is unique and he is eminently well served by the engineers.

Piano Concertos 1 in E min.; 2 in F min.

☛ 🏵 **** MDG 340 1267-2. Zacharias, Lausanne CO

⊶ Ⓜ *** RCA (ADD) **SACD** 82876 67902-2. Rubinstein, London New SO, Skrowaczewski, or Symphony of the Air, Wallenstein

Ⓜ *** EMI 5 03412-2. Argerich, Montreal SO, Dutoit

ⒷⒷ *** Regis RRC 1096. Tirimo, Philh. O, Glushchenko

Zacharias directs the **Lausanne Chamber Orchestra** from the keyboard, and the opening tuttis of both first movements have never been more commandingly full of life and grace. Zacharias finds new insights in both works and notably in the development section of the *F minor Concerto*. Both slow movements are magical and the finales sparkle, without putting virtuosity before musical values. The sound is well up to MDG standards. A disc to treasure.

Rubinstein's shaping of the main theme of the *E minor Concerto* is memorable and in the *Larghetto* his control of colour and rubato are inimitable. Again in the *F minor Concerto*, although the Carnegie Hall acoustic proved less than ideal, Rubinstein's contribution is an object lesson in the delicate playing of Chopin's poetic moments; his rubato is so natural that the music sounds as if it were extemporized and the new SACD transfer makes the very most of the sound.

In **Martha Argerich's** newest EMI coupling her pianism remains as mercurial and her virtuosity as incandescent as ever; indeed, she has rarely sounded as captivating or characterful. **Charles Dutoit** gets good playing from the **Montreal Orchestra**.

Martino Tirimo's readings often bring exquisite delicacy and they are totally without barnstorming, yet there is spontaneity in every bar, and both slow movements bring playing where one has an impression of musing reverie. In outer movements passagework is scintillatingly alive, and finales have a beguiling rhythmic lift.

Piano Concerto 1 in E min., Op. 11

⊶ **** DG 477 640-2. Li, Philh. O, A. Davis – LISZT: *Piano Concerto 1* ****

Ⓜ *** DG (ADD) 449 719-2. Argerich, LSO, Abbado – LISZT: *Concerto 1* ***

ⒷⒷ **(*) Naxos 8.550292. Székely, Budapest SO, Németh – LISZT: *Concerto 1* **(*)

(i) Piano Concerto 1. Ballade 1; Nocturnes 4 & 5, Op. 15/1–2; 7, Op. 27/1; Polonaise 6, Op. 53

⊶ Ⓜ *** EMI (ADD) 5 67548-2. Pollini, (i) Philh. O, Kletzki

(i) Piano Concerto 1. Berceuse; Fantaisie in F min., Op. 49; Fantaisie-impromptu

*** DG 457 585-2. Pires, (i) COE, Krivine

Yundi Li won the Chopin Warsaw competition in 2000 when he was still a teenager. Thus he is in the lineage of Pollini, Argerich and Zimerman, and he lives up to it in this, his debut concerto disc. His playing is so fresh and natural and his virtuosity is worn so lightly.

Pollini's classic recording still remains among the best available of the *E minor Concerto*. This is playing of such total

spontaneity, poetic feeling and refined judgement that criticism is silenced. The additional items come from Pollini's first EMI solo recital, and the playing is equally distinguished, the recording truthful.

Maria João Pires's concerns centre on the more inward-looking side of Chopin rather than its incandescence or brilliance, but this is a performance of substance and she is given eminently responsive support from the **Chamber Orchestra of Europe** and **Emmanuel Krivine**. The solo pieces are thoughtful, sensitive accounts and there are no quarrels with the DG recording.

With persuasive support from **Abbado**, **Martha Argerich** provides some lovely playing, especially in the slow movement. Perhaps in the passagework she is rather too intense, but this is far preferable to the rambling style we are sometimes offered.

Piano Concerto 2 in F min., Op. 21

ⒷⒷ (***) Naxos mono 8.110612. Cortot, O, Barbirolli – SCHUMANN: *Concerto* (***)

(i) Piano Concerto 2. Ballades 1–4; Barcarolle, Op. 60; Berceuse (2 versions); Chants polonais (trans. Liszt); Etudes, Op. 10/1–12 (2 versions); Op. 25/1–12 (2 versions); Nouvelles études; Impromptus, Op. 29, 36; Nocturnes Op. 9/2; 15/1–2; 27/1; 55/1–2; 24 Preludes; Prelude in C sharp min., Op. 45; Piano Sonatas 2; 3; Waltzes 1–14

Ⓜ (***) EMI mono 7 67359-2 (6). Cortot, (i) with O, Barbirolli

Cortot, who recorded so much Chopin between the wars and for so many embodied the spirit of Chopin at that period, never committed the *E minor Concerto* to disc. The *Second*, recorded in 1935 at the Abbey Road Studios, sounds wonderfully fresh and is as individual as one would expect from this great artist. Mark Obert-Thorn gets a very good sound from the shellac originals.

Cortot's spontaneity, poetic feeling and keyboard refinement are also heard to prodigal effect on the six EMI CDs.

Les Sylphides (ballet; orch. Douglas)

⊶ ✸ Ⓑ **** DG (ADD) 459 645-2 (2). BPO, Karajan (with DELIBES: *Coppélia*: suite; OFFENBACH: *Gaîté parisienne*: excerpts and music by GOUNOD; PONCHIELLI; TCHAIKOVSKY***)

Karajan conjures consistently beautiful playing from the **Berlin Philharmonic Orchestra**, and he evokes a delicacy of texture which delights the ear throughout. The sound is full and atmospheric, and this is one of Karajan's very finest recordings. The couplings are hardly less impressive.

CHAMBER MUSIC

Cello Sonata in G min., Op. 65; Grand duo concertante in E on Themes from Meyerbeer's 'Robert le Diable'; Nocturne in C sharp min., Op. posth. (arr. Piatigorsky); Etudes: in E min., Op. 25/7; D min., Op. 10/6 (arr. Glazunov; ed. Feuermann); Waltz in A min., Op. 34/3 (arr. Ginsburg)

☛—⊞ (BB) *** Naxos 8.553159. Kliegel, Glemser

Fresh and ardent performances of the *Sonata* and the remaining two pieces that comprise Chopin's complete output for cello and piano. These gifted and accomplished young artists are very well recorded indeed.

Cello Sonata, Op. 63. Etudes: Op. 10/3; Op.10/5 (trans. Glazunov). Op. 23/7; Introduction & Polonaise Brillante, Op. 3; Nocturnes: 16, Op. 35/2; 19, Op. 72/1 (arr. Mørk/Stott); 20, Op. posth. Preludes: 4 (arr. Mørk/Stott); 6. Waltz 3, Op. 14/2

*** Virgin Classics 385784-2. Mørk, Stott

This collection of cello music centres on the two original cello works that Chopin wrote, one from either end of his career, the very early *Introduction and Polonaise brillant*, written when he was still in his teens, and the *Cello Sonata*, which was one of his last works, much influenced in its dark intensity by the break-up of his deep relationship with the novelist George Sand. It would be hard to imagine a more powerful account of the *Sonata* than this one from the superb Norwegian cellist, **Truls Mørk**, well matched by the pianist **Kathryn Stott**. There is similar rhythmic resilience in Mørk's performance of the *Andante and Grande Polonaise brillante*, with a delicious spring in the main polonaise theme, and with a thrilling speeding-up in the final coda. The cello transcriptions that make up the rest of the programme are also very effective. Most haunting is the *Valse melancolique* which the *Waltz*, Op, 14, No. 2 becomes. The recording helps, made in collaboration with Norwegian Radio in the warm acoustic of Ostre Fredikstad Church in Norway, which suggests a substantial scale in the cello sound.

Cello Sonata in G min., Op. 65

(N) **** Hyp. CDA 67624. Gerhardt, Osborne – ALKAN: *Cello Sonata* ***

(B) *** EMI Debut 3 59645-2. Harwood, Berner (with GLAZUNOV: *Chant du Ménestral*; POPPER: *Elfentanz.*; OFFENBACH: *Les Larmes de Jacqueline* ***) – BEETHOVEN: *Cello Sonata 3* ***

(B) *** EMI 5 74333-2 (2). Tortelier, Ciccolini – FAURÉ; MENDELSSOHN; RACHMANINOV: *Cello Sonatas* ***

A lovely, rapt, beautifully played and recorded account of Chopin's surprisingly complex *Cello Sonata* on Hyperion. Both soloist and accompanist seem to perform as one and both artists' immaculate phrasing amazes. The rare coupling makes this disc especially appealing and the sleeve notes by Kenneth Hamilton are fascinating.

    Richard Harwood, one of the outstanding young cellists of his generation, gives a compelling reading of the Chopin *Cello Sonata*, bringing out the qualities which – perhaps surprisingly – link it with the Beethoven *Sonata*, which provides the principal coupling. His expressive rubato is never excessive, yet the warmth of the inspiration is carried over strongly, with incisive attack in the *Allegros*.

    Tortelier's recordings of the Chopin and Rachmaninov *Sonatas*, which were made in the 1960s in the Salle Wagram,

come up sounding fresh. They occupied a commanding position in the catalogue during the early 1970s, and rightly so!

Piano Trio in G min., Op. 8

(BB) *** Warner Apex 0927 40822-2. Trio Fontenay – SMETANA: *Piano Trio* **

The **Trio Fontenay** give a vividly characterized and well-projected account of the *Piano Trio*, written when Chopin was 18 and not exactly one of his greatest works. Good, clear recording.

PIANO MUSIC

Vladimir Ashkenazy Chopin Edition

Albumblatt in E; Allegro de concert in A, Op. 46; Barcarolle; Berceuse; Boléro in A min., Op. 19; 2 Bourrées; Cantabile in B flat; Fugue in A min.; Galop marquis; Hexameron: Variation in E min.; Largo in E flat; 3 Nouvelles études; Rondo in E flat, Op. 16; Souvenir de Paganini; Tarantelle in A flat, Op. 43; Variations brillantes in B flat, Op. 12; Wiosna (Spring) from Op. 74/2. Ballades 1–4; Scherzi 1–4. 12 Etudes, Op. 10; 12 Etudes, Op. 25. Impromptus 1–3; 4 (Fantaisie-impromptu). 24 Preludes, Op. 28; Preludes: in C sharp min., Op. 45; in A flat. Mazurkas 1–29; 30–68 (including 2 versions of Op. 68/4). Nocturnes 1–12; 13–21. Polonaises 1–6; 7, Polonaise-fantaisie; 8–16. Sonatas 1–3; Contredanse in G flat; 3 Ecossaises; Marche funèbre in C min., Op. 72/2; Rondos: in C min., Op. 1; à la Mazur in F, Op. 5; in C, Op. 73; Variations on a German National Air; Variations in D (for piano duet – with Vovka Ashkenazy). Sonatas; Fantaisie in F min. Waltzes 1–19

(B) *** Decca (ADD/DDD) 443 738-2 (13)

Ashkenazy made his Chopin recordings for Decca over a decade from 1974 to 1984, using seven different locations, yet the recorded sound is remarkably consistent, always natural in colour and balance and with a good presence, whether from an analogue or a digital source. Consistently persuasive, these readings combine poetry with flair and (as in the *Ballades*) often bring a highly communicated warmth. The bravura brings genuine panache, whether in the large-scale, virtuoso pieces like the *Scherzi* or in the chimerical approach to a miniature like the *Souvenir de Paganini*. At bargain price this set makes an unbeatable investment.

Allegro de concert, Op. 46; Etudes, Opp. 10 & 25; 3 Nouvelles Etudes

(M) (***) EMI (mono) 3 79888-2. Arrau

Immaculately cultured playing distinguishes these celebrated 1956 recordings which well deserve their legendary status. Remarkably fresh sound.

Andante spianato & Grande Polonaise brillante, Op. 22; Ballades 1–4; Mazurkas, Op. 24/2; Op. 56/3; Op.

59/1–3; 3 Nouvelles Etudes; Nocturne in B, Op. 62/1; Polonaise fantaisie, Op. 61; Scherzos 1–3

(M) *** RCA 82876 72554-2 (2). Ax

Emanuel Ax is much less well-known in England than he is in the USA, where he has the highest reputation, especially in the music of Chopin. This two-disc recital shows why. Although recorded at different times, between 1975 and 1987, and at different venues, the playing has the vibrant projection of a live recital, with a consistent flow of spontaneous feeling, only very occasionally affected by touches of self-consciousness. The recording is at times a little hard, but the piano is given striking presence and realism.

Andante spianato & Grande Polonaise brilliante; Barcarolle in F sharp; Berceuse in D flat; Nocturnes 1–19; Scherzi 1–4; Waltz in A flat, Op. 34/1

⊕ 🌑 (M) (***) EMI (mono) 5 09668-2 (2). Rubinstein

Just as **Rubinstein's** later RCA stereo set of *Nocturnes* have (temporarily, we hope) vanished from the British catalogue, EMI have chosen to reissue some of his earlier Chopin recordings, made between 1928 and 1937, as (rightly) one of their 'Great Recordings of the Century'. They are indeed the lynchpin of the recorded Chopin repertoire and many of these performances have not been equalled or surpassed, even by Rubinstein himself. The current remastering by Andrew Walter has removed almost all the background noise, and the mono piano recording is miraculously real and vivid.

(i) Andante spianato & Grande Polonaise brillante; (ii) Polonaises 1–7; (iii) 3 Polonaises, Op. 71; 6 Polonaises, Op. posth.; Album Leaf in E; 2 Bourrées; Cantabile in B flat; Fugue in A min.; Galop marquis in A flat; Largo in E flat

(M) *** DG (DDD/ADD) 2-CD 477 5430 (2). (i) Argerich; (ii) Pollini; (iii) Ugorski

This is a straight reissue of Volume 5 from DG's Chopin Edition. **Pollini** offers magisterial playing, in some ways more commanding than Rubinstein (and better recorded) though not more memorable. **Argerich's** *Andante spianato* (1974) is everything it should be: wonderfully relaxed to start with and extrovertly sparkling in the *Grande Polonaise*. **Ugorski** fills in the gaps with some of Chopin's early works: interesting to hear, sometimes entertaining, but containing only glimpses of the greatness that was to emerge. Excellent value.

Ballades 1–4, Op. 23; Op. 38; Op. 47; & Op. 52; Barcarolle, Op. 60; Fantasia, Op. 49; Scherzo 2 B flat min., Op. 31; Nocturne F sharp, Op. 15/2

(N) *** DG DVD 40 073 4449. Krystian Zimerman – SCHUBERT: 4 *Impromptus, D. 899* ***

Krystian Zimerman's pianism has exceptional control and tonal subtlety and his account of the *Ballades* has an aristocratic polish and an authority that silences criticism. Flawless playing which to quote Jeremy Siepman, 'never courts the listener with effects'. The recital comes from February 1987 and is directed by Humphrey Burton and Horant Holfelt without recourse to any eccentric camera angles or other visual gimmicks that detract from the musical effects. They are unafraid to leave the camera angle in the same place for as long as the eye requires. The sound has clarity and presence. The Schubert *Impromptus* are every bit as distinguished as the Chopin.

Ballades 1–4; Barcarolle; Fantaisie in F min.

⊕ *** DG 423 090-2. Zimerman

Ballades 1–4; Nocturnes 1–21 (complete)

(B) *** Double Decca (ADD) 452 579-2 (2). Ashkenazy

Ballades 1–4; Scherzi 1–4

⊕ (M) *** RCA **SACD** (ADD) 82876 61396-2. Rubinstein

*** Hyp. CDA 67456. Hough

Ballades 1–4; Scherzi 1–4; Prelude, Op. 45

⊕ (M) *** Decca (ADD) 466 499-2. Ashkenazy

Krystian Zimerman's impressive set of the *Ballades* and the other two works on this disc are touched by distinction throughout and have spontaneity as well as tremendous concentration to commend them, and the modern digital recording is of fine DG quality.

However, **Rubinstein's** readings are unique and the digital remastering has been highly successful. The performances of the *Ballades* are a miracle of creative imagination, with Rubinstein at his most inspired. The *Scherzi*, which gain most of all from the improved sound (they were originally very dry), are both powerful and charismatic, and the recording is further enhanced on SACD.

Among present-day pianists, **Stephen Hough** has not only the keyboard virtuosity but also the vision and poetic insight this music calls for. His playing serves as a reminder of just what an original master Chopin was and how vital was his genius. One of the best modern versions of either sets of pieces.

Ashkenazy's readings of the *Ballades* are thoughtful and essentially unflashy; the rubato arises naturally from his personal approach to the music. The intimacy of the recording allows him to share this with the listener. The recording is admirably natural and satisfying. The *Nocturnes* were recorded over a decade, from 1975 to 1984. The playing is splendidly imaginative and atmospheric.

Those wanting the alternative coupling with the *Scherzi* will find the reissue in Decca's 'Legends' series equally attractive. In the *Scherzi* the playing is chimerically dazzling, and the isolated Op. 45 C *sharp minor Prelude*, a pianistic tone-poem in its own right, makes an ideal interlude before the *B minor Scherzo* bursts in on the listener. Very good recording, particularly impressive in the *Scherzi*, which have a fine depth of sonority.

Berceuse; Fantaisie in F min.; Scherzi 1–4

*** Chan. 9018. Shelley

Howard Shelley has the advantage of a sympathetic recording. But there is freshness and tenderness about his approach and, though he is obviously totally inside this music, he manages to convey the feeling that he is discovering it for the first time.

(i) *Berceuse in D flat, Op. 57;* (ii) *Cantabile in B flat; Contredanse in G flat;* (iii) *Etudes, Op. 10/1–10; Op. 25/1–10;* (iv) *3 Nouvelles Etudes;* (v) *Impromptus 1–3; Fantaisie impromptu, Op. 66; 19 Waltzes*

(BB) *** EMI Gemini (ADD/DDD) 3 50874-2 (2). (i) Barenboim; (ii) Barto; (iii) Gavrilov; (iv) Laval; (v) Anievas

Gavrilov's *Etudes* bring an exuberant virtuosity that it is impossible to resist, even if some of the tempi are breathtakingly fast. Yet the sustained legato of the famous *3 in E major* is lovely, and Gavrilov's poetic feeling, both here and in *6 in E flat minor*, is indisputable. For the three *Nouvelles Etudes* EMI turn to Danielle Laval, who is less extrovert than Gavrilov but no less convincing.

Anievas gives us all the *Waltzes*. His playing is quite different from Gavrilov's and has a mellower, beautiful, analogue piano recording to match. Yet his technique is absolutely secure, and there is much to enjoy. He is also very successful in characterizing the three *Impromptus*, and the *Fantaisie-impromptu* (which is used to open the second disc) certainly does not lack panache. The two miniatures, *Cantabile* and the *Contredanse in G flat*, which come at the end of the recital, are inconsequential, but **Tzimon Barto** brings out their guileless charm, and the second disc ends with a simple, poetic account of the lovely *Berceuse* from **Daniel Barenboim**, very naturally recorded.

24 Etudes, Op. 10 & Op. 25

(N) (M) *** Decca (ADD) 478 0350 Ashkenazy

Etudes, Op. 10/1–12; Op. 25/1–12; 3 Nouvelles études

⊕─ 🏵 **** Erato 8573-80228-2 (2). Lugansky

⊕─ (BB) *** Warner Apex 8573 89083-2. Berezovsky

*** Chan. 8482. Lortie

Etudes, Op. 10/1–12; Op. 25/1–12; Impromptus 1–3; Fantaisie-impromptu

⊕─ 🏵 (M) *** Sony SK61885. Perahia

*** DG (ADD) 413 794-2. Pollini (*Études* only)

Etudes, Op. 10/1–12; Op. 25/1–12; Fantaisie in F min., Op. 49; Sonatas 1–3

⊕─ (BB) *** Double Decca (ADD) 466 250-2 (2). Ashkenazy

Murray Perahia's expressive range, variety of keyboard colour and musical imagination are of exceptional quality. His virtuosity is totally self-effacing, so that the listener's engagement with Chopin's world is complete. The value of the set is further enhanced by the outstanding quality of the recorded sound.

Nikolai Lugansky produces a beautiful sound at every

dynamic and is unconcerned with showmanship or high-voltage display. He is a real artist with consummate delicacy of fingerwork and fluidity of phrasing. A most distinguished and valuable recording.

Ashkenazy recorded his Chopin survey as far as possible in chronological order. The sets of *Etudes* from 1975 offer playing of total mastery and are also available separately (478 0 350). The *C minor Sonata* (No. 1) is an early work (1827) and not deeply characteristic. Ashkenazy's account (1976) enjoys classic status. His 1980 performance of the *Funeral March Sonata* (No. 2) is no less dazzling than his earlier live recording of 1972 and in some respects surpasses it. It has wonderful panache. The *B minor Sonata*, recorded a year later, is also memorable and involving. An authoritative account of the *F minor Fantasy* provides an excellent makeweight in very realistic sound.

Marvellous playing, too, from the 23-year-old **Boris Berezovsky** in 1991. Just try the dazzling Op. 10/2 or the gentle poetry of the famous *E major Etude* which follows, while the three final *Studies* of Op. 25 show his wide range of dynamic, natural sensitivity and compelling power. In short this is a thrilling disc, and would be highly recommendable even if it cost far more.

Louis Lortie's set of the 24 *Etudes* can also hold its own with the best. His playing has a strong poetic feeling and an effortless virtuosity. He is beautifully recorded at The Maltings, Snape (the acoustics of which occasionally cloud the texture).

Pollini's record comes from 1975 and sounds splendidly fresh in its digitally remastered form. These are vividly characterized accounts, masterly and with the sound eminently present, although not as full in sonority as the more recent versions.

(i) *Études, Opp. 10 & 25;* (ii) *24 Preludes, Op. 28;* (iii) *Sonata 2 in B flat min., Op. 35*

*** BBC/Opus Arte **DVD** OA 0893 D. (i) Freddy Kempf; (ii) Perl; (iii) Hewitt

The *Preludes* were recorded by **Alfredo Perl** in Hopetoun House, Edinburgh, **Kempf's** *Etudes* in France at Château de Neuville, Gambais, and **Angela Hewitt's** Op. 35 at Wimbledon Theatre. In all three instances the performances are of quality and are free from any intrusive idiosyncrasies. Moreover, the camerawork in each location is of the old school, never fussy or wanting to draw attention to itself, but managed with discretion and taste. This DVD is very modestly priced, given the amount of music offered, and will give much pleasure.

Etudes, Op. 10/6; Op. 25/3–4, 10–11; 4 Mazurkas, Op. 17; Piano Sonata 3 in B min., Op. 58

(B) *** Virgin 4 82120-2. Andsnes

Andsnes proves as impressive an interpreter of Chopin as he is of Grieg, and here he has the advantage of state-of-the-art piano-sound. The programme here is arbitrary, but every piece is illuminatingly played.

Etudes, Op. 25/1–12; 24 Preludes, Op.28; Sonata 2 in B flat min., Op. 35 (Funeral March)

*** Opus 111 OP 30-289 (2). Sokolov

Grigory Sokolov's electrifying playing of the *Etudes*, Op. 25, and of the *Second Piano Sonata* is something of a must: he is a virtuoso whose technique is matched by real insight.

Fantasy in F min., Op. 49; Piano Sonata 3, Op. 38

Ⓜ *** EMI (ADD) 5 62884-2. Arrau (with MENDELSSOHN: *Andante and Rondo capriccioso*; WEBER: *Konzertstück****)

Arrau was on his finest form in 1960 when he recorded the *B minor Sonata* and the forthright reading of the *Fantasy in F minor*. In the Sonata he evokes a dreamy quality in the quieter music – the *Largo* is especially beautiful – yet he can find plenty of vigour for stronger writing. This is a very fine performance indeed and he is very seductive in the delightful fairy world of Mendelssohn's *Andante and Rondo capriccioso*, an excellent mono recording from 1951.

Mazurkas 1–59, Op. 6/1–4; Op. 7/1–5; Op. 17/1–4; Op. 24/1–4; Op. 30/1–4; Op. 33/1–4; Op. 41/1–4; Op. 50/1–3; Op. 56/1–3; Op. 59/1–3; Op. 63/1–3; Op. 67/1–4; Op. 68/1–4 & Op. 68/4 (revised version); 60–68, Op. posth.

🅑 *** Double Decca DDD/ADD 448 086-2 (2). Ashkenazy

As can be seen, **Ashkenazy's** survey of Chopin's *Mazurkas* is the most comprehensive available. They are finely articulated, aristocratic accounts and he includes all the posthumously published *Mazurkas*. The Decca recordings (often digital) are more modern and more natural than that afforded to Rubinstein.

Nocturnes 1–21

*** DG 447 096-2 (2). Pires

🅱🅱 *** Arte Nova 74321 82185-2 (2). Castro

🅑 *** DG 453 022-2 (2). Barenboim

Nocturnes 1–21; Barcarolle; Fantaisie in F min.

Ⓜ *** Ph. (ADD) 464 694-2 (2). Arrau

Nocturnes 1–21; Impromptus 1–3, 4 (Fantaisie-impromptu)

*** Hyp. CDA 67371/2. Hewitt

Pires gives performances of great character, her playing often bold as well as meltingly romantic and brings the right poetic feel to this music. Hers is the art that conceals art, and that serves the composer to perfection. She uses the widest dynamic range and is recorded with a brilliant presence as well as a basically warm sonority. A well chosen selection is also available (477 7583).

Angela Hewitt is so established in the public consciousness as an eminent Bach interpreter that the idea of her playing anything else seems as unlikely as it was with Rosalyn Tureck. This Chopin is no less authentic in feeling and magisterial in accomplishment. A very satisfying collection and beautifully recorded too.

Ricardo Castro offers a series of performances to compete with almost any in the catalogue. The degree of concentration and thoughtful simplicity of approach is consistent throughout both discs, his nuancing and rubato managed with convincing spontaneity. The recording, made in two quite different venues, is of high quality, clear and natural.

Barenboim recorded the *Nocturnes* in 1981 and he was very beautifully recorded. Phrasing is beautifully moulded, seemingly spontaneous, thoughtful and poetic, and becoming really impetuous only in the music's more passionate moments.

Arrau's approach creates tonal warmth coupled with inner tensions of the kind one expects in Beethoven and this is a very compelling cycle, full of poetry, the rubato showing an individual but very communicable sensibility. Although Arrau's Chopin is seldom mercurial, it is never inflexible, and it has its own special insights.

Nocturnes 1–21; 24 Preludes, Op. 28; Preludes 25–6

🅱🅱 **(*) EMI Gemini (ADD) 5 86507-2 (2). Ohlsson

Garrick Ohlsson recorded the *Polonaises*, then the *Preludes* (in 1974), and between 1977 and 1979 the *Nocturnes*, all at Abbey Road. He is thoughtful and often engagingly poetic. He is always at the service of the composer and is seldom wilful. The penultimate *Prelude in C sharp minor*, Op. 45, is particularly beautiful; then he throws off the brief, posthumous *A flat* work to make a neat conclusion. He is at his very best in the *Nocturnes*, played with pleasing flexibility and control of colour, the rubato spontaneous and nicely judged. He is well recorded, with the sound in the *Nocturnes* often very good indeed.

Nocturnes 1–19; Scherzi 1–4

🅱🅱 (**(*)) Naxos mono 8.110659/60. Rubinstein

The Naxos transfers are of **Rubinstein's** London recordings made at Abbey Road in 1932 (the *Scherzi*) and 1937 (the *Nocturnes*). They are transferred from 78-r.p.m. originals (in excellent condition) by Stuart Rosenthal, with some background noise still present at times. One also feels that in the *Nocturnes* a little more space could have been allowed between each piece. But although the sound is less impressive, not as wide-ranging as EMI's own transfers, this is fair value at the Naxos price.

Nocturnes in E flat, Op. 9/2; F, F sharp & G min., Op. 15/1–3; C sharp min., Op. 27/1; B, Op. 32/1; G, G min., Op. 37/1–2; C min., F sharp min., Op. 48/1–2; F min., Op. 55; E, Op. 62/2; E min., Op. 72/1 (posth.)

Ⓜ *** DG Entrée 471 743-2. Barenboim

This well-chosen collection of 13 *Nocturnes* drawn from **Barenboim's** 1980 complete survey is eminently recommendable. But Ricardo Castro offers all 21 on Arte Nova – see above – for the same cost, and his admirably recorded performances are every bit as enticing as these.

Polonaises 1–16, Op. 26/1–2; Op. 40/1–2; Op. 44; Op. 53; Polonaise-fantaisie, Op. 61; Op. 71/1–3; Op. posth./1–6. Albumblatt; Allegro de concert, Op. 46;

Barcarolle; Berceuse; 2 Bourrées; 3 Nouvelles études; Fugue in A min.; Galop marquis; Tarantelle in A flat; Wiosna (arr. from Op. 74/2)

⊕ (B) *** Double Decca ADD/DDD 452 167-2 (2). Ashkenazy

Polonaises 1–7; Andante spianato et Grande Polonaise brillante

⊕ (M) *** RCA (ADD) 09026 63048-2. Rubinstein

⊕ *** DG SACD 471 648-2; (M) CD 457 711-2. Pollini

Ashkenazy's performances of the *Polonaises* are of the highest calibre and the recording is of Decca's best. The second CD contains some items that are quite short (the piano transcription of Chopin's song *Wiosna* lasts for barely a minute, but it is very fetching). But there are substantial works too: the *Barcarolle* and *Berceuse*, the latter meltingly done, and the *Allegro de concert* and *Nouvelles études* also show Ashkenazy at his finest. At Double Decca price this pair of CDs is self-recommending.

Master pianist that he was, **Rubinstein** seems actually to be rethinking and re-creating each piece, even the hackneyed *Military* and *A flat* works, at the very moment of performance in this recording, made in Carnegie Hall. His easy majesty and natural sense of spontaneous phrasing give this collection a special place in the catalogue, and the *Andante spianato and Grande Polonaise* obviously inspire him.

Pollini's set offers playing of outstanding mastery as well as subtle poetry, and the DG engineers have made a satisfactory job of the new transfer, although the hardness on top remains something to which the ear must adjust.

24 Preludes, Op. 28; Ballades 1 G min. Op. 23; 2 F, Op. 38; 3 A flat, Op. 47; 4 F min., Op. 52. Fantaisie-impromptu in C sharp min., Op. 66

(N) (BB) (***) Naxos mono 8.111118 Moiseiwitsch

24 Preludes, Op. 28; Preludes 25–26; Scherzi 1–4; Waltzes 1–19

⊕ (B) *** Double Decca (ADD) 460 991-2 (2). Ashkenazy

24 Preludes, Op. 28; Prelude in C sharp min., Op. 45. Andante spianato et Grande Polonaise, Op. 22; Polonaise-fantaisie in A flat, Op. 61

⊕ *** Chan. 9597. Lortie

24 Preludes, Op. 28; Scherzi 1–4

*** Naim NAIMCD 028. Gimse

26 Preludes; Berceuse in D flat; Polonaise-fantaisie, Op. 61; Souvenir de Paganini; Introduction & Variations on a theme from Herold's Ludovic

(N) (B) *** CfP (ADD) 5 21849-2 Barenboim

Ashkenazy's 1979 set of the *Preludes* combines drama and power with finesse and much poetic delicacy when called

for. The *Waltzes* were recorded over the best part of a decade. There is an impressive feeling for line throughout, an ability to make each waltz seem spontaneous and yet as carefully wrought as a tone-poem. The *Scherzi* have characteristic panache, the playing imbued with imaginative insights and spontaneity. Again excellent recording.

Louis Lortie's expertly recorded account of the *Preludes* is among the best we have had in recent years. He has poetic feeling, character and finesse in equal measure. Not all his interpretative decisions will convince everyone, but on the whole this is enjoyable and distinguished Chopin playing.

Håvard Gimse is a cultured player whose talent is primarily lyrical. He is at his best in the self-communing, poetic side of these wonderful pieces but there is no want of fire, though perhaps more could be made of the dramatic and dynamic contrasts in the *B minor Scherzo*. The Sofienberg Church in Oslo offers an excellent acoustic and the recording is pleasingly natural.

Moiseiwitsch's Chopin was issued on plum-label 78 rpm discs but there is nothing here that is anything other than top-drawer. The *Preludes* were recorded in 1948–9, the first three *Ballades* in 1939 and the last in 1948. The *Fantaisie-impromptu* which he often programmed, comes from 1952. Ward Marston gets exemplary results and gets freshness and colour into the sound. There are excellent and well-researched notes by Jonathan Summers, a model of their kind. Not to be missed.

Recorded in 1976, **Barenboim's** account of the *Preludes* is thoroughly satisfying, even if it does not quite match Ashkenzay or Lortie, and the two rarities which complete the disc are sparklingly played. Excellent value

Scherzi 1–4; Introduction & Variations on a German Air; Variations on 'Là ci darem la mano', Op. 2

(BB) **(*) Hyp. Helios CDH 55181. Demidenko

Nikolai Demidenko plays with magisterial keyboard authority and command of colour. There are narcissistic and idiosyncratic touches to which not all listeners will respond; all the same, there is still much that will (and does) give pleasure.

Scherzi 1–4; Preludes; Op. 28/2; 4–10; 11; 19; 21 & 23

⊕ ✸ (BB) **** Regis RRC 119. Sviatoslav Richter

This Regis coupling derives from two separate **Richter** recitals of 1977 and 1979, originally published by Olympia. There is some marvellous playing in the *Préludes*. These obviously derive from a public concert, as there is applause at the end. He is distinctly ruminative and wayward at times, but always poetically so. As for the *Scherzi*, they are inspired: there are no more imaginatively spontaneous performances in the catalogue. Everywhere there are fresh insights that seize the listener by the ear, none more frisson-creating than the centrepiece of the *Third Scherzo*, when simple chords are answered by a magical filigree in the right hand. This is Chopin playing of a truly remarkable calibre, and fortunately the remastering by Paul Arden-Taylor is of a high order: the piano quality is very real, full and immediate.

Scherzi 1–4; Piano Sonata 2 (Funeral March)

⊕–Ⓜ**** EMI 5 18171-2. Trpceski

The brilliant young Macedonian pianist **Simon Trpceski** offers dazzling performances of the *Second Sonata* as well as all four of Chopin's *Scherzos*, adopting extreme speeds which may initially seem too hectic but which, thanks to the pianist's virtuosity and his charismatic presence, are most compelling. His feeling for rubato is natural and spontaneous-sounding, in performances which consistently convey the sense of live communication. Excellent sound.

Piano Sonatas 1 in C min., Op. 4; 2 in B flat min. (Funeral March), Op. 35; 3 in B min., Op. 58

Ⓜ*** Decca (ADD) 448 123-2. Ashkenazy

Ashkenazy's accounts enjoy classic status, and they are certainly well recorded, with very vivid sound. They are also available as part of a Double Decca combined with the *Etudes* and *Fantasy in F minor* – see above.

Piano Sonata 2 in B flat min., Op. 35

Ⓜ*** DG 463 678-2. Pogorelich – PROKOFIEV: *Sonata 6*; RAVEL: *Gaspard* ***❀

(***) Testament mono SBT 1089. Gilels – MOZART: *Sonata 17*; SHOSTAKOVICH: *Preludes & Fugues 1, 5 & 24* (***)

Ivo Pogorelich possesses an outsize personality and a keen awareness of colour. He is a commanding artist of undoubted charisma, and his playing has temperament and fire in abundance. There are many wilful touches here and some agogic mannerisms that will not have universal appeal. All the same, these are performances to be reckoned with, and he went on a year later to record the outstanding Prokofiev and Ravel couplings. Here the balance is close and probably does not do full justice to the quality of his *pianissimo* tone, which nevertheless sounds remarkable.

Gilels's account of the *B flat minor Sonata* was recorded in New York and first appeared in 1984. The passage of time has not dimmed its classic status or its poetic intensity and, although some allowances have to be made for the recorded sound, they are few.

Piano Sonatas 2 in B flat min. (Funeral March); 3

*** DG (ADD) 415 346-2. Pollini

Pollini's performances are commanding; his mastery of mood and structure gives these much-played *Sonatas* added stature. The slow movement of Op. 35 has both drama and atmosphere, so that the contrast of the magical central section is all the more telling. Both works are played with distinction, but the balance is just a shade close.

Piano Sonata 2 in B flat min., Op. 35; Fantaisie-impromptu, Op. 66; Polonaises 3 in A, Op. 30/1; 5 in F sharp min., Op. 44; 6 in A flat, Op. 53; 7 (Polonaise-fantaisie), Op. 61; Scherzo 1 in B min., Op. 20

⊕–*** Sony (ADD) 82876 78769-2. Horowitz

A stunning recital by any standards, assembled from various CBS/Sony collections recorded over a decade between 1962 and 1972, when the great pianist was still at the very peak of his form. The playing is dazzling; its virtuosity is enormously refreshing and is illuminated by the sense of poetry and fine musical judgement that **Horowitz** so abundantly commanded. The *Fantaisie-impromptu* was recorded at a Carnegie Hall recital, the rest in the studio.

Piano Sonata 3; Barcarolle; Impromptus 1–3; Fantaisie-impromptu

*** Chan. 9175. Shelley

Piano Sonata 3; Mazurkas: in A min., Op. 17/4; in B flat min., Op. 24/4; in D flat, Op. 30/3; in D, Op. 33/2; in G; in C sharp min., Op. 50/1 & 3; in C, Op. 56/2; in F sharp min., Op. 59/3; in B; in F min.; in C sharp min., Op. 63/1–3; in F min., Op. 68/4

⊕–*** RCA 09026 62542-2. Kissin

Piano Sonata 3; Prelude in C sharp min., Op. 45; Scherzo 4 in E, Op. 54

(***) BBC mono/stereo BBCL 4138-2. Perlemuter

Evgeny Kissin plays not only with an effortless mastery but with a naturalness and freshness that silence criticism. His sense of poetry and his idiomatic rubato are combined with impressive technical address and impeccable taste.

An outstanding Chopin recital from **Howard Shelley**, whose interpretative powers continue to grow in stature. His playing has poetic feeling and ardent but well-controlled temperament. Very good sound.

Considering his standing in the musical world, **Vlado Perlemuter** made relatively few commercial recordings. The *Sonata* comes from a 1964 recital and is mono, while the *E major Scherzo* and the *Prelude* (both stereo) are from the early 1970s, when Perlemuter was already in his late sixties. There is some wonderfully perceptive music-making here and the musical importance of this disc is enhanced by exceptionally good notes by Jeremy Siepmann. Strongly recommended.

Waltzes 1–14; Impromptus 1–4 (Fantaisie-impromptu)

⊕–Ⓜ*** RCA (ADD) 82876 59422-2. Rubinstein

Waltzes 1–14; Barcarolle; Mazurka in C sharp min., Op. 50/3; Nocturne in D flat, Op. 27/2

❀Ⓜ(***) EMI mono 5 66904-2. Lipatti

Rubinstein's performances of the *Waltzes* have a chiselled perfection, suggesting the metaphor of finely cut and polished diamonds, and his clear and relaxed accounts of the *Impromptus* make most other interpretations sound forced by comparison. The digital remastering has softened the edges of the sound-image, and there is an illusion of added warmth.

Dinu Lipatti's classic performances were recorded by Walter Legge in the rather dry acoustic of a Swiss Radio studio at Geneva in the last year of Lipatti's short life, and with each CD reincarnation they seem to have grown in wisdom and subtlety.

RECITAL COLLECTIONS

Andante spianato et Grande Polonaise brillante, Op. 22; Ballade 1 in G min., Op. 23; Berceuse in D flat, Op. 57; Fantasia in F min., Op. 49; Mazurkas: in D flat, Op. 30/3; in B min., Op. 33/4; in A min., Op. 68/2; Scherzo 2 in B flat min., Op. 31; Sonata 2 in B flat min., Op. 35; Waltzes: in A flat, Op. 34/1; in A flat, Op. 69/1; in E flat, Op. posth.

(N) *** Opus Arte **DVD** OA6904 D. Michelangeli

This is in black-and-white, taking from a live 1962 RAI recital in Turin, the colour being provided by the playing! **Michelangeli** is, as always, aloof and totally absorbed in his music making. But with immaculate pianism and compelling artistry, this casts a strong spell.

Allegro de Concert in A, Op. 46; Berceuse in D flat, Op. 57; Boléro in A min., Op. 19; 6 Polonaises, Op. posth.; Tarantella in A flat, Op. 43

(BB) *** Hyp. Helios CDH 55183. Demidenko

Most of these pieces are early works: the *Polonaises in G minor* and *B flat major* (with which he frames the recital) date from 1817, that in *G sharp minor* from 1822, the *G flat major* from 1829 and the *Boléro* from 1833, while the *Allegro de Concert* and *Tarantella* were composed at the beginning of the 1840s. The two masterpieces, the *Berceuse* and *Polonaise-fantasy* (both superbly played) date from 1843–4 and 1846; so here **Nikolai Demidenko** demonstrates Chopin's progress from youthful precociousness to genius. Yet he plays the earliest pieces with such winning affection and idiomatic feeling.

Andante spianato et Grande Polonaise brillante; Fantaisie-impromptu; 3 Mazurkas, Op. 59; Nocturne in E flat, Op. 9/2; Piano Sonata 3

⊶ *** EMI 5 57702-2. Lim

Dong-Hyek Lim's range of colour and command of dynamic nuance are masterly and he has a strong and individual musical personality. Apart from his effortless technical fluency, he brings a rich poetic imagination to this music and, in the *Sonata*, no mean command of structure. This signals the arrival of an outstanding and exciting pianistic talent. EMI give him an excellent and very natural recording.

Ballades 1 & 4; Barcarolle; Etudes: Op. 10/5; Op. 25/7; Nocturnes: Op. 9/2–3; Op. 15/1; Op. 27/1; Polonaise-fantaisie; Waltz in A flat, Op. 16/1

(BB) *** RCA stereo/mono 74321 68008-2. Horowitz

All these performances derive from live recitals. *The Nocturnes* (in *E flat major*, Op. 23/2, and *C sharp minor Etude*, Op. 25/7) are in excellent mono from 1957, with the rest coming from between 1979 and 1982. The performances are fabulous; to the end of his career **Horowitz's** technique was transcendental and his insights remarkable. There is much

excitement, but even more that is unforgettably poetic, and not a bar that is predictable. With the sound so realistic, his presence is very tangible.

Ballade 1; Mazurkas: 19 in B min., 20 in D flat, Op. 30/2–3; 22 in G sharp min., 25 in B min., Op. 33/1 & 4; 34 in C, Op. 56/2; 43 in G min., 45 in A min., Op. 67/2 & 4; 46 in C; 47 in A min., 49 in F min., Op. 68/1–2 & 4; Prelude 25 in C sharp min., Op. 45; Scherzo 2

(*) DG (ADD) 477 7563. Michelangeli

Although this recital somehow does not quite add up as a whole, the performances are highly distinguished. **Michelangeli's** individuality comes out especially in the *Ballade* and is again felt in the *Mazurkas*, which show a wide range of mood and dynamic. The *Scherzo* is extremely brilliant, yet without any suggestion of superficiality. The piano tone is real and lifelike.

Ballade 2 in F, Op. 38; Impromptu 2 in F sharp, Op. 36; 4 Mazurkas, Op. 33; Sonata 2 in B flat min. (Funeral March), Op. 35; 3 Waltzes, Op. 34

(N) **** DG 477 7626 Pollini

Pollini recorded this outstanding studio recital in the Munich Herculessaal in 2008. The playing is dazzling and poetic by turns, astonishingly live and spontaneous as if an audience were present which it is not. Chopin-playing of a very high calibre indeed. Not to be missed.

Ballade 3 A flat, Op. 47; Sonata 2 (Funeral March), Op. 35; Nocturne E flat, Op. 9/2; Waltzes in C sharp min., Op. 64/2; A flat, Op. 64/3; E min., Op. posth. Chants polonais 1 & 6 (arr. LISZT)

(N) (BB) (***) Naxos mono 8.112020. Rachmaninov – SCHUMANN: *Carnaval, Op. 9; Spanisches Liederspiel* (***)

Most of this repertoire was recorded in the mid-to-late 1920s (the *Spanisches Liederspiel* and the *Chants polonais* come from 1942, the year before **Rachmaninov's** death). Ward Marston produces very fine results in his transfers and brings presence to these unique performances.

Ballades 3–4; Mazurkas 1–3, Op. 59/1–3; Op. 63; in F min., Op. 68/4; Polonaises 5 in F sharp min., Op. 44; 6 in A flat

⊶ *** Virgin 5 45620-2. Anderszewski

Piotr Anderszewski's Chopin recital along with Dong-Hyek Lim's recital discussed above has the right blend of sensibility and poetic feeling with classical finesse. Anderszewski is obviously an artist of quality, whose Chopin has a sense of real flair and vision as well as splendid control.

Ballade 3; Barcarolle; Berceuse; Etudes 13 in A flat; 21 in G flat, Op. 25/1 & 9; Fantaisie in F min.; Impromptu 1 in A flat; Mazurka 13 in A min., Op. 17/4; Nocturnes 5 in F sharp min., Op. 15/2; 20 in C sharp min., Op. posth.; Preludes: in A flat & C min., Op. 28/17 & 20; Scherzo 2 in B flat min., Op. 31; Waltzes 5 in A flat, Op. 42; 14 in E min. (op. posth.)

☁ ⇥ (BB) *** Naxos 8.555799. Idil Biret

Idil Biret's impetuosity and brilliance both combine to make the *E minor Waltz* which opens this recital arresting in its bravura, but she plays with both character and poetry in the *Barcarolle* and the two *Ballades*, while the *Berceuse* has a touching simplicity worthy of a young pupil of Wilhelm Kempff ('Uncle Kempff' as she called him). Indeed, overall this admirably planned recital demonstrates what a natural feeling Biret has for Chopin. The recording is excellent, with a real sense of presence.

Ballade 4; Berceuse; Etudes: Opp. 10/3, 8 & 9; 25/1–3; Fantaisie in F min.; Mazurka in A min., Op. 68/2; Nocturne: in E flat, Op. 9/2; D flat, Op. 27/2; Polonaise in A, Op. 40/1; A flat, Op. 53; Waltzes: in A flat, Op. 42; E min., Op. posth.

(**(*)) Testament mono SBT 1030. Solomon

This anthology affords ample proof of **Solomon's** power to distil magic in pretty well whatever composer he touched. Most of these 78-r.p.m. recordings were made between 1942 and 1946; the *F minor Fantaisie* is pre-war (1932), a wonderfully searching account, and the sheer delicacy and poetry of the playing shine through the often frail recorded sound. Good transfers.

Barcarolle in F sharp min., Op. 60; Berceuse in D flat, Op. 57; 2 Nocturnes, Op. 27; Piano Sonatas 2 (Funeral March) & 3

(N) *** Hyp. CDA 67706 Hamelin

Marc-André Hamelin's opening *Berceuse* is appealingly gentle, and the pair of *Nocturnes* are beautifully played, particularly the *D flat*. The *Barcarolle* finds a well-judged balance between poetry and intensity of feeling. Both *Sonatas* are bold, direct interpretations, with the *Marche funèbre* felt but gently withdrawn. There is some dazzling playing in the *Presto* finale of *No. 2* and in the *Scherzo* and *Finale* of *No. 3*. If sometimes one feels Hamelin presses a little hard, as in the opening movement of the *B flat minor Sonata*, overall the readings of the *Sonatas* are very impressive, as is the recording.

Barcarolle. Op. 60; Etudes Op. 10/4 & 5; Op. 25/1 & 5; Impromptu in G flat, Op.51; Sonata 2 (Funeral March) Polonaises in A flat, Op. 53; in F sharp min., Op. 64; Waltz in A min., Op. 34/2

(N) (**) Medici Arts DVD 3078458 Artur Rubinstein (with
DEBUSSY: *Ondine*; SCHUMANN: *Des Abends*; VILLA-LOBOS: *Polichinelle*)

Here is the historic Moscow recital **Rubinstein** gave in the Grand Hall of the Conservatoire on 1 October, 1964. The bulk of the great pianist's records were made in the studio so it is particularly valuable to see him live under recital conditions interacting with a highly responsive audience. In addition to his Chopin he includes among his encores, two that were great favourites with him, the Debussy *Ondine* from the Second Book of Preludes and Villa-Lobos's exuberant *O Polichinelle*. The monochrome picture betrays its age and is very grainy and wanting in sharp focus. The camera work is fairly static which is not a bad thing but it is stiff and the sound is primitive. The 'bonus' offers two fragments of silent film from 1929 which are also monochrome. Recommendable only to hardened Rubinstein enthusiasts.

Etudes: in G flat, Op. 10/5; in G sharp min.; in C sharp min., Op. 25/6–7; 3 Ecossaises, Op. posth. 72/3; Fantasy in F min.; Impromptu in A flat, Op. 29; Sonata 3; Waltzes: in A flat; A min., Op. 34/1–2; in E min., Op. posth.

*** DG 453 456-2. Pletnev

Opening with the great *F minor Fantasy* and closing with the *B Minor Sonata*, both superbly done, **Pletnev's** well-planned recital has all the hallmarks of a live recital, plus the technical advantage of studio recording. Such is his command of tonal colour elsewhere that one is scarcely aware of the piano's hammers even in fortissimo passages. But interpretatively things are less straightforward and he is often wilful. His rubato in the *B minor Sonata* is at times intrusive. The *G flat* and *G sharp minor Etudes* are dazzling, as is the famous *E minor Waltz* (written when the composer was twenty); and the *Ecossaises*, which are even earlier, are deliciously frothy. Yet the *C sharp minor Etude* takes the listener into a wholly different world and is very touching, as is the slow movement of the *Sonata*. For all one's reservations about the personal element, this is very distinguished playing indeed.

Fugue in A min., Op. posth.; Lento con gran espressione in C sharp min., Op. posth.; Nocturnes: in E flat, Op. 9/2; in C min., Op. posth.; Polonaise in B flat min., Op. posth.; Waltzes: in A min., Op. 34/2; in A min.; in E min.; in F sharp min., Op. posth.

**(*) Etcetera KTC 1231. Antoni – FIELD: *Largo; Nocturnes*, etc.
***

The primary purpose of this CD is to make a direct comparison with similar works, written even earlier, by John Field, who invented the *nocturne* in the year Chopin was born. **Helge Antoni** plays simply and poetically, and this serves to point up his comparisons. He is naturally recorded in a pleasing acoustic.

VOCAL MUSIC

Songs: The bridegroom; Drinking song; Faded and vanished; Reverie (Dumka); Handsome lad; Hymn from the tomb; Lithuanian song; The maiden's wish; Melodia (Elegy; Lamento); The messenger; My darling; Out of my sight; The ring; Sad river; Spring; There where she loves; The two corpses; The warrior; Witchcraft. Songs arr. Pauline Viardot from Chopin Mazurkas: Berceuse (from Op. 33/3); Faible cœur (from Op. 7/3); La Danse (from Op. 50/1); La Fête (from Op. 6/4); Plainte d'amour (from Op. 6/1)

💿 (BB) *** Hyp. Helios CDH 55270. Kryger, Spencer

Chopin wrote these songs for relaxation, just to please himself, never publishing them, and that may explain why the Polish flavour is so strong. He was reflecting his own early background, and the results are charming. *Mazurka* rhythms abound, as in the haunting *Handsome lad*, with the collection rounded off in the one song which goes deeper, *Melodia*, the heartfelt lament of an exile. **Urszula Kryger**, with her vibrant Slavonic tone well controlled, makes the most sympathetic interpreter, sensitively accompanied by **Charles Spencer.**

CILEA, Francesco (1866–1950)

Adriana Lecouvreur (DVD version)

🎭→ *** Opus Arte **DVD** OA LS 3011 D. Freni, Dvorský, Mingardo, Cossotto, La Scala, Milan, Ch. & O, Gavazzeni

Recorded in 1989, when Lamberto Puggelli's lavish production was new, this version of *Adriana Lecouvreur* from La Scala is far more successful than the recording of the same production made for TDK 11 years later. That is largely because the original cast is so much more assured and vocally well focused than the later replacements, and the veteran **Gianandrea Gavazzeni** is a masterly conductor in this music. **Mirella Freni** in the title-role as the great singing actress might easily have been overparted, but her projection is strong and positive, with the tenderness of her two big arias well caught. **Peter Dvorský** is first rate as Maurizio, strong, firm and unstrained, and **Fiorenza Cossotto** with her rich mezzo makes a splendid foil for Freni. Visually, with Brian Large as video director, the extravagance of the elaborate and ultra-realistic sets and costumes is wonderfully brought out.

Adriana Lecouvreur (CD version)

🎭→ Ⓜ **** Decca 475 7906 (2). Sutherland, Bergonzi, Nucci, d'Artegna, Ciurca, Welsh Nat. Op. Ch. & O, Bonynge

On CD **Sutherland's** performance in the role of a great tragic actress could not be warmer-hearted. She impresses with her richness and opulence in the biggest test, the aria *Io son l'umile ancella*, an actress's credo, and her formidable performance is warmly backed up by the other principals, and equally by **Richard Bonynge's** conducting, not just warmly expressive amid the wealth of rich tunes, but light and sparkling where needed, easily idiomatic.

CIMAROSA, Domenico
(1749–1801)

Piano Sonatas, Volumes I–III, 1–62 (complete)

*** Arcobaleno AAOC 93672 (2). Crudelli

Cimarosa's sonatas have a good deal in common with Scarlatti's sonatas, offering considerable variety of mood and style, although they are not as searching. **Crudelli** uses a modern piano and plays stylishly with crisp, clear timbre and articulation. But there is charm as well as scholarship in her advocacy. The recording gives the piano a clean, clear image so that these performances are both authentic and

spontaneous and it is a pity that the documentation is so limited.

18 Keyboard Sonatas, R. 1–18

Ⓝ ⒝⒝ **** Naxos 8.570718 Sangiorgio (piano)

Cimarosa's keyboard sonatas are a real find, and they sparkle delightfully in the hands of **Victor Sangiorgio.** As presented here, each is in three (or occasionally two) brief sections. Sometimes all three are brisk, at others there is a central *Andante*, with each work adding up to about three minutes of music in total. We'll say no more, but urge readers to discover them by acquiring this highly rewarding disc for themselves.

Il Maestro di Cappella

Ⓜ **** Decca 2-CD (ADD) 475 8490 (2). Corena, ROHCG O, Quadri – DONIZETTI: *Don Pasquale* ***

Corena's classic assumption of the role of the incompetent Kapellmeister makes a most welcome return to the catalogue after being unavailable for far too long. The Decca stereo allows his orchestral rehearsal to come over most vividly, with the poor man dashing first to the left then to the right, to one instrument after another, trying to keep each in order. Corena shows complete mastery of the *buffo* bass style, and he is so little troubled by the florid passages that he can relax and bring out the fun. The vintage 1960 recording is clear and atmospheric, with the directional effects naturally conveyed.

Dixit Dominus

**(*)CPO 999 988-2. Rizzone, Rottensteiner, Bonfatti, Coro I Musici Cantori de Trento & Voci Roveretane, Orchestra Haydn di Bolzano e Trento, Pirona

The tuneful, bubbling invention we know from Cimarosa's operas and concertos is also found in his appealing *Dixit Dominus*, from 1796. The performance is reasonably well done, but a sharper sound would have given it more impact.

CLEMENS NON PAPA, Jacob (c. 1510/15–c. 1555/6)

Missa and Motet: Ecce quam bonum. Motets: Accesserunt ad Jesum; Carole, magna est; Job tonso capite; Pascha nostrum; Veni electa mea

*** Signum SIGCD 045. Brabant Ens., Rice

Jacob Clement or Clemens non Papa was jokingly known as Clement-not-the-Pope, so as to distinguish him from either Pope Clement VII or the Flemish poet, Jacobus Papa. However, we know very little about him. It seems likely that he was in Bruges from 1544–5, and he certainly spent most of his life in the Low Countries. However, he was very prolific and much respected in his time (over a dozen of his Masses have survived, over 200 motets and many chansons).

Based on the composer's own motet, the *Mass Ecce quam bonum* is in five parts, extended to six from the *Sanctus* onwards, and is an essentially joyful celebration of the unity of the church, and God's benediction on those who lead a peaceful life. Glorious singing throughout and outstandingly fine recording in the chapel of Merton College, Oxford, where the impressive conductor of the **Brabant Ensemble** is based; and it is he who provides the notes. Full texts and translations are provided.

Missa Pastores quidnam vidistis; Motets: Pastores quidnam vidistis; Ego flos campi; Pater peccavi; Tribulationes civitatum

✹ **** Gimell CDGIM 013. Tallis Scholars, Phillips

The beauty of line and richness of texture in the masterly *Missa Pastores quidnam vidistis* are unforgettable in this superb performance by the **Tallis Scholars**. The programme opens with the parody motet associated with the Mass, which has a glorious eloquence. Of the other motets, *Pater peccavi*, solemnly rich-textured, is especially memorable; but the whole programme is designed to reveal to modern ears another name hitherto known only to scholars. The recording is uncannily real and superbly balanced.

CLEMENTI, Muzio (1752–1832)

Symphonies: 1; in B flat & D, Op. 18/1–2
*** Chan. 9234. LMP, Bamert

Symphonies: 1 in C; 2 in D; 3 in G (Great National Symphony); 4 in D

(BB) *** Warner Apex (ADD) 2564 62762-2 (2). Philh. O, Scimone

Six of Clementi's 20 symphonies survive. The four numbered works are all scored for much larger forces than the Op. 18 set and even include trombones. Their musical content explains Clementi's high reputation in his lifetime as a composer for the orchestra, not just the piano. If the *Great National Symphony* is the most immediately striking, with *God save the King* ingeniously worked into the third movement, the other works are all boldly individual.

Bamert's performances are on a chamber scale and are refreshingly alive and polished. They are given top-class Chandos sound.

Scimone's Philharmonia performances are both lively and sympathetic, the recording is excellent, and this set is well worth its modest cost.

PIANO MUSIC

Capriccio in B flat; Fantasia with Variations on 'Au clair de la lune', Op. 48; Preludio 1 alla Haydn in C; Preludio 1 alla Mozart (both from Op. 19); Sonatas: in F min., Op. 13/6; in F, Op. 33/11; in G min., Op. 34/11

▬ (M) *** Warner Elatus 2564 60676-2. Staier (fortepiano)

The reissue of **Andreas Staier's** splendid recital gives it a fair claim to being the most desirable introduction to the music of Clementi in the catalogue. The anticipation of Beethoven appears in nearly all this music. The *Sonatas* are all considerable works, and Staier's flexibility of style brings out their individuality strongly.

6 Piano Sonatas, Op. 1; in G, WoO 14 (Alternative first movement for Op. 1/2); 3 Sonatas, Op. 2; 3 Sonatas, Op. 7; 3 Sonatas, Op. 8; Sonatas: in A flat, WoO 13

(B) **** Hyp. CDA 67632 (2). Shelley

3 Piano Sonatas, Op 9; 3 Sonatas Op. 10; Sonata Op. 1; Sonatas, Op 12/1-4; Toccata, Op. 11/2

(N) (B) *** Hyp. CDA 67717 (2). Shelley

3 Piano Sonatas, Op. 13; Sonata in C, Op.20; 3 Sonatas, Op. 23; 2 Sonatas, Op. 24; in F, WoO 3

(N) (B) *** Hyp CDA 67729 (2). Shelley

Howard Shelley includes here the *Sonata in A flat*, WoO 13, composed in Rome when Clementi was only 13, but he begins the collection with Opus 1, where the opening allegro of the first of the set immediately shows the music's attractively spontaneous early style, with its flavour of Mozart. The layout then follows the approximate order of composition. Shelley's performances are full of life and sparkle, the virtuosity effortless, the developing character and expressive range of the later works of Opus 7 and 8 fully realized. Not surprisingly, the Hyperion recording is in the demonstration bracket. Each of these pairs of CDs is offered for the price of one. Throughout this series Shelley's artistry and finesse are heard to fine effect and readers can invest in the set with confidence.

Piano Sonatas in A, Op. 2/4; G min., Op. 8/1; B flat, Op. 8/3; F min., Op. 13/6; G, WO14

▬ (BB) *** Naxos 8.555808. Alexander-Max (piano)

The American pianist, **Susan Alexander-Max**, gives magnetic performances of five sparkling and original early sonatas by Clementi, on what one hopes is the start of a series from Naxos.

Piano Sonatas: in F min., Op. 13/6; in B flat, Op. 24/2; in F sharp min., Op. 25/5; in G, Op. 37/1

*** Accent ACC 67911D. van Immerseel (fortepiano)

Very fleet and brilliant performances from **Jos van Immerseel**. The slow movements of these *Sonatas* have considerable expressive depth, and the outer ones are full of a brilliance that is well served by this eminently skilful and excellent artist.

Piano Sonatas: in B flat, Op. 24/2; in G; in F sharp min., Op. 25/2 & 5; in D, Op. 37/2; 6 Progressive Sonatinas, Op. 36

(BB) *** Naxos 8.550452. Szokolay

Balázs Szokolay's Naxos anthology is very successful and his playing inspires enthusiasm. Decent recording; excellent value.

Piano Sonatas, Op. 24/2; Op. 25/5; Op 40/2–3

⟿ (BB) **** Hyp. Helios CDH 55227. Demidenko (piano)

The spirit of Beethoven undoubtedly hangs over the dramatic opening of the *D major Sonata*, Op. 40/3, with which **Demidenko** begins his recital, and his performances of both this and the closing Op. 40/2 (both published in 1802) are very arresting. The *Molto adagio sostenuto*, which acts as a prelude to this *B minor Sonata*, is played with moving serenity, and both the central *Largo mesto e patetico* and the *Lento patetico* of the *F sharp minor*, Op. 25/5, are very beautiful in Demidenko's hands. The *Allegro confuoco* of Op. 40/2 brings dazzling virtuosity, while he provides his own cadenza for the first movement of Op. 24/2. Recorded at the Snape Maltings, Aldeburgh, in 1994, this reissue is a fine bargain.

Piano sonatas: in D, Op. 25/6; in A, Op. 33/1; in A, Op. 50/1; in G min. (Didone abbandonata), Op. 50/3

Ⓜ *** CRD 3500. Roscoe

Martin Roscoe makes a very persuasive case for playing these sonatas on a modern instrument. He is particularly searching in the *Adagio sostenuto* of the late *A major Sonata*, Op. 50/1, and how impressively he pedals in the dolorous *Introduzione (Largo patetico e sostenuto)* of the *G minor Sonata (Didone abbandonata)*, then presenting the *Adagio dolente* most touchingly and finding plenty of drama in the agitated finale. Yet the gallant early *D major* work is joyfully spirited and full of charm. The recording is very natural, well up to the high standard we expect from this label.

Piano Sonatas in G; B min.; D, Op. 40/1–3

⟿ (BB) *** Naxos 8.553500. de Maria

Pietro de Maria's account of the three sonatas of Op. 40 is impeccable not only in terms of virtuosity but in musicianship and artistry. He is accorded first-class sound, fresh and present.

CLIFFE, Frederic (1857–1931)

Symphony 1 in C min., Op. 1; Cloud and Sunshine (Orchestral Picture)

✿ *** Sterling CDS 1055-2. Malmö Opera O, Fifield

Frederic Cliffe was born in Bradford in 1857 and is thus contemporary with Elgar. On the staff of the Royal College of Music, he suddenly came to the fore when his *First Symphony* was premièred in 1889, receiving enthusiastic plaudits from every quarter. The symphony is indeed an astonishing achievement for a young composer and gives absolutely no impression of inexperience. It is readily comparable in warmth and constructional skill with, for instance, the *First Symphony* of Gounod, but it has a much greater affinity with the early symphonies of Dvořák. The orchestration throughout is vivid, showing a natural flair, especially in its richly Wagnerian scoring for the horns and brass. In short, this is a remarkably inventive and fluent work, which one returns to with much pleasure.

The orchestral picture of *Cloud and Sunshine* is equally confident in its pictorial evocation, if not as memorable thematically as the symphony. Both are played with zest, warmth and spontaneity by the fine **Malmö orchestra**, under their dedicated and understanding conductor, **Christopher Fifield.**

CLIFFORD, Hubert (1904–59)

Serenade for Strings

*** Dutton CDLX 7174. BBC Concert O, Wordsworth – HARRISON: *Brendon Hill; Worcestershire Suite*, etc. ***

Hubert Clifford's *Serenade for Strings* was written in 1943 for the BBC Empire String Orchestra. The first movement became well known in its own right as a popular light encore, but the other movements are no less appealing. Both the Scherzo and the *Molto Allegro* finale are certainly lively, but they always possess a light touch which is very pleasing; the slow movement has just the right amount of depth and is memorable. This makes an original and enjoyable bonus following on from Julius Harrison's delightful music (see below).

String Quartet in D

Ⓜ *** Dutton CDLX 7163. Locrian Ens. – BAINTON: *String Quartet* ***

Born in Australia, Hubert Clifford came to Britain in 1930 to study with Vaughan Williams and never returned home. The *String Quartet in D* comes from 1935 and was broadcast twice in the following year and again (twice) in 1946. It is a well-fashioned piece whose discourse is civilized and pleasing, very much pre-war in feeling. There is some Gallic influence and evidence of his Irish origins, some generations back. The material does not quite sustain its length, but all the same it is well served by the **Locrian Ensemble**, and the Dutton recording is very truthful.

COATES, Eric (1886–1957)

(i) *By the Sleepy Lagoon;* **(ii)** *Calling all Workers: March;* **(iii)** *Cinderella (Phantasy); From Meadow to Mayfair: Suite; London Suite; London Again Suite;* **(i)** *The Merrymakers Overture;* **(iii)** *Music everywhere: March;* **(iii; iv)** *Saxo-Rhapsody;* **(i)** *The Three Bears (phantasy);* **(ii)** *The Three Elizabeths: Suite;* **(i)** *The Three Men: Man from the Sea (only);* **(iii)** *Wood Nymphs (valsette)*

⟿ Ⓑ *** CfP (ADD) 3 52356-2 (2). RLPO, Groves; CBSO, Kilbey; or LSO, Mackerras

It is good to welcome back this key collection of the music of Eric Coates, 'the man who writes tunes', much loved by orchestral players as he also writes so gratefully for their instruments, being an ex-orchestral player himself. On the whole, **Groves**, who has the lion's share of the repertoire here, proves a persuasive advocate, although occasionally his approach is slightly bland. **Jack Brymer** is the excellent soloist in the *Saxo-Rhapsody*; and the other piece with a diluted jazz element, *Cinderella*, also goes with a swing. However, not surprisingly, the performances from **Sir Charles Mackerras** and the **LSO** are even more lively, and there are also several really outstanding ones from the **CBSO** under **Reginald Kilbey**. He proves the ideal Coates conductor, with a real flair for catching the sparkle of the composer's leaping *allegro* figurations, notably in the first movement of *The Three Elizabeths*, where also his shaping of the central, slow movement – one of the composer's finest inspirations, dedicated to the late Queen Mother – has an affectionate grace. The marches are splendidly alive and vigorous.

Ballad; By the Sleepy Lagoon; London Suite; The Three Bears (phantasy); The Three Elizabeths (suite)

(M) *** ASV CDWHL 2053. East of E. O, Nabarro

Malcolm Nabarro has the full measure of Coates's leaping *allegros* and he plays the famous marches with crisp buoyancy. *The Three Bears* sparkles humorously, as it should; only in *By the Sleepy Lagoon* does one really miss a richer, more languorous string-texture. Excellent, bright recording, and the price is right.

Cinderella (Phantasy); Dam Busters March; Joyous Youth (Suite); London Suite; Miniature Suite; The Selfish Giant (Phantasy); The Three Bears (Phantasy)

⊕– ❀ *** Chan. 9869. BBC PO, Gamba

It is a joy to hear his imaginatively coloured orchestration on a full-sized orchestra with an ample string-group splendidly served by these superb performances and Chandos's demonstration-worthy recordings. The finest of the three *Phantasies* is *The Three Bears*, with its opening rhythmic phrase, 'Who's been sleeping in my bed?' and its later, utterly beguiling waltz theme. *Cinderella* boasts another richly romantic example, and two more, both deliciously lightweight, close the *Joyous Youth Suite* and the *Miniature Suite*, which shows the composer at his most elegant and graceful. More robust is the *London Suite*, with its vigorous, pacy evocation of the old Covent Garden Market, followed by a romantic portrayal of *Westminster*, complete with chimes. The *Knightsbridge March* finale was famous as a signature tune for the BBC. The programme ends appropriately with *The Dam Busters*. All orchestral musicians love playing Coates's music and this is conveyed by the orchestra throughout this wonderfully enjoyable CD.

Cinderella (Phantasy); Footlights (Concert Waltz); London Again Suite; The Selfish Giant (Phantasy); Summer Days Suite; Three Men Suite; TV March

*** Avie AV 2070. RLPO, Wilson

The **Liverpool Phil.** have not recorded Eric Coates since the days of Sir Charles Groves, but they have not lost their touch, and under the excellent **John Wilson** they play this attractively tuneful music with verve and affection. How well Coates builds the introduction to the *Footlights Waltz* before the beguiling tune arrives, and how effectively Wilson and

his players respond! Alongside the waltz, the engaging *Three Men Suite* (as distinct from the catchy finale) and the charmingly scored lightweight *Summer Days* are new to the CD catalogue and they are most winningly played and recorded here.

The Dam Busters: March. From Meadow to Mayfair: Suite. The Merrymakers: Overture. Summer Days: Suite. Three Bears (Phantasy); Three Elizabeths Suite: March

*** Lyrita (ADD) SRCD 246. New Philh. O or LPO, Boult (with GRAINGER: *Over the Hills and Far Away*; DELIUS: *Marche Caprice*; WALTON: *Hamlet: Funeral March*; VAUGHAN WILLIAMS: *The Wasps: March past of the Kitchen Utensils*; ROSSINI, arr. BRITTEN: *Soirées musicales: March*; HOLST: *Suite in E flat, Op. 28/1: March*)

As ever, Coates's music has great craftsmanship as well as good tunes and, lightweight though it is, it lies firmly within the English tradition. Here **Boult** finds its affinities with Elgar in delicacy of scoring and hints of nostalgia. *Summer Days*, written in the summer of 1919, was the first work that Coates composed as an ex-orchestral player. It includes a justly famous waltz, *At the Dance*, graciously elegant and with hardly any Viennese influence. The lollipops added for this reissue are equally welcome, particularly *The March past of the Kitchen Utensils*, the hit number from Vaughan Williams's incidental music for *The Wasps*. The late-1970s recording is splendid, matching Lyrita's predictable high standard.

Dancing Nights (Concert Waltz); The Enchanted Garden (Ballet); Footlights (Concert Valse); The Four Centuries (Suite): Rhythm (20th Century). London Bridge March; 2 Symphonic Rhapsodies: Pitch my Lonely Caravan; Birdsongs at Eventide/I heard You Singing; The Three Men: Suite; Summer Afternoon (Idyll)

⊕– *** Lyrita SRCD 213. LPO, Wordsworth

A fine vintage collection from the **LPO**, directed with élan by **Barry Wordsworth**, is shrewdly chosen to include some less familiar repertoire, notably the inventively tuneful ballet score, *The Enchanted Garden* (at 21 minutes the composer's longest single movement, it includes, of course, a foxtrot theme among more traditional rhythms). Other highlights include the finale of the *Three Men Suite* with its witty quotation of 'Johnny come down from Hilo'. Fine, lively performances, the orchestra obviously enjoying themselves, and vivid recording.

COLERIDGE-TAYLOR, Samuel (1875–1912)

4 Characteristic Waltzes, Op. 22; Gipsy Suite, Op. 20; Hiawatha Overture, Op. 30; Othello Suite, Op. 79; Petite Suite de concert, Op. 77; Romance of the Prairie Lilies, Op. 39

*** Marco 8.223516. Dublin RTE Concert O, Leaper

Coleridge-Taylor wrote much delightful orchestral music, the most famous being the charming *Petite Suite de concert*. The composer's feeling for the genre is also apparent in the *Four Characteristic Waltzes*. Each is nicely coloured: there is a nostalgic *Valse bohémienne*, a countrified *Valse rustique* (the oboe so easily conjuring up the countryside), a stately *Valse de la reine*, and a lively *Valse mauresque*. The *Gipsy Suite* is a piquantly coloured four-movement work of considerable appeal, while the *Othello Suite*, beginning with a lively dance, has an engaging *Willow Song* and ends with a stirring *Military March*. Performances and recording are excellent, and this is altogether a winning if essentially lightweight collection, perhaps more for aficionados than for the general collector.

Violin Concerto in G min., Op. 80

*** Hyp. CDA 67420. Marwood, BBC Scottish SO, Brabbins –
SOMERVELL: *Violin Concerto in G* ***

Violin Concerto in G min., Op. 80; Legend, Op. 14; Romance in G, Op. 39

B—❀ **** Lyrita SRCD 317. McAslan, LPO, Braithwaite (with
HARRISON: *Bredon Hill* ****)

Coleridge-Taylor's beautiful *Violin Concerto* was one of the great discoveries of the Lyrita catalogue, although, recorded in 1994, it was not issued until 2007 (after two other versions had appeared). **Lorraine McAslan's** warmly lyrical performance is fully worthy of it and **Nicholas Braithwaite** and the **LPO** give her passionate support. McAslan provides poetic performances of the *Legend* and *Romance*, both with memorable main themes, the *Legend* especially captivating. Then for a valuable bonus we are given the richly atmospheric *Bredon Hill* rhapsody of Julius Harrison, a lovely piece, obviously influenced by Vaughan Williams's *Lark Ascending*, but also by Butterworth, another memorable performance, admirably recorded.

Anthony Marwood is an accomplished advocate and a convincing exponent of this worthwhile score. The **BBC Scottish Orchestra** is polished, although perhaps it could do with greater fervour. But the Lyrita CD is the one to go for.

African Dances, Op. 58; Hiawatha Sketches, Op. 16; Petite suite de concert, Op. 77; Violin Sonata, Op. 28

Ⓜ *** Dutton CDLX 7127. Juritz, Dussek

Coleridge-Taylor's *Violin Sonata* of 1897 (premièred by Albert Sammons) has much of the easy melodic facility of the *Violin Concerto* with a readily appealing central *Larghetto*. The engaging *Petite suite de concert*, familiar from its orchestral version, works just as well in this format. The *Hiawatha Sketches*, also inspired by Longfellow, pre-date the famous cantata by two years, and are pleasing light music, as are the later *African Dances*. All agreeable music, very well played by **David Juritz** and **Michael Dussek**, while the Dutton recording balance cannot be faulted.

Ballade in C min., Op. 73; Clarinet Quintet in F sharp min., Op. 10; Piano Quintet in G min., Op. 1

**** Hyp. CDA 67590. Nash Ens.

The *Piano Quintet*, written at the age of 18, is an astonishingly precocious work. It brims with assurance in its melodic sweep, and it is remarkable that this is probably its first performance since its première in 1893. Both Schubert's and, especially, Dvořák's influence can clearly be heard in this work. The *Clarinet Quintet*, written shortly afterwards, is perhaps the greater work. Again, the influence of Dvořák is most apparent. The *Ballade* is a later work, written for the violinist Michael Zacherewitsh and first performed in Leeds in 1907. It is a wonderfully romantic, brooding work, with the spirit of Tchaikovsky (whom Coleridge-Taylor admired) and even of Rachmaninov. It is all masterfully performed by the **Nash Ensemble**, whose unforced yet vital performances are a constant source of joy. Immaculate recording.

(i-iii) Hiawatha's Wedding Feast. (ii; iv) Petite Suite de Concert, Op. 77 (v) La Bamboula (Rhapsodic Dance)

B—Ⓑ *** CfP 587 0242. (i) Richard Lewis & Royal Choral Soc.
(ii) Philh. O; (iii) Sargent; (iv) Weldon; (v) Bournemouth SO, Alwyn

HMV's budget reissue of **Sargent's** splendid 1961 Abbey Road recording of just *Hiawatha's Wedding Feast*, with the **Royal Choral Society** is a real success, including of course Richard Lewis's stylish performance of *Onaway! Awake, Beloved!* The CD transfer is not sharply focused, but the sound remains warmly atmospheric. The *Petite Suite de Concert* is the composer's best-known orchestral work a salon pastiche of great charm. **George Weldon's** polished **Philharmonia** performance is wholly sympathetic and not in the least sentimental, and it is given first-class sound. *La Bamboula*, which the composer wrote for his third visit to the USA in 1910, is a 'series of evolutions' on a West Indian dance also used by Gottschalk, and it makes an attractive encore.

COLLINS, Anthony (1893–1963)

Eire; Festival Royal Overture; The Lady with the Lamp; Louis XV Silhouettes; Symphony 1 for Strings; The Saga of Odette; Santa Cecilia; Vanity Fair; Victoria the Great

❀ Ⓜ **** Dutton CDLX 7162. BBC Concert O, Wilson

Anthony Collins was the ideal recording conductor, as he was able to bring music vividly to life in the studio, and his Decca Sibelius cycle was a classic of the post-war LP era. This is the first CD devoted to his own highly enjoyable music. It opens with the patriotic *Festival Royal Overture* (first performed in 1956) and, while it uses such obvious quotations as *God save the Queen* and the 'Big Ben' chimes, it builds its own themes into a most entertaining work. The same patriotic spirit pervades his music to the 1937 film *Victoria the Great*.

Ear-tickling colours run through the delightful pastiche, *Louis XV Silhouettes*. The three-movement suite, *Eire*, based on Irish folk-tunes, is equally attractive, especially the toe-tapping final Reel, *Fluter's Hooley. Valse Lente* is a short and nostalgic evocation, originally used in the 1950 film *Odette*; and from the 1951 film *The Lady with the Lamp* the composer extracted the title theme and the music from the ball scenes to produce the *Prelude and Variations* included here. In the *Symphony for Strings* (1940), Collins's penchant for pastiche is to the fore. His most famous piece of all is the disarmingly simple *Vanity Fair*. First performed in 1952, this is the composition he most wanted to be remembered for, and indeed it is an exquisite little miniature of the sort that cheers you up every time you hear it.

John Wilson and the **BBC Concert Orchestra** play all his music with great affection and style, and they are well supported by Dutton's engineering team.

CONFREY, Edward (1895–1971)

African suite; Amazonia; Blue Tornado; Coaxing the Piano; Dizzy Fingers; Fourth Dimension; Jay Walk; Kitten on the Keys; Meandering; Moods of a New Yorker (suite); Rhythm Venture; Sparkling Waters; Stumbling Paraphrase; 3 Little Oddities; Wisecracker Suite

*** Marco 8.223826. Andjaparidze

Older collectors will surely remember *Kitten on the Keys* and perhaps *Dizzy Fingers* and *Coaxing the Piano* (all dazzlingly played here). Confrey established his international fame as a precocious virtuoso pianist/composer in the early 1920s. His music has a witty charm and is clearly influenced by French impressionism as well as by Gershwin and the Scott Joplin rags. The Georgian pianist **Eteri Andjaparidze** gives engagingly sparkling performances of the bravura pieces, including the ingenious closing *Fourth Dimension* with its amazingly virtuosic cross-hand accents, and she is equally at home in the more relaxed ragtime of *Jay Walk*, *Stumbling* and the sauntering gait of *Meandering*. But she also relishes the atmosphere and charm of the gentler pieces among the *Oddities* and the suites (two of the *Moods of a New Yorker* recall the tranquil simplicity of MacDowell's *To a wild rose*). A most entertaining collection, given excellent piano recording.

COOKE, Arnold (1906–2005)

Clarinet Concerto

(BB) *** Hyp. Helios CDH 55069. King, Northwest CO of Seattle, Francis – JACOB: *Mini-Concerto*; RAWSTHORNE: *Concerto* ***

Arnold Cooke's music contains an element of Hindemithian formalism, carefully crafted, but the slow movement of this *Concerto* soars well beyond. **Thea King** makes a passionate advocate, brilliantly accompanied by the **Seattle Orchestra** in excellent (1982) analogue sound, faithfully transferred.

Symphony 1; Concerto in D for String Orchestra; Jabez and the Devil (Ballet Suite);

*** Lyrita SRCD 203. LPO, Braithwaite

The first symphony may not break new ground, but on record it can provide genuine refreshment. The expansive first movement has a swinging 9/8 theme and a neatly managed false ending; the slow movement is a deeply expressive elegy which turns into a touching processional, and the finale is festive with fanfares. The *Concerto for Strings* is neo-classical, somewhat lean-textured but never dry, with a pensive slow movement and a bouncing finale. The ballet from which the suite is taken was written for the Royal Ballet in 1961 and is both atmospheric and colourful. Performances and recording are excellent: **Braithwaite** really feels this music and the **LPO** responds committedly.

Symphony 3 in D

*** Lyrita (ADD) SRCD 295. LPO, Braithwaite – BRIAN: *Symphonies 6 & 16* ***

This is also a well-made, highly enjoyable symphony which deserves more than the occasional airing. If there is, as in his other works, a whiff of Hindemith in his writing, there is far more of Cooke himself, confident and positive in theme and argument. Performances and recording are excellent and the coupling, too, is well worth exploring.

(i) Cello Sonata 2; (ii) Viola Sonata; (iii) Violin Sonata 2

*** British Music Soc. BMS 432CD. Terroni, with (i) Wallfisch; (ii) Goff; (iii) Stanzelett

The *Viola Sonata* of 1936/7 is comparatively sinewy, yet has a deeply felt *Andante*, and plenty of vitality in the finale. The *Cello Sonata* was written in 1979/80 (and received its concert première by **Raphael Wallfisch** and **Raphael Terroni** on 4 November 2006, the centenary of the composer's birth). The *Lento*, improvisatory in feeling, has a touching lyricism, and the jolly, very rhythmic finale bounces along with great confidence.

But undoubtedly the most attractive of these three works is the *Violin Sonata* of 1980, which sets off with a buoyant main theme and a skipping impetus, and has a yearning melody for its *Andante*. The finale, with its cross-rhythms, also has an underlying lyrical impetus and is capped by a neatly managed fugato. All three performances are most persuasive and truthfully recorded, if lacking a little in resonant warmth.

Clarinet Quintet

(BB) *** Hyp. Helios CDH 55105. King, Britten Qt – HOLBROOKE: *Eilean Shona*; HOWELLS: *Rhapsodic Quintet*; FRANKEL; MACONCHY: *Clarinet Quintets* ***

Like his *Clarinet Concerto*, Arnold Cooke's *Quintet* has a slightly sinewy lyrical flow in the manner of Hindemith but, though the composer does not always seek to 'charm', **Thea King's** playing is so seductive in the *Andante* that the listener is aurally cajoled. The first movement is characteristically unpredictable in line and flow, but the performance here finds its slightly wan melodic appeal and the perky finale is most winning. Excellent recording.

COPLAND, Aaron (1900–90)

Appalachian Spring (complete recording of full score); Billy the Kid (ballet suite); Rodeo: 4 Dance Episodes

𝄞 ✿ (M) **** RCA 82876 65840-2. San Francisco SO, Tilson Thomas

It was Eugene Ormandy who in 1954 persuaded Copland to score the complete *Appalachian Spring* – hitherto available only in its original chamber version – for full orchestra. It is still not in print, existing only in manuscript, but **Michael Tilson Thomas's** superb recording confirms Ormandy's view that the work would expand magnificently. In the ballet the variations on *Simple Gifts* which form the climax are presented in, and interrupted by, an additional episode in which a revivalist appears and warns the central couple in the story of what Copland called 'the strange and terrible aspects of human fate'.

The complete ballet here runs to 36 minutes, and in this magnificently played and very moving performance is revealed as a 20th-century masterpiece to rank alongside the three key Stravinsky ballets, including *The Rite of Spring*. The opening is wonderfully serene, and Tilson Thomas finds infinite detail and colour throughout, while creating a richly evocative tapestry of great beauty, helped by a recording of extraordinary breadth. The performances of the two cowboy ballets are similarly imaginative and compelling, giving the impression of coming to the music for the first time. This is not to be missed, even if you already have other versions of this vivid music.

Appalachian Spring (ballet) Suite

(B) *** DG 477 6352-2. LAPO, Bernstein – BARBER: *Adagio for Strings* ***; GERSHWIN: *Rhapsody in Blue* **(*)

Bernstein's DG version of *Appalachian Spring* was recorded at a live performance, and the conductor communicates his love for the score in a strong yet richly lyrical reading and the compulsion of the music-making is obvious. The recording is close but not lacking in atmosphere, and it sounds extremely vivid, reissued in DG's Critics' Choice series.

Appalachian Spring (ballet) Suite; Billy the Kid: Suite; Fanfare for the Common Man; Rodeo (4 Dance Episodes)

(BB) **(*) Naxos 8.550282. Slovak RSO (Bratislava), Gunzenhauser

(i) Appalachian Spring (ballet) Suite; (ii) Billy the Kid (suite); Rodeo (4 Dance Episodes)

(*) Telarc **SACD 60648 or CD 80078. Atlanta SO, Lane – HINDEMITH: *Symphonic Metamorphoses on Themes of Weber* **(*)

The **Bratislava orchestra** play with such spontaneous enjoyment in *Rodeo* and *Billy the Kid* that one cannot help but respond. If some of the detail in *Appalachian Spring* is less sharply etched than with Bernstein, the closing pages are tenderly responsive. The recording is admirably colourful and vivid, with a fine hall ambience, and the spectacle of the *Fanfare for the Common Man* is worth anybody's money. A bargain.

Louis Lane's performances on Telarc were given recording of demonstration quality. Lane's account of *Appalachian Spring*, without missing the score's lyrical qualities, has an attractive feeling of the ballet theatre about it. *Rodeo* is not as bitingly dramatic as with Bernstein, but it is folksy and enjoyable. The recording is very slightly enhanced on the SACD, and this includes the – not particularly appropriate – Hindemith coupling. The CD version, with little loss of fidelity, is at mid-price. But both are upstaged by the Tilson Thomas RCA collection.

(i) Appalachian Spring (ballet) Suite; (ii) Ceremonial Fanfare; (iii) Dance Symphony; El salón México; (i) Fanfare for the Common Man; (i; iv) Lincoln Portrait; (v) Music for Movies; (vi) Quiet City; (iii) Rodeo: 4 Dance Episodes; (vii) Old American Songs (excerpts): Simple gifts; Ching-a-ring-chaw; Long time ago; I bought me a cat; At the river

𝄞 (B) *** Double Decca ADD/DDD 448 261-2 (2). (i) LAPO, Mehta; (ii) Philip Jones Brass Ens.; (iii) Detroit SO, Dorati; (iv) Peck; (v) L. Sinf., Howarth; (vi) ASMF, Marriner; (vii) Horne, ECO, C. Davis

Mehta's performance of *Appalachian Spring* is one of the most distinguished of several fine recordings he made for Decca in the late 1970s, which also included the spectacular *Fanfare for the Common Man* and the *Lincoln Portrait*, with **Gregory Peck** a comparatively laid-back narrator who speaks Lincoln's prose with dignity and restraint. **Dorati's** performances of the *Dance Symphony*, *El salón México* and *Rodeo* are notable for their bright, extrovert brilliance, and the only reservation is that, somewhat surprisingly, Dorati's treatment of jazzy syncopations is rather literal. The evocative opening picture of the *New England Countryside* occupies the same musical world as *Appalachian Spring*. Again, fine playing from the **London Sinfonietta** under **Elgar Howarth**, and vivid recording. **Marriner's** account of *Quiet City* is second to none, but the highlight of the second CD is **Marilyn Horne's** delightful performances of five *Old American Songs*. Excellent value.

(i) Appalachian Spring; (ii) El salón México; (iii) Fanfare for the Common Man; (iv) Old American Songs

(N) (M) *** EMI 2 06634-2 (i) Saint Louis SO, Slatkin; (ii) Dallas SO, Mata;(iii) Mexico PO, Bátiz; (iv) Hubbard, O of St Luke's, Russell Davies

A first-class collection. **Slatkin** is naturally at home in *Appalachian Spring* and the sound is first class. **Bátiz's** orchestra doesn't have the technical excellence of Slatkin's but he is a lively and persuasive interpreter of Copland. **Mata's** Dallas performance of *El salón México* is as good as any – brilliant playing in demonstration sound, and **Hubbard** is a fine folksy exponent of the attractive *American Songs*.

Appalachian Spring (original chamber version); *Nonet for Strings; 2 Pieces for String Quartet*

Ⓝ Ⓜ *** Nimbus NI 2506 St Luke's Chamber Ens (or Qt.) Russell Davies

(i) *Clarinet Concerto. Music for Movies; Music for the Theatre; Quiet City*

Ⓝ Ⓜ *** Nimbus NI 2522 (i) Blount; O of St Luke's, Russell Davies

Apart from *Appalachian Spring* (beautifully played and very balletic), glowing in its original version, and the atmospheric *Quiet City*, most of this music is lesser-known Copland. **William Blount** is a rich-toned soloist in the *Clarinet Concerto*, languid in the first movement, but contrasting with the roisterous jazzy finale. The vibrant *Music for the Theatre* with its brash *Prologue* and *Dance* and ironic *Burlesque* nicely offsets the mellower New England evocations of *Music for Movies*, although here *Sunday Traffic* makes another lively contrast and the *Threshing Machines* are very busy too. The *Nonet* is more demanding, more severe, with the first three chords generating most of its melodic and harmonic material. But it rewards the listener who returns to it. These excellent performances directed by **Dennis Russell Davies** come from the MusicMasters Catalogue and were very well recorded at the end of the 1980s.

Billy the Kid (excerpts); *Down a Country Lane;* (i) *Old American Songs* (Sets 1–2); (ii) *8 Poems of Emily Dickinson*

⊖— ⒷⒷ *** Warner Apex 2564 62089-2. St Paul Chamber O, Wolff, with (i) Hampson; (ii) Upshaw

Hugo Wolff and his fine **St Paul Chamber Orchestra** are completely at home here, and it is good to have the composer's own scoring of *Down a Country Lane* (originally a piano piece). However, the highlights are the two superbly sung song-cycles. In the *Old American Songs*, **Thomas Hampson** is in a special class, and he includes both sets. So is **Dawn Upshaw's** eloquent set of the *Emily Dickinson Poems*, now easily the finest version on record.

Billy the Kid (Ballet) *Suite & Waltz; Rodeo: 4 Dance Episodes & Honky Tonk Interlude*

(*) RCA **SACD (ADD) 82876 67904-2. O, Gould – GROFÉ: *Grand Canyon Suite* **(*)

Although you would never guess it from the richness of the sound of this new Living Presence SACD, **Morton Gould's** recordings of Copland's two cowboy ballets (in three-track stereo) date from 1957. Gould's performances are vividly characterized and full of vitality, and the expressive music (the *Corral Nocturne* in particular) has a romantically luxuriant languor, all this emphasized by the warmly atmospheric recording. While Bernstein's versions have a more idiomatic, abrasive bite, Gould's vigour and his natural affinity (as a ballet composer himself) with Copland's rhythmic style is infectious, and he includes the *Honky Tonk* piano sequence and *Saturday Night Waltz* in *Rodeo*. The technicolor sound is

gorgeous, if perhaps a shade over-resonant for music designed for the ballet pit.

Clarinet Concerto

ⒷⒷ *** ASV COE CD COE 811. Hosford, COE, Fischer – MOZART: *Clarinet Concerto*; R. STRAUSS: *Duet Concertino* ***

*** Chan. 8618. Hilton, SNO, Bamert – NIELSEN: *Concerto*; LUTOSŁAWSKI: *Dance Preludes* ***

Richard Hosford's performance of Copland's masterly concerto is second to none, with the strings and harp of the **Chamber Orchestra of Europe** warmly and seductively atmospheric at the opening, while the jazzy syncopations of the work's second section are vibrantly pointed, with the witty clarinet contribution which follows quite delectable. Excellent, atmospheric recording too, and highly recommendable couplings. A true bargain.

Janet Hilton's performance is soft-grained and has a light touch, yet she finds plenty of sparkle for the finale and her rhythmic felicity is infectious. She is at her very finest, however, in the gloriously serene opening, where her tender, poetic line is ravishing.

(i) *Clarinet Concerto. Dance Panels; Music for Theatre; Quiet City*

Ⓝ Ⓜ *** EMI 2 34439-2. NY Chamber Symphony, Schwarz with (i) David Shifrin

David Shifrin's account of the *Clarinet Concerto* is among the best, the opening radiant in timbre and showing a natural fluency of phrasing, the later jazzy elements also well caught. What makes this collection especially attractive, apart from the beautifully played and evocative account of *Quiet City*, is the inclusion of the rare *Dance Panels*. Those, who enjoy *Appalachian Spring*, will surely respond to this inspired and diverse score, which typically moves with great ease from lyric tonal painting to jazzy dance rhythms. The *Music for the Theatre* has comparable contrasts, The performances are of a high standard and the recording vivid and with a particularly attractive ambience. Now offered at mid-price.

(i) *Piano Concerto; The Tender Land* (opera): *Suite;* (ii) *Old American Songs, Volumes 1–2*

Ⓝ ⒷⒷ **** Naxos 8.5529297 (i) Benjamin Pasternack; (ii) St Charles Singers, Elgin SO, Hanson

Benjamin Pasternack is a persuasive soloist in the *Piano Concerto*, a fine performance contrasting the lyrical first section with a glittering account of the jazzy finale. *The Tender Land Suite* (which stands up well, independently from the opera) moves from the characteristically atmospheric *Introduction* and *Love music* to a boisterous party scene and back to the lyrical finale, *The Promise of Living*. But the highlight of the disc is the full set of *Old American Songs* which sound even more captivating in their choral versions, which especially suit *Simple Gifts*, *At the River*, *I Bought me a Cat* and the superb pay-off number, *Ching-a-ring Chaw*.

Letter from Home; Prairie Journal; The Red Pony (film score): *Suite; Rodeo: 4 Dance Episodes*

⊟ ⚙ (BB) **** Naxos 8.559240. Buffalo PO, Falletta

A Copland collection not to be missed, for it contains much rare and inspired music, notably the nostalgic wartime *Letter from Home* and *Prairie Journal*, commissioned by the Columbia Broadcasting Network in 1936, predating *Billy the Kid* and *Rodeo*, and just as evocative of the Western landscapes. But even more valuable is Copland's enchanting score for the 1948 film of John Steinbeck's *The Red Pony* about life on a Californian ranch. **JoAnn Falletta** is totally in tune with the Copland ethos and the excellent **Buffalo Philharmonic** play all this music with a natural understanding of the idiom: they are wonderfully boisterous in the *Hoe Down* from *Rodeo*. Splendidly vivid and atmospheric recording, too. Not to be missed.

Quiet City

⊟ (M) **** Decca 475 8237 – ASMF, Marriner – BARBER: *Adagio*; COWELL: *Hymn & Fuguing Tune*; CRESTON: *A Rumor*; IVES: *Symphony 3* ****

Marriner's 1976 version is both poetic and evocative, and the playing of the trumpet and cor anglais soloists is of the highest order. The digital remastering has brought about added clarity without loss of atmosphere.

Quiet City; (i) 8 Poems of Emily Dickinson

⊟ (BB) *** EMI Encore 3 45287-2. (i) Hendricks; LSO, Tilson Thomas – BARBER: *Adagio*, etc. ***

This is an intensely beautiful disc that in deep thoughtfulness belies the conventional idea of American culture being brash. *Quiet City* is memorable with solo trumpet and cor anglais (superbly played by **Maurice Murphy** and **Christine Pendrill**) adding atmospheric intensity. Copland himself orchestrated eight of his twelve settings of Emily Dickinson poems for chamber orchestra for his seventieth birthday concert, and **Tilson Thomas** as a young conductor was in charge. The freshness and sharp imagination of the accompaniments are enhanced in support of vocal lines lovingly matched to Dickinson's distinctive poetic style. Radiant singing from **Barbara Hendricks**, and equally sensuous sounds from the orchestra.

Clarinet Sonata; Nocturne for Clarinet and Piano

(N) (BB) ⊟ **** Naxos 8.572240 Emma Johnson, Lenahan – BERNSTEIN: *Sonata*; DANKWORTH: *Suite for Emma*; *Picture of Jennie* ****

The opening four-note figure immediately and indelibly reveals the identity of the composer of this very appealing sonata. The 'singing simplicity' of the opening melts into busy dancing, but there is still more folksy melody to come and in the slow movement the clarinet soliloquizes against a repeated serene scalic piano figure. The finale is jazzily high spirited, but the first movement is recalled before the close. This is a masterwork and should be much better known. It is superbly played here, followed by the nostalgically gentle, sleepy *Nocturne*.

PIANO MUSIC

Piano Fantasy

*** Mode 93. Laimon – IVES: *Piano Sonata 3* ***

Sara Laimon certainly seems to be right inside this initially intractable work, following the composer's continually changing directives as written on the score with apparent spontaneity, right through to the reflective closing pages. She is very well recorded, so if you are musically adventurous you might try this example of Copland's music, which could not be further removed from *Billy the Kid*! (The disc can be obtained from Mode, PO Box 1262, New York 10009 or www.mode.com)

Piano Fantasy; Passacaglia; Piano Sonata; Piano Variations

(M) *** Divine Art 25016. Clarke

Raymond Clarke opens with the early *Passacaglia*, composed in 1921–2 while the composer was in Paris and dedicated to Nadia Boulanger. It is a self-consciously serious work, easy to follow, and in Clarke's hands attractively diverse. The 'craggy' *Piano Variations* of 1930 follow on naturally after it (even the keys are related). Clarke then proves completely at home in the *Sonata*. The *Fantasy* is handled with equal understanding, especially in its changes of mood and tempo, and the recording is outstandingly vivid and realistic, with a full sonority in the bass. A most satisfying and rewarding collection.

Piano Sonata; 4 Piano Blues; Scherzo humoristique: The Cat and the Mouse

*** Nim. NI 5585. Anderson – GERSHWIN: *3 Preludes*; *Arrangements of Songs*; *An American in Paris* ***

Mark Anderson also gives an outstanding account of the *Piano Sonata*, making it seem emotionally warmer and texturally and harmonically less spare than usual. His reading will surely make new friends for the work; it is 'freely expressive' (as the first movement is marked by the composer) and with the restless rhythmic mood of the central *Vivace* spontaneously caught, with even a brief jazz inflexion. The *Four Piano Blues* are in Copland's easily accessible style and are also very well characterized, while the witty portrait of *Le Chat et la souris* makes a brilliant encore for what is a live recital in Nimbus's own concert hall.

VOCAL MUSIC

(i) In the Beginning. Help us, O Lord; Have mercy on us, O my Lord; Sing ye praises to our King

*** Hyp. CDA 66219. (i) Denley; Corydon Singers, Best – BARBER: *Agnus Dei*; BERNSTEIN: *Chichester Psalms* ***

In the Beginning is a large-scale, 15-minute motet for unaccompanied chorus and soprano solo, written in 1947, and the long span of the work is well structured with the help of the soprano soloist, here the fresh-toned **Catherine Denley**. The chorus is just as clear and alert in its singing, not only in the big motet but also in the three delightful little pieces which come as an appendix. Vivid recording, full of presence.

(i) In the Beginning. 5 Old American Songs; Motets: Have mercy on us; Help us, O Lord; Sing ye the Praises to our King; Thou, O Jehova

*** Gloriae Dei Cantores GDCD 029. (i) Bybee; Gloriae Dei Cantores, Patterson – VIRGIL THOMSON: Hymns; Mass, etc. ***

An outstanding account of In the Beginning with warmly expressive singing from this splendid choir, based in Cape Cod, Massachusetts. The mezzo, **Luretta Bybee**, is an eloquent, full-voiced soloist, though her vibrato is somewhat intrusive. Five favourite American Songs follow. Then come four equally diverse miniature motets, ending with the joyful Sing ye the praises, which show the choir at their very finest. Excellent recording, and an even more imaginative Virgil Thomson programme as coupling, make this a very desirable issue indeed.

(i; ii) Old American Songs (Sets I & II); 12 Poems of Emily Dickinson. (ii) 4 Piano Blues

⊕ *** Black Box BBM 1074. (i) Chilcott; (ii) Burnside

Susan Chilcott's superb collection of Copland songs, bringing together 25 of his most approachable pieces, plus the Four Piano Blues, is beautifully recorded as well as masterfully performed. Though the Old American Songs with their openair, folk-based inspiration are more readily suited to a man's voice, Chilcott is strong and magnetic in each one, and she equally relishes the touching simplicity of the Emily Dickinson Poems, with **Burnside** the ideal accompanist, crisp and pointed in the songs as well as in his solo pieces.

CORELLI, Arcangelo (1653–1713)

Ciaconna, Op. 2/12; Concerto grosso, Op. 6/5; Sonate da chiesa, Op. 1/9–10; Op. 2/4; Op. 3/5; Op. 4/2; Trio Sonata, Op. 5/3

(BB) **(*) Virgin 2x1 4 82097-2 (2). L. Bar. – PURCELL: Fantasias & In nomines **(*)

The **London Baroque** collection mixes church and chamber sonatas with an impeccable feeling for the style of the period and a continuo which includes archlute and organ, appropriately. Ornamentation is judicious and intonation is secure. The Abbey Road recording is admirably transparent and vivid.

Concerti grossi, Op. 6/1–12

⊕ (B) *** Hyp. Dyad CDD 22011 (2). Brandenburg Consort, Goodman

⊕ (M) *** DG 459 451-2 (2). E. Concert, Pinnock

⊕ *** Naïve OP 30-147 and 30-155. Europa Galante, Biondi

⊕ (BB) *** Naxos 8.550402/3. Capella Istropolitana, Krechek

Corelli's glorious set of Concerti grossi, Op. 6, is now very well represented in the catalogue in all price-ranges. For those who prefer period performances there is plenty of choice. **Roy Goodman** and the **Brandenburg Consort** use 17 string players plus harpsichord continuo, archlute and organ; however, there is a sense of style and a freshness of approach in the Goodman version that is very persuasive. The recorded sound is first class.

Pinnock and his **English Concert** bring not only an enthusiasm for this music but a sense of grandeur. They are entirely inside its sensibility, and the playing of the concertino group (**Simon Standage, Micaela Comberti** and **Jaap ter Linden**) is wonderfully fresh-eyed and alert, yet full of colour.

But the newest set, from the appropriately named **Europa Galante**, is as fine as any. The chamber-sized ripieno of period instruments (2,2,2,1,1) offers crisp detail yet no feeling of any lack of sonority, and the elegant playing is alert and vital yet smiles pleasingly: these musicians are obviously enjoying the music, and so do we. The soloists are excellent, as is the recording.

For those preferring the richer textures of modern instruments, the Naxos set by the **Capella Istropolitana** under **Jaroslav Krechek** represents very good value indeed.

Oboe Concerto (arr. Barbirolli)

(B) *** Dutton Lab./Barbirolli Soc. CDSJB 1016. Rothwell, Hallé O, Barbirolli – HAYDN; MARCELLO: Oboe Concertos *** (with Recital C. P. E. BACH; LOEILLET; TELEMANN: Sonatas, etc. **)

Barbirolli's Concerto is cunningly arranged from a Trio Sonata and in its present form it makes one of the most enchanting works in the oboe repertoire. The performance here is treasurable and the clear, natural recording projects the music admirably.

CHAMBER MUSIC

Sonate da chiesa, Op. 1/1–12; Op. 3/1–12; Sonate da camera (Trio Sonatas), Op. 2/1–12; Op. 4/1–12

*** Chan. 0692 (4).   Purcell Qt

The admirable **Purcell Quartet** (joined by **Catherine Weiss** in Op. 4), with a continuo from **Jakob Lindberg**, theorbo and archlute, plus **Robert Woolley** (organ in Opp. 1 and 3 and harpsichord in Opp. 2 and 4) surveys all Corelli's Sonatas of Opp. 1–4. Their playing is vibrant and stylish, and expressive in slow movements, and in that respect, although allegros are admirably spirited, makes somewhat less of the lighter character of the Sonate da chiesa, than Medlam and the London Baroque, although the difference is hardly consequential. The Chandos recording is first rate, and this complete set is highly recommendable.

Trio Sonatas, Op. 1/9; Op. 2/4 & 12 (Ciacona); Op. 3/12; Op. 4/3; Op. 5/3, 11 & 12 (La Folia)

⊕ *** Hyp. CDA 66226. Purcell Qt

The Hyperion disc is one of six designed to illustrate the widespread use in the 18th century of the famous La Folia theme. It includes a varied collection of *sonate da chiesa* and *sonate da camera*. Excellent performances from all concerned, and recording to match.

Violin Sonatas, Op. 5/1–12

⊶ 🏵 *** HM HMU 907 298.99 (2). Manze, Egarr

(BB) *** Naxos 8.557165 (1–6); 8.557799 (7–12) (available separately). Fernandez, Wilson

Corelli's twelve *Violin Sonatas*, Op. 5, were published in 1700. Nos. 1–5 are in five-movement *sonata la chiesa* form, Nos. 7–11 are *sonate da camera*, usually in four movements, although Nos. 10 and 11 each includes a brief additional section. Corelli's invention is inexhaustible and the set closes with perhaps the most celebrated set of variations on the traditional *La Folia* theme. **Andrew Manze** is in his element here. Dazzling playing on a baroque instrument, with slow movements touchingly lyrical, full of subtle detail, and plenty of gusto and character in *allegros*, yet with unwanted acerbities banished. **Richard Egarr** is a true partner, and there are countless felicities. The balance is natural, with the violin obviously dominating, yet the harpsichord comes through.

The performances by **François Fernandez** (playing a baroque violin – a Guarneri) and **Glen Wilson** (using a Dutch copy of a Ruckers harpsichord), are also stylish, fresh and spirited and very well recorded, and make an admirable bargain alternative.

CORIGLIANO, John (born 1938)

Circus Maximus (Symphony 3 for Large Wind Ensemble); Gazebo Dances for Band

(N) (BB) **(*) Naxos 8.559601 University of Texas Wind Ens., Junkin

Circus Maximus is scored for a very large wind ensemble and as it pictures the famous venue in ancient Rome it is meant to be performed with the players positioned surrounding the audience, and in all sections of the hall. This is not possible without surround sound but the Naxos recording does quite well with a normal stereo effect. In between the big climaxes come *Night Music* and *Prayer Music*, but the resulting spectacle is hardly subtle. The *Gazebo Dances* are much more rewarding, particularly the closing jolly *Tarantella*.

3 Hallucinations. (i) Mr Tambourine Man: Seven Poems of Bob Dylan

(N) (BB) *** Naxos 8.559331. Buffalo PO, Falletta with (i) Plitmann

Written at the request of Sylvia McNair, who wanted a song cycle for Carnegie Hall, she asked that only American texts were used. In the end, Corigliano used the texts from Bob Dylan's songs – without having heard Dylan's musical treatment. The songs were subsequently orchestrated and performed by **Hila Plitman** – an 'amplified' soprano in 2003. Corogliano's style suits the imagination of Dylan's texts very well, and the opera-cum-music-theatre style of the singing

admirably fits the style of the music. '*Blowin' in the Wind*' is particularly haunting number but it is all enjoyable, even if it doesn't really plumb any great emotional depth. The 3 *Hallucinations* derive from Ken Russell's film *Altered States* (1980), three colourful and atmospheric pieces in a somewhat horror-music style. It is all vividly performed and recorded, and full texts are included.

(i) The Red Violin Concerto; (ii) Violin Sonata

*** Sony/BMG 82876 88060-2. Bell, with (i) Baltimore SO, Alsop; (ii) Jeremy Denk

John Corigliano wrote the film score for *The Red Violin* (about a violin travelling through three centuries) and he had Joshua Bell as the 'voice' of the violin. He then decided to transform the *Chaconne* of the film score, first into a concert piece for violin and orchestra, then later to expand it into a full-length concerto by adding a wild *pianissimo* Scherzo, with the soloist playing 'high, ethereal and dance-like'. A lyrical *Andante flautando* follows, with the soloist joining in a duet with the orchestra flute. The finale is 'a rollicking race in which the opposed forces of soloist and orchestra vie with each other' against extraneous non-musical sounds. There is a melancholy lyrical counterpart, before the *Chaconne* returns to complete the work. It is an unpredictable but fascinating work, and it could surely not be presented more excitingly than by **Joshua Bell** with **Marin Alsop** and the excellent **Baltimore Orchestra**. The recording is extremely vivid. The *Violin Sonata*, written much earlier (in 1962/3) is even more unpredictable, rhythmic patterns constantly changing, with two central slow movements framed by outer allegros. The performance here is again surely definitive.

The Red Violin: Chaconne

(BB) **(*) Naxos 8.559302. Hanslip, RPO, Slatkin (with WAXMAN: *Tristan Fantasia* – ADAMS: *Violin Concerto* **(*)

The 17-minute *Chaconne* which John Corigliano has fashioned from the main theme of his film score opens seductively, reaches an explosive climax and, after a cadenza, ends decisively. The performance and recording here can hardly be faulted.

Symphony 2; (i) The Red Violin: Suite from the film

*** Chan. **SACD** CHSA 5035. I Musici de Montréal, Yuli Turovsky, (i) with Eleonora Turovsky & Ch.

Symphony 2 for String Orchestra; The Mannheim Rocket

*** Ondine ODE 1039-2. Helsinki PO, Storgårds

John Corigliano's *Second Symphony*, commissioned by the Boston Symphony Orchestra, draws on his 1996 *String Quartet*, but the adaptation involved rewriting three of the five movements. The opening *Prelude* combines synchronous threads of sound which oscillate hauntingly, leading to a climax and a serene chordal apotheosis. The Scherzo is slashingly aggressive, but the middle section is gentle, bearing a lyrical *passacaglia*. The *Nocturne* opens ethereally and creates a richly sustained string tapestry to picture a serene Moroccan night, interrupted by a pattern of muezzin calls from the city's many mosques. Then comes a complex *Fugue*, which the composer describes as 'anti-contrapuntal'. He uses a single theme in separate voices moving at different tempi; the work closes with a *Postlude* in valedictory mood, with a high solo violin 'meant to impact a feeling of farewell'. The synchronous sound threads of the *Prelude* return, and the symphony ends as it began, fading into silence. It is a remarkably imaginative piece, not nearly as difficult to follow as it sounds.

The Mannheim Rocket is a phantasmagorical orchestral picture of Baron von Munchausen's Wedding Cake Rocket taking off, but it is also a pun on a musical term made famous by the Mannheim orchestra in the 18th century to describe a rising musical sequence that speeded up and grew louder as it went higher. The performances here are first class and so is the spectacular recording. This is all real music and well worth trying.

The alternative Chandos version is also very well played and recorded under the composer's supervision. Those with SACD facilities will find the sound very impressive indeed. The suite drawn from the composer's music for the François Giraud film, *The Red Violin*, is in 11 brief sections, in effect a violin concerto, with the solo violin emerging ever more prominently in writing both brilliant and lyrical, with a gypsy cadenza towards the end. The *Suite* is rounded off with a beautiful development of the main theme, representing the heroine Anna, not just on the violin and the orchestra but briefly with a wordless chorus (unidentified on the disc). Whether you choose this coupling or *The Mannheim Rocket* on Ondine, the symphony itself is well worth having.

The Red Violin Caprices (for violin solo); (i) Sonata for Violin & Piano

(N) (BB) *** Naxos 8.559364 Quint; (i) with Wolfram – v. THOMSON: *Portraits* ***

The *Caprices for solo violin* are yet another extension of music from the film of that name and they are brilliantly and expressively played by **Philippe Quint**. The *Sonata* (where William Wolfram also participates expertly) is more unpredictable but certainly inventive.

A Dylan Thomas Trilogy: (i) Author's Prologues; (ii) Fern Hill; (iii) Poem in October; (ii) Poem on his Birthday

(N) (BB) *** Naxos 8.559394. Nashville Symphony Co. & O, Slatkin with (i) Allen; (ii) Jackson; (iii) Tessier

Written over many years, the Dylan poems Corigliano chose reflected the circumstances of his own life, from the relatively untroubled poem of youth which is *Fern Hill*, to his 'crisis' of turning thirty in *Poem in October*, to the far darker *Poem on his Birthday* (age thirty-five) and the three were thus presented in 1976. However, Corigliano felt the trilogy was not quite complete and Dylan's *Author's Prologue* was added, heard at the beginning and in between *Fern Hill* and *Poem in October*. The result is a rather compelling 'three ages of man' story, with bold, imaginative orchestrations and Corigliano's music skilfully reflecting the nuances of the texts. It is hard to imagine better performances than the superb ones they

receive here and the recording is excellent. The sleeve notes are by the composer and texts are included.

CORNYSH, William (c. 1468–1523)

Ave Maria, mater Dei; Gaude, virgo, mater Christi; Salve regina

⊶ 🌸 (B) **** Gimell 2 CD CDGIM 209 (2). Tallis Scholars, Phillips – BROWNE: *Motets*; TAVERNER, TYE: *Western Wind Mass* ***

Cornysh's music is quite unlike much other polyphony of the time and is florid, wild, complex and, at times, grave. The **Tallis Scholars** give a magnificent, totally committed account of these glorious pieces – as usual their attack, ensemble and true intonation and blend are remarkable. Excellent recording.

Ave Maria, mater Dei; Gaude, virgo, mater Christi (motets); Magnificat; Salve regina

*** Gaudeamus CDGAU 164. Cardinall's Musick, Carwood – TURGES: *Magnificat*; PRENTES: *Magnificat* ***

In his survey of early Tudor polyphony, **Andrew Carwood**, with his keenly responsive group, **Cardinall's Musick**, here presents all four of Cornysh's surviving liturgical works, including a fine *Magnificat* and a radiant *Salve regina*, alongside even more elaborate *Magnificats* by two composers far less well-known but just as inspired. Complex and beautiful, the *Magnificat* of Turges is the most expansive of all, while Prentes's *Magnificat*, closely following Cornysh's, even outshines that model in both scale and sublimity.

COUPERIN, Armand-Louis (1725–89)

(i) Violin Sonata 3. Pièces de clavecin, Book 1: Suites in B flat & G: excerpts

⊶ (BB) *** Virgin 3 85806-2 (2). Curtis; (i) Lucy van Dael (with Claude-Bénigne BALBASTRE: *Pièces de clavecin* ***) – François COUPERIN: *Pièces de clavecin* ***

This two-disc set is especially attractive and valuable in including music by both Armand-Louis and François Couperin, plus four attractive pieces from the *First Book* of Claude-Béninge Balbastre (1725–99) of which *La Courteille* is particularly winning. All the items by Armand-Louis are well chosen for variety and character and **Alan Curtis** plays them with flair. He is joined by **Lucy van Dael** in the *Sonata*. The recording is first class.

Pièces de clavecin: excerpts

*** Chan. 0718. Yates (harpsichord)

Armand-Louis Couperin was distantly related to both François and Louis. His *Pièces de clavecin* were published in 1751 in two books, and here we are offered a good selection of 21 pieces, almost all with sobriquets. Some, such as the

Allemande and *La Grégoire*, show a debt to Rameau; but others, such as *L'Affligée* and *La Chéron*, are more forward-looking. **Sophie Yates** is an admirable exponent, using a copy by Andrew Garlick of a Parisian Goujon harpsichord dating from 1749. The recording is fairly resonant, so it is important to get the volume setting right – not too loud and not too soft – and then the results are very impressive.

Pièces de clavecin: L'Affligée; La du Breüil; Les Tendres Sentimens

(*) BIS CD 982. Hirosawa (harpsichord) – François
   COUPERIN; Louis COUPERIN: *Pièces de clavecin **(*)***

Another thunderous harpsichord so closely balanced that immediate action is called for to reduce the level setting. No quarrels however with **Asami Hirosawa's** playing, which has great expressive feeling. Her account of *L'Affligée* has greater poignancy than Harald Hoeren's, and if the volume is turned down a satisfactory result can be secured.

COUPERIN, François
(1668–1733)

Les Apothéoses: L'Apothéose composé à la mémoire immortelle de l'incomparable M. de Lully; La Parnasse ou l'Apothéose de Corelli

⚭ (M) *** Astrée ES 9947. Hespèrion XX, Savall

Couperin's two great linked instrumental works, both called *Apothéoses*, between them ardently espouse the virtues of the conflicting French and Italian influences on early 18th-century music. The composers Lully and Corelli are thus united in the Elysian fields, with the French and Italian muses playing each other's music. It is a delightful concept. Each work has a sequence of stylized classical vignettes. *L'Apothéose de Lully* is programmatic and evokes Apollo and Mercury; *L'Apothéose de Corelli* is an eloquent Trio sonata, but also with titled movements, grave, expressive and lively by turns. The performances by **Savall** and **Hespèrion XX** have splendid life, grace and refinement of feeling.

Concerts royaux 1 in G; 2 in D; 3 in A; 4 in E min.

⚭ *** Alia Vox **SACD** AVSA 9840. Le Concert des Nations, Savall

*** ASV CDGAU 101. Trio Sonnerie

The *Concerts royaux* can be performed in a variety of forms. On the ASV Gaudeamus disc, the **Trio Sonnerie** give them in the most economical fashion (violin, viola da gamba and harpsichord) and the contribution of all three musicians is unfailingly imaginative. Excellent recording.

However, the Trio Sonnerie are upstaged by **Jordi Savall** (bass viol and director) whose period-instrument ensemble, **Le Concert des Nations**, includes flute, oboe, violin, bassoon and continuo. They play this music delightfully, with warmth and spirit, and the recording has an ideal ambience and fine presence. On four-channel SACD, the illusion of sitting in the concert hall is very real.

Les Nations, Vol. 1: Première Ordre (La Français); Deuxième Ordre (L'espagnole); Concerts royaux: Deuxième Concert à deux violes ou autres instruments à l'unisson; La Sultana

*** Chan. 0684. Purcell Qt

Les Nations, Vol. 2: Troizième Ordre (L'Impériale); Quatrième Ordre (La Pièmontoise); L'Art de Toucher le Clavecin: 2nd & 3rd Préludes. Concerts royaux: Treizième Concert à deux instruments à l'unisson

*** Chan. 0729. Purcell Qt

These four collections, published in 1726, were composed over a considerable period. Their fusion of French and Italian styles proves greatly rewarding in what are essentially greatly varied collections of dance movements. The period performances by these excellent players are as stylish as one could wish, and they fill out the two discs appropriately with duets from the *Concerts royaux*. An important addition to the catalogue.

Pièces de violes: Les Goûts Réunis (1724): excerpts: 10th, 12th & 13th Concerts; 2 Suites (1728)

*** Avie AV 2132. Luolajan-Mikkola, Perkola, Häkkinen

This expert Finnish trio (two bass violists and a harpsichordist) offer here a collection of what they call 'private music', written for the French court. Of the two mature *Suites* the first has the expected layout of *Prélude, Allemande, Courant, Sarabande grave, Gavotte gracieusement, Gigue gayment*, finishing with a spirited *Passacaille*; the second is in four movements, with the noble and dignified third named *Pompe funèbre*, perhaps in memory of Marais, who had died the year the *Pièces* were published. The music from the earlier *Les Goûts Réunis* is equally varied, and its movement titles often convey their character: *Air Tendre, La Tromba, Sarabande tendrement, Air agréable* and so on. The performances are authentic and very responsive to the music's expressive moods; but the viola da gamba timbre is something of an acquired taste, so this is perhaps a disc to approach with a degree of caution. The recording is certainly real and present.

KEYBOARD MUSIC

Livres de pièces de clavecin 1–4; Ordres 1–27

(B) *** Warner 2564 64176 (10). Baumont

For his magisterial traversal of the 27 *Ordres*, the French harpsichordist **Olivier Baumont** has used five different instruments and has elected to record each *Ordre* on the same harpsichord, giving the full details of each in his eminently scholarly and thorough notes. The recordings were made at various times in the 1990s, mostly in the studios of Radio France. He penetrates the soul of this music and conveys his love for it. (A worthwhile selection is available on Apex 2564 62089.)

Harpsichord Suites, Book 1: Ordre 1; Concerts royaux 1–2

(BB) *** Naxos 8.550961. Cummings (harpsichord)

Harpsichord Suites, Book 3: Ordre 13

(*) BIS CD 982. Hirosawa (harpsichord) – ARMAND-LOUIS COUPERIN; LOUIS COUPERIN: *Pièces de clavecin* **(*)**

Laurence Cummings plays a modern instrument by Michael Johnson modelled on a Taskin, and he produces pleasing and musical results.

Asami Hirosawa couples the marvellous *Treizième ordre* with two of Louis Couperin's *Suites* and three pieces by Armand-Louis. She is thoroughly inside the French style and shows a natural feeling for its rhythmic flexibility. A very close microphone-balance produces pretty deafening results, but a drastic reduction of volume makes for more satisfactory listening.

Harpsichord Suites, Book 3 (excerpts)

⊶ (BB) *** Virgin 3 85806-2 (2). Curtis (with Lucy van Dael, Brüggen, Haynes) (with Claude-Bénigne BALBASTRE: *Pièces de clavecin* ***) – Armand-Louis COUPERIN: *Sonata; Pièces de clavecin* ***

Alan Curtis provides a splendid survey of Couperin's Book 3 and is joined by **Frans Brüggen** (recorder) in *Le Rossignol-en-amour, Double du Rossignol* and *La Juilliet*, by **Lucy van Dael** (violin) in *La Létville* and by **Bruce Haynes** (baroque oboe) in the two *Musettes* with drone basses. Excellently recorded, and with its enterprising couplings this stands out among Couperin collections.

Harpsichord Suites, Book 2: Ordres 6 & 8; Book 3: Ordre 18

*** Hyp. CDA 67440. Hewitt (piano)

Having had a great success with Bach's keyboard music, **Angela Hewitt** now turns to Couperin, and the present disc is the first of three in which she has chosen music that she feels is best suited to the piano. In her admirable accompanying notes she comments on the composer's extensive and explicit ornaments: 'Leaving them out is not an option! It is all related to gesture: ornamentation is there for an expressive purpose, to emphasize one note, to make you wait for another. It is all part of the melodic line.' Certainly, in her hand the ornamentation is both crisply decorative and flexible and always inherent in the music's forward flow. In short, this playing is endlessly diverting and the piano is most naturally recorded.

Harpsichord Suites, Book 3: Ordre 13: Les Lis naissans; Les Rozeaux; L'Engagement; Les Folies françoises ou Les Dominos; L'âme-en-peine; Ordre 14: Le Rossignol-en-amour; La Linote-éfarouchée; Les Fauvètes plaintives; Le Petit-rien; Ordre 15: Le Dodo, ou L'amour au Berceau; Ordre 16: La Distraite; L'Himen-amour; Ordre 19: La Muse-Plantine (with excerpts from Books I and II)

⊶ **** Hyp. CDA 67520. Hewitt (piano)

Angela Hewitt centres her third Couperin collection on the *Treizième Ordre* of Book III, which she considers one of Couperin's finest suites. It includes *Les Folies françoises ou Les Dominos*, a miniature theme-and-variations on the

famous *La Folia* bass, with each variation depicting a different character arriving at a masked ball in an invisible cloak (domino).

Harpsichord Suites, Book 4, Ordres 21, 24–7

*** Hyp. CDA 67480. Hewitt (piano)

Angela Hewitt's selection from Book 4 (with the Ordres not played consecutively) is even more enticing than her first collection from Books 2 and 3. All the pieces have intriguing titles and not all of them are obviously reflected in the mood of the music. Among the most enigmatic are *Les Ombres errantes* ('Wandering souls'), the rondeau *L'Epineuse* ('The Thorny One'), which in the event is most engaging, and the poised and friendly representation of the composer's own name, which may or may not be intended as a self-portrait. The four pieces from the 17th *Ordre* (all in the key of B minor) are kept until last and make a splendidly satisfying closing set. Splendid alive and sensitive performances, really fine recording and excellent documentation.

ORGAN MUSIC

Messe des Paroisses; Messe des couvents

⊶ (BB) *** Naxos 8.557741/42. Robin (organ of Poitiers Cathedral)

Couperin's pair of *Organ Masses* each consist of 21 versets, which are intended to alternate with the text of the Mass, sung in plainchant. Only in two, for the *Offertory* and *Deo Gratias*, could the composer expand himself, and Couperin chooses to do this only in the *Offertory*. His Masses have been recorded in the past with the sung plainchant included, but the organ versets stand up well independently, and the recording here has dispensed with the plainchant. **Jean-Baptiste Robin's** splendid performances of just the *Masses*, given magnificent, modern, digital recordings, will be an obvious choice.

VOCAL MUSIC

Laudate pueri Dominum; Motet à Sainte Suzanne; 4 Versets d'un Motet composé de l'ordre du Roy (1703); 7 Versets d'un Motet composé de l'ordre du Roy (1704); 7 Versets d'un Motet composé de l'ordre du Roy (1705); Verset du motet de l'année dernière: Qui dat nivem

⊶ (BB) *** Virgin 2x1 5 62419-2 (2). Piau, Pelon, Fouchécourt, Corréas, Les Talens Lyriques, Rousset – HENRI DU MONT: Motets ***

Although the overall standard of solo singing and instrumental playing here is high, **Sandrine Piau** is the star of the occasion. She takes the place of her agile and apparently ethereal-voiced predecessor, Marguerite-Louise, Couperin's cousin, for whom the music was written, and is the leading soloist in the first of the psalm versets (1702) 'composed by order of the King'. Here in the exquisite *'Adolescent sum ego'* she is in duet with the hardly less impressive **Caroline Pelon** and a pair of celestial flutes, but she also contributes to the other versets and the closing *Laudate pueri Dominum* (the earliest of Couperin's motets written for the Chapel Royal). But perhaps the finest work of all here is the joyful *Motet à Sainte Suzanne*, written much later and showing the composer's mature style at its most persuasive. With first-class recording this is an outstanding disc in every way, and it is linked inexpensively to a rewarding collection of music by Couperin's much lesser-known predecessor, Henry du Mont.

Leçons de ténèbres pour le Mercredi Saint 1–3

⊕– *** BIS CD 1575. Kirkby, Mellon, Medlam, Charlston – DELALANDE: *Leçons de ténèbres* ***

Leçons de ténèbres pour le Mercredi Saint, 1–3; 4 versets du motet

⊕– *** Erato 0630 17067-2. Daneman, Petibon, Les Arts Florissants, Christie

Of available performances, **Sophie Daneman, Patricia Petibon** and **Les Arts Florissants** must probably rank highly. The first two *Leçons* are divided between the two sopranos, who join together for the last. As the *Trois leçons de ténèbres* take less than 40 minutes, the *Quatre versets du motet* (eight minutes) make an ungenerous fill-up. However, these are exquisite performances and are beautifully recorded.

Yet **Emma Kirkby** and **Agnès Mellon** also blend the voices together with sweetness and light, and their performances are hardly less delightful, with **Charles Medlam** and **Terence Charlston** (organ) providing admirable continuo support. The BIS recording too is first class, and the coupling with Delalande's equally beautiful settings is substantial, giving more than twenty minutes extra music.

COUPERIN, Louis (c. 1626–61)

Pièces de clavecin: Galliarde in G; 5 Pièces in D; 6 Pièces in C; Preludes in F, A, G & F sharp min.; Preludes (Toccades) in A min. & D min.; Tombeau de M. Blancrocher

⊕– (BB) *** Naxos 8.555936. Wilson

Louis Couperin wrote far less than his celebrated nephew, but his small output is of great quality. And indeed there is a greater eloquence and more feeling in many of these miniatures than in much of the comparable output of François. These are intimate and often inward-looking pieces, and **Glen Wilson**, who has recently published a reconstruction of Couperin's lost *Préludes non mesurés*, brings us totally inside their world. He plays a copy of a 1628 instrument by Rückers the Younger and is expertly recorded. This fine disc leaves one wondering whether it is not Louis who deserves to be called 'le-grand'.

Harpsichord suites: in A min.; in C; in D; in F (including Le Tombeau de M. Blancrocher)

(BB) *** Naxos 8.550922. Cummings (harpsichord)

Pièces de clavecin: Suites in A min. & C

**(*) BIS CD 982. Hirosawa (harpsichord) – Armand-Louis COUPERIN; François COUPERIN: *Pièces de clavecin* **(*)

Laurence Cummings plays a modern copy of a Rückers, which is very well recorded by Naxos. His selection is generous and he arranges his own groupings. His decoration is convincing and he plays with much spontaneity and flair. The CD offers some 75 minutes of music and is one of Naxos's best bargains.

Asami Hirosawa couples two of Louis Couperin's suites with pieces by Armand-Louis, and the *Treizième ordre* by Couperin-le-grand. She is an impressive advocate, admirably flexible in such pieces as the *Prélude à l'imitation de M. Froberger*. We occasionally felt the need for greater variety of colour, though in this respect she is not helped by a very close microphone-balance.

COUPERIN, Marc Roger Normand (1663–1734)

Livre de tablature de clavecin (c. 1695): complete

*** Hyp. CDA 67164. Moroney (harpsichord)

Marc Roger Normand's book contains 57 pieces – many attributed to other composers, including Chambonnières, Le Bègue and Lully. His choice is unerringly perceptive. Virtually all these miniatures are very personable, especially those by Paul de la Pierre and members of his family. Normand was a first cousin of François Couperin and was clearly a first-rate musician. Apart from his own works he includes an extended set of variants (27 couplets) on the famous *Folies d'Espagnes*. **Moroney** is a persuasive advocate. He plays with style and spontaneity and consistently entertains the listener. He uses a splendid Italian virginal dating from the 17th century, which is beautifully recorded, and this collection can be very highly recommended.

COWELL, Henry (1897–1965)

Hymn & Fuguing Tune

⊕– (M) **** Decca 475 8237. ASMF, Marriner – BARBER: *Adagio;* COPLAND: *Quiet City;* CRESTON: *A Rumor;* IVES: *Symphony 3* ****

The likeable *Hymn and Fuguing Tune*, by a composer otherwise little known, is well worth having, and it is superbly played and recorded here.

CRESTON, Paul (1906–85)

A Rumor

⊕– (M) **** Decca 475 8237. ASMF, Marriner – BARBER: *Adagio;* COPLAND: *Quiet City;* COWELL: *Hymn & Fuguing Tune;* IVES: *Symphony 3* ****

A Rumor is a witty and engaging piece and it is played here with plenty of character by **Marriner's Academy**. It completes a thoroughly rewarding and approachable disc of 20th-century American music that deserves the widest currency. The sound is first class.

Symphonies 1, Op. 20; 2, Op. 35; 3 (Three Mysteries), Op. 48

⏻— (BB) *** Naxos 8.559034. Ukraine Nat. SO, Kuchar

Paul Creston was among the most approachable of American symphonists. The *First* is exuberantly colourful and strongly rhythmic, with clean-cut themes. The titles of the four compact movements – *With Majesty*, *With Humour*, *With Serenity* and *With Gaiety* – reflect the openness of the emotions. 2 is much darker, with each of its two substantial movements moving from darkness towards a lightened mood. 3 outlines the life of Christ with a peaceful opening, almost pastoral, representing the Nativity and leading to a joyful *allegro*. The second movement, representing the Crucifixion, is a heartfelt lament, avoiding bitterness and anger, before the Resurrection finale, where Creston is at his most specifically American, almost Copland-like, with jagged syncopations leading to a triumphant close. The **Ukraine Orchestra**, very well rehearsed, plays with warmth and an idiomatic flair surprising from a non-American band, and it is very well recorded.

Symphony 2, Op. 35

*** Chan. 9390. Detroit SO, Järvi – IVES: *Symphony 2* ***

Järvi's well-recorded and excellently performed Chandos version of 2 can be recommended if the Ives coupling is desired.

Symphony 5, Op. 64; Invocation and Dance, Op. 58; Out of the Cradle, Op. 5; Partita, Op. 12; Toccata, Op. 68

⏻— (BB) *** Naxos 8.559153. Seattle SO, Schwarz

The *Toccata* from 1957 has much of the same vitality and rhythmic flair as the symphonies, and the wild clarinet solos we recall in the *Second Symphony* resurface here, calling to mind the *Danse générale* from *Daphnis et Chloé*. The *Fifth Symphony* (1956) is a three-movement work, exuberant and full of spirit, and as expertly fashioned as most of Creston's music. Readers who respond to Barber and Copland will find themselves at home in Creston's world. Splendid performances and recording.

String Quartet, Op. 8

(***) Testament mono SBT 1053. Hollywood Qt – DEBUSSY: *Danse sacrée*, etc.; RAVEL: *Introduction & Allegro*; TURINA: *La oración del torero*; VILLA-LOBOS: *Quartet 6* (***)

The *String Quartet*, Op. 8, is a pleasing, well-fashioned piece, slightly Gallic in feeling. The *Adagio* unfolds with eloquence. It could not be better served than it is by the **Hollywood Quartet**, recorded in 1953: the playing is stunning, and the recording, too, is very good for its period, even if the acoustic is on the dry side.

CROSSE, Gordon (born 1937)

(i) Ariadne: Concertante for solo oboe and 12 Players, Op. 31; (ii) Changes

*** Lyrita (ADD) SRCD 259. (i) Francis, LSO Ens., Lankester; (ii) Vyvyan, Shirley-Quirk, Orpington Junior Singers, Highgate School Boys' Ch., L. Symphony Ch., LSO, Del Mar

Ariadne is in effect a sustained one-movement oboe concerto, vividly dramatic in its eventful span, with an implied programme to illustrate the legend, the invocation of the Cretan caves of the Minotaur, atmospherically recaptured. The performance by **Sarah Francis**, for whom the work was written, is superb, helped by brilliant, committed playing from the **LSO Ensemble**. The title of the coupled work, *Changes*, is a pun, referring not merely to the transience of nature but to the tolling of bells. This is a work which can be appreciated at different levels, whether by children or by sophisticated listeners. A good piece to have on record, particularly when it is so well performed and recorded.

Purgatory (opera): complete

(N) *** Lyrita (ADD) SRCD 313. Bodenham, Hargreaves, Royal Northern College of Music Ch. & O, Lankester

Yeats's grim dialogue of the murderous father confessing his crimes to his son is set by Crosse with a simple devotion to the text. It is less effective dramatically on CD than in the theatre, but this student performance rises far above what you would expect from young performers – splendidly conveys the concentration of this retrained score. Both the soloists use their voices most intelligently and the recording (originally Argo), from 1975, emerges with great vividness on CD. Worth exploring.

CROSSLEY-HOLLAND, Peter (1916–2001)

Symphony in D

(N) (M) *** Dutton CDLX 7215. RSNO, Yates (with GOOSSENS: *Variations on Cadet Rousselle*; IRELAND: *Bagatelle*, *Cavatina* etc. (***))

Peter Crossley-Holland was a respected BBC administrator and from the late 1950s until 1963 in charge of music for the Third Programme. In 1969 he became a professor in the music faculty of the University of California, Los Angeles. This rather overshadowed his creative output even though he was a prolific composer. After embarking on medicine at Oxford, he changed course and studied with John Ireland, Mátyás Seiber and Edmund Rubbra. The *Symphony* occupied him from 1988 to 1994 and is a four-movement work lasting some thirty-seven minutes. The writing has the breadth of a symphonist, the ideas unfolding inevitably and organically. The idiom is distinctly diatonic but there is individuality and a real sense of purpose. He writes well for the orchestra and always holds the listener. The John Ireland pieces and Sir Eugene Goossens'

Variations on Cadet Rouselle, once a popular feature of BBC programmes, make excellent makeweights. Very good playing from the **Royal Scottish National Orchestra** under **Martin Yates**.

CRUSELL, Bernhard (1775–1838)

Clarinet Concertos in E flat. Op. 1. F min., Op. 5; B flat, Op. 11

Ⓝ **** BIS-SACD1723 Martin Fröst, Gothenburg SO, Okku Kamu

The Swedish clarinettist, Bernhard Crusell was considered a supreme virtuoso/composer of his time and he left us three highly appealing and very tuneful concertos for his instruments. They are most elegantly played by the young Swedish clarinettist, **Martin Fröst** and the fine **Gothenburg Orchestra** under **Okku Kamu**. There have been previous excellent versions by Emma Johnson (ASV), Antony Pay on a period instrument (Virgin) and a dazzling virtuoso account by Kari Kriikku (Ondine). All are highly enjoyable but this new BIS SACD seems to trump the others (except perhaps for Emma Johnson). Strongly recommended.

CURZON, Frederick (1899–1973)

The Boulevardier; Bravada (Paso doble); Capricante (Spanish Caprice); Cascade (Waltz); Dance of an Ostracised Imp; Galavant; In Malaga (Spanish Suite); Punchinello: Miniature Overture; Pasquinade; La Peineta; Robin Hood Suite; (i) Saltarello for Piano & Orchestra; Simonetta (Serenade)

*** Marco 8.223425. (i) Cápová; Slovak RSO (Bratislava), Leaper

The best-known piece here is the *Dance of an Ostracised Imp*, a droll little scherzando. But the *Galavant* is hardly less piquant and charming, the delicious *Punchinello* sparkles with miniature vitality, and the *Simonetta* serenade is sleekly beguiling. Curzon liked to write mock Spanishry, and several pieces here have such a Mediterranean influence. Yet their slight elegance and economical scoring come from cooler climes further north. The performances throughout are played with the finesse and light touch we expect from this fine **Slovak** series, so ably and sympathetically conducted by **Adrian Leaper**. The recording is admirable.

CZERNY, Carl (1791–1857)

Piano Sonatas 5 in E, Op. 76; 6 in D min., Op. 124; 8 in E flat, Op. 144; 9 in B min., Op. 145; Nocturne in E flat, Op. 647

Ⓝ **** Nimbus NI 5832/3 Martin Jones

Carl Czerny has the reputation of an educational pedagogue of the piano. Yet, as this Nimbus set demonstrates, he was an excellent composer in his own right and these *Sonatas* are full of attractive ideas. A torchbearer at Beethoven's

funeral, he was famous as an interpreter of the latter's piano music. His own certainly has a Beethovenian flavour at times, but moves between a late classic and early romantic styles. His *Sonatas* each have five or six movements and comparable diversity. The pleasing *Adagio con sentimento*, brilliant *Scherzo* and diverting closing *Rondo* of the *E flat Sonata* are good examples of his stature and the *Andantino and Variations* which ends the *E major* work is another example of his ready musical imagination. **Martin Jones** is a splendid advocate of his music, plying with ideal simplicity of style and ready virtuosity. He is very well recorded and this Volume I is highly recommendable. We hope more will follow.

DALE, Roger (1885–1943)

(i; ii) English Dance (arr. Bowen); (i; iii) Introduction & Andante for 6 Violas, Op. 5; (i; ii) Phantasy for Viola & Piano; Suite for Viola & Piano, Op. 2

Ⓝ Ⓜ *** Dutton CDLX 7204. (i) Chase with (ii) Otaki; (iii) Shaw, Opie, Beer, Cvetkov, Cininx

Roger Dale was a London born pianist/composer who, from 1900, studied at the RAM where, for the last 35 years of his life, he was on the staff. His music received some strong support during his life, with Lionel Tertis championing the *Suite for Viola and Piano*, often making the central *Romance* one of his encores. It is indeed a lovely piece, with gorgeous lyrical melodies, and is flanked by a highly expressive first movement and a finale of much virtuoso brilliance. Tertis commissioned the *Introduction and Andante*, another highly appealing work with all the individual parts beautifully weaving around one another. The *Phantasy for Viola and Piano* is in a single movement, but offers a great variety of mood with its essentially folk-like theme running through the score. The *English Dance* is a delightfully nostalgic piece, heard here in the arrangement by York Bowen for the first time. Superb recordings and performances and Lewis Foreman's sleeve notes are typically informative.

DAMASE, Jean-Michel (born 1928)

Piano Music: Apparition; Introduction et Allegro; 8 Etudes; Sonate; Sonatine; Thème et Variations

Ⓜ *** Somm SOMMCD 034. Unwin

Damase's piano music is witty, elegant and, above all, unpredictable, with the *Apparition* opening in a vision of delicacy and, after constantly shifting visions and textures, closing a little less enigmatically. The *Etudes* are chimerical. The *Sonata* too, with its gruff opening toccata, moves from the bell-like sonority of the *Andante* to a turbulent finale which suddenly changes gear in midstream, to end reflectively. The *Sonatine* epitomizes the composer's finest features, neatly crafted and unostentatiously charming, especially the winningly debonair finale. The *Theme and (15) Variations* alternate beween slow and fast variants very engagingly. All in all, a delectable cocktail of French pianistic *bon-bons*, played with affection and nimble dexterity by a pianist who always anticipates the surprises around the corner.

DANCLA, Jean Baptiste Charles (1817–1907)

Petite Ecole de la mélodie, Op. 123

(N) *** Chan. 10510. Rimonda, Canziana – SAINT-SAËNS: *Violin Sonata 1*; MASSENET: *Méditation from Thaïs* ***

Charles Dancla has the reputation of being the last exponent of the classical French tradition of violin-playing and these 12 trifles make a delightful rarity, with **Rimonda** and **Canziona**, talented young artists playing with such rhythmic zest it could easily have listeners dancing. This is light music at its most attractive, with the pieces nicely varied.

DANKWORTH, John (born 1927)

Suite for Emma; Picture of Jeannie

(N) (BB) **** Naxos 8.572240. Emma Johnson, Lenehan – BERNSTEIN: *Sonata*; COPLAND: *Sonata; Nocturne* ***

A leading figure in the jazz world for fifty years, (Sir) Johnny Dankworth shows his skill in writing 'straight' music for **Emma**, the clarinettist he so rightly admires. The five pieces include a charmingly nostalgic *Waltz* and a gentle *Pavane*, and then the music takes off with a catchy *Scherzo* which sits astride both 'classical' and jazz idioms. The finale fully exploits the virtuosity of both his soloists.

DANZI, Franz (1763–1826)

(i) Wind Quintets, Op. 56/1–3; Wind Sextet in E flat, Op. 10; (ii) Wind Quintets, Op. 67/1–3; Horn Sonata 1, Op. 28; (iii) Wind Quintets, Op. 68/1–3; Horn Sonata 2, Op. 44

(BB) *** Naxos (i) 8.553076; (ii) 8.553570; (iii) 8.554694. Michael Thompson Wind Quintet; Thompson (horn), Fowke (piano)

Wind Quintets, Op. 56/1–3; Op. 67/1–3; Op. 68/1–3; (i) Piano & Wind Quintets, Op. 41; Op. 53; Op. 54

(M) *** BIS-CD 1581/2. BPO Wind Quintet; (i) with Derwinger

Danzi was one of the first composers to cultivate the wind quintet; these diverting pieces offer unexpected pleasure. On Naxos the horn soloist **Michael Thompson** has gathered round him a superbly balanced group of London's leading wind players and they combine to give polished and beautifully blended performances. The *Wind Sextet* is in the tradition of wind Harmoniemusik and is fluently appealing. The second disc also includes Danzi's *First Horn Sonata*, probably modelled on Beethoven's similar work, although the style is more romantic. The *Second Sonata* is even more lyrically gal-

lant, particularly in the theme and variations finale. But any one of these three discs will give much enjoyment.

The reissued BIS collection which costs about the same, is also played with much distinction and recorded with great clarity and presence. Although the *Piano Quintets* are less substantial, they are rather delightful all the same.

DAQUIN, Louis-Claude (1694–1772)

12 Noëls for Organ

⌐ **** Hyp. Helios CDH 55319. Herrick (organ of Church of St Rémy, Dieppe, France)

If you haven't discovered Daquin's *Douze* engaging *Noëls* before now, you are in for a treat. These 12 brief chorales are charmingly diverse in invention, from the buoyant imitation of *Le Noël en duo* to the piquant colouring of *Noël sur les flutes* and the lively closing *Noël Suisse*. **Christopher Herrick** registers them piquantly on this perfectly chosen French organ with its true Gallic accent, and plays with great spirit. The Hyperion recording could hardly be bettered.

DARNTON, Christian (1905–81)

Piano Concertino in C

(BB) *** Naxos 8.557290. Donohoe, Northern Sinfonia – ROWLEY; GERHARDT; FERGUSON: *Piano Concertos* ***

Warmly lyrical, with a touch of Stravinskian neoclassicism and a dash of Shostakovich, and ending with a bravura display in the finale, Christian Darnton's *Concertino* for piano and strings makes a valuable addition to this imaginative collection of four British concertos, superbly performed by **Peter Donohoe** directing the **Northern Sinfonia** from the keyboard.

D'ASTORGA, Emanuele (c. 1680–1757)

Stabat Mater

✪ (M) *** DHM/BMG 82876 60145-2. Monoyios, Mammel, Happel, Balthazar-Neumann Ch., Freiburg Bar. O, Hengelbrock – DURANTE: *Magnificat in B flat*; PERGOLESI: *Confitebor tibi Domine* *** ✪

*** Hyp. CDA 67108. Gritton, Bickley, Agnew, Harvey, King's Consort Ch., King's Consort, King – BOCCHERINI: *Stabat Mater* ***

D'Astorga's setting was justly renowned in its time for its intensity of lyrical feeling and its broad flow of lyrical melody, notably in the solos and duets. Yet, unusually, it ends exultantly, celebrating Christ's 'victory' over the cross, with a lively if unadventurous extended final chorus. The German performance here is in every way persuasive, beautifully sung and played, and directed with much spirit by **Hengelbrock**. The recording is first class, and texts and translation are included.

Emanuele d'Astorga's *Stabat Mater* predates Boccherini's – with which it is coupled on Hyperion – by nearly a century and, unlike that work (and the Pergolesi setting on which it is based), is written like a miniature oratorio with soloists and chorus. The chorus opens and closes the work – the opening with touching melancholy, but the closing *Christe quam sit hinc exire* much more upbeat. In between, the various solos and duets are expressively quite intense, and overall this is a remarkably accomplished and rewarding piece, especially when sung as eloquently as it is on Hyperion, with excellent soloists and a fine choral contribution, all very well recorded.

DAVIES, Sir Henry Walford
(1869–1941)

Everyman (oratorio; complete)

(M) *** Dutton CDLX 7141. Putnins, Staples, Ferrari, Johnston, London Oriana Ch., Kensington SO, Drummond

Written in 1904, *Everyman* follows the progress of Everyman from earth to heaven, a theme which echoes Elgar's *Dream of Gerontius* of four years earlier in a more homespun way. The impact of this performance is greatly enhanced by the clarity of the words, both from the four excellent soloists and from the vigorous chorus. It is true that Davies makes Death, a tenor-role, into rather too amiable a figure, and the melodic material could be more striking, but this is a powerful piece that richly deserves revival, here well directed by **David Drummond** in full, brilliant sound.

DAVIS, Carl (born 1936)

Aladdin (ballet; complete)

(BB) *** Naxos 8.557898/9. Malaysian PO, composer

Carl Davis's score was written for the London Contemporary Dance Company in the 1990s, intended as a Christmas ballet. The music is colourful and melodic, somewhat after the style of film music, but it certainly doesn't lack inventive imagination. It is very well played by the **Malaysian Philharmonic Orchestra** and the composer ensures plenty of sparkle and expressive warmth. Very good recording, too. We hope there may be a DVD, which would be even more enjoyable.

DEBUSSY, Claude (1862–1918)

Concertante and Orchestral Music (almost complete)

(B) *** Chan. X10144 (4). Queffélec, Masters, Bell, King, McChrystal, Ulster O, Y. P. Tortelier

Chandos have now assembled Debussy's orchestral music (previously coupled with Ravel) in a bargain box of recordings which generally reflect the state of the art. There are excellent soloists in the concertante works. The subtlety and atmosphere of *La Boîte à joujoux* are captured splendidly, and the concertante works are equally sensitive. Not all the per-

formances are a first choice, but the shorter works come off particularly well.

(i) Berceuse héroïque; (ii; iii) Danses sacrée et profane (for harp and strings); (ii) Images; Jeux; Marche écossaise; La Mer; (ii; iv) Nocturnes; (ii) Prélude à l'après-midi d'un faune; (ii; v) Première Rapsodie for Clarinet & Orchestra

🎵 ⚙ (B) **** Ph. Duo (ADD) 438 742-2 (2). Concg. O, (i) Van Beinum; (ii) Haitink; with (iii) Badings; (iv) Women's Ch. of Coll. Mus.; (v) Pieterson

This Duo ranks as probably the finest Debussy collection in the CD catalogue. Although the programme as a whole is directed by **Haitink**, it is good that his distinguished predecessor, **Eduard van Beinum**, is remembered by the opening *Berceuse héroïque*, played with great delicacy and a real sense of mystery, with the early (1957) stereo highly effective. For the *Danses sacrée et profane* Haitink takes over, with elegant playing from the harpist, **Vera Badings**, who is excellently balanced. Haitink's reading of *Images* is second to none and is beautifully played by the wonderful Dutch orchestra; this applies equally to *Jeux*, while in the *Nocturnes* the choral balance is judged perfectly, and few versions are quite as beguiling and seductive as Haitink's. His *La Mer* is comparable with Karajan's 1964 recording. The hazily sensuous *Prélude à l'après-midi d'un faune* and the undervalued *Clarinet Rhapsody* are also played atmospherically, although the former is more overtly languorous in Karajan's hands. Again, the Philips recording is truthful and natural, with beautiful perspectives and realistic colour, a marvellously refined sound.

Berceuse héroïque; Images; Jeux; Marche écossaise; La Mer; Musiques pour le Roi Lear; Nocturnes; Prélude à l'après-midi d'un faune; Printemps

(BB) *** EMI Gemini (ADD) 3 65235-2 (2). Fr. R. & TV Ch. & O, Martinon

Martinon's is a very good *Images*, beautifully played, with the orchestral detail vivid and glowing. *Jeux* is also very fine, with the sound attractively spacious. *La Mer* enjoys the idiomatic advantage of fine French orchestral playing, even if it does not quite match Karajan or Haitink. The *Musiques pour le Roi Lear* is a real rarity; the colourful *Fanfare* remains impressive, and *Le Sommeil de Lear* is highly evocative. The *Nocturnes* are beautifully played, as indeed is *Printemps*, with Martinon penetrating its charm. At budget price these are competitive recommendations, and the current transfers are warmly atmospheric; even if the upper end of the range is rather brightly lit, there is plenty of depth in the sound.

Berceuse héroïque; 3 Etudes (arr. Jarrell); (i) 3 Nocturnes; Pelléas et Mélisande: Symphonic Suite (arr. Constant). Suite bergamasque: Clair de lune (arr. Caplet)

(N) (BB) *** Naxos 8.570994. Lyon Nat O, Märkl; (i) with Leizig R. Ch.

The two major items here are the set of three *Nocturnes*, central in Debussy's output, and the substantial *Symphonic Suite* from the opera, *Pelléas et Mélisande*, which Marius Constant put together using almost entirely the evocative orchestral interludes from the opera. **Märkl's** performances are warm and idiomatic, and the only reservation is that almost inevitably there is rather a lack of contrast in the opera suite which moves slowly. The three *Nocturnes* are the high-spot of the whole collection. The passage in *Fêtes* where one hears a procession from afar on muted trumpets is magically achieved, while *Sirènes* brings a vital yet languorous contribution from the **Leipzig Radio Choir**. The Caplet orchestration of *Clair de lune* is probably the best-known item, sumptuously wrought and the *Berceuse héroïque*, written as a tribute to King Albert of the Belgians in the First World War, is similarly evocative. The orchestration of the *3 Etudes*, made by Michael Jarrell as recently as 1991, represents a different approach to orchestration, a degree sharper, appropriate enough in some of Debussy's more advanced music. Altogether a rewarding collection, immaculately recorded, showing Märkl as a sensitive Debussian.

La Boîte à joujoux; Children's Corner* (orch. Caplet); *Danse* (orch. Ravel); (i) *Danses sacrée et profane*; (ii) *Fantaisie for Piano & Orchestra; La Plus que lente; Khamma; Petite suite* (orch. Büsser); (iii) *Première rapsodie for Clarinet & Orchestra*; (iv) *Rapsodie for Saxophone

(BB) *** EMI Gemini (ADD) 3 65240-2 (2). Fr. R. & TV O, Martinon; with (i) Jamet; (ii) Ciccolini; (iii) Dangain; (iv) Londe

Children's Corner and *La Boîte à joujoux* contain much to enchant the ear, as does the tuneful *Petite suite*. The rarity here is *Khamma*. This and the two *Rapsodies* are underrated and, although there are alternative versions of all these pieces, none is more economically priced. The performances are sympathetic and authoritative, and the recordings have been remastered successfully. The sound is full and spacious, with an attractive ambient glow. A bargain.

***La Boîte à joujoux* (orch. Caplet); *La Mer; Prélude à l'après-midi d'un faune; 3 Préludes: Ce qu'a vu le vent d'ouest; Feuilles mortes; Feux d'artifice* (orch. Colin Matthews)**

✿ (B) **** EMI 5 58045-2. (i) BPO, Rattle

Recorded live, with all the extra tension that brings, this is one of **Sir Simon Rattle's** most outstanding CDs. The *Prélude à l'après-midi d'un faune* opens with a deliciously translucent flute solo, and Rattle brings a richly sensuous allure and a warm flexibility of phrasing to its central climax that is quite irresistible. *La Boîte à joujoux* is quite magical in its subtle rhythmic feeling and luminous detail, quite the finest account in the catalogue, with all the quotations wittily observed. *La Mer* is unforgettable, and again unsurpassed, not even by Karajan. The opening is extraordinarily atmospheric, the play of the waves shimmering in the sunlight, and the closing dialogue between wind and sea gathers in tension to produce a thrillingly ferocious closing storm. Colin Matthews's Debussian scoring in his orchestration of the three piano *Préludes* is uncannily accurate: *Feuilles mortes* is hauntingly evocative and *Feux d'artifice*, with its spluttering

sparkle, all but trumps the piano original. Throughout the disc, the recording, balanced by Mike Clements, is very much in the demonstration bracket. (The contents of this CD, plus the contents of the Encore disc over the page (*Images; Jeux* and *Le Roi Lear*), have also been reissued in a five-CD bargain boxed set, coupled with a Ravel programme – EMI 5 14565-2 – see under the coupling, below.) But the present disc is unmissable on its own.

Children's Corner* (orch. Caplet); *Jeux; La mer; Prélude à l'après-midi d'un faune

(N) (BB) *** Naxos 8.570759 Lyon Nat. O, Märkl

If anything, **Märkl's** second Debussy collection is even finer than the first. Once again he proves a natural Debussian, and the Lyon auditorium's warmly glowing acoustics are ideal for the music. *La mer* is placed seductively in southern climes, yet the force of the wind in the finale is not diminished. The *Prélude à l'après-midi d'un faune* really captures the sensuous afternoon rapture of the faune, and the sensuous playing from strings and woodwind alike also illuminates *Jeux*. Debussy's *Poème danse* is expertly paced, the forward momentum most tellingly controlled, the luminous orchestral colouring very seductive, while the climax evolves passionately. The orchestra then clearly relishes Caplet's vivid scoring of *Children's Corner* and captures all its considerable charm, with the *Golliwog's Cakewalk* ending the programme vigorously.

***Danse* (*Tarantelle styrienne*); *Sarabande* (orch. Ravel)**

**(*) Australian Decca Eloquence 476 2452. Concg. O, Chailly – RAVEL: *Boléro*; MUSSORGSKY: *Pictures at an Exhibition* **(*)

Ravel's orchestrations of two Debussy piano pieces, the *Sarabande* from the suite *Pour le piano*, and *Danse*, an arrangement of the early *Tarantelle styrienne*, make delightful and comparatively rare items in **Chailly's** disc demonstrating Ravel's genius as an orchestrator. Ripely brilliant recording.

***Danse sacrée et danse profane* (for harp and string orchestra)**

(***) Testament mono SBT 1053. Mason Stockton, Concert Arts Strings, Slatkin – CRESTON: *Quartet*; RAVEL: *Introduction & Allegro*; TURINA: *La oración del torero*; VILLA-LOBOS: *Quartet 6* (***)

Felix Slatkin and his Hollywood colleagues give as atmospheric an account of the *Danse sacrée et danse profane* as any on record, and **Anne Mason Stockton** is the excellent harpist. The mono recording dates from 1951 but is uncommonly good. This comes as part of a remarkably fine anthology of Hollywood Quartet recordings.

Danses sacrée et profane; Images; Jeux; Prélude à l'après-midi d'un faune

(M) *** Sup. (ADD) SU 3478-2 011. Czech PO, Baudo (with Patras)

Jeux is clothed in richly glowing colours, with ravishingly seductive string-textures, while **Baudo** displays a subtle feeling for the music's ebb and flow. He also lets the famous *Prélude* unfold with a natural progress and the central climax of the piece flowers quite spontaneously. At the very opening of *Images* the piquant oboe solo is ear-catching. *Les Parfums de la nuit* waft languorously in the evening breeze, and the opening of *Le Matin d'un jour de fête* is hauntingly evocative before the orchestra blazes into life. This, like the *Danses sacrée*, was recorded a decade later with comparable success.

(i) *Danses sacrée et profane*; (ii) *3 Ballades de François Villon; Le Jet d'eau*

*** DG 471 614-2. Cleveland O, Boulez, with (i) Wellbaum; (ii) Hagley – RAVEL: *Menuet antique*, etc. ***

An evocative account of the *Danse sacrée et danse profane*, ideal listening to cool you on a summer evening, perfectly done by **Lisa Wellbaum** and the **Cleveland Orchestra**. **Alison Hagley**, the Mélisande in Boulez's Welsh National Opera DVD of *Pelléas*, gives highly appealing accounts of the Baudelaire setting, *Le Jet d'eau* and the *Trois Ballades de François Villon*. Altogether a lovely recital.

6 Epigraphes antiques (orch. Ansermet); *Jeux*

(***) Testament mono SBT 1324. SRO, Ansermet – SAINT-SAËNS: *Danse macabre;* – DUKAS: *L'Apprenti Sorcier*, etc. **(*)

Ansermet's scoring of the *Six Epigraphes Antiques* is most felicitous. The performances have great atmosphere and real style; and it is good to have the Ansermet account of his own transcription, whose tempi are so perfectly judged and textures so perfectly balanced, back in circulation. Very decent mono sound. A most winning reissue, well worth investigating.

6 Epigraphes antiques (orch. Ansermet); *Estampes: Pagodes* (orch. André Caplet); *Printemps* (suite symphonique; original (1887) choral version, reconstructed Emil de Cou); *Prélude: La puerta del vino* (orch. Henri Büsser); *Suite bergamasque* (orch. Gustave Cloez & André Caplet)

**(*) Ara. Z 6734. San Francisco Ballet O, De Cou; (i) with soloists and Ch.

A fascinating disc, and most fascinating of all is the original choral version of *Printemps*, which sounds positively voluptuous in this superbly rich recording. The result will intrigue all Debussians and its seductive impact will surely thrill all listeners. The orchestrated piano pieces are also very successful. The fastidiously scored *Epigraphes antiques* are very beguiling; and the whole set is made to sound lustrous in its impressionistic colouring. The **San Francisco Ballet Orchestra** plays very well indeed, and the spacious acoustic provides an impressively full and naturally balanced sound-picture.

Fantaisie for Piano & Orchestra

☌ **BB** *** Warner Apex (ADD). 8573 89232-2. Queffélec, Monte Carlo Op. O, Jordan – RAVEL: *Piano Concertos* ***

The Warner Apex disc offers an inexpensive coupling of

the major works for piano and orchestra by both Debussy and Ravel, and in **Anne Queffélec's** hands the *Fantaisie* makes a very pleasing impression indeed and is very well recorded.

(i) *Fantaisie for Piano and Orchestra. Solo Piano Music*

(N) ☌ **** Ph. 475 7301 (4) Kocsis; (i) Budapest Fest. O, Ivan Fischer –RAVEL: *Piano Concertos* (***)

Kocsis's recital of some of Debussy's shorter pieces (included here) won the Gramophone 1990 instrumental award. Now his subsequent recordings have been added to make up this cherishable complete survey. It is in every way outstanding. The recording of the piano is still among the most realistic we have ever heard and artistically this collection is even more distinguished in terms of pianistic finesse, sensitivity and tonal refinement.

Images: Ibéria (only)

☌ (M) *** Telarc CD 80574. Cincinnati SO, López-Cobos – TURINA: *Danzas fantásticas* etc. ***

Images: Ibéria. La Mer; (i) *Nocturnes. Prélude à l'après-midi d'un faune*

(M) *** RCA **SACD** 82876 66374-2. Boston SO, Munch – RAVEL: *Boléro*, etc.

(M) *** Ph. (ADD) 464 697-2. Concg. O, Haitink; (i) with female Ch.

Images; Jeux; Le Roi Lear (incidental music)

(BB) *** EMI Encore 5 75218-2. CBSO, Rattle

Images; La Mer; Nocturnes: Nuages; Fêtes (only); *Prélude à l'après-midi d'un faune*

(M) *** RCA (ADD) 82876 59416-2. Boston SO, Munch

Images; La Mer; Prélude à l'après-midi d'un faune

(B) *(**) DG Entrée 477 5014. Santa Cecilia Nat. Ac. O, Bernstein

Images; (i) *Nocturnes; Le Martyre de Saint–Sébastien:* (symphonic fragments); *La Mer; Prélude à l'après-midi d'un faune; Printemps* (orch. Büsser)

(BB) *** Universal 476 5882(2). Montreal SO, Dutoit; (i) with chorus

Images; (i) *Nocturnes; Prélude à l'après-midi d'un faune*

☌ (M) *** EMI 3 91967-2. LSO, Previn; (i) with Amb. Ch.

Haitink's magical performances and recordings (from the mid- to late-1970s), extracted from Haitink's Duo above, have stood the test of time and remain unsurpassed. Indeed, the allure of the orchestral sound as remastered here is quite unforgettable. An admirable choice for Philips's set of '50 Great Recordings'.

Previn's account of *Images* was the first EMI digital record to appear, and every colour and sonority, however subtle, registers. There is much to admire in Previn's performance, too. Dynamic nuances are carefully observed; there is much felicitous wind playing and no want of intelligent and musical phrasing, and the *Prélude à l'après-midi d'un faune* is equally vividly captured by the engineers. The *Nocturnes*, recorded five years later, also have great spontaneity. Some might feel that the *Sirènes* are too voluptuous, but this matches Previn's extrovert approach. The spectacular qualities of the EMI sound-picture certainly provide comparably clear definition and no lack of ambient atmosphere. This reissue is certainly an apt candidate for EMI's 'Great Recordings of the Century'.

Jesus López-Cobos manages the colour nuancing impressively in *Ibéria*, and if he is not quite a match for Reiner, he finds a fragrant allure in *Les parfums de la nuit* and plenty of glitter in *Le matin d'un jour de fête*. The warm ambience of Cincinnati Music Hall is splendidly caught in the first-class Telarc recording, the balance wholly natural. With outstanding Turina couplings, this disc can certainly be recommended in its new mid-price format.

In *Images* **Rattle** is memorably atmospheric, while in *Jeux* he is just a touch more expansive than most rivals and also more evocative. The *King Lear* excerpts sound splendid. First-rate recording, very vivid but beautifully balanced. At Encore price this is a truly remarkable bargain.

Munch's vintage accounts of Debussy were transformed on CD, with the acoustic now casting a wonderfully warm aura over the orchestra, the sound gloriously expansive and translucent. Munch's inclination to go over the top may not appeal to all listeners, but the results are compelling and the orchestral bravura is thrilling. The *Prélude à l'après-midi d'un faune* makes a ravishing interlude, expanding to a rapturous climax. As can be seen, *Ibéria* has been reissued separately in SACD format, coupled with Ravel's *Boléro*, *Rapsodie espagnole* and *La Valse*, with the sound even more glamorous, but losing something in the upper range.

In *Images* and the *Nocturnes* **Dutoit** is freer than some with rubato, as well as in his warm, expressive moulding of phrase. His sharp pointing of rhythm, as in the Spanish dances of *Ibéria* or the processional march in *Fêtes*, is also highly characteristic of his approach to French music. By contrast, the remaining works are strong rather than evocative. However the documentation is non-existent.

A recording from 1989 which we have not discovered before shows **Bernstein** at his most atmospherically seductive in *Images*, alluring in *Les parfums de la nuit*, glittering elsewhere. However, the account of the *Prélude à l'après-midi d'un faune* must be the longest on record, beautifully played, especially at the opening and close, but indulgently expanded. He attempts a Canute too on *La Mer*, and undoubtedly is more successful than the king in wilfully controlling the ocean's behaviour, especially in the closing section. The concentration of the playing is undoubtedly gripping, but this is not an ideal choice for DG's Entrée label designed for inexperienced listeners.

Jeux; La Mer; Nocturnes: Nuages, Fêtes (only)

(***) Testament mono SBT 1108. St Cecilia Ac., Rome O, De Sabata – RESPIGHI: *Fountains of Rome* (***)

Victor de Sabata's 1947 account with his Rome orchestra of *Jeux* brings great character and atmosphere to this wonderful score. Although the two purely orchestral *Nocturnes* first appeared on record in 1948, de Sabata's account of *La Mer* did not; it makes its first appearance now, but it is still music-making of quality that deserves a place in any Debussy collection.

(i) *Jeux;* (ii) *La Mer;* 24 *Préludes* (arr. & orch. Colin Matthews)

Ⓝ Ⓜ **** Hallé (i) CDHLL 7518; (ii) CDHLL 7513 Hallé O, Elder

These are highly compelling **Hallé** accounts of *Jeux* and *La Mer*, both played with subtle rubato, infinitely varied dynamic and much seductive atmosphere. Tension is high throughout both works while the transparent acoustic of Manchester's splendid Bridgewater Hall brings diaphanous atmospheric detail and helps climaxes to expand superbly. The same comments apply to Colin Matthews's highly imaginative orchestration of Debussy's piano *Préludes*, which have shimmering textures and are, if anything even more impressionistic than the piano originals. Only *Feux d'artifice* and the rather pompous *S. Pickwick Esq* are less than ideally transcribed, but *Danseuses de Delphes*, *Des pas sur la neige* and *Les fée sont d'exquises danseuses* (on CDHLL 7518) and *Le vent dans la plaine*, *Les sons et les parfums*, and *Feuilles mortes* (on CDHLL 7513) are magically evoked, with Andrew Keener's balancing skill ensuring a first class sound balance. The two CDs are available separately.

Jeux; Prélude à l'après-midi d'un faune; (i) *La Chute de la maison Usher* (ed. & orch. Robert Orledge; DVD version)

*** Cap. **DVD** 93517. Dancers, VSO, Foster, (i) with Soloists

Here is an interesting production from the Bregenz Festival of 2006. Debussy toyed for some 15 years with plans for two Poe operas, *The Devil in the Belfry* (which came to nothing) and *The Fall of the House of Usher*, on which he worked between 1908 and 1917, but which he never finished. Robert Orledge has prepared a remarkably effective performing version of the score (he is a brilliant orchestrator). The present highly imaginative staging assigns the four main roles not only to singers but also to some dancers of the Royal Ballet. It casts a strong spell, as do the performances of *Prélude à l'après-midi d'un faune* and *Jeux* in the choreography of Kim Brandstrup. Generally fine playing from the **Vienna Symphony Orchestra**, even if they are not always successful in producing a really idiomatic Debussy sonority.

Le Martyre de Saint-Sébastien: La Cour des lys; Danse extatique (DVD version)

*** Arthaus **DVD** 100 314. Rotterdam Philh. O, Gergiev (V/D: Bob van den Burg) – PROKOFIEV: *Scythian Suite;* STRAVINSKY: *Piano Concerto*, etc. ***

This DVD shows something of the breadth of **Gergiev's** musical sympathies (and, in the rehearsal sequences, his charm, which persuades his players to give of their best). He has a genuine feeling for Debussy and we can imagine him directing a distinguished *Pelléas*.

Le Martyre de Saint-Sébastien (symphonic fragments); Prélude à l'après-midi d'un faune (DVD version)

*** MDG Audio **DVD** 9371099-5; CD 337 1099-2. Orchester der Beethovenhalle, Bonn, Soustrot – RAVEL: *Ma Mère l'Oye; La Valse* ***

Soustrot gives highly atmospheric, slightly understated but not under-characterized accounts of these scores, with no exaggerated nuances, only unforced music-making. The recorded sound is beautifully balanced too, with the details emerging with both clarity and subtlety. Altogether a most distinguished coupling. It sounds particularly real in its Audio DVD format – this is one of the finest Debussy recordings in the catalogue.

La Mer (DVD version)

(N) **(*) EuroArts **DVD** 2050136. Chicago SO, Barenboim (with BOULEZ: *Notations I – IV*) – FALLA: *El sombrero de tres picos*

A fluent, lucid account of *La Mer* from the **Chicago Orchestra** captured during their European tour in April 2000 and recorded in the Philharmonie in Cologne. Expert camera work and excellent sound. The DVD also includes a twenty-minute conversation between **Barenboim** and Pierre Boulez, whose *Notations I–IV* opens the programme.

La mer; Prélude á l'après-midi d'un faune (DVD version)

(N) **** Sony **DVD** 88697202449 Berlin PO, Karajan – RAVEL: *Daphnis et Chloë –Suite 2* ****

Glorious performances of both masterpieces which would be difficult to surpass. Perhaps **Karajan's** DG recordings on LP during the mid-1960s are even more sumptuous but these superbly controlled accounts are both beautifully recorded and expertly directed for the cameras. The performances were recorded at the Philharmonie in 1987, two years before Karajan's death.

La Mer (CD versions)

⊶ (M) **** RCA (ADD) 82876 71614-2. Chicago SO, Reiner – RESPIGHI: *Fountains & Pines of Rome* ****

⊶ (M) *** DG (ADD) 447 426-2. BPO, Karajan – MUSSORGSKY: *Pictures*; RAVEL: *Boléro* ***

⊶ (M) *** RCA **SACD** (ADD) 82876 61387-2. Boston SO, Munch – IBERT: *Escales* ***; SAINT-SAËNS: *Symphony 3 in C min.* ***✿

(N) (M) *** RCO 08001. Concg. O, Jansons – DUTILLEUX: *L'Arbre des Songes*; RAVEL: *La Valse* ***

*** Naïve V 4946. O. Nat. de France, Svetlanov – SCRIABIN: *Poème de l'extase* ***

La Mer; Nocturnes

✿ (M) *** EMI 5 62746-2 . Philh. Ch. & O, Giulini – RAVEL: *Alborada; Daphnis et Chloé: Suite 2* ***✿

La Mer; (i) Nocturnes; Prélude à l'après-midi d'un faune; Printemps

(BB) *** Regis RRC 1177. LSO; (i) L. Symphony Ch.; Frühbeck de Burgos (without *Printemps*)

La Mer; Nocturnes: Nuages; Fêtes (only); Le Martyre de Saint-Sébastien (symphonic fragments); Prélude à l'après-midi d'un faune

(***) Testament mono SBT 1011. Philh. O, Cantelli

La Mer; Prélude à l'après-midi d'un faune

⊶ (M) **** DG (ADD) 477 7161. BPO, Karajan – RAVEL: *Boléro, etc.* ***

*** Atma **SACD** 2 2549 Metropolitan O of Montreal, Nezet-Seguin – BRITTEN: *Four Sea Interludes* ***; MERCURE: *Kaleidoscope* ***;

The **Metropolitan Orchestra of Montreal** may not be so well known outside Canada as the great Montreal Symphony Orchestra, but here under its Music Director, **Yannick Nézet-Séguin** it shows what a formidable band it is, offering performances both incisive and refined, notably in the two evocative Debussy masterpieces, reflecting the acoustic of the Church of Saint-Nom-de-Jesus in Montreal, the recording venue. Woodwind solos are clean and atmospheric, with the warm flute soloist in *L'après-midi* specially named, Marie Andrée Benny.

Reiner's 1960 recording has all the atmosphere that makes his version of *Ibéria*, recorded at the same time, so unforgettable. Of course the marvellous acoustics of the Chicago Hall contribute to the appeal of this superbly played account: Reiner's record gives great pleasure: the effect is just a bit more lustrous than Karajan's remastered DG version, although the upper range is more brightly lit.

After more than four decades **Karajan's** 1964 account of *La Mer* is still very much in a class of its own. It enshrines the spirit of the work as effectively as it observes the letter, and the superb playing of the **Berlin Orchestra**, for all its virtuosity and sound, is totally self-effacing. It is now available, coupled with Karajan's outstanding (1966) record of Mussorgsky's *Pictures at an Exhibition* and a gripping account of Ravel's *Boléro*, but we prefer the original coupling of the *Prélude à l'après-midi d'un faune* and Ravel's *Daphnis et Chloé*, which are equally unforgettable.

Munch's account of *La Mer* dates from 1956, yet this new transfer makes it sound better then ever, incredibly vivid for its period (or any period, for that matter). Even though the sound is close-miked, the Boston acoustic provided plenty of atmosphere to match the performance's undoubted excitement. Outstanding couplings and expanded sound on offer to those with SACD systems.

Largely thanks to the Concertgebouw acoustic and the richness of the orchestra's string section the opening of *La Mer* in **Jansons'** recording is exceptionally warm, and it is only with the second section that the chill of the English Channel is conveyed in Debussy's magical orchestral effects. The final section, the dialogue of the wind and the sea, brings a thrilling final build-up.

Giulini's early stereo recordings of Debussy (from 1962) remain very distinguished indeed. It would be difficult to fault his reading of *La Mer*, and the *Nocturnes* are played with great delicacy of feeling and refinement of detail, with a fine contribution from the **Philharmonia Chorus**, which gives the final movement great allure. Both works here are beautifully recorded. The Ravel coupling is equally fine, and this CD is fully worthy of its inclusion among EMI's 'Great Recordings of the Century'.

Cantelli's account of the four symphonic fragments from *Le Martyre de Saint-Sébastien* is one of the most beautiful performances he ever committed to vinyl; the textures are impeccably balanced and phrases flawlessly shaped. Its atmosphere is as concentrated as that of the legendary first recording under Coppola. *La Mer* and the *Prélude à l'après-midi d'un faune* are hardly less perfect, and the transfers are excellent.

Although strong in Mediterranean atmosphere, **Frühbeck de Burgos's** account of *La Mer* has an underlying grip, so he can concentrate on evocation at the opening and continue to lead the ear on spontaneously. Overall there is plenty of excitement and much subtlety of detail, both here and in the *Nocturnes*, where textures again have the sensuousness of southern climes, and no lack of glitter. The *Prélude à l'après-midi d'un faune* brings lovely, delicate flute-playing from **Paul Edmund-Davies** and a richly moulded string climax. If these are not conventional readings, they are full of impulse and are superbly recorded.

Svetlanov obviously has an intuitive feeling for Debussy's *La Mer*, and he established excellent rapport with these fine players. A very atmospheric account, which is finely paced and superbly played. This is a performance of stature, as is that of the Scriabin. An excellent note by Marc Vignal and very good sound.

Prélude à l'après-midi d'un faune; La Cathédrale engloutie (orch. Stokowski)

Ⓜ (**(*)) Cala mono CACD 0526. NBC SO, Stokowski –
   GOULD: *2 Marches for Orchestra*; HOLST: *The Planets* (***)

The *Prélude à l'après-midi d'un faune* derives from an NBC broadcast dating from March 1943. Apart from a couple of blemishes (the opening has a fair amount of swish), the sound is acceptable, but the performance is more than that: it is individual and compelling, with the faun's reverie celebrated with some particularly lush string-playing. The same comments apply to **Stokowski's** superb account of his transcription of *La Cathédrale engloutie*, dating from a February 1944 broadcast but sounding rather shrill. There are some technical faults: a sudden brief drop in level quite early on, some pitch fluctuation, etc., but the magnetism of the performance is never in doubt. Two attractive fill-ups for an individual account of *The Planets*.

COLLECTIONS

Orchestral Transcriptions & Arrangements: *Children's Corner; Clair de lune* (2 versions: by **André Caplet & Stokowski**); *Danse* (Ravel); *6 Épigraphes antiques* (Ansermet); *Estampes: La Soirée dans Grenade; Petite Suite* (Henri Büsser); *Sarabande* (Ravel)

(*) ATMA Surround Sound **SACD SACD2 2377. Quebec SO, Talmi

Yoav Talmi and his fine **Orchestre Symphonique de Québec** present these arrangements with rich, sensuous feeling, especially effective in Stokowski's luscious arrangement of *Clair de lune*, where by contrast André Caplet's simple scoring hardly alters its original character; both versions are beautifully played. The *Six Épigraphes antiques*, alluring in their atmospheric warmth, are also without quite the clarity of detail Ansermet brought to them himself. The two Ravel transcriptions are among the highlights, the noble *Sarabande* and the colourful *Danse*. This is vivaciously performed but might have had more sparkle; this can be partly attributed to the recording, the empty-hall effect obvious if you bring in the back speakers (very subtly) and then luxuriate in the glowing string and woodwind sounds. Undoubtedly this is a beguiling collection, but its voluptuousness may not suit all tastes.

CHAMBER MUSIC

Cello Sonata in D min.

Ⓜ *** Decca (ADD) 475 8239 Rostropovich, Britten –
   SCHUBERT: *Arpeggione Sonata* **(*); SCHUMANN: *3 Stucke in Volkston* ***

ⒷⒷ *** Warner Apex 0927 40599-2. Noras, Rigutto – FRANCK; FAURÉ: *Cello Sonatas* ***

**(*) ASV CDDCA 796. Gregor-Smith, Wrigley – BRIDGE; DOHNANYI: *Sonatas* **(*)

The classic version by **Rostropovich** and **Britten** leads the field. It has a clarity and point which suits the music perfectly and the recording is first class.

From **Arto Noras** and **Bruno Rigutto** comes as fine a performance of the *Cello Sonata* as any in the catalogue (excepting Rostropovich and Britten). Noras was recorded in 1995, and the sound is good. At the price it is a real bargain.

Bernard Gregor-Smith and **Yolande Wrigley** play with great refinement and authority, as well as much sensitivity. They are perhaps too closely balanced but this does not prevent their record being highly desirable.

Le Petit Nègre; Petite pièce; Première rapsodie; Rapsodie for Cor Anglais; Rapsodie for Saxophone; Sonata for Flute, Viola & Harp; Syrinx

Ⓜ *** Cala CACD 1017 (2). Bennett, Daniel, Campbell, Gough, Watkins, Haram, Tapping, Jones – SAINT-SAËNS: *Chamber Music* ***

The *Rapsodie for Cor Anglais*, with which this Cala Duo opens, is more familiar in its form for alto saxophone; it was originally to have been called *Rapsodie mauresque*. **Nicholas Daniel** plays it with great sensitivity. It is also heard in its alternative form, splendidly played by **Simon Haram**. The performance of the *Sonata for Flute, Viola & Harp* is also highly sensitive.

Piano Trio in G (1880)

☞— *** Hyp. CDA 67114. Florestan Trio – FAURÉ; RAVEL: *Piano Trios* ***

Debussy's *Piano Trio*, a product of his teenage years, may reveal few signs of his mature style but it makes a very apt and delightful coupling for the Ravel and Fauré works. With personnel led by the pianist **Susan Tomes**, the **Florestans** follow up the success of their prize-winning Schumann disc for Hyperion in a strong and urgent reading, at once highly polished and flexibly expressive. Vivid sound.

The **Joachim Trio** (coupled with Ravel) play with consistent sensitivity and finesse. This is a thoroughly musical account and beautifully recorded; but it would not necessarily be a first choice, though the attractive price-tag (and the agreeable Schmitt bonus) makes it competitive. (Naxos 8.550934)

String Quartet in G min., Op. 10

☞— (M) *** Ph. 464 699-2. Italian Qt – RAVEL: *Quartet* ***

(B) *** EMI 3 66557-2. Formosa Qt – MOZART: *String Quartet 14 in G*; SCHUBERT: *Quartettsatz*; WOLF: *Italian Serenade* ***

(M) *** Biddulph WH 0012. Ysaÿe Qt – FAURÉ: *String Quartet*; STRAVINSKY: *Concertino 3 Pieces; Double Canon* ***

(i) String Quartet; (ii) Syrinx

☞— (B) **** CfP (ADD) 3 82231-2. (i) Chilingirian Qt; (ii) Philippa Davies – RAVEL: *Introduction and Allegro; String Quartet* ****

The **Chilingirian** coupling is in every way competitive. They give a thoroughly committed account with well-judged tempi and very musical phrasing. The Scherzo is vital and spirited, and there is no want of poetry in the slow movement. The recording has plenty of body and presence and has the benefit of a warm acoustic. The coupling is now made triply attractive by the inclusion of not only a fine account of *Syrinx* for solo flute, which opens the disc, but also an outstanding version of Ravel's intoxicating *Introduction and Allegro*, making this Classics for Pleasure reissue a bargain of the highest order and sounding very good indeed.

It need hardly be said that the playing of the **Quartetto Italiano** is outstanding. Perfectly judged ensemble, weight and tone still make this a most satisfying choice and, even if it is rather short measure, the Philips recording engineers have produced a vivid and truthful sound-picture. However, it has now been promoted from bargain to mid-price.

The **Formosa Quartet Taiwan**, give masterly performances of all four items on their disc in EMI's Debut series. The Debussy develops into a searchingly intense performance, with the third movement *Andantino* hushed and with an inner depth that makes it the emotional centre of the

work. Refined and polished playing in all four movements that yet captures the tensions of live performance. Excellent sound.

The **Ysaÿe Quartet**, captured in 2005 and 2006, are noted interpreters of the Debussy, and their Fauré and Stravinsky couplings are hardly less satisfying.

As we know from their Haydn recordings, the **Kodály Quartet** are an excellent ensemble, and they too give a thoroughly enjoyable account. This music-making has the feel of a live performance; these players also have the benefit of a generous fill-up and very good recorded sound. Excellent value. (Naxos 8.550249)

Syrinx; Bilitis (arr. Lenski); (i) La Plus que lente

*** EMI 5 56982-2. Pahud; (i) Kovacevich – PROKOFIEV: *Flute Sonata*; RAVEL: *Chansons madécasses* ***

Syrinx has rarely sounded more erotic or other-worldly. The *Bilitis* is a transcription by Karl Lenski of the *Six épigraphes antiques* for piano duet (1914). **Emmanuel Pahud** is sensitive both to every nuance and dynamic subtlety and to the spirit of this highly effective transcription. **Stephen Kovacevich** gives a beautifully characterized account of Debussy's satire of a salon waltz, *La plus que lente*, as good as any and better than most.

Violin Sonata

☞— 🏵 (M) **** Decca (ADD) 460 006-2. Chung, Lupu – FRANCK: *Violin Sonata* ****🏵 ; CHAUSSON: *Poème* ****

(M) *** DG 477 5448 (2). Mintz, Bronfman (with *Recital of Encores* by ALBÉNIZ; COUPERIN; GLAZUNOV; GRANADOS; KREISLER; WEBER; WIENIAWSKI) – FAURÉ; FRANCK; RAVEL: *Violin Sonatas* ***

*** DG 445 880-2. Dumay, Pires – FRANCK: *Violin Sonata*; RAVEL: *Berceuse*, etc. ***

(B) *** CfP 575 80422. Little, Lane – POULENC: *Violin Sonata*; RAVEL: *Violin Sonata*, etc. ***

Kyung-Wha Chung plays with marvellous character and penetration, and her partnership with **Radu Lupu** could hardly be more fruitful. Nothing is pushed to extremes and everything is in perfect perspective. The recording sounds admirably real.

Shlomo Mintz gives a performance which gives much pleasure. This can be recommended alongside – though not in preference to – Chung and Lupu. However, Mintz and **Bronfman** have the additional advantage of offering fine accounts of the Fauré and Ravel *Sonatas* and a magnificent one of the Franck, with an attractive collection of encores thrown in for good measure.

Augustin Dumay and **Maria João Pires** give as idiomatic and sensitive an account of the Debussy *Sonata* as one could wish for, and those wanting their particular coupling with Franck and Ravel need not really hesitate.

Tasmin Little and **Piers Lane** also give a highly dedicated performance which tautly holds together the often fragmentary argument, making the result sound spontaneous in its total concentration. Excellent sound and a first-rate coupling.

Violin Sonata; Nocturne et Scherzo; Beau soir; La fille aux cheveux de lin; Minstrels; Il pleure dans mon coeur

*** Avie AV 2059. Graffin, Désert – ENESCU: *Impressions d'enfance*; RAVEL: *Sonata; Tzigane* ***

The performance of the *Violin Sonata* from **Philippe Graffin** and **Claire Désert** is delightfully chimerical, sensitively small-scaled. But this very musical partnership offers also the early *Nocturne et Scherzo*. The other transcriptions are by Arthur Hartmann, except *Minstrels*, which Debussy himself arranged in 1914. The recording throughout has an attractive intimacy, and the couplings are all well worth having.

PIANO MUSIC

Music for Piano Duet and Two Pianos

Danses sacrée et profane; En blanc et noir; Lindaraja; Nocturnes (trans. RAVEL); Prélude à l'après-midi d'un faune

(BB) *** Hyp. Helios CDH 55014. Coombs, Scott

Stephen Coombs and **Christopher Scott** made an outstanding début with this fine recording, which leads the field in this repertoire. Very highly recommended.

6 Épigraphes antiques; Marche écossaise sur un thème populaire; La Mer; Petite Suite; Symphonie in B min.

*** Quartz QTZ 2048. Piano Four Hands (Tong & Hasegawa)

La Mer comes off here with astonishingly effective brilliance. Of course Debussy finished it first in a four-handed piano arrangement, and although the orchestration obviously adds a great deal, it stands up well in the present format, with remarkable inner detail, and the exciting performance by **Joseph Tong** and **Waka Hasegawa** makes a vivid impact. The delightful *Petite Suite* (more familiar in Büsser's elegant orchestral transcription) is an equal success. But the entirely uncharacteristic *Symphonie* has little to recommend it. The clumsily thick-textured opening is unrecognizable as Debussian; only the more lyrical central section offers any degree of interest. The *Marche écossaise* is exuberant and the *Six Épigraphes antiques* are mysterious in their delicate evocation. Altogether an excellent collection, played with persuasively spontaneous feeling, and well (if fairly resonantly) recorded.

Solo piano music

2 Arabesques; Ballade; Berceuse héroïque; Children's Corner; Danse; Danse bohémienne; D'un cahier d'esquisses; Estampes; 12 Etudes; Hommage à Haydn; Images 1–2; L'Isle joyeuse; Masques; Mazurka; Nocturne; Le Petit Nègre; La plus que lente; Pour le piano; Préludes, Books 1–2; Rêverie; Suite bergamasque; Valse romantique. (i) Fantaisie for piano & orchestra

⊶ (M) (***) EMI mono 5 65855-2 (4). Gieseking; (i) with Hessischen R. O, Schröder

The two sets of *Préludes* date from 1953 and 1954, as indeed do most of the recordings collected here. The earliest is *Children's Corner* from 1951, which is also the date of the Frankfurt recording of the *Fantaisie*. The latter calls for some (albeit not great) tolerance, but the remaining performances sound better than ever. Gieseking's artistry is too well known to need further exegesis or advocacy. A marvellous set which all pianists should investigate.

Complete Works for Solo Piano

**** Decca 452 022-2 (2) (Volume 1); 460 247-2 (2). Thibaudet

Beautifully recorded, **Jean-Yves Thibaudet's** wide range of tone and dynamic is used with great imagination, and his playing often suggests an improvisatory quality. The music's subtlety of colour, with half-lights as well as sudden blazes of light (as in the stunning *Feux d'artifice*), is fully understood by this fine artist, and there is no question as to the spontaneity of his playing. The *Préludes* are among the finest on record.

But most impressive are the *Etudes*, unsurpassed on record in their strong characterization, flair and virtuosity – not even by Mitsuko Uchida's famous Philips set – and, with Decca's recording so real and immediate, they project with vivid spontaneity as at a live recital. These four CDs make a clear first choice among modern digital recordings of this totally absorbing repertoire.

2 Arabesques; Ballade; Children's Corner; Estampes; Mazurka; Le Petit nègre; La Plus que lente; Suite bergamasque

⊶ *** Onyx ONYX 4018. Rogé

Pascal Rogé is now embarking on a second survey of this repertoire for Onyx. He has already given us a superb set of the *Préludes* (see below) and this follow-up disc is every bit as fine. This is playing of real distinction, equally impressive in its articulation and in the control of colour, phrasing and dramatic projection; in this latter respect he surpasses his early, Decca series. The recording is very real indeed: he might be in the room with you.

2 Arabesques; Ballade; Danse bohémienne; Danse (Tarantelle styrienne); Mazurka; Nocturne; Pour le piano; Rêverie; Suite bergamasque; Valse romantique

*** Simax PSC 1297. Austbø

Haakon Austbø concentrates on the (for the most part) slighter pieces which are less readily found in single-disc collections of Debussy's piano music. There are obvious exceptions, including the *Suite bergamasque* (where Austbø plays the *Clair de lune* gently and exquisitely) and the closing *Passpied*, which has appealing elegance, and *Pour le piano*, where the performance is as fine as any available. Altogether this is a persuasively played recital, full of Debussian insights, and showing that Austbø has a natural affinity with this repertoire. He is truthfully recorded in a well-chosen acoustic.

2 Arabesques; Berceuse héroïque; Children's Corner; Danse bohèmienne; Élégie; Hommage à Haydn Mazurka; Morçeau de coucous; Nocturne; Pages d'album; Le Petite Nègre; La plus que lente; Rêverie; Suite bergamasque

(N) ⌐→ **** Chan. 10467. Bavouzet

Ballade; D'un cahier d'esquisses; Estampes; Images oubliées; L'isIe joyeuse; Masques; Pour le piano; Tarantelle styrienne; Valse romantique.

**** Chan. 10443. Bavouzet.

Etudes, Books I & II; Images, Series I & II

(N) ⌐→ **** Chan 10497. Bavouzet

Préludes Books; 1 & 2.

**** Chan. 10421 (2). Jean-Efflam Bavouzet.

Although there have been many outstanding Debussy recitals over the years from the likes of Zoltan Kocsis, Pascal Rogé, Noriko Ogawa and Jean-Philippe Collard, **Jean-Efflam Bavouzet's** survey lives up to the promise of the first two issues. Indeed we are inclined to consider it as a first choice were it not for the fact that the claims of rival versions are so strong. But Debussy playing does not come any better than this, and anyone collecting this excellently recorded Chandos series need not really look any further.

2 Arabesques; Children's Corner; Clair de lune; Images: Books 1 & 2; L'Isle joyeuse

(M) *** EMI 5 00272-2. Simon Trpčeski

This remarkable player goes from strength to strength. His is individual and intelligent Debussy that grips the listener throughout. As one expects from the acoustic of Potton Hall, Suffolk, the recorded sound is excellent. EMI have recorded a feature on this artist and his home town, Ohrid in Croatia, which can be accessed on a website to which the booklet directs us.

2 Arabesques; Children's Corner; Estampes; Images, Books 1–2; L'Isle joyeuse; Pour le piano; Préludes, Book 1; Rêverie; Suite bergamasque

(B) *** Double Decca (ADD) 443 021-2 (2). Rogé

Pascal Rogé's playing is distinguished by a keen musical intelligence and sympathy, as well as by a subtle command of keyboard colour, and this Double Decca set must receive the warmest welcome. *Children's Corner* is played with neat elegance and the characterization has both charm and perception, while the *Suite bergamasque, Pour le piano* and *Images* are no less distinguished. In *Estampes* there are occasional moments when the listener senses the need for more dramatic projection, but Rogé brings genuine poetic feeling to the first book of the *Préludes*. The CD transfers are clear and firm.

2 Arabesques; Children's Corner; Estampes; L'Isle joyeuse; Le Petit Nègre; La Plus que lente; Rêverie; Suite bergamasque: Clair de lune

*** Chan. 9912. Tabe

Among newer recordings of Debussy piano music **Kyoko Tabe's** recital is eminently successful. She has a good feeling for atmosphere and a keen musical intelligence. This is a fine issue on every count.

Berceuse héroïque; La Boîte à joujoux; Elégie; Pièce pour l'oeuvre du Vêtements du blessé; Préludes, Book II (complete)

*** BIS CD 1355. Ogawa

Children's Corner; D'un cahier d'esquisses; Hommage à Joseph Haydn; Morceau de concours; Le Petit Nègre; La Plus que lente; Préludes, Book 1

*** BIS CD 1205. Ogawa

6 Epigraphs antiques; Etudes, Books I & II; Etude retrouve'e; Intermède; Les soirs illuminées par l'ardeur du Charbon

(N) **** BIS CD 1655. Ogawa

Estampes; Images, Books 1–2; Images oubliées; L'Isle joyeuse; Masques pour piano

*** BIS CD 1105. Ogawa

Noriko Ogawa has an unerring feeling for the Debussy sound world and the delicacy and refinement of touch to do it full justice. This Japanese pianist is the equal of Thibaudet, and her elegance and finesse are matched by a magnificent sense of atmosphere. The recorded sound is in the best tradition of the house, and the accompanying notes by Leif Hasselgren are first class. Strongly recommended.

Bruyères; Canope; Children's Corner; Images, Books I & II (DVD version)

*** Opus Arte **DVD** OA 0941 D. Arturo Benedetti Michelangeli (plus documentary: 'Maestro di Maestri')

This recital was filmed and recorded by RAI at Turin in 1962 and is in black-and-white. The playing is anything but. **Michelangeli** plays with an amazingly wide range of colour and refinement of dynamics and touch. His concentration, sense of atmosphere and pianism are at their finest. Forget the feeble documentary of 1959 – not for the hagiography, but for the crass questions of the self-satisfied interviewer. However, it does give us a glimpse of the pianists who take part in the annual festival in Arrezo, including **Adam Harasiewicz**, who had won the Chopin Prize a few years earlier. But, as Debussy playing, Michelangeli's performances take some beating.

Children's Corner Suite

(BB) **(*) Naxos 8.550885. Biret – SCHUMANN: *Kinderszenen*; TCHAIKOVSKY: *Album for the Young* ***

Idil Biret takes the opening movement very briskly and

impetuously, but the performance then settles down and is sensitive and well characterized, especially the closing *Golliwog's Cakewalk*. Good recording and recommendable couplings too.

Children's Corner; Images, Books 1–2; Préludes, Books 1–2

**(*) DG (ADD) 449 438-2 (2). Michelangeli

There is no doubt that these performances of *Children's Corner* and the two sets of *Images* are very distinguished. The *Préludes* undoubtedly bring piano playing which is pretty flawless. At the same time, it is very cool and detached and, although Book 2 excited enormous enthusiasm in some quarters, both Books here will strike many as somewhat glacial and curiously unatmospheric.

Children's Corner; Estampes; L'Isle joyeuse; Images I & II; La Plus que lente; Suite bergamasque

⊶ (M) (***) EMI mono 5 62798-2. Gieseking

A self-recommending disc, drawing on **Walter Gieseking's** four-disc survey listed above. The mono recordings are of excellent quality.

Etudes, Books 1–2

⊶ ✿ (M) **** Ph. 475 7559. Uchida

Etudes, Books 1–2; Estampes; L'Isle joyeuse

(BB) *** Regis RRC 1091. Tirimo

12 Etudes; Images, Books 1–2

*** Warner 8573 83940-2. Aimard

Mitsuko Uchida's remarkable account of the *Etudes* on Philips is not only one of the best Debussy piano records in the catalogue and arguably her finest recording, but also one of the best ever recordings of the instrument. It is even more attractive at mid-price and is certainly worthy of inclusion as one of Philips's Originals.

Debussy playing of some stature from **Pierre-Laurent Aimard**, though his playing does not project the mists and atmosphere of this music so much as its extraordinary colour, inner vitality and originality. The *Images* are vibrant and as good as any in the catalogue, and the musical and technical challenges of the *Etudes* are surmounted with magisterial aplomb. This holds its own even alongside the wonderful Uchida set. Crystalline, clean recording that is in the demonstration category.

Martino Tirimo offers not only the *Etudes*, played with imagination and much subtlety of colour, but he also includes a set of *Estampes* and *L'Isle joyeuse*, neither quite as impressive, but still worth having. He is very well recorded and this Regis reissue is very competitive in the cheapest price-range.

Hommage à Rameau

(M) (**(*)) BBC mono BBCL 4064-2. Michelangeli –

BEETHOVEN: *Sonatas 4 & 12* **(*); RAVEL: *Gaspard de la nuit* (***)

The Debussy *Hommage à Rameau* is beautifully delivered and controlled. It comes with an almost miraculous account of Ravel's *Gaspard*, which alone is worth the price of the disc. The notes by William Robson, **Michelangeli's** BBC producer, serve to bring the whole occasion vividly to life.

Préludes, Books 1–2 (complete)

⊶ ✿ (M) (****) EMI mono 5 67233-2. Gieseking

*** Hyp. CDA67530. Osborne

*** Onyx 4004. Rogé

(BB) *** Regis RRC 1111. Tirimo

Gieseking's classic set of both Books of the Debussy *Préludes* takes its rightful place as one of EMI's 'Great Recordings of the Century' and now has proper documentation. The current remastering again confirms the natural realism of the 1953–4 Abbey Road recording.

Steven Osborne has a real feeling for keyboard colour, a keen imagination and an effortless technique. A very well-balanced recording from the Henry Wood Hall.

When **Pascal Rogé** embarked on his Debussy recordings for Decca in the 1970s, he did not include the Second Book of *Préludes*. He is among the finest exponents of this inexhaustible and fascinating repertoire now before the public, and his expertly recorded performances are totally gripping.

No grumbles about value for money or quality from **Martino Tirimo** on Regis. His playing is very fine indeed and can withstand comparison with most of his rivals – and, apart from the sensitivity of his playing, the recording is most realistic and natural.

VOCAL MUSIC

Le Martyre de Saint-Sébastien; (i) 3 Ballades de François Villon

(**) Testament mono SBT 1214. Collart, Collard, Gayraud, Falcon; (i) Plantey; French R.O & Ch., Inghelbrecht

Inghelbrecht's performance is totally dedicated and refreshingly wanting in glamour, and such is the sense of authenticity it communicates that its want of finish seems of no account. Readers who really care about Debussy should seek this out.

Early Songs: Poèmes de Théodore de Banville

*** Deux-Elles DXL 1052. Keith, Lepper

Gillian Keith proves a sensitive interpreter of these early Debussy songs. Keith with her fine control of dynamic does wonders in shading her tone in songs which demand subtlety above all. There is a sensuous element even in Debussy's earliest songs, and this generous selection gets one marvelling at the range and finesse of the composer even in his teens.

3 Ballades de François Villon

(***) Testament mono SBT 1312. Souzay, Bonneau – DUPARC: *Chanson triste; Elégie*, etc.; CHAUSSON: *Songs*; RAVEL: *Don Quichotte à Dulcineé* (***)

The *Villon Ballades* are heard in their orchestral form (*Le Promenoir des deux amants* and *La Grotte* in the orchestration by Louis Beydts) although, as in the Ravel *Don Quichotte*, the balance is not ideal. **Souzay** is very close to the microphone and masks some of the orchestral detail. But this is superb singing by a master of this repertoire, and **Jacqueline Bonneau** is an ideal partner.

3 Ballades de François Villon; Fêtes galantes (2nd series); Fleur des blés; Mandoline; 3 Mélodies; Nuit d'étoiles; 5 Poèmes de Baudelaire; Voici que le printemps

*** Hyp. CDA 67357. Maltman, Martineau

Christopher Maltman proves himself equal to the challenges of Debussy, Verlaine and Baudelaire, and in no small measure the success of his recital resides in the superb support of **Malcolm Martineau**. This is a most successful and enjoyable recital.

3 Chansons de Charles d'Orléans

*** Ph. 438 149-2. Monteverdi Ch., ORR, Gardiner – FAURÉ: *Requiem*; RAVEL; SAINT-SAËNS: *Choral Works* ***

With **Gardiner** and his period forces bringing out the medieval flavour of these charming choral settings, this adds to a generous and unusual coupling for Gardiner's expressive reading of the Fauré *Requiem*.

La Damoiselle élue

(***) Testament mono SBT 3203 (3). De los Angeles, Boston SO, Munch – BERLIOZ; *Les Nuits d'été*; MASSENET: *Manon* ***

The combination of **Munch's** purposeful understanding of this wayward work, together with the charm of **Victoria de los Angeles**, make this an exceptional performance, even though in limited (1955) mono sound. As in the Berlioz song-cycle, the RCA recording may not capture the full golden beauty of the singer's voice, but these two works make a valuable bonus for the classic Monteux version of Massenet's *Manon*.

4 Poèmes de Charles Baudelaire (orch. John Adams)

*** Warner 2564 61938-2. Graham, BBC SO, Yan Pascal Tortelier – CHAUSSON: *Poème de l'amour et de la mer*; RAVEL: *Shéhérazade* ***

It was surely an extraordinary venture of John Adams to orchestrate four of these songs; he omits *La mort des amants*. The result is to give the words an entirely new atmosphere, a richer background patina, and in *Recueillement* he even brings in horns, apparently to suggest a Wagnerian ethos. Certainly **Susan Graham** responds to this new backcloth, so different from a piano, and she sings tenderly and often very

beautifully indeed. A fascinating and daring experiment, well brought off by conductor and singer alike.

OPERA

Pelléas et Mélisande (DVD versions)

*** DG **DVD** 073 030-9. Hagley, Archer, Maxwell, Cox, Walker, Welsh Nat. Op. Ch. & O, Boulez (V/D: Peter Stein)

Boulez's account of *Pelléas* with the Welsh National Opera was much acclaimed at the time, and, judging from the 1992 DVD recording, rightly so. Boulez produces much greater atmosphere than he did in his CD version. The soloists are impressive; **Alison Hagley's** Mélisande especially is both good to look at and to listen to. Her vocal and stage characterization are excellent, and she conveys an appealing sense of innocence. **Neill Archer's** Pelléas is no less intelligently projected, and **Kenneth Cox's** Arkel is splendidly sung and finely acted. Peter Stein's production is effective, simple and beautifully lit. This is infinitely more satisfying than the alternative Lyons production with its perverse setting.

Pelléas et Mélisande (CD versions)

⊖ *** DG 435 344-2 (2). Ewing, Le Roux, Van Dam, Courtis, Ludwig, Pace, Mazzola, Vienna Konzertvereinigung, VPO, Abbado

Ⓜ *** Naïve Radio FranceV4923 (3). Von Otter, Holzmair, Naouri, Schaer, Vernhes, Couderc, R. France Ch. & Nat. O, Haitink

ⒷⒷ *** Naxos 8.660047-9 (3). Delusch, Theruel, Arapian, Bacquier, Jessoud, Ch. Regional Nord/Pas de Calais, O Nat. de Lille, J.-C. Casadesus

ⓃⓂ(***) Glyndebourne Festival Opera GFOCD 003-63. Duval, Wilbrink, Roux, Glyndebourne Ch., RPO, Gui

Claudio Abbado's outstanding version broadly resolves the problem of a first CD recommendation in this opera, which has always been lucky on record. If among modern versions the choice has been hard to make between Karajan's sumptuously romantic account, almost Wagnerian, and Dutoit's clean-cut, direct one, Abbado satisfyingly presents a performance more sharply focused than the one and more freely flexible than the other, altogether more urgently dramatic. The casting is excellent, with no weak link.

Haitink even in the opening prelude establishes the dedication of his reading, spacious, capturing an intensity that unmistakably evokes a great live event. **Holzmair** is a fresh, lyrical Pelléas, believably ardent in his obsession with Mélisande, and with **von Otter** also characterizing superbly, tender and subtle, not just an innocent. The Golaud of **Laurent Naouri** is the more moving when with his youngish baritone he is such a believable lover, not merely a predator. The others too are first rate, with firmness and clarity the keynote, with the soprano of **Florence Couderc** fresh and bright if obviously feminine in this young boy's role. The CD index points are limited to the beginnings of scenes, not even separating the preludes and interludes, so that the third disc, containing just Act V, has only a single index point.

Casadesus's Naxos set is most compelling, with fresh, young voices helping to make the drama more involving. **Mireille Delusch** is a bright and girlish Mélisande, well matched against the high baritone of **Gérard Theruel** as a boyish Pelléas. The others are first rate too, including the veteran, **Gabriel Bacquier**, aptly sounding old as Arkel. The orchestra, with a modest band of strings, adds to the chamber-scale intimacy. The libretto comes in French only, but with good notes and a synopsis in English. An outstanding bargain nevertheless.

The 1963 Glyndebourne performances of *Pelléas* is particularly treasurable for the beautifully characterized Mélisande of **Denise Duval** and the elegant Pelléas of **Hans Wilbrink**. The Golaud of **Michel Roux** is no less powerfully projected as indeed was the Arkel of **Guus Hoeckman**. Above all it is the atmosphere which **Vittorio Gui** distilled from the **LPO** that makes this account so special. His tempi are very broad and spacious, and the singers are well integrated into the sound balance. Naturally the orchestral texture is not transparent and the sound is typical of broadcast relays, even if this is Glyndebourne's own and not necessarily the BBC's balance. The presentation is very handsome with the 200-page libretto flanked by the discs themselves. Devotees of *Pelléas* should not miss this.

Pelléas et Mélisande (excerpts from the opera, arr. Marius Constant)

(M) *** Sup. SU 3899-2 (2). Czech PO, Baudo – FAURÉ: *Pelléas Suite*; SCHOENBERG: *Pelleas: Tone poem*; SIBELIUS: *Pelléas: Suite* ***

In order to make a quartet of works inspired by *Pelléas et Mélisande* **Baudo** has included Marius Constant's tone-poem using music from the opera in a continuous flowing stream. Those who know the opera well will recognize his sources, and certainly it is beautifully played and recorded here and makes a fascinating novelty.

Rodrigue et Chimène (opera; completed Langham Smith; orch. Denisov)

*** Erato 4509 98508-2 (2). Brown, Dale, Jossoud, Van Dam, Bastin, Le Texier, Lyon Op. Ch. & O, Nagano

In the years immediately before he started work on his masterpiece, *Pelléas et Mélisande*, Debussy all but completed this opera to a much more conventional libretto, telling the story of El Cid. Richard Langham Smith reconstructed the rest, and Edison Denisov did the inspired orchestration, adding music from other sections to fill in a few gaps. The best comes first, with radiant singing from **Laurence Dale**, ideal as Rodrigue, and the fresh and expressive soprano, **Donna Brown**, as Chimène. Atmospheric off-stage choruses are distinctive too, but little of Act III gives much clue as to the identity of the composer, enjoyable though it is. **Kent Nagano's** superb recording brings vividly atmospheric sound. **José van Dam** sings strongly and clearly as the heroine's father, Don Diègue, with the veteran, **Jules Bastin**, in splendid voice as Don Gomez.

DECAUX, Abel (1869–1943)

Clairs de lune

*** Hyp. CDA 67513. Hamelin – DUKAS: *Piano Sonata* ***

These four extraordinarily forward-looking and imaginative pieces by Decaux are the only works of his that are known, though sketches for a fifth, *La forêt*, exist. They make a fascinating makeweight for Marc-André Hamelin's masterly account of the Dukas *Sonata*.

DELAGE, Maurice (1879–1961)

4 Poèmes hindous

(***) Testament mono SBT 1135. Micheau, Fr. R. O, Cluytens – STRAVINSKY: *Le Rossignol* *** 🏵

The *Quatre Poèmes hindous* make an ideal coupling for *Le Rossignol*. These four songs are very much in the received post-Debussian tradition and are exquisitely sung by **Janine Micheau**. While the mono sound is less transparent than is ideal, the recording is expertly transferred and gives great pleasure.

DELIBES, Léo (1836–91)

Complete ballets: (i) Coppélia; (ii) Sylvia; (iii) La Source (CD versions)

⊛– (B) *** Decca (ADD/DDD) 460 418-2 (4). (i) Nat. PO; (ii) New Phil. O; (iii) ROHCG O Bonynge

Bonynge's digital *Coppélia* recording sparkles from start to finish. There is tremendous energy in the many vigorous numbers and the contribution of the woodwind is a continual delight. Not as consistently inspired as *Coppélia*, *Sylvia* is more serious and symphonic in approach but there are many exciting set-pieces, much piquant colouring and a haunting *leitmotif* which runs throughout. The **New Philharmonia** play with tremendous energy and style, and the 1972 recording is as brilliant as you could wish. *La Source* was the composer's first ballet, though he wrote only Acts II and III. The complete ballet is given here, with Acts I and IV written by Minkus, whose contribution is rather more melancholy than Delibes's but is well written and enjoyable. The **ROHCG Orchestra** plays with great style and the digital recording is warm and detailed – well up to the house standard. At bargain price, this set is exceptional value.

Coppélia (ballet; complete)

(B) *** Double Decca (ADD) 444 836-2 (2). SRO, Bonynge – MASSENET: *Le Carillon* ***

Coppélia (ballet; complete); La Source: Suites 2 & 3; Intermezzo: Pas de fleurs

(BB) *** Naxos 8.553356/7. Slovak RSO (Bratislava), Mogrelia

On the Double Decca reissue of his earlier (1969) analogue set, **Bonynge** secures a high degree of polish from the **Suisse**

Romande Orchestra, with sparkling string- and wind-textures, and with sonority and bite from the brass. The Decca recording sounds freshly minted and, with its generous Massenet bonus, little-known music of great charm, this set remains competitive.

The **Bratislava** orchestra plays with characteristic finesse and grace and with glowing lyrical feeling. Other versions may have more surface brilliance, but most lovers of ballet music will enjoy the naturalness of perspective and the attractively smooth string-quality. *La Source* comes off equally well. The *Pas de fleurs grande valse* is a real lollipop and in the two suites the music (selected rather arbitrarily) has plenty of colour and rhythmic life.

Coppélia (ballet; highlights)

⌐ BB *** Warner Apex 2564 60365-2. Lyon Opéra O, Nagano

A very generous and comprehensive selection from Delibes's delightful score for *Coppélia*, which Tchaikovsky admired so much. Every bar of the music-making is of the highest quality, and the recording with its nicely judged acoustic is as attractive as the playing. Self-recommending, unless you want the complete score, which costs twice as much.

Coppélia: extended excerpts; Sylvia: extended excerpts

⌐ B *** EMI (ADD) 5 69659-2 (2). Paris Op. O, Mari

Jean-Baptiste Mari uses ballet tempi throughout, yet there is never any loss of momentum, and the long-breathed string-phrasing and felicitous wind solos are a continual source of delight. Mari's natural sympathy and warmth make the very most of the less memorable parts of the score for *Sylvia* (and they are only slightly less memorable). Seventy-five minutes are offered from each ballet. The sound is fresh.

Coppélia: suite; Kassya: Trepak; Le Roi s'amuse: suite; La Source: suite; Sylvia: suite

BB **(*) Naxos 8.550080. Slovak RSO (Bratislava), Lenárd

An attractive hour of Delibes, with five key items from *Coppélia*, including the *Music for the Automatons* and *Waltz*, four from *Sylvia*, not forgetting the *Pizzicato*, and four from *La Source*. Perhaps most enjoyable of all are the six pastiche ancient 'airs de danse', provided for a ballroom scene in Victor Hugo's play, *Le Roi s'amuse*. They are played most gracefully, and the excerpts from the major ballets are spirited and nicely turned. Vivid sound.

Sylvia (ballet): complete (CD version)

⌐ BB *** Naxos 8.553338/9. Razumovsky Sinfonia, Mogrelia – SAINT-SAËNS: *Henry VIII Ballet Music* ***

Mogrelia's performance of *Sylvia* is above all spacious, bringing out the music's pastel-shaded lyricism yet finding plenty of weight for the more vigorous music depicting the hunters. The performance as a whole, glowing sentience takes precedence over vitality, and some might find the atmosphere a little sleepy at times. Excellent, naturally balanced recording.

OPERA

Lakmé (complete)

B *** Double Decca 460 741-2 (2). Sutherland, Berbié, Vanzo, Bacquier, Monte Carlo Op. Ch. & O, Bonynge

BB (**(*)) Naxos (mono) 8.111235/6. Robin, De Luca, Disney, Borthayre, Collart, Ch. & O of Opéra Comique, Sébastien (with additional arias sung by Villabella, Couzinou & Ben Sedira)

M (**) Decca mono 475 6793 (2). Robin, De Luca, Disney, Collart, Lemaître, Luca, Borthayre, Jansen, Perriat, Opéra Comique O, Sébastien – BELLINI: Arias from: *La sonnambula*; PROCH: *Theme & Variations, Op. 164, Deh, torna mio bene* (LPO, Fistoulari)

The performance on Decca seizes its opportunities with both hands. **Sutherland** swallows her consonants, but the beauty of her singing, with its ravishing ease and purity up to the highest register, is what matters; and she has opposite her one of the most pleasing and intelligent of French tenors, **Alain Vanzo**. Excellent contributions from the others too, spirited conducting and brilliant, atmospheric recording. The reissue as a Double Decca makes a splendid bargain and the new-style synopsis will prove especially helpful for newcomers to this opera.

The **Sébastien** performance dates from 1952 and the voices – very much in front of the orchestra – are warmly and vividly caught by Decca (John Culshaw was the producer). **Mado Robin's** highly individual timbre is certainly affecting and her amazing vocal agility and freak high notes are used to predictably impressive effect in the *Bell Song*. The rest of the cast, if not outstanding, are characterful and, with French forces, it sounds vividly theatrical. The bonus material is well worth having, with Robin's speciality, final high notes – and they have to be heard to be believed – as startling as ever! Highlights are available on 475 6158.

However, Ward Marston's Naxos transfer restores all the bloom of John Culshaw's original excellent sound-balance, including that on Mado Robin's voice. This set is well worth having at budget price, more especially as the bonus is a trio of arias splendidly sung by famous French singers from the late 1920s and early 1930s. These include **Miguel Villabella's** honeyed *Prendre le dessin d'un bijou . . . Fantaisie aux divins mensonges* (1931), **Robert Couzinou's** ardent and very French *Lakmé, ton doux regard se voile* (1927), and another spectacular *Bell Song* from **Leila Ben Sedira** (1929). The transfers are again very real and vivid.

DELIUS, Frederick (1862–1934)

(i) *Air & Dance;* (ii) *Florida Suite; North Country Sketches;* (iii) *2 Aquarelles; Fennimore & Gerda: Intermezzo; Hassan: Intermezzo & Serenade; Irmelin: Prelude; Late Swallows; On Hearing the First Cuckoo in Spring; A Song before Sunrise; Summer Night on the River;* (iv) *In a Summer*

Garden; A Village Romeo & Juliet: Walk to the Paradise Garden

Ⓜ *** Chan. (ADD/DDD) 2x1 241-37 (2). (i) LPO; (ii) Ulster O; (i–ii) Handley; (iii) Bournemouth Sinf., Del Mar; (iv) Bournemouth SO, Hickox

A splendidly comprehensive collection from three fine Delians. **Handley** includes the comparatively rare *Florida Suite* (written in America) and the *North Country Sketches* (which evoke the seasons on the Yorkshire moors). **Del Mar** then creates a mood of serene, atmospheric evocation – into which Eric Fenby's arrangement of *Late Swallows* from the *String Quartet* fits admirably; then **Hickox** takes over flexibly. *In a Summer Garden* is both ardent and luxuriant in its shimmering summer heat haze and the **Bournemouth Symphony Orchestra** play passionately for him in the *Walk to the Paradise Garden*.

2 Aquarelles (arr. Fenby); Brigg Fair; Dance Rhapsodies 1-2 (ed. Beecham); Florida Suite; In a Summer Garden; North Country Sketches; On Hearing the First Cuckoo in Spring; Summer Night on the River (both edited Beecham); The Walk to the Paradise Garden

Ⓑ **(*) Double Decca 460 290-2 (2). Welsh Nat. Op. O, Mackerras

Mackerras is just as warmly sympathetic in these Delius orchestral pieces as in his complete opera recording, *A Village Romeo and Juliet*. The *Dance Rhapsodies*, music which is far from rhapsodic, here receive fresh, taut performances. In the shorter works **Mackerras** is warmly sympathetic, with the woodwind playing particularly excellent. But the recording, made in the Brangwyn Hall, Swansea, is less spacious, less sensuous than the Austrian-made one of the opera, lacking Delian mystery. The massed strings in particular have too much brightness; one requires more lambent textures in this music.

Brigg Fair

Ⓜ (**(*)) BBC mono BBCL 4113. RPO, Beecham – BERLIOZ: *The Trojans: Royal Hunt and Storm*; CHABRIER: *España; Gwendoline Overture*; DEBUSSY: *L'Enfant prodigue: Cortège et Air de danse*; MASSENET: *La Vierge: Le dernier sommeil de la vierge*; SAINT-SAËNS: *Le rouet d'Omphale* (with MOZART: *Divertimento in D, K.131: excerpts* (**(*))

Beecham's BBC recording of *Brigg Fair* comes from a live broadcast concert of 1956. The playing of **Gerald Jackson** (flute), **Terence MacDonagh** (oboe), **Jack Brymer** (clarinet) and **Gwydion Brooke** (bassoon) ensures its evocative delicacy, but the recording itself leaves something to be desired, and the EMI stereo version is preferable.

(i) Brigg Fair; La Calinda (arr. Fenby); In a Summer Garden; Fennimore and Gerda: Intermezzo. Hassan: Intermezzo and (iii) Serenade (arr. Beecham); (ii) Irmelin: Prelude; (i) Late Swallows (arr. Fenby); On Hearing the First Cuckoo in Spring; A Song before Sunrise; (ii) A Song of Summer; (i) Summer Night on the River; (ii) A Village Romeo and Juliet: Walk to

the Paradise Garden (arr. Beecham); (i; iv) Appalachia (with brief rehearsal sequence)

Ⓜ *** EMI (ADD) 5 65119-2 (2). (i) Hallé O; (ii) LSO; (iii) with Tear; (iv) Jenkins, Amb. S; all cond. Barbirolli

Sir John Barbirolli shows an admirable feeling for the sense of light Delius conjures up and for the luxuriance of texture his music possesses. The gentle evocation of *La Calinda* contrasts with the surge of passionate Italianate romanticism at the climax of the *Walk to the Paradise Garden*. Barbirolli's style is evanescent in repose and more romantic than the Beecham versions but, with lovely playing from both the **Hallé** and the **LSO**, the first-rate analogue sound from the mid- to late-1960s adds to the listener's pleasure. *Appalachia* is given an admirably atmospheric reading that conveys the work's exotic and vivid colouring.

Brigg Fair; Dance Rhapsody 2; Fennimore and Gerda: Intermezzo (arr. Fenby); Florida Suite: Daybreak - Dance (La calinda) (revised & edited Beecham); Irmelin: Prelude; On Hearing the First Cuckoo in Spring; Sleigh Ride; Song before Sunrise; Summer Evening (arr. Beecham); Summer Night on the River

Ⓜ **** EMI 5 67552. RPO, Beecham

The further remastering of **Beecham's** stereo Delius recordings, made at Abbey Road at the end of the 1950s, continues to demonstrate a technological miracle. The result brings these unsurpassed performances into our own time with an uncanny sense of realism and presence. The delicacy of the gentler wind and string textures is something to marvel at, as is the orchestral playing itself. Beecham's fine-spun magic, his ability to lift a phrase is apparent from the very opening of *Brigg Fair*, which shows Delius at his most inspired and Beecham's orchestra at their most incandescent. The admirable documentation is by Lyndon Jenkins. Sheer magic, and fully worthy to be included in EMI's 'Great Recordings of the Century'.

(i) Brigg Fair; Eventyr; In a Summer Garden; (ii) A Song before Sunrise; (i) A Song of Summer; (ii) Summer Night on the River; A Village Romeo and Juliet: Walk to the Paradise Garden

Ⓑ *** CfP (DDD/ADD) 575 3152. (i) LPO; (ii) Hallé O, Handley

Vernon Handley's beautifully played **Hallé** performances were recorded in 1981, and the digital sound is of EMI's best quality, matching clarity of definition with ambient lustre and rich colouring. This very generous reissue adds three hardly less fine **LPO** performances recorded in the Henry Wood Hall three years earlier, where the analogue quality is very nearly as good.

Brigg Fair; In a Summer Garden; On Hearing the First Cuckoo in Spring; Paris (The Song of a Great City); Summer Night on the River; A Village Romeo and Juliet: Walk to the Paradise Garden

Ⓑ **** Warner Apex 8573 89084-2. BBC SO, A. Davis

A superb disc. Beecham may be very special in these lovely scores but it is good to have state-of-the-art modern recordings, admirably spacious and atmospheric and with an excitingly wide dynamic range. In short this is post-Beecham Delius with a new approach from a conductor who feels this music in his very being.

La Calinda; In a Summer Garden; Irmelin Prelude; Song of Summer; A Village Romeo & Juliet: Walk to the Paradise Garden

⊕—Ⓜ **** EMI (ADD) 3 79983-2. LSO, Barbirolli – BAX: *Tintagel*; IRELAND: *London Overture* ****

These are richly romantic rather than delicately subtle performances. **Sir John Barbirolli** does not provide here the limpid, evanescent textures for which Beecham was famous, but brings instead his almost Italianate feeling to Delius's passionate arching string-phrases. Lovely playing throughout, and first-rate, analogue (mid-1960s) sound.

(i) Caprice & Elegy; (ii–iii) Piano Concerto; (iv–v) Violin Concerto; (vi–iii) Hassan: Intermezzo & Serenade; Koanga: La Calinda; (v) On Hearing the First Cuckoo in Spring; (vii) Legend for Violin & Piano

(***) Testament mono SBT 1014. (i) Harrison, CO, Fenby; (ii) Moiseiwitsch, Philh. O; (iii) Lambert; (iv) Sammons; (v) Liverpool PO, Sargent; (vi) Hallé O; (vii) Holst, Moore

The greatest treasure is the first ever recording of the *Violin Concerto*, made in 1944 and featuring the original soloist, **Albert Sammons**, arguably the most eloquent and moving account of the work ever committed to disc. **Moiseiwitsch's** recording of the *Piano Concerto*, also the first ever, is hardly less powerful, making a very good case for this warm but less cogent piece. The other items range from the 1930 recording of the *Caprice and Elegy* by **Beatrice Harrison**, the dedicatee, with suspect intonation and plentiful portamento, to **Sargent's** 1947 recording of the *First Cuckoo*, very warm and free in its rubato. **Constant Lambert** is also a first-rate interpreter of Delius, as the *Hassan* and *Koanga* excerpts show. This transfer has higher surface-hiss than later issues on this label, but the disc must be strongly recommended.

Cello Concerto

*** EMI 5 55529-2. du Pré, RPO, Sargent (with Recital) ***

The EMI disc offers what was **du Pré's** first concerto recording, and the recital is a transfer of the material mainly from her very first EMI sessions in 1962 which gave such clear promise of glories to come. Most recommendable, although readers will note that it remains at full price.

(i) Cello Concerto; (ii) Double Concerto for Violin & Cello; Paris (The Song of a Great City)

Ⓑ *** CfP 575 8032. (i; ii) Wallfisch; (ii) Little; RLPO, Mackerras

This superb recording of the *Double Concerto*, with soloists who easily outshine their predecessors on record (however distinguished), confirms the strength of a piece which establishes its own logic, with each theme developing naturally out of the preceding one. **Raphael Wallfisch** is just as persuasive in the *Cello Concerto*, and **Mackerras** proves an understanding interpreter of the composer in the big tone-poem, *Paris, The Song of a Great City*. The recording is comparably full and atmospheric.

Piano Concerto in C min.

Ⓑ *** CfP 575 9832. Lane, RLPO, Handley – FINZI: *Eclogue*; VAUGHAN WILLIAMS: *Piano Concerto* ***

ⒷⒷ (***) Naxos mono 8.110689. Moiseiwitsch, PO, Lambert (with solo pieces by DEBUSSY; GODOWSKY; GRANADOS; IBERT; POULENC; PROKOFIEV; RAVEL; STRAVINSKY (***))

Piers Lane gives a masterly performance of the Delius *Piano Concerto*, weighty without pomposity, which effectively counters ideas of being 'sub-Grieg', early though it is. Lane's measured, concentrated reading of the slow movement is particularly compelling.

Benno Moiseiwitsch was a keen advocate of the *Piano Concerto*. It is not the greatest Delius but has wonderful moments, which Moiseiwitsch plays with great sensitivity and imagination.

Violin Concerto

ⒷⒷ (**(*)) Naxos mono 8.110951. Sammons, Liverpool PO, Sargent – ELGAR: *Violin Concerto* (**(*))

Albert Sammons's première account of the Delius *Violin Concerto*, recorded in 1944, is by general consent still unsurpassed even by the likes of Ralph Holmes and Tasmin Little, except in terms of recording quality and readers may now turn with confidence to the Naxos transfer.

Fennimore and Gerda: Intermezzo; Irmelin: Prelude; Koanga: La Calinda (arr. Fenby); On Hearing the First Cuckoo in Spring; Sleigh Ride

Ⓑ *** CfP (ADD) 575 3162. LPO, Handley – VAUGHAN WILLIAMS: *Lark Ascending; Wasps Suite*, etc. ***

These five favourite Delius items belong to the same 1977 Henry Wood Hall sessions as the **LPO** items included in the companion **Handley** collection above. The playing is equally sensitive and the warm, spacious analogue recording is most attractively transferred. The Vaughan Williams items are hardly less attractive.

Florida Suite; Idylle de printemps; Over the Hills and Far Away; La Quadroone; Scherzo; (i) Koanga: Closing Scene

⊕—ⒷⒷ **** Naxos 8.553535. E. N. Philh. O, Lloyd-Jones; (i) with Glanville, Lees, Evans, Francis, Peerce, Thomas

Several of the works here are new to disc, including the *Idylle de printemps*, fresh and charming, leading to an ecstatic climax. *La Quadroone* and *Scherzo* were originally planned as movements in a suite. **Lloyd-Jones** has clearly learnt from Beecham's example in his glowing and intense readings of the other three works, with the orchestra's woodwind soloists excelling themselves in delicate pointing, not least in the haunting *La Calinda*, included in the *Florida Suite. Over the Hills and Far Away*, raptly done, is richly evocative too, and the epilogue to the opera, *Koanga*, rounds off a generously filled disc with music both sensuous and passionate, featuring six female vocal soloists from Opera North, three sopranos and three mezzos.

CHAMBER MUSIC

Cello Sonata

*** Chan. 8499. R. and P. Wallfisch – BAX: *Rhapsodic Ballad*; BRIDGE: *Cello Sonata*; WALTON: *Passacaglia* ***

In the Chandos version of the *Cello Sonata* the performers give as strong and sympathetic an account as is to be found. They are also excellently recorded.

(i) Cello Sonata; (ii) String Quartet

(*) Australian Decca Eloquence (ADD) 442 9486. (i) Isaac, Jones; (ii) Fitzwilliam Qt – SIBELIUS: *String Quartet* *

The *Quartet* is rarely heard, either in the concert hall or on record. The **Fitzwilliam Quartet** make a very convincing case for it and their performance is committed and imbued with evident affection. The 1978 recording is superb. As one might expect, Delius's *Cello Sonata*, written in 1916, is a flowing, endlessly lyrical work. It is good to have this version restored to the catalogue, even though **George Isaac** and **Martin Jones** interpret it not so much with love as with literal freshness. The 1971 sound is not as sumptuous as for the *Quartet*, but is more than acceptable.

String Quartet

*** ASV CDDCA 526. Brodsky Qt – ELGAR: *Quartet* ***

In this music, the ebb and flow of tension and a natural feeling for persuasive but unexaggerated rubato is vital; with fine ensemble but seeming spontaneity, the **Brodsky** players consistently produce that. First-rate recording.

PIANO DUET

Dance Rhapsodies 1 & 2; In a Summer Garden; North Country Sketches; On Hearing the First Cuckoo in Spring; A Song before Sunrise; Summer Night on the River (arranged for piano, four hands, by Peter Warlock)

*** BIS CD 1347. Ogawa, Stott

Noriko Ogawa and **Kathryn Stott** have formed a most sensitive duo partnership. *Summer Night on the River*, acquires an attractive freshness transferred to the piano, as does *In a Summer Garden* with its flickering imitations of birdsong. Generally the more rhythmic the writing the more effective it is in piano transcription, as in the 6/8 of *A Song before Sunrise*. When it comes to the *North Country Sketches*, which Warlock transcribed somewhat later in 1921, these arrangements sound like original piano music.

VOCAL MUSIC

(i) Appalachia; Sea Drift; (ii) A Song before Sunrise; Koanga: La Calinda

*** Australian Decca Eloquence (ADD) 467 601-2. (i) Shirley-Quirk, L. Symphony Ch., RPO, Hickox; (ii) ASMF, Marriner

Hickox's 1977 LP of *Appalachia* and *Sea Drift* is an early example of this conductor's natural affinity with Delius. These are fresh and dedicated performances, urgent in their expressiveness rather than lingering. **John Shirley-Quirk** sings with characteristic sensitivity, and the chorus is outstanding. The trusty **Marriner** items are always good to hear, and the sound throughout this generous CD is superb. Texts are included in this Eloquence release, as are excellent notes by Christopher Palmer.

(i) An Arabesk; A Mass of Life: Prelude. (ii) Songs of Sunset, Parts 1-7; (iii) Part 8; Songs: (iv) I-Brasil; Le ciel est pardessus le toit; Cradle Song; Irmelin Rose; Klein Venevil; The Nightingale; Twilight Fancies; The Violet; Whither

Ⓜ(***) Somm mono BEECHAM 8. (i, ii) Henderson, L. Select Ch.; (ii) Haley; (iii) Evans, Llewellyn, BBC Ch.; (iv) Labbette; LPO or RPO, Beecham (or (iv) Beecham, piano)

In the live recording of the *Songs of Sunset* Beecham conveys a virile thrust and energy in the writing, partly by opting for faster speeds. Both in this, with its seven linked sections, and in the single span of *An Arabesk*, the line of the argument is clarified. **Roy Henderson** is the clean-cut, sensitive baritone soloist in both, sounding very English, with **Olga Haley** a fresh, bright mezzo soloist in the *Songs of Sunset*. The test pressings sadly lack the final section, but a substitute is provided for that section, taken from a 1946 recording with **Nancy Evans** and **Redvers Llewellyn** which Beecham initially rejected. The ends of 78-r.p.m. sides tend to have a noisy surface, but there is ample body in the sound. **Dora Labbette** is the enchanting soprano soloist in all the separate songs. Four of the ten come in the beautiful orchestral versions, with the rest accompanied at the piano by Beecham himself. He may have been only a good amateur pianist, but his natural magnetism still shines out.

(i) A Mass of Life (sung in German); (ii) Requiem

☒ *** Chan. 9515 (2). (i) Rodgers, Rigby, Robson; (ii) Evans; (i-ii) Coleman-Wright; Waynflete Singers, Bournemouth Ch. & SO, Hickox

Hickox gives a glowing account of this ambitious setting of a German text drawn from Nietzsche's *Also sprach Zarathustra*. He is helped by excellent singing and playing from his **Bournemouth** forces, and by fine solo singing, notably from the soprano, **Joan Rodgers**. The full and atmospheric Chandos recording confirms the primacy of this version even over the excellent previous recordings. The *Requiem*, half an hour long, makes the ideal coupling, emerging as a fine example of Delius's later work, not as distinctive in its material as the *Mass*, but with an element of bleakness tempering the lushness of the choral writing.

Here too – with **Rebecca Evans** this time as soprano soloist – Hickox conducts a most persuasive performance, ripely recorded.

(i) *Sea Drift; Songs of Farewell;* (i; ii) *Songs of Sunset*

🎧 *** Chan. 9214. (i) Terfel; (ii) Burgess; Bournemouth Symphony Ch., Waynflete Singers, Southern Voices, Bournemouth SO, Hickox

In this second recording of Delius's masterpiece **Hickox** finds even more magic, again taking a spacious view – which keeps the flow of the music going magnetically. **Bryn Terfel** adds to the glory of the performance, the finest since Beecham, as he does in the *Songs of Sunset*, with **Sally Burgess** the other characterful soloist. The *Songs of Farewell*, helped by incandescent choral singing, complete an ideal triptych, presented in full and rich Chandos sound.

(i) *The Song of the High Hills; Hassan: Intermezzo & Serenade; Irmelin: Prelude;* (ii) *Koanga: Final Scene;* (ii; iii) *A Village Romeo and Juliet*

🅑🅑 (***) Naxos mono 8.110982-3 (2). RPO, Beecham, with (i) Hart, Jones, Luton Ch. Soc.; (ii) RPO Ch.; (iii) Dyer, Soames, Dowling, Sharp, Ritchie, Bond

In 1946 **Beecham** made an important first recording of Delius, *The Song of the High Hills*. Written in 1911, it is one of his most ambitious choral works, very evocative in its use of wordless chorus to represent man in nature, while expressing the composer's 'joy and exhilaration one feels in the Mountains'. That is a spirit which Beecham captures perfectly, again never letting the music meander.

A Village Romeo and Juliet was recorded two years later. **René Soames** was a tenor with a very English sound; to say the least, he does not sound sufficiently ardent, and his dry, thin tone is somewhat uningratiating, making his portrayal of Sali seem a little stiff, though musically the clarity and precision are impressive. **Lorely Dyer** as Vreli is fresh and bright, but she has a small voice and her intonation at the beginning of Scene 4 is vulnerable. However, the Naxos transfer captures the voice better than the 1992 EMI transfer of this historic Beecham recording, with less emphasis on her rapid vibrato. It is also good to hear such vintage singers of the period as **Dennis Dowling** and **Frederick Sharp** as the respective fathers of the hero and heroine, with an excellent line-up of soloists in the many incidental roles. The extra items are very welcome too.

OPERA

Fennimore and Gerda (complete)

🎧 *** Chan. 9589. Stene, Howarth, Tucker, Coleman-Wright, Danish Nat. R. Ch. & SO, Hickox

Fennimore and Gerda, the sixth and last of Delius's operas, may suffer from a lopsided libretto but it has some of his most inspired vocal music. Using the original German, **Hickox's** reading is aptly sensuous – far warmer than the only previous recording on EMI, conducted by Meredith Davies – with fresh-voiced principals headed by **Randi Stene**

as Fennimore, **Judith Howarth** as Gerda and **Peter Coleman-Wright** and **Mark Tucker** as rivals in this very Scandinavian love-tangle.

(i) *Koanga* (opera; complete); (ii) *Song of the High Hills*

Ⓜ *** EMI (ADD) 5 85142-2 (2). (i) Holmes, Lindsay, Herincx, Erwen, Allister, Estes, Alldis Ch., LSO; (ii) RLPO & Ch., Groves

With big Verdian ensembles and Puccinian ariosos (the style is still unmistakably Delian) *Koanga* is a big, red-blooded opera, which makes a striking impact on record. The recording uses a revised libretto, much more effective than the original. When it first appeared in 1974, **Groves's** powerful reading plus excellent singing from the whole cast makes this reissue uniquely valuable. The splendid analogue recording has transferred most vividly and atmospherically to CD, and the set is well documented. *The Song of the High Hills*, with its wordless chorus, was recorded in the same year, and is perceptively interpreted, but here Groves is inclined to understatement.

A Village Romeo and Juliet (complete)

🎧 Ⓜ *** EMI (ADD) 5 75785-2 (2). Luxon, Mangin, Harwood, Tear, John Alldis Ch., RPO, M. Davies (includes illustrated talk by Eric Fenby)

Meredith Davies's great quality is his inspired pacing of a score that can easily stagnate. Davies sets the love-duets in dramatic contrast to the vigorous writing, above all in the lively fair scene. The plot is made to unfold with a feeling of inevitability. **Elizabeth Harwood** and **Robert Tear** are both excellent as Vreli and Sali, winningly characterful and clearly focused, with the role of Sali as a boy in the opening scene taken by a bright treble, **Corin Manley**, against the fresh soprano of **Wendy Eathorne** for Vreli as a child. **Benjamin Luxon** and **Noel Mangin** can hardly be bettered as the warring fathers, dark and incisive, while **John Shirley-Quirk** in the equivocal role of the Dark Fiddler – representing the spirit not of evil but of raw nature – is firm and forthright with an apt hint of the sinister. Eric Fenby provides a very detailed synopsis and (as a supplement on the second disc) the recorded talk on Delius and his career.

(i) *A Village Romeo and Juliet* (complete); (ii) *Songs of Sunset*

Ⓜ (***) Somm mono BEECHAM 12 (2). (i) Soames, Hambleton, F. Smith, Sharp, Clinton, Terry, Davies; (ii) Haley, Henderson; BBC Theatre Ch., RPO, L. Select Ch.; LPO, Beecham

Beecham's radio recording of Delius's opera, *A Village Romeo and Juliet*, was made for the BBC Third Programme only a week before he went to the EMI studio to record the opera with substantially the same cast. The wonder is how different it is interpretatively. The timing alone provides an indication of the contrast, with the studio recording some 11 minutes shorter than the radio recording in an opera lasting under two hours. Surprisingly, the more expansive radio recording is the one which sounds more passionate at almost every point, with the spontaneity of the live performance far outweighing any advantages of precision and balance in the studio version. Though the studio recording is better balanced, it is the radio version which, despite flaws, is the more atmospheric, with more air round the voices. The revised version of **Beecham's** 1934 Leeds Festival performance of the *Songs of Sunset* makes a welcome bonus on the second disc, an astonishingly vivid and atmospheric live performance of these sensuous settings of poems by Ernest Dowson, with **Olga Haley** and **Roy Henderson** the excellent soloists.

DEL TREDICI, David
(born 1937)

Paul Revere's Ride

*** Telarc CD 80638. Plitmann, Clement, Polegato, Atlanta Ch. & SO, Spano (with BERNSTEIN: *Lamentation* from *Symphony 1*) – THEOFANIDIS: *The Here and Now* **(*)

David Del Tredici's dramatic – indeed thrilling – setting is fully worthy of Longfellow's much-loved poem describing a legendary event that took place at the very beginning of the American War of Independence, here most vividly pictorialized. This première performance is fully worthy of Del Tredici's splendidly spontaneous piece, with **Hila Plitmann** a most eloquent soloist, with a lovely voice, alongside a superb choral and orchestral response. It will surely be a hit wherever it is performed in the USA. The recording is spectacular, although the richly resonant chorus could be more sharply focused.

DEVIENNE, François
(1759–1803)

Clarinet Sonata 1

*** EMI 3 79787-2. Meyer, Maisenberg – MILHAUD: *Scaramouche*; POULENC; SAINT-SAËNS: *Sonatas* ***

François Devienne belongs to the last half of the 18th century. He was a celebrated flautist (and published a treatise for the one-key instrument), but he wrote equally well for the clarinet, the C clarinet in this instance. His style anticipated Weber but was rather more amiably classical, certainly virtuosic and pleasing, but not truly memorable. However, **Sabine Meyer** makes a persuasive case for this agreeable work, well partnered by **Oleg Maisenberg**, and their couplings are all much more characterful. Excellent recording.

DIAMOND, David (1915–2005)

(i) Violin Concerto 2. The Enormous Room; Symphony 1

☞ ⒝⒝ *** Naxos 8.559157. Seattle SO, Schwarz, (i) with Talvi

The *First Symphony* was composed after the outbreak of war had forced Diamond to abandon his studies with Nadia Boulanger in Paris and return to America, and the piece is undoubtedly an auspicious beginning to his impressive symphonic portfolio. The lyrical *Second Violin Concerto* (1947) is a bit Stravinskian with a dash of Walton. It is finely played by the Finnish-born **Ilkka Talvi**; and the fantasia, *The Enormous Room* (1948), takes its inspiration from the e. e. cummings description of his incarceration in a French detention camp in 1918. Diamond's score is rhapsodic in feeling, with orchestral textures of great luxuriance; it is both imaginative and atmospheric, and throughout he is well served by **Gerard Schwarz**, the **Seattle Orchestra** and the Delos team who originally recorded it. Indeed, the recording is outstanding.

(i) Kaddish for Cello & Orchestra. Psalm; Symphony 3

⒝⒝ *** Naxos 8.559155. (i) Starker; Seattle SO, Schwarz

The *Third Symphony* is a four-movement work of no mean power. This and the *Psalm* show Diamond as a real man of the orchestra; and the **Seattle Orchestra** proves an eloquent advocate. *Kaddish* is a more recent piece and is played here by its dedicatee, **János Starker**. A highly recommendable Naxos reissue.

Symphonies 2 & 4

⒝⒝ *** Naxos 8.559154. Seattle SO, Schwartz

The *Fourth Symphony* is very diatonic, tonal, impeccably crafted and sophisticated. The *Second Symphony* is a large-scale work, lasting nearly three-quarters of an hour, written in 1942–3 at the height of the war, and it has great sweep and power. It is beautifully crafted and evinces a continuity of musical thought that defines the real symphonist. These excellent performances, at bargain price, with such dedicated and expert playing, all set in a spacious and well-balanced, ventilated acoustic (though some may find it too reverberant), represent good value at the asking price.

Symphony 8; Suite 1 from the Ballet, Tom; (i) This Sacred Ground

⒝⒝ *** Naxos 8.559156. Seattle SO, Schwarz; (i) with Parce, Seattle Girls' Ch. & NorthWest Boychoir

The *First Suite from the Ballet, Tom* inhabits much the same musical world as Aaron Copland. The *Eighth Symphony* makes use of serial technique but will still present few problems to those familiar with Diamond's earlier music, for it remains lyrical and thought-provoking. It culminates in a double fugue of considerable ingenuity. *This Sacred Ground* is a short setting for soloist, choirs and orchestra of the Gettysburg Address, and it may not travel so well. Committed performances and excellent, natural, recorded sound.

Piano Sonata

(***) VAI mono VAIA 1124. Tureck – DALLAPICCOLA: *2 Studies for Violin & Piano* (***); SCHUMANN: *Piano Concerto* (*(**))

David Diamond wrote his *Sonata* especially for **Rosalyn Tureck**, bearing in mind her special experience in contrapuntal playing which was to prove very telling in the double fugue of the powerful finale. But her light, clear articulation gives a splendid sparkle to the Scherzo, which comes as the centrepiece of the highly expressive *Adagio*. This is the work's world première performance, in front of an audience in New York's Town Hall, and it has great intensity and power. The recording is very close and is hard in *fortissimo*, but acceptable. Miss Tureck especially requested that her CD should be included in our *Guide*, and understandably so.

DITTERSDORF, Carl Ditters von (1739–99)

Double-Bass Concertos 1 in D; 2 in D (Krebs 171/2)

*** Hyp. CDA 67179. Nwanoku, Swedish CO, Goodwin –
VANHAL: *Double-Bass Concerto in D* ***

The double-bass can make a cumbersome concerto soloist, but **Chi-Chi Nwanoku**, regular member of distinguished ensembles ever since her student days, makes light of any problems in these concertos. She is amazingly agile and incisive in allegros, well tuned and expressive in lyrical slow movements. The Va hal is charming enough, but the two Dittersdorf works are more distinctive, making up an ideal coupling, very well recorded.

Harp Concerto in A (arr. Pilley)

B—⚙ (M) **** Decca (ADD) 425 723-2. Robles, ASMF, Brown
– BOIELDIEU; HANDEL: *Harp Concertos*, etc. **** ⚙

Dittersdorf's *Harp Concerto* is a transcription of an unfinished keyboard concerto with additional wind parts. It is an elegant piece, thematically not quite as memorable as the Boieldieu coupling, but captivating when played with such style.

6 Symphonies after Ovid's Metamorphoses

**(*) Chan. 8564/5 (2). Cantilena, Shepherd

All the *Ovid Symphonies* have a programmatic inspiration and relate episodes from the *Metamorphoses* of Ovid, such as *The Fall of Phaeton*, which are vividly portrayed. *The Rescue of Andromeda by Perseus* is a particularly effective work (it has an inspired *Adagio*) and the slow movement of the *D major, The Petrification of Phineus and his Friends*, is a delight. *The Transformation of the Lycian Peasants into Frogs* could hardly be more graphic and is full of wit. This is inventive and charming music that will give much pleasure, and it is generally well served by **Cantilena** under **Adrian Shepherd**. There is also a set on Naxos (8.553368/9) acceptably performed by the **Failoni Symphony Orchestra** under **Hanspeter Gmür**, but the Chandos versions have much more character and are worth the extra cost.

Symphonies in A; D; & E flat

(BB) *** Naxos 8.570198. Lisbon Metropolitan O, Cassuto

These symphonies are every bit as enjoyable as those associated with Ovid and clearly have a good deal in common with Haydn and Mozart, with surprise reminders of both those composers. They are well crafted and neatly scored, and these well-recorded performances do them full justice.

DOHNÁNYI, Ernst von (1877–1960)

(i) Harp Concertino, Op. 45; (ii) Piano Concerto 2 in B min., Op. 42; (iii) Violin Concerto 2 in C min., Op. 43

*** Chan. 10245. (i) Lantaff; (ii) Shelley, (iii) Ehnes; BBC PO, Bamert

The latest issue in the ongoing Chandos series brings the *Second Piano Concerto*, played with great panache by **Howard Shelley**, and the soloists in the other works are hardly less fine; the *Harp Concertino* is a most engaging work in **Lantaff's** hands. Chandos and the BBC team at Manchester provide excellently balanced sound.

Piano Concertos 1 in E min., Op. 5; 2 in B min., Op. 42

*** Hyp. CDA 66684. Roscoe, BBC Scottish SO, Glushchenko

These concertos are well wrought, with a melodic warmth that fails to be indelible, but they provide bravura for the soloist and contrast for the orchestra. The present performances are surely unlikely to be surpassed for their commitment, and the playing is finished as well as ardent; the recording, too, is excellent.

Piano Concerto 1 in E min., Op. 5; Ruralia Hungarica

*** Chan. 9649. Shelley, BBC PO, Bamert

Howard Shelley magnetically sustains the massive length of the outer movements of the *First Piano Concerto* relishing the Lisztian fluency of the improvisatory writing and bringing a natural gravity to the chorale theme of the Bruckner-like central *Andante*. As an attractive coupling Bamert conducts the five movements of the orchestral version of *Ruralia Hungarica*, just one of the five folk-based works to which he gave this title. Full, vivid recording, not always ideally clear on detail.

Konzertstück for Cello & Orchestra, Op. 12

*** Chan. 8662. Wallfisch, LSO, Mackerras – DVOŘÁK: *Cello Concerto* ***

Dohnányi's *Konzertstück* has many rich, warm ideas, not least a theme in the slow movement all too close to *Pale hands I loved beside the Shalimar*, and none the worse for that. **Wallfisch's** performance, as in the Dvořák, is strong, warm and committed, and the Chandos sound is first rate.

Violin Concertos 1 in D min., Op. 27; 2 in C min., Op. 43

(N) (BB) **** Naxos 8.570833. Ludwig, R SNO, Falletta

It is remarkable that these two rewarding concertos are not more familiar. Admittedly the *D minor Concerto* (1915) is perhaps a shade over extended, with four movements and a playing time of 41 minutes. But after its Brahmsian opening it produces memorable lyrical secondary material, and has a most eloquent slow movement. This is followed by a dashing scherzo and a variations finale in which the main theme of the first movement returns strikingly before the close. The *Second Concerto* written much later (1949) has Hungarian influences, a warm *molto sostenuto* Adagio and a memorably catchy *giocoso* finale (the best movement). **Michael Ludwig's** performances combine virtuosity and a rich lyrical feeling, at times producing exquisitely gentle playing. It is good to see Naxos have taken up **JoAnn Falletta**, another outstanding young American female conductor, who has established herself, following alongside the success of Marin Alsop, and she provides admirably sensitive accompaniments. The Naxos recording, too is first class.

Serenade in C, Op. 10

*** Hyp. CDA 67429. Leopold String Trio – MARTINŮ; SCHOENBERG: *Trios* ***

This delightful *Trio* with its overtones of Brahms and Dvořák always gives pleasure. Its famous première recording with Heifetz, Primrose and Feuermann has never been equalled or surpassed, but this superb account by the **Leopold Trio** will do very nicely. They play with great conviction and convey much pleasure in their music-making.

Symphony 1; American Rhapsody, Op. 47

*** Chan. 9647. BBC PO, Bamert

Dohnányi's *First Symphony* is something of a find. It is not just accomplished; the scoring shows real flair. A large-scale piece, some 55 minutes in duration, it reveals a strong sense of form. **Matthias Bamert** directs both works impressively and has the advantage of the **BBC Philharmonic** and excellent engineering from the BBC/Chandos team. You will find this most rewarding music.

Symphony 2, Op. 40; Symphonic Minutes, Op. 36

*** Chan. 9455. BBC PO, Bamert

Dohnányi's *Symphonic Minutes* are richly inventive and have enormous charm. The *Second Symphony* is a generally well-argued and finely crafted piece and is well worth getting to know, even if (at nearly 50 minutes) it rather outstays its welcome. The playing of the **BBC Philharmonic** under **Matthias Bamert** is vital and sensitive, and the Chandos recording is in the best traditions of the house.

Variations on a Nursery Tune, Op. 25; Suite in F sharp min., Op. 19; The Veil of Pierrette: Suite, Op. 18

⊶ *** Chan. 9733. Shelley, BBC PO, Bamert

For all their popularity, Dohnányi's variations on 'Twinkle, twinkle, little star', with their witty parodies, have been meanly treated on disc. The brilliant version with **Howard Shelley** the sparkling soloist is especially welcome when it offers two other examples of Dohnányi the charmer. The *Wedding Waltz* from the mimed entertainment, *The Veil of Pierrette*, was once well known, dashingly Viennese, as are the other three movements, previously unrecorded, including a *Merry Funeral March* which parodies Mahler. The *Suite* too is engagingly colourful. Brilliant performances, sumptuously recorded.

Piano Quintets 1; 2 in E flat min., Op. 26; Serenade in C, Op. 10

*** Hyp. CDA 66786. Schubert Ens. of London

(i-ii) Piano Quintets 1-2; (i) Suite in the Old Style, Op. 24

*** ASV CDDCA 915. (i) Roscoe; (ii) Vanbrugh Qt

Dohnányi wrote the first of his two *Piano Quintets* when still in his teens; it is ripely Brahmsian, built strongly on memorable themes. The *Second Quintet*, dating from 20 years later, just after the *Nursery Variations*, is sharper and more compact, with Hungarian flavours more pronounced, if never Bartókian. The *Suite in the Old Style*, for piano alone, is an amiable example of pre-Stravinsky neoclassicism, again beautifully written for the instrument. The **Vanbrugh Quartet** is well matched by **Martin Roscoe** in keen, alert performances, warmly recorded.

The **Schubert Ensemble** give us in addition the *Serenade for String Trio*. A clear three-star recommendation for the Hyperion disc and their excellent pianist, **William Howard**.

Serenade for String Trio

Ⓑ *** Virgin 2x1 5 61904-2 (2). Domus – MARTINŮ: *Piano Quartet 1*, etc.; DVOŘÁK: *Bagatelles*; KODÁLY: *Intermezzo*; SUK: *Piano Quartet* ***

The Dohnányi *Serenade for String Trio* comes from 1902. The three players from the **Domus** team meet its demands with admirably alert and sensitive playing. This performance comes as part of a rewarding and inexpensive programme from Domus which has an eminently natural recorded sound.

Serenade for String Trio; Sextet

⊶ ✿ ⒷⒷ *** Naxos 8.557153. Spectrum Concerts Berlin, Dodge

The *Serenade for String Trio* is Dohnányi's most popular chamber work but the *Sextet* is even more distinctive, with a strong first movement prominently featuring the horn, and a slow movement which builds up powerfully, before the two lighter movements which follow. The delicately pointed Scherzo leads to an exuberant finale, with jagged cross-rhythms, comic false entries and deliciously surreal waltz-references. It is played here breathtakingly fast, with the waltz parodies wittily highlighted, and the fun of the final 'wrong-key' cadence nicely pointed under the direction of the cellist, **Frank Sumner Dodge**. Brilliant, full-bodied sound to match.

Violin Sonata in C sharp min., Op. 21; Andante rubato (Ruralia Hungarica)

**(*) Biddulph LAW 015. Shumsky, Lipkin – WEINER: *Violin Sonatas 1 & 2* **(*)

Oscar Shumsky and **Seymour Lipkin** were recorded in New York in 1993 and they make an excellent case for this neglected but fine sonata. Shumsky's playing is not quite as polished or masterly as it was in the early 1980s, but it is still supremely musical. A worthwhile addition to the catalogue.

PIANO MUSIC

6 Concert Etudes, Op. 28; Pastorale; Ruralia Hungarica, Op. 32a; Variations on a Hungarian Folk Song, Op. 29

🎵 ⚙ (BB) *** Naxos 8.553332. Pawlik

The *Six Concert Etudes*, Op. 28, of 1916 are among the most technically demanding pieces in the repertoire. **Markus Pawlik** was still in his twenties when he recorded these pieces, and his playing is remarkable for its dazzling virtuosity, sensitivity, finesse and good taste. His dexterity and wonderful clarity of articulation in the *D flat Etude* are exceptional. His is a formidable talent, and we hope to hear much more of him. Decent recorded sound. Recommended with all enthusiasm.

DONIZETTI, Gaetano
(1797–1848)

(i) *Clarinet Concertino in B flat*; (ii) *Cor Anglais Concertino in G*; (iii) *Flute Concertino in C min.*; (iv) *Oboe Concertino in F*; (v) *Double Concertino in D min. for Violin & Cello*; (vi) *Sinfonia a soli instrumenti di fiato in G min. Sinfonia in D min; per la Morte di Capuzzi*

🎵 ⚙ (BB) **** Naxos 8.557492. (i) B. Kovács; (ii) Girgás; (iii) I. Kovács; (iv) J. Kiss; (v) A. Kiss, J. Kiss Domonkos; (vi) Soloists, Budapest Camerata, L. Kovács

All these concertos are most winning, as elegant as they are inventive, and all the expert soloists (several of whom seem to be interrelated) smilingly convey the music's Italian sunshine. The concertos are framed by two contrasting *Sinfonias*. Both are played very persuasively, and throughout the collection **László Kovács** and his **Budapest Chamber Orchestra** provide supportive and stylish accompaniments. The recording could hardly be bettered, and the result is a collection which will give great and repeated pleasure. Now at Naxos price it is a great bargain.

Overtures: Linda di Chamounix; Maria di Rohan; Marino Faliero; Les Martyres; Don Pasquale

(BB) *** Warner Apex (ADD) 2564-62418-2. Monte Carlo Op. O, Scimone – CIMAROSA: *Il fanatico per gli antichi romani; Il matrimonio segreto: Overture* **(*); MERCADANTE: *Sinfonia sopra i motive dello Stabat mater di Rossini* ***

These sprightly performances of Donizetti overtures make an attractive and entertaining collection. Both the lightness and the energy of the writing are presented with flair, with Donizetti's melodies and his rumbustious brand of drama enjoyably conveyed. The characteristic Monte Carlo acoustic adds to the theatricality of the music.

CHAMBER MUSIC

String Quartets 7-9

*** CPO 999 170-2. Revolutionary Drawing Room

Introduzione for Strings; String Quartets 10 in G min.; 11 & 12 in C

(M) *** CPO 999 279-2. Revolutionary Drawing Room

String Quartets 13 in A; 14 in D; 15 in F

(M) **(*) CPO 999 280-2. Revolutionary Drawing Room

String Quartets 16 in B min.; 17 in D; 18 in E min.

(M) *** CPO 999 282-2. Revolutionary Drawing Room

This excellent CPO series reveals Donizetti to be a considerable contributor to the string quartet medium, offering works that in their craftsmanship and quality of invention can stand comparison with all but the very finest of Haydn. These six and the following four, Nos. 13–16, all date from around 1821, when the composer was in his early twenties. They are very much Haydn-influenced (in the best sense). These players are completely at home on their period instruments: their execution is fresh, vital and expressive, without any linear eccentricities.

No. 14 in D is programmatic, and we hear the storm gathering immediately at the opening: its full force is soon sweeping through the music. The hushed *Adagio* sadly contemplates the havoc left behind, but the genial Minuet suggests that life goes on, with repairs carried out in the Trio, while the hammering workmen sing to themselves.

Finest of the whole series is the mature *E minor Quartet* of a decade later, splendidly assured in its light-hearted first movement, which the composer used as a basis for his *Linda di Chamounix Overture*. It is splendidly played; indeed, the performances throughout this CD are among the finest in the series, and the recording is first class, too.

String Quartet 13 in A

(M) *** CRD 3366. Alberni Qt – PUCCINI: *Crisantemi*; VERDI: *Quartet* ***

This is an endearing work with a Scherzo echoing that in Beethoven's *Eroica* and with many twists of argument that are attractively unpredictable. It is given a strong, committed performance and is well recorded.

ORATORIO

Il diluvio universale (oratorio; complete)

**(*) Opera Rara ARC 31. Palazzi, Cullagh, Lee, Custer, Geoffrey Mitchell Ch., LPO, Carella

Donizetti's rare oratorio tells the story of Noah and the Flood in operatic terms. Recorded in Conway Hall, the sound is a little dry, but clearly separated. The vocal cast is strong, with **Mirco Palazzi** in the role of Noah a light-voiced bass, though surprisingly Donizetti does not give him an aria to sing. The rest of the cast make a good team, but the work relies on the strong chorus, who contribute one of the main sources of enjoyment.

OPERA

Anna Bolena (complete)

⊕–Ⓜ **** Decca 475 7910 (3). Sutherland, Ramey, Hadley, Mentzler, Welsh Nat. Op. Ch. & O, Bonynge

Ⓜ (**(*)) EMI mono 5 66471-2 (2). Callas, Simionato, Rossi-Lemeni, G. Raimondi, Carturan, La Scala, Milan, Ch. & O, Gavazzeni

In this 1987 recording of *Anna Bolena* **Joan Sutherland** crowns her long recording career with a commanding performance. Dazzling as ever in coloratura, above all exuberant in the defiant final cabaletta, she poignantly conveys the tragedy of the wronged queen's fate with rare weight and gravity. **Samuel Ramey** as the king is outstanding in a fine, consistent cast. Excellent recording, and this reissue includes a full libretto.

The **Callas** recording was made live at La Scala in 1957, with the great diva at her most searingly magnetic. **Gavazzeni** proves a most sympathetic conductor and, though the rest of the cast is no match for Callas, there is characterful if rather inflexible singing from **Simionato** as Giovanna and a fresh, clear contribution from **Gianni Raimondi** in the relatively small tenor role of Percy, here made the smaller by cuts. **Nicola Rossi-Lemeni** as Henry VIII is positive but gritty of tone in a less than convincing characterization. The radio sound is dry and limited and with occasional interference, but for Callas fans this is well worth hearing.

L'assedio di Calais (complete)

*** Opera Rara (ADD) OR 9 (2). Du Plessis, D. Jones, Focile, Serbo, Nilon, Platt, Glanville, Smythe, Treleaven, Harrhy, Bailey, Mitchell Ch., Philh. O, Parry

The Opera Rara set is one of the most invigorating of all the complete opera recordings made over the years by that enterprising organization. With **Della Jones** and **Christian du Plessis** in the cast, as well as a newcomer, **Nuccia Focile**, as Queen Eleanor, **David Parry** conducts the **Philharmonia** in a fresh, well-sprung performance which gives a satisfying thrust to the big ensembles. The one which ends Act II, including a magnificent sextet and a patriotic prayer for the chorus, brings the opera's emotional high point. When, in Act III, Edward III's big aria turns into a sort of jolly waltz song, the music seems less apt.

Dom Sebastien, Roi de Portugal

⊕–*** Opera Rara ORC33 (3). Kasarova, Filianoli, Miles, Keenlyside, Caruso, ROHCG O, Elder

Recorded at live concert performances in 2005, this Opera Rara recording of Donizetti's last completed opera, first heard in 1943, gives the lie to the idea that his powers of invention faded as his health deteriorated. It is not only his last opera, but his most ambitious, adopting the five-act form that was coming to be popular in Paris, thanks to Meyerbeer. Not only is there a fine sequence of arias for each character, the ensembles are generally superb, often based on tunes that could easily be mistaken for early Verdi. **Mark**

Elder conducts a vigorous and thrustful performance, with an excellent cast, led by the mezzo, **Vesselina Kasarova**, as a Zayda with a very Slavonic timbre, and the high Italian tenor, **Giuseppe Filianoli**, as Sebastien, coping very well with some of the stratospheric writing, and with **Alastair Miles** as the Grand Inquisitor and **Simon Keenlyside** as Abayaldo both outstanding. **Carmelo Corrado Caruso** sings the incidental role of the poet, Camoens, author of the great Portuguese poem, the *Lusiad*.

Don Pasquale (complete; DVD versions)

⊕–**** Arthaus **DVD** 101 303. Desderi, Giordano, Gatell, Cassi, Teatro Municipale di Piacenza Ch., Luigi Cherubini O, Muti (Dir: Andrea De Rosa; V/D: Gabriele Cazzola)

⊕–*** TDK **DVD** DVWW-OPDPSC. Furlanetto, Focile, Kunde, Gallo, La Scala, Milan, Ch. & O, Muti

Ⓝ ** Decca **DVD** 074 3202. Raimondi, Flórez, Rey, Widner, Zurich Opera Ch. & O, Santi (Dir: Grischa Asagaroff; V/D Felix Breisach) (with *La fille du régiment* Ⓑ *** Decca 074 3287 (3))

Both **Muti's** performances are very enjoyable indeed. But the Arthaus version, a live recording from the 2006 Ravenna Festival, is rather special. First, it includes an unforgettable characterization of Don Pasquale himself from the veteran *buffo*, **Claudio Desderi**, now in his sixties but still in fine voice, warm-toned in lyrical passages and with wonderful articulation in the famous patter-duet with the excellent Dottore Malatesta, **Mario Cassi**, at the end of Act III. Norina (**Laura Giordano**, who studied with Maria Chiara) enters the action as a demure, pretty young thing, but becomes increasingly formidable as the opera progresses. But she is fully equal to the vocal bravura demanded of her, particularly in the closing scene. **Francisco Gatell** is her very convincing lover: he has a pleasingly light tenor voice which is heard at its finest in the nocturnal serenade of the last Act. But the opera is dominated by Desderi's dignified portrayal of Pasquale, and it is given greater pathos than usual by his touching dismay at his increasingly untenable position, especially after Norina has slapped him. The Ravenna production is handsome, traditional in the best sense, and Muti keeps the action alive through every moment of Donizetti's miraculous score, which seems to get better and better as the opera proceeds. The recording and camerawork cannot be faulted.

As a more consistently light-hearted version, with delightful La Scala sets and colourful costumes, the 1994 TDK *Don Pasquale* will also be hard to beat. Visually it is a joy, and with three outstanding principals the performance sparkles from start to finish. By not seeming too old, **Ferruccio Furlanetto's** portrayal of Don Pasquale is the more convincing, but he has no chance against **Nuccia Focile's** minx of a Norina and one certainly feels sorry for him at his discomfiture. **Gregory Kunde** is an appropriately ardent Ernesto; his voice isn't creamy but he sings passionately and has good comic timing, and **Lucio Gallo** enters into the spirit of the story as a wily Dottore Malatesta. But once more it is **Muti's** direction that keeps the action fizzing and the ensembles sparkling, and ensures that the resolution of the plot takes its natural course. Again excellent sound and camerawork.

It is **Juan Diego Flórez** (on top form) as the hero, Ernesto, who dominates the Decca Zurich set, rather than **Ruggero Raimondi's** somewhat nonplussed Don Pasquale. Moreover **Isabel Rey** is hardly a deliciously pretty Norina, and although her *coloratura* is brilliant enough, some of her top notes are inclined to be squally. Indeed she is obviously not young and would seem to be a more suitable wife for Pasquale than for Ernesto who is too obviously much more youthful than her. **Oliver Widmer** is very convincing as Dottor Malatesta, the opera's staging cannot be faulted with a superb circular triple set, and **Santi** conducts with brio. But even though this performance is given as a free bonus with a fine set of *La fille du regiment* it is far from a first choice among available DVD versions.

Don Pasquale (complete; CD versions)

*** EMI 7 47068-2 (2). Bruscantini, Freni, Nucci, Winbergh, Amb. Op. Ch., Philh. O, Muti

(M) *** Decca 2-CD (ADD) 475 8490 (2). Corena, Sciutti, Oncina, Krause, V. State Op. Ch. & O, Kertész – CIMAROSA: *Il maestro di cappella* ****

Muti's is a delectably idiomatic-sounding reading, one which consistently captures the fun of the piece. **Freni** is a natural in the role of Norina, both sweet and bright-eyed in characterization, excellent in coloratura. The *buffo* baritones, the veteran **Bruscantini** as Pasquale and the darker-toned **Leo Nucci** as Dr Malatesta, steer a nice course between vocal comedy and purely musical values. Muti is helped by the beautifully poised and shaded singing of **Gösta Winbergh**, honey-toned and stylish as Ernesto. Responsive and polished playing from the Philharmonia, and excellent studio sound.

Kertész's performance with the **Vienna State Opera Chorus** and **Orchestra** brings moments that suggest operetta rather than Italian opera, but it is full of high spirits, with much laughter and jollity expressed along with the singing. **Fernando Corena** is an attractive *buffo*, even if his voice is not always well focused enough to sing semiquavers accurately. **Juan Oncina** sounds rather strained, not least in his serenade, but he captures the spirit of the piece; and **Tom Krause** makes an incisive Malatesta. **Graziella Sciutti** is charming from beginning to end, bright-toned and vivacious, and remarkably agile too. The 1964 Decca recording is excellent, with plenty of atmosphere as well as sparkle, and the Originals reissue includes full documentation.

Don Pasquale (complete; in English)

(M) *** Chan. 3011 (2). Shore, Dawson, Banks, Howard, Mitchell Ch., LPO, Parry

David Parry and a lively team of soloists, using Parry's own translation, deliver a well-paced, jolly and amiable performance. The interplay of characters is caught well and the celebrated patter-duet between Don Pasquale and Dr Malatesta, wonderfully articulated, brings none of the traditional comic wheezing at the end – on the whole, an advantage. **Andrew Shore** and **Jason Howard** are good *buffo* singers, characterful if a little gruff, with Howard's Malatesta

rather younger-sounding than usual, a believable brother of Norina. **Lynne Dawson** is fresh, sweet and agile as the heroine, and **Barry Banks** is a clear and unstrained Ernesto. Full sound, atmospheric enough to give warmth to the voices without obscuring words. If your preference is for opera in English, you can't go wrong with this.

L'elisir d'amore (complete; DVD versions)

🎬 *** Decca DVD 074-103-9. Gheorghiu, Alagna, Scaltriti, Alaimo, Lyon Op. Ch. & O, Pido

**(*) Decca DVD 074 3226. Blegen, Pavarotti, Ellis, Bruscantini, Met. Opera Ch. & O, Rescigno

Updated to the 1920s with jolly sets in primary colours, Frank Dunlop's production for Lyon Opéra on Decca makes an attractive DVD, very well produced by Brian Large, involving the same cast as on the excellent Decca CD recording, also made in 1996. **Angela Gheorghiu** as Adina emerges in Act I brandishing a riding-crop, more than a match for Belcore, let alone Nemorino, and singing enchantingly. As Belcore **Roberto Scaltriti** is young and virile, with Dulcamara equally impressive, arriving in a vintage Rolls-Royce drawing a streamlined caravan. Under **Evelino Pido** the comedy of the piece fizzes winningly, with something of a circus atmosphere created by the staging.

Pavarotti takes the role of Nemorino fairly boisterously; one cannot think that he won't get the girl in the end. He sings ardently, although *Una furtiva lagrima* is bold rather than especially sweet-voiced. Similarly, **Judith Blegen** is an appealing Adina, if a little mature for the role, but her *Prendi, per me sei libero* is still impressive. **Brent Ellis** is a suitably bumptious Belcore, and the old hand **Sesto Bruscantini** is a characterful Dr Dulcamara. The stage direction is often very busy, with the big Met. area bustling with the chorus, who sing well enough; but the direction of **Nicola Rescigno** is not as vivacious as one might ideally want; the recording too could be more sharply focused. Altogether enjoyable, but not really distinctive, apart of course for Pavarotti.

L'elisir d'amore (CD versions)

🎬 (M) *** Erato 4509 98483-2 (2). Devia, Alagna, Spagnoli, Praticò, Tallis Chamber Ch., ECO, Viotti

🎬 (M) *** Decca 475 7514 (2). Sutherland, Pavarotti, Cossa, Malas, Amb. S., ECO, Bonynge

(M) *** Sony (ADD) 827969645826 (2). Cotrubas, Domingo, Evans, Wixell, Watson, Rohcg Ch. & O, Pritchard

(B) **(*) Double Decca (ADD) 443 542-2 (2). Gueden, Di Stefano, Corena, Capecchi, Mandelli, Maggio Musicale Fiorentino Ch. & O, Molinari-Pradelli

(BB) (***) Naxos mono (ADD) 8.110125/26 (2). Sayao, Tagliavini, Valdengo, Baccaloni, Lenchner, Met. Op. Ch. & O, Antonicelli (with excerpts from LEONCAVALLO: *Pagliacci*; PUCCINI: *La Bohème* (**))

The mid-priced Erato set is a light, generally brisk account of the score, and it provides an ideal modern alternative to Richard Bonynge's version. **Mariella Devia** cannot match

Sutherland for beauty of tone in the warmly lyrical solos but she sparkles more, bringing out what a minx of a heroine this is. **Roberto Alagna's** tenor timbre was then lighter, if not quite so firm, and, like Devia, he brings out the lightness of the writing delectably. His performance culminates in a winningly hushed and inner account of the soaring aria, *Una furtiva lagrima*. Rounding off an excellent cast, **Pietro Spagnoli** is a fresh, virile Belcore, and **Bruno Praticò** a clear, characterful Dr Dulcamara, an excellent *buffo* baritone, making the very most of a voice on the light side. The sound is first rate. Highlights are available on an Apex disc (2564 61496-2) which makes a good sampler.

Joan Sutherland makes Adina a more substantial figure than usual, full-throatedly serious at times, at others jolly like the rumbustious Marie; in the key role of Nemorino, **Luciano Pavarotti** proves ideal, vividly portraying the wounded innocent. **Spiro Malas** is a superb Dulcamara, while **Dominic Cossa** is a younger-sounding Belcore, more of a genuine lover than usual. **Bonynge** points the skipping rhythms delectably and the recording is sparkling to match, with striking presence. Now reissued in Decca's series of Originals, it is offered at mid-price for the first time, with full text and translation.

Originating from a successful Covent Garden production recorded at Abbey Road, this newly remastered Sony reissue centres very much on the delectable Adina of **Ileana Cotrubas**. Quite apart from the delicacy of her singing, she presents a sparkling, flirtatious character to underline the point of the whole story. **Plácido Domingo** by contrast is a more conventional hero and less the world's fool than Nemorino should be. **Sir Geraint Evans** gives a vivid characterization of Dr Dulcamara, though the microphones sometimes bring out roughness of tone. **Ingvar Wixell** is an upstanding Belcore; the stereo staging is effective, and the remastering has plenty of atmosphere. Alas, the lack of a printed libretto is a drawback. The only way to obtain this is via a computer CD-ROM drive. Otherwise full marks.

With **Hilde Gueden** at her most seductive, the very early (1955) Decca stereo recording offers a delightful, spontaneous-sounding performance. Not just Gueden but the other soloists too are strikingly characterful, with **Giuseppe di Stefano** at his most headily sweet-toned, singing with youthful ardour, **Fernando Corena** a strong and vehement Dulcamara and **Renato Capecchi** well contrasted as Sergeant Belcore, though not quite so firm of tone, but both splendidly comic. Even without a libretto it makes a good bargain, with two CDs offered for the price of one.

Bidu Sayao on Naxos is perfectly cast here as Adina, giving a sparkling portrayal opposite the young, golden-toned **Tagliavini** as Nemorino. Like all Italian tenors of his generation, he has his unstylish habits, but echoing Gigli he gives a winningly delicate account of *Una furtiva lagrima*, as well as entering into the fun of the piece. **Giuseppe Valdengo** could hardly be stronger as a firm, powerful Belcore, and the veteran, **Salvatore Baccaloni**, in traditional *buffo* bass style milks every comic point as the quack, Dulcamara, with **Antonicelli** timing the comedy to a nicety. Clear, if limited, mono sound. As a supplement come two delightful live recordings of Sayao: Nedda's communing with the birds in *Pagliacci* and the *Bohème* duet, *O soave fanciulla*, with Giuseppe di Stefano.

The Elixir of Love (complete; in English)

Ⓜ **(*) Chan. 3027 (2). Banks, Plazas, Holland, Shore, Williams, Mitchell Ch., Philh. O, Parry

This lively account in English under **David Parry** brings out the high spirits of the piece, even if inevitably there are resulting echoes of Gilbert and Sullivan. Central to the performance's success is the vivacious Adina of **Mary Plazas**, sparkling and sweet-toned, guaranteed to ensnare any man around. **Barry Banks** gives a forthright performance as the innocent hero, Nemorino, even if the tone is not really Italianate enough for this music, whatever the language. **Ashley Holland** as Sergeant Belcore and **Andrew Shore** as Dr Dulcamara are lively and characterful, agile in rapid patter, even if their voices could be more sharply focused.

Elvida (complete)

*** Opera Rara ORC 29. Massis, Spagnoli, Larmore, Ford, LPO, Allemandi

Written in 1826, when Donizetti was still in his twenties, *Elvida* is his only serious one-Act opera. The one-Act format was dictated by the royal timetable, and it results in a delightfully compact *dramma per musica*, involving the conflict of Castilian and Moorish forces in Spain. With a cast of principals identical to those in Opera Rara's recording of *François di Foix*, the performance is similarly strong and lively under the direction of **Antonello Allemandi**. **Annick Massis** is again outstanding in the title-role. Though the invention is not quite as striking as that in *François di Foix*, there are many delightful passages, such as the galloping 6/8 stretta which rounds off the Act I duet of Elvida and Zeidar.

Emilia di Liverpool (complete); L'eremitaggio di Liverpool (complete)

🔊 *** Opera Rara (ADD) OR 8 (3). Kenny, Bruscantini, Merritt, Dolton, Mitchell Ch., Philh. O, Parry

The very name, *Emilia di Liverpool*, makes it hard to take this early opera of Donizetti seriously. In this set, sponsored by the Peter Moores Foundation, we have not only the original version of 1824 but also the complete reworking of four years later, which was given the revised title noted above. Such a veteran as **Sesto Bruscantini** makes an enormous difference in the *buffo* role of Don Romualdo in *Emilia*, a character who speaks in Neapolitan dialect. His fizzing duet with Federico (the principal tenor role, sung superbly by **Chris Merritt**) sets the pattern for much vigorous invention. With fresh, direct conducting from **David Parry**, this is a highly enjoyable set for all who respond to this composer.

La favorita (complete)

Ⓜ **(*) Decca (ADD) 430 038-2 (3). Cossotto, Pavarotti, Bacquier, Ghiaurov, Cotrubas, Teatro Comunale Bologna Ch. & O, Bonynge

La favorita may not have as many memorable tunes as the finest Donizetti operas, but red-blooded drama provides ample compensation. Fernando is strongly and imaginatively sung here by **Pavarotti**. The mezzo role of the heroine is taken by **Fiorenza Cossotto**, formidably powerful if not quite at her finest, while **Ileana Cotrubas** is comparably imaginative as her confidante, Ines, but not quite at her peak. **Bacquier** and **Ghiaurov** make up a team which should have been even better but which will still give much satisfaction. Bright recording.

La Fille du régiment (DVD versions)

(N) 🔊⟵ ✿ ******** Virgin **DVD** 5 19002-9. Dessay, Flórez, Corbelli, Palmer, Maxwell, ROHCGO, Campanella; (Dir: Laurent Pelly; V/D Robin Lough)

(N) ******* Decca **DVD** 074 3146. Ciofi, Flórez, Ulivieri, Franci, Benini, Ch. & O of Teatro Carlo Felice di Genova, Frizza ; Director Emilio Sagi (with *Don Pasquale* (B) ****** Decca 074 3287 (3))

*(*) TDK **DVD** DV-OPLFDR. Devia, Kelly, Podles, Pratico, La Scala Ch. & O, Renzetti (Dir. Crivelli, TV Dir. Protasoni)

Virgin and Decca each offer a DVD of *La fille du régiment* which feature today's star tenor, **Juan Diego Flórez** as the opera's hero, Tonio. He sings and acts superbly in both sets, throwing off his famous nine repeated high Cs in '*Pour mon âme*' effortlessly and in the Decca version even singing an encore. He creates an appealing lover-figure for both **Natalie Dessay** at Covent Garden, and the boyish **Patrizia Ciofi** in Geneva. They are both attractive heroines and each creates an individual personality for the characterization of the regiment's adopted daughter. Both are live performances and the Decca Geneva set brings the action forward to the final days of World War II and dresses the soldiers in American uniforms, even though their dialogue and choruses continue to suggest they are French! However this typical director's whim is harmless enough as the action is unaffected. What makes this production especially effective is the singing and acting of **Nicola Ulivieri** as a fatherly Sulpice and **Francesca Franci** is a suitably aristocratic Marquise de Berkenfield. The chorus is excellent in depicting their ingenuous admiration and support for the heroine, and Patrizia Ciofi takes her famous role with personality and vocal virtuosity. The overall result is certainly enjoyable and the set comes with a free documentary disc (about the opera, the theatre and with a portrait of Flórez) in a two-for-one package with *Don Pasquale* – also starring Flórez.

But Ciofi is no match for **Natalie Dessay** who establishes her star quality from her very first entry and vivaciously dominates the opera throughout. She is deliciously funny, and often audacious in her various comic business – and she sings both brilliantly and movingly too. In short she is an unforgettably enchanting Marie, unlikely to be surpassed. Moreover Laurent Polly's production and staging is full of imaginative detail without making the comedy too broad. Coupled with unexpectedly original sets, excellent costuming and splendidly alive musical direction from Bruno Campanella this version is for DVD what the famous Sutherland/Pavarotti version is for CD.

Recorded live at La Scala, Milan, in June 1996, the DVD of *La Fille du régiment* is taken from a film for Italian televi-sion (RAI) with pretty sets and costumes by Franco Zeffirelli using flat, bright colours echoing those in an 18th-century print. The performance centres round the characterful Marie of **Mariella Devia**, a diminutive figure, bossy in a military way, who, defying her size, sings with a loud, penetrating voice, agile up to the highest register but not very steady in the middle. Opposite her, the Tonio of **Paul Austin Kelly** is a handsome roly-poly figure, sporting a great cushion of fuzzy hair. What matters is that he has a clear, firm, lyrical tenor, with a formidably unstrained top register, so that he copes superbly with the notorious arietta, *Pour mon âme*, in the finale of Act I with its clutch of high Cs. **Eva Podles** is magnificent in the character role of the Marquise de Berkenfield, commanding both in her singing and in her acting, completely dominating the compliant Sulpice of **Bruno Pratico** in Act II. The ensembles both with and without the chorus are brilliantly done, though the reunion trio, *Tous les trois réunis*, is taken absurdly fast. Otherwise the conducting of **Donato Renzetti** is warm and idiomatic. Note that nowadays even La Scala prefers the French text of this opera to the Italian version of Donizetti's score.

La Fille du régiment (CD version)

🔊⟵ (M) ******** Decca (ADD) 478 1366 (2). Sutherland, Pavarotti, Sinclair, Malas, Coates, ROHCG Ch. & O, Bonynge

It was with the Decca cast that *La Fille du régiment* was revived at Covent Garden, and **Sutherland** immediately showed how naturally she takes to the role of Marie, a *vivandière* in the army of Napoleon. She is in turn brilliantly comic and pathetically affecting, and **Pavarotti** makes an engaging hero. **Monica Sinclair** is a formidable Countess in a fizzing performance of a delightful Donizetti romp that can confidently be recommended both for comedy and for fine singing. Recorded in Kingsway Hall, the CD sound has wonderful presence and clarity of focus. This set now returns to the catalogue as one of Decca's 'Originals'.

François di Foix (complete)

🔊⟵ ******* Opera Rara ORC 28. Massis, Spagnoli, Larmore, Ford, Antoniozzi, LPO, Allemandi

Patric Schmid of Opera Rara has produced a splendid account of one of Donizetti's one-Act operas, 75 minutes long, *François di Foix*, described as a *melodramma giocoso*. This story of the Countess mistreated by her husband inspired Donizetti to write a sparkling sequence of numbers which never outstay their welcome, with one bright idea leading on to another, including a chorus which anticipates one in *L'elisir d'amore*. The piece ends, after many duets and ensembles, in a big tournament scene. This first recording, well paced by the conductor, **Antonello Allemandi**, is also notable for bringing forward an outstanding young coloratura soprano, **Annick Massis**, who takes the title-role, wonderfully bright and agile, rising up to the challenge of her big numbers. **Jennifer Larmore** sings warmly as the Page, with the bass, **Alfonso Antoniozzi**, aptly gritty as the malicious Count, the tenor, **Bruce Ford**, lyrical as the attendant Duke, and **Pietro Spagnoli** magisterial as the King.

(i) *Gabriella di Vergy* (1838 version); (ii) Scenes from 1826 version

**(*) Opera Rara ORC 3 (2). (i) Andrew, du Plessis, Arthur, Tomlinson, J. Davies, Winfield; (ii) Harrhy, Jones; RPO, Francis

Dating from 1979 and transferred well to CD, this Opera Rara set of *Gabriella di Vergy* (not to be confused with *Gemma di Vergy*) presents the rediscovered score, written in the composer's hand, of a piece which Donizetti himself never heard with its many sparkling cabalettas and superb Act II finale. The cast is a capable one, with **Alun Francis**, as ever, a sympathetic conductor; it is interesting to hear **John Tomlinson** early in his career, slightly miscast. It is fascinating to have as appendix three excerpts from the original, 1826 score, with **Della Jones** taking the role of the hero, Raoul, later rewritten for tenor.

Linda di Chamonix (complete; DVD version)

** TDK **DVD** DV-OPLDC. Gruberová, Van der Walt, Will, Ariostini, Kallisch, Zurich Opera Ch. & O, A. Fischer (V/D: A. Bernard-Leonardi)

With **Edita Gruberová** still in reasonably good voice in the coloratura, undoubtedly touching in the Mad Scene, this is an impressive if uneven performance, and of course Gruberová hardly looks like a young country girl. But **Deon van der Walt** looks good as Carlo and he sings ardently, and the rest of the cast are vocally reliable, **Jacob Will** as the Marquis and **Cornelia Kallisch** as Pieretto much more than that. The staging with its drapes is not too distracting and the video direction is acceptable. Best of all is the splendid contribution of chorus and orchestra, stylishly and vividly directed by **Adam Fischer** and very well recorded. A stopgap, perhaps, but a generally enjoyable one.

Lucie de Lammermoor (complete; in French; DVD version)

*** TDK **DVD** DV OPLDL. Ciofi, Alagna, Tezier, Laho, Cavallier, Saelens, Lyon Op. Ch. & O, Pidò (V/D: Don Kent)

It was bold of the **Lyon Opéra** to revive the French version of *Lucia di Lammermoor* that Donizetti originally prepared for Paris. The differences from the original are not great, but for the Donizetti devotee they provide a new insight into the working of the composer, with even some of the passage-work in Lucia's Mad Scene modified. **Patrizia Ciofi** is a bright, agile heroine who sings brilliantly. **Roberto Alagna** as Edgard is outstanding and **Ludovic Tezier** is impressively dark and firm as Henry, with the rest of the cast generally reliable. The production has traditional costumes, set against darkly sinister backgrounds, with the Video Director tending to steal attention with his odd camera effects. **Evelino Pidò** controls the ensembles well but lets the Mad Scene move on rather slowly. However it is thrillingly sung by Ciofi.

Lucia di Lammermoor (complete)

⊗— *** Decca (ADD) 410 193-2 (2). Sutherland, Pavarotti, Milnes, Ghiaurov, Davies, Tourangeau, ROHCG Ch. & O, Bonynge

⊗— (***) Royal Opera House ROH (mono) Sl002 (2). Sutherland, Gibin, Shaw, Rouleau, MacDonald, Elkins, ROHCG O & Ch., Serafin

⊗— Ⓑ *** Double Decca (ADD) 460 747-2 (2). Sutherland, Cioni, Merrill, Siepi, St Cecilia Ac., Rome, Ch. & O, Pritchard

ⒷⒷ (***) EMI mono 5 86197-2 (2). As below, with Callas, Di Stefano, Gobbi, Serafin

⊗— Ⓜ (***) EMI mono 5 66438-2 (2). Callas, Di Stefano, Gobbi, Arie, Ch. & O of Maggio Musicale Fiorentino, Serafin

**(*) EMI 5 56284-2 (2). Callas, Tagliavini, Cappuccilli, Ladysz, Philh. Ch. & O, Serafin

(i) *Lucia di Lammermoor* (complete); (ii) Highlights (from Historical Recordings)

ⒷⒷ (***) Naxos mono 8.110131/2. (i) Callas, Di Stefano, Gobbi, Arie, Ch. & O of Maggio Musicale Fiorentino, Serafin; (ii) Merrill, Pinza, Vellicci (1952); Galli-Curci, Schipa (1928); Barrientos, Hackett, Stracciari, Mardones, Meader, Noé, Pinza (1920); Dal Monte (1926); Gigli (1925); McCormack (1910)

Though some of the girlish freshness of voice which marked the 1961 recording had disappeared by the 1971 set, **Sutherland's** detailed understanding was intensified. Power is there as well as delicacy, and the rest of the cast is first rate. **Pavarotti**, through much of the opera not as sensitive as he can be, proves magnificent in his final scene. The sound-quality is superb on CD. In this set the text is absolutely complete.

Rarely has the Royal Opera House seen quite so historic an occasion as the overnight emergence of **Joan Sutherland** as a superstar in February, 1959. This live recording captures the thrill of the occasion vividly, with Sutherland not only fresh and bright throughout, but technically flawless, with crisp trills and coloratura and seamless legato. Not only that, her vocal acting is magnetic, not least in Lucia's two big scenes, the Fountain Scene in Act I as well as in the Mad Scene. Gibin may not be an ideal Donizetti singer, too heavyweight, but he is capable, and both **Joseph Rouleau** as Raimondo and **John Shaw** as Enrico, stalwarts of the company, are first rate. **Serafin** is wonderfully vigorous and supremely understanding of the Donizetti style.

The 1961 **Sutherland** version of *Lucia* is a bargain in Double Decca format. Though consonants were being smoothed over, the voice is obviously that of a young singer, and dramatically the performance was close to Sutherland's famous stage appearances of that time, full of fresh innocence. Her coloratura virtuosity remains breathtaking, and the cast is a strong one, with **Pritchard** a most understanding conductor. The reissue has Decca's new-style synopsis, with a 'listening guide' for newcomers to the opera.

Callas's earlier, mono set dates from 1953. The diva is vocally better controlled than in her later, stereo set (indeed some of the coloratura is excitingly brilliant in its own right), and there are memorable if not always perfectly stylish contributions from **Di Stefano** and **Gobbi**. As in the later set, the text has the usual stage cuts, but the remastered sound is impresssive. This (5 66438-2) has been newly remastered for the reissue. However, EMI have brought out an alternative budget version (5 86197-2) to compete with Naxos; it comes without libretto but with an acceptable booklet with a cued synopsis. Naxos (who also include a cued synopsis) offer not only the complete opera but seven fascinating historical recordings. Among the historical recordings, the **Galli-Curci/Tito Schipa** duet and **Toti Dal Monte's** pristine Mad Scene stand out, and it is always a pleasure to hear **Gigli's** golden tenor. The famous Sextet was recorded primitively in New York in 1920, and is for aficionados of acoustic recordings only! Comparison with the budget EMI transfer reveals a somewhat smoother upper focus on Naxos, both on voices and on orchestra, which we are inclined to prefer, although some might think that Callas is given slightly more presence on EMI.

The **Callas** stereo version was recorded in Kingsway Hall in 1959, with her edgy top notes cleanly caught. Her flashing-eyed interpretation of the role of Lucia remains unique, though the voice has its unsteady moments. One instance is at the end of the Act I duet with Edgardo, where Callas on the final phrase moves sharpwards and **Tagliavini** – here past his best – flatwards. **Serafin's** conducting is ideal, though the score, as in Callas's other recordings, still has the cuts which used to be conventional in the theatre. An hour of highlights from this set is available on EMI 5 66664-2.

Lucrezia Borgia (complete)

(M) *** Decca (ADD) 421 497-2 (2). Sutherland, Aragall, Horne, Wixell, London Op. Voices, Nat. PO, Bonynge

Sutherland is in her element here. **Aragall** sings stylishly too, and although **Wixell's** timbre is hardly Italianate he is a commanding Alfonso. **Marilyn Horne** in the breeches role of Orsini is impressive in the brilliant *Brindisi* of the last Act, but earlier she has moments of unsteadiness. The recording is characteristically full and brilliant.

Maria Padilla (complete)

(*) Opera Rara (ADD) ORC 6 (3). McDonall, Jones, Clark, Du Plessis, Earle, Caley, Kennedy, Davies, Mitchell Ch., LSO, Francis

Maria Padilla even matches *Lucia di Lammermoor* in places, with the heroine ill-used by the prince she loves, Pedro the Cruel. When the obligatory mad scene is given not to the heroine but to her father, even a tenor such as **Graham Clark** – future star in Bayreuth – can hardly compensate, however red-blooded the writing and strong the singing. In the title-role **Lois McDonall** is brightly agile, if at times a little raw. **Alun Francis** directs the LSO in a fresh, well-disciplined performance and, as ever with Opera Rara sets, the notes and commentary contained in the libretto are both readable and scholarly.

Maria Stuarda (DVD versions)

(N) (B) *** Naxos Dynamic **DVD** 2.110268. Piscitelli, Polverelli, De Biasio, Alberghini, Cassi, Marchigiana Ch. & O, Frizza (Dir: Lier Luigi Pizzi; V/D: Davide Crescendi)

(N) *** Arthaus **DVD** 101 361. Antonacci, Devia, Meli, Alberghini, Terranova, La Scala, Milan Ch. & O, Fogliani (V/D: Carlo Tagliabue)

Why is it that operatic stage designers want to mount colourful operas against such austere staging? Pier Luigi Pizzi's set for the 2007 Marchigiano production offers a combination of ramps, plus a bare set of steps, centre stage. Fortunately the costumes are pleasingly colourful (Elisabetta's headdress in Act I is impressive), and reasonably in-period and the performance itself more than compensates. The cast is dominated by **Maria Pia Piscitelli's** moving portrayal of the condemned Queen Maria. She sings with much lyrical beauty and is a true star, all but matched by **Laura Polverelli's** imperious portrayal of Elisabetta. The men are good too, especially **Roberto de Biasio's** Conte di Leicester, and the many male/female duets are very telling. The big scene when the queens meet, with its splendid quintet, and Maria's furious denunciation of Elisabetta as a bastard, is a thrilling highlight. **Riccardo Frizza** directs throughout with plenty of vitality, yet gives the singers persuasively lyrical support. All in all a considerable success, although not visually entrancing.

The minimalist but undistracting La Scala stage design, a mixture of grilles and grids, highlight the superb costumes in **Fogliani's** excellent performance dating from 2008. **Mariella Devia**, at the age of 60, shows remarkably few signs of her age and she makes a compelling Maria Stuarda, whilst **Anna Caterina Antonacci** makes an excellent Elisabetta, both coping well with their high-flying *coloratura*. The great confrontation between the queens at the climax of Act I is superbly dramatic, while the men, particularly **Francesco Meli** in the role of Leicester, are very good indeed. There are some textual differences in this score, some slighter than others, than the versions we are used to with Bonynge and Mackerras, (the finale in Act I, as well as the final aria, for example). Excellent conducting, chorus and orchestra, expert camera-work and a sharp picture complete the package. A backstage documentary is included as a bonus.

Maria Stuarda (CD version)

(M) *** Decca (ADD) 425 410-2 (2). Sutherland, Tourangeau, Pavarotti, Ch. & O of Teatro Comunale, Bologna, Bonynge

In the Decca set of Donizetti's tellingly dramatic opera on the conflict of Elizabeth I and Mary Queen of Scots, the contrast between the full soprano Maria and the dark mezzo Elisabetta is underlined by some transpositions, with **Tourangeau** emerging as a powerful villainess in this slanted version of the story. **Pavarotti** turns Leicester into a passionate Italian lover, not at all an Elizabethan gentleman. As for **Sutherland**, she is at her most fully dramatic too, and the great moment when she flings the insult *Vil bastarda!* at her cousin brings a superb snarl; **Richard Bonynge** directs an urgent account of an unfailingly enjoyable opera. Unusually for Decca, the score is slightly cut. The recording is characteristically bright and full.

Mary Stuart (in English)

🔊 **** Warner **DVD** 50467 8028-2. Baker, Plowright, Rendall, Tomlinson, Opie, ENO Ch. & O, Mackerras (V/D: Peter Butler)

Ⓜ *** Chan. 3017 (2). Baker, Plowright, Rendall, Tomlinson, Opie, ENO Ch. & O, Mackerras

Dame Janet Baker chose this opera for her farewell to the operatic stage in London in 1982, understandably when the role of the tragic queen was one of her most powerful assumptions. Her deeply moving performance, with her voice ringing gloriously, is well known from the audio version, but this video greatly intensifies the experience. John Copley's inspired production, with evocative sets and costumes by Desmond Heeley, makes the perfect background for her brilliant acting. The joyful mood of her first aria is powerfully transformed into anger as she confronts Queen Elizabeth. That leads to resigned dedication as she sings her prayer in the last scene. **Rosalind Plowright** in her prime makes an excellent, statuesque foil as Elizabeth, and the other principals are first rate too – the young **John Tomlinson** as Talbot, **David Rendall** a ringing tenor as Leicester and **Alan Opie** characterful as Cecil. **Sir Charles Mackerras** as conductor strongly underlines the drama of the piece.

Poliuto (complete)

🔊 Ⓜ (***) EMI mono 5 65448-2 (2). Callas, Corelli, Bastianini, Zaccaria, La Scala Ch. and O, Votto

In 1960 **Maria Callas** returned to **La Scala**, having missed the two previous seasons, and had a triumph. This live recording, made at the time, demonstrates the scale of that triumph, with Callas's musical imagination and intensity of communication at their very peak. **Corelli** gives a heroic performance, noticeably subtler and more sensitive in scenes opposite Callas than when he is on his own. **Bastianini** and **Zaccaria** complete the top Scala team of principals and, though the chorus is often rough, **Votto** heightens the dramatic impact in his conducting. Variable and limited mono sound, now effectively remastered.

Roberto Devereux (complete)

**(*) Opera Rara ORC24 (2). Miricioiu, Bros, Ganassi, Frontali, ROHCG Ch. & O, Benini

Central to the success of this new set is the singing of the Romanian, **Nelly Miricioiu**, as Elizabeth, a fine, characterful soprano who has been unjustly neglected on disc. With a voice far warmer than Sills', yet just as flexible in coloratura, she gives a most moving account of the key role of the Queen, and she is well matched by the fresh, young tenor, **José Bros**, as Essex, who, instead of belting his words out like his predecessor on disc, shades his tone with a delicacy all too rare with tenors today in this repertory. The contrast of youth and maturity is equally effective in the casting of the clear-toned **Sonia Ganassi** as Sara, while **Maurizio Benini** draws warmly dramatic, idiomatic singing and playing from the **Covent Garden Chorus** and **Orchestra**. The only snag of this live performance is that the audience is so enthusiastic

that wild applause punctuates the performance all too often. As usual with Opera Rara, the booklet is a model of scholarship, with profiles and portraits of great singers of the past who have sung the principal roles, though curiously nothing about the present cast except their photos.

Rosmonda d'Inghilterra (highlights)

🔊 *** Opera Rara ORR 214. Fleming, Ford, Miricioiu, Miles, Montague, Philh. O, Parry

It was in 1994, just before her spectacular rise to international superstar status, that **Renée Fleming** contributed to Opera Rara's splendid recording of this long-neglected Donizetti opera. Shrewdly that company here offers 76 minutes from the opera, covering substantially all the vocal high spots involving the heroine. The result is a formidable demonstration of Fleming's art, with her sumptuous voice then at its freshest. With starry casting for the other characters too, the quality of her contribution, far from being dimmed, is enhanced still further, with **Nelly Miricioiu** and **Diana Montague** nicely contrasted, and with **Bruce Ford** and **Alastair Miles** ideally cast. Strong, purposeful direction from **David Parry** and full, vivid sound. Unlike most Opera Rara issues, this one does not provide texts, only a summary of plot for each item.

Ugo, conte di Parigi (complete)

*** Opera Rara (ADD) (3). D. Jones, Harrhy, J. Price, Kenny, Arthur, du Plessis, Mitchell Ch., New Philh. O, Francis

The 1977 recording of *Ugo, conte di Parigi* was the result of formidable detective work, revealing in this early opera of 1832 a strong plot and some fine numbers, including excellent duets. Matching such singers as **Janet Price** and **Yvonne Kenny**, **Maurice Arthur** sings stylishly in the title-role with a clear-cut tenor that records well. **Della Jones** and **Christian du Plessis**, regular stalwarts of Opera Rara sets, complete a stylish cast. Reissued on CD, thanks to the Peter Moores Foundation, it offers a fresh and intelligent performance under **Alun Francis**, and the scholarly, readable notes and commentary, as well as libretto and translation, are models of their kind.

Collection: 'Donizetti Divas': excerpts from: (i) *Alfredo il Grande*; (ii) *L'assedio di Calais*; (iii) *Chiara e Serafina*; (iv) *Dom Sébastien de Portugal*; (v) *Emilia di Liverpool*; (vi) *Gabriella di Vergy*; (vii) *Maria De Rudenz*; (viii) *Maria Padilla*; (ix) *Rosmonda d'Inghilterra*; (x) *Ugo, Conte di Parigi*; (xi) *Zoraisa di Granata*

🔊 *** Opera Rara (ADD) ORR 213. (i; iii) D. Jones; (ii) Focile, du Plessis; (iii; v) Kenny; (iii) Davies; (iv) Elkins; (vi) Andrew; (vii; ix) Miricioiu; (vii) MacFarland, Ford; (viii) McDonall; (ix) Fleming; (x) Price, Harrhy; (xi) Cullagh, Montague; with variations orchestras & conductors

Recorded with various singers and orchestras between 1977 and 1990, this collection of Donizetti rarities brilliantly exploits the sparkling style of **Della Jones** as exponent of Donizetti. The various items have been compiled from earlier recordings from Opera Rara, complete operas as well as the earlier volumes of the '100 Years of Italian Opera' series, yet in sound and above all in vocal quality the results are splendidly consistent. Anyone looking to explore the neglected side of Donizetti's vast output without venturing into complete operas will find this most illuminating.

Arias from: (i; ii) *Belisario;* **(ii; iii)** *Gemma di Vergy;* **(i)** *Parisina d'Este. Torquato Tasso*

Ⓜ ******* RCA (ADD) 82876 62309-2 (2). Caballé, Amb. Op. Ch., LSO, Cillario, with (i) Elkins; (ii) McDonnell; (iii) Fyson, Mauro – ROSSINI; VERDI: *Arias* *******

Three famous LP recital 'rarities' discs are generously brought together here for the first time. **Caballé's** conviction as well as her technical assurance makes for highly dramatic results in these still rare Donizetti scenas. The placing of the voice in the *Belisario* item is superbly assured, as is the control of tone, with never a hint of forcing, even in the most exposed *fortissimo*. The cabaletta from *Torquato Tasso* goes equally impressively, helped by **Cillario's** sympathetic conducting; and there is much elsewhere to enjoy, for these late-1960s recordings display some of Caballé's finest qualities. The recording is full and vivid, though there is some minor distortion when the voice presses hard. Texts and translations included.

DOVE, Jonathan (born 1959)

The Adventures of Pinocchio **(DVD version)**

Ⓝ ******* Opus Arte **DVD** OA 101 D2 (2). Simmonds, Summers, Plazas, Bottone, Broadbent, Clayton, Chorus & Orch of Opera North, Parry (Dir: Martyn Duncan. Sets and Costumes, Francis O'Connor)

Jonathan Dove with his librettist, Alasdair Middleton, in this operatic version in two substantial acts, gives a much fuller idea of the story of Pinocchio, as told by Carlo Collodi, starting with the moment when Geppetto the woodman finds a talking log in the forest. Geppetto is about to chop it up, when it speaks to him demanding that he preserve it, later demanding that he should bring out the secret it contains, nothing less than the puppet, Pinocchio, who kicks him as his legs appear.

Generally the scenes follow the development of Pinocchio from rebellious puppet to kind and considerate boy. One important detail in the story, much exploited by Disney, that the opera ignores completely is the varying length of Pinocchio's nose, depending on the lies he is telling: in the opera, no doubt for the convenience of the costume department, Pinocchio's nose remains long from beginning to end.

Dove's writing characteristically is colourful and vigorous, with inventive instrumentation and the sharp jazzy syncopations add to the attractions of the writing, which is generally easily lyrical. The performance, filmed live is excellent, and conducted very ably by **David Parry**. **Victoria Simmonds** is excellent in the title role, wearing a very convincing costume, with **Jonathan Summers** as Geppetto. A very welcome issue of a most attractive new opera.

DOWLAND, John (1563–1626)

CONSORT MUSIC

Consort music

*** Hyp. CDA 66010. Extempore String Ens.

The **Extempore Ensemble's** technique of improvising and elaborating in Elizabethan consort music is aptly exploited here in an attractively varied selection of pieces by Dowland; on record, as in concert, the result sounds the more spontaneous. Excellent recording.

Consort music, lute solos and songs

🎧 Ⓑ ******* Naxos 8.553326. Rose Consort of Viols, with Heringman and King

Catherine King's fresh voice and simplicity of line are all her own and she is very touching in the melancholy songs. The **Rose Consort**, lively enough in the galliards, also show their sensitivity to Dowland's doleful moods, notably in the famous *Semper Dowland semper dolens*, but also in the lament for Oliver Cromwell (not the famous Oliver Cromwell), played sombrely on bass viol and lute. The two lute solos, very well played by **Jacob Heringman**, offer further contrast, and the whole programme is recorded most naturally.

Consort Pieces; Lute Fancies and Lute Songs

Ⓝ ******** Sony/BMG 88697225022. Dorothy Mields, Santana (lute), Herl (viola da gamba), Sirius Viols

This is a particularly successful and rewarding collection entitled 'The Seven Shades of Melancholy'. Yet it has no lack of variety and there are songs (*Clear or Cloudy* and *Time Stands Still*, for instance) which are only on the edge of melancholy. **Dorothy Mields**, who introduces the programme herself, has a particularly rich and lovely soprano voice, and sings with great sensitivity. In between come beautifully played consort items by the **Sirius Viols** (a sextet) and the whole programme is framed by two lute solos by **Lee Santana**. The disc is handsomely packaged and well documented. Recommended.

Lachrimae, or Seaven Teares

*** BIS CD 315. Dowland Consort, Lindberg

Jakob Lindberg and his consort of viols give a highly persuasive account of Dowland's masterpiece. The texture is always clean and the lute clearly present.

Lachrimae: 7 Passionate pavans. **(ii) Consort settings**

🎧 ******* Virgin 5 45005-2. Fretwork, with Wilson

This is a reissue of **Fretwork's** 1989 recording of excerpts from the *Lachrimae*, for which the 'passionate' pavans serve as introduction. They are distinguished also by their pervading melancholy but are followed by a newly recorded collection of Dowland's own galliards, so one can choose to move over to more cheerful music at any time. All the performances are of undoubted merit and are well recorded.

(i) *Lachrimae: 7 Passionate Pavans.* Consort settings

**(*) HM HMU 907275. (i) The King's Noyse, Douglass; (ii) Hargis, O'Dette (lute)

The King's Noyse also give a very affecting performance of the *Lachrimae*, plus a generous programme of other pieces for viols. In a similarly dolorous mood, **Ellen Hargis** contributes just five lute songs, which she sings touchingly and beautifully, and they are expertly accompanied by **Paul O'Dette**. They are interspersed with the instrumental music, and one could have wished that the balance was more even between vocal and instrumental items. However, the recording is most natural and full texts are included.

Complete Solo Lute Music (Collection)

(N) ⎘– (B) **** BIS-SACD 1724. Jacob Lindberg (8-course or 10-course lute or 8-course orpharion)

(BB) *** Naxos 8.557586 (Vol.1); 8.557862 (Vol.2); 8570449 (Vol.3); 8570284 (Vol.4). Nigel North (lute)

Jacob Lindberg, a superb lutenist now provides us with the complete solo lute and orpharion music of John Dowland including two closing *Pavans* from J. D. Mylius's *Thesaurus gratiarum* which he has only recently discovered. The orpharion, a flat-backed wire-strung instrument, is used to atmospheric effect in the 11 works for which it was intended. This music can be dipped into at pleasure for it is offered on a single SACD with a playing time of four-and-a-quarter hours (achieved apparently by using DVD technology for an audio-only SACD). Lindberg's playing is peerless and the result is totally realistic. One can pick out any one of the 92 items virtually instantaneously. A remarkable achievement, very well documented. We feel that this ease of access gives Lindberg a lead over his competitors.

Nigel North has also just completed a comprehensive coverage of this repertoire for Naxos. He plays with perception and skill and no lack of spontaneity and is given fine presence by the recordings. Volume 1 tends to concentrate on the livelier pieces; Volume 2 includes the famous *Lachrimae Pavan* and the *Semper Dowland semper dolens* although the programme offers sprightly numbers too. Volume 3 concentrates on the three principal Elizabethan dances movements - *almains, galliards* and *pavans* of which the *Melancholy Galliard* and *Pavana doulant* are most typical of the composer's melancholy, even in dance forms. In the fourth and final volume North combines dances, including many favourite galliards, plus some transcribed songs. This coverage is altogether excellent and will suit those who may not want to have the whole collection, but would prefer to enter Dowland's world a disc at a time.

VOCAL MUSIC

Ayres (with viols); Lute Solos and Songs

(BB) **** Hyp. Helios CDH 55241. Bowman, King's Consort or D. Miller (lute) – CAMPION; FORD; JOHNSON; DANYEL; FERRABOSCO; HUNNIS: *Ayrs; Lute Songs & Solos* ***

A particularly attractive collection, offering maximum variety. **James Bowman** has exactly the right alto voice for this repertoire and he sings very beautifully, while the lutenist **David Miller** (who introduces four different lutes during the course of the programme) and the quartet of viols from the **King's Consort** are equally memorable. The recording is well up to Hyperion's usual high standard. A true bargain.

Lute songs, Book I (1597); Book II (1600)

*** Metronome METCD 1010. Agnew, Wilson

Lute songs, Book III (1603); Book IV (1610); Book V (1612)

*** Metronome METCD 1011. Agnew, Wilson

Paul Agnew's tenor voice has a certain darkness of colouring in the middle range that seems just right for the dolour of such songs as *Come ye heavie states of night* and *Flow not so fast ye fountaines*, or the despondent *If that a sinners sighes be angels foode* (a lovely performance), yet he can lighten it attractively for lively numbers like *What if I never speede* or *Fine knacks for ladies*. **Christopher Wilson's** intimate accompaniments could not be more gently supportive, and the recording balance is admirable within a pleasingly atmospheric acoustic. Each disc is handsomely presented with a beautifully printed booklet containing full texts and illustrations, all within a slipcase.

First Booke of Songes (1597)

*** Decca O/L (ADD) 475 9114. Consort of Musicke, Rooley

Here **Rooley** and the excellent **Consorte of Musicke** have recorded all the contents of the *First Booke of Songes* in the order in which they are published, varying the accompaniment between viols, lute and bass viol, but also offering voices and viols, and even voices alone. There is hardly any need to stress the beauties of the music itself, which is eminently well served by this stylish ensemble, and beautifully recorded. This L'Oiseau-Lyre disc returns to the catalogue using the original logo and artwork and including full texts.

Four-part lute songs

**(*) Lyrichord LEMS 8031. Saltire Singers, Dupré

The **Saltire Singers** are a superb vocal group from the early 1960s. **Patricia Clark** and **Edgar Fleet** were both performers with Deller's Consort, and **Desmond Dupré** was Deller's lutenist. The vocal blend here is ravishing. Seldom have individual singers matched their voices more richly in this repertoire, with Patricia Clark leading with a sweet, soaring soprano, her gentle touch of vibrato ideal for Dowland's melodic lines. The choice of songs too is admirable, offering some of Dowland's very finest inspirations. The extended *Tell me true love* brings opportunities for lovely solo contributions from each member of the team; but most touching of all is the melancholy *Wherever sin sore wounding*, which shows Dowland at his most profound. The recording of the voices could hardly be bettered, except that at times they tend to overwhelm the lute. The only other small caveat is the relatively short measure (44 minutes), but the quality of the singing more than compensates. Full texts are provided.

Lute Songs

(BB) **(*) Virgin 2x1 5 62410-2 (2). Kirkby, Rooley – JONES: *Lute Songs* ***

Emma Kirkby seldom disappoints, and she sings these songs with simple beauty, often touching. But her white, pure timbre does not always find quite enough variety of colour and intensity in Dowland's more poignant expressions of dolour. **Anthony Rooley** accompanies very supportively on either his lute or a 7-course orpharion. What makes this inexpensive double especially attractive is the coupled selection of songs by Robert Jones, which suit Kirkby's voice very persuasively. Excellent balance and truthful recording.

Lute Songs

(*) BIS **SACD 1475. Kirkby, Rooley (lute)

If you enjoy the freshness of **Emma Kirkby's** singing, with its total freedom from artifice, this programme can certainly be recommended, with its naturally balanced and beautifully played accompaniments from **Anthony Rooley**. But, as with the earlier Virgin collection with Rooley, Kirkby does not find quite enough variety of expression to uncover the fullest depth of some of these songs. The recording is enhanced on surround sound SACD: if the back speakers are judiciously balanced, the sense of presence is very natural.

Elizabethan Lute Songs

*** RCA 886970 49272. Pears, Bream (with Songs by MORLEY; ROSSETTER & FORD)

The selection of Dowland's songs dominates this recital, which **Peter Pears** sings with his usual blend of intelligence and lyrical feeling. His very individual timbre readily identifies with the underlying melancholy which characterizes so many Elizabethan songs, and **Bream** accompanies impeccably on the lute. The recordings were made in 1963 in London's Wigmore Hall and 1969 in the Conway Hall.

Lute Songs & Lute Solos

*** Hyp. CDA 67648. Padmore , Kenny – BRITTEN: *Nocturnal after John Dowland*: Ogden, guitar ***

Mark Padmore's tenor voice is rich-timbred as well as deeply expressive, and he can sparkle too (sample *Sorrow stay*, followed immediately by *Away with these self-loving lads*). **Elizabeth Kenny** plays her solo items just as beautifully as she accompanies the singer. The disc is very well planned so that as a centrepiece the lute solo, *Sleep, wayward thoughts*, is followed by the song *Come heavy sleep* to introduce Britten's guitar *Nocturnal* (*Reflections on 'Come, heavy sleep'*) with its eight fascinatingly diverse variations, including an extended closing *Passacaglia* – brilliantly and imaginatively played by **Craig Ogden**. The programme then ends with eight more well-chosen items from Padmore and Kenny.

Lute Songs and Lute Solos (with *Galliards* by Mary, Queen of Scotts. Attrib. FRANCIS CUTTING: *Greensleeves (Divisions)*. Anon.: *Bonny Sweet Robin; Callino; Kemp's Jig*)

(BB) *** Naxos 8.553381. Rickards, Linell (lute)

Steven Rickards has a light, precise counter-tenor voice which he uses very imaginatively in this sequence of 19 songs, including many of Dowland's finest. There are also well-chosen lute solos from **Dorothy Linell**, supplementing her excellent accompaniments. The recording, made in New York, is clear and well balanced. Full texts and good notes are provided.

Lute Songs

*** Lyrichord (ADD) LEMS 8011. Oberlin, Iadone (lute)

One can hardly believe that this recital was recorded in 1958, so fresh and vivid is the sound. **Russell Oberlin's** very special counter-tenor timbre is beautifully caught. *I saw my lady weep* is most moving, while *Flow my tears* soars; but most touching of all is the closing *In darkness let me dwell*. **Joseph Iadone** contributes two of Dowland's most famous instrumental pieces. The only drawback to this disc is the comparatively short playing-time of 48 minutes.

DRAESEKE, Felix (1835– 1913)

Piano Concerto in E flat., Op. 36

(N) *** Hyp. CDA 67636. Becker, Berlin RSO, Michael Sanderling – JADASSOHN: *Piano Concertos 1 & 2* ***

Draeseke is hardly a household name these days, but in his day, he did acquire a certain reputation. His *Piano Concerto* of 1885–6 is Beethovenian in scope and Lisztian in spirit. Its exceptionally lively and colourful outer movements make for entertaining listening, along with the colourful orchestrations, though the music lacks melodic memorability.

DREYSCHOCK, Alexander (1818–69)

Piano Concerto in D min., Op. 137

*** Hyp. CDA 67086. Lane, BBC Scottish SO, Willén – KULLAK: *Piano Concerto in C min.* ***

This is one of the very finest of Hyperion's 'Romantic Piano Concerto' series. **Piers Lane** rises to the occasion with glittering dexterity and fine romantic flair, while the orchestra provides enthusiastic support, introducing the endearing main theme of the *Andante* with affectionate warmth. The splendidly balanced recording presents the polished dialogue between solo piano and the often flamboyant orchestra in an ideal perspective.

DUFAY, Guillaume (c. 1400–74)

Sacred Music from the Bologna Manuscript

*** Signum SIGCD 023. Clerks' Group, Wickham

Edward Wickham and his excellent **Clerks' Group** here explore the Bologna Manuscript, Q15, which is one of the great surviving collections of fifteenth-century music. Their selection aims to show the changes in Dufay's style. The Clerks'

Group always seem completely at home in this repertoire and Wickham's pacing is always convincing. A fine and beautifully recorded collection.

Ave regina celorum; Missa Puisque je vis (attrib.)

*** Hyp. CDA 67368. Binchois Cons., Kirkman – LOYSET COMPÈRE: *Omnium bonorum plena*; ANON.: *Concede nobis domine; Salve maris stella*

The *Missa Puisque je vis* has, for some half a century, been thought to have been written by Dufay, and recent scholarship has all but confirmed the attribution. It may well date from about the same time as the better-known *Missa Ecce ancilla domini*. It is based on a rather engaging courtly song about an unattainable lady, of which the text can be read to have a double meaning. It makes a useful basis for the Mass as its melody remains in the mind. It is sung here simply and beautifully by this group of eight singers. However, it does not match the richness of Dufay's *Ave regina celorum*, which was his own personal intercession with the Virgin, and he requested that it should be sung at his bedside at the moment of his death. The anonymous *Salve maris stella* is also impressive and Loyset Compère's motet, *Omnium bonorum plena*, flows agreeably, as does *Concede nobis domine*, but none of these motets, though sympathetically performed, matches the quality of the two Dufay works, authentic or not. The recording, made in All Saints, Tooting, is first class.

Missa L'homme armé; Motet: Supremum est mortalibus bonum

🎵 (BB) *** Naxos 8.553087. Oxford Camerata, Summerly

Jeremy Summerly and his **Oxford Camerata** give a powerfully expressive and wholly convincing account of Dufay's masterly cyclic *Mass* using a Burgundian chanson as its basis. We hear this sung first in its original format as an introduction, and its message, 'The armed man should be feared', makes a dramatically appropriate contrast with the motet, *Supremum est mortalibus*, which is a peace song. The latter was written some 30 years earlier, yet it shows just as readily the remarkable inventiveness and eloquence of this 15th-century French composer. The *Mass* movements are interspersed with plainchant in the same Dorian mode. With vivid yet atmospheric recording this can be given the strongest recommendation.

Missa Santi Anthoni de Padua. Motet: O proles Hispaniae / O sidus Hispaniae

(B) *** Hyp. Helios CDH 55271. Binchois Cons., Kirkman

Through clever detective work this fine 10-movement plenary *Mass* (with four sections of the Ordinary – *Introit, Gradual, Alleluia* and *Offertory* – added to the Proper) is now attributed with fair confidence to Dufay. Sensitive singing from the six singers of the **Binchois Consort** under **Andrew Kirkman**, and a splendid coupling in the five items by Dufay's contemporary, Gilles Binchois, all very well recorded. The Binchois Consort also performs a motet with two texts associated with St Anthony. The recording is first class and the disc is highly recommendable.

Mass for St James the Greater. Motets: Apostolo glorioso; Balsamus et munda cera; Gloria; Credo; Rite majorem Jacobum canamus/Arcibus summis miseri reclusi

(N) (BB) **** Hyp. Helios CDH 55272. Binchois Consort, Kirkman

St James the Greater was remembered as an important mystical figure in medieval times. Closely associated with Christ and the Virgin Mary, brother of St John the Evangelist, he was the first Bishop of Jerusalem and martyred by Herod Agrippa. The 9-part *Mass* he inspired is one of Dufay's most ambitious, eloquently beautiful and stylistically varied, created from the richness of the melodic chants the composer drew on. The accompanying contemplative *Rite majorem* is linked with the *Mass*, but the other motets here have different associations, and provide further variety in one of the finest examples of Dufay's genius on disc. This CD has rightly been highly praised, for **Kirkman's** performances with the **Binchois Consort** are very compelling and beautifully recorded.

Mass Se la face ay pale (with Propers from the end of the 1440s); Ballade Se la face ay pale. Motets: O tres piteux; Magnanime gentis

(N) **** Hyp. CDA 67715. Binchois Consort, Kirkman

For their recording of the most famous of Dufay's masses, being a celebrated example of one of the earliest works to use a unified *cantus firmus* structure. But here it is presented as it would have been performed in its time, with a set of *Propers* from the same period (found in manuscript of the late 1450s). **Kirkman** also offers as a postlude the ballad which supplied the composer with his *cantus firmus* for the *Mass*, plus two motets of the same period. Thus the overall sequence is one of considerable variety of music of striking expressive depth and as usual with this superb group, the performances could not be more eloquent and dedicated.

DUKAS, Paul (1865–1935)

L'Apprenti sorcier (The Sorcerer's Apprentice)

🎵 *** DG 419 617-2. BPO, Levine – SAINT-SAËNS: *Symphony 3* ***

(***) Testament mono SBT 1017. Philh. O, Cantelli – CASELLA: *Paganiniana*; FALLA: *Three-Cornered Hat*; RAVEL: *Daphnis et Chloé: Suite 2* (***)

(M) **(*) Chan. 6503. SNO, Gibson – ROSSINI (arr. Respighi): *La Boutique fantasque*; SAINT-SAËNS: *Danse macabre* **(*)

Levine chooses a fast basic tempo, though not as fast as Toscanini (who managed only two 78 sides), but achieves a deft, light and rhythmic touch to make this a real orchestral Scherzo. Yet the climax is thrilling, helped by superb playing from the **Berlin Philharmonic**. The CD has an amplitude and sparkle which are especially telling.

Cantelli's 1954 mono account still remains one of the very best performances ever recorded, and it is splendidly transferred.

Gibson secures excellent playing from the **SNO**, if without the sheer panache of some of his competitors. The recording (made in City Hall, Glasgow, in 1972) is less overtly brilliant than Levine's but has plenty of atmosphere. The Chandos disc, however, is ungenerous in playing time (37 minutes).

L'Apprenti sorcier (The Sorcerer's Apprentice) (with spoken introduction)

(BB) **(*) Naxos 8.554463. Morris (nar.), Slovak RSO, Jean – RAVEL: *Ma Mère l'Oye* *** ; SAINT-SAËNS: *Carnival of the Animals* **(*)

In this Naxos triptych clearly aimed at young children, **Johnny Morris** provides a concise and effective narrative introduction. The performance is alive and well paced; it takes a while to generate the fullest tension, but any child should respond to this imagery. The recording is excellent, spacious and vivid.

L'Apprenti sorcier; La Péri

**(*) Testament SBT 1324. Paris Conservatoire O, Ansermet – SAINT-SAËNS: *Danse macabre*; DEBUSSY: *Jeux; 6 Epigraphes antiques*, etc. (***)

L'Apprenti sorcier; La Péri: Poème dansé (with Fanfare); Symphony in C

(BB) *** Warner Apex 0927 48725-2. (i) Nouvel PO; (ii) SRO, Jordan

L'Apprenti sorcier; La Péri (with Fanfare); Polyeucte: Overture

(M) *** Sup. (ADD) SU 3479-2 011. Czech PO, Almeida

The super-bargain Apex disc offers a reissue of what were the first accounts of the Dukas *Symphony* and *La Péri* to reach CD, and the 1985 recording sounds splendid in this new transfer, especially in *La Péri*, which is spectacular, atmospheric and clear. **Jordan's** reading of the *Symphony* has both vitality and musical conviction, and he is equally sensitive to the richly languorous evocation of *La Péri*, while building a thrilling climax. An outstanding bargain: indeed this would be recommendable if it cost far more.

Almeida's Dukas collection, made in 1973, is hardly less successful. Almeida's performance of *La Péri* is sensuous and gripping, and the orchestral playing has both intensity and allure. *Polyeucte*, an early work with Wagnerian echoes, is also extremely successful, especially the closing *Andante tranquillo*. But what makes this Supraphon disc very competitive is the sparkling *L'Apprenti sorcier*, the main theme winningly jaunty and ideally paced, and reaching a brilliant climax, with superb roistering horns and the whole orchestra on its toes.

Ansermet's 1954 recording of *La Péri* with the Paris Conservatoire Orchestra, which was originally coupled with Rachmaninov's *Isle of the Dead*, omits the *Fanfare*. The sound, in this transfer of the experimental stereo master (made alongside the mono but never released at the time), is obviously more detailed, and the earlier version is a reading of

great breadth and style. *L'Apprenti sorcier* is also very successful, and there is an added bonus of Saint-Saëns's *Danse macabre*. Well worth investigating.

(i) L'Apprenti sorcier; La Péri (with Fanfare); (ii) Polyeucte Overture; Symphony in C; (iii) Piano Sonata; La Plainte, au loin, du faune; Prélude élégiaque

⊕– (B) *** Chan. 2 for 1 241-32. (i) Ulster O; (ii) BBC PO, Y. P. Tortelier; (iii) Fingerhut

Yan Pascal Tortelier gives a very good performance of *La Péri*, with plenty of atmosphere and feeling, and *L'Apprenti sorcier* is equally successful. Tortelier's account of the *Symphony* is a clear primary recommendation, as is *Polyeucte*, an early piece with Wagnerian echoes. Excellent Chandos rcording in all four works ensures their success.

Margaret Fingerhut's collection of the piano music is recommendable too, a distinguished survey, with the large-scale *Sonata* particularly authoritative. The *Prélude élégiaque*, and *La Plainte, au loin, du faune* both move into the world of Debussian impressionism. They are both played very evocatively. Again very good sound.

La Péri (with Fanfare)

(BB) **(*) Naxos 8.557274. Nat. O de Lille-Région Nord, Jean-Claude Casadesus – BERLIOZ: *Nuits d'été*; CHAUSSON: *Poème* **(*)

Jean-Claude Casadesus with his fine **Lille Orchestra** conducts a warmly atmospheric reading of Dukas's 'poem for orchestra', introduced (as it should be) by the fanfare written as a brief prelude. The recording is both warm and clear, with the brass beautifully caught. Not perhaps a first choice, but an excellent supplement to the two vocal pieces.

Piano Duet

L'Apprenti sorcier (arr. for 2 pianos)

(BB) **(*) EMI Gemini (ADD/DDD) 5 86510-2 (2). Collard, Béroff – DEBUSSY & RAVEL: *Music for piano, 4 hands & 2 pianos*; BIZET: *Jeux d'enfants* **(*)

The composer's own piano-duet transcription of his most famous work is surprisingly successful, particularly the opening and closing pages; but **Collard** and **Béroff** are spirited throughout and the digital recording is fully acceptable.

Piano Sonata in E flat min.

⊕– *** Hyp. CDA 67513. Hamelin – DECAUX: *Clairs de lune* ***

(BB) **(*) Warner Apex 0927 48996-2. Hubeau

The Dukas *Sonata* has always hovered on the periphery of the catalogue. However, with this mighty performance by **Marc-André Hamelin**, earlier versions are all but swept aside. Hamelin has the full measure of this extraordinary work and he is blessed with first-rate recorded sound from the Henry Wood Hall by Simon Eadon and Andrew Keener.

Ariane et Barbe-Bleu (opera; complete)

*** Telarc CD-80680 (2). Lori & Peter Phillips, Bardon, Rose, BBC SO, Botstein

Originally broadcast on BBC Radio 3, this account of Dukas's exotic opera about Bluebeard is strong and sympathetic. **Lori Phillips** sings with bright, fresh tone as Ariane and, though **Peter Phillips's** baritone is hardly sinister in the role of Bluebeard, it is a strong, cleanly focused performance. This fills an important gap very effectively.

DU MONT, Henry (1610–84)

Allemande à 3; Pavane à 3; Saraband à 3; Symphonie à 3 (for 2 violins & continuo); Allemande en tablature; Allemande grave; Allemande sur les anches (all for organ); Pavane pour clavecin; Dialogue motets: Dialogue angelis et peccatoris; Dialogus de Anima; In lectulo meo; In te Domine; Litanies à la Vierge

— (BB) *** Virgin 2x1 5 62419-2 (2). Les Talens Lyriques, Rousset – COUPERIN: *Motets* ***

Rousset, in his diverse collection with **Les Talens Lyriques**, introduces some of the chamber and instrumental music, in which a noble expressive gravity predominates, although there are engaging dance-like interludes. The harpsichord *Pavane* with which Rousset closes the concert himself is one of its highlights, and the other is the echo motet, *In lectulo meo*, in which **Sandrine Piau** shines radiantly in a duet with herself. But the most important and striking of these dialogue motets is the ambitious *Dialogus de Anima* – almost an oratorio – for five singers, in which God, a sinner and an angel converse, with the piece ending with a splendid five-part chorus. This is most vividly performed and recorded, and with full texts and translations this Virgin bargain Double can be recommended highly.

DUNHILL, Thomas (1877–1946)

Symphony in A min., Op. 48.

(M) *** Dutton CDLX 7195. RSNO, Yates – ARNELL: *Lord Byron* ***

Thomas Dunhill was a pupil of Stanford in the 1890s and became best known for his light music and as a song composer. His *Symphony* was written in 1914–16 and first given in 1922 in Belgrade, and again in Bournemouth in 1924. It fell out of the repertoire and this is its first revival since the 1930s. The three stars are for the excellent performance and recording; the work itself is genial and likeable enough but wanting in individuality and cogency.

DUNSTABLE, John (d. 1453)

Missa Rex seculorum. Motets: Albanus roseo rutilat – Quoque ferundus eras – Albanus domini Laudus; Ave maris stella; Descendi in ortum meum; Gloria in canon; Preco preheminence – Precursor premittur – textless – Inter natos mulierum; Salve regina mater mire; Specialis Virgo; Speciosa facta es; Sub tuam protectionem; Veni sancte spiritus – Veni creator spiritus

— **** Metronome METCD 1009. Orlando Cons.

The **Orlando Consort** present their generous, 74-minute survey with an impressive combination of direct, impassioned feeling and style. If the splendid *Missa Rex seculorum* is of doubtful attribution, every piece here, motets and antiphons alike, is clearly by a major composer with a highly individual voice. The recording is excellent in every way and this CD, which won the *Gramophone*'s Early Music Award in 1996, offers the collector an admirable and highly rewarding entry into this composer's sound-world.

Mass movements: Kyrie; Gloria a 4; Credo a 4; Gloria Jesus Christi Fili Dei (2 settings); Sanctus; Credo: Da gaudiorum premia; Agnus Dei; Quam pulchra es; Veni sancte spiritus; Gloria in Canon (arr. Pitts)

— (BB) **** Naxos 8.557341. Tonus Peregrinus, Pitts

Dunstable's most famous piece (and justly so) is the isorhythmic motet, *Veni sancte spiritus*, in which a comparatively enigmatic formal structure becomes totally dwarfed by the music's expressive beauty. But the *Mass* movements here are, if anything, more beautiful. The eight singers of **Tonus Peregrinus** sing all this music with richly blended tone and deep feeling, and **Antony Pitts**, their director, has arranged a little encore with a performace of Dunstable's four-part *Gloria in Canon* to which he has added a two-part canon underneath, as 'in the original work there must have been some kind of harmonic support'. Altogether a superb disc, fully worthy of a great but still little-known musician from the distant past.

DUPARC, Henri (1848–1933)

Mélodies (complete)

— *** Hyp. CDA 66323. Walker, Allen, Vignoles

The Hyperion issue is as near an ideal modern Duparc record as could be. **Roger Vignoles** is the ever-sensitive accompanist, and the recording captures voices and piano beautifully, bringing out the tang and occasional rasp of **Sarah Walker's** mezzo and the glorious tonal range of **Thomas Allen's** baritone.

Mélodies

— (***) Testament mono SBT 1312. Souzay, Bonneau – RAVEL: *Don Quichotte à Dulcineé*; DEBUSSY: *3 Ballades* *** ; CHAUSSON: *Mélodies* (***)

*** Nim. (ADD) NI 5736/7 (2). Cuénod, Parsons – FAURÉ: *Mélodies* ***

Souzay's recordings of 12 of Duparc's 16 songs, made with **Jacqueline Bonneau** for Decca, comes from 1953 and is superior, both vocally and interpretatively, to his 1970 set for HMV. The voice has a wonderful freshness and bloom, and the monaural sound is also remarkably good – and not just for its period. The balance is well judged and every syllable registers. Some of the songs have never been surpassed, even by Bernac or Panzera. These are very special performances and exquisitely accompanied.

Hugues Cuénod was already 70 when he made these recordings, though this hardly shows: the voice is light and steady, and his sense of style impeccable. Both the accompanists (the documentation does not indicate who accompanies what) are highly sensitive and match the refined intelligence that this great artist brings to this repertoire.

DUPRÉ, Marcel (1886–1971)

ORGAN MUSIC

6 Chorales, Op. 28; 2 Chorales, Op. 59; 24 Inventions, Op. 50; 4 Modal Fugues, Op. 63

(BB) *** Naxos 8.553862. Biery

The 24 *Inventions*, Op. 50, which are divided to begin and end this CD, are, like Bach's *Well-Tempered Clavier*, composed in all the major and minor keys. They are distinguished by fastidious craftsmanship and considerable imagination, as are the 6 *Chorales*, Op. 28 (1930). The *Chorales*, Op. 59, and the *Four Modal Fugues* come from the 1960s. **James Biery** is an excellent advocate and the recording, made on the Casavant organ of the Cathedral of Saints Peter and Paul, in Providence, Rhode Island, is splendidly lifelike and has great clarity and definition. A rewarding issue.

Choral et Fugue, Op. 57; Cortège et Litanie, Op. 19/2; 3 Esquisses, Op. 41; Évocation, Op. 37; Allegro deciso. Preludes & Fugues, Op. 7/1–3; Le Tombeau de Titelouse: Te lucis ante terminum; Placare Christie servuli, Op. 38/6 & 16; Symphonie 2; Symphonie-Passion; Variations sur un vieux Noël, Op. 20

⊶ (M) *** Hyp. Dyad CDD 22059 (2). Scott (organ of St Paul's Cathedral)

John Scott's recording of this collection on the organ of St Paul's Cathedral is one of the most impressive reissues of recent times. His playing is more spontaneous and convincing than many of the composer's own recordings in the past. Dupré's music is revealed as reliably inventive and with an atmosphere and palette all its own. Scott is a splendid advocate and the St Paul's Cathedral organ is unexpectedly successful in this repertoire.

DURUFLÉ, Maurice (1902–86)

COMPLETE ORGAN MUSIC

Chant Donné (Hommage à Jean Gallan); Fugue sur le thème du Carillon des Heures de la Cathédrale de Soissons, Op. 12; Méditation; Prélude, Adagio et Choral varié sur le thème du 'Veni Creator', Op. 4; Prélude sur l'Introit de l'Épiphanie, Op. 13; Scherzo, Op. 2; Suite, Op. 5

⊶ *** CPO compatible Surround Sound SACD 777 042-2. Flamme (Mülheisein organ, Stiftskirche, Bad Gandersheim)

(BB) *** Naxos 8.557924. Fairs (organ of Notre-Dame d'Auteuil, Paris)

Previous recordings of Duruflé's organ music are now upstaged by this superb new CPO SACD, in surround sound. If a suitable player is available, linked to back speakers, one has the extraordinary feeling of sitting in the Stiftskirche, where the recording was made. Not only is the climax of the Op. 5 *Toccata* overwhelming but in the gentler music the pedals still make their presence felt, even on a normal CD playback. **Friedhelm Flamme** plays a magnificent new organ, installed in 2000, for which the *manufacturer d'orgue*, Mülheisein, was awarded the *Meilleurs Ouvriers de France* prize. Flamme's playing is highly sensitive, and he can articulate with great delicacy when needed, as in the *Scherzo* and the *Prélude*, Op. 4, while he creates a fine climax for the *Carillon des Heures*. Very highly recommended.

Henry Fairs has twice won the Prix Maurice Duruflé at Chartres, so he is well fitted for this repertoire. He plays a restored Cavaillé-Coll organ – impressively pictured, although not described here. It can be heard at its most spectacular in the *Toccata* from the *Suite*, Op. 5, but its colour palette is impressive and is well handed by Fairs. This is not as spectacular a survey as Flamme's on CPO, but Fairs is very well recorded and this Naxos CD is well worth its modest cost.

Danse lente, Op. 6/2; Prélude et Fugue sur le nom d'Alain, Op. 7

*** Chan. 10315. Whitehead (organ of Saint Étienne Cathedral, Auxerre, France) – ALAIN: *Aria; Danses*, etc. ***

The well-known *Prélude et Fugue* weaves the name, Alain, into both sections and even quotes from the composer's *Litanies* at the conclusion of the *Prélude*. The transcribed *Danse lente* is the middle movement of Duruflé's orchestral *Trois Danses*, and almost turns the organ into an orchestra in its own right. In this spendidly played recital, both pieces are interwoven with a highly stimulating programme of music by Alain on an organ ideal for this repertory.

Organ Music: *Fugue sur le carillon des heures de la Cathédrale de Soissons, Op. 12; Méditation, Op. posth.; Prélude, adagio et choral varié sur le 'Veni Creator', Op. 4; Prélude et fugue sur le nom d'Alain, Op. 7; Prélude sur l'introit de l'Epiphanie; Scherzo, Op. 2; Suite, Op. 5*

*** BIS CD 1304. Fagius

Hans Fagius uses the four-manual 89-stop 1928 Frobenius organ of Aarhus Cathedral in Denmark for his recital, and a particularly fine instrument it is. Apart from his good musicianship and taste, Fagius has the additional advantage of authority, since he also studied with the composer. Fagius's liner-notes are also exemplary and he has the additional advantage of superbly realistic BIS recording.

Requiem, Op. 9

◑— (M) *** Warner Elatus 0927 49001-2. Larmore, Hampson, Amb. S., Philh. O, Legrand – FAURÉ: *Requiem* ***

(B) *** Decca Eclipse 448 711-2. Palmer, Shirley-Quirk, Boys of Westminster Cathedral Ch., L. Symphony Ch., LSO, Hickox – FAURÉ: *Pavane*; POULENC: *Gloria* ***

(M) *** EMI (ADD) 3 79994-2. Baker, Roberts, King's College, Cambridge, Ch., Butt, Ledger – FAURÉ: *Requiem; Pavane* ***

Requiem, Op. 9; Messe Cum jubilo, Op. 11; 4 Motets sur les thèmes grégoriens, Op. 10; Notre père, Op. 14 (both for a cappella choir)

*** Chan. 10357. Trinity College, Cambridge, Ch., Marlow; with Wilkinson; Herford; Williams (organ)

(i; ii; v) Requiem, Op. 9; (iii; iv; v) Messe cum jubilo, Op. 11; (iii) 4 Motets on Gregorian Themes, Op. 10; (v) (Organ) Prélude et fugue sur le nom d'Alain, Op. 7

◑— (BB) **** Warner Apex 2564 61139-2. (i) Bouvier, Depraz, Philippe Caillard Ch., LAP; (ii) Stéphane Caillat Ch.; (iii) Soyer; (iv) O Nat. de l'ORTFM; all cond. composer; (v) Duruflé-Chevalier (organ)

Requiem, Op. 9 (3rd version); 4 Motets, Op. 10

*** Hyp. CDA 66191. Murray, Allen, Corydon Singers, ECO, Best; Trotter (organ)

(i–iii) Requiem. Op. 9; (ii) 4 Motets, Op. 10; (iii) (Organ) Prélude et fugue sur le nom d'Alain

(B) *** Double Decca (ADD) 436 486-2 (2). (i) King, Keyte; (ii) St John's College, Cambridge, Ch.; (iii) Cleobury (organ); Guest – FAURÉ: *Requiem*, etc.; POULENC: *Messe*, etc. ***

Duruflé wrote his *Requiem* in 1947, overtly basing its layout and even the cut of its themes on the Fauré masterpiece. A clear first choice is almost impossible to make; however, the Apex budget reissue is particularly valuable as it offers a spontaneous dedicated performance under the direction of the composer that blossoms into great ardour at emotional peaks. The less familiar but no less beautiful *Messe cum jubilo* receives a comparatively inspirational account, its gentler passages sustained with rapt concentration, with beautiful playing from the **French Radio Orchestra**. The soloists in both works rise to the occasion, and the choral singing combines passionate feeling with subtle colouring. The composer proves a splendid exponent of his own works, as does his daughter playing the *Prélude et Fugue* on the organ of Soissons Cathedral. The spaciously atmospheric recordings were made between 1959 (the *Requiem*) and 1971. Not to be missed.

Michel Legrand uses the full orchestral version and makes the most of the passionate orchestral eruptions in the *Sanctus* and *Libera me*. He strikes a perfect balance between these sudden outbursts of agitation and the work's mysticism and warmth. The **Ambrosian Choir** sing ardently yet find a treble-like purity for the *Agnus Dei* and *In Paradisum*, while **Jennifer Larmore** gives the *Pie Jesu* more plangent feeling than its counterpart in the Fauré *Requiem*. The recording, made in Watford Town Hall, is spacious and most realistically balanced.

Using the chamber-accompanied version, with strings, harp and trumpet – a halfway house between the full orchestral score and plain organ accompaniment – **Best** conducts a deeply expressive and sensitive performance. With two superb soloists and an outstandingly refined chorus, it makes an excellent recommendation, well coupled with the motets, done with similar freshness, clarity and feeling for tonal contrast. The recording is attractively atmospheric yet quite clearly focused.

Hickox tempers the richness of the orchestral version by using boys' voices in the choir. He relishes the extra drama of orchestral accompaniment with biting brass at the few moments of high climax. **Felicity Palmer** and **John Shirley-Quirk** sing with deep feeling and fine imagination, if not always with ideally pure tone. The recording has a pleasantly ecclesiastical ambience, which adds to the ethereal purity of the trebles, and the stereo spread is wide.

Philip Ledger's 1980 version of the *Requiem* uses organ rather than orchestral accompaniment. Yet such is the clarity of the recording and the sense of atmosphere engendered by the performance (and enhanced by the King's acoustic) that one scarcely misses the additional dimension of colour that the orchestra provides. The singing is splendid and the grave beauty and emotional restraint of Duruflé's music is movingly conveyed. Many will find this version satisfying, as it is so beautifully recorded.

The (originally Argo) **St John's** version also uses boy trebles instead of women singers, even in the solo of the *Pie Jesu* – exactly parallel to Fauré's setting of those words, which was indeed first sung by a treble. The alternative organ accompaniment is used here, not as warmly colourful as the orchestral version, but very beautiful nevertheless. The 1974 recording is vividly atmospheric. To this have been added the *Four Motets*, on plainsong themes, which are also finely sung. The organ piece, another sensitive example of Duruflé's withdrawn genius, makes a further bonus, especially when one realizes that this generous pair of CDs includes also the *Mass* and *Salve Regina* of Poulenc.

The Chandos CD collects together Duruflé's complete choral works, including the touching setting of *Notre père* which the composer dedicated to his wife. The three major works are well represented on CD, but the **Trinity College Choir** sing very responsively, and **Richard Marlow** has the advantage of a very wide-ranging Chandos recording, which creates warmly atmospheric, seemingly distanced choral *pianissimos* and highly dramatic climaxes. Those who are satisfied with the organ version and who enjoy the high drama which such contrasts bring will find this very satisfying, for the soloists are excellent and **Clare Wilkinson's** contribution to the *Pie Jesu* is most affecting.

DUSSEK (Dusik), Jan Ladislav
(1760–1812)

Piano Sonatas, Op. 9/1-3; Op. 77 (L'Invocation)

(N) *** CPO 777 323-2. Becker

Dussek holds only a peripheral place in the catalogue. Andreas Staier has been his champion on the fortepiano in the past. Meanwhile **Markus Becker** offers us three early sonatas, first published in 1789 and his last, somewhat Beethovenian sonata, Op. 77 written twenty years later. Very much of their period, they are always interesting and inventive, with classicism making way for romanticism. They are well played here (especially the *prestissimo* finale of Op. 7/3) and well recorded.

DUTILLEUX, Henri (born 1916)

Cello Concerto (Tout un monde lointain)

☞ **** EMI (ADD) 5 67867-2. Rostropovich, O de Paris, Baudo – LUTOSŁAWSKI: *Cello Concerto* ***

(i) Cello Concerto (Tout un monde lointain); (ii) Métaboles; (iii) The Shadows of Time

(M) *** Warner Elatus 0927 49830-2. (i) Noras, Finnish RSO, Saraste; (ii) O Nat. de France, Rostropovich; (iii) Boston SO, Ozawa

(i) Cello Concerto. Métaboles; Mystères de l'instant

*** Chan. 9565. (i) Pergamenschikov; BBC PO, Y. P. Tortelier

The *Cello Concerto* is intense in feeling and rich in those glowing timbres and luminous textures which he is so successful in creating. **Rostropovich** plays the work with enormous virtuosity and feeling; the **Orchestre de Paris** under **Serge Baudo** gives splendid support, while the 1975 recording is immensely vivid, with Rostropovich looming larger than life but given great presence. This has now rightly been reissued as one of EMI's 'Great Recordings of the Century'.

The Finnish cellist, **Arto Noras**, is a committed and authoritative soloist and is given excellent support from **Saraste** and the **Finnish Radio Orchestra**. Both performances and recordings of the *Métaboles* and *The Shadows of Time* have been recommended in earlier editions of the *Guide* and make an excellent coupling.

Boris Pergamenschikov rises to the challenge and, although Rostropovich's remains an almost mandatory recommendation, thanks to the composer's authority, the excellence of the orchestral playing under **Yan Pascal Tortelier** and the Chandos recording earn it a three-star grading. The *Métaboles* and the *Mystères de l'instant* are played expertly and persuasively.

(i) Cello Concerto (Tout un monde lointain); Symphony No. 1; Timbres, espace, mouvement (La Nuit etoilée)

(BB) **(*) Arte Nova 74321 92413-2. O Nat. Bordeaux Aquitaine, Graf; (i) with Queyras

A fine performance of the *Cello Concerto*, too, from **Jean-Guihen Queyras** and the sound is most vivid and present; this can certainly be recommended and is well worth acquiring, even at the risk of duplication.

(Violin Concerto) L'Arbre des Songes

(N) (M) *** RCO 08001. Sitkovetsky, Concg. O, Jansons – DEBUSSY: *La Mer*; RAVEL: *La Valse* ***

L'Arbre des Songes, the 'Tree of Dreams', is Dutilleux's unconventional violin concerto in four main sections with three important *Interludes*. **Dmitri Sitkovetsky** proves the most persuasive soloist, with **Jansons** masterly in his shaping of the accompaniment, bringing out the beauty of the scoring, helped by the unique quality of the **Concertgebouw's** different sections, notably the incomparable strings. It is good to have the orchestra promoting live recordings of this quality, though it seems a pity that such a disc does not appear on one of the regular international labels.

(i) (Violin Concerto) L'Arbre des songes; (ii) La Geôle; 2 Sonnets de Jean Cassou; Mystère de l'instant

☞ (BB) *** Arte Nova 82876 63825-2. O Nat. Bordeaux Aquitaine, Graf, with (i) Charlier; (ii) Le Roux

In *L'Arbre des songes* **Charlier** has commanding authority and unforced eloquence, shaping every phrase and balancing each texture to perfection, and this newcomer with the **Orchestre National Bordeaux Aquitaine** is very recommendable. New to the catalogue is *La Geôle*, composed in 1944 during the war to a text by Jean Cassou, two of whose sonnets he set 10 years later. Good sound and excellent value.

(i) Violin Concerto (L'Arbre des songes); Timbres, espace, mouvement; (ii) 2 Sonnets de Jean Cassou

*** Chan. 9504. (i) Charlier; (ii) Hill, N. Davies; BBC PO, Y. P. Tortelier – ALAIN: *Prière* ***

In terms of artistry and musicianship **Charlier** yields nothing to his rivals, and **Yan Pascal Tortelier** gives us the *Timbres, espace, mouvement* (*La Nuit étoilée*) from 1979 as a makeweight. The *Deux Sonnets de Jean Cassou* come in Dutilleux's own orchestral transcription, in which **Martyn Hill** and **Neal Davies** are effective soloists.

Métaboles

☞ (BB) *** Warner Apex (ADD) 0926 48686-2. O Nat. de l'ORTF, Munch – HONEGGER: *Symphony 4* ***

Métaboles was commissioned in 1964 by the Cleveland Orchestra and only three years later taken into the studio by **Charles Munch**, one of Dutilleux's most notable champions. In its day (1967) it was a state-of-the-art recording, and though there are many more recent accounts, it still sounds vivid and exhilarating. Munch's account of the Honegger symphony is also outstanding.

Métaboles; The Shadows of Time; Symphony 2 (Le Double)

(BB) **(*) Arte Nova 74321 80786-2. O Nat. Bordeaux Aquitaine, Graf

The **Bordeaux Orchestra** play with finesse and sensitivity throughout this disc and those above, though in the two symphonies (which are separated on Arte Nova) they do not supersede the performances by the BBC Philharmonic under Yan Pascal Tortelier on Chandos. However, given the price and the excellence of the recorded sound, they make a perfectly valid alternative recommendation, and the other orchestral works are impressive too.

Sur le même accord

(M) *** DG 477 5376. Mutter, O Nat. de France, Masur –
BARTÓK: *Violin Concerto 2*; STRAVINSKY: *Violin Concerto in D* ***

Dutilleux's *Sur le même accord* is a short work (under nine minutes) and was commissioned for **Mutter** by Paul Sacher when she was 16; she was in her thirties when the score finally arrived. This performance was recorded at its Paris première in 2003, and very fine it is too. *Sur le même accord* is 'on the same chord' and the music is derived from the six plucked notes heard at the beginning. Like all Dutilleux's music, it is highly imaginative and atmospheric, and makes a welcome addition to his growing discography.

Symphonies 1–2

⊕– ❀ **** Chan. 9194. BBC PO, Y. P. Tortelier

Marvellously resourceful and inventive scores, which are given vivid and persuasive performances by **Yan Pascal Tortelier** and the **BBC Philharmonic Orchestra**. The engineers give us a splendidly detailed and refined portrayal of these complex textures – the sound is really state-of-the-art.

Ainsi la nuit (String Quartet)

⊕– (B) *** EMI Début 5 74020-2. Belcea Qt – DEBUSSY, RAVEL: *String Quartets* ***

The **Belcea** accounts of the Debussy and Ravel quartets are pretty impeccable, and their Dutilleux is hardly less sensitive. One's first impression of *Ainsi la nuit* is of fragmentation and delicate wisps of texture, but gradually its power and logic emerge. The Belcea players are extraordinarily sensitive to its dynamic range and produce a performance of great finesse. At budget price and with good sound, this enjoys a strong competitive advantage.

Piano music: Au gré des ondes; Bergerie; Blackbird; Mini-Prélude en éventail; Petit air à dormir debout; 3 Preludes; Resonance; Sonata; Tous les chemins mènent a Rome

(BB) *** Naxos 8.557823. Chen

The *Piano Sonata* of 1948 was one of the composer's first works to attract wide attention, and it remains the most important, thoughtful and beautifully written. Yet each of the smaller pieces makes its mark crisply and without inflation, consistently inventive, with intriguing titles adding to their charms. Chen's playing is magnetic and well controlled, but giving the impression of a pianist improvising. There have been excellent accounts of these pieces before, including one of the *Sonata* by its dedicatee, Geneviève Joy, the composer's wife, but this is now a first recommendation. Very good sound.

DVOŘÁK, Antonín (1841–1904)

'Deo Gratias': A documentary on the life of Dvořák (written and directed by Martin Suchanek)

*** Sup. **DVD** SU 7007-9. (includes performances of the composer's music by various Czech artists)

Dvořák's own final comment on his life was '*Deo Gratias*', 'Thanks be to God'. That makes an apt title for this admirably direct and informative documentary surveying the composer's career. It is fascinating to find that Dvořák's reports from his first music school were unflattering, with the exception that he was 'strong on counterpoint'; that in London he would get up at 6 a.m. to wander round the city; and that the salary he received in New York as Director of the Conservatoire was 30 times higher than what he was getting at home.

The biography is illustrated with a sequence of performances, filmed live, single movements rather than complete works. The selection is fair enough, with **Vaclav Neumann** warmer in his conducting than he has often been in his studio recordings. Those items – the finale of the *New World Symphony* and the first movement of the *Cello Concerto* with **Gustav Rivinius** as soloist – are vintage recordings, but the brilliantly played finale of the *Piano Concerto* dates from only three years ago, from the same performance (with **Martin Kasik** as soloist and with **Jiri Kout** conducting) that Supraphon has also issued complete on CD.

American Suite, Op. 98b

*** Sup. SU 3882-2. Prague Philh., Hrusa – SUK: *Scherzo fantastique; Serenade for Strings* ***

Jakob Hrusa draws superb playing, polished, refined and intense, from the **Czech Philharmonia Orchestra**, which Bělohlávek founded. He directs a magical performance, utterly charming in all five movements of Dvořák's *American Suite*, one of his last orchestral works. Well coupled with the two Suk pieces, it comes in full, clear sound.

Warner 100th Anniversary Edition: (i) American Suite in A, Op. 98b; (ii) Carnival Overture; (iii) Czech Suite; (iv) The Golden Spinning Wheel; (ii) In Nature's Realm, Op. 91; (i) Legends, Op. 59a; (ii) Othello, Op. 93; (iv) The Noon Witch, Op. 108; The Water Goblin, Op. 107; The Wild Dove, Op. 110; Symphonies: 7; 8; 9 (New World)

(BB) *** Warner 2564 61530-2 (5). (i) Rochester PO, Zinman; (ii) NYPO, Masur; (iii) Lausanne CO, Jordan; (iv) Concg. O, Harnoncourt

The collection here is not altogether predictable, with the *American* and *Czech Suites* especially welcome. With **Harnoncourt** conducting the last three symphonies (including a first-class account of the *New World*) and the four key symphonic poems, this is certainly excellent value, and the standard of recording is high.

(i) *American Suite, Op. 98b*; (ii) *Czech Suite, Op. 39; Nocturne for Strings in B, Op. 40; Polka for Prague Students in B flat, Op. 53a; Polonaise in E flat; Prague Waltzes*; (i) *Slavonic Dances 1–16, Op. 46/1–8, Op. 72/1–8*; (ii) *Slavonic Rhapsody 3, Op. 45*

(B) *** Double Decca (DDD/ADD) 460 293-2 (2). (i) RPO; (ii) Detroit SO; Dorati

Dvořák's *American Suite* has clear influences from the New World. **Dorati** has its measure and the **RPO** are very responsive. The Kingsway Hall recording balance suits the scoring rather well, but the *Slavonic Dances*, recorded at the same time (1983), are not so sweet here in the upper range of the strings, although otherwise the sound is full and pleasing. Dorati's performances have characteristic brio, the RPO response is warmly lyrical when necessary and the woodwind playing gives much pleasure. The *Czech Suite* can sometimes outstay its welcome, but certainly not here. The other items too have the brightness and freshness that mark out the *Slavonic Dances*, especially the *Polka* and *Polonaise* with their attractive rhythmic spring. The most charming piece of all is the set of *Waltzes*, written for balls in Prague – Viennese music with a Czech accent – while the lovely *Nocturne* with its subtle drone bass makes a winning interlude. The *Slavonic Rhapsody*, with its opening suggesting a troubadour and his harp, makes a vivacious end to what the documentation rightly describes as 'two-and-a-half hours of Dvořák's most tuneful orchestral music'.

(i) *American Suite, Op. 98b*; (ii) *Czech Suite, Op. 39; Overtures*: (i) *Carnival, Op. 92*; (ii) *In Nature's Realm, Op. 91; My Home, Op. 62; Otello, Op. 93*; (i) *Scherzo capriccioso, Op. 66; The Wild Dove (symphonic poem), Op. 110*

🔑 (BB) *** Virgin 2x1 3 49943-2 (2). (i) RLPO, or (ii) Czech PO; Pešek

The **Czech Philharmonic** always have something individual to say in Dvořák's music, and their playing here, especially in the lyrically jubilant *My Home Overture*, and the five folk-influenced pastoral movements of the *Czech Suite*, is very appealing.

It must remembered that **Pešek** was also for a decade Musical Director of the **Royal Liverpool Philharmonic Orchestra**, and he left an idiomatic Czech character on their woodwind playing which one can hear in the central movements of the *American Suite*, and a certain rhythmic freshness that is very obvious in the *Carnival Overture*, with its dazzling close, and again in the sparkling *Scherzo capriccioso*, in which he observes the central repeat. Excellent recording throughout makes this a very attractive collection.

American Suite; 7 Interludes for Small Orchestra; (i) *Mazurka for Violin & Orchestra. Nocturne in B; Polka in B flat; Polonaise in E flat; 5 Prague Waltzes*; (ii) *Rondo for Cello & Orchestra; Silent Woods for Cello & Orchestra*

(BB) *** Naxos 8.557352. (i) Trostianski; (ii) Yablonsky; Russia PO, Yablonsky

This is a tidying-up compilation, offering just short of 80 minutes of lesser-known Dvořák. The highlight is the *American Suite*. The *Seven Interludes* were written much earlier, in 1867: they are agreeable enough, but very slight. The *Mazurka* (1879) for violin and orchestra has something of the flavour of the *Slavonic Dances*. The dance movements are jolly and infectious, the *Polonaise* suitably boisterous. The performances here are all of good quality, as is the recording, and with good documentation the disc earns its three stars for enterprise as well as enjoyment.

Cello Concerto in B min., Op. 104 (CD versions)

🔑 ✿ (M) **** DG (ADD) 447 413-2. Rostropovich, BPO, Karajan – TCHAIKOVSKY: *Rococo Variations* **** ✿

🔑 (N) *** Virgin 50999 510 035 2 7. Gautier Capuçon, Frankfurt RSO, Paavo Järvi – HERBERT: *Cello Concerto 2* ***

*** BBC (ADD) BBCL 4156-2. Du Pré, RLPO, Groves – IBERT: *Cello and Wind Concerto* ***

*** Chan. 8662. Wallfisch, LSO, Mackerras – DOHNANYI: *Konzertstück* ***

(M) *** RCA **SACD** 82876 66375-2. Piatigorsky, Boston SO, Munch – WALTON: *Concerto* ***

*** Teldec 8573-85340-2. Du Pré, Swedish RSO, Celibidache – SAINT-SAËNS: *Cello Concerto 1* ***

The intensity of lyrical feeling and the spontaneity of the partnership between **Karajan** and **Rostropovich** ensures the position of their DG disc at the top of the list of recommendations for this peer among 19th-century cello concertos. The orchestral playing is glorious. Moreover, the analogue recording, made in the Jesus-Christus-Kirche in September 1969, is as near perfect as any made in that vintage analogue era, and the CD transfer has freshened the original.

This coupling of the Dvořák *Cello Concerto* with the second and finer of Victor Herbert's *Cello Concertos* is specially apt when it prompted Dvořák to write his masterpiece in America. **Gautier Capuçon** gives a distinctive, characterful and intense performance, well supported by **Paavo Järvi** and the **Frankfurt Orchestra** – the fruity-toned Frankfurt horn gives a beautiful account of the great second subject. It is Capuçon's gift to play with warm intensity while keeping a relatively steady pulse. As in the Herbert the slow movement is deeply elegiac, while the incisive finale leads to a dedicated account of the beautiful epilogue. Altogether a version of this much-recorded work which stands comparison with any in the catalogue, made the more attractive by the coupling.

On the BBC Legends label comes a live broadcast recording, made in July 1969 at the Proms, which thrillingly captures **Jacqueline du Pré's** astonishing range of expression and tone-colour in this masterpiece, with **Charles Groves** warmly supportive. There are some magical things and a liberal use of portamento. This may have fallen out of fashion now, but hers is a big-hearted reading, full of passion and sensitivity; her natural freedom sounds totally spontaneous and persuasive, bringing out a poignancy in the work to tug at the heart. The lightweight Ibert *Concerto*, recorded in 1962, with the cello the first among many soloists, makes a welcome coupling, a work that du Pré never otherwise recorded.

Rafael Wallfisch's is also an outstanding version, strong and warmly sympathetic, masterfully played. The excitement as well as the warmth of the piece comes over as in a live performance, and Wallfisch's tone remains rich and firm in even the most taxing passages. The orchestral playing, the quality of sound and the delightful, generous and unusual coupling all make it a recommendation which must be given the strongest advocacy.

Piatigorsky's superb (1960) recording is praised below in its normal CD coupling with the *Eighth Symphony*. But in the new SACD transfer, the orchestral sound is transformed, richer and fuller in colour, worthy of the composer's vivid scoring. Of course the balance of the cello remains too forward, but in all other respects the recording is greatly improved, and the coupling with Walton is most welcome.

Jacqueline du Pré's Swedish Radio recording brings excellent sound, even better than on her EMI studio recording made in Chicago two years later. Her reading here is even more warmly spontaneous than the later one. Evidently, du Pré did not just tolerate the typical exaggerations of a **Celibidache** reading, but responded positively to them.

Casals plays with astonishing fire and the performance seems to spring to life in a way that eludes many modern artists. This performance is one of the classics of the gramophone. There is not a great deal to choose between Mark Obert-Thorn's transfer of the Dvořák and the EMI version – both have been done with great care – though if pressed to a choice, we would prefer the slightly more detailed Naxos. (8.110930)

Jacqueline du Pré's celebrated early recording with **Barenboim** conveys the spontaneous passion that marked her playing in public, and it is a performance that captures very vividly the urgent interpretative flair of both husband and wife, conductor and soloist. Though the exaggeratedly forward balance of the cello remains very noticeable, in the new transfer the sound has filled out nicely and is clearly detailed. The recoupling with Elgar is also sensible. (EMI 5 55527-2)

(i) *Cello Concerto;* (ii) *Piano Concerto, Op. 33*

𝄞 Ⓜ (***) Sup. mono SU 3825-2. (i) Rostropovich; (ii) Maxián; Czech PO, Talich

Rostropovich has recorded the Dvořák concerto seven times in all, but he professed his 1952 collaboration with **Václav Talich** to be the finest – and despite the mono sound he is probably right. No one plays the concerto better than he and no one conducted Dvořák better than the great Czech conductor. **František Maxián** was a pupil of Vilém Kurz, whose version of the piano part he plays. Despite its age, the 1951 recording has always sounded fresh, even in its LP form, and the digital remastering enhances it further. Self-recommending.

(i) *Cello Concerto, Op. 104; Symphonic Variations, Op. 78*

*** Channel Classics CCSSA 25807. Budapest Festival O, I. Fischer, (i) with Pieter Wispelwey.

Channel Classics here offers an outstanding version of the much-recorded Dvořák *Cello Concerto*, one to rival any version already in the catalogue, very well and imaginatively coupled with the much earlier *Symphonic Variations*. The outstanding Dutch cellist **Pieter Wispelwey** crowns the previous discs he has made for the label in this electrifying live recording, brilliantly accompanied by the **Budapest Festival Orchestra** under **Ivan Fischer**. In the *Symphonic Variations* Fischer holds the structure cleanly together, crisply defining each of the 27 brief variations and the fugal finale. One marvels afresh at the composer's inventiveness in elaborating on the simple theme, on a par with that of the *Slavonic Dances*, and the performance is crowned with a thrilling climax in the finale. Altogether an outstanding new version of an imaginative Dvořák coupling.

(i) *Cello Concerto;* (ii) *Symphony 8 in G, Op. 88*

Ⓜ **(*) RCA (ADD) 82876 55302-2. Boston SO, Munch, (i) with Piatigorsky

Piatigorsky's classic 1960 account of the *Cello Concerto* emerges again on RCA's Red Seal label – remastered and sounding better than ever – though that cannot alter a balance which places the cello too close, not always flattering to the soloist. There is no lack of orchestral colour and the acoustic of Symphony Hall is well conveyed behind the music-making. The performance is the very opposite of routine, with Piatigorsky and **Munch** in complete rapport, producing a totally spontaneous melodic flow. Although there are moments when intonation is less than immaculate, the inspiration of the performance carries the day. The *Symphony* was recorded a year later but sounds better than in earlier transfers. Munch's reading is strongly characterized and, though he occasionally presses hard, the thrust comes from a natural ardour. In short, a fresh, individual account and a desirable coupling.

(i) *Cello Concerto;* (ii) *Symphony 9 (New World)*

𝄞 ⒷⒷ *** Warner Apex (ADD) 0927 49919-2. (i) Hoelscher, Hamburg PO, Keilberth; (ii) NW German Philharmonie, Lindenberg

Ludwig Hoelscher has a really big, resonant tone and a big, heroic sense of style to go with it. With Hoelscher one has a sense of real striving, and that is just how it should be. The 1958 recording, full and warm and vivid, is astonishingly good. If the balance favours the soloist unduly, the tone he gives us is so glorious that one finds it hard to carp over such a matter. **Lindenberg's** account of the *New World Symphony* is not quite on this level, but it is a direct, persuasively simple reading, again with a beautifully played slow movement. Again, good sound (from 1969). This is a bargain disc to seek out, even if duplication is involved.

(i) *Cello Concerto;* (ii) *Piano Trio 4 (Dumky)*

*** HMC 90 1867. Queyras; (i) Prague Philh., Bělohlávek; (ii) Faust, Melnikov

The linking of the *Cello Concerto* and the *Dumky Trio* is particularly apt when the cello plays such a salient role in the *Trio*. The young cellist **Jean-Guihen Queyras** takes up that positive role with power and deep expressiveness from his very first solo, just as he does in the *Concerto*. These may not be Czech artists, but their feeling for the idiom is unerringly magnetic. So far from the *Piano Trio* falling short in any way after the mastery of the *Concerto*, it emerges as a work of comparable stature, benefiting greatly from refined digital sound. In the *Cello Concerto* **Jiří Bělohlávek** and the **Prague Philharmonia** prove incisive and warmly sympathetic accompanists, matching the youthful urgency of Queyras's solo performance.

Piano Concerto in G min., Op. 33

⊶ (M) *** EMI (ADD) 5 66895-2. Richter, Bav. State O, C. Kleiber – SCHUBERT: *Wanderer Fantasia* ***

(i) *Piano Concerto;* (ii) *Violin Concerto*

*** Chan. 10309. (i) Hayroudinoff; (ii) Ehnes; BBC PO, Noseda

Richter plays the solo part in its original form (and not the more pianistically 'effective' revision by Wilém Kurz which is published in the Complete Edition), and his judgement is triumphantly vindicated. This is the most persuasive and masterly account of the work ever committed to disc; its ideas emerge with an engaging freshness and warmth, while the greater simplicity of Dvořák's own keyboard writing proves in Richter's hands to be more telling and profound. **Carlos Kleiber** secures excellent results from the **Bavarian Orchestra**, and the 1977 recording has clarity and good definition to recommend it.

The Canadian violinist, **James Ehnes**, gives a strong, incisive performance of the *Violin Concerto*, with speeds on the fast side in the first two movements and the *furiant* finale bitingly fresh. His rapid vibrato gives a distinctive timbre to his playing, making the slow movement less warmly romantic than it often is, and the recording, generally well balanced, is yet less full and warm than in the *Piano Concerto*. That receives a superb performance from the Russian, **Rustem Hayroudinoff**, one which stands the closest comparison with the classic version by Sviatoslav Richter. Even more than Richter, Hayroudinoff brings out the joyful, carefree quality of Dvořák's inspiration, bringing home what a wonderful fund of good melodies it contains. The clarity of his articulation in the often tricky passagework is phenomenal. Helped by full, rich sound which yet allows fine detail, **Noseda** and the **BBC Philharmonic** match the subtlety and point of the soloist's playing, establishing this as an outstanding modern version.

(i) *Piano Concerto;* (ii) *Violin Concerto;* (iii) *Silent Woods* (for cello & orchestra)

(B) *** Virgin 3 91346-2. (i) Désert, Strasbourg SO, Guschlbauer; (ii) Tetzlaff, Czech PO, Pešek; (iii) Walden, RLPO, Pešek

Tetzlaff's performance of the *Violin Concerto*, distinguished by quicksilver lightness in the passagework, is both full of fantasy and marked by keen concentration and a sense of

spontaneity. With the violin balanced naturally, not spotlit, the slow movement has a hushed intensity at the opening, which gives extra poignancy to Tetzlaff's tender, totally unsentimental phrasing. In romantic freedom of expression **Pešek** makes orchestral textures clear, bringing out extra detail even in the heaviest tuttis, despite reverberant recording.

Claire Désert's account of the *Piano Concerto* is hardly less telling, bold and vibrant in the first movement, but with the secondary theme pointed with much charm. **Guschlbauer** provides a strong backing and is an equally sympathetic partner in the lovely *Andante*, where Désert plays with much poetic feeling to provide a perfect foil for sparkling articulation in the zestful furiant finale with its exciting barnstorming close. First-class recording gives the piano a realistically scaled profile in relation to the orchestra. Then, for a bonus, **Timothy Walden** and Pešek provide the warmly atmospheric *Silent Woods* as a touching encore.

(i) *Piano Concerto in G min.* *Symphony 8 in G* (DVD versions)

(N) *** Arthaus Musik **DVD** 102 139. Prague SO, Altrichter with (i) Ardašev

Violin Concerto in A min., Op. 53; (ii) *Biblical Songs, Op. 99;* (iii) *Te Deum, Op. 103* (DVD versions)

(N) *** Arthaus Musik **DVD** 102 137. Prague SO, Jírí Belohlávek with (i) Zenaty; (ii) Eva Randová; (iii) Livia Aghova, Ivan Kusnjer; Prague Ph. Ch.

These performances took place at a Dvořák Festival at the Alte Oper in Frankfurt in 1993 and were recorded for BBC TV and Unitel. The camerawork is directed by Rodney Goldberg, a guarantee of good musical judgment and visual discretion. Indeed it is hard to imagine them being bettered visually and the performances, too, are refreshingly idiomatic with good orchestral playing from the **Prague Symphony Orchestra**. **Ivan Zenaty** is a superb soloist in the *Violin Concerto* as indeed is **Igor Ardašev** in the more problematic *Piano Concerto*, and we have no quarrel with **Petr Altrichter's** reading of the *G major Symphony*.

(i) *Piano Concerto in G min., Op. 33; The Golden Spinning Wheel*

⊶ (M) *** Warner 8573 87630-2. (i) Aimard; Concg. O, Harnoncourt

Harnoncourt has consistently proved himself an understanding conductor of Dvořák, and here he directs an outstandingly imaginative account of the *Piano Concerto* (using the original score) in partnership with the scintillating pianism of **Pierre-Laurent Aimard**. *The Golden Spinning Wheel* with its opening horn fanfares, the most enticing of the composer's symphonic poems, makes an attractive coupling.

(i) *Piano Concerto, Op. 33; The Water Goblin (symphonic poem), Op. 107*

(BB) *** Naxos 8.550896. (i) Jandó; Polish Nat. RSO, Wit

An infectiously fresh and warmly lyrical account from **Jandó** and the highly supportive **Polish National Radio Orchestra** under **Antoni Wit**. Jandó conveys his own pleasure, and Wit's accompaniment glows with colour; he then offers a splendidly vibrant and colourful portrayal of *The Water Goblin*, one of the composer's most vividly melodramatic symphonic poems. The violins are a shade overbright but otherwise the sound is excellent. Very enjoyable and well worth its modest cost.

Violin Concerto in A min., Op. 53

🎵— Ⓜ *** Warner Elatus 2564 60806-2. Vengerov, NYPO, Masur – BRAHMS: *Violin Concerto* **(*)

🎵— Ⓑ *** CfP 575 8062. Little, RLPO, Handley – SIBELIUS: *Concerto 1* ***

🎵— Ⓜ *** DG (IMS) 449 091-2. Mintz, BPO, Levine – BRUCH: *Concerto 1* ***

(i) Violin Concerto; Romance in F min., Op. 11; (ii) Sonatina in G, Op. 100; 4 Romantic Pieces, Op. 75

Ⓜ **(*) EMI 5 62595-2. Perlman; (i) LPO, Barenboim; (ii) Sanders

Maxim Vengerov performs not only with the effortless brilliance and dazzling technical command that one expects but with poetic feeling, freshness and spontaneity. He receives splendid support from **Kurt Masur** and the **New York Philharmonic** (they are recorded at a concert performance) and the balance between the soloist and orchestra is judged expertly. However, there are some reservations about the Brahms coupling.

Tasmin Little brings to this concerto an open freshness and sweetness, very apt for this composer, that are extremely winning. She establishes her place firmly with full-ranging, well-balanced sound that coordinates the soloist along with the orchestra.

There is dazzling playing from **Shlomo Mintz**, whose virtuosity is effortless and his intonation astonishingly true. There is good rapport between soloist and conductor, and the performance has the sense of joy and relaxation that this radiant score needs. The digital sound is warm and natural in its upper range.

The **Perlman** and **Barenboim** partnership is at its peak in the both the *Concerto* and the delectable *Romance*, and this coupling remains very competitive, the more so in that this reissue in the 'Perlman Edition' is at mid-price, and now offers the double bonus of the enchanting *Sonatina* plus the hardly less attractive set of *Four Romantic Pieces*. Both are beautifully played and well recorded, save for the imbalance between the celebrated violinist and the more recessed pianist.

(i) Violin Concerto; (ii) Piano Quintet, Op. 81

🎵— Ⓜ *** EMI 503415-2. Chang, with (i) LSO, C. Davis; (ii) Kerr, Christ, Faust, Andsnes

It makes a very attractive and unusual disc to have the brilliant young violinist, **Sarah Chang**, coupling her warm and powerful account of the Dvořák *Violin Concerto* not with another concerto but with one of the composer's most popular chamber works, with the pianist **Leif-Ove Andsnes** sharing the leadership of the group in equally inspired playing in the *Piano Quintet*. As though making music for fun, they are freely spontaneous-sounding in their expressiveness, with the *Dumka* slow movement seemingly improvisatory, and the Scherzo very light, taken at a challengingly fast tempo. The performance of the *Concerto*, with **Sir Colin Davis** a powerful and understanding Dvořákian, similarly draws freely expressive playing from Chang. The recording, made at the Watford Colosseum, enhances the feeling of a big-scale performance, with full-bodied sound set in a lively acoustic.

(i) Violin Concerto; (ii) Violin Sonata; Sonatina for Violin & Piano

🎵— Ⓝ **** Sony 88697 499632. Liebeck with (i) RSNO, Walker (ii) Apekisheva

This neatly gathers together Dvořák's three principle works for violin solo. **Liebeck**, a Londoner trained at the RAM, has an easy, warm and fluent style, well-displayed in this debut concerto record for Sony. His expressiveness never runs into self-indulgence, remaining spontaneous-sounding. **Garry Walker** and the **RSNO** make the idiosyncratic structure of the *Concerto* very clear, leading on to the delightful Slavonic dance of the finale. The *Sonata* has many of the same qualities, but it is the *Sonatina*, product of the composer's later period when he was influenced by American music which brings the most attractive music of all, a masterpiece that has rarely been appreciated as it deserves.

Czech Suite; A Hero's Song, Op. 111; Festival March, Op. 54; Hussite Overture, Op. 67

ⒷⒷ **(*) Naxos 8.553005. Polish Nat. RSO (Katowice), Wit

Antoni Wit is most impressive in *A Hero's Song*. There is an outburst of patriotic hyperbole towards the close (with thundering trombones), but Wit generates excitement without letting things get out of hand. The performance of the *Czech Suite* is warm and relaxed, nicely rustic in feeling, but again is affected by the resonance.

Czech Suite; Polonaise in E flat; 8 Prague Waltzes

*** Sup. SU 3867-2. Prague Philh., Hrusa

Exploiting the Czech idiom, on the whole these are gentle, easy-going pieces, notably the *Czech Suite*. The *Polonaise* opens brassily, with splendid panache, introducing a strongly rhythmic piece, full of vigour. The *Eight Waltzes* then prove amazingly varied, with no sense that waltz-time is outstaying its welcome. All the performances are excellent, with **Jakub Hrusa**, still in his mid-twenties, drawing colourful and alert playing from the **Prague Philharmonia**. First-rate sound.

Overtures: Carnival; Hussite; In Nature's Realm; My Home; Othello. Symphonic Poems: The Golden Spinning Wheel; The Noonday Witch; The Wood Dove; Symphonic Variations, Op. 78; Slavonic Dances 1–16, Op. 46/1–8; Op. 72/1–8

🎵— Ⓑ *** DG Trio (ADD) 469 366-2 (3). Bav. RSO, Kubelik

Kubelik has a special feeling for Dvořák, and these performances are among his finest on record and they are superbly played, with the *Slavonic Dances* displaying both virtuosity and panache. He is also splendidly dashing in *Carnival*; and the other two overtures, Opp. 91 and 93 – all three linked by a recurring main theme – are comparably successful and full of colouristic subtlety.

Overture: *The Cunning Peasant*

(M)(**) Sup. mono SU 1914 011. Czech PO, Sejna – SKROUP: *The Tinker Overture*; SMETANA: *Festive Symphony, etc.* (***)

Overture: *My Home.* Symphonic Poems: *The Golden Spinning Wheel; A Hero's Song, Op. 111; The Noonday Witch; The Water Goblin; The Wood Dove, Op. 110*

(B) **(*) Chan. 2-for-1 241-3 (2). RSNO, Järvi

Many will be attracted to **Neeme Järvi's** collection by the modern, digital sound, warmly atmospheric in typical Chandos style, not always clean on detail but firmly focused. These recordings were all fill-ups for Järvi's integral set of the symphonies. The real rarity here is *A Hero's Song*, Dvořák's very last orchestral work. Järvi's strongly committed, red-blooded performance minimizes any weaknesses. *My Home* is given an exuberant performance, bringing out the lilt of the dance rhythms, and Järvi is a dramatic advocate of *The Water Goblin*. He also brings out the storytelling vividly in *The Noonday Witch*, while the most memorable of all the symphonic poems, *The Golden Spinning Wheel*, has plenty of drama and atmosphere, helped by the fine bloom of the recording. The only snag here is the relative short measure.

The Cunning Peasant is not one of Dvořák's greatest overtures, though **Karel Sejna** makes the most positive case for it in his mono recording. Acceptable sound and a useful fill-up to Smetana's exhilarating *Festive Symphony*.

The Golden Spinning Wheel; The Noonday Witch; The Water Goblin; The Wild Dove

⊶ 🏵 (M) **** Teldec 2-CD 2564 60221-2 (2). Concg. O, Harnoncourt

(M)(***) Sup. mono SU 3827-2. Czech PO, Talich

Harnoncourt's collection of Dvořák's four most vivid symphonic poems is one of his finest pairs of records and one of Teldec's most realistic recordings. The performances offer superlative playing from the **Concertgebouw Orchestra**, and Harnoncourt's direction is inspired, lyrical and dramatic by turns, ever relishing Dvořák's glowing scoring for woodwinds and, in the famous *Spinning Wheel*, the horns and, towards the close, a gloriously sonorous passage for the trombones. The end of *The Water Goblin* is superbly melodramatic and *The Golden Spinning Wheel* is unsurpassed on record, even by Beecham. The recording and ambience are so believable that one feels one has the famous Dutch concert hall just beyond the speakers.

Talich's famous mono set comes from 1950. The performances have great electricity and excitement and a uniquely idiomatic Czech feeling. The sound is fully accept-able, although the dynamic range is limited, and because Talich uses the traditional cuts in *The Golden Spinning Wheel* Supraphon have managed to fit them all on to a single disc.

The Golden Spinning Wheel, Op. 109; The Noonday Witch, Op. 108; The Wood Dove, Op. 110

(BB) *** Naxos 8.550598. Polish Nat. RSO (Katowice), Gunzenhauser

The **Polish Orchestra** seem thoroughly at home in Dvořák's sound-world and **Gunzenhauser** gives warm, vivid performances and is especially evocative in the masterly *Golden Spinning Wheel*. There is shapely string phrasing and a fine, sonorous contribution from the brass. The concert hall of Polish Radio in Katowice has expansive acoustics – just right for the composer's colourful effects.

Serenade for Strings; Serenade for Wind in D min.

(N) *** Sup. SU3932-2. Prague Philharmonia, Hrusa – SUK: *Meditation on an Old Czech Hymn*

*** Ph. (ADD) 400 020-2. ASMF, Marriner

Marriner's Philips performances are direct without loss of warmth, with speeds ideally chosen, refined yet spontaneous-sounding; in the *Wind Serenade* the **Academy** produce beautifully sprung rhythms, and the recording has a fine sense of immediacy.

Fine playing from the **Capella Istropolitana** on Naxos, and flexible direction from **Jaroslav Krček**. His pacing is not quite as sure as in the delightful Suk coupling, and the *Adagio* could flow with a stronger current, but this is still an enjoyable and well-recorded performance. (8.550419)

Jakub Hrusa conducts outstanding performances of the two Dvořák *Serenades*, for strings and wind respectively, coupled with a rarity by Josef Suk. The *String Serenade* is easily lyrical, the *Larghetto* slow movement brings the most refined string playing at the most hushed *pianissimos* with idiomatic dynamic shading. The finale is then a Slavonic dance with exciting cross-rhythms until the first movement is momentarily recalled, tender and nostalgic. The *Wind Serenade* brings clean separation of voices and crisp rhythms, while the *Menuetto* second movement is quite different from the equivalent movement in the *String Serenade*, with a dashing furiant as its middle section. The third movement marked *Andante* is warmly moulded with dynamic shading exceptionally subtle, while the finale is a rousing piece with a look back at the first movement and glorious whoops on the horns in the coda. Hrusa in all this demonstrates his ability to draw the most idiomatic playing from his brilliant band.

Serenade for Wind in D min., Op. 44 (DVD version)

⊶ *** Arthaus DVD 100 725. Members of BPO Wind (V/D: Klaus Lindemann) – BEETHOVEN: *Octet in E flat, Op. 103* ***

The blending of the **Berlin Philharmonic Wind** is richly urbane, but this does not mean their performance of Dvořák's delightful *Serenade* is in any way lacking in vitality and spirit; indeed, the *Allegro molto* finale is irresistibly zestful, bubbling over with bravura. The Beethoven *Wind Octet* is rightly treated in a more robust fashion, presented with the freshness of a masterpiece. The ensemble is recorded within the Jaspissaal of the Neue Kammern (new chambers) of the summer palace of Frederick the Great in Potsdam-Sanssouci, which is a visual delight and has a superb acoustic for a wind ensemble: the sound is in every way first class. The camera follows individual players and the whole ensemble in alternation and is usually just where you would want it to be.

Serenade for Wind in D min., Op. 44 (CD versions)

(M) *** CRD (ADD) CRD 3410. Nash Ens. – KROMMER: *Octet-Partitas* ***

(BB) *** Naxos 8.554173. Oslo PO Wind Soloists – ENESCU: *Dixtuor*; JANÁČEK: *Mládí* ***

(**(*)) Testament mono SBT 1180. L. Bar. Ens., Haas –
MOZART: *Serenades 11 & 12* (**(*))

The **Nash Ensemble** can hold their own with the competition in the *D minor Serenade*, and their special claim tends to be the coupling, a Krommer rarity that is well worth hearing. The CRD version of the Dvořák is very well recorded and the playing is very fine indeed, robust yet sensitive to colour, and admirably spirited.

The **Oslo Wind Soloists** on Naxos give us a genuine bargain. Here is a performance of real quality that can stand alongside the finest on offer. Crisp rhythms predominate, and a good sense of line and tonal finesse. These artists recorded this repertoire on the Victoria label in the early 1990s under a conductor. These are different and better accounts in every way. No need to hesitate.

Karl Haas's preference for fast speeds and metrical rhythms is well illustrated in this reading of Dvořák's *Wind Serenade*, in which the opening march has more of a military flavour than usual. As a generous supplement to Mozart's two great serenades for wind octet, this makes an ideal coupling of three of the greatest of all wind works, performed by an ensemble that included some of the finest British players of the post-war period, including **Dennis Brain**, **Frederick Thurston** and **Terence Macdonagh**. Vivid, immediate sound, well transferred.

Slavonic Dances 1–16, Op. 46/1–8; Op. 72/1–8

(&) **** Teldec 8573 81038-2. COE, Harnoncourt

(&) (BB) *** Sony 69699894523. Cleveland O, Szell

(M) *** DG (ADD) 457 712-2. Bav. RSO, Kubelik

Slavonic Dances, Op. 46 & 72; Carnival Overture

(N) (BB) (***) Naxos mono 8.111331. Czech PO, Talich

Harnoncourt's excitingly uninhibited new set of the *Slavonic Dances*, with the **Chamber Orchestra of Europe**, combines great exuberance and virtuosity with vivid colouring. Harnoncourt's direction has tremendous zest and vitality.

In **Szell's** exuberant, elegant and marvellously played set of the *Slavonic Dances* the balance is close (which means *pianissimos* fail to register) but the charisma of the playing is unforgettable and, for all the racy exuberance, one senses a

predominant feeling of affection and elegance. The warm acoustics of Severance Hall ensure the consistency of the orchestral sound.

Kubelik's set, now issued as one of DG's 'Originals', offers polished, sparkling orchestral playing. The sound has greater refinement and a rather wider range of dynamic than the competing Sony disc and for that reason many will choose it in preference to Szell, for Kubelik has a very special feeling for Dvořák, and the playing of the **Bavarian Orchestra** brings a thrilling virtuosity and a special panache of its own.

Legendary performance from EMI Abbey Road sessions dating from 1935 from the master of Czech music, **Václav Talich**. These performances have marvellous authority and freshness which cuts through the limited sound. The *portamento* in the *Carnival* overture is not only charming, it sounds absolutely right, whilst the vigour of the playing is exhilarating. Excellent notes by Tully Potter.

Slavonic Dances 1–8 & 15, Op. 46/1–8; Op. 72/7

(B) *** Decca Eloquence (ADD) 476 2742. LSO, Martinon –
MASSENET: *Le Cid*; MEYERBEER: *Les Patineurs* *** ●

An exuberantly vivacious collection of the *Slavonic Dances*, with **Martinon** adding a touch of Gallic wit to make these performances unique in every way. Full, warm sound from 1959, making this a fine bonus to the outstanding Massenet/Meyerbeer coupling.

(i) Slavonic Dances 1, 3 & 8, Op. 46/1, 3 & 8; 9–10, Op. 72/1–2; (ii) Symphonic Variations, Op. 78

(M) *** Decca (ADD) 475 7730. (i) Israel PO; (ii) LSO; Kertész –
SMETANA: *Bartered Bride Overture & Suite*; *Vltava* ***

Kertész's *Slavonic Dances* from the 1960s are here reissued for Decca's series of Originals, with the *Symphonic Variations* added for good measure. The **Israel Orchestra** is not one of the world's finest, but here the playing is irresistible in its gaiety and vivacious colouring. The *furiants* go with the wind, but Kertész maintains the underlying lyricism of the music. The recording is marginally over-reverberant and may need a slight treble control, but it is otherwise excellent. The comparatively unfamiliar *Symphonic Variations* makes a highly desirable bonus, with playing and recording well up to the standard the **LSO** consistently achieved in their Dvořák series.

(i) 3 Slavonic Rhapsodies, Op. 45; (ii) Rhapsody in A min., Op. 14

(&) (BB) *** Naxos 8.550610. Slovak PO, (i) Košler; (ii) Pešek

Dvořák's three *Slavonic Rhapsodies* of 1878 are much more like symphonic poems without a programme and, while overflowing with characteristic ideas and colourful scoring, they are also loosely constructed and melodramatic. But it is the earlier *Rhapsody in A minor* that is the most ambitious work here. **Libor Pešek's** performance is splendid, with a vigorous response from the orchestra, who even bring off the bombastic, patriotic coda. This is every bit as enjoyable as the Op. 45 *Rhapsodies*, although it is not as sophisticated as No. 3. This Naxos collection would be recommendable even if it cost far more.

Suite in A, Op. 98b

Ⓜ (***) Sup. mono SU 1924-2 001. Czech PO, Sejna – MARTINŮ: *Concerto for Double String Orchestra*, etc. (***)

A lovely performance of the beautiful *A major Suite*, recorded in mono in 1956; but the real attraction on this disc is the Martinů pieces – especially the *Third Symphony* – which are very special.

Symphonic Variations

*** Australian Decca Eloquence (ADD) 467 608-2. LSO, Kertész – BRAHMS: *Haydn Variations* ***

Kertész's account of the underrated *Symphonic Variations* is outstanding, with the conductor bringing out all the Brahmsian overtones as well as the Czech composer's freshness of spirit. The 1970s recording remains vivid and full, and with two excellent couplings this is certainly a desirable CD.

SYMPHONIES

Symphonies 1–9

🎵 Ⓜ *** Chan. 9991 (6). SNO, Järvi

Ⓑ *** Sup. SU 3802-2 (6). Prague RSO, Vladimir Valek

Symphonies 1–9; Overtures: Carnival; In Nature's Realm; My Home. Scherzo capriccioso

🎵 ✿ Ⓑ *** Decca (ADD) 430 046-2 (6). LSO, Kertész

Symphonies 1–9; Overture: Carnival. Scherzo capriccioso; The Wood Dove

Ⓑ **(*) DG 463 158-2 (6). BPO, Kubelik

Now reissued at mid-price, Järvi's Chandos set makes a good choice for those wanting first-class digital recordings of these symphonies, the sound full and naturally balanced. There are no fillers, as with Kertész on Decca (and there would have been room for some on the first, second and sixth CDs), but each symphony can now be heard without a break, and Järvi is a consistently persuasive Dvořákian.

In the bargain range, the Supraphon box is very welcome when, with refined, finely detailed recording, it makes a formidable rival to the long-established Kertész, LSO set on Decca. Valek's preference is for brisk speeds which yet allow ample lift to Czech dance-rhythms. Helped by clean, well-balanced recording, this goes with admirably clear textures, even in the heaviest tuttis. Throughout all these performances, there is a natural, idiomatic feeling of players tackling works they already know well, even in the rarer early symphonies. The only seriously questionable tempo is in the first movement of No. 6, which is on the slow side, but there an initial heaviness quickly evaporates when the playing is so crisp and well sprung. Nos. 5 and 7 gain in many ways from having been recorded live in the Rudolfinum in Prague, but there is no lack of tension in

any of these performances, whether recorded live or in the studio.

For those not wanting to go to the expense of the digital Chandos/Järvi set, **István Kertész's** bargain box is a strong recommendation among the remaining collections of Dvořák symphonies. The CD transfers are of Decca's best quality, full-bodied and vivid, with a fine ambient effect. It was Kertész who first revealed the full potential of the early symphonies, and his readings gave us fresh insights into these often inspired works. To fit the symphonies and orchestral works on to six CDs, some mid-work breaks have proved unavoidable; but the set remains a magnificent memorial to a conductor who died sadly young.

Kubelik's set from the late 1960s and early 1970s has much to recommend it, first and foremost being the glorious playing of the **Berlin Philharmonic** and the natural idiomatic warmth Kubelik brings to his music-making. He seems less convinced by the earlier symphonies, and in No. 3 there is an element of routine, something which does not happen with Kertész on Decca. In spite of some idiosyncratic touches, however, Kubelik achieves glowing performances of Nos. 6–9, and especially No. 7; in No. 8 he is also more compelling than his Decca competitor. The remastered DG sound is impressively wide-ranging and is especially fine in the last (and greatest) three symphonies. Many will also be glad to have his memorable account of *The Wood Dove*.

Symphony 1; A Hero's Song, Op. 111

*** Chan. 8597. SNO, Järvi

Symphony 1; Legends, Op. 59/1–5

ⒷⒷ *** Naxos 8.550266. Slovak PO or Slovak RSO, Gunzenhauser

The first of Dvořák's nine symphonies is on the long-winded side. Yet whatever its structural weaknesses, it is full of colourful and memorable ideas, often characteristic of the mature composer. **Järvi** directs a warm, often impetuous performance, with rhythms invigoratingly sprung in the fast movements and with the slow movement more persuasive than in previous recordings. The recording is warmly atmospheric in typical Chandos style.

Though on a super-bargain label, the competing Bratislava version rivals Järvi's Chandos disc both as a performance and in sound. The ensemble of the **Slovak Philharmonic** is rather crisper, and the recording, full and atmospheric, has detail less obscured by reverberation. The first five of Dvořák's ten *Legends* make a generous coupling: colourful miniatures, colourfully played.

Symphony 2 in B flat, Op. 4; Legends, Op. 59/6–10

ⒷⒷ *** Naxos 8.550267. Slovak PO or Slovak RSO, Gunzenhauser

Symphony 2; Slavonic Rhapsody 3 in A flat, Op. 45

**(*) Chan. 8589. SNO, Järvi

With speeds more expansive than those of Neeme Järvi, his Chandos rival, **Gunzenhauser** gives a taut, beautifully textured account, very well played and recorded, clearly preferable in every way, even making no allowance for price. The completion of the set of *Legends* makes a generous coupling (73 minutes).

Järvi's performance, characteristically warm and urgent, is let down by the reverberant Chandos sound, here missing the necessary sharpness of focus, so that the tangy Czech flavour of the music loses some of its bite. The *Slavonic Rhapsody* is done with delicious point and humour, with the sound back to Chandos's normal high standard.

Symphony 3 in E flat, Op. 10; Carnival Overture, Op. 92; Symphonic Variations, Op. 78

*** Chan. 8575. SNO, Järvi

Järvi's is a highly persuasive reading, not ideally sharp of rhythm in the first movement but totally sympathetic. The recording is well up to the standards of the house, and the fill-ups are particularly generous.

Symphonies 3; 6 in D, Op. 60

(BB) *** Naxos 8.550268. Slovak PO, Gunzenhauser

These exhilarating performances of the *Third* and *Sixth Symphonies* are well up to the standard of earlier records in this splendid Naxos series. **Gunzenhauser's** pacing is admirably judged through both works, and rhythms are always lifted. Excellent, vivid recording in the warm acoustics of the Bratislava Concert Hall.

Symphony 4 in D min., Op. 13; (i) Biblical Songs, Op. 99

*** Chan. 8608. SNO, Järvi, (i) with Rayner Cook

Järvi's affectionate reading of this early work brings out the Czech flavours in Dvořák's inspiration and makes light of the continuing Wagner influences, notably the echoes of *Tannhäuser* in the slow movement. This is a performance to win converts to an often underrated work. The recording is well up to the Chandos standard.

Symphonies 4–6; Overtures: Carnival; In Nature's Realm; Scherzo capriccioso

(B) *** Double Decca (ADD) 473 798-2 (2). LSO, Kertész

Kertész gives a good dramatic account of the *Fourth Symphony*, accepting the Wagner crib in the slow movement and making the most of the Scherzo. No. 5, with its pastoral atmosphere and further echoes of Wagner, is particularly successful and full of vitality. No. 6 clearly reflects the influence of Brahms, particularly of the *Second Symphony*, but Kertész's performance effectively underlines the individuality of the writing as well. Outstanding versions of the dashing *Carnival Overture*, an equally sparkling *Scherzo capriccioso* and the colourful *In Nature's Realm* make admirable bonuses.

Symphonies 4; 8 in G, Op. 33

(BB) **(*) Naxos 8.550269. Slovak PO, Gunzenhauser

Gunzenhauser's *Fourth* is very convincing. In his hands the fine lyrical theme of the first movement certainly blossoms, and the relative lack of weight in the orchestral textures brings distinct benefit in the Scherzo. The slow movement, too, is lyrical without too much Wagnerian emphasis. The naturally sympathetic orchestral playing helps to make the *Eighth* a refreshing experience, even though the first two movements are rather relaxed and without the impetus of the finest versions. The digital sound is excellent, vivid and full, with a natural concert-hall ambience.

Symphony 5 in F, Op. 76; The Water Goblin, Op. 107

*** Chan. 8552. SNO, Järvi

Järvi is most effective in moulding the structure, subtly varying tempo between sections to smooth over the often abrupt links. His persuasiveness in the slow movement, relaxed but never sentimental, brings radiant playing from the **SNO**, and Czech dance-rhythms are sprung most infectiously, leading to an exhilarating close to the whole work, simulating the excitement of a live performance.

Symphonies 5; 7 in D min., Op. 70

(BB) *** Naxos 8.550270. Slovak PO, Gunzenhauser

Gunzenhauser's coupling is recommendable even without the price advantage. The beguiling opening of the *Fifth*, with its engaging Slovak wind solos, has plenty of atmosphere, and the reading generates a natural lyrical impulse. The *Seventh*, spontaneous throughout, brings an eloquent *Poco adagio*, a lilting Scherzo and a finale that combines an expansive secondary theme with plenty of excitement and impetus.

Symphonies 5; 7–8; 9 (New World); Othello Overture; Scherzo capriccioso

⊕ (B) **(*) EMI 5 00878-2 (3). Oslo PO, Jansons –SMETANA: *Vltava* ***

Mariss Jansons's readings of Nos. 5, 7 and 8 are still among the finest in the catalogue. Indeed, No. 5 is the most delectable account of this radiant symphony and was given a 🌑 on first appearance. Nos. 7 and 8 are also key versions, both outstandingly fine, with the dramatic tensions of the D minor work bitingly conveyed, yet with detail treated affectionately and with rhythms exhilaratingly sprung. No. 8 is given a performance of high contrasts too, with the slow movement warmly expansive and the whole crowned by a winningly spontaneous-sounding account of the finale, rarely matched in its exuberance. Unfortunately, Jansons's direct view of the *New World Symphony* (the first of the series to be recorded) hardly matches the earlier works (or, indeed, its excellent Smetana *Vltava* coupling) in vigour, warmth and fantasy. It is rather undermined by the earlier recorded sound, which does not match its companions. However, this inexpensive reissue is well worth having for the other three symphonies alone, and also for the *Scherzo capriccioso*, which brings another exuberant performance while the superb *Othello Overture* makes an additional generous bonus.

Symphony No.6; Water Goblin, Op.107

Ⓝ *** Pentatone SACD PTC 5186 302. Netherlands PO,
Kreizberg

Symphony 6 in D, Op. 60; The Wood Dove, Op. 110

⊞ *** Chan. 9170. Czech PO, Bělohlávek

Bělohlávek conducts a glowing performance of No. 6, rich
in Brahmsian and Czech pastoral overtones, helped by satisfyingly full and immediate Chandos sound. This easily
takes precedence over the Järvi version (CHAN 8350). His
reading of the late symphonic poem is comparably warm
and idiomatic in a relaxed way.

Kreizberg's reading consistently brings out the fact that
not a bar could have been written by any other composer
but Dvořák. The Water Goblin makes an ideal coupling, the
first of the five graphic symphonic poems on folk stories
that Dvořák wrote when he returned from his three years in
America, and Kreizberg, helped by the engineers, brings out
the extra elaboration of the orchestration. As usual with
Pentatone issues the quality of sound is outstanding, depending on the engineering of technicians formerly with
Philips: there is fine separation and clarity which yet allows
for a warm overall ensemble.

The LSO Live disc of No. 6 is an admirable and infectiously spirited performance. Sir Colin Davis and his fine
players are wonderfully idiomatic and offer a performance
of exceptional clarity of detail. For the Scherzo, Davis adopts
a fastish tempo, and the snapping rhythms come out with
extra sharpness, leading to a light, delicate account of the
Trio section. In the finale he brings out the warmly
Brahmsian qualities. Not a first choice perhaps, but a stimulating one. (LSO Live 0059)

Symphonies 6; 8 in G, Op. 88

⊞ **** DG 469 046-2. VPO, Chung

The first movement of No. 6 surpasses in breadth and power
(and in the natural way in which it unfolds) almost anything
between the C major (Great) of Schubert and the Second of
Brahms, the shadows of both of which are clearly visible. It
is luminous and innocent, as is the Eighth, another glowing
and life-enhancing score, generously coupled here. Both
symphonies are served supremely well by Chung and the
Vienna Orchestra and the DG engineers.

Symphony 7 in D min., Op. 70; (i) Romance for Violin & Orchestra, Op. 11; Slavonic Dances, 9–16, Op. 72/1–8 (DVD versions)

⊞ **** Arthaus DVD 102135. (i) Zenaty; Prague SO,
Bělohlávek (Dir: Rodney Greenberg)

This is undoubtedly one of the key Dvořák recordings on
DVD. As we have commented below, Bělohlávek's natural
affinity with the composer means that his reading of the
Seventh Symphony is outstanding in every way and the Prague
Orchestra play with natural idiomatic warmth and plenty of
vitality. The complete set of the eight Op. 72 Slavonic Dances
is similarly idiomatic and vivacious, and the Romance, with

Ivan Zenaty a persuasive soloist, is a splendid bonus. The
recording too is first class, as is the camerawork.

Symphony 7 in D min., Op. 70

⊞ ⒃ *** LSO 0014. LSO, C. Davis

Sir Colin Davis's live recording of the Seventh with the LSO
was made at the Barbican in March 2001, a powerful reading,
a shade freer and more warmly expressive than his earlier
(1975) version for Philips with the Concertgebouw Orchestra
(see below), with more immediate sound, the power and expressive range are intensified, culminating in a towering account of the finale which, unlike many, here emerges as a
fully satisfying conclusion, after the masterly originality of
the earlier movements.

Symphony 7 in D min., Op. 70; Nocturne for Strings, Op. 40; The Water Goblin, Op. 107

*** Chan. 9391. Czech PO, Bělohlávek

Bělohlávek knows better than his direct rivals how to draw
out idiomatic warmth from the Czech Philharmonic, and
he is helped by satisfyingly full and glowing Chandos
sound. Fresh, well paced and intelligently shaped, this is a
thoroughly recommendable reading, paired with an excellent account of The Water Goblin and the eloquent, poignant
Nocturne for Strings. In this spacious reading of the Nocturne
the Czech strings produce ravishing sounds, and The Water
Goblin is similarly relaxed and warm rather than sharply
dramatic.

Symphonies 7 in D min., Op. 70; 8 in G, Op. 88

⒃ (***) Naxos mono 8.111045. Czech PO, Talich

Older collectors who grew up in wartime England will remember Talich's accounts of the D minor and G major
Symphonies, then known as Nos. 2 and 4. They were recorded
when the great Czech orchestra visited London in 1935 and
1938, and they still remain the classic accounts to have. Some
later accounts have come close, but none has surpassed
them. Good sound for the period.

Symphonies 7–9; American Suite

Ⓝ ⒃ **(*) Virgin 5 22039-2. (2) RLPO, Pešek

Symphonies 7–9; Overture Carnival

Ⓑ **(*) Sony (ADD) 074646315125 (2). Cleveland O, Szell –
SMETANA: Bartered Bride Overture; String Quartet 1 (From
My Life): orchestral version, arr. Szell

(i) Symphonies 7–9; (ii) Romance in F min., Op. 11. (i) Symphonic Variations

⊞ Ⓑ *** CfP 2-CD 575 7612 (2). (i) LPO, Mackerras; (ii)
Gonley, ECO

At bargain price Mackerras's triptych offers performances
of all three symphonies which are among the finest ever,
with first-rate digital recording throughout. With
Mackerras, tragedy is not uppermost in the D minor Seventh
Symphony, but rather Dvořákian openness. No. 8 easily

matches its companion in effervescence. The colour and atmosphere of the piece are brought out vividly and with a lightness of touch that makes most rivals seem heavy-handed. Mackerras takes a warmly expansive view of the *New World*, remarkable for a hushed and intense account of the slow movement and superb playing from the **LPO**. In the *Symphonic Variations*, too, his relaxed treatment is consistently winning. **Stephanie Gonley**, the leader of the ECO (who take over for this one item), is a sensitive and characterful soloist in the haunting *Romance in F minor*, originally coupled with the *Legends* and added for this generous and highly recommendable reissue.

Szell's performances of the last three symphonies come from the late 1950s. The recordings have a characteristically forward balance; although brightly lit, the sound is full-bodied in its current transfer, with the Severance Hall ambience well caught. Throughout, the playing combines polish with vitality. No. 7 has a strong forward impulse. It may be lacking in geniality but it has plenty of character: the slow movement has a strong foward impulse and there is no lack of sparkle elsewhere. No. 8 is superbly played, the pick of the bunch, and no one should be disappointed with the *New World* with taut outer movements, a responsive yet refined *Largo* and an attractive rhythmic lilt in the Scherzo. The *Carnival Overture* (from 1963) is predictably super-brilliant, as is Smetana's *Bartered Bride Overture*. The surprise bonus is Szell's fully scored orchestral transcription of Smetana's *First String Quartet*, which is made to sound more like a symphony. It is played spontaneously and with much zest and brings a passionately felt slow movement. The 1949 mono recording is a bit fierce in *fortissimo* but has supporting weight and warmth. The result is memorable.

Pešek's recordings of nos. 7 and 8, made at the end of the 1980s, are among the most refreshing of his recordings, persuasive in a light, relaxed way, slow movements warm, with the folk element brought out. However the *New World* is a little lacking in spontaneity and grip, a reading which could use a bit more adrenalin. The coupled *American Suite*, however, is presented with a beguilingly affectionate touch. The sound is full and clear.

Symphony 8 in G, Op. 88; The Noonday Witch, Op. 108

⊕–(M) **** Warner 3984 4487-2. Concg. O, Harnoncourt

Symphony 8; The Wood Dove, Op. 110

*** Chan. 8666. SNO, Järvi

Harnoncourt's *G major* is the finest of the three **Concertgebouw** recordings of the late Dvořák symphonies he made between 1997 and 1999. It opens richly and expansively, yet has all the extra tension and spontaneity one expects from a live performance, and an ongoing drama, to match the underlying warmth, especially in the slow movement, which is wonderfully detailed. The orchestral playing is superb, as is the recording: rich, brilliant and ideally balanced in the glowing Concertgebouw acoustic. The tone-poem is equally fine, and this is now a top recommendation for this symphony.

Järvi's highly sympathetic account of the *Eighth* underlines the expressive lyricism of the piece, the rhapsodic freedom of invention rather than any symphonic tautness, with the **SNO** players reacting to his free rubato and affectionate moulding of phrase with collective spontaneity. The warm Chandos sound has plenty of bloom, with detail kept clear, and is very well balanced.

Symphonies 8 in G, 9 in E min. (From the New World) (DVD version)

⊕–(N) **** Sony **DVD** 8697202409. VPO, Karajan

Karajan recorded the *New World* way back in 1940 with the Berlin Philharmonic and another version in 1958 in stereo, the latter sounding exhilaratingly fresh. He returned to it in 1977 but did not record the *G major* commercially until the present issue. The present performances come from 1985 and were recorded at concerts in the Grossesaal of the Musikverein. They capture the verdant freshness of this music but also show their sense of structure in a strong light. An imposing set and for many will be a first choice.

Symphonies 8 in G; 9 (New World) (CD version)

⊕–**** Ph. **SACD** 470 617-2; 464 640-2. Budapest Festival O, I. Fischer

⊕–(M) *** Decca (ADD) 475 7517. LSO, Kertész

Symphonies 8 in G, Op. 88; 9 in E min. (From the New World), Op. 95

(M)(***) Sup. mono SU 3833-2 001. Czech PO, Talich

**(*) Signum SIGCD 110. Sapporo SO, Otaka

Among their reissues in the Originals series, Philips and Decca vie with each other by both coupling together outstanding performances of the two favourite Dvořák symphonies. Philips have chosen a fairly recent pairing by the **Budapest Festival Orchestra** under **Iván Fischer** which combines freshness with refinement and thoughtfulness with passion, and is currently at the top of our list of recommendations, with the additional advantage of outstanding, modern, digital recording. Iván Fischer includes the exposition repeat of the *New World*, and both performances are uncommonly imaginative and marvellously played. The recording is of Philips's very finest and also available in surround sound on compatible CD.

Decca have paired together (for the first time) **Kertész's** much-admired accounts of the same two symphonies with the **LSO**, recorded three decades earlier. Kertész's reading of the *G major Symphony* has long been famous for its freshly spontaneous excitement, with well-judged tempi throughout, and an affectionately expressive account of the slow movement. Kertész's *New World*, too, offers one of the finest performances ever committed to disc, with a most exciting first movement (exposition repeat included) and a *Largo* bringing playing of hushed intensity to make one hear the music with new ears. Tempi in the last two movements are perfectly judged, and the (1967) recording quality was of Decca's finest of the period.

These Supraphon versions are post-war accounts recorded in the Rudolfinium in 1951 (*No. 8*) and 1954 (*No. 9*) during a turbulent period when Talich was being harassed by the Czech communist regime. They are both concentrated and vivid accounts, which bring these scores wonderfully to life.

Enjoyably warm and lyrical readings from **Otaka**, who in the *Eighth* brings pleasingly idiomatic woodwind playing. Similarly, in the first movement of the *New Word* the second subject is introduced very tenderly. By contrast, the cor anglais theme of the *Largo* could ideally be a fraction more relaxed. The orchestral playing is very sympathetic throughout, but these performances are not quite distinctive enough to be front runners, although they are most naturally recorded.

Symphony 9 in E min. (From the New World), Op. 95

🔑 (M) *** Warner 3984 25254-2. Concg. O, Harnoncourt (with *The Water Goblin* ***)

✿ *** BBC (ADD) BBCL 4056-2. BBC SO, Kempe – BEETHOVEN: *Overture: Leonore 3*; PROKOFIEV: *The Love for Three Oranges: Suite* ***

*** Telarc CD 80616. Cincinnati SO, Paavo Järvi – MARTINŮ: *Symphony 2* ****

(N) **(*) Naïve V 5132. La Chambre Philharmonique, Krivine – SCHUMANN: *Konzertstuck in F for Four Horns* ***

(N) **(*) Ondine ODE 1141-2. Curtis SO, Eschenbach – HINDEMITH: *Piano Music with Orchestra* ***

Symphony 9; Overture: Carnival

(M) *** RCA **SACD** 82876 66376-2. Chicago SO, Reiner – SMETANA: *Bartered Bride Overture*; WEINBERGER: *Schwanda Polka & Fugue*

Symphony 9. Overtures: Carnival; In Nature's Realm; Othello

🔑 (M) **** Ondine Double ODE 962-2 (2). Czech PO, Ashkenazy

(i) *Symphony 9*; (ii) *Czech Suite; Prague Waltzes*

🔑 (B) *** Decca 448 245-2. (i) VPO, Kondrashin; (ii) Detroit SO, Dorati

Symphony 9; Slavonic Dances 1, 3 & 7, Op. 46/1, 3 & 7; 10 & 15, Op. 72/2 & 7

(M) *** DG (ADD) 435 590-2. BPO, Karajan

Symphony 9 (New World); Symphonic Variations

(N) (BB) *** Naxos 8. 570714. Baltimore SO, Alsop

Ashkenazy's Ondine recording is not only an outstanding recommendation, but it also makes an excellent coupling, offering Dvořák's trilogy of overtures, originally conceived as a group under the title of 'Nature, Life and Love', together with his most popular symphony in a two-for-the-price-of-one package. Ashkenazy follows the instruction from Dvořák to ignore the first-movement exposition repeat. Textures are not ideally transparent, largely a question of the immediate recorded sound, warm rather than clear.

Recorded live, **Harnoncourt's** first movement, with its bold, clipped rhythms and a nice relaxation for the lyrical second group, generates plenty of excitement, with exposition repeat made part of the structure. The *Largo* by contrast is gentle, with the cor anglais solo very delicate, almost like an oboe, and with some superb *pianissimo* string-playing to follow. The Scherzo lilts as it should, and the finale is well thought out so that it moves forward strongly, yet it can look back to the composer's reprise of earlier themes with touching nostalgia. This CD is made the more attractive by the superbly atmospheric and magnetic account of *The Water Goblin*, one of Dvořák's most colourful symphonic poems. It is even more recommendable at mid-price.

Marin Alsop makes the *New World* very much her own, with the fine **Baltimore Orchestra** responding in an account full of warmth, moments of high drama, and above all finely paced with a spontaneous forward flow. Yet the luminous grace of the strings is immediately apparent at the affectionate opening of both first and second movements. The delicate close of the *Largo*, after the songful repeat of the lovely cor anglais melody is memorable. Yet the movement's central episodes are equally poetic. The Scherzo then bursts in on the listener, and the finale has all the impetus one could want. But what makes this disc doubly recommendable is the superb account of the coupled *Symphonic Variations*, inspired but surprisingly neglected. The extraordinary variety of invention and scoring captivates the ear, until it reaches its genial fugal apotheosis and the performance sweeps to its folksy, grandiloquent ending. Throughout, the recording is outstanding in every way, well balanced and vivid in detail, heard within the naturally captured acoustic of Baltimore's excellent Symphony Hall.

Kempe's *New World Symphony* brings another memorable performance, dedicated, with *pianissimos* of breathtaking delicacy. This is a quite exceptional account, and while they make a curious mixture for a single disc, each of the three contrasted works on this CD has a rare intensity, coming from the two Prom concerts that Kempe conducted in August 1975 on the eve of his taking over as Chief Conductor of the **BBC Symphony Orchestra** in succession to Pierre Boulez.

Kondrashin's Vienna performance of the *New World Symphony* was one of Decca's first demonstration CDs. Recorded in the Sofiensaal, every detail of Dvořák's orchestration is revealed within a highly convincing perspective. Other performances may exhibit a higher level of tension but there is a natural spontaneity here. The budget-priced Eclipse CD is enhanced by **Dorati's** bright, fresh versions of the *Czech Suite* and the even rarer *Prague Waltzes* (Viennese music with a Czech accent).

Reiner's 1957 *New World* is an essentially lyrical performance without idiosyncratic disturbances. There is no first-movement exposition repeat, but how naturally the second subject is ushered in, and how well the music flows, both here and in the *Largo*, with consistently lovely playing, especially in the rapt closing section. The Scherzo sparkles and its lilting rustic interlude is especially beguiling, while there is plenty of excitement in the finale. As with all these RCA SACD reissues, one notices the added warmth of the sound and firm but resonant bass. What makes this disc the more attractive are the fill-ups, and not just the brilliant *Carnival Overture*, which bursts with energetic orchestral bravura and yet has a ravishing Slavonic feeling in the middle section.

Having the most popular of Dvořák's symphonies in coupling with one of the most approachable of symphonies by a twentieth-century Czech composer is a neat and original idea, particularly apt when both works were written in the United States. **Paavo Järvi** not only reveals his own keen imagination and sharp concentration in both performances, he demonstrates consistently the excellence of the **Cincinnati Orchestra** under his guidance: ensemble in both works is first rate, readily matching the finest rival versions. The quality of the playing, warmly idiomatic both in Martinů and Dvořák, is enhanced by the refinement and clarity of the brilliant Telarc recording.

Karajan's 1964 DG analogue recording has a powerful lyrical feeling and an exciting build-up of power in the outer movements. The *Largo* is played most beautifully, and Karajan lets the orchestra speak for itself, which it does, gloriously. The rustic qualities of the Scherzo are brought out affectionately, and altogether this is very rewarding. The recording is full, bright and open. This is now reissued, sounding as good as ever, coupled with five favourite *Slavonic Dances*, given virtuoso performances.

La Chambre Philharmonique, founded by **Emmanuel Krivine**, prides itself on being less like a regular orchestra than a chamber group, and the results on this first-rate coupling of popular Dvořák and rare Schumann certainly bear that out. Krivine secures biting attack in both works using a reduced body of strings, 8. 8. 7. 6. 5, which undoubtedly helps in securing great clarity, with timpani standing out cleanly – particularly important in the Dvořák, and encouraging Krivine to opt for fast *allegros*, although perhaps the lyrical side of the work is less emphasized. First-rate sound, recorded in Grenoble, to bring out the quality of the playing.

Eschenbach's reading of the *New World* is comparably small-scale, with some lovely wind solos, as in the great cor anglais melody of the slow movement, and with plenty of bite in the last two movements. Eschenbach favours a very plain approach, with even the clarinet counter-subject in the finale played with little magic. The coupling, however, is fascinating.

CHAMBER AND INSTRUMENTAL MUSIC

Piano Quartets 1 in D, Op. 23; 2 in E flat, Op. 87

🎧 🌸 ******** Hyp. CDA 66287. Domus

*** Australian Ph. Eloquence (ADD) 470 6622. Beaux Arts Trio, Trampler

The Dvořák *Piano Quartets* are glorious pieces, and the playing of **Domus** is little short of inspired. This is real chamber-music playing: intimate, unforced and distinguished by both vitality and sensitivity. They are recorded in an ideal acoustic and in perfect perspective; they sound wonderfully alive and warm.

The playing of the **Beaux Arts Trio** is as fresh and spontaneous as the music itself, and the early 1970s recording still sounds remarkably well – warm and beautifully balanced.

Piano Quartet 2 in E flat, Op. 87; Piano Quintet, Op. 81

Ⓜ ****(*)** Warner Elatus 2564 60336-2. Schiff, Panocha Qt

András Schiff and the **Panocha Quartet** offer a welcome pairing, particularly at so competitive a price. The performances are musical and very well recorded and, though neither is a first choice if price is no object, they are both very enjoyable.

(i) Piano Quintet in A, Op. 81. String Quartets 5, Op. 9: Romance; 10 in E flat, Op. 51; 12 in F (American), Op. 96; 13 in G, Op. 106; 14 in A flat, Op. 105; String Quintet in E flat, Op. 97; 5 Bagatelles for 2 Violins, Cello & Harmonium, Op. 47; Cypresses; 2 Waltzes (for string quartet); Terzetto (for 2 violins & viola in C), Op. 74

🎧 Ⓜ ******* ASV CDDCS 446 (4). The Lindsays, with (i) P. Frankl

A splendid compilation, gathering together many of Dvořák's key chamber works and including not only the *American Quartet* but also the lovely *Quintet*, which has similar transatlantic connections. Incidentally and importantly, they include the repeat in the first movement of this work, with its lead-back. None of this music is uninspired and most of it shows the composer at his finest. The performances are characteristically warm and vital, and the recording is first class, clearly focused but with a pervading bloom.

Piano Quintet in A, Op. 81

🎧 ******** ASV CDDCA 889. Frankl, Lindsay Qt – MARTINŮ: *Piano Quintet 2* ********

*** Mer. CDE 84459. Denk, Concertante (members) – BRAHMS: *Piano Quintet* ****(*)**

Piano Quintet in A; 5 Bagatelles, Op. 47.

*** HM HMC 901880. Braley, Ens. Expectations

(i) Piano Quintet in A; String Quartet 12 in F (American), Op. 96

*** Testament (ADD) SBT 1074. (i) Stepán; Smetana Qt – JANÁČEK: *String Quartet 1* *******

(i) Piano Quintet in A; (ii) String Quintet in A min., Op. 1.

*** Sup. SU 3909-2. Skampa Quartet, with (i) Stott; (ii) Durantel

(i) Piano Quintet in A; String Quintet 2 in G, Op. 77

🎧 ******* Hyp. CDA 66796. Gaudier Ens., (i) with Tomes

This ASV account of Dvořák's glorious *Piano Quintet* by the **Lindsays** with **Peter Frankl** can readily stand comparison with the famous early Decca account with Clifford Curzon. Apart from Peter Frankl's fine contribution, one especially responds to **Bernard Gregor-Smith's** rich cello-line. Because of the resonance, the recording is full and warm, and if there is just a hint of thinness on the violin timbre the balance with the piano is particularly well managed.

With **Susan Tomes** the inspired pianist, the **Gaudier Ensemble** give a sparkling performance of the *Piano Quintet*, full of mercurial contrasts that seem entirely apt and with rhythms superbly sprung. The *G major String Quintet* is lighter than most rival versions, with speeds on the brisk side and with **Marieke Blankestijn's** violin pure rather than rich in tone. Very well recorded, this makes an excellent recommendation if you fancy the coupling. In neither work are the exposition repeats observed.

Concertante is a group of musicians from the Juilliard School; they offer the rare coupling of the *Piano Quintets* of Brahms and Dvořák. This latter is a particularly fine performance, full of passionate spontaneity in the opening movement and with a balancing warmth throughout. Here the lead violin is **Colin Jacobson**, while **Xiao-Dong Wang** (who leads in the Brahms) is on the second desk; and this may account for the even greater impetus, although the well-balanced pianist, **Jeremy Denk**, also makes a first-class contribution. The closing pages are most beautifully managed.

In terms of tonal finesse and bloom, the **Smetana Quartet** had few peers, and their ensemble is perfect. Moreover the quality of the mid-1960s recorded sound is as good as many being produced today. The *Piano Quintet*, in which they are joined by **Pavel Štěpán**, is glorious, even if the acoustic is slightly drier than is ideal. No quarrels with the *F major Quartet* either. The sound is analogue and has great warmth.

Recorded in warm, full sound, the pianist **Frank Braley** leads an often fiery and impulsive account of Dvořák's masterly *Piano Quintet* of 1887, using a vintage Steinway of 1874. The clarity of his articulation adds sparkle to his freely romantic reading, matched by the talented string-players of the **Ensemble Expectations**. The coupling brings a welcome rarity, written in 1878, the year of the first set of *Slavonic Dances*, for the rare combination of two violins, cello and harmonium, an instrument popular at the time, particularly in America. The sequence is delightful in its exploitation of fresh ideas, and Braley readily adapts to the demands of the harmonium.

Recorded in the Rudolfinum in Prague, the **Skampa Quartet**, with respectively **Laurene Durantel** on the double-bass and **Kathryn Stott** on the piano, give bright, idiomatic performances of both these attractive *Quintets*, making an excellent coupling. The *String Quintet* with double-bass as the extra instrument is the first of the two string quintets that the composer wrote, the second having an extra viola instead. The relatively fast speeds chosen by the Skampas seem to enhance the rhythmic resilience of these performances, with the light, bright recording enhancing the impact of both works. The freshness and clarity of the Supraphon performance is also helped by the bright recording, with a

sense of fun conveyed in the finale, with deliciously lifted rhythms.

(i) Piano Quintet in A. String Quintets 1–3, Opp. 1, 77 & 97; String Sextet in A, Op. 46

Ⓑ *** Ph. (ADD) Duo 462 284-2 (2). (i) Kovacevich; BPO Octet (members)

This is the first time all these works have been gathered together on CD, and they make up a very enticing Duo. The **Berlin Philharmonic** soloists play most eloquently; these performances are both musical and polished. They are splendidly matched in the *Piano Quintet* by **Stephen Kovacevich** whose clarity of articulation is a marvel. The recordings, from 1968 and 1972, occasionally show their age just a little in the upper range of the string-timbre in *fortissimos*. But there is a pleasing ambient fullness and the sound is generally well balanced.

Piano Trio 1 in B flat, Op. 21.

*** Sup. SU 3927-2. Smetana Trio – FIBICH: *Piano Trio in F* ***; MARTINŮ: *Piano Trio 2 in D min.* ***

The **Smetana Trio**, led by the cellist **Jan Páleníček**, son of Josef Páleníček, one of the founders of the original Smetana Trio in 1931, give inspired, totally idiomatic performances of these nicely contrasted Czech works. Much the most ambitious work on the disc is this first of Dvořák's four *Trios*, written when he was 34 and with his Czech idiom firmly established. One could never mistake this music for Brahms or for any composer but Dvořák. The other two *Trios*, each barely 15 minutes long, are fascinating rarities, well worth hearing. The Smetanas give a wonderfully refined performance of the present work, which is strong and energetic.

Piano Trios 1 in B flat, Op. 21; 2 in G min., Op. 26; 3 in F min., Op. 65; 4 in E min. (Dumky), Op. 90

ⒷⒷ **** Warner Apex 2564 69984-8 (2). Trio Fontenay

Ⓑ *** Chan. 2x1 241-24 (2). Borodin Trio

*** Ara. Z 6726-2 (2). Golub, Kaplan, Carr

Piano Trios 1 in B flat, Op. 21; 3 in F min., Op. 65

🎧 *** MDG 342 1261-2. V. Piano Trio

Piano Trios 2 in G min. Op. 26; 4 (Dumky), Op. 90

🎧 *** MDG 342 1262-2. V. Piano Trio

In reissuing the **Trio Fontenay's** set of Dvořák *Piano Trios* at budget price, Warner tend to sweep the board. First-class playing and expertly balanced modern recording combine to make this very attractive indeed. **Wolf Harden**, the pianist, dominates – but only marginally so: his colleagues match him in lyrical ardour, and they are as sympathetic to Dvořák's warm lyricism as to the Czech dance characteristics of the livelier allegros.

The **Borodin** performances, recorded live at various venues between 1983 and 1985, have all been issued previously, and the *Dumky* remains as a separate issue, coupled with Smetana (see below). There is characteristic ardour and fire;

such imperfections as there are arise from the natural spontaneity of live music-making. The recording varies a little from venue to venue but gives a very real illusion of presence. Although we have a special regard for the newest MDG set from the Vienna Piano Trio, this Chandos bargain reissue remains strongly recommendable in Chandos's two-for-the-price-of-one series.

The talented young players of the **Vienna Piano Trio** bring out to the full the dramatic contrasts of Dvořák's writing. They are not just sharp in attack but rapt and intense in bringing out the mystery of the slow movement. The performance of the *F minor Trio* has similar contrasts of light and shade, with the Brahmsian weight of the piano-writing powerfully brought out and with the expressive range of the violin and cello similarly wide in performances that consistently give the illusion of a live experience. On the second disc, the ear immediately registers the wide range of dynamic of the playing. The constant changes of mood and tempo in the *Dumky* are handled with chimerically spontaneous Slavonic feeling, and the playing is superb.

David Golub, **Mark Kaplan** and **Colin Carr** make an ideally balanced group; Golub produces a wide range of keyboard colour and combines subtlety with a vital yet flexible rhythmic grip. Splendidly characterized playing and totally idiomatic in style. Throughout there is feeling and freshness, yet nothing is overstated. An altogether delightful set which gives great pleasure.

The **Beaux Arts'** earlier versions of the *Piano Trios* come from the end of the 1960s. The *F minor* is played with great eloquence and vitality. And what sparkling virtuosity there is in the Scherzo of the *G minor, Op. 26*. The splendours of the *Dumky* are well realized in an account of great spontaneity and freshness. The recording is naturally balanced and splendidly vivid; only a degree of thinness on the violin-timbre gives any grounds for reservation. At Duo price this is excellent value. (Ph. 454 259-2)

Piano Trios 1–2

(BB) *** Naxos 8.55439. Joachim Trio

Piano Trios 1; 4 (Dumky)

*** Nim. NI 5472. V. Piano Trio

The **Vienna Piano Trio** show admirable musicianship and sensitivity in the *B flat Trio* and in the famous *Dumky Trio*, and they are very well recorded too.

Fresh, vital playing from this excellent Naxos group. Very good recording too, and though not to be preferred to the Beaux Arts, this is eminently recommendable and worth the money.

Piano Trio 2 in G min., Op. 26

(N) **(*) Sup. SU 3949-2. Smetana Trio – TCHAIKOVSKY: *Piano Trio* **(*)

The **Smetana Trio** offers Dvořák's *Second G minor Piano Trio* with its warmly appealing *Largo*, delicious *Scherzo* and *Finale*, played here with an idiomatic lightness of touch. The performance of the coupled Tchaikovsky *Trio* is also a fine one, rather more intimately balanced than its competitors, and

with its pianist, although well placed in the integrated overall sound picture, less dominant.

Piano Trios 2 in F min, Op 65; 3 in E min. Op 90 (Dumky)

(N) *** Cobra 0025. Osiris Piano Trio

The first point to note in this coupling of the second and third of Dvořák's three mature piano trios is the phenomenal precision of the playing of the Dutch **Osiris Trio**. Not only that, they have a lightness of touch, notably in the dance rhythms of the so-called *Dumky Trio*. They winningly bring out the folk-dance element in this highly original work in six sections, with laments set in sharp contrast with vigorous dances, reflecting the traditional Dumka form. The dance rhythms all go with a swing. The *F minor Trio*, written after the death of Dvořák's mother, is altogether different, weighty in its traditional structure in four movements. The first movement is given a surging strength, with the lyrical second subject offering a clear contrast. Most impressive of the movements in this performance is the *Poco Adagio* third movement which has an inner intensity: the high violin is ravishingly beautiful, no doubt reflecting the composer's mourning for his mother.

Piano Trios 3–4 (Dumky)

*** Hyp. CDA 66895. Florestan Trio

Piano Trio 4 in E min. (Dumky), Op. 90

*** Arco Diva UP 0098 131. Max Brod Trio – BEETHOVEN: *Piano Trio 1* ***

*** Warner 2564 61492-2. Beaux Arts Trio – MENDELSSOHN: *Piano Trio 1* ***

With two Czech string-players joined by a German pianist, the **Max Brod Trio** gives a winningly idiomatic account of Dvořák's *Dumky Trio*, with the typical alternations of slow and fast sounding totally natural and spontaneous, to reflect Czech folk music. The slow sections are warm and tender in their meditative intensity, perfectly contrasted with the jaunty rhythms of the fast sections. Excellent, well-balanced sound, if a little dry.

The Hyperion disc also offers musicianly and refined performances that will give much pleasure, and the recording, too, is excellent.

The **Beaux Arts** made their début on LP some 36 years ago with their performance of the *Dumky Trio* (alone, on one full-priced LP) and, although some of the personnel has changed, the youthfulness and grace of the playing has not. **Menahem Pressler** is every bit as sensitive and fleet of finger as he was in the mid-1950s. The new Warner recording is of course more realistic and wide-ranging. It is splendidly balanced and makes a very happy tribute to this wonderful ensemble. The recording is naturally balanced and the illusion of a live occasion is striking.

4 Romantic Pieces, Op. 75; Slavonic Dance, Op. 46/2 (original version); Violin Sonatina in G, Op. 100

&—(M) *** Sup. SU 3772. Suk, Holec – SMETANA: *From the Homeland*; SUK: *Ballade; 4 Pieces* ***

4 Romantic Pieces, Op. 75; Violin Sonatina in G, Op. 100; Humoresque (for solo piano)

*** Analekta FL2 3191. Ehnes, Laurel – JANÁČEK: *Violin Sonata 1*; SMETANA: *From the Homeland* ***

Idiomatic and beautifully turned performances, as one would expect from the composer's grandson and his accomplished partner. The *Sonatina* is an utterly delightful work, particularly the slow movement, which is played exquisitely. It is good, too, to hear the *E minor Slavonic Dance* in its original form, before Dvořák scored it for orchestra. The 1971 recording is excellent and the faithful CD transfer quite transforms the original LP sound.

On Analekta, the collection of violin and piano music by the three greatest Czech composers inspires not just the brilliant Canadian violinist, **Ehnes**, but his piano-partner, **Eduard Laurel**, to performances which with rare understanding bring out the special, most winning qualities of each work. As a charming coda, Ehnes, switching to the piano, offers a reading, albeit a little wayward, of Dvořák's ever-popular *Humoresque*.

Serenade/Octet, Op. 22 (original version); Serenade for Wind, Op. 44 (trans. for Octet); Slavonic Dances, Op. 72/2, 3 & 8 (trans. for double wind quintet)

*** Praga PRD 350021. Czech Nonet

The original (1873) version of Dvořák's *Serenade*, Op. 22, was scored for clarinet, horn, bassoon, two violins, viola and double bass, plus piano. It sounds most engaging, altogether more folksy and rural. The *Wind Serenade* has also been transcribed by František Hertl for a similar group, and the three *Slavonic Dances* for double wind quartet by a member of the **Czech Nonet**. The result in all this music is delightful, beautifully played and recorded – a refreshing change from the normal versions.

String Quartets 1–14; Cypresses, B.152; Fragments in A min.; F, B.120; 2 Waltzes, Op. 54, B.105

(B) *** DG (ADD) 463 165-2 (9). Prague Qt

Dvořák's *Quartets* span the whole of his creative life. The glories of the mature *Quartets* are well known, though it is only the so-called *American* which has achieved real popularity. The beauty of the present set, made in 1973–7, is that it offers more *Quartets* (not otherwise available) plus two *Quartet Movements*, in A minor (1873) and F major (1881), plus two *Waltzes* and *Cypresses* for good measure, all in eminently respectable performances and decent recordings. The present transfers are managed most satisfactorily, with a nice balance between warmth and presence. At bargain price, neatly packaged and with good documentation, this is self-recommending.

String Quartets 5 in F min., Op. 9; 7 in A min., Op. 16

0→ (BB) *** Naxos 8.553377. Vlach Qt

String Quartets 8 in E., Op. 80; 11 in C, Op. 61

0→ (BB) *** Naxos 8.553372. Vlach Qt

String Quartet 9 in D min., Op. 34; Terzetto in C (for 2 violins and viola), Op. 74

0→ (BB) *** Naxos 8.553373. Vlach Qt

String Quartets 10 in E flat, Op. 51; 14 in A flat, Op. 105

0→ (BB) *** Naxos 8.553374. Vlach Qt

String quartets 12 in F (American), Op. 96; 13, in G, Op. 106

0→ (BB) *** Naxos 8.553371. Vlach Qt

Although there is stiffer competition now that DG have reissued the Prague Quartet set of the Dvořák canon at budget price, the **Vlach** is as good a way of exploring this repertoire as any. Their tonal matching seals their claims to be an outstanding international group, and there is nothing 'bargain basement' about the performances except their price. The playing is cultured and has warmth and vitality, and there can be no grumbles so far as the quality of the recorded sound is concerned; it is natural, well focused and warm. The dark intensity on a whispered *pianissimo* which marks the hushed opening of Op. 105, one of Dvořák's masterpieces, leads on to performances of exceptional strength and refinement, and throughout the series the vigorous movements bring exhilaratingly sprung rhythms and slow movements that are deeply expressive. The Vlach are as fresh and persuasive as any of their rivals on premium-priced labels.

String Quartets 8 in E, Op. 80; 9 in D min., Op. 34

*** Praga HMCD 90. Kocian Qt

Outstanding performances from the **Kocian Quartet**, naturally idiomatic and full of vitality. Both slow movements are played most beautifully, the *Adagio* of the *D minor* is very tender, and both Scherzos have a real Slavonic rhythmic feel. The outer movements of the *E major* are particularly appealing. The recording is real and present, perhaps a shade close (there is a hint of shrillness on the violins) but well balanced. This is much more characterful and authentic than the coupling of the same two works by the Chilingirians on Chandos.

String Quartets 9, Op. 34; 14 in A flat, Op. 105

(M) *** Somm SOMMCD 231. Delmé Qt

With this issue the **Delmé Quartet** celebrate their fortieth birthday (they were founded in 1962). They are a refreshingly musical ensemble, unglamorous and free from gloss, and though there are some infelicities, both quartets are very well served. The sublime slow movement of Op. 34 is eloquently played, and the recording, made in Leiston Abbey, is eminently truthful and well balanced.

String Quartet 12 in F (American), Op. 96

(B) *** Calliope CAL 6262. Annesci Qt – GLAZUNOV: *Quartet 3* ***

*** EMI 7 54215-2. Alban Berg Qt – SMETANA: *Quartet* ***

Ⓜ *** Classic fM 75605 57027-2. Chilingirian Qt – BORODIN: *Quartet 2*; SHOSTAKOVICH: *Quartet 8* ***

ⒷⒷ (***) Dutton mono CDBP 9713. Griller Qt – BLOCH: *Quartet 2; Night*; MOZART: *Adagio & Fugue* (***)

(***) Testament mono SBT 1072. Hollywood Qt – KODÁLY; SMETANA: *Quartets* (***)

Ⓜ **(*) Virgin 2x1 5 62437-2 (2). Endellion Qt – SMETANA: *String Quartet 1*; MARTINŮ: *Double Concerto*, etc. ***

A warmly refined account from the rich-timbred **Annesci Quartet**. This is essentially a mellow performance (helped by richly atmospheric recording), but there is no lack of underlying impulse, and there is plenty of dash in the sparkling finale. The Glazunov coupling is equally recommendable.

The **Alban Berg** have their finger on the vital current that carries its musical argument forward. Phrasing is shaped dextrously and the polish and elegance of their playing are never in danger of diminishing the spontaneous-seeming character of this music.

On Classic fM, the **Chilingirian Quartet** give powerful, incisive performances, though they are recorded a bit too forward. **Levon Chilingirian's** violin-tone is given a slight edge by the full, immediate recording. In the Dvořák the big contrasts of mood and atmosphere are brought out, with the slow movement yearningly beautiful and the fast movements given an infectious spring.

When this brilliant version of Dvořák's *American Quartet* was recorded in 1948, the **Grillers** were at their peak, unassailably the leading such group in Britain. Perfectly matched, they bring out the exhilaration of the fast music, notably in a dazzling account of the finale and the yearning beauty of the slow movement. This was a fine early example of Decca's prowess in using its *ffrr* process, and Dutton in the CD transfer secures astonishingly vivid results. Well coupled with the masterly but neglected Bloch *Quartet* and the Mozart masterpiece.

The **Hollywood Quartet** is pretty well self-recommending, and their account of the *F major Quartet* is everything one would expect: impeccable in terms of execution, ensemble and taste. This was a quartet which brought real artistry to everything they played.

The **Endellion Quartet** give a generally excellent account. Mind you, one is pulled up with a start at the second theme of the first movement which the leader, **Andrew Watkinson**, pulls out of shape. However, these players are robust in style, their music-making has conviction, they are eminently well recorded, and the couplings are as generous as they are unexpected.

String Quartets 12 (American); 13 in G, Op. 106

🎧 *** ASV CDDCA 797. Lindsay Qt

In the *American Quartet* the **Lindsays'** account is certainly among the very best in terms of both performance and recording. The *G major* is also played very well, with much the same dedication and sensitivity. An outstanding coupling.

String Quartet 12 (American); (i) String Quintet in E flat, Op. 97

🎧 ⒷⒷ **** Warner Apex 0927 44355-2. Keller Qt, with (i) Deeva

Dvořák wrote the second of his string quintets (the one with the extra viola) in the same period as the popular Op. 96 *Quartet*, similarly using thematic material with American inflexions, so that the two works make an apt and attractive coupling. The **Keller Quartet** give outstanding readings of both works, crisp and fanciful, with light, clear textures and speeds generally on the fast side. A real bargain.

String Quartet 14; Terzetto in C, Op. 74

**(*) BBC Legends BBCL 4180-2. Smetana Qt – JANÁČEK: *Quartet 1 (Kreutzer Sonata)* **(*)

*** Testament SBT 1075. Smetana Qt – JANÁČEK: *String Quartet 2* ***

(*) Avie AV 2092. Szymanowski Qt – BACEWICZ: *Quartet 4*; HAYDN: *Quartet* *

The **Smetanas** are unrivalled in Czech repertoire and their account of the *A flat Quartet* was given at London's Queen Elizabeth Hall in 1975. It is as persuasive an account as any in the catalogue. The *Terzetto* for two violins and viola is a studio recording from 1969 and makes an excellent makeweight to a rewarding and compelling recital.

The **Smetanas** (on Testament) observe the traditional cut in the finale of Op. 105, from 11 bars before fig. 11 until 4 bars after fig. 12. This is a wonderful performance. Moreover it also comes with the *Terzetto in C* for two violins and viola, a rarity in the concert hall, played freshly and elegantly, and with their outstanding account of Janáček's *Intimate Letters*, which is new to the British catalogues.

The performance by the **Szymanowski Quartet** is excellent, sensitive and polished, with the *furiant* Scherzo full of life and the slow movement warmly played. Yet some ears may find the blend of tone these players achieve at times a little too sensuously smooth and suave, for they are very flattered by the recording.

String Quintets in A min., Op. 1; E flat, Op. 97

🎧 ⒷⒷ *** Naxos 8.553376. Vlach Qt, with L. Kyselac

An intelligent coupling by the **Vlach** of the earliest *Quintet*, coupled with one of the most masterly of all his chamber works, the *E flat*, Op. 97. No need to worry about this performance or recording, for both are excellent and, although there are alternatives of quality, none is priced so competitively.

String Quintets: (i) in G, Op. 77; (ii) in E flat, Op. 97

*** Bayer BR 100 184CD. Stamitz Qt, with (i) Hudec; (ii) Talich

String Quintets: in G, Op. 77; in E flat, Op. 97; Intermezzo in B, Op. 40

*** Chan. 9046. Chilingirian Qt, with D. McTier

The **Stamitz Quartet** is perhaps balanced more forwardly but is recorded pleasantly, and the **Chilingirian** set on Chandos has more air round the sound but without any loss of focus. Both performances have the warmth and humanity that Dvořák exudes, but the Chilingirians undoubtedly score in including the beautiful *B major Intermezzo* that the composer had originally intended for the *G major Quintet* and which he subsequently expanded into an independent work for full strings, the *Nocturne*, Op. 40. This tips the balance in their favour.

String Quintet in E flat, Op. 97; String Sextet in A, Op. 48

☛ *** Hyp. CDA 66308. Raphael Ens.

The *E flat major Quintet*, Op. 97, is one of the masterpieces of Dvořák's American years, and it is most persuasively given by the **Raphael Ensemble**, as is the coupled *Sextet*. It is also very well recorded, though we are placed fairly forward in the aural picture.

String Quintet, Op. 77; String Sextet, Op. 48; Intermezzo, Op. 40

☛ *** ASV GLD 4011. Nash Ens.

The **Nash Ensemble** prove to be most persuasive advocates of both these fine ensemble works for strings, beautifully matched and with a fine feeling for the Czech idiom. The *Sextet* too brought Dvořák to international notice. The *Intermezzo* which comes as supplement, here given with single strings, is especially apt, when this was originally intended as an extra slow movement for the *String Quintet*, a gentle, intimate piece. First-rate sound.

String Sextet in A, Op. 48 (DVD Version)

(*) Sup. **DVD SU 7004-2. Augmented Smetana Qt –
  SMETANA: *String Quartets 1–2 (plus documentary on the Smetana Quartet)* **(*)

The *Sextet* makes an admirable fill-up for the two Smetana *Quartets* and is given without intrusive camerawork. Musically very satisfying, though the documentary in which the members of the quartet look back over their career is curiously stiff.

Violin Sonatina in G, Op. 100 – see also under Violin Concerto

☛ *** Praga PRD 250 153. Remés, Kayahara – JANÁČEK;
  MARTINŮ; SMETANA: *Violin Sonatas* ***

*** Avie Crear Classics AV 0037. Gleusteen, Ordronneau –
  FRANCK: *Violin Sonata*; GRIEG: *Violin Sonata 3* ***

Dvořák's *Violin Sonatina* is full of charm, its four movements are by no means diminutive in character, and the composer probably chose the title to emphasize its unpretentiousness. This splendidly sensitive account from **Václav Remés**, admirably partnered by **Sachiko Kayahara**, is sheer delight from beginning to end and has an authentic Czech lilt, yet is full of character. The recording is very good indeed, and so are the couplings.

  Kai Gleusteen and **Catherine Ordronneau** also share the pleasures of playing this delightful *Sonatina*, written in New York in 1893, and in particular bring out the charm of its recognizable melodic connection with the composer's 'New World' era. An altogether winning performance of a captivating work, naturally recorded in a concert hall acoustic at Crear in the Scottish Highlands, with a visual backcloth as memorable as the music.

Slavonic Dances 1–16, Op. 46/1–8; Op. 72/1–8

☛ *** Mirare MIR042. Désert, Strosser

☛ (BB) *** Naxos 8.553138. Matthies, Köhn

Recorded at a music festival in Nantes early in 2007, **Claire Désert** and **Emmanuel Strosser** give fluent, nicely sprung readings. The fact that these are live recordings intensifies the dynamic shading, which is subtler than in the Naxos version, and Désert and Strosser relish the stylistic contrast in the second set of eight dances, when Dvořák went outside the world of Czech music for his inspiration and drew on dances from other Slavonic countries.

  The brilliant piano duo of **Silke-Thora Matthies** and **Christian Köhn** are most persuasive performers, radiating their own enjoyment, bringing out inner parts, giving transparency to even the thickest textures, subtly shading their tone and, above all, consistently springing rhythms infectiously, with an idiomatic feeling for Czech dance music. The forwardly balanced recording brings out the brightness of the piano while letting warmth of tone come forward in such gentler dances as *No. 3 in D*. An excellent bargain.

Poetic Tone Pictures, Op. 85; Theme & Variations, Op. 36

(BB) **(*) Regis RRC 1171. Kvapil

Dvořák is not best known as a composer for the piano, yet his set of *Poetic Tone Pictures* has great charm, and the influences of folksong are striking: these pieces have much in common with the *Lyric Pieces* of Grieg. The *Theme and Variations*, Dvořák's one major solo work, followed after the *Piano Concerto* of 1876 and is stronger and more classical in feeling. **Radoslav Kvapil** has the full measure of this music and plays the gentler evocations very persuasively. He is truthfully recorded, but the sound is a bit dry and *forte* passages tend to harden. Nevertheless, this disc is well worth having at its modest price. It is available either separately or within a four-CD Czech Piano Anthology, which also includes music by Janáček, Smetana and Suk (Regis 4005).

7 Organ Preludes & Fugues

**(*) BIS CD 1101. Ericsson – GLAZUNOV: *Preludes & Fugues*,
  etc.; SIBELIUS: *Intrada*, etc. ***

These pieces – five preludes, a fughetta and two fugues – are graduation exercises that Dvořák wrote on leaving the Prague Organ School. They are played very well here and show the fluency and technical proficiency you would expect from any gifted student, but no sign of individuality.

VOCAL AND CHORAL MUSIC

Cypresses ((i) Instrumental and (ii) Vocal Versions), B11 & B152

*** Somm SOMMCD 236. (i) Delmé Qt; (ii) Robinson, Johnson

The charming sequence of 12 pieces for string quartet that Dvořák entitled *Cypresses* has been recorded fairly often, but the set of 18 songs on which they are based has been seriously neglected. Here, as an ideal and generous coupling, comes a disc setting the two cycles side by side, with illuminating results. Both sets in their reflection on youthful love provide a touching portrait of the composer. Though the present recording of the song versions sets the singer at a slight distance, with occasional roughness at the top disturbing the general sweetness of tenor-tone, **Timothy Robinson's** performances are warmly sympathetic, helped by ever-responsive accompaniment from **Graham Johnson**. The **Delmé Quartet** plays the instrumental versions with exceptionally sweet matching, generally opting for relatively broad speeds and warmly expressive phrasing. The disc also offers excellent detailed notes and full texts and translations.

Biblical Songs, Op. 99; Gipsy Melodies, Op. 55; In Folk Tone, Op. 73; Love Songs, Op. 83

*** Sup. SU 3437-2. Peckova, Gage

Dagmar Pecková's is an ideal voice for this repertory, unmistakably Slavonic in timbre, yet firm and pure as well as rich. She retains a freshness that is specially apt for the songs inviting a girlish manner, including the most famous of this composer's songs, the fourth of the seven *Gipsy Songs, Songs my Mother taught me*, sounding fresh and new. Full texts are given, but translations in German and French as well as English come on separate pages, making it far more difficult to follow songs line by line. Clear, well-balanced sound.

Requiem (DVD version)

☛ *** Arthaus DVD 102 063. Be ačková, Kirilová, Protschka, Vele, Prague Philharmonic Ch., Czech PO, Neumann

Recorded (in association with Bavarian Radio) against the glorious backcloth of St Vitus Cathedral, Prague, **Neumann's** inspired performance is more spacious and has a less fiery drive than Ančerl's celebrated DG audio version, but the conductor creates a sustained intensity from the very opening, and the **Czech Philharmonic Chorus** reaches heights of fervour in both the *Offertorium* and the resplendent *Sanctus*, while the second *Pie Jesu* (which moved the composer himself so much when he conducted the work's première at the Birmingham Festival in 1891) and the *Agnus Dei* make an equally poignant climax at the work's close. The soloists make a good team; the women are not without the occasional wobble, but they sing committedly and ensure that the work's Czech character is fully maintained. The recording is first class and the video direction admirably straightforward, using the cathedral interior very effectively for visual variety.

(i) Requiem, Op. 89; (CD versions) (ii) 6 Biblical Songs from Op. 99

☛ 🌐 (M) *** DG 453 073-2 (2). (i) Stader, Wagner, Haefliger, Borg, Czech PO & Ch., Ančerl; (ii) Fischer-Dieskau, Demus

This superb DG set from 1959 brings an inspired performance of Dvořák's *Requiem* which here emerges with fiery intensity, helped by a recording made in an appropriately spacious acoustic that gives an illusion of an electrifying live performance, without flaw. The passionate singing of the chorus is unforgettable and the German soloists not only make fine individual contributions but blend together superbly in ensembles. DG have added **Fischer-Dieskau's** 1960 recordings of six excerpts from Op. 99. He is at his superb best in these lovely songs. **Jörg Demus** accompanies sensitively, and the recording-balance is most convincing.

(i) Requiem, Op. 89; (ii) Mass in D, Op. 86

(B) *** Double Decca (ADD) 448 089-2 (2). (i) Lorengar, Komlóssy, Isofalvy, Krause, Amb. S., LSO, Kertész; (ii) Ritchie, Giles, Byers, Morton, Christ Church Cathedral Ch., Oxford, Cleobury (organ), Preston

Kertész conducts with a total commitment to the score and he secures from singers and orchestra an alert and sensitive response. The recording, which has the advantage of the Kingsway Hall ambience, has a lifelike balance, and for this Double Decca reissue the work has been sensibly recoupled with **Simon Preston's** beautifully shaped **Christ Church** account of the *Mass in D*, recorded six years later. In both works the CD remastering shows how good were the original recordings.

Saint Ludmila (oratorio), Op. 74

*** Orfeo C 513992H (2). Aghová, Breedt, Beczala, Vele, Prague Chamber Ch., WDR Cologne Ch. & SO, Albrecht

Saint Ludmila is a winningly vigorous, dramatic work, reflecting the composer we know from the symphonies in its rhythmic strength and lyrical warmth. It is a piece full of white-hot inspiration, punctuated with lively choruses and arias, often feeling operatic. This Orfeo issue offers a strong, colourful performance which points the drama well, using four first-rate Czech-speaking soloists and with the **Cologne Choir** augmented by the **Prague Chamber Choir**. The result is both polished and idiomatic, helped by warm, full sound, even though the chorus is set behind the orchestra.

Stabat Mater, Op. 58 (DVD version)

(N) *** Arthaus DVD 102 143. Urbanová, Kachlíková, Margita, Mikuláš, Prague Ph. Ch; Prague SO, Pešek

This performance took place at a Dvořák Festival at the Alte Oper in Frankfurt in 1993 and was recorded for BBC TV and Unitel. The performance is attractively idiomatic with good choral singing from the **Prague Chorus** and fine orchestral playing from the **Prague Symphony Orchestra**. **Libor Pešek** conducts with dedication in this choral piece and with excellent camerawork it is most rewarding.

Stabat Mater; Psalm 149, Op. 79 (CD version)

(BB) **(*) Naxos 8.555301/2 (2). Brewer, Simpson, Aler, Gao, Washington Ch. & O, Shafer

(i) Stabat Mater; (ii) Legends 1–10, Op. 59

(B) *** DG Double (ADD) 453 025-2 (2). (i) Mathis, Reynolds, Ochman, Shirley-Quirk, Bav. R. Ch. & SO; (ii) ECO; Kubelik

The *Stabat Mater* blazed the trail for Dvořák's cause during his lifetime. **Kubelik** is consistently responsive and this is a work which benefits from his imaginative approach. The recording, made in the Munich Herkulessaal, is of very good quality. The ten *Legends* are beautifully played by the ECO. This music ought to be better known, with its colourful scoring and folksy inspiration of a high order. Again very good recording.

Robert Shafer conducts his chorus and the **Washington Orchestra** in a fresh, well-disciplined reading. The chorus is rather backwardly placed, but Shafer's clean-cut directness helps to avoid any feeling of sentimentality. Outstanding among the soloists is **Christine Brewer**, and **John Aler**, though not as sweet-toned as usual, sings very sensitively too. The mezzo, **Marietta Simpson**, is tremulous as recorded, and **Ding Gao** is clear and reliable in the bass solos.

OPERA

Dimitrij

*** Sup. SU 3793-2 (3). Vodička, Drobková, Hajóssyová, Aghová, Mikulaš, Kusnjer, Prague Philharmonic Ch., Prague R. Ch., Czech PO, Albrecht

This first complete recording of Dvořák's ambitious historical opera was made in 1989, an opera memorable for carrying on the story of Boris Godunov after the Tsar died. This is a fine recording, idiomatically conducted by **Gerd Albrecht**, with the choirs from Prague making the most of the many ensembles, not least the double-choruses representing the conflicting Polish and Russian forces. As has regularly been pointed out, Dvořák was less influenced in these by the rugged example of Mussorgsky than by the grand operas written for Paris by Meyerbeer. In the title-role **Leo Vodička** is a strong, very Slavonic-sounding tenor, singing sensitively if at times with strain. Sweetest on the ear among the women is **Livia Aghová** as Xenia, pure, fresh and precise in attack. As Marina, **Magdalena Hajóssyová** is bright and fresh, if with an occasional edge on the voice; and the contralto, **Drahomira Drobková**, is a warm, rich-toned Marfa. Good sound, with the singers' diction admirably clear.

The Jacobin

Ⓜ *** Orfeo C641 043F (3). Bronikowski, Lehotsky, Aghová, Stephinger, Holland, Danková, Mikulaš, Lorenz, Georg, Cologne Children's Ch., Prague Chamber Ch., Cologne R. Symphony Ch. & O, Albrecht

*** Sup. (ADD) 11 2190-2 (2). Zítek, Sounová, Přibyl, Machotková, Blachut, Průša, Tuček, Berman, Katilena Children's Ch., Kuhn Ch., Brno State PO, Pinkas

This opera is a strange but attractive mixture. The main plot involves the hero, Bohuš, son of Count Vilém, being falsely accused of being a revolutionary Jacobin. But Dvořák – having made him a baritone, not a tenor – centres his emotions on the subplot involving village life and the love between the gamekeeper, Jiří, and Terinka. Terinka's father, the village musician-schoolmaster, Benda, is the focus of delectable rehearsal scenes with the schoolchildren and villagers. **Gerd Albrecht**, the conductor who has recorded

so many of Dvořák's major works, is warmly understanding of the Czech folk idiom, and he points rhythms delectably; set in an open acoustic, using large forces both in the orchestra and in the multiple choruses, the Orfeo version achieves a fine balance between high drama and rustic colour. One is forced to take the mortal threat to Bohuš from the evil Adolf very seriously.

Michal Lehotsky, a tenor, sweetly Slavic in timbre, takes the role of Jiří, as he does on the **Wexford** set from Fone, and again he gives an animated performance. Opposite him is the soprano, **Lívia Aghová**, as Terinka, again both Slavic in timbre and sweet-toned, charmingly provocative. Though **Andrea Danková**, as Bohuš's wife Julie, is more variable and with a more pronounced vibrato and a tendency to shrillness under pressure on top, the apt weight of the voice establishes the character well, making the necessary contrast with Terinka. As Bohuš, the baritone **Marcin Bronikowski**, lyrical in his early scenes, rises splendidly to the challenge of the final scene when he appeals to his father, convincing him of his innocence, so bringing the happy ending. In the key role of Benda the character tenor, **Eberhard Francesco Lorenz**, paints a colourful portrait of the schoolmaster without caricaturing him, and the fine bass, **Christoph Stephinger**, sings nobly as the Count, with **Peter Mikulaš** strongly cast as the Count's Burgrave. As Adolf, **Mark Holland** sounds gritty at times, but that is only apt for so villainous a character, and he sings with fine projection in his big moments. The important choruses – with big ensembles ending each Act – are superbly sung too. This is a piece that by rights should have become a far closer rival to *The Bartered Bride* than it has. Though the set takes three discs instead of two for rival versions, that brings the advantage of having each Act complete on a single disc.

On Supraphon **Jiří Pinkas** draws lively and idiomatic performances from a first-rate cast, including such stalwarts as **Vilem Přibyl** as the hero (a little old-sounding but stylish) and the veteran tenor **Beno Blachut** giving a charming portrait of the heroine's father. **Václav Zítek** sings the heroic part of the Jacobin himself with incisive strength and **Daniela Sounová** is bright and clear as the heroine. The analogue sound is clear and firmly focused. A full libretto/translation is included.

Kate and the Devil (complete)

**(*) Sup. (ADD) 11 1800-2 (2). Barová, Ježil, Novák, Sulcová, Suryová, Horáček, Brno Janáček Op. Ch. & O, Pinkas

This is a charming comic fantasy about the girl who literally makes life hell for the devil who abducts her. It inspired a score that might almost be counted an operatic equivalent of his *Slavonic Dances*, full of sharply rhythmic ideas, colourfully orchestrated. The role of Kate is very well taken by **Anna Barová**, firm and full-toned, with Jirka sung attractively by **Miloš Ježil**, though his Slavonic tones are strained on top. The snag is the ill-focused singing of **Richard Novák** as the Devil, characterful enough but wobbly. **Jiří Pinkas** persuasively brings out the fun and colour of the score, drawing excellent singing from the chorus; and the 1979 recording has plenty of space, agreeably warm and atmospheric. The libretto is well produced and clear, but it assumes that the set is on three CDs instead of two, with Acts II and III together on the second.

The King and the Charcoal Burner

*** Orfeo C678 06214 (2). Jenis, Mikuláš, Aghová, Breedt, Lehotsky, Jindrich, Cologne West German R. Ch. & O, Albrecht

The King and the Charcoal Burner was the second opera that Dvořák wrote and the first to be staged. In its first form it was abandoned during rehearsal as being too complex and Wagnerian, which led the composer to rewrite the piece completely, simplifying its textures and material. There followed two more versions, which together form the basis of the present recording, recorded at concert performances with **West German Radio** forces in Cologne and an excellent cast of young Czech singers under the ever-sympathetic advocate, **Gerd Albrecht**. As it is, the piece vies with Smetana's *The Bartered Bride* in the freshness of the Czech flavours, from the opening *Overture*. Very attractive it is, if without the sharp memorability of Smetana's most striking numbers. Well-balanced sound, with voices exceptionally clear and well defined, with clear diction.

Rusalka (DVD version)

(*) Sup. **DVD SU 7008-9. Subrtová, Zidek, Miková, Mixová, Haken, Ovčačiková, Prague Nat. Ch. & O, Chalabala (V/D: Bohumil Zoul)

What the film director Bohumil Zoul has done in the Supraphon DVD is to use the 1961 Supraphon audio recording as the soundtrack for an imaginative re-creation of the story, using actors chosen for their looks. So Rusalka, sung freshly and brightly by **Milada Subrtová**, is played by a very pretty young girl, Katerina Machackova, and the Prince, sung by the legendary **Ivo Zidek**, has film-star good looks in the person of Miroslav Nohinek. The Foreign Princess, formidably sung by **Alena Miková**, is portrayed by the handsomely implacable Marie Malkova, while the Turnspit, sung by a girl, **Ivana Mixová**, is played by a young boy (Michal Mikes). Among the principals, only the old Watersprite is sung and played by the same artist, **Eduard Haken**.

The opening scene between Rusalka and the Watersprite makes clear their supernatural character by using superimposed images, making their green complexions and bodies transparent. The superimposed images continue until the Prince arrives on his horse, and we see the transformation of Rusalka into a human being, so losing her fussy green complexion and acquiring a blouse and skirt. Though the camerawork tends to be fussy, the result is certainly evocative. One trouble, which increases towards the end of the film, is the coordination of words and lips, and the 1961 audio recording, clear and full on voices, tends to have rather thin orchestral sound. That said, this is a most traditional presentation following the composer's vision, with a first-rate performance allied to an idealized setting of the story.

Rusalka (complete; CD versions)

**** Chan. **SACD** 10449 (3). Barker, La Spina, Martin, Whitehouse, Owens, Crane, Fiebig, Matthews, Pendry. Opera Australia Ch., Australian Opera & Ballet O, Hickox

**** Decca 460 568-2 (3). Fleming, Heppner, Hawlata, Zajick, Urbanová, Kusnjer, Kloubová, Kühn Mixed Ch., Czech PO, Mackerras

There is a strong case for this new version from Chandos, recorded in SACD. **Cheryl Barker** may not have so creamily beautiful a voice as Renée Fleming on Decca, but she sounds more aptly girlish and fresh. Her big solo in Act I, the *Invocation to the Moon*, flows far more easily than in Fleming's very beautiful but very expansive version on Decca, an obvious advantage. The tenor **Rosario La Spina**, as the Prince is younger sounding, more obviously virile and more expressive than the Heldentenor Ben Heppner on Decca. As for Hickox himself, he conducts this magical score with a bite that brings out the elements so closely related to the *Slavonic Dances*, and the recording, made live in the Sydney Opera House (a difficult venue), is aptly clean and fresh. **Bruce Martin** as the Water Goblin may not have as rich or well focused a voice as Franz Hawlata on Decca, but it is a strong and characterful performance, and as the witch, Jezibaba, **Anne-Marie Owens** is satisfyingly rich and fruity, where her Decca counterpart is relatively thin-toned.

The Decca CD set is in every way a satisfying musical experience. This offers not only ripely atmospheric sound but what in almost every way is the ideal cast, with the **Czech Philharmonic** incandescent under **Sir Charles Mackerras**. **Renée Fleming** gives a heartfelt, sharply detailed performance, with the voice consistently beautiful over the widest range. **Ben Heppner** too, with his powerful tenor at once lyrical and heroic, is ideally cast as the Prince. **Franz Hawlata** as the Watergnome, Rusalka's father, and **Dolora Zajick** as the witch, Ježibaba, are both outstanding too, with even the smaller roles cast from strength, using leading singers from the **Prague Opera**. In his inspired conducting Mackerras does not resist the obvious Wagnerian overtones, yet Czech flavours are never underplayed in the many colourful dance rhythms. Highlights are available on 466356-2.

Rusalka (sung in English) (DVD version)

*** Arthaus **DVD** 102 019. Hannan, Macann, Howard, Treleaven, Cannan, ENO Ch. & O, Elder (Stage Dir: David Pountney; V/D: David Bailey)

The ENO concept was to set this fairy-tale piece in an Edwardian nursery full of toys, with the Watergnome as Rusalka's grandfather in a wheelchair, and Rusalka herself first seen on a swing with her feet bound together, very much an Alice in Wonderland figure. The Witch is a wicked aunt, dressed in sinister black as she pronounces her curses on Rusalka, as when, with Rusalka opting for human form, she snarls, 'You'll be dumb for ever more!' In the title-role **Eilene Hannan** sings powerfully with her clear, bright soprano, **John Treleaven** as the Prince sings with unstrained clarity, even if he does not cut a very romantic figure, and **Rodney Macann** as the Grandfather/Watergnome tends to steal the show, very characterful with his dark, incisive bass. **Ann Howard** is wonderfully menacing as the Aunt/Witch with her firm mezzo, while the fluttering vibrato of **Phyllis Cannan** as the Foreign Princess even adds to her exotic image. Unlike most of the others in Act II, who are dressed white, she stands out in her fashionable crimson gown. The three Watersprites, Rusalka's sisters, are all wonderfully lively, and incidental characters are all very well taken. **Mark Elder**, an inspired conductor, draws warm, incisive playing from the orchestra, adding to the dramatic impact. A unique entertainment, well worth trying.

The Stubborn Lovers (complete)

*** Sup. SU 3765-2. Janál, Březina, Sýkorová, Kloubová, Beláček, Prague Philharmonic Ch. & Philh., Bělohlávek

This sparkling one-Act comic opera with an amiably non-sensical plot is guaranteed to delight all lovers of Dvořák's music. In a sequence of 16 brief scenes it gives an amusing picture of village life, mainly in brisk ensembles. This splendid account of an opera otherwise unrecorded, very well sung and played, with **Jiří Bělohlávek** a most persuasive conductor, makes its mark tellingly, with one winning tune after another from the Overture onwards.

Rather like Alfonso in *Così fan tutte*, Rericha is the manipulator, contributing to almost every number, a role strongly taken here by the bass, **Gustáv Beláček**, coping splendidly with solos rather like patter-songs. The mellifluous light tenor **Jaroslav Březina** is splendid as Toník, characterizing well and making his change of heart convincing, as **Zdena Kloubová** does as Lenka when, seeing Toník as the choice of her mother, she wonders why tears have come into her eyes. The respective parents, Vávra and Ríhová, are well taken too, though they have less opportunity to establish positive characters. A welcome rarity.

Wanda (complete)

**(*) Orfeo C149003F (3). Romanko, Tchistjakova, Straka, Daniluk, Kusnjer, Breedt, Prague Chamber Ch., WDR Ch. & SO Cologne, Albrecht

In five Acts, *Wanda* dates from 1876, the year after Dvořák composed his eternally fresh *Fifth Symphony*, and much of that freshness is carried over to the opera, with orchestration light and transparent. On disc it is well worth investigating, and **Gerd Albrecht**, using a revised and expanded edition of a score thought to be lost in the Second World War, conducts a strong, purposeful performance, with fine teamwork in the ensembles. The principal male soloists, **Peter Straka** as Slavoj and **Ivan Kusnjer** as Roderick, are both first rate, but the warm, idiomatic singing of the principal women, **Olga Romanko** in the title-role and **Irina Tchistjakova** as her sister, Božena, is marred by the unevenness of their very Slavonic voices. Excellent singing from the joint Czech and German choirs, and full, well-balanced radio recording.

DYSON, George (1883–1964)

(i) *Concerto leggiero* (for piano & strings); *Concerto da camera*; *Concerto da chiesa* (both for string orchestra); **(ii)** *Violin Concerto*; *Children's Suite* (after Walter de la Mare)

●—Ⓜ *** Chan. 10337X (2). (i) Parkin; (ii) Mordkovich; City of L. Sinfonia, Hickox

It was an excellent idea to couple this pair of concertante discs at mid-price, the *Violin Concerto* richly inspired, the *Piano Concerto* lighter textured, the two string works in the great tradition of English string music. All are splendidly played and recorded – the second disc is discussed separately in more detail below.

Symphony in G; At the Tabard Inn: Overture; Concerto da chiesa for Strings

●—Ⓑ *** Naxos 8.557720. Bournemouth SO, Lloyd-Jones

(i) *Symphony in G;* **(ii)** *At the Tabard Inn: Overture;* **(ii; iii)** *In Honour of the City*

Ⓜ **(*) Chan. 10308X. (i) City of L. Sinfonia; (ii) LSO; (iii) L. Symphony Ch.; Hickox

First heard in 1937, Dyson's *Symphony in G* is the most ambitious of his orchestral works, using ideas from *The Canterbury Pilgrims*, with majestic scoring for the brass. Helped by clear, well-balanced recording, **David Lloyd-Jones** conducts a brilliant performance which clarifies often heavy textures. In the *Concerto da chiesa for strings* of 1949, each of the three movements develops a medieval hymn melody, with *Veni Emmanuel* inspiring a darkly dedicated slow first movement, among Dyson's finest inspirations. That melody returns, transformed, at the end of the finale which is based on the vigorous psalm-tune, *Laetatus sum*. With solo strings atmospherically set against the full string band, this is a neglected masterpiece. *At the Tabard Inn* was originally designed as an overture for his choral work, *The Canterbury Pilgrims*, and completes a first-rate disc, superbly played.

By its side, the more expensive **Hickox** version, although very well played, seems less convincing, especially the first movement, which tends to flag a little. The Chandos disc also includes two fill-ups, originally issued with *The Canterbury Pilgrims*, *At the Tabard Inn* and the choral *In Honour of the City*, both excellently performed; they are discussed below. But the Naxos CD is first choice for the symphony.

CHAMBER MUSIC

(i) *Cello Sonata;* **(ii)** *3 Lyrics for Violin & Piano; 3 Violin Pieces; Bach's Birthday; Epigrams for Piano; My Birthday; Prelude & Ballet for Piano; Primrose Mount; Twilight; 3 War Pieces*

Ⓜ *** Dutton CDLX 7137. Owen Norris, with (i) Spooner; (ii) Juritz

With **Owen Norris** an ideal interpreter, pointing rhythm and phrase seductively, the wit of the ten tiny *Epigrams* at the start has one appreciating Dyson's lightness of touch. Just as witty are the four pieces entitled *Bach's Birthday*, with counterpoint that strays into atonality, intended as a joke for his friend, the pianist and scholar Harold Samuel. *Three War Pieces*, unpublished until now, were written when Dyson was in service in the trenches in the First World War, while other groups of pieces like *Twilight* and *My Birthday* from the 1920s were designed for amateurs to play, as are the two sets of violin pieces.

3 Rhapsodies (for string quartet)

(BB) *** Hyp. Helios CDH 55045. Divertimenti – HOWELLS: *In Gloucestershire (String Quartet 3)* ***

Although its spirit is lighter, more capricious, the first of Dyson's *Rhapsodies* follows on quite naturally after the gentle close of Howells's haunting portrayal of the Gloucestershire countryside. The second, a dark elegy, makes a haunting contrast, but the third is again essentially light-hearted in its lyrical grace. Surprisingly, the work was inspired by Dante and written after a Mediterranean holiday. Its changing moods are caught most sensitively by this excellent group, and the Hyperion recording is of high quality.

VOCAL MUSIC

Benedicite; Evening Service in D; Hail Universal Lord; Live forever, glorious Lord; Te Deum; Valour; (i) (Organ) Prelude; Postlude; Psalm-tune Prelude (I was Glad); Voluntary of Praise

🔊 (BB) *** Regis RRC 1161. St Catherine's College, Cambridge, Ch., Owen Rees; (i) Rees (organ) – HOWELLS: *Dyson's Delight*

There are some well-made organ pieces here (plus an admiring contribution from Herbert Howells, based on two themes from Dyson's *Canterbury Pilgrims*), but it is the vocal music that is the more memorable. It is all sung with striking freshness by choristers who seem to have its inflexions in their very being. Excellent recording in a spacious acoustic, though the words come over well. Even so, there is an excellent leaflet with this reissue (of an originally Unicorn disc), setting them out and giving much useful information about the composer and his music, a model of its kind.

3 Choral Hymns; (Organ) Fantasia & Ground Bass; Hierusalem; Psalm 150; 3 Songs of Praise

*** Hyp. CDA 66150. Hill, St Michael's Singers, Trotter, RPO, Rennert

Where the organ piece unashamedly builds on an academic model, *Hierusalem* reveals the inner man more surprisingly, a richly sensuous setting of a medieval poem inspired by the thought of the Holy City, building to a jubilant climax. It is a splendid work and is backed here by the six hymns and the Psalm setting, all of them heart-warming products of the Anglican tradition. Performances are outstanding, with Jonathan Rennert drawing radiant singing and playing from his team, richly and atmospherically recorded.

(i–ii) The Canterbury Pilgrims. Overture At the Tabard Inn; (i) In Honour of the City

🔊 *** Chan. 9531 (2). (i) Kenny, Tear, Roberts; (ii) London Symphony Ch.; LSO, Hickox

Dyson's best-known work is preceded by the *Overture* based on its themes. Here the soloists all have major contributions to make, for Dyson's characterization of the individual pilgrims is strong; but the glory of the piece is the choruses, which are splendidly sung here. In *Honour of the City*, Dyson's setting of William Dunbar, appeared in 1928, nine years before Walton's version of the same text; Dyson, however, unlike Walton, uses a modern version of the text, as he does in *The Canterbury Pilgrims*, and to fine, direct effect. The splendid Chandos recording is fully worthy of the vibrant music-making here.

(i) Nebuchadnezzar; (ii) Confortare; O Praise God in His Holiness. 3 Songs of Praise; Woodland Suite

**** Chan. 10439. BBC SO, Hickox, with (i) Padmore, N. Davies; (i; ii) BBC Symphony Ch.

It was bold of Sir George Dyson in 1934, when commissioned to write a choral work for the Three Choirs Festival, to choose a subject which immediately invited comparison with Walton's *Belshazzar's Feast*, first performed with great success three years earlier. Needless to say, it cannot compare with the Walton masterpiece in memorability, but it is a fine work nonetheless, very well written for the forces used and similarly relying on clean-cut chordal choral writing, as in the unaccompanied passage at the start, very similar to the first chorus of *Belshazzar*. The fine tenor **Mark Padmore** sings beautifully in the role of the Herald, comparable with the baritone soloist in Belshazzar, while the baritone **Neal Davies** sings strongly too as Nebuchadnezzar himself. **Richard Hickox** draws warmly committed playing and singing from the **BBC Symphony Orchestra** and **Chorus**. The shorter works which make up the rest of the disc are well worth hearing too, most of them designed for use in schools, reflecting Dyson's role as a schoolmaster and, later, an inspector of schools. A very agreeable collection, an excellent addition to the series of Dyson recordings that Chandos has sponsored, very well recorded.

Quo Vadis

*** Chan. 10061 (2). Barker, Rigby, Langridge, Williams, Royal Welsh College of Music & Drama Chamber Ch., BBC Nat. Ch. & O of Wales, Hickox

In *Quo Vadis*, Dyson draws on the widest array of sources, rearranging texts from such poets as Campion, Vaughan, Herrick, Shelley, Newman and Bridges in an elaborate kaleidoscope of words, mixing different sources together in all but one of the nine substantial movements, even rearranging individual lines from Wordsworth's *Intimations of Immortality*. The warm but well-defined Chandos recording helps to heighten the impact of the incandescent singing of the **Welsh Choristers**, semi-chorus as well as full choir, inspired by the dedicated direction of **Richard Hickox**. Each of the four soloists – here a strong, firm and characterful quartet – in turn takes a leading role in the nicely balanced sequence of movements. They also sing as a quartet in the movements ending each half. Dyson's idiom may not be strikingly original but, with its lyrical warmth and fine control of texture, and with emotions often heightened by striking key-changes, the result will delight all devotees of the British choral tradition.

ELGAR, Edward (1857–1934)

(i–ii) *Adieu; Beau Brummel: Minuet;* (i; iii) *3 Bavarian Dances, Op. 27; Caractacus, Op. 35: Woodland Interlude. Chanson de matin; Chanson de nuit, Op. 15/1–2; Contrasts, Op. 10/3; Dream Children, Op. 43;* (iv) *Enigma Variations, Op. 36;* (i; iii) *Falstaff, Op. 68: 2 Interludes.* (iv) *Pomp and Circumstance Marches 1–5, Op. 39;* (i; iii) *Salut d'amour; Sérénade lyrique;* (i; iii; v) *Soliloquy for Oboe* (orch. Gordon Jacob); (i–ii) *Sospiri, Op. 70; The Spanish Lady: Burlesco. The Starlight Express: Waltz. Sursum corda, Op. 11*

Ⓑ *** Chan. 2-for-1 241-4 (2). (i) Bournemouth Sinf.; (ii) Hurst; (iii) Del Mar; (iv) RSNO, Gibson; (v) with Goossens

Sir Alexander Gibson's reading of *Enigma* has stood the test of time and remains very satisfying, warm and spontaneous in feeling, with a memorable climax in *Nimrod*. The 1978 recording, made in Glasgow's City Hall, remains outstanding. The *Pomp and Circumstance Marches*, too, have fine *nobilmente* and swagger. The rest of the programme is a collection of miniatures directed by either **George Hurst** or **Norman Del Mar**, both understanding Elgarians. Elgar wrote the *Soliloquy* for Leon Goossens, who plays it with his long-recognizable tone-colour and feeling for phrase. Most of the other pieces in Norman Del Mar's programme are well known, but they come up with new warmth and commitment here, and the 1976 recording, made in the Guildhall, Southampton, has an appealing ambient warmth and naturalness. George Hurst recorded his Elgar rarities a year earlier in Christchurch Priory, and again the recording has plenty of body, but there is more thinness in the sound of the violins in these items than with Del Mar.

Orchestral Miniatures: *3 Bavarian Dances; Carissima; Chanson de Matin; Chanson de Nuit; 3 Characteristic Pieces, Op. 10; Froissart Overture; May Song; Mazurka; Minuet, Op. 21;* (i) *Romance for Bassoon & Strings*

ⒷⒷ *** Naxos 8.557577. (i) Tilson; New Zealand SO, Judd

James Judd has always been a most understanding Elgarian, and here he conducts an attractive selection of shorter pieces as well as the early overture *Froissart*, all in understanding performances. The miniatures, at which Elgar was such a dab hand, are presented delightfully and with much affection, while *Froissart* is ripely passionate. First-rate sound.

'A Portrait of Elgar': *3 Bavarian Dances, Op. 27; Carissima; Chanson de matin; Chanson de nuit, Op. 15/1–2; Cockaigne Overture, Op. 40; Dream Children, Op. 43; Enigma Variations, Op. 36; Froissart Overture, Op. 19; Gavotte (Contrasts), Op. 10/3; Introduction & Allegro for Strings, Op. 47; May Song; Mazurka, Op. 10/1; Nursery Suite; Pomp and Circumstance Marches 1–5, Op. 39; Rosemary (That's for remembrance); Sérénade lyrique; Serenade for Strings, Op. 20; Salut d'amour, Op. 12;*

Spanish Lady (suite); The Wand of Youth Suite 2, Op. 1b

Ⓑ **(*) Nim. NI 1769 (4). E. SO or E. String O, Boughton

This very inexpensive four-disc set is made up of four separate Elgar collections, and Disc 3 duplicates the *Chanson de matin* and *Chanson de nuit*, already included on Disc 2. However, the latter collection (including the *Nursery Suite* plus *Dream Children* and most of the miniatures) is particularly attractive, for **William Boughton's** performances are graceful and sympathetic and have plenty of character. The *Enigma Variations* have many pleasingly delicate touches of colour, with the brass and organ making a fine effect in the finale. There is an easy swagger about the *Pomp and Circumstance Marches*. The warmly reverberant acoustic of the Great Hall of Birmingham University gives the performances of these larger-scale works a spaciousness that is entirely apt. What is more questionable is the scale conveyed by the recording (in the same acoustic) for the other, lighter and more intimate pieces, the large scale implied tends to inflate the music, particularly in the *Wand of Youth* excerpts.

'The Lighter Elgar': (i) *Beau Brummel: Minuet;* (ii) *Carissima;* (i) *Chanson de matin, Op. 15/2;* (ii) *3 Characteristic Pieces, Op. 10: Mazurka; Sérénade mauresque; Contrasts: The Gavotte AD 1700 & 1900.* (i) *Dream Children, Op. 43;* (ii) *May Song; Mina; Minuet, Op. 21; Rosemary (That's for remembrance);* (ii–iii) *Romance for Bassoon & Orchestra, Op. 62;* (i) *Salut d'amour, Op. 12;* (ii) *Sevillana, Op. 7; Sérénade lyrique;* (i; iv) *The Starlight Express, Op. 78:* Organ grinder's songs: *My old tunes; To the children.* (i) *The Wand of Youth Suite 1: excerpt: Sun Dance*

⊶ ✲ Ⓜ **** EMI (ADD) 5 65593-2. (i) RPO, Collingwood; (ii) N. Sinfonia, Marriner; with (iii) Chapman; (iv) Harvey

This beautifully recorded CD combines almost all the contents of two LPs. In the first, **Frederick Harvey** joins the orchestra for two organ grinder's songs from the incidental music for *The Starlight Express*, and they have seldom been sung more winningly on record. It is these items one remembers most, but the second collection under **Sir Neville Marriner** is hardly less successful. All the music is pleasingly delightful in its tender moods and restrained scoring, favouring flute, bassoon and the clarinet in middle or lower register. Very much worth having is the rhapsodic *Romance for Bassoon and Orchestra* with **Michael Chapman** the elegant soloist. The **Northern Sinfonia** play with style and affection. Throughout, EMI have provided that warm, glowing sound that is their special province in recording Elgar's music.

Caractacus: March. Coronation March; Empire March; Grania and Diarmid: Funeral March. March of the Moghul Emperors. Polonia; Pomp and Circumstance Marches 1–5, Op. 39

ⒷⒷ *** Naxos 8.557273. New Zealand SO, Judd

The five *Pomp and Circumstance Marches* in brisk, well-sprung readings are flanked by four rather longer pieces – three more extended marches plus, as a final item, *Polonia*, Elgar's

First World War tribute to Poland, with its sequence of Polish martial themes made to sound very British. The clarity and crisp ensemble of the *Pomp and Circumstance* pieces (as well as speeds on the brisk side) give them a winning freshness, with the brass particularly impressive. *Grania and Diarmid*, is here enhanced when it includes not just the march itself but the substantial introduction, usually labelled 'Incidental Music'. *March of the Moghul Emperors*, with its exotic percussion, is a welcome rarity too. The *Triumphal March* from *Caractacus* has the brassiest opening of any of the marches, and Judd makes it swagger infectiously. Warm, clear, well-balanced recording.

(i) *Chanson de matin; Chanson de nuit;* (ii) *Characteristic Piece: Contrasts (Gavotte), Op. 10/3;* (iii) *Cockaigne Overture;* (i; vii) *Cello Concerto;* (i; viii) *Violin Concerto;* (iv) *Coronation March;* (ii) *Elegy for Strings;* (v) *Enigma Variations;* (i) *Falstaff;* (ii) *Froissart Overture;* (v) *Imperial March;* (iii) *In the South;* (i) *Introduction and Allegro for strings;* (ii) *Serenade for Strings;* (i) *The Sanguine Fan (Suite). Symphonies:* (iii) *1 in A flat;* (vi) *2 in E flat;* (vi; ix) *Sea Pictures*

Ⓑ *** LPO (mono/stereo) (ADD/DDD) LPO 0016/20 (5). LPO, cond. (i) Boult; (ii) composer; (iii) Solti; (iv) Ronald; (v) Mackerras; (vi) Handley; (vii) with Tortelier; (viii) with Campoli; (ix) with J. Baker

This is a fascinating anthology, representing the **LPO's** coverage on record of Elgar's music over half a century, from recordings with the composer (1933) and **Sir Landon Ronald** (1935), through to **Sir Charles Mackerras's** *Enigma* Variations in 1985. The composer's own recordings have come up surprisingly well, particularly the *Elegy for Strings*, which is very moving. Most of these are key recordings and it is good to be reminded of **Alfredo Campoli's** memorable if not entirely idiomatic recording of the *Violin Concerto*. But the most valuable inclusion has not been published before: **Dame Janet Baker's** live concert performance of the *Sea Songs* in the Royal Festival Hall in 1984, two decades after her more famous recording with Barbirolli. The singing is as moving as ever, and it has the added intensity of live music-making with the ever-sympathetic **Handley** finding remarkable orchestral detail, so that at times one is reminded of *Gerontius*. The box comes with an excellent note by Andrew Neil, Chairman of the Elgar Society, and includes the text of the *Sea Songs*.

(i) *Cockaigne;* (i; ii) *Cello Concerto;* (i) *Elegy; Enigma Variations; Falstaff; Froissart; Introduction & Allegro for Strings; Pomp & Circumstance Marches 1–5; Serenade for Strings; Sospiri; Symphonies 1–2;* (iii) *3 Bavarian Dances; Caractacus: Triumphal March; Carillon; Chanson de matin; Chanson de nuit; Empire March; Grania and Diarmid (incidental music); Imperial March; In the South; Polonia; The Sanguine Fan; arr. Fantasia & Fugue in C min. (Bach); Overture in D min. (Handel).* (iv; v) *Violin Concerto;* (iv) *Nursery Suite; Severn Suite; Coronation March; Crown of India Suite;* (vi) *Organ*

Sonata (orch. Jacob); Wand of Youth (Suites 1–2); (vii) *Beau Brummel; Carissima; 3 Characteristic Pieces; Minuet; Dream Children; May Song; Mina; Minuet; Romance for Bassoon & Orchestra* (with Chapman); *Rosemary; Salut d'amour; Sérénade lyrique; Sevillana.* (viii) **The Composer conducts:** *Chanson de matin; Chanson de nuit; Cockaigne Overture; Land of Hope & Glory* (introduced by Elgar); *Pomp & Circumstance Marches 1–5; Salut d'amour; Serenade for Strings; Dream of Gerontius: Prelude. Piano Improvisation 4* (composer, piano **Chamber Music;** (ix; x) *Piano Quintet;* (xi) *String Quartet in E min.;* (v; xii) *Violin Sonata in E min.* **Piano Music:** (ix) *Concert Allegro; Serenade;* (xiii) *Organ Sonata in G* **Vocal Music** (with soloists & ch.): (iii) *The Apostles; The Kingdom* (with illustrated introduction by Boult); (xiv) *The Banner of St George; Great is the Lord; National Anthem.* (iv) *The Black Night;* (iv) *Caractacus;* (xv) *Coronation Ode;* (i) *Dream of Gerontius* (with J. Baker); (xvi) *From the Bavarian Highlands;* (iv) *The Light of Life;* (iii) *The Music Makers* (with J. Baker); (vi) *Scenes from the Saga of King Olaf;* (i) *Sea Pictures* (with J. Baker). (xiv) *The Spirit of England; Te Deum & Benedictus;* (vi) *The Starlight Express* **Choruses:** (xvii) *Angelus; Ave Maria; Ave maris stella; Ave verum corpus; Give unto the Lord; O Hearken Thou; Te Deum & Benedictus;* (xviii) *Deep in my soul;* (xix) *5 Part Songs from the Greek Anthology; Reveille; The Wanderer;* (xx) *Fly Singing Bird; The Snow; Spanish Serenade;* (xxi) *My love dwelt in a northern land; The Shower;* (xxii) arr. *Jerusalem* (Parry); (xxiii) *Songs, Op. 48/1; Op. 59/1, 3; Op. 60/1–2*

ⒷⒷ *** EMI 5 03603-2 (30). Various Os & Chs., cond. (i) Barbirolli; (ii) with Du Pré; (iii) Boult; (iv) Groves; (v) with Hugh Bean; (vi) Handley; (vii) Mariner or Collingwood; (viii) composer. (ix) Ogdon; (x) Allegri Qt; (xi) Music Group of London; (xii) Parkhouse; (xiii) Sumsion; (xiv) cond. Hickox. (xv) Ledger; (xvi) Del Mar; (xvii) Worcester Cathedral Ch., Robinson; (xviii) King's Singers; (xix) Bacholian Singers; (xx; iv) Liverpool Philh. Ch.; Tear; (xxi) CBSO Ch., Halsey; (xxii) Goldsmith's Choral Union, Orwell Hughes; (xxiii; vi) Tear, CBSO

This extraordinary collection covers the remarkable anthology of EMI recordings of Elgar's music made during the analogue era in the 1960s and 1970s, with a few digital CDs stretching into the 1980s. They are grouped (and we have listed them) under the key Elgar conductors of the time, notably **Barbirolli, Boult, Handley** and **Groves**, but room has been found for a final disc of the composer's own electrical mono recordings, dating from between 1926 and 1933. Chamber and instrumental music has also been included, and some fascinating miscellaneous vocal items. The transfers are of the highest quality and show that EMI, above all other recording companies, captures the true Elgar sound with its special combination of opulent *nobilmente* and brilliance. Many of these recordings are four-star and all are indispensable. The documentation is limited to titles and performers, but altogether this set is a bargain of bargains.

(i) *Cockaigne Overture*; (ii; iii) *Cello Concerto*; (iv) *Elegy*; (i) *Enigma Variations*; (v) *Falstaff*; (iv) *Froissart*; (vi; vii) *Introduction and Allegro for Strings*; (i) *Pomp & Circumstance Marches 1–5*; (vi) *Serenade for Strings*; (iv) *Sospiri*. Symphonies: (i) 1 in A flat; (v) 2 in E flat; (ii; viii) *Sea Pictures*

☛ (B) *** EMI 3 67918-2 (5). Barbirolli, with (i) Philh. O; (ii) LSO; (iii) Du Pré; (iv) New Philh. O; (v) Hallé O; (vi) Sinfonia of L.; (vii) Allegri Qt; (viii) with J. Baker

As an Elgarian **Sir John Barbirolli** was unsurpassed (not even by Boult), and EMI's budget box gathers together his key recordings of the orchestral works: the justly famous pairing of the *Cello Concerto* and *Sea Pictures* (with **Jacqueline du Pré** and **Dame Janet Baker** respectively) and the two miniatures, the *Elegy* and *Sospiri*, so touching in Sir John's hands. The analogue Kingsway Hall recordings, made between 1962 and 1966, are of EMI's ripest and are splendidly transferred to CD. The versions of the symphonies are the 1962 **Philharmonia** account of No. 1 and the 1964 **Hallé** performance of No. 2, both very personal and wayward readings. At the moment, many of these recordings are not available separately, so this box is doubly valuable.

Cockaigne Overture, Op. 40; Enigma Variations, Op. 36; Introduction & Allegro for Strings; Serenade for Strings, Op. 20

☛ 🌑 (BB) *** Warner Apex 0927 413712-2. BBC SO, A. Davis

Andrew Davis's collection of favourite Elgar works is electrifying. The very opening of *Cockaigne* has rarely been so light and sprightly, and it leads on to the most powerful characterization of each contrasted section. The two string works are richly and sensitively done. Similarly, the big tonal contrasts in *Enigma* are brought out dramatically, notably in Davis's rapt and spacious reading of *Nimrod*, helped by the spectacular Teldec recording. This is surely a worthy successor to Barbirolli in this repertoire and is an outstanding disc in every way. At its new Apex price it is one of the great Elgarian bargains.

(i) *Cockaigne Overture* (including an 'accidental stereo' excerpt); (ii) *Enigma Variations*; *Pomp and Circumstance Marches 1–2*; (iii) *3–5*

(BB) (***) Naxos mono 8.111022. Composer, with (i) BBC SO; (ii) Royal Albert Hall O; (iii) LSO

The novelty on this CD is a highly controversial 'accidental stereo' excerpt of the *Cockaigne Overture*, much talked about in 78-r.p.m. circles. The apparent stereo seems to have been made possible because, as was normal in recordings of this time, two turntables would be running during the cutting of the wax recording master discs, usually fed from the same microphone. Sometimes, as appears to be the case here, two separate microphones were used and (to cut a long story short) were in effect left and right channels. When synchronized together, they give a crude but discernible stereo effect. The producer of this CD, Mark Obert-Thorn, who has written a fascinating note included in the booklet, has made a superb job of this process. It undoubtedly adds another dimension to Elgar's recorded legacy.

Cockaigne Overture; Enigma Variations; Serenade for Strings, Op. 20.

(M) **(*) Telarc CD 80192. Baltimore SO, Zinman

David Zinman is a persuasive Elgarian, though his readings are affectionate rather than dramatically robust, and the cockney spirit of *Cockaigne* seems a little undercharacterized. However, the fine **Baltimore** string playing is idiomatically warm and expansive: the opening of *Enigma* has a gentle, touching lyricism, *Nimrod* is almost elegiac, while the great cello variation (B.G.N.) is gloriously rich. The Telarc recording is magnificent, with superbly resonant brass: the Guards ride by in *Cockaigne* grandiloquently, and the close of both the *Overture* and the *Variations* are sonically thrilling (bass drum and organ come through splendidly). The *Serenade* is beautifully played, the *Larghetto* touchingly nostalgic, and again the sound is first class.

Cockaigne Overture; Falstaff; Introduction and Allegro for Strings; Serenade for Strings

(B) *** CfP (ADD/DDD) 575 3072. LPO, Handley

Vernon Handley directs a superb performance of *Falstaff*, and the achievement is all the more remarkable because his tempi are unusually spacious (generally following the composer's markings). The playing of the **LPO** is warmly expressive and strongly rhythmic. *Cockaigne* is also given a performance that is expansive yet never hangs fire. The *Introduction and Allegro* and *Serenade* are digital and date from 1983. They were made in Watford Town Hall, but the balance is closer, the string outline more brightly lit. The *Introduction and Allegro* is passionate, yet with lyrical contrasts tenderly made; the *Serenade* brings a somewhat indulgent treatment of the *Larghetto*, and here comparison with Boult is not in Handley's favour. Nevertheless this reissue is a real bargain.

(i) *Cockaigne Overture*; (ii) *Froissart Overture*, Op. 19; *Pomp and Circumstance Marches*, Op. 39: (i) 1 in D; (ii) 2 in A min.; 3 in C min.; (i) 4 in G; (ii) 5 in C*

☛ (M) *** EMI (ADD) 5 66323-2. (i) Philh. O; (ii) New Philh. O; Barbirolli

It is good to have *Cockaigne*, **Barbirolli's** ripe yet wonderfully vital portrait of Edwardian London, back in the catalogue – one of the finest of all his Elgar records. *Froissart* is very compelling too (though the CD transfer is slightly less flattering here), and Barbirolli makes a fine suite of the five *Pomp and Circumstance Marches*. The lesser-known Nos. 2 and 5 are particularly gripping, with plenty of contrast in No. 4 to offset the swagger elsewhere. Here the sound is as expansive as you could wish.

Cello Concerto in E min., Op. 85 (original version)

*** Nim. NI 5763. Wallfisch, RLPO, Dickins – BRIDGE: *Oration*; HOLST: *Invocation* ***

The edition used here is marked as carrying Elgar's final instructions in every detail. Only a single note has had to be corrected (and that all but inaudible), but there are many differences in detail (dynamics, articulation, note lengths). There is also evidence available as to the composer's wishes concerning phrasing in the two recordings he conducted himself with Beatrice Harrison as soloist; and in two cases there are striking tempi changes (based on Elgar's own practice): in the *appassionato* section of the slow movement and at the end of the main quick section of the finale. But none of this would be effective were the soloist and conductor here not passionately involved in the music as they feel it. After the commanding opening flourish, **Wallfisch** and **Dickins** set off very gently indeed, and the cello and the orchestral strings sing their song with touching restraint. The finale unleashes the music's energy joyously, with more brilliant solo playing; but the return to the intensity of the slow movement has a heartfelt, elegiac feeling, before the abrupt surge to the coda. The recording is spacious, richly realistic and ideally balanced and, with its enterprising couplings, this CD is very desirable indeed.

Cello Concerto in E min., Op. 85

⊶ 💮 Ⓜ **** EMI (ADD) 5 62886-2. Du Pré, LSO, Barbirolli (with *Cockaigne Overture*) – *Sea Pictures* *** 💮

*** EMI (ADD) 5 55527-2. Du Pré, LSO, Barbirolli – DVOŘÁK: *Cello Concerto* **(*)

Ⓜ *** Sony 0746443954129. Ma, LSO, Previn – WALTON: *Cello Concerto* ***

**** Testament SBT 1388. Du Pré BBC SO, Barbirolli – BACH: *Cello Suites 1–2* ****

*** Virgin 5 45356-2. Mørk, CBSO, Rattle – BRITTEN: *Cello Symphony* ***

(i) Cello Concerto; (ii) Enigma Variations

*** Australian Decca 450 021-2. (i) Harrell, Cleveland O, Maazel; (ii) LAPO, Mehta

(i) Cello Concerto. Falstaff; (ii) Romance for Bassoon; (iii) Smoking Cantata

Ⓜ *** Hallé CD HLL 7505. (i) Schiff; (ii) Salvage; (iii) Shore; Hallé O, Elder

Jacqueline du Pré was essentially a spontaneous artist. Her style is freely rhapsodic, but the result produced a very special kind of meditative feeling; in the very beautiful slow movement, brief and concentrated, her inner intensity conveys a depth of *espressivo* rarely achieved by any cellist on record. Brilliant virtuoso playing too in the Scherzo and finale. CD brings a subtle extra definition to heighten the excellent qualities of the 1965 recording, with the solo instrument firmly placed. Alongside the original pairing with **Janet Baker's** *Sea Pictures* comes **Barbirolli's** superb account of *Cockaigne*, and the disc is now offered at mid-price.

EMI have now given an alternative coupling with the Dvořák *Concerto*, and this much-loved recording is given extra warmth and clarity in the new transfer. However, we retain our allegiance to the original pairing, which has been revamped as one of EMI's 'Great Recordings of the Century'.

Recorded in Prague in good stereo, this live recording of the Elgar *Cello Concerto* on Testament is just as fine as **Du Pré's** classic studio version, perhaps even finer, although the EMI recording and coupling with the *Sea Pictures* still makes for a first choice. In the earlier account the speeds are very similar with characteristically expansive treatment of the slow movement and *Epilogue* finale, with the cello-tone down to the subtlest *pianissimo*. The current pairing with her début recording of two Bach *Cello Suites* makes this Testament issue even more valuable.

In its rapt concentration **Yo-Yo Ma's** recording with **Previn** is second only to du Pré. The first movement is lighter, a shade more urgent than the du Pré/Barbirolli version, and in the Scherzo he finds more fun, just as he finds extra sparkle in the main theme of the finale. The key movement with Ma, as with du Pré, is the *Adagio*, echoed later in the raptness of the slow epilogue, poised in its intensity. Warm, fully detailed recording, finely balanced, with understanding conducting from Previn. At mid-price a splendid bargain.

It is quite a coup for **Mark Elder** to have so masterly a cellist as **Heinrich Schiff** in the *Cello Concerto*, with the first movement played with patrician nobility, very Elgarian, yet without inflation. *Falstaff* brings a thrustful account that carries one magnetically over the many contrasted sections, giving the illusion of a live performance; and the *Romance for Bassoon* makes an attractive supplement, with **Graham Salvage**, the orchestra's principal bassoon, as soloist, bringing out the glowing lyricism. As a tiny extra squib comes the first ever performance and recording of one of Elgar's 'japes', a protest for baritone and orchestra against a ban on smoking in the hall, imposed in his home by the composer's host and close friend, Edward Speyer.

Truls Mørk has the requisite blend of fervour and dignity, yet there is a freshness and directness here which is affecting. **Rattle** and the **Birmingham Orchestra** give excellent support, and the recording has excellent internal balance and naturalness of perspective.

Lynn Harrell's deeply felt reading balances a gentle nostalgia with extrovert brilliance. The slow movement is tenderly spacious, the Scherzo bursts with exuberance and, after a passionate opening, the finale is memorable for the poignantly expressive reprise of the melody from the slow movement. In the *Enigma Variations*, **Mehta** proves a strong and sensitive Elgarian, and this is a highly enjoyable performance which has long been admired. The vintage Decca recording, with the organ entering spectacularly in the finale, is outstanding in its CD transfer.

Other versions by **Rostropovich** (BBC Legends Mono 6198-2), **Anne Gastinel** (Naïve V 4961), the Finnish cellist, **Arto Noras** (Warner Apex 0927 40600-2) and his Sweish colleague, **Torleif Thedéen** (BIS 480) all have their merits but, are not among the primary recommendations.

(i) Cello Concerto; (ii) Violin Concerto

Ⓑ (***) Avid mono AMSC 587. (i) Casals, BBC SO, Boult; (ii) Sammons, New Queen's Hall O, Wood

In some ways **Albert Sammons's** 1929 recording of the *Violin Concerto* has never been surpassed. The first Avid CD transfer of these recordings was singularly unsuccessful. But the second, current version is infinitely superior. The sound in both works is now excellent, the *Cello Concerto* full and with the soloist firmly focused, the *Violin Concerto* even more remarkable in its warmth and natural clarity, with the solo violin caught vividly and cleanly. Sammons's high level of concentration and the atmospheric magnetism generated in the unsurpassed account of the finale come over very directly to complete a remarkably compelling listening experience.

(i; ii) *Cello Concerto;* (iii) *Dream Children: 2 Pieces for small orchestra, Op. 43;* (i) *Enigma Variations; Froissart Overture;* (iii) *Wand of Youth Suites 1 & 2;* (iii; iv) *Starlight Express: highlights*

Ⓜ **(*) Australian Decca Eloquence 442 8280 (2). Mackerras, with (i) RPO; (ii) Cohen; (iii) Welsh Nat. Op. O; (iv) Hagley, Terfel

This two-CD set includes **Robert Cohen's** later (1992) recording of the *Cello Concerto*, in which he imbued it with extra weight and gravity, masterfully sustaining slower speeds in the first and third movements, though the latter is marginally marred by some excessive coloration on the flat side. The finale, faster than before and more volatile, crowns the whole performance. The bright, up-front recording brings out the brash rather than the mellow qualities in the *Froissart Overture. Enigma* is rather sluggish at the start and in *Nimrod*, but erupts in a superb, impulsive finale, bold and brassy. The *Wand of Youth Suites* are superbly done, with **Mackerras** bringing out all the nostalgic charm of the gentler numbers and ending in a riotous version of *The Wild Bears*, brilliantly recorded. Brilliant can also describe the vivacious items from *The Starlight Express* which also offer exceptionally rich and vivid Decca sound (with a wonderfully resonant bass drum), and a pair of excellently characterful soloists. The haunting *Dream Children* pieces make a fine bonus.

(i; ii) *Cello Concerto;* (iii) *Enigma Variations;* (ii) *Pomp and Circumstance Marches 1 & 4*

⊶ Ⓜ **(*) Sony 82876 78737-2, (i) Du Pré; (ii) Phd. O; (iii) LPO; cond. Barenboim

Jacqueline du Pré's second recording of the Elgar *Cello Concerto* was taken from live performances in Philadelphia in November 1970, and this is a superb picture of an artist in full flight, setting her sights on the moment in the *Epilogue* when the slow-movement theme returns, the work's innermost sanctuary of repose. **Barenboim's** most distinctive point in *Enigma* is in giving the delicate variations sparkle and emotional point, while the big variations have full weight, and the finale brings extra fierceness at a fast tempo. The *Pomp and Circumstance Marches* are comparably lively and colourful, but the new Sony transfer still lacks something in body and amplitude.

(i) *Cello Concerto;* (ii) *Falstaff; Nursery Suite*

Ⓑ (***) Dutton mono CDBP 9776. Composer with (i) Harrison, New SO; (ii) LSO

Dutton's revised transfers of these three works are especially valuable, particularly the 1928 recording of the *Cello Concerto*

with **Beatrice Harrison** as soloist, which now has a satisfying weight and body, though Harrison's wiry tone is not to everyone's taste, and the intonation is occasionally suspect. The recording of *Falstaff*, made at the opening of the EMI Abbey Road Studios in 1931, has always been impressive in transfers, and the equally historic 1931 recording of the *Nursery Suite*, made in the presence of the dedicatees, the Duke and Duchess of York, as well as Princesses Elizabeth and Margaret Rose, comes out very brightly and clearly.

(i) *Cello Concerto;* (ii) *Symphony 2 in E flat, Op. 63*

⊶ ⒝Ⓑ (***) Naxos mono 8.111260. (i) Harrison, LSO; (ii) New SO; cond. composer

Mark Obert-Thorn's new transfers of Elgar's own recordings, made in 1930 in London's Queen's Hall and in 1928 in Kingsway Hall, also bring the music-making to life with astonishing realism. Especially in the symphony, one soon sits back and listens to Elgar's own electrifying performance. The composer's sense of line, his ability to mould rhythms, with speeds often faster than usual today, regularly brings an extra emotional thrust and the most poignant intensity in *pianissimos*. This applies also to the *Cello Concerto*, with **Beatrice Harrison's** simple eloquence and delicacy of feeling matched by the composer, although here the recording balance is more confined. As an unusual bonus we are offered the first (unused) take of the Scherzo of the symphony.

(i) *Piano Concerto* (realized Walker). *Adieu* (orch. Geehl); *Suite of Four Songs* (transcribed for orchestra, Haydn Wood); (ii) *Choral Music: The Immortal Legions; So Many True Princesses* (orch. Payne); *Spanish Serenade*

Ⓜ *** Dutton CDLX 7148. (i) Owen Norris; (ii) BBC Singers; BBC Concert O, Lloyd-Jones – COLLINS: *Elegy in Memory of Elgar* ***

Like the *Symphony No. 3*, the Elgar *Piano Concerto*, 40 minutes long, has been realized from the composer's sketches, written between 1913 and his death. Robert Walker has ingeniously put together a host of fragments, but the result fails to hang together in the way the *Symphony No. 3* does in Anthony Payne's realization. Nevertheless, Walker has done an excellent job so that, with **Owen Norris** displaying formidable concentration and virtuosity and **David Lloyd-Jones** drawing warmly idiomatic playing from the **BBC Concert Orchestra**, the result is always enjoyable.

The other items make a charming supplement, not just the *Suite* compiled by Haydn Wood and *Adieu*, a late piano piece orchestrated by Henry Geehl, but the three choral items. The Anthony Collins piece, based on a motif in the sketches for the *Third Symphony*, is another enjoyable rarity for Elgarians. First-rate sound.

Violin Concerto (original version)

*** Avie AV 2091. Graffin, RLPO, Handley – CHAUSSON: *Poème* (original version) ***

It is thanks to the enterprise of the violinist **Philippe Graffin** that we now also have this première recording of the Elgar *Violin Concerto* in its original form. There is some evidence that Elgar himself had reservations about some of Kreisler's suggested changes, even though he went along with them. That said, Graffin's performance with the ever-understanding backing of **Vernon Handley** and the **Royal Liverpool Philharmonic** is a most distinguished one, magically exploiting the range of *pianissimo* that the score asks for, not least in the accompanied cadenza, which is yearningly beautiful in this performance. The sound is first rate, and the disc comes with comprehensive notes, not just those of Graffin but also a reproduction of the script of a 1937 broadcast by W. H. Reed, Elgar's violinist friend, about the creation of the *Concerto*.

Violin Concerto in B min., Op. 61 (DVD version)

(N) *** Medici Arts **DVD** 3085228. Perlman, BBC SO, Rozhdestvensky – SAINT-SAËNS: *Introduction & Rondo capriccioso* ***; PROKOFIEV: *Violin Concerto 1* ***

Perlman's magisterial reading of the Elgar *Concerto* was recorded at the Royal Albert Hall during the 1981 Proms, the period when **Gennady Rozhdestvensky** was the **BBC Symphony Orchestra's** chief conductor. With a Russian conductor and an American soloist, the performance remains quintessentially English. A triumph all round. Discreet and intelligent camerawork from Peter Butler.

Violin Concerto in B min., Op. 61 (CD versions)

(M) *** EMI 5 03417-2. Kennedy, CBSO, Rattle – VAUGHAN WILLIAMS: *The Lark Ascending* ***

(N) *** Canary Classics CC06. Shaham, Chicago SO, Zinman

(BB) (***) Naxos mono 8.110902. Menuhin, LSO, composer – BRUCH: *Concerto 1* (**)

(BB) (**(*)) Naxos mono 8.110951. Sammons, Liverpool PO, Sargent – DELIUS: *Violin Concerto* (**(*))

(BB) (***) Naxos mono 8.110939. Heifetz, LSO, Sargent – WALTON: *Violin Concerto* (***)

(***) Beulah mono 1PD 10. Campoli, LPO, Boult – MENDELSSOHN: *Violin Concerto* (***)

(i) Violin Concerto; (ii) Cockaigne Overture; Froissart Overture; Imperial March

⊕—(B) *** EMI (ADD) 3 82156-2 (i) Y. Menuhin, New Philh. O; (ii) LPO, Boult

(i) Violin Concerto; Introduction and Allegro for Strings

⊕—(M) *** EMI 3 45792-2. (i) Kennedy; LPO, Handley

With this impressive remake of the Elgar *Violin Concerto*, **Kennedy** launched masterfully into his new career, refreshed after years of self-imposed exile from the regular concert platform. He made this new recording in Birmingham immediately after giving his first live concerto performance in years, and the reading has extra thrust and passion compared with his earlier recording of this epic work. The outer movements are faster and more freely expressive than before, the slow movement more expansive, with *pianissimos* of magical intensity, qualities equally impressive in the evocative Vaughan Williams piece.

But for many ears, **Nigel Kennedy's** earlier (1984) recording of the *Violin Concerto* has an even greater freshness than his later recording in Birmingham with Rattle. It is certainly commanding, and with **Vernon Handley** as guide it is centrally Elgarian in its warm expressiveness. This is particularly striking in the first movement and, both here and in his urgent account of the *allegros* in the finale, Kennedy shows that he has learnt more than any recorded rival from the example of the concerto's first great interpreter, Albert Sammons. Yet the influence of Yehudi Menuhin is also apparent, not least in the sweetness and repose of the slow movement and in the deep meditation of the accompanied cadenza which comes as epilogue. The recording is outstandingly faithful and atmospheric, coupled with Handley's passionate yet tender 1983 account of the *Introduction and Allegro*.

It is good to welcome an all-American performance of this most British of concertos that is so thrillingly passionate. **David Zinman** draws from the **Chicago Symphony** playing notable for its richness as well as its characteristic polish and detail. The playing of the orchestra finds a perfect counterpart in **Gil Shaham's** performance. His range of tone and of dynamic is extreme – some might feel too much so, when some of his *pianissimos*, as in the second subject of the first movement, are so gentle that they can barely be heard against the orchestra. But there is nothing self-indulgent or sentimental in his playing. Equally, Shaham's pronounced vibrato is always perfectly controlled. The slow movement brings refinement and purity, while the main *allegro* in the finale is fast and light, leading to a deeply dedicated account of the long accompanied cadenza. The recording on the Canary Classics label (personal to the soloist, Gil Shaham) is taken from live performances, and that adds to the impact, with the opulent sound matching the playing.

Mark Obert-Thorn's transfer of the classic first **Menuhin** recording with the composer is taken from what he describes as pre-war RCA Victor 'Z' shellac pressings, and the result is surprisingly successful, the soloist truthfully caught with a minimum of background noise, and the orchestral strings given plenty of body. The coupled Max Bruch, recorded the previous year, is less successful.

Menuhin's second recording (in stereo) in partnership with **Sir Adrian Boult** is hardly less moving and inspirational than his first. Boult directs the performance with a passionate thrust in the outer movements and with the warmest Elgarian understanding in the beautiful slow movement. The 1966 Kingsway Hall recording is characteristically warm and atmospheric, yet vividly focused by the CD transfer. Boult's personal insight into the problems of Elgar interpretation is well illustrated in the pair of overtures offered as coupling, and the early-1970s sound is well up to EMI's high analogue standard.

It is difficult to imagine the concerto being better played than it is in this inspired 1928 recording by **Albert Sammons**, who had recorded it in abridged form in the days of acoustic recording. Even the classic Menuhin–Elgar version, made four years later, wonderful though it is, is in some ways outclassed and collectors may now turn with confidence to the Naxos transfers.

Jascha Heifetz's unique reading of the Elgar is well transferred on Naxos in mellower sound than on previous RCA transfers. The ease of his virtuosity leads to dazzling bravura at speeds faster than usual, bringing a rare volatile quality in music that can easily seem a struggle. Yet that ease goes with a passionate warmth in Elgar's great lyrical moments. Heifetz treats the slow movement as a lyrical interlude, before the brilliant display of the finale leads to a deeply reflective account of the unaccompanied cadenza. Good (1949) mono sound.

Campoli gives a deeply felt but highly individual account of Elgar's great concerto. One can judge one's reaction to this performance by the control of vibrato on the opening phrase of his first entry. This is an essentially romantic approach, full of warmth; but Campoli applies himself here with dedication to a work he obviously loves, and the result – with Boult securely and compellingly at the helm – is most rewarding.

Other versions by Dong-Suk Kang on Naxos and Perlman on DG are less distinctive.

(i) Violin Concerto in B min., Op. 61; (ii) Enigma Variations, Op. 36

(M) (***) EMI mono 5 66979-2. (i) Menuhin, LSO; (ii) Royal Albert Hall O; composer

The 1932 Menuhin/Elgar recording of the Violin Concerto emerges on this newly remastered EMI CD with a fine sense of presence and plenty of body to the sound. As for the performance, its classic status is amply confirmed. Elgar's own 1926 recording of Enigma is too well known for much further comment. The engineers have done wonders with the current remastering, and this coupling is surely worthy to take its place among EMI's 'Great Recordings of the Century'.

(i) Violin Concerto; Serenade for Strings

**** Onyx 4025. Ehnes, Philh. O, A. Davis

James Ehnes is the soloist in this exceptionally subtle and understanding account of the Elgar Violin Concerto. His half-tones are ravishing, and though he uses a wide vibrato the result is anything but sentimental. The second subject in the first movement is deeply expressive but not rhythmically distorted, and the whole performance benefits from Ehnes's flawless intonation. The final epilogue of the unaccompanied cadenza is deeply meditative, crowning a performance that stands out among recent recordings. Andrew Davis's lilting account of the Serenade for Strings makes an excellent fill-up.

(i; ii) Violin Concerto in B min.; (iii; iv) Piano Quintet in A min.; (v) String Quartet in E min.; (i; vi) Violin Sonata in E min; (iii) (Piano): Concert Allegro; Serenade

(B) **(*) CfP 585 9082 (2). (i) Bean; (ii) RLPO, Groves; (iii) Ogdon; (iv) Allegri Qt; (v) Music Group of L.; (vi) Parkhouse

Hugh Bean recorded the Violin Concerto in 1972 in the wake of Menuhin's re-recording and, if his performance does not quite match that, it is still a very fine one and – as the splendid opening tutti immediately shows – it is strongly and authoritatively conducted by Sir Charles Groves; it has a warmth and simplicity that are disarming, with the first movement's second subject beautifully played, and the serene beauty of the slow movement well caught, followed by a successful finale with some very fine moments, especially in the closing pages. Not quite a first choice then, but well worth having when the rest of this collection is so desirable, including the Piano Quintet, the most ambitious of Elgar's three major chamber works. John Ogdon and the Allegri Quartet gives considerable satisfaction. The String Quartet is well done too. The Violin Sonata has both an autumnal quality and a Brahmsian flavour, and it responds to ripe treatment such as Hugh Bean and David Parkhouse provide. The Concert Allegro for piano is a valuable oddity, rescued by John Ogdon (the music was long thought to be lost) and splendidly played, while the Serenade brings some charming ideas, even if it reveals Elgar's obvious limitations when writing for the keyboard.

Dream Children, Op. 43; Nursery Suite; Wand of Youth Suites 1 & 2, Op. 1a and 1b

(B) (BB) *** Naxos 8.557166. New Zealand SO, Judd

(M) *** Chan. (ADD) 10422 X. (i) Bournemouth Sinf., Del Mar; (ii) Ulster O, Thomson

It makes an ideal coupling on Naxos to have the two Wand of Youth Suites, using themes Elgar had written in boyhood for a family play, alongside his other two works inspired by childhood, Dream Children of 1902 and the Nursery Suite of 1930. The freshness of inspiration is a delight, superbly brought out in these fine performances from New Zealand, recorded in Wellington in full, well-balanced sound, with James Judd always an idiomatic Elgarian. The Wand of Youth Suites in particular range wonderfully wide in mood and invention, culminating in the most brilliant movement of all, The Wild Bears, an orchestral showpiece here given a spectacular performance.

The Ulster Orchestra plays most beautifully and the ambience of the recording is well suited to the music's moments of gentle nostalgia. In the Wand of Youth the playing in Ulster is attractively spirited, and in the gentle pieces, the music-making engagingly combines refinement and warmth. The Nursery Suite is strikingly well characterized. Del Mar's account of the Dream Children dates from 1976 and the recording is analogue but still sounds well. But the more modern Naxos disc is even more tempting.

Enigma Variations: 'A Hidden Portrait' (with complete performance; DVD version)

*** BBC Opus Arte DVD OA 0917D. nar. A. Davis; BBC SO, A. Davis (V/D: Diana Hill)

Sir Andrew Davis's fine performance of the Enigma Variations, with Nimrod hushed, slow and steady, was recorded in the atmospheric surroundings of Worcester Cathedral, where Elgar said everyone should hear his music. Davis introduces a highly enjoyable documentary about the work and 'the friends pictured within'. He sets the work clearly against the composer's career, 'the masterpiece that catapulted him to fame in 1899', and each section is illustrated with archive material and in-period reconstructions, happily with no dialogue, only Davis's narration. Though the visual illustrations are fussy and irrelevant at times, the actual performance has no unwanted intrusions, just a sepia photo of the subject as each variation begins.

Enigma Variations (Variations on an Original Theme), Op. 36

(B) *** EMI (ADD) 3 82157-2. LSO, Previn – BUTTERWORTH: Banks of Green Willow; VAUGHAN WILLIAMS: Fantasias: on a Theme of Tallis; Greensleeves; The Wasps Overture ***

(***) BBC Legends mono BBCL 4172-2. LSO, Monteux – RAVEL: Le tombeau de Couperin; CHABRIER: Fête Polonaise; WEBER: Jubel Overture; PIJPER: Symphony 3 ***

**(*) Cala (ADD) CACD 0524. Czech PO, Stokowski – BRAHMS: Symphony 1 in C min., Op. 68 **(*)

(M) *** EMI 5 67748-2. LSO, Boult – HOLST: Planets ***

André Previn uniquely but imaginatively couples Elgar's most popular orchestral work with the three most popular pieces of Vaughan Williams, and for this reissue EMI have appealingly thrown in the Butterworth idyll for good measure. The Enigma is not entirely idiomatic, but it is refreshingly spontaneous. In some ways it is a similar reading to Monteux's with the same orchestra, strong and consistent, noble rather than passionate. The recording is impressively ample.

Pierre Monteux in his late eighties as principal conductor of the LSO made a classic recording of the Enigma Variations for RCA, but this recording, made in mono in 1962, is if anything even more intense, offering a noble, steadily paced account of Nimrod and erupting brilliantly in the final variation, representing Elgar himself. The coupling with the Third Symphony of Willem Pijper a welcome rarity.

Stokowski adroitly guides the players of the Czech Philharmonic through Elgar's masterpiece, illuminating every bar with his special affection, and the result is gloriously rich in spontaneous feeling, casting an entirely new slant on a work that one felt one knew very well indeed. Stokowski's insights are special to himself. The coupling is a splendid version of Brahms's First Symphony, recorded live with the LSO at the Royal Festival Hall in 1972.

Boult's Enigma comes from the beginning of the 1970s, but the recording has lost some of its amplitude in its transfer to CD: the effect is fresh, but the violins sound thinner. The reading shows this conductor's long experience of the work, with each variation growing naturally and seamlessly out of the music that has gone before. Yet the livelier variations bring exciting orchestral bravura and there is an underlying intensity of feeling that carries the performance forward.

With the BBC engineers capturing the atmospheric thrill of a Prom performance in the Royal Albert Hall, Sir Malcolm Sargent's 1966 account may be a degree less polished, but its thrust and urgency are irresistible, building up superbly to the final variations, in which the BBC brass and the obbligato organ convey an extra frisson, even if the sound is pretty opaque and there are too many extraneous noises.

Enigma Variations; Coronation March, Op. 65; In the South (Alassio), Op. 50

🔊 (BB) *** Naxos 8.553564. Bournemouth SO, Hurst

George Hurst with the Bournemouth Orchestra inspires richly expressive playing, full of subtle rubato which consistently sounds natural and idiomatic, never self-conscious. Like Elgar himself, he tends to press ahead rather than linger, as in the great climactic variation in Enigma, Nimrod, as well as in the finale and in the overture, In the South. The Coronation March also inspires an opulent, red-blooded performance, and the recording throughout is rich and sumptuous.

Enigma Variations; Elegy for Strings (2 versions); Introduction & Allegro for Strings (2 versions); Symphony 1 in A flat, Op. 55

(B) (***) Dutton Double mono/stereo CDSJB 1017 (2). Hallé O, Barbirolli

Barbirolli recorded both the Enigma Variations and the beautiful Elegy (for which he had a special affection) three times, and the Introduction and Allegro six times! Here we are offered the third (1947 – mono) and fifth (1956 – stereo) versions of the latter. In the earlier, mono account the recapitulation of the big striding theme in the middle strings already has superb thrust and warmth. The Enigma recording is the first (in mono), also from 1947, and it sounds very well in the present transfer, though the later and very exciting Pye stereo version, and the 1962 HMV version (see below) are finer on both performance and sonic grounds. Which is not to say that this strikingly fresh, earlier version is not worth having. But what makes the present collection special is the inclusion of the first (1956), originally Pye, stereo account of the First Symphony. The Hallé plays at a good sparkling allegro, and the remaining movements have comparable intensity, and in this new Dutton transfer the sound, though not as ripe as the later, EMI version, is much more than acceptable.

Enigma Variations; Falstaff, Op. 68

(N) ** Lyrita (ADD) SRCD 301. New Philh. O, A. Davis

Andrew Davis's performances are freshly thought, intelligent readings which lack the last ounce of magic to make them truly memorable. However, with excellent sound and top-notch playing, they are far from unenjoyable; and the mid-1970s sound is excellent.

Enigma Variations; Falstaff; Grania and Diarmid: Incidental Music & Funeral March

*** EMI 5 55001-2. CBSO, Rattle

In Enigma, Rattle and the CBSO are both powerful and refined, overwhelming at the close, and they offer a generous and ideal coupling. Falstaff is given new transparency in a spacious reading, deeply moving in the hush of the final death scene, with the Grania and Diarmid excerpts as a valuable makeweight. However this CD is still at full price.

Enigma Variations; In the South; Introduction and Allegro for Strings

Ⓑ **(*) CfP (mono/stereo) 3 52394-2. LPO, Boult

Anyone who thinks **Boult** could not let himself go in surging, passionate music should hear this thrilling mono version (from 1956) of *In the South*. As sound it is pretty good too, as the recording was made in the Kingsway Hall. The stereo recording of *Enigma* (where, from the opening bars, Boult shows how naturally he can inflect and shape an Elgarian melodic line) and the athletic and thrillingly strong version of the *Introduction and Allegro* could not be more enjoyable.

Enigma Variations; Introduction and Allegro for Strings

Ⓜ *** LPO LPO 0002. LPO, Haitink – BRITTEN: *Our Hunting Fathers* ***

Bernard Haitink's live recordings of the *Enigma Variations* and the *Introduction and Allegro*, dating respectively from 1986 at the Royal Albert Hall and 1984 at the Royal Festival Hall, make an excellent coupling for his outstanding Prom performance of the rare Britten cantata. Characteristically, his speeds are on the broad side but never involve a loss of tension, with nobility the keynote, not least in the radiant account of *Nimrod*. Well recorded, the **LPO** strings, with David Nolan as leader, are in first-rate form.

(i) Enigma Variations; Pomp and Circumstance Marches 1 & 4; Salut d'amour, Op. 12; (ii) Serenade for Strings in E min., Op. 20

Ⓑ *** Naxos 8.554161. (i) Czecho-Slovak RSO; (ii) Capella Istropolitana; Leaper

Though **Leaper's** slow account of the 'Enigma' theme makes an unpromising start, his reading of the *Variations* is most beautiful, with ripely resonant string-playing and with warmly expressive rubato in *Nimrod* suggesting that the **Slovak** players had been won over to Elgar by Leaper's advocacy. Most refined of all is the **Capella Istropolitana's** account of the *Serenade*, with the slow movement specially beautiful, finely shaded. An excellent compilation of Elgar's most popular orchestral pieces, brilliantly recorded.

Falstaff, Op. 68; Elegy, Op. 58; The Sanguine Fan (ballet), Op. 81

⊶ Ⓑ *** Naxos 8.553879. N. Philh., Lloyd-Jones

Rich, full Naxos sound with high dynamic contrasts adds satisfying weight to **David Lloyd-Jones's** taut and dramatic account of Elgar's elaborate Shakespearean portrait. Speeds are often on the fast side, but idiomatically so, with a natural feeling for Elgarian rubato and sprung rhythms. Both in *Falstaff* and in *The Sanguine Fan*, Lloyd-Jones draws fragmented structures warmly and persuasively together so that the late ballet-score emerges strongly, not just a trivial, occasional piece. The beautiful *Elegy* is most tenderly done, modest in length but no miniature. An outstanding bargain, competing with all premium-price rivals.

Falstaff; Froissart; (i) Romance for Bassoon & Strings; Grania and Diarmid: Incidental Music

⊶ Ⓑ *** Warner Apex 2564 62200-2. (i) Sheen; BBC SO, A. Davis

After the superb collection comprising *Cockaigne*, the *Enigma Variations* and the two key string works, this is **Sir Andrew Davis's** finest Elgar disc. *Falstaff* is a richly detailed, deeply affectionate performance, poignant too, and has much of the warmth of the Barbirolli version, yet it has a superbly expansive, modern, digital recording. *Froissart* too, without being pressed too hard, has a real Elgarian sweep and *nobilmente*. The bassoonist **Graham Sheen** is a most sensitive soloist in the *Romance*, and the *Grania and Diarmid* incidental music is delightfully presented, with much fine wind and string playing.

Falstaff, Op. 68; Symphony 1

Ⓝ Ⓑ (***) Naxos 8.111256. LSO, composer

Elgar recorded the *First Symphony* in 1930 (in Kingsway Hall) and *Falstaff* between November 1931 and February 1932. Those who invested in the Dutton transfers on EMI (now withdrawn) will not need this newcomer, good though it is, but anyone seeking this particular coupling will not be disappointed by Mark Obert-Thorn's excellent Naxos disc.

(i–ii) Introduction & Allegro for Strings; (i) Serenade for Strings; (iii) Elegy, Op. 58; Sospiri, Op. 70

⊶ ✿ Ⓜ **** EMI 5 67240-2. (i) Sinfonia of L.; (ii) Allegri Qt; (iii) New Philh. O; Barbirolli – VAUGHAN WILLIAMS: *Greensleeves & Tallis Fantasias* **** ✿

Barbirolli's famous record of English string music (the *Elegy* and *Sospiri* were added later) might be considered the finest of all his records, and it remained in the catalogue at full price for over three and a half decades. Now not only does it cost less, it rightly takes its place as one of EMI's 'Great Recordings of the Century', with the current remastering of an originally magnificent recording losing nothing, combining bite and excellent inner definition with the fullest sonority.

King Arthur: Suite; (i) The Starlight Express (suite), Op. 78

Ⓜ **(*) Chan. 6582. (i) Glover, Lawrenson; Bournemouth Sinf., Hurst

The *King Arthur Suite* is full of surging, enjoyable ideas and makes an interesting novelty on record. The *Starlight Express* Suite is taken from music Elgar wrote for a children's play, with a song or two included. Though the singers here are not ideal interpreters, the enthusiasm of **Hurst** and the **Sinfonietta** is conveyed well, particularly in the *King Arthur Suite*. The recording is atmospheric if rather over-reverberant, but the added firmness of the CD and its refinement of detail almost make this an extra asset in providing a most agreeable ambience for Elgar's music.

Serenade for Strings in E min., Op. 20

⊶ Ⓑ *** Warner Apex 2564 61437-2. RPO, Warren-Green – BRITTEN: *Simple Symphony*; BUTTERWORTH: *Banks of*

Green Willow; HOLST: *St Paul's Suite*; VAUGHAN WILLIAMS: *Fantasia on a Theme of Tallis* ***

With the **RPO** players ever responsive, **Warren-Green's** performance – part of an outstanding anthology of English music – is even finer than his earlier, deleted Virgin account in bringing out the grace of Elgar's string writing and the tender feeling of the *Larghetto*.

Symphonies 1, Op. 55; 2, Op. 63

▬ Ⓑ **** Lyrita (ADD) SRCD 221 (2). LPO, Boult

In 1968, at the time when **Sir Adrian Boult** recorded the two Elgar *Symphonies* for Lyrita, he wrote an open letter to *Gramophone*, couched diplomatically, but in fact reflecting his fury that at the sessions his recording manager had forced him on technical grounds to abandon his habit of a lifetime and have all the violins of the **LPO** on the left instead of divided right and left between the two sections. Now the comparisons with Boult's other recordings of the Elgar *Symphonies* demonstrate very clearly how fine they are – arguably the finest versions he ever recorded. Compared with the EMI versions of both works, which he recorded less than five years later, they are altogether tauter, with the ensemble of the orchestra noticeably crisper. The recording too is brighter and clearer as transferred on this CD. The idea of having the symphonies on two discs in a two-for-the-price-of-one package adds to the attractions of the new issue.

Symphonies 1–2; Cockaigne; In the South

Ⓑ **** Double Decca (ADD) 443 856-2 (2). LPO, Solti

Symphonies 1–2; Grania and Diarmid (incidental music), Op. 42; In the South (Alassio) Concert Overture; Introduction and Allegro for Strings; Serenade for Strings in E min.

▬ Ⓑ *** EMI (ADD) 3 82151-2 (2). LPO, Boult

Before **Solti** recorded the *First* he made a searching study of Elgar's own 78-r.p.m. recording, and Solti seems freed from emotional inhibitions, with every climax superbly thrust home and the hushed intensity of the glorious slow movement captured magnificently on CD. The *Second* receives an equally incandescent reading, once again closely modelled on Elgar's own surprisingly clipped and urgent performance, but benefiting from virtuoso playing and, as with the *First*, vintage Decca sound. Fast tempi bring searing concentration and an account of the finale that for once presents a true climax. The original **LPO** couplings of the *Cockaigne* and *In the South* overtures were logical, even if *In the South*, recorded in 1979, is over-tense.

  Sir Adrian Boult's final version of the *First Symphony*, made when he was 87, emerges here with splendid freshness. But Boult is less thrustful than Solti, with speeds less extreme in both directions. Most clearly distinctive is the lovely slow movement, presented as a seamless flow of melody, less 'inner' than with Solti, and, above all, glowing with untroubled sweetness. This HMV set is however completely superseded by the earlier Lyrita versions, made with the same orchestra. For his fifth recording of the *Second Symphony* Sir Adrian has mellowed a degree. The tempo is a shade slower

than before (and much slower than Solti's or the composer's own on the great leaping 12/8 theme). The peak comes in the *Funeral March*, where the concentration of the performance is still irresistible. In the finale, firm and strong, Boult cleverly conceals the repetitiveness of the main theme and gives a radiant account of the lovely epilogue. The companion performances of the two major string works and *In the South* are all strongly committed, and the early-1970s recording has plenty of breadth and range.

Symphonies 1–2; Cockaigne Overture; (i) Sea Pictures

*** Australian Decca Eloquence 442 8277 (2). RPO, Mackerras, (i) with D. Jones

Mackerras's performance of the *First Symphony* is one of the most bitingly passionate readings since Elgar's own, brilliantly recorded, and Mackerras's account of the brassy final coda is the most stirring yet, a thrilling culmination. In the outer movements of the *Second Symphony*, Mackerras's speeds are markedly faster than on most modern versions, yet there is no feeling of rush. It may not be the most brilliantly played version of the *Second Symphony*, but the energetic thrust goes with an idiomatic feeling for Elgarian rubato. And though the recording is finely detailed, it still has plenty of body. **Della Jones** gives a commanding performance of the *Sea Pictures*. The *Cockaigne Overture* is brilliantly done, with high contrasts and an incisive attack. Superb Decca sound.

Symphony 1 in A flat, Op. 55

ⒷⒷ *** LSO Live LSO 0017. LSO, C. Davis

Symphony 1; Imperial March, Op. 32

ⒷⒷ *** Naxos 8.550634. BBC PO, Hurst

Symphony 1; In the South, Op. 50

Ⓜ *** Decca (ADD) 475 8226. LPO, Solti

(***) Testament mono SBT 1229. LPO, Boult

(i) Symphony 1; In the South Overture; (ii) Canto popolare: In Moonlight

▬ Ⓜ *** Hallé CD HLL 7500. (i) Hallé O, Elder; (ii) Rice, Elder

Symphony 1 in A flat; Introduction and Allegro for Strings, Op. 47

▬ ✸ **** BBC (ADD) BBCL 4106-2. Hallé O, Barbirolli

Symphony 1, Op. 55; Organ Sonata Op. 28 (orch. Jacob)

**** Chan. SACD CHSA 5049. BBC Nat. O of Wales, Hickox

Symphony 1; Pomp and Circumstance Marches 1–5

▬ Ⓑ *** CfP (ADD/DDD) 575 3052. LPO, Handley

On 24 July 1970 **Sir John Barbirolli** conducted (and recorded) an inspired **Hallé** performance of Elgar's *First Symphony* in St Nicholas's Chapel as his major contribution to the King's

Lynn Festival. Four days later he suffered a fatal heart attack. There could be no finer memorial. But this final version has not only great depth of feeling but also the frisson of live music-making: it matches and even surpasses that first venture in its surging forward momentum, and the acoustic of the chapel provides a wonderfully warm glow and the richest amplitude for the Hallé brass and strings, without blunting the *fortissimos*. Most memorable of all is the sheer richness of the opening of the *Adagio*, sustained throughout with Barbirolli's characteristic warmth of feeling, while the impassioned Hallé string playing is as rich in tone as it is heartfelt. Everyone has their favourite version of the *Introduction and Allegro*, but no Elgarian will be disappointed with the present account, which still has the Hallé strings sitting on the edge of their seats, responding to the ardour of 'Glorious John'.

Richard Hickox and the **BBC National Orchestra of Wales** follow up their earlier recording of Elgar's *Second Symphony* with this impressive version of No.1, in many ways even finer than that earlier offering. It helps that the *Symphony* is most generously coupled with, the *Organ Sonata No.1* orchestrated by Gordon Jacob. As with No. 2, the SACD recording is spectacular in its range and clarity. Cunningly, Hickox has a wonderful way of presenting the great Elgarian melodies simply, starting with the spacious march of the introduction, setting out the motto theme. His control of the big 'gulp' moments, so important in this work, is masterly.

Solti's unsurpassed account of the *First Symphony* (see above) now arrives separately as one of Decca's 'Originals'. However, *In the South* is less successful, over-taut, if still exciting. Here Solti is not helped by a Decca recording on which brilliance is not quite matched by weight or body (an essential in Elgar).

Vernon Handley directs a beautifully paced reading which can be counted in every way outstanding. It is in the slow movement above all that Handley scores; his account is spacious and movingly expressive. The coupled *Marches* are exhilaratingly brilliant and if Nos. 2 and (especially) 3 strike some ears as too vigorously paced, comparison with the composer's own tempi reveals an authentic precedent. Certainly the popular *First* and *Fourth* have an attractive, gutsy grandiloquence. With very good sound, well transferred to CD, this is highly recommendable indeed.

Mark Elder's pacing is ideal, building the symphonic structure unerringly, with the slow movement bringing playing of exceptional refinement and beauty, with breathtaking *pianissimos*, and with the finale, taken fast, leading to a movingly triumphant return of the motto theme. *In the South* brings an equally compelling performance, again with textures remarkably clear. As a bonus, a first recording is included of the haunting *Canto popolare* from the overture in a vocal version, *In Moonlight*, with the mezzo, **Christine Rice**, as soloist and Mark Elder at the piano.

Reflecting the emotions of a live event, **Colin Davis's** use of rubato and expressive hesitations on **LSO** Live is greater than it might have been in a studio performance, notably in the tender account of the slow movement, but the concentration of the playing is so intense that the results are magnetic, not self-conscious. The performance builds up to a thrilling account of the finale, which prompts wild applause. Excellent sound.

On the bargain Naxos label comes a warmly sympathetic version of the *Symphony No. 1* from the **BBC Philharmonic** under **George Hurst**. Masterly with Elgarian rubato, he refreshingly chooses speeds faster than have become the norm, closer to those of Elgar himself. No one will be disappointed with Hurst's powerful reading, well coupled with the *Imperial March*.

The first wonder of the superb transfer of **Boult's** 1949 version of Elgar's *First Symphony* from Testament is the astonishing quality of the sound: mono only but full-bodied and finely detailed to give a keen sense of presence, with a surprisingly wide dynamic range. As to interpretation, the heavenly *Adagio* has an extra meditative intensity in the way that Boult presents each of the great lyrical themes, pure and poignant in their beauty. Nobility is the keynote of the whole interpretation. Boult's recording of the overture, *In the South*, made in 1955, brings out his thrustful side even more strikingly, with urgent speeds giving way in the lovely *Canto popolare* section to a honeyed beauty, with **George Alexander** the superb viola soloist. Sadly, the 1955 sound is shallower than that of six years earlier for the *Symphony*.

Symphony 2 in E flat, Op. 63

(BB) *** LSO Live LSO 0018. LSO, C. Davis

Symphony 2; In the South (Alassio)

*** Chan. **SACD** CHSA 5038. BBC Nat. O of Wales, Hickox

Symphony 2; Introduction and Allegro for Strings

⊶ Ⓜ *** Hallé CDHLL 7507. Hallé O, Elder

Symphony 2; (i) Sea Pictures

⊶ Ⓑ **** CfP (DDD/ADD) 575 3062. LPO, Handley; (i) with Greevy

Handley's remains the most satisfying modern version of a work which has latterly been much recorded. What Handley conveys superbly is the sense of Elgarian ebb and flow, building climaxes like a master and drawing excellent, spontaneous-sounding playing from an orchestra which, more than any other, has specialized in performing this symphony. The sound is warmly atmospheric and, at the peak of the finale, vividly conveys the added organ part in the bass (which Elgar himself suggested 'if available'): a tummy-wobbling effect. As a generous coupling **Bernadette Greevy** – in glorious voice – gives the performance of her recording career in *Sea Pictures*. Handley's sympathetic accompaniments are no less memorable, with the **LPO** players finding a wonderful rapport with the voice. In the last song Handley uses a telling ad lib. organ part to underline the climaxes of each stanza.

Mark Elder follows up his brilliantly successful earlier Elgar recordings on the **Hallé Orchestra's** own label with this glowing account of the *Second Symphony*. With speeds on the broad side in the first two movements, he draws muscular playing from the orchestra, taut and compelling, with the brass particularly impressive. Elder's control in the gradual building of climaxes is splendidly demonstrated in the Funeral March slow movement, helped by full, clear sound, recorded in the BBC's Manchester studios. The finale, rather brisker than usual, rounds off a deeply satisfying performance. As a pendant, Elder reads the Shelley poem, *Song*, from which Elgar's superscription is taken, 'Rarely, rarely comest thou, Spirit of Delight'. The *Introduction and Allegro*, recorded in the helpful acoustic of Bridgewater Hall, brings a performance of big, dramatic contrasts, with the Hallé strings ideally refined.

Hickox's version for Chandos was the first recording of an Elgar symphony in Surround Sound SACD, a very impressive pioneering effort, bringing out the glory of Elgar's orchestration. Interpretatively, Richard Hickox with the excellent **BBC National Orchestra of Wales** steers a distinctive course on the key question of the tempo for the surging 12/8 rhythms of the first movement, not as alarmingly fast as Elgar himself in both his recordings but faster than those, like Vernon Handley, in the noble Boult tradition. In the slow movement, by contrast, Hickox adopts a broad tempo and sustains it well. The transparency of sound also brings extra benefits in the Scherzo, as daringly fast as Elgar's own; in the finale too, the lightness and transparency of many passages, not least the epilogue, bring out the tenderness behind this ultimately elegiac movement. The *Overture, In the South* makes a valuable supplement, and the ripeness of the thrilling coda brings a final demonstration of this orchestra's impressive quality.

Recorded live in the autumn of 2001 as part of his Elgar series, **Sir Colin Davis's LSO** account of No. 2 follows a similar pattern to No. 1 in a spacious, refined reading that readily sustains speeds broader than usual. Particularly for a live recording, the dynamic range is remarkable, with whispered *pianissimos* of breath-taking gentleness, set against ripe *fortissimos* with glorious brass sounds. Though in the finale Davis adopts a fast speed, his account of the lovely epilogue with its hushed reference back to the opening theme of the whole work is exceptionally spacious and tender, making a haunting close.

(i) Symphony 1; Imperial March; (ii) Symphony 2; (iii) Symphony 3 (completed Anthony Payne)

(BB) *** Naxos 8.503187 (3). (i–ii) BBC PO; (i) Hurst; (ii) Downes; (iii) Bournemouth SO, Daniel

The three individual recordings of the Elgar *Symphonies* make a suitable budget commemorative boxed set, all individually recommendable. The three CDs in individual jewel cases are packaged in a slip-case. This set is available only in the UK.

Symphony 3 (from the composer's sketches, realized by Anthony Payne)

◷ (BB) *** Naxos 8.554719. Bournemouth SO, Daniel

(BB) *** LSO Live LSO 0019. LSO, C. Davis

Symphony 3 (completed from sketches, elaborated by Payne)

*** NMC NMCD 053. BBC SO, A. Davis

Symphony 3: (sketches and commentary by Payne)

(B) *** NMC NMCD 052. Gibbs, Norris, BBC SO, A. Davis

Symphony 3; Pomp and Circumstance March 6; (i) Queen Alexandra's Memorial Ode (all realized Anthony Payne)

**** Chan. **SACD** CHSA 5057. BBC Nat. O of Wales, Hickox; (i) with Adrian Partington Singers

Anthony Payne's realization of Elgar's sketches for the *Third Symphony* is so assured that it has already attracted a series of fine recordings. On the original disc **Andrew Davis** undoubtedly gives an inspired performance, the playing of the **BBC Symphony Orchestra** is thoroughly committed and the symphony is very well recorded. His illustrated talk, which comes as a supplement, gives precise details of his thinking and procedures, and this bargain-price CD makes a splendid addition to whichever recording of the complete work is chosen.

The following performance from the **Bournemouth Symphony Orchestra** under **Paul Daniel** matches Davis's earlier performance, and the leaner sound of the Bournemouth orchestra brings out the originality more, while the Naxos price gave this disc, with its first-rate sound, a competitive edge.

Colin Davis's LSO version then offered direct rivalry to its predecessors, bringing a performance just as powerful and concentrated, marked by refined string playing with *pianissimos* magically caught, even if the weight of tuttis is not quite as great as in the more forwardly balanced Naxos recording.

Richard Hickox's version tends to cap what has gone before. This is special, and not only in the quality of the performance, which is very compelling indeed. His reading is not only marginally stronger and more dramatic than the others, but it has the advantage of superb SACD surround sound and exceptionally attractive couplings. The *Memorial Ode for Queen Alexandra* as orchestrated by Payne, with the **Adrian Partington Singers**, is a tenderly moving piece, with Elgar in his role as Master of the King's Music setting a text by John Masefield. The *Pomp and Circumstance March No. 6*, like the symphony, was reconstructed and orchestrated by Payne, and in some ways is the most complex of all the *Pomp and Circumstance Marches*, a fine and valuable addition to an outstanding disc.

MUSIC FOR BRASS

Severn Suite, Op. 87

(BB) **(*) Hyp. CDH 55070. L. Brass Virtuosi, Honeyball – IRELAND: *Downland Suite*, etc.; VAUGHAN WILLIAMS: *Prelude on 3 Welsh Hymns* **(*)

Elgar was commissioned to write his *Severn Suite* for the 1930 Crystal Palace Brass Band Festival. It was scored by Henry Geehl, who apparently also had quite a hand in its construction (he complained that the composer's sketches were inadequate). Elgar later orchestrated it, but the original is very effective indeed, with the characteristic flourish of the opening *Prelude* (the theme of which returns at the work's close) contrasting with the sombre *Elegy* – all highly telling on brass alone. This is an excellent performance, though it could perhaps have had more swagger at the end, and ideally one would have liked a full-sized brass band, instead of this more modest-sized group of players, fine as they are. Excellent recording.

CHAMBER AND INSTRUMENTAL MUSIC

(i) Piano Quintet in A min., Op. 84; String Quartet in E min., Op. 83

🎵– *** Chan. 9894. Sorrel Qt, (i) with Brown

(BB) *** Naxos 8.553737. Maggini Qt, (i) with Donohoe

(BB) *** Discover DICD 920485. Aura Ens., (i) with Fink

Piano Quintet; Violin Sonata in E min., Op. 82

*** Hyp. CDA 66645. Nash Ens. (members)

The **Sorrel Quartet**, perfectly matched by Ian Brown in the *Piano Quintet*, give exceptionally searching readings of these two late chamber works of Elgar. These are dedicated performances which understandingly bring out the contrast between the expansive *Quintet*, bold in its rhetoric, and the more intimate *Quartet*, with its terse, economical structure. The breadth of expression, using the widest dynamic range down to the most delicate *pianissimos*, intensifies the impact of each performance, magnetic and concentrated as if recorded live.

The Naxos and Discover versions appeared simultaneously, both at super-bargain price, both very recommendable. The Naxos issue with the young British **Maggini Quartet**, joined by **Peter Donohoe**, offers stylish, nicely pointed, slightly understated readings. Yet it is the **Aura Ensemble** of Switzerland which, perhaps surprisingly, offers even more red-blooded, urgently expressive readings, helped by rich, forward sound.

With the violinist, **Marcia Crayford**, and the pianist, **Ian Brown**, both as the duo in the *Sonata* and as the key players in the *Quintet*, the performances on Hyperion are more volatile than usual; but it is the slow movements above all that mark these performances as exceptional. The central *Adagio* of the *Quintet*, far slower than usual, then brings the most dedicated playing of all, making this not just a lyrical outpouring but an inner meditation. Warm, immediate recording.

String Quartet in E min., Op. 83

*** Regis RRC 1015. Britten Qt – WALTON: *Quartet* ***

*** Discrete disc 0701. Pavão Qt – BAX: *Quartet 1* ***

*** ASV CDDCA 526. Brodsky Qt – DELIUS: *Quartet* ***

(*) Hyp. CDA 66718. Coull Qt – BRIDGE: *3 Idylls*; WALTON: *Quartet* *

There is a poignancy in this late work which the beautifully matched members of the **Britten Quartet** capture to perfection. Not only do they bring out the emotional intensity;

they play with a refinement and sharpness of focus that give superb point to the outer movements. With more *portamento* than one would normally expect today, the result is totally in style.

The ladies of the **Pavão Quartet** are completely inside the idiom of this work and give as thoughtful and concentrated a performance as one could wish for, even if the Britten Quartet on Regis, coupled with Walton, probably remains a first choice.

The young players of the **Brodsky Quartet** take a weightier view than usual of the central, interlude-like slow movement, but they amply justify it. The power of the outer movements, too, gives the lie to the idea of this as a lesser piece than Elgar's other chamber works. First-rate recording.

Though in the Elgar the **Coulls** sound almost too comfortable, less successful at conveying the volatile mood-changes, their relaxed warmth is still very persuasive; and the Walton performance, with the melancholy of the slow movement intensified, is very fine. Excellent sound.

Violin Sonata in E min., Op. 82

🎵– **** Challenge CC 72171. Van Keulen, Brautigam – GRIEG: *Sonata 1*; SIBELIUS: *Humoresques* ****

🎵– *** Globe Musical Network GMN CO113. Little, Roscoe – BAX: *Violin Sonata 2* ***

*** Nim. NI 5666. Hope, Mulligan – FINZI: *Elegy*; WALTON: *Violin Sonata* ***

(BB) (***) Naxos mono 8.110957. Sammons, Murdoch – SCHUBERT: *Rosamunde: Entr'acte*; DVOŘÁK: *Humoresque, Op. 101/7*; MASSENET: *Thaïs: Méditation*; NACHEZ: *Passacaglia on a Theme of Sammartini*; SAMMONS: *Bourrée*; TRAD.: *Londonderry Air*; MOZART: *Sinfonia Concertante in E flat*

(**(*)) Testament mono SBT 1319. Rostal, Horsley – DELIUS; WALTON: *Violin Sonatas* (**(*))

Violin Sonata; Canto popolare; La Capricieuse, Op. 17; Chanson de matin, Op. 15/2; Chanson de nuit, Op. 15/1; Mot d'amour, Op. 13/1; Offertoire, Op. 11 (arr. Schneider); Salut d'amour, Op. 12; Sospiri, Op. 70; Sursum corda, Op. 11

🎵– ✵ *** Chan. 9624. Mordkovitch, Milford

Violin Sonata; Canto popolare; Chanson de matin; Chanson de nuit; Mot d'amour; Salut d'amour; Sospiri; 6 Easy Pieces in the First Position

*** Chan. 8380. Kennedy, Pettinger

Along with the *Cello Concerto*, the *Piano Quintet* and the *String Quartet*, the *Sonata* belongs to Elgar's last creative period; all were composed at Brinkwells during 1918–19. Considering its quality, it is surprising how rarely it is given in the concert hall, though it has fared better on record. It is a work of striking power and eloquence and not the least of these four great pieces. **Isabelle van Keulen** and **Ronald Brautigam** are artists of keen insight, immaculate musicianship and culture, and they penetrate to its very core. Moreover, they are accorded first-rate sound, well balanced and very lifelike. A strong first recommendation.

Lydia Mordkovitch here transforms the elusive Elgar *Violin Sonata*. In rapt and concentrated playing she gives it new mystery, with the subtlest pointing and shading down to whispered *pianissimos*. The shorter works include not only popular pieces like *Salut d'amour, Chanson de matin* and *Sospiri*, but rarities like a version of *Sursum corda* never previously recorded and a little salon piece of 1893 which Elgar inexplicably published under the pseudonym, Gustav Francke.

Tasmin Little gives a warmly romantic, freely expressive reading of the *Sonata*, presenting it as a big-scale virtuoso work, where so often it has been underplayed. She allows herself fair freedom over tempo, so that the second subject conveys spontaneity in every phrase. Her volatility in the finale leads up to a magnificent conclusion. Very well recorded, with the Bax *Sonata No. 2* an excellent coupling, dating as it does from exactly the same period as the Elgar.

On Nimbus the Elgar *Sonata* brings a performance of high contrasts both in dynamic range – with **Daniel Hope** using daringly extreme *pianissimos* – and in flexibility of tempo. Hope then treats the enigmatic slow movement as more than an interlude, bringing out gravity through his dark violin-tone. In the finale, too, Hope conveys an improvisational quality, again using the widest dynamic range, finely matched by **Simon Mulligan**. Warm, atmospheric recording, less reverberant than many from this source.

At the start of the *Sonata*, **Kennedy**, also on Chandos, establishes a concerto-like scale, which he then reinforces in a fiery, volatile reading of the first movement, rich and biting in its bravura. The elusive slow movement, *Romance*, is sharply rhythmic in its weird Spanishry, while in the finale Kennedy colours the tone seductively. As a coupling, Kennedy too has a delightful collection of shorter pieces, not just *Salut d'amour* and *Chanson de matin* but other rare chips from the master's bench, although here he is less subtle than Mordkovitch. Kennedy is matched beautifully throughout the recital by his understanding piano partner, **Peter Pettinger**, and the recording is excellent.

Originally linked with the Dvořák *Violin Concerto* and now recoupled with Brahms, **Vengerov's** performance is at once passionate and large scale. He also brings out the thoughtful poetry of the piece, with a vein of fantasy in the elusive slow movement. (Warner Elatus 2564 60661-2)

Music for wind

Adagio cantabile (Mrs Winslow's Soothing Syrup); Andante con variazione (Evesham Andante); 4 Dances; Harmony Music I–IV; 5 Intermezzos; 6 Promenades

Ⓑ *** Chan. (ADD) 241-33 (2). Athena Ens.

This is a reissue of a pair of discs which originally appeared separately at mid-price. Elgar's 'Shed Music', as he called it, was written, when he was a budding young musician, for himself and four other wind-players to perform, and here it is presented very appealingly and excellently recorded.

PIANO MUSIC

Solo piano music

Adieu; Carissima; Chantant; Concert Allegro; Dream Children; Griffinesque; In Smyrna; May Song; Minuet; Pastorale; Presto; Rosemary; Serenade; Skizze; Sonatina

**(*) Chan. 8438. Pettinger

The Chandos record includes nearly all of Elgar's piano music. This has not established itself in the piano repertoire but, as **Peter Pettinger** shows, there are interesting things in this byway of English music (such as the *Skizze* and *In Smyrna*). We get both the 1889 version of the *Sonatina* and its much later revision. Committed playing from this accomplished artist, and a pleasing recording too, with fine presence on CD.

Carissima; Dream Children, Op. 43; Douce Pensée; Echo's Dance; Enigma Variations (trans. Elgar); Sérénade Mauresque; Sonatina in G; Une Idylle, Op. 4/1

ⒷⒷ *** Naxos 8.570166. Wass

This collection of some of the lighter piano pieces (as well as the piano transcription of the *Enigma Variations*) are treasurable, particularly in such sensitive hands as those of **Ashley Wass**. First-rate sound.

ORGAN MUSIC

Organ Sonata 1 in G, Op. 28

*** Priory PRDC 401. Scott (organ of St Paul's Cathedral) – HARRIS: *Sonata* ***; BAIRSTOW: *Organ Sonata* ***

Elgar's *Organ Sonata* is a ripely expansive piece, a richly inspired work, more of a symphony than a sonata. **John Scott** gives an excitingly spontaneous performance and the St Paul's Cathedral organ seems an ideal choice, although some of the *pianissimo* passages become rather recessed. The recording has plenty of spectacle and the widest dynamic range.

VOCAL AND CHORAL MUSIC

Angelus; Ave Maria; Ave maris stella; Ave verum corpus; Ecce sacerdos magnus; Fear not, O land; Give unto the Lord; Great is the Lord; I sing the birth; Lo! Christ the Lord is born; O hearken thou; O salutaris hostia 1–3

ⒷⒷ *** Hyp. Helios CDH 55147. Worcester Cathedral Ch., Hunt; A. Partington (organ)

Though in the grand setting of Psalm 48, *Great is the Lord*, one misses the impact of a big choir, the refinement of **Dr Hunt's** singers, their freshness and bloom as recorded against a helpful acoustic are ample compensation, particularly when the feeling for Elgarian phrasing and rubato is unerring. The coronation anthem *O hearken thou* would also benefit from larger-scale treatment, convincing as this refined performance is; but most of these 14 items are more intimate, and the **Worcester** performances are near ideal, with clean ensemble, fine blending and taut rhythmic control. Vividly atmospheric recording, which still allows for full detail to emerge.

Ave Maria; Ave maris stella; Ave verum corpus; Benedictus, Op. 34/2; Give unto the Lord (Psalm 29), Op. 74; Go song of mine, Op. 57; Great is the Lord (Psalm 48), Op. 67; The Light of Life, Op. 29; Seek Him that maketh the seven stars; Light of the world. O hearken Thou, Op. 64; O salutaris hostia; Te Deum laudamus, Op. 34/1; The Apostles: The Spirit of the Lord is upon me

🎵 (BB) *** Naxos 8.557288. St John's, Cambridge, College Ch., Robinson; J. Vaughan (organ)

Elgar's shorter Latin settings, *Ave verum corpus, Ave Maria, Ave maris stella, O hearken Thou* and *O salutaris hostia*, are all quite lovely. The more ambitious *Te Deum* and *Benedictus* was written for the Hereford Three Choirs Festival of 1897 and, like the Psalm setting *Great is the Lord* (first heard at Westminster Abbey in 1912), shows Elgar at full stretch. It is also good to have the serene *Prologue* to *The Apostles* (1903), *The Spirit of the Lord*, and, finally, the two memorable excerpts from Elgar's first oratorio, *The Light of Life*, notably the stirring *Light of the world*, which is the exultant closing chorus. Splendid singing throughout and excellent recording make this a collection to treasure.

The Apostles, Op. 49

*** Chan. 8875/6. Hargan, Hodgson, Rendall, Roberts, Terfel, Lloyd, L. Symphony Ch., LSO, Hickox

(M) *** EMI (ADD) 7 64206-2 (2). Armstrong, Watts, Tear, Luxon, Grant, Carol Case, Downe House School Ch., LPO Ch., LPO, Boult (with *Light of Life: Meditation*)

Where Boult's reading has four-square nobility, **Hickox** is far more flexible in his expressiveness, drawing singing from his chorus that far outshines that on the earlier reading. Most of his soloists are preferable too, for example **Stephen Roberts** as a light-toned Jesus and **Robert Lloyd** characterful as Judas. Only the tenor, **David Rendall**, falls short, with vibrato exaggerated by the microphone. The recording, made in St Jude's, Hampstead, is among Chandos's finest, both warm and incandescent, with plenty of detail.

Boult's performance gives the closing scene great power and a wonderful sense of apotheosis, with the spacious sound-balance rising to the occasion. Generally fine singing – notably from **Sheila Armstrong** and **Helen Watts** – and a 1973/4 Kingsway Hall recording as rich and faithful as anyone could wish for. The powerfully lyrical *Meditation* from *The Light of Life* makes a suitable postlude without producing an anticlimax, again showing Boult at his most inspirational.

The Black Knight, Op. 3; Scenes from the Bavarian Highlands, Op. 27

🎵 ⚙ *** Chan. 9436. L. Symphony Ch., LSO, Hickox

The cantata *The Black Knight* is based on a similar story to that of Mahler's early cantata, *Das klagende Lied*. **Hickox**,

helped by exceptionally rich and full recording, with vivid presence, consistently brings out the dramatic tensions of the piece as well as the refinement and beauty of the poetic sequences, to make the previous recording under Sir Charles Groves sound too easy-going, enjoyable though it is. The part-songs inspired by the composer's visit to Bavaria then add even more exhilaration, with the vigour and joy of the outer movements – better known in Elgar's orchestral version – brought out winningly, and with the **London Symphony Chorus** at its freshest and most incisive. A disc to win new admirers for two seriously neglected works.

(i) Caractacus (complete); Coronation March; Imperial March; Enigma Variations

(M) *** EMI 7 63807-2 (2). (i) Armstrong, Tear, Glossop, Rayner Cook, King, Stuart, RLPO Ch.; RLPO, Groves

(i) Caractacus, Op. 35. Severn Suite (full orchestral version)

*** Chan. 9156/7. (i) Howarth, Wilson-Johnson, Davies, Roberts, Miles, L. Symphony Ch.; LSO, Hickox

Caractacus, based on the story of the ancient British hero pardoned by the Emperor Claudius, dropped out of the regular repertory long ago, forgotten except for the rousing *Triumphal March* and some notorious lines about the nations 'standing to hymn the praise of Britain like brothers hand in hand'. **Groves** offers a very fine performance with consistently excellent soloists and fine choral singing which with ripe recording brings out all the Elgarian atmosphere (even if it does not manage the clearest projection of the words).

Elgar's *Caractacus* draws from **Hickox** and his splendid **LSO** forces a fresh, sympathetic reading, generally very well sung, with **David Wilson-Johnson** in the title-role, recorded in opulent Chandos sound. The only reservation is that the earlier, EMI recording conducted by Sir Charles Groves was crisper in ensemble and even better sung, with even more seductive pointing of rhythm. For coupling, Hickox has the full orchestral arrangement of Elgar's very last work, originally for brass band, the *Severn Suite*.

(i) Coronation Ode, Op. 44; The Spirit of England, Op. 80

🎵 (M) *** Chan. 6574. Cahill, SNO Ch. and O, Gibson; (i) with Collins, Rolfe Johnson, Howell

Gibson's performances combine fire and panache, and the recorded sound has an ideal Elgarian expansiveness, the choral tone rich and well focused, the orchestral brass given plenty of weight, and the overall perspective highly convincing. He is helped by excellent soloists, with **Anne Collins** movingly eloquent in her dignified restraint when she introduces the famous words of *Land of Hope and Glory* in the finale; and the choral entry which follows is truly glorious in its power and amplitude. *The Spirit of England*, a wartime cantata to words of Laurence Binyon, is in some ways even finer, with the final setting of *For the fallen* rising well above the level of his occasional music.

(ii; iii; iv) Coronation Ode, Op. 44; (i; ii) The Spirit of England, Op. 80; (i) O hearken thou, Op. 64 (with (iv) Land of Hope and Glory (arr. Elgar))

Ⓜ *** EMI (ADD/DDD) 5 85148-2. (i) L. Symphony Ch., N. Sinfonia, Hickox; (ii) Lott; (iii) Hodgson, Morton, Roberts, Cambridge University Musical Soc.; (iv) Ch. of King's College, Cambridge, Band of the Royal Military School of Music, New Philh. O, Ledger – PARRY: *I Was Glad* ***

Ledger is superb in capturing the swagger and panache of the *Coronation Ode*, flouting all thoughts of potentially bad taste. There is excellent singing and playing, although the male soloists do not quite match their female colleagues. The spectacular (1969) recording, made in King's College Chapel with extra brass bands, makes a splendid impact, with the resonant acoustics creating a jumbo *Land of Hope and Glory* at the close. The remastering does not seem to make the sound as ideally sharp as it might be, but it remains a compulsive listening experience nevertheless. **Hickox** conducts a rousing digital version of *The Spirit of England*, magnificently defying the dangers of wartime bombast, with the **London Symphony Chorus** on radiant form. With a beautiful performance of *O hearken thou*, Elgar's rousing version of the *National Anthem*, and Parry's *I was glad*, this CD is a must for all Elgarians.

The Dream of Gerontius (DVD version)

🔗 🗝️ **** Warner **DVD** 3984 22351-2. Langridge, Wyn-Rogers, Miles, BBC Ch. & SO, A. Davis

Andrew Davis is one of the most recent conductors in a distinguished line (including Sargent, Boult and Barbirolli, and even Britten) for whom *Gerontius* has a special place in his affections. In the introduction to this performance, created to celebrate the BBC's 75th anniversary, he tells us that the work has always been part of his being, and his dedication surely comes out in every bar of the music. It is a truly inspired account with a wonderfully flexible forward momentum – in the great *Praise to the Holiest in the Height* chorus, the acceleration to the climax and the final pulling back is breathtaking. The **BBC Chorus** sings superbly, and the close of the work, illuminated by **Catherine Wyn-Rogers's** infinitely touching 'Farewell' makes an even more moving apotheosis. **Philip Langridge** is at his very finest as Gerontius, deeply involved and colouring the words with remarkably controlled intensity; and **Alastair Miles**, resonantly combining the roles of Priest and Angel of Agony, is tremendously commanding, with the augmented **BBC Chorus** on top form, joining him to make the 'Go forth' sequence at the end of Part One a truly riveting conclusion. Here the rich reverberation of St Paul's Cathedral adds to the magnificence of the climax, underpinned by the organ pedals; and in the infamous Demons' chorus the clouding of the resonance adds to the atmospheric impact when Davis takes it so breathtakingly fast. Altogether this is the finest recorded *Gerontius* ever, and not only is it an advantage to follow the words of Cardinal Newman's poem in the surtitles, but Bob Coles's imaginative camera placement means that the text is poignantly illustrated by images from the glorious interior of the cathedral itself. Altogether

a magnificent achievement, and James Naughtie's introduction is well worth having too.

The Dream of Gerontius, Op. 38 (CD versions)

Ⓝ 🔗 🌼 Ⓜ **** Hallé CDHLD 7520 (2). Groves, Coote, Terfel, Hallé Ch. & Youth Ch., Hallé O, Elder

*** Chan. 8641/2. Palmer, A. Davies, Howell, L. Symphony Ch. & LSO, Hickox – PARRY: *Anthems* ***

Ⓑ (***) CfP mono 585 9042 (2). Lewis, Thomas, Cameron, Huddersfield Ch. Soc., RLPO, Sargent – WALTON: *Belshazzar's Feast* (**)

(i) The Dream of Gerontius; (ii) Cello Concerto

(***) Testament mono SBT 2025 (2). (i) Nash, Ripley, Noble, Walker, Huddersfield Ch. Soc., Liverpool PO; (ii) P. Tortelier, BBC SO, Sargent

(i) The Dream of Gerontius; (ii) The Music Makers, Op. 69

Ⓜ *** EMI (ADD) 5 66540-2 (2). (i) Gedda, Watts, Lloyd, Alldis Ch., LPO Ch., New Philh. O; (ii) Baker, LPO Ch., LPO, Boult

Ⓜ *** EMI (ADD) 3 91978-2 (2). (i; ii) Baker, (i) Lewis, Borg, Hallé & Sheffield Philh. Ch., Hallé O, Barbirolli; (ii) LPO Ch., LPO, Boult

(i) The Dream of Gerontius; (ii) Sea Pictures

Ⓑ *** EMI (ADD) 5 73579-2 (2). (i) Baker, Lewis, Borg, Hallé & Sheffield Philharmonic Ch., Amb. S., Hallé O; (ii) Baker, LSO, Barbirolli

Mark Elder's Hallé recording of *Gerontius* now goes straight to the top of the list, alongside Andrew Davis's DVD version, which has an added dimension. But Elder conjures consistently inspired playing from the **Hallé Orchestra** and magnificent singing from the choir, creating remarkable warmth and tension in *pianissimos* and wonderfully expansive climaxes in a recording which has the widest possible dynamic range. One has only to sample the 'Demons' Chorus', *Go forth*, or *Praise to the Holiest* to experience the power and weight of the vocal projection. But the wonderful acoustics of Manchester's Bridgewater Hall and Andrew Keener's engineering also come into the matter, adding a bloom to the overall sound, yet (with Mark Elder's direction) showing countless detail in Elgar's wonderfully imaginative score, hardly realized before on record. The soloists are splendid too and every word is clear. **Paul Groves** is a most affecting Gerontius, warm-toned and intense, and (while one does not forget Janet Baker), **Alice Coote** sings radiantly as the Angel, especially in her gentle 'Farewell'. **Bryn Terfel** is predictably commanding in both his roles, while not eclipsing memories of either Alastair Miles (with Andrew Davis) or Robert Lloyd (with Boult). But one of the most memorable parts of the performance is the superbly played *Prelude*, in which Mark Elder manages to encapsulate the whole work in ten and a half minutes. This is well worth playing separately on its own.

Boult's total dedication is matched by his powerful

sense of drama. **Robert Lloyd** is a magnificent Priest and Angel of Agony and the spiritual feeling is intense throughout, but the human qualities of the narrative are also fully realized. **Nicolai Gedda** in the role of Gerontius brings a new dimension to this characterization. He is perfectly matched by **Helen Watts** as the Angel. It is a fascinating vocal partnership and is matched by the commanding manner which Robert Lloyd finds for both his roles. The orchestral playing is always responsive, and often, like the choral singing, very beautiful, while the dramatic passages bring splendid incisiveness and bold assurance from the singers. The 1976 Kingsway Hall recording has been remastered quite stunningly: the sound has great presence as well as ideal ambient warmth and atmosphere. It is technically, as well as musically, a truly great recording. The performance and recording of *The Music Makers*, made at Abbey Road a decade earlier, is also very successful. If only the whole piece lived up to the uninhibited choral setting of the *Nimrod* variation from *Enigma*, it would be another Elgar masterpiece. Nevertheless, Boult's dedication, matched by **Janet Baker's** masterly eloquence, holds the listener throughout, and the current transfer has brought a new vividness to the choral contribution.

Barbirolli's red-blooded reading of *Gerontius* is among the most heart-warmingly dramatic ever recorded; here it is offered, in a first-rate CD transfer, in coupling with **Janet Baker's** rapt and heartfelt account of *Sea Pictures*. No one on record can match her in this version of *Gerontius* for the fervent intensity and glorious tonal range of her singing as the Angel, one of her supreme recorded performances; and the clarity of CD intensifies the experience. In terms of pure dedication the emotional thrust of Barbirolli's reading conveys the deepest spiritual intensity. The recording may have its hints of distortion, but the sound is overwhelming. **Richard Lewis** gives one of his finest recorded performances, searching and intense, and, though **Kim Borg** is unidiomatic in the bass role, his bass tones are rich in timbre, even if his projection lacks the dramatic edge of Robert Lloyd on the reissued Boult set. The alternative coupling of **Boult's** *Music Makers* and **Barbirolli's** *Gerontius* (with **Janet Baker** common to both) now comes in EMI's 'Great Recordings of the Century'.

Sir Malcolm Sargent in 1945 paced the score perfectly, drawing incandescent singing from the **Huddersfield Choral Society**. The soloists too, superbly led by **Heddle Nash** as Gerontius, have a freshness and clarity rarely matched, with Nash's ringing tenor consistently clean in attack. Though **Gladys Ripley's** fine contralto is caught with a hint of rapid flutter, she matches the others in forthright clarity, with **Dennis Noble** as the Priest and **Norman Walker** as the Angel of the Agony both strong and direct. The mono recording captures detail excellently; even if inevitably the dynamic range is limited and the chorus lacks something in body, such a climax as *Praise to the Holiest* has thrilling bite. The first and finest of **Paul Tortelier's** three recordings of the Elgar *Cello Concerto* makes an ideal coupling, emotionally intense within a disciplined frame.

Hickox's performance is deeply understanding, not always ideally powerful in the big climaxes but paced most sympathetically, with a natural understanding of Elgarian rubato. The soloists make a characterful team. **Arthur Davies** is a strong and fresh-toned Gerontius; **Gwynne Howell** in the bass roles is powerful if not always ideally steady; and **Felicity Palmer**, though untraditionally bright of tone with her characterful vibrato, is strong and illuminating. Though on balance Boult's soloists are even finer, Hickox's reading in its expressive warmth conveys much love for this score, and the last pages with their finely sustained closing *Amen* are genuinely moving.

The outstanding alternative **Sargent** performance of *The Dream of Gerontius* brings a great spiritual perception and, as with Boult, the closing pages of the first and second parts have a rapt intensity that is very moving, without any hint of emotional indulgence. EMI chose the excerpt of *Go Forth Upon Thy Journey* (with **John Cameron** in superb voice) to include in their anthology tribute to Sir Malcolm Sargent and this shows, as does the whole performance, an inspiration which this conductor only rarely found in the recording studio. **Richard Lewis** is a fine Gerontius and his dialogues with **Marjorie Thomas** have a beauty and stillness that is totally memorable. The one failure of the Sargent performance is the *Demons' Chorus*, in which the **Huddersfield Chorus** fail to let themselves go. But everywhere else the singing is magnificent, one of their finest achievements on disc, and the mono recording is generally worthy of it.

(i) *The Kingdom, Op. 51*; (ii) *Coronation Ode, Op. 34*

(M) *** EMI (ADD) 7 64209-2. (i) M. Price, Minton, Young, Shirley-Quirk, LPO Ch., LPO, Boult; (ii) Lott, Hodgson, Morton, Cambridge University Music Soc., King's College, Cambridge, Ch., New Philh. O, Band of Royal Military School of Music, Kneller Hall, Ledger

The Kingdom; Sursum corda; Sospiri

*** Chan. 8788/9. Marshall, Palmer, A. Davies, Wilson-Johnson, L. Symphony Ch., LSO, Hickox

Boult was devoted to *The Kingdom*, identifying with its comparative reticence, and his dedication emerges clearly throughout a glorious performance. The melody which Elgar wrote to represent the Holy Spirit is one of the noblest that even he created, and the soprano aria, *The sun goeth down* (beautifully sung by **Margaret Price**), leads to a deeply affecting climax. The other soloists also sing splendidly, and the only reservation concerns the chorus, which is not quite as disciplined as it might be and sounds a little too backward for some of the massive effects which cap the power of the work. The coupling of the *Coronation Ode* is handy and certainly welcome, rather than particularly appropriate. Both works are generously cued.

Hickox proves a warmly understanding Elgarian and his manner is ripely idiomatic. His soloists make a characterful quartet. **Margaret Marshall** is the sweet, tender soprano, rising superbly to a passionate climax in her big solo, *The sun goeth down*, and **Felicity Palmer** is a strong and positive – if not ideally warm-toned – Mary Magdalene. **David Wilson-Johnson** points the words of St Peter most dramatically, and **Arthur Davies** is the radiant tenor. The fill-ups are not generous: the intense little string adagio, *Sospiri*, and the early *Sursum corda*.

The Light of Life (Lux Christi), Op. 29

*** Chan. 9208. Howarth, Finnie, A. Davies, Shirley-Quirk, L. Symphony Ch., LSO, Hickox

Notably more than Sir Charles Groves in the earlier, EMI recording, **Hickox** conveys the warmth of inspiration of *The Light of Life* in glowing sound, with the chorus incandescent. The solo singing is richly characterful, even if the microphone catches an unevenness in the singing of the mezzo, **Linda Finnie**, and of **John Shirley-Quirk**; nevertheless he sings nobly as Jesus in the climactic 'Good Shepherd' solo. **Arthur Davies**, as the blind man, and the soprano, **Judith Howarth**, are both excellent, singing with clear, fresh tone.

The Music Makers; Sea Pictures, Op. 37

🔑 (BB) *** Naxos 8.557710. Connolly, Bournemouth Ch. & SO, Wright

Any new recording of either of these works invites immediate comparison with the classic versions with Dame Janet Baker, and **Sarah Connolly** comes nearer than any current British mezzo to offering a modern alternative, not only in the rich, firm quality of her voice but in the dedication of her singing. In each of the songs of *Sea Pictures* she brings out the distinctive qualities of Elgar's writing, each one so well contrasted with the others, with finely controlled legato phrasing and shading of dynamic. In her contribution to the big cantata, *The Music Makers*, she offers the element of dedication so essential, with the chorus singing purposefully and **Simon Wright** drawing strong playing from the **Bournemouth Symphony Orchestra**. Excellent sound.

The Spirit of England

(M) *** Dutton CDLX 7172. Gritton, Kennedy, BBC Ch. & SO, Lloyd-Jones – KELLY: *Elegy: In Memoriam Rupert Brooke*; ELKINGTON: *Out of the Mist* ***; GURNEY: *War Elegy*; PARRY: *The Chivalry of the Sea* ***

In *The Spirit of England* Elgar's original intention was to have two soloists, giving the outer movements ('The Fourth of August' and 'For the fallen') to a soprano and the middle movement ('To women') to a tenor. Here, for the first time, a tenor, the talented young **Andrew Kennedy**, takes over for the central setting, and certainly the result is a degree more effective than with a single soloist. **David Lloyd-Jones** conducts a powerful performance, bitingly dramatic in 'The Fourth of August', with the chorus in superb form, and with the setting of 'For the fallen' – its words much the best known – aptly elegiac, the more powerful for being taken at a flowing speed. **Susan Gritton** sings brightly and with clarity.

3 Partsongs, Op. 18; 4 Partsongs, Op. 53; 2 Partsongs, Op. 71; 2 Partsongs, Op. 73; 5 Partsongs from the Greek Anthology, Op. 45; Death on the hills; Evening scene; Go, song of mine; How calmly the evening; The Prince of Sleep; Weary wind of the West

*** Chan. 9269. Finzi Singers, Spicer

Elgar's partsongs span virtually the whole of his creative career, and the 22 examples on the **Finzi Singers'** disc range from one of the most famous, *My love dwelt in a northern land*, of 1889 to settings of Russian poems (in English translation) written during the First World War. The Finzi Singers under **Paul Spicer** give finely tuned, crisp and intense readings of all the pieces.

Sea Pictures (song-cycle), *Op. 37*

🔑 ❀ (M) **** EMI (ADD) 5 62886-2. Baker, LSO, Barbirolli – *Cello Concerto* (with *Cockaigne Overture*) *** ❀

** ABC Classics (ADD) 461 922-2. Elkins, Queensland SO, Albert – SHIELD: *Rosina*; WILLIAMSON: *The Growing Castle* ***

Like du Pré, **Baker** is an artist who has the power to convey on record the vividness of a live performance. With the help of **Barbirolli** she makes the cycle far more convincing than it usually seems, with often trite words clothed in music that seems to transform them. On CD, the voice is caught with extra bloom, and the beauty of Elgar's orchestration is enhanced by the subtle added definition. This unique coupling has now been reissued at mid-price as one of EMI's 'Great Recordings of the Century'.

Albert's warm-hearted, atmospheric and beautiful account of the *Sea Pictures* makes an unexpected fill-up to Shield's sparkling rustic opera, *Rosina*. Margreta Elkins's voice is well captured in the 1983 recording. Though the orchestra lacks richness, it is perfectly acceptable. Texts are included, along with very full documentation.

The Starlight Express (incidental music), *Op. 78*

(B) *** CfP (ADD) 585 9072. Masterson, Hammond-Stroud, LPO, Handley

It has been left to latter-day Elgarians to revive a 1916 score (incidental music for a children's play) that was not a success in its day but that reveals the composer at his most charming. But the ear is constantly beguiled. Much of the orchestral music has that nostalgically luminous quality that Elgarians will instantly recognize. Both soloists are excellent, and the **LPO** plays with warmth and sympathy. The 1976 recording is excellent and it matters little that, in order to fit the piece complete on to a single CD, some minor cuts have had to be made.

EL-KHOURY, Bechara
(born 1957)

(i) *Piano Concerto, Op. 36*; (ii) *Méditation poétique for Violin & Orchestra, Op. 41*; (iii) *Poèmes for Piano & Orchestra: 1, Op. 11; 2, Op. 22; Sérénades for Strings: 1: Feuilles d'Automne; 2, Op. 20*

(BB) *** Naxos 8.557692. (i) El Bacha; (ii) Poulet; (iii) Lively; Cologne O, Dervaux

The *Piano Concerto* is very approachable, with its varying conflicting moods well projected by the excellent soloist; it brings opportunities for virtuoso rhetoric. Both here and in the two *Poèmes* for piano and orchestra, played by a different but equally persuasive soloist, the combination of vividly coloured orchestral drama and lyricism reminds one of film music. But undoubtedly the finest concertante work here is the comparatively innocent *Méditation poétique* for violin and orchestra, which is beautifully played by **Gérard Poulet**. (Incidentally, these performances were recorded 'live', which accounts for a couple of slips from the horns.) The two amiable *String Serenades*, the first autumnal, the second more searching and ardent, would – like the *Méditation* – be welcome at any concert.

Danse des aigles, Op. 9; Les Dieux de la terre (Image symphonique); Le Liban en flammes (Lebanon in Flames), Op. 14; La Nuit et le fou (Night and the Fool): Suite Symphonique, Op. 29; Le Regard de Christ, Op. 2; Requiem pour orchestre, Op. 18

(BB) *** Naxos 8.557691. Cologne O, Dervaux

The CD of orchestral works opens with a catchy and brightly scored *Danse des aigles*, followed by the darker symphonic poem, *Les Dieux de la terre*, and the suite, *La Nuit et le fou*, both highly atmospheric and imaginatively scored. The other two symphonic poemes, *Le Liban en flammes* (inspired by the same events as the *Requiem*) and the shorter and much more dramatic *Regard du Christ*, are full of incident. El-Khoury's orchestral sound-world is very much his own: he uses a remarkable range of orchestral effects. Undoubtedly the finest of these orchestral works is the *Requiem* of 1980 with its subtitle ('For the Lebanese Martyrs of the War'). Opening like a traditional funeral march, it even quotes briefly the rhythm of Siegfried's funeral music and develops into an agonized lament, interrupted by warlike reminiscences; but it remains affirmative, ending with a dramatic final gesture of regret. **Pierre Dervaux** is a highly sympathetic exponent of this repertoire and these are all fine, dedicated performances.

(i; ii) Les Fleuves englouties (The engulfed rivers), Op. 64; (i; iii) New York, Tears and Hope, Op. 65; Sextuor (arr. for 24 violins), Op. 58. (iv) (Piano) Fragments oubliées, Op. 66; (v) Waves, Op. 60

(BB) *** Naxos 8.570134. (i) LSO; (ii) Harding; (iii) Brabbins; (iv) Dimitri Vassilakis; (v) Hideki Nagano

In many ways this is the finest of these El-Khoury compilations, and in *New York, Tears and Hope* offers the first major orchestral piece concisely reflecting the human experience of 9/11. Opening poignantly, it moves to a petrifying climax, and ends elegiacally, but without a trace of despair. The intensely concentrated *Sextet* (arranged for full string ensemble at the request of Shlomo Mintz) is only five minutes in length, and might be regarded as a companion work, a wistfully dark lamentation, but suddenly quickening and moving out of the clouds. *Les Fleuves englouties* is a series of impressionistic miniatures, contrasting serenity and struggle with confident life-assertion. The two closing piano pieces similarly move from reflection to responses which are more fragmented but positive. The performances are very persuasive indeed and excellently recorded.

Symphony (The Ruins of Beirut); Hill of Strangeness; Twilight Harmonies; Wine of the Clouds

(BB) **(*) Naxos 8.557043. Nat. SO of Ukraine, Sirenko

The *Symphony* was composed (in 1985) in the wake of the civil war in the Lebanon and is a powerful, tragically arresting work, laid out in four fairly traditional movements. But it is without any kind of conventional development of ideas; in essence it is a kaleidoscopic set of brief variants. Even more than the vividly scored symphony, the three shorter works rely a great deal on orchestral textures, with contrasting sonorities, dynamics, mood and colouring, all skilfully manipulated to give an illusion of forward movement (rather than development). The brass scoring is emphatic, with exuberant use of the horns. The restless symphonic meditation, *Hill of Strangeness* ('Colline de l'étrange') 'is a journey through a fog pierced by glimpses of light' and is concerned with 'solitude and the struggle of the light to come through dark clouds'. It is certainly enigmatic. *Harmonies crépusculaires* was written in memory of the conductor Pierre Dervaux and is essentially valedictory in feeling, but the finality of death is powerfully conveyed by more shattering brass interruptions, with an answering tolling bell. The dream-like *Wine of the Clouds* ('Le Vin des nuages') 'is a confrontation between silence and the violence of nature', opening impressionistically and ending with a torrent of sound, including the composer's characteristic horn glissandi.

EMMANUEL, Maurice
(1862–1938)

6 Chansons bourguignonnes du Pays de Beaune

*** Erato 0630 17577-2 (2). Upshaw, Lyon Op. O, Nagano –
  CANTELOUBE: *Songs of the Auvergne: Series 1–5* ***

Maurice Emmanuel's attractive orchestral arrangements enhance these Burgundian songs from the Beaune region, in very much the same way as Canteloube's *Chants d'Auvergne*. The six included here are nicely contrasted, and they are delightfully sung and most idiomatically accompanied. *Le Pommier d'août* and *Noël* are particularly engaging, but most memorable of all is the haunting closing *Farewell to the shepherdess*.

ENESCU, Georges (1881–1955)

Romanian Rhapsodies 1–2, Op. 11/1–2

(M) *** Chan. 6625. RSNO, Järvi – BARTÓK: *Hungarian Pictures*; WEINER: *Hungarian Folkdance Suite* ***

Järvi has a warmly idiomatic feeling for these amiable, peasant-inspired rhapsodies, moulding phrases and linking passages with spontaneity, drawing committed playing, with plenty of subtle touches from the **Royal Scottish National Orchestra**, ripely recorded. Although the first of the two rhapsodies is much the more popular, and justly so, the second is also lively and colourful. They are now aptly coupled with comparably entertaining and colourful folk-inspired music by Bartók and Weiner.

Romanian Rhapsodies 1–2; (i) Symphonie concertante for Cello & Orchestra, Op. 8; Suites for Orchestra: 1 & 2 in C, Opp. 9 & 20; 3 (Villageoise) Op. 27; (ii) Poème roumaine, Op. 1

(BB) **(*) Warner Apex 2564 62032-2 (2). Monte Carlo PO, Foster, with (i) Maggio-Ormezowski; (ii) Male Ch. of Colonne O, & Ens. Audita Nova

The *Symphonie concertante* is an attractively written piece, again using national dances. The cello soloist is excellent. The first two of the *Three Suites for Orchestra* are well crafted without being in the very first rank, yet they are expertly laid out for the orchestra and have a charm and appeal that ought to ensure them a wider following. The *Third (Village) Suite* brings a series of pastoral scenes and more national dances to conclude. The *Poème roumaine* has lyrical appeal and uses an evocative wordless male chorus with bells at the opening, and later a solo violin; it features the Romanian national anthem as its finale. All this is well enough served by the **Monte Carlo Orchestra** under **Lawrence Foster** and is given the benefit of natural, spacious recording.

Symphonies (i) 1 in E flat, Op. 13; 2 in A, Op. 17; (ii; iii) 3 in C, Op. 21; (ii; iii; iv) Vox Maris (Symphonic Poem), Op. 31

(B) *** EMI 5 86604-2 (2). (i) Monte Carlo PO, (ii) O Nat. de Lyon; Lawrence Foster; with (iii) Les Eléments Chamber Ch.; (iv) Brenciu; Sydney

The *First* and *Second Symphonies* are scored with great flair. They have never been played with such vigour and conviction as here, nor as well recorded. **Lawrence Foster**, who has recorded a good deal of Enescu, directs the **Monte Carlo Orchestra** with tremendous fire and an infectious enthusiasm, and the players respond as if their lives depended on it. The even more opulent *Third Symphony* (1918) is more intractable; but Foster sustains the fullest tension in the ecstatic finale with its wordless chorus (helped by the passionate singing of the Les Eléments Choir). *Vox Maris* takes the unearthly evocation a stage further, using offstage soprano and tenor soloists and chorus, and even drawing on a motif borrowed from *Oedipe*. Performance and recording show Lawrence Foster again at his finest, with another impressive choral contribution, although the wobbly soprano soloist is not an asset.

CHAMBER MUSIC

Cello Sonatas 1 in F min., 2 in C, Op. 26

(N) (BB) *** Naxos 8.570582. Buruiana, Tchiba

Although published together as Op. 26, the *First Sonata* comes from 1898 (between the first two violin sonatas) and the *Second*, written for Casals, from 1935. The *First* is a long work, a little short of 40 minutes, and is somewhat Brahmsian in character, while its successor lasts half an hour. Both are beautifully crafted, inventive and thoroughly rewarding musically. They are expertly played by the young

Romanian cellist **Laura Buruiana** with her German-based Hungarian partner, **Martin Tchiba**, and are recorded with great presence and clarity, though the cellist is at times balanced too reticently. Nonetheless strongly recommended.

(i) String Octet in C, Op. 7 (trans. for O by Lawrence Foster); (ii) Violin Sonata 3, Op. 25

(N) **(*) Virgin 9 519331-2. (i) Monte Carlo PO, Foster; (ii) Sokolov, Kosenko

The *Octet* is effectively transcribed for strings and expertly played by the **Monte Carlo Orchestra**. Readers may well have preferred it in the composer's original form. It is all very musically done, as indeed is the familiar *Sonata No. 3* in the Romanian style.

Dixtuor, Op. 14

**** Naxos 8.554173. Oslo PO Wind Soloists – DVOŘÁK: *Wind Serenade*; JANÁČEK: *Mládí* ***

The *Dixtuor* or *Decet* is one of Enescu's most glorious scores: its sophisticated counterpoint and idyllic charm are most appealing. The plaintive slow movement is haunting. The **Oslo Wind Soloists** are artists of quality whose reading challenges the finest at any price. Crisp rhythms, a good sense of line and tonal finesse. These artists recorded this piece on the Victoria label in the early 1990s, but these are different and better accounts in every way.

Impressions d'enfance (for Violin & Piano), Op. 28

*** Avie AV 2059. Graffin, Désert – DEBUSSY: *Violin Sonata; Nocturne et Scherzo*, etc.; RAVEL: *Sonata; Tzigane* ***

Impressions d'enfance is a series of charming nostalgic glimpses of the composer's childhood, beautifully evoked in the performance here. Opening with the sound of a fiddler on the street, there follow brief portraits, first a melancholy old beggar, then a stream trickling at the bottom of a garden, a bird in its cage and a cuckoo clock, a cricket; then, more atmospherically, moonlight and the wind in the chimney; and, finally sunrise, with night-time banished in a rhapsodic finale in which one feels the composer returning forcefully to the present.

Piano Quartet 2 in D min., Op. 30; Piano Quintet, Op. 29

(BB) **(*) Naxos 8.557159. Solomon Ens.

The *Piano Quartet No. 2* (1943–4) has something of the subtlety and finesse of late Fauré and, like the *Quintet*, is a work of real substance which rewards the serious listener. This music does not try to impress with effect or originality but by its continuity of thought and finely paced musical development. The **Solomon Ensemble** play well but the balance is not ideal: there is not enough air round the sound and the first violin is placed too reticently, hence the reservation. Strongly recommended all the same, particularly at its competitive price.

String Quartets 1 in E flat; 2 in G, Op. 22/1–2

(BB) *** Naxos 8.554721. Ad Libitum Qt

The Enescu quartets share the same opus number but are separated by over three decades. Few works by this extraordinary musician are without their rewards, and although neither quartet rises to the same imaginative heights as *Oedipe* or the *Dixtuor* they are full of good things. They are well played by this fine Romanian team and priced at the right level. The adventurous collector will not baulk at a fiver for repertoire that he or she does not know and will find the outlay worthwhile.

Violin Sonatas 2, Op. 6; 3, Op. 25; Torso

(BB) *** Hyp. Helios CDH 55103. A. Oprean, J. Oprean

Enescu's *Second Violin Sonata* is an early work, written in 1899 when he was 17 and still studying in Paris with Fauré. The *Third* (1926), together with the opera, *Oedipe*, is his masterpiece and shows an altogether different personality; the difference in stylistic development could hardly be more striking. **Adelina Oprean** is thoroughly inside the idiom, as befits a Romanian, and she deals with its subtle rubati and quarter-tones to the manner born. She exhibits excellent musical taste but her partner (and brother) is somewhat less scrupulous in his observance of dynamic nuance. The additional *Torso* is a sonata movement from 1911, which was published only in the 1980s.

Violin Sonata 3 in A min., Op. 25

(BB) (***) Naxos mono 8.111127. Y. & H. Menuhin – BACH: *Unaccompanied Violin Sonata in C*; PIZZETTI: *Violin Sonata 1 in A* (***)

Yehudi Menuhin and his sister **Hephzibah** recorded this wonderful *Sonata* in Paris in 1936 in the presence of the composer. Their evident love for the piece shines through. Yehudi was 19 at the time and Hephzibah 15, and they both possess a captivating youthful ardour – and the sound is remarkably fine for the period.

Violin Sonata 3 in A min., Op. 25/1 (excerpt; DVD version)

**(*) EMI DVD 4904529. Y. & H. Menuhin (bonus:
MENDELSSOHN: *Variations sérieuses, Op. 54*) – BARTÓK: *Contrasts for piano, violin & cello*, etc.; FRANCK: *Violin Sonata in A*; SCHUBERT: *Piano Trio 1 in B flat* **(*)

The ORTF recording was made presumably at the Maison de la Radio in 1972 and, like the Bartók *Contrasts*, is in colour. We are given just the *Moderato malinconico*, which is a pity. On the whole the camerawork serves us well, though there is some superimposition of the two artists which may not please all tastes, and the colour is a little faded.

PIANO MUSIC

Piano Sonatas: 1 & 3, Op. 24/1 & 3; Nocturne in D flat; Pièce sur le nom de Fauré; Prelude & Fugue in C; Scherzo

*** Avie AV 2081 (2). Borac

Suites 1–3

*** Avie AV 0013. Borac

Luiza Borac won the 1991 Enescu International Prize. She proves a dedicated and authoritative interpreter of this interesting and rewarding music. This repertoire is rarely (if indeed ever) encountered in the recital room or in broadcast programmes, which enhances the importance of this set. Luiza Borac covers the formative years in the *Prelude and Fugue* of 1903 through to the *Third Sonata* of 1934. The *First Sonata* shows the influence of Debussy and Ravel, while the *Third* (written after the completion of his masterpiece, the opera *Oedipe*) will come as something of a revelation to the listener. The three *Suites* are equally rewarding. Borac plays with total commitment and is well served by the recording, made in St Dunstan's Church, Mayfield.

Oedipe (complete)

(N) (B) *** EMI 2 08833-2 (2). Van Dam, Hendricks, Fassbaender, Lipovšek, Monte-Carlo PO, Foster

This is an almost ideal recording (from 1990) of a rare and long-neglected masterpiece, with a breathtaking cast of stars backing up a supremely fine performance by **José van Dam** in the central role Oedipus. The idiom is tough and adventurous, as well as warmly exotic, with vivid choral effects, a revelation to anyone who knows Enescu only from his *Romanian Rhapsody*. The only reservation is that the pace tends to be on the slow side; but the incandescence of the playing of the **Monte Carlo Philharmonic** under **Lawrence Foster** and the richness of the singing and recorded sound amply compensate for that, making this a musical feast. Fortunately the set is reissued with a full libretto and translation.

FALLA, Manuel de (1876–1946)

(i; ii) Harpsichord Concerto; (iii; iv; v) El amor brujo; (iv, vi, vii) Nights in the Gardens of Spain; (viii) The Three-Cornered Hat; (ix) La vida breve: Interlude and Dance; (x) Homenaje 'Le tombeau de Claude Debussy'; (vii) 4 Spanish Pieces; (xi) 7 Canciones populares españolas; (ii; xii) Psyché

🔔 ⚙ (B) **** Double Decca (ADD/DDD) 466 128-2 (2). (i) Constable; (ii) L. Sinf., Rattle; (iii) New Philh. O; (iv) Frühbeck de Burgos; (v) Mistral; (vi) LPO; (vii) De Larrocha; (viii) Montreal SO, Dutoit; (ix) SRO, Ansermet; (x) Fernández; (xi) Horne, Katz; (xii) with Jennifer Smith

A myriad of performances have been perceptively gathered together for this 'Essential Falla' compilation, which is surely rightly named. **Dutoit's** 1984 complete version of *The Three-Cornered Hat* is wonderfully atmospheric as well as brilliantly played. Recorded in 1966, **Frühbeck de Burgos's** *El amor brujo* also enjoys exceptionally vivid sound, yet with plenty of light and shade, and the control of atmosphere in the quieter passages is masterly, while **Nati Mistral** has the vibrant, open-throated production of a real flamenco singer.

Alicia de Larrocha's later digital version of *Nights in the Gardens of Spain* is unsurpassed among modern recordings. Her playing of the *Four Spanish Pieces* glitters. The other shorter works are equally worthwhile. **Ansermet's** *Interlude and Dance* from *La vida breve*, with its melodramatic opening and lively dance section, is always enjoyable, and **Marilyn Horne's** *Spanish Folksongs* are vibrantly idiomatic. **John Constable's** crisply vivid account of the delightful *Harpsichord Concerto* (with Rattle) and the haunting rarity, *Psyché*, for voice – **Jennifer Smith** a fine soloist – and orchestra complete an extraordinarily generous survey.

(iv; vii) *Harpsichord Concerto;* (i–iii) *El amor brujo;* (iv–vi) *Nights in the Gardens of Spain;* (i; ii; v) *The Three-cornered Hat;* (iv) *Piano: Fantasia bética;* 4 *Piezas espanolas;* (i; viii–ix) *Psyché;* (i; viii) *Soneto a Córdoba;* (i; iv) *7 Spanish Popular Songs*

(N)(B) *** EMI (ADD) 2 CD 237595-2 (2)

(i) De los Angeles; (ii) Philh. O; (iii) Giulini; (iv) Soriano; (v) Frühbeck de Burgos; (vi) O de la Société des Concerts du Conservatoire; (vii) Debost, Casier, Boutard, Nérini, Cordier; (viii) Challan; (ix) Gérard, Trio à cordes français

Not too much to grumble about here. **Giulini's** *El amor brujo* dates from the early 1960s, the **Philharmonia's** playing is polished, and Guilini produces civilized, colourful performances. The recording too is brightly coloured, although noticeably resonant in *The Three Cornered Hat* where, although the performance (under **Frühbeck de Burgos**) is excellent, it has not the red-blooded vigour which others have brought to it. **Victoria de los Angeles's** contribution is an undoubted point in its favour. She finishes off the first CD with *7 Spanish Popular Songs*, colourfully and idiomatically sung, dating from 1962. *Nights in the Gardens of Spain*, which opens CD 2, is superbly done, with both atmosphere and brilliance in equal amount. The splendid *Harpsichord Concerto* makes for a sharply piquant contrast, and then de los Angeles returns for a beautiful performance of the comparatively rare *Psyché*, with the delicious accompaniment of string trio, flute and harp. The piano items are played with much relish by **Soriano**. Very good 1960s sound throughout, well transferred.

El amor brujo (complete)

⌐● 🔑 **** BBC (ADD) BBCL 4005-2. Lane, BBC SO, Stokowski – BEETHOVEN: *Symphony 7* *(**); BRITTEN: *Young Person's Guide to the Orchestra* **(*)

Stokowski's BBC account of Falla's *El amor brujo* was given at a Prom in 1964 and has all the electricity of a live occasion. This is an outstanding and thrilling performance. In almost every movement Stokowski opts for fast speeds, with the players of the **BBC Symphony Orchestra** challenged to the limit, as in the *Ritual Fire Dance*, which is electrifying. Consistently Stokowski finds colour and atmosphere, and his soloist, **Gloria Lane**, with her fruity mezzo tone-colours, sounds comparably idiomatic. In short, this is the most gripping and hypnotic performance on or off record, and the recording quality is very good indeed.

(i) *El amor brujo* (complete); (ii) *Nights in the Gardens of Spain. La vida breve: Interlude and Dance*

(M) *** Chan. 10232X. (i) Walker; (ii) Fingerhut; LSO, Simon

The brightly lit Chandos recording emphasizes the vigour of **Geoffrey Simon's** very vital account of *El amor brujo*, and **Sarah Walker's** powerful vocal contribution is another asset, her vibrantly earthy singing highly involving. The **Simon/Fingerhut** version of *Nights in the Gardens of Spain* also makes a strongly contrasted alternative to Alicia de Larrocha's much-praised reading, and the effect is more dramatic, with the soloist responding chimerically to the changes of mood. The *Interlude and Dance* from *La vida breve* make a very attractive encore.

(i) *El amor brujo* (Love, the Magician); (ii) *The Three-Cornered Hat* (ballets; both complete)

(M) *** EMI (ADD) 5 67587-2 (2). De los Angeles, Philh. O, (i) Giulini; (ii) Frühbeck de Burgos – *La vida breve* ***

(i) *El amor brujo* (Love, the Magician); (ii) *The Three-Cornered Hat* (ballet); *La vida breve: Interlude and Dance*

(M) *** Decca (ADD) 466 991-2. SRO, Ansermet, with (i) De Gabarain; (ii) Berganza

Listening to **Ansermet's** early 1960s version of *The Three-Cornered Hat*, you understand why his recordings are cherished by audiophiles: the sound is glitteringly brilliant and full. The performance has lots of character and shows the conductor and his orchestra on top form. *El amor brujo* is not quite so brilliant as a recording, or as a performance, but it is still very good, with plenty of nice touches and the *Interlude and Dance* from *La vida breve* is especially vivid here. A very colourful and worthy addition to Decca's 'Legends' label.

A beautifully civilized and atmospheric account of *El amor brujo* from **Giulini**, warmly and atmospherically recorded. Thoroughly enjoyable, even if the performance is not as vivid and red-blooded as **Frühbeck de Burgos's** *Three-Cornered Hat*, where the *'Olés'* were recorded separately and dubbed on, but which has greater high spirits. **Victoria de los Angeles** does not sound quite earthy enough, but she sings splendidly throughout and the CD transfers are excellent. This is now recoupled with *La vida breve* as one of EMI's 'Great Recordings of the Century'.

(i) *El amor brujo* (complete); *The Three-Cornered Hat: 3 Dances; La vida breve: Interlude & Dance*

⌐● **** RCA **SACD** (ADD) 88697 04607-2. (i) L. Price; Chicago SO, Reiner (with GRANADOS: *Goyescas: Intermezzo*) – ALBÉNIZ: *Iberia* (excerpts) ****

Reiner's complete *El amor brujo*, from a vintage period with the **Chicago Symphony Orchestra**, is a fiery and colourful account, yet totally seductive in its nudging of rhythms in *The Magic Circle* and in the languorous *Pantomime*. **Leontyne Price's** contribution is riveting: it has all the dark, guttural fire you could ask for, flamenco singing to the manner born, the operatic voice almost unrecognizable. The excerpts from *La vida breve* and three dances from *The Three-Cornered Hat* are both sultry and gripping; they have far more sparkle than many recordings made since, and the final dance brings really exciting virtuosity. The recordings from 1958 and 1963 (*El amor brujo*) have been vividly remastered in their new SACD format, giving sound in the demonstration bracket.

The account of the *Goyescas Intermezzo* is full of temperament. However, this disc has been reissued at premium price.

Nights in the Gardens of Spain

🎵 (BB) *** Warner Apex 8573 89223-2. Heisser, Lausanne CO, López-Cobos – ALBENIZ: *Concierto fantástico*, etc.; TURINA: *Rapsodia sinfónica* ***

The performance by **Jean-François Heisser** (with **López-Cobos** a highly idiomatic partner) is first class in every way, combining warm evocation, brilliant colouring and excitement. The playing could hardly be more grippingly spontaneous, and the modern (1996) digital sound is vividly real. The couplings are equally attractive and this comes in the lowest price range.

The Three-Cornered Hat (complete; DVD version)

(N) *** EuroArts DVD 2050136. Chicago SO, Barenboim – BOULEZ: *Notations I–IV*; DEBUSSY: *La Mer* ***

The concert comes from the **Chicago Symphony Orchestra's** European tour in April 2000 and was recorded in the Philharmonie in Cologne. The Falla is obviously close to **Barenboim's** heart for he gives as sympathetic and convincing a performance of it as we have ever heard. The Chicago orchestra responds with playing of virtuosity and character, as indeed they do in the couplings, *La Mer* and the Boulez *Notations I–IV*. Expert camerawork and excellent sound throughout. The DVD also includes a 20-minute conversation between Barenboim and Boulez.

The Three-Cornered Hat (complete; CD version)

🎵 *** Chan. 8904. Gomez, Philh. O, Tortelier – ALBENIZ: *Iberia* ***

Yan Pascal Tortelier is hardly less seductive than Dutoit in handling Falla's beguiling dance-rhythms, bringing out the score's humour as well as its colour. The fine Chandos recording is full and vivid, if rather reverberant, and **Jill Gomez's** contribution floats within the resonance; but the acoustic warmth adds to the woodwind bloom, and the strings are beguilingly rich. The closing *Jota* is joyfully vigorous.

The Three-Cornered Hat (ballet): 3 Dances

(***) Testament mono SBT 1017. Philh. O, Cantelli – CASELLA: *Paganiniana*; DUKAS: *L'Apprenti sorcier*; RAVEL: *Daphnis et Chloé: Suite 2* (***)

It is good that **Cantelli's** excellent (1954) performances of these vivid dances are back in such fine transfers. Elegant, polished accounts, given very good mono sound.

The Three-Cornered Hat (ballet): Miller's Dance, Danse finale

*** BBC (ADD) BBCL 4123-2. Philh. O, Giulini – BRUCKNER: *Symphony 7*; MUSSORGSKY: *Khovanshchina: Prelude* ***

The Falla dances, recorded live, make a lively contrast to **Giulini's** dedicated reading of Bruckner's *Seventh Symphony*, the main work on the disc.

VOCAL MUSIC

Siete canciones populares españolas (7 Spanish Popular Songs)

🎵 (BB) **** EMI Encore 5 86985-2. Monoyios, Barrueco (guitar) – GRANADOS: *12 Danzas españolas* ****

🎵 (***) Testament mono SBT 1311. Souzay, Bonneau – FAURÉ: *Mélodies* *** 🏵; RAVEL: *Histoires naturelles* (***)

The late **Gérard Souzay** is wonderfully captured here in this 1951 set, made only six years after his Paris début and finding the youthful bloom of his voice at its peak. Highly characterized performances, and expertly accompanied by **Jacqueline Bonneau**. No need to make any allowances for the age of the Decca recording in Paul Baily's scrupulous remastering.

OPERA

La vida breve (complete)

(M) *** EMI (ADD) 5 67587-2 (2). De los Angeles, Higueras, Rivadeneyra, Cossutta, Moreno, Orféon Donostiarra Ch., Nat. O of Spain, Frühbeck de Burgos – *El amor brujo*; *Three-Cornered Hat* ***

La vida breve is a kind of Spanish *Cavalleria rusticana* without the melodrama. Unquestionably the opera's story is thin but if the music for the final scene is weakened by a fundamental lack of drama in the plot, **Frühbeck de Burgos** makes the most of the poignancy of the closing moments. **Victoria de los Angeles** deepened her interpretation over the years and her imaginative colouring of the words gives a unique authority and evocation to her performance. The flamenco singer in Act II (**Gabriel Moreno**) also matches the realism of the idiom with an authentic 'folk' style. The recording remains atmospheric but has increased vividness and presence.

FASCH, Johann Friedrich
(1688–1758)

Andante in D, FWVL: D 15; Concertos (for wind and strings): in B flat, FVWL: B3; in D, FVWL: D15; Ouverture grosso in D, FWKV: D8

(N) *** Chan. 0751. Tempesta di Mare, Ngai

Concertos: for 2 flutes, 2 oboes, bassoon & strings; for 2 corni da Caccia, 2 oboes, bassoon, violin & strings; Overtures in F, A; Sinfonias in A, G

(N) *** CPO 777 424-2. Les Amis de Philippe, Rémy

Johann Fasch was Bach's predecessor at the Leipzig Thomasschule and a considerable composer in his own right. Here are two very agreeable collections of his orchestral music. The *Andante* on Chandos is very gracious, sounding like Handel with a touch of Gluck, and the *Overture grosso* is exceptionally lively and colourful – in five movements with often elaborate horn parts. Both *Concertos* (in B flat and D) are richly scored.

On CPO the *Overtures* in three movements offer substantial first movements of lively invention, graceful slow movements and light-hearted finales. The *Sinfonias* offer nicely contrasted movements too: the *Andante* of the G major is unexpectedly dark and ominous, but the work ends in a joyful manner. As on Chandos, the multi-instrument concertos are most enjoyable, and the florid writing in the *D major Concerto* is very beguiling, as is the piquant writing for the flutes and bassoon in the finale. The CPO CD offers over 70 minutes of this attractive, rarely performed baroque music, stylishly played and well recorded. The Chandos disc is even more vividly recorded, but offers a playing time of only 60 minutes.

Overture (Suite) in D min.; (i) Passio Jesu Christi (Brockes-Passion)

🔊 **ⒷⒷ** **** Naxos 8.570326. Capella Savaria Bar. O; (i) with Zádori, Megyesi, Cser, Budapest Schola Cantorum, Térey-Smith

The *Passio Jesu Christi* is a real discovery – a truly remarkable work, in many ways anticipating Bach. The text is a substantially shortened version of the Gospel story as told by the poet Barthold Brockes, frowned on by the Church authorities for being too theatrical and sentimental. However, in Fasch's setting it is neither, but it is musically very rewarding, particularly when as beautifully sung and played as it is here. Throughout the work Fasch intersperses eight Lutheran chorales, beautifully sung by the **Budapest Schola Cantorum**. Before the choral work, the lively **Capella Savaria Baroque Orchestra** show their excellence in a polished and spirited performance of the sprightly *Suite in D minor* for two oboes, bassoon, strings and continuo. The recording is in the demonstration class and this is a disc worth seeking out.

FAURÉ, Gabriel (1845–1924)

Ballade for Piano & Orchestra, Op. 19

🔊 **✿** **ⒷⒷ** (***) Dutton mono CDBP 9714. K. Long, Nat. SO, Boyd Neel – LEIGH: *Concertino*; MOZART: *Piano Concertos 15 & 24* (***)

*** Chan. 8773. Lortie, LSO, Frühbeck de Burgos – RAVEL: *Piano Concertos* **(*)

ⒷⒷ **(*) Naxos 8.550754. Thiollier, Nat. SO of Ireland, De Almeida – FRANCK: *Symphonic Variations*; D'INDY: *Symphonie sur un air montagnard français* **(*)

Recorded in 1944, **Kathleen Long's** classic recording of Fauré's *Ballade* remains among the most inspired ever, at once subtle and immediate in its communication, a perfect demonstration of Long's refined artistry. A fine supplement to the equally subtle readings of Mozart *Concertos* and the hauntingly effective Leigh *Concertino*. A magical (and very generous) CD, very well recorded and transferred.

Louis Lortie is a thoughtful artist and his playing has both sensitivity and strength. This is as penetrating and well recorded an account of Fauré's lovely piece as any now avail-

able; however, the coupling is not one of the preferred versions of the Ravel concertos.

Naxos offer an intelligently planned triptych. **François-Joël Thiollier** shows some imagination and sensitivity in Fauré's lovely *Ballade*. The orchestral playing is perfectly acceptable, without being in any way out of the ordinary; likewise the recording. All the same, it is worth the money.

Ballade for Piano & Orchestra, Op. 19; Berceuse for Violin & Orchestra, Op. 16; Caligula, Op. 52; Les Djinns (orchestral version), Op. 12; Elégie for Cello & Orchestra, Op. 24; Fantaisie for Piano & Orchestra, Op. 111; Masques et bergamasques, Op. 112; Pelléas et Mélisande, Op. 80; Pénélope: Prélude; Shylock, Op. 57

🔊 **Ⓑ** *** EMI 3 97722-2 (2). Collard, Y. P. & P. Tortelier, Von Stade, Gedda, Bourbon Vocal Ens., Toulouse Capitole O, Plasson

This set of Fauré's orchestral music contains much that is very rewarding indeed. It includes the delightful *Masques et bergamasques* and the *Pelléas et Mélisande* and *Shylock* music, as well as such rarities as *Les Djinns* and *Caligula*. **Plasson** gets an alert and spirited response, and the recordings are very good. Although the vocal items no longer have texts and translations, as on the original issues, the set is now offered at bargain price. Altogether this is a lovely collection in every way, offering many delights, and it cannot be too warmly recommended.

(i) Ballade for Piano & Orchestra, Op. 19; Dolly Suite; (ii) Elégie for Cello & Orchestra; (iii) Fantaisie for Flute & Orchestra (orch. I. Aubert); Masques et bergamasques; Pavane (orch. H. Rabaud); Pénélope: Prelude

🔊 **** Chan. 9416. (i) Stott; (ii) Dixon; (iii) Davis; BBC PO, Tortelier

The celebrated *Elégie* is here tenderly played by **Peter Dixon**. **Kathryn Stott** brings out not only the poetry in the *Ballade for Piano and Orchestra*, but also the scherzando sparkle of the virtuoso passages. Just as convincing are the *Fantaisie for Flute* (soloist **Richard Davis**) and the ever-popular *Dolly Suite*, both arranged by other hands. The four brief movements of *Masques et bergamasques* are charmingly done and Tortelier's account of the *Overture* to *Masques et bergamasques* is second to none. Indeed, he has the measure of all the music on this disc, be it the poignancy of the *Pénélope Prelude* or the delicacy of the *Dolly Suite*.

(i) Berceuse, Op. 116; Dolly Suite, Op. 56; Masques et bergamasques, Op. 112; Pelléas et Mélisande (suite), Op. 80; (ii) Shylock (suite), Op. 57

ⒷⒷ *** Naxos 8.553360. Dublin RTE Sinf., Georgiadis, with (i) Healy; (ii) Russell

John Georgiadis with his rhythmic flair not only brings out the colour and vigour of the fast movements but, as a fine violinist himself, persuades his Irish players to draw out the expressive warmth of such numbers as *Tendresse* in the *Dolly Suite*. *Masques et bergamasques*, the *Dolly Suite* and the incidental music to *Pelléas et Mélisande* are all among Fauré's best-loved works, and it is good too to have the rarer music for the Shakespeare-based play, *Shylock*, complete with two vocal movements sweetly sung by **Lynda Russell**. **Michael Healy** is the expressive violin soloist in the lovely *Berceuse*. Warm, atmospheric recording, transferred at rather a low level.

Dolly Suite, Op. 56 (orch. Rabaud)

⊕– Ⓜ *** EMI 3 79986-2. Fr. Nat. R. O, Beecham – BIZET: *Carmen Suite 1*, etc.; CHABRIER: *España*, etc.; SAINT-SAËNS: *Le rouet d'Omphale* ***

The consistently imaginative and poetic phrasing that distinguished **Beecham's** best performances is very apparent here – the *Bercesue*, *Le Jardin de Dolly* and *Tendresse* (in Rabaud's orchestration) are exquisite, while *Le Pas espagnole* has the kind of dash we associate with Beecham's Chabrier. The 1961 stereo has come up impressively.

Fantaisie for Piano & Orchestra, Op. 111

⊕– *** Australian Decca Eloquence (ADD) 476 235-2. De Larrocha, LPO, De Burgos – FRANCK: *Symphonic Variations*; RAVEL: *Piano Concertos in G & for the Left Hand* ***

The Fauré *Fantaisie* is a late work, but an aristocratic one of great distinction, beautifully played and recorded in this 1972 performance. The couplings are recommendable too: altogether this is an impressive anthology.

Masques et bergamasques; Pavane

Ⓑ *** CfP (ADD) 575 1382. LPO, Handley – CANTELOUBE: *Chants d'Auvergne* *** 🏵

These performances under **Vernon Handley** are very enjoyable, fresh and sympathetic, with excellent recording to add bloom to the fine playing. A fine bonus for the outstanding Canteloube coupling.

Pelléas et Mélisande (Suite)

Ⓜ *** Sup. SU 3899-2 (2). Czech PO, Baudo – DEBUSSY: *Pelléas: Tone poem*; SCHOENBERG: *Pelléas: symphonic poem*; SIBELIUS: *Pelleas & Melisande: Suite* ***

Baudo's performance, beautifully played by the **Czech Philharmonic Orchestra** and very well recorded, comes appropriately coupled with music by Schoenberg and Sibelius, plus an orchestral arrangement of music from Debussy's opera.

Pelléas et Mélisande Suite, Op. 80; (i) Pavane, Op. 50

*** Chan. 8952. (i) Renaissance Singers; Ulster O, Tortelier – CHAUSSON: *Poème*, etc. ***

These finely finished and atmospheric Chandos performances come in harness with a fine account from the soloist-conductor of Chausson's *Poème* and a perceptive and idiomatic performance of the *Poème de la mer et de l'amour*. Very good orchestral playing and exemplary recording.

CHAMBER MUSIC

(i) Allegretto Moderato for 2 Cellos; (ii) Andante. Elégie, Op. 24; Papillon, Op. 77; Romance, Op. 69; Sérénade, Op. 98; Sicilienne, Op. 78; Sonatas 1 in D min., Op. 109; 2 in G min., Op. 117

**(*) RCA 09026 68049-2. Isserlis, Devoyon; with (i) Waterman; (ii) Greer

Steven Isserlis understands the essential reticence and refinement of Fauré's art. Perhaps he is at times a shade too reticent in the music and could allow himself to produce a more ardent and songful tone. The balance, which slightly favours his partner, contributes to this impression. **Pascal Devoyon** is a no less perceptive and sensitive artist. A welcome, then, for the artistry of these performances, but tinged with slight disappointment at the less than ideal balance.

Cello Sonata 1 in D min., Op. 109

ⒷⒷ *** Warner Apex 0927 40599-2. Noras, Rigutto – DEBUSSY, FRANCK: *Cello Sonatas* ***

Cello Sonatas 1 in D min., Op. 109; 2 in G min., Op. 117

⊕– Ⓑ *** EMI (ADD) 5 74333-2 (2). Tortelier, Heidsieck – CHOPIN; MENDELSSOHN; RACHMANINOV: *Cello Sonatas* ***

Cello Sonatas 1–2; Après un rêve, Op. 7/1; Berceuse, Op. 16; Elégie, Op. 24; Papillon, Op. 77; Romance, Op. 69; Sérénade, Op. 98; Sicilienne, Op. 78

Ⓝ ⒷⒷ *** Naxos 8.557889. Kliegel, Tichman

Cello Sonatas 1–2; Elégie; Sicilienne

Ⓜ *** CRD (ADD) CRD 3316. Igloi, Benson

Noble performances from both **Tortelier** and **Heidsieck**, who play with fervour and eloquence within the restrained expressive limits of the music. The fine EMI recording brings both instruments into the living room most vividly.

The two cello sonatas are among the most sublime creations of Fauré's later years and **Maria Kliegel** and **Nina Tichman** give warmly sensitive and intelligent accounts of them. They do not displace Tortelier but do compensate by including other cello works by Fauré, including the notably popular *Elégie*. Collectors needing this repertoire should find this well-recorded set well worth having.

Moving performances from the late **Thomas Igloi** and **Clifford Benson** that do full justice to these elusive and rewarding Fauré sonatas, and the recording is clear, if not one of CRD's finest in terms of ambient effect.

An eloquent performance too on Warner Apex of the wonderful *D minor Sonata* by this aristocratic Finnish cellist, who plays with subtlety and finesse. If the couplings appeal, this makes an excellent bargain.

(i) Cello Sonatas 1–2; (ii) Andante in B flat, Op. 75; Berceuse, Op. 16; Elégie; (iii) Fantaisie, Op. 79; Morceau de concours; (ii) Morceau de lecture; (i)

Papillon, Op. 77; (i–ii) Piano Trio in D min., Op. 120; (ii) Romance, Op. 28; (i) Serenade in B min., Op. 98; Sicilienne, Op. 78; (ii) Violin Sonatas 1 in A, Op. 15; 2 in E min., Op. 108

Ⓑ *** EMI (ADD) 5 85279-2 (2). Collard; with (i) Lodéon; (ii) Dumay; (iii) Debost

Piano Quartets (i; ii) 1 in C min., Op. 15; (i; iii) 2 in G min., Op. 45; Piano Quintets 1 in C min., Op. 89; 2 in C min., Op. 115; (iii) String Quartet in E min., Op. 121

Ⓑ **(*) EMI (ADD) 5 85282-2 (2). (i) Collard; (ii) Dumay, Pasquier, Lodéon; (iii) Parrenin Qt

Dumay and **Collard** bring different and equally valuable insights, and the performances of the *Piano Quartets* are masterly. In addition, there are authoritative and idiomatic readings of the two *Piano Quintets*, the enigmatic and otherworldly *Quartet* and, on the first set above, the *Piano Trio*, the two *Cello Sonatas* (what a fine player **Lodéon** is!), plus all the smaller pieces. However, one has to accept that, because the Paris Salle Wagram was employed for the recordings (made between 1975 and 1978), close microphones have been used to counteract the hall's resonance.

Cello Sonatas 1 & 2; Piano Trio, Op. 120; Nocturne 13, Op. 119

*** Chan.10447. Priya Mitchell, Christian Poltéra, Kathryn Stott

What hypnotic and subtle works these are! Tortelier and Heidsieck are strong contenders in the *Cello Sonatas* and there are plenty of others (see above), but the present performances are hardly less persuasive and the late *Piano Trio* enhances the disc's attractions.

Piano Quartet 1 in C min., Op. 15

*** Aeon AECD 0540. Schumann Qt – CHAUSSON: *Piano Quartet* ***

The **Quatuor Schumann's** precision of ensemble adds greatly to the impact of the early Fauré *Piano Quartet*, as it does with the Chausson, making an apt and attractive coupling. As in the Chausson, the most compelling playing of all comes in the Schumann Quartet's account of the *Adagio* slow movement, hushed in deep meditation, leading to an incisive account of the brilliant finale with its dashing triplet rhythms. One looks forward to more discs from this fine group.

Piano Quartets 1 in C min., Op. 15; 2 in G min., Op. 45

◧– ✸ **** Hyp. CDA 66166. Domus

Domus have the requisite lightness of touch and subtlety, and just the right sense of scale and grasp of tempi. Their nimble and sensitive pianist, **Susan Tomes**, can hold her own in the most exalted company. The recording is excellent, too, though the balance is a little close, but the sound is not airless.

Piano Quartets 1 in C min., Op. 15; 2 in G min., Op. 45; Piano Quintets 1 in D min., Op. 89; 2 in C min., Op. 115

Ⓑ *** Double Decca 475 187-2 (2). Rogé, Ysaÿe Qt

It goes without saying that **Pascal Rogé** and the **Ysaÿe Quartet** give performances of great finesse and sensitivity. On the first CD they are more successful in the *Quintet No. 1* than in the early *Quartet No. 1*, where they must yield to Domus (Hyperion), who find greater delight and high spirits in the Scherzo. The recording here is very good, though there is an occasional moment when the reverberant acoustic affects the focus. The *Second Quintet* and *Quartet* were recorded in a different location a year later – though, curiously, the aural image is still not quite perfect. That said, the playing of all concerned is excellent, alive and subtle, with expert and sensitive contributions from the distinguished pianist.

Piano Quintets 1–2

◧– ✸ **** Hyp. CDA 66766. Domus, with Marwood

The playing of **Domus** in these two masterpieces is as light, delicate and full of insight as one would expect. They make one fall for this music all over again. The second is among the masterpieces of Fauré's Indian summer as he approached his eighties. Excellent sound.

Piano Trio in D min., Op. 120

*** Ara. Z 6643. Golub/Kaplan/Carr Trio – DEBUSSY: *Piano Trio* ***; SAINT-SAËNS: *Piano Trio* **(*)

*** Hyp. CDA 67114. Florestan Trio – DEBUSSY; RAVEL: *Piano Trios* ***

Piano Trio; (i) La Bonne Chanson, Op. 61

Ⓜ *** CRD (ADD) CRD 3389. Nash Ens., (i) with Walker

David Golub, **Mark Kaplan** and **Colin Carr** give as understanding and idiomatic a performance of the sublime Fauré *Trio* as is to be found. The recording is very good indeed, with plenty of warmth.

The **Florestans** offer a very apt coupling of three sharply contrasted French works. Fauré is represented in mellow old age, Debussy as a teenager and Ravel in high maturity. With personnel drawn from the piano quartet group Domus, led by the pianist **Susan Tomes**, they give an exceptionally strong, unapologetic reading, at once highly polished and flexibly expressive, revealing what power Fauré retained to the end of his life. Vivid sound.

The members of the **Nash Ensemble** also give a dedicated performance of the late, rarefied *Piano Trio*, capturing both the elegance and the restrained concentration. They are hardly less persuasive in the song-cycle, where the characterful warmth and vibrancy of **Sarah Walker's** voice, not to mention her positive artistry, come out strongly in this beautiful reading of Fauré's early settings of Verlaine, music both tender and ardent. The atmospheric recording is well up to CRD's high standard in chamber music.

String Quartet in E min., Op. 121

◧– ✸ ⒷⒷ *** Naxos 8.554722. Ad Libitum Qt – RAVEL: *Quartet* ***

(N) *** Hyp. CDA 67664. Dante Qt – FRANCK: *String Quartet in D* ***

(M) *** Wigmore Live 0012. Ysaÿe Qt – DEBUSSY: *String Quartet;* STRAVINSKY: *Concertino 3 Pieces; Double Canon* ***

*** HM Aeon AECD 0426. Ysaÿe Qt – MAGNARD: *String Quartet, Op. 16* ***

The **Ad Libitum Quartet** are from Romania. Their ensemble and intonation are perfect, their tone is silken and they give a wonderfully expressive and beautifully characterized account of Fauré's elusive late *String Quartet* – one of the best we have ever heard and one of the best in the catalogue. It is recorded in the Moldava Philharmonic Hall in Iasi and is very natural and lifelike.

The *E minor Quartet* has an almost detached beauty in its minor-keyed, melancholic way and the **Dantes** find much nuance in the score. This impressive performance is coupled to an outstanding version of the Franck *Quartet*. The recording is superb.

There is not a great deal to choose between the Wigmore and Harmonia Mundi performances, so that choice of coupling may be a decisive factor for collectors. The acoustic of the Abbey of L'Epau where the Harmonia Mundi recording was made is particularly warm and rich. But the Naxos disc is a splendid bargain.

Violin Sonatas 1 in A, Op. 13; 2 in E min., Op. 108

(BB) *** Hyp. Helios CDH 55030. Osostowicz, Tomes

(M) *** DG 477 5448 (2). Mintz, Bronfman (with Recital of Encores by ALBENIZ; COUPERIN; GLAZUNOV; GRANADOS; KREISLER; WEBER; WIENIAWSKI) – DEBUSSY; FRANCK; RAVEL: *Violin Sonatas* ***

Violin Sonatas 1–2; Andante in B flat, Op. 75; Berceuse, Op. 16; Romance in B flat, Op. 28

(BB) *** Naxos 8.550906. Kang, Devoyon

Dong-Suk Kang, splendidly partnered by **Pascal Devoyon**, gives us performances which are very fine indeed. This is most welcome – and very good value for money.

Krysia Osostowicz and **Susan Tomes** bring an appealingly natural, unforced quality to their playing and they are completely persuasive, particularly in the elusive *Second Sonata*. The acoustic is a shade resonant but, such is the eloquence of these artists, the ear quickly adjusts. At Helios price, this is highly recommendable.

Splendid playing, too, from **Shlomo Mintz**, who is also rather swamped by the pianist, **Yefim Bronfman**, though his virtuosity and sensitivity are not in question, nor is the lyrical intensity of Mintz's playing. It is the resonant acoustic of the Deutschlandfunk Sendesaal which takes some getting used to.

PIANO MUSIC

Solo piano

Ballade in F sharp, Op. 19; Barcarolles 1–13; (i) Dolly Suite, Op. 56; Impromptus 1–5; Impromptu,

Op. 86; Mazurka in B flat, Op. 32; 13 Nocturnes; Pièces brèves 1–8, Op. 84; 9 Préludes, Op. 103; Romances sans paroles 1–3; (i) Souvenirs de Bayreuth; Theme & Variations in C sharp min., Op. 73; Valses-caprices 1–4

⊕ *** Hyp. CDA 66911/4 (4). Stott, (i) with Roscoe

(B) *** CRD (ADD) 5006 (5). Crossley (without *Dolly Suite; Souvenirs de Bayreuth*)

Both the *Thirteen Barcarolles* and the *Thirteen Nocturnes* give a most illuminating view of Fauré's career, gentle and unsensational like the music itself, but with the subtlest of developments towards a sparer, more rarefied style. That comes out all the more tellingly when, as here, they are given in succession and are played with such poetry and spontaneous-sounding freshness. Each of the four discs contains well over 70 minutes of music, logically presented, with the *Nocturnes* spread between the third and fourth discs, framing the lighter pieces, including such duets as the witty Wagner quadrille, *Souvenirs de Bayreuth*, and the ever-fresh *Dolly Suite*, both with **Kathryn Stott** ideally partnered by **Martin Roscoe**. A masterly set.

Paul Crossley's recordings come from the 1980s. He shows an instinctive feeling for Fauré's elusive, expressive language and subtle artistry. A drawback to the CRD set is that five CDs are involved, and the piano duet items are not included. Stott must remain a first recommendation. Those who do not want to buy the complete oeuvre but are looking for a very well-recorded anthology of Fauré's piano music should investigate Kun-Woo Paik's Decca CD.

Ballade in F sharp, Op. 19; Barcarolle 1, Op. 26; Impromptu 2, Op. 31; Improvisation (8 Pièces brèves), Op. 84/5; Nocturnes 1; 3, Op. 33/1 & 3; 6, Op. 63; 11, Op. 104/1; 13, Op. 119; Préludes, Op. 103, 2 & 7; Romance sans paroles, Op. 17/3

*** Decca 470 246-2. Paik

Kun-Woo Paik continues to impress in French music. This Fauré recital is the finest single-disc anthology of this great composer's music to have appeared for some time. Even if Fauré is well represented in your library, you should add this excellently recorded recital, which would make a fine introduction for those new to this repertoire.

Barcarolles 1–13 (complete); Theme and Variations in C sharp min., Op. 73

(***) Testament mono SBT 1215

Nocturnes 1–13 (complete)

(***) Testament mono SBT 1262

Impromptus 1–5; Impromptu, Op. 86; 8 Pièces brèves; Valses-caprices 1–4

(***) Testament mono SBT 1263. Thyssens-Valentin

These three Testament CDs, superbly transferred from Ducretet-Thomson discs in mono, offer Fauré interpretations that have rarely been matched for their poetry and natural spontaneity of expression, coupled with a flawless technique. These discs, recorded respectively in 1955, 1956 and 1959, consistently have one marvelling at the fluidity of **Thyssens-Valentin's** playing, which yet is combined with sparkling control, in a way that few rival versions can begin to match. It almost feels as though she herself is actually creating this music as she plays.

Barcarolles 1, 5 & 6; Nocturnes 1, 8 & 13; Romance sans paroles 1–3; Valse-caprice 1; Theme and Variations

🅑—, (BB) *** Regis (ADD/DDD) RRC 1187. Crossley

This makes an admirable 75-minute recital, taken from **Paul Crossley's** five-disc coverage for CRD. The engaging *Theme and Variations* is especially welcome. Crossley never forces the music, yet his purity of style is never chaste and his concentration and sense of scale demonstrate his full understanding of this repertoire. The recorded sound is consistently good, though reflecting slightly different recording balances between 1983 and 1987. A bargain.

Barcarolles 1, Op. 26; 6, Op. 70; Impromptus 2, Op. 31; 3, Op. 34; Nocturnes 1, 3, Op. 33/1 & 3; 4, Op. 36; 6, Op. 63; 13, Op. 119; 8 Pièces brèves, Op. 84; Romance sans paroles 3, Op. 17/3

🅑—, *** Hyp. CDA 67074. Stott

An admirably chosen collection, arranged in the form of a recital, taken from **Kathryn Stott's** complete survey. A pity the C sharp minor *Theme and Variations* was not included, but what is (69 minutes) is well worth having when played and recorded so persuasively.

Nocturnes 1–13 (complete)

Ⓝ **** Avie AV 2133. Owen

The *Nocturnes* span Fauré's whole composing career and, while the earlier works inherit a moonlight romanticism from Chopin (although the second includes a turbulent centrepiece), the *Fourth in E flat* is deliciously sensuous, with a specially Fauréan delicacy. The *Ninth in B minor* is modally haunting, and the later works are rather more harmonically adventurous and develop an added internal intensity. All, however, are among his most rewarding piano miniatures and could not have been written by any other composer. **Charles Owen** is obviously completely at home in these sometimes elusive works and plays them beautifully, with subtle feeling for their colour. He is very well recorded.

VOCAL MUSIC

Complete Mélodies

Vol. 1

*** Hyp. CDA 67333. Lott, J. Smith, McGreevy, Doufexis, Mark Ainsley, Maltman, Varcoe; Johnson

Vol. 2

*** Hyp. CDA 67334. McGreevy, J. Smith, Lott, Doufexis, Mark Ainsley, Fouchécourt, Maltman, Varcoe; Johnson

Graham Johnson's Hyperion survey of the Fauré songs is quite masterly. They are shared among a distinguished team of mainly British singers. As ever in these Hyperion song surveys, the piano accompaniments are highly sensitive and imaginative in their use of keyboard colour while, as so often, Graham Johnson provides immaculate documentation which greatly enhances the value of each volume. The singing radiates a love for and dedication to these wonderful songs, and no one with an interest in Fauré (or in good singing) should miss them.

Mélodies: (i) Après un rêve; Arpège; Automne; Au bord de l'eau; (ii) C'est l'extase langoureuse; Clair de lune; En sourdine; Green; L'Horizon chimérique (cycle); Mandoline; Prison; Spleen

✿ (***) Testament mono SBT 1311. Souzay, (i) Bonneau or (ii) Baldwin – FALLA: *Canciónes populares españolas*; RAVEL: *Histoires naturelles* ***

Writing in 1955, the authors of *The Record Guide* spoke of **Souzay** surpassing his earlier achievements, and they hailed these Fauré songs on Decca LXT 2543 (from which this Testament issue in part derives) as 'one of the most satisfactory LP song recitals yet issued'. Half a century later it has lost none of its ability to enchant and remains one of the most eloquent of all Souzay's song records.

Mélodies: Après un rêve; Aurore; Automne; La bonne chanson; Au bord de l'eau; Clair de lune; L'Horizon chimérique; Lydia; 5 Mélodies 'de Venise'; Mirages; Nell; Le Parfum impérissable; Le plus doux; Les Présents; Prison; Les Roses d'Ispahan; Soir; Spleen

*** Nim. (ADD) NI 5736/7 (2). Cuénod, Isepp – DUPARC: *Mélodies: Chanson triste*, etc. ***

Hugues Cuénod was already 70 when he made these well-balanced recordings, though this hardly shows: the voice is light and steady and his sense of style impeccable. Both the accompanists (the documentation does not indicate who accompanies what) are highly sensitive and match the refined intelligence this great artist brings to this repertoire.

Mélodies: Après un rêve; Au bord de l'eau; Les Berceaux; Clair de lune; Lydia; Mandoline; Le Papillon et la fleur; Sylvie

*** Virgin 5 45360-2. Gens, Vignoles – DEBUSSY; POULENC: *Mélodies* ***

Véronique Gens is a highly accomplished artist and certainly makes a beautiful sound. She allows Fauré's art to speak for itself, although there are times when you feel stronger characterization would not come amiss. She is sensitively accompanied by **Roger Vignoles** and recorded with great naturalness.

La Chanson d'Eve, Op. 95; Mélodies: Après un rêve; Aubade; Barcarolle; Les Berceaux; Chanson du pêcheur; En prière; En sourdine; Green; Hymne; Des Jardins de la nuit; Mandoline; Le Papillon et la fleur;

Les Présents; Rêve d'amour; Les Roses d'Ispahan; Le Secret; Spleen; Toujours!

🎵— ⚙ *** Hyp. CDA 66320. Baker, Parsons

Dame Janet Baker gives magical performances of a generous collection of 28 songs, representing Fauré throughout his long composing career, including many of his most winning songs. **Geoffrey Parsons** is at his most compellingly sympathetic, matching every mood. Many will be surprised at Fauré's variety of expression over this extended span of songs.

Requiem, Op. 48

🎵— Ⓜ *** Teldec 0927 49001-2. Bonney, Hampson, Amb. S., Philh. O, Legrand – DURUFLÉ: *Requiem* ***

(i) Requiem; (ii) Pavane

Requiem (1893 version); Ave Maria, Op. 67/2; Ave verum corpus, Op. 65/1; Cantique de Jean Racine, Op. 11; Maria, Mater gratiae, Op. 47/2; Messe basse; Tantum ergo, Op. 65/2

🎵— **** Coll. (ADD) COLCD 109. Ashton, Varcoe, Cambridge Singers, L. Sinfonia (members), Rutter

Requiem (1893 version); Ave verum corpus; Cantique de Jean Racine; Messe basse; Tantum ergo

*** Hyp. CDA 66292. Seers, Poulenard, George, Corydon Singers, ECO, Best

Requiem; Cantique de Jean Racine; La Naissance de Vénus, Op. 29

*** Australian ABC Classics 472 045-2. Macliver, Tahu Rhodes, Cantillation, Sinf. Australis, Walker

(i; ii; iv) Requiem; (ii; iii) Les Djinns, Op. 12; (ii) Madrigal, Op. 35

*** Ph. 438 149-2. (i) Bott, Cachemaille; (ii) Monteverdi Ch., Salisbury Cathedral Boy Choristers; (iii) Vatin; (iv) ORR, Gardiner – DEBUSSY: *3 Chansons de Charles d'Orléans*; RAVEL: *3 Chansons*; SAINT-SAËNS: *3 songs* ***

John Rutter's inspired reconstruction of Fauré's original 1893 score, using only lower strings and no woodwind, opened our ears to the extra freshness of the composer's first thoughts. Rutter's fine, bright recording includes the *Messe basse* and four motets, of which the *Ave Maria* setting and *Ave verum corpus* are particularly memorable. The recording is first rate but places the choir and instruments relatively close.

Michel Legrand uses the full orchestral version of 1900 in the most dramatic way possible, yet the delicacy of the *In paradisum* reflects an equally sympathetic response to the gentler, mystical side of the music. **Barbara Bonney's** *Pie Jesu* with its simplicity and innocence is very touching. **Thomas Hampson** makes an eloquent contribution to the *Libera me*, and after the climax the flowing choral line shows the subtle range of colour and dynamic commanded by the **Ambrosian Singers** (as well as the orchestra). With superb, spacious recording this performance is very compelling indeed, and it is coupled with an equally fine account of the Duruflé work which was inspired by Fauré's masterpiece.

John Eliot Gardiner, like Rutter but with period forces, also chooses the version of the *Requiem* with the original instrumentation. The darkness matches Gardiner's view of the work, which he makes more dramatic than it often is. The mellow recording takes away some of the bite but, with excellent soloists – **Catherine Bott** radiantly beautiful in the *Pie Jesu*, **Gilles Cachemaille** vividly bringing out word-meaning – it makes an excellent choice. *Les Djinns* is specially welcome, with piano accompaniment on a gentle-toned Erard of 1874; and all the other pieces, including Fauré's enchanting *Madrigal*, are in various ways inspired by early French part-songs, with the medieval overtones brought out in the Debussy and with the humour of the Ravel nicely underlined.

Matthew Best's performance with the **Corydon Singers** also uses the Rutter edition but presents a choral and orchestral sound that is more refined, set against a helpful church acoustic. *In paradisum* is ethereally beautiful. Best's soloists are even finer than Rutter's, and he too provides a generous fill-up in the *Messe basse* and other motets, though two fewer than Rutter.

The Australian artists on ABC give a translucent, sensuous performance, and their well-blended sound and fine balance are enhanced by the singing of **Cantillation**, which is a relatively small choir. **Teddy Tahu Rhodes** is a bass-baritone with a slightly grainy finish to his voice, but an uncommon agility, while **Sara Macliver's** lovely *Pie Jesu* is effortless and pure. The performance of the *Cantique de Jean Racine* is very fine too. However, the special interest of this release is the inclusion of *La Naissance de Vénus*, in essence a single-scene mythological opera, intended for the concert hall. Again Tahu Rhodes, in the role of the deity Jupiter, shows considerable agility, this time in a high baritone register. A worthwhile addition to the catalogue. Full texts and translations are included, with excellent documentation.

FAYRFAX, Robert (1464–1521)

Missa Albanus; Missa O bone Ihesu (with Elevation Motet: Anima Christi … Resurrexio Christi); Missa O quam glorifica; Missa Regali ex progenie; Missa Tecum principium

Ⓜ *** Gaudeamus CDGAX 353 (3). Cardinall's Musick, Carwood

This fine mid-priced set gathers together all Fayrfax's known *Masses*, plus a bonus in the newly discovered and magnificent *O bone Ihesu* and an incomplete four-part setting of *Anima Christi* (an 'elevation motet' sung during the elevation of the host). The surviving text begins with '*Resurrexio*' and David Skinner, whose editions are used throughout, tells us in the notes that there is no doubt about the connection of this motet with the *Mass*. The performances and recordings are of outstanding quality, and anyone who has not yet sampled this glorious music could do no better than start here.

FERGUSON, Howard (1908–99)

Piano Concerto (for piano and strings)

⊕— ⑧⑧ *** Naxos 8.557290. Donohoe, Northern Sinfonia –
DARNTON; GERHARD; ROWLEY: *Piano Concertos* ***

This *Concerto for Piano and Strings*, written in 1951, is conceived in structure on neoclassical lines, with an opening orchestral tutti, but it follows the warmly attractive idiom that is typical of the composer, very British, with brilliant writing for the soloist, not least in the finale with its jazzy syncopations, slightly Waltonian, leading to a climax in waltz time. The central *Theme and Variations* comes nearer to the pastoral tradition, building up powerfully. **Peter Donohoe**, directing the **Northern Sinfonia** from the keyboard, is the most persuasive interpreter. Well-balanced sound. An excellent, varied and imaginative coupling.

Overture for an Occasion, Op. 16; Partita, Op. 5a; (i) 2 Ballads, Op. 1; (ii) The Dream of the Rood, Op. 19

⊕— *** Chan. 9082. (i) Rayner Cook; (ii) Dawson, L. Symphony Ch.; LSO, Hickox

This collection includes a striking setting of the *Lyke-Wake dirge*, written in 1928, long before Britten. The *Partita* of 1935–6 is surprisingly dark until the last movement, with a weirdly enigmatic second movement and a lamenting slow movement. The *Overture for an Occasion*, written for the Queen's coronation, has the warmth and colour of comparable Walton works, and further echoes of Walton flavour the *Dream of the Rood*, a setting of an Anglo-Saxon poem with a radiant soprano solo introducing a sequence of richly atmospheric choruses. **Hickox** proves an ideal advocate, drawing incandescent singing and playing from his performers, with rich and clear Chandos sound to match.

(i) Octet; (ii; iii) Violin Sonata 2, Op. 10; (iii) 5 Bagatelles

⊕— *** Hyp. CDA 66192. (i) Nash Ens.; (ii) Chilingirian; (iii) Benson – FINZI: *Elegy* ***

Ferguson's *Octet* is written for the same instruments as Schubert's masterpiece, a delightful counterpart. Those seeking a first-class modern version will find that the **Nash Ensemble** fill the bill admirably. The other works on the Hyperion disc display the same gift of easy, warm communication, including the darker *Violin Sonata* and Finzi's haunting *Elegy for Violin & Piano*.

(i) Violin Sonatas 1, Op. 2; 2, Op. 10; (ii) 4 Short Pieces; (iii) 3 Sketches, Op. 14; (iv) Discovery (song-cycle), Op. 13; (v) 5 Irish Folksongs, Op. 17; (vi) Love and reason; (iv) 3 Mediaeval Carols, Op. 3

*** Chan. 9316-2. (i) Mordkovitch; (ii) Hilton; (iii) Butt; (iv) Mark Ainsley; (v) Burgess; (vi) Schneider-Waterberg; all with Benson

This generous collection of Ferguson's chamber music, beautifully performed, provides a fine counterpart to Hickox's orchestral and choral disc. It is framed by the two

Violin Sonatas (1931 and 1946), both powerful works, with **Lydia Mordkovitch** a rich and persuasive interpreter. **Clifford Benson** is the linchpin among the performers, contributing to all the works here. The *Four Short Pieces* for clarinet and the *Three Sketches* for flute are delightful miniatures, as is the counter-tenor song, *Love and reason*, and the *Carols* and the *Discovery* cycle for tenor. Best of all is the colourful cycle of Irish folksongs for mezzo, vividly performed by **Sally Burgess**. Excellent, well-balanced sound.

(i) Partita for 2 Pianos, Op. 56; Piano Sonata in F min., Op. 8

*** Hyp. CDA 66130. Shelley, (i) Macnamara

Ferguson's *Sonata* is here given a powerful and intense performance, a work which, for all its echoes of Rachmaninov, is quite individual. The *Partita* is also a large-scale work, full of good ideas, in which **Howard Shelley** is joined for this two-piano version by his wife, **Hilary Macnamara**. Excellent, committed performances and first-rate recording, vividly transferred to CD.

5 Bagatelles; Sonata in F min.

Ⓜ *** Somm SOMMCD 038. Bebbington – GURNEY: *Nocturnes* ***

Ferguson's muscular *Piano Sonata* (1938–40), written in memory of his teacher, Harold Samuel, is a work of deep, controlled, yet passionate intensity. Its language is frankly romantic and splendidly laid out for the piano, at times even reminding the listener of Brahms, Rachmaninov or, nearer home, Bliss – and none the worse for that! **Mark Bebbington** gives convincing performances, though the recording is decent rather than distinguished.

FESCA, Friedrich Ernst (1789–1826)

Symphony 1 in E flat, Op. 6; Omar & Leila Overture; Overtures in D, Op. 41; C, Op. 43

*** CPO 999 889-2. N. German R. Philharmonie, Beermann

Symphonies 2 in D, Op. 10; 3 in D, Op. 13; Overture Cantemire

*** CPO 999 869-2. N. German R. Philharmonie, Beerman

This disc follows on from **Beermann's** CD of the highly entertaining *Second* and *Third Symphonies* of Fesca, and this new CD proves every bit as entertaining. Not that this *First Symphony* is as individual as the two later ones. Indeed, the first movement is clearly modelled on Mozart's *No. 39*, but it is no less enjoyable with its elegant, tuneful writing, particularly when the performance is so sympathetic. The two concert overtures were originally *entr'actes* at the court theatre, and both feature slow introductions leading on to exceptionally bright and lively *allegros*. The dramatic overture to his opera, *Omar und Leila*, features some pleasing 'exotic' touches in the orchestration. A first-class recording completes the attractiveness of both issues.

FIBICH, Zdeněk (1850–1900)

Symphonies 1 in F, Op. 17; 2 in E flat, Op. 38; 3 in E min., Op. 53

⊕ Ⓑ *** Chan. Double 9682 (2). Detroit SO, Järvi

There is a strong Bohemian feel to these works and if, like so much of Fibich's music, the *First Symphony*, which opens so invitingly, is a little square, such is the excellence of **Neeme Järvi's** performance that it does not feel so. The performances of the *Second* and *Third* come into competition with a Supraphon issue from the Brno Orchestra under Jiří Waldhans and Bělohlávek (11 0657-2). But the Chandos recording scores in terms of fidelity and space, and the **Detroit Orchestra** respond with enthusiasm to these scores. Overall this set is well worth exploring and far preferable to the Naxos alternative. (8.553699)

Piano Quintet, Op. 42

*** ASV CDDCA 943. Endymion Ens. – DOHNÁNYI: *Sextet* ***

Fibich's *Piano Quintet* is a relatively late piece; it comes from the last decade of his life and has much lively invention and no mean charm. The **Endymions** give a first-rate account of it and are excellently recorded.

Piano Trio in F

*** Sup. SU 3927-2. Smetana Trio – DVOŘÁK: *Piano Trio in B flat*; MARTINŮ: *Piano Trio 2* ***

With its positive ideas the *Trio* by Zdeněk Fibich, starting with a bold opening gesture, the urgency of the outer movements very much reflects a young man's inspiration. It is all the more attractive in such a compact format, though the Czech flavours are not very strong.

Moods, Impressions & Reminiscences, Opp. 41, 44, 47 & 57; Studies of Paintings

ⒷⒷ **(*) Regis RRC 1221. Kvapil

These small vignettes are touching – they are a forerunner of Janáček's *Leaves from an overgrown path* and most are full of strong poetic feeling and beauty of melodic line. They are played with great subtlety by **Radoslav Kvapil**. The piano-timbre is a little hard and lacking bloom; nevertheless, the gentler pieces work their full magic and this is a worthwhile disc at its new budget price. It also comes as part of a four-disc Regis anthology of Czech piano music (RRC 4006).

Sarka (complete)

*** Orfeo C 541 002H (2). Urbanová, Lotric, Kirilova, Jenis, Vienna Concert Ch., Vienna RSO, Cambreling

**(*) Sup. (ADD) SU 0036-2 612 (2). Depoltavá, Pribyl, Randová, Zítek, Brno Janáček Op. Ch., Brno State PO, Stych

Fibich's *Sarka* is based on the Czech legend of the predatory Sarka and her fellow Amazons. Fibich was aiming directly at writing a Wagnerian opera, especially in his echoes of *Tristan und Isolde* in the love duet for Sarka and Ctirad, the knight with whom she falls in love against her will. The weakness lies in melodic material that only fitfully sticks in the memory. On Orfeo **Sylvain Cambreling** conducts a strong and purposeful performance in a good, well-balanced radio recording. Both the principals, **Eva Urbanová** as Sarka and **Janez Lotric** as Ctirad, are outstanding, with their characterful Slavonic voices that yet focus beautifully, and the others make a strong team.

The Supraphon version dates from 1978, with warmly atmospheric analogue sound. Its great strength is the idiomatic conducting of **Jan Stych**, even though **Eva Depoltavá** in the title-role is less characterful than Urbanová on Orfeo. **Vilem Pribyl** is a first-rate Ctirad, but the most outstanding singing comes from **Eva Randová** as the leader of the Amazons, Vlasta, rich and distinctive.

FIELD, John (1782–1837)

(i) Piano Concertos 1–7; Divertissements 1–2; Nocturne 16 in F; (ii) Quintetto

Ⓝ Ⓜ *** Chan. 10468 (4). O'Rourke; (i) LMP, Bamert; (ii) Juritz, Godson, Bradley, Desbruslais

The music of these concertos is uneven, but they are all easy to enjoy, and most have their fair share of winning themes, with scintillating passagework, persuasively nocturnal slow movements, and often a catchy closing rondo. The soloist, **Míceál O'Rourke**, is very persuasive and he receives admirable support from **Bamert** and the **London Mozart Players**, and first-class recording. The extra items which complete the CD containing the *Seventh Concerto* – the two *Divertissements* and *Nocturne* – all include a really good tune, while the serene single-movement *Piano Quintet* is also delicately charming. The concertos are all available on separate discs: Nos. 1 & 2 (Chan. 9368); 3 & 5 (Chan. 9495); 4 & 6 (Chan. 9442); and 7 plus encores (Chan. 9534).

Piano Concertos 1 in E flat; 3 in E flat

⊕ ⒷⒷ *** Naxos 8.553770. Frith, Northern Sinfonia, Haslam

Benjamin Frith has the bargain field to himself. His playing is characteristically sensitive and fresh, and he is well supported by the **Northern Sinfonia** and **David Haslam**. Very good, warm recording, in a decent acoustic.

Piano Concertos 2 in A flat; 3 in E flat

Ⓜ **** Telarc CD 80370. O'Conor, SCO, Mackerras

These Telarc performances are beautifully recorded and are distinctly superior. **John O'Conor** plays throughout with great distinction and always displays the lightest touch – his softly gleaming roulades are very fetching – and **Mackerras** accompanies with warmth and character. A delightful disc in every respect.

Piano Concertos 5 (L'Incendie par l'orage); 6 in C

⊕ ⒷⒷ **** Naxos 8.554221. Frith, Northern Sinfonia, Haslam

These two concertos are exhilaratingly performed by **Benjamin Frith** with the **Northern Sinfonia**, with Frith's sparklingly clear articulation in rapid scales and figuration magnetizing the attention in music that can easily seem just trivial. The title of the *Fifth Concerto, L'Incendie par l'orage* ('Fire from Lightning'), reflects a dramatic storm passage in the long and ambitious first movement, while the lovely slow movement of the *Sixth Concerto* is a nocturne in all but name, with the outer movements full of bright ideas.

Nocturnes 1–9; Piano Sonatas 1 in E flat; 2 in A, Op. 1/1–2

🎧— (BB) **** Naxos 8.550761. Frith

Nocturnes 10–17; 18 (Midi); Piano Sonata 3 in C min., Op. 1/3

🎧— (BB) **** Naxos 8.550762. Frith

Benjamin Frith's playing is delectably coaxing, and he makes these *Nocturnes* so often seem exquisitely like Chopin, yet still catches their naïve innocence, especially in the *A flat major* work. He hops, skips and jumps delightfully in the Irish *Rondo* finale of the *First Sonata* and is hardly less beguiling in the rather more imposing opening movement of the *Second*.

The second CD includes the famous *Nocturne 18* whose original title was *Midi* (or 'Twelve O'clock Rondo'). The *Third Sonata* occupies the midway point in the recital. Its first movement is just a little hectoring (Beethovenian *con fuoco* was not Field's natural element) but the closing *Rondo* simulates another popular air for its basis. As before, the recording is very natural.

Largo in C min.; Nocturnes in B flat; C min.; E min.; Prelude in C min.; Romance in E flat; Waltzes: in A; E (Sehnsucht)

*** Etcetera KTC 1231. Antoni – CHOPIN: *Recital* **(*)

Under the title 'Crossfire' this fascinatingly devised recital readily demonstrates links and influences between the music of John Field (who invented the Nocturne) and Chopin, his young Polish successor. **Helge Antoni** is a notably sensitive advocate of Field's music, and his simple style readily draws parallels with alternated pieces by Chopin. A recital that is both stimulating and musically enjoyable too, as it is naturally recorded.

Piano Sonatas 1–3, Op. 1/1–3; 4 in B; Collection of Piano Airs; Fantaisire; Rondos and Variations

(M) *** Chan. 2x1 241-38. O'Rourke

Míceál O'Rourke plays these two-movement *Sonatas* with some flair. This disc is now joined with a (nearly 80-minute) recital of shorter pieces, and much of it has that quiet charm one expects from this delightful composer. O'Rourke again proves a dedicated interpreter of real artistry, playing with intelligence and taste. Recorded at The Maltings, Snape, he is admirably served by the Chandos team.

FINZI, Gerald (1901–56)

(i) Cello Concerto, Op. 40; (ii) Concerto for Small Orchestra & Solo Violin; Prelude, Op. 25; Romance, Op. 11 (both for strings)

(M) *** Chan. 10425X. (i) Wallfisch; (ii) Little; City of L. Sinfonia., Hickox

(i) Cello Concerto; (ii) Eclogue for Piano and Strings; Grand Fantasia & Toccata

🎧— (BB) *** Naxos 8.555766. (i) Hugh; (ii) Donohoe; N. Sinfonia, Griffiths

The *Cello Concerto* is arguably Finzi's greatest work, not just ambitious but deeply moving, written under the stress of knowing he was terminally ill. **Wallfisch** finds all the dark eloquence of Finzi's central movement, and the performance overall has splendid impetus, with **Hickox** providing the most sympathetic backing. The Chandos recording has a very natural balance.

The Naxos version, with **Tim Hugh** a most sensitive soloist, has the advantage not only of bargain price but of a very apt coupling in two of Finzi's concertante works with piano, originally designed for a concerto. **Peter Donohoe** is the powerful soloist, not always as tender as he might be, but still very sympathetic. A good bargain alternative choice.

(i) Cello Concerto; (ii) Clarinet Concerto

🌼 **** Lyrita SRCD 236. (i) Ma, New Philh. O.; (ii) Denman, RPO, Handley

In the *Cello Concerto* **Yo Yo Ma**, in his début recording, responds with the utmost sensitivity, sometimes playing on a mere thread of tone in his magical account of the *Andante quieto*. His is not a big performance but a gently inspired one, and many will like his lightness of touch in the finale. The *Clarinet Concerto* is a comparable masterpiece. If it lacks the contemplative qualities of the *Cello Concerto*, its more extrovert character and consistent charm are no less compelling. **John Denman's** performance is entirely seductive, and in both works **Vernon Handley's** sensitive accompaniments bring first-rate playing while the recording is of Lyrita's usual excellence. A treasurable disc.

Clarinet Concerto, Op. 31

(BB) *** Hyp. Helios CDH 55101. King, Philh. O, Francis – STANFORD: *Clarinet Concerto* ***

(i) Clarinet Concerto, Op. 31; 5 Bagatelles for Clarinet & Strings (arr. Ashmore), Op. 23a; Love's Labour's Lost: 3 Soliloquies, Op. 28; (ii) Introit in F for Solo Violin & Small Orchestra, Op. 6; Romance in E flat for String Orchestra, Op. 11; A Severn Rhapsody, Op. 3

🎧— (BB) *** Naxos 8.553566. (i) Plane; (ii) Hatfield; N. Sinfonia, Griffiths

(i) Clarinet Concerto; (ii) Eclogue for Piano & Strings; Love's Labour's Lost: Suite; Prelude for String Orchestra; Romance for Strings

(M) *** Nim. NI 5665. (i) Hacker; (ii) Jones; E. String O, Boughton

(i) Clarinet Concerto; (ii) Introit for Violin & Orchestra

(M) **** BBC (ADD) BBCM 5015-2. (i) Hilton, BBC N. SO, Thomson; (ii) Jarvis, LPO, Boult – LEIGH: Harpsichord Concertino **** (with Concert: 'English Music' ***)

(i) Clarinet Concerto, Op. 31; (ii) 5 Bagatelles for Clarinet & Piano

*** ASV CDDCA 787. Johnson; (i) RPO, Groves; (ii) Martineau – STANFORD: Clarinet Concerto, etc. ***

Emma Johnson is even more warmly expressive in the concerto than Thea King on her Helios disc, and with **Sir Charles Groves** and the **RPO** ideally sympathetic accompanists. Finzi's sinuous melodies for the solo instrument are made to sound as though the soloist is improvising them.

Thea King also gives a definitive performance, strong and clean-cut. Her characterful timbre, using little or no vibrato, is highly telling against a resonant orchestral backcloth. **Alun Francis** is a most sympathetic accompanist. With Stanford's even rarer concerto this makes a most attractive bargain reissue, and the sound is excellent.

Finzi's Concerto is also played most nimbly by **Janet Hilton**, admirably supported by **Bryden Thomson**, especially in the lovely Adagio, which is memorably intense. The Introit for Violin and Orchestra, which brings another memorable theme, is a meditative, thoughtful piece, very well played by **Gerald Jarvis** and the **LPO** under **Sir Adrian Boult** in 1969. This is part of a 77-minute concert of English music, including the delicious Harpsichord Concertino of Walter Leigh.

Robert Plane's highly responsive performance of the concerto also uses a wide range of dynamic, and movingly brings out the work's sense of improvisatory lyricism. Not to be outdone, the Naxos collection offers the Three Soliloquies, plus an orchestration of the five lovely Bagatelles, which is even more evocative than the original version with piano. The Introit for Violin and Orchestra is most sensitively played by **Lesley Hatfield**. The Romance is hardly less engaging, while Severn Rhapsody shows its composer spinning his pastoral evocation in the manner of Butterworth. All this music is most persuasively presented by the **Northern Sinfonia** under **Howard Griffiths** and the Naxos recording has plenty of warmth and atmosphere.

Alan Hacker's reading of the Concerto is also improvisatory in style and freely flexible in tempi, with the slow movement at once introspective and rhapsodic. The concert suite of incidental music for Shakespeare's Love's Labour's Lost is amiably atmospheric and pleasing in invention and in the colour of its scoring. The two string-pieces are by no means slight and are played most expressively; the Romance is particularly eloquent in **William Boughton's** hands. For the reissue a sensitive account of the Eclogue has been added.

(i) Concerto for Violin & Small Orchestra; Prelude, Op. 25; Romance, Op. 11 (both for strings); (ii) In Years Defaced (song-cycle, orchestrated by Finzi, Alexander, Roberts, Matthews, Payne and Weir)

🎧 *** Chan. 9888. (i) Little; (ii) Mark Ainsley; City of L. Sinfonia, Hickox

The Concerto for Violin and Small Orchestra draws on Finzi's distinctive brand of pastoral writing, the outer movements are strong and vigorous, the central slow movement ethereally reflective. The warmly expressive Prelude for Strings was salvaged from a Chamber Symphony that was never completed, while the Romance is the most ravishing piece of all.

Taking their cue from Finzi's own setting of When I set out for Lyonnesse, the five other composers involved, all Finzi admirers, offer sensitive settings of a sequence of poems (four by Hardy) which together form a satisfying cycle, designed to celebrate the composer's centenary in 2001, sympathetically sung by **John Mark Ainsley**. Colin Matthews brings out the mystery of Flecker's evocative poem, To a Poet a Thousand Years Hence, while Anthony Payne (the understanding 'realizer' of Elgar's Third Symphony) provides a brilliant conclusion, more radical than the rest, with the compound-time setting of Hardy's Proud Songsters, quite different from Britten's setting of the same poem in Winter Words.

Eclogue for Piano & String Orchestra

(B) *** CfP 575 9832. Lane, RLPO, Handley – DELIUS: Piano Concerto; VAUGHAN WILLIAMS: Piano Concerto ***

This is the central movement of an uncompleted piano concerto which the composer decided could stand on its own. It was Howard Ferguson who edited the final manuscript and set the title. The mood is tranquil yet haunting, and **Piers Lane** gives it a tenderly sympathetic reading.

(i) Eclogue for Piano & String Orchestra, Op. 10; (ii) The Fall of the Leaf (Elegy), Op. 20; (i) Grand Fantasia & Toccata for Piano & Orchestra, Op. 38; (ii; iii) Introit for Small Orchestra and Violin; (ii) Nocturne (New Year Music), Op. 7; A Severn Rhapsody, Op. 3; Prelude, Op. 25; Romance, Op. 11; 3 Solitudes (all for string orchestra), Op. 11

🎧 *** Lyrita (ADD) SRCD 239. (i) Katin, New Philh. O, Handley; (ii) LPO, Boult; (iii) with Friend

This collection of shorter orchestral works has some charming miniatures, the music reflecting the wistful, often death-obsessed side of Finzi's character; thus in the Nocturne the New Year brings regret rather than celebration. The pure beauty of the Introit (a surviving movement from a violin concerto whose outer movements were withdrawn) and the easy Englishness of the Severn Rhapsody are equally characteristic, implying more than they seem to. Boult's affectionate performances are superbly recorded and **Rodney Friend** is an understanding soloist in the concerto movement. The two recordings for piano and orchestra are very well played by **Peter Katin** and the orchestra under **Vernon Handley**, and again are very well recorded.

(i) Music for 'Love's Labour's Lost' (for string orchestra); (ii) Farewell to Arms; (iii) In terra pax; (iv) Let us Garlands bring, Op. 18; (v) 2 Sonnets by John Milton

*** Lyrita (DDD/ADD) SRCD 237. (i) RPO; (ii–v) New Philh. O; both cond. Handley; with (ii; v) Partridge; (iii) Manning, Noble, John Alldis Ch.; (iv) Carol Case

Finzi here sets highly compressed Milton sonnets in a way that genuinely intensifies the words, reflecting the composer's own intimations of death at the time of composition. They are beautifully sung by **Ian Partridge**, who is also the soloist in the introduction and aria, *Farewell to Arms*. *In terra pax* is a Christmas cantata in miniature, charming in Finzi's most relaxed folk-based style. **John Carol Case** is the soloist in five Shakespeare lyrics, delicate and individual. The collection is prefaced by *Love's Labour's Lost*, a vivid suite for strings. Altogether a valuable collection which helps to fill in the complex personality of a minor composer of distinction. Excellent recording.

Elegy for Violin & Piano

*** Nim. NI 5666. Hope, Mulligan – ELGAR: *Violin Sonata*; WALTON: *Violin Sonata* ***

*** Hyp. CDA 66192. Chilingirian, Benson – FERGUSON: *Octet*, etc. ***

The Finzi *Elegy* is a very apt makeweight for the Elgar and Walton sonatas, the only surviving movement from a projected violin sonata written in a hectic period for Finzi at the beginning of the Second World War.

Finzi's moving little *Elegy* also makes an apt fill-up for the record of chamber music by his friend, Howard Ferguson.

VOCAL MUSIC

Song-cycles: Before and after Summer, Op. 16; I said to Love, Op. 19b; Let us garlands bring, Op. 18

(BB) *** Naxos 8.557644. Williams, Burnside

Before and after Summer consists of 10 Hardy songs which Finzi assembled in 1949, notably the dark, powerful setting of *Channel Firing* which comes as a centrepiece. *I said to Love* is a collection of five settings assembled after the composer's death by his widow and son, three dating from the 1930s when he was at his most creative, and two, far darker, dating from his last months before he died in 1956. *Let us garlands bring*, better known, consists of five Shakespeare settings, dedicated to Vaughan Williams, which bring refreshing new illumination to texts set many times before, with *Come away Death* and *Fear no more the Heat of the Sun* among the finest of all Finzi songs. Firm, even tone from Roderick Williams and beautifully clear diction, with immaculate playing from **Iain Burnside**.

Dies natalis; Intimations of Immortality

**(*) Hyp. CDA 66876. Mark Ainsley, Corydon Singers & O, Best

Matthew Best, with **John Mark Ainsley** as soloist in both works, uses a relatively small orchestra. Mark Ainsley has a sweet if small voice, very apt for both works, even if under pressure there is some unevenness. The chorus sings with

feeling, though the recording is not as vividly immediate as the Lyrita recording.

God is gone up; Magnificat; Let us now praise famous men; Lo, the full final sacrifice; My Lovely One; Thou didst delight my eyes; Welcome, Sweet and Sacred Feast; 7 Unaccompanied Part-Songs, Op. 17.

⊕ (BB) *** Naxos 8.555792. St John's College, Cambridge, Ch., Robinson

Gerald Finzi wrote a handful of anthems and motets for the Anglican Church, here freshly and warmly sung by the choir of **St John's College, Cambridge**, under their choirmaster, **Christopher Robinson**. Crowning the collection is the extended setting of Richard Crashaw's poem, *Lo, the full final sacrifice*, ending on an ecstatic 'Amen' with scrunching harmonies. Unlike most offerings in this excellent St John's series from Naxos, this one includes secular items, unaccompanied part-songs, beautifully wrought, setting poems by Robert Bridges.

Intimations of Immortality (Ode)

*** Lyrita SRCD 238. Partridge, Guildford Philharmonic Ch. & O, Handley – HADLEY: *Symphonic Ballad: The Trees so High* ***

Finzi's music, which is in the richest English choral tradition is here performed with a passionate sense of commitment. In this the beauty and intensity of **Ian Partridge's** singing are a key factor, and equally the choral singing is richly committed, while the **Guildford Philharmonic Orchestra** is challenged to playing that would not disgrace a much more famous orchestra. Excellent recording too, and a most enterprising coupling.

Oh Fair to See; Till Earth Outwears; A Young Man's Exhortation

*** Linn CKD 253. Gilchrist, Tilbrook

(N) (BB) **(*) Naxos 8.570414. Mark Ainsley, Burnside

James Gilchrist's fine disc of Finzi, with **Anna Tilbrook** the most sensitive accompanist, makes the perfect complement to the Naxos issue of Finzi songs, with very few duplications. Gilchrist with his clear tenor tone brings out the reflective beauty of Finzi's response to words, and brings vitality to the relatively few vigorous songs. Well-balanced sound.

John Mark Ainsley comes into direct competition with James Gilchrist on Linn, and it has to be said that the Linn performances are even more characterful. Mark Ainsley is at home in this repertoire and his singing is naturally expressive; although his voice is of modest size, he projects it well and his diction is clear. He is persuasively accompanied by **Iain Burnside**, but the piano is balanced rather closely.

A Young Man's Exhortation

*** Hyp. CDA 67459. Padmore, Vignoles – TIPPETT: *Boyhood's End*; BRITTEN: *7 Hölderlin-Fragmente; Um Mitternacht*, etc. ***

Finzi's delightful cycle, dating from 1933, offers 10 more

settings of Hardy poems, which are among the most warmly lyrical songs he ever wrote, with the poet's often earthy verse matched by the composer's English pastoral idiom. **Mark Padmore** is an ideal interpreter, warmly accompanied by **Roger Vignoles**, who provides a perceptive commentary in the notes. Well coupled with other cycles on the theme of youth and friendship.

FOERSTER, Josef Bohuslav (1859–1951)

Symphony 4 in C min. (Easter Eve), Op. 54; My Youth, Op. 44; Festive Overture, Op. 70

(BB) *** Naxos 8.557776. Slovak RSO, Friedel

Foerster's *Fourth Symphony* is one of the best-kept secrets of Czech music. Composed, like its two companions on this CD, during the early part of Foerster's stay in Vienna, it shows the influence of Bruckner and Mahler. It is a long work, some 47 minutes in length, and of striking quality. Its Scherzo is worthy of Dvořák himself and is among the most captivating movements of its kind composed anywhere at this period. The opening of the work has great nobility and depth, and it leaves the listener in no doubt that this is a symphony of real substance. The *Festive Overture* of 1907 and the somewhat earlier Op. 44 symphonic poem, *My Youth*, are both first recordings and are well worth a place in the repertory. The American conductor **Lance Friedel** is obviously committed to this music and gets a very good response from the **Slovak Orchestra**. Recommended with enthusiasm.

Symphony 4 in C min. (Easter Eve), Op. 54; Springtime and Desire, Op. 93

(M) *** Sup. (ADD/DDD) 111 822-2. Prague SO, Smetáček

This beautiful if overlong symphony is both dignified and noble; its Scherzo is infectiously memorable and could be as popular as any of the *Slavonic Dances* if only it were known. All the same, the symphony wears well. To this analogue recording Supraphon add a 1985 account, digitally recorded, of *Springtime and Desire*, a symphonic poem with a strong emphasis on the symphonic, and this, like the symphony, is a most welcome addition to the catalogue. Good performances, decent recording.

FÖRSTER, Christoph (1693–1745)

Horn Concerto in E flat

*** Ara. Z 6750. Rose, St Luke's Chamber Ens. – HAYDN; L. MOZART; TELEMANN: *Horn Concertos* ***

Christoph Förster was a contemporary of Bach and this, the earliest of the four concertos in this outstanding collection, is no less demanding of the soloist's virtuosity. **Stewart Rose** is a splendid player, secure in technique, his style buoyant and expressive by turns, and the orchestra of which he is principal provides him with warmly stylish accompaniments. The recording is first class.

FOSS, Lukas (1922–2009)

3 American Pieces

(BB) *** Encore 2 08124-2. Perlman, Boston SO, Ozawa – BARBER: *Violin Concerto*; BERNSTEIN: *Serenade after Plato's 'Symposium'* ***

As the title suggests, Foss's *Three American Pieces* have a strong element of Copland-like folksiness, married to sweet, easy lyricism and with some Stravinskian echoes. Skilfully orchestrated for a small orchestra with prominent piano, all three of the pieces, not just the final *Allegro, Composer's Holiday*, but also the first two, *Early Song* and *Dedication*, have a way of gravitating into hoe-down rhythms, often with a surprising suddenness.

Fantasy Rondo; For Lenny; Grotesque Dance; Four 2-Part Inventions; Passacaglia; Prelude in D; Scherzo ricercato; Solo

(BB) *** Naxos 8.559179. Scott Dunn

An impressive pianist, Lukas Foss was also a prolific composer, and the *Inventions* and *Grotesque Dance* were written when he was 16. This disc collects all his piano music from his teens through to *Solo* (1981) and *For Lenny* (1987). They are inventive and at times delightful pieces. Highly recommended.

String Quartet 1

☗—*** Crystal CD 836. American Art Qt – STRAVINSKY: *Divertimento; Duo concertante* ***

Written at the age of 23, Lukas Foss's essentially lyrical *First String Quartet* is a masterpiece, and it is marvellously played here. The **American Art Quartet** give it a superb performance, playing it without a break. The ethereal opening matches the slow movement in beauty and intensity. The recording is too close and is rather dry, but the music's extraordinary originality comes over unfettered.

FOULDS, John (1880–1939)

Dynamic Triptych for Piano & Orchestra

*** Lyrita SRCD 211. Shelley, RPO, Handley – VAUGHAN WILLIAMS: *Piano Concerto* ***

John Foulds was working in Paris in the late 1920s when he wrote this ambitious concerto, and the profusion of memorable ideas, not always well disciplined, makes for an attractive piece, particularly so in the last of the three movements, *Dynamic Rhythm*, with its extrovert references to Latin-American rhythms and the American musical. Played with dedication and beautifully recorded, it makes an interesting coupling for the masterly and underestimated Vaughan Williams *Piano Concerto*. **Howard Shelley** and the **RPO** under **Vernon Handley** give a highly persuasive account of the *Triptych*, and the 1984 recording is well up to the usual high Lyrita standard.

April – England; (i) Dynamic Triptych (Piano Concerto), Op. 88; Music-Pictures (Group III), Op.

33; Lament from A Celtic Suite, Op. 29; The Song of Ram Dass

🎵— ******* Warner 2564 62999-2. CBSO, Oramo; (i) with Donohoe

April – England finds Foulds in pastoral mood, while *The Song of Ram Dass* shows something of his feeling for the East. But the most important piece here is the *Dynamic Triptych*, for piano and orchestra, deploying the composer's interest in unorthodox scales and rhythms. **Donohoe's** recording offers a challenge to Howard Shelley's pioneering Lyrita version and makes a competitive alternative. The **City of Birmingham Symphony Orchestra** under **Sakari Oramo** are persuasive advocates of this highly interesting figure and in *Music-Pictures (Group III)* offer a valuable première recording. Excellent notes from Malcolm Macdonald and first-rate recording.

Cello Sonata

*** British Music Soc. BMS 423CD. Cole, Talbot – BOWEN; WALKER: *Cello Sonatas* *******

Foulds's *Cello Sonata* is a passionately romantic work with memorable invention, notably the *dolce con semplicita* secondary theme in the first movement, and the ardent melody of the *Lento*, which is surrounded by pizzicatos, with the closing *Molto brioso* the most original of the three movements. The performance here could not be more expressively dedicated and, if the recording is rather over-resonant, its warmth suits the rich musical flow.

String Quartets 9 (Quartetto intimo), Op. 89; 10 (Quartetto geniale), Op. 97; Aquarelles, Op. 32

✳ ******* Pearl SHECD 9564. Endellion Qt

The *Quartetto intimo*, written in 1931, is a powerful five-movement work in a distinctive idiom more advanced than that of Foulds's British contemporaries, with echoes of Scriabin and Bartók. Also on the disc is the one surviving movement of his tenth and last quartet, a dedicated, hymn-like piece, as well as three slighter pieces which are earlier. Passionate performances and excellent recording, which is enhanced by the CD transfer. A uniquely valuable issue.

PIANO MUSIC

April, England; Egoistic; English Tune with Burden, Op. 89; Essays in the Modes, Op. 78; Music-Pictures Groups VI (Gaelic Melodies), Op. 81; VII (Landscapes), Op. 13; Variations & Improvisations on an Original Theme, Op. 4

*** BIS CD 933. Stott

Kathryn Stott proves brilliant and persuasive in this repertoire. She also has the advantage of quite exceptionally truthful and vivid recording quality. The *Essays in the Modes* (1928), which opens the disc, is interesting stuff; one is reminded of *Petrushka* in the first and of Busoni elsewhere. Stott characterizes these pieces and everything here with strong personality. Try *Prismic*, the last of the *Essays*, and the intelligence and wit of her playing will make a striking im-

pression. Not great music but, played like this, one is almost persuaded that it is.

A World Requiem

**** Chan. **SACD** CHSA 5058. Charbonnet, Wyn-Rogers, Skelton, Finley, Trinity Boys' Ch., Crouch End Festival Ch., Philh. Ch., BBC Symphony Ch. & O, Botstein

Foulds wrote his *A World Requiem* for the 1923 Festival of Remembrance, using over a thousand performers. The music is eclectic, with many derivations, and is essentially a cry for world peace. The work subdivides and opens darkly, but the call for deliverance in the second half is exuberant in its message that Christ's promise to mankind is the world's salvation. With these huge forces and four soloists, the vocal spectacle obviously recalls Mahler's *Third, Resurrection* and *Eighth Symphonies*, and certainly this performance exerts a gripping hold on the listener. The recording is very much in the demonstration bracket.

FRANÇAIX, Jean (1912–97)

(i) Piano Concertino; Les Bosquets de Cythère; Les Malheurs de Sophie

🎵— ******* Hyp. CDA 67384. (i) Cassard; Ulster O, Fischer

This new account of the *Piano Concertino* by **Philippe Cassard** on Hyperion is to be warmly welcomed. The first-movement *Presto* is exhilaratingly brisk, yet Cassard's articulation is immaculate, and the other three movements are full of the delicacy and charm for which the work is celebrated, especially the whimsical finale. *Les Bosquets de Cythère* might have been a ballet but is in essence a suite of waltzes. The island of Cythère was traditionally the birthplace of Aphrodite and it is celebrated as the home of intoxicating sensual pleasure. *Les Malheurs de Sophie* depicts the misadventures of the ill-behaved three-year-old heroine and her cousin, Paul, who is two years older. Like the other works here, the score is played with great affection and elegant attention to detail by the **Ulster Orchestra** under **Thierry Fischer**, and the Hyperion recording is in the demonstration class.

(i; ii) L'Horloge de Flore (for oboe & orchestra); (i; iii) Cor anglais Quartet; (iii) String Quartet; (iv) Trio for Oboe, Bassoon & Piano

🎵— ******** CPO 999 779-2. (i) Lencsés; (ii) Stuttgart RSO, SWR, Segal; (iii) Parissii Qt; (iv) Françaix Trio

L'Horloge de Flore is captivating. Inspired by the Linnaeus Flower Clock (which ingeniously conveys the time by its formation from different floral species, each of which blossoms at a different hour of the day or night) the music forms a suite of seven miniature movements, mainly gentle. It is beautifully played by **Lajos Lencsés** and the accompaniment is admirably tasteful. In short, this is a miniature treasure and it is supported by other inconsequential chamber works, all playful and presented with much finesse, and each as personable as it is slight. The closing *String Quartet* is full of whimsy and ends very gently with a *molto sostenuo*.

*Ouverture anacréonique; Pavane pour un génie
vivant; Scuola de ballo; Sérénade; Symphony 3 in G*

**** Hyp. CDA 67323. Ulster O, Fischer

Françaix did not number his symphonies, but this amiable
G major work is his *Third* (1953), composed light-heartedly
in memory of Papa Haydn. What a happy work this is! The
Sérénade, written 20 years earlier, is even more jocular, opening with fake-rhythmic abrasiveness before a melancholy
bassoon introduces the *Andantino*. But high spirits return
in the chirping *Poco Allegretto* and dashingly ribald finale.

A touching calm then dominates the rather lovely opening of the *Ouverture anacréonique* (1978). But the music soon
livens up vivaciously and reaches a confident, jazzy climax.
The exquisite *Pavane pour un génie vivant*, a homage to Ravel,
evokes that composer's world idyllically. The programme
then ends winningly with a pastiche *Scuola de ballo*, based
on the music of Boccherini. The whole programme is played
with warmth, polish and vitality in equal measure, the
recording is first class and this is very highly recommended.

Les Demoiselles de la nuit; Le Roi nu (ballets;
complete)

*** Hyp. CDA 67489. Ulster O, Thierry Fischer

Le Roi nu is based on Hans Andersen's story, 'The Emperor's
New Clothes', and after an imposing fanfare launches into
brilliant, illustrative music, light and varied. *Les Demoiselles
de la nuit* of 1948 is much darker, a surreal story based on a
scenario of Jean Anouilh, described as 'a cat ballet in one
Act'. Starting with a wonderfully evocative *Nocturne* (repeated
later), the predominantly melancholy tone is dotted with
lighter passages typical of Françaix, always keenly illustrative. **Thierry Fischer** conducts the **Ulster Orchestra** in compellingly idiomatic performances, vividly recorded.

CHAMBER MUSIC

*À huit (Octet); Clarinet Quintet; Divertissement for
Bassoon & String Quintet; (i) L'Heure du berger*

⊕— *** Hyp. CDA 67036. Gaudier Ens., (i) with Tomes

*À huit (Octet); Clarinet Quintet; Divertissement for
Bassoon & String Quintet*

**(*) MDG MDGL 3300. Charis Ens.

À huit, written for the Vienna Octet in 1972 and dedicated to
the memory of Schubert, is a delight. The *Clarinet Quintet* is
a relatively late work (1977) but full of the beguiling charm
that distinguishes so much of Françaix's invention. Despite
its wartime provenance, the *Divertissement for Bassoon and
String Quintet* manages to smile, while *L'Heure du berger*, background music for a brasserie, comes off equally well. Highly
polished and characterful playing from all concerned on
Hyperion and excellent recording.

Wind Quintets 1 & 2; (i) L'Heure du berger

*** MDG 603 0557-2. Kammervereinigung Berlin; (i) with
Zichner

These Berliners put over Françaix's delightful *Wind Quintets*

with great charm and delicacy. These are performances that
radiate freshness and fun and, apart from the virtuosity of
the performances, the naturalness of the recording and the
balance are a continuing source of delight. *L'Heure du berger*
is a piano and wind sextet, but this is as good in its different
way. Delicious playing and enchantingly light-hearted
music.

FRANCK, César (1822–90)

**(i) *Le Chasseur maudit*; (ii) *Les Eolides*; (i) *Psyché*;
Rédemption; (i; iii) *Nocturne***

*** Australian DG Eloquence (ADD) 476 2800. (i) O de Paris,
Barenboim; (ii) SRO, Ansermet; (iii) Ludwig

What a good idea to gather together **Barenboim's** 1976
Franck recordings, yet not include the obvious *Symphony*
(which was not one of his recording successes) instead of
the rarer works here. *Rédemption* is given a splendidly convincing performance, with glorious brass antiphonies. *Le
Chasseur maudit* opens with a most evocative Sunday morning ambience, and the devilish chase which follows, with its
arresting horn calls, is vividly exciting. The orchestral sections of *Psyché* are richly done, showing real *tendresse*, and
the relatively simple and brief *Nocturne*, beautifully sung by
Christa Ludwig, makes a beguiling bonus. The 1967 sound
for **Ansermet's** *Les Eolides* is even more vivid, a work that
suits him well, with much expressive feeling in the ebb and
flow of the string writing of this haunting piece.

Symphonic Variations for Piano & Orchestra

*** Decca 475 8764. Thibaudet, SRO, Dutoit – SAINT-SAËNS:
Piano Concertos 2 & 5 ***

⊕—Ⓜ *** Decca (ADD) 466 376-2. Curzon, LPO, Boult –
BRAHMS: *Piano Concerto 1*; LITOLFF: *Scherzo* ***

*** Australian Decca Eloquence (ADD) 476 235-2. De Larrocha,
LPO, Frühbeck de Burgos – FAURÉ: *Fantasie* ***; RAVEL:
Piano Concertos in G and for the Left Hand ***

*** Sup. SU 3714-2. Moravec, Prague Philh. O, Bělohlávek –
BEETHOVEN: *Piano Concerto 4* ***; RAVEL: *Piano Concerto
in G* **(*)

ⒷⒷ **(*) Naxos 8.550754. Thiollier, Nat. SO of Ireland, De
Almeida – FAURÉ: *Ballade*; D'INDY: *Symphonie sur un chant
montagnard français* **(*)

Once played to death, the lovely *Variations symphoniques* are
rarely encountered in the concert hall these days and are relatively seldom committed to disc. **Jean-Yves Thibaudet** plays
them with affection and style, and effortlessly conveys their
charm. He receives admirable support from the **Geneva
Orchestra** under **Dutoit** and splendid recorded sound. This
is now first choice among modern recordings.

Clifford Curzon's 1959 recording of the Franck *Variations*
has stood the test of time. It is an engagingly fresh reading,
as notable for its impulse and rhythmic felicity as for its poetry. The vintage Decca recording is naturally balanced and
has been transferred to CD without loss of bloom.

The Spanish interpreters, **Alicia de Larrocha** and

Frühbeck de Burgos, provide a reading that (perhaps surprisingly) brings out the French delicacy of the *Variations* more than usual. It is most enjoyable, very well recorded (1972), and makes a very welcome return to circulation in this very recommendable anthology.

François-Joël Thiollier shows imagination, and the orchestral playing is perfectly acceptable without being in any way distinguished. All the same, many will find it tempting at this price.

Moravec's ability to convey expressive warmth without exaggeration comes out in the Franck *Symphonic Variations*, with the improvisatory writing for the soloist sounding totally natural and spontaneous in free rubato. The faster variations bring bright, clear textures, not just in the piano part but also in the orchestral writing, with Bělohlávek drawing the most responsive playing from the orchestra he founded.

Symphonic Variations; Les Djinns

*** Alpha 104. Biret, Bilkent SO, Páris – MASSENET: *Piano Concerto* ***

Refinement is the keynote of Idil Biret's performance of Franck's *Symphonic Variations*. The orchestra does not open dramatically but sets a gentler romantic mood which permeates Birit's relaxed performance, full of poetic touches. But when the music gathers pace, rhythms are sparkling, and the closing section is admirably spirited. *Les Djinns* arrive darkly and sombrely, but Biret enters with great dash to chase after the phantoms, and it is her ready virtuosity which carries the music forward, with warm lyrical contrast and glowing dexterity in the delectable coda, where the apparitions are finally banished by gentleness. An imaginatively contrasted pair of performances in which Alain Páris is an excellent partner and the recording does the performers full justice.

Symphony in D min.

🔊 ✺ Ⓜ **** RCA (ADD) SACD 82876 67897-2. Chicago SO, Monteux – STRAVINSKY: *Petrushka* ***

🔊 **** PentaTone SACD Surround Sound PTC 5186 078. SRO, Janowski – CHAUSSON: *Symphony* ***

Ⓜ *** DG (ADD) 449 720-2. Berlin RSO, Maazel – MENDELSSOHN: *Symphony 5* ***

*** Universal Accord 476 8069. Liège PO, Langrée – CHAUSSON: *Symphony* ***

Ⓝ Ⓜ **(*) Medici Arts (ADD) MM 028. Netherlands RPO, Stokowski – RAVEL: *Fanfare: L'Eventail de Jeanne* ***; PROKOFIEV: *Alexander Nevsky* ***

(i) Symphony in D min.; Le Chasseur maudit; (ii) Symphonic Variations for Piano & Orchestra

Ⓑ **(*) RCA 82876 65833-2. (i) Boston SO, Munch; (ii) Pennario, Boston Pops O, Fiedler

Symphony in D min.; Les Eolides; (i) Symphonic Variations for Piano & Orchestra

🔊 *** Chan. 9875. (i) Lortie; BBC PO, Tortelier

Symphony in D min.; Psyché: Four Orchestral Extracts

🔊 *** Avie AV 003. Strasburg PO, Latham-König

Symphony in D min.; (i) Symphonic Variations for Piano & Orchestra

Ⓝ Ⓑ *** CfP 5 21854-2. Toulouse Capitole SO, Plasson; (i) with Collard

Monteux exerts a unique grip on this highly charged Romantic symphony, and his control of the continuous ebb and flow of tempo and tension is masterly, so that any weaknesses of structure in the outer movements are disguised. The splendid playing of the Chicago Orchestra is ever responsive to the changes of mood, and the most recent remastering for SACD brings a further improvement; indeed, now the quality reflects the acoustics of Chicago's Orchestra Hall in the same way as the Reiner recordings, with textures full-bodied and glowing, without loss of detail. The newest coupling is Monteux's uniquely authoritative 1962 Boston recording of *Petrushka*.

Marek Janowski gives us what must be one of the finest accounts of the Franck masterpiece since Beecham and Monteux. The playing of the Geneva Orchestra has richness and an expressive power that do full justice to this score, whose stature is often underrated, thanks to its over-familiarity. Very rich recorded sound, especially for those with a surround sound facility.

With brilliantly full Chandos recording enhancing Tortelier's warm, urgent reading of the *Symphony*, this CD makes another outstanding recommendation for Franck's two most popular orchestral works, an ideal coupling not as common as one might expect. Louis Lortie is the excellent soloist in the *Symphonic Variations*, spontaneously poetic in the slow sections, sparkling and light in the scherzando finale.

Plasson's 1985 performance of the *Symphony* has conviction and genuine lyrical fervour, equally strikingly in the secondary theme of the first movement and the impulsive gusto of the finale. This may not seem as individual an account as that by Monteux but it is certainly both exciting and satisfying, and the EMI recording is much more impressive than the RCA recording for Monteux, even if it is not top-drawer EMI. Jean-Philippe Collard's performance of the *Symphonic Variations* is characteristically sensitive, full of imaginative colouring and touched by distinction. Those looking for a budget coupling of these two works should be well satisfied.

Munch's 1957 performance of the *Symphony in D minor* was always among the finest ever recorded. It is held together very tautly. But it suffered – as it still does – from the internal balance of the orchestra, which lets the trumpets (with a nasal edge to their tone) coarsen the texture of the loud moments. Otherwise the warm Boston acoustics are heard to good effect, although in the slow movement the harp is very forward. The finale begins with tremendous élan, and the quotations from previous movements are not allowed to halt the onward flow of the music. *Le Chasseur maudit* here sounds spectacular: the horn calls come over arrestingly. The *Symphonic Variations* are brilliantly played by **Leonard Pennario**, and if **Fiedler's** support is strong rather than subtle this is still very enjoyable. A thoroughly worthwhile reissue.

Stokowski's moulding of the basic tempo of the first movement varies with the music's flow, but with the tension highly maintained the performance is easy to enjoy in spite of its indulgences. The *Allegretto* is beautifully played, its delicacy well maintained, and then the finale produces a thrilling forward impulse which carries the performance to an exciting conclusion. The engaging Ravel *Fanfare* acts as a piquant prelude. The recording (of a broadcast), made in Rotterdam's De Doelen concert hall, is warmly atmospheric, and the Prokofiev coupling is highly recommendable.

Latham-König also daringly uses constantly varying tempi and the widest dynamic range. His reading is wayward but full of warmth, and he keeps a splendid grip on the structure. He then offers Franck's second orchestral version of *Psyché* (omitting the chorus), which languorously captures the music's sensuous evocation while the thrilling climax of the third section, *Le Jardin d'Eros*, is later to be ardently capped by the strings. The recording is spaciously spectacular – very much in the demonstration bracket.

Maazel's DG account is beautifully shaped, both in its overall structure and in incidental details. He adopts a fairly brisk tempo in the slow movement, which, surprisingly enough, greatly enhances its poetry and dignity; his finale is also splendidly vital. The work gains enormously from strong control and deliberate understatement, as well as from the refinement of tone and phrasing which mark this reading, for there is no lack of excitement. The recording is admirably well blended and balanced.

It is good too that the Franck *Symphony* should be coupled with Chausson's Opus 20 and under **Louis Langrée** the interpretation of the Franck could hardly be more idiomatic, with subtle nuances of phrasing and variations of tempo consistently reflecting the players' affection for the music and, helped by well-balanced recording, the playing has splendid dramatic bite.

CHAMBER MUSIC

Cello Sonata in A (trans. of Violin Sonata)

🎵 (BB) *** Warner Apex 0927 40599-2. Noras, Rigutto – DEBUSSY; FAURÉ: *Cello Sonatas* ***

🎵 (B) *** EMI Gemini (ADD) 5 82633 (2). Du Pré, Barenboim – BRAHMS: *Sonatas 1 & 2* *(*); CHOPIN: *Sonata* **(*)

**(*) CRD (ADD) CRD 3391. Cohen, Vignoles (with DVOŘÁK: *Rondo*) – GRIEG: *Cello Sonata* **(*)

Franck's *Violin Sonata* when translated to the cello is mellower, less extrovert, but its originality of structure, based on strikingly memorable material, is underlined all the more.

Arto Noras's performance is as good as any, particularly at this competitive price. He is an elegant player of much finesse, and both the Debussy and Fauré sonatas come off well.

Du Pré and **Barenboim** also give a fine, mature, deeply expressive reading of a richly satisfying work, beautifully recorded. However, their couplings are uneven in appeal.

Robert Cohen gives a firm and strong rendering of the Franck *Sonata* in its cello version, splendidly incisive and dashing in the second-movement *Allegro*, but the recording is more limited than one expects from CRD, a little shallow.

Piano Quintet in F min.

🎵 (BB) *** Naxos 8.553645. Levinas, Quatuor Ludwig – CHAUSSON: *Quartet in C min.* ***

(***) Testament mono SBT 1077. Aller, Hollywood Qt – SHOSTAKOVICH: *Piano Quintet* (***)

Michaël Levinas and the **Quatuor Ludwig** give a very impressive account of 'the king of piano quintets' (the phrase is Tournemire's). Both the playing and the recorded sound are of a high standard.

Edward Sackville-West and Desmond Shawe-Taylor, the authors of *The Record Guide*, spoke of the **Aller/Hollywood** version five decades ago as a 'clean-limbed performance ... the players' attack is extraordinarily vivid and the instrumental balance beautifully maintained'. Even if there is no mistaking the (1953) mono sound as being of its time, the performance has such eloquence and power that the music leaps out of the speakers with a vibrant intensity.

The rather high-powered account from **Heifetz** and his starry team of soloists – which is strongly projected and marvellously played, of course, conveys little of the intimacy of chamber music. The same goes for the Dvořák coupling, but not the Françaix *Trio*, which is enchanting. (RCA 74321 909652)

(i) Piano Quintet in F min. String Quartet in D

(N) *** Phoenix ED. 142. Petersen Qt, (i) with Pizarro

At one time a warhorse, the *F minor Quintet* of 1879 is nowadays a rarity in the concert hall and is not generously represented on disc. The *Quartet*, written in the year before his death, was always a rarity and, although there have been impressive recordings (the Fitzwilliams' CD among them), they have been even more elusive. And so this coupling is particularly valuable since **Pizarro** is a sensitive and imaginative player and the **Petersen** a masterly ensemble. Those wanting both works will find this coupling very recommendable.

String Quartet in D

(N) *** Hyp. CDA 67664. Dante Qt – FAURÉ: *String Quartet in E min* ***

(i) String Quartet in D; (ii) Violin Sonata in A

🎵 *** Australian Decca Eloquence (ADD/DDD) 476 8463. (i) Fitzwilliam Qt; (ii) Amoyal, Rogé

Franck's *Quartet*, highly ambitious in its scale, its almost orchestral texture and its complex use of cyclic form, contains some of the composer's most profound, most compelling thought, and this magnificent performance by the **Fitzwilliam Quartet**, superbly triumphing over the technical challenges with totally dedicated, passionately convinced playing, completely silences any reservations. Richly recorded, with the thick textures nicely balanced, this was one of the finest chamber records of the late 1970s. **Amoyal** and **Rogé**, richly recorded in 1995, provide a superb account of the *Violin Sonata*, a performance full of fantasy and giving the impression of music emerging spontaneously on the moment.

The **Dante** offer a freshly vibrant account of the Franck *String Quartet* which brings out all the drama of the score as well as its beauty. It opens with a rich boldness, superbly captured by the Hyperion engineers, and one is instantly grabbed by the intensity of the playing. The *Scherzo* is very delicately done, and the slow movement hauntingly beautiful. The finale, taken at a fast tempo, is strikingly dramatic in its contrasts between the lyrical and the dramatic writing – as well as the wide range of colours brought out by the four players – and this is one of the finest accounts of this work on CD, if not eclipsing the Fitzwilliam version.

Viola Sonata in A (transcription of Violin Sonata)

*** Chan. 8873. Imai, Vignoles – VIEUXTEMPS: *Viola Sonata*, etc. ***

*** Simax PSC 1126. Tomter, Gimse – VIEUXTEMPS: *Viola Sonata*, etc. ***

An all-Belgian coupling from these two violists, **Imai** and **Tomter**. The Franck loses a certain amount of its flamboyance and passion, and gains in a kind of measured dignity. Both performances listed above are exemplary if you want it in this form. There is absolutely nothing to choose between them; both are commanding performances and have an impressive eloquence.

Violin Sonata in A (DVD version)

(*) EMI **DVD 4904519. Y. & H. Menuhin (bonus: Mendelssohn: *Variations sérieuses, Op. 54* – BARTÓK: *Contrasts; Violin Sonata 1: Finale*; SCHUBERT: *Piano Trio 1* **(*)

The **Menuhins** must have performed this *Sonata* many times, but they succeed in making it sound very fresh. The recording comes from the BBC studios in early 1960 and is in black-and-white, and the camerawork is predictably restrained and finely judged.

Violin Sonata in A

⊶ 🌑 Ⓜ **** Decca (ADD) 460 006-2. Chung, Lupu – DEBUSSY: *Violin Sonata* **** 🌑 ; CHAUSSON: *Poème* ****

Ⓜ **** Decca 475 8246. Perlman, Ashkenazy – BRAHMS: *Horn Trio in E flat* **(*)

⊶ ⒝⒝ *** EMI 208122-2. Chang, Vogt – SAINT-SAËNS: *Violin Sonata 1*; RAVEL: *Violin Sonata* ***

⊶ Ⓜ *** DG (ADD) 477 5903. Danczowska, Zimerman – SZYMANOWSKI: *Mythes*, etc. ***🌑

*** EMI 5 56815-2. Perlman, Argerich – BEETHOVEN: *Violin Sonata 9 in A (Kreutzer)* ***

*** DG 445 880-2. Dumay, Pires – DEBUSSY: *Violin Sonata in G min.*; RAVEL: *Berceuse*, etc. ***

*** Avie Crear Classics AV 0037. Gleusteen, Ordronneau – DVOŘÁK: *Violin Sonatina*; GRIEG: *Violin Sonata 3* ***

Ⓝ (***) Testament mono SBT 1442. D. Oistrakh, Yampolski – RAVEL: *Tzigane*; SCHUMANN: *Fantaisie, Op. 131* (arr. Kreisler); SZYMANOWSKI: *Myths, Op. 30* (***)

The Franck *Sonata* is exceptionally well served on CD. **Kyung-Wha Chung** and **Radu Lupu** give a glorious account, full of natural and not over-projected eloquence, and most beautifully recorded. The slow movement has marvellous repose and the other movements have a natural exuberance and sense of line that carry the listener with them. The 1977 recording is enhanced on CD and, with an apt Chausson coupling, this reissue remains very desirable indeed.

With **Perlman** and **Ashkenazy**, after a magical opening, the first movement catches the listener by the ears with the thrust of the forward impulse and the intensity of its lyrical flow. Yet there is no lack of flexibility and the sheer ardour of this interpretation makes it a genuine alternative to the Chung/Lupu account, and worthy of inclusion among Decca's 'Originals'. There are, however, problems with the focus of the (splendidly played) Brahms coupling.

Sarah Chang and **Lars Vogt** also make a winning partnership and give a commanding account of the *Sonata*. Vogt proves particularly impressive in the challenging piano part, and if the coupling appeals (and it should) readers need not hesitate. Good recorded sound too.

Kaja Danczowska's account of the Franck *Sonata* – now reissued as one of DG's Originals – is distinguishd by a natural sense of line and great sweetness of tone, and she is partnered superbly by **Krystian Zimerman**. Indeed, in terms of dramatic fire and strength of line, this version can hold its own alongside the finest on record, while its Szymanowski coupling is outstanding in every way.

As in the Beethoven *Kreutzer Sonata*, **Perlman** and **Argerich** challenge each other to thrilling effect in this live EMI recording, made in Saratoga in 1999. Some may resist the expressive freedom, whether in phrasing, rubato or in fluctuations of speed, but the magnetism will for most be irresistible. As in the Beethoven coupling, audience noises are intrusive at times.

Kai Gleusteen is a winningly natural player with a lovely tone, and he phrases Franck's melodies with warm lyricism. His partnership with **Catherine Ordronneau** is one of complete musical affinity, and their account of this much-played sonata can rank with the best, with all four movements bringing playing of sympathetic lyrical feeling and fervour.

The distinguished partnership of **Augustin Dumay** and **Maria João Pires** offers as assured and powerful an interpretation of Franck's indestructible *Sonata* as any now in the catalogue. The DG recording is more than acceptable, and readers wanting this particular coupling need not hold back.

David Oistrakh's performance comes from 1958. It finds **Yampolski** in tremendous form, with both ardour and virtuosity in abundant supply. The *Myths* are characteristic and highly individual and make an appealing coupling.

ORGAN MUSIC

3 Chorals (in E; B min.; A min.); 3 Pièces (Fantaisie in A; Cantabile; Pièce héroïque); 6 Pièces (Fantaisie 1 in C, Op. 16; Grande pièce symphonique, Op. 17;

Prélude, fugue et variation, Op. 18; Pastorale, Op. 19; Prière, Op. 20; Final, Op. 21)

⊕—🌼 (BB) **** Warner Apex 2564 61428-2 (2). Alain (Cavaillé-Coll organ of the Eglise Saint-François de Sales, Lyon)

(B) *** Cal. (ADD) CAL 5920/21. Isoir (Cavaillé-Coll organ of Luçon Cathedral)

(BB) *** Regis RRC 2054 (2). Bate

Marie-Claire Alain recorded all these works on a Cavaillé-Coll organ at Lyon. These performances are full of spontaneous feeling, and the registration brings some glorious sounds, with the detail quite remarkably clear.

André Isoir's performances are also recorded on a Cavaillé-Coll organ (in 1975), and very impressively too. His performances, with their improvisatory character, are just as authentic as Marie Claire Alain's and his recording justly won a Grand Prix du Disque. The *Grande pièce symphonique* is especially successful, the *Chorals* are appropriately cool, and the *Pièce héroïque* is also strikingly spontaneous. However, the digitally recorded Warner Apex set remains first choice on grounds of both excellence and economy.

Jennifer Bate plays the Danion-Gonzalez organ at Beauvais Cathedral and is given the benefit of an excellent digital recording. The spacious acoustic contributes an excellent ambience to the aural image, and Bate's brilliance is always put at the service of the composer. The *Pièce héroïque* seems rather well suited to the massive sounds which the Beauvais organ can command and all the music chosen here – the content of three CDs, previously available on the Unicorn label – shows the instrument to good advantage. The only small criticism is that Bate rushes the opening of the *A minor Choral*, some of whose detail does not register in this acoustic at the speed. However, this is a splendid bargain issue by any standards.

Choral 2

*** Chan. 9785. Tracey (organ of Liverpool Cathedral) – GUILMANT: *Symphony 2 for Organ & Orchestra*; WIDOR: *Symphony 3 for Organ & Orchestra* ***

Franck's *Second Choral* is an expansive *Passacaglia* which reaches a great climax and then gently fades away in the valedictory closing bars. Although the Liverpool organ is not entirely right for it (one needs better definition), **Ian Tracey's** performance can hardly be faulted, and the result is nothing if not spectacular, enough to make a suitable encore for the two concertante works.

PIANO MUSIC

Choral 3; Danse lente; Grand caprice; Les Plaintes d'une poupée; Prélude, aria et final; Prélude, choral et fugue

⊕—, *** Hyp. CDA 66918. Hough

Stephen Hough's impressive *Prélude, choral et fugue* is worthy to rank alongside Murray Perahia's account (currently withdrawn), and no praise could be higher. In addition to the piano music, Hough gives us his own transcription of the *Third* of the organ *Chorals*, which in his hands sounds as if it

had been written for the piano, so splendidly is it played. A most distinguished record in every way.

Eglogue (Hirtengedicht), Op. 3; Les Plaintes d'une poupée; Prélude, aria et final; Prélude, choral et fugue; Premier grand caprice, Op. 5

(BB) *** Naxos 8.554484. Wass

What **Wass** brings out in the major items is the technical brilliance of the keyboard writing. He uses a ravishing range of tone, lightening the *Prélude, aria et final* with a flowing speed in the *Prélude* and a mysterious opening for the *Final*. The two lyrical miniatures are charmingly done, but most impressive is the finest of Franck's piano works, the *Prélude and Choral*, leading to a powerful, clean-cut account of the *Fugue*, which makes one want to hear Wass in Bach. Heavy *fortissimos* tend to clang – partly the eager pianist's fault – but otherwise the sound is full and vivid.

VOCAL MUSIC

Psyché (symphonic fragments)

(***) Testament mono SBT 1128. René Duclos Ch., Paris Conservatoire O, Cluytens – RAVEL: *Daphnis et Chloé* ***

It is logical that **André Cluytens's** sensitive account of *Daphnis* should be coupled with Franck's most sumptuous and imaginative score. Both are inspired by classical mythology. The 1954 recording is mono but the transfer is of high quality and no collector will fail to respond.

FRANKEL, Benjamin (1906–73)

(i) Viola Concerto, Op. 45; (ii) Violin Concerto (In Memory of the Six Million), Op. 24; (iii) Serenade Concertante for Piano Trio & Orchestra, Op. 37

⊕—(M) *** CPO 999 422-2. (i) Dean; (ii) Hoelscher; (iii) Smith, Lale, Emmerson; Queensland SO, Albert

The *Violin Concerto's* emotional core is the expressive and eloquent slow movement. Yet apart from its elegiac centre, the overwhelming impression the work leaves is powerful and positive, a testament to the strength of the human spirit. The *Viola Concerto* is much later and is hardly less memorable. Frankel's lyricism and his musical ingenuity are always in evidence. The composer describes the *Serenata concertante*, which is for piano trio and orchestra, as 'a street scene' in which passing traffic, a distant jazz band, lovers dancing and much else besides can be heard. It wears its serial organization lightly. Both **Ulf Hoelscher** and **Brett Dean** are impressive soloists in the two concertos and the **Queensland Orchestra** respond with supportive playing. The recording engineers serve these fine players faithfully and produce an impressive and wide-ranging sound. Strongly recommended.

Symphonies 1–8; Overtures; Mephistoteles Serenade and Dance

(B) *** CPO 999 661-2 (4). Queensland SO, Albert

Benjamin Frankel is a master of the orchestra, and the *First Symphony* (1959) leaves no doubt that he was also a master symphonist. The music develops organically; Frankel has something of the strength of Sibelius combined with a Mahlerian anguish, and his serialism, like that of Frank Martin, never undermines tonal principles. The *Fourth Symphony* is arguably one of the very finest of Frankel's works. It has a more restrained palette than its predecessors, yet its invention is both powerful and distinctive. The *Fifth Symphony*, too, is a well-argued and impressive score. The *Sixth* is dark and powerfully argued and gets very persuasive advocacy. The *Seventh* was commissioned by the Peter Stuyvesant Foundation for the LSO, who gave its première under André Previn in 1970. A thoughtful and searching piece, it was underrated at the time and we now have the opportunity of getting to know it for ourselves. The opening of the *Eighth* (1971) is vintage Frankel and the work as a whole has a sense of logic and purpose that marks his best music. The **Queensland Orchestra** play with dedication, and are very well recorded.

Clarinet Quintet, Op. 28

(BB) *** Hyp. Helios CDH 55105. Thea King, Britten Qt – COOKE: *Clarinet Quintet*; HOLBROOKE: *Eilean Shona*; HOWELLS: *Rhapsodic Quintet*; MACONCHY: *Clarinet Quintet* ***

Frankel's *Clarinet Quintet* (1956) was a BBC commission for the Cheltenham Festival. It is perhaps the least harmonically tractable work in **Thea King's** Helios anthology, but it communicates strongly in a performance as strong as this, especially the quirky central *Scherzo*, while the elegiac finale, written in memory of the distinguished clarinettist, Frederick Thurston, is utterly haunting.

FRESCOBALDI, Girolamo
(1583–1643)

Keyboard Music: *Capriccios; Canzonas; Correntes; Partite sopra un aria Romana detta la Manista Ricercare cromatico; Toccatas*

(N) (BB) **** Naxos 8. 570717. Folts (harpsichord)

Martha Folts here provides an admirable survey of the keyboard music of a highly influential composer whose music demands a free, improvisatory style of performance, of which she is obviously a master. She plays a most attractive instrument made by Jerome de Zentis in 1658, restored by Keith Hill. The programme is nicely varied between dance-movement *Capriccios* (including a set of variations using the two-note call of the cuckoo) and *Toccatas*, and includes also a particularly attractive *Partita*. The recording is most realistic, but it is important to keep the volume level low.

FURTWÄNGLER, Wilhelm
(1886–1954)

Symphonic Concerto: Adagio

(**) Testament mono SBT 1170. Fischer, BPO, Furtwängler – BRAHMS: *Piano Concerto 2* (**(*))

(BB) (**) Naxos mono 8.110879. Fischer, BPO, Furtwängler – BEETHOVEN: *Symphony 5*; WAGNER: *Parsifal: Preludes* (***)

Edwin Fischer's sympathetic account of the *Adagio solenne* from the B minor *Symphonic Concerto* is available on both Naxos and Testament. While Mark Obert-Thorn's Naxos transfer is not as full-blooded as Paul Baily's, it is eminently serviceable if the couplings are preferred. The *Adagio* is a noble piece, with an autumnal feel to it. It may not be great music, but with its echoes of Bruckner leading to passionate climaxes it makes agreeable listening in the 1939 studio recording, even with limited sound.

Symphony 2 in E min.

(***) DG mono 457 722-2 (2). BPO, Furtwängler – SCHUMANN: *Symphony 4* (***) ✹

Furtwängler spoke of his *Second Symphony* as his spiritual testament. It is Brucknerian in its dimensions and sense of space. The first movement, lasting 24 minutes, is accommodated on the first CD, and the remaining three on the second. Furtwängler himself thought the present studio recording, made in the Jesus-Christus-Kirche, Berlin, in 1950 'stilted', but it sounds amazingly clear and warm in this transfer and readers should not be put off acquiring it. The Schumann coupling – one of Furtwängler's very finest mono records – makes a superb coupling.

GABRIELI, Andrea (1510–86)

Canzon in the 1st tone for 10 parts; Canzons in the 7th & 9th tone for 8 parts; Canzon in the 7th, 8th & 9th tones for 12 parts; Canzon in the 12th tone for 10 Parts; Sonata for 3 Violins & Organ; Intonations for Organ in the 1st, 2nd, 3rd, 4th, 7th, 8th, 9th, 10th & 11th Tones; Ricercar for Organ; 3 Mass Movements; Motets: Anglus ad pastores ait; Deus, qui beatum Marcum; Hodie Christus natus est; In eccelsiis; O magnum mysterium; Plaudite, psallite, Jubilate Deo omnis terra; Regina coeli laetare

(M) *** Sony 82876 78762-2. Gabrieli Consort La Fenice; E. Power Biggs (organ); Gregg Smith Singers; Fort Worth Texas Boys' Ch.; Edward Tarr Brass Ens., Negri

E. Power Biggs pioneered more than one stereo recording of the music of Andrea Gabrieli, enlisting the expertise of the late Professor Denis Stevens to edit the scores and instrumental material. Biggs then hired musicians who were equally at home on modern and antique instruments. 'We then mixed purity with common sense. Some pieces sounded very beautiful on old trombones, while some needed the extra power and brilliance that would set the basilica's acoustics ringing.' The result, recorded in the fine sonority of San Marco, Venice, in 1967, is a great success. The singing of the combined choral and brass groups here, admirably directed by **Vittorio Negri** and excellently balanced, is a total success, and Power Biggs's own organ *Intonations* make noble interludes. This is indeed worthy of inclusion among Sony's 'Great Performances'.

(i) Ricercar a 4 del primo tuono; Ricercar a 4 del sesto tuono; Ricercar a 4 del duodecimo tuono; Ricercar per sonar a 8. (ii) (Organ) Canzon alla Francese: Petit Jacquet; Intonazione del sesto tuono; Madrigal: Ancor che co'l partire; Ricercar del settimo tuono; (i; ii; iii) Missa Pater peccavi; Motets: (i; iii) De profondis clamavi; (iv; i) O sacrum convivium

ⒷⒷ *** Hyp. Helios CDH 55265. (i) His Majesty's Sackbutts & Cornets; Roberts (organ); (iii) His Majesty's Consort of Voices, Roberts, (iv) with Pickard

It is good to have first-class performances of some of Andrea Gabrieli's *Ricercari* on record, even if they are less spectacular and, indeed, less varied than those of his nephew, Giovanni. The *Mass* setting (based on Andrea's own motet, *Pater peccavi in coelum*) settles for very simple counterpoint but springs to life in the *Sanctus*.

The solo motet, *O sacrum convivium*, is simply and beautifully sung by **Anna Sarah Pickard**, whose vocal line is integrated within the 'accompaniment' by four sackbuts. The organ interludes are played by the group's director, **Timothy Roberts**, and the concert closes with the eight-part *Ricercar per sonar*, which is rather impressive. Excellent recording in a well-judged acoustic.

Madrigals: Amami, vita mia, ch'io t'amo anchora; Ancor che col partire; Asia felice hor ben posso chiamarmi; Caro dolce ben mio, perche fuggire; Chi'nde darà la bose al solfizar; etc. Instrumental Pieces: Amami, vita mia, ch'io t'amo anchora; Dunque il comun poter; Fuor fuori a sì bel canto

⌖ *** Chan. 0697. I Fagiolini, Hollingworth – GIOVANNI GABRIELI: Madrigals: *Sacri di Giove augei sacre Fenici* (2 versions). Instrumental Pieces: *Canzon I: La Spiritata*

Andrea Gabrieli has been somewhat overshadowed by his nephew Giovanni, yet his music has an expressive character and colour very much its own. These little-known madrigal settings show a ready musical response to the Renaissance poetic vision of love which, although embroidered with elegant words, is quite explicit in its expressions of earthly desire. The lovely Petrarch setting, *Lasso, Amor mi transporta ov'io non voglio*, makes it plain that love carries the lover 'where I do not wish to go', while in the intense dialogue between Cloris and Adonis, *Io mi sento morire*, ecstatic 'death' does not quite mean what it says!

Gabrieli was nothing if not versatile, and his touching tribute on the death of Willaert contrasts with *Asia felice*, depicting a celebration of the Turkish defeat at the Battle of Lepanto (with cornett, three trombones, organ and percussion), while the love songs could hardly be sung with greater longing. Excellent recording, and full texts and translations are included in this very valuable addition to Renaissance repertoire.

Benedictus Dominus Deus a 8; Gloria in excelsis Deo a 16; Magnificat a 12; O crux splendidior a 8; Ricercar del duodecimo tuono a 4

Ⓑ *** CfP (ADD) 586 0492. Amb. S., String & Brass Ens., Stevens – Giovanni GABRIELI: *Angelus ad pastoris ait*, etc. ***

There are some splendidly grandiloquent gestures here and the massive sonorities of the *Gloria in excelsis Deo*, with voice and brass textures interweaving, move towards their climax without strain. The textures in *O crux splendidior* are lighter and the *Ricercar* for brass is particularly successful. The singing is impressive throughout and the brass playing has the proper richness of sonority. A pioneering collection that is still highly recommendable.

Psalmi Davidici 6; 31; 37; 50; 101; 129; 143; Antiphon: Ne remimiscaris Domini

Ⓜ **(*) CPO 999 863-2. Capella Ducale Venetia, Picotti

Andrea Gabrieli's setting of the *Seven Penitential Psalms* of David, published in 1583, shows a deeper, more expressive side of a composer nearly always twinned with his nephew, Giovanni, with his spectacular brass writing. **Picotti** has settled for darker brass sonorities, which are blended in with the homophonic choral sound in a resonant acoustic. The singing is warmly mellifluous and the sombre character of the music is preserved throughout; one might have liked more variety of dynamic range and (at times) more vigour, but the beauty of the simple vocal lines is well sustained. The recording is warmly atmospheric rather than clear.

GABRIELI, Giovanni (1554–1612)

Canzoni da sonare: I (La spiritata) a 4; I a 5 (1615); I toni a 10 (1597); II a 4 (1606); III a 6 (1615); VII a 7 (1615); XII toni a 10 (1597; 2 versions); XXIV a 8 (1608); XXVII a 8 (1608); Ricercar sopra 'Re fa me don' a 4

⌖ ⒷⒷ *** Virgin 2x1 5 62028-2 (2). Hespèrion XX, Savall – A. GABRIELI: *Canzon sopra 'Qui la dira'*; GUAMI: *Canzon: 'La accorta' a 4; Canzon sopra 'La battaglia' a 4; Canzon 'La cromatica' a 4; Canzon 'La guamina'; Canzon XXIV a 8; Canzon XXV a 8*; SCHEIN: *Banchetto musicale*; SCHEIDT: *Ludi Musici* ***

A fine selection of Giovanni Gabrieli's *Canzonas*, together with half a dozen more by his contemporary Giuseppe Guami, which are in much the same style. Also included is a *Canzon sopra 'Qui la dira'* by Giovanni's uncle, Andrea (with whom he studied), based on a song. This is played on the harpsichord and makes an attractive interlude. But **Jordi Savall** varies the scoring throughout, so that some works are for strings (including the solemn *Ricercar*), others include brass to splendid effect. Guami's *'La accorta'* is melancholy, and his *'Battaglia'* is disappointingly low key, but many of the others are very jolly, notably Giovanni's dancing *Canzon VII a 7* and Guami's *Canzon XXV a 8*. This and Giovanni's florid closing *Canzon XII toni* in ten parts demand great bravura from all concerned. The performances are splendid, and so is the recording. This is one of the finest collections of Renaissance music in the catalogue.

Music for Brass, Vol. 1

ⒷⒷ *** Naxos 8.553609. LSO Brass, Crees

Music for Brass, Vol. 2

(BB) *** Naxos 8.553873. LSO Brass, Crees

Music for Brass, Vol. 3

(BB) *** Naxos 8.554129. LSO Brass, Crees

Starting with the *Canzon XVII* of 1615 in 12 parts, involving three choirs of instruments, **Eric Crees** and his brilliant players from the brass section of the **LSO** demonstrate at once what variety of tone they can produce, with the finest shading of timbre and texture. In the great *Sonata pian' e forte* of 1597 in eight parts and the even more striking *Double Echo Canzon in 12 Parts*, the playing is remarkable as much for its restraint and point as for its dramatic impact. Beautiful sound, both clear and atmospheric, not aggressive.

The *Canzon in echo duodecimi toni à 10* in Volume 3 is obviously the most spectacular piece, but the paired *Sonatas XX* and *XXI* (with organ) thrillingly combine rich sonorities with complex decoration, and in Volume 2 there are several very striking pieces, notably *La Spiritata* and *Canzon XVI à 12*, which closes the disc.

Sonata pian' e forte

(***) BBC BBCL mono 4059-2. LSO, Stokowski – LISZT: *Mephisto Waltz 1*; NIELSEN: *Symphony 6*; TIPPETT: *Concerto for Double String Orchestra* ***

The *Sonata pian' e forte* was a repertory piece in the 1940s and '50s, before the period-instrument movement got under way, and **Stokowski** evokes a rich individual sonority from his fine players.

(i) Angelus ad pastoris ait a 12; Buccinate in neomenia tuba; Canzon septimi toni a 8; Hodie Christus natus est a 10; Hodie completi sunt a 8; O Domine Jesu Christe a 8; O magnum mysterium a 8; Omnes gentes plaudite manibus a 16; (ii) Buccante in neomenia tuba a 19; Canzon septimi toni; In eccelessis a 14; Timor et tremor

(B) *** CfP (ADD) 586 0492. (i) King's College, Cambridge, Ch., Cambridge University Musical Soc., Bach Ch., Wilbraham Brass Soloists, Willcocks; (ii) Amb. S., String & Brass Ens., Stevens – ANDREA GABRIELI: *Benedictus Dominus Deus*, etc. ***

This generous Classics for Pleasure reissue combines the above impressive performances, directed by **Sir David Willcocks** in 1973, with a pioneering stereo programme from 1966, recorded at Abbey Road. The latter collection, directed by **Denis Stevens**, pioneered these multi-voiced works; if the massive sonorities of *Buccinate in neomenia*, with its 19-part ensemble divided into four separate choirs, sounds a little too close, the sound is otherwise very impressive. The lighter vocal texture of *Timor et tremor* is very successful, and *In eccelessis*, with its attractive answering between higher and lower voices, is more expansive. The **King's** recordings have much more space, and performances and recordings are of the quality we would expect from this source. A fine disc, and a bargain too.

'A Venetian Christmas'

*** DG 471 333-2. Gabrieli Consort and Players, McCreesh – DE RORE: *Missa praeter rerum serie*

Paul McCreesh adds to his evocative series re-creating great religious occasions with what might have been heard at Christmas in St Mark's in Venice around the year 1600. Punctuated by chant, a variety of pieces by Giovanni Gabrieli for choir, for organ and for brass ensemble sets the central liturgy in context. Gabrieli characteristically exploits the wide-ranging antiphonal effects inspired by St Mark's, with the first motet, *Audite principes*, involving no fewer than 16 parts, divided into three separate groups, each led by a solo voice. Most striking is the setting of the *Mass* chosen, dating from half a century earlier, a so-called parody *Mass* by Cipriano de Rore in seven parts (one more than the complex motet by Josquin Des Prez on which it is based), a magnificent example of polyphony, superbly performed here.

GADE, Niels (1817–90)

Symphonies 1; 8 (* BIS CD 339); 2; 7 (**(*) BIS CD 355); 3–4 (*** BIS CD 338); 5–6 (*** BIS CD 356)**

(N) Stockholm Sinf., Järvi

The Gade symphonies are well worth exploring. Their debt to Mendelssohn aside (especially in the first two and No. 4), there is still a sense of real mastery throughout the cycle. No. 3 in particular has great freshness and a seemingly effortless flow of ideas. The *Fifth* is a delightfully sunny piece and the *Sixth* is rather more academic, but the *Seventh* has great geniality and charm, and the *Eighth* is very civilized. The **Stockholm Sinfonietta** and **Neeme Järvi** give very fresh and lively performances, and the recording is natural and truthful.

Violin Sonatas 1 in A, Op. 6; 2 in D min., Op. 21; 3 in B flat, Op. 59

(N) *** Da Capo 8.226066. Christina Åstrand, Per Salo

Gade was by training a violinist, though his prowess in this field was overshadowed by his achievements as a conductor in his native Copenhagen and in Leipzig where he succeeded Mendelssohn at the Gewandhaus Orchestra. The first two sonatas come from the 1840s, the second composed immediately after his time in Leipzig in 1849, and the third in 1885. Appealing and fresh if, like the symphonies, Mendelssohnian in idiom, and heard in very accomplished performances by these two artists, both prominent members of the Danish Radio Symphony Orchestra.

GÁL, Hans (1890–1987)

Piano Music

24 Fugues, Op. 108; 3 Sketches, Op. 7; 3 Preludes, Op. 64; 24 Preludes, Op. 83; 3 Small Pieces, Op 64; Sonata, Op. 28; Sonatinas 1 & 2, Op. 58; Suite, Op. 24

Ⓜ *** Avie AV 2064 (3). McCawley

Like his slightly older contemporary, Egon Wellesz, Hans Gál composed in a wide variety of genres, and this three-CD set covers his piano music, from his earliest *Three Sketches* (1910–11) through to the *Twenty-Four Fugues* of 1980, completed when he was ninety. The music deserves and receives dedicated advocacy from **Leon McCawley**, who brings this inventive and individual body of music to life and puts us all in his debt by so doing. The Avie recording is lifelike and full-bodied.

GALUPPI, Baldassarre
(1706–85)

8 Keyboard Sonatas

Ⓝ **** Sony/BMG RCA 88697367932. Bacchetti (piano)

Andrea Bacchetti has already uncovered for us some remarkable piano music of Cherubini. Now he turns to Galuppi, who wrote over 100 sonatas, most of which are still unknown. Those here are of high quality. They are almost always in two movements, usually slow then fast, and playing together for about nine or ten minutes, although the work in B flat included here has an opening *Andante* which extends to ten minutes in itself. Galuppi's invention is delightful and by no means stereotyped and his music is fully worthy of a modern piano. Bacchetti brings each work to life with his pellucid articulation and always charms the ear. He is very well recorded too. A disc not to be missed, even though it is not key repertoire.

Motets: *Laetatus Sum; Lauda Jerusalem; Nisi Dominus*

*** DG 477 6145. Invernizzi, Cirillo, Mingardo, Agnew, Cooley, Foresti, Zeppenfeld, Körnerscher Singverein, Dresden, Dresden Instrumental Concert, Kopp – VIVALDI: *Dixit Dominus* ***

These three choral works (première recordings) make for delightful listening, with their florid, Italianate melodies, beautifully and sensitively performed. The darker *Nisi Dominus* has some splendidly dramatic writing, from the minor-keyed introduction with its scurrying strings to its vivacious aria, *Sicut sagittae*. This is music which looks forward to the church music of the classical era of Haydn and his contemporaries.

GARDNER, John (born 1917)

(i) *Piano Concerto 1. Symphony 1; Overture (Midsummer Ale), Op. 71*

ⒷⒷ *** Naxos 8.570406. (i) Donohoe; RSNO, Lloyd-Jones

This coupling of two of John Gardner's major works, plus a sparkling comedy overture, could not be more welcome, brilliantly played and recorded. Here is one of the most unjustly neglected composers of his generation. The *Symphony No.1*, the most extended of the works on the new disc, is in four movements, spanning over 40 minutes. The *Piano Concerto*

No. 1 of 1957 offers a contrasted idiom in its percussive echoes of the Bartók *Piano Concertos*, suiting **Peter Donohoe's** strong style admirably in another performance brilliantly backed by **David Lloyd-Jones** and the **Royal Scottish National Orchestra**. The disc is dazzlingly rounded off with a rumbustious Comedy Overture, *Midsummer Ale*, written for the orchestra of Morley College, of which Gardner was music director. By rights this disc will bring renewed attention to the music of a most attractive composer.

GAY, John (1685–1732)

The Beggar's Opera (Benjamin Britten version; DVD version)

Ⓝ *(**) Decca DVD 074 3329. Baker, Pollak, Harper, Coates, Kelly, Jerome, Hartley, Dickerson, McKellar, ECO, M. Davies (V/D: Charles Rogers)

How splendid that this 1963 performance is available on DVD. True, Britten's version of Gay's *Beggar's Opera*, with Britten adding his own musical personality to the simplicity of the 18th-century writing, does rob the music of some of its intrinsic charm, but the vibrancy of the performance is utterly compelling. Indeed, with such great personality singers as **Edith Coates** (Mrs Trapes) and **Anna Pollak** (Mrs Peachum), the results are very characterful indeed. **Janet Baker** as Polly and **Heather Harper** as Lucy are other highlights; and all the men, who include the splendid **Kenneth McKellar** as Macheath, are excellent. The production is first rate and the camerawork very sympathetic. The picture quality is fair for its period but the sound is good.

The Beggar's Opera (arr. Pepusch and Austin)

🎭 ⒷⒷ *** CfP 575 9722 (2). Morison, Cameron, Sinclair, Wallace, Brannigan, Pro Arte Ch. & O, Sargent – GERMAN: *Tom Jones* ***

The Beggar's Opera was the 18th-century equivalent of the modern American musical. It was first produced in 1728 and caused a sensation with audiences used to the stylized Italian opera favoured by Handel. This performance under **Sargent** is in every way first class, and the soloists could hardly be bettered, with **Elsie Morison** as Polly, **John Cameron** as MacHeath and **Owen Brannigan** a splendid Peachum. The linking dialogue is spoken by actors to make the result more dramatic, with every word crystal clear. The chorus is no less effective and the 1955 recording has a most appealing ambience. It was one of EMI's first great stereo successes and the chorus 'Let us take the road' (where the singers recede into the distance) was understandably included on their Stereo Demonstration disc. It now returns to the catalogue, coupled with a delightful selection from Edward German's *Tom Jones* which is hardly less vivid.

GEMINIANI, Francesco
(1687–1762)

Concerti grossi, Op. 2/1–6; Op. 3/1–4

🎭 ⒷⒷ *** Naxos 8.553019. Capella Istropolitana, Kreček

Concerti grossi, Op. 3/5–6; Op. 7/1–6

🛢 ⓑⓑ *** Naxos 8.553020. Capella Istropolitana, Kreček

This is part of an ongoing Naxos project to record all Geminiani's *Concerti grossi* using modern instruments but in a style which clearly reflects the freshness and vitality of period-instrument practice. The **Capella Istropolitana** offer excellent accounts of Op. 2, Op. 3, and include the whole of Op. 7. The performances are striking for their freshness and vitality, and they are very well recorded. Bargain-hunters need not hesitate.

Concerti grossi, Op. 3/1–6

Ⓝ Ⓜ *** Decca (ADD) 478 0024. AAM, Hogwood

Hogwood's approach reveals the vigour and freshness of Geminiani's melodious and resourceful invention. The Opus 3 *Concerti* are given performances of genuine quality and readers normally resistant to the cult of authentic instruments can be reassured that there is no lack of body and breadth here. They are also extremely well recorded (analogue, 1976), though the CD transfer picks up some studio noise and on our copy there was a curious moment of background hum which comes up suddenly and disappears on track 8 (Op. 3/2). But that may have now been cured.

(i) 12 Concerti grossi, Op. 5 (after Corelli); (ii; iii) Cello Sonata in D min., Op. 5/2; Ornamented arrangement of Corelli's Sonata in A for Violin & Cello

**** HM HMU 907261/62 (2). (i) AAM, Manze; (ii) Watkin; (iii) McGillivray

The period-instrument performance by the players of the **Academy of Ancient Music** are led from the bow by **Andrew Manze**. He is a superb soloist, but so are his colleagues. *Allegros* are full of vigour (and bravura) while the exquisite delicacy of the solo contribution to slow movements makes the strongest possible case for authenticity in this music. As a bonus, two further arrangements are offered, equally persuasive in performance. The recording is excellent and this makes a clear first choice for Op. 5.

Concerti grossi: in D min. (La folia, from CORELLI: Sonata in D min., Op. 5/12); in G min., Op. 7/2; Trio Sonatas 3 in F (from Op. 1/9); 5 in A min. (from Op. 1/11); 6 in D min. (from Op. 1/12); Violin Sonatas: in E min., Op. 1/3; in A, Op. 4/12

🛢 ⓑⓑ *** Hyp. Helios CDH 55134. Purcell Band & Qt

This record comes from Hyperion's '*La folia*' series, though the only piece here using that celebrated theme is the arrangement Geminiani made of Corelli's *D minor Sonata*. Apart from the *G minor Concerto*, Op. 7, No. 2, the remainder of the disc is given over to chamber works. The **Purcell Quartet** play with dedication and spirit and convey their own enthusiasm for this admirably inventive music to the listener.

6 Cello Sonatas, Op. 5

**(*) Decca/O-L 475 9108. Pleeth, Hogwood, Webb

Geminiani's six *Sonatas*, Op. 5, appeared first in Paris in 1746 and then in London the following year. The present recording is based on the London edition and, as is the practice in this (originally Oiseau-Lyre) series, uses a replica of an 18th-century cello and bow and a 1766 Kirckman harpsichord. The admirable players do their best to reproduce contemporary practice, though the absence of vibrato (and the prominence of the cello continuo) tends to tire the ear. The music itself is often rewarding and imaginative, and the recording is in the high traditions of this series. The disc is reissued with the original sleeve presentation.

GERHARD, Roberto (1896–1970)

(i) Violin Concerto. Symphony 4 (New York)

*** Lyrita SRCD 274. (i) Neaman; BBC SCO, C. Davis

The *Violin Concerto* dates from Gerhard's early years in Cambridge and, rather like the violin concerto of a fellow pupil of Schoenberg, Alban Berg, it successfully combines a lyrical style with serial method, though the virtuoso writing has one thinking of the violin pyrotechnics of another Spaniard, Sarasate. A brilliant performance from **Yfrah Neaman** and **Colin Davis**, who provides highly sympathetic direction, with the **BBC Symphony Orchestra** playing superbly both here and in the *Fourth Symphony*. This was written in Gerhard's seventieth year and shows him at his most imaginatively adventurous. The work, bearing the subtitle *New York* and written for that city's Philharmonic Orchestra, is brilliant and colourful. Gerhard resorts to crypto-electronic sounds which delight the ear rather than baffling it.

GERMAN, Edward (1862–1936)

VOCAL MUSIC

Merrie England (complete; without dialogue)

ⓑⓑ **(*) CfP Double 575 7672 (2). McAlpine, Bronhill, Glossop, Glynne, Sinclair, Kern, Rita Williams Singers, O, Collins

Although this recording dates from 1960, it cannot compare in stereo sophistication with EMI's *Beggar's Opera* of five years earlier. All the solo voices are close-miked, usually in an unflattering way, and too often they sound edgy, while the chorus is made artificially bright; the orchestra is lively enough, but the violins are thin. However, it must be said that **Michael Collins** directs the proceedings in an attractively spirited fashion. Among the soloists, **Howell Glynne** is splendid as King Neptune, and **Monica Sinclair** sings with her usual richness and makes *O peaceful England* more moving than usual. **Patricia Kern's** mezzo is firm and forward, while **William McAlpine** as Sir Walter Raleigh sings with fine, ringing voice. The **Rita Williams Singers** are thoroughly professional even if just occasionally their style is suspect. However, another recording seems unlikely so this is acceptable, *faute de mieux*.

Tom Jones (operetta: highlights)

⌕━ (BB) *** CfP 575 9722 (2). Harvey, Minty, Glover, Riley, Nigel Brooks Ch., O, Gilbert Vinter – GAY: *The Beggar's Opera* *** 🌸

Listening to this sparkling selection, one's first impression is how like Sullivan is the basic idiom. The opening chorus might have come straight out of *Patience*, and there are many ensembles and solos that have a distinct reminder of one or other of the Savoy operas. The librettist here even uses one of Gilbert's rhymes '*Festina lente*' as part of a song-title. But there is music, too, that could have come only from German's own pen, the really charming *Here's a paradox for lovers* and of course the delicate *Dream O'day Jill* and the famous *Waltz Song*. They are all extremely well sung here by a solo group who, like the conductor, **Gilbert Vinter**, convey real enthusiasm for this tuneful score. The 1966 recording is excellent and has transferred vividly to CD. Splendidly coupled, this inexpensive set is not to be missed.

GERSHWIN, George (1898–1937)

An American in Paris; Catfish Row (Suite); (i) Concerto in F. Cuban Overture; Lullaby; Mexican Dance; (i) Rhapsody in Blue (original, 1924 version); (ii) Second Rhapsody; (i) Variations on 'I got Rhythm'; Walking the Dog; (Piano Solo) (i) Rialto Ripples; (ii) O Land of mine, America

(M) **(*) Telarc 2-CD 80445. Cincinnati Pops O, Kunzel; with (i) Tritt; (ii) Goodyear; (iii) Central State University Ch., Caldwell

The Telarc two-disc anthology, originally assembled for the Gershwin Centenary in 1998, is pretty comprehensive and includes the 1924 Whiteman scoring of the *Rhapsody*, with **William Tritt** lively enough, yet without the breathless momentum of the famous piano-roll account with the composer. The *Concerto* has a nostalgically memorable slow movement, but the outer movements are somewhat lacking in sheer verve. However, **Stewart Goodyear** makes a surprising success of the *Second Rhapsody* and both the *Rialto Ripples* rag and the engaging '*I got Rhythm*' *Variations* are played with stylish flair by his colleague. The other main items are also available differently coupled, and nearly all the shorter pieces are worth having. The sentimental choral work which ends the concert, although sung ardently, needs more Sousa-like pep than it receives here; the recording, too, is not up to the usual Telarc standard.

(i) An American in Paris; Catfish Row (Suite from Porgy and Bess); (ii) Cuban Overture; (i) Lullaby; (iii) Rhapsody in Blue

(N) (M) **(*) EMI 2 06628-2. (i) St Louis SO, Slatkin; (ii) LSO, Previn; (iii) Donohoe, L. Sinfonia, Rattle

Slatkin is clearly at home in Gershwin, and the gloriously ample acoustic of Lovell Hall, St Louis, makes everything seem opulent, although *American in Paris* could be more extrovert. However, Catfish Row, Gershwin's own suite from *Porgy and Bess*, is played with relish. **Donohoe** plays brilliantly in the *Rhapsody in Blue* and **Rattle's** coaxing of jazz rhythms is agreeably affectionate, but the result is just a little British.

An American in Paris; Piano Concerto in F; Rhapsody in Blue

⌕━ 🌸 (M) *** Sony 82876 78768-2. (i) NYPO, Bernstein; (ii) Previn, O, Kostelanetz; (iii) Bernstein (piano) with Columbia SO

⌕━ (M) *** EMI 5 66891. Previn (piano & cond.), LSO

Bernstein's outstanding 1960 coupling of *An American in Paris* and *Rhapsody in Blue* has stood the test of time. Bernstein's approach in the *Rhapsody*, which he directs from the keyboard, is exceptionally flexible but completely spontaneous. It is a masterly account in every way, quixotic in mood, rhythmically subtle and creating a great surge of human warmth at the entry of the big central tune. The performance of *An American in Paris* is vividly characterized, brash and episodic, an unashamed American view, with the great blues tune marvellously phrased as only an American orchestra can do it. Both recordings still sound very good indeed. For this reissue, **André Previn's** account of the *Concerto in F* (made at the same time) with **Kostelanetz**, not surprisingly, has more pizazz and is more telling stylistically than his later HMV version with the LSO. Kostelanetz and his orchestra play a major part in the interpretation, especially in the brilliant finale. Once again, the remastered sound is remarkably vivid. Altogether these classic versions remain unsurpassed.

The digital remastering of Previn's EMI set, made at the beginning of the 1970s, has brought a striking enhancement of the recording itself; there is now much more sparkle. The performance of the *Concerto* was always an outstanding one by any standards, but now in the *Rhapsody* one senses many affinities with the famous Bernstein account. *An American in Paris* is exuberantly volatile, and the entry of the great blues tune on the trumpet has a memorable rhythmic lift.

An American in Paris; (i) Piano Concerto in F; Cuban Overture; (i) Rhapsody in Blue; Variations on 'I got Rhythm'

(M) *** RCA SACD 82876 61393-2. (i) Wild; Boston Pops O, Fiedler

The RCA SACD, with just short of 80 minutes' playing time, offers the contents of two 'Living Stereo' LPs, recorded in 1959 and 1961 respectively, now with enhanced sound. Besides the usual triptych, **Fiedler's** *Cuban Overture* is added, which has great élan, and **Earl Wild** includes a bouncy account of the '*I got Rhythm*' *Variations*, given plenty of rhythmic panache and a nice touch of wit. The outer movements of the *Concerto* are comparably volatile and the blues feeling of the slow movement is strong. In *An American in Paris* Fiedler adds to the exuberance by bringing in the bevy of motor horns indicated in the original score (though Paris is without them these days). The slightly brash recording sounds newly minted.

An American in Paris; (i) Rhapsody in Blue

** Telarc SACD 60646. Cincinnati SO, Kunzel, (i) with Eugene
List – TCHAIKOVSKY: *Capriccio Italien; 1812*, etc. **(*)

Eugene List is as always an impressive soloist in Gershwin,
and the Telarc performance using the full symphonic scoring is recorded very sumptuously indeed. The rich sound is
ideal for those who like to wallow in the melodic richness of
An American in Paris. The blues tune certainly sounds expansive and there is no real lack of vitality, although in both
works there seems an over-prominence of the bass drum (a
characteristic of Telarc CDs). Originally issued on their own,
these Gershwin performances now come with an even more
spectacular Tchaikovsky triptych.

(i–ii) An American in Paris; (ii–iii) Rhapsody in Blue; (ii; iv) Overtures: Funny Face; Girl Crazy; Let 'em eat Cake; Of thee I sing; Oh Kay!; Strike up the Band; (ii; v) Promenade (Walking the Dog); (ii; v; vi) Fascinatin' Rhythm

🅑–🅑 **** Sony 8277969301821. (i) NYPO; (ii) Tilson Thomas;
(iii) composer (from 1925 piano roll), Columbia Jazz Band;
(iv) Buffalo PO; (v) LAPO; (vi) Sarah Vaughan

This remarkable re-creation of the composer's own performance was taken from a 1925 piano roll, using Ferdé
Grofé's initial scoring for Paul Whiteman. A group of eminent musicians was then gathered in the studio to play
Grofé's scoring. **Gershwin's** solo performance was recorded
from the pianola, and the tape was then used by **Michael
Tilson Thomas** and his '**Columbia Jazz Band**', who skilfully
fitted the accompaniment around it. The spontaneity of the
finished performance is quite riveting.

Fortunately the main coupling is a very fine account of
An American in Paris with the **NYPO** on top form, while the
excellent **Buffalo Philharmonic** are equally on their toes
and enjoying themseleves in sparkling performances of
the six overtures. The two bonuses are also splendidly
done, with **Sarah Vaughan's** *Fascinatin' Rhythm* a great closing
encore.

Catfish Row (suite from Porgy and Bess)

*** Telarc CD 80086. Tritt, Cincinnati Pops O, Kunzel –
GROFE: *Grand Canyon Suite* ***

Catfish Row was arranged by the composer after the initial
failure of his opera. It includes a brief piano solo, played
with fine style by **William Tritt** in the highly sympathetic
Telarc performance, which is very well recorded.

Porgy and Bess Symphonic Picture (arr. Robert Russell Bennett)

🅱🅱 **(*) Resonance CDRSN 3042. Bournemouth SO, Farrer –
COPLAND: *Billy the Kid; Rodeo* **(*)

John Farrer presents the famous Robert Russell Bennett
Symphonic Picture with some panache, and the **Bournemouth**
players respond with spirited flair, the brass especially.
However, the orchestral sound could ideally be more sumptuous. Dorati's famous Detroit version is not upstaged – see
above.

Rhapsody in Blue – see also above

🅑 **(*) DG 477 6362. Bernstein (piano & cond.), LAPO –
BARBER: *Adagio for Strings*; COPLAND: *Appalachian
Spring* ***

In his last recording of this work for DG, **Bernstein** rather
goes over the top with his jazzing of the solos in Gershwin.
Such rhythmic freedom was clearly the result of a live rather
than a studio performance. This does not match Bernstein's
(1959) analogue coupling on Sony.

Piano Music (Collection)

🅱🅱 *** Hyp. CDH 55006. Brownridge

Angela Brownridge offers Gershwin's meagre output of solo
concert pieces for piano, opening with a Joplinesque early
rag, *Rialto Ripples*, Gershwin's first instrumental number
from 1916. She plays the *Three Preludes* very well indeed, and
also includes piano interludes from various shows, like the
pair of *Waltzes in C* which the composer and Kay Swift played
as a piano duet in *Pardon My English*.

There are also two pot-pourri *Overtures* which are very
spirited and then – by offering just chorus and verse – she
finds room for 18 of Gershwin's finest song-arrangements,
her playing scintillating and romantic by turns, yet always
stylish. The recording is excellent. A bargain.

3 Preludes; An American in Paris (arr. Daly); Songs (arr. Gershwin): Fascinatin' rhythm; I got rhythm; I'll build a stairway to paradise; The man I love; Oh, lady be good; Liza; Somebody loves me; Sweet and low down; 'Swonderful; Who cares?

**(*) Nim. NI 5585. Anderson – COPLAND: *Piano Sonata*, etc.
***

Recorded at a live recital in Nimbus's own concert hall, this
is an enjoyable enough collection of Gershwin favourites.
Mark Anderson plays very well, if without those subtle rhythmic inflexions that mark most American performances and
especially Gershwin's own piano-roll recordings. But why
transcribe *An American in Paris*? It sounds so much better in
its full orchestral costume.

Piano Rolls

'The Piano Rolls': (i) An American in Paris; (ii) Idle dreams; Kicking the clouds away; Novelette in fourths; On my mind the whole night long; Rhapsody in Blue; Scandal walk; So am I; Swanee; Sweet and lowdown; That certain feeling; When you want 'em you can't get 'em, when you've got 'em you don't want 'em

*** None. 7559 79287-2. (i) Milne and Leith; (ii) composer

This series, recorded by the composer between 1916 and 1926
using the Welte-Mignon and Duo-Art piano-roll systems,
was reproduced through a 1911 pianola (operated by Artis
Wodehouse) and then recorded in digital stereo – with the
utmost realism. The result is as if **Gershwin** himself was
playing in the studio. The four-handed arrangement of *An
American in Paris* is a marvellous 'orchestral' performance
and matches the composer in its flamboyance and breadth

of style. *Rhapsody in Blue* is the composer's special arrangement. The sound is first class and admirably present.

VOCAL MUSIC

'Kiri Sings Gershwin': Boy wanted; But not for me; By Strauss; Embraceable you; I got rhythm; Love is here to stay; Love walked in; Meadow serenade; The man I love; Nice work if you can get it; Somebody loves me; Someone to watch over me; Soon; Things are looking up; Porgy and Bess: Summertime

**(*) EMI 7 47454-2. Te Kanawa, New Theatre O, McGlinn (with chorus)

In **Dame Kiri's** gorgeously sung *Summertime* from *Porgy and Bess*, the distanced heavenly chorus creates the purest kitsch. But most of the numbers are done in an upbeat style. Dame Kiri is at her most relaxed and ideally there should be more variety of pacing: *The man I love* is thrown away at the chosen tempo. But for the most part the ear is seduced; however, the pop microphone techniques bring excessive sibilants on CD.

OPERA AND MUSICALS

Girl Crazy (musical)

Ⓜ *** None. 7559-79250-2. Blazer, Luft, Carroll, Korbich, O, Mauceri

Girl Crazy, despite its hit numbers – *Embraceable you*, *I got rhythm* and *Bidin' my time* – has always been counted a failure; but this lively recording, with an ensemble of distinguished New York musicians conducted by **John Mauceri**, gives the lie to that. The casting is excellent and the only serious reservation is that the recording is dry and brassy, aggressively so – but that could be counted typical of the period too.

Lady Be Good (musical)

*** None. 7559 79308-2. Teeter, Morrison, Alexander, Pizzarelli, Blier, Musto, Ch. & O, Stern

This charming score, dating from 1924 (just after *Rhapsody in Blue*), emerges as one of the composer's freshest. *Lady Be Good* was the piece originally written for the brother-and-sister team of Fred and Adele Astaire, and the casting of the principals on the disc is first rate. These are not concert-singers but ones whose clearly projected voices are ideally suited to the repertory, including **Lara Teeter** and **Ann Morrison** in the Astaires' roles and **Michael Maguire** as the young millionaire whom the heroine finally marries. The score has been restored by Tommy Krasker, and an orchestra of first-rate sessions musicians is conducted by **Eric Stern**.

Oh Kay!

⊶ *** None. 7559 79361-2. Upshaw, Ollman, Arkin, Cassidy, Westenberg, Larsen, Ch. & O of St Luke's, Stern

The last in this splendid Nonesuch series of Gershwin musicals is in many ways the finest of all. With the music (including hits like *Someone to watch over me*, *Clap yo' hands*, *Do do do* and the very catchy *Fidgety feet*) fitting neatly on to one CD, this is a fizzing entertainment. **Dawn Upshaw** is a highly enticing Kay, and she gets vivid support from **Kurt Ollman** as Jimmy, **Adam Arkin** as Shorty McGee and **Patrick Cassidy** as Larry. The cast could hardly be more naturally at home in Gershwin's sparkling score. **Eric Stern** directs with great flair and the recording is admirably vivid. Not to be missed.

Porgy and Bess (opera; complete published score)

⊶ ✹ *** EMI DVD 4 92496-9. White, Haymon, Blackwell, Hubbard, Baker, Clarey, Evans, Glydebourne Ch., LPO, Rattle

Ⓜ ✹ *** EMI 234430-2 (3). Details as above

Ⓜ **(*) Decca (ADD) 475 8663 (3). White, Mitchell, Boatwright, Quivar, Hendricks, Clemmons, Thompson, Cleveland Children's Ch., Cleveland O, Maazel

After the huge success of the Glyndebourne production of *Porgy and Bess*, EMI took the whole cast to the Shepperton Studios, where it was produced for video by Trevor Nunn and Yves Baignere, using the giant stage to move the actions around freely as in a film. The result is stunningly successful, bringing the story to life with extraordinary vividness. This is one of the most creative of all such productions so far, fully worthy of Gershwin's masterly score.

On CD, **Simon Rattle** conducts the same cast and orchestra as in the opera house, and the EMI engineers have done wonders in establishing more clearly than ever the status of *Porgy* as grand opera. By comparison, **Lorin Maazel's** Decca CD version sounds a degree too literal, Rattle and the **LPO** capture Gershwin's rhythmic exuberance with the degree of freedom essential if jazz-based inspirations are to sound idiomatic. The chorus is the finest and most responsive, and **Willard White** is superbly matched by the magnificent Jake of **Bruce Hubbard** and by the dark and resonant Crown of **Gregg Baker**. As Sportin' Life, **Damon Evans** gets nearer than any of his rivals to the original scat-song inspiration. **Cynthia Haymon** as Bess is movingly convincing in conveying equivocal emotions, **Harolyn Blackwell** as Clara sensuously relishes Rattle's slow speed for *Summertime* and **Cynthia Clarey** is an intense and characterful Serena. EMI's digital sound is exceptionally full and spacious.

Maazel, like Rattle, includes the complete text. The vigour and colour are irresistible, and the recording is of Decca's most spectacular mid-seventies quality. **Willard White** is again a magnificent Porgy, dark of tone; while **Leona Mitchell's** vibrant Bess has a moving streak of vulnerability, and **François Clemmons** as Sportin' Life achieves the near impossible by singing the role and making one forget Cab Calloway. But above all it is Maazel's triumph, and he produces dazzling playing from the **Cleveland Orchestra**. Full texts are included; even so, this is now upstaged by Rattle's EMI set.

Porgy and Bess (original 1935 Broadway score)

*** Decca 475 7877 (2). Powell, Lister, Lynch, McDonald, Mack, Thompson Williams, Rowe, Blair Children's Ch., Tennessee State University Band, Nashville Symphony Ch. & O, Mauceri

This is a new-look (or, rather, old-look) *Porgy and Bess*, for **John Mauceri** and Wayne Shirley have here reassembled Gershwin's score as the composer used it in the initial Broadway performances. This version puts aside about 40 minutes of music, something that often happens to a musical during its initial provincial run. Mauceri's new performance has a spicy Broadway atmosphere, and the new principals, **Alvy Powell** as Porgy and **Marquita Lister** as Bess, bring a real, idiomatic feel to the music, with no flavour of the opera house. **Lester Lynch** as Crown is aggressively impressive too, and Clara's *Summertime* (**Nicole Cabell**) is truly seductive. Even more compelling is **Robert Mack's** Sportin' Life, a truly unattractive character. The rest of the cast also measure up, and the back-up accompaniments, chorus and orchestra add plenty of colloquial bite. This is how *Porgy and Bess* sounded on Broadway in 1935.

Porgy and Bess: Symphonic Picture (arr. Bennett)

**** Australian Decca Eloquence 442 9496. Detroit SO, Dorati
– GROFE: *Grand Canyon Suite*, etc. **(*)

Robert Russell Bennett's famous arrangement of Gershwin melodies has been recorded many times, but never more beautifully and sumptuously than on this Decca digital version from Detroit. The performance is totally memorable and the sound quite superb. A real demonstration CD.

Strike Up the Band (musical)

**(*) None. 7559 79273-2 (2). Barrett, Luker, Chastain, Graae, Fowler, Goff, Lambert, Lyons, Sandish, Rocco, Ch. & O, Mauceri

Strike Up the Band was the nearest that George and Ira Gershwin ever came to imitating Gilbert and Sullivan, although its two hit numbers, *The man I love* and *Strike up the band*, are entirely characteristic. For all its vigour, the performance lacks something of the exuberance which marks the recordings of musicals conducted by John McGlinn for EMI. It may be correct to observe the dotted rhythms of *The man I love* as precisely as this performance does, but something is lost in the flow of the music, and to latter-day ears the result is less haunting than the customary reading. The singers are first rate, but they would have been helped by having at least one of their number with a more charismatic personality. The second disc includes an appendix containing seven numbers used in the abortive 1930 revival.

GESUALDO, Carlo (c. 1561–1613)

Ave, dulcissima Maria; Ave, regina coelorum; Maria mater gratiae; Precibus et meritus beatae Mariae (motets). *Tenebrae responsories for Holy Saturday*

🎧 *** Gimell CDGIM 015. Tallis Scholars, Phillips

Ave, dulcissima Maria; Peccantem mei quotidie; Tribularer si nescirem; Tribulationem et dolorem (motets). *Tenebrae responsories for Holy Saturday*

Ⓑ *** HM Musique d'abord HMA 1951320. Ens. Vocal Européen, Herreweghe – GORLI: *Requiem*

The astonishing dissonances and chromaticisms may not be as extreme here as in some of Gesualdo's secular music but, as elaborate as madrigals, they still have a sharp, refreshing impact on the modern ear which recognizes music leaping the centuries. The **Tallis Scholars** give superb performances, finely finished and beautifully blended; superbly recorded, this is another of the Tallis Scholars' ear-catching discs, powerful as well as polished.

Herreweghe's performances with his European group of singers are also very fine, not as volatile as those by the Tallis Scholars, but serenely intense and moving. Apart from *Ave dulcissima Maria*, which he shares with Phillips, he chooses three different motets, all suitably penitential. Moreover, he offers a bonus of an extraordinary, even bizarre *Requiem* by Sandro Gorli (born in Como in 1948). The composer has provided his own text, and the music's modern dissonances, although even more flagrantly pungent, are curiously in the spirit of medieval writing; and the work ends in a desperately wild call of 'Father, why hast thou forsaken me?'

Leçons de ténèbres: Responsories for Holy Week

ⒷⒷ ** Warner Apex 2564 62782-2 (2). A Sei Voce

The performances on Warner Apex cover the complete *Tenebrae responsories* for Maundy Thursday, Good Friday and Holy Saturday. They are smoothly and expressively sung but are on a fairly unvaried dynamic level, refined in feeling and without drama. Other performances find more depth in this music, and the Apex issue has no texts and translations.

Leçons de ténèbres: Responsories for Maundy Thursday

🎧 *** Signum SIGCD 048. King's Singers

Gesualdo's *Responsories for Maundy Thursday* of 1611, with their surprising chromatic dissonances, are among the most remarkable and original of all *Ténèbre* settings. Immediately, as *In Monte Oliveti* opens, the **King's Singers** demonstrate a very flexible approach to tempo and dynamic that is to characterize their whole performance. The impeccable intonation and tonal matching also give a special richness to the chordal writing; and its moments of dissonance. The performance closes simply with the chant, *Christus factus est*, and this is treated as a brief recessional. In short, this is a superbly sung performance, expressively poignant but dramatic too, which brings a new dimension to this remarkable music; and the recording is outstanding.

Madrigals, Books I–III (complete)

*** CPO 777 138-2 (2). Gesualdo Consort, Amsterdam, Van der Kamp

Madrigals, Book V (1611)

*** Glossa GCD 920935. La Venexiana

It is against the background of the peak period of his extraordinary life that Gesualdo wrote his madrigals. Obviously the 1590s were an extraordinarily creative period for Gesualdo, and the five-part madrigal settings clearly reflected the emotional turmoil of his own life. Their extraordinary unpredictability of feeling, with pain and joy side by side, was exhibited in their chromatic intensity, and the spread of dissonances, the desperation in love of many of their texts, must relate to the composer's personal experiences. We now, at last, have the beginnings of two complete collections on CD, as we assume the disc from **La Venexiana** is the first of a series. In each case the madrigals are sung by a beautifully blended group of five voices, with **Harry van der Kamp's Amsterdam** ensemble slightly more robust (and pleasingly so) in tone. Gesualdo's madrigals are essentially *a cappella* works, but in the First Book of the Amsterdam series a lute or archlute is sometimes discreetly introduced; the Second Book includes a soprano solo with harpsichord, and in the Third a harpsichord is more often featured, and a single madrigal is heard as a harpsichord solo. The recording throughout both sets is excellent, with the acoustic very pleasing in each. Full texts and translations are included, and the documentation is first class.

GIBBONS, Orlando (1583–1625)

Consorts for Viols: *Fantasies a 3, 1–4; Fantasies a 6, 1–5; In Nomines a 5, 1–2.* **Keyboard Pieces arranged for Viols:** *Fantasia; Galliard; Go from my Window; Pavan; Pavan Lord Salisbury; Peascod Times.* **Vocal works arranged for Viols:** *Hosanna to the son of David; O Lord, in thy wrath; The Silver Swan*

⊕—, *** Avie AV 0032. Phantasm

The *Fantasies* for viol consort by Orlando Gibbons are among the most sublime works in the string repertory, leading on to the *Fantasias* of Purcell, even breathing the same air as the late Beethoven *Quartets*. Sadly, on disc they have too often been treated to performances that slice your ears off in period abrasiveness; happily, the group, **Phantasm**, is different, at once authoritative and beautifully matched. The complexity of the *Fantasies in six parts*, presented here as a cohesive group, is astonishing both in rhythm and in counterpoint, and the two six-part *In Nomines*, more austere, have a similar intensity. Four *Fantasies in three parts* demonstrate Gibbons's contrapuntal mastery just as clearly. Quoting the composer, Phantasm supplement this music written specifically for viols with transcriptions of such keyboard pieces as the superb *Lord Salisbury Pavan*, as well as three of Gibbons's greatest vocal pieces, the anthems *O Lord, in thy wrath* and *Hosanna to the son of David*, as well as the lovely madrigal, *The Silver Swan*. Well-balanced sound, though with a limited dynamic range.

Consort Music: *Fantasias a 4: 1–2 in C; In Nomines: a 4 in D min.; a 5: 1 in C; 2 in G min.* (i) *Ye Sacred Muses (Elegy on the Death of Thomas Tallis)*

*** Globe GLO 5159. Royal Consort, (i) with Cordier – BYRD: *Consort Songs* ***

These *Fantasias* and *In Nomines* are played with warmth and refinement, and with subtle variations of dynamic light and shade. As we have commented on the Byrd couplings, a consistent atmosphere of dolour pervades. But that lies within the music itself, and **David Cordier's** sensitive account of Gibbons's posthumous tribute to Tallis, *Ye Sacred Muses*, is most touchingly sung.

Consort and vocal music

⊕—, ⒝⒝ *** Naxos 8.550603. (i) Rose Consort of Viols; (ii) Roberts; with (iii) Red Byrd; (iv) Bonner

This makes the perfect supplement to the excellent Naxos issue of Gibbons's church music (see below), with 22 items that cover a wide range of songs as well as instrumental music. The players of the **Rose Consort**, with agreeably tangy string-tone, contribute most of the instrumental pieces, culminating in two magnificent *Fantazias* in six parts: No. 3 with ear-catching harmonic clashes, No. 5 with side-slipping chromatic writing, pointing forward to later centuries. **Timothy Roberts** is the soloist in keyboard music on harpsichord, virginals and organ, while the soprano, **Tessa Bonner**, is the bright-toned soloist in a sequence of songs with consort accompaniment. Also standing out are two fine anthems, one written for the funeral of a Dean of Windsor, with **Red Byrd** accompanied by the consort, five voices and five instruments.

Keyboard Music: *Almans; The King's Jewel; Coranto; Fancy; Fantasias; Galliards; Grounds; Lincoln's Inn Masque; Pavans; Lord Salisbury Prelude; The Queens Command; Verse*

⊕—, Ⓜ *** Explore EXP 0006. Hogwood (cabinet organ, Italian spinet, harpsichord)

An admirable anthology, thoroughly enjoyable, of Gibbons's keyboard music, very well played and recorded (originally on L'Oiseau-Lyre in 1975). **Christopher Hogwood** uses period instruments, and much variety is obtained by the contrasting colours of the instruments; and the recording does full justice to their sound and character, with the CD transfer completely faithful. An invaluable addition to the repertoire.

Anthems and verse anthems

*** Gaudeamus CDGAU 123. King's College Ch., L. Early Music Group, Ledger; Butt

This invaluable anthology was the first serious survey of Gibbons's music to appear on CD. It contains many of his greatest pieces. Not only are the performances touched with distinction, the recording too is in the highest flight and the analogue sound has been transferred to CD with complete naturalness. Strongly recommended.

Anthems and Verse Anthems: *Hosanna to the Son of David; In nomine a 4; O clap your hands; O Lord in thy wrath; This is the record of John*

*** EMI 3 94430-2. King's College, Cambridge, Ch., with Fretwork – TOMKINS; WEELKES: *Anthems*

Orlando Gibbons was a chorister at King's College in the 1590s and he served the Crown as court musician for over 20 years. This rich collection is made doubly fascinating by its coupling with the music of his contemporaries, Tomkins and Weelkes, with examples of two or three different settings of the same text by more than one of the three composers. *O clap your hands* and the six-voice *Hosanna to the Son of David* show Gibbons at his most exultant, *O Lord in thy wrath* at his most penitent. *This is the record of John* and the *In nomine* setting have accompaniments from **Fretwork**. Splendid singing and recording.

Anthems

⟠ **BB** *** Naxos 8.553130. Oxford Camerata, Summerly; Cummings

Using his small professional choir, 12 singers at most, and often fewer, **Jeremy Summerly** directs fresh, finely focused readings of an outstanding collection of Gibbons's anthems. That is particularly so in the six magnificent unaccompanied full anthems which are included, where the astonishing harmonic clashes and progressions in the counterpoint come out with wonderful impact, generally with just a single voice per part.

In addition there are three fine verse anthems, drawing on the full complement of singers, with organ accompaniment, plus Gibbons's two evening services, the short one much simpler than the second one. Three organ pieces are also included, though Laurence Cummings's account of the extended *Fantazia* in four parts is not as varied as it might be. Fine, clear, atmospheric sound.

Anthems and verse anthems: *2nd Evening Service: Magnificat; Nunc dimittis. Organ Fantasia in A min (MB XX/12)*

⟠ **BB** *** Hyp. Helios CDH 55228. Blaze, Varcoe, Winchester Cathedral Ch., Hill; Farr or Baldock

Orlando Gibbons's *Hosanna to the son of David* is among the very finest anthems of the period, a glory of English music, and aptly that is the opening item for this excellent collection of Gibbons's church music, very well performed and recorded. **Robin Blaze** is an outstandingly sweet-toned counter-tenor soloist, well matched by **Stephen Varcoe** in the verse anthems. The only pity is that the collection concentrates on verse anthems, nine of them plus the *Second Evening Service*, as against only three full anthems with their excitingly elaborate counterpoint. The *Fantasia in A minor* for organ makes an apt supplement.

Hymnes and Songs of the Church (1623)

BB *** Naxos 8.557681. Tonus Peregrinus

This Naxos disc collects all Gibbons's *Hymnes and Songs of the Church* as published in 1623, and arranged for this recording by **Antony Pitts**, the director of **Tonus Peregrinus**. They are divided into eight groups, Songs of Joy, Love, Sacrifice, Lamentation, Triumph, Unity, Faith and Hope. Each Hymne is brief, and each is based on one of 'fifteen or so' tunes 'depending on how you count them', and underpinned by simple bass lines. Tonus Peregrinus can be relied on for scholarship and vocal excellence; even so, the result is unexpectedly rewarding. Excellent documentation too.

GILLIS, Don (1912–78)

The Alamo; (i) The Man Who Invented Music; Portrait of a Frontier Town; Saga of a Prairie School; Symphony 5½ (for Fun)

Ⓜ (***) Dutton mono CDLK 4163. New SO, composer, (i) with Kilty (nar.)

Don Gillis had a long and active career in America from the 1930s to the 1970s. His *Symphony No. 5½* is undoubtedly his best-known piece, enjoying quite a vogue in the 1950s. It is indeed a fun work, brightly and wittily scored. *The Alamo* is a 1947 tone-poem depicting the dramatic events associated with the famous fort in San Antonio, Texas. The folk-like atmosphere of the opening and closing sections is nostalgically caught here, contrasting with the later melodrama. The *Saga of a Prairie School* is overtly sentimental, but it similarly shows the composer's skill at evocative scene-painting, with the reflective 'prayful' scenes set against more vigorous writing where one marvels at the brilliance of the orchestral playing under the composer, especially the brass. The *Portrait of a Frontier Town* is a bright and breezy portrayal of Fort Worth, Texas, including everything you would expect to find, from square-dancing to 'Prairie Sunsets', scenes of *Night Life* as well as (less believably) a portrait of *The Chamber of Commerce!* The *Man Who Invented Music* acts as a kind of young person's guide to the orchestra. It is a charming period piece. The performances on this CD can be thought of as definitive, and the (originally Decca) sound is remarkably bright and vivid, with Dutton's remastering technique heard at its finest.

GINASTERA, Alberto (1916–83)

Cello Sonata, Op. 49; 5 canciones populares argentinas, Op. 10; Pampeana 2; Puneña 2, 'Hommage à Paul Sacher'

Ⓝ **BB** *** Naxos 8.570569. Kosower, Jee-Won Oh

The prolific Argentine composer Alberto Ginastera (not to be confused with Fred Astaira) had a vivid sense of colour, as the orchestral *Pampeana No. 3*, once available on Chandos, displays. The more restrained palette of cello and piano still shows him as unfailingly inventive and these fine soloists argue his case most persuasively. All these pieces are diverting and this makes a most attractive introduction to his music.

GIORDANO, Umberto (1867–1948)

Andrea Chénier (DVD versions)

**** TDK **DVD** DVWW OPACH. Guleghina, Cura, Guelfi, Ch. & O Teatro comunale di Bologna, Rizzi (Dir: Giancarlo di Monaco, V/D: Paula Langobardo)

⟠ *** Warner NVC Arts **DVD** 5050466-8357-2-7. Tomowa-Sintow, Domingo, Zancanaro, ROHCG Ch. & O, Rudel (V/D: Humphrey Burton)

Dating from 1985, the DVD of Michael Hampe's production offers a traditional staging that vividly captures the atmosphere of Giordano's melodramatic presentation of Revolutionary France. Under the experienced conducting of **Julius Rudel**, the three principal characters are powerfully drawn, all three at the peak of their powers. **Plácido Domingo** cuts a flamboyant figure as Chénier, with the widest range of tone and expression in his key monologues. Though **Anna Tomowa-Sintow's** creamy soprano grows a little rough under pressure, she makes a tenderly sympathetic Maddalena; but it is **Giorgio Zancanaro** as Gérard who emerges as the most powerful figure, singing gloriously and bringing out the more human side of this revolutionary leader, convincingly making the transition from the defiant flunky he is in Act I. Other roles are well taken, too. No booklet is provided and no synopsis, with no indication on the box who is singing which roles.

Recorded in Bologna in 2006, the DVD from TDK offers a traditional production with handsome stage pictures, strongly conducted by **Carlo Rizzi**. Act II even includes a statue of Marat murdered in his bath. **José Cura** in the title-role of the poet is not always as refined as he can be, though his singing in the big numbers is powerful, and for *Come un bel dì di maggio* in Act IV he does find a gentle half-tone. **Maria Guleghina** as Maddalena sings with tender beauty, though she grows unsteady under pressure, as does the powerful **Carlo Guelfi** in the key role of Gérard, the proud servant in Act I who, after the French Revolution, becomes a leader. Very impressive among the lesser characters is **Carlo Cigni** as Roucher.

Andrea Chénier (CD versions)

Ⓜ **(*) EMI (ADD) 358676-2 (2). Corelli, Stella, Sereni, Rome Op. Ch. & O, Santini

Ⓜ (***) Orfeo mono C 682 062 (2). Tebaldi, Corelli, Bastianini, V. State Op. Ch. & O, Matačić

The glory of the 1964 EMI version is the Chénier of **Franco Corelli**, one of his most satisfying performances on record, with heroic tone gloriously exploited. The other singing is less distinguished. Though **Antonietta Stella** was never sweeter of voice than here, she hardly matches such rivals as Scotto. The 1960s recording is vivid, with plenty of atmosphere, and has been transferred to CD most naturally, but the deleted RCA set in the same price range, with Domingo and Scotto, remains a clear first choice.

This broadcast recording of 1960 from the Vienna State Opera may have thinnish (mono) sound, but the performance is often electrifying. **Ettore Bastianini** is superb as Gérard, the servant who becomes an official in the government after the French Revolution. Not only is his voice rock-steady in its darkness, he characterizes vividly, above all in his two big arias, at the start and in *Nemico della patria* in Act III. Though **Renata Tebaldi's** voice as Maddalena lacks its full warmth thanks to the recording, she sings beautifully, while **Franco Corelli** in the title-role is at his peak, singing totally without strain, if sounding heavy-handed in his Act IV aria, *Come un bel dì di maggio*. **Lovro von Matačić** conducts powerfully, bringing out the many moments of high drama,

not least in the final duet when Chénier and Maddalena face the guillotine.

Fedora (complete; DVD versions)

🔊➔ *** TDK **DVD** DVWW OPFED. Freni, Domingo, Scarabelli, Corbelli, Ch. & O of La Scala, Milan, Gavazzeni (Dir: & V/D: Lamberto Puggelli)

(*) DG **DVD 073 2329. Freni, Arteta, Domingo, Croft, Hartman, Met. Op. Ch. & O, R. Abbado (V/D: Brian Large)

Recorded at La Scala in 1993, the TDK version of Giordano's *Fedora* is valuable for capturing not only the moving characterization of the heroine, Fedora, by **Mirella Freni**, but also the glorious singing of **Plácido Domingo** as the hero, Loris. It is he who has the one sure-fire hit item, the brief aria, *Amor ti vieta*. The two other principals, Olga and De Siriex, are strongly taken by **Adelina Scarabelli** and **Alessandro Corbelli**, if with limited beauty of tone. The production is grandly traditional, with the darkness of the first two Acts giving way to lightness and beauty in the Alpine scene of Act III. Freni gives herself totally to the culminating scene, when she poisons herself rather than reveal that it is she who has betrayed Loris as a revolutionary to the police. The veteran conductor, **Gianandrea Gavazzeni**, is brilliant at bringing out the colour and drama of the piece.

The DG video, taken from a live performance in 1997, offers a typically lavish production by Beppe de Tomasi from the Met. in New York with a cast as starry as could be assembled anywhere. **Mirella Freni** in 1997 was vocally past her best but the voice is still very beautiful, and maturity is an apt quality for a singer characterizing the beautiful widow, Fedora. **Plácido Domingo** makes a handsome Loris, relishing his big moment in *Amor ti vieta*. In the subsidiary roles **Ainhoa Arteta** as Countess Olga and **Dwayne Croft** as the diplomat, De Siriex, both sing with clear, firm tone, while **Roberto Abbado** paces the work well. The big snag is that the enthusiasm of the Met. audience involves prolonged applause at Freni's entrance and after the big moments of both Freni and Domingo. Brian Large's sensitive video direction homes in on the principals effectively but fails to display the grandeur of Ferruccio Villagrossi's sets fully enough.

GIPPS, Ruth (born 1921)

Horn Concerto, Op. 58

*** Lyrita SRCD 316. Pyatt, LPO, Braithwaite – ARNOLD; BOWEN; JACOB: *Horn Concertos*; VINTER: *Hunter's Moon* ***

In its sense of fantasy, Ruth Gipps's *Concerto* is quite different from its companions in this collection of British horn concertos, opening with gentle orchestral radiance and a largely reflective mood. Throughout, passages demanding dashing virtuosity are made subservient to the atmospheric feeling created by the rich but often delicate colouring of the orchestral tapestry. The finale could not be more infectiously good-humoured and buoyant, but it also has a magical, tenderly lyrical interlude before the rumbustious return of the jaunty main theme.

Symphony 2, Op. 30

*** Classico CLASSCD 274. Munich SO, Bostock –
BUTTERWORTH: *Symphony 1* ***

Ruth Gipps studied with Vaughan Williams and during the war years played the oboe in the City of Birmingham Symphony Orchestra. She became a tireless champion of neglected repertoire and an excellent teacher. Her *Second Symphony* comes from 1945 and, though indebted to Vaughan Williams, is well argued and inventive. It is decently played and recorded.

GIULIANI, Mauro (1781–1829)

(i; ii) *Guitar Concertos 1 in A, Op. 30; 2 in A, Op. 36; 3 in F, Op. 70; Introduction, Theme with Variations & Polonaise (for Guitar & Orchestra), Op. 65;* (i) *Grande ouverture, Op. 61; Gran sonata eroica in A; La Melanchonia; Variations on 'I bin a Kohlbauern Bub', Op. 49; Variations on a Theme by Handel, Op. 107;* (i; iii) *Variazioni concertanti, Op. 130*

🎵 Ⓑ *** Ph. Duo (ADD) 454 262-2 (2). (i) Pepe Romero, (ii) with ASMF, Marriner; (iii) with Celedonio Romero

Pepe Romero is a first-rate player, and his relaxed music-making and easy bravura bring an attractive, smiling quality. But what makes these *concertos* so distinctive are the splendid accompaniments provided by the **Academy of St Martin-in-the-Fields** under **Marriner**, and throughout there are many delightful touches from the orchestra. The *Variations concertanti* for two guitars, in which Pepe is joined by **Celedonio**, is played with affection and ready virtuosity. The mid-1960s recording is warm and refined throughout, very easy on the ear.

GLASS, Philip (born 1937)

(i) *Cello Concerto;* (ii) *Concerto Fantasy for 2 Timpanists and Orchestra*

🎵 *** Dunvagen Music (ASCAP) 0014. (i) Julian Lloyd Webber; (ii) Glennie, Haas; RLPO, Schwarz

Glass's *Cello Concerto* opens darkly and atmospherically; but the work's warmly lyrical strain is immediately apparent, and Glass's writing is genuinely melodic, hauntingly so, especially in the central movement, which brings what the soloist describes as 'an almost trance-like serenity'. A remarkable work, marvellously played.

The *Concerto Fantasy* is in four movements, all dominated by thundering timpani, with the third a cadenza duet for the two soloists. It is very noisy and invigorating. You will find it either thrilling or sonically overwhelming. Both performances here are surely definitive.

(i; ii) *Concerto for Saxophone Quartet & Orchestra;* (ii) *Symphony 2;* (iii) *Orphée, Act II, scene III: Interlude*

*** None. 7559 79496-2. (i) Rascher Saxophone Qt; (ii) Stuttgart CO; (iii) V. RSO; composer

Philip Glass's *Symphony No. 2*, in three substantial movements, represents his music at its most mellifluous, his second-generation brand of minimalism. Written in 1993, it uses polytonality as a basic element, to a degree taking the place of contrasts traditional in symphonic form. The *Interlude* from *Orphée* is vintage Glass, while the more compact *Saxophone Quartet Concerto* brings the liveliest music, with jazzy syncopations in the second movement and Spanish-American flavours in the finale varying Glass's persistent *moderato* writing. Excellent performances and well-balanced recording.

Violin Concerto

🎵 *** Telarc CD 80494. McDuffie, Houston SO, Eschenbach – ADAMS: *Violin Concerto* ***

(i) Violin Concerto; Company; Akhnaten: Prelude & Dance

ⒷⒷ **(*) Naxos 8.554568. (i) Anthony; Ulster O, Yuasa

Glass's *Violin Concerto*, with its hypnotic minimalist exploration of simple basic material, is one of his best and most approachable works. The repeated four-note downward scale on which the soloist weaves his serene soliloquy in the slow movement is particularly haunting, the effect very like a chaconne, which links it readily to the coupled Adams concerto. On Telarc **McDuffie** gives a first-class performance and is very well recorded indeed.

Adele Anthony is a talented violinist from Tasmania, who here gives a sweetly expressive reading, despite a rather plodding account of the very opening. In the central movement she finds a rare tenderness, as well as on the high harmonics at the end of the whole work. The concerto makes an excellent centrepiece for a complete disc of Glass's music, with **Yuasa** and the **Ulster Orchestra** equally persuasive in the four brief movements of *Company* and the two orchestral passages from the opera, *Akhnaten*.

Company; Façades

🎵 Ⓑ *** EMI 2 06624-2. LCO, Warren-Green – ADAMS: *Shaker Loops* ***; REICH: *8 Lines* ***; HEATH: *Frontier* ***

Company consists of four brief but sharply contrasted movements for strings; *Façades* offers a haunting cantilena for soprano saxophone, suspended over atmospherically undulating strings. The performances are full of intensity and are expertly played, and the recording is excellent.

Heroes Symphony; The Light

🎵 ⒷⒷ *** Naxos 8.559325. Bournemouth SO, Alsop

The Light is an undulating, minimalist piece, with changing orchestration eventually leading to a 'transformation' of the initial motive and a final cessation of the pulsing. It lasts for 24 minutes and some listeners may find it difficult to stay the course. The *Heroes Symphony*, however, has six movements (chosen from ten) to make a varied but fairly cohesive structural whole with attractive and changing invention and imaginative scoring and percussive detail to match the character of the six named sections. The result is hardly a masterpiece, but is undoubtedly entertaining in **Marin Alsop's** persuasive performance, excellently played by the **Bournemouth Symphony Orchestra**, and very well recorded.

Symphonies 2 & 3

🎵 ⏺ (BB) *** Naxos 8.559202. Bournemouth SO, Alsop

Marin Alsop's accounts of these two symphonies are magnetically performed and brilliantly recorded. No. 2, much the longer work in three substantial movements, dates from 1994 and this is unreconstructed minimalism with unrelenting kaleidoscopic repetitions. No. 3, first heard in 1995, is little more than half the length, a piece for 19 strings and optional percussion, with the gentle opening movement serving as prelude to the second and third movements, the one fast, the other a measured chaconne. The fourth movement is brief and brilliant, drawing threads together.

String Quartets 2 (Company); 3 (Mishima); 4 (Buczak); 5

*** None. 7559 79356-2. Kronos Qt

Happily, the *quartets* here are presented in reverse order, for the last of the four, No. 5, dating from 1991, presents Glass at his most warmly expressive and intense. Textures are luminous, shimmering in their repetitions rather than thrusting them home relentlessly. The **Kronos Quartet**, for whom the work was written, give a heartfelt performance, as they do of the *Quartet No. 4* (1990), written in memory of Brian Buczak, who died of Aids. The valedictory mood is intensified by a lyrical and poignantly beautiful middle movement, leading to a noble finale. Though Nos. 4 and 5 most clearly reveal the hand of a master, the earlier works also represent Glass at his most approachable, the more so when they are treated to magnetic performances by the Kronos Quartet, superbly recorded.

ORGAN MUSIC

(i) Dances 2 & 4; (ii) Duets & Canons (suite); (i) Satyagraha (opera), Act III: Finale

*** Nim. NI 5664. (i) Broadbent; (ii) Bowyer (Marcusson organ in St Augustin's Chapel, Tonbridge School, Kent)

Dance 2 represents the most basic form of minimalism, offering a hypnotically relentless ostinato for nearly 25 minutes, with very minor changes of the harmonic implications in the pedals. *Dance* 4 is more musically eventful. Below the toccata-like sequence there is a galumphing figure in the bass and frequent if repetitious harmonic movement. The shorter (seven-minute) *Satyagraha* finale is sandwiched in between the two *Dances*, more lyrical in feeling, but hardly more motivated. All three pieces are played with devoted determination by **Christopher Bowers Broadbent**, who never puts a foot or finger wrong. **Kevin Bowyer** takes over for the *Duets and Canons* (1996) creating a thoughtful, improvisatory feeling. All ten are brief and have liturgical titles, which the composer tells us are based on the plainsong of the Third

Mass of the Nativity, but the closing *Agnus Dei and Benedictus* finally leave the listener in mid-air. The recording of the fine Marcusson organ at Tonbridge cannot be faulted.

OPERA

La Belle et la bête (opera based on the film of Jean Cocteau; complete)

*** None. 7559 79347. Felty, Purnhagen, Kuether, Martinez, Neill, Zhou, Philip Glass Ens., Riesman

What Glass has done here is to provide a new musical accompaniment to a showing of Cocteau's 90-minute film, *La Belle et la bête*, dispensing with Auric's original film-music and synchronizing the singing-parts with the speech of the actors in the film. In the opening scenes the music is far lighter and more conventionally beautiful than most Glass, but then the poignancy of the story is more and more reflected in the score, both tender and mellifluous. Glass's justification lies in the intensity of the score overall, with **Janice Felty** and **Gregory Purnhagen** both clearly focused in the central roles, though Purnhagen's baritone suggests from the start a heroic, not a bestial, figure. Vividly atmospheric sound.

Einstein on the Beach (complete)

*** None. 7559 79323-2 (3). Soloists, Philip Glass Ens., Riesman

Glass himself explains the need for a new recording of this bizarre and relentless opera – as the surreal title implies, more dream than drama. Where the earlier recording had an abrasive edge, this new one is more refined, melding the different elements, electronic alongside acoustic, more subtly and persuasively than before. Even so, the first train episode, over 20 minutes long, remains mind-blowing in its relentlessness. The impact is heightened by the vividness of the recording, with spoken voices in particular given such presence that they startle you as if someone had burst into your room. The vision remains an odd one, but with a formidable group of vocalists and instrumentalists brilliantly directed, often from the keyboard, by **Michael Riesman**, the new recording certainly justifies itself.

Satyagraha (DVD version)

*** Arthaus **DVD** 100 136. Goeke, Harster, Danniker, Nielsen, Greiwe, Württemburg State Theatre O, Russell Davis

Philip Glass's second opera, *Satyagraha*, is a curiosity, an opera with virtually no plot, using a text in Sanskrit, a tribute to Mahatma Gandhi as peace-maker. The title *Satyagraha* means 'dedication to the truth', and each of the three long Acts, almost an hour each, has a superscription paying tribute to other leaders, Tolstoy, the poet Rabindranath Tagore, and Martin Luther King. Reflecting Glass's minimalist score, the dream-like staging involves little movement, though Glass's detailed inventiveness induces a hypnotic effect, clearly related to oriental meditation. **Dennis Russell Davis** with an excellent cast, led by three singers sharing the role of Gandhi, conducts a persuasive performance.

GLAZUNOV, Alexander
(1865–1936)

A la mémoire de Gogol, Op. 86; A la mémoire d'un héros, Op. 8; (i) Chant du ménestrel for Cello & Orchestra, Op. 71; Concerto ballata for Cello & Orchestra, Op. 108; 2 Pieces for Cello & Orchestra, Op. 20

(BB) *** Naxos 8.553932. Moscow SO, Golovschin, (i) with Rudin

The *Chant du ménestrel* has an easy charm that delights the ear. *A la mémoire de Gogol* is a dignified, well-shaped piece which belies (as does the *Concerto ballata*) Glazunov's reputation for scoring too thickly. **Alexander Rudin's** playing here is eloquent. The **Moscow Orchestra** plays well for **Igor Golovschin** and the sound has pleasing warmth and clarity.

Carnaval Overture, Op. 45; Concert Waltzes 1–2, Opp. 47 & 51; Spring, Op. 34; Salomé (incidental music), Op. 90: Introduction; Dance

(BB) **(*) Naxos 8.553838. Moscow SO, Golovschin

There are some attractive ideas in *Spring* (*Vesna*), a charming work, refined and transparent in its orchestration, playing on birdsong and building to a sensuous climax. The more familiar *Concert Waltzes* contain some of Glazunov's most winning tunes. The novelty most likely to excite curiosity here is Glazunov's music for Oscar Wilde's *Salomé*, with Salome's dance leading to a Polovtsian climax. Salome sheds her veils in a most unerotic fashion. But this cannot be blamed on the conductor, and generally these are warm, idiomatic performances, richly recorded.

(i) Concerto ballata for Cello & Orchestra, Op. 108; (ii) Piano Concerto 1, Op. 92

*** Chan. 9528. (i) Dyachkov; (ii) Pirzadeh; I Musici de Montréal, Turovsky – ARENSKY: *Violin Concerto* ***

The highly romantic *First Piano Concerto* is already well served by Stephen Coombs (see below). The *Concerto ballata* is also available on Naxos, but **Yegor Dyachkov** is a fine soloist, and the young Iranian-born Canadian pianist, **Maneli Pirzadeh**, proves a most poetic and brilliant exponent of the *Piano Concerto*. All in all, this makes a highly recommendable coupling.

Piano Concertos 1 in F min., Op. 92; 2 in B flat

**(*) Hyp. CDA 66877. Coombs, BBC Scottish SO, Brabbins – GOEDICKE: *Concertstück* **(*)

These two *piano concertos* are ripely lyrical, like a mixture of Brahms and Rachmaninov, but the inspiration is anything but tired or faded. As in his survey of Glazunov's piano music for the same label, **Stephen Coombs** is a persuasive advocate, and he always leaves one with the feeling that this music means more than it does. The **BBC Scottish Symphony Orchestra** under **Martyn Brabbins** give sympathetic support, and the only serious reservation one might make concerns the over-resonant recording acoustic.

Piano Concerto 2 in B flat, Op. 100

**(*) Chan. 9622. Herskowitz, I Musici de Montréal, Turovsky – DAVIDOV: *Cello Concerto 2* **(*); CONUS: *Violin Concerto* **(*)

Matthew Herskowitz is not quite as persuasive an artist as, say, Stephen Coombs on Hyperion. However, the merit of this record is to explore Russian concertos of the second rank which deserve a place in your library.

Violin Concerto in A min., Op. 82

🎵—**** Pentatone SACD PTC 5186 059. Fischer, Russian Nat. O, Kreizberg – KHACHATURIAN: *Violin Concerto* ***; PROKOFIEV: *Violin Concerto 1* ***

🎵— 🌸 *** RCA 74321 87454-2. Znaider, Bav. RSO, Jansons – PROKOFIEV: *Violin Concerto 2*; TCHAIKOVSKY: *Méditation* ***🌸

🎵— (M) *** DG 457 064-2. Shaham, Russian Nat. O, Pletnev – KABALEVSKY: *Concerto*; TCHAIKOVSKY: *Souvenir d'un lieu cher, etc.* ***

🎵— (M) *** Warner Elatus 0927 49567-2. Vengerov, BPO, Abbado – PROKOFIEV: *Concertos 1–2* ***

*** BIS SACD 1432. Gluzman, Bergen PO, Litton – TCHAIKOVSKY: *Violin Concerto; Souvenir* ***

The unique coupling of three Russian *violin concertos* on Pentatone could hardly be more recommendable, with warmly compelling performances from the brilliant young German virtuoso, superbly recorded in full, bright, clear sound, given added sonority in SACD. In the Glazunov *Concerto* it is the clarity and subtlety of **Julia Fischer's** playing that marks her reading out, in rivalry with even the finest. She finds yearning tenderness in the slow middle section of this one-movement work and gives an easy swing to the bouncy rhythms of the final section.

Nikolaj Znaider's Glazunov reveals an artist who not only has commanding technical address but eloquence and taste. His approach is fresh and so he makes one fall for this glorious work all over again. He is given splendid support by **Mariss Jansons** and the excellent **Orchester des Bayerischen Rundfunks**. A special mention should be given to the recording engineer, Wolfgang Karreth, who gets the ideal balance between soloist and orchestra and a very natural and lifelike sound.

Gil Shaham gives a pretty dazzling account of the Glazunov *Concerto* with **Mikhail Pletnev** and the **Russian National Orchestra** which can well hold its own with the current opposition. The couplings are unusual, and this is an enterprising choice for Universal's 'Critics' Choice' series.

Originally coupled with Tchaikovsky, **Vengerov's** version is now paired, even more attractively, with his outstanding Prokofiev performances. His account of the Glazunov is hardly less exceptional, for again he gives a familiar concerto extra dimensions, turning it from a display piece into a work of far wider-ranging emotions, when he contrasts and shades the tone-colours so magically, keeping the richest tone in reserve for the third theme. Predictably, his dashing final section is breathtaking in its brilliance.

Born in the Ukraine, **Vadim Gluzman**, moved to Israel

in 1990, where Isaac Stern befriended him, and then on to the USA. His performance of the engaging Glazunov *Concerto* has a pleasing simplicity, and there is no absence of virtuosity, so that he can be brilliant and touching by turns. He has a fine supportive accompanist in **Andrew Litton** and a truthful balance in first-class surround sound from BIS. The Tchaikovsky couplings show him at his finest.

In the winter of 1934 **Heifetz** came to London to record the Glazunov, a work previously unrecorded. The exuberance of his playing, well matched by **Barbirolli's** sympathetic accompaniment, makes it a uniquely compelling version, freely improvisational, with a dedicated account of the *Andante sostenuto* and an exuberant one of the swaggering finale. The Naxos transfer (8.110940) is well balanced, if not quite as sophisticated as the previous, EMI remastering (7 64030-2), with surface hiss occasionally intrusive.

For those who accept slightly dated 1963 stereo sound, **Heifetz** is again incomparable, his later account among the strongest and most passionate in the catalogue, and the RCA orchestra under Hendl gives fine support. The remastered recording sounds really good in its new SACD format. (8287 6 66372-2)

From the Middle Ages, Op. 79; Scènes de ballet, Op. 52

*** Chan. 8804. SNO, Järvi – LIADOV: *A Musical Snuffbox* ***

From the Middle Ages (suite), Op. 79; The Sea, Op. 28; Spring, Op. 34; Stenka Razin, Op. 13

(M) *** Chan. 7049. SNO, Järvi

Järvi makes out an excellent case for these charming Glazunov suites. Although this music is obviously inferior to Tchaikovsky, Järvi has the knack of making you think it is better than it is, and the Chandos recording is up to the best standards of the house. The disc also includes a fine account of Liadov's delightful *A Musical Snuffbox*.

The tone-poem *Spring* was written two years after *The Sea* and is infinitely more imaginative; in fact it is as fresh and delightful as its companion is cliché-ridden. At one point Glazunov even looks forward to *The Seasons. Stenka Razin* makes a colourful enough opening item for this alternative collection.

Raymonda – 'Dancer's Dream' (Documentary)

(N) Arthaus DVD 107 015. Principal Dancers & Corps de Ballet, with Paris Nat. Opéra O, Anissimov (Dir. François Roussillon)

A fascinating documentary (from 1999) about Glazunov's colourful ballet *Raymonda*, and its comparatively recent success with Rudolf Nureyev. The documentary is dedicated to the great ballet productions Nureyev created at the Opéra National de Paris, of which he was its artistic director from 1983. The documentary focuses on both the history of the ballet and Nureyev's work on it, and offers a fascinating series of interviews interspersed with scenes from the ballet. Some of the material is archival, but the majority is of very beautiful recent productions, where both the colour of the music and the beauty of the dancing are well conveyed. The

picture- and sound-quality are both first class. A thoroughly rewarding and civilized documentary – and a must for balletomanes.

Raymonda (ballet; complete; DVD version)

⊕—*** Arthaus DVD 100 719. Bessmertnova, Vasyuchenko, Taranda, Nobrova, Bolshoi Ballet, directed Grigorovich; Bolshoi Theatre O, Zhuraitis (V/D: Shuji Fujii)

Glazunov's *Raymonda* (his first major theatrical score, premièred in 1898) is a traditional romantic ballet with a simple story and a happy ending; and this admirable DVD is especially valuable for preserving a lavish (1989) **Bolshoi** production which draws on the original choreography (*Raymonda* was the last ballet in which Petipa participated). Undoubtedly this is the Bolshoi at their peak, and the orchestral playing under **Algis Zhuraitis** is first class, as is the recording. The camerawork cannot be faulted, although the Bolshoi stage is huge, and some of the long shots are inevitably rather distantly focused.

Raymonda (complete; CD version)

(BB) **(*) Naxos 8.553503/4. Moscow SO, Anissimov

This Naxos version is played elegantly and affectionately, and the Moscow upper strings are full and warm as recorded. It does not lack life. But in seeking atmosphere, the playing creates a less than vibrant effect, although this is partly caused by **Alexander Anissimov's** tendency to luxuriant tempi.

The Seasons (ballet; complete), Op. 67

⊕—(B) **** Double Decca 455 349-2 (2). RPO, Ashkenazy – PROKOFIEV: *Cinderella* ****

(M) **(*) Decca 460 315-2. SRO, Ansermet – KHACHATURIAN: *Gayaneh; Spartacus*: excerpts ***

(BB) **(*) Naxos 8.550079. Czech RSO (Bratislava), Lenárd – TCHAIKOVSKY: *Sleeping Beauty Suite* **

(BB) (***) Dutton mono CDBP 9754. SO, composer – PROKOFIEV: *Romeo and Juliet: Suite 2* (***)

The Seasons; Concert Waltzes 1 & 2; Stenka Razin

(N) **(*) Australian Decca Eloquence 480 038 (2). SRO, Ansermet – GLINKA: *Jota argonesa*, etc.; LIADOV: *Baba-Yaga*, etc. ***; SCHUMANN: *Carnaval* **(*)

The Seasons (ballet; complete); Scènes de ballet, Op. 52

⊕—(M) *** Telarc CD 80347. Minnesota O, Edo de Waart

Ashkenazy's account of Glazunov's delightful ballet is the finest it has ever received. The **RPO** playing is dainty and elegant, refined and sumptuous, yet the strings respond vigorously to the thrusting vitality of the Autumnal *Bacchanale*. The Decca engineers, working in Watford Town Hall, provide digital sound of great allure and warmth, very much in the demonstration bracket. As can be seen, this recording is available on a Double Decca, coupled with Prokofiev's *Cinderella* ballet.

The very attractive Minnesota performances of *The*

Seasons and the delightful *Scènes de ballet* make an ideal coupling, and this is doubly attractive now it has been reissued at mid-price.

Ansermet's recording dates from 1966 and is of vintage Decca quality. The performance takes a little while to warm up, but perhaps that is not inappropriate in the opening *Winter* sequence, where the conductor's meticulous ear for detail is a plus point, for the wind playing throughout is engagingly pointed. At the opening of *Summer* one might wish for a richer, more sumptuous sound from the **Suisse Romande** violins, but the zestful opening of *Autumn* is firm to the point of fierceness.

Ansermet's *Seasons* is also available on an Australian import, differently coupled. Indeed, the alternative couplings are all worth having and the two *Concert Waltzes* are as delightful as ever.

Ondrej Lenárd gives a pleasing bargain account of Glazunov's delightful score, finding plenty of delicacy, while the entry of Glazunov's most famous tune at the opening of the *Autumn Bacchanale* is very virile indeed. The sound is atmospheric, yet with plenty of fullness.

Recorded for the Columbia label in 1929, the composer's own reading of *The Seasons* brings a vigorous and colourful performance, with surprisingly good ensemble from what was evidently a pick-up orchestra. The impact of the performance, not least in the exuberant *Bacchanale* for *Autumn* with lifted rhythms, is greatly heightened by the vivid and full-bodied transfer by Michael Dutton.

Symphonies 1–8; Ballade in F, Op. 78; From Darkness to Light; Mazurka in G, Op. 38

(B) *** BIS CD 1663/4 (5). BBC Nat. O of Wales, Otaka

A valuable set, offering all eight symphonies on five CDs for the price of two. They span just over two decades; the *First* being composed when Glazunov was a boy of sixteen and the *Eighth* completed when he was just forty. The symphonies are very consistent, both in substance and in character: if you have heard and liked one, its companions will offer few surprises and much satisfaction. The ideas are appealing and the craftsmanship and orchestration show an impressive mastery. Arnold Bax used to play them in duet form – understandably, for they are musically rewarding and are unlikely to be encountered in concert programmes. But they are decently represented on CD and have been out on individual discs for some time. The present issue represents a true bargain and the performances and recordings can hold their own against the Polyansky cycle on Chandos and other rivals.

Symphonies 1 in E, Op 5; 5 in B flat, Op. 55

(*) Orfeo C 093101A. Bav. RSO, Neeme Järvi

Symphony 2 in F sharp min., Op. 16; Concert Waltz 1

(*) Orfeo C 148101A. Bamberg SO, Järvi

Symphony 3 in D, Op. 33; Concert Waltz 2

*** Orfeo C 157101A. Bamberg SO, Järvi

Symphonies 4 in E flat, Op. 48; 7 in F, Op. 77

(*) Orfeo C 148201A. Bamberg SO, Järvi

Symphony 6 in C min., Op. 58; Poème lyrique, Op. 12

*** Orfeo C 157201A. Bamberg SO, Järvi

Symphony 8 in E flat, Op. 83; Overture solennelle, Op. 73; Wedding Procession

(*) Orfeo C 157201A. Bav. RSO, Järvi

Neeme Järvi's cycle of the Glazunov *Symphonies* has been restored to the catalogue. Alas, they are all still at full price, but they are also all available separately, and they include some attractive bonuses. The *Third* and *Sixth Symphonies* are among the finest of the set, full of vigour and benefiting from the polish of the **Bambergers'** playing. But all these performances are cultivated. No. 1 is highly sympathetic in Järvi's hands, cogent and engagingly fresh. No. 2 is comfortable, both in music and in sound, but is undoubtedly enjoyable; and Järvi brings out the full charm of No. 4. No. 5 (like No. 8 played by the **Bavarian Radio Orchestra**) may lack something in glitter, but the balance is full and pleasing. Above all, Järvi avoids bombast which can too easily take over in these works, which are nothing if not civilized.

Symphony 1; (i) Violin Concerto, Op. 82

*** Chan. 9751. Russian State SO, Polyansky, (i) with Krasko

What a remarkable and delightful work the Glazunov *First Symphony* is! **Polyansky's** pacing keeps the music alive throughout, and manages the tempi changes in an engagingly spontaneous way, and the Chandos sound, full and with glowing wind colouring, is flattering. **Julia Krasko** plays the *Violin Concerto* warm-heartedly and with confidence and ready bravura, and she receives fine support from the Russian orchestra. The Chandos sound is well up to standard.

Symphony 2 in F sharp min., Op. 16. (i) Coronation Cantata, Op. 56

*** Chan. 9709. Russian State SO, Polyansky, (i) with Lutiv-Ternovskaya, Kuznetsova, Grivnov, Stepanovich, Russian State Symphonic Capella

Though **Polyansky's** performance loses some concentration in the finale, it is warmly expressive and colourful, helped by rich, full recording. What makes the disc especially attractive is the substantial fill-up, the première recording of the *Coronation Cantata* which Glazunov wrote to celebrate the coronation of the last Tsar, Nicolas II. A winning rarity, very well performed, with a strong team of soloists, all attractively Slavonic in timbre, even if the soprano grows edgy under pressure.

Symphonies 4 in E flat, Op. 48; 5 in B flat, Op. 55

*** Chan. 9739. Russian State SO, Polyansky

*** ASV CDDCA 1051. Philh. O, Butt

The *Fourth Symphony* is a charming and well-composed work, held together structurally by a theme which Glazunov uses in all three movements. The *Fifth*, written two years later, is more imposing, but not so very different really, although the first movement is more vigorous. Throughout both works the **Philharmonia** playing under **Butt** is persuasively warm and sympathetic, helped by the spacious, well-balanced recording.

However, **Polyansky's** Chandos competitor has the advantage of a fine **Russian Orchestra** which immediately establish a richly Slavonic atmosphere of melancholy for the languorous opening theme of No. 4. The Chandos recording is glowingly warm in capturing string and woodwind timbres alike, yet the Scherzos of both symphonies sparkle translucently. The resonance means that the finales have less bite than with the ASV recording and, while they are played with robust, Russian-dance vigour, Butt is exceptionally spirited in the finale of No. 5. It is a case of swings and roundabouts, for the ASV recording is clearer, if not more lustrous.

Symphonies 4; 7 in F, Op. 77

⊕ *** Warner 2564 63236-2. RSNO, Serebrier

Serebrier gets very characterful and brilliant performances from the **Royal Scottish National Orchestra** and his account of No. 4 in particular has a good claim to be a first recommendation. What a charming work the *Seventh* is, sometimes dubbed the *Pastoral* after the similarity of the opening to the opening of Beethoven's *Sixth*. It never fails to captivate. The writing for horns is striking in all four movements, with the RSNO's soloists outstandingly fine, as are the woodwind. The finale brings together ideas from all the preceding movements in a Lisztian transformation. Very good recorded sound too.

Symphony 5 in B flat; The Seasons (ballet; complete)

⊕ *** Warner 2564 61434-2. RSNO, Serebrier

Jose Serebrier with the **Royal Scottish National Orchestra** here couples two of Glazunov's most warmly attractive works. The one-Act ballet *The Seasons* is the most popular of his orchestral works, deservedly so. The *Fifth Symphony*, here given an exhilarating performance. With outstanding recorded sound giving clarity and weight, the refinement and power of the performance are superbly caught.

Symphonies 5; 8 in E flat, Op. 83

⊕ (BB) *** Naxos 8.553660. Moscow SO, Anissimov

Alexander Anissimov does his best to make the textures as clear and well ventilated as possible, and pays great attention to details of dynamics and balance. Try the Scherzo of the *Fifth Symphony* and you will find much lightness of touch and a greater transparency than is often encountered in records of these works. Strongly recommended, especially at such a modest cost.

Symphony 6 in C min., Op. 58; Characteristic Suite in D, Op. 9

⊕ *** Chan. 10238. Russian State SO, Polyansky

Symphony 6; The Forest (tone-poem), Op. 19

(BB) **(*) Naxos 8.554293. Moscow SO, Anissimov

Polyansky's reading of the *Sixth Symphony* has plenty of impetus and excellent detail, and the *Characteristic Suite* is well worth having on disc. Very good playing from the **Russian State Symphony Orchestra** and excellent Chandos recording make this another desirable addition to the catalogue.

Anissimov also handles the symphony admirably and, with the Moscow players responding persuasively, the performance is a great success. However, *The Forest* is an over-extended pantheistic tone-poem with an ingenuous programme. Yet the work is rarely if ever performed, and the fine account of the symphony is worth its modest Naxos price.

Symphony 8, Op. 83; Poème lyrique, Op. 65; (i) Commemorative Cantata, Op. 65

⊕ *** Chan. 9961. Russian State SO, Polyansky; (i) with Kuznetsova, Grivnov, Russian State Symphonic Capella

Symphony 8 in E flat; Raymonda (Ballet Suite), Op. 57a

**(*) Warner 2564 61939-2. RSNO, Serebrier

Polyansky's performance of the *Eighth Symphony* is thoroughly persuasive throughout, especially in the finale, which is both exciting and satisfyingly cumulative. The *Poème lyrique*, too, is given a rapturous account, with Polyansky revelling in the Russianness of the melodic line. But what makes this disc especially compelling is the lovely cantata commemorating the centenary of the birth of Pushkin. Soloists, chorus and orchestra combine to give a passionately dedicated performance of what is surely one of the composer's finest choral works. The recording is well up to Chandos's excellent standard.

Serebrier pairs the *Eighth* with an attractive selection from the *Raymonda* ballet. The symphony comes off very well, although the Scottish performance is rather less vibrant than Polyansky's Chandos version. However, the *Raymonda Suite* shows the composer at his finest, with consistently more memorable writing than in the symphony, full of melodic charm and felicitous scoring. The orchestral playing here is most sympathetic and the sound very pleasing.

CHAMBER MUSIC

5 Novelettes, Op. 15

(***) Testament mono SBT1061. Hollywood Qt – BORODIN: *String Quartet 2*; TCHAIKOVSKY: *String Quartet 1* (***)

The **Hollywood Quartet** bring a freshness and ardour to these charming compositions that are most persuasive.

String Quartets 2 in F, Op. 10; 4 in A min., Op. 64; Elegy, Op. 105

*** MDG 603 1237-2. Utrecht Qt

String Quartets: 3 in G (Slave), Op. 26; 5 in D min., Op. 70

*** MDG 603 1236-2. Utrecht Qt

Both *Quartets* on MDG 603 1237-2 are youthful. The 'Slavonic' influences in the *Mazurka* third movement of Op. 26 and the *Fête slave* finale bring Russian dance influences at their most civilized, while the slow movement of the *A minor Quartet* is particularly beautiful. What elegantly written music this is! For those starting to collect these works, the **Utrecht** versions can be thoroughly recommended. They are warmly and pleasingly recorded.

String Quartet 3 in G (Slavonic)

(B) *** Cal. CAL 6262. Annesci Qt – DVOŘÁK: *String Quartet 12 (American)* ***

Glazunov's *Slavonic Quartet* is so named because of its finale ('*Une fête slave*'), which the **Annesci** players despatch with attractive geniality, neatly catching the dance rhythms. They are equally fetching in the *Alla Mazurka*, with its underlying drone, while the first two movements are full of lyrical warmth. A first-rate coupling, for the Dvořák performance is no less endearing.

String Quintet in A, Op. 39

*** Chan. 9878. ASMF Chamber Ens. – TCHAIKOVSKY: *Souvenir de Florence* ***

Glazunov's *String Quintet* (with second cello) is a work of characteristic warmth and lyricism. The performance is thoroughly committed and persuasive, and very well recorded too.

(i) String Quintet, Op. 39; 5 Novelettes

(BB) *** Naxos 8.570256. Fine Arts Qt, (i) with Rosen

Glazunov's warmly attractive lyricism as well as his technical mastery come out winningly in both these works, not least the *Novelettes*, charming genre pieces, each echoing a different national dance, Spanish, Hungarian, Oriental, and so on. The *String Quintet* is beautifully fashioned and mellifluous, with the first movement introduced by the viola unaccompanied, a sonata movement full of attractive themes. The **Fine Arts Quartet** plus **Nathanial Rosen** on the second cello give brilliant performances, warmly understanding as well as polished, and very well recorded in New York.

Piano Music

Piano Sonata 1 in B flat min., Op. 74; Grande valse de concert, Op. 41; 3 Miniatures, Op. 42; Petite valse, Op. 36; Suite on the name 'Sacha'; Valse de salon, Op. 43; Waltzes on the Theme 'Sabela', Op. 23

(BB) *** Hyp. Helios CDH 66833. Coombs

Easy Sonata; 3 Etudes, Op. 31; Miniature in C; 3 Morceaux, Op. 49; Nocturne, Op. 37; 2 Pieces, Op. 22; 2 Preludes-improvisations; Sonatina; Theme & Variations, Op. 72

(BB) *** Hyp. Helios CDH 55222. Coombs

Marking the start of a Russian series, each of these two discs contains a major work, the *Piano Sonata No. 1* on the first and the *Theme and Variations*, Op. 72, on the second. For the rest, you have a dazzling series of salon and genre pieces, full of the easy charm and winning tunefulness that mark Glazunov's ballet, *The Seasons*. **Stephen Coombs** proves a most persuasive advocate, consistently conveying sheer joy in keyboard virtuosity to a degree rare in British pianists.

(i) Piano Sonata 2 in E min., Op. 75; Barcarolle sur les touches noires; Idyll, Op. 103; 2 Impromptus, Op. 54; In modo religioso, Op. 38; Prelude & 2 Mazurkas, Op. 25; Song of the Volga Boatmen, Op. 97 (arr. Siloti); (ii) Triumphal March, Op. 40

(BB) *** Hyp. Helios CDH 55224. (i) Coombs; (ii) Holst Singers, Layton

The most substantial work here is the *Second Sonata* of 1901, which is better played than by any of its rivals we have heard. The most unusual piece is the transcription of a Wagnerian *Triumphal March*, written for the Chicago Exposition, which eventually introduces *Hail Columbus*, sung in Russian! Not all the music on this generously filled CD is of equal merit but most of it is rewarding, and the recording serves the music well.

4 Preludes & Fugues, Op. 101; Prelude & Fugue in D min., Op. 62; in E min. (1926)

(BB) *** Hyp. Helios CDH 55223. Coombs

One does not think of Glazunov in terms of preludes and fugues, but these are all impressive pieces and this Helios reissue is most welcome.

ORGAN MUSIC

Fantasy, Op. 110; Preludes & Fugues: in D, Op. 93; in D min., Op. 98

*** BIS CD 1101. Ericsson – DVOŘÁK: *Preludes & Fugues* **(*); SIBELIUS: *Intrada*, etc. ***

The *Prelude and Fugue in D* was composed in the immediate wake of the *Eighth Symphony*, and the *D minor* (which also exists in a version for piano), with its powerfully wrought fugue, will surprise those who think of Glazunov as a dyed-in-the-wool conservative. The *Fantasy* is well worth getting to know. **Hans Ola Ericsson** produces some splendid effects from the powerful new Gerald Woehl organ at St Petrus Canisius, Friedrichshafen. The recording is in the demonstration class and has tremendous presence and range.

VOCAL MUSIC

Tsar Iudesyskiy (King of the Jews)

*** Chan. 9467. Russian State Symphony Ch. & SO, Rozhdestvensky

Tsar Iudesyskiy (King of the Jews); Salome (incidental music): Introduction and Salome's dance

*** Chan. 9824. (i) Russian State Symphonic Capella; Russian State SO, Polyansky

Glazunov's incidental music to Konstantin Romanov's *Tsar Iudesyskiy* (*King of the Jews*) offers considerable artistic rewards. **Rozhdestvensky** shapes each phrase with feeling and imagination, and he gets good results from his chorus and orchestra. Moreover, the quality of the recorded sound is first rate in every respect.

Astonishingly Chandos have followed up Rozhdestvensky's CD with another, using similar forces conducted by **Valéry Polyansky**. His version is hardly less compelling, although perhaps Rozhdestvensky is that bit more dramatic at the opening, and in portraying the Levites' trumpets (actually horns). But Polyansky's account is richly atmospheric and his singers are splendid. There is little in it, although some may be swayed by the more recent CD's inclusion of the music that Glazunov wrote in 1908 for a production of Oscar Wilde's *Salome*.

GLIÈRE, Reinhold (1875–1956)

(i) *Concerto for Coloratura Soprano, Op. 82*; (ii) *Harp Concerto, Op. 74*

🎵 *** Chan. 9094. (i) Hulse; (ii) Masters; City of L. Sinfonia, Hickox – GINASTERA: *Harp Concerto* ***

This digital recording of Glière's lush concertos is highly competitive in both works. The recording is suitably rich and opulent, yet every detail is audibly in place. **Eileen Hulse** is an impressive soloist with excellent control, well-focused tone and a good sense of line, and she is excellently supported by the **City of London Sinfonia** and **Richard Hickox**. Nor need **Rachel Masters** fear comparison with her predecessor, Osian Ellis; so, given such excellent sound, this is all highly self-indulgent and sybaritic.

Symphony 3 in B min. (Ilya Mourometz), Op. 42

🎵 *** Telarc CD 80609. LSO, Botstein

*** Chan. 9041. BBC PO, Downes

Fine as its Chandos competitor is, this new Telarc recording of Glière's *Ilya Mourometz Symphony* is even more impressive. **Botstein** uses the uncut original score of 1911, and even though both outer movements run to over 22 minutes, their length is well sustained. What Botstein also does is to bring out the underlying Russian folksong inspiration of the writing. The spaciously spectacular recording is well up to the high standard we expect from this label.

Downes and the **BBC Philharmonic** in magnificent form give an urgently passionate performance of this colourful programme piece. Downes, taut and intense, relates the writing very much to the world of Glière's close contemporary, Rachmaninov. The recording, made in the concert hall of New Broadcasting House, Manchester, is one of Chandos's finest, combining clarity and sumptuousness. But the new Telarc recording is even finer.

Octet, Op. 5; Sextet, Op. 11

*** MDG 308 1196-2. Berlin Philharmonic String Octet

Glière's *Octet* comes from 1900, when the composer was in his mid-twenties, and the *Sextet*, his third essay in the medium, was composed five years later. Both works show a mastery not only of the genre (Glière was a fine violinist) but the impeccable craftsmanship that one would expect from a pupil of Taneyev, while the melodic ideas are both beautifully fashioned and finely paced. The **Berlin Philharmonic String Octet** play with enthusiasm and persuasiveness, and the MDG sound is very lifelike. An appealing and welcome issue.

GLINKA, Mikhail (1804–57)

Capriccio brillante on the Jota aragonesa (Spanish Overture 1); Kamarinskaya; Souvenir of a Summer Night in Madrid (Spanish Overture 2); Valse-fantaisie; A Life for the Tsar: Overture & Suite (Polonaise; Krakowiak; Waltz; Mazurka; Epilogue)

*** ASV CDDCA 1075. Armenian PO, Tjeknavorian

Capriccio brillante on the Jota aragonesa (Spanish Overture 1); Kamarinskaya; Overture in D; Ruslan and Ludmilla: Overture & Suite; Souvenir of a Summer Night in Madrid (Spanish Overture 2); Symphony on Two Russian Themes; Valse-Fantaisie

🎵 **** Chan. 9861. BBC PO, Sinaisky

Kamarinskaya is a kaleidoscopic fantasy on two Russian folksongs. Tchaikovsky said it contained 'the whole of Russian music, just as the acorn holds within itself the oak tree'. The two Spanish overtures created another genre, the orchestral 'picture postcard', which Russian composers brought home from their travels abroad. Glinka's two pieces have a glitter and atmospheric appeal all of their own, especially the *Capriccio brillante*, featuring a 'jota aragonesa' also used by Liszt. But the seductive scoring of *Summer Night in Madrid* was in some ways even more influential. The *Valse-fantaisie* is a charmer, but the overture and suite from *A Life for the Tsar* are more conventional. The whole programme is played under **Tjeknavorian** with a natural vitality and a delightful feeling for its Russianness under a conductor who is a composer himself. The bright recording, full-bodied and glowing, is one of the finest we have received from ASV.

Sinaisky duplicates the main items in Tjeknavorian's programme, but includes also the seductive *Symphony on Two Russian Themes*. Many will also prefer the fizzingly brilliant *Overture*, *March* and *Dances* (effectively a charming ballet suite) from *Ruslan and Ludmilla* to the excerpts from *A Life for the Tsar*. Moreover, not only is the playing of the **BBC Philharmonic** under Sinaisky both warmly responsive and sparkling, but the state-of-the-art Chandos recording (brass, woodwind and strings alike) is even finer than the ASV alternative. Highly recommended.

Jota aragonesa; Kamarinskaya; A Life for the Tsar: Overture. Ruslan and Ludmilla: Overture; Valse-Fantasie

Ⓝ *** Australian Decca Eloquence 480 038 (2). SRO, Ansermet – GLAZUNOV: *The Seasons* etc.; LIADOV: *Baba-Yaga*, etc.; SCHUMANN: *Carnaval* **(*)

This is real **Ansermet** repertoire. All the Glinka items on this 2-CD set are highly enjoyable: *Ruslan and Ludmilla* is given a relaxed outing compared to Solti's LSO version, but is no less enjoyable for that, while in the rarer *Kamarinskaya* and *A Life for the Tsar Overture*, Ansermet brings all the bright colours of the score to vivid life. The *Valse-Fantasie* is delightful indeed, and its tune hard to get out of one's head. The lively *Jota aragonesa* is especially enjoyable, with its glittering castanets and percussion, and the crescendo starting at 7 minutes 18 seconds is most excitingly played.

Polka 1 (orch. Balakirev); Spanish Overtures 1 (Jota aragonesa); 2 (Summer Night in Madrid); Waltz Fantasia; Ivan Susanin (A Life for the Tsar): Overture. Prince Kholmsky: Overture and Entr'actes to Acts II–IV; Ruslan and Ludmilla: Overture; Chernamor's March

(BB) *** Regis (ADD/DDD) RRC 1142. USSR SO & Bolshoi Theatre O, Svetlanov

These Russian recordings have been selected from a two-disc Melodiya set that last appeared on BMG/RCA. The performances embrace a considerable time-span (1963–84). The playing of the **USSR Symphony Orchestra**, which provides the majority of the items, is nothing if not expert and idiomatic, and the remastered recordings, though variable in quality, are generally very good indeed.

CHAMBER MUSIC

Grand Sextet in E flat

(BB) *** Hyp. Helios CDH 55173. Capricorn – RIMSKY-KORSAKOV: *Quintet for Piano & Wind* ***

Glinka's *Sextet* is rather engaging, particularly when played with such aplomb as it is here. The contribution of the pianist, **Julian Jacobson**, is brilliantly nimble and felicitous. The balance places the piano rather backwardly, but the CD provides good detail and presence.

Trio pathétique in D min.

*** Chan. 8477. Borodin Trio – ARENSKY: *Piano Trio* ***

Glinka's *Trio* is prefaced by a superscription: *'Je n'ai connu l'amour que par les peines qu'il cause'* ('I have known love only through the misery it causes'). It is no masterpiece – but the **Borodins** almost persuade one that it is. The Chandos recording is vivid and has excellent presence.

OPERA

A Life for the Tsar (Ivan Susanin)

(BB) (***) Naxos mono 8.111078/80. Mikhailov, Spiller, Antoneva, Yelepp, Hosson, Skobtsov, Svetlanov, Bolshoi Ch. & O, Melik-Pasheyev (Acts I–IV); Nebolsin (Epilogue)

The bass **Maxim Mikhailov** was the finest Ivan Susanin of his day and he sang the role some 400 times. **Natalia Spiller**, who sings his daughter, Antonida, was one of the greatest of the Bolshoi's heroines. The singing is superb and it is difficult to imagine a vocally or dramatically finer cast or finer conducting. The Epilogue was recorded in 1950 and is conducted by **Vasili Nebolsin**. The third CD is completed by some isolated arias sung by **Antonina Nezhdanova** (1913),

Chaliapin (recorded in London in 1923) and **Helge Rosvænge** (in Berlin, 1940). Readers who can remember what Soviet recordings sounded like in the days of 78s and LP will be amazed at the quality of this set.

Ruslan and Ludmilla (complete; DVD versions)

⊕→ *** Ph. **DVD** 075 096-9 (2). Ognovienko, Netrebko, Diadkova, Bezzubenkov, Gorchakova, Kirov Op. Ch. & O, Gergiev – (Prod: Wilson, V/D: Hulscher) (Bonuses: Gergiev: '*Introducing Ruslan*' and '*Catching up with Music*' – biographical tour)

⊕→ *** Ph. **DVD** 075 099-9 (6). As above – BORODIN: *Prince Igor*; MUSSORGSKY: *Boris Godunov*

Gergiev in his Kirov recording, done live on stage, launches into this classic Russian opera with a hair-raisingly fast and brilliant account of the overture, and then characteristically brings out the subtlety of much of the writing, as well as the colour. The voices come over well, with **Vladimir Ognovienko** characterful as Ruslan, bringing out word-meaning, most impressively in his big Act II aria. **Anna Netrebko** is fresh and bright as Ludmilla, as well as agile, not as shrill as many Russian sopranos, but it is **Galina Gorchakova** as Gorislava who takes first honours; she is rich and firm, as is **Larissa Diadkova** in the travesti role of Ratmir, especially impressive in the delightful duet with Finn (**Konstantin Pluzhnikov**). In addition there are two bonuses, the first an introduction to the opera of some 18 minutes and a 50-minute feature about Gergiev. The staging is colourful, if at times a bit static, and the whole production will give much pleasure.

GLUCK, Christoph (1714–87)

Don Juan (ballet; complete)

*** Australian Decca Eloquence (ADD) 476 2440. ASMF, Marriner – HANDEL: *Ariodante; Il Pastor Fido (suites)* ***

(BB) *** Warner Apex 8573 89233-2. E. Bar. Sol., Gardiner

Gluck's *Don Juan* is a wonderful score, revolutionary in its day, and it comes across to modern ears as a tuneful work full of striking ideas, with plenty of charm and drama. This classic 1967 recording has great lightness of touch, beautiful playing and vintage Decca sound. If Gardiner's (Erato) version brought out more of the work's drama, there is nothing in the least bland about **Marriner's** direction and, with its very enjoyable coupling, this makes a welcome return to circulation.

Originally part of the Collection, the alternative **Gardiner** version has much to recommend it at Apex price. The 1981 recording is full and modern. The performance too has a clean and dramatic profile.

OPERA

Alceste (DVD version)

(*) Arthaus **DVD 101 251. Naglestad, Kaasch, Rydh, Ch. & O of Stuttgart Opera, Carydis (Dirs: Jossi Wieler, Sergio Morabito, V/D: Nele Munchmeyer)

The Arthaus DVD of Gluck's *Alceste* in the 1776 Paris version offers a performance in modern dress, mainly impressive for the fine singing of **Catherina Naglestad** in the title-role and the strong support given by the chorus, a key player in this reform opera. Naglestad rises splendidly to the challenge of the big numbers, not least *Divinités du Styx*. The conductor **Constantinos Carydis** draws playing from the orchestra that has clearly been influenced by period practice and though the stylized movements of the chorus in a modern setting are not always effective the result is strong and convincing, with the incidental roles also well sung.

Alceste (Vienna version 1767; complete; CD version)

(B) *** Naxos 8.660066/68 (3). Ringholz, Lavender, Degerfeldt, Treichl, Martinsson, Drottningholm Theatre Ch. & O, Östman

This is the first recording of the Vienna version of *Alceste*, rather simpler and more direct in manner than the far–better-known French version of 1776. Here, Alceste's powerful aria *Divinités du Styx* becomes *Ombre, larve*, less imposing, and the intimate scale of the **Drottningholm** presentation reflects that, with a cast of young singers remarkable for their freshness rather than for their power. At the Naxos price one can hardly complain that the opera is laid out rather extravagantly on three discs, when in any case that brings the advantage of one disc per Act. Well-balanced sound, with voices well to the fore. Full libretto, synopsis and translation are provided.

Armide (complete)

⊕–– *** DG 459 616-2. Delunsch, Workman, Podles, Naouri, Ch. & Musiciens du Louvre, Minkowski

Using a libretto set by Lully almost a century earlier, Gluck develops a compellingly flexible structure, with arias, duets and recitatives merging in quick succession. **Minkowski's** treatment could not be more dramatic, persuasively leading one on at speeds on the brisk side. The cast is strong, powerfully led by **Mireille Delunsch** in the title-role, singing with rich, firm tone, and with **Charles Workman** fresh and clean-cut as the tenor hero, Renaud. In the brief but important role of La Haine, **Ewa Podles** sings with commanding intensity, and the minor roles are also well taken. The live recording gives weight and bite to the substantial instrumental band.

Iphigénie en Aulide (complete)

⊕–– (M) *** Erato 2292 45003-2 (2). Van Dam, Von Otter, Dawson, Aler, Monteverdi Ch., Lyon Op. O, Gardiner

Gardiner here reconstructs the score as presented in the first revival of 1775; the recording conveys the tensions of a live performance without the distractions of intrusive stage noise. The darkness of the piece is established at the very start, with men's voices eliminated, and a moving portrait built up of Agamemnon, here sung superbly by **José van Dam**. In the title-role **Lynne Dawson** builds up a touching portrait of the heroine. Her sweet, pure singing is well contrasted with the positive strength of **Anne Sofie von Otter**

as Clytemnestra, and **John Aler** brings clear, heroic attack to the tenor role of Achilles. The performance is crowned by the superb ensemble-singing of the **Monteverdi Choir** in the many choruses. A highlights disc is also available on Apex (2564 61507-2).

Iphigénie en Tauride (complete; CD versions)

*** DG 471 133-2 (2). Delunsch, Keenlyside, Beuron, Naouri, Louvre Ch. & O, Minkowski

*** Telarc CD 80546 (2). Goerke, Gilfry, Cole, Salters, Baker, West, Boston Baroque, Pearlman

Marc Minkowski launches into his characterful, highly distinctive reading in a performance of the overture with characteristically extreme speeds in both directions. It sounds idiomatic, thanks to having a cast almost entirely made up of French speakers, who enunciate their words clearly to heighten the meaning. That is especially true of **Mireille Delunsch** in the title-role, golden-toned and deeply affecting in her great aria, *O malheureuse Iphigénie!* **Simon Keenlyside** as Oreste is hardly less idiomatic and characterful, with his sharply focused baritone. **Yann Beuron** as Pylade and **Laurent Naouri** as Thoas complete an outstanding team. Balance of merits between Minkowski and Pearlman could not be closer.

With an excellent cast, led by **Christine Goerke** radiantly pure-toned in the title-role, **Martin Pearlman** directs his Boston forces in a fresh, direct reading of the last of Gluck's 'reform' operas, which unaffectedly brings out the dramatic bite as well as the beauty. Pearlman's choice of speeds is never extreme, always natural, and, besides Goerke, **Rodney Gilfry** as Oreste and **Vinson Cole** as Pylade with clean, heady tenor tone are both excellent. An excellent, safe choice for anyone wanting this masterpiece in a period performance.

Orfeo ed Euridice (DVD versions)

**(*) Warner DVD 5050467-3921-2-0. Baker, Speiser, Gale, Glyndebourne Festival Ch., LPO, Leppard (V/D: Rodney Greenberg)

Peter Hall's classic Glyndebourne production of *Orfeo*, here recorded in 1982, is valuable above all for marking one of **Dame Janet Baker's** last operatic appearances. It is good to be reminded how powerful the result is when her passionately intense singing is matched by her equally involved and compelling acting. To see her cradling the dead Euridice in her arms as she sings *Che farò* is deeply moving. **Raymond Leppard** draws biting attack and warm expressiveness from the **LPO**, though the impact of the musical clarity is slightly muted by the rather soft focus of the camerawork. Leppard has opted for a version of the score broadly based on the composite Berlioz edition, but using the Italian rather than the French text, including at the end Gluck's sequence of ballet numbers as a grand finale, here imaginatively staged. John Bury's sets are stylized and evocative. As Euridice, **Elisabeth Speiser** sings powerfully but has an edge on her voice, less noticeable on video than on the Erato CD. As Amor, **Elizabeth Gale** sings brightly, seemingly unhampered by being suspended at a height, pantomime-wise, throughout the opera. The **Glyndebourne Chorus** sings with superb attack.

Orfeo ed Euridice (complete; CD versions)

Ⓜ *** EMI 2165779 (2). Hendricks, Von Otter, Fournier, Monteverdi Ch., Lyon Op. O, Gardiner

Ⓜ *** Erato 2292 45864-2 (2). J. Baker, Speiser, Gale, Glyndebourne Ch., LPO, Leppard

*** Teldec 4509 98418-2 (2). Larmore, Upshaw, Hagley, San Francisco Op. Ch. & O, Runnicles

EMI have reissued **Gardiner's** earlier recording of the Berlioz edition of Gluck's opera, sung in French. It is now at mid-price and many will be glad to have this set, which aimed at combining the best of both the Vienna and Paris versions, although he omits the celebratory ballet at the end of the opera. **Anne Sofie von Otter** is a superb Orphée; and both **Barbara Hendricks** as Euridice and **Brigitte Fournier** as Amour are also excellent. The chorus is Gardiner's own **Monteverdi Choir**, superbly clean and stylish, and the recording is full and well balanced.

Leppard presents the score with freshness and power, indeed with toughness. Nowhere is that clearer than in the great scene leading up to the aria, *Che farò*, where Baker commandingly conveys the genuine bitterness and anger of Orpheus at Eurydice's death. **Elisabeth Speiser** as Eurydice and **Elizabeth Gale** as Amor are both disappointing but, as in the theatre, the result is a complete and moving experience centring round a great performance from Dame Janet. The complete ballet-postlude is included, delightful celebration music. The recording has been enhanced in the CD transfer, bright and vivid without edginess, and there is an excellent (74-minute) budget CD of highlights, including the Ballet Music, on Apex (2564 61497-2).

Donald Runnicles also conducts a performance based on the 1869 Berlioz edition, generally adopting speeds a degree broader than those preferred by Gardiner in his EMI set, and with a smoother style. **Jennifer Larmore** makes a strong and positive Orphée, brilliant in the aria which in this edition ends Act I, rich and warm in rather broad treatment of the big aria, *J'ai perdu mon Eurydice*. Next to Von Otter for Gardiner she sounds very feminine, and not quite as flexible. **Dawn Upshaw** is a charming Eurydice, and **Alison Hagley** a sweet-toned Amour, though she is balanced very backwardly, as is the chorus at times in what is otherwise a good recording. Unlike Gardiner, but like Leppard on Erato, Runnicles includes ballet music at the end.

Using the original Italian text of the first Vienna version of 1762, **Östman's** Naxos version offers a refreshingly robust account using period forces, recorded live in the beautiful Drottningholm Theatre near Stockholm. Without any of the extra items that Gluck composed for Paris, the result fits neatly on a single CD, which, unlike many bargain opera issues, includes a complete libretto and translation. The performance has its uneven moments, but all three soloists have fresh, clear voices, with the warm mezzo, **Ann-Christine Biel**, sustaining the title-role well, even if she is not specially characterful. Clear, undistracting sound. Not a first choice, but well worth having. (Naxos 8.660064)

Orphée et Eurydice (1774, Paris version)

🔊 ⒷⒷ *** Naxos 8.660185/86 (2). Fouchécourt, Dubose, Le Blanc, Lafayette Ch. & O, Brown

Ryan Brown's set, recorded at the University of Maryland in 2002, uses the 1774 Paris version of the score, with a tenor in the title-role. Lightness is the keynote of the whole performance, with rhythms crisp, textures sparklingly clear, and speeds which never fall into heaviness or sentimentality, flowing easily. Not only that, Brown has the great advantage of having in the title-role one of the finest tenors in the French 18th-century tradition, **Jean-Paul Fouchécourt**. Having too few tracks is one of the very few flaws in an outstandingly stylish set, with **Catherine Dubosc** as Eurydice and **Suzie Le Blanc** as Amour, both sweet-toned but nicely contrasted, as with Fouchécourt benefiting from being native French-speakers. Though the 1774 text is complete, Brown omits the ballet music at the end, pointing out in his excellent note that Gluck drew it largely from other sources after the initial performances. Clear, fresh sound.

Paride ed Elena (complete)

🔊 *** DG 477 5415 (2). Kožená, Gritton, Sampson, Webster, Gabrieli Consort & Players, McCreesh

First heard in 1770, *Paride ed Elena* remains a masterpiece, as **Paul McCreesh** amply demonstrates in his starrily cast version with the **Gabrieli Consort and Players**. In the castrato role of Paris, **Magdalena Kožená** sings ravishingly, not least in the glorious finale of Act II, with comments not just from Helen (the excellent, characterful **Susan Gritton**) but from Cupid, here called Amore. **Carolyn Sampson** sings that role very sweetly, and **Gillian Webster** is well cast too as Pallas Athene, the goddess predicting doom at the end. This ideal set includes two versions of the final scene, the revised and shortened version as well as the published one. Beautifully balanced sound.

Arias from: Iphigénie en Tauride; Orphée et Eurydice; Paride ed Elena

*** Erato 8573 85768-2. Graham, OAE, Bicket – MOZART: *Arias* ***

Masterly as is **Susan Graham's** singing of Mozart, in a wide range of arias, her Gluck performances are if anything even more revelatory, making one of the outstanding recital discs of recent years. These are all characters that she has portrayed on stage, and the characterization and ease with French words could not be more compelling, particularly in the three contrasted *Iphigénie* arias. The voice is creamily beautiful, and though the best known of these items, Orpheus's *J'ai perdu mon Eurydice*, is on the slow side, Graham sustains her line flawlessly. Polished playing and well-balanced sound.

Arias: Orfeo ed Euridice: Che farò; Che puro ciel. Telemaco: Se per entro

*** Virgin 5 45365-2. Daniels, OAE, Bicket – MOZART; HANDEL: *Arias* ***

Even in a generation that has produced an extraordinary crop of fine counter-tenors, the American **David Daniels** stands out for the clear beauty and imagination of his singing. The best-known items here – the two principal solos from Gluck's *Orfeo* – are done with a tender expressiveness that matches any performance by a mezzo, with Daniels's natural timbre, at once pure and warm, completely avoiding counter-tenor hoot. Not only that, his placing of the voice is flawless, with the florid singing equally impressive in its brilliance and precision.

GODARD, Benjamin (1849–95)

(i) Concerto romantique for Violin & Orchestra, Op. 35; Violin Concerto 2, Op. 131; Scènes poétiques for Orchestra, Op. 46

(BB) *** Naxos 8.570554. Slovak State PO, Trevor, (i) with Hanslip

The *Violin Concerto No. 2* begins in a dramatic manner, though richly romantic melodies quickly take over. A brooding slow movement follows, followed by an exceptionally gay and vivacious finale – where the sprit of Offenbach enters. The much earlier *Concerto Romantique* has a lively, rustic quality which is very appealing, while the two slower central movements have much sentimental charm. The finale begins dramatically with the orchestra, but the violin enters, contrastingly, and the work ends brilliantly with a riot of double-stops and the like from the soloist. The *Scènes poétiques* are four bucolic movements depicting outdoor scenes. They are delightfully picturesque, in the manner of Massenet's *Scènes* for orchestra. Whilst none of the music on this CD is especially deep, or even great music, it is all thoroughly entertaining and tuneful, made all the more enjoyable when so persuasively presented. Well worth the asking price.

GOEDICKE, Alexander (1877–1957)

Concertstück in D (for piano and orchestra), Op. 11

**(*) Hyp. CDA 66877. Coombs, BBC Scottish SO, Brabbins – GLAZUNOV: *Piano Concertos 1 & 2* **(*)

Alexander Goedicke's *Concertstück* is far from negligible, both in its melodic invention and in its musical structure. **Stephen Coombs** is a brilliant and sympathetic interpreter of this music and the **BBC Scottish Symphony Orchestra** under **Martyn Brabbins** give every support. The recording is too reverberant – and this perhaps inhibits a full three-star recommendation.

GOEHR, Alexander (born 1932)

(i) Little Symphony; (ii) PianoTrio; (iii) String Quartet 2

(N) *** Lyrita (ADD) SRCD 264. (i) LSO, Mar; (ii) Orion Trio; (iii) Allegri Qt

The *Piano Trio* and *String Quartet* – two powerful and individual works - were originally released on Argo in 1973, and the quality of the performances readily communicates their distinction to any open-minded listener. The *Quartet*, written for Lord Dyvenor in 1967, is the tougher and more challenging work, but the serene finale has obvious links with late Beethoven. The *Trio*, written for the Menuhins at Bath in 1966, is rather less introspective, with dance rhythms and bell effects prominent. The *Little Symphony* (originally released on Philips in 1965) is 'little' only in the forces required. Each strand tends to be thought of as a solo, and the result is a virtuoso piece for any orchestra, lasting well over half an hour. In keeping with so many composers at that time who relied on twelve-note techniques, Goehr seems to be reluctant to let his powers of invention have full freedom. **Norman Del Mar** conducted the first performance at the York Festival, and the **LSO** responds here magnificently. The transferred sound is very good indeed, though the 1973 recordings are even finer.

GOLDMARK, Karl (1830–1915)

Violin Concerto in A min., Op. 28

🎵 ❀ *** Delos DE 3156. Hu, Seattle SO, Schwarz – BRUCH: *Violin Concerto 2* ***

(BB) *** Naxos 8.553579. Tsu, Razumovsky Sinfonia, Yu Long – KORNGOLD: *Violin Concerto* ***

(M) *** EMI 5 09676-2. Perlman, Pittsburgh SO, Previn – KORNGOLD: *Violin Concerto*; SINDING: *Suite in A min.* ***

The Taiwanese soloist **Nai-Yuan Hu** (pronounced Nigh-Yen Who) makes an outstanding début on CD with a coupling of two underrated concertos which on his responsively lyrical bow are made to sound like undiscovered masterpieces. The Goldmark is a tuneful and warm-hearted concerto that needs just this kind of songful, inspirational approach: Hu shapes the melodies so that they ravishingly take wing and soar. Moreover, **Schwarz** and the **Seattle Orchestra** share a real partnership with their soloist and provide a full, detailed backcloth in a natural concert-hall framework.

Vera Tsu is another outstanding soloist. Her tone is rich, bringing out to the full the ripe romanticism of the Goldmark *Concerto*. Her attack is fearless in the many bravura passages, so that the dance rhythms of the dance-finale have a rare sparkle, and her hushed playing in the central slow movement at a very broad speed movingly demonstrates her inner concentration, helped by the equally beautiful, finely varied playing of the **Razumovsky Sinfonia** of Bratislava. Rich, full, open sound.

Goldmark's attractive concerto is also beautifully played by **Itzhak Perlman**, whose effortless virtuosity and lyrical pulse challenge all-comers. He is balanced very much in the foreground, but the sound-quality is fresh and **Previn** accompanies sympathetically. This is very charming and likeable music and Perlman plays it most winningly. Moreover, with his new coupling he includes the attractive Sinding *Suite*.

Rustic Wedding Symphony, Op. 26

(B) **(*) Decca Eloquence 476 8743. LAPO, López-Cobos –
GRIEG: Symphony ***

Rustic Wedding Symphony, Op. 26; Overtures: In Italy, Op. 49; In the Spring, Op. 36

(BB) **(*) Naxos 8.550745. Nat. SO of Ireland, Gunzenhauser

Rustic Wedding Symphony, Op. 26; Sakuntala Overture, Op. 13

*** ASV CDDCA 791. RPO, Butt

Yondani Butt and the RPO clearly enjoy themselves. The recording has brightly lit violins, but plenty of bloom on the woodwind, and the only miscalculation of balance concerns the trombone entry in the first movement, which is too blatant and too loud. Otherwise this is in every way enjoyable. The Overture Sakuntala opens impressively but does not quite sustain its 18 minutes. Butt presents it with persuasive vigour and lyrical feeling, and does not shirk the melodrama.

López-Cobos directs a refreshing and attractively spirited reading. As with Gunzenhauser, below, his generally fast tempi detract somewhat from the charm of the piece, but the wide-ranging sound, which presents the Los Angeles orchestra untypically at a distance, means that this is a more than acceptable bargain coupling for the rare Grieg Symphony.

Gunzenhauser gives a fresh, bright-eyed account. He takes both the opening movement and the Andante (In the Garden) appreciably faster than does Butt, and he loses something in poise and spacious eloquence in consequence. But the overall performance is spontaneous and enjoyable. It is well recorded and, although the violins sound thin, that is almost certainly not the fault of the engineers. Of the two jaunty overtures, In Italy is especially vivacious and sparkling.

Symphony 2 in E, Op. 35; In Italy Overture, Op. 49; Prometheus Bound, Op. 38

*** ASV CDDCA 934. Philh. O, Butt

Goldmark's Second Symphony is a highly confident piece with a strong opening movement, an ambivalent but appealing Andante, a vivaciously delicate Scherzo which is Mendelssohn undiluted, and a characteristically folksy, dance-like finale. Yondani Butt has the work's full measure. The Lisztian Prometheus Bound on the other hand is overlong and melodramatic, and the main Allegro is routine in its working out. Yet it has some winning lyrical ideas and Butt does his very best for it. The Italian Overture is genuinely vivacious, though not especially Italianate: it has a rather beautiful nocturnal sequence as a central episode. The ASV recording is in every way excellent.

String Quartet in B flat, Op. 8; (i) String Quintet in A min., Op. 9

**(*) ASV CDDCA 1071. Fourth Dimension String Qt, (i) with Smith

Goldmark's String Quartet in B flat is a fluent, beautifully fashioned piece, very much in the Schumann and Mendelssohn tradition, though one is in no doubt that the musical argument is guided by a sense of purpose. The String Quintet is an even stronger piece, sure in its feeling for musical movement and with some good ideas. The Fourth Dimension String Quartet makes its début, with David Smith as the second cello in the Quintet. Decent performances, though the tonal blend leaves something to be desired, and one would welcome greater richness of timbre.

GOODALL, Howard (born 1958)

Missa Aedis Christi; Ecce Homo; In Memoriam Anne Frank; Marlborough Canticles; Psalm 23; They were not here

(N) *** Universal 476 3331. Christ Church Cathedral Ch., Oxford, Darlington; String Quartet, David Goode (organ)

Requiem (Eternal Light); Love Divine; Psalm 23; Spared

(N) **(*) EMI 215047-2. Marsh, Boe Maltman, Christ Church Cathedral Ch., Oxford, Darlington

Howard Goodall really came to the fore when his catchy setting of Psalm 23 was used for the remarkably successful 'Vicar of Dibley' TV series. He has also contributed Ecce Homo to 'Mr Bean'. He writes in an easy, flowing, melodic style, which many enjoy and others find a trifle bland. Yet his In Memoriam Anne Frank has a plangent climax and They were not here is a rather striking setting of a poem by David Geraint Jones commemorating VE Day in Europe. The Missa Aedis Christi has many telling moments too, not least the echo effects in the Sanctus, while the closing Nunc Dimittis from the Marlborough Canticles is richly expansive. The Christ Church performances are committed and eloquent, and very well recorded, so if you are intrigued to find more music like the Vicar of Dibley theme, this CD will meet that need admirably.

The Requiem (Eternal Light) is even more eclectic, unashamedly drawing on a variety of popular styles, the opening Kyrie and the Agnus Dei (which could easily become another Goodall hit) both contemporary-romantic in different ways, while the second section (Revelation – Factum est silentium) even has a flavour of Carl Orff. The hymn Lead kindly light is attractively upbeat, and the closing In Paradisum is unexpectedly full-throated and passionate, and brings another striking melody. There is no doubt that, whatever one's preconceptions, all this music communicates, and Goodall's ready tunefulness underpins his great skill in vocal writing, while there are many imaginative touches in the simple accompaniments. The Requiem is followed by Love Divine, a luscious hymn setting, and the 23rd Psalm returns (in the performance used on TV) before the final haunting Spared, a poignant setting of a poem by Wendy Cope, recalling the experience of the telephone farewell by a separated couple in New York on 9/11. Throughout these fine Oxford performances, the sincerity of Howard Goodall's writing shines through. It may at times be simplistic but is far preferable to atonal, barbed-wire music. The recording is excellent.

GÓRECKI, Henryk
(born 1933)

(i) Harpsichord Concerto; (ii) Little Requiem for a Polka (Kleines Requiem für eine Polka); (iii) Good Night (In Memoriam Michael Vyner) for soprano, alto flute, 3 tam-tams and piano

*** None. 7559 79362-2. L. Sinf.; (i) Zinman; (ii) Chojnacka, cond. Stenz; (iii) Upshaw, Bell, Constable, Hockings

The *Little Requiem* (1993) opens with a single quiet bell-stroke; a piano (**John Constable**) then engages in a tranquil dialogue with the violins, to be rudely interrupted by a burst of bell-ringing; the energetic, marcato *Allegro impetuoso* follows. The piece ends with a raptly sustained elegiac *Adagio*, still dominated by the quietly assertive tolling bells. The two-movement *Harpsichord Concerto*, written a decade earlier, combines soloist and strings in a vibrant, jangly ménage. *Good Night* is nocturnally serene. The soprano voice enters only in the third movement, with a cantilena to Shakespeare's words from *Hamlet*: 'Good night ... and flights of angels sing thee to thy rest!' Both here and in the *Little Requiem* the very atmospheric recording brings an added dimension to the communication from performers who are obviously totally committed to the composer's cause.

Symphony 3 (Symphony of Sorrowful Songs), Op. 36

*** None. 7559 79282-2. Upshaw, L. Sinf., Zinman

*** Australian ABC Classics 472 040-2. Kenny, Adelaide SO, Yuasa

Symphony 3 (Symphony of Sorrowful Songs), Op. 36; 3 Pieces in the Olden Style

⊕→ (BB) *** Naxos 8.550822. Kilanowicz, Polish Nat. RSO, Wit

Scored for strings and piano with soprano solo in each of the three movements, all predominantly slow, Górecki's *Symphony 3* sets three laments taking the theme of motherhood. The **London Sinfonietta's** fine performance, beautifully recorded, is crowned by the radiant singing of **Dawn Upshaw**.

Zofia **Kilanowicz** on Naxos has also obviously become immersed in the word-settings. In the work's closing section, with its hint of a gentle but remorseless tolling bell, **Wit** achieves a mood of simple serenity, even forgiveness. The *Three Pieces in Olden Style* make a fine postlude, the second with its dance figurations, the third with its fierce tremolando violins, like shafts of bright light, suddenly resolving to a very positive ending. All in all, this seems in many ways a 'best buy'.

Despite its several predecessors, this Australian recording of Górecki's *Third Symphony* finds new things to say. **Yvonne Kenny** treats the work almost like an opera, comprising three very distinct dramatic soliloquies and she is well supported by the **Adelaide Symphony Orchestra**. However, there is no coupling, whereas the fine Naxos version includes also the *Three Pieces in the Olden Style*.

VOCAL MUSIC

(i) Good Night (Requiem for soprano, alto flute, 3 tam-tams and piano), Op. 63; (ii) Little Requiem for a Polka (for piano & 13 instruments), Op. 64; 3 Pieces in Old Style for Strings

*** Telarc CD 80417. I Flamminghi, Werther; with (i) Szmytra, Edmund-Davis, Righarts; (ii) Gleizes

Górecki's *Requiem* was written for and dedicated to Michael Vyner. He died in 1989, and Górecki immediately set about writing this simple valedictory piece for solo soprano, darkly resonant alto flute and, in the epilogue, three tam-tams (gongs of indefinite pitch), played very gently indeed. The quotation in the title is from Shakespeare's *Hamlet* – 'Good night ... flights of angels sing thee to thy rest' – and the work's prevailing elegiac quietness has much in common with the *Little Requiem*, written three years later. The *Three Pieces in Old Style* make a perfect foil and are beautifully played by this excellent group under **Roldof Werther**. Needless to say, the Telarc recording is in the demonstration bracket.

(i) Miserere, Op. 44; Amen, Op. 35; Euntes ibant et flebant, Op. 32; (ii) Wuslo moja (My Vistula, Grey Vistula), Op. 46; Szeroka woda (Broad Waters): Choral Suite of Folksongs, Op. 39 (Oh, our River Narew; Oh, when in Powistle; Oh, Johnny, Johnny; She picked wild roses; Broad waters)

*** None. 7559 79348-2. (i) Chicago Symphony Ch. & Lyric Op. Ch., Nelson; (ii) Lyra Chamber Ch., Ding

Górecki's powerful *Miserere* was prompted by the political upheaval in Poland in 1981. The combined **Chicago** choirs maintain the sombrely atmospheric opening *pianissimo* with impressive concentration, and the dynamic climax of the piece, when they sing in 10 parts, is very compelling. The following *Euntes ibant et flebant* (for unaccompanied chorus) is simpler, more serene. The five folksong settings are also essentially expressive (even *Oh, Johnny, Johnny* is marked *Molto lento – dolce cantabile*) and all are harmonically rich. They are beautifully sung by the smaller group. The recording, made in the Church of St Mary of the Angels in Chicago, is admirable.

GOTTSCHALK, Louis
(1829–69)

(i) La Casa del Joven Enrique por Méhul – Gran overture; (ii) Célèbre tarentelle pour piano & orchestre; Symphonies 1 (Romantique); 2 (A Montevideo); (ii) Variations de concert sur l'hymne portugais du Roi Louis; (iii) Ave Maria; (iv) Escenas Campestres Cubanas – Opéra en 1 acte

(BB) **(*) Naxos 8.559320. Hot Springs Festival O, Rosenberg, with (i) John & Richard Contiguglia, Draghícescu, Lin, Pepper; (ii) Gurt; (iii) Barrick; (iv) Noggle, Taylor, Ziebarth

A very appealing disc of Gottschalk's attractive orchestral music, much of it available (in these versions) for the first time. As the sleeve-note writer says, in his *Escenas Campestres*

Cubanas (Cuban Country Scenes), Gottschalk 'combines high art, populist sensibilities and mass appeal'. The music is tuneful and catchy, even if the singing is rather wild. **Melissa Barrick** sounds like a boy treble in the *Ave Maria*.

PIANO MUSIC

Complete solo piano music: 'An American Composer, bon Dieu!'

Vol. 1 *** Hyp. CDA 66459.; Vol. 2 Hyp. CDA 66697.; Vol. 3 Hyp. CDA 66915.; Vol. 4 Hyp. CDA 67118.; Vol. 5 Hyp. CDA 67248.; Vol. 6 Hyp. CDA 67349.; Vol. 7 Hyp. CDA 67478.; Vol. 8 Hyp. CDA 67536. Philip Martin

Gottschalk invented the conception of the composer/recitalist in America, just as Liszt had in Europe. As a touring virtuoso he had great audience appeal, and if his music is lightweight it is well crafted and tuneful, paying homage to both Liszt and Chopin. Its exotic folk-influences are drawn colloquially and naturally from the Deep South, with syncopated rhythms the strongest feature.

   Philip Martin's complete survey on Hyperion is in every way distinguished. He is naturally sympathetic to the transatlantic idioms, yet he treats the music as part of the romantic mainstream, bringing out its various derivations. He plays with elegance, brilliance, style and, above all, spontaneity. He is very well recorded in an ideal acoustic.

Bamboula; Le Banjo; Le Bananier; The Dying Poet; L'Etincelle; La Gallina; La jota aragonesa; Manchega; Pasquinade; La Savane; Souvenirs d'Andalousie; Souvenir de Porto Rico, Marche des Gibarois; Suis-moi!; Tremolo; Tournament Galop; The Union: Paraphrase de Concert on the national airs, Star-Spangled Banner, Yankee Doodle and Hail Columbia

🎧 (BB) *** Naxos 8.559145. Licad

If you want a single representative disc of Gottshalk's music, this is it. **Cecile Licad** is right inside this repertoire. She obviously enjoys every bar and conveys her enthusiam to us, playing with character, polish and rhythmic gusto. *Le Banjo*, which opens the programme, has great zest, *Bamboula* (the 'Danse de nègres') thumps vigorously, and the *Tournament Galop* chases along with infectuous bravura. Yet *Le Bananier* has an almost sinuous charm and *La Savane* is played with winning delicacy. Even *The Dying Poet* is made to sound delicate rather than too overtly sentimental, partly because here, as elsewhere, Licad's rubato is naturally spontaneous. The programme closes with the spectacular *Union Paraphase*, presented with genuine bravdo. Very well recorded, this disc is irresistible.

GOUGH, John (1903–51)

Serenade for Small Orchestra

*** Chan. 9757. BBC PO, Handley – BAINTON: *Symphony 2 in D min.*; CLIFFORD: *Symphony* ***

The short but charming *Serenade for Small Orchestra* reveals a genuine creative talent and was written in 1931 for Hubert Clifford's wedding. Exemplary playing and first-rate recorded sound.

GOULD, Morton (1913–96)

Fall River Legend (ballet; complete)

🎧 *** Albany TROY 035. Peters, Nat. PO, Rosenstock (with recorded conversation between Agnes de Mille and Morton Gould)

This complete recording of *Fall River Legend* opens dramatically with the Speaker for the Jury reading out the Indictment at the trial, and then the ballet tells the story of Lizzie Borden in flashback. Gould's music has a good deal in common with the folksy writing in Copland's *Appalachian Spring*, and it is given a splendidly atmospheric performance and recording by the **New York orchestra** under **Rosenstock**. There is also a 26-minute discussion on the creation of the ballet between Agnes de Mille and the composer.

2 Marches for Orchestra

(M) (***) Cala mono CACD 0526. NBC SO, Stokowski – DEBUSSY: *Prélude à l'après-midi d'un faune*, etc. (**(*)); HOLST: *Planets* (***)

These two stirring wartime marches were 'written in tribute to two of our gallant allies': the first is Chinese in character (complete with marching effects), the second colourfully employs two Red Army songs. An enjoyable end to a fascinating **Stokowski** disc; and the sound, emanating from an NBC broadcast from March 1943, is fully acceptable.

Symphony 3

**(*) Albany SACD TROY 515. Albany SO, Miller – HARRIS: *Symphony 2* **(*)

Morton Gould proves to be a symphonist of quality, though his musical personality is too indebted to Stravinsky, Copland, Roy Harris and William Schuman for a distinctive and individual voice to be discerned. But there is an engaging vigour and a keen feeling for the cut-and-thrust of the musical argument. Decent, well-characterized playing, though the strings could perhaps have greater richness of sonority.

GOUNOD, Charles (1818–93)

Faust: Ballet music

(B) *** Australian Decca Eloquence (ADD) 476 2724. ROHCG O, Solti – OFFENBACH: *Gaîté Parisienne* ***; RESPIGHI: *Rossiniana* **(*)

Solti's 1959 account of the *Faust* ballet music is undoubtedly one of the liveliest (and most vividly recorded) versions committed to disc. While Beecham *et al.* have offered more elegance in this repertoire, no one beats Solti for sheer energy; he has a style all his own, and the final *Entrée de Phryné* almost goes off the rails with its hard-driven but exciting brilliance.

Symphonies 1 in D; 2 in E flat

☐—*** ASV CDDCA 981. O of St John's, Smith Square, Lubbock

The beautifully sprung and subtly phrased performances from **John Lubbock** and the **Orchestra of St John's** bring out the charm of these delightful symphonies. Lubbock's care for detail and the refreshingly polished playing is matched by a pervading warmth. We hope ASV will decide to reissue the Gounod pairing on their bargain label, when it would again be fully competitive.

Petite symphonie in B flat (for 9 wind instruments)

☐—Ⓜ *** Chan. (ADD) 6543. Athena Ens. – IBERT: 3 *Pièces brèves*; POULENC: *Sextet ****

An astonishingly fresh and youthful work, the *Petite symphonie* in fact has impeccable craftsmanship and is witty and civilized. It makes ideal listening at the end of the day, and its charm is irresistible in a performance as full of *joie de vivre* as that provided by the **Athena** group, who are particularly light-hearted in the finale.

Mélodies and songs

*** Hyp. CDA 66801/2. Lott, Murray, Rolfe Johnson, Johnson

Graham Johnson here devises an enchanting programme of 41 songs, presenting the full span of Gounod's achievement not just in French *mélodie* (on the first of the two discs) but also in songs Gounod wrote during his extended stay in England. The soloists here are at their very finest. So on the first disc, after charming performances of the opening items from **Felicity Lott**, **Ann Murray** enters magically, totally transforming the hackneyed lines of *Ave Maria*, before tackling the most joyous of Gounod songs, the barcarolle-like *Sérénade*. **Anthony Rolfe Johnson** is comparably perceptive in *Biondina*, bringing out the Neapolitan-song overtones, as well as in six of the English settings. As in the Schubert series, Johnson's notes are a model of scholarship, both informed and fascinating.

Messe Chorale

ⒷⒷ *** Warner Apex 8573 89235-2. Lausanne Vocal Ens., Corboz; Alain (organ) – SAINT-SAËNS: *Mass ***(*)*

Gounod's *Messe Chorale*, an early work, could not be more different from his *Messe solennelle de Sainte-Cécile*. Drawing on the 18th-century tradition of French organ Mass, it intersperses choral sections with organ interludes, all based on the chosen Gregorian theme which acts as a leitmotif, reaching an expressive peak in the *Hosanna in excelsis* of the *Sanctus*. Gounod's setting has an endearing simplicity, and it is beautifully sung and recorded here under **Michel Corboz**, with **Marie-Claire Alain** making a splendid foil for the choir on the magnificent organ of Lausanne Cathedral.

Messe solennelle de Sainte-Cécile

*** EMI 7 47094-2. Hendricks, Dale, Lafont, Ch. and Nouvel O Philharmonique of R. France, Prêtre

Ⓜ *** DG 477 7114. Seefried, Soltze, Uhde, Czech Ch. & PO, Markevitch

Gounod's *Messe solennelle*, with its blatant march setting of the *Credo* and sugar-sweet choral writing, may not be for sensitive souls, but **Prêtre** here directs an almost ideal performance, vividly recorded, with glowing singing from the choir as well as the three soloists. However this is still at premium price.

Reissued in DG's Originals series, **Markevitch's** vintage version, recorded in the mid-1960s, still sounds remarkably well. In his straight-faced way Markevitch makes the incongruity of Gounod's jolly and vulgar tunes all the more delectable; soloists, chorus and orchestra are all first rate. A good alternative to Prêtre's more modern EMI account.

Faust (complete)

☐—✿ *** Teldec 4509 90872-2 (3). Hadley, Gasdia, Ramey, Mentzer, Agache, Fassbaender, Welsh Nat. Op. Ch. & O, Rizzi

*** EMI 5 56224-2 (3). Leech, Studer, Van Dam, Hampson, Ch. & O of Capitole de Toulouse, Plasson

Ⓜ **(*) EMI (ADD) 5 67967-2 (3) [5 67975-2]. De los Angeles, Gedda, Blanc, Christoff, Paris Nat. Op. Ch. & O, Cluytens

Ⓜ **(*) Ph. 475 7769 (3). Te Kanawa, Araiza, Nesterenko, Schmidt, Coburn, Bav. R. Ch. & SO, C. Davis

ⒷⒷ (***) Naxos mono 8.111083/85 (3). Bjoerling, Kirsten, Siepi, Met. Op. Ch. and O, Cleva (Appendix: Bjoerling: SCHUBERT: *Ständchen*; SIBELIUS: *Var det en dröm?*; *Svarta rosor*; *Säv, saäv, susa*; HERBERT: *Princess Pat: Neapolitan Love Song*. Excerpts from: PUCCINI: *La Bohème* (with Anna-Lisa Bjoerling); GOUNOD: *Roméo et Juliette*; DONIZETTI: *L'elisir d'amore*; MASCAGNI: *Cavalleria rusticana*; WAGNER: *Lohengrin*)

Rizzi, with an outstanding cast and vividly clear recording, makes the whole score seem totally fresh and new. **Jerry Hadley** as Faust has lyrical freshness rather than heroic power, brought out in his headily beautiful performance of *Salut! demeure* and, like Rizzi's conducting, his singing has more light and shade in it than that of rivals. The tenderness as well as the bright agility of **Cecilia Gasdia's** singing as Marguerite brings comparable variety of expression, with the *Roi de Thulé* song deliberately drained of colour to contrast with the brilliance of the *Jewel Song* which follows. Her performance culminates in an angelic contribution to the final duet, with Rizzi's slow speed encouraging refinement, leading up to a shattering moment of judgement and a fine apotheosis. **Alexander Agache** as Valentin may be less characterful than Hampson on the EMI Toulouse set, but his voice is caught more richly; but it is the commandingly demonic performance of **Samuel Ramey** as Mephistopheles that sets the seal on the whole set, far more sinister than José van Dam on EMI. Like that EMI set, the Teldec offers a valuable appendix, not just the full ballet music but numbers cut from the definitive score – a drinking song for Faust and a charming aria for Siebel. EMI's supplementary items, four, all different, are more generous but musically less interesting.

On EMI, **Plasson** comes near to providing another recommendable *Faust*, even if **José van Dam's** gloriously dark, finely focused bass-baritone does not have the heft of a full-blooded bass voice such as is associated with the role of Mephistopheles. **Cheryl Studer** conveys the girlishness of Marguerite, using the widest range of dynamic and colour. If **Richard Leech's** voice might in principle seem too light-weight for the role of Faust, the lyrical flow and absence of strain make his singing consistently enjoyable. As Valentin, **Thomas Hampson** is strongly cast, with his firm, heroic baritone. The sound has a good sense of presence, set in a pleasantly reverberant acoustic which does not obscure necessary detail. In addition to supplementary numbers, the appendix offers the complete ballet music.

In the reissued **Cluytens** set, the seductiveness of **Victoria de los Angeles's** singing is a dream and it is a pity that the recording hardens the natural timbre slightly. **Christoff** is magnificently Mephistophelian. **Gedda**, though showing some signs of strain, sings intelligently, and among the other soloists **Ernest Blanc** has a pleasing, firm voice, which he uses to make Valentin into a sympathetic character. Cluytens's approach is competent but somewhat workaday. The set has been attractively repackaged and remastered to make a good mid-priced choice for this popular opera. There is a particularly generous set of highlights (75 minutes) on CfP 3 93376-2.

Davis's *Faust* may not always be idiomatic but, with fine singing from most of the principals, it is a refreshing version. **Dame Kiri**, more than you might expect, makes a light and innocent-sounding Marguerite, with the *Jewel Song* made to sparkle in youthful eagerness, leaping off from a perfect trill. **Evgeni Nesterenko** as Mephistopheles is a fine, saturnine tempter. **Andreas Schmidt** as Valentin sings cleanly and tastefully in a rather German way, while **Pamela Coburn** as Siebel is sweet and boyish. The big snag is the Faust of **Francisco Araiza**, a disappointing hero, with a voice, as recorded, gritty in tone and frequently strained. He underlines the simple melody of *Salut, demeure*, for example, far too heavily, not helped by a syrupy violin solo.

Taken from a Metropolitan Opera broadcast in 1950, the Naxos historical set offers a vividly dramatic performance under **Fausto Cleva** featuring three of the star singers of the time in a theatre sometimes dubbed the *Faustspielhaus*. **Jussi Bjoerling** as Faust is in ringing voice, full-bloodedly caught at full throttle, firm and clear. **Cesare Siepi**, a pillar of the Met., sings magnificently as Mephistopheles, happier in French than most Italian singers, while **Dorothy Kirsten** makes a clear, firm Marguerite, fresh and forthright rather than charming. The voices come over superbly, and one quickly adjusts to the limited orchestral sound. Exceptionally, the ballet music is included in Act IV, and as a supplement on the third disc there are arias and songs from Schubert and Wagner to Sibelius and Victor Herbert, recorded by Bjoerling in American and Swedish broadcasts.

Faust (complete; in English)

⊕─Ⓜ *** Chan. 3014 (3). Clarke, Plazas, Miles, Magee, Montague, Walker, Geoffrey Mitchell Ch., Philh. O, Parry

Faust, in a good English translation by Christopher Cowell, works brilliantly. The dramatic intensity is consistently heightened by **David Parry's** lively conducting, with the music paced to bring out the full impact of the big climaxes,

and with freshness and sparkle given to such familiar numbers as the *Soldiers' Chorus*. The chorus is electrifying, and the cast of principals is first rate. **Paul Charles Clarke** sings strongly in the title-role (if not always sweetly), well experienced from appearing in the Welsh National Opera production. **Alastair Miles**, who also sang with WNO, is outstanding in every way as Mephistopheles, dark, firm and incisive, if not always sinister. **Mary Plazas** brings out the girlish innocence in Marguerite, sweet and pure, making light of the vocal challenges, above all giving joy to the *Jewel Song*. With singers as characterful as **Diana Montague** and **Sarah Walker** in smaller roles, this is one of the finest issues yet in the excellent 'Opera in English' series promoted by the Peter Moores Foundation. The third disc includes the complete ballet music as a supplement.

Roméo et Juliette (complete)

⊕─Ⓜ **** EMI 3 58624-2. Alagna, Gheorghiu, Vallejo, Van Dam, Keenlyside, Capitole de Toulouse Ch. & O, Plasson

With **Gheorghiu** and **Alagna** inspired as the lovers, the EMI **Toulouse** set offers the finest performance on disc yet, in almost every way. Gheorghiu does not just sing sweetly, without strain, the subtlety of her expression and her ability to rise to the demands of tragedy set her apart, and Alagna – who made such an impact in this role at Covent Garden early in his career – is youthfully ardent and unstrained. The rest of the cast is generally excellent too, with **José van Dam** as Frère Laurent and **Simon Keenlyside** as Mercutio both outstanding, though **Marie-Ange Todorovitch**, bright and agile as Stephano, is rather shrill. Given absolutely complete with the Act IV ballet music (not a dramatic gain) the set takes three discs instead of two, but is well worth it. Warm, atmospheric sound.

GRAINGER, Percy (1882–1961)

Blithe Bells; Colonial Song; English Dance; Duke of Marlborough's Fanfare; Fisher's Boarding House; Green Bushes; Harvest Hymn; In a Nutshell (Suite); Shepherd's Hey; There Were Three Friends; Walking Tune (symphonic wind band version); We Were Dreamers

*** Chan. 9493. BBC PO, Hickox

Hickox is masterly here, with rhythms always resilient, both in bringing out the freshness of well-known numbers like *Shepherd's Hey* and in presenting the originality and charm of such little-known numbers as *Walking Tune*. The **BBC Philharmonic** is in superb form, warmly and atmospherically recorded. By far the longest item is the suite, *In a Nutshell*, which includes pieces like the *Arrival Platform Humlet*, well known on their own, and which has as its core a powerful and elaborate piece, *Pastoral*, which with its disturbing undertow belies its title.

Blithe Bells (Free Ramble on a Theme by Bach: Sheep may safely graze); Country Gardens; Green Bushes (Passacaglia); Handel in the Strand; Mock Morris; Molly on the Shore; My Robin is to the

Greenwood Gone; Shepherd's Hey; Spoon River; Walking Tune; Youthful Rapture

🎵 Ⓜ *** Chan. 6542. Bournemouth Sinf., Montgomery

For those wanting only a single Grainger orchestral collection, this could be first choice. Among the expressive pieces, the arrangement of *My Robin is to the Greenwood Gone* is highly attractive, but the cello solo in *Youthful Rapture* is perhaps less effective. Favourites such as *Country Gardens, Shepherd's Hey, Molly on the Shore* and *Handel in the Strand* all sound as fresh as new paint. The 1978 recording, made in Christchurch Priory, has retained all its ambient character in its CD transfer.

Irish Tune from County Derry; Lincolnshire Posy (suite); Molly on the Shore; Shepherd's Hey

Ⓜ *** ASV (ADD) CDWHL 2067. L. Wind O, Wick –
MILHAUD; POULENC: *Suite française* ***

First-class playing and vivid recording, with the additional attraction of delightful couplings, make this very highly recommendable.

(i) Ye Banks and Braes o' Bonnie Doon; (ii) Colonial Song; Country Gardens; (i) The Gum-Suckers' March; Faeroe Island Dance; Hill Song 2; (ii) Irish Tune from County Derry; (i) The Lads of Wamphray March; (ii) Lincolnshire Posy; (i) The Merry King; Molly on the Shore; (ii) Shepherd's Hey

*** Chan. 9549. Royal N. College of Music Wind O, with (i) Rundell, (ii) Reynish

Even more than most issues in the Chandos Grainger series, this is a fun disc, with the brilliant young players of the **Royal Northern College** relishing the jaunty rhythms. Many of the pieces are well known in Grainger's alternative arrangements, but this version of Grainger's most popular piece, *Country Gardens*, is not just an arrangement of the piano version, but, as he explained himself, 'a new piece in every way'. The *Faeroe Island Dance* in this late band version of 1954 has a pivoting ostinato for horns that echoes the opening of Vaughan Williams's *Fifth Symphony*, before launching into the dance proper with echoes of *The Rite of Spring*.

PIANO MUSIC

Country Gardens; In a Nutshell (suite): Gay but Wistful; The Gum-Suckers' March; Jutish Medley; March-Jog (Maguire's Kick); Molly on the Shore; One More Day My John; Ramble on the Last Love-Duet from Strauss's 'Der Rosenkavalier'; Sheep and Goat Walkin' to the Pasture; Shepherd's Hey; Spoon River; Sussex Mummers' Christmas Carol; Turkey in the Straw; The Warriors. STANFORD: *Irish Dances*, arr. GRAINGER: *Leprechaun's Dance; A Reel*

🎵 *** Nim. NI 8809. Grainger (from Duo-Art piano rolls)

We have always been admirers of the Duo-Art player-piano recording system, and here **Grainger's** personality leaps out from between the speakers, yet the original rolls were cut between 1915 and 1929! It is good to have such a winningly

vigorous *Country Gardens* and such a characterful *Shepherd's Hey*, while *Sheep and Goat Walkin' to the Pasture* has rhythmical character of the kind that makes one smile. *Gay but Wistful* is neither – nonchalant, rather – but endearing. The lyrical numbers like the touching *Sussex Mummers' Christmas Carol*, *One More Day My John* and the lilting *Zanzibar Boat-Song* have a winningly relaxed flair, and Grainger makes his arrangement of the Richard Strauss love-duet from *Der Rosenkavalier* sound intimately luscious and deliciously idiomatic. The recording is first class.

Complete: 'Dished up for Piano', Volumes 1–5

Volume 1: Andante con moto; Bridal Lullaby; Children's March; Colonial Song; English Waltz; Handel in the Strand; Harvest Hymn; The Immovable 'Do'; In a Nutshell (Suite) (Arrival Platform Humlet; Gay but Wistful; The Gum-Suckers' March; Pastoral); In Dahomey; Mock Morris; Peace; Sailor's Song; Saxon Twi-Play; To a Nordic Princess; Walking Tune

Volume 2: Arrangements

Volume 3: Folksong arrangements

Volume 4: Arrangements

Volume 5: Arrangements: Original works for up to six hands

Ⓑ *** Nim. NI 5767 (5). Martin Jones (with McMahon; Martin)

Martin Jones's splendid Nimbus survey of Grainger's piano music is no longer available on separate CDs, but they do now come together in a slip-case at bargain price. The playing is refreshingly alive and spontaneous and splendidly secure technically, and the performances not only have panache but also readily convey the enjoyment of the participants. The pianos are recorded reverberantly in the Nimbus manner – but it rather suits this repertoire, and the image is absolutely truthful.

VOCAL MUSIC

Anchor song (setting of Rudyard Kipling); Thou gracious power (setting of Oliver Wendell Holmes); Arrangements of folksongs

*** Chan. 9499. Padmore, Varcoe, Joyful Company of Singers, City of L. Sinf., Hickox; Thwaites

In the darkly intense *Shallow Brown* **Hickox** has a clear advantage in opting for an excellent baritone soloist (**Stephen Varcoe**), with an equally fine choral ensemble. In Hickox's version of the *County Derry* (the 'Londonderry air') he has chosen an extended, elaborate setting. *Ye banks and braes* is another item given in a version previously unrecorded, with a whistled descant. Among the pieces completely new to disc are the *Marching tune* and *Early one morning*. Also most striking is the brief, keenly original choral piece, *The lonely desert-*

man sees the tents of the Happy Tribes, here given a dedicated performance, with the tenor intoning a theme from Grainger's orchestral piece, *The Warriors*, and the distant chorus chattering a chant borrowed from his *Tribute to Foster*.

(i) Bell Piece. Blithe Bells; (ii) Children's March; Hill Songs I & II; The Immovable 'Do'. Irish Tune from County Derry; Marching Song of Democracy; The Power of Rome and the Christian Heart

*** Chan. 9630. Royal N. College of Music Wind O, Reynish or Rundell; with (i) Gilchrist; (ii) vocal group from band

Where in their first collection (above) the splendid players of the **Royal Northern College of Music Wind Orchestra** clearly so enjoy Grainger's rhythmic buoyancy, here they equally relish his feeling for wind colour, as in the engaging *Hill Songs*, and rich sonorities, as in the powerful and remarkable *The Power of Rome and the Christian Heart*, and equally so in this characteristically imaginative arrangement of the *Londonderry Air* for band and pipe organ. *Bell Piece* (a 'ramble' on Dowland's melancholy air, *Now, O Now I Needs Must Part*) begins with a tenor solo with piano, before the wind players gently steal in. In the *Children's March* members of the band are invited twice to sing a vocalise when they are not playing. Altogether a fascinating and greatly enjoyable programme, strikingly well directed by **Timothy Reynish** and **Clark Rundell**.

The Crew of the Long Serpent; Danish Folk Song Suite; Kleine Variationen-Form; Stalt Vesselil (Proud Vesselil); To a Nordic Princess; (i) (Vocal) Dalvisa; Father and Daughter (Fadit og Dóttir); The Merry Wedding; The Rival Brothers; Song of Värmland; Under un Bro (Bridge)

*** Chan. 8721. Danish Nat. RSO, Hickox; (i) with Stephen, Reuter, Danish Nat. R. Ch.

From his earliest years Grainger was drawn to Scandinavian and Icelandic literature. This stimulating and rewarding collection centres on music directly influenced by his immersion in those cultures, all little known, except perhaps the *Danish Folk Song Suite*, with its highly exotic orchestration, winningly presented here. Among the other orchestral items the rollicking *Crew of the Long Serpent*, the colourful *Variations*, and the much more extended and lusciously scored *Tribute to a Nordic Princess* stand out. In the complex opening choral piece, *Father and Daughter*, a traditional Danish folk dance is mixed up with a theme of Grainger's own. The jolly, concerted *Merry Wedding* is sung in English: it draws on a folk poem for its text, but is musically original. *Dalvisa* is a delightful vocalise, using the same melody Alfvén featured as the centrepiece in his *Midsummer Rhapsody*. Splendid performances and top-class Chandos sound.

Bold William Taylor; Colonial song; The Bridegroom Grat; Died for love; Free music; Harvest hymn; Hubby and Wifey; The Land o' the Leal; Lisbon; Lord Maxwell's goodnight; Lord Peter's Stable-Boy; Molly on the Shore; The Nightingale; The old woman at the christening; The only son; The power of love; The shoemaker from Jerusalem; The

twa corbies; The two sisters; Walking tune; Willow willow; Ye Banks and Braes O' Bonnie Doon

**(*) Chan. 9819. D. Jones, Hill, Varcoe, ASMF Chamber Ens.

The present volume of the Chandos Grainger series is devoted to pieces (with or without vocal contributions) accompanied by various chamber ensembles. Grainger's scoring is as vividly captivating as ever, and never more so than in his arrangements of *Lisbon* and *Walking tune* (both for wind quintet), or in accompanying the delightful melody of *The shoemaker from Jerusalem* (with flute, trumpet, strings and piano (four hands)). Excellent recording, as usual from this source.

Duke of Marlborough Fanfare; Green Bushes (Passacaglia); Irish Tune from County Derry; Lisbon; Molly on the Shore; My Robin is to the Greenwood Gone; Shepherd's Hey; Piano Duet; Let's Dance Gay in Green Meadow. Vocal and Choral: Bold William Taylor; Brigg Fair; I'm Seventeen Come Sunday; Lord Maxwell's goodnight; The Lost Lady Found; The Pretty Maid Milkin' Her Cow; Scotch Strathspey and Reel; Shallow Brown; Shenandoah; The Sprig of Thyme; There Was a Pig Went Out to Dig; Willow Willow

🎵 *** Australian Decca Eloquence (ADD) 467 234-2. Pears, Shirley-Quirk, Amb. S. or Linden Singers, Wandsworth Boys' Ch., Britten or Bedford

This collection is one of the best single-disc anthologies of Grainger's music. The bulk of the collection derives from Britten's 1969 LP, and the sound in this transfer is extraordinarily full and vivid: indeed, the clarity of *There Was a Pig Went Out to Dig* has uncanny presence. It is altogether a delightful anthology, beautifully played and sung throughout. If Grainger's talent was smaller than his more fervent advocates would have us believe, his imagination in the art of arranging folksong was prodigious. The *Willow* song is a touching and indeed haunting piece and shows the quality of Grainger's harmonic resource. The *Duke of Marlborough Fanfare* is strikingly original, and so is *Shallow Brown*. Vocal and instrumental items are felicitously interwoven, and Decca's Australian team are to be congratulated in making this CD available.

GRAM, Peder (1881–1956)

Symphonies 2, Op. 25; 3, Op. 35; (i) Avalon, Op. 16

*** DaCapo 8.224718. (i) Andrea Pellegrini; Danish PO, Matthais Aeschbächer

Even for those with a keen interest in Danish music, Peder Gram is just a name among the younger contemporaries of Carl Nielsen. He was an influential figure and administrator in his day and ended up as the wartime head of music at Danish Radio. His pre-war *Second Symphony* caused something of a stir. though after its completion he felt that his creative fires were beginning to cool. And so, as a retirement present and to encourage him to continue to compose, his colleagues and friends gave him a sumptuously bound volume of scoring pages with the words *Symphony No. 3* handsomely engraved on the spine! Both symphonies are inventive and well worth recording and they encourage curiosity as to his other work. Eminently serviceable performances and recording.

GRANADOS, Enrique
(1867–1916)

(i) *Dante* (symphonic poem); *Goyescas: Intermezzo*; (ii) *La maja y el ruiseñor; 5 Piezas sobre cantos populares españolas* (arr. Ferrer)

*** ASV CDDCA 1110. Gran Canaria PO, Leaper; with (i) Herrera; (ii) Lucey

Dante is unexpectedly confident in its use of the orchestral palette. Granados evokes his narrative using luscious post-Wagnerian chromaticism and even introduces voluptuous hints of Scriabin and early Schoenberg. *Francesca's Story* is a straightforward setting of Canto V of Dante's poem, and here there are even hints of Puccini's *Madame Butterfly*. The vocal line is affectingly sung by **Nancy Herrera**, her fully coloured mezzo darkening the lower notes entreatingly. **Adrian Leaper** and the excellent **Gran Canaria Orchestra** play this remarkable score with languorous intensity. The enchanting highlight of *Goyescas*, *La maja y el ruiseñor*, is simply and beautifully sung by **Frances Lucey**, and the opera's *Intermezzo* follows vibrantly. Anselm Ferrer's orchestration of five of the *Piezas sobre cantos populares* skilfully re-creates the music orchestrally – sultry and sparkling by turns. They are most winningly and flexibly presented, to make an entertaining centrepiece in a first-class collection, atmospherically and vividly recorded.

12 *Danzas españolas* (orch. Ferrer)

☞ (BB) *** Naxos 8.555956. Barcelona SO & Catalonia Nat. O, Brotons

This overtly nationalistic music, using original tunes, has encouraged various composers to orchestrate them, of which this set by Rafael Ferrer is colourful and effective. The flutes and oscillating strings in No. 2 have a haunting atmosphere, and the delicacy of writing in the central sections of No. 5, flanked with its strong, brooding theme, is imaginative also. If, in its orchestral format, this is hardly the most subtle music, it is all colourful and enjoyable. The recording is vivid and bright, matching the performance, and this inexpensive CD is worth its modest price.

12 *Danzas españolas; Escenas poeticas*, Book I (arr. for guitar and orchestra)

(BB) *** Naxos 8.553037. Kraft, Razumovsky Sinf., Breiner

These are attractive transcriptions for guitar and orchestra of Granados's piano pieces. The Canadian guitarist **Norbert Kraft** is a brilliant and effective player. If you want to try Granados in this orchestral garb rather than in its original, keyboard form, you can invest in this with confidence.

(i) *Piano Quintet in G min.* Piano music: *A la Cubana*, Op. 36; *Aparición; Cartas de amor – Valses íntimos*, Op. 44; *Danza caracteristica; Escenas poéticas* (2nd series)

(M) *** CRD (ADD) CRD 3335. Rajna; (i) with Alberni Qt

The *Piano Quintet* is a compact work, neat and unpretentious, in three attractive movements, including a charming lyrical *Allegretto* and a vigorous finale where the piano is most prominent. Among the solo items, the evocative pieces in the *Escenas poéticas II* are the most valuable, but even the more conventional colour-pieces that make up the rest of the disc are worth hearing in such perceptive readings. The CRD analogue recording is very good indeed and so are the CD transfers.

GUITAR MUSIC

Cuentos de la juventud, Op. 1: *Dedicatoria. Danzas españolas 4 & 5*, Op. 37/4–5; *Tonadillas al estilo antiguo: La maja de Goya. Valses poéticos*

☞ ✦ (BB) **** RCA 74321 68016-2. Bream (guitar) – ALBENIZ: *Collection* (with pieces by MALATS and PUJOL) **** ✦

Like the Albéniz items with which these Granados pieces are coupled, these performances show **Julian Bream** at his most inspirational. The illusion of the guitar being in the room is especially electrifying in the middle section of the famous *Spanish Dance No. 5*, when Bream achieves the most subtle *pianissimo*. Heard against the background silence, the effect is quite magical. But all the playing here is wonderfully spontaneous. This is one of the most impressive guitar recitals ever recorded, and for this super-bargain reissue RCA have generously added the *Tres piezas españolas* of Rodrigo, recorded a year later and no less distinguished.

PIANO MUSIC

Piano Music (complete)

(BB) *** Nim. NI 1734 (6). M. Jones

Allegro de concierto; Escenas románticas; Goyescas (complete); *Goyescas: Intermezzo. Goyesca (El pelele); Oriental, canción, variada, intermedio y final; Rapsodia aragonesa; Valse de concert; Reverie* (Improvisation; transcribed from a Duo Art piano roll)

(BB) *** Nim. NI 5595/8 (4). M. Jones – ALBENIZ: *Iberia*, etc. ***

The Nimbus six-disc set is described as 'the complete published works for the piano', but you will look in vain in the contents list for the *Goyescas*: as they are listed (on the second CD) as *Los majos enamorados*, Parts I and II. The *Libro de horas* come between the two Books (which works well enough), with *El pelele* played quite separately. No reason is given for this in the sparse notes, the one drawback to the set which is otherwise highly recommendable at its modest price. As can be seen, there is an equally recommendable shorter collection (which includes the *Goyescas* and also the Duo Art piano-roll transcription of the composer playing an improvisation).

A la pradera; Barcarola, Op. 45; Bocetos; Cuentos de la juventud, Op. 1; Mazurka, Op. 2; Moresque y Arabe; Sardana; Los soldados de cartón

Ⓜ *** CRD (ADD) 3336

Allegro de concierto; Capricho español, Op. 39; Carezza vals, Op. 38; 2 Impromptus; Oriental; Rapsodia aragonesa; Valses poéticos

Ⓜ *** CRD (ADD) 3323

Danzas españolas, Op. 37

Ⓜ *** CRD (ADD) 3321

Escenas románticas; 6 Piezas sobre cantos populares españolas; Danza lenta

Ⓜ *** CRD (ADD) 3322

6 Estudios espresivos; Estudio, Op. posth.; Impromptu, Op. 39; 3 Marches militaires; Paisaje, Op. 35; Pequeña suite (In the garden of Elisenda)

Ⓜ *** CRD (ADD) 3337

Goyescas; Escenas poéticas (1st series); Libro de horas

Ⓜ *** Rajna CRD (ADD) 3301

Thomas Rajna plays with great sympathy and flair. Apart from the *Danzas españolas*, some of the finest music is to be found in the *Escenas románticas* and in the other pieces on CRD 3322 and 3323. The later volumes, however, excellently played and recorded, are well worth considering, and not merely for the sake of completeness. The eight pieces on CRD 3336, opening with the beguilingly innocent *Moresque y Arabe*, are delightful, pleasingly contrasted in style and played with great character and spontaneity. The *Six Estudios* serve to point the formative influences in Granados's style – Schumann and, to a lesser extent, Fauré – while the other pieces, including the *Marches militaires* (in which Rajna superimposes the second piano part) are unfailingly pleasing. His account of *Goyescas* must yield to **Alicia de Larrocha**, but his interpretations are clear and persuasive and the music's greatness does not elude him. The fill-ups, more immediately charming, less ambitious, are valuable, too. A distinguished set, welcome in the CD catalogue at mid-price.

12 Danzas españolas; Goyescas (complete);

Ⓜ *** RCA 82876 60863-2. De Larrocha

Alicia de Larrocha has recorded much of this repertoire before, both for Spanish Hispavox and later, perhaps definitively, for Decca (see below). Her view of these pieces has not changed substantially since, although her responses in the earlier recordings are sometimes marginally fresher. However, her newest, RCA set of the *Danzas españolas* is every bit as perceptive and sparkling, and her Spanish temperament remains naturally attuned to this music. The RCA recording is natural, fully coloured and with fine sonority; it is very present and vivid: the listener is closer to the instrument than with Decca.

Goyescas (complete)

⊕–⦿✸ Ⓑ *** Double Decca 448 191-2 (2). De Larrocha – ALBÉNIZ: *Iberia*, etc. ***

Ⓜ *** EMI (ADD) 3 61514-2 (2). De Larrocha – ALBÉNIZ: *Iberia; Navarra* ***

Goyescas: Los majos enamorados, Parts I–II

Ⓑ *** Nim. 2-CD NI 7718/9. Martin Jones – ALBÉNIZ: *Iberia* ***

Alicia de Larrocha brings special insights and sympathy to the *Goyescas* (given top-drawer Decca sound in 1977); her playing has the crisp articulation and rhythmic vitality that these pieces call for, while she is hauntingly evocative in *Quejas ó la maja y el ruiseñor*. The overall impression could hardly be more idiomatic in flavour or more realistic as a recording. This Double Decca coupling with Albéniz's *Iberia* is very distinguished.

Alicia de Larrocha's EMI set of *Goyescas* derives from the Spanish Hispavox catalogue and was made in 1962, a decade before her Decca set. The performance is more impulsive, at times more intensely expressive, if less subtle in feeling than the later version, and the recording, if not as fine as the Decca, is eminently realistic.

As in the coupled *Iberia* of Albéniz, **Martin Jones's** instinctive sympathy with the Spanish idiom brings a remarkable freshness to the music of Granados, and the recording is very real and natural.

GREENE, Maurice (1696–1755)

Hearken unto Me, ye Holy Children (motet)

*** Hyp. CDA 67298. Blaze, Daniels, Harvey, King's Consort Ch. & O, King – HANDEL: *The Choice of Hercules* ***

Maurice Greene, Handel's contemporary and for many years his unfriendly rival, cannot compare with that master in originality of invention, but this extended motet makes an attractive and valuable fill-up for the rare Handel cantata, equally well performed by the **King's Consort**.

GREGSON, Edward (born 1945)

(i) *Concerto for Piano & Wind (Homages); (ii) Saxophone Concerto; (iii) Trumpet Concerto*

Ⓝ *** Chan. 10478. (i) Goerner; (ii) Sugawa; (iii) Antonsen; BBC PO, Rundel

Edward Gregson tells us that he is particularly attracted to the concerto form. The *Concerto for Piano and Wind* uses Stravinsky as model without losing its own originality. Its central *Passacaglia* is capped by the rhythmic impetus of the *Rondo Burlesque* finale, which then by sleight of musical hand transforms itself into an anonymous twelfth-century carol.

The *Trumpet Concerto* is also full of sparkle, based on a three-note motif heard at the opening on the timpani; but it too has an elegiac, haunting soliloquy for a slow movement, followed by a vibrant rondo-capriccio finale demanding and receiving great virtuosity from the soloist, **Ole Edvard Antonsen**.

Perhaps most remarkable of all is the *Saxophone Concerto* (written for its soloist, **Nobuya Sugawa**), a dazzling cornucopia of ideas and jazzy dance episodes, even reaching pandemonium at times, but again with a lyrical core and another haunting slow movement. All three performances here are outstanding and show the bravura and sensitivity of the three soloists while **Clark Rundell** directs the accompaniments with spirit and sensuous warmth. The recording is of Chandos's demonstration standard.

GRIEG, Edvard (1843–1907)

'Ballad for Edward Grieg': DVD Documentary, with Leif Ove Andsnes; includes *Arietta*, Op. 12/1; *At Your Feet*, Op. 68/3; *Ballade in G min.*, Op. 24; *Folk Tune*, Op. 12/5; *Homesickness*, Op. 57/6; *Wedding Day at Troldhaugen*, Op. 65/6; (i) *Piano Concerto in A min.*

➻—**** EMI **DVD** 5 12128-9. Andsnes, (i) with Bergen PO, Ruud; Richard Peel (narrator) (Dir: Thomas Hellum, DVD prod: Jans Saure)

In this documentary we accompany **Leif Ove Andsnes** as he prepares to record the *Ballade in G minor*, which Grieg himself felt unable to play in public, because of its personal associations with the death of his parents. We follow the pianist as he travels the world, following in the composer's footsteps, preparing himself to play the *Ballade*. Grieg was very restless and visited many of the major European capital cities (including a very successful visit to London), but then he usually became homesick and returned to Troldhaugen, where we also return, to hear Andsnes play some *Lyric Pieces*, introducing and using the composer's own Steinway piano (which he greatly likes) in his living room, with comments between each of the pieces. En route we learn a great deal about Grieg and his music, and if this is not a documentary to return to more than once or twice, the performances which follow are all outstanding, and are not duplicated on Andsnes's other CDs. The performance of the *Concerto* includes encores. The recording is of high quality and the video direction is excellent.

Complete Orchestral Music: Bell Ringing; (i) Piano Concerto; 2 Elegiac Melodies; Funeral March in memory of Rikard Nordraak (2 versions); Holberg Suite; In Autumn; 2 Lyric Pieces; Lyric Suite; 2 Melodies; 2 Nordic Melodies; 4 Norwegian Dances; Old Norwegian Melody with Variations; 4 Symphonic Dances; Symphony in C; (ii) Bergliot (Melodrama). Vocal works: At the Cloister Gate; At Rondane; Den Bergtekne (The Mountain Thrall); Landkjenning (Land Sighting); Peer Gynt (concert version; complete + Suites 1–2); Sigurd Jorsalfar (incidental music); 6 Songs with Orchestra. Olav Trygvason (Opera fragment)

Ⓝ Ⓑ *** BIS CD 1740/2 (8). (i) Ogawa; (ii) Mauseth (nar.); soloists, including Hagegård, Kringelborn, Solberg, Bergen Vocal Ens., Philharmonic Ch. & O, Ruud

This valuable collection of Grieg's music is offered very inexpensively (8 discs for the price of 3), handsomely packaged and well documented.

(i) Bergliot (melodrama for orchestra), Op. 42; (ii) Piano Concerto in A min.; 2 Elegiac Melodies, Op. 34; Funeral March in Memory of Richard Nordraak; Holberg Suite, Op. 40; In Autumn, Op. 11; 2 Lyric Pieces, Op. 68; Lyric Suite, Op. 54; Norwegian Dances, Op. 35; 2 Norwegian Folk Melodies, Op. 53; 2 Nordic Melodies, Op. 63; Old Norwegian Romance with Variations, Op. 51; Sigurd Jorsalfar (suite) Op. 56; 4 Symphonic Dances, Op. 64; Symphony in C min.; Choral: (iii) Before a Southern Convent, Op. 30; (iv; v) Orchestral Songs: The First Meeting; From Monte Pincio; Henryk Wergeland; Spring; A Swan; (v; vi) Landkjenning, Op. 31; (v) The Mountain Thrall, Op. 32; (v; vii) Olav Trygvason (scenes), Op. 50; (viii) Peer Gynt (complete incidental music); (ix) Sigurd Jorsalfar (incidental music)

Ⓑ *** DG 471 300-2 (6). Gothenburg SO (& Ch.), Järvi; with (i) Tellefsen (nar.); (ii) Zilberstein; (iii) Bonney, Stene, Women's Ch.; (iv) Bonney; (v) Hagegård; (vi) with Men's Ch.; (vii) Stene, Gjevang & Ch.; (viii) Bonney & Soloists

This comprehensive coverage of Grieg's 'music with orchestra', with many of the performances unsurpassed, would make an ideal basis for any Grieg collection. Most are discussed below, although not **Lilya Zilberstein's** account of the *Piano Concerto*, one of the few disappointments. It is a good narrative performance and could never be called routine, but her reading is comparatively conventional, with few fresh insights. The documentation is excellent but the surprise is the omission of texts and translations for the vocal music, with only synopses deemed necessary. But the standard of recording is consistently high, and this six-disc bargain box is still remarkable value.

(i) Piano Concerto in A min. (original 1868/72 version); Larviks-polka (1858); 23 Small Pieces (1859)

*** BIS CD 619. Derwinger, (i) Norrköping SO, Hirokami

This CD offers us a fascinating glimpse of how the concerto must have sounded to its contemporaries. **Love Derwinger** is the intelligent and accomplished soloist with the **Norrköping Orchestra**, and he proves a sensitive guide in the collection of juvenilia that completes the disc. The concerto is well balanced and Derwinger's solo pieces are well recorded too.

Piano Concerto in A min., Op. 16

➻—✹ Ⓜ **** EMI 5 03419-2. Andsnes, BPO, Jansons – SCHUMANN: *Piano Concerto* ***✹

➻—Ⓜ **** Ph. (ADD) 475 7773. Kovacevich, BBC SO, C. Davis – SCHUMANN: *Piano Concerto* *** ᵇ→ Ⓜ *** Sony 518810-2 [SK 92736]. Perahia, Bav. RSO, C. Davis – MENDELSSOHN: *Concerto 2: Finale*; SCHUMANN: *Concerto* ***

Ⓝ ᵇ→ **** Chan.10509. Shelley, Opera N. O – SAINT-SAËNS: *Concerto 2*; SCHUMANN: *Piano Concerto* ****

*** EMI 7 54746-2. Vogt, CBSO, Rattle – SCHUMANN: *Concerto* ***

Ⓜ *** Decca (ADD) 466 383-2. Lupu, LSO, Previn – SCHUMANN: *Concerto* ***

Ⓝ Ⓑ *** CfP 2 28368-2. Devoyon, LPO, Maksymiuk – SCHUMANN: *Piano Concerto* ***

(i) Piano Concerto; Ballade in G min.; (ii) Lyric Pieces, Op. 57/6; Op. 62/6; Op. 65/6; Wedding Day at Troldhaugen, Op. 68/5; Evening in the Mountains, Op. 68/4; Remembrances, Op. 71/7

Ⓜ *** EMI 3 94399-2. Andsnes; (i) BPO, Jansons; (ii) Recorded on the composer's own piano

It was with the Grieg *Concerto* that **Leif Ove Andsnes** made his concerto début in 1990 on the Virgin label. This new version, recorded live in Berlin, is just as spontaneous-sounding, with soaring flights of imagination, while the **Berlin Philharmonic** is at its warmest under **Mariss Jansons**; his virtuosity is commanding, but it is never at the expense of tenderness and poetic feeling. The Schumann too brings glorious playing from both soloist and orchestra, with both offering warm, clear sound; in short, this is a gramophone classic for the present decade.

The G minor *Ballade* was written in the wake of Grieg's parents' death. Much of his grief was poured into the *Ballade*, a set of variations on an old Norwegian folk song. Poignant and deeply felt, it is among his greatest works and, such was the emotion it aroused and the pain which accompanied its composition, that Grieg himself could hardly bear to play it in later life. **Leif Ove Andsnes** has the full measure of its depth and his beautifully recorded account must be a mandatory acquisition.

Whether in the clarity of virtuoso fingerwork or the shading of half-tone, **Kovacevich** is among the most illuminating of the many great pianists who have recorded the Grieg *Concerto*. He plays with bravura and refinement, the spontaneity of the music-making bringing a sparkle throughout, to balance the underlying poetry. The 1972 recording has been freshened most successfully and this now returns to the catalogue, effectively remastered as one of the finest of Philips's Originals.

Perahia revels in the bravura as well as bringing out the lyrical beauty in radiantly poetic playing. He is commanding and authoritative when required, with the blend of spontaneity, poetic feeling and virtuoso display this music calls for. He is given sympathetic support by **Sir Colin Davis** and the fine **Bavarian Radio Symphony Orchestra**, and it now comes at mid-price with the finale of the *Second* Mendelssohn *Concerto* as an encore.

Howard Shelley is gifted with keen intelligence and consummate artistry, and his accounts of the Grieg and Schumann (which he directs from the keyboard) belong in the most exalted company. Shelley succeeds in balancing the concerto's overall structure without ever sacrificing the lyrical freshness and poetry of its invention. The disc is particularly generous in including the extra work by Saint-Saëns. Fine orchestral playing and excellent recording add to the attractions of this coupling.

Lars Vogt never allows his personality to obtrude; he colours the familiar phrases with great subtlety yet without the slightest trace of narcissism. He is very well supported by **Rattle** and the **CBSO**, and excellently recorded. An unusually sensitive player, his version, with the inevitable Schumann coupling, is eminently satisfying.

Decca's remastering of **Radu Lupu's** fine (1973) Kingsway Hall recording, one of Decca's very best of the period, suits the style of the performance, which is boldly compelling in the outer movements, but has warmth and poetry too, especially striking in the slow movement, where **Previn's** hushed opening is particularly telling. Indeed, the orchestral contribution is a strong one throughout, while Lupu's playing has moments of touching delicacy, and this Decca performance must stand high on the list of mid- and bargain-priced recommendations.

Devoyon's account is characteristic of him: aristocratic without being aloof, pensive without being self-conscious, and brilliant without being flashy. He is a poetic artist whose natural musicianship shines through, and this excellent account is very competitive, with fine, supportive playing from the **LPO** under **Jerzy Maksymiuk**.

Dinu Lipatti's classic 1947 version of the Grieg *Concerto*, intensely poetic, like the Schumann with which it is coupled, has been a staple of the catalogue from when it was made, but here in the superb Dutton transfer the sound is fuller and clearer than ever before, preferable to the EMI remastering, with the additional advantage that the disc comes at super-bargain price. (Dutton CDBP 9717)

Piano Concerto; 6 Lyric Pieces, Op. 65/1–6

Ⓑ *** Virgin 391369-2. Andsnes, Bergen PO, Kitayenko – LISZT: *Piano Concerto 2* ***

In his earlier (1991) Virgin recording, **Andsnes** again wears his brilliance lightly. There is no lack of display and bravura here, but no ostentation. Indeed, he has great poetic feeling and delicacy of colour, and Grieg's familiar warhorse comes up with great freshness. His piano is perfectly balanced in relation to the orchestra and anyone wanting the Liszt coupling should be well satisfied.

2 Elegiac Melodies, Op. 34; Erotik; 2 Melodies, Op. 53; 2 Norwegian Airs, Op. 63

ⒷⒷ **(*) Naxos 8.550330. Capella Istropolitana, Leaper – SIBELIUS: *Andante festivo*, etc. **

Adrian Leaper secures responsive and sensitive playing from the **Capella Istropolitana** in this Grieg collection, the recording is very good indeed and the balance natural.

(i) 2 Elegiac Melodies, Op. 34; Holberg Suite; (ii) In Autumn, Op. 11; (iii) Lyric Suite, Op. 54; Norwegian Dances, Op. 35; (iv) Old Norwegian Romance with Variations; Symphonic Dances, Op. 64; (iii) Sigurd

Jorsalfar: Homage March; (Piano): (v) Lyric Pieces, Op. 12 & Op. 28

(BB) *** EMI Gemini (ADD) 5 86513-2 (2). (i) N. Sinfonia, Tortelier; (ii) RPO, Beecham; (iii) Hallé O, Barbirolli; (iv) Bournemouth SO, Berglund; (v) Adni

A most attractive bargain anthology, recorded over 25 years. Yet how well the very first recording, **Beecham's**In Autumn, still sounds. (It was made in the Kingsway Hall in 1955.) **Tortelier** gives most affecting performances of the *Elegiac Melodies* and *Holberg Suite*, very well recorded and still among the best in the catalogue. **Barbirolli's** three items are also available on a Dutton CD (see below). How delightfully he presents the *Allegretto tranquillo*, the second of the *Four Norwegian Dances*. **Berglund's** highly dramatic *Symphonic Dances* are also available on an Encore disc, but his highly sympathetic and imaginatively volatile performance of the delightful *Old Norwegian Romance with Variations* (all separately cued) are well worth having. **Daniel Adni's**Lyric Pieces, which act as an appendix, are most beautifully played and very well recorded indeed. All the CD transfers are excellent.

2 Elegiac Melodies; Holberg Suite, Op. 40; 2 Lyric Pieces, Op. 68; 2 Melodies, Op. 53; 2 Nordic Melodies, Op. 63

(✿) **** BIS SACD 1491. Bergen PO, Ruud

This is simply the most beautiful record of Grieg's string music in the catalogue, and one of the most beautiful and realistic recordings of strings we have ever heard – made appropriately in the Grieg Hall in Bergen. The wonderfully vital account of the *Holberg Suite* is unsurpassed, not even by Karajan's famous account, and the gentler pieces are exquisite, especially the *Two Nordic Melodies*, which are Elysian, and the closing *At the Cradle* from the *Lyric Pieces*, Op. 68. Truly marvellous playing from the **Bergen Orchestra** and inspired conducting from **Ole Kristian Ruud**, while the BIS producers, Hans Kipfer and Thore Brinkmann, and sound engineer Jens Braun deserve to share the Rosette and the fourth star unique to this volume. Try and hear the disc on SACD equipment with four speakers, and you will be amazed; but it sounds pretty marvellous through just two.

Holberg Suite, Op. 40

(M) *** Decca (ADD) 470 262-2. ASMF, Marriner – TCHAIKOVSKY: *Serenade* *** ; DVOŘÁK: *Serenade* **(*)

(BB) *** Warner Apex 0927 43075-2. Norwegian R. O, Rasilainen – NIELSEN: *Little Suite;* STENHAMMAR: *Serenade* ***✿

Marriner's richly lyrical account of the *Holberg Suite* is outstanding in every way: the *Air* has a pleasing graciousness and the *Rigaudon* plenty of sparkle. The 1970 (Argo) recording remains splendidly fresh.

An unaffected account of the *Holberg Suite* from **Ari Rasilainen** and his Norwegian players that serves to enhance the attractions of the coupling, Stenhammar's glorious *Serenade for Orchestra.*

Holberg Suite, Op. 40; Peer Gynt Suites 1–2

*** DG 439 010-2. BPO, Karajan – SIBELIUS: *Finlandia*, etc. ***

Holberg Suite, Op. 40; Peer Gynt Suites 1–2; Sigurd Jorsalfar: Suite, Op. 56

(B) *** DG 2-CD (DDD/ADD) 474 269-2 (2). BPO, Karajan – SIBELIUS: *Finlandia*, etc. ***

Karajan's performance of the *Holberg Suite* has wonderful lightness and delicacy, with cultured phrasing not robbing the music of its immediacy, while in *Peer Gynt* many subtleties of colour and texture are revealed by the vividly present recording, clear and full and with a firm bass-line, especially in the thrillingly gutsy *In the Hall of the Mountain King*. The digital recording now proves to be one of the best to have emerged from the Philharmonie in the early 1980s. For their 'Karajan Collection' reissue, DG have added the three pieces from *Sigurd Jorsalfar* and joined this CD economically to an equally outstanding Sibelius programme. This is Karajan and the **BPO** at their very finest, and the coupling is outstanding in every way. Very fine sound, too.

In Autumn Overture; Lyric Piece: Erotik, Op. 43/5; Norwegian Dances; Old Norwegian Romance with Variations

*** Chan. 9028. Iceland SO, Sakari – SVENDSEN: 2 *Icelandic Melodies* for strings ***

The **Icelandic orchestra** play very responsively for their Finnish conductor, **Petri Sakari**, who gives very natural and straightforward accounts of this endearing music. Highly musical performances, with no lack of personality, truthfully recorded. Very recommendable.

Old Norwegian Romance & Variations, Op. 51; Sigurd Jorsalfar: Suite, Op. 56; Symphony in C min.

(BB) *** Naxos 8.557991. Malmö SO, Engeset

Bjarte Engeset makes an excellent case for the Grieg *Symphony* – not one of his most characteristic works, but it has many pleasing qualities. Engeset injects plenty of vigour into his performance, making it seem more dramatic than usual. The *Variations* are superbly done, with plenty of the fresh charm and detail brought out. No complaints about the *Sigurd Jorsalfar* items, which are as enjoyable as ever, with the *Intermezzo* wonderfully atmospheric. Good, well-balanced sound.

Symphony in C min.

(B) *** Decca Australian Eloquence 476 8743. Bergen SO, Anderson – GOLDMARK: *Rustic Wedding Symphony* **(*)

The *Symphony* is a student work, written while Grieg was living in Denmark, but he forbade performances of the work after hearing Svendsen's *First Symphony* in 1867, and the score was bequeathed to Bergen Public Library on the understanding that it was never to be performed. The work takes just over 37 minutes, and those expecting characteristic Grieg will be disappointed. In some ways the finale is the most confident of the four movements, though its seams are clearly audible. The ideas are fresher than in the inner movements and, although it is no masterpiece, the work is uncommonly assured for a youth of 20. It is persuasively played in Bergen, and the Decca recording is truthfully balanced, with good perspective and colour.

CHAMBER MUSIC

Andante con moto (for piano trio)

(N) *** Simax SACD PSC 1279 (2). Grieg Trio – SMETANA: *Piano Trio, Op. 15*; TCHAIKOVSKY: *Piano Trio* ***

Grieg's *Andante* for piano trio was only published posthumously and is virtually unknown. But it is a substantial movement (perhaps intended as part of a major work), opening and closing evocatively but with an ardently passionate central section. Very well played here, it is well worth having as a bonus in this two-disc package. The surround sound adds to the presence (and resonance) of the recording.

Cello Sonata in A min., Op. 36

**(*) CRD 3391. Cohen, Vignoles – FRANCK: *Cello Sonata* **(*)

Cello Sonata in A min.; Intermezzo in A min.; Piano Sonata, Op. 7

🎵 (BB) *** Naxos 8.550878. Birkeland, Gimse

Oystein Birkeland and Håvard Gimse give the *Sonata* an alive and sensitive account, coupled with the early and unrepresentative *Intermezzo in A minor*. They are both imaginative players and are decently recorded. Given the modest outlay involved, this competes very strongly with its rivals, but even if it were at mid- or full-price it would be highly recommendable. Gimse's performance of the early *Piano Sonata*, Op. 7, is also very good indeed. Altogether a first-rate bargain.

In the folk element **Cohen** might have adopted a more persuasive style, bringing out the charm of the music more, but certainly he sustains the sonata structures well. The recording presents the cello very convincingly. It has been most naturally transferred to CD.

(i) Cello Sonata; (ii) String Quartet 1

*** Virgin 5 45505-2. (i) Mørk, Gimse; (ii) Sigerland, Sponberg, Tomter, Mørk

Like Leif Ove Andsnes's recent set of *Lyric Pieces*, the *Cello Sonata* was recorded at Grieg's home, Troldhaugen, on his own piano. It is **Truls Mørk's** second recording and he plays with characteristic sensitivity and refreshing ardour. **Håvard Gimse** is an impeccable partner: he has the keenest musical instincts and great keyboard finesse. This is arguably the best and most compelling account of the *Sonata* to be had. Apart from the *Ballade*, Op. 24, the *String Quartet*, also in G minor, is Grieg's most deeply felt instrumental piece. The four artists assembled for the excellent Virgin recording can hold their own with the best, and they bring an intensity, freshness and imagination to this fine score.

String Quartets 1–2 in F (unfinished)

🎵 (BB) *** Naxos 8.550879. Oslo String Qt – JOHANSEN: *String Quartet* ***

(BB) *** Hyp. Helios CDH 55299. Chilingirian Qt

String Quartets 1–2; (i) Andante con moto for Piano Trio. Fugue in F min.

(BB) *** Regis RRC 1279. Raphael Qt; (i) with Röling

The Naxos account of the quartets from the **Oslo String Quartet**, a relatively new group, proves the best of the lot – indeed it is the best version we have had since the Budapest. They would easily sweep the board even at full price, on account of their sensitivity, tonal finesse and blend, and the keenness of their artistic responses. They play only the first two movements of the *F major Quartet*, leaving room for a fine quartet by Grieg's biographer, David Monrad Johansen. The recording balance, made in the Norwegian Radio studios, is excellent, neither too forward nor too recessed.

The **Chilingirians** leave off where Grieg did, just as the Oslo Quartet do on Naxos. They have lavished much care on it and their disc is expertly engineered by Arne Kaselborg and Andrew Keener. Recommended alongside the Naxos.

The **Raphael Quartet** performances of these two *Quartets* are spirited and well recorded. If the *F major* is not quite in the class of the account by the Oslo Quartet, their Regis CD enjoys two points of special interest: they give us Julius Röntgen's conjectural realization of the sketches of the remaining two movements Grieg had planned for the *Second Quartet*, and they also include another rarity in the shape of the *Andante con moto* for piano trio, which is worth having on disc.

The version of the *First Quartet* from the **New Helsinki Quartet** couples it with the Sibelius *Quartet*. It is dramatic, well shaped and vital, yet full of sensitivity, and can be strongly recommended among modern recordings, and the disc now comes in the lowest price-range. (Warner Apex 0927 40601-2)

The **Budapest Quartet's** recording dates from 1936, but its attractions in terms of coupling here are strong. The Sibelius *Voces intimae* and the Hugo Wolf *Italian Serenade* are both superb performances and still remain unsurpassed. The Biddulph transfer is excellent. (Biddulph mono LAB 098)

Violin Sonata 1 in F, Op. 8

🎵 *** Challenge CC 72171. Van Keulen, Brautigam – ELGAR: *Sonata*; SIBELIUS: *Humoresques* ***

The Op. 8 *Sonata* comes between the *E minor Piano Sonata* and the *Piano Concerto*. But to present-day ears it has the perennial freshness and immediacy of all Grieg and sounds fresher than ever in the hands of this masterly partnership. The Elgar *Sonata* is equally desirable, while the Sibelius wartime *Humoresques* are captivating, and the three they give us are beautifully played.

Violin Sonatas 1 in F, Op. 8; 2 in G, Op. 13; 3 in C min.

🎵 *** Simax PSC 1162. Tonnesen, Smebye

*** Chan. 9184. L. and E. Mordkovitch

In each sonata **Terje Tonnesen** plays with much sweetness of tone and tenderness of feeling. His virtuosity is disarmingly effortless and there is a lyric and expressive grace that is captivating. His partner, **Einar Henning Smebye**, is sensitive and responsive, and the balance is excellent. For many this will be a first choice.

Yet the same goes for **Lydia** and **Elena Mordkovitch** (*mère* *et fille*) on an admirably recorded Chandos CD. They, too, give splendidly fresh and well-shaped accounts of all three sonatas which give much pleasure in music-making. Affectionate yet virile performances – thoroughly recommendable.

Violin Sonata 3 in C min., Op. 45

*** Avie Crear Classics AV 0037. Gleusteen, Ordronneau – DVOŘÁK: *Violin Sonatina*; FRANCK: *Violin Sonata* ***

Kai Gleusteen and **Catherine Ordronneau**, Canadian- and French-born respectively, have teamed up to make an impressively close partnership, and their performance of the Grieg *C minor Sonata* has plenty of vitality and is especially successful in sharing its endearingly warm lyricism. They are recorded at Crear, a centre for the arts in the Scottish Highlands (in Argyle) with a wonderful view of the 'Paps' of Jura as a backcloth. The recording is resonant but gives an impression of live music-making, and the couplings are equally enjoyable.

PIANO MUSIC

Old Norwegian Romance with Variations (for 2 pianos), Op. 51; arr. for 2 Pianos of Mozart's Fantasia in C min., K.475

(N) *** Blu-ray Lindberg Lyd **SACD** Surround Sound 2L57SABD. Dena Piano Duo – MOZART: *Sonata for 2 Pianos, K.448* ****

The Blu-ray recording process (played through an SACD system) produces a piano image of exceptional clarity and presence, and these performances by the **Dena Piano Duo** are of high quality. It cannot be said that Grieg's eclectic but diverting variations are as effective in a piano duet format as they are in their orchestral form, but the music-making here is certainly spontaneously enjoyable. Grieg however blotted his copybook by making a clumsy and thick-textured transcription of Mozart's solo piano *Fantasia in C minor* for piano duo and, although the Dena Duo do their best with it, it still sounds much less effective than Mozart's original version for just one instrument.

Einar Steen-Nøkleberg Complete Naxos Series

(BB) *** Naxos 8.550881. Vol. 1: *Early and Late Pieces*

(BB) *** Naxos 8.550882. Vol. 2: *19 Norwegian Folksongs*

(BB) *** Naxos 8.550883. Vol. 3: *Ballade; Melodies of Norway*

(BB) *** Naxos 8.550884. Vol. 4: *17 Norwegian Peasant Dances*

(BB) **(*) Naxos 8.553391. Vol. 5: *Norway's Melodies 1–63*

(BB) **(*) Naxos 8.553392. Vol. 6: *Norway's Melodies 64–117*

(BB) **(*) Naxos 8.553393. Vol. 7: *Norway's Melodies 118–52*

(BB) **(*) Naxos 8.550394. Vol. 8: *Lyric Pieces, Books 1–4*

(BB) **(*) Naxos 8.550395. Vol. 9: *Lyric Pieces, Books 5–7*

(BB) **(*) Naxos 8.550396. Vol. 10: *Lyric Pieces, Books 8–10*

(BB) **(*) Naxos 8.550397. Vol. 11: *Orch. Transcriptions, I*

(BB) **(*) Naxos 8.550398. Vol. 12: *Orch. Transcriptions, II*

(BB) **(*) Naxos 8.550399. Vol. 13: *Orch. Transcriptions, III*

(BB) **(*) Naxos 8.550400. Vol. 14: *Sketches: Concerto; Sonata*

Einar Steen-Nøkleberg has recorded every note of music Grieg composed for the piano. He has impressive musical credentials and is, among other things, the author of a book on Grieg's piano music and its interpretations. His survey displaces earlier sets in quality: he is responsive to mood and is searchingly imaginative in his approach. He is beautifully recorded throughout in the Linderman Hall of the Norwegian State Academy of Music.

Lyric Pieces: Op. 12/1; Op. 38/1; Op. 43/1–2; Op. 47/2–4; Op. 54/4–5; Op. 57/6; Op. 62/4 & 6; Op. 68/2, 3 & 5; Op. 71/1, 3 & 6–7

⊕ (M) **** DG (ADD) 449 721-2. Gilels

With **Gilels** we are in the presence of a great keyboard master whose characterization and control of colour and articulation are wholly remarkable. An altogether outstanding record in every way. This recording has been admirably remastered for reissue in DG's 'Originals' series and now sounds better than ever.

Lyric Pieces, Op. 12/1, 2, 3 & 6; Op. 18/6–8; Op. 47/1; Op. 54/3–4; Op. 57/2, 3 & 6; Op. 62/1, 4–6; Op. 65/6: Wedding Day at Troldhaugen; Op. 68/3; Op. 71/2, 6–7

⊕ ✿ *** EMI 5 57296-2. Andsnes

The Op. 65 *Lyric Pieces* on the **Andsnes** bargain recital derive from the young Norwegian pianist's début recordings of the Grieg *A minor* and Liszt *A major Concertos*, while the remainder come from the following year when he was 22 years old. The playing has great freshness, and Andsnes almost succeeds in making listeners feel that they have not heard such oft-played pieces as *Butterfly*, *Solitary Wanderer*, *To Spring* or *Shepherd Boy* before. Andsnes commands great tonal subtlety and a wonderful range of keyboard colour, yet there is no pursuit of surface beauty at the expense of artistic truth. At its price, this is outstanding.

Lyric Pieces, Opp. 12/8; 38/1 & 6; 43/1 & 2; 47/1, 3 & 7; 54/3–4; 57/4, 5 & 6; 62/4; 68/2; 71/2–3

(B) *** CDK CDKM 1003. Pletnev

It is good to see this masterly Grieg recital return to circulation, as it contains playing of great poetic feeling and keen sensibility. It was briefly available on Melodiya in the late 1980s and, though by no means the equal of Gilels's famous anthology on DG in terms of recorded sound, was artistically a worthy successor. As usual with **Pletnev** nothing is routine and there is a concentration that gives these miniatures a freshness and depth that few artists can match. One had forgotten just how good this revealing recital is. If the distinction of the playing is not matched by the quality of the recorded sound, it is still eminently serviceable.

25 Norwegian Folk-Songs and Dances, Op. 17/1, 5, 7–8, 10, 12, 18, 19, 22, 24–25; Norwegian Folk Dances, Op. 66/1, 7–8, 12, 14–15, 18–19; Norwegian

*Peasant Dances, Op. 72/2, 7, 8, 14–16; Songs, Op.
41/1, 4, 6; Op. 52/1–3*

Ⓑ *** Naim CD 059. Gimse

Håvard Gimse is among the most impressive and imaginative of Norwegian pianists, and he offers an expertly chosen
anthology of dances from the Op. 17 set of 1870 and a handful
of pieces from the much later Op. 66 and Op. 72 collections
from 1896 and 1902. He also gives us half a dozen of Grieg's
own song transcriptions. The lifelike recording (if slightly
closely balanced) is made on a well-regulated Steinway in
the fine acoustic of the Sofienberg Church in Oslo, and this
is a most distinguished and satisfying addition to the Grieg
discography.

VOCAL MUSIC

**A cappella choral music: (i) *At the Halvdan Kjerulf
monument; Ave maris stella; Dona nobis pacem;* (ii)
*4 Psalms, Op. 74; Holberg Cantata. Male-voice
choruses: Election song; Impromptu; Inga Litamor;
The late rose; Westerly wind***

*** Simax PSC 1187. (i) Sandve; (ii) Vollestad; Oslo
 Philharmonic Ch., Skiöld

Grieg's *a cappella* output is among the least known. This disc
by the **Oslo Philharmonic Choir** offers a generous helping
of it and presents it persuasively. His last work, the *Four
Psalms*, Op. 74, dates from 1906 and is based on traditional
tunes of popular Norwegian origin. The Oslo Philharmonic
Choir produce a beautiful and well-blended sound. Good
recording.

**Orchestral songs: *Album lines, Departed; En svane
(The swan); Eros; Fra Monte Pincio; Spillemænd
(Fiddlers);The mountain thrall, Op. 26; The
Princess; 4 Songs, Op. 60; 6 Songs, Op. 48; To the
motherland. A vision; With a water-lily; Peer Gynt:
Solveig's cradle song***

*** Dinemec DCCD022. Farley, LPO or Philh. O, Serebrier

This anthology collects 23 Grieg songs, three in the composer's own orchestrations but the vast majority in transcriptions by the conductor, **José Serebrier**. Some of them, like
Prinsessan (The Princess) do not gain in the process, but the
vast majority do, and Serebrier's orchestrations are both expert and idiomatic. **Carole Farley** does not use the white-
toned, vibrato-free style favoured by some of the younger
generation of Norwegian singers, but her disc is none the
worse for that. Only occasionally is her vibrato obtrusive.
For the most part she commands a wide expressive range
and exhibits considerable feeling for the character of each
of the songs. Moreover the orchestral support is sensitive
and the recording well balanced.

**Songs: *At Rodane; A bird song; The first primrose;
From Monte Pincio; Hope; I love but thee; I walked
one balmy summer evening; Last spring; Margreta's
cradle song; On the water; The Princess; Spring
showers; A swan; To her II; Two brown eyes; Upon a
grassy hillside; 4 Poems from Bjørnstjerne***

**Bjørnson's Fishermaiden, Op. 21; 6 Songs, Op. 48;
Peer Gynt: Solveig's song; Solveig's cradle song**

ⒷⒷ **(*) Naxos 8.553781. Arnesen, Eriksen

An inexpensive and, at 70 minutes, well-filled CD, beautifully
recorded and pleasingly sung. **Bodil Arnesen** has a voice of
great purity and radiance. She sings marvellously in tune,
though some may find that in this repertoire she has something of a 'little-girl', innocent quality that does not give the
whole picture. This perhaps is troubling when you are listening to all the songs straight off. Taken a group at a time,
she will touch most hearts, particularly in the setting of
Bjørnson's *Prinsessen* and *Det første møte*. **Erling Eriksen** is
an excellent accompanist.

**6 Elegiac Songs of John Paulsen, Op. 59;
Fædrelangssang (National Song); Gentlemen-
menige (Gentlemen Rankers); Norway, 5 Songs of
John Paulsen, Op. 58; Soldaten (The Soldier); 9
Songs, Op. 18; Taaren (Tears); Vesle Gut (Little Lad)**

BIS-CD-1657. Groop, Vignoles

**10 Songs by Otto Benzon, Op. 69/70; Clara's Song;
Easter Song; Election Song; The Fair-Haired Maid
(2 versions); Morning Prayer at School; The
Mountain Thrall; The Princess; Ragnhild; Sighs;
The Singing Congregration; To a Devil The Tryst**

Ⓝ *** BIS CD 1757. Groop, Vignoles

The Finnish mezzo **Monica Groop** is a supremely polished
artist and penetrates the very essence of the Grieg songs with
an artlessness that conceals art. **Roger Vignoles** is a masterly
accompanist who matches her artistry.

**Haugtussa (song-cycle), Op. 67; Hjertets melodier,
Op. 5; 6 Ibsen Poems, Op. 25; 6 Lieder, Op. 48;
Prinsessen, EG133**

Ⓝ *** Hyp. CDA 67670. Karnéus, Drake

The Grieg songs are well served already, but this recital by
Katarina Karnéus and **Julius Drake** makes a most desirable
supplement. Karnéus was the Cardiff Singer of the World
way back in 1995 and she made a much-admired Sibelius
song recital. The highlight of the present issue is *Haugtussa*,
Grieg's masterpiece among his song output, and these artists
prove worthy of it. Excellent sound and authoritative notes
by Robert Matthew-Walker.

**Haugtussa (song-cycle), Op. 67; 6 Songs, Op. 48;
Songs: Beside the stream; Farmyard song; From
Monte Pincio; Hope; I love but thee; Spring; Spring
showers; A swan; Two brown eyes; While I wait;
With a waterlily (sung in Norwegian)**

🔊 ✿ Ⓜ *** DG 477 6326. Von Otter, Forsberg

This recital of Grieg's songs by **Anne Sofie von Otter** and
Bengt Forsberg is rather special. Von Otter commands an
exceptionally wide range of colour and quality, and in
Forsberg she has a highly responsive partner. Altogether a
captivating recital, and beautifully recorded, too; it rightly
won the *Gramophone* Solo Vocal Award in 1993 and was also

the magazine's 'Record of the Year'. It now reappears in Universal's '*Gramophone* Award Collection' at mid-price, with full documentation included.

Peer Gynt (Concert version by Alain Perroux; complete)

🎙️ **** Aeon ACD 0642 (2). Actors: Jennings, Gwynn; D. Jacobi (narrator); Singers: Henschel, Dam-Jensen, Koch; Le Motet de Genève Ens. Vocale, SRO, Tourniaire

Ibsen's epic play *Peer Gynt* in a complete performance, with Grieg's incidental music, can run to more than five hours. In achieving this concert version, Alain Perroux gave top priority to the 26 numbers of Grieg's complete score, presented in the context of a concise version of the dramatized story. So he devised a narrative to link the episodic story – superbly spoken here by **Sir Derek Jacobi**. The play itself is simply and sparsely dramatized and is here acted out in English translation, with Peer and the other characters brought convincingly to life in a folksy dialect. Peer himself is excellently played by **Alan Jennings**, while **Inger Dam-Jensen** sings Solveig's role. The musical performances include other soloists, an impressive choir of Trolls, and fine orchestral playing from the **Suisse Romande Orchestra** under **Guillaume Tourniaire**. With the most vivid recording Tourniaire's performance must be counted a great success – not the only way to approach this music (see below) but a convincing musical and dramatic experience. This, in spite of the inevitable fragmentation of a concise version which, inevitably, misses out much detail in the interest of a viable time-span of rather more than two hours. Full documentation includes a complete text of the vocal numbers, which are sung in Norwegian. A remarkable achievement.

Peer Gynt (complete dramatized version); *Before a Southern Convent, Op. 20; Bergliot, Op. 42*

Ⓝ ⒷⒷ ***(*) Naxos 8.570871/2. Actors: Sand, Jacobson, Gericke, Hivju, Galdos, Boys' & Girls' Choruses of Lund Cultural School, Malmö Chamber Ch. & SO, Engset

This is a full dramatized version like the Aeon set above, but with the spoken text pruned and spoken in Norwegian. This seems perverse in a recording designed for a market where most of the customers will understand English. Even so, it must be said that, even without a translation, this epic drama projects very well indeed when the music itself is played with the utmost freshness and is most vividly recorded.

Peer Gynt: extended excerpts

🎙️ *** Virgin 5 45722-2. Mattei, Tilling, Hellekant, Ellerhein Girls' Ch., Estonian Nat. SO & Male Ch., Paavo Järvi

Peer Gynt: extended excerpts; *Bridal Procession, Op. 19/2; 4 Norwegian Dances*

Ⓜ *** RCA 82876 65834-2. Dam-Jensen, L. Symphony Ch., RPO, Temirkanov

Paavo Järvi conducts his **Estonian** forces in warmly expressive, full-blooded readings of 20 items from Grieg's com-

plete *Peer Gynt* music. There are several discs which offer more than the two popular orchestral suites, but Järvi's selection is more generous than most of them, simply omitting the items where spoken words predominate. The extra warmth of his performance is helped by full, forward sound, recorded in a rather reverberant acoustic. His account of the celebrated number, *In the Hall of the Mountain King*, is very exciting, with a wild accelerando and vigorous vocal contributions. Though their roles are limited, the three soloists are first rate, with the baritone, **Peter Mattei**, giving a virile portrait of Peer Gynt in his *Serenade*.

Even though this repertoire is so well served on CD, **Temirkanov's** fine RCA disc should not be passed by. He seems to have an innate feeling for Grieg, and this is one of his very finest records. He offers 16 numbers from *Peer Gynt* and has a vigorous response from the **London Symphony Chorus** (who are enthusiastically angry trolls in *The Hall of the Mountain King*), while he conjures most sensitive playing from the **RPO**. Moreover, he also includes sprightly, colourful and dramatic accounts of the *Four Norwegian Dances*, while the delightful *Bridal Procession* is a closing lollipop. The resonance means that the choral focus is not absolutely sharp, but in all other respects the recording is excellent.

(i) Peer Gynt: excerpts; *In Autumn (overture); An Old Norwegian Romance with Variations; Symphonic Dance 2*

🎙️ ✿ Ⓜ *** EMI 5 66914-2. (i) Hollweg, Beecham Ch. Soc., RPO, Beecham

Beecham showed a very special feeling for this score, and to hear *Morning*, the gently textured *Anitra's Dance* or the eloquent portrayal of the *Death of Aase* under his baton is a uniquely rewarding experience. **Ilse Hollweg** makes an excellent soloist. The recording dates from 1957 and, like most earlier Beecham reissues, has been enhanced by the remastering process. The most delectable of the *Symphonic Dances*, very beautifully played, makes an ideal encore after *Solveig's Lullaby*, affectingly sung by Hollweg. The *In Autumn* overture, not one of Grieg's finest works, is most enjoyable when Sir Thomas is so persuasive, not shirking the melodramatic moments. Finally for the present reissue, we are offered *An Old Norwegian Romance with Variations* (not previously released in its stereo format). It is a piece of much colour and charm, which is fully realized here.

Peer Gynt: Suites 1 & 2; *Bell Ringing, Op. 54/6; Funeral March in Memory of Rikard Nordraak; Old Norwegian Romance with Variations*

🎙️ **** BIS-SACD 1591. Bergen PO, Ruud

Ole Ruud's BIS SACD is now a clear first choice for the two *Peer Gynt Suites*. The freshness of *Morning* recalls Beecham, and the string playing in the *Death of Aase*, *Anitra's Dance* and *Solveig's Song* has exquisite delicacy of feeling; yet *In the Hall of the Mountain King*, opening gently, accelerates to a terrific climax, demonstrating the recording's wide range. The *Funeral March* is powerfully and sombrely played and the charming *Old Norwegian Melody with Variations* (another

Beecham speciality) makes a vivid contrast, with *Bell Ringing* a spectacular encore. Excellent playing and superb recording, especially when heard in surround sound.

Peer Gynt: Overture; Suites 1–2; Lyric Pieces: Evening in the Mountain; Cradle Song; Sigurd Jorsalfar: Suite, Op. 56; Wedding Day at Troldhaugen, Op. 65/6

(BB) **(*) Naxos 8.550140. CSSR State PO, Košice, Gunzenhauser

A generous Grieg anthology on Naxos (70 minutes, all but 3 seconds) and the performances by the **Slovak State Philharmonic Orchestra** in Košice are very fresh and lively and thoroughly enjoyable. There is wide dynamic range both in the playing and in the recording, and sensitivity in matters of phrasing.

GRIFFES, Charles Tomlinson
(1884–1920)

Bacchanale; Clouds; The Pleasure-Dome of Kubla-Khan; (i) Poem for Flute and Orchestra; 3 Tone-Pictures (The Lake at Evening; The Vale of Dreams; The Night Winds); The White Peacock. (ii) 3 Poems of Fiona McLeod (The Lament of Ian the Proud; The Dark Eyes to Mine; The Rose of the Night)

🎵 (BB) *** Naxos 8.559164. Buffalo PO, Falletta; with (i) Wincenc; (ii) Quintiliani

This invaluable disc gives a warm and colourful portrait of this late-romantic American composer, sadly short lived. It includes not only his three best-known orchestral works, but a clutch of rarities as well, otherwise unavailable on disc. The shimmering beauty of his writing matches that of Debussy on the one hand, Delius on the other, with his inspiration regularly coming from English literature. Apart from Debussy and Ravel, Griffes was drawn to Mussorgsky and Scriabin, as well as to oriental music. *The White Peacock* (1915) comes from a suite for piano (*Four Roman Sketches*), which he later scored for orchestra. *The Pleasure-Dome of Kubla Khan* (1919) and the *Poem for Flute and Orchestra* (1918) are probably his masterpieces. Performances here are outstanding and very well recorded, with **JoAnn Falletta** as music director of the **Buffalo Philharmonic** drawing refined and atmospheric performances from her players, with **Barbara Quintiliani** as the bright soloist in the songs and **Carol Wincenc**, principal flute in the orchestra, a most sympathetic soloist in the *Poem*. This fine compilation fills an important gap in the catalogue.

Roman Sketches: The White Peacock; Nightfall; The Fountain of the Acqua Paola; Clouds

🎵 *** ASV Gold GLD 4020. LSO, Pittau – KORNGOLD: *Symphonic Serenade* ***

Charles Griffes, the American impressionist composer, is most remembered for *The White Peacock*, but all four of the richly evocative miniature tone-poems here have the shim-

mering, sensuous textures that made that piece famous, with influences from Debussy, Delius and Respighi glowingly apparent. Yet the music is still all his own, and it is very beautifully played and recorded here, with the similarly luscious Korngold *Symphonic Serenade* as an ideal coupling. Demonstration sound quality.

GROFÉ, Ferde (1892–1972)

Grand Canyon Suite

🎵 (M) *** Telarc CD 80086 (with additional cloudburst, including real thunder). Cincinnati Pops O, Kunzel – GERSHWIN: *Catfish Row* ***

(M) **(*) RCA (ADD) 82876 67904-2. O, Gould – COPLAND: *Billy the Kid ; Rodeo* **(*)

The Cincinnati performance is played with great commitment and fine pictorial splendour. What gives the Telarc CD its special edge is the inclusion of a second performance of *Cloudburst* as an appendix with a genuine thunderstorm laminated on to the orchestral recording. The result is overwhelmingly thrilling, except that in the final thunderclap God quite upstages the orchestra, who are left trying frenziedly to match its amplitude in their closing peroration.

Morton Gould's account of the *Grand Canyon Suite* is as spectacular as you could want. The 1960 recording was made in RCA Victor's ballroom studio in New York's Manhattan Center, with the orchestra repositioned during the recording for maximum sonic effect. The horns, for instance, were separated and relocated round the room for the succession of horn calls which open the *Sunset movement*, and elsewhere echo-chamber effects were used, notably for the trombone duet in *On the Trail*, during which the players used megaphones. A similar treatment was given to the strings at the opening of the *Cloudburst* sequence.

(i) Grand Canyon Suite; (ii) Mississippi Suite

(*) Australian Decca Eloquence (ADD/DDD) 442 9496. (i) Detroit SO, Dorati; (ii) Eastman-Rochester O, Hanson – GERSHWIN: *Porgy & Bess Symphonic Picture* *

Antal Dorati has the advantage of a superlative Decca recording, very much in the demonstration class, with stereoscopically vivid detail. Yet the performance combines subtlety with spectacle, and this version is very much in a class of its own. The *Mississippi Suite*, a much lesser piece, is also persuasively presented, in the vivid Mercury manner, especially the exuberant portrait of *Huckleberry Finn*. But the canyon storms rage much more spectacularly on the Telarc version.

GUARNIERI, Carmargo
(1907–93)

Symphonies 2 (Uirapuru); 3. Abertura Concertante

(N) *** BIS CD-1220. São Paulo SO, John Neschling

Guarnieri was a native of São Paulo, though he studied briefly in Paris with Koechlin. Best known for his piano music (which aspiring pianists used to play at BBC auditions), his symphonies are colourful and exuberant, full of vitality and impetus. They are very well played and recorded here, and this CD is worth exploring.

GUERRERO, Francisco
(1528–99)

Missa Sancta et Immaculata; Hei mihi, Domine; Lauda mater ecclesia; Magnificat septimi toni; O lux beata Trinitas; Traha me post te, virgo Maria; Vexilla Regis

(N) (BB) *** Hyp. Helios CDH 55313. Westminster Cathedral Ch., O'Donnell

A boy chorister and brilliant instrumentalist in his youth, Guerrero spent virtually his entire career as maestro at Seville Cathedral. His *Missa Sancta et immaculata* is based on the celebrated four-part motet of that name by his one-time master, Christobel de Morale. The two serene motets, *Hei mihi, Domine* and *Trahe me post te, virgo Maria*, and the three hymns composed for Passion Sunday are of striking quality and character. The **Westminster Cathedral Choir** and **James O'Donnell** give performances of quite outstanding eloquence and poetry and the recording is first class.

GUILMANT, Félix Alexandre (1837–1911)

Symphony 1 for Organ & Orchestra, Op. 42

⊕-*** Chan. 9271. Tracey (organ of Liverpool Cathedral), BBC PO, Tortelier – WIDOR: *Symphony 5* *** ; POULENC: *Organ Concerto* **(*)

This Guilmant *Symphony* (the composer's own arrangement of his *First Organ Sonata*) is a real find, with all the genial vigour of the famous work of Saint-Saëns. The first movement has a galumphing main theme and an equally pleasing secondary idea. It is followed by a tunefully idyllic *Pastorale* (with some delicious registration from **Ian Tracey**) and a rumbustiously grandiloquent finale. All great fun, and well suited to the larger-than-life resonance of Liverpool Cathedral with its long reverberation period.

Symphony 2 for Organ & Orchestra, Op. 91

*** Chan. 9785. Tracey (organ of Liverpool Cathedral), BBC PO, Tortelier – FRANCK: *Choral 2*; WIDOR: *Symphony 3* ***

Guilmant's *Second Symphony* is a hugely effective transcription of his *Eighth Organ Sonata*. It opens gently with an anticipatory, fanfare-like figure on the violins; then, after the grandiose organ entry with tutti, the *allegro* sets off with infectious vigour. The *Adagio con affetto* is romantic but still reminds us we are in a cathedral, as does the shorter *Andante sostenuto*, which follows the rumbustious Scherzo. The finale opens evocatively and then becomes instantly animated, working towards a splendidly grandiloquent

ending. The performance has great gusto and, if the wide resonance of Liverpool Cathedral prevents any chance of internal clarity, it certainly gives the music a superb impact. Full marks to the Chandos engineers.

GURNEY, Ivor (1890–1937)

Songs: All night under the moon; An epitaph; Bread and cherries; By a bierside; The cloths of Heaven; Cradle song; Desire in spring; Down by the Salley Gardens; Epitaph in old mode; 5 Elizabethan Songs; Even such is time; The fields are full; The folly of being comforted; Hanacker mill; In Flanders; I will go with my father a-ploughing; Most holy night; Nine of the clock; Severn Meadows; The singer; You are my sky

*** Hyp. CDA 67243. Agnew, Drake

Ivor Gurney was born in Gloucester and became a chorister at the cathedral, later studying composition under Stanford and (after his wartime service) Vaughan Williams. Soldiering in the trenches in the First World War ruined his physical health, and probably led to a later mental deterioration and eventually complete mental collapse. But during his comparatively short creative life he composed over 300 songs, the best of which are among the finest settings in the English language, their pervasive dolorous mood often drawing parallels with Dowland. **Paul Agnew** moulds the melodic lines with great sensitivity, his use of vocal colour illuminating the words, and **Julius Drake** accompanies with natural understanding. The recording is excellent, and this is another fine addition to the Hyperion treasure-house of vocal recordings.

War Elegy

⊕-(M) *** Dutton CDLX 7172. BBC SO, Lloyd-Jones – KELLY: *Elegy: In Memoriam Rupert Brooke*; ELKINGTON: *Out of the Mist* ***; ELGAR: *The Spirit of England*; PARRY: *The Chivalry of the Sea* ***

This deeply moving orchestral piece offers a totally new view of the tragic Ivor Gurney. It is quite different from the charming songs and poems he wrote, even after he had been incarcerated in a mental home for 20 years of his life. That mental illness had been brought about by his terrible experiences in the trenches in the First World War, something which this piece directly reflects in a powerful funeral march. After a single rehearsal run-through in 1920, it was totally neglected, and here it receives its very first professional performance, superbly conducted. On a fascinating disc of war-inspired pieces it stands out as a heart-stopping work, chilling in its power.

PIANO MUSIC

Nocturnes: in A flat; B. 4 Unpublished Pieces: Despair; The Sea; Sehnsucht (Longing); Song of the Summer Woods. Preludes 1–9

(M) **(*) Somm CD038. Bebbington – FERGUSON: *Bagatelles; Sonata* ***

Ivor Gurney is remembered more for his songs (he was also a poet) than for his piano music. The four unpublished pieces written when he was in his late teens show a strong poetic feeling and, though the idiom is eclectic, there is a real emerging musical personality and a strong sense of Englishness. Most of these pieces cast a certain spell, despite a limited range of moods. **Mark Bebbington** plays them very sensitively.

HAAS, Pavel (1899–1944)

String Quartets 1, Op. 3; 3, Op. 15

*** Sup. SU 3922-2. Pavel Haas Qt – JANÁČEK: *String Quartet 1* ***

String Quartet 2 (From the Monkey Mountains), Op. 7

*** Sup. SU 3877-2. Pavel Haas Qt – JANÁČEK: *String Quartet 2* ***

Pavel Haas was destined to die in Auschwitz in 1944, so these superb recordings of his three *Quartets* by the eponymous Czech quartet are particularly welcome. The *First*, written in 1921, is short, powerful in utterance and succinct. The *Second*, subtitled *From the Monkey Mountains* and written four years later, has a distinctly bizarre flavour, and goes over the top in its finale with its jazz drumming. The *Third Quartet* (1938) is undoubtedly the finest of the three, passionate, pungent and heartfelt, with a closing set of variations, plus fugue, and has great vitality. Marvellous performances and the couplings are equally impressive both as performances and as recordings.

HAHN, Reynaldo (1875–1947)

Le Bal de Béatrice d'Este (ballet suite)

(BB) *** Hyp. Helios CDH 55167. New L. O, Corp – POULENC: *Aubade; Sinfonietta* ***

Le Bal de Béatrice d'Este is a charming pastiche, dating from the early years of the century and scored for the unusual combination of wind instruments, two harps, piano and timpani. **Ronald Corp** and the **New London Orchestra** play it with real panache and sensitivity.

Piano Concerto in E

⊕ *** Hyp. CDA 66897. Coombs, BBC Scottish SO, Ossonce – MASSENET: *Piano Concerto* ***

Entitled *Improvisation*, the opening movement of this charming work starts with a theme which surprisingly has an English flavour, easily lyrical, leading on to variations full of sharp, sparkling contrasts. A brief, light-hearted Scherzo leads to a combined slow movement (*Reverie*) and finale (*Toccata*). What **Stephen Coombs's** inspired performance demonstrates is that, though no deep emotions are touched, this is a delightful piece, well worth reviving.

CHAMBER MUSIC

Nocturne in E flat for Violin and Piano; Piano Quartet 3 in G; Romance; Si mes vers avaient des ailes (trans. for cello and piano); Soliloque et Forlane for Viola and Piano; Violin Sonata in C

⊕ *** Hyp. CDA 67391. Room-Music

Stephen Coombs, who is the pianist of **Room-Music**, here plays with great sensitivity and intelligence. So, too, do his companions, the violinist **Charles Sewart**, violist **Yuko Inoe** and **Philip de Groote**, cellist of the Chilingirian Quartet. The C major *Violin Sonata* of 1926 breathes much the same air as the Fauré of the *Piano Quartets* and the A major *Sonata*; and much the same goes for the shorter pieces: the *Romance* and the *Nocturne*. The *Piano Quartet No. 3* reflects nothing of the darkness of the times. Its slow movement has all the enchantment of a balmy Mediterranean night. It has fluency and grace, and an innocent delight in life.

Piano Quintet in F sharp min.

*** Hyp. CDA 67258. Coombs, Chilingirian Qt – VIERNE: *Piano Quintet* ***

Hahn's *Piano Quintet* is both compelling and fresh, although the debt to Fauré (not so much the later music as the Fauré of the A major *Sonata* and the *Piano Quartets*) is pervasive. **Stephen Coombs** and the **Chilingirians** play with conviction and character, and are given the benefit of present and vivid recorded sound.

Mélodies

L'Air; A Chloris; L'Automne; 7 Chansons grises; La Chère Blessure; D'une prison; L'Enamourée; Les Etoiles; Fêtes galantes; Les Fontaines; L'Incrédule; Infidélité; Offrande; Quand je fus pris au pavillon; Si mes vers avaient des ailes; Tyndaris

(BB) *** Hyp. Helios CDH 55040. Hill, Johnson

If Hahn never quite matched the supreme inspiration of his most famous song, *Si mes vers avaient des ailes*, the delights here are many, the charm great. **Martyn Hill**, ideally accompanied by **Graham Johnson**, gives delicate and stylish performances, well recorded.

Melodies

*** Hyp. CDA 67141/2. Lott, Bickley, Bostridge, Varcoe, L. Schubert Chorale, Layton, Johnson

This is the most comprehensive collection of Hahn songs ever recorded. As in his Schubert edition for Hyperion, **Graham Johnson** masterminds the project to give endless new insights, whether in his ideal choice of soloists, his inspired playing or his illuminating notes. Specially valuable are the ten *Etudes latines*, both pure and sensuous in their classical evocation. Fine, atmospheric sound.

'La Belle Epoque': Mélodies: A Chloris; L'Automne; D'une prison; L'Enamourée; Dans la nuit; Fêtes galantes; Les Fontaines; Fumée; L'Heure exquise; Infidélité; Je me souviens; Mai; Nocturne; Offrande;

Paysage; Le Printemps; Quand je fus pris au pavillon; Quand la nuit n'est pas étoilée; Le Rossignol des lilas; Si mes vers avaient des ailes; Trois jours de vendange; Etudes Latines: Lydé; Phyllis; Tyndaris

⊙— *** Sony SK 60168. Graham, Vignoles

The solemnity of **Susan Graham's** first song, *A Chloris*, with its Bachian pastiche may surprise those who think of Hahn as merely a dilettante tunesmith, and Graham finds the fullest range of expression in this charming collection. A good single-disc choice, made the more attractive by the glowing beauty of Graham's voice, sensuous in the most famous song, *Si mes vers avaient des ailes*. Fine, sensitive accompaniment from **Roger Vignoles**.

HALÉVY, Jacques Fromental
(1799–1862)

La Juive (complete; DVD version)

*** DG **DVD** 073 4001 (2). Shicoff, Stoyanova, Ivan, Zhang, Fink, Daniel, V. State Op. Ch. & O, Sutej (V/D: Johannes Muller – described as the DVD Producer, no video director identified)

Recorded at the Vienna State Opera in 2003, Gunter Kramer's production of Halévy's most famous opera seeks to make the story of Jewish persecution in 1414 relevant to today by updating it broadly to the 20th century. With Gentile characters and the chorus wearing Austrian traditional costume, '*Trachten*', the date becomes slightly ambiguous. The central character of Eleazar, the Jew, is very much a figure such as the Nazis might have condemned, a characterization that **Neil Shicoff** relishes (as he does in the earlier CD set), singing nobly. His daughter, Rachel (touchingly sung by **Krassimira Stoyanova**), is later revealed to be adopted and in fact a Gentile, daughter of Eleazar's enemy, Cardinal de Brogni, powerfully sung by **Walter Fink**. Though **Jianyi Zhang** as Leopold is hardly a romantic figure, he sings with freshness and clarity, his tenor well contrasted with that of Shicoff. **Simina Ivan** as Princess Eudoxie sings with sweetness and poise, and **Boaz Daniel** is fine as Ruggiero, firm and dark. **Vjekoslav Sutej** draws warmly expressive playing and singing from the orchestra and chorus, making the most of melodramatic situations even when backed by less than inspired music. Bright, forward sound. The second disc contains an hour-long bonus in two films, 'Finding Eleazar', a portrait of Shicoff, and a film of Shicoff singing one of his big arias as directed by Sidney Lumet in New York.

HALVORSEN, Johan (1864–1935)

Air norvégien, Op. 7; Danses norvégiennes

⊙— (BB) *** Naxos 8.550329. Kang, Slovak (Bratislava) RSO, Leaper – SIBELIUS: *Violin Concerto;* SINDING: *Légende;* SVENDSEN: *Romance ***

Dong-Suk Kang plays the attractive *Danses norvégiennes* with great panache, character and effortless virtuosity, and delivers an equally impeccable performance of the earlier *Air norvégien*.

Askeladden: Suite; Gurre (Dramatic Suite), Op. 17; The Merchant of Venice: Suite

*** Simax PSC 1198. Latvian Nat. SO, Mikkelsen

Festival March; Kongen (The King): Suite; Tordenskjold (Suite); Vasantasena: Suite

*** Simax PSC 1199. Latvian Nat. SO, Mikkelsen

Halvorsen composed extensively for the stage. The suite from *The Merchant of Venice* on the first CD is second-rate salon stuff, but that is the only disappointment. The music to Holger Drachmann's play *Gurre* is not only expertly laid out for the orchestra but delightfully fresh. The idiom is indebted to Grieg but he obviously knew his Berlioz and Svendsen. *Sommernatsbryllup* ('Summer night's wedding') has much charm and brilliance and so has the opening *Aftenlandskap* ('Evening scene'), an atmospheric and appealing piece. *Askeladden* is a play for children, and the suite recorded here has abundant charm. The second disc brings music for Bjørnstjerne Bjørnson's play, *Kongen* ('The King'), whose delightful second movement, *Hyrdepigernes Dans* ('Dance of the Shepherdesses') is quite irresistible; it is difficult to get it out of your head. *Vasantasena* aspires to an oriental exoticism which is quite endearing and charming. The **Latvian National Orchestra** play splendidly for **Terje Mikkelsen**, and the recording is state of the art, with beautifully transparent strings and with plenty of space round the sound.

HANDEL, George Frideric
(1685–1759)

'Masterworks': (i) *Concerti grossi, Op. 3/1–6; Op. 6/1–12;* (ii) *Concerto grosso in C (Alexander's Feast);* (iii) *Concerti a due cori 1–3;* (iv; i) *Oboe Concertos 1–3; Largo in F; Arrival of the Queen of Sheba (Solomon);* (v; i) 12 *Organ Concertos, Op. 4/1–6; Op. 7/1–6; 13 (Cuckoo & Nightingale); 14–16; Sonata: Il Trionfo del Tempo e del Disinganno;* (i) *Music for the Royal Fireworks; Water Music (Suites 1–3);* (vi) *Flute Sonatas: in E min. & D; Halle Flute Sonatas 1–3;* (vii) 6 *Trio Sonatas, Op. 2; Trio Sonatas in F & G min.;* (viii) 4 *Coronation Anthems;* (viii–ix) *Dixit Dominus;* (viii; x) *Nisi Dominus;* (viii; xi) *Dettingen Anthem & Te Deum;* (xii) *Giulio Cesare in Egitto* (complete); (xiii) *Hercules* (complete); (xiv) *Israel in Egypt* (complete); (xv) *Judas Maccabaeus* (complete); (xvi) *Messiah* (complete; 1739 version); (xvii) *Ode for St Cecilia's Day;* (viii; xviii) *Salve Regina;* (xix) *Solomon* (complete)

Ⓝ (BB) **** Decca (ADD/DDD) 478 1190 (30). (i) ASMF, Marriner; (ii) L. Philomusica, Granville Jones; (iii) AAM, Hogwood; (iv) R. Lord; (v) Malcolm; (vi) Bennett, Kraemer, Vigay; (vii) Bennett, Latchem or Petri, with Sillito, Cuckson or Malcolm; (viii) Westminster Abbey Ch. & O, or E.

Concert, Preston; (ix) Augér, Dawson, Montague, Nixon, Birchall; (x) Montague, Mark Ainsley, Birchall; (xi) Tipping, H. Christophers, Varcoe, Pearce; (xii) Mijanovi , Koẑená, Hellekant, Von Otter, Mehta, Ewing, Bertin, Ankaous, Musiciens du Louvre, Minkowski; (xiii) Tomlinson, Walker, Rolfe Johnson, J. Smith, Denley, Savidge, Monteverdi Ch., E. Bar. Sol., Gardiner; (xiv) Gritton, Crabtree, Chance, Ogden, Bostridge, Varcoe, Vivian, East, King's College, Cambridge, Ch., Brandenburg Consort, Cleobury; (xv) R. Davies, Palmer, J. Baker, Shirley-Quirk, Keyte, Esswood, Wandsworth School Ch., ECO, Mackerras; (xvi) Ameling, Reynolds, Langridge, Howell, ASMF & Ch., Marriner; (xvii) Lott, Rolfe Johnson, E. Concert Ch. & O, Pinnock; (xviii) Augér; (xix) Scholl, Dam-Jensen, Gritton, Hagley, Bickley, Agnew, Harvey, Gabrieli Consort & Players, McCreesh

The Decca bargain 'Masterworks' 30-disc compilation consists primarily of vintage modern-instrument recordings of the highest quality which we have continued to praise over the years. The contribution of **Marriner** and the **ASMF** is considerable, and the chamber music, with many top musicians contributing, is also highly distinguished. As for the vocal section, there are countless starry names here, and the selection includes complete versions of six key operas and oratorios. Of course, such a compilation cannot begin to cover the amazing range of Handelian repertoire now on record, but there are many favourite works here, and virtually nothing to disappoint. This would certainly make a fine basis for a Handelian library and, while texts are not included, the documentation is otherwise excellent. Highly recommended.

Ariodante (suite): Overture; Sinfonia pastorale; Ballo. Il Pastor Fido (suite): Overture; March: Air pour les chasseurs I & II

*** Australian Decca Eloquence (ADD) 476 2440. ASMF, Marriner – GLUCK: Don Juan *******

These two highly attractive suites are played with grace and fine rhythmic point by **Marriner** and his splendid orchestral group. A fine bonus for the superb Gluck ballet, with vintage Argo (1971) sound.

Concerti grossi, Op. 3/1–6 (including 4b), HWV 312–17

⌐ (BB) ******* Hyp. Helios CDH 55075. Brandenburg Cons., Goodman

Roy Goodman's set achieves the best of both worlds by including the spurious (but very engaging) No. 4b and, like Hogwood, using an authentic version of No. 6, yet featuring the concertante organ at its close as a bonus. The playing is rhythmically spirited and enjoyably light and airy: this is period-instrument music-making at its most seductive, helped by some delightfully sensitive flute and oboe contributions from **Rachel Brown** and **Katharina Arfken** respectively. First-class recording, natural and transparent, with a pleasing ambience. A fine bargain.

Concerti grossi, Op. 3/1–6

⌐ ******** HM HMU 907 415. AAM, Egarr

(BB) ******* Naxos 8.553457. N. Sinfonia, Creswick

Richard Egarr's Gramophone Award-winning performance with the freshly minted Academy of Ancient Music now takes its place at the top of the list of recommendations for those wanting period instruments. Ignoring his predecessor Christopher Hogwood's suggestions about the finale being inauthentic, he returns to the usual two-movement Sixth Concerto with its concertante organ and even interpolates an 'improvised' middle section which he plays himself. The other attraction of the disc is the bonus encore, a lively 'concerto' for solo violin and strings which **Pavlo Beznosiuk** despatches with aplomb, especially the sparkling finale. Throughout, the Academy play with characteristic athleticism, but with no suggestion of acid in the strings, and there is also a total lack of sentimental feeling in the espressivo of slow movements. Excellent recording.

Barry Creswick and his excellent **Northern Sinfonia** provide a most enjoyable modern-instrument version of Op. 3. They do not include No. 4b, nor give us the revised version of No. 6, but neither do most of their competitors, and with excellent playing throughout, freshly paced and most truthfully recorded, this is excellent value.

Concerti grossi, Op. 3/1–6; Op. 6/1–12

(M) ******* Avie AV 2065 (3). Handel & Haydn Soc., Boston, Hogwood

(M) ******* Decca 475 8673 (3). ASMF, Marriner

Avie have taken over from Decca/Oiseau-Lyre **Hogwood's** recordings of Opp. 3 and 6, recorded in 1988 and 1991/2 respectively, and have reissued the whole series very economically on three discs. The performance of Op. 3 with his excellent Boston players has no lack of energy and life and a fairly high degree of polish. Hogwood's characteristically astringent rhythmic style is then heard at its most vital in Op. 6. The playing brings bracingly brisk tempi and here there is no question of any lack of refinement, with transparency of texture rather than sonority paramount. Two harpsichords and an arch-lute are used as continuo.

The integral Decca recording of the Handel Concerti grossi makes a permanent memorial of the partnership formed by the inspired scholarship of **Thurston Dart** and the interpretative skill and musicianship of **Neville Marriner** and his superb ensemble, at their peak in the late 1960s. Dart planned a double continuo of both organ and harpsichord, used judiciously to vary textural colour and weight. Alas, the first-class CD transfer for this reissue among Decca's Originals brings no cues for individual movements, only one band for each work.

Concerti grossi, Op. 6/1–12

⌐ ******* Chan. 9004/6. I Musici de Montréal, Turovsky

(N) (B) ****(*)** Decca O-L 478 0319 (3). Il Giardino Armonico, Antonini

**(*) Telarc CD 80253 (Nos. 1–6); CD 80688 (Nos. 7–12). Boston Bar., Pearlman

I Musici de Montréal offer a refreshing and stimulating set of Handel's Opus 6. The group uses modern instruments and **Yuli Turovsky's** aim is to seek a compromise between modern and authentic practice by paring down vibrato in some of the expressive music. The concertino, **Eleonora** and **Natalya Turovsky** and **Alain Aubut**, play impressively, while the main group (6.3.1.1) produces full, well-balanced tone, and Handel's joyous fugues are particularly fresh and buoyant. Turovsky paces convincingly, not missing Handel's breadth of sonority and moments of expressive grandeur.

Antonini's new set of Opus 6 has been enthusiastically received in some quarters, but for us it has an aspect which prevents an unqualified recommendation. Antonini restores ('and expands') the oboe parts in Nos. 1, 2, 5, and 6 and the playing throughout is dramatic, full of vitality and certainly responsive to the music's expressive qualities. If one samples the famously melodic aria: *Larghetto e piano* in No.12, one finds it is gently paced to uncover its simple charm. But **Il Giardino Armonico** here consists of only eight players (including a continuo of archlute and tripleharp), and one listens in vain for the richness of sonority found in the competing set from Turovsky and earlier versions featuring the ASMF. Moreover, *fortissimos* and frequent *sforzandos* have a sharp cutting edge, which we found becomes tiring to listen to. The recording itself cannot be faulted.

Pearlman's set was recorded in two groups, Nos. 1–6 in 1992 and the remainder in 2007. But the recording quality is consistently fine, as we would expect from Telarc. The performances are consistently warm and elegant, polished, without loss of vitality, and undoubtedly enjoyable. Yet in spite of the use of period instruments there is an absence of exhilaration and bite in the playing, and the full grandeur of Handel's inspiration only partly emerges.

Concerto grosso in B flat, Op. 6/7

*** Ara. Z 6723. San Francisco Ballet O, Lark Qt, Le Roux – SCHOENBERG: *Concerto for String Quartet & Orchestra after Handel's Op. 6/7*; ELGAR: *Introduction & Allegro for Strings*; SPOHR: *Concerto for String Quartet & Orchestra* ***

What a pleasure to hear a Handel *Concerto grosso* played for once on a full body of modern strings, emphasizing its warmth of sonority. But this is included as part of an imaginative concert of string music so that the listener can compare the original with Schoenberg's bizarre but aurally fascinating recomposed pastiche.

(i) Harp Concerto, Op. 4/6; Variations for Harp

&—❀ (M) **** Decca (ADD) 425 723-2. Marisa Robles, (i) ASMF, Iona Brown – BOIELDIEU; DITTERSDORF: *Harp Concertos, etc.* **** ❀

Handel's Op. 4/6 is well known in both organ and harp versions. **Marisa Robles** and **Iona Brown** make an unforgettable case for the latter by creating the most delightful textures, while never letting the work sound insubstantial. The **ASMF** accompaniment, so stylish and beautifully balanced, is a treat in itself, and the recording is well-nigh perfect.

Oboe Concertos 1, HWV 301; 2, HWV 302a; 3, HWV 287; Sonatas for Oboe & Continuo in B flat, HWV 357; in F, HWV 363a; in G min., Op. 1/6,

HWV 364a; in C min., Op. 1/8, HWV 366; Sonata in G min. for Oboe, Violins & Continuo, HWV 404

&—❀ (BB) **** Regis RRC 1106. Francis, L. Harpsichord Ens.

Oboe Concertos 1–3; Air & Rondo (ed. Camden); (i) Suite in G min. (ed. Camden); Otho: Overture

(BB) *** Naxos 8.553430. Camden, (i) Girdwood; City of L. Sinfonia, Ward

Sarah Francis is a superb baroque oboist, at the same time directing the members of the **London Harpsichord Ensemble** with spirit and finesse. These performances are not only delightful but a model of style. A collection that leads the field, not least for its excellent sound. At its new Regis price it is a remarkable bargain.

Anthony Camden, for years principal oboe of the LSO, here makes a very welcome solo appearance on disc, playing with typical point and style, using his attractively reedy tone. The regular oboe concertos are well supplemented by the *Suite in G minor* as edited by Camden, where he is joined by the prize-winning **Julia Girdwood** on the second oboe. The *Otho Overture* too features prominent roles for oboes in duet. **Ward** and the **City of London Sinfonia** are sympathetic accompanists using modern instruments. First-rate sound from All Saints, East Finchley.

Organ concertos

Organ Concertos, Op. 4/1–6; Op. 7/1–6

&—❀ (BB) **** Warner Apex 2564 62760-2 (2). Koopman, Amsterdam Bar. O

Organ Concertos, Op. 4/1–6; Op. 7/1–6; in F (The Cuckoo and the Nightingale), HWV 295; in A, HWV 296; in D min., HWV 304

&—❀ (BB) *** DG Trio 469 358-2 (3). Preston; Holliger (harp in Op. 4/6), E. Concert, Pinnock

Ton Koopman's paired sets of Opp. 4 and 7 now reappear on the Apex super-bargain label, complete on two CDs. They take precedence over all the competition, both as performances and as recordings. The playing has wonderful life and warmth, tempi are always aptly judged and, although original instruments are used, this is authenticity with a kindly presence, for the warm acoustic ambience of St Bartholomew's Church, Beek-Ubbergen, Holland, gives the orchestra a glowingly vivid coloration and the string timbre is particularly attractive. So is the organ itself, which is just right for the music.

Simon Preston's set of the major organ concertos returns to the catalogue, economically priced on a DG Archiv Trio. **Ursula Holliger's** solo contribution on a baroque harp is memorable, for she creates some delicious sounds. For those wanting a complete coverage of these engaging works this should serve admirably.

Organ Concertos, Op. 4/1–6

(BB) *** Naxos 8.553835. Lindley, N. Sinfonia, Creswick

A most enjoyable and inexpensive modern-instrument performance of Op. 4 on Naxos, rhythmically jaunty and warmly expressive by turns and the piping reeds of the organ at Holy Cross Church, Fenham, seem very apt for the music. Not a first choice overall but an undoubted bargain.

Organ Concertos, Op. 4/1–6 (Chamber versions)

🔑 Ⓜ **** Avie AV 2055. Halls, Sonnerie, Huggett

Ⓝ *** Decca 478 1465. Dantoni, Accademia Bizantina

Ⓝ *** HM HMU 807466. Egarr, AAM

Matthew Halls presents these works on a Dutch Fama/Klop instrument, with a specification to meet all of Handel's demands. **Monica Huggett's** period-instrument accompaniments are similarly on a chamber scale, using a small string group, plus a pair of oboes (as used by Handel) in Nos. 1 and 4. The result is delightful. Matthew Halls is a superb soloist, improvising and decorating genially and stylishly without ever overdoing it. Moreover, the recording is beautifully balanced, the sound throughout wholly beguiling. The documentation is first class.

Two competing new versions of the Opus 4 *Concertos* bring a further choice, as both soloists direct the music from the keyboard. **Dantoni** uses the organ in Bartholomäuskirche in Handel's home city of Halle. It is a positive organ with six stops, built in the style of a small Bohemian instrument in 2007. Its characteristic sound is piquant but relatively more robust than the instrument used on Harmonia Mundi and balanced by his accompanying group of 16 players (with recorders used in No. 6).

Using a four-stop chamber organ built by Robin Jennings, **Richard Egarr** offers a pleasing set of smaller-scale performances, with his organ producing an even more piquant and modest timbre. He includes a special arrangement of the final concerto to accommodate a lute, as was included for the first performance in 1736 (together with *Alexander's Feast*). Overall these performances are more lightweight, but certainly not less appealing.

Organ Concertos: in G, Op. 4/1; in B flat, Op. 4/2

Ⓝ (***) Australian Decca Eloquence mono 480 0833. Demessieux, SRO, Ansermet – VIVALDI: *Bassoon Concertos* **; MARCELLO: *Oboe Concerto* (***)

The two organ concertos here in well-balanced mono sound, dating from 1952, are performed with distinction by the distinguished **Jeanne Demessieux** – these are baroque concerto performances in unashamedly modern-instrument style at their best, now enjoying a new – and well-deserved – return to the catalogue.

Music for the Royal Fireworks (original wind scoring)

🔑 **** Telarc CD 80038. Cleveland Symphonic Winds, Fennell – HOLST: *Military Band Suites* **** ❀

Music for the Royal Fireworks (original wind version; complete); *Water Music Suite* (arr. Harty); *Concerto a due cori in F; Concertos 1 in F; 3 in D*

🔑 ❀ *** Testament SBT 1253. L. Wind Ens., Pro Arte O, LSO, Mackerras

For a recording well over forty years old, this historic Testament (originally Pye) account of Handel's *Fireworks Music* is astonishing. **Charles Mackerras** in 1959 followed up the adventurous idea of using a band of no fewer than 62 wind players plus nine percussionists, echoing Handel's original Hyde Park ensemble in 1749. The result hits you between the ears, especially the rasping horns in the overture, thanks to full and spacious sound with a wide stereo spread. But far from sounding jaded, these leading players were challenged to give an electrifying performance. As a supplement comes a mono recording of the *Minuets I* and *II* with fireworks and cannon effects as background, a fun item demonstrating how important stereo is. The other items, more traditional in style, find Mackerras also blowing away cobwebs. Even the *Water Music Suite* as arranged by Harty sounds brighter and fresher than usual.

In 1978, in Severance Hall, Cleveland, Ohio, **Frederick Fennell** gathered together the wind and brass from the **Cleveland Symphony Orchestra** and recorded a performance to demonstrate spectacularly what fine playing and digital sound could do for Handel's open-air score with the sharpness of focus matched by the presence and amplitude of the sound-image.

Music for the Royal Fireworks; Water Music (complete)

🔑 ❀ Ⓜ **** DG Entrée 474 168-2. Orpheus CO

Ⓝ Ⓜ ***DG 477 7562. E. Concert, Pinnock

Ⓝ ⒷⒷ *** Hyp. Helios CDH55375. King's Consort, King

Ⓑ *** Virgin 545266-2. LCP, Norrington

ⒷⒷ *** Naxos 8.550109. Capella Istropolitana, Warchal

Although modern instruments are used, such is the **Orpheus'** sense of baroque style, so crisp and buoyant are the rhythms, that the effect has much in common with a period performance without any of the snags. How warmly and elegantly they play the colourful and more intimate dances in the central *G major Suite* of the *Water Music*, and they begin with a riveting account of the *Royal Fireworks Music*, catching its sense of spectacle. Strings are used as Handel wished, but the wind and brass dominate. Alas, this outstandingly recorded CD has just been withdrawn.

Pinnock's *Fireworks Music* has tremendous zest and the *Water Music* too is very enticing. Speeds are consistently well chosen. One test is the famous 'Air', which here remains an engagingly gentle piece. The recording is beautifully balanced and clear and this 'Originals' reissue is a first choice for those wanting period-instrument performances.

Robert King was the first in 1989 to record a period performance of the *Royal Fireworks Music* using the full complement of instruments Handel demanded. It was quite an achievement assembling no fewer than 24 baroque oboists ('foreman Paul Goodwin') and 12 baroque bassoonists, nine trumpeters, nine exponents of the hand horn and four timpanists. It all makes for a glorious noise, and King's Handel style has plenty of rhythmic bounce, and the recording gives ample scale. The *Water Music* dates from 1997 and this is above all a performance of contrasts – between the elegant lighter dance movements with the playing warmly refined, and the set-piece *allegros* where the baroque horns and trumpets burst forth exuberantly. They always play with joyful vigour, and with as much weight and with more brightness than modern instruments. The strings are never edgy and often quite mellow, as in the famous 'Air'. The result is both successful and pleasing.

Norrington uses a full orchestra but highlights the bright trumpets and braying horns to give both works a vividly robust open-air flavour. The dance movements have grace, but a lively grace, and it is the consistent vitality that makes these performances so stimulating.

Bohdan Warchal directs the Capella Istropolitana in bright and lively performances of the complete *Water Music* as well as the *Fireworks Music*, well paced and well scaled, with woodwind and brass aptly abrasive, and with such points as double-dotting faithfully observed.

CHAMBER MUSIC

Sinfonia in B flat (for 2 flutes & continuo) (*HWV 338*); *Flute Sonatas, Halle 1–3* (*HWV 374/376; 378*), *Op. 1/1a* (*HWV 379*); *Oboe Sonatas in B flat* (*HWV 357*), *Op. 1/5 & 8* (*HWV 363a & 366*); *Recorder Sonatas, Op. 1/2, 4, 7, 8a & 11* (*HWV 360, 362, 365, 367a & 369*); *in B flat* (*HWV 377*); *Violin Sonatas in D min.* (*HWV 359a*); *Op. 1/3, 6, 9, 10, 12–15* (*HWV 361, 364a, 367a, 368, 370/373*); *Fantasia in A* (for violin & continuo), *HWV 406*; *Trio Sonatas* (for flute, violin & continuo), *Op. 2/1–2* (*HWV 386b & 387*); (for 2 violins & continuo), *Op. 2/3* (*HWV 388*); (for recorder, violin & continuo), *Op. 2/4*; (for 2 violins & continuo), *Op. 2/5* (*HWV 390a*); (for 2 flutes & continuo), *Op. 2/6* (*HWV 391*); *3 Dresden Trio Sonatas* (for 2 violins & continuo), (*HWV 392/3*); *in E* (*HWV 394*); *Trio Sonatas in E min.*, (*HWV 395*); (for 2 oboes & continuo), *Op. 5/1* (*HWV 396*); *Op. 5/2* (for 2 violins & continuo); *Op. 5/3* (for flute, violin & continuo); *Op. 5/4–5* (for 2 violins & continuo) (*HWV 396/400*); *Op. 5/6* (for 2 oboes and continuo); *Op. 5/7* (for 2 violins & continuo) (*HWV 401/402*); *in C* (*Saul*) (*HWV 403*); *in F* (for 2 recorders & continuo) (*HWV 405*)

(B) *** Ph. (ADD/DDD) 470 893-2 (9). Academy Chamber Ens.

This remarkable achievement of Philips in recording virtually all Handel's chamber music in London between 1982 and 1984 with a group of outstanding instrumentalists has lain dormant in the catalogue for two decades. Yet it is an enterprise that can be compared with the Beaux Arts' set of Haydn's *Piano Trios* in both its enterprise and its excellence in terms of performance and outstandingly natural recording quality. As can be seen below, many of the wind sonatas are available separately on a Duo set and are discussed there, but now the whole survey arrives in a bargain box, admirably documented. In short, this set is an endless source of stimulation and pleasure and can be very strongly recommended.

Flute Sonatas; Oboe Sonatas & Violin Sonatas; Recorder Sonatas; Trio Sonatas (complete)

(BB) **(*) CRD (ADD) CRD 5002 (6). L'Ecole d'Orphée

The complete period-instrument recording by L'Ecole d'Orphée of Handel's chamber music involves outstanding artists like Stephen Preston (flute) and David Reichenberg (oboe), and the string players are led by John Holloway. The playing is distinguished, the recording excellent, and the new bargain box is handsomely packaged. The one great snag, carried over from the separate CD issues, is the absence of cues for individual movements, so these records are more difficult to delve into than the original LPs. They are very good value just the same, and the documentation cannot be faulted.

Flute Sonata in D, Op. 2/4, HWV 378; Oboe Sonata in C min., Op. 1/8, HWV 366; Recorder Sonata in A min., Op. 4, HWV 362; Trio Sonatas in F, Op. 2/4, HWV 389; in F, Op. 5/6, HWV, 401; Violin Sonata in D, Op. 1/13, HWV 371

(N) (BB) *** Regis (ADD) RRC 1294. L'Ecole d'Orphee

An attractively chosen selection from the CRD complete set of Handel's chamber music praised by us above, and with the cue points missing from the original discs now added.

Sonatas for Flute, Oboe, Recorder or Violin & Continuo, Op. 1/1, 1a, 1b, 2–8, 9a, 9b, HWV 359 a & b, 361/2; 363b, 364a, 365–6, 367a & b, 369, 371, 379; Halle Sonatas 1–3 (*HWV 374–6*); & *HWV 357–8 & 377*

*** Hyp. CDA 66921/3. Beznosiuk, Beckett, Goodwin, Tunnicliffe, Wallfisch, Nicholson

The Hyperion set concentrates on Opus 1 although, illogically, four of the violin sonatas previously counted as being part of Handel's opus have been omitted as spurious (HWV 368 and 372–3). The fine *Halle Sonatas* have been included, plus some other miscellaneous works now considered to be authentic. The performances use period instruments and have the advantage of current practice, so both flute and oboe timbres have a strong baroque flavour, but the violins are less raw-timbred than the quality offered by L'Ecole d'Orphée; on the other hand, the playing itself is mellower and perhaps at times slightly less vital than on the more comprehensive CRD set.

Flute Sonatas: Op. 1/a; Halle Sonatas 1–3; Oboe Sonatas 1–2, HWV 357, 363a; Op. 1/5 & ; Recorder Sonatas, Op. 1/2, 4, 7 & 11 & HWV 367a & 377; Sinfonia in B flat for 2 Violins & Continuo, HWV 338; Trio Sonatas for 2 Flutes & Continuo & 2 Recorders & Continuo, HWV 395 & 405

⇌ (BB) **** Ph. Duo (ADD) 446 563-2 (2). ASMF Chamber Ens.

This superb Philips Duo assembles virtually all the important *Sonatas* for wind instruments and continuo, plus a single (*Sinfonia*) *Trio Sonata* for two violins and continuo, on a pair of discs offered for the price of one. William Bennett uses a modern flute very persuasively in the *Flute Sonatas* and includes, besides the work from Opus 1 and the three *Halle Sonatas*, a more recent discovery from a Brussels manuscript.

Nicholas Kraemer and Denis Vigay provide admirable support, and the recording is most realistic and present. In the *Recorder Sonatas* Michala Petri plays with her customary virtuosity and flair, and Neil Black is marvellously accomplished in the *Oboe Sonatas*. Both artists share an excellent rapport with their continuo players, who include George Malcolm (harpsichord), Denis Vigay (cello) and Graham Sheen (bassoon), and again the sound is exemplary, natural and spacious. Only those seeking original instruments need look elsewhere.

Flute or Alto Recorder Sonatas: Op. 1/2, 4, 7, 9 & 11; in B flat

*** HM HMU 907151. Verbruggen, Koopman, Linden

Marion Verbruggen uses modern copies of two alto recorders from the early 18th century and a similar voice flute in D; the sounds here are appealingly mellow, with the continuo featuring cello, harpsichord and chest organ. The effect is intimate, expressive and lively by turns, but with no attempt at self-conscious bravura. The recording is beautifully balanced.

(i; ii) Recorder Sonatas, Op. 1/2, 4, 7, 9 & 11; 7 in B flat; (ii) Harpsichord Suite 7 in G min.

*** Guild GMCD 7301. (i) Davis; (ii) Ponsford

Alan Davis's piping recorder is robust in colour, his playing most engaging, and he does not over-ornament, so the melodic line is never fussy. He is very well accompanied by David Ponsford, who also gives a fine performance of the *G minor Harpsichord Suite*.

Recorder Sonatas, Op. 1/2, 4, 7, 11; HWV 367a, 377

*** BIS CD 955. Laurin, Masaaki & Hidemi Suzuki

Dan Laurin is a virtuoso recorder player to match Michala Petri (although with less charm), and his decoration is ever impressive. He is readily matched by Hidemi Suzuki on his baroque cello (their performance of the *Furioso* movement in HWV 367a is hair-raising), and Masaaki Suzuki completes the partnership on the harpsichord. The balance is excellent, within a pleasing acoustic. However the content is ungenerous for a full-priced CD.

Recorder Sonatas, Op. 1/2, 4, 7, 11; in D min. (Fitzwilliam), HWV 367a; Trio Sonata in F, HWV 405; Favourite Air (Lelio's Aria from 'Scipio'); Gavotte, HWV 604; Gigue, HWV 599; Minuet, HWV 603

⊕ (BB) *** Naxos 8.550700. Czidra, Harsányi, Pertis, Keleman

A particularly attractive and generous anthology. These Hungarian musicians are first-class players and their accounts of the sonatas from Op. 1 and the *Trio Sonata* (for two recorders and continuo) are second to none. The encores (for various combinations) are most engaging, especially the *Gavotte* and *Gigue*. The recording is excellent.

Trio Sonatas, Op. 2/1–6 (HWV 386–91) (complete)

*** Avie AV 0033. Huggett, Benjamin, Crouch, Hazelzet, Halls

Handel's set of *Trio Sonatas*, Opus 2, was published by Walsh as being suitable for a pair of violins, oboes or flutes, but this was a publishing gambit to secure more sales, and they are best suited for a pair of violins. The *First Sonata* is available in an alternative version, often performed on oboes; however, here Wilbert Hazelzet plays the upper part on a flute, and this works admirably. Not surprisingly with this cast list, these period performances are of high quality, catching the Handelian sprightliness and nobilty of melodic line (especially when Matthew Halls chooses an organ for the continuo) and yet retaining the character of the Corellian *Sonate da chiesa* which was Handel's compositional pattern. First-class recording.

(i) Trio Sonatas, Opp. 2/5; 5/4 & 7 for 2 Violins & Continuo; Italian cantatas: (i; ii) Notte placida e cheta; (i; ii; iii) Tra la fiamme

⊕ *** Chan. 0620. (i) Purcell Qt (members); (ii) Bott; (iii) with Kershaw, Downer, Amherst, Manson

An entirely delightful recital. The *Trio Sonatas* are full of attractive invention, notably an impressive passacaglia in Op. 5/4, and they are used to frame and act as an interlude between the two Italian cantatas, ravishingly sung by Catherine Bott. The recording is ideally balanced.

Violin Sonatas, Op. 1/3, 6, 10, 12–13; in G, HWV 358; D min., HWV 359a; Allegro in C min., HWV 408; Andante in A min., HWV 412

⊕ **** HM HMU 907259. Manze, Egarr (harpsichord)

Anyone looking for a complete set of Handel's *Violin Sonatas* on period instruments need look no further. The performances are buoyant and full of life. They have undoubted panache and easy virtuosity, and the eloquence of Andrew Manze's lyrical phrasing is immediately demonstrated by the opening *Affetuoso* of the D major, Op. 1/13, with which the programme begins. The period violin is vividly caught and the harpsichord is well placed in the attractively resonant sound-picture. Highly recommended.

KEYBOARD MUSIC

Keyboard Suites Sets 1 & 2: (i) 1 in A; (ii) 2 in F; 3 in D min.; (i) 4 in E min.; (ii) 5 in E; (i) 6 in F sharp min.; 7 in G min.; (ii) 8 in F min.

⊕ ✪ (BB) **** EMI Gemini (ADD) 5 86540-2 (2). (i) Gavrilov; (ii) Richter

Keyboard Suites (i) 9 in G min.; (ii) 10 in D min.; 11 in D min.; (i) 12 in E min.; (ii) 13 in B flat; (i) 14 in G; (ii) 15 in D min.; (i) 16 in G min.

⊕ ✪ (BB) **** EMI Gemini (ADD) 5 86543-2 (2). (i) Richter; (ii) Gavrilov – BEETHOVEN: *Piano Sonata 17* *** ✪

These superb recordings of the Handel *Keyboard Suites* were recorded by Sviatoslav Richter and Andrei Gavrilov at the Château de Marcilly-sur-Maulne during the 1979 Tours Festival. EMI have issued the set in first-class transfers, and in an economical format with Richter's famous 1961 account of Beethoven's *D minor Sonata*, Op. 31, No. 2, thrown in for good measure. The serenity and tranquillity of the slow movements and the radiance of the faster movements have never before been so fully realized.

Harpsichord Suites, Set 1: 1–8, HWV 426/433; 6 Fugues or Voluntariess for Organ or Harpsichord, HWV 605/10; Fugues: in F; E, HWV 611/12

🎧 Ⓜ *** Hyp. Dyad CDD 22045 (2). Nicholson (harpsichord)

Paul Nicholson's playing is admirable, full of life yet with a degree of intimacy that is very appealing. He has an ideal (unnamed) harpsichord, which is perfect for this repertoire and which is superbly recorded. Nicholson's crisp and stylish ornamentation is never fussy, and he is generous with repeats.

Harpsichord Suites, Set 1 (1720): 1–8; Set 2 (1733) 7–8; 9: Preludio (only)

*** Chan. 0669 (Set 1, 1–5); Chan. 0688 (Set 1, 6–8; Set 2, 7–8; 9: Preludio). Yates (harpsichord)

Harpsichord Suites, Set 1 (1735): 1–6

*** Chan. 0644 (3). Yates

Sophie Yates offers both sets of the *Harpsichord Suites*. She plays with flair and vivacity and has the exuberance and bravura – and, above all, the sense of style – that this music calls for.

Harpsichord Suites, Sets 1 & 2: 3; 8; 11; 13; 14; 15

Ⓜ *** Lyrichord LEMS 8034 (2). Wolfe (harpsichord)

The Texan harpsichordist **Paul Wolfe** was a pupil and protégé of Wanda Landowska. He had a harpsichord specially built for him by Frank Rutkowski of Stoney Creek, Connecticut. It is a magnificent creature, dubbed by its maker 'the *Queen Mary*' because of its length – nine feet! It has two manuals with a range of just over five octaves, and seven pedals to alter and mute the timbre, and it includes a buff (or lute) stop which creates a dry, pizzicato sound. The range of colour is aurally fascinating and Wolfe makes the very most of the tonal and dynamic contrasts possible in Handel's music, especially in the variations. The playing itself is infectiously full of life; one's only comment is that Wolfe usually chooses to pace the *Allemandes* very slowly and grandly, even the *Sarabande variée* in the 11th Suite, which is based on *La folia*. The deep bass stop (also favoured by Landowska) can be heard to its fullest effect in the *Prelude* of the *F minor Suite* (No. 8), which provides a lively end to the second disc. The two-CD set, which has 85 minutes of music, is offered at a special price.

Keyboard Suite, Set 2, 1 in B flat (HWV 434)

Ⓜ *** Warner Elatus 2564 61762-2. Schiff (piano) – BRAHMS: Variations & Fugue on a Theme of Handel; REGER: Variations and Fugue on a Theme of Bach ***

This is the *Harpsichord Suite* from which Brahms drew the theme of Handel's third-movement *Aria con variationi* for his own *Variations and Fugue*. **András Schiff** plays the Handel very stylishly, and then moves with hardly a pause straight on to the opening of the Brahms, presumably to avoid any interruption of applause, as these performances are taken from a live recital at the Concertgebouw in 1994. Excellent recording.

VOCAL MUSIC

Aci, Galatea e Polifemo (complete)

🎧 *** Virgin 2CD 5 45557-2 (2). Piau, Mingardo, Naouri, Le Concert d'Astrée, Haïm

A delightful new version of *Aci, Galatea e Polifemo*. **Sandrine Piau** gives the role a strong profile, and **Sara Mingardo**, a true Handelian, sings gloriously. What caps the newest version is **Laurent Naouri's** superbly resonant bass as the one-eyed giant, Polifemo. The Virgin recording is first class.

Acis and Galatea (complete)

*** Erato 3984-25505-2 (2). Daneman, Petibon, Agnew, Cornwell, Ewing, Sinclair, Piolino, Le Monnier, Les Arts Florissants, Christie

Acis and Galatea; Il pastor fido: Hunting Scene

Ⓑ *** Double Decca 452 973-2 (2). Tear, Gomez, Langridge, Luxon, Ch. & ASMF, Marriner – Tear: 'Baroque Recital'***

(i) Acis and Galatea; (ii) Cantata: Look Down, Harmonious Saint

*** Hyp. CDA 66361/2. (i; ii) Mark Ainsley; (i) McFadden, Covey-Crump, George, Harre-Jones; King's Cons., King

Christie gives us a chamber performance with forces similar to those Handel used for the Canons performances. Tempi are inclined to be brisk and rhythms crisp but he has marshalled expert singers; **Alan Ewing's** Polyphemus is particularly good, well characterized and spirited. Indeed, the whole performance is full of life and personality, and William Christie holds everything together with finesse and grace. The sound, too, is well balanced and natural.

Robert King directs a bluff, beautifully sprung reading that brings out its domestic jollity. Using the original version for five solo singers and no chorus, this may be less delicate in its treatment but it is just as winning. The soloists are first rate, with **John Mark Ainsley** among the most stylish of the younger generation of Handel tenors, and the bass, **Michael George**, characterizing strongly. **Claron McFadden's** vibrant soprano is girlishly distinctive. This Hyperion issue provides a valuable makeweight in the florid solo cantata, thought to be originally conceived as part of *Alexander's Feast*, nimbly sung by **Mark Ainsley**.

The refinement and rhythmic lift of the Academy's playing under **Neville Marriner** make for a lively, engaging performance, marked by characterful solo singing from a strong team. The choruses are sung by a quartet drawn from a distinguished vocal sextet (Jennifer Smith, Margaret Cable, Paul Esswood, Wynford Evans, Neil Jenkins and Richard Jackson) and, with warmly atmospheric recording, the result is a sparkling entertainment. **Robert Tear's** tone is not always ideally mellifluous (for instance in *Love in her eyes sits playing*) but, like the others, he has a good feeling for Handelian style; the sweetness of **Jill Gomez's** contribution is a delight. The 1977 (originally Argo) recording is of vintage quality and this Double Decca reissue is made the more attractive by the inclusion of a further solo recital from Robert Tear of rare English baroque repertoire – music by Arne, Boyce and Hook, as well as Handel.

Agrippina condotta a morire; Figlio d'alte speranze; Notte placida e cheta; Un'alma innamorata (Italian Cantatas). Concerto a quattro

(N) **** BIS-SACD 1695. Kirkby, L. Baroque

Emma Kirkby's bright, pure voice is perfectly suited to these brilliant but generally lightweight inspirations of the young Handel's Italian period. The cantatas chosen are all for solo voice with modest instrumental forces. She is at her finest in *Agrippina condotta a morire* and brings real bravura to *Figlio d'alte speranza*. Light-hearted and sparkling performances to match. The *Concerto a Quattro* offered as a bonus is of doubtful authenticity.

Alexander's Feast; Concerto grosso in C (Alexander's Feast)

(M) **(*) Ph. 475 7774 (2). Watkinson, Robson, Brown, Stafford, Varcoe, Monteverdi Ch., E. Bar. Sol., Gardiner

Gardiner's version of *Alexander's Feast* was recorded live at performances given at the Göttingen Festival. The sound is not distractingly dry, but it is still harder than usual on singers and players alike, taking away some of the bloom. What matters is the characteristic vigour and concentration of Gardiner's performance. **Stephen Varcoe** may lack some of the dark resonance of a traditional bass, but he projects his voice well. **Nigel Robson's** tenor suffers more than do the others from the dryness of the acoustic. The soprano **Donna Brown** sings with boyish freshness, and the alto numbers are divided very effectively between **Carolyn Watkinson** and the soft-grained counter-tenor **Ashley Stafford**. The *Concerto grosso in C* was given with the oratorio at its first performance.

L'allegro, il penseroso, il moderato

(M) *** Erato (ADD) 2292 45377-2 (2). Kwella, McLaughlin, Smith, Ginn, Davies, Hill, Varcoe, Monteverdi Ch., E. Bar. Sol., Gardiner

Taking Milton as his starting point, Handel illustrated in music the contrasts of mood and character between the cheerful and the thoughtful. Then, prompted by his librettist, Charles Jennens, he added compromise in *Il moderato*, the moderate man. The sequence of brief numbers is a delight, particularly in a performance as exhilarating as **Gardiner's**, with excellent soloists, choir and orchestra. The recording is first rate.

Alla caccia Diana; Armida abbandonata; Notte placida e cheta; Tu fedel? tu costante; Un'alma innamorata (Italian Cantatas, Volume 2)

*** Glossa GCD 921522. Galli, Invernizzi, La Risonanza, Bonizzoni (harpsichord)

Aminta e Fillide, Arresta il passo; Clori, mia bella Clori (Italian Cantatas, Volume 4)

(N) *** Glossa GCD 921 524. Rial, Schiavo, La Risonanza, Bonizzoni

Figlio d'alte speranze; Il delirio amaroso (Da quel giorno fatale); Pensieri notturno di Filli (Nel dolce dell'oblio); Tra le fiamme (Il consiglio) (Italian Cantatas, Volume 1)

*** Glossa GCD 921521. Invernizzi, La Risonanza, Bonizzoni

Roberta Invernizzi has Volume 1 to herself, and she sings with a striking mixture of expressive feeling, even passion, and refinement. Her coloratura is as firm as her phrasing is stylish. In Volume 2 she is joined by **Emanuela Galli** who sings four of the five solo cantatas very dramatically and with finely nurtured intensity. Like her colleague, she has a natural, Italianate feeling for the words. Invernizzi joins her for Diana's lively hunting cantata (*Alla caccia Diana*) and again **Bonizzoni** directs the music with refreshing spontaneity. The pair of sopranos (**Maria Grazia Schiavo** and **Nurial Rial**) who take on Volume 4 of this rewarding series give an entirely delightful account of Aminta's wooing of Fillide, and Schiavo continues with an equally refined account of *Clori, mia bella Clori*. Both cantatas enjoy engagingly delicate support from the accompanying group, including some impressive contributions from the solo violins.The documentation too is excellent. This series sets a very high standard, and we look forward to further issues.

(i; ii) Amarilli vezzosa (Il duello amoroso); Clori, mia bella Clori; (i) O come chiare e belle (Italian Cantatas)

(BB) *** Hyp. Helios CDH 55136. Kwella, L. Handel O, Darlow; with (i) Fisher, (ii) Denley

The most ambitious work here is *O come chiare e belle*, a half-hour piece with allegorical overtones using three voices and written to compliment Pope Clement XI during the War of the Spanish Succession. As in most of the cantatas, some of the ideas are familiar from later versions, as in the aria, *Tornami a vagheggiar*, later used in *Alcina*, and here brilliantly sung by **Gillian Fisher**. The two shorter cantatas are equally charming, *Clori, mia bella Clori* for solo voice, the other a duet for soprano and contralto, well sung by **Patrizia Kwella** and **Catherine Denley**. Though **Denys Darlow** does not always lift rhythms enough, the freshness of the music is well caught.

(i) Amarilli vezzosa (Il duello amoroso); Mi palpita il cor; Nel dolce tempo; Vedendo Amor; Trio Sonata, Op. 2/1

*** HM HMC 90 1957. (i) Scholl; Accademia Bizantina, Dantone; (i) with Guilmette

Andreas Scholl has chosen three pastoral cantatas composed by Handel while he was in Italy (where at the time opera was banned) and a fourth composed in London. He sings them very beautifully indeed with much subtlety of colour and dynamic. In *Amarilli vezzosa* he is joined in duet (between shepherd and shepherdess) with **Hélène Guilmette**, who sings with comparable refinement. The accompaniments are imaginatively supportive, and this will give pleasure to all admirers of this remarkable counter-tenor.

Aminta e Fillide (cantata)

⊶ (BB) *** Hyp. Helios CDH 55077. Fisher, Kwella, L. Handel O, Darlow

In writing for two voices and strings, Handel presents a simple encounter in the pastoral tradition over a span of ten brief arias which, together with recitatives and final duet, last almost an hour. The music is as charming and undemanding for the listener as it is taxing for the soloists. This lively performance, beautifully recorded with two nicely contrasted singers, delightfully blows the cobwebs off a Handel work hitherto totally neglected. It is even more attractive on the bargain Helios label.

Apollo e Dafne (cantata); The Alchemist (incidental music)

(BB) *** Naxos 8.555712. Pasichnyk, Pomakov, European Union Bar. O, Goodman

Roy Goodman, an alert, stylish interpreter of Handel, draws from his baroque orchestra, with its team of international players, a lively reading of this dramatic cantata on a classical theme, written by Handel at the beginning of his career during his stay in Italy. The Overture used here is the Allegro from the Concerto grosso Op. 3, No. 1, with the brisk sequence of brief arias and duets culminating in the longest aria, Cara pianta, with its expansive phrases well sustained by the young baritone, Robert Pomakov. As Dafne, Olga Pasichnyk sounds fresh and girlish. Voices are balanced, forward with the orchestra cleanly focused behind, despite distantly distracting reverberation. But with the attractive suite of incidental music from The Alchemist thrown in for good measure this is a good Naxos bargain.

Athalia (complete)

(BB) *** Naxos 8.554364/5. Scholl, Schlick, Holzhausen, Reinhold, Brutscher, MacLeod, Junge Kantorei, Frankfurt Bar. O, Martini

Very well cast and stylishly performed, using period instruments, the Naxos set makes an excellent bargain. Outstanding among the singers is Barbara Schlick as Josabeth, pure, sweet and expressive, and though Elisabeth Scholl in the title-role provides too little contrast with her rather boyish tone not really apt for this 'Jewish Clytemnestra', her attack is clean and fresh. The castrato role of Joad is taken by Annette Reinhold, who sounds uncannily like a low counter-tenor, firm and secure, with little vibrato. Good, undistracting recording.

Belshazzar (complete)

⊶ (B) **** DG Trio 477 037-2 (3). Rolfe Johnson, Augér, Robbin, Bowman, Wilson-Johnson, E. Concert Ch. & O, Pinnock

(M) **(*) Teldec 0630 10275-2 (3). Palmer, Lehane, Tear, Esswood, Van der Bilt, Stockholm Chamber Ch., VCM, Harnoncourt

Handel modified Belshazzar over the years, and Pinnock has opted not for the earliest but for the most striking and fully developed text. The cast is starry, with Arleen Augér at her most ravishing as the Babylonian king's mother, Nitocris, Anthony Rolfe Johnson in the title-role, James Bowman as the prophet Daniel and Catherine Robbin as King Cyrus, all excellent. Full, well-balanced sound. This reissued Trio is a real bargain.

The drama is the more pointed when the soloists on Teldec, led by Felicity Palmer and Robert Tear, keep the story-line clearly in mind with their expressive enunciation of the words. The other soloists, too, are excellent, notably Paul Esswood with his fresh counter-tenor tone, and the bass, Peter van der Bilt. Most enjoyable of all is the singing of the fine Stockholm Choir, delectably light and pointed in some of the end-of-scene choruses.

Carmelite Vespers

(BB) *** Virgin 2x1 5 61579-2 (2). Feldman, Kirkby, Van Evera, Cable, Nichols, Cornwell, Thomas, Taverner Ch. & Players, Parrott

What Andrew Parrott has recorded here is a reconstruction by Graham Dixon of what might have been heard in July 1707 at the church of the Carmelite Order in Rome for the Festival of Our Lady of Mount Carmel. Dixon has put the motets and Psalm settings in an order appropriate for the service of Second Vespers, noting that it is not the only possible reconstruction. Of these, the only unfamiliar Handel piece is Te decus Virgineum – which makes this not quite the new experience promised but nevertheless an enjoyable way of hearing a magnificent collection of Handel's choral music. In a liturgical setting in 1707, women's voices would not have been used, but the sopranos and altos of the Taverner Choir produce an aptly fresh sound, as does the fine group of soloists, headed by an outstanding trio of sopranos: Emma Kirkby, Jill Feldman and Emily van Evera. The recording, made in St Augustine's, Kilburn, London, has a pleasant and apt ambience, which, however, does not obscure detail. At its modest price this reissue is well worth having.

Chandos Anthems 1–11, HWV 246–256 (complete)

⊶ (M) *** Chan. 0554/7. Dawson, Kwella, Partridge, Bowman, George, Sixteen Ch. & O, Christophers

It is appropriate that a record label named Chandos should record a complete set of Handel's Chandos Anthems. This is now available on four CDs in a box (at mid-price) and marks one of the most successful and worthwhile achievements of The Sixteen on CD. From the first of these fine works, which Handel based on his Utrecht Te Deum, to the last with its exuberant closing Alleluja the music is consistently inspired; it has great variety of invention and resourceful vocal scoring. The recordings are well up to the house standard.

Chandos Anthems 7: My song shall be alway; 9: O praise the Lord with one consent; 11a: Let God arise

(N) *** Hyp. CDA 67737. Kirkby, Iestyn Davies, Gilchrist, Neal Davies, Trinity College Ch., AAM, Layton

It looks as if Hyperion are beginning a new series of the *Chandos Anthems* with an excellent quartet of soloists (each of the four has a solo or duet spot in all three works, while the chorus is used to open and close each anthem). The modestly scaled performances are authentic in the best sense (the accompanying strings are sweet rather than edgy) and notable for their freshness: the present disc can be warmly recommended alongside the Chandos versions.

The Choice of Hercules (cantata)

*** Hyp. CDA 67298. Gritton, Coote, Blaze, King's Consort Ch. & O, King – GREENE: *Hearken unto Me* ***

The Choice of Hercules is unique among Handel's works, a dramatic cantata to an English text in a single Act lasting 50 minutes, crisply telling the story of Hercules (taken by a counter-tenor, here the excellent **Robin Blaze**) making his choice between Virtue (the rich, firm mezzo, **Anna Coote**) and Pleasure (**Susan Gritton**, equally radiant). **Robert King**, in this work otherwise unavailable on disc, brings out the unquenchable freshness of invention that Handel retained even in his last years, with the choir and players of the **King's Consort** consistently responsive and resilient. The extended anthem by Handel's contemporary and rival, Maurice Greene, makes a valuable extra.

Coronation Anthems (complete). (i) Organ Concerto, Op. 4/4. Jephtha: Overture. Messiah: Worthy is the Lamb; Amen. Solomon: Arrival of the Queen of Sheba

(N) ☸➛ **** Coro COR 16066. The Sixteen, Christophers; (i) with Ross

(i) Coronation Anthems (complete); (ii) Concerti a due cori 2–3, HWV 333/4

(M) *** DG 447 280-2. (i) Westminster Abbey Ch., Preston; (i–ii) E. Concert; (ii) Pinnock

(i) Coronation Anthems (complete); (ii) Ode for the Birthday of Queen Anne

*** Australian Decca Eloquence (ADD) 466 676-2. (i) King's College, Cambridge, Ch., ECO, Willcocks; (ii) Kirkby, Nelson, Minty, Bowman, Hill, Thomas, Christ Church Cathedral Ch., Oxford, AAM, Preston

A splendid new set of the *Coronation Anthems* from **Christophers** and his fine chorus and orchestral group, with a nice set of encore lollipops to fill out the disc, including Alastair Ross's lively account of the most attractive of the Opus 4 *Organ Concertos*. Christophers opens the famous *Zadok the Priest* almost *sotto voce* and the choral entry is thus made the more cutting and resplendent.

Willcocks's famous 1961 recording of these four anthems sounds much better on CD than it ever did on LP, and is greatly enjoyable. They are coupled with a fine performance of the *Ode for the Birthday of Queen Anne*, recorded in the late 1970s, and sound very good indeed. An excellent CD from Australian Decca.

Those who like sparer, period textures will favour **Preston** in the *Coronation Anthems* where, although the result is less grand, the element of contrast is even more telling. To have the choir enter with such bite and impact underlines the freshness and immediacy, with characterful period playing. An exhilarating version. The new coupling of the two *Concerti a due cori* is welcome, with the performances full of rhythmic vitality.

Deborah (complete)

☸➛ *** Hyp. CDA 66841/2. Kenny, Gritton, Denley, Bowman, George, New College Ch., Oxford, Salisbury Cathedral Ch., King's Consort, King

Handel's 1733 oratorio, *Deborah* opens spectacularly with a fine trumpet overture which borrows fom the *Fireworks Music*. The cast is strong, with clear, bright singing from **Yvonne Kenny** in the name-role and **Susan Gritton** as Jael. **James Bowman** as Barak and especially **Michael George** as Abinoam make impressive contributions, and **Catherine Denley** is even more striking as Sisera. But what gives the set its distinction is the fine singing from the combined choristers of **Salisbury Cathedral** and the **Choir of New College, Oxford**, although the resonance does take some of the edge off the sound. Nevertheless, **Robert King's** direction is assured and stylish and this is most enjoyable.

Dettingen Te Deum; Dettingen Anthem

*** DG 410 647-2. Westminster Abbey Ch., E. Concert, Preston

The *Dettingen Te Deum* is a splendid work, continually reminding one of *Messiah*, written the previous year. **Preston's** Archiv performance with the **English Concert** makes an ideal recommendation, with its splendid singing, crisp but strong, excellent recording and a generous, apt coupling. This setting of *The King shall rejoice* should not be confused with the *Coronation Anthem* of that name. It is less inspired, but has a magnificent double fugue for finale. The recording is first class.

Dixit Dominus; Coronation Anthem: Zadok the Priest

☸➛ (BB) *** Warner Apex (ADD) 0927 48683-2. Palmer, Marshall, Brett, Messana, Morton, Thomson, Wilson-Johnson, Monteverdi Ch. & O, Gardiner

Dixit Dominus; Nisi Dominus; Salve Regina

(M) *** DG 477 6729. Westminster Abbey Ch. & O, Preston

Dixit Dominus; Nisi Dominus; Silete venti

*** Chan. 0517. Dawson, Russell, Brett, Partridge, George, Sixteen Ch. & O, Christophers

Handel's *Dixit Dominus* is extremely florid and requires bravura from soloists and chorus alike. **John Eliot Gardiner** catches all its brilliance and directs an exhilarating performance, marked by strongly accented, sharply incisive singing from the choir and outstanding solo contributions. In high contrast with the dramatic choruses, the duet for two sopranos, *De torrente*, here beautifully sung by **Felicity Palmer** and **Margaret Marshall**, is languorously expressive, but stylishly so. Other soloists match that, and the analogue recording is first rate, making this reissue a real bargain.

Simon Preston draws ideally luminous and resilient singing from the **Westminster Abbey Choir**, with a fine team of soloists in which **Arleen Augér** and **Diana Montague** are outstanding. The playing of the orchestra of period instrumentalists, led by **Roy Goodman**, in every way matches the fine quality of the singing. However, this *al fresco* reissue omits any serious documentation.

Christophers's speeds tend to be more extreme, slow as well as fast, and the recorded sound, though full and well detailed, is less immediate. The Chandos issue gains from having a third item. *Silete venti* allows the silver-toned **Lynne Dawson** to shine even more than in the other items, ending with a brilliant *Alleluia* in galloping compound time.

Esther (1732 revised version; complete)

*** Somm SOMMCD 238/9. Joshua, Outram, Osmond, Bickley, Bowman, Angus Smith, Kennedy, Watson, Purves, L. Handel Ch. & O, Cummings

Handel composed *Esther* for the Duke of Chandos-to-be – James Brydges. In 1732 he revised and expanded it to become a full-length oratorio, inserting the two best-known *Coronation Anthems*, including *Zadok the Priest* (with a new text), which are superbly performed here by the excellent **London Handel Choir**. Among the soloists are **Susan Bickley** and **James Bowman** (who has to cope with considerable complex coloratura), and the superb **Christopher Purves**. This is a live concert performance, and with **Laurence Cummings** directing such an impressive cast it cannot fail to be thoroughly rewarding.

(i) Gloria in B flat; (ii) Dixit Dominus

🎵 Ⓜ *** BIS CD 301235. (i) Kirkby, Royal Ac. of Music Bar. O, Cummings; (ii) Martinpelto, Von Otter, Stockholm Bach Ch.; Drottningholm Bar. Ens., Ohrwall

The existence of the *Gloria* has been known for some time. But only in September 2000 was it positively identified as a work by Handel, and an inspired one too. It was appropriate that **Emma Kirkby**, the reigning queen of baroque, was given the privilege of making the first recording, accompanied by an excellent modern-instrument chamber group. She sings the florid opening exultantly and is even more impressive in the heady bravura of the closing *Cum sancto spirito*. Yet it is the beauty of her lyrical singing which stands out even more, and indeed her stylish control of ornamentation. The recording is vividly forward.

The performance of *Dixit Dominus* also has very fine soloists, although none quite to match Kirkby in easy flowing lines. But the chorus is equally important here and the singing of the **Stockholm Choir** has splendid vigour and bite.

(i) Gloria in B flat; Italian Cantatas: (ii) Mi palpita il cor; (iii) Pastorella vagha bella; (iv) Harpsichord Suite 3 in D min.

**(*) Lyrichord LEMS 8055. (i; iii) Baird; (i) Queen's Chamber Band; (ii) Coid, Heller; (ii; iii) Seidenberg; (ii–iv) Comparone

The Lyrichord disc offers an attractively planned recital called '*Handel in Rome*', combining vocal and instrumental music, and including the newly discovered *Gloria*, which is most stylishly accompanied by the **Queen's Chamber Band**. **Julianne Baird** has a warm, rich soprano voice, but it proves just a fraction unwieldy (especially heard alongside Dame Emma Kirkby) in the coloratura runs which end this work and also the charming *Pastorella vagha bella*. Both this and *Mi palpita il cor* have a neatly played continuo, and the latter includes a pleasing oboe obbligato from **Marsha Heller**. The counter-tenor **Marshall Coid**, who has a highly individual alto voice, also sings expressively, but again is a little insecure in his upper tessitura. However, this is still a rewarding programme, made the more so by the splendid account of the *D minor Harpsichord Sonata* by **Elaine Comparone**. (Its seven movements are split into three groups to make interludes between the vocal items.)

Israel in Egypt

Ⓝ Ⓑ🅑 ** Naxos 8.570966/7. Albino, Nils Brown, Modolo, Mahon, McLeod, Nedecky, Roach, Such, Watson, Aradia Ens., Mallon

(i) Israel in Egypt; Coronation Anthems: Zadok the Priest; The King shall Rejoice

🎵 Ⓜ **** Decca 4781374 (2). (i) Holton, Priday, Deam, Stafford, Chance, Collin, Kenny, Robertson, Salmon, Tindall, Tusa, Clarkson, Purves; Monteverdi Ch., E. Bar. Sol., Gardiner

(i) Israel in Egypt: Lamentations of the Israelites for the Death of Joseph; (ii) The Ways of Zion do Mourn (funeral anthem)

🎵 *** Erato (ADD) 2292 45399-2 (2). (i) Knibbs, Troth, Greene, Priday, Royall, Stafford, Gordon, Clarkson, Elliott, Kendall, Varcoe, Stewart; (ii) Burrowes, Brett, Hill, Varcoe; Monteverdi Ch. & O, Gardiner

In his originally Philips version of *Israel in Egypt* **Gardiner** secures subtler playing from his period instruments, not just more stylish and generally more lightly sprung than in the earlier, Erato version, but conveying more clearly the emotional and dramatic thrust. So the start is more mysterious, and such illustrative numbers as the hopping of the frogs during the Plague choruses are even more delightfully pointed than before. As before, first-rate soloists have been chosen from the chorus, and the digital recording is full and well balanced. The *Coronation Anthems* are also winningly performed. At Duo price, this is even more of a first choice.

Using modern instruments, **Gardiner** made his Erato recording in 1978. The singing both of the chorus and of the 12 soloists chosen from its members is excellent, though, like all other modern recordings, this one slightly falls down in resonance on the most famous number, the duet for basses, *The Lord is a Man of War*. In almost every way Gardiner gains by presenting the *Lamentations* not as an introduction to the main oratorio, but as a supplement, with the same music given in its original form, with text unamended, as written for the funeral cantata for Queen Caroline. Excellent, full-bodied, analogue sound.

The Toronto performance by the excellent **Aradia Ensemble**, with its cast of experienced young soloists, is well sung and very well recorded, but the choral singing lacks the extra bite and vitality that bring this work, so dependent on choruses, vividly alive in the way that Gardiner's performances do.

Jephtha (CD versions)

Ⓜ *** Decca 478 0398 (3). Robson, Dawson, Von Otter, Chance, Varcoe, Holton, Monteverdi Ch., E. Bar. Sol., Gardiner

Ⓜ ** Warner Teldec 2564 69258-7. Hollweg, Gale, Linos, Esswood, Thomaschke, Arnold Schoenberg Ch., Mozart-Sangerknaben, VCM, Harnoncourt

Gardiner's recording was made live at the Göttingen Festival in 1988, and though the sound does not have quite the bloom of his finest studio recordings of Handel, the exhilaration and intensity of the performance come over vividly, with superb singing from both chorus and an almost ideal line-up of soloists. **Nigel Robson's** tenor may be on the light side for the title-role, but the sensitivity of expression is very satisfying. **Lynne Dawson**, with her bell-like soprano, sings radiantly as Iphis, and the counter-tenor **Michael Chance** as her beloved, Hamor, is also outstanding. **Anne Sofie von Otter** is powerful as Storge, and **Stephen Varcoe**, with his clear baritone, again on the light side, is a stylish Zebul. As for the **Monteverdi Choir**, their clarity, incisiveness and beauty are a constant delight.

Harnoncourt's pursuit of extra authenticity, using original instruments, has its snags, and not just in the acid timbre of the strings. He takes a comparatively operatic view of the work, but he mars the impact of that by too frequently adopting a mannered style of phrasing. The soloists too are far less impressive than those on the Gardiner edition, and altogether this is hardly at all competitive.

Joshua (complete)

⊶ ✪ **** Hyp. CDA 66461/2. Kirkby, Bowman, Mark Ainsley, George, Oliver, New College, Oxford, Ch., King's Consort, King

Ⓝ **(*) MDG 332 1532-2 (2). Myung-Hee Hyun, Gilchrist, Wolff, Potter, Poplutz, Cologne Chamber Ch., Collegium Cartusianum, Neumann

Emma Kirkby is here ideally sparkling and light in the role of Achsah, daughter of the patriarchal leader, Caleb (taken here by the bass, **Michael George**). Her love for Othniel, superbly sung by **James Bowman**, provides the romantic interest in what is otherwise a grandly military oratorio, based on the Book of Joshua. The singing is consistently strong and stylish, with the clear, precise tenor **John Mark Ainsley** in the title-role. **Robert King** and his **Consort** crown their achievement in other Hyperion issues, and the choir of **New College, Oxford**, sings with ideal freshness. Warm, full sound.

The star of **Peter Neumann's** Cologne set is undoubtedly the sweet-voiced **Myung-Hee Hyun** as Achsah, who virtually dominates the proceedings. **James Gilchrist** is effective in the title-role, but **Konstantin Wolff** is rather ill-focused as

Caleb, and neither he nor **Alex Potter** as Othnieldo quite match their opposite numbers on Hyperion. The **Cologne Chamber Choir** sing clearly and confidently but could be more dramatic in the stirring choruses of the Israelites.

Judas Maccabaeus (complete)

⊶ Ⓜ *** DG (ADD) 447 692-2 (3). Palmer, Baker, Esswood, Davies, Shirley-Quirk, Keyte, Wandsworth School Ch., ECO, Mackerras

⊶ ⒝⒝ *** Regis Alto (ADD) ALC 2002 (2). Harper, Watts, Young, Shirley-Quirk, Amor Artis Ch., Wandsworth School Boys' Ch., ECO, Somary

**(*) Hyp. CDA 66641/2 (2). Kirkby, Denley, Bowman, MacDougall, George, Birchall, Ch. of New College, Oxford, King's Consort, King

Judas Maccabaeus may have a lopsided story, but the sequence of Handelian gems is irresistible, the more so in a performance as sparkling as DG's reissued 1976 recording under **Sir Charles Mackerras**. Though not everyone will approve of the use of boys' voices in the choir, it gives an extra bit of character. Hearing even so hackneyed a number as *See, the conqu'ring hero* in its true scale is a delightful surprise. **Ryland Davies** and **John Shirley-Quirk** are most stylish, while both **Felicity Palmer** and **Janet Baker** crown the whole set with glorious singing. The recording quality is outstanding in its CD format, fresh, vivid and clear.

Regis have had the excellent idea of licensing **Somary's** splendid (1971) Vanguard set, and at budget price this reissue is very recommendable indeed. With **Alexander Young** a ringing tenor (his *Sound the Alarm* is a highlight) and **Helen Watts** singing the opening aria in Act III exquisitely, this is all most enjoyable, a traditional account that is full of life. The choruses are especially good: no one will be disappointed with *See the conqu'ring hero* (nor the horn accompaniment). The recording is wholly natural and there is a sense of commitment throughout from all departments. Modern instruments are used, but the harpsichord continuo comes through well.

With some superb solo singing and refined instrumental textures, **Robert King's** performance can be recommended warmly, even though it is not as lively as some of his Purcell recordings. It is partly that the chorus is not as forward or as bright-toned as one wants in Handel; but there is much to enjoy, with **Jamie MacDougall** clean and bright if not always ideally firm in the title-role, and with the pure-toned **Emma Kirkby** well contrasted with the much warmer mezzo of **Catherine Denley**. **Michael George** gives splendid weight to the bass arias so central to Handel oratorio.

Sacred cantatas: *Laudate pueri (Psalm 112); Coelestis dum spirat aura; O qualis de coelo sonus; Salve Regina; Trio Sonata in G min., HWV 27*

⊶ ✪ **** BIS CD 1065. Kirkby, L. Baroque, Medlam

Emma Kirkby is in glorious voice throughout this splendid recital, floating the opening line of *Salve Regina* most beautifully, and then dashing away to a sparkling accompaniment in *Eja ergo*. Her closing *Alleluja!* in *O qualis de coelo sonus* is wonderfully nimble, as is the flowing *Felix dies* ('Happy day') of *Coelestis dum spirat aura*. Finest of all is the setting of *Psalm 112*, where she soars up to the heavens on a characteristic repeated phrase and sings flowingly and ravishingly against a particularly attractive accompaniment – in which the continuo with organ is delightfully conceived – capped by the spirited runs of the *Gloria Patri*. This is one of Kirkby's very finest Handel records. Her voice is caught with a lovely bloom, and the balance with the accompaniment is just about perfect. Not to be missed.

Messiah (complete DVD version)

🎬 ⊕– **** Warner **DVD** 0630 17834-2. Nelson, Kirkby, Watkinson, Elliott, Thomas, Westminster Abbey Ch., AAM, Hogwood; Simon Preston (organ) (V/D: Roy Tipping)

Hogwood's DVD *Messiah* dates from 1982, the same period as his Oiseau-Lyre audio recording, and it has the appealing advantage of the warm acoustic of Wesminster Abbey. He uses a chorus of fewer than thirty, and his **Academy of Ancient Music** are in first-class form, with an an excellent unnamed trumpet soloist in *And the trumpet shall sound*. There are a pair of sopranos, **Judith Nelson** and a very young **Emma Kirkby**, both contributing superbly. Indeed, there is no flaw in the solo team, and **David Thomas** is particularly strong in the bass arias. Hogwood uses the 1754 Foundling Hospital score, and the result is an enjoyably fresh 'traditional-period' performance which is beautifully sung and a pleasure to watch but one can hear every word and the backcloth of Westminster Abbey is well used by the camera to provide a visual treat.

Messiah (complete CD versions)

⊕– **** DG **SACD** Surround Sound 477 066-2 (2) / 453 464-2 (2) CD. Röschmann, Gritton, Fink, Daniels, Neal Davies, Gabrieli Consort & Players, McCreesh

⊕– Ⓜ **** DG 477 5904 (2). Augér, Von Otter, Chance, Crook, Tomlinson, E. Concert Ch., E. Concert, Pinnock

⊕– *** BIS CD 891/892 (2). Midori Suzuki, Mera, Elwes, Thomas, Bach Collegium Japan, Masaaki Suzuki

Ⓜ *** LSO Live SACD 0607 (2). Gritton, Padmore, Mingardo, Miles, L. Symphony Ch., LSO, C. Davis

Ⓜ *** COLCD 132 (2). Lunn, Marshall, Gilchrist, Purves, Cambridge Singers, RPO, Rutter

Ⓜ *** Hyp. Dyad CDD 22019 (2). Dawson, Denley, James, Davies, George, Sixteen Ch. & O, Christophers

*** DHM/BMG **SACD** Surround Sound 82876 64070-2 (2). Schäfer, Larsson, Schade, Finley, Arnold Schoenberg Ch., VCM, Harnoncourt

*** HM HMC 901498.99 (2). Schlick, Piau, Scholl, Padmore, Berg, Les Arts Florissants, Christie

*** Ph. 434 297-2 (2). Marshall, Robbin, Rolfe Johnson, Brett, Hale, Shirley-Quirk, Monteverdi Ch., E. Bar. Sol., Gardiner

*** Decca 414 396-2 (2). Te Kanawa, Gjevang, Lewis, Howell, Chicago Ch. & SO, Solti

Ⓜ *** Ph. Duo (ADD) 464 703-2 (2). Harper, Watts, Wakefield, Shirley-Quirk, L. Symphony Ch., LSO, C. Davis

ⓃⓂ *** Coro 16062 (3). Sampson, Wyn-Rogers, Padmore, Purves, The Sixteen, Christophers

**(*) HM HMC 90 1928/9. Avemo, Bardon, Zazzo (countertenor), Neal Davies, Clare College, Cambridge, Ch., Freiburg Bar. O, Jacobs

Using the Foundling Hospital version of the score, **McCreesh**, in re-creating the sort of performance Handel supervised there in 1754, seeks to present a 'thoroughly modern performance – A *Messiah* for the Millennium' as he puts it. It is a bright and individual reading, bringing out the drama of the music with extreme speeds in both directions. The chorus copes well with all his bracing tempi, and the result is both expressive and vital. He is lucky to have an excellent team of young soloists, with both sopranos singing with appealing freshness and the splendid contralto, **Bernarda Fink**, touchingly simple in *He was despised*. The golden-voiced tenor opens the performances with a warmly lyrical account of *Comfort ye my people*, and the resonant bass, **Neal Davies**, shakes with the best of them in *Thus said the Lord of Hosts*. It is altogether a most stimulating performance, and for collectors with surround sound facility will probably be a first choice, even before Pinnock and Suzuki.

Trevor Pinnock presents a performance using authentically scaled forces which, without inflation, rise to grandeur and magnificence, qualities Handel himself would have relished, and Pinnock (more than his main rivals) balances his period instruments to give a satisfying body to the sound. There is weight too in the singing of the bass soloist, **John Tomlinson**, firm, dark and powerful, yet marvellously agile in divisions. **Arleen Augér's** range of tone and dynamic is daringly wide, with radiant purity in *I know that my Redeemer liveth*. **Anne Sofie von Otter** sustains *He was despised* superbly with her firm, steady voice. Some alto arias are taken just as beautifully by the outstanding counter-tenor, **Michael Chance**. The tenor, **Howard Crook**, is less distinctive but still sings freshly and attractively.

With his excellent Japanese singers and players, **Masaaki Suzuki** here excels himself. His crisp, sharp manner goes with transparent textures and sprung rhythms, and though modest forces are used the result has natural dramatic weight. The consistent alertness of the chorus is a delight but the fast speeds he tends to prefer never sound breathless, and he is never afraid to choose a spacious tempo, if the mood of the music demands it – as in the aria, *He was despised*, sung with seamless beauty by the male alto, **Yoshikazu Mera**. The soprano **Midori Suzuki** sings with radiant purity, notably in *I know that my Redeemer liveth*, and the two British soloists are excellent too, with **John Elwes** bright and eager and **David Thomas** caught at his warmest.

It was **Colin Davis**, early in his career, who made a breakthrough in recording the *Messiah* using a small professional chorus and adopting speeds far faster than was then the custom. His new LSO Live version, recorded at the Barbican, has a comparably distinguished team of soloists and they make an excellent team, with clean, clear voices, well focused. **Mark Padmore** is outstanding as the tenor soloist, and **Sara Mingardo** is a fine, firm mezzo, not at all fruity, singing *He was despised* movingly at a steady tempo. She contrasts well with the soprano, **Susan Gritton**, in *He shall feed his flock*. The *Hallelujah Chorus* is bright and forward, with timpani prominent, and in the *da capo* arias, like the beautifully sung *I know that my Redeemer liveth*, ornaments are added in the repeats.

Not surprisingly, **John Rutter's** is essentially a traditional performance, but with lively tempi and no lack of expressive feeling; and it is very well recorded indeed. The tenor **James Gilchrist** sings his opening *Comfort ye ... Every valley* beautifully, with a rich-timbred legato; and the alto **Melanie Marshall** is extremely articulate, although in her runs some might feel she points consonants too sharply. **Joanne Lunn** has a full, rich timbre, creating a clarion call in *There were shepherds abiding* and she manages *Rejoice greatly* impressively at Rutter's swift pacing. **Christopher Purves** is a real bass as *The people that walked in darkness* readily shows. Altogether a fine set which will give much pleasure.

Harry Christophers on Hyperion consistently adopts speeds more relaxed than those we have grown used to in modern performances, and the effect is fresh, clear and resilient. Alto lines in the chorus are taken by male singers; a counter-tenor, **David James**, is also used for the *Refiner's fire*, but *He was despised* is rightly given to the contralto, **Catherine Denley**, warm and grave at a very measured tempo. The team of five soloists is as fine as that on any rival set, with the soprano, **Lynne Dawson**, singing with silvery purity. The band of 13 strings sounds as clean and fresh as the choir. The sound has all the bloom one associates with St John's recordings. Now offered as a two-for-one Dyad, this is a real bargain.

Harnoncourt's *Messiah* is full of eccentricities, yet he is never, never dull, and his performance is endearingly enjoyable and beautifully sung, and gloriously recorded in totally believable, spectacular surround sound, with the **Arnold Schoenberg Choir** matching their similarly fine singing in Harnoncourt's memorable account of Haydn's *Creation*. The soprano **Christine Schäfer** is radiant throughout, and especially so in *I know that my Redeemer liveth*. Harnoncourt's accompaniments are always alive and often dramatic; yet *All we like sheep* has an engagingly light touch. *Hallelujah* brings another surprise, opening quite gently and generating a full head of steam only as it proceeds and the brass enter. It's different, but it works well, and *Worthy is the Lamb* is suitably majestic, the fugal entries all splendidly incisive, with a dramatic brass entry, and capped with a satisfying, culminating *Amen*.

William Christie's preference for fast, resilient speeds and light textures, not least in choruses, never prevents him from giving due emotional weight to such key numbers as *He was despised*. That is superbly sung, with touching simplicity, firm tone and flawless intonation, by the counter-tenor, **Andreas Scholl**. The other singers too sound fresh and young. Excellent sound, though the chorus is placed a little backwardly.

John Eliot Gardiner chooses bright-toned sopranos instead of boys for the chorus and he uses, very affectingly, a solo treble to sing *There were shepherds abiding*. Speeds are fast and light, and the rhythmic buoyancy in the choruses is very striking, though idiosyncratically Gardiner begins

Hallelujah! on a *pianissimo*. *Why do the nations* and *The trumpet shall sound* (both sung with great authority) come over dramatically, and the soloists are all first class, with the soprano **Margaret Marshall** finest of all, especially in *I know that my Redeemer liveth*. Other highlights include Marshall's angelic version of *Rejoice greatly*, skipping along in compound time.

Sir Georg Solti inspires a vital, exciting reading. The **Chicago Symphony Orchestra and Chorus** respond to some challengingly fast but never breathless speeds, showing what lessons can be learnt from authentic performance in clarity and crispness. Yet the joyful power of *Hallelujah* and the *Amen* chorus is overwhelming. **Dame Kiri Te Kanawa** matches anyone on record in beauty of tone and detailed expressiveness, while the other soloists are first rate too, though **Anne Gjevang** has rather too fruity a timbre. Brilliant, full sound.

It has to be said that, although it is very enjoyable in a traditional way, **Harry Christophers'** third (2008) recording is a little disappointing, by comparison with his earlier Hyperion Dyad version. Again he favours spacious tempi and there is some alteration in the allocation of solos, but this time without using a counter-tenor. Certainly the solo singing is impressive, especially **Christopher Purves**, **Carolyn Sampson** and **Catherine Wyn-Rogers**, although *He was despised* is not as memorable as with Catherine Denley. The choral response, using a fairly big group, is impressive, with *Unto us a child is born* (for instance) nicely paced, but overall the earlier set is the more memorable for its fresh resilience. The new one comes with a sampler bonus disc including nine items as diverse as the *Arrival of the Queen of Sheba* and **Lynne Dawson's** *Let the bright seraphim*.

René Jacobs has the advantage of the excellent choir Rutter trained at **Clare College**, one of the best in the country. They sing superbly, and the **Freiburg Baroque Orchestra** also make an impressive contribution. Jacobs's solo team are excellent but his dramatic and often eccentric approach is often undiomatic and will not appeal to all listeners, and sometimes his tempi are pressed too hard. He uses a harp for the angel's recitative, which seems to carry angelic symbolism too far, and there are other alterations too which are difficult to accept. All in all, a disappointment.

Robert Shaw's *Messiah* dates from 1966. It is another fairly traditional performance, using a relatively small, professionally trained chorus, and four top American soloists. We know how good **Judith Raskin** and **Richard Lewis** are from their other records, but **Florence Koploff**, 'a Shaw regular', is a genuine contralto with another fine voice, and the bass, **Thomas Paul**, is excellent too: the key solos here do not disappoint. Altogther this is very enjoyable, and although not a first choice, will be of special interest to American listeners, for whom Shaw has been a key figure in choral performance and recording in the USA – admired by Toscanini, as well as many others. (RCA 82876 62317-2)

Messiah (1751 version)

⊛→ Ⓑ **** Naxos 8.570131/2. Jenkinson, Jones, Brooks, I. Davies, Spence, Dougan, Ch. Of New College, Oxford, AAM, Higginbottom

In his 1751 reconstruction **Higginbottom** used boy trebles not only for the choruses but for the soprano arias as well. *Rejoice greatly* is, however, allotted to the solo tenor, **Toby Spence**, who sings very pleasingly throughout. Higginbottom also uses the period-instrument **Academy of Ancient Music**, now producing orchestral sound of great transparency and refinement, and also the sweetest of string sounds. Tempi are lively and the whole performance goes with a swing, with warmth and vitality the keynotes. *For unto us a child is born* sparkles, but *Hallelujah* has all the weight one could want. The solo trebles cover themselves with glory. **Otta Jones** is most engaging in *How beautiful are the feet* and **Henry Jenkinson**, who is allotted *I know that my Redeemer liveth*, sings with the utmost simplicity and purity. It is the male alto **Iestyn Davies**, however, who is very touching in *He was despised*, decorating the *da capo* reprise very gently. Throughout the performance, which is superbly recorded, the feeling is one of freshness, and this recording has the strongest recommendation, quite irrespective of price.

Messiah (reorchestrated by Sir Eugene Goossens)

⚙ Ⓜ *** RCA (ADD) 09026 61266-2 (3). Vyvyan, Sinclair, Vickers, Tozzi, RPO Ch. & O, Beecham

This is a performance flamboyantly reorchestrated, both dramatic and moving, which at every point radiates the natural flair of the conductor. Many of **Beecham's** tempi are slower than we expect today, but not the *Hallelujah Chorus*, which is fast and resilient. The third disc with its 17-minute appendix of eight items – normally cut at the time this recording was made – comes as a bonus, as the set is priced as for two mid-range CDs.

Messiah (slightly abridged)

⚙ Ⓑⓑ (***) Dutton Lab. mono 2CDEA 5010 (2). Baillie, Ripley, Johnson, Walker, Huddersfield Ch. Soc., Liverpool PO, Sargent

Sargent's first recording of Handel's *Messiah* is not complete. Following his usual performance practice, three numbers are cut from Part II and four from Part III. The recording venue was Huddersfield Town Hall in 1946, when that great Choral Society was still at its peak, and Handel's masterpiece is here brought vividly to life in a brilliant Dutton transfer from the 78s. What is so involving is the way this remarkably realistic and present recording (in many ways more vivid than the later, stereo set), made in a series of four-minute takes, comes over with the tension of a live performance. The star of the performance is **Isobel Baillie**. Her first entry in *There were shepherds* is a moment of the utmost magic, and what follows is utterly ravishing, while her gloriously beautiful *I know that my Redeemer liveth* has never been surpassed on record. **Gladys Ripley** sings *He was despised* with moving simplicity and restraint, and she warmly introduces *He shall feed His flock*, sharing it with Baillie, who re-enters exquisitely.

Der Messias (arr. & orch. Mozart, K.572: DVD version in German)

(*) Arthaus **DVD 101 175. Donna Brown, Kallisch, Sacca, Miles, Stuttart Gächinger Kanorei, Rilling (V/D: Helmut Rost)

Messiah (Mozart's version in English)

♫ Ⓜ *** Signum SIGCD 074 (2). Lott, Palmer, Langridge, Lloyd, Huddersfield Ch. Soc., RPO, Mackerras

It is curious that the first DVD of *Messiah* should be Mozart's German version, and the additional scoring for woodwind, horns and brass certainly gives the orchestra an 18th-century sound, while the three trombones add to the weight of the choruses. Ironically, in the truncated *Sie schalft die Posaun* the trumpet sounds only very modestly and much of the instrumental obbligato is given to the horn, for there were no solo performers readily available on high baroque trumpets in Mozart's time. Quite reasonably, the conductor here, **Helmuth Rilling**, has opted for a traditional rather than a period-style performance, and he deliberately opts for spacious, though not leaden, tempi. The result remains enjoyable and quite fresh. Rilling has a splendid team of soloists, and an excellent chorus, and the backcloth of the Stadtkirche Ellwangen in Stuttgart is visually pleasing.

Sir Charles Mackerras is obviously happy to return to Mozart's additional orchestration, and it is notable that Handel's original trumpet solo has here been restored to *And the trumpet shall sound*. Mackerras offers a more-or-less traditional approach, with a first-class team of soloists, and no male alto. The **Huddersfield Choral Society** returns to the stage, singing as richly as ever, but now more athletically and with crisper enunciation. Tempi are brisker than in Sargent's day, but not so brisk that any of the work's grandeur and nobility is lost, and there is weight without unwieldiness. Above all, Mackerras has gathered a solo team that can make the arias – taken at spacious tempi – into the radiant creations Handel envisaged. **Felicity Palmer's** moving *He was despised* is matched by **Felicity Lott's** serenely lovely *I know that my Redeemer liveth*. The choruses have plenty of bite and in *Worthy is the Lamb* and the final *Amen* there is a noble majesty. The **RPO** accompaniments are rewarding in their own right, and altogether this is very satisfying indeed, especially when it is so splendidly recorded.

Ode for the Birthday of Queen Anne (Eternal source of light divine); Sing unto God (Wedding Anthem); Te Deum in D (for Queen Caroline)

*** Hyp. CDA 66315. Fisher, Bowman, Mark Ainsley, George, New College, Oxford, Ch., King's Consort, King

Handel's *Birthday Ode for Queen Anne* combines Purcellian influences with Italianate writing to make a rich mixture. **Robert King's** performance is richly enjoyable, with warm, well-tuned playing from the **King's Consort** and with **James Bowman** in radiant form in the opening movement. The other two items are far rarer. Warmly atmospheric recording, not ideally clear on detail.

Ode for St Cecilia's Day

♫ *** ASV CDDCA 512. Gomez, Tear, King's College, Cambridge, Ch., ECO, Ledger

♫ Ⓜ *** DG Blue 474 549-2. Lott, Rolfe Johnson, Ch. & E. Concert, Pinnock

Ode for St Cecilia's Day; Cecilia volgi un sguardo

🎵➔ **** Hyp. CDA 67463. Sampson, Gilchrist, Ch. & King's Consort, King

Robert King's outstanding version of the *St Cecilia's Day Ode* gains even over the finest rivals by also including as a generous fill-up a half-hour cantata, far less well known but a fine piece, equally dedicated to St Cecilia. Helped by the recording, King's reading is crisp and clear, with textures transparent. **Carolyn Sampson** sings with radiant purity, not least in the lovely aria, *The soft complaining flute*, while **James Gilchrist** confirms his status as among the very finest British tenors of his generation, his clear, firm voice beautifully projected. The chorus of the **King's Consort** sings with comparable freshness. The same two soloists feature in the cantata, *Cecilia volgi un sguardo*, written in 1736 to be interpolated in a performance of the oratorio, *Alexander's Feast*. The two tenor arias are followed by one for the soprano in three sections. The piece ends triumphantly with a fine duet.

Those seeking a version with modern instruments will find **Philip Ledger's** ASV version a splendid one. With superb soloists – **Jill Gomez** radiantly beautiful and **Robert Tear** dramatically riveting in his call to arms – this delightful music emerges with an admirable combination of freshness and weight. Ledger uses an all-male chorus; the style of the performance is totally convincing without being self-consciously authentic. The recording is first rate: rich, vivid and clear.

Trevor Pinnock's account of Handel's magnificent setting of Dryden's *Ode* comes near the ideal for a performance using period instruments. Not only is it crisp and lively, it has deep tenderness too, as in the lovely soprano aria *The complaining flute*, with **Lisa Beznosiuk** playing the flute obbligato most delicately in support of **Felicity Lott's** clear singing. **Anthony Rolfe Johnson** gives a robust yet stylish account of *The trumpet's loud clangour*, and the choir is excellent, very crisp of ensemble. Full, clear recording with voices vivid and immediate.

Parnasso in Festa (Serenata)

Ⓝ **** Hyp. CDA 67701/2. Moore, Sampson, Crowe, Outram, Clegg, Moore, Harvey, King's Consort & Ch., Halls

Parnasso in Festa was an extended celebratory serenata (essentially an opera devised for concert performance) designed to celebrate Princess Anne's marriage to William of Orange, and the court attended its première on 13 March 1734, the day before the wedding. Handel greatly admired the Princess, who had been his favourite pupil, and he was inspired to create a superb mélange of arias and choruses of his finest quality. *Parnasso in Festa* is set on Mount Parnassus, associated in Greek mythology with Apollo, the God of the Arts, and home of the nine sacred muses. In the serenata, Handel ingeniously draws a parallel with the real-life event. Three of the Muses, Apollo, Orpheus and Mars, and the huntress Clori join the celebrations of the nuptials of the mortal king, Peleus and the sea-nymph, Thetis. For the score Handel drew partly on the music for *Athelia*, but he also composed much that is new; and there are many fine choruses.

The orchestra was expanded to include flutes, recorders, and both horns and trumpets, plus timpani. The result is splendidly sung by a virtually all-female cast of soloists: **Diana Moore** (Apollo), **Carolyn Sampson** (Clio), **Lucy Crowe** (Orfeo), **Rebecca Outram** (Calliope) and **Ruth Clegg** (Clori), all especially fine. With an exuberant chorus and orchestra under Mathew Halls, this makes an irresistible entertainment, very well recorded. The documentation, too, is excellent, including a full libretto. Not to be missed.

La Resurrezione

*** DG 447 767-2 (2). Massis, Smith, Maguire, Mark Ainsley, Naouri, Les Musiciens du Louvre, Minkowski

Marc Minkowski brings out the dramatic bite of this early Handel oratorio, often opting for extreme speeds, particularly fast ones, challenging his excellent soprano **Annick Massis** to the limit in the Angel's brilliant first aria. He may rarely relax in the way that Ton Koopman did on his earlier Erato version (currently withdrawn), but in this episodic piece there is much to be said for such a taut approach, with fine, clean-textured playing from **Les Musiciens du Louvre**.

Samson (complete)

🎵➔ Ⓜ *** Teldec 2564 69260-2 (2). Rolfe Johnson, Alexander, Kowalski, Miles, Prégardien, Venuti, Blasi, Arnold Schoenberg Ch., VCM, Harnoncourt

Harnoncourt here conducts a Handel performance in which Handelian grandeur shines out from the opening overture with its braying horns and genially strutting dotted rhythms. He is altogether warmer than before, and a fine team of singers, led by **Anthony Rolfe Johnson** in the title-role, is allowed full expressiveness, with speeds in slow numbers broader than one might expect. So the blind Samson's first aria, *Total eclipse*, is very measured, with Rolfe Johnson using the widest tonal and dynamic range. Though the recording catches some flutter in **Roberta Alexander's** voice as Dalila, she gives a characterful performance, well contrasted with **Angela Maria Blasi**, her attendant, who sings the lovely aria, *With plaintive note*, most beautifully. **Maria Venuti** in the climactic *Let the bright seraphim* at the end is not ideally pure-toned, but she sings strongly and flexibly. Other fine singers include **Alastair Miles**, magnificent in the bass role of the giant, Harapha, not least in *Honour and arms*, as well as the rich-toned counter-tenor, **Jochen Kowalski** as Micah and **Christoph Prégardien** in the tenor role of the Philistine. With the **Schoenberg Choir** singing incisively, Harnoncourt presents the work not only with period instruments but on an authentic scale.

Saul (complete)

Ⓜ **** Ph. 475 8256. (3) Miles, Dawson, Brown, Ragin, Ainsky, Mackie, Monteverdi Ch., E. Bar Soloists, Gardiner

**(*) DG 474 510-2 (3). Neal Davies, Scholl, Padmore, Gritton, Argenta, Agnew, Lemalu, Gabrieli Consort and Players, McCreesh

Central to the success of **Paul McCreesh's** version of *Saul* is the warmly characterful singing of the counter-tenor

Andreas Scholl, in the role of David, in effect the central character in this dramatic oratorio even more than the king himself. That said, none of the other soloists quite matches their counterparts on the Gardiner version on Philips, a recording made live in Gottingen in 1989 and still sounding well, with an acoustic less reverberant than that of All Saints, Tooting, where this DG Archiv recording was made. So **Neal Davies** as Saul is less cleanly focused than Alastair Miles on Philips, and Neil Mackie is fresher and firmer as the High Priest than **Paul Agnew** here, while even **Nancy Argenta** as Saul's daughter, Michal, sounds less sweet than usual, hardly a match for Lynne Dawson on Philips. The tautness of McCreesh's direction and the precision of the choral singing, all the crisper in a studio performance, make it a strong alternative, but the Gardiner version remains first choice, an outstanding version in every way.

Joachim Carlos Martini on Naxos offers a clear, fresh, lively reading using period instruments, very well recorded, making an excellent bargain version. Outstanding among the soloists is the creamy-toned **Barbara Schlick**, who sings the role of Michal, Saul's daughter and David's wife. The **Frankfurt chorus** sing well, but are not ideally focused. Otherwise the sound is fresh and clear. (Naxos 8.554361/3)

Solomon (complete)

B—❀ Ⓜ **** Ph. 475 7561 (2). Watkinson, Argenta, Hendricks, Rolfe Johnson, Monteverdi Ch., E. Bar. Sol., Gardiner

**** HM HMC 90 1949/50. Sampson, Gritton, Connolly, Padmore, Wilson-Johnson, Berlin RIAS Chamber Ch., Akademie für Alte Musik, Reuss

(i) *Solomon* (ed. & arr. Beecham). *Love in Bath* (ballet music, arr. Beecham)

Ⓜ **(*) EMI Gemini (ADD) 5 86516-2 (2). (i) Cameron, Young, Morison, Lois Marshall, Beecham Choral Soc.; RPO, Beecham

Gardiner's *Solomon* is among the very finest of all Handel oratorio recordings. With panache, he shows how authentic-sized forces can convey Handelian grandeur even with clean-focused textures and fast speeds. The choruses and even more magnificent double choruses stand as cornerstones of a structure which may have less of a story-line than some other Handel oratorios – the Judgement apart – but which Gardiner shows has consistent human warmth. The Act III scenes between Solomon and the Queen of Sheba are given extra warmth by having in the latter role a singer who is sensuous in tone, **Barbara Hendricks. Carolyn Watkinson's** pure mezzo is very apt for Solomon himself, while **Nancy Argenta** is clear and sweet as his Queen; but the overriding glory of the set is the radiant singing of Gardiner's **Monteverdi Choir**. Its clean, crisp articulation matches the brilliant playing of the **English Baroque Soloists**, regularly challenged by Gardiner's fast speeds, as in *The Arrival of the Queen of Sheba*; and the sound is superb, coping thrillingly with the problems of the double choruses.

Daniel Reuss uses a chorus of 40 and the **Akademie für Alte Musik** play with great expressive vitality, with the brass braying when called for. But above all he has a superb team of soloists: **Carolyn Sampson** is at her lyrical finest, **Sarah Connolly** seems ideally cast in the mezzo name-role, and **Susan Gritton** is hardly less impressive as the Queen. **Mark Padmore** and **David Wilson-Johnson** give appropriate male support and Padmore manages his coloratura with aplomb. All in all an impressive achievement.

In his revision and re-orchestration of *Solomon*, **Sir Thomas Beecham** boldly left out sections which hold up the central plot involving the Queen of Sheba, omitting the Judgement Scene but using the double chorus *From the censer curling rise* after the entertainment for the Queen. With Beecham magicking the music – however inauthentically – the performance can be warmly recommended to devotees of the conductor – and to Handelians too, as long as they are tolerant.

The EMI Gemini set finds room for *Love in Bath*, the title of which conceals the identity of **Beecham's** ballet, first performed just before the end of the war, called *The Great Elopement*. Needless to say, the **Royal Philharmonic Orchestra** play like angels – if occasionally not perfectly disciplined angels. However, the transfer of *Solomon* produces rather fierce violin-sound in the *Overture*, and the spikiness is again noticeable in the *Arrival of the Queen of Sheba*; and there is a thinness too on the violins in the ballet suite.

Theodora (complete; DVD version)

*** Warner DVD 0630-15481-2. Upshaw, Daniels, Olsen, Croft, Hunt-Lieberson, OAE, Christie (V/D: Peter Sellars)

The Glyndebourne staging of Handel's oratorio, *Theodora*, was recorded in June 1996. Peter Sellars himself has directed the video as well as acting as stage director, heightening the impact of this updated production. Though the original is set in AD 304, Sellars updates the story to the present day, with the Roman Governor, Valens, becoming an American-style President. At the end, when Theodora and Didymus are martyred, Sellars has them strapped down and lethally injected, a chilling dénouement. The staging involves a stylized set so as to cope with the changes of scene normal in a Handel oratorio. What makes the result so compelling is not just the inspired direction of William Christie with the **Orchestra of the Age of Enlightenment**, but above all a cast that it would be hard to match. **Dawn Upshaw** in the title-role is tenderly appealing, and her sweet, pure singing is matched by that of **Lorraine Hunt Lieberson** as her friend, Irene, conveying a depth of feeling if anything even greater in wonderful arias. In the castrato role of Didymus, the counter-tenor **David Daniels** gives a masterly performance, brilliant technically and moving too, and the tenor, **Richard Croft**, is equally stylish as Septimius, with **Frode Olsen** powerful as the unyielding Valens. Generous measure, with three and a half hours of music on a single disc – though the documentation is sketchy, with no booklet and only a brief synopsis of the plot.

Theodora (complete; CD versions)

B—**** DG 469 061-2 (3). Gritton, Bickley, Blaze, Agnew, N. Davies, Gabrieli Cons. & Players, McCreesh

Ⓜ *** MDG 332 1019-2 (3). Somer, Buwalda, Rasker, Schoch, Sol, Schweiser, Cologne Chamber Ch., Coll. Cartusianum, Neumann

Paul McCreesh's version sweeps the board. Beautifully recorded in a sympathetic acoustic it offers an outstandingly sensitive, well-paced reading, ideally cast, using a text which gives alternative versions of numbers that Handel revised. Using a relatively large string section (26 players), McCreesh brings out the dramatic contrasts vividly. In the title-role **Susan Gritton** sings radiantly, unaffectedly compassing the widest range of expression, a moving central focus to the drama, with the even-toned counter-tenor, **Robin Blaze**, equally impressive as Didymus, the Roman officer who becomes her fellow martyr. The mezzo, **Susan Bickley**, sings with simple dedication as Irene, with **Paul Agnew** elegant in the role of Septimius and **Neal Davies** an authoritative Valens, President of Antioch.

    Peter Neumann's version on MDG, well played and sympathetically paced, would be very welcome but for the formidable competition from McCreesh on DG Archiv. The German cast is first rate, admirably coping with an English text, led by the warm-toned **Johanette Somer** as Theodora and the excellent counter-tenor, **Sytse Buwalda**, as Didymus. The three discs come for the price of two.

The Triumph of Time and Truth

Ⓜ *** Hyp. Dyad CDD 22050 (2). Fisher, Kirkby, Brett, Partridge, Varcoe, L. Handel Ch. and O, Darlow

Darlow's performance of Handel's very last oratorio is broad and strong and very enjoyable. The soloists have all been chosen for the clarity of their pitching – **Emma Kirkby**, **Gillian Fisher**, **Charles Brett** and **Stephen Varcoe**, with the honey-toned **Ian Partridge** singing even more beautifully than the others, but with a timbre too pure quite to characterize 'Pleasure'. Good atmospheric recording.

Il tronfo del tempo e del Disinganno

Ⓝ **(*) Hyp. CDA 67681/2. Invernizzi, Aldrich, Oro, Dürmüller, Academia Montis Regalis, De Marchi

    Roberta Invernizzi's clear, pleasing soprano dominates the full-price Hyperion version, with plenty of bravura coloratura to catch the ear. **Kate Aldrich** is the mezzo Piacere representing 'Pleasure', while the counter-tenor **Martin Oro** is perhaps not entirely enlightened. **Jörg Dürmüller** has less to contribute (especially in Part II) as the tenor representative of Tempo ('Time'), but he sings ardently and strongly throughout. On the whole they are a good team, and the **Academia** provide an acceptable period-instrument backing.

'Great Oratorio Duets' from Alexander Balus; Alexander's Feast; Belshazzar; Deborah; Esther; Jephtha; Joshua; Saul; Solomon; Susanna; Theodora

⊶ *** BIS **SACD** 1236 (Surround Sound). Sampson, Blaze, OAE, Kraemer

We usually get plenty of compilations of opera arias and duets on disc, but almost never a comparable oratorio selection. But BIS have had the inspired idea of putting together two of the finest baroque soloists of our time, and they prove a truly distinctive partnership. The voices of **Robin Blaze** and **Carolyn Sampson** were surely made for each other, and they blend quite perfectly, particularly when they trill together or answer each other in a conversational style. Not surprisingly, **Nicholas Kraemer's** accompaniments are most stylish, and if you have facilities for SACD surround sound, the realism of a most vivid recording is greatly enhanced.

OPERA

Acis and Galatea (complete; CD version)

⊶ Ⓜ **** Chan. (ADD) Chan 3147. Sutherland, Pears, Galliver, Brannigan, St Anthony Singers L. Philomusica, Boult

In 1959, originally from Decca (Oiseau-Lyre), **Boult** provided the début stereo recording of Handel's masque. **Joan Sutherland** in fresh, youthful voice makes a splendid Galatea, sparkling in the florid passages, warmly sympathetic in the lyrical music. **Peter Pears**, too, is at his finest, and although **David Galliver** is less striking, his contribution is still a good one; while **Owen Brannigan** was surely born to play Polyphemus, and he comes over as a very genial one-eyed giant, the villainy muted. His lusty account of *O ruddier than the cherry* (heard in the version with treble recorder), where he makes a positive virtue of intrusive aspirates, is alone worth the cost of the disc. Anyone hearing it who can resist a smile must be stony-hearted indeed. Although tempi are more relaxed than we would expect today, Boult's sympathetic direction ensures that the music-making has a lift throughout. The documentation includes a full text.

Admeto, re di Tessaglia (complete)

Ⓜ *** Virgin (ADD) 5 61369-2 (3). Jacobs, Yakar, Gomez, Bowman, Cold, Dams, Van Egmont, Il Complesso Barocco, Curtis

Admeto is among the very greatest of Handel's operas, and this recording, made in 1977 in Holland, was one of the first complete recordings of a Handel opera to attempt an authentic approach, and the most successful up to that time. Though recitatives are on the slow side, it stands the test of time, a fine performance, very well cast, played with refinement on period instruments and excellently recorded. Here the counter-tenor **René Jacobs** gives an understanding and characterful performance in the title-role, but it is **Jill Gomez** as Antigona who steals first honours, with magnificent singing, sweet, pure and strong of tone, with ornamentation beautifully crisp. **Rachel Yakar** is not so sweetly caught by the microphones, but hers is a stylish performance too, and the rest of the cast has no weak link, with **James Bowman** outstanding as Admeto's brother, Trasimede.

Agrippina (complete; DVD version)

(*) EuroArts **DVD 2054538. Daniels, Hall, Von Kannen, Kuebler, Nicolai, Hielscher, Katz, Lesbo, L. Bar. Players, Östman (Dir: Michael Hampe)

Michael Hampe's production involves handsome baroque sets by Mauro Pagano and traditional costumes. *Agrippina* is an opera set in the early years of Imperial Rome, with

Agrippina the centre of intrigues, opposed by another great manipulator, Poppea. **Barbara Daniels** is agile, strong and bright in the title-role, with **Janice Hall** first rate as Poppea. The snag of the performance is that two of the principal castrato roles, those of Nero and Narciso, are here taken by baritones instead of counter-tenors, reflecting the date of the production (before period performance was fully accepted).

(i) *Alceste: Overture & Incidental Music;* (ii) *Anthem for the Foundling Hospital;* *Ode for the Birthday of Queen Anne;* (iii) *Utrecht Te Deum & Jubilate in D*

Ⓑ *** Double Decca 458 072-2 (2). (i; ii; iii) Kirkby, Nelson, D. Thomas, AAM; (i) Cable, Elliott, Ch., Hogwood; (ii) Minty, Bowman, Hill; (ii; iii) Christ Church Cathedral Ch., Preston; (iii) with Brett, Covey-Crump, Elliott

Handel left us much to enjoy in the impressively dramatic *Alceste Overture* in D minor and the *Grand entrée* for Admetus, Alceste and their wedding guests, which get the proceedings off to a fine start. There follows a series not just of solo items but also some simple tuneful choruses in which a small secondary vocal group participates. There is nearly an hour of freshly enjoyable music and **Hogwood** draws lively, sympathetic performances from his team. The *Ode* has its Italianate attractions and opens with a splendid counter-tenor aria from **James Bowman**, with an elaborate trumpet obbligato, superbly played here. But it is the much later *Foundling Hospital Anthem* that is the more memorable, not just because it concludes with an alternative version of the *Hallelujah Chorus*, but also because the other borrowed numbers are also superb. The *Utrecht* pieces were written just before Handel came to London and were intended as a sample of his work. **Preston** directs performances which are characteristically alert and vigorous, particularly impressive in the superb closing *Glory be to the Father* with its massive eight-part chords. Throughout the team of soloists regularly associated with the Academy give of their best, and the recordings, made in 1977 and 1979 are splendidly transferred, clean and clear yet not losing their analogue atmosphere.

Alcina (CD versions)

☍— *** Erato 8573 80233-2 (3). Fleming, Graham, Dessay, Kuhlmann, Lascarro, Robinson, Naouri, Les Arts Florissants, Christie

☍— Ⓜ *** EMI 3 58681-2 (3). Augér, D. Jones, Kuhlmann, Harrhy, Kwella, M. Davies, Tomlinson, Opera Stage Ch., City of L. Bar. Sinf., Hickox

Ⓝ *** DG 477 7374 (3). DiDonato, Gauvin, Beaumont, Prina, Van Rensburg, Preiante, Cherici, Il Complesso Barocco, Curtis

Alcina is among the finest of Handel's operas. The fine Erato set was recorded live at the Paris Opéra. Only in recitatives do stage noises ever intrude, and the tensions of a live recording help to minimize the drawback of an opera containing only one ensemble number (the Act III terzetto) in addition to the traditional brief choral finale. **Christie** too is masterly at avoiding any monotony in the long sequence of *da capo* arias, with recitative superbly timed and reprises beautifully decorated. **Renée Fleming** is in glorious voice as

Alcina, with **Susan Graham** characterizing well in the trouser-role of Ruggiero. **Natalie Dessay** as Alcina's sister, Morgana, relishes the challenge of the brilliant *Tornami a vagheggiar* (appropriated by Joan Sutherland in the inauthentic Decca set), helped by Christie's relatively relaxed tempo. He also sets relaxed speeds in some of the great slow arias such as *Verdi prati*, encouraging an expressive approach which yet remains within the bounds of period style. Highlights are available on 857385356-2.

It would be hard to devise a septet of soloists more stylish than those on the reissued EMI set, with **Arleen Augér** brilliant and warm-toned, singing warmly in the great expansive arias. **Della Jones** stands out in the breeches role of Ruggiero and **Eiddwen Harrhy** as Morgana is no less brilliant, while **Kathleen Kuhlmann**, **Patrizia Kwella** and **John Tomlinson** all sing with a clarity and beauty to make the music sparkle. **Hickox** underlines the contrasts of mood and speed, conveying the full range of emotion. The reissue provides a cued synopsis with a list of tracks. A fine alternative to Christie's version.

Alan Curtis's account is on a more intimate scale than its two major competitors, and his period-instrument accompanying group is considerably less robust. This means great transparency of detail but less sonority. His vocal team is led by the excellent **Joyce DiDonato**, dramatically very impressive, while **Maite Beaumont** is a strong Ruggiero and **Karina Gauvin** a seductive Morgana. **Sonia Prina** as Bradamente and **Laura Cherici's** Oberto make up a strong team, if not one that overall is preferable to the starry casts enjoyed by Christie and Hickox. This is essentially for authenticists.

Almira (complete)

Ⓜ **(*) CPO 999 275-2 (3). Monoyios, Rozario, Gerrard, D. Thomas, Nasrawi, MacDougall, Elsner, Fiori Musicale, Lawrence-King

Almira was Handel's first opera, written in Hamburg in 1704. Even so, one regularly detects a genuine Handelian flavour in the themes, and he himself borrowed a fair measure of the material here in later works. This recording, with three discs offered for the price of two, was made after a staging presented in both Halle and Bremen in 1994. **Andrew Lawrence-King** secures a fresh and well-paced – if rather plain – performance, with deft playing from the German period orchestra. **Ann Monoyios** is a light, bright Almira, with **Patricia Rozario**, taxed a little by the high tessitura, equally stylish as Edilia. The two principal tenor roles are very well taken by **Jamie MacDougall** and **Douglas Nasrawi**, with the third tenor, **Christian Elsner**, taking the comic servant role. **David Thomas** sings with clean attack in the bass role of the Prince of Segovia. Good, undistracting and well scaled in an intimate acoustic.

Amadigi di Gaula (complete)

*** Erato 2292 45490-2 (2). Stutzmann, J. Smith, Harrhy, Fink, Musiciens du Louvre, Minkowski

Minkowski's electrifying performance is one of his sharpest, dominated vocally by the magnificent young French contralto (no mere mezzo) of **Nathalie Stutzmann** in the title-role. She sings Amadigi's gentle arias most affectingly, notably the lovely *Sussurrate, onde vezzose*, and the two women characters, Amadigi's lover Melissa and Princess Oriana, are well taken by **Eiddwen Harrhy** and **Jennifer Smith**, with the brilliant arias for Prince Dardano of Thrace superbly sung by **Bernarda Fink**. It is a performance on an intimate scale, and the more involving for that.

Ariodante (complete; DVD version)

(*) Dynamic **DVD 33559 (2). Hallenberg, Cherici, Iorio, Nesi, Lepore, Stains, Prato, Il Complesso Barocco, Curtis (Dir: John Pascoe, V/D: Matteo Ricchetti)

This is a very impressively sung DVD set of *Ariodante*, led by **Ann Hallenberg** in the castrato title-role, who manages her complex divisions with aplomb. **Laura Cherici**, Ariodante's beloved Ginevra, also has a lovely voice when singing expressively, while **Marta Vandoni Iorio** sings and characterizes Dalinda, the heroine's lady-in-waiting admirably. She is eventually to love Captain Luciano (the pleasant-voiced tenor, **Zachary Stains**) but through the machinations of the villain Polinesso (**Mary-Ellen Nesi**), she compromises her mistress. All ends well, however, and the King of Scotland gives his blessing to the match of his daughter and Ariodante (who hails from Fife!) and pardons Dalinda. The music is ever rewarding, but to watch the performance is complicated when two of the male characters are played by women, and the costumes are wholly inappropriate, approximating to fairly modern English dress (around the middle of the 20th century), with not a suspicion that the opera is set in Scotland. One needs the (excellent) booklet to follow what is going on. But the singing and playing of **Il Complesso Barocco** under **Alan Curtis** is of a high standard.

Ariodante (complete; CD versions)

🎵 *** DG 457 271-2 (3). Von Otter, Dawson, Podles, Croft, Musiciens du Louvre, Minkowski

🎵 (M) *** Ph. Trio (ADD) 473 955-2 (3). J. Baker, Mathis, Burrowes, Bowman, Rendall, Ramey, L. Voices, ECO, Leppard

On DG Archiv, with an outstanding, starry team of soloists, **Marc Minkowski** conducts a high-powered reading, urgently dramatic and a compelling set in every way. Though **Anne Sofie von Otter** in the title-role is not quite at her freshest, and Dame Janet Baker on the rival set gives an even more moving performance, her characterization is as strong as ever. Among the others **Lynne Dawson** and **Ewa Podles** are outstandingly fine.

In the colourful, urgent performance under **Raymond Leppard**, the castrato role of Ariodante is a challenge for **Dame Janet Baker**, who responds with singing of enormous expressive range, from the dark, agonized moments of the C minor aria early in Act III to the brilliance of the most spectacular of the three display arias later in the Act. Baker's duets with **Edith Mathis** as Princess Ginevra, destined to marry Prince Ariodante, are enchanting too, and there is not a single weak member of the cast, though **James Bowman** as Duke Polinesso is not as precise as usual, with words often

unclear. However, this now returns as a mid-priced Trio, which means that it is without a translated text, and a cued synopsis is offered as a poor alternative. In all other respects it is an outstanding set.

Arminio (complete)

*** Virgin 5 45461-2 (2). Genaux, McGreevy, Labelle, Custer, Petroni, Buwalda, Ristori, Il Complesso Barocco, Curtis

Standing out in the cast is **Geraldine McGreevy**, who takes the key role of the heroine, Tusnelda, daughter of the German prince, Segeste. Tusnelda has far more arias than anyone else, many of them vigorous, but including such deeply reflective numbers as the ravishing *Rendimi il dolce sposo*, which ends Act II. In Act III she has (in addition to another reflective aria) two charming duets with voices in chains of thirds. **Vivica Genaux** as Arminio is not caught quite so well by the microphone, but the whole cast, including **Dominique Labelle**, an excellent second soprano as Sigismondo, are commendably agile in the florid writing, with the fresh-toned period band, **Il Complesso Barocco**, ever-responsive. Clear, well-balanced sound.

Ezio (complete)

(N) *** DG 477 5073. Hallenberg, Prina, Gauvin, Giustiniani, Il Complesso Barocco, Curtis

Handel's *Ezio* has been described as 'a depressing tale of envy, betrayal and egoism', yet it contains much glorious music, starting off with an overture very much in *Water Music* mode with trumpets and drums prominent. Historically, the opera is based on the exploits of the Roman General Aetius (Ezio translated) who, in the last days of the Empire, defeated Attila the Hun on the Catalaunian Plain, with the military and personal muddles effectively sorted out to give a happy ending. In fact Aetius was murdered in 454 by the Emperor Valentinian III, who feared him as a rival. The performance under **Alan Curtis**, recorded in the Teatro Comunale of Lonigo, relies on fresh, mainly young voices, cleanly focused, notably on **Ann Hallenberg** in the title-role and **Sonia Prina** as Valentiniano. Curtis with his period-performance forces is also fresh and lively, with the acoustic of a theatre nicely caught. A valuable set of an enjoyable rarity.

Faramondo (complete)

(N) *** Virgin 5 099 2 216611-2 (3). Cencic, Jaroussky, Karthauser, de Liso, Sin, R. Svizzera Ch., I Barocchisti, Fasolis

Faramondo is another of Handel's rarest operas, written in 1738, performed here by a cast of fresh young singers giving stylish performances, with no suspicion of aspirated coloratura. The period-performance players of **I Barocchisti** are strongly directed by **Diego Fasolis**. The title-role of Faramondo, King of the Franks, is very well taken by **Max Emanuel Cencic**, coping well with the exceptionally low-lying register, reflecting the qualities of the singer who originally took the part. Faramondo is at war with Gustavo, King of the Cimbrians, a role given to a bass, who sings the first of the many arias. The plot from then on is typically complex, involving Clotilde, Faramondo's sister, who has been taken captive, and Adolfo, Gustavo's son, who is in love with Clotilde. Rosimonda, Gustavo's daughter, then arrives, and in the end she is offered to Faramondo as a sign of peace, the happy ending typical of *opera seria*. The oddity of the plot did not prevent Handel from writing inspired music, and yet again, we have it confirmed in a recording that shows it was largely accidental whether these Handel operas became successful or not. But this is another valuable set, very well recorded.

Fernando (complete)

🎧 *** Virgin 3 65483-2 (2). Zazzo, Cangemi, Pizzolato, Abete, Cencie, Adami, Bannerjee, Il Complesso Barocco, Curtis

Alan Curtis offers the first recording of the opera which Handel developed into *Sosarme*, changing the characters from historical figures to classical ones from ancient history. The result is arguably fresher and more immediate than in *Sosarme*. Curtis draws lively playing from his period band, with a first-rate line-up of soloists. In the title-role **Lawrence Zazzo** is a masterly counter-tenor, coping superbly with the elaborate divisions, while **Veronica Cangemi**, as Elvida, Dionisio's daughter, with whom Fernando is in love, has a gorgeously creamy soprano which is not only beautiful in her lyrical numbers but also flexible in the brilliant ones. She is well contrasted with **Marianna Pizzolato** as Isabella, wife of Dionisio. The two tenors in the cast, **Filippo Adami** as Dionisio, and **Neal Bannerjee** as Alfonso, his son, have less distinctive voices which are yet admirably agile, as is the bass. First-rate recording, made in St Gallen, Switzerland.

Flavio (complete)

Ⓑ *** HM HMX 2901312.3 (2). Gall, Ragin, Lootens, Fink, Högman, Fagotto, Messthaler, Ens. 415, Jacobs

Handel's score was brilliantly written for some of the most celebrated singers of the time, including the castrato, Senesino. His four arias are among the high spots of the opera, all sung superbly here by the warm-toned and characterful counter-tenor, **Derek Lee Ragin**; almost every other aria is open and vigorous, with the whole sequence rounded off in a rousing ensemble. **René Jacobs's** team of eight soloists is a strong one, with only the strenuous tenor of **Gianpaolo Fagotto** occasionally falling short of the general stylishness. Full, clear sound, and text and translations included.

Floridante

🎧 *** DG 477 6566 (3). Mijankovic, DiDonato, Priante, Zamir, Invernizzi, Novaro, Il Complesso Barocco, Curtis

As is well known, Handel regularly adapted his operas to suit the needs of the individual singers available for each revival. Here, the role of the heroine, Elmira, was switched even before the first performance, but here Curtis has restored what Handel originally wanted, a role for soprano. Conversely, he keeps the role of Rossana, natural daughter of Otone, King of Persia, as a soprano, fresh and bright in her relatively short, tuneful arias. The great glory of the set is the singing of **Joyce DiDonato** as Elmira, not just fresh-toned, with flawless legato in her lyrical arias, but dazzlingly brilliant in the florid ones. **Marijana Mijankovic** in the castrato role of Floridante, Prince of Thrace, sings warmly but with a slightly unsteady tone. The role of Oronte is sung with clean attack by the baritone **Vito Priante**; **Roberta Invernizzi** is firm and flexible as the Prince of Tyre, and the counter-tenor **Riccardo Novaro** is excellent as the satrap, Timante. First-rate sound, recorded in a church in Viterbo.

Giulio Cesare in Egitto (complete; DVD versions)

🎧 *** Opus Arte DVD OA 0950 D (3). Connolly, Bardon, Kirchschlager, De Niese, Dumaux, Maltman, Glyndebourne Ch., OAE, Christie (Dir: David McVicar, V/D: Robin Lough)

**(*) EuroArts DVD 2053599 (2). Pushee, Alexander, Gunn, Campbell, Kenny, Dalton, Bennett, Gilchrist, Australian Op. & Ballet O, Hickox (V/D: Peter Butler)

William Christie conducts the **Orchestra of the Age of Enlightenment** and an outstanding cast in an account at once scholarly, lively and refreshing, a live recording of the 2005 production at Glyndebourne. **Sarah Connolly** sings superbly in the title-role, looking very boyish, opposite **Danielle de Niese** as Cleopatra, a soprano brighter-toned than usual for this role, a provocative figure. **Patricia Bardon** is an excellent Cornelia and **Christophe Dumaux** a characterful Tolomeo. Like most other versions, the action is updated, with the Roman army presented in the uniforms of the Britsh army in India in the 19th century. Action is effectively presented against a permanent set, involving a sequence of classical arches seen in perspective.

Francisco Negrin's production of *Giulio Cesare* for the Sydney Opera House with walls of hieroglyphics often superimposed, is updated from Roman times to a kind of Ruritanian state, with colourful uniforms involving cuirasses. By contrast, the Egyptian characters, not just Cleopatra but the others too, wear timeless robes, sharply distinguishing them. The counter-tenor **Graham Pushee** sings powerfully in the title-role with his cleanly focused voice, offering immaculate articulation and phenomenal agility in the many formidable divisions. Opposite him is the superb Cleopatra of **Yvonne Kenny**, glamorous of person and voice. Happily, Hickox allows her big arias full expansiveness, bringing out their beauty. **Rosemary Gunn** is a fine Cornelia, statuesque in her bearing and rich of voice, with **Andrew Dalton** a characterful Tolomeo and the dark-toned **Stephen Bennett** a formidable Achilla. The Sesto of **Elizabeth Campbell** is bright and clear if shrill at times.

Giulio Cesare (complete; CD versions)

🎧 Ⓑ **** HM HMX 2901 385.7 (3). Larmore, Schlick, Fink, Rorholm, Ragin, Zanasi, Visse, Concerto Köln, Jacobs

*** Astree E 8558 (3). Bowman, Dawson, Laurens, James, Visse, La Grande Ecurie et la Chambre du Roy, Malgoire

**(*) DG 474 210-2 (3). Mijanovic, Kožená, Von Otter, Hellekant, Bejun Mehta, Ewing, Bettini, Ankaoua, Musiciens du Louvre, Minkowski

The casting of the pure, golden-toned **Barbara Schlick** as Cleopatra on Harmonia Mundi proves outstandingly successful. **Jennifer Larmore** too, a fine, firm mezzo with a touch of masculine toughness in the tone, makes a splendid Caesar. Together they crown the whole performance with the most seductive account of their final duet. **Derek Lee Ragin** is excellent in the sinister role of Tolomeo (Ptolemy); so are **Bernarda Fink** as Cornelia and **Marianne Rorholm** as Sesto, with the bass, **Furio Zanasi**, as Achille. **René Jacobs's** expansive speeds mean that the whole opera will not fit on three CDs, but the fourth disc, at 18 minutes merely supplementary, comes free as part of the package, and includes an extra aria for the servant, Nireno, delightfully sung by the French counter-tenor, **Dominique Visse**. Firm, well-balanced sound. This now comes at bargain price with texts and translations included.

The counter-tenor **James Bowman** in the **Malgoire** set is strongly contrasted against the firm and purposeful mezzo, Jennifer Larmore. The contrast between **Lynne Dawson** as Cleopatra and Barbara Schlick is a key one too, for Dawson, following Malgoire's general approach, concentrates on beauty and classical poise, whereas Schlick brings out greater depth of expression. The contrast is similar over **Giullemette Laurens** as Cornelia as against Bernarda Fink, the one poised, the other more deeply expressive, often at broader speeds. By contrast, the counter-tenor, **Dominique Visse**, is the more actively characterful as the villainous Tolomeo, where Derek Lee Ragin for Jacobs combines sharp characterization with cleaner vocalization. Malgoire's text is not quite as complete as Jacobs's, with cuts in recitative.

As he establishes in the Overture, Minkowski prefers speeds on the fast side, sometimes very fast, with playing clear and clipped from the **Musiciens du Louvre**. That regularly sets a challenge to his singers as well as the players, very well taken. So Cleopatra's first aria in Act I sounds rushed despite the brilliant, characteristic singing of **Magdalena Kožená**, and sadly her second Act I aria is cut. Otherwise, hers is a commanding performance, deeply moving in her big lyrical numbers, *V'adoro pupille* and *Piangero*, for which Minkowski allows full warmth and tenderness at aptly spacious speeds. **Marijana Mijanovic** sings powerfully in the title-role, with **Anne Sofie von Otter** a poised Sesto and **Charlotte Hellekant** a firm, clear Cornelia.

Julius Caesar (Giulio Cesare; complete, in English)

(*) Arthaus **DVD 100 308. Details as below (Dir: John Copley, V/D: John Michael Phillips.)

Ⓜ *** Chan. 3019 (3). J. Baker, Masterson, Walker, D. Jones, Bowman, Tomlinson, ENO Ch. & O, Mackerras

Taken from Channel 4's TV presentation of the English National Opera production, the Arthaus DVD offers a studio performance with the original staging modified. **Janet Baker** sings and acts commandingly in the title-role, with **Valerie Masterson** a sympathetic if hardly sensuous Cleopatra, and **Sarah Walker** as Pompey's widow, Cornelia, matching even Baker in the intensity of her singing and acting. **Della Jones** as Sextus, **James Bowman** as the scheming Ptolemy and **John Tomlinson** as Achillas are all ideal in their roles, with Michael Stennett's sumptuous costumes adding to the success of the production. **Sir Charles Mackerras** paces the

music masterfully, but sadly the orchestral sound on DVD is thinner than in the audio recording, with an edge to it. So the CDs remain first choice. On CD the ravishing accompaniments to the two big Cleopatra arias amply justify the use by the excellent **ENO Orchestra** of modern rather than period instruments. The full, vivid studio sound makes this one of the very finest of the invaluable series of ENO opera recordings in English sponsored by the Peter Moores Foundation (excerpts are available on Chan 3072).

Giustino (complete)

*** HM HMU 907130/32. Chance, Röschmann, Kotoski, Gondek, Lane, Padmore, Minter, Cantamus Halle Chamber Ch., Freiburg Bar. O, McGegan

First heard in 1737 and never revived until 1967, the opera *Giustino* has been consistently underestimated. **Nicholas McGegan**, with his fast, crisp manner and fondness for extra decoration in *da capo* repeats, brings out the element of sparkle and irony implied in the improbable story, treated refreshingly in dozens of brief arias. **Michael Chance** is outstanding in the title-role originally written for a castrato, and **Dorothea Röschmann** sings most movingly in the key role of Arianna. **Drew Minter**, stylish and intelligent as he is, fails to give enough bite to the villainous role of Amanzio; but there are few other disappointments, and the tenor, **Mark Padmore**, sings with virtuoso flair in the military role of Vitaliano. The German string-players are more abrasive than one expects nowadays, but this is a set to delight all Handelians, filling in an important gap.

Hercules (complete)

*** DG 469 532-2 (3). Saks, Von Otter, Croft, Dawson, Daniels, Pujol, Ch. & Musiciens du Louvre, Minkowski

Ⓜ *** DG 447 689-2 (2). Tomlinson, Walker, Rolfe Johnson, J. Smith, Denley, Savidge, Monteverdi Ch., E. Bar. Sol., Gardiner

Mark Minkowski conducts an urgently dramatic account of Handel's music-drama in English on a classical theme. **Anne Sofie von Otter** gives a vividly characterful performance which, with fine gradation of tone and expression, brings out the full range of emotion implied. She is specially moving at the end when she realizes that her jealousy has brought the death of her husband. As Hercules, **Gidon Saks** sings with fine, clear focus, not as weighty as many a traditional Handel bass, but firm and dark. Excellent contributions too from **Lynne Dawson** as a bright, charming Iole, from the counter-tenor, **David Daniels**, peerless as the herald, Lichas, and from **Richard Croft**, elegant in the music of Hyllus, Hercules's son. The French chorus is not quite as idiomatic as the Monteverdi Choir in the rival Gardiner version.

Gardiner's brisk performance of *Hercules* using authentic forces may at times lack Handelian grandeur in the big choruses, but it conveys superbly the vigour of the writing, its natural drama; and the fire of this performance is typified by the outstanding singing of **Sarah Walker** as Dejanira. **John Tomlinson** makes an excellent, dark-toned Hercules. Fresh voices consistently help in the clarity of the attack – **Jennifer**

Smith as Iole, **Catherine Denley** as Lichas, **Anthony Rolfe Johnson** as Hyllus and **Peter Savidge** as the Priest of Jupiter. Refined playing and outstanding recording quality make this most welcome at mid-price.

Imeneo (complete)

(B) *** CPO 999 915-2 (2). Hallenberg, Stojkovic, Thornhill, Stiefermann, Chung, Cologne Vocal Ens., Capella Augustina, Spering

This late opera by Handel, one of the last two Italian operas he ever wrote, has been inexplicably neglected on disc, and this lively version, recorded in Cologne in collaboration with West German Radio, admirably fills the gap, well sung and well played, even if **Andreas Spering's** direction brings some plodding continuo. The story inspires Handel to a sequence of fine numbers, notably for Rosmene and Tirinto. **Johanna Stojkovic** sings strongly, bright and clear in the most taxing divisions, while **Anna Hallenberg** as Tirinto is equally commanding with her warm, firm mezzo, rising superbly to the challenge of her big showpiece aria, *Sorge nell'alma*, which anticipates *Why do the nations* in *Messiah*. Finer still is her tragic minor-key aria in Act III, *Pieno il core*, by far the most extended number. Also impessive is the trio for Rosmene and the rival suitors, while Rosmene's final aria is the most original of all, with curious stops and starts, and bald octave writing in the accompaniment. The original version of the text is used, with the role of Imeneo taken by a baritone – impressively sung by **Kay Stiefermann** – where Handel's revision for Dublin uses a tenor instead. Clear, well-balanced sound.

Orlando (DVD version)

(N)(***) Arthaus **DVD** 101 309 (also Blu-ray version 101310). Mijanovič, Janková, Peetz, Clark, Wolff, Zürich Op. La Scintilla O, Christie

The magician Zoroastro oversees the action of this remarkable opera, concerned that its hero, Orlando (tempted by the allure of Angelica, Queen of Catlai), is possibly becoming dedicated to love rather than to the glory of battle. But she in turn loves Medoro, an African prince; and Medoro is also involved with the shepherdess Dorinda. So Act I ends with a glorious 'romantic triangle' trio as fine as anything Handel ever wrote. Orlando is famously unstable and is consumed with jealousy, which leads to a striking Mad scene at the end of Act II. However, all ends well with Orlando a hero again, and Dorinda reconciled to Medoro's unfaithfulness.

In Handel's conception, *Orlando* takes place partly in a wood, with the magical appearance of a fountain transforming the scene to a garden, but returning to the woodland in Act II, when Medoro carves his name and that of his beloved Angelica on a tree. Act III shifts to Dorinda's cottage, then moves to a 'horrid' cavern, and back to Dorinda's cottage for the final reconciliation.

However Jens-Daniel Herzog's staging for the Zürich opera perversely places the action in a World War II sanatorium, with Zoroastro in a white cloak manipulating the action within a set of moving screens and walls. Orlando is costumed as a wounded army officer, and Medoro appears

to be a womanizing spiv. Angelica looks attractive in modern costume, as does the delightful Dorinda, who sings with great charm, and they (all but Orlando) make love quite sexily. But, most importantly, the singing of all five principals is quite beautiful. Whether with ravishing lyrical lines or spectacular vocal fireworks (a speciality of Orlando), every inspired number is a pleasure to listen to, to the extent that one watches the ridiculous action without distraction, including one scene when the sanatorium staff are seen hanging out their patients' trousers on a series of washing lines, which Dorinda can fondle as she sings about Medoro! The three stars are only for the singing and, of course, **Christie's** excellent orchestral backing.

Orlando (complete; CD versions)

🎵 **** O-L 430 845-2 (3). Bowman, Augér, Robbin, Kirkby, D. Thomas, AAM, Hogwood

*** Erato 0630 14636-2 (3). Bardon, Mannion, Summers, Joshua, Van der Kamp, Les Arts Florissants, Christie

Handel's *Orlando* was radically modified to provide suitable material for individual singers, notably in the magnificent Mad scene which ends Act II on the aria, *Vaghe pupille*. That number, superbly done on Oiseau-Lyre by **James Bowman**, with appropriate sound effects, is only one of the virtuoso vehicles for the counter-tenor. For the jewelled sequences of arias and duets, **Hogwood** has assembled a near-ideal cast, with **Arleen Augér** at her most radiant as the queen, Angelica, and **Emma Kirkby** characteristically bright and fresh in the lighter, semi-comic role of the shepherdess, Dorinda. **Catherine Robbin** assumes the role of Prince Medoro strongly and **David Thomas** sings stylishly as Zoroastro. This is one of Hogwood's finest achievements on record, taut, dramatic and rhythmically resilient. Vivid, open sound.

William Christie's Erato recording of *Orlando* makes a valuable alternative. The most obvious difference is that, where Hogwood has a male alto singing the title-role, Christie here opts for a fine mezzo, **Patricia Bardon**. Her approach is more overtly dramatic than James Bowman's for Hogwood, with moods and passions more positively characterized. The celebrated Mad scene ending Act II illustrates the point perfectly, with Christie and Bardon more violent, using bigger contrasts, ending in a scurrying *accelerando*. His other soloists are all excellent, readily matching their rivals, not least the contralto, **Hilary Summers**, as Prince Medoro.

Ottone, re di Germania (complete)

*** Hyp. CDA 66751/3. Bowman, McFadden, Smith, Denley, Visse, George, King's Cons., King

Robert King and his **King's Consort** offer a version on Hyperion with **James Bowman** as Ottone. The women principals do not have sufficiently pure, firm voices, but when it comes to the key castrato roles taken by counter-tenors, it is quite different. Bowman, with his rich tone, continues to sing with enormous panache and virtuoso agility. **Dominique Visse** as the duplicitous Adalberto tends to overcharacterize, but the singing is full of colour. Added to that is the richness and bloom on the instrumental sound.

Partenope (complete)

⊕ₘ*** Chan. 0719 (3). Joshua, Summers, Wallace, Zazzo, Streit, Foster-Williams, Early Op. Co., Curnyn

Partenope is a fine piece that moves swiftly in a story ranging wide from despair to witty innuendo, ending happily on a double wedding. Central to the success of **Christian Curnyn's** well-paced performance is the glorious singing of **Rosemary Joshua** in the title-role of Partenope. Set against her in the role of the mischievous Rosmira, Princess of Cyprus (for most of the time disguised as a man), is the ripe-toned contralto, **Hilary Summers**. Other principals in the excellent **Early Opera Company** cast include two outstanding counter-tenors, **Stephen Wallace** as Armindo and **Lawrence Zazzo** as Arsace, suitors to the Queen, with the warlike Emilio, the third suitor, strongly taken by the tenor, **Kurt Streit**. Handsomely packaged, with each of the three Acts complete on a single disc, it is among the most attractive of rarities among Handel operas.

Radamisto (complete; CD version)

*** Virgin 5 45673-2 (2). DiDonato, Ciofi, Beaumont, Labelle, Cherici, Stains, Lepore, Il Complesso Barocco, Curtis

Cast from strength, **Alan Curtis's** stylish reading of *Radamisto* with **Il Complesso Barocco** is based on a stage production at the Viterbo Festival, given in 2003. The three principal sopranos are all outstanding – **Joyce DiDonato** in the title-role powerful and agile, **Patrizia Ciofi** lighter and brighter and well contrasted as Polissena, and **Dominique Labelle** as Fraarte warm and fruity. Where at one point in haste Handel gave Polissena an inappropriate aria from the opera *Rodrigo*, Curtis then opts for the alternative from the second version of the opera, *Barbaro, partiro*, effectively so.

Rinaldo (complete; CD versions)

⊕ₘ**** Decca 467 087-2 (3). Daniels, Bartoli, Fink, Finley, Orgonasova, Taylor, AAM, Hogwood

BB **(*) Naxos 8.660165/7 (3). Barber, Whalen, Hannigan, Watson, Opera in Concert, Aradia Ens., Mallon

The inspired and characterful counter-tenor, **David Daniels**, makes an ideal choice for the castrato role of Rinaldo, strong and imaginative in martial music, tenderly expressive in such a poignant aria as *Cara sposa*. **Cecilia Bartoli** rightly preferred the gentler role of Rinaldo's wife, Almirena, and makes *Lascia ch'io pianga* one of the high points of the performance. **Luba Orgonasova** is wonderfully contrasted in the fire-eating role of the sorceress, Armida, with **Bernarda Fink** bringing character to the recessive role of Goffredo, the Christian captain-general, and **Gerald Finley** firm and positive as Argante, King of Jerusalem. Above all, Christopher Hogwood brings out not only the colour but the vigour of Handel's inspiration, with speeds on the fast side but never rushed, always sounding fresh.

Mallon opts for the first version of the score, even though Handel later added alternative numbers. Following that decision, he has women instead of counter-tenors for the castrato roles of Rinaldo and Eustazio, giving the small castrato role of the magician, Mago, to a bass. The cast is made up of fresh, youthful-sounding singers, none of them

strikingly characterful but all stylish, with clean, fresh voices and immaculate techniques. Despite the dictates of period performance Mallon takes the most famous number, the aria *Lascia ch'io pianga*, exceptionally slowly, allowing the excellent soprano **Laura Whalen** to ornament the reprise with great delicacy. Vivid, open sound. An excellent bargain, despite the lack of a full libretto.

Rodelinda, Regina de Langobardi (complete; CD versions)

⊕ₘ *** DG 477 5391 (3). Kermes, Mijanovi , Davislim, Prina, Lemieux, Priante, Il Complesso Barocco, Curtis

For the excellent DG Archiv version of *Rodelinda* the conductor, **Alan Curtis**, has prepared a version of the score primarily based on the original production in 1725 but with important additions from later versions, including the superb aria for the main castrato role of Bertarido, *Vivi Tiranno*. In the title-role of Rodelinda, **Simone Kermes** copes splendidly with the enormous range demanded and the feats of coloratura, if with a slight edge at the top of the voice. For the castrato roles of Bertarido and Unulfo, Curtis has opted to have mezzos, with **Marijana Mijanovi** and **Marie-Nicole Lemieux** both excellent, and with Mijanovi singing nobly in the most celebrated number, *Dove sei*. Outstanding even in this cast is the Australian tenor, **Steve Davislim**, as Grimoaldo, betrothed to Eduige, sister of Bertarido, well taken by **Sonia Prina**. First-rate sound.

(i) Rodelinda; (ii) Theodora (DVD versions; complete)

Ⓝ *(**) Warner **DVD** 50-1865-3273-2-5. (i) Antonacci, Scholl, Streit, Chiummo, Winter, Stefanowicz, Siese, OAE, Christie (Director: Jean-Marie Villégier); (ii) Upshaw, Daniels, Olsen, Croft, Hunt, OAE, Christie (Dir: Peter Sellars)

Both these Glyndebourne productions are very well sung by excellent casts, and **Christie's** direction cannot be faulted. But, as with so many Handel opera recordings, the staging is perverse, so that the words of the arias, although relating to the interplay between the characters, have no connection with the costumes and sets. Jean-Marie Villégier's production of *Rodelinda* is set in the silent movie era and, although the costumes are totally out of period, they are plain and pleasing and the simple sets work well enough, with **Anna Caterina Antonacci** in the title-role, **Andreas Scholl** (making his stage début) as Bertarido (apparently dead at the beginning of the opera) and **Kurt Streit** as Grimoaldo, who wants Rodelina for himself.

Peter Sellars's staging of *Theodora* transfers the action to modern-day America and the opening scene, with the chorus in red T-shirts, is ridiculously at odds with Valens's (**Frode Olsen**) proclamation about worshipping the Roman Gods. Once again the casting is impressive, with **Dawn Upshaw** a fine Theodora and **David Daniels** an equally impressive Didimus, **Richard Croft** as Septimus and **Lorraine Hunt** as Irene. But visually this all leaves much to be desired. The set provides a third disc, 'A Night with Handel', linking a series of arias sung by half a dozen different singers with locations in present-day London.

Semele (complete)

*** Chan. 0745 (3). Joshua, Summers, Sherratt, Croft, Wallace, Early Opera Company Ch. & O, Curnyn

*** DG 435 782-2 (3). Battle, Horne, Ramey, Aler, McNair, Chance, Mackie, Amb. Op. Ch., ECO, Nelson

(N) (BB) *** Naxos 8.570431/3. Scholl, Schmidt, Markert, Schoch, Schwarz, Popken, Junge Kantorei, Frankfurt Bar. O, Martini

If *Semele* is known as a rule only by its most celebrated aria, *Where'er you walk*, it contains many other superb numbers. In this fine new Chandos version **Rosemary Joshua**, with her crystal-bright soprano, sings brilliantly in her famous big aria, *Myself I shall adore*, crisply pointed with neat triplets. **Richard Croft** as Jupiter sings with a pleasant light tenor and similarly gives a virtuoso performance of the brilliant passage work of the aria, *No, no I'll take no less*, and each of them has added ornaments for *da capo* repeats. **Christian Curnyn** directs the whole opera stylishly and his cast is uniformly strong. With excellent recording this can certainly be recommended.

The DG recording turns away from current fashion in using modern rather than period instruments, but the balance of advantage is in its favour. **Nelson's** performance is briskly paced, with rhythms sprung infectiously, and he has a strong cast, all of whom distinguish themselves.

There are also many pleasures to be had in the bargain Naxos account, given a generally enjoyable performance, stylishly accompanied by the excellent **Frankfurt Baroque Orchestra**, directed with spirit by **Joachim Carlos Martini**. The chorus also sings vigorously but seems to be in a different, more resonant acoustic. **Elisabeth Scholl's** dashing coloratura in the name role certainly carries the part, and she is delightful in her portrayal of the morning lark, gently touching in *O sleep why dost thou leave me*, and she shows her virtuosity in *Myself I shall adore*. She gets appealing support from the other female participants, notably **Julia Schmidt's** charming joint assumption of the roles of Iris and Cupid. **Annette Markert's** clear alto makes for a strong portrayal of Juno, and the bass **Klaus Mertens'** portrayal of Somnus at the opening of Act III is another striking scene. **Knut Schoch** has a fine, resonant tenor voice as Jupiter, and his *Where'er you walk* is a highlight in an opera overflowing with memorable numbers.

Serse (Xerxes; complete; CD version)

⊶ *** Conifer 75605 51312-2 (3). Malafronte, J. Smith, Milne, Bickley, Asawa, D. Thomas, Ely, Ch. & Hanover Band, McGegan

**(*) Virgin 5 45711-2 (3). Von Otter, Norberg-Schulz, Zazzo, Piau, Tro Santafé, Abete, Furlanetto, Les Arts Florissants, Christie

McGegan, with light textures and generally brisk speeds, gives necessary momentum while allowing his principals full expressiveness in such deeper numbers as the hero's Act II aria, *Il core spera e teme*, warmly sung by **Judith Malafronte**, as is *Ombra mai fù*. The counter-tenor **Brian Asawa**, in the role of Xerxes' brother, Arsamene, is equally expressive with rich, even tone and fine agility, and **Jennifer Smith** as the heroine, Romilda, is particularly effective in her dramatic arias. **Lisa Milne** as her sister, Atalanta, nicely catches an ironic tone, with **Susan Bickley** fresh and agile as Amastre. Characterful baritone contributions from **David Thomas** (as a comic servant) and **Dean Ely**, with the chorus's brief interjections adding brightness and sparkle. Full, open sound.

Surprisingly, **Anne Sofie von Otter**, although she characterizes strongly in the title-role, is less sweet of tone than usual, and **Elizabeth Norberg-Schulz** too is not at her best as Romilda. Fortunately the counter-tenor **Lawrence Zazzo** is in superb voice as Arsamene; **Sandrine Piau** too is in excellent voice as Atalanta. **Christie** directs the proceedings spiritedly and you won't be disappointed with his warmly expressive tempo for the famous *Ombra mai fù.*

Silla (complete)

⊶ (M) *** Somm SOMMCD 227-8 (2). Bowman, Lunn, Marsh, Baker, Nicholls, Cragg, Dixon, London Handel O, Darlow

Handel's early opera, *Silla*, is a curiosity, but it has one delightful number after another, all relatively brief with no longueurs anywhere. Silla's slumber aria, *Dolce nume*, is ravishing, as is the touching aria for Silla's estranged wife, Metella, *Io noin chiedo più*, while Silla's aria, *La vendetta*, and that of his enemy, Claudio, *Con tromba guerriera*, with trumpets blazing, are fine examples of the martial Handel.

Denys Darlow conducts a fresh, stylish performance with his **London Handel Festival** forces, recorded live at the Royal College of Music. Textures are clean and rhythms light and resilient, with **James Bowman** in the title-role leading a consistently reliable team. **Rachel Nicholls** as Metella is not as steady as the rest, but everyone copes very well with florid vocal writing, and with a live occasion, well caught, adding to the magnetism.

Tamerlano (complete; DVD version)

⊶ **** Arthaus **DVD** 100 702 (2). Bacelli, Randle, Norberg-Schulz, Pushee, Bonitatibus, Abete, E. Concert, Pinnock (V/D: Jonathan Miller)

This is an instance where the DVD, recorded live in the small and ideal Goethe theatre in Bad Lauchstädt, is greatly preferable to the CDs, with solo voices naturally caught and strongly projected against the beautifully recorded and balanced orchestra. It is a strong team of soloists, with **Monica Bacelli** in the title-role controlling her full, firm contralto well, the counter-tenor, **Graham Pushee**, light and free as Andronico and **Anna Bonitatibus** a charming Princess Irene. **Thomas Randle** gives a vigorously resonant account of the role of Bazajet, and **Elizabeth Norberg-Schulz** is most resonant as Bazajet's daughter, Asteria. The production is simple and very effective, and Judy Levine's vivid costumes create a colourful contrast. The DVD set is splendidly documented, and includes a 'read the score' facility, with the action taking place behind the music – of course one can alternatively have the subtitles. The additional features include a retrospective review of 50 years of the Handel Festivals, from which this comes, and rehearsal sequences of the present performance.

Tamerlano (complete; CD versions)

**(*) Avie AV 0001. (Cast as above), E. Concert, Pinnock

Ⓜ *** Erato 2292 454908-2 (2). Ragin, Robson, Argenta, Chance, Findlay, Schirrer, E. Bar. Sol., Gardiner

On CD **John Eliot Gardiner's** live concert performance of *Tamerlano* presents a strikingly dramatic and immediate experience. Leading the cast are two outstanding counter-tenors whose encounters provide some of the most exciting moments: **Michael Chance** as Andronicus, firm and clear, **Derek Lee Ragin** in the name-part equally agile and more distinctive of timbre, with a rich, warm tone that avoids womanliness. **Nigel Robson** in the tenor role of Bajazet conveys the necessary gravity, not least in the difficult, highly original G minor aria before the character's suicide; and **Nancy Argenta** sings with starry purity as Asteria. The only snag is the dryness of the sound, which makes voices and instruments sound somewhat aggressive.

Teseo (complete; DVD version)

*** Arthaus **DVD** 100 708. Laszczkowski, Rostorf-Zamir, Riccarda Wessling, Berlin Lautten Compagney, Katschner (Dir: Axel Kohler, V/D: Ute Feudel)

Teseo was an adaptation of Racine's play on the confrontation of Theseus and Medea. In five Acts, the two protagonists do not appear until Act II, and for much of the opera Theseus hardly emerges as the central character. This Berlin production of 2004 by Axel Kohler offers a stylish reading on period instruments, with an excellent line-up of principals. As Agilea, **Sharon Rostorf-Zamir** with her rich mezzo establishes the quality in the first three arias, and the three counter-tenors in the cast – taking the roles of Theseus, Egeo and Arcane – are all first rate, a plus point for this version. Kohler's production involves broadly traditional costumes and the simplest of sets.

Teseo (complete; CD version)

*** Erato 2292 45806-2 (2). James, D. Jones, Gooding, Ragin, Napoli, Gall, Les Musiciens du Louvre, Minkowski

Marc Minkowski, among the liveliest of period-performance specialists, brings out the inventiveness, helped by an excellent cast, dominated by British and American singers. These include **Della Jones** as Medea, **Eirian James** in the castrato role of Teseo, **Julia Gooding** as Agilea and characterful counter-tenors **Derek Lee Ragin** and **Jeffrey Gall** as Egeo and Arcane.

Tolomeo (complete; CD version)

*** DG 477 7106 (3). Hallenberg, Spagnoli, Il Complesso Barocco, Curtis

Tolomeo, a *dramma per musica*, written in 1728, may not be well known but it has many fine numbers. **Ann Hallenberg** is warm and firm in the title-role and **Pietro Spagnoli** as Araspe, King of Cyprus, gives a strong and vigorous characterization, with bright and clean sopranos taking smaller roles, each coping well with the florid divisions. **Alan Curtis**, who has already given us a fine DVD performance of *Ariodante* (also with Ann Hallenberg in the lead), is equally

impressive here, and **Il Complesso Barocco** serves the singers well. Fine DG recording.

VOCAL COLLECTIONS

(i) 9 German Arias; (ii) Oboe Sonatas, HWV 357; 363a; 366

*** Hyp. CDA 67627. (i) Sampson; (ii) Bellamy; King's Consort

(i) 9 German Arias; Trio Sonatas, Op. 2/1 & 4

Ⓝ *** Chan. 0743. (i) Baird; Tempesta di Mare Chamber Players

The *Nine German Arias* (written between 1724 and 1726) are the nearest Handel came to writing an intimate song-cycle. All the lyrics derive from Heinrich Brockes' set of poems ('Earthly delight in God') designed to be set as cantatas (with recitatives, which Handel chose not to use). Many of the poems are poetic paraphrases of Bible texts, and these have been identified in the CD's notes, with their translations. The accompaniments include obbligati for solo flute and violin, and every one of these arias has a winning Handelian flavour. **Julianne Baird** sings them very appealingly, and by grouping them in three sets of three, interspersed by a pair of *Trio Sonatas*, elegantly played by **Tempesta di Mare**, the listener's enjoyments is enhanced.

Carolyn Sampson's performances are as fresh as they are tonally beautiful and musically phrased, and using ornamentation judiciously. But to be on the safe side and to avoid monotony, Hyperion have interspersed the arias with three *Oboe Sonatas*, stylishly played by **Alexandra Bellamy**, with **Robert King** as part of the continuo.

'Handel Gold': Arias: Alcina: (i) Tornami a vagheggiar; (ii) Verdi prati. Ariodante: (iii) Dopo notte, altra e funesta. Atalanta: (iv) Care selve. (v) Coronation Anthem: Zadok the Priest. Floridante: (vi) Ma che vuoi piú da me. (vii) Giulio Cesare; Piangerò la sorte mia; (viii) V'adoro pupile. (ix) Hercules: Where shall I fly! Jephtha: (x) Waft her, angels. Joshua: (xi) Oh! Had I Jubal's lyre. (xii) Judas Maccabaeus: See the Conqu'ring Hero comes; (xiii) Father of Heav'n. Messiah: (xiv) He was despised; (xv) I know that my Redeemer liveth; (xvi) The People who walked in the darkness; (xvii) Behold I tell you a mystery – The Trumpet shall Sound; (xviii) Hallelujah Chorus. Muzio Scevola: (xix) Ah, dolce nome. Samson: (xx) Let the bright seraphim. Semele: (xxi) Hence, Iris, hence away; (xxii) Myself I shall adore; (xxiii) Where'er you walk. Serse: (xxiv) Frondi tenere; Ombra mai fu. Solomon: (xxv) Almighty pow'r! Tamerleno: (xxvi) Ciel e terra armi di sdegno. Theodora: (xxvii) Angels, ever bright and fair. Il Trionfo del Tempo e del Disinganno: (xxviii) Lascia la spina

Ⓝ ✿ Ⓑ **** Decca 478 1460 (2). (i) Sutherland; (ii) Wunderlich; (iii) Von Otter; (iv) Pavarotti; (v) Westminster Abbey Ch.., E. Concert, Pinnock; (vi) DiDonato; (vii) Berganza; (viii) Fleming; (ix) J. Baker; (x) Robson; (xi)

Kožená; (xii) ASMF Ch. & O, Marriner; (xiii) Bumbry; (xiv) Ferrier; (xv) McNair; (xvi) Tomlinson; (xvii) Quasthoff; (xviii) E. Concert Ch. & O, Pinnock; (xix) Oberlin; (xx) Te Kanawa; (xxi) Horne; (xxii) Danielle de Niese; (xxiii) Terfel; (xxiv) Domingo; (xxv) Scholl; (xxvi) Villazón; (xxvii) Gritton; (xxviii) Bartoli

Vividly recorded and with the items presented in an expertly chosen sequence, this 'Decca Gold' collection is fully worthy of its name. Not only does it show Handel, in 28 varied arias, as a great tunesmith worthy to be placed alongside Schubert and Tchaikovsky but, with this remarkably starry cast, the performances are all fully worthy of this great music. Whether in the brilliant coloratura of **Bartoli**, **Sutherland**, **Janet Baker**, **Marilyn Horne**, or **Danielle de Niese** (whose engaging *Myself I shall adore* is a surprise highlight), the sparkle of **Kiri Te Kanawa**, the vitality and drama from **Rolando Villazón**, these are all memorable performances. One is also ravished by the lyrical beauty of line from **Pavarotti**, **Renée Fleming** and especially **Bryn Terfel** and **Russel Oberlin**, while of the items from *Messiah* one relishes **John Tomlinson's** sombre *People who walked in darkness*, **Sylvia McNair's** delightfully fresh *I know that my Redeemer liveth* and, above all, **Kathleen Ferrier's** unforgettable *He was despised*.

Arias & excerpts from: *Alceste*; (i) *L'allegro, il penseroso ed il moderato*; *Esther*; *Jephtha*; *Rodelinda*; *Samson*; *Il trionfo del tempo e del disinganno*; *Semele*; (i; ii) *Tamerlano*

*** HM HMU 90 7422. Padmore, E. Concert, Manze; with (i) Crowe; (ii) Blaze

All today's singers seem to want to aspire to a collection of Handel arias, and there are plenty to choose from. These include such favourites as *Waft her, angels*, *Total eclipse* and *Where'er you walk* and much that is unfamiliar besides, including a duet from *L'allegro, il penseroso ed il moderato* with **Lucy Crowe**, and a scena from *Tamerlano* in trio with Crowe and **Robin Blaze**. But the solos are all full of magical sensitivity and intimacy, while *da capos* are tellingly recoloured. Altogether a superb collection, with the **English Concert** under **Andrew Manze** providing equally intimate accompaniments.

Arias & Overtures (1704–1726): *Almira*; *Amadigi di Gaula*; *Giulio Cesare in Egitto*; *Rinaldo*; *Rodelinda*; *Rodrigo*; *Scipione* (with *March*); *Silla*; *Tamerlano*. Arias & Duets (1726–1728) from: (i) *Alessandro*; *Admeto*; *Riccardo primo*; *Serse*; *Tolomeo*. Arias & Overtures (1729–41) from: *Alcina*; *Ariana in Creta*; *Atalanta*; *Berenice, regina d'Eggito*; *Deidamia*; *Ezio*; *Lotario*; *Partenope*; *Sosarme, re di Media*

⌕– Ⓜ *** Hyp. CDS 44271/3. Kirkby, (i) with Bott; Brandenburg Cons., Goodman

This three-disc survey covers the astonishingly wide operatic range of Handel's career from 1704 to 1726, nearly two dozen operas in all. In between these two collections comes a third, dealing with the middle-period operas which Hyperion describe as 'the era of the Rival Queens', as the lead roles were

originally sung by the two sopranos, Francesca Cuzzoni and Faustina Bordoni. They were given this title as they first appeared together playing the rival lovers of Alessandro (the Great). So for this programme the baroque queen **Emma Kirkby** is joined by the rich-voiced and equally regal **Catherine Bott** in a programme which appropriately includes a particularly generous selection from the opera with which the sobriquet is associated. With full documentation, texts and translations, this is an unmissable set for lovers of Handel's Italian operas.

Airs, 'scènes célèbres', sinfonias and instrumental music from: *Admeto*; *Alcina*; *Giulio Cesare*; *Radamisto*; *Rodelinda*; *Serse*; *Concerto grosso* (*Alexander's Feast*)

⌕– ✿ **** HM HMC 901685. Scholl, Berlin Akademie für Alte Musik

Handel's most celebrated aria, *Ombra mai fù*, is radiantly sung here, with firm, golden tone, alongside the equally lovely *Chiudetevi, miei lumi* from *Admeto*, and the glorious *Dove sei* from *Rodelinda*, with the programme capped by an unforgettably beautiful *Verdi prati* from *Alcina*. There are lively moments too, notably the genial *Va tacito*, which has a jolly horn obbligato. The splendid period-instrument **Berlin Akademie für Alte Musik** end the programme with a superb account of the *Alexander's Feast Concerto grosso*, light and airy. But it is **Andreas Scholl's** wonderfully stylish and moving singing that makes this record indispensable. The recording is full and immediate.

Arias from: *Ariodante*; *Theodora*

Ⓜ *** Wigmore Hall WH Live 0013. Hunt Lieberson, Vignoles – MAHLER: *5 Ruckert Lieder*; LIEBERSON: *O ihr Zatlichen*, etc. ***

The untimely death from cancer of **Lorraine Hunt Lieberson** makes one value the relatively few recordings she made, including this live recording, taken at a Wigmore Hall recital in 1998. Having Handel arias accompanied on the piano may not be ideal, but the brilliance and agility of this singing is magnetic.

Operatic Duets from: *Admeto*; *Atalanta*; *Faramondo*; *Flavio*; *Muzio Scevola*; *Orlando*; *Poro*; *Re dell'Indie*; *Rinaldo*; *Serse*; *Silla*; *Sosarme*; *Teseo*

Ⓜ *** Virgin 5 18179-2. Ciofi, DiDonato, Il Compresso Barocco, Curtis

We have already had a stimulating and highly successful collection of duets from Handel's oratorios (see above, on BIS), and here is a comparable operatic selection, in which situations are usually more theatrical and produce dramatic or intensely expressive interchanges between the characters. So it is here, and there are plenty of novelties, not least the rewarding selection from *Poro*, *Re dell'Indie*, or, on a lighter note, the delightful excerpts from *Atalanta* and *Faramondo* and deeply touching ones from *Teseo* and *Silla*. All these duets and more are engagingly and beautifully sung by **Patrizia Ciofi** and **Joyce DiDonato**, soprano and mezzo respectively, with ornamentation nicely managed. **Il Compresso Barocco**, directed by **Alan Curtis**, provide most sensitive accompaniments, and the recording is warm and vivid.

Arias from: *Agrippina; Orlando; Partenope; Rinaldo; Serse*

🅱🅱 **(*) Warner Apex 2564 60519-2. Horne, Sol. Ven., Scimone

Here is a dazzling demonstration of **Marilyn Horne** singing a varied compilation of Handel arias. The flexibility of her voice in scales and trills and ornaments of every kind remains formidable, and the power is extraordinary down to the tangy chest-register. The voice is spotlit against a reverberant acoustic. Purists may question some of the ornamentation, but voice-fanciers will not worry.

Arias from: *Agrippina; Alexander Balus; Giulio Cesare; Lotario; Orlando; Rinaldo; Rodelinda; Samson; Scipione; Semele; Serse*

*** Decca **SACD** 475 6186 / CD 475 547-2. Fleming, OAE, Bicket

Accompanied by the fine period players of the **Orchestra of the Age of Enlightenment** under **Harry Bicket**, **Renée Fleming** has taken scholarly advice over such matters as ornamenting *da capo* repeats, not making them too intrusive. The 16 items range wide, with favourites like *Ombra mai fù*, *Let the bright seraphim* and Cleopatra's arias in *Giulio Cesare*, set against rarities like Adelaide's Act II aria in *Lotario* and, best of all, Cleopatra's touching aria, *Calm thou my soul*, from the oratorio, *Alexander Balus*.

Arias from: *Alessandro; Amadigi; Arianna in Creta; Deidamia; Faramondo; Giulio Cesare; Orlando; Partenope; Rodelinda; Scipione; Tamerlano*

⊶ *** Naïve E 8894. Piau, Les Talens Lyriques, Rousset

The French soprano, **Sandrine Piau**, has few rivals today in the phenomenal agility she brings to these 12 arias, each from a different *opera seria*, starting with a breathtaking display in Berenice's aria from *Scipione*. Her control of coloratura is complete, with never a hint of any intrusive aitches, and that goes with a voice that is bold, fresh and clear, beautiful in such darkly intense slow arias such as those from *Amadigi* and *Deidamia*. The arias are each linked to a series of six great prima donnas of the 18th century, and Piau amply demonstrates that in every way she is a modern match for any of them.

Arias: *Alexander's Feast: The Prince, unable to conceal his pain; Softly sweet in Lydian measures; Atalanta: Care selve; Giulio Cesare: Piangerò; Messiah: Rejoice greatly; He shall feed his flock; Rinaldo: Lascia ch'io pianga; Samson: Let the bright Seraphim*

*** Delos D/CD 3026. Augér, Mostly Mozart O, Schwarz –
    BACH: *Arias* **(*)

Arleen Augér's bright, clean, flexible soprano is even more naturally suited to these Handel arias than to the Bach items with which they are coupled. The delicacy with which she tackles the most elaborate divisions and points the words is a delight.

Overtures and Arias (1704–1726) from: *Almira; Amadigi di Gaula; Giulio Cesare in Egitto; Rinaldo; Rodelinda; Rodrigo; Scipione* (with *March*); *Silla; Tamerlano*

*** Hyp. CDA 66860. Kirkby, Brandenburg Cons., Goodman

Overtures and Arias (1729–1741) from: *Alcina; Arianna in Creta; Atalanta; Berenice, regina d'Egitto; Deidamia; Ezio; Lotario; Partenope; Sosarme, re di Media*

*** Hyp. CDA 67128. Kirkby, Brandenburg Cons., Goodman

It might be thought that a collection interspersing Handel arias and overtures would not be particularly stimulating, but **Emma Kirkby** (in glorious voice) and **Roy Goodman** directing invigorating playing by the **Brandenburg Consort** prove just how enjoyable such a concert, or pair of concerts, can be. The first disc covers the first half of Handel's operatic career. Volume 2 deals with Handel's later operas and opens with the virtually unknown overture to *Lotario* (1729). Queen Adelaide's feisty aria which follows shows Emma Kirkby at her nimblest, although she is hardly less dazzling in *Dite pace* from *Sosarme*. Perhaps the most delightful item here is *Chi t'intende?* from *Berenice*, where Kirkby clearly enjoys her continuing duet with the solo oboe.

Arias from: *Amadigi; Ariodante; Deidamia; Giulio Cesare; Lotario; Radamisto; Rinaldo; Rodelinda; Scipione*

*** Linn CKD252. Bell, SCO, Egarr

Emma Bell's superb collection of soprano arias covers the full span of the Italian operas that Handel wrote for London, from *Rinaldo* in 1711 to *Deidamia* 30 years later in 1741. Here is a voice of glowing quality, at once bright yet creamy in texture, weighty yet pure, which is matched by fine musical imagination and a masterly control of technique. The collection begins with one of the most brilliant arias, *Destero dall empia dite* from *Amadigi*, with two trumpets obbligato setting the pattern in the instrumental introduction, dazzlingly played by members of the **Scottish Chamber Orchestra**. Though modern instruments are used, **Richard Egarr** effectively adopts an apt degree of period style for Handel.

Arias from: *Ariodante; Rodelinda; La Resurrezione; Serse; Tamerlano*

Ⓝ **** DG 477 8056. Villazón, Gabrieli Players, McCreesh

Rolando Villazón shows himself here just as much a master of Handel as he is of Donizetti. He opens commandingly with *Tamerlano*, the spirited *Ciel e terra di sdegno*, and returns to this opera later with a dramatic scene, including the touching arioso, *Figlia mia, non pianger*. The recitative, *Fatto inferno è il mio petto* from *Rodelinda*, then contrasts with the lovely *Pastorello d'un povero Armento* from the same opera. Whether in spectacular bravura runs (as in *Crude furie degl'orridi abissi* from *Serse* and *Dopo notte atra e funesta* from *Ariodante*) or in tender lyricism (as in the very beautiful *Scherza infida* from the same opera), his lovely voice and gently stylish vocal line give great pleasure. Not surprisingly, he also magics the famous *Ombra mai fu* from *Serse*. He is sympathetically accompanied by **McCreesh** and his **Gabrieli Players**, and is vividly recorded.

Arias from: *Belshazzar; Jephtha; Messiah; Saul; Semele; Theodora*

♪– ******** Virgin 5 45497-2. Daniels, Ens. O de Paris, Nelson

Even **David Daniels** has rarely matched the brilliance, beauty and expressive intensity of this superb collection of arias from Handel oratorios, starting with two arias from *Belshazzar*, the one exuberant in vigour, a display aria for Cyrus with trumpets and timpani, the other noble and deeply felt for Daniel, *O Sacred Oracles of Truth*. Similarly a light and brilliant aria from *Semele* is set against one in a poignant minor key, while the four arias from *Theodora*, all for the character Didymus, similarly cover a wide range. Those from *Saul* have David singing his lament for Jonathan set against a noble prayer, while Hamor's arias from *Jephtha* lead to the noblest performance of all, *He was despised* from *Messiah*. **John Nelson** draws electric playing from his period orchestra, starting brilliantly on the first *Belshazzar* aria.

Arias from: *Flavio*: (i) *Amor, nel mio penar; Giulio Cesare in Eggitto: Va tacito e nascosto; Hercules*: (ii) *Turn thee, youth to joy and love* (with Chorus); (iii) *This manly youth's exalted mind; Mount, mount the steep ascent* (with Chorus). *Messiah*: (iv; v) *He shall feed his flock;* (v) *Rejoice greatly;* (vi) *Why do the nations?... Let us break* (with Chorus); *Orlando*: (i) *Fammi combattere; Rinaldo*: (vii) *Or la tromba in suon festante; Rodelinda: Vivi tirrano; Xerxes: Frondi tenere... Ombra mai fù;* (viii) *9 German Arias: Süsse Sille, sanfte Quelle;* (ix) *Silete venti* (Motet, with Flute & Continuo)

♪– ✿ ******** Capriccio Surround Sound **SACD** 71 024. (i) Axel Köhler; (ii) Hruba-Freiberger; (iii) Arleen Augér; (iv) Charles Humphries; (v) Max Emanuel Cencic; (vi) Robert Torday, V. Boys' Ch.; (vii) Jochen Kowalski; (viii) Ann Monoyios & Berlin Bar. Co.; (ix) Emma Kirkby; (with various orchestras & conductors)

This is simply the most thrilling collection of miscellaneous Handel arias in the catalogue, and the Rosette must be shared equally by the perceptive unnamed compiler, the artists for their inspired contributions, and to Capriccio's Surround Sound for providing such an extraordinary communication of the artists' presence and of the feeling of actually sitting in the concert hall. It is not possible to do justice to the many fine performances here. Opening with resplendent trumpets, as only Handel knows how to write for them, the programme begins with the clarion call from *Rinaldo, Or le tromba in suon festante*, dramatically sung by **Jochen Kowalski**, who is later to be equally commanding in the bravura aria from *Rodelinda*, and then melts the listener with a glorious *Ombra mai fù*.

After **Axel Köhler** has sung the virtuoso aria from *Orlando* with alomb, she is joined in duet in the *Julius Caesar* excerpt by a remarkably characterful unnamed period-horn soloist. Our own **Emma Kirkby** is as ravishing as ever in the celestial motet, *Silete venti*, and **Ann Monoyios** shares her lovely German aria, *Süsse Stille*, with the flute d'amour. And it is the delicate opening and closing writing for flutes that helps to make **Arleen Augér's** first aria from *Hercules* so haunting. There are, alas, no texts and translations – but, for once, one is lost for words anyway.

Arias from: *Giulio Cesare; Rinaldo; Rodelinda; Serse; Tamerlano*

*** Virgin 5 45326-2. Daniels, OAE, Norrington

Here again, **David Daniels** stands out for the evenness and beauty of his voice, with an exceptionally rich lower register. Though the orchestra is not always as alert as it might be, his singing in this challenging group of arias, starting with *Ombra mai fù* from *Serse*, is warmly expressive in slow numbers and brilliantly dramatic in fast ones like *Al lampo dell'armi* from *Giulio Cesare*. Well-balanced sound.

Arias from: *Israel in Egypt; Messiah; Radamisto; Rodelinda; Muzio Scavelo*

✿ ******* DG 477 6541. Oberlin, Fuller, Bar. Ch. O, Dunn

This disc is quite sensational. When it appeared in 1960, first on American Decca and subsequently on DG, it was hailed as 'a tour de force, one of the most amazing demonstrations of vocal homogeneity on record'. **Russell Oberlin** had a relatively short career: Londoners may remember that he appeared briefly at Covent Garden as Oberon in Britten's *Midsummer Night's Dream*. He produces a thrilling sonority and lets us hear arias that Handel would have written for alto castratos or *fema le mezzo* sopranos very much as they might have sounded in Handel's lifetime. In terms of both virtuosity and artistry this singing really is amazing. No less amazing is the fact that this is its first (belated) appearance on CD.

Arias: *Judas Maccabaeus: Father of heaven; Messiah: O Thou that tellest; He was despised; Samson: Return O God of Hosts*

♪– ✿ Ⓜ (*******) Decca mono 475 6411. Ferrier, LPO, Boult – BACH: *Arias* (*******)

Kathleen Ferrier had a unique feeling for Handel; these performances are unforgettable for their communicative intensity and nobility of timbre and line. She receives highly sympathetic accompaniments from **Boult**, another natural Handelian.

Arias: *Partenope: Sento amor; Ch'io parta?; Furibondo spira il vento; Tolomeo: Stille amare*

*** Virgin 5 45365-2. Daniels, OAE, Bicket – GLUCK, MOZART: *Arias* *******

One of the *Partenope* arias provides the title for this third exceptional disc of counter-tenor arias, ranging widely in its expressiveness, with **David Daniels** using his extraordinarily beautiful voice, clear and pure with none of the usual counter-tenor hoot, with the keenest artistry. Whether in deeply expressive lyrical numbers or in brilliant florid passages, his technique is immaculate, with the voice perfectly placed.

Duets: *A mirarvi io son intento; Conservate, raddoppiate; Fronda leggiera e mobile; Langue, geme, sospira e si lagna; Nò, di voi non vo' fidarmi; Se tu non lasci amore; Sono liete, fortunate; Tanti strali al sen mi scocchi; Troppo cruda, troppo fiera*

Ⓑ**(*) Hyp. Helios CDH 55262. Fisher, Bowman, King's Consort

About half of Handel's Italian duets are included here. All are engagingly intimate works, flowing readily between the two voices, here the admirably matched soprano of **Gillian Fisher** and the alto of **James Bowman**. Fisher sings so musically and sweetly and with an appealing simplicity. Bowman is his inimitable self, and the accompaniments use a varied continuo of cello, archlute, harpsichord and chamber organ. Texts and translations are provided.

HANSON, Howard (1896–1981)

Symphony 1; Merry Mount (suite); Pan and the Priest, Op. 26; Rhythmic Variations on Two Ancient Hymns

ⒷⒷ**(*) Naxos 8.559072. Nashville SO, Schermerhorn

Schermerhorn gives a relaxed account of the *First Symphony*, notably slower than the composer's own deleted thrusting Mercury account, but this warmer approach offers its own rewards, especially in some of the more lyrical passages. The two tone-poems are rarities: *Pan and the Priest*, written during 1925–6, begins quite mournfully on a solo cor anglais, and is passionate and reflective in turn, with the orchestra (including a piano) used colourfully. The *Rhythmic Variations* are melancholic and contemplative in nature, but appealing also, and the colourful *Merry Mount* suite (one of Hanson's best works) is splendidly done. The **Nashville SO** play well for Schermerhorn, and the sound is warm and reasonably vivid. Good value.

Symphony 2 (Romantic)

Ⓝ Ⓑ *** EMI 2 06612-2. St Louis SO, Slatkin – VIRGIL THOMSON: *Autumn; Plow that broke the Plains*, etc. ***

Symphony 2 (Romantic), Op. 30; Bold Island Suite; Merry Mount Suite; Fanfare for the Signal Corps

▣ *** Telarc CD 80649. Cincinnati Pops O, Kunzel

With the Mercury anthologies currently unobtainable (temporarily, we hope) this Telarc issue must now be regarded as the key Howard Hanson CD. It is magnificently played and gloriously recorded in ideally full and spacious Telarc sound. Apart from the richly persuasive performance of the composer's most memorable symphony, so hauntingly melodic, the *Merry Mount Suite* is also played outstandingly, especially the engaging *Children's Dance* and the expansive *Love duet*. This, like the central *Summer Seascape* of the fine *Bold Island Suite* (a recording première), has the full patina of rich scoring so characteristic of this endearing composer. A splendid disc in every way.

Slatkin's performance is also a very satisfying one, responding to the expressive nostalgia of the slow movement

and bringing an exhilarating attack to the finale. The full, atmospheric recording, beautifully balanced and rich in washes of string-tone, is a pleasure in itself, and the Virgil Thomson couplings are well worth having.

Symphony 3

(***) Biddulph mono WHL 044. Boston SO, Koussevitzky – MUSSORGSKY: *Khovanshchina: Prelude*; LIADOV: *The Enchanted Lake*; RIMSKY-KORSAKOV: *Legend of the Invisible City of Kitezh: Entr'acte; Dubinushka*; FAURÉ: *Pelléas et Mélisande: Prélude; La Fileuse; Mort de Mélisande* **(*)

With passionate playing from the **Boston Orchestra**, **Koussevitzky's** reading is powerfully committed, immediately establishing the northern atmosphere of Hanson's sound-world and building the finale steadily to its final climax with gripping concentration. The Biddulph transfer is very good, with sonic inadequacies easily forgotten. The other pieces, which come before the symphony, are all played superbly, but the sound is more variable. Highlights include the Mussorgsky *Khovanshchina Prelude*, sombrely paced, and the Liadov *Enchanted Lake*, both highly evocative and the latter remarkably full and atmospheric. The excerpts from Fauré's *Pelléas et Mélisande* are delicately done, although here climaxes are less refined.

HARRIS, Roy (1898–1979)

Symphonies 2 and 3

(*) Albany **SACD TROY 515. Albany SO, Miller

Here is something of special interest and value. It fills in the gap between Harris's *First Symphony* of 1933, and the celebrated *Third*. Although Koussevitzky had commissioned it, the first performance was conducted by his concert-master, Richard Burgin, and Harris never attended it. He subsequently seems to have disowned the piece, except for the middle movement, which is undoubtedly the finest. It is fascinating to hear the harmonic language of the *Third* taking shape and the sinewy counterpoint and Gregorian-like melodies unfold so naturally. One is occasionally reminded of Vaughan Williams. The first movement is less convincing, although Harris already shows his firmness of grip and purpose; the finale makes a strong ending. The orchestral playing is committed, though the string tone is lacking in weight. The SACD recording is perfectly acceptable, if not outstanding; but the sheer interest of the work carries the day.

Symphonies 3; (i) 4 (Folk Song Symphony)

▣ ⒷⒷ *** Naxos 8.559227. (i) Colorado Symphony Ch.; Colorado SO, Alsop

Good news. This issue heralds the appearance of a complete cycle of the 13 symphonies of Harris, which Naxos are undertaking. The *Third* gets a rousing performance. The *Fourth, Folk Song Symphony*, offers colourful settings for chorus and orchestra of five traditional songs, with two purely instrumental numbers, livelier than the rest, as interludes. An attractive novelty, but not the equal of either of its immediate neighbours.

Symphonies 7; 9; Epilogue to Profiles in Courage –
J.F.K.

(BB) **(*) Naxos 8.559050. Nat. SO of Ukraine, Kuchar

Kuchar and the **Ukraine Orchestra** offer powerfully idiomatic accounts of these two symphonies, and they are
recorded vividly, though the upper strings are lacking real
body and weight. The writing, open and strong, with antiphonal effects between massed strings and brass is recognizably from the same pen as the *Third*, well worth
investigating. No. 7, like that celebrated work, is in a single
20-minute movement of contrasted sections.

Commissioned for Philadelphia, No. 9 takes its inspiration from the American Constitution and is in three substantial movements, each with a quotation from the
Constitution as a superscription. Surprisingly, the opening,
'*We, the people*', brings a jolly waltz motif with whooping
brass, and it is only in the second and third movements,
much more extended, that the composer takes on a solemn
mood, with the pavane-like second movement leading to a
strong finale with martial overtones. The *Epilogue* in memory
of President Kennedy is elegiac, dignified without quite becoming a funeral march, gritty at times, leading to a meditative close.

Symphonies (i) 8 (San Francisco Symphony) for
Orchestra with Piano; 9; Memories of a Child's
Sunday

*** Albany TROY 350. Albany SO, Miller, (i) with Feinberg

The *Eighth Symphony* is a one-movement piece in five sections, Harris provides a virtuoso piano part, and tubular
bells. Dan Stehman speaks of the chorale-like slow movement of the *Ninth Symphony*, along with the slow movement
of the *Fifth*, as being Harris's finest. Its sound-world is fresh
and there is a Gallic transparency of texture. *Memories of a
Child's Sunday* is a slight piece written much earlier, in 1945,
for Rodzinski and the New York Philharmonic. The **Albany
Orchestra** plays very well for **David Alan Miller** and in the
Ninth they are to be preferred to their Ukrainian colleagues.
Very fine recorded sound.

HARRISON, Julius (1885–1963)

(i) Bredon Hill; Prelude-Music; Romance (A Song of
Adoration); Troubadour Suite; Widdicombe Fair;
Worcestershire Suite

(M) *** Dutton CDLX 7174. BBC Concert O, Wordsworth, (i)
with Trusler – CLIFFORD: *Serenade for Strings* ***

Julius Harrison was a well-regarded conductor. In the 1940s,
his increasing deafness forced him to stop conducting and
concentrate on composing. His two most famous works are
included in this splendid new CD: the *Worcestershire Suite*
and *Bredon Hill*. The former comprises four descriptive
movements, full of good tunes, scene-painting and a pleasing outdoor atmosphere. *Bredon Hill*, with its soaring solo
violin lines, rather like *The Lark Ascending*, is beautifully
evocative and pastoral in feeling. The *Troubadour Suite* has a
nicely flavoured medieval spirit, piquantly orchestrated, very

much in the tradition of Holst's *St Paul's Suite* and Warlock's
Capriol Suite. *Prelude-Music* is a very pleasing piece of romantic 'light music', as are both the *Romance* and *Widdicombe
Fair*. **Barry Wordsworth** and his orchestra have brought it
back to life. Highly recommended in every way, including
the excellent sound.

HARRISON, Lou (born 1917)

Symphony 2 (Elegiac)

(N) (M) ***Nim. NI 2512. American Composers O, Russell
Davies – HOVHANESS: *Symphony 2; Lousadzak* ***

Lou Harrison's remarkable *Second Symphony* is an ideal coupling for the Hovhaness *Second*. Although for the most part
scored frugally, it uses a large orchestra, including a piano
and two harps. It creates the same feeling of space, only more
intangibly, and its textures are comparably haunting. The
five movements are all named and the first, '*Tears of the angel,
Israfel*', is delicately scored and deeply evocative. After a bold,
uncomfortable Scherzo, the feeling of serenity returns, to be
interrupted by the calamitously dissonant '*Praises for Michael
the Archangel*'. With the closing '*Sweetness of Epicurus*' the elegiac feeling returns, creating a gently glowing sense of ecstasy. The work is superbly played, and stays in the memory
long after the last two-note figure has become silence.

HARTMANN, Karl Amadeus (1905–63)

(i) Concerto funèbre (for Violin & Strings). Sonatas
1–2; Suites 1–2 (for Solo Violin)

(N) *** Hyp. CDA 67547. Ibragimova; (i) Britten Sinfonia,
Shave

The *Concerto funèbre* – for violin and strings – very much
reflects in its dark moods, often passionately disconsolate,
the troubled period 1939, when it was written. **Alina
Ibragimova's** very responsive performance is movingly intense and committed, and she plays the *Adagio* and closing
Chorale with poignant feeling. This is a troubling but very
rewarding work to which one is drawn to return. The solo
violin *Sonatas* and *Suites* are quite remarkable. Obviously
they pay a debt of inheritance to Bach, but they also have a
distinct personal profile. They date from 1927 and represent
the first of the composer's works to survive. Each *Sonata*
and *Suite* offers four or five contrasted movements of great
character, and it is difficult to find many other modern
works for unaccompanied violin that offer such a depth of
feeling (often plangent) or such attractive and original opportunities for virtuosity, which the soloist here clearly relishes. The recording is excellent and this disc is very much
worth exploring.

HARTY, Hamilton (1879–1941)

A Comedy Overture; (i) Piano Concerto; (ii) Violin
Concerto; (iii) In Ireland (Fantasy); An Irish

Symphony; (ii) Variations on a Dublin Air; With the Wild Geese; (iv) The Children of Lir; Ode to a Nightingale. Arrangement: The Londonderry Air

Ⓜ *** Chan. 10194X (3). (i) Binns; (ii) Holmes; (iii) Fleming, Kelly; (iv) Harper; Ulster O, Thomson

Bryden Thomson's reissued box gathers togther Harty's orchestral and concertante works with great success. The *Piano Concerto* has strong Rachmaninovian influences, and if the *Violin Concerto* is less individual it is often touched with poetry. **Ralph Holmes** gives a thoroughly committed account of the solo part and is well supported by an augmented **Ulster Orchestra** under Bryden Thomson. The *Irish Symphony*, built on traditional themes, is best known for its Scherzo, entitled *A Fair Day*, but it is brilliantly scored and enjoyable throughout. It is extremely well played by the Ulster Orchestra, while the *In Ireland Fantasy* is full of delightful Irish melodic whimsy. Melodrama enters the scene in the symphonic poem, *With the Wild Geese*, but its Irishry asserts itself immediately in the opening theme. All these performances are highly sympathetic and there is a high standard of digital sound throughout. The three discs are no longer available separately.

(i) Piano Concerto; Comedy Overture; Fantasy Scenes

⊶ ⒷⒷ *** Naxos 8.557731. Ulster O, Yuasa, (i) with Donohoe

Peter Donohoe offers a faster, fresher version of Harty's very appealing *Piano Concerto* than the Chandos rival with **Malcolm Binns**, though the latter remains enjoyable in its richer sound. Similarly, the *Comedy Overture* is much faster than on Chandos's version, and it sparkles in its wit and easygoing energy. The *Fantasy Scenes* is attractive, light, 'postcard' music with a vaguely exotic feel, and prettily scored. This CD is recommended in every way and the sound, though without the sumptuous quality which Chandos obtained with the same orchestra, is very good.

An Irish Symphony; In Ireland; With the Wild Geese

⊶ ⒷⒷ *** Naxos 8.554732. Nat. SO of Ireland, O Duinn

The *Irish Symphony* has won great acclaim for its brilliant scoring and craftsmanship. The brief, dancing Scherzo entitled *The Fair Day* is the more exciting for being taken at breathtaking speed. The players of the **National Symphony Orchestra of Ireland** take up the challenge brilliantly, and bring all the necessary warmth to the other evocative movements, which, like the two tone-poems, a generous fill-up, are atmospheric programme–pieces inspired by Irish legends and places. Full, clear sound.

Music for cello and piano: Butterflies; Romance & Scherzo, Op. 8; Wood-stillness

Ⓜ *** Dutton CDLX 7102. Fuller, Dussek – HURLSTONE: *Cello Sonata;* PARRY: *Cello Sonata* ***

Slight but quite pleasing pieces that are fill-ups for the two cello sonatas by Hurlstone and Parry. Effective and accomplished playing from **Andrew Fuller** and **Michael Dussek** – and very well recorded too.

3 Pieces for Oboe & Piano

ⒷⒷ *** Hyp. Helios CDH 55008. Francis, Rasumovsky Qt – BOUGHTON: *Pastorale;* HOWELLS: *Sonata;* RUBBRA: *Sonata* ***

Harty's three oboe *Pieces*, played here with piano, were written for Henry Wood's 1911 Proms with an orchestral accompaniment. They are utterly charming in this more intimate version, and both artists respond to their disarming melodiousness, especially in the very Irish tune of the closing *A la campagne*. The balance is too forward but the playing has delicacy of feeling and, if you turn the volume down, the effect is very pleasing.

VOCAL MUSIC

(i) The Children of Lir; Ode to a Nightingale; (ii) Variations on a Dublin Air. Arrangement: Londonderry Air

Ⓜ *** Chan. 7033. Ulster O, Thomson, with (i) Harper; (ii) Holmes

Harty's setting of Keats's *Ode to a Nightingale* is richly convincing, a piece written for his future wife, the soprano, Agnes Nicholls. The other work, directly Irish in its inspiration, evocative in an almost Sibelian way, uses the soprano in wordless melisma, here beautifully sung by **Heather Harper**. The performances are excellent, warmly committed and superbly recorded. The *Variations on a Dublin Air*, for violin and orchestra, and Harty's arrangement of the *Londonderry Air* have been added for the reissue.

HAYDN, Joseph (1732–1809)

Complete Concertos

Concertos (i) for Cello, in C, Hob VIIb:1; in D, Hob VIIb 2 & 4; (ii) for Horn in D, Hob VIId:3; (iii) for Keyboard (Organ): in C, Hob XVIII:1, 8 & 10; (iv) for Harpsichord in D, C & F, Hob XVIII: 2, 5 &7; (v) for Piano: in F, Hob XVIII:3; in G, Hob XVIII:4 & 9; in D, Hob XVIII:11; (vi) for 2 Lyre Organizzate, Hob VIIh:1 in C (arr. 2 recorders); Hob VIIh:2 in G (arr. flute & oboe); HobVIIh:3 in G (arr. for 2 flutes); HobVIIh:4 in F (arr. for flute & oboe); HobVIIIh:5 in F (arr. for 2 recorders); (vii) for Trumpet in E flat, Hob VIIe:1; (viii) for Violin in C, A & G, Hob VIIa:1, 3 & 4. (ix) Double Concerto for Violin & Fortepiano, Hob XVIII:6

Ⓝ ⒷⒷ *** Naxos 8.506019 (6). (i) Kliegel; (ii) Babanov; (iii) Hoeren; (iv) Haugsand; (v) Knauer; (vi) Rothert & Spätling (recorders), Fromanger & Nelken (flutes), Hommel; (vii) Schuster; (viii) Hadelich; (ix) Daskalakis & Hoeren (fortepiano); Cologne CO, Müller-Brühl

This Naxos tercentenary box, containing just Haydn's authenticated concertos, is particularly inviting. All are fine recordings, underpinned by stylish and lively accompaniments by the excellent **Cologne Chamber Orchestra**, sensitively directed by **Helmut Müller-Brühl**, and the separate

CDs are discussed below. If the *Trumpet Concerto* (still the finest ever written for this instrument, and brilliantly played here) stands out, the fine *D major Cello Concerto*, Hob XVIIb:2, is also superbly presented by Naxos's star cellist, **Maria Kliegel**, who then goes on to give a most persuasive account of the *Adagio* of the early *C major concerto* (only discovered in 1961).

Of the *Piano Concertos*, only the justly popular *D major*, with its striking opening theme, could readily be placed alongside those of Mozart, especially in this winning performance by **Sebastian Knauer**, but he plays its companions very stylishly. The *Organ* (with no pedals required) and *Harpsichord Concertos* are virtually interchangeable, with sparkling *allegros*, the baroque scoring brightened by horns or trumpets, framing appealingly expressive slow movements, with the performances so alive. The *Horn Concerto* is florid and demands and receives ready virtuosity, especially in the slow movement, which soars up romantically high.

The three *Violin Concertos* are not distinctive, although **Augustin Hadelich** plays them spontaneously and with much finesse. However, the delicate little *Double Concerto for Violin and Harpsichord* is a surprise. Perfectly balanced, the interplay between the two instruments catches the ear engagingly, especially in the slow movement.

Finally, and also unexpectedly, the transcribed works for a pair of lire organizzate are most inventively sprightly. They were commissioned by the King of Naples to be played in duet with his teacher on a curious hybrid combination of hurdy-gurdy and organ. It's obsolete now, but the alternative transcriptions for varying woodwind instruments in pairs are most effective (as Haydn intended), and the music is by no means trivial. Altogether this is a most rewarding compilation, with performances and recording of high quality and a handsome accompanying booklet offered within a most presentable box.

Cello Concerto 1 in C

(***) BBC Legends (mono) BBCL 4198-2. Rostropovich, LSO – ELGAR: *Cello Concerto*; SAINT-SAËNS: *Cello Concerto 1* (***)

Directing the **LSO** from his cello, **Rostropovich** gives a dashing interpretation of the *Concerto in C*. It was one of the items in his mammoth sequence of over 30 concertos that he performed in London in 1965. At that time this work was only just becoming familiar, having been buried for centuries, and this came as a revelation. Rostropovich plays the Britten cadenza, as he did on other occasions. The main interest of the disc is the Elgar, which he never recorded otherwise.

Cello Concertos 1–2; Violin Concertos: in D, Hob VIIb: Adagio (only); in G, Hob VIIa: 4 (transcribed for cello) (DVD version)

☍– 🏵 **** DG DVD 073 4351. Maisky, with VSO – SCHUMANN: *Cello Concerto* ****

What a joy, as **Maisky's** performance of Haydn's *C major Cello Concerto* opens in the beautiful concert room of the Schloss Hetzendorf in Vienna, to hear the rich-timbred soloist and the lovely sounds of the **Vienna** strings playing on modern instruments, which Maisky himself directs with a combina-

tion of bow and body movements. He is a pleasure to watch, and these are simply glorious performances, beautifully photographed, and if Maisky sounds a little indulgent in the *Adagio* he has transcribed from the *C major Violin Concerto*, this and the complete G major work add to the pleasures of this superb DVD, one of the finest in the catalogue.

Cello Concertos 1 in C; 2 in D, Hob VIIb/1–2

Ⓜ *** EMI (ADD) 5 66896-2. Du Pré, ECO, Barenboim; or LSO, Barbirolli – BOCCHERINI: *Cello Concerto in B flat* (arr. GRUTZMACHER) ***

Ⓝ Ⓜ *** Decca 478 0025. Coin, AAM, Hogwood

🅱🅱 *** Naxos 8.550059. Kanta, Capella Istropolitana, Breiner – BOCCHERINI: *Cello Concerto* ***

(i) Cello Concertos 1–2; Symphony 104 (arr. Salomon)

☍– *** Channel Classics CCS 7395. (i) Wispelwey; Florilegium

Pieter Wispelwey is an inspired soloist in the period performance with **Florilegium**, at times abrasive but always transparent in texture, with the soloist's clean articulation allowing fast speeds in outer movements with no feeling of rush. The central *Adagios* by contrast are surprisingly slow, not as elegant as some, but deeply felt. Salomon's arrangement of Haydn's last symphony for flute, string quartet and piano makes an unusual if lightweight coupling.

Jacqueline du Pré's recording of the *C major Concerto* in April 1967 was the first she made with her husband, **Daniel Barenboim**, and she gives a performance of characteristic warmth and intensity. Equally, with **Barbirolli** scaling his accompaniment to match the inspirational approach of his young soloist, the performance of the better-known *D major Concerto* is just as warm and expressive, and the romantic feeling is matched by an attractively full, well-balanced sound-picture.

Christophe Coin, too, is a superb soloist and, provided the listener has no reservations about the use of original instruments, **Hogwood's** accompaniments are equally impressive. Excellent sound.

Ludovít Kanta is a fine artist. The excellent Naxos recording is made in a bright, resonant acoustic in which every detail is clearly registered, though the players are perhaps forwardly placed. The accompaniments are alert and fresh. Kanta plays contemporary cadenzas. An excellent bargain.

(i) Cello Concertos 1–2 Hob VIIb/1–2; (ii) Piano Concerto in D, Hob XVIII/11 (DVD version)

☍– 🏵 **** EuroArts DVD 2072068. ASMF, (i) with Rostropovich; directed Iona Brown; (ii) Francesch, cond. Marriner

Here is as perfect a coupling as you will ever find on record: Haydn's three finest concertos, given outstanding performances, with the **ASMF** in sparkling form, the *Cello concertos* led by **Iona Brown** and the *D major Piano Concerto* with **Marriner** conducting. **Rostropovich** is unsurpassed in the works for cello, playing with great warmth and with many subtle touches, using the widest range of dynamic. **Homero Francesch** articulates with buoyant crispness of style and no less sophistication of detail. In short, this is wonderfully enjoyable, both to watch and to be involved in, for Rostropovich in particular is always fascinating visually, as he is so completely involved in the music. The *Cello Concertos* were recorded in 1975 (in the London Henry Wood Hall) and the *Piano Concerto* in 1982 against the rich backcloth of the Bayreuth Opernhaus, and the sound is splendidly clear and vivid. This is among the most recommendable of all concerto DVDs.

(i) *Cello Concertos 1–2; (ii; iii) Piano Concerto in D, Hob XVIII/11; (iv) Trumpet Concerto in E flat; Violin Concertos Nos. (v) 1 in C; (vi; iii) 4 in G, Hob XVIIa/1 & 4; (vii) Flute Trios (London), Hob IV/1–3*

⊕ Ⓑ *** Sony 517 485-2. (i) Ma; (ii) Ax; (iv) Marsalis; (v) Lin, Minnesota O, Marriner

An excellent compilation, well worth collecting if you want all these works. In the *Cello Concertos* **Ma's** refinement of approach brings its own rewards, though some may prefer a bolder approach to music that belongs firmly to the classical 18th century. The well-transferred analogue recording is clean and full. **Ax** plays the finest of Haydn's piano concertos on a modern piano and does so with great style; he is splendidly accompanied and recorded. **Marsalis's** invigorating account of the *Trumpet Concerto* is second to none, and, aided by **Leppard** and the **ECO**, the result is both brilliant and stylish. **Cho Liang Lin's** account of the *C major Violin Concerto* also has plenty of classical strength and drive; the slow movement is perhaps a little lacking in charm but is nevertheless enjoyable: the playing is by no means insensitive. The recording is again excellent.

(i) *Cello Concertos 1–2; (ii) Violin Concertos 1, 3 & 4; (ii; iii) Double Concerto for Violin & Harpsichord in F, Hob XVIII/6*

Ⓑ *** Ph. Duo (ADD) 438 797-2 (2). ECO, with (i) Walevska, De Waart; (ii) Accardo; (iii) Canino

Christine Walevska presents the two cello concertos freshly, well partnered by **Edo de Waart** and the **ECO**. She is balanced almost within the orchestra, to give an agreeable chamber-like quality to the music-making. The three *Violin Concertos* are all early; the *C major*, written for Tomasini, is probably the best. The other two have come into the limelight fairly recently. **Accardo** plays with great elegance and charm. It would be idle to pretend that either they or the *Double Concerto for Violin and Harpsichord* are great music, in that the soloists are rather forward, but the 1980 recording has been well transferred.

(i) *Flute Concerto in D (attrib., but probably by Leopold Hoffmann); Scherzandi 1–6*

⊕ Ⓜ **** EMI 4 76863-2. (i) Pahud; Berlin Haydn Ens., Schellenberger – M. HAYDN: *Flute Concerto* ***

This is an enchantingly light-hearted record, displaying the supreme musicianship of **Emmanuel Pahud** as one of EMI's 'Great Artists of the Century' and the **Berlin Haydn Ensemble** in Haydn's six *Scherzandi*, unexpected treasures, dating from Haydn's early Esterházy years.

(i) *Harpsichord Concerto in D, Hob XVIII:2; (ii) Horn Concerto 1 in D, Hob VIId:3; (iii; i) Double Concerto in F for Violin & Fortepiano, Hob XVIII:6; (iv) Trumpet Concerto in E flat, Hob VIIe:1*

Ⓝ Ⓑ *** Naxos 8.570482. (i) Hoeren; (ii) Babanov; (iii) Daskalakis; (iv) Schuster; Cologne CO, Müller-Brühl

The *Harpsichord Concerto* (well balanced here) is a pleasing miniature work of comparatively little consequence; the *Horn Concerto* is much more difficult to play than any of the four Mozart concertos and is most notable for its eloquent, wide-ranging *Adagio*. The *Double Concerto* is an unexpected pleasure, especially the slow movement; but the only masterpiece here is the *Concerto for Trumpet*. **Dmitri Babanov** plays it with a fine open tone and engagingly crisp articulation in the famous rondo finale. Again excellent accompaniments throughout and first-class recording.

Horn Concerto 3 in D, Hob VII/d3

*** Ara. Z 6750. Rose, St Luke's Chamber Ens. – FORSTER; LEOPOLD MOZART; TELEMANN: *Horn Concertos* ***

Ⓑ *** Teldec (ADD) 0630 12324-2. Baumann, Concerto Amsterdam, Schröder – DANZI; ROSETTI: *Concertos* ***

Stewart Rose plays the outer movements ebulliently and, like Dennis Brain, phrases the eloquent slow movement richly, yet sonorously relishing the passages where the melodic line dips down into the horn's lower register. He has the big, broad tone typical of a modern wide-bore instrument. The **St Luke's Chamber Orchestra** provide a lively, supportive accompaniment and the recording is excellent, as are the couplings. A first-rate disc in every way.

Baumann's 1969 account has firm classical lines. The *Adagio* is rather sombre here but brings some splendidly resonating low notes from the soloist, and the finale is attractively spirited. The recording has been attractively remastered and has more bloom than on its last appearance.

Horn Concertos 3 in D, Hob VII/d3; 4 in D, Hob VII/d4

⊕ Ⓑ *** Warner Apex 0927 40825-2. Clevenger, Franz Liszt CO, Rólla – M. HAYDN: *Concertino* ***

Dale Clevenger gives superb accounts of the two surviving *Horn Concertos* attributed to Haydn (the fourth is of doubtful lineage). He is especially good in slow movements, like Baumann a little solemn in No. 3, but eloquently so, with the *Adagio* of No. 4 given a gentle melancholy. The accompaniments are supportive, polished and elegant. These performances have fine spirit and spontaneity and the recording, made in a nicely judged and warm acoustic, approaches the demonstration class.

Oboe Concerto in C, Hob VIIg/C1

Ⓜ *** Dutton Lab./Barbirolli Soc. (ADD) CDSJB 1016. Rothwell, Hallé O, Barbirolli – CORELLI; MARCELLO: *Oboe Concertos* *** (with Instrumental Recital: C. P. E. BACH; LOEILLET; TELEMANN: *Sonatas*, etc. **)

Haydn's *Oboe Concerto* is of doubtful authenticity, but in this account played by **Evelyn Rothwell**, deftly accompanied by her husband, Haydn would surely have welcomed the attribution. The orchestra is given a very positive classicism by **Barbirolli's** firmness, and in the opening movement his wife's delicacy makes a delightful foil for the masculine orchestral presentation. The slow movement is well brought off and the delicacy of articulation returns in the finale. The 1958 recording is resonant and the skilful Dutton transfer almost entirely disguises its age.

Piano Concertos in F; G; G; D, Hob XVIII/3, 4, 9 & 11

Ⓝ ⓑⓑ *** Naxos 8.570485. Knauer (piano), Cologne CO, Müller-Brühl

Piano Concertos: in F; in G; in D, Hob XVIII/3, 4 & 11

⟿ Ⓜ **** EMI 2 28527-2. Andsnes, Norwegian CO

*** HM HMC 90 1854. Staier (fortepiano), Freiberg Bar. O, Von der Golz

ⓑⓑ *** Arte Nova 74321 51635-2. Smirnova, Sinfonia Varsovia, Schmidt-Gertenbach

Leif Ove Andsnes gives inspired performances of the three Haydn piano concertos that are fully authenticated. Andsnes justifies his generally brisk speeds for outer movements in subtle pointing of rhythm and phrase, articulating crisply – always individual without being self-conscious. His preference is for speeds on the slow side in middle movements, but rapt and naturally expressive; in his hands and those of the **Norwegian Chamber Orchestra**, which he directs from the keyboard, these concertos blossom.

However if you enjoy 18th-century music on a fortepiano, **Staier** is your man. He adds decoration and ornamentation very skilfully, especially in slow movements, and he plays his own cadenzas. So this is very much his disc. The **Freiburg Baroque Orchestra** is the best in the authentic business, and **Gottfried von der Golz's** accompaniments are a joy in themselves. So this Harmonia Mundi disc has a special place in the Haydn discography and is very enjoyable indeed.

These works are also played with freshness and point by **Lisa Smirnova** and admirably accompanied with a sure sense of style and a nice feeling for light and shade by **Volker Schmidt-Gertenbach** and the excellent **Sinfonia Varsovia**. The recording is beautifully balanced.

Sebastian Knauer adds an extra concerto, so he has an advantage over both Andsnes and Pletnev. But listen to his response in the opening movement of the *F major* and the delicacy of his account of the following *Largo cantabile*, which is then followed by the memorable *Adagios* of both the *G major* and *D major* works. Moreover, he plays with great freshness and sparkle in finales, offering cadenzas of his own. The **Cologne Chamber Orchestra** give attentive support without adding anything especially individual to their accompaniments. However, with naturally balanced recording this is very good value.

Piano Concertos in G; F; D, Hob XVIII/4, 7 & 11

⟿ ⓑⓑ *** Virgin 2×1 5 61881-2 (2). Pletnev, Deutsche Kammerphilharmonie – *Piano Sonatas 33, 60 & 62, etc.* ***

(i) Piano Concertos in G, F & D, Hob XVIII/4, 7 & 11; Piano Sonatas 33, Hob XVI/20; 60 (English), Hob XVI/50; 62, Hob XVI/52; Andante & Variations in F min., Hob XVII/6

⟿ ⓑⓑ **** Virgin 4-CD 5 62259-2 (4). Pletnev; (i) Deutsche Kammerphilharmonie – MOZART: *Piano Concertos 9, 20, 23 & 24* ***

Mikhail Pletnev offers playing of great character and personality. He obviously enjoys a splendid rapport with the **Deutsche Kammerphilharmonie**, and the colour and feeling Pletnev discovers in these pieces is a source of wonder, both distinctive and distinguished. This now comes inexpensively coupled on a Virgin Double with Pletnev's accounts of three key piano sonatas – a superb bargain.

The sonatas too are full of personality and character. The *C major*, the so-called *English Sonata*, is given with great elegance and wit, and the great *E flat Sonata*, Hob XVI/52, is magisterial. The playing has a masterly authority and Pletnev is well recorded throughout.

Trumpet Concerto in E flat

⟿ ✹ Ⓑ *** Sony 516 233 (2). Marsalis, Nat. PO, Leppard – MICHAEL HAYDN: *Concerto in D;* VIVALDI: *Double Concerto, RV 537;* BACH: *Brandenburg Concerto 2*

Ⓑ *** CfP 3 82227-2. Balmain, RLPO, Kovacevich – MOZART: *Horn Concertos 1–4* ***

The **Hardenberger** and **Wynton Marsalis** performance has been reissued within a well-chosen collection, worthy of its Rosette. The Marsalis 2-disc set includes also concertos by Michael Haydn, Vivaldi and Bach's *Second Brandenburg*. Marsalis is splendid, his bravura spectacular, with the finale a tour de force, yet never aggressive in its brilliance. His way with Haydn is eminently stylish, as is **Leppard's** lively and polished accompaniment.

Ian Balmain, at the time principal trumpeter of the **Royal Liverpool Philharmonic Orchestra**, favours extreme speeds for Haydn's delectable *Concerto*, playing brilliantly. It makes an apt coupling for **Claire Briggs's** fine recordings of the Mozart *Horn Concertos* which also favour brisk tempi.

Violin Concertos: in C; A; & G, Hob VIIa:1, 3 & 4

Ⓝ ⓑⓑ *** Naxos 8.570483. Hadelich, Cologne CO, Müller-Brühl

Violin Concertos (i) 1 in C; (ii) 4 in G, Hob VIIa/1 & 4

*** Australian Ph. Eloquence (ADD) 442 8294. Grumiaux, with (i) ECO; (ii) New Philh. O; Leppard – M. HAYDN: *Violin Concerto in A;* MOZART: *Adagio in E; Rondo in C* ***

Violin Concertos 1 in C; 4 in G, Hob VIIa/1 & 4; (i) Double Concerto for Violin & Piano, Hob VIII/6

ⓑⓑ *** Hyp. Helios CDH 55007. Adelina Oprean, European CO; (i) with Justin Oprean

Violin Concertos 1 in C; 4 in G, Hob VIIa/1 & 4; (i) Sinfonia concertante in B flat for Violin, Cello, Oboe, Bassoon & Orchestra, Hob I/105

🎵→ Ⓑ *** Virgin 2x1 5 61800-2 (2). Wallfisch, OAE; (i) with
Watkin, Robson, Warnock – *Symphonies 26; 52; 53* ***

Elizabeth Wallfisch leads the **Orchestra of the Age of Enlightenment** from her bow and proves a highly sensitive soloist. In the *Sinfonia concertante* the smiling interplay of the various wind and string soloists has never been bettered on record and the use of period instruments brings a pleasing intimacy and plenty of spirit. The recording is truthfully balanced and vivid. These performances now come on a Virgin Double, coupled with three symphonies admirably played by Kuijken's Petite Bande.

Grumiaux shows a real feeling for this repertoire. Although played on modern instruments, there is an admirable feeling of lightness, helped by **Leppard's** stylish accompaniments. In the slow movements, Grumiaux's style suits it especially well, and the broad, rich tone he finds is highly pleasing. Excellent mid-1960s sound.

On Naxos, excellent performances of three pleasing but not distinctive works, played very musically and appealingly. **Augustin Hadelich** phrases the *Adagio* of the C *major* exquisitely so that this work stands out among its companions. It is a delightful serenade-like movement, which he obviously relishes and he plays exquisitely. **Müller-Brühl's** accompaniments are stylish and the recording is first class.

The Helios disc makes a good modern-instrument alternative for those interested in the well-crafted (and very well played) *Double Concerto for Violin and Piano*, which has a particularly striking dialogue between the two soloists in the central *Largo*. In the two solo concertos, **Adelina Oprean** proves a persuasive soloist with a dulcet but not over-opulent timbre. The central cantilena of the G *major Concerto*, with its pizzicato accompaniment, is delightful, and she directs the orchestra in outer movements with vigour and point. The sound is good too.

24 Minuets

*** Decca Australian Eloquence (ADD) 476 7693. Philh.
Hungarica, Dorati

This collection of 24 *Minuets*, amazingly varied and imaginative, was written late in Haydn's career and, though few of them have the symphonic overtones of the minuets in the late symphonies, they represent the composer at his most inspired. Haydn's own definition of a good composer was 'one who can write a brand new minuet'. **Dorati's** classic performances are characteristically genial, and the excellent (1975) sound emerges freshly on this reissued CD, with plenty of weight in the orchestral sound.

The Seven Last Words of Our Saviour on the Cross (Orchestral version; DVD version)

*** EMI **DVD** 5 99400-9. La Scala, Milan, PO, Muti (V/D:
Pierre Cavassilas)

The performance of the orchestral version of the *Seven Last Words* by **Riccardo Muti** and the **Filharmonica della Scala** is recorded in the Chiesa di San Francesco, Arezzo, and sets Haydn's masterpiece against the backcloth of the frescoes of Piero della Francesca. A very well-shaped performance which Muti controls sensitively. The menu enables you to access descriptions of the various frescoes and also a commentary on the music. The full score can also be accessed, but it masks the performers and the other visual delights completely. A marvellous set.

SYMPHONIES

Austro-Hungarian Haydn Orchestra Series, cond. Adám Fischer

Symphonies: Nos. 1 in D; 2 in C; 3 in G; 4 in D; 5 in A; 6 in D (Le Matin); 7 in C (Le Midi); 8 in G (Le Soir); 9 in C; 10 in D; 11 in E flat; 12 in E; 13 in D; 14 in A; 15 in D; 16 in B flat; 17 in F; 18 in G; 19 in D; 20 in C; 21 in A; 22 in E flat (Philosopher); 23 in G; 24 in D; 25 in C; 26 in D min. (Lamentatione); 27 in G; 28 in A; 29 in E; 30 in C (Alleluja); 31 in D (Horn Signal); 32 in A; 33 in C; 34 in D min.; 35 in B flat; 36 in E flat; 37 in C; 38 in C (Echo); 39 in G min.; 40 in F; 41 in C; 42 in D; 43 in F (Mercury); 44 in E min. (Trauer-symphonie); 45 in F sharp min. (Farewell); 46 in B; 47 in G; 48 in C (Maria Theresa); 49 in F min. (La Passione); 50 in C; 51 in B flat; 52 in C min.; 53 in D; 54 in G; 55 in E flat (School-Master); 56 in C; 57 in D; 58 in F; 59 in A (Fire); 60 in C (Il distratto); 61 in D; 62 in D; 63 in C (La Roxelane); 64 in A; 65 in A; 66 in B flat; 67 in F; 68 in B flat; 69 in C (Laudon); 70 in D; 71 in B flat; 72 in D; 73 in D (La Chasse); 74 in E flat; 75 in D; 76 in E flat; 77 in B flat; 78 in C min.; 79 in F; 80 in D min.; 81 in G; (82–87 'Paris Symphonies') 82 in C (The Bear); 83 in G min. (La Poule); 84 in E flat; 85 in B flat (La Reine); 86 in D; 87 in A; 88 in G; 89 in F; 90 in C; 91 in E flat; 92 in G (Oxford); (93–104 'London Symphonies') 93 in D; 94 in G (Surprise); 95 in C min.; 96 in D (Miracle); 97 in C; 98 in B flat; 99 in E flat; 100 in G (Military); 101 in D (Clock); 102 in B flat; 103 in E flat; 104 in D (London) (complete)

🅱🅱 *** Nimbus NI1722. (8) MP3 Files

🅱🅱 *** Brilliant 99925 (53)

Adam Fischer's series was recorded for Nimbus over 14 years in the Esterházy Palace, where Haydn himself worked. The final box of 20 symphonies was the finest of all, a superb culmination to a great project, covering the *Symphonies Nos. 21–39* plus *A* and *B*. But throughout the series the virtuosity of individual players in this orchestra of carefully selected Austrian and Hungarian musicians fully matches Haydn at his most demanding, with soloists challenged to the limit by fast speeds.

In the symphonies recorded at the beginning of the project (from 1987 to 1990) comparisons with Dorati's earlier Decca series generally have the merits of each balanced fairly evenly, but the advantage tips in favour of Fischer as the project develops. In those early recordings too the slow movements tend to be taken at the sort of broad speeds of tradition, with warmly expressive phrasing.

Over the years it took to complete the project Fischer, following period practice, increasingly opts for faster speeds for both slow movements and Minuets (which begin to acquire a Scherzo-like flavour), giving him a clear advantage over Dorati. Also the string playing comes closer to period practice, with lighter phrasing and less marked use of vibrato. That development is noticeable as early as the recordings made in 1994 and 1995, when most of the *Sturm und Drang Symphonies* were covered – broadly those in the late 40s and early 50s in the regular Breitkopf numbering. Finales in particular, taken fast, have all the bite and wildness one could want, with pinpoint attack.

This set is now available on the Brilliant label on 53 CDs costing about £55 or in a special Nimbus re-issue – a boxed set of 8 CDs as MP3 files with excellent documentation. A pair of Violin Concertos and two Overtures are offered as a bonus with the Nimbus set.

Philharmonia Hungarica Series, cond. Dorati

Symphonies 1–104; Symphonies A; B. Alternative versions: Symphony 22 (Philosopher), 2nd version. Symphony 63 (La Roxelane), 1st version. Symphony 53 (L'Impériale): 3 alternative Finales: (i) A (Capriccio); (ii) C (Paris version, attrib. Haydn); D: Overture in D (Milanese version); Symphony 103: Finale (alternative ending); (i) Sinfonia Concertante in B flat for Oboe, Bassoon, Violin & Cello

❀ **(BB)** *** Decca (ADD) 478 1221 (33). (i) with Engl, Baranyai, Ozim, Rácz

Dorati was ahead of his time as a Haydn interpreter when, in the early 1970s, he made this pioneering integral recording of the symphonies. Superbly transferred to CD in full, bright and immediate sound, the performances are a consistent delight, with brisk *allegros* and fast-flowing *Andantes*, with textures remarkably clean. The slow, rustic-sounding accounts of Minuets are more controversial, but the rhythmic bounce makes them attractive too. The set includes not only the *Symphonies A* and *B* (Hoboken Nos. 106 and 108) but also the *Sinfonia concertante in B flat*, a splendidly imaginative piece with wonderful unexpected touches. Dorati's account – not surprisingly – presents the work as a symphony with unusual scoring, rather than as a concerto. As H. C. Robbins Landon tells us in the accompanying notes, the *Symphonies A* and *B* were omitted from the list of 104 authentic symphonies by error, as the first was considered to be a quartet (wind parts were discovered later) and the second a divertimento. Dorati also includes as an appendix completely different versions of *Symphony No. 22 (The Philosopher)*, where Haydn altered the orchestration (a pair of flutes substituted for the cor anglais, entirely removed the first movement and introduced a new *Andante grazioso*; plus an earlier version of No. 63, to some extent conjectural in its orchestration, for the original score is lost. Of the three alternative finales for *L'Impériale* (No. 53), the first (A) contains a melody which, Robbins Landon suggests, 'sounds extraordinarily like Schubert'; the second (C) seems unlikely to be authentic; but the third (D) uses an overture which was first published in Vienna. 'In some respects,' Robbins Landon suggests, 'this is the most successful of the three concluding movements.' He feels the same about the more extended finale of the

Drum Roll Symphony, which originally included 'a modulation to C flat, preceded by two whole bars of rests'. But Haydn thought that this made the movement too long and crossed out the whole section. Robbins Landon continues: 'Perhaps Haydn was for once in his life too ruthless here.' Dorati's set is being re-issued for the bi-centenary on 33 CDs at about £45.

Symphonies A in B flat; B in B flat; Nos. 1-104; Overtures: Lo speziale; La vera costanza; Sinfonia concertante in B flat

(N) **(BB)** *** Naxos 8 503400 (34). Capella Istropolitana, Wordsworth; Cologne CO, Müller-Brühl; Northern CO, Ward; Nicolas Esterházy Sinf. & Swedish CO, Drahos; Sinfonia Finlandia Jyväskylä, Patrick Gallois; Toronto CO, Mallon

Naxos have used a number of orchestras in building up their survey of the Haydn symphonies, the latest being the excellent **Sinfonia Finlandia Jyväskylä** and **Toronto Chamber Orchestra** (see below). The standard has been high and anyone wanting an inexpensive complete set with good documentation should find this a very satisfactory investment. The standard of playing and recording is high.

Hanover Band Series, cond. Goodman

Symphonies 1–5 (Hyp. Helios CDH 55111)

Symphonies 6 (Le Matin); 7 (Le Midi); 8 (Le Soir) (Hyp. Helios CDH 55112)

Symphonies 9–12 (Hyp. Helios CDH 55113)

Symphonies 13–16 (Hyp. Helios CDH 55114)

Symphonies 17–21 (Hyp. Helios CDH 55115)

Symphonies 22 (Philosopher); 23–25 (Hyp. Helios CDH 55116)

Symphonies 42; 43 (Mercury); 44 (Trauer) (Hyp. Helios CDH 55117)

Symphonies 45 (Farewell); 46; 47 (Hyp. Helios CDH 55118)

Symphonies 48 (Maria Theresa); 49 (Passione); 50 (Hyp. Helios CDH 55119)

Symphonies 70–72 (Hyp. Helios CDH 55120)

Symphonies 73 (La Chasse); 74–75 (Hyp. Helios CDH 55121)

Symphonies 76–78 (Hyp. Helios CDH 55122)

Symphonies 82 (The Bear); 83 (The Hen); 84 (Hyp. Helios CDH 55123)

Symphonies 85 (La Reine); 86; 87 (Hyp. Helios CDH 55124)

Symphonies 90; 91; 92 (Oxford) (Hyp. Helios CDH 55125)

Symphonies 93; 94 (Surprise); 95 (Hyp. Helios CDH 55126)

Symphonies 101 (Clock); 102 in B flat; Overture: Windsor Castle (Hyp. Helios CDH 55127)

⊕—(BB) ***

From the very outset of his Hyperion project, **Roy Goodman**, who began at the beginning with the low-numbered symphonies, established a winning manner in early Haydn and, as the series progressed, he showed that his dramatic approach was being fruitful in the middle-period and later works. The recording is resonant, giving bloom to the strings, yet oboes and horns (and other wind and brass, when used) come through vividly. Goodman's distinguished series was never completed. There is no longer space to detail all the individual performances but we have commented about performances of special interest, although every disc is worth having.

The performances of the linked Esterházy works (Nos. 6–8) are characteristically lively and fresh, bringing out the colour of all three works.

No. 20 includes trumpets and drums, dating it to Haydn's pre-Esterházy years (for those forces were not available to the composer in his early Esterházy period); the wind are silent in the slow movement. Goodman's account of the *Philosopher*, with its pair of cor anglais, is predictably bold and rhythmic, with an exhilarating finale (superb horn triplets!) to cap what has gone before. No. 43 has a three-note linking figure, which unites the first three movements, and it is the finale that develops Mercurial vigour. The *Trauersinfonie* opens tersely; but it is the contemplative *Adagio* that gives the symphony its sobriquet, followed by the powerfully cogent finale, which is full of nervous rhythmic energy. The famous *Farewell Symphony*, with its rare key of F sharp minor, follows on naturally after the *Sturm und Drang* of the finale of No. 44. The famous finale here opens vivaciously, then makes its abrupt change of mood and tempi so that the players can depart one-by-one, with Goodman himself relinquishing his place at the harpsichord at bar 205 to play the solo violin part in duet with his leader, Pavlo Beznosiuk. The horns immediately play a strong role in No. 47, but this time crooked in G, opening and dominating the first movement with an arresting fanfare, answered engagingly by dancing strings and woodwind. There follows a slow movement with a cantabile theme and four variations, where the melody and bass line are later inverted. Even more ingenious is the 'reversible Minuet', in which each section is followed by its exact mirror image; the horns again feature in the *Trio*. No. 72 is now known to have been written during the composer's earliest years at Eisenstadt, and the work becomes something of a display piece for the horn quartet, for which the *Horn Signal* (No. 31) was also written. From the very opening, the horns are spectacularly featured and return in

the Minuet and are afforded antiphonal echo effects, and then they take a back seat for the agreeable theme and variations finale, until their flourishes in the coda. The toughness of Goodman's approach to Haydn comes out strikingly in the *Paris Symphonies*. Indeed a little more charm would have been welcome, even though the playing is always polished and neatly articulated. *La Reine* and Nos. 86 and 87 are large-scale performances, often weighty, but slow movements are most elegantly played, especially the delightful *Capriccio Largo* of No. 86, while the *Vivace* finale of No. 87 is superbly spirited. *Symphonies 90–92* are engagingly lightweight performances, though full of character and vitality. But the first three *London Symphonies* are immediately weightier. In No. 94 the *Surprise* is beautifully prepared with a *pianissimo* repeat of the main theme before the *fortissimo* chord. The Minuet (more a Scherzo) is then a real *Allegro molto*. The Hyperion recordings maintain the highest standard throughout. At the opening of the *Clock Symphony* one's ears pick up the harpsichord continuo from which Roy Goodman directs his vivacious performances of Nos. 101 and 102. Highlights include the *Andante* of the *Clock*, which is delightfully pointed, and full of charm. But No. 102 is even finer, with a slow movement full of refined detail and a crisply buoyant Minuet and finale.

Other Recordings

Symphonies A; B, Hob 1:107/8; Symphony 62 in D; Overtures: Lo speciale; La vera costanza

(N) ⊕—(BB) *** Naxos 8.572130. Toronto CO, Mallon

The so-called *Symphonies A* and *B* are early works, written in the late 1750s, before the young composer moved to Esterházy. Both are scored for oboes, horns and strings, with harpsichord continuo, and it is the second of the two works which looks forward most readily, with a bassoon solo for the Trio of the Minuet and the light-hearted closing *Presto*. The two *Overtures* are virtually sinfonias, *Lo speciale* with three movements, the centrepiece a charming Minuet; but *La vera costanza* is more like a divertimento with five, all very brief. The *Symphony No. 62* dates from 1780 and deserves to be much better known. Scored for flute, as well as oboes, bassoons, horns and strings, it has a jaunty first movement with a really catchy secondary theme; the second movement (featuring the flute), is an unconventional *Allegretto*, the Minuet has a bassoon solo at its centre, and the very rhythmic, dashing finale completes a work which shows the composer at his most searching, never willing to work to a formula. It is splendidly played by this excellent Canadian group under their young conductor, **Kevin Mallon**, as is the rest of the programme. This is a key disc in the Haydn repertoire.

Symphonies 6 (Le Matin); 7 (Le Midi); 8 (Le Soir)

⊕—(BB) *** Naxos 8.550722. N. CO, Ward

These were almost certainly the first works that Haydn composed on taking up his appointment as Kapellmeister to the Esterházys. The **Northern Chamber Orchestra** under **Nicholas Ward** has wind players who relish their solos, the strings create a chamber-music atmosphere, and it is the intimate scale of these performances that is so attractive. Modern instruments are used, but textures are fresh and the ambience of the Concert Hall of Broadcasting House, Manchester, adds the right degree of warmth.

Symphonies 9–12

(BB) *** Naxos 8.557771. Sinfonia Finlandia, Gallois

These are lively, spontaneous performances from **Gallois** on modern instruments, only slightly marred by the recording which, though full and warm, could be slightly sharper in detail. The fast string passages are especially vivacious and enjoyable, and this CD is well-worth the asking price.

Symphonies 22 (Philosopher); 29; 60 (Il Distratto)

(BB) *** Naxos 8.550722. N. Co., Ward

Symphonies 23; 24; 61

(BB) *** Naxos 8.550723. N. CO, Ward

The fresh, stylish approach of the **Northern Chamber Orchestra** is entirely suited to these symphonies, and here **Nicholas Ward** makes a persuasive case for the use of modern instruments. No. 24 includes a leading semi-concertante flute part (nicely managed) and the G major has a wistful Andante for strings alone, and a vital Presto finale, well sprinkled with strongly accented quadruplets. The opening movement of No. 61 is obviously more mature and is presented with both character and charm. Excellent recording.

Symphonies 25 in C; 42 in D; 65 in A

(N) (BB) *** Naxos 8.570761. Sinfonia Finlandia Jyväskylä, Gallois

We have already met **Patrick Gallois** and his excellent **Sinfonia Finlandia Jyväskylä** near the very beginning of the Haydn series, and here they give perceptive and highly responsive performances of three more rare and fascinating works, including the early Symphony No. 25, in which Haydn replaces the slow movement with a gracious slow minuet featuring sonorous horns. No. 42 comes from 1771 and has a particularly eloquent Adagio, with one of Haydn's most gracious themes, introduced first on strings alone, with the wind joining in later. Gaiety returns in the lively Minuet and the spirited Scherzando e Presto finale. No. 65, from a similar period, lifts off immediately Vivace e con spirito, and the simple string tune of the following Andante is frequently interrupted for no apparent reason. After a Minuet framing a Trio in which the principal violin is marked acciaccatura, the hunting finale has the horns leading the way boisterously.

Sturm und Drang Symphonies 26; 35; 38; 39; 41; 42; 43 (Mercury); 44 (Trauer); 45 (Farewell); 46; 47; 48 (Maria Theresia); 49 (La Passione); 50; 51; 52; 58; 59 (Fire), 65

(B) **(*) DG 463 731-2 (6). E. Concert, Pinnock

Pinnock's forces are modest (with 6.5.2.2.1 strings), but the panache of the playing conveys any necessary grandeur. It is a new experience to have Haydn symphonies of this period recorded in relatively dry and close sound, with inner detail

crystal clear (harpsichord never obscured) and made the more dramatic by the intimate sense of presence, yet with a fine bloom on the instruments. Some may find a certain lack of charm at times, and others may quarrel with the very brisk one-in-a-bar Minuets and even find finales a little rushed.

Symphonies 26 (Lamentatione); 35; 49 (La Passione)

(BB) **(*) Naxos 8.550721. N. CO, Ward

Although enjoyable, this disc from **Nicholas Ward** and his **Northern Chamber Orchestra** is not quite as fresh-sounding as his first. The playing remains elegant and the horns (in B flat alto) are splendid in the Minuet of No. 35. But the opening Allegro assai con spirito of the Lamentatione could do with a shade more bite, and in the Adagio the warm resonance makes the finely played oboe solo almost a cor anglais and the melodic line like a Handel aria. The resonance of the BBC's Studio 7 in Manchester brings a pleasingly mellow sound-picture, but the string detail is not sharply defined.

Symphonies 26 (Lamentatione); 52; 53 (L'Impériale)

(B) *** Virgin 2x1 5 61800-2 (2). La Petite Bande, Kuijken – Violin Concertos 1 & 4; Sinfonia Concertante ***

These are fresh, vital, cleanly articulated performances which wear their authenticity lightly and even indulge in speeds for slow movements that are more expansive and affectionate than many purists would allow. These three symphonies now appear on a Virgin Double, coupled with two key violin concertos and the Sinfonia concertante in B flat.

Symphonies 30 in C (Alleluja); 53 in D (L'Imperiale); 69 in C (Laudon)

(BB) **** Warner Apex 2564 60520-2. VCM, Harnoncourt

The first movement of No. 30 is based on an Alleluja that formed part of the Mass for Easter week. The work features unusually prominent writing for the trumpets in the outer movements. No. 53 has a vigorous first movement with dancing strings, and the Andante features characteristically inventive variations on one of the composer's most engaging themes.

The sobriquet of No. 69, Laudon, was appended by Haydn himself and celebrates a highly successful field marshal of that name. The vigorous rhythms of the opening movement certainly have a military flavour. But it is the unpredictable finale with its fiercely contrasting dynamics (and a violin solo to introduce the return of the main theme) that gives the work its individuality. All three performances here are quite splendid, with outstandingly brilliant music-making that makes an unanswerable case for playing Haydn on period instruments. The recording is first class.

Symphonies 30 (Alleluja); 55 (Schoolmaster); 63 (La Roxelane)

(BB) *** Naxos 8.550757. N. CO, Ward

An entirely winning triptych of named Haydn symphonies, spanning a highly creative period from the three-movement Alleluja (1765), with its delightful woodwind contribution in the Andante, to La Roxelane (1780), where the Allegretto paints an engaging portrait of a flirtatious character in a play and the finale fizzes with energy. In between comes *The Schoolmaster*, whose *Adagio* brings a theme and variations of disarming simplicity. Alert and vivacious playing from all concerned; admirable pacing and first-class sound.

Symphonies 31 (Horn Signal); 59 (Fire); 73 (La Chasse)

⊕– Ⓜ **** Warner Elatus 2564 60033-2. VCM, Harnoncourt

This is one of Harnoncourt's very best records. All three symphonies are notable for their spectacular horn parts. The playing here – using natural horns – is superb, with throatily exuberant braying at the opening of the *Horn Signal*, an equally striking contribution throughout the *Fire Symphony* (where the horns are crooked in A), and more cheerful hunting-calls in the spirited finale of *La Chasse*. The playing is not only extremely vital and polished but even has an element of charm (not something one can always count on from this source). The orchestra communicate their involvement throughout.

Symphonies 32 in A; 33 in C; 34 in D min

ⒷⒷ *** Naxos 8.554154. Cologne CO, Mühler-Brühl

Symphonies 37 in C; 38 in C (Echo); 39 in G min; 40 in F

ⒷⒷ *** Naxos 8.557093. Cologne CO, Mühler-Brühl

Helmut Mühler-Brühl and the **Cologne Chamber Orchestra** take over on this pair of discs with generally excellent results.

Symphonies 41 in C; 58 in F; 59 in A (Fire)

ⒷⒷ **(*) Naxos 8.557002. Cologne CO, Mühler-Brühl

Symphonies 43 (Mercury); 46–47

⊕– ⒷⒷ *** Naxos 8.554767. Cologne CO, Mühler-Brühl

Haydn's *Symphonies Nos. 41, 58* and *59* are beautifully played here, but one feels that a work with the sobriquet 'Fire' might have been a bit fierier in the opening *Presto*. However, the splendid horn playing in the finale more than compensates, and this is certainly an enjoyable disc.

The nickname 'Mercury' for No. 43 probably relates to a stage work, with a fine A flat slow movement opening on muted strings. No. 47 brings striking military horn-calls at the start, beautifully caught in this recording; but the most memorable of the three is No. 46, with its lilting B minor slow movement. Its extraordinary finale is then punctuated by sudden silences, with sharp modulations and an unexpected quotation from the preceding Minuet. **Mühler-Brühl's** choice of speeds cannot be faulted, with *allegros* crisp and alert and slow movements kept flowing.

Symphonies 44–49

⊕– Ⓑ *** Artemis/Van. (ADD) ATM-CD 1495 (3). Zagreb RSO, Janigro

Janigro's 1963 Vanguard collection of the six *Sturm und Drang Symphonies* stands as one of the early treasures of the bargain shelf, serving in the early stereo era to confirm what sharp,

vital work Haydn was producing long before the famous symphonies written for London. Throughout, the modern-instrument performances with a modest-sized ensemble are exemplary; the first-rate analogue recording sounds excellent in this new CD transfer, and there are fine notes by Christa Landon, wife of H. Robbins Landon.

Symphonies 44 (Trauer); 88; 104 (London); Symphonies 45 (Farewell); 48 (Maria Theresi); 102; Symphonies 82 (The Bear); 96 (Miracle); 100 (Military); Symphonies 83 (The Hen); 94 (Surprise); 101 (The Clock); Symphonies 85 (La Reine); 92 (Oxford); 103 (Drum Roll)

ⒷⒷ *** Naxos 8.505006 (5). Capella Istropolitana, Wordsworth

Like **Barry Wordsworth's** recordings of Mozart symphonies, with the **Capella Istropolitana** on the Naxos label, this Haydn collection provides a series of outstanding bargains at the lowest budget price. The sound is not quite as clean and immediate as in the Mozart series, a little boomy at times in fact, and Wordsworth's preference for relatively relaxed speeds is a little more marked here than in Mozart, but the varied choice of works on each disc is most attractive. At their modest cost, these are well worth collecting.

Symphonies 54; 56; 57

⊕– ⒷⒷ *** Naxos 8.554108. Cologne CO, Müller-Brühl

In vivid, full-ranging recordings made by German Radio, **Müller-Brühl** conducts lively performances with his excellent chamber orchestra of three symphonies from around 1774. Müller-Brühl, using modern instruments, yet reflects period practice in asking for very limited vibrato and light articulation from the strings.

Symphonies 64 in A; 84 in E flat; 87 in A

ⒷⒷ *** Naxos 8.550770. Nicolaus Esterházy Sinfonia, Drahos

Symphonies 66 in B flat; 67 in F; 68 in B flat

ⒷⒷ *** Naxos 8.554406 Nicolaus Esterházy Sinfonia, Drahos

The Budapest **Nicolaus Esterházy Sinfonia** under **Béla Drahos** now takes over in the Naxos series with generally excellent results although they are rather reasonably recorded.

Symphonies 69 (Laudon); 89; 91

ⒷⒷ **(*) Naxos 8.550769. Budapest Nicolaus Esterházy Sinfonia, Drahos

The resonance of the Reformed Church, Budapest, prevents the sharpest definition here. The orchestra is set back and the internal balance is natural: the strings have bloom without edginess. This is alert, thoroughly musical playing with apt tempi. The *Andante con moto* of No. 89 is elegantly done, and the variations of the *Andante* of No. 91 are neatly handled (with an elegant bassoon solo). All in all this gives pleasure, but more brightness on top would have been welcome.

Symphonies 72; 93; 95

⊕– ⒷⒷ *** Naxos 8.550797. Nicolaus Esterházy Sinfonia, Drahos

These performances are polished, warm and spirited and, if the Naxos recording is on the reverberant side, it does not cloud textures. Four horns are featured prominently in No. 72 and provide many bravura flourishes and virtuoso scales in the opening movement; the playing here is first class. The orchestral response is equally impressive in the fine slow movements of these later works, and throughout **Béla Drahos's** pacing is matched by the overall sense of spontaneity and style.

Symphonies 74–76

🎼 (BB) *** Naxos 8.554109. Cologne CO, Müller-Brühl

The three symphonies dating from the early 1780s make an attractive group, characteristically lively in outer movements but each with slow movements involving the use of mysterious muted strings. **Müller-Brühl**, as in his other Haydn recordings, favours broad *adagios* and Minuets that retain the idea of a stately dance. Yet the freshness and rhythmic resilience never fail to bring the performances to life. Like its companions, an excellent recommendation.

Symphony 76 in E flat (DVD version)

*** TDK **DVD** DV-COWAND2. NDR SO, Wand (V/D: Andreas Missler-Morell) – BRUCKNER: *Symphony 6* **(*)

A very straight and straightforward account of this Haydn symphony both from **Wand** and the orchestra and from the camera team. A pleasure to watch and hear.

Symphonies 77–79

🎼 (BB) *** Naxos 8.553363. N. CO, Ward

For these three little-known but most engaging symphonies, written in 1782–3, **Nicholas Ward** could hardly be more persuasive. The colourful charm of Haydn's scoring in the *B flat Symphony* is most sensitively caught, the *Vivace* opening of *No. 78 in C minor* is highly dramatic, while both slow movements are eminently graceful. The Minuets, though not rushed, are suitably spirited and finales are deft and lively, especially the winning monothematic *Presto* of the *C minor* work, which includes some of the composer's genial pauses.

Symphonies 80; 81; 99

(BB) *** Naxos 8.554110. Cologne CO, Müller-Brühl

Müller-Brühl here couples two symphonies of 1783–4 with the first of the masterpieces which Haydn wrote for Salomon for the second of his two visits to London. No. 80 is remarkable for the dark intensity of the minor-key opening with its dramatic use of tremolo. Chromatic touches break in later too. In these later symphonies, unlike the earlier ones, Müller-Brühl does allow Minuets to acquire a hint of the Scherzo at brisker speeds. No. 99 is remarkable for Haydn's inclusion for the first time in a symphony of a pair of clarinets.

Symphonies 80; 83 (Hen); 84; 87–89

🎼 (BB) *** ASV Resonance CD RSB 203 (2). LMP, Glover

Jane Glover's very winning Haydn recordings with the **London Mozart Players** have been consistently underrated since they first appeared in the late 1980s. They are consis-

tently strong and energetic and fully characterized. Throughout outer movements these modern-instrument performances are as lively as you could wish, and the recording with its warm ambience is excellent. A genuine bargain.

Symphonies 82 (The Bear); 83 (The Hen); 84; 85 (La Reine); 86; 87 (Paris)

🎼 ❀ (BB) **** Virgin 2x1 5 61659 (2). OAE, Kuijken

(B) *** Double Decca (ADD) 473 801-2 (2). Philh. Hungarica, Dorati

**(*) DHM/BMG 82876 60602-2 (3). VCM, Harnoncourt

Kuijken and his players wear their authenticity lightly and the slow movements are allowed to relax beautifully, while the one-in-a-bar treatment of the Minuets produces a delightful Ländler-like swing. With dynamic contrasts underlined, the grandeur of Haydn's inspiration is fully brought out, along with the rigour. Above all, he and his players convey the full joy of Haydn's inspiration in every movement, and the reissue at bargain price is surely irresistible.

Dorati's set of *Paris Symphonies* are well up to the high standard of his integral Haydn series, freshly stylish performances with plenty of vigour. The only point of controversy here is Dorati's consistently slow tempi for the Minuets, nicely pointed as they are.

Harnoncourt is nothing if not unpredictable, and this set of the Haydn *Paris Symphonies* bears this out in the most exciting fashion. First, he takes every repeat in sight (even the second parts of main movements), including of course every section of the Minuets and Trios, and even the measured introduction to *La Reine*. These performances show this always vigorous and alive conductor at his most characterful and stimulating and, above all, both dramatic and warmly expressive in Haydn's always memorable slow movements. Tempi take unexpected turns, especially in Minuets and Trios, but the individuality of this music-making and its vitality are difficult to resist, though seriously lacking in charm.

Symphonies 82–87 (Paris); 93–104 (London)

(N) (B) **(*) DG 477 7917 (7). BPO, Karajan

There is much in **Karajan's** combined *Paris* and *London Symphonies* that commands attention. Like the Davis London set on Philips, this is big-band Haydn – but what a band! But of course the Orchestra of the Concert de la Loge Olympique, for which Haydn wrote the *Paris Symphonies*, was large, consisting of 40 violins and no fewer than 10 double-basses! It goes without saying that the quality of the orchestral playing here is superb, and Karajan is meticulous in his attention to detail. However, the Paris group are rather heavy-handed accounts – the slow movements are kept moving but the Minuets are very slow indeed, full of pomp and majesty, and at times too grand and lacking charm and grace. But Karajan seems more responsive to the *London Symphonies*, and there is evidence of tenderness in some slow movements, witness the close of *No. 98 in B flat*. Again the Minuets are wanting in sparkle, but there is no lack of breadth and dignity, and the sound of the **Berlin Philharmonic** itself is a joy.

Symphony 83 in G min. (La Poule)

🎵 **** BBC (ADD) BBCL 4038. Hallé O, Barbirolli – LEHAR: *Gold and Silver*; JOHANN STRAUSS JR: *Emperor Waltz*, etc.; R. STRAUSS: *Der Rosenkavalier Suite* ***

This is one of **Barbirolli's** most cherishable records. The account of *Symphony No. 83* is delightful, with the 'Hen' clucking to the manner born. There is grace and simplicity in the *Andante* and exuberance in the finale, and the couplings are unmissable.

Symphonies 83 (La Poule); 88; 96 (Miracle)

BB (***) Dutton mono CDBP 9750. Hallé O, Barbirolli

Barbirolli's mono recording of No. 83 (*The Hen*), made in 1949, was the very first in the catalogue. Characteristically, he gives it an energetic reading full of fun and high dramatic contrasts. So the clucking of the second subject has rarely been pointed with more wit. No. 96, with which *The Hen* was originally coupled on LP, has freer, more open sound. The playing is a degree more polished and elegant, with no diminution of energy or wit, and again the flute and oboe emerge as stars in the **Hallé** team. Barbirolli sustains the great, sensuously tuneful melody of the *Largo* of No. 88 at a slow speed, with elegance as well as warmth, and the fun of the finale is delightfully caught. Michael Dutton's transfers are a model of their kind, full-bodied and warm.

Symphonies 85 in B flat (La Reine); 86 in D

BB **(*) Warner Apex 2564 60451-2. St Paul CO, Wolff

The excellent **St Paul Chamber Orchestra** give polished, animated accounts of two of the finest *Paris Symphonies*. No. 85 (*La Reine*) includes the slow-movement variations on *La petite gentille et jeune Lisette*, so admired by Queen Marie-Antoinette, here played most elegantly. The *Capriccio* slow movement of No. 86 is perhaps a little staid, but the finale is infectiously spirited. Excellent, natural recording with the concert-hall acoustic on the resonant side, adding to the weight of the first movement of the *D major* work.

Symphony 88

🎵 🌟 (M) (****) DG mono 474 988-2. BPO, Furtwängler – SCHUMANN: *Symphony 4* ***🌟

Even those who usually find **Furtwängler's** interpretations too idiosyncratic will be drawn to this glowing performance. The beauty of his shaping of the main theme of the slow movement is totally disarming, and the detail of the finale, lightly sprung and vivacious, is a constant pleasure. The **Berlin Philharmonic** plays marvellously well for him, and the 1951 recording in its remastered form sounds admirably fresh, yet has plenty of body. DG have now reissued the original coupling, a uniquely inspired performance of Schumann's *Fourth Symphony*, which also has a Rosette, so collectors should seek this wonderful disc out without delay.

Symphonies 88–92

*** EMI 3 94237-2 (2). BPO, Rattle

It is good to see and hear that **Sir Simon Rattle** is keeping big-band Haydn symphonies going, with modern instruments, but using narrow-bore valve horns and antiphonally separating first and second violins, and featuring embellished repeats. These live performances are full of character and individuality, and reveal Haydn as a symphonist on the fullest scale. The **Berlin Philharmonic** too plays superbly and is very impressively recorded.

Symphonies 88 in G; 92 in G (Oxford); 95 in C min.; 98 in B flat; 100 in G (Military); 101 in D (Clock); 102 in B flat; 104 in D (London)

(N) (B) ** EMI 2 15300-2 (3). Philh. or New Philh. O, Klemperer

Klemperer, not the likeliest conductor in Haydn, in his broad, measured view yet shows his mastery in structuring and rhythmic pointing. With good analogue sound, an interesting historical document.

Symphonies (i) 88 in G; (ii) 95 in C min.; 101 (Clock)

🎵 *** Testament SBT 1411. (i) Chicago SO; (ii) Fritz Reiner SO; Reiner

The *G major Symphony* (No. 88) comes from Chicago, but its companions with the orchestra **Reiner** drew from players in the Met. and New York freelancers, together with some of the **Chicago Symphony**, was recorded in Manhattan in 1963. These are performances of style, eloquent and beautifully finished, a model of Haydn playing. Originally issued on RCA, they sound wonderfully fresh in Paul Baily's restorations. Whatever other Haydn readers may have collected in recent years, this is not to be passed over.

Symphonies 88; 104 (London)

(M) *** CRD (ADD) CRD 3370. Bournemouth Sinf., Thomas

With an orchestra on a chamber scale, the playing has great freshness and vitality; indeed it is the urgency of musical feeling that **Ronald Thomas** conveys, which makes up for the last ounce of finesse.

Symphonies 91 in E flat; 92 (Oxford); (i) Scena di Berenice

🎵 **** HM HMC 901849. (i) Fink; Freiburg Bar. O, Jacobs

As in their exuberant account of Haydn's *Seasons*, **René Jacobs** and the **Freiburg Baroque Orchestra** (currently the finest of all period-instrument groups of this size) find a sense of joy, of carefree intensity in the playing of the two *Symphonies*. As in the oratorio, Jacobs is well aware of Haydn's sense of humour, pointing rhythms to bring it out in such a movement as the *Andante* in No. 91. The other distinctive point about this issue is the inclusion of Haydn's *Scena di Berenice* as a coupling, the most powerful bonus. Here **Bernarda Fink** is searingly dramatic, freely varying the pace and tone-colours of the recitatives to bring out the meaning of the words (included, along with translations, in the booklet) and rising superbly to the challenge of the two arias, slow and fast.

Symphonies 92 (Oxford); 94 (Surprise); La fedelta premiata: Sinfonia

🎵 **** MDG **SACD** Surround Sound 1325-6. Austro-Hungarian Haydn O, A. Fischer

This coupling of two of the best known of the later nick-named symphonies is not a spin-off from this orchestra's complete set of the Haydn symphonies for Nimbus but a live recording, made in Graz in 2004. The playing is out-standingly lively and alert, bringing out the drama of both works in high dynamic contrasts. The impact of the cele-brated surprise, *fortissimo* on the timpani, in the fast-flowing *Andante* of No. 94 has rarely been as great. The galloping rhythms of the overture to *La fedelta premiata* are as exhila-rating as anything in the symphonies, with valveless horns braying away. As a separate showcase for the conductor and orchestra, the disc readily wins its place, vividly recorded in Multichannel SACD.

Symphonies 92 (Oxford); 104 (London)

(BB) *** Regis RRC 1084. E. Sinfonia, Groves – MOZART: *Symphony 31 (Paris)* ***

Sir Charles Groves's performances are robust yet elegant; both slow movements are beautifully shaped, with Haydn's characteristic contrasts unfolding spontaneously. In the last movement of the *Oxford* the dancing violins are a special de-light in what is one of the composer's most infectious finales. Excellent recording, and this budget Regis reissue has an equally recommendable Mozart bonus.

Symphony 92 (Oxford); (i) Arianna a Naxos (Cantata); Scena di Berenice (DVD version)

(*) BBC Opus Arte **DVD OA 0821 D. (i) Bartoli; VCM, Harnoncourt at the 2001 Syriarte Festival, Graz, Austria (includes discussion of the music of Haydn between Bartoli and Harnoncourt, and a brief depiction of the Festival) (TV Dir: Brian Large)

We already have a Decca recording of *Arianna a Naxos* by **Cecilia Bartoli** with András Schiff, but this splendidly sung version with string accompaniment is even more telling, even though the orchestral transcription was not Haydn's own. Moreover, the performance is especially vivid in the singer's visual presence, while **Harnoncourt** accompanies with great sensitivity.

The equally inspired *Scena di Berenice* is set to a text taken from Metastasio's *Antigono*. It has a direct affinity with *Arianna*. Bartoli's performance is again very moving, and is most expressively accompanied. The two vocal items are pre-ceded by a vibrant performance of Haydn's *Oxford Symphony* which, like *Arianna*, was very well received during Haydn's visits to London in the 1790s. This is a characteristic Harnoncourt performance with a rather gruff, even abrasive, first movement that not all will take to. He is more persua-sive in the central movements, and the sparkling finale is a joy. Certainly the performance gains from watching the con-ductor, whose facial expressions are so mobile.

Symphonies 93–104 (London Symphonies)

(B) **(*) Decca 475 551-2 (4). LPO, Solti

Symphonies 93; 94 (Surprise); 97; 99; 100 (Military); 101 (Clock) (London Symphonies)

8—1 (B) **** Ph. Duo (ADD/DDD) 442 614-2 (2). Concg. O, Davis

Symphonies 95; 96 (Miracle); 98; 102; 103 (Drum Roll); 104 (London) (London Symphonies)

8—1 (B) **** Ph. Duo (ADD/DDD) 442 611-2 (2). Concg. O, Davis

Symphonies 93–98 (London Symphonies)

8—1 (BB) **** EMI Gemini (ADD) 5 85770-2 (2). RPO, Beecham

Symphonies 99–104 (London Symphonies)

8—1 (BB) **** EMI Gemini (ADD) 5 85513-2 (2). RPO, Beecham

(i) Symphonies 93–104 (London Symphonies); with extra performances of Nos. (ii) 88 in G; (iii) 91 in E flat; (ii) 98 in B flat

8—1 (B) **** DG (ADD) 474 364-2 (5). (i) LPO; (ii) BPO; (iii) Bav. RSO, Jochum

Sir Colin Davis's Haydn series (recorded between 1975 and 1981) is one of the most distinguished sets he has given us over his long recording career, and its blend of brilliance and sensitivity, wit and humanity gives these two-for-the-price-of-one Duo reissues a special claim on the collector. There is no trace of routine in this music-making and no failure of imagination. The excellence of the playing is matched by Philips's best recording quality, whether ana-logue or digital. The **Concertgebouw** sound is resonant and at times weighty, but has good definition.

Jochum's exhilarating set of Haydn's *London Symphonies* (1972/3) is consistently stylish, and the challengingly fast tempi in the outer movements bring an athletic exuberance which is highly infectious. The conductor moulds the slow movements with a tenderness that never spills over to un-stylish mannerisms and handles the sets of themes and vari-ations to bring great diversity of atmosphere and mood, all of which combine to make these wonderfully satisfying readings. The recordings have never sounded better than in these new transfers, with sound that is both full and vivid. To make this set even more appealing, DG have added an extra disc containing an earlier recording. No. 98 is a per-formance of equal distinction, perhaps a degree more mel-low. In No. 88 the **Berlin Orchestra** is even more polished than the **LPO**, and Jochum brings his characteristic warmth and humanity to both these scores. No. 91, with the **Bavarian Orchestra**, was recorded in 1958 and sounds only fractionally less full-bodied than its 1960s companions.

The paired EMI collections of **Beecham's** recordings sound admirably full-bodied and have been transferred amazingly successfully. The performances are sensitive and invigorating. The art of phrasing is one of the prime secrets of great music-making, and no detail in Beecham's perform-ances of the *London Symphonies* goes unattended. They have also great warmth, drama too, and perhaps a unique genial-ity. The sound throughout is full and fresh (it's the 1992 re-mastering), with plenty of body, sweet violin-timbre and no edge. These performances possess an inner life and vitality that put them in a class of their own and are wonderful value in this bargain Gemini-double format.

While it might be felt that **Solti's** way with some of the symphonies is sometimes a bit too uptight for Haydn, others unexpectedly glow in his hands, with the coupling of Nos. 93 and 99 (recorded in 1987) proving the pick of the bunch. The lovely slow movement of No. 93 has both delicacy and gravitas, and that of No. 99 is serenely spacious. The *Miracle* and the *Clock*, although brilliantly played by the **LPO**, were rather too taut to convey all Haydn's charm; in Nos. 102 and 103 the tensions speak of the 20th century rather than the 18th. In the *Surprise* and *Military Symphonies*, the conductor stresses the brilliance and fire of the outer movements, which are again a bit hard-driven, but there is no lack of *joie de vivre*. In Nos. 95 and 104 Solti found the perfect balance between energy and repose. The final symphonies, Nos. 97 & 98, were released in 1992, and they maintained the balance between Solti's boundless energy and Haydn's warmth and humour. These symphonies, now released in a bargain box (on four instead of five CDs) make a very stimulating set.

Symphonies 93; 96 (Miracle); 98 in B flat
(BB) *** EMI Encore 3 41428-2. ECO, Tate

Symphonies 94 (Surprise); 95; 97; 99; 101 (Clock)
(N) (B) **** CfP 5 21855-2 (2). ECO, Tate

Symphonies 100 (Military); 102 in B flat; 103 (Drum Roll); 104 (London)
(N) (B) **** CFP 2 28369-2 (2). ECO, Tate

Consistently **Tate** chooses speeds that allow the sparkle and wit of Haydn's writing to come out naturally throughout all these performances. There are many such examples, as in the first movements of Nos. 96 and 98 and in the finales too. Tate's pacing brings out Haydn's humour far more than anything faster and fiercer would do, as in the second subject of the *Military* or in the joyful lilt of the 6/8 rhythms of the first-movement *allegro* in the *Drum Roll*. Slow movements too are admirably paced and imaginative in detail, and each of these works has a fine tone, beautifully played. Warm, well-balanced sound means that these inexpensive reissues are among the supreme bargains among the late Haydn symphonies.

Symphonies 93; 96 (Miracle); 98; 100 (Military); 101 (Clock); 102; 103 (Drum Roll); Sinfonia concertante; Overture: Il mondo della luna
(N) (M) **(*) DG 477 8117 (2). COE, Abbado

Recorded between 1986 and 1995 in Vienna, Berlin (the Jesus-Christus-Kirche), and Ferrara, **Abbado's** performances with the **Chamber Orchestra of Europe** with their polish and natural elegance could not be more removed from period-instrument style. The orchestra provides expansive tuttis, although detail in wind and strings is always refined and polished. The 'ticking' *Andante* of the '*Clock*' (for instance) is gently played with a bold contrast in the first tutti, and the Scherzo is a vigorously buoyant three-in-a-bar. But mostly the result is traditional and the performances, although not

inflated, are not chamber-scale. At times one feels even more bite and vitality would have been an advantage, but this music-making is easy to enjoy when the recording is so warm and naturally balanced.

Symphonies 94 in G (Surprise); 96 in D (Miracle)
⊕–⊕ (M) **** Decca O/L 475 9111. AAM, Hogwood

Hogwood's 1984 coupling is welcome back to the catalogue in its original L'Oiseau-Lyre presentation. Moreover, the playing itself is superb: polished, feeling, and full of imaginative detail. The acid bottle has been abandoned by the strings, who play expressively, without squeezing the timbre unmercifully. The account of No. 94 is particularly dramatic, and in the *Andante* there is not just one 'surprise' (and that pretty impressive, with the contrast afforded by the gentle strings at the opening) but two more *forte* chords to follow at the beginning of each subsequent phrase – a most telling device. With superb recording, full yet transparent, this can be strongly recommended. An issue to make converts to the creed of authenticity.

Symphonies 94 (Surprise); 96 (Miracle); 97
✸ (B) (****) Decca Australian Eloquence (mono) 476 8483. Concg. O, Van Beinum

A treasurable reissue from the early 1950s. **Van Beinum** conducts exceptionally poised and vivacious performances in the very best **Concertgebouw** tradition of Haydn playing. The personality of the orchestra comes through in every bar, in both the woodwind solos and the pointed string bowing. In the *Surprise Symphony* particularly, the acoustic adds a nobility of sound to the already well-balanced ensemble, and the tempi throughout are, almost without exception, perfectly chosen and safely maintained. The recording as produced by John Culshaw and engineered by Kenneth Wilkinson is a marvellous example of Decca *ffrr* (mono) excellence. Snap this up before it disappears!

Symphonies 100 (Military); 101 (Clock)
*** BBC Legends BBCL 4176-2. LPO, Jochum – HINDEMITH: *Symphonic Metamorphosis on Themes of Weber* ***

These Haydn performances of the *Military* and *Clock Symphonies* were given at the Royal Festival Hall in coordination with a series of recording sessions that DG was holding, in which Jochum recorded all 12 of the *London Symphonies*. It is fascinating to compare the results of the studio recordings and these live versions. As one might expect, the studio recordings are a degree more polished, a fraction more precise in ensemble; yet in compensation the joy of Haydn's inspiration, above all the rhythmic lift that Jochum was able to draw from the players, is even more striking in the live accounts.

Symphony 104 in D (London)
(M) *** Decca (ADD) 470 256-2. VPO, Karajan – BEETHOVEN: *Symphony 7* **(*)

A really noble account, powerful and forward-looking, of the *London Symphony* from **Karajan** and the **Vienna Philharmonic** on their finest form. As in Karajan's later, DG account, the first-movement repeat is observed and detail is etched with loving care, the delicate passages perfectly balanced with the bold tuttis. The slow movement, without any self-conscious mannerisms, is shaped warmly and graciously, and the Minuet sparkles, taken at a brisk pace, while the outer movements have splendid life and impetus. The 1959 recording, produced by John Culshaw, is extremely fine for its period (indeed any period) and has been transferred to CD without loss of the ambient bloom of the Sofiensaal.

CHAMBER MUSIC

Baryton (Divertimenti) Octets, Hob X/1–6, 10 &12; Concerti a due Lire for the King of Naples, Hob VIIh/1–6; 8 Notturni for the King of Naples, Hob II/25–32; 6 Scherzandi, Hob II/33–8

(N) *** BIS CD 1796/8. V. Haydn Sinf., Huss

Prince Esterházy was particularly fond of the baryton, whose delicate sonorities appealed to him. The instrument belongs to the gamba family. It is strung with six silver-covered gut strings, which are played with a bow, and it is equipped with nine drone metal strings which serve as a sympathetic counterpart, but can also be plucked with the thumb of the left hand. The constant resonance of these strings produces the baryton's singing tone and its reverberance. Haydn himself practised to master the instrument, but it took him six months to achieve competence. Yet the instrument never really became established, and Haydn's Baryton Octets are among the few works featuring the instrument to have survived. But they make a fascinating inclusion here, as the character of the instrument dominates the texture, although Haydn often provides bravura horn writing to give the music a lift.

The Concerti for lire and charming Notturni were commissioned by King Ferdinand of Naples, who himself played the lira organizzata, a hybrid of the hurdy-gurdy with small organ pipes. Haydn's works were written for two such instruments, and (as revised by the composer) their music is now assigned to a sextet of wind and string instruments, engagingly scored. They are elegantly played here and this is a most valuable collection.

There is also a separate collection of the Notturni on CPO in which **Dieter Klöcker** and the **Consortium Classicum** get round the textural problem by using a pair of chamber organs besides the basic instrumental ensemble, but this is a less satisfactory solution and produces a degree of monotony (CPO 999 741-2).

Baryton Trios 71 in A; 96 in B min.; 113 in D; 126 in C

*** ASV Gaudeamus CDGAU 109. Hsu, Miller, Arico

Baryton Trios 87 in A min.; 97 in D (Fatti per la felicissima nasetta de S:ai:S); 101 in C; 111 in G

*** ASV Gaudeamus CDGAU 104. Hsu, Miller, Arico

These are most beguiling performances, which have subtlety and finesse, and the music itself is consistently inventive and attractive. Natural and well-balanced recorded sound,

too. The second collection is no less desirable than the first. Well worth exploring.

Cassations in E flat & D, Hob II/21–22 (arr. for String Quartet, as Op. 2/3 & 5)

(BB) *** Naxos 8.555703. Kodály Qt – HOFFSTETTER: String Quartets ***

The original versions of these five-movement Cassations were scored for two horns and strings, and the arranger of the string quartet versions is unknown, but they transcribe very effectively. The E flat Quartet is notable for its charming serenade-like slow movement, pizzicato second Minuet and cheerful finale; the D major has a winningly energetic opening movement, another graceful slow movement and a racy finale. They are admirably played here and splendidly recorded.

8 Divertimenti (Feldparthie) (for Wind Sextet)

**(*) Testament (ADD) SBT 1346. L. Wind Soloists, Brymer

By comparison with Mozart, Haydn's writing is much more earthy, suggesting (like the original title of these works, 'Feldparthie') that they were written for a private wind band. Moreover the bravura of the horn writing suggests the availability of local virtuosi of a high calibre, and this applies equally to the superb playing here. The music has elegance too, as the very first of the series immediately displays; but it makes its effects more from the spirited brilliance of the playing (particularly in the vigorous 'hunting' finales of Nos. 1 to 3) than for subtlety of colour. Excellent (originally Decca) recording from 1968, immaculately transferred to CD.

(i) Flute Trios for 2 Flutes & Cello 1–4 (London), Hob IV/1–4; (ii) Flute Quartets, Op. 5, 1 in D, Hob II/D9; 2 in G, Hob II/G4; 3 in D, Hob II/D10; 4 in G, Hob II/1; 5 in D, Hob II/D11; 6 in C, Hob II/11

(B) *** Accent ACC 30083 (2). (i) Bernard Kuijken, Mark Hantaï, Wieland Kuijken; (ii) Bernard, Siegfried & Wieland Kuijken, François Fernandez

The London Trios date from 1794 during Haydn's visit to England and the first two include variations on the song, Trust not too much. They are delightful works and receive felicitous performances from this authentic group on Accent who make the most winning sounds. The Flute Quartets, Op. 5, in the view of H. C. Robbins Landon may not all be by Haydn. It seems fairly certain, however, that the first two, also known as Divertimenti, are authentic, very early works from the 1750s. All the music is engaging when played with such finesse and warmth, although this is a set to be dipped into rather than taken in large doses. The recording is admirably fresh and realistic.

Flute Trios: in D, F & G, Hob XV/15–17

(BB) **(*) Warner Apex 0927 40602-2. Helasvuo, Hakkila, Kartunnen

These three Flute Trios were written together in the summer of 1790. They are slight but have a simple charm which is well caught by these unpretentious performances by this Finnish team, **Mikael Helasvuo** (flute), **Tuija Hakkila** (fortepiano), and **Anni Kartunnen** (cello). The recording is clear and truthful.

Piano Trios 1–46, Hob XV:1–41; Hob XIV:C1 in C; Hob XV:C1 in C; Hob XIV6/XVI6 in G; Hob XV:f1 in F min.; Hob deest in D (complete)

🎗 🏵 Ⓑ **** Ph. 454 098-2 (9). Beaux Arts Trio

It is not often possible to hail one set of records as a 'classic' in quite the way that Schnabel's Beethoven sonatas can be so described. Yet this set can be described in those terms, for the playing of the **Beaux Arts Trio** is of the very highest musical distinction. The contribution of the pianist, **Menahem Pressler**, is inspired, and the recorded sound on CD is astonishingly lifelike. The CD transfer has enhanced detail without losing the warmth of ambience or sense of intimacy. Offered in a bargain box of nine CDs, this is a set no Haydn lover should miss: it is desert island music.

Piano Trios: Hob XV, 5; 18; 19; 20

Ⓜ **(*) CPO 999 468-2. Trio 1790

Piano Trios, Hob XV, 6–10

Ⓜ **(*) CPO 999 466-2. Trio 1790

Piano Trios, Hob XV, 11–14

Ⓜ **(*) CPO 999 467-2. Trio 1790

Piano Trios, Hob XV, 21–23

Ⓜ **(*) CPO 999 731-2. Trio 1790

Piano Trios, Hob XV, 24–26; 31–32

Ⓜ **(*) CPO 999 828-2. Trio 1790

Piano Trios: Hob XV: 34–35; 38; 40; f1

Ⓜ **(*) CPO 777 243-2. Trio 1790

The Beaux Arts Trio have long reigned supreme in this repertoire but those who are attracted by the idea of original instruments might well consider this expert group, **Trio 1790**, which is based in Cologne and was recorded there in the WDR studios. They are intelligent players, and their discs are priced economically. The performances sparkle; there is plenty of wit and character, and the Cologne Radio recordings are first class. All the same this will remain an adjunct rather than a replacement for the Beaux Arts and the sublime Menahem Pressler.

Piano Trio in A, Hob XV 18

*** Daphne DAPHNE 1026. Trio Poseidon – BRAHMS: *Piano Trio No.1*; IRELAND: *Phantasie Trio* ***

Formed in 2002, the **Trio Poseidon** brings together three talented Swedish musicians who had already established high reputations. In Haydn the sound of the piano seems rather light, almost like a fortepiano, but is very acceptable. The work is marked by a central *Andante* on the slow side, which allows ample time for the decorations to be articulated cleanly, leading to a jaunty account of the finale.

Piano Trios, Hob XV, 18, 19; (i) Andante with Variations in F min., Hob XVII; (ii) Cantata: The Battle of the Nile, Hob XXVIb4; 2 Italian Duets, Hob XXVa1–2; The Spirit's Song, Hob XXVIa41

*** Gaudeamus CDGAU 219. Four Nations Ens., with (i) Appel; (ii) Monoyios, Nils Brown

The Battle of the Nile, from which the CD takes its title, was occasioned by Nelson and Lady Hamilton's visit to Esterháza. The Princess Esterházy arranged for Haydn and some musicians to entertain the guests and Haydn was persuaded to compose this cantata to words by Cornelia Knight, who accompanied them on the visit, celebrating Nelson's victory. This expert group play the two 1794 *Trios* with exemplary taste and vitality and **Andrew Appel** gives us a sensitive account of the *Andante with Variations in F minor* on a fine copy of an instrument by Anton Walter. *The Battle of the Nile* is a rarity and is currently available in only one alternative. An enjoyable, well-played and beautifully recorded disc.

Piano Trios, Hob XV, 24, 25 (Gypsy), 26, 27

Ⓝ 🎗 **** Hyp. CDA 67719. Florestan Trio

With **Susan Tomes** in the lead, these **Florestan** performances are wonderfully fresh and appealing, alive, full of subtle detail and indeed of joy in the music. This is the first of a series. They are vividly recorded.

Piano Trio, Hob XV, 25 in G (Gypsy)

ⒷⒷ (***) Naxos mono 8.110188. Thibaud, Casals, Cortot – BEETHOVEN: *Kakadu Variations* (***); SCHUBERT: *Piano Trio 1* (***)

Few Haydn trios – apart from this one in G major, the so-called *Gypsy* – were played in the 1920s and 1930s. This famous recording, made in 1927, has been lovingly restored by Ward Marston even if it undoubtedly shows its age.

String quartets

String Quartets 1–83 (including Op. 2/1–6: Cassations; Op. 3/1–6, attrib. Hoffstetter); The Seven Last Words of Jesus Christ, Op. 51

Ⓝ 🎗 🏵 ⒷⒷ *** Naxos 8.502400 (25). Kodály Qt

String Quartets 1–10; 19–83 (complete)

Ⓑ *** Ph. 464 650-2 (21). Angeles Qt

This complete survey by the **Angeles Quartet** comes on 21 CDs and was made over a period of five years (1994–9). Both the playing and the sound quality are of a consistently high standard: generally speaking, the set is beautifully balanced without excessive reverberation and with great clarity; the players have warmth, intelligence and a refined tonal blend and their readings are full of character and wit. They leave you in no doubt that they have thought deeply about this music, but at the same time they never leave the impression that they are too studied or wanting in spontaneity. The internal balance is very good indeed, even if one might occasionally welcome greater projection from the cellist. Tempos are finely judged, and there is a keen awareness of Haydn's developing stature throughout. One never gets the feeling that one is hearing the earlier quartets through the eyes and ears of the later quartets. The group's sense of characterization is pretty unerring, and it leaves you marvelling anew at the quality of Haydn's musical invention.

It is difficult to generalize about so vast an output or so ambitious a recording enterprise, but the Angeles Quartet brings greater transparency of texture than the **Kodály Quartet**, on Naxos and arguably greater finish. The Kodály does not lack warmth or a sense of style, and the consistently friendly warmth of these players' approach to Haydn's music is always endearing. The result almost always sounds spontaneous and usually carries the feeling of 'live' music-making. The Kodály's playing was flattered by the warm acoustics of the Budapest Unitarian Church, which suited its mellow, civilized approach, although at times the engineers slightly miscalculated the microphone balance and captured a little too much resonance, bringing a degree of textural inflation. But the sound is always natural, the performances do not miss Haydn's subtleties or his jokes, and the group always communicates readily.

The reissued Kodály set is absolutely complete, including the early *Cassations*, the engaging works by Hoffstetter, for long wrongly attributed to Haydn, and the *Seven Last Words* in its string quartet transcription. The set comes in a handsome box with a first-class booklet of documentation covering the String Quartets, Symphonies, Concertos and Piano Sonatas (designed, no doubt, to tempt the collector into exploring further). It is undoubtedly a splendid bargain.

String Quartets: Op. 1/0; 43, Op. 42; 83, Op. 103

**(*) Mer. (ADD) ECD 88117. English Qt

These fine players rise to all the challenges posed by this music, and the recorded sound is eminently truthful. There would have been room for another *Quartet* on this disc, which offers rather short measure at 43 minutes.

String Quartets 1–4, Op. 1/1–4

(BB) **(*) Naxos 8.550398. Kodály Qt

String Quartets 5–6, Op. 1/5–6; 7–8, Op. 2/1–2

(BB) **(*) Naxos 8.550399. Kodály Qt

The Opp. 1 and 2 *Quartets* are in essence five-movement divertimenti scored for four string players. These earliest works have not quite the unquenchable flow of original ideas that the early symphonies have but, in such fresh performances as these, they make easy and enjoyable listening even if, with the performances generous in observing repeats, some movements outstay their welcome. The resonant ambience of the Unitarian Church in Budapest seems not unsuitable for works which lie midway between divertimenti and quartets, and the focus seems brighter and sharper on the second CD, recorded in June 1991, two months after the first.

String Quartets 9–10, Op. 2/4 & 6 (Le Matin); 35, Op. 42

(BB) **(*) Naxos 8.550732. Kodály Qt

The Unitarian Church, Budapest, continues to provide a warm, flattering tonal blend but a texture that is a little too ample for early Haydn, while the fairly close microphones reduce the dynamic range. However, the **Kodály's** friendly style and elegant finish suit early Haydn. These performers find exactly the right degree of expressiveness for the *Adagio* of Op. 2/4 and are equally at home in the engaging *Andante ed innocentemente* which opens the first movement of Op. 42, a splendid work, written a quarter of a century later.

String Quartets 15 in G, Op. 3/3; 16 in B flat, Op. 3/4; 17 in F (Serenade), Op. 3/5; 18 in A, Op. 3/6 – see HOFFSTETTER

String Quartets 19; 21–22, Op. 9/1, 3 & 4

(BB) *** Naxos 8.550786. Kodály Qt

String Quartets 20; 23; 24, Op. 9/2, 5 & 6

(BB) *** Naxos 8.550787. Kodály Qt

The **Kodály Quartet** are in excellent form throughout Opus 9. Their simple eloquence in all three slow movements on the first disc serves Haydn well: the *Largo* of Op. 9/3 is ideally paced and beautifully poised. The players then go on to give a captivating account of the finale. Indeed, all the finales here are superb, showing Haydn at full stretch. The last of the set in A major opens with a very attractive *Presto* in 6/8, which is delightfully buoyant here. Fortunately, the Naxos recording team (in December 1992 and January 1993) have mastered the acoustics of the Unitarian Church in Budapest. The microphones are in the right place and the sound is not inflated.

String Quartets 25–26; 28, Op. 17/1, 2 & 4

(BB) *** Naxos 8.550853. Kodály Qt

The **Kodály Quartet** seem very much at home in this music, which they approach with affection, yet with an appealing directness which leads to playing which is perfectly integrated, yet fresh. The recording could hardly be bettered: the balance is most natural.

String Quartets 27; 29; 30, Op. 17/3, 5 & 6

(BB) *** Naxos 8.550854-2. Kodály Qt

While the other works here are also played with pleasing warmth and finesse, the highlight of the second Naxos disc of Op. 17 is the *D major Quartet*, which has a searching, aria-like slow movement, dominated by the principal violin, which is played most eloquently here. This is the last of the set, and appropriately the last to be recorded in this highly distinguished Naxos series. The recording balance is quite admirable.

String Quartets 31–36 (Sun Quartets), Op. 20/1–6

(N) ⊕– **** CPO **SACD** 777 173-3 (2). Pellegrini Qt

⊕– **** Astrée E 8802 (2). Mosaïques Qt

The so-called 'Sun' *Quartets* mark a real step forward in Haydn's development of the medium. The most famous is Opus 20, No. 4 with its *Minuet alla Zigarese* and brilliant finale; but all six have something individual to say. They are played here with much vitality and pleasing intimacy between the **Pellegrini** players, and the surround sound is very realistic. But the slightly resonant acoustic means that one must be careful to set the volume level not too high on both pairs of speakers in order to give a completely realistic perspective.

Using period instruments, the four players of the **Mosaïques Quartet** create individual timbres which are pleasing to the ear and which have body and transparency, are perfectly matched and never edgy. There is no squeezed phrasing, and the use of vibrato is as subtle as the control of colour and dynamic. Intonation and ensemble are remarkably exact. Such is the calibre of this music-making and the strength of insight of these players that the character of these fine, relatively early works is communicated with seemingly total spontaneity. This is playing of rare distinction which is immensely revealing and rewarding, helped by state-of-the-art recording of complete realism and presence within an acoustic that provides the necessary intimacy of ambience.

String Quartets 31; 33; 34 (Sun), Op. 20/1, 3, & 4

**(*) ASV CDDCA 1027. Lindsay Qt

The **Lindsays** are at their finest in *No. 34 in D major* and make much of its theme and variations slow movement, brief Gypsy Minuet and scherzando finale. These recordings were apparently made under studio conditions and the playing in the slow movements of the other two *Quartets* has slightly less concentration than one has come to expect from their 'live' recordings. The sound is first class, and the extra finish of the ensemble brings its own rewards.

String Quartets 32; 34; 35, Op. 20/2, 5 & 6

☛ **** ASV CDDCA 1057. Lindsay Qt

These are three of Haydn's very greatest mid-period quartets, and the **Lindsays** have their full measure, with the feeling of 'live' music-making persisting throughout. The rich-textured opening of *No. 32 in C major* is immediately inviting, and the *Capriccio* second movement is most sensitively done, as is the lovely, rocking siciliano *Adagio* of *No. 34 in F minor*. The *Allegro di molto e scherzando* character of the first movement of the *A major* is perfectly caught. All three finales are fugal, and the lightness and keenness of articulation here is a joy. Excellent, truthful recording. Very highly recommended.

String Quartets 32, 34 (Sun), 35, Op. 20/2, 4 & 5; 40, Op. 33/4; 43, Op. 42; 44, 47, Op. 50/1 & 4; 67 (Lark), Op. 64/5; 70, Op. 71/2; 76 (Fifths), 77 (Emperor), 79, Op. 76/2, 3 & 5

Ⓑ *** ASV CDRSB 407 (4). Lindsay Qt

This rather arbitrary **Lindsay** collection consists of four separate live recitals, recorded at public performances at the 'Genius of Haydn' Festival at the Wigmore Hall in 1987.

String Quartets 32, Op. 20/2; 35, Op. 20/5; 39 (Bird), Op. 33/3; 43, Op. 42; 57–8, Op. 54/1 & 2; 79, Op. 76/5 (DVD version)

(*) Opus Arte **DVD OA 0920D. Lindsay Qt

The **Lindsays** were recorded and filmed at the 2004 Kuhmo Festival in Finland, with two of the seven *Quartets* (Nos. 35 and 43) caught at live performances. As always, the visual element increases the intensity of communication between performers and listeners, although here the camera moves from shot to shot rather arbitrarily and not always perceptively and is sometimes too close. Members of the quartet introduce each work, but the credits follow each performance, which is less than ideal for continued watching. A documentary film follows: '*4 Better or 4 Worse – The Anatomy of a String Quartet*' by Reiner Moritz, in which these players discuss the problems of quartet playing, with excerpts from rehearsals, including those of other comparable ensembles. In this instance we are probably best to stick to some of the Lindsays' audio recordings.

String Quartets 34 (Sun), Op. 20/4; 38 (Joke), Op. 33/2; 39 (Bird), Op. 33/3; 61 (Razor), Op. 55/2; 67 (Lark), Op. 64/5; 77 (Emperor), Op. 76/3

☛ Ⓜ *** ASV CDDCS 236 (2). Lindsay Qt

All these performances show the **Lindsays** on top form; indeed the *Sun Quartet* is the finest performance on the full-priced CD from which it comes. Anyone wanting a grouping of these named quartets (all masterpieces) cannot go wrong here as the recordings are all vividly real: the *Emperor*, for instance, which was recorded live, is very present indeed. The only snag is that a compilation like this cuts across other collections which group together works of a single Opus number.

String Quartets 34, Op. 20/4; 47, Op. 50/4; 77 (Emperor), Op. 76/3

*** ASV CDDCA 731. Lindsay Qt

The **Lindsays'** performances were again recorded at public performances, on this occasion in London's Wigmore Hall. The advantages this brings are twofold: higher spontaneity and a greater propensity to take risks. In all three performances the gains outweigh any loss, though the balance tends to cause some coarse-sounding tone in *fortissimo* passages.

String Quartets 37; 38 (Joke); 40, Op. 33/1–2 & 4

**(*) ASV CDDCA 937. Lindsay Qt

String Quartets 37–42, Op. 33/1–6

**** Astrée E 8801 (2). Mosaïques Qt

String Quartets 37–38 & 41, Op. 33/1–2 & 5

ⒷⒷ **(*) Naxos 8.550788. Kodály Qt

String Quartets 39–40 & 42, Op. 33/3–4 & 6

ⒷⒷ **(*) Naxos 8.550789. Kodály Qt

String Quartets 39 (Bird); 41 in G; 42, Op. 33/3, 5 & 6

☛ *** ASV CDDCA 938. Lindsay Qt

String Quartets 40; 41; 42 (How do you do?), Op. 33/4–6

*** Kingdom KCLCD 2015. Bingham Qt

The **Lindsays** are vividly alert and their playing is full of tension, emphasized by the recording, where the microphones are close, giving striking presence and stressing the bite on the timbre of the leader, **Peter Cropper**. Fortunately, the superb ensemble stands up to such scrutiny. No one could say that the Lindsays miss the wit inherent in the finale of the *Joke*; yet, in spite of the gentle ending, the smile is weakened by the vibrant purposefulness. The performances here use the Henle Urtext edition, which differs quite substantially in phrasing and, in places, even in notes from the more familiar Peters Edition, especially at the opening of Op. 33/1. The second disc includes a Rosette-worthy account of Op. 33/3 with Haydn's birdsong exquisitely simulated.

Those wanting Op. 33 on period instruments can be recommended without reservation to the **Mosaïques Quartet**, whose performances are more penetrating than any of their competitors. Indeed the intensity of the playing is remarkable, with concentration held throughout the widest range of dynamic, and constantly uncovering hidden depths in these works, even in the *Joke Quartet*. There are touches of darkness, as well as serenity, in *adagios*; and finales dance with fairy lightness, while the crisply pointed *Allegretto* which ends Op. 33/6 has a Beechamesque rhythmic panache. Marvellous playing throughout, with every detail revealed in sound which is both transparent, yet never in the least texturally meagre. The superb recording is perfectly balanced.

The tonal matching and ensemble of the **Bingham Quartet** are most impressive, with the leader, Stephen Bingham, a remarkably stylish player who really understands how to shape a Haydn phrase. Above all the Binghams convey their pleasure in the music, and every performance here sounds fresh. The recording was made at the Conway Hall, London, in 1990. The balance is a shade close, but the instruments are naturally focused, individually and as a group. Even if the range of dynamic is a little affected, the playing itself is full of light and shade so that if the volume level is carefully set one soon forgets this reservation in the sheer pleasure this music affords.

The **Kodály Quartet** play Op. 33 with an easy, relaxed warmth. Their style is low-key so that the 'Joke' finale of Op. 33/2 is rather gentle and muted; on the other hand, the reason for the sobriquet of the *Bird Quartet* is affectionately conveyed and the finale is delightfully light-hearted. Slow movements are serene and quietly musical. Minuets are generally full of character, with the Trios nicely realized, and this applies especially to the charming middle section of the Scherzo in the *Joke Quartet*. In short these are performances which convey the players' affection for this wonderful music, with no possible desire to put their own personalities between composer and listener. The Naxos recording is wholly natural, with the acoustics of the Budapest Unitarian Church beautifully caught without any textural inflation.

String Quartet 39 in C (Bird), Op. 33/3

🎞️ 🌑 (BB) **** Dutton mono CDBP 9702. Griller Qt –
MOZART: *String Quartets 14–15 (Haydn Quartets)* **** 🌑

This simply is one of the finest Haydn quartet recordings ever put on disc, and the Dutton transfer from the 1946 Decca *ffrr* 78s miraculously provides a sound–quality superior to many modern digital stereo recordings. The **Griller** were in their absolute prime at the time. You need only sample the grace and finesse of the first movement, with its engaging chirping, the serene blending of timbre in the *Adagio* and the elegance of the closing *Rondo* to realize that this playing is very special indeed, as is the recording.

String Quartets 43 in D min., Op. 42; 81; 82, Op. 77/1–2; 83, Op. 103

🎞️ 🌑 **** ASV Gold GLD 4010. Lindsays Qt

Haydn's last three *Quartets* are exceptionally well served on CD, with outstanding versions by the Kocian Quartet (Praga PR 250157) and by the Mosaïques on period instruments (Astrée E 8800). But these 'swan song' versions by the **Lindsays** are outstanding in every way and, with an engaging account of Op. 42 thrown in for good measure, this is not only generous but also one of their most cherishable records.

But it is in the Op. 77 *Quartets* that the Lindsays' response is most fully stretched. The bouncing lift of the opening *Allegro moderato* of the G major is irresistible, and the *Adagio* has wonderful expressive delicacy and dynamic subtlety, with the buoyant Minuet producing a surge of dancing energy in the remarkable Trio, and the rustic finale brimming with imaginative contrasts. Altogether this is a splendid collection that, with Opus 42 placed third in the programme, makes a very satisfying concert. The recording is very real and immediate.

String Quartets 44–49, Op. 50/1–6

(BB) *** Naxos 8.553983 (Nos. 44–46); 8.553984 (Nos. 47–49) (available separately). Kodály Qt

*** ASV Gold GLD 4007 (1–3); GLD 4008 (4–6). Lindsays Qt

The **Kodály Quartet** are back to their finest form in Op. 50 and they are most naturally recorded. These are mellow performances, warm and polished, with perfect blending of timbre, yet refined detail. Slow movements are beautifully shaped, with the leader, **Attila Falvay**, frequently distinguishing himself with the graceful finish of his phrasing. *Allegros* are spirited but unforced, Minuets have an affectionate modicum of wit, and finales are never rushed.

The **Lindsays'** set of Op. 50 are superbly played and recorded. Their approach is less mellow, less affectionate than that of the Kodály Quartet, who are not surpassed, but the playing is very stimulating indeed.

String Quartets 50–56 (The Seven Last Words of Our Saviour on the Cross), Op. 51

🎞️ 🌑 **** ASV CDDCA 853. Lindsay Qt

**** Astrée E 8803. Mosaïques Qt

🎞️ (BB) **** Naxos 8.550346. Kodály Qt

The recording by the **Lindsay Quartet**, while offering all the devotional gravity that Haydn demands, brings not just an illuminating variety but also a sense of drama, and the performance makes no compromise for, unlike some others, the Lindsays observe the first-half repeats in each movement, extending the work to a full 70 minutes, instead of under an hour. After the long sequence of slow movements, the Lindsays' account of the final, brief *Presto, Il terremoto*, then conveys the full, elemental force of the earthquake. It is thrilling with so elusive a work to have so complete an answer in a single recording, with sound both well defined and glowingly beautiful, set against an apt church acoustic.

The slightly austere style of the **Mosaïques Quartet** is perfectly suited to the sometimes withdrawn, expressive intensity of Haydn's collection of seven *Adagios*. The Introduction is immediately commanding, and throughout the playing combines strength with subtlety, with the fifth and sixth movements gaining from the lean timbre, delicacy of feeling and great concentration, and the seventh (which Haydn marks 'Pater in tuas manus commendo spiritum meum') finding a natural resolution. The final 'earthquake' could hardly be more forcefully telling. Excellent, vivid recording within a well-judged ambience.

The **Kodály Quartet**, too, give a memorable performance, strongly characterized and beautifully played, with subtle contrasts of expressive tension between the seven inner slow movements. They also offer an appropriate bonus in Haydn's last, unfinished, two-movement *Quartet*. The recording is first rate, vividly present yet naturally balanced.

String Quartets 57–59, Op. 54/1–3

⊕ *** HM Aeon AECD 0313. Ysaÿe Qt

*** ASV CDDCA 582. Lindsay Qt

(BB) *** Naxos 8.550395. Kodály Qt

*** Hyp. CDA 66971. Salomon Qt

These **Ysaÿe** performances can rank with the very best. Playing and ensemble are first class and there is plenty of warmth: the *Adagio* of the *C major*, Op. 54/2, is particularly fine, and the finale is most impressively handled. The slow movement of the *E major*, too, is beautifully judged, and the finale is both graceful and spirited. Excellent, well-balanced recording and a friendly atmosphere to make this a most enjoyable disc.

The playing of the **Lindsay Quartet** is splendidly poised and vital, and the recording is very fine indeed.

The **Kodály** players enter animatedly into the spirit of the music; the leader, **Attila Falvay**, shows himself fully equal to Haydn's bravura embellishments in the demanding first violin writing. The Naxos sound is fresh and truthful.

The **Salomon Quartet**, led by **Simon Standage**, play on period instruments, but there is nothing anaemic or edgy about the body of tone they command, and the pervading feeling here is of freshness, with finales spirited without being rushed off their feet. This is one of the very best records from these excellent players, and the recording is first class.

String Quartets 57–59, Op. 54/1–3; 72; 73; 74, Op. 74/1–3

(BB) *** Virgin 2x1 5 61436-2 (2). Endellion Qt

The **Endellion Quartet** were recorded in The Maltings, Snape (in 1988 and 1990 respectively), which provides an ideal acoustic environment. The playing is bright-eyed, fresh and vital, and in both sets they prove a sound guide to this repertoire. The sound is strikingly immediate but is beautifully integrated, and there are many moments of musical insight. With the two discs offered for the cost of a single mid-priced CD, this set is very competitive.

String Quartet 58 in C, Op. 54/2

⊕ *** Avie AV 2092. Szymanowski Qt –– BACEWICZ: *Quartet 4* ***; DVOŘÁK: *Quartet 14* **(*)

A wonderfully polished account of the *C major Quartet* from the **Szymanowski Quartet**; indeed, their playing in the first movement can only be described as exquisite. The *Adagio* too is gently intense, but some listeners might find here that the players' warmth of response is almost too sensuously expressive for Haydn. But they are beautifully recorded, and this is difficult to resist.

String Quartets 60; 61 (Razor); 62, Op. 55/1–3 (Tost Quartets)

*** ASV CDDCA 906. Lindsay Qt

(BB) **(*) Naxos 8.550397. Kodály Qt

Here the **Lindsays** are heard under studio conditions, but in Holy Trinity Church, Wentworth, and the results, on the second set of *Tost Quartets*, are marginally less chimerical than in their live recordings, but not less dedicated or less vital. There is of course greater polish, as the fizzing finale of Op. 55/3 readily demonstrates. The recording is lifelike and vivid without excessive resonance.

Opus 55 brings playing from the **Kodály Quartet** which is undoubtedly spirited and generally polished, but the music-making at times seems plainer than usual in the Naxos series. The recording is bright and clear, with a realistic presence.

String Quartets 63–65, Op. 64/1–3

⊕ *** ASV CDDCA 1083. Lindsay Qt

*** Hyp. CDA 67011. Salomon Qt

(BB) *** Naxos 8.550673. Kodály Qt

String Quartets 66; 67 (Lark); 68, Op. 64/4–6

*** Hyp. CDA 67012. Salomon Qt

(BB) *** Naxos 8.550674. Kodály Qt

Op. 64 are splendidly played by the **Lindsays**. The slow movements of the *B minor* and *B flat major* are particularly searching. First-class recording.

The **Salomon** performances are well up to the standard of their versions of the earlier works. Their timbre is leaner than that of the estimable Kodály Quartet on Naxos but they blend beautifully and have their own insights to offer: their precise ensemble in no way inhibits commitment and feeling. The second of the two discs is particularly rewarding, with the famous opening movement of the *Lark* readily taking flight and the *Adagio* poised and intense. The Hyperion recording is admirably truthful.

These **Kodály** performances are all enjoyable, but the set seems to get better and better as it progresses. Op. 64/1–3 were recorded on 25–29 April 1992; the last to be done, the *B flat major*, is remarkably successful, with a vigorous opening *Vivace assai* and a rapt *Adagio*. The other three works were taped on 1–3 May, and clearly the group had found its top form. The *Adagio cantabile e sostenuto* of No. 4 finds them at their most concentrated: the *Lark* has never soared aloft more spontaneously and the Minuet and finale of No. 6 close the set in a winningly spirited fashion. The warm acoustics of the Budapest Unitarian Church provide a mellow and expansive sound-image, but not an orchestral one, and detail remains clear. A most enjoyable set.

String Quartets 63, 65 & 68, Op. 64/1, 3 & 6

*** Astrée E 8886. Mosaïques Qt

Immaculate period-instrument performances from the **Mosaïques**, with absolutely no rough edges. They are beautifully played in every respect, but are a little cool by the side of the Lindsays. However, admirers of 'authentic' Haydn will find this well up to standard, and the recording is very lifelike.

String Quartets 67 in D (Lark), Op. 64/5; 76 in D min. (Fifths), Op. 76/2; 81 in G, Op. 77/1

**** HM HMC 901823. Jesusalem Qt

The **Jerusalem Quartet** is a first-class group and they give outstanding performances of these three masterpieces. In the *D major*, the 'Lark' soars aloft sweetly and disarmingly, and after a beautifully played *Adagio* the finale has the lightest possible touch. The first movement of the *Fifths* is faster than usual, but convincingly so, and the following *Andante* is delightfully elegant. Similarly, the opening movement of the *G major* dances along with engaging rhythmic pointing, and the *Adagio* that follows is comparably searching. The recording is beautifully balanced and sounds very real in a most suitable acoustic. Highly recommended (alongside the Lindsays on ASV).

String Quartets 69–71 (Apponyi Quartets), Op. 71/1–3; 72–74 (Rider), Op. 74/1–3

⊕➝ (BB) **** Naxos 8.550394 (69–71); 8.550396 (72–74). Kodály Qt

(M) *** Arcana A 918 (2). Festetics Qt

The Naxos recordings by the **Kodály Quartet** are outstanding in every way and would be highly recommendable even without their considerable price advantage. The digital recording has vivid presence and just the right amount of ambience: the effect is entirely natural.

The **Festetics Quartet** continue their period-instrument Haydn series with beautifully judged performances of Opp. 71 and 74. The playing has the customary animation and finish, with detail perceptively observed, and well-blended yet beautifully transparent textures. As before, there is nothing vinegary here, and phrasing and line are impeccably musical. Minuets are pleasing, without heaviness (sample the

Trio of Op. 71/3 for delectable articulation) and finales sparkle. These are three-star performances without a doubt, and the recording could hardly be better judged. One's only reservation concerns slow movements, sometimes a little solemn.

String Quartets 72–74, Op. 74/1–3

⊕➝ *** Sup. Praga **SACD** Surround Sound PRD/DSD 250 212. Kocian Qt

*** ASV Gold GLD 4013. Lindsays Qt

As usual, the **Lindsays** are on top form with their vital, imaginative and highly spontaneous performances, which are among the best on record, and excellently balanced.

But the **Kocians** are pretty marvellous too. Their blending is a joy, without any loss of individuality among the players, and they are vital too, with finales sparkling irresistibly, especially the famous *Rider* rhythm of the *G major*. But what caps these performances are the beautifully played slow movements, especially of Nos. 73 and 74. Moreover, the realism of the Praga recording, with the back speakers carefully balanced to add just ambient effect, is astonishingly realistic.

String Quartets 75; 76 (Fifths); 77 (Emperor); 78 (Sunrise); 79; 80, Op. 76/1–6 (Erdödy Quartets)

⊕➝ ✿ **** ASV CDDCA 1076 (75–77); CDDCA 1077 (78–80). Lindsay Qt

*** Astrée E 8665 (2). Mosaïques Qt

(BB) **** Naxos 8.550314 (75–77); 8.550315; (78–80). Kodály Qt

String Quartets 76 (Fifths); 77 (Emperor); 78 (Sunrise), Op. 76/2–4

⊕➝ (BB) *** Naxos 8.550129. Kodály Qt

(M) *** EMI 5 56166-2. Alban Berg Qt

(BB) *** Warner Apex 0927 40824-2. Eder Qt

The **Lindsays** crown their series of Haydn recordings with this superb set of the supreme masterpieces from Op. 76, marvellously played and truthfully recorded. In their hands these *Quartets* are made to sound among the greatest ever written, which of course they are. The Lindsays have covered three of these works before, in live recordings, but this time not only is the sound more refined, the performances are too, while keeping the strength and warmth which characterize all the Lindsays' playing. The later quartets are equally fine. Very highly recommended.

The **Kodály Quartet** too are fully worthy of the composer's inexhaustible invention and make a splendid bargain recommendation. Their playing brings a joyful pleasure in Haydn's inspiration and there is not the slightest suspicion of over-rehearsal or of routine: every bar of the music springs to life spontaneously, and these musicians' insights bring an ideal combination of authority and warmth, emotional balance and structural awareness.

The leonine style and comparatively spare textures that are the essential feature of the playing of the **Mosaïques Quartet** are immediately apparent at the opening of the first of the *Erdödy* set and undoubtedly cast a new and different light on Haydn's supreme masterpieces in this genre. Every detail of the polyphonic emerges clearly, but with no sense of didacticism. The recording could hardly be bettered, transparent and beautifully focused within a pleasing ambience. If you already have a modern-instrument recording of these marvellous works, this is surely an essential supplement.

The **Alban Berg Quartet's** recordings of Op. 76 offers peerless playing, with poised slow movements, simply and beautifully played, yet with every note perfectly in place. At times one might venture a suspicion that everything is too perfectly calculated, but such a judgement would be unfair, for Haydn's spirit hovers over this music-making. Perhaps they could smile a little more here. Nevertheless this is playing of distinction, bringing impeccable blending and ensemble. Although the recording is brightly lit and the effect a shade too up-front, it is realistic and admirably balanced.

The **Eder** is a Hungarian Quartet which came to the fore in the early to mid-1980s, when these recordings were made. The players command a refined and beautiful tone, with generally excellent ensemble and polish. These are elegant performances that are unlikely to disappoint even the most demanding listener, save perhaps in the finale of the *Emperor*, which they take a little too quickly. They are unfailingly thoughtful players whose internal balance and tonal blend are practically flawless. The recording is altogether excellent and this reissue is a bargain.

String Quartets 75–80, Op. 76/1–6; 81–2, Op. 77/1–2; 83, Op. 103

(M) *** DG (ADD) Trio 471 762-2 (3). Amadeus Qt

Haydn's late quartets have much the same expansiveness and depth as the symphonies, and here the **Amadeus** succeed in conveying both their intimacy and their sense of scale. The recordings are bright and truthful. Those who invest in this Trio will find much to reward them, though in Op. 76 the Kodály Quartet are even finer. However, the Amadeus accounts of the two Op. 77 *Quartets* are outstanding, as is the unfinished *D minor*, Op. 103. They are on their finest form here. There is a sense of spontaneity as well as a genuine breadth to these readings. The recordings have a warm acoustic and plenty of presence.

String Quartet 76, Op. 76/2

(**(*)) Testament mono SBT 1085. Hollywood Qt – HUMMEL: *Quartet in G* *(*); MOZART: *Quartet 17* **(*)

The **Hollywood Quartet** were recorded at a memorable concert in London's Royal Festival Hall in September 1957. These recordings have never been available before. The playing can only be described as impeccable, not surprisingly so, given the tonal beauty and musical sophistication these artists commanded; and the sound is astonishingly good for the period. There are a couple of minutes of balance test and a brief exchange among the players.

String Quartet 79 in D, Op. 76/5

*** Telarc CD 80415. Cleveland Qt – CORIGLIANO: *Quartet* ***

This is a superb performance, the noble simplicity of the slow movement gravely and movingly caught, and the racy

finale as spick and span as it is exhilarating. Outstandingly fine recording, too, and if the coupling is unexpected it is certainly rewarding.

String Quartets 81; 82, Op. 77/1–2; 83, Op. 103

🎧—**** Astrée E 8800. Mosaïques Qt

🎧—*** HM PRD 250 157. Kocian Qt

*** Australian Decca Eloquence 476 2575. Takács Qt

*** Hyp. CDA 66348. Salomon Qt

String Quartets 81; 82, Op. 77/1–2

(BB) ** Naxos 8.553146. Kodály Qt

Using period instruments to totally convincing effect, the **Mosaïques Quartet** give outstanding performances of Haydn's last three *Quartets*. They play with much subtlety of colour and dynamic and bring total concentration to every bar of the music. The *D minor Quartet*, Haydn's last, is beautifully judged. The recording is absolutely real: the sound is transparent as well as immediate. This is among the finest of all Haydn quartet records.

Those preferring modern-instrument performances could hardly do better than invest in the **Kocian Quartet**. *Allegros* sparkle, ensemble is clean and true, and slow movements are beautifully played, notably the eloquent variations of Op. 77/2, but also the *Andante grazioso* of Haydn's last *Quartet*, where the hint of melancholy is nicely understated. The recording is very real, the players not too close in an attractive acoustic.

The **Takács Quartet** play with warmth, expressive refinement and vitality, and the Decca recording has clean, well-focused sound, with just about the right degree of resonance. Though this is not perhaps a first choice, their admirers need not hesitate.

The **Salomon**, recorded in a less ample acoustic, produce an altogether leaner sound but one that is thoroughly responsive to every shift in Haydn's thought. They seem to have great inner vitality and feeling.

The **Kodály Quartet** give comparatively robust performances of both works, made to seem even more robust by the close balance which reduces the dynamic range – not that the playing is notable for *pianissimo* contrast. This is warm, friendly music-making and in that respect (and in that respect only) preferable to the Mosaïques; but the latter's playing has considerably more subtlety, and they offer an extra work.

PIANO MUSIC

(i) Divertimento (The Master and his Pupil) for piano duet, Hob XVII/2; Arietta with 12 Variations, Hob XVII/3; Capriccio in G, Hob XVII/1; Theme & Variations in C, Hob XVII/5; 20 Variations in G, Hob XVII/2; Variations on the Austrian Anthem (after Hob XIII/77)

(BB) *** Naxos 8.553972. Jandó (piano), (i) with Kollár

A fascinatingly diverting disc in all respects. The engaging if over-long piano duet, *Il Maestro lo Scolare* (with the two-part dialogue nicely separated on a single piano in the recording) was transcribed from a baryton trio in 1766/8. It opens with an echo of Handel's *Harmonious Blacksmith* and (obviously a teacher–pupil exercise) gets progresssively more difficult. The closing section is a Minuet. The *Arietta* is also based on a Minuet – from Haydn's *String Quartet No. 20*, Op. 9/2, while the *Capriccio* takes a folk song as its basis with the unlikely title of *Acht Sauschnider müssen sein* ('It takes eight to castrate a boar') and the variations on the famous *Emperor* theme are a transcription of the slow movement of the string quartet with that nickname, Op. 76/1. **Jenö Jandó** plays everything in his freshly direct, classical manner and he is expertly joined by **Zsuzsa Kollár** in the four-handed work. The recording is clear and clean.

PIANO SONATAS

Piano Sonatas 1–16; 17–19 (Hob Deest) 20; 28, Hob XIV/5; 29–62, Hob XVI/1–52 & G1; Hob XVII/D1; The Seven Last Words on the Cross; Adagio in F; Capriccio in G on the song 'Acht Sauschneider müssen sein'; Fantasia in C; 7 Minuets from 'Kleine Tänz für die Jugend'; Variations in F min.; 5 Variations in D; 6 Variations in C; 12 Variations in E flat; 20 Variations in A

Ⓑ *** Decca (ADD) 443 785-2 (12). McCabe (piano)

Two things shine through **John McCabe's** performances: their complete musicianship and their fine imagination. In presenting them as he does on a modern piano, McCabe makes the most of the colour and subtlety of the music, and in that respect his style is more expressive, less overtly classical than Jandó's (see below) while the recording is made to sound somewhat softer-grained by the acoustic of All Saints' Church, Petersham. Given phrasing so clearly articulated and alertly phrased, and such varied, intelligently thought-out and wholly responsive presentation, this set can be recommended very enthusiastically. The recordings are of the very highest quality, truthful in timbre and firmly refined in detail. The set is most reasonably priced and the pianist provides his own extensive and illuminating notes. To sample the calibre of this enterprise, begin with *The Seven Last Words* – playing of unexaggerated expressive feeling that almost makes one believe this was a work conceived in pianistic terms.

Piano Sonatas 1–62 (complete); Seven Last Words of our Saviour on the Cross; Miscellaneous Solo Works, including Fantasia in C; German Dances & Minuets. Variations

Ⓝ ℗→ ⒝⒝ *** BIS CD 1731/3 (15). Brautigam (fortepiano)

Ronald Brautigam's survey has great vitality and spontaneity and he is most realistically recorded. If you want a complete set of the Haydn piano sonatas, this would probably be a first choice. The documentation is excellent and the 15 discs come for the price of three.

Piano Sonatas 1-61 (complete); Adagios in F & G; 2 Allegrettos in G; Arietta with 12 Variations in A;

Fantasia in C; Variations (Sonata un piccolo divertimento) in F min.

Ⓝ ℗→ ⒝⒝ *** Naxos 8.51042 (10). Jandó

Jenö Jandó, too, seems to be in his element throughout his Haydn survey. His freshness of approach and stylistic confidence are consistently striking. The recording also is excellent, and overall this Naxos series can be recommended with equal confidence to its competitor on BIS. It comes with the comprehensive booklet detailing the Piano Sonatas, String Quartets, Concertos and Symphonies.

Keyboard (Divertimento) Sonatas 1–20, Hob XVI/1–16 & G1; D1; 17–18, Hob Es2 & 3; 19, Hob XVI/47; 20, Hob XVI/18

Ⓜ *** BIS CD 1293/4 (3). Brautigam (fortepiano)

Ronald Brautigam here turns to the early 'Divertimeno' sonatas that were written in the 1750s and 1760s for the clavichord or harpsichord. Brautigam uses a fortepiano, a copy by Paul McNulty of a mid-1790s instrument by Walter. Many of the earlier sonatas are of little consequence and Haydn did not include them in his list of complete keyboard works that he made for Breitkopf. The more individual sonatas, such as the *E minor*, No. 19, Hob XVI/47, and the *B flat*, No. 20, Hob XVI/18, come from the 1760s and are played with imagination and delicacy. Good playing and exemplary recording, but ultimately the set is for completists.

Piano Sonatas 1, Hob. XVI/8; 2, Hob XVI/7; 3, Hob XVI/9; 4, Hob XVI/G1; 5, Hob XVI/11; 6, Hob XVI/10; 7, Hob XVII/D1; 8, Hob XVI/5; 9, Hob XVI/4; 10, Hob XVI/1

⒝⒝ *** Naxos 8.553824. Jandó

There are no autograph manuscripts of Haydn's earliest sonatas, which were all written before 1766. The authenticity of No. 1 (Hob XVI/8) is certain, and many of the others of these three-movement works bear the same musical fingerprint and a characteristic simplicity of style. Doubts have been expressed about No. 8 (Hob XVI/5), but it is presented attractively enough here.

Piano Sonatas 11, Hob XVI/2; 12, Hob XVI/12; 13, Hob XVI/6; 14, Hob XVI/3; 15, Hob XVI/13; 16, Hob XVI/14; 18, Hob XVI deest

⒝⒝ *** Naxos 8.553825. Jandó

These early sonatas are all played freshly in **Jandó's** pleasingly direct style. All but one are simple, three-movement works; the exception is *No. 13 in G*, which has an appealing additional *Adagio* which Jandó treats simply but appealingly. The recording is truthful and this issue, Volume 8 in the series, cannot be faulted.

Piano Sonatas 20, Hob XVI/18; 30, Hob XVI/19; 31, Hob XVI/46; 32, Hob XVI/44

⒝⒝ **(*) Naxos 8.553364. Jandó

The first movement of the *G minor Sonata* is particularly appealing, with its neat articulation and tight little runs, and the same might be said of the opening movement of the *A flat major* (No. 31), while its finale is similarly bright and sparkling. But first prize goes to the closing movement of the *D major*, which skips along delightfully and brings quite dazzling dexterity. The thoughtful *Adagio* of the *B flat major*, however, is just a little too studied; but this is not enough of a disadvantage to prevent a recommendation. The piano recording is very realistic.

Piano Sonatas 22 in D; 38 in F; 42 in G ; 48 in C, Hob XVI/37; 23; 27; 35; Divertimento in A flat, Hob XVI/46; Parthia in E flat, Hob XVI/Es3

(N) *** Nim. NI 5847. Lester (historic fortepianos)

The interest of this collection is to compare the sound of the different instruments on which **Richard Lester** plays these six works so brightly and freshly. The *Sonatas in D, F, G* and *C* are performed on a Schantz instrument now in the Holbourne Museum in Bath, very like the one Haydn purchased himself in 1788. Of the four the *C major* seems especially suited to the drier timbre. The other two pieces are played on an unidentified instrument from northern Italy dating from around 1790 and restored by Michael Cole. This has a sonority more closely comparable with a modern piano and suits the music very well indeed.

Piano Sonatas 23 in F; 24 in D; 32 in B min.; 37 in D; 40 in G; 41 in B flat; 43 in A flat; 46 in A flat; 50 in C; 52 in E flat

🎧 **** Hyp. CDA 67554 (2). Hamelin

Hamelin till now has excelled in his recordings in the high romantic virtuoso repertory; but here he reveals himself as a fine classicist, fresh and stylish and always conveying the feeling of live communication. His speeds for *Allegros* are phenomenally fast, yet the clarity of articulation and the springing of rhythms prevent them from sounding breathless, and in slower movements he allows himself full breadth over tempo without ever resorting to unstylish phrasing. From beginning to end in these ten sonatas (and three of the very finest among them) Hamelin has one spellbound over the boundless inventiveness of Haydn as keyboard composer. A superb pair of discs, standing out in this repertoire.

Piano Sonatas 24, Hob XVI/26; 30, Hob XVI/19; 32, Hob XVI/44; 33, Hob XVI/20; 44, Hob XVI/29

🎧 ✿ **** EMI 5 56756-2. Andsnes

Playing of great elegance and consummate artistry, the finest Haydn sonata recording to have appeared for a long time. Very different in approach from Pletnev's 1989 recital (see below) – the repertoire does not overlap – but no less individual or persuasive. The young Norwegian pianist plays with rare imagination and keyboard colour, and the EMI sound is first class. The recordings are all made in Abbey Road, save for the *E flat* (No. 44), which was recorded in Oslo.

Piano Sonatas 28 in D, Hob XVI/5a; 29 in E flat, Hob XVI/45; 30 in D, Hob XVI/19

*** BIS CD 1174. Brautigam

Piano Sonatas 35 in A flat, Hob XVI/43; 36 in C, Hob XVI/21; 37 in F, Hob XVI/22; 38 in F, Hob XVI/23

*** BIS CD 1095. Brautigam

Ronald Brautigam continues his much and rightly admired Haydn odyssey. We can only re-echo our continued enthusiasm for this set. Brautigam has tremendous life and combines apparent spontaneity of expression and scholarship. The recordings are altogether exemplary.

Piano Sonatas 29; 31; 34; 35; 49, Hob XVI/45, 46, 33, 43 & 36

🎧 **** Sony SK 89363. Ax

These elegant accounts by **Emanuel Ax** are fluent and unmannered, sensitive and vital, and they are very well recorded. An excellent sampler for some of the composer's most attractive keyboard works.

Piano Sonatas 29, Hob XVI/45; 33, Hob XVI/20; 34, Hob XVI/33; 35, Hob XVI/43

(BB) *** Naxos 8.553800. Jandó

Jandó is on very good form here. His style is a little plain and classical but never insensitive, and he is well recorded. A useful addition to a fine series.

Piano Sonatas 31, Hob XVI/46; 45–47, Hob XVI/30–32

*** BIS CD 1094. Brautigam

Piano Sonatas 32, Hob XVI/44; 34, Hob XVI/33; 42–4, Hob XVI/27–29

*** BIS CD 1093. Brautigam

These two recordings in **Ronald Brautigam's** ongoing Haydn cycle are devoted to the sonatas of 1776, and they are as refreshing and alive as earlier issues in this eminently collectable series. He uses a copy made in 1992 by Paul McNulty of a fortepiano by Anton Gabriel Walter from about 1795. Wonderful recorded sound.

Piano Sonatas 32 in G min., Hob XVI/44; 33 in C min., Hob XVI/20; 53 in E min., Hob XVI/34; 54 in G, Hob XVI/40; 58 in C, Hob. XVI/48

🎧 (M) *** Warner Elatus 2564 60677-2. Schiff

Piano Sonatas 59–62, Hob XVI/49–52; Fantasia in C, Hob XVII/4

🎧 (M) *** Warner Elatus 2564 60807-2. Schiff

András Schiff's Haydn recordings were recorded in the Berlin Teldec studios by Christopher Raeburn, one of Decca's most distinguished producers, this is a collection issue of high quality.

Piano Sonatas 32 in G min.; 49 in C sharp min.; 59 in E flat; 62 in E flat

*** Signum SIGCH 0097. Lill

It is good to see **John Lill** returning to the recording studio in very good form and in a well-chosen selection of Haydn sonatas. His style is plain, but none the worse for that, for the *Adagio* slow movements of both the two *E flat Sonatas* are particularly fine, and in all these works his poise and clear articulation give much pleasure. He is excellently recorded too.

Piano Sonatas 33, Hob XVI/20; 39, Hob XVI/39; 40, Hob XVI/25; 41, Hob XVI/26

*** BIS CD 1163. Brautigam (fortepiano)

Piano Sonatas 35, Hob XVI/43; 36, Hob XVI/21; 37, Hob XVI/22; 38, Hob XVI/23

*** BIS CD 1095. Brautigam (fortepiano)

With the present pair of CDs **Brautigam** reaches the *Esterházy Sonatas* (Nos. 36–41), dating from 1773. The additional sonatas, *No. 33 in C minor* (Hob XVI/20) and *No. 35 in A flat* (Hob XVI/43) come from 1771 and the period 1771–3 respectively.

Piano Sonatas 33, Hob XVI/20; 47, Hob XVI/32; 53, Hob XVI/34; 50, Hob XVI/37; 54, Hob XVI/40; 56, Hob XVI/42; 58–62, Hob XVI/48–52; Adagio in F, Hob XVII/9; Andante with Variations in F min., Hob XVII/6; Fantasia in C, Hob XVII/4

🎧 **** Ph. (ADD/DDD) 478 1369 (4). Brendel

This collection offers some of the best Haydn playing on record – and some of the best **Brendel**, too. The eleven sonatas, together with the *F minor Variations* and the *C major Fantasia* are splendidly characterized and superbly recorded. The first is analogue, the remainder digital.

Piano Sonatas 33, Hob XVI/20; 60, Hob XVI/50; 62, Hob XVI/52; Andante & Variations in F min., Hob XVII/6

🎧 (BB) **** Virgin 2x1 5 61881-2 (2). Pletnev – *Piano Concertos, Hob XVIII/4, 7 & 11* ****

Pletnev's reading of the *Sonatas* is full of personality and character. The *C major* is given with great elegance and wit, and the great *E flat Sonata* is magisterial. This playing has a masterly authority, and Pletnev is very well recorded. Now coupled with his equally memorable accounts of Haydn's three finest piano concertos, this reissue is a splendid bargain and one not to be missed.

Piano Sonatas 36, Hob XVI/21; 37, Hob XVI/22; 38, Hob XVI/23; 39, Hob XVI/24; 40, Hob XVI/25; 41, Hob XVI/26

(BB) *** Naxos 8.553127. Jandó

The sonatas in Volume 5 of the Naxos series form a set of six, written in 1773 and dedicated to Prince Nikolaus Esterházy. They are all attractive works and they inspire **Jandó** to consistently fine performances. This is one of the most rewarding issues in this admirable series. Excellent piano sound.

Piano Sonatas 42, Hob XVI/27; 43, Hob XVI/28; 44, Hob XVI/29; 45, Hob XVI/30; 46, Hob XVI/31; 47, Hob XVI/32

(BB) *** Naxos 8.550844. Jandó (piano)

The last work here, in B minor, opens with perhaps the most striking idea of all and, after the gracious central Minuet, ends in a flurry of precocious virtuosity, with **Jandó** clearly in his element. He shows himself a complete master of this repertoire, and the recording, crisp and clean but not too dry, is first class.

Piano Sonatas 48, Hob XVI/35; 49, Hob XVI/36; 50, Hob XVI/37; 51, Hob XVI/38; 52 in G, Hob XVI/39

(BB) *** Naxos 8.553128. Jandó

The opening movement of No. 49 and the memorable *Largo e sostenuto* of No. 50 (and its infectious finale) show **Jandó** in top form; in the other works his bright, stylish playing is always responsive to Haydn's direct, lively manner. The recording is well up to the high standard of this series.

Piano Sonatas 48, Hob XVI/35; 49, Hob XVI/36; 50, Hob XVI/37; 51, Hob XVI/38; 52, Hob XVI/39

*** BIS CD 992. Brautigam (fortepiano)

Piano Sonatas 53, Hob XVI/34; 54, Hob XVI/40; 55, Hob XVI/41; 56, Hob XVI/42; 57, Hob XVI/47; 58, Hob XVI/48

(M) *** BIS CD 300993. Brautigam (fortepiano)

Piano Sonatas 59, Hob XVI/49; 60, Hob XVI/50; 61, Hob XVI/51; 62, Hob XVI/52

*** BIS CD 994. Brautigam (fortepiano)

Ronald Brautigam's first disc here is given over to five of the so-called *Auenbrugger Sonatas*. Brautigam is hardly less vital and imaginative here than in Mozart. Apart from his technical virtuosity, his playing has tremendous flair and sparkle. The second disc (CD 300993) includes the *Bossler Sonatas* (Nos. 54–6). Brautigam gives them with tremendous flair and, in fact the whole disc is a delight from beginning to end. The third (CD 994) brings the *Genzinger Sonata* (No. 59), so named because Marianne von Genzinger was its dedicatee, and three *London Sonatas*, composed in 1794–5, when Haydn was in his early sixties. Exhilarating playing which augurs well for the rest of the series.

Piano Sonatas 53, Hob XVI/34; 54, Hob XVI/40; 55, Hob XVI/41; 56, Hob XVI/42; 58, Hob XVI/48; Variations in F min. (Sonata, un piccolo divertimento), Hob XVII/6

(BB) *** Naxos 8.550845. Jandó (piano)

These are appealing performances of the three *Sonatas*, Hob XVI/40–42, dedicated to Princess Marie Esterházy. **Jandó** also gives a splendid account of the more ambitious three-movement *Sonata in E minor*, Hob XVI/34. He is a true Haydn player, and this is in every way recommendable, particularly as the recording is so vivid and clean: just right for the repertoire.

Piano Sonatas 58–62, Hob XVI/48–52

(M) *(**) Sony SMK 87857. Gould

Glenn Gould recorded Haydn's last five *Piano Sonatas* in 1981/2 and his clean, classical style is often refreshing, but after a while his squeaky-clean articulation, although quite remarkably crisp, becomes a little wearing and the ear craves less staccato and a less percussive approach to *allegros* and the irritating vocalise is always there to disturb the otherwise silent background. The digital recording is clear and truthful.

Piano Sonatas 59–62, Hob XVI/49–52

(BB) *** Naxos 8.550657. Jandó

Jandó here shows himself a thoughtfully imaginative player as well as a bold one, and the finale of the great *E flat Sonata* has splendid, unforced bravura.

Piano Sonata 62 in E flat

(**) BBC Legends (mono) BBCL 4201-2. Hess – BACH: *English Suite 2* (**(*)); SCHUMANN: *Carnaval* (***)

Recorded for the BBC in 1962 when **Dame Myra Hess** was recovering from a stroke, this account of Haydn's *Sonata No. 62* was the very last performance she ever gave. Though the result is not quite as fluent as it would have been earlier, the intensity of her playing makes this historic recording most valuable, well coupled with Bach and Schumann.

VOCAL MUSIC

Arianna a Naxos; Scena di Berenice (DVD version) – see under Symphony 92 (Oxford)

*** Opus Arte **DVD** OA 821D. Bartoli, VCM, Harnoncourt

Cecilia Bartoli's fine DVD performances are discussed under their coupling.

Arianna a Naxos (orchestral version); Scena di Berenice; Miseri noi, miserata patria!; Son pietosa, son bonina; Solo e pensoso

⊕— *** Avie AV 2066. Augér, Handel & Haydn Society O, Hogwood

Augér holds the contrasted sections of the two big cantatas, the *Scena di Berenice* and *Arianna a Naxos*, firmly together. The third cantata, *Miseri noi*, like the *Scena di Berenice*, is another jewel not published until well on in the 20th century. Those and the two arias – *Solo e pensoso* is a setting of a Petrarch sonnet – inspire Augér to heartfelt singing, helped by immaculate recording, engineered by a Decca team. Full texts are provided.

Birthday Cantatas: Destatevi o miei fidi; Qual dubbio ormai. Celebration cantata: Da qual gioia improvvisa; Symphony 12 in E flat

*** HM HMC 90 1768. Stojkovic, Sunhae Im, Ciolek, Cologne Vocal Ens., Capella Coloniensis, Spering or Kraemer

Haydn was only deputy Kapellmeister at Esterházy when he wrote the two birthday cantatas to celebrate the name–day of his princely employer – in 1763 and 1764 respectively – with the texts offering the usual unalloyed praise. The third cantata celebrates the Prince's safe return from a distant journey and even includes a welcome chorus. With good solo singing, this is enjoyable enough; and if, like the *Symphony* from the same period, it is not great music, it shows how resourceful the budding young composer was.

The Creation (complete; in English; DVD version)

(N) ⊕— **** Decca O/L **DVD** 071 1269. Kirkby, Rolfe Johnson, George, New College, Oxford, Ch., AAM Ch. & O, Hogwood (Producer & Director: Chris Hunt)

Hogwood uses the English text which Haydn himself recognized as having equal validity with the German. Moreover Hogwood defies what has become the custom in period performances and opts for large forces such as Haydn – who during his trips to London was most impressed by large-scale performances of Handel oratorios – would have welcomed. The result, recorded in Gloucester Cathedral (which offers much visual pleasure), for all its weight retains an attractive freshness. The **Choir of New College, Oxford**, with its trebles, adds to the brightness of the choral sound and the trio of soloists is admirably consistent. A young **Emma Kirkby** (this was filmed for TV in 1990) is brightly distinctive, and **Anthony Rolfe Johnson** is comparably sweet-toned. **Michael George** is wonderfully intense in the hushed opening recitative before the blazing outburst on the creation of light, even if later the voice emerges less beautifully. Hogwood may lack some of the flair and imagination of Rattle (on CD), but as a period DVD performance this makes a perfect counterpart to Gustav Kuhn's alternative version in German. During the opening 'Representation of Chaos' we are shown dramatic film of the universe in its earliest formation, followed by the creation of life, with plants growing as the viewer watches (drawn from the BBC Natural History Unit). Then the producer, Chris Hunt, concentrates on the performers and the beauty of the cathedral itself, plus classic paintings by Blake and Turner.

The Creation (complete; in English; CD versions)

⊕— **** DG 477 7361 (2). Piau, Padmore, N. Davies, Harvey, Persson, Chetham's Chamber Ch., Gabrieli Consort & Players, McCreesh

*** EMI 7 54159-2 (2). Augér, Langridge, Thomas, CBSO & Ch., Rattle

**(*) Telarc CD 80298 (2). Upshaw, Humphrey, Cheek, Murphy, McGuire, Chamber Ch. & SO, Shaw

Paul McCreesh takes a refreshingly vibrant and joyous new look at Haydn's masterpiece, revising large parts of the English–language text, also rewriting the recitatives 'as Haydn might have done had he been more familiar with the English language'. However, McCreesh assures us that his revision happily does not omit favourite phrases like 'the flexible tiger' and 'With verdure clad'. McCreesh uses five soloists (with **Sandrine Piau** and **Mark Padmore** standing out in Parts I and 2), almost 100 singers in the chorus, and the **Gabrieli Consort** expanded to over 100 players as used by Haydn for the 1799 première of the German version. The performance is not short on drama, as the thundering timpani anticipate at the very opening, and the closing choruses of Part 1, *The Heavens are Telling*, and Part 2, *Achieved is the* *glorious work*, are thrilling. But the lyrical side of the music comes over too, with excellent solo singing. In Part 3, **Peter Harvey** and **Miah Persson** are a radiant Adam and Eve, and McCreesh ensures that the closing chorus, *Praise the Lord uplift your voices*, brings a moving apotheosis. The set is offered (with full texts provided) at a special price as Part 3 on the second CD only runs for about half an hour.

Rattle brings out the illustrative colour with exceptional vividness: birdsong, lion-roars and the like. He has plainly learnt from period performance, not only concerning speeds – often surprisingly brisk, as in the great soprano aria, *With verdure clad* – but as regards style too. The male soloists sound none too sweet as recorded, but they characterize positively; and there is no finer account of the soprano's music than that of **Arleen Augér**. The weight of the **Birmingham Chorus** is impressive, achieved without loss of clarity or detail in a full, well-balanced recording.

Robert Shaw with his keenly disciplined chamber choir conducts a strong, clean-cut performance, using an English translation modified from the traditional one. Though Shaw's generally broad speeds show little influence from period performance, his concern for clarity of texture is very different from old-style performances, and the Telarc engineers help with full, immediate sound, bringing out sharp dynamic contrasts. **Dawn Upshaw** adopts too romantically expressive a manner, but the solo singing is good, with **Heidi Grant Murphy** and **James Michael McGuire** brought in for the Adam and Eve numbers of Part 3.

The Creation (*Die Schöpfung*; complete; in German; DVD versions)

🎬 ✱ **** TDK **DVD** DVWW-COCREA. Augér, Sima, Schreier, Berry, Hermann, Arnold Schoenberg Ch., Coll. Aur., Kuhn (introduced by a documentary on the work and the occasion, by the Video Director, Franz Kabelka)

*** Capriccio **DVD** Surround Sound 93 507. Cencic, Schmidt, Bauer, Jankowitsch, V. Boys' Ch., Ch. Viennensis, V. Volksoper SO, Marschik (V/D: Axel Stummer)

It is difficult to imagine a finer filmed and recorded account of Haydn's *Creation* than this TDK DVD version, made doubly moving by the date of the performance: 31 March 1982, the 250th anniversary of the day of Haydn's birth. Moreover, the event took place in the Great Hall of the Old Vienna University where, on 27 March 1808, Haydn had attended a gala performance of his already celebrated masterpiece, under the direction of Antonio Salieri. All this and more is related in a splendid documentary about the history and composition of the work.

As for the performance, it is quite electrifying, but in the right way, for **Gustav Kuhn**, with his lively temperament, conducts with an ideal combination of zest and depth of feeling. He opens with a true *pianissimo* and at the word 'light' produces an overwhelming *fortissimo*. The soloists are unsurpassed on record. **Arleen Augér** (Gabriel) is at her glorious best, **Peter Schreier** (Uriel) sings with honeyed ardour, and **Walter Berry** is a powerfully resonant Rafael, with some wonderfully telling low notes. In Part Three **Gabriele Sima** and **Roland Hermann** (looking at his partner with a benev-

olent twinkle) are perfectly cast as Adam and Eve. Throughout, the singing of the **Arnold Schoenberg Choir** is superb, the playing of the **Collegium Aureum**, using original instruments, gives consistent aural pleasure, and the work ends in a spirit of radiant joy, which is just what Haydn intended. The unfussy video direction by Franz Kabelka concentrates on the performers, so it is very like sharing the occasion with them.

The 1994 Capriccio DVD of Haydn's *Creation* can also be most cordially recommended. It may not have soloists of quite the individuality of the top CD versions, notably Karajan's, but they are a fine team, with the rich-voiced bass, **Ernst Jankowitsch**, dominating, first as a resonant Rafael, and in Part 3 as a fine, mature Adam, where he is an excellent match for **Gertraud Schmidt**. She is not a young Eve, but she has a lovely voice and sings impressively. **Christian Bauer** is a fresh-voiced Uriel who discards his glasses not long before the interval, and the male soprano, **Max Emanuel Cencic**, deals with Gabriel's coloratura with ease, even if he has a curious lip-vibrato. The choral singing is first class and the conductor has the performance firmly in his grip: at the opening, the 'Representation of Chaos' is powerfully evoked. The visual backcloth and the atmospheric acoustics of the Grosser Saal of the Musikverein add to one's pleasure, for the Surround Sound is full and vivid, well balanced, with an impressive dynamic range and good clarity.

The Creation (*Die Schöpfung*; in German; CD versions)

🔊 **** DHM/BMG 82876 58340-2 (2). Röschmann, Schade, Gerhaher, Arnold Schoenberg Ch., VCM, Harnoncourt

🔊 (BB) *** EMI Gemini 3 50842-2 (2). Bonney, Blochwitz, Rootering, Wiens, Bär, Stuttgart RSO & Ch., Marriner

🔊 (M) *** DG (ADD) 449 761-2 (2). Janowitz, Ludwig, Wunderlich, Krenn, Fischer-Dieskau, Berry, V. Singverein, BPO, Karajan

🔊 *** DG 477 6327-2 (2). McNair, Brown, Schade, Finley, Gilfry, Monteverdi Ch., E. Bar. Sol., Gardiner

(N) (M) *** Decca (ADD) 478 1377. Popp, Hollweg, Moll, Döse, Luxon, Brighton Festival Ch., RPO, Dorati

(N) **(*) Virgin 3 95235-2 (2). Karthäuser, Kühmeier, Spence, Werba, Henschel, Les Arts Florissants, Christie

Celebrating their fiftieth anniversary at the Musikvereinsaal in Vienna, **Nikolaus Harnoncourt** and the **Concentus Musicus** give an incandescent account of Haydn's *Creation*, recorded live. Harnoncourt inspires a natural warmth that infects all the performers, the outstanding **Arnold Schoenberg Choir** as well as the three splendid soloists, the soprano **Dorothea Röschmann** at once full and clear, the tenor **Michael Schade** heady and unstrained and the finely focused bass **Christian Gerhaher** plainly benefiting from his experience as a Lieder singer. The live atmosphere adds to the dramatic bite of the performance from the start. The recording, well forward with weighty brass, adds to the drama, not least with the great entry of the chorus on the word, *Licht* ('Light'), thrillingly powerful. A triumphant celebration of 50 years' achievement.

What distinguishes **Sir Neville Marriner's** 1989 Stuttgart recording is the truly outstanding contribution of the soloists. Each in turn enters singing most beautifully, **Hans Peter Blochwitz** as Uriel, **Jan Henrik Rootering** as Raphael, and **Barbara Bonney** a radiant-voiced Gabriel. And how delightfully they combine in their Trios in Part II. In Part III **Edith Wiens** is a hardly less delightful Eve, and her duets with the warm-voiced Adam of **Olaf Bär** are similarly memorable. The chorus is comparatively lightweight in *Die Himmel erzählen*, but they sing with vigour and conviction and the finale of Part III, *Singt dem Herrn*, combined with the soloists, is exhilarating. Throughout, the orchestral playing is first rate, and the recording excellent. A splendid bargain version that can be ranked alongside the best.

Among regular versions of *The Creation* sung in German, **Karajan's** 1969 set remains unsurpassed, despite two small cuts (in Nos. 30 and 32). The combination of the **Berlin Philharmonic** at its most intense and the great **Viennese Choir** makes for a performance that is not only polished but warm and dramatically strong too. The soloists are an extraordinarily fine team, more consistent in quality than those on almost any rival version.

It is good to have **Dorati's** 1976 set back in the catalogue as one of Decca's 'Originals'. It is a characteristically lively and well-sprung account. The very opening is magnetic, and its imaginative touches and joyfulness of spirit more than compensate for any minor lapses in crispness of ensemble. The soloists are a splendid team. The chorus is as gusty as you like in *Die Himmel erzälen*, with the soloists nicely balanced. While among the earlier recordings Karajan is not superseded, Dorati's enjoyably spontaneous music-making is very attractive.

Characteristically, **Gardiner** takes a dramatic view, overtly expressive, vividly pointing the highlights of the Creation story, but the exhilaration and power of Haydn's inspiration, as well as its lyrical beauty, have never been conveyed more tellingly in a period performance on disc. The soloists are outstanding too, though the silvery soprano, **Sylvia McNair**, does not always sing full out.

Christie's fresh and often exuberant account of *The Creation*, readily showing his fine ear for detail, has none of the drawbacks of period performance and most of the advantages, notably the delicacy of colouring provided by his period orchestra. The choir sings freshly and vividly, and certainly produces a suitably spectacular response to the appearance of light. The star among the soloists is **Sophie Karthäuser's** ravishing portrait of Eve, and **Markus Werba** makes a sympathetic partner. **Genia Kühmeier** (Gabriel), **Dietrich Henschel** (Raphael), and **Toby Spence** complete a good team. But this is not a primary recommendation.

(i) *The Creation;* (ii) *The Seasons;* (iii) *Il Ritorno di Tobia* (complete; in German)

(N) (BB) *** Naxos 8.507008 (6). (i) Im, Kobow, Müller-Brachmann, Wehler, Cologne Vocal Ens., Capella Augustina, Spering; (ii) Karasiak, MacLeod, Rubens, Gewandhaus Chamber Ch., Leipzig CO, Schuldt-Jensen; (iii) Borchev; Dahlin; Hallenberg; Invernizzi; Karthäuser, Cologne Vocal Ens., Capella Augustina, Spering

Available separately (*The Creation* on 8.557380/81; *The Seasons* on 8.557600/01; and *Il Ritorno di Tobia* on 8.570300/02) or as a compilation, this inexpensive Naxos set offers strong, reliable and thoroughly enjoyable versions not just of *The Creation* and *The Seasons*, but of the little-known, much earlier oratorio of 1775 with the subject taken from the Apocrypha, *Il Ritorno di Tobia*. It may not have the full mastery of the last works, but it is well worth hearing in a performance as fine as this with Leipzig forces. The soprano singing the archangel Raffaele, **Roberta Invernizzi**, is outstanding in her agility, and **Anders Dahlin** is a pleasant, clear tenor; but all the singing is never less than very good and often outstanding, particularly from the choirs, both from Leipzig and Cologne. First-rate sound too.

The Creation is another first-rate period performance. After the extreme hush of the opening, the choral cry of *Licht!* (*Light!*) is then shattering in its impact. Generally **Spering's** speeds are on the fast side, yet with no feeling of rush. The three soloists too are all excellent and youthful sounding, and the **Cologne Vocal Ensemble** is an incisive ensemble with ample power for the dramatic moments.

The Seasons has the splendid **Gewandhaus Chamber Choir** and the **Leipzig Chamber Orchestra**, directed with plenty of vitality by **Morten Schuldt-Jensen**. The *Autumn Hunting Chorus*, with roistering horns, shows them at their most vivid. Again, all three soloists are excellent, with the rich-voiced soprano **Sibylla Rubens** and pleasing tenor **Andreas Karasiak** matched by the resonant bass, **Stephan MacLeod**. Again first-class recording.

Masses

Hickox Chandos Recordings

Masses 1–14 (complete). *Alfred, König der Angelsachsen* (incidental music: excerpts); *Ave Regina; Salve Regina; Te Deum*

(B) *** Chan. 0734 (8). Soloists, Coll. Mus. 90, Hickox

One of **Richard Hickox's** major achievements on record is his glorious complete coverage of the Haydn late *Masses*. If you have not already collected some of these CDs, this box is self-recommending in every respect.

Masses 1 in F (Missa brevis), Hob XXII/1; 11 in D min. (Nelson), Hob XXII/11; Ave Regina in A, Hob XXIIIb/3

⊗ *** Chan. 0640. Gritton, Stephen, Padmore, Varcoe, Coll. Mus. 90, Hickox

Masses 1a in G (Rorate coeli desuper), Hob XXII/3; (i) 13 in B flat (Schöpfungsmesse), Hob XXII/13 (with Haydn's alternative Gloria)

⊗ *** Chan. 0599. (i) Gritton, Stephen, Padmore, Varcoe; Coll. Mus. 90, Hickox

It is a great merit of this series that early *Masses* and shorter choral works are included as couplings for the late, great *Masses* written for the name-days of the Princess Esterházy. Those extra items include some masterly works, and it is fascinating to hear Haydn's very first *Mass* – the coupling for the *Nelson Mass*, most popular of all – which he wrote in his teens, a wonderfully fresh, bright inspiration. It is good too as one of the couplings for the *Schöpfungsmesse* to have the alternative setting of the *Gloria*, with the quotation from Haydn's oratorio, *The Creation* ('*Schöpfung*'), removed in deference to an objection from the Austrian Empress.

Masses 2a: Sunt bona mixta malis; 3 in C: Missa Cellensis in honorem Beatissimae Virginis Mariae

*** Chan. 0667. Gritton, Stephen, Padmore, Varcoe, Coll. Mus. 90, Hickox

Masses 4 in E flat: Missa in honorem Beatissimae Virginis Mariae (Great Organ Mass); 8 in C (Mariazellermesse)

*** Chan. 0674. Gritton, Winter, Padmore, Varcoe, Watson, Coll. Mus. 90, Hickox

The *Great Organ Mass*, dating from 1768–9, is unique among Haydn's earlier *Masses*, with a pair of cor anglais instead of oboes bringing a darkness to the textures, and with the organ adding delicate baroque tracery, beautifully played with light registration by **Ian Watson**. A devout Catholic, Haydn's joy in the liturgy bubbles out, as in the wildly syncopated *Amen* at the end of the *Sanctus*.

The *Mariazeller Mass*, written in 1782, was the last *Mass* setting that Haydn composed before the final six masterpieces. Adventurous modulations of key relate to Haydn's symphonic writing, leading to an exuberant setting of the final *Dona nobis pacem*, so syncopated it is almost jazzy. There and throughout, **Hickox**, with bouncing rhythms, inspires performances that convey the pure joy of Haydn.

Masses 6 in G (Missa Sanctae Nicolai), Hob XXII/6; 9 in B flat (Missa Sancti Bernardi de Offida (Heiligmesse))

*** Chan. 0645. Anderson, Stephen, Padmore, Varcoe, Coll. Mus. 90, Hickox

The so-called *Heiligmesse*, dating from 1796, was the first of the great sequence of six Masses, written annually for the name-day of Princess Esterházy, that crowned Haydn's composing career. **Hickox** and his fine team of soloists, choir and period orchestra bring out the exuberance of inspiration that marks this and the other works in the series. Equally, the *St Nicolai Mass*, written in 1772, points forward to his later achievements, though the conclusion on *Dona nobis pacem* more conventionally brings a radiantly lyrical close, all beautifully achieved here by Hickox and his team, vividly recorded.

Masses 7 in B flat: Missa brevis Sancti Joannis de Deo (Little Organ Mass); 12 in B flat (Theresienmesse)

⏣— *** Chan. 0592. Watson, Stephen, Padmore, Varcoe, Coll. Mus. 90, Hickox

What distinguishes **Richard Hickox's** version of the *Theresienmesse* is the way he brings out the joyful exuberance of inspiration. At each turn Haydn surprises his listeners

with new approaches, from the symphonic setting of the *Kyrie* with contrapuntal entries and side-slipping harmonies to the trumpets and drums of the final *Dona nobis pacem*. The excellent coupling is the *Little Organ Mass* – so-called because of the elaborate organ accompaniment for the soprano solo in the *Benedictus*, with **Janice Watson** a radiant soloist.

Mass 10 in C: Missa in tempore belli (Paukenmesse), Hob XXII/9; Alfred, König de Angelsachsen (incidental music): Aria of the Guardian Spirit; Chorus of the Danes; 2 Te Deums in C, Hob XXIIIc/1–2

⏣— **** Chan. 0633. Argenta, Denley, Padmore, Varcoe, Coll. Mus. 90, Hickox

The impact of war is reflected not just in the title, *Missa in tempore belli*, of the second of Haydn's final choral masterpieces, but in the writing, with the hushed *Kyrie* dramatically interrupted by trumpets and timpani. **Hickox's** outstanding performance offers fascinating couplings, not only the two brilliant settings of the *Te Deum*, with celebratory trumpets and timpani, but the two completed items that Haydn wrote for the production of a German play about Alfred the Great, written in the same year as the *Mass* and with similarities of style. Exuberant performances under Hickox and brilliant recording.

Mass 14 in B flat (Harmoniemesse); Salve regina in E

⏣— *** Chan. 0612. Argenta, Stephen, Padmore, Varcoe, Coll. Mus. 90, Hickox

Hickox's superb disc aptly couples the *Harmoniemesse*, the last major work that Haydn ever wrote, with his first important work, the *Salve Regina*, written in his twenties, when he was still an assistant to the composer Porpora and echoing his style. Nonetheless, there are plenty of distinctive points in the young composer's vigorous writing, simple as it is compared with his mature work. The *Harmoniemesse* is a favourite with Hickox, with Haydn's final fling as a composer bringing more elaborate orchestral writing. That was thanks to Prince Esterházy hiring a full *Harmonie* (wind section), while in unflagging inspiration Haydn delivers characteristic surprises in the setting with Hickox fully relishing the composer's humour.

Other recordings

Masses 9 in B flat (Missa Sancti Bernadi von Offida) (Heiligmesse); 10 in C (Missa in tempore belli) (Paukenmesse); Insanae et vanae curae

*** Ph. 470 819-2. Lunn, Mingardo, Lehtipuu, Sherratt, Monteverdi Ch., E. Bar. Sol., Gardiner

This Philips coupling follows after **Gardiner's** outstanding pairing of the *Nelson* and *Theresienne Masses* (470 286-2 – see below), similarly dramatic and incisive, and his fine team of soloists and the **Monteverdi Choir** are again on top form. For his bonus this time, he gives us the motet, *Insanae et vanae curae*, which originally belonged with the oratorio *Il* *ritorno di Tobia* and now, sung in Latin instead of German, is given a spirited, biting performance to match the two main works. The Philips recording is admirably clear and clean, bringing splendid detail.

Mass 11 (Nelson); Te Deum in C, Hob XXIIIc/2

₿─ *** DG 423 097-2. Lott, Watkinson, Davies, Wilson-Johnson, Ch. & E. Concert, Pinnock

The *Nelson Mass* (*Missa in angustiis*: 'Mass in times of fear') brings a superb choral offering from **Trevor Pinnock** and the **English Concert**. With incandescent singing from the chorus and fine matching from excellent soloists, Pinnock brings home the high drama of Haydn's autumnal inspiration. Similarly, the *Te Deum* leaps forward from the 18th century all the more excitingly in an authentic performance such as this. Excellent, full-blooded sound, with good definition.

Mass 13: Schöpfungsmesse (Creation Mass)

*** Teldec 3984 26094-2. Oelze, Von Magnus, Lippert, Finley, Arnold Schoenberg Ch., VCM, Harnoncourt – SCHUBERT: *Magnificat, D.486; Offertorium in B flat, D.963 (Intende voci)* ***

Marked by lightness, resilience and transparency, speeds are moderate in both directions, easily flowing with rhythms well sprung. That is, until the final *Dona nobis pacem*, where **Harnoncourt** opts for a very fast speed, rounding off this celebration of the *Mass* in exhilaration – as Haydn himself used to put it, *Laus Deo*, 'Praise to God'. The four soloists are excellent, as is the chorus. The recording is warmly atmospheric, though the backward balance of the choir prevents it from having quite the impact its incisive singing deserves. An unexpected coupling, but an illuminating one.

Masses 13 in B flat: Schöpfungsmesse (Creation Mass) 14 in B flat (Harmoniemesse)

*** Ph. 470 297-2 (2). Ziesak, Lunn, Gruffydd Jones, Fink, Spicer, Mingardo, Prégardien, Butterfield, Busher, Lehtipuu, Widmer, Sherratt, Monteverdi Ch., E. Bar. Sol., Gardiner

This was the first of **Gardiner's** three Philips couplings of Haydn's last six great *Masses* and it set the seal on the excellence of the series, with its starry group of soloists and brightly dramatic choral singing. Comparison with Hickox on Chandos shows the latter the more infectious interpreter, Gardiner the more sharply dramatic, often with faster pacing to match. Yet both are very rewarding in their own chosen way. The recording is excellent.

The Seasons (complete; in English)

Ⓑ *** Somm Beecham (ADD) 16-2 (2) (arr. and orch. Beecham). Morison, Young, Langdon, Beecham Choral Soc., RPO, Beecham

ⒷⒷ *** EMI Gemini (ADD) 5 86118-2 (2) (as above). Morison, Young, Langdon, Beecham Choral Soc., RPO, Beecham

Beecham's approach to Haydn's score was somewhat cavalier. He used orchestrations of the keyboard accompaniments for the recitatives, and (as with his RCA recording of Handel's *Messiah*) added percussion effects, including cymbals. A bell was added to the horns striking eight o'clock in *Summer*, and extra shots to the bass's hunting aria in *Autumn*. Yet he obviously revelled in Haydn's expressive tone-painting and he chose a fine solo team, led by **Elsie Morison**, who sings with tender flexibility and charm. The fresh-voiced tenor, **Alexander Young**, and the vibrant bass, **Michael Langdon**, are equally strong, and the three singers match their voices very musically in the various trios. The choral singing is not as polished as we would expect today from an entirely professional chorus, but the hearty vigour and commitment carry the day, while the **RPO**, and especially the strings, play with both warmth and stylish delicacy of feeling. In short, this is as spirited and individual as one would expect from Beecham, and the early Abbey Road stereo is full and clear. The remastering on Somm cannot be faulted, and a full text is provided of Dennis Arundell's new translation, which was especially commissioned for this recording.

On the EMI budget Gemini set the recording has again been remastered quite splendidly, but there is no libretto.

The Seasons (Die Jahreszeiten; complete; in German)

₿─ ⊛ **** HMC 801829.30 (2). Petersen, Gura, Henschel, RIAS Chamber Ch., Freiburg Bar. O, Jacobs

*** DG 431 818-2 (2). Bonney, Rolfe Johnson, Schmidt, Monteverdi Ch., E. Bar. Sol., Gardiner

Ⓑ *** Ph. 438 715-2 (2). Mathis, Jerusalem, Fischer-Dieskau, Ch. & ASMF, Marriner

More than any other version, the period performance under **René Jacobs** brings out the joy of this piece, based on James Thomson's poem, as he nudges the music persuasively when Haydn has fun in imitating the lowing of cattle, the cry of the quail and the chirping of the cricket. With recording of ideal clarity and immediacy Jacobs also brings out the boldness of the writing for brass and timpani in the finales of each section, notably the drinking chorus which rounds off *Autumn*. **Marlis Petersen** is the fresh, agile soprano, **Werner Gura** the light, heady tenor and **Dietrich Henschel** the fine baritone, singing with a Lieder-singer's concern for detail. Excellent contributions too from the **RIAS Chamber Choir** and the splendid **Freiburg Baroque Orchestra**.

Gardiner here almost always gets the best of both worlds in intensity of communication, whatever the purists may say. Even more than usual, this studio performance conveys the electricity of a live event. The silver-toned **Barbara Bonney** and **Anthony Rolfe Johnson** at his most sensitive are outstanding soloists, and though the baritone, **Andreas Schmidt**, is less sweet on the ear, he winningly captures the bluff jollity of the role of Simon.

Marriner directs a superbly joyful performance of Haydn's last oratorio, effervescent with the optimism of old age. **Edith Mathis** and **Dietrich Fischer-Dieskau** are as stylish and characterful as one would expect, pointing the words as narrative. The tenor too is magnificent: **Siegfried Jerusalem** is both heroic of timbre and yet delicate enough for Haydn's most elegant and genial passages. The chorus and orchestra, of authentic size, add to the freshness. The recording, made in St John's, Smith Square, is warmly reverberant without losing detail.

The Seven Last Words of Our Saviour on the Cross

*** Naïve V 5045. Piau, Sandhoff, Getchell, Van der Kamp, Accentus, Akademie für alte Musik, Berlin, Equilbey

Returning from England after his second visit to London, Haydn stayed in the Bavarian city of Passau, and there he heard a performance of his own *Seven Last Words*, which he had written in orchestral form, in an arrangement by the local Kapellmeister, Joseph Friebert, for voices and orchestra. Impressed, Haydn asked for a copy of the transcription and, returning to Vienna, he set about making his own version for soloists, chorus and orchestra, adding parts for clarinets and trombones, but using Friebert's devotional texts. He also added a second instrumental *Introduzione* between the fourth and fifth 'Words', scored for wind instruments alone. Later, he asked Baron Gottfried van Sweeten, director of the Imperial Library, to revise the texts for a first performance in Vienna in 1796. The result is the work on the present CD, far more eloquent and expressively powerful than the orchestral original. It is superbly sung and played here, and beautifully recorded, to make an important addition to the Haydn discography.

Stabat mater

*** Griffin GCCD 4029. Bern, Ager, Carwood, Underwood, Christ Church Cathedral Ch., L. Musici, Darlington, Goode (organ)

Haydn's *Stabat mater* was the first of his vocal works to establish his reputation internationally, an ambitious cantata written in 1767, soon after Haydn took over responsibility for Prince Esterházy's church music. Even against strong competition, the Griffin issue finds a distinctive place. It uses an orchestra of modern instruments; but **Stephen Darlington** takes note of period practice, lightening string textures and finding extra detail. He also tends to adopt fast speeds, at times challengingly so, as in the big tenor aria, *Vidit sum*, stylishly sung by **Andrew Carwood**. The other striking quality of this set, besides the use of a church choir with boy trebles, is the warmly atmospheric cathedral acoustic, which yet allows ample detail.

OPERA

L'anima del filosofo (Orfeo ed Euridice; complete)

*** O-L 452 668-2 (2). Bartoli, Heilmann, D'Arcangelo, Silvestrelli, AAM, Hogwood

Cecilia Bartoli is in her element, passionately expressive, creating a larger-than-life character, in Euridice's death scene, Orfeo's agony of lament (agitated, and very different from Gluck's *Orfeo* aria, *Che farò*), and a brilliant coloratura aria for the Sybil. Though Orfeo's death comes as an anticlimax, the final chorus for the Bacchantes is most memorable, in a minor key, dark and agitated, then fading away to the close. **Uwe Heilmann** is a most sympathetic Orfeo, musically stylish, even if the microphone catches the hint of a flutter, as it does too with the well-contrasted voices of **Ildebrando**

d'Arcangelo as King Creonte, Euridice's father, and **Andrea Silvestrelli** as Pluto. The chorus, so important in this work, is fresh and well disciplined.

(i) Armida; (ii) La fedeltà premiata; (iii) Orlando paladino; (iv) La vera costanza (all complete)

Ⓑ ******* Ph. (ADD) 473 476-2 (10). (i) Burrowes, Ramey, Leggate; (i; iii; iv) Ahnsjö; (i; iv) Norman, Rolfe Johnson; (ii) Terrani, Landy, Von Stade, Titus, Cotrubas, Alva, Mazzieri, SRO Ch.; (ii; iv) Lövaas; (iii) Augér, Ameling, Killebrew, Shirley, Luxon; (iii; iv) Trimarchi; (iv) Donath, Ganzarolli; Lausanne CO, Dorati

(i) L'incontro improvviso; (ii) L'infedeltà delusa; (iii) L'isola disabitata; (iv) Il mondo della luna (all complete). (v) Cantata: Miseri noi! misera patria; Petrarch's Sonnet from 'Il Canzionieri': Solo e pensoso. (vi) Terzetto and (vii) Aria from PASTICCIO: La Circe, ossia L'isola incantata. Arias for: (viii) Acide e Galatea. (ix) SARTI: I finti erede. (x) TRAETTA: Ifigenia in Tauride. (xi) BIANCHI: Alessandro nell'Indie. CIMAROSA: I due supposti conti. GAZZANIGA: L'isola di Alcina. GUGLIELMI: La Quakera spiritosa. PAISIELLO: La Frascatana

Ⓑ ******* Ph. (ADD) 473 851-2 (10). (i) Luxon, M. Marshall, D. Jones, Prescott; (i; ii; vi; x) Ahnsjö; (i; iii) Zoghby; (i, iv) Trimarchi; (ii) Hendricks; (ii; iv; v; vii; xi) Mathis; (ii; vi; vii; ix) Baldin; (ii; vi; viii) Devlin; (iii) Lerer; (ii; iv) Alva, Bruson; (iv) Von Stade, Augér, Valentini Terrani, Rolfe Johnson; Lausanne CO, Dorati

Haydn is not celebrated as an operatic composer, yet in many ways his contribution to this genre is underrated, and for those drawn to **Dorati's** vintage series, these two boxes, each of ten CDs, in the Philips bargain Collector's Edition, provide an economical way to explore this repertoire. Each opera is also available separately. With fine soloists there will be much here to delight the ear, and Dorati conducts brightly and resiliently; although he tends to flag in the recitatives, these performances still offer much to relish. The presentation offers good documentation, but keyed synopses in place of full libretti. Also included is an additional programme of miscellaneous arias by Haydn and substitution arias by other composers, the latter (for the most part) sung by **Edith Mathis**. The analogue recording from the late 1970s is excellent and the CD transfers first class. Try the first box and you will surely want the second.

(i) L'isola disabitata (complete); (ii) Cantata: Arianna a Naxos

*** Ara. Z 6717-2 (2). Mentzer, with (i) Huang, Aler, Schaldenbrand, Padova CO, Golub; (ii) Golub (piano)

L'isola disabitata is a lightweight, relatively brief work, involving only four characters, performing seven arias and a final quartet, with copious recitative in between. The set numbers are typically fresh in their inspiration, and the final quartet is a delight in offering solo roles not just to the three singers but to a quartet of obbligato instruments echoing each character: violin and flute for the women, cello and bassoon for the men, with horns and timpani adding to the brilliance of the orchestra.

David Golub and his orchestra from **Padua** give a warm, relaxed reading, with speeds consistently slower than on the rival Dorati version. The soloists are all first rate, with **Susanne Mentzer** warm and firm as Costanza, **Ying Huang** fresh and girlish as Silvia and **John Aler** clear-toned as Gernando. **Christopher Schaldenbrand** jibs at singing trills but is stylish otherwise. Well-balanced sound. *Arianna a Naxos* has Mentzer accompanied by Golub at the piano (unidentified in the booklet) to make a very welcome fill-up, to give a substantial advantage over the Dorati set.

'Haydn & Mozart Discoveries': Arias from: *Acide e Galatea; Il desertore; La scuola de' gelosi; La vera costanza*

Ⓜ **(*) Decca (ADD) 475 7169. Fischer-Dieskau, V. Haydn O, Peters – MOZART: *Arias* **(*)

'Haydn and Mozart Discoveries', the disc claims – and very delightful they are too, even if Haydn gets much less attention, with comparatively lightweight and simple pieces.

HAYDN, Michael (1737–1806)

Flute Concerto in D

⊕↴ Ⓜ **** EMI 4 76863-2. Pahud, Berlin Haydn Ens. – J. HAYDN: *Flute Concerto; Scherzandi* ***

Emmanuel Pahud's superbly played account of Michael Haydn's enchanting little work is now reissued to represent Pahud as one of EMI's 'Great Artists of the Century'.

Horn Concertino in D

ⒷⒷ *** Warner Apex 0927 40825-2. Clevenger, Franz Liszt CO, Rolla – J. HAYDN: *Horn Concertos 3 & 4* ***

Michael Haydn's *Concertino* is attractive; the second-movement *Allegro* is played in fine style by **Dale Clevenger**, whose articulation is a joy in itself. An outstanding bargain coupling.

Violin Concerto in A

Ⓜ *** Australian Ph. Eloquence (ADD) 442 8294. Grumiaux, New Philh. O, Leppard – J. HAYDN: *Violin Concertos 1 & 4*; MOZART: *Adagio; Rondo* ***

The outer movements of this concerto have perky, attractive melodies which are very enjoyable, especially when so stylishly played, both by soloist and conductor. The 1970 recording emerges superbly in this new transfer.

Symphonies 1 in C, P.35; 2 in C, P.2; 3 (Divertimento) in G; 4 in B flat, P.51; 5 in A, P.3; 6 in C, P.4; 7 in E, P.5; 8 in D, P.38; 9 in D, P.36; 10 in F, P.45; 11 in B flat, P.9; 12 in G, P.7; 15 in D, P.41; 16 in A, P.6; 18 in C, P.10; 25 in G, P.16; 26 in E flat, P.17; 27 in B flat, P.18; 28 in C, P.19. Sinfonia (Divertimento) in G, P.8

ⒷⒷ **(*) CPO 999 591-2 (6). Slovak CO, Warchal

Michael Haydn's 41 symphonies were composed over three decades from 1760 until 1789. The early three-movement works are comparatively straightforward and seldom adventurous, usually simply scored for oboes, horns and strings; sometimes flutes were added. The invention, too, though often quite endearing, is not particularly individual. Even so, almost all the symphonies written in the 1760s have at least one memorable movement and sometimes two. The **Slovak Chamber Orchestra** is an excellent modern-instrument ensemble and performances throughout are lively in the traditional sense, warm and committed. **Warchal** phrases most musically, but generally observes repeats, which makes some slow movements seem rather long.

Symphonies 11, P.9; 16, P.6; 25, P.16; 34, P.26; 40, P.32

*** Chan. 9352. LMP, Bamert

Bamert's programme is very well chosen and makes a fine sampler for this repertoire. None of this is great music, but all of it is enjoyable and the composer's penultimate *F major* work (1789) brings a strong, impressively constructed opening movement and a tender *Adagio* with muted strings. The well-detailed recording is pleasingly full and resonant.

Missa in honorem Sanctae Ursulae; Requiem pro defuncto Archiepiscopo Sigismondo

Ⓑ *** Hyp. CDA 67510 (2). Sampson, Summers, Gilchrist, Harvey, King's Consort & Ch., King

The *Requiem*, written on the death of Archbishop Siegmund of Salzburg in 1771, reflects not only the sadness Michael Haydn felt for a much-loved cleric, but his deep grief over the death of his daughter earlier in the year. The *Mass*, dating from much later, 1783, was written for a Benedictine Abbey near Salzburg, a fine example of Michael Haydn's late style, with thematic links between the movements. In complete contrast with the *Requiem*, the opening *Kyrie* is an elegant piece expressing happiness, while the *Sanctus*, very brief, is gentle and reflective, expanding into joy for *Pleni sunt coeli*. The *Benedictus* is the longest movement, a soprano solo, beautifully sung by **Carolyn Sampson**, punctuated by the chorus. **Robert King** conducts a fresh, lively performance, with **Hilary Summers** and **James Gilchrist** also outstanding among the soloists, as they are again in the *Requiem*, though here the ensemble is not always as crisp as in the *Mass*. First-rate sound.

HEATH, Dave (born 1956)

The Frontier

Ⓑ *** Virgin 3 63308-2. LCO, Warren-Green – ADAMS: *Shaker Loops* *** ✿ ; GLASS: *Company*, etc. *** ; REICH: *8 Lines* ***

In *The Frontier* Heath's incisive rhythmic astringency is tempered by an attractive, winding lyrical theme which finally asserts itself just before the spiky close. The work was written for members of the **LCO**, and their performance, full of vitality and feeling, is admirably recorded.

HENSELT, Adolf von (1814–89)

Piano Concerto in F min., Op. 16; Variations de Concert on 'Quand je quittai la Normandie' from Meyerbeer's 'Robert le Diable', Op. 11

*** Hyp. CDA 66717. Hamelin, BBC Scottish SO, Brabbins – ALKAN: *Concerti da camera* ***

Henselt's *F minor Concerto* is fiendishly difficult (Egon Petri thought it one of the hardest pieces he had ever played) but it seems to present few problems for **Marc-André Hamelin**, who is more than equal to its challenges. The idiom, as one might expect, is greatly indebted to Mendelssohn and Chopin, but there is much to give delight, quite apart from the virtuosity of the playing. Stunning playing throughout from this remarkable Canadian pianist, and very good recorded sound.

HENZE, Hans Werner (born 1926)

'Henze: Portrait of an Outsider'; Requiem

🔑 ✹ *** Arthaus **DVD** 100 360. Wiget, Hardenberger, Bostridge, Kaune, Drake, Frankfurt RSO, Stenz; CBSO, Rattle; Ens. Modern, Metzmacher (Prod: Dennis Marks, Dir: Barrie Gavin)

The portrait must be one of the best documentary productions of its kind committed to video. There are contributions from **Simon Rattle**, Oliver Knussen and (albeit briefly) William Walton, and excerpts from the *Third* and *Eighth Symphonies*, the haunting *La selva incantata*, the *Nachtstücke und Arien*, *Undine* (with Fonteyn in the first production) and the *Arabian Songs* he composed for Ian Bostridge. The programme is strongly atmospheric and never indulges in excessive explanation or talking down (it is indeed far more ambitious than anything we are likely to find on BBC TV nowadays). It is a reflective and moving programme, which brings us close to this remarkable composer. The *Requiem*, which is dedicated to the memory of his friend Michael Vyner of the London Sinfonietta, occupied him during 1990–92 and receives as definitive a performance as any can be. Henze himself spoke of the work as a search for 'a new key to these dark rooms we have to go to find our way and to find ourselves', and the work is among his most deeply felt and personal utterances.

(i) Barcarola; Symphonies 7; (ii) 9; (iii) 3 Auden Songs

Ⓝ Ⓑ *** EMI 2-CD 2 37601-2 (2). (i) CBSO, Rattle; (ii) Berlin R. Ch., BPO, Metzmacher; (iii) Bostridge, Drake

This two-CD set is invaluable while the DG box of the first six symphonies conducted by the composer is deleted. The *Seventh Symphony*, written for **Simon Rattle** and the **CBSO** in 1983/4, is not only the longest Henze has written, it is also the weightiest and most traditionally symphonic, Beethoven-like, in four substantial movements. Rather belying its title, the *Barcarola* presents a similarly weighty and massive structure, an elegiac piece of over 20 minutes, written in memory of Paul Dessau, and inspired by the myth of the ferryman, Charon, crossing the Styx. Henze refers to his

Ninth Symphony as a *summa summorum* of his musical output. It is choral throughout, a setting of seven poems by Hans-Ulrich Treichel based on Anna Segher's *The Seventh Cross*, and there is no doubting the intensity and depth of feeling that lie behind the symphony. The recording derives from the première at the Philharmonie in 1997, and the singing of the **Berlin Radio Choir** is superb in every way. Powerful and impressive. When Henze heard **Ian Bostridge** singing his *Three Auden Songs* he was so impressed that he wrote further settings for him. Listening to these compelling performances, one can understand why the composer was attracted to Bostridge's unique vocal qualities and timbre. The one serious drawback to this reissue is that its presentation is remiss in omitting the texts.

Violin Concertos 1; (i) 2; 3

🔑 *** MDG 601 1242-2 (2). Janicke, Madgeburg PO, Ehwald; (i) with Mädler

The *First Concerto* was written when Henze had worked out his combination of 12-tone serialism and neoclassicism. Though the orchestral textures have a Stravinskian clarity, the harmonic idiom echoes that of Berg over its four clearly defined movements. The *Second Concerto* of 1971 comes from the period when Henze was profoundly influenced by left-wing politics and, in a far wilder idiom over its six movements, with surreal diatonic passages, brings a linking of concerto form and music-theatre. It involves not just the solo violin and 33 instruments, but also recorded tape and a baritone soloist, the whole work powerfully presented in **Torsten Janicke's** fine performance. The *Third Concerto* of 1997, here given in the composer's 2002, more elaborate revision, offers in its three movements portraits of characters in Thomas Mann's *Dr Faustus*, a novel about musical creation centring on the composer Adrian Leverkuhn. First-rate performances, vividly recorded.

3 Symphonische Etüden; (i) Nachtstücke und Arien; Quattro Poemi; La selva incantata

*** Wergo WER 6637-2. NDR SO, Ruzicka, with (i) Kaune

Nachtstücke und Arien of 1957 is one of Henze's most seminal works. Three of the four pieces come from the 1950s, and the inspired *Nachtstücke und Arien* are beautifully given by **Michaele Kaune** and the **NDR Orchestra** under **Peter Ruzicka**. What a powerful spell the much later *La selva incantata* casts! It must be among Henze's most atmospheric and imaginative scores.

INSTRUMENTAL MUSIC

Royal Winter Music: Guitar Sonatas 1 & 2

*** MDG MDGL 3110. Evers

Music for 2 guitars: Memorias se El Cimarrón; Minette (Canti e rimpianti ariosi); 3 Märchenbilder from the Opera 'Pollicino'

*** MDG 304 0881-2. Ruck, Càsoli

The *Royal Winter Music Sonatas* are based on Shakespearean

characters from *Romeo and Juliet* and *A Midsummer Night's Dream*, together with personifying Ariel, Ophelia, Richard III and Lady Macbeth, portraits which **Reinbert Evers** creates with great virtuosity and brilliance. On the second disc, *Memorias se El Cimarrón*, is the most immediately striking item, exploiting an extraordinarily wide range of sonorities and expressive devices, which **Jürgen Ruck** and **Eleana Cásoli** of the **Ensemble Musica** bring vividly to life. For the *Märchenbilder* from *Pollicino* Henze returns to a delightful children's opera he composed for Montepulciano. All this music is played with effortless mastery and imagination.

VOCAL MUSIC

Die Bassariden (opera; complete)

🅱– Ⓜ(**(*)) Orfeo mono C605032I (2). Driscoll, Paskalis, Lagger, Melchert, Dooley, Meyer, V. State Op. Ch., VPO, Dohnányi

The Bassarids represents a synthesis of Henze's symphonic and operatic writing, its single 2½-hour Act being divided into four movements: a first-movement sonata form, a Scherzo, an *Adagio* and a passacaglia finale. The plot (after Euripides's *The Bacchae*) concerns the conflict between Pentheus, the new king of Thebes, and the god Dionysus, and the king's subsequent murder at the hands of Dionysus's drunken followers, among them Pentheus's own mother. It contains some of Henze's most imaginative and compelling invention. This Orfeo performance is of the première on 6 August 1966 and is an impressive one. **Loren Driscoll's** Dionysus is very good indeed, and the remainder of the cast could hardly be bettered. **Christoph von Dohnányi** gets first-class results from the **Vienna Philharmonic**. The recording is pretty monochrome but generally well balanced, and it makes an important contribution to the Henze discography.

Boulevard Solitude (opera; complete; DVD version)

*** EuroArts **DVD** 2056 358. Aikin, Lindskog, Fox, Canturri, Delamboye, Putnins, Cor Vivaldi, Cambra del Palau de la Música Catalana Ch., Gran Teatre dei Liceu, Barcelona, O, Peskó (Dir: Nicholas Lehnhoff)

Henze's *Boulevard Solitude*, a re-working of the Manon of Abbé Prevost, was his first opera, produced in 1952 in Hanover, when the audience included Nicholas Lehnhoff, the director of the present staging, a co-production with the Royal Opera House, Covent Garden. In London it was hailed as an outstanding production; as theatre it worked perfectly and was a gripping operatic experience. The cast here differs from London with the sole exception of **Pär Lindskog's** Armand, but the Manon of **Laura Aikin** is no less convincing and the opera has masterly musical direction, too, from **Zoltán Peskó**. Very good sound and video direction.

Der junge Lord (opera: complete; DVD version)

Ⓝ*** Medici **DVD** 2072398. McDaniel, Driscoll, Little, Röhrl, Sardi, Krubowsk, Krebs, Johnson, Otto, Mathis, Schönberg Boys' Ch.; Ch. and O of Deutsche Oper, Berlin, Dohnányi

Der junge Lord is an ape, disguised as an English aristocrat and introduced into a smug early-nineteenth-century German community to teach it some lessons about acceptable and unacceptable social behaviour. The ape ultimately reverts from 'artificial human eloquence to crude animal violence'. Henze has a wonderful sense of theatre and an unfailing fund of musical invention, even if much of it in *Der junge Lord* is pastiche. This DVD derives from the original telecast and is directed with great aplomb and flair. Henze is impressively served here by **Christoph von Dohnányi**, who keeps the climaxes in view without starving instrumental detail of musical point. A most welcome issue.

Voices

*** Berlin Classics (ADD) 2180-2 BC (2). Trexler, Vogt, Leipzig RSO Chamber Ens., Neumann

Ⓜ*** Explore (ADD) EXP 007/8. Walker, Sperry, L. Sinf., composer

This massive and wide-ranging song-cycle of 22 numbers, lasting over 90 minutes, is among Henze's most inspired and characterful works, even including ironic songs echoing Kurt Weill, several of them setting poems by Bertolt Brecht. The wonder is that, so far from seeming too disparate a sequence, *Voices* gathers in richness as it progresses, with instruments including ocarina, accordion, mouth organ and electric guitar, as well as a large percussion section. Some of the episodes are violent, but the work is rounded off with the most beautiful and most extended piece, a duet, *Blumenfest* ('Carnival of flowers'), which seems to suggest a final ray of hope, with bitterness gone. Neumann's analogue recording, made in Germany in 1980, presents a sharply focused performance, strong and dramatic, with two excellent, clean-cut soloists.

On the appropriately named Explore label, the virtuosity of the writing is matched by the brilliance of the performance, designed as a whole evening of entertainment, here crisply caught, with the **London Sinfonietta** most inspired under the composer's baton adding to the impact. **Sarah Walker** and **Paul Sperry** are excellent soloists. First-rate Decca sound. Texts and translations are included and this makes a fine alternative to the Berlin Classics version and is probably a first choice.

HERBERT, Muriel (1897–1984)

36 Songs

Ⓝ*** Linn CKD 335. Tynan, Gilchrist, Owen Norris

Claire Tomalin movingly describes how her mother, Muriel Herbert, struggled against the problems of her life as a single mother to write these songs. She was trained at the Royal Academy of Music, and she skilfully backs up the distinctive lyricism of each song with inventive accompaniments, which **David Owen Norris** praises for their individuality. In her Hardy setting, *Faint Heart in a Railway Train*, she reflects the rhythm of the train, just as Britten does in *Winter Words*, only a generation or two earlier. There are point numbers like *Jenny Kissed Me* and some movingly simple songs, such as *David's Lament for Jonathan* in Peter Abelard's words as translated by Helen Waddell, and also in a charming Swinburne *Cradle Song*. Her setting of *Carmina Burana* is also taken from a translation of the 13th-century original by Helen Waddell. Her choice of poets ranges wide, not just among recognized classics but to Joyce and her favourite, Yeats. A charming group of tiny children's songs have words by Ada Harrison. Those are sung with clear fresh tone by **Aylish Tynan**, as is the *Cradle Song*, but most of the songs are sung by **James Gilchrist** at his most sensitive.

HERBERT, Victor (1859–1924)

Cello Concerto 2 in E min., Op 109

(N) ⊶ *** Virgin 5 0999 510 035-2. Gautier Capuçon,
Frankfurt RSO, Paavo Jäarvi – DVOŘÁK: *Cello Concerto* ***

Victor Herbert was a multi-talented musician, one of the world's leading cello virtuosos of his time and the composer of two cello concertos, which greatly influenced Dvořák in the United States to write his supreme masterpiece. That makes this coupling of the Dvořák *Cello Concerto* with the second and finer of Herbert's specially apt, and **Gautier Capuçon** gives distinctive, characterful and intense performances of both works, well supported by **Paavo Järvi** and the **Frankfurt Orchestra**, specially strong in its brass section. It is Capuçon's gift to play with warm intensity while keeping a relatively steady pulse. That makes the central slow movement of the Herbert deeply elegiac.

HÉROLD, Ferdinand (1791–1833)

La Fille mal gardée (ballet; complete; DVD version; choreography: Frederick Ashton)

⊶ *** Warner NVC Arts **DVD** 0630 19395-2. Collier,
Coleman, Shaw, L. Edwards, Grant, Royal Ballet, ROHCG
O, Lanchbery (Design: Osbert Lancaster, V/D: John Vernon)

La Fille mal gardée (ballet; new version adapted by Peter Hertel; DVD version; (choreography: Heinz Spoerli, after Jean Dauberval)

*** DG **DVD** 073 4158. Kozlova, Jensen, Ris, Schläpfer, Spoerli,
Basle Ballet, VSO, Lanchbery (Dir: José Montes-Baquer)

The ballet *La Fille mal gardée* has had a fascinatingly long and varied history, and its origins as a subject for dance pantomime go back over two centuries. The first version was created by the French choreographer, Jean Dauberval, with the familiar plot and farmyard setting, but initially with a different title; and it was taken to London in 1791. The music included popular French folk material and operatic airs of the time. But when it reached Paris in 1828 a new score was written for it by Hérold. Much of the music was his own, but he also borrowed from Rossini and later Donizetti. In 1864 yet another new score was commissioned from Peter Ludwig Hertel, which still included a good deal of Hérold's music. For the **Spoerli Basle** production, yet another score was confected by Michel Damase, based on both Hérold and

Hertel; it includes some of the original French folk and 'military' music. While the story remains broadly the same, the new music allows for varied and pretty added dances with something of a pastoral French folk style, and the soldiers too make their entry. Indeed, this Spoerli version is visually most attractive, allowing the principal dancers opportunities to mime the narrative pleasingly, and it provides plenty of leeway for charming and spectacular solos and *pas de deux*. The famous drag part of the heroine's continually thwarted mother, angrier than ever, remains, as does her famous *Clog Dance*. But the part of the rich farmer's son, Alain, is expanded and is made more appealing, an innocent rather than a simpleton. The dancing of the principals is splendid throughout, the farm scene makes a convincing and beautiful backcloth, and altogether this is a most enjoyable entertainment, with quite a few differences from the Frederick Ashton version. **John Lanchbery** conducts with flair, the orchestra plays very elegantly and is very well recorded. With excellent video direction, this is altogether recommendable.

However, the Royal Ballet *La Fille mal gardée*, with costumes and scenery by Osbert Lancaster, is a visual delight from beginning to end. Frederick Ashton's ever-inventive choreography is both witty and charming, and **Lesley Collier** and **Michael Coleman** are a most engaging pair of lovers and dance with nimble grace. **Brian Shaw's** Widow Simone is the perfect foil, with the famous *Clog Dance* a captivating highlight, and **Garry Grant** is by no means outshone as the goofy Alain: he remains in our affections when his inept wooing comes to naught. The orchestra is again conducted by **John Lanchbery**, who has arranged this complex score so that it naturally follows every move of the dancers, while his constant drawing on familiar passages by Rossini adds to the listener's pleasure. The recording too is excellent, and the slight touch of thinness on the violin timbre is not a problem when the overall sound is so rich and resonantly full.

La Fille mal gardeé (ballet, arr Lanchbery): complete

⊶ *** Australian Decca Eloquence 442 9048 (2). ROHCG O,
Lanchbery – LECOCQ: *Mam'zelle Angot* ***

Lanchbery himself concocted the score for this fizzingly comic and totally delightful ballet. Here, with sound of spectacular Decca fidelity, Lanchbery conducts a highly seductive account of the complete ballet with an orchestra long familiar with playing it in the theatre. It is coupled with Gordon Jacob's equally delicious confection, based on the music of Lecocq.

La Fille mal gardée (arr. Lanchbery): extended excerpts (CD versions)

(B) *** CfP 2-CD 586 1782 (2). RLPO, Wordsworth –
MESSAGER: *Deux Pigeons; Isoline* ***

(M) *** Decca (ADD) 430 196-2. ROHCG O, Lanchbery

Barry Wordsworth's scintillating CD account of a generous extended compilation from the ballet includes all the important sequences and the EMI digital recording is still in the demonstration bracket. With playing from the **Royal Liverpool Philharmonic** that combines refinement and delicacy with wit and humour, this is very recommendable indeed, especially in its inexpensive CfP reissue, coupled with Messager's delectable *Two Pigeons Ballet*.

The earlier extended selection on Decca has a vintage Kingsway Hall recording. One cannot believe that it dates from 1962, for the combination of ambient bloom and the most realistic detail still places it in the demonstration bracket. The performance is also wonderfully persuasive and brilliantly played, displaying both affection and sparkle in ample quantity.

Overture: Zampa

**** Chan. 9765. RLPO Ch., BBC PO, Tortelier (with Concert: *French Bonbons* ****)

Hérold's famous bandstand overture is played here with fine panache and given first-class recording. The rest of the programme of 'French Bonbons' is equally diverting, part of a concert of French orchestral lollipops.

HERRMANN, Bernard
(1911–75)

Film Scores: Five Fingers; The Snows of Kilimanjaro

(BB) *** Naxos 8.570186. Moscow SO, Stromberg

Two quite different films: the one, *Five Fingers*, dramatic – even melodramatic – the other, *The Snows of Kilimanjaro*, romantic, atmospheric and something of an epic; between them they show just how consistently and lyrically inventive Herrmann could be, whatever the challenge. Excellent performances in Moscow (of all places!) and good recording.

Film Score: The Egyptian

(BB) *** Naxos 8.557705. Moscow Symphony Ch. & O., Stromberg

John Morgan has done a characteristically superb job in reconstructing the music from the forgotten 1955 epic, *The Egyptian*, presenting the best of the 100-minute score for a 71-minute CD. The music is, of course, well worth saving. Excellent performances and sound.

HIGDON, Jennifer (born 1962)

Concerto for Orchestra; Cityscape

ⵔ– *** Telarc CD 80620. Atlanta SO, Spano

Jennifer Higdon's *Concerto* is an astonishingly alive and fertile work in five movements, summoned by bells, and opening with a whirlwind on the strings, soon joined by woodwind, and introducing glowing brass sonorities. The second movement is a sprightly Scherzo, the animation undiminished. The third movement, which is most imaginatively scored, introduces each section of the orchestra in turn, with the string chords giving a distinct whiff of Copland (which is to return in the finale). The fourth belongs to the percussion. With sounds both exotic and ear-tweaking, it gathers

momentum, helped by the drummers, to lead to the exhilarating finale with its stabbing rhythmic ostinato on the violins, which becomes more and more jubilant.

Cityscape, commissioned by the orchestra, is a portrait of Atlanta, first its vibrant *Skyline*, the centrepiece a haunting pastoral evocation as the 'river sings a song to the trees', and finally a kaleidoscopic evocation of the city's main thoroughfare. The performances here are outstanding, the *Concerto* resplendent with orchestral virtuosity, the *Cityscape* conveying an unmistakable American panorama. The Telarc engineers rise to the occasion, yet they have the advantage of the superb acoustics of Atlanta's Symphony Hall.

HILDEGARD of Bingen
(1098–1179)

(i) Ordo Virtutum; (ii) In Portrait (DVD version)

ⵔ *** BBC **DVD** Opus Arte OA 0874 D (2). (i) Boothroyd, Hancorn, Mayfield, Chamber Op. Ch., Vox Animae, Fields, Adams, Devine (Dirs: Michael Fields & Evelyn Tubb)

Confidante of popes, Hildegard was a genius in almost every field – composer, playwright, author, poet, artist, theologian, philosopher, visionary and prophet; and she taught that the world should be enjoyed by man and woman together – 'Only thus is the earth fruitful'. Her views were so remarkable in their time that it is a wonder they could be expressed and she survive. Because her mystic visions (in which she believed that God was communicating directly to her) were accepted by the Church as genuine, her power was remarkable and far-reaching. Moreover, she could speak plainly to those in authority above her and her criticisms would be accepted.

Her extraordinarily sung and spoken mystery play, *Ordo Virtutum* ('The Play of the Virtues') celebrates her philosophy, based on the love of God and the enjoyment of life, alongside resistance to sin. Even with the music alone (which has been imaginatively recorded by Sequentia) this is a remarkable achievement, but to see it played out in glowing colours, imaginatively performed and beautifully sung, partly outside and partly inside, in splendidly chosen natural settings, adds an extra dimension to the drama, particularly in the dramatic passages in Scenes I and IV, where the Devil enters. The music, simple but soaring monody but with sparingly used harp, recorder and percussion accompaniments, is very beautiful in itself; its flowing lines haunt the memory and it is radiantly sung, while the drama of the piece comes over splendidly.

The accompanying second DVD includes a compulsive BBC 'Omnibus' dramatization of Hildegard's early life, before she set up her own order; and no better choice for the role of Hildegard could have been found than **Patricia Routledge**, who conveys the warmth and spiritual essence of her character. The additional items include 'A Real Mystic' (an interview and lecture with Professor Matthew Fox, author of *Illuminations*, supplemented with an illustrative art gallery tour), while Mary Grabowsky considers Hildegard's spiritual significance for the 21st century.

Canticles of Ecstasy

✦ ❀ *** DHM/BMG 05472 77320-2. Sequentia, Thornton

This first instalment makes a splendid introduction, a collection of Marian antiphons, sequences, and responsories, plus eulogies to the Holy Spirit where the poetic imagery is often drawn from nature. At speeds more spacious than those of the Gothic Voices, with women's voices alone, the elaborate monodic lines soar heavenwards even more sensuously, matching the imagery of Hildegard's poetry.

Chants

*** Lyrichord LEMS 8027. Gentile, Drone Ch.

The famous medieval legend of Saint Ursula, daughter of a British king, tells of a three-year pilgrimage to Rome with 11,000 other women (in fact more likely a party of 11, expanded in the storytelling), who were slaughtered on their return journey by Attila the Hun for refusing to become concubines, and were thus martyred. Hildegard's chants in this collection reflect her response to their sacrifice. **Norma Gentile** sings them radiantly, and they soar up over a constantly sustained drone choral pedal. Beautifully recorded.

Hymns and sequences: *Ave generosa; Columba aspexit; O Ecclesia; O Euchari; O Jerusalem; O ignis spiritus; O presul vere civitatis; O viridissima virga*

✦ *** Hyp. CDA 66039. Gothic Voices, Muskett, White, Page

This Hyperion CD by the **Gothic Voices** was the disc which put Hildegard firmly on the map. It draws widely on the Abbess of Bingen's collection of music and poetry, the *Symphonia armonie celestium revelationum* – 'the symphony of the harmony of celestial revelations'. These hymns and sequences, most expertly performed and recorded, have excited much acclaim – and rightly so. A lovely CD.

O Jerusalem; Voice of the Blood

Ⓑ *** DHM/BMG 2-CD 74321 88689-2 (2). Sequentia
    Women's and Men's Vocal & Instrumental Ens., Thornton

The present pairing offers two collections. The first is called 'O Jerusalem'. The bells of Bamberg Cathedral toll through the opening title-piece, which also has simple instrumental backing, and there is more purely instrumental music here than in previous collections, joining flute, rebec, organ and vielle (hurdy-gurdy). There follows a lively *Magnificat* for St Rupert. The following music, beginning with *O tu illustrata*, soaringly evokes a radiantly mystical image of the Virgin Mary, to stand as symbol for the consecration of the women who were to renounce the physical world and join Hildegard's order; but for the hymn to the Holy Spirit a male group enters impressively, before the closing rapturous Marian testament from the women.

As leader of a spiritual community of women, Hildegard felt a strong identification with Ursula, and the opening lament of the cycle, *O rubor sanguinis*; and later her purity is compared with apple-blossoms. After a reference to the Trinity, the fifth piece is an address to Ecclesia, a female personification of the heavenly community, and this symbolic (and vulnerable) figure is to return in the closing pieces, of

which the antiphon, *Nunc gaudeant*, brings an extraordinary burst of spiritual energy. Two purely instrumental interludes add variety to a carefully planned collection which is, understandably, often rather sombre in its basic mood. Unfortunately, no texts or translations are offered.

The Origin of Fire (Music and Visions)

✦ *** HM Surround Sound **SACD** HMU 807327.
    Anonymous 4

Hildegard of Bingen's celestial music is well suited to SACD, offering the listener the ability to use the controls for the sound to float all around, while staying well focused. The present collection explores the theme of the 'fiery spirit' and climaxes with the extended hymn, *O ignee spiritus*, with the melismas of this central sequence and the following vision of Love particularly memorable. The **Anonymous 4** are ideal exponents, blending together and soaring up and over Hildegard's curving lines, the effect at once ecstatic and serene in a well-judged, spacious ambience.

HILLIER, Ferdinand (1811–85)

Piano Concertos 1 in F min., Op. 5; 2 in F sharp min., Op. 69; 3 in A flat, Op. 170

Ⓝ *** Hyp. CDA 67655. Shelley, Tasmanian SO

Ferdinand Hillier was immensely famous in his day, and it is no surprise to learn that he was a pupil of Hummel; but he is now merely a footnote in history. The early *First Concerto* dates from 1831, and its brilliance was designed to show off the composer's prowess at the keyboard. The *Second Concerto*, considered his finest, was premièred in 1843 and is a more complex work with some quite original touches: the pianist launches in without any introduction, for example, and one's ear is constantly tickled by the many keyboard embellishments of the thematic material. The finale with its occasional Hungarian colouring is most enjoyable. The *Third Concerto* lives up to its subtitle (*Concerto espressivo*) at the opening, but when the piano enters the *Allegro con anima* score-marking is apt, with its crisp and perky writing, and the movement as a whole is very charming indeed. The following *Andante* has a pleasing and gentle melancholy about it, and the finale is spirited and sometimes offers unexpected interruptions – such as the two fermentas which hold up the movement's progress. That this record is so successful must be attributed to **Howard Shelley's** sparkling playing, and his direction adds much to the intrinsic value of the music – as does Hyperion's excellent balance and recording.

HINDEMITH, Paul (1895–1963)

Complete Orchestral Works, Volume 1: *Amor and Psyche; Nobilissima Visione; Philharmonic Concerto; Symphonic Metamorphosis on Themes of Carl Maria von Weber* (CPO 999 004-2). *Lustige Sinfonietta; Rag Time; Symphonic Dances* (CPO 999 005-2). *Concert Music for Strings & Brass;*

Nusch-Nuschi Dances; Symphony Die Harmonie der Welt (CPO 999 006-2). Symphony in E flat; Symphony in B flat for Concert Band; Overture, Neues vom Tage ((***) CPO 999 007-2). Mathis der Maler (Symphony); Sinfonia Serena. Prelude: When Lilacs Last in the Door-yard bloom'd (CPO 999 008-2). Concerto for Orchestra; Pittsburgh Symphony; Sinfonietta in E; Marsch über den alten Schweizerto (CPO 999 014-2)

(M) *** CPO 999 248-2 (6). Queensland SO, Melbourne SO, or Sydney SO, Albert (no longer available separately)

Werner Andreas Albert's survey of the Hindemith canon was recorded between 1987 and 1992, and some of the individual discs have been discussed in earlier volumes. Both the playing of the various Australian orchestras and the radio recordings are of a high standard. The set serves as a reminder of the vigorous and lively creative imagination this (at present) underrated master possessed and the treasures that abound in his output. The *Sinfonia serena*, the *Nobilissima visione* and the *Die Harmonie der Welt Symphony* are masterpieces.

'Hindemith Conducts Hindemith' (complete DG recordings): *Amor und Psyche: Overture; Concerto for Orchestra, Op. 38; (i) The Four Temperaments (Theme and Variations for Piano and Strings); (ii) Konzertmusik for Harp, Piano & Strings, Op. 49; Symphonic Dances; Symphonic Metamorphosis on Themes of Carl Maria von Weber; Symphony (Die Harmonie der Welt); Symphony (Mathis der Maler)*

(***) DG mono 474 770-2 (3). BPO, composer; with (i) Otte; (ii) Haas

Hindemith made a number of records for Deutsche Grammophon in the early 1950s, before transferring his allegiance to EMI. Works like the exhilarating *Symphonic Dances*, the *Konzertmusik for Harp, Piano and Strings*, and the *Harmonie der Welt Symphony* have not been in currency since the days of vinyl. DG certainly lavished first-class sound on them and the *Mathis Symphony* and the *Weber Metamorphosis* are impressively detailed and full-bodied, given their date. Those who have treasured their LPs of these pieces can rest assured that a great deal of trouble has been taken over these transfers, and it is particularly good to have Hindemith's own thoughts on the *Harmonie der Welt Symphony*, one of his greatest works.

Concert Music for Brass & Strings, Op. 50; (i) Clarinet Concerto; (ii) Horn Concerto; Nobilissima visione (Suite); Symphonia serena; Symphony in B flat for Concert Band

(B) *** EMI 3 77344-2 (2). Philh. O, composer, with (i) Cahuzac; (ii) Brain

Hindemith's own performances with the **Philharmonia Orchestra** of half a dozen of his most characteristic works come out with astonishing vividness. Particularly welcome is the *Clarinet Concerto*, played here by the French virtuoso, **Louis Cahuzac**. The *Horn Concerto* dazzlingly played by its original performer, **Dennis Brain**. But it is a revelation to have the other works. *Nobilissima visione*, the fine ballet score

on the theme of St Francis, shows Hindemith at his most inspired. There is dignity and nobility in its splendid opening, and the slow movement has a grave beauty that is quite haunting. The *Concert Music* is characteristic of Hindemith's early music and the *Symphonia serena* is a splendid affair. The composer proves a most persuasive interpreter in his own music, drawing refined and committed performances and finding wit in the *Symphony for Concert Band*.

(i; ii) Concert Music for Brass and Strings; (iii) Mathis der Maler (Symphony); (i; iv) Nobilissima visione (Suite); (v) Der Schwanendreher (Viola Concerto); (vi) Symphonia Serena; (i; iv) Symphonic Metamorphosis on Themes of Weber

(N) 🕮 (B) *** EMI (ADD/DDD) 2 06863-2 (2). (i) Phd. O; (ii) Ormandy; (iii) BPO, Karajan; (iv) Sawallisch; (v) Zimmerman, Bav. R. O, Shallow; (vi) Philh., composer

As a vintage collection of the composer's key works this EMI two-CD set is hard to beat. The *Concert Music for Strings and Brass* is given a superb performance and recording by **Ormandy** and the **Philadelphia Orchestra**, who bring virtuosity and opulent tone to this score. **Karajan's** 1957 account of *Mathis der Maler* is equally impressive. It was made in the Berlin Jesus-Christus-Kirche and the sound is impressively spacious, the strings gloriously full. The full-blooded performance is remarkably dramatic and convincing, the central movement very touching. Karajan is convincing in everything he does. In the *Nobilissima visione* **Sawallisch** also draws a warm, rich-texture sound from the Philadelphia Orchestra, giving a performance that does full justice to its breadth and dignity, and if his account of the *Symphonic Metamorphosis on Themes of Weber* could be sharper and more fleet of foot, it is still very well characterized. Moreover, everything about the performance of *Der Schwanendreher* is excellent – indeed it is arguably the best before the public: the artistic and technical quality are equally fine. To cap the compilation, the composer's own account of the *Symphonia serena* is a splendid affair.

Concert Music for Strings & Brass; (i) Violin Concerto. Symphonic Metamorphosis on Themes of Weber

*** Chan. 9903. (i) Kavakos; BBC PO, Tortelier

The *Concert Music for Strings and Brass* is superbly played here. The *Violin Concerto* of 1939 has been memorably recorded by David Oistrakh and the composer but this newcomer by **Leonidas Kavakos** is without doubt the best since then.

Cello Concertos 1 in E flat, Op. 3; 2 (1940); Kammermusik 3, Op. 36/2

(BB) *** CPO 999 375-2. Geringas, Queensland SO, Albert

The *Cello Concerto*, Op. 3, is naturally a derivative piece, with a lot of Reger and Strauss and not too much of the Hindemith we know. The 1940 *Second Concerto* is a fine piece, though not the equal of the *Violin Concerto* of the previous year, and the programme is completed by the little concerto from the *Kammermusik*. **David Geringas** is a generally impressive soloist and the orchestral response maintains the eminently respectable standard we have come to expect from this series.

(i) *Cello Concerto 2*; (ii) *The Four Temperaments* (theme and variations for piano and strings)

🔊 *** Chan. 9124. (i) Wallfisch; (ii) Shelley; BBC PO, Tortelier

Both the *Cello Concerto* and *The Four Temperaments* are vintage Hindemith. The four variations of the latter are ingenious and subtle and are splendidly realized by **Howard Shelley** and the **BBC Philharmonic** under **Yan Pascal Tortelier**. **Raphael Wallfisch** is the eloquent soloist in the *Cello Concerto*. The Chandos recording is very good indeed.

Complete Orchestral Works, Volume 2: (i; ii) *Cello Concertos 1–2*; (iii; ii) *Piano Concerto*; (iii; ii) *Der Dämon, Op. 28*; (v) Film Music: *In Sturm und Eise*; (ii; iii) *Four Temperaments*; (ii) *Hérodiade* (2 versions); (v) *Kammermusik 1, Op. 24*; (ii; iv) *2, Op. 36/1*; (i; ii) *3, Op. 36/2*; (v) *5 Pieces for String Orchestra*; (v) *Plöner Musiktage: excerpts*; *Suite französischer Tänz*

Ⓑ *** CPO 999 783-2 (5). (i) Geringas; (ii) Frankfurt RSO; (iii) Mauser; (iv) Queensland SO, Albert; (v) Tasmanian SO

Apart from the *Cello Concertos*, which are still available separately, among the key works here is the *Piano Concerto*, and *The Four Temperaments*, one of the composer's most immediately accessible works, both equally successful here in the hands of **Siegfried Mauser**. *Der Dämon* ('The Demon') is an early ballet; it has great resourcefulness in matters of colour and is full of imaginative, original textures. *Hérodiade* derives its inspiration from Mallarmé's poem and is another beautiful score. It is an excellent idea to have it first with the text, then again without it, and **Annie Giequel** speaks it in exemplary fashion. The *Kammermusik 1–3* are well represented by Chailly's Decca set, but are no less effective here. The *Konzertmusik* is as original as its instrumental setting for piano, brass and harps might suggest. Throughout, **Werner Albert** gets excellent results from his forces in Frankfurt, Tasmania and Queensland, and the CPO engineering team produce recordings that are a model of good balance.

Complete Orchestral Works, Volume 3: (i) *Clarinet Concerto*; *Concerto for Flute, Oboe, Clarinet, Bassoon, Harp & Strings*; (ii) *Horn Concerto*; (iii) *Organ Concerto*; (iv) *Concerto for Trumpet, Bassoon & Strings*; (v) *Violin Concerto*; *Kammermusik 4–5, Op. 36/3–4*; *6 & 7, Op. 46/1–2*; (vi) *Konzertmusik, Op. 48*; *Der Schwanendreher (Viola Concerto)*; *Trauermusik (for viola and strings)*; *Tuttifäntchen Suite*

Ⓑ *** CPO 999 784-2 (2). (i) Mehlhart; (ii) Neuncker; (iii) Haas; (iv) Friedrich, Wilkening; (v) Olding; (vi) Dean; Frankfurt RSO or Queensland SO, Albert

The *Clarinet Concerto* was written for Benny Goodman; here the soloist is placed rather too forwardly; the *Horn Concerto* is equally familiar and both performances are eminently acceptable. The *Organ Concerto* was the composer's last work and is a rarity. To be frank it is a rather manufactured piece,

not by any means vintage Hindemith. The *Kammermusik No. 7*, also for organ, is infinitely more rewarding; its austere contrapuntal slow movement is particularly impressive. But it is the *Violin Concerto* which is the main work, and here **Dene Olding** acquits himself well. He is particularly impressive in the slow movement, which is thoughtful and inward-looking. The *Concerto for Woodwinds, Harp and Strings* is the more rewarding of the other two composite works, and is also more varied in texture. The viola was Hindemith's own instrument and he writes gratefully for it. The *Kammermusik No. 5* is fairly generously represented on disc, while the *Konzertmusik, Op. 48* has a particularly engaging first movement and an imaginative and deeply felt slow movement. It operates at a higher level of inspiration than *Der Schwanendreher*, good though that is, or the *Trauermusik* that Hindemith composed at high speed on the death of George V. The Australian violist and composer **Brett Dean** gives masterly accounts of all four pieces, and the **Queensland Symphony Orchestra** plays with excellent ensemble and precision for **Werner Albert**. This CD is the highlight of the present collection.

(i) *Horn Concerto*; *Concert Music for Brass and Strings*

🔊 Ⓜ *** EMI 5 67782-2. (i) Brain; Philh. O, Sawallisch – R. STRAUSS: *Horn Concertos 1–2* (***) ✧

The Hindemith *Horn Concerto* at first seems lyrically much less voluptuous than its Strauss couplings, but it is very atmospheric and has a brief but witty central Scherzo which **Brain** articulates very winningly. Towards the close of the haunting palindromic finale the soloist imaginatively declaims a short poem – written by the composer – in such a way that the horn's note values match the syllables of the words (which are not intended to be spoken). Brain's performance is incomparable, with splendid support from **Sawallisch**, a superb Straussian, who also directs a fine account of the *Concert Music for Brass and Strings*. Both were recorded in the Kingsway Hall in 1956 and the early stereo is clear and full.

(i) *Organ Concerto*; (ii) *Organ Sonatas 1–3*

🔊 ⒷⒷ *** Warner Apex (ADD) 2564 60227-2. (i) Heiller, Austrian RSO, Hórvat; (ii) Ullmann

The *First* and *Second Organ Sonatas* are both exhilarating and masterly. The *Third Sonata* was written shortly after Hindemith had settled in Yale. The *Organ Concerto* is not to be confused with the last of the *Kammermusik* of 1927, but is the larger-scale four-movement score, commissioned by the New York Philharmonic in 1962 and which was to prove the composer's last work. The performance by **Anton Heiller** and **Austrian Radio** forces under **Milan Hórvat** is authoritative and well recorded, and the sonatas are also finely played on the organ of the Brucknerhaus, Linz.

Violin Concerto

🔊 Ⓜ *** Decca (ADD) 470 258-2 (2). D. Oistrakh, LSO, composer – MOZART: *Sinfonia concertante, etc.* **(*); BRUCH: *Scottish Fantasia* ***

David Oistrakh's 1962 reading of the *Violin Concerto* is still first choice. It was a revelation on its release: the work has never before or since blossomed into such rewarding lyricism on record. The orchestral contribution, under the composer himself, is strikingly passionate, with the soloist providing many moments when the ear is ravished by the beauty of phrasing and inflexion. The superb sound emerges freshly in the transfer.

Concerto for Winds, Harp & Orchestra; Konzertmusik for Brass & Strings, Op. 50; Mathis der Maler: Symphony

Ⓑ *** Chan. 9457. Czech PO, Bělohlávek

The *Concerto for Winds, Harp and Orchestra* has never been heard to better effect on record. The *Konzertmusik for Brass and Strings* is hardly less imposing. **Bělohlávek** takes a broad and spacious view that is most impressive. Competition is of course much keener in the *Mathis der Maler Symphony*, and here Bělohlávek is a little more detached and wanting in intensity. The playing of the **Czech Philharmonic** is as expert and responsive as one might expect, and the Chandos engineers cope well with the reverberant acoustic.

Kammermusik 1 for 12 Instruments, Op. 24/1; (i) 2 (Piano Concerto), Op. 36/1; (ii) 3 (Cello Concerto), Op. 36/2; (iii) 4 (Violin Concerto), Op. 36/3; (iv) 5 (Viola Concerto), Op. 36/4; (v) 6 (Viola d'amore Concerto), Op. 46/1; (vi) 7 (Organ Concerto), Op. 46/2; Kleine Kammermusik for Wind Quintet, Op. 24/2

Ⓑ **** Double Decca 473 722-2 (2). (i) Brautigam; (ii) Harrell; (iii) Kulka; (iv) Kaskhashian; (v) Blume; (vi) Van Doeselaar; Concg. O, Chailly

The Decca set is complete and includes the delightful little *Wind Quintet (Kleine Kammermusik)*. The playing of the distinguished soloists and the members of the **Concertgebouw** is beyond praise, so is the Decca recording.

Kammermusik 5, Op. 36/4; Konzertmusik for Viola & Orchestra, Op. 48; Viola Concerto (Der Schwanendreher)

*** ASV CDDCA 931. Cortese, Philh. O, Brabbins

Paul Cortese is the accomplished soloist in all three works, including the fifth of the *Kammermusik*. The **Philharmonia** respond with some enthusiasm to **Martyn Brabbins's** direction, and although there are finer recordings of *Der Schwanendreher* (above all, Tabea Zimmermann on EMI, now deleted) this disc gives undoubted pleasure. The recording is very good indeed, with great presence and body.

5 Pieces for strings, Op. 44/4

*** Australian Decca Eloquence (ADD) 442 8414. ASMF, Marriner – BARTÓK: *Divertimento for Strings* ***; PROKOFIEV: *Visions Fugitives*; VIVALDI: *Concertos* ***

With finely etched playing in precise ensemble, **Marriner** and the **Academy** transform the Hindemith *Pieces* from exercises to works of genuine imagination. Also included on this disc is the **Moscow Chamber Orchestra's** classic (1962) recording of Bartók's *Divertimento for strings*: the ensemble and intonation are faultless. This is a performance of extreme brilliance and, if emotionally it is driven very hard, it is quite appropriate in such music.

Pittsburgh Symphony; Ragtime; Symphonic Dances

*** Chan. 9530. BBC PO, Tortelier

The *Symphonic Dances* is one of Hindemith's most inventive and enjoyable works and it is full of resource and imagination and deserves to be as popular as the *Symphonic Metamorphosis on Themes of Weber*. The *Pittsburgh Symphony* is a rewarding piece full of good ideas. **Yan Pascal Tortelier** and the **BBC Philharmonic** give meticulously prepared and committed performances, and the Chandos sound is above reproach. Strongly recommended.

Sinfonia serena; Symphony (Die Harmonie der Welt)

Ⓑ *** Chan. 9217. BBC PO, Tortelier

The *Sinfonia serena* (1946) is a brilliant and inventive score. The scoring is inventive and imaginative. The *Symphony, Die Harmonie der Welt* (1951), is another powerful and consistently underrated score. These well-prepared and finely shaped **BBC** performances are given state-of-the-art recording quality. An outstanding issue.

Symphonic Metamorphosis on Themes of Weber

*** BBC Legends BBCL 4176-2. LSO, Jochum – HAYDN: *Symphonies 100 & 101* ***

(*) Telarc **SACD 60648. Atlanta SO, Shaw – COPLAND: *Appalachian Spring*, etc. **(*)

Jochum brings out the joy of what might be regarded as Hindemith's most extrovert work. What he relishes is the colour, brilliance and humour in the way Hindemith orchestrates the Weber themes, giving the music swaggering flamboyance, underlining the sharp contrasts of timbre. The **LSO**, then as now acknowledged as the most brilliant of the London orchestras, respond with virtuoso playing, with horn and timpani in particular having a wonderful time.

Robert Shaw treats Hindemith's colourful variations almost neoclassically. His is a sharp, incisive performance that misses some of the bounce and charm but is very well recorded – although the SACD enhancement is marginal. A curious coupling for the three Copland ballet scores.

Symphony in E flat; Overture Neues vom Tage; Nobilissima visione

*** Chan. 9060. BBC PO, Tortelier

The *Symphony in E flat* is an inventive and resourceful score and is well worth investigating. **Yan Pascal Tortelier** gets excellent results from the **BBC Philharmonic**. Good, musicianly performances of *Nobilissima visione* and the much earlier *Neues vom Tage Overture* complete an admirable addition to the Hindemith discography.

Trauermusik

*** Cal. CAL 9364. Bukac, Czech RSO, Válek – BARTÓK: *Viola Concerto*; MARTINŮ: *Rhapsody-Concerto* ***

When Hindemith came to London to perform his *Schwanendreher Concerto*, he was greeted by the news that King George V had died. The BBC commissioned him to write his *Funeral Music*, which he accomplished in a few days: a poignant seven-minute piece which **Vladimir Bukac**, the violist of the Talich Quartet, plays with feeling and dignity.

CHAMBER MUSIC

Bassoon Sonata; Harp Sonata; Horn Sonata; Sonata for 2 Pianos; Sonata for Piano, 4 Hands

*** MDG 304 0694-2. Ens. Villa Musica, with Thunemann, Storck, Vlatkovic, Piret, Randalu

These are not only well-fashioned but often very satisfying pieces. **Klaus Thunemann** is an expert and persuasive advocate of the *Bassoon Sonata* and its companions here receive highly accomplished performances. Throughout the **Ensemble Villa Musica's** Hindemith series we have heard so far, the recording is very faithful and lifelike.

(i) *Double-bass Sonata;* (ii) *Trombone Sonata;* (iii) *Tuba Sonata;* (iv) *Cello Sonata; Small Sonata for Violoncello; A Frog He Went A-courting*

🔑 *** MDG 304 0697-2. Randalu, with (i) Güttler; (ii) Slokar; (iii) Hilgers; (iv) Ostertag

This collection is both artistically rewarding and technically excellent. The sound is very vivid and present and the programme intelligently laid out. Hindemith was enormously prolific and often composed on automatic pilot, but these pieces are fresh and inventive.

Horn Sonata

(M) (***) BBC mono BBCL 4164-2. Brain, Mewton-Wood – BEETHOVEN: *Quintet* (**); JACOB: *Wind Sextet*; VINTER: *Hunter's Moon* (***)

Dennis Brain gives a masterly account of the lyrically unpredictable and at times marmoreal Hindemith *Sonata* which, like the *Concerto*, was written for him. His outstanding partner, **Noel Mewton-Wood**, is a strong musical personality in his own right: in the slow movement his delicate, bravura articulation is memorable, and elsewhere his playing is truly authoritative. The mono recording is well balanced.

Kleine Kammermusik for Wind Quintet, Op. 24/2

*** Nim. NI 5728. V. Quintet – LIGETI: *6 Bagatelles*; NIELSEN: *Wind Quintet* ***

(BB) **(*) Naxos 8.553851-2. Thompson Wind Quintet – BARBER: *Summer Music* **(*); JANÁČEK: *Mládí* **(*); LARSSON: *Quattro tempi* **

The **Vienna Quintet** fully convey the wit and lightness of touch that distinguish Hindemith's writing in this entertaining *Kleine Kammermusik*. The playing is a delight from first to last and is beautifully recorded in the Wiener Konzerthaus. The coupling, too, is logical in giving us an exact contemporary, the Nielsen *Wind Quintet*.

The **Michael Thompson Wind Quintet** give an excellently spirited and alert performance with plenty of wit but the close balance is a distinct handicap. If you think this would not worry you, it is worth the modest outlay.

String Quartet 3, Op. 22

❀ (***) Testament mono SBT 1052. Hollywood Qt – PROKOFIEV: *Quartet 2*; WALTON: *Quartet in A min.* (***) ❀

The **Hollywood Quartet** possessed extraordinary virtuosity and perfection of ensemble, and it is difficult to imagine more persuasive advocacy. The transfer is excellent and, although the mono sound is less than ideal, the performance still sweeps the board.

String Quartet 4, Op. 22

*** ECM 1874 476 5779. Zehetmair Qt – BARTÓK: *Quartet 5* ***

Those who find Hindemith's music ugly should hear the **Zehetmair Quartet's** refined and commanding account of the *Fourth Quartet*. They are totally inside this idiom.

Viola Sonata in F, Op. 11/4

(***) Biddulph mono LAB 148. Primrose, Sandromá – BAX: *Fantasy Sonata for Viola & Piano*; BLOCH: *Suite* (***)

The classic 1938 Primrose recording of Hindemith's most lyrical sonata, with **Jesús María Sandromá**, probably remains unsurpassed for sheer style and refinement of tone. Given the date, the sound is very acceptable.

(Unaccompanied) *Viola Sonatas 1; 2, Op. 11/5; 3, Op. 25/1; 4, Op. 31/4*

*** ASV CDDCA 947. Cortese

(i) *Viola Sonatas* (for viola and piano) *Op. 11/4; Op. 25/4;* (Unaccompanied) *Viola Sonatas: Op. 11/5; Op. 25/1; Op. 31/4*

🔑 *** ECM 833 309-2 (2). Kashkashian, (i) with Levin

The solo sonatas are played with superb panache and flair – and, even more importantly, with remarkable variety of colour – by **Kim Kashkashian**, who has an enormous dynamic range. The performances of the sonatas with piano are hardly less imaginative and the recording is good.

Violin Sonatas 1 in E flat, Op. 11/1; 2 in D, Op. 11/2; 3 in E; 4 in C

*** BIS CD 761. Wallin, Pöntinen

As with most Hindemith, both the Op. 11 *Sonatas* are well crafted and inventive. The finest of the four is the last, in C major, which is both individual and finely wrought. **Ulf Wallin** and **Roland Pöntinen** play this repertoire with real dedication and conviction, and the BIS recording is very lifelike and present. They include a fragment of an alternative finale for the *E flat Sonata*, Op. 11/1, that Hindemith subsequently discarded.

PIANO MUSIC

Piano Sonatas 1–3; Variations

** Marco 8.223337. Petermandl

Hindemith's crisply contrapuntal piano writing brings a strong consistency to the three contrasted works. No. 1 is the most challengingly ambitious, with the compact No. 2 more easily lyrical. Yet it is No. 3, directly echoing the first of Beethoven's late sonatas, Opus 101, which is the clearest masterpiece. Built on strikingly memorable themes and ending with a formidable double fugue, it inspires **Petermandl Hans**, to a powerful performance, very well recorded.

Ludus tonalis; Suite (1922), Op. 26

**(*) Hyp. CDA 66824. McCabe

Hindemith's *Ludus tonalis* has been recorded before, but not with more concentration and authority than it is on Hyperion by **John McCabe**. He offers also the *Suite 1922* which, if anything, is thornier still. So if you are a Hindemith addict, this is surely a disc you will want to explore.

Organ Sonatas 1–3

*** Chan. 9097. Kee – REGER: *4 Organ Pieces* ***

Piet Kee plays on the Müller organ of St Bavo in Haarlem, an instrument more suited to Hindemith than the somewhat spacious acoustic in which it is recorded. This small point apart, Kee plays with his customary distinction and character. All three sonatas are rewarding, and no one investing in this disc is likely to be disappointed on either artistic or technical grounds.

VOCAL MUSIC

When Lilacs Last in the Dooryard Bloom'd (Requiem)

Ⓜ *** Telarc CD 80132. DeGaetani, Stone, Atlanta Ch. & SO, Shaw

This 'Requiem for those we loved' is one of the composer's most deeply felt works and one of his best. **Shaw** gives a performance of great intensity and variety of colour and nuance. Both his soloists are excellent, and there is both weight and subtlety in the orchestral contribution. Splendid recording.

OPERA

(i; ii) Sancta Susanna (complete). Das Nusch-Nuschi: Dances, Op. 20; Tuttifäntchen: Suite; (i) 3 Songs, Op. 9

*** Chan. 9620. (i) Bullock; (ii) D. Jones, Gunson & Soloists, Leeds Festival Ch.; BBC PO, Y. P. Tortelier

In the one-Act opera *Sancta Susanna* Hindemith's musical language is distinctly expressionist, lyrical and atmospheric, though with traces of Gallic influence (and in particular Debussy) and Puccinian elements happily intermingled. It is a far cry from the austere, monochrome contrapuntalist of the later symphonies. Written immediately after the end of the First World War, it scandalized its first audiences by its erotic-cum-blasphemous character. It is a short piece, some 23 minutes in length, but enormously intense and con-

centrated in feeling. The performance is gripping, splendidly sung and expertly played by **Yan Pascal Tortelier** and the **BBC Philharmonic Orchestra**.

The oriental elements in the *Nusch-Nuschi Dances* simply adorn a 1920s-style score, while the suite from the children's pantomime, *Tuttifäntchen*, of 1922 is delightful in its use of tunes from children's games, with ragtime introduced in the *Dance of the Dolls*. The Straussian *Drei Gesänge*, Op. 9, written earlier, in 1917, are luxuriant and rich, and again unlike anything we know from the mature composer. **Susan Bullock** sings them with great conviction and flair.

HODDINOTT, Alun
(1929–2008)

(i) Clarinet Concerto, Op. 3; (ii) Harp Concerto, Op. 11; Piano Concertos: (iii) 1, Op. 19; (iv) 2, Op. 21

*** Lyrita (ADD/DDD) SRCD 330. (i) De Peyer; (ii) Ellis; (i; ii) LSO, cond. Atherton; (iii) Fowke, RPO, Wordsworth; (iv) M. Jones, RPO, A. Davis

The *Clarinet Concerto* is an early work which (in 1954) put Hoddinott on the map. Fluent as it is, it does not match the *Harp Concerto* in the quality of its invention or the intensity of its atmosphere. The *Harp Concerto*, written for **Osian Ellis** in 1957, is a most beautiful work, strongly individual in feeling and quite haunting. The textures are splendidly lucid and transparent, and the recording is a model of its kind in the balance between solo instrument and orchestra. The two *Piano Concertos* were written one after the other in 1960, although the *Second* was revised in 1969. Both have strongly motivated themes and each makes use of the device of a palindrome. These recordings were made by Decca engineers and are of the most spectacular realism.

(i; ii) Concertino for Viola & Small Orchestra, Op. 14; (iii; iv) Nocturnes & Cadenzas for Cello & Orchestra, Op. 62; (v; ii) Dives and Lazarus (cantata), Op. 39; (vi; iv) Sinfonia Fidei (for soprano, tenor, chorus & orchestra), Op. 95

*** Lyrita (ADD/DDD) SRCD 332. (i) Erdélyi; (ii) New Philh. O, Atherton; (iii) Welsh; (iv) Philh. O, Groves; (v) Palmer, Allen, Welsh Nat. Op. Ch.; (vi) Gomez, Burrowes, Philh. Ch.

Csaba Erdélyi, the superb principal viola of the **New Philharmonia** in the mid-1970s, makes an admirable advocate in the imaginatively conceived *Viola Concertino* of 1958, the point of the argument made sharper by the lightness of the string section against a normal woodwind group. By comparison the *Nocturnes and Cadenzas* is less easy to come to grips with, presenting a more withdrawn face. Nevertheless **Moray Welsh** excels himself as the cello soloist, making his soliloquy seemingly improvisational, and **Sir Charles Groves** draws excellent playing from the **Philharmonia Orchestra**. *Dives and Lazarus* is highly individual, especially in the dramatic closing section, *When Lazarus died*, with its exultant 'Allelujas'. *Sinfonia Fidei* (1977) returns to a more conservative idiom than that contained in Hoddinott's purely serial music, but the result is hardly less passionately compelling. Soloists, chorus and orchestra join to project all this music with the most ardent advocacy; and the recordings, spaciously atmospheric, whether analogue or digital, are in every respect first rate.

Symphonies (i; ii) 2, Op. 29; (i; iii) 3, Op. 61; (iv) 5, Op. 81

*** Lyrita (ADD) SRCD 331. (i) LSO; (ii) Del Mar; (iii) Atherton; (iv) RPO, A. Davis

The *Second Symphony* dates from 1962 and is clearly the work of a composer who, though a serialist, still retains an allegiance to tonal centres and who uses twelve-note technique as a spur rather than a crutch. Its arguments are not difficult to follow and there is a great outburst of passionate lyricism from the strings at the climax of the *molto adagio*. **Norman Del Mar** directs the work confidently, and the **LSO** respond with eloquence. The *Third Symphony* is even more powerfully wrought, dark in colouring and deeply imaginative. **David Atherton's** performance (again using the LSO) is wholly convincing. The *Fifth Symphony* is a more abrasive work than the *Third* and less immediately approachable, although the second of its two movements is laid out in six clearly differentiated sections. The vintage recordings of both the *Third* and *Fifth Symphonies* were made by a Decca engineering team in the early 1970s and are spectacularly vivid in their presence, range and definition.

HOFFSTETTER, Romanus
(1742–1815)

String Quartets: 1 in C; 2 E (attrib. Haydn as Op. 3/1–2)

(BB) *** Naxos 8.555703. Kodály Qt – HAYDN: *Cassations, Hob II/21–22* (arr. for *String Quartet*) ***

String Quartets 3 in G; 4 in B flat; 5 in F (Serenade); 6 in A (attrib. HAYDN, as Op. 3/3–6)

⌐ (BB) *** Naxos 8.555704. Kodály Qt

Romanus Hoffstetter, if it was he who composed these works, seems fated never to have his name on them, even though H. C. Robbins Landon discovered that 'Signor Hoffstetter' was inscribed on the plates from which the original parts were printed. Haydn never questioned their authenticity when Pleyel included them in the complete edition of his string quartets. They are elegant, neatly composed works with lively outer movements, gentle, graceful slow movements and the kind of lilting, intoxicating Minuets that are an integral part of Austrian music of this period. The *C major* stands out for its resourceful opening *Fantasia con variazioni* and its charmingly wistful *Andante*. But it is the *F major* that is justly the most famous, for not only does it have the unforgettable 'Serenade' for its *Andante cantabile*, but also another *galant* lilting tune as the second subject of the opening movement, and another amiable *Scherzando* finale.

The **Kodály Quartet's** performances are in every way first class, treating the music with all the finesse that is its due,

and winningly acknowledging its vitality and charm. The recording is most real and vivid.

HOLBORNE, Antony
(c. 1560–1602)

Pieces for bandora: Almain: The Night Watch; Fantazia; A Ground; for cittern: A French Toy; A Horne Pype; The Miller; Praeludium; Sicke Sicke and Very Sicke; (i) for cittern with a bass: Galliard; Maister Earles Pavane; Queenes Galliard; for lute: Almains: Almaine; The Choice. Fantasia. Galliards: As it fell on a holie yve; The Fairy-rownde; Holburns passion; Muy linda; Responce; The teares of the muses. Pavans: Heres paternus; Pavan, and Galliard to the same; Posthuma; Sedet sola. A French Toy. Variations: Il Nodo di gordio

⌐ ✪ *** Gaudeamus CDGAU 173. Heringman, (i) with Pell

An entirely delightful representation on CD of an Elizabethan lutenist, composer and poet, now totally overshadowed by Dowland. Indeed, his melancholy pavane, *Posthuma*, has as much 'dolens' as almost anything by Dowland. It is this meditative quality which **Jacob Heringman** catches to perfection and which makes this collection so appealing. He improvises his own divisions when needed, as was expected by the composer, and his playing is appealingly spontaneous. But there is lively writing too, like *The Miller* and *A French Toy*; and how well they sound on the cittern, a robust-timbred instrument favoured mainly by the lower classes, and which came to be much played in barber's shops. Heringman is beautifully recorded in a most suitable ambience, providing the ideal CD for a late-evening reverie.

Lute pieces

(BB) **(*) Naxos 8.553974. Wilson (lute) – ROBINSON: *Lute Pieces & Duets* ***

Christopher Wilson plays these pieces very well, notably the lively items like *The Fairy Round* and *Wanton*, with *Muy Linda* a highlight. But he does not penetrate the inner core of the ruminative pieces as touchingly as Jacob Heringman. However, there is not too much duplication here and this inexpensive Naxos disc is well worth obtaining for the coupled repertoire (including duets) by Holborne's contemporary, Thomas Robinson.

Pavans, Galliards, Almains

*** HM HMX 2907238. The King's Noyse, O'Dette

In 1599 Antony Holborne published a collection of his 'Pavans, Galliards, Almains and other Short Airs', containing 65 dances for five-part consort, which he suggested could be played on 'viols, violins, or other musical wind instruments'. Most of the pieces on this CD come from this anthology and are stylishly and warmly played by a string group, but with the occasional solo from **Paul O'Dette** on lute or cittern. The programme is arranged under the title 'My Self' and is subdivided into biographical sections. But this is just a charming conceit for, although the titles of many of the pieces reflect the described events, they are not directly associated with them. Nevertheless, it makes for an attractive and varied programme, very well played and recorded.

HOLBROOKE, Josef (1878–1958)

The Birds of Rhiannon, Op. 87

*** Lyrita SRCD 269. LPO, Handley –BANTOCK: *Overture to a Greek Tragedy: Oedipus at Colonus*: Philh. O, Braithwaite; ROOTHAM: *Symphony 1* ***

The Birds of Rhiannon is a shortish piece, lasting about 15 minutes and drawing on Holbrooke's operatic trilogy on Welsh legends that occupied him from 1912 to 1920. The piece ends with birdsong. The level of inspiration of Holbrooke's piece does not quite rise to the theme and it would be idle to pretend that it is a masterpiece. But the playing of the **LPO** under **Handley** is excellent, as it is also in the rather more interesting coupling.

HOLMBOE, Vagn (1909–96)

(i) Cello Concerto, Op. 120; (ii) Brass Quintet, Op. 79; (iii) Triade, Op. 123; (iv) Benedic Domino, Op. 59

☞ *** BIS (ADD/DDD) CD 078. (i) Bengtsson, Danish RSO, Ferencsik; (ii) Swedish Brass Quintet; (iii) Tarr, Westenholz; (iv) Camerata Ch., Enevold

Vagn Holmboe's magificent *Cello Concerto* is given an excellent performance here, and the account of the choral piece, *Benedic Domino*, has an austere beauty and elevation of feeling that are rare in contemporary music. The *Brass Quintet* is effective and stirring; and the *Triade* for trombone and organ is hardly less striking. Only the *Quintet* is a digital recording, but its companions here are also strikingly good as sound.

Chamber Concertos (i) 1, Op. 17; (ii) 3, Op. 21; (iii) 7, Op. 37; (iv) Beatus Parvo for Choir & Orchestra, Op. 117

*** BIS CD 1176. Aalborg SO, Hughes, with (i) Ogawa; (ii) Fröst; (iii) Hunt; (iv) Danish Nat. Op. Ch.

The *Beatus Parvo* (1971), composed for an amateur music society in southern Sweden, has clarity of texture and immediacy of response. Readers coming to this repertoire afresh will find the present issue and its companions bring performances of real distinction and very vivid recorded sound.

Chamber Concertos 8 (Sinfonia concertante), Op. 38; 10 (Woodwind, Brass and Gut), Op. 40; Concerto giocondo e severo, Op. 132; Den Galsindede Tyrk (The Ill-tempered Turk): Ballet Suite, Op. 32b

*** BIS CD 917. Aalborg SO, Hughes

There is a strongly neoclassical flavour to both scores, and those who enjoy the exhilarating *Fifth Symphony* will derive much pleasure from both, and particularly the resourceful theme-and-variations that comprise the second movement of the *Eighth*.

The *Concerto giocondo e severo* is scored for much larger forces than its predecessors but it has much of their ambience and spirit and is every bit as rewarding. His ballet *Den Galsindede Tyrk* ('The Ill-tempered Turk') was never mounted. In 1970 Holmboe returned to the score and fashioned a five-movement work of quality from the original, recasting and rescoring much of it. **Owain Arwel Hughes** and his fine **Aalborg** musicians are completely attuned to Holmboe's world and the recording has all the realism, clarity and presence one has come to expect from BIS.

Chamber Concertos (i) 11 for Trumpet & Orchestra, Op. 44; (ii) 12 for Trombone, Op. 52; (iii) Tuba Concerto, Op. 152; Intermezzo Concertante, Op. 171

☞ *** BIS CD 802. (i) Hardenberger; (ii) Lindberg; (iii) Larsen; Aalborg SO, Hughes

The noble neo-baroque *Concerto No. 11 for Trumpet* (1948) could hardly be better served than by **Håkan Hardenberger's** account with the **Aalborg Orchestra**, and any newcomer will have to be pretty good to match **Christian Lindberg's** account of the *Twelfth Chamber Concerto*. These are inspiriting and inspiring pieces. The one-movement *Tuba Concerto* explores the virtuoso possibilities of this instrument as do few others; so does the *Intermezzo Concertante*. These are dazzling performances and the orchestral support under **Owain Arwel Hughes** is first class. The recording is state of the art. Highly recommended.

Epilog, Op. 80; Epitaph (Symphonic Metamorphosis), Op. 68; Monolith, Op. 76; Tempo variabile, Op. 108

☞ ✹ *** BIS CD 852. Aarhus SO, Hughes

The first of Vagn Holmboe's *Symphonic Metamorphoses* brings musical ideas that unfold, change shape and assume new identities without losing sight of their individuality, in much the same way as does, say, the *Seventh Symphony* of Sibelius. The playing of the **Aarhus Orchestra** is excellent and **Owain Arwel Hughes** is in total sympathy with these magnificent scores. The recording is state of the art.

Flute Concertos 1, Op. 126; 2, Op. 147; (i) Concerto for Recorder, Strings, Celesta & Vibraphone, Op. 122

*** BIS CD 911. Wiesler, (i) with Laurin; Aarhus SO, Hughes

The *Flute Concertos* and the *Concerto for Recorder, Strings, Celesta and Vibraphone* are wonderfully inventive scores whose luminous, shining textures captivate the mind and reaffirm the conviction that Holmboe stands head and shoulders above his contemporaries in the North. Strong performances from all concerned, and splendid recording too. Don't miss this.

Symphonies 1, Op. 4; 3 (Sinfonia rustica), Op. 25; 10, Op. 105

*** BIS CD 605. Aarhus SO, Hughes

Symphony 2, Op. 15; Sinfonia in memoriam, Op. 65

*** BIS CD 695. Aarhus SO, Hughes

Symphonies (i) 4 (Sinfonia sacra), Op. 29. 5, Op. 35

**(*) BIS CD 572. (i) Jutland Op. Ch.; Aarhus SO, Hughes

Symphonies 6, Op. 43; 7, Op. 50

**(*) BIS CD 573. Aarhus SO, Hughes

Symphonies 8, Op. 56 (1951); 9 (1968)

🎧—🏵 **** BIS CD 618. Aarhus SO, Hughes

Symphonies 11, Op. 141; 12, Op. 175; 13, Op. 192

*** BIS CD 728. Aarhus SO, Hughes

The general outlook of the *First Symphony* (*Sinfonia da camera*) is neoclassical and its proportions are modest, but one recognizes the vital current of the later Holmboe, the lucidity of thinking and the luminous textures. The last movement has an infectious delight in life; so, too, has the exhilarating finale of the *Third* (*Sinfonia rustica*), the first of his three wartime symphonies. The *Tenth* is dark, powerful and imaginative: altogether one of the Danish composer's most subtle and satisfying works. The performances and recordings are altogether first class.

The *Second Symphony* with its imaginative middle movement and its vital companions is a splendid piece. The *Sinfonia in memoriam* is a dark work of striking power and imaginative breadth and is masterly in every way.

The *Fifth Symphony* makes a good entry point into Holmboe's world. The only word to describe its outer movements is exhilarating. The slow movement has a modal character, but an anguished outburst in the middle serves as a reminder that this is a wartime work, composed during the dark days of the Nazi occupation. The *Fourth* (*Sinfonia sacra*) is a six-movement choral piece. It encompasses a bracing vigour and underlying optimism alongside moments of sustained grief.

Holmboe's *Sixth Symphony* is a much darker piece than its predecessor. Its distinctively Nordic world is established by the brooding, slow-moving fourths of the long introduction; there is writing of great luminosity too. The one-movement *Seventh Symphony* is a highly concentrated score, individual in both form and content, which encompasses great variety of pace and mood.

This conductor penetrates the spirit of the score of the *Eighth Symphony*. The *Ninth Symphony* is a dark, powerful work, among the finest Holmboe has given us. This is music which, one can feel with some certainty, future generations will want to hear. The **Aarhus Orchestra** are equally persuasive in the *Ninth* as in the *Eighth*, and the recording is the best so far in the cycle.

The *Thirteenth Symphony* is an astonishing achievement for a composer in his mid-eighties. It is a veritable powerhouse. The *Twelfth* is tautly structured and well argued, though less inspired than the *Eleventh Symphony*, which finds Holmboe at his most visionary. Every credit is owed to **Owain Arwel Hughes** and the **Aarhus Symphony Orchestra** for their fervent advocacy of all this music and to the splendid BIS engineers for the vivid and superbly natural sound.

PIANO MUSIC

Romanian Suite; Sonatina Briosa (symphonic suite); Suono da bardo; Suite, Op. 4

*** Danacord DACOCD 502. Blyme

Suono da bardo is Holmboe's most important piano piece and comes from the same period as the *Seventh Symphony*. Subtitled 'Symphonic Suite', it is undoubtedly more symphonic than pianistic. Holmboe's composer-pianist colleague, Niels Viggo Bentzon, gave its first performance, and **Anker Blyme** made its first LP recording a few years later, in 1956. He returned to it some four decades later to give this admirable account; the rest of the programme is equally impressive.

HOLST, Gustav (1874–1934)

Beni Mora (Oriental Suite); Egdon Heath; Fugal Overture; Hammersmith; (i) Invocation for Cello & Orchestra; Somerset Rhapsody

🎧—**BB** *** Naxos 8.553696. RSNO, Lloyd-Jones; (i) with Hugh

The six works here are neatly balanced, three dating from before the climactic period of *The Planets* and three after. So the generously lyrical *Somerset Rhapsody*, *Beni Mora* and the long-neglected *Invocation for Cello and Orchestra* (with **Timothy Hugh** a moving soloist) lead on to the tauter and more astringent post-war works: the Hardy-inspired *Egdon Heath*, the darkly intense prelude and fugue, *Hammersmith*, and the *Fugal Overture*. Fresh and idiomatic performances, superbly recorded in full and brilliant sound.

(i) Beni Mora (Oriental Suite), Op. 29/1; A Fugal Overture, Op. 40/1; Hammersmith – A Prelude & Scherzo for Orchestra, Op. 52; (ii) Japanese Suite; (i) Scherzo (1933/4); A Somerset Rhapsody, Op. 21

*** Lyrita (ADD) SRCD 222. (i) LPO; (ii) LSO; Boult

Beni Mora (written after a holiday in Algeria) is an attractive, exotic piece that shows Holst's flair for orchestration vividly. **Boult** clearly revels in its sinuousness. The *Japanese Suite* is not very Japanese, although it has much charm, particularly the piquant *Marionette Dance* and the innocuous *Dance under the cherry tree*. The most ambitious work here is *Hammersmith*, far more than a conventional tone-picture, intensely poetic. As with other records in this Lyrita series, the first-class analogue recording has been splendidly transferred to CD.

(i) Brook Green Suite for String Orchestra; (ii) Fugal Concerto for Flute and Oboe; The Perfect Fool (Ballet Suite); St Paul's Suite for String Orchestra; Somerset Rhapsody, Op. 21/2; (iii) Six Choruses for Male Voices, excerpts: Good Friday; Love Song; Intercession; Before Sleep; Drinking Song; A Dirge for Two Veterans

🎧—**B** *** CfP (DDD/ADD) 575 9812. ECO, (i) Menuhin; (ii) with Snowden, Theodore; (iii) with Baccholian Singers, Humphries

There are a number of collections of Holst's shorter orchestral works currently available on CD, but none is better played or recorded than this and none is better value. There is some delightful solo playing from **Jonathan Snowden** and **David Theodore** in the *Fugal Concerto*. Even if the suite from *The Perfect Fool* involves duplication, this is still a disc well worth having, the more so as EMI have now added a short but memorably beautiful collection of Holst's shorter choral pieces, beautifully sung and warmly recorded two decades earlier. Most memorable of all is the darkly compressed *A Dirge for Two Veterans*, a processional setting with brass and percussion, written in 1914.

Brook Green Suite; (i) Double Violin Concerto, Op. 49; (ii) Fugal Concerto for Flute, Oboe & Strings, Op. 40/2; (iii) Lyric Movement for Viola & Small Orchestra; 2 Songs Without Words, Op. 22; St Paul's Suite, Op. 29/2

*** Chan. 9270. (i) Ward, Watkinson; (ii) Dobing, Hooker; (iii) Tees; City of L. Sinfonia, Hickox

The most striking piece here, a fine example of Holst's later, sparer style, is the *Double Concerto* for two violins and small orchestra, very taut and intense. The delicacy of the solo playing in the central *Lament* of this fine work is matched by the ethereal *pianissimo* from **Stephen Tees** at the opening of the *Lyric Movement*. The woodwind playing is delightful here too, as is the gentle clarinet solo which opens the *Country Song*, the first of Holst's two *Songs Without Words*. What matters throughout this programme is the surging warmth that **Richard Hickox** draws from his modest forces. The recording is superb – very real indeed.

Brook Green Suite; (i; ii) Double Violin Concerto, Op. 49; (iii) Fugal Concerto for Flute, Oboe & Strings, Op. 40/2; (iv) Lyric Movement for Viola & Chamber Orchestra; (i) A Song of the Night (for violin & orchestra), Op. 19/1. St Paul's Suite

⊶ (BB) *** Naxos 8.570339. E. Sinfonia, Griffiths, with (i) Graham; (ii) Ewins; (iii) Pyne, Harmer; (iv) Viytovych

An outstandingly imaginative collection of Holst's shorter works, four of them in concertante style, with excellent soloists from the orchestra. New to the catalogue is the beautiful *Song of the Night* for violin and orchestra, written in 1905 but not published until 50 years after the composer's death. It is beautifully played here, but then the solo contributions to the other works are hardly less memorable, and **Howard Griffiths** displays his Holstian credentials with vigorously expressive accounts of the better-known *Brook Green* and *St Paul's Suites*, extremely well played by the **English Sinfonia**. The recording has splendid body and atmosphere.

Cotswolds Symphony in F (Elegy: In memoriam William Morris), Op. 8; Indra (Symphonic Poem), Op. 13; (i) Invocation (for cello & orchestra), Op. 19/2; (iii) The Lure (ballet music); The Morning of the Year: Dances, Op. 45/2; Sita: Interlude from Act III, Op. 23; (ii) A Song of the Night (for violin & orchestra), Op. 19/1; A Winter Idyll

*** Lyrita (DDD/ADD) SRCD 209. (i) Baillie; (ii) McAslan; LPO, or (iii) LSO; Atherton

The earliest work here, *A Winter Idyll*, was written in 1897 when Holst was in his early twenties. Both in this work and in the *Elegy*, which is a slow movement originally forming part of a *Cotswolds Symphony*, one can detect little of the mature Holst. The familiar fingerprints do surface, however, in *Indra* (1903) and *A Song of the Night* (1905), which is among the scores Colin Matthews has edited. *The Lure* (1921) was written at short notice for Chicago and is characteristic, but the inspiration is not of the quality of *The Perfect Fool*. The *Dances* from *The Morning of the Year* enjoy the distinction of being the very first commission made by the BBC Music Department. Holstians will need no urging to acquire this interesting, well-played and well-recorded disc. None of the music is Holst at his best, but it usefully fills in our picture of him.

(i) Egdon Heath; (ii) Fugal Concerto, Op. 40/2

(M) (***) BBC mono/stereo BBCB 8007-2. (i) LSO, Britten; (ii) Adeney, Graeme, ECO, I. Holst – BRITTEN: *The Building of the House Overture*; BRIDGE: *Enter Spring; The Sea* ***

Though the 1961 mono recording is dry, with the limited dynamic range sabotaging *pianissimos*, the concentration of **Britten** interpreting *Egdon Heath*, one of Holst's most inspired works, makes this well worth hearing, particularly with such excellent couplings.

Imogen Holst's urgent, robust reading of her father's *Fugal Concerto* comes from 1969 in much finer sound, also recorded at the Aldeburgh Festival. She brings out a bluff honesty in Holst's very English neoclassical writing. Fine solo work, too, from **Richard Adeney** on the flute and **Peter Graeme** on the oboe.

Egdon Heath; The Perfect Fool (ballet suite)

(M) *** EMI 5 62615-2. LSO, Previn – BRITTEN: *Sinfonia da Requiem*, etc. ***❀

Previn's account of *Egdon Heath* is full of dark intensity and his *Perfect Fool* ballet suite makes a colourful, extrovert contrast. First-class recording makes this an excellent bonus for Previn's outstanding Britten coupling.

Hammersmith: Prelude & Scherzo, Op. 52; Marching Song, Op. 22; Military Band Suites 1 in E flat; 2 in F, Op. 28/1–2; arr. of BACH (attrib.): Fugue à la gigue

*** Chan. 9697. Royal N. College of Music Wind O, Reynish – VAUGHAN WILLIAMS: *English Folksongs Suite*, etc. ***

Truly marvellous bravura playing from the **Royal Northern College of Music's Wind Orchestra** in the *Second Military Band Suite*. **Timothy Reynish** catches the jaunty quality of this attractive music and is especially perceptive in the way he sneaks the *Greensleeves* melody into the *Fantasia on the Dargason*. The only slight disappointment is the climax of the great *Chaconne*, at the opening of the *First Suite*, and the bass drum is submerged – not nearly as telling as on the Telarc recording. As a compensation we are given an inspired account of *Hammersmith*, the finest performance on record. The work's haunting atmosphere is fully captured. It is good, too, to have Holst's effective arrangement of the spirited *Fugue à la gigue*. Apart from the matter of the bass drum, the vivid Chandos recording is demonstration-worthy, with splendid range, detail and a rich underlying sonority. Most enjoyable!

Invocation for Cello and Orchestra, Op. 19/2

*** Nim. NI 5763. Wallfisch, RLPO, Dickins – BRIDGE: *Oration*; ELGAR: *Cello Concerto* ***

Holst's *Invocation* is a highly attractive and lyrical piece, with a big central climax, finely realized here, and a valuable addition to the catalogue, with some touching solo playing from **Wallfisch**, and it is splendidly recorded.

Military Band Suites 1 in E flat; 2 in F

⊕– ❀ **** Telarc CD 80038. Cleveland Symphonic Winds, Fennell – HANDEL: *Royal Fireworks Music* ****

Frederick Fennell's Telarc versions of Holst's two *Military Band Suites* have more gravitas though no less *joie de vivre* than his old Mercury set. They are magnificent, and the recording is truly superb – digital technique used in a quite overwhelmingly exciting way. The *Chaconne* of the *First Suite* makes a quite marvellous effect here. The playing of the **Cleveland** wind group is of the highest quality.

Military Band Suites 1–2, Op. 28/1–2; Moorside Suite for Brass Band (all orch. Gordon Jacob); Suite de Ballet in E flat, Op. 10; Walt Whitman Overture, Op. 7

*** Lyrita (ADD/DDD) SRCD 210. LPO, Braithwaite

The *Suite de Ballet*, written in 1910, is Holst's earliest published instrumental work, and already in this sequence of engaging genre pieces – *Danse rustique*, *Valse*, *Scène de nuit* and *Carnival* – he showed his flair for brilliant and often unexpected orchestration. The even earlier and resourcefully melodic *Walt Whitman Overture* of 1899, with its bold Wagnerian influences, again shows Holst's assurance in writing for brass and indeed his natural orchestral skill. Although repetitive, its jolly progress to a strong climax is well caught in this very lively performance. As a brass player himself, Holst welcomed the chance to compose the *Moorland Suite* as a test piece for the National Brass Band Festival Championships at Crystal Palace in 1928. For all the skill of Gordon Jacob's orchestration, with the view of giving the music a wider circulation, the original scores are superior. Nevertheless, **Nicholas Braithwaite's** performances are freshly appealing and very well recorded. The *Moorland Suite* is the most successful transcription, especially the lovely central *Nocturne* and the grandiloquent closing *March*.

The Planets (suite), Op. 32

⊕– Ⓜ **** Decca 417 5532. Montreal Ch. & SO, Dutoit

⊕– Ⓜ **** Decca (ADD) 475 8225. V. State Op. Ch., VPO, Karajan – STRAUSS: *Don Juan* ***

*** DG CD 445 860-2. Monteverdi Ch. women's voices, Philh. O, Gardiner – GRAINGER: *The Warriors* ***

Ⓜ *** EMI 5 67748-2. Geoffrey Mitchell Ch., LPO, Boult – ELGAR: *Enigma Variations* ***

*** DG 439 011-2. Berlin Ch., BPO, Karajan

(i) The Planets; Beni Mora; (ii) The Perfect Fool (Ballet Suite)

Ⓑ *** CfP 585 9132. (i) BBC SO; (ii) RPO; Sargent

(i) The Planets (suite); (ii) Brook Green Suite; (i) St Paul's Suite

ⒷⒷ *** Regis Alto ALC 1013. Amb S., RPO; (i) Handley; (ii) Wordsworth

The Planets (suite); Egdon Heath, Op. 47

⊕– ⒷⒷ *** Warner Apex 8573 89087-2. BBC SO, with women's chorus & organ, A. Davis

Charles Dutoit's natural feeling for mood, rhythm and colour, so effectively used in his records of Ravel, here results in an outstandingly successful version of *The Planets*, both rich and brilliant, and recorded with an opulence to outshine almost all rivals. It is remarkable that, whether in the relentless build-up of *Mars*, the lyricism of *Venus*, the rich exuberance of *Jupiter* or in much else, Dutoit and his Canadian players sound so idiomatic. It won the *Gramophone* Engineering Award in 1987, as well it might, and now appears in Universal's 'Gramophone Awards Collection' at mid-price.

With **Karajan** at his peak, his extraordinarily magnetic and powerful (1961) Decca account of *The Planets* is still uniquely individual, bringing a rare tension, an extra magnetism, projected by superb Decca recording, produced by John Culshaw in the Sofiensaal.

With speeds never exaggerated, **John Eliot Gardiner** avoids vulgarity, yet with his rhythmic flair he gives *The Planets* a new buoyancy. The offstage women's chorus at the end of *Neptune* has seldom been more subtly balanced.

With spectacularly brilliant and wide-ranging digital recording, engineered by Tony Faulkner, **Andrew Davis's** set of *Planets* is among the finest of modern recordings, and this Apex disc is a first choice among super-bargain versions. *Egdon Heath* then follows on very effectively, another intense performance, but here the spectacular recording at climaxes sounds more uninhibited, less in character than in the older Boult and Previn versions.

Sir Adrian Boult with the **LPO** gives a performance at once intense and beautifully played, spacious and dramatic, rapt and pointed. The great melody of *Jupiter* is calculatedly less resonant and more flowing than previously but is still affecting, and *Uranus* as well as *Jupiter* has its measure of jollity.

After a sinister opening, **Handley** builds up the climax of *Mars* impressively and the well-separated closing chords have malignant impact. The noble tune of *Jupiter* develops a similar build-up of intensity; *Saturn* too has a well-graduated melancholy climax and the choral diminuendo to silence is beautifully managed by the **Ambrosians**. *Venus* is warm and beautiful rather than sensuous or withdrawn, and the resonance provides a lustrous *Mercury*, undoubtedly chimerical if less sharply etched than in some versions. But the sound overall is attractively rich, giving glowing orchestral colour, the horns expansively opulent. What makes this budget version well worth considering is the bracingly fresh account of the *St Paul's Suite* which Handley offers as a bonus, while **Barry Wordsworth's** *Brook Green Suite* is hardly less appealing.

Sir Malcolm Sargent introduced many of us to *The Perfect Fool* and, like *The Planets*, his performance is full of character. *Mars*, taken fast, like *Uranus*, has plenty of clarity and bite and the organ pedals come through well in the sombre portrayal of *Saturn*, while the central tune in *Jupiter* is given special dignity. Sargent is equally at home in *Beni Mora*, an attractively exotic piece that shows Holst's flair for orchestration in a different but equally vivid way. Altogether a splendid collection, showing Sargent at his most charismatic

Karajan's early (1981) digital DG recording is spectacularly wide-ranging, while the marvellously sustained *pianissimo* playing of the **Berlin Philharmonic** – as in *Venus* and the closing pages of *Saturn* – is very telling indeed. *Mars* has great impact, and the sound, full and firm in the bass, gives the performance throughout a gripping immediacy and presence. In short this is a thrilling performance and highly recommendable, but it remains at full price and without a coupling.

The Planets (suite, including Colin Matthews: Pluto and Neptune with original ending); Lyric Movement

(BB) *** Hyp. Helios CDH 55350. Hallé O, Elder

**** EMI 3 59382-2. Berlin R. Ch., BPO, Rattle – DEAN: *Komarov's Fall*; PINTSCHER: *Towards Oasis*; SAARIAHO: *Asteroid 4179*; TURNAGE: *Seres*

The Planets (suite; including Matthews: Pluto); The Mystic Trumpeter

🔊 (BB) *** Naxos 8.555776; also Audio **DVD** 5.11004. RSNO, Lloyd-Jones

Sir Simon Rattle's latest recording of *The Planets* is not only superbly played, but it has state-of-the-art sound, with radiant orchestral textures and very beautiful string *pianissimos*, although the wide dynamic range may offer problems domestically. But with this recording we have to accept a second (free) disc, including four short works commissioned by the conductor. These are vividly scored, evocative, colourful and rhythmic, even jazzy by turns; but, like Matthews' *Pluto*, they are musically no match for Holst's masterpiece.

Mark Elder conducts the **Hallé Orchestra** in a warm rather than bitingly dramatic reading of *The Planets*, which ends in Colin Matthews's extra movement, *Pluto – The Renewer*. It was the idea of Kent Nagano as Elder's predecessor with the Hallé to add such a movement, with Matthews proving the ideal composer for a seemingly impossible task. Though the tempo is very fast, the rapid scurrying seems to move round in circles, evoking an atmosphere of mystery apt for the smallest, remotest planet.

Since it emerges out of Holst's last movement, *Neptune*, involving a slight modification of the score, Elder conducts a second performance of that movement with the original ending of offstage women's choir fading into nothing. The tender, reflective *Lyric Movement*, with **Timothy Pooley** a fine viola soloist, makes a generous bonus.

David Lloyd-Jones's reading with the **Royal Scottish National Orchestra** is even finer than Elder's, more spontaneous-sounding if not always quite so polished. Where Lloyd-Jones scores is in bringing out the contrasted character of each movement, starting with an account of *Mars* which in its urgency and menace contrasts strongly with the strangely relaxed view of Elder. Where Elder has for coupling a rare late work, Lloyd-Jones and Matthews have unearthed a very early work of Holst's that was never performed, a *Scena* to a text by Walt Whitman, which may reveal little of Holst's mature style, but which is colourful and atmospheric and well worth hearing. Full, vivid sound.

(i; ii) The Planets (suite, arr. 4 hands), Op. 32; (i) Christmas Day in the Morning; Jig; Nocturne; O! I Hae seen the Roses Blaw; The Shoemaker; Toccata

*** Black Box BBM 1041. (i) John York; (ii) Fiona York

Holst's own arrangement of *The Planets* for piano duet may lack the atmospheric warmth and rich orchestral colours of the original, but in this alert reading by the **York** duo the clarity is refreshing and there is plenty of magnetism in the rhythmic writing. It follows that the fast movements are much more effective than the three slow movements, *Venus*, *Saturn* and *Neptune*, even if the fading of the alternating chords at the end, originally given to offstage women's chorus, is persuasively done. The delight of the disc is to have this major work preceded by six pieces for piano duet, which sparkle from first to last, ranging from the vigorous *Toccata* of 1924 to the tonally equivocal *Jig* of 1932, all brilliantly played and very well recorded.

St Paul's Suite

🔊 (BB) *** Warner Apex 2564 61437-2. RPO, Warren-Green – BRITTEN: *Simple Symphony*; BUTTERWORTH: *Banks of Green Willow*; ELGAR: *String Serenade*; VAUGHAN WILLIAMS: *Fantasia on a Theme of Tallis* ***

Warren-Green's strongly characterized performance is second to none, with the outer movements characteristically full of joyous energy and a wide range of dynamic used to charm the listener with the wistful delicacy of the engaging second-movement *Ostinato*. Fine playing and first-class recording.

Air & Variations; 3 Pieces for Oboe & String Quartet, Op. 2

*** Chan. 8392. Francis, English Qt – BAX: *Quintet*; MOERAN: *Fantasy Quartet*; JACOB: *Quartet* ***

The three pieces here are engagingly folksy, consisting of a sprightly little *March*, a gentle Minuet with a good tune, and a Scherzo. Performances are first class, and so is the recording.

VOCAL MUSIC

Part Songs

🔑 (BB) *** Hyp. Helios CDH 55171. Holst Singers, Layton (with Theodore, Truman, Williams)

A wholly delightful collection: it has so many treasures and the music and singing (and recording) are of such quality that, as the original *Gramophone* review rightly commented, it is 'a joy to listen through without interruption'. The sheer technical excellence of the singing is remarkable, as is **Stephen Layton's** absolute control: the blending peerless, partly because the choir's intonation is absolutely secure.

The programme opens with carols (the eight-part double-choir setting of *Ave Maria* has an extraordinarily rich interplay of harmony, and the two linked numbers – *A Welcome Song* and *Terlyi, terlow* – both with **David Theodore** (oboe) and **Robert Truman** (cello) – are enchanting). A passage which has been used elsewhere (this time by Holst himself, in one of the *Military Band Suites*) pictures the syncopated hammering of *The Song of the Blacksmith* with its refrain, *Kiki, kikki, kang, kang,* which sounds for all the world like 'Chitty, chitty, bang, bang', and with the same rhythm.

The radiant *Sweet and low* and *The splendour falls* have superbly evocative imitative effects. The lovely *Now sleeps the crimson petal* brings delightful overlapping of parts, and the unpronounceable Welsh folksong translates as 'My sweetheart's like Venus'. Holst's imagination knows no bounds and this is altogether a superb reminder of his remarkable versatility.

(i) *Ave Maria, H.49*; (ii–iv; viii) *A Choral Fantasia, Op. 51 (H.177)*; (iii–iv; viii) *A Dirge for Two Veterans, H.121*; (v–viii) *The Cloud Messenger, Op. 30 (H.111)*; (i) *The Evening Watch, H.159*; (vi–viii) *The Hymn of Jesus, Op. 37 (H.140)*; (iv; vi; viii) *Ode to Death, Op. 38 (H.144)*; (i) *4 Partsongs*; (ii–iv; viii) *7 Partsongs, H.162*; (i) *This have I done for my true love, H.128*

🔑 (B) *** Chan. 2-for-1 241-6 (2). (i) Finzi Singers, Spicer; (ii) Rozario; (iii) Joyful Company of Singers; (iv) City of L. Sinfonia; (v) D. Jones; (vi) L. Symphony Ch.; (vii) L. Symphony Ch.; (viii) Hickox

Richard Hickox proves a passionate advocate of the shorter choral works of Holst, demonstrating that the two Whitman settings, *A Dirge for Two Veterans* and *Ode to Death*, are among his finest pieces for voices: the *Dirge*, written just after war had started in 1914, a grim processional for male voices, brass and percussion, and the *Ode* in 1919 when it was over and his disillusion was even more intense. That second work is in very much the same vein of inspiration as his masterpiece, the *Hymn of Jesus*, and, with the larger forces of the **London Symphony Chorus**, brings the most powerful performance here. It easily outshines even Sir Adrian Boult's vintage version for Decca. Hickox secures tauter and crisper ensemble, as well as treating the sections based on plainchant with an aptly expressive freedom.

The long-neglected choral piece, *The Cloud Messenger*, may lack the concentration of the *Hymn of Jesus*, but it brings similarly incandescent choral writing. Warmly and positively realized by Hickox and his powerful forces, with **Della Jones** a fine soloist, it makes a major discovery. Both the later works, the *Seven Partsongs* of 1925 as well as the *Choral Fantasia* of 1930, set poems by Robert Bridges, with the choral writing fluently beautiful. Though **Patricia Rozario** is not on her finest form, the **Joyful Company of Singers** sing superbly in intense and moving performances, helped by rich and full Chandos sound.

4 Canons for Equal Voices; 6 Choral Folk Songs; Choral Hymn from the Rig Veda: Hymn to Manas. The Homecoming

(N) (B) *** EMI (ADD) 2 16155-2. Baccholian Singers, Ian Humphries – VAUGHAN WILLIAMS: *Folk Songs* ***

A beautiful and memorable collection of Holst's smaller choral pieces coupled with equally memorable Vaughan Williams folksong arrangements. Holst's highly original Hardy setting, *The Homecoming*, stands out with its stark narrative and dialogue.

A Choral Fantasia, Op. 51; Choral Symphony, Op. 41

(BB) **(*) Hyp. Helios CDH 55104. Dawson, Guildford Choral Society, RPO, Davan Wetton

Though the ensemble of the **Guildford Choral Society** is not ideally crisp, and one really wants more weight of sound, the originality of Holst's choral writing and the purposeful nature of the argument are never in doubt in this surprisingly rare coupling, with **Lynne Dawson** the radiantly beautiful soprano soloist in both works. Holst is nothing if not daring in using well-known texts by Keats in the *Choral Symphony*, adding a new dimension even to the 'Ode on a Grecian Urn'. This is well worth considering in its bargain-priced reissue.

(i) *A Choral Fantasia, Op. 51*; (ii) *Psalm 86*

🔑 (M) *** EMI (ADD) 5 65588-2. (i) Baker; (ii) Partridge; Purcell Singers, ECO, Imogen Holst – FINZI: *Dies natalis*; VAUGHAN WILLIAMS: *5 Mystical Songs*, etc. ***

In Holst's *Choral Fantasia* **Dame Janet Baker** once again shows her supreme quality as a recording artist. The recording, though not lacking ambient warmth, is admirably clear (indeed the organ pedals are only too clear). The setting of *Psalm 86*, with its expressive tenor part sung beautifully by **Ian Partridge**, is also included in this generous compilation. The recording here is outstanding, and the success of both these performances owes much to the inspired direction of the composer's daughter.

Choral Hymns from the Rig Veda (Group 3), *H. 99, Op. 26/3*

*** Hyp. CDA 66175. Holst Singers & O; Davan Wetton; Owen – BLISS: *Lie Strewn the White Flocks*; BRITTEN: *Gloriana: Choral Dances* ***

The third group of *Choral Hymns from the Rig Veda*, like the whole series, reveals Holst in his Sanskritic period at his most distinctively inspired. In this responsive performance, it makes an excellent coupling for the attractive Bliss and Britten items, atmospherically recorded.

(i) Choral Hymns from the Rig Veda; (ii) 6 Early Songs; (ii; iii) 4 Songs for Voice & Violin; (iv) 12 Humbert Wolfe settings; (ii) The Heart Worships; Margret's Cradle Song

(BB) *** Naxos 8.557117. (i) Maltman; (ii) Gritton; (iii) Fuller (violin); (iv) Langridge; all with Steuart Bedford (piano)

Naxos have enterprisingly picked up a disc of rare Holst vocal repertoire, originally issued on the Collins label. Apart from the comparatively well-known, very Holstian and mystically atmospheric *Hymns from the Rig Veda*, sung sensitively (if with a slightly intrusive vibrato) by **Christopher Maltman**, the most striking songs are the Humbert Wolfe settings, in which **Philip Langridge** is in his element. But the star performer here is **Susan Gritton**, persuasive in the early songs but at her very finest in the *Four Songs for Voice and Violin*, set to medieval lyrics, with **Louisa Fuller** a responsive partner. Throughout, **Steuart Bedford** is thoroughly at home in the piano accompaniments, and the recording is excellent.

The Evening Watch, H.159; Six Choruses, H.186; Nunc dimittis, H.127; 7 Partsongs, H.162; 2 Psalms, H.117

*** Hyp. CDA 66329. Holst Singers & O, Davan Wetton

Hilary Davan Wetton's performance of the comparatively austere but no less inspired *Evening Watch* creates a rapt, sustained *pianissimo* until the very closing bars, when the sudden expansion is quite thrilling. The *Six Choruses* for male voices show the composer at his most imaginative, while the comparable *Partsongs* for women often produce a ravishingly dreamy, mystical beauty. The final song, *Assemble all ye maidens*, is a narrative ballad about a lost love, and its closing section is infinitely touching. The performances are gloriously and sensitively sung and unerringly paced.

The Mystic Trumpeter

*** Lyrita (ADD) SRCD 270. Armstrong, LSO, Atherton –
     PARRY: *Ode on the Nativity*; VAUGHAN WILLIAMS: *Sons of Light* ***

The Mystic Trumpeter is a setting of Whitman. There are some striking things in it and in both its harmonic language and metrical freedom it looks forward to things to come. **Sheila Armstrong** gives an impressive account of this rarity and she is given sympathetic support from **Atherton** and the **LSO**.

OPERA

(i) Savitri (complete); (ii) Dream City (song-cycle, orch. Matthews)

(BB) **(*) Hyp. Helios CDH 55042. (i) Langridge, Varcoe, Palmer, Hickox Singers; (ii) Kwella, City of L. Sinfonia; Hickox

The simple story of *Savitri* is taken from a Sanskrit source. **Felicity Palmer** is earthy, vulnerable as Savitri, her grainy mezzo caught well. **Philip Langridge** and **Stephen Varcoe** both sing sensitively with fresh, clear tone, though their

timbres are rather similar. **Hickox** is a thoughtful conductor both in the opera and in the orchestral song-cycle arranged by Colin Matthews (with Imogen Holst's approval) from Holst's settings of Humbert Wolfe poems. **Patrizia Kwella's** soprano at times catches the microphone rather shrilly.

HONEGGER, Arthur (1892–1955)

Les Aventures du Roi Pausole: Overture; Ballet; (i)Cello Concerto; Pastoral d'été; Pacific 231; Rugby; The Tempest: Prélude

(BB) (***) Dutton mono CDBP 9764. Grand SO, composer, (i) with Marechal – JAUBERT: *Ballade*. PIERNÉ: *Ramuntcho*

Apart from the *Cello Concerto*, which was recorded in Paris during the war, these recordings were all made in 1930 and have great immediacy of feeling, in particular the *Prélude* to *The Tempest*, which has a frenzied intensity that is thrilling. **Maurice Marechal** was the dedicatee of the concerto, composed in 1928, and he plays it committedly. After the Second World War Honegger recorded the *Symphonie liturgique*, and we hope that Dutton will turn their attention to that in due course.

(i) Cello Concerto, H72; (ii) Cello Sonata, H32; Sonatina, H42; (iii) Sonatina for violin & cello, H80

**** BIS-CD-1617. Poltéra, with (i) Malmö SO, Ollila-Hannikainen; (ii) Stott; (iii) Tetzlaff

Christian Poltéra proves an eloquent and sweet-toned soloist, and he is well supported by the fine **Malmö Orchestra**. **Kathryn Stott** proves highly sympathetic in the 1920 *Sonata*, and the *Sonatina* of 1922, originally for clarinet, is new to the catalogue in this form. This repertoire is neglected – quite unjustly so – and readers should investigate it urgently, particularly as it is so well played and recorded.

Symphonies 1; 2 for Strings with Trumpet Obbligato; 3 (Symphonie liturgique); 4 (Deliciae Basiliensis); 5 (Di tre re); Symphonic movements: 1, Pacific 231; 2, Rugby

⊕ (BB) *** Warner Apex 2564 62687-2 (2). Bav. RSO, Dutoit

Symphonies 1; 2 for Strings with Trumpet Obbligato; 3 (Symphonie liturgique); 4 (Deliciae Basilienses); 5 (Di tre re); 3 Symphonic Movements: 1, Pacific 231; 3; The Tempest: Prelude

(M) *** Sup. (ADD) 11 1566-2 (2). Czech PO, Baudo

Duitoit's inexpensive Apex set is an appealingly economical way of acquiring excellent, modern, digital recordings (dating from 1982) of the five symphonies, plus two of the *Symphonic Movements* (recorded three years later). In Dutoit's hands the phrasing of the **Bavarian Orchestra** has both dignity and eloquence. He gives thoroughly idiomatic accounts of both the *Liturgique* and '*Di tre re*' *Symphonies*. In the *Fifth* he does not galvanize the orchestra into playing of the same volcanic fire and vitality that Serge Baudo secures from the Czech Philharmonic Orchestra in the alternative

Supraphon set (11 1566-2), but the Warner recording is fresher and more detailed. Both *Pacific 231* and *Rugby* are well done; although the latter may be found a little genteel, the playing and recording are more than adequate compensation.

The Supraphon performances come from the 1960s, but they are more than merely serviceable. The sound comes up very well indeed and the playing of the **Czech Philharmonic** for **Baudo** is totally committed. The performance of the *Fifth Symphony* has never been surpassed (except possibly by the pioneering Munch recording) and has amazing presence and detail for its period.

Symphony 2 for Strings & Trumpet

Ⓜ *** EMI (ADD) 5 67595-2. O de Paris, Munch – RAVEL: *Boléro*, etc. ***

Honegger's wartime *Second Symphony*, scored for strings to which an obbligato trumpet is added at the very end of the work, commands a genuine intensity of feeling with a strong and vital imagination. **Munch** conducted the work's French première and made the pioneering set of 78s. The present version is his finest account of this dark and haunting score, and he secures first-class playing from the strings of the **Orchestre de Paris**. The naturally balanced recording is lively and has atmosphere as well as opulence.

Symphonies 2 for Strings with Trumpet Obbligato; 3 (Symphonie liturgique)

🗝 ❀ Ⓜ **** DG (ADD) 447 435-2. BPO, Karajan – STRAVINSKY: *Concerto in D* ***

Karajan's accounts of these magnificent symphonies come from 1973 and still remain in a class of their own, luminous, incandescent and moving (one of DG's 'Legendary Originals').

Symphony 3 (Symphonie liturgique); Rugby; Mouvement symphonique 3; Pacific 231; Pastoral d'été

ⒷⒷ *** Naxos 8.555974. New Zealand SO, Yuasa

Takuo Yuasa, currently principal conductor of the Ulster Orchestra, gets impressive results from the New Zealanders, and the recording has great presence and detail. This is not perhaps a first choice but, taken on its own merits, is a perfectly viable one and at its modest price will give much satisfaction.

Symphonies 3; 5; Pacific 231

*** Chan. 9176. Danish Nat. R. O, Järvi

The *Symphonie liturgique* has stiff competition to meet in the classic Karajan account, but **Neeme Järvi** and the **Danish Orchestra** serve it very well indeed, and the digital Chandos recording is even more detailed and present, and certainly fuller, than the DG version. Järvi's version of the *Fifth Symphony* is also masterly, even if it does not match the hell-for-leather abandon of Baudo's Supraphon version (see above). But that is now over 30 years old and, though it still sounds pretty amazing, this is undeniably superior.

VOCAL MUSIC

Une Cantate de Noël

🗝 Ⓑ *** CfP 586 1722 (2). Sweeney, Waynflete Singers, Winchester Cathedral Ch., ECO, Neary – BERLIOZ *L'enfance du Christ* **(*) ; POULENC: *Mass; Motets* ***

At last a recording of Honegger's charming *Christmas Cantata* to do it full justice. It was the composer's last completed work and deserves to be more popular in the festive season outside France. The performance here is superior in every way and the recording is impressively wide-ranging and well defined.

Le Roi David (complete)

ⒷⒷ **(*) Naxos 8.553649. Martin, Fersen, Borst, Todorovitch, Ragon, Guedj, Ch. Régional Vittoria d'Ile de France, O de la Cité, Piquemal

The Naxos set gives us the original scoring of *Le Roi David* for 17 instruments, the double bass being the only string instrument. In 1923, Honegger scored it in the familiar concert version, adding the narration which Naxos use here. **Michel Piquemal's** performance is a good one and, though there are certain weaknesses (the tenor's vibrato will not be to all tastes), there is a good feeling for the dramatic shape of the work. Piquemal keeps a firm grip on the proceedings and the instrumentalists play with real commitment, while the recording is very adequate.

HOROVITZ, Joseph (born 1926)

(i) Clarinet Concerto; (ii) Euphonium Concerto; (iii) Jazz Concerto for Piano, Strings & Percussion; (iv) Violin Concerto

Ⓜ *** Dutton CDLX 7188. (i) Cross; (ii) Mead; (iii) Owen Norris; (iv) Haveron; Royal Ballet Sinfonia, composer

Joseph Horovitz stands out among today's composers for writing approachable music beautifully crafted. These four compact concertos are prime examples, colourful and attractive. The *Concerto for Clarinet and Strings* is tuneful and lively, while the *Concerto for Euphonium and Chamber Orchestra* handles a tricky instrument imaginatively, even more tuneful than the clarinet work, with a warm melody in the slow movement. The *Violin Concerto* brings a jaunty first movement, while the *Concerto for Jazz Band and Orchestra* winningly draws on jazzy syncopations. Brilliant performances, strongly conducted by the composer.

HOVHANESS, Alan (1911–2000)

(i) Guitar Concerto 1; (ii) Khrimian Hairig, Op. 49; Symphony 60 (To the Appalachian Mountains), Op. 396

🗝 ⒷⒷ *** Naxos 8.559294. Berlin RSO, Schwarz, with (i) Leisner; (ii) Ranch

The *Guitar Concerto* uses the orchestra vividly, but for the most part consists of long, ruminative passages for the soloist, often interrupted by haunting instrumental solos, or indeed by the full orchestra. *Khrimian Hairig* was originally the slow movement of a trumpet concerto and consists of a melismatic soliloquy from the soloist, which reaches a striking apotheosis. The *Symphony*, with its magical opening for woodwind which leads to a chorale, is richly melodic, using Appalachian folk idioms. The second movement evokes a square dance, but all the other themes are both appealing and original. The performances here are of the highest quality and are superbly recorded.

(i) *Guitar Concerto 2. Fanfare for the New Atlantis; Symphony 63 (Loon Lake)*

(N) (BB) *** Naxos 8.559336. RSNO, Robertson; (i) with Calderón

The *Second Guitar Concerto* was commissioned by Narciso Yepes. The solo guitarist (here the excellent **Javier Calderón**) dominates a kaleidoscope of orchestral chorale sonorities, pizzicati and fugati, in the most inventive way. The *Fanfare* moves from a solo trumpet to the climax of the rebirth of Atlantis in the full orchestra. The *Symphony 63 (Loon Lake)* is characteristically evocative, spectacular in its washes of orchestral colour both from the strings and the woodwind alike. Hovhaness's music is strangely haunting, when the performers are as dedicated and responsive as they are here and the recording worthy of the complex scoring.

Symphony 2 (Mysterious Mountain), Op. 132; (i) *Lousadzak*

(N) (M) *** Nim. NI 2512. American Composers O, Russell Davies; (i) with Jarrett – HARRISON: *Symphony 2* ***

The music of the *Second Symphony* is spacious, amiably melodic and easy to come to terms with. It begins with pastoral, modal writing, leading to a central fugal climax and returning compulsively to rich, expressive serenity. *Lousadzak* (a made-up word meaning 'dawn of light') is dominated by a throbbing, complex ostinato which moves through the piano's various registers in a most haunting way, with the accompaniment varied and the basic rhythmic figure steadily expanded and varied. This is far more than minimalism. The performances and recording could hardly be more inviting and the coupled symphony by Harrison is even finer.

HOWELLS, Herbert (1892–1983)

(i) *Piano Concertos 1 in C min., Op. 4* (completed Rutter); *2 in C, Op. 39; Penguinski*

⊶ *** Chan. 9874. (i) Shelley; BBC SO, Hickox

Long buried, Herbert Howells's *First Piano Concerto*, with its final pages now restored by John Rutter, is a revelation. With Grieg and Rachmaninov among the models, the piano writing is bold and powerful, full of strong themes, set in a warmly English idiom. **Howard Shelley** as soloist and **Richard Hickox** as conductor hold the expansive structure superbly together. The *Second Concerto* of 1925, more modest

in scale but more advanced in idiom with its echoes of Debussy, Ravel and Stravinsky, is equally attractive, and the jolly occasional piece *Penguinski* makes a delightful encore.

Concerto for Strings; Elegy for Viola, String Quartet & Strings; Suite for String Orchestra; Serenade

⊶ ✪ *** Chan. 9161. City of L. Sinfonia, Hickox

These three splendid and inspired works are all in the great and ongoing tradition of English string-writing. The *Concerto* (1938) opens with a great burst of energy, but the secondary theme is hauntingly nostalgic, and the elegiac character of the slow movement establishes the music's character. The viola *Elegy*, written much earlier (1917), is clearly modelled on Vaughan Williams's *Tallis Fantasia*, yet it is masterly in its own right and very moving. The delicate one-movement *Serenade*, which also features a solo quartet, dates from the same year. The *Allegro deciso* and *Rondo* which open and close the *Suite* (1938) are rhythmically extrovert in a Holstian 'St Paul's' manner, but then, after a gentle, rapturous *Siciliano*, the Minuet opens with a deeper-voiced pizzicato. The performances here are exemplary, superbly played and conducted by **Hickox** with deep commitment and understanding. The recording is warm, sonorous and clearly detailed.

The 'B's' (Suite for Orchestra); (i) *3 Dances for Violin & Orchestra;* (ii) *Fantasia; Threnody* (both for cello & orchestra); *The King's Herald; Paradise Rondel, Op. 40;* (iii) *In Green Ways* (Song Cycle); *Pastoral Rhapsody; Procession, Op. 36*

⊶ (BB) *** Chan. 2 for 1 CHAN 241-20 (2). (i) Mordkovitch; (ii) Welsh; (iii) Kenny; LSO, Hickox

The inspired suite, *The Five 'B's*, celebrates the composer's musician friends and colleagues at the Royal College of Music at the beginning of the 1914–18 war. As such it has something in common with Elgar's *Enigma Variations*, although Howells clearly identified each dedicate. 'Blissy' (Arthur Bliss) inspires a dainty, chimerical Scherzo on the first disc, with the piano an orchestral soloist. The shorter evocations are framed by an exuberant *Overture* with a *nobilmente* lyrical expansiveness representing the composer himself ('Bublum') and the finale ('Benjee' – Arthur Benjamin), which begins lightheartedly but ends grandiloquently, recalls the composer's own themes from the overture. The *Three Dances for Violin and Orchestra*, another wartime work (1915), are in the best English folk/pastoral tradition, with **Lydia Mordkovitch** as a brilliant violin soloist; and the song-cycle, *In Green Ways*, with **Yvonne Kenny** also includes poignant elegies. The English countryside is strikingly evoked in this group of five songs, using lyrics by Shakespeare and Goethe. Yvonne Kenny sings the whole group most affectingly and **Richard Hickox** and the **LSO** are ardent and communicative advocates of all this fine music.

The most personal works on the second disc are the *Fantasia* and *Threnody*, both for cello and orchestra, together forming a sort of rhapsodic concerto. The other major piece is the *Pastoral Rhapsody*, written in 1923. Similarly pastoral but predominantly vigorous, the *Paradise Rondel* of 1925 is full of sharp contrasts, with one passage offering clear echoes of the *Russian Dance* from *Petrushka*. The collection opens with the boldly extrovert *King's Herald*, bright with Waltonian fanfares. *Procession* brings more echoes of *Petrushka*, again reflecting Howells's response to the Diaghilev Ballets Russes' appearances in London. Helped by rich, atmospheric sound, Richard Hickox draws performances that are both brilliant and warmly persuasive from the LSO, with **Moray Welsh** a movingly expressive soloist in the concertante works.

CHAMBER MUSIC

Clarinet Sonata; A Near-Minuet for Clarinet & Piano; Prelude for Harp; Rhapsodic Clarinet Quintet; Violin Sonata 3

(BB) **** Naxos 8.557188. Mobius

Howells's *Rhapsodic Quintet* for clarinet and string quartet is one of the most beautiful clarinet works of the 20th century. **Robert Plane**, the clarinet of the talented group **Mobius**, plays with a ravishing range of tone and natural warmth, well supported by the string quartet led by **Philippe Honore**. Plane is also the brilliant soloist in Howells's even more ambitious *Clarinet Sonata* of 1946, more angular and percussive than one expects from Howells. Honore is the violinist with the pianist **Sophia Rahman** in the powerful *Violin Sonata 3*, written for Albert Sammons in 1923 after a visit by the composer to Canada, inspired by the rugged grandeur of the Rockies. The *Prelude for Harp* and the *Near-Minuet for Clarinet and Piano* are attractive make-weights for a superb disc, compelling in every way and vividly recorded.

(i) Fantasy String Quartet, Op. 25; (ii) Piano Quartet, Op. 21; (i; iii) Rhapsodic Quintet for Clarinet and Strings

🔈 *** Lyrita (ADD) SRCD 292. (i) Richards Ens.; (ii) Richards Piano Qt; (iii) King

The *Piano Quartet* was written in 1916, when Howells, still in his early twenties, was studying with Stanford. It may have its roots in a Brahmsian conception of the genre but the inspiration is gloriously vital, and anyone not afraid to enjoy music composed without concern for fashion should sample a work that is far more than derivative and hardly immature. Within a year or so, when the young Howells had composed the other two works on the disc, the influence of the folk-song movement had become more dominant. Though some of the youthful buoyancy had gone, this too is splendid music, warmly recommendable to anyone sympathetic to the English revival. The committed performances and fine recording add to the real joy of his disc.

Oboe Sonata

(BB) *** Hyp. Helios CDH 55008. Francis, Dickinson –
BOUGHTON: *Pastoral*; HARTY: *3 Pieces*; RUBBRA:
Sonata ***

Howell's *Oboe Sonata* is a florid work, but **Sarah Francis** surmounts its complexities very musically, echoed by her pianist, **Peter Dickinson**. She provides a full, singing tone. The

balance is forward, within a resonant acoustic, and it is important not to set the volume control too high.

In Gloucestershire (String Quartet 3)

(BB) *** Hyp. Helios CDH 55045. Divertimenti – DYSON: 3
Rhapsodies ***

Howells's *Third String Quartet* is permeated with the spirit of Vaughan Williams; the opening movement, treating the first violin as a soloist, mistily yet radiantly evokes the Gloucestershire countryside. After the windswept Scherzo, the slow movement is elegiac; but the finale, jauntily alive and folksy in flavour, is drawn back eventually to the gently atmospheric mood of the work's opening. The performance by **Divertimenti** is deeply expressive and beautifully played and recorded.

Rhapsodic Clarinet Quintet, Op. 31

(BB) *** Hyp. Helios CDH 55105. King, Britten Qt – COOKE:
Clarinet Quintet; HOLBROOKE: *Eilean Shona*; HOWELLS:
Rhapsodic Quintet; FRANKEL; MACONCHY: *Clarinet
Quintets* ***

Howells's inspired single-movement *Rhapsodic Quintet*, which dates from 1919, is one of his very finest works, opening arrestingly with rich string harmonies and based on two utterly haunting, very English themes. **Thea King**, who plays ravishingly and with great poetic feeling, reckons its closing section 'to be one of the loveliest moments in music – the peace of ages is in it'. The performance here is fully responsive to this mood, and the recording is first class.

Violin Sonatas 1 in E, Op. 18; 2 in E flat, Op. 26; 3 in E min., Op. 38; Cradle Song, Op. 9/1; 3 Pieces, Op. 28

🔈 ⚙ (BB) **** Hyp. Helios CDH 55139. Barritt, Edwards

The three *Violin Sonatas* come from an intensely creative period. The *First* (1917) opens delicately and romantically, darkens a little in the *Meno mosso*, then, after a brief, unbridled Scherzo, ends in ravishing tranquillity. The *Second*, with a lovely, simple, folk-like slow movement, bursts into sparkling vitality in the finale. The *Third Sonata* maintains the English pastoral character in its underlying lyricism, but erupts with energy in the pizzicato centrepiece, which carries through into the restless finale: both are marked *assai ritmico*. The main theme of the delightful *Cradle Song* is rather like a Slavonic folk-tune, and while the first two of the *Three Pieces* are richly English in feeling, the haunting finale is actually based on a Russian folksong. **Paul Barritt** and **Catherine Edwards** are right inside this music and play together with a passionate and moving single voice; moreover, they are superbly balanced and recorded.

ORGAN MUSIC

Psalm Preludes, Sets I & II; 3 Rhapsodies, Op. 17; Rhapsody 4

*** Priory PRCD 480. Cleobury (organ of King's College, Cambridge)

The *Psalm Preludes* are rich in ideas and powerfully communicative, each being a musical meditation on a single verse. The *Rhapsodies*, not surprisingly, are more powerfully romantic in a Lisztian way, with big, dramatic swells of tone. The *Third* was written in York during a Zeppelin raid in the First World War, and the malignant writing depicts the tumult of the experience and the composer's passionate reaction. The *Fourth* was written in 1958, some 40 years after the first three, and is actually marked *turbulento*. The climax is tremendous, with thundering pedals, and as a sonic experience it is overwhelming. **Stephen Cleobury's** performances have great vitality and passion (and delicacy when required), and the recording is quite superb.

VOCAL MUSIC

Anthems: *The fear of the Lord; Like as the hart; Hymn: All my hope on God is founded; Sacred Part-Song; Long, long ago; Magnificat (Gloucester Service); Requiem*

*** Coll. COLCD 118. Soloists, Cambridge Singers, Rutter; Marshall (organ) – STANFORD: *Anthems; Canticles*, etc. ***

Rutter's programme opens with three very fine *Magnificat* settings, Howells's the most ambitious, framed by two of Stanford's, while a pair of Stanford's anthems also enclose two quite contrasted anthems of Howells: the comparatively gentle *Like as the hart*, and the more robust *The fear of the Lord*. All this music is rewarding and is capped by the lovely *Requiem* for *a cappella* double choir, which above all is thoughtful and serene. Its highly unconventional layout includes Psalms 23 and 121 (*I will lift mine eyes unto the hills*), surrounded by two different settings of the *Requiem aeternam*. John Rutter's performance is movingly dedicated and radiantly sung. The concert ends rousingly with a hymn, *All my hope on God is founded*. The recording is very fine.

Antiphon; 3 Carol-Anthems; Even such is Time; God is gone up; Haec Dies; The House of the Mind; Long, Long ago; 2 Madrigals; Mass in the Dorian Mode; Regina Coeli; Requiem; Salve Regina; A Sequence for St Michael; Take him, Earth, for cherishing; The Summer is coming; Sweetest of Sweets; Nunc Dimittis; Te Deum; Thee will I love

Ⓑ ***** Chan. 241-34 (2). Soloists, Finzi Singers, Spicer**

The *Requiem* is the one large-scale work here; but many of the shorter settings, like the *Mass in the Dorian Mode*, *A Sequence for St Michael* and the *Te Deum*, are also among Howells's masterpieces. Many of them are available in fine alternative performances from other cathedral choirs, but they are also splendidly sung here and this collection inexpensively explores much else among Howells's choral output, from the early *Even such is time* to the ravishing *Carol Anthems* and the much later thrilling motet, *God is gone up*. The singing throughout is well up to the eloquent, finely blended and characterfully expressive performances we expect from this fine vocal group, while the Chandos recording is well up to the house standard.

Canticles for Morning and Evening Services, Vol. 1

*** Priory PRCD 748. Collegiate Singers, Millinger, Moorhouse (organ)

Canticles for Morning and Evening Services, Vol. 2

*** Priory PRCD 759. Collegiate Singers, Millinger, Moorhouse (organ)

Howells composed some 20 settings of the *Magnificat* and *Nunc dimittis* and, while it is not difficult to pick one's favourites, the amazing consistency of inspiration shines out again and again through these two collections, making his contribution to the Anglican Matins and Evensong uniquely special, astonishing when one realizes that he was himself an agnostic.

The 1941 settings for men's voices and organ are here sung by women, with tonally lavish and at times radiantly ethereal effect. Similarly Howells's writing for the upper voices is richly harmonized for Oxford in 1970, showing that the composer's touch remained as sure as ever three decades later. Also included on the second CD is the brief but memorable *Hymn for St Cecilia* and the luminous unaccompanied *Salve Regina* which is so poignant in its emotional pull, for all its underlying serenity. The performances here are splendidly sung by the **Collegiate Singers**, under **Andrew Millinger**, while **Richard Moorhouse's** organ contribution always makes its mark. The recording, made in Marlborough College Chapel, could hardly be bettered.

3 Children's Songs; 4 French Chansons, Op. 29; A Garland for de la Mare (group of 11 unpublished songs); In Green Ways (song-cycle), Op. 43; Peacock Pie (song-cycle), Op. 33; 2 South African Settings; 4 Songs, Op. 22 (Madrigal); Miscellaneous songs

*** Chan. 9185/6 (2). Dawson, Pierard, Mark Ainsley, Luxon, Drake

This two-disc collection covers virtually all of Howells's completed songs. One of the driving forces behind the project is the pianist **Julius Drake**, who plays the accompaniments with a consistent rhythmic spring and a sense of fantasy. Two of the finest songs are among the best known, *King David* and *Come sing and dance*, and such a group of miniatures as *Peacock Pie*, settings of Walter de la Mare written early in Howells's career, have a characteristic point and charm. Far more searching are the 11 much longer settings of de la Mare poems. Among the other fascinating examples are two South African settings to words by the Afrikaner poet, Jan Celliers, including one still very topical, *Spirit of freedom*. The sopranos, **Catherine Pierard** and **Lynne Dawson**, both have aptly fresh, English-sounding voices, with **John Mark Ainsley** as the thoughtful tenor and **Benjamin Luxon** the characterful baritone; a fine team, even though the recording brings out some unevenness in the vocal production of both Mark Ainsley and Luxon.

3 Carol Anthems: A Spotless Rose; Sing lullaby; Here is the little door; Collegium regale: Magnificat; Nunc dimittis; Hymn for St Cecilia; O love all beauteous

things; O Pray for the Peace of Jerusalem; A Sequence for St Michael; Salve Regina; Service for New College, Oxford: Magnificat; Nunc dimittis; Service for St George's Chapel, Windsor: Te Deum; Benedictus

☙→ *** Hyp. CDA 67494. Wells Cathedral Ch., Archer; M. Gough

Like the CRD New College, Oxford, collection below, this splendid programme from **Wells Cathedral** includes three of Howells's finest short choral works, and here **Malcolm Archer** uses them to open his programme. *A Sequence for St Michael*, a supreme masterpiece, is underpinned emotionally by the resonance of the tragic death of the composer's child, whose name was also Michael. Yet Howells invokes the Archangel himself as he stands in both mystery and glory on the Western cliffe of Paradise. It is work of grandeur and passion as well as beauty, and this is marvellously conveyed in the profoundly fervent performance here. *A Hymn for St Cecilia* is more direct and hymn-like, but it gathers intensity as it proceeds; *O Pray for the Peace of Jerusalem* is, by contrast, meditative and is sung with affecting simplicity.

The anthem, *O love all beauteous things*, set to a poem of Robert Bridges, is another small-scale masterpiece, with characteristic moments of both sensuousness and passion, and there is to be a passionate response again from the choir in the rich St George's *Te Deum* and the vibrant Oxford *Magnificat*. The three delightful and tender carol settings come towards the end of the recital, to be followed by the most famous of Howells's settings of the *Magnificat* and *Nunc dimittis*, drawn from the *Collegium regale*, less extrovert than those written for Oxford, but no less moving, with the *Nunc dimittis* ending the programme in a burst of glory. The choir is superbly recorded within the cathedral ambience, yet is not too backwardly placed, with words clear and plenty of edge to the climaxes. With a playing time of nearly 80 minutes, this must be a prime choice among collections of Howells's church music.

Collegium regale: Office of Holy Communion; Requiem. St Paul's Service: Magnificat; Nunc dimittis. Motets: Like as the hart; Long, long ago; Take him, earth. Organ music: Paean; Rhapsody 3

☙→ (BB) **** Naxos 8.554659. St John's College Ch., Robinson, Farrington

No composer this century has surpassed Herbert Howells in the beauty and imagination of his Anglican church music. Naxos here offers a generous selection, in seductive performances from the **Choir of St John's College, Cambridge**, that match and almost surpass any previous versions. This will have King's Choir down the road looking to its laurels, helped by immaculate sound, at once atmospheric and cleanly focused.

(i) Hymnus paradisi; (ii) A Kent Yeoman's Wooing Song

*** Chan. 9744. Rodgers, BBC Symphony Ch. & O, Hickox, with (i) Rolfe Johnson; (ii) Ogston

Hymnus Paradisi; An English Mass

*** Hyp. CDA 66488. Kennard, Mark Ainsley, RLPO Ch., RLPO, Handley

(i) Hymnus paradisi; (ii) Sir Patrick Spens

(BB) *** Naxos 8.570352. Gilchrist, Bach Ch., Bournemouth SO, Hill, with (i) C. Rutter; (ii) R. Williams

In *Hymnus Paradisi* **Handley** conveys a mystery, a tenderness rather missing from the previous recording, made by Sir David Willcocks for EMI, strong as that is. Handley's soloists bring a moving compassion, as in the haunting setting of the 23rd Psalm which makes up the third movement. The Hyperion digital recording is warm, full and atmospheric. *An English Mass* is simpler yet also hauntingly beautiful.

Hickox gives a deeply felt performance of *Hymnus Paradisi*, not as forthright as David Hill's on Naxos, but still with great warmth and power. He similarly has a rarity for a coupling in the form of the *Kent Yeoman's Wooing Song*. It was intended as a wedding present (in the end a very belated one) for two friends. Written in four parts, it finds the composer in an unexpectedly light-hearted mood, with the four sections of the score going through the mating process: in Part One the soprano announces she is 'on the market', and this is followed by the baritone stating his case. The third section is a love song, while the fourth brings things to a triumphant conclusion – but not, as the sleeve-note writer points out, before the soprano has played hard to get! The soloists are uniformly excellent, as is the warm Chandos sound.

David Hill directs a superb version of Howells's *Hymnus Paradisi*, with excellent soloists, choir and orchestra. His account is direct and fresh, exciting in the more flamboyant parts of the score, such as in the *Sanctus*, yet relaxing beautifully in the reflective passages. *Sir Patrick Spens*, written at the age of 25, was Howells's first major large-scale choral work. It opens with tremendous gusto, a bracing, briny, swashbuckling adventure which befits the nautical story of the text. It is excitingly and vividly performed here, with a superb recording to match.

Missa Sabrinensis

☙→ (B) *** Chan. 2 for 1 241-27 (2). Watson, D. Jones, Hill, Maxwell, L. Symphony Ch., LSO, Rozhdestvensky – *Stabat Mater* ***

Rozhdestvensky here conducts a passionate account of what in many ways is the most powerful of all the composer's major works. There is little of the restraint that is typical of much of Howells's choral writing. Rather he exploits the lushest, most passionate elements in his richly postimpressionist style, and he hardly lets up over the whole span. It would be hard to imagine a more inspired performance than Rozhdestvensky's. Over the incandescent singing of the choir, the four excellent soloists give radiant performances, with the golden-toned soprano, **Janice Watson**, regularly crowning the mood of ecstasy in her solos. Full, glowing, atmospheric sound to match, and a superb coupling.

(Organ) De la Mare's Pavane; Flourish for a Bidding; Jacob's Brawl; St Louis Come to Clifton;

Walton's Toye. (Choral): House of the Mind; Hymn for St Cecilia; King of Glory; New College Service: Magnificat & Nunc Dimittis; O Pray for the Peace of Jerusalem; A Sequence for St Michael

(M) *** CRD CRD 3454. New College, Oxford, Ch., Higginbottom

Higginbottom opens with the inspired *Sequence for St Michael*, a setting of a medieval lyric which was originally intended as part of *Hymnus paradisi* and is connected with the death of the composer's nine-year-old son. This beautiful and very dramatic motet is most movingly sung. The *Hymn to St Cecilia* is more direct yet, set to a poem by Ursula Vaughan Williams, and has increasing radiance. *O Pray for the Peace of Jerusalem* was written during the war, while Howells and his wife were snowbound in a cottage in the Cotswolds. It has a magnetic, tranquil stillness. These are all fine performances, beautifully sung, with the choir more recessed, less dramatically projected, than with the Wells Cathedral Choir on Hyperion. The organ pieces act as contrasting interludes. The programme ends with a thrillingly unrestrained setting of George Herbert's *King of Glory*. Howells believed there was no dividing line between spiritual tranquillity and God-given ecstasy, and this remarkable piece carries both expressions of human experience. The whole programme is very well sung, played and recorded, and shows the composer at his most inspirational.

(Organ) Psalm-preludes, Set 1/1; Paen; Prelude: Sine nomine. (Vocal): Behold, O God our defender; Here is the door; Missa Aedi Christi: Kyrie; Credo; Sanctus; Benedictus; Agnus Dei; Gloria; Sing lullaby; A spotless rose; Where wast thou?

(M) *** CRD 3455. New College, Oxford, Ch., Higginbottom (organ)

A further collection of the music of Herbert Howells, splendidly sung by **Edward Higginbottom's** fine choir, while he provides the organ interludes in addition. Among the shorter pieces, the carol-anthem *Sing lullaby* is especially delightful, and the programme ends with the motet *Where wast thou?*, essentially affirmative, in spite of the question posed at the opening. Beautifully spacious sound makes this a highly rewarding collection.

Requiem. Motets: The House of the Mind; A Sequence for St Michael

*** Chan. 9019. Finzi Singers, Spicer – VAUGHAN WILLIAMS: *Lord thou hast been our refuge*, etc. ***

Requiem; Take him, earth, for cherishing

*** United Recordings 88033. Barber, Field, Johnstone, Angus, Vasari, Backhouse – MARTIN: *Mass* ***

Howells's *Requiem* is the work which prepared the way for *Hymnus Paradisi*, providing some of the material for it. For unaccompanied chorus, it presents a gentler, compact view of what in the big cantata becomes powerfully expansive. The **Finzi Singers**, 18-strong, give a fresh and atmospheric, beautifully moulded performance, well coupled with two

substantial motets with organ by Howells, as well as choral pieces by Vaughan Williams.

On United the soloists and **Vasari**, a choir conducted by **Jeremy Backhouse**, are absolutely first class and give a well-nigh exemplary performance, possibly finer than its immediate rival. Doubtless couplings will resolve the matter of choice. The present disc offers the *Requiem* in harness with another *Mass* from the inter-war years by Frank Martin.

Stabat Mater

⊷ (B) *** Chan. 2 for 1 247-27 (2). Archer, L. Symphony Ch., LSO, Rozhdestvensky – *Missa Sabrinensis* ****

The *Stabat Mater* was Howells's last major work. Though the ecstasy is not as consistently sustained as in the earlier *Missa Sabrinensis*, with which it is now coupled; with many more passages of hushed devotion, one registers with new intensity the agony of St John the Divine at the foot of the Cross, the companion of the Virgin Mary. The saint is personified in the tenor solos, here sung superbly by **Neill Archer** with a clear, heady tone, starting with his first thrilling entry on *O quam tristis*. As in the *Missa*, **Rozhdestvensky** proves the most passionate advocate, magnetically leading one through the whole rich score. Though ensemble sometimes suffers, it is a small price to pay for such thrusting, spontaneous-sounding conviction. Glowing, rich sound.

HUMMEL, Johann (1778–1837)

Bassoon Concerto in F

*** Chan. 9656. Popov, Russian State SO, Polyansky – MOZART; WEBER: *Bassoon Concertos* ***

A first-class modern recording of Hummel's genial *Bassoon Concerto* was needed, and **Valeri Popov** fits the bill, twinklingly good-natured and elegant, especially in the swinging 6/8 finale. His woody timbre (a French instrument perhaps) is most appealing, and **Polyansky** provides a warmly polished accompaniment, helped by the resonant, but not clouded, recording.

Piano Concerto in A; L'Enchanment d'Oberon; Rondo brillant, 'Le Retour à Londres'; 8 Variations & Coda on 'O du lieber Augustin'

**** Chan. 10374. Shelley, LMP

By far the earliest work here is the *A major Piano Concerto*, written, like another unnumbered A major concerto (already recorded by Shelley), in about 1798 when the composer was still in his teens. It is **Shelley's** gift that with his phenomenal agility and clarity of articulation he can make Hummel's decorative writing a delight. The slow movement of the concerto is a lyrical *Romanze*, again with plentiful keyboard decoration, leading to a charming Rondo finale with a lightly skipping main theme and with one more serious episode in the middle, when the key switches to the relative minor key of F sharp minor.

L'Enchanment d'Oberon (with that French word spelt incorrectly) not only echoes Weber's one-movement *Konzertstück* of six years earlier, but in its five sections it relates to the opera, if with few direct quotations. This is unashamedly light music, designed for immediate appeal, with a march in lightly dotted rhythm leading to a storm episode. *Le Retour à Londres* of 1831 was expressly designed as a tribute to the British capital on the first of his 'grand farewell tours'. A cadenza links the slow, ruminative introduction to the main body of the *allegro*, featuring a jaunty Rondo theme over an oompah rhythm, leading to an equally jaunty march. Shelley again proves an ideal soloist. As a tailpiece comes the purely orchestral set of variations and coda on the tinkling little German folksong, *O du lieber Augustin*. The tune may be unremittingly corny in its three-in-a-bar Laendler rhythms, but it is liable to stick in the mind for hours afterwards. First-rate recording, clear and vivid, warm and full.

Piano Concerto in C, Op. 34; Rondos brillants in A, Op. 56 & B flat, Op. 98

*** Chan. 10216. Shelley, LMP

This disc from **Howard Shelley**, with full, open, well-balanced sound and sparkling performances, rounds off the Chandos series with the C major work, the earliest of Hummel's mature piano concertos, written in 1809, the year of Beethoven's *Emperor Concerto*. The two works labelled *Rondo brillant* were written later, in 1814 and 1822 respectively, each with a lyrical introduction of roughly five minutes leading on to a rondo finale, full of elaborate passagework for the soloist – both rather like concertos without a first movement.

Piano Concertos: in A min., Op. 85; B min., Op. 89

⊶ **** Chan. 8507. Hough, ECO, Thomson

The *A minor* is Hummel's most often-heard piano concerto, never better played, however, than by **Stephen Hough** on this prize-winning Chandos disc. The coda is quite stunning; it is not only his dazzling virtuosity that carries all before it but also the delicacy and refinement of colour he produces. The *B minor*, Op. 89, is more of a rarity, and is given with the same blend of virtuosity and poetic feeling which Hough brings to its companion. He is given expert support by **Bryden Thomson** and the **ECO** – and the recording is first class.

Piano Concerto in A flat, Op. 113; Concertino in G, Op. 73; Gesellschafts Rondo, Op. 117

*** Chan. 9558. Shelley, LMP

The *Concertino* is slight and frothy but is played with elegance and virtuosity by **Howard Shelley**, who directs from the keyboard. The *A flat major Concerto* comes from 1827 and was written for the composer's concert tours of 1828–30. It is well scored and the solo part is brilliantly decorative. Some have found the final *Rondo alla Spagniola* prophetic of Chopin's *E minor Concerto*. The *Gesellschafts Rondo (Society Rondo)* from 1829 is a 12-minute piece consisting of a slow introduction and a dashing vivace. It is all fresh and delightful, even if it plumbs no depths. Brilliant playing from Shelley.

Double Concerto for Piano & Violin, Op. 17; Violin Concerto (completed by Gregory Rose)

(BB) **(*) Naxos 8.557595. Trostiansky, Osetinskaya, Russian PO, Rose

Hummel echoes Mozart's great *Sinfonia concertante* in his *Double Concerto* of 1805, a charming work with elegant interplay between the soloists, particularly in the playful Rondo finale. The great merit of this Russian performance is the piano contribution of **Polina Osetinskaya**, with Hummel's rippling passagework played with crystal-clear articulation. The violinist, **Alexander Trostiansky**, is a fluent and able artist, but sadly his tone is unpleasantly acid, a failing which also mars the *Violin Concerto*. This is a piece that the Hummel scholar, Joel Sachs, has counted 'doubtful or unverifiable', though there are plenty of characteristic touches.

Grand Rondeau brillant; Oberon's Magic Horn; Variations & Finale in B flat, Op. 115; Variations in F, Op. 97

(BB) *** Naxos 8.557845. Hinterhuber, Gävle SO, Grodd

The four concertante pieces on this imaginative disc were written between 1820 and 1833, primarily as vehicles to show off Hummel's virtuosity at the keyboard. **Christopher Hinterhuber**, who has already recorded piano music by C. P. E. Bach for Naxos, is a first-rate soloist, accompanied by the **Gävle Symphony Orchestra**, one of the oldest in Sweden, under its German music director, **Uwe Grodd**. An excellent disc of long-buried rarities, well worth hearing.

Trumpet Concerto in E flat

⊶ (M) *** Sony SMK 89611. Marsalis, Nat. PO, Leppard – HAYDN: *Concerto* *** (with concert: *Trumpet Concertos* ❀ ***)

The **Hardenberger** and **Wynton Marsalis** performance has been reissued within a well-chosen collection heard in the familiar brass key of E flat. Marsalis (and his accompanists) do not miss the genial lilt inherent in the dotted theme of the first movement, and the finale captivates the ear with its high spirits and breezy bravura. Marsalis's approach is straight and classical. In matters of bravura, however, he relishes the sparkling finale.

(i) Violin Concerto in G; Adagio and Rondo alla Polacca in A (for violin & orchestra); Potpourri for Viola and Orchestra in G min., Op. 94; Variations, Op. 115 (for piano & orchestra)

*** Chan. 10255. Shelley, LMP, (i) with Ehnes

The Hummel scholar Joel Sachs lists the composer's *G major Violin Concerto* among the 'doubtful or unverifiable works', but it has many characteristic touches, built as it is on warmly lyrical themes, starting with a clean-cut march tune marked by dotted rhythms. The Canadian violinist, **James Ehnes**, is the brilliant and persuasive soloist. The *Variations in B flat* for piano and orchestra finds the soloist, **Howard Shelley**, in peak form, dazzlingly finger-perfect, and the result is a delight. Played and recorded like this, all these works are immensely enjoyable.

Sappho von Mitilene (ballet), Op. 68; Die Zauberschloss: Suite; 12 Waltzes & Coda

**** Chan. 10415. LMP, Shelley

The ballet *Sappho von Mitilene*, based on the Sapphic legend from ancient Greece, is here represented by 12 movements lasting a full 47 minutes. The scoring adds to the charming sequence, with weighty brass including alto, tenor and bass trombones as well as trumpet, timpani and horn. **Howard Shelley** draws beautifully sprung rhythms from the **London Mozart Players** who, as recorded, sound rather large for such a work. *Die Zauberschloss* ('The Magic Castle') is much more clearly illustrative and again nicely varied, with a Minuet, a *Tarantella* and a *Laendler* ending the work with fine panache. On a very well-filled disc the extra item is a charmer too, with 12 tiny waltzes, all of them less than a minute long. One hopes more Hummel ballet music will now be unearthed.

CHAMBER MUSIC

Amusement for Piano & Violin in F min., Op. 108; Violin Sonatas: in F, Op. 5/2; C, Op. 14; Variations 'alla Monferina' in D, Op. 54 for Piano & Cello

*** Mer. CDE 84439. Triangulus

The title *'Amusement'* for the first of the four works on this Meridian disc could not be more apt. This is in effect a compact sonatina for violin and piano, which brings out the open, unpretentious qualities of Hummel's writing at their most appealing. Though longer and structurally more elaborate, the two *Sonatas* are hardly more ambitious, two works similarly designed to entertain without making too many demands on the listener.

The *Variations 'alla Monferina'* for cello and piano, varied and inventive, have a haunting little refrain in 6/8 which recurs at various points. After ten variations the piece is rounded off with a galloping 6/8 coda. Though **Alison Moncrieff's** cello is not helped by the recording, which underlines some minor flaws, this is another engaging example of Hummel's attractive and undemanding writing. In both the works with violin and those with cello, **Lyn Garland** at the piano is the prime mover, as Hummel would have expected, always fresh and lively.

Flute Sonatas 1 in G, Op. 2/2; 2 in D, Op. 50; 3 in A, Op. 64; (i) Flute Trio in A, Op. 78; Grand rondeau brillant for Flute & Piano in G, Op. 126

⊟ (BB) *** Naxos 8.553473. Daoust, Picard, with (i) Dolin

Hummel's elegant, easy-going melodic style seems custom-made for the flute, and his three lightweight sonatas are lacking in neither diversity nor charm. The *Grand rondeau brillant* is entertainingly like a Weber display piece. The performances on Naxos are both sunny and technically felicitous, and are warmly recorded. The *Trio* is an ingenuous set of variations on a Russian folk tune which lends itself to sparkling divisions. Here there is plenty of bustle before the work ends peacefully.

Piano Quintet in E flat, Op. 87; Piano Septet in D min., Op. 74

(B) *** Decca Australian Eloquence (ADD) 476 2447. Melos Ens. – WEBER: Clarinet Quintet ***

These two highly engaging works show the composer at his most melodically fecund and his musical craftsmanship at its most apt. His skill at shaping and balancing a movement can be impressive: it is the ideas themselves (as in all music) that can make or break a structure, and here they are entirely appropriate to music designed to entertain. This these works certainly do in such spontaneous and polished performances. The 1965 sound is warm, full and rich, and this is a vintage recording in every way; and this version of the *Piano Quintet* is preferable to that on its Hyperion Dyad competitor. The Weber coupling is a charmer too.

Piano Trios 1–7

(M) *** MDG 3307/8 (2). Trio Parnassus

Comparing the first with the last of the trios shows no marked development of style of the kind one expects with the very greatest composers, but all seven works are individually rewarding in their diverse ways, and the composer's fund of ideas never dries up for a moment. The **Trio Parnassus** play throughout with consistent zest and spontaneity and they obviously enjoy the simple lyrical melodies. They are admirably recorded and this box can carry a strong recommendation.

Septet in D min., Op. 74

⊟ (M) *** CRD 3344. Nash Ens. – BERWALD: Septet ***

Hummel's *Septet* is an enchanting and inventive work with a virtuoso piano part, expertly dispatched here by **Clifford Benson**. A fine performance and excellent recording make this a highly desirable issue, particularly in view of the enterprising coupling.

Serenades, Op. 63 & 66; Potpourri, Op. 53

*** MDG 301 1344-2. Consortium Classicum (Dieter Klocker, Helman Jung, Andreas Krecher, Sonja Prunnbauer, Thomas Duis)

This, unashamedly, is a collection of fun music, performed by the members of **Consortium Classicum** with the sort of exuberance that Hummel and his friends must have brought to these confections, designed for relaxed festive evenings in the Imperial Gardens in Vienna or in private houses. Rounding things off comes a jaunty contredanse-cum-waltz, evidently Hummel's own invention. These evidently are the first ever recordings of light music from another age, and they can still give much pleasure in performances like these.

String Quartets: in C; in G; in E flat, Op. 30/1–3

⊟ (BB) *** Hyp. Helios CDH 55166. Delmé Qt

Hummel's three quartets are closer to Haydn than Beethoven, though the first of the set in C major with its impressive opening *Adagio e mesto* in the minor key, and fine *Adagio*, obviously leans towards the influence of the later composer, while the audacious quotation of *Comfort ye* from Handel's *Messiah* in the preceding *Andante* brings yet another example of Hummelian sleight of hand. In short these are fascinating works, highly inventive, and crafted with the composer's usual fluent charm. They are splendidly played by the **Delmé** group, who provide plenty of vitality and warmth. The Hyperion recording is fresh and believable.

Piano Sonata 2, Op. 13; La bella capricciosa (Polonaise), Op. 55; Caprice, Op. 49; La contemplazione (Una fantasia piccola), Op. 107/3; Hungarian Rondo, Op. 107/6; Rondo, Op. 11; Variations on a Theme from Gluck's Armide, Op. 57

*** Chan. 9807. Shelley

Starting with a wittily pointed account of the *Rondo*, Opus 11, **Howard Shelley** gives the most persuasive accounts of piano music by this leading virtuoso of his time. He may never have developed towards free Romanticism as Beethoven, Schubert and Weber did, but such stylish performances as Shelley's, beautifully recorded, bring many delights, as in the sparkling *Gluck Variations*, the well-constructed *Sonata*, Opus 13, and the late, polka-like *Hungarian Rondo*.

Piano Sonatas 3 in F min., Op. 20; 5 in F sharp min., Op. 81; 6 in D, Op. 106

⊕— **** Hyp. CDA 67390. Hough

These three *Sonatas* are arguably the finest of the series, and **Hough** gives the most characterful performances, beautifully recorded. The most radical of the three, written in 1819, is in F sharp minor, in which Hummel fully embraces the new romantic movement, with a first movement that brings a very free rendering of sonata form, full of contrasts and surprises, built on a striking, angular main theme. The slow movement after a weighty introduction then anticipates Chopin's *Nocturnes*, leading to an energetic Slavonic dance finale. *No. 6 in D* marks a return to a more classical manner, at times like Weber, with a fast mazurka for Scherzo, while *No. 3 in F minor* of 1807 has a quirkiness typical of the composer, with a central slow movement marked to be played 'majestically'. In its way this makes as much of a discovery as Richard Hickox's revelatory recordings of Hummel *Masses*.

VOCAL MUSIC

Masses in B flat, Op. 77; D, Op. 111; (i) Alma Virgo

⊕— *** Chan. 0681. Gritton, Collegium Musicum 90, Hickox; (i) with Gritton

Like Haydn's last six settings of the *Mass* they were written for the name-day of the Princess Esterházy, and they have inspired Hickox and his team to performances just as electrifying as those they have given of those Haydn *Masses*. These Hummel *Masses*, unlike Haydn's, are for chorus alone without soloists. The *Mass in D* (1808) begins in sombre mood with some adventurous harmonies, but Hummel in both *Masses*, like Haydn, prefers vigorous movement to meditation, often in fugal writing with sharply syncopated rhythms, which makes for exhilarating results.

As with Haydn, the settings of the final *Dona nobis pacem* in both *Masses*, far from conveying peace, are joyfully energetic, though, unlike Hummel, Hummel fades down to a gentle close in each. **Susan Gritton** is the pure-toned soloist in the fill-up, *Alma Virgo*, an aria in two sections, with the chorus joining in for the culminating *Alleluia* with whooping horns.

Mass in D min., S67/W13; Salve Regina

*** Chan. 0724. Gritton, Nichols, Helen Stephen, Padmore, Varcoe, Coll. Mus. 90 Ch. & O, Hickox

In the *D minor Mass* of 1805 Hummel seems intent on taking the listener by surprise, with the *Credo* starting lyrically in a flowing triple time, the opposite of a positive affirmation of belief. Throughout the *Mass* Hummel demonstrates that he is intent on writing a thoughtful rather than a sharply dramatic setting, with the soloists generally treated as a corporate team, set against the full choir, and the triumphant setting of *Dona nobis pacem* ends not on a fugue such as Haydn preferred but on powerful homophonic writing. The *Salve Regina* is hardly elegiac in its operatic style with elaborate coloratura for the soprano soloist, here glowingly sung by **Susan Gritton**. **Richard Hickox** again proves an ideal interpreter, drawing superb playing and singing from **Collegium Musicum 90**.

(i) Mass in E flat, Op. 80; Quod in urbe, Op. 88; Te Deum

⊕— *** Chan. 0712. Coll. Mus. 90, Hickox, (i) with Gritton, Murray, Gilchrist, Varcoe

The *Mass in E flat* has a winning freshness, with a setting of the *Kyrie* which, after opening gently, promptly expands into a joyful *Allegro*. The performance consistently captures the joy of Hummel's inspiration, with clean attack and fine diction from the chorus as well as the soloists. That clarity extends to the superb setting of the *Te Deum*, written at high speed to celebrate peace with Napoleon in 1805. *Quod in urbe*, written as a gradual for inclusion in services, also starts strikingly, with timpani alone in fanfare rhythm, another fine work neglected for far too long. With full, clear sound, recorded in the Blackheath Concert Hall, Hickox must again be congratulated.

Missa Solemnis in C; Te Deum

⊕— (BB) *** Naxos 8.557193. Wright, McKendree-Wright, Power, Griffiths, Tower Voices, New Zealand SO, Grodd

Here with New Zealand forces, including the brilliant professional chamber choir, **Tower Voices**, we have the longest of Hummel's five *Masses* in coupling with an electrifying setting of the *Te Deum*. Both were written in 1806, and one is constantly reminded that this was the period of the Napoleonic wars, when each of these works so often features martial music with fanfares, trumpets and drums. Unlike most Anglican settings, this *Te Deum* ends on a grand *fortissimo*. A thrilling issue, all the more recommendable at super-bargain price.

HUMPERDINCK, Engelbert (1854–1921)

Hänsel und Gretel (complete; DVD version)

**** EuroArts DVD 2055888. Papoulkas, Gabler, Vermillion, Ketelsen, Vilsmaier, Teuscher, Female & Children's Ch. of Saxon State Op., Dresden, Hoffstetter (Stage Director: Katharina Thalbach, V/D: Andreas Morell)

This is a wholly enchanting production of Humperdinck's wonderfully tuneful children's opera that cannot be recommended too highly. It was the Dresden Semperoper's Christmas presentation in 2006 and it would be an ideal Christmas gift for any musical youngster – and it is very entertaining for adults too. There are no voices here of the calibre of Schwarzkopf and Grümmer, but **Hans-Joachim Ketelsen** (as Peter, the children's Father) sings his 'Tra-la-la-las' with richly resonant amiability, and **Irmgard Vilsmaier** as their Mother is unusually convincing dramatically. **Iris Vermillion** is a gloriously camp Witch (she enters glamorously and then changes into a seedier costume). But vocally the children dominate. Their *Dance Duet* is a real highlight, and **Anna Gabler** is vocally and dramatically strong as Gretel, while **Lydia Teuscher** sings charmingly as the Sandman and Dew Fairy. **Michael Hoffstetter** directs with flair, pacing the opera spontaneously, yet finding much glowing detail in Humperdinck's score, especially the strings and horns, helped by demonstration-worthy sound in the lively opera-house acoustic. But it is **Katharina Thalbach's** production that makes this such an enchanting entertainment, full of imaginative detail, from the angels who either swing in on wires or come down a chute, to the Witch's house, made of eatable biscuits, which conveniently turns into the oven. And one must not forget the hugely real giant tortoise who stays around to guard the children; and the happy ending is exhilaratingly staged, with glorious singing from the chorus of women and children.

Hänsel und Gretel (complete; CD versions)

⊶— ⛭ BB (***) Naxos mono 8.110897/8. Schwarzkopf, Grümmer, Metternich, Ilosvay, Schürhoff, Felbermayer, Children's Ch., Philh. O, Karajan (with additional excerpts sung by Supervia, Ferraris, Hüsch, Seinemeyer, Jung)

Ⓜ (***) EMI mono 5 67061-2 (2). Schwarzkopf, Grümmer, Metternich, Ilosvay, Schürhoff, Felbermayer, Children's Ch., Philh. O, Karajan

Ⓜ *** Sony (ADD) S2K 96455 (2). Cotrubas, Von Stade, Ludwig, Nimsgern, Te Kanawa, Söderström, Cologne Op. Children's Ch., Gürzenich O, Pritchard

Ⓝ Ⓜ **(*) Decca (ADD) 478 0143 (2). Fassbaender, Popp, Berry, Hamari, Burrowes, Gruberová, Schlemm, V. Boys' Ch., VPO, Solti

Karajan's classic 1950s set of Humperdinck's children's opera, with **Schwarzkopf** and **Grümmer** peerless in the name-parts, is enchanting; this was an instance where everything in the recording went right. The original mono LP set was already extremely atmospheric. In most respects the sound has as much clarity and warmth as rival recordings made in the 1970s. There is much to delight here; the smaller parts are beautifully done and **Else Schürhoff's** Witch is memorable.

This is now reissued as one of EMI's 'Great Recordings of the Century', but there is no doubt that the alternative Naxos set is the one to go for. This is one of the finest transfers Mark Obert-Thorn has achieved to date. Moreover, as a bonus on the second disc we are offered a series of historical recordings of excerpts dating from 1928, with **Conchita**

Supervia rattling away as Hansel, partnered by **Maria Ferraris** as Gretel singing the *Dance Duet* in Italian; **Meta Seinemeyer** and **Helen Jung** in 1929; **Gerard Hüsch** as Peter (in 1937); and three excerpts from 1935, with **Elisabeth Schumann** as the Sandman singing a duet with herself, accompanied by Ernest Lush.

Beautifully cast, the **Pritchard** version from Sony was the first in genuine stereo (in 1978) to challenge the vintage Karajan set. **Cotrubas** – sometimes a little grainy as recorded – and **Von Stade** both give charming characterizations, and the supporting cast is exceptionally strong, with **Söderström** an unexpected but refreshing and illuminating choice as the Witch. Pritchard draws idiomatic playing from the **Gürzenich Orchestra**, and the recording is pleasingly atmospheric. This is, however, another of those Masterwork reissues in which the libretto is only available via a CD-ROM and a personal computer.

Solti with the **Vienna Philharmonic** directs a strong, spectacular version, emphasizing the Wagnerian associations of the score. Solti does the *Witch's Ride* very excitingly, and the VPO are encouraged to play with consistent fervour throughout. The result, although rather lacking in charm, is well sung, with the two children (**Brigitte Fassbaender** and **Lucia Popp**) both engagingly characterized. **Edita Gruberová** is an excellent Dew Fairy and **Walter Berry** is first rate as Peter. **Anny Schlemm's** Witch is memorable if vocally unsteady, and there are some imaginative touches of stereo production associated with *Hocus pocus* and her other moments of magic. The recording is characteristically vivid. A full libretto accompanies the reissue.

Hänsel und Gretel: highlights

BB *** EMI Encore 586097-2. Von Otter, Bonney, Lipovšek, Schwarz, Schmidt, Hendricks, Lind, Tölz Boys' Ch., Bav. RSO, Tate

It is good to have a set of highlights from the deleted Bavarian set conducted, fairly briskly but sympathetically, by **Jeffrey Tate**. **Barbara Bonney** as Gretel and **Anne Sofie von Otter** as Hänsel are hardly less fine than the exceptionally strong duos on rival sets, and the chill that **Marjana Lipovšek** conveys as the Witch, using the widest range of expression, is equally telling. The recording has plenty of warmth and atmosphere. A bargain.

Hansel and Gretel (complete; in English)

**** Chan. 3143 (2). Larmore, Evans, Henschel, Plowright, Hayward, Tynan, Montague, New London Children's Ch., Philh. O, Mackerras

Ⓑ *** CfP (ADD) 5 75993-2 (2). Kern, Neville, Howard, Hunter, Herincx, Robinson, Sadler's Wells Op. O, Bernardi – WAGNER: *Siegfried Idyll*: L. Sinf., C. Davis ***

Useful as the old Classics for Pleasure set has been, **Mackerras's** new English version of *Hansel and Gretel* trumps it on almost every point. With Chandos's digital recording clear and beautifully separated, yet with an agreeable bloom on voices, the version, sponsored by the Sir Peter Moores Opera in English Foundation, brings an exceptional, lively performance with Sir Charles Mackerras the inspired conductor. The new David Pountney translation is used, fresher and more naturally idiomatic, and the cast of soloists is distinguished, with even **Jane Henschel** as the Witch refusing to caricature the role. **Jennifer Larmore** and **Rebecca Evans** sing delightfully in the title-roles, their voices properly contrasted. **Rosalind Plowright** and **Robert Harwood** make an impressive Mother and Father, and the Dew Fairy (**Sarah Tynan**) and Sandman (**Diana Montague**) also create pleasingly different images. Mackerras directs the **Philharmonia Orchestra** with his usual vitality. This is a set that will clearly stand the test of time as an English version, in every way rivalling even the best of versions in the original German, with the fresh young voices of the **New London Children's Choir** beautifully caught.

From CfP, this was the first full-length Sadler's Wells Opera recording in English, and it proved to be one of the finest of all the company's ventures into the recording studio. It was also the first complete foreign opera in English on record since way back in the days of early operatic 78s. The result is warm and atmospheric and not at all artificial sounding.

HURLSTONE, William
(1876–1906)

(i) Piano Concerto in D; Fantasie-Variations on a Swedish Air; (ii) Piano Quartet in E min., Op. 43; Piano Trio in G

*** Lyrita (ADD) SRCD 2286 (2). (i) Parkin, LPO, Braithwaite; (ii) Tunnell Piano Qt

Hurlstone's was a tragic career. He was a prodigy as a composer, sensitive and imaginative; his teacher, Stanford, thought him more promising than his contemporary, Vaughan Williams. He was also a fine pianist, but ill-health and poverty prevented him from developing these talents, and he died at the age of thirty. Neither of the two concertante works has the formal strength of his chamber music, but they are both distinctive, the *Concerto* the more positive, the *Variations* the more quirkily individual. Both performances do the music full justice and they sound excellent. The two chamber works offered here are characteristic, superficially Brahmsian in manner, as with Stanford, but with a winning Englishry. The *Piano Quartet* is the more vital of the two, but both are richly rewarding and very well played and recorded.

The Magic Mirror: Suite; Variations on a Hungarian Air; Variations on an Original Theme

*** Lyrita (ADD) SRCD 208. LPO, Braithwaite

The *Variations on an Original Theme* date from 1896, though the theme on which they are based comes from a *Trio*, written two years earlier. They show considerable inventive resource and although, like the *Variations on a Hungarian Air*, there is also a certain debt to Brahms, they have a lightness of touch and a feeling for the orchestra which is marked. *The Magic Mirror Suite* of 1900 also offers reminders of the Elgar of *The Wand of Youth*. But it is not long before one can sense something quietly individual beginning to surface.

The **LPO** and **Nicholas Braithwaite** give lively, cultured performances of this eminently well-crafted, immaculately scored and civilized music, and they are beautifully recorded.

Cello Sonata in D

Ⓜ *** Dutton CDLX 7102. Fuller, Dussek – HARTY: *Butterflies*, etc.; PARRY: *Cello Sonata in A* ***

Hurlstone's *Cello Sonata* is as well fashioned and musicianly as you would expect from this gifted composer. It receives excellent advocacy from **Andrew Fuller**, who also writes the intelligent notes, and his fine pianist, **Michael Dussek**. At the same time it is not easy to discern a distinctive voice here beneath the Brahmsian veneer. The recording is excellent, well balanced and present.

(i) Piano Quartet in E min.; Piano Trio in G; Adagio (arr. from (i) Cello Sonata 2)

Ⓜ *** Dutton CDLX 7128. Dussek Piano Trio; (i) with Boyd

The idiom in both the *Piano Trio* and the *Piano Quartet* is conservative, with echoes of Mendelssohn and Brahms as much as of Stanford. What raises them above the level of imitations is the fluent memorability of both the material and the arguments, as in the jig-like Scherzo and jaunty finale of the *Trio* and the sweetly tuneful *Andante cantabile* of the *Quartet*. The moving *Adagio lamentoso* slow movement of the *Cello Sonata No. 2* was arranged for viola by Hurlstone's fellow composer, Frank Bridge, and it makes a fine supplement to the major works. It is played beautifully here by **James Boyd**, who also joins the excellent **Dussek Trio** for the *Piano Quartet*. When tunes sprang from Hurlstone's imagination so fluently, it would be good to hear some of his dozens of songs and the cantata, *Alfred the Great*.

HYDE, Miriam (1913–2005)

(i) Piano Concertos 1 in E flat min.; 2 in C sharp min.; (ii) Village Fair

**(*) Australian Universal ABC Classics (ADD) 465 735-2. (i) Hyde; Australian SO, Simon; (ii) Sydney SO, Franks

Miriam Hyde was a well-respected composer and teacher in Australia, and we have here her early *Piano Concertos*, written in 1932–3 and 1934–5 respectively. They are unashamedly romantic in tradition, with bold writing and rich orchestration – Brahms and Rachmaninov being obvious models. The tunes are memorable and each work has many felicities, not least in the touches of folk-like melody and colour. It is all very enjoyable and the music is instantly appealing. These are excellent performances, though the 1975 recording is a little thin. With an attractive fill-up in the form of *Village Fair*, once again with folk-like themes, this is a valuable addition to the catalogue. Miriam Hyde certainly deserves wider recognition.

IBERT, Jacques (1890–1962)

(i) Bachannale; Bostoniana; (ii) Flute Concerto; (i) Divertissement; (iii) Escales; (i) Louisville Concerto;

(iii) Ouverture de fête; (i) Symphonie marine; (iii) Tropismes pour des amours imaginaires; (iv) 4 Chansons de Don Quichotte

🅑🅑 **(*) EMI Gemini (ADD/DDD) 5 17639-2 (2). (i) CBSO, Frémaux; (ii) Pahud, Zürich Tonhalle O, Zinman; (iii) French Nat. R. O, Martinon; (iv) van Dam, Lyon Opéra O, Nagano

A generous and interesting collection. Even if some of it does not show the composer at his best, it is all played idiomatically under **Frémaux**, and is well recorded in the early 1970s. *Escales*, the *Ouverture de fête* and *Tropismes* have genuine atmosphere in **Martinon's** hands. But the highlights of the collection are the virtuosic and stylish account of Ibert's delightful *Flute Concerto* by **Emmanuel Pahud** and the **Zürich Tonhalle Orchestra** under **David Zinman**, superbly recorded, and **José Van Dam's** fine performances of the rare *Quatre chansons de Don Quichotte* in which the closing *Chanson de la mort* is most movingly sung and **Kent Nagano's** accompaniment is very sensitive.

La Ballade de la Geôle de Reading; (i) Persée et Andromède (opera; compléte); Sarabande pour Dulcinée

*** Avie AV 0008. (i) Massis, Rouillon, Beuron; Strasbourg PO, Latham-Koenig

The *Ballade de la Geôle de Reading*, inspired by passages from Oscar Wilde's poem, ignores the text in a purely orchestral evocation, with echoes of Ravel's *Daphnis et Chloé* hardly suggesting the rigours of prison life. *Persée et Andromède* is a miniature opera in two compact Acts, telling of Andromeda and the monster Cathos who eventually, after being slaughtered by Perseus, rises from his remains to become a handsome prince. The opening immediately establishes an exotic atmosphere, very French and when Cathos is finally transformed, his music grows more sensuous too, culminating in a love duet. All three principal soloists are first rate, with fresh, youthful-sounding voices. The *Sarabande pour Dulcinée*, taken from Ibert's ballet *Don Quichotte*, is an attractive makeweight. Sensitive direction from **Jan Latham-Koenig** throughout and very well recorded, warmly responsive playing from the **Strasbourg Philharmonic**.

Concertino da camera for Saxophone & Orchestra

✿ **** BIS CD-1357. Delangle, Singapore SO, Shui (with: MILHAUD: *Scaramouche*; Paule MAURICE: *Tableaux de Provence*; RAVEL: *Pavane pour une infante défunte*; Florent SCHMITT: *Légende, Op. 66*; Henri TOMASI: *Saxophone Concerto ***)

Ibert's charming *Concertino* comes first and encapsulates the spirit of the disc. Two pieces are new to the catalogue: the *Tableaux de Provence* by the little-known woman composer Paule Maurice (1910–67) and the *Concerto* for alto saxophone and orchestra by the Corsican, Henri Tomasi (1901–72). In addition to the familiar Ravel *Pavane pour une infante défunte* in the arrangement by Tami Nodaira and Milhaud's *Scaramouche*, the Tomasi and Maurice have charm and atmosphere and radiate the sunny ambience of Provence. The Florent Schmitt *Légende, Op. 66*, is a strong piece, inventive

and resourceful. **Claude Delangle** is a most distinguished exponent of this delightful repertoire and is eminently well supported by the **Singaporeans** under **Lan Shui**, and the BIS team.

Concerto for Cello & Wind Instruments

(***) BBC (mono) BBCL 4156-2. du Pré, Michael Krein Ens., Krein – DVOŘÁK: *Cello Concerto* **(*)

Jacqueline du Pré probably took Ibert's delightful concerto into her repertory for a BBC studio concert in 1962 with the **Michael Krein Ensemble**, whose enterprising and expert programmes were frequent at this period. A splendid performance and a worthwhile and welcome, if all too brief, supplement to her superb Prom performance of the Dvořák, superbly played, with the cello the first among many soloists.

Flute Concerto

🎧 *** BIS SACD 1559. Bezaly, São Paulo SO, Neschling (with BORNE: *Carmen Fantasy*) – RODRIGO: *Concierto pastoral* ***

Sharon Bezaly's account is very much the equal of Pahud's, ravishing in the reverie of the slow movement, and wonderfully exuberant in the finale, with its unbuttoned reminder of the *Divertissment*. Her Rodrigo coupling, too, is more tempting than Pahud's Khachaturian transcription, and the BIS programme includes also François Borne's seductive and dazzling *Fantaisie brillante on airs from 'Carmen'*, played equally bewitchingly. The BIS multi-channel recording too is in the demonstration bracket.

Divertissement

🎧 **** Chan. 9023. Ulster O, Tortelier – MILHAUD: *Le Bœuf; Création*; POULENC: *Les Biches* ****

(***) Testament mono SBT 1309. Paris Conservatoire O, Désormière – IPPOLITOV-IVANOV: *Caucasian Sketches*; DOMENICO SCARLATTI (arr. Tommasini): *The Good-Humoured Ladies*; TCHAIKOVSKY: *Sleeping Beauty Suite* (***)

🅑🅑 **(*) Virgin 2x1 4 82103-2. City of L. Sinfonia, Hickox (with FAURÉ: *Pavane*) – BIZET: *Symphony in C*; RAVEL: *Tombeau de Couperin*; TCHAIKOVSKY: *Serenade for Strings; Souvenir de Florence* **(*)

Yan Pascal Tortelier provides at last a splendid, modern, digital version of Ibert's *Divertissement*. There is much delicacy of detail, and the coupled suite from Poulenc's *Les Biches* is equally delectable. Marvellous, top-drawer Chandos sound.

Désormière was a stylist, and it shows in every bar. This 1951 recording, produced (like the rest of the programme) by John Culshaw, remains unsurpassed in terms of sheer character and style, though there have been many since that have been played with greater polish and better recorded. Lovers of French music of the 1920s should not miss it.

Hickox presents the *Divertissement* with both style and gusto, and the **City of London players** respond with much spirit, especially in the finale, complete with police whistle. The recording is a shade over-resonant but fully acceptable when the proceedings have moments of riotous vigour. If you want the rest of the programme, this is enjoyable enough.

Escales (Ports of Call)

⌐ Ⓜ *** RCA (ADD) **SACD** 82876 61387-2. Boston SO, Munch – DEBUSSY: *La Mer* **(*)** ; SAINT-SAËNS: *Symphony 3* ❀ ***

Munch's *Escales* brings some ravishing textures from the Boston violins, and the finale, *Valencia*, has sparkling dance rhythms. The 1956 recording, if balanced rather closely, has brilliance and transparency; and it sounds much fuller in this new SACD transfer.

CHAMBER MUSIC

3 Pièces brèves

⌐ Ⓜ *** Chan. 6543. Athena Ens. – GOUNOD: *Petite symphonie in B flat;* POULENC: *Sextet* ***

(***) BBC mono BBCL 4066-2. Dennis Brain Wind Quintet (with instrumental recital (***))

Ibert's *Trois pièces brèves* could hardly be played with more polish, wit and affection than in this brilliantly realized performance by the Athena group, the effect enhanced when they are recorded so realistically.

The characterful blend of **Dennis Brain** and his colleagues in his **Wind Quintet** (Gareth Morris, Leonard Brain, Stephen Waters and Cecil James) is fully captured in the BBC mono recording, and the warm, spirited geniality of their ensemble brings a delightful bonhomie to the music's wit – the pastoral opening is captivating.

INDIA, Sigismondo d' (1582–1629)

Amico hai vinto; Diana (Questo dardo, quest'arco); Misera me (Lamento d'Olympia); Piangono al pianger mio; Sfere fermate; Torna il sereno zefiro

*** Hyp. CDA 66106. Kirkby, Rooley (chitarone) – MONTEVERDI: *Lamento d'Olympia, etc.* ***

Sigismondo d'India was in the vanguard of the new movement founded by Monteverdi, and his laments show him to be a considerable master of expressive resource. His setting of the *Lamento d'Olympia* makes a striking contrast to Monteverdi's and is hardly less fine. This is an affecting and beautiful piece, and so are its companions, particularly when they are sung as freshly and accompanied as sensitively as here.

Madrigals & Canzonettes: Arditi baci miei; Cara mia cetra; Infelice Didone; Intenerite voi, lagrime mi; La mia Filli crudel; Mentre che'l cor; Mormora seco alquanto; Odi quel Rossignolol; Piange Madonna; Questa mia aurora; Scherniscimi, crudele; Sfere, fermate li giri sonori; Sù, sù prendi la cetra; Torna il sereno zfiro; Un di soletto; La Virtù; Vorrei baciarti, o Filli

⌐ *** HM HMC 901774. Kiehr, Concerto Soave, Aymes (with: GIOVANNI-MARIA TRABACI: *Gagliarda; Partita prima*

sopra Ruggiero; Partita sesta Cromatica sopra Ruggiero; Seconda Stravaganza; ASCANIO MAYONE: *Toccata V per il cimbalo cromatico*)

This is a superb disc and bears out the promise of the earlier Hyperion collection, above. Sigismondo d'India's madrigals undoubtedly rank alongside those of Monteverdi, both in the quality of their melodic lines and in their expressive, chromatic richness. And there could be no more ideal performer for them than **Maria Cristina Kiehr**. Her vocal beauty and ravishing phrasing have long been apparent from her previous records. Her vocal decoration is astonishing. But she is also infinitely touching in the songs of unrequited love. She closes the recital with the soaringly joyful *La Virtù*, a number to confirm d'India's mastery if one were needed. Three instrumental or keyboard pieces by contemporary composers, Giovanni-Maria Trabaci, Ascanio Mayone and Giovanni de Macque, are used as pleasing interludes. The accompaniments, employing a small instrumental ensemble including lute, guitar, harp and organ (or one of these), are just about perfect, and the recording is first class. Full texts and translations are included. A disc to put straight away at the top of your list.

Il primo libro de madrigali (1606): Interdette speranz'e van desio. Ottavo libro de madrigali: Il pastor fido, Act IV, Scene 9: Se tu, Silvio crudel, mi saetti (five madrigal cycle)

⌐ ❀ Ⓜ *** Virgin 5 61165-2. Chiaroscuro, L. Bar., Rogers – MONTEVERDI: *Madrigals* *** ❀

It is in the cycle from his Eighth Book of Madrigals, *Se tu, Silvio crudel, mi saetti*, that one experiences not only the composer's lyrical originality to the full but also his affinity with the operatic writing of his greater contemporary, Monteverdi. The vocal dialogue, which alternates solo and ensemble singing, is touching and dramatic by turns, and requires effortless vocal virtuosity. The quality of the performances is superlative, refined without a hint of preciosity, and always alive, while the accompaniments on the oboe and harpsichord are delicately balanced. An outstanding collection in every way.

INDY, Vincent d' (1851–1931)

(i) Choral varié; Lied. Saugefleurie; Wallenstein

Ⓝ *** Hyp. CDA 67690. BBC Nat. O of Wales, Fischer, (i) with Power

Memories of the old EMI recording of *Wallenstein* are not completely erased by this newcomer, but this is certainly a better played and recorded version of this rather enjoyable work. **Thierry Fischer** brings plenty of energy to this early but ambitious tone-poem, and the final and longest movement, *La mort de Wallenstein*, is very impressively done. The fill-ups are all rarities and well worth having: the two works for viola and orchestra are beautifully played by **Lawrence Power** (both very lovely works) while the tone-poem *Saugefleurie* is a typical mixture of the composer's Wagnerian influence mixing with his own very French style and producing some very beautiful, luminous colours from the orchestra. Very good sound, as usual, from this source.

Diptyque méditerranéen; Istar; Poème des rivages

⊕↝ *** Timpani 1C1101. Luxembourg PO, Krivine

The *Poème des Rivages* was the product of d'Indy's late love affair with a student, Caroline Janson, 36 years his junior. She returned his feelings, and d'Indy suddenly acknowledged the underlying sensuality of his own nature. The rich orchestral colours of these four seascapes develop an expressive radiance in his luminous scoring. The work is not another *La Mer*, but the final scene, *Le mystère de l'océan*, certainly depicts the sea's unpredictability and violence, returning at last to the gentle calm of the work's introduction.

The *Poème des rivages* followed in 1925/6 and reflects even more balmily the composer's new contentment with his young wife. *Istar* dates from 1896 and tells of the Assyrian goddess who (like Orfeo and Eurydice, only in reverse) seeks to retrieve her lover from the realm of the dead. **Krivine** makes the most of its sensuous feeling, and all three performances are of a high order. The **Luxembourg Orchestra** are obviously at home in these scores, and their conductor finds moments of genuine rapture in all three works, and he controls their differing structures admirably. The recording, too, is warmly atmospheric, and this disc should make new friends for the composer.

La forêt enchantée, Op. 8; Jour d'été à la montagne, Op. 61 ; Souvenirs, Op. 62

⊕↝ **** Chan. 10464. Iceland SO, Gamba

These are three of d'Indy's most remarkable works; they reveal him not only as an impressionist in a Debussian mould, but also as influenced by both Wagner and folk-dance melodies from his own culture. *La Forêt enchantée* of 1878 is described as a *Légende-symphonique*; it is based on an epic romantic ballad by Ludwig Uhland. The orchestral writing is vividly melodramatic and the music is both sensuous and exciting. By the time the masterly *Jour d'été à la montagne* was written, some 30 years later, d'Indy's style had matured, and while the Wagnerian opulence remains this is written very much in the manner of Debussy and Ravel, with even a daybreak and chorus of birds at the opening. The sultry central section is entitled *Après-midi sous les pins*, but includes lively folk dancing before the weather clouds over with rumbles of thunder. *Souvenirs* followed almost immediately (in 1906) and was written in memory of his late wife (represented by an *idée fixe – Bien-Aimée*), romantically recalling their happy summers together and again evoking the countryside. The rich orchestration of the music in all three works is superbly realized by the excellent **Iceland Symphony Orchestra** under **Rumon Gamba** and the superbly expansive yet vivid Chandos recording, and this a very much a key record of d'Indy's orchestral music.

Jour d'été à la montagne, Op. 61; (i) Symphonie sur un chant montagnard (cévenole), Op. 25

ⓑⓑ **(*) Warner Apex 0927 49809-2. R. France PO, Janowski; (i) with Collard

This inexpensive Apex reissue is worth having for the sake of *Jour d'été à la montagne*, one of d'Indy's most inspired pieces. This version is artistically superior to most rivals, though the late lamented **Catherine Collard's** version of the *Symphonie sur un chant montagnard français*, sometimes known as the *Symphonie cévenole*, is handicapped by some unsympathetic accompanying from **Janowski**, while the 1991 recording's synthetic balance does not allow the sound to expand. Good playing from the **Orchestre Philharmonic de Radio France** makes this disc value for money.

Karadec, Op. 34; Symphony 2; Tableaux de voyage

Ⓝ *** Chan. 10514. Iceland SO, Gamba

D'Indy's *Second Symphony* remains one of the neglected masterpieces of turn-of-the-century French music. True, at almost 45 minutes it can seem a rather sprawling proposition, but **Rumon Gamba's** fresh, bracing performance brings out all the score's rich qualities, making one relish the many incidental delights this work offers. The melancholy and rather haunting theme played at the opening of the third movement, for example, is beautifully done here, but the standard of the playing from the Icelanders is generally very high. This is the finest performance of the score to date. The *Tableaux de voyage*, orchestrations by the composer of his piano music, makes an atmospheric and rather beautiful suite, and one relishes the exotic elements of the highly entertaining *Karadec Suite*.

Symphonie sur un chant montagnard français (Symphonie cévenole)

ⓑⓑ **(*) Naxos 8.550754. Thiollier, Nat. SO of Ireland, De Almeida – FAURÉ: *Ballade*; FRANCK: *Symphonic Variations* **(*)

On Naxos the French-born but American-trained **François-Joël Thiollier** gives an intelligent performance, perfectly well accompanied and decently recorded, and with an interesting coupling. It is worth the money.

String Quartet 1

*** Hyp. CDA 67097. Chilingirian Qt – CHAUSSON: *String Quartet* (completed D'INDY)

Among the string quartets which French composers wrote in the last years of the 19th century those of Vincent d'Indy are the most unjustly neglected, as this outstanding performance of 1 demonstrates. It is a striking work which in its bold thematic material often echoes Beethoven. A powerful first movement leads to an ecstatic slow movement, an elegant interlude and an exuberant finale. The Chausson quartet makes a very apt coupling here, completed by d'Indy after the composer's tragic death in a road accident.

IPPOLITOV-IVANOV, Mikhail (1859–1935)

Armenian Rhapsody, Op. 48; Caucasian Sketches, Set II: Iveria, Op. 42; Jubilee March (Voroshilov), Op. 67; (i) Mtzyri, Op. 54; Turkish Fragments, Op.

62; Turkish March, Op. 55; (ii) Aria: Assya: I wonder if it is misfortune

*** ASV CDDCA 1102. Armenian PO, Tjeknavorian; with (i) Hatsagortsian; (ii) Khachaturian

Tjeknavorian and ASV have turned up a second set of *Caucasian Sketches*, called *Iveria*, with a jubilant closing *Georgian March* that might become popular, like the *Procession of the Sardar*, given sufficient exposure. The *Turkish Fragments* describe the progress of an Eastern caravan, opening with a processional, and including a nocturnal sequence with a sultry Rimskian oboe melody. The symphonic poem *Mtzyri* is most notable for its interpolated ballad from the nymph who finds the young hero of the story wounded by a leopard in the forest. This is touchingly sung by **Hasmit Hatsagortsian**, if with a very characteristic Russian vibrato. **Vardouhi Khachaturian's** performance of the mezzo scena from *Assya* has no lack of temperament or eloquence, and the other (*Turkish March*) is enjoyably ebullient. Very well recorded, this CD is worth exploring if you enjoy this kind of undemanding and tuneful Russian orchestral music.

Caucasian Sketches (suite), Op. 10

*** Chan. 9321. BBC PO, Glushchenko – KHACHATURIAN: *Symphony 3*, etc. ***

*** ASV CDDCA 773. Armenian PO, Tjeknavorian – KHACHATURIAN: *Gayaneh*, etc. **(*)

Once a popular repertory piece, the colourful *Caucasian Sketches* have fallen out of favour; only the final *Procession of the Sardar* is generously represented on CD. The present version by the **BBC Philharmonic** under **Fedor Glushchenko** is generally superior to the alternative on ASV.

The *Procession of the Sardar* is played by the Armenians with great brio. The other items rely mainly on picaresque oriental atmosphere for their appeal, which **Tjeknavorian** also captures evocatively in this brightly lit recording.

IRELAND, John (1879–1962)

Concertino pastorale; A Downland Suite (arr. composer and Geoffrey Bush); Orchestral Poem; 2 Symphonic Studies (arr. Bush)

🎵–♩ *** Chan. 9376. City of L. Sinfonia, Hickox

The valedictory *Threnody* of the *Concertino pastorale* and the lovely *Elegy* from the *Downland Suite* show the composer at his most lyrically inspired, and the rapt playing here does them full justice. The early *Orchestral Poem* (1904) is a surprisingly powerful work as presented here with great passion, with splendid brass writing at its climax. The two *Symphonic Studies* come from film music Ireland wrote for *The Overlanders*, not incorporated into the concert suites: the brass chromatics in the first have a familiar ring; the second has a wild momentum, recalling the cattle stampede in the film, but both stand up well as independent concert pieces.

Piano Concerto in E flat

Ⓝ ♩–Ⓜ **** Dutton CDLX 7223. Stott, RPO, Handley – BRIDGE: *Phantasm*; WALTON: *Sinfonia concertante* ****

Piano Concerto in E flat; Legend for Piano & Orchestra; Mai-Dun (symphonic rhapsody)

*** Chan. 8461. Parkin, LPO, Thomson

(i) Piano Concerto; Legend for Piano & Orchestra. Overture: Satyricon; 2 Symphonic Studies; (ii) These Things Shall Be

**(*) Lyrita (ADD) SRCD 247. LPO, Boult, with (i) Parkin; (ii) Carol Case, LPO Ch.

John Ireland's *Piano Concerto* is unaccountably neglected in the concert hall, for it has an immediate and lasting appeal, and it is one of the very few true masterpieces among piano concertos by English composers. **Kathryn Stott** gives the most sympathetic reading of this delightful work on record since the original interpreter on disc, Eileen Joyce. Spaciously expressive in the lyrical passages and crisply alert in the jazzy finale, Stott plays with a sense of spontaneity, using freely idiomatic rubato. Very well recorded and well coupled, this version makes an easy first choice for this work.

The alternative versions include **Eric Parkin's** splendidly refreshing and sparkling performance, with excellent support from **Bryden Thomson** and the **LPO**, and they include the beautiful *Legend* and *Mai-Dunn* which are equally successful. It was also Parkin who was chosen for the 1968 Lyrita version, and here there is obviously dedicated playing by the **LPO** under **Boult**. The snag is the recording acoustic, opulent enough, but the reverberation blows up the textures of the music, piano and orchestra alike. However, the other works are worth having on disc, particularly *These Things Shall Be*, a choral work with a mixture of Elgarian nobilmente and Waltonian declamation which is very effective, although the lack of bite in the sound is a drawback.

A Downland Suite; Elegiac Meditation; The Holy Boy

*** Chan. 8390. ECO, Garforth – BRIDGE: *Suite for Strings* ***

A Downland Suite was originally written for brass band. However, the present version was finished and put into shape by Geoffrey Bush, who also transcribed the *Elegiac Meditation*. **David Garforth** and the ECO play with total conviction and seem wholly attuned to Ireland's sensibility. The recording is first class, clear and naturally balanced.

A London Overture

♩–Ⓜ *** EMI (ADD) 3 79983-2. LSO, Barbirolli – BAX: *Tintagel*; DELIUS: *Collection* ***

Barbirolli's performance of the *London Overture* is a great success. The pithy main theme has character and the warm romanticism of the middle section is not allowed to overwhelm the work's conciseness. First-class recording means that this is unsurpassed.

A London Overture; Epic March; The Holy Boy; (i–ii) Greater love hath no man; These things shall be; (i; iii) Vexilla Regis

♩–Ⓜ *** Chan. 10110X. LSO, Hickox, with (i) L. Symphony Ch.; (ii) Terfel; (iii) Bott, Shaw, Oxley

Richard Hickox is a sympathetic interpreter of Ireland's music and he obtains sensitive results (and good singing) in *The Holy Boy* and *These things shall be*. The CD is of particular interest in that it brings a rarity, *Vexilla Regis*, for chorus, brass and organ, composed when Ireland was 19 and still a student of Stanford. First-class recorded sound.

MUSIC FOR BRASS

Comedy Overture; A Downland Suite (for Brass Band); The Holy Boy (arr. Cameron)

(BB) **(*) Hyp. Helios CDH 55070. L. Brass Virtuosi, Honeyball
– ELGAR: *Severn Suite*, etc.; VAUGHAN WILLIAMS: *Prelude on 3 Welsh Hymns* **(*)

John Ireland's *Downland Suite* and what was later – in its orchestral form – to become the *London Overture* were both conceived for brass band. The two central movements of the suite (*Elegy* and *Minuet*) and indeed the main 'Piccadilly' theme of the *Overture* sound especially well on brass, as does David Cameron's arrangement of *The Holy Boy*. Excellent performances and recording, but one could wish the ensemble was larger: these are first-rate players, but we need more of them.

CHAMBER MUSIC

(i) Cello Sonata; (ii) Fantasy-Sonata for Clarinet & Piano; (iii) Phantasie Trio in A min; Piano Trios 2–3; (iv) Sextet for Clarinet, Horn & String Quartet; (v) Violin Sonatas 1–2

**(*) Lyrita (ADD) SRCD 2271 (3). (i) Navarra; (ii) de Peyer; (iii; v) Neaman, (iii) Lloyd Webber; (i–iii; v) Parkin; (iv) Melos Ens. (members)

The *Cello Sonata* is both passionate and rhapsodic in feeling, and the performance here catches its romantic flair, even though Lloyd Webber's ASV version is finer. However, the performance of the *Fantasy Sonata* is marvellously persuasive, and this emerges as the most memorable of the three works recorded by the **Melos** group. The *Sextet* is an early work (1898), inspired by Brahms; its Brahmsian flavour is unmistakable, and the music has an attractive autumnal mood. The early *First Violin Sonata* is an attractive, spontaneous piece with a fine slow movement and a characteristically gay, dance-like finale. The *Second* (1917) is a splendid work, and admirers of the *Piano Concerto* are urged to discover its qualities in this very fine, dedicated performance, which catches its inspiration so well. Excellent recording throughout.

(i) Cello Sonata; (ii) Fantasy Sonata for Clarinet & Piano; (i) The Holy Boy (for cello & piano); (iii) Phantasie Trio; Piano Trios 2–3; (iv) Violin Sonatas 1–2

(N) (B) *** Chan. 241-40 (2). (i; iii) Georgian; (i; iii–iv) I. Brown; (ii) de Peyer, Pryor; (iii–iv) Mordkovitch

Few British composers have written with quite such easy lyricism as John Ireland. The first two of the *Piano Trio*s, well contrasted, are warmly appealing, but the masterpiece is the four-movement *Piano Trio 3* of 1938, passionately intense. The two *Violin Sonata*s are both superb works too, masterfully played here by **Lydia Mordkovitch** with **Ian Brown**, who also accompanies **Karine Georgian** in the *Cello Sonata*. Completing the set, the recording of the *Fantasy Sonata* of 1943 for clarinet dates from earlier, with **Gervase de Peyer** and **Gwenneth Pryor** playing with equal commitment.

(i) Cello Sonata in G min.; The Holy Boy; (ii) Violin Sonata 1 in D min.; (i; ii) Piano Trio 2 in E

☞ *** ASV Gold GLD 4009. McCabe; with (i) J. Lloyd Webber; (ii) Hope

Inspired performances, all with **John McCabe** at the piano. The *First Violin Sonata*, with **Daniel Hope** a masterly violinist, may not be as well known as the *Second*, but it is just as skilfully written, with a tenderly meditative slow movement between powerful outer movements. In a single movement, compact but well varied, the *Piano Trio 2* is one of Ireland's tautest works, inspired by the horrors of the First World War, while the *Cello Sonata* of 1923 is stylistically more adventurous in its chromatic writing, rounded off with a vigorous finale that anticipates the jazzy rhythms of the comparable movement in Ireland's popular *Piano Concerto*. That and *The Holy Boy* in its cello version were recorded well before the rest, but the sound remains consistent, and the performances with **Julian Lloyd Webber** are characteristically sensitive.

Clarinet Trio in D (reconstructed Stephen Fox); Fantasy Sonata for Clarinet & Piano; The Holy Boy for Clarinet & Piano; Sextet for Clarinet, French Horn & String Quartet

(N) (BB) **** Naxos 8.570550. Plane, Rahman, Neary, Pyatt, Maggini Qt

All these works are available elsewhere in different permutations, except the delightful *Clarinet Trio* which the composer left unfinished. As the work used material from an early piano trio Stephen Fox has been able to rewrite the missing sections. It is ingeniously done and the result is most attractive. The other works also show the composer at his best and are beautifully played, with **Robert Plane** a characterful and sensitive clarinettist, and **David Pyatt** making an impressive horn contribution to the *Sextet*, underpinned by the excellent **Maggini Quartet**. With excellent recording this is a most desirable disc.

Phantasie Trio

*** Daphne DAPHNE 1026. Trio Poseidon – BRAHMS: *Piano Trio 1*; HAYDN: *Piano Trio 32* ***

The Ireland performance here demonstrates how fluent his writing already was, as he makes the transitions from one section to another with a warmly lyrical central sequence and dazzlingly brilliant conclusion. It makes one wish that the Poseidon Trio had recorded more Ireland, but much of the attraction of this disc is the very variety of the programme.

Violin Sonatas 1 in D min.; 2 in A min.; Bagatelle; Berceuse; Cavatina; The Holy Boy

(BB) *** Hyp. Helios CDH 55164. Barritt, Edwards

Paul Barritt and **Catherine Edwards** make an effective partnership and give very persuasive accounts of both these fine sonatas. An excellent, well-balanced recording earns this a strong recommendation to those wanting just this repertoire alone on a single (budget) disc.

(i) The Holy Boy; (ii) Phantasie Trio; (iii) Violin Sonatas 1–2

(M) (***) Dutton mono CDLX 7103. (i–ii) Hooton; (i) Pratt; (ii–iii) Grinke; (ii) Taylor; (ii–iii) composer; (iii) Sammons

We have long treasured **Frederick Grinke's** 78-r.p.m. set of the *Violin Sonata 1* with the composer at the piano, and can confirm that the Dutton transfer of this 1945 recording brings its sound to life with striking effect. The *Violin Sonata 2*, on the other hand, again with **John Ireland** at the piano but with its dedicatee, the legendary **Albert Sammons**, recorded in 1930, also sounds very well for its age, as does the *Phantasie Trio*. An invaluable and self-recommending set which readers should cherish. Outstanding transfers.

String Quartets 1 in D min.; 2 in C min.; The Holy Boy

**(*) ASV CDDCA 1017. Holywell Ens.

Both quartets come from 1897, when Ireland was 18, and were published posthumously. There is little sign of individuality but each work is beautifully crafted and gives much pleasure. The idiom is close to Dvořák and the ideas are fluent and pleasing. The **Holywell Ensemble** offer decent performances and are well recorded.

PIANO MUSIC

Complete Piano Music

(N) (M) (***) Lyrita mono REAM 3112 (3). Rowlands

Alan Rowlands's survey is distinctly authoritative, as he studied with the composer at length during the 1950s and Ireland recommended him to Lyrita for the first mono recording of the complete piano music. That these are dedicated performances is indisputable, and the mono recordings are fully acceptable. But Lyrita then re-recorded the music equally successfully with Eric Parkin in stereo, so now it is difficult to recommend the earlier set except to completists.

Piano Music: Ballade; The Darkened Valley; Decorations; Equinox; Greenways (The Cherry Trees; Cypress; The Palm and May); London Pieces (Chelsea Reach; Ragamuffin; Soho Forenoons); Merry Andrew; Month's Mind; On a Birthday Morning; 2 Pieces (For Remembrance; Amberley Wild Brooks); 2 Pieces (February's Child; Aubade); 2 Pieces (April; Bergomask); 4 Preludes (The Undertone; Obsession; The Holy Boy; Fire of Spring); Prelude in E flat; Rhapsody; Sarnia – An Island Sequence; Soliloquy; Sonata; Sonatina; Summer Evening; The Towing-Path

8— (M) *** Lyrita (ADD) SRCD 2277 (3). Eric Parkin

Ireland was at his most natural writing for the piano. He seems fully to have understood the instrument and he poured into it some of his finest invention. **Eric Parkin's** sympathy with the music is in no doubt and his technique is no less impressive. The first disc is framed by the *Decorations* and the equally delightful *London Pieces*. The second includes the *Sonata*, rightly admired as one of the composer's finest works. The third recital opens with the engaging *Sonatina* and concludes with *Sarnia*. But throughout the set there are many other indelible miniatures. The *Holy Boy* (the second of the *Four Preludes*) is justly the most famous, but try also *Soliloquy*, *The Towing-Path* and *Merry Andrew*. It is difficult to imagine Parkin's performances being surpassed, for he brings a command of colour and a temperamental affinity to the music, and the piano recording is very real indeed. Parkin went on to re-record much of this repertoire digitally on three CDs for Chandos (Chan. 9056, 9140 and 9250) and he included a few pieces not offered in the earlier survey. It goes without saying that he remains completely inside the composer's idiom and he is again very well recorded. But the earlier, analogue recordings have a feeling of discovery and indeed a very special magic.

Piano Music, Volume 1: Piano Sonata; Ballade; Decorations; London Pieces; Sonatina

(N) (B) *** Somm SOMMCD 074. Bebbington

Mark Bebbington has now begun a new survey of this repertoire to offer the collector an embarrassment of riches. Sufficient to say that his performance of the *Sonata* is most convincing and the *Decorations* and *London Pieces* as admirably evocative and beautifully played and recorded.

Aubade; February's Child; The Darkened Valley; Decorations; April; Leaves from a Child's Sketchbook; Merry Andrew; 3 Pastels; Rhapsody; Sonatina; Summer Evening; The Towing-Path

(BB) *** Naxos 8.553889. Lenehan

Ballade; Columbine; In Those Days; London Pieces; Prelude in E flat; Sarnia

(BB) *** Naxos 8.553700. Lenehan

Piano Sonata 1; The Almond Tree; Ballad of London Nights; Equinox; Green Ways (The Cherry Tree; Cypress; The Palm and May); On a Birthday Morning; 2 Pieces (Amberley Wild Brooks; For Remembrace); Preludes (The Undertone; Obsession; The Holy Boy; Fire of Spring); Soliloquy; Spring will not wait

(N) (BB) *** Naxos 8.570461. Lenehan

John Lenehan is making a complete survey for Naxos and he too proves the most persuasive advocate, warmly expressive, using rubato in a totally idiomatic way. The most ambitious work is the three-movement suite, inspired by Guernsey, *Sarnia*, far more than a set of atmospheric colour pieces and its last movement has echoes of the *Piano Concerto in E flat*.

The second programme offers a score of miniatures, including two of Ireland's most hauntingly atmospheric pieces, *The Towing-Path* and *The Darkened Valley*, a Blake inspiration. The longest work here is the *Sonatina* in three short movements, with the opening *Moderato* bringing echoes of Ireland's colourful *Piano Concerto*, the second a dark meditation leading to a galloping finale. Impeccable performances, vividly recorded.

The third programme includes the *Piano Sonata* and the *Four Preludes*, the third of which, *The Holy Boy*, is justly one of the composer's most famous and touching miniatures.

VOCAL MUSIC

(i) Baritone Songs, including: *I have twelve oxen; Marigold; 5 Poems by Thomas Hardy; 6 Sacred and Profane Songs; Sea Fever; Spring Sorrow; 5 16th-Century Songs; Santa Chiara; Songs of a Wayfarer; We'll to the woods no more.* **(ii) Contralto Songs, including:** *Earth's Call; The 3 Ravens; 3 Arthur Symons Songs; Mother and Child; 3 Thomas Hardy Songs;* **(iii) Tenor Songs, including:** *The East Riding; Heart's desire; Love is a sickness; The Land of Lost Content; My true love hath my heart*

Ⓜ *** Lyrita (ADD) SRCD 2261 (3). (i) Luxon; (ii) Hodgson; (iii) Mitchinson; (i–iii) Alan Rowlands

Benjamin Luxon's understanding performances of these baritone songs, splendidly accompanied, form the main part of the collection and, though the ever-popular *Sea Fever* and *I have twelve oxen* may still strike most indelibly, many of the others also have vigorous memorability. *Earth's Call* is the most ambitious of the contralto songs – almost a dramatic scena – but most of both these and the tenor songs reflect the tinge of melancholy that was an essential part of Ireland's temperament, subtle miniatures which sensitively follow the cadences of English lyric poetry. **Alfreda Hodgson's** and **John Mitchinson's** performances (with the piano balanced rather backwardly) are admirably responsive.

Songs: *5 Poems by Thomas Hardy; 3 Songs to Poems by Hardy; The Bells of St Marie; The cost; During Music; If there were dreams to sell; I have twelve oxen; Marigold – Youth's spring; Palm Sunday, Naples; Penumbra; Salley Gardens; Santa Chiara; Sea Fever; Spleen; Tryst in a Fountain Court; The Vagabond; We'll to the woods no more; When I am dead my dearest; Tutto è scolto; Great things*

Ⓝ ⒷⒷ *** Naxos 8.570467. Williams, Burnside

John Ireland's settings of English poems are among the most sensitive of the early 20th century, as this fine collection makes plain. They include one of the best known of all songs of the period, his setting of John Masefield's *Sea Fever*, a haunting tune that completely transcends the genre of the drawing-room ballad. But there is much else to treasure here, notably Masefield's *The Vagabond*, the Thomas Hardy settings and, of course, *I have twelve oxen*, and *If there were dreams to sell*. **Roderick Williams's** voice seems ideally focused for this repertoire and in this respect is preferable to

a more extended collection with Christopher Maltman (together with John Mark Ainsley and Lisa Milne) on Chandos CDA 67261/2.

IVES, Charles (1874–1954)

'An American Journey': *From the Steeples and the Mountains; Symphony 4: 3rd Movement: Fugue; Three Places in New England; The Unanswered Question.* **Choral: (i)** *The Circus Band;* **(i; ii)** *General William Booth Enters into Heaven;* **(i)** *The Pond (Remembrance); Psalm 100; They are There!* **Songs: (ii)** *Charlie Rutlage; In Flanders Field* (orch. David Tredici); *Memories; Serenity* (orch. John Adams); *The Things our Fathers Loved; Tom Sails Away*

🔑 🏵 **** RCA 09026 63703-2. (i) San Francisco Girls' Ch.; (ii) Hampson; San Francisco Symphony, Tilson Thomas

Michael Tilson Thomas's programme opens with one of Ives's most succinct and evocative orchestral explosions of dissonant polyphony, *From the Steeples and the Mountains*, and ends with his most beautiful, enigmatic and visionary work, *The Unanswered Question*.

Tilson Thomas places Ives's other out-and-out masterpiece, *Three Places in New England*, at the centre of a collection of vocal music. The choral items range from the mystically brief evocation of *The Pond* (subtitled *Remembrance*) for female voices, and a heartfelt setting of *Psalm 100*, to the rumbustiously syncopated *Circus Band* and the enthusiastically patriotic but characteristically zany *They are There!*

Thomas Hampson is obviously in his element in this repertoire. But the vocal highlight is *General William Booth Enters into Heaven*, where soloist and the excellent choruses exultantly combine in Ives's glorious portrayal of Booth and his Salvation Army leading his assembly of converted drunks and floozies into heaven, to the discomfiture of the angels. Not to be missed.

Instrumental Pieces for Small Orchestra: (i; ii) *Aeschylus and Sophocles.* **(i)** *All the Way Round and Back.* **(i; ii)** *The Bells of Yale or Chapel Chimes.* **(i)** *From the Steeples and the Mountains; The Gong on the Hook and Ladder; Mists;* **(i; ii)** *On the Antipodes.* **(i)** *Over the Pavements; The Pond; The Rainbow; Sets 1–3; Tone Roads 1 & 3.* **Songs: (iii)** *Ann Street; At the River; The Cage; Charlie Rutlage; A Christmas Carol; Evening; Farewell to Land; from 'The Swimmers'; General William Booth enters into Heaven; The Greatest Man; Side Show; Soliloquy; West London*

Ⓝ Ⓜ *** EMI 2 06631-2. (i) Ens. Modern, Metzmacher ; (ii) with Herford; (iii) Nixon, McCabe

The Ives discography which has deluged on us over the last few years has tended to show a brilliant imagination, plus a remarkably original mind and a daunting exploration of discord. But then Ives himself could afford to be daring, for he was also a very successful businessman, and although he was disappointed by his musical neglect he said 'If a composer has a nice wife and some nice children, how can he let the children starve on his dissonance.' Yet the *Tone Roads* are atonal and way ahead of their time in their rhythmic unpredictability, and all these instrumental pieces, which are daringly full of both vitality and originality, are not designed for musical fainthearts. Many of them are pictorially evocative; many of them are also essentially vocal in conception, and the texts which inspired them are given here in the accompanying booklet. They are played and presented with great élan. As for the group of songs, they lay claim to Ives being considered one of the greatest twentieth-century song writers; many of them are worthy of Schubert in their marriage of vocal line and pianistic partnership. **Marni Nixon** sings them superbly and with the right simplicity of approach and a voice of consistent tonal beauty. **John McCabe** accompanies splendidly and the spacious stereo is suitably atmospheric.

(i) *Central Park in the Dark*; (ii) *Holidays Symphony*; *Symphonies 2 & 3* (*The Unanswered Question*) (original version for Trumpet, Flute Quartet & Strings)

🎵 (M) *** Sony (ADD) 516023-2 (2). NYPO, Bernstein; with (i) Ozawa & Peress (assistant conductors); (ii) Camerata Singers, Kaplan (with talk: 'Leonard Bernstein discusses Charles Ives')

Central Park in the Dark, as the title implies, provides a brilliant collection of evening sounds, evocative yet bewildering. The first three sections of the so-called *Holidays Symphony*, with their still-startling clashes of impressionistic imagery, are well enough known. The fourth – full title: *Thanksgiving and/or Forefathers' Day* – is more of a rarity, bringing in a full chorus to sing a single verse of a hymn at the close. The performance is red-bloodedly convincing yet has remarkably clear detail. *The Unanswered Question* is probably the most purely beautiful music Ives ever wrote, with muted strings (curiously representing silence) set against a trumpet representing the problem of existence. Superb playing (the trumpeter is **William Vacchiano**) and vivid recording, but the forward balance means the lack of a true *pianissimo*, especially noticeable in *The Unanswered Question*.

Bernstein's earlier, CBS/Sony recordings of the *Symphonies* have characteristic conviction and freshness. The remastered sound is amazingly improved over the old LPs, full and atmospheric. The balance is too close, but the dynamics of the playing convey the fullest range of emotion. This reissue includes Bernstein's illustrated lecture on Ives (recorded in 1966).

Three Orchestral Sets: 1 (3 *Places in New England*: original version, ed. Sinclair); (i) 2 (complete). 3 (includes *During Camp Meetin' Week – One Secular Afternoon in Bethel* (ed. Porter); *Andante* (realized Josephson))

(N) 🎵 ✿ (BB) **** Naxos 8.559353. Malmö SO, Sinclair; (i) with Chamber Ch.

Ives created his *Sets* by assembling a trio of independent short pieces to make a composite work. The *Three Places in*

New England (of 1913–14) is a prime example, and many consider it among his very greatest music, with its extraordinary pictorialism enhanced by popular musical quotations, followed by an ecstatic climax in the finale. Here we are offered the work's first draft, less complex than the finished *Set*, but introducing the hauntingly weird and beautiful string writing which is common to all three *Sets*. It opens the *Second* with its *Elegy to our Forefathers*, which again has an exuberant closing movement. Ives didn't finish his *Third Set* (1927). He had gathered the material together in sketches, but, sapped by a heart attack and diabetes, he had lost the concentration to pull the disparate material into a single work. Thus, the first two movements have been put together by David Gray Porter, climaxed with a cacophonous mêlée of popular tunes, while the utterly haunting closing section has been ethereally realized by Nors Josephson. The result, played with marvellous intensity and dedication by the **Malmö Symphony Orchestra** under **James Sinclair** (and superbly engineered by Mike Hatch), is unforgettable. As Jan Swafford says in his excellent note, 'it is like one of Michelangelo's unfinished sculptures'.

Symphonies 1–4; *Central Park in the Dark*; (i) *General William Booth enters into Heaven*

🎵 **** Hyp. **SACDA** or CDA 67540 (*Symphonies 1, 4 & Central Park*); **SACDA** or CDA 67525 (*Symphonies 2 & 3 & General Booth*). Dallas SO, Litton; (i) with Albert

Recorded live in Dallas in January 2006, **Andrew Litton's** two discs cover the symphonies of Ives in the most logical way, with the four main works supplemented by two of his most striking shorter pieces, a coupling offering an advantage over rival versions. Litton is totally in sympathy with Ives's distinctive use of hymns and marches. The *First Symphony*, with its echoes of Dvořák's *New World*, already points forward to the composer's later radical development. The *Fourth Symphony* emerges as a masterpiece, amazing music to have been conceived as early as it was, with the contrapuntal element so important in Ives's writing clarified, and the hilarious introduction of 'Yankee Doodle' in the fourth movement given delightful point. The *Second Symphony* is distinctively Ivesian in many of its procedures, with hymns and marches superimposed on more conventional passages, often celebrating the American brass band. The finale is a quodlibet with one theme piled on another, erupting finally in a shattering *fortissimo* account of *Columbia Queen of the Ocean*. The *Third Symphony*, on the face of it less radical than the others, is entitled *The Camp Meeting*, with the three movements based on organ pieces Ives wrote early in his career. *General William Booth Enters Heaven* develops to a massive climax, vividly caught in Litton's performance with **Donnie Ray Albert** as soloist. The sound, though not the most immediate, is vivid too, and is particularly spacious on SACD, with textures commendably clear, as in Ives's use of the piano as part of the orchestra in 4.

Symphony 1 in D min.

*** Chan. 9053. Detroit SO, Järvi – BARBER: *Essays 1–3* ***

Neeme Järvi gives a very persuasive account of the *First*

Symphony, and there is a fresh and unforced virtuosity from the Detroit orchestra. Excellent, very natural recorded sound, excellently balanced.

Symphonies (i) 1 in D min.; 2; (ii) 3; (iii; iv) 4; (iii) Orchestral Set 1; (iii; iv) Orchestral Set 2; (iii) Three Places in New England

Ⓑ **(*) Double Decca (ADD) 466 745-2 (2). (i) LAPO, Mehta; (ii) ASMF, Marriner; (iii) Cleveland O, Dohnányi; (iv) Cleveland Ch.

Mehta's Los Angeles recordings of the first two symphonies are very well recorded indeed. The *First* is superbly played, but the drawback here is a substantial cut in the last movement. **Marriner's** account of the *Third Symphony* is first rate in every way, just as successful as Bernstein's account, and much better recorded. For the *Fourth Symphony*, *Orchestral Sets 1 & 2* and the masterly *Three Places in New England* we move into the digital era with **Dohnányi's** Cleveland forces: these performances are very fine, and the sound is superb. In short, if you don't mind about the cut mentioned above, this is an inexpensive way of making a representative collection of Ives's major works at a modest outlay.

Symphony 2

*** Chan. 9390-2. Detroit SO, Järvi – CRESTON: *Symphony 2* ***

Symphony 2; Central Park in the Dark; The Gong on the Hook and Ladder; Hallowe'en; Hymn for Strings; Tone Roads 1; The Unanswered Question

🎧 **** DG 429 220-2. NYPO, Bernstein

Bernstein's DG disc brings one of the richest offerings of Ives yet put on record, offering *Symphony 2* plus six shorter orchestral pieces. They include two of his very finest, *Central Park in the Dark* and *The Unanswered Question*, both characteristically quirky but deeply poetic too. The extra tensions and expressiveness of live performance here heighten the impact of each of the works. The difficult acoustic of Avery Fisher Hall in New York has rarely sounded more sympathetic on record.

The Chandos CD offers a very good performance, and has the great advantage of also offering **Neeme Järvi's** account of Paul Creston's vital and invigorating *Second Symphony*.

(i) Symphony 2; (ii) The Unanswered Question

Ⓝ 🎧 ✦ ****DVD DG 073 4513. (i) Bav. RSO; (ii) NYPO; Bernstein (with GERSHWIN: *An American in Paris*; *Rhapsody in Blue*; Bernstein, piano & NYPO ****✦)

An indispensable DVD. To watch **Bernstein** conduct these supreme masterpieces of American music is a joy and a privilege in itself, his face expressing almost every emotion and his communication with the orchestral players absolute. The richly resonant acoustic of the Royal Albert Hall casts a glow on the glittering rhythmic detail of *An American in Paris* from every member of the **NYPO** (especially the solo brass), which is as unforgettable as the arrival of the great blues centrepiece. Taking the solo role in the *Rhapsody*, Bernstein dom-

inates completely, playing with unfettered freedom of tempo and nuance (his virtuosity is tangible), while in the Ives *Symphony* he produces radiantly expressive string textures from the **Bavarian** strings and captivates the ear with the composer's kaleidoscopic quotations of popular tunes. The symphony's close is all but overwhelming, to be followed by the epilogue of the *Unanswered Question* with its insistent, haunting trumpet solo. At a Harvard University lecture Bernstein said 'I'm no longer sure what the question is, but I do know the answer is Yes.' After the music drifts into silence he leaves the podium to delay any applause. (The DVD includes a talk about the symphony by Bernstein himself.)

Symphony 3

🎧 Ⓜ **** Decca 475 8237. ASMF, Marriner – BARBER: *Adagio*; COPLAND: *Quiet City*; COWELL: *Hymn & Fuguing Tune*; CRESTON: *A Rumor* ****

Marriner's vintage account still stands up against all the competition and it sounds excellent in the current transfer for Decca's 'Originals'. The couplings are all highly recommendable.

Variations on America (orch. Schuman)

Ⓑ🅱 *** Naxos 8.559083. Bournemouth SO, Serebrier – SCHUMAN: *Violin Concerto*, etc. ***

Ives's *Variations on America* is an apt coupling for two outstanding works of William Schuman, who proves an infinitely imaginative colourist in orchestrating the former's brilliant and sometimes whimsical variations on the national melody, which has quite different words and implications in the USA and Britain. **Serebrier's** performance with the excellent **Bournemouth Orchestra** has subtlety of detail as well as gusto, and the recording is first class.

Instrumental Pieces: The Gong on the Hook and Ladder (Original version); Hallowe'en; In Re Con Moto; (Piano) 5 Take-offs: The Seen and Unseen? (Sweet and Tough); Rough and Ready et al. and/or The jumping Frog; Song without (Good) Words; Scene Episode; Bad Resolutions and Good WAN! (Jan 1, 1907); 3 Quarter-Tone Pieces; Songs: Aeschylus and Sophocles; The Housatonic at Stockbridge; On the Antipodes; The Pond; Remembrance; Soliloquy or A Study in Sevenths and Other Things; Sunrise

🎧 Ⓑ🅱 **** Naxos 8.559194. Continuum (members), Seltzer & Sachs (directors & pianists)

The opening song-group, very well sung, begins lyrically with *The Housatonic at Stockbridge*, but at its climax the piano accompaniment goes wild; the following *Soliloquy* explodes similarly, and the dissonant, untamed accompaniment continues its conflict to underline *On the Antipodes*. *Sunrise* (Ives's final song) initially brings relative peace and an Elysian violin solo but still has an agitated climax.

The first of the instrumental pieces, *The Gong on the Hook and Ladder*, pictures the annual parade of the neighbourhood Fire Company, for the appliance was heavy and had to be held in check manually down the hill, while the violent clanging gong on the hand wheel 'must ring steady'. *Hallowe'en* is a busy, dissonant Scherzo (the strings playing in different keys), suggesting the growing flames of the bonfire, with children running round it. *In Re Con Moto et al.* brings the most ferocious dissonance of all 'to stretch ear muscles', as Ives suggested. The piano pieces, *Five Take-offs* (implying improvisatory freedom, but in fact highly organized), were published as recently as 1991, and would make a stimulating centrepiece for any modern piano recital. The untamed, feral *Jumping Frog* has an underlying boldly controlled cantus firmus. Then, astonishingly, *Song without (Good) Words* is quite beautiful – very romantic, but with wrong notes – and *Scene Episode* begins in much the same mood of emotional serenity, which is not quite sustained.

The *Three Quarter-Tone Pieces* are aurally the most fascinating of all, more remarkably so as they are very listenable. They really do 'tweak the ear muscles'. All in all, this makes a fine, characteristic anthology, splendidly realized by artists not named individually, except for the pair of director/pianists. The *Take-offs* (an expression Ives used as meaning improvisation) are simpler but just as original, the two excellent pianists are **Joel Sachs** and **Cheryl Seltzer**, and the sopranos, both projecting well, are **Victoria Villamil** and **Sheila Schonbrun**. This collection shows the composer as slightly off the beam at times, but endearingly so. The recording is excellent and the (essential) documentation praiseworthy, including the words of the songs.

(i) *Piano Trio;* (ii) *Violin Sonatas 2 & 4 (Children's Day at the Camp Meeting);* (iii) *Largo for Violin, Clarinet & Piano;* (iv) *7 Songs*

(N) (M) *** EMI 2 34450-2. (i–iii) Dicterow; (i) Stepansky (i–iii) Margalit; (iii) Drucker; (iv) Voigt, Zeger

This is all vintage Ives material, very well played, especially the *Piano Trio*, although the *Violin Sonatas* bring a fine partnership between **Glenn Dicterow** and **Israela Margalit**. **Deborah Voigt** also has the measure of the songs now added to the reissue as a bonus.

String Quartets 1–2

(BB) *** Naxos 8.559178. Blair Qt

The *Second Quartet* (written between 1911 and 1913) still draws on popular material, but used in densely polyphonic bursts so that the themes are fragmented and difficult to recognize, while the weird harmonies and moments of fierce dissonance in the argument become all but atonal in the finale. The Scherzo – not quite two minutes long – treats its popular material more recognizably but with intense unpredictabilty. Superb performances here and fine recording: the disc is worth having for the student quartet; but only the aurally brave will venture to return to the later work very frequently.

Violin Sonatas 1–4

🎧— (BB) *** Naxos 8.559119. Thompson, Waters

Ives's four extraordinary *Violin Sonatas* were written between 1902 and 1906, and are quite a find. Their erratically stimulating originality is in no doubt, but they are also among his most immediately appealing works, with the usual tan-talizing snatches of hymns and popular tunes to spice the melodic flow.

There is no doubt that the full-timbred **Curt Thompson** and **Rodney Waters** are excellent artists. It is difficult to imagine this music being played better or more idiomatically, and the daunting bravura is readily forthcoming. The recording too is most realistic.

PIANO MUSIC

Piano Sonata 1

*** Mode 93. Laimon – COPLAND: *Piano Fantasy* ***

Ives's five-movement *First Piano Sonata* was composed over a long period and finally put together in 1919. The result is a series of events, the piano writing is alternately lyrically expressive or hard-hitting, and often chromatically dense. The boldly discursive finale, the longest movement, recaptures some of the evocative mood of the opening, and the work ends enigmatically, as it began. **Sara Laimon** obviously has the full measure of the piece and certainly demonstrates its intractable nature and its compulsive originality.

Piano Sonata 2 (Concord, Mass., 1840–1860)

🎧— *** Hyp. CDA 67469. Hamelin – BARBER: *Piano Sonata* ***

(i) *Piano Sonata 2 (Concord, Mass.);* (ii) *Three Quarter-tone Pieces*

(BB) *** Warner Apex 0927 49515-2. Lubimov; with (i) Verney, Cherrier; (ii) Aimard

Piano Sonata 2 (Concord, Mass.); Celestial Railroad; Emerson Transcriptions 1; Varied Air & Variations

(BB) *** Naxos 8.559127. Mayer

As with the Barber coupling, **Marc-André Hamelin** is completely at home in Ives's eccentric, discursive *Sonata* whose four movements are each inspired by key 19th-century literary figures in Concord, from Emerson to Thoreau. The second movement (Hawthorne), which brings oscillation between thunderous complexity and tender lyricism, is superbly played, so that the touching and boldly romantic picture of the Alcotts that emerges in the third movement leads easily into the finale, with its flute solo stealing in beguilingly. (When asked why he put in this interlude, Ives suggested that as no one was likely to play his sonata he saw no reason not to include a flute when required.) Well, he was wrong about the performances, and Hamelin's account of this fascinatingly eccentric and rewarding work shows why. The recording is first class.

Alexei Lubimov and Pierre-Laurent Aimard (see below), both also include Ives's brief (and optional) obbligatos for viola and flute in the first and fourth movements respectively. **Steven Mayer**, who omits them, is also remarkably lucid and sympathetic, and he ends the finale most movingly and memorably. As couplings he offers also the tough, though briefly soft-centred, *Varied Air and Variations* and *The Celestial Railroad*, a nightmarish, noisy train journey, a trip to a promised land which never materializes. The *Emerson*

Transcription is essentially a reworking of the opening material of the *Sonata*, and of less general interest.

Lubimov on Apex offers as his bonus the remarkable *Quarter-tone Pieces*, in which he is joined by **Aimard** at the second piano. Whether or not they achieve identical tuning with Seltzer and Sachs on the Naxos/Continuum anthology (above), they produce a more lyrically romantic effect in the opening *Largo* and are less dauntless in the fantasia on *America/God save the King*.

(i) Piano Sonata 2; (ii) Songs: Ann Street; The Cage; The Circus Band; A Farewell to Land; From The Swimmers; The Housatonic at Stockbridge; The Indians; Like a sick eagle; Memories: Very pleasant; Rather sad; 1, 2, 3; September; Serenity; Soliloquy (or A Study in 7ths and other things); Songs my mother taught me; The sound of a distant horn; The Things our Fathers Loved; Thoreau

⊕–*** Warner 2564 60297-2. Aimard, with (i) Zimmerman, Pahud; (ii) Graham

Pierre-Laurent Aimard's reading of the *Sonata* ranks with the best in all respects and it is beautifully recorded. Aimard also provides outstanding accompaniments for the equally recommendable song selection. **Susan Graham's** voice is not quite as richly alluring as Roberta Alexander's, but her singing is truly idiomatic and has moments of real beauty; moreover, her selection is balanced to include more of the rugged numbers like the hair-raising *Soliloquy*, while she is at her best in the contrasts of *Memories, Very pleasant* and *Rather sad*.

Songs (complete recording; recorded and listed in alphabetical order)

Vol. 1: 1, 2, 3; Abide with me – Cradle Song (8.559269)

Vol. 2: December – Gruss (8.559270)

Vol. 3: Harpalus – Luck and Work (8.559 271)

Vol. 4: Majority – Over all the Treetops (8.559272)

Vol. 5: Paracelsus – Swimmers (8.559273)

Vol. 6: Tarrant Moss – Yellow Leaves (8.559274)

Ⓝ ⒝⒝ *** Naxos 8.559269/74. Various Singers, Instrumental Ens.; Dickson, Garrison, Pennna, Trudel (piano), Kabaoka (glockenspiel), Teardo (organ)

What can we say about such an enterprise as this – a recording of *all* of Ives's songs, listed in alphabetical order on each disc so that one can easily retrieve any single item? The cast of singers includes some stalwarts, such as **Lielle Berman**, **Jennifer Casey Cabot**, **Patrick Carfizzi**, **Michael Cavalieri**, **Robert Gardner**, and **Tamara Mumford**; others come to the fore as necessary. As one progresses through the series one is amazed, not only by the quality of the songs (and their remarkable variety) but the skill of the casting of both singers and accompanists. Altogether a fascinating survey, well worthy of its modest cost. The documentation is excellent, although no texts are given.

Allegro; At the River; The Children's Hour; The Circus Band; A Christmas Carol; Down East; Evening; Evidence; Ilmenau; In Flanders Fields; In the Alley; The Last Reader; The Light that is Felt; Mists; My Native Land; Night Song; Omens and Oracles; On the Counter; Premonitions; Romanzo (di Central Park); The See'r; Slow March; Songs my mother taught me; The South Wind; They are There!; Those Evening Bells; To Edith; Two Little Flowers (and dedicated to them); Watchman!; The World's Wanderers

⊕– ✿ *** Hyp. CDA 67644. Finley, Drake

The very opening song here, *On the Counter*, is totally nostalgic, and this is immediately followed by his vociferous reaction to *The Circus Band*. Then comes *Two little flowers*, which he wrote with his wife as a sentimental tribute to his adopted daughter and her playmate, while *Mists*, also written jointly, is an elegy after her mother's sudden death. Both are touchingly beautiful. The closing song here *Romanzo (di Central Park)* sets Leigh Hunt's succinct *Love Song* with its dozen words, written vertically and rhyming in pairs, yet telling their story of a lover's tryst, the last four being 'Kiss, Bliss, Blest, Rest.' The performances here from **Gerald Finley** and **Julius Drake** are wonderfully characterful and warmly sympathetic. This is a disc one can enjoy right through without stopping, and if you respond to it as we have, there is a companion, by the same artists (CDA 67516).

JACOB, Gordon (1895–1984)

Mini-Concerto for Clarinet & String Orchestra

⊕– ⒝⒝ *** Hyp. Helios CDH 55069. King, Northwest CO of Seattle, Francis – COOKE: *Concerto*; RAWSTHORNE: *Concerto* ***

Gordon Jacob in his eighties wrote this miniature concerto for **Thea King**, totally charming in its compactness. She proves the most persuasive of dedicatees, splendidly accompanied by the orchestra from Seattle and treated to first-rate (1982) analogue sound, splendidly transferred. An enticing bargain reissue.

Horn Concerto

⊕–*** Lyrita SRCD 316. Pyatt, LPO, Braithwaite – ARNOLD; BOWEN; GIPPS: *Horn Concertos*; VINTER: *Hunter's Moon* ***

This is one of Gordon Jacob's best concertos, a highlight of this collection of works by British composers and, like several of its companions, first performed by Dennis Brain. Opening with a hint of neoclassicism, the work's ripe romanticism soon emerges with a particularly successful interplay between bravura passagework and lyrical melody. A daunting cadenza acts as an intermezzo, before the haunting nocturnal slow movement contrasts with a brilliant finale demanding (and receiving here) crisply pointed virtuosity from the soloist; yet again there is a contrasting evocative lyrical element. **David Pyatt's** performance is superbly confident and assured and, with **Braithwaite** in partnership, the work's touches of gentler nostalgia are well realized. Demonstration sound.

Symphonies 1; 2 in C

**** Lyrita SRCD 315. LPO, Wordsworth

The two symphonies recorded here were separated by fifteen years. The opening movement of the *First* (1929) is full of great energy and drive, with contrasting themes strongly and convincingly developed. The composer wrote of the second movement, '[it is] elegiac in character and is somewhat in the style of a funeral march'. The finale, with its striking opening four downward leaps of a fifth, is also full of energy and drive, and is generally optimistic in spirit. The *Second Symphony* (1944–5) is spirited and outgoing. The first movement is followed by an intense, searching *Adagio* which opens plangently on high strings, but later assumes the character of a threnody, and was written in memory of the composer's brother, who was killed on the Somme. The composer called it 'a meditation on war, suffering and victory'. Recording of great clarity and richness of sonority.

Clarinet Quintet in G min.

⊕— (BB) *** Hyp. Helios (ADD) CDH 55110. King, Aeolian Qt – SOMERVELL: *Clarinet Quintet ***

Gordon Jacob wrote his fine *Clarinet Quintet* for Frederick Thurston. It is essentially pastoral, even autumnal, in feeling but has an engaging second movement Scherzo, a *Rhapsody* for slow movement and a chirpy *Theme and Variations* for finale. **Thea King** plays with deep understanding and much character, and she is strongly matched by the **Aeolian Quartet**, led by Emmanuel Hurwitz. The fine 1979 analogue recording is impeccably transferred to CD, and this reissue is a worthwhile bargain

Divertimento for Harmonica & String Quartet

*** Chan. 8802. Reilly, Hindar Qt – MOODY: *Quintet; Suite ***

Gordon Jacob's set of eight sharply characterized miniatures shows the composer at his most engagingly imaginative and the performances are deliciously piquant in colour and feeling. The recording could hardly be more successful.

Oboe Quartet

*** Chan. 8392. Francis, English Qt – BAX: *Quintet*; HOLST: *Air & Variations*, etc.; MOERAN: *Fantasy Quartet ***

Gordon Jacob's *Oboe Quartet* is well crafted and entertaining, particularly the vivacious final Rondo. The performance could hardly be bettered, and the recording is excellent too.

(i; ii) Oboe Quartet; (i; iii) Oboe Sonata; (ii) 6 Shakespearian Sketches; (i; iv; v) Trio for Flute, Oboe & Harpsichord; (i) Sonatina for Solo Violin

(M) *** Dutton CDLX 7177. (i) Francis; (ii) Tagore String Trio; (iii) Dussek; (iv) Fitton; (v) Beach; (vi) Mason

The *Oboe Quartet* is most appealing in its essentially pastoral nature, with some gorgeously lyrical passages, often very

haunting, or in the bubbling vitality of the Scherzo and the catchy *Rondo* finale. The *Oboe Sonata* establishes a rather more serious mood from the word go, but a mood which is curiously hypnotizing. The *Sonatina for Violin Solo* (1954) is a tour de force for the soloist and highlights the composer's skill at providing enormous variety with a single instrument. The *Six Shakespearian Sketches* (1946) opens with an exquisite atmosphere which pervades much of this work's six movements, though it ends with rumbustious humour. The *Trio for Flute, Oboe and Harpsichord* dates from 1958, and there is much wit and delight – and certainly quirky humour – in this offbeat score, not least in the finale, where the flautist changes to a piccolo. Superb performances and recording.

Piano & Wind Sextet, Op. 3

(M) (**) BBC mono BBCL 4164-2. Malcolm, Dennis Brain Wind Quintet – BEETHOVEN: *Quintet* (**) ; HINDEMITH: *Horn Sonata*; VINTER: *Hunter's Moon* (***)

Gordon Jacob's *Piano and Wind Sextet* is most delightfully scored and full of attractive invention. The opening and closing of the work are elegiac, and there is a sparkling Scherzo for which the forward recording is very close indeed! The slow movement, a B flat minor *Cortège*, is imbued with a gentle melancholy; the Minuet is an engaging highlight, and the buoyant, syncopated finale is joyously zestful, but with a recurring lyrical horn theme, of which Dennis makes the very most.

JADASSOHN, Salomon
(1831–1902)

Piano Concertos 1 in C min., Op. 89; 2 in F min., Op. 90

(N) *** Hyp. CDA 67636. Becker, Berlin RSO, Michael Sanderling – DRAESEKE: *Piano Concerto in E flat ***

Jadassohn was known in his day mainly as a composition teacher in Leipzig, and he counted many famous names among his pupils, including Grieg, Delius and Busoni. Unlike his more famous pupils, however, Jadassohn was unable to provide truly memorable themes. That is not to say that his music is unenjoyable – it is far from that. Liszt is an obvious role-model for him in both form and temperament; and with first-rate performances and recordings it is good, for those curious about musical byways, to be able to assess this music again for themselves.

JANÁČEK, Leoš (1854–1928)

(i) Capriccio for Piano (left hand) & 7 Wind Instruments; Concertino for Piano & Chamber Orchestra; (ii) Sinfonietta; (iii) Violin Sonata; (iv) 7 Piano Pieces; (iv; v) The Diary of One who Disappeared; (vi) Glagolitic Mass

(N) (B) *** EMI 2-CD 2 37606-2 (2). (i) Rudy, Paris Op. Nat. (members), Mackerras; (ii) Philh. O, Rattle; (iii) Amoyal, Rudy; (iv) Adès; (v) Bostridge, Philogene, Diane Atherton,

Flannery, Edwards; (vi) Palmer, Gunson, Mitchinson, King, CBSO Ch. & O, Rattle

An outstanding two-CD anthology, with **Rattle's** memorable coupling of the *Sinfonietta* and *Glagolitic Mass* as its centre-piece. **Mikhail Rudy** is completely inside the quirky left-hand *Capriccio* and also gives a totally idiomatic account of the *Concertino*. The uniquely involving song-cycle, *The Diary of One who Disappeared*, was prompted by the composer's passionate unrequited love for a young married woman, Kamila Stosslova, and the wildness of the writing – spontaneous, electric, for both voice and piano – reflects the urgency of his inspiration, with **Ian Bostridge** taking the central role. This is a performance which fully exploit's Bostridge's great gift for conveying nervily intense emotion, with nervous tension giving way to moments of ecstasy. The mezzo, **Ruby Philogene**, is also ideally cast, sensuously rich-toned, and the offstage trio is atmospherically caught. **Thomas Adès** accompanies with comparable inspiration and completes the anthology with seven of the composer's piano miniatures. The volatile *Violin Sonata* is hardly less successful.

(i) *Capriccio for Piano & Wind; Concertino for Piano & Chamber Ensemble;* (ii) *Lachian Dances;* (iii) *Sinfonietta;* (iv) *Suite for String Orchestra;* (iii) *Taras Bulba;* (v) *Mládí* (suite for wind)

(B) *** Double Decca (ADD) 448 255-2 (2). (i) Crossley, L. Sinf., Atherton; (ii) LPO, Huybrechts; (iii) VPO, Mackerras; (iv) LACO, Marriner; (v) Bell, Craxton, Pay, Harris, Gatt, Eastop

On this Double Decca, **Paul Crossley** is the impressive soloist in the *Capriccio* and the *Concertino*, performances that can be put alongside those of Firkušný – and no praise can be higher. This account of *Mládí* is among the finest available; the work's youthful sparkle comes across to excellent effect here. In **Mackerras's VPO** coupling of the *Sinfonietta* and *Taras Bulba* the massed brass of the *Sinfonietta* has tremendous bite and brilliance as well as characteristic Viennese ripeness. *Taras Bulba* is also given more weight and body than usual, the often savage dance-rhythms presented with great energy. The performance of the *Lachian Dances* under the Belgian conductor, **François Huybrechts**, is highly idiomatic and effective, and he is helped by fine playing from the **LPO**. The *Suite for String Orchestra* was **Marriner's** first recording with the **Los Angeles Chamber Orchestra**, and the sound is characteristically ripe. The *Suite* is an early and not entirely mature piece but, when played as committedly as it is here, its attractions are readily perceived, and it certainly does not want character. Excellent sound throughout.

(i; ii) *Capriccio; Concertino;* (iii) *Lachian Dances;* (iv) *Sinfonietta;* (v) *Suite for String Orchestra;* (iv) *Taras Bulba;* (vi; vii) *Dumka* (for violin & piano); (viii) *Mládí;* (ix; vi) *Pohádka; Presto* (for cello & piano); (vi; vii) *Romance* (for violin & piano); (x) *String Quartets 1; 2;* (v; vi) *Violin Sonata;* (i) *In the Mist; On an overgrown Path; Teme con variazioni (Variations for Zdenka);* (xi) *Glagolitic Mass;* (xii) *Říkadla*

(B) *** Decca (ADD/DDD) 475 523-2 (5). (i) Crossley; (ii) L. Sinf.

(members); (iii) LPO, Huybrechts; (iv) VPO, Mackerras; (v) LAPO, Marriner; (vi) Atherton; (vii) Sillito; (viii) Bell, Craxton, Pay, Harris, Gatt, Eastop; (ix) van Kampen; (x) Gabrieli String Qt; (xi) Urbanová, Be aková, Bogachov, Novák, Slovak Phil. Ch., VPO, Chailly; (xii) London Sinf. Ch.

This set adds to the Double Decca collection of orchestral and concertante works above and proves a useful and inexpensive way of acquiring a lot of Janáček. The two *String Quartets* are among the composer's most deeply individual works and are profoundly impassioned utterances. The **Gabrieli Quartet** have the measure of this highly original music and give an idiomatic account of these masterpieces, playing with clarity as well as warmth, and with the advantage of vintage (1978) Decca sound. In the account of *Mládí*, the work's youthful sparkle comes across to excellent effect here. **Crossley's** survey of the piano music is both poetic and perceptive. The set brings a number of rarities, including the *Violin Sonata* and the *Říkadla* for chamber choir and ten instruments, both works very much worth getting to know. Finally, **Chailly's** strong and refined reading of the *Glagolitic Mass* makes a splendid finale, with fine detail emerging in the glowing Decca recording (1998), the emotional depth is fully brought out, with fine, idiomatic singing and a virtuoso display from Thomas Trotter in the final organ solo.

(i) *Capriccio for Piano; Concertino; (Piano) Sonata (1.x.1905); Along an Overgrown Path I & II; In the Mist; Reminiscences; Zdenka Variations*

⊕—(M) **** DG (ADD) 449 764-2 (2). Firkušný; (i) Bav. RSO (members), Kubelik

Capriccio; Concertino; Mládí (Youth) for wind sextet; *March of the Blue Boys* for piccolo & piano; (i) *Nursery Rhymes (Říkadla)* for chamber ch. & chamber ens.

*** Chan. 9399. Berman, Netherlands Wind Ens., Fischer; (i) with Prague Music Ac. Ch.

Kubelik partners **Rudolf Firkušný** in his thoroughly idiomatic earlier account of the *Concertino*. Now reissued in DG's series of 'Originals', this collection is eminently recommendable. Firkušný has long been regarded as the most authoritative exponent of the piano music. He recorded these pieces in the early 1970s, and he produces seamless *legato* lines, hammerless tone and rapt atmosphere. The recordings are all of high quality.

Though Firkušný remains in a class of his own, **Boris Berman** is a good soloist in both the *Concertino* and *Capriccio*. The astonishing *Říkadla* are given with great character by the **Netherlands Wind Ensemble** and the **Prague Academy Choir**. **Thierry Fischer** directs the proceedings impressively: the playing throughout is full of life and sensitivity. Vibrant recorded sound – every detail tells.

Violin Concerto (Pilgrimage of the Soul) (reconstructed Faltus & Stědrů)

(BB) *** Warner Apex 0927 40812-2. Zehetmair, Philh. O, Holliger – BERG: *Violin Concerto;* HARTMANN: *Concerto funèbre ***

This is highly original music, with some delightful lyrical ideas, imaginatively scored, albeit also with moments of top-heavy orchestral writing, searing in its intensity – particularly as played here by **Thomas Zehetmair** and the **Philharmonia** under **Heinz Holliger**. Excellent recorded sound. A most rewarding triptych, well worth exploring at budget price.

(i) Violin Concerto (Pilgrimage of the Soul); (ii) Danube Symphony; Sinfonietta; (iii) Schluck und Jau (incidental music): excerpts

(N) *** Sup. 11 1422-2. Brno State O, Jílek, with (i) Zenatý; (ii) Dvořáková; (iii) Beneš

Ivan Zenatý is an aristocrat of the violin and his performance of the concerto is tenderly affecting. The incidental music to *Schluck und Jau* is a two-movement piece about as long as the *Violin Concerto* and likewise full of characteristic ideas. **Jílek's** performance of the *Sinfonietta* can hold its own with the best, as can the *Danube Symphony* which has invention of great imagination. Altogether a highly recommendable disc.

(i) The Fiddler's Child; (ii) Idyll for String Orchestra; (i) Jealousy: Overture; Sinfonietta; (ii) Suite for Strings; (i) Taras Bulba; The Cunning Little Vixen: Suite

(B) *** Chan. 2-for-1 241-7 (2). (i) Czech PO, Bělohlávek; (ii) Jupiter O, Rose

Idyll; Suite for String Orchestra

⊕ 🏵 **** Chan. 9816. Norwegian CO, Brown – BARTÓK: *Divertimento for Strings* 🏵 ****

In the *Idyll* the **Norwegian Chamber Orchestra** and **Iona Brown** sweep the board. Their playing is vibrant, full of enthusiasm and vitality, and yet finding also a touching nostalgia in the slow sections of the *Idyll* and an even more subtle and haunting espressivo in the two lovely *Adagios* of the *Suite*. The recorded sound is absolutely state-of-the-art and the Bartók coupling quite outstanding.

The *Idyll* and the *Suite for Strings* are also ravishingly played by the **Jupiter Orchestra** under **Gregory Rose**, who shows himself completely at home in the lilting Czech idiom and who achieves rapt concentration in the touching slow movements. The rest of the Chandos programme is also very stimulating. This splendidly vivid account of the *Sinfonietta* is unsurpassed, and throughout all these performances the beauty of the orchestral playing, and opulence and detail of the recordings add to the attractions of a very well-chosen compilation.

Sinfonietta

⊕ (M) *** EMI 5 66980-2. Philh. O, Rattle – *Glagolitic Mass* ***

⊕ *** Chan. 8897. Czech PO, Bělohlávek – MARTINŮ: *Symphony 6*; SUK: *Scherzo* ***

Sinfonietta; Lachian Dances; Taras Bulba

(BB) *** Naxos 8.550411. Slovak RSO (Bratislava), Lenárd

Rattle gets an altogether first-class response from the orchestra and truthful recorded sound from the EMI engineers, and his coupling with the *Glagolitic Mass* is very attractive indeed.

Jiří Bělohlávek's exultant and imaginative account of the *Sinfonietta* is one of the best currently on offer and is coupled with an outstanding version of Martinů's *Sixth Symphony*, the recording, made in the Smetana Hall, Prague, is impressive.

On Naxos we have the normal LP coupling of the *Sinfonietta* and *Taras Bulba*, but with the *Lachian Dances* thrown in for good measure, all played by musicians steeped in the Janáček tradition – and all at a very modest cost. These are excellent performances; the recording, made in a fairly resonant studio, is natural and free from any artificially spotlit balance.

Sinfonietta; Preludes: From the House of the Dead; Jealousy (original Overture to Jenůfa); Katya Kabanova; The Makropulos Affair

(N) (B) **(*) EMI (ADD) 2 35720-2. Pro Arte O, Mackerras (with WEINBERGER: *Schwanda the Bagpiper: Polka & fugue*; SMETANA: *The Bartered Bride: Overture* ***)

Sir Charles Mackerras's 1959 version of the *Sinfonietta* was the first of his many recordings. This performance has a fire and bite that were not even matched by his later, Decca recording. The playing of the **Pro Arte Orchestra** is immensely vivid; its lack of the last degree of refinement seems to increase its forceful projection. The brass sonorities (the work used 12 trumpets) are pungent, and elsewhere the recording has striking detail and colour. The original coupling of the four operatic *Preludes* was an imaginative choice, and similar comments apply to the vibrant playing here. Both the Weinberger and Smetana fill-ups are lively and engaging, and the remastering in this bargain CD seems more successful than in its last incarnation, although the recording sounds its age.

Sinfonietta; Taras Bulba; Jealousy Prelude; The Cunning Little Vixen: Suite; Káta Kabanová: Overture & Interludes; Šárka Overture; Schluck und Jau (incidental music): excerpts: Andante & Allegretto

⊕ **** Sup. SU 3739-2 (2). Czech PO, Mackerras

No one can match **Sir Charles Mackerras** as an inspired and dedicated advocate of the music of Janáček. *Šárka* is represented by the *Overture*, and the *Káta Kabanová* excerpts (including the two delightful little *Interludes* that Mackerras himself discovered in Prague) similarly come from his complete recording. The other items all come in new recordings, with the **Czech Philharmonic** responding warmly. Apart from *Jealousy*, the original prelude to *Jenůfa*, the rarity in the collection are the two pieces from the incidental music for a play by Gerhardt Hauptmann, *Schluck und Jau*. The first of the two completed movements brings some intriguing echoes of the fanfares in the *Sinfonietta*, and the second in 5/8 time is equally original in its unexpected instrumentation. The suite taken from *The Cunning Little Vixen*, consisting of virtually the whole of Act I without the voices, is here given in Janáček's own sharply original orchestration. Best of all, the two central orchestral works, the *Sinfonietta* and *Taras Bulba*, come in live recordings which are even warmer and more idiomatic, crowning the whole collection, helped by full and spacious recording.

Taras Bulba

*** Australian Decca Eloquence 467 602-2. Cleveland O, Dohnányi – KODÁLY: *Concerto for Orchestra*; BARTÓK: *Concerto for Orchestra* ***

Dohnányi's warmly expressive reading of *Taras Bulba* is recorded in Decca's finest digital Cleveland style, and is imaginatively coupled on this excellent Australian Eloquence CD.

CHAMBER MUSIC

(i; iii) Allegro; Dumka; Romance; Sonata (for violin & piano); (ii; iii) Pohádka (Fairy Tale); Presto (for cello & piano); (iii) (Piano) Along an Overgrown Path, Series I–II; In the Mists; 3 Moravian Dances; Paralipomena; Reminiscence; Piano Sonata in E flat min. (I. X. 1905); Theme & Variations (Zdenka's Variations)

*** BIS CD 663/664. (i) Wallin; (ii) Rondin; (iii) Pöntinen

This excellent collection ranges from the *Romance* for violin and piano from the late 1870s, to the much later *Reminiscence* for piano. **Pöntinen** is an unfailingly intelligent player. **Ulf Wallin** proves a strong yet sensitive advocate of the *Violin Sonata*, and the cellist **Mats Rondin** is no less admirable in the *Pohádka* (*Fairy Tale*) and the *Presto* for cello and piano. Readers wanting this whole collection may rest assured that both playing and recording are of a generally high standard.

Concertino; Mládí

🅱🅱 *** HM HMA 1901399. Walter Boeykens Ens. – DVOŘÁK: *Serenade in D min. for Wind* ***

The **Walter Boeykens Ensemble** is a most distinguished group, and anyone wanting this coupling need have no qualms about investing in it. Both the *Concertino*, with **Robert Groslot** as the soloist, and *Mládí* are as fresh and compelling as any currently on disc. The 1991 recordings from Antwerp have worn well.

Mládí

*** Nim. NI 5812. Quintett Wien (with PIRCHNER: *String Quartet: Variations on a Tyrolean Slave Song*) – MOZART: *Serenade 12* ***

🅱🅱 **(*) Naxos 8.553851-2. Michael Thompson Wind Quintet – BARBER: *Summer Music* **(*); HINDEMITH: *Kleine Kammermusik* **(*); LARSSON: *Quattro tempi* **

Mládí, scored for wind sextet including bass clarinet, is a spirited and atmospheric piece. The splendid Vienna Ensemble makes the very most of the music's changing moods and is very well recorded. The Pirchner *Quartet/Variations* is audacious and resourceful; even if the music itself is not of the quality of either of the major

works on this disc, it is expertly played and makes a diverting encore.

Janáček's *Mládí* is superbly played by the **Michael Thompson Wind Quintet**, who are sensitive to every nuance of this glorious and haunting score. Wonderfully accomplished and sensitive though they are, they are let down by a close balance, which robs the music of atmosphere.

String Quartet 1 (Kreutzer Sonata)

*** Sup. SU 3922-2. Pavel Haas Qt – HAAS: *String Quartets 1 & 3* ***

*** Testament (ADD) SBT 1074. Smetana Qt – DVOŘÁK: *Piano Quintet, etc.* ***

**(*) BBC Legends BBCL 4180-2. Smetana Qt – DVOŘÁK: *String Quartet 14, etc.* **(*)

The new Supraphon account by the **Pavel Haas Quartet** now leads the field, superbly played and most realistically recorded, and the Haas couplings are equally illuminating.

The **Smetana Quartet's** account of the *First Quartet* (*Kreutzer Sonata*) is also one of the very best versions of the work ever committed to disc. There is a wonderful feeling that these players have lived with this music all their lives – and in fact live *for* it, so committed do they sound. Worth every penny of its full price.

The **Smetana Quartet** was recorded at London's Queen Elizabeth Hall in February 1975. The BBC recording sounds very acceptable, and the performance has a powerful involvement and intensity, and the presence of an audience always draws something extra from the players.

String Quartet 2 (Intimate Letters)

*** Sup. SU 3877-2. Pavel Haas Qt – HAAS: *String Quartet 2* ***

*** Testament (ADD) SBT 1075. Smetana Qt – DVOŘÁK: *String Quartet 14, etc.* ***

Like its companion, coupled with the equally stimulating music of Haas, this performance by the **Pavel Haas Quartet** is passionately convincing and very well recorded indeed. Recommended, alongside the Smetana Quartet's version.

The **Smetana** account deserves the same accolade. In terms of subtlety, tonal finish and technical polish, this is absolutely flawless – and the 1960s sound is superb, and not just for its period. Strongly recommended alongside its companion.

String Quartets 1 (Kreutzer); 2 (Intimate Letters)

*** Cal. CAL 9333. Talich Qt – SCHULHOFF: *Quartet 1*

*** ASV CDDCA 749. Lindsay Qt – DVOŘÁK: *Cypresses* ***

Ⓝ **(*) DG 477 8093. Emerson Qt (with MARTINŮ: *3 Madrigals for violin & viola*)

EMI Encore 2 08121-2. Alban Berg Qt (with DVOŘÁK: *Piano Quintet, Op. 81: Dumka only* ***)

(i) String Quartets 1 (Kreutzer Sonata); 2 (Intimate Letters); (ii) Allegro for violin and piano; Violin Sonata

*** Meridian CDE 84560. (i) Dante Qt; (ii) Ososiowicz, Rados

(i) String Quartets 1–2; (ii) On an Overgrown Path: Suite 1

⊛→ Ⓜ *** Cal. CAL 5699. (i) Talich Qt; (ii) Kvapil

(i) String Quartets 1–2; (ii) Pohádka for Cello & Piano; (iii) Violin Sonata

⊛→ ⒷⒷ *** Naxos 8.553895. (i) Vlach Qt; (ii) Ericsson; (ii–iii) Maly; (iii) Vlachová

*** Brodsky BRD 3503. (i) Brodsky Qt; (ii) Cousin (ii; iii) Thomas; (iii) Haveron

Pride of place must go to the **Talich Quartet** on Calliope, not because their recording is the best, but because of their extraordinary qualities of insight. They play the *Intimate Letters* as if its utterances came from a world so private that it must be approached with great care. The disc's value is much enhanced by a fill-up in the form of the *First Suite, On an Overgrown Path*. **Radoslav Kvapil** is thoroughly inside this repertoire.

The latest coupling from the **Talichs** is also among the very finest available. This Talich is a different ensemble from the recording we list on CAL 5699. Their leader, Jan Talich, is the son of the Talich, violist and violinist, of the previous quartet. In any event, this is big-boned and impassioned playing that carries the listener with it. The recording is a little forward, but not unacceptably so.

The **Lindsays** on ASV are also eminently competitive and have the right blend of sensitivity and intensity. Theirs must certainly rank very highly among current recommendations. They play with the same concentration and sensitivity they bring to all they do, and are recorded with great naturalness.

Immaculately prepared accounts by the **Dante Quartet**, which are among the best to have appeared recently and can hold their own with the finest. Their coupling is a splendid and persuasive account of the *Violin Sonata* from **Krysia Osostowicz** and the Hungarian pianist **Ferenc Rados**, with whom she also gives us the *Allegro* originally a sketch for the last movement of the violin sonata but eventually formed the basis for the third movement.

The **Vlach Quartet** on Naxos give well-played, impassioned accounts of both **Quartets** and are warmly recorded. Moreover, the account of the *Violin Sonata* by **Jana Vlachová** and **František Maly** is very fine, and the *Pohádka for Cello and Piano* is given as touching and imaginative a performance by **Mikael Ericsson** as any in the catalogue. Good recordings and excellent value for money.

The **Brodsky Quartet** also play the two Janáček *String Quartets*, both of them masterly examples of the composer's late style, with characteristic flair and drive, with richness as well as power and with a natural feeling for their lyrical qualities. They readily rival other quartets in that coupling but, like the Vlach Quartet on Naxos, they generously add the fairy-tale suite for cello and piano, *Pohádka*, and the *Violin Sonata*, also very well played. Excellent sound.

From the **Emerson Quartet**, magnificent playing, awe-inspiring in its ensemble and tonal subtleties. However, it is wanting in the real intensity and spontaneity that these works demand. Listen to an excerpt and one is bowled over by the Emersons' mastery; listen to either of the complete quartets and one realizes that there is something missing in terms of character. Superb sound.

The **Alban Berg** coupling was made at public performances in the Mozartsaal and the Konzerthaus in Vienna in 1993. They play with enormous and at times almost frenzied intensity and are not frightened to produce rough, gutsy sound. Indeed, that impression is possibly enhanced by the fierce, strident recording. Although the reissue is inexpensive, the fill-up is a curious choice.

Violin Sonata

⊛→ *** Praga PRD 250 153. Remés, Kayahara – DVOŘÁK: *Sonatina*; MARTINŮ, SMETANA: *Violin Sonatas* ***

⊛→ *** Analekta FL2 3191. Ehnes, Laurel – DVOŘÁK: *Romantic Pieces; Sonatina in G; Humoresque*; SMETANA: *From the Homeland* ***

*** HM HMC 901793. Faust, Kupiec – LUTOSŁAWSKI: *Partita; Subito*; SZYMANOWSKI: *3 Mythes* ***

**(*) Avie AV0023. Gleusteen, Ordonneau – PROKOFIEV: *Violin Sonata 1*; SHOSTAKOVICH: *19 Preludes* **(*)

This newest Praga account from **Václav Remés** and the rich-timbred **Sachito Kayahara** is fiercely intense, yet warmly affectionate, the questing closing *Adagio* highly dramatic, and with the closing pages creating a mood of tender intensity. The playing itself is superbly assured and characterful, and the recording first class.

In the equally fine collection of violin and piano music by the three greatest Czech composers on Analekta, **Ehnes** and **Laurel** make light of the technical and interpretative problems of the Janáček *Sonata*, always an elusive work. Playing with ease and warmth, they are persuasively spontaneous-sounding, with Ehnes using the widest tonal range, as in an ecstatic *pianissimo* at the end of the second-movement *Ballada*.

The programme on the Harmonia Mundi disc may seem an odd mixture, but it works well. There is a spontaneous sense of fantasy in all these performances which lightly brings out the quirky side of the Janáček. In the lyrical *Ballata* second movement, **Isabelle Faust's** *pianissimo* playing is breathtaking.

The similarly mixed bag of Slavonic works on the Avie disc makes an impressive showcase for the talents of the Canadian-born violinist, **Kai Gleusteen**, and his French accompanist, **Catherine Ordonneau**. Their account of the quirky Janáček *Violin Sonata* is most compelling. The recording, one of a series made in the 'inspirational and innovative working space' of Crear, on the west coast of Scotland, is on the reverberant side, but there is no lack of detail.

PIANO MUSIC

Along an Overgrown Path, Books I & II; In the Mists; Piano Sonata (1.x.1905); Reminiscence

⊛→ Ⓜ *** SOMMCD 028. Owen

⊛→ ⒷⒷ *** Regis RRC 1172. Kvapil

Along an Overgrown Path: Suite 1; In the Mists; Piano Sonata (1.x.1905)

Ⓑ *** Virgin 2x1 3 49913-2 (2). Andsnes – NIELSEN: *Chaconne*, etc. ***

It says much for **Charles Owen** and his understanding of Janáček, that he should present this music with such a distinctive voice. Here and throughout the disc Owen is helped by the clarity of the well-balanced recording. The qualities that make Owen's performance of the *Sonata* so impressive recur in the other works here. So *Along an Overgrown Path* reflects the composer's folk influences in lyrical freshness. *In the Mist* conveys the impression of improvisations caught on the wing, again gaining from the extra clarity and range of the Somm recording. The tiny *Reminiscence*, product of the year the composer died, makes a moving supplement.

Radoslav Kvapil is naturally at home in this engaging music, and he is very well recorded. So you cannot go wrong with this 1994 Regis CD (originally issued on the Unicorn label). It is also available in a first-class Regis compilation of Czech piano music, together with works by Dvořák, Smetana & Suk (RRC 4005).

Leif Ove Andsnes, too, is a first-class exponent of this repertoire and, if you are tempted by the equally fine Nielsen coupling, this can also be strongly recommended, although he offers less music.

Piano Sonata (1.x.1905)

*** MDG 604 1141-2. von Eckardstein – MESSIAEN: *La Rousserolle effarvatte*; PROKOFIEV: *Piano Sonata 8* ***

Severin von Eckardstein's approach is extremely sensitive and thoughtful. As fine an account of the work as we have encountered.

VOCAL MUSIC

Glagolitic Mass (original version, ed. Wingfield)

Ⓑ— **** Chan. 9310. Kiberg, Stene, Svensson, Cold, Danish Nat. R. Ch. & SO, Mackerras – KODÁLY: *Psalmus hungaricus* ****

The added rhythmic complexities of this original version, as interpreted idiomatically by **Mackerras**, encourage an apt wildness which brings an exuberant, carefree quality to writing which here, more than ever, seems like the inspiration of the moment. The chorus sings incisively with incandescent tone, and the tenor soloist, **Peter Svensson**, has a trumpet-toned precision that makes light of the high tessitura and the stratospheric leaps that Janáček asks for. The soprano **Tina Kiberg**, also bright and clear rather than beautiful in tone, makes just as apt a choice. Recorded sound of a weight and warmth that convey the full power of the music.

Glagolitic Mass

Ⓑ— Ⓜ *** EMI 5 66980-2. Palmer, Gunson, Mitchinson, King, CBSO & Ch., Rattle – *Sinfonietta* ***

*** Australian Decca Eloquence (ADD) 466 902-2. Kubiak, Collins, Tear, Schöne, Brighton Festival Ch., RPO, Kempe – KODÁLY: *Laudes organi; Psalm 114* ***

Rattle's performance of the standard published score, aptly paired with the *Sinfonietta*, is strong and vividly dramatic, with the Birmingham performers lending themselves to Slavonic passion. The recording is first class and is now reissued as one of EMI's 'Great Recordings of the Century'.

Kempe stresses the lyrical elements of the score rather than going for outright fervour, but the orchestra and chorus are fully committed, and the solo singing is first rate too, with **Teresa Kubiak** particularly impressive. Everything is helped by the most realistic recording, which has transferred very well to CD. The unusual Kodály coupling is appropriate and adds to the interest of this reissue on Australian Decca's Eloquence label.

OPERA

(i) The Cunning Little Vixen (with Orchestral Suite); (ii) From the House of the Dead; (iii) Jenůfa; (iv) Káta Kabanová; (v) The Makropulos Affair; Sinfonietta; Taras Bulba; Zárlivost: Overture

Ⓑ **(*) Decca (ADD/DDD) 475 6872 (9). (i) Bratislava Children's Ch.; (i; ii) Jedlická; (ii) Zídek; (i; iii) Popp, Randová, (ii; iii) Zahradníček; (iii) Ochman; (iii; iv; v) Söderström, Dvorský; (iv) Kniplová, Krejčik, Márová; (v) Blachut; (i–v) V. State Op. Ch., VPO, Mackerras

Sir Charles Mackerras's recordings of Janáček's five key operas are one of the outstanding achievements of the Decca operatic catalogue and cannot be too highly praised. In a bargain box, with three orchestral works thrown in for good measure, the attraction is obvious. However, although synopses are provided, they are not cued. These are operas where the libretti with translations are almost essential, and it is a pity that they are not made available separately – perhaps at extra cost.

The Cunning Little Vixen (complete; DVD version)

**(*) Arthaus DVD 100 240. Allen, Jenis, Minutillo, O de Paris, Mackerras

With **Sir Charles Mackerras** again bringing out the characteristic sharpness of Janáček's writing in this fantasy opera, the power of the score as well as its charm comes over strongly in this DVD production at the Châtelet Theatre in Paris with Nicholas Hytner as stage director. Central to the production's success are the designs of Bob Crowley which take one into a toytown world with stylized, brightly coloured sets in angular shapes, and costumes to match. Musically, the singing of **Thomas Allen** as the Forester focuses the whole performance, strong and sympathetic in conveying this character's devotion to the life of the forest. He is one of the few singers who dominate the orchestra in a recording which favours instruments against voices. The bright, penetrating voices of **Eva Jenis** as the Vixen and **Hana Minutillo** as the Fox also defy the recording balance. With Czech titles for individual tracks it is not always easy to identify which character is singing.

The Cunning Little Vixen (complete; CD version); The Cunning Little Vixen (suite, arr. Talich)

⊶ Ⓜ *** Decca 417129-2 (2). Popp, Randová, Jedlická, V. State Op. Ch., Bratislava Children's Ch., VPO, Mackerras

*** Sup. SU (ADD) 3071/2 612 (2) (without suite). Tattermuschová, Zikmundová, Kroupa, Hlavsa, Prague Nat. Ch. & O, Gregor

Mackerras's thrusting, red-blooded CD reading on Decca is spectacularly supported by a digital recording of outstanding, demonstration quality. The inspired choice of **Lucia Popp** as the vixen provides charm in exactly the right measure: sparkling and coquettish, spiteful as well as passionate. The supporting cast is first rate, too. Talich's splendidly arranged orchestral suite is offered as a bonus in a fine new recording.

Janáček's opera is given on Supraphon with plenty of idiomatic Slavonic feeling by the composer's compatriots, with the part of the little vixen here charmingly sung by **Helena Tattermuschová**. The recording is evocatively warm and atmospheric. While the digitally recorded Decca Mackerras set (with Lucia Popp) remains a more obvious first choice, this earlier Czech version can hold its own.

The Cunning Little Vixen (sung in English)

Ⓜ *** Chan. 3101 (2). Watson, Allen, Tear, Knight, Howell, ROHCG Ch. & O, Rattle

The **Rattle** set gains from having been recorded as a spin-off from a highly successful Covent Garden production with the same excellent cast. In interpretation, Rattle's approach provides a clear alternative to that of Sir Charles Mackerras on his classic Decca version with a Czech cast. Where Mackerras characteristically brings out the sharp, angular side of Janáček's writing, the distinctly jagged element, Rattle's manner is more moulded, perhaps more immediately persuasive, if less obviously idiomatic. The recording is beautifully balanced, and this is important in the ensembles. What matters is that the words are ideally clear, with excellent diction from everyone.

The Excursions of Mr Brouček (complete)

⊶ **** DG 477 7387 (2). Vacík, Straka, Janál, Haan, Plech, BBC Singers, BBC SO, Bělohlávek

⊶ *** Sup. (ADD) 11 2153-2 (2). Přibyl, Svejda, Jonášová, Czech PO Ch. & O, Jílek

Mr Brouček is a delightful piece (to quote John Warrack, 'a genuinely amusing and a touching and most original work'). This DG version comes from a concert performance mounted by the BBC at the Barbican in 2007 with Czech soloists, a Czech conductor and the **BBC Singers** and **Symphony Orchestra**. The result is a thoroughly idiomatic performance and an excellent balance. Although the second half ('Mr Brouček's Excursion to the fifteenth century') is less well sustained than the first, his excursion to the Moon, **Jirí Bělohlávek** gives a persuasive account of it. The two parts are accommodated on a CD each, and the DG production offers elegant results in the best traditions of the company.

This Supraphon performance comes over with real charm, thanks to the understanding conducting of **Jílek**, but also to the characterization of the central character, the bumbling, accident-prone Mr Brouček (literally Mr Beetle).

Vilém Přibyl portrays him as an amiable, much-put-upon figure as he makes his excursions. The big team of Czech singers (doubling up roles in the different parts, with **Vladimir Krejčik** remarkable in no fewer than seven of them) are outstanding, bringing out both the warmth and sense of fun behind the writing. The result is a delight, as sharp and distinctive as any Janáček opera. The analogue recording, made in Prague in 1980, is full and atmospheric, with a fine sense of presence on CD.

Orchestral Suites: *The Excursions of Mr Brouček; Jenůfa* (arr. Breiner)

Ⓝ Ⓑ Ⓑ *** Naxos 8.570555. New Zealand SO, Breiner

An ideal disc for those who like Janáček's musical language, but not opera. Both these *Suites* are very well compiled, keeping faithfully to the composer's orchestrations, though substituting the vocal lines to the orchestra and providing concert endings. These two contrasted suites – 70 minutes of first-rate music – are most enjoyable and the performances and recording very good.

From the House of the Dead (complete; DVD version)

*** DG **DVD** 073 4426. Bär, Stocklossa, Margita, Sulzeno, Mark Ainsley, Haberfield, Arnold Schoenberg Ch, Mahler CO, Boulez

Patrice Chéreau was just the man to produce and direct this intensely powerful account of what must be one of the most depressing opera scenarios in the repertoire. Certainly Dostoevsky's original memoirs, on which the opera is based, do have an upbeat ending, as the central character, Goryanchikov – the excellent **Olaf Bär** – is released (alongside the eagle the prisoners have tended), and the young Alyeya (the very believable **Eric Stocklossa**) shows he is now able to read. Nevertheless, the narrative is fascinating, and here, with excellent characterization from all the main characters, and powerful musical direction from **Boulez** (bringing out what he calls the 'primitivism' in Janáček's score), the narrative is brought vividly to life throughout by Stéphane Merge's film direction. There is excellent documentation. And the bonus includes much extra material about the rehearsals, plus a discussion between Patrice Chéreau and Boulez on Dostoevsky's text.

(i) *From the House of the Dead*; (iii) *Mládí* (for wind sextet); (ii; iii) *Říkadla* (for chamber ch. & 10 instruments)

⊶ *** Decca DDD/ADD 430 375-2 (2). (i) Jedlička, Zahradníček, Janska, Zídek, Zítek, V. State Op. Ch., VPO, Mackerras; (ii) L. Sinf. Ch.; (iii) L. Sinf., Atherton

With one exception, the Decca cast is superb, with a range of important Czech singers giving sharply characterized vignettes. The exception is the raw Slavonic singing of the one woman in the cast, **Jaroslav Janska**, as the boy Alyeya, but even that fails to undermine the intensity of the innocent relationship with the central figure which provides an emotional anchor for the whole piece. The chamber-music items added for this reissue are both first rate.

Jenůfa (complete; DVD version)

🎞 ****** Arthaus DVD 100 208. Alexander, Silja, Langridge, M. Baker, Glyndebourne Ch., LPO, A. Davis (V/D: Nikolaus Lehnhoff)

**(*) TDK DVD DVWW-OPJENU. Stemme, Marton, Silvasti, Lindskog, Gran Teatre del Liceu Ch. & SO, Schneider (Stage Director: Olivier Tambosi, V/D: Pietro d'Agostino)

The impact of Nikolaus Lehnhoff's production of Jenůfa was always strong and positive, with the stark yet atmospheric designs of Tobias Hoheisel adding to the sharpness. On DVD, with close-ups in this television film of 1989 adding to the impact, the result is even more powerful. This visual treatment exactly matches the sharp originality of Janáček's score, with its often abrasive orchestration heightened by passages of surging beauty, superbly realized by **Andrew Davis** and the **LPO**.

Roberta Alexander makes a warm, slightly gawky Jenůfa, with **Philip Langridge** as the frustrated lover, Laka, making this awkward character totally believable, an object for sympathy, finally fulfilled. Both sing superbly, and so do the rest of the cast, including **Mark Baker** as the wastrel, Steva, a tenor well contrasted with Langridge. Yet dominating the cast is the Kostelnicka of **Anja Silja**. The abrasiveness in her voice, which with Wagner heroines was often obtrusive, is here a positive asset, and her portrayal of this formidable character, positive and uncompromising yet ultimately an object of pity, is totally convincing in all its complexity. The way she delivers Kostelnička's apprehensive cry at the end of Act II was 'as if death were peering into the house'. Full, vivid sound very well transferred, if with an edge that suits the music.

Olivier Tambosi's production on TDK sets the major part of the action on a raised portion of the stage against a rather effective, plain but pastoral, backcloth, showing the growing corn. He places a symbolic rock at centre stage to suggest the foetus of the child which dominates the opera's narrative, which grows in size in Act II to dominate the scene and is then broken up into rocky terrain in the third Act. **Nina Stemme's** vulnerable portrayal of Jenůfa is warmly sympathetic, and she is at her finest at the close of the opera when the story reaches its climax, with the discovery of the frozen body of her child. The men in her life, step-brothers **Jorma Silvasti** as Laca and **Pär Lindskog** as Steva, sing passionately and are convincingly characterized. But, of course, the key to the opera is the Kostelnička, and there is no doubt that **Eva Marton** gives a strongly dominating performance; and herein lies the flaw. She sings powerfully and emotionally but with a consistently wide vibrato which for some ears will be a deterrent to listening to her voice. Overall, the performance is gripping and **Peter Schneider's** musical direction is admirable, as is Pietro d'Agostino's camerawork. The very necessary documentation is excellent.

Jenůfa (complete; CD versions)

🎞 ✿ Ⓜ ***** Decca 475 8227 (2). Söderström, Ochman, Dvorský, Randová, Popp, V. State Op. Ch., VPO, Mackerras

*** Erato 0927 45330-2 (2). Mattila, Silja, Silvasti, Hadley, Randová, ROH Ch. & O, Haitink

The Decca CDs bring a performance from **Mackerras** and his team which is deeply sympathetic, strongly dramatic and superbly recorded. **Elisabeth Söderström** creates a touching portrait of the girl caught in a family tragedy. The two rival tenors, **Peter Dvorský** and **Wieslav Ochman** as the half-brothers Steva and Laca, are both superb; but dominating the whole drama is the Kostelnicka of **Eva Randová**. Some may resist the idea that she should be made so sympathetic but the drama is made stronger and more involving.

Haitink's version, recorded live at Covent Garden in October 2001, is distinguished not only by the warm, intense conducting but by the fine singing of the principals, notably **Karita Mattila** in the title role. Mattila with her fresh, girlish tone combined with great emotional depth, outshines even Elisabeth Söderström, whose more mature voice is less appropriate for the role, warmly expressive as she is. **Anja Silja** also gives a most memorable performance. **Randová** is here masterly in the much smaller role of Grandmother Buryja, and both tenor roles are very well taken, too, with **Jorma Silvasti** as Laca rising most movingly to the challenge of the final scene and the reconciliation with Jenůfa, while **Jerry Hadley** sings with comparable freshness as Steva. Though the sound on this live recording does not have the weight and power of the Decca digital studio recording and stage noises inevitably intrude at times, it is finely detailed, and the atmosphere adds to the compulsion of the performance, with refined playing from the orchestra.

Handsomely repackaged, with full libretto and translation, the 1979 Supraphon set, while lacking the concentration of Mackerras's set for Decca, is fresh, sharp and enjoyable. A strong cast is headed by two veteran singers, **Vilém Přibyl** as Laca and **Nadejda Kniplová** as the Kostelnitčka; their singing is most assured, but their voices are often raw for the gramophone. So too with most of the singers in the smaller parts, though the role of Jenůfa went to the now famous, creamy-toned **Gabriela Beňačková**, with no hint of a Slavonic wobble. As Stewa, the tenor **Vladimir Krejčík** makes an excellent impression. (SUP SU 3869-2)

Jenůfa (sung in English)

Ⓜ *** Chan. 3106 (2). Watson, Barstow, Wedd, Robson, Davies, WNO Ch. & O, Mackerras

Based on the acclaimed production of Jenůfa from **Welsh National Opera**, **Sir Charles Mackerras's** Chandos set offers an important alternative to the classic, prize-winning version he conducted in 1982 for Decca. The benefit of the Chandos sound is that the colour and originality of Janáček's orchestral textures come over even more vividly than on the brilliant Decca set, at once opulent and well defined, with each strand clarified and the exotic percussion effects brought out. Helped by a few sound-effects, the result is generally more atmospheric.

When it comes to the rival casts on CD, they are both very strong, with no weak links. **Janice Watson** on Chandos has a beautiful voice, sounding aptly young, fresh and girlish, and deeply expressive too. As the Kostelnička, **Dame Josephine Barstow** is edgier and more abrasive, and with that she conveys not only the obsessive side of this powerful character but an element of vulnerability, apt for the story. The two tenor roles are also very well taken, with **Peter Wedd** as Steva and **Nigel Robson** as Laca nicely contrasted, effectively bringing out the sharp differences of character between the half-brothers. **Elizabeth Vaughan** as Grandmother Buryja and **Neal Davies** as the Foreman complete a formidable line-up of principals. Not surprisingly, words are much clearer from the male singers than from the female but the final duet between Jenůfa and Laca is even more tender than it was in the Vienna performance, bringing out all the subtlety of Janáček's evocative writing.

Káta Kabanová (complete; DVD versions)

🎬 *** Arthaus **DVD** 100 158. Gustafson, Palmer, R. Davies, McCauley, Graham-Hall, Winter, Glyndebourne Ch., LPO, A. Davis (V/D: Nikolaus Lehnhoff)

(i) Káta Kabanová (complete; CD version); (ii) Capriccio for Piano & 7 Instruments; Capriccio for Piano & 6 Instruments

🎵 *** Decca (ADD) 475 7518 (2). (i) Söderström, Dvorský, Kniplová, Krejčik, Márová, V. State Op. Ch., VPO, Mackerras; (ii) Crossley, L. Sinf., Atherton

First seen at Glyndebourne in 1988, this Arthaus DVD offers the ground-breaking production by Nikolaus Lehnhoff with stark, striking designs by Tobias Hoheisel, which led to a whole sequence of memorable Janáček productions. It remains one of the most powerful, with **Nancy Gustafson** tenderly moving as the heroine starved of love, constantly frustrated by her implacable mother-in-law, the deeply unsympathetic Kabanicha, brilliantly portrayed and sung by **Felicity Palmer**, with a powerful cutting edge. The production, too, is exactly suited to the distinctive idiom of Janáček, with its contrasts of abrasiveness and rich beauty. Strong contributions too from **Ryland Davies** as Tichon, Káta's husband, **Barry McCauley** as Boris, and **John Graham-Hall** as Kudrjas, with characterful contributions too from such a veteran as **Donald Adams** as Boris's father, Dikoj. Bright, forward sound adds to the impact.

It was understandable that Decca should have chosen *Káta Kabanová* for one of their new series of Originals, for **Elisabeth Söderström** dominates the opera as Káta in one of her finest and most moving recorded performances. The rest of the cast is Czech and, with **Mackerras** at the helm, the performance overall can hardly fail. The two concertante works, with **Paul Crossley** also on top form, were added for the original reissue.

Though **Mackerras's** Supraphon set offers digital sound and has an excellent Czech cast, it cannot match his earlier, Decca version in colour or bite. Though his speeds are a degree faster than before, the result is less violent and less involving, thanks partly to the low-level recording, set in a reverberant acoustic. **Be ačková**, rich and vibrant, is an exceptionally characterful Káta, arguably more idiomatic than Söderström on Decca, and the other principals are first rate too, but at every point this pales before its rival. (SU 3291-2632)

Kátya Kabanová (sung in English)

Ⓜ *** Chan. 3145 (2). Barker, Henschel, Brubaker, Hoare, Wedd, Howell, WNO Ch. & O, Rizzi

Carlo Rizzi, who conducted the live performances for WNO, is a persuasive Janáček interpreter, and it is fascinating to compare this English version with the Decca recording made by Mackerras with the Vienna Philharmonic and an excellent, mainly Czech, cast but with the title-role taken by the Swedish soprano, Elisabeth Söderström. Taking the title-role is **Cheryl Barker**, again fresh, clear and powerful, more girlish-sounding than Söderström on Decca and, when in Act III Emilia Marty is at last given a sustained solo, the new version is even more powerful than the old one, aptly abrasive and less moulded. **Jane Henschel** is outstanding as Marfa Kabanová, the rich widow who persecutes her daughter-in-law, Katya, wonderfully rich and firm throughout her range. It is remarkable too that, as in the Czech cast for Mackerras, the three tenor roles are exceptionally well taken, even if the contrast between **Robert Brubaker** as Boris, **Peter Wedd** as Kudryash and **Peter Hoare** as Tichon, husband of Katya and son of Marfa, is not ideally marked. **Gwynne Howell** as the merchant, Dikoi, uncle of Boris, is also excellent. Another outstanding issue in the Opera in English series.

The Makropulos Affair (DVD version)

🎬 ✱ *** Warner **DVD** 0630 14016-2. Silja, Begley, Braun, Shore, LPO, A. Davis (Director: Nikolaus Lehnhoff, V/D: Brian Large)

Now comes the 1995 Glyndebourne production by Nikolaus Lehnhoff, whose *Káta Kabanová* we so much admired, and with an astonishingly powerful account of the heroine from **Anja Silja**. In fact, it is difficult to flaw this production on any count. It is excellently cast, with **Kim Begley** as Gregor, **Viktor Braun** as Pruš and **Andrew Shore** as Dr Kolenaty, and it is conducted with a sense both of atmosphere and of pace by **Sir Andrew Davis**. He is hardly less idiomatic and sensitive than Mackerras. Those who were privileged to see this will not forget the commanding portrayal of Emilia by Silja. As usual, Brian Large brings everything to the screen with scrupulous care and taste to make this a very special contribution to the Janáček DVD discography.

(i) The Makropulos Affair (CD version): complete; (ii) Lachian Dances

🎵 *** Decca (ADD) 430 372-2 (2). (i) Söderström, Dvorský, Blachut, V. State Op. Ch., VPO, Mackerras; (ii) LPO, Huybrechts

Mackerras and his superb team provide a thrilling new perspective on this opera, with its weird heroine preserved by magic elixir well past her 300th birthday. **Elisabeth Söderström** is not simply malevolent: irritable and impatient rather, no longer an obsessive monster. Framed by richly colourful singing and playing, Söderström amply justifies that view, and **Peter Dvorský** is superbly fresh and ardent as Gregor. The recording, like others in the series, is of the finest Decca analogue quality. The performance of the *Lachian Dances* is highly idiomatic and makes a good bonus.

The Makropulos Case (sung in English)

(M) *** Chan. 3138 (2). Barker, Brubaker, Graham-Hall, Xanthoudakis, Wegner, Walker, Clark, ENO Ch. & O, Mackerras

It says much for the quality of the **English National Opera Orchestra** that for this new version in English, the playing is just as polished as that of the Vienna Philharmonic, with the benefit of extra dramatic bite, thanks to experience in the opera house. The recording of the new set brings an advantage too with extra separation, suiting Janáček's music better, as Sir Charles says in his conversation with Rodney Milnes. Also, the words are astonishingly clear, even more so than in other recordings in the Moores series. As to the Chandos cast, **Cheryl Barker** rivals Elisabeth Söderström on Decca in the dramatic bite of her singing, fresh and clean-cut, and when in Act III Emilia Marty at last given a sustained solo, the new version is even more powerful than the old one, aptly abrasive and less moulded. Though the American, **Robert Brubaker**, cannot quite match Peter Dvorský on Decca in the key role of Albert Gregor, and in some of the smaller roles the Czech singers have an advantage too in sharper characterization, all give strong, firmly focused performances.

Osud (complete, in English)

(M) *** Chan. 3029. Langridge, Field, Harries, Bronder, Kale, Welsh Nat. Op. Ch. & O, Mackerras

Though this recording was made with **Welsh National Opera** forces, its success echoes the ENO production. **Philip Langridge** is again superb in the central role of the composer, Zivny, well supported by **Helen Field** as Mila, the married woman he loves, and by **Kathryn Harries** as her mother – a far finer cast than was presented on a short-lived Supraphon set. **Sir Charles Mackerras** captures the full gutsiness, passion and impetus of the composer's inspiration, from the exhilarating opening waltz ensemble onwards, a passage that vividly sets the scene in a German spa at the turn of the century. The warmly atmospheric recording brings out the unusual opulence of the Janáček sound in this work, written immediately after *Jenůfa*, yet it allows words to come over with fine clarity.

Šárka (complete)

*** Sup. SU 3485-2. Urbanová, Straka, Kusnjer, Brezina, Prague Philharmonic Ch., Czech PO, Mackerras

Šárka, written originally in 1887, was Janáček's very first opera. Though the idiom has more echoes of Dvořák and Smetana than anticipations of the mature Janáček, its dramatic point comes over strongly, with the legend reduced to bare essentials to give it a dream-like quality, making it a Freudian fantasy before its time. Janáček regarded this as his Wagnerian opera, ending as it does with the immolation of the formidable heroine, Šárka (an Amazonian figure sworn to avenge herself on man) on the funeral pyre of Ctirad, the hero-figure with whom, against her will, she falls in love. It is not just an immolation, but a Liebestod, or love-death. This first stereo recording could hardly be finer, with **Mackerras** inspiring his Czech singers and players to give

an incandescent performance, with **Eva Urbanová** and **Peter Straka** ideally cast, both characterfully Slavonic and clean in attack. First-rate sound, with atmospheric choral effects beautifully caught.

JAUBERT, Maurice (1900–40)

Ballade

(BB) (***) Dutton (mono) CDBP 9764. SO, composer –
    HONEGGER: *Cello Concerto*, etc.; PIERNÉ: *Ramuntcho* (***)

Maurice Jaubert graduated from the Nice Conservatoire and practised law before turning to music. He is best remembered for his film music; he wrote the scores for *Un Carnet de Bal* and *La Fin du Jour* in the late 1930s. The *Ballade* was recorded in 1934. But the attraction of this issue is naturally the Honegger, for which this makes a pleasing makeweight.

JENKINS, John (1592–1678)

Consort Music: Ayres a 4 in D min. & G min. (Ayre; Almaine; Couranto); Divisions for 2 Basses in C; Fantasia: in C min.; D; E min.; Fantasias in C min. (2); Fantasia in F (All in a Garden Green); Fantasy-suite in A min.; In nomine in G min.; Newarke Seidge (Pavan; Galliard); Pavan in F

(BB) *** Naxos 8.550687. Rose Consort of Viols, with Roberts

Consort Music: Divisions for 2 Bass Viols in D; Fantasias: a 4 in D; in F (2); a 5 in C min. (2); & D; a 6 in A min. & C min.; In nomines: a 6 in E min. & G min.; Pavan for 2 Bass Viols; Pavan a 6 in F; Pieces for Lyra Viol; Suites 4 in C for 2 Trebles, Bass & Organ; 7 in D min., for Treble, 2 Basses & Organ in D min.

*** Virgin 5 45230-2. Fretwork, with Nicholas

John Jenkins spent his life in Norfolk and lapsed into obscurity. Yet on the evidence of these two fine, complementary CDs his viol music is of high quality and well worth rediscovering. It does not seek great profundity, although the beautiful *Pavan in F major*, common to both discs, is memorable, and all the *Fantasias* are well crafted – their invention appealingly immediate. Although they overlap, both collections are thoroughly recommendable, with the difference between them accentuated by the difference in performance pitch, with **Fretwork** slightly higher, giving a brighter, fresher impression, whereas the **Rose Consort** have a somewhat warmer tonal blend, especially noticeable in that fine *Pavan*.

Consort Music for Violins in 6 Parts: Fantasies 1–11; Bell Pavan; In nomines 1–2

*** Astrée ES 9962. Hespèrion XX, Savall

The performances here are richly blended and bring out the full, expressive depth of this music. At times one feels that the playing of the faster pieces could have produced a brighter projection, but viols are not violins and have a more limited dynamic range, so this remains a highly recommendable anthology. The recording itself, warm and full and not too close, cannot be faulted.

12 Fantasies in 6 parts; Bell Pavan in A min.; In nomines in G min. and E min.; Pavan in F

B—, *** Avie AV 2099. Phantasm

With their elaborate counterpoint, these pieces – all but one in the minor mode – hark back to the Golden Age of Elizabethan music, even though they probably date from the 1620s, after the great queen died, early in the long career of John Jenkins. The writing is masterly and the performances consistently sympathetic; but, with music with little variation of dynamic or texture, this is not a disc to play all the way through at one go, but to sample appreciatively. Well recorded.

17 Fantasies & 3 Pavans in 5 parts

B—, *** Avie 2120. Phantasm

Phantasm, the outstanding viol consort, here offers the first complete recording of all 20 of Jenkins's works in five parts. These outstanding performances help in offering beautifully tuned instruments, which might otherwise sound edgy. Phantasm bring out the drama of much of the writing, a biting quality which hardly matches the portrait of the composer that has been handed down.

An earlier pioneering collection from the 1980s comes from the **Consort of Musicke**, directed by **Trevor Jones**, including *Fantasias, Fantasy-Suites* and dances, all played with dedication, communicating the music's freshness and lyricism and worth its mid-price. The (originally Oiseau-Lyre) recording is excellent. (Explore EXP 0010)

JENKINS, Karl (born 1944)

'Quirk': Allegretto from Palladio for Strings. (i) Concerto for Flutes, Keyboards & Percussion (Quirk); (ii) Concerto for 2 Harps & Orchestra (Over the Stone); (iii) Concerto for Marimba & Orchestra (La Folia); (iv) Concerto for Violin & Orchestra (Sarikiz)

(N) B—, **** EMI 5 00235-2. (i) Davies, Alley, Percy; (ii) Finch; (iii) Percy; (iv) Bisengalliev; LSO, composer

'Quirk' is the title chosen by the composer for this delightful collection of miniature concertos and which he has also given to the lively *Double Flute Concerto* with its finale entitled 'Chasing the Goose'. Vivaldi is the comparison who springs to mind, for although the Jenkins style is light-hearted, his inspiration and communicative musical skills easily match those of the baroque concerto composer. Moreover, he includes a haunting set of variations on the baroque favourite theme, *La Folia*, but scored for solo marimba, a remarkably apt choice. The other works captivate the ear with equal felicity, the sparkling *Violin Concerto* has a memorably expressive central *Romanza* and the gentle, evocative *Concerto for Two Harps* is so written that both instruments can be played by a single harpist, in this instance the very sensitive **Catrin**

Finch. The programme ends with the catchy *Allegretto ostinato* from *Palladio* (originally the first movement of a concerto grosso) which has since become a top popular hit, difficult to dislodge from the memory. All the performances are enticing, and the recording is excellently balanced.

The Armed Man (A Mass for Peace)

(*) EMI **DVD DVB3 32345-9. John S. Davies Singers, Serendipity, Welsh Nat. Op. O, composer

The special interest of Jenkins's Mass is that it thematically draws on a famous 15th-century Burgundian popular song, *L'Homme armé* (translated as 'The armed man is to be feared'), which had been used as a basis for a Mass by countless medieval composers before him, so establishing a link with a long tradition, instantly recognizable at the opening. The DVD performance, filmed live, is illustrated by back-projections of a daunting series of war images, mostly in black and white, taken from various cinema newsreels and TV broadcasts, giving added point to the composer's music. This is at its most moving in the penultimate triptych, the *Agnus Dei, Now the guns have stopped*, and *Benedictus*, before the optimistic and blander closing *Better is Peace*. The well-recorded performance under the composer is unambitious visually, but otherwise cannot be faulted.

Stabat Mater

B—, **** EMI 5 00283-2. Adamonyte, Sykes, EMO Ens., RLPO Ch. & O, composer

It is obvious that with the *Stabat Mater* Karl Jenkins has another big hit with the public on his hands. The whole work is communicatively tuneful in a way that most music-lovers can respond too. The composer has interpolated six texts not in the *Stabat Mater* liturgy, including a previously composed *Ave verum. Incantation*, the second section, is in early Arabic, with **Belinda Sykes** singing idiomatically. Then the following *Vidit Jesum in tormentis* is a simple and rather lovely chorale, magnetically elaborated. The fourth-movement *Lament* (with a text especially written by Carol Barratt), with another memorable theme, is touchingly sung by **Jurgita Adamonyte**, and the *Sancta Mater* creates an explosive contrast in its choral response to the Crucifixion. *Are you lost out in the darkness?*, the ninth section, is a lament drawing on a story from the *Epic of Gilgamesh*, and the *Paradisi gloria* makes a thrilling close, building with its closing 'Alleluias' to a great climax. The soloists and Liverpool forces respond to the composer's direction passionately, and the recording is excellent.

JOACHIM, Joseph (1831–1907)

Hamlet Overture, Op. 4

*** Simax PSC 1206. Oslo PO, Jansons – BRAHMS: Symphony 1 ***

Though this first of Joachim's two Shakespearean overtures (the second being *Heinrich IV*) cannot compare in quality of material with the Brahms symphony, it makes an apt and enjoyable coupling, when the young Brahms admired it so much that he made a piano transcription. Excellent performance and fine sound.

Heinrich IV Overture, Op. 7

*** Simax PSC 1205. Olso PO, Jansons – BRAHMS: *Symphony 4* ***

Joachim wrote the second of his Shakespearean overtures, based on *Henry IV*, over a prolonged period in 1853 and 1854, reacting to the adverse criticism of Schumann that it was too gloomy. Whether or not through Joachim's revisions, it is certainly not that, with its fanfares and marches a sharper, more inventive piece than the earlier *Hamlet Overture*, making an interesting coupling for the Brahms symphony, similarly well recorded.

JOHANSEN, David Monrad
(1888–1974)

String Quartet, Op. 36

(BB) *** Naxos 8.550879. Oslo String Qt – GRIEG: *String Quartets* ***

David Monrad Johansen's *String Quartet*, composed in 1969 when in his early eighties, is persuasively played by the **Oslo String Quartet** and is impeccably recorded. It is a well-crafted piece but not as distinctively personal as *Pan* or the best of his mature works.

JOHNSON, Robert (c. 1563–1633)

Lute Pieces: Almaynes 1–4; Fantasia; The gipsies dance; My Lady Mildmay's Delight (Gallyard); Pavans 1–3; Songs: (i) As I walked forth; Away delights; Care-charming sleep; Come heavy sleep; Come hither you that love; Hark! hark! the lark; Have you seen the bright lily grow?; How wretched is the state; Oh let us how; Tell me dearest; Where the bee sucks; With endless tears; Woods, rocks and mountains

**(*) Avie 2053. (i) Sampson; Wadsworth, Levy

Robert Johnson, son of John Johnson, lutenist to Queen Elizabeth I, became in his turn lutenist to King James I, also serving under Prince Charles and remaining with him after he became Charles I. Johnson was later to provide songs for Shakespeare's plays, notably *The Tempest*. His writing has a wider range of mood than Dowland's, although he can certainly achieve movingly expressive dolour, as in *Care-charming sleep*, *With endless tears* and *Come heavy sleep*, which are as fine as any of Dowland's songs. The delightful *Have you seen the bright lily grow?*, with its upward leap, is a number that ought to be really famous. **Carolyn Sampson** has a sweet but full voice and sings most pleasingly and stylishly, and she is felicitously accompanied by **Matthew Wadsworth** (and occasionally by Mark Levy's bass viol); the lute solos are also attractively played. The one snag to the recording is the resonance of St Mary's Church, South Crake, Norfolk, which has not been fully controlled by the recording engineer and sometimes catches the voice slightly on louder climaxes.

JONES, Daniel (1912–93)

Symphonies (i) 4 (In Memory of Dylan Thomas); 7; (ii) 8

*** Lyrita (ADD) SRCD 329. (i) RPO, Groves; (ii) BBC Welsh SO, Thomson

There is no doubt, listening to these symphonies, that Daniel Jones is a genuine symphonic thinker, capable of arguing in long, coherently related paragraphs. The *Fourth Symphony*, written in memory of Dylan Thomas, is powerfully atmospheric; and the *Seventh* is strong in feeling and organically conceived. 8, too, is finely crafted and tersely argued. These symphonies are worth hearing and, given such fine playing and recording, they can certainly be recommended.

Symphonies (i) 6; (ii) 9; (i; iii) The Country beyond the Stars (cantata)

*** Lyrita (ADD) SRCD 326. (i) RPO, Groves: (ii) BBC Welsh O, Thomson; (iii) with Welsh Nat. Op. Ch.

The *Sixth Symphony* (1964) is certainly one of his finest, eclectic in style; but the cogency of the argument is matched by his ability to communicate emotional experience. The *Ninth Symphony*, written a decade later, is in normal four-movement form, finely crafted and tersely argued, but its material is not quite so strongly personalized. It is very well played by the **BBC Welsh Orchestra** under **Bryden Thomson** and truthfully recorded. *The Country beyond the Stars* is the earliest work here (1958) and is obviously designed to suit the traditional qualities of Welsh choirs: warm, relaxed writing with bursts of eloquent fervour, but always easy on the ear. The **Welsh National Opera Chorus** do it full justice and the sound, like Groves's performance, is very fine.

String Quartets 1–8

*** Chan. 9535 (2). Delmé Qt

The *First Quartet* is a particularly impressive work, with a certain cosmopolitanism and a distinctly French tinge to its atmosphere. But Jones is always his own man. 2 is exploratory and has a characteristically concentrated *Lento espressivo*. 3–5 are distinguished by seriousness of purpose and fine craftsmanship. The last three quartets are even more succinct (each lasting about a quarter of an hour). 6 marked the 250th birthday of Haydn and uses two of that master's themes. Its mood is strongly focused, moving from a solemn introduction (and back again) via the Haydnesque Scherzo and a simple slow movement. 7 is masterly, intensely concentrated: its central movement is marked *Penseroso*. The last quartet, full of memorable ideas, was left unfinished; it was skilfully completed from the composer's sketches by Giles Easterbrook. Appropriately, it has a hauntingly elegiac close. It is played here with enormous dedication and, like 7, holds the listener in a powerful emotional spell. A fitting conclusion to a splendid series, given definitive readings from a quartet closely identified with the music, and first-class Chandos sound.

JONES, Robert (1570–1615)

Lute Songs

(BB) *** Virgin 2x1 5 624 10-2 (2). Kirkby, Rooley – DOWLAND: *Lute Songs* **(*)

Robert Jones was a younger contemporary of John Dowland of whom we know little, except that he never enjoyed the same acclaim. Yet his songs, if seldom exploring the greater depths of emotion (there is little or no despair in his amorous encounters), have great charm and are often very touching. These songs suit **Emma Kirkby's** voice and her simplicity of style to perfection. She catches their mood admirably and is especially delightful in the more optimistic celebrations of love from the Second Book: *Love wing'd my hopes, Love is a bable*, and *Love's god is a boy*, with its pretty refrain. In short, this recital is most rewarding, and it suggests that Robert Jones was a finer composer than his reputation suggests. **Anthony Rooley** accompanies most supportively, and voice and lute are admirably balanced.

JONGEN, Joseph (1873–1953)

Symphonie Concertante for Organ & Orchestra, Op. 81

*** Telarc CD 80096. Murray, San Francisco SO, de Waart – FRANCK: *Fantaisie*, etc. ***

Anyone who likes the Saint-Saëns *Third Symphony* should enjoy the Jongen *Symphonie Concertante*. Even if the music is on a lower level of inspiration, the passionate *Lento misterioso* and hugely spectacular closing *Toccata* make a favourable impression at first hearing and wear surprisingly well afterwards. **Michael Murray** has all the necessary technique to carry off Jongen's hyperbole with the required panache. He receives excellent support from **Edo de Waart** and the **San Francisco Symphony Orchestra**, and Telarc's engineers capture all the spectacular effects with their usual aplomb. A demonstration disc indeed.

JOSQUIN DESPRÉZ (died 1521)

Chansons; Instrumental pieces (viols or lute): *Adieu mes amours; Fors seulment; Fortuna desperata; Ile fantazies; Mille regretz; La plus des plus; Si j'ay perdu mon amy*

⊗ – **(B)** *** HM Musique d'Abord HMA 1951279. Ens. Clément Janequin

'*Un magnifique condensé de l'art de Josquin*', justly commented *Le Monde* about this disc. The vocal numbers are sung with dolour or vitality as required, and the blending of the two, three, four, five or even six voices is as admirable as the intonation is secure. Lute and viol pieces provide interludes. The programme ends with the sparkling six-voice *Allégez*

moy, followed by the infinitely touching tribute to Ockeghem. A pity there are texts but no translations, but that is the French way. A marvellous disc just the same, and very well recorded.

Missa Ad fugam; Missa Sine nomine

(N) *** Gimell CDVGIM 039. Tallis Scholars, Phillips

It seems likely that the *Missa Ad fugam* is either a very early work or not by Josquin at all, but the *Missa Sine nomine* shows the composer at his very finest, holding the listener in its grip by its sheer intensity through textures of great variety. The **Tallis** performances ensure that the music unfolds with a kind of inevitable spontaneity and they are, as usual, beautifully recorded.

Chansons; Mass Movements; Motets

(M) *** Gaudeamus CDGAU 361. Clerks' Group, Wickham

The very opening *Tu solus qui facis* grabs the attention, and the following five-voice setting of *Salve Regina* is equally beautiful. The three chansons, *Adieu mes amours, Bergerette Savoysienne* and *Baisés moi*, make an apt contrast, and the excerpts from the four Masses included are also well chosen to show the eloquence of the composer's writing. The collection ends with *Ave Maria . . . Virgo serena* which **Edward Wickham** suggests in his accompanying note 'has come to represent the quintessence of Josquin'. The performances could hardly be bettered, and the recording too is of very high quality, so if you want a Josquin sampler, this is ideal.

(i) Messe Ave Maris Stella; Missa de Beata Virgine; Missa Gaudeamus; Missa L'homme armé sexti toni; Missa lLhomme armé super voces musicales; Missa Pange lingua; Motets; Motets à la Vierge; (ii) Missa Hercules dux Ferrariae; Motets: Inviolata, integra, et casta es, Maria; Miserere mei, Deus. Instrumental pieces: Chi à Martello Dio Gu'il Toglia; Deus, in nomine tuo salvum me fac

❀ **(B)** **** Naive Astrée Auvidis E 8906 (6). A sei voci (i) Maîtrise des Pays de Loire (members); (ii) Maîtrise Notre-Dame de Paris, Les Saqueboutiers de Toulouse, Ens. Labyrinthes; all directed Fabre-Garrus

Bernard Fabre-Garrus's pacing and flexibility of line are masterly. Five of the six discs include a major Mass setting, together with a group of motets, of which the Paris recording is the most spectacular. This CD (E 8601) offers the *Mass for Hercules, Duke of Ferrara*, which is supported throughout by a brass group, who play an introduction and postlude (for sackbuts and drums) and include also a specially sung and played tribute to the Duke, plus memorable performances of the *Misere mei, Deus* and an invocation to the Virgin, *Inviolata, integra, et casta es, Maria*.

The disc including the beautiful *Missa de Beata Virgine* (in six parts, richly sung by twelve voices) includes five appropriate linking motets *à la Vierge*, including a fine *Ave Maria* and *Stabat Mater* (E 8560). The *Missa Gaudeamus* (E 8612) with its soaring soprano line also stands out as among Josquin's most beautiful Mass settings, while it is fascinating to hear both versions of *L'homme armé* where Josquin draws on his cantus firmus so subtly that one has to listen very hard to spot it. Altogether a superb set, faithfully recorded in a warm but not clouding acoustic, and well documented, if in very small print.

Motetti de Passione … B (1503): Ave verum corpus; Christem ducem/Qui velatus; Domine, non secundum; O Domine Jesu Christe; Tu solus, qui facis mirabilia; Missa Faisant regretz

🎧📀 ❋ *** Gaudeamus CDGAU 302. Clerks' Group, Wickham (with FRYE: *Tut a par moy* ***)

Josquin's compact but characteristically fluent and appealing four-part Mass setting, *Faisant regretz*, is based on a four-note motif taken from Walter Frye's rondeau for three voices, *Tut a par moy*, which is also included on this CD. This dolorous song must have been very famous in its day and Josquin ingeniously weaves the very striking motto theme (always easy to recognize) into his vocal texture with great imaginative resource – right through to the *Agnus Dei*.

But even more striking in this outstanding collection is the cycle of five motets largely based on the readings in Petrucci, *Motetti de Passione … B* of 1503. They are arrestingly chordal in style, the opening declamatory *Tu solus, qui facis mirabilia*, with its bare harmonies, arrestingly so. The extended *Christem ducem/Qui velatus* (a setting of Passiontide hymns by St Bonaventure) which Wickham rightly places last, is the most movingly expressive of all. Superb performances, given an uncanny presence in an ideal acoustic.

Ave Maria (for 4 voices); Chanson: L'homme armé; Missa l'homme armé super voces musicales; Missa l'homme armé sexti toni; Missa la sol fa re mi; Plainchant: Pange lingua; Missa Pange lingua; Praeter rerum serium

🎧📀 Ⓑ **** Gimell CDGIM 206 (2). Tallis Scholars, Phillips

This two-for-the-price-of-one offer generously combines nearly all the contents of two outstanding Josquin CDs, including two of the most famous Mass settings of the medieval era, both based on a familar chanson, *L'homme armé*, also used by other composers. The recordings of the *Missa Pange lingua* and the ingenious *Missa la sol fa re mi* are also unsurpassed and won a *Gramophone* award in 1987. The motet *Ave Maria* makes a beautiful closing item. The recordings are as outstanding as the perfectly blended flowing lines of the singing.

Motets: Inter natos mulierum; Pater noster/Ave Maria; Planxit autem David; Recordare, virgin mater

*** Hyp. CDA 67183. Binchois Cons., Kirkman (with BAULDEWEYN: *Ave caro Christi cara*; CHAMPION (or JOSQUIN): *De Profundis*; FORESTIER (or JOSQUIN): *Veni sancte spiritus*; CRAEN: *Tota pulchra est*; WILLAERT: *Verbum bonum et suave*)

What the disc amply demonstrates is that, though Josquin's fame and reputation are securely based (a supreme master of the period – witness the lovely *Recordare* for upper voices), there was much superb music being written by less celebrated composers from the early 16th century. Willaert's six-part *Verbum bonum* is wonderfully inventive, and Forestier's *Veni sancte spiritus*, long thought to be by Josquin, is equally powerful. Under **Andrew Kirkman** the Binchois Consort sing with fine, beautifully matched ensemble, and are treated to finely balanced recording.

Antiphons, motets and sequences: Inviolata; Praeter rerum serium; Salve regina; Stabat mater dolorosa; Veni, sancte spiritus; Virgo prudentissima; Virgo salutiferi

*** Mer. (ADD) ECD 84093. New College, Oxford, Ch., Higginbottom

The Meridian anthology collects some of Josquin's most masterly and eloquent motets in performances of predictable excellence by **Edward Higginbottom** and the **Choir of New College, Oxford**. An admirable introduction to Josquin, and an essential acquisition for those who care about this master.

Chanson: Fortuna desperata (probably by BUSNOIS); Missa Fortuna desperata; Adieu mes amours; Bererette savoysienne; Consideres mes incessantes (Fortuna); La plus des plus

*** Gaudeamus CDGAU 220. Clerks' Group, Wickham (with ISAAC: *Bruder Conrat/Fortuna*; SENFL: *Herr durch dein Bluet/Pange lingua/Fortuna*; ANON.: *Fortuna Zibaldone*; GREITER: *Passibus ambiguis/Fortuna valubis errat* ***)

The fascination of the collection from the **Clerks' Group** is the inclusion of not just the chanson on which Josquin's Mass was based, probably by Antoine Busnois (1430–92) but also eight further treatments and rearrangements of a song which in its time was obviously as popular as *L'Homme armé* – including four by Josquin himself. Most striking of all is the anonymous Florentine *Fortuna Zibaldone*, in which one really needs the provided translation, for the four voices sing three different light-hearted texts simultaneously, together with the original chanson, with the whole performance taking just over a minute! As usual, the singing here is admirable in its blending and clarity of line, and the recording quite excellent.

Missa Faisant regretz; Missa di dadi

Ⓜ 🎧 **** Decca O/L 475 9112. Medieval Ens. of London, P. & T. Davies

The two Josquin Masses recorded here are both parody Masses, based on English music of the period. The *Missa di dadi* is among the earliest of Josquin's Masses and takes its cantus firmus from the tenor part of the chanson, *N'aray-je jamais mieulx* by Robert Morton; its companion, the *Missa Faisant regretz*, draws for its cantus firmus on another by Walter Frye. The latter is among the shortest of Josquin's Masses and acquires its name from the fact that its four-part cantus firmus occurs on the words 'Faisant regretz' in the chanson *Tout a par moy*. They are both ingenious works and, more to the point, very beautiful, particularly when sung with such dedication and feeling as they are here. The **Medieval Ensemble of London** sing superbly; they not only blend perfectly but are blessed with perfect intonation.

Missa Hercules dux Ferrariae; Miserere mei Deus. Motets; Chansons: Le Déploration de la mort de Johannes Ockeghem; El grillo; En l'hombre d'ung buissonet au matinet; Je me complains; Je ne me puis tenir d'aimer; Mille regretz; Petite camusette; Scaramella va' alla guerra – Loyset Compère: Scaramella fa la galla; GOMBERT (attrib. JOSQUIN): Motet: Lugabet David Absalon

🅱🅱 *** Virgin 2x1 5 62346-2 (2). Hilliard Ens., Hillier

The **Hilliard Ensemble** find the full measure of Josquin's Mass, *Hercules dux Ferrariae*, probably written just before the composer's appointment to Ferrara in 1505, and featuring a cantus based on the letters of the work's title, paying homage to the composer's future employer, Duke Ercole d'Este. The performance revels in the rich flowing lyricism of the *Kyrie* and *Agnus Dei*, whose second section includes a fascinating three-in-one canon, yet bringing passionate ardour to the climaxes of the *Sanctus* and *Benedictus*.

The motets are sung with dignity and feeling, but the chansons display infinite variety and colour. *Petite camusette* ('Little Snubnose') has a winning charm to set against the deeply touching *Mille regretz*, while the sparkling Italian frottola, *Scaramella va' alla guerra* and the witty portrait of a cricket, *El grillo*, show Josquin in lighter vein. The disc ends movingly with an elegiac tribute to Ockeghem, who succeeded Josquin in Ferrara after only a year, only to perish later in the plague. Expertly balanced and eminently truthful, these discs make an admirable pair (at budget price) to kindle the enthusiasm of the uninitiated. But it is a pity there are no texts and translations.

Missa l'homme armé sexti toni. Motets: Absalom, fili mi; Ave Maria

⊶ ✸ 🅱🅱 *** Naxos 8.553428. Oxford Camerata, Summerly
– VINDERS: *Lament on the Death of Josquin* ***

An interesting feature of the Josquin setting is his interpolation of a trope (*Laeta dies*) following the *Credo* and before the *Sanctus* using a non-liturgical text. The effect is undoubtedly dramatic at the centre of a work where the flowing lines of the polyphony have such a rich harmonic implication. The long *Credo* breaks free, with the polyphony becoming more animated, and so becomes the central focus of the whole Mass – and what a beautiful Mass it is; very beautifully sung and recorded here. The *Ave Maria* is used to create a tranquil mood before the Mass itself begins, and the very touching motet, *Absalom, fili mi*, makes a poignant coda. This is followed by the radiant elegy of Josquin's contemporary, Jheronimus Vinders, with its soaring treble line, surely a fitting tribute. With full texts provided, this CD is one of the very finest of this distinguished Naxos series.

JOUBERT, John (born 1927)

Sinfonietta, Op. 38; Temps perdu (Variations for String Orchestra), Op. 99; (i) The Instant Moment, Op. 110

** British Music Society BMS 419CD. E. String O, Boughton; (i) with Herford

John Joubert was born in Cape Town but settled in Britain during the early years of apartheid. He taught at the Universities of Hull and Birmingham, but his large output has received scant recognition in the record catalogues. All three works are unfailingly inventive and don't waste notes. Those who feel at home in the worlds of Sibelius or Britten will respond to these fine scores. Joubert's is a quiet but distinctive voice. The performance, alas, is no more than adequate: the strings are lacking in body and tonal bloom. Nevertheless, this is recommended, for we are unlikely to have an alternative.

Symphony 1, Op. 20

Ⓜ *** Lyrita SRCD 322. LPO, Handley

Finely crafted and cogently argued, the symphony receives excellent advocacy from **Handley** and the **LPO**, and first-rate recording. It comprises a traditional four-movement structure and is scored for a classical symphony orchestra (with piano) and is largely tonal in nature. All in all, it is a fine symphony, with echoes of the music of Bax, Alwyn, Walton – and, in the finale, even Poulenc. The CD lasts just over half an hour and is offered at mid-price.

(i) Piano Trio; (ii) String Quartet 2; (iii) Piano Sonatas 1, Op. 24; 2, Op. 72; 3, Op. 57; (iv) Lyric Fantasy on themes from 'Jane Eyre'; (v) Landscapes (for soprano & piano trio)

Ⓜ *** Somm Céleste SOMMCD 060 (2). (i; iv; v) Bebbington; (i; v) Chadwick; Anna Joubert; (ii) Brodsky Qt; (iii) McCabe; (v) Rozario

The *Piano Trio* is a most inventive work ending with a fine *Passacaglia*, and **Patricia Rozario** passionately joins the group for *Landscapes*, a group of five poems imaginatively set. (The personnel of the Trio, incidentally, includes the composer's daughter as cellist.) The *Second Quartet*, while being very much Joubert's own creation, quotes ingeniously from both Beethoven and Shostakovich. It is superbly played by the ever reliable **Brodskys**. **John McCabe** proves thoroughly at home in the three *Piano Sonatas* (2 brings another Passacaglia, while 3 is inspired by an anti-war Hardy poem), and the *Lyric Fantasy*, offered as a bonus, is endearingly melodic, played sensitively by **Mark Bebbington**, who also leads the trio. Excellent recording throughout makes this a thoroughly recommendable set to explore.

Choral music: *How are my Foes increased, Lord, Op. 51; 3 Hymns to St Oswald, Op. 74; Nowell, Op. 58; O Praise God in his Holiness, Op. 52; 3 Pro Pace Motets; (i) Sleep Canticle, Op. 18*

**(*) British Music Society (ADD) BMS 012CDH. Louis Halsey Singers, Halsey; Martin Neary (organ), (i) with J. Knibbs, Covey-Crump

John Joubert writes tonally in an individual, somewhat plangent harmonic style, well demonstrated by the music performed here, which includes the *Pro Pace Motets*, three powerful Latin motets, of which *Solus ad Victimam* is the most ambitious, and a trio of hymns, also in Latin, where the harmonic style is plainer. The *Sleep Canticle* effectively uses tenor and soprano soloists to dramatize its theme (described by the composer as 'a meditation on the subject of sleep as a kind of rehearsal for the experience of death'). The **Louis Halsey Singers** perform all this music with fervour and they close with an attractive *Nowell* setting in English, but again with a medieval text. The 1975 recording is good without being outstanding, but the composer's strong personality comes over in every item here.

KABALEVSKY, Dmitri
(1904–87)

Colas Breugnon: Overture & Suite; The Comedians (Suite); Romeo and Juliet (Suite)

*** ASV CDDCA 967. Armenian PO, Tjeknavorian

(BB) *** Naxos 8.553411. Moscow SO, Jelvakov

The suite from *The Comedians*, music for a play called *The Inventor and the Comedian*, is cheap and cheerful, quite attractive and very well laid out for the orchestra – though, as in the score for *Romeo and Juliet* (which derives from 1956), some of its faster movements are tiresomely scatty. Still, there are others which are inventive and atmospheric. **Tjeknavorian's** performances are characterized more sharply than **Jelvakov's** and in *Romeo and Juliet* these fine Armenian players find echoes of Prokofiev. Both *The Comedians* and *Colas Breugnon* are exceptionally vivid, for the ASV recording projects the orchestra in the brightest hues and with a striking presence.

The Comedians (suite), Op. 26

☙ (M) *** RCA (ADD) 09026 63302-2. RCA Victor SO, Kondrashin – KHACHATURIAN: *Masquerade Suite*; RIMSKY-KORSAKOV: *Capriccio espagnol*; TCHAIKOVSKY: *Capriccio italien* *** ⊙

On the RCA collection the *Comedians' Galop* follows on almost immediately after the finale of Khachaturian's *Masquerade*, and the impetuous stylistic link is obvious. **Kondrashin's** performance is affectionate and colourful as well as lively, and the warm resonance of the recording helps to prevent the music from sounding too brash. The Tchaikovsky and Rimsky-Korsakov couplings are marvellous.

(i) Cello Concertos 1 in G min., Op. 49; 2 in C min., Op. 77; Spring (symphonic poem), Op. 65

(BB) **(*) Naxos 8.553788. (i) Rudin; Moscow SO, Golovschin

The enchanting *First Concerto in G minor* was written in 1949 for Kushevitzky, and it wears well. **Alexander Rudin** is a first-rate soloist who yields nothing to the majority of his full-priced rivals. The orchestral playing is decent and acceptable but falls short of distinction. Good recording. The short, slight and charming symphonic poem is not otherwise available.

Cello Concerto 2, Op. 77

☙ (BB) *** Virgin 5 61490-2 (2). Isserlis, LPO, Litton – BLOCH:

Schelomo; ELGAR: *Cello Concerto*; R. STRAUSS: *Don Quixote*; TCHAIKOVSKY: *Rococo Variations*, etc. ***

**(*) BIS CD 719. Lindström, Gothenburg SO, Ashkenazy – KHACHATURIAN: *Cello Concerto* **(*)

Steven Isserlis on Virgin gives a compelling and ardent account of the concerto and the **LPO** play well for **Andrew Litton**. As far as recorded sound is concerned, it is impressive.

Mats Lindström also proves an admirably sensitive soloist in Kabalevsky's *Second Concerto*. The recording is of high quality and well balanced but is a shade over-resonant, although the ear adjusts.

Piano Concertos 1, Op. 9; 2, Op. 23

(BB) *** Naxos 8.557683. Banh, Russian PO, Yablonsky

(i) Piano Concertos 2 in G min., Op. 23; 3 in D, Op. 50; Colas Breugnon: Overture. The Comedians, Op. 26; Suite

*** Chan. 10052. BBC PO, Sinaisky with (i) Stott

It is good to have Kabalevsky's enjoyable *Piano Concertos* at bargain price for those who wish to explore this characterful if uneven composer. The (sub-Rachmaninov) *First Concerto* and (Prokofievian) *Second* have nice dashes of colour and melody, even if neither is a masterpiece. These performances are thoroughly committed and idiomatically Russian.

The *Third*, his 'Youth' Concerto is simple and direct in style, rather like the *Second Piano Concerto* of Shostakovich. **Miss Stott** brings both wit and charm to this slight if often predictable piece – not a work that many people will want to revisit very often – and gives a no less outstanding account of the *Second*. The **BBC Philharmonic** under **Vassily Sinaisky** give admirable support and lively and well-characterized accounts of the popular *Colas Breugnon* and *The Comedians Suite*, and the Chandos/BBC recording is first class.

(i) Piano Concerto 1; The Comedians: Suite; Pathétique Overture; (i) Rhapsody for Piano & Orchestra on the Theme of 'School Years'; Spring

(BB) *** Regis RRC 1287. Russian Cinematographic SO, Mnatsakanov; (i) with Sheludiakov

A bargain introduction to the tuneful charm of Kabalevsky. Beginning with the melodically melodramatic *Pathétique Overture*, the more substantial *First Piano Concerto* follows, offering easy-going invention with an obvious Russian flavour. The symphonic poem *Spring* is attractive enough, while the *Rhapsody for Piano and Orchestra* is wittier and more inventive. *The Comedians* finds the composer at his best: a suite which brims and sparkles with good tunes. Excellent, authentic-sounding performances and decent sound.

(i) Piano Concertos 1; 4 (Prague); Symphony 2

☙ *** Chan. 10384. BBC PO, Sinaisky, (i) with Stott

The *Fourth Concerto*, written for a piano competition in 1979, brings together three miniature movements based on Czech themes – hence its nickname of 'Prague' Concerto. **Kathryn Stott** is the brilliantly persuasive soloist, with **Sinaisky** warm and idiomatic in his conducting of the **BBC Philharmonic**. As to the *Symphony*, it is consistently refreshing in its strongly rhythmic writing and striking themes, a fine work representing Soviet music at its best. Brilliant, vivid sound, typical of this source.

(i) Piano Concerto 3 (Dedicated to Soviet Youth); Rhapsody for Piano & Orchestra on a Theme of the Song 'School Years'; (ii) Poem of Struggle for Orchestra & Chorus

(N) (BB) *** Naxos 8.557794. RPO, Yablonsky, with (i) Liu; (ii) Gnesin Ac. Ch. – RIMSKY-KORSAKOV: *Piano Concerto* ***

The light and cheerful *Third Piano Concerto* receives a sparkling performance here and is very well recorded. The *Rhapsody*, premièred in 1964, is based on a popular song Kabalevsky wrote called *School Years* in 1957. It is unashamedly tuneful and unpretentious, and its simple and catchy tunes are irresistible in this lively performance. The *Poem of Struggle*, written in 1931, is more serious, with the composer intending to portray contemporary modern reality. It is no masterpiece, but the rousing chorus at the end is quite effective.

Violin Concerto in C, Op. 48

𝄞 (M) *** DG 457 064-2. Shaham, Russian Nat. O, Pletnev – GLAZUNOV: *Concerto*; TCHAIKOVSKY: *Souvenir d'un lieu cher*, etc. ***

*** Chan. 8918. Mordkovitch, SNO, Järvi – KHACHATURIAN: *Violin Concerto* ***

Kabalevsky's *Violin Concerto* has never enjoyed the same popularity among players as either of the *Cello Concertos*. However, its effortless invention and Prokofievian charm lend it a genuine appeal. **Gil Shaham's** brilliant account of the piece, in partnership with **Pletnev** should win it many more friends.

    Lydia Mordkovitch also plays with great flair and aplomb and is given first-class recording. This is coupled with an equally fine version of the Khachaturian concerto, which collectors who already have the Glazunov might prefer.

Cello Sonata in B flat, Op. 71

*** Simax PSC 1146. Birkeland, Gimse – MARTINŮ: *Cello Sonata 1; Variations* ***

(M) *** Somm CD 029. Walton, Grimwood – MIASKOVSKY: *Cello Sonata 2*; PROKOFIEV: *Cello Sonata* ***

Øystein Birkeland and **Håvard Gimse** offer a Kabalevsky rarity: his *Sonata in B flat*. It is one of Kabalevsky's better pieces. This version is a first recommendation. Excellent, full-bodied and well-balanced sound, as well as being artistically impeccable. A rewarding issue.

    Jamie Walton and **Daniel Grimwood** are young artists, and Somm deserve credit for giving them their début. Their playing is fresh and in every way unaffected.

Piano Sonatas 1–3; Piano Sonatinas 1–2

(N) (BB) **(*) Naxos 8.570822. Dossin

The *First Sonata in F* is early but has a memorable *Andantino semplice*; the *Second in E flat* is famous for demanding much bravura from its performer, and also again for its delectable *Andante sostenuto*. But we were even more taken with the pair of *Sonatinas*, smaller in scale, but most attractively neo-classical, particularly the *First in C major* which is most winning. **Alexandre Dossin's** performances all rise to the occasion, but the piano *fortissimos* are inclined to sound rather percussive.

KAJANUS, Robert (1856–1933)

Sinfonietta in B flat, Op. 16; Finnish Rhapsody 1 in D min., Op. 5; Kullervo's Funeral March, Op. 3; (i) Aino (Symphonic Poem for male chorus and orchestra)

*** BIS CD 1223. Lahti SO, Vänskä, (i) with Helsinki University Ch.

As a conductor Kajanus was Sibelius's most fervent advocate, interpreting all his major works and directing those premières that the composer himself didn't conduct. It was a performance that Kajanus gave in Berlin of his *Aino Symphony* that inspired Sibelius to compose his *Kullervo Symphony*. Before Sibelius burst on the scene with *Kullervo* and *En Saga*, Kajanus made a considerable name for himself as a composer, but his energies became increasingly consumed by conducting. His music is typical of the national romanticism of the period and, although few would make great claims for its individuality, it is always finely crafted and, in the case of the *Sinfonietta* of 1915, often arresting. **Osmo Vänskä** and the **Lahti orchestra** play it with fervour and conviction, and the BIS team serves them well.

KALLIWODA, Johann (1801–66)

String Quartets 1–3, Opp. 61/2 & 90

𝄞 *** Call. CAL 9357. Talich Qt

Johann Kalliwoda was a Bohemian court musician of considerable talent, and these three *String Quartets* make delightful listening. They are very much post-Haydn, but they brim over with attractive invention, freely distributed between the players, and formally they are impressively cultivated. The performances here are superbly polished, the soul of finesse, yet they are imbued with expressive feeling and vitality. The recording is most realistic, and this engaging disc is highly recommended to anyone who enjoys the string quartets of Haydn.

KÁLMÁN, Emmerich (1882–1953)

Countess Maritza (highlights; in English)

**(*) TER CDTER 1051. Hill-Smith, Remedios, Livingstone, Moyle, Rice, Martin, Barber, Bullock, New Sadler's Wells O, Wordsworth

Set in the Hungarian countryside, *Countess Maritza* gave Kálmán plenty of chances to display his skill in writing memorable numbers with a Hungarian flavour. The plot is slight, but the nostalgic *Luck is a Golden Dream*, sung by **Lynn Barber** as a gypsy girl, sets the scene, followed by the delightful *How Do You Do*, characterfully sung by Count Tassilo, the opera's hero, with children's chorus. But the score's highlight must be the evocative *Vienna Mine*, one of the composer's most catchy melodies, although **Remedios** has not quite the easy smoothness of a Tauber to make it as captivating as it might be. **Marilyn Hill-Smith** as the Countess, singing with her customary style, is charming in the sentimental duet with the Count, *Be Mine, My Love*, as well as in the aria, *Set the Gypsy Music Playing* – another popular hit. The opera ends with a swinging waltz. **Barry Wordsworth** conducts securely and catches the spirit of Kálmán's world with a fair degree of success. The recording, though perhaps not ideally atmospheric, is reasonably full and bright.

Die Csárdásfürstin (The Gypsy Princess)

(BB) *** Naxos 8.660105/6 (2). Kenny, Roider, Erdmann, Kathol, Slovak Philh. Ch., Slovak RSO, Bonynge

Die Csárdásfürstin tells an improbable tale of the mismatch between a showgirl, Sylva, and an aristocrat, Prince Edwin. **Richard Bonynge** conducts a lively, beautifully sprung performance, made the more idiomatic by using an East European orchestra. **Yvonne Kenny** as Sylva gives a characterful, idiomatic performance, well supported by singers very much in the operetta tradition, and by **Michael Roider** as Edwin and **Mojca Erdmann** and **Marko Kathol** as the second couple. Well produced, the numbers are introduced by a sprinkling of dialogue. The first-rate sound brings out the beauty of Kálmán's orchestration.

Die Csárdásfürstin (highlights)

(B) *** EMI (ADD) 5 86875-2. Rothenberger, Brokmeier, Anheisser, Gedda, Miljakovic, Bav. State Op. Ch., Graunke SO, Mattes

Launching straight away into a spectacular opening number, this highly attractive selection from 1915 is full of excellent tunes, with plenty of Hungarian spice; all served up, one after another, in the live (1971) performance. A bargain, even without any texts and translations. Warm yet lively sound.

Der Zigeunerprimas (complete)

** CPO 777 058-2 (2). Lienbacher, Rossmanith, Todorovich, Saccà, Stiefermann, Slovak R. Ch., Bav. State Op. Children's Ch., Munich R. O, Flor

The composer's trademark Hungarian writing is given full rein in this operetta, a sort of Hungarian *Die Meistersinger*, of which Hungarian gypsy music is very much part of the work's essence. Kálmán supplied his operettas with attractive waltzes and other dances, but he is really seductive in such numbers as Pali Rácz's Lied, *Auf dem dolg'nem* . . . where the theme is hummed over shimmering strings and a harp. None of the singers is outstanding; one or two (such as the bass) are rather wobbly, but most are acceptable. **Flor** conducts warmly and sympathetically, with plenty of energy in the lively numbers which, like the Act II duet, *Ich schau hin*, go with a real swing; yet he is beautifully relaxed in the lyrical central section. The sound is warm and atmospheric. The main drawback is that there is no libretto, and the track analysis is not exactly crystal clear. The notes are plentiful, but heavy-going.

KARLOWICZ, Mieczyslaw
(1876–1909)

Symphonic Poems: Episode at a Masquerade, Op. 14; Lithuanian Rhapsody, Op. 11; Stanislav and Anna Oswiecimowie, Op. 12

(N) (BB) *** Naxos 8.570452. Warsaw PO, Wit

Symphonic Poems: Eternal Songs, Op. 10; Returning Waves, Op. 9; A Sorrowful Tale (Preludes to Eternity), Op. 13

(N) (BB) *** Naxos 8.570295. New Zealand SO, Wit

Born some months after Ravel, Karlowicz's life was cut short in his early thirties when he was engulfed in an avalanche in the Tatra mountains. He is a composer of some substance who bridges the gap between Moniuszko and Szymanowski. At times there is a Straussian opulence (Karlowicz writes well for the orchestra) and, given the modest price, readers with an adventurous taste and a liking for post-romanticism might well want to investigate the six symphonic poems here, written between 1904 and 1909. They are colourfully scored and their melodic inspiration varies between brooding melancholy, delicate evocation, and more positive life affirmation: the climax of *Song of Love and Death* generates real excitement. Indeed, **Antoni Wit** gets playing of considerable ardour from both the **Warsaw Philharmonic** and the **New Zealand Symphony Orchestra**, and detail is persuasively warm and polished. The recording is excellent. Well worth trying.

Violin Concerto in A, Op. 8

(N) *** EMI 3 79034-2. Kennedy, Polish CO, Kaspszyk (with CHOPIN: *Nocturnes, Op. 9/1 & 2*) – MŁYNSARSKI: *Violin Concerto 2* ***

Good to see that, instead of another Bruch or Mendelssohn, **Nigel Kennedy** has chosen to champion the Karlowicz Concerto along with the *Second Concerto* of his contemporary, Emil Młynsarski (1870–1935). Those willing to explore music off the beaten track will find their enterprise well rewarded; both composers have their own voice. A pity about the gaudy front cover, but that is of no real moment.

KELLY, Bryan (born 1934)

(i) Crucifixion; Missa brevis; Magnificat from the Emanuel Evening Service; Like as the Hart; O Clap your Hands; Praise his Name in the Dance; The Lovely Lady

*** Priory PRCD 755. (i) Manahan Thomas, Mulroy; Clare College, Cambridge, Ch., Brown, Reid (organ)

It is good to have a *Crucifixion* setting so powerful and immediate in its appeal, completely removed from the

Victorian heritage of Stainer, while still featuring simple sung chorales. The bold contrasts between soprano and tenor soloists are a strong feature of a work which intersperses biblical texts with poems by George Herbert, the librettist, Anne Ridler and W. H. Auden's 'Shield of Achilles', and the touching solo dialogue, *A Ragged Urchin*, makes a poignant interlude after Jesus' final cry of despair to God.

Kelly's *Missa brevis* is equally compelling, with the chorus later joyfully moving into waltz tempo without a suggestion of triviality. The exuberant *Magnificat* is trumped in rhythmic energy by *Praise His Name in the Dance*, and while *O Clap your Hands* is more tranquil, the use of a 5/8 time signature gives the melodic lines a subtle lift. Neither the lovely medieval carol setting, *The Lovely Lady Sat and Sang*, nor the passionate closing, *Like as the Hart*, is in the least predictable, but both show the composer at his imaginative best. The **Clare College Choir** under their current conductor, **Timothy Brown**, are naturally at home in this moving, highly communicative music, while the organist **John Reid's** contribution is in every way admirable. They are excellently recorded.

KERLL, Johann Kasper (1627–93)

Complete Free Organ Works

Ⓜ *** Oehms OC 362. Kelemen (Ededacher organ, Schlägl Abbey)

Joseph Kelemen has here collected Kerll's complete solo works suitable for the organ, including seven *Toccatas*, which are clearly influenced by Froberger, and six spirited *Canzonas*. But to cap the programme there is a fine *Ciaccona*, a spectacular *Battaglia* (which Kelemen makes the very most of), and he ends with a very impressive *Passacaglia*, which shows how resourceful Kerll could be. In short, this music is highly inventive, and most enjoyable when played with such lively spontaneity. Kelemen's documentation is extensive, discussing the composer, the organ and traditional performance practice. An off-the-beaten-path disc, well worth exploring.

KERN, Jerome (1885–1945)

Show Boat (complete recording of original score)

⊕– ✿ *** EMI 3 61543-2 [3 61554-2] (3). von Stade, Hadley, Hubbard, O'Hara, Garrison, Burns, Stratas, Amb. Ch., L. Sinf., McGlinn

In faithfully following the original score, this superb set at last does justice to a musical of the 1920s which is both a landmark in the history of Broadway and musically a work of strength and imagination hardly less significant than Gershwin's *Porgy and Bess* of a decade later. The original, extended versions of important scenes are included, as well as various numbers written for later productions. As the heroine, Magnolia, **Frederica von Stade** gives a meltingly beautiful performance, totally in style, bringing out the beauty and imagination of Kern's melodies, regularly heightened by wide intervals to make those of most of his

Broadway rivals seem flat. The **London Sinfonietta** play with tremendous zest and feeling for the idiom; the **Ambrosian Chorus** sings with joyful brightness and some impeccable American accents. Opposite von Stade, **Jerry Hadley** makes a winning Ravenal, and **Teresa Stratas** is charming as Julie, giving a heartfelt performance of the haunting number, *Bill* (words by P. G. Wodehouse). Above all, the magnificent black bass, **Bruce Hubbard**, sings *Ol' man river* and its many reprises with a firm resonance to have you recalling the wonderful example of Paul Robeson, but for once without hankering after the past. Beautifully recorded to bring out the piece's dramatic as well as its musical qualities, this is a heart-warming issue.

(i) Show Boat (highlights); (ii–v) Music in the Air (excerpts); (ii, v; vi) Roberta (excerpts)

⊕– Ⓑ *** CfP (ADD) 3 35980-2. (i) Watters, McKay, Bassey, Te Wiata, Bryan, Webb, Rita Williams Singers, O, Collins; (ii) Cole, Fitzgibbon; (iii) Grimaldi; (iv) Linden Singers; (v) New World Show O; (vi) Bronhill, Scott, O, Ornadel

These highlights from 1959 were reviewed in the first *Stereo Record Guide* in 1960. That review itself is a period piece now, with the text referring to the artists as belonging to 'the current hit parade'. There is also advice to 'sample **Miss Shirley Bassey** and **Don McKay** before purchasing the record'. Indeed, their singing style sounds more of the late 1950s than of the 1920s, but it is still very enjoyable. All the cast have music-theatre voices, and all are obviously enjoying themselves. **Inia Te Wiata** is outstanding in *Ol' man river*: he does not over-sentimentalize it, as many others do. Other highlights include the memorable **Dora Bryan** – always an entertaining actress – as Ellie, singing *Life upon the wicked stage*.

The excerpts from the other two musicals are very attractive too. *Music in the Air* remains one of Kern's finest lesser-known scores, with the songs worked skilfully into the plot. *I've told every little star* is one of its more famous numbers, but the four others, including *When the spring is in the air* (difficult to get out of your head) and *I'm alone*, make one long to hear the rest of the show. It is very well performed and recorded (1961). Hardly less appealing is the music to *Roberta*, dating from 1933 (filmed in 1935 and 1952) and similarly containing some vintage hits: *Smoke gets in your eyes* and *Yesterdays* (both sung gorgeously by **June Bronhill**, though the latter was recorded a couple of years earlier). Excellent sound from 1961.

KETÈLBEY, Albert (1875–1959)

'Appy 'Ampstead; Bells across the Meadows; In a Chinese Temple Garden; In a Monastery Garden; In a Persian Market; In the Mystic Land of Egypt; The Phantom Melody; Sanctuary of the Heart; Wedgwood Blue

Ⓜ *** Decca (ADD) 444 786-2. RPO & Ch., Rogers (with *Concert of Gypsy Violin Encores*: Sakonov, L. Festival O. ***)

Eric Rogers and his orchestra present the more famous pieces with both warmth and a natural feeling for their flamboyant style, and the tunes throughout come tumbling out, vulgar but irresistible when played so committedly.

Bells Across the Meadow; Chal Romano (Gypsy Lad); The Clock and the Dresden Figures; In a Chinese Temple Garden; In a Monastery Garden; In a Persian Market; In the Moonlight; In the Mystic Land of Egypt; Sanctuary of the Heart

⊕↻ Ⓑ *** CfP (ADD) 3 52399-2. Midgley, Temperley, Pearson (piano), Amb. S., Philh. O, Lanchbery (with LUIGINI: *Ballet Egyptien ***)

A splendid collection in every way. **John Lanchbery** uses every possible resource to ensure that, when the composer demands spectacle, he gets it. In the *Monastery Garden* the distant monks are realistically distant, in *Sanctuary of the Heart* there is no mistaking that the heart is worn firmly on the sleeve. The recording is excellent, full and brilliant. Luigini's *Ballet Egyptien* is equally successful.

KHACHATURIAN, Aram
(1903–78)

The Battle of Stalingrad (film score: Suite); Dance Suite, excerpts: Caucasian Dance; Uzbek Dance; Masquerade Suite; The Valencian Window (Incidental Music): Suite

ⒷⒷ ** Regis Alto ALC 1019. Armenian PO, Tjeknavorian

The Battle of Stalingrad (a film score for which its composer won a Stalin Prize) is very much Soviet popular music, although it draws on a folk tune, 'There's a Crag on the Volga'. It is suitably illustrative and it has a lively march, *Forward into Victory* which, although presented with conviction, is hardly distinguished. The *Masquerade Suite* is played with vigour and has plenty of local colour, but the highlight of this reissue is the early suite from the incidental music to the Spanish comedy, *The Valencian Widow* (1940), which is probably the composer's first major score. It is brimming over with striking tunes: this is the Khachaturian of *Gayaneh*. **Tjeknavorian** and his orchestra play all this music with great spirit and they relish its Armenian flavours.

Cello Concerto in E min.

(*) BIS CD 719. Lindström, Gothenburg SO, Ashkenazy (with RACHMANINOV: *Vocalise *) – KABALEVSKY: *Cello Concerto **(*)

Khachaturian's *Cello Concerto* of 1946 has some sinuous Armenian local colour for its lyrical ideas, but none of the thematic memorability of the concertos for violin and piano and the *Gayaneh Ballet* score, on which Khachaturian's reputation must continue to rest. The combined concentration of **Lindström** and **Ashkenazy** prevents the writing from sounding too inflated. The recording is a bit over-resonant, but otherwise faithful and well balanced.

Cello Concerto in E min.; Concerto-Rhapsody for Cello & Orchestra in D min.

ⒷⒷ **(*) Regis (ADD) RRC 1094. Tarasova, Russian SO, Dudarova

Marina Tarasova plays both works with great eloquence and expressive vehemence; she has a big tone and impeccable technique. The orchestral playing is gutsy and sturdy without, perhaps, the finesse that might have toned down some of the garishness of the orchestral colours. The recording is bright and breezy – not worth a three-star grading and nor is the orchestral contribution, though Tarasova certainly is.

Piano Concerto in D flat

⊕↻ *** Warner 2564 63074-2. Berezovsky, Ural PO, Liss – TCHAIKOVSKY: *Piano Concerto 1 ***

ⒷⒷ (***) Naxos mono 8.110673. Kapell, Boston SO, Koussevitzky – PROKOFIEV: *Piano Concerto 3* (***); SHOSTAKOVICH: *3 Preludes; Piano Concerto 3* (***)

(i) Piano Concerto in D flat; Dance Suite; Polka & Waltz (both for wind band)

*** ASV CDDCA 964. (i) Servierian-Kuhn; Armenian PO, Tjeknavorian

(i) Piano Concerto in D flat; Gayaneh (ballet) Suite; Masquerade: Suite

**(*) Chan. 8542. (i) Orbelian; SNO, Järvi

Berezovsky's is the most electrifying account of the Khachaturian *Piano Concerto* on disc. For once, not only does the opening movement not sag, it moves forward irresistibly, and Berezovsky and **Liss** can even relax in the lyrical central section without letting the tension subside, for the orchestral playing brings out all the sinuous, Armenian colour in the scoring. The slow movement opens and closes with a creepy bass clarinet and moves towards its passionate climax with a real romantic sweep. The finale sets off thrillingly at a furious pace, and once again the performers can relax in the central cadenza-interlude before Berezovsky is dazzling us again with his digital brilliance, and the reprise of the first movement's opening theme is unashamedly raucous. The recording is first class, too.

The **Kapell** performance is quite electrifying and inspiriting, although **Koussevitzky's** presence at the helm also has something to do with it. The same must also be said for the Prokofiev. The Naxos transfer gives us the Prokofiev, which is equally remarkable.

The Armenian partnership of **Dora Servierian-Kuhn** and **Loris Tjeknavorian** provides another recommendation for a modern version of Khachaturian's somewhat uneven *Piano Concerto*. The other pieces on the ASV disc are very slight but lively enough; easily the most memorable item is the second *Uzbek Dance* in the *Dance Suite*, quite extended and touchingly atmospheric.

The Chandos recording is splendid technically, well up to the standards of the house. **Constantin Orbelian**, an Armenian by birth, plays brilliantly, and **Järvi** achieves much attractive lyrical detail. The couplings, sumptuously played, are both generous and appealing.

Violin Concerto in D min.

⊕✿ Ⓜ **** RCA [ADD] 09026 63708-2. Kogan, Boston SO, Monteux – PROKOFIEV: *Alexander Nevsky ****✿

⊟➡ ******** Pentatone **SACD** PTC 5186 059. Fischer, Russian Nat. O, Kreizberg – GLAZUNOV: *Violin Concerto* ********; PROKOFIEV: *Violin Concerto 1* ********

⊟➡ Ⓜ (***) EMI mono 3 61570-2. D. Oistrakh, Philh. O, composer – TANEYEV: *Suite de Concert* ***

*** HM Naïve V 4959. Sergey Khachaturian, Sinfonia Varsovia, Krivine – SIBELIUS: *Violin Concerto* ***

*** Chan. 8918. Mordkovitch, SNO, Järvi – KABALEVSKY: *Violin Concerto* ***

Leonid Kogan's powerfully direct approach to this once-popular concerto, aided by superlative playing from the **Boston Symphony Orchestra** under **Monteux**, is electrifying. Together, they make it sound like an unqualified masterpiece, and the astonishingly vivid (1958) recording puts many digital recordings to shame with its vivid presence. This is the most exciting performance of Khachaturian's underrated concerto that you can buy.

Julia Fischer offers the first Surround Sound SACD of this attractive concerto, made in May 2004 in Moscow – and very impressive it is in its vividness and presence and in the clarity of the orchestral sound. The clarity and freshness of her performance are what immediately strike home in the chattering figuration at the start, with a rare tenderness developing in the lyrical second subject. The yearning tenderness of the slow movement confirms that this was one of the composer's most inspired works in a performance of high contrasts, while the biting clarity of Fischer's performance in the finale brings lightness and sparkle.

Khachaturian wrote his *Violin Concerto* (perhaps his finest work) for **David Oistrakh**, and here the composer provides a brilliant and warmly sympathetic backing for the great violinist's masterly and, indeed, definitive performance, with the central *Andante* ravishingly phrased and the finale sparkling with effortless brilliance. It is very sad that orchestral tuttis are often fierce. Truly a great recording spectacular, and the coupling too is uniquely valuable.

The young **Sergey Khachaturian** has found an ideal partner in **Emmanuel Krivine**, who brings out all the colourfully imaginative orchestral detail to match the soloist's commanding lyrical flow, especially in the unforgettable, sinuous main theme of the first movement. Splendid recording, spacious, open and wide-ranging.

Among other recent performances of this attractively inventive concerto, **Lydia Mordkovitch** is probably the most competitive. She plays with real abandon and fire, and Chandos balance her and the orchestra in a thoroughly realistic perspective.

(i) *Gayaneh* (ballet; original, 1942 score), Op. 50; (ii) *Masquerade* (Suite); *Spartacus* (excerpts); *Russian Fantasy*

⊟➡ Ⓑ *** RCA 82876 65836-2 (2). (i) Nat. PO; (ii) LSO, Tjeknavorian

Khachaturian began his score for *Gayaneh* in 1939 but later revised it during the period which also produced the *Violin Concerto*. It was completed in 1942 and is among his finest works. It is admirably played here under a conductor (himself an Armenian, like the composer) who has a natural feel-ing for Khachaturian's music. So we must be grateful that this well-balanced recording of the original is now available again, coupled to naturally sympathetic performances of the *Masquerade Suite* and excerpts from *Spartacus* (with the great *Adagio* splendidly expansive and passionate), recorded a decade later. The *Russian Fantasy* is not memorable, but the set as a whole is indispensable.

Gayaneh (ballet; excerpts); Spartacus (ballet; excerpts)

⊟➡ Ⓜ *** Decca (ADD) 460 315-2. VPO, composer – GLAZUNOV: *The Seasons* **(*)

Gayaneh (ballet): Suite; Masquerade: Suite; Spartacus (ballet): Suite

(*) ASV (ADD) CDDCA 773. Armenian PO, Tjeknavorian – IPPOLITOV-IVANOV: *Caucasian Sketches* *

Gayaneh (ballet): Suite; Masquerade: Waltz & Mazurka; Spartacus (ballet): Suite

⊟➡ ⒷⒷ *** Warner Apex 8573 89237-2. Bolshoi SO, Lazarev

Gayaneh (ballet; highlights); Spartacus (ballet; highlights)

Ⓑ *** CfP (ADD) 3 93229-2. LSO, composer (with GLAZUNOV: *The Seasons: Autumn*: Philh. O, Svetlanov ***)

Khachaturian came to Vienna in 1962 to record these inspired performances of the most popular numbers from his two ballets, and this Decca record (reissued in Decca's 'Legends' series) is the one to go for. It is superbly remastered to restore and even improve on the demonstration quality of the original LP, recorded in the Sofiensaal. Like the sound, the performances are very fresh.

The composer's later, EMI Classics for Pleasure selections from his two famous ballets offer one more item from *Gayaneh* than on his earlier, Decca coupling. The EMI sound, more modern than the Decca, is a shade reverberant for the more vigorous numbers. The **LSO** play excitingly throughout. The inclusion of only *Autumn* from Glazunov's *Seasons* decreases the appeal of this CD, when the competing Decca disc offers the whole ballet.

At the opening of **Alexander Lazarev's Bolshoi** CD, the famous *Sabre Dance* bursts into the room spectacularly, with thumping drums and blazing percussion, and the *Lezginka* is similarly vibrant and exciting. Yet *Ayshe's awakening* could not be more evocative with its growling bass clarinet. The two best-known *Masquerade* items are brightly done, but with plenty of dynamic shading to counter the ebullience. Then Lazarev opens his *Spartacus* selection with the famous *Adagio*, and the gentle oboe solo and languorous Bolshoi strings soon expand passionately. In short, with extremely spectacular, if reverberant, recording, this super-bargain reissue makes an easy first choice for those wanting a modern digital selection of this music.

The **Armenians** also clearly relish the explosive energy of this music. The *Masquerade Suite* relies rather more on charm for its appeal, but **Tjeknavorian** and his players bring a determined gusto, even to the *Waltz* and certainly to the ebullient closing *Galop*.

Masquerade Suite

8—**Ⓜ** *** RCA (ADD) 09026 63302-2. RCA Victor SO, Kondrashin – KABALEVSKY: *The Comedians Suite*; RIMSKY-KORSAKOV: *Capriccio espagnol*; TCHAIKOVSKY: *Capriccio italien* 🏵 ***

Kondrashin certainly knows how to play this music, with warmth as well as sparkle, and even a touch of romantic elegance when **Oscar Shumsky** plays the violin solo in the *Nocturne*. Yet the final *Galop* is as boisterous as one could wish. The resonant recording gives the orchestra a pleasing ambience.

Spartacus (ballet; complete. Choreography: Yuri Grigorovich)

(***) Arthaus **DVD** 101 115. Mukhamedov, Verrov, Semenyaka, Belova, Bolshoi Ballet & Theatre O, Zhuraitis (V/D: Shuji Fujii)

Khachaturian's ballet *Spartacus* has had a very chequered history. After four years in gestation, the huge score was ready in 1954. But it was never to be performed in its original form.

Finally, in 1968 Yuri Grigorovich started afresh. He centred the narrative on the conflict between the two main characters and their lovers. The action is framed by the military scenes, with Act I opening spectacularly, Crassus and his legions filling the huge Bolshoi stage with their visceral prowess, and the choreography full of stabbing swords and goose-stepping to show they are fascists.

Alas, one wants to laugh for the wrong reasons. It is all rather crass, and one soon realizes that this is the Soviet equivalent of a second-rate Hollywood epic movie. Khachaturian's music, with its continuous sequential climaxes which almost never produce a distinctive melody, is no better than a low-grade film score, with the orchestration carrying the main interest. The dancing of the principals, however, is very impressive and their stamina extraordinary, when the choreography is so continuously athletic. Spartacus's continuous leaps are amazing, and Aegina and Phrygia's solos are as graceful as the (often curiously awkward) movements they are given to dance will allow. We get just a hint of the score's single really inspired number in Phrygia's *Monologue*, but for the ravishing full *Adagio* sequence we have to wait until Act II, and it is worth waiting for.

Spartacus (ballet): Suites 1–3

*** Chan. 8927. RSNO, Järvi

The ripe lushness of Khachaturian's scoring in *Spartacus* narrowly skirts vulgarity. **Järvi** and the **RSNO** clearly enjoy the music's primitive vigour, while the warmly resonant acoustics of Glasgow's Henry Wood Hall bring properly sumptuous orchestral textures, smoothing over the moments of crudeness without losing the Armenian colouristic vividness.

Symphonies 1 in E min.; 3 in C (Symphonic Poem)

*** ASV CDDCA 858. Armenian PO, Tjeknavorian

The *First Symphony* was Khachaturian's exercise on graduating from Miaskovsky's class in 1934. It is far from negligible and in some ways is superior to some of his later work – certainly to the bombastic *Third*. Now there is a modern account which enjoys the advantage of good digital recording. The **Armenian Orchestra** play well for Tjeknavorian, and his is a safe recommendation.

Symphony 2 (original version); Gayaneh: Suite (excerpts)

*** Chan. 8945. RSNO, Järvi

Neeme Järvi and his Scottish forces give a very fine account of themselves and they enjoy the benefit of a superb recording. It runs to some 51 minutes.

(i) Symphony 3 (Symphonic Poem); Triumphal Poem

*** Chan. 9321. BBC PO, Glushchenko, (i) with Lindley – IPPOLITOV-IVANOV: *Caucasian Sketches* ***

If the *Third Symphony* was as strong on musical substance as it is on decibels, it would be something to reckon with. But, alas, it is garish and empty; there are no fewer than 18 trumpets in all! Analgesics and earplugs will be in brisk demand in its vicinity. The **BBC Philharmonic**, spurred on by their Russian conductor, play as if they believe in it, and the Chandos recording is in the demonstration category. The three stars are for the performance and the recording – not for the music!

PIANO MUSIC

10 Children's Pieces; 2 Pieces; Poem; Sonata; Sonatina; Toccata; Waltz (from Masquerade)

ⒷⒷ **(*) Regis RR 1184. McLachlan

Apart from the *Toccata* (1932), which is a frequent encore, Khachaturian's piano music rarely features in piano recitals. At 80 minutes, this CD offers all of it with the exception of the *Scenes from Childhood* and the *Recitative and Fugues*. The early pieces, *Poem* (1927) and the *Valse-caprice* and *Dance* (1926), are much like the *Toccata*, pretty empty, but the later pieces including the *Sonatina* (1959), the *Ten Children's Pieces* (1964) and the *Sonata* (1961) are worth a hearing, even though they are limited in range and rely on a small vocabulary of musical devices. **Murray McLachlan** is a persuasive guide. His recording, made at All Saints' Church, Petersham, is eminently serviceable, though there are times when the attentions of a tuner would not have come amiss (particularly in the garrulous first movement of the *Sonata*).

KLAMI, Uuno (1900–61)

Kalevala Suite, Op. 23; Karelian Rhapsody, Op. 15; Sea Pictures

Ⓑ **(*) Chan. 10427X. Iceland SO, Sakari

The *Kalevala Suite* is Klami's best-known work but, like the other two pieces on this disc, it is highly derivative. Ravel and Schmitt mingle with Falla, Sibelius and early Stravinsky; while there are some imaginative and inspired passages (such as the opening of the *Terheniemi* or Scherzo), there is some pretty empty stuff as well. The performances under **Petri Sakari** are very good indeed, and the recording has a good perspective and a wide dynamic range. The reissue is well worth its bargain price.

Lemminkäinen's Island Adventures; (i) Song of Lake Kuujärvi; Whirls: Suites 1 & 2

*** BIS CD 656. (i) Ruuttunen; Lahti SO, Vänskä

Klami was a master of orchestral colour. *Lemminkäinen's Island Adventures* dates from 1934 and is more Sibelian than is usual with this composer, but its musical substance does not really sustain its length. There is quite a lot of Prokofiev and Shostakovich in the ballet, *Whirls*, and in *Song of Lake Kuujärvi*, and greater depth in the orchestral song. The performances are good and **Esa Ruuttunen** is an excellent baritone; and the recording offers wide dynamic range and natural perspective.

KODÁLY, Zoltán (1882–1967)

Concerto for Orchestra

*** Australian Decca Eloquence (ADD) 467 602-2. Philh. Hungarica, Dorati – JANÁČEK: *Taras Bulba*; BARTÓK: *Concerto for Orchestra* ***

Concerto for Orchestra; Dances of Marosszék; Symphony in C; Theatre Overture

🎧 *** Chan. 9811. BBC PO, Y. P. Tortelier

Concerto for Orchestra; Dances of Galánta; Dances of Marosszék; Háry János: Suite; Symphony in C; Summer Evening; Theatre Overture; Variations on a Hungarian Folksong (The Peacock)

(B) *** Double Decca (ADD) 443 006-2 (2). Philh. Hungarica, Dorati

Yan Pascal Tortelier and the **BBC Philharmonic** prove a superb partnership here, while the Chandos and BBC engineering team have surpassed themselves to produce demonstration quality. Kodály's *Concerto for Orchestra* was written for the Chicago orchestra and Bartók actually took it with him to America in 1940. This, the *Dances of Marosszék* and the *Theatre Overture* leave no doubt that Kodály was a past-master of the orchestra.

The *Symphony* comes from the composer's last years and lacks real concentration and cohesion. Even so, in **Dorati's** hands the passionate *Andante* is strong in gypsy feeling and the jolly, folk-dance finale, if repetitive, is colourful and full of vitality. *Summer Evening*, too, is warmly evocative, but in the *Theatre Overture*, brightly and effectively scored, the invention is thin. The 1973 sound remains of vintage quality, and the CD transfers are first rate.

Dorati's warmly committed performance of Kodály's *Concerto for Orchestra* in fine analogue sound is also available in Australia with the more obvious coupling of Bartók's *Concerto*, while Janáček's *Taras Bulba* is equally worth having.

Dances of Galánta

*** Linn CKD 234. Scottish CO, Mackerras – BARTÓK: *Divertimento; Music for Strings, Percussion & Celesta* ***

On Linn, the *Dances from Galánta* make a valuable supplement for **Sir Charles Mackerras's** warm, refined readings of the two great Bartók works. In this genial work he brings out the dance element delectably, and the recording brings out the colourfulness of Kodály's orchestration.

Dances of Galánta; Dances of Marosszék; Háry János Suite; (i) Psalmus hungaricus, Op. 13

(M) *** DG mono/stereo 457 745-2. Berlin R.I.A.S., Fricsay, (i) with Ernst Haefliger, St Hedwig's Cathedral Ch.

Dances of Galánta; Dances of Marosszék; (i) Háry János Suite, Instrumental Excerpts & Singspiel; Gergély-Járás; (ii) Táncnóa; Túrót eszik a cigány

🎧 **** Ph. 462 824-2. Budapest Festival O, Ivan Fischer; with (i) Children's Ch. Magnificat, Budapest; (ii) Children's Ch. Miraculum, Kecskemét

(i) Dances of Galánta; (ii) Dances of Marosszék; Háry János Suite; (i) Variations on a Hungarian Folksong (The Peacock)

**(*) BIS CD 875. (i) Brno State PO; (ii) SWF SO, Baden-Baden; Serebrier

Dances of Galánta; Háry János Suite; Variations on a Hungarian Folksong (The Peacock)

(M) **** Nim. NI 7081. Hungarian State SO, A. Fischer

Iván Fischer's Kodály is no less successful than his Bartók records. His set has the advantage of totally idiomatic playing from a very fine orchestra and superbly well-defined recording from the Philips engineers. This Budapest collection is now the front-runner in the Kodály discography and the point from which lovers of this genial composer should set out. The extra items are very enticing.

The Nimbus CD also has the advantage of totally idiomatic playing. The detail in *Háry János* is a delight, not least the sensitive cello playing in the central song, while the cimbalom is perfectly balanced. The *Galánta Dances* rise to a thrilling *vivace* close, and the *Peacock Variations*, too, are full of colour and vitality. An excellent alternative collection, with demonstration sound in a warmly resonant but unclouded acoustic.

José Serebrier gets very good playing from the **Brno Orchestra** in both the *Dances of Galánta* and the *Peacock Variations*, and the remaining two works with the **Südwestfunk Orchestra** in Baden-Baden are, if anything, even better and the recording warmer. There is plenty of character in the orchestral playing of both ensembles, and the BIS recordings are up to house standard.

Fricsay's performances are crisp and exciting, the orchestra superbly on its toes, a notable passage being the beautifully managed horn solo in the central trio of the intermezzo in *Háry János*. The mono recording was demonstration-worthy in its day and is still pretty remarkable.

Háry János Suite

(BB) *** Naxos 8.550142. Hungarian State O, Mátyás Antal
(with Concert: 'Hungarian Festival' ***)

The Naxos Hungarian performance of the *Háry János Suite* is also wonderfully vivid, with the cimbalom – here perfectly balanced within the orchestra – particularly telling. The brilliant digital sound adds to the vitality and projection of the music-making, yet the lyrical music is played most tenderly.

(i) *Hungarian Rondo. Summer Evening; Symphony*

**(*) ASV CDDCA 924. (i) Warren-Green; Philh. O, Butt

The *Summer Evening* is a beautiful piece, eminently well served by **Yondani Butt**. It comes with a well-characterized account of the *Symphony*, not more impressive than Dorati's version but, of course, a more up-to-date recording. Very good indeed, albeit not quite three-star.

(Unaccompanied) *Cello Sonata, Op. 8*; (i) *Cello Sonata* (for cello and piano), *Op. 4*

🎧 *** Sup. SU 3515-2. Barta, (i) with Cech – NOVAK: *Cello Sonata* ***

(Unaccompanied) *Cello Sonata, Op. 8*; *Cello Sonata, Op. 4; Adagio* (both for cello and piano)

(B) *** EMI Debut 5 75685-2. Yang, Moon

(Unaccompanied) *Cello Sonata, Op. 8*; (i) *Cello Sonata* (for cello & piano), *Op. 4; 3 Chorale Preludes* (arr. from Bach, BWV 743, 747 & 762)

(BB) *** Naxos 8.553160. Kliegel, (i) with Jandó

(Unaccompanied) *Cello Sonata, Op. 8*; (i) *Duo for Violin & Cello, Op. 7*

🎧 **** Delos D/CD 1015. Starker, (i) with Gingold

When, not long before the composer's death, Kodály heard **Starker** playing this *Cello Sonata*, he apparently said: 'If you correct the ritard in the third movement, it will be the Bible performance.' The recording is made in a smaller studio than is perhaps ideal; the *Duo*, impressively played by **Starker** and **Josef Gingold**, is made in a slightly more open acoustic. There is a small makeweight in the form of Starker's own arrangement of the Bottermund *Paganini Variations*.

Kodály's *Solo Cello Sonata* also receives a performance of exceptional power, precision and clarity from the Czech cellist **Jiří Barta**. Deeply reflective, the intensity of his performance never flags, with a rare depth of concentration in the darkly intense central *Adagio*. In both movements of the Op. 4 *Sonata*, Barta and his pianist, **Jan Cech**, make the switches of speed seem natural as though part of an improvisation, and the folk element is aptly heightened by an element of rawness, with the players striking sparks off each other in fiery fantasy. The Novák *Sonata* makes a welcome and substantial supplement.

Maria Kliegel in Kodály's magnificent solo *Cello Sonata* offers a warm and fanciful performance, powerful and flowing. **Jenö Jandó** is an outstandingly sympathetic partner in the two-movement Op. 4 *Sonata*, a performance deeply in-trospective in the slow first movement and full of fantasy in the *Allegro con spirito* of the finale. The three *Chorale Preludes* are romantic arrangements – with the cello generally underlining the chorale melodies – of organ pieces attributed to Bach but now thought spurious.

The two Korean musicians introduced on EMI's Debut label are very impressive, and **Sung-Won Yang's** account of the *Solo Cello Sonata* can withstand the most elevated comparisons and must receive the strongest recommendation, particularly as the disc includes the 1905 *Adagio for Cello and Piano*, which was originally intended to serve as a movement of the Op. 4 *Sonata* and is of considerable quality. The expertise and warmth of both players is matched by first-rate recording.

String Quartet 2, Op. 10

🎧 *** DG 419 601-2. Hagen Qt – DVOŘÁK: *String Quartet 12*, etc. ***

🎧 *** Testament (ADD) SBT 1072. Hollywood Qt – DVOŘÁK; SMETANA: *Quartets* (***)

The **Hagen** give a marvellously committed and beautifully controlled performance of the *Second* – indeed as quartet playing it would be difficult to surpass. In range of dynamic response and sheer beauty of sound, this is thrilling playing and welcome advocacy of a neglected but masterly piece. The recording is well balanced and admirably present.

The **Hollywood Quartet's** was recorded in 1958 and, unlike the Dvořák and Smetana with which it is coupled, is in stereo. The present performance can only be described as masterly, enhancing the attractions of an already excellent issue.

VOCAL MUSIC

Laudes organi (Fantasia on a 12th-Century Sequence); Psalm 114 (from the Geneva Psalter)

*** Australian Decca Eloquence (ADD) 466 902-2. Brighton Festival Ch., Heltay, Weir – JANÁČEK: *Glagolitic Mass* ***

These works were written towards the end of Kodály's career; they are richly rewarding and show that even when the composer took on dramatic subjects, his was a relatively gentle art (in contrast to his friend Bartók). **Heltay** directs persuasive performances, with **Gillian Weir** brilliant as the organ soloist (the *Laudes organi* performance receives its CD début here). The recording is excellent, and these works make a fine bonus for the Janáček coupling.

Psalmus hungaricus, Op. 13

🎧 **** Chan. 9310. Svensson, Copenhagen Boys' Ch., Danish Nat. R. Ch. & SO, Mackerras – JANÁČEK: *Glagolitic Mass* ****

As the unusual but refreshing coupling for the Janáček *Mass*, the *Psalmus hungaricus* is infected by **Mackerras** with an element of wildness that sweeps away any idea of Kodály as a bland composer. As in the Janáček, the tenor **Peter Svensson** is an excellent, clear-toned and incisive soloist, if here rather more backwardly balanced. The glory of the performance lies most of all in the superb choral singing, full, bright and superbly disciplined, with the hushed *pianissimos* as telling as the great *fortissimo* outbursts. It is a mark of Mackerras's understanding of the music that the many sudden changes of mood sound both dramatic and natural. Full, warm and atmospheric recording, with plenty of detail.

KOECHLIN, Charles (1867–1950)

Le Buisson ardent; The Jungle Book (Le Livre de la Jungle); La Course de printemps

⌂₁ *** Häns. CD 93.045. SWR Stuttgart SO, Holliger

La Course de printemps is astonishingly atmospheric and its range of sonorities bold and forward-looking. Holliger has also recorded *Le Buisson ardent* ('The Burning Bush'), another luminous and evocative score, the composer's last symphonic poem, which calls for a huge orchestra, including ondes martenot, five saxophones, piano and organ. It is an evocation of rebirth – at times ardently intense in the strings but with the ondes martenot later used to represent the incorporeal manifestation of the reborn spirit. The sense of ecstasy then gives way to the vigour and potency of life itself, but closing temperately. Koechlin is one of the most remarkable figures in French music after Debussy, a master of the orchestra and completely original.

Les Heures persanes, Op. 65

*** Marco Polo 8.223504. Reinland-Pfalz PO, Segerstam

Koechlin's powers as an orchestrator are evident in these 16 exotic mood-pictures, which were originally composed for the piano in 1913. They evoke a journey recorded by Pierre Loti in 1900: 'He who wants to come with me to see at Isfahan the season of roses should travel slowly by my side, in stages, as in the Middle Ages.' The work is generally slow-moving, but this music has tremendous atmosphere and exotic colours. In the hands of **Leif Segerstam** and the **Reinland-Pfalz orchestra** this music casts a powerful spell. It is also beautifully recorded.

The Jungle Book (Le Livre de la jungle)

⌂₁ **** Marco Polo 8.223484. Reinland-Pfalz PO, Segerstam

Koechlin's lifelong fascination with Kipling's *Jungle Book* is reflected in this four-movement tone-poem whose composition extended over several decades. *La Course de printemps*, Op. 95, the longest of them, is extraordinarily imaginative and pregnant with atmosphere: you can feel the heat and humidity of the rainforest and sense the presence of strange and menacing creatures. *La Loi de la jungle* is the most static and the least interesting. **Leif Segerstam** is excellent in this repertoire and with his refined ear for texture distils a heady atmosphere and he is beautifully recorded. Anyone with a feeling for the exotic will respond to this original and fascinating music.

CHAMBER MUSIC

L'Album de Lilian, 1st Series, for Voice, Flute & Piano; 2nd Series, for Flute & Piano, Op. 149;

Morceau de lecture, Op. 217; 14 Pièces, Op. 157b (both for flute & piano); (i) Sonata for 2 Flutes; Sonata for Piano & Flute, Op. 52

⌂₁ **(BB)** **** Hyp. Helios CDH 55107. Fenwick Smith, West, Amlin; (i) with L. Buyse

Charles Koechlin's writing for the flute is very French, very delicate and very special. The *Quatorze Pièces*, which open this programme, are enchanting and show his supreme gifts as a miniaturist. The Première Série of *L'Album de Lilian* is slightly more substantial, but only slightly. Only two have lyrics, the first translates as 'Keep that schoolgirl complexion', the second, *Tout va bien*, suggests 'All is well because love's sorrow lasts but a moment'. The others are for piano solo and are slightly Satiesque, while the delicious *Skating – Smiling*, and *En route vers le bonheur* are for voice and piano, but without words. Two of the *Quatre Pièces* of the magical Second Series, *Swimming* and *Le Jeux du clown*, are worthy of Debussy in their simple impressionism, while *Le Voyage chimérique* could only be Koechlin himself. The *Flute Sonata* opens with tranquillity, moves on to a wistful *Sicilienne* and closes in vivid animation. The *Sonata for Two Flutes* begins very sadly, but after a cheerful little Scherzando moves to a perky allegro and then, inevitably, back to the mood of the opening. These top Boston musicians play all this music with supreme understanding and elegance: indeed, the performances here are little short of exquisite and full of life. They are beautifully recorded. If you only buy one disc of the music of Charles Koechlin, this is the one to get.

Cello Sonata, Op. 66; Chansons bretonnes, Book 1, Op. 115

*** Hyp. CDA 66979. Lidström, Forsberg – PIERNE: *Cello Sonata* ***

Koechlin's sonata is pensive and introspective, ruminative in character, and **Mats Lidström** and **Bengt Forsberg** give a cultured, finely controlled performance of compelling subtlety. The sound is natural and lifelike. In every respect this is a disc of quality.

Chansons bretonnes (for cello & piano), Book 3

*** Hyp. CDA 67244. Lidström, Forsberg – MAGNARD & WIDOR: *Sonatas* ***

The Koechlin *Chansons bretonnes* have the charm and imagination one associates with this composer. **Lidström** and **Bengt Forsberg** play all these pieces, which are quite short, with eloquence and flair. The sound is excellent.

Horn Sonata, Op. 70; 15 Pieces, Op. 180; Morceau de lecture (for horn); Sonneries

*** ASV CDDCA 716. Tuckwell, Blumenthal

The *Sonata* is a richly conceived three-movement work, linked by its evocative opening idea. The *Morceau de lecture* is freer, more rhapsodic, immediately stretching up ecstatically into the instrument's higher tessitura. The *15 Pieces* are delightful vignettes, opening with a rapturous evocation, *Dans la forêt romantique*. While some of them are skittish, notably the muted Scherzo (4) or jolly *Allegro vivo* (11), many explore that special solemn melancholy which the horn easily discovers in its middle to lower register, as in 10 and 12 (both marked *doux*). Two others are for hunting horns, and they robustly use the open harmonics which are naturally out of tune (an effect Britten tried more sparingly), while the 11 brief *Sonneries* are all written for cors de chasse in two, three or four parts, which **Tuckwell** plays by electronic means. This is a collection to be dipped into rather than taken all at once, but Tuckwell's artistry sustains the listener's interest; and the fine pianist, **Daniel Blumenthal**, makes the most of his rewarding part in the *Sonata*. The recording is excellent.

String Quartets 1, Op. 51; 2, Op. 57

(N) *** Arrese AR2006-3. Ardeo Qt

Like Milhaud, Koechlin studied at the conservatoire with André Gedalge, the '*cher maître*' of the dedication, and also with Fauré, whose influence can be felt here. The *First Quartet* occupied him between 1911 and 1913 and the *Second*, which was to be the basis of his *First Symphony*, during 1915–16. Both are products of an inquiring and cultivated intelligence and make compelling listening. Decent playing from the all-female quartet.

PIANO MUSIC

Les Heures persanes, Op. 65 (16 Pieces for Piano)

*** Chan. 9974. Stott

This is the original piano score of *Les Heures persanes* ('The Persian Hours') of which the orchestral version is praised above. Almost all this music is seductively unhurried. The listener is thus made to linger in scenery that is often picturesque in a gently evocative way. The closing number speaks for itself: *Derviches dans la nuit. Assez animé, nocturne mystérieuse – Variante – Clair de lune sur a place désert*, ending the journey mystically as it began, *after the legendary roses have blossomed*. **Kathryn Stott's** pianistic colours are sensuously warm and often exotic, and she is very atmospherically recorded.

KORNGOLD, Erich (1897–1957)

'Erich Wolfgang Korngold – The Adventures of a Wunderkind': A Portrait; with Concert: (i) Cello Concerto; (ii) Violin Concerto; (iii) Don Quixote: excerpt; 2 Fairytale Pictures, Op. 3

*** Arthaus **DVD** 100 362. (i) Frankfurt RSO, Wolff; with (i) Viersin; (ii) Kavakos; (iii) Frey (Producers: Axel Hempel, Klaus Helmbold, Director: Barrie Gavi)

The feature on Korngold's career in Vienna and then Hollywood comes from Hessischen Rundfunk and is enriched with rare archive material from the family archives and Warner Brothers' films. It is intelligently directed. Korngold's life unfolds in a leisurely and effortless way and the biography includes musical illustrations by **Anne Sofie von Otter, Bengt Forsberg** and **Mats Lindström**. The *Cello* and *Violin Concertos* are expertly played and the **Frankfurt Orchestra** responds well to **Hugh Wolff's** direction. Those

with an interest in the composer or in music in pre-war Vienna should not hesitate to get this.

Baby Serenade, Op. 24; Sursum corda (Symphonic Overture), Op. 13; Der Schneemann: Prelude & Serenade; Die tote Stadt: Prelude; Das Wunder der Heliane: Interlude

B–– *** ASV CDDCA 1074. Bruckner O, Richter

This is a delightful disc, centring on a work new to the catalogue, the *Baby Serenade*, providing a musical evocation of family life with a baby, charmingly unpretentious. The Overture, *Sursum corda*, is like Respighi with a German accent, and even the excerpts from *The Snowman*, an opera written when Korngold was only eleven, are rich and lush, though the orchestration is by Zemlinsky, a point not mentioned in the booklet. The other two operatic excerpts make up the warmly enjoyable programme, helped by excellent playing and recording.

(i) Cello Concerto in C, Op. 37; (ii) Piano Concerto in C sharp for the Left Hand, Op. 17; Symphonic Serenade for Strings, Op. 39; Military March in B flat

B–– (M) *** Chan. 10433X. (i) Dixon; (ii) Shelley; BBC PO, Bamert

The *Cello Concerto* is an adaptation of a short piece Korngold composed in 1946 for the film *Deception* starring Bette Davis and Claude Rains. The *Concerto in C sharp for Piano Left Hand* (1924) is an altogether different matter. Composed, like Ravel's concerto, for the one-armed pianist Paul Wittgenstein, who had lost his right arm during the First World War, it is an extraordinarily imaginative and resourceful work. Although it springs from a post-Straussian world, it is full of individual touches. **Howard Shelley** gives it a radiant performance and is given splendid support. To complaints that the *Military March* (1917) was rather fast, Korngold is said to have replied that it was intended to be played for the retreat! The *Symphonic Serenade for Strings* is a very beautiful (as well as beautifully crafted) work with a highly inventive Scherzo and an eloquent, rather Mahlerian slow movement. First-rate playing and opulent, well-balanced recording. Well worth exploring.

Violin Concerto in D, Op. 35

⚜ **** Onyx 4016. Ehnes, Vancouver SO, Tovey – BARBER; WALTON: *Violin Concerto* ⚜ ****

B–– *** DG **SACD** 474 874-2; CD 474 515-2. Mutter, LSO, Previn – TCHAIKOVSKY: *Violin Concerto in D* ***

(M) *** EMI 5 62590-2. Perlman, Pittsburgh O, Previn – SIBELIUS: *Concerto*; SINDING: *Suite in A min.* ***

(M) *** EMI 5 09676-2. Perlman, Pittsburgh SO, Previn – GOLDMARK: *Violin Concerto*; SINDING: *Suite in A min.* ***

(BB) *** Naxos 8.553579. Tsu, Razumovsky Sinfonia, Yu Long – GOLDMARK: *Violin Concerto* ***

(i) Violin Concerto; (ii) Much Ado About Nothing (suite), Op. 11

☾┄ *** DG 439 886-2. Shaham; (i) LSO, Previn; (ii) Previn (piano) – BARBER: *Violin Concerto* ***

In this inspired and generous coupling, **James Ehnes** gives one of the finest performances of the concerto, bringing out its full emotional thrust without vulgarity or exaggeration. His playing has always been impressive on disc, but here he excels himself in the expressive range as well as the tonal beauty of his performance, with expressive rubato perfectly controlled, drawing from Ehnes some ecstatic playing of the many stratospheric melodies above the stave. The opening oboe solo of the slow movement is radiantly played and later Ehnes takes it up with ravishing warmth, as does the orchestra. The finale is dazzling and this unsurpassed, spectacular recording is made the more indispensable by its Barber and Walton couplings.

The Israeli violinist **Gil Shaham** gives a performance of effortless virtuosity and strong profile. Shaham is warm and committed. The suite from Korngold's incidental music to *Much Ado About Nothing* provides a delightful and apt makeweight, with Shaham yearningly warm without sentimentality, clean and precise in attack.

In another outstanding performance, **Mutter** adopts a freely expressive style, almost improvisatory in the way she inflects the ripe melodies drawn from the composer's scores for Hollywood films. Plainly, for her, this is the music of love, reflected in having her husband, **André Previn**, conducting. The inner depth of her playing at the end of the central slow movement is magical, and her dazzling virtuosity in the dashing finale is breathtaking.

Perlman, dashing and romantic, also gives a superlative account, and though he is placed too close to the microphone the recording overall is vivid, and the couplings are very recommendable.

This now comes alternatively coupled with Goldmark's engaging *Concerto* (besides the Sinding *Suite*), which is perhaps a more apt choice of coupling.

Vera Tsu, born in Shanghai and trained in America, is another outstanding soloist. In every way this ripely romantic version of the Korngold is a match for other full-price rivals, thanks to Tsu's rich, ample tone and her flawless intonation, as well as her fearless attack in bravura writing. In the quality of sound the recording outshines most other versions, rich and free, both immediate and atmospheric, with fine dynamic range and with the Chinese conductor, **Yu Long**, drawing beautiful, refined playing from the Bratislava orchestra.

There is also a very fine recording by **František Novotný** (on Arco Diva UP0108-2131) with the **Philharmonia Orchestra** under **Martin Turnovský**, catching both its lyrical nostalgia and its brilliance. But the couplings seem less suitable: **Karla Bytnatová** sings the Mahler *Rückert Lieder* ravishingly, but Turnovský's coupled, vividly played account of Strauss's *Don Juan* is not as voluptuous as the finest versions.

(i; ii) *Violin Concerto*; (ii) *Much Ado About Nothing: Suite*; (iii) *Symphony in F sharp*; (ii) *Theme and Variations, Op. 42*; (iv) *Piano Trio*. *Die tote Stadt*: (v) *Mariettas Lied*; (vi) *Pierrots Lied*

Ⓝ ⒷⒷ ** EMI Gemini 2 17650-2 (2). (i) Hoelscher; (ii)

Stuttgart RSO, Mattes; (iii) Phd. O, Welser-Möst; (iv) Margalit, Dicterow, Stepansky; (v) Te Kanawa, Philh. O, Rudel; (vi) Hampson, Munich RSO, Luist

A good if perhaps not distinctive anthology including **Hoelscher's** enjoyable account of the *Violin Concerto*, and the engaging *Much Ado About Nothing Suite*. The key work here is the *Symphony*, a work of real substance. **Welser-Möst** secures an excellent account of it, although the Chandos version directed by Edward Downes is an even finer recording.

Film scores: *Captain Blood; Elizabeth and Essex; The Prince and the Pauper; The Sea Hawk* (all arr. Russ)

☾┄ *** DG 471 347-2. LSO, Previn

He thought of the ripely romantic film scores for these four swashbucklers starring Errol Flynn as 'operas without singing'. Considering how quickly he had to work, the complexity of the writing is astonishing, with Korngold closely supervising sumptuous orchestrations by associates such as Hugo Friedhofer and Milan Roder. The sequence culminates in *The Sea Hawk* of 1940, with over 100 minutes of music deftly compressed into a colourful 18-minute suite of highlights, the most substantial of the four here, each with scores reconstructed and reassembled by Patrick Russ. Such a haunting movement as *Sold into Slavery* from the *Captain Blood* suite fully matches in originality anything Korngold ever wrote. **André Previn**, nurtured in Hollywood and himself the winner of four Oscars for his film music, proves the ideal interpreter, with the **LSO** both brilliant and passionate.

Film Scores: *Deception; The Sea Hawk* (arr. Morgan)

*** Naxos 8.570110/1. Moscow Symphony Ch. & O, Stromberg

John Morgan has restored Korngold's amazing complete score for the famous Errol Flynn vehicle, *The Sea Hawk*, continually bursting with musical ideas, and Naxos have coupled it with the score for *Deception*, including a famous concertante cello part (warmly played here by **Alexander Zagorinsky**) which was to form the nucleus of the later cello concerto. The Russian performances have appropriate Hollywood-styled hyperbole, even if there is some lack of refinement in the sumptuous recording. But this is a unique set, showing the sheer fertility of the composer's imagination.

(i) *Much Ado About Nothing (Suite), Op. 11*; (ii) *Abschiedslieder (Songs of Farewell), Op. 14*; *Einfache Lieder (Simple Songs), Op. 9*; (iii) *Prayor*; (ii) *Tomorrow*

*** ASV CDDCA 1131. Linz Mozart Female Ch., Bruckner O, Linz, C. Richter with (i) Hochstenbach; (ii) Mitchell-Velasco; (iii) Gould

The suite that Korngold provided for *Much Ado About Nothing* is richly orchestrated and includes the première recording of his *Garden Music*. The film *The Constant Nymph* (1942) centred on the life of a composer and needed an original composition for the climax. Korngold provided *Tomorrow*, a characteristically flamboyant work, in his lushest style, for large orchestra, female choir and mezzo soprano soloist, here the excellent **Gigi Mitchell-Velasco**. She also sings with great sensitivity in the two Mahlerian song-cycles, bringing much charm to the earlier – but by no means immature – Op. 9 set (the evocative *Night Wanderer* is another first recording), and she is no less successful in the moving *Songs of Farewell* of 1920–1. The *Prayor* is a short but effective liturgical work, dating from 1940, for female choir, organ and orchestra, though it is slightly marred by a solo tenor who is somewhat wobbly and not producing the sweetest of sounds. Otherwise, all the performances are warmly sympathetic, as is the sound, with a full amplitude and plenty of range to suit the music. Texts and translation are included.

Sinfonietta, Op. 5; Sursum corda, Op. 13

(M) ******** Chan. 10432X. BBC PO, Bamert

Korngold's *Sinfonietta* is a four-movement symphony in all but name, betraying a prodigious expertise both in the organization of musical ideas of real quality and individuality. At 43 minutes, it is an extraordinary achievement for a 14-year-old – an adolescent composer springing as it were fully equipped on to the musical scene. *Sursum corda*, an early virtuoso showpiece lasting 20 minutes, is finer than one might expect, an extraordinarily sumptuous piece that in its wide range of moods keeps suggesting that it will turn into the *Pines of Rome*. The present performance of the *Sinfonietta* is a clear front-runner, and the Chandos recording is altogether superb in terms of definition and opulence. A ripely enjoyable disc of beautifully played performances, with a sumptuous sound-picture.

Symphonic Serenade, Op. 39

ᴮ—******* ASV Gold GLD 4020. LSO, Pittau – GRIFFES: *Roman Sketches: The White Peacock* *******

Korngold's *Symphonic Serenade*, lusciously memorable, ought by now to be a repertoire work. But there is no justice in music, and dreadful stuff is regularly heard, while this small-scale masterpiece languishes unplayed in concert halls. With its sensuous, glowing textures it has much in common with its Griffes couplings, but it has great vitality too, especially in its sparkling Scherzo, while the beautiful slow movement is written in the spirit of Mahler. It is superbly played here and the recording is in the demonstration bracket.

Symphony in F sharp, Op. 40; (i) Abschiedslieder, Op. 14

ᴮ—(M) ******* Chan. 10431X. (i) Finnie; BBC PO, Downes

The *Symphony* is a work of real imaginative power. It is scored for large forces – a big percussion section including piano, celeste, marimba, etc. – and the orchestra is used with resource and flair. The **BBC Philharmonic** play with enthusiasm and sensitivity for **Edward Downes**. The *Abschiedslieder* are much earlier and were completed in 1920; there is a great deal of Strauss, Mahler and Zemlinsky here. **Linda Finnie** is a persuasive soloist, and the balance is eminently well judged. The Chandos recording is wide-ranging and lifelike.

Piano Music, 4 Hands: (i) *Piano Trio in D, Op. 1.* **Solo Piano Music:** *Piano Sonatas 1–3; Don Quixote: 6 Character Pieces after Cervantes; 4 Little Caricatures for Children, Op. 19; Much Ado About Nothing (3 Pieces); Märchenbilder, Op. 3; Potpourri aus der Oper 'Der Ring des Polykrates'; The Snowman (Pantomime in 2 Scenes); Die tote Stadt: Schach Brugge; What the Woods Tell Me; 4 Waltzes; Das Wunder der Heliane: Intermezzo*

(B) ******* Nim. NI 5705/8 (4). Jones, (i) with McMahon

Martin Jones has always been one of the most exploratory of pianists and his four-CD set of the Korngold piano music is a valuable addition to the catalogue. The early music is of astonishing precocity and pianistic assurance – and some of it (such as the second of the *Four Waltzes*) touching. The *Four Little Caricatures for Children* in the style of Schoenberg, Bartók and others are quite elegant. The *Second Sonata*, composed when Korngold was 13, is a finely wrought piece, played with great conviction by Martin Jones. The *Piano Trio*, written when he was only 12, is given in its transcription for piano, four hands (the original was premièred by Bruno Walter, Arnold Rosé and Friedrich Buxbaum). There are some delightful shorter pieces, such as *Heinzelmännchen* ('The Imps'), which are quite haunting. A worthwhile set with well-balanced and truthful recorded sound.

SONGS

4 Abschiedslieder, Op. 14; 3 Lieder, Op. 18; 3 Lieder, Op. 22; 5 Lieder, Op. 28; 4 Shakespeare Songs, Op. 31; Songs of the Clown, Op. 29; Sonnets for Vienna, Op. 41; Unvergänglichkeit, Op. 27

(N) ****** Signum SIGCD 160. Connolly, Dazeley, Burnside

Korngold's flair for combining music with drama and his natural melodic gift made him a natural contributor to German Lieder, and many of these settings appear drawn on his own personal experiences, although the Shakespeare songs in English evolved from his incidental music for Max Reinhardt's film of *A Midsummer Night's Dream*. To have so many of his settings on record is bounty indeed, but we found a problem with the performances. **Sarah Connolly** has a wide range and ability to slip up easily to Korngold's top notes, but she also has an intrusive vibrato. **William Dazeley** is inclined to over-dramatize and turn drama into melodrama. The Shakespearean English songs are more successful (especially those sung by Dazeley), but the vibrato problem still remains with Connolly's contributions. **Ian Burnside** accompanies well throughout and the recording cannot be faulted.

CHAMBER MUSIC

(i) Piano Quintet in E, Op. 15; (ii) Suite for 2 Violins, Cello & Piano Left Hand, Op. 23

*** ASV CDDCA 1047. (i) Schmolk; (ii) McFarlane; Schubert Ens. of London

The *Piano Quintet* is powerfully wrought and superbly laid

out for the medium, and rightly enjoyed much exposure in the 1920s. Its resurrection in this fine new recording is more than welcome, for it reaffirms the fertility of Korngold's imagination and the quality of his invention. The *Suite*, Op. 23, one of six works written for Paul Wittgenstein, has some splendid ideas: the third-movement *Grotesquerie* is particularly striking.

String Sextet, Op. 10

*** Hyp. CDA 66425. Raphael Ens. – SCHOENBERG: *Verklaerte Nacht* ***

*** Kleos KL 5142. Concertante – BRIDGE: *Sextet* ***

The Korngold *Sextet* is an amazing achievement for a 17-year-old. Not only is it crafted with musicianly assurance and maturity, it is also inventive and characterful. The **Raphael Ensemble** play it with great commitment and the Hyperion recording is altogether first class.

Yet again the *Sextet* comes over as a splendid piece when played with such conviction, subtlety and feeling as by this fine American string group, **Concertante**. They are superbly recorded, and the Bridge coupling is equally persuasive.

OPERA

Die Kathrin (complete)

*** CPO 999 602-2 (2). Diener, Rendall, Hayward, Watson, D. Jones, BBC Singers, BBC Concert O, Brabbins

Die Kathrin is a far warmer and more relaxed piece than Korngold's other operas. The opulent scoring and ripe lyricism go with a novelettish story of Kathrin, a servant-girl, and her wandering minstrel of a sweetheart. With echoes of Strauss's *Arabella*, Puccini's *Suor Angelica* and even Humperdinck's *Hänsel und Gretel*, **Martyn Brabbins** draws aptly sumptuous sounds from the **BBC Concert Orchestra**, in a recording taken from a BBC radio production. A characterful cast, including **Della Jones** and **Lillian Watson** in small roles, is headed by the radiant young German soprano, **Melanie Diener**, but with **David Rendall** rather strained as the hero, François.

Die tote Stadt (complete)

🎧 (M) *** RCA (ADD) GD 87767 (2). Neblett, Kollo, Luxon, Prey, Bav. R. Ch., Tölz Ch., Munich R. O, Leinsdorf

At the age of 23 Korngold had his opera, *Die tote Stadt*, presented in simultaneous world premières in Hamburg and Cologne! The score again includes many echoes of Puccini and Richard Strauss, but its youthful exuberance carries the day. Here **René Kollo** is powerful, if occasionally coarse of tone, **Carol Neblett** sings sweetly in the equivocal roles of the wife's apparition and the newcomer, and **Hermann Prey**, **Benjamin Luxon** and **Rose Wagemann** make up an impressive cast. **Leinsdorf** is at his finest.

Recorded live at the Royal Swedish Opera in 1996, the Naxos version offers a warmly expressive reading, bringing out the ripeness of melodic writing. The recording too is admirably clear, with more orchestral detail than in the vintage first recording under Leinsdorf. The tenor, **Thomas Sunnegardh**, sings cleanly and freshly in the central role of

Paul, with **Anders Bergstrom** youthfully convincing as his friend, Frank. Yet the glory of the set is the singing of **Katarina Dalayman** as Marietta – radiantly pure and tender in Marietta's song in Act I – which even outshines the model of **Carol Neblett** on RCA. The snag is that **Segerstam** observes various cuts in the score, omitting some 15 minutes of music. Naxos provide a detailed synopsis and a German libretto, but no translation. (8.660060/1)

KOŽELUCH, Leopold
(1747–1818)

Clarinet Concerto 2 in E flat

🎧– *** ASV CDDCA 763. Johnson, RPO, Herbig – CRUSELL; KROMMER: *Concertos* ***

Leopold Koželuch's concerto is a highly agreeable work, especially when performed so magnetically by **Emma Johnson**. There is plenty of Johnsonian magic here to light up even the most conventional passage-work and the 'naturally flowing melodies' (the soloist's own description), and she is accompanied well and recorded admirably, with the slow movement made to sound recessed and delicate.

Symphonies in D; F; & G min.

*** Chan. 9703. LMP, Bamert

These symphonies are pleasingly crafted, sub-Mozart; but each is distinguished by a graceful and appealing slow movement and a vigorous, light-hearted finale. They are very well played on Chandos, and the fairly resonant recording ensures their weight and substance.

KRAMÁŘ, František

see KROMMER, FRANZ

KRAUS, Joseph Martin (1756–92)

Azire: ballet music; (i) Violin Concerto in C, VB 151. Olympie: incidental music

(BB) *** Naxos 8.570334. New Zealand SO, Grodd, (i) with Nishizaki

The lively invention we know from the 'Swedish Mozart's' symphonies is found in this substantial 30-minute *Violin Concerto*. Classically elegant it may be, but it also contains passages of virtuosic brilliance. The slow movement (strings alone) has much relaxed charm, as has the rondo-finale. The *Olympie* incidental music is rather darker, as befits the rather grim story. It consists of a rather *Sturm und Drang* overture, a march, and four *Entr'actes* and a *Postlude* which is rather beautiful. The five short numbers form Kraus's 1779 Swedish opera *Azire* are all that survive from the work, and delightful they are too. Decent performances and sound.

Fiskarena (ballet; complete), VB 40; Ballet music for Gluck's 'Armide', VB 39; 2 Pantomimes, VB 37 & 38

(BB) *** Naxos 8.557498. Swedish CO, Sundkvist

Kraus wrote his ballet *Fiskarena (The Fishermen)* for the Royal Stockholm Opera. It includes a familiar hornpipe and its melodic flow is disarmingly attractive, 18th-century light music at its most appealing. The two *Pantomimes* are like miniature symphonies. All this music is elegantly played by the **Swedish Chamber Orchestra** under its highly sympathetic conductor, **Petter Sundkvist**, and the recording is up to the best Naxos standard.

Symphonies: in A, VB 128; F (Buffa), VB 129; F, VB 130; C (Violin obbligato), VB 138; C, VB 139; C min., VB 142; E flat, VB 144; Olympie Overture; Symphonies in C sharp min., VB 140; E min., VB 141; in C min. (Funèbre), VB 148; Overture in D min.; Symphonies: in D, VB 143; in F, VB 145; Riksdagsmusiken Sinfonia per la Chiesa in D, VB 146; Miksdagsmarsh

(BB) **** Naxos 8.554472 (VB 128–30; 138); 8.553734 (VB 139, 142, 144 & Olympie); 8.554 777 (VB 140, 141, 148 & Overture); 8.555305 (VB 143, 145, 146 & Marsh) (available separately). Swedish CO, Sundkvist

Born in the same year as Mozart, Kraus was dubbed the 'Swedish Mozart', but these lively symphonies, freshly performed by the **Swedish Chamber Orchestra**, suggest that his music has more in common with that of Haydn (who praised his music highly), above all in the *Sturm und Drang* period. Kraus was drawn to the minor keys (especially the *Symphony in C sharp minor* and the *Symphonie funèbre*), and the tough streak in his writing is emphasized by the sharpness of syncopated rhythms. The major-key symphonies are marginally less striking, although *Allegros* still have plenty of vitality. Indeed, the fourth volume (8.555305) contains all the positive qualities that mark the other three volumes, the major-key symphonies combining classical elegance with Kraus's more dramatic style. The music is animated and inventive, often with a compelling edge, with the spirit of Haydn strongly felt in the major-keyed works. First-class recording and lively, fresh playing complete the picture.

KREISLER, Fritz (1875–1962)

Violin Concerto in the Style of Vivaldi

*** DG 439 933-2. Shaham, Orpheus CO – VIVALDI: *Four Seasons* ***

An amiable pastiche, which sounds almost totally unlike Vivaldi as we experience his music performed today. It is warmly played and clearly enjoyed by its performers, and the sumptuousness of the sound is the more striking, coming, as it does, immediately after Vivaldi's wintry winds.

Violin Music (complete)

Vol. 1: Viennese styled music; Works 'in the style of' . . . Dvořák arrangements

Vol. 2: Original Pieces; Tartini/Corelli *Pastiches.* TARTELLI: *Concerto in the Style of Vivaldi; Devil's Trill Sonata*

Vol. 3: Tchaikovsky/Grainger arrangements; Trad. (*Londonderry air*); Works '*in the style of*' . . . *Tambourin Chinois*

Vol. 4: Classical arrangements: Schubert; Weber; Haydn; Gluck; Mozart

(N) (B) *** Nimbus NI 2529/32. Shumsky, Wolfram

Oscar Shumsky has a gorgeous tone and is a supreme stylist in this repertoire – an ideal performer if you want a complete coverage of Kreisler's own music, which was both tuneful and elegant, to say nothing of demanding considerable bravura. For many, Kreisler fooled his public into believing in the authenticity of the encores '*in the style of* . . . and certainly they are clever pastiches. Here Shumsky parades the whole collection in front of the listener, admirably accompanied by **Milton Kaye** and **William Wolfram** and most truthfully recorded (in 1983/4), originally on the MusicMasters label.

Allegretto in the Style of Boccherini; Aucassin & Nicolette; Berceuse romantique; Caprice viennois; La gitana; Liebesfreud; Liebeslied; Marche miniature viennois; Menuett in the Style of Porpora; Polichinelle; Praeludium & Allegro in the Style of Pugnani; La Précieuse in the Style of Louis Couperin; Rondino on a Theme of Beethoven; Schön Rosmarin; Sicilienne & Rigaudon in the Style of Francoeur; Syncopation; Tambourin chinois; Tempo di Minuetto in the Style of Pugnani; Toy-Soldiers' March

(B) *** Decca 2-CD 475 6715 (2). Bell, Paul Coker (with 'Violin Favourites': BLOCH: *Nigun (Baal Shem)*; BRAHMS: *Hungarian Dance 1* (arr. Joachim); FALLA, arr. Kreisler: *La vida breve: Spanish Dance*; GRASSE: *Wellenspiel*; NOVÁČEK: *Perpetuum mobile*; PAGANINI: *Cantabile, Op. 17*; SARASATE: *Carmen Fantasy, Op. 25*; SCHUMANN: *Vogel als Prophet*; SIBELIUS: *Romance, Op. 78/2; Mazurka, Op. 81/1*; WIENIAWSKI: *Scherzo-tarantelle, Op. 16; Thème original varié, Op. 15* (with Sanders))

As readily shown by the opening *Praeludium & Allegro*, **Joshua Bell** refuses to treat this music as trivial, and there is a total absence of schmaltz. *Tambourin chinois*, impeccably played, lacks something in charm, but not the neatly articulated *La Précieuse*. And what lightness of touch in *Schön Rosmarin*, what elegance of style in the *Caprice viennois*, what panache in the paired *Liebesfreud* and *Liebeslied*, and how seductive is the simple *Berceuse romantique*, one of the novelties here, like the winning *Toy-Soldiers' March* and the unexpected, almost Joplinesque rag, *Syncopation*. The recording is completely realistic. This recital has now been reissued as a Double with a further disc of encores, of which the most substantial item is the luscious *Carmen Fantasy* of Sarasate. They are played with similar elegance and flair, and equally persuasively accompanied by **Samuel Sanders**. If you want 2 hours and 9 minutes of violin lollipops, very realistically recorded, this reissue could prove ideal.

Encores: *Andantino in the style of Martini; Caprice Viennois; Liebeslied; Recitative & Scherzo*

capriccioso, Op. 6; Schön Rosmarin; Siciliano & Rigaudon in the Style of Francoeur; Tempo di minuetto in the Style of Pugnani; Syncopation; Toy Soldiers' March; Tambourin chinoise.
Arrangements: ALBENIZ: *Tango;* CHAMINADE: *Sérénade espagnole;* DVOŘÁK: *Slavonic Dances 2 in E min.; 3 in G; Songs my Mother taught me;* GLUCK: *Mélodie;* GRAINGER: *Molly on the Shore;* GRANADOS: *Spanish Dance 5;* CHOPIN: *Mazurka 45 in A min., Op. 67/4;* LEHÁR: *Frasquita: Serenade;* SCHUMANN: *Romance in A, Op. 94/2*

⊶ Ⓜ *** EMI (ADD/DDD) 5 62601-2. Perlman, Sanders

Perlman's supreme mastery has rarely been demonstrated more endearingly than in the collection of arrangements, where the partnership with **Samuel Sanders** has the intimacy of equals rather than that of star soloist and accompanist. The original pieces here include such artless charmers as *Syncopation* (jauntily relaxed), and the inclusion of Grainger's *Molly on the Shore* in the transcriptions is both unexpected and successful. The recording is vivid and realistic, the balance placing Perlman well forward but with the piano well in the picture.

KREUTZER, Conradin
(1780–1849)

Septet (for clarinet, horn, bassoon, violin, viola, cello & double-bass), Op. 62

*** MDG 308 0232. Charis-Ens. – WITT: *Septet* ***

A beautifully played and recorded version of Kreutzer's infectiously enjoyable *Septet* on MDG; it is full of lovely tunes and invention, all bubbling along with witty and felicitous writing for each of the seven instruments, and the Witt coupling is also delectable.

KREUTZER, Joseph (1778–1832)

Grand Trio for Flute, Clarinet & Guitar, Op. 16

*** Mer. CDE 84199. Conway, Silverthorne, Garcia – BEETHOVEN: *Serenade;* MOLINO: *Trio* ***

Joseph Kreutzer, thought to be the brother of Rodolphe, dedicatee of Beethoven's *A major Violin Sonata*, wrote many works for the guitar, of which this is a delightful example. The guitar, given at least equal prominence with the other instruments, brings an unusual tang to the textures of this charming piece, ending with a rousing *Alla polacca*. A nicely pointed performance on Meridian, very well recorded in warm, faithful sound.

KREUTZER, Rodolphe
(1766–1831)

Grand Quintet in C

ⒷⒷ **(*) Hyp. Helios CDH 55015. Francis, Allegri Qt – CRUSELL: *Divertimento;* REICHA: *Quintet* **(*)

This is the Kreutzer of the Beethoven sonata. The *Grand Quintet* is thought to date from the 1790s; it is somewhat bland but rather enjoyable when played as beautifully as it is here. This is part of an attractive triptych, now offered by Hyperion at bargain price. However, the CD plays for under 50 minutes.

KROMMER, Franz (Kramář, František) (1759–1831)

Clarinet Concerto in E flat, Op. 36

⊶ *** ASV CDDCA 763. Johnson, RPO, Herbig – CRUSELL: *Concerto 1;* KOZELUCH: *Concerto 2* ***

Ⓜ *** Warner Elatus 0927 49558-2. Kam, Württemberg CO, Heilbronn, Faerber – MOZART: *Clarinet Concerto* ***

Emma Johnson is at her most winning in this attractive concerto, which is made to sound completely spontaneous in her hands, particularly the engaging finale, lolloping along with its skipping main theme. The *Adagio* is darker in feeling, its mood equally well caught. Excellent accompaniments and warm, refined recording make this a most engaging triptych.

Sharon Kam's performance is also very attractive and full of personality, and she is well accompanied by **Faerber**. If you prefer the Mozart *Concerto* as a coupling, she plays that very well too and with real charm.

Double Clarinet Concerto

**** EMI 3 79786-2. Meyer, Bliss, ASMF, Sillito – SPOHR: *Clarinet Concertos 2 & 4* ****

Krommer's *Double Clarinet Concerto* starts in such a cheerful manner that it is hard not to smile, and the smile grows broader on hearing the delightful interplay between the two soloists, **Sabine Meyer** and **Julian Bliss**. The slow movement possesses, as the sleeve-note writer says, 'pathos and operatic passion', while the finale, beginning unexpectedly with pizzicato strings, is full of delightful invention and much brilliance. Superb performances and very natural recording.

Oboe Concertos in F, Op. 37 & 52

⊶ ⒷⒷ *** Hyp. Helios CDH 55080. Francis, LMP, Shelley – MOZART: *Oboe Concerto* ***

These two concertos were published in 1803 and 1805 respectively. Needless to say, **Sarah Francis** winningly essays all the music's changes of mood and style: her exquisite timbre and elegant phrasing would surely have delighted this attractively inventive Bohemian composer, as would **Howard Shelley's** polished accompaniments, delicate or full-blooded as necessary.

Symphonies 2 in D, Op. 40; 4 in C min., Op. 102

*** Chan. 9275. LMP, Bamert

The two symphonies played here by the **London Mozart Players** under **Matthias Bamert** present a different picture of Krommer: the *D major Symphony* (1803) opens in something of the manner of *Don Giovanni*, while much else conveys a distinctly Beethovenian visage. The *C minor*, Op. 102, composed towards the end of the second decade of the 19th century, already has a whiff of the changing sensibility that we find in Schubert and Weber. Very interesting and refreshing music, played with evident enthusiasm, and well recorded.

Divertimento in F, Op. 96; (i) Piano Quintet in E flat, Op. 95

(N) *** Phoenix 106. Kontraste Köln, (i) with Pullaev (fortepiano)

The six-movement *Divertimento* for string trio is a late work, lightweight but with a strikingly rhythmic second *Minuet* and two slow movements, of which the *Adagio* has a touch of melancholy and the *Andante* a lightweight charm. The *Piano Quintet*, however, is a work of stronger character, with a catchy scalic main theme for the first movement, an eloquent central *Largo* and a pulsing, energetic finale. Both works are very persuasively played and **Alexander Pullaev** brings much added character to the *Quintet* by using a fortepiano which seems just right for the music.

Oboe Quartets 1–2, IX: 21/2; 2 Oboe Quintets in C, VII:12/13

(BB) *** Regis RRC 1201. Francis, Tagor String Trio, with Barritt

Krommer's music is slight, but its charm is as undeniable as its craftsmanship. Sample the simple interplay of parts at the opening *Quintet in C* or the wistful *Adagio* of the *First Quartet* to be instantly won over, while the Rondo finales are engagingly light and vivacious in the hands of the stylish **Sarah Francis**. She dominates the performances without swamping her companions, and the recording has an agreeable intimacy.

Partitas: in E flat; in B flat, Op. 45/1–2; in E flat with 2 Horns, FVK 2d

(BB) *** Naxos 8.553868. Michael Thompson Wind Ens.

Partitas: in F, Op. 57; E flat, Op. 71; B flat, Op. 78; Marches, Op. 31/3–5

(BB) *** Naxos 8.553498. Budapest Wind Ens.

Franz Krommer specialized in music for wind instruments, of which the two *Partitas*, Op. 45, were always among his most popular works, exploiting the conventional wind band (or *Harmonie*) of flutes, oboes, horns and bassoons in pairs, plus trumpet on occasion. Even more striking – and not published till this century – is the third *Partita* here, with the two horns given virtuoso solo roles, a concerto in all but name. Vividly recorded, this Naxos issue offers masterly performances from the ensemble of leading London performers previously led by Barry Tuckwell.

The second Naxos disc is just as successful as its predecessor. The **Budapest Wind Orchestra**, led by their exuberant clarinettist **Kálmán Berkes**, are a first-rate ensemble, full of spirit and personality. They yield nothing in terms of artistic excellence or recording quality to any rivals.

Octet-Partitas in B flat, Op. 67; in E flat, Op. 79

(M) *** CRD (ADD) CRD 3410. Nash Ens. – DVOŘÁK: *Serenade for Wind* ***

The **Nash Ensemble** give excellent and lively accounts of both these attractive pieces. This is not great music, but it is highly agreeable (the main theme of the first movement of Op. 67 is engagingly ingenuous) and the Nash Ensemble readily demonstrate their charms in a direct way, for which the bright recording is admirably suited.

KUHLAU, Friedrich (1786–1832)

Overtures: *Elisa; Elverhøj (The Elf's Hill); Hugo and Adelheid; Lulu; The Magic Harp; The Robber's Castle; The Triplet Brothers from Damask; William Shakespeare*

⊕—. *** Chan. 9648. Danish Nat. RSO, Schønwandt

Lulu is a fairy-tale opera from the same source as *Zauberflöte*, while *William Shakespeare* is based on the Bard's (alleged) youthful exploit of poaching deer. This delightful disc, brilliantly played and recorded, offers all seven of Kuhlau's opera overtures, plus his most famous work: the overture to the classic Danish play, *Elverhøj (Elf's Hill)*.

CHAMBER MUSIC

Flute Quintets 1–3, Op. 51

*** ASV CDDCA 979. Stinton, Prospero Ens.

(BB) *** Naxos 8.553303. Rafn, Sjogren, Rasmussen, Andersen, Johansen

Kuhlau's *Flute Quintets* are charmingly amiable works, well crafted, with fresh invention, the slow movements having surprising expressive depth. We are marginally inclined to prefer the playing of **Jennifer Stinton**, and she gets excellent support from the **Prospero Ensemble**, but their Scandinavian competitors are also first class, and **Eyvind Rafn** is also a soloist of personality. Both recordings are vivid and present.

Duo brillante in D, Op. 110/3; Introduction & Rondo on the Chorus 'Ah! quand il gèle', from Onslow's Opera 'Le Colporteur'; Grande Sonata concertante in A min., Op. 85

*** Globe GLO 5180. Root, Egarr (fortepiano)

Flute Sonatas: in E flat, Op. 64; in G, Op. 69; in E min., Op. 71; in G, C & G min., Op. 83/1–3; in E min., Op. 71; Grande Sonata Concertante in A min., Op. 85

*** Dacapo 8.224071/72. Rafn, Vagning

Flute Sonatas in G, C & G min., Op. 83/1–3

(BB) *** Naxos 8.555346. Grodd, Napoli

The *Grand Sonata in A minor* has a Hummelian first movement with an engaging dotted secondary theme, followed by a bouncing Scherzo, a serene *Adagio* and a gay, chirping closing Rondo. The *Duo brillante* is in much the same vein as the *Sonata*. The *Introduction and Rondo* opens dramatically and is instantly more operatic in its melodic flow. All these works are of quality but essentially lightweight. They are admirably played and recorded here. **Marten Root** uses a copy of an early 19th-century German flute, and **Richard Egarr** a bright-toned 1825 fortepiano.

It is when we turn to the trio of Opus 83 *Sonatas*, published in Bonn in the same year, that we discover why their composer was regarded at the time as 'the Beethoven of the flute'. These are three of the very finest flute sonatas of the early 19th century and are fully worthy of the present, highly sympathetic performances on modern instruments, which do not try to over-dramatize or trivialize the music with exaggerated bravura. The recording is excellent and this disc is another real Naxos discovery.

However, the excellent Dacapo set offers all seven of Kuhlau's *Flute Sonatas* which he began writing in 1824. While the *Grande Sonata Concertante* represents the peak of his output, the earlier *Sonatas* of Opus 64 and 69 are also fine works. The very first uses an *Ancien air danois* for an engaging set of variations as its central movement, while the finale reminds one of Schubert as well as Beethoven; the G major work is lyrically appealing throughout, and again has a perky finale. Opus 71 is the only work of the seven (other than the *Grande Sonata*) to have four movements, including a lively Scherzo with a *Ländler* trio. Its slow movement has a touching simplicity and the finale sparkles irrepressibly. All six sonatas are most sympathetically played on modern instruments by **Eyvind Rafn** (a superb flautist) and **Esther Vagning** (an excellent pianist), and the recording gives them a vivacious presence.

OPERA

Lulu (opera; complete)

*** Kontrapunkt/HM 32009/11. Saarman, Frellesvig, Kiberg, Cold, Danish R. Ch. & SO, Schønwandt

This *Lulu* comes from 1824 and is surely too long: the spoken passages are omitted here – but, even so, the music takes three hours. The opening of Act II has overtones of the Wolf's Glen scene in *Der Freischütz* and the dance of the black elves in the moonlight is pure Mendelssohn – and has much charm. The invention is generally fresh and engaging, though no one would claim that it has great depth. The largely Danish cast cope very capably with the not inconsiderable demands of Kuhlau's vocal writing, the Danish Radio recording is eminently truthful and vivid, and **Michael Schønwandt** draws excellent results from the **Danish Radio Chorus and Orchestra**.

KUHNAU, Johann (1660–1722)

Magnificat in C

⊕ *** EuroArts **DVD** 2053419. York, Bartosz, Dürmüller, Mertens, Amsterdam Bar. Ch. & O, Koopman – BACH: *Magnificat, BWV 243a; Cantata 10* ***

⊕ *** BIS CD 1011. Persson, Tachikawa, Türk, Urano, Bach Coll., Japan, Suzuki – BACH: *Magnificat in D;* ZELENKA: *Magnificats in C & D* ***

Johann Kuhnau died the year before the Bach *Magnificat* came into being in its first (E flat) incarnation. Kuhnau's own setting is his most ambitious work and calls for large forces and is thought to have been composed for a Christmas service at Leipzig. It is not otherwise available on CD and any rival will have to be pretty stunning to match this version from **Masaaki Suzuki** and his largely Japanese forces. Apart from the excellence of his singers and instrumentalists, the recorded sound is quite exemplary.

Koopman's DVD has the added advantage of the visual imagery in the beautiful St Thomas's Church, Leipzig, where both this setting and Bach's follow-up version were first heard. In all respects the performance is first class, and the recording is wonderfully vivid. DVD collectors need not hesitate: it stands out among recordings in this medium.

KULLAK, Theodor (1818–82)

Piano Concerto in C min., Op. 55

*** Hyp. CDA 67086. Lane, BBC Scottish SO, Willén – DREYSCHOCK: *Piano Concerto* ***

Theodor Kullak, on the evidence of this most attractive concerto, was a very gifted composer, with melody coming easily to him. A strong march-like theme dominates the first movement and, when the piano enters, the glittering passage-work lies somewhere between that in the Liszt and Chopin concertos, while the romantic secondary tune has a comparable heritage. The central movement is equally engaging, with bursts of energy, never languishing, and the glittering Weberian finale makes one smile with pleasure at the witty audacity of the main theme. The work is given a scintillating performance by **Piers Lane**, vigorously and sensitively supported by the **BBC Scottish players** under **Niklas Willén**. The recording is first class.

LALO, Edouard (1823–92)

Cello Concerto 1 in D min., Op. 33

*** ASV CDDCA 867. Rolland, BBC PO, Varga – MASSENET: *Fantaisie;* SAINT-SAËNS: *Cello Concerto 1* ***

*** EMI (ADD) 5 55528-2. Du Pré, Cleveland O, Barenboim – R. STRAUSS: *Don Quixote* ❀ ***

Sophie Rolland plays with effortless eloquence and is given responsive support from the **BBC Philharmonic** under **Gilbert Varga**, though he is a little brusque in the *Intermezzo*. An enjoyable and convincing performance. The excellence of the BBC/ASV recording makes for a strong recommendation.

Jacqueline du Pré's recording of the Lalo *Concerto* was taken live from a broadcast in Cleveland in January 1973, right at the end of du Pré's playing career, in one of her last remissions from multiple sclerosis. It is a masterly performance and is totally involving, even though the cello is balanced rather more backwardly than in du Pré's studio recordings. In spite of that, her fire at the opening grabs the attention, leading on to a performance that is both passionate and poetic.

(i) Cello Concerto 1, Op. 33; Symphony in G min.; Namouna (ballet): excerpts

*** BIS CD 1296. (i) Thedéen; Malaysian PO, Bakel

Torleif Thedéen isn't a Rostropovich, but his playing is spontaneously persuasive and his wistful *espressivo* is very appealing in the secondary material of the first movement of the *Cello Concerto*. The *Intermezzo* is also touchingly responsive, and the performance ends triumphantly.

Kees Bakel proves a most sensitive exponent of Lalo's *Symphony*, and he opens the work evocatively. The main *allegro* has plenty of impetus, and after an eloquently shaped *Adagio*, the finale is vibrant and rhythmically not too heavy, so it does not sound Schumannesque. The bonus is a suite of six movements from *Namouna*, again played with plenty of spirit and colour. But here the full and resonant orchestral sound, is less ideal for light-textured dance music. Even so, this is still very enjoyable, and overall the disc is very recommendable, and especially so for the *Symphony*.

(i) Concerto russe; Violin Concerto in F. Scherzo; Le Roi d'Ys Overture

⏴–•• *** Chan. 9758. (i) Charlier; BBC PO, Y. P. Tortelier

Yan Pascal Tortelier opens with a marvellously rumbustious account of *Le Roi d'Ys Overture*. But the main value of this disc is **Olivier Charlier's** seductive accounts of the two concertante works. The *Violin Concerto* is engagingly songful and ought to be better known, but the real find is the *Concerto russe*, in essence a sister work to the *Symphonie espagnole*, but with Slavonic rather than sultry Spanish inspiration. Tortelier – with the help of Lalo – provides a vivid orchestral backcloth, and the opulent, well-balanced Chandos recording adds to the listener's pleasure.

Concerto Russe, Op. 9; Symphonie espagnole

⏴–• Ⓜ **** HM PRD 350 017. Poulet, Prague RSO, Válek

A superb disc. **Gérard Poulet** gives a highly individual account of the *Symphonie espagnole*, to which he brings many inimitable personal touches. But the performance of the *Concerto Russe* is full of warmth and tender lyrical finesse, revealing it as a true masterpiece, with the central movements particularly seductive, and with a finale which opens rapturously and the Russian dance finale scintillating. In both works Poulet is helped by the strong contribution of **Vladimir Válek**, whose orchestral backing is full of character, matching the soloist at every turn. The recording is in the demonstration bracket.

Namouna (ballet): extended excerpts (Suites 1–2 & Allegro Vivace; Tambourin; La Gitane; Bacchanale)

**(*) Auvidis V 4677. Monte Carlo PO, Robertson

Namouna (ballet): Suites 1–2; Valse de la cigarette

**(*) ASV CDDCA 878. RPO, Butt – GOUNOD: *Mors et Vita: Judex*

There is no complete version available of Lalo's ballet, but **David Robertson** has added four more items to the content of Lalo's two *Suites*, plus the charmingly Gallic *Valse de la cigarette* (which the composer extracted as a separate number). He has also re-established the music in ballet-order, whereas in the *Suites* Lalo reassembled the items for concert performance. Robertson secures sensitive, polished playing from his **Monte Carlo Orchestra**, who resound with warmth, and the recording has plenty of colour and ambience.

Yondani Butt achieves performances of the *Suites* and the *Valse de la cigarette* which have comparable colour and finesse, and the **RPO** play extremely well. Even so, they don't necessarily upstage their French competitors and they offer less music. The ASV disc offers a big *religieuse* Gounod tune as an encore, but more of *Namouna* would have been preferable.

Symphonie espagnole (for violin and orchestra), Op. 21

*** Claudio CB 5256-2. Jin, LSO, Wordsworth – SARASATE: *Carmen Fantasy* ***; PROKOFIEV: *Solo Violin Sonata* *** (with KROLL: *Banjo and Fiddle* orch. BRADBURY; TARREGA: *Recuerdos de la Alhambra*, arr. RICCI**(*))

Ⓜ **(*) Sony 88697 99817-2. Stern, Phd. O, Ormandy – BRUCH: *Violin Concerto 1* **(*)

Min Jin's essentially delicate approach is very appealing. **Barry Wordsworth's** spacious opening sets the mood for her warm yet gently lyrical entry, and how delicately and seductively she introduces the secondary theme. The *Andante* then becomes the heart of the performance. The chirping woodwind opens the finale invitingly, and again she displays airily blithe phrasing in her lilting bowing. Among the encores the *Recuerdos* of Tárrega is a distinct novelty, but the transcription is not really convincing. Kroll's *Banjo and Fiddle* (with orchestra) is more successful.

Isaac Stern gives a rich, red-blooded performance, but one which does not lack rhythmic subtlety. He is recorded very close in relation to the orchestra, but **Ormandy** is not upstaged and otherwise the sound is vivid and still commendably opulent. A totally memorable performance.

Heifetz's 1951 account has superb panache and there are no complaints about the mono recording. Alas, he omitted the *Intermezzo* (a practice curiously common in his time), which is our loss, but the performance of the rest, like all the music on this CD, is dazzling. (RCA 09026 61753-2)

Zukerman's performance (coupled with Vieuxtemps) is also outstandingly successful. He plays with great dash and fire yet brings a balancing warmth. (Sony SBK 48274)

Piano Trios 1 in C min., Op. 7; 2 in B min.; 3 in A min., Op. 26

*** ASV CDDCA 899. Barbican Piano Trio

As always with Lalo, this is the kind of unpretentious, inventive, well-crafted and delightful music which 19th-century civilization seemed able to foster and their composers to produce – and of which the late 20th was conspicuously and lamentably bare. There is not much to say about the performances, except to note their excellence and poise.

Le Roi d'Ys (complete; DVD version)

Ⓝ *** Dynamic DVD 33592. Piunti, Girard, Martin-Bonnet, Guèze, Van Mechelen, Graus, Tissons Ch. & O of Opéra Royal de Wallonie, Davin (Director: Jean-Louis Pichon; V/D: Matteo Ricchetti)

Lalo's melodramatic overture to *Le Roi d'Ys* is comparatively well known, but not the opera from which it derives, so congratulations to the Belgian Royal Walloon Opera for mounting the work so successfully in 2008, as a co-production with the Opéra Théâtre de Saint-Etienne. First and foremost, it has costumes in the period of the story, and a convincing set which can handle the mystical appearance of the city's Patron St Corentin and the opera's spectacular watery climax convincingly. Secondly, the opera is strongly cast with the two sisters, Margared (**Giuseppina Piunti**) and Rozenn (**Guylaine Girard**), carrying their key parts dramatically. **Sébastien Guèze**, with a pleasingly French tenor voice, is an excellent hero, Mylio, loved by both sisters. **Eric Martin-Bonnet** as Le Roi holds his own with dignity, and **Werner Van Mechelen** is a splendid villain (Karnac), who is obsessed with Margared. She doesn't want him, but is furious not to have secured Mylio for herself. She persuades Karnac into helping her open the locks which will cause the sea to flood the city, and so have her revenge on the happy lovers immediately after their wedding. The score is pleasingly melodic, the opera has plenty of action and is altogether most entertaining in this excellent video presentation.

LAMBERT, Constant (1905–51)

Apparitions (Ballet; arr. of Liszt); Mars & Venus (Ballet; arr. of Scarlatti)

Ⓜ *** Dutton CDLX 7149. Royal Ballet Sinfonia, Wordsworth (with LANCHBERY: *Tales of Beatrix Potter:* Excerpts) – L. BERKELEY: *Judgement of Paris: Suite* ***

Constant Lambert's delightful arrangements of four Scarlatti *Keyboard Sonatas*, chosen by Marie Rambert, for a ballet strangely entitled *Mars and Venus*, managed to retain much of the character and charm of the originals, to make entertaining listening. But finer still was *Apparitions*, created jointly with Gordon Jacob. Lambert's scenario was derived from Berlioz's *Symphonie fantastique*, for which he chose the music of Liszt with great skill, and it was brilliantly orchestrated by Jacob. The music is superbly played and recorded, and this CD, which celebrates the choreography of Sir Frederick Ashton and includes also a suite from Lanchbery's *Tales of Beatrix Potter*, is far more than a nostalgic memento.

Aubade héroïque; (i) The Rio Grande; (ii) Summer's Last Will and Testament

🗝 *** Hyp. CDA 66565. E. N. Philh. O, Lloyd-Jones; (i) with Gibbons; (ii) Burgess, Shimell, Ch. of Opera North & Leeds Festival

The Rio Grande, Lambert's jazz-based choral concerto setting of a poem by Sacheverell Sitwell, is one of the most colourful and atmospheric works from the 1920s. The *Aubade héroïque* is an evocative tone-poem inspired by Lambert's memory of a beautiful morning in Holland in 1940. *Summer's Last Will and Testament* is a big, 50-minute choral work, setting lyrics by the Elizabethan, Thomas Nashe, on the unpromising subject of the threat of plague. **Lloyd-Jones** and his outstanding team, mainly from **Opera North**, bring out the vitality and colour of the writing, with each of the nine substantial sections based on Elizabethan dance-rhythms. The recording in all three works is full, vivid and atmospheric.

The Bird Actors Overture; Pomona (ballet); Romeo and Juliet (ballet)

*** Chan. 9865 Victoria State O, Lanchbery

Pomona is well served by **John Lanchbery** and his **Victoria State Orchestra**, even if it does not quite command the elegance of the David Lloyd-Jones account on Hyperion. This present issue also brings *Romeo and Juliet*, which Lambert composed for Diaghilev. *The Bird Actors* is a short overture of some three minutes, originally intended for an earlier ballet called *Adam and Eve*. Recommended to all with a taste for this engaging composer.

(i; ii) Piano Concerto (for piano & 9 players); (iii) The Rio Grande; (i) Elegiac Blues; Elegy; Old Sir Faulk (arr. Rodney Bennett)

🗝 Ⓑ *** EMI (ADD) 5 86595-2. (i) Bennett; (ii) E. Sinfonia (members), Dilkes; (iii) Ortiz, Temperley, L. Madrigal Singers, LSO, Previn – WALTON: *Symphony 2* ***

Richard Rodney Bennett's solo recording of the *Piano Concerto*, with **Dilkes** and members of the **English Sinfonia** (plus the three piano pieces) makes the music sparkle with wit. The key item among the shorter works is the *Elegiac Blues*, which Bennett presents rather slowly and expressively; the *Elegy*, more ambitious in scale, is less sharply inspired, but *Old Sir Faulk* shines out as the finest of these three delightful genre pieces. The pairing with **Previn's** equally persuasive 1973 account of *The Rio Grande* could not be more apt, with its colourful and genial jazz references in a setting of Sacheverell Sitwell's exotic poem.

(i) Piano Concerto (1924); The Bird Actors Overture; Elegiac Blues; Prize Fight; Romeo and Juliet (ballet)

*** Hyp. CDA 67545. (i) Plowright; E. N. Philh., Lloyd Jones

This is not the *Piano concerto with 9 players* listed above but the 1924 work, altogether more characteristically life-enhancing, which was reconstructed from the piano duet short score by Edward Shipley and Giles Easterbrook. **Jonathan Plowright** gave the work its first performance in 1988 and he plays it here with panache, the freshness of new discovery still permeating the music-making. *Prize Fight* is as rumbunctious as it sounds, while the *Elegiac Blues* was a moving threnody for Lambert's favourite black singer, Florence Mills (written for piano, and not orchestrated until 1928). This is a key item in the Lambert discography, splendidly played and recorded, and highly recommended.

(i) Piano Concerto (1924); Merchant Seamen (Suite); Pomona; Prize Fight

☐➡ Ⓜ *** ASV CD WHL 2122. BBC Concert O, Wordsworth, with (i) Owen Norris

The *Piano Concerto* is very characteristic, with something of the spirit of Milhaud, jazzy and entertaining. Lambert's score for the documentary, *Merchant Seamen*, dates from 1940 and he drew on this for a five-movement suite two years later. The most familiar of the pieces here is the ballet *Pomona*, which receives a most sympathetic performance at the hands of the excellent **BBC Concert Orchestra** and **Barry Wordsworth**. In fact, the playing throughout is very good indeed, and so is the ASV/BBC recording.

Horoscope (complete ballet)

*** ASV CDDCA 1168. BBC Concert O, Wordsworth – WALTON: *Wise Virgins* ***

Like *The Wise Virgins*, Lambert's *Horoscope*, a colourful work on an astrological theme, dates from a vintage period of the Sadler's Wells ballet company at the beginning of the Second World War. Until now it has appeared on disc only as an orchestral suite, but on this ASV issue **Barry Wordsworth** has resurrected four extra items to make up the complete ballet. Though the newly restored movements are not as striking as those we already know, Wordsworth's warmly sympathetic readings make a strong case for the revival of the original ballets.

Horoscope: Suite

☐➡ ✿ ⒷⒷ **** Hyp. Helios CDH 55099. E. N. Philh. O, Lloyd-Jones – BLISS: *Checkmate*; WALTON: *Façade* ****

The suite from *Horoscope* is sheer delight. **David Lloyd-Jones** is very sympathetic to its specifically English atmosphere. He wittily points the catchy rhythmic figure which comes both in the *Dance for the Followers of Leo* and, later, in the *Bacchanale*, while the third-movement *Valse for the Gemini* has a delectable insouciant charm. Excellent playing and first-class sound, perhaps a shade resonant for the ballet pit, but bringing plenty of bloom. A superb bargain.

(i; iii) Horoscope (ballet suite); (iii; iv) The Rio Grande. Arrangements: (ii; iii) CHABRIER: Ballabile; LISZT: Apparitions (ballet): Galop; (iii; v) MEYERBEER: Les Patineurs (ballet Suite) (with (vi) WALTON: Façade (original version): excerpts)

ⒷⒷ (***) ASV Living Era mono AJC 8558. (i) RLPO; (ii) Philh. O; (iii) cond. Lambert; (iv) Harty (piano), St Michael Singers; Hallé O; (v) Sadler's Wells O; (vi) Lambert or Dame Edith Sitwell (reciters), Ens., cond. Walton

A unique and treasurable memento of **Constant Lambert** as composer, conductor *and reciter* – heard alongside the equally remarkable **Dame Edith Sitwell** in the first recorded performance of extended excerpts from *Façade*. Every word of the daft poetry is crystal clear, and **Walton** himself conducts with élan, coordinating text and music with remarkable precision. That was in 1929, the same year that Lambert's masterpiece, *The Rio Grande*, was recorded with the original performers, **Sir Hamilton Harty** playing the solo piano part with the **Hallé Orchestra**, and the composer conducting. Lambert himself also conducts the sparkling account of

Horoscope, and the jazzy syncopations are caught in both works with splendid lift and panache. Lambert's own arrangement of Meyerbeer's *Les Patineurs* follows (long a key item in the Decca ballet catalogue under Martinon), alongside Chabrier's *Ballabile*, while the *Galop* is a brief reminder of his equally colourful scoring of the Lisztian ballet, *Apparitions*. The transfers throughout are vividly clear, but with thin and scrawny violin-tone at higher dynamic levels, though the gentler music glows pleasingly. All the same, an indispensable disc for admirers of this key figure in English music-making in the first half of the 20th century. Full texts of *The Rio Grande* and *Façade* are included. What a bargain!

(i) King Pest: Rondo Burlesca; (ii) Music for Orchestra; (iii) Pomona (ballet); Romeo and Juliet (ballet)

☐➡ *** Lyrita (DDD/ADD) SRCD 215. (i) RPO, Joly; (ii) LPO, Wordsworth; (iii) ECO, Del Mar

The sparky invention of the precocious Lambert is well represented here and makes this another key disc. In the two ballet scores (he wrote most of *Romeo and Juliet* before he was twenty) he showed how cleverly he could pick up tricks from those fashionable in Paris at the time, including Milhaud and others. **Del Mar** directs bright and persuasive performances, well recorded. The *King Pest Rondo Burlesca* is a danse macabre from a much longer work, *Summer's Last Will and Testament*. It is brilliantly scored and reaches a demonic climax. *Music for Orchestra* is an early work, written soon after Lambert was a student at the RCM, but again shows his skills of orchestral evocation. The performances here are excellent and the recording is spectacular in range, body and colour.

Pomona (ballet); Tiresias (ballet)

*** Hyp. CDA 67049. E. N. Philh. O, Lloyd-Jones

Pomona, written for Diaghilev in 1927, finds Lambert deftly echoing the neoclassical Stravinsky and Les Six in his sequence of formal dances. *Tiresias*, completed not long before Lambert died, is more ambitious, the work of a composer steeped in the dramatic needs of ballet. The thematic material may not be so memorable as in Lambert's finest works, but with strong rhythmic invention and rich sounds – the piano often prominent – it is most attractive, only disappointing in the downbeat ending.

CHAMBER MUSIC

(i; ii) Concerto for Piano & 9 Players; (i) Piano Sonata; (iii; i) 8 Poems of Li-Po; (iv; i) Mr Bear Squash-you-all-flat

*** Hyp. CDA 66754. (i) Brown; (ii) Nash Ens., Friend; (iii) Langridge; (iv) Hawthorne

Constant Lambert's remarkable qualities are in excellent evidence here in the **Nash Ensemble's** anthology which brings the *Eight Poems of Li-Po*, in a lovely performance from **Philip Langridge**. **Ian Brown** proves an equally exemplary advocate in the *Concerto* and the *Piano Sonata*, which is not generously represented on disc. *Mr Bear Squash-you-all-flat* is Lambert's first composition, an entertainment written at roughly the same time as Walton's *Façade*, when Lambert was still in his teens, and based on a Russian fairy story. It is not certain whether Lambert meant the text to be spoken, but **Sir Nigel Hawthorne** speaks it excellently; he is balanced somewhat reticently (a fault on the right side).

Salomé (incidental music): Suite

*** Hyp. CDA 67239. Nash Ens., Lloyd-Jones – WALTON: *Façade* ***

The three items drawn from Constant Lambert's incidental music for Oscar Wilde's *Salomé* make a pleasing extra for the excellent Hyperion version of Walton's *Façade* entertainment. Giles Easterbrook confected this suite of two atmospheric scene-setting fragments, followed by Salomé's dance and sudden demise, a long way after Strauss. With **Richard Hosford** on clarinet and **John Wallace** on trumpet, the performance is exemplary and very well recorded.

Piano Sonata; Elegiac Blues; Elegy; Suite in 3 Movements

*** Somm SOMMCD 062. Bebbington – ARNOLD: *Piano Sonata, etc.* ***

Even though the outer movements are comparatively prolix, Lambert characteristically insinuates jazz-derived syncopations and harmonic influences into the impressive *Sonata*, and indeed into all the music here; and very attractive it is, especially the engagingly inventive and unpredictable *Suite in Three Movements*. The *Elegy* muses memorably and poignantly; the nonchalant *Elegiac Blues* is purely jazz-derived and makes a winning encore. **Mark Bebbington** is in his element in all this music, and he is splendidly recorded.

LANCHBERY, John (1923–2003)

Tales of Beatrix Potter (ballet)

Ⓑ *** CfP (ADD) 3 93230-2. ROHCG O, Lanchbery

This is a companion score to **John Lanchbery's** arrangement of *La Fille mal gardée*. The composer-arranger used Victorian popular tunes (including some by Sullivan) of the period of the Beatrix Potter stories, and they are linked so skilfully that one would think the score had been composed as original music. The ballet itself has a visual appeal for children but can prove boring for adults. But not the music when it is played as spiritedly and affectionately as here. This was top-drawer analogue Abbey Road recording from the beginning of the 1970s.

LANDINI, Francesco (c. 1335–97)

Love Songs

*** HM HMU 907269. Anonymous 4

Francesco Landini was a key figure of his period, made the more so by the number of his songs (*ballate*) which have survived. Rather more that 150 of his works have survived, 140 are unaccompanied *ballate* in two or three voices, virtually

all dealing with love (mostly unrequited), desire and rejection, but a very few, like *Echo la primavera*, considering the beauty of a lover's surroundings. **Anonymous 4** have chosen 18 of the finest and sing them beautifully. The result is hypnotic: they have a lyrical atmosphere all their own, and they are very pleasingly recorded in a warm acoustic. Full texts and translations are provided.

LANGLAIS, Jean (1907–91)

Chant de paix; Chant héroïque; Paraphrase grégorienne: Hymne d'Actions de grâces (Te Deum); Improvisation on Veni creator spiritus; (i) Messe solennelle

*** Priory PRDC 597. Lee (organ); (i) with Gloucester Cathedral Ch., Briggs – VIERNE: *Messe solennelle* ***

These four organ pieces sum up the style of Langlais's organ music admirably. He likes to contrast big swathes of organ sound with gentler textures – dramatically demonstrated in the *Improvisation on Veni creator spiritus* with its spectacular *fortissimos* framing the central evocation using the quiet *vox humana* stop. Bold contrasts are even more striking in the *Te Deum*, with the gentle opening chords immediately interrupted by powerful *fortissimos*, and the piece is dominated by loud, gleaming fanfares.

The *Messe solennelle* is similarly dramatic, with the organ thundering out in the *Kyrie*, the choir's response ecstatic but acting as a rich emotional foil to the organ turbulence. It is remarkable that the Gloucester Cathedral organ should be so suitable for this repertoire, every bit as much as a French organ, but **Mark Lee's** playing is gutsy, revelling in the plangent registration, and the **Cathedral Choir** under **David Briggs** rises excitingly to the musical challenges. A superb disc.

5 Méditations sur l'Apocalypse; Suite Médiévale

ⒷⒷ *** Naxos 8.553190. Mathieu (Cavaillé-Coll organ at Saint-Brieuse Cathedral)

With his *Cinq Méditations* Langlais finds a partial affinity with Messiaen, although his writing is infinitely more direct and his theological conclusion, unlike Messiaen's, totally nihilistic. It is an extraordinary vision and one seemingly founded in despair. The organ registrations here are extraordinarily bizarre, the picaresque grotesquerie wholly original; and it ends the work in a cruel, pessimistic nightmare. By its side, the *Suite Médiévale* is comparatively innocuous. So these two remarkable works balance each other in their opposing responses to Christian belief. Performances and recording are of the highest quality.

(Organ) Symphonies 1; 2 (Alla Webern); Poem of Happiness; Suite brève; Suite française: Nazard; Arabesque for flutes

🎹 *** Nim. NI 5408. Bowyer (Carthy organ, Concert Hall, Calgary, Canada)

The *First Symphony* was composed during the dark period of the German occupation of France. Its first movement is angrily aggressive and dissonant, although its structure is comparatively traditional. The composer suggested that the second movement, *Eglogue*, reflected 'consolation', yet it includes a brief scherzando section. The tension continues to haunt the arch-like, emotionally ambivalent *Choral*, but lifts in the finale, marked *Vif et joyeux*. Langlais described it as a 'celebration', obviously looking to a brighter future: the music thrillingly extrovert, brilliant in the manner of a Widor Toccata, only more astringent.

The two *Suites* were composed after the Liberation, with the four-movement *Suite brève* opening with a characteristically full-throated *Grand jeux* and closing with a jolly and very French *Dialogue sur les mixtures*. The *Poem of Happiness* (1967) is by contrast unexpectedly vigorous, scurrying unpredictably, unfettered – exuberant rather than contented.

The *Second Symphony 'Alla Webern'* (1977) is a serial work with the serial theme immediately spelled out in the pedals. But (bearing in mind the sobriquet) each movement is very brief (the whole work lasts little more than five minutes), while the listener's interest lies with the ear-tickling registration.

(i) *Messe solennelle*; (i; ii; iii) *Missa salve regina*; (Organ): (i) *Paraphrases grégoriennes, Op. 5*; *Te Deum. Poèmes évangéliques, Op. 2*; *La Nativité*; *Triptyque grégorien: Rosa mystica*

⊕━ *** Hyp. CDA 66270. Westminster Cathedral Ch., Hill, (i) with O'Donnell; (ii) Lumsden; (iii) ECO Brass Ens.

Jean Langlais's organ music owes much to Dupré's example, and the two Masses are archaic in feeling, strongly influenced by plainchant and organum, yet with a plangent individuality that clearly places the music in the 20th century. The style is wholly accessible and the music enjoys fervent advocacy from these artists, who are accorded sound-quality of the high standard one expects from this label.

LANNER, Joseph (1801–43)

Galops: *Amazonen; Jägers Lust; Malapou; Ländler: Neue Wiener. Polonaise: Bankett. Polka: Cerrito. Waltzes: Marien-Walzer; Steyrische Tänze; Die Weber*

ⒷⒷ **(*) Naxos 8.555689. Vienna Tanzquartett – J. STRAUSS: *Pariser-Polka; Wiener Blut Walzer*, etc. **(*)

The arrangements, for string quartet, would have been heard all over Austria's coffee-houses and restaurants in the 19th century, and the **Tanzquartett Wien** easily evoke that period. This CD sensibly mixes some energetic polkas with the more leisurely waltzes and a single Ländler to make a good representative programme. The recording and performances are both good, if not quite in the superlative league.

LA RUE, Pierre de (c. 1460–1518)

Antiphons: *Bene omnia fecit; Dedit mihi Dominus pennas; Dum medium silentium; O quam gloriosum est regnum; Sancta Maria succurre miseris; Tribus miraculis; Virgo gloriosa; Magnificats Tone I, II, IV, V, VI, VII, VIII; Salve Regina II, IV & V*

ⒷⒷ **** Naxos 8.557896/7. VivaVoce, Peter Schubert

This is the first complete recording of Pierre de la Rue's seven surviving *Magnificats* as well as three of his settings of *Salve Regina*. *Salve Regina* IV quotes from chansons of Dufay and Binchois. All the *Magnificats* and two of the *Salve Reginas* alternate verses of chant with verses of polyphony, using the same melodic material. The music itself is glorious, and is gloriously sung and recorded. Dipped into, this pair of discs will give much musical satisfaction, for there are excellent notes by Julie Cumming, and full texts and translations.

Missa de Sancta Cruce; Motets: *Considera Israel; Salve Regina III; Vexilla Regis*

*** ASV Gaudeamus CDGAU 307. Clerks' Group, Wickham (with Johann de QUADRIS: *Lamentations****)

Pierre de la Rue travelled little and was not exposed to outside influences as was his more famous contemporary, Josquin. In his Masses his polyphony is complex and swift moving, the harmonic implications relatively plain, although the *Salve Regina* and *Vexilla Regis* are richer in texture. **Edward Wickham** and his **Clerks' Group** negotiate the intricacies of the imitative writing with skill, especially the triple-time writing in the *Gloria* and *Credo*. The two-part *Lamentations* of Johannes de Quadris are further examples of the spare vocal writing of the mid-15th century, but this is a specialist collection rather than one for the general collector.

Requiem

⊕━ *** ASV Gaudeamus CD GAU 352. Clerks' Group, Wickham – BRUMEL: *Requiem* ***

Requiem; *Missa L'Homme armé*

ⒷⒷ *** HM Musique d'Abord HMA 1951296. Ens. Clément Janequin, Visse

Pierre de la Rue's *Requiem* is an ideal coupling for Brumel's masterpiece, for not only is it sombre, and is performed solemnly by the **Clerks Group**, but it employs remarkably low ranges for the bass voices. This makes the contrasting entry of the trebles in the Gradual Psalm *Sicut cervus* the more celestial. However, the main influences come from the *Requiem* of Ockeghem, and La Rue's dark sonorities here are balanced by less predictable melodic writing which is both communicative and moving in its serenity. Performance and recording are outstanding, as usual from this group.

Dominique Visse's approach to the *Requiem* brings a lighter touch and considerably faster tempi throughout than the performance from the Clerks' Group. The result is still solemn but less grave, and undoubtely freshly enjoyable. But Edward Wickham's approach is even more convincing. Similarly, the **Clément Janequin Ensemble's** singing of the Mass based on the chanson, *L'Homme armé*, flows forward in a similar way. Again, excellent recording.

LASSUS, Orlandus (1532–94)

Il Canzoniere di Messer Francesco Petrarca: excerpts

🎵 *** HM HMC 901828. Huelgas Ens., Van Nevel

Francesco Petrarca's 14th-century collection of 366 poems called *Il Canzoniere* caught the imagination of Orlandus Lassus in Venice, and he set more than 60 of them. Ten of them are here. The music's richness is deeply felt in these moving performances, and the varied and refined accompaniments are part of the pleasure this collection brings. Most are in five parts, but *S'una fede amorosa* (celebrating constancy and passion in love) is in eight and is particularly rich in texture. However, a touching sadness is the pervading mood, even *Là ver l'aurora* ('Around dawn') about the coming of spring. But they are sung, played and recorded so beautifully that one's mood is elevated rather than cast down.

Le lagrime di San Pietro a 7

🅱🅱 *** Naxos 8.553311. Ars Nova, Holten

*** HM HMC 901483. Kiehr, Koslowsky, Berridge, Türk, Lamy, Koay, Peacock, Ens. Voc. Européen, Herreweghe

Le lagrime di San Pietro (*The Tears of St Peter*) is a late work, a setting of 21 verses of the poet, Luigi Transillo (1510–68), Howard Mayer Brown calls it a work of 'almost Baroque religious fervour'. The Naxos performance by a first-class Danish choir is comparatively robust yet offers singing of great sensitivity and a wide dynamic range. The recording, made at the Copenhagen Grundtvigskirken, has a properly spacious ambience, yet is admirably clear.

The *Lagrime di San Pietro* is also performed by **Herreweghe's** forces with dedication and perfection in the matter of intonation. Excellent recording.

9 Lamentationes Jeremiae

🅱🅱 *** Regis RRC 1123. Pro Cantione Antiqua, Turner

*** HM HMC 901299. Paris Chapelle Royale Ens., Herreweghe

The performances under **Bruno Turner** are expressive and vital. The recording too is spacious and warm. So for that matter is the Harmonia Mundi recording for the Chapelle Royale and **Philippe Herreweghe**, whose performances of the *Lamentations* are hardly less admirable. However the Regis reissue has a considerable price advantage.

Lamentationes Jeremiae Prophetae (Prima Diei) (for Thursday in Holy Week). Tract: Absolve Domine; Missa pro defunctis (Requiem); Motets: In monte Oliveti; Vide homo

🎵 *** Signum SIGCD 076. Coll. Regale, Cleobury

The pairing of the *Lamentations attributed to Jeremiah*, for Maundy Thursday of 1585, with the *Missa pro defunctis* (one of three) of 1578 has been chosen by **Stephen Cleobury** to 'represent Lassus's treatment of death': both the sacrifice of Christ and human mortality. Of the two linked motets, the text of *In monte Oliveti* is also associated with Maundy Thursday, but *Vide homo* (which closes the programme) brings a text which is the most profoundly moving of all, as Christ accuses mankind with the words, 'See, O man, what things I endure for you; To you I cry, I who am dying for you.' This beautiful setting was the composer's own swansong, for he died three weeks after he completed it, in May 1594. Performances and recording are, as to be expected with Cleobury, of the very finest quality.

Missa bell'amfitrit'altera

🎵 🅱🅱 *** Naxos 8.550836. Oxford Schola Cantorum, Summerly – PALESTRINA: *Missa hodie Christus natus est,* etc. ***

Missa bell'amfitrit'altera (including music by Hans Leo HASSLER & Christian ERBACH)

🅱🅱 *** Hyp. Helios CDH 55212. Westminster Cathedral Ch., His Majesty's Sackbutts & Cornetts, O'Donnell

This magnificent Mass of Palestrina's great Flemish contemporary, Lassus, makes a superb coupling for the outstanding performances of Palestrina masterpieces on the Naxos disc. This is the full **Schola Cantorum of Oxford**, not just the smaller Camerata group, and arguably it is too large for the dedicated, intimate polyphony of Lassus; but the singing is superb and the recording is warm and atmospheric. Yet another outstanding Naxos issue of early music.

The Westminster Cathedral version of the glorious *Missa bell'amfitrit'altera* imaginatively simulates a re-creation of how 'it might have been performed on the Feast Day of a Martyr-Bishop, around 1600', with added music by two other contemporary composers. The Mass propers are given a rich instrumental accompaniment and interspersed with organ *Toccatas* and other music, and the performance concludes with the spectacular Canzon, *La Paglia*, of Erbach and the exultant *Domine Dominus noster* of Hassler for the full ensemble. A most successful venture, on all counts.

Marian Vespers

🎵 ***(*) CPO 777 182-2. Weser-Renaissance, Bremen, Cordes

Manfred Cordes has assembled here a complete service of *Marian Vespers* as performed at the Munich court of Duke Albrecht V, where Lassus took the post of Music Director in 1563. The sequence, after the *Introitus*, includes five psalms for the feasts *Beatae Mariae Virginis*, performed with their antiphons, sung before and after the psalms. These *Introits* are also sung polyphonically. In the cathedral, instruments (usually trombones and cornets) were also used. The *Responsory* followed, then the *Hymn* (here *O glorioso Domina*), with the *Magnificat octavi toni a 8* and its antiphons forming the climax. Finally came the *Benediction*. The singing of the **Weser-Renaissance** group is of high quality and during the *Psalms*, *Hymnus* and *Magnificat* the brass sonorities are richly impressive, although in the resonance of the Stiftskirche, where the recording was made, the brass sometimes all but overwhelms the voices. With this reservation, this is a four-star CD.

Missa Entre vous filles; Missa Susanne un jour; Motet: Infelix ego

♦ **(BB)** **** Naxos 8.550842. Oxford Camerata, Summerly

With its radiant presentation of the opening *Kyrie*, the *Missa Entre vous filles* is Lassus at his freshest and most telling, and the *Sanctus* is particularly beautiful. The *Missa Susanne un jour*, however, is more ambitious, based on what **Jeremy Summerly** describes as 'the most famous song of the 16th century – the *l'Homme armé* of its day'. Moreover, as it deals with the Apocryphal Susanna who was accused of wanton behaviour by two elders after she had spurned their sexual advances, this was just the sort of parody model that had caused the Council of Trent to be upset, two decades ealier. The motet, *Infelix ego*, is a sombre yet very touching meditation on Psalm 51, the words of which seem appropriate under the circumstances: 'Unhappy I, of all help bereft, who, against heaven and earth have offended'. The 12 voices of the **Oxford Camerata** under **Jeremy Summerly** are beautifully blended here, and they sing with dedication and feeling throughout. Excellent recording. A bargain.

Missa osculetur me; Motets: Alma redemptoris mater; Ave regina coelorum; Hodie completi sunt; Osculetur me; Regina coeli; Salve regina; Timor et tremor

♦ *** Gimell CDGIM 018. Tallis Scholars, Phillips

Lassus learned the technique of double-choir antiphonal music in Italy. The Mass is preceded by the motet, *Osculetur me* (*Let him kiss me with the kisses of his lips*), which provides much of its motivic substance and is glorious in its sonorities and expressive eloquence. The singing of the **Tallis Scholars** under **Peter Phillips** is as impressive as it was on their earlier records, and the recording is beautifully present.

(i) Missa pro defunctis (Requiem) for 4 voices; (ii) Aurora lucis rutilat (hymn for Lauds); Magnificat on Aurora lucis rutilat. Motets: Christus resurgens; Regina coeli laetare; Surgens Jesus

♦ **(BB)** *** Regis RRC 1124. Pro Cantione Antiqua, Brown; (ii) Turner

The **Pro Cantione Antiqua's** selection of music for Easter Sunday includes a glorious *Aurora lucis rutilat* for two five-part choirs and the *Magnificat* based on the motet, plus **Mark Brown's** fine performance of the four-part *Requiem*. The performances are of high quality, as is the recording.

Magnificat quarti toni; Missa Surge Propera. Motets from The Song of Songs: Osculetur me; Quam pulchra es; Surge propera amica mea; Tota pulchra es; Veni dilecti mi; Veni in hortum meum; Vulnerasti cor meum

**** ASV Gaudeamus CS GAU 310. Cardinall's Musick, Carwood

Andrew Carwood is very adept at arranging a programme combining a Mass with motets, and here he has imaginatively framed the *Missa Surge Propera* with seven motets from the 'Song of Songs', or *Canticum Canticorum*, with the eight-part *Magnificat* making a rich-voiced finale. The texts of the 'Song of Songs' revel in the sensuous and uninhibited phys-

ical love of man for woman. Of course, Lassus's music is not sensual, but he does vividly pick up the expessive feeling of the text – just sample *Vulnerasti cor meum* ('You have ravished my heart'). Fine singing, of course, recorded in the warm acoustic of the Chapel at Arundel Castle. Excellent documentation, too, and full texts and translations.

Missa: Tous les regretz; Motets, Hymns & antiphons: Aurora lucis rutilat; Ave verum corpus; Domine convertere; Salve regina; Surgens Jesus; Timor et tremor; Tristis est anima meo; Veni creator

*** CRD CRD 3517. New College, Oxford, Ch., Higginbottom

The *Mass Tous les regretz* is based on a six-voice chanson by Nicholas Gombert, and in this performance the Mass movements are interspersed with some of Lassus's finest shorter pieces, including the Eastertide hymn and motet, *Aurora lucis rutilat* and *Surgens Jesus*, with its joyous 'Alleluias' stirringly sung here, while *Timor et tremor* and *Tristis est anima meo* show the despairing and apprehensive side of the composer's faith. However, after the lovely, serene *Benedictus* and *Agnus Dei* of the Mass, **Higginbottom** ends his programme with the Marian antiphon, *Salve regina*, and the Pentecostal hymn, *Veni creator*, with its glowing confidence in salvation. Whether liturgically correct or not, this musical sequence works well, and the performances could not be more dedicated or more beautifully sung. The recording, too, is first class.

7 Penitential Psalms

♦ **(B)** *** Hyp. Dyad CDD 22056 (2). Henry's Eight, Jonathan Brown

The *Seven Penitential Psalms* (6, 32, 38, 51, 102, 130, 148, 150 (the last two are combined as the Laudate Psalms)) were recited after Lauds on Fridays in Lent. Lassus's simple but touchingly plaintive settings first appeared soon after his appointment at the Munich court, although they were probably composed a few years earlier. **Henry's Eight**, directed by **Jonathan Brown**, sing unaccompanied; their ensemble, tonal blend and intonation are immaculate and the music is admirably paced; moreover, the singing has a richness of line and tone which is deeply felt but never overstated. The recording, made in St Jude-on-the-Hill, Hampstead, London, is beautifully balanced and has admirable clarity within an ideal acoustic. Full texts and translations and excellent notes accompany this mid-priced reissue.

LAURIDSEN, Morton
(born 1943)

Choral Music (collection)

*** Hänssler CD 98272. Chamber Ch. Of Europe, Matt, with composer (piano); Halubek (organ)

**(*) Hyp. CDA 67580. Polyphony, Britten Sinfonia, Layton

Morton Lauridsen, though less well known in Britain, is in some ways the American equivalent of John Rutter, if perhaps without the same melodic individuality. Yet he writes music that ordinary music lovers want to hear. His choral music is much performed in the USA, and there is no doubt that *Lux aeterna* and *O magnum mysterium* (which are offered only by the **Chamber Choir of Europe**) are memorably communicative and rewarding. **Polyphony**, alternatively, offer the fine *Ave dulcissima Maria*, the *Mid-Winter Songs* and *Nocturnes*. Both groups include *Les chansons des roses*, which have a charm of their own. However, although both sets of performances are admirable, the edge goes to the Hänssler CD, for the composer is present as pianist, the singing is very fresh and **Nicol Matt** catches the music's atmosphere and comparative simplicity of utterance uncommonly well.

LAWES, Henry (1596–1662)

Songs

*** Hyp. CDA 66315. Kirkby, Consort of Musicke, Rooley

The Lawes songs were enormously popular in their time. Today their direct, declamatory style seems comparatively unsubtle alongside Purcell. The melancholy is tangible, but not overtly expressive. The brief but effective *Tavola* is like an arietta from an Italian opera. The Hyperion collection is fairly wide in its range: the title-number (*Sitting by the streams*) is a verse anthem. There are plenty of secular songs too, notably the engaging *Angler's song*, and admirers of **Emma Kirkby** – here in radiant voice – and **Anthony Rooley's** immaculately stylish **Consort of Musicke** will find much to enjoy.

LAWES, William (1602–45)

Consort Setts a 5 1–5; Consort Setts a 6 1–5

*** Alia Vox AV 9823 (2). Hespèrion XXI, Savall

Consort Setts a 5 1–5; Consort Setts a 6 1–5; 2 Airs for Lyra Viol; Airs for 3 Lyra Viols; 5 Dances for Lyra Viol

Ⓑ **(*) Virgin 2x1 5 62001-2 (2). Fretwork, Nicholson (organ)

The *Consort Setts* reveal a distinct musical personality, not as strong as Purcell's, but with an individual lyrical gift, a propensity for moments of dissonance and the skill of a craftsman. Like Dowland, Lawes also had a penchant for melancholy. Scored for viols with an underlying organ continuo, they are through-composed – each of the movements draws on the same thematic material, and Lawes weaves his part-writing to achieve the fullest possible sonorities. The *Fantazies* are searching, usually melancholy or sombre in feeling, while the *Airs* provide lighter contrast. **Jordi Savall** and **Hespèrion XXI** give well-paced, expressive performances, often intense, and the balance of the viols with the organ avoids making the texture opaque. However, unlike Fretwork, they offer no bonus items, which makes the Allia Vox issue less competitive, even though the Hespèrion performances would be a first choice for the complete set.

The **Fretwork** viols are closely balanced, which reduces the dynamic range of the playing, while the organ integrates so well with the vibrato-less string texture that there seems a lack of contrast in colour, if not in feeling. The pieces for lyra bring a livelier 'country dance' feel, but when one turns to the Concordia collection below, the effect is undoubtedly fresher.

Consort Setts a 6 in B flat; in F; in D; Lyra Viol Trios in D; in D min.; Catches; Come my Lads, Hark Jolly Lads; Whither go Ye?; The Wise Men were but Seven

𝄞 *** Metronome METCD 1045. Concordia, Levy

Mark Levy and **Concordia** also give stylish and appealing performances of these three well-chosen *Consort Setts* in six parts. The playing is alert and sensitive, and the recording is very successful with a pleasing freshness of string texture attractively underpinned by the organ. The pacing here is exceptionally well judged to reveal the full character of all these works. It is good to have the *Lyra Viol Trios*: the *D major*, with its central movement entitled *Humor* and with a closing *Saraband*, is a striking little work. The catches, which act as interludes, are paired, in each case alternating slow and fast examples. The curious title of the collection, *Knock'd on the Head*, refers to the composer's death at the siege of Chester; but as the 'knock' came from a bullet, it hardly seems an appropriate description.

Fantasia Suites for 2 Violins, Bass Viol & Organ 1–8

*** Chan. 0552. Purcell Qt

Lawes studied with Coperario, and Lawes's own *Fantasia Suites* are based on those of his mentor but are simpler, usually more extrovert works than the *Consort Suites*. They are in three movements, in each case a *Fantazy* followed by two *Aires*, in essence dance movements, *Alman* and *Galliard*, later *Corant* or *Saraband*. The organ does not just play a continuo role but is important in its own right. The music itself is lively in invention and by no means predictable, with surprise moments of passing dissonance, and the composer's individuality comes out in his special brand of lyricism. The performances here have plenty of life, and the recording balance is very successful: the result is enjoyably fresh.

Royal Consorts 1–10

*** Chan. 0584/5. Purcell Consort

*** Gaudeamus CDGAU 146/7. Greate Consort, Huggett

The 10 *Royal Consorts*, even though they are in four rather than five or six parts like the *Setts*, in many ways represent Lawes's most ambitious undertaking. Each suite is in six or seven movements, the first of which is the most extended, sometimes taking as long as the remaining charming *Aires* and increasingly lively *Almans*, *Corants* and *Sarabands*, all put together. Indeed, these opening expressive *Fantazies* or *Pavanes* offer the kernel of the arguments and contain the most adventurous music, combining nobility of feeling with ear-catching contrapuntal lines.

The playing of the **Purcell Consort** is notably sprightly, the recording fresh and vividly clear, but within an open acoustic of some depth. The brightness and transparency of the sound, without loss of sonority, means that the individual instruments are cleanly delineated, although blending well together, never better demonstrated than in the splendidly managed *Echo* movement that ends the first work of the series.

Monica Huggett and her Greate Consort are very slightly recessed; their sound is warmer and the expressive music is given a fuller texture by the resonance. Some will feel that, presented in this way, this music is afforded more atmosphere. They also play at a slightly lower pitch, which means that the effect is inevitably mellower when compared directly with the brighter Chandos sound, although on ASV detail is by no means unclear. Both sets of performances are very rewarding, and if we are inclined, marginally, to favour the bright projection and added transparency of Chandos, many collectors will surely respond differently.

Consort Setts a 5: in A; C (2); F & G; Consort Pieces a 4: 2 Aires in C; 2 Aires in C min.; Aire (Fantazy) in C; Fantazy in C min. (VdGS 108/113)

⊶ **** Channel Classics CCS 15698. Phantasm

The playing of Phantasm explores a wide dynamic range and is beautifully blended in its delicacy and warmth, in no way edgy or acerbic. The group is most naturally recorded and this disc is as fine an introduction to Lawes's consort music as any in the catalogue.

Songs

**(*) Hyp. CDA 67589. Blaze, Outram, MacDonald; Kenny and/or Carter (lute or theorbo) – HENRY LAWES: *Songs* **(*)

This collection of songs by Henry and William Lawes opens with William's charming *Gather ye rosebuds while ye may*, which Robin Blaze sings as a duet with Rebecca Outram (soprano). Robert MacDonald (bass) contributes *When shall I see my captive heart?* and four more come from Robin Blaze, with Elizabeth Kenny (lute or theorbo). *Oh, let me still and silent be* and *When man for sin thy judgment feels* are among the most deeply expressive in the collection, which suggests that William was the finer song composer of the two. The programme is given variety by items for solo lute and lute duets with William Carter. But one wishes the other vocal soloists had contributed more to the recital. The documentation is excellent.

LECLAIR, Jean-Marie
(1697–1764)

Complete Flute Chamber Music: Sonatas, Op. 1/2 & 6; Op. 2/1, 3, 5, 7 & 11; (i) Trio Sonata, Op. 2/8; Flute Sonata, Op. 9/7; (ii) Second Récréation de musique for 2 Flutes & Continuo, Op. 8

Ⓝ ⒝⒝ *** Naxos 8.557440/1. Fenwick Smith, Gibbons, Blustein; with (i) Jeppesen (viola da gamba); (ii) Krueger

Violin Sonatas, Op. 5/1, 3, 4, 7 & 8

Ⓝ *** ECM 476 6280. Holloway, Jaap ter Linden, Mortensen

The music of Jean-Marie Leclair hops in and out of the catalogue at regular intervals. His music tends to be underrated, yet its merits are considerable; although his lyricism is not strongly individual, it often has considerable charm and

never more so than in the so-called *Récréation de musique* for *two flutes*, a seven-movement suite with a celebrated and diverting *Chaconne* for its penultimate movement and a *Tambourin* to finish. The *Flute Sonatas* each have four movements, with usually half of them dances: Correntes, Gavottas, Sarabandas. Their style, however, is distinctly French in its elegance and finish. The sonatas are fresh, well constructed and often highly expressive, even if the ideas are not in themselves always especially memorable.

Leclair wrote well for the flute, but in the main he dedicated himself to the violin, for which he wrote 40 sonatas against only the present collection for the flute. John Holloway has chosen five *Violin Sonatas*, all taken from Opus 5 which he and his colleagues consider among the finest in Leclair's output. 4 brings yet another *Chaconne* of considerable merit. Certainly the performances from Holloway, Jaap ter Linden and Lars Mortensen are very well played and impressively dedicated, so you can make a choice between flute and violin for approximately the same cost.

LECOCQ, Alexandre (1832–1918)

Mam'zelle Angot (ballet, arr. Gordon Jacob)

*** Australian Decca Eloquence 442 9048 (2). Nat. PO, Bonynge – HEROLD: *La Fille mal gardée* ***

Mam'zelle Angot is a jolly, vivacious score with plenty of engaging tunes, prettily orchestrated in the modern French style. Richard Bonynge offers the first recording of the complete score, and its 39 minutes are consistently entertaining, especially with orchestral playing of such polish and wit. The Kingsway Hall recording is warm and vivid, bringing sharp detail and tangibility, especially at lower dynamic levels. A winner in every way, with an outstanding coupling to match.

LEHÁR, Franz (1870–1948)

Chinese Ballet Suite; Fata morgana; Korallenlippen; Ein Märchen aus 1001 Nacht; Marsch und Palótas; Peter and Paul in Cockaigne: Ballet Music; Preludium religioso; Resignation; Suite de danse; Zigeunerfest (ballet scene)

*** CPO 999 761-2. German (Berlin) RSO, Jurowski

A delightful concoction of unfamiliar Lehár, most of it stemming from his stage works. It is all highly tuneful and vivacious in the Viennese manner, with splashes of local colour – such as the delightful *Chinese Ballet Suite* and the very Hungarian-sounding *Fata morgana* – with lively orchestrations adding spice. Lehár's inventive ideas always engage the ear, helped by enthusiastic performances and a warm recording.

Gold and Silver Waltz, Op. 79

⊶ **** BBC (ADD) BBCL 4038. Hallé O, Barbirolli – HAYDN: *Symphony 83 in G min. (La Poule);* JOHANN STRAUSS JR: *Emperor Waltz,* etc.; R. STRAUSS: *Der Rosenkavalier Suite* ****

Lehár's finest waltz acts as an unforgettable encore for **Barbirolli's** 1969 Promenade Concert. He encourages the Prommers to hum along gently, yet not overwhelm the famous tune, and they even manage a *pianopianissimo* at the reprise. The result is magical.

Overtures: *Clo-clo; Der Göttergatte; Die lustige Witwe*; Waltzes: *Adria; Altwiener; Grützner; Valse Boston (Wilde Rosen)*

(*) CPO 999 891-2. Berlin RSO, Jurowski

These are large-scale performances of generally little-known Lehár, with the exception of the *Merry Widow Overture* (here in the composer's 1940 version). The less well-known concert waltzes are enjoyable. It is hard to understand why the *Grützner Waltz*, with its beautiful opening building up to a fine waltz, very much in the Strauss tradition, was never published. The *Valse Boston* dispenses with the Strauss-like introduction and replaces it with a short *maestoso* to call the dancers to the floor. The overtures to *Clo-Clo* and *Der Göttergatte* are lively works and full of delightful ideas. It is all very enjoyable, and the orchestra play to the manner born. The only reservation is the recording, which, although it allows details to emerge well, is just a bit too reverberant.

(i) *The Count of Luxembourg*: highlights; (ii) *The Land of Smiles*: highlights; (iii) *The Merry Widow*: highlights

Ⓑ ** CfP (ADD) 575 9962 (2). (i–iii) Bronhill; (i) Jason, Fyson, McCarthy Singers, Studio 2 Concert O; (ii) Craig, Fretwell, Grant, Sadler's Wells Op. O; (i; ii) cond. Tausky; (iii) Round, McAlpine, Lowe, Sadler's Wells Op. Ch. & O, Reid

The Sadler's Wells pioneering recording of *The Merry Widow* in English with the excellent **June Bronhill** both stylish and charming in the lead is strongly characterized; only in **Howard Glynne's** Baron Zeta is there a suspicion of Gilbert and Sullivan. **Thomas Round** is an appropriately raffish Danilo, although it is a pity that the recording tends to accentuate the unevenness in his voice. **William McAlpine** as Camille de Rosillon comes over much better, and his *Red as the Rose* is exquisitely sung. The chorus is outstandingly good and these excerpts are most entertaining: the *March Septet* is a riot (if a well-drilled riot), and **William Reid** conducts with sensitivity, obvious affection and a real feeling for the music's idiom, and the recording is vividly atmospheric.

In *The Land of Smiles* **June Bronhill** takes the supporting role of Mi (the heroine's sister), and though **Elizabeth Fretwell** is less rich-timbred she sings sweetly enough. **Charles Craig**, as ever, is outstanding as Sou-Chong, with his rich, fine tenor voice sounding out gloriously in 'You are my heart's delight' (with different words). The recording has a good balance between brilliance on the one hand and warmth and resonance on the other.

The Count of Luxembourg is generally less distinguished, and although Tausky conducts just as understandingly as he does in *The Land of Smiles*, and **Neville Jason** makes an engaging Count, the singing overall is less impressive than before and the effect is often unflattering to the voices. Nevertheless, this inexpensive two-CD reissue makes a good sampler of a Sadler's Wells vintage period.

The Czarevitch (in English)

*** Telarc CD 80395. Gustafson, Hadley, Itami, Atkinson, Carl, ECO, Bonynge

Though it lacks the really memorable melodies which make the finest Lehár operettas so winning, *The Czarevitch* is a delightful piece which, with **Richard Bonynge** as a most understanding conductor, is full of charm and sparkle, with Russian colour from balalaikas nicely touched in. Anyone wanting this in English translation will not be disappointed, with the second couple of principals readily matching up to **Jerry Hadley** and **Nancy Gustafson**.

(i) *Friederike*; (ii) *Giuditta*; (iii) *Der Graf von Luxemburg*; (iv) *Das Land des Lächelns*; (v) *Die lustige Witwe*; (vi) *Paganini*; (vii) *Der Zarewitsch* (all complete; in German)

ⒷⒷ **(*) EMI (ADD/DDD) 585997-2 (13). (i) Kalenberg, Datz, Stadler, Fuchs, Donath, Dallapozza, Bav. R. Ch., Munich RSO, Wallberg; (ii) E. Moser, Hirte, Gedda, Baumann, Munich Conzert Ch. & R. O, Boskovsky; (iii) Gedda, Böhme, Litz, Brokmeier, Popp, Holm, Bav. State Op. Ch., Graunke SO, Mattes; (iv) Rothenberger, Gedda, Holm, Friedauer, Moeller, Bav. RSO Ch., Graunke SO, Mattes; (v) Lott, Hampson, Szmytka, Aler, Azesberger, Glyndebourne Ch., LPO, Welser-Möst; (vi) Rothenberger, Lenz, Gedda, Sachtleben, Dieberitz, Zednik, Bav. State Op. Ch., Bav. SO, Boskovsky; (vii) Gedda, Söhnker, Reimer, Streich, Friedauer, Relchart, Bav. State Op. Ch., Graunke SO, Mattes

This is a bumper bargain box for Lehár aficionados and, with the exception of *The Merry Widow*, all the performances here are recommendable. Unfortunately, for Lehár's most popular work, EMI opted to use the 1993 **Welser-Möst** recording, which is far from ideal for, though he has a fair idea of the idiom, his slowish speeds often diminish the sparkle, as in the *March Septet* in Act II. **Thomas Hampson** makes a handsome, swaggering Danilo, but he is not vocally at his sweetest, and the other three principals all sing with more uneven production than usual, so that their duets lose much of their appeal. **Felicity Lott** has both charm and dignity as the widow herself, but her voice is given an unpleasant edge at times.

There is plenty to enjoy in the lively and well-recorded (1980) version of *Friederike*, a delightful performance, with **Helen Donath** charming in the name-part, and **Dallapozza**, a light, heady tenor, perhaps a bit stressed by the weight in his title-role but rising to the great Tauber number *O Mädchen, mein Mädchen!*

Das Land des Lächelns dates from 1967, and after the rather thin-sounding overture the recording has plenty of theatrical presence. The cast is strong: **Gedda** is in excellent form and, besides **Anneliese Rothenberger**, **Renate Holm** makes a charming contribution as Mi. The most famous numbers, such as *You are my heart's delight*, are splendidly done.

In *Giuditta* **Gedda** hardly shows his years in the Tauber role, with half-tones honeyed as ever, but **Edda Moser** is disappointing in the name-part, rarely sounding seductive as

Schwarzkopf and Gueden did in this role. **Boskovsky** conducts with his usual sympathy and the sound is decent.

Willy Mattes presents a bright and breezy version of *Der Graf von Luxemburg*, recorded in 1969. **Gedda** and **Holm** (who has many delightful numbers to sing) are once again on form, and most of the rest of the cast carry the lively spirit of the performance. Recorded around the same time, **Mattes's** account of *Der Zarewitsch* is hardly less impressive. **Gedda** is once again in the lead and, with such delightful artists as **Rita Streich** (whose singing is as charming and stylish as ever), it is impossible not to enjoy this.

Choosing the romanticized demon violinist Paganini as a subject for an operetta gave Lehár a chance to exploit a plot full of court intrigue, with the celebrated court violinist in love with the crown princess. All that is missing is a score overflowing with memorable musical ideas, though the piece is hardly tuneless. In this red-blooded performance from 1977 **Boskovsky** makes an excellent case for the work, especially as the singing is generally first rate, as is the recording.

The one snag for non-German speakers throughout these performances is the large amount of dialogue. Translations are not included, but there is a track-by-track outline included with the synopses, as well as the background for each opera as a guide. However, this is an inexpensive way to acquire all the composer's key works.

The Land of Smiles (in English)

🎧 *** Telarc CD 80419. Gustafson, Hadley, Itami, Atkinson, ECO, Bonynge

Richard Bonynge proves as warmly understanding of the Lehár idiom as he is in Bellini, while **Jerry Hadley** winningly takes the Tauber role of Prince Sou-Chong. He also provides a new translation, with the hit-number, *You are my heart's delight*, becoming *My heart belongs to you*, with diction commendably clear. **Nancy Gustafson** makes a bright heroine, and **Lynton Atkinson** sings with winning lightness in the second tenor role. Recommended.

The Land of Smiles (Das Land des Lächelns); The Merry Widow (Die lustige Witwe) (both complete in German)

🎧 Ⓜ (***) EMI mono 5 85822-2 (2). Schwarzkopf, Kunz, Gedda, Loose, Philh. Ch. & O, Ackermann

As Hanna Glawari in *The Merry Widow* (which she was to record again in stereo) **Schwarzkopf** has both sparkle and youthful vivacity, and the *Viljalied* – ecstatically drawn out – is unique. Some may be troubled that **Kunz** as Danilo sounds older than the Baron (**Anton Niessner**), but it is still a superbly character cast.

The Land of Smiles has a comparably glamorous roster, and if here **Gedda** does not have quite the passionate flair of Tauber in his famous *Dein ist mein ganzes Herz*, his thoughtful artistry matches a performance which effortlessly brings out the serious parallels without weighing the work down. **Schwarzkopf** and **Kunz** again sing delectably, and the CD transfers are lively and full of presence. Dialogue is included, but separately cued.

(i) The Land of Smiles (Das Land des Lächelns) (complete in German). Excerpts from: (ii) Eva; (iii) Frasquita; (iv) Friederike; (v) Der Fürst der Berge; (vi) Giuditta; (vii) Das Land des Lächelns; Paganini; (viii; ix) Schön ist die Welt; (viii) Der Zarewitsch

ⒷⒷ (***) Naxos mono 8.111016/17. (i) Schwarzkopf, Kunz, Gedda, Loose, Kraus, Philh. Ch. & O, Ackermann; (ii) Lehmann; (iii) Tauber; (iv) Aramesco; (v) Eisinger; (vi) Rosvaenge; (vii) Schwarzkopf, Glawitsch; (viii) Rethy; (ix) Wittrich

Ackermann's mono recording of *The Land of Smiles* is available above on EMI, coupled with *The Merry Widow*. Naxos offer it separately, together with a generous collection of Lehár arias sung by a galaxy of great operetta singers from the past. Mark Obert-Thorn's transfer is every bit as good as EMI's, and (praise be!) the dialogue is all separately cued. **Schwarzkopf** not only sings delightfully in the main work but also contributes in 1939 (alongside the stirring **Rupert Glawitsch**) to excerpts from *Paganini* and (in 1940) *Das Land des Lächelns*, where the voice sounds young and sweet, almost soubrettish. Other highlights are provided by heady tenor contributions from **Leonardo Aramesco** and **Marcel Wittrich**, almost trumped by **Helge Rosvaenge** in *Giuditta* and the delightful soprano **Irene Eisinger** in *Der Fürst der Berge*. Ward Marston's faithful transfers show just how good were the original masters.

The Merry Widow (complete; DVD version; in English)

🎧 *** Opus Arte **DVD** OA 0836 D. Kenny, Skovhus, Kirchschlager, Turay, San Francisco Op. Ch. & O, Kunzel (V/D: Gary Halvorson)

It would be hard to imagine a more extravagant production of *The Merry Widow* than Lotfi Mansouri's for the San Francisco Opera, recorded live on this DVD in December 2001. Michael Yeargan's sets faithfully echo the 1890s designs at Maxim's in Paris, Thierry Bosquet's costumes are comparably lavish, and the text is unusually full. The dialogue – with Christopher Hassall's translation expanded by Ted and Deena Puffer – is wittier and truer to the Parisian atmosphere than the original German. **Yvonne Kenny** as the heroine not only sings beautifully but is both vivacious and provocative. **Bo Skovhus** makes a handsome Danilo, determined not to be putty in her hands, and their final reconciliation to the *Merry Widow Waltz* could not be more moving. **Angelika Kirchschlager** makes a charming Valencienne, opposite the Camille of **Gregory Turay**, with **Carlo Hartmann** as Baron Mirko, Valencienne's husband, strong and characterful, relishing the humour.

The Merry Widow (Die lustige Witwe; complete; in German; CD versions)

🎧 *** DG 439 911-2. Studer, Skovhus, Bonney, Trost, Terfel, Monteverdi Ch., VPO, Gardiner

ⒷⒷ (***) Regis mono RRC 1163. Schwarzkopf, Gedda, Kunz, Loose, Philh. Ch. & O, Ackermann

Ⓝ Ⓑ ** EMI 5 20974-2 (2). Lott, Hampson, Szmytka, Aler,

Bogarde (nar.), Glyndebourne Ch., LPO, Welser-Möst (with Collection of JOHANN STRAUSS: *Waltzes* **)

John Eliot Gardiner has the bonus of the **Vienna Philharmonic** very much on home ground, playing not only with a natural feeling for the idiom but with unrivalled finesse and polish. As Hanna Glawari **Cheryl Studer** gives her most endearing performance yet and the gentle half-tone on which she opens the soaring melody of the *Viljalied* is ravishing. Consistently she sings with sweet, firm tone and the Danish baritone, **Boje Skovhus**, as Danilo makes an animated, raffish hero. The second couple, Valencienne and Camille, are delectably taken by **Barbara Bonney** and **Rainer Trost**, clear and youthful-sounding, outshining all rivals. The rest make an outstanding team, with **Bryn Terfel**, ripely resonant, turning Baron Mirko into more than a *buffo* character, while the choristers of Gardiner's **Monteverdi Choir**, obviously enjoying their Viennese outing, bring to Lehár the point and precision they have long devoted to the baroque repertory.

Those collectors wanting just **Schwarzkopf's** celebrated earlier mono recording of the *Merry Widow* will find the Regis transfer smooth and pleasing, with the voices truthfully caught. There is no translation but a good synopsis, and the dialogue is separately banded. A genuine bargain.

The live **Welser-Möst** set, recorded in the Royal Festival Hall in July 1993, proves a disappointment. **Dirk Bogarde's** narration, which punctuates separate numbers, is delivered with an unenticing, arch knowingness and, while **Thomas Hampson** is a swaggering Danilo and **Felicity Lott** has both charm and dignity as the Widow herself, overall the singing lacks appeal, not helped by Welser-Möst's slowish speeds, which diminish the sparkle, as in the *March septet*. The rather edgy recording is another minus point, and the collection of five Johann Strauss waltzes and two overtures which acts as a filler is not any real compensation.

LEIGH, Walter (1905–42)

(i) *Agincourt Overture*; (ii; iii) *Concertino for Harpsichord & Strings*; (ii) *The Frogs; Overture & Dance*; (i) *Jolly Roger Overture*; (ii) *A Midsummer Night's Dream: Suite for Small Orchestra; Music for String Orchestra*

*** Lyrita (ADD) SRCD 289. (i) New Philh. O; (ii) LPO; Braithwaite; (iii) with Pinnock

Walter Leigh was a craftsman composer of the finest kind, one who aimed to make his music useful, hence his frequent essays in incidental music. His personal style remained very English, with frequent but gentle neoclassical overtones. His masterpiece remains the *Harpsichord Concertino*, which has been recorded three times before this Lyrita version, but never so persuasively as by Kathleen Long in the days of 78s (see below), using a piano. **Pinnock's** sensitive performance is among the finest using the harpsichord, though the balance places the solo instrument rather close. Otherwise the recording is excellent, as are all the performances. A most worthwhile disc.

Concertino for Harpsichord & String Orchestra

🎵 Ⓜ **** BBC BBCM 5025-2. Malcolm, ASMF, Marriner – FINZI: *Clarinet Concerto; Introit* **** (with Concert: *English Music* ****)

Walter Leigh's *Concertino for Harpsichord and String Orchestra*, with its heavenly slow movement has surely never been played more winningly than it is here by **George Malcolm**. The balance with **Marriner** and his **Academy** is perfectly judged, so that the appearance of so lively a performance (from 1972), expertly engineered by the late James Burnett, is most welcome. This is a highlight of a desirable bargain collection of English music, by Butterworth, Finzi, Vaughan Williams and Warlock.

Concertino for Piano & String Orchestra

Ⓑⓑ (***) Dutton CDBP 9714. K. Long (piano), Boyd Neel String O, Boyd Neel – FAURÉ: *Ballade in F sharp*; MOZART: *Piano Concertos 15 & 24* (***)

Though this charming *Concertino* was primarily designed for harpsichord, the piano is given as an option, chosen here for the première recording in 1946. In subtlety and feeling **Kathleen Long's** reading has never been surpassed. It makes a fine tribute to a superb pianist long under-appreciated. The transfer is excellent.

Music for Strings; Air (for treble recorder & piano); 3 Movements for String Quartet; Recorder Sonatina; Reverie (for violin & piano); Romance (for 2 violins, viola, cello & piano); Trio for Flute, Oboe & Piano; Viola Sonatina

Ⓜ *** Dutton CDLX 7143. Lochrian Ens., Student String Qt

Because of his early death, Walter Leigh did not realize the full potential of the splendid *String Quartet* of 1929, with its sinewy, Hindemithian influences. Earlier (in 1922) he wrote the easily communicative *Reverie*, while the *Romance* is even more appealingly languorous. But by 1930 Leigh was writing his *Three Movements* in an expressively direct style. The *Music for String Orchestra* is in the same popular vein and of warm appeal. If the *Viola Sonatina* of 1932 returns to more astringent, Hindemithian lyricism, the *Flute, Oboe and Piano Trio* is unashamedly genial, while the delectably tranquil recorder *Air* and 1939 *Recorder Sonatina* finally established the pastoral English neoclassicism that is the true hallmark of Leigh's style. A most attractive and varied collection, very well played and recorded.

LEIGHTON, Kenneth (1929–88)

(i) *Cello Concerto*; (ii) *Symphony 3 (Laudes musicae), Op. 80*

🎵 Ⓜ *** Chan. 10307X. (i) Wallfisch; (ii) Mackie; RSNO, Thomson

Though not as powerful or deeply moving as the superb Finzi *Cello Concerto*, this Leighton work is tautly argued and thoughtful. **Raphael Wallfisch** plays it as if his life depended on it. The *Symphony* draws the same complete dedication from its performers. The recording is very immediate and has splendid clarity and definition.

(i) Concerto for Organ, Strings & Timpani, Op. 58. Concerto for Strings, Op. 39; Symphony for Strings, Op. 3

(N) *** Chan. 10461. BBC Nat. O of Wales, Hickox, (i) with John Scott

Kenneth Leighton's *Symphony for Strings* is a work of astonishing maturity. Written when he was nineteen, its opening has a gravity and depth reminiscent of Rubbra, though even at this stage Leighton was very much his own man. After some years spent in Deal and Oxford, he was appointed professor of music in Edinburgh, where he passed the remainder of his life. His music is expressive and lyrical: 'All my days are spent trying to find a good tune', he once said; and this shines through both in the Op. 3, which Finzi first championed, its successor of 1961, and the later *Organ Concerto* of 1970. Here is a composer of real substance played with great dedication and conviction by the **BBC National Orchestra of Wales** under the late lamented **Richard Hickox**. The recording is in the best traditions of the house.

Veris gratia (for cello, oboe & strings), Op. 9

*** Chan. 8471. Wallfisch, Caird, RLPO, Handley – FINZI: *Cello Concerto* ***

Finzi is the dedicatee of Kenneth Leighton's *Veris gratia*, and so it makes an appropriate coupling for his *Cello Concerto*, more particularly as its English pastoral style nods in his direction. The performance is highly sympathetic, **George Caird** the excellent oboist, and the naturally balanced recording is first class.

(i; iii) Elegy for Cello & Piano, Op. 5; (ii; iii) Metamorphoses for Violin & Piano, Op. 48; (ii; iii) Partita for Cello & Piano, Op. 35; (i–iii) Piano Trio, Op. 46

(M) *** Dutton CDLX 7118. (i) Fuller; (ii) McAslan; (iii) Dussek

The *Piano Trio* (1965) is a work of real substance, which grows with repeated hearing. The *Partita for Cello and Piano* (1959) is another searching, thoughtful piece with an impassioned opening *Elegy* and an inventive Scherzo. All three works are deeply felt and serious, concentrated in utterance, and all deserve to be more widely known. These are committed and powerful performances from all three artists, who are completely inside this fine music, and the cellist, **Andrew Fuller**, provides the excellent and informative notes. This is a first-rate recording, and the recorded sound is in the top flight.

Piano Quartet in 1 Movement (Contrasts & Variants), Op. 63; Piano Quintet, Op. 34; Piano Trio, Op. 46

*** Mer. CDE 84465. Markham, Edinburgh Qt

We have already had a fine recording of the *Piano Trio* of 1965, and the *Piano Quartet* and *Quintet* confirm what a strongly individual contribution Kenneth Leighton has made to mid-20th-century English chamber music. Both establish his concentrated polyphonic style and the structural unity of his conceptions, the early *Piano Quintet* of 1959 growing out of a four-note theme at the opening, which returns in the finale as a splendidly developed *Passacaglia*. The elegiac *Adagio* contrasts with a vibrant Scherzo to match that in the *Piano Trio*. The single-movement *Piano Quartet* of 1972 is a concentrated kaleidoscope of mood and tempo contrasts, yet ends in calm serenity, confirming the underlying lyricism of all Leighton's music. The performances are first class.

PIANO MUSIC

(i) Sonata for Piano, 4 Hands, Op. 92; (Solo Piano) 4 Romantic Pieces, Op. 95

*** BMS CD 408R. Composer, (i) with Kingsley

Kenneth Leighton was a formidable pianist and wrote for the instrument with consummate mastery. Both performances were recorded at the Wigmore Hall and are expertly engineered by Mike Skeet. This is approachable music, yet challenging and thoughtful, and these performances obviously enjoy a special authority.

Conflicts, Op. 51; Fantasia contrappuntistica, Op. 24; Household Pets, Op. 86; Sonatina 1; 5 Studies, Op. 22

**(*) Abacus ABA 402-2. Parkin

The *Household Pets* is a sensitive piece, refined in craftsmanship, and the *Fantasia contrappuntistica* is comparably powerful. **Eric Parkin** plays it with total sympathy, and the recording is eminently serviceable.

VOCAL MUSIC

3 Carols, Op. 23 (The Star Song; Lully, lulla, thou tiny child; An ode to the birth of our Saviour); The Christ Child lay on Mary's lap; Hymn of the Nativity; Of a rose is all my song

*** Regent REGCD 243. Christ's College, Cambridge, Ch., Rowland – BRITTEN: *Ceremony of Carols* ***

A delightful collection of carols showing that Kenneth Leighton can attractively evoke the nativity scene in lyrical music of the finest English tradition. The setting of *Lully, lulla, thou tiny child* is particularly memorable. The performances are freshly spontaneous and the warm acoustic of the chapel adds to the atmosphere. A fine coupling for Britten's famous *Ceremony of Carols*.

Crucifixus pro nobis; An Easter Sequence; Evensong Services: Magnificat & Nunc Dimittis; Magnificat & Nunc Dimittis (Collegium Magdalenae Oxoniense); Give Me the Wings of Faith; Rockingham: Chorale Prelude on 'When I Survey the Wondrous Cross'; Veni, creator spiritus; What Love of this is thine?

(BB) *** Naxos 8.555795. Durrant, Oxley, Steele-Perkins, Whitton, St John's College, Cambridge, Ch., Robinson

Leighton was steeped in the Anglican tradition in his youth

as a cathedral chorister, and he contributed to its repertory throughout his life. There are two settings here of the Evening Canticles, framing the sequence, one for Magdalen College, Oxford (1959), and the *Second Service* (1971) composed in memory of the organist Brian Runnett, who died tragically in his mid-30s. They are among the most powerful since those of Herbert Howells, vividly and thoughtfully illustrating each verse, the *Second Service* ending with a hushed *Gloria*. The *Easter Sequence*, with trumpet obbligato, here played superbly by **Crispian Steele-Perkins**, is wonderfully written for trebles, and the cantata, *Crucifixus pro nobis*, using 17th-century texts by Patrick Carey and Phineas Fletcher, is a movingly spare and compressed setting of the Passion story. **Robinson** obtains very good singing from **St John's College Choir** and the acoustic of St John's College Chapel is splendidly captured in this fine Naxos recording.

(i; ii) *Morning Canticles; O God, enfold me in the sun; Sequence for All Saints; The World's Desire;* (ii) *Chorale prelude on Rockingham for organ*

Ⓝ *** Hyp. CDA67641. (i) Wells Cathedral Ch. & School Chapel Ch., Matthew Owens, (ii) David Bednall

Kenneth Leighton's upbringing as a chorister in Wakefield Cathedral inspired him in much of his subsequent career; he composed an enormous amount for the church though he was never in fact a traditional believer. But this music has a serenity and lyricism that are unfailingly satisfying – as indeed is the singing of the **Wells Cathedral Choir**. The problems of recording in Wells Cathedral are solved with mastery.

Sinfonia mistica (Symphony 2); Te Deum laudamus

Ⓝ ✺ **** Chan. 10495. Fox, BBC Nat. Ch. of Wales & Nat. O of Wales, Hickox

This is a hauntingly compelling recording of some of Kenneth Leighton's most inspired music. Written in the mid-1970s as a response to the death of his mother, the *Sinfonia mistica* is, in the composer's words, 'a requiem or a meditation on the subject of death which usually becomes so more real to us in the second half of life'; yet the music is inspiring rather than depressing. It is music of a profoundly spiritual nature, and its six movements provide music of much imagination as well as musical logic. The texts are taken from the great metaphysical poets such as John Donne and George Herbert, and they are beautifully sung by **Sarah Fox**. The orchestral version of his magnificent *Te Deum laudamus* makes a fine bonus to an outstanding CD. The orchestra and chorus were inspired to great heights in this recording, and the sound itself is of demonstration quality.

LEONCAVALLO, Ruggiero
(1858–1919)

Pagliacci (complete; DVD versions)

**** DG **DVD** 073 4389. Vickers, Kabaivanska, Glossop, Panerai, Lorenzi, La Scala, Milan, Ch. & O, Karajan

(Director: Herbert von Karajan, V/D: Ernst Wild) – MASCAGNI: *Cavalleria rusticana* **(*)

🎜– **** Ph. **DVD** 070 428-9. Domingo, Stratas, Pons, Rinaldi, La Scala, Milan, Ch. & O, Prêtre (Dir: Franco Zeffirelli) – MASCAGNI: *Cavalleria rusticana* ****

(*) DG **DVD 073 4295. Alagna, Vassileva, Mastromarino, Marrucci, Ch. & O of the Verona Arena, Sutej (Dir: Alagna, V/D: Paula Langobardo)

(*) Opus Arte **DVD OA0983D. Galouzine, Bayo, Guelfi, Gandia, Ch. & O of Teatro Real, Madrid, López-Cobos (Director: Giancarlo del Monaco, V/D: Angel Luis-Ramírez) – MASCAGNI: *Cavalleria rusticana* **(*)

In his 1968 *Pagliacci* **Karajan** not only gave an inspired account of the opera, so imaginatively staged by Paul Hager, but also directed the performance himself. Of course he had a superb Canio in **Jon Vickers**, and the glamorous Bulgarian soprano **Raina Kabaivanska** sang and acted the part of Nedda splendidly. **Peter Glossop** not only introduces himself tellingly in the *Prologue*, singing directly to the camera, but then gives a clumsily oafish portrayal of the deformed Tonio, with sinister flashes of his determination on revenge. **Rolando Panerai** is a convincing Silvio and **Sergio Lorenzi** excellent as Peppe. But is it Jon Vickers' powerfully brooding portrayal of Canio which dominates the performance, visually as well as vocally, and his *Vesti la giubba* is truly memorable. With traditional sets and costumes, the production itself is spectacular, and the action never sags, undoubtedly a tribute to Karajan himself.

Each half of this Philips double bill is announced as 'A Film by Franco Zeffirelli', but where *Cavalleria rusticana* was recorded on location in Sicily, *Pagliacci* uses open sets as realistic as possible. Here, too, the singers mime to an audio recording, with Zeffirelli's camerawork generally helping to disguise any discrepancies between sound and vision. **Juan Pons** sings the Prologue – very powerfully – before a genuine audience including children, and that set reappears in the staging of Act II. The preliminary drama of Act I involves a more informal set, equally naturalistic, with the company of actors using an ancient van in this updating to the 1930s. Nedda's communing with the birds is introduced by offstage tweeting, as she plays with her children. **Teresa Stratas** sings brilliantly if with some edge at the top, and **Alberto Rinaldi** makes a very convincing Silvio. Yet it is **Plácido Domingo** who dominates, singing superbly in this 1981 recording.

Recorded live in 2006 in the open-air Arena di Verona, the alternative DG version offers a colourfully traditional production, well cast but with lamentably little background information given with the disc, not even a list of tracks. **Roberto Alagna** is very much the star of the show, in ringing voice, stressed only in his final *No pagliaccio non son*. He is well matched by the rich-toned **Alberto Mastromarino** as Tonio, well contrasted with the handsome Silvio of **Enrico Marrucci**. **Svetla Vassileva** as Nedda is more variable. Her basically beautiful voice grows shrill under pressure, disappointingly so when she communes with the birds. The production is strong and straightforward, and equally the conducting of **Viekoslav Sutej** underlines the melodramatic strength of the piece, recorded in surprisingly good sound.

In the Opus Arte coupling with *Cavalleria rusticana*, the opening Prologue, reliably sung by **Carlo Guelfi**, begins as the earlier opera ends. The travelling theatrical players arrive in a lorry, and the performance is truly *verismo*, with the tragic story unfolding very dramatically indeed. **Maria Bayo** as Nedda rather steals the show; she is dominated by Canio, who is boldly sung and strongly acted by **Vladimir Galouzine**, even if his voice is without the most flexible upper range. But with the whole cast on top form, including the chorus, and with gripping overall direction from **Jesus López-Cobos**, this is a very successful entertainment.

Pagliacci (complete; CD versions)

(M) *** RCA (ADD) 74321 50168-2. Caballé, Domingo, Milnes, John Alldis Ch., LSO, Santi

(***) EMI mono 5 56287-2 (2). Callas, Di Stefano, Gobbi, La Scala, Milan, Ch. & O, Serafin – MASCAGNI: *Cavalleria rusticana* (***)

(M) **(*) EMI (ADD) 7 63650-2 (2). Scotto, Carreras, Nurmela, Amb. Op. Ch., Philh. O, Muti – MASCAGNI: *Cavalleria rusticana* **(*)

For those who do not want the obvious coupling, the Caballé/Domingo RCA set is a first-rate recommendation, with fine singing from all three principals, vivid playing and recording, and one or two extra passages not normally included – as in the Nedda–Silvio duet. **Milnes** is superb in the Prologue.

It is thrilling to hear *Pagliacci* starting with the Prologue sung so vividly by **Tito Gobbi**. **Di Stefano**, too, is at his finest, but the performance inevitably centres on **Callas** and there are many points at which she finds extra intensity, extra meaning. **Serafin's** direction is strong and direct. The mono recording is greatly improved in the new transfer, with voices well forward, but this set is overpriced.

Regis provide an excellent and inexpensive transfer of the **Serafin** set, where the diva is all but upstaged by **Gobbi**. **Di Stefano** too is at his finest. A bargain. (RRC 1235)

Under **Muti's** urgent direction both *Cav.* and *Pag.* represent the music of violence. In both he has sought to use the original text, which in *Pag.* is often surprisingly different, with many top notes eliminated and Tonio instead of Canio delivering (singing, not speaking) the final *La commedia è finita*. Muti's approach represents the antithesis of smoothness. **Scotto's** Nedda goes raw above the stave, but the edge is in keeping with Muti's approach, with its generally brisk speeds. **Carreras** seems happier here than in *Cav.*, but it is the conductor and the fresh look he brings that will prompt a choice here. The sound is extremely vivid.

I *Pagliacci* (in English; complete)

(M) *** Chan. 3003. Opie, Mannion, O'Neill, Bronder, Dazeley, Geoffrey Mitchell Ch., Peter Kay Children's Ch., LPO, Parry

David Parry conducts a powerful performance in the Peter Moores Foundation's 'Opera in English' series, building the drama persuasively. The cast is one of the finest in the series yet, with **Rosa Mannion** a touching Nedda, and **Alan Opie** and **William Dazeley** both outstanding and well contrasted

in the baritone roles. **Dennis O'Neill** sings very well too as Canio, but he faces greater problems with translating the tragic clown into an English-speaking hero. No longer *On with the motley* but *Put on your costume*. Warm, atmospheric sound, with voices beautifully focused.

LEONIN (c. 1163–90)

Organa: *Alleluya, Epulemur Azamis; Gaude Maria; Propter veritatem; Viderunt omnes*

*** Lyrichord LEMS 8002. Oberlin, Bressler, Perry – PEROTINUS: *Organa* ***

Over eight centuries have passed since the construction of the Cathedral of Notre Dame began and Leonin, the cathedral's composer, was writing this music. It is in two parts, with the top voice moving in unison or octaves, or over a sustained or only occasionally moving second part. Sometimes both voices sing in unison. The present performances are extraordinarily convincing and take us back in time to the very beginning of written music. Excellent recording.

Organa: *Alleluya, Dies sanctificatus; Alleluya, dulce lignum; Alleluya, inter natos mulierum; Alleluya, Paraclitus Spiritus Sanctus; Alleluya, Pascha nostrum; Alleluya, Spiritus Sanctus procedens; Priusquam te formarem; Viderunt omnes*

*** Hyp. CDA 66944. Red Byrd, Capella Amsterdam

This is a more extensive selection of Leonin's organa than the Lyrichord disc above. The recordings include compositions for the main feasts from the first part of the liturgical year. Much of the music brings elaborate, rhapsodic melodic lines which are quite haunting in these atmospheric and confidently sung performances, admirably recorded. Full texts, translations and good documentation, as we expect from Hyperion.

Viderunt omnes

(BB) *** Naxos 8.557340. Tonus Peregrinus (with Clausulae Motet on *Non nobis Domine*) – PEROTIN: *Beata viscera; Viderunt omnes* ***

We are always fascinated by the richness of Leonin's two-part organa duplum, in which the plainchant melody is slow and the second part provides a more elaborate solo line (*organum purum*), or with the two parts moving together sonorously in an identical rhythm. Here, both male and female voices are used to vary the colour, and there is nothing dull whatsoever about the result; indeed, the bare consecutive intervals are magnetic. Also included is an earlier, simpler parallel organum, taken from the ninth-century treatise, 'Scolica euchiriadis', setting the Psalm, *Non nobis Domine*, which is equally magnetic, ending evocatively with the tolling cathedral bell. The singing of **Tonus Peregrinus** directed by **Antony Pitts** is resonantly convincing, as is the acoustic of the Abbaye de Chancelade. The superb documentation includes full texts and photographs of the original manuscripts. Coupled with the more complex organa of Perotin, this disc is an amazing bargain.

LIADOV, Anatol (1855–1914)

Baba-Yaga, Op. 56; Ballade, Op. 21b; The Enchanted Lake, Op. 62; From the Apocalypse, Op. 66; Intermezzo, Op. 8; Kikimora, Op. 63; Mazurka, Op. 19; Nénie, Op. 67; Polonaises, Opp. 49 & 55

🅑🅑 **(*)** Naxos 8.555242. Slovak PO, Gunzenhauser

Baba-Yaga; Chants Populairs Russes; Kikimora

***Australian Decca Eloquence 480 038 (2). SRO, Ansermet –
GLAZUNOV: *The Seasons; Concert Waltzes 1 & 2* **(*)**;
GLINKA: *Ruslan and Ludmilla,* etc. ***; SCHUMANN:
Carnaval **(*)**

*Baba-Yaga, Op. 56; The Enchanted Lake, Op. 62;
From the Apocalypse, Op. 66; Kikimora, Op. 63;
Mazurka: Village Scene by the Inn, Op. 19;
Polonaise, Op. 49; 8 Russian Folksongs, Op. 58;
Scherzo in D, Op. 16*

🎧 *** Chan. 9911. BBC PO, Sinaisky

The *Enchanted Lake* and *Kikimora* are wonderfully atmospheric, and the performances by **Vassily Sinaisky** and the **BBC Philharmonic** are pure magic. Although they are the best known, a piece like *From the Apocalypse* is hardly less inspired. The performances are matched by recording of equal richness and luminosity.

These Liadov items gave both Decca and **Ansermet** a good opportunity to show off their prowess. Indeed, one is swept into the evil world of *Baba-Yaga* from the word go and *Kikimora* is no less intense. The eight items of Liadov's *Chants Populairs Russes* are very pleasing, with the Russian colours producing some wonderful sonorities. The 1960s recordings are superbly transferred.

It is good that **Gunzenhauser's** comprehensive Liadov collection has been transferred from full-price Marco Polo to bargain-price Naxos. They are well played and recorded versions of this colourful and imaginative music, and certainly worth the very modest cost. The new full-price Chandos version under Sinaisky, with slightly different programming, offers more sophisticated playing and outstandingly atmospheric recording and is obviously preferable, though the Naxos has the brighter focus.

PIANO MUSIC

Barcarolle in F sharp min.; Marionettes; Little Waltz in G; Musical Snuffbox; 3 Pieces, Op. 11; 2 Pieces, Op. 24; 3 Pieces, Op. 57; 4 Pieces, Op. 64; 3 Preludes; Variations on a Polish Folk Theme, Op. 51; Variations on a Theme by Glinka, Op. 35

Ⓝ 🅑🅑 *** Hyp. Helios CDH 55309. Coombs

Framed by two more ambitious sets of variations (of equal attraction) these miniatures have much of the charm, elegance and melodic facility of Liadov's better-known orchestral vignettes based on Russian folk tunes. The composer's piano music represented the largest part of his output and,

as **Stephen Coombs** points out in his note with this disc, though often small in scale each jewelled piece is immaculately finished. Coombs plays all of them with affectionate style and soon captures the listener's response to music of skilled melodic and gently moving craftsmanship. The recording is excellent.

LIGETI, György (1923–2006)

(i) *Cello Concerto;* (ii) *Piano Concerto;* (iii) *Violin Concerto*

🎧 *** DG 439 808-2. (i) Queyras; (ii) Aimard; (iii) Gawriloff;
Ens. InterContemporain, Boulez

This concertante triptych won the *Gramophone* magazine's Contemporary Music Award in 1996. The composer's imaginative inventiveness is never in doubt, but his musical purpose is not always easy to fathom. All the performers believe that this music has an underlying profundity; all three performances are musically and technically impressive and communicate strongly.

6 Bagatelles for Wind Quintet

*** Nim. NI 5728. V. Quintet – HINDEMITH: *Kleine
Kammermusik;* NIELSEN: *Wind Quintet* ***

*** Crystal CD 750. Westwood Wind Quintet – CARLSSON:
Nightwings; MATHIAS: *Quintet;* BARBER: *Summer
Music* ***

Ligeti's folk-inspired *Bagatelles* are highly inventive and very attractive; and on Crystal they are played with dazzling flair and unanimity of ensemble by this American group.

The **Vienna Quintet** give as persuasive an account of the lighthearted 1953 *Bagatelles* as any we have had in the past. They are subtle, witty and effervescent and a delight from first to last – and they are beautifully recorded in the Wiener Konzerthaus. Choice here will depend on couplings.

Horn Trio

*** Chan. 9964. Danish Horn Trio – BRAHMS: *Horn Trio* ***

Ligeti entitled his Trio 'Homage to Brahms', and he follows Brahms's four-movement layout, though with a *Passacaglia-Lament* placed as the finale, rather than an eruption of exuberance. It would seem an obvious coupling, yet the composer said of his work that 'the only thing reminiscent of Brahms is perhaps a certain smilingly conservative comportment – with distinctly ironic distance' (whatever that implies). It is an individual and challenging work, played with extraordinary commitment and expertise, but one wonders whether many Brahms lovers will take to it!

String Quartet 2

Ⓜ *** Wigmore Hall Live WHLive 003. Arditti Qt –
DUTILLEUX: *Ainsi la nuit;* NANCARROW: *Quartet 3* ***

Ligeti's *String Quartet 2* opens *Allegro nervosa* with a dramatic single pizzicato pluck; then, after whistly harmonics, the figuration is spontaneously impulsive and fragmentary, but not in any way melodic. The whole of the following *Sostenuto, molto calmo* is a variation of the fabric of the first movement, and the *Presto furioso* opens with repeated pizzicatos (remembering Bartók's *First Quartet*). The composer likens this movement to the *Poème symphonique for hundred metronomes!* Then follows a *Presto furioso, brutale, tumultuoso*, which speaks for itself. The fifth and final movement, *Allegro con delicatezza*, begins like the buzzing of flies, but then creates a remarkable atmosphere of mysticism, 'like a memory seen through mist', the composer tells us, 'the whole of the previous progress of the work is recapitulated but in a gentler form', even with wisps of what is almost, but not quite, a melodic fragment. This live Wigmore Hall performance builds up great tension so that even if you cannot follow the argument the finale is electrifying, and there is a distinct silence after the work's close, before the audience responds with applause.

Le Grand Macabre (complete opera)

*** Sony S2K 62312 (2). Ehlert, Clark, White, Nes, Ragin, Cole, Suart, L. Sinf. Voices, Philh. O, Salonen

It is the revised version of *Le Grand Macabre* that is recorded here under supervision from the composer, using an English text. Set in Breughelland, this apocalyptic vision lightens its macabre theme – of the ending of the world – with humour, viciously satirical and anarchic, setting out from a witty prelude for tuned motor-horns, with tongue-in-cheek echoes of a baroque toccata. **Salonen** is a brilliant advocate, drawing colourful playing from the **Philharmonia**. **Sibylle Ehlert** is dazzling in the coloratura role of Gepopo, **Graham Clark** a characterful Piet the Pot, and **Willard White** aptly baleful as the *grand macabre* himself, the sinister Nekrotzar. This may be an offbeat piece, but as audiences have found, it has a sparkle which has one simultaneously laughing and thinking. Atmospheric sound, recorded live at the Théâtre du Chatelet.

LILBURN, Douglas (1915–2001)

Aotearoa Overture; Birthday Offering; Drysdale Overture; Festival Overture; Forest (Tone Poem); Processional Fanfare; Song of Islands

(BB) *** Naxos 8.557697. New Zealand SO, Judd

James Judd and the **New Zealand Symphony Orchestra** followed up their CD of Lilburn's three symphonies (see below) with this collection of shorter works. *Aotearoa* is the Maori name for New Zealand and the engaging overture is worthy of its name. *Forest* is an early tone-poem with a brooding northern atmosphere, while the *Drysdale Overture* is pictorial in a more pastoral way. *A Song of Islands* is similarly rewarding, but perhaps the most inventive work is *A Birthday Offering*, written in 1956 as a tenth birthday tribute to the New Zealand orchestra, a kind of concerto for orchestra, none too predictable. The *Processional Fanfare*, for three trumpets and organ, is an exuberant arrangement of *Gaudeamus igitur*, played with real flair; but then throughout the disc the New Zealand Symphony Orchestra are on their best form, which is considerable, while the Naxos recording is first rate.

Symphonies 1–3

⌐ (BB) *** Naxos 8.555862. New Zealand SO, Judd

Douglas Lilburn is a true symphonist: his structures are not inflated, and the orchestral colouring is an integral part of the musical argument. Inspired by the spacious landscapes and mountain ranges of his homeland, the first two are heavily influenced by Sibelius; indeed the slow movement of 1 (1949) includes a direct quotation. Vaughan Williams (under whom the composer studied in England) makes his presence felt in the slow movement of 2 and perhaps also in the folksy flavour of the Scherzos. In the *Third Symphony* (1961) Lilburn finds an even more individual voice. Although there are aspects of serialism here, one would hardly guess, so spontaneously appealing is the writing. Indeed, all three symphonies are splendid works, immediately drawing the listener in to their special world, and they could not have a more committed advocate. **Judd's** performances are vigorously alive, gripping, and splendidly played, and the Naxos recording is vividly detailed, with plenty of warmth and atmosphere.

LINDE, Bo (1933–70)

(i) Cello Concerto; (ii) Violin Concerto

⌐ 🌐 (BB) **** Naxos 8.557855. (i) Kliegel; (ii) Gomyo; Gävle SO, Sundkvist

Make no mistake this violin concerto, first performed in 1958, is a work of quite striking beauty and full of a gentle melancholy. Linde's craftsmanship is thoroughly assured, the invention warm and lyrical, and the writing for the orchestra highly imaginative and luminous. Its final touching coda is altogether magical. The young Tokyo-born, Canadian violinist **Karen Gomyo** is the elegant and expressive soloist and the orchestral playing is first class. The somewhat later *Cello Concerto* is a somewhat darker but no less intense piece, with a powerful *Lento* finale. This music has real nobility and a natural eloquence, and it inspires a totally committed performance from **Maria Kliegel** and the orchestra, from whom **Petter Sundkvist** draws an excellent response. The recording is of demonstration standard, lifelike and with a truthful perspective between soloist and orchestra.

A Merry Overture; Musica Concertante; Suite Variée; Suite Boulogne

*** Swedish Society SACD 1132. Gävle SO, Sundkvist

This music may not be in quite the same bracket as the *Violin Concerto*, but it is well worth investigating all the same. *A Merry Overture* is an early work, written when Linde was twenty-one, and it was much performed in Sweden in the 1950s. The *Musica Concertante* of 1963 is a lively piece which dates from the period of the *Cello Concerto*. **Petter Sundkvist** gets good results from his players and the recording is every bit as good as it is in the concertos.

LINLEY, Thomas, Jr (1756–78)

The Song of Moses (oratorio); Let God arise (anthem)

Ⓝ ⒷⒷ **** Hyp. Helios CDH 55302. Gooding, Daneman, King, Dale Forbes, Holst Singers, Parley of Instruments, Holman

Thomas Linley, born in Bath, came from a musical family. He was an exact contemporary of Mozart, who, after Linley's early death, declared he was 'a true genius'. Both the early anthem (written for the 1773 Three Choirs Festival at Worcester) and his splendid oratorio (which triumphs over its undistinguished libretto, using the same material as Handel's *Israel in Egypt*) show his skill in vocal and orchestral writing and fresh melodic gifts, drawing on the styles of both Handel and J. C. Bach. Both oratorio and anthem are framed with spectacular choruses, fully scored with trumpets, and the closing *Wonderful art thou* from the latter is a magnificent double fugue. But it is the solo writing, and especially the airs and duets for one or two sopranos, that stands out, and it is delivered with lyrical purity, virtuosity and aplomb by both the fine soloists here, **Julia Gooding** and **Sophie Daneman**. With superb performances of both works under **Peter Holman**, this is a disc not to be missed – you will be surprised at the exuberant and individual lyrical qualities of the music.

LISZT, Franz (1811–86)

(i–ii) Piano Concertos 1–2; Fantasia on themes from Beethoven's 'The Ruins of Athens'; Grande fantaisie symphonique on themes from Berlioz's 'Lélio'; Hungarian fantasia for Piano & Orchestra; Malédiction; Totentanz; (i) Ce qu'on entend sur la montagne; Die Ideale; Festklänge; 2 Episodes from Lenau's 'Faust'; Héroïde funèbre; Hamlet; Hungaria; Hunnenschlacht; Mazeppa; Mephisto Waltz 2; Orpheus; Les Préludes; Prometheus; Tasso; Von der Wiege bis zum Grabe; (i; iii) Dante Symphony; (i; iv) A Faust Symphony; (i) Concert Paraphrases: SCHUBERT: Wanderer-Fantasie; WEBER: Polonaise brillante

⊶ ⒷⒷ *** EMI (ADD) 5 85573-2 (7). (i) Leipzig GO, Masur, with (ii) Béroff; (iii) Leipzig Thomaner-chor; (iv) Leipzig R. Ch. male voices

Béroff has justly won acclaim for his superb technique and his refined poetic sense, and these recordings show him to be a Lisztian of flair. His accounts of the much-recorded concertos can hold their own with most of the competition: these are exhilarating performances and are given the extra attraction of fine orchestral playing and vivid (late 1970s) recording. The same comments apply to the other piano concertante works: they are all superbly done, with ample brilliance, yet are musical and stylish, with a sense of fun in the virtuosic fireworks. As for the tone-poems, Masur makes the strongest possible case for them. He proves as persuasive

an advocate as any on record. The rich sonority on the lower strings, the dark, perfectly blended woodwind tone and the fine internal balance of the **Leipzig Gewandhaus Orchestra** hold the listener's attention throughout – for in the weaker pieces Liszt benefits from all the help his interpreters can give him. Only in *Orpheus* does Masur let us down: he breezes through it at record speed and misses the endearing gentleness that Beecham brought to it in the early 1960s. In the two *Symphonies*, Masur is again impressive, though even in the *Gretchen* movement of the *Faust Symphony* he moves things on, albeit not unacceptably, and there is no want of delicacy and ardour. The *Faust Symphony* can certainly hold its own, and the same may be said of the *Dante Symphony*. The recordings are well balanced and refined throughout, emerging more freshly than ever on CD. A very considerable achievement.

Piano Concertos 1–2; Concerto 3 (ed. Jay Rosenblatt); Concerto pathétique; De profundis; Fantasia on a Theme from Beethoven's 'Ruins of Athens'; Fantasy on Hungarian Folk Tunes; Grande fantaisie symphonique on themes from Berlioz's 'Lélio'; Méditation; Polonaise brillante; Totentanz; Wandererfantaisie

Ⓜ *** Chan. 10371X (3). Lortie, Hague Residentie O, Pehlivanian

Louis Lortie's accounts of the two known concertos with the **Hague Residentie Orchestra** under **George Pehlivanian** are very impressive and can hold their own with all but the very best. But these are better recorded than any of their rivals and bring poetic insights as well as virtuosity. There is less competition in the *Hungarian Fantasia* and *Totentanz*, and these Chandos versions rank with the best from the past. The so-called *Third Concerto*, first given in 1990, and the *Concerto pathétique* are reconstructions and are of interest to Lisztians rather than the wider musical public. Liszt's transcription of Schubert's *Wanderer Fantasia* for piano and orchestra is another matter, and Lortie's performance is second to none. The transcriptions of the Weber *Polonaise brillante*, the *Fantasia on a Theme from Beethoven's 'Ruins of Athens'*, and the *Grande fantaisie symphonique on Berlioz's 'Lélio'* are all equally desirable, and once again the fine playing of the Residentie Orchestra under Pehlivanian contributes to making this an exhilarating collection, with consistently excellent Chandos recording.

Piano Concertos 1–2

⊶ Ⓜ *** Ph. (ADD) 464 710-2. S. Richter, LSO, Kondrashin – BEETHOVEN: *Piano Sonatas 10; 19–20* ***

Ⓜ (***) DG mono 474 024-2 (5). Kempff, LSO, Fistoulari – BEETHOVEN: *Piano Concertos 1–5*; BRAHMS: *Piano Concerto 1*; MOZART: *Piano Concertos 9 & 15*; SCHUMANN: *Piano Concerto* (***)

Piano Concertos 1–2; Hungarian Fantasia

(***) BBC mono BBCL 4031-2. S. Richter, LSO, Kondrashin (with CHOPIN: *Andante spianato & grande polonaise, Op. 22* (***))

(i) *Piano Concertos 1; 2;* (ii) *Malédiction;* (iii) *Dante Sonata* (orch. Lambert)

🅱🅱 (***) Dutton mono CDBP 9742. (i) Sauer, Paris Conservatoire O, Weingartner; (ii) Osborn, Boyd Neel SO, Boyd Neel; (iii) Kentner, Sadler's Wells O, Lambert

Piano Concertos 1–2; Totentanz

🎵— 🌼 **** DG 423 571-2. Zimerman, Boston SO, Ozawa

🎵— 🅱🅱 **** Warner Apex 2564 62044-2. Berezovsky, Philh. O, Wolff

**** BIS **SACD** 1530. Cohen, São Paulo SO, Neschling

(i) *Piano Concertos 1–2; Sonata in B min.*

Ⓜ **(*) Sony SK 94746. Ax; (i) Philh. O, Salonen

Krystian Zimerman's record of the two *Concertos* and the *Totentanz* is altogether thrilling, and he has the advantage of excellent support from the **Boston Orchestra** under **Ozawa**. It has poise and classicism and, as one listens, one feels this music could not be played in any other way – surely the mark of a great performance! This record is outstanding in every way, and still remains a first choice for this repertoire.

Boris Berezovsky's extrovert yet highly musical accounts of the two *Concertos* and the rumbustious *Totentanz* make a superb alternative super-bargain issue. Berezovsky plays throughout with enormous panache and bravura, yet with melting poetic feeling. **Hugh Wolff** proves a splendid partner, and the **Philharmonia Orchestra** play with great gusto. The full-blooded, resonantly spacious recording was made at Aldeburgh in 1994.

Yet another fine triptych comes from **Arnoldo Cohen** with the **São Paulo Symphony Orchestra** and **John Neschling**, and they have the advantage of spectacular BIS surround sound. Superb solo contributions (especially in the thrilling bravura of the *Totentanz*), splendid orchestral support, and a real feeling for Liszt. Perhaps this is not an ultimate first choice but it ranks with the finest.

Emanuel Ax and **Esa-Pekka Salonen** also create a memorable partnership for a splendid modern coupling of the two Liszt *Piano Concertos*, with a spectacularly vivid recording to match performances which have all the bravura qualities one might have expected from the composer himself. Yet the lyrical interludes are played most sensitively. Ax's account of the *Sonata* is equally arresting, but it is a highly personal reading, impetuous and wilful. Even so, this is a remarkable disc that cannot fail to hold the listener from the first note to the last, and the sound, though forward, is in the demonstration bracket.

Sviatoslav Richter's playing is unforgettable and so is his rapport with **Kondrashin** and the **LSO**, whose playing throughout is of the very highest order. The sound is vivid and present but the acoustic is rather dry for full comfort. However, given playing of this calibre, one soon adjusts. The reissue is now available as one of Philips's '50 Great Recordings', curiously recoupled with three of Beethoven's least ambitious early piano sonatas, beautifully played and recorded.

Kempff recorded the two Liszt Concertos for Decca in 1954 in totally distinctive performances, remarkable for the diamond clarity of textures and rhythmic sparkle. The inflation so easily suggested in these works is completely avoided, so the results are uniquely fresh, helped by clean Decca sound engineered by Kenneth Wilkinson. Mono recordings too long unavailable.

This Dutton reissue is of special documentary interest. **Emil Sauer** and **Felix Weingartner** were the last surviving members of Liszt's circle so they knew his musical intentions well. Their recording affords a rare opportunity to relish the artistry of Sauer, then 76 but still a commanding, authoritative virtuoso. **Franz Osborn** gave us the very first recording of the *Malédiction*, which comes from 1945, his only appearance as a concerto soloist on records. The sound is very natural indeed for the period and the playing magisterial. So, too, is **Louis Kentner's** *Dante Sonata* in the arrangement that Constant Lambert made of *Après une lecture de Dante*. Again, the 1940 recording wears its years lightly in this fine Dutton transfer. A valuable set that all Lisztians will want.

The BBC Legends CD is a memento of **Richter's** first major concert in London in the Royal Albert Hall in 1961. Broadly the interpretations reveal little difference between live and studio, with the important exception that the rush of adrenalin at the end of each finale brings speeds a fraction more urgent, with virtuosity even more daring. But the disc is a must for the *Hungarian Fantasia*. This is electrifying playing with the music presented with power rather than wit. Moreover, the BBC CD captures a real sense of occasion. The Chopin, recorded at a concert two days earlier, provides a delightful bonus.

Piano Concerto 1 in E flat

*** DG 477 640-2. Yundi Li, Philh. O, A. Davis – CHOPIN: *Piano Concerto 1* ***

Ⓜ *** DG (ADD) 449 719-2. Argerich, LSO, Abbado – CHOPIN: *Piano Concerto 1* ***

Ⓝ *** Naïve V5053. de la Salle, Gulbenkian Foundation O, Lisbon, Foster – PROKOFIEV: *Concerto 1;* SHOSTAKOVICH: *Concerto 1* ***

Yundi Li's Liszt concerto is pretty stunning. He won the Chopin Warsaw Competition in 2000 when he was still in his teens. Thus he is in the Pollini, Argerich, Zimerman lineage and lives up to it in this, his début concerto disc. His playing is fresh and natural, and his virtuosity is lightly worn. **Sir Andrew Davis** and the **Philharmonia Orchestra** give excellent support and the sound is first rate.

Martha Argerich (in 1968) recorded only Liszt's *First Concerto* and not the *Second*. However, there is an excellent partnership between the pianist and **Abbado**, and this is a performance of flair and high voltage which does not ever become vulgar. It is very well recorded, and in this reissue, coupled with Chopin, it sounds better than ever.

Lise de la Salle, accompanied with typical flair by **Lawrence Foster**, makes a charismatic début with this triptych of brilliant performances. Her Liszt glitters and thrills with bravura, yet she finds the full expressive range of the *Adagio*, and she is certainly a match for her more familiar competitors. The couplings are equally remarkable and this is a disc to look out for.

Piano Concerto 2 in A

(B) *** Virgin 3 91369-2. Andsnes, Bergen PO, Kitayenko –
GRIEG: *Piano Concerto; Lyric Pieces, Op. 65* ***

Leif Ove Andsnes is a real musician who plays with great tenderness and poetic feeling, as well as bravura. Marvellous sound too, and an excellent balance.

(i) Dante Symphony; (ii) Années de pèlerinage, Book 2: Après un lecture du Dante (Fantasia Quasi Sonata)

(M) *** Warner Maestro 256469368-9. (i) Women's Voices of Berlin R. Ch., BPO, Barenboim; (ii) Barenboim (piano)

(i) Dante Symphony; (ii; iii) A Faust Symphony, G.108; (ii; iv) Les Préludes; Prometheus

(B) **(*) Double Decca (ADD) 466 751-2 (2). (i) Voltaire College Ch., SRO, López-Cobos; (ii) Solti; (iii) Jerusalem, Chicago Ch. & SO; (iv) LPO

Barenboim really has the measure of this overextended but remarkable work and controls its rhapsodic structure admirably, holding the tension throughout the first movement and creating enormous visceral excitement at the close. He is helped by marvellous playing from the **BPO**, who really sound as if they believe in it all, and the radiant choral effects are superbly brought off. The resonant acoustic of Berlin's Schaulspielhaus lets everything expand with Wagnerian amplitude and the result is very impressive indeed. As an encore, Barenboim leaves the rostrum for the piano and offers the *Dante Sonata*, which has the same literary basis but offers a quite different musical treatment. The performance is flamboyantly arresting, but the piano recording is curiously shallow.

López-Cobos's account of the *Dante Symphony* comes with Liszt's alternative conclusion, a sudden loud outburst of 'Hallelujahs' from the trebles after the usual *pianopianissimo* ending. It is most effective, crowning a performance which is more remarkable for its refinement of sound and balance than for its dramatic thrust. **Solti's** Liszt is almost always successful. His performance of the *Faust Symphony* is spacious, yet brilliant, with superb playing from his **Chicago Orchestra**, though the bright recording underlines the fierce element in his reading and removes some of the warmth. The Mephistophelean finale brings the most impressive playing of all, with Solti's fierceness chiming naturally with the movement's demonic quality. The two tone-poems, recorded in the 1970s, are brilliantly played and recorded. Even with the reservations expressed, this is excellent value.

(i) Fantasia on Hungarian Folk Tunes; Malédiction; Totentanz; (ii) Arr. of Schubert: Wanderer Fantasia (all for piano and orchestra); Années de pèlerinage (complete); Ballade 2; Concert paraphrases: Bellini: Réminiscences de Norma; 12 Schubert Songs; Mozart: Réminiscences de Don Juan; Verdi: Rigoletto; 2 Concert studies (Waldesrauschen; Gnomenreigen); 3 Concert studies (Il lamento; La reggierezza; Un sospiro); Consolations 1–6; 12 Etudes d'exécution transcendante; Etudes

d'exécution transcendante d'après Paganini: La campanella; Grand galop chromatique; Harmonies poétiques et religieuses: Funérailles; Hungarian Rhapsody 12; Liebesträume 1–3; Mephisto Waltz 1; Sonata; Valse impromptu

(B) *** Decca 467 801-2 (9). Bolet; with (i) LSO, Iván Fischer; (ii) LPO, Solti

The full range of the late **Jorge Bolet's** achievement for Decca in the music of Liszt is admirably surveyed in this bargain box, all splendidly recorded, and there are two other shorter surveys below. One or other should be in every representative collection.

Fantasia on Hungarian Folk Themes (for piano & orchestra)

(BB) (***) Naxos mono 8.110683. Moiseiwitsch, LPO, Lambert –
GRIEG: *Piano Concerto*; SAINT-SAËNS: *Piano Concerto 2*
(***)

A useful reminder of **Moiseiwitsch's** virtuosity and Lisztian prowess. His account with Constant Lambert still gives much pleasure.

(i) Fantasia on Hungarian Folk Tunes; Hungarian Rhapsodies 2, 4–5; Mazeppa; Mephisto Waltz 2; Les Préludes; Tasso, lamento e trionfo

⊶ (B) **** DG Double (ADD) 453 130-2 (2). BPO, Karajan; (i) with Cherkassky

Shura Cherkassky's glittering (1961) recording of the *Hungarian Fantasia* is an affectionate performance with some engaging touches from the orchestra, though the pianist is dominant and his playing is superbly assured. The rest of the programme is comparably charismatic. The cellos and basses sound marvellous in the *Fifth Rhapsody* and *Tasso*, and even the brashness of *Les Préludes* is a little tempered. *Mazeppa* is a great performance, superbly thrilling and atmospheric – with a riveting coda – worthy of a Rosette. A set showing **Karajan** and his **Berlin Orchestra** at their finest.

A Faust Symphony (DVD version)

⊶ ✪ **** EuroArts DVD 2072078. Riegel, Tanglewood Festival Ch., Boston SO, Bernstein (V/D: Humphrey Burton)

A Faust Symphony (CD versions)

(M) *** DG (ADD) 447 449-2. Riegel, Tanglewood Festival Ch., Boston SO, Bernstein

(BB) *** EMI Encore 5 090172-2. Winbergh, Westminster Choir College Male Ch., Phd. O, Muti

A Faust Symphony; Hunnenschlacht; Mephisto Walt. 1; Nocturnal Procession

(N) **(*) Australian Decca Eloquence 442 9992 (2). SRO, Ansermet – MAGNARD: *Symphony 3* ***

Bernstein conducts this riveting (1976) Boston performance, so thrillingly captured on DVD – and one of his very finest recordings, with all the added stimulus of live music-making, and splendidly photographed under the direction of

Humphrey Burton. Fine as the CD version is, it is not its match. Bernstein seems to possess the ideal temperament for holding together grippingly the melodrama of the long first movement, taking it spaciously but building up the great excitement in the closing pages, while in the lovely *Gretchen* movement he draws exquisite playing from the **Boston Symphony Orchestra**, both the woodwind and the strings in the many chamber-music passages. The *Mephistofelean* finale, with its anticipations of the orchestral wildness of Berlioz and the brass sonorities of Wagner, is held together superbly, with the tension building all the time, to be capped by the magnificent entry of the chorus, and sustained to the final profound apotheosis. **Kenneth Riegel's** impressive tenor contribution to the CD version is again surpassed by his ardent singing in the live performance, and throughout the playing of the Boston orchestra is superb, especially the strings, helped in their sonority and radiance by the unsurpassed acoustic of Symphony Hall.

Muti shows a natural sympathy for a piece that can readily seem overlong. Some might feel that he is too overtly melodramatic in the finale, yet his pacing of the first movement is admirable, finding tenderness as well as red-blooded excitement. In the *Gretchen* movement, he conjures the most delicately atmospheric playing from the orchestra, the vocal contributions are sound, and throughout he is helped by the ambience of the Old Met. in Philadelphia, which seems especially suitable for this score. The early digital recording is brilliant yet full-blooded, and on EMI's super-budget Encore label this remains very competitive.

The opening of the *Faust Symphony* sounds especially haunting in **Ansermet's** hands, and although his orchestra lacks the virtuoso brilliance of rival recordings, this performance is hardly wanting in drama. Indeed, the impassioned string-writing in the opening *Faust* movement is surprisingly forceful, rich and full. The delicacy in the *Gretchen* movement is particularly striking, even if the woodwind playing is scarcely the last word in orchestral refinement. In the finale, Ansermet really tells a story through this music with excellent characterization, and it ends in a blaze of sound with a full chorus and organ included. **Werner Krenn** is the superb tenor soloist. The *Dance of the Village Inn* (*Mephisto Waltz 1*) is lusty enough – and again the sound is very rich and full (incidentally, Ansermet uses the *pianissimo* ending of this work). The *Nocturnal Procession* is full of brooding atmosphere. Ansermet's was the work's première recording on LP, and it stands up very well. The flamboyant *Battle of the Huns* was recorded earlier (in 1959) yet still sounds most vivid. Here Ansermet matches the flamboyance of the writing with a spontaneous, hell-for-leather performance which is exciting from first note to last – and Liszt's use of the organ is most effective.

(i–iv) *A Faust Symphony;* (i; ii) *Orpheus;* (i; v) *Les Préludes; Tasso;* (i–iii; vi) *Psalm XIII*

🔊 ⓑⓑ ******** EMI Gemini (ADD) 4 76927-2 (2). (i) RPO; (ii) Beecham; (iii) with Beecham Choral Soc. (iv) A. Young; (v) cond. Silvestri; (vi) W. Midgley

Beecham's classic (1958) Kingsway recording of the *Faust Symphony*, very well transferred to CD, shows this instinctive

Lisztian at his most illuminatingly persuasive. His control of speed is masterly, spacious and eloquent in the first two movements, without dragging, and with the central portrait of *Gretchen* ravishingly played. The finale is brilliant and urgent, without any hint of breathlessness. The Beecham CD is unlikely to disappoint anyone wanting to enjoy a uniquely warm and understanding reading of an equivocal piece, hard to interpret. *Orpheus*, the original coupling for the two-disc LP set, is also played very beautifully. The performance of *Psalm 13* is slightly less impressive. It is sung in English, with the legendary **Walter Midgley**, but is drier and more monochrome. For the additional fillers here, EMI have chosen **Silvestri's** highly distinguished Philharmonia accounts of *Les Préludes* and *Tasso*. *Tasso* is less easy to bring off and Silvestri has its full measure and gives it great intensity. Again, the recordings from 1957/8 are amazingly full and vivid.

Hungarian Rhapsodies 1–3

(*******) Cala (mono) CACD 0545. NBC SO, Stokowski – BEETHOVEN: *Symphony 6* (*******)

Recorded in February 1955, **Stokowski's** performances of the first three Liszt *Hungarian Rhapsodies* have the same glowing qualities as the Beethoven, with which they are coupled. This is music of a flamboyance that chimes exactly with the conductor's unique qualities.

Hungarian Rhapsodies 1–6

(*) Mercury (ADD) **SACD 432 015-2. LSO, Dorati – ENESCU: *Romanian Rhapsody 1* *******

Dorati's is undoubtedly the finest set of *Hungarian Rhapsodies*. He brings out the gypsy flavour and, with lively playing from the **LSO**, there is both polish and sparkle. The new SACD transfer further enhances the sound although the upper range betrays the age of the recordings.

Mephisto Waltz 1

(*******) BBC mono BBCL 4059-2. LSO, Stokowski – GABRIELI: *Sonata pian'e forte*; NIELSEN: *Symphony 6*; TIPPETT: *Concerto for Double String Orchestra* *******

Stokowski's zestful and vibrant account of the first *Mephisto Waltz* comes with two rarities of the Stokowski discography, Nielsen's *Sixth Symphony* and the Tippett *Double Concerto*.

SYMPHONIC POEMS

Ce qu'on entend sur la montagne; Festklänge; Hunnenschlacht

ⓑⓑ ****(*)** Naxos 8.557846. New Zealand SO, Halász

Both Chandos and Naxos are making a survey of Liszt's symphonic poems, and while in this instance **Halász** and his New Zealand forces don't quite equal the outstanding excellence of the Chandos recording, this collection is still impressively played and recorded, and many collectors may feel that the Naxos price is about right for these works. They are by no means top-quality Liszt but are still worth having on disc when the performances are so idiomatically committed.

Ce qu'on entend sur la montagne; Orpheus; Les Préludes; Tasso: Lamento e Trionfo (Symphonic Poems)

*** Chan. 10341. BBC PO, Noseda

Ce qu'on entend sur la montagne, beginning with its murmuring violins, is most atmospheric, and **Noseda** generates plenty of inner tension in this somewhat episodic score. The huge dynamic range of the recording is very effective, with all departments of the orchestra responding to the vivid scoring with warm enthusiasm. *Tasso* brings some very beautiful playing, with Noseda coaxing ravishing sounds in the evocative passages, but also rising to the climaxes superbly.

Les Préludes is perhaps a shade too delicate, lacking the gravitas – and, indeed, electricity – of Karajan's famous DG account, but it has an alternative subtlety of nuance to make it compelling in its own way. The richly expressive writing in *Orpheus* is much better suited to Noseda's expansive approach. A promising start to the series.

Festklänge; Héroïde funèbre; Mazeppa; Prometheus

*** Chan. 10417. BBC PO, Noseda

The highlight here is *Mazeppa*, one of Liszt's finest symphonic poems, alongside *Orpheus* and *Les Préludes*. While Karajan's electrifying version is not surpassed (and probably never will be), **Noseda** and the **BBC Philharmonic Orchestra** give it plenty of life and vividly recreate the evocation of the horse galloping across the countryside with the eponymous hero strapped to its back. The other works are more uneven, but Noseda is suitably exuberant in *Festklänge* and he catches the sombre atmosphere of the *Hérodïade funèbre* eloquently. The BBC orchestra is again on its toes throughout and the Chandos recording is in the demonstration bracket.

Héroïde Funèbre; Hungaria; Le triomphe funèbre

(BB) *** Naxos 8.557847. New Zealand SO, Halász

Michael Halász here offers three rarities, each with a valedictory theme. *Hungaria*, dating from 1856, was inspired by the Hungarian uprising of 1848, with a funeral march at its heart. *Héroïde funèbre* of 1848 was similarly inspired by the revolution in France, also in 1848, and again with funeral music, this time set against beautiful lyrical ideas and passing quotation from the *Marseillaise*. *Le triomphe funèbre*, shorter than the other two, is tauter, with greater use of chromatic ideas, but including a patriotic march before the final, sombre funeral march. Halász draws committed performances from his orchestra, very well recorded.

Hunnenschlacht (Symphonic Poem); Hungarian March

(M) ** Telarc CD 80079. Cincinnati SO, Kunzel – BEETHOVEN: *Wellington's Victory* **

From **Kunzel** a direct, unsubtle performance of a rarely recorded piece, not one of Liszt's finest works in the genre. The Telarc sound, however, is highly spectacular, with the organ interpolation adding to the expansiveness of texture. The *Hungarian March* is Liszt's own orchestration of a piano piece written in 1843; it is rather jolly and is played with much spirit here to make a good encore.

(i) Hunnenschlacht; Mazeppa; Orpheus; (ii) Les Préludes (symphonic poems)

*** Australian Decca Eloquence 466 706-2. (i) LAPO; (ii) VPO; Mehta

Zubin Mehta is in his element here. The performances are red-blooded and tremendously exciting. Liszt's vulgarity is played up in a swaggeringly extrovert way, but there is plenty of character too. The rich, vibrant recording is an audiophile's delight – the staggered entries throughout the strings in *Mazeppa* are thrilling. Equally praiseworthy is the pastoral atmosphere Mehta creates in *Orpheus* – with real sensitivity from the **Los Angeles Orchestra**. Those who like Liszt with all the stops out will certainly enjoy this Australian reissue, especially when the CD transfer is so vivid.

Les Préludes; Mazeppa; Prometheus; Tasso, lamento e trionfo (symphonic poems)

⑧→ (BB) **** Naxos 8.550487. Polish Nat. RSO (Katowice), Halász

Michael Halász too has the full measure of this repertoire, and this is one of the most successful collections of Liszt's symphonic poems to have emerged in recent years. He draws some remarkably fine playing from the **Katowice Radio Orchestra**. The brass playing is very impressive throughout, especially the trombones and tuba, who have the epic main theme of *Mazeppa*, but its grandiloquence is no less powerful in *Les Préludes*, weighty and never brash. The recording is spacious, with full, natural string-textures, but it is the resounding brass one remembers most.

Tasso, lamento e trionfo

**(*) Testament mono SBT 1129. Philh. O., Silvestri – TCHAIKOVSKY: *Manfred Symphony* *(*)

Silvestri's version of *Tasso* was one of his best recordings (second only perhaps to his account of Elgar's *In the South*). It comes up well in this new transfer but the Tchaikovsky coupling does not show the Romanian maestro at his best.

Totentanz (for piano and orchestra)

(B) (**(*)) Australian Decca Eloquence mono 476 7671. Katin, LPO, Martinon – (with DOHNANYI: *Variations on a Nursery Song* **(*)); LUTOSŁAWSKI: *Paganini Variations* ***; RACHMANINOV: *Paganini Variations* **(*)

Katin's dashing performance of the *Totentanz* with **Martinon** is full of demonic urgency and, despite rather thin (but not unattractive) 1954 sound, this classic account remains highly enjoyable.

PIANO MUSIC

Complete piano music (57 volumes) and supplement
Hyperion. Leslie Howard

Leslie Howard's ambitious project to record all the piano music of Liszt is now complete and has been generally well received internationally, with several issues collecting a Grand Prix du Disque in Budapest. The set has great documentary interest and has been listed and discussed in several earlier editions. The performances are very capable and musicianly, and there are many moments of poetic feeling, but for the most part his playing rarely touches distinction. The kind of concentration one finds in great Liszt pianists such as Arrau, Kempff and Richter (and there are many younger artists whose names spring to mind) only surfaces occasionally. Howard's technique is formidable, but poetic imagination and the ability to grip the listener are here less evenly developed. However the coverage is remarkable and if this playing rarely takes the breath away by its virtuosity or its poetic insights, it is unfailingly intelligent and the Hyperion recordings are consistently first class.

A full listing will be found in the Hyperion Catalogue, meanwhile we would wish to draw readers' attention to some of the rarer and more outstanding issues, such as Liszt's transcription of the *Bunte Reihe* (originally for violin and piano) of Ferdinand David (1810–70) in Volume 16 (CDA 66506). Leslie Howard plays them beautifully, as he does the two Liszt Songbooks of early Lieder in Volume 19 (CDA 66593).

Volume 26 (CDA 66771/2) is almost entirely devoted to music which Liszt wrote as a teenager, and has obvious interest, as has Howard's pioneering recording of the 12 *Grandes Etudes* in Volume 34. They were pilot versions of the *Etudes d'exécution transcendante*, and Leslie Howard plays them with remarkably confident bravura (CDA 66973). Many of the Russian and Hungarian novelties in Volume 35 (CDA 66984) are also ear-tickling.

One of the most valuable discs of the series is Volume 47 (CDA 67187), which includes unpublished music which Liszt intended for a first cycle of *Harmonies poétiques et religieuses*, while Volume 51 (CDA 67233/4), which Howard calls 'Paralipomènes', has early drafts of other famous works including three different versions of the *Dante Sonata*. The 18 *Hungarian Romances* presented on Volume 52 are equally fascinating, in essence a manuscript notebook of Hungarian themes, which in Volume 57 (CDA 67418/19), in their final form, became the 19 *Hungarian Rhapsodies*, growing out of those early collected ideas.

Alternative versions of six of those *Rhapsodies* appear in the penultimate volume (56), which consists of four CDs of 'Rarities, Curiosities, and Fragments' (CDA 67414/7) plus 23 *Album Leaves*, simple romantic pieces, which Liszt dedicated to his friends. And if you are drawn by a collection of rare operatic Concert Paraphrases, Volume 54 admirably features some rare examples (CDA 67406/7).

Crowning the whole series are the two volumes (53a/b) of the complete music for piano and orchestra (CDA 67401/2 and 67403/5) in which Howard tackles no fewer than 15 different works, admirably accompanied by the **Budapest Symphony Orchestra**. He plays them all with flair and dedication and is, as usual, very well recorded. In the final Volume (57) (CDA 67418/20) he caps the series with a dazzlingly spontaneous account of the nineteen *Hungarian Rhapsodies*.

Supplement

'New Discoveries': *Années de pèlerinage*: early drafts: *Aux anges gardiens; Sunt lacrymae rerum; Postludium: Nachtspiel: Sursum corda. Célèbre mélodie hongroise; From the Album of Princess Marie zu Sayn-Wittgenstein: Album-Leaf; Lilie; Hryá; Mazurek; Krakowiak; La lugubre gondola (original Venice manuscript); 11 Zigeuner-Epos*

*** Hyp. CDA 67346. Howard

This supplementary disc brings together two dozen items, many of them charming 'album leaves', which Liszt wrote for various admirers, including the ten-year-old Princess Marie of Sayn-Wittgenstein. Such trifles, some only a few seconds long, and a series of 11 tuneful gypsy pieces reveal Liszt at his most unpretentious, fresh and direct, and so do the newly discovered early drafts of pieces, which he later elaborated, such as *La Lugubre gondola*, with strikingly bald textures. Howard is here at his warmest and most persuasive, bringing out how Liszt's genius developed.

Other recordings of piano music

Années de Pèlerinage (Book 1, 1st Year: Switzerland; Book 2, 2nd Year: Italy) (DVD version)

⊕→ **** DG **DVD** 073 4146. Brendel (V/D: Humphrey Burton)

Alfred Brendel is at his finest in these 1986 performances of the first two books of pieces inspired by Liszt's years of travel, and he is recorded most realistically. He introduces each of the items individually, although his comments are separately cued, so that one can enjoy the music alone. Brendel's body language is very much part of his playing and he communicates with intense feeling, though never at the expense of the evocation. Humphrey Burton's video direction is admirable and there is no doubt that Brendel's playing is afforded an added dimension when he can be closely, though not too closely, observed.

Années de pèlerinage: Book 1, 1st Year: Switzerland; 2nd & 3rd Years: Italy; Supplement: Venezia e Napoli (complete)

⊕→ Ⓑ **** DG (ADD) 471 447-2 (3). Berman

Berman's technique is fabulous, more than equal to the demands made by these 26 pieces. The playing is enormously authoritative and quite free of empty display or virtuoso flamboyance, even though its brilliance is never in question. Indeed Berman brings searching qualities to this music; much of the time he is thoughtful and inward-looking, while the power of the *Dante Sonata* is equalled by the coruscating glitter of his articulation of the *Tarantella* from the *Supplément: Venezia e Napoli*. The recording is firmly and faithfully transferred to CD and does full justice to Berman's range of colour and dynamics. Moreover this box is remarkably inexpensive and well documented.

Années de pèlerinage, 1st Year (Switzerland)

ⒷⒷ **** Naxos 8.550548. Jandó

Even remembering his excellent Beethoven and Haydn recordings, **Jandó's** performances of the Liszt *Années de pèlerinage* are an impressive achievement. The solemn opening of *La Chapelle de Guillaume Tell* immediately shows the atmospheric feeling he can generate in this remarkable music, and its later, more grandiose rhetoric is handled with powerful conviction.

Années de pèlerinage, 2nd Year (Italy); Supplement: Venezia e Napoli

⊕━ 🌑 🅑🅑 ******** Naxos 8.550549. Jandó

Sposalizio is superbly evoked, and the three contrasted *Petrarch Sonnets* bring the most imaginatively varied characterization, with No. 123 especially chimerical. But clearly Jandó sees the *Dante Sonata* as the climactic point of the whole series. His performance has tremendous dynamism and power. One has the sense of Liszt himself hovering over the keyboard.

Années de pèlerinage, 3rd Year (Italy) (complete)

⊕━ 🅑🅑 ******** Naxos 8.550550. Jandó

The opening *Angelus* shows **Jandó** at his most imaginatively expansive and commanding, while *Les Jeux d'eau à la Villa d'Este* sparkles and glitters: this is playing of great appeal. The secret of Jandó's success is that he is deeply involved in every note of Liszt's music. First class recording too.

Ballade 2; Harmonies poétiques et religieuses; Rêves d'amour; Romance oubliée; Romance: O pourquoi donc

Ⓝ ******* Calliope CAL 9371/2. Amoyel

An outstanding collection of little-known Liszt, including a highly individual characterization of the complete *Harmonies poétiques et religieuses*, music that in **Pascal Amoyel's** hands emerges as both romantically inspired and remarkably forward-looking. The *Drei Liebesträume* (only one of which is well known) are ripely romantic and yet still refined in feeling, the *Romance oubliée* hauntingly nostalgic; and the *Second Ballade* has all the Lisztian bravura you could want. The recording is most real and vivid, and this is a set for Lisztians who want to further explore the music of this unpredictable composer.

Concert Paraphrases of Beethoven's 'An die ferne Geliebte'; Mignon; Schumann Lieder: Widmung; Frühlingsnacht

*** Chan. 9793. Lortie – SCHUMANN: *Fantaisie in C, Op. 17* *******

Louis Lortie's Chandos recital appears under the title 'To the Distant Beloved', after Beethoven's song-cycle, *An die ferne Geliebte*, which he plays in Liszt's transcription (together with a pair of Schumann Lieder), and very impressively too. But collectors will want this for the Schumann *Fantasy*, which is the centrepiece of the recital and is given an outstanding performance.

Concert Paraphrases of Beethoven's Symphonies 2 & 5

🅑🅑 ******* Naxos 8.550457. Scherbakov

It is **Scherbakov's** achievement that he makes Liszt's piano transcriptions of these Beethoven symphonies sound so pianistic. With wonderfully crisp articulation and fluent passage-work, textures are clarified, and the freshness and energy of the writing are strongly brought out both in the exuberantly youthful 2 and the darkly dramatic 5. He is, so to speak, more of a Weingartner than a Toscanini (as was Katsaris) but his *Fifth* still has that barnstorming quality that arrests your attention. At super-bargain price, well worth investigating even by those who shy away from transcriptions. Excellent, clear piano sound.

Concert paraphrases of Rossini: Soirées musicales; Overture William Tell

⊕━ 🅑🅑 ******* Naxos 8.553961. Geki

Liszt made his Rossini transcriptions in 1836, and they are rarely heard in the recital room or on record. The only rival is Leslie Howard's set on Hyperion, and this performance by the Yugoslav-born **Kemal Geki** at super-bargain price has infinitely more wit, lightness of touch and subtlety of articulation. In fact this is dazzling playing that sparkles when required and has an effortless brilliance that is quite captivating.

Concert paraphrases of Schubert Lieder: Auf dem Wasser zu singen; Erlkönig; In der Ferne; Ständchen

⊕━ 🌑 ******* Sony SK 66511. Perahia – BACH/BUSONI: *Chorales*; MENDELSSOHN: *Songs without Words* 🌑 *******

Murray Perahia brings to these transcriptions a poetic finesse that is very much his own. Impeccable artistry and taste are blended with a wonderful naturalness.

12 Etudes d'exécution transcendante (DVD version)

Ⓝ ******** Avie **DVD** AV 2174. Sherman

Russell Sherman, recorded live in New York City, shows his mastery of the piano and of Liszt in this for the most part assured and poetic performance of what must be one of the supreme examples of pianistic virtuosity in the whole repertoire. The venue, the Angel Orensanz Center for the Arts, is attractive and intimate; but we do not see a great deal of it, as the producer Chris Williamson rightly ensures that for the most part the camera fascinatingly focuses on the pianist's hands, and we see his amazing dexterity, mercurial suppleness, and ability to move both hands about independently with unbelievable speed and assurance – never more so than in *Mazeppa*, an extraordinarily descriptive odyssey. But he is equally compelling in the more delicate filigree of *Chasse-neige* and *Feux follets*. The DVD includes conversations with Craig Smith, a Boston musician, and with Christopher Lydon, a radio journalist, plus some teaching excerpts. But its Sherman's pianism that counts here. He also provides flowery programme notes, added to by Smith.

12 Etudes d'exécution transcendante (complete)

⊕━ Ⓜ ******** Warner Elatus 2564 69369-3. Berezovsky

Boris Berezovsky shows astonishing flair and technical assurance, yet in *Feux follets* he plays with the utmost delicacy, and the ruminative poetry of *Ricordanza* is melting. The piano is recorded boldly and brilliantly, not as full and sonorous as with Arrau, but there is no lack of pianistic colour in the gentler lyrical writing. The colour portrait of Liszt on the back of the accompanying booklet demonstrates why so many women succumbed to his physical charms!

(i) 12 Etudes d'exécution transcendante; (ii) 6 Etudes d'exécution transcendante d'après Paganini; (i) 3 Etudes de concert (Il lamento; La leggierezza; Un sospiro); 2 Etudes de concert (Waldesrauschen; Gnomenreigen)

(B) **(*) Ph. (ADD) Duo 456 339-2 (2). (i) Arrau; (ii) Magaloff

Arrau always played with great panache and musical insight, which more than compensates for the occasional smudginess in the recorded sound. He produced a wonderfully distinctive tone, and his enormous range of keyboard colour was splendidly captured by the Philips engineers of the day. Arrau's playing is most masterly and poetic, and the recording, if too reverberant, is admirably truthful and rich in timbre. However, his bravura in Gnomenreigen is riveting. So too is Nikita Magaloff's virtuosity in the Paganini Studies, and here the bright, less sumptuous piano-tone projects his digital dexterity with fine glitter. Overall this is most impressive and can be recommended enthusiastically.

Collection: 12 Etudes d'exécution transcendante; Hungarian Rhapsodies 1–19; Rapsodie espagnole; Sonata in B min. Recital: Années de pèlerinage: Les Jeux d'eau à la Villa d'Este; Ballade 2; Etudes de concert: 1, Ronde des lutins; 2, Danse le bois; Grand études après Paganini: La campanella; La Chasse; Grand galop chromatique; Harmonies poètiques et religieuse: Funérailles; 2 Légendes; Liebestraum 3; Mephisto Waltz; Polonaise 1; Valse-impromptu; Valse oubliée 1

(B) (***) EMI mono/stereo 5 74512-2 (5). Cziffra

12 Etudes d'exécution transcendante; Mephisto Waltz 1

(M) (***) EMI mono 5 62799-2. Cziffra

This five-disc set gathers together the recordings made by the celebrated virtuoso, Georges Cziffra, over three decades between the mid-1950s and the mid-1980s. He began with a chimerically brilliant set of the Etudes d'exécution transcendante and the equally legendary Hungarian Rhapsodies. Both were made in faithful if slightly restricted mono sound in the Hungaroton studio in Budapest in 1956. The result is strikingly fresh and the easy technical dexterity is astonishing. Much of the rest of the repertoire appears here for the first time. Cziffra remained at the height of his powers throughout, and the shorter bravura pieces, most recorded in stereo, display the same enormous technical command and delectably clean, light articulation as the earlier sessions, the playing volatile and charismatic, the recordings clear and forward. The recordings have been effectively remastered, the sound variable, often good, very good in the Sonata. But the panache of the playing triumphs over the early technology.

Hungarian Rhapsodies 1–19; Rapsodie espagnole

🎧 (B) *** DG Double (ADD) 453 034-2 (2). Szidon

Roberto Szidon offers Liszt playing of the highest order. He has flair and panache, genuine keyboard command and, when required, great delicacy of tone. He is well recorded too, and this DG Double is not only inexpensive but also provides (as does Cziffra on EMI) an excellent version of the Rapsodie espagnole. Cziffra's performances are from an artist of an even more volatile personality, but Szidon is by no means upstaged: his style is equally valid and his approach is always imaginatively illuminating.

Hungarian Rhapsodies 2, 6, 8 (Capriccio), 9 (Carnival in Pest), 10 (Préludio), 12–15 (Rákoczy March)

(M) *** EMI (ADD) 5 67554-2. Cziffra

As can be heard in the most famous C sharp minor Rhapsody (2), Cziffra's reckless impulsiveness is matched by his breathtaking bravura in the closing section, and it was an excellent idea to issue a selection from his deleted complete set as one of EMI's 'Great Recordings of the Century'. The remastered recordings from the early 1970s have fine realism and presence.

Piano Sonata in B min.; Concert Paraphrase on Verdi's 'Rigoletto'

*** DG DVD 073 4079. Yundi Li – CHOPIN: Piano Concerto 1: Rondo, etc. ***

Yundi Li's playing has delicacy and finesse, and a pretty flawless technique. He has an appealing personality that puts the listener very much on his side, and he gives a very fine account of the B minor Sonata. Nor does his version of the Rigoletto Paraphrase lack virtuosity or panache. Perhaps the Sonata has yet to exhibit the command and personality of a great pianist, but this recital certainly indicates that his is a formidable talent with enormous potential whose future will blossom.

Piano Sonata; Années de pèlerinage, 2nd Year: Après une lecture du Dante (Fantasia Quasi Sonata); Concert Study: Gnomenreigen; Harmonies poétiques et religieuses: Funérailles

🎧 (M) **** DG 457 6292. Pletnev

Piano Sonata; 3 Concert Studies

🎧 *** Chan. 8548. Lortie

Piano Sonata in B min.; Consolation 3; 6 Etudes d'exécution transcendente d'après Paganini; Mephisto Waltz

(N) (BB) *** EMI Encore (ADD) 2 35733-2. Anievas

Piano Sonata in B min.; En rêve; 4 Little Piano Pieces; La lugubre gondola; Nuages gris; Richard Wagner – Venezia; Schlaflos! Frage und Antwort; Sinistre, disastro; Trübe Wolken; Unstern!

🎧 **** HM HMC 901845. Lewis

Piano Sonata; 2 Legends (St Francis of Assisi Preaching to the Birds; St Francis of Paola Walking on the Waves); Scherzo & March

⊕—(BB) **** Hyp. Helios CDH 55184. Demidenko

Pletnev's earlier account of the B minor Sonata, made when he was in his 20s and briefly available on Olympia, had dazzling virtuosity and brilliance. This newcomer has even greater tonal finesse, articulation and control of keyboard colour; there is a tremendous grip, depth and majesty, and the breadth of the Sonata is deeply impressive. A performance of stature among the very best that this great pianist has yet given us. The remainder of the programme is hardly less gripping; reservations concerning the close balance do not obscure the artistry and distinction of this recital.

Paul Lewis's version of the Liszt Sonata stands out, even among the many dozens of rival recordings, for its power and clarity, enhanced by full, immediate sound. Lewis with masterly control brings out the structural strength. For coupling he has an illuminating group of late pieces, including two written as elegies for Wagner, not just La lugubre gondola (in the second and more extended version) but RW – Venezia, building up powerfully over the briefest span. Also two pieces, Nuages gris and Unstern!, which find the composer at his most adventurous.

Nikolai Demidenko's is a keenly dramatic and powerfully projected account of the Sonata that has the listener on the edge of his or her seat. It must be numbered among the finest performances he has given us. The excitement and virtuosity are second to none and almost call to mind Horowitz. He has the advantage of exceptionally vivid recorded sound, and the remainder of the recital goes equally well.

Anievas gives a fine and memorable performance of the Sonata, notable for its thoughtfulness and its subtlety in the control of tension. The lyrical impulse is finely balanced to bring out the music's poetry as well as its fire and strength. There may be more flamboyant interpretations available which more readily project the music's bravura, but only a few recorded performances are as satisfying as this, or more successful in revealing the work's stature. The recording too is very good, although the reverberation prevents absolute clarity in the bass in florid passages.

Louis Lortie gives almost as commanding a performance of the Liszt Sonata as any in the catalogue; its virtuosity can be taken for granted and, though he does not have the extraordinary intensity and feeling for drama of Pletnev, he has a keen awareness of its structure and a Chopinesque finesse that win one over. The Chandos recording, though a shade too reverberant, is altogether natural.

Piano Sonata; Années de pèlerinage, 1st Year: Au bord d'une source; 2nd Year: Sonetto 104 del Petrarca; 3rd Year: Les Jeux d'eau à la Villa d'Este; Concert Paraphrases: Die Forelle; Erlkönig (Schubert); Réminiscences de Don Juan (Mozart); Rigoletto (Verdi); Consolation 3; Etudes d'exécution transcendante d'après Paganini: La campanella; Etudes de concert: Gnomenreigen; Un sospiro; Harmonies poétiques et religieuses: Funérailles;

Hungarian Rhapsody 12 in C sharp min.; Liebestraum 3 in A flat; Mephisto Waltz 1

⊕—(B) **** Double Decca 444 851-2 (2). Bolet

The full range of **Jorge Bolet's** achievement for Decca in the music of Liszt is admirably surveyed here, ending with his commanding account of the Sonata, a performance combining power, imagination and concentration. He can be romantic without sentimentality, as in the Consolation, Un sospiro or the most famous Liebestraum, yet can dazzle the ear with bravura or beguile the listener with his delicacy of colouring, as in the Années de pèlerinage. All the recordings here, save the Mozart Concert Paraphrase, are digital and are as clear and present as one could wish.

Miscellaneous recitals

Années de pèlerinage, 1st Year: Vallée d'Obermann; 2nd Year: Sposalizio; Il penseroso; Bagatelle without tonality; En rêve; Funérailles; Hungarian Rhapsody 13 (arr. Volodos); Legend: St Frances of Assisi Preaching to the Birds; La lugubre gondola; Weinen, Klagen, Sorgen, Zagen (Prelude after Bach)

⊕—**** Sony SACD 88697 06500-2. Volodos

Arcadi Volodos's playing must be the nearest we can get to hearing Liszt himself give a recital. And indeed a splendidly programmed recital too, with everything from the Années de pèlerinage (played with enormous flair) to the weird Bagatelle without tonality. There is excitement in plenty (as in the Vallée d'Obermann and the Hungarian Rhapsody), magical evocation and colour of St Francis and his birds, and much poetry everywhere. He is splendidly recorded. A recital not to be missed.

Années de pèlerinage, 2nd Year: 3 Sonetti di Petrarca (47, 104 & 123); Dante Sonata; Concert Paraphrases on Verdi: Aida: Danza sacra e duetto finale; Quartet from Rigoletto; Miserere from Trovatore; Legend: St Francis of Assisi Preaching to the Birds

**(*) EuroArts DVD 2056748. Barenboim

Daniel Barenboim communicates readily, especially in live performance as here (in May 2007), and he is always a pleasure to watch and listen to in Liszt. He is particularly evocative in the portrait of St Francis Preaching to the Birds, but plays impressively throughout. However, the acoustic of La Scala is a little dry and does not flatter his piano tone; although this does not prevent enjoyment, the DG recital below is even more rewarding.

Années de pèlerinage, 2nd Year: 3 Sonetti di Petrarca (47, 104 & 123); Concert Paraphrase on the Quartet from Verdi's 'Rigoletto'; Consolations 1–5; Liebesträume 1–3

⊕—(M) *** DG (ADD) 435 591-2. Barenboim

Daniel Barenboim proves an ideal advocate for the Consolations and Liebesträume, and he is highly poetic in the Petrarch Sonnets. His playing has an unaffected simplicity that is impressive and throughout there is a welcome understatement and naturalness, until he arrives at the Rigoletto

Paraphrase, which is played with plenty of flair and glitter. The quality of the recorded sound is excellent.

Recital I: *Années de pèlerinage, 3rd Year: Tarantella; Harmonies poétiques et religieuses: Pensées des morts; Bénédiction de Dieu dans le solitude; Legend: St Francis of Assisi Preaching to the Birds; Mephisto Waltz 1; Rapsodie Espagnole*

Recital II: *Années de pèlerinage, 2nd Year: Après une lecture du Dante (Dante Sonata); 3rd Year: Aux cyprès de la Villa d'Este I & II; Les Jeux d'eau à la Villa d'Este; Ave Maria; Ave Maria (Die Glocken von Rom); La lugubre gondola (2 versions); Recueillement*

⌥ ✹ **(BB)** *** Virgin 2x1 Double 5 61439-2. Hough

Few pianists of the younger generation have quite such a magic touch as **Stephen Hough**, and this budget-priced Virgin Double rescues two of his finest recitals. The performances are all magnetic. On the first disc, he brings sparkle and wit to the fireworks of the *Mephisto Waltz* and the *Tarantella* from the third year of the *Années de pèlerinage* with phenomenal articulation, and he plays the extended slow movement of the *Bénédiction* with velvety warmth. The second collection is mainly of rarer music and is imaginatively chosen to include two different versions of both *Aux cyprès de la Villa d'Este* and the darkly original *La lugubre gondola*, in each case with the second version longer and more elaborate than the first. The cascades of *Les Jeux d'eau à la Villa d'Este* make a glittering centrepiece. The recording is excellent, but the documentation is abysmal. Nevertheless the concentration of the playing here is unforgettable.

Ave Marias in D flat; G; E; d'Arcadelt; 6 Consolations; Harmonies poétiques et religieuses, 7–10; Ungarns Gott (left-hand)

(BB) *** Naxos 8.553516. Thomson

Concert paraphrases of sacred music: Alleluja; Ave maris stella; 11 Chorales; Hungarian Coronation Mass: Benedictus; Offertorium; L'Hymne du pape; In festo transfigurationis; O Roma nobilis; Sancta Dorothea; Stabat Mater; Urbi et orbi; Weihnachtslied; Zum Haus des Herrn ziehen wir

(BB) *** Naxos 8.553659. Thomson

Harmonies poétiques et religieuses 1–6; Les morts; Resignazione; Ungarns Gott (two-hand)

(BB) *** Naxos 8.553073. Thomson

Philip Thomson is a Canadian pianist who has specialized in Liszt. He exhibits considerable artistry in the three discs listed above and commands not only the virtuosity which this repertoire calls for in abundance but also great poetic feeling. He commands a wide range of keyboard colour and refinement of *pianissimo* tone and has the benefit of very good recorded sound as well. All of his Liszt recitals are touched by distinction and are a real bargain.

Ballade 2; Harmonies poétiques et religieuses: Bénédiction de Dieu dans la solitude; Mephisto Waltz 1; Sposalizio; En rêve; Schlaflos!; Unstern!

(M) *** Oehms OCD 228. Perl

In his rapt concentration **Perl** brings weight to Liszt's sequential arguments, underlining the link between the magnificent *Ballade* over its 15-minute span and Liszt's sonata in the same key. Even more expansive is the surgingly lyrical *Bénédiction*, with the first *Mephisto Waltz* bringing virtuoso fireworks at the end. Excellent, well-balanced sound.

Concert paraphrase of Wagner's Tannhäuser Overture; Etudes de concert, 1st Set, 3: Un sospiro; 2nd set, 1: Waldesrauschen; 2: Gnomenreigen; Etudes d'exécution transcendante d'après Paganini, 3: La campanella; Grand galop chromatique; Harmonies poétiques et religieuses: Funérailles; Liebestraum 3; ;spagnole

(M) *** RCA (ADD) 82876 63310-2. Bolet

Here is a real find, a recital recorded by **Jorge Bolet** in the early 1970s, when he was at the very peak of his form, a decade before he made his series of digital recordings for Decca, and just before his Carnegie Hall début in 1974. The playing in *Gnomenreigen* and the exuberant *Grand galop chromatique* is dazzling, while *La campanella* is articulated with crystal clarity, and there is more glittering fingerwork in the *Rapsodie espagnole*.

The famous *Liebestraum* and *Un sospiro* are romantically charged, without a hint of sentimentality, while the darker atmosphere of *Funérailles* is powerfully caught. Even the almost unplayable finale of Liszt's arrangement of Wagner's *Tannhäuser Overture* is made coherent by the clear separation of the chorale from the decorative cascades – a *tour de force* of pianism. The analogue recording is excellent and the CD transfer faithful (perhaps a fraction hard) and gives him a most realistic presence.

ORGAN MUSIC

Concertstück in A; Fantasia and Fugue on 'Ad nos salutarem, undam'; Orpheus (Symphonic Poem); Prelude on 'Weinen, Klagen, Sorgen, Zagen'; Trauerode (Les Morts: Oraison)

⌥ **(BB)** **** Naxos 8.554544. Rothkopf (Sauer organ, Evangelische Stadtkirche, Bad Homberg)

Consolations in D flat; E (Tröstung); & E (Andantino); Evocation à la Chapelle Sistine; Prelude and Fugue on the name 'BACH'; Legend: St Francis of Assisi Preaching to the Birds; Variations on 'Weinen, Klagen, Sorgen, Zagen'

⌥ **(BB)** **** Naxos 8.555079. Rothkopf (Sauer organ, St Petri Dom, Bremen)

The key Liszt works which were originally written for organ include the *Prelude and Variations on 'Weinen, Klagen, Sorgen, Zagen'*, the *Prelude and Fugue on the name 'BACH'* and *Fantasia and Fugue on 'Ad nos salutarem, undam'*. **Andreas Rothkopf** opens the first disc with the last-named piece, and gives a magnificent account: the delayed entry of the pedals is a thrilling moment and the climactic fugue no less exciting. The *Prelude and Fugue on 'BACH'* and the *'Weinen, Klagen'* *Variations* are similarly spectacular and demand great virtuosity, which is fully forthcoming here. The other pieces are transcriptions, some made by the composer, some by others. But they all take full advantage of the rich palette of these two magnificent organs, from the dark-hued *Trauerode*, to the romantic *Consolations*. But the most surprisingly effective transcription here is of the *Legend of St Francis Preaching to the Birds*, where the organ effects are more exotically descriptive than in the piano version, while the chorale sounds richly expansive on the organ. Throughout both CDs the performances are very fine indeed and the recording in the demonstration bracket. The back-up documentation, too, is excellent.

VOCAL MUSIC

Christus (oratorio)

ⓑⓑ *** Warner Apex 2564 61167-2 (3). Valente, Lipovšek, Lindroos, Krause, Slovak Philharmonic Ch., Rotterdam PO, Conlon

Liszt's *Christus* is less an oratorio than an episodic sequence of contrasted pieces, many of them very beautiful, inspired by the person of Christ. It is not part of the scheme to personify Christ in the way that Bach does in the Passions, but to intersperse devotional hymns – such as *The Three Kings* or the carol-like *O filii et filiae* – between atmospheric scene-paintings such as *The Beatitudes* or *The Miracle Depicting Christ Walking on the Waters*. **James Conlon** and his Rotterdam forces give a dedicated reading, full of warmth and understanding. The liveliness of the acoustic and the distancing of the sound may obscure some detail, but this is an account, recorded at a live concert, that brings out the beauties and expressiveness of the writing to the full. Tiny mishaps, inevitable in a live performance, are not likely to undermine enjoyment, and the reissue is very reasonably priced.

LITOLFF, Henri (1818–91)

Concerti symphoniques 2 in B min., Op. 22; 4 in D min., Op. 102

*** Hyp. CDA 66889. Donohoe, Bournemouth SO, Litton

The *Fourth Concerto Symphonique* is the source of the famous Litolff Scherzo, so often heard in the days of 78s. The first movement is rhetorical but opens with endearing flamboyance under the baton of **Andrew Litton**, while the passage-work scintillates in the hands of **Peter Donohoe**. The secondary material has both delicacy and charm. The famous Scherzo which follows is taken a fraction too fast and loses some of its poise, the articulation not always absolutely clean; but one adjusts to the breathless virtuosity, and it remains the work's finest inspiration. The *Adagio religioso* opens with some lovely horn-playing, its solemn mood nicely offset later by the pianistic decoration. The finale,

marked *Allegro impetuoso*, is certainly all of that, with more twinkling bravura from Donohoe.

The *Second Concerto* is also well worth while. True, its opening *Maestoso* is hopelessly inflated, but in the Chopinesque secondary material Donohoe finds an engaging charm as well as brilliance. The second movement is another scintillating Scherzo and, if not quite as memorable as its more famous companion, it has a tripping centrepiece worthy of Saint-Saëns, especially as presented here. With a warm, naturally balanced recording, this entertaining Hyperion CD is very much worth having.

Concerti symphoniques 3 in E flat (National hollandais), Op. 45; 5 in C min., Op. 123

*** Hyp. CDA 67210. Donohoe, BBC Scottish SO, Litton

Overall, this pair of engaging works are much more consistently inspired than the more famous 4. Litolff incorporates two old Dutch tunes into 3 (hence the work's subtitle). After an opening movement with a zestful military flavour, the rollicking Scherzo includes one of these; the following nocturnal *Andante* makes a touching, songful interlude before the dazzling finale, which is to introduce the second in the form of a patriotic chorale. The brilliant dénouement is fully worthy of Liszt.

The opening mood of the *Fifth Concerto* seems darker, dispelled by another jauntily memorable Scherzo. The finale opens with a whiff of Beethoven and has unexpected weight, with the contrasting lyrical material moving into a world somewhere between Liszt and Mendelssohn. Both performances have great flair, with **Donohoe** playing brilliantly throughout, and **Litton** and his Scottish players giving splendid support. The recording is first class. A most enjoyable and recommendable coupling, notable for its ready fund of memorable melody.

Concerto symphonique 4: Scherzo

⊶ Ⓜ *** Decca (ADD) 466 376-2. Curzon, LPO, Boult – BRAHMS: *Piano Concerto;* FRANCK: *Symphonic Variations* ***

Curzon provides all the sparkle Litolff's infectious Scherzo requires, and the 1958 Walthamstow Town Hall recording makes a delightful encore for the Brahms *Concerto* and the Franck *Symphonic Variations* in this reissue in Decca's 'Classic Sound' series. The fine qualities of the original sound, freshness and clarity, remain impressive.

LLOYD, George (1913–98)

(i) Cello Concerto; The Serf (opera): Orchestral Suite 1

⊶ *** Albany TROY 458. (i) Ross; Albany SO, Miller

Like the comparable work of Elgar, George Lloyd's poignant *Cello Concerto* was a late composition. It was completed in July 1997, a year before his death at the age of 85, and its ethos clearly reflects the composer's frustration at the rejection of his work by the musical establishment. The work is in seven continuing sections, all based on the opening lyrical theme.

Anthony Ross is clearly very committed to this highly emotional work and, with strong support from the **Albany Symphony Orchestra** under **David Miller**, he gives a performance of moving eloquence.

The Serf is a colourful score, but its touches of melodrama are not wholly convincing, and the extended *Love Duet* is without a sufficiently memorable melodic line for its purpose. First-class recording throughout.

(i) *Piano Concerto 4; The Lily-Leaf and the Grasshopper; The Transformation of That Naked Ape*

*** Albany AR 004. Stott; (i) LSO, composer

The *Fourth Piano Concerto* is a romantic, light-hearted piece with a memorable 'long singing tune' (the composer's words), somewhat Rachmaninovian in its spacious lyricism contrasting with a 'jerky' rhythmic idea. The performance by **Kathryn Stott** and the **LSO** under the composer is ardently spontaneous from the first bar to the last. The solo pieces are eclectic but still somehow Lloydian. The recording is first rate.

Concerto for Violin & Strings; Concerto for Violin & Winds

(key) **** Albany TROY 316. Anghelescu, Philh. O, Parry

George Lloyd's *Concerto for Violin and Strings* is very much in the great English tradition of writing for string orchestra, with or without a soloist. Its plaintive opening develops a plangent melancholy in the first movement. The rhythmically quirky Scherzo which follows is more cheerful, but the clouds do not lift entirely and it is left to the dancing finale to round off the work, but the closing bars are curiously equivocal. The *Concerto for Violin and Winds* is more robustly extrovert, neoclassical, acerbic, and brilliantly and originally scored. Its slow movement is bitter-sweet, very touching, but again producing an ambivalence of feeling, which strays into the initially light-hearted, dancing finale. In both works the Romanian soloist **Cristina Anghelescu** has just the right temperament for the music's quixotic changes of mood. **David Parry** directs, in partnership with his soloist, definitive recorded performances. The recording too is first class and most realistically balanced.

Symphonies 1 in A; 12

(key) **** Albany TROY 032-2. Albany SO, composer

The pairing of George Lloyd's first and last symphonies is particularly appropriate, as they share a theme-and-variations format. The *First* is relatively lightweight. The mature *Twelfth* uses the same basic layout but ends calmly with a ravishingly sustained *pianissimo*, semi-Mahlerian in intensity, that is among the composer's most beautiful inspirations. At the beginning of the work, the listener is soon aware of the noble lyrical theme which is the very heart of the *Symphony*. The **Albany Symphony Orchestra** gave the work its première and they play it with enormous conviction and eloquence, helped by the superb acoustics of the Troy Savings Bank Music Hall, which produces sound of demonstration quality.

Symphonies 2; 9

*** Albany TROY 055. BBC PO, composer

Lloyd's *Second Symphony* is a lightweight, extrovert piece, conventional in form and construction, though in the finale the composer flirts briefly with polytonality, an experiment he did not repeat. The *Ninth* (1969) is similarly easy-going; the *Largo* is rather fine, but its expressive weight is in scale, and the finale, 'a merry-go-round that keeps going round and round', has an appropriately energetic brilliance. Throughout both works the invention is attractive, and in these definitive performances, extremely well recorded, the composer's advocacy is very persuasive.

Symphony 3 in F; Charade (suite)

*** Albany TROY 90. BBC PO, composer

The *Third Symphony* clearly subdivides into three sections, and it is the central *Lento* which has *the* tune, a winding, nostalgic theme that persists in the memory. It is atmospherically prepared and eventually blossoms sumptuously. *Charade* dates from the 1960s and attempts to portray the London scene of the time, from aggressive *Student Power* and *LSD* to *Flying Saucers* and *Pop Song*. The ironic final movement, *Party Politics*, is amiable rather than wittily abrasive. The composer is good at bringing his music vividly to life, and he is very well recorded indeed.

Symphony 4

(key) **** Albany AR 002. Albany SO, composer

George Lloyd's *Fourth Symphony* was composed during his convalescence after being badly shell-shocked while serving in the Arctic convoys of 1941/2. The first movement is directly related to this period of his life, and the listener may be surprised at the relative absence of sharp dissonance. After a brilliant Scherzo, the infectious finale is amiable, offering a series of quick, 'march-like tunes', which the composer explains by suggesting that 'when the funeral is over the band plays quick cheerful tunes to go home'. Under Lloyd's direction, the **Albany Symphony Orchestra** play with great commitment and a natural, spontaneous feeling. The recording is superb.

Symphonies 4; 5; 8

(M) *** Lyrita (ADD) SRCD 2258 (3). Philh. O, Downes

Here are three of George Lloyd's most representative symphonies, including the five-movement *Fifth*, opening with a deceptively simple *Pastorale*, but with two intensely expressive slow movements, a *Chorale* and *Lamento*; and the *Eighth*, the first to be heard in public after the composer's recovery from his wartime experiences. The performances are excellent and the Lyrita recording is in every way first class, making this set a very generous sampler for this repertoire.

Symphony 5 in B flat

(key) *** Albany TROY 022-2. BBC PO, composer

The *Fifth Symphony* is a large canvas, with five strong and contrasted movements, adding up to nearly an hour of music. It was written during a happy period spent living simply on the shore of Lac Neuchâtel, during the very hot summer of 1947. In the finale, the composer tells us, 'everything is brought in to make as exhilarating a sound as possible – strong rhythms, vigorous counterpoints, energetic brass and percussion'. The symphony is played with much commitment by the **BBC Philharmonic** under the composer, who creates a feeling of spontaneously live music-making throughout. The recording is first class.

Symphonies (i) 6; (ii) 10 (November Journeys); (i) Overture: John Socman

**(*) Albany TROY 15-2. (i) BBC PO; (ii) BBC PO Brass; composer

The bitter-sweet lyricism of the first movement of *November Journeys* is most attractive, but the linear writing is more complex than usual in a work for brass. In the finale a glowing *cantando* melody warms the spirit, to contrast with the basic *Energico*. The *Calma* slow movement is quite haunting, no doubt reflecting the composer's series of visits to English cathedrals, the reason for the subtitle. The *Sixth Symphony* is amiable and lightweight; it is more like a suite than a symphony. **Lloyd's** performances are attractively spontaneous and well played, and the equally agreeable *John Socman Overture* also comes off well, although it is rather inconsequential.

Symphony 7

☚━ **** Albany TROY 057. BBC PO, composer

The *Seventh Symphony* is a programme symphony, using the ancient Greek legend of Proserpine. The slow movement is particularly fine, an extended soliloquy of considerable expressive power. The last and longest movement is concerned with 'the desperate side of our lives – "Dead dreams that the snows have shaken, Wild leaves that the winds have taken" – ' yet, as is characteristic with Lloyd, the darkness is muted; nevertheless the resolution at the end is curiously satisfying. Again he proves an admirable exponent of his own music. The recording is splendid.

Symphony 8

*** Albany TROY 230. Philh. O, composer

After his severe depression and nervous breakdown, Lloyd gave up composing entirely for many years, earning his living instead as a mushroom farmer, only gradually turning back to composition. The *Eighth Symphony*, written in 1961 – the first to be heard in public – is a product of that long recuperative period, and in the openness of inspiration (passionately English) it both belies earlier depression and testifies to the success of composition as therapy. Linked by a six-note leitmotif, the work holds well together. Even if the scherzando finale is arguably a little too long for its material, the elliptical first movement (opening and closing atmospherically and with a richly memorable secondary theme) and the eloquently sustained *Largo* both show the composer at his finest. The recording, made in the spacious acoustics of Watford Town Hall, is first class.

Symphony 11

*** Albany TROY 060. Albany SO, composer

The urgently dynamic first movement of the *Eleventh Symphony* is described by the composer as being 'all fire and violence', but any anger in the music quickly evaporates, and it conveys rather a mood of exuberance, with very full orchestral forces unleashed. With the orchestra for which the work was commissioned, Lloyd conducts a powerful performance, very well played. The recording, made in the Music Hall of Troy Savings Bank near Albany, is spectacularly sumptuous and wide-ranging.

PIANO MUSIC

Aubade (fantasy suite); Eventide; The Road through Samarkand

☚━ *** Albany Troy 248. Goldstone and Clemmow (piano duet)

Aubade, written in 1971, is a substantial suite of some 38 minutes' length, a dream-like fantasy, with pictures flitting through his mind at dawn. Its evocations are impressionistic, its flavour distinctly Gallic. It is all brilliantly imagined and its colourful imagery is vividly realized in a bravura performance by **Anthony Goldstone** and **Caroline Clemmow**. *Eventide* is a touching re-presentation and elaboration of a carol from the composer's youth – a simple melody which is charmingly ingenuous and not sentimentalized. *The Road through Samarkand* is a virtuoso toccata dominated by a simple motto theme. It is full of rhythmic interest, often syncopated, and the players clearly relish the virtuosity it demands. In short these are first-rate performances of highly communicative music which shows the composer at his most successfully spontaneous. The recording is vivid but somewhat over-reverberant.

VOCAL MUSIC

(i) Requiem; Psalm 130

☚━ ✦ **** Albany TROY 450. (i) Wallace; Exon Singers, Owens

The *Requiem* was George Lloyd's final work and it represents the composer's infinitely touching farewell to life, which he always celebrated with vigour in spite of his many disappointments. It is written for counter-tenor and small chorus, although the choral writing is as rich in melody and harmony as anything in the *Symphonic Mass*. Indeed at 50 minutes the *Requiem* is hardly less ambitious, and one does not sense a smaller scale. Because of his realization that he would not have enough time to complete a large orchestral score, Lloyd turned to the organ, and that proved one of the work's principal strengths, for the organ writing is often thrilling and always imaginatively resourceful. The work is splendidly sung and played (the organist, **Jeffry Makinson**, deserves his own Rosette). It is inspirational in feeling, with that special quality that almost always comes with a first recording. The simple *a cappella* setting of *Psalm 130*, written in 1995, makes an apt coupling. The recording itself, made in the Church of St Alban the Martyr, Holborn, is first class, but black marks for the documentation, which provides no translation of the Latin text of the *Requiem* and omits the words of the *Psalm* altogether.

A Symphonic Mass

🎚–⭘ ✱ **** Albany TROY 100. Brighton Festival Ch., Bournemouth SO, composer

George Lloyd's *Symphonic Mass* is his masterpiece. Written for chorus and orchestra (but no soloists) on the largest scale, the work is linked by a recurring main theme, a real tune which soon lodges insistently in the listener's memory, even though it is modified at each reappearance. It first appears as a quiet setting of the words *Christe eleison*, nearly four minutes into the *Kyrie*. The climax of the whole work is the combined *Sanctus* and *Benedictus*, with the latter framed centrally. To the words, *Dominus Deus*, the great melody finds its apotheosis in a passage marked *largamente con fervore*. Then the *Sanctus* reasserts itself dramatically and, after a cry of despair from the violins, the movement reaches its overwhelmingly powerful and dissonant dénouement. Peace is then restored in the *Agnus Dei*, where the composer tells us the words *Dona nobis pacem* became almost unbearably poignant for him. The performance is magnificent and the recording is fully worthy, spaciously balanced within the generous acoustic of the Guildhall, Southampton, and overwhelmingly realistic, even in the huge climax of the *Sanctus* with its shattering percussion.

Iernin (opera; complete)

*** Albany TROY 121/3 (3). Hill Smith, Pogson, Herford, Rivers, Powell, BBC Singers & Concert O, composer

George Lloyd was only 21 when in the early 1930s he wrote this ambitious opera, and there is an open innocence in the warmly atmospheric, lyrical score. The piece was inspired by an ancient Cornish legend about ten maidens turned into a circle of stones, one of whom, Iernin (pronounced Ee-er-nin), returns in human form. Though this is ostensibly an old-fashioned opera, it deserves revival, and on the recording – taken from a BBC Radio 3 presentation in 1988 – the composer conducts a red-blooded, warmly expressive reading. Though some of the ensemble writing is less distinguished, the offstage choruses of faery folk are most effective. As to the soloists, **Marilyn Hill Smith** sings brightly in the title-role with all the agility needed, and the tenor, **Geoffrey Pogson**, copes well with the hero's role, if with rather coarse tone. The most distinguished singing comes from the rich-toned contralto, **Claire Powell**, as Cunaide. The third disc includes a half-hour interview with the composer, which makes up in part for the absence of background notes in the booklet with the libretto. Excellent, well-balanced BBC sound.

LLOYD WEBBER, Andrew

(born 1948)

Requiem

Ⓝ Ⓜ *** Decca 478054-2. Brightman, Domingo, Winchester Cathedral Ch., ECO, Maazel

This *Requiem* may be derivative at many points, with echoes of Carl Orff – not to mention the *Requiems* of both Verdi and Fauré – but with **Maazel** conducting a performance of characteristic intensity, it certainly has a life of its own. The *Pie Jesu* is a model of bridge-building, a melody beautiful and individual by any standard, which yet has all the catchiness of one of Lloyd Webber's tunes in a musical. Plainly the high, bright voice of **Sarah Brightman** was the direct inspiration, and the beauty of her singing certainly earns her her place alongside **Plácido Domingo**, contributing in a rather less prominent role. Radiant sounds from the **Winchester Cathedral Choir**, not least the principal treble, Paul Miles-Kingston. Above all, this is music to which one returns with increasing appreciation and pleasure. The sound is excellent, with good presence.

LÔBO, Alonso (c. 1555–1617)

Motets: Audivi vocem de coelo; Pater peccavi

Ⓑ🅑 *** Naxos 8.553310. Ars Nova, Holten (with Concert of Portuguese Polyphony ***) – CARDOSO: *Motets*; MAGALHAES: *Missa O Soberana luz*, etc. ***

Lôbo's two beautiful motets, *Audivi vocem de coelo* ('I heard a voice from heaven') and *Pater peccavi* ('Father, I have sinned'), confirm the individuality of his writing. They are part of an outstandingly sung collection which is among the most desirable records of its kind in the catalogue.

Motets: Ave Maria; Credo quod redemptor; Versa est in Luctum; Vivo ego, dicit Dominus

Ⓑ *** Gimell CDGIM 205 (2). Tallis Scholars, Phillips – CARDOSO: *Requiem*; Duarte LÔBO: *Requiem*; VICTORIA *Requiem* ***

These four motets by Alonso Lôbo (not related to Duarte) include a striking setting of *Versa est in Luctum*, also set by Victoria in connection with his *Requiem*, although Lôbo's piece is not associated with a *Missa pro defunctis*. But *Credo quod redemptor* is also memorable, and so is the beautiful *Ave Maria*, which is complex in structure but sounds richly serene, with a lovely final *Amen*.

LÔBO, Duarte (c. 1565–1646)

Missa pro defunctis

🎚–Ⓑ *** Gimell CDGIM 205 (2). Tallis Scholars, Phillips – CARDOSO: *Requiem*; Alonso LÔBO: *Motets*; VICTORIA *Requiem* ***

🎚–🅑 *** Naxos 8.550682. Oxford Schola Cantorum, Summerly – CARDOSO: *Missa pro defunctis* ***

Missa pro defunctis (Requiem); Audivi vocem de coelo

Ⓑ *** Hyp. Helios CDH 55138. William Byrd Ch., G. Turner – Filip de MAGALHÁES; *Missa Dilecus meus* ***

Duarte Lôbo's *Requiem* for double choir (eight voices) is an exceptionally rich and firmly harmonized work. The general effect is homophonic, but there is some simple polyphonic interplay in the *Gradual* and the *Offertory*. This is a work of dignity and deep feeling, and it is superbly sung by the **William Byrd Choir**, who also offer the celestial motet, *Audivi vocem de coelo*. Their coupling is music by Lôbo's Portuguese contemporary, Filip de Magalháes, which is hardly less beautiful.

Undoubtedly the **Tallis Scholars** are also completely at home in this music, and the smaller scale of their performances brings added clarity without too much loss of atmosphere. The singing itself is radiantly pure and beautiful. If you want the Victoria *Requiem* also, this Gimell Double is the version to go for.

Lôbo's *Missa pro defunctis* for double choir is a work of beautiful flowing lines (following directly on from Palestrina), bold dramatic contrasts and ardent depth of feeling. The *Agnus Dei* is particularly beautiful. A solo treble briefly introduces each section except the *Kyrie*, which adds to the effect of the presentation. This is another triumph from **Jeremy Summerly** and his excellent Oxford group (38 singers), who catch both the Latin fervour and the underlying serenity of a work which has a memorably individual voice.

LOCATELLI, Pietro (1695–1764)

L'Arte del violino (12 Violin Concertos), Op. 3

♫— ******** Hyp. CDA 66721/3. E. Wallfisch, Raglan Bar. Players, Kraemer

12 Concerti grossi, Op. 1

♫— (BB) ******** Naxos 8.553445/6. Capella Istropolitana

Concerti grossi, Op. 1/2, 4, 7, 8 (Christmas Concerto), 9 & 10

♫— ******** HM HMC 90 1889. Freiburg Bar. O, von der Goltz

Pietro Locatelli was a younger contemporary of Handel and Vivaldi. It was in 1733 that he wrote *L'Arte del violino*. In its outer movements each of the twelve concertos includes an extended *Capriccio* of enormous technical difficulty, with fast, complicated, sometimes stratospheric, upper tessitura. The slow movements, by contrast, produce a series of flowing ideas that have an inherent Handelian grace. **Elizabeth Wallfisch** not only throws off the fireworks with ease but produces an appealingly gleaming lyrical line. With excellent, vital and stylish support from **Kraemer** and his **Raglan Baroque Players**, this may be counted a stimulating authentic re-creation of a set of concertos which had a profound influence on the violin technique of the time.

Locatelli's set of Opus 1 *Concerti grossi*, although indebted to Corelli (with the *Eighth* of the set ending with a *Christmas Pastorale*), similarly has a style and personality all its own. The invention is vigorous, the expressive range appealing. The **Capella Istropolitana** play with crisp attack, plenty of sparkle and resilient rhythms, while slow movements reveal a keen identity with the lessons of period performance, even though modern instruments are used. The Naxos recording is admirable.

Alternatively, the superb period-instrument group, the **Freiburg Baroque Ensemble**, give us what they consider are the six best of the concertos on a single disc. Their superb playing makes this CD a clear first choice among Locatelli issues, even finer than the Naxos complete Opus 1, which offers twice as much music for less cost.

LOCKE, Matthew (c. 1621–77)

Consort of Fower Parts: Suites 1 in D min.; 2 in D min./maj.; 3 & 4 in F; 5 in G min.; 6 in G

*** Astrée ES 9921. Hespèrion XX

Consort of Fower Parts: Suites 1–6; Flatt Consort a 3 'for my cousin Kemble'

*** Global Music Network GMNC 0109. Phantasm

Matthew Locke, born in Devon, was a choirboy at Exeter Cathedral, but when Charles II was restored to the throne of England, Locke became Master of the King's Music at the royal court; but he probably wrote the *Consort of Fower Parts* earlier, in the 1650s. If they are not ambitious in instrumentation, they are much more so in musical achievement. Each suite opens with a *Fantazie* and then follows a standard sequence of *Courante*, *Ayre* and *Saraband*. Locke's suites were regarded at the time as being composed, 'after the old style', but the music itself is forward-looking and by no means predictable. It seems likely that they would have been performed with continuo, a practice followed sparingly in the Hespèrion performance, using a double harp and organ.

Both sets of performances are highly musical, scholarly and well recorded, but there is a first choice. In the dance movements there is an extra rhythmic vigour and buoyancy with **Hespèrion**, and in the *Ayres* of the *First* and *Second Suites*, for instance, there is extra expressive warmth.

However, **Phantasm** also play this music delightfully. Their approach is intimate yet also reveals the music's expressive qualities as being considerable, while the dance movements are very sprightly. They are admirably recorded and they also include the ambitious suite of six movements which the composer wrote for his cousin which includes no fewer than three *Fantazies*.

Anthems: *Be thou exalted Lord; How doth the city sit solitary; Lord let me know mine end; O be joyful in the Lord, all ye lands*. Oxford Ode: *Descende caelo cincta sororibus*. Latin Motets: *Audi, Domine, clamantes ad te; Jesu, auctor clementie*

♫— (BB) ******* Hyp. Helios CDH 55250. New College, Oxford, Ch., Parley of Instruments, Higginbottom

Like others of his era Matthew Locke (although he was a Catholic himself) wrote Anglican music, including some fine anthems, as well as concerted Latin works. Apart from demands on his time at the court, he had a strong connection with Oxford and he wrote the so-called *Oxford Ode* for an academic celebration. There is plenty of variety here. *Super flumina Babylon*, a setting of Psalm 136, opens with a solemn two-movement Sinfonia. *O be joyful in the Lord* is as good-tempered as it sounds, with an attractive string accompaniment. Yet *How doth the city* (with an almost orchestral organ accompaniment) is a melancholy setting of verses from the *Lamentations of Jeremiah*. *Lord let me know mine end* has a diminuendo at the close. But the collection ends on a triumphant note, with full choir and orchestra in *Be thou exalted Lord*. Male voices are used throughout, as women began to sing in English choirs only in the 1770s. A most worthwhile collection, well sung throughout, and recorded in a comparatively dry acoustic to match the sound the composer would have expected both in Oxford and in London.

LOEWE, Carl (1796–1869)

9 Ballads

Ⓜ *** EMI (ADD) 3 91990-2 (2). Fischer-Dieskau, Moore –
    MENDELSSOHN: *Lieder* ***

Loewe, born the year before Schubert, lived on into the age of Wagner. This excellent collection, recorded in 1967, shows why his reputation stood so high, and could readily do so again. Last century there were many who preferred Loewe's setting of the *Erlking* to Schubert's, and here **Fischer-Dieskau** uses all his tonal virtuosity to underline the contrasted characterization, bringing the hair-raising story vividly to life. The ballad *Edward* too is most memorably done, and other items like *Der Schatzgräber* ('The Treasure-Seeker') and *Tom der Reimer* are also memorable. Throughout, **Gerald Moore** uses all his art in the accompaniments, and full texts and translations are included.

LOEWE, Frederick (1901–88)

with LERNER, Alan Jay (1918–86)

My Fair Lady (Musical)

☇ ❀ Ⓜ (***) Sony mono SMK 89997. Andrews, Harrison, Holloway, King and original cast, Ch. & O, Allers (with Post-Recording Conversations and Playback)

There are many who count *My Fair Lady* as the greatest musical of all, with a script by George Bernard Shaw and brilliantly apt lyrics by Alan Jay Lerner, and who can argue with them, for Frederick Loewe's score was no less inspired. There are sixteen numbers here, and not a dud among them, when most modern musicals manage with one or two hits, endlessly reprised.

This is not the later, stereo recording (which is far inferior) but the original mono LP, recorded in 1956 and vividly transferred to CD; moreover it includes the witty original orchestrations by Robert Russell Bennett and Phil Lang, which apparently are no longer in use today in the interests of theatrical economy and a smaller orchestra.

LOMBARDINI, Maddelena

Laura see Sirmen, Maddelena

LORTZING, Albert (1801–51)

Der Wildschütz (operetta) complete

Ⓑ **(*) EMI (ADD) 3 81837-2. Rothenburger, Litz, Wunderlich, Prey, Bav. State Op. Ch. & O, Heger

Der Wildschütz ('The Poacher') is an engaging piece that aims merely to charm and delight in an idiom that echoes Mendelssohn and Weber. The tangle of plot is improbable, a storm in a rustic teapot, but the characters are sharply and endearingly delineated, and one can readily understand why the operetta has never been out of the repertory in Germany and remains a firm favourite. The key recording of the work under Bernard Klee on DG is at present withdrawn, but **Robert Heger's** EMI/Electrola set, dating from 1963, is most enjoyable too, and is well cast, though the performance sparkles less and the recording is more limited. But it is still worth considering (now reissued with a good keyed synopsis) for the singing of the late **Fritz Wunderlich** in the role of the hero, even finer than Peter Schreier on DG.

Zar und Zimmermann (DVD version)

*** Arthaus DVD 101 269. Wolansky, Haage, Sotin, Popp, Fliether, Hamburg State Ballet, Ch., Hamburg Philharmonic State O, Mackerras (Dir: Rolf Liebermann, V/D: Joachim Hess)

Zar und Zimmermann ('The Tsar and the Carpenter') is a frothy, comic romp of mistaken identities, centring around Tsar Peter the Great who is working in the shipyards of Saardam under an assumed name. All sorts of complications ensue but, of course, all ends happily. Written in 1837, it was the work which marked Lortzing's maturing in terms of sophistication and musical personality. There is plenty of characterization and variety in the parts, and the construction of the finales is especially impressive (they have been likened to those of Mozart). The opera brims with good tunes. This DVD is an early colour television production, dating from 1969, and both the picture and sound-quality are very good for the period. The cast is excellent, featuring such a starry name as **Lucia Popp**, and the conducting under **Mackerras** has tremendous zing. Indeed, the sense of fun is conveyed splendidly. The sets and costumes are attractive and unpretentious, rare commodities in many of today's opera productions.

LÜBECK, Vincent (1654–1740)

Chorales: Ich ruf zu dir, Herr Jesu Christ; Nun Last uns Gott den Herren; Preludes: in C; D min.; E; G; G min.; Preludes & Fugues in C min. & F min.

Ⓜ *** Oehms SACD Surround Sound OC 507. Kelemen (Huss-Schnitger organ of St Cosmae et Damiani zu Stade)

The magnificent organ of St Cosmae et Damiani is the star of this disc, magnificently recorded, which in surround sound makes one think one is sitting in the church itslf. **Joseph Keleman** contributes, of course, for he brings all this music fully to life, revelling in the bravura, and especially in using the pedals. This is the perfect instrument for this repertoire, for Vincent Lübeck was appointed organist at St Cosmae in 1674, although he would not have known the sound of the present instrument. The music included here has only recently come to light and it all sounds pretty marvellous in Kelemen's hands, with the registration consistently imaginative. The opening *Preludium in C minor* has a thundering pedal solo, with three fugues following, and there are more spectacular pedal solos in the *Preludes in D, G minor* and *D minor*. Contrast is provided by the *Choral Prelude, Nun Last uns Gott den Herren*, in which Kelemen invests the variations with piquant colouring. He is equally imaginative in the *Choral fantasia, Ich ruf zu dir, Herr Jesu Christ*, using echo effects in the reeds, while the closing *D minor Prelude*, which has one of the longest fugues in North German organ writing, ends with a virtuoso toccata. All in all, a pretty stimulating recital.

LUDFORD, Nicholas (1485–1557)

Masses; Magnificat benedicta & Motets (as listed below)

🎧–✹ Ⓜ *** Gaudeamus CDGAX 426 (4). Cardinall's Musick, Carwood

Missa Benedicta et venerabilis; Magnificat benedicta

*** Gaudeamus CDGAU 132. Cardinall's Musick, Carwood

Missa Christi Virgo dilectissima; Motet: Domine Ihesu Christie

*** Gaudeamus CDGAU 133. Cardinall's Musick, Carwood

Missa Lapidaverunt Stephanum; Ave Maria ancilla trinitatis

*** Gaudeamus CDGAU 140. Cardinall's Musick, Carwood

Missa Videte miraculum; Motet: Ave cuius conceptio

*** Gaudeamus CDGAU 131. Cardinall's Musick, Carwood

This four-CD box gathers together the four splendid discs of Ludford's music performed by **Andrew Carwood** and his excellent group of singers, who are individually as impressive as in the blended whole. This is music of remarkably passionate feeling, and it brings to life a composer who spent much of his working life in St Stephen's Chapel at St Margaret's, Westminster. He was an ardent Catholic and was very happily married – he paid for his wife to have her own pew and gave her an elaborate ceremonial burial. He then married again, and his second wife was instructed to prepare something more modest for his interment alongside his beloved first spouse. His music is little short of extraordinary, and we hope our Rosette will tempt collectors to explore it, either through this comprehensive box, or by trying one of the individual issues.

LUIGINI, Alexandre (1850–1906)

Ballet Egyptien, Op. 12 (suite)

Ⓑ *** CfP (ADD) 352399-2. RPO, Fistoulari – KETÈLBEY: Collection ***

Because of its bandstand popularity, Luigini's amiable and tuneful *Ballet Egyptien* has never been taken very seriously. However, the four-movement suite is highly engaging (both the two central sections have good tunes), especially when played as affectionately and stylishly as here under that master conductor of ballet, **Anatole Fistoulari**. The 1958 recording has come up remarkably freshly, and this makes an excellent bonus for an outstanding Ketèlbey concert.

LULLY, Jean-Baptiste (1632–87)

Lés Comédies Ballets: excerpts from: (i) Les Amants magnifiques; L'Amour Médecin; Le Bourgeois Gentilhomme; Georges Dandin (Le Grand Divertissement royal de Versailles); Monsieur de Pourceaugnac (Le Divertissement de Chambourd); Pastoral comique; Les Plaisirs de l'île enchantée; (ii) Phaéton (tragédie en musique; complete)

🎧–ⒷⒷ *** Warner Apex 2564 62184-2 (2). (i) Poulenard, Mellon, Ragon, Laplénie, Verschaeve, Delétré, Cantor; (ii) Crook, Yakar, J. Smith, Gens, Thereul, Sagittarius Vocal Ens.; Musiciens du Louve, Minkowski

The series of comédies-ballets represented here were written between 1663 and 1670, and their tuneful and often outrageous burlesque represents an unparalleled comic partnership between composer and playwright – French insouciance combined with witty *bucolique* music which obviously reflects the influence of Italian comic opera, yet never loses its Gallic character, especially in the charming and often beautiful pastoral airs.

The ensemble of 'Ironic salutation to Men of Medicine' (Lully despised doctors) in *L'Amour médecin* is matched by the robust male interchanges while wallowing in the hedonistic pleasures of *L'île enchantée*, and there are similar comically boisterous ensembles in the divertissement, *Georges Dandin*, although they are perhaps capped by the extraordinary excerpt from *Monsieur de Pourceaugnac*, which makes fun of polygamy. The two longest selections come from *Le Bourgeois Gentilhomme*, and, finally, the masterly third *intermède* of *Les Amants magnifiques*, which combines a gentler humour with graceful lyricism. The team of soloists clearly relishes every humorous situation, and the presentation has consistent sparkle and spontaneity, while the lyrical music is most persuasively phrased by singers and orchestra alike.

Phaéton tells the famous story of the attempt of the son of Jupiter to drive across the heavens in his father's chariot. The horses bolt and Jupiter strikes him dead, to the apparent rejoicing of everyone. When Lybye can then be partnered by her beloved Epaphus, it is hardly a tragedy at all, with their love celebrated earlier in two brief but intensely beautiful duets. The cast is strong – **Véronique Gens** is most affecting as Lybye, with **Rachael Yakar** and **Jennifer**

Smith impressive too, and **Howard Crook** clean-focused and stylish in the name-part. Throughout the two discs, **Marc Minkowski's** direction is compellingly fresh and resilient. Both recordings are co-productions between Erato and Radio France and are strikingly vivid and immediate. One laments the appalling documentation, or lack of it, but this set is not to be missed.

Motets: *Benedictus; Exaudi Deus; O dulcissime; Notus in Judaea Deus*

🎵 ⏵ (BB) *** Naxos 8.554389. Concert Spirituel, Nicquet

Master of the King's Music in the golden age of Louis XIV, Lully dominated French music for over 30 years, carefully keeping such composers as Charpentier in the background. Though in depth he may not quite match Charpentier, let alone Purcell, he was consistently lively and inventive. This excellent Naxos issue offers three of the larger-scale, multi-movement motets with choir and soloists, set against two of the best-known 'little' motets for soloists alone, including the beautiful *O dulcissime*. First-rate French performances, with no singers individually named.

OPERA

Atys (opera; complete)

*** HM HMC 901257/9 (3). de Mey, Mellon, Laurens, Gardeil, Semellaz, Rime, Les Arts Florissants Ch. & O, Christie

Christie and his excellent team give life and dramatic speed consistently to the performance of *Atys*, and there are many memorable numbers, not least those in the sleep interlude of Act III. Outstanding in the cast are the high tenor, **Guy de Mey**, in the name-part and **Agnès Mellon** as the nymph, Sangaride, with whom he falls in love.

Persée (DVD version; complete)

*** EuroArts **DVD** 2054178. Auvity, Lenormand, Novacek, Whicher, Laquerre, Coulombe, Ainsworth, Tafelmusik Chamber Ch. & Bar. O, Niquet (V/D: Marc Stone)

Set in the historic Elgin Theatre in Toronto, Marshall Pynkoski's production for Tafelmusik under its lively music-director, **Hervé Niquet**, offers a staging as close as possible to the original (1682) presentation of the opera in the Palace of Versailles. Costumes are sumptuously baroque, and the sort of stage effects popular at the time, with gods coming down from the flies, add to the effectiveness. The work itself is a traditional *tragédie lyrique* in five acts, lasting just over two hours, with arioso taking the place of set numbers, punctuated in each act by dances – cue for ballet from the Atelier Company. The plot involves the linking of two classical legends, taken from Ovid's *Metamorphoses*: Perseus's slaying of Medusa, and his rescue of Andromeda, daughter of the King of Ethiopia. The title-role of Persée – who appears for the first time only in Act III – is very well taken by the high tenor, **Cyril Auvity**, and though the other principals are variable the piece moves swiftly. The role of Medusa is taken by a bearded baritone, **Olivier Laquerre**, rather roughish for this repertory, if characterful, particularly in the solo of lamentation for loss of his/her beauty.

LUMBYE, Hans Christian
(1810–74)

Amelie Waltz; Britta Polka; Champagne Galop; Columbine Polka Mazurka; Concert Polka (for 2 violins and orchestra); Copenhagen Steam Railway Galop; Dream Pictures (fantasy); The Lady of St Petersburg (polka); The Guards of Amager: Final Galop; My Salute to St Petersburg (march); Napoli (ballet): Final Galop; Polonaise with Cornet Solo; Queen Louise's Waltz; Salute to August Bournonville; St Petersburg Champagne Galop

🎵 ⏵ (BB) *** Regis RRC 1155. Odense SO, Guth

The superb Regis collection (originally on Unicorn) offers 75 minutes of the composer's best music, with wonderfully spontaneous performances demonstrating above all its elegance and gentle grace. It opens with a vigorous *Salute to August Bournonville* and closes with a *Champagne Galop* to rival Johann junior's polka. In between comes much to enchant, not least the delightful *Amelie Waltz* and the haunting *Dream Pictures Fantasia* with its diaphanous opening texture and lilting main theme. But Lumbye's masterpiece is the unforgettable *Copenhagen Steam Railway Galop*. This whimsical yet vivid portrayal of a local Puffing Billy begins with the gathering of passengers at the station – obviously dressed for the occasion in a more elegant age than ours. The little engine then wheezingly starts up and proceeds on its short journey, finally drawing to a dignified halt against interpolated cries from the station staff. Because of the style and refinement of its imagery, it is much the most endearing of musical railway evocations, and the high-spirited lyricism of the little train racing through the countryside, its whistle peeping, is enchanting. This is a superbly entertaining disc, showing the **Odense Symphony Orchestra** and its conductor **Peter Guth** as naturally suited to this repertoire as was the VPO under Boskovsky in the music of the Strauss family. The recording has a warm and sympathetic ambience which gives a lovely bloom to the whole concert. This reissue is a bargain if ever there was one.

LUTOSŁAWSKI, Witold
(1913–94)

Cello Concerto

🎵 ⏵ (M) **** EMI (ADD) 5 67867-2. Rostropovich, O de Paris, composer – DUTILLEUX: *Cello Concerto* ****

The *Cello Concerto* was written in response to a commission by **Rostropovich**. As in some other Lutosławski pieces, there are aleatory elements in the score, though these are carefully controlled. The sonorities are fascinating and are heard to good advantage on the EMI CD. The soloist is rather forward, but in every other respect the recording is extremely realistic. Rostropovich is in his element and gives a superb account of the solo role, and the composer's direction of the accompaniment is grippingly authoritative.

(i; ii; iii) *Cello Concerto*; (i; ii; iv) *Concerto for Oboe, Harp & Chamber Orchestra*; (v) *Concerto for*

Orchestra; (i; ii; ix) Dance Preludes; (i; vi; vii) Les Espaces du sommeil; (v) Funeral Music; (i; vii) Symphony 3; (viii) Variations on a Theme by Paganini; (v) Venetian Games

Ⓑ **** Ph. Duo (ADD) 464 043-2 (2). (i) composer; (ii) Bav. RSO; (iii) Schiff; (iv) H. and U. Holliger; (v) Nat. SO of Warsaw, Rowicki; (vi) Fischer-Dieskau; (vii) BPO; (viii) Argerich, Freire; (ix) Brunner

This is an excellent bargain-price introduction to Lutosławski which includes many of his most important works. The *Third Symphony* is given an authoritative performance under the direction of the composer, while *Les Espaces du sommeil* is performed by its dedicatee, **Dietrich Fischer-Dieskau**, and more definitive versions could hardly be imagined. Recorded around the same time in equally impressive performances was the *Cello Concerto* with **Heinrich Schiff**, a fine work, while the *Concerto for Oboe, Harp and Chamber Orchestra* was written for the **Holligers**, who perform it here; it mingles charm, irony and intelligence in equal measures. The *Dance Preludes* date from 1953 and were later scored for clarinet and orchestra, as recorded here. They are more folk-like in idiom and are attractively presented by **Eduard Brunner** (clarinet). The *Paganini Variations*, a piano duo dating from 1941, is exhilarating and is played with great virtuosity by **Martha Argerich** and **Nelson Freire**. The *Funeral Music* is an angular work which makes some impression, but is rather empty. *Venetian Games* is music of wider appeal, while the famous *Concerto for Orchestra* – a brilliant and highly attractive work – is thoroughly idiomatic. All the **Rowicki** performances are excellently recorded and have transferred very well to CD. A bargain set in every way.

(i; ii) Cello Concerto; (ii) ;(iii) 7 Preludes & Fugue for 13 Solo Strings; (iv) String Quartet; (v; ii) Paroles tissées; (ii; vi) 3 Poèmes d'Henri Michaux; (vii; ii) 5 Songs for Soprano & Orchestra (The Sea; Storm; Winter; Knights; Church Bells)

Ⓑ *** EMI Gemini (ADD) 5 85773-2 (2). (i) Jablonski; (ii) Polish R. Nat. SO; (iii) Polish CO; all cond. composer; (iv) Alban Berg Qt; (v) Louis Devos; (vi) Kraków R. Ch.; (vii) Lukomska

This valuable collection was recorded under the auspices of the composer in the Polish Radio Studios in Kraków in 1976–7, with the *String Quartet* added much later, in 1995. **Roman Jablonski's** account of the *Cello Concerto* still stands up well against the competition, though it is not a first choice. The searching *Seven Preludes and Fugue for Strings* (1970–2) show the mature Lutosławski and are vividly played by the Polish orchestra, as is the short, elliptical *Postlude* (1958). The choral *Poèmes d'Henri Michaux* date from the early 1960s. With their variety of effects, including whispering and syllabic monotones, the writing readily contrasts with the atmospheric *Paroles tissées* ('Woven Words') with its mystical feeling and remarkable word-imagery. The equally atmospheric *Five Songs* (written in 1957 and orchestrated the following year) find a highly sympathetic and idiomatic soloist in **Halina Lukomska**, with the texturally intriguing accompaniments catching the ear quite as much as the vocal line.

In his two-movement *String Quartet* Lutosławski tells us that he uses 'chance elements to enrich the rhythmic and expressive character of the music without in any way limiting the authority of the composer over the final shape of the piece'. Altogether this inexpensive survey offers a well-conceived demonstration of the composer's breadth of achievement. As might be expected, performances are of a generally high standard and the analogue recordings have been transferred very well to CD.

Concerto for Orchestra; Mi-parti; Overture for Strings; (i) 3 Poems by Henri Michaux

Ⓑ🎵 ⒷⒷ *** Naxos 8.553779. (i) Camerata Silesia Ch., Szostak; Polish Nat. RSO, Wit

The settings of the surrealist poet, Henri Michaux, dating from the early 1960s, are highly original in their use of choral textures, and *Mi-parti* in a single span, slow then fast, points forward in the brilliance and originality of its interplay of instruments to the later symphonies. Strong and purposeful performances, vividly recorded in full, immediate sound.

(i) Piano Concerto; Little Suite; Symphonic Variations; Symphony 2

ⒷⒷ *** Naxos 8.553169. (i) Paleczny; Polish Nat. RSO, Wit

The early, tonal *Symphonic Variations* make an attractive introduction to the second of Naxos's discs in what aims to cover his complete orchestral music. The *Little Suite* is an approachable work too, before the much tougher and more substantial symphony and concerto, which make up the greater part of the disc. In two massive movements, *Hesitant* and *Direct*, *Symphony 2* is an uncompromising piece, and here it is helped by a purposeful, very well-rehearsed performance. The *Piano Concerto* is even more elusive, often fragmentary, but again the performance is magnetic: **Paleczny** plays with a clarity and brilliance that sound totally idiomatic. Excellent sound, with good presence.

Dance Preludes (for clarinet & orchestra)

ⒷⒷ *** Hyp. Helios CDH 55068. King, ECO, Litton – BLAKE: *Clarinet Concerto*; SEIBER: *Concertino* ***

*** Chan. 8618. Hilton, SNO, Bamert – COPLAND; NIELSEN: *Concertos* ***

Lutosławski's five folk-based vignettes are a delight in the hands of **Thea King** and **Andrew Litton**, who give sharply characterized performances, thrown into bold relief by the bright, clear recording. An excellent bargain reissue.

Janet Hilton also emphasizes their contrasts with her expressive lyricism and crisp articulation in the lively numbers. Excellent recording.

Paganini Variations for Piano & Orchestra

*** Australian Decca Eloquence (mono/stereo/DDD) 476 7671. Jablonski, RPO, Ashkenazy – DOHNÁNYI: *Variations on a Nursery Song* **(*); LISZT: *Totentanz* (**(*)); RACHMANINOV: *Paganini Variations* **(*)

The *Paganini Variations* for two pianos, one of Lutosławski's earliest works (1941), is heard here in the much later orchestral transcription, with evident pleasure and delight.

Symphony 3; (i) Variations on a Theme of Paganini; (ii) Les Espaces du sommeil; (iii) Paroles tissées

(BB) *** Naxos 8.553423. (i) Glemser; (ii) Kruszewski; (iii) Kusiewicz; Polish Nat. RSO (Katowice), Wit

The earliest piece on Naxos, the *Paganini Variations* for two pianos, comes from 1941, but in 1978 the composer re-arranged the piece for piano and orchestra. This and the *Third Symphony* from 1982 are well played and recorded. Less persuasive, perhaps, is *Les Espaces du sommeil* (the soloist is a bit forward, though he sings well). In the *Paroles tissées* the singer is less at ease both with the musical idiom and with the French language. All the same, this well-filled CD is recommendable in every other respect.

Symphony 4; (i) Chain II; Interlude; Partita; Musique funèbre

🎁 (BB) **** Naxos 8.553202. (i) Bakowski; Polish Nat. RSO, Wit

Symphony 4 is Lutosławski's culminating masterpiece which, in its concentration over two linked movements, seems to echo Sibelius's *Seventh*. The darkly intense *Funeral Music* in memory of Bartók is another beautiful and concentrated work, while the two violin concertante works, *Chain II* and *Partita*, here come with the separating *Interlude*, similarly thoughtful, which Lutosławski wrote as a link. In almost every way, not least in the playing of the violinist, **Krzysztow Bakowski**, these Polish performances match and even outshine earlier recordings conducted by the composer, helped by full, brilliant sound.

Variations on a Theme of Paganini

(M) *** Ph. 475 8520. Argerich & Freire – RACHMANINOV: *Suite 2, Op. 17*; RAVEL: *La valse* ***

Lutosławski's *Variations* for piano duo are exhilarating and are played here with great virtuosity. The recording is very natural, but makes obvious the rather reverberant acoustic of the recording location.

Paganini Variations (arr. Ptasazynska)

*** Chan. 9398. Safri Duo & Slovak Piano Duo – BARTÓK: *Sonata for 2 Pianos & Percussion* ***; HELWEG: *American Fantasy* **

A slight piece from Lutosławski's youth, dressed up by Marta Ptasazynska for the same forces as the Bartók *Sonata*. It is brilliantly played and no less remarkably recorded at a Danish Radio concert. There is enthusiastic applause, which is understandable, and whistling, which is unfortunate.

LUTYENS, Elisabeth (1906–83)

(i; ii) And Suddenly it's Evening; (iii) Quincunx

(N) ***Lyrita (ADD) SRCD 265. (i) Handt; (ii) BBC SO (members); (iii) Nendick, Shirley-Quirk, BBC SO, Del Mar; (iv) Manning, Carewe (with (ii; iv) BEDFORD: *Music for Albion Moonlight* ***)

Quincunx is a hauntingly original work. The setting of lines by Sir Thomas Browne forms only a central vocal oasis (unaccompanied) in the middle of a complex series of instrumental pieces, until the music grows slower and stiller at the end, and one is reminded in the brass solos of the more direct Stravinsky. Generally with twelve-note serialism thoroughly absorbed, Elisabeth Lutyens's idiom comes closer to that of Berg in flavour, though any parallel is misleading with a work that is original in its own right. *And Suddenly it's Evening* is not quite so successful. There are many interesting touches in this score, but the impact of this setting of words by the poet Salvatore Quasimodo (translated by Jack Bevan) is blunted when the music is so unrelievedly slow. Like *Quincunx*, the performances and recording are as brilliant as can be imagined. Her music is coupled with David Bedford's the (in many ways) extraordinary *Music for Albion Moonlight*. With words by Kenneth Patchen, it is rather like a development of Schoenberg's *Pierrot Lunaire* that goes way beyond anything the Second Viennese School ever conceived of, and listeners should be warned of excruciating semi-tone glissandos on an instrument known as the alto-melodica. There are also sudden shrieks on the words 'Hell!' and 'Mad!' which are not recommended to those of a nervous disposition. Beautifully performed and recorded and, like the Lutyens, originally released on Argo.

MCCABE, John (born 1939)

Arthur Pendragon (ballet): Suite 1; (i) Piano Concerto 1. Pilgrim for Double String Orchestra

(N) (M) *** Dutton CDLX 7179. BBC Scottish SO, Austin, (i) with composer

Arthur Pendragon is a colourful ballet score, premièred in 2000, from which the composer compiled this four-movement *Suite*. The music is lively and inventive, using a battery of percussion instruments, and the composer offers a new take on the Arthurian legend. In 1998, as a result of a commission from the Brunel Ensemble, McCabe rearranged his music for *The Pilgrim's Progress* for double string orchestra and dedicated it to the conductor on this recording. It is an imaginative piece, written in the English string-music tradition, generally slow in pulse, but with enough variation in texture to keep the listener interested. The *Piano Concerto*, commissioned for the 1967 Southport Centenary Festival, is written in four movements, the first slow and brooding, which builds up to an impressive climax then launches into a brilliant but short vivo second movement. The long third movement is divided into several sections, ranging from slow and atmospheric to angrily dramatic, while the finale is generally the lightest in spirit. Elements of Vaughan Williams and Tippett run though this work (and the others on this CD) as well as Stravinsky; but McCabe does possess a distinctive voice.

(i) Flute Concerto; Symphony 4 (Of Time and the River)

🎁 **** Hyp. CDA 67089. BBC SO, Handley; (i) with Beynon

Completed in 1994, his *Fourth Symphony*, entitled *Of Time and the River* after Thomas Wolfe's novel, is a magnificent work in two substantial movements – fast to slow, then slow to fast. The idiom is warmer and more approachable than in McCabe's earlier music, echoing in its atmospheric orchestration and some of the melodic lines Britten on the one hand and Sibelius on the other, while remaining distinctive and new. Superb performances and vivid recording, not just of the *Symphony* but of the large-scale *Flute Concerto* McCabe wrote for James Galway. Ideal notes as well.

Edward II (ballet; complete)

🎵 *** Hyp. CDA 67135/6 (2). Royal Ballet Sinfonia, Wordsworth

McCabe's score is at once colourfully atmospheric as well as symphonic in its thinking, vividly telling the story in mood and action, drawing on medieval sources for themes and for the 'tuckets and alarums' which add point to such a plot. Having abandoned the more severely serial stance of his earlier music. There have been few full-length ballet scores as impressive as this since Prokofiev and Britten, inspiring **Barry Wordsworth** and the **Royal Ballet Sinfonia** to a strong and colourful performance, vividly recorded.

CHAMBER MUSIC

Concerto for Piano & Wind Quintet; Fauvel's Rondeaux; Musica notturna; Postcards for Wind Quintet

Ⓜ *** Dutton CDLX 7125. Fibonacci Sequence

This fresh and alert piece in four linked sections dates from 1969, early in McCabe's career, a concerto, he explains in his own illuminating note, as much for the members of the wind quintet as for the virtuoso piano soloist. The *Musica notturna*, dating from even earlier (1964), has a comparable sharpness in exploiting the changing moods and aspects of a great city at night, while the third of these works in linked sections dates from much more recently, *Fauvel's Rondeaux* of 1995. *Postcards*, dating from 1991, is a set of eight striking miniatures, including a *bossa nova* and a *fugato*, reworked for wind quintet from *Eight Bagatelles* for two clarinets, originally written in 1965. The bite and brilliance of the performances by the **Fibonacci Sequence** are ideal for this music, helped by full, immediate sound.

Maze Dances; (i) Star Preludes

*** Metier MSV CD 92029. Sheppard Skaerved; (i) with Honma – RAWSTHORNE: *Violin Sonata*, etc. ***

These two substantial works by McCabe make an ideal coupling for the two fine violin pieces by Rawsthorne, a fellow composer he has long championed. *Maze Dances* is a brilliant and varied fantasia for unaccompanied violin, inventive and ingenious in exploiting this limited medium, while *Star Preludes* for violin and piano, just as varied in expression, equally reveals the composer's deep understanding of string technique. Flawless performances, beautifully recorded.

String Quartets 3, 4 & 5

🎵 *** Hyp. CDA 67078. Vanbrugh Qt

Few 20th-century string quartets have such a haunting opening as John McCabe's masterly *Third*, and the work ends with a *Passacaglia* which 'derives its overall shape and flow from the concept of a lakeland stream', tumbling down in irregular patterns until the return of that memorable opening motif leads to a wonderful sense of calm. The single-movement *Fourth Quartet* (1982) is hardly less compelling. Once again the close is comparatively peaceful, with an expressive cello soliloquy. The *Fifth Quartet* (1989) is programmatic and, as the very beginning makes plain, was inspired by a series of Graham Sutherland's aquatints called *The Bees*. These three remarkable works could hardly be presented with greater concentration or more commitment, and the recording is first class.

5 Bagatelles; Haydn Variations; Studies 3 (Gaudi); 4 (Aubade); 6 (Mosaic); Variations, Op. 22

*** British Music Society BMS 424DC. Composer

The British Music Society have here published a major survey of McCabe's piano music, from the early *Variations* (1963) to the much more complex *Haydn Variations* of 1983, while the pianistically exploratory *Studies* span the decade between 1970 and 1980. The *Bagatelles*, five brief vignettes, in the words of the composer 'were written to a request for not-too-difficult 12-notes pieces', but the third and sixth *Studies* are extended works, architecturally inspired. McCabe is a formidable pianist and is obviously an ideal exponent of his own music. Excellent recording.

3 Folk Songs, Op. 19: Johnny was gone for a soldier; Hush-a-by Birdie; John Peel (for tenor, clarinet & piano)

*** Campion Cameo 2001. Hindmarsh, Turner, Cuckson – BUSH: *Prison Cycle*; RAWSTHORNE: *Songs* **(*)

The *Three Folk Songs*, by John McCabe, very well sung by **Martin Hindmarsh**, have a neatly tailored clarinet obbligato, and the recital closes with a droll arrangement of *John Peel*, with its witty hornpipe pay-off.

MACCUNN, Hamish (1868–1916)

Concert overture: The Land of the Mountain and the Flood; The Dowie Dens o' Yarrow; The Ship o' the Fiend; Cantata; (i) The Lay of the Last Minstrel: Breathes There the Man; O Caledonia!; Jeannie Deans (opera; excerpts)

🎵 *** Hyp. CDA 66815. BBC Scottish SO, Brabbins; (i) with Watson, Milne, MacDougal, Sidholm, Gadd, Danby, Scottish Opera Ch.

The Land of the Mountain and the Flood is a very well-constructed piece, with a memorable tune. **Martyn Brabbins** and the **BBC Scottish Symphony Orchestra**, in a brilliant new performance, give it fresh life, and the Hyperion recording has range and sparkle. *The Dowie Dens o' Yarrow* is a very similar piece, with comparable rhythmic impetus and another attractive secondary theme, given to the oboe. The even more atmospheric *Ship o' the Fiend* introduces another endearing lyrical cello theme reminiscent of *The Land of the Mountain and the Flood*.

MacCunn's opera *Jeannie Deans* is a tuneful and colourful piece with plenty of musical vitality. Effie's aria, *Oh that I again could see* (she is imprisoned in the Tolbooth), and the following *Lullaby* are touchingly sung here by **Janice Watson**, and the choral contribution is very spirited. The excerpt from the cantata *The Lay of the Last Minstrel* brings a suitably vigorous closing chorus, *O Caledonia!*

Piano music: 6 Scottish Dances; Valse

*** Divine Art 2-5003. McLachlan – MCEWEN: *La Côte d'Argent*, etc. *** ; MACKENZIE: *Chasse aux papillons*, etc. **(*)

The subtitle of this Scottish collection is 'Impressionistic piano works', but that hardly applies to these simple miniatures by Hamish MacCunn, engaging though they are. They include one real lollipop: the *Plaid Dance* (track 5) which, with its gentle Scottish snaps, haunts the memory beguilingly. **Murray McLachlan** plays most sympathetically and is well recorded.

MACDOWELL, Edward
(1860–1908)

(i) Piano Concertos 1–2; Second Modern Suite, Op. 14

☷– *** Hyp. CDA 67165. Tanyel; (i) with BBC Scottish SO, Brabbins

Seta Tanyel gives sparkling performances of these attractive works, relishing the pianistic fireworks typical of this lyrical American composer. The fill-up, involving piano alone, offers a sequence of six colourful and unpretentious genre pieces. Tanyel's characterful playing, full of sparkle and imagination, is well matched by the playing of the **BBC Scottish Orchestra** under **Martyn Brabbins**, helped by full-bodied, well-balanced recording.

2 Fragments after the Song of Roland, Op. 30: The Saracens; The Lovely Aldä; Hamlet/Ophelia, Op. 22; Lancelot and Elaine, Op. 25; Lamia, Op. 29

*** Bridge 9089. RPO, Krueger

The two *Fragments after the Song of Roland* are the middle movements of what was intended as a programme-symphony, and *The Lovely Aldä* is a gentle portrait which has something in common with MacDowell's *Wild Rose*, if not as melodically memorable. The portraits of *Hamlet* and *Ophelia* are highly romantic and, like both the symphonic poems, the lyrical writing is very appealing. *Lancelot and Elaine* (drawing on Tennyson's *Idylls of the King*) is particularly evocative. *Lamia* is based on a poem by Keats. MacDowell's music resourcefully varies the theme representing Lamia to indicate the events of the narrative, which ends badly for both characters. The performances here are

very persuasive. **Karl Krueger** is a splendid and dedicated advocate and the **RPO** playing is warmly seductive and beautifully recorded.

Suites 1, Op. 42; 2 (Indian); Hamlet and Ophelia (tone-poem), Op. 22

☷– ⒷⒷ *** Naxos 8.559075. Ulster O, Yuasa

The *Indian Suite* opens with a dramatic horn call and its first movement (*Legend*) is a grandiose evocation of the 'once-great past of a dying race' and draws on folk themes from the Iowas and Kiowas. The closing *Village Festival* expands energetically in the brass, finally returning to the mood of the opening movement. The *First Suite* (actually the second in order of composition) is a comparable series of genre evocations, and the suite ends with a winning dance from the *Forest Spirits*. The performances here are outstanding in every way, full of colour, warmth and vitality, and the recording is state-of-the-art.

PIANO MUSIC

Fireside Tales, Op. 61; New England Idylls, Op. 62; Sea Pieces, Op. 55; Woodland Sketches, Op. 51

**(*) Marco Polo 8.223631. Baragallo

MacDowell's most famous piano piece opens this recital: *To a Wild Rose* (named by his wife) is the first of the 10 *Woodland Sketches*. They are all pleasant if not distinctive vignettes, most lasting a little over a minute. The other three suites are very similar. Not a CD to listen to all at once but to be dipped into; one can appreciate that **James Baragallo** is a thoroughly sympathetic exponent, and he is well recorded.

MCEWEN, John Blackwood
(1868–1948)

A Solway Symphony; (i) Hills o' Heather; Where the Wild Thyme Blows

☷– **** Chan. 9345. (i) Welsh; LPO, Mitchell

McEwen's highly evocative *Solway Symphony* is a triptych of seascapes marked by magically transparent orchestration and crisply controlled argument. Above all, this is warm-hearted music. *Hills o' Heather* is a charming movement for cello and orchestra, while *Where the Wild Thyme Blows* uses slow pedal points to sustain harmonically adventurous arguments. The performances, conducted by **Alasdair Mitchell**, who edited the scores, are outstanding, a well-deserved tribute to a neglected composer who was far more than an academic. The recording is sumptuously atmospheric.

CHAMBER MUSIC

String Quartets 4; 7 (Threnody); 16 (Quartette provençale); 'Fantasia' for String Quartet, 17

*** Chan. 9926. Chilingirian Qt

McEwen remained true to his Scottish roots. The *Fourth*

Quartet in its chromatic writing yet brings in a Scottish flavour, while 7 is a moving response to the tragedy of the First World War. 16 is openly evocative in its often Debussian response to the countryside of Provence, and the *Fantasia Quartet*, 17, his last, written the year before he died, in a single substantial movement of five linked sections, reaffirms his romantic allegiances with echoes of Dvořák in the meditative central section. Superb, warmly expressive performances and full, warm Chandos sound.

Violin Sonatas 2; 5 (Sonata-Fantasia); 6; Prince Charlie – A Scottish Rhapsody

⌒-,******* Chan. 9880. Charlier, Tozer

McEwen's *Second Violin Sonata* (1913–14) shows the influence of both Debussy and Chausson. All the works recorded here show him to be a polished craftsman and a composer of real culture. The *Fifth Sonata* (1921), written for Albert Sammons, said to be his finest in this genre, recalls John Ireland and, like everything on this disc, holds the listener. Very good playing from **Olivier Charlier** and **Geoffrey Tozer**, excellent and vivid sound from Chandos and informative notes by Bernard Benoliel.

PIANO MUSIC

La Côte d'Argent: 5 Vignette; 3 'Keats' Preludes; On Southern Hills; 4 Sketches; Sonatina

*** Divine Art 2-5003. McLachlan – MACKENZIE: *Chasse aux papillons*, etc. ****(*)** ; MACCUNN: *6 Scottish Dances* *******

John Blackwood McEwen shows distinct French influences in his piano music. Not so much in the *Four Sketches*, which includes a brief 5/4 'Minuet', and a dazzling closing *Humoresque*, or the *Sonatina* which, with its Celtic flavours, is very much his own – especially the charming central *Andante semplice* – but in the *Three 'Keats' Preludes* (each prefaced by a fragment of the poet's verse) and even more in the atmospheric triptych, *On Southern Hills*, the influences of Debussy and Ravel are clear. The *Five Vignettes*, are lighter, but still evocative. Excellent performances from **Murray McLachlan** and good recording.

MACHAUT, Guillaume de
(c. 1300–1377)

Ballades, rondeaux, virelais

⌒-,******** Hyp. CDA 66087. Kirkby, Gothic Voices, Page

The ballades and virelais included here are written imploringly, and in elaborate admiration, to ladies of great beauty and of all other virtues, except apparently a willingness to respond. The fluid part-writing of the ensemble pieces is unique, but the solo pieces are very appealing, especially when sung, as two of them are here, by an artist of the calibre of **Emma Kirkby**. One wishes she had played a larger part in the programme, but **Rogers Covey-Crump**, **Colin Scott-Mason**, **Emily van Evera** and **Margaret Philpot** all make sympathetic individual contributions. As a group the **Gothic Voices** certainly know how to shape the melancholy melis-

mas of the concerted items: they blend beautifully together, giving effective, unexaggerated tweaks to the passing moments of dissonance. The closing four-part motet, a Triplum, celebrates the Virgin Mary and is perhaps the most beautiful work on the disc. Excellent recording.

Ballades; Chansons; Rondeaux; Virelais

Ⓜ ****(*)** DG 477 6731. Orlando Cons.

The **Orlando Consort** blend beautifully together, led by **Robert Harre-Jones**, whose richly coloured alto line is most appealing. But the snag is the basic sameness of colour inevitable with two, three or four unaccompanied male voices, however expressively they sing and however pleasingly recorded. In that respect the Hyperion disc above is much more appealing, and the DG issue has no texts and translations.

Un Lay de consolation; Le lay de la fonteigne

Ⓝ Ⓜ ******* Decca 478 8026. L. Medieval Ens., Peter & Timothy Davies

The lai emerged at the end of the twelfth century and differs from the rondeau and ballade in that it has many stanzas; indeed, all but two of the 19 lais of Machaut have 12 stanzas, including the two recorded here. In *Le lay de la fonteigne*, written during the period 1349–63, each of the even-numbered stanzas is a canon in three parts at the unison. *Un lay de consolation* is a work of the last decade of Machaut's life and survives only as a monophonic piece. However, the American scholar Richard Hoppin discovered that two halves of each stanza fit to produce two-part polyphony, and it is performed like this, the second part being assigned to instruments. *Le lay de la fonteigne* is the longer of the two, lasting nearly half an hour, and it is sung by three singers, only one of whom has the text in the canonic sections; the others vocalise. Music of specialist appeal but undoubted beauty. The recording and presentation are altogether exemplary.

Motets

*** Signum SIGCD 011. Clerks' Group, Wickham

This collection is doubly valuable, as it includes not only three-part motets from early in Machaut's career (1320–50), which he composed over French love-song melodies, but also a group of Latin motets which are later (1360) and are set in four parts to religious and more serious secular texts and are written over a plainchant melody. They use an isorhythmic style, that is regularly repeating combinations of rhythm and harmony, after each voice has entered singly. Moreover, **Edward Wickham** has also included five anonymous independent Mass movements, simple and beautiful in their austerity, taken from the Ivrea Codex. The performances are exemplary.

Messe de Nostre Dame; Le Livre dou Voir dit (excerpts): Plourez dames; Nes qu'on porroit (ballades); Sans cuer dolens (rondeau); Le Lay de bonne esperance; Puis qu'en oubli (rondeau); Dix et sept cinq (rondeau)

⌒-, Ⓑ Ⓑ ******** Naxos 8.553833. Oxford Camerata, Summerly

With his *Messe de Nostre Dame* (dedicated to the Virgin Mary), Guillaume de Machaut wrote the first known complete setting of the Ordinary of the Mass: *Kyrie, Gloria, Credo, Sanctus* and *Agnus Dei*. He chose to finish with his own simple interpolation: *Ite missa est*, which very briefly tells us, 'The Mass is ended; thanks be to God.' Machaut's writing is full of extraordinary, dissonant clashes and sudden harmonic twists which are immediately resolved, so the music is both serene and plangently stimulating: here is an epoch-making work of great originality.

Jeremy Summerly's account is undoubtedly eloquently serene; it is beautifully controlled and modulated, rather after the fashion of the famous Willcocks/King's College accounts of the Byrd Masses.

On Naxos the chansons were recorded, equally effectively, at the BBC's Maida Vale studio; they celebrate Machaut as poet/lover as well as composer and, at its modest price, the disc is worth having for these alone. The solo singing in the extra items on the Hyperion disc is very impressive indeed. *Le Lai de la Fonteinne* is another elaborate poem of 12 stanzas in praise of the Virgin, six polyphonic, six monodic, beautifully sung by **Rogers Covey-Crump** and **John Potter**, while the shorter rondeau, an expressive piece if restlessly so, is ingeniously constructed, and is a 'crab' canon by inversion, in that the imitating part, instead of being presented straightforwardly, is written backwards and upside down – appropriately so, to fit the text: 'My End is my Beginning.'

MACKENZIE, Alexander
(1847–1935)

Benedictus, Op. 37/3; Burns – 2nd Scottish Rhapsody, Op. 24; Coriolanus (incidental music): *Suite, Op. 61; The Cricket on the Hearth: Overture, Op. 62; Twelfth Night* (incidental music): *Overture/Suite, Op. 40*

🎵 *** Hyp. CDA 66764. BBC Scottish SO, Brabbins

Mackenzie, in the *Burns Rhapsody* uses three Scottish folk tunes quite felicitously, notably '*Scots! wha hae*', which is very emphatic. The second movement has charm, and indeed Mackenzie's own lyrical gift is quite striking in the jolly, at times Sullivanesque *Cricket on the Hearth Overture* (which also shows his deft orchestral skill), and of course the *Benedictus* with a melody typical of its time. The incidental music for *Twelfth Night* is in the form of an overture, subdivided into six sections, with a Shakespeare quotation for each to identify its mood. The whole programme is presented with commitment and polish by the **BBC Scottish Symphony Orchestra** and makes a very agreeable 75 minutes of not too demanding listening. The recording is excellent.

Scottish Concerto, Op. 55

*** Hyp. CDA 67023. Osborne, BBC Scottish SO, Brabbins – TOVEY: *Piano Concerto in A* ***

Built on Scottish themes, Mackenzie's *Concerto*, premièred by Paderewski, centres round its lyrical slow movement, framed by a rhapsodic first movement and a dance finale based on *Green Grow the Rushes O*. The young Scottish pianist **Steven Osborne** is a brilliant advocate, **Brabbins** a natural partner.

Piano music: *Chasse aux papillons; Harvest Home; Odds and Ends: High Spirits; Refrain 3 Morçeaux*

(*) Divine Art 2-5003. McLachlan – MACCUNN: *6 Scottish Dances;* MCEWEN: *La Côte d'Argent*, etc. *

Mackenzie's genre piano vignettes are derivative but hardly draw on the French impressionist school, as their inclusion in this collection might imply. It is the music of the other two composers on this enterprising collection that makes it worth exploring.

MACMILLAN, James
(born 1959)

(i) *Clarinet Concerto (Ninian);* (ii) *Trumpet Concerto (Epiclesis)*

🎵 **** BIS CD 1069. RSNO, Lazarev, with (i) Cushing; (ii) Wallace

The *Clarinet Concerto* is a celebration of the early Scottish St Ninian, with three of his miracles each inspiring a movement. The third and last, much the longest, brings another depiction of the Eucharist, with a joyful brassy chorale as a final climax. The soloist has a virtuoso role, but many of the most memorable moments come in hushed lyrical passages, with the clarinet bringing a resolution after orchestral violence. *Epiclesis*, the *Trumpet Concerto*, meaning prayer or invocation, leads the composer to attempt a musical equivalent to the Eucharist, the act of communion, in what he describes as 'the transformation of musical substances'. The free-flowing, almost improvisatory writing for the solo trumpet, with much fluttering figuration, is punctuated by big orchestral outbursts, leading at the most moving moment to a simple chorale, played *pianissimo* on the trumpet as though in purification. After that the jazzy syncopations of the final section sound almost like Charles Ives in brash contrast, leading finally to the most powerful climax and a fading away as the soloist departs. The performances of both works are not just brilliant but totally committed in bringing out the drama of this music, with BIS recording of demonstration quality.

Cumnock Fair; Sinfonietta; Symphony 2

*** BIS CD 1119. SCO, composer

MacMillan's *Second Symphony*, written in 1999, builds on ideas from an early piano sonata. A massive central movement is flanked by an evocative prelude, with bird-twittering ostinatos, a slow chorale and a reflective postlude, in which the chorale returns. The *Sinfonietta* starts mysteriously with a hypnotic slow section, which is brutally interrupted by violent *fortissimo* chords. It is almost Ives-like in its terracing of contrasted ideas, while *Cumnock Fair* is even more so in its kaleidoscopic quotations of dances with a Scottish flavour, wilder and wilder. Strong, intense performances, flawlessly balanced.

The Confession of Isobel Gowdie; The Exorcism of Rio Sumpul; Tuireadh

♦– **** BIS CD 1169. BBC Scottish SO, Vänskä

The Confession of Isobel Gowdie, and two other substantial works of the same period, were similarly inspired by events which moved the composer deeply. *Tuireadh* is a lament inspired by the Piper Alpha oil-rig disaster. The writing, originally for clarinet and string quartet, is here reassigned to orchestral strings, with the clarinet vividly conveying the agony of the bereaved. The *Exorcism of Rio Sumpul* was inspired by an atrocity in El Salvador in 1986, with the music illustrating the violence as well as the menace, and unexpectedly erupting into a final dance of joy and thanksgiving when it was revealed that by some miracle no one was killed. MacMillan's direct, intensely communicative style is well illustrated in all three works, with **Osmo Vänskä** drawing powerful performances from the **BBC Scottish Symphony Orchestra**, very well recorded.

The Confession of Isobel Gowdie; Symphony 3

*** Chan. 10275. BBC PO, composer

As the composer describes it, *The Confession of Isobel Gowdie* is the Requiem that Isobel Gowdie, a Catholic martyr accused of witchcraft, never had. In a single 25-minute span it begins in deep meditation, then the central section, by far the longest, brings a violence reflecting the brutality with which the martyr was treated. The beauty of the final section, in which she seems to find peace, with its references to plainsong is all the more affecting here in the composer's own performance.

Symphony 3 (2002) follows a comparable pattern of slow, inexorable build-up over a massive span, this time far bigger still. The work's paradoxical subtitle, 'Silence', was inspired by the work of the Japanese author Shusaku Endo, whose novel with that title has had a profound influence on the composer. The concentration of the playing of the **BBC Philharmonic** under **MacMillan** adds to the tautness in both works, and the performances are brilliant in every way and superbly recorded.

Triduum, an Easter Triptych, Part 1: (i) The World's Ransoming (for cor anglais and orchestra); Part 2: (ii) Cello Concerto

*** BIS CD 989. (i) Pendrill; (ii) R. Wallfisch; BBC Scottish SO, Vänskä

The World's Ransoming and the *Cello Concerto*, each self-contained, are the first two in a sequence of three related works representing MacMillan's response to Christ's Passion and the Easter story. *The World's Ransoming*, with its poignant writing for cor anglais set against violent interruptions, provides the emotional prelude and is intensely involving music, often wild in its expressionism. **Christine Pendrill** is the superb soloist, and though **Raphael Wallfisch** is just as expressive as the soloist in the *Cello Concerto*, conveying Christ's agony, sadly the balance sets him at a distance. This three-movement work, is even more violent, the embodiment of earthquake and storm, both physical and spiritual. Brilliant performances, spaciously recorded.

Triduum, an Easter Triptych, Part 3: Symphony (Vigil)

*** BIS CD 900. Fine Arts Brass Ens., BBC Scottish SO, Vänskä

The *Symphony (Vigil)* in three movements – *Light*, *Tuba insonet salutaris* and *Water* – forms the climax of the *Triduum* triptych, longer than either of the preceding works. Predictably it moves from darkness to light, with violence at the start of the first movement echoing the music of the *Cello Concerto*. The second movement brings fanfares spread spaciously, the last trump graphically portrayed, while the resolution of the final movement, longer than the other two put together, brings no easy salvation. **Vänskä** draws brilliant, warmly committed playing from the **BBC Scottish Symphony Orchestra**, vividly recorded.

Veni, veni, Emmanuel; Tryst

♦– (BB) **** Naxos 8.554167. Currie, Ulster O, Yuasa

With **Colin Currie**, the young prizewinning percussionist, matching his compatriot predecessor, Evelyn Glennie, in flair and panache, the Naxos version of the brilliant and dramatic percussion concerto, *Veni, veni, Emmanuel*, cannot be recommended too highly. **Takuo Yuasa** is a strong and persuasive conductor, not just in *Veni, veni, Emmanuel*, but in the earlier work, *Tryst*, an extended and colourful fantasy in five sections built on a setting of a Scottish song. Recorded in the helpful acoustic of the Ulster Hall, Belfast, the sound is exceptionally full and vivid, matching the excellent playing of the orchestra.

(i) Piano Sonata; Barncleupedie; Birthday Present; For Ian; (ii) Raising Sparks (cantata)

*** Black Box BBM 1067. (i) York; (ii) Rigby, Nash Ens., Brabbins

The *Piano Sonata* of 1985 in three movements is much the most demanding work here, far grittier than the rest, inspired by the extreme winter of that year and later the source of the *Second Symphony*. *For Ian* then brings total release into pure tonality and lyricism, a strathspey full of Scottish-snap rhythms. *Birthday Present* seems a very sombre gift, musically striking nonetheless, and the final *Barncleupedie* (1990) rounds things off light-heartedly with a piece which in slow barcarolle rhythm supports the melody, *Will Ye No Come Back Again*.

Like so much of MacMillan's music, *Raising Sparks* has a profoundly religious base, this time from a Jewish inspiration. The opening incantation by the mezzo-soprano soloist, low and sustained in the chest register with occasional ornamentation, immediately makes the Jewish associations clear enough, leading to a sequence of five songs setting poems by Michael Symmons Roberts on the theme of creation and redemption. The vocal line, though taxing, is more lyrical than in many new works, superbly sung by **Jane Rigby**, while the instrumental accompaniment is endlessly inventive, with the piano (the masterly **Ian Brown**) generally the central instrument in the ensemble.

VOCAL MUSIC

Cantos Sagrados; Christus vincit; Child's Prayer; Divo Aloysio Sacrum; The Gallant Weaver; Seinte Mari moder milde; So Deep; Tremunt vidente angeli

*** Signum SIGCD 507. L. Elysian Singers, Laughton; Jackson

A fascinating pot-pourri of James MacMillan's choral music called *Santos Sagrados* ('Sacred Songs'), which ranges from Latin motets to Scottish traditional settings or arrangements, including a pair of Robert Burns songs. The two major pieces offer a striking contrast, with the title number for choir and organ (the excellent **Carl Jackson**) in which MacMillan brings moments of intimidating darkness to the radiantly celestial *Tremunt vidente angeli*. Fine singing throughout from the excellent **Elysian Singers** (appropriately named for some of these dedicated religious settings) under their persuasive conductor, **Sam Laughton**.

Christus vincit; . . . here in hiding . . .; Nemo te condemnavit; Seven last Words from the Cross

Ⓝ ⒝⒝ *** Naxos 8.570719. Dmitri Ens., Ross

James MacMillan originally wrote his *Seven Last Words from the Cross* for BBC Television for 8-part chorus and strings, with each section shown on a separate night. That device failed to recognize that the impact of these pieces gains enormously from being heard in sequence with a powerful build-up, starting with Christ's words to the robber being crucified with him, through *Eli, eli lama sabachtani* and ending with *Father, into thy hands*. MacMillan's dedicated writing can also be most dramatic if often pauseful in a way most effective in a live performance. The three extra items – two of them in first recordings – make a valuable supplement. *Christus vincit* is a motet for double chorus, written for St Paul's Cathedral. The **Dmitri Ensemble** under **Graham Ross** gives immaculate performances, with the young voices of the choir well supported by the strings.

Mass; A Child's Prayer; Changed; Christus vincit; A New Song; Seinte Mari moder milde; (i) Gaudeamus

⊖͞ *** Hyp. CDA 67219. Westminster Cathedral Ch, Baker; (i) Reid

It would be hard to think of any recent music that so intensely conveys religious ecstasy as James MacMillan's *Mass*. MacMillan is yet distinctive in his brilliant use of choral effects, with surging crescendos up to glowing *fortissimos* to stir the blood. Two of the extra sections, taken from the Eucharistic Liturgy, largely involve solo chanting, but the fervour of MacMillan's inspiration as a devout Catholic himself makes for music of high voltage from first to last. Equally the shorter choral works on the disc, all written in the 1990s, have a rare freshness and concentration, often involving powerful slabs of sound.

The singing of the **Westminster Cathedral Choir** is electrifying, with **Martin Baker** directing his first recording as choirmaster. The solo singing, too, deserves special mention, with a solo treble negotiating a spectacular upward leap at the close of *Christus vincit*. *Gaudeamus* is a brief organ solo involving bird-noises, rather different from Messiaen's, beautifully played by **Andrew Reid**.

O bone Jesu, Mairi

Ⓝ *** Hänssler SACD 93.250. SW R. Vocal Ens., Creed – VAUGHAN WILLIAMS: *Mass in G min.; Silence and Music*

The **Stuttgart choir** gives strong and precise performances of English works for mixed choir by MacMillan and Vaughan Williams, defying the idea that they do not understand the idiom. The *Mass* is particularly successful. *O bone Jesu* is a motet inspired by the 15th-century Scottish composer, Robert Carver, setting a Gaelic poem, featuring bold choral effects with clashing intervals. The SACD gives superb, spacious sound.

Missa brevis; Strathclyde Motets; Tenebrae responsories; Introit: Give me Justice

*** Linn CKD 301.Cappella Nova, Tavener

The *Missa brevis* is early, composed when MacMillan was just seventeen and already showing an original musical personality. But the key work here is the set of seven comparatively straightforward but distinctly expressive *Strathclyde Motets*, unaccompanied except for a trumpet obbligato in the second, intended (as the composer has told us) for church use, by non-professional choirs, rather than for concert performance. The *Tenebrae responsories* understandably are darker and more plangent as sung by a small group from the **Cappella Nova**, whose singing under **Alan Tavener** throughout in an ideal kirk acoustic is very fine indeed.

MACMILLAN, Kenneth
(1929–92)

Mayerling (complete ballet; DVD version)

**** Opus Arte OA R3101D. Royal Ballet (members), ROHCG O, Wordsworth

This was MacMillan's last full-length ballet, and arguably his masterpiece. It has long been in circulation on video and LaserDisc, but this DVD scores even over the latter, excellent though it was. The plot concerns the events that led up to the joint suicide of Crown Prince Rudolf of Austria-Hungary (Irek Mukhamedov) and the 17-year-old Mary Vetsera (Viviane Durante) at Mayerling and evokes the claustrophobic and oppressive atmosphere at the Court of the Emperor Franz Joseph to vivid and compelling effect. MacMillan's superb choreography is well served by the recording team and the main dancers, with Darcy Bussell as Mitzi Caspar, the Prince's regular mistress and Matthew Hart as Bratfisch, his private cab-driver, and the rest of the cast, are (as so often nowadays with the Royal Ballet) flawless. There is no weakness anywhere in the company. The score draws on Liszt, in particular the *Faust Symphony*, and the compilation with various piano pieces was made and expertly orchestrated by John Lanchbery. We have returned to this 1994 recording (and various revivals at Covent Garden) with undiminished and ongoing admiration and pleasure.

MACONCHY, Elizabeth
(1907–94)

Clarinet Concertinos 1 (1945); 2 (1984)

ⓑⓑ *** Hyp. Helios CDH 55060. King, ECO, Wordsworth –
ARNOLD: *Clarinet Concertos 1–2; Scherzetto*; BRITTEN:
Clarinet Concerto Movement ***

The two Maconchy *Concertinos*, each in three movements and under ten minutes long, have a characteristic terseness, sharp and intense, that runs no risk whatever of seeming short-winded. Not only **Thea King** but the **ECO** under **Barry Wordsworth** bring out the warmth as well as the rhythmic drive, as in the other attractive works on this disc.

(i) Music for Strings; (ii) Overture, Proud Thames; (iii) Serenata concertante for Violin & Orchestra; (iv) Symphony for Double String Orchestra

*** Lyrita (DDD/ADD) SRCD 288. (i–ii) LPO; (iii–iv) LSO; (iii)
with Parikian; (i) Wordsworth; (ii–iv) Handley

These works all testify to the strength of Elizabeth Maconchy's imagination, the *Overture*, in the words of the composer, inspired by the river itself 'from its trickling source among green fields to the full tide of life in London'; the *Music for Strings* has the widest variety of tempo and texture in its four movements, with the finale 'an extrovert happy-go-lucky movement'. The *Symphony for Double String Orchestra* is very much in the tradition of British string music, with a flavour not too distant from Tippett's concerto for a similar ensemble. The *Serenata concertante* – a violin concerto in all but name – is grittier and less lyrical, at least until you come to the slow third movement, which builds up in simple lyricism to a grinding climax like that of Walton's *First Symphony*. **Handley** directs superb, committed performances, vividly recorded, and **Barry Wordsworth** is equally impressive in the *Music for Strings*.

Clarinet Quintet

ⓑⓑ *** Hyp. Helios CDH 55105. King, Britten Qt – COOKE;
FRANKEL: *Clarinet Quintets*; HOWELLS: *Rhapsodic Quintet*;
HOLBROOKE: *Eilean Shona* ***

Elizabeth Maconchy's *Clarinet Quintet*, with its bright, acerbic wit, makes a perfect foil for the other works in **Thea King's** fine anthology, its dancing, racy finale contrasting with her special brand of poignant lyricism in the slow movement. King's sprightly playing is admirably supported by the **Britten Quartet**, and the recording is outstandingly vivid.

String Quartets 1–13

⊗ Ⓜ *** Regis Forum FRC 9301 (3). Hanson, Bingham or
Mistry Qts

The first four *Quartets* were recorded by the **Hanson Quartet** and the **Bingham Quartet** seem equally at home in this

repertoire. The third CD includes the final *Quartetto Corto*, a miniature piece, dating from 1984, all persuasively played by the **Mistry Quartet**. All these works testify to the quality of Maconchy's mind and her inventive powers. She speaks of the quartet as 'an impassioned argument', and there is no lack of either in these finely wrought and compelling pieces. Though the playing may occasionally be wanting in tonal finesse, each group plays with total commitment and is well recorded.

(i) The Sofa; (ii) The Departure

Ⓝ *** Chan. 10508. Independent Opera, Wheeler; with (i)
Sharratt, Tynan, Thorpe, von Borden; Orr, Kozari, Leese; (ii)
Poole, Vramsmo

Elizabeth Maconchy's two one-act operas make up an excellent disc, the works nicely contrasted. *The Sofa* starts very much in comic-opera mode with amiably chattering music, but the story turns sour with the arrival of the sinister grandmother of the central character, Prince Dominic, an unapologetic hedonist who is seeking to seduce the heroine, Monique. The grandmother controls Dominic's money, and she disapproves of his philandering. With her magic powers, she decides to turn him into a sofa: he will be released only if a couple seek to make love while sitting on the sofa.Everyone wonders where Dominic has gone to, but in the end Edward makes love to Monique on the sofa, and Dominic is restored, a wiser man. With Maconchy's deft scoring, the impossible story works well, even if one would welcome a few more obvious tunes.

The *Departure* involves only two main characters, Julia, a mezzo-soprano, and Mark, a tenor. The point of the story is that Julia has been killed in a car crash, and she sees in her imagination her own funeral. The role of Julia is superbly taken by **Louise Poole**, an outstanding young artist whose pinpoint accuracy is a delight to the ear. Much of the score is devoted to a monologue for the dead Julia, but the climax to the opera comes in a long and sensuous duet between Julia and Mark, with that tenor role very well taken by **Håkan Vramsmo**. They obviously cannot meet and finally have to say goodbye, with offstage voices adding to the atmosphere of poignancy. The tenderness of the emotions contrasts well with the high spirits of *The Sofa*. **Dominic Wheeler** is the understanding conductor, by turns lively and sensitive, with the company of Independent Opera at Sadler's Wells.

MADETOJA, Leevi (1887–1947)

Symphonies 1 in F, Op. 29; 2, Op. 35; 3 in A, Op. 55; Comedy Overture, Op. 53; Okon Fuoko, Op. 58; Pohjalaisia Suite, Op. 52

⊗ Ⓜ **** Chan. 7097 (2). Iceland SO, Sakari

Apart from Sibelius himself, with whom Madetoja briefly studied, there are many influences to be discerned in the *First Symphony* (1915) – figures like Strauss, the Russian post-nationalists, Reger and above all the French, for whom Madetoja had a lifelong admiration. The *Second Symphony* (1917–18), composed at about the same time as Sibelius was working on the definitive version of his *Fifth*, is expertly fashioned and despite the obvious debts there is some individuality too. The *Third* was written in the mid-1920s while Madetoja was living in Houilles, just outside Paris. Gallic elements surface most strongly in this piece. The *Comedy Overture* (1923) is an absolute delight, and both the suite from the opera *Pohjalaisia (The Ostrobothnians)* and the ballet–pantomime *Okon Fuoko* show an exemplary feeling for colour and atmosphere. Both the performances and the spacious natural recordings are exemplary.

OPERA

The Ostrobothnians (Pohjalaisia) (complete); Suite from the opera, Op. 52a

🎵 Ⓜ *** Finlandia 3984 21440-2 (2). Hynninen, Sirkiä, Groop, Auvinen, Finnish R. Ch.; Finnish RSO, Saraste

Madetoja's opera dates from the early 1920s and is set in the western Finnish plains of Ostrobothnia which Madetoja knew well, and its central theme is the Bothnian farmer's love of personal liberty and his abhorrence of authoritarian restraints. Against this background of tension, there is a simple love story. The opera is also interspersed with humorous elements that lighten the mood and lend the work variety. Madetoja's language springs from much the same soil as most Scandinavian post-nationalists. However, the score makes often imaginative use of folk material and Madetoja's sense of theatre and his lyrical gift are in good evidence. *Pohjalaisia* is effective theatre and this recording completely supersedes the 1975 set under Jorma Panula – also with **Hynninen** as the hero – both artistically and technically. Like its predecessor it offers excellent teamwork from the soloists, and keen, responsive playing from the **Finnish Radio** forces under **Saraste**. The work lasts barely two hours, and the fill-up derives from a 1993 recording.

MAGALHÃES, Filipe de
(1571–1652)

Missa Dilecus meus; Commissa mea pavesco

🎵 Ⓑ🅱 *** Hyp. Helios CDH 55138. William Byrd Ch., Gavin Turner – D. LÔBO: *Missa pro defunctis* ***

Most of Magalhães's surviving works are found in two books dated 1636, including the present beautiful Mass for five voices. The music flows richly but with rather more impetus than in the coupled Lôbo *Requiem*, until the simple *Benedictus* and double *Agnus Dei* which has an additional voice, with the altos divided. The following funeral motet, *Commissa mea pavesco*, is similarly serene and also richly harmonized in six parts. A splendid coupling, beautifully sung and recorded.

Missa O Soberana luz; Motets: Commissa mea pavesco; Vidi aquam

🅱🅱 *** Naxos 8.553310. Ars Nova, Holten – CARDOSO; LÔBO: *Motets* ***

Filipe de Magalhães was the youngest of the three great Portuguese composers who all became pupils of Manuel Mendes (c. 1547–1605) at Evora in eastern Portugal. The others, Cardoso and Lôbo, are also represented in this outstanding concert, but Magalhães was reputedly the favourite pupil. One can see why, listening to his highly individual writing in both the Mass *O Soberana luz* and the two hardly less memorable motets, *Vidi aquam* ('I beheld the water') and *Commissa mea pavesco* ('I tremble at my sins') with its instantly poignant opening. In the Mass the *Sanctus* soars radiantly and the lovely *Benedictus* is equally affecting, only to be capped by the *Agnus Dei*. The Danish performances are wonderfully eloquent and the recording, made at Kasterskirken, Copenhagen, has an ideal ambience and is beautifully clear.

MAGNARD, Albéric (1865–1914)

Symphonies 1 in C min., Op. 4; 2 in E, Op. 6; Symphonies 3 in B flat min., Op. 11; 4 in C sharp min., Op. 21

🎵 Ⓜ *** Hyp. Dyad CDD 22068 (2). BBC Scottish SO, Ossone

Symphonies 1–4; Chant funèbre; Hymne à la justice; Ouverture

Ⓑ *** EMI (ADD) 5 72364-2 (3). Capitole Toulouse O, Plasson

The *First Symphony* (1889–90) was composed in the shadow of Magnard's friend and mentor, Vincent d'Indy, and follows more strictly cyclical principles. Yet its ideas still show individuality of character and, despite the debt to Wagner and Franck, the last two symphonies have distinct personalities; they are separated by 17 years. The *Fourth* has an impressive intellectual power and is well crafted, with no shortage of ideas. For all the appearance of academicism, there is a quiet and distinctive personality here, and dignity too. The *Chant funèbre* is an earlier work that has a vein of genuine eloquence.

The superb Hyperion set of his four symphonies, neatly fitted on two inexpensive CDs, easily outshines earlier rivals, with warm, cleanly focused sound.

The **Toulouse Capitole Orchestra** under **Michel Plasson** also play this music as if they believe every note, as indeed they should, and the recording is sonorous and well defined. Plasson spreads to three CDs but offers extra items, and the EMI set is at bargain price and is excellent value.

Symphony 3, Op. 11

Ⓝ *** Australian Decca Eloquence 442 9992 (2). SRO, Ansermet – LISZT: *Faust Symphony*, etc. **(*)

Magnard's *Third Symphony*, perhaps the best of his four, doesn't have the memorability of, for example, Chausson's, but it is very accomplished and has few longueurs. It was one of **Ansermet's** last recordings (September 1968) and is extremely well recorded. Its rather imposing introduction is well controlled by Ansermet and the ensuing *Allegro* is given plenty of vigour. The second movement, *Danses*, is full of vitality, with the strings impressively articulated; the slow movement is a rather uneasy pastorale, and the finale has great forward momentum. This work is used as a fill-up to Ansermet's 1967 Liszt recordings.

Cello Sonata in A, Op. 20

*** Hyp. CDA 67244. Lidström, Forsberg – KOECHLIN: *Chansons Bretonnes*; WIDOR: *Sonata****

Magnard's music has an unfailing nobility as well as a distinction in terms of line and form. The *Cello Sonata*, which dates from 1910–11, is a big work lasting half an hour. **Mats Lidström** and **Bengt Forsberg** play it with eloquence and feeling, and are very well recorded.

String Quartet, Op. 16

*** HM Aeon AECD 0426. Ysaÿe Qt – FAURÉ: *String Quartet in E min.* ***

Magnard was a highly self-critical composer, and his *Quartet*, a long work of some 40 minutes, shows an original mind at work. Its chromaticism encouraged one critic to place him closer to Reger than any of his Gallic contemporaries. His is an individual voice and an interesting one. The present performance and recording do the work full justice.

MAHLER, Gustav (1860–1911)

Symphonies 1–10; Das Lied von der Erde (DVD versions)

**(*) DG DVD 73 4088 (9). J. Baker, Armstrong, Ludwig, Kollo, VPO, LSO or Israel PO, Bernstein

As David Gutman points out in the perceptive essay which comes with each of these boxes of DVDs, the cycle here which **Bernstein** recorded for video in the early 1970s comes neatly between his early CBS cycle with the New York Philharmonic from the 1960s and the late cycle he recorded for DG with the Vienna Philharmonic in the 1980s, which is discussed further below. If the one was sharp and intense in its approach to Mahler, the later cycle represented a more reflective Bernstein. Arguably this midway view on video is the finest of the three, and certainly the addition of video to the formula adds another layer of intensity, when here is a conductor who, almost Christ-like, physically seemed to suffer as he conducted, so dedicated was he.

The four double-disc boxes contain the sequence of the symphonies, with an extra disc devoted to rehearsals with the Vienna Philharmonic in the *Fifth* and the *Ninth* and two feature films, *Four ways to say farewell*, a study of the *Ninth Symphony*, and a personal introduction to *Das Lied von der Erde*, which **Bernstein** regards as Mahler's greatest symphony. Those last two are wonderfully revealing of Bernstein the man, and of his intellectual brilliance, but the rehearsal sequences will be disappointing to non-German speakers, as his comments to the Vienna Philharmonic in German completely defeat the writer of subtitles, and he omits them.

Symphonies: 1 in D; (i) 2 (Resurrection)

*** Ph. DVD 074 3131. BPO, Haitink; (i) with McNair, Van Nes, Ernst Senff Ch. (Director: Barrie Gavin)

Symphony 3 in D min.

*** Ph. DVD 074 3132. Quivar, Tölz Boys' Ch., Women of Ernst-Senff Ch., BPO, Haitink (Director: Barrie Gavin)

Symphonies: (i) 4 in G.; 7 in E min.

** Ph. DVD 074 3133. BPO, Haitink; (i) with McNair

Haitink made these, his third set of recordings of the Mahler symphonies, between 1991 and 1993, live in the Berlin Philharmonie. The **Berlin Philharmonic** plays superbly for him while the recording itself is very much in the demonstration bracket on CD (especially with the optional 5.1 DTS surround sound), and there is no doubt that the visual element adds enormously to their impact and communication. In the *First Symphony* Haitink builds the first-movement climax slowly, with increasing tension; and at its peak the camera focuses directly on him, and the sheer intensity of that moment is quite remarkable. There is greater gravity in his view than in earlier recordings, to bring out the full weight of this ambitious early work, and a greater freedom of expression, although Haitink was never one to wear his heart on his sleeve.

The *Resurrection Symphony* also brings one of his very finest Mahler recordings, weighty and bitingly powerful. The sound of the **Berlin Philharmonic** is again caught with a vividness and presence rarely matched. The equivalent CDs were studio recordings, but here all the tensions of a live performance are conveyed, leading up to a glorious apotheosis in the Judgement Day finale. The soloists are outstanding, and the chorus immaculately expands from the rapt, hushed singing of their magical first entry to incandescent splendour.

The *Third Symphony* is no less powerful and spacious, with the **Berlin Philharmonic** again producing glorious sounds. Once again, the finale is a superb culmination, glowing and concentrated, and **Haitink** gives the work a visionary strength often lacking. The mysery of *Urlicht* is then beautifully caught by the mezzo soloist, **Jard van Nes**.

The key to **Haitink's** Mahler 4 is simplicity, and here he conducts a warm, polished reading that can hardly be faulted, except that it does not quite catch the innocent freshness lying behind this of all Mahler's symphonies. The slow movement is poised and gentle, not quite as rapt as some versions but still very beautiful. The child-heaven finale, too, at a comparatively slow tempo is smoother than usual, with **Sylvia McNair** a light, boyish soloist.

Haitink's reading of the *Seventh* is not as evocative as others in his cycle, even the *Nachtmusiks* are less magical than they might be. The Berlin Orchestra play well but there is not the conviction and concentration of the other symphonies in the cycle.

Symphonies 1–9

(B) *** Decca (DDD/ADD) 430 804-2 (10). Buchanan, Zakai, Chicago Ch. (in 2); Dernesch, Ellyn Children's Ch., Chicago Ch. (in 3); Te Kanawa (in 4); Harper, Popp, Augér, Minton, Watts, Kollo, Shirley-Quirk, Talvela, V. Boys' Ch., V. State Op. Ch. & Singverein (in 8); Chicago SO, Solti

(i) Symphonies 1–9; (ii) Kindertotenlieder; (iii) Kindertotenlieder; 3 Rückert Lieder; Das irdische Leben

(B) **(*) Sony (ADD) SX12K 89499 (12). Spoorenberg, Annear, Procter, Mitchinson, McIntyre, Venora, Tourel, Lipton, Israel PO, LSO or NYPO, Bernstein; (ii) J. Baker; (iii) J. Tourel

(i) Symphonies 1–10; 6 Early Songs; Kindertotenlieder; (ii) Das Lied von der Erde; (i) Lieder eines fahrenden Gesellen; Das Klagende Lied

(BB) **(*) DG 471 451-2 (15). Studer, Meier, Goldberg, Allen, Fassbaender, Plowright, Schwartz, Keikl, Gruberová, Terfel, Vermillion, Lewis; (i) Philh. O; (ii) Dresden Staatskapelle; all cond. Sinopoli

Solti's achievement in Mahler has been consistent and impressive, and this reissue is a formidable bargain that will be hard to beat. 1–4 and 9 are digital recordings, 5–8 are digitally remastered analogue. Solti draws stunning playing from the **Chicago Symphony Orchestra**, often pressed to great virtuosity, which adds to the electricity of the music-making; if his rather extrovert approach to Mahler means that deeper emotions are sometimes understated, there is no lack of involvement; and his fiery energy and commitment often carry shock-waves in their trail. All in all, an impressive achievement.

The 12-disc Sony compilation includes not only **Bernstein's** historic pioneering cycle of the Mahler symphonies for CBS but a number of valuable supplements. With the nine completed symphonies recorded between 1960 and 1967 and the *Adagio* from 10 added in 1975, the cycle has never sounded fresher or clearer, with sound less coarse than originally. Though Bernstein's later cycle (459 080–2) for DG brings more refined sound, these earlier interpretations, all but 8 with the **New York Philharmonic**, are generally more thrustful and dramatic. The reading of No. 9 is far less expansive in the last movement but is still deeply meditative, so that the whole symphony can be fitted on to a single disc. The valuable supplements include a live recording of the *Adagietto* of 5 played at the funeral of Robert Kennedy and two versions of *Kindertotenlieder*, not just the one recorded in Israel in 1974 with **Dame Janet Baker**, but the earlier studio recording of 1960 with **Jenny Tourel**, a favourite singer with Bernstein, brisker, less reflective, as well as Tourel in three of the *Rückert Lieder* and *Das irdische Leben* from *Des Knaben Wunderhorn*.

Giuseppe Sinopoli's individual, sometimes wilful readings of Mahler, but ones which with full-blooded recording bring out the warmth as well as the power. One is never in doubt as to the greatness of the music, or the dedication with which the conductor approaches each work. Just occasionally Sinopoli chooses a tempo that is not just wilful but perverse – as in the snail-pace for the second *Nachtmusik* of 7, and he generally favours speeds on the broad side, but magnetism is a consistent quality, and so it is in the other Mahler works which make up this 15-disc set. *Das Klagende Lied* – with a starry quartet of soloists – is taken from a live concert which the Philharmonia gave in Tokyo in November

1990, while the song-cycles were recorded as adjuncts to the symphonies. *Das Lied von der Erde* is the odd one out, recorded in Dresden with the **Staatskapelle** five years after the rest had been completed, but just as persuasive in its Mahlerian manners, with **Iris Vermillion** and **Keith Lewis** strong and reliable soloists, if not as characterful as some.

Symphonies 1–9; 10 (Revised Performing Edition by Deryck Cooke)

🔊— (B) *** Decca 475 6686 (12). Concg. O (Berlin RSO in 10), Chailly; with Diener, Lang, Prague Philharmonic Ch. in 3; Bonney in 4; Eaglen, Fulgoni, Schwanewilms, Siezak, Larrson, Heppner, Mattei, Rootering, Prague Philharmonic Ch., Netherlands R. Ch., Children of Kathedrale Ch. St Bavo & Breda in 8

Chailly's strong, satisfying overall approach to Mahler, without eccentricity, is supported by the superb playing of the **Royal Concertgebouw Orchestra** throughout and the demonstration quality of the Decca sound, never more remarkable than in the dedicated account of the *Resurrection Symphony*. The *Third* also has comparably weighty intensity, but the spacious account of *4* has rather less depth of inner feeling. The *Fifth* more than compensates and is perhaps the highlight of the cycle, although the *Sixth* also conveys great concentration and is marvellously played. In the spectacular *Symphony of a Thousand* the Decca engineers more than rise to the challenge, as they do again in the *Ninth*. Chailly is lucky in his soloists, all of whom sing beautifully, and the choral contributions are of the highest quality too. Overall, this box is strongly recommendable, particularly if demonstration recording quality is a priority. It comes with full texts and translations.

Symphony 1 in D (Titan)

🔊— (M) **** Decca 458 622-2. LSO, Solti

(M) *** Decca 475 8230. Chicago SO, Solti

(BB) *** Sony SBK 89783. VPO, Maazel

(N) (M) **(*) LSO Live SACD LSO0663. LSO, Gergiev

The **London Symphony Orchestra** play Mahler's *First* like no other orchestra. They catch the magical opening, with its bird sounds and evocatively distanced brass, with a singular ambience, at least partly related to the orchestra's characteristic blend of wind timbres. Throughout there is wonderfully warm string-playing and the most atmospheric response from the horns. **Solti's** tendency to drive hard is felt only in the second movement, which is pressed a little too much, although he relaxes beautifully in the central section. Especially memorable are the poignancy of the introduction of the *Frère Jacques* theme in the slow movement and the exultant brilliance of the closing pages, helped by the wide range of dynamic and the wonderfully clear inner detail of the newly remastered, 1964 Kingsway Hall recording.

Because of the excellence of the 1964 LSO version, which has been a prime choice for many years and still is, it was hard for **Solti** and the Decca engineers to match his earlier achievement, even with exceptionally high-powered playing from the **Chicago Symphony Orchestra** and brilliant, crystal-clear digital recording. On CD, that very clarity takes away some of the atmospheric magic – the feeling of mists dispersing in the slow introduction, for example – but charm and playfulness in this *Wunderhorn* work emerge delightfully; one of the happiest of Solti's records, tinglingly fresh, with perfectly chosen speeds.

With superb playing and refined recording, **Maazel's** account of the *First* has an authentic Viennese glow. Though there are other versions which point detail more sharply, this performance has a ripeness and an easy lyricism that place it among the most sympathetic bargain versions. The sound too is full and atmospheric as well as brilliant. A fine bargain alternative to Solti.

Gergiev's live account of Mahler's *First Symphony* is extrovert and flamboyant, with plenty of drama, particularly in the outer movements. At times it almost feels aggressive (the Ländler movement could do with a bit more charm), underlined by the rather dry but certainly vivid acoustic of the Barbican, where it was recorded in January 2008, faithfully caught on SACD. Yet, by the same token, there is some superbly hushed playing too, and the **LSO** play magnificently throughout. Not everyone will respond to Gergiev's way with Mahler but this is certainly a distinctive version.

(i) *Symphony 1 in D* (Original (1893) version with *Blumine*); (ii) *Lieder eines fahrenden Gesellen*

⊕ (M) *** RCA (ADD) 82876 76233-2. (i) Phd. O, Ormandy; (ii) von Stade, LPO, A. Davis

The score of the early version of Mahler's *First Symphony* contained the *Blumine* movement. **Ormandy's** was its first recording (in 1968) and the arrival of the *Blumine* section at the close of the first movement, with its appealing trumpet melody so beautifully played, is a frisson-creating moment and, while its inclusion alters the character and scale of the work overall, any true Mahlerian should enjoy it in a performance as warm-hearted as this. Ormandy is rather relaxed at the very opening of the symphony and his tempi are very flexible elsewhere, notably in the Scherzo and finale. But the glorious playing of the Philadelphia strings is very seductive indeed, and the remastered recording has splendid richness and bloom.

The coupling (which comes from the CBS/Sony archive) is a highly enjoyable account of the *Wayfaring Lad* cycle from **Frederica von Stade** and **Andrew Davis**, recorded a decade later with a refreshing hint of youthful ardour, which contrasts with most other performances. The recording is close but has a most attractive ambience and is very well transferred.

Symphonies 1; (i) 2 *(Resurrection)*

⊕ (B) *** Double Decca (ADD) 448 921-2 (2). (i) Harper, Watts, L. Symphony Ch.; LSO, Solti

(B) *** Ph. Duo 475 6222 (2). BPO, Haitink; (i) with McNair, Van Nes, Ernst-Senff Ch.

Solti's 1964 LSO account of 2 remains a demonstration of the outstanding results Decca were securing with analogue techniques at that time, although on CD the brilliance of the *fortissimos* may not suit all ears. **Helen Watts** is wonder-

fully expressive, while the chorus has a rapt intensity that is the more telling when the recording perspectives are so clearly delineated. Coupled with his outstanding version of 1, it makes a genuine bargain at Double Decca price.

There is greater gravity in **Haitink's** view now, to bring out the full weight of this ambitious early work and a greater freedom of expression. The *Resurrection Symphony* dates from six years later and brings another of Haitink's finest Mahler recordings. Above all, Haitink conveys the tensions of a live occasion. Outstanding in every way, this can be placed alongside Rattle's superb CBSO set.

Symphonies (i) 1; (ii) 3

(N) *(**) Australian Decca Eloquence 480 1133 (2). Mehta, with (i) Israel PO; (ii) Forrester, Los Angeles Master Chorale, LAPO

Mehta's version of the *First Symphony* is brilliantly recorded (in 1974) but the hard-driving, frenetic quality of the outer movements will not appeal to everyone, though the warmth of the slow movement does offer some compensations. Mehta in his years in Los Angeles, however, rarely recorded a performance so authentically Viennese as this Decca account of the *Third Symphony* (1978). The crisp spring of the first movement leads to a fruitily Viennese view of the second and a carefree account of the third in which the *Wunderhorn* overtones come out vigorously. The singing is excellent, and the sharpness of focus of the reading as a whole is impressive, underlined by brilliant (if a bit too close) recording. However, it must be admitted that the performance leaves a certain feeling of aggressiveness which detracts from the warmer side of the reading.

Symphony 2 in C min. *(Resurrection)*

⊕ ✹ (M) **** EMI 3 45794-2 (2). Augér, J. Baker, CBSO Ch., CBSO, Rattle

⊕ ✹ (M)(****) BBC Legends (mono) BBCL 4136-2. Woodland, Baker, BBC Ch. & Choral Soc., LSO, Stokowski

⊕ (M)(***) Testament mono SBT2 1320 (2). Stader, J. Baker, St Hedwig's Cathedral Ch., BPO, Barbirolli

⊕ (M) *** EMI (ADD) 5 67235-2. Schwarzkopf, Rössl-Majdan, Philh. Ch. & O, Klemperer

(M) *** Chan. 6595/6. Lott, Hamari, Latvian State Ac. Ch., Oslo Philharmonic Ch., Oslo PO, Jansons

*** DG 477 5082 (2). Gvazava, Larsson, Orfeon Donostiarra, Lucerne Festival O, Abbado – DEBUSSY: *La Mer***(*)

Sir Simon Rattle's reading of Mahler's *Second Symphony* is among his very finest records, superlative in its breadth and the vividness of its sound. The inspired orchestral playing and beautifully balanced choral singing are matched by the heartfelt response of the soloists, **Arleen Augér** and **Dame Janet Baker**. EMI have now understandably chosen the set for inclusion in their 'Great Recordings of the Century'.

For the first ever Prom performance of the *Resurrection Symphony* **Leopold Stokowski** had a triumph, for here was a larger-than-life reading of an apocalyptic work. The response of the audience at the end was so prolonged and so enthusiastic that, against the strict Prom rule of the time,

Stokowski gave an encore, repeating the final visionary choral sequence. Now at last on disc in this BBC Legends recording of the broadcast, we have the legend vividly confirmed, for though the sound is in mono the immediacy and sense of presence, as well as the atmosphere of the hall, are vividly caught: full, bright and clear, giving the illusion of stereo. **Janet Baker**, the dedicated mezzo soloist, is joined by the fresh-toned **Rae Woodland**. Stokowski is more urgent than Barbirolli, lighter in the second-movement *Andante*, more sinister in the Scherzo, leading to a shattering rendering of the Judgement Day finale, with the **BBC Chorus**, **Choral Society** and attendant choirs as intense in their dedicatedly hushed singing as in the extrovert power of the climaxes. It makes an overwhelming experience, marred only slightly by inevitable audience noises.

Barbirolli's long-buried radio recording from Berlin will be a revelation even to the many admirers of this great Mahlerian, and the result is electrifying from beginning to end. Helped by full, vividly immediate sound, this is an impassioned, freely volatile performance, massively powerful in the outer movements while setting in contrast the '*Wunderhorn*' playfulness of the third movement against the darkness of the *Urlicht* slow movement, sung by **Dame Janet Baker** with heartfelt intensity. The vision of Judgement Day in the long choral finale is then cataclysmic, so shattering that one readily forgives the out-of-time chimes at the very end. Just too long for a single CD, this issue is offered on two discs for the price of one.

Klemperer's performance – one of his most compelling on record – comes back to the catalogue on a single CD as one of EMI's 'Great Recordings of the Century', sounding better than ever. The remastering of the Kingsway Hall recording is impressively full and clear, with a real feeling of spectacle in the closing pages. The first movement, taken at a fairly fast tempo, is intense and earth-shaking; though in the last movement (which incidentally is generously cued) some of Klemperer's speeds are designedly slow, he conveys supremely well the mood of transcendent, heavenly happiness in the culminating passage, with the **Philharmonia Chorus** and soloists themselves singing like angels.

The crisp attack at the start of the opening funeral march sets the pattern for an exceptionally refined and alert reading of the *Resurrection Symphony* from **Jansons** and his **Oslo Orchestra**. During the first four movements, this may seem a lightweight reading, but at the finale the whole performance erupts in an overwhelming outburst for the vision of Resurrection. That transformation is intensified by the breathtakingly rapt and intense account of the song, *Urlicht*, which precedes it. The choral singing is heartfelt, to crown a version which finds a special place even among the many distinguished readings on a long list.

Abbado's 2004 version of the *Resurrection Symphony* was recorded live at the Lucerne Festival, using an orchestra of specially chosen players. The thrust and tautness of the performance are established from the very start, with speeds faster than usual and generally faster than those which Abbado adopted in his two previous recordings of the work. The exception is the third-movement Ländler, where at a relatively relaxed speed he brings out the *Des Knaben*

Wunderhorn associations. The mezzo soloist, **Anna Larsson**, gives a satisfyingly weighty performance, with warm contralto timbre in the chest register, and though the microphone brings out the vibrato of the soprano, **Eteri Gvazava**, she is a first-rate soloist too, while the choral singing is focused with exceptional clarity. The closeness of the well-detailed recording adds to the impact.

Symphony 3 in D min.

*** Decca SACD 470 652-2; CD 475 514-2. Lang, Prague Philharmonic Ch., Netherlands Children's Ch., Concg. O, Chailly

Ⓝ Ⓜ **(*) LSO Live **SACD** LSO 0660 (2). Larsson, Tiffin Boys' Ch., L. Symphony Ch., LSO, Gergiev

(i) Symphony 3 in D min.; (ii) Kindertotenlieder

Ⓝ (***) Testament mono SBT2 1422. Ferrier, with (i) BBC SO, Boult; (ii) Concg. O, Klemperer

(i) Symphony 3; (ii) Des Knaben Wunderhorn: 8 Lieder

🏷 **** EMI 5 56657-2 (2). (i) Remmert, CBSO Women's Ch.; (ii) Keenlyside; CBSO, Rattle

Rattle conducts an outstanding version of 3, magnetic from the very start, rich, bold and opulent, and very well recorded with an exceptionally full bass. The subtlety of Rattle's phrasing and rubato not only brings out the work's deeper qualities, with the visionary intensity of the long finale superbly caught, but – far more than most – the joy and humour of the lighter movements. **Simon Keenlyside's** beautiful, finely detailed readings of the *Knaben Wunderhorn* songs make a very welcome bonus, with an extra song, *Ablösung im Sommer* (which is quoted in the third movement of the *Symphony*) aptly included in an arrangement by Berio.

Characteristically strongly characterized and brilliantly played, with the second and fourth movements even more sharply rhythmic than with Abbado, **Chailly's** account is among the finest. He has a warmly sensitive mezzo soloist in **Petra Lang**, and the reading is heightened by his dedicated account of the finale with its easy flowing tempo. The Decca SACD recording is among the finest this symphony has yet received.

In the first days of the Third Programme after the war, the BBC programmed its first complete cycle of Mahler symphonies. **Sir Adrian Boult** conducted the *Third* with **Kathleen Ferrier** as soloist in 1947. This was its first performance in England, and it was not given again until 1960. These acetates show that Sir Adrian was an *echt*-Mahlerian and completely inside the idiom. Older listeners will be delighted with this (RL remembers hearing the broadcast), in spite of the imperfections of the recorded sound. The *Kindertotenlieder* come from a Dutch broadcast made in 1951: Ferrier recorded the cycle with Bruno Walter, who perhaps evinces greater warmth and poetry than **Klemperer** but no less control. An important document for both Mahlerians and Ferrier aficionados.

Gergiev is intensely theatrical in Mahler's *Third Symphony* – a work which has always been quite elusive in the recording studio. The sharp dynamic contrasts were well brought out in the first movement, with all the colourful woodwind writing well highlighted and pointed. The slow movement is sensitively done, if without the sublime heights of the best versions available, though the rather dry acoustic doesn't always help, even if it allows plenty of detail to emerge. The following *Scherzando* doesn't have the proper lightness of touch, and if **Anna Larsson**, the alto soloist, has a bit of a wobble in the next movement, she is very expressive and is beautifully supported by the orchestra. The chorus and boys' choir are both excellent. The long finale is beautifully played and moulded, even if, again, it fails to reach the tension of the finest versions available. The audience from this live performance in 2007 are unbelievably quiet.

Symphony 4 in G

(M) *** RCA (ADD) 82876 59413-2. Blegen, Chicago SO, Levine

*** EMI 5 56563-2. Roocroft, CBSO, Rattle

(M) *** RCA **SACD** 82876 67901-2. della Casa, Chicago SO, Reiner

(B) *** Virgin 3 63277-2. Murray, RPO, Litton

(M) *** DG (ADD) 419 863-2. Mathis, BPO, Karajan

(N) *** RCA 16852-2. Orgonášová, Tonhalle O, Zürich, Zinman

(BB) *** Naxos 8.550527. Russell, Polish Nat. RSO, Wit

(N) ** BBCL (ADD) 4248-2. Lott, BBC N. SO, Sanderling (with *Don Giovanni Overture*)

(i) Symphony 4; (ii) Lieder eines Fahrenden Gesellen

(B) *** Sony SBK 46535 (i) Raskin, Cleveland O, Szell; (ii) von Stade LPO, A. Davis

George Szell's 1966 record of Mahler's *Fourth* represented his partnership with the **Cleveland Orchestra** at its highest peak, and the digital remastering for CD brings out the very best of the original recording. The performance remains uniquely satisfying: the music blossoms, partly because of the marvellous attention to detail (and the immaculate ensemble), but more positively because of the committed and radiantly luminous orchestral response to the music itself. In the finale Szell found the ideal soprano to match his conception. An outstanding choice, generously coupled. In contrast with most other recorded performances, **Frederica von Stade** insinuates a hint of youthful ardour into her highly enjoyable account of the *Wayfaring Lad* cycle.

James Levine draws a superlative performance from the **Chicago orchestra**, one which bears comparison with the finest versions, bringing out not merely the charm but also the deeper emotions. The subtlety of his control of tempo, so vital in Mahler, is superbly demonstrated and, though he may not quite match the nobility of Szell's famous analogue Sony version in the great slow movement, he has the advantage of a more modern (1975) recording. **Judith Blegen** makes a fresh, attractive soloist.

Simon Rattle's performance begins with an idiosyncratic but valid reading of the opening bars, at first very slow then brisk for the main *Allegro*. It reflects the thoughtfulness on detail of his approach to Mahler, reflected in an unusually

refreshing account, youthfully urgent, which rises to a spacious, songful reading of the long slow movement. **Amanda Roocroft** sings with warm, creamy tone in the finale. Refined recording to match. This also stands high among modern recordings of this beautiful symphony.

On RCA the SACD remastering has brought a glowing warmth to the 1958 Chicago recording. **Reiner's** performances is wayward, but lovingly so; and everything he does sounds spontaneous. There is a mercurial quality in the first movement and plenty of drama too; the second is engagingly pointed but with a balancing warmth, the Viennese element strong. The slow movement has striking intensity, and in its rapt closing pages leads on gently to the finale in which **Lisa della Casa**, in ravishing voice, matches Reiner's mood.

Recorded in 1990, Virgin's captivatingly fresh account from **Andrew Litton** and the **RPO** has lain forgotten in the EMI vaults until now. It is a consistently flexible, highly spontaneous, vibrant account with lovely warm playing, rich in colour and full of individual touches, and drama too, especially in the slow movement which has one of the most spectacular climaxes on disc. **Ann Murray** then puts the seal on the performance with the touching simplicity of her contribution to the finale. Demonstration sound adds to the many pleasures this CD offers. Finer than many more famous versions, it comes very high on the list of recommendations.

Karajan's refined and poised, yet undoubtedly affectionate account remains among the finest versions of this lovely symphony, and **Edith Mathis's** sensitively composed contribution to the finale matches the conductor's meditative feeling. With glowing sound, this makes another outstanding mid-priced recommendation.

Zinman offers a bracing and fresh version of Mahler's *Fourth Symphony* in first-class sound. The orchestra play superbly, and if they are not quite in the league of the BPO in terms of having this repertoire under their skin, many will respond to their sensitively direct approach. Indeed, the slow movement in very beautifully done indeed, and the soprano soloist **Luba Orgonášva** is superb in the finale, which Zinman conducts supremely well.

Antoni Wit conducts a fresh, spontaneous-sounding reading, beautifully played and recorded, that can be warmly recommended at Naxos's bargain price. **Lynda Russell** is a pure-toned soprano soloist in the finale, both fresh and warm, with Wit giving a good lilt to the rhythm. Excellent sound, which gives a good bite and focus to the woodwind, so important in Mahler.

Good though it is to hear **Sanderling's** level-headed approach to this work, and **Felicity Lott's** fine contribution in the finale, neither the 1978 recording nor the orchestral playing are good enough to make it a top choice.

Symphonies: (i) 4; (ii) 8 (Symphony of 1000)

(M) **** EMI 3 61572-2 [3 61580-2] (2). (i) Popp; (ii) Connell, Wiens, Lott, Schmitt, Denize, Versalle, Hynninen, Sotin, Tiffin School Boys' Ch., LPO Ch.; LPO, Tennstedt

Tennstedt conducts a strong, spacious reading of the *Fourth Symphony* which yet conveys an innocence entirely in keeping with this most endearing of the Mahler symphonies. He makes the argument seamless in his easy transition of speed, yet he never deliberately adopts a coaxing, charming manner; in that he is followed most beautifully by **Lucia Popp**, the soloist in the finale. For its reissue among EMI's 'Great Recordings of the Century' this is aptly coupled with Tennstedt's magnificent recording of the *Eighth*, the finest of his whole Mahler cycle. His soloists are a strong and characterful team. The great glory of the set is the singing of the **London Philharmonic Choir**, assisted by the **Tiffin School Boys' Choir**. With the extra range and richness of the 1986 Walthamstow recording coping superbly with even the heaviest passages, it will for many listeners be even more satisfying than the Decca version.

Symphony 5 in C sharp min. (DVD version)

🎬 *** EMI **DVD** 490325-2. BPO, Rattle – ADÈS: *Asyla* (V/D: Bob Coles)

Rattle's fine version of Mahler's *Fifth* was recorded in November 2002 at his inaugural concert as music director of the Berlin Philharmonic. The video fully captures the atmospheric excitement of that occasion in a reading which brings out the work's lyrical qualities. It is also a version which demonstrates the joyfulness of much of the writing, notably in the finale. The DVD has a clear advantage over the CD issue in that it also contains the other work in the concert, Thomas Adès's brilliant showpiece, *Asyla*. The package also contains a second disc with an extended interview with Rattle by Nicholas Kenyon, his biographer and a former Controller of Music at the BBC.

Symphony 5 in C sharp min.

🎬 **** Decca 458 860-2. Concg. O, Chailly

**** EMI 5 57385-2. BPO, Rattle

*** DG 437 789-2 BPO, Abbado

🏵 Ⓜ *** EMI (ADD) 5 66910-2. New Philh. O, Barbirolli

Ⓝ **(*) RCA **SACD** 31450-2. Tonhalle O, Zürich, Zinman

Ⓝ Ⓑ LPO 0033. LPO, Zweden

Chailly excels himself in his strong, clear-sighted, but deeply felt reading of 5, with his concentration reflected in superlative playing from the **Concertgebouw**, caught with exceptional clarity in the full and brilliant Decca recording. The beauty of Mahler's orchestration has rarely been conveyed so vividly, with the hushed intensity of the *Adagio* the more moving for its reticence, and with the joyful finale dazzling in its crisp detail. Other, more personal readings may be more distinctive, but none is more widely recommendable.

One element which **Rattle** brings out more than his rivals is the exuberance of Mahler's writing. In this live recording one vividly registers the excitement of the occasion. The emotional climax of the performance comes, as it should, in the great *Adagietto*. Yet Rattle, looking at the evidence, treats it differently from most latter-day interpreters who make it expansively elegiac. By contrast he responds to it with the music emerging tenderly, as though from another world. This above all is a songful vision full of tenderness, with phrasing affectionately moulded in spontaneous warmth.

Abbado's is another outstanding version, recorded live in the Philharmonie, Berlin, with the dramatic tensions of a concert performance vividly captured. The great *Adagio* is raptly done, wistful rather than openly romantic, and the *Wunderhorn* finale is at once refined and exuberant. With excellent sound this is Abbado at his peak.

Barbirolli's famous analogue 1969 recording (made in Watford Town Hall) has now been splendidly remastered for EMI's 'Great Recordings of the Century' series and sounds fuller, clearer, more atmospheric than ever. On any count this is one of the greatest, most warmly affecting accounts ever committed to disc, expansive, yet concentrated in feeling: the *Adagietto* is very moving indeed. A classic version which many will prefer even to Abbado's newer digital account.

With very fine playing from the **Tonhalle Orchestra** and state-of the art SACD recording, **Zinman** offers a direct approach to Mahler to which many will respond. It has to be admitted, though, that in the last analysis it is a little undercharacterized and classic accounts from the VPO, Berlin Symphony Orchestra, et al., offer the greater Mahlerian experience.

Zinman's performance, however, is far preferable to another new version on LPO, which is given a somewhat superficial performance with the conductor failing to galvanize the **LPO** to meet the demands of this symphony. The orchestra play well, of course, in the *Adagietto* especially so, but neither as a performance nor as a recording is this a viable choice.

Symphony 6 (DVD version)

**** EuroArts **DVD** 2055648. Lucerne Festival O, Claudio Abbado

Abbado's electrifying account of the *Sixth Symphony* was recorded on 10 August 2006 with the **Lucerne Festival Orchestra**: this is composed primarily of the Mahler Chamber Orchestra, to which were added leading players from the Berlin and Vienna Philharmonic, members of the Alban Berg and Hagen Quartets and the Sabine Meyer Ensemble – quite a line-up! The playing is of the highest order of virtuosity and, for all his apparent frailty, Abbado conducts like a man possessed. The camerawork is discreet and always places the eye where the ear wants it directed. This must be to the DVD catalogue what Karajan's account with the Berlin Philharmonic was to the CD lists. Powerful and gripping, and vividly recorded.

Symphony 6 in A min.

🎬 *** DG 445 835-2. VPO, Boulez

🅱🅱 *** Naxos 8.550529 (2). Polish Nat. RSO (Katowice), Wit

Ⓑ *** Double Decca (IMS) (ADD) 444 871-2 (2). Concg. O, Chailly – ZEMLINSKY: *Maeterlinck Lieder* ***

Ⓝ Ⓜ *** LSO Live LSo 0661. LSO, Gergiev

With superlative playing from the **Berlin Philharmonic**, **Karajan's** reading of the *Sixth* is a revelation, above all in the slow movement, which emerges as one of the greatest of Mahler's slow movements. Though the outer movements firmly stamp this as one of the darkest of the Mahler symphonies, in Karajan's reading their sharp focus makes them both compelling and refreshing. The fine, mid-1970s DG recording, with its wide dynamic, adds enormously to the impact. **Christa Ludwig's** moving account of the *Kindertotenlieder* has been added to the previously coupled *Rückert Lieder*: fine, positive performances with comparative distinction and refinement in the orchestral playing.

Boulez conducts a performance of the most enigmatic symphony which in its power and sharpness of focus transcends almost any rival. Boulez's control of speeds is masterful, never rushed, even though this is a performance squeezed on to a single disc, and the slow movement brings hushed, ravishingly beautiful playing of a refinement it would be hard to match. The finale is rugged and weighty, with crisp pointing of rhythms, making this an outstanding recommendation.

The excellent quality of the **Katowice Orchestra** of Polish Radio is impressively demonstrated in all four movements of this difficult symphony. The ensemble can hardly be faulted, and the full, atmospheric recording enhances that quality with string-sound that is fresh and radiant. **Wit** conducts a spacious performance, clean and well sprung, with the varying moods sharply contrasted. On two full discs it becomes less of a super-bargain than some Naxos issues, but it stands comparison with any rival.

Chailly's version with the **Concertgebouw** offers brilliant playing and spectacular sound in a reading remarkable for its broad, rugged approach in the outer movements. There is relentlessness in the slow speed for the first movement, with expressive warmth giving way to a square purposefulness, tense and effective. The third movement brings a comparably simple, direct approach at a genuine flowing *Andante*. In its open songfulness it rouses *Wunderhorn* echoes. Anyone fancying the unexpected but attractive Zemlinsky coupling need not hesitate.

Gergiev places the *Scherzo* after the slow movement as Mahler did at the work's première, though it was originally placed second (Gergiev's way is now becoming more common). Gergiev's approach to Mahler's *Sixth* is bold and dramatic and his performance has a total conviction not always apparent in his controversial cycle. Even in the slow movement, the climax is driven, but relaxes beautifully in all the key moments. He goes for an almost brutish energy in this dark symphony of Mahler, and the results are compelling. The sound is bold and vivid, if lacking somewhat in space around the instruments. The audience are quiet as can be.

Symphony 7 in E min. (DVD version)

*** DG **DVD** 2054629. Lucerne Festival O, Abbado

An impressive and well-presented account from **Abbado** in a most persuasive reading, originally televised in August 2005. However, those who remember Abbado in his days with the LSO or the Berlin Philharmonic should be warned that, although his spirit is untamed, his failing health has left him looking a shadow of his former self, gaunt and haggard.

Symphony 7 in E min. (CD versions)

⊕– Ⓜ **** DG 445 513-2. Chicago SO, Abbado

*** RCA 09026 63510-2 (2). LSO, Tilson Thomas

ⒷⒷ **(*) Naxos 8.550531. Polish Nat. RSO, Halász

Abbado's command of Mahlerian characterization has never been more tellingly displayed than in this most problematic of the symphonies; even in the loosely bound finale Abbado unerringly draws the threads together. The precision and polish of the **Chicago Symphony Orchestra** go with total commitment, and the recording is one of the finest DG has made with this orchestra.

Michael Tilson Thomas conducts a strong, purposeful reading of the *Seventh*, with polished and refined playing from the **LSO** and recording to match. His terracing of textures and dynamics is perfectly judged. The result may be less atmospheric and evocative than in some readings, but the relative coolness of the second *Nachtmusik*, for example, makes one appreciate the work the more keenly for its symphonic qualities. Although the fragmentary structure of the finale is in no way disguised, the pointedness of the playing holds it firmly together. A strong contender in a hotly competitive field.

Symphony 8 (Symphony of 1000)

⊕– Ⓜ **** Decca (ADD) 475 7521. Harper, Popp, Augér, Minton, Watts, Kollo, Shirley-Quirk, Talvela, V. Boys' Ch., V. State Op. Ch. & Singverein, Chicago SO, Solti

⊕– Ⓜ *** EMI 2 28529-2. Brewer, Isokoski, Banse, Rammert, Henschel, Villars, Wilson-Johnson, Relyea, L. Symphony Ch., CBSO Ch., Youth Ch. & O, Rattle

Ⓝ Ⓜ *** LSO Live LSO 0669. Yastrebova, Tynan, Dudinova, Passikivi, Bulycheva, Semishkur, Markov, Nikitin, Etham College Ch., Chora Arts Society of Washington, LSO Ch., LSO, Gergiev

(*) PentaTone **SACD Surround Sound PTC 5186 166. Cotrubas, Harper, Van Bork, Finnilä, Dielman, Cochran, Prey, Soltin, Amsterdam Choruses, Concg. O, Haitink

*** Decca 467 314-2. Eaglen, Schwarnewilms, Ziezak, Fulgoni, Larsson, Heppner, Mattri, Rootering, St Bavo's Cathedral Boys' Ch., Breda Sacraments Ch., Prague Philharmonic Ch., Netherlands R. Ch., Concg. O, Chailly

In interpretation, **Solti's** famous (1971) Mahler *Eighth* is outstanding in every way, extrovert in display but full of dark implications, and this is one of his finest Mahler records. It now comes on a single mid-priced CD as one of Decca's new series of Originals.

Recorded live in Symphony Hall, Birmingham, in June 2004, **Rattle** completes his Mahler symphony cycle with a powerful, urgent reading of the *Symphony of a Thousand*. The performance gains enormously from the liveness of the occasion, with high-voltage electricity generated from first to last. Added to that, his relatively fast tempi for the long expanses of the second movement, setting Goethe, mean that, as with Solti, the whole work is on a single disc, an obvious advantage. The soloists are an excellent team, headed by the superb American soprano **Christine Brewer**, and the massed choruses match the orchestra in the bite and power of their singing, leading up to a thrilling account of the final sequence. The recording is not quite as full or open in atmosphere as some rivals, but that never masks the power of the performance.

This LSO Live version is at once the most ambitious and the most impressive in **Gergiev's** variable Mahler series. This so-called *Symphony of a Thousand* was recorded live in St Paul's Cathedral and, thanks to clever microphone placing, the sound is admirably clear, if with a reverberant background. The atmosphere of a great occasion is caught admirably, with the timpani and organ very impressive, even if the soloists are placed rather backwardly. The dynamic range is most impressive too. The climactic chorus on *Alle vergangliche* in this setting of the final section of Goethe's *Faust* makes a thrilling conclusion. The soloists are good, with the bright high soprano of **Viktoria Yastrebova** sounding ethereal. A most competitive version.

Haitink's 1971 recording of Mahler's *Eighth Symphony* was recorded in four channels for quadraphonic issue, and on this SACD using four speakers the performance is revealed in its full glory, and Haitink's spacious and certainly powerfully sustained interpretation is heard as never before within the superb acoustics of the Concertgebouw, whose ambience is ideal for Mahler's music. The dynamic range is remarkable, and there are few recordings of any music more spectacularly compelling than the work's closing 'Hymnenartig', with the words 'Alles Vergängliche' of the final section tremendously expressive and moving, proceeding to an overwhelming climax as the brass and timpani cap the last words of the chorus. The only snag to this reissue is the lack of text and translation.

Though it features multiple choirs and spectacular recording, **Chailly's** version is distinctive for underplaying the grandeur of the opening movement, *Veni creator spiritus*. He has deliberately sought to make the long second movement with its Faust setting – a sequence of dramatic scenes culminating in the chorus, *Alles vergängliche* – the true climax of the work. The team of soloists is outstanding, with the recording vividly catching the detail and perspectives of the massive ensemble.

Symphony 9 in D min.

🔗 (M) **** DG 439 024-2. BPO, Karajan

(M) *** EMI (ADD) 5 67925-2 [567926]. BPO, Barbirolli

*** Decca SACD 475 6191. Concg. O, Chailly

(M) *** EMI (ADD) 3 8008-2 (2). New Philh. O, Klemperer – R. STRAUSS: *Death and Transfiguration; Metamorphosen***

Symphony 9; (i) Kindertotenlieder; 5 Rückert Lieder

🔗 (B) *** DG Double (ADD) 453 040-2 (2). BPO, Karajan; (i) with Ludwig

Fine as **Karajan's** other Mahler recordings have been, his two accounts of the *Ninth* transcend them. In the earlier, analogue version (453 040-2) it is the combination of richness and concentration in the outer movements that makes for a reading of the deepest intensity, while in the middle two movements there is point and humour as well as refinement and polish. Helped by full, spacious recording, the sudden *pianissimos* that mark both movements have an ear-pricking realism such as one rarely experiences on record, and the

unusually broad tempi are superbly controlled. In the finale Karajan is not just noble and stoic; he finds the bite of passion as well, sharply set against stillness and repose.

Within two years **Karajan** went on to record the work even more compulsively at live performances in Berlin. The major difference in that later recording (439 024-2) is that there is a new, glowing optimism in the finale, rejecting any Mahlerian death-wish and making it a supreme achievement. Yet the earlier (1980) analogue performance makes a remarkable alternative, reissued as a DG Double. Moreover the performances of the *Kindertotenlieder* and *Rückert Lieder* have a distinction and refinement of playing which stand out above all.

Barbirolli greatly impressed the Berliners with his Mahler performances live, and this recording reflects the players' warmth of response. He opted to record the slow and intense finale before the rest, and the beauty of the playing makes it a fitting culmination. The other movements are strong and alert too, and the sound remains full and atmospheric, though now even more clearly defined in its current remastering for reissue as one of EMI's 'Great Recordings of the Century'. An unquestionable bargain.

The great glory of the **Chailly** version is the spectacular SACD recording, which is very full-bodied and almost larger than life, with the widest dynamic range. The playing of the **Royal Concertgebouw** is spectacular too, with details clearly in place and rhythms crisp and sharp in the middle two movements. If, next to the finest live recordings, this studio account sounds a degree too metrical in the massive outer movements, the power of the work has never come over with greater impact.

Klemperer's refusal to languish pays tribute to his spiritual defiance, and the physical power is underlined when the sound is full-bodied and firmly focused. The sublimity of the finale comes out the more intensely, with overt expressiveness held in check and deep emotion implied rather than made explicit. Now recoupled both with the Strauss *Metamorphosen* and with *Death and Transfiguration*, this is one of the more important reissues in EMI's 'Great Recordings of the Century'.

Symphony 10 in F sharp (Unfinished) (revised performing edition by Deryck Cooke)

🔗 (M) **** EMI 5 034220-2. BPO, Rattle

(B) **(*) CfP 585 901-2. Bournemouth SO, Rattle

In 1980, at the beginning of his recording career, **Simon Rattle** recorded this inspired realization of Mahler's five-movement concept. With the **Bournemouth Symphony Orchestra**, that remains an electrifying account, weightily recorded now on CfP, but his new version with the **Berlin Philharmonic**, recorded live, transcends it in almost every way. It is not only the extra refinement of the Berliners but also the extra detail that Rattle brings out in almost every phrase that goes with an even greater concentration.

VOCAL MUSIC

(i) Kindertotenlieder; (ii) Des Knaben Wunderhorn (excerpts); (i) Lieder eines fahrenden Gesellen

(N) **(*) Phoenix 105. Köln RSO, Bertini; with (i) Quasthoff;
(ii) Hagegård

These performances date from the early 1990s, with the
Kindertotenlieder recorded live in 1993. As in the *Lieder eines
fahrenden Gesellen*, **Thomas Quasthoff** is predictably impressive at this early stage of his career, before he became famous.
His is a young man's portrayal of these works, but by no
means an undeveloped one: he brings out plenty of subtle
nuance in his phrasing and is compelling throughout.
Håkan Hagegård gives an impassioned account of the *Des
Knaben Wunderhorn* excerpts, which are most enjoyable. The
recorded sound is excellent throughout, though **Bertini** delivers not the most inspired of accompaniments. Alas, no
texts provided.

(i) Kindertotenlieder; (ii) Des Knaben Wunderhorn; (i) Lieder eines fahrenden Gesellen; Rückert-Lieder

*** DG **DVD** 073 4167. (i) Hampson, VPO; (ii) Popp, Grönroos,
Israel PO; Bernstein

Thomas Hampson gives us a beautifully controlled account
of the *Lieder eines fahrenden Gesellen* which find **Bernstein** and
the **Vienna Philharmonic** at their finest – subtle, delicate
colourings and strong atmosphere; indeed, quite glorious
orchestral playing throughout. No quarrels either with
Kindertotenlieder or the *Rückert* songs. **Lucia Popp** and the
Finnish baritone, **Walton Grönroos**, are also given excellent
support by **Bernstein** and the **Israel Philharmonic Orchestra**
(even if it is no Vienna Philharmonic) in the 12 *Wunderhorn*
songs. The performances come from the late 1980s and the
video direction is refreshingly natural, even if the picture is
not as fresh in colouring or as fine in focus as more modern
recordings.

(i) Kindertotenlieder; Des Knaben Wunderhorn: Des Antonius von Padua Fischpredigt; Das irdische Leben; Urlicht; (ii) Das klagende Lied; (i) Lieder eines fahrenden Gesellen; 5 Rückert Lieder

(B) *** Double Decca 473 725-2 (2). (i) Fassbaender, Berlin
Deutsche SO; (ii) Dunn, Baur, Hollweg, Schmidt,
Düsseldorf State Musikverein, Berlin RSO; Chailly

Fassbaender gives fearless, vividly characterized performances of *Kindertotenlieder*, the *Lieder eines fahrenden Gesellen*,
the *Five Rückert Lieder*, and three songs from *Des Knaben
Wunderhorn*. The strength of **Chailly's** *Das klagende Lied* lies
with the splendid singing of the Düsseldorf choir and the
demonstration-worthy Decca recording, full of presence.
While not quite upstaging Rattle in revealing the music's
imaginative detail, Chailly pulls one special trick out of the
hat in *Waldmärchen* by using a boy alto (**Markus Baur**) to
represent the voice from the grave, a tellingly sepulchral
effect. Full texts and translations are provided, and this
makes an impressive and generous Double Decca anthology.

Kindertotenlieder; Lieder eines fahrenden Gesellen; Lieder und Gesänge: 1, 3, 5, 10–13; 5 Rückert Lieder

*** Hyp. CDA 67392. Genz, Vignoles

Stephan Genz gives sensitive, finely detailed readings of

Mahler's three most popular cycles in their piano versions,
adding for good measure seven of Mahler's Youth songs,
Lieder und Gesänge. It says much for **Roger Vignoles's** accompaniments that he finds such fantasy in the piano writing,
with the sparer textures of the accompaniments for
Kindertotenlieder made to reflect the pain of bereavement in
their bareness.

(i) Kindertotenlieder; Lieder eines fahrenden Gesellen; (ii) 5 Rückert Lieder

⊙ ✸ (M) **** EMI (ADD) 5 66981-2. Baker, Hallé or New
Philh. O, Barbirolli

**(*) Australian Decca Eloquence 442 8287. Horne, with (i)
RPO, Lewis; (ii) LAPO, Mehta

(BB) **(*) Naxos 8.554156. Greevy, Nat. SO of Ireland, with (i)
Fürst; (ii) Decker

Dame Janet Baker's collaboration with **Barbirolli** represents
the affectionate approach to Mahler at its warmest: intensely
beautiful, full of breathtaking moments. The spontaneous
feeling of soloist and conductor for this music comes over
as in a live performance and brings out the tenderness to a
unique degree. An indispensable CD.

Horne is not ideally recorded: the microphones are too
close in the **Mehta** items, accentuating the impression of a
lack of subtlety. But her wonderfully rich mezzo is a joy to
hear in its own right, and the sheer power of her voice can
be very exciting, as in the climax of *Um Mitternacht*. In
Kindertotenlieder, Horne has a statuesque quality which does
not ideally suit Mahler's intensely personal inspiration. But
there is much to admire, much that is beautiful.

Bernadette Greevy may lack a degree of vitality in such a
song as the second of the *Wayfaring Lad* cycle, the song that
gave Mahler his first theme in his *First Symphony*, but her
poise in such a great song as the Rückert setting, *Ich bin in
der Welt abhanden gekommen*, is most satisfying, readily compensating for any lack of emotional weight compared with the
finest interpretations. The **Irish National Symphony
Orchestra** play with rich, velvety tone in every section,
helped by the warmly atmospheric recording, made in the
National Concert Hall in Dublin.

Kindertotenlieder; 3 Rückert Lieder: Ich atmet' einen linden Duft; Ich bin der Welt abhanden gekommen; Um Mitternacht

⊙ ✸ (BB) (***) Regis mono RRC 1153. Ferrier, VPO, Walter –
BRAHMS: *Vier ernste Gesang, etc.* (***)

Kathleen Ferrier's radiant *Kindertotenlieder* (from 1949) are
wonderfully moving, and the three *Rückert Lieder* from 1952,
heartfelt and monumental, are magically intense, with
Bruno Walter and the **Vienna Philharmonic Orchestra**
adding a special affectionate glow to the music-making.
Indeed, the orchestra sounds far better here than on the
original Decca LPs. These two artists worked wonderfully
well together and this Regis coupling, transferred warmly
and smoothly, is a very real bargain.

Das klagende Lied (complete: Part 1, Waldmärchen; Part 2, Der Spielmann; Part 3, Hochzeitsstücke)

⊕→ *** EMI 5 66406-2. Döse, Hodgson, Tear, Rea, CBSO Ch., CBSO, Rattle

Rattle brings out the astonishing originality of Mahler's cycle, but adds urgency, colour and warmth, not to mention deeper, more meditative qualities. So the final section, *Wedding Piece*, after starting with superb swagger in the celebration music, is gripping in the minstrel's sinister narration and ends in the darkest concentration on a mezzo-soprano solo, beautifully sung by **Alfreda Hodgson**. This is one of Rattle's earliest Mahler recordings, but it sounds excellent in what appears to be a new transfer.

Des Knaben Wunderhorn

⊕→ (M) **** EMI 5 67236-2. Schwarzkopf, Fischer-Dieskau, LSO, Szell

Des Knaben Wunderhorn; Das himmlische Leben; Urlicht

*** Decca 467 348-2. Bonney, Fulgoni, Winbergh, Goerne, Concg. O, Chailly

Szell's 1968 Kingsway Hall recording of *Des Knaben Wunderhorn* rightly joins EMI's 'Great Recordings of the Century'. The superb singing of **Schwarzkopf** and **Fischer-Dieskau** is underpinned by wonderfully sensitive playing from the **LSO** under Szell.

Strongly characterized, **Chailly's** disc of the *Des Knaben Wunderhorn* songs is also among the most distinctive versions available. The soloists are an outstanding team, with **Matthias Goerne** exceptionally perceptive, **Barbara Bonney** equally individual in characterization. Fresh and girlish, she also sings one of the two extra songs added to the usual 12, the child–heaven finale to the *Fourth Symphony*. The other extra song is the meditative *Urlicht* from the *Resurrection Symphony*, with the rich-toned **Sara Fulgoni** as mezzo soloist. The late **Gösta Winbergh** is also brought in as tenor soloist, when Chailly opts for having the military song, *Revelge*, in a higher key than usual.

Des Knaben Wunderhorn: 12 Lieder; Lieder eines fahrenden Gesellen; Lieder und Gesänge 1–14; 5 Rückert Lieder

(BB) *** EMI 4 76780-2 (2). Fischer-Dieskau, Barenboim

The piano versions of Mahler's songs may not match in colour his orchestral versions, but with **Daniel Barenboim** imaginatively accompanying **Dietrich Fischer-Dieskau** the subtlety of Mahler's word-setting and of his piano writing is most compelling. This two-disc compilation at bargain price brings together a series of recordings they made in Berlin in 1978, classic performances, even if Fischer-Dieskau's baritone is not quite as fresh as it was earlier. Texts and translations are provided, though in minuscule type.

Lieder eines fahrenden Gesellen

(M) *** Orfeo C 522 991B. Ludwig, VPO, Boehm –
BEETHOVEN: *Symphony 4*; SCHUMANN: *Symphony 4* ***

As the chosen soloist in an electrifying concert conducted by **Karl Boehm** in August 1969, **Christa Ludwig** excels herself in a deeply moving, strongly characterized reading of the *Wayfaring Lad* songs. The spontaneity of the performance makes up for any incidental flaws of the moment, with the voice gloriously firm and rich. No texts or translations of the songs are given, but every word is clear in this helpfully balanced radio recording.

Lieder eines fahrenden Gesellen; Lieder und Gesänge (aus der Jugendzeit); Im Lenz; Winterlied

⊕→ 🌟 (BB) **** Hyp. Helios CDH 55160. J. Baker, Parsons

Janet Baker presents a superb collection of Mahler's early songs with piano, including two written in 1880 and never recorded before, *Im Lenz* and *Winterlied*; also the piano version of the *Wayfaring Lad* songs in a text prepared by Colin Matthews from Mahler's final thoughts, as contained in the orchestral version. The performances are radiant and deeply understanding from both singer and pianist, well caught in atmospheric recording. A heart-warming record.

(i) Lieder eines fahrenden Gesellen; (ii) 3 Rückert Lieder: Ich atmet' einem linden Duft; Ich bin der Welt abhanden gekommen; Um Mitternacht

(***) BBC mono/stereo BBCL 4107-2. Christa Ludwig, with (i) Philh. O, Cluytens; (ii) Parsons (with: BRAHMS: *Ständchen; Wiegenlied* ***) – R. STRAUSS: *Four Last Songs* ***

The mono recording for Ludwig's 1957 account of the Mahler *Wayfaring Lad* cycle captures the richness of the voice vividly, with changing emotions clearly conveyed. The other songs, with **Geoffrey Parsons** at the piano, come from a Wigmore Hall recital given 21 years later, with the glorious voice still flawless in poised legato.

Das Lied von der Erde

⊕→ (M) *** BBC (ADD) BBCM 5012-2. Baker, Mitchinson, BBC N. SO, Leppard

(M) *** EMI (ADD) 5 66892-2. Ludwig, Wunderlich, Philh. & New Philh. O, Klemperer

(M) **(*) Sony (ADD) 82876 78752-2. Miller, Haefliger, NYPO, Walter

(*) RCA **SACD 88697 08281-2. Forrester, Lewis, Chicago SO, Reiner

(i) Das Lied von der Erde; 3 Rückert Lieder

(M) (***) Decca mono 466 576-2. Ferrier; (i) Patzak; VPO, Walter

(BB) (***) Naxos mono 8.110871. Ferrier; (i) Patzak; VPO, Walter

Taken from a performance for radio in the Free Trade Hall, Manchester, the **Leppard** version offers **Baker** in 1977, giving another of her moving and richly varied readings of the contralto songs. The final *Abschied* has a depth and intensity, a poignancy that sets it alongside Dame Janet's earlier recordings. **John Mitchinson** may not have the most beautiful tenor, but his voice focuses ever more securely through the work, with many cleanly ringing top notes. Raymond Leppard draws fine playing from the orchestra, now renamed the **BBC Philharmonic**, though the body of strings is thin for Mahler. Acceptable BBC sound, with the voices naturally placed, not spotlit.

The latest Decca remastering of the famous (1952) Ferrier–Patzak version of *Das Lied* is a revelation. At the very opening the orchestral strings are not ideally focused, but Ferrier's voice is warmly and vividly caught, as is the characterful Patzak. Even more remarkable is the transfer of the three Rückert songs recorded at the same time (*Ich bin der Welt abhanden gekommen, Ich atmet' einen linden Duft* and *Um Mitternacht*).

Mark Obert-Thorn's transfers on Naxos are also admirable, slightly less open than the Decca in *Das Lied*, but somewhat smoother in focus. The *Rückert Lieder*, which come first, sound particularly beautiful. However, the Naxos disc, though it is less expensive than the Decca, unusually for this label does not include texts or translations.

Though **Bruno Walter's** 1960 New York version does not have the tear-laden quality in the final *Abschied* that made his earlier Decca Vienna account (in mono) with Kathleen Ferrier unique, that is its only serious shortcoming. The performances are bursting with vitality, **Ernst Haefliger** sparkles with imagination and **Mildred Miller** is a warm and appealing mezzo soloist, lacking only the ultimate depth of feeling you find in a Ferrier; while Walter himself has rarely sounded so happy on record. The recording, made in New York's Manhattan Center, is spacious and lively, although it has an element of coarseness.

Klemperer's way with Mahler is at its most individual in *Das Lied von der Erde* – and that will enthral some, as it must infuriate others. With slower speeds, the three tenor songs seem initially to lose some of their sparkle and humour; however, thanks to superb, expressive singing by the late **Fritz Wunderlich** – one of the most memorable examples of his artistry on record – and thanks also to pointing of rhythm by Klemperer himself, subtle but always clear, the comparative slowness will hardly worry anyone intent on hearing the music afresh. As for the mezzo songs, **Christa Ludwig** sings them with a remarkable depth of expressiveness; in particular, the final *Abschied* has the intensity of a great occasion. Excellent digitally remastered recording.

Reiner's approach too has delicacy, drama and feeling. He follows the letter of the score exactly. For instance, at the climactic point of the closing 'Abschied' he and **Maureen Forrester** create tension with their gentle tenderness. The whispered murmurs of 'Ewig' at the end have not quite the heart-searching intensity one remembers with Ferrier or Baker, but their touching understatement may be nearer to the meaning of the poem and thus to Mahler's intention. Forrester is on top form throughout, and **Richard Lewis** sings passionately and is both imaginative and musicianly: the whole performance is full of spontaneity. An SACD reissue worth seeking out.

5 Rückert Lieder

(M) *** Wigmore Hall WH Live 0013. Hunt Lieberson, Vignoles – HANDEL: Arias from *Ariodante; Theodora;* LIEBERSON: *O ihr Zatlichen*, etc. ***

The untimely death from cancer of **Lorraine Hunt Lieberson** makes one value the relatively few recordings she made, including this live recording taken at a Wigmore Hall recital in 1998. Here is a mezzo who more than any of

her generation bade fair to rival Janet Baker in the warmth, beauty and intensity of her singing, most strikingly in these songs with which Baker was so closely associated. They are the more poignant when the very texts have death as a theme.

MALIPIERO, Gian Francesco (1882–1973)

Violin Concerto

*** Sup. (ADD) SU 3904-2. Gertler, Prague SO, Smetáček – CASELLA: *Violin Concerto* ***

Malipiero and Casella were born within a year of each other and their *Violin Concertos* were composed at roughly the same period in their careers. The Malipiero has fallen out of the repertory, so it is good to have **André Gertler's** 1971 recording back in circulation. It is a finely wrought piece, at times almost reminiscent of the pastoral quality of Vaughan Williams. An enterprising and welcome reissue.

Symphonies 3 (Delle Campane); 4 (In Memoriam); Sinfonia del mare

(N) (BB) *(*) Naxos 8.570878. Moscow SO, Almeida

It is good to have Malipiero symphonies available at bargain price. 3 and 4 were composed during the Second World War, the former inspired by the tolling of bells of St Mark's Basilica to signify the German invasion of Italy in 1943; and stylized bell evocations run throughout this work. The *Fourth Symphony* is dedicated to Koussevitzky and contains a particularly beautiful slow movement. His *Sinfonia del mare* ('Sea Symphony') is very evocative and displays the composer's gift for orchestral colour. It is a great pity that neither the performances (which sound somewhat scrappy) nor the sound are first rate.

MANFREDINI, Francesco (1684–1762)

Concerti grossi, Op. 3/1–12

☞─ 🕸 (BB) *** Naxos 8.553891. Capella Istropolitana, Krček

This splendid set of 12 concertos, published in Bologna in 1718, was dedicated to Prince Antoine I of Monaco, with whose court orchestra Manfredini was associated. The most famous of them is 12, a *Christmas Concerto* in the style of Torelli and Corelli, opening with a delightful *Pastorale* in siciliano rhythm. And if there are other influences here too, of Vivaldi in particular, and even anticipations of Handel, the music has its own individuality and is endlessly inventive. *Allegros* are vital and buoyant, slow movements tenderly touching, often featuring one or two solo violins. The Naxos performances here are both fresh and penetrating, with bouncing outer movements and expressive *Adagios*. Moreover the playing is perfectly in style, demonstrating how using modern instruments can be just as authentic as period manners in baroque music. The recording is absolutely natural, very much in the demonstration bracket.

MANKELL, Henning
(1868–1930)

Piano Music: *Ballad 7, Op. 77; 3 Preludes, Op. 54; 3 Legends, Op. 59; 4 Pieces (Barcarolle; Evening Mood; Tempest Mood; Slow Waves), Op. 60; Valse mesto, Op. 58; Fantasy Sonatas: 1, Op. 69, 3, Op. 72; 6, Op. 76*

(N) *** Phoenix 184 (2). Christensson

Henning Mankell was born into a musical family in northern Sweden and, after a period teaching the piano in the provinces, in 1917 was elected a fellow of the Royal Swedish Academy of Music, where he continued to teach and also began composing. The works represented in this recording are from his later period (1922–30) and, with increasing familiarity, it is being recognized that some of the finest Swedish piano music derives from his hand.

The sets of *Preludes* and *Legends* are all impressionistic and have something of the atmosphere of Debussy, although Mankell's treatment of harmony was individual. Evocations like *Waves* (from the *Preludes*) and the *Legend, Atlantis*, are particularly evocative, although most striking of all are the *Four Pieces*, with the penultimate *Tempest Mood* and closing *Slow Waves* showing Mankell at his most imaginative. The three *Fantasy Sonatas* are essentially rhapsodical, with the third especially successful; but the closing *Ballade* is a remarkable work, with something of the variety of a Chopin *Ballade*, only twice as extended. **Anna Christensson** is thoroughly at home in this repertoire and plays with great confidence and poetic feeling. She is very well recorded, and anyone who is looking for a new composer in the field of early twentieth-century piano music and who has flatly refused to indulge in atonalism, should find this collection very rewarding.

MARAIS, Marin (1656–1728)

Pièces a deux viole, Book I (1686): Chaconne in G; Suites in D min. & G

*** Astrée Naïve ES 9963. Savall, Coin, Koopman, Hopkinson Smith

Pièces de viole, Book II (1701)

*** Astrée Naïve ES 9978. Savall, Gallet, Hopkinson Smith

Pièces de viole, Book II: Couplets de folies; Fantaisie pièces in D min.; E; Suite in E; Tombeau de Monsieur Ste Colombe

⊖– **** BIS CD 909. Luolajan-Mikkola, Haavisto, Palviaininen

Pièces de viole, Book II: Suite in D min.; Couplets de folies; Book III: Suites in G & A min.

*** Glossa GCD 920406. Pandolfo, Balestracci, Boysen, Costoyas, Meyerson

Marais wrote his five books of *Pièces de viole* over four decades – between 1686 and 1725 – and as time went by he moved on-

ward from the standard dance pattern of allemande, courante, sarabande, gigue, gavotte and minuet. The First Book introduces a fine *Chaconne*, an *Echo fantaisie*, and ends with a deeply expressive *Tombeau*. The Second Book is mainly famous for its *Follie d'espagne*, 32 bravura variations on an Iberian dance we know as *La folia*. But it also includes *La Voix humaine* and another *Tombeau*, remembering Lully. The Third Book includes a *Gigue à l'anglais*, a *Muzette*, a *Grand ballet* and another *Chaconne*.

There is no questioning **Jordi Savall's** authority in these pieces, and he leads a dedicated team. But his manner is somewhat austere, the colouring is comparatively dark, and some may well prefer the lighter touch and textures of **Paolo Pandolfo** and his colleagues. The Glossa issue is particularly well documented, and it includes *Folies d'espagne* separately on a bonus disc.

However, our favourite among these issues is the BIS CD, which is particularly attractively recorded. **Markku Luolajan-Mikkola's** full timbre is warmly caught, and he plays with plenty of expressive feeling and flexibility and a wide range of dynamic. In essence, this is very friendly playing which wins the ear without abrasiveness, and his continuo group is just as excellent.

Pièces de viole, Book II (1701): Les Folies d'Espagne; Suite in E min.; Book IV (1717): La Labyrinthe

⊖– **** HM Zig-Zag Territoires ZZT 060801. Ens. Spirale, Muller

This Zig-Zag collection from the excellent **Ensemble Spirale** is particularly attractive in including *Les Folies d'Espagne*, and the similarly celebrated virtuoso piece, *La Labyrinthe*. But the centrepiece is the complete *Suite in E minor* from Book II, with its 13 varied movements, ending with the *Tombeau pour M. de Sainte-Colombe*, which is played very touchingly. Indeed, the gamba playing of **Marianne Muller**, the group's director, and of her colleague **Sylvia Abramowicz** and of their excellent continuo of harpsichord, baroque guitar and theorbo is first class, with sensitive phrasing and warm tone. Moreover the recording too is state-of-the-art: the viola da gamba sound is particularly firm and well focused.

Pièces de viole; 4 Suites from Books II & III

(N) (BB) *** Virgin 69321320. Jerome & Pierre Hantai, Verzier

This is another particularly attractive collection, inexpensive, very well played and vividly and smoothly recorded.

Pièces de viole, Book IV (1717): Suite d'un goût étranger (complete)

⊖– **** Alia Vox AVSA 9854I (2). Savall, Hantaï, Pierlot, Lislevand, Diaz-Latorre, Lawrence-King, Estevan

Jordi Savall now gives us a complete coverage of Marais's Book IV, including the *Suite d'un goût étranger*, using a varied continuo. He is a complete master of this repertoire, and famous virtuoso items like *Le Tourbillon* and the *Labyrinth* are superbly played. The recording balance too is excellent, and the pair of discs is very handsomely packaged and presented.

Pièces en Trio: Sonnerie de Sainte-Geneviève du Mont de Paris (for Violin, Bass Viol &

Harpsichord (1723); Suites: 1 in C (for Flute, Violin, Bass Viol & Harpsichord) (1692); Pièces de Viole, Book II (1711): 4 in D (for Bass Viol & Harpsichord)

(B) *** HM Musique d'Abord HMA 195414. Alice & Nikolaus Harnoncourt, Stastny, Tachezi

The *Trio Sonata* here in which the flute dominates has great charm and above all delicate and elegant in feeling rather than effervescent. The *D major Viola da Gamba Suite*, played with aplomb by **Nikolaus Harnoncourt** (in 1973), has a dozen movements, with half of them given names. But they are not as striking as the *Sonnerie de Sainte-Geneviève du Mont de Paris*, composed much later. This is a set of variations in the style of a chaconne, and led by a violin rather than a treble viol. It simulates church bells and also supposedly evokes city life around the church, although it is the bells which dominate. First-class performances and recording.

Pièces de violes: L'Arabesque; Le Badinage; Le Labyrinthe; Prélude in G; La Rêveuse; Sonnerie de Sainte-Geneviève du Mont de Paris; Suite in G; Tombeau pour Monsieur de Sainte-Colombe

⊛ (BB) *** Naxos 8.550750. Spectre de la Rose – SAINTE-COLOMBE: *Le Retour*, etc. ***

Naxos have stepped in enterprisingly and chosen a programme that is not only most attractive in its own right, but which also includes the key items used in the fascinating film about the conjectural relationship between Marin Marais and his reclusive mentor, Sainte-Colombe (*Tous les matins du monde*). **Spectre de la Rose** consists of a first-rate group of young players, led by **Alison Crum**, who plays in a dignified but austere style which at first seems cool but which is very effective in this repertoire. *Le Badinage* is perhaps a little stiff and unsmiling, but the key item, Marais's eloquent lament for his teacher, *Tombeau pour Monsieur de Sainte-Colombe*, is restrained and touching. Good, bright, forward recording, vividly declaiming the plangent viola da gamba timbre. But be careful not to play this record at too high a volume setting.

Pièces de violes: Book I (1686): Tombeau de M. Meliton. Book II (1701): Couplets de folies; Les Voix humaines. Book III (1711): Suite in D. La Gamme et autres Morceaux de Simphonie (1723): Sonate à la Marésienne

⊛ (BB) *** Naxos 8.553081. Spectre de la Rose

The second Naxos collection from **Spectre de la Rose** even includes a rare work in which the violin takes the lead (the *Sonate à la Marésienne*), although the embroidering gamba partner takes the lion's share of bravura. It is a most attractive work and is played here with real sparkle, while the following *Suite in D* also shows Marais at his most attractively inventive. *Les Voix humaines* is deeply pitched, and even the *Couplets de folies* is far from light-hearted. Spectre de la Rose are experts in this field and play most persuasively throughout.

Sémélé (Tragédie lyrique; complete)

(N) **** Glossa GCD 921614 (2). Mercer, Dolié, Thébault,

Dahlin, Labonette, Azzaretti, Tauran, Abadie, Le Concert Spirituel, Niquet

Marais's 1709 setting of *Sémélé* used a libretto by Houdar de la Motte in which the basic classical storyline and nature of the characterization are often different from Handel's *Semele*. The drama of Jupiter's unfaithfulness to his angry wife Juno is common to both settings, but the principal alternative twist of the plot comes at the end: Prince Adraste (whom Semele was originally to marry, to please her father Cadmus, King of Thebes) fails to survive the final earthquake and conflagration. Instead of being consumed by Jupiter's fire, Semele is restored to life by the god, who installs her in heaven as his mistress instead!

Houdar de la Motte's portrait of Semele is nowhere near as self-admiring and resourceful as Handel's character, but she is obviously gently desirable, and is given two beautiful, expressive arias: *Amour régnez en paix* in Act III, and *Descendes cher amant* in Act IV, both delicately accompanied by flutes. Alongside the arias for the other principal characters there also numerous brief duos. However, the real glory of Marais's setting lies in his fine choruses and his delightful writing for the orchestra, often with enchanting textures. This is immediately apparent in the opening extended prologue, a Bacchanalia, with Apollo appearing to announce the opera's storyline. The instrumental writing reaches a climax in the great *Chaconne* in Act II, the most ambitious ever composed in France; but the accompaniment throughout lights up the dialogue in the most colourful way. The singing cast here is excellent, but the playing of **Le Concert Spirituel** is even more so, making this a most rewarding listening experience. Full texts and translations are included.

MARCELLO, Alessandro
(1669–1747)

6 Oboe Concertos (La Cetra)

(M) *** Chan. 0744X. Robson, Latham, R. Brown, Coll. Mus. 90, Standage

The six concertos of *La Cetra* reveal a pleasing mixture of originality and convention; often one is surprised by a genuinely alive and refreshing individuality. **Standage's** set with **Collegium Musicum 90** makes the most of Marcellos's solo scoring, finding plenty of colour and nuance in these highly inventive works, not only for one or two oboes (or flutes) but for solo violin (Standage himself). Slow movements often possess real poignancy and the fast movements bubble and sparkle. Moreover he includes an additional *Concerto con l'Eco* that is well worth having. Performances are appealingly stylish and beautifully recorded.

Oboe Concerto in C min. (arr. Rothwell)

⊛ (M) *** Dutton Lab./Barbirolli Soc. CDSJB 1016. Rothwell, Hallé O, Barbirolli – CORELLI; HAYDN: *Oboe Concertos* *** (with Recital: C. P. E. BACH; LOEILLET; TELEMANN: *Sonatas*, etc. **

Sir John's subtlety in matters of light and shade within an orchestral phrase brings this music immediately alive, and at the same time prevents the rather jolly opening tune from sounding square. The exquisitely beautiful *Adagio* is followed by a gay finale, both showing the soloist at her finest, and the well-balanced (1969) recording and excellent transfer add to one's pleasure.

Oboe Concerto in D min.

(BB) **(*) Naxos 8.550556. Kiss, Erkel CO – C. P. E. BACH: *Concertos* **(*)

This enjoyable concerto, once attributed (in a different key) to Benedetto Marcello, is given a good performance here by **József Kiss** and is very well recorded. One might have preferred more dynamic contrast from the soloist, but his timbre is right for baroque music and he plays with plenty of spirit. This disc is well worth its modest cost for the C. P. E. Bach couplings.

10 Keyboard Sonatas, Op. 3; Labarinto sopra il clavicembalo; La stravaganza in C (ciaccona con variazione)

*** Chan. 0671 (2). Loreggian (harpsichord)

Marcello's invention is usually common to all the movements of each sonata, and though infinitely varied in treatment the basic ideas remain intact and attractively recognizable throughout. The *Labarinto* (in two sections) is a free, fantasy-like piece, with the bold rhythms and repeated notes of the closing section catchily bizarre. The C major ciaccona, *La stravaganza*, was Marcello's most famous harpsichord piece, and its 38 variations produce an expansive 15-minute work which rather outstays its welcome. Not the fault of the performance, one hastens to say, for the playing here is full of life and sparkle. The instrument itself is a reconstruction of a late-17th-century Italian harpsichord, and it is vividly recorded.

MARCELLO, Benedetto
(1686–1739)

Oboe Concerto in C min. (trans. BONELLI)

Australian Decca Eloquence mono 480 0833. Reversy, SRO, Ansermet – VIVALDI: *Bassoon Concertos* **(*); HANDEL: *Organ Concertos* ***

The lovely *C minor Oboe Concerto* of Marcello was recorded in 1951, and although the oboe, played by **Roger Reversy**, is rather startlingly upfront, it doesn't distract too much from the poised music-making. The finale is a toe-tapping delight.

MARENZIO, Luca (1553–99)

Madrigals (1580): Excerpts from Book I; Book II; Book IV; Book V; Book VI; Book VII; Book IX. (with PHILIPS: *Tirsi morir vola*; TERZI: *Intavolatura di liuto, libro primo: Liquide perle Amor, da gl'occhi sparse*)

🌓 *** Naïve OP 30245. Concerto Italiano, Alessandrini

Rinaldo Alessandrini here demonstrates the claims as a madrigalist of Luca Marenzio, born 14 years before Monteverdi, concentrating in his choice on the madrigals Marenzio wrote early in his life in a fresh, open style that attracted listeners with its sweetness. A good selection from those written later in the composer's brief career complete the picture. Very well paced, with structures clearly presented, they make a superb sequence in these beautifully recorded, finely detailed performances. Adding to the variety, Alessandrini adds discreet instrumental continuo to many of the items.

MARINI, Biagio (1594–1663)

Sinfonias for Strings 2 & 5; Sonatas for Strings 1–4; Balletto primo; (i) La lagrimo d'Erminia

(N) (M) *** Decca O/L 478 0020. Consorte of Musicke, Rooley or Trevor Jones; (i) with Kirkby and Rogers

Marini was a younger contemporary of Monteverdi, his life spanning the first half of the seventeenth century. The prize discoveries here are the *String Sonatas*, lively and imaginative; the other instrumental items too are far from routine. The songs are less interesting, but with fresh, characterful singing from **Emma Kirkby** and **Nigel Rogers**, they help to fill out the picture of an interesting historical figure, long neglected. Performances and recording are typical of the excellent Florilegium series which Decca/Oiseau-Lyre have resurrected for this welcome reissue.

MARKEVITCH, Igor (1912–83)

(i) Partita; (ii) Le Paradis Perdu

(N) (BB) **(*) Naxos 8.570773. Arnhem PO, Lyndon-Gee; with (i) Hoek; (ii) Shelton, Walker, Garrison, Netherlands Concert Ch.

A fascinating disc, beginning with Markevitch's early *Partita* of 1931, where one is swept immediately into a vigorous *Allegro risoluto*, full of fascinating rhythms and harmonies, and tremendous forward impulse. It is in effect a piano concerto with a brilliant part for the soloist, not least the brilliantly fast finale which follows from a mysterious and memorable slow movement. The oratorio *Le Paradis Perdu* is even more ambitious; based on Milton's *Paradise Lost*, it was completed in 1935, and this, like the *Partita*, is its first recording. From the very opening, Markevitch creates a gripping atmosphere, often other-worldly, especially with the chorus halfway though Part I. The soloists are good, even if they all have a bit of a wobble, and the orchestra, though not always totally immaculate, plays with enthusiasm. The chorus is excellent, and their often heady passages are particularly exciting. The sound is generally very acceptable, even if in the loud, massed passages it feels a little compressed. There are copious notes, but it is a pity the texts were not included. At bargain price, well worth acquiring.

MARSH, John (1752–1828)

Symphonies 1, 3, 4 & 6; Conversation Symphonie for 2 Orchestras

(N) (BB) *** Regis Alto ALC 1017. Chichester Concert, Graham-Jones

John Marsh was innovative: because of the continuing influence of Handel, the symphony format was not fashionable in England at his time; for the most part they each consisted of three short movements and, while the tunes sometimes have a whiff of Handel, there is a strong element of the English village green. The *Conversation Symphony* does not divide into two separate ensembles but makes contrasts between higher and lower instrumental groupings. Five of Marsh's works are presented here by an aptly sized authentic baroque group: they play well and the (originally Olympia) recording is effectively balanced. Well worth exploring at budget price.

Symphonies 2, 6, 7 (La Chasse), 8, Conversation Symphony for 2 Orchestras

*** Chan. 10458. LMP, Bamert

John Marsh was self-taught, and was sometimes dismissed by his contemporaries as an amateur. Yet these lively and inventive works demonstrate his imaginative qualities, well brought out in these excellent performances from **Matthias Bamert** and the **London Mozart Players**. The most colourful of the symphonies is 7 entitled *La Chasse*, with its big horn solo at the start, followed by two movements in a galloping triple time. The *Conversation Symphony* is original in dividing the orchestras not into two equal groups but by pitch, a device that works surprisingly well. An outstanding disc in the Contemporaries of Mozart series.

MARTIN, Frank (1890–1974)

Ballades for: (i) Cello & Small Orchestra; (ii) Flute, Strings & Piano; (iii) Piano & Orchestra; (iv) Saxophone & Small Orchestra; (v) Viola, Wind, Harpsichord, Timpani & Percussion; (vi) Trombone & Piano

*** Chan. 9380. (i) Dixon; (ii) Chambers; (ii–iii; v–vi) Elms; (iv) Robertson; (v) Dukes, Masters; (vi) Bousfield; LPO, Bamert

The *Ballades* are among Martin's most personal utterances, so the present issue is a most valuable addition to the Martin discography, particularly in view of the excellence and commitment of the performances. Subtle, state-of-the-art recording with no false 'hi-fi' brightness, but a natural and unobtrusive presence. An indispensable disc for admirers of this subtle and rewarding master.

(i) Ballade for Piano & Orchestra; Piano Concertos 1; (ii) 2; (i; ii) Danse de la peur for 2 Pianos & Small Orchestra

⌐ 🕸 **** ASV CDDCA 1082. (i) Sebastian Benda; (ii) Badura-Skoda; O della Svizzera Italiana, Christian Benda

The *First Piano Concerto* of 1933–4 anticipates many of the characteristic fingerprints of the *Petite symphonie concertante* and the *Concerto for Seven Wind Instruments*. The pale, haunting instrumental colourings of the slow movement evoke Martin's own special world. The ASV CD brings the *Danse de la peur*, also from the 1930s, a highly imaginative, dramatic and above all atmospheric score which is new to the Martin discography. Good performances and decently balanced recordings, which are recommended with the strongest enthusiasm.

(i) Ballade for Piano & Orchestra; (ii) Ballade for Trombone & Orchestra; (iii) Concerto for Harpsichord & Small Orchestra

**(*) Jecklin-Disco (ADD) JD 529-2. (i) Benda; (ii) Rosin; (iii) Jaccottet; Lausanne CO, composer

(i; ii) Ballade for Cello & Piano; (i; iii) Ballade for Flute & Piano; (i) 8 Préludes pour le piano; (i; iv) Drey Minnelieder; (i; iv) 6 Monologues from Jedermann; (ii; v) 3 Chants de Nöel

(M) **(*) Jecklin (ADD) 563-2. (i) Composer; (ii) Honegger; (iii) Willoughby; (iv) Rehfuss; (v) Ameling, Odé

JD 529-2 brings the *Harpsichord Concerto* with **Christiane Jaccottet**, who took part in the première recording of the *Petite Symphonie Concertante* in the early 1950s. Like the companion works, it derives from the Swiss Radio Archives and comes from 1971. **Sebastian Benda** gives just as powerful and imaginative account of the *Ballade for Piano and Orchestra*. This is quintessential Martin: music from another world.

JD 563-2 restores to circulation a memorable (1955) recording of the *Jedermann Monologues* with **Heinz Rehfuss** and the composer, originally made for Decca, as well as a 1952 broadcast with **Henri Honegger** for the Süddeutscher Rundfunk, Stuttgart. **Martin** is the pianist throughout this disc, and just how formidable a player he is emerges in the eight *Préludes* he wrote for Lipatti. An essential acquisition for all admirers of the composer.

(i; ii) Cello Concerto; (i; iii) Ballade for Cello & Piano; (iii) 8 Preludes for Piano

⌐ 🕸 **** BIS CD 1637. (i) Poltéra; (ii) Malmö SO, Ollila-Hannikainen (iii) Stott

Christian Poltéra's superb recorded account of Frank Martin's glorious *Cello Concerto* with the **Malmö Symphony Orchestra** under **Tuomas Ollila-Hannikainen** has an inspirational intensity to compare with the famous du Pré/Barbirolli account of the Elgar *Concerto*. The works share a deep, meditative, expressive feeling, although Martin's concerto also has a poignant valedictory character to suggest personal loss. Then follows the much earlier *Ballade* which is a fantasia-like interplay between cello and piano, in which **Kathryn Stott** proves a natural partner. Martin produced little piano music, yet the *Eight Preludes* are masterly, dallying with Schoenberg's 12-note formula, but never dispensing with tonality. The result is a highly rewarding set of pieces, resourcefully pianistic and richly inventive, compellingly played by Stott. With state-of-the art recording throughout, this disc makes a perfect introduction to Martin's music and cannot be recommended too highly.

(i) Harpsichord Concerto. Passacaglia; (ii) Polyptyque (for violin & 2 string orchestras)

(N) **** MDG 901 1539-6. (i) Rudolf Scheidegger; (ii) Zimmermann, Musikkollegium Winterthur, van Steen

The *Harpsichord Concerto* is played marvellously and it has great breadth; it feels wonderfully natural and unhurried. The rarity here is the *Polyptyque* for violin and two string orchestras, which comes from the penultimate year of Martin's life. It was inspired by a polyptych, a set of very small panels he saw in Siena depicting the Passion story, from Christ's entry into Jerusalem through to his final resurrection, but missing out the crucifixion. The pattern of an active movement followed by a reflective one is followed throughout. It is played with consummate artistry by **Willi Zimmermann** and the **Winterthur** ensemble under **Jac van Steen**. Martin's own transcription for strings of the noble organ *Passacaille* completes an outstanding addition to his discography.

Concerto for 7 Wind Instruments, Percussion & Strings; (i) Erasmi monumentum (for organ and orchestra); Etudes for Strings

*** Chan. 9283. (i) Pearson; LPO, Bamert

Erasmi monumentum is a substantial piece of some 25 minutes. The first movement, *Homo pro se* ('The Independent Man'), alludes to the name given to Erasmus by his contemporaries; the second is *Stulticiae Laus* ('In Praise of Folly'), and the third is *Querela Pacis* ('A Plea for Peace'). The outer movements are pensive and atmospheric; the middle movement is less convincing. **Matthias Bamert's** account of the *Concerto for Seven Wind Instruments* is very assured, relaxed and animated; although thoroughly persuasive, he makes rather heavy weather of the *Etudes*.

Concerto for 7 Wind Instruments, Timpani, Percussion and Strings; (i) Petite symphonie concertante; (ii) 6 Monologues from Jedermann

⊶ (BB) **** Warner Apex 0927 48687-2. (i) Guibentif, Jaccottet, Riuttimann; (ii) Cachemaille; SRO, Jordan

In *Petite symphonie concertante*, **Armin Jordan** has atmosphere and an unhurried sense of pace, and the soloists and orchestra are very well balanced. It is excellently played (with **Christiane Jaccottet**, who took part in the first performance). The account of the *Concerto for Seven Wind Instruments* is also a fine one. The *Six Monologues* from Hofmannsthal's *Everyman*, written at the height of the Second World War, are subtle and profound. Their concentration of mood is well conveyed by **Gilles Cachemaille**, and the orchestral detail is well captured. Eminently recommendable and an inexpensive entry into Martin's world.

The Four Elements; (i) In terra Pax

⊶ **** Chan. 9465. (i) Howarth, Jones, Hill, Williams, Roberts, Brighton Festival Ch.; LPO, Bamert

Les Quatre Eléments, written for Ansermet's 80th birthday in 1967, is a highly imaginative work which exhibits to striking effect Martin's feeling for the orchestra and his subtle mastery of texture. *In terra Pax* is a noble work, and this makes a distinguished addition to the growing Martin discography. The singers are not perhaps quite as impressive as in the deleted Ansermet set, but in every other respect the new recording is superior.

Passacaglia; (i; ii) Maria-Triptychon; (i) Polyptyque

(N) ⊶ **** ECM 173 3930. (i) Cantoreggi; (ii) Banse; German R. PO, Poppen

These three key Martin works make an alternative indispensable triptych in performances as fine as these. The *Passacaglia* was written for organ and orchestrated in 1962, with grippingly powerful results. The pictorial *Polyptyque* for violin and double string orchestra comes from a decade later and is a work of powerful vision and spirituality. The *Maria-Triptychon* for solo soprano, violin and orchestra, combining the *Ave Maria, Magnificat* and *Stabat mater dolorosa*, culminates powerfully with the *Magnificat*. First-class recording makes this another very enticing example of Frank Martin's charismatic genius.

Symphonie concertante (arr. of Petite symphonie concertante for full orchestra); Symphony; Passacaglia

⊶ ⊛ **** Chan. 9312. LPO, Bamert

The *Symphony* is a haunting and at times quite magical piece. The two pianos are effectively used and although, as in the *Petite symphonie concertante*, lip service is paid to the 12-note system, the overall effect is far from serial. Its main companion here is the transcription Martin made for full orchestra of the *Petite symphonie concertante* the year after its first performance. Harp and piano are used for colouristic effects but completely relinquish any hint of soloist ambitions. The *Passacaglia* is Martin's 1962 transcription for full orchestra of his organ piece. Sensitive playing from the **LPO** under **Matthias Bamert** and exemplary Chandos recording.

CHAMBER MUSIC

(i) Ballade for Cello & Piano; (ii) Ballade for Flute & Piano; Piano Quintet; (iii) Violin Sonata; (iv) 4 Sonnets à Cassandre

*** ASV CDDCA 1010. Burnside, Pears-Britten Ens.; (i) Watkins; (ii) K. Jones; (iii) Jackson; (iv) Rearick

This rewarding issue brings us the rarely heard *Piano Quintet*, in which Martin's debts to Ravel and Fauré are clearly evident. The *Violin Sonata* is a three-movement piece, much indebted to the Debussy *G minor Sonata*. All these pieces, save for the *Ballades* for flute and cello, pre-date the period in which Martin found his true idiom – in such works as *Le Vin herbé* and *Der Cornet*. The performances are as alert and sensitive as one could wish, and the recordings are very good too.

Piano Trio on Irish Folktunes

*** Simax PSC 1147. Grieg Trio – BLOCH: *3 Nocturnes*; SHOSTAKOVICH: *Piano Trios* ***

The *Piano Trio* is expertly played here and the interest of the couplings further enhances the value of this issue, arguably the best the **Grieg Trio** has given us. The Simax recording is first rate.

PIANO MUSIC

(i) Music for Piano Duet: *Études pour 2 pianos: Ouverture et foxtrot; Pavane couleur du temps (à 4 mains); 2 pièces faciles (à 2 pianos)*. Piano music: *Au Clair de lune; Étude rythmique; Esquisse; Guitare; Fantaisie sur des rythmes flamenco; 8 Préludes*

*** ABC Classics 476 2601 (2). Adam, (i) with Logan

This enterprising issue brings his complete piano music, including the transcription for two pianos of the well-known *Études pour cordes* that Martin composed for Paul Sacher in the mid-1950s. **Julie Adam** proves a capable and convinced advocate of this music. On the second CD she is admirably partnered by **Christine Logan**. They sensitively convey the Ravel-like delicacy of the *Pavane couleur du temps* and the robust rhythms of the *Études*. The delightful wit of *Les Grenouilles, le Rossignol et la Pluie* makes one regret that, despite his distinction as a pianist, Martin did not write more for the instrument. The recording is eminently truthful and well balanced. A rewarding issue in every respect.

VOCAL MUSIC

Der Cornet

🔶 **** Orfeo S 164881A. Lipovšek, Austrian RSO, Zagrosek

Der Cornet or, to give it its full title, *Die Weise von Liebe und Tod des Cornets Christoph Rilke* ('The Lay Song of the Love and Death of Cornet Christoph Rilke'), is one of Martin's most profound and searching works. Martin's setting for contralto and small chamber orchestra was written at the height of the war and in the immediate wake of *Le Vin herbé*, his oratorio on the Tristan legend. The shadowy, half-real atmosphere often reminds one of the world of *Pelléas*; and the restrained, pale colourings provide an effective backcloth to the vivid and poignant outbursts which mark some of the settings. The performance by **Marjana Lipovšek** is remarkable. Sensitive orchestral playing and faithfully balanced, well-recorded sound. This music casts a powerful spell and is strongly atmospheric.

Golgotha (oratorio; complete)

🔶 **** Cascavelle VEL 3004. Locher, Graf, Dami, Fink, Brodard, Baghdassarian, Antoniotti, Ens. Voc. de Lausanne & Sinf., Corboz

(i) Golgotha; (ii) Mass for Double Choir

🅱🅱 *** Warner Apex (ADD/DDD) 2564 64398-2 (2). (i) Staempfli, De Montmollin, Tappy, Mollet, Huttenlocher, Faller Ch. & SO, Faller; (ii) Choeur de Chambre du Midi, Martin

The Cascavelle performance is magnificent, admirably paced

by **Michel Corboz**, and with some fine solo singing. **Elisabeth Graf** in the *Méditation* that opens the second half sings with much feeling though it is almost invidious to single out any of the fine soloists. The recording, made in Lausanne Cathedral in 1994, has greater presence and depth than its Erato predecessor, and there is plenty of space around the aural image. Full documentation is provided.

The eloquence, power and dignity of this music are also well conveyed by the conviction of **Faller's** performance, and this makes a good budget alternative to the Corboz version. The *Mass* is a digital recording, and the singing of the **Choeur de Chambre du Midi** under **Denis Martin** is very good indeed. While the Cascavelle version of *Golgotha* is undoubtedly superior, this Apex coupling remains very good value, with the text and translation of *Golgotha* available on www.warnerclassics.com/sungtexts.php.

Mass for Double Choir; Passacaille for Organ

🔶 💿 **** Hyp. CDA 67017. Westminster Cathedral Ch., O'Donnell – PIZZETTI: *Messa di requiem; De profundis* 💿 ****

The *Mass for Double Choir* is one of Martin's purest and most sublime utterances. The latest version from the **Westminster Cathedral Choir** under **James O'Donnell** is the most outstanding. The boys produce marvellously focused tone of great purity and expressive power, and the tonal blend that O'Donnell achieves throughout is little short of miraculous. This won *Gramophone* magazine's 'Record of the Year' award in 1998, and deservedly so. As a fill-up O'Donnell offers the *Passacaille* for organ, together with two magnificent Pizzetti works.

6 Monologues from 'Jedermann' (Everyman)

Ⓜ *** Virgin 3 63310-2. van Dam, Lyon Nat. Op. O, Nagano – IBERT: *4 Chansons de Don Quichotte*; POULENC: *Le Bal masqué*; RAVEL: *Don Quichotte à Dulcinée* ***

(i) 6 Monologues from Everyman; (ii) Maria Triptychon; (i) The Tempest (3 excerpts)

*** Chan. 9411. (i) Wilson-Johnson; (ii) Russell; LPO, Bamert

Kent Nagano directs powerfully sustained accompaniments for what is perhaps the most enterprising item in this imaginatively chosen quartet of French song groupings, all written around the third decade of the 20th century. **Van Dam's** singing, like Nagano's orchestral backcloth, is impressively felt, and his darkness of colour in the penultimate monologue prepares the way movingly for the ardently sombre closing prayer. A full text and translation is provided, and this collection can be strongly recommended.

Chandos couples the excerpts from *The Tempest* with the *Everyman Monologues*; **David Wilson-Johnson** sings with intense – but not excessive – dramatic feeling and total commitment and conviction. The extra rarity on this disc is the *Maria Triptychon*. **Linda Russell** and the violinist **Duncan Riddell** give a totally dedicated account of it. **Bamert** and the **LPO** generate a keen sense of atmosphere, and the Chandos recording is every bit as good as the other issues in this splendid series.

Requiem

🎵 **** Jecklin-Disco (ADD) JD 631-2. Speiser, Bollen, Tappy, Lagger, Lausanne Women's Ch., Union Ch., SRO, composer

This is arguably the most beautiful *Requiem* to have been written since Fauré's and, were the public to have ready access to it, would be as popular. The recording, made at a public performance that the (then 83-year-old) composer conducted in Lausanne Cathedral, is very special. The analogue recording is not in the demonstration class, but this music and performance must have three stars.

Le Vin herbé (oratorio)

🎵 **** HM HMC 901035-2. Piau, Davislim, Böhnert, RIAS Chamber Ch., Scharoun Ens., Reuss

Daniel Reuss has shown his sympathies with the Swiss master in earlier recordings. His singers and instrumentalists show themselves to be both completely attuned to this exalted score and sensitive to its luminous textures and powerful sense of mystery. The work casts a strong spell; its colours are delicate in shade, pastel and half-lit. Its debt to Debussy's *Pelléas* is obvious enough in its strong atmosphere and dramatic understatement as well as in its sensitivity to language, yet its world is quite unlike anything else. The choir has perfect intonation and tonal blend. Expertly balanced recording, too. In all, a wonderful issue.

MARTINI, Johannes
(c. 1440–97/8)

Ave maris stella; Magnificat terti toni; O beate Sebastiane; Salve regina

*** Gaudeamus CDGAU 171. Clerks' Group, Wickham –
    OBRECHT: *Laudes Christo; Missa Malheur me bat* ***

Though Martini cannot compare with Obrecht in imagination, the motets recorded here have a simple beauty, made the more compelling by the dedicated performances of the **Clerks' Group**, atmospherically recorded.

MARTINŮ, Bohuslav (1890–1959)

The Amazing Flight (Podivuhodný Let); On tourne! (Natáči se!); La Revue de cuisine (Kuchynska Revue)

🎵 *** Sup. SU 3749-2. Czech PO, Hogwood

La Revue de cuisine stands up rather well against *La Création du monde* or any other of Milhaud's jazz-inspired pieces, and the present performance is second to none. The **Czech Philharmonic** play every note with great zest. *Natáči se!* is quite irresistible in its freshness and innocence, and its seventh movement, once played, is difficult if not impossible to get out of one's head. And what harmonic subtlety there is elsewhere in this wonderfully inventive and imaginative score. This is music which infectiously communicates its love of life and high spirits – and leaves you feeling better! Very good and well-detailed recorded sound.

La Bagarre; Half-Time; Intermezzo; The Rock; Thunderbolt

*** Sup. (ADD) 001669. Brno State O, Vronsky

La Bagarre and *Half-Time* are early evocations, the latter a Honeggerian depiction of a roisterous half-time at a football match that musically doesn't amount to a great deal. The three later works are much more interesting – *Intermezzo* is linked to the *Fourth Symphony* – and the collection as a whole will be of great interest to Martinů addicts, if perhaps not essential for other collectors. All the performances are alive and full of character, and the recording is vividly immediate.

(i) Concertino in C min. for Cello, Wind Instruments & Piano; (ii) Harpsichord Concerto; (iii) Oboe Concerto

🎵 **** Sup. 11 0107-2 031. (i) Večtomov, Topinka, members of Czech PO; (ii) Růžičková, Rehák; (iii) Krejči; (ii; iii) Czech Philharmonic Chamber O; (i, iii) Skvor; (ii) Neumann

Zuzana Růžičková has made a number of recordings of the *Harpsichord Concerto* but this is her most successful. The sound is agreeably spacious, though the balance is synthetic and the piano has equal prominence with the solo harpsichord. However, the playing is spirited and sympathetic; and the *Oboe Concerto* is heard to excellent advantage too, with very good playing and a well-laid-out sound-picture. The early *Concertino for Cello with Piano, Wind and Percussion* is more than acceptably played and recorded.

Cello Concertos 1–2; Concertino in C min. for Cello, Wind Instruments, Piano & Percussion

*** Chan. 9015. Wallfisch, Czech PO, Bělohlávek

Cello Concerto 1 was composed in 1930 but has been revised twice. *Cello Concerto 2* is the bigger of the two. It opens with a very characteristic and infectiously memorable B flat tune, and there is much of the luminous orchestral writing one associates with the *Fourth* and *Fifth Symphonies*. It is a warm-hearted, lyrical score with a Dvořák-like radiance.

(i) Concerto da camera (for violin & orchestra with piano & percussion), H285; Concerto for violin, piano & orchestra, H342; Czech Rhapsody, H307A (arr. for violin & orchestra by Jirí Temí)

*** Hyp. CDA67672. Matoušek, Czech PO, Hogwood; (i) with Košárek

The *Concerto da camera* is inventive and radiates vitality, but it is the later *Concerto for Violin, Piano and Orchestra* which is the more captivating. It strides out in the manner of the celebrated pre-war *Double Concerto* and maintains a striking momentum. The *Czech Rhapsody* is a slighter piece, dedicated to Kreisler, though he never played it.

Concerto for Double String Orchestra, Piano & Timpani; Symphony 1

🎵 **** Chan. 8950. Czech PO, Bělohlávek

The *Double Concerto* is one of the most powerful works of the present century, and its intensity is well conveyed in

Bělohlávek's vital, deeply felt performance. His dedicated and imaginative account of the *First Symphony* is very good indeed. Bělohlávek is totally inside this music, and the recording, made in the agreeably resonant Spanish Hall of Prague Castle, is very natural. Strongly recommended for both works.

(i) *Double Concerto for Flute, Violin & Orchestra, H252; (ii) Duo concertante for two violins & orchestra, H264; (iii) Double Violin Concerto in D, H329*

*** Hyp. CDA67671. Matoušek, with (i) Thomsen; (ii) Pasquier, (iii) Koh; Czech PO, Hogwood

The delightful *Concerto for Flute, Violin and Orchestra* must be numbered among the most inventive and rewarding of Martinů's concerto grosso conceptions. Nor is the *Duo concertante*, composed the following year, less inventive. The *D major Concerto* is vintage Martinů and well worth having on disc. Strongly recommendable performances and good, if reverberant, sound.

Concerto grosso; Overture for Orchestra; The Parables; Rhapsody for Large Orchestra; Sinfonia concertante for 2 Orchestras

*** Sup. SU 3743-2. Czech PO, Bělohlávek

The set of *Parables* is among the composer's last works and is vintage Martinů. The *Rhapsody* of 1928 was written for Koussevitzky, but the *Sinfonia concertante* and the *Concerto grosso* are both from the 1930s and are good examples of Martinů's neo-baroque style. The *Overture* is something of a rarity, and this is the only recording currently available. The resonant acoustic of the Dvořák Hall of the Rudolfinum, Prague, slightly muddies detail, but this will not put off admirers of the composer, for the performances by the **Czech Philharmonic** under **Jiří Bělohlávek** are exhilarating and idiomatic. The artwork (including the CD label itself) has a childlike, paintbox quality that is highly attractive.

Oboe Concerto

⊶ *** Nim. NI 5330. Anderson, Philh. O, Wright – FRANÇAIX: *L'Horloge de flore*; R. STRAUSS: *Concerto* ***

Ⓝ Ⓜ ** Sup. (ADD) SU 3955. Hanták, Brno PO, Turnovsky (with MOZART: *Oboe Concerto*) – R. STRAUSS: *Oboe Concerto* **

Martinů's *Oboe Concerto* is a splendid addition to the modern repertory for the oboe. While the writing is not as florid as that in the coupled Richard Strauss *Concerto*, it still needs considerable flexibility of technique on the part of the soloist if the work's essential lyricism is to flow through the decoration. The basic quality of the music is high-spirited and confident. The soloist here, **František Hanták**, meets the music's needs well, but the recording is somewhat close and the Nimbus collection is far preferable.

The account by **John Anderson**, principal of the Philharmonia, is outstanding in every way, with the *Andante* quite ravishing when the soloist's timbre is so rich. The recording is first class and the couplings particularly attractive.

(i) *Piano Concertos 2, 3 & 4 (Incantation). Piano music: Etudes and Polkas; Fantasy and Toccata; Julietta, Act II: Moderato; Les Ritournelles; Piano Sonata 1*

⊶ ❋ Ⓜ **** RCA 2 CD 74321 88682-2 (2). Firkušný; (i) with Czech PO, Pešek

Rudolf Firkušný premièred all three *Concertos* here and was the dedicatee of 3; and his recordings are very special. The finest of them is 4 (*Incantation*), which here receives a performance that is unlikely to be surpassed. Its exotic colourings and luminous, other-worldly landscape, with its bird cries and extraordinary textures, have never been heard to better advantage. It is a work of strong atmosphere and mystery. Firkušný is its ideal advocate. In the *Fourth Concerto* nothing is hurried and every phrase is allowed to breathe – and the same goes for its two companions. The 1988 recording is very good indeed.

Firkušný also gave the first performances of many of these solo piano pieces and his playing could not be more delicate in its keyboard colouring, more authoritative or refined. The recording is not made in a large enough acoustic but is otherwise truthful, and this set is not to be missed, even though the presentation and documentation leave much to be desired.

(i) *Piano Concerto 3; (ii) Bouquet of Flowers*

Ⓜ *** Sup. stereo/mono SU 3672-2 901. (i) Páleníček; (ii) Domanínská, Cervená, Havlák, Mráz, Prague Philharmonic Ch., Kühn Children's Ch.; Czech PO, Ančerl

Martinů's highly eclectic *Third Piano Concerto* displays an infectious and lively facility, but (the slow movement especially) is rather too long for its content. The 1961 stereo recording has transferred well to CD. But what makes this disc special is the inclusion of the exuberant *Bouquet of Flowers* (1937). The text is taken entirely from Czech poetry, the music echoes the wild speech-rhythms, and the orchestration (with prominent parts for two pianos) is most colourful. The performance here is magnificent. No apologies whatsoever need to be made for a 1955 mono recording which is very good indeed: atmospheric, yet with incisive choral tone.

(i) *Piano Concerto 4 (Incantations); (ii) Symphony 4; Tre Ricercari*

ⒷⒷ *** Warner Apex 0927 49822-2. (i) Páleníček, Brno State PO, Pinkas; (ii) Czech PO, Turnovsky

The *Fourth Piano Concerto*, written in the mid-1950s for Firkušný, is a highly imaginative and original score, presented most persuasively here. The *Fourth Symphony* dates from 1945 and is written in a readily accessible style, and throughout the work one feels a strong thematic unity. The *Three Ricercari* are less substantial but attractive enough; the outer movements rattle along with characteristic toccata-like brilliance, the piano strongly featured in the rhythmically beguiling finale. The performances of both works, but especially the symphony, are first rate and the recording, one of Supraphon's best, has transferred vividly to CD with only slight loss of body.

Rhapsody-Concerto for Viola & Orchestra; Suite concertante for Violin & Orchestra (2 versions)

(N) *** Hyp. CDA 67673. Matoušek, Czech PO, Hogwood

Matoušek, changing from his usual violin to viola, gives a first-class account of the *Rhapsody-Concerto*, one of the composer's most rewarding and characteristic scores, and, with **Hogwood** and the **Czech Philharmonic** accompanying, this can be recommended alongside Suk. But the couplings make the Hyperion disc even more enticing: two almost completely different versions of the *Suite concertante* (commissioned by Dushkin) with only the first movement of each sharing much music in common. Both versions are rewarding in different ways, and to have them together, so well played and recorded by a soloist who was closely involved with both of them, is bounty indeed.

Violin Concertos 1 & 2

(N) *** Hyp. CDA 67674. Matoušek, Czech PO, Hogwood

Violin Concertos 1–2; Rhapsody-Concerto for Viola & Orchestra

(M) **(*) Sup. (ADD) 11 1969-2 Suk, Czech PO, Neumann

The *First Concerto* comes from 1931 and was intended for Samuel Dushkin. However, the performance never came off. The *Second* was written for Mischa Elman in 1943 and was first given in Boston under Koussevitzky. They are both delightful works and **Bohuslav Matoušek** plays them with much style and virtuosity. As in earlier issues in the series, **Christopher Hogwood** reveals a total sympathy with the composer's sensibility. By far the most poignant and eloquent of these works is the *Rhapsody-Concerto* for viola and orchestra, in which **Suk** is also the soloist and which dates from the period of the *Fantaisies symphoniques*. Suk is a masterly player, of course, and the **Czech Philharmonic** play with obvious pleasure. The recordings are analogue and inner detail is not quite as sharply focused as in the very best discs from the 1970s.

Violin Concerto 1; Suite concertante for Violin and Orchestra (2nd version; 1945)

**(*) Sup. SU 3653-2-031. Matoušek, Czech PO, Hogwood

The *Suite concertante* is characteristic Martinů, neoclassical, fresh and vital. Its second movement is one of his most inspired and radiant pieces, and is as luminous as Dvořák. The third movement, too, is infectiously high-spirited. The disc runs to just under 48 minutes, so room could have been found for the *Second Violin Concerto*. Characterful performances from **Bohuslav Matoušek** and the **Czech Philharmonic**, and **Christopher Hogwood** has shown himself a committed advocate of this composer. The recorded sound is a little glassy and reverberant, in the Supraphon manner, but very serviceable.

(i) Violin Concerto 2; (ii) Toccata e due Canzoni. Serenade 2

(N) *** HM HMC 90 1951. (i) Faust; (ii) Tiberghien; Prague Philh., Bělohlávek

The *Second Violin Concerto* is an appealing and inventive score of much greater substance than its predecessor from the 1930s, and it finds Martinů very much in *concerto grosso* mode. It is splendidly played by **Isabelle Faust**, idiomatically compelling, with fine support from **Bělohlávek**. The *Toccata e due Canzoni* is also a kind of *concerto grosso*, with an obbligato piano part (played here by Cedric Tiberghien). The *Second Serenade* (for strings) is lightweight and folksy and the **Prague Philharmonia** have its full measure. Well worth investigating.

Rhapsody-Concerto for Viola and Orchestra

*** Call. CAL 9364. Bukac, Czech RSO, Válek – BARTÓK: *Viola Concerto*; HINDEMITH: *Trauermusik* ***

The *Rhapsody-Concerto* was written for the violist of the Cleveland Orchestra and was premièred under Szell in 1953. It is one of Martinů's most rewarding pieces, written in the vintage years which saw the creation of the *Fantaisies symphoniques* and the *Sixth Symphony*. Eloquent playing from all concerned, and fine recording.

Spalíček (ballet; complete); Dandelion (Romance); 5 Duets on Moravian Folksongs

*** Sup. 11 0752-2 (2). Soloists, Kantilena Children's Ch., Kühn Mixed Ch., Brno State PO, Jílek

The original of Martinů's engaging ballet *Spalíček* dates from 1931–2. The dances, familiar from the suites, are interspersed with vocal episodes, both solo and choral. For the most part this music is quite captivating, particularly given the charm of this performance. Two shorter works complete the set: *Dandelion Romance* for mixed chorus and soprano, and *Five Duets on Moravian Folksong Texts* for female voices, violin and piano, both of which come from his last years. All in all, a delightful addition to the Martinů discography.

Symphonies 1–6

(M) **** BIS CD 1371/2. Bamberg SO, N. Järvi

Martinů always draws a highly individual sound from his orchestra. On hearing the *First Symphony*, Virgil Thomson wrote, 'the shining sounds of it sing as well as shine', and there is no doubt this music is luminous and life-loving. The BIS recording is in the demonstration class yet sounds completely natural, and the performances under **Neeme Järvi** are totally persuasive and have a spontaneous feel for the music's pulse. BIS have Järvi's set of the six *Symphonies* in a box, with the three CDs offered for the price of two, making a clear first choice for modern recordings of this repertoire.

Symphony 2

**** Telarc CD 80616. Cincinnati SO, Paavo Järvi – DVOŘÁK: *Symphony 9* ***

Like Dvořák's *New World Symphony*, Martinů's *Second* was written when the composer was in the United States, making it an apt if unusual coupling for that much-recorded work. The refinement and clarity of the Telarc recording enhance an outstanding performance, with **Paavo Järvi** even outshining his father's excellent version of this same work, thanks to the excellence of the **Cincinnati orchestra's** playing. The Czech flavour in all four movements is enhanced by the genial warmth of phrasing and the rhythmic lift.

Symphony 4; Memorial to Lidice; (i) Field Mass

⌐ⁿ *** Chan. 9138. (i) Kusjner, Czech Ph. Ch.; Czech PO, Bělohlávek

There is a radiance about this work that is quite special, and **Bělohlávek's** account of it is quite the best that has appeared in recent years. The *Memorial to Lidice*, composed in response to a Nazi massacre, is a powerful and haunting piece, and so is the *Field Mass*, which receives its best performance until now – by far.

Symphonies 5; 6; Memorial to Lidice

Ⓜ (***) Sup. mono SU 3694-2. Czech PO, Ančerl

Ančerl's are classic accounts from the era of mono LP. The *Fifth* is the work's première recording, made in 1955, while the *Sixth* was recorded in the following year. The *Memorial to Lidice* (1943), was recorded in 1957. These performances have an authenticity of feeling that still remains special, even though there are many fine new versions. The sound is better than ever.

Symphony 6 (Fantaisies symphoniques)

⌐ⁿ *** Chan. 8897. Czech PO, Bělohlávek – JANÁČEK: *Sinfonietta*; SUK: *Scherzo* ***

This Chandos version of 6 has great dramatic strength and is fully characterized; undoubtedly these players believe in every note. It is an outstanding performance that does full justice to the composer's extraordinarily imaginative vision and is very well recorded.

CHAMBER MUSIC

Cello Sonatas 1 (1939); 2 (1942); 3 (1952)

ⒷⒷ *** Hyp. Helios CDH 55185. Isserlis, Evans

Martinů's three *Cello Sonatas* span the period 1939–52 and are full of rewarding musical invention. **Steven Isserlis** and **Peter Evans** offer very good playing and very acceptable recording, and this can be strongly recommended, especially at Helios price.

Cello Sonata 1; Variations on a Theme of Rossini; Variations on a Slovak Theme

*** Simax PSC 1146. Birkeland, Gimse – KABALEVSKY: *Cello Sonata 2* ***

Diverting though they are, the two sets of *Variations* are not top-drawer Martinů even if they do sound at their freshest and most charming in the hands of this Norwegian partnership. The powerful *Cello Sonata 1*, however, is another matter and **Oystein Birkeland** and **Håvard Gimse** play it wonderfully, with splendid rhythmic vitality, lyrical fervour and abundant imagination. The recorded sound is exceptionally truthful and lifelike, sonorous and marvellously balanced. A most rewarding issue in every way.

(i) Madrigal Sonata for Flute, Violin & Piano; (ii) 5 Madrigal Stanzas for Violin & Piano; (i) Promenades for Flute, Violin & Harpsichord; (iii) Scherzo for Flute & Piano; Sonata for Flute & Piano; (i) Sonata for Flute, Violin & Piano

⌐ⁿ **** Fleurs de Lys FL 2 3031. (i–ii) Dubeau; (i–iii) Hamelin; (i; iii) Marion

The performances are as fresh and exhilarating as the music itself, delightfully inventive and vital. All three artists play with imagination and virtuosity, and the recording has exemplary clarity and presence. The jazz-like Scherzo from the late 1920s comes off particularly well.

4 Madrigals for Oboe, Clarinet & Bassoon; 3 Madrigals for Violin & Viola; Madrigal Sonata for Piano, Flute & Violin; 5 Madrigal Stanzas for Violin & Piano

*** Hyp. CDA 66133. Dartington Ens.

These delightful pieces exhibit all the intelligence and fertility of invention we associate with Martinů's music. The playing of the **Dartington Ensemble** is accomplished and expert, and the recording, though resonant, is faithful.

Nonet; Trio in F for Flute, Cello & Piano; La Revue de cuisine

**** Hyp. (ADD) CDA 66084. Dartington Ens.

Only one of these pieces is otherwise available on CD and all of them receive first-class performances and superb recording. The sound has space, warmth, perspective and definition. An indispensable issue for lovers of Martinů's music.

Oboe Quartet (for oboe, violin, cello & piano); Piano Quartet; String Quintet; Viola Sonata

ⒷⒷ *** Naxos 8.553916. Artists of 1994 Australian Festival of Chamber Music

The best thing here is the captivating *Oboe Quartet*, which is quite a discovery. Like the fine *Viola Sonata* and the early *String Quintet*, whose slow movement is crossed by the shadow of Martinů's master, Roussel, its appearance at budget price is doubly welcome in that the performances are lively and spirited and the recording eminently natural.

Piano Quintets 1 & 2; Sonata for Two Violins & Piano

ⒷⒷ *** Naxos 8.557861. Kosárek, Martinů Qt

The *First Quintet* and the *Sonata for Two Violins and Piano* both come from the early 1930s, when Martinů was living in Paris, and they are slight pieces. The weightiest and most substantial work is the *Second Quintet*, composed in 1944 in America. Very fine playing from these artists, and good recorded sound.

Piano Quintet 2

⌐ⁿ **** ASV CDDCA 889. Frankl, Lindsay Qt – DVOŘÁK: *Piano Quintet* ***

Martinů's *Second Piano Quintet* is a remarkably successful

piece, characteristically original in its content and rhythmic style. The **Lindsays** with **Peter Frankl** have its full measure. The recording is lively and present, with the piano well integrated, although there is just a touch of thinness on the strings. An outstanding coupling.

Piano Trio 2 in D min.

*** Sup. SU 3927-2. Smetana Trio – DVOŘÁK: *Piano Trio in B flat*; FIBICH: *Piano Trio* ***

The Martinů *Trio* dates from the composer's last years after the Second World War, when his style had mellowed and become more traditional once more. Again the layout is fast–slow–fast, urgently purposeful in the first movement and with a *moto perpetuo* main theme in the finale. The central slow movement has some gritty writing in the middle, with one weird, hushed passage in which the violin plays in an ethereal *pianissimo*. But overall this is a very stimulating work and the performance and recording cannot be faulted.

String Quartets 1–7

Ⓜ **(*) Sup. (ADD) SU3917-2 (3). Panocha Qt

The *First* of the quartets is both the longest and the most derivative; it is heavily indebted to the world of Debussy and Ravel. The *Third* is by far the shortest (it takes barely 12 minutes) and has the nervous energy and rhythmic vitality characteristic of the mature composer. The *Fourth* and *Fifth* are close to the *Double Concerto for Two String Orchestras, Piano and Timpani*. The *Fifth* is the darkest of the quartets and in its emotional intensity is close in spirit to Janáček's *Intimate Letters*. The *Sixth* – and in particular its first movement – is a powerful and disturbing piece, and there is a sense of scale and a vision that raise it above its immediate successor. The **Panocha** set is eminently recommendable, even though the recordings are a bit two-dimensional.

String Quartets 1–2; Tri jezdci (Three Horsemen)

ⒷⒷ **(*) Naxos 553782. Martinů Qt

The *First Quartet* lasts almost 40 minutes and is known as the 'French' (the nickname was Martinů's own) and what it lacks in individuality it makes up for in craftsmanship. The *Second Quartet* (1925) is more concentrated and more complex, and its greater density of incident reflects the influence of Roussel, with whom Martinů was studying. The fill-up is a remarkably accomplished first recording of *Tri jezdci*, which was written when the composer was twelve. The **Martinů Quartet** play with spirit and the recording is decent: fresh and lifelike without being outstanding.

String Quartets 3, 4 & 5

⊶ *** BIS CD 1389. Emperor Qt

Using new, critically revised scores, the **Emperor String Quartet** present their refreshing interpretations of three works that give a fascinating picture of an exciting era in 20th-century music. Fine recording too.

String Quartets 4–5; 7 (Concerto da camera)

ⒷⒷ *** Naxos 8.553784. Martinů Qt

The *Fourth* and *Fifth Quartets* come from the period 1937–8.

The *Seventh*, subtitled *Concerto da camera*, is less concentrated in feeling. It is finely crafted and very much in Martinů's neoclassical vein, if less memorable and spontaneous. Anyway, they are all well played and recorded and can be confidently recommended.

String Sextet; 3 Madrigals for violin & viola

Ⓝ *** Hyp. CDH 55321. Raphael Ens. – SCHULHOFF: *String Sextet* ***

The *Sextet* for two each of violins, violas and cellos was for many years, during the 1950s and '60s, Martinů's calling card in the concert hall but is now rather a rarity. It comes from 1932 and was written rather quickly – in the course of one week. It is a strikingly assured piece in which the musical argument unfolds with a natural sense of organic growth. Rather to his surprise, it earned Martinů the Elizabeth Sprague Coolidge Medal, winning first prize out of 145 entries. The *Madrigals* are post-war, very typical Martinů, and are despatched with great virtuosity. The **Raphael Ensemble** give a masterly account of it, and the 1991 recording is truthful and lifelike.

String Trio 2

*** Hyp. CDA 67429. Leopold String Trio – DOHNÁNYI: *Serenade in C*; SCHOENBERG: *Trio* ***

Martinů's *Second String Trio* comes from his Paris years, 1934 in fact, by which time he had made a name for himself in the musical world. Much of the writing is in the composer's neoclassical manner, and the **Leopold String Trio** make a strong case for the piece. Exemplary recorded sound.

Violin Sonata 1, H182; Sonatas in C, H120; D min., H152; Concerto, H13; Elegy, H3; Impromptu, H166; 5 Short pieces, H184

⊶ Ⓜ *** Sup. SU 3410-2 (2). Matoušek, Adamec

Violin Sonatas 2, H308; 3, H303; Sonatina in G, H262; 7 Arabesques, H201A; Arietta, H188A; Czech Rhapsody, H307; Intermezzo, H261; 5 Madrigal Stanzas, H297; Rhythmic Etudes, H202

⊶ Ⓜ *** Sup. SU 3412-2 (2). Matoušek, Adamec

Martinů's output for violin and piano is fairly extensive. The two handsomely produced and well-recorded double-CD sets cover his whole output, through to his mid-fifties and *Sonata 3* (1944) and the *Czech Rhapsody* written for Kreisler (1945). The *Third Sonata* in particular is very impressive. **Bohuslav Matoušek** and **Petr Adamec** are completely inside the idiom, having played Martinů virtually from the cradle.

Violin Sonata 3 in G, Op. 100

*** Praga PRD 250 153. Remeš, Kayahara – DVOŘÁK: *Sonatina*; JANÁČEK, SMETANA: *Violin Sonatas* ***

Václav Remeš and **Sachito Kayahara** combine to give a superb account of Martinů's passionate *Third Sonata*, fiery and intense, yet relaxing warmly for the composer's moments of gentler lyricism: the opening of the *Finale* has a lovely rapt serenity.

Sonata for 2 Violins & Piano

**(*) Hyp. CDA 66473. Osostowicz, Kovacic, Tomes –
MILHAUD: *Violin Duo*, etc. **(*); PROKOFIEV: *Violin
Sonata* ***

Martinů's *Sonata for Two Violins and Piano* finds him full of invention and vitality. **Krysia Osostowicz, Ernst Kovacic** and **Susan Tomes** play it with all the finesse and sensitivity you could wish for, and they are excellently recorded. The disc would be even more recommendable if it had a longer playing time than 46 minutes.

PIANO MUSIC

Les bouquinistes du Quai Malaquais; Butterflies and Birds of Paradise; The Fifth Day of the Fifth Moon; Film en miniature; Puppets; Spring in the Garden

(BB) *** Naxos 8.557918. Koukl

This is part of a new Naxos survey of the composer's 'complete piano music'. Much of it is early, but no one could say that the three sets of *Puppets* (written between 1912 and 1924) are not both engaging and original; and the same could be said of the suite for children, *Spring in the Garden* (1920). The highlights of the programme, however, are *Butterflies and Birds of Paradise*, written in the same year, and *Les bouquinistes* (booksellers) *du Quai Malaquais*. **Giorgio Koukl** might at times have produced a lighter touch, but he is very well recorded and this looks to be an indispensable new series. Three other volumes in the Naxos survey are now available (8.557914; 8.557919 and 8.570215) which can also be recommended to the composer's admirers.

Dumka; 3 Esquisses; Fantaisie et Toccata; Fenêtre sur le jardin; Sonata 1

*** Tudor 7054. Kaspar

Études and Polkas (Books 1–3); Borová (7 Czech Dances); Butterflies and Birds of Paradise

*** Tudor 7125. Kaspar

Paul Kaspar is a Czech pianist, born in Ostrava, who is completely inside the idiom and plays with persuasiveness and exuberance throughout. Martinů's piano music always impresses with its freshness, energy, and abundant intelligence. Kaspar serves it with dedication, and in turn he is well served by the Bavarian recording team; if the balance is a shade close, the present set still serves us well. It is far preferable to the selection recorded by **Eleonora Bekova** (on Chandos 9655), whose playing is serviceable without being really distinguished.

VOCAL MUSIC

The Epic of Gilgamesh (oratorio)

*** Marco Polo 8.223316. Depoltová, Margita, Kusnjer, Vele, Karpílšek, Slovak Philh. Ch. & O, Košler

*** Sup. SU 3918-2. Machotková, Zahradníček, Zítek, Průša, Brousek, Czech Philh. Ch., Prague SO, Bělohlávek

The Epic of Gilgamesh comes from Martinů's last years and is arguably his masterpiece. It evokes a remote and distant world, full of colour and mystery. Gilgamesh is the oldest poem known to mankind. The work abounds with invention of the highest quality and of consistently sustained inspiration. The Marco Polo performance is committed and sympathetic and the recording very natural in its balance.

Bělohlávek's version can hold its own artistically with the excellent Marco Polo account. It does not displace it but can certainly be recommended alongside it and now has a price advantage.

OPERA

Ariane (complete; in French)

*** Sup. SU 3524-2 6312. Lindsley, Phillips, Doležal, Burun, Novák (bass), Czech PO & Ch., Neumann

As with his earlier operatic masterpiece, *Julietta*, Martinů based his one-act opera *Ariane* on a play, *Le Voyage de Thésée*, by his friend Georges Neveux. In making his adaptation Martinů treats it as baroque monody, interspersed with three sinfonias, three self-contained dramatic sequences and a closing aria. The pastiche elements have great lightness of touch; it seems that the bravura of Ariane herself, sung excellently by the American soprano **Celina Lindsley**, was inspired by Callas. **Richard Novák's** vibrato may be too wide for some, but generally speaking the performance is sung well (in French), and **Václav Neumann** gets alert and sensitive playing from the **Czech Philharmonic**. The recording (from 1987) is eminently serviceable. The opera has both freshness and charm and devotees of Martinů need not hesitate.

The Greek Passion (DVD version)

(*) Sup. **DVD SU 7014-9. Mitchinson, Field, Tomlinson, Savory, Kühn Children's Ch., Czech PO Ch., Brno PO, Mackerras

With a few small cuts, this derives from a CD recording of the complete work made in Brno in 1981. It tells in an innocent, direct way of a village where a Passion play is to be presented; the individuals – tragically, as it proves – take on qualities of the New Testament figures they represent. **Mackerras** made an ideal advocate and the recording was excellent. Now it has been turned into a filmed video by Czech TV, set around a real village and church. The Czech cast act out the story, miming to the English words (often not very closely) and there is no doubt that the result is both musically and dramatically compelling. The sound is still excellent, so this undoubtedly adds an extra dimension to the music.

Julietta (complete)

🎧 *** Sup. (ADD) 3626-2 612 (2). Tauberová, Zídek, Zlesák, Otava, Bednář, Mixová, Jedenáctík, Procházková, Hanzalíková, Soukupová, Jindrák, Veverka, Svehla, Zlesák, Lemariová, Berman, Prague Nat. Theatre Ch. & O, Krombholc

Described by the composer as a Dreambook, *Julietta* was

given first in Prague in March 1938. This vintage Supraphon recording, made in 1964, captures that surreal quality vividly, for the ear is mesmerized from the very start, when the howling of a high bassoon introduces the astonishingly original prelude. The voices as well as the orchestra are then presented with a bright immediacy which reinforces the power and incisiveness of **Krombholc's** performance. The sharpness of focus adds to the atmospheric intensity, as when in the first Act The Man in the Window plays his accordion. **Ivo Zídek** gives a vivid portrait of the central character, Michel, perplexed by his dream-like search, and there is no weak link in the rest of the cast. The three CDs of the 1993 transfer are now reduced to two (the break coming at scene V of Act II) and the sound is brighter and more firmly focused, with a very marginal loss of the gentler sonority that distinguished the LP set. Informative notes and libretto come with multiple translations.

Les Larmes du couteau; The Voice of the Forest

*** Sup. SU 3386-3 631. Jonášová, Smidová, Janál, Prague Philharmonia, Bělohlávek

The two one-Act operas recorded here are both short, roughly half an hour each. With the Dadaist Les Larmes du couteau (or The Knife's Tears) we are close to the world of L'Histoire du soldat, Les Six and Kurt Weill. It is entertaining if insubstantial and diverts the listener. Good soloists and recording, with the musical and speech elements well balanced. The Voice of the Forest offers a more familiar Martinů. It is far more individual in style and, like the ballet Špalíček, draws on Czech folklore and melody. In it, Martinů's invention is unfailingly fresh and although one can see why it has never made waves it has much to offer. The set is packaged as one disc in a box for two, so as to accommodate the copious and handsomely produced documentation.

MARTUCCI, Giuseppe
(1856–1909)

Symphony 1 in D min., Op. 75; Andante, Op. 69/2 (arr. cello and orchestra); Giga, Op. 61/3; Canzonetta, Op. 65/2; Notturno, Op. 70/1 (all arr. For orchestra)

(N) (BB) *** Naxos 8.570929. Roma SO, La Vecchia

Symphony 2 in F, Op. 81; (i) Theme & Variations for Piano & Orchestra, Op. 58. Gavotta, Op. 55/2; Tarantella, Op. 44/6

(N) (BB) *** Naxos 8.570930. Roma SO, La Vecchia, (i) with Lya De Barberiis

Martucci was a contemporary of Elgar and gained distinction both as a pianist (appearing in London, Paris and other European centres) and a conductor. In his later years he was a great champion of Wagner and gave the first Italian performance of Götterdämmerung. His own music is finely wrought and, though conservative in outlook, its fine craftsmanship and quiet individuality exert a certain spell. The **Roma Symphony Orchestra** under **La Vecchia**

obviously believe in this music and serve it well. Well worth investigating.

MASCAGNI, Pietro (1863–1945)

L'amico Fritz (complete)

🎵–(M) *** EMI 5 67376-2 (2). Pavarotti, Freni, Sardinero, ROHCG Ch. & O, Gavazzeni

The haunting Cherry Duet from this opera whets the appetite for more, and it is good to hear so rare and delightful a piece, one that is unlikely to enter the repertory of our British opera houses. The performance could not be more refined, and **Freni** and **Pavarotti** were both at their freshest in 1969 when it was recorded. While the dramatic conception is at the opposite end of the scale from Cavalleria rusticana, one is easily beguiled by the music's charm. The **Covent Garden Orchestra** responds loyally; the recording is clear, warm and atmospheric and has transferred beautifully to CD. Though perhaps not a 'Great Recording of the Century', this mid-priced reissue is very winning. The documentation includes a full libretto and attractive sessions photographs.

Cavalleria rusticana (complete; DVD versions)

🎵– **** Ph. DVD 070 428-9. Obraztsova, Domingo, Bruson, La Scala, Milan, Ch. & O, Prêtre (Dir: Franco Zeffirelli) – LEONCAVALLO: Pagliacci****

(N) *** TDK DVD DVWW-OPCAV. Komlosi, Sung Kyu Park, De Mola, Di Felice, Di Castri, San Carlo Ch. & O, Zhang Jiemin

(*) DG DVD 073 4389. Cossotto, Cecchele, Guelfi, Martino, La Scala, Milan, Ch. & O, Karajan (Director: Giorgio Strehler, V/D: Ernst Wild) – LEONCAVALLO: Pagliacci **

**(*) Opus Arte DVD OA0983D (2). Urmana, La Scola, Jugovic, Ch. & SO of Teatro Real, Madrid, López Cobos (Director: Giancarlo del Monaco, V/D: Angel Luis Ramirez) – LEONCAVALLO: Pagliacci **(*)

Franco Zeffirelli has here (in 1981) opted to film Cavalleria rusticana on location in Sicily, with wonderfully evocative results. The camerawork brilliantly heightens the drama too, with long shots used for such key moments as the final fight between Turiddù and Alfio, which in the theatre always takes place offstage. He also uses close-ups very effectively to bring out the conflicting emotions of Santuzza and Turiddù in their big duet. Authentic costumes augment the local colour, and the handling of the chorus adds to the realism. As in Pagliacci, Zeffirelli regularly conceals any problem of coordination between sound and vision as the singers mime their words. **Plácido Domingo** is in superb voice as Turiddù, singing and acting with total command, and **Renato Bruson** makes a strong, characterful Alfio. As Santuzza, **Elena Obraztsova** sings warmly, with a rich and fruity mezzo, if with too insistent a vibrato. Stealing the scene in the far smaller role of Mamma Lucia, the veteran mezzo **Fedora Barbieri** is superb, wonderfully characterful and still in fine voice.

A truly verismo performance from San Carlo on TDK, conducted with great vitality and warm expressive feeling by the excellent female conductor, **Zhang Jiemin**. The background is the spectacular castellated Antiche Terme Romane, near Naples, an open-air theatre (once associated with the Roman emperor Nero). With high walls, the (visible) orchestra becomes a centrepiece beneath the action, which is on several levels. Indeed, at the end of her big scene with Turiddù, Santuzza rushes right down past the orchestra almost into the audience. The only miscalculation is Turiddù's opening 'Siciliana', which is too distantly placed. But when the opera gets under way the cameras move in to give the viewer plenty of close-ups. **Ildiko Komlosi** uses her big, rich voice powerfully, and the superbly passionate interchanges with Turridù are as thrilling as the *Easter Hymn* with the chorus. The acoustic is slightly dry so the orchestral sound has splendid projection and clarity (and the best cymbals in Italy!) and the set certainly adds to the atmospheric feeling of the performance.

Karajan recorded *Cavalleria Rusticana* in video in 1968, with three of these artists, **Cossotto**, **Martino** and **Guelfi**, but Turiddù (**Gianfranco Cecchele**), although lusty enough, was not their equal. Moreover, **Fiorenza Cossotto**, who sang the part of Santuzza superbly, proved much less successful as an actress, and her melodramatic portrayal is not kindly observed by the camera in close-up, especially as the singers have to mime their parts to a prerecording. The production, staged by Giorgio Strehler, was filmed spectacularly – seemingly in the open air – on a large set, back to back with *Pagliacci*. The action is comparatively static, although musically impressive. Karajan at the helm conducts spaciously and with rich romantic feeling (especially in the *Prelude* and *Intermezzo*). The video direction by Ernst Wild is competent but, despite Cossotto's glorious singing, as an overall production this does not match the coupled *Pagliacci*, completely overseen by Karajan himself.

There are no starry names in the Madrid production, but it is well sung and convincingly acted against a bare but realistic set. **Violeta Urmana** and **Vincenzo La Scola** are a very convincing Santuzza and Turiddù, and the Lola of **Dragana Jugovic** is pretty enough to seduce the most resistant lover. The climax, with the fight between Alfio and Turiddù, is presented on stage, and at Turiddù's death the production moves without a break into the Prologue of *Pagliacci*. The opera is strongly directed by **Jesús López-Cobos** and its very directness gives it a strong appeal.

Cavalleria rusticana (complete; CD versions)

🎵 (M) **** RCA (ADD) 74321 39500-2. Scotto, Domingo, Elvira, Amb. Op. Ch., Nat. PO, Levine

🎵 (***) EMI mono 5 56287-2 (2). Callas, Di Stefano, Panerai, Ch. & O of La Scala, Milan, Serafin – LEONCAVALLO: *I Pagliacci* (***)

(M) **(*) EMI (ADD) 7 63967-2 (2). de los Angeles, Corelli, Sereni, Rome Op. Ch. & O, Santini – LEONCAVALLO: *I Pagliacci* ***

(M) **(*) EMI (ADD) 7 63650-2 (2). Caballé, Carreras, Hamari, Manuguerra, Varnay, Amb. Op. Ch., Southend Boys' Ch., Philh. O, Muti – LEONCAVALLO: *I Pagliacci* **(*)

Now reissued at mid-price (pleasingly presented in a slip-case with libretto), the **Scotto–Domingo** set now stands as a first recommendation for Mascagni's red-blooded opera, with Domingo giving a heroic account of the role of Turiddù, full of defiance. Scotto is strongly characterful too, and **James Levine** directs with a splendid sense of pacing, by no means faster than his rivals (except the leisurely Karajan) and drawing red-blooded playing from the **National Philharmonic**. The recording is vivid and strikingly present in its CD transfer.

Dating from the mid-1950s, **Callas's** performance as Santuzza reveals the diva in her finest form, with edginess and unevenness of production at a minimum and with vocal colouring at its most characterful. The singing of the other principals is hardly less dramatic and **Panerai** is in firm, well-projected voice.

Though not as vibrant as von Matači's *Pagliacci* coupling, this beautifully sung, essentially lyrical **Santini** performance could give considerable satisfaction, provided the bitterness of Mascagni's drama is not a first consideration. Like the coupling, it shows **Corelli** in good form; both he and **de los Angeles** are given scope by Santini to produce soaring, Italianate singing of Mascagni's richly memorable melodies. The recording is suitably atmospheric.

Muti's EMI *Cav.* is comparably biting and violent, brushing away the idea that this is a sentimental score. The result is certainly refreshing, with **Caballé** – pushed faster than usual, even in her big moments – collaborating warmly. So *Voi lo sapete* is geared from the start to the final cry of *Io son dannata*, and she manages a fine snarl on *A te la mala Pasqua*. **Carreras** does not sound quite so much at home, though the rest of the cast is memorable, including the resonant **Manuguerra** as Alfio and the veteran **Astrid Varnay** as Mamma Lucia, wobble as she does. The recording is forward and vivid.

MASSENET, Jules (1842–1912)

Le Carillon (ballet; complete)

(B) *** Double Decca 444 836-2 (2). SRO, Bonynge – DELIBES: *Coppélia* ***

Le Carillon was written in the same year as *Werther*. The villains of the story who try to destroy the bells of the title are punished by being miraculously transformed into bronze jaquemarts, fated to continue striking them for ever! The music of this one-Act ballet makes a delightful offering – not always as lightweight as one would expect. With his keen rhythmic sense and feeling for colour, **Bonynge** is outstanding in this repertory, and the 1984 Decca recording is brilliant and colourful. A fine bonus (37 minutes) for a desirable version of Delibes' *Coppélia*, at the cheapest possible price.

Le Cid: ballet suite

🎵 ✹ *** Australian Decca Eloquence (ADD) 476 2742. Israel PO, Martinon – DVOŘÁK: *Slavonic Dances*; MEYERBEER: *Les Patineurs* ✹ ***

In **Martinon's** hands, Massenet's tunes fizz and effervesce like the best champagne, while the more reflective numbers have colourful, picture-postcard atmosphere. Equally remarkable is the astonishingly vivid Decca recording, the sort of brilliant yet warm sound for which the company became famous, and it is superbly transferred to CD.

Piano Concerto in E flat

*** Hyp. CDA 66897. Coombs, BBC Scottish SO, Ossonce – HAHN: *Piano Concerto in E* ***

*** Alpha 104. Biret, Bilkent SO, Páris – FRANCK: *Symphonic Variations; Les Djinns* ***

Massenet unexpectedly completed this substantial concerto at the age of 60. It regularly reveals his love of the keyboard, and in a performance like **Stephen Coombs's** the result is a delight, the writing full of attractive ideas. **Jean-Yves Ossonce** is a most sympathetic accompanist, drawing idiomatic playing from the **BBC Scottish Symphony**, helped by warm, well-balanced sound.

Idil Biret strikes the right degree of flamboyance. But it is the romantic delicacy of her playing that one remembers, and the finale gambols along infectiously and spiritedly. In short, this engaging work is played with great imagination and flair, and is very well recorded.

Fantaisie (for Cello & Orchestra)

*** ASV CDDCA 867. Rolland, BBC PO, Varga – LALO: *Cello Concerto*; SAINT-SAËNS: *Cello Concerto 1* ***

Massenet's *Fantaisie for Cello and Orchestra* is music for the sweet-toothed. The Canadian cellist, **Sophie Rolland**, and the BBC forces under **Gilbert Varga** play it with total commitment and fervour as if they believe every note. Excellent recording.

Hérodiade (ballet) Suite; Orchestral Suites 1; 2 (Scènes hongroises); 3 (Scènes dramatiques)

(BB) **(*) Naxos 8.553124. New Zealand SO, Ossonce

The ballet suite from *Hérodiade* comes in the final scene of the opera and the five movements are nicely scored. The other orchestral suites offer Massenet's ready store of tunes and his charmingly French orchestral palette. The playing of the **New Zealand Orchestra** is first class, polished and vivid, though it is a pity that the microphones are somewhat close.

Scènes alsaciennes

*** Talent SACD DOM 2929. Nice PO, Guidarini (with Gustav CHARPENTIER: *Impressions d'Italie* ***) – SAINT-SAËNS: *Suite algérienne* ***

The *Scènes alsaciennes* are full of charm in this most engaging performance from **Marco Guidarini** and his excellent **Nice Orchestra**. The opening picture of a leisurely Sunday morning after Matins is evoked most atmospherically, and the vibrant horns in *Au cabaret* really catch the ear. In the finale, *Dimanche soir*, the soldiers' evening retreat is vividly caught, especially if you have back speakers to create the surround sound which this SACD provides so naturally. Gustav Charpentier was a pupil of Massenet and his *Impressions d'Italie* follow in his master's footsteps, if rather more impressionistically, particularly in the graceful second move-

ment, *A la fontaine*. But the lively closing picture of *Napoli* brings a colourful kaleidoscope of folk melodies.

Scènes alsaciennes; Scènes de féerie; Scènes napolitaines; Scènes pittoresques

⊕ – (BB) **** Naxos 8.553125. New Zealand SO, Ossonce

Best known are the somewhat ingenuous *Scènes pittoresques* and the *Scènes alsaciennes*. The most touching movement is the beautiful *Sous les tilleuls* ('Under the Lime Trees'), with its wilting dialogue between cello and clarinet, played here with an affectionate finesse worthy of a Beecham. With full, sparkling, yet warmly atmospheric recording, this is a first-class disc in every way.

La Vierge: Le Dernier sommeil de la vierge (The Last Sleep of the Virgin)

(M) (**(*)) BBC mono BBCL 4113. RPO, Beecham (with spoken introduction) – BERLIOZ: *The Trojans: Royal Hunt and Storm*; CHABRIER: *España; Gwendoline Overture*; DEBUSSY: *L'Enfant prodigue: Cortège et Air de danse*; DELIUS: *Brigg Fair*; SAINT-SAËNS: *Le Rouet d'Omphale*; (with MOZART: *Divertimento in D, K. 131: excerpts*) (**(*))

This was one of **Sir Thomas's** most celebrated 'lollipops' and it comes from a live broadcast concert of 1956, complete with a characteristic spoken introduction. It is beautifully played but the recording, although warm and pleasing, is rather restricted.

OPERA

Esclarmonde (complete)

⊕ – (B) **** Decca 475 7914 (3). Sutherland, Aragall, Tourangeau, Davies, Grant, Alldis Ch., Nat PO, Bonynge

Joan Sutherland's performance of the central role of *Esclarmonde* is in its way as powerful as it is in Puccini's last opera. **Aragall** proves an excellent tenor, sweet of tone and intelligent, and the other parts are well taken too. **Richard Bonynge** draws passionate singing and playing from chorus and orchestra, and the recording has both atmosphere and spectacle to match the story, based on a medieval romance involving song-contests and necromancy. This makes a fine bargain for those wanting to explore Massenet's lesser-known operas.

(i) Le Jongleur de Notre-Dame; (ii) La Navarraise (also includes excerpts from 1933 recording of Le Jongleur with Vezzani, O cond. Dumazert)

(M) ** Gala (ADD; stereo/mono) GL 100.747 (2). (i) Vanzo, Massard, Bastin, Dupouy, Ch. & O de l'ORTF, Dervaux; (ii) Moizan, Vanzo, Mars, Lovano, Vigneron, Lyrique Ch. & O de la RTF, Hartemann

Alain Vanzo makes these radio recordings especially valuable, even though *La Navarraise*, recorded in 1963, is in mono only. *Le Jongleur de Notre-Dame*, written in 1900, is one of Massenet's most charming pieces. As a single-sex piece in a religious setting with the Virgin intervening, it evidently influenced Puccini's *Suor Angelica*. Vanzo dominates this broadcast recording, but the others in the cast (as well as the mixed chorus) all sing well, with the 1973 sound nicely atmospheric. In *La Navarraise* the performances (not just of Vanzo but of **Geneviève Moizan** in the title-role as well as of **Jean Peyron** as the second tenor) make it well worth hearing.

Le Jongleur de Notre-Dame (complete)

(B) **(*) EMI (ADD) 5 75297-2 (2). Vanzo, Bastin, Vento, Raffali, Frémeau, Monte-Carlo Op. Ch. & O, Boutry

Le Jongleur de Notre-Dame, written in 1900, was composed entirely for male voices (with the exception of the chorus of angels). The images of rustic village and abbey life are colourfully contrasted. **Alain Vanzo** as the juggler, Jean, is at his stylish best – his drinking song (an 'Alleluia' to wine!) with its rustic violin obbligato is a highlight. The rest of the French cast is idiomatic and convincing. In the comic role of the Abbey's cook, Bonaface, the robust humour is brought out well by **Jules Bastin**. **Roger Boutry** provides sympathetic support with his Monte Carlo forces, and the 1978 sound is warmly atmospheric. There are no texts to help non-French speakers, but the set is inexpensive and has undoubted period charm.

Manon (complete; DVD versions)

(N) ⛐ **** DG DVD 073 4431. Netrebko, Villazón, Fischesser, Daza, Corazza, Kataja, Berlin State Op. Ch. & O, Barenboim (Producer: Bernhard Fleischer; V/D: Andreas Morell)

**** TDK DVD DVOPMANON (2). Fleming, Alvarez, Chaignaud, Sénéchal, Paris Nat. Op. Ch. and O, López-Cobos (Dir: Deflo, DVD Dir: François Roussillon)

**** Virgin DVD 50999 50506897 (2). Dessay, Villazón, Ramey, Lanza, Vas, Henry, Gran Teatre del Liceu Ch. & SO, Pérez (Director: David McVicar, V/D: François Roussillon) (with documetary on rehearsals for the opera)

*** DG DVD 073 4207. Gruberová, Araiza, Thau, Helm, Gahmlich, Tichy, V. State Op. Ch. & O, A. Fischer (Dir: Jean-Pierre Ponnelle, V/D: Brian Large)

We are particularly well served with outstanding versions of *Manon*. Apart from Renée Fleming's memorable assumption of the role on TDK, Natalie Dessay is wonderfully characterful in her partnership with Villazón on Virgin. But now **Villazón** (at his finest) is re-partnered with **Anna Netrebko**, singing gloriously on DG, in a passionate liaison that proves most moving of all. Moreover, whereas David McVicar's production on Virgin from the very beginning underlines the seamy side of the world into which the young Manon enters, the producer of the Berlin version, Bernhard Fleischer, emphasizes its glamour, underpinned by luscious costuming (from Susan Hilferty) in 1950s style. But Manon herself is totally charismatic as she moves from innocent ingénue on a bench waiting for a train, to a glamorous blonde of Marilyn Monroe vintage in the Hôtel de Transylvanie. The spectacle of the Cours-la-Reine scene is dazzling, but what one remembers most is the tenderly sensuous love scenes between the two principals, notably the delightful aria when Manon nostalgically serenades her little table, and the great emotional climax when she seduces her lover to abandon his plan to enter the church. With **Alfredo Daza** a fine, dignified

Lescaut and **Rémy Corazza** most convincing as the villain, Guillot, the close of the opera is handled most movingly. Throughout, **Barenboim** (who stepped in at the last moment to conduct) achieves first-class orchestral playing and keeps the tension high, and overall the performance is quite unforgettable.

Gilbert Deflo's production for the National Opera in Paris is refreshingly direct in its presentation of the story over the five acts, using apt in-period costumes set in contrast with the simple stylized sets, both designed by William Orlandi. **Renée Fleming** not only sings superbly, she acts with total conviction, brilliantly making the transition from the vivacious seventeen-year-old of Act I, inexperienced yet wilful, to the mature, even more wilful figure of the later acts, making one understand her dilemma over her love for Des Grieux. It is well matched by the upstanding, slightly awkward Des Grieux of **Marcelo Alvarez**, also singing splendidly with a wide tonal range down to a fine head-voice in *Ah fuyez douce image*. Equally fine is the magnificent singing of the baritone **Jean-Luc Chaignaud** readily commanding the stage. With **Jésus López-Cobos** drawing idiomatic playing and singing from chorus and orchestra, it makes a splendid addition to the DVD catalogue.

This live recording of an outstanding production by David McVicar at the Liceu Theatre in Lisbon featured an exceptionally strong leading duo in **Natalie Dessay** as Manon and **Rolando Villazón** as Des Grieux. The rest of the cast is comparably characterful, though **Samuel Ramey** as the Count Des Grieux is not very steady. No matter, the performance is altogether gripping. **Victor Pablo Pérez** conducts strongly and the stylized production, using traditional costumes, works exceptionally well, not least in creating the scene of corruption into which the young Manon, so simply dressed, makes her initial entry. Villazón is an ardent lover and creates a perfect partnership with Dessay. The ballet scenes, too, are splendidly danced and visually delightful, to make a neat foil for the narrative. The camerawork is admirable, the sound is excellent, and in every way this is an intensely satisfying DVD version of a memorable production.

Adam Fischer conducts a 1983 performance from the **Vienna State Opera**, with sets and costumes by Jean-Pierre Ponnelle – and what gorgeous sets and costumes they are: the period detail is superb and the performance is a joy to watch. It is a joy to hear also, with an excellent cast, the leads giving characterful and intelligent portrayals. **Gruberová** is suitably sparkling in her showy numbers and equally successful in conveying Manon's less than cheerful fate at the end. Fischer conducts his Vienna forces urgently but not insensitively. If not as fine as the TDK set with Renée Fleming, this makes an enjoyable alternative choice – what a wonderful score it is!

Manon (complete; CD versions)

⛐ (M) **** EMI 3 81842-2 (2). Gheorghiu, Alagna, Patriarco, van Dam, La Monnaie Op. Ch. & O, Pappano

⛐ (***) Testament mono SBT 3203 (3). de los Angeles, Legay, Dens, Paris Opéra-Comique O, Monteux – BERLIOZ: *Les Nuits d'été*; DEBUSSY: *La Demoiselle élue* (***)

**(*) EMI 7 49610-2 (2). Cotrubas, Kraus, Quilico, van Dam, Toulouse Capitole Ch. & O, Plasson

(BB) (***) Naxos mono 111268/70. de los Angeles; cond Monteux (as above, with DEBUSSY: *La demoiselle élue* & BERLIOZ: *Les nuites d'été* (***))

In Act I **Gheorghiu** instantly establishes the heroine as a vivacious, wilful character with a great sense of fun, and her singing is both imaginative and technically flawless. The aria, *Adieu, notre petite table*, is tenderly affecting, shaded down to a breathtaking *pianissimo* at the end. A fine actress, she develops the character too, while **Alagna**, always at his happiest in French-language opera, portrays Des Grieux as full of eager innocence as well as passion. The other La Monnaie soloists make a splendid team under **Antonio Pappano**, with **José van Dam** impressively cast as Des Grieux's father. Pappano himself is as understanding an interpreter of Massenet as he is of Puccini, drawing warmly committed playing and singing from the whole company. Available also at mid-price.

No one has recorded the role of Manon in Massenet's opera quite so bewitchingly as **Victoria de los Angeles** in this historic EMI recording of 1955, girlishly provocative at the start, conveying tragic depth later. The voice is at its most golden, and this vivid new transfer from Testament gives the mono sound extra warmth and immediacy. **Henri Legay** as Des Grieux also sings with honeyed tones, a believable young lover ensnared, and **Pierre Monteux** in one of his rare opera recordings is masterly in his timing and phrasing. As a splendid bonus you also have RCA recordings of Berlioz and Debussy, similarly persuasive, recorded in Boston, also in 1955.

The **Plasson Toulouse** set is a stylish performance, well characterized and well sung. **Ileana Cotrubas** is a charming Manon, more tender and vulnerable than de los Angeles but not so golden-toned and with a more limited development of character, from the girlish chatterbox to the dying victim. **Alfredo Kraus** betrays some signs of age, but his is a finely detailed and subtle reading. **Louis Quilico** has a delightfully light touch as Lescaut, **José van Dam** is a superb Comte Des Grieux, and, although Plasson is rougher with the score than Monteux was, his feeling for French idiom is very good.

The Naxos set has a considerable price advantage, although the transfer (while projecting the voices vividly) is thinner in the orchestra. However, its trump card is a brief spoken introduction by **Pierre Monteux**, recalling Massenet himself directing all aspects of an early performance, from which he learned a good deal.

Thaïs (complete)

**** Decca 466 7662 (2). Fleming, Hampson, Sabbatini, Bordeaux Op. Ch. & O, Abel

The character of Thaïs in Massenet's opera finds an ideal interpreter in **Renée Fleming**. After making the heroine's unlikely conversion to virtue totally convincing, she crowns her performance with a deeply affecting account of her death scene, ending with a ravishing *pianissimo* top A. **Thomas Hampson** as Athanaël, a character working just as improbably in the opposite direction, cannot quite equal her in such

total conviction but he is vocally ideal. The others are well cast too, notably **Giuseppe Sabbatini** as Nicias, and though the **Bordeaux Opera Orchestra** is not quite as refined as some, **Yves Abel** draws warmly sympathetic playing from them throughout, with the young French virtuoso, **Renaud Capuchon**, luxuriously cast in the big violin solo of the *Méditation*. Excellent sound. A clear first choice.

Thaïs: *Méditation*

(N) *** Chan. 10510. Rimonda, Canziana – DANCLA: *Petite Ecole de la mélodie*; SAINT-SAËNS: *Violin Sonata 1 in D min.* ***

The popular *Méditation* from Massenet's *Thaïs* comes in a beautifully judged performance, not too slow, and with magical half-tones from **Rimonda's** violin. It makes a welcome filler to two exceptionally attractive works for violin and piano.

Werther (complete; DVD version)

(N) ** Arthaus DVD 101 317. Purdy-Ikaia, Hablowetz, Kolarczyk, Schlingensiepen, Badische Staatskapelle Karlsruhe, Children's Ch., Carlberg (Director: Robert Tannenbaum; V/D: Brooks Riley)

With the several star-studded CD versions of *Werther* available, not many collectors are likely to be attracted to this sombre video production from Arthaus. **Keith Purdy-Ikaia's** portrayal of Werther is certainly true to the character created in Goethe's novel, with his obsession with the idea that 'except for ourselves, nothing else exists, everything is void', and he sings strongly, if with an intrusive vibrato. **Silvia Hablowetz** is a sympathetic Charlotte, singing well but with little seductive charisma, and **Ina Schlingensiepen** is a charming Sophie, although she too is shown as an unfortunate, crippled girl in the hands of fate. **Armin Kolarczyk's** Albert is certainly convincing, again appropriately, with no sex appeal. The set is contrived, but the scenes with the children do at least bring contrasting light relief. Much of Massenet's vocal score is projected well and **Daniel Carlberg** creates considerable intensity in the orchestra. But this is not an uplifting operatic experience.

Werther (complete; CD versions)

(M) **** EMI 3 81849-2 (2). Alagna, Gheorghiu, Hampson, Petibon, Tiffin School Children's Ch., LSO, Pappano

*** RCA 74321 58224-2 (2). Vargas, Kasarova, Schaldenbrand, Kotoski, Berlin Knabenchor & Deutsche SO, Jurowski

(M) *** DG (ADD) 477 5652 (2). Domingo, Obraztsova, Augér, Grundheber, Moll, Cologne Children's Ch. & RSO, Chailly

(M) **(*) EMI (ADD) 5 62627-2 (2). Gedda, de los Angeles, Soyer, Benoit, Grigoriou, Mallabrera, Mesplé, ORTF Children's Ch., O de Paris, Prêtre

Though **Alagna** with his French background is an ideal choice for Werther himself, **Gheorghiu** with her bright soprano is a less obvious one for the role of the heroine, Charlotte, normally given to a mezzo. But as a magnetic actress she conveys an extra tenderness and vulnerability, with no lack of weight in such a solo as *Laisse couler mes larmes* in Act III. **Thomas Hampson** is outstanding as Albert and **Patricia Petibon** a sweet-toned Sophie. As in Puccini, **Pappano** is subtle as well as powerful, using rubato idiomatically and with refinement to heighten the drama and point the moments of climax. Good warm sound.

The RCA set makes the perfect alternative to the EMI version. Here is casting of the two principals that in every way is centrally satisfying. With her vibrant mezzo, **Vesselina Kasarova** is a natural choice for Charlotte, full and intense at the big moments, even if the vibrancy, as caught by the microphone, turns into unevenness under pressure. **Ramon Vargas** with his clear, precise tenor is the perfect hero here. He may not be as distinctive as Alagna, but he sings such a solo as *Pourquoi me reveiller* with greater purity, shading the voice down most sensitively. The other principals are not so strongly cast, with **Dawn Kotoski** rather shrill as Sophie, but **Jurowski's** conducting is warm and dramatic, even if it lacks the distinctive subtleties of Pappano. The sound is brilliant and clear.

Chailly proves a sharply characterful conductor, one who knows how to thrust home an important climax as well as to create evocative textures, varying intensity positively. **Plácido Domingo** in the name-part sings with sweetness and purity as well as strength, coping superbly with the legato line of the aria, *Pourquoi me réveiller*. **Elena Obraztsova** is richer and firmer than she usually is on record, but it is a generalized portrait, particularly beside the charming Sophie of **Arleen Augér**. The others make up a very convincing team, and this inexpensive reissue is well worth considering, even though the documentation has only a track-by-track synopsis.

Victoria de los Angeles's golden tones, which convey pathos so beautifully, are ideally suited to Massenet's gentle melodies and, although she is recorded too closely (closer than the other soloists), she makes an appealing heroine. **Gedda**, too, makes an intelligent romantic hero, though **Prêtre's** direction could be more subtle. This set now reappears, excellently remastered, as one of EMI's 'Great Recordings of the Century'.

Werther (complete; in English)

(M) *** Chan. 3033 (2). Brecknock, Baker, Wheatley, Blackburn, Roberts, Tomlinson, ENO Ch. & O, Mackerras

Mackerras's version offers an exceptionally warm reading in English which is strong in dramatic thrust. The cast too is exceptionally strong, with **John Brecknock** clear, fresh and firm in the title-role. Yet it is the performance of **Janet Baker** as Charlotte that provides the linchpin, rising to great heights in the tragedy of Act IV. **Joy Roberts** is a bright, agile Sophie, and the other male singers can hardly be faulted. Remarkably, this was taken from a single performance, not edited from a series. Voices are close enough for every word of Norman Tucker's excellent translation to be heard.

MATHIAS, William (1934–92)

(i) *Clarinet concerto*; (ii) *Harp concerto*; (iii) *Piano concerto 3*

*** Lyrita (ADD) SRCD 325. (i) de Peyer; (ii) Ellis; (iii) Katin; LSO or New Philh. O, Atherton

Helped by vividly immediate recording, the *Clarinet Concerto* with its clean-cut, memorable themes sparks off an inspired performance from **Gervase de Peyer**, not just in the lively outer movements but also in the poignant *Lento espressivo* in the middle. The *Harp Concerto* (1970) is less outward-going, but it prompts Mathias to create evocative, shimmering textures, very characteristic of him. The harp, superbly played by the dedicatee, **Osian Ellis**, is set alongside exotic percussion, with the finale a snappy jig that delightfully keeps tripping over its own feet. In *Piano Concerto 3* of 1968 the outer movements bring jazzily syncopated writing, like Walton with a difference, here incisively played by **Peter Katin**. They frame an atmospheric central *Adagio* with echoes of Bartókian 'night music', like Bartók with a difference.

(i; ii) *Dance Overture, Op. 16*; (iii; ii) *Divertimento for String Orchestra, Op. 7*; (i; ii) *Invocation & Dance, Op. 17*; (iv; ii) '*Landscapes of the mind*': *Laudi, Op. 62*; *Vistas, Op. 69*; (iii; ii) *Prelude, Aria & Finale for String Orchestra, Op. 25*; (v) *Sinfonietta, Op. 34*

*** Lyrita (ADD) SRCD 328 [id.]. (i) LSO; (ii) Atherton; (iii) ECO; (iv) New Philh. O; (v) Nat. Youth O of Wales, Davison

The joyful *Dance Overture* is vividly scored, rather after the manner of Malcolm Arnold, and the *Invocation and Dance* has genuine spontaneity. The *Divertimento* and *Prelude, Aria and Finale* have a family likeness in presenting workmanlike Hindemithian arguments in fast movements and warm lyricism in slow ones, although the *Aria* is restrained and ethereal. The colourful, extrovert *Sinfonietta* has a *Lento* with a delectable blues flavour, and the finale too is popularly based rhythmically, with its lively and sometimes pungent syncopations. Undoubtedly the two most remarkable works here are the two pieces described by their composer as 'Landscapes of the mind'. *Laudi*, written in 1973, somewhat after the manner of Messiaen. The even more mystically evocative *Vistas* was inspired by the composer's visit to the USA in 1975. Here an Ivesian influence is unmistakable. Performances throughout are of the highest calibre, with **David Atherton** at his most perceptive, and the recordings (engineered by Decca for the most part) are outstanding.

String Quartets 1–3

B–*** Metier MSVCD 92005. Medea Qt

Spanning the years 1967–86, Mathias's three string quartets make a fine sequence, illuminating his whole achievement. The *Third Quartet* brings together elements of both the earlier works, with the first of its three movements developing from a deceptively light opening into a taut, large-scale structure comparable with *Quartet 1*. All three quartets, very well recorded, are outstandingly well performed by the young **Medea Quartet**.

Wind Quintet

*** Crystal CD 750. Westwood Wind Quintet – CARLSSON:

Nightwings; LIGETI: *Bagatelles*; BARBER: *Summer Music* ***

Of the five movements of this spirited *Quintet* the Scherzo is particularly felicitous and there is a rather beautiful *Elegy*. The playing of the **Westwood Wind Quintet** is highly expert and committed, and the recording is very good indeed.

VOCAL MUSIC

(i–iii) *Ave Rex, A Carol Sequence, Op. 45*; (iv; v; iii) *Elegy for a Prince, Op. 59*; (v; vi) *This Worlde's Joie, Op. 67*

🎵 **** Lyrita (ADD) SRCD 324. (i) Welsh Nat. Op. Ch.; (ii) LSO; (iii) Atherton; (iv) G. Evans; (v) New Philh. O; (vi) J. Price, Bowen, Rippon, Bach Ch., St George's Ch., Willcocks

Ave Rex, Mathias's fine *Carol Sequence* (quoting the medieval *Alleluya, a new work is come on hand*, and *Sir Christemas*) has the robust inspiration of Britten's *Ceremony of Carols*, with which it has much in common, while *This Worlde's Joie* is Mathias's interpretation of the 'Four Seasons' and is in four comparatively short, lyrical sections, lightweight in style, but with the composer's usual direct appeal 'intended to be enjoyed by both listeners and performers', says the composer. And enjoyable it is, from the very opening bars, with their felicitous orchestration. In between the major works comes Mathias's setting – in English translation – of the medieval Welsh *Elegy for a Prince* (Llywelyn, the last native Prince of Wales, killed by the soldiers of Edward I in 1282), eloquently sung by **Geraint Evans**. The performances throughout are first class and the recordings, made by Decca engineers, are very fine (spectacularly vivid and wide-ranging in the choral works).

Ave verum corpus; A babe is born; All wisdom is from the Lord; Festival Te Deum; In excelsis gloria; Let the people praise thee; Lift up your heads; Magnificat & Nunc dimittis; Missa brevis; O be joyful in the Lord; O Nata lux. Organ: Carillon; Processional

Ⓝ **** Hyp. CDA 67740. Wells Cathedral Ch., Matthew Owens; J. Vaughn (organ)

Both the opening anthem on this disc, *Let the people praise thee, O God*, and the *Magnificat* (from the 'Jesus College Service') are exuberantly thrilling. But Mathias can be equally moving in his gentle writing as the *Nunc dimittis*, which follows, shows so readily. The spirited carol, the gently syncopated *A babe is born*, has a Rutterish flavour; the *Missa brevis*, more plangent in its harmony, is all Mathias's own, and its moving *Agnus Dei* opens *pianopianissimo*. But the organ unleashes its full glory in the *Festival Te Deum* and sets the dancing mood of the last item here, *O be joyful in the Lord*. The **Wells Cathedral Choir** sings superbly throughout this 76-minute collection which lifts the listener's spirits throughout. The recording, made in the Cathedral Church of St Andrew, is outstanding too, and this CD collection is an ideal way to enjoy the full range of the composer's vocal writing.

Missa brevis; Rex gloriae; Anthems: Ad majorem Dei gloriam; Angelus; Alleluia; Doctrine of Wisdom; Except the Lord build the house; Hodie Christus natus est; The Lord is my Shepherd; Veni sancte spiritus

✤ **** Paraclete Press GDCD 026. Gloriæ Dei Cantores, Patterson

This splendidly sung programme comes from **Gloriæ Dei Cantores**, a 44-voice choir from Cape Cod, Massachusetts, directed by **Elizabeth Patterson**. The thrilling opening of *Sanctus* establishes this as the emotional kernel of the work, with the organ then creating darker woodwind colours to introduce the very touching *Agnus Dei*. The anthems are hardly less individual and inspired. *The Lord is my Shepherd* is very Welsh in feeling, a passionate declaration of faith; *The Doctrine of Wisdom* again uses the organ very atmospherically, and its melodic simplicity is telling. With singing of such commitment and intensity, yet exploiting the widest range of dynamics, every piece here is memorable. Mathias could hardly have hoped for more persuasive advocacy or finer recording. If you have difficulty in getting this disc, the Choir's website address is: www.paracletepress.com.

MATTHEWS, Colin (born 1946)

(i) *Horn Concerto*; (ii) *Alphabicycle Order*

Ⓝ Ⓜ *** Hallé CDHLL 7515. (i) Watkins; (ii) Goodman (narrator); Hallé O, (i) Elder; (ii) Gardner

We know Colin Matthews mainly from his brilliant orchestrations of Debussy's piano *Préludes*. Now he shows his paces with a highly original *Horn Concerto* which is mostly gently expressive, but also momentarily boldly forceful. It has a superbly confident soloist in **Richard Watkins**. Now for something entirely different. *Alphabicycle Order* is an engagingly friendly but never bland setting, spiced with wit, of Christopher Reid's encapsulation of the alphabet. Narrator **Henry Goodman**, the **Hallé Children's Chorus** and the **Orchestra**, under **Edward Gardner**, clearly enjoy themselves, and so do we.

MAUNDER, John (1858–1920)

***Olivet to Calvary* (cantata)**

Ⓑ **(*) CfP (ADD) 575 779-2 (2). Mitchinson, Harvey, Guildford Cathedral Ch., Rose; Morse (organ) – STAINER: *The Crucifixion* ***

It is easy to be patronizing about music like this but, provided one accepts the conventions of style in which it is composed, the music is effective and often moving. The performance has an attractive simplicity and genuine eloquence. **Frederick Harvey** is particularly moving at the actual moment of Christ's death; in a passage that, insensitively handled, could be positively embarrassing, he creates a magical, hushed intensity. The choir sing beautifully, and in the gentler, lyrical writing (the semi-chorus *O Thou whose sweet compassion*, for example) sentimentality is skilfully avoided.

The 1964 recording is first class in every way, and it has been admirably transferred to CD. This now comes aptly paired with Stainer's *Crucifixion*.

MAW, Nicholas (1935–2009)

Violin Concerto (1993)

☞ *** Sony SK 62856. Bell, LPO, Norrington

Maw here excels himself in a work specifically written for **Joshua Bell**, who responds superbly with playing of heartfelt warmth as well as brilliance. The opening *Moderato* movement has something of the fervour of the Walton *Violin Concerto*, with Maw firmly establishing his personal approach to tonality in seamless lyricism, leading up to a grinding climax. Coming second, the Scherzo is the longest movement, with Walton again brought to mind in the spiky brilliance, set against a central section with a ripe horn solo. The third movement, *Romanza*, is then a calm interlude before the carefree surging thrust of the finale, leading to a bravura conclusion, not the slow fade so often favoured latterly by concerto composers. **Roger Norrington** and the **LPO** are strong and sympathetic partners, with warm, full recording to match.

(i) Dance Scenes; (ii) Odyssey

☞ Ⓜ *** EMI 5 85145-2 (2). (i) Philh. O, Harding; (ii) CBSO, Rattle

Spanning 90 minutes, Nicholas Maw's *Odyssey* has been counted the biggest continuous orchestral pieces ever written. The slow movement alone lasts for over half an hour, while the *allegros* bring a genuine sense of speed, thrusting and energetic. The result is astonishingly fine, with the engineers totally disguising the problems of recording in Birmingham Town Hall. For its mid-priced reissue, EMI have added his brilliantly orchestrated and virtuosic *Dance Scenes* (which at times remind one of Respighi's orchestrations), superbly played and recorded.

Sinfonia

Ⓝ *** Lyrita (ADD) SRCD 307. ECO, Del Mar (with ADDISON: *Divertimento for Brass Qt*; J. GARDNER: *Theme and Variations for Brass Qt*; DODGSON: *Sonata for Brass Quintet* ***)

Nicholas Maw's *Sinfonia* is by far the longest work on this CD, lasting half an hour. **Norman Del Mar** has a remarkable sense of colour in his textures, but this work is not a bath of self-indulgence. Indeed, in some ways it is a tough work and its argument is certainly closely wrought. But an unprejudiced listener would find an immediate and lasting enjoyment. It was written in the mid-1960s and has echoes of Britten and late Strauss, but still presents an individual idiom in its extended three-movement structure. A superb, committed performance from 1971 is coupled with three brilliantly played and recorded works for brass ensemble, generally lighter in spirit, especially John Addison's delightful *Divertimento*.

(i) Flute Quartet; (ii) Piano Trio

*** ASV CDDCA 920. Monticello Trio, with (i) Pearce; (ii) Coletti

Commissioned by the Koussevitzky Foundation, the *Piano Trio* was written in 1991 for the **Monticello Trio**, who here record it in a warmly expressive performance, fiery where necessary. The *Flute Quartet* of 1981 was written for **Judith Pearce** of the Nash Ensemble, who plays it most beautifully here; it is another fine example of Maw's broad romanticism, powerful and lyrical, often sensuous, approachable yet clearly contemporary. Though the central slow movement opens as a fugue, it develops emotionally to become an atmospheric nocturne, leading to a scurrying finale. Excellent performances and sound.

Scenes and Arias

*** Lyrita (ADD) SRCD 267. Manning, Howells, Proctor, BBC SO, Del Mar – MILNER: *Roman Spring; Salutatio Angelica* ***

Scenes and Arias is a setting of medieval love-letters that unexpectedly explodes into soaring, passionate music of a richness such as you would expect in a Richard Strauss opera. The parallel with Strauss is inevitable when Maw uses women's voices with an intertwining mellifluousness one associates above all with *Rosenkavalier*. Maw has a habit of setting elaborately decorated figures to long-sustained chords, but he avoids the charge of writing in too static a way with vigorous *allegros* full of jagged syncopations. Lovely singing from the soloists, passionately committed conducting from **Norman Del Mar** and first-rate recording.

MAXWELL DAVIES, Peter (born 1934)

(i) Antechrist; (i; ii) Missa super 'L'Homme armé'; (iii) Second Fantasia on John Taverner's 'In nomine'; (iv) Seven In Nomine; (v) Lullaby for Ilian Rainbow; (i; vi) From Stone to Thorn; Hymn to St Magnus; (vi) O magnum mysterium

☞ Ⓜ **** Decca (ADD) 475 6166 (2). (i) Fires of London, composer; (ii) V. Redgrave (speaker); (iii) New Philh. O, Groves; (iv) London Sin., Atherton; (v) Walker (guitar); (vi) Thomas (soprano); Cirencester Grammar School Ch. & O, composer

Antechrist is a sort of exuberant overture. *L'Homme armé*, a more extended but comparable work, similarly working on a medieval motif, is also most approachable, while *From Stone to Thorn*, a work much thornier in argument, directly displays the formidable talents of – among others – the soprano **Mary Thomas**. Two years later, the **Fires of London** recorded the *Hymn to St Magnus*, a powerful and uncompromising piece lasting over 36 minutes, one of the finest works inspired by the composer's flight to Orkney. Mary Thomas, helps to build the concentration, particularly in the hypnotic repetitions of the plea, *St Magnus, pray for us* (in Latin), which punctuate the long third movement.

Groves's 1972 performance of *The Second Fantasia on John*

Taverner's 'In nomine', in good sound, is not ideally incisive or polished; but anyone willing to accept a challenge will find this work very rewarding. O magnum mysterium was written for the Cirencester Grammar School, where the composer once taught, and his pupils sing this brilliantly.

Seven in Nomine is an early work, full of the composer's fascinating experiments in textures and form, often reflecting and using music from the 16th and 17th centuries. The 1979 performance under **David Atherton** is excellent. All in all, this is an ideal introduction to Maxwell Davies's music, and represents superb value for money.

Sinfonia; Sinfonia concertante

(BB) *** Regis RRC 1148. SCO, composer

A welcome bargain reissue. In his Sinfonia of 1962 Peter Maxwell Davies took as his inspiration Monteverdi's Vespers of 1610, and the dedication in this music, beautifully played by the **Scottish Chamber Orchestra**, is plain from first to last. The Sinfonia concertante is a much more extrovert piece for strings plus solo wind quintet and timpani. In idiom this is hardly at all neoclassical and, more than usual, the composer evokes romantic images, as in the lovely close of the first movement. Virtuoso playing from the Scottish principals, not least the horn. Well-balanced recording too.

CHAMBER MUSIC

Ave maris stella; Dove, Star-Folded; Economies of Scale; Psalm 24

**(*) Divine Art/ Metier MSV 28503. Gemini, Ian Mitchell

Of these four chamber works the most immediately approachable is the first on the disc, Psalm 24 (a Motet for Instrumental Ensemble), hauntingly dominated by a medieval cantus firmus. The valedictory Dove, Star-Folded, for string trio, is similarly based on a Greek Byzantine hymn and combines 'inward-looking slow music' with 'dance-like quick music' with considerable intensity. Economies of Scale, for clarinet, piano, violin and cello, has a parallel with Messiaen's Quartet for the End of Time, and although the writing is far wilder and more complex than anything Messiaen wrote,it has a 'beautifully poised ending'. Ave maris stella (loosely based on the plainsong) is a virtuoso sextet with much the same instrumentation as the Psalm. The work opens and closes in a contemplative fashion, but in between the writing is kaleidoscopically fragmentary and intensely complex; it is certainly not easy listening, although it is remarkably stimulating when played with such assurance and very clearly recorded.

Naxos Quartets 1 & 2 (Naxos 8.557396)

Naxos Quartets 3 & 4 (Naxos 8.557397)

Naxos Quartets 5 (Lighthouses of Orkney and Shetland); 6 (Naxos 8.557398)

Naxos Quartets 7 (Metafore sul Borromini); 8 (Naxos 8.557399)

(BB) *** Maggini Qt

Naxos Quartets 9 & 10

(N) (BB) *** Naxos 8.557400. Maggini Qt

Maxwell Davies's projected series of 10 Quartets on Naxos starts impressively in 1, with movements that combine structural and thematic ingenuity, typical of the composer, with emotional weight. The first of the four movements in Quartet No. 2 opens with an impressive slow introduction, leading to an energetic Allegro. The middle two movements are linked as a pair, with the recitative in the first echoing ideas in Quartet 1, while the finale is slow and deeply meditative, a movingly serene conclusion.

The very opening of the third of Maxwell Davies's Quartets on Naxos may be dauntingly thorny, but that leads quickly to meditative music which is plainly from the heart. The second movement, In Nomine, the longest of the four, is even more deeply intense, with plainsong an underlying element, leading to a sharply rhythmic Scherzo, and a Fugue which starts in echo of late Beethoven. 4, lighter in tone and more direct, was inspired by Brueghel's picture of children's games. In a single massive movement of 25 minutes it switches between passages of manic energy and dark meditation, with quirky twists and turns.

The Fifth Quartet's title refers to the sweep of the beam of the North Ronaldsay light, which moves from the beginning to the end of the two-movement work, and also to the different flashing 'calls' of lighthouses (so that mariners can identify any particular one). 6 is more ambitious in its six movements, the second and fifth of which draw on Advent and Christmas chant, and the first of a pair of Scherzos is a pizzicato. The Adagio turns into recitative towards the close.

The Seventh Quartet, intended to celebrate the work of the 17th-century architect Francesco Borromini, is a sequence of seven slow movements connected with seven of Borromini's most impressive buildings. The Eighth Quartet is in one movement and draws on Dowland's Queen Elizabeth's Galliard; it is described by the composer as an 'Intermezzo' in the cycle. Obviously the **Maggini** players have fully grasped all this writing and there is no doubting their identification and concentration. The Naxos recording is well up to the usual high standard on both discs.

The Ninth Quartet is cast in six movements, in two groups, the first pair (allegro and slow movement concentratedly joined in content) then three less formidable to follow, and a powerful finale. 10 has five movements with an Adagio at the centre, hardly less probing and not providing a conclusive end. 'I needed to leave the door open,' suggests the composer, curiously as it is the close of this highly demanding cycle. The **Maggini** performances are as concentrated as ever and very well recorded.

(i; ii) Mass; (i) Missa parvula; Dum complerentur; Veni Sancta Spiritus. Organ pieces: (i) Reliquit domum meum; Veni Creator Spiritus

*** Hyp. CDA 67454. Westminster Cathedral Ch., Baker; with (i) Quinney; (ii) Houssart (organ)

Where the Missa parvula is a setting for boys' voices in unison with organ accompaniment, the Mass is for full choir and with organ accompaniment involving a second instrument in two of the sections. The lyrical directness of the *Missa parvula*, with the final *Agnus Dei* sounding almost like a carol, is immediately attractive, touching in its simplicity. Maxwell Davies, with roots in medieval music, tends to avoid making the liturgy dramatic, so that even the setting of *Et resurrexit* in the *Credo* hardly stands out from the lyrical flow. Similarly, in the *Mass* for full choir, using a much more elaborate idiom, the composer even more strikingly draws on medieval techniques, basing it on two Whitsun plainsong chants. Complementing the two settings of the Mass come two motets, *Veni Sancta Spiritus*, slow and devotional, and *Dum complerentur*, a Pentecostal piece involving triumphant 'Alleluias', and two organ pieces, the valedictory *Reliquit domum* and the penitential *Veni Creator Spiritus*. **Martin Baker** draws radiant singing from his fine choir, atmospherically recorded.

MAYERL, Billy (1902–50)

Piano Miscellany

(N) (M) **** Dutton CDLX 7211. De'ath

Billy Mayerl was the most popular English composer/performer of light music in the syncopated style in the 1920s and '30s. It is indeed a very English style; he never went to America, not sure if he would be welcome there, with Gershwin reigning. But that only makes his music the more individual. *Marigold* was his most famous piece and that, alas, is not included here, but much else is, and **Leslie De'ath** knows just how to play it, with crisp fingers, a swinging rhythm and a light touch. There are two-dozen delectable pieces to choose from and the collection is of such a quality that you can play it right through, or pick and choose. Try the opening and closing Irishry, the charming *Meadowsweet* and *Alpine Bluebell* from 'In my Garden' or the deliciously frivolous *Milkman's Scherzo* and *Clowning*, and the two 'Insect oddities', *Ladybird Lullaby* and *Praying Mantis*. For gentle poetry, sample *The Forgotten Forest* and you will surely be hooked. The recording is excellent.

MAYR, Simon (1763–1845)

L'amor coniugale (Farsa sentimenal)

(BB) **(*) Naxos 8.660198/9. Rizzone, Bille, Charalgina, Machej, Bellavia, Trammell, Württemberg PO, Franklin

The *farsa sentimental*, an amalgamation of *opera buffa* and *opera seria* into what might be described as *opera semiseria*, arrived in the 1790s, and it is into this category that Mayr's *L'amor coniugale* slips neatly. More remarkable is its plot, derived from the same source as Beethoven's *Fidelio*, which it pre-dates, arriving in Dresden in 1804, shortly before Beethoven's *Leonora*. However, Mayr's libretto places the action in 17th-century Poland. The characters are much the same as in Beethoven's opera, only with different names. The soprano role of Leonora is exchanged for Zeliska; her imprisoned husband Florestan becomes the tenor role,

Amorveno. Rocco the gaoler is now Peters; his daughter is now Floreska and the governor is Moroski. The narrative however is sentimentalized. Amorveno is in prison and left to starve to death, as the governor wants to seduce his wife who, although in disguise, is no longer the heroic rescuer, and the plot is resolved (after a modest brass fanfare) by the appearance of Ardelao (the hero's brother) who arrives after neither gaoler nor governor is willing to kill their prisoner. However weak the plot, the music itself has much charm, and it is most enjoyably sung by all concerned, with **Cinzia Rizzone** a delightful Zeliska. **Christopher Franklin** directs the piece with plenty of life and sparkle, and the **Württemberg Philharmonic Orchestra** play stylishly. The recording is excellent and the only reservation (and it is a big one) is that the accompanying notes give just over half a page to a synopsis which is not cued to the individual numbers. Even so, this is easy to enjoy.

David in spelunca Engaddi (David in the Cave of Engedi): Oratorio

(N) (BB) *** Naxos 8.570366/67. Ostermann, Horak, Ichihara, Duffe, Schneider, Simon Mayr Ch. & Ens., Hauk

Johann Simon Mayr's oratorio was written in 1795 and was first performed in Venice at the Ospedale dei Mendicanti, where there were plenty of female singers available. Here David is sung by a mezzo-soprano, and the other four members of the cast are also sopranos, which makes following the action a little difficult! However, there is a good synopsis, the music is lyrically appealing, and the singing is uniformly of a high standard (as is the chorus and orchestra). So this makes entertaining listening, even if it would have been far more enjoyable with a libretto and translation. However, one can get this from www.naxos.com/libretti/570366.htm

MEDTNER, Nikolai (1880–1951)

(i) *Piano Concertos 1 in C min., Op. 33; 2 in C min., Op. 50; 3 in E min. (Ballade), Op. 60; (Piano) Sonata-ballade in F sharp, Op. 27*

*** Chan. 9040 (2). Tozer; (i) LPO, Järvi

Piano Concerto 1 in C min. Op. 33; Liebliches Kind (arr. Sudbin)

*** BIS SACD 1588. Sudbin, São Paulo SO, Neschling –
TCHAIKOVSKY: *Piano Concerto 1* ***

(i) *Piano Concerto 1; Sonata-ballade*

*** Chan. 9038. Tozer, (i) LPO, Järvi

Piano Concertos 1; 3

⊗→ (BB) *** Naxos 8.553359. Scherbakov, Moscow SO, Ziva

(i) *Piano Concerto 2; (ii) Piano Quintet in C*

⊗→ (BB) *** Naxos 8.553390. Scherbakov, with (i) Moscow SO, Golovschin; (ii) Danel, Tedla, Bourová, Pudhoransk

Piano Concertos 2–3

*** Hyp. CDA 66580. Demidenko, BBC Scottish SO, Maksymiuk

*** Chan. 9039. Tozer, LPO, Järvi

Piano Concertos 2–3; Arabesque in A min., Op. 7/2; Tale in F min., Op. 26/3

(***) Testament mono SBT 1027. Composer, Philh. O, Dobrowen

Konstantin Scherbakov is highly sympathetic and offers very musical playing. He strikes us as more imaginative and subtle in both his range of dynamics and diversity of colour than any of his rivals. True, Geoffrey Tozer (Chandos) has the finer recording, but taken all round Scherbakov would make an eminently satisfactory first choice: artistically it is impeccable, as a recording it is very natural and well balanced and, not least, the price is right.

Yevgeny Sudbin takes on the recondite one-movement Medtner *Concerto*, coupling it with the Tchaikovsky *B flat minor*. This is commanding playing and inspires only the most exalted comparisons. It is good to see Medtner enjoy such youthful and brilliant advocacy, and with such impressive SACD sound too.

Tozer has obvious feeling for this composer and his playing has no lack of warmth and virtuosity. **Demidenko** has the greater fire and dramatic flair, and his performance with the **BBC Scottish Orchestra** under **Jerzy Maksymiuk** has one very much on the edge of one's chair. He is by no means as well recorded as Tozer: the sound of the piano is shallow and the orchestra lacks real transparency and is a bit two-dimensional in terms of front-to-back perspective.

On Testament we have two of the celebrated set of **Medtner's** own concerto recordings which the Maharajah of Mysore funded in the late 1940s. Medtner was then in his sixties but his playing is still pretty magisterial. These concertos and the early miniatures still possess an aristocratic allure and a musical finesse that it is difficult to resist. The performances were never reissued in the UK in the days of LP, and their reappearance at long last is as welcome as it is overdue. Good transfers.

Violin Sonatas 1 in B min., Op. 21; 2 in G, Op. 44

*** Chan. 9293. Mordkovitch, Tozer

The first two of Medtner's three *Violin Sonatas* come on a well-recorded Chandos release. **Lydia Mordkovitch** proves a most imaginative and thoughtful advocate of the sonata, betraying an effortless expressive freedom. Both she and her partner are well recorded.

Violin Sonata 3 (Sonata Epica), Op. 57

*** Erato 0630 15110-2. Repin, Berezovsky – RAVEL: *Violin Sonata* ***

Vadim Repin and **Boris Berezovsky** make a formidable partnership, and they give what is arguably the most sensitive and certainly the most persuasive account of the *Sonata Epica* since David Oistrakh and Alexander Goldweiser's celebrated Melodiya LP. They bring to it a wide range of colour and dynamics and infuse every phrase with life. Very natural recording-balance adds to the pleasure this CD gives.

PIANO MUSIC

Piano duet: Russian Round Dance; Knight Errant, Op. 58/1–2

*** Hyp. CDA 66654. Demidenko, Alexeev – RACHMANINOV: *Suite*, etc. ***

The Russian round-dance or *khorovod* was written in 1946 and Medtner and Moiseiwitsch recorded it the same year for EMI. Here it is given with great lightness of touch, though this partnership loses beauty of tone-production above *fortissimo*.

Dithyrambe, Op. 10/2; Elegy, Op. 59/2; Skazki (Fairy Tales): 1 (1915); in E min., Op. 14/2; in G, Op. 9/3; in D min. (Ophelia's Song); in C sharp min., Op. 35/4; Forgotten Melodies, 2nd Cycle, 1: Meditation; Primavera, Op. 39/3; 3 Hymns in Praise of Toil, Op. 49; Piano Sonata in E min. (The Night Wind), Op. 25/2; Sonata Triad, Op. 11/1–3 (CRD (ADD) CRD 3338/9)

Improvisation 2 (in Variation Form), Op. 47; Piano Sonata in F min., Op. 5 (CRD (ADD) CRD 3461)

3 Novelles, Op. 17; Romantic Sketches for the Young, Op. 54; Piano Sonatas in G min., Op. 22; A min., Op. 30; 2 Skazki, Op. 8 (CRD (ADD) CRD 3460)

Forgotten Melodies, Op. 39; 2 Skazki, Op. 48; Etude in C min.; I Loved Thee, Op. 32/4; Sonata minacciosa, Op. 53/2 (CRD (ADD) CRD 3509)

4 Skazki, Op. 34; Sonata-Ballade in F sharp, Op. 27; Sonata romantica in B flat min., Op. 53/1 (CRD (ADD) CRD 3498)

🅑 🅜 *** Milne

Medtner's art is subtle and elusive. He shows an aristocratic disdain for the obvious, a feeling for balance and proportion and a quiet harmonic refinement that offer consistent rewards. There is hardly a weak piece here, and **Milne** is a poetic advocate whose technical prowess is matched by first-rate artistry. Such is the quality of his playing that one is never tempted to think of this music as pale Rachmaninov. Milne has lived with Medtner for the best part of a lifetime, and this tells. His playing has refinement and authority, and the transcription he has made of the Pushkin setting, *I Loved Thee*, is quite magical. In the *Sonata minacciosa*, though Milne's playing might be more mercurial and incandescent, he brings valuable insights of his own. The *Sonata-Ballade* and *Sonata romantica* are also finely and perceptively played. Very good recording.

Skazki (Fairy Tales), Opp. 8, 9, 14, 20, 26, 31/3, 34, 35, 42, 48, 51; Skazka (1915); Romantic Sketches for the Young, Op. 54

🎕—*** Hyp. CDA 67491/2 (2).Milne

The present issue collects the numerous *Skazki*, or 'Fairy Tales', which Milne has already recorded for CRD. Milne makes out the strongest case for these imaginative pieces, both at the keyboard and in his excellent notes.

Forgotten Melodies, Opp. 38–9; 3 Marches, Op. 8; Sonata-Ballade in F sharp, Op. 27; Sonata Idylle in G, Op. 56; Sonata Skazka in C min., Op. 25/1; Sonata Triad, Op. 11; Sonatas in A min., Op. 30; in B flat min. (Sonata romantica), Op. 53/1; in E min. (Night Wind), Op. 25/2; in F min., Op. 5; in F min. (Sonata minacciosa), Op. 53/2; in G min., Op. 22

🎕—**** Hyp. CDA 67221-4 (4). Hamelin

Marc-André Hamelin's artistry is to be found at its most consummate in this four-CD set of the sonatas and miscellaneous piano music. If you find Medtner just a little bland or predictable, then try this set, for in Hamelin's hands it is neither. Playing touched by distinction.

Forgotten Melodies, Cycles I & II Opp. 38–9; 2 Marches, Op. 8

🎕—*** Hyp. CDA 67578. Hamelin

This is a reissue from **Marc-André Hamelin's** outstanding four-disc boxed set of Medtner's piano music (above) which was a *Gramophone* 'Critics' Choice', and also won a Diapason d'Or. If you have not yet tried this repertoire, this is a good sampler.

Sonata-Reminiscenza in A min., Op. 38/1

**(*) RCA 82876 65390-2. Kissin – SCRIABIN: *5 Preludes*, etc.; STRAVINSKY: *3 Movements from Petrushka* **(*)

Kissin is a wonderful pianist, of that there is no question. However, those who recall the celebrated Gilels account of this score will find a certain self-awareness here that inhibits him from finding the same depth. He is better in the virtuoso shallows of *Petrushka*.

MENDELSSOHN, Fanny
(1805–47)

Piano Trio in D, Op. 11

🅱🅱 *** Hyp. Helios CDH 55078. Dartington Piano Trio – Clara SCHUMANN: *Trio in G min* ***

Like Clara Schumann's *G minor Trio* with which it is coupled, the *Piano Trio* has impeccable craftsmanship and great facility. Its ideas are pleasing, though not strongly individual. The **Dartington Piano Trio** play most persuasively and give much pleasure. Excellent recording.

Lieder

*** Hyp. CDA 67110. Gritton, Asti

Fanny Mendelssohn's response to German poets from Goethe to Heine is at least the equal of her brother's, at once memorably tuneful and subtle in her illumination of the texts, adding distinctively to the Lieder tradition. Her writing is not just poetic but often vigorous, with fine accompaniments to match. **Susan Gritton**, sweet if just a little unvaried in tone, and **Eugene Asti** are refreshing, consistently sympathetic interpreters. They provide their own perceptive notes: Fanny's caustic comments on the poet Heine bring the man vividly to life.

MENDELSSOHN, Felix
(1809–47)

(i) Capriccio brillant, Op. 22; (i; ii) Double Concerto for Violin & Piano; (i) Rondo brillant, Op. 29; Serenade & Allegro giocoso, Op. 43 (BIS CD 713); Piano Concertos 1 in G min., Op. 25; 2 in D min., Op. 40; Piano Concerto in A min. (BIS CD 718); (iii) Double Piano Concertos: in A flat; E (BIS CD 688); (ii) Violin Concerto in D min.; Violin Concerto in E min., Op. 64 (1844 version); Octet, Op. 20: Scherzo (orchestral version) (BIS CD 935)

Ⓑ *** BIS CD 966/68. (i) Brautigam; (ii) van Keulen; (iii) Derwinger, Pöntinen, Amsterdam New Sinf., Markiz

Ⓑ *** BIS **SACD** 1766 (equivalent to 4 CDs) (artists as above)

These are exemplary recordings of exemplary performances. Indeed it is difficult to flaw them. They are available separately (the individual catalogue numbers are listed within the titles above), but there is a price advantage in purchasing them all together. The interesting account of the *E minor Violin Concerto* in its original form (beautifully played by **Isabelle van Keulen**) is of particular interest. Mendelssohn spent seven years (1838–45) working over what is perhaps his most successful concertante work and this is its earlier draft. Its gestation is discussed in greater detail in the accompanying notes for the individual disc, but the notes here are still pretty copious.

This extraordinary alternative 'single layer' SACD – obviously the shape of things to come, plays normally on any SACD player (but not on a CD deck). The quality is comparable with the normal CDs but there are 4 hours, 16 minutes playing time on this single disc, with cues for all the individual movements of the concertos incorporated.

(i) Piano Concerto in A min. (for piano and strings); (iv) Piano Concertos 1 in G min; 2 in D min.

🎕—🅱🅱 **** Warner Apex 8573 89088-2. Katsaris; (i) Franz Liszt CO, Rolla; (ii) Leipzig G. O, Masur

It was a happy idea to couple the early *A minor Concerto* at budget price with the two major works in this form. It is impossible not to respond to **Katsaris's** vitality, even if at times there is a feeling of rushing his fences. He plays with enormous vigour in the outer movements of the later works and receives strong support from **Masur**. There is nothing heavy, yet the music is given more substance than usual, while the central slow movements bring a relaxed lyrical *espresso* which provides admirable contrast. The full, well-balanced recording has attractive ambience and sparkle.

(i) Piano Concerto in A min. (for piano & strings); String Symphonies 9 in C min.; 10 in B min.; 12 in G min.

*** Australian Decca Eloquence (ADD) 476 8460. ASMF, Marriner, (i) with Ogdon

The remarkable and ambitious *A minor Concerto* is played with great verve and spirit by **John Ogdon**. The *String Symphonies*, written around the same time, are no less remarkable. All the music is splendidly brought to life by committed, vivacious playing and excellent, vintage 1960s (Argo/Decca) sound.

Piano Concerto 1 in G min., Op. 25

*** DG 474 291-2. Lang Lang, Chicago SO, Barenboim – TCHAIKOVSKY: *Piano Concerto 1* **(*)

Piano Concerto 1, Op. 25; Capriccio brillant, Op. 22

(BB) *** Warner Apex 0927 99842-2. Huang, NYPO, Masur – MOZART: *Piano Concerto 21* ***

The close balance of the piano establishes this as a big-scale performance, with the minor-key bite of the opening strongly presented. In the slow movement **Lang Lang** opts for a tempo on the broad side, lessening its role as a song without words. With sparkling playing, the performance erupts into a winningly joyful account of the finale. A rare and attractive coupling for the distinctive account of the Tchaikovsky.

A fresh and pleasing account of 1 plus a sparkling *Capriccio* from **Helen Huang**, and the Mozart coupling is enjoyable, too. Excellent value.

(i) Piano Concerto 1 in G min.; Symphonies (ii) 4 (Italian); (iii) 5 (Reformation)

(BB) (***) Dutton mono CDBP9780. (i) Dorfman, LSO, Goehr; (ii) Hallé O, Harty; (iii) Paris Conservatoire O, Munch

Good to have the opportunity of hearing **Sir Hamilton Harty's** account of the *Italian Symphony* with the **Hallé Orchestra**, recorded in the early 1930s, when he was its permanent conductor. RL has long treasured Charles Munch's 78-r.p.m. set of the *Reformation* and has never quite understood why it was never transferred to LP. It is a vibrant and sensitive performance and it finds the **Paris Conservatoire Orchestra** in top form. Exemplary transfers.

Piano Concertos 1–2; Capriccio brillant

⊕ ✿ **** Chan. 9215. Shelley, LMP

Piano Concertos 1–2; Capriccio brillant; Rondo brillant

⊕ (BB) **** Naxos 8.550681-2. Frith, Slovak State PO (Košice), Stankovsky

Piano Concertos Nos 1–2; Capriccio brillant; Rondo brillant; Serenade & Allegro Giocoso in B min., Op. 43

⊕ **** Hyp. CDA 66969. Hough, CBSO, Foster

(i) Piano Concertos 1–2; Prelude & Fugue, Op. 35/1; Sonata in E, Op 6

⊕ (M) **** Sony (ADD) 88697 00818-2. Perahia; (i) ASMF, Marriner

(i) Piano Concertos 1–2, Songs without Words, Op. 19/1, 2, & 6 (Venetian Gondola Song); Op. 30/4 & 6; Op. 38/6; Op. 53/1; Op. 62/1 & 6 (Spring Song); Op. 67/4 (Spinning Song) & 6; Op. 85/6; Op. 102/5

(M) *** Decca 466 425-2. Schiff, (i) with Bav. RSO, Dutoit

Stephen Hough treats these compact minor-key works with a biting intensity. Yet with freer expressiveness and bigger contrasts he also brings out extra poetry, and in the finales a sparkling wit. He also has the advantage of the most generous and very apt couplings, three other, rare, concertante piano works by Mendelssohn. The point and delicacy of Hough's passage-work are a constant delight.

Howard Shelley offers marvellous playing in every respect: fresh, sparkling and dashing in the fast movements, poetic and touching in the slower ones. The **London Mozart Players** are a group of exactly the right size for these works and they point rhythms nicely and provide the necessary lift. Shelley dispatches the *Capriccio brillant* with similar aplomb, and the recording-balance is admirably judged, with rich, truthful recorded sound.

Benjamin Frith on Naxos is a hardly less personable and nimble soloist: he is sensitively touching in the slow movements. The **Slovak Orchestra** accompany with vigour and enthusiasm, and if the effect is at times less sharply rhythmic this is partly the effect of a somewhat more reverberant acoustic. What makes the Naxos disc very competitive is the inclusion of the *Rondo brillant*, which Frith dispatches with admirable vigour and sparkle. This disc is very good value indeed.

András Schiff also plays both concertos marvellously, with poetry, great delicacy and fluency, while his virtuosity is effortless. He is given excellent acccompaniments by **Dutoit** and the Bavarian players, and the Decca recording is first class. His simplicity of style suits the *Songs without Words*, although some might find his approach a little cool. Yet the famous *Spring Song* shows him at his best. The recording is again most natural and realistic.

Murray Perahia's playing catches the Mendelssohnian spirit with admirable perception. There is sensibility and sparkle, the slow movements are shaped most beautifully and the partnership with **Marriner** is very successful, for the **Academy** give a most sensitive backing. The recording could be more transparent but it does not lack body, and the piano timbre is fully acceptable. At mid-price, a very recommendable issue.

Double Piano Concertos: in A flat; in E

⊕ *** Hyp. CDA 66567. Coombs, Munro, BBC Scottish SO, Maksymiuk

(BB) *** Naxos 8.553416. Frith, Tinney, Dublin RTE Sinf., O'Duinn

Mendelssohn's *Double Concerto in A flat* is the most ambitious of all his concertante works, and the work in E brings an expansive first movement too; they provide formidable evidence of the teenage composer's fluency and technical finesse. **Stephen Coombs** and **Ian Munro** prove ideal advocates, playing with delectable point and imagination, finding a wit and poetry in the writing that might easily lie hidden, with even the incidental passage-work magnetizing the ear. The recording of the pianos is on the shallow side, and the string-tone is thin too, but that is not inappropriate for the music.

The Naxos disc challenges the outstanding Hyperion issue coupling these same two charming double concertos. If the Irish players are not quite as persuasive as their Scottish counterparts on Hyperion, their playing is just as refined, and **Frith** and **Tinney** are a fair match for Coombs and Munro, less powerful but just as magnetic and even more poetic. The transparent recording helps, very appropriate for such youthful music.

Double Piano Concerto in E.

*** Chan. 9711. Güher and Süther Pekinel, Philh. O, Marriner – BRUCH; MOZART: *Double Concertos* ***

Mendelssohn wrote his *Double Piano Concerto* when he was only fourteen, yet it contains many ideas that are entirely characteristic of his mature style. In such a performance as this its freshness justifies the length, for it brings an accompaniment from **Marriner** and the Academy, finely pointed, which does not inflate the piece. The **Pekinel** sisters, as in the other two works, give a fresh, alert performance with pinpoint ensemble. Warm, full sound.

Violin Concerto in D min.; (i) Double Concerto in D min. for Violin, Piano & Strings; Violin Concerto in E min., Op. 64

(BB) *** Naxos 8.553844. Bisengaliev, N. Sinfonia, Penney; (i) with Frith

Two juvenilia are here dispatched with zest and freshness by these excellent musicians, even if in the *D minor Violin Concerto* **Bisengaliev's** finale is a bit headlong. Spirited playing from the **Northern Sinfonia** under **Andrew Penney** and a predictably stylish contribution from **Benjamin Frith**.

Violin Concerto in E min., Op. 64 (DVD version)

(*) EMI **DVD 490445-9. Grumiaux, O. Nat. de l'ORTF, Rosenthal (with BACH: *Violin Partita 2, BWV 1004: Sarabande & Chaconne*; BLOCH: *Baal Shem: Il Nigun* (with André Chometon)) – BEETHOVEN: *Violin Concerto* **(*)

The **Grumiaux** DVD account of the Mendelssohn *Concerto* was made in the Palais de la Méditerranée in Nice in January 1961. In his day Grumiaux was an aristocrat of violinists, and his tonal refinement and selfless artistry made his achievement quite special. The sound is somewhat wanting in bloom and climaxes are wanting in transparency, but the essential qualities of this great violinist emerge in this work and in the various shorter pieces listed above. The Paganini was an encore at the Mendelssohn concert, while the Bach and Bloch pieces were recorded variously at the ORTF studios and in the Netherlands.

(i) Violin Concerto in E min. Op. 64 (Original Version); (ii) Octet in E flat, Op. 20 (Revised Version); (iii) 3 Lieder

*** DG 477 6634. Hope, with (i) COE, Hengelbrock; (ii) COE soloists; (iii) Knauer

This is **Daniel Hope's** début recording for DG, and very good it is too. He plays the *Violin Concerto* in its original (1844) form, which DG claim as a 'world première recording': it was in fact recorded in 1998 by Isabella van Keulen on the BIS label (see the collection of concertos, above). The playing both of Hope and of the **Chamber Orchestra of Europe** under **Thomas Hengelbrock** is first class and the *Octet*, heard in its critically revised 1832 version (which is a première recording), has great lightness of touch and character.

Violin Concerto in E min., Op. 64 (CD versions)

🎧 (M) **** Decca 460 976-2. Chung, Montreal SO, Dutoit – BRUCH: *Violin Concerto 1; Scottish Fantasy* ****

🎧 *** EMI 5 56418-2. Chang, BPO, Jansons – SIBELIUS: *Violin Concerto* ***

🎧 *** Telarc CD 80507. McDuffie, SCO, Swensen – BRUCH: *Violin Concerto 1* ✿ ***

*** Teldec 2564 69366-8. Perlman, Chicago SO, Barenboim – BRAHMS: *Double Concerto* ***

(M) *** EMI (ADD) 5 62591-2. Perlman, LSO, Previn – TCHAIKOVSKY: *Concerto* **(*)

*** Virgin 545663-2. Capuçon, Mahler CO, Harding – SCHUMANN: *Violin Concerto in D min.****

(B) *** DG Double (ADD) 453 142-2 (2). Milstein, VPO, Abbado – BEETHOVEN: *Concerto* *** ; BRAHMS: *Concerto* **(*) ; TCHAIKOVSKY: *Concerto* ***

(BB) (***) Naxos mono 8.110977. Milstein, Philharmonic-Symphony O, New York, Barbirolli – BRUCH: *Violin Concerto 1*; TCHAIKOVSKY: *Violin Concerto* (***)

(BB) *** Naxos 8.550153. Nishizaki, Slovak PO, Jean – TCHAIKOVSKY: *Concerto* ***

(M) *** CRD (ADD) CRD 3369, R. Thomas, Bournemouth SO – BEETHOVEN: *Romances 1–2*; SCHUBERT: *Konzertstück* ***

(M) *** DG 445 515-2. Mutter, BPO, Karajan – BRAHMS: *Violin Concerto* ***

(M) *** DG 463 641-2. Mutter, BPO, Karajan – BRUCH: *Concerto 1* ***

(M) *** EMI 5 18173-2. Kennedy, ECO, Tate – BRUCH: *Concerto 1*; SCHUBERT: *Rondo* ***

(M) *** EMI (ADD) 5 66906-2. Menuhin, Philh. O, Kurtz – BRUCH: *Concerto 1* ***

(M) *** EMI Legend (ADD) 5 57766 (with bonus **DVD**: MOZART: *Violin Concerto 3, K. 216*). Menuhin, Philh. O, Kurtz – BRUCH: *Violin Concerto****

(M) *** RCA **SACD** (ADD) 82876 61391-2. Heifetz, Boston SO, Munch – BEETHOVEN: *Violin Concerto****

(M) **(*) DG (ADD) 477 6349. Mintz, Chicago SO, Abbado (with KREISLER: *Caprice Viennoise; Liebeslied; Liebesfreud*, with Benson, piano) – BRUCH: *Violin Concerto 1* ***

Ⓜ **(*) RCA 09026 61743-2. Heifetz, Boston SO, Munch –
TCHAIKOVSKY: *Concerto, etc.* **(*)

Kyung Wha Chung favours speeds faster than usual in all
three movements, and the result is sparkling, with the lovely
slow movement fresh and songful, not at all sentimental.
With warmly sympathetic accompaniment from **Dutoit** and
the **Montreal orchestra**, amply recorded, the result is one of
Chung's happiest records. The coupling of Bruch's *G minor
Concerto* and *Scottish Fantasy* in Decca's 'Legends' series is
ideal.

Unlike the Sibelius with which it is coupled, **Sarah
Chang's** account of the Mendelssohn was recorded under
studio conditions in the Philharmonie, Berlin. Here too she
offers an astonishingly mature reading, more restrained
than some, but still magnetic in its thoughtfulness and
spontaneous poetry. Warm, atmospheric sound.

McDuffie's Mendelssohn is a performance of disarming
simplicity, with natural phrasing and the most beautiful
tone. This is a less passionate work than the Bruch coupling,
and **Swensen** provides an orchestral backcloth on a comparable scale, but, as with the Bruch, the interchanges between
soloist and orchestra have the natural spontaneity of live
music-making, and the slow movement brings a flowing
cantilena of touching beauty and raptly gentle feeling at the
close, before the finale dashes off, the orchestra matching
McDuffie's sparkle with comparable vivacity and colour. The
Telarc recording, full textured and with a believable perspective, is well up to the high standards of the house.

Perlman's 1993 Chicago version, strong and volatile, was
recorded live and originally issued in coupling with the second Prokofiev. It makes an excellent, more generous coupling in the new format with the powerful Perlman/Ma
version of the Brahms *Double Concerto*.

Perlman's 1972 recording was very highly regarded in its
day. He gives a performance as full of flair as almost any,
and he is superbly matched by the **LSO** under **Previn**, at that
time at their very peak. With ripe recording, this remains
competitive in its mid-priced reissue in the 'Perlman
Edition', although the Tchaikovsky coupling is not quite its
match.

The lightness and resilience of **Renaud Capuçon's** playing at the very start of the Mendelssohn, matched by the
transparent textures of the **Mahler Chamber Orchestra**
under **Daniel Harding**, instantly establish the distinctive
character of his version of a much-recorded concerto. The
urgency of the main *Allegro* still allows the crystalline precision of Capuçon's playing of rapid passage-work to come
over without any hint of rush. The chamber scale works well,
but Capuçon's formidable virtuosity ensures that there is no
feeling of a small-scale performance. With free, open sound,
recorded in the Jugendstilltheater in Vienna, this makes
an outstanding version of an apt and rare coupling.

Milstein's later DG version is a highly distinguished performance, very well accompanied. His account of the slow
movement is more patrician than Menuhin's and his slight
reserve is projected by sound which is bright, clean and clear
in its CD remastering. This now comes on a DG Double
which also includes the Beethoven and Brahms concertos.

Milstein made four recordings of the Mendelssohn, and

this Naxos reissue, his first, comes from May 1945. There is
a sense of exhilaration and a freshness that is very persuasive
and the engineers capture Milstein's tone with great fidelity.
When transferred to LP in the early 1950s there was a much
wider frequency-range as well as quieter surfaces. Mark
Obert–Thorn's transfers are exemplary; the performance
should be snapped up, particularly at so competitive a price.

Takako Nishizaki gives an inspired reading of the concerto, warm, spontaneous and full of temperament. The central *Andante* is on the slow side, but well shaped, not
sentimental, while the outer movements are exhilarating,
with excellent playing from the **Slovak Philharmonic**.
Though the forwardly placed violin sounds over-bright, the
recording is full and warm. A splendid coupling at super-
bargain price.

Ronald Thomas's account is in many ways the opposite
of a dashing virtuoso approach, yet his apt, unforced choice
of speeds, his glowing purity of intonation and the fine coordination with the orchestra he leads (an amazing achievement in this often complex, fast-flowing music) put this
among the most satisfying versions available. It is intensely
refreshing from first to last, and is helped by excellent
recording and fine couplings.

The freshness of **Anne-Sophie Mutter's** approach communicates vividly to the listener, creating the feeling of hearing the work anew. Her gentleness and radiant simplicity in
the *Andante* are very appealing, and the light, sparkling finale
is a delight. Mutter is given a small-scale image, projected
forward from the orchestral backcloth; the sound is both
full and refined. This fine performance comes alternatively
coupled with either Brahms or Bruch.

Kennedy establishes a positive, masculine view of the
work from the very start, but fantasy here goes with firm
control. The slow movement brings a simple, songful view
of the haunting melody, and the finale sparkles winningly,
with no feeling of rush. With a bonus in the rare Schubert
Rondo and clear, warm recording, it makes an excellent recommendation.

The restrained nobility of **Menuhin's** phrasing of the famous principal melody of the slow movement has long been
a hallmark of his reading with **Efrem Kurtz**, who provides
polished and sympathetic support. The sound of the CD
transfer is bright, with the soloist dominating but the orchestral texture well detailed.

Menuhin's coupling with Bruch also comes in EMI's new
Legend series with a bonus DVD of Mozart's *Third (G major)
Concerto*, which was filmed with the Orchestre de Chambre
de l'ORTF in Paris in 1967 and makes an interesting, but not
exceptional, bonus.

As one might expect, **Heifetz** gives a fabulous performance. His speeds are consistently fast, yet in the slow movement his flexible phrasing sounds so inevitable and easy that
it is hard not to be convinced. The finale is a tour de force,
light and sparkling, with every note in place, and **Munch's**
accompaniment throughout is outstanding. The 1959
recording is very good for its period and sounds well on CD,
where it is paired with Tchaikovsky. But the new SACD transfer brings an added warmth, and the new coupling, the
Beethoven *Concerto*, is eminently recommendable.

Mintz's version is powerfully conceived, less reticent than Mutter, less spontaneous than Perlman. It is not quite the equal of the Bruch coupling, although **Abbado** gives fine support. The Kreisler encores make a welcome bonus.

Jaime Laredo's version on a budget CD brings an attractively direct reading, fresh and alert but avoiding mannerism, marked by consistently sweet and true tone from the soloist. The orchestral ensemble is amazingly good when you remember that the soloist himself is directing. Vivid recording. (Regis RRC 1152)

2 Concert Pieces for Clarinet & Basset Horn: in F min., Op. 113; in D min., Op. 114

⊕₋ *** EMI 5 57359-2. S. Meyer, W. Meyer, ASMF, Sillito – BAERMANN: *Clarinet Quintet 3*; WEBER: *Clarinet Quintet* ***

Ⓑ *** Hyp. Dyad CDD 22017 (2). King, Dobrée, LSO, Francis (with Concert – see below ***)

*** Sup. SU 3554-2. Peterkova, Prague Philh. O, Bělohlávek – BRUCH: *Double Concerto*; ROSSINI: *Introduction, Theme and Variations; Variations in C* ***

These two delightful pieces for clarinet and basset horn are miniature concertos in all but name, each in three tiny movements. They are perfect vehicles for the brother-and-sister team of **Sabine** and **Wolfgang Meyer**, here opting for string orchestra accompaniment rather than the original piano. The perfect coupling for the Weber and Baermann *Quintets*, very well recorded.

They are also played with a nice blend of expressive spontaneity and high spirits by **Georgina Dobrée**, who proves a nimble partner for the ever-sensitive **Thea King**. This is part of an excellent two-disc set, including other attractive concertante works by Max Bruch, Crusell, Spohr and other less familar names.

Ludmila Peterkova also brings out the charm of these two miniature concertos as well as the wit, with **Jiří Bělohlávek** and the **Prague Philharmonia** sensitive partners. Excellent, full-bodied sound.

The Hebrides (Fingal's Cave) Overture

Ⓜ (**) Beulah mono 3PD12. BBC SO, Boult – SCHUBERT: *Symphony 9* (**(*)); WAGNER: *Die Meistersinger: Overture* (**)

Boult, recording the *Hebrides Overture* in 1933 with the recently founded **BBC Symphony Orchestra**, takes a fresh, generally brisk view, which allows a degree of flexibility in the build-up of ostinatos and in the lovely reprise of the second subject, but with no romantic excess. The Beulah transfer is dry, with no added reverberation, not helped by a high but even surface hiss; but the body of sound makes one readily forget the limitations.

Symphonies for Strings 1–12; 13 in C min. (single movement)

*** BIS CD 938/940. Amsterdam New Sinf., Markiz

*** BIS-**SACD** 1738 (equivalent to 3 CDs) as above: Amsterdam New Sinf., Markiz

Symphonies for Strings 1–12

⊕₋ Ⓜ *** Hyp. CDS 44081/3. L. Festival O, Pople

Symphonies for String Orchestra 1–6 (Naxos 8.553161)

Symphonies for String Orchestra 7–9 (Naxos 8.553162)

Symphonies for String Orchestra 10–13 (Sinfoniesatz) (Naxos 8.553163)

⊕₋ ⒷⒷ *** N. CO, Ward

Mendelssohn's early symphonies for strings, lost for 150 years, were rediscovered in 1950. The first ten were student works and the last two, together with the virtually unknown *Symphony Movement in C minor* (13), had all been completed before their young composer reached the age of 14. The playing of the **Amsterdam New Sinfonietta** is vibrant and alive, and the recording has a warmth and clarity that give the set the edge over almost all its current rivals. This music is full of charm, and the quality of Mendelssohn's youthful invention is little short of astonishing.

Like the BIS collection of concertos above, this extraordinary alternative 'single layer' SACD (obviously the shape of things to come) plays normally on any SACD player (but not on a CD deck). The quality is comparable with that of normal CDs but there are 4 hours, 16 minutes playing time on this single disc, with cues for all the individual movements of the symphonies included.

Originally issued in 1991/2 on three separate discs, **Ross Pople's** set is among his finest recordings. He achieves modern-instrument performances that are as polished and spirited as they are lyrically persuasive and dramatic. Slow movements are both gracious and with genuine gravitas and much depth of feeling, often elegiac (sample 9). The contrapuntal interplay of the *Allegros* has an attractive lightness of touch (as in the splendid opening movement of 12), yet the music is never made to sound trivial. The recordings, made between 1985 and 1990 in the Church of Edward the Confessor, Mottingham, Kent, are warm and natural, and detail is not clouded.

Nicholas Ward and the **Northern Chamber Orchestra** match rivals at whatever price. The freshness and incisiveness of the performances are enhanced by bright, clean recording, made in the Concert Hall of Broadcasting House in Manchester. Not only does Ward bring out the exhilarating sparkle and vigour of the fast movements – with Mendelssohn, even at the age of 11, giving clear anticipations of his mature style – but he also gives apt emotional weight to such beautiful lyrical movements as the *Andante* of 2 or the darkly slow introduction to the one-movement 10 *in B minor*. All three discs can be warmly recommended to everyone.

Symphonies 1 in C min., Op. 11; (i) 2 in B flat, Op. 52 (Hymn of Praise); 3 in A min. (Scottish), Op. 56; 4 in A (Italian), Op. 91; 5 in D min. (Reformation), Op. 107

(N) (B) *** DG 477 7581. BPO, Karajan; (i) with Mathis, Rehmann, Hollweg, Deutschen Op. Ch.

(B) *** Decca Trio 470 946-2 (3). (i) Banse, Rubens, Cole, Berlin R. Ch.; Deutsches SO, Berlin, Ashkenazy

Symphonies 1–5; Overture: The Hebrides

(M) *** Chan. 10224X (3). Philh. O, Weller (with Haymon, Hagley, Straka, Philh. Ch. in Symphony 2)

Karajan's distinguished set of the Mendelssohn *Symphonies* was recorded in 1971/2 in the Berlin Jesus-Christus-Kirche. The early C minor work sounds particularly fresh and the *Hymn of Praise* brings the fullest sound of all; the very fine choral singing is vividly caught. The soloists make a good team, rather than showing any memorable individuality; but overall Karajan's performance is most satisfying. The *Scottish Symphony* is a particularly remarkable account and the *Italian* shows the **Berlin Philharmonic** in sparkling form; the only drawback is Karajan's characteristic omission of both first-movement exposition repeats. There are few reservations to be made about the *Reformation Symphony* and the sound has been effectively clarified without too much loss of weight.

Weller's set of the Mendelssohn symphonies can stand comparison with the finest alternatives. Certainly it is the most beautifully recorded, the Chandos sound richly full-bodied, though not sharply defined.These are warm, affectionate readings which include exposition repeats and build excitingly to climaxes. In the *Reformation Symphony* and in *Fingal's Cave*, which follows, there is an emotional thrust that is very involving, leading to a joyfully exultant conclusion in the finale. Again in the *Hymn of Praise* (2) from the opening trombone solo onwards it is the warmth and weight of the recorded sound that tells, with a large chorus set against full-bodied, satisfyingly string-based orchestral sound. Though again speeds are often dangerously slow, the sense of spontaneity in the performance makes it compelling throughout. A considerable achievement.

The alternative tastefully presented Trio box collects **Ashkenazy's** Decca Mendelssohn symphonies, recorded at various times between 1993 and 1997 with the **Deutsches Symphonie-Orchester, Berlin** (the reborn Radio Symphony Orchestra). The set has a great deal going for it, particularly at this attractive price, with characterfully shaped phrasing and vital playing. Ashkenazy is unfailingly musical and fresh in his approach, and both the playing of this fine orchestra and the Decca recording are first rate.

Symphonies 1; 5 (Reformation)

(BB) *** Warner Apex 256460370-2. Leipzig GO, Masur; (i) with Bonney, Schönheit, Leipzig R. Ch.

Masur's mastery in his later Mendelssohn recordings is due in good measure to his ability to adopt relatively fast speeds and make them sound easy and relaxed, not hurried and breathless, and in both symphonies here Masur is faster than his principal rivals on disc, not just in *Allegros* but in slower movements too. In 1 and 5 that works very well indeed, bringing an alert freshness with no hint of sentimentality.

(i) Symphony 2 (Hymn of Praise); Psalm 114; A Midsummer Night's Dream: Overture

*** EuroArts **DVD** 2054668. Leipzig GO, Chailly; (i) with Schwanewilms, Schnitzer, Seifert, Leipzig Ch. (Dir: Michael Beyer) (with Documentary film: *Chailly in Leipzig*; RIHM: *Verwandlung*)

The EuroArts DVD offers the same performances as on the (deleted) Decca disc of the *Hymn of Praise*, but adds the other items in the concert celebrating **Riccardo Chailly's** arrival in Leipzig as the new music director of the **Leipzig Gewandhaus Orchestra** and of the opera. The original version of *Lobgesang* is in some ways disappointing next to Mendelssohn's own revised version. But seeing the performance as well as hearing it in the handsome modern Gewandhaus Hall minimizes the disappointment and, though the final chorus cannot match the revision, the visible enthusiasm of the singers and of the conductor (mouthing the words) makes it much more enjoyable. The extra items are also well worth hearing, Mendelssohn's strong and forthright setting of *Psalm 114* for chorus and orchestra and the thoughtful and beautifully written orchestral work, composed expressly for this occasion by the distinguished German composer, Wolfgang Rihm. Even the sound seems better when accompanied by vision.

Symphony 2 (Hymn of Praise)

*** DG 423 143-2. Connell, Mattila, Blochwitz, L. Symphony Ch., LSO, Abbado

*** Naïve OP 30-98. Isokoski, Bach, Lang, Ch. Musicus Köln, Das neue Orchester, Spering

(N) **(*) Carus 83.213. Karg, Gura, Maria Bernius, Stuttgart Ch., Deutsche Chamber Philharmonie Bremen, Frieder Bernius

Abbado's full-price digital version is very fine, brushing aside all sentimentality, both fresh and sympathetic and, though the recording is not ideally clear on inner detail, the brightness reinforces the conductor's view. The chorus, well focused, is particularly impressive, and the sweet-toned tenor, **Hans-Peter Blochwitz**, is outstanding among the soloists.

Spering presents a performance of the *Hymn of Praise* in period style. With clean, crisp textures this is most refreshing, full of incidental beauties. For example, the once-celebrated duet for the two soprano soloists, *Ich harrete des Herrn* ('I waited for the Lord'), is intensely beautiful in its simplicity, with **Soile Isokoski** (also in Herreweghe's *Elijah*) and **Mechthild Bach** both angelically sweet yet nicely contrasted. The tenor soloist, **Frieder Lang**, is also exceptionally sweet-toned, though his projection is keen enough to make the *Huter, ist die Nacht bald hin?* ('Watchman, what of the night?') episode very intense and dramatic. Though not always clear in inner definition, the freshness of the choral singing matches that of the whole performance.

In the Carus recording, though the soprano of **Christiane Karg** initially sounds too shallow in her first solo, she comes into her own in the duet, set to the words 'I waited for the Lord'. The great moment which follows is set to the words *Die Nacht ist vergangen* ('the night has departed'), a moment which sends a thrill through all performers, as it certainly does in this recording. The final fugue is impressive too, very clearly defined here, with a final resounding reference to the 'All that has life and breath' theme. The choral singing is of high quality throughout, but overall this Carus version would not be a first choice.

Symphony 3 (Scottish); Overtures: Calm Sea and Prosperous Voyage; The Hebrides; Ruy Blas

(BB) **(*) Naxos 8.550222. Slovak PO, Dohnányi

Symphony 3 in A min. (Scottish); (i) A Midsummer Night's Dream: Overture & Incidental Music

●━ 🌸 (M) **** Decca (ADD) 466 990-2. LSO, Maag; (i) with Vyvyan, Lowe, ROHCG female ch.

Maag's classic account of the *Scottish Symphony* is remarkable for its freshness and natural spontaneity. The opening cantilena is poised and phrased very beautifully and sets the mood for what is to follow. A pity that the exposition repeat is not included, and though in the last movement the final *Maestoso* is measured, the effect remains most compelling, almost Klemperian in manner, with superb horn-playing. The *Midsummer Night's Dream* excerpts date from 1957 and sound equally fresh, and this new Legends mastering includes the vocal and choral numbers on the original LP, which were not included on the previous reissue. Strongly recommended – a wholly delightful disc.

Oliver Dohnányi conducts a joyful account of the *Scottish Symphony* on Naxos, given the more impact by forward recording. Mendelssohn's lilting rhythms in all the fast movements are delightfully bouncy, and though the slow movement brings few hushed *pianissimos*, its full warmth is brought out without sentimentality. The three overtures, also very well done, not least the under-appreciated *Ruy Blas*, make an excellent coupling.

Symphonies 3 in A min. (Scottish); 4 (Italian)

(M) *** DG 427 810-2. LSO, Abbado

(BB) **** ASV Resonance CD RSN 3018. O of St John's, Lubbock

*** Mer. CDE 84261. Apollo CO, Chernaik

(B) *** Virgin 2x1 3 49983-2 (2). LCP, Norrington – SCHUMANN: *Symphonies 3 & 4* **(*)

Symphonies 3 (Scottish); 4 (Italian); Overture, Athalia

●━ (M) **** RCA 82876 76234-2. Bamberg SO, Flor

Symphonies 3 (Scottish); 4 (Italian); Hebrides Overture

●━ (M) **** DG (ADD) 449 743-2. BPO, Karajan

Karajan's 1971 account of the *Scottish* is justly included among DG's 'Originals', as it is one of his finest recordings. The coupling was originally the *Fingal's Cave*, a characterful and evocative account, but now the *Italian Symphony* has been added, recorded two years later. This is also played very beautifully and brilliantly but, good though the performance is, it does not quite match that of the *Scottish* and it is just a shade wanting in spontaneity and sparkle.

As we have often said, **Claus Peter Flor** is a truly natural Mendelssohnian, and in this coupling of the two favourite symphonies he finds every bit of charm in the composer's delightful scoring, notably so in the lead-back in the first-movement exposition repeat of the *Italian*, and in the delectable Scherzo of the *Scottish*, where every detail is remarkably clear – you can even hear the horn arpeggios. He brings an easy warmth throughout, his pacing is nigh on perfect, there is sparkle and energy here, without the music ever being over-driven, the coda is beautifully prepared, then the horns sing out with great richness and dignity leading firmly to the symphony's very satisfying close. The *Athalia Overture* makes an exciting pendant, but the symphonies are truly memorable.

Abbado's fine DG digital recordings of the *Scottish* and *Italian Symphonies*, coupled together from his complete set, make a splendid mid-price bargain. The recording is admirably fresh and bright – atmospheric, too – and the ambience, if not absolutely sharply defined, is very attractive. Both first-movement exposition repeats are included.

Lubbock's coupling of the *Scottish* and *Italian Symphonies* makes an outstanding super-bargain reissue, offering performances of delightful lightness and point, warmly and cleanly recorded. The string section may be of chamber size but, amplified by a warm acoustic, the result sparkles, with rhythms lifted exhilaratingly. The slow movements are both on the slow side but flow easily with no suspicion of sentimentality, while the *Saltarello* finale of the *Fourth*, with the flute part delectably pointed, comes close to Mendelssohnian fairy music.

David Chernaik, gives performances of these two symphonies which in their vitality and freshness are second to none. Although the recording is live, the audience is notably quiet and shows its presence only by clapping perfunctorily at the end of each work, a distraction which could and should have been edited out. The London-based **Apollo Chamber Orchestra**, on its toes throughout, is exactly the right size for these two symphonies, and the recording (in St John's, Smith Square) has been beautifully balanced. Chernaik includes the essential exposition repeats in both symphonies.

When it appeared in 1990, **Norrington's** was the first CD to offer both the *Scottish* and *Italian Symphonies* on period instruments. As in the Schumann coupling, Norrington opts for unexaggerated speeds in the outer movements, relatively brisk ones for the middle movements. The results are similarly exhilarating, particularly the clipped and bouncy account of the first movement of the *Italian*. The *Scottish Symphony* is far lighter than usual, with no hint of excessive sweetness. The Scherzo has rarely sounded happier, and the finale closes in a fast *galop* for the 6/8 coda, with the horns whooping gloriously. Good, warm recording, only occasionally masking detail in tuttis.

(i) Symphonies 3 (Scottish); 4 (Italian); 5 (Reformation); (ii) Overtures: Athalie; Calm Sea and Prosperous Voyage; Son and Stranger (Die Heimkehr und gluckliche Fahrt); Ruy Blas

🔊 **(BB)** **** EMI Gemini (ADD) 381788-2 (2). New Philh. O, (i) Muti; (ii) Atzmon

In his performances of the three key symphonies **Muti** emerges as a natural interpreter of this composer. He gives a smiling performance of the *Scottish Symphony*, with delicate rhythmic pointing, but one which with its wide dynamic range gives Mendelssohn his due weight. The glowing, exhilarating performance of the *Italian Symphony*, with well-chosen tempi – not rushed in the neatly articulated first movement – is also among the finest accounts available. If his relatively fast view of the third movement (marked *con moto*) allows less shaping, he takes a strikingly effective view of the finale, underlining a diabolic quality in the tarantella (*Saltarello*) of legend rather than giving the movement wit. Then to cap his triptych, Muti gives one of the most commanding accounts of the *Reformation Symphony* in the catalogue, again given the composer due weight in the outer movements, but finding an elegantly light touch for the Scherzo, and an expansive dignity for the apotheosis of the great chorale in the finale. Throughout the 1970s recordings are rich and warm. The set is completed with **Moshe Atzmon's** outstanding collection of *Overtures*, including two favourites and a pair of relatively rare offerings, all beautifully played and recorded.

Symphony 4 (Italian)

🔊 **(M)** **** Cala CACD 0531. Nat. PO, Stokowski – BRAHMS: *Symphony 2* ****

(***) Testament mono SBT 1173. Philh. O, Cantelli – BRAHMS: *Symphony 3* (***)

(BB) **(*) EMI Encore 5 09022-2. BPO, Tennstedt – SCHUBERT: *Symphony 9 (Great)* ***

Like the coupled Brahms, this was one of the last recordings **Stokowski** made, with a first-class orchestra of London's top musicians. The result is a fizzingly brilliant account of the *Italian Symphony*, exhilarating, yet with never any sense of the music being rushed. Stokowski observes the all-important first-movement exposition repeat, and the elegant *Andante* and the colourful Minuet, with delightful playing from the horns in the Trio, show him at his most beguiling. The new transfer of the 1978 recording is splendidly done.

Cantelli recorded Mendelssohn's *Italian Symphony* twice with the Philharmonia and this 1951 version on Testament is even finer than the later version, a degree more biting and urgent in the first movement with more light and shade, more spontaneously expressive in the middle movements, and clearer and lighter in the *Presto* finale. In first-rate mono sound it makes a very welcome coupling for Cantelli's glowing account of the Brahms.

Tennstedt's account of the *Italian* is vividly articulated and obviously felt. He is not quite as spontaneous as Stokowski, though the quality of the Berliners' playing is very fine. The early digital recording has admirable body and clarity to commend it, and at Encore price this version is well worth considering for its outstanding Schubert coupling.

Symphonies 4 (Italian; original & revised versions); 5 (Reformation)

*** DG 459 156-2. VPO, Gardiner

In both versions of the *Italian* and in the live recording of the *Reformation* – with all Victorian cobwebs blown away – **John Eliot Gardiner** brings out both the transparency and the urgency of Mendelssohn's inspiration, generally preferring fast but never breathless speeds. The *coup* is that the revised versions of the last three movements of the *Italian* have never been recorded before. The composer made the revisions in the year following the London première. Surprisingly for so discriminating a composer, he undermined the exuberant inspiration of the original, smoothing over melodic lines (as in the *Pilgrim's March*) and extending linking passages. Even so, a fascinating insight into the creative process and the danger of second thoughts on what was originally white-hot inspiration.

Symphony 5 (Reformation)

(M) *** DG (ADD) 449 720-2. BPO, Maazel – FRANCK: *Symphony in D min.* ***

The *Reformation Symphony* springs grippingly to life in **Maazel's** hands. The **Berlin Philharmonic** brass make an immediate impact in the commanding introduction and the orchestral playing throughout continues on this level of high tension. The finale is splendidly vigorous, the chorale, *Ein' feste Burg is unser Gott*, ringing out resplendently. Maazel's interpretation was aptly chosen for reissue in DG's series of 'Originals', and the Franck coupling is hardly less impressive. The recording is spacious and has been vividly enhanced by the DG CD transfer.

CHAMBER MUSIC

Cello Sonatas 1 in B flat, Op. 45; 2 in D, Op. 58

(B) *** EMI (ADD) 5 74333-2 (2). Tortelier, De la Pau – CHOPIN; FAURÉ; RACHMANINOV: *Cello Sonatas* ***

Cello Sonatas 1–2; Assai tranquillo; Songs without Words, Op. 109; Frühlingslied, Op. 19a/1 (arr. Piatti); Jägerlied Op. 19a/3; Venetian Gondola Song, Op. 19a/6 (arr. Piatti); Variations concertantes

*** Avie AV 2140. Meneses, Wyss

Cello Sonatas 1–2; Assai Tranquillo; Song without Words, Op. 109; Variations concertantes, Op. 17

🔊 **(BB)** **** Hyp. Helios CDH 55064. Lester, Tomes

Cello Sonatas 1–2; Song without Words, Op. 109; Variations concertantes, Op. 17

🔊 **(BB)** *** Naxos 8.550655 (without *Assai tranquillo*). Kliegel, Merscher

It was an excellent idea for **Antonio Meneses**, cellist of the Beaux Arts Trio since 1998, with his regular chamber-music partner, the pianist **Gerard Wyss**, to offer the collected cello music of Mendelssohn. The *Sonatas* are arguably the greatest works in the genre written between those of Beethoven and

Brahms, notably 2 with its skipping compound time in the first movement, exhilaratingly done in this performance at brilliant high speed. The clarity of articulation in the virtuoso piano part is astonishing. The *Variations Concertantes*, the other substantial piece Mendelssohn wrote specifically for cello and piano, is straightforward in its use of variation form, and the Opus 109 *Song without Words*, the only one not designed for piano solo, is fresh and vigorous, and the Piatti transcriptions are strong in their adaptation for the medium. The playing of both cello and piano is immaculate, with a clean balance between the instruments, nicely separated.

Susan Tomes, the inspired pianist of the group Domus, and her cellist colleague, **Richard Lester**, give performances full of flair on this ideally compiled disc of Mendelssohn's collected works for cello and piano, brimming with charming ideas. As well as the works with opus number they include a delightful fragment, *Assai tranquillo*, never previously recorded.

Naxos's star cellist, **Maria Kliegel**, together with **Kristine Merscher** also give enjoyably fresh and spontaneous accounts of the two *Sonatas*, and they certainly charm the ear with the *Variations concertantes*. Their naturally recorded Naxos disc is every bit as enjoyable as the Helios collection, except, of course, they omit the *Assai tranquillo*.

Paul Tortelier is wholly in sympathy with these two sonatas, and even if he is partnered less expertly by his daughter **Maria de la Pau** this is still a thoroughly worthwhile collection. Good recording.

Cello Sonata 2 in D, Op. 58

(N) *** Testament SBT 1419. Piatigorsky, Pennario (with
CHOPIN: *Sonata in G min., Op. 65*) – STRAUSS: *Cello Sonata* ***

Gregor Piatigorsky was the greatest cellist of his generation. The first movement of the *D major Sonata* has something of the atmosphere of the *Italian Symphony*, though it is the middle movements that offer Mendelssohn at his best. The playing is of the highest quality. In the Chopin coupling the pianist is **Firkušný** and, leaving aside the Rostropovich–Argerich set on DG, this has an unsurpassed eloquence.

Octet in E flat, Op. 20

(M) *** Wigmore Hall Live WHLive 001. Nash Ens. (with
BEETHOVEN: *Clarinet Trio in B flat, Op. 11* ***)

(BB) *** Hyp. Helios CDH 55043. Divertimenti – BARGIEL:
Octet ***

(BB) ** EMI Gemini (ADD) 3 50864-2 (2). Melos Ens. of L. –
BEETHOVEN: *Octet & Septet*; SCHUBERT: *Octet* ***

The **Nash** performance offers the most vivid and warmhearted playing, and all the live communication that one expects from music-making in this ideal-sized venue for chamber and instrumental music. The delicate Scherzo truly evokes the 'swirling mists' and 'sighing breezes' that Mendelssohn pictured in his imagination. The recording's producer, Andrew Keener placed his microphones fairly close, and the effect is to rob the sound of a good deal of its natural hall ambience in order to give the group a clearer projection.

Divertimenti give a very natural and unforced account of the celebrated *Octet* which, though it may not be the most distinguished in the catalogue, still gives great pleasure. Excellent recorded sound.

The EMI **Melos** recording dates from the late 1960s, but it has a rather hard, bright edge on the leader's tone, immediately noticeable in the first movement. The stereo is remarkably clear and detailed, without loss of warmth. The finale is bright and gains from the clear recording, but the edge on the sound remains a drawback.

Octet in E flat, Op. 20; String Quintets 1 in A, Op. 18; 2 in B flat, Op. 87; String Quartet 2 in A min., Op. 13

⊕ (M) *** Virgin 2x1 5 61809-2 (2). Hausmusik

A highly desirable bargain set. The *Octet* and *String Quintet* 1 were recorded in the Concert Hall of York University in 1989, and the recording, balanced by Mike Hatch, is outstanding, clear and transparent, with an attractively warm ambience giving extra weight to the lower lines. The period-instrument performance of the *Octet*, with **Monica Huggett** leading the violins and **Anthony Pleeth** the cellos, is most refreshing, as is the account of the *Second String Quintet*, another miraculous masterpiece of Mendelssohn's boyhood. The coupling of the *Second Quartet* and *Second Quintet* was made four years later in an ecclesiastical acoustic, and the balance engineer, Mike Clements, had to put his microphones closer to the players. Playing is alert and, above all, these players communicate delight in all this music, and their account of the *Octet* is second to none.

Piano Quartet 1 in C min., Op. 1; Piano Sextet in D, Op. 110

(BB) **(*) Naxos 8.550966. Bartholdy Piano Qt (augmented)

Piano Quartets 2 in F min., Op. 2; 3 in B min., Op. 3

(BB) **(*) Naxos 8.550967. Bartholdy Piano Qt

The **Bartholdy Quartet** have an excellent pianist in **Pier Narciso Masi**, and his mercurial style is just right for these early works. The string players are always fluent and show a light-hearted vivacity in Mendelssohn's scherzos (especially in the very winning *Allegro molto* of 3) and finales, and they play the simple slow movements gracefully. The *Piano Sextet* has an engaging immediacy and the piano well caught.

Piano Trio 1 in D min., Op. 49

⊕ *** Warner 2564 61492-2. Beaux Arts Trio – DVOŘÁK: *Piano Trio 4 (Dumky)* ***

(BB) (***) Naxos mono 8.110185. Thibaud, Casals, Cortot –
SCHUMANN: *Piano Trio 1* (***)

When the **Beaux Arts Trio** made their début on LP, some fifty years ago, it was with this coupling and, although the personnel has changed, the youthfulness and grace of the playing has not. **Menahem Pressler** is every bit as mercurial and fleet-of-finger as he was in the mid-1950s. The new recording is, of course, far more realistic and wide-ranging, balanced and is a very happy tribute to this wonderful ensemble.

The partnership of **Jacques Thibaud, Pablo Casals** and **Alfred Cortot** was perhaps the most celebrated of its kind – and certainly the most famous pre-war trio. They are technically immaculate, supremely lyrical, and their apparent spontaneity of feeling is born of firm musical discipline. Ward Marston's transfer gives this exalted performance, with its miraculously characterized Scherzo, a new lease of life.

Piano Trios 1 in D min., Op. 49; 2 in C min., Op. 66

℗ **** Hyp. CDA 67485. Florestan Trio

℗ (BB) **** Naxos 8.555063. Gould Piano Trio

Dazzling playing from this ensemble puts the **Florestan** at the very top of the list in this repertoire. The freshness of response and the virtuosity of the pianist **Susan Tomes** make this pretty irresistible. Excellent recorded sound, too.

The young players of the **Gould Trio** give performances as fine as any on disc. Not just the violinist, **Lucy Gould**, but the cellist, **Martin Storey**, and above all the pianist, **Benjamin Frith**, prove to be inspired recording artists, offering passage-work of sparkling evenness and clarity. At Naxos price an outstanding bargain.

String Quartets: in E flat; 1–6; 4 Pieces, Op. 81

(M) *** Hyp. CDS 44051/3. Coull Qt

String Quartets 1–6; 4 Pieces, Op. 81

℗ (M) **** Decca Trio 473 255-2 (3). Ysaÿe Quartet

(B) *** Arte Nova 82876 64009-2 (3). Henschel Qt

The fine Decca set from the **Ysaÿe Quartet** in its new Trio box format becomes a marginal first choice for the *Quartets* alone, though the three Naxos discs (below) remain a highly recommendable alternative and they include more extra items (see below). In essence these Decca performances are warm, urbane and cultured, as befits this civilized and endearing music, and the recording is eminently satisfactory, with fine presence set within a warm acoustic.

The three **Henschel** siblings also rank with the very finest, so that, for instance, the *Adagio* and *Intermezzo* of Op. 13 have an endearing simplicity, and the *Adagio* of Op. 44/3 has a touching depth of feeling, readily contrasting with the dancing Scherzo and bravura virtuosity of the finale. The third disc pairs the remaining Op. 44 *Quartets*, adding the *Four Movements* of Op. 81, played with similar perception. Decent sound and handsome packaging too.

The **Coull** survey is also eminently satisfactory and includes the early (1823) *Quartet in E flat*, the playing alive and spontaneous, well paced and musically penetrating. The quietly intense playing in slow movements shows the group's affinity with this repertoire. The recording is realistic and well balanced.

String Quartets: in E flat; 1 in E flat, Op. 12; 4 in E min., Op. 44/2 (Naxos 8.550862)

String Quartets 2 in A min., Op. 13; 5 in E flat, Op. 44/3; Scherzo in A min., Op. 81/2; Theme & Variations in E, Op. 81/1 (Naxos 8.550863)

String Quartets 3 in D, Op. 44/1; 6 in F min., Op. 80; Capriccio in E min., Op. 81/3; Fugue in E flat, Op. 81/4 (Naxos 8.550861)

℗ (BB) **** Aurora Qt

At Naxos price, the new **Aurora** set of Mendelssohn's complete music for string quartet is a genuine bargain. The performances have a natural Mendelssohnian charm and elegance, but their strength and passion acknowledge the fact that the young composer in his teens wrote them under the influence of the Beethoven quartets. Indeed, the account of the *F minor* work, composed after his sister Fanny's death, is perhaps the highlight of the set. The recording is first class.

String Quartets 1 in E flat, Op. 12; 2 in A min., Op. 13 (MDG 307 1055-2)

String Quartets 3–4; Capriccio (1843); Fugue (1827) (MDG 307 1168-2)

String Quartets 5 in E flat, Op. 44/3; 6 in F min., Op. 80; Scherzo & Theme and Variations, Op. 81 (MDG 307 1056-2)

**** Leipzig Qt

String Quartet in E flat; Octet, Op. 20.

**(*) MDG 307 105-2. (Augmented) Leipzig Qt

The excellent **Leipzig Quartet**, with their warm, richly blended tone and natural finesse, give superbly polished accounts of these delightful works. Their lightness of touch and elegance are balanced by great (but not exaggerated) depth of feeling. They also have a naturalness and warmth that is most satisfying. Their performances serve as a reminder that this is great music which is all too often taken for granted by critics. Not surprisingly, the Leipzig players also give a beautifully turned and graceful account of the remarkable early *Quartet in E flat* without opus number, but when they are joined by four undoubtedly excellent colleagues for the *Octet*, the effect is less refined, not helped by a recording which tends to emphasize both treble and bass at the expense of a detailed overall sound-picture. The central movements are the most successful, with the Scherzo fleet and delicate and the *Andante* appealingly phrased.

String Quartets 1 in E flat, Op. 12; 4 in E min., Op. 44/2; 6 in F min., Op. 80

℗ **** Naxos 8.570001. New Zealand Qt

The **New Zealand Quartet's** performances are very compelling indeed, distinctly looking forward to Beethoven in their urgency and strength. However, they don't miss the charm of the *First Quartet* (especially the engagingly played *Canzonetta*), although by no means do they treat it as an immature work. They are enormously arresting in the *F minor Quartet*. The recording is state-of-the-art. We hope this is to be the first of a complete survey; if so, it will be hard to beat.

String Quartets 1–6; 4 Pieces, Op. 81; (with CD-ROM: Quartet in E flat (1823); Octet for Strings in E flat, Op. 20 and DVD documentary: Recording the Octet)

**(*) DG 477 5370 (4). Emerson Qt

The **Emerson Quartet** are flawless in their unanimity of ensemble and tonal finesse. Indeed, in terms of technical prowess and sheer polish, all these Mendelssohn performances could hardly be bettered, and the DG recording is bright and well focused. If there is any reservation, it is a certain want of period sensibility. The playing is virtuosic – Manhattan rather than Weimar. The performances have the public profile of modern concert-giving and convey little sense of intimacy and too little sense of grace. But, of course, they are expert and masterly.

String Quintets 1 in A, Op. 18; 2 in B flat, Op. 87

****SACD** BIS-SACD 1254. Mendelssohn Qt with R. Mann

Ⓝ ⒃ *** Naxos 8.570488. Fine Arts Qt, Danilo Rossi

Ⓝ *** CPO 777 389-2. Augmented Mannheim Qt

Anyone wanting modern-instrument recordings of two of Mendelssohn's finest chamber works could not better this BIS-SACD. The performances are full of sparkle and vitality: the outer movements have great spirit and energy while the finales with their brilliant contrapuntal writing are played with thrilling virtuosity, and the Scherzo of Op. 87 is like quicksilver. Yet the *Intermezzo* of the same work is touchingly simple in its natural warmth. On a DVD/SACD player there is added fullness and resonance in the bass, at the same time producing a very slightly less transparent blend of timbre.

The performances by the **Mannheim Quartet** are of fine quality, cultured, full of character and presence. But they are upstaged by the augmented **Fine Arts Quartet** on Naxos, who have the advantage of economy and strike a splendid balance between vitality and elegance, The *Intermezzo* of the *A major Quartet* is engagingly played, the Scherzo is crisp and brilliant, and the *Adagio* of the *B flat Quartet* is most warmly and stylishly played, and both finales sparkle. The recording is excellent.

Violin Sonatas: in F (1820); in F min., Op. 4 (1823); in F (1838); Allegro in C; Andante in D min.; Fugues: in C min.; in D min.; Movement in G min.

⒃ *** Naxos 8.554725. Nomos Duo

Two of these *Sonatas* date from Mendelssohn's early years, but are attractively crafted. The mature work is notable for its brilliant *vivace* finale in which the **Nomos Duo** (Nicholas Milton and Nina-Margret Grimsdóttir) really let rip. Some may feel that a little more poise here would have been welcome, but that is the only reservation. They are a fine team and make a good case for the earliest work (more of a *Sonatina*), especially the closing *moto perpetuo Presto*, which is neatly paced. The shorter pieces come from a book of exercises but are rather pleasing miniatures. Excellent recording in a friendly acoustic.

PIANO MUSIC

Capriccio in F sharp min., Op. 5; 7 Characteristic Pieces, Op. 7; Fantasia (Sonata écossaise) in F sharp min., Op. 28; Prelude & Fugue in E min.; Sonata Movement in B flat

⊶ ⒃ *** Naxos 8. 553541. Frith

This collection gives a very different idea of Mendelssohn's piano-writing from that in the *Songs without Words*. The *Characteristic Pieces* present fascinating evidence of the influence of Bach on the young composer, with some impressive contrapuntal writing in fugues both brilliant and thoughtful. Also some echoes of Scarlatti. The three-movement *Fantasia* and the *Capriccio*, as well, inspire **Benjamin Frith** to sparkling playing, vividly recorded.

Preludes & Fugues 1-6, Op. 35; 3 Caprices, Op. 33; Perpetuum mobile in C, Op. 33

⊶ ⒃ *** Naxos 8.550939. Frith

Benjamin Frith offers a highly imaginative set of the Op. 35 *Preludes and Fugues*, full of diversity, from the flamboyant opening *Prelude in E minor* to the expansive *Prelude 6 in B flat*. The three *Caprices* are equally varied in mood and colour and are most sensitively presented. The *Perpetuum mobile* makes a scintillating encore. Acceptably full if not remarkable piano-sound.

Scherzo from A Midsummer Night's Dream, Op. 61 (trans. Rachmaninov)

**** Hyp. CDA 66009. Shelley – RACHMANINOV: *Variations*, etc. ****

Howard Shelley, with fabulously clear articulation and delectably sprung rhythms, gives a performance of which Rachmaninov himself would not have been ashamed.

Piano Sonatas: in E, Op. 6; in G min., Op. 105; in B flat, Op. 106; Rondo capriccioso, Op. 14

⒃ *** HM HMX 395117. Chiu

Frederic Chiu is a delightful Mendelssohnian and he plays these three early *Piano Sonatas* with a winning mixture of brilliance and tranquillity, and the more familiar *Rondo capriccioso* sparkles with wit. The recording is too close and a bit hard, but one can accept this at budget price when the playing is as remarkable as the control of colour.

Piano Sonata in G min., Op. 105; Capriccio in E, Op. 118; Etude in F min.; Fantasia on 'The Last Rose of Summer', Op. 15; 2 Pieces: Andante cantabile; Presto agitato; Scherzo a capriccio in F sharp min.; Variations in B flat, Op. 83

⊶ ⒃ *** Naxos 8.553358. Frith

The *G minor Sonata*, Op. 105, is distinctly Haydnesque, and there is perhaps more charm than individuality. Although the *Fantasia on 'The Last Rose of Summer'* is pretty thin stuff, in such imaginative fingers, it sounds delightful and marvellously fresh. Naxos provide quite excellent recording, and the series so far is touched with distinction.

Piano Sonata in B flat, Op. 106; Albumblatt, Op. 117; Andante cantabile e presto agitato in B; 3 Fantasies et Caprices, Op. 16; Rondo capriccioso in E, Op. 14; Variations in E flat, Op. 82

⊕→ (BB) *** Naxos 8.553186. Frith

The *B flat Sonata* has been called 'a comfortable and domestic' version of Beethoven's *Hammerklavier*. However, **Benjamin Frith** is so persuasive that he dispels this impression. His playing is nothing less than a delight, and in the celebrated *Rondo capriccioso* and the more conventional *Variations in E flat* of 1841 he is as light of touch as one could possibly wish.

Songs without Words, Books 1–8 (complete); Albumblatt, Op. 117; Gondellied; Kinderstücke, Op. 72; 2 Klavierstücke

⊕→ (B) **** DG Double (ADD) 453 061-2 (2). Barenboim

This 1974 set of Mendelssohn's complete *Songs without Words*, which **Barenboim** plays with such affectionate finesse, has dominated the catalogue for nearly two decades. The sound is first class. At DG Double price, this sweeps the board in this repertoire.

Songs without Words, Opp. 19/1, 3, 5; 30/2, 4, 6; 38/2, 3, 6; 53/4; 62/2; 67/1–2, 4; 103/5

⊕→ ✿ *** Sony SK 66511. Perahia – BACH/BUSONI: *Chorales*; LISZT: *Concert Paraphrases of Schubert Lieder* *** ✿

As his earlier records have so amply demonstrated, **Murray Perahia** has a quite unique feeling for Mendelssohn. He invests these pieces with a depth of poetic feeling that is quite special.

VOCAL MUSIC

Choral Music: 6 Anthems for different times of the year; Ave Maria; Ehre sei Gott in der Höh; Heilig, heilig is Gott, der Herr Zebaoth; Hör mein Bitten; Kyrie eleison; Mein Gott, warum hast du?; Mitten wir im Leben sind; Richte mich Gott; Verleih' uns Freiden; Warum toben die Heiden?

⊕→ (BB) **** Hyp. Helios CDH 55268. Dawson, Covey-Crump, Scott, Corydon Singers, ECO, Best

We missed this record on its original, premium-priced issue, but the reviewer in the *American Record Guide* did not, declaring it 'One of the most enriching listening experiences I have had for some time.' In short, the singing here is glorious, and so is the music. One of the surprises is the three-section *Ave Maria*, its radiant outer sections framing an exultant, contrapuntal middle section, which here springs thrillingly into life after the serenity of the opening. But every number shows Mendelssohn's inspiration at its most endearing, ending with a ravishing performance of the justly famous *Hör mein Bitten* ('Hear my Prayer') in which **Ann Dawson** soars heavenwards (translated here as 'Ah could I fly away with the dove'). Truly splendid singing throughout from the **Corydon Singers** and their soloists, and fine accompaniments from the **ECO** with **Matthew Best** directing

the whole programme with exactly the right touch. Excellent recording, as one would expect from this source, and full texts and translations provided.

(i) Ave Maria; Beati mortui; Die deutsche Liturgie; Hear my Prayer; 100th Psalm (Jauchzet dem Herrn, alle Welt); (i; ii) Laudate pueri; Magnificat (My Soul doth Magnify the Lord); 3 Psalms (2, 22 & 43), Op. 78; 6 Sprüche (Maxims for the Church Year), Op. 79

**** Chan. 10363. Trinity College, Cambridge, Ch., Marlow; with (i) Bennett; (ii) Cheng, Wilkinson

Although *Hear my Prayer* is justly top favourite (with 'O for the wings of a dove' sung by **Rachel Bennett** with glorious confidence, especially the gentle coda), there is much other truly memorable choral music here, not least the beautiful motet, *Laudate pueri*, for female choir, contrasted with a celestial trio of soloists. The three sections of the *German Liturgy* for a cappella double choir are hardly less memorable, featuring a quartet of soloists. Most ambitious of all is the a cappella English *Magnificat*, opening quite jauntily and, after changing mood flexibly, the penultimate section moves into a fugato, before the majestic closing *Amen*. **Richard Marlow** directs this Mendelssohnian choral galaxy with sure understanding, not a hint of sentimentality and superb control. Needless to say, the Chandos recording is first class, and so is the documentation, with full texts and translations.

6 Choruses, Op. 88; 4 Choruses, Op. 100; Der Erste Frühlingstag; Im Freinen zu singen; In Grünen

(N) *** HM HMC 90 1992. Berlin RIAS Chamber Ch., Rademann

Mendelssohn was particularly adept at writing a cappella choral music, as this collection shows admirably, centring on pastoral inspirations and with unfailingly attractive invention for every item. They are superbly sung and excellently recorded and Mendelssohnians should not miss this anthology.

Elijah (oratorio), Op. 70

⊕→ *** Chan. 8774/5. White, Plowright, Finnie, A. Davies, L. Symphony Ch., LSO, Hickox

(BB) *** EMI Gemini (ADD) 5 86257-2 (2). G. Jones, J. Baker, Gedda, Fischer-Dieskau, Woolf, Wandsworth School Boys' Ch., New Philh. Ch. & O, Frühbeck de Burgos

(BB) *** EMI Gemini 3 50884-2 (2). Schmidt, Rost, Kallisch, Van der Walt, Dietzel, Düsseldorf State Musikvereins Ch., Cologne Gürzenich O, Conlon

**(*) Decca 455 688-2 (2). Terfel, Fleming, Bardon, Mark Ainsley, Edinburgh Festival Ch., OAE, Daniel

Richard Hickox with the **London Symphony Chorus** and the **LSO** secures a performance that both pays tribute to the English choral tradition in this work and presents it dramatically as a kind of religious opera. **Willard White** may not be ideally steady in his delivery, sometimes attacking notes from below, but he sings consistently with fervour. **Rosalind Plowright** and **Arthur Davies** combine purity of tone with operatic expressiveness, and **Linda Finnie**, while not matching the example of Dame Janet Baker in the classic EMI recording, sings with comparable dedication and directness in the solo, O rest in the Lord. The chorus fearlessly underlines the high contrasts of dynamic demanded in the score. The Chandos recording, full and immediate yet atmospheric too, enhances the drama.

Frühbeck de Burgos proves an excellent Mendelssohnian. The choice of Fischer-Dieskau as the prophet is more controversial. His pointing of English words is not always idiomatic, but his sense of drama is infallible and goes well with this Mendelssohnian new look. Gwyneth Jones and Nicolai Gedda similarly provide mixed enjoyment, but the splendid work of the chorus and, above all, the gorgeous singing of Dame Janet Baker make this a memorable and enjoyable set, very well recorded (in the late 1960s) and spaciously and realistically transferred to CD. A real bargain.

James Conlon's Elijah comes directly into competition with the Frühbeck de Burgos New Philharmonia set, also reissued on EMI's budget Gemini label. That has rather more famous soloists, but not necessarily more successful ones, except for Dame Janet Baker, whose contribution is unique. Even so, Cornelia Kallisch's O rest in the Lord is beautifully sung, as is Elijah's affecting It is enough O Lord (the excellent Andreas Schmidt). Above all else, Elijah depends on the chorus and, from the opening Help Lord!, the choral singing in Cologne, digitally recorded and superbly present, has tremendous drama and bite, and throughout Conlon's vibrant direction easily matches that of Frühbeck de Burgos. So, unless the presence of Dame Janet is essential, then the newer bargain version wins on points, though first choice at premium price rests with Richard Hickox on Chandos.

The glory of Paul Daniel's Decca set is the fiercely dramatic portrayal of the central character by Bryn Terfel. This Elijah is the very personification of an Old Testament prophet. Renée Fleming sings most beautifully as the principal soprano, strong rather than reflective in Hear ye, Israel. There are no weak links among the others, even if there are no stars either, with Patricia Bardon'sO rest in the Lord sounding rather matter-of-fact. Many will find it refreshing that with a period orchestra Paul Daniel takes a crisp, direct view of the work, helped by fresh, cleanly focused singing from the Edinburgh Festival Chorus. Yet Daniel is at times too metrical to conceal the squareness of some of the work's weaker passages. Clean, well-separated sound.

Hymn: Hor mein Bitten, Herr (Hymn of Praise); Motets: Ehre sei Gott in der Höhe; Herr, nun lässest du deinen Diener in Frieden fahren; Mein Gott, warum hast du mich verlassen; Mitten wir im Leben sind; Warum toben die Heiden; 6 Sprüche, Op. 79

(BB) *** HM (ADD) HMA 1951142. Paris Chapelle Royale, Coll. Voc. de Ghent, Herreweghe; Huys

Herreweghe's motet performances are splendidly fresh and vital, bringing out the composer's acknowledged debt to earlier models. Mitten wir im Leben sind features antiphonal alternation of male and female choirs and uses a chorale previously used by Bach. The part-writing is made admirably clear. Their account (in German) of the famous Hymn of Praise is very dramatic, shedding Anglican sentimental associations, with the excellent soloist, Greta de Reyghere, clear and true in the famous 'Oh for the wings of a dove'. The recording is excellent, cleanly focused within a non-blurring ecclesiastical ambience. The documentation is good, but the German texts and the English translations are not placed side by side. This now comes at budget price.

Infelice; Psalm 47 (As pants the hart), Op. 42

(BB) *** Virgin 2x1 5 61469-2 (2). Baker, City of L. Sinfonia, Hickox – BERLIOZ: Les Nuits d'été, etc.; BRAHMS: Alto Rhapsody, etc.; RESPIGHI: La sensitiva ***

The scena, Infelice – a piece that harks back to an earlier tradition – and the Psalm-setting both have the solos prescribed for soprano, but they suit Dame Janet Baker well, here making a welcome foray out of official retirement for a recording. The voice is in superb condition, with the weight of expressiveness as compelling as ever. The Psalm sounds very like an extra item from Elijah.

40 Lieder

(M) **(*) EMI (ADD) 3 91990-2 (2). Fischer-Dieskau, Sawallisch – LOEWE: Ballads ***

Though Mendelssohn generally reserved his finest song-like inspirations for the Songs without Words, the lyrical directness of these varied settings of Heine, Ebert, Eichendorff, Lenau, Lichtenstein, Klingmann and others (there are three settings of Frühlingslied and two of Reislied) assures him of a niche of his own among contemporary composers of Lieder. Fischer-Dieskau, recorded at his finest in 1970, conveys the joy of fresh discovery; but in some of the well-known songs, Grüss or Auf Flügeln des Gesanges, he tends to overlay his singing with heavy expressiveness. Lightness should be the keynote, and that happily is wonderfully represented in the superb accompaniments of Sawallisch. Excellent, natural recording. This reissue, as one of EMI's 'Great Recordings of the Century', brings full texts and translations.

Lieder

(BB) *** Hyp. Helios CDH 55150. M. Price, Johnson

There is a delightfully light touch to the famous 'On Wings of Song' (Auf Flügeln). Frühlingslied ('Spring Song') is equally appealing, and Minnelied soars. The vivid portrayal of a witches' dance (Hexenlied) and Neue Liebe with its 'riding elves in the moonlight' are both very much in the spirit of the Midsummer Night's Dream music, even if the former, with the fiendishly complex piano part so brilliantly played by Graham Johnson, has a slightly sinister air. In between comes the lovely Gruss, a gentle 'Greeting'. In short, this is a particularly rewarding collection, with Margaret Price and her partner Graham Johnson in splendid form and made vividly present by the recording. Even though this is a bargain reissue, full texts and translations are provided, plus excellent notes by Richard Wigmore.

A Midsummer Night's Dream (ballet; complete; choreography by George Balanchine)

🎬 **** BBC Opus Arte **DVD** OA 0810D. Pacific Northwest Ballet, BBC Concert O, Steven Kershaw. Producer: Francia Russell (V/D: Nigel Shepherd)

Balanchine's 1962 ballet was created for the New York City Ballet, and based not only on the inspired score to Shakespeare's play of Mendelssohn's *A Midsummer Night's Dream* but also on other Mendelssohn scores, including the overtures *Athalia*, *Die schöne Melusine* and *Son and Stranger*, plus two movements of the *Ninth* of his early symphonies for strings.

This performance was recorded in 1999 at the then newly reopened Sadler's Wells Theatre while the Pacific Northwest Ballet were on tour. It is a fine company with an enviable reputation and some altogether excellent principal dancers: Lisa Apple's Helena and Julie Tobiason's Hermia are particularly fine, and the scene between Titania and Bottom is most affecting. The fairy scenes are imaginatively handled and staged.

Mendelssohn's music is well served by the ever underrated **BBC Concert Orchestra**, who always excel when given a chance to play repertoire of quality. The camerawork and the quality of colour are very high. An enchanting ninety minutes.

A Midsummer Night's Dream: Overture, Op. 21; Incidental Music, Op. 61 (complete; with melodramas and text)

🎬 **** DG 439 897-2. Battle, von Stade, Tanglewood Festival Ch., Boston SO, Ozawa (with excerpts from play spoken by Dame Judi Dench)

A Midsummer Night's Dream: Overture, Op. 21; Incidental Music, Op. 61 (complete)

Ⓑ *** CfP 575 142-2. Wiens, Walker, LPO Ch. & O, Litton (with GRIEG: *Peer Gynt*: excerpts; cond. Pritchard **)

A Midsummer Night's Dream: Overture, Op. 21; Incidental Music, Op. 61 (complete); Overtures: Calm Sea and Prosperous Voyage; The Hebrides; Ruy Blas.

Ⓜ *** RCA 82876 60864-2. Popp, Lipovšek, Bamberg Ch. & SO, Flor

Ozawa's virtually complete performance presents Mendelssohn's enchanting incidental music – which is most beautifully played throughout by the **Boston Symphony Orchestra** – complete with the Shakespearean text, which is spoken over the melodramas by **Judi Dench**. With two excellent soloists and a fine choral contribution, the only omission here is the brief excerpt which is No. 6 in the score; but the fragmentary reprise of the *Wedding March*, and the two little comic snippets, the Bergomask (*Dance of the Clowns*) and ironic little *Funeral March*, intended for the Rude Mechanicals' 'Pyramus and Thisbe' playlet are included. Judi Dench speaks the Shakespeare text in the simplest way, and in her performance Shakespeare's words seem to glow as magically as Mendelssohn's music. The recording is first

class, and the balance, with Dench's narration quite intimate but with every word clear, is very well judged indeed.

The RCA disc is **Claus Peter Flor's** finest record. His account of the incidental music omits the little melodramas, which is a pity, but otherwise this could be a first choice, particularly as the three Overtures are equally recommendable. Recorded in the warmly resonant acoustics of the Dominikanerbau, Bamberg, the orchestra is given glowingly radiant textures; but Flor's stylish yet relaxed control in *A Midsummer Night's Dream* brings the kind of intimacy one expects from a chamber ensemble. **Lucia Popp's** vocal contribution is delightful, especially when she blends her voice so naturally with that of **Marjana Lipovšek** in *You spotted snakes*.

Andrew Litton also includes the melodramas and, like Previn, he uses them most effectively as links, making them seem an essential part of the structure. He too has very good soloists; in the Overture and Scherzo he displays an engagingly light touch, securing very fine wind and string playing from the **LPO**. The wide dynamic range of the recording brings an element of drama to offset the fairy music. Both the *Nocturne*, with a fine horn solo, and the temperamental *Intermezzo* are good examples of the spontaneity of feeling that permeates this performance throughout and makes this disc another bargain. However, Sir John Pritchard's account of the excerpts from *Peer Gynt*, although well played, is rather matter-of-fact.

St Paul, Op. 36

Ⓝ Ⓜ *** Chan. 10516 (2). Gritton, Rigby, Banks, Coleman-Wright, BBC Nat. Ch. & O of Wales, Hickox

Ⓝ *** Carus CARUS 83214 (2). Kiehr, Güra, Volle, Stuttgart Chamber Ch., Deutsch Kammerphilharmonie, Bremen, Bernius

Richard Hickox's version, recorded live in Cardiff with BBC Welsh forces, completely avoids sentimentality, finding a freshness which effectively echoes the Bach *Passions* in punctuating the story of St Paul with chorales and the occasional 'turba' or crowd chorus. In brushing any Victorian cobwebs away Hickox tends to favour speeds on the fast side, never sounding hurried but, more importantly, never sounding heavy or pompous as other German versions often do. Choral singing is excellent and, among the soloists, **Susan Gritton** and **Jean Rigby** are first rate, though the tenor, **Barry Banks**, is a little strained and **Peter Coleman-Wright** sounds rather gritty as recorded, though never wobbly. The warmth and clarity of the recording add to the freshness. It is now offered at mid-price with full texts and translations.

The Bremen performance conducted by **Frieder Bernius** is also enjoyably fresh, both in the choral singing and in the orchestral backing. Among the soloists, **Maria Cristina Kiehr** stands out for her vocal purity and depth and, with no contralto, she takes over the alto solos, which is the set's one drawback. However, the tenor **Werner Güra** sings beautifully, and his colleague **Michael Volle** is also excellent – which gives the Carus set one advantage over the Chandos. The recording is excellent too, but Hickox remains a first choice.

MENOTTI, Gian-Carlo
(1911–2007)

(i) *Violin Concerto; Cantatas; (ii) The Death of Orpheus; (iii) Muero porque no muero; (iv) Oh llama de amor viva*

*** Chan. 9979. (i) Koh; (ii) MacDougall; (iii) Melinek; (iv) Roberts; Spoleto Ch. & O, Hickox

Richard Hickox once more draws from his fine Spoleto team warmly persuasive readings of eclectic works which are powerfully convincing in committed performances like these. The young American violinist, **Jennifer Koh**, is the excellent soloist in the *Concerto*. The slow movement, played with hushed dedication, has a tender poignancy, while the vigorous finale with its jaunty main theme predictably ends with virtuoso fireworks.

The two cantatas, using Spanish texts by the mystics St Teresa of Avila and St John of the Cross, offer sensuous music closer to Puccini's opera, *Suor Angelica*, than to any religious model. The chorus in each dramatically enhances the meditative solos representing each saint. **Julia Melinek** is the vibrant soloist in the St Teresa cantata, though **Stephen Roberts** is sadly unsteady in the St John of the Cross setting. *The Death of Orpheus*, to an English text by Menotti himself, is similarly dramatic. Orpheus's song emerges as a broad diatonic melody, with choral writing of Delian sensuousness. **Jamie MacDougall** is the expressive soloist, with the chorus fresh and incisive in all three cantatas.

OPERA

Amahl and the Night Visitors (opera; complete)

⊕— *** That's Entertainment CDTER 1124. Haywood, Dobson, Watson, Painter, Rainbird, ROHCG Ch. & O, Syrus

Recorded under the supervision of the composer himself, this is a fresh and highly dramatic performance, very well sung and marked by atmospheric digital sound of striking realism. Central to the success of the performance is the astonishingly assured and sensitively musical singing of the boy treble, **James Rainbird**, as Amahl, while **Lorna Haywood** sings warmly and strongly as the Mother, with a strong trio of Kings.

The Consul (complete)

⊕— *** Chan. 9706 (2). Bullock, Otley, Kreitzer, Livengood, Austin, Broadbent, 1998 Spoleto Festival O, Hickox

This ripely red-blooded performance, recorded live at the Spoleto Festival in 1998, finds **Richard Hickox** a passionate interpreter of this early response to the Cold War and the human tragedies involved. Hickox builds the structure masterfully, firmly controlling tension. He is helped by an excellent orchestra and a good cast, led by **Susan Bullock** in the central role of Magda. Her big outburst against bureaucracy at the end of Act II brings the emotional high point of the whole opera, an overwhelming moment worthy of Puccini. None of the others quite matches Bullock vocally, with some voices rather unsteady. **Jacalyn Kreitzer** is warmly

affecting as the Mother, and **Charles Austin** sings strongly as the Secret Agent, giving a rounded portrait. Full-toned, vivid recording, with ample detail.

(i) *Martin's Lie* (complete); (ii) *Canti della lontananza: Impossible Lovers; The Letter; Pegasus Asleep; Resignation; The Seventh Glass of Wine; Snowy Morning; The Spectre; (iii) 5 songs: The eternal prisoner; My ghost; The idle gift; The longest wait; The swing*

*** Chan. 9605. (i) Tees Valley Boys' Ch., N. Sinfonia, Hickox; (ii) Leggate, Martineau; (iii) Howarth, Martineau

Martin's Lie was written as a follow-up to the children's piece for TV, *Amahl and the Night Visitors*, a sinister medieval story with a moral, fluently told in 45 minutes; warmly involving singing and playing. **Judith Howarth** and **Robin Leggate** are the singers in the two brief song-cycles, with Menotti's writing all the richer in the Italian settings.

The Saint of Bleecker Street (opera; complete)

*** Chan. 9971(2). Melinek, Richards, Stephen, Bindel, Zeltzer, Farrugia, Howard, Rozynko, Spoleto Festival Ch. & O, Hickox

Overlook the melodramatic plot, even forget the variable casting of solo singers – not Italianate enough with too many wobblers – for this pioneering recording of Gian-Carlo Menotti's opera, *The Saint of Bleecker Street*, demonstrates that this is one of the composer's most powerful scores, colourful, atmospheric and tuneful, with telling dramatic effects, often involving genuine Italian tunes. Set in New York's Little Italy, it revolves round the dying Annina, a would-be nun with a gift for faith-healing, and her boorish agnostic brother, Michele. For Menotti, a Catholic who lost his faith, the story aims to symbolize the clash between faith and doubt. In this performance, recorded live, the red-blooded feelings involved are passionately brought out by **Richard Hickox**, with talented young performers from the **Festival Choir and Orchestra** of Menotti's summer music festival at Spoleto. Full, brilliant sound.

MESSAGER, André (1853–1929)

Les Deux Pigeons

*** Australian Decca Eloquence 476 2448. Welsh Nat. Op. O, Bonynge

Messager's charming gypsy ballet was premièred at the Paris Opéra in 1886 on the same bill as Donizetti's *La Favorita*. But it swiftly established its independence, to remain on the repertoire and be revived (with new choreography by Fredrick Ashton) by the Sadler's Wells Company in 1961. The music is light but cleverly scored, after the manner of Delibes; agreeably tuneful, it does not wear out its welcome. **Bonynge** secures playing from the **Welsh National Opera Orchestra** that is consistently graceful and sparkling, and if the sound is vivid and naturally balanced, it is not quite out of Decca's very top drawer.

Véronique (opera; complete)

(BB) **(*) EMI (ADD) 5 74073-2 (2). Mesplé, Guiot, Benoit, Dens, Dunand, Pruvost, René Duclos Ch., LOP, Hartemann

Messager's gentle charms are well displayed in his 1898 opera, *Véronique*. The story of Hélène de Solanges, who works in disguise in a Parisian florist's in the 1840s under the assumed name Véronique, produces plenty of romantic complications, which are all sorted out by the end. There are several numbers that understandably became Edwardian favourites, including the two duets from Act I: the 'Donkey duet' (*De ci, de l'*) and the 'Swing duet' (*Poussez, poussez, l'escarpolette*). The Act I quartet with the refrain '*Charmant, charmant*' is another highlight of the utmost piquancy. The performance here is excellent, **Mady Mesplé** again showing her supremacy in this repertoire, while the rest of the cast and the conductor understand Messager's idiom perfectly. The 1969 recording has transferred very well to CD, with the voices clear and vivid. But as ever in this bargain operetta series, no texts or translations are provided, which will be a distinct drawback for many collectors.

MESSIAEN, Olivier (1908–92)

(i) *L'Ascension;* (ii) *Couleurs de la cité céleste; Et exspecto resurectionem mortuorum*

*** Erato (ADD) 2564 60225-2. (i) French R. & TV O, Constant; (ii) Loriod, Strasbourg Instrumental & Percussion Group, Boulez

L'Ascension (an early work from 1933) may be static in feeling but it is highly personal in flavour. The performance from **Marius Constant** and the **French Radio Orchestra** is most persuasive, and they are admirably served by the engineers. *Et exspecto* draws liberally on the composer's beloved birdsong, *Les Couleurs de la cité céleste* represented the composer's ideal of 'stained-glass music' and 'ends no more than it begins, and turns on itself like a rose-window of blazing and invisible colours'. It sounds very impressive here in demonstrating the extraordinary sonorities the composer draws from piano, wind and percussion, with **Boulez** ensuring that every detail is clear.

(i) *L'Ascension; Et exspecto resurectionem mortuorum;* (ii) *Turangalîla Symphony;* (iii) *Quatuor pour la fin du temps;* (iv) (2 Pianos) *Visions de l'amen;* (Piano) (v) *Rondeau;* (vi) *Chants de terre et de ciel;* (vii) *Cinq Rechants;* (vi) *Harawi. Poèmes pour Mi* (with (viii) orchestra and with (vi) piano); (ix) *La Transfiguration de Notre seigneur Jesus Christ*

(B) *** Decca 478 0352 (6). (i) LSO, Stokowski; (ii) Thibaudet, Harada, Concg. O, Chailly; (iii) Bell, Collins, Isserlis, Mustonen; (iv) Ogdon, Lucas; (v) Crossley; (vi) Barker, Sherlaw Johnson; (vii) Alldis Ch.; (viii) Palmer, BBC SO, Boulez; (ix) Loriod & instrumental soloists, Westminster Symphony Ch., Washington Nat. SO, Dorati

Decca have decided to issue a pair of centenary boxes, and

this is devoted to orchestral and instrumental works. The performances are virtually all noteworthy and (like its companion below) this could make a useful cornerstone of any Messiaen collection.

Des Canyons aux étoiles

⊶ (M) **** DG 471 617-2 (2). Muraro, Justafre, Fr. R. PO, Chung

Myung-Whun Chung, who studied with the composer, conducts a warmly expressive, free-flowing reading of Messiaen's tribute to the United States on its bicentenary in 1976. The set offers a striking contrast with the now deleted Sony version under Salonen, which is more severe in its precise registering of Messiaen's evocation of birdsong in each movement. Chung, together with his brilliant soloists, is freer and therefore more evocative in his readings of movements directly inspired by a sequence of venues in the American south-west, mainly the deserts and canyons of Utah and Arizona. In place of weight **Jean-Jacques Justafre** offers a volatile reading which spans an extraordinary tonal and dynamic range. Like the others, he brilliantly demonstrates that this is music to love and embrace. The DG two-disc package comes at upper mid-price.

(i) *Chronochromie;* (ii) *Eclairs sur l'au-delà;* (iii) *Et exspecto resurectionem mortuorum; Les offrandes oubliées;* (iv) *Turangalîla Symphony;* (v) *Le merle noir;* (vi) *Quatuor pour la fin du temps;* (vii) *Theme & Variations;* 2-Piano music: (viii) *Visions de l'amen;* Piano music: (ix) *Cantéyodjayâ;* (x) *4 Etudes de rhthme; Préludes; Vingt regards sur l'enfant Jésus.* Organ music: (xi) *Apparition de l'église éternelle; L'Ascension; Le banquet céleste; Le corps glorieux; Diptyque; Livre d'orgue; Messe de la Pentecôte; La Nativité du Seigneur.* Vocal music: (xii) *Chants de terre et de ciel;* (xiii) *Cinq rechants;* (xii) *Harawi;* (xiv) *3 Mélodies; La mort du nombre;* (xiii) *O sacrum convivium!; 3 Petites Liturgies de la Présence divine;* (xii) *Poèmes pour Mi*

(N) (BB) *** EMI Stereo/mono 2 17466-2 (14). (i) BBC SO, Dorati; (ii) BPO, Rattle; (iii) O de Paris, Baudo; (iv) Loriod, Beroff, LSO, Previn; (v) Pahud; (vi) Loriod, Poppen, M. Fischer-Dieskau, Meyer; (vii) Poppen, Loriod; (viii) Rabinovitch, Argerich; (ix) Ogdon; (x) Béroff; (xi) composer; (xii) Command & Petit; (xiii) L. Sinf. Ch. & Voices, L. Sinf., Edwards

This is EMI's budget compilation for the Messiaen centenary. The performances and recordings are of a generally high standard, although the *Quatuor pour la fin du temps* is not high on the list of recommendations. But the box is well worth its modest cost, if you don't mind limited documentation.

Couleurs de la cité céleste; Hymne pour grand orchestre; (i) *3 Petites Liturgies de la Présence divine*

(N) **** DG 477 7944. R. France PO, Myung Wha-Chung, with Maîtrise de R. France

This is the first of two outstanding single-CD collections of

Messiaen's music especially recorded by DG for the centenary of the composer's birth. (The other is a recital by Pierre-Laurent Aimard – see below.) We already know the extraordinary patina of *Couleurs de la cité céleste* from the Boulez version, but **Myung Wha-Chung's** version is if anything even more multi-coloured and atmospheric. The *Hymne*, with its long serene opening theme on the strings, in the words of Paul le Flem, 'evokes a mysticism where ecstasy and fervour are combined'. The *Trois Petites Liturgies* are even more ambitious, intended, in the composer's words, 'to bring a kind of organized act of praise into the concert room', dominated by ecstatic singing from the female chorus, but bringing in a repeated chorale on the strings based on the love theme we know in *Turangalîla*. The scoring includes tuned percussion, the gamelan, ondes martenot and piano and, in the finale, semi-spoken incantations. The work shows the composer at his most imaginative and most haunting, and it is given an inspired performance and superb recording, appropriately in Radio France's Salle Olivier Messiaen.

Turangalîla Symphony

🔑 Ⓜ ******** RCA (ADD) 82876 59418-2. Leanne Loriod (ondes martenot), Yvonne Loriod (piano), Toronto SO, Ozawa

*** Decca 436 626-2. Thibaudet, Harada, Concg. O, Chailly

*** Erato 8573 82043-2. Almard, Kim, BPO, Nagano

(i; ii) *Turangalîla Symphony*; (i; iii; iv; v) *Quatuor pour la fin du temps*; (i; iv) *Theme & Variations*

Ⓝ Ⓑ ****** EMI 2-CD 20686727. (i) Loriod; (ii) Béroff, LSO, Previn; (iii) Meyer; (iv) Poppen; (v) Manuel Fischer-Dieskau

Previn made two recordings of *Turangalîla* but in his **LSO** version his vividly direct approach, helped by spectacular recording, has much electricity. He is at his best in the work's more robust moments, for instance the jazzy fifth movement, and he catches the wit at the beginning of the *Chant d'amour 2*. The idyllic *Garden of the Sleep of Love* is both serene and poetically sensuous, and the apotheosis of the love theme in the closing pages is both jubilant and life-enhancing. Unfortunately, although the composer was supposed to have been present at the recording, the *Quatuor* performance is disappointing. This a work that depends on atmosphere and dynamic contrast, and the other recordings listed below do the music much greater justice in this respect. The *Theme and Variations* are much more successful, but are not as fine as the Chandos version listed below.

Ozawa's performance comes from 1967, but you would never guess that from the brilliantly atmospheric sound, which is just as vivid as some of the newer versions, such as Nagano's Erato version, and has that bit more warmth and atmosphere. **Yvonne Loriod's** piano is placed too forward, but her contribution is undoubtedly seminal, and the overall balance is otherwise well managed. The performance itself is brilliantly played: it has plenty of electricity, and a warm sensuality too. It was and remains one of Ozawa's best recordings and is now economically reissued on a single CD as part of RCA's 'Classic Collection'.

Chailly's full-priced Decca account may have the advantage of even finer, digital recording, but it costs more; being (just) fitted on to a single full-priced CD; however, it is without Rattle's considerable bonus.

Simon Rattle conducts a winning performance of *Turangalîla*, not only brilliant and dramatic but atmospheric and convincing. The recording is warm and richly coordinated, while losing nothing in detail. **Peter Donohoe** and **Tristan Murail** play with comparable warmth and flair. The performance of the *Quatuor pour la fin du temps*, led by **Erich Gruenberg** and with **Gervase de Peyer** the inspirational solo clarinettist, is in the very highest class, the players meeting every demand the composer makes on them, and the fine, clear, Abbey Road recording gives the group striking presence while affording the proper background ambience. The bonus, *Le Merle noir*, exploits the composer's love of birdsong and is splendidly played and recorded here.

Nagano seems determined to emphasize all the bizarre qualities of the score, including glissando whoops among the brilliant percussive effects. The *Joie du sang des étoiles* is jazzily, joyously extrovert, and this high level of tension (and noise) persists throughout. The *Final* is almost overwhelming in its energetic flamboyance and its culmination certainly has the sense of absolute finality. But although the sensuous aspects of the score are fully realized in the *Jardin du sommeil d'amour*, the contrasting element of repose seldom surfaces, and such a consistent clamour for most of the 73 minutes needs a fair degree of stamina. The recording itself has remarkable range and vividness.

Quatuor pour la fin du temps

🔑 ******** DG 469 052-2. Shaham, Meyer, Jian Wang, Chung

*** Call. CAL 9898. Sajot, Naganuma, Broutin, Gastaldi

*** Delos D/CD 3043. Chamber Music Northwest – BARTÓK: *Contrasts* *******

(i) *Quatuor pour la fin du temps*; (ii) *Chronochromie*

Ⓝ Ⓜ ******* EMI (ADD) 2 12688-2. (i) Gruenberg, de Peyer, Pleeth, Béroff; (ii) BBC SO, Dorati

Quatuor pour la fin du temps; Fantaisie for Violin & Piano; Piece for Piano Quintet; Morceau de lecture à vue

Ⓝ ******* Signum SIGCD 126. Soloists of the Philh. O

(i; ii) *Quatuor pour la fin du temps*; (i) *Les offrandes oubliées*; (i; ii) *Theme and Variations*

Ⓝ ******* Chan. 10480. (i) Plane; (ii) Gould Piano Trio

Messiaen's visionary and often inspired piece was composed during his days in a Silesian prison camp. Among his fellow-prisoners were a violinist, a clarinettist and a cellist, who, with the composer at the piano, made its creation possible. The newest DG account must now take pride of place among its rivals. It is a performance of the highest quality, with a level of concentration and intensity that grips the listener from first to last, and is superbly recorded. There are notes by both Messiaen and the cellist Etienne Pasquier, who was interned with Messiaen and took part in the première at the German prisoner-of-war camp in January 1941.

The EMI account, now reissued at mid-price as one of the 'Great Recordings of the Century', is led by **Erich Gruenberg** and, with **Gervase de Peyer** the inspirational clarinettist, is also in the very highest class, the players meeting every demand the composer makes upon them; and the fine, clear, Abbey Road recording gives the group striking presence, while affording the proper background ambience. **Dorati's** fine performance of *Chronochromie* has been added as an apt bonus. The work has its inspiration in nature, the composer's long established preoccupation with birdsong and the culminating *Epode*, readily understandable as a climactic representation of the birds' dawn chorus. The immensely vivid recording is worthy of the music.

Both Signum and Chandos have also issued outstanding new recordings of the *Quatuor*, each full of intensity and sensitively meeting the music's atmospheric needs and contrasts. In each case the clarinettist (**Barnaby Robson** on Signum, **Robert Plane** on Chandos), plays very sensitively, and with both CDs there are generous bonuses. The *Theme and Variations* and *Fantaisie* (each for violin and piano) were written in consecutive years (1931 and 1932). They are immature but rewarding short works and, while the *Variations* are also characteristically inventive, we are inclined to like the *Fantaisie* better. On Chandos *Les offrandes oubliées* is heard in an effective piano transcription by the composer; on Signum, *Le merle noir* is one of the most catchy of Messiaen's bird simulations, while the *Piece for Piano Quartet* and the tiny *Morceau* are attractive rare miniatures.

Like the DG version, which it readily matches, the Calliope performance is inspirational. The CD plays for only just over 43 minutes, which makes it very expensive; but many will think it worth it. **Jean-Louis Sajot's** clarinet tone is not soft-centred, but he plays with great character, and **Yuriko Naganuma's** violin solos are very beautiful, with the work closing in Elysian serenity. It is these two players who dominate the ensemble, without dwarfing their fine colleagues. The recording is very immediate and real.

David Shifrin, like his colleagues, fully captures the work's sensuous mysticism, while the solos of **Warren Lash** (cello) and **Williams Doppmann** have a wistful, improvisatory quality: both *Louange à l'éternité de Jésus* and the closing *Louange à l'immortalité de Jésus* are played very beautifully. The Delos recording is naturally balanced and very realistic, while the ambience is suitably evocative.

(i) *Oiseaux exotiques* **(for piano and orchestra). Piano music: (ii)** *Cantéyodjayâ; Catalogue d'oiseaux* **(complete);** *4 Etudes de rythme;* **(iii)** *Vingt regards sur l'enfant Jésus.* **Organ music: (iv)** *Apparition de l'église éternelle; L'Ascension; Le banquet céleste; Les corps glorieux; Diptyque; Messe de la Pentocôte;* **(v)** *La Nativité du Seigneur;* **(iv)** *Verset pour la fête de la dédicace;* **(v) (Vocal)** *O sacrum convivium!*

(N) (B) *** Decca (ADD/DDD) 478 0353 (7). (i) Thibaudet, Concg. O, Chailly; (ii) Sherlaw Johnson; (iii) Ogdon; (iv) Trotter; (v) Preston; King's College, Cambridge, Ch., Guest

This is Decca's other back-catalogue collection reissued for the Messiaen centennial, including the rare *Oiseaux exotiques* for piano and orchestra with **Thibaudet** and **Chailly** making

a fine partnership. **Robert Sherlaw Johnson** contributes a good deal of the piano music, including the *Cantéyodjayâ* with its serial influences, but also with a distinct association with Debussy. The opening of the work immediately introduces a striking idea, which is used as a kind of refrain against a collage of other ideas. The basic raw material of the *Catalogue d'oiseaux* is birdsong, as heard and remembered by the composer in his homeland, but what we hear is far removed from an imitative set of bird calls. Sherlaw Johnson's playing is poetic in feeling, and with a natural understanding of the music's atmosphere. The (originally Argo) recording is very fine. **John Ogdon** is allotted the *Vingt regards sur l'enfant Jésus* and while he is thoughtful and unfailingly conscientious, other versions have more spontaneity and insight. **Simon Preston**, however, is a convinced advocate of *La Nativité du Seigneur* and conveys its hypnotic power most successfully, and the (again Argo) recording reproduces with great fidelity. **Thomas Trotter**, too, is thoroughly at home in this repertoire and is an organ virtuoso of the highest order, while the **King's** performance of *O sacrum convivium!* completes a remarkably wide-ranging selection.

PIANO MUSIC

Complete piano music

Disc 1: *Catalogue d'oiseaux, Books 1–3* (RRC 1108)

Disc 2: *Catalogue d'oiseaux, Books 4–6* (RRC 1109)

Disc 3: *Catalogue d'oiseaux, Book 7; Supplément: La Fauvette des jardins; Petites esquisses d'oiseaux* (RRC 1110)

Disc 4: *20 Regards sur l'enfant-Jésus* (RRC 2055 (2))

Disc 5: *Cantéyodjayâ; 4 Etudes de rythme; Fantaisie burlesque; Pièce pour le tombeau de Paul Dukas; Préludes; Rondeau;* **(i)** *Visions de l'Amen* (RRC 2056 (2))

(BB) **** Regis RRC 7001 (7). Hill; (i) with Frith

Catalogue d'oiseaux

(BB) **** RRC 3008 (3). Hill (from above set)

Peter Hill made his outstanding collection of Messiaen's piano music between 1986 and 1992 for Unicorn. Those recordings now appear at bargain price on the Regis label, admirably documented. They come complete in a slip-case, but are available separately as listed above. The complete *Catalogue d'oiseaux* is also available as a separate collection. Peter Hill prepared this music in Paris with the composer himself and thus has his imprimatur. The *Petites esquisses d'oiseaux*, written in 1985, formed a belated postlude to the series.

With his inherent feeling for the colour and atmosphere of Messiaen's sound-world, Hill makes an excellent case for all this repertoire, save perhaps for the somewhat repetitive *Fantaisie burlesque* of 1932, which outstays its welcome. His playing is consistently sensitive and has great finesse, with the *Cantéyodjayâ* (1948) particularly refined. For the *Vingt regards sur l'enfant-Jésus*, recorded in 1991 in St Paul's, Southgate, it is the contemplative, lyrical writing that one remembers, the moments of calm, rather than the vibrant climaxes. Which is not to say that the playing is not vividly alive, but rather that bravura is never the first consideration, even though the pianism shows complete mastery. The composer himself has spoken with great warmth of the artist and he has every reason. Bob Auger's recordings, too, are a splendid memento of one of Britain's most musically perceptive sound-engineers.

Cantéyodjayâ; 4 Etudes de rythme; Préludes: Chant d'extase dans une paysage triste; Cloches d'angoisse et larmes d'adieu; La Colombe; Instants défunts; Le Nombre léger; Plainte calme; Un Reflet dans le vent; Les Sons impalpables du rêve (Naxos 8.554090)

Fantaisie burlesque; La Fauvette des jardins; Les Offrandes; Pièce pour le tombeau de Paul Dukas; Prélude; Rondeau (Naxos 8.554655)

Catalogue d'oiseaux (complete); Petites esquisses d'oiseaux (Naxos 8.553532/4 (3))

(BB) *** Austbø

This impressive Norwegian pianist (who is domiciled in the Netherlands) is totally in sympathy with Messiaen's elusive idiom.

Whatever one's reactions to Messiaen's music, he creates a world entirely his own. Håkan Austbø is completely attuned to this sensibility, and the recording is exemplary. Aficionados of Messiaen need not hesitate.

Catalogue d'oiseaux, Book 3: L'alouette lulu. Book 5: La bouscarle. Etudes de rythme: Île de feu I & II. 8 Préludes

(N) 🎧— **** DG 477 7452. Aimard

This is another of the key records of the Messiaen centenary celebrations. **Pierre-Laurent Aimard** had a personal relationship with the composer and studied with Yvonne Loriod, and his performances have rare authority. He plays all eight of the early *Préludes* (of 1928–9), readily finding Messiaen's special brand of intimate and extrovert impressionism, both highly original and underpinned by a Debussian inheritance; but *Song of ecstasy in a sad landscape*, *The impalpable sounds of a dream* and *A reflection in the wind* are very much Messiaen's own conceptions. The two excerpts from *Catalogue d'oiseaux* are completely contrasted, both unpredictable and both requiring real virtuosity; they are marvellously played. Similarly, the extraordinary, exotic, even jazzy rhythms of *Île de feu* are controlled with amazing sharpness of articulation. The piano recording is wonderfully clear – very much in the demonstration bracket.

Catalogue d'oiseaux: La Rousserolle effarvatte

*** MDG 604 1141-2. von Eckardstein – JANÁČEK: *Sonata 1.X.1905*; PROKOFIEV: *Sonata 8* ***

Severin von Eckardstein's account of *La Rousserolle effarvatte*, the seventh of the *Catalogue d'oiseaux*, is both sensitive and brilliant.

8 Préludes pour piano; 20 Regards sur l'enfant-Jésus

(BB) **(*) EMI Gemini (ADD) 4 76915-2 (2). Béroff

Béroff is totally at home in this repertoire and his performances are inspirational. Clean, well-focused sound – but a little wanting in richness and clarity. However, this set is very tempting at Gemini price.

20 Regards sur l'enfant-Jésus

🎧— **** Teldec 3984 26868-2 (2). Aimard (piano)

🎧— *** Hyp. CDA 67351/2. Osborne

*** Erato (ADD) 4509 91705-2 (2). Y. Loriod

(M) *** RCA 82876 62316-2 (2). Serkin

(BB) *** Naxos 8.550829/30. Austbø

Pierre-Laurent Aimard has received the composer's praise for his 'magnifique technique, sonorité claire et timbrée, et interprétations d'une rare intelligence'. Aimard's performance on disc is technically remarkable (although the virtuosity is always at the service of the music) and atmospherically perceptive. Fascinatingly, he is very relaxed at the opening, but evocation is in no doubt and the concentration steadily grows and with it the tension. The piano is very well recorded indeed, and this can be strongly recommended.

Steven Osborne's performance has much in common with that of Pierre-Laurent Aimard. It too is deeply sensitive and full of atmospheric feeling. The Hyperion recording is first class, and to make a choice between these two versions is almost impossible: both are very distinguished indeed.

The 1973 recording by **Yvonne Loriod** – the composer's second wife – of *Vingt regards* has long been considered very special in its understanding and feeling for the composer's musical sound-world. The piano recording is full but is otherwise acceptable rather than outstanding – yet the magnetism of the playing overcomes the lack of the sharpest focus.

Peter Serkin's remains among the finest versions at mid-price. He has an intense feeling for atmosphere and superb keyboard control. His recording is well lit and clear.

Håkon Austbø has excellent credentials in this repertoire. His is an individual view, with a wider range of tempi and dynamic than Loriod. His account of the opening *Regard du père* and the later *Regard du fils sur le fils* is paced much more slowly, but his playing has great concentration and evocative feeling so that he readily carries the slower tempo, and in *Par lui tout a été fait* articulation is bolder, giving the music a stronger profile, helped by the clearer, Naxos digital focus. This is undoubtedly a performance that grips the listener and can be strongly recommended as an alternative view.

ORGAN MUSIC

Complete Organ Music: (i) Apparition de l'église éternelle; L'Ascension; Le banquet céleste; Les corps glorieux; Diptyque; Livre d'orgue; Livre du Saint

Sacrement; *Méditations sur le mystère de la Sainte Trinité; Messse de la Pentecôte; La Nativité du Seigneur; Verset pour la fête de la dédicace;* (ii) 3 Posthumous works: *Monodie; Offrande au Saint Sacrement; Prélude* (with Birdsong in Messiaen's music)

(Ⓝ) ⏛→ (Ⓑ) **** BIS CD 1770/72 (7). Ericsson ((i) Grönlund organ of Luleå Cathedral, Sweden; (ii) Gerald Woehl organ of Katharinenkirche in Oppenheim, Germany)

The outstanding new complete survey of Messiaen's organ music by **Hans-Ola Ericsson** on BIS is of outstanding quality, musically and technically. It includes recordings of the three posthumous pieces, a 232-page booklet documenting the music; and as an appendix there are recordings of the bird calls indicated in Messaien's organ scores. The seven CDs come for the cost of three.

Complete organ music (including unpublished works): *Monodie; Prélude; Offrande du Saint Sacrement*

(Ⓜ) *** DG 471 480-2 (6). Latry (organ of Notre-Dame de Paris)

Disc 1: *L'Apparition de l'église éternelle; Le Banquet céleste; La Nativité du Seigneur (9 Méditations)* (RRC 1086)

Disc 2: *L'Ascension (4 Méditations); Les Corps glorieux (7 Visions de la vie des ressuscités)* (RRC 1087)

Discs 3–4: *Livre d'orgue (1951); 9 Méditations sur le mystère de la Sainte Trinité; Messe de la Pentecôte* (RRC 2051) (2)

Discs 5–6: *Diptyque (Essai sur la vie terrestre);* (i) *Livre du Saint Sacrement; Verset pour la Fête de la Dédicace* (RRC 2052) (2)

(Ⓑ) **** Regis RRC 6001 (6). Bate (organ of Cathedral of Saint-Pierre, Beauvais, or (i) L'Eglise de la Sainte-Trinité, Paris)

Volume 1: *Apparition de l'église éternelle; Le Banquet céleste; La Nativité du Seigneur* (Priory PRCD 921)

Volume 2: *Méditations sur le mystère de la Sainte Trinité* (Priory PRCD 922)

Volume 3: *Le Corps glorieux; Messe de la Pentecôte* (Priory PRCD 923)

Volume 4: *L'Ascension; Livre d'orgue* (Priory PRDC 924)

Volumes 5 & 6: *Livre du Saint Sacrement. Early Pieces: Diptyque; Monodie; Offrande au Saint Sacrement; Prélude; Verset pour la Fête de la Dédicace* (Priory Double PRDC 925/6)

Volumes 1–6 (complete) (PRMESSIAENSET (6))

(Ⓜ) **** Weir

'C'est vraiment parfait!' said Messiaen after hearing **Jennifer Bate's** recording of *La Nativité du Seigneur,* one of his most extended, most beautiful and most moving works, with the nine movements each hypnotically compelling in their atmospheric commentaries on the Nativity story. But the composer also gave his imprimatur to every one of these recordings, all but one of which were made between 1979 and 1981 on the Beauvais organ, endorsing the performances with great enthusiasm. He then sent Jennifer Bate the manuscript of his last masterpiece, *Livre du Saint Sacrement,* which she premièred at Westminster Cathedral in 1986 and went on to record at Sainte-Trinité in 1987. Of the other pieces, *Le Banquet céleste* and *Diptyque* are both early works, the former already intense in its religious feeling, the latter dedicated to Messiaen's teachers, Dukas and Dupré.

The recordings were superbly engineered by the late Bob Auger and are all in the demonstration bracket. Jennifer Bate is completely at home in Messiaen's sound-world and readily identifies with the religious experience which has inspired all of the composer's organ music. In every way this inexpensive reissue of recordings originally made by Unicorn is definitive.

Gillian Weir's magnificently recorded coverage of Messiaen's organ music was recorded on the superb organ of Aarhus Cathedral, Denmark, in association with BBC Radio 3, and was originally issued on Collins. Now it returns on Priory, and its excellence is confirmed. Like Jennifer Bate, Weir was a personal friend and confidante of the composer, and the authority and conviction of her playing shines out through the entire project: its concentration and power are immediately apparent in the opening *Apparition de l'église éternelle,* while *Le Banquet céleste* and the remarkably diverse *Le Corps glorieux* show the strength of her characterization. Only in the *Méditations sur le mystère de la Sainte Trinité* does one feel that, although she still holds the music in a firm grip, her approach is a little static. But this remains very compelling, if only for the rich and sometimes piquant palette of sound she commands on her Danish organ. The records are available individually at mid-price (with the fourth and fifth discs together, treated as a double), whereas Bate's recording is on the budget Regis label. But Gillian Weir's set is in every way a recommendable alternative, and it is well documented, including her personal reminiscences of the composer.

Olivier Latry's survey is also distinguished and is very well recorded indeed in Notre-Dame. The result has great atmosphere, especially effective in conveying the composer's spiritual mysticism which is at the heart of Latry's essentially thoughtful interpretations. Jennifer Bate is more vividly extrovert and this is clear when comparing the two accounts of *La Nativité du Seigneur,* which also demonstrates the special suitability of the Beauvais organ. Both approaches are valid, of course, and the DG set has the advantage of offering some more unpublished items. But it is offered on six mid-priced CDs, whereas Bate's Regis reissue is in the budget range, and Gillian Weir is at mid-price.

L'Apparition de l'église éternelle; L'Ascension (4 Méditations); Le Banquet céleste; Le Corps glorieux (7 Visions de la vie des ressuscités); Diptyque (Essai sur la vie terrestre et l'éternité religieuse); Livre d'Orgue (Reprises par interversion; Première pièce en trio; Les Mains de l'abîme; Chants des oiseaux; Deuxième pièce en trio; Les Yeux dans les roues; Soixante-quatre durées); Messe de la Pentecôte; La Nativité du Seigneur (9 Méditations)

Ⓜ *** EMI mono 7 67400-2 (4). Composer (Cavaillé-Coll organ of L'Eglise de la Sainte-Trinité, Paris)

In an intensive series of sessions which began at the end of May and continued through June and July of 1956, **Olivier Messiaen** returned to the organ in Sainte-Trinité, with which all his music is associated, and recorded everything he had written and published before that date. These performances not only carry the imprint of the composer's authority but also the inspiration of the occasion. The large-scale works have a concentration and compelling atmosphere that are unforgettable. No apologies at all need be made for the range, breadth and faithfulness of the recording, although some must be made for the organ itself, which is not always perfectly tuned. There is minor background hiss, which is not troublesome, and technically the CD transfers are a remarkable achievement.

VOCAL MUSIC

Cinq Rechants; O sacrum convivium

*** HM HMC 901834. RIAS Kammerchor, Reuss – MARTIN: *Mass for Double Choir; Songs of Ariel* ***

The *Cinq Rechants* or 'Refrains' of 1948 is the last element in Messiaen's so-called Tristan trilogy, which includes *Turangalîla*. It is his last *a cappella* work, and he thought of it as one of his very finest. It embraces elements of Peruvian folksong, the *alba* or dawn songs of the troubadours and the chansons of Claude le Jeune, as well as Indian rhythms. The **Berlin Choir** meet its formidable vocal demands with a performance of remarkable virtuosity, and add a serene account of the earlier *O sacrum convivium*. Superb and responsive singing throughout.

OPERA

Saint François d'Assise (complete)

*** DG 445 176-2 (4). van Dam, Upshaw, Aler, Krause, Arnold Schoenberg Ch., Hallé O, Nagano

It was a labour of love over a full eight years, writing this massive four-hour opera. The live recording, made in the Felsenreitschule in Salzburg during the 1998 Festival, is astonishingly vivid, with voices and orchestra clear and immediate but with ample bloom in the helpful acoustic. The discs actually improve on the live experience, not only in the extra clarity but in the audibility of words, with the libretto an extra help in following the measured progress of a work that tells the story of St Francis in eight tableaux that fight shy of conventional dramatic design, predominantly medi-

tative at measured speeds. In such a performance as this the result is magnetic, with **Nagano** drawing inspired playing from the **Hallé**, with **José van Dam** masterly in the title-role and **Dawn Upshaw** radiant in the role of the Angel. The rest of the cast is comparably strong. Messiaen himself regarded this as his greatest achievement, a synthesis of what he represented musically and a supreme expression of his Catholic faith. His characteristic use of birdsong here reaches its zenith – aptly so with such a subject – when in his hypnotic patterning he claims to have used every example he had ever notated.

MEYER, Edgar (born 1960)

Violin Concerto

*** Sony SK 89029. Hahn, St Paul CO, Wolff – BARBER: *Violin Concerto* ***

Edgar Meyer wrote this *Violin Concerto* specially for **Hilary Hahn**, providing an unusual but apt coupling for the Barber *Concerto*, equally an example of American late romanticism. Unashamedly tonal and freely lyrical, it opens with a yearning folk-like melody that echoes Vaughan Williams, and there is also a folk-like pentatonic cut to some of the writing in both of the two substantial movements. The first is a free set of variations, leading to a virtuoso exercise in using a persistent pedal note, while avoiding monotony. The second movement, in clearly defined sections, easily erupts at times into a rustic dance, and ends on a dazzling coda. Hahn plays with passionate commitment, amply justifying her choice of coupling.

MEYERBEER, Giacomo (1791–1864)

Les Patineurs (ballet suite; arr. & orch. Lambert)

🎵❋ **** Australian Decca Eloquence (ADD) 476 2742. Israel PO, Martinon – DVOŘÁK: *Slavonic Dances*; MASSENET: *Le Cid Ballet Music* ❋ ***

This 1958 coupling of Meyerbeer and Massenet was justly famous in its day. The sheer vividness of the opening number, with its growling cellos, the swagger of the string rhythms and the thundering timpani strokes, are still startling – and, praise be, the CD transfer is superb. No less astonishing is the quality of the playing, with **Martinon** inducing the **Israeli Orchestra** to catch the full inflexion of the French ballet style: the performance overflows with colour, and the tunes come tumbling out, bursting with *joie de vivre*.

Il Crociato in Egitto (complete)

*** Opera Rara (ADD) OR 10 (4). Kenny, Montague, D. Jones, Ford, Kitchen, Benelli, Platt, Geoffrey Mitchell Ch., RPO, Parry

This was the sixth and last opera which Meyerbeer wrote for Italy. The musical invention may not often be very distinctive, but the writing is consistently lively, notably in the ensembles. With one exception – **Ian Platt**, ill-focused in the role of the Sultan – the cast is a strong one, with **Diana Montague** outstanding in the castrato role of the Crusader-Knight, Armando. **Della Jones**, too, in the mezzo role of Felicia, whom Armando has abandoned in favour of Palmide, the Sultan's daughter, sings superbly, with agile coloratura and a rich chest register. **Yvonne Kenny** is brilliant as Palmide. **Bruce Ford**, with his firm, heroic tone, and **Ugo Benelli** are very well contrasted in the two tenor roles. Though the chorus is small, the recording is clear and fresh.

Margherita d'Anjou (complete)

**(*) Opera Rara ORC 25 (2). Massis, Ford, Barcellona, Miles, Previati, LPO, Parry

Dating from 1820, *Margherita d'Anjou*, set on the Scottish borders in 1462, was a milestone in Meyerbeer's career, pointing forward not only to the last of his Italian operas, *Il Crociato in Egitto*, but to the grand historical epics of his Paris years. The heroine of the title is Margaret of Anjou, widow of Henry VI, a formidable role commandingly taken in this recording by **Annick Massis**. Starting with a military overture, the piece involves many lively choruses and ensembles, well controlled by **David Parry**, who has an excellent team. Opposite Massis as Lavarenne, Grand Senechal of Normandy, is the tenor **Bruce Ford**, exploiting his impressive vocal range, if sometimes with rough tone, while the mezzo **Daniella Barcellona** is strongly cast as Lavarenne's wife, and **Alastair Miles** is impressive too as the banished general, Belmonte. The full, clear sound is marred by piano continuo in recitative, set far too close.

Semiramide (complete)

BB ****** Naxos 8.660205/6. Riedel, Adami, James, Gierlach, Peretyatyarko, Silva, Altensteig, Rossini Ch., Württemberg PO, Bonynge

Who would have expected to see **Bonynge** conducting a new recording on Naxos? But he is directing a first recording of a recently rediscovered score, not a masterpiece by any means, but agreeable enough. **Deborah Riedel** is impressive in the title-role, in vocal partnership with **Fiona James** as Prince Scitalce, while her other suitor, Prince Ircano (**Filippo Adami**), sings ardently enough. The rest of the cast are sound, and Bonynge, as is his gift, keeps the pot on the boil throughout, and gets good support from the men's chorus. A worthwhile novelty, competitively priced.

MIASKOVSKY, Nikolay

(1881–1950)

Cello Concerto in C min., Op. 66

⊶ ✸ **** EMI (ADD) 3 80013-2. Rostropovich, Philh. O, Sargent – PROKOFIEV: *Sinfonia concertante*; RACHMANINOV: *Vocalise* ********

*** Signum SUGCD116. Walton, Philh. O, Briger (with ELGAR: *Cello Concerto* *******)

The *Cello Concerto* of 1944 is one of Miaskovsky's most poignant works. It radiates an all-pervasive nostalgia, a long-

ing for a world lost beyond recall, and its gentle, elegiac sentiment is haunting. **Rostropovich** remains its most persuasive and authoritative exponent, and he is given sensitive support from the **Philharmonia Orchestra** under **Sir Malcolm Sargent**.

On Signum a highly appropriate coupling of two profoundly elegiac (and, for that matter, simply profound) concertos by two major composers, and **Jamie Walton's** recording is a welcome and eloquent newcomer.

(i) Cello Concerto; Symphony 27 in C min., Op. 85

*** Chan. 10025. (i) Ivashkin; Russian State SO, Polyansky

Alexander Ivashkin's is another eloquent account which judges to perfection the concerto's melancholy and nobility, and the recording is very natural. As a coupling, Chandos offer the *Twenty-Seventh Symphony*, his last, completed in 1949, less than a year before he died. Yet it is a work which, far from reflecting the approach of death (he was already suffering from cancer), conveys an amiable warmth in the outer movements and a moving serenity in the lovely central slow movement, only briefly interrupted by a tender violin melody that is almost Elgarian in its nobility, while Miaskovsky paid necessary homage to his Soviet masters in the stirring march themes of the extrovert finale.

Violin Concerto

BB ******* Naxos 8.557194. Grubert, Russian PO, Yablonsky – VAINBERG: *Violin Concerto* *******

Miaskovsky's *Violin Concerto* of 1939 is one of the most appealing and lyrical of all Russian concertos. Its neglect is quite unaccountable. The Lithuanian violinist **Ilya Grubert** offers the *Concerto* coupled enterprisingly with the Vainberg and at a remarkably competitive price. Grubert plays it with appropriate affection and grace, and he is well supported by his Russian players. At the price this must be self-recommending, and readers who have not acquired the even finer deleted Repin version should lose no time in snapping this up.

Divertissement, Op. 80; Silence, Op. 9; Sinfonietta in B min., Op. 32/2

(N) **BB** ******* Regis Alto ALC 1042. Russian Federation Ac. SO, Svetlanov

Silence is an early tone-poem based on Edgar Allan Poe and dating from 1909. Miaskovsky played it through with his friend Prokofiev. The influence of Wagner and Rachmaninov (particularly *Isle of the Dead*) is to be felt. The *Sinfonietta for strings* of 1929 acted as a kind of calling card for him during the 1930s and was widely heard in Europe and America. The *Divertissement* comes from 1948, the year in which Zhdanov launched his attack on all the leading Soviet composers of the day including Miaskovsky. There is a poignant lyricism here and in the first movement an endearing waltz theme that recalls those in Prokofiev's *War and Peace*. Dedicated performances. The disc is well worth its modest cost.

Lyric Concertino, Op. 32/3; Salutation Overture, Op. 48; Serenade in E flat, Op. 32/1; Sinfonietta in B min., Op. 32/2

⊕— ⓑⓑ *** Regis RRC 1244. Soloists, Moscow New Opera O, Samoilov

The *Serenade* has great charm and strong lyrical appeal; the *Lyric Concerto* (for flute, clarinet, horn, bassoon, harp and strings), and particularly its slow movement, has considerable harmonic subtlety. The performances under **Yevgeny Samoilov** are of fine quality and he gives a sensitive reading of the *Sinfonietta* for strings. These are enduring pieces; not so the *Salutation Overture*, written for Stalin's 6oth birthday, which is worth giving a miss. Very good recording. A bargain.

Sinfonietta for Strings in B min., Op. 32/2; Theme & Variations; 2 Pieces, Op. 46/1; Napeve

⊕— *** ASV CDDCA 928. St Petersburg CO, Melia

The *Sinfonietta for Strings* will appeal to anyone of a nostalgic disposition. The players give an affectionate, well-prepared account of it and convey the wistful, endearing nature of the slow movement to perfection. The *Theme and Variations* (on a theme of Grieg) also has the same streak of melancholy. The first of the *Two Pieces*, Op. 46, No. 1, is a transcription and reworking for strings of the inner movements, reversing their order, of Miaskovsky's *Symphony 19 for Military Band*, composed in 1939. The **St Petersburg Chamber Orchestra** is an expert and responsive ensemble, and the ASV recording does them proud.

Symphonies (complete). Divertimento, Op. 80; Silence, Op. 9; Sinfonietta in B min., Op. 32/2

Ⓝ *** Warner Classics 256469689-8. Russian Federation SO, Svetlanov

A warm welcome for the complete Miaskovsky cycle – or, rather, not-quite-complete cycle, as the *Eighteenth Symphony* is missing in all of the sets we have seen. Not that Warner seemed particularly concerned, for when the omission was pointed out, they did not even bother to return the call. The set went on to collect an award – and rightly so, for Miaskovsky is a master symphonist and **Yevgeni Svetlanov** believes in this music ardently. This empathy shines through all these performances. (But the *Eighteenth* in C major, composed in 1937, was recorded digitally by Svetlanov and coupled with the *Second Symphony* in C sharp minor, a big piece twice as long as its companion, on Olympia OCD732. It may still be possible to find this in some outlets.)

The *First Symphony* (also recorded by Rozhdestvensky), is very much in the received tradition, as are its immediate successors; it is in the massive hour-long *Sixth* of 1922 with a choral finale that Miaskovsky finds his real voice: the delicacy and intense nostalgia of the trio section of the Scherzo is wonderfully affecting and unlike any of his contemporaries. Explore its successors from the interwar years, and each has its own distinctive sound-world. 22, '*Ballade*' in B minor, has a combined richness of vision and breadth of canvas. The pervasive melancholy of 25 (a close neighbour of the *Cello Concerto*) and one of the finest and most expressive is totally and refreshingly out-of-keeping with the spirit of its times, though it is 27, which the composer never lived to hear, that sounds as if it is a contemporary work of Borodin

or Arensky – and none the worse for that! In its separate format, the series had extensive and authoritative notes by Per Skans but the boxed set has only the sketchiest of presentation. But this is a treasure house that will reward the exploratory listener: dedicated performances, music of great humanity and integrity and acceptable if not distinguished recorded sound. Many of the symphonies are also available separately on the Regis Alto label.

Symphonies (i) 1 in C min., Op. 3; (ii) 19 in E flat for Wind Band, Op. 46

**(*) Russian Disc (ADD) RDCD 11 007. (i) USSR MoC SO, Rozhdestvensky; (ii) Russian State Brass O, Sergeyev

Miaskovsky's *First Symphony* is very much in the received tradition. It is obvious from the very start that Miaskovsky was a composer who could think on a big scale. The *Nineteenth Symphony in B flat* for military band is a slighter piece, worth hearing for its inner movements, a wistful *Moderato* and a well-written *Andante*. The *First Symphony* is well played by the **Ministry of Culture Orchestra** under **Gennady Rozhdestvensky**, though the brass sound a bit raw, as indeed do the upper strings. The *Nineteenth* is played with great brio and genuine affection. The less-than-three-star recording-quality should not deter collectors from investigating this work.

Symphonies 5 in D, Op. 18; 9 in E min., Op. 28

**(*) Marco Polo 8.223499. BBC PO, Downes

The *Fifth Symphony* is a sunny, pastoral score dating from 1918, very much in the tradition of Glazunov and Glière. **Downes's** recording with the **BBC Philharmonic**, recorded in an admittedly over-resonant venue in Derby, is to be preferred both artistically and sonically to its earlier rival by the USSR Symphony Orchestra under Ivanov on Olympia (now deleted). The *Ninth Symphony* is somewhat better served than 5 so far as the sound is concerned. It is vintage Miaskovsky, more cogently argued and more interesting in thematic substance than the *Eighth*. Very good performances and good enough recording – just – to make three stars.

Symphony 6 in E flat min. (Revolutionary), Op. 23

(**(*)) Russian Disc mono RDCD 15008. Yurlov Russian Ch., USSR SO, Kondrashin

The *Sixth* is Miaskovsky's longest symphony (it takes nearly 65 minutes) and is arguably his masterpiece. The work occupied him over a two-year period (1921–3). It encompasses a wide range of feeling and has dignity and an epic sweep reminiscent of Eisenstein. Miaskovsky subsequently retouched its scoring and made further revisions in 1947. The 1959 **Kondrashin** recording had a special authority and dramatic intensity; it is still in circulation and remains a benchmark account.

Symphony 12 in G min., Op. 35; Silence (symphonic poem after Poe), Op. 9

**(*) Marco Polo 8.223302. Slovak RSO (Bratislava), Stankovsky

The *Twelfth Symphony* is endearingly old-fashioned. It is highly enjoyable, particularly when it is as well played as it is here by the **Bratislava Radio Orchestra** under their gifted young conductor, **Robert Stankovsky**. The tone-poem *Silence* draws for its inspiration on Edgar Allan Poe's *The Raven* and has a strongly atmospheric quality with a distinctly *fin-de-siècle* air: if you enjoy Rachmaninov's *Isle of the Dead*, you should investigate it. The orchestra play with enthusiasm and they are decently recorded.

Symphonies 24 in F min., Op. 63; 25 in D flat, Op. 69

🔾 (BB) *** Naxos 8.555376. Moscow PO, Yablonsky

Very worthwhile accounts of both symphonies from **Dmitri Yablonsky** and the **Moscow Philharmonic**. Yablonsky's account of 25, Miaskovsky's first post-war symphony, holds up well against Svetlanov's (coupled with 1). He is less expansive in the glorious first movement but no less heartfelt. This is particularly haunting and moving, full of the all-pervasive melancholy which is *echt*-Miaskovsky. The recording is decent and, although those collecting the Svetlanov cycle will want to complete it, those who cannot wait will find the modest outlay here well worth while.

Symphony 27 – see *Cello Concerto*

CHAMBER MUSIC

Cello Sonata 1 in D, Op. 12

🔾 (BB) **** Virgin 2x1 4 82067-2 (2). Mørk, Thibaudet – PROKOFIEV; RACHMANINOV; SHOSTAKOVICH: *Cello Sonatas*; STRAVINSKY: *Suite italienne* ***

This is an outstandingly desirable and generous bargain collection. The Norwegian cellist **Truls Mørk** plays the lovely Miaskovsky *Sonata* with both feeling and restraint, and the couplings are no less desirable. The recording is truthful and well balanced.

Cello Sonata 2 in A min., Op. 81

🔾 (M) *** Somm CD 029. Walton, Grimwood – KABALEVSKY: *Sonata in B flat*; PROKOFIEV: *Cello Sonata* ***

What a glorious work the *Second Sonata* of 1949 is! Its invention flows freely and naturally, and although the idiom was thought of as highly conservative (and it would have been for 1890, let alone the 1940s) the ideas are distinguished and have an eloquence that is most appealing. The trouble is that the opening tune is difficult to dislodge from the memory, as is the Fauréan contrasting idea. Impeccable playing from these little-known young artists, who more than repay the confidence Somm has placed in them. Good recording.

PIANO MUSIC

Piano Sonatas: 4 in C min., Op. 27; 5 in B, Op. 64/1; Sonatine in E min., Op. 57

(BB) *** Regis RRC 1245. McLachlan

It is good to see that Regis are beginning to reissue (at budget price) **Murray McLachlan's** survey of the piano music of Miaskovsky. In a scholarly note he tells us that 2 was actually

the *Seventh* and that many more may come to light. If they are as interesting as the *Fourth* or the *E minor Sonatine*, so much the better. The middle movement of the latter, marked *Narrante e lugubre*, is dark and pessimistic, and quite haunting. McLachlan speaks of the 'enormous tactile pleasure' it gives to the performer, but it also grips the listener. This gifted young artist readily communicates his own enthusiasm for this music, and his playing is both authoritative and persuasive. Good recording, too.

Piano Sonatas 6 in A flat, Op. 62/2; 7 in C, Op. 82; 8 in D min., Op. 83; 9 in F, Op. 84

**(*) Marco Polo 8.223178. Hegedüs

The Marco Polo disc brings the last four sonatas. The young Hungarian pianist, **Endre Hegedüs**, is an imaginative interpreter: he colours the second theme of the *Barcarolle* section of the *Eighth Sonata* with great tenderness and subtlety. The sound is a little wanting in bloom.

MILHAUD, Darius (1892–1974)

L'Apothéose de Molière, Op. 286; Le Bœuf sur le toit, Op. 58; (i) Le Carnaval d'Aix, Op. 83b; Le Carnaval de Londres, Op. 172

🔾 (BB) *** Hyp. Helios CDH 55168. (i) Gibbons; New L. O, Corp

Le Carnaval d'Aix is a carefree work, full of high spirits, and is very expertly played by **Jack Gibbons** and the **New London Orchestra** under **Ronald Corp**. They also convey the Satie-like circus-music character of *Le Bœuf sur le toit* to excellent effect. What delightful music this is, and so expertly fashioned by this lovable composer. The Molière pastiche and the arrangement of melodies from *The Beggar's Opera* are not top-drawer Milhaud, but they are still worth having. Very good recording from the Hyperion team.

(i) Ballade for Piano and Orchestra; Piano Concerto 4, Op. 295; (ii) Symphonies 4, Op. 281; 8 in D (Rhodanienne), Op. 362

🔾 (BB) **** Warner Apex 0927 49982-2. (i) Helffer, O Nat. de France, Robertson; (ii) Fr. R. & TV PO, composer

An immensely valuable budget reissue. The *Ballade* (1920) was composed for Roussel, and Milhaud made his piano début at its première in New York: its languorous opening seems to hark back to his days in Brazil. The *Fourth Piano Concerto* (1949), written for the virtuoso, Sadel Zkolowsky, is an inventive piece of some substance, with a particularly imaginative and evocative slow movement. **Claude Helffer** is an admirable exponent of both works, and he and **David Robertson** readily catch the music's special atmosphere.

The *Fourth Symphony* was commissioned by French Radio in commemoration of the centenary of the 1848 uprising and revolution, and its four movements offer a vivid portrayal of those events. It is scored for unusually large forces, including two saxophones and a vast array of percussion, all heard to good effect in the first movement, which depicts the uprising with massive polytonal and dissonant clashes; the second laments the fallen, the third describes liberty rediscovered, and the finale is almost festive. The *Eighth Symphony*, written in the late 1950s for a new concert hall at the University of California, is subtitled *Rhodanienne* and evokes the course of the river Rhône from its beginnings in the Alps down to the Carmargue. Rich in instrumental resource, it is full of imaginative colours and textures, and the playing of the **Orchestre Philharmonique de l'ORTF** for **Milhaud** himself is absolutely first rate. These performances date from 1968, and the sound is much cleaned up for this CD, which commands an unqualified recommendation.

(i) *Le Boeuf sur le toit*, Op. 58; (iv; ii) *Le Carnaval d'Aix*, Op. 83b; (i) *La création du monde*, Op. 81a; *Saudades do Brasil*, Nos. 7–9 & 11; (ii) *Suite française*, Op. 248; *Suite provençale*, Op. 152b; (iii) *Le bal martiniquais*, Op. 249; (iii–v) *Paris*, Op. 284; (iii) *Scaramouche*, Op. 165b

(N) (BB) *** Brilliant 90071/2. (i) O Nat. de France, Bernstein; (ii) Monte Carlo O, Prêtre; (iii) Lee, Ivaldi; (iv) Béroff, (v) Collard

An ideal introduction to this genial composer at a very modest outlay. It brings **Bernstein's** exhilarating 1971 HMV recordings of *La création du monde* and *Le Boeuf sur le toit*, still unsurpassed in their flair, together with slightly later recordings by four distinguished French pianists. In the adorable *Carnaval d'Aix*, **Michel Béroff** is the soloist with the **Monte Carlo Orchestra** under **Georges Prêtre**, an ideal conductor in this repertoire. Altogether outstanding value.

Le Bœuf sur le toit; Concertino de printemps; (i) Violin Concertos 1, Op. 93; 2, Op. 263; Op. 135

*** Orfeo C646051A. (i) Steinbacher; Munich R. O, Steinberg

The *First* and *Second Violin Concertos* return to the catalogue to be strongly welcomed, particularly in such fluent performances by **Suzanne Steinbacher** and these Bavarian musicians. These are both inventive and finely wrought pieces that deserve a place in the wider concert repertoire, not just in the CD catalogue. The adorable *Concertino de printemps* and *Le Bœuf sur le toit* are splendid makeweights.

Le Bœuf sur le toit, Op. 58; La Création du monde, Op. 81

**** Chan. 9023. Ulster O, Y. P. Tortelier – IBERT: *Divertissement*; POULENC: *Les Biches* ****

Le Bœuf sur le toit; La Création du monde; (i) L'Homme et son désir; Suite provençale

⊗— (BB) **** Naxos 8.557287. Lille Nat. O, Casadesus; (i) with Makuuchi, Zhao, Vidal, Deletre

The Naxos issue, vividly recorded, makes an ideal Milhaud collection, surveying a wide range of his long career. **Jean-Claude Casadesus** conducts the **Lille Orchestra** in warmly idiomatic performances which combine refinement with rhythmic bite. The rarity is an even earlier ballet, *L'Homme et son désir*, written in 1917–18 to a scenario by Paul Claudel, set in the primeval Amazonian forest. The exotic scoring is for solo wind and strings, with a very large percussion section and four solo voices singing wordlessly. The atmospheric colours of the piece are brilliantly caught, with the eight brief movements of the *Suite provençale* as an attractive makeweight, taken in 1936 from incidental music to a play.

A most engaging account of *Le Bœuf sur le toit* from **Yan Pascal Tortelier** and his **Ulster players**, full of colourful detail, admirably flexible and infectiously rhythmic. Perhaps *La Création du monde* is without the degree of plangent jazzy emphasis of a French performance, but its gentle, desperate melancholy is well caught, and the playing has plenty of colour and does not lack rhythmic subtlety. The Chandos recording, although resonant, is splendid in every other respect, and so are the couplings.

Le Carnaval d'Aix, Op. 83b; Ballade, Op. 61; Piano Concertos 1, Op. 127; 2, Op. 228; 3, Op. 270; 4, Op. 295; 5, Op. 346; 5 Études for Piano & Orchestra, Op. 63; Fantaisie Pastorale, Op. 188

*** CPO 777 162-2 (2). Korstick, Basle RSO, Francis

Milhaud recorded the *First Concerto* with Marguerite Long in the days of 78-r.p.m. discs but there are few alternative versions of the remaining four. Together, the pieces on these two CDs comprise Milhaud's complete output for piano and orchestra. At its best it is sunny and irresistible music, though elsewhere it is fluent rather than inspired. Very persuasive and strongly recommended.

(i; ii) Concertino de printemps (2 versions); (iii) Piano Concerto; (ii) Violin Concerto 2; (iv) Suite française; (v) Scaramouche (suite for 2 pianos)

(BB) (***) Dutton mono CDBP 9711. (i) Astruc with O; (ii) Kaufman, French R. O (members); (iii) Long, O Nat. de France; (iv) NYPO; all cond. composer; (v) Sellick and Smith

Milhaud regarded melody as 'the only living element in music' and turned all his resources to the expression of melodic ideas, often spring-like in their freshness and charm. No more so than in the vivacious *Concertino de printemps* which, in a Dutton scoop, is given here, first in its brilliant (1933) première recording by **Yvone Astruc**, and also in an even more breathtaking later version (1949), dazzlingly played by **Louis Kaufman**. Yet both performances reveal the music's underlying expressive nostalgia, and this is found again in the 'Slow and sombre' middle movement of the *Second Violin Concerto*, which Kaufman also plays superbly, delivering the finale with sparkling virtuosity. He is recorded closely but truthfully.

Marguerite Long (in 1935) scintillates in the small-scale *Piano Concerto*, and the composer delivers the full bonhomie of the *Suite française*, even if here the dated New York recording is brash and two-dimensional. For the most part, however, the splendid Dutton transfers make one forget the early provenance of these always vivid recordings. The performance of *Scaramouche* by **Cyril Smith** and **Phyllis Sellick** is unsurpassed, with the light-hearted Brazilian syncopations of the finale especially infectious, and here the 1948 Abbey Road recording sounds very realistic.

(i; ii) *5 Études for Piano & Orchestra, Op. 63*; (ii) *Sérénade, Op. 62*; (iii) *Symphony 3 (Sérénade), Op. 71*; (ii) *Suite de l'opéra, Maximilien, Op. 110b*; (iv) *Suite symphonique 2 (Protée)*; (v) *Suite for Violin, Clarinet & Piano, Op. 157b*; (i) *3 Rag Caprices, Op. 78*

Ⓜ (***) Divine Art CD 27807. (i) Badura-Skoda; (ii) VSO, Swoboda; (iii) Ens., Goehr; (iv) San Francisco SO, Monteux; (v) Parrenin, Delécluse, Haas-Hamburger

The *Sérénade, Op. 71*, with **Walter Goehr** conducting an eminent group of soloists including Jean Pougnet, Anthony Pini, Reginald Kell, Paul Draper and George Eskdale, was first issued in the 'Columbia History of Music' and, so far as we know, was never reissued on LP or CD. **Monteux's** account of *Protée* comes from his time with the San Francisco orchestra in 1945, and the **Swoboda** records, made in Vienna in 1950, originally appeared on Westminster and have an authentic feel to them.

Symphonies: 1, Op. 10; 2, Op. 247; 3 (Te Deum), Op. 271; 4, Op. 281; 5, Op. 322; 6, Op. 343; 7, Op. 344; 8 (Rhodanienne), Op. 362; 9, Op. 380; 10, Op. 382; 11 (Romantique), Op. 384; 12 (Rurale), Op. 390

Ⓜ *** CPO 999 656-2 (5). Basle RSO, Francis

Although he was celebrated for his *Petites symphonies*, Milhaud did not turn to the large-scale form until 1939 after the outbreak of war. The *First* was written in response to a commission from the Chicago Symphony Orchestra; Milhaud conducted its première recording after he had fled France in 1940. The *Second* was composed for Boston in 1944, a work of great resource and diversity. With the liberation of France in the same year, the composer Henri Barraud, then head of French Radio, commissioned the *Third* and *Fourth*, which celebrated the hard-won peace. Of the symphonies that were to come over the next two decades, it was the *Sixth* that has created the most lasting impression. Written for Charles Munch and the Boston Orchestra, it enjoyed consistent exposure during the 1950s – Milhaud conducted it with the BBC Symphony at that time – and it is like so much of Milhaud's best music, relaxed and sunny, like his native Aix-en-Provence, but a work of compelling substance. During the 1990s **Alun Francis** recorded all the symphonies with the **Basle Radio Symphony Orchestra**, and with the deletion of the individual CDs they are now gathered in this five-CD set. Get it while it is still in circulation, for the music is rewarding and the performances very well prepared and convincingly delivered. Good sound too.

CHAMBER MUSIC

La Cheminée du Roi René

(***) BBC mono BBCL 4066-2. Dennis Brain Wind Quintet (with instrumental recital (***))

The account by the **Dennis Brain Wind Quintet** of Milhaud's *Cheminée du Roi René*, with its pastiche Provençal flavour, is sheer delight, making it seem like a minor masterpiece. How beguiling are the *Aubade*, *La Maousinglade* and the finale, a *Madrigal-nocturne*. The sound too has a pleasing ambient glow.

Duo for 2 Violins, Op. 243; (i) *Sonata for 2 Violins & Piano, Op. 15*

(*) Hyp. CDA 66473. Osostowicz, Kovacic, (i) with Tomes – MARTINŮ: *Violin Sonata **(*)*; PROKOFIEV: *Violin Sonata **

The *Sonata for Two Violins and Piano* of 1914 is beautifully crafted and has a charming slow movement but is very slight. Not as slight, though, as the *Duo*, the first two movements of which were composed at a dinner party; the finale was written the following morning. Elegant performances from **Krysia Osostowicz** and **Ernst Kovacic** and, in the *Sonata*, **Susan Tomes**.

Music for wind: La Cheminée du Roi René, Op. 105; Divertissement en trois parties, Op. 399b; Pastorale, Op. 47; 2 Sketches, Op. 227b; Suite d'après Corrette, Op. 161b

Ⓜ **(*) Chan. 6536. Athena Ens., McNichol

Though none of this is first-class Milhaud, it is still full of pleasing and attractive ideas, and the general air of easy-going, life-loving enjoyment is well conveyed by the alert playing of the **Athena Ensemble**. One's only quarrel is with the somewhat close balance.

Scaramouche (arr. for clarinet & piano)

*** EMI 3 79787-2. Meyer, Maisenberg – DEVIENNE; POULENC; SAINT-SAËNS: *Sonatas ****

Written for piano duo, *Scaramouche* is one of Milhaud's audacious minor masterpieces, and it is irresistible here with **Sabine Meyer** leading the piano with her dashing roulades. There is wit, too, plus captivating élan in its infectious Brazilian finale. A most winning performance, realistically recorded, with the clarinet dominating.

String Quartets 1, Op. 5; 7 in B flat, Op. 87; 10, Op. 218; 16, Op. 303

*** Cybella CY 804. Aquitaine Nat. Qt

The *Seventh Quartet* speaks Milhaud's familiar, distinctive language; its four short movements are delightful, full of melody and colour. The *Tenth*, too, is attractive; the *Sixteenth* was a wedding anniversary present for his wife: its first movement has great tenderness and warmth. The **Aquitaine Quartet** have excellent ensemble, intonation is good and their playing is polished. The recording has a wide dynamic range and a spacious tonal spectrum.

String Quartets 5, Op. 64; 8, Op. 121; 11, Op. 232; 13, Op. 268

*** Cybella CY 805. Aquitaine Nat. Qt

The *Fifth Quartet* is not one of Milhaud's most inspired; the *Eighth*, on the other hand, has much to commend it, including a poignant slow movement. 11 has a splendid pastoral third movement and a lively jazzy finale; 13 has overtones of Mexico in its finale and a beguiling and charming *Barcarolle*. Both performance and recording are very good.

PIANO MUSIC

Music for 2 pianos: *Le Bal martiniquais, Op. 249;* ***Le Bœuf sur le toit, Op. 58a; Carnaval à la Nouvelle-Orléans, Op. 275; Kentuckiana, Op. 287; La libertadora, Op. 236; Scaramouche, Op. 165b; Songes, Op. 237***

🎵 **** Hyp. CDA 67014. Coombs, Pizarro

Hyperion assemble the bulk of Milhaud's music for two pianos from the popular and irresistible *Scaramouche* through to the duet arrangement of *Le Bœuf sur le toit*. An entertaining and delightful issue which brings some high-spirited pianism from these fine players and very good recorded sound.

MILNER, Anthony (1925–2002)

Roman Spring (cantata); *Salutatio Angelica, Op. 1*

*** Lyrita (ADD) SRCD 267. Hodgson, Palmer, Tear, L. Sinf. & Ch., Atherton – MAW: *Scenes and Arias* ***

Anthony Milner, an academic and lecturer as well as a composer, writes civilized, well-constructed music that deserves a place in the catalogue. *Salutatio Angelica* uses the text of the *Angelus*, with each of the three settings of the *Ave Maria* given to the mezzo soloist (most beautifully sung by **Alfreda Hodgson**). The other cantata, written 21 years later, is more ambitious and more lively, a setting of five well-contrasted Latin poems, grouped in three separate movements. The writing is generously lyrical and often vigorously rhythmic – no suspicion here that Latin is a dead language. Excellent performance and recording.

MINKUS, Léon (1826–1917)

La Bayadère (ballet; complete. Choreography: Natalia Makarova after Marius Petita)

**** TDK **DVD** DVWW-BLLBSC. Zakharova, Bolle, Brusson, Hewison, Sutera, La Scala, Milan, Ballet & O, Colman (V/D: Tina Protasoni)

**** TDK **DVD** DVWW-BLLBM. Asylmuratova, Mukhamedov, Bussell, Dowell, Kumakawa, Royal Ballet, ROHCG O, Lanchbery

La Bayadère (which may be translated as 'The Temple Dancer') arrived in St Petersburg in 1877, three decades after Adam's *Giselle*. Musically it is not its match, and the plot is unconvincingly melodramatic (drawing on both *Giselle* and *Aida!*). But for balletomanes the galaxy of marvellous choreography is a continual visual delight, for Petipa was at his peak and his invention throughout is constantly and engagingly fresh. So this is an ideal work for DVD, as Minkus's score, for all its moments of charm, does not really stand up on its own. The ballet's narrative line with its melodramatic climaxes needs a good deal of mime, and Natalia Makarova's Covent Garden production treats it in a stylized way (to match the handsome, stylized decor), whereas Olga Evreinoff at La Scala goes for realism, to match the more traditionally realistic La Scala settings. As for the dancing, it is superlative both at Covent Garden and at La Scala, with **Altynai Asylmuratova** and **Svetlana Zakharova** equally ravishing as Nikita. **Darcey Bussell** (at the Garden) is a particularly seductive Gamzatti, but **Isabelle Brusson** is sensuous too; and some may like **Roberto Bolle's** athletic, long-legged bravura portrayal of Solor, rather than **Irek Mukhamedov's** more overtly masculine persona. In both productions the corps de ballet are eye-catchingly graceful and elegantly precise as they make their patterned movements. One final point that tips the balance towards the Scala version is that **David Colman's** reading of the score comes over as that bit more racily romantic than **Lanchbery's**; but he is helped by a more open acoustic and a recording of greater range, giving the strings more radiance and bite.

La Bayadère (complete; arr. Lanchbery)

*** Decca 436 917-2 (2). ECO, Bonynge

Lanchbery has provided the present score, and he is responsible for the orchestration. Unlike Adam's rather disappointing *Le Corsaire* (also recorded by the same forces), this work is full of pleasing melody and first rate orchestral effects. If you like late 19th-century ballet music, then here is nearly two hours of it, played with much vivacity, elegance and drama, and given Decca's top-quality sound.

Don Quichotte (ballet: complete, with music arr. John Lanchbery). Choreography Rudolf Nureyev, after Maris Petipa

Ⓝ **(*) Arthaus **DVD** 107 009. Dupont, Legris, Bart, Didière, Corps de Ballet & O de l'Opéra Nat. de Paris, Florio

Minkus created his ballet *Don Quichotte* in 1869, but in 1966 Rudolf Nureyev staged a new, abbreviated version, reducing the original five Acts to three and a Prologue. But, like Petipa, the original choreographer, he concentrated on episodes from the second part of the novel, centring on the loving couple, Kitri and Basile. The Don becomes a minor, rather grotesque and peripheral figure introduced in the Prologue. However, in Act II he believes the heroine is his Dulcinea and, coming to her rescue, he attacks the windmill which dominates the stage, while in Act III he fights a brief duel to aid the loving couple as they prepare for their wedding. The ballet itself, for the most part, exists outside the story, with Act I virtually a continuing divertissement. It is full of lively dances to conventional choreography, and the two principals here, **Aurélie Dupont** as Kitri and **Manuel Legris** as Basile, have plenty of spectacular solos and *pas de deux*, supported by the Paris Opéra Corps de Ballet. Don Quixote, rather well portrayed by Jean-Marie Didière, is essentially a non-dancing role and remains his rather melancholy self. The score is agreeably melodic if not distinctive. Well crafted and colourfully orchestrated, it has a few set-pieces, including a group of Spanish Dances, but is without the genius of Tchaikovsky or Delibes. Those wanting just the music alone can get an acceptable Naxos CD set of the full original (1869) score, played by the **Sofia National Opera Orchestra** (8.557065/6).

MOERAN, Ernest J. (1894–1950)

(i) Cello Concerto; (ii; iii) Violin Concerto; (iii) 2 Pieces for Small Orchestra: Lonely Waters; Whythorne's Shadow

🎵 Ⓜ ******** Chan. 10168X. (i) Wallfisch, Bournemouth Sinf., Del Mar; (ii) Mordkovitch; (iii) Ulster O, Handley

The *Cello Concerto* (1945) is a pastoral work with elegiac overtones, save in its rather folksy finale. **Raphael Wallfisch** brings an eloquence of tone and a masterly technical address to this neglected piece, and he receives very responsive orchestral support from **Norman Del Mar** and the Bournemouth players. The *Violin Concerto* is also strongly lyrical in feeling. The first movement is thoughtful and rhapsodic, its inspiration drawn from Moeran's love of the west coast of Ireland; the middle movement makes use of folk music; while the finale, a ruminative elegy of great beauty, is the most haunting of the three. **Lydia Mordkovitch** plays with great natural feeling for this music and, quite apart from his sensitive support in the *Concerto*, **Vernon Handley** gives an outstanding account of *Lonely Waters*. Superb recording.

(i) Cello Concerto; (ii) Cello Sonata in A min.; Prelude for Cello & Piano

Ⓝ ****** Lyrita (ADD) SRCD 299. Coetmore, with (i) LPO, Boult; (ii) Parkin

Peers Coetmore, widow of E. J. Moeran, is the dedicatee of the *Cello Concerto*, a fine lyrical work written as a wedding present in 1945, the year of their marriage. One cannot miss the intensity of feeling in her playing. This is a deeply felt offering to a once long-neglected composer, but the solo playing falls short of the virtuoso standard one demands on record. One has to listen with a sympathetic ear. In the *Cello Sonata*, the soloist brings a dedicated intensity to the work, also written for her (in 1948), not long before he died. It is a thoughtful, introspective piece, well worth getting to know. The *Prelude for Cello and Piano* makes a nice bonus, though the soloist's intonation is not totally secure. First-class late-1960s sound.

Violin Concerto

Ⓜ (***) Divine Art mono 27806. Campoli, BBC SO, Boult – DOUGLAS COATES: *Violin Concerto* (**)

In his accompanying note, Andrew Rose makes strong claims for **Alfredo Campoli's** reading of the Moeran *Concerto* – and rightly so! There is an inwardness, a rhapsodic freedom and intensity about his playing which makes this a moving experience, and **Sir Adrian Boult** and the **BBC Symphony Orchestra** also play with great sensitivity. The recording comes from 1954 and calls for tolerance, but it is very acceptable, and the performance is really quite special. What a wonderful player Campoli was when he was at his best. He was never better than at this exalted level.

(i) Violin Concerto; (ii) Rhapsody for Piano & Orchestra; (iii) Rhapsody 2

*** Lyrita (ADD) SRCD 248. (i) Georgiadis, LSO, Handley; (ii) McCabe, New Philh. O, Braithwaite; (iii) LPO, Boult

Moeran's delectable *Violin Concerto*, dating from 1942, reflects the composer's devotion to Delius more than most; two lyrical movements frame a central Scherzo with something of an Irish flavour. It receives a superb performance from **John Georgiadis**, strongly backed by the **LSO** under **Vernon Handley**. The *Rhapsody for Piano and Orchestra* is fresh and spontaneous, as one would expect from this composer. His art offers directness of utterance and a disarming sincerity, and he is well served by **John McCabe** and the **New Philharmonia** under **Nicholas Braithwaite**. The colourful *Second Rhapsody* (for orchestra only) is an early work, dating from 1924. **Boult** proves, as always, an intensely sympathetic conductor, and the recording quality matches Lyrita's excellent standards throughout.

In the Mountain Country; Rhapsodies 1–2; Serenade in G; (i) Nocturne

Ⓜ ******* Chan. 10235X. Ulster O, Handley, (i) with Mackey, Renaissance Singers – WARLOCK: *Capriol Suite*, etc. *******

The *Serenade in G* has a good deal in common with Warlock's *Capriol Suite*. Both use dance forms from a previous age and transform them with new colours and harmonic touches. **Handley** and the **Ulster Orchestra** present it with striking freshness and warmth in its original version. *In the Mountain Country* and the pair of *Rhapsodies* (the *First* Holstian in its quirky rhythms and colourful brass, the *Second* Irish in inflexion with a memorable main tune) are unashamedly folk-inspired and have great vitality and lyrical appeal. The *Nocturne*, a setting of a poem by Robert Nichols for baritone and eight-part chorus, much admired by Britten, receives a wholly sympathetic performance and recording here, and the resonant acoustics of the Ulster Hall, Belfast, provide a warmly atmospheric ambient glow.

Symphony in G min.; Overture for a Masque; (i) Rhapsody for Piano & Orchestra

Ⓜ ******* Chan. 10169X. (i) Fingerhut; Ulster O, Handley

Symphony in G min.; Sinfonietta

ⒷⒷ ******* Naxos 8.555837. Bournemouth SO, Lloyd-Jones

(i) Symphony in G min.; (ii) Sinfonietta; (i) Overture for a Masque

🎵 ❋ ******** Lyrita (ADD) SRCD 247. (i) New Philh. O; LPO; Boult

Built confidently on strikingly memorable ideas, and first heard in 1937, Moeran's *G minor Symphony* is in the best English tradition of symphonic writing and is worthy to rank with the symphonies of Vaughan Williams and Walton. But for all the echoes of these composers, and of Sibelius too, it has a strongly individual voice. **Boult's** radiant mid-1970s performance is spacious, the recording not as opulent as Handley's Chandos version (very much cast in the Boult mould) but still very impressive. Characteristically, he refuses to push too hard too soon, but the ebb and flow of tension are superbly controlled to build the most powerful possible climaxes. Rarely, even in Vaughan Williams, has Boult adopted so overtly expressive a style, especially in the glorious slow movement, and the 1975 recording quality, although refined, allows the widest dynamic range down to the gentlest *pianissimo* for the hushed, intense opening of the slow movement. The *Sinfonietta* is a fresh and attractive work, written a decade later. More extrovert than the symphony, it shows its composer as less ready to write in long paragraphs. It is nevertheless an attractive work and, alongside the *Overture*, given Boult's persuasive advocacy it makes an apt coupling.

Chandos have reissued at mid-price **Vernon Handley's** compelling performance with the exuberant, syncopated *Overture* thrown in for good measure. An outstanding disc in every way, with superb recording sounding better than ever.

The Naxos version, warmly and idiomatically conducted by **David Lloyd-Jones**, could hardly be more persuasive, well played by the **Bournemouth Orchestra** and treated to a full-range recording, with transparent textures bringing out the fine detail of the orchestration. The jolly, vigorous *Sinfonietta*, equally well played, makes an apt coupling. In the *Symphony*, Handley might be marginally more bitingly powerful, but this new version has a considerable price advantage and is certainly not second best.

(i) Symphony in G min.; (ii) String Trio; (iii) Can't you Dance the Polka; Sheep sheering; Sweet fa's the eve

(***) Divine Art mono 27808. (i) Hallé O, Heward; (ii) Pougnet, Riddle, Pini; (iii) Goss, H. Nash, Cathedral Male Voice Ch., Moore

Dutton originally transferred **Leslie Heward's** pioneering recording of the Moeran *Symphony* to CD, coupling it with the John Ireland *Piano Concerto*, but this issue is no less valuable, for much trouble has been taken over it, and it brings the 1941 records of the *String Trio* and **Heddle Nash** singing *Diaphenia* and *The Sweet of the Year* in 1945. As one returns to Moeran's music, the fresher it seems, and the performances are wonderfully invigorating.

Fantasy Quartet for Oboe & Strings

*** Chan. 8392. Francis, English Qt – BAX: *Quintet*; HOLST: *Air & Variations*, etc.; JACOB: *Quartet* ***

Moeran's folk-influenced *Fantasy Quartet*, an attractively rhapsodic single-movement work, is played admirably here, and the recording is excellent, well balanced too.

(i) Fantasy Quartet for Oboe & Strings; (ii) String Quartet 2 in A min.; (iii) Violin Sonata

(M) *** Chan. 10170X. (i) Francis, English String Qt (members); (ii) Melbourne Qt; (iii) Scotts, Talbot

Sarah Francis's admirable account with the **English String Quartet** of Moeran's *Fantasy Quartet* is here re-coupled with the *String Quartet in A minor* of 1921, together with the more intense and forward-looking *Violin Sonata* (written a year later). The performance from **Donald Scotts** and **John Talbot** is full of rough-hewn energy, with plenty of contrast in the central *Lento*. While the Maggini–Naxos coupling with the earlier *E flat Quartet* is more logical, the Chandos disc is very attractive in its own right.

String Quartets 1 in E flat; 2 in A min.; String Trio

◉– (BB) *** Naxos 8.554079. Maggini Qt

The *String Quartet in A minor* (1921) has a certain pastoral quality, with Irish echoes in the dance rhythms and ending on a flamboyant Rondo. The *String Trio* of 1931, beautifully written with no feeling of thinness, is even subtler, with the pastoral idiom more equivocal in its tonal shiftings. The Naxos CD also offers something of a discovery in the form of an earlier *Quartet in E flat*. Although it is not a masterpiece, there are some quite inspired things in it and the **Maggini** play throughout with great dedication and commitment. The recording is very lifelike and present. A first-class bargain.

COMPLETE PIANO MUSIC

Bank Holiday; 3 Fancies (Windmills; Elegy; Burlesque); 2 Legends (Folk Story; Rune); On a May Morning; 3 Pieces (The Lake Island; Autumn Woods; At a Horse Fair); 2 Pieces (Prelude; Berceuse); Stalham River; Summer Valley; Theme and Variations; Toccata. Trad. arr. Moeran: Irish Love Song; The White Mountain

*** ASV CDDCA 1138. Hunt

Moeran was born in Middlesex but was buried in County Kerry in his beloved Ireland. Much of this music is unashamedly folksy. *Bank Holiday*, which opens the programme genially, 'tips its hat' to Percy Grainger, but most of the pieces are evocative and atmospheric, even the arrangement of the Irish tune, best known as 'Star of the County Down', which he called *The White Mountain*. The other arrangement, *Irish Love Song*, is simpler, a lovely melody which was later to become an *Irish Lament* for cello and piano. *On a May Morning* opens dreamily but has a lively central dance; on the other hand, the iridescent *Toccata* has a soft centre. *Summer Valley*, in lilting 6/8, has a Delian air. The most ambitious piece here is the *Theme and* (six) *Variations*. The theme is reminiscent of another folk tune, the variations flow into each other naturally and the work is in some ways more like a Fantasia. Fine, sensitive performances throughout from **Una Hunt**, well recorded. Generous measure too (77 minutes): a delightful disc to dip into rather than play all through.

Piano pieces: Bank Holiday; 2 Legends; Prelude and Berceuse; Stalham River; Toccata; The White Mountain

*** Lyrita (ADD) SRCD 266. Parkin – BAINES: *Piano music* ***

These piano pieces, which date from the 1920s, are highly agreeable, fresh and enjoyable in their English adaptation of Debussian trends. *The White Mountain* is a charmingly simple setting of a very familiar Irish folk tune. Excellent recording.

MOMPOU, Federico (1893–1987)

Complete Piano Music

*Canciónes y danzas 1–12, 14; Cants mágics;
Chanson de berceuse; Charmes; Dialogues; Fêtes
lointaines; Impresiones intimas; Musica callada,
Books 1–4; Pessebres; Préludes; Scènes d'enfants;
Souvenirs de l'Exposition; Surburbis; 3 Variations;
Variations sur un thème de Chopin*

Ⓑ **(*) Nim. NI 5724/7 (4). M.Jones

Martin Jones has already given us some fine recordings, including a first-rate set of the piano music of Percy Grainger. Now he turns to another miniaturist. Born in Barcelona, Mompou studied in Paris and his music is a fascinating mixture of Catalan and French influences, though in its colouring and textures the French influence is strong. There are plenty of fine individual CDs of this composer's music, but for collectors who want to explore the entire repertoire, Jones is a sound guide, at home in its diverse moods and colours. One feels at times he could be more chimerical and seek more translucent textures, but his simplicity of approach is a plus point and, with truthful recording, this can certainly be recommended to musical explorers.

*Canciónes y danzas 1–12; 14; Cants mágics;
Suburbis*

ⒷⒷ *** Warner Apex 8573 89228-2. Heisser

Jean-François Heisser displays a natural sympathy for Mompou's elusive world, and besides the *Canciónes y danzas* and *Cants mágics* he offers also the rarer early work, *Suburbis* (1916/17), which evokes the suburbs of Barcelona. The second and third of the five pieces are concerned with the gypsies, followed by a touching portrait of a little blind girl (*La ceguetta*), while the last is a lively picture of a street organ player. At its modest cost and very well recorded, this is well worth having.

*Canciónes y danzas 1–12, 14; Charmes; Scènes
d'enfants*

ⒷⒷ *** Naxos 8.554332. Masó

In many ways **Jordi Masó's** excellent Naxos collection is not upstaged by the competition. Moreover this is to be the first of a continuing series. He gives us the complete *Canciónes y danzas* (except for 13, which is for guitar), plus the engagingly diverse, but at times almost mystical *Charmes*, and his playing is imbued with gentle poetic feeling. Masó's pianistic sensibility is never self-aware, always at the service of the composer, and the music's soft-hued colours are perceptively graduated. The unostentatious innocence of the *Scènes d'enfants* is beautifully caught. Excellent recording makes this a disc to recommend even if it cost far more than it does.

*Canciónes y danzas 1, 3, 5, 7, 8–9; Cants mágics;
Charmes; Dialogues I–II; Paisajes; Preludios 1, 5
(Palmier d'étoiles), 6 (for the left hand), 7, 9–10; 3
Variations*

☕ ❀ **** Hyp. CDA 66963. Hough

This exceptionally generous (77 minutes) and wide-ranging *Gramophone* Award-winning recital makes an obvious first choice for those wanting to explore, on a single CD, the fullest possible range of Mompou's piano music. **Stephen Hough**, who provides the illuminating notes, imaginatively describes this as 'the music of evaporation ... There is no development of material, little counterpoint, no drama or climaxes to speak of; and this simplicity of expression – elusive, evasive and shy – is strangely disarming.' He is completely inside Mompou's fastidious, Satie-esque sound-world and understands the absorbed influences which make this music as much French as Spanish. The recording too is excellent if a little reverberant. Not even Mompou himself equalled, let alone surpassed, Hough in this repertoire.

Musica callada, Books I–IV; 3 Variations

Ⓜ *** HM HMI 987070. Perianes

*Musica callada, Books I–IV; El pont; Muntanya
(Dansa)*

ⒷⒷ **(*) Naxos 8.554727. Masó

Jordi Masó's survey of Mompou's piano music continues with the *Musica callada* – 28 pieces which appeared in four volumes between 1959 and 1967. The title comes from the *Cántico espiritual* and means 'music without sound' although this is complemented with the additional description *Soledad sonora* ('insistent solitude'). The very first piece, *Angelico*, creates the work's atmosphere and other pieces are called *Placid, Tranquillo – trè calme, Luminoso* and so on. The problem for the performer is that almost all this music is slow and reflective (the Lento marking reappears frequently), and it has to be said that this is not entirely solved here. Jordi Masó is by no means insensitive, but although he is well recorded, the colouring remains monochrome. The two impressionistic pieces which close the recital are *El pont* ('The Bridge') and *Muntanya* ('Mountain'). They have not been recorded before and make successful encores.

The Spanish pianist **Javier Perianes** is obviously completely at home in this extraordinarily static repertoire and – provided one does not listen to more than a few of the pieces at a time – he holds the listener's attention and is very well recorded. Moreover, he finds more colour in the music than his Naxos competitor.

MONDONVILLE, Jean-Joseph Cassanéa de (1711–72)

VOCAL MUSIC

*Grands motets: De profundis; Venite exultemus;
Petits motets: Benefac Domine; In decachordo
psalterio; Regna terrae*

☕– ⒷⒷ *** Hyp. Helios CDH 55038. Fisher, Daniels, Varcoe, New College, Oxford, Ch., L. Bar. Ens., Higginbottom

Mondonville's *Grands Motets* were modelled on those of

Delalande, but are even finer and more individual. This outstanding CD includes his *De profundis*, a remarkably diverse setting of verses 1–8 of Psalm 129. The performance is of very high quality. The opening *De profundis clamavi* is wonderfully ethereal, with boy trebles set back in the atmospheric Oxford acoustic. Their refined approach is matched by the ravishingly pure soprano line of **Gillian Fisher**, while the closing *Requiem aeternam* floats celestially.

Higginbottom's Helios collection then offers another rather less grand motet, but one which alongside *De profundis* was greatly popular and frequently performed in its day. It is more lyrical, less dramatic and textually simpler – a radiant expression of praise.

The three solo *Petits motets* with their modest harpsichord and continuo accompaniments are altogether more intimate but no less valuable, each showing **Gillian Fisher** in glorious voice (indeed this CD is worth having for her contribution alone), while Edward Higginbottom exchanges his baton for the harpsichord keyboard. Altogether this is a delightful bargain collection, given state-of-the-art sound.

MONIUSZKO, Stanislaw
(1819–72)

The Haunted Manor (opera; complete)

Ⓜ *** EMI 5 57489-2 (2). Kruszewski, Hossa, Lubańska, Stachura, Nowacki, Toczyska, Polish Nat. Op. Ch. & O, Kaspszyk

Moniuszko, the leading Polish romantic after Chopin, is generally remembered, if at all, by his opera *Halka*, a tragic story set against a peasant background. Yet in almost every way *The Haunted Manor*, one of the hidden treasures of Polish opera, is more original, more inventive and, above all, more attractive with its tuneful sequence of ensembles.

Two shuddering chords at the very start reflect the title, but then the first scene sets quite a different tone of voice in a rousing military ensemble, when two brothers, Stefan and Zbigniev, on leaving their comrades, swear they will never marry, so as always to be ready to fight for their country. The manner is as close to Gilbert and Sullivan as to Smetana, with a dash of Donizetti thrown in. The main haunting scene anticipates the G. & S. 'Ghosts' High Noon Scene' in *Ruddigore*, with portraits coming to life. The brothers wake up to the fact that they are both in love, Stefan with Hanna, Zbigniev with Jadwiga.

Though ensembles predominate, each of the main characters is given a big showpiece aria. The one for Hanna is particularly impressive, with its Donizettian coloratura brilliantly sung by the bright-toned **Iwona Hossa**. **Anna Lubańska** with her firm, warm mezzo is also impressive as Jadwiga; but the casting of the two brothers is not so strong, with the lusty tenor **Dariusz Stachura** strained as Stefan, not attacking notes cleanly, and **Piotr Nowacki** as Zbigniev happier in fast music than sustained melody. Best of all is **Adam Kruszewski** in the central role of Miecznik, the Sword-Bearer, a fine baritone with a timbre not unlike Sir Thomas Allen's. Add on a few *buffo* characters and a formidable aunt figure, strongly taken by **Stefania Toczyska**, and you have a

splendidly successful entertainment, with superb playing and singing from the **Polish National Opera Chorus and Orchestra**, dynamically conducted from first to last by **Jacek Kaspszyk**.

MONTEVERDI, Claudio
(1567–1643)

'The Full Monteverdi' (A film by John La Bouchardière), including Madrigals: Book IV

Ⓝ Ⓑ **** Naxos DVD 2.110224. I Fagiolini, Hollingworth
(Director of photography: Nick Gordon Smith)

Do you want to listen to Monteverdi's *Fourth Book of Madrigals* – superbly sung as it is by I Fagiolini – against a film backcloth centring on six vulnerable couples in a restaurant (and elsewhere) whose relationships are falling apart? Each couple features a singer and a (non-singing) actor, with the singer miming to the music. Amazingly (or perhaps not amazingly) the singers are often as dramatically convincing as their theatrical partners, and the result can be very touching, particularly as the cameras are beautifully handled. Subtitles are available.

Canzonette (1584)

🎵 ⒷⒷ *** Naxos 8.553316. Concerto delle Dame di Ferrara, Vartolo

Monteverdi's very first publication in 1582 was the *Sacrae cantiunculae tribus vocibus*, and a collection of *Madrigali spirituali* in four parts followed in 1585. The following year brought the present set of *Canzonette*, delightful works for three voices. Their title-page makes the point that Monteverdi was just 17, and they are dedicated to the composer's 'master and patron', Pietro Ambrosisi of Cremona, and the music itself is fresh and engaging, as indeed are all these comparatively simple settings of poems about love (mostly unrequited) and consequent desperate longing. But Monteverdi has a twinkle in his eye in giving *Godi pur dei bei sen* an appropriate jumping rhythm, for the poem begins: 'Delight, happy flea, in the fair bosom where you leap and ever sweetly bite.'

This is very lightweight repertoire, to be sure, but the performances by the singers and string ensemble of **Concerto delle Dame di Ferrara**, directed by **Sergio Vartolo**, are most felicitous. A most enjoyable introduction to the early music of a composer who was later to write much greater music, but none with more charm. Excellent recording and full documentation, with texts and translations provided.

Madrigals, Books 1 (1587); 2 (1590); 3 (1592); 6 (1614) (all complete); 7, excerpts: Tempo la cetra; Tirsi e Clori. 8: Madrigali guerrieri; Madrigali amorosi; Opera-ballets: Il ballo delle ingrate; Il combattimento di Tancredi e Clorinda; Volgendo il ciel (1638) (complete)

ⒷⒷ **(*) Virgin 5 62268-2 (7). Kirkby, Tubb, Nichols, Agnew, King, Ewing and soloists, Cons. of Musicke, Rooley

Anthony Rooley recorded almost all the Monteverdi

Madrigals between 1990 and 1996. Two-thirds of the texts in Book 1 are concerned with love's disappointments, the words full of torments, which gives Monteverdi plenty of opportunity for expressive dolour. This first disc also includes two excerpts from Book 7, including the charming pastoral ballet, *Tirsi e Clori*, written for the Mantuan court and extolling the joys of requited love and faithfulness. Book 2 is also more simple in its appeal and imagery than the later writing but, like Book 1, it all comes to life freshly, including the very effective Tasso settings.

With Books 3 and 4 we move to some of Monteverdi's finest madrigals, often dazzling, in which his originality began to make itself felt to the full. Moreover these are masterly performances, the flexibility and control of dramatic contrasts conveying consistent commitment. Book 6 includes the five-part transcription of the *Lamento d'Arianna* and *Zefiro torno*, two of the composer's masterpieces, and also works from Monteverdi's years at Mantua.

Monteverdi published his ambitious Volume 8 after a long gap in his madrigal output. It includes one of the very greatest examples in *Lamento della ninfa*, in what the composer described as the *stile rappresentativo* or theatre style, plus the well-known opera-ballets. The performances here continue to be polished and distinctive, and the cast-list is strong.

For the most part, however, this reissued collection represents a considerable achievement for **Rooley** and his singers and instrumentalists, with first-class recording throughout. The set is most inexpensive, but the documentation is sparse, with no texts and translations.

Madrigals, Book 2 (complete)

⊶ **** Opus 111 OP 30-111. Concerto Italiano, Alessandrini
*** Glossa GCD 920922. La Venexiana, Cavina

Rinaldo Alessandrini and his superb **Concerto Italiano** are singing their sunny Italianate way through Monteverdi's complete madrigal sequence. Apart from being of Italian birth, all the performers here have studied early Italian and therefore bring a special idiomatic feeling to the words. The Second Book, about half of whose five-part settings are from Tasso, demands and receives a simpler style of presentation than the later works, and there is radiant freshness about the singing here which is particularly appealing. The recording has the most pleasing acoustic.

The alternative performances from **La Venexiana** directed by **Claudio Cavina** have similar Italian flair and hardly less eloquence. They are particularly strong in bringing out the rich lyricism of the Second Book with its poetic evocations of nature, yet the love songs have a fine delicacy of passionate feeling (*Dolcemente, dormiva la mia Clori* is delightful), while the depth of distress expressed in *Crudel, perché mi fuggi?* is truly poignant. The generously expansive acoustic provides an admirable setting for a group in which individual voices can soar and blend with equal felicity. Excellent documentation and pleasing packaging.

Madrigals, Book 3 (complete)

*** Glossa GCD 920910. La Venexiana, Cavina

At the heart of Book III is the so-called 'nuovo stile' which anticipates operatic recitativo and aria. The two dramatically expressive highlights of the Book are *Vattene pur cudel*, the lament of Armida, abandoned by Rinaldo, while the declamatory *Vivrò fra i mieie tormenti* (also a setting of Tasso) is the continuation of the celebrated *Combattimento di Tancredi e Clorinda*, which Monteverdi was to set in full in Book VIII. These are sung quite dramatically by **La Venexiana** and with deep feeling, but their style is less histrionic than one would expect from the Concerto Italiano.

Madrigals, Book 4 (complete)

⊶ *** Naïve OP 30-81. Concerto Italiano, Alessandrini

Madrigals, Books 4–5 (complete). *Book 7: Con che soavità, labbra odorate; Tempro la cetra. Book 8: (Madrigali guerrieri et amorosi): Mentre vaga; Ogni amante è guerrier*

Ⓑ *** O-L Double 455 718-2 (2). Consort of Musicke, Rooley

Madrigals, Book 5 (complete)

⊶ ✿ **** Naïve OPS 30-166. Concerto Italiano, Alessandrini

The Fourth Book, published in 1603 and again for five voices, marks an added richness of expressive feeling over Monteverdi's earlier settings, well recognized by **Rinaldo Alessandrini** and his superbly blended vocal group. This series goes from strength to strength and can be strongly recommended. The recording continues to match the singing in excellence.

Under **Anthony Rooley**, the well-integrated singers of the **Consort of Musicke**, led by **Emma Kirkby**, give masterly performances of the Fourth Book, which suits their vocal style especially well. Book 5 marked a turning point in Monteverdi's madrigal output, for the last six works bring an obligatory continuo and are much freer in style than their predecessors, even semi-operatic in their use of freely individual vocal solos. It might be said that the change of style in the singing from the Consort of Musicke is less marked than in the competing (full-priced) collection of these works by the **Concerto Italiano** directed by **Rinaldo Alessandrini**, whose singing is distinctly Italianate and more extrovert. Nevertheless the comparatively restrained approach of Rooley's group brings its own rewards, and their refinement is reflected in the delicate lute continuo in the later numbers.

Madrigals, Book 6 (1614)

⊶ **** Naïve OP 30423. Concerto Italiano, Alessandrini

In Book VI **Rinaldo Alessandrini** and the **Concerto Italiano** come completely into their own with their passionate account of the opening four-part scena, the famous *Lamento d'Arianna*, especially in their arrestingly plangent singing of Part 3: 'Where is the fidelity that so often you swore to me . . . Are these the crowns you place upon my brow?' The second number is the equally famous *Zefiro torna*, which with its dancing rhythms provides a lighter expressive contrast, but then produces an astonishingly dissonant ending, very powerfully sung. *A Dio torna* is a touching operatic dialogue between a pair of lovers with the larger concerto group giving the central narration and an encouraging comment, before the final parting. *Batto, qui pianse Ergaste* brings even more contrasts of mood and tempo, with the heroine, Clori (represented by a pair of sopranos in duet), chasing a fleeing doe, her devoted swain following. This is an outstanding disc in every way which it will be difficult to match, let alone surpass.

Madrigals, Book 7 (1619) (complete)

*** Glossa GCD 920927 (2). La Venexiana, Instrumental Ens., Cavina

To describe the new style of his madrigals in Book 7 of 1619, Monteverdi used the term *'stile concitato'* or concerto, and departed from his previous standard five-part format to embrace a wide variety of voicing: works for a solo voice are found alongside settings for two, three, four and six voices, with the duets often for two of the same genre: soprano, contralto or tenor. To introduce the listener to his use of instrumental accompaniments, he opens with a brief sinfonia, and to point to the future, he closes with a charming extended pastoral dance cantata, *Tirsi e Clori*, which is delightfully sung here. Indeed the enlarged **La Venexiana** and their accompanying instrumental group obviously relish the expanded style and the wide variety of mood, impassioned, joyful, dolorous and sensuous by turns; and again their standard of performance is consistently high, as is the quality of the warmly atmospheric recording. Full texts and translations are included.

Madrigals, Book 8: *Madrigali guerrieri et amorosi: Volume I: Sinfonia: Altri canti d'amor; Lamento della ninfa; Vago augelletto; Perchè t'en fuggi, o Fillide?; Altri canti a Marte; Due belli occhi fur l'ami; Ogni amante è guerrier; Hor che'l ciel e la terra; Gira il nemico, insidioso Amore; Dolcissimo usignolo; Ardo, ardo avvampo*

🔊 🌑 **** Naïve OP 30435 (3). Concerto Italiano, Alessandrini

*** HM HMC 90 1736/7. Kiehr, Haller, Martins, Fink, Laporte, Bowen, Ovenden, Zeffiri, Rensberg, Torres, Abete, Delaigue, Concerto Vocale, Jacobs

Ⓑ **(*) Virgin 2x1 5 61570-2 (2). Soloists, Consort of Musicke, Rooley

Rinaldo Alessandrini and his **Concerto Italiano** continued their superlative series of recordings of Monteverdi's madrigals with Book 8, *Madrigals of War and Love*. As before, the singing combines Italianate fire and lyricism in ideal proportions and the instrumental accompaniments could hardly be finer. The disc includes famous items like the three-part *Lamento della ninfa* and the two-part *Hor che'l ciel el la terra*. The recording too is first class. The second disc also includes the three-part *Lamento della ninfa* and the two-part *Hor che'l ciel e la terra*. Finally, the third disc includes some of Monteverdi's most adventurous and dramatically varied settings, ending with the spectacular *Mentre vaga Angioletta* and the equally complex *Ninfa che scalza il piede*

('Nymph who, barefoot, loose-locked and carefree') with its many changes of mood and metre. The recording is first class and this now makes a clear first choice.

René Jacobs and his **Concerto Vocale**, with a host of outstanding singers led by **Maria Cristina Kiehr**, now make a major contribution in this increasingly competitive field, and they come out with flying colours. That is not to say that they surpass Alessandrini and his Italian group, but they are very impressive in their own right, even in the demanding *Lamento della ninfa* and *Hor che'l ciel et la terra*. Jacobs and his singers are at their most dramatic in the famous opéra-ballets, *Il ballo delle ingrate* and *Il combattimento*. But here **Alessandrini** and his **Concerto Italiano** are even finer, a clear primary choice. However, overall this Harmonia Mundi set is very rewarding.

The *Madrigali guerrieri* are very theatrical and include *Il ballo delle ingrate* and *Il combattimento di Tancredi e Clorinda*, which are also available separately in other individual versions (see below). The performances on Virgin are impressive, and anyone collecting **Rooley's** series should find this inexpensive Double well worth its modest cost. The cast list is strong, including **Emma Kirkby** and **Evelyn Tubb**, but **Andrew King** is the narrator in *Il combattimento* and his approach is less than robustly full-blooded, while in both works the performances under Christie (see below) are more dramatically arresting.

Madrigals, Book 8 (excerpts): *Madrigali guerrieri et amorosi: Altri canti d'amor; Altri cante di marte; Il Gira il nemico; Hor che'l ciel e la terra; Lamento della ninfa; 2 Sinfonias; Volgendo il ciel movete al mio bel suon* (Ballo)

Ⓜ *** Astrée ES 9944. Figueras, Tiso, Banditelli, Climent, Carnovich, Garrigosa, Costa, La Capella Reial de Catalunya, Savall

Savall's way with Monteverdi's Book 8 is, above all tremendously vital: his singers emphasize the strong rhythmic contrasts of the *Madrigali guerrieri*. There are some very fine voices in his team, none lacking individuality of character, yet blending splendidly, as at the opening of *Hor che'l ciel e la terra*. **Montserrat Figueras**, **Lambert Climent** (tenor) and **Daniele Carnovich** (bass) stand out, and Figueras is at her glorious best in the famous *Lamento della ninfa*. This is an excellent anthology in all respects and full translations are included.

Madrigals, Book 8: Opera-Ballet

Altri canti d'Amor; Il ballo delle ingrate; Il combattimento di Tancredi e Clorinda; Volgendo il ciel (Ballo movt)

Ⓑ *** Hyp. Helios CDH 55165. Red Byrd, Parley of Instruments, Holman

(i) *Il ballo delle ingrate*; (ii) *Il combattimento di Tancredi e Clorinda*

🔊 **** Naïve OP 30-196. (i) Ermolli, Dominguez, Carnovich, Franzetti; (ii) Franzetti, Ferrarini, Abbondanza; Concerto Italiano, Alessandrini

Il ballo delle ingrate; Il combattimento di Tancredi e Clorinda; Tirsi e Clori; Tempo la cetra

(BB) **** Warner Apex 2564 6181-2. Tragicomedia, Stubbs

Il combattimento di Tancredi e Clorinda

(B) *** HM HMA 195 1626. Semeliaz, Brand, Rovenq, Les Arts Florissants, Christie

Il combattimento di Tancredi e Clorinda; Arias and Duets

🎧 **** Virgin 3 63350-2. Villazón, Ciofi, Lehtipuu, Le Concert d'Astrée, Haim

There is no more commandingly dramatic account of *Il combattimento* on record than this Italianate version from **Rinaldo Alessandrini**, with superb singing from all three principals. **Roberto Abbondanza** is a splendidly histrionic narrator, and in the death scene **Elisa Franzetti**, singing her farewell, is exquisitely moving. Franzetti returns at the end of *Il ballo delle ingrate* to bid an eloquent adieu on behalf of the ungrateful souls, condemned for rebelling against earthly love, to be echoed by Monteverdi's infinitely poignant closing chorus from her companions. The performance overall is cast from strength. **Daniele Carnovich** is a true basso profundo and makes a superb Pluto, but **Francesca Ermolli** and **Rosa Dominguez** are equally fine as Amor and Venus, respectively. The vivid recording is warmly atmospheric.

Red Byrd is an impressive vocal group and in *Il combattimento* **John Potter** narrates more colloquially than his competitors, yet builds up plenty of excitement in the heat of the battle, while **Catherine Pierard** as Clorinda sings her closing threnody very touchingly. *Il ballo* is also characterized most effectively. **Richard Wistrech** makes a striking Pluto, his low notes resonating tellingly, and at the close, after the beautiful lament from Pierard's Ungrateful Spirit, the charming little closing chorus is made to fade into the distance as the Lost Souls (who were 'so esteemed in the world' for their chaste purity) return to their dark abode in Pluto's kingdom. The major works are interspersed with two short but unexpectedly appealing works, written in praise of the Austrian Emperor Ferdinand III, 'Let others sing of Love . . . You whose immortal crown is woven from the laurels of Caesar' and a light-hearted ballet with a Poet as soloist and chorus: 'Turning in the sky along its immortal path the wheels of glorious and serene light, the sun brings back the age of peace under the new King of the Roman Empire.' Excellent recording, and full texts and translations.

Besides *Il ballo* and *Il combattimento*, **Stephen Stubbs** and **Tragicomedia** offer another opera-ballet written for the Mantuan court, *Tirsi e Clori*, a dialogue between two lovers celebrating both the spirit of love and the dance, while the solo madrigal, *Tempro la cetra*, eloquently sung by **John Potter**, acts as a dramatic prelude, 'I tune the lyre', though it lines up with *Il combattimento* rather than *Il ballo*. These two major works are strongly cast: the female dialogues are delightfully sung, and **Harry van der Kempe** is a dramatically commanding Pluto, with splendid lower tessitura. *Il combattimento* could not be more moving, with **Douglas Nasrawi's** narration rising to fever-pitch at the climax of the battle itself, then eloquently expressing the tragedy of the result. Excellent recording and full texts and translations make this irresistible at super-budget price.

Rolando Villazón is a superbly histrionic narrator in *Il combattimento*, and there is thrilling vocal virtuosity at the climax of the battle, with Clorinda's poignant dying words sung very gently. This is as fine as any version on record, but it is surprising that *Il ballo delle ingrate* is not offered as a coupling. Instead, we have a spectacularly sung collection of arias and duets in which all three singers, Villazón, **Patrizia Ciofi** and **Topi Lehtipuu**, have ample opportunities to show their vocal prowess in some marvellously varied music. Standing out is Villazón's movingly expressive *Sì dolci è 'l tormento* with its melancholy downward scale, and Patrizia Ciofi's contrasting *Ohimè ch'io cado Ohimè*.

Christie's account of *Il combattimento* is also very dramatic, with the storytelling vividly projected and with **Françoise Semeliaz** a touching Clorinda in the tragic closing scene. The recording is admirably vivid too. The libretto is in Italian and French only, but the narrative is easy enough to follow.

Other Madrigal collections

Madrigals from Books 4, 5, 7 & 8; Orfeo: Prologue & Sinfonia

🎧 **** Chan. 0730. I Fagiolini, Hollingworth

Madrigals from Books 3, 4, 5, 6, 7 & 8; Ballo: Tirsi e Clori; Ballo delle ingrate: Sinfonia

🎧 **** Chan. 0749. I Faglioni, Hollingworth

In this new Chandos series, **Robert Hollingworth** and his vocal and instrumental group, **I Fagiolini**, have sought an individual approach to presenting Monteverdi's wealth of secular madrigals. Hollingworth argues that recordings of complete volumes of Monteverdi's madrigals is not the ideal way for the listener to approach them. He suggests instead creating individual programmes 'juxtaposing masterworks for different dispositions and, in so doing, aiming to keep the aural palette refreshed'. In addition care has been taken over the choice of continuo for individual items. For instance, one of the highlights of the first disc is *Con che sovità*, written for solo voice and three instrumental groups. There is not space to dwell on the beauty of individual madrigals. All of those here are gloriously sung and played. The second collection is, if anything, finer than the first, ranging from the sensuously explicit *Sì ch'io vorrei morire*, where the lover wishes to die in his moment of ecstasy, the adoring *Chiome d'oro* ('Golden tresses'), the ardent *Ogni amante è guerrier* ('Every lover is a warrior') to the extended lament at the beloved's tomb, *Lagrime d'amante al sepolcro dell'amata*. The collection ends with the familiar ballo, *Thirsis and Cloris*, where the pair unendingly dance together in increasing joy in the world around them.

Madrigals: *Ab aeterno ordinata sum; Confitebor tibi, Domine* (3 settings); *Deus tuorum militum sors et corona; Iste confessor Domini sacratus; Laudate*

Dominum, O omnes gentes; La Maddalena: Prologue: Su le penne de venti; Nisi Dominus aedificaverit domum

☛⚙ ******** Hyp. CDA 66021. Kirkby, Partridge, Thomas, Parley of Instruments

There are few recordings of Monteverdi's solo vocal music as persuasive as this. The three totally contrasted settings of *Confitebor tibi* (Psalm 110) reveal an extraordinary range of expression, each one drawing out different aspects of word-meaning. Even the brief trio, *Deus tuorum militum*, has a haunting memorability – it could become to Monteverdi what *Jesu, joy of man's desiring* is to Bach – and the perform-ances are outstanding, with the edge on **Emma Kirkby's** voice attractively presented in an aptly reverberant acoustic. The accompaniment makes a persuasive case for authentic performance on original instruments. The CD sounds su-perb (but has been withdrawn).

Madrigals: Addio Florida bella; Ahi com'a un vago sol; E cosi a poco a poco torno farfella; Era l'anima mia; Luci serene e chiare; Mentre vaga Angioletta ogn'anima; Ninfa che scalza il piede; O mio bene, a mia vita; O Mirtillo, anima mia; Partenza amorosa; Se pur destina; Taci, Armelin deh taci; T'amo mia vita; Troppo ben può questo tiranno amore

Ⓑ ******* HM (ADD) HMC 1951084. Concerto Vocale, Jacobs

A highly attractive collection of generally neglected items, briskly and stylishly performed. The most celebrated of the singers is the male alto, a fine director as well as a soloist. But since this disc was first issued in 1983, **Barbara Schlick**, **Marius van Altena** and **Guy de Mey** have also established themselves. With continuo accompaniment – the common factor in this programme, in which no *a cappella* madrigals are included – the contrasting of vocal timbres is superbly achieved. An excellent recording, well transferred to CD.

Madrigali concertati: Augelin, che la voce; Eccomi pronta ai baci; Ecco vicine, o belle tigre; Gira il nemico insidioso; Lamento della ninfa; Mentre vaga Angioletta; Ninfa, che scalza il piede; Ogni amante è guerrier; Perché fuggi; S'ei vostro cor, Madonna; Soave libertate; Tornate, o cari baci; Vaga su spina ascosa; Zefiro torna (Ciaccona)

ⒷⒷ ******* Warner Apex 2564 60710-2. Soloists, Tragicomedia, Stubbs

These concerted madrigals come from the Seventh and Eighth Books. Those from the Seventh are written in from one to six concerted parts, with the theme of love predomi-nating. Such as the masterly vocal chaconne *Zefiro torna* ('Summer breezes'), which seems to be in all such collections. The madrigals from the Eighth Book include the extended *Ogni amante è guerrier* ('Every lover is a warrior') with its mar-tial oratory, and the melancholy *Lamento della ninfa*, with its stabs of dissonance at the loss of a beloved. The members of **Tragicomedia** never disappoint, and this is a well-chosen collection, readily demonstrating the amazing range of Monteverdi's madrigals. As the essential texts and transla-tions are included, this well-recorded disc is a bargain.

Madrigals (duets and solos): Chiome d'oro, bel thesoro; Il son pur vezzosetta pastorella; Non è gentil core; O come sei gentile, caro angellino; Ohimé dov'é il mio ben?; Se pur destina e vole il cielo, partenza amorosa. Sacred music: Cantate Domino; Exulta, filia Sion; Iste confessione II; Laudate Dominum in sanctis eius; O bone Jesu, o piissime Jesu; Sancta Maria, succurre miseris; Venite, siccientes ad aquas Domini. Opera: Il ritorno d'Ulisse in patria: Di misera regina (Penelope's Lament)

☛ⒷⒷ ******* Regis RRC 1060. Kirkby, Tubb, Consort of Musicke, Rooley

Admirers of **Emma Kirkby** will surely revel in this collection, mostly of duets, in which she is joined by **Evelyn Tubb**. The two voices are admirably matched and both artists ornament their lines attractively and judiciously. Tubb is given a solo opportunity in Penelope's lament from *Il ritorno d'Ulisse*, which she sings dramatically and touchingly. **Anthony Rooley's** simple accompaniments with members of the **Consort of Musicke** are also imaginatively stylish. We are pleased to report that this inexpensive reissue has been properly documented.

Lamento d'Olympia; Maladetto sia l'aspetto; Ohimè ch'io cado; Quel sdengosetto; Voglio di vita uscia

*** Hyp. CDA 66106. Kirkby, Rooley (chittarone) – D'INDIA: *Lamento d'Olympia, etc.* *******

A well-planned recital from Hyperion contrasts the two set-tings of *Lamento d'Olympia* by Monteverdi and his younger contemporary, Sigismondo d'India. The performances by **Emma Kirkby**, sensitively supported by **Anthony Rooley**, could hardly be surpassed. Her admirers can be assured that this ranks among her best records.

Sacred Music, Vol. I: Beatus vir I; Christe redemptor omnium; Confitebor Primo; Dixit [Dominus] Primo; Laudate Dominum omnes gentes; Laudate pueri Primo; Magnificat Primo; Missa a 4

*** Hyp. **SACDA**; CDA 67428. Outram, Covey-Crump, Mulroy, Auchincloss, Daniels, Gilchrist, Harvey, Evans, King's Consort Ch. & O, King

Sacred Music, Vol. II: Cantate Domino; Currite populi; Ego dormio; Exultent caeli; Laudate Dominum; Letaniae della Beata Vergine; Messa a 4 voci; O beatae viae; Venite, siccientes

*** Hyp. **SACDA**; CDA 67438. Sampson, Outram, Covey-Crump, Daniels, Gilchrist, Harvey, King's Consort Ch. & O, King

Sacred Music, Vol. III: Cantate Domino; Christe, adoramus te; Confitebor tibi III alla francese; Dixit Dominus II; Ecca sacrum paratum; Gloria in excelsis Deo; Lauda Jerusalem; Memento Domine David; Nisi Dominus I; Salve Regina II; Sancta Maria

*** Hyp. **SACDA**; CDA 67487. Sampson, Outram, Auchincloss,

Covey-Crump, Daniels, Gilchrist, Harvey, Evans, King's Consort Ch. & O, King

Sacred Music, Vol. IV: *Adoramus te, Christe; Beatus vir II; Dixit Dominus II; Domine, ne in furore tuo; Exulta, filia Sion; Laetatus sum I; Laudate Dominum omnes gentes III; Magnificat II; Salve, o Regina, o Mater; Salve Regina; Salve Regina I; Sanctorum mritis II*

*** Hyp. **SACDA**; CDA 67519. Sampson, Outram, Osmond, Covey-Crump, Daniels, Auchincloss, Gilchrist, Harvey, Evans, King's Consort Ch. & O, King

Robert King and his **King's Consort** here offer their invaluable and comprehesive series of a relatively neglected part of Monteverdi's output, with masterpieces well sprinkled throughout these four volumes. Most of the works are motets, i.e. not part of the fixed church liturgy, and might be sung as interludes within a Mass or between the Psalms of a Vespers service, as with *Laetatus sum*. This is spectacularly set and, while based on a four-note ostinato, yet expands gloriously and at times reminds the listener of other, more familiar works, like the *Beatus vir* (included in Volume I) and the well-known *Gloria*. The fourth volume also includes a fascinating echo *Salve Regina*, very effectively realized here. Performances and recording throughout this fine series are of the highest quality and, as can be seen, each volume also comes as an SACD with the sound further expanded.

Mass of Thanksgiving (Venice 1631)

(BB) *** Virgin 2x1 3 49993-2 (2). Taverner Consort Ch. & Players, Parrott

Andrew Parrott here presents a reconstruction of the *Mass of Thanksgiving* as performed in Venice on 21 November 1611. At the heart of the celebration lies Monteverdi's magnificent seven-part *Gloria* from his great collection, *Selva morale e spirituale*. The *Kyrie* sections of the *Credo* (including an amazing chromatic *Crucifixus*), the *Offertory*, *Sanctus*, *Agnus Dei* and a final *Salve regina* also come from that great collection. The only parts of the actual Mass written by another composer are the sections of the *Credo* that Monteverdi did not set. They are by Giovanni Rovetta, while other contemporaries of Monteverdi contributed the additional items, including Girolami Fantini, Giuseppe Scarani and Francesco Usper, to make a very grand whole. The recording is warmly atmospheric, with the brassy music at the opening and close approaching and receding, and with appropriate sound effects punctuating the ceremony. The performance is superb; the only reservation to make is that with only a little less linking material it would have been possible to fit the whole on to a single CD.

Motets: *Cantate domino a 6; Domine ne in furore a 6; Missa da cappella a 4; Missa da cappella a 6 (in illo tempore)*

(BB) *** Hyp. Helios CDH 55145. The Sixteen, Christophers; Phillips

Harry Christophers draws superb singing from his brilliant choir, highly polished in ensemble but dramatic and deeply

expressive too, suitably adapted for the different character of each Mass-setting, when the four-part Mass involves stricter, more consistent contrapuntal writing and the six-part, in what was then an advanced way, uses homophonic writing to underline key passages. Vivid, atmospheric recording.

Motets for solo voice: '*Pianto della Madonna*': *Confitebor tibi Domini (Missa a 4 voci e salmi, 1650); Currite populi; Ecce sacrum paratum; O quam pulchra es (Ghirlanda sacra, 1645); Exulta, Filia Sion (Sacri canti, 1629); Jubilet a voce sola in dialogo; Lamento dell'Arianna: Pianto della Madonna; Laudate Dominum (all from Selva morale e spirituale, 1640); Salve, O Regina (Sacre canti, 1624); Venite, videte (1625)*

🔑 🔆 (M) **** HM HMC 901680. Kiehr, Concerto Soave, Aymes (with MARINI: 2 *Sinfonias* (from *Church Sonatas*); Costanto ATEGNATI: *Ricercar*; Claudio MERULO: *Toccata con minute****)

Maria Cristina Kiehr's compilation is very beautiful. With the vocal items contrasted with short instrumental ritornellos by other musicians from the same period, we cannot praise this recital too highly. Every work is glorious and is ravishingly sung. *Currite populi* introduces a lovely flowing *Alleluia*; *O quam pulchra es* ('How fair thou art, my love') is permeated with an exquisite melancholy which returns in several later items, and especially the famous excerpt from the *Lamento dell'Arianna*, which gives the CD its title. The fresh, spring-like *Jubilet* has a delightful echo effect, with a nice touch of added resonance, and *Exulta, Filia Sion* is another joyful song, with florid runs and a jubilant closing *Alleluia*. The closing *Laudate Dominum* makes a wonderful apotheosis, with alleluias and echoing phrases adding to its paean of praise. Superb music, superb singing and playing, and warmly atmospheric recording all here combine to bring the listener the very greatest musical rewards.

Selva morale e spirituale (complete)

*** HM HMC 901718/20 (3). Cantus Cöln, Concerto Palatino, Konrad Junghänel

These are performances marked by keen perception as well as energy. In his presentation Junghänel effectively solves one of the main problems of the whole: the very variety of the pieces, which range widely in their styles from pure polyphony to the latest developments of the mid-17th century, plainly drawn from all periods of Monteverdi's career. The original publication also had them in higgledy-piggledy order, and Junghänel has perceptively reordered them to present the first and third of the three CDs roughly as *Vespers* collections, with miscellaneous items on the second disc. It works well, with the 12 singers of **Cantus Cöln** led by the fine soprano, **Johanna Koslowsky**, offering ample variety of colour and expression to keep concentration. A superb achievement, helped by fine, atmospheric recording.

Selva morale e spirituale: excerpts: *Adoramus te; Beatus vir a 6 voci; Chi vol che m'innamori; Confitebor terzo alla francese; Confitebor tibi*

Domine; E questa vita un lampo; Gloria a 7 voci; Laudate Dominum; O ciechi ciechi

(B) *** HM HMA 195 1250. Les Arts Florissants, Christie

Christie's programme here gives an idea of its range, from Beatus vir, the vivid large-scale Psalm-setting for six voices and violins, and the splendid seven-voiced Gloria, with its burst of vocal virtuosity at the opening, to the succinct Adoramus te, and the more modest Laudate Dominum for bass voice with continuo. All the performances here are imbued with a flowing vitality and combine breadth and devotional feeling with vocal and instrumental refinement. As usual from this source, the recording is admirably clear and spacious.

Vespro della Beata Vergine (Vespers) (DVD version)

☚─✿ **** DG DVD 073 035-9; CD 429 565-2 (2). Monoyios, Pennicchi, Chance, Tucker, Robson, Naglia, Terfel, Miles, H.M. Sackbutts & Cornetts, Monteverdi Ch., L. Oratory Ch., E. Bar. Sol., Gardiner

When in 1989 John Eliot Gardiner made his live recording in the grand setting of St Mark's, Venice, this film was made for BBC television. If on CD the reverberation and occasionally the balances of voices do not suit every listener, the video version makes everything plain, and the beauty and grandeur of the setting exactly match the glories of the music, superbly interpreted. It is good to find the young Bryn Terfel among the soloists, one of an outstanding team. Among the bonus items is an illuminating 20-minute introduction by Gardiner himself, also filmed in Venice. He outlines the music and its composition, with a brief portrait of the composer, and emphasizes his own devotion to this of all works, which played a key part in his emergence as a conductor, evoking a sense of joy in him whenever he returns to it.

Vespro della Beata Vergine (Vespers) (CD versions)

*** DG 477 6147 (2). Gabrieli Consort & Players, McCreesh

*** BIS CD 1071/2 (2). Midori Suzuki, Nonoshita, Hatano, Türk, Van Dyke, Taniguchi, MacLeod, Ogasawara, Bach Coll. Japan Ch. & O, Masaaki Suzuki

*** Hyp. CDA 67531/2 (2). Sampson, Daniels, Gilchrist, Harvey, King's Consort and Ch., Robert King

(N)(M) *** EMI 2 12685-2 (2). Kirkby, Covey-Crump, Rogers, Thomas, Taverner Consort & Players, Parrott

(BB) *** Hyp. Dyad CDD 22028 (2). The Sixteen, Christophers

Like Sir John Eliot Gardiner on his version recorded in the ample acoustic of St Mark's, Venice, Paul McCreesh and the Gabrieli Consort offer a performance of the Vespers that attempts to follow liturgical practice. Yet where Gardiner's ample acoustic brings its inconsistencies of balance, McCreesh, recording in the helpful acoustic of Tonbridge Hall, has a much more controllable acoustic, while still conveying the impression of a live event. The result is a smaller-scale, more intimate reading of this iconic work, very well recorded.

Suzuki's fine set aims to include not just the Vespers, complete with the grand Magnificat in seven voices, but the other items in the collection which Monteverdi published in 1610. Following the example of Andrew Parrott, Suzuki has chosen to transpose the music down a fourth not only for the two settings of the Magnificat, but for the Mass and the Lauda Jerusalem, each written in a combination of high clefs. It makes a satisfying and generous package, very well performed and warmly recorded. The scale is not as grand as in Gardiner's version nor as intimate as Philip Pickett's. The reverberation often obscures detail in the big choral numbers, but the balance is excellent between solo voices and choir, and the approach is characteristically lively and well sprung in the way one expects of this fine choral conductor. A first-rate recommendation, particularly with such generous bonuses.

Robert King crowns his Monteverdi series for Hyperion including not only the usual text but also the other two works that appeared in the same 1610 publication, the six-part Magnificat and the Missa illo tempore. The six-part work is less elaborate than the seven-part Magnificat from the Vespers proper, but it offers a valuable alternative. As King points out, the six-part work offers the alternative of organ accompaniment on its own, instead of orchestral accompaniment. The opening may seem disconcertingly bare, when King rejects the idea of using material from the prelude to the opera, Orfeo, yet the result is tautly dramatic too. The soloists make an excellent team, all singers regularly associated with King and his outstanding work, notably Carolyn Sampson and James Gilchrist. Warmly atmospheric recording, that yet allows plenty of detail to be heard.

Though Andrew Parrott uses minimal forces, with generally one instrument and one voice per part, so putting the work on a chamber scale in a small church setting, its grandeur comes out superbly through its very intensity. Brilliant singing here by the virtuoso soloists, above all by Nigel Rogers, whose distinctive timbre may not suit every ear but who has an airy precision and flexibility to give expressive meaning to even the most taxing passages. Fine contributions too from Parrott's chosen groups of players and singers, and warm, atmospheric recording. This now at mid-price is one of EMI's 'Great Recordings of the Century'.

The Sixteen's version presents a liturgical performance of what Graham Dixon suggests as Monteverdi's original conception. In practice the occasional changes of text are minimal; the booklet accompanying the set even includes an order of tracks if anyone wishes to hear the Vespers in traditional form. As it is, the performance includes not only relevant Gregorian chant but antiphon substitutes, including a magnificent motet of Palestrina, obviously relevant, Gaude Barbara. The scale of the performance is very satisfying, with The Sixteen augmented to 22 singers (7.4.6.5) and with members of the group taking the eight solo roles.

OPERA

L'Incoronazione di Poppea; L'Orfeo; Il Ritorno d'Ulisse in Patria (complete; DVD version)

**(*) DG DVD 734 278 (5). Huttenlocher, Schmidt, Hermann, Linos; Hollweg, Schmidt, Estes, Perry, Huttenlocher; Tappy, Yakar, Schmidt, Esswood, Perry, Oliver; Zürich Op.,

Monteverdi Ensemble, Harnoncourt. (Dir: Jean-Pierre Ponnelle, V/D: Roland Ott)

DG's five-disc set brings together the three ground-breaking productions presented at the Zürich Opera House in 1978/9 with **Nikolaus Harnoncourt** conducting and with production and lavish designs by Jean-Pierre Ponnelle. They were each filmed in Vienna, with the sound recordings made in Zürich and with the singers miming to the film. These productions and performances are very much of their period. With a whole range of star singers in each opera, not normally associated with period performance, the results are still very involving. In *L'Orfeo*, Harnoncourt has in the title-role a weighty baritone, **Philippe Huttenlocher**, stylish but not the sort of voice one would latterly expect. **Trudeliese Schmidt** sings warmly as the allegorical figure of Music, and **Detlinde Turban** is a bright, pure Euridice. **Roland Hermann** is a fine Apollo, and the incidental roles of the Shepherds and others are well-taken. *Il Ritorno d'Ulisse* has **Werner Hollweg** expressive in the title-role, with Trudeliese Schmidt as a fresh, youthful Penelope, and with **Simon Estes** as Antinoo. The final reunion duet of Ulisse and Penelope is most moving.

Most successful of the three performances is *L'Incoronazione di Poppea*. Here even more strikingly there is an impressive line-up of stars not normally associated with period performance, led by the Swiss tenor, **Eric Tappy**, as Nerone and **Rachel Yakar** as Poppea, with Trudeliese Schmidt weightily tragic as Ottavia and **Matti Salminen** darkly intense as Seneca. The jolly duet of celebration between Nerone and Lucano after Seneca's suicide is sparkingly done. Memorable too is the singing of the counter-tenor, **Paul Esswood** as Ottone, one of the few counter-tenors in these productions. Excellent too are **Janet Perry** as Drusilla and above all **Alexander Oliver**, a favourite at Glyndebourne in the drag part of the Nurse Arnalta. Setting the seal on a fine performance is the final duet between Nerone and Poppea, the loveliest (and most immoral) in all Monteverdi.

L'Incoronazione di Poppea (complete DVD versions)

🎞–******** Bel Air **DVD** BAC 004. Delunsch, von Otter, Brunet, Hellekant, Sedov, Fouchécourt, Les Musiciens du Louvre, Minkowski (V/D: Vincent Bataillon)

🎞–******** Warner NVC Arts **DVD** 0630 16914-2. Ewing, Bailey, Clarey, Duesing, Lloyd, Gale, Glyndebourne Ch., LPO, Leppard (V/D: Peter Hall & Robin Lough)

(*) Arthaus **DVD 100 108. Schumann, Croft, Kuhlmann, Gall, Peeters, Brooks, Concerto Köln, Jacobs. (Dir: Michael Hampe, V/D: José Montes-Baquer)

With an outstanding cast, Klaus Michael Gruber's production offers a staging with stylized sets and timeless costumes, effectively clarifying the story of the love of Nero and Poppea. Minkowski has opted basically for the Venice version of the score, but has added three instrumental interludes by Monteverdi's associate, Biagio Marini, to facilitate scene-changes. He has chosen instrumentation with ample bass continuo to suit the venue, and the result is a moving and beautiful account, which heightens the love scenes between Poppea and Nero, not least the ecstatic final duet – when, curiously, they are not seen to embrace – and the monologues of the deserted wife, Ottavia, powerfully sung by **Sylvie Brunet**. She emerges as an equal star with **Anne Sofie von Otter** as Nero and **Mireille Delunsch** ravishing as Poppea. Other roles are strongly taken by **Charlotte Hellekant** as Ottone, **Denis Sedov** as a handsome, young-looking Seneca and **Jean-Paul Fouchécourt** comically in drag as the nurse, Arnalta. A presentation that very effectively brings out the sharp contrasts of pathos and comedy in this masterpiece.

We have a very soft spot for the richly opulent **Leppard** version of Monteverdi's opera, at a far remove from today's scrupulously authentic versions. Here, not only are the strings gorgeous-sounding, but the castrati roles have been transposed, and the original three acts condensed into two. The cast of this faithful (1984) Glyndebourne production are watched by characters from the Prologue, Fortune, Virtue and Cupid, and, with Peter Hall directing, the drama is vividly projected (often with the camera observing the characters individually). **Maria Ewing** as a boldly self-confident Poppea is well matched vocally by **Dennis Bailey's** Nero, and **Robert Lloyd** is a tower of strength as Seneca. **Cynthia Clarey**, singing with passionate espressivo, is a sympathetic Ottavia and **Dale Duesing** completes a thoroughly convincing cast as Ottone. The setting is visually sumptuous, to match Leppard's luxurious conception, and he directs the proceedings with panache. For those who don't care for authenticity in early opera, with all its visual contradictions concerning male and female personae, this well-recorded version should prove very rewarding.

The Arthaus performance from the 1993 Schwetzingen Festival is far more severe, both artistically and as a visual experience. It suffers from a less than ideal Poppea in **Patricia Schumann** but both **Kathleen Kuhlmann's** Ottavia and **Darla Brooks's** Drusilla are expressive and intelligent singers, and the Seneca of **Harry Peeters** is exemplary.

L'incoronazione di Poppea (opera; CD versions)

🎞–******** DG 447 088-2 (3). McNair, von Otter, Hanchard, Chance, d'Artegna, E. Bar. Sol., Gardiner

Ⓜ ******* Virgin 5 61783-2 (3). Augér, D. Jones, Hirst, Reinart, Bowman, City of L. Bar. Sinfonia, Hickox

Ⓝ Ⓜ ****(*)** Warner 2564 69261-1 (3). Donath, Söderström, Berberian, Esswood, Luccardi, Hansmann, Langridge, VCM, Harnoncourt

With an exceptionally strong and consistent cast in which even minor roles are taken by star singers, **Gardiner** presents a purposeful, strongly characterized performance. He is helped by the full and immediate sound of the live recording, made in concert at the Queen Elizabeth Hall, London. **Sylvia McNair** is a seductive Poppea and **Anne Sofie von Otter** a deeply moving Ottavia, both singing ravishingly. **Francesco d'Artegna**, a robustly Italian-sounding bass, makes a stylish Seneca, and there are clear advantages in having a counter-tenor as Nero instead of a mezzo-soprano, particularly one with a slightly sinister timbre like **Dana Hanchard**. So in the sensuous duet which closes the opera, the clashing intervals of the voices are given a degree of abrasiveness, suggesting that, though this is a happy and beautiful ending, the characters still have their sinister side. The text has been modified with newly written ritornellos by Peter Holman, using the original, authentic bass-line, and aiming to be 'closer to what Monteverdi would have expected' than the usual flawed text.

On Virgin, the tender expressiveness of **Arleen Augér** in the title-role of Monteverdi's elusive masterpiece combines with a performance from **Richard Hickox** and the **City of London Baroque Sinfonia** which consistently reflects the fact that it was recorded in conjunction with a stage production in 1988. Hickox daringly uses a very spare accompaniment of continuo instruments, but he overcomes the problems of that self-imposed limitation by choosing the widest possible range of speeds. The purity of Augér's soprano may make Poppea less of a scheming seducer than she should be, but it is Monteverdi's music for the heroine which makes her so sympathetic in this oddly slanted, equivocal picture of Roman history, and one that has seldom sounded subtler or more lovely on record than this. Taking the castrato role of Nero, **Della Jones** sings very convincingly with full, rather boyish tone, while **Gregory Reinart** is magnificent in the bass role of Seneca. **James Bowman** is a fine Ottone, with smaller parts taken by such excellent singers as **Catherine Denley**, **John Graham-Hall**, **Mark Tucker** and **Janice Watson**. **Linda Hirst** sounds too raw of tone for Ottavia, making her a scold rather than a sympathetic suffering widow. Fitted on to three well-filled mid-priced CDs, the opera comes with libretto and translation and can be recommended alongside the Gardiner set.

Harnoncourt's pioneering version, dating from the 1970s, had the dual advantage of being both complete, and – according to the standards of the time – authentic. There is no question that the dramatic power of the music comes across. **Helen Donath** is commanding as Poppea, and she is extremely well supported by **Paul Esswood** as Ottone and **Cathy Berberian**, whose characterization of Ottavia is an imaginative one. Donath's singing has not the richness and dignity that Janet Baker gives to this role, but she brings the character fully to life. **Elisabeth Söderström** has the almost impossible task of creating a heroic image in the role of Nero, written for a high castrato, but her performance is excellent, even if she fails wholly to submerge her femininity. Harnoncourt brings plenty of vitality to the performance as a whole, and his instrumental group provide impressive and some times beautiful, if over-decorative accompaniments.

Orfeo (CD version; complete)

⊖— Ⓜ *** Decca 476 7213-2 (2). Mark Ainsley, Gooding, Bott, Bonner, George, Grant, New L. Cons., Pickett

*** DG 419 250-2 (2). Rolfe Johnson, Baird, Dawson, von Otter, Argenta, Robson, Monteverdi Ch., E. Bar. Sol., Gardiner

Pickett has not tried to treat *Orfeo* with kid gloves but has aimed above all to bring out its freshness. So, in the dark *Sinfonia* with its weird chromatic writing, which at the opening of Act III represents Orfeo's arrival in the underworld, Pickett cuts out strings and uses brass instruments alone. As Orfeo, **John Mark Ainsley** may have a less velvety tenor than Anthony Rolfe Johnson on the Gardiner set, but his voice is more flexible in the elaborate decorations of *Possente spirito*, Orfeo's plea to Charon. Outstanding among the others is **Catherine Bott**. In *Orfeo* she not only sings the elaborate role given to La Musica in the Prologue, sensuously beautiful and seductive in her coloration, but also the part of Proserpina and the key role of the Messenger who graphically describes the death of Euridice. This has now been reissued in Universal's 'Critics' Choice' series with full documentation including text and translation.

John Eliot Gardiner very effectively balances the often-conflicting demands of authentic performance – when this pioneering opera was originally presented intimately – and the obvious grandeur of the concept. So the 21-strong **Monteverdi Choir** conveys, on the one hand, high tragedy to the full, yet sings the lighter commentary from nymphs and shepherds with astonishing crispness, often at top speed. However, Gardiner is strong on pacing. This is a set to take you through the story with new involvement. Though editing is not always immaculate, the recording on CD is vivid and full of presence.

Il ritorno d'Ulisse in patria (DVD versions)

⊖— **(*) Arthaus **DVD** 101 101. Luxon, J. Baker, Howles, Lloyd, Burrows, Popova, Caley, Glyndebourne Ch., LPO, Leppard (Director: Peter Hall, V/D: David Heather)

Raymond Leppard's lush arrangements of Monteverdi and Cavalli operas may have fallen completely out of fashion in an age devoted to period performance but, as with *L'Incoronazione di Poppea* (above), there is a great deal to enjoy in his account, recorded in 1973, with **Benjamin Luxon** robust as Ulisse, still in excellent voice, and, most strikingly of all, **Dame Janet Baker** as the ever-patient Penelope. Hers is a deeply moving performance, masterfully acted and sung. Others making strong contributions include **Robert Lloyd** as the Old Shepherd and **Ian Caley** as Ulisse's son, Telemaco. For Baker alone the DVD is worth hearing, and John Bury's stylized sets, with flying gods and goddesses, are a delight to the eye, backing up Peter Hall's stage direction. That said, the presentation on DVD is inadequate there is not even a complete cast list, except in the filmed credits at the end of the performance.

MONTSALVATGE, Xavier
(1912–2002)

Concerto brève for Piano & Orchestra

*** Australian Decca Eloquence (ADD) 476 2971. Larrocha, RPO, Frühbeck de Burgos – ALBENIZ: *Rapsodia Española*; SURINACH: *Piano Concerto*; TURINA: *Rapsodia sinfónica* ***

Xavier Montsalvatge's *Concerto brève* is dedicated to **Alicia de Larrocha**, who plays it here with authority and conviction. While no masterpiece – there is no really memorable theme – it is nevertheless entertaining, especially with its colourful orchestration, which is well brought out by the first-class (1977) Decca engineering. The **RPO** under **Frühbeck de Burgos** are excellent, and this rarity makes a good bonus for the other concertante works offered here.

MOODY, James (1907–95)

(i) Quintet for Harmonica & String Quartet; (ii) Suite dans le style français

*** Chan. 8802. Reilly; (i) Hindar Qt; (ii) Kanga – JACOB: *Divertimento* ***

James Moody's *Suite in the French Style* may be pastiche but its impressionism is highly beguiling. The *Quintet* is more ambitious, less charming perhaps, but likely to prove even more rewarding on investigation, especially the very diverse theme and variations of the finale, the longest movement. The performance and recording are hardly likely to be bettered.

MORALES, Cristóbal de
(c. 1500–53)

Missa Si bona suseptimus

**(*) Gimell CDGIM 033. Tallis Scholars, Phillips (with CRECQUILLON: *Andreas Christi famulus*; VERDELOT: *Si bona suseptimus*)

The Spanish Renaissance master Cristóbal de Morales began and ended his career in Spain, but he spent the decade between 1535 and 1545 singing with the Sistine Chapel Choir in Rome. The *Missa Si bona suseptimus* was almost certainly composed during this period, and its opulence of line owes something to Italian influence, yet Morales retained his own fluid style, as comparison with *Mille regretz* shows. The present Mass is a parody mass, using as its source Verdelot's motet, *Si bona suseptimus*, which is concerned with the theme of Job ('The Lord giveth and the Lord taketh away'), although Morales's texture and polyphony are richer than his model. The **Tallis Scholars'** performance is appropriately prefaced by its source motet and followed by another work long credited to Morales, but now thought to be by Thomas Crecquillon. It is the splendid eight-part motet, *Andreas Christi famulus*, but its layout is denser, less supple than that of Morales. These are fine performances, beautifully and passionately sung and recorded, but in the main work the lack of variety of dynamic (though not of tempo) is a drawback for the non-specialist listener.

MORENO TORROBA, Federico (1891–1982)

Sonatina for Guitar & Orchestra; Interludes I & II

*** Analekta Fleur de Lys FL 2 3049. Boucher, Amati Ens., Dessaints – ABRIL: *Concierto Mudéjar* ***

Moreno Torroba's *Sonatina* was written in the early years of the 20th century for Segovia; the composer made the concertante arrangement of the solo work not long before he died. The outer movements, with their Castilian atmosphere, are gay and engaging, and the Romance, which forms the central *Andante*, is quite captivating, especially when the performance has such a simple spontaneity and is not too overladen with expressive feeling. The two *Interludes* are also both highly evocative and they are most winning in their present format. **Rémi Boucher** is a splendid soloist, and **Raymond Dessaints** gives him affectionate support. The warmth of the truthful and very well-balanced recording adds to the listener's pleasure.

Luisa Fernanda (complete)

*** Valois V 4759. Domingo, Villaroel, Pons, Rodrigo, Madrid University Ch., Madrid SO, Marba

This is an ideal recommendation for anyone wanting to investigate the zarzuela, the Spanish genre of operetta. Moreno Torroba, best known for his guitar music, here offers in three compact Acts a sequence of catchily tuneful numbers, brightly orchestrated. Led by **Domingo** in glowing form as the hero, Javier, an army colonel, the cast is as near ideal as possible, with **Veronica Villaroel** in the title-role and **Juan Pons** as Javier's rich rival. Bright, immediate sound.

MOSCHELES, Ignaz (1794–1870)

Piano Concertos 1 in F, Op. 45; 6 in B flat (Fantastique); 7 in C min. (Pathétique), Op. 93

*** Hyp. CDA 67385. Shelley, Tasmanian SO

The *First Piano Concerto* arrived in 1818. It is not a particularly flamboyant work, and is not really distinctive until the jolly finale. The *Sixth Concerto* (1834) is altogether more fluent and mature, with all three sections planned to be played without interruption, the gentle slow movement joined to the rollicking gypsy finale by an agitato bridge passage derived from the opening movement. The *Seventh Concerto* dates from the following year and is notable in that the central movement is a Scherzo with the slow movement ingeniously interwoven. The reason for the nickname *Pathétique* is not clear, but in **Howard Shelley's** hands it emerges as an attractively inventive work. Indeed, all the concertos are entertaining when the solo playing is so brilliantly persuasive, the orchestra supportive, and the recording excellent.

Piano Concertos 2 in E flat, Op. 56; 3 in G min., Op. 58; Anticipations of Scotland (Grand Fantasia), Op. 75

*** Hyp. CDA 67276. Shelley, Tasmanian SO

Both these piano concertos appeared in 1825. *2 in E flat* is particularly attractive, with one striking idea after another bubbling up in the substantial outer movements – the finale a Chopin-like Polacca – and with a deeply meditative central *Adagio*. Though the thematic material of *3 in G minor* is not so memorable, with passage-work that involves note-spinning reminiscent of a study by Czerny, the finale makes amends with a jolly Rondo in a galloping 6/8 time. *Anticipations of Scotland*, as the title suggests, was written before Moscheles ever visited the country. Scottish songs were freely available to him, however, and in this fantasia he uses three in particular, with characteristic Scottish snap-rhythms – *Kelvin Grove, Auld Robin Gray* and *Lord Moira's Strathspey* – for a sequence of variations. Again, this is a piece full of conventional passage-work, this time helped by the underlying melodies. Moscheles's writing is always winningly fluent, so that even when it is at its most predictable, it sparkles away in the hands of a fine pianist like **Howard Shelley**, who draws lively playing from the **Tasmanian Orchestra**, with vivid, immediate recording.

Piano Concertos 2 in E flat, Op. 56; 4 in E, Op. 64

⊕ᵣ *** Zephyr Z 116-99. Hobson, Sinfonia da Camera

The *E flat Concerto* opens with the timpani setting the mood for an imposing march, with a Hummelian dotted rhythm, and they later set off the jolly *Polonaise* of the finale. The E major work has a more expansively ambitious opening tutti, and its slow movement centres on a romantic horn solo. The horns then announce the closing set of bold variations on 'The British Grenadiers', which gives **Ian Hobson** plenty of opportunities for glittering bravura. He plays spiritedly throughout both works, yet obviously relishes their *galant* lyricism, while effectively directing the accompaniments from the keyboard. The recording is truthful and well balanced, and altogether this is a most enjoyable coupling.

MOZART, Leopold (1719–87)

Horn Concerto in D

*** Ara. Z 6750. Rose, St Luke's Chamber Ens. – FORSTER;
   HAYDN; TELEMANN: *Horn Concertos* ***

Leopold Mozart's *Horn Concerto* of 1755 is enormously demanding of its soloist – far more difficult than the later concertos of Wolfgang Amadeus. The first movement gambols in a sprightly 6/8, but soon takes the horn up into its highest register, where it remains for the expressive minor-key *Romanza*. The third movement then sets off lustily and demands that the soloist trill his way up a major arpeggio. **Stewart Rose's** trills, whether relaxed as in the slow movement, or buoyant as here, are impressively clean: he is a true virtuoso and establishes the difference between this essentially classical work and the earlier Baroque concerto of Telemann. A supplemental Minuet completes the piece traditionally and offers more opportunities for bravura. This performance will be hard to surpass, and the recording is excellent.

Symphonies in C (C 1, C 4 & D 1); in D (D 17 & D 25); in G (G 14)

Ⓝ **** Chan. 10496. LMP, Bamert

Leopold Mozart was a highly respected composer of symphonies before his famous son arrived on the scene and soon virtually eclipsed his output. But these excellent, lively and very well played performances show how inventive he was. All but two are in three movements, but the *Andantes* in the C major, C 4 (subtitled Partita), and the D major, D 25, are most engaging, while his very effective writing for horns in all four movements of the C major, D1, adds much to the music. The opening symphony here, again in C major and with four movements, is a most satisfyingly balanced work. Obviously young Wolfgang learned much from his father, but Leopold's symphonies are by no means a carbon copy of junior's music. A most attractive disc, full of elegant ideas and vitality, and very well recorded.

Symphonies in A (A 1); D (D 15); G (G 8); G (New Lambach); Toy Symphony

Ⓝ ⒷⒷ ** Naxos 8.570499. Toronto CO, Mallon

A somewhat disappointing collection, surprising from a group who have already given us some enjoyable Haydn symphonies. But **Mallon** treats these works almost as if they were divertimenti, playing them elegantly and in lively fashion, but with not quite enough robust vitality. Best is the *Lambach Symphony*, which is one of Leopold's finest. However, the *Toy Symphony* is meant to be fun and it is hardly that here, with little attempt to make the special effects sparkle.

MOZART, Wolfgang Amadeus (1756–91)

EMI COLLECTOR'S EDITION (50 CDS)

Bassoon Concerto, K.191 (Nakanishi); *Clarinet Concerto, K.622* (A. Marriner; both with LMP, Glover); *Flute Concerto 1, K.313* (Snowdon, LPO, Mackerras); *Flute & Harp Concerto, K.299* (Snowdon, Thomas); *Oboe Concerto, K. 314* (Hunt; both with LPO, Litton); *Piano Concertos 9, 11–27; Concert Rondo 1 in D, K.382* (Barenboim, ECO); *Violin Concertos 1–5; Rondo in C, K.373* (D. Oistrakh, BPO); *Horn Concertos 1–4; Rondo, K.371* (Vladković, ECO, Tate); *3 String Divertimenti, K.136/8* (LMP, Glover); *Serenades: 6 (Serenata notturna); 7 (Haffner)* (Bath Festival O, Menuhin); *13 (Eine kleine Nachtmusik)* (all LMP, Glover); *10–12. Symphonies 1; 4; in F, K19a; 5; 7a (Lambach), K.45a; '43' in F, K.76; 25–30; 31 (Paris); 32–5 (Haffner); 36 (Linz); 38 (Prague); 39–41 (Jupiter)* (ECO, Tate); *Wind Divertimenti: 8, K.213; 9, K.240; 12, K.252; 14, K.270* (all Consortium Classicum); *Clarinet Quintet* (A. Marriner); *Oboe Quartet* (Hunt; both with Chilingirian Qt); *String Quartets: 15–17* (Hunt); *18–19 (Dissonance); 22* (Heutling Qt); *String Quintets: 3 in C, K.515; 4 in G min., K.516;* (with Graf, viola); *Violin Sonatas: 23 in D, K.306; 24 in B flat, K.372; 26 in B flat, K.378; Andante & Allegretto, K.404* (Kagan & S. Richter); *Piano Sonatas: 10–17; Variations, K.24–5; 54; 179–180; 264–5; 352–4; 398; 455; 500; 573; 613* (Barenboim); *Cantatas & Concert Arias: 12 Lieder* (Hendricks, Pires or Söllscher (guitar)); *Ch'io mi scordi* (with Lausanne CO, Eichenholtz); *Exsultate jubilate* (with ASMF, Marriner); *Ave verum corpus* (V. Singverein, Philh. O, Karajan); *Masses: 14 (Coronation) & Vesperae solennes de confessore* (Soloists, Bav. R. Ch. & SO, Jochum); *18 in C min.* (Soloists, Alldis Ch., New Philh. O, Leppard); *19 (Requiem)* (Soloists, New Philh. Ch. & O, Frühbeck de Burgos); *Vesperae de Domenica* (Soloists, King's College Ch. & Cambridge Classical Players, Cleobury). Complete operas: *Così fan tutte* (Vanesse, Ziegler, Watson, Aler, Duesing, Desderi, Glyndebourne Ch., LPO, Haitink); *Don Giovanni* (Soyer, Sgourda, Harper, Donath, G. Evans, Rinaldi, Alva, Scottish Op. Ch., ECO, Barenboim); *Die Entführung aus dem Serail* (Rothenberger, Popp, Gedda, Unger, Frick, V. State Op. Ch., VPO, Krips); *Le nozze di Figaro* (Fischer-Dieskau, Harper, Blegen, G. Evans, Berganza, John Alldis Ch., ECO, Barenboim); *Die Zauberflöte* (Rothenberger, Schreier, Moser, Moll, Berry, Miljacovik, Brokmeier, Bav. State Op. Ch. & O, Sawallisch)

(BB) **** EMI (ADD) 3 87894-2 (50) Artists as above

This extraordinary set of 50 CDs is the Mozartian bargain of all time and would serve admirably to accompany a castaway to a desert island. Alas, there is no documentation except titles and cast lists, but one can't have everything at this modest cost, and the set is still very desirable indeed – worthwhile alone for **Barenboim's** recordings of the piano music (concertos, sonatas and variations), and **Jeffrey Tate's** superb modern-instrument recordings of the symphonies with the ECO; and there is much else besides which is equally treasurable. Not all the artists are obvious choices, but the coverage is amazingly complete, including the five greatest operas (Barenboim's *Don Giovanni* is a disappointment, but he compensates with a first-rate *Nozze di Figaro*). Altogether this is very desirable indeed, with recording of excellent quality throughout.

Adagio and Fugue in C min., K.546; Violin Concerto 3 in G; Symphony 41 in C (Jupiter)

**(*) EMI 5 57418-2. Perlman, BPO

Recorded in upfront sound, this vividly captures the atmosphere of a great occasion, defying received taste in offering unashamedly 'big-band' performances of Mozart. Weighted with double-basses, the opening of the *Adagio and Fugue* has a magnificence worthy of Stokowski, apt enough for such a massive inspiration, and the *Jupiter Symphony*, too, is Beethovenian in scale. In the *G major Violin Concerto* **Perlman** is even more persuasively spontaneous, directing from the violin, than he was in his 20-year-old studio recording with a conductor.

Cassations 1–3

(BB) *** Naxos 8.550609. Salzburg CO, Nerat

All three early *Cassations* are given lively, nicely turned performances, very well – if resonantly – recorded. This admirable disc is certainly worth its modest cost and nicely fills a gap in the catalogue.

CONCERTOS

(i) Bassoon Concerto, K.191; (ii) Clarinet Concerto, K.622; (iii) Flute Concerto 1, K.313; Andante, K.315; (iii; iv) Flute and Harp Concerto in C, K.299; (v) Horn Concertos 1–4; (vi) Oboe Concerto, K.314; Sinfonia concertante, K.297b

(B) *** DG Trio 469 362-2 (3). (i) Morelli; (ii) Neidich; (iii) Palma; (iv) Allen; (v) Jolley or Purvis; (vi) Wolfgang; Orpheus CO

Frank Morelli chortles his way engagingly through the outer movements of the *Bassoon Concerto* and is contrastingly doleful in the *Andante*; **Charles Neidich** uses a basset clarinet in K.622 and his timbre is very appealing; **Randall Wolfgang's** plaintive, slightly reedy tone is especially telling in the *Adagio* of the *Oboe Concerto* and he plays the finale with the lightest possible touch, as does **Susan Palma** the charming Minuet which closes the *Flute Concerto*. The *Sinfonia concertante* for wind is pleasingly fresh; the players match their timbres beautifully in the *Adagio*, and again the last movement is delightful with its buoyant rhythmic spirit. The *Divertimenti* and *Serenades* also bring highly admirable performances. Alert, crisply rhythmic, with much finesse and imaginative use of light and shade. *Eine kleine Nachtmusik* is wonderfully light-hearted and fresh and among the finest on record; the *Serenata notturna*, which can easily sound bland, has a fine sparkle here, while the B flat *Wind Divertimento*, K.270, is notable for some felicitous oboe playing. All the works are given excellent recordings, probably a 'best buy' for all wanting this music in a digital format.

Bassoon Concerto in B flat, K.191

*** Chan. 9656. Popov, Russian State SO, Polyansky – HUMMEL; WEBER: *Bassoon Concertos* ***

*** Caprice CAP 21411. Sönstevold, Swedish RSO, Comissiona – PETTERSSON: *Symphony 7* ***

Valeri Popov's playing has character and warmth. He is at his most personable in the Minuet Rondo finale. **Polyansky's** accompaniment is warmly supportive, and the Chandos recording is well up to standard.

Knut Sönstevold's is a good, big-band performance which gives pleasure, and is very well recorded.

(i; ii) Bassoon Concerto; (iii; iv) Clarinet Concerto; (v) Flute Concerto 1; (vi; iv) Horn Concertos 1–4; (vii; ii) Oboe Concerto

**** (B) Double Decca (DDD/ADD) 466 247-2 (2). (i) McGill; (ii) Cleveland O, Dohnányi; (iii) de Peyer; (iv) LSO, Maag; (v) Bennett, ECO, Malcolm; (vi) Tuckwell; (vii) Mack

These recordings readily demonstrate the ongoing excellence of the Decca coverage of the Mozart wind concertos over three decades. **Gervase de Peyer** is admirable in the *Clarinet Concerto*, and his account remains as fine as any available, fluent and lively, with masterly phrasing in the slow movement and a vivacious finale. **Barry Tuckwell** at the time was proving a natural inheritor of the mantle of Dennis Brain. His easy technique, smooth, warm tone and obvious musicianship command allegiance and give immediate pleasure. **William Bennett** a decade later, but again in the Kingsway Hall, is hardly less impressive in the *G major Flute Concerto*. For the *Bassoon* and *Oboe Concertos* we turn to Cleveland. The oboist, **John Mack**, has an appealingly sweet (but not too sweet) timbre; then **David McGill**, in the work for bassoon, immediately establishes his keen individuality. He does not overdo the humour in the finale. All in all, very enjoyable music-making by musicians from both sides of the Atlantic who are equally at one with Mozart.

(i) *Bassoon Concerto*; (ii) *Clarinet Concerto*; (iii) *Flute Concerto 1*

🎵 (M) **** DG 457 719-2. VPO, Boehm; with (i) Zeman; (ii) Prinz; (iii) Tripp

These are meltingly beautiful accounts. All three soloists perform with the utmost distinction under **Boehm**, who lets the music unfold in an unforced way, relaxed yet vital. Excellent mid-1970s sound makes this a highly recommendable DG 'Originals' disc.

(i) *Bassoon Concerto*; (ii) *Flute Concerto 1*; (ii; iii) *Concerto for Flute & Harp*

🎵 (BB) **** ASV COE 813. (i) Wilkie; (ii) Fischer; (iii) Sprenkels; COE, cond. (i; ii) Végh; (iii) Fischer

On ASV comes the first of an outstanding series of bargain reissues of Mozart's wind concertos, recorded by soloists from the **Chamber Orchestra of Europe** on modern instruments in the early 1990s; they share an inimitable feeling for Mozartian grace and manners. In the *Bassoon Concerto*, the Australian soloist **Matthew Wilkie** immediately makes his mark with his engaging timbre and witty articulation, and in the *Andante* he is matched in graceful phasing by **Sandor Végh** in the orchestral accompaniment. **Thierry Fischer** plays the work for flute with captivating delicacy, with the closing Minuet quite delightful. He also directs as well as taking the solo role in the celestial work for flute and harp, where the balance is particularly felicitous. A most rewarding triptych, beautifully recorded.

(i) *Bassoon Concerto, K.191*; (ii) *Flute Concerto 1*; (ii; iii) *Concerto for Flute & Harp*; (ii) *Andante for Flute & Orchestra, K.315*

(N) (M) *** Decca O/L 478 0021. (i) Bond; (ii) Beznosiuk; (iii) Kelly; AAM, Hogwood

This is another of Decca's Oiseau-Lyre reissues (from 1988), and very good it is too. The performances are peerless and have 'authentic' timbres, notably **Danny Bond's** bassoon. The *Flute and Harp Concerto* is remarkably and appealingly clear in texture, but the sound overall has plenty of body.

Clarinet Concerto in A, K.622 (DVD versions)

(*) EuroArts DVD 2055158. Kam (basset clarinet), Czech PO, Honeck (with *Don Giovanni Overture*; *Symphony 38 (Prague)* *) (Director: Adam Rezek)

**(*) EuroArts DVD 2072088. Schmidl, VPO, Bernstein (with *Symphony 25 in G min., K.183*) (Director: Humphrey Burton)

There is no doubt that **Sharon Kam's** live performance of the *Clarinet Concerto* is the primary DVD recommendation. She plays a basset clarinet beautifully and with character. Her phrasing in the slow movement has an appealing simplicity, and her tone has the extra focus that the alto instrument can provide in the lower register, without losing the richness in the middle and upper range. The snag is visual. Throughout, she plays while moving her body in a circular movement with the music; at a concert-hall distance this would be acceptable, but in close-up it soon becomes distracting. **Manfred Honeck** opens the concert with a thrillingly dramatic account of the *Don Giovanni Overture* and closes it with a superb *Prague Symphony*, as vital and arresting as any in the catalogue. The camera angles, apart from dwelling on the soloist in the concerto, are acceptable, but the bird's-eye view of the performers, which is regularly featured, adds nothing to the music-making.

Although both **Bernstein's** performances are recorded live, they come from two separate concerts, the *Clarinet Concerto* recorded in the Vienna Konzerthaus in 1987, the *Symphony* in the Musikvereinsaal a year later. Humphrey Burton ensures that we see a great deal of Bernstein (even in the concerto) who continually conveys his sheer pleasure in the music, but the *Adagio* of the *Clarinet Concerto* is languorously slow. **Peter Schmidl** is the principal clarinet of the orchestra, and his mellow but patrician contribution, using a modern clarinet, is smoothly articulate and very warm and musical. The orchestral sound is rather more open and wider in range in the early symphony, which receives an affectionate performance but one with real vitality in the outer movements, even though the sound itself could have more bite.

Clarinet Concerto in A, K.622 (CD versions)

(BB) *** ASV COE CD COE 811. Hosford, COE, Schneider – COPLAND: *Clarinet Concerto*; R. STRAUSS: *Duet Concertino* ***

*** DG 457 652-2. Collins, Russian Nat. O, Pletnev – BEETHOVEN: *Clarinet (Violin) Concerto in D, Op. 61* ***

(***) Testament mono SBT 1381. B. Walton, Philh. O, Karajan – BRAHMS: *Clarinet Quintet* ***

(i) *Clarinet Concerto*; (ii) *Flute Concerto 1 in G*; (ii; iii) *Flute & Harp Concerto*

**** EMI 5 57128-2. (i) Meyer; (ii) Pahud; (iii) Langlamet, BPO, Abbado

(i) *Clarinet Concerto*; (ii) *Flute & Harp Concerto*

(BB) *** Regis RRC 1061. (i) Campbell; (ii) Davies, Masters; City of L. Sinfonia, Hickox

David Campbell's agile and pointed performance of the clarinet work brings fastish speeds and a fresh, unmannered style in all three movements. His tonal shading is very beautiful. The earlier work for flute and harp is just as freshly and sympathetically done, with a direct, unmannered style sounding entirely spontaneous. A bargain.

Richard Hosford plays the basset clarinet most beautifully and clearly relishes its chalumeaux. His is an essentially lyrical approach and his *Adagio* is most sensitively phrased, especially the gentle reprise, while the finale is delightfully bouncy, the performance helped throughout by **Schneider's** elegantly matched backing and the first-rate sound. If the couplings are suitable, this is a fine bargain recommendation.

Michael Collins also uses a basset clarinet, relishing the extra downward range and richness of timbre. His speeds in the outer movements are fast, wonderfully agile and with the cleanest articulation and crisp rhythmic pointing, as well as fine detail. It is a reading not just elegant but powerful too, as well as deeply poetic in the slow movement. The playing of the **Russian National Orchestra** under **Pletnev** is refined and elegant to match, but the coupling is controversial.

Sabine Meyer's 1998 performance brings out how much her individual artistry has intensified. She also opts for speeds faster than usual, but finds time to point phrasing and shade dynamics with keen imagination and a feeling of spontaneity; where appropriate, she adds cadenza-like flourishes, as in the honeyed lead-back to the reprise in the central *Largo*. The two concertos with **Pahud** reveal him as an outstandingly individual artist, light and athletic, dominant over the rather reticent harpist in the *Double Concerto*, so the present triptych is highly recommendable.

Karajan recorded the *Clarinet Concerto* on three occasions (the other two with Leopold Wlach and Karl Leister) but the present (1957) version has strong claims to be considered the finest. Karajan's admiration for **Bernard Walton** is well known and his artistry shines through in this selfless and eloquent account. This cannot be too strongly recommended.

(i) Clarinet Concerto; (ii) Oboe Concerto; (iii) Sinfonia concertante for Violin, Viola & Orchestra, K.364

(*) Guild GMCD 7181. (i) Lluna; (ii) Knights; (iii) Studt, Jvania; Bournemouth Sinf., Studt

(i) Clarinet Concerto; (ii) Oboe Concerto; (i–iii) Sinfonia concertante, K.297b

(BB) *** ASV COE CD COE 814. (i) Hosford (basset clarinet); (ii) Boyd; (iii) O'Neill, Williams; COE, Schneider

(i) Clarinet Concerto in A, K.622; (ii) Piano Concerto 27 in B flat, K.595; Symphony 25 in G min., K.183

(M)(**(*)) Dutton mono CDSJB 1026. NYPO, Barbirolli, with (i) Goodman; (ii) Casadesus

(i) Clarinet Concerto; (ii) Clarinet Quintet, K.581

∅—**** Hyp. CDA 66199. King; (i) ECO, Tate; (ii) Gabrieli Qt

∅—(M) **** RCA 82876 60866-2. Stoltzman; (i) ECO; (ii) Tokyo String Qt

*** PentaTone **SACD** PTC 5186 048. Andrew Marriner; (i) ASMF, N. Marriner; (ii) ASMF Chamber Ens.

(i) Clarinet Concerto; (ii) Clarinet Quintet

*** ASV Gold GLD 4001. Johnson; (i) ECO, Leppard; (ii)

Takács-Nagy, Hirsch, Boulton, Shulman (with BAERMANN: *Adagio* ***) – WEBER: *Clarinet Concertino* ***

(i) Clarinet Concerto; Overture: Die Entführung aus dem Serail (arr. Sargent)

(B) (***) BBC Classics mono BBCM 5014-2. (i) Brymer; BBC SO, Sargent (with MENDELSSOHN: *A Midsummer Night's Dream: Nocturne; Wedding March* (**)) – SCHUBERT: *Symphony 8 (Unfinished)* (**)

(i) Clarinet Concerto, K.622; (ii) Clarinet Quintet, K.581; (iii) Exsultate, Jubilate, K.165

∅—(M) **** ASV Platinum PLT 8514. (i) Johnson, ECO, Leppard; (ii) Hilton, Lindsay Qt; (iii) Lott, LMP, Glover

Thea King's coupling brings together winning performances of Mozart's two great clarinet masterpieces. She steers an ideal course between classical stylishness and expressive warmth, with the slow movement becoming the emotional heart of the piece. The **Gabrieli Quartet** is equally responsive in its finely tuned playing. For the *Clarinet Concerto* Thea King uses an authentically reconstructed basset clarinet. With **Jeffrey Tate** an inspired Mozartian, the performance – like that of the *Quintet* – is both stylish and expressive, with the finale given a captivating bucolic lilt. Excellent recording.

Richard Stoltzman gives equally outstanding performances of both works. The *Concerto*, full of spontaneity, brings a comparatively brisk, sparkling tempo in the first movement and a contrasting, leisurely *Adagio*, deeply felt, in which Stoltzman produces the most beautiful timbre and gently embroiders the reprise of the main theme. The Rondo is high-spirited, with the clarinet roulades delightfully bucolic. By directing the **ECO** himself, the soloist controls the work's structure as he wants, and then in the *Quintet* the silky-toned **Tokyo Quartet** provide a seductive backing tapestry and a performance equally full of subtle light and shade, especially striking in the finale. The recording is first class, bright and glowing in both works and admirably balanced.

The smiling faces of **Sir Neville** and **Andrew Marriner** shine forth on the front of their SACD, which offers performances of a comparably gracious warmth, full of affectionate touches and tender nuances. Tempi are relaxed, the lovely *Larghetto* of the *Quintet* is exquisitely and balmily played; but the effect is never bland and the finale has a pleasingly light rhythmic touch. The producer, Andrew Keener, has made good use of the acoustic of the Henry Wood Hall, and the SACD envelops the listener in its friendly ambience. The overall musical tapestry is richly upholstered, not as bright and transparent as the RCA/Stoltzman version, but very beguiling.

This Platinum collection fascinatingly contrasts the styles of two young British clarinettists. **Emma Johnson** has a sense of spontaneity, of natural magnetism which traps the ear from first to last, whether in the sparkle and flair of the outer movements or the inner intensity of the central slow movement. **Leppard** and the **ECO** are in bouncing form, and the recording is first rate. **Janet Hilton** then gives a disarmingly unaffected account of the *Clarinet Quintet* and gets excellent support from the **Lindsays**. The recording is forward, but well balanced and vivid. There are many delights in **Felicity Lott's** *Exsultate, Jubilate*: her clean and stylish singing is well supported by **Jane Glover's** sympathetic conducting, which elicits poised playing from the **LMP**.

This pairing has now been reissued on ASV's Gold label, more generously with Baermann's lovely *Adagio* (once attributed to Wagner) and Weber's delightful *Concertino*.

On the COE disc, **Richard Hosford's** fine account of the *Clarinet Concerto* (see above) is part of an all-Mozart collection where it would be hard to imagine an account of the *Oboe Concerto* that conveys more fun in the outer movements, infectiously pointed and phrased, both by the ever-imaginative **Douglas Boyd** and by his colleagues. The wind soloists in the live recording of the *Sinfonia concertante* are four COE artists who know when to take centre stage and when to hold back in turn. The variations of the finale are a delight.

Recorded live at a Promenade Concert in the 1960s, **Jack Brymer** gives a characteristically luscious account of the *Clarinet Concerto*, with his chalumeau delectably rich. The Mendelssohn encores are well played too, although the *Wedding March* has much more spirit than the comparatively lethargic *Nocturne* (well recognized by the Promenaders). But the surprise here is what appears to be **Sargent's** own arrangement of the *Entführung Overture*, to which is added an elaborately extended coda, exciting enough but sounding more like Beethoven than Mozart.

Joan Enric Lluna's basset-clarinet sounds fascinatingly different, with the lower chalumeau range drier and with more point on the articulation, the effect aurally intriguing. **Andrew Knights's** *Oboe Concerto* is both nimble and full-timbred, enjoyably vivacious. But what makes this triptych especially attractive is the outstanding account of the *Sinfonia concertante*, with **Richard Studt** leading persuasively on the violin and **Nodar Jvania** a most sympathetic partner. The **Bournemouth Sinfonietta** provide excellent accompaniments, but the one drawback here is the close balance, especially of the soloists.

More transfers from Dutton for the **Barbirolli** label, rescuing valuable performances from Sir John's years with the New York Philharmonic. Both the *B flat Concerto*, K.595, with that great Mozartian **Robert Casadesus**, and the 'little' *G minor Symphony*, K.183, recorded on 3 November 1940, were issued commercially on 78-r.p.m. discs, but the *Clarinet Concerto*, with **Benny Goodman** as soloist, from December of that year, has not been available before.

(i) *Flute Concertos 1–2*; (ii) *Flute & Harp Concerto*

(M) *** RCA 82876 59409-2. Galway; (ii) Robles; ASMF, Marriner

(M) *** Decca (ADD) 440 080-2. (i) Bennett, ECO, Malcolm; (ii) Tripp, Jellinek, VPO, Münchinger

James Galway and **Marisa Robles** take an expansive, warmly expressive view of the slow movement of the *Flute and Harp Concerto*; she also matches him in a delightfully bouncy account of the finale. In the solo concertos, too, Galway takes an expansive, expressive view of the slow movements and a winningly relaxed one of the *Allegros*.

William Bennett gives a beautiful account of the concertos, among the finest in the catalogue. Every phrase is shaped with both taste and affection, and the playing of the **ECO** under **George Malcolm** is fresh and vital. The earlier, Vienna recording of the *Flute and Harp Concerto* has also stood the test of time. Refinement and beauty of tone and phrasing are a hallmark throughout, and **Münchinger** provides most sensitive accompaniments.

(i; ii) *Flute Concertos 1–2*; (i–iii) *Flute & Harp Concerto*; (iv) *Divertimento for Strings 1, K.136; 2 Marches, K.335; Serenades 6 (Serenata notturna); 9 (Posthorn)*; (v) *Symphonies 35 (Haffner); 36 (Linz); 38 (Prague); 39 in E flat, K.543; 40 in G min., K.550; 41 in C (Jupiter)*

🗝 ✱ (BB) **** Virgin Classics 5×1 5 61678-2 (5). (i) Coles; (ii) ECO; (iii) Yoshino; (iv) Lausanne CO; (v) Sinfonia Varviso; Menuhin

This is an outstanding Mozartian CD bargain – five discs for the price of one! Moreover, the set would be highly desirable if it cost several times as much. Both the *Flute Concertos* are stylishly and pleasingly played by **Samuel Coles**, and when **Naoko Yoshino** joins him in the delectable *Flute and Harp Concerto* the interplay is fluently appealing. No complaints about the sound either and there is no doubting the character of these performances. The *Serenata notturna* and the *Divertimento* are graceful and fresh, and so is the *Posthorn Serenade*. Menuhin's approach is above all elegantly light-hearted and **Crispian Steele-Perkins** has his brief moment of glory as the posthorn soloist in the Minuet.

Yet when we turn to the last six symphonies, we encounter playing and interpretations of a very special order. The **Sinfonia Varviso** responds warmly to **Menuhin** as the group's chosen President. Though modern instruments are used, the scale is intimate, with textures beautifully clear, and the fresh, immediate sound highlights the refined purity of the string playing. In the last four symphonies speeds are on the fast side, yet he does not sound at all rushed. The *G minor* is especially memorable – among the finest ever recorded. With playing of precision, clarity and bite, one constantly has the feeling of live music-making. Exposition repeats are observed in both first and last movements of the *Jupiter* and this performance, like its partner, takes its place as a top recommendation for the two last symphonies, irrespective of cost.

Flute Concertos 1–2; (i) *Flute & Harp Concerto; Andante in C, K.315; Rondo in D, K.Anh.184*

(N) 🗝 **** BIS SACD 1539. Bezaly, (i) with Palloc; Ostrobothian CO, Kangas

If you begin listening to this superb BIS SACD with the opening *G major Concerto*, using the surround sound, you will surely be immediately seduced by the exquisite solo playing of **Sharon Bezaly**, most persuasively accompanied, and offered within a glowing acoustic. The *Flute and Harp Concerto* which follows, with **Julie Palloc's** delicate harp image, is equally captivating, the whole programme beautifully played and recorded; and it sounds pretty good, too, on normal CD equipment. Comparison with the equally natural Oiseau-Lyre recording of the *Flute and Harp Concerto* (see above) is fascinating, the latter sounding more transparent but not as resonantly seductive as the BIS textures.

(i) *Flute Concertos 1–2;* (ii) *Flute Sonatas 4–6, K.13–15*

(BB) *** Regis RRC 1151. Hall; (i) Philh. O, Thomas; (ii) Alexander-Max

Judith Hall produces a radiantly full timbre; moreover she is a first-class Mozartian, as she demonstrates in her cadenzas as well as in the line of the slow movement, phrased with a simple eloquence that is disarming. There is plenty of vitality in the *allegros* and **Peter Thomas** provides polished, infectious accompaniments to match the solo playing. For the Regis reissue, three of the *Flute Sonatas* have been added. Once again Judith Hall's instrumental personality dominates the music-making, and she is appropriately accompanied by **Susan Alexander-Max** on an Erard pianoforte (*c.* 1846).

(i) *Flute Concertos 1 & 2; Symphony 41 (Jupiter)*

⊕–┐ *** Telarc CD 80624. Boston Bar., Pearlman; (i) with Zoon

Jacques Zoon gives readings of both works that it would be hard to match for both sheer virtuosity and imagination, making the baroque flute sound more like a flute and less like a recorder than usual. Stylishly, he adds substantial cadenzas in both works to slow movements as well as to the first, with **Martin Pearlman** and the **Boston Baroque** sympathetic accompanists. In the *Jupiter Symphony* they come into their own in a most refreshing performance, with the snapping rhythms of the opening motif given a dry, military flavour, and with a military flavour returning at the very end of the finale. The woodwind are cleanly defined, with the strings relatively reticent, but the reading is far from small-scale. An unusual coupling, but a highly enjoyable disc.

(i; iii) *Flute Concerto 1 in G, K.313; Andante in C, K.315;* (ii; iii) *Oboe Concerto in C, K.314;* (iv) *Sinfonia concertante in E flat, K.297b; Serenade 10 in B flat for 13 Wind Instruments, K.361*

(BB) *** EMI Gemini 4 76918-2 (2). (i) Debost; (ii) Bourgue; (iii) O de Paris; (iv) ECO; all cond. Barenboim

Michel Debost gives a charming, sprightly account of the *Flute Concerto* and **Maurice Bourgue** is hardly less appealing in the *Oboe Concerto*, although the resonant sound of the string tuttis tends to spread a little too much. But the importance of this reissue lies with Mozart's less well-known *Sinfonia concertante* and especially the so-called 'Gran Partita'. Here we have expertly blended wind-tone, free from the traces of self-indulgence that occasionally mar **Barenboim's** music-making. Tempi are a little on the brisk side, especially in the first movement – but none the worse for that when the playing itself is so resilient and the quality of the recorded sound so well focused, with excellent body and definition.

Flute & Harp Concerto in C, K.299

(M) *** DG (ADD) 463 648-2. Zöller, Zabaleta, BPO, Märzendorfer – REINECKE: *Harp Concerto*; RODRIGO: *Concierto serenata* ✿ ***

Karlheinz Zöller is a most sensitive flautist, his phrasing a constant source of pleasure, while **Zabaleta's** contribution is equally distinguished. The 1963 recording is clear and clean, if not quite as rich as we would expect today.

(i) *Flute & Harp Concerto in C, K.299;* (ii) *Oboe Concerto*

*** Chan. 9051. (i) Milan, Kanga; (ii) Theodore; City of L. Sinfonia, Hickox – SALIERI: *Double Concerto* ***

A warmly elegant modern-instrument account of this beguiling concerto, with the delicate interweaving of flute and harp given a delightful bloom by the resonant recording. The *Oboe Concerto* is equally sensitive, again with the line of the *Adagio* delectably sustained by **David Theodore**, whose creamy tone is so enticing. Both soloists play their own cadenzas.

(i) *Flute & Harp Concerto; Overture Die Zauberflöte; Symphony 39 in E flat, K.543 (DVD version)*

*** EuroArts DVD 2054678. (i) Patrick Gallois, Fabrice Pierce; O della Svizzera Italia, Marriner (V/D: Mando Bernardinello)

The *Flute and Harp Concerto*, recorded live at the Palazzo dei Congressi in Lugano in 2005, makes a very winning visual experience, with the two distinguished soloists close alongside each other, warmly exchanging the phrases of Mozart's delectable dialogue. **Marriner** looks a shade stern, but the playing itself is elegant and smiling: both the *Overture* and *Symphony* are splendidly alive, and the whole concert is well recorded and perceptively photographed.

(i) *Flute & Harp Concerto; Sinfonia concertante, K.297b*

(BB) *** Naxos 8.550159. (i) Válek, Müllerová; Capella Istropolitana, Edlinger

Richard Edlinger's account of the *Flute and Harp Concerto* is thoroughly fresh and stylish, and the two soloists are excellent. Although the *Sinfonia concertante in E flat, K.297b,* is not quite so successful, it is still very impressive, and it gives much pleasure. Both performances are very decently recorded; in the lowest price-range they are a real bargain.

Horn Concertos 1 in D, K.412; 2–4 in E flat, K.417, 447 & 495

(B) *** CfP 3 82227-2. Briggs, RLPO, Kovacevich – HAYDN: *Trumpet Concerto* ***

Horn Concertos 1 (with alternative versions of Rondo); 2–4; Allegro, K.370b & Concert Rondo in E flat (ed. Tuckwell); Fragment in E, K.494a

(BB) *** Regis RRC 1007. Tuckwell, Philh. O

Horn Concertos 1–4; Concert Rondo in E flat, K.371 (ed. Civil or E. Smith)

*** Chan. 9150. Lloyd, N. Sinfonia, Hickox

Horn Concertos 1–4; Concert Rondo in E flat, K.371; Fragment in E flat, K.494a; (i) Concerto 4, K.495: Rondo (transcribed Flanders & Swan): Ill Wind

(M) **** Telarc CD 80367. Ruske, SCO, Mackerras, (i) with Suart

Horn Concertos 1–4; Concert Rondos: in E flat, K.371 (completed John Humphries); in D, K.514 (completed Süssmayr); Fragment for Horn & Orchestra in E flat, K.370b (reconstructed Humphries)

(BB) **** Naxos 8.553592. Thompson, Bournemouth Sinf.

Horn Concertos 1–4; Rondo, K.514 (completed by both Süssmayr & Tuckwell)

*** ABC Classics ABC 476 5745. Jiang, West Australian SO, Tuckwell

Horn Concertos 1 (including Rondo in D, K.514, completed Süssmayr); 2–4; Concert Rondos in E flat, K.371; in D (alternative finale to K.412, completed Humphries)

*** Häns. 98.316. T. Brown, ASMF, I. Brown

Horn Concertos 1–4; Concert Rondo in E flat, K.371 (reconstructed Greer); Rondo in D, K.485 (reconstructed Jeurisson)

(BB) **** HM HCX 3957012. Greer, Philh. Bar. O, McGegan

Horn Concertos 1–4; Concert Rondo, K.371; Fragments: in E, K.Anh.98a; in E flat, K.370b; in D, K.514 (all ed. Tuckwell)

(M) **** Decca 458 607-2. Tuckwell, ECO

As well as offering superb performances of the four regular concertos using revised texts prepared by John Humphries, the outstanding Naxos issue includes reconstructions of two movements designed for a horn concerto dating from soon after Mozart arrived in Vienna. It is fascinating too to have extra passages in 4, again adding Mozartian inventiveness. **Michael Thompson** plays with delectable lightness and point, bringing out the wit in finales, as well as the tenderness in slow movements. He also draws sparkling and refined playing from the **Bournemouth Sinfonietta**, very well recorded in clear, atmospheric sound.

Another first-class super-bargain set comes from **Lowell Greer**, who uses a modern copy of a Raoux Parisian cor of 1818, which has a most attractive timbre. He plays with complete freedom, disguising the stopped notes skilfully, and his Mozartian line is impeccable. Slow movements are phrased with appealing simplicity and the rondo finales have splendid buoyancy. **McGegan** and his chamber orchestra accompany very stylishly and the recording is excellent.

Born in Shanghai, but a resident of Australia since he was five, **Lin Jiang** has become, under the tutelage of the veteran horn-player Barry Tuckwell, one of the leading instrumental soloists in Australia. Here, using a modern instrument, with **Tuckwell** taking on the role of conductor, he plays the four Mozart *Horn Concertos*, adding a rare alternative version of the *Rondo* finale of the so-called '1', in the key of D. Tuckwell here offers his own completion as well as Süssmayr's. Jiang plays with a rich, opulent sound, beautifully rounded, displaying fine tonal contrasts. His fluency is phenomenal with even the most elaborate passage-work cleanly articulated. There is an easy swing to the *Rondo* of the suspect 1 which is most engaging, and it is good to compare the two different versions offered here. The orchestral sound is fresh and clear, with the strings of the **West Australian Symphony Orchestra** playing with commendable refinement and purity.

For Hänssler, **Timothy Brown** chooses a modern instrument, and his persuasive lyrical line, imaginative phrasing and neat use of cadenzas show him as a true Mozartian. Another of the memorable features of this fine Hänssler disc is the warmth and finesse of **Iona Brown's** stylish accompaniments. The recording too is most natural in balance and sound-quality, and this CD stands high among modern versions of these ever-fresh concertos.

Eric Ruske, principal horn of the Cleveland Orchestra, gives outstandingly fresh performances of the four Mozart *Concertos*. Not only are the famous *Rondos* exceptionally buoyant and sharply rhythmic, but first-movement *allegros* combine elegance with a comparatively swift pacing which is naturally Mozartian in feeling. Slow movements, too, have an equally agreeable lift, as in the *Larghetto* of K.447, while the pointed articulation in the finale is a joy. Ruske is helped by truly vivacious accompaniments from **Mackerras** and the **Scottish Chamber Orchestra**. But what makes this special is the inclusion of *Ill Wind*, the famous Flanders and Swan poem, which exactly fits the *Rondo* of the *Fourth Concerto*. Here the reciter is the celebrated Gilbertian, **Richard Suart**. We feel sure that Mozart himself would have been delighted with the line 'I've lost my horn, lost my horn, found my horn . . . gorn!'

The Decca Ovation reissue (458 607-2) offers **Barry Tuckwell's** third set of the four concertos in excellent digital sound, recorded in the Henry Wood Hall in 1983. The orchestra provides crisp, polished and elegant accompaniments to make a perfectly scaled backcloth for full-timbred solo playing which again combines natural high spirits with a warmly expressive understanding of the Mozartian musical line. This reissue now includes the rest of Mozart's concertante horn music.

Barry Tuckwell's Regis (originally Collins) CD, his fourth recording of the Mozart *Horn Concertos*, remains a splendid alternative choice. They are fresh, without a suspicion of routine, and are played with rounded tone and consistently imaginative phrasing. Moreover the collection is complete.

Tuckwell's EMI Encore 1971 set offers strong, warm performances which have stood the test of time with Marriner's beautifully managed accompaniments. At budget price, with the two short fill-ups, this CD is well worth its modest cost. (EMI 5 74966-2)

Among the more recent versions is a fine Chandos set by **Frank Lloyd**, an outstanding soloist of the new generation. Like Tuckwell, he uses a modern German double horn with great skill and sensitivity. **Hickox** provides admirable accompaniments, and the Chandos recording is well up to the high standards of the house. (Chan. 9150)

Claire Briggs (at the time principal horn of the CBSO) gives brilliant performances of all four concertos, with the celebrated finale of 4 taken exceptionally fast. Even that is superbly articulated without any feeling of breathlessness, though it lacks some of the fun others have brought. This inexpensive disc also includes a first-class account of Haydn's *Trumpet Concerto*.

(i) *Horn Concertos 1–4*; (ii) *Piano & Wind Quintet in E flat, K.452*

🔑 (B) (****) EMI mono 3 38603-2. Brain; (i) Philh. O, Karajan; (ii) Horsley, Brain Wind Ens. (members)

(***) Naxos mono 8.111070. (i) Brain, Philh. O, Karajan; (ii) Gieseking, Philh. Wind Ens.

An EMI bargain reissue of **Dennis Brain's** famous (1954) mono record of the concertos, coupled with the *Quintet*, and this is self-recommending.

The Naxos coupling chooses a different but no less attractive early version of the *Quintet* with **Gieseking**, which many will prefer. Good transfers of these still unsurpassed classic performances.

Oboe Concerto in C, K.314

🔑 (BB) *** ASV CD COE 808. Boyd, COE, Berglund – R. STRAUSS: *Oboe Concerto* ***

(B) *** Hyp. Helios CDH 55080. Francis, LMP, Shelley – KROMMER: *Oboe Concertos* ***

Anyone wanting the delightful and very apt coupling of *Oboe Concertos* by Mozart and Richard Strauss will find **Douglas Boyd** infectiously imaginative in both works – see above. The sound is full and vivid.

Sarah Francis has already given us distinguished performances of oboe concertos by Handel and Telemann. Here she turns to Mozart with equal elegance and is persuasively accompanied by **Howard Shelley** and the **London Mozart Players** who, like their soloist, are completely satisfying in their stylish playing using modern instruments. The closing Rondo is particularly engaging.

Keyboard concertos

(i) *Harpsichord Concertos 1–3, K.107; 2 Klavierstück, K.33b; Minuets, K.1–5; Sonatas: in E flat, K.26; in D, K.29 in B flat, K.31*

*** Naïve OPS 30-9003. Fernandez, (i) with Le Concert Français, Hantaï

Very slight pieces by the child Mozart, but very elegantly played and decently recorded.

Piano concertos

(with list of keys and Köchel numbers)

1 in F, K.37; 2 in B flat, K.39; 3 in D, K.40; 4 in G, K.41; 5 in D, K.175; 6 in B flat, K.238; 8 in C, K.246; 9 in E flat, K.271; 11 in F, K.413; 12 in A, K.414; 13 in C, K.415; 14 in E flat, K.449; 15 in B flat, K.450; 16 in D, K.451; 17 in G, K.453; 18 in B flat, K.456; 19 in F, K.459; 20 in D min., K.466; 21 in C, K.467; 22 in E flat, K.482; 23 in A, K.488; 24 in C min., K.491; 25 in C, K.503; 26 in D, K.537 (Coronation); 27 in B flat, K.595; 2 Pianos: E flat, K.365; 3 Pianos: F, K.242; Concert Rondo in D, K.382; in A, K.386

Piano Concertos 1–6; 8–9; 11–27; Rondo in D, K.382

🔑 (BB) *** EMI (ADD) 5 72930-2 (10). Barenboim, ECO

(B) **(*) DG 469 510-2 (without *Rondo*) (8). Anda, Salzburg Mozarteum O

(i) *Piano Concertos 1–6; 8–9, 11–27; Concert Rondos 1*; (ii) *2*; (iii) *Double Piano Concerto in E flat, K.365*; (iii; iv) *Triple Piano Concerto in F, K.242*

🔑 ❀ (B) **** Sony (ADD/DDD) 82876 872302 (12). Perahia, Lupu, ECO

(B) *** Decca (ADD/DDD) 443 727-2 (10). Ashkenazy, with (i) Philh. O; (ii) LSO, Kertész; (iii) Barenboim, ECO; (iv) Fou Ts'ong

The **Perahia** cycle is a remarkable achievement; in terms of poetic insight and musical spontaneity the performances are in a class of their own. There is a wonderful singing line and at the same time a sensuousness that is always tempered by spirituality. About half the recordings are digital and of excellent quality and, we are glad to report, the earlier, analogue recordings have been skilfully remastered with first-class results, both in this complete set and in the separate issues below. This is an indispensable set in every respect.

Ashkenazy's set with the **Philharmonia** appeared over more than a decade. The account of the *E flat Concerto*, K.365, with **Barenboim** and the **ECO**, and the *Triple Concerto*, with **Fou Ts'ong** to complete the trio, is earlier still (1972). These performances have won golden opinions over the years, and the clarity of both the performances and the recordings is refreshing: indeed, the fine Decca sound is one of their strongest features.

The sense of spontaneity in **Barenboim's** EMI performances of the Mozart concertos, his message that this is music hot off the inspiration line, is hard to resist, even though it occasionally leads to over-exuberance and idiosyncrasies. These are as nearly live performances as one could hope for on record, and the playing of the **English Chamber Orchestra** is splendidly geared to the approach of an artist with whom the players have worked regularly, and the sound is generally freshened very successfully in the remastering.

EMI are now beginning to reissue these recordings separately on Classics for Pleasure, and so far *20 in D min.*, K.466, and *24 in C min.*, K.491, plus the *Piano Sonata in C*, K.545, are available on 2 28278-2; and 22 *in E flat*, K.482, and 23 *in A*, K.488, are on CfP 5 21868-2.

Were the competition not so fierce, **Anda's** often very fine performances could carry a stronger recommendation. They are beautifully poised and have excellent feeling for style; some are quite memorable for their unidiosyncratic freshness. The recordings, made between 1962 and 1969, do not quite match those of Barenboim (the violin timbre is more dated) and Anda is a less individual artist, but the sound is clean and well balanced and the set gives consistent enjoyment.

Piano Concertos 5–6; 8–9; 11–27

(M) *** Decca 448 140-2 (9). Schiff, Salzburg Mozarteum Camerata Academica, Végh

András Schiff's cycle with the **Salzburg Mozarteum Camerata Academica** under **Sándor Végh** proves to be one of the most satisfying and arguably the finest since Murray Perahia's cycle of the late 1970s. Schiff plays a Bösendorfer piano, and its relatively gentle, cleanly focused timbre has something of the precision of a fortepiano without any loss of the colour which comes with a more modern instrument. The recording is consistently more beautiful than in Perahia's Sony set. Just occasionally Schiff dots his 'i's and crosses his 't's a little too precisely, but for the most part he is so musically and perceptive that this seems unimportant. In short, these are lovely performances, enhanced by the quality of the accompaniment under Végh, who is unfailingly supportive. For the most part Schiff plays his own cadenzas, but in the first movement of K.466 he uses a cadenza by Beethoven, and the finale of K.488 brings one by George Malcolm.

Piano Concertos 5–6; 8–9; 11–27; Rondo in D, K.382

(B) **(*) Ph. 475 7306 (8). Uchida, ECO, Tate

(i) Piano Concertos 5–6; 8–9; 11–27; Rondo in D, K.382. Bonus DVD: (ii) Double Piano Concerto in E flat, K.365; (ii; iii)Triple Piano Concerto in F, K.242

(B) *** Warner 2564 61919-2 (8 + Bonus DVD). Barenboim; (i) BPO; (ii; iii) Solti; (iii) Schiff, with ECO

Barenboim rerecorded the *Piano Concertos* for Warner Classics between 1986 and 1998, a number of them at live concerts. The performances are consistently of the highest quality, the earlier concertos made to sound both fresh and mature by the distinction of the playing, not only of Barenboim but also the **Berlin Philharmonic Orchestra**, which he directs from the keyboard. In some of the later works the result is weighty in a way which sometimes makes the music look forward to Beethoven. Overall these performances, which have rather more gravitas than his EMI series, yet remain spontaneous-sounding, are very satisfying in a different way. Moreover to make a very special bonus for this well-documented boxed set Warner have provided a splendid DVD of the *Double* and *Triple Concertos* with **Solti** and **András Schiff** as Barenboim's excellent colleagues. Barenboim leads in the Double Concerto and Solti conducts. Solti leads in the *Triple Concerto* and persuades the **ECO** to play very beautifully indeed. Excellent recording and effectively straightforward camera-work.

Mitsuko Uchida's cycle, which she began in 1985, is now complete, with playing of considerable beauty and performances of the earlier concertos guaranteed never to offend and most likely to delight. She is unfailingly elegant but a little over-civilized, consistently alive and imaginative, although at times one would welcome a greater robustness of spirit, a livelier inner current. Throughout, **Jeffrey Tate** draws splendid playing from the **ECO**, and these artists have the benefit of exceptionally good recorded sound; although the perspective favours the piano, the timbre of the solo instrument is beautifully captured. As one would expect from two artists of this calibre, there are many felicities, but individually none of the performances of the major works here would be a first choice, and 16 is split between two CDs after the first movement.

Piano Concertos (i) 5 in D, K.175; (ii) 8 in C, K.246; (iii) 17 in G, K.453; (iv) 27 in B flat, K.595 (DVD Recordings)

🎬 *** EuroArts DVD 2010248. (i) Frager, Swiss R. & TV O, Andreae (recorded in Teatro Bibiena, Mantua); (ii) Zacharias, Stuttgart RSO, Gelmetti (recorded at the Schwetzingen Palace); (iii) Ránki, ECO, Tate; (iv) Aleksandar Madžar, RPO, Previn (both recorded at the Imperial Palace of Schönbrunn, Vienna) (V/D: János Darvas)

This is one of a series of DVD groups of live Mozart piano concerto recordings using different soloists, conductors, orchestras and venues, with stimulating results. The present collection happily frames early and middle-period works with the composer's very first, entirely original concerto. The partnership of **Malcolm Frager** and **Marc Andreae** seems ideal for the earliest concerto, while the playing of the **Swiss Orchestra** is fresh, polished and vibrant, and the lively recording, brightly transferred, is just right for the music. When we turn to the C major, the bearded conductor, **Gianluigi Gelmetti**, has a rather imposing image, but he is a natural Mozartian and persuasively matches the warmly sensitive Stuttgart accompaniment to **Christian Zacharias's** comparatively intimate style, within a mellower acoustic, so suitable for the graceful *Andante* and delectable finale.

Jeffrey Tate provides a strong, vivid opening ritornello for the G major work, and **Deszö Ránki's** playing has both vitality and delicacy, especially in the exquisite *Andante*, where the fine woodwind playing of the **ECO** so sensitively creates the opening mood. Mozart's last concerto shares the same venue but features the **Royal Phiharmonic Orchestra**, directed by **André Previn** in relaxed rather than valedictory mood. In this work, the camera often centres on the pianist, **Aleksandar Madžar**. All four concertos are beautifully recorded and the camerawork varies in emphasis, but generally the shots of the orchestra, pianist and conductor are well judged. A most rewarding collection in every respect.

Piano Concertos 5, K.175; 9 (Jeunehomme), K.271; 16, K.451

(M) *** Warner Elatus 0927 49827-2. Barenboim, BPO

Barenboim opens his cycle with the **Berlin Philharmonic** with these three comparatively early concertos which show him at his very finest form, free from affectation, both at the keyboard and in directing the Berlin Philharmonic, who are also on top Mozartean form.

Piano Concertos 6, K.238; 8, K.246; 19, K.459

(BB) *** Naxos 8.550208. Jandó, Concentus Hungaricus, Antal

19 in F is a delightful concerto and it receives a most attractive performance, aptly paced, with fine woodwind playing, the finale crisply sparkling. 6 is hardly less successful; if 8 seems plainer, it is still admirably fresh. With excellently balanced recording this is a genuine bargain.

Piano Concertos in B flat: 6, K.238; 15, K.450; 27, K.595

*** Warner 2564 62259-2. Aimard, COE

It is not often one gets three Mozart piano concertos on a single disc – and all in the same key, too. They are all engagingly spontaneous works, and the performances sunny and cultivated to match. **Pierre-Laurent Aimard** directs the orchestra from the keyboard, but the only way that shows is in the unity with the soloist and this collection is very easy to enjoy.

Piano Concertos 6, K.238; 17, K.453; 21, K.467

(M) *** DG (ADD) 447 436-2. Anda, Salzburg Mozarteum Camerata Academica

Géza Anda's poetic account of the *C major Concerto*, K.467, is one of the most impressive from his cycle, notably for a beautifully poised account of the slow movement. In the *G major*, K.453, there is both strength and poetry, while the DG recording is excellent in both balance and clarity. The *B flat Concerto*, K.238, is played simply and eloquently and this remains a most enjoyable triptych.

Piano Concertos (i) 6 in B flat, K.238; (ii) 19 in F, K.459; (iii) 20 in D min., K.466 (DVD Recordings)

*** EuroArts **DVD** 2010238. (i) Zacharias, Stuttgart RSO, Gelmetti (recorded at the Schwetzingen Palace); (ii) Lupu, Deutsche Kammerphilharmonie, Zinman (recorded at the Sophiensaal, Munich); (iii) Ivan Klánský, Virtuoso di Praga, Jiří Bělohlávek (recorded at the Rittersaal of Palais Waldstein) (V/D: János Darvas)

Zacharias and **Gelmetti** have already given us a fine account of K.246, and their performance of the comparatively mild K.238 is hardly less felicitous.

It is then a great pleasure to sit and identify with the audience's welcome for **Radu Lupu** when he comes on to the platform for his distinguished account of the *F major Concerto*. We see a great deal of him (and of his hands) during the performance, and his intensity of concentration is formidable. The conductor **David Zinman** is a pleasure to watch too, as he conjures wonderfully sensitive playing from the **Deutsche Kammerphilharmonie**.

After this excellence, the *D minor* could well have been an anticlimax, but **Bělohlávek's** intense, stormy opening sets the scene dramatically so that **Ivan Klánský's** piano entry can provide the poetic contrast mirrored in his calm facial expression. The same contrast between serenity and turbu-

lence is caught in the *Romance*, and the finale then overflows with energy.

Piano Concertos 8 in C, K.246; 9 (Jeunehomme), K.271

⊕→ (M) *** Ph. 475 7777. Uchida, ECO, Tate

This is one of the most successful of **Mitsuko Uchida's** Mozart concerto couplings and, as it happens, the so-called *Jeunehomme Concerto*, K.271, was written for a woman pianist of that name. But these are works that suit Uchida's flowing style, with both slow movements sensitively played and no lack of momentum in outer movements. Some may like greater robustness, but there is no lack of freshness or subtlety of colour. The recording too is first class, beautifully balanced, with a very real piano image. It is now reissued in Universal's series of Originals.

Piano Concertos (i) 9 in E flat (Jeunehomme), K.271; (ii) 12 in A, K.414; (i) 17 in G, K.453; (ii) 19 in F, K.459; Rondos: in D, K.382; A min., K.511

(B) *** Erato (ADD) 0927 41397-2 (2). Pires, with (i) Gulbenkian Foundation O, Guschlbauer; (ii) Lausanne CO, Jordan

Piano Concertos 12, K.414; 19, K.459

(BB) *** Warner Apex 2564 60161-2. Pires, Lausanne CO, Jordan

Piano Concertos 13 in C, K.415; 14 in E flat, K.449; 21 in C, K.467; 23 in A, K.488; 26 in D (Coronation), K.537; Rondo in A, K.386

(B) *** Erato (ADD) 0927-41396-2 (2). Pires, Gulbenkian Foundation O, Guschlbauer

Maria João Pires recorded these Mozart concertos in the 1970s, before fame had overtaken her. They are refreshingly musical and full of character, and no allowances need be made for the sound. Readers wanting bargain accounts of these concertos can rest assured that these are far more than serviceable – indeed, they have style as well as the accomplished musicianship one expects from her. Eminently recommendable.

Piano Concertos (i) 9 in E flat (Jeunehomme), K.271; (ii) 12 in A, K.414; (iii) 26 (Coronation), K.537 (DVD Recordings)

*** EuroArts **DVD** 2010218. (i) Uchida, Salzburg Mozarteum O, Tate (recorded at the Mozarteum, Salzburg); (ii) Ashkenazy, RPO (recorded at Hampton Court Palace, London); (iii) Francsch, Deutsche Kammerphilharmonie, Albrecht (V/D: János Darvas)

We already have a recording of the *Jeunehomme Concerto* from **Uchida**, on CD, but this Salzburg account with **Jeffrey Tate** is finer. She is at her freshest and plays with appealing simplicity. Tate and the **Salzburg Mozarteum Orchestra** are splendid partners, and Uchida can concentrate on her own solo role, and here she is a pleasure to watch.

Pianists almost always tend to look awkward conducting from the keyboard when the camera takes a frontal view. But **Ashkenazy** manages better than most in the introduction to the *A major Concerto*, K.414, and of course the orchestra plays very stylishly, with the full beauty of the *Andante* shared equally by the keyboard and the orchestra. The finale is rhythmically irresistible in its light-hearted brio, and the recording is remarkably successful, considering the venue.

Homero Francsch is the least known of the soloists in this series so far, but, although he is visually a little restless to watch, he is an excellent Mozartian, and so is **Gerd Albrecht**, who draws elegant and polished playing from the **Deutsche Kammerphilharmonie** in the *Coronation Concerto*. The performance is beautifully proportioned, with a serene slow movement framed by outer movements of striking vitality.

Piano Concertos (i) 9 (Jeunehomme), K.271; (ii) 14, K.449; (iii) 22, K.482; (iv) 27, K.595; Serenade 13 (Eine kleine Nachtmusik), K.525

(***) Pearl mono GEMS 0167 (2). Perpignan Festival O, Casals, with (i) Hess; (ii) Istomin; (iii) Serkin; (iv) Horszowski

A welcome two-CD set of four Mozart concertos from the 1951 Perpignan Festival with **Horszowski** and **Dame Myra Hess** both inspired, with **Casals** conducting. Casals brought humanity and wisdom to all his music-making.

Piano Concertos 9, K.271; 15, K.450

Ⓜ (***) DG mono 474 024-2 (5). Kempff, SRO, Munchinger – BEETHOVEN: *Concertos 1–5*; BRAHMS: *Concerto 1*; LISZT: *Concertos 1–2*; SCHUMANN: *Concerto* (***)

These long-forgotten mono recordings, made in 1953 for Decca, provide a valuable successor to DG's limited-edition box of **Kempff's** 1950s concerto recordings. The clarity and sparkle of his playing, making for consistently transparent textures, is matched by the tender poetry of such movements as the C minor slow movement of K.271.

Piano Concertos 9, K.271; 15, K.450; 22, K.482; 25, K.503; 27, K.595

⊛ Ⓑ **** Ph. Duo (ADD) 442 571-2 (2). Brendel, ASMF, Marriner

The account of the opening *Jeunehomme* is finely proportioned and cleanly articulated, with a ravishing account of the slow movement. **Brendel** is hardly less fine in K.450, and the E flat *Concerto* has both vitality and depth. 25 (there is well-deserved applause at the close) was recorded at a live performance and has life and concentration, and a real sense of scale. Here as elsewhere the playing of the **ASMF** under **Marriner** is alert and supportive. K.595 is also among Brendel's best Mozart performances, with a beautifully poised *Larghetto* and a graceful, spirited finale. Highly recommended.

Piano Concertos 9, K.271; 17, K.453

⊛ Ⓜ **** Chan. 9068. Shelley, LMP

Howard Shelley's playing is a delight and is possessed of a refreshing naturalness which should win many friends. There is spontaneity and elegance, a strong vein of poetic feeling and extrovert high spirits. His *G major Concerto* belongs in the most exalted company and can withstand comparison with almost any rival. But both performances

are touched by distinction, and they are beautifully recorded too.

Piano Concertos 9 (Jeunehomme); 18 in B flat, K.456

⊛ ❋ **** EMI 5 57803-2. Andsnes, Norwegian CO

Outstanding Mozart playing from **Leif Ove Andsnes** and the **Norwegian Chamber Orchestra**, and first-rate sound too. This is one of the most natural in style and completely musical accounts of Mozart that we have had recently.

Piano Concertos 9 in E flat (Jeunehomme), K.271; 20 in D min., K.466; 23 in A, K.488; 24 in C min., K.491

⊛ ⒷⒷ **** Virgin 4-CD 5 62259-2 (4). Pletnev, Deutsche Kammerphilharmonie – HAYDN: *Piano Concertos & Sonatas* ****

Piano Concertos 9 in E flat (Jeunehomme), K.271; 24 in C min., K.491

Ⓑ **** Virgin 3 65467. Pletnev, Deutsche Kammerphilharmonie

Pletnev and the **Deutsche Kammerphilharmonie** have obviously established a close rapport, and each of these performances is individually and positively characterized. The *Jeunehomme* certainly sounds youthful, bringing crisp, precise articulation in the first movement and a poised *Andante*, yet with real expressive depth, followed by a brisk, attractively jaunty finale. The cadenzas are Mozart's own.

The uneasy, *sotto voce* opening of the D minor, K.466, is full of underlying tension, which is maintained throughout the strong tuttis, but **Pletnev** relaxes completely for the delicate lyrical secondary theme. In this concerto he uses Beethoven's cadenzas, which bring a sudden striking change of mood in the finale, otherwise light-hearted. In Pletnev's hands the slow movement of K.488 is among the most beautiful on record, the finale the most rushed. Here he returns to Mozart's cadenzas. But in the *C minor Concerto* (K.491) he is again intensely dramatic, Beethovenian in feeling and powerful in conception. Excellent recording throughout. This now comes recoupled in a budget box with equally impressive performances of piano concertos and sonatas of Haydn.

Piano Concertos 9, K.271; 25, K.503

**** None. 7559 79454-2. Goode, Orpheus CO

Richard Goode is now embarking on a Mozart concerto series. The **Orpheus Chamber Orchestra** are consistently at one with him in matters of phrasing and style, and they immediately establish the boldly expansive character of the great *C major Concerto*, K.503. These are performances of much character, beautifully recorded. Mozart's cadenzas are used in K.271, but Goode uses his own in K.503.

Piano Concertos 9 in E flat (Jeunehomme), K.271; 25 in C, K.503; Rondo in A, K.386

*** Onyx 4013. Rogé, Indianapolis SO, Leppard

Pascal Rogé is sensitive and a subtle Mozartian – as, it goes without saying, is **Raymond Leppard**. A thoroughly recommendable disc, which will give much musical satisfaction to those who invest in it.

Piano Concertos 11 in F, K.413; 12 in A, K.414; 13 in C, K.415 (chamber versions)

*** Hyp. CDA 67358. Tomes, Gaudier Ens.

There are few recording pianists to match **Susan Tomes** in clarity of articulation, and here she leads performances which sparkle from beginning to end, with every note cleanly defined. Speeds are relatively fast, with slow movements kept moving to bring out their soaring lyricism.

Piano Concertos 11, K.413; 14, K.449; 15, K.450

🎔 🌸 (M) *** Warner Elatus 2564 60116-2. Barenboim, BPO

All three works show **Barenboim** in his very finest Mozartian style, both at the keyboard and in directing the **Berlin Philharmonic**. The orchestral contributions in opening movements are imposing without being too heavy, and they bring much grace to slow movements. Finales are no less engaging, particularly in K.413; and witness the string-playing at the opening of the superb Rondo of K.449. The *B flat Concerto* is a live performance, but the others are by no means studio-bound. Barenboim's keyboard articulation is a constant joy, as is his pearly tone; and somehow he manages to give the first movement of the *F major*, K.413, an extra youthful freshness that places it before the others in the development of the composer's style. But it is the joyous spontaneity of the music-making throughout that makes this triptych so cherishable.

Piano Concertos 12, K.414; 14, K.449; 21, K.467

(BB) *** Naxos 8.550202. Jandó, Concentus Hungaricus, Ligeti

In **Jenő Jandó's** hands the first movement of K.449 sounds properly forward-looking; the brightly vivacious K.414 also sounds very fresh here, and its *Andante* is beautifully shaped. The excellent orchestral response distinguishes the first movement of K.467: both grace and weight are here, and some fine wind-playing. An added interest in this work is provided by Jandó's use of cadenzas provided by Robert Casadesus. Jandó is at his most spontaneous throughout these performances and this is altogether an excellent disc, well recorded.

Piano Concertos 12, K.414; 19, K.459

🎔 (M) *** Chan. 9256. Shelley, LMP

Another fine disc in **Howard Shelley's** musically rewarding and beautifully recorded series. Admirers of this artist need not hesitate in investing here, with the music's expressive range fully encompassed without mannerism, slow movements eloquently shaped and outer movements aptly paced and alive with vitality.

Piano Concertos 12, K.414; 20, K.466; Rondo in D, K.382

*** RCA 09026 60400-2. Kissin, Moscow Virtuosi, Spivakov

The *D major Rondo*, K.382, has an elegance and delicacy worthy of the greatest Mozart players of the day. The *A major Concerto*, K.414, shows the same immaculate technical finesse

and musical judgement (save, perhaps, in the slow movement, which some could find a little oversweet). There are perhaps greater depths in the *D minor Concerto* than **Kissin** finds but, even so, the playing is musical through and through and gives unfailing pleasure. The recorded sound is very good and the disc as a whole deserves the attention of any Mozartian.

Piano Concerto 13 in C, K.415 (DVD version)

🎔 🌸 **** TDK **DVD** DV-VERSA. Barenboim, BPO (with Concert ***)

This outstanding DVD brings a captivating account of this early concerto, greatly enhanced on video, with the empathy between pianist/conductor and his players communicating directly and magically to the viewer. The other works in the programme are Ravel's *Le Tombeau de Couperin* and Beethoven's *Eroica Symphony*, also very finely played.

Piano Concertos 13, K.415; 14 in E flat, K.449; 23 in A, K.488

(BB) *** Warner Apex 2564 60448-2. Pires, Gulbenkian Foundation CO of Lisbon, Guschlbauer

Maria João Pires, in a triptych of her earliest recordings (1973–4) for Erato, plays with spirit and taste as well as immaculate small-scale fingerwork. Her playing at that time reminds one a little of Ingrid Haebler's earliest records for Vox, and she offers many personal insights. **Guschlbauer** gives her most musical support and provides robust orchestral tuttis in the outer movements of the two early concertos. The recording can hardly be faulted, for the engineers provide a realistic balance and the sound is warm and pleasingly intimate. An enjoyable bargain.

Piano Concertos 13, K.415; 24, K.491

🎔 (M) **** Chan. 9326. Shelley, LMP

Howard Shelley has immaculate keyboard manners and his strong, natural musicianship is always in evidence. An instinctive yet thoughtful Mozartian whose consummate artistry places his cycle among the very finest now on the market.

Piano Concertos 14, K.449; 17, K.453; 21, K. 467

(M) *** DG 477574-7. Pires, COE or VPO, Abbado.

This is a reissue of Pires's coupling of Concertos 17 and 21 (see below) with the E flat major concerto, added, and a reduction to mid-price in the Mozart Collection.

Piano Concertos 14 in E flat, K.449; 21 in C, K.467; 6 German Dances, K.571; March, K.335

(***) BBC Legends mono BBCL 4227-3. Serkin, ECO, Schneider

Rudolf Serkin's performance, along with the *Dances*, comes from the 1964 Edinburgh Festival, and is full of delight and freshness. The *C major Concerto* comes from the Guildhall two years later and also conveys the lightness of touch and depth you would expect. **Alexander Schneider** is as always a supreme Mozartian and the sound, if a little distant in balance, is still very acceptable.

Piano Concertos 14, K.449; 27, K.595

⊶ Ⓜ **** Chan. 9137. Shelley, LMP

Admirable performances, stylish and with a fine Mozartian sensibility. This is altogether most refreshing, and the recording is very good indeed.

Piano Concertos 15 in B flat, K.450; 23 in A, K.488

**(*) Arte Nova 82876 64014-2. Kirschnereit, Bamberg SO, Bermann

The *B flat Concerto* is one of the finest performances so far in **Matthias Kirschnereit's** Bamberg cycle. The opening movement is attractively spirited and robust, while the central theme and variations is played with warmth and elegance, and the bouncing finale is highly infectious. The first movement of the *A major*, too, is fresh and strong rather than mellow, but the lovely *Adagio*, taken very gently and slowly, makes the fullest contrast; and the finale again sparkles, with attractive woodwind detail, yet with no lack of weight. Throughout, **Frank Bermann** provides a vivid orchestral profile, with a realistic balance.

Piano Concertos (i) 15 in B flat, K.450; (ii) 23 in A, K.488; 24 in C min., K.491

⊶ ✸ **** Testament mono SBT 1222. Solomon, Philh. O; (i) Ackermann, (ii) Menges

This is quite exceptional Mozart playing: it has depth and serenity, impeccable grace and wit, and an incomparable sense of style. Almost half a century has passed since these recordings were made, and they have been out of circulation most of that time. They are in a class of their own. Remarkably good sound.

Piano Concertos (i) 15, K.450; (ii) 24, K.491

Ⓑ (***) Dutton mono CDBP 9714. Kathleen Long; (i) Nat. SO, Boyd Neel; (ii) Concg. O, Van Beinum – FAURÉ: *Ballade*; LEIGH: *Concertino* (***)

These two vintage recordings of Mozart concertos, together with the works by Fauré and Walter Leigh, provide a superb memorial to a British pianist who has not been given credit for her inspired artistry. In Mozart the pearly clarity of her articulation is a delight throughout, not least in the lilting finale of K.450. Excellent Decca *ffrr* sound, superbly transferred.

Piano Concertos 16, K.451; 24–5; 26 (Coronation); 27

Ⓑ **(*) Double Decca 475 181-2 (2). Schiff, Camerata Academica des Mozarteum, Salzburg, Végh

András Schiff's playing has exemplary taste and is distinguished by refined musicianship. There is a wonderful unanimity of phrasing and musical thinking from the strings and some superb wind-playing, every note finely placed and every phrase shaped with keen sensitivity. One snag is that the rare *D major Concerto*, K.451, is split between the two CDs.

Piano Concertos 16, K.451; 25, K.503; Rondo in A, K.386

Ⓑ *** Naxos 8.550207. Jandó, Concentus Hungaricus, Antal

Jenő Jandó gives a very spirited and intelligent account of the relatively neglected *D major Concerto*, K.451, in which he receives sensitive and attentive support from the excellent **Concentus Hungaricus** under **Mátyás Antal**. The players sound as if they are enjoying themselves and, although there are greater performances of the *C major Concerto*, K.503, on record, few are at this extraordinarily competitive price.

(i) Piano Concerto 17 in G, K.453; Symphony 39 in E flat, K.543 (DVD version)

✸ **** EuroArts DVD 2072098. Bernstein, VPO (Director: Humphrey Burton)

Bernstein's approach is different in each work. He plays the concerto with wonderfully affectionate warmth, indulging himself in the sheer pleasure of the music, especially in the magically seductive slow movement, and, with a minimum of gesture, encouraging the great Vienna orchestra to match his response. Then the finale unwinds into sheer joy with one of Mozart's most engaging rondo themes. The *Symphony* then follows, bursting with incandescent energy and power (all repeats taken) and, in the *Andante*, rich, expressive feeling. Fortunately, Humphrey Burton is in charge and he directs the cameras with characteristic prescience (at one point he catches Bernstein when he stops conducting altogether and lets the orchestra play on by themselves). The sound is absolutely first class and this is not to be missed.

Piano Concertos 17, K.453; 18, K.456

ⒷⒷ *** Naxos 8.550205. Jandó, Concentus Hungaricus, Antal

This is one of the finest in **Jandó's** excellent super-bargain series. Tempi are admirably judged and both slow movements are most sensitively played. Jandó uses Mozart's original cadenzas for the first two movements of K.453 and the composer's alternative cadenzas for K.456. Excellent sound.

Piano Concertos 17 in G, K.453; 20 in D min., K.466

⊶ ✸ *** EMI 5 00281-2. Andsnes, Norwegian CO
*** Virgin 3 44696-2. Anderszewski, Scottish CO

Andsnes's account of the *G major*, K.453, has everything that this glorious score calls for: sparkle in its first movement, poignancy in the second and a sense of joy in the finale. It has been hailed as 'great playing by any standards' and ranks among the most exalted company, Edwin Fischer and Perahia. Similarly the *D minor* is a performance of stature and depth. The recording is expertly balanced, lifelike and natural.

Piotr Anderszewski is an artist whose approach to music-making is fresh yet well thought out, sensitive, touched by distinction and without the slightest trace of fussiness or preciosity. There is a blend of musical imagination and pianistic finesse that makes this unfailingly illuminating.

Piano Concertos 17 in G, K.453; 21 in C, K.467

*** DG 439 941-2. Pires, COE, Abbado

Maria João Pires's playing, both in the mercurial *G major Concerto* and in its more ceremonial *C major* companion, is elegant, searching and intelligent. She has taste and fine musicianship, and the **Chamber Orchestra of Europe** under

Abbado give excellent support. Good recording. But see also under *Concerto 14.*

Piano Concertos 17, K.453; 27, K.595

(BB) *** Regis (ADD) RRC 1154. Brendel, V. Volksoper O, Angerer

Brendel was an inspired Mozartian when he made his earlier Mozart recordings for the Vox Turnabout label at the end of the 1950s and beginning of the 1960s; these performances have a radiant freshness and spontaneity which he did not always match in his later, Philips versions. The recording is thin in the matter of violin-tone, though it has good ambience, and at Brendel's first entry one forgets this fault, for the piano is realistically recorded and convincingly balanced in relation to the orchestra. Brendel is helped by a vivacious orchestral contribution in both works. 27 is very distinguished and can be spoken of in the same breath as Gilels's version.

Piano Concertos 18, K.456; 19, K.459

*** HM HMX 3957138. Tan (fortepiano), Philh. Bar. O, McGegan

Piano Concertos 18 in B flat, K.456; 19 in F, K.459; Rondo in D, K.382

🎵 ❀ (M) *** Warner Elatus 2564 60810-2. Barenboim, BPO

Barenboim immediately puts his personal seal on this CD with his captivating account of the *D major Rondo*, a work of much charm but also repetitive, which lends itself to flexibility. Here, by imaginative variation of tempo and dynamic, it sounds wonderfully fresh. But so do both the Concertos. They are brimming over with Barenboim's joy in the music, with delightfully sprung rhythms and winningly felicitous slow movements. The totally infectious finales end each work in a mood of blissful happiness. The **Berlin Philharmonic** respond to Barenboim's flair and affectionate elegance with especially elegant woodwind playing, and the recording balance could not be improved on. A treasure of a disc – and Barenboim uses Mozart's own cadenzas.

No one is more convincing on the fortepiano than **Melvyn Tan**. The pointedly rhythmic main theme of the *F major Concerto* suits the fortepiano particularly well – which is not to say that the *Allegretto* isn't equally winning, with some delightful wind-playing from these characterful period instrumentalists. The *B flat Concerto* is hardly less successful. **McGegan** and his players are clearly completely at one with their soloist. The recording is more intimate, slightly drier than in Malcolm Bilson's DG series, and the result is most persuasive.

Piano Concertos 18, K.456; 20, K.466

🎵 **** None. 7559 79439-2. Goode, Orpheus CO

Yet another entirely captivating coupling in **Richard Goode's** outstanding series with the **Orpheus Chamber Orchestra**. The lightly sprung opening movement of the *B flat Concerto*, K.456, is sheer delight. There is no finer performance in the catalogue. The mood then changes completely for the dark opening of the *D minor Concerto*. The piano enters simply, but then engages in a dialogue which readily hints at the music's histrionic associations with *Don Giovanni*, and the dynamic finale is suitably impassioned. Goode uses Mozart's second cadenza in the first movement of K.456 and Beethoven's in the equivalent movement of K.466, composing one of his own for the finale. A superb disc, splendidly balanced and recorded.

Piano Concertos 19, K.459; 23, K.488 (DVD Recording)

**(*) DG DVD 073 4097. Pollini, VPO, Boehm – BEETHOVEN: *Piano Concertos 3 & 5;* BRAHMS: *Piano Concerto 2* **(*)

Pollini's Mozart always has style and pianistic distinction, and Böhm was a wonderful Mozartian. These recordings were made at the Musikvereinsaal in April 1976 and the video direction of Hugo Käch is eminently discreet and unobtrusive. It is difficult to find fault with playing of this distinction and dedication, shorn as it is of any expressive exaggeration, but it is not always possible to warm to it. There is no want of pianistic or orchestral beauty, but there is an aloof quality to which not everyone will respond.

Piano Concertos 19 in F, K.459; 27 in B flat, K.595

🎵 **** None. 7559 79608-2. Goode, Orpheus CO

What shines out here is the illusion of live performance, even though these come from the studio. Goode's approach is purposeful and direct, as well as magnetically individual, with natural weight and gravity reflecting his equivalent mastery as a Beethovenian. At such a moment as the hushed B minor opening of the development in the first movement of K.595, Goode has you marvelling afresh at a modulation that is quite extraordinary for a movement in B flat major. Not that Goode's Mozart has anything heavy about it, with the finales of both works marked by lightness, wit and sparklingly clear passage-work. The piano-tone is firm and full, though the orchestra could be more forwardly placed after the opening tuttis.

Piano Concerto 20 in D min., K.466

(M) *** DG (ADD) 463 649-2. S. Richter, Warsaw PO, Wislocki (with BEETHOVEN: *Piano Concerto 3; Rondo* *(*))

Richter proves his virtuosity by restraint, and this is the quality running right through his extremely fine performance of the *D minor Concerto*. He lets Mozart's music speak for itself, but whether in the choice of tempo, a touch of rubato or some finely moulded phrase, his mastery is always apparent. The slow movement is beautifully shaped, its opening theme phrased with perfect grace, and the closing pages are exquisite. The buoyancy of the finale is a joy. **Wislocki** and the **Warsaw Orchestra** provide an accompaniment of character, and although the recording sounds dated in the matter of string-tone, the piano image remains realistic. This reissue is fully worthy to take a place among DG's 'Originals', and it is a pity that the coupling is so disappointing.

Piano Concertos 20, K.466; 21, K.467; 23, K.488; 24, K.491; 25, K.503

Ⓑ *** Double Decca (DDD/ADD) 452 958-2 (2). Ashkenazy, Philh. O

This Double Decca set, reissued for **Ashkenazy's** sixtieth birthday, now includes both the D minor and C minor masterpieces, but not K.595 (27), which, however, remains available on a slightly different permutation at a similar cost – see below. K.491 and K.503 are among the finest in his series, so the present grouping is particularly attractive. The Kingsway Hall recordings cannot be faulted. They were made between 1977 and 1983; 20, 23 and 25 are digital.

(i) Piano Concertos 20–21; 23; 27; Sonata 17 in D; Rondo in A min., K.511

Ⓑ *** Double Decca (ADD/DDD) 436 383-2 (2). Ashkenazy, (i) Philh. O

This alternative set, with slightly different contents, is also highly recommendable on all counts, with the four favourite Mozart *Piano Concertos* included, plus a splendid *Sonata* and a charming *Rondo*. **Ashkenazy's** performance of the *B flat Concerto* is as finely characterized as one would expect. The *Sonata* and *Rondo* were recorded earlier (in 1967); the playing is equally fine.

Piano Concertos 20 in D min., K.466; 22 in E flat, K.482

🎧 Ⓑ **** Regis RRC 1273. Tirimo, Prague CO

There is no other bargain coupling of Mozart piano concertos to surpass this Regis disc, splendidly recorded in Athens in 2004. In both the *D minor Concerto*, with its atmospheric *sotto voce* opening, and the winningly fresh *E flat Concerto*, the slow movements are played by **Tirimo** with an appealing delicacy of feeling, yet not a hint of precocity, and outer movements are crisply articulated and full of vitality. The finale of K.482 is irresistibly vivacious, helped by superb accompaniments from the **Prague Chamber Orchestra** (the woodwind excel themselves), directed with élan from the keyboard by the pianist. Not to be missed, even if duplication is involved.

Piano Concertos 20, K.466; 23, K.488

🎧 Ⓜ **** Chan. 8992. Shelley, LMP

Those wanting this coupling with modern instruments will find **Howard Shelley's** performances immensely rewarding. Characterization is strong, yet the slow movement of K.488 is very beautiful and touching. Splendid Chandos recording.

Piano Concertos (i) 20; (ii) 23; 24; 26 (Coronation); (i) 27

Ⓜ *** Decca (ADD) 468 491-2 (2). Curzon; (i) ECO, Britten; (ii) LSO, Kertész

Always a perfectionist and especially so in Mozart, **Curzon** was seldom satisfied with his performances, always feeling he could do better. Initially only K.466 and K.491 were approved by the soloist for release, yet K.595 was hardly less distinguished, while K.488 and K.491 were eventually released together. Even if they are slightly less fine and as such bear out Curzon's doubts, by any normal standards this is

pianism of distinction. The additional attraction of the present set is the inclusion of K.537 (hitherto unavailable on CD) where Curzon is completely seductive in the *Larghetto* and sparkles happily in the finale. Strong support from the **LSO**, although **Kertész** perhaps proved a rather less imaginative accompanist than **Britten**. The recordings, made in the Kingsway Hall or the Maltings, are up to Decca's highest standards.

Piano Concertos 20, K.466; 24, K.491

🎧 **** Sony 82876 73714-2. Stadtfeld, NDR SO, Weil

*** Ph. 462 622-2. Brendel, SCO, Mackerras

The prize-winning German pianist, **Martin Stadtfeld**, gives electrifying accounts of both these concertos in a true partnership with **Bruno Weil** and the **North German Symphony Orchestra**. Both concertos here have darkly dramatic openings, the *C minor* work especially so, and Weil brings out their tragic feeling with orchestral tuttis of great power and tempi which carry the music strongly forward. When Stadtfeld enters in K.491, the tension is maintained, yet the secondary theme emerges with true Mozartian lyricism. At the end of the first movement he plays a subjective and musing cadenza of his own, slowing the tempo right down, which some may feel is intrusive. But the performance has such conviction and character that it is easy to forgive this indulgence which would be fully acceptable at a concert. The *Larghetto* has an appealing simplicity, while the mood of the finale is perfectly judged.

Brendel recorded this coupling with Neville Marriner in 1974 and now, more than a quarter of a century later, he gives accounts that are hardly less thoughtful without being wanting in spontaneity and which, if anything, are more searching and articulate. Moreover, in **Mackerras** he here has a partner who is one of the most experienced of Mozartians. This is a popular coupling: it is recorded with great realism and can be accommodated among top recommendations.

(i) Piano Concerto 20 in D min., K.466; (ii) Triple Piano Concerto in F, K.242; (iii) Symphony 32 in G, K.318; (iv) Rondo in C, K.373; Adagio in E, K.261

Ⓝ *** Opus Arte DVD OA 1004D. (i–ii) Argerich, (ii) Paul & Rico Gulda; (i–iii) New Japan PO, Arming; (iv) Renaud Capuçon

Martha Argerich and her musical companions radiate a delight in music-making that makes this concert, recorded in Tokyo, a highly enjoyable and satisfying musical experience. The camerawork is devoid of gimmickry and places the listener to good advantage throughout. What a fine and expressive player **Renaud Capuçon** is! In the *D minor Concerto* Argerich is magisterial.

Piano Concertos 21, K.467; 22 in E flat, K.482

🎧 **** Chan. 9404. Shelley, LMP

Ⓜ *** EMI (ADD) 5 62750-2. Fischer, Philh. O, Sawallisch

Ⓝ Ⓜ **(*) EMI 2 17270-3. Biss, Orpheus CO

Howard Shelley's cycle continues to delight, and the *C major* has dignity, intelligence and poetic feeling. The *E flat* has poise and breadth, and the winds of the **London Mozart**

Players are heard to good advantage. These performances can be confidently recommended alongside the very finest rivals.

Miss **Fischer's** gentle, limpid touch, with its frequent use of half-tones, still gives much pleasure. The slow movements of both concertos are beautifully done, and the pianist's intimate manner is often shared by the Philharmonia wind soloists, who offer playing of polish and delicacy. **Sawallisch's** contribution is also considerable, and his firm directing hand ensures that neither performance becomes effete and the recording is nicely balanced, the piano full in tone, and the orchestra does not sound too dated.

Jonathan Biss has been collecting golden opinions in recent years, and this coupling of two Mozart concertos will enhance his standing. He has good taste and fine musicianship, and though this splendidly recorded disc would not supplant our top recommendations, it is certainly worth considering alongside them.

Piano Concertos 21, K.467; 23, K.488

(B) *** Virgin 3 63292-2. Pommier, Sinfonia Varsovia

Piano Concertos 21; 23; Rondos for Piano & Orchestra 1 in D, K.382; 2 in A, K.386

●━ (M) **** Sony (DDD/ADD) SMK 89876. Perahia, ECO

Both concertos capture **Perahia's** very special Mozartian sensibility and are beautifully recorded. The C major, K.467, is given delicacy and charm with an exquisite slow movement and spirited finale. The slow movement of K.488 has an elevation of spirit that reaffirms one's conviction that this is indeed a classic recording. The two Concert Rondos incorporated for the first time on record the closing bars newly rediscovered by Professor Alan Tyson.

Both Virgin performances have plenty of sparkle in outer movements – the first movement of K.467 is particularly arresting – and both slow movements are played simply and beautifully. **Jean-Bernard Pommier's** Adagio in K.488 compares favourably with Brendel's, and the string-playing at the famous opening of the Andante of K.467 is ravishing in its transparent delicacy and gentle warmth. The finale of the same work is brisk but never sounds rushed. The sound is first class.

Piano Concertos 21, K.467; 24, K.491

(BB) *** Regis RRC 1067. Shelley, City of L Sinfonia

Howard Shelley's delightfully fresh and characterful readings of these fine concertos are outstanding value at budget price.

Piano Concertos (i) 21 in C; (ii) 24 in C min., K.491

(M) (*(**)) EMI mono 4 76884-2. (i) Lipatti, Lucerne Festival O; (ii) Gieseking, Philh. O; both cond. Karajan

Lipatti's performance derives from a broadcast from the 1960 Lucerne Festival; the orchestral sound is not well focused and there is some discoloration and distortion at climaxes. However, nothing can detract from the distinction of Lipatti's playing or its immaculate control. This is now reissued with **Gieseking's** poised, aristocratic (1953) account

of the C minor Concerto, K.491. Here the Kingsway Hall recording is excellent. But it would surely have been better to keep this an all-Lipatti CD.

Piano Concertos 21, K.467; 26 (Coronation)

(M) *** DG Entrée 471 738-2. Pires, COE or VPO, Abbado

Pires's playing in the C major Concerto is elegant, searching and intelligent. She has taste and fine musicianship, and the **Chamber Orchestra of Europe** under **Abbado** give excellent support. The Coronation Concerto is, if anything, even finer. Recorded at a live performance (with a virtually silent, spellbound audience), this is completely captivating, especially the slow movement.

(i) Piano Concertos 21, K.467; 26 (Coronation), K.537; (ii) 12 Variations on 'Ah, vous dirai-je, Maman', K.265

●━ ✿ (BB) *** Sony SBK 67178. (i) Casadesus, Columbia SO or Cleveland O, Szell; (ii) Previn (piano)

The ravishing slow movement of K.467 has never sounded more magical than here, and **Robert Casadesus** then takes the finale at a tremendous speed; but, for the most part, this is exquisite Mozart playing, beautifully paced and articulated. Casadesus's Mozart may at first seem understated, but the imagination behind his readings is apparent in every phrase.

(i) Piano Concerto 22, K.482; Adagio & Fugue in C min., K.546; (ii) Sinfonia concertante, K.364

*** BBC (ADD) BBCB 8010-2. (i) Richter; (ii) Brainin, Schidlof; ECO, Britten

With **Britten** as partner, **Sviatoslav Richter** gives an inspired reading of the Mozart concerto, for which Britten specially wrote new cadenzas, which are in use here. Though the sound is not as cleanly focused as in a studio recording, it is warmly atmospheric, as it is in the other two works. In the Sinfonia concertante Britten equally charms his two soloists from the **Amadeus Quartet**, making them relax in spontaneously expressive playing, with the lightness of the finale a special delight.

Piano Concertos 22 in E flat, K.482; 27 in B flat, K.595; Adagio & Fugue in C min.

●━ (****) BBC Legends (mono) BBCL 4206-2. Richter, ECO, Britten

Recorded at Aldeburgh Festivals these two BBC radio recordings, superbly engineered by James Burnett are far more revealing than any of **Richter's** studio recordings. Not only are his agility and clarity of articulation a marvel, the beauty of his legato is magical. In this he is accompanied by **Benjamin Britten**, always an inspired partner of artists he admires, fresh and vigorous. The great C minor Adagio and Fugue, with Britten conducting the **ECO**, is darkly tragic in its power.

(i) Piano Concerto 23 in A, K.488; Adagio in B min. K.540; Rondo in D, K.485

(**(*)) BBC mono BBCL 4111-2. Hess, (i) with LPO, Boult – BEETHOVEN: Piano Concerto 4 **(*)

Dame Myra Hess recorded disappointingly little commercially. Dating from October 1961, the Mozart concerto performance was her very last in public, following her decision after a stroke to retire. You would never know that she was in anything but the most robust health from the vigour of her performance, with the finale taken at such a lick that the **LPO** under **Boult** finds it hard to keep up. The two separate solo pieces, which come as a valuable makeweight, are taken from studio recordings made in 1958.

Piano Concertos 23, K.488; 24, K.491

☞ ******** None. 7559 79489-2. Goode, Orpheus CO

Richard Goode gives an outstandingly fresh and satisfying account of Mozart's most lovable *A major Concerto*, the slow movement serenely beautiful and the finale delightfully vivacious. The opening tutti of K.491 is formidably strong and forward-looking, but the movement unfolds with a natural Mozartian flexibility, and Goode's playing in the *Larghetto* has a ravishing simplicity. The jaunty finale is nicely paced and gets attractively bolder as it proceeds. Throughout both works, the ear notices the sensitive contributions of the **Orpheus** woodwind as well as the elegant finish and warmth of the strings. Goode uses Mozart's cadenza in K.488 and, enterprisingly, one by Paul Badura-Skoda in K.491.

Piano Concerto 24 in C min., K.491

(****(*)**) VAI mono VAIA 1192-2 (2). Tureck, Oslo PO, Güner-Hegge – BACH: *Clavier Concertos 1, 5 & 7; in D min.* ****(*)**

Needless to say, **Rosalyn Tureck's** account, recorded live, is full of character, as is the accompaniment, although the actual orchestral playing could be more polished. Her style is both direct and flexible. She plays her own cadenzas and overall this is certainly an enjoyable account, the solo part beautifully articulated, if not as distinctive as her Bach. The finale is particularly strong. The mono recording is in every way excellent and well balanced too.

Piano Concertos 24 in C min., K.491; 25 in C, K.503. Fantasia in D min., K.397

Ⓝ ☞ ******** Avie AV 2175. Cooper, N Sinf., Creswick

This is certainly one of the key Mozart concerto couplings of 2008. **Imogen Cooper** plays with ravishing delicacy and refinement, and many engaging touches of detail. She is listed as co-director of the orchestra with **Bradley Creswick**, and certainly the orchestra plays very beautifully too. The account of the (solo) *Fantasia in C minor* is equally magical, taken at a hauntingly slow tempo. Outstanding recording too: this is a CD not to be missed.

Piano Concertos 24 in C min., K.491; 27 in B flat, K.595

Ⓜ ******* Medici Masters MM010-2. Casadesus, Cologne RSO, Szell (with WEBER: *Konzertstück in F min.*, cond. Hubertus (*******))

Casadesus and **Szell** often recorded Mozart together in Cleveland during the 1950s and early '60s, but these two concertos were made in 1958 and 1960 with the **Cologne Radio Orchestra** and have the same distinction and aristocratic grace that we find in their collaboration for CBS. The Weber *Konzertstück* is marvellously done with wit, finesse and felicitous finger-work and comes from 1954 (in mono) with the same orchestra under **Romanus Hubertus**. The sparkle of the performances outweighs the inevitable sonic limitations.

(i) Piano Concerto 25, K.503; Symphony 38 (Prague); (i; ii) Concert aria: Ch'io mi scordi di te

*** MDG 340 0967-2. (i) Zacharias (piano); Lausanne CO, Zacharias; (ii) with Fink

Christian Zacharias, in consistently refreshing performances, relishes his multiple roles, not just conducting a fresh and lively account of the *Prague Symphony*, but also acting as piano soloist; in the *Concerto*, he directs the weighty K.503 from the keyboard and also provides a crisply pointed obbligato in the most taxing of Mozart's concert arias, *Ch'io mi scordi di te*. **Bernarda Fink** with her firm, creamy voice, officially a mezzo, is untroubled by the soprano tessitura, giving the most characterful interpretation, imaginatively pointing words and phrases. The sense of freedom and spontaneous enjoyment is here enhanced by the clarity of the recording, made in the Metropole, Lausanne.

Piano Concertos 25 in C, K.503; 27 in B flat, K.595; Rondo in A, K.386

ⒷⒷ ******* Arte Nova 82876 64016-2. Kirschnereit, Bamberg SO, Beerman

Matthias Kirschnereit plays with vitality and elegance and **Frank Beerman** and the **Bamberg Symphony Orchestra** give him persuasive support. The playing is full of spontaneous vitality and the recording is excellent. With a vivacious account of the *Rondo* for good measure, this is excellent value.

Piano Concerto 26 (Coronation), K.537

*** BBC (ADD) BBCL 4020-2. Curzon, BBC SO, Boulez – BEETHOVEN: *Piano Concerto 5 (Emperor)* *******

Curzon and **Boulez** in this 1974 Prom performance of the *Coronation Concerto* make rewarding partners. The combination of introspection and intellectual rigour results in an inspired reading of one of the more problematic Mozart piano concertos, fresh, bright and resilient in the outer movements with pearly passage-work, and thoughtfully unmannered in the slow movement. Full-bodied sound, set in the warm acoustic of the Royal Albert Hall.

Piano Concertos 26, K.537; 27, K.595

☞ Ⓜ ******* Warner Elatus 2564 60679-2. Barenboim, BPO

This 1988–9 coupling from **Barenboim** is first class in every way, beautifully played, with warm, vigorous accompaniments from the **Berlin Philharmonic** which do not sound inflated. There is a hint of sobriety in both slow movements, but they are both memorable and each is perfectly offset by the light-hearted contrast of the finale which follows. A most enjoyable coupling, drawn from a highly distinguished cycle.

Piano Concerto 27; (i) Double Piano Concerto, K.365

☞ 🏵 Ⓜ ******** DG (ADD) 463 652-2. Emil Gilels, VPO,

Boehm, (i) with Elena Gilels (with SCHUBERT: *Fantasy in F min., D. 940*)

Gilels's is supremely lyrical playing that evinces all the classical virtues. All the points are made by means of articulation and tone, and each phrase is marvellously alive, while **Boehm** and the **Vienna Philharmonic** provide excellent support. The performance of the marvellous *Double Concerto* is no less enjoyable. Its mood is comparatively serious, but this is not to suggest that the music's sunny qualities are not brought out. The Schubert bonus has been added for the CD's rightful reissue as one of DG's 'Legendary Originals'.

(i; iv) *Piano Concerto 27, K.595;* (i; ii; iv) *Double Piano Concerto, K.365;* (i; iii) *Double Piano Sonata in D, K.448*

(***) BBC (ADD) stereo/mono BBCL 4037-2. (i) Curzon; (ii) Barenboim (piano); (iii) Britten; (iv) ECO, Barenboim

The two concertos, set in the warm Royal Albert Hall acoustic, come from a Prom concert in 1979, with **Barenboim** directing from the keyboard in the *Double Concerto* and conducting in Mozart's last *Piano Concerto, K.595,* **Curzon's** favourite. This is Mozart at his most joyous. The *Duo Sonata* finds Curzon in 1960 in a partnership with **Britten** at Jubilee Hall, Aldeburgh, and though the mono sound is far drier, it is firm and immediate, letting one appreciate another exuberant performance with the middle movement bringing delectable interplay between the players.

(i) *Piano Concerto 27, K.595;* (ii) *Double Piano Concerto in E flat, K.365. Rondo in A min., K.511*

(N) (BB) (***) Naxos mono 8.111294. Schnabel, with (i) LSO, Barbirolli; (ii) Karl-Ulrich Schnabel, LSO, Boult

Artur Schnabel's account of the *B flat Concerto* with **Barbirolli** conducting the **LSO** was one of the mainstays of the prewar HMV catalogue, and it is good to hear its virtues so vividly restored. Good, too, to have the 1936 version of the *Double Concerto* with Schnabel's son, **Karl-Ulrich,** and **Boult.** The *A minor Rondo* was a post-war recording, marvellously played, and one of the products of Schnabel père's 1946 visit to London. Mandatory listening.

(i; ii) *Piano Concerto 27, K.595;* (iii) *Piano Quartet in G min., K.478;* (iv; ii) *Exsultate, jubilate, K.165*

*** BBC (ADD) BBCB 8005-2. (i) S. Richter; (ii) ECO, Britten; (iii) Britten, Sillito, Aronowitz, Heath; (iv) Ameling

Britten as conductor in **Richter's** reading of K.595 is warmer in his Mozart style than his soloist, just as persuasive as he is in his recording with Clifford Curzon. Best of all is the *Piano Quartet,* where Britten's expressiveness even in the simplest scale passage has one magnetized, a great performance. Though the string sound in the concerto is a little thin, the other two recordings are excellent. As an encore **Elly Ameling** has never sounded more sweetly radiant on disc than in this account of *Exsultate, jubilate,* technically immaculate.

Double Piano Concerto in E flat, K.365

*** Chan. 9711. G. and S. Pekinel, Philh. O, Marriner – BRUCH; MENDELSSOHN: *Double Piano Concerto* ***

This unique coupling of the *Double Piano Concertos,* devised by the **Pekinel** sisters, is an inspired one, even though the Mozart is the only masterpiece among the three works. It receives a fresh, alert reading, marked by superb ensemble from the two soloists, helped by vivid Chandos sound.

(i) *Double Piano Concerto in E flat, K.365; Triple Piano Concerto in F (Lodron), K.242* (arr. for 2 pianos); *Andante & Variations in G, K.501; Fantasia in F min., K.608* (arr. Busoni)

⊛ (M) *** Sony 518811 [SK 92735]. Perahia, Lupu; (i) with ECO

Murray Perahia and **Radu Lupu** are in good form in both concertos. The performances emanated from public concerts at The Maltings, Snape, between 1987 and 1990, and they have much of the excitement and spontaneity of live music-making. The two pianists are beautifully matched in both works, and again in the *Variations* and Busoni's transcription of the *F minor Fantasy,* originally written for a musical clock.

(i) *Double Piano Concerto in E flat, K.365;* (ii) *Sinfonia concertante for Violin, Viola & Orchestra, K.364a*

(N) ⊛ (M) **** Chan. 10507X. (i) Gimse, Anvik; (ii) Iona Brown, Tomter; Norwegian CO, I. Brown

It is surprising that these two greatest of Mozart's 'double concertos' are not more regularly coupled, occupying adjacent Köchel numbers, both dating from 1779. Before she left us, **Iona Brown** built the **Norwegian Chamber Orchestra** into a superb body. It is good to welcome two brilliant young Norwegian pianists in K.365, light and agile, each articulating with refreshing clarity, relishing the antiphonal effects. In the elegant, spontaneously expressive account of the *Sinfonia concertante* the contrast between the soloists is more striking, when Iona Brown's clear, bright violin tone is set against the nut-brown warmth of **Lars Tomter's** viola. They make the slow movement the central point of their interpretation, with the closing section particularly moving, and the sparkling finale then follows on naturally. Full, clear Chandos sound. Highly recommended, especially at mid-price.

Violin concertos

Violin Concertos 1–5 (DVD and CD versions)

⊛ **** DG DVD 073 4210 (2); CD 474 215-2 (2). Mutter, Camerata Salzburg (V/D: Andy Sommer)

Violin Concertos 1–5; (i) *Sinfonia concertante for Violin, Viola & Orchestra, K.364* (DVD version)

⊛ *** DG DVD 073 4157 (2). Kremer, VPO, Harnoncourt; (i) with Kashkashian (V/D: Klaus Lindemann, Rodney Greenberg or Horant Hohfeld)

Anne-Sophie Mutter has had the *Violin Concertos* of Mozart as part of her very being since the beginning of her career. 'He's the composer I have grown up with, who was always there waiting for me, at every juncture of my career.' But these recordings (made live in December 2005 in the

Salzburg Mozarteum at the end of a long tour) are special. She hardly conducts at all, except to start a concerto; her body movements are enough, for she has already established a complete rapport with the players of the **Salzburg Camerata**, whose ensemble is marvellously crisp and who are at one with her expressively in every bar of the music. Her performances, as before, show complete mastery and total freshness, yet they have the added maturity of long experience without loss of spontaneity. The audience is remarkably silent, but the drawback is that the camera angles are very restless, constantly changing shots of her from various positions, as well as observing key parts of the orchestral contribution. But one adjusts, and this set can be strongly recommended. In a bonus film she talks about her performing life, and members of the orchestra comment on their experience of working with her.

Gidon Kremer unites exceptionally well with the wild-eyed but visibly involved **Nikolaus Harnoncourt** and, with the **Vienna Philharmonic** playing superbly, this is exceptionally vivid music-making. The solo concertos are played simply and stylishly, but Harnoncourt's always alive and richly expressive accompaniments give the music-making the kind of lift which ensures that Kremer's playing never slips into routine. But the highlight of the set is Mozart's masterly *Sinfonia concertante*, where **Kim Kashkashian** joins the partnership and adds to the intensity of feeling. She has a glorious tone and the interplay between the soloists in the slow movement is ravishing, followed by the gloriously infectious finale. The recording is splendidly balanced.

Adagio for Violin and Orchestra in E, K.261; Rondo for Violin and Orchestra in C, K.373

BB (***) Naxos mono 8.110975. Milstein, RCA Victor SO, Golschmann – DVOŘÁK; GLAZUNOV: *Violin Concerto* (***)

These Mozart pieces are given with all the elegance and finesse – and purity – that **Milstein** commanded, and make a splendid foil to the Dvořák and Glazunov *Concertos*.

Violin Concertos 1–5; Adagio in R, K.261; Rondo Concertante in B flat, K.268

☰— **** PentaTone Surround Sound **SACD** PTC 5186 044 (1,2,5); PTC 5186 064 (3-4 and *Adagio*, K.261; *Rondo*, K.269). Julia Fischer, Netherlands CO, Kreizberg

Violin Concertos 1–5; Adagio in E, K.261; Rondo in C, K.373; Rondo Concertante in B flat, K.269

☰— **B** **** O-L Double 455 721-2 (2). Standage, AAM, Hogwood

(i) Violin Concertos 1–5; (ii) Adagio in E, K.261; Rondo in C, K.373; (i; iii) Sinfonia concertante, K.364

☰— **B** **** Ph. (ADD) Duo 438 323-2 (2). Grumiaux, (i) LSO, C. Davis; (ii) New Philh. O, Leppard; (iii) with Pellicia

Violin Concertos 1–5; Adagio in E, K.261; Rondo Concertante in B flat, K.269

BB *** Virgin 2x1 Double 5 61576-2 (2). Huggett, OAE

Violin Concertos 1–5; (i; ii) Concertone in C, K.190; (i) Sinfonia concertante for Violin, Viola & Orchestra, K.364

☰— **M** **** Avie AV 2058 (3). Mintz, with (i) Shaham; (ii) Anderson; ECO

Violin Concertos 1–5; Rondos 1–2, K.269 & K.373

M *** Sony SM2K 89983 (2). Lin, ECO, Leppard

Violin Concertos 1–5; (i) Sinfonia concertante, K.364

N *** DG 477 371 (2). Carmignola, O Mozart, Abbado; (i) with Waskiewicz

(i) Violin Concertos 1–5; (ii) Violin Sonatas 32 in B flat, K.454; 34 in A, K.526

M *** Ph. (ADD) stereo/mono 464 722-2 (2). Grumiaux, (i) LSO, C. Davis; (ii) Haskil

Shlomo Mintz's naturally flowing classical simplicity of line and gleaming tone are a joy throughout, yet these performances are deeply felt. Mintz directs the **ECO** himself from the bow, and they provide the most polished, elegant and supportive accompaniments, with bouncing rhythms in *Allegros* and lovely, warm phrasing of slow movements. (One notices in passing the glowing contribution of the horns.) The *Concertone*, with a delightful oboe contribution from **John Anderson**, is captivating, agreeably lightweight, while both here and in the lyrically flexible account of the inspired *Sinfonia concertante* **Hagai Shaham** proves an admirable violin partner. Mintz chooses himself to take the viola part in the latter, which brings an almost improvisatory feeling. The recordings bring a clarity and intimacy as well as warmth in the sound which, thanks to clean separation, never feels constricted.

Masterly playing from the magnificent Netherlands ensemble and the impeccable **Julia Fischer**. Wonderfully musical performances, exceptionally well recorded, too. They have been highly praised, and rightly so, as splendid modern-instrument recordings, full of style and beautifully phrased, with ravishing slow movements especially in K.261 and K.281 (which makes the second CD particularly memorable). The recording, made in the Waalse Kerk, Amsterdam, has a pleasingly warm acoustic without blurring detail. Whether heard through two or four speakers, the expansive sound is very persuasive, with the soloist ideally balanced. The back speakers add a fine sense of sitting within the church itself.

The young Italian virtuoso **Giuliano Carmignola** was a semi-finalist at the 1974 International Tchaikovsky Competition, and members of the Orchestra della Scala who were there alerted Abbado to his talent. They played the Mozart concertos with the period-instrument **Orchestra Mozart**, and established a close rapport; and **Carmignola** joined them to record these concertos in 2007. With Abbado's agreement, he decided to choose bright tempi throughout and articulation which is 'very clean and spare', while vibrato had 'to be used in a controlled way and never as an end in itself'. Both soloist and conductor sought 'to convey a new feeling of energy, vitality and freshness'. Carmignola's partner in the *Sinfonia concertante*, **Danushka Waskiewicz**, is hardly less accomplished. These recordings were made at Bologna in 2007 and must be ranked among the finest in this repertoire, whether on period or modern instruments. Impeccable recording.

Grumiaux's accounts of the Mozart *Violin Concertos* come from the early 1960s and are still among the most beautifully played in the catalogue at any price. The orchestral accompaniments have sparkle and vitality, and Grumiaux's contribution has splendid poise and purity of tone. For this generous reissue on their bargain Duo label, Philips have added the *Adagio*, K.261, and *Rondo*, K.373, recorded later in 1967, and also a fine performance of the great *Sinfonia concertante*, K.364, with **Arrigo Pellicia** proving a sensitive partner for Grumiaux, especially in the *Andante*. Grumiaux's set comes alternatively with two late *Violin Sonatas*, where he is admirably partnered by **Clara Haskil**. This was a celebrated partnership and these classic vintage accounts are of the highest calibre. The recordings from the late 1950s are mono, and although the sound is remarkably vivid and true, this is not made clear on the packaging. Nevertheless these are treasurable performances.

Anyone seeking period-instrument performances need look no further than **Standage's** superb Oiseau-Lyre set. Standage's beautifully focused, silvery tone is a constant joy. **Hogwood's** accompaniments are beautifully sprung, with no lack of warmth, the orchestral violins articulating neatly and gracefully to match the soloist and the transparent textures revealing every detail of the orchestral scoring. The shorter pieces are also given fine performances and are never treated just as encores. The 1990 Abbey Road recording is first rate throughout, beautifully balanced and with not a trace of edginess anywhere.

Monica Huggett provides an admirable alternative. She directs from the bow and she is a superb soloist: spontaneous, vital, warm and elegant. She plays her own cadenzas, and very good they are too. Orchestral textures are fresh and transparent, ensemble is excellent, and the solo playing is without even a drop of vinegar; indeed, the violin timbre, if not opulent, is firm, well focused and sparkling.

Cho-Liang Lin creates a ready partnership with **Leppard** and the **ECO**, and his persuasive style brings a combination of effervescence and delicacy matched by the orchestra, with appealing tenderness in slow movements and plenty of dash in finales. Lin is full of fancy and imagination; there is an element of youthful lightness running through these performances, though there is no lack of bite or point either. But this is essentially sweet, elegant playing in a traditional but uninflated style. First-class recording.

Violin Concertos 1 in B flat, K.207; 2 in D, K.211; 3 in G, K.216

*** Virgin 3 44706-2. Biondi, Europa Galante

Fabio Biondi's Virgin disc, almost certainly part of a projected complete cycle, is a stimulating demonstration of period performance of these concertos. Biondi plays with great vivacity and a balancing expressive feeling, and **Europa Galante**, which he directs from the bow, match his vitality

and lyrical intensity. The recording has great presence and realism, and this is very recommendable indeed.

Violin Concertos (i) 1 in B flat, K.207; (ii) 2 in D, K.211; 4 in D, K.218; (i) Adagio in E, K.261

(M) *** EMI 5 62825-2. Mutter; (i) ASMF, Marriner; (ii) Philh. O, Muti

Anne-Sophie Mutter was given very sensitive support from both **Muti** and **Marriner**. Her playing combines purity and classical feeling, delicacy and incisiveness, and is admirably expressive. Its freshness is also most appealing. Moreover, the digital recording is consistently good, the images clearly defined and the balance very satisfactory.

Violin Concertos 1 in B flat, K.207; 3 in G, K.216; 5 in A, K.219

*** Australian Decca Eloquence (ADD/DDD) 476 2748. Brown, ASMF

Violin Concertos 1 in B flat, K.207; 3 in G, K.216; (i) Sinfonia concertante for Violin, Viola & Orchestra, K.364

(N) (M) *** Virgin 502112-2. Renaud Capuçon, SCO, Langrée; (i) with Tamestit

Violin Concertos 2 in D, K.211; 4 in D, K.218; (i) Sinfonia concertante in E flat, K.364

*** EMI 3 78374-2. Vengerov, UBS Verbier O, (i) with Power

*** Australian Decca Eloquence (ADD/DDD) 476 2747. Brown, ASMF; (i) with Suk

Maxim Vengerov here beautifully scales his powerful tone down to suit the talented young players of the **UBS Verbier Orchestra**. Vengerov's rapport with them results in fresh and spontaneous-sounding performances throughout, very distinctive, if occasionally including idiosyncratic interpretative points, as in the slow start of the *Sinfonia concertante*. Vengerov builds a beautifully balanced partnership with the superb viola-player, **Lawrence Power**, in the *Sinfonia concertante*. Warm and full recording.

Renaud Capuçon favours brisk tempi – the finale of the *B flat major Concerto* in particular is played with sparkling bravura – but these are enjoyably alive performances, and in the *Sinfonia concertante* he is well partnered by **Antoine Tamestit** who has an attractively full viola timbre. They play the slow movement expressively, but not quite as movingly as Iona Brown and Lars Tomter on Chandos (see above).

Iona Brown's accounts of the Mozart *Violin Concertos* (originally on Argo) have the advantage of including another fine account of the great *Sinfonia concertante*, in which she is joined by **Josef Suk**. The performances of the solo concertos have a freshness and vigour that are winning, and, like the newer Avie set, the participants convey a sense of pleasure in what they are doing. There is a spring-like quality to this music-making. The only slight reservation concerns the *Sinfonia concertante*, where there is an element of restraint in the slow movement, which does not quite blossom here as it does in the finest versions. Nevertheless, these two CDs fully deserve a three-star recommendation.

Violin Concerto 3 in G

☦ (BB) *** EMI Gemini (ADD) 3 81487-2 (2). D. Oistrakh, Philh. O – BEETHOVEN: *Triple Concerto*; BRAHMS: *Double Concerto*; PROKOFIEV: *Violin Concerto 2* ***

*** Warner 2564 61561-2. Rachlin, Bav. RSO, Jansons – BRAHMS: *Violin Concerto in D* ***

David Oistrakh's supple, rich-toned yet essentially classical style suits the melodic line of this youthful work and gives it the stature of maturity. The orchestral contribution is directed by the soloist himself and is eminently polished. EMI provide admirably smooth yet vivid sound, and this is just one of four marvellous performances which make up this superb Gemini compilation.

In **Rachlin's** version of K.216 it is striking that, though a full symphony orchestra is involved, **Jansons** keeps it in scale with the music. Even before the soloist enters, the brisk tempo and the lightness of texture establish the qualities of the reading, and despite the speed there is no feeling of rush, just of a persuasively taut interpretation. The central *Adagio* is marked by ultra-refined playing from soloist and orchestra alike. The finale, like the first movement, is fast, light and transparent, with a winning lilt.

Violin Concertos 3; 5 (Turkish)

Ⓜ *** DG (ADD) 457 746-2. Mutter, BPO, Karajan

(BB) *** Naxos 8.550063. Nishizaki, Capella Istropolitana, Gunzenhauser

Extraordinarily mature and accomplished playing from **Anne-Sophie Mutter**, who was a mere fourteen years old when her recording was made. The instinctive mastery means that there is no hint of immaturity: the playing has polish, but fine artistry too and remarkable freshness. **Karajan** is at his most sympathetic and scales down the accompaniment to act as a perfect setting for his young soloist. The recording has been transferred brilliantly to CD, though some might feel that the orchestral strings are a shade too brightly lit.

This is the finest of **Nishizaki's** three discs of the Mozart *Violin Concertos* on Naxos. The readings are individual and possess the most engaging lyrical feeling and the natural response of the soloist to Mozartian line and phrase. A good balance, the soloist forward, but convincingly so, and the orchestral backcloth in natural perspective. A real bargain.

Violin Concerto 4, K.218

(BB) (***) Naxos mono 8.110946. Szigeti, LPO, Beecham – BEETHOVEN: *Violin Concerto* (***)

Szigeti's account of this Mozart concerto comes in harness with his memorable Beethoven with Bruno Walter. Szigeti was in his prime when this was made, and his individuality shines through.

Violin Concertos (i) 4, K.218; (ii) 5 (Turkish) K.219

Ⓑ *** Nim. NI 1735 (3). Shumsky, SCO, Y. P. Tortelier – BACH: *Concertos*; YSAŸE: *Sonatas* ***

Shumsky's performances are of the highest calibre. They are totally unaffected, spontaneous, and full of character. He has an excellent rapport with **Yan Pascal Tortelier**, who secures a warm, very alive and musical response from the **Scottish Chamber Orchestra**, with the players themselves conveying enthusiasm and pleasure. The recording is natural and nicely balanced. This now comes as part of a memorial box to profile the three major recordings which Shumsky made for Nimbus before he died in 2000. It is inexpensive and with good documentation; it is well worth acquiring.

Violin Concerto 5 (Turkish)

Ⓜ *** DG (ADD) 447 403-2. Schneiderhan, BPO, Jochum – BEETHOVEN: *Violin Concerto* *** ✦

(***) Testament mono SBT 1228. Kogan, Conservatoire O, Vandernoot – BEETHOVEN: *Violin Concerto* (***)

Ⓝ (BB) (***) Naxos 8.111288. Heifetz, LSO, Sargent – BACH: *Violin Concertos* (****)

This was perhaps the finest of the complete set of Mozart's *Violin Concertos* which **Schneiderhan** recorded with the **Berlin Philharmonic** in the late 1960s. The recording is realistically balanced, and this makes a generous coupling for his famous record of the Beethoven, made six years earlier.

Matching the outstanding account of the Beethoven *Concerto* with which it is coupled, **Kogan's** 1957 version of Mozart, recorded later in the same month, is comparably strong and purposeful in the first movement, positive in the expressive contrasts. The slow movement is sweet and tender, poetic without self-indulgence, and the finale sparkles in its contrasting sections. Excellent transfer to make one forget the absence of stereo.

Heifetz recorded the *Turkish Concerto* at least three times, once with Barbirolli and once with a chamber orchestra which he directed himself. The present account is predictably memorable, and **Sargent** proves a supportive partner. Mark Obert-Thorn's transfer of the 1951 Abbey Road recording is clear and clean but a little thin on top.

Concertone in C., K.190; Sinfonia concertante, K.364

☦ ✦ Ⓜ **** DG 477 575-5. Perlman, Zukerman, Israel PO, Mehta

The DG version of the *Sinfonia concertante* is in a special class and is an example of 'live' recording at its most magnetic, with the inspiration of the occasion caught on the wing. **Zubin Mehta** is drawn into the music-making and accompanies most sensitively. The *Concertone* is also splendidly done; the ear notices the improvement in the sound-balance of the studio recording of this work. But the *Sinfonia concertante*, with the audience incredibly quiet, conveys an electricity rarely caught on record.

Concertone; Sinfonia concertante, K.364; Rondo, K.373

☦ ✦ **** Pentatone Surround Sound **SACD** PTC 5186 098. Fisher, Nikoli , Netherlands CO, Kreizberg

The Pentatone coupling does not have the advantage of live recording in the *Sinfonia concertante*, but the surround sound is glorious, and **Julia Fischer** and **Gordan Nikolić** give a totally memorable account, easily matching that of Perlman and Zukerman on DG, fine as they are. So we see no reason for our ✿ not to be shared by both discs. The *Concertone* (where Nikolić changes to violin) is plainer, but still most enjoyable, and Fischer offers the *C major Rondo* as a bonus between the two major works.

DANCES AND MARCHES

12 German Dances, K.586; 6 German Dances, K.600; 4 German Dances, K.602; 3 German Dances, K.605

(BB) *** Naxos 8.550412. Capella Istropolitana, Wildner

Fresh, bright, unmannered performances of some of the dance music Mozart wrote right at the end of his life. The playing is excellent and the recording is bright and full. An excellent super-bargain.

DIVERTIMENTI

Divertimenti and serenades

Divertimenti for Strings 1–3, K.136–8; Serenades 6 in D (Serenata notturna), K.239; 13 in G (Eine kleine Nachtmusik), K.525

(M) **(*) Classic fM 75605 57024-2. City of L. Sinfonia, Watkinson

These are delightful performances from the **City of London Sinfonia**: fresh, warm and polished. *Eine kleine Nachtmusik* is elegant, graceful and nicely paced, and the same can be said of the three engaging *String Divertimenti*. The *Serenata notturna* features the leaders of each section (two violins, viola and double bass) as a solo concertino group, and with the timpani not over-dominant. The resonance of the recording is rather excessive but, if you don't mind that, this Classic fM programme is very recommendable.

Divertimento 1 in D, K.236; Serenade in D (Serenata notturna), K.239; Serenade in D (Posthorn), K.328

🎧➔ (BB) *** Virgin 2x1 4 82112-2 (2). Lausanne CO, Y. Menuhin – SCHOENBERG: *Verklaerte Nacht*; WAGNER: *Siegfried Idyll*; WOLF: *Italian Serenade* ***

An exceptionally attractive anthology of what is all essentially string music. The little *Divertimento* sparkles in **Menuhin's** hands and the *Serenades* are equally light-hearted and fresh, with **Crispian Steele-Perkins** in his element in his brief appearance in the Minuet of the *Posthorn Serenade*.

Divertimento 2 in D, K.131; 15 in B flat, K.287

(BB) *** Naxos 8.550996. Capella Istropolitana, Nerat

The playing of the **Capella Istropolitana** under **Harald Nerat** is beautifully turned and polished. The *D major Divertimento* is charmingly scored for flute, oboe, bassoon, four horns and strings, but it has a gracious second-movement *Adagio* cantilena of disarming simplicity for strings alone. The *B flat Divertimento* was written five years later, in Salzburg, and is scored more simply for two horns and strings.

Divertimento 17 in D, K.334 (DVD version)

(*) Sony **DVD SVD 46388. BPO, Karajan – RICHARD STRAUSS: *Also sprach Zarathustra* ***

By the time **Karajan** conducted these two celebratory concerts he was already ailing, but, once there, the electric intensity of his conducting is as striking as ever. Karajan gives brightly refreshing accounts of the outer movements, and determinedly traditional readings of the three middle movements omitting the march movement, K.445, latterly thought to belong to the piece. The celebrated Minuet, which comes third, prompts Karajan to a reading so slow and moulded one is reminded of Beecham's more eccentric interpretations of Mozart. The orchestra responds with total loyalty, and the wit and exhilaration of the finale make a delightful conclusion.

Wind divertimenti and serenades

Divertimenti for Wind 3, K.166; 4, K.186; 8, K.213; 9, K.240; 12, K.252; 13, K.253; 14, K.270; Serenades 10, K.361; 11, K.375; 12, K.388

(M) *** Auvidis E 8627/29 (3). Zefiro Ens.

Astrée Auvidis offer a digital set at mid-price (three records for the cost of two), offering three major *Serenades*, plus seven of the *Divertimenti*, played on period instruments by a highly sensitive Italian group. The performances are very recommendable on all counts. The sounds of the period instruments are delightfully fresh and the blending of timbres most felicitous. The playing itself brings a characteristic Italianate sunny quality to Mozart yet is remarkably subtle in detail. The *Gran Partita* is particularly seductive, with only one tiny flaw. At the opening of its eloquent *Adagio* the initial oboe entry begins a little below the note: some ears might find this disturbing on repetition. Otherwise intonation is impeccable and the brilliant playing on natural horns by Raul Diaz and Dileno Baldin is most infectious; overall the **Zefiro** group play with such glowing finesse and spontaneity that this Auvidis set must marginally take pride of place.

Divertimenti in B flat, K.Anh.227 (K.196f); 12 in E flat, K.252; 13 in F, K.253; Serenade 12 in C min., K.388

🎧➔ (BB) **** Naxos 8.555943. Oslo PO Wind Ens.

These 1997 performances show the **Oslo Philharmonic** wind on top form. They give the two Salzburg *Divertimenti* with finesse and grace, and bring great intensity to the *C minor Serenade*. The recording, made at the Lommedalen Church at Baerun, has splendid presence and bloom. An outstanding bargain.

6 German Dances, K.571; Les Petits riens: ballet music, K.299b; Serenade (Eine kleine Nachtmusik)

🎧➔ (BB) *** Warner Apex 0927 48691-2. SCO, Leppard

The performance of *Les Petits riens* is delightful, spirited and polished, and the *German Dances* are no less lively and elegant; the famous *Nachtmusik* is nicely proportioned and very well played. The sound too is most believable, giving a tangible impression of the players sitting together out beyond the speakers.

A Musical Joke, K.522; Notturno in D for 4 Orchestras, K.286; Serenade 6 (Serenata notturna); 13 (Eine kleine Nachtmusik)

⊕ 🌑 **** Alia Vox **SACD** Surround Sound AVSA 9846. Le Concert des Nations, Savall

An outstanding disc in every way, which includes (by the grace of SACD) the first really convincing recorded performance of the Notturno for Four Orchestras, scored for four separate groups, each consisting of first and second violins, viola and double bass, plus a pair of horns. Mozart left the first group unnamed, but called the others 'Echo Primo', 'Echo Duo' and 'Echo Trio', and the music is written so that the first orchestra announces each theme and the others repeat it in increasingly brief and shortened echoes, while it is the resonant horns that bring the remarkable atmospheric effects. With SACD surround sound, the effect is greatly enhanced and would surely have brought a twinkle of pleasure to Mozart's eye if he could have heard it.

Musically it is a very fine performance, as indeed is the Musical Joke, played deadpan so that the jokey dissonances are all the more arresting. The performance of Eine kleine Nachtmusik is also refreshingly spirited and eloquent, with the use of one instrument to a part producing a pleasingly full texture; while in the equally successful Serenata notturna the balance with the timpani is splendidly managed, so that they outline the music without drowning it.

Masonic Music: Adagio & Fugue in C min., K.546 (arr. for strings); Adagios in F & B flat, K.410/11; Maurerische Trauermusik, K.477; Cantata: Eine kleine Freimaurer, K.623; Choruses: Die Maurerfreude, K.471; Dir, Seele des Weltalls, K.429; 4 Lieder

Ⓝ ⒷⒷ *** Naxos 8.570897. Heo Young-Hoon, Kassel State Op. Ch. Male Voices, Kassel Spohr CO, Paternostro

A pleasing collection of music Mozart wrote after he joined the Viennese Lodge in 1784. The Adagio and Fugue is the most celebrated piece (arranged here for string orchestra) while the other two Adagios are for woodwind; the F major is very brief. The Trauermusik, also of modest length, for strings and woodwind; is rather fine. The collection opens with a jolly chorus (a hymn to the sun), and closes with a 'Little Masonic Cantata', Loudly proclaim our joy, for two tenors and chorus; the Lieder are well sung by a capable tenor, **Heo Young-Hoon**. **Roberto Paternostro** directs the **Kassel Spohr Chamber Orchestra** and **Chorus** persuasively, and the recording is most natural. Not essential repertoire, but still of interest.

Overtures

Overtures: Apollo et Hyacinthus; Bastien und Bastienne; La clemenza di Tito; Così fan tutte; Don Giovanni; Die Entführung aus dem Serail; La finta giardiniera; Idomeneo; Lucio Silla; Mitridate, re di Ponto; Le nozze di Figaro; Il re pastore; Der Schauspieldirektor; Die Zauberflöte

⊕ ⒷⒷ *** Naxos 8.550185. Capella Istropolitana, Wordsworth

Barry Wordsworth follows up his excellent series of Mozart symphonies for Naxos with this generous collection of overtures, no fewer than 14 of them, arranged in chronological order and given vigorous, stylish performances. In Italian overture form, Mitridate and Lucio Silla, like miniature symphonies, have separate tracks for each of their three contrasted sections. Very well recorded, the disc is highly recommendable at super-bargain price.

Overtures: Bastien und Bastienne; La clemenza di Tito; Così fan tutte; Don Giovanni; Die Entführung aus dem Serail; La finta giardiniera; Idomeneo; Lucio Silla; Le nozze di Figaro; Il re pastore; Der Schauspieldirektor; Die Zauberflöte

Ⓜ *** RCA 82876 76235-2. Dresden State O, C. Davis

A self-recommending set of Mozart overtures from **Colin Davis** here reappears in RCA's 'Classic Library' series at mid-price. Davis perfectly balances the full weight of the dramatic moments with the sparkle of the lighter ones, and the dynamic contrasts are very well judged. The recording is good. If occasionally the tuttis can seem a little bass-heavy because of the resonant Dresden acoustic, this is not a serious problem, and anyone wanting a budget collection of Mozart overtures on modern instruments in digital sound cannot go far wrong here.

Overtures: Bastien und Bastienne; Così fan tutte; La clemenza di Tito; Don Giovanni; Die Entführung aus dem Serail; La finta giardiniera; Idomeneo; Le nozze di Figaro; Il re pastore; Lucio Silla; Der Schauspieldirektor; Die Zauberflöte

⊕ Ⓑ *** Virgin 3 63284-2. Lausanne CO, Y. Menuhin

Menuhin's 1990 Lausanne collection is predictably stylish, the performances elegantly turned, with neat articulation from the strings. Yet there is ample life and drama, and very well recorded indeed, with textures clean, yet with a fine overall sonority. The order is felicitous, so it is possible to play the programme straight through and enjoy every piece.

Overtures: La clemenza di Tito; Così fan tutte; Don Giovanni; Die Entführung aus dem Serail; La finta giardiniera; Idomeneo; Lucio Silla; Le nozze di Figaro; Der Schauspieldirektor; Die Zauberflöte

Ⓜ *** Warner Elatus 2564 60122-2. Zürich Opera House O; or Concg. O; or VCM; Harnoncourt

Harnoncourt draws splendidly polished and spirited playing from all these orchestras, and the result is consistently dramatic and satisfying, even if the CD is played straight through. And although the most familar overtures (Don Giovanni and Così fan tutte for instance) come up freshly, the lesser-known ones, for example La clemenza di Tito and the three-part Lucio Silla, are among the most stimulating. Of course, because many of these performances derive from his opera recordings, some are without their concert endings. But no matter; this is an excellent disc, and consistently well recorded too.

Serenades

Serenades 1 in D, K.100; 10 in B flat for 13 Wind Instruments (Gran Partita), K.361

⊕┄ *** BIS CD 1010. Tapiola Sinf., Kantorow

The **Tapiola Sinfonietta** under **Jean-Jacques Kantorow** gives a finely paced and splendidly phrased account of the great *Wind Serenade* and a delightfully vital account of the *D major Serenade*, K.100, lightly accented and full of character and wit. They make more of this piece than many of their rivals, and they get superb recording from the BIS team. Very recommendable.

Serenades 3, K.185; 4 (Colloredo), K.203

🅑🅑 *** Naxos 8.550413. Salzburg CO, Nerat

Well-played, nicely phrased and musical accounts on Naxos, recorded in a warm, reverberant acoustic, but one in which detail clearly registers. The **Salzburg Chamber Orchestra** has real vitality, and most readers will find these accounts musically satisfying and very enjoyable.

Serenades (i) 6 (Serenata notturna), K.239; 7 (Haffner), K.250; 9 (Posthorn), K.320

*** Telarc CD 80161. Prague CO, Mackerras

In **Mackerras's** coupling the playing is lively and brilliant, helped by warm recorded sound, vivid in its sense of presence, except that the reverberant acoustic clouds the tuttis a little. The violin soloist, **Oldrich Viček**, is very much one of the team under the conductor rather than a virtuoso establishing his individual line. By omitting repeats in the *Haffner*, Mackerras leaves room for the other delightful *Serenade*, just as haunting, with the terracing between the solo string quartet (in close focus) and the full string band aptly underlined.

Serenade 7 (Haffner), K.250; Symphony 35 (Haffner), K.385

⊕┄ *** Häns. CD 98.173. ASMF, I. Brown

The coupling of the *Haffner Symphony* and *Haffner Serenade*, especially apt, is surprisingly rare. In the *Symphony* **Iona Brown**, unlike Marriner, follows the autograph in omitting an exposition repeat. Brown herself is the virtuoso soloist in the *Serenade*, as she was in the Marriner version on Philips, lighter than ever in the *moto perpetuo* scurryings of the fourth movement Rondo.

Serenades 9 (Posthorn), K.320; 13 (Eine kleine Nachtmusik), K.525

**(*) Telarc CD 10108. Prague CO, Mackerras

(i) Serenades 9 (Posthorn), K.320; 13 (Eine kleine Nachtmusik), K.525; (ii) 6 German Dances, K.509; Minuet in C, K.409

🅑 **(*) Sony (ADD) SBK 48266. (i) Cleveland O, Szell; (ii) LSO, Leinsdorf

Serenade 9 (Posthorn), K. 320; Symphony 33, K 319

⊕┄ *** Häns. CD 98.129. ASMF, I. Brown

Iona Brown here offers another popular *Serenade* alongside a symphony contemporary with it. The sound is outstandingly good, with plenty of bloom but with no excessive reverberation. These are attractively fresh Mozart performances, using modern instruments, which have concern for the crisper manners encouraged by period performance. Speeds are consistently brisker than those of the Marriner versions which we have used for comparison. The finale of *Symphony 33*, for example, brings a hectic speed which does not sound at all breathless, with feather-light triplets, and similarly in the finale of the *Posthorn Serenade* with which it is coupled.

The Prague strings have great warmth and **Mackerras** gets vital results from his Czech forces. Rhythms are lightly sprung and the phrasing is natural in every way. The Telarc acoustic is warm and spacious with a wide dynamic range (some might feel it is too wide for this music), though most ears will find the effect agreeable.

Marvellously vivacious playing from the **Clevelanders** in the *Posthorn Serenade*, especially in the exhilarating *Presto* finale, yet there is no lack of tenderness in the *concertante* third movement. *Eine kleine Nachtmusik* is similarly polished and vital, and in both works the Severance Hall acoustic provides a full ambience, but it is a pity that the close balance means a reduced dynamic range. Even so, this is music-making of great character. **Leinsdorf's** *German Dances* make a lively bonus, if not as distinctive as the Szell performances.

Serenade 10 in B flat for 13 wind instruments (Gran Partita), K.361

🅑🅑 **(*) Hyp. Helios CDH 55093. Albion Ens.

Ⓜ **(*) Telarc CD 80359. St Luke's O (members), Mackerras

**(*) Accent ACC 68642D. Octophorus, Kuijken

Serenade 10 in B flat (Gran Partita), K.361; Adagio in B flat for 2 Clarinets and 3 Basset Horns, K.484a

⊕┄ *** MDG 301 1077-2. Consortium Classicum

The **Consortium Classicum's** performance of the *Gran Partita* is among the finest on disc. The CD begins with a rarity, the *Adagio in B flat for Two Clarinets and Three Basset Horns*, K.484a, and K.361 is a serenade with a difference. There are unusual touches: the first trio of the second movement and the theme in the variation movement are for strings alone. They are very well recorded, too.

The **Albion Ensemble** give a most enjoyable account of Mozart's large-scale *Serenade*, finely blended and polished, and with the outer movements enjoyably robust and spirited. There is some very fine oboe-playing, and **Andrew Marriner's** clarinet is noticeably elegant in the penultimate *Theme and Variations*. Elsewhere there are moments when the mellifluous playing has rather less character, although it never becomes bland.

Sir Charles Mackerras here turns to an excellent group of players from Purchase, New York. They play expertly together, with good ensemble. The performance is warm and relaxed above all, with the penultimate set of variations particularly colourful and chirpy, and the closing *Rondo* (which Mozart marks *Allegro molto*) by contrast rumbustiously exhilarating. Excellent Telarc recording but, at 50 minutes 37 seconds, a coupling should surely have been added, even at mid-price.

On period instruments **Barthold Kuijken** directs his talented team in an authentic performance where the distinctive character of 18th-century instruments brings a sparer, lighter texture, as it should. Speeds tend to be on the cautious side but the liveliness of the playing makes up for that. The recording adds to the clarity but, again, there is no coupling.

Serenades 10, K.361; 11, K.375; 12, K.388; Wind Divertimenti: K.240; K.252; K.253; K.270

(B) *** Double Decca 458 096-2 (2). Amadeus Winds, Hogwood

Anyone wanting period performances of Mozart's three supreme *Serenades for Wind* will find that this collection offers a fascinating aural comparison. K.375 and K.388 were recorded first in 1985 in New York, and the effect is undoubtedly more plangent than in the later performances recorded in Boston in 1987 (K.361) and 1989 (the four *Divertimenti*). In the *C minor Serenade* the extra darkness of colour adds to the character of the music. The speeds are perhaps a recognition of the players' technical problems, coping with intonation and less sophisticated mechanisms, a point brought home in the clear, full, digital recording, with much clicking of keys. By the time they came to record the *Gran Partita*, two years later, the group's integration was much smoother and the effect is much more sophisticated. Indeed, this is an outstandingly characterful account, not lacking finesse, and making the strongest possible case for authenticity. Both the *Adagio* and *Romance* are lyrically mellow, and the *Theme and Variations* is almost Schubertian in its innocent charm. The jocular finale goes like the wind, pressed home with a virtuosity surmounting almost all difficulties. The four *Divertimenti* are also very successful, with the vivid colouring preventing any possible feeling of blandness.

Serenades for Wind Instruments: 10 in B flat (Gran Partita), K.361; 11 in E flat, K.375; 12 in C min., K.388; Sinfonia Concertante for Wind, K.297b

⊶ (BB) **** COE CD COS 242 (2) (with *Concert Rondo in E flat, K.371*) – COE Wind Soloists, Schneider

The brilliant young wind soloists of the **Chamber Orchestra of Europe**, with **Alexander Schneider** a wise and experienced guide, give unusually positive and characterful readings of these supreme examples of wind music, performances which combine brilliance with warmth and a feeling of spontaneity. The only controversial point is that the second *Adagio* of K.361, phrased subtly, sounds rather heavier than usual, at a comparatively relaxed speed. The C minor opening of K.388 might have been more menacing; K.375, however, is a special delight, as genial as it is characterful. The *Sinfonia concertante* is a live performance, less immaculate than the rest of the collection; but it is a lively, stylish account, with atmospheric if imperfectly balanced sound, not helped by audience noises. However, this hardly detracts from the value of the reissued set as a whole, as elsewhere the sound is most persuasive, vivid and faithful, and set against a warm acoustic. The *Gran Partita* is also available

separately on CD COE 804, and the *E flat* and *C minor Serenades* on CD COE 802.

Serenades 10 (Gran Partita), K.361; 13 (Eine kleine Nachtmusik)

(BB) (***) Naxos mono 8.110994. VPO, Furtwängler (with GLUCK: *Overture Alceste*, BPO)

Furtwängler's 1947 recording of the great *B flat Wind Serenade* is a performance of enormous warmth, lightness of touch and tonal richness, which we have long treasured on the five original 78s. It is a reading of depth and, although the sonorities are at times weightier than we are used to nowadays, the phrasing of the Viennese players has enormous delicacy and grace. The *Eine kleine Nachtmusik* comes from 1949 and there is a bonus in the form of the Gluck *Alceste Overture*, one of the few wartime records Furtwängler made with the **Berlin Philharmonic** for the Telefunken label. A must.

Serenades 11, K.375; 12, K.388

(**(*)) Testament mono SBT 1180. L. Bar. Ens., Haas – DVOŘÁK: *Serenade* (**(*))

Serenades 11, K.375; 12, K.388; Overtures: Le nozze di Figaro (arr. Vent); Don Giovanni (arr. Triebensee); Die Zauberflöte (arr. Heidenreich)

⊶ (BB) *** Hyp. Helios CDH 55092. E. Concert Winds

Both *Serenades* on Helios are among the finest on disc and the *Overtures* are great fun. Fresh, spirited playing throughout, firmly focused and well-blended sound, both from the players and from the engineers. A delight.

This historic reissue of pioneering recordings from **Karl Haas** and the **London Baroque Ensemble** of three of the greatest of all wind works is valuable for performances that are ahead of their time in their brisk, no-nonsense manners and fast speeds, with the works often tackled impromptu. There is a brisk, military flavour in *allegros*, yet the mastery of individual players still defies the idea of over-rigid performances, with delectable interplay between the principals. Vivid and immediate transfers of recordings, set in a dry acoustic.

Sinfonias Concertantes and Epistle Sonatas – *see also* Concertone above

Sinfonia concertante for Violin, Viola & Orchestra, K.364 (DVD version)

(*) EMI **DVD 490449-9. I. Oistrakh, D. Oistrakh, Moscow PO, Menuhin – BACH: *Double Violin Concerto*, etc.; BRAHMS: *Double Concerto* **(*)

Mozart's heavenly *Sinfonia concertante* is wonderfully played by **Oistrakh** *père et fils* at the Royal Albert Hall in September 1963 when the **Moscow Philharmonic** was on tour here, and in this item **Menuhin** rather than Kondrashin conducts. It is a valuable document and is splendidly produced by Anthony Craxton with appropriately discreet camera-work. David Nice's notes speak of 'the elegance and focused tone David Oistrakh draws from the viola', and this is a joy in itself. A moving record, in spite of the inevitable limitations of the sound.

Sinfonia concertante for Violin, Viola & Orchestra, K.364 (CD versions)

(M) **(*) RCA (ADD) SACD 88697 04605-2. Heifetz, Primrose, RCA Victor SO, Izler Solomon – BACH: *Double Concerto*; BRAHMS: *Double Concerto* ***

(***) BBC (ADD) BBCL 4019-2. D. and I. Oistrakh, Moscow PO, Menuhin – BEETHOVEN: *Violin Concerto in D, Op. 61* (***)

(BB) (***) Naxos mono 8.110957. Sammons, Tertis, LPO, Harty (with: ELGAR: *Violin Sonata in E min., Op. 82* (with Murdoch); SCHUBERT: *Rosamunde: Entr'acte*; DVOŘÁK: *Humoresque, Op. 101/7*; MASSENET: *Thaïs: Méditation*; NACHEZ: *Passacaglia on a theme of Sammartini*; SAMMONS: *Bourrée*; TRAD.: *Londonderry Air* (all with Moore))

(**(*)) Testament mono SBT 1157. Brainin, Schidlof, LMP, Blech – SCHUBERT: *String Quintet in C.* (**)

The **Heifetz/Primrose** partnership is too closely balanced and the brisk pace of the finale may not suit all tastes, but the crisp interchange is fresh and joyful, and in the slow movement the warmly responsive interchange between the two great soloists is genuinely moving, with the cadenza outstanding. The SACD remastering has greatly improved the sound.

With **David Oistrakh** playing the viola and his son, **Igor**, the violin, the Mozart *Sinfonia concertante* under **Menuhin's** baton is a most spontaneous and vivid performance, and the BBC recording gives us truthful and natural sound. Self-recommending.

Albert Sammons was the greatest English violinist of his day, and he possessed a wonderful breadth of phrasing and sensitivity. His account of the *E flat Sinfonia concertante*, K.364 with **Tertis**, remains one of the greatest performances of this masterpiece on record. It comes closer to Mozart than most subsequent recordings, particularly in the rapt, inward exchanges between the two soloists in the slow movement. Quite wonderful in fact. The fill-ups complete a splendid further tribute to Sammons's artistry.

The Testament version of the *Sinfonia concertante* was recorded at Abbey Road in 1953. The studio recording, cleanly transferred, focuses the soloists sharply, giving warmth and body to the tone – exceptionally rich from **Peter Schidlof** on the viola. If the slow movement is a degree broad and heavy with **Blech**, the finale is jollier, at a marginally more relaxed tempo.

(i; ii) Sinfonia concertante in E flat, K.364; (ii) Duo for Violin and Viola in G, K.423

(M) **(*) Decca (ADD) 476 7288-2 (2). D. Oistrakh; (i) Moscow PO, Kondrashin; (ii) I. Oistrakh – BRUCH: *Scottish Fantasia*; HINDEMITH: *Violin Concerto* ***

The performance by the **Oistrakh** duo is not notable for its relaxed manner. Everything is shaped most musically, but sometimes the listener may feel that the performers in their care for detail and concern for the balance are less involved in the music itself. However, with solo playing of a high cal-

ibre the music-making is still rewarding, and the 1963 recording sounds well in this new transfer. This is now reissued in Universal's 'Critics' Choice' series.

Sinfonia concertante, K.297b

(a)–*** Warner 2564 621791-2. Saleh, Azmeh, Biron, Polyak, West-Eastern Divan O, Barenboim – BEETHOVEN: *Symphony 5* ****

(M) (***) Cala mono CACD 0523. Tabuteau, Portnoy, Schoenbach, Jones, Phd. O, Stokowski – BEETHOVEN: *Symphony 6 (Pastoral)* (***)

With the brilliantly talented young players of the **West-Eastern Divan Orchestra**, both Arab and Israeli, **Barenboim** directs an unashamedly traditional reading of Mozart's concertante masterpiece, with a relatively large body of strings. In this live recording, made in the Palestinian town of Ramallah, the buoyancy of the playing is firmly established in the opening orchestral tutti, bright and brisk. The four wind soloists enhance that impression in the resilience and fine coordination of their interplay, led by the outstanding oboist, **Mohamed Saleh**. A delectable performance. Like the orchestra's first disc, this one is backed up by a documentary on DVD, this time issued separately.

Stokowski recorded the *Sinfonia concertante* in December 1940; it was his first and only Mozart recording made in his quarter-century directing the **Philadelphia Orchestra**. The result is sheer joy. His graceful string-phrasing may have romantic elements, but the warmth is ever persuasive. His expert group of orchestral soloists (balanced forwardly and clearly) blend well together – with the single proviso that the bassoonist at times produces a rather close vibrato. The transfer is excellent and the sound, though a bit subfusc, is always fully acceptable, with a wider dynamic range than on the coupled Beethoven. A disc to treasure for all Stokowskians.

(i) Sinfonia concertante, K.297b; (ii) Piano & Wind Quintet in E flat, K.452

(a)– ❀ (***) Testament mono SBT 1091. (i) Brain, James, Sutcliffe, Walton, Philh. O, Karajan; (ii) Gieseking, Philh. Wind Ens. – BEETHOVEN: *Piano & Wind Quintet* ❀ (***)

The Mozart *Quintet* is one of the classic chamber-music recordings of all time. Gieseking and members of the **Philharmonia Wind** (**Dennis Brain**, **Sidney Sutcliffe**, **Bernard Walton** and **Cecil James**) recorded it over 40 years ago, and in terms of tonal blend and perfection of balance and ensemble it has few rivals. To the original quintet coupling Testament have added the *Sinfonia concertante* for wind, which these distinguished players recorded with **Karajan** in 1953, a performance of comparable stature. Not to be missed. The mono sound comes up wonderfully fresh in this Testament transfer. This is a full-price reissue and is worth every penny of the asking price.

Sonatas 1–17 (Epistle Sonatas)

(BB) **(*) Naxos 8.550512. Sebestyén, Budapest Ferenc Erkel CO

** MDG 605 0298. Ullman, V. Concillium Mus., Angerer

The *Epistle Sonatas* derive their name from the fact that they were intended to be heard between the Epistle and Gospel in the Mass. Admittedly they are not great music or even first-class Mozart; however, played with relish they make a strong impression. The final *Sonata*, K.263, becomes a fully fledged concerto.

While it is understood that, apart from *16 in C*, K.329, which has a specific solo part, the organ is not intended as a solo instrument in these *Chiesa Sonatas*, it seems perverse to balance the instrument so that it blends in completely with the orchestral texture, as the Naxos engineers have done. Otherwise these alert, polished and nicely scaled performances could hardly be improved on and, apart from the controversial matter of the relationship of the organ to the orchestra, the recording is first class.

On the alternative MDG versions (as in the Naxos alternative recording) the organ is very much in the background. They are well played and recorded.

SYMPHONIES

Symphonies 1 in E flat, K.16; in F, K.19a; 4 in D, K.19; 5 in B flat, K.22; 6 in F, K.43; 7 in D, K.45; 7a (Alte Lambacher) in G, K.45a; in B flat, K.45b; 8 in D, K.48; 9 in C, K.73; 10 in G, K.74; in F, K.75; in F, K.76; in D, K.81; 11 in D, K.84; in D, K.95; in C, K.96; in D, K.97; in C, K.102; 12 in G, K.110; 13 in F, K.112; 14 in A, K.114; in D, K.120 & K.121; 15 in G, K.124; 16 in C, K.128; 17 in G, K.129; 18 in F, K.130; 19 in E flat, K.132; 20 in D, K.133; 21 in A, K.134; in D, K.161; 22 in C, K.162; 23 in D, K.181; 24 in B flat, K.182; 25 in G min., K.183; 26 in E flat, K.184; 27 in G, K.199; 28 in C, K.200; 29 in A, K.201; 30 in D, K.202; 31 in D (Paris), K.297; 32 in G, K.318; 33 in B flat, K.319; 34 in C, K.338; 35 in D (Haffner), K.385; 36 in C (Linz), K.425; 38 in D (Prague), K.504; 39 in E flat, K.543; 40 in G min., K.550; 41 in C (Jupiter), K.551

⌾ (BB) **** EMI 5 85589-2 (12). ECO, Tate

Jeffrey Tate's survey of the Mozart symphonies is one of the finest things he has done for the gramophone. Recorded over a long period, from 1984 to 2003, his inspiration remained constant. Tate jumped in at the deep end by starting with 40 and 41, and they remain very impressive accounts. In the *Jupiter*, the apt scale of the **ECO** fully allows the grandeur of the work to come out: on the one hand, it has the clarity of a chamber orchestra performance, but on the other, with trumpets and drums, its weight of expression never underplays the scale of the argument, which originally prompted the unauthorized nickname. In both symphonies, exposition repeats are observed in outer movements, particularly important in the *Jupiter* finale which, with its miraculous fugal writing, bears even greater argumentative weight than the first movement, a point firmly established by Tate.

The first three CDs in the boxed set concentrate on his earliest symphonies, including many of the unnumbered symphonies (here given supplementary numbers, 42–52).

Some of the rarer unnumbered works are adaptations of early opera overtures, and all of them are colourful pieces. These early works are full of vitality (even if the authenticity of one or two of them is doubtful). Tate finds fresh exhilaration in these scores where the young Mozart was finding his feet, exploring possibilities all the time. From 25 onwards, itself very well done, Tate's detailed articulation and fine detail are always telling. In all these works, he provides a winning combination of affectionate manners, freshness and elegance.

Both the *Linz* and the *Prague* receive strong but elegant readings, bringing out the operatic overtones in the latter, not just in the *Don Giovanni*-like progressions in the slow introduction, but also in the power of the development section and in the wonder of the chromatic progressions in the slow movement, as well as the often surprising mixture of timbres. In the *Linz*, Tate is attractively individual, putting rather more emphasis on elegance and finding tenderness in the slow movement, taken (like the *Adagio* of the *Prague*) at a very measured speed.

The recordings are fresh and warm throughout this stimulating and enjoyable set, which is strongly recommended, especially at super-bargain price.

Symphonies 1 in F, K.19a; 5 in G, K.45a; 6 ; 7 – 9 in F, K.75; in F, K.76; in B flat, K.45b; in D, K.81; in D, K.95; in D, K.97; 10 – 11 in B flat, K.Anh.214; in C, K.96; 12 – 29 ; 31 – 36; 38 – 41

(B) **** DG 471 666-2 (11). E. Concert, Pinnock

Pinnock's Mozartian enterprise has the advantage of some years' experience of authentic performance, and certain exaggerated elements have been absorbed into a smoother, but not less vital, playing style. In the invigorating 'Salzburg' Symphonies (16–29) the playing has polish and sophistication, fine intonation, spontaneity and great vitality, balanced by warm, lyrical feeling in the slow movements. Indeed, the account of *29 in A* is among the finest available and the earlier *A major* work (21) is very impressive too, as is the *G minor*, K.183, and the very 'operatic' *23 in D*. In the later symphonies, the masterpieces from the *Paris* to the *Jupiter* can be warmly recommended, and not only to period enthusiasts. It is the joy and exhilaration in Mozart's inspiration that consistently bubble out from these accounts, even from the dark *G minor* or the weighty *Jupiter*. The rhythmic lift which Pinnock consistently finds is infectious throughout, and it is a measure of his mastery that when in a slow movement such as that of the *Prague* he chooses an unusually slow speed, there is no feeling of dragging. Clear, well-balanced sound throughout the series makes this set an obvious primary recommendation for those wanting period-instrument performances, especially at its new bargain price.

Symphonies 1; 4; in F, K.19a; 5; in G, K.45a; 6-36; 38–41

⌾ (M) *** Telarc CD 80300 (10). Prague CO, Mackerras

Mackerras's is an outstanding series, with electrifying performances of the early as well as the later symphonies. There is not a suspicion of routine, with the playing full of dramatic contrasts in rhythm, texture or dynamic. Mackerras has a keen feeling for Mozart style, not least in the slow movements and minuets, which he regularly takes faster than usual. His flowing *Andantes* are consistently stylish too, with performances on modern instruments regularly related to period practice. An outstanding instance comes in the G minor *Andante* of *5 in B flat*, K.22, where Mackerras, fastish and light, makes others seem heavy-handed in this anticipation of romanticism, underlining the harmonic surprises clearly and elegantly. Consistently Mackerras finds light and shade in Mozart's inspirations, both early and late, though some may feel that, with warm reverberation characteristic of this Prague orchestra's recording venue, the scale is too large, particularly in the early symphonies. Harpsichord continuo, where used, is usually well balanced.

Symphonies 6, K.43; 48, K111/120; 50, K161/163; 51 K.121; 52, K.208/102; 55 K.App.2140

(key) **** Pentatone **SACD** PTC 5186 139. ASMF, Marriner

Symphonies 7a in G, K.45a (Alte Lambacher); in G (Neue Lambacher); 12 in G, K.110; 18 in F, K.130

(key) **** Pentatone **SACD** PTC 5186 112. ASMF, Marriner

Symphonies 7 in D, K.45; 8 in D, K.48; 9 in C, K.72; 19 in E flat, K.132; Andante grazioso, K.132

(key) **** Pentatone **SACD** PTC 5186 138. ASMF, Marriner

Symphonies 20 in D, K.133; 45 in D, K.95; 46 in C, K.96; 47 in D, K.97; 51 in D, K.196

(key) **** Pentatone **SACD** PTC 5186 113. ASMF, Marriner

Marriner and the **ASMF** were at the top of their form in the early 1970s when they recorded these juvenile Mozart symphonies in London (in Brent Town Hall, Wembley). The Philips recordings have long been famous for their naturalness, and now we discover that they were originally 4-channel recordings; when heard in SACD format, with the back speakers properly balanced, the spatial effect of the sound is amazing. Marriner's survey has a splendid Mozartian vitality and yet has all the grace of Karl Boehm's early DG survey of the Mozart symphonies, yet with more freedom and sparkle. The Academy play with great style, warmth and polish, and the effect with such realistic sound is splendidly alive and vivid. These delightful recordings are thus given a wholly new lease of life. It has recently been confirmed that both the *Lambach Symphonies* were written in 1766 by Mozart *père* and *fils* when the latter was ten years old. Wolfgang then wrote K.45 alone, during a trip to Vienna in 1767/8, and K.48 at the end of 1768. But it is in K.132, composed in Salzburg in 1772, that Mozart's true symphonic style emerges, and included here too is its alternative slow movement, a delightful *Andante grazioso*. The symphonies on the third disc also come from the 1770s, probably written during the teenage composer's visit to Italy: distinct Italian influences can be discovered in the writing. 51 is identical to the *Overture La finta giardiniera*, with an added finale. It is all delightful music, and especially rewarding when played with such grace and spontaneous feeling.

Symphonies 14–18

*** Telarc CD 80242. Prague CO, Mackerras

14 in A is a particularly fine work (as indeed are all Mozart's A major symphonies) and, like the others here, it receives an invigorating account with brisk *Allegros* and a strong, one-in-a-bar tempo for the Minuet (this suits the Minuet of *18 in F* even better as it is very folksy). Slow movements, however, are very direct and are pressed onwards slightly unbendingly; here some might find **Mackerras's** approach too austere. The bright recording is resonant, which prevents absolute clarity, but the clean lines of the playing ensure plenty of stimulating impact.

Symphonies 15–18

(BB) **(*) Naxos 8.550874. N. CO, Ward

Symphonies 19; 20; 37 in G: Introduction only (with remainder of the symphony by Michael Haydn)

(BB) *** Naxos 8.550875. N. CO, Ward

Nicholas Ward's stylish Mozart series here offers six symphonies written in 1772. The orchestral string-phrasing is particularly elegant in slow movements (notably the wistful *Andante* of *15 in G* and the charming melody which forms the centrepiece of 17), while the lively first movement of *18 in F* effervesces neatly. Elsewhere *Allegros* are alert and strong. Excellent, full and well-balanced recording, though not ideally sharply detailed. 19 is scored for four horns, two in E flat *alt*, and they give added weight and character to the orchestral texture in outer movements. 20 is given extra brightness by a pair of trumpets. But it is the delectable *Andante* that catches the ear with its charming flute solo over muted violins. Mozart contributed just the rather grand opening *Adagio maestoso* to the symphony once mistakenly regarded as his 37. It is played most persuasively: this disc is well worth having on all counts.

Symphonies 19–23

(key) *** Telarc CD 80217. Prague CO, Mackerras

Mackerras is equally lively in these early works from Mozart's Salzburg period. The surprising thing is how fast his speeds tend to be. In one instance the contrast is astonishing, when at a very brisk *Andantino grazioso* Mackerras turns the slow middle movement of 23 into a lilting Ländler, quite different from other performances. The recording is reverberant, as in the later symphonies, giving relatively weighty textures; with such light scoring, however, there is ample clarity, with braying horns riding beautifully over the rest.

Symphonies 24, K.173; 26, K.161a; 27, K.161b; 30, K.202

(key) *** Telarc CD 80186. Prague CO, Mackerras

Where in later symphonies **Mackerras** chooses more relaxed speeds, here he tends to be more urgent, as in the finale of 26 or the *Andantino grazioso* slow movement of 27, where he avoids the questionable use of muted strings. The reverberation of the recording gives the impression of a fairly substantial orchestra, without loss of detail, and anyone fancying this particular group of early Mozart symphonies need not hesitate.

Symphonies 25, K.183; 32, K.318; 41 (Jupiter), K.551 (Naxos 8.550113)

Symphonies 27, K.199/161b; 33, K.319; 36 (Linz), K.425 (Naxos 8.550264)

Symphonies 28, K.200; 31 (Paris), K.297; 40, K.550 (Naxos 8.550164)

Symphonies 29, K.201; 30, K.202; 38 (Prague), K.504 (Naxos 8.550119)

Symphonies 34, K.338; 35 (Haffner), K.385; 39, K.543 (Naxos 8.550186)

Symphonies 40, K.550; 41 (Jupiter), K.551 (Naxos 8.550299)

⊕ (BB) *** Capella Istropolitana, Wordsworth

The **Capella Istropolitana** consists of leading members of the Slovak Philharmonic Orchestra of Bratislava; though their string-tone is thinnish, it is very much in scale with the clarity of a period performance but tonally far sweeter. The recording is outstandingly good, with a far keener sense of presence than in most rival versions and with less reverberation to obscure detail in tuttis. **Wordsworth** observes exposition repeats in first movements, but in the finales only in such symphonies as 38 and 41, where the movement particularly needs extra scale. In slow movements, as is usual, he omits repeats. He often adopts speeds that are marginally slower than we expect nowadays in chamber-scale performances; but, with exceptionally clean articulation and infectiously sprung rhythms, the results never drag, even if 29 is made to sound more sober than usual. In every way these are worthy rivals to the best full-priced versions, and they can be recommended with few if any reservations. Anyone wanting to sample might try the coupling of 34, 35 and 39 – with the hard-stick timpani sound at the start of 39 very dramatic. The *Linz* too is outstanding. For some, the option of having the last two symphonies coupled together will be useful.

Symphonies 25, K.183; 28, K.200; 29, K.201

⊕ *** Telarc CD 80165. Prague CO, Mackerras

If you want performances on modern instruments, these are as fine as any, fresh and light, with transparent textures set against a warm acoustic and with rhythms consistently resilient. **Mackerras's** speeds are always carefully judged to allow elegant pointing but without mannerism, and the only snag is that second-half repeats are omitted in slow movements, and also in the finale of 29.

Symphonies 38 (Prague); 39; Serenata notturna

(***) Testament mono SBT 1094. Philh. O, Klemperer

Symphonies 29; 41 (Jupiter); Serenade 13 (Eine kleine Nachtmusik)

(***) Testament mono/stereo SBT 1093. Philh. O, Klemperer

Klemperer's 1954 Mozart symphony recordings of 29 and 41 on Testament, unavailable for many decades, marked the turning-point in his accident-prone career. They were the very first recordings which he made with the **Philharmonia Orchestra**. Only the first movement of 29 bears out the later image of Klemperer as slow and rugged. After that, all is exhilaration, with superlative playing from the Philharmonia, with rhythms beautifully sprung and phrases elegantly turned. The *Jupiter* in particular is electrifying, one of the very finest versions on disc, both powerful and polished, while *Eine kleine Nachtmusik* (in stereo) for once is made to sound like late Mozart, both strong and elegant. Outstanding transfers.

The mono version of the *Prague Symphony* is strong and rugged, but finely sprung and phrased, with the *Don Giovanni* relationship firmly established. This mono version of 39 too is fresher than the stereo remake, while the *Serenata notturna* brings a typical Klemperer contrast, with the orchestra providing four-square support for the soloists, who by contrast are allowed their measure of charm and elegance.

Symphonies 25 in G min., K.183; 31 (Paris); 41 (Jupiter)

(BB) **(*) Warner Apex 0927 49045-2. Amsterdam Bar. O, Koopman

The highlight here is the early *G minor Symphony*, where original instruments, with their extra cutting edge, are ideal for expressing the *Sturm und Drang* neurosis of the first movement with its thrilling octave upward thrusts, and this degree of tension is maintained throughout the work. In comparison, the *Paris Symphony* lacks the balancing elegance that modern instruments can bring, but the *Jupiter* receives another powerfully energetic reading, with all important repeats included. When the finale reaches its vibrant apotheosis, the enthusiastic applause confirms that this has the vigour and spontaneity of live music-making. Good (rather than outstanding) recording, but this is excellent value.

Symphonies 28–36; 38–41 (Jupiter)

(B) **(*) Decca 475 9120 (5). Dresden State O, C. Davis

Colin Davis's performances reflect little or no influence from period performance. With the full-bodied, resonant Dresden recording and with vital and imaginative playing from the **Dresden Orchestra**, the set will undoubtedly be enjoyed by Mozartians who are committed to big-band Mozart. The survey got off to a good start with a sparkling and delightful account of 28, coupled with an alert, sensitive and perceptive *Jupiter*, played with vitality and finesse. Alongside it came a pairing of another two of Mozart's greatest symphonies, one of the finest accounts of No. 39 *in E flat* then currently on the market, and an impressive version of 29 *in A*. Though Davis favours big-scale Mozart – the dramatic opening of the *Haffner* is very weighty – he opts for fastish *allegros* in this work; and the *Prague*, *Linz* and *40 in G minor* are elegant and refined, but still on a big, traditional scale. However, the earlier symphonies in the cycle are smoother and gentler in their manners than we expect from this conductor, and some may well prefer the same conductor's earlier, L'Oiseau-Lyre recordings, reissued on Australian Decca Eloquence, even if that survey is less complete (see below).

Symphonies: 28; 33; 35 (Haffner); Serenade (Eine kleine Nachtmusik); Overture: Le nozze di Figaro

🔚 (M) *** Sony 82876 78765-2. Cleveland O, Szell

Szell and his **Clevelanders** are shown at their finest here. All three symphonies sparkle, with light, airy playing from the strings in outer movements in 28, and 33 which is consistently exhilarating, while the *Haffner* is equally polished and strong. Yet there is a tranquil feeling to *Andantes* which shows Szell as a Mozartian of undoubted sensibility, and this is just as striking in the nicely paced *Eine kleine Nachtmusik* with its engagingly light-hearted finale, while the fizzing account of the *Figaro Overture* readily demonstrates the orchestral brilliance. The 1960s sound is fresh, a little thin on top but full-bodied and clean.

Symphonies 28; 33; 36 (Linz); 38 (Prague); Divertimenti 10; 11 (Nannerl Septet)

🔚 *** Australian Decca Eloquence (ADD) 442 8149 (2). ECO, C. Davis

It is astonishing that these much-admired Mozart recordings from **Colin Davis** have had to wait so long to emerge on CD. In *28 in C* Davis is infectiously inspired and, despite the use of a comparatively small-scaled band, he captures the strength of the *Prague Symphony*, with its obvious links with *Don Giovanni*. His treatment of the slow movements steers an admirable course between severity and affectionate treatment. 33 was the work's first stereo recording, and the crisp strings and clean-sounding woodwind of his orchestra respond immediately to Davis's direction, and the performance has wit as well as breadth. The *Linz* is very appealing in its direct but unforced way, and the decorous shaping of its slow movement's contours is superbly done. These transfers bring out all the detail of the original recordings without any loss of the warm ambience which was one of the recording's best features. A thoroughly recommended set on modern instruments, and the two attractive *Divertimenti* are equally sparkling, containing many felicities in the playing.

Symphony 29 in A, K.201

(**(*)) Testament mono SBT 2242 (2). Royal Danish O, Klemperer – BEETHOVEN: *Symphony 3; Leonore 3*; BRAHMS: *Symphony 4* (**(*))

**(*) Testament SBT2 1217 (2). BPO, Klemperer – BACH: *Suite 3 in D*; BEETHOVEN: *Symphony 6 (Pastoral)* **(*)

In **Klemperer's** live recording of 29 with the Royal Danish Orchestra, made in 1954, the opening *Allegro moderato* is characteristically slow and square, heavy despite the thin orchestral sound. But the last three movements are quite different, with the *Andante* refined and beautifully moulded at a flowing tempo, the Minuet light and tripping and the finale ex-

hilarating in its energy. However, as in the other two items from the same concert on the first of the discs in this set, the coughing of the audience is distracting.

In May 1964 **Otto Klemperer**, aged 79, returned to Berlin to conduct the **Berlin Philharmonic** in three works that were favourites with him, determined above all to get Karajan's orchestra to produce a distinctive Klemperer sound. Though the Mozart brings characteristically broad speeds, it erupts into an exuberant account of the finale. First-rate transfers of radio sound.

Symphonies 29–31 (Paris); 33–34; 38 (Prague); 39

(BB) *** EMI (ADD) Gemini 3 50917-2 (2). ECO, Barenboim

Symphonies 32; 35 (Haffner); 36 (Linz); 40 in G min.; 41 (Jupiter); Divertimento 7 in D, K.205; 2 Marches in D, K.335

(BB) *** EMI (ADD) Gemini 3 50922-2 (2). ECO, Barenboim

Barenboim's recordings were made at Abbey Road over a five-year span, between 1966 and 1971. With fine rhythmic pointing and consistently imaginative phrasing, these performances certainly still have a place in the catalogue. 29 and 34 are particularly successful, and the *Paris* (31) is also given an outstanding performance, the contrasts of mood in the first movement underlined and the finale taken at a hectic tempo that would have sounded breathless with players any less brilliant than those of the **ECO**. The *D major Serenade* also responds well to Barenboim's affectionate treatment, while the two *Marches* are attractively jaunty and colourful.

Symphonies 29; 31 (Paris); 34

🔚 (BB) (***) Dutton Lab. mono CDEA 5008. LPO, Beecham

These incomparable performances date from between 1937 and 1940. **Beecham's** are elegant and cultivated accounts which in many ways are unique, though 29 brings one of his most controversial readings, where the pace of the opening movement is eccentrically slow, even if he is very persuasive in his pointing. In the finales, by contrast, Beecham prefers really fast speeds, exhilarating in all three here. The superb new transfers are fuller and have much finer presence, transparency and, above all, body than the earlier, EMI versions that appeared some years ago.

Symphonies 29; 32; 33; 35 (Haffner); 36 (Linz); 38 (Prague); 39; 40; 41(Jupiter)

(N) (B) *** DG (ADD) 477 7925(3). BPO, Karajan

It is difficult to conceive of better big-band Mozart than these beautifully played and vitally alert readings, recorded between 1966 and 1968. There are details about which some may have reservations. 29 certainly sparkles, but textures may be a trifle too smooth for some tastes The same comments apply to 33, although the orchestral playing is, of course, superlative, resilient as well as strong. There is a broadening of tempo at bar 71 in the first movement of the *Linz*, and the Minuet and Trio may seem too slow, while the opening of the *G minor* may not be dark enough for some listeners. In general, however, these are finely proportioned readings, so naturally paced and shaped . As recordings they are well balanced, alive and yet smooth.

Symphonies 29; 35 (Haffner); 38; 39; 40; 41 (Jupiter)

(M) **(*) EMI (ADD) 3 45810 2 (2). Philh. O or New Philh. O, Klemperer

Klemperer's monumentally characterful recordings of the key Mozart symphonies still hold their place in the catalogue and probably deserve their position among EMI's 'Great Recordings of the Century', even if there are some reservations.

Symphony 31 in D (Paris), K.297

(BB) *** Regis RRC 1084. E. Sinfonia, Groves – HAYDN: Symphonies 92 (Oxford); 104 (London). ***

Sir Charles Groves's account of the *Paris Symphony* is mellow and relaxed, with a beautifully played slow movement and finely observed detail. The playing is alert, but the unhurried pacing brings out the music's breadth. The Abbey Road recording is excellent: warm yet clear.

Symphonies 31 (Paris); 33; 34

**(*) Telarc CD 80190. Prague CO, Mackerras

Mackerras and the **Prague Chamber Orchestra** give characteristically stylish and refined performances, clean of attack and generally marked by brisk speeds. As in their accounts of the later symphonies, all repeats are observed – even those in the *da capos* of Minuets. However, the reverberant Prague acoustic, more than in others of the Telarc series, clouds tuttis: the *Presto* finale of the *Paris* brings phenomenal articulation of quavers at the start, which then in tuttis disappear in a mush.

Symphonies (i) 31 in D (Paris); (ii) 40 in G min., K.550

**(*) Arthaus DVD 100 073. (i) Salzburg Mozarteum O, Tate; (ii) Stuttgart RSO, Gelmetti (V/D: Jànos Darvas)

These two live performances were recorded two years apart, the *Paris Symphony*, in the beautiful Mozarteum, at the Salzburg Festival in 1989, the *G minor* in the Rokokotheatre, Schloss Schwetzingen, where the backdrop is plain but the acoustics far superior. Indeed, the performance of the *40th Symphony* is quite glorious; so beautiful is the playing on modern instruments and so warmly appealing and musically detailed is **Gianluigi Gelmetti's** interpretation that one realizes afresh as one listens that this is one of Mozart's supreme masterpieces. Gelmetti's control of light and shade is absolute, and as the music continues his style becomes more dramatic, and it is obvious that as he turns over the pages of the score he is totally within the music, and his little smiles of pleasure at the response of his fine orchestra communicate to us.

Needless to say, **Jeffrey Tate** also gives a very fine account of the symphony Mozart wrote for a comparatively large orchestra (55 strong) to impress the jaded Parisians in 1778, with its strong tutti opening and tenderly playful secondary theme, which Tate and his orchestra contrast so effectively. Tate's conducting technique is infinitely more athletic than

that of his colleague, and it suits the brilliance of Mozart's writing. But the three-movement *Paris Symphony* needs sharper definition, and it should have been first in the programme.

Symphonies 32, K.318; 35 (Haffner), K.385; 39, K.543

*** Telarc CD 80203. Prague CO, Mackerras

On Telarc, **Mackerras** is fresh rather than elegant, yet with rhythms so crisply sprung that there is no sense of rush. His whirling one-in-a-bar treatment of Minuets may disconcert traditionalists, but brings exhilarating results. The third movements of both the *Haffner* and 39 become Scherzos, not just faster but fiercer than regular Minuets, and generally his account of 39 is as commanding as his outstanding versions of the last two symphonies.

Symphony 33 in B flat, K.319 (DVD version)

(*) DG DVD 073 4017. Bav. State O, Kleiber (Producer: Harald Gerick) (with BEETHOVEN: *Overture Coriolan* *) – BRAHMS: *Symphony 4* **(*)

Kleiber's reading is a direct, classical one, firm in contour, and the Bavarian orchestra play very stylishly and responsively, though it is the genial finale that remains most vividly in the memory. The camera moves around the orchestra discerningly but often stays to watch the conductor, who seems very relaxed (but at times obviously conscious that he is being observed).

Symphonies 33 in B flat, K.319; 35 in D (Haffner), K.385

(M) *** Häns. CD 94.003. ASMF, I. Brown

These are spirited, sparkling performances, full of life and warmth. They were recorded in the Henry Wood Hall in 1997, and Andrew Keener has succeeded in getting a very good, natural and well-balanced sound. This CD delights, though it is short measure at 40 minutes even at mid-price. There are no liner notes.

Symphonies 33 in B flat, K.319; 39 in E flat, K.543; Adagio & Fugue, K.546; Serenade 13 in G (Eine kleine Nachtmusik); Divertimento for Strings in D, K.334; Adagio; Overture 'Le nozze di Figaro'

(M) (***) EMI mono 4 76876-2. VPO, Karajan

The *B flat Symphony* (33) was committed to disc in 1946 and the great *E flat* (39) in 1949, and they were rightly hailed in their day for their lightness of touch and perfection of style. They still sound wonderfully fresh, and the recorded sound is still impressively balanced. A very desirable reissue.

Symphony 35 in D (Haffner), K.385

(**(*)) Naxos mono 8.110841. NYPO & NYSO, Toscanini – HAYDN: *Symphony 101* **(*)

Toscanini conducted the amalgamated **New York Philharmonic and Symphony Orchestras** from 1928 to 1936 (the NBC Symphony was created specially for him in 1937). There is a wonderful sparkle about these 1929 records, Mark Obert-Thorn includes an alternative take of the finale. Remarkably good sound, considering their age.

Symphonies 35–36; 38–41 – see also *Flute Concertos 1–2* **(above)**

Symphonies 38 (Prague); 39; 40; 41 (Jupiter)

Ⓜ **(*) DG (ADD) 447 416-2 (2). BPO, Boehm

Ⓑ **(*) EMI 5 00836-2 (3). ASMF, Marriner

Karl Boehm's way with Mozart in the early 1960s was broader and heavier in texture than we are used to nowadays, and the exposition repeats are the exception rather than the rule; but these **Berlin Philharmonic** performances are warm and magnetic, with refined and strongly rhythmic playing, and there is an attractive honesty and strength about them. The *Linz*, for instance, is an example of Boehm at his finest, with an agreeable, fresh vitality; but overall there is a comfortable quality of inevitability here, perpetuating a long Mozart tradition. The recordings sound full, vivid and well balanced in the new transfers.

Marriner's third (1986/7) set of the Mozart symphonies is the most beautifully recorded of all. The playing too is graceful and elegant. With bracing rhythms and brisker pacing than in his earlier, Philips set, these readings are positive yet unidiosyncratic. Phrasing is supple and the Mozartian spirit is always alive here. There is not quite the incandescent freshness of his earliest Decca/Argo series, and there is a degree of disappointment in the *Haffner* and *Jupiter Symphonies*, which are slightly undercharacterized. For the most part, however, this is music-making that will give a great deal of pleasure.

Symphony 35 (Haffner)

*** BBC BBCL 4076-2. Hallé O, Barbirolli – BEETHOVEN: *Symphony 7* ***; WAGNER: *Siegfried Idyll* (***)

(**) BBC mono BBCL 4016-2 (2). BBC SO, Toscanini – BEETHOVEN: *Missa solemnis; Symphony 7* (**(*)); CHERUBINI: *Anacréon Overture* ***

Barbirolli's view of the *Haffner Symphony* is just as characterful as the Beethoven *Seventh* with which it is coupled on this BBC Legends issue. Recorded at the Royal Albert Hall during the Prom season, the sound is rather thick and dull, due in part to the string section being larger than we might expect today. Even so, Barbirolli's characteristic pointing of phrase and rhythm remains very compelling, leading to an effervescent account of the finale. The Wagner item also adds to this striking portrait of the conductor.

Mozart's *Haffner Symphony* was always a favourite with **Toscanini**, and this live performance, recorded in London, is warmer and more sympathetic than either his early version with the New York Philharmonic or his later performance with the NBC Symphony. Though the recording is rather rougher than on the rest of the two-disc set, it makes a valuable bonus to the Beethoven items.

Symphonies 35 (Haffner), K.385; 38 (Prague), K.504; 39, K.543; 40, K.550; 41 (Jupiter), K.551

Ⓑ *** Ph. Duo 470 540-2 (2). Dresden State O, C. Davis

Though **Colin Davis** favours big-scaled Mozart, he opts for fastish *allegros*, and the refinement of the playing helps to make up for the bass-heavy thickness of the Dresden sound as recorded by the engineers. The dramatic opening of the *Haffner* is made very weighty indeed. In the slow movements of both the *Haffner* and *Prague*, Davis is more obviously affectionate, yet without sentimentality. The *Jupiter* is all one would expect: alert, sensitive, perceptive and played with vitality and finesse by the **Dresden Orchestra**. The *E flat Symphony* is one of the finest on the market. If the *G minor* may seem a little weighty to some, its relaxed manner and the superbly refined and elegant playing ensure the power of the work is fully conveyed.

Symphonies 35 (Haffner); 40; 41 (Jupiter)

⊕ ⒷⒷ *** Sony (ADD) SBK 46333. Cleveland O, Szell

Szell and his Clevelanders are shown at their finest here. The sparkling account of the *Haffner* is exhilarating, and the performances of the last two symphonies are equally polished and strong. Yet there is a tranquil feeling to both *Andantes* that shows Szell as a Mozartian of striking sensibility and finesse. He is at his finest in the *Jupiter*, which has great vigour in the outer movements and a proper weight to balance the rhythmic incisiveness; in spite of the lack of repeats, the work's scale is not diminished. Here the sound is remarkable, considering the early date (late 1950s), and the remastering throughout is impressively full-bodied and clean.

Symphony 36 in C (Linz), K.425

(*) Ph. DVD 070 161-9. VPO, Kleiber (Director: Horant Hohlfeld) (with BEETHOVEN: *Overture Coriolan* *) – BRAHMS: *Symphony 2* **(*)

The **Vienna Philharmonic** always have something special to contribute to Mozart, and the *Linz* is a direct account, not as individual as one might expect, but well recorded. The performance of *Coriolan* is especially fine.

Symphonies 36 (Linz); 38 (Prague); 39; 40; 41 (Jupiter)

⊕ Ⓑ *** Ph. (ADD) Duo 438 332-2 (2). ASMF, Marriner

In terms of finesse and elegance of phrasing, the orchestral playing on the Philips Duo is of very high quality and **Marriner's** readings are satisfyingly paced, full of vitality and warmth. There is not a whiff of original-instrument style here, but those who enjoy the sound of Mozart in a modern orchestra of a reasonable size should be well satisfied.

Symphonies 36 (Linz); 41 (Jupiter)

⊕ *** Arthaus DVD 100 081. ECO, Tate (V/D: Jànos Darvas)

This the finest of the three Arthaus DVDs of Mozart symphonies. Once again the two symphonies are placed in the wrong order, but in this instance **Tate's** affectionate reading of the *Linz*, full of Beechamesque Mozartian detail in the woodwind (which the camera delights to pick up), is engaging in a quite different way from the powerful *Jupiter*. Tate plays repeats in the outer movements, and there is little sense of a smaller scale. But it is the *Jupiter* that stands out. It is on the largest scale (35 minutes, with all essential repeats included) and, as it happens, the sound here is more immediate and vivid to suit the music. Like Gelmetti's DVD account of the *G minor Symphony* (see above), it is among the finest performances on DVD, commandingly rhythmic in the first movement and with a tremendous head of steam built up in the finale.

Symphonies (i) 38 (Prague); (ii) 39 in E flat, K.543 (DVD versions)

(*) Arthaus **DVD 100 083. Deutsche Kammerphilharmonie, (i) Albrecht; (ii) Zinman

Gerd Albrecht directs an enjoyably polished but essentially direct and straightforward account of the *Prague*, recorded in the Christian Zaiss Saal, Wiesbaden, where the acoustic provides a well-integrated but not very transparent sound-picture. One's pleasure comes from the superb response of the **Deutsche Kammerphilharmonie**. But then we have a chance to observe **David Zinman** at the helm, a wholly different visual and musical experience. He offers all possible repeats, and his characterization of every movement of this masterpiece is always stimulating. The recording, made in the Munich Sophiensaal, is excellent, vivid, with far more range than its companion.

Symphonies 38 (Prague); 39 in E flat, K.543 (CD versions)

(BB) *** ASV CD COE 806. COE, Schneider

Schneider's might be counted old-fashioned readings by not observing exposition repeats, with the recording set in a warm, helpful acoustic, bringing out the sweetness of the **COE** violins. But the constant rhythmic resilience of his direction and the superb response of the COE, the solo wind-playing a delight, lightens everything; and this is a most rewarding coupling.

Symphonies 38 (Prague); 39; 40; 41 (Jupiter)

🔗 **** Linn CD 308 (2). SCO, Mackerras

🔗 (BB) *** Virgin 2x1 5 62428-2 (2). Sinfonia Varsovia, Y. Menuhin

*** Warner 2564 63067-2 (2) + bonus sampler. COE, Harnoncourt

Sir Charles Mackerras conducts the **SCO** in outstanding performances of Mozart's last six symphonies with the lesson of period performance sharpening the impact of traditional instruments. The strings play with little vibrato, the brass rasps boldly and the timpani are always dramatically prominent. The result is joyful in its freedom, making this one of the top recommendations for this much-recorded repertoire.

Menuhin reveals himself as very much a classicist, with speeds on the fast side, notably in the *Andante* of the *Prague*, giving the movement a free, song-like lyricism. He treats the third movement of No. 39 as a brisk Ländler, almost hurdy-gurdy-like, refusing – after consultation with the autograph – to allow a rallentando at the end. Otherwise the only other oddity is his omission of the exposition repeat in the first movement, when as a rule he is generous with repeats, observing them in both the first movement and finale of the *Jupiter*. With such vivid sound, this is a

strong recommendation for those collectors wanting all four symphonies.

Harnoncourt has re-recorded the last four symphonies of Mozart yet again, still in proper scale, but this time with the modern-instrument **Chamber Orchestra of Europe**, who play superbly for him. Nevertheless, Harnoncourt's period-performance influences remain, including brisk tempi, with often fierce accents, and explosive timpani with hard sticks. The performances are consistently vibrant, but with elegant playing in slow movements. The *Prague* has a feeling of bravura throughout, and 39 too has plenty of spirit, especially in the sparkling finale, even if Harnoncourt misses its geniality. But the first movement of the *G minor* is very successful, and the set is crowned by a thrilling account of the *Jupiter* with all repeats included (as elsewhere), to lead to a remarkably powerful final apotheosis, carrying all before it. There is a free bonus disc, offering samples (complete movements) from 15 of his other recordings, covering the music of eight different composers.

Symphony 40 in G min., K.550

(***) BBC mono BBCL 4120-2. Hallé O, Barbirolli –
    SCHUBERT: *Symphonies 5 & 8 (Unfinished)* (***)

Recorded in 1962 in the BBC studios, **Barbirolli** conducts a strong, finely shaped performance of the *G minor Symphony*. The middle two movements are rather broader than one would expect today, and there is no repeat of the first-movement exposition, but this is a fine example of the **Hallé Orchestra's** playing as Barbirolli developed it. The mono sound is limited but undistracting.

Symphonies 40; 41 (Jupiter)

🔗 ✦ (M) **** DG 445 548-2. VPO, Bernstein

*** DG 477 5798. Musiciens du Louvre, Minkowski (with *Idomeneo Ballet Music, K.367*)

*** Telarc CD 80139. Prague CO, Mackerras

Bernstein's electrifying account of 40 is keenly dramatic, individual and stylish, with the finale delightfully airy and fresh. If anything, the *Jupiter* is even finer: it is exhilarating in its tensions and observes the repeats in both halves of the finale, making it almost as long as the massive first movement. Bernstein's electricity sustains that length, and one welcomes it for establishing the supreme power of the argument, the true crown in the whole of Mozart's symphonic output. This mid-price reissue on DG's Masters label now takes its place again at the top of the list of recommendations for this coupling.

Minkowski's period-instrument coupling of the last two Mozart symphonies is truly individual and very much forward-looking. The account of the *G minor* is very persuasive, helped by his warm acoustic, and the string playing of the **Musiciens du Louvre** in the slow movement is lyrically beautiful; but it is in the *Jupiter Symphony* that Minkowski triumphs, the first movement pressed forward vigorously with hard-edged timpani strokes, the slow movement very expressive, yet with uneasy undercurrents. The powerful finale is taken briskly, but with plenty of weight. All necessary repeats are used, to build to a massive and thrilling apotheosis, with the recording outstandingly vivid. The *Idomeneo Ballet Music* is rather like a sinfonia and makes an attractive bonus.

On Telarc, with generally fast speeds, so brisk that he is able to observe every single repeat, **Mackerras** takes a fresh, direct view which, with superb playing from the **Prague Chamber Orchestra**, is also characterful. On the question of repeats, the doubling in length of the slow movement of 40 makes it almost twice as long as the first movement, a dangerous proportion – though it is pure gain having both halves repeated in the magnificent finale of the *Jupiter*.

THEATRE AND BALLET MUSIC

Theatre Music: Ballet music: *Idomeneo; Les Petits riens;* Incidental music: *Thamos, King of Egypt;* Music for *Pantalon and Columbine; Sketches for a Ballet Intermezzo*

Ⓑ *** Ph. (ADD) 464 940-2 (5). Various artists including ASMF, Marriner & Netherlands CO, Zinman

Zinman and his Netherlanders give a neatly turned account of the ballet from *Idomeneo*, musical and spirited. **Marriner** takes over with modern, digital sound for *Les Petits riens* and the two novelties, and the **ASMF** playing has characteristic elegance and finesse. The music for *Pantalon and Columbine* (more mime than ballet) survives in the form of a first violin part, and Franz Beyer has skilfully orchestrated it for wind and strings, using the first movement of the *Symphony*, K.84, as the overture and the last movement of *Symphony*, K.120, as the finale. Beautifully played as it is here, full of grace and colour, this is a real find and the digital recording is first rate. *Thamos, King of Egypt* is marvellous music which it is good to have on record, particularly in such persuasive hands as these. The choral singing is impressive and the orchestral playing is excellent.

CHAMBER MUSIC

Adagio & Fugue in C min., K.546 – see also Clarinet Quintet

ⒷⒷ (***) Dutton Lab. mono CDBP 9713. Griller Qt – BLOCH: *String Quartet 2; Night;* DVOŘÁK: *String Quartet 12 (American)* ***

Played by a string quartet, Mozart's masterly *Adagio and Fugue* are if anything even tauter and stronger than when played by full strings. The **Griller Quartet**, at the peak of their form in 1948, give a fresh, purposeful reading, very well recorded, a welcome supplement to the equally fine readings of popular Dvořák and neglected Bloch.

Adagio & Rondo for Flute, Oboe, Viola, Cello & Piano, K.617; (i) *Clarinet Trio (Kegelstatt);* (ii) *Flute Quartets 1–4;* (iii) *Horn Quintet;* (iv) *Oboe Quartet*

Ⓑ ⒷⒷ *** Virgin 2x1 5 61448-2 (2). Nash Ens., with (i) Collins; (ii) P. Davies; (iii) Lloyd; (iv) Hulse

In the *Adagio and Rondo*, originally written for glass harmonica, the wind instruments blend together most felicitously.

Michael Collins proves a winningly personable soloist in the *Clarinet Trio*. **Gareth Hulse** plays exquisitely in the *Oboe Quartet* and the **Nash Ensemble** blend in most sensitively, and give excellent support to **Frank Lloyd's** warmly lyrical account of the *Horn Quintet*. The second disc contains the four *Flute Quartets*, with **Philippa Davies** both a nimble and a highly musical flautist. She is very well balanced with her Nash colleagues and these are pleasingly warm, intimate performances.

(i) *Clarinet Quartet in B flat* (trans. of *Violin Sonata, K.327d*); (ii) *Oboe Quartet in F, K.370; String Quartet 21 in D, K.575*

ⒷⒷ **(*) HM Classical Express HCX 3957 107. (i) Hoeprich; (ii) Schachman; Artaria Qt

The transcription of the *Violin Sonata*, K.327d, into a *Clarinet Quartet* is a surprising success, and the work sounds for all the world as if it was written for the present combination, particularly in the jocular finale. The more so as the clarinettist, **Erich Hoeprich**, is a most personable and musical player. **Marc Schachman's** creamy yet nicely pointed oboe-playing is also just right for the *Oboe Quartet*, a most spirited, expressive performance that is among the best on record. Without soloists the **Artaria Quartet** give an accomplished account of the *First Prussian Quartet*, enjoyable if not distinctive. But the recording is first class, and the other two works make this disc well worth investigating at bargain price.

Clarinet Quintet in A, K.581

ⒷⒷ **** Warner Apex 0927 44350-2. Leister, Berlin Soloists – BRAHMS: *Clarinet Quintet* ***

Ⓑ *** HM HMN 911 691. Carbonare, Hery, Binder, Bone, Pouzenc – BRAHMS: *Clarinet Quintet* ***

(**(*)) Testament mono SBT 1282. Boskovsky, V. Octet (members) – BRAHMS: *Clarinet Quintet* ***

Simplicity is the keynote of **Karl Leister's** 1988 performance, but in the lovely slow movement he gives a gentle reflective serenity that creates a mood of Elysian rapture, with his string group supporting him most sensitively. The Minuet makes a strong rhythmic contrast so that the final variations can again charm the ear with their combination of lyricism and high spirits. The coda is then presented as a light-hearted culmination. Very good recording and a modest price make this coupling, with an equally fine account of the Brahms, very recommendable indeed.

Alessandro Carbonare, principal clarinet of the Orchestre National de France, produces exceptionally beautiful, liquid tone-colours over the widest dynamic range. Clear and fresh as the outer movements are, the high point is the *Larghetto*, magically gentle and with the main melody tastefully elaborated on its reprise. The four string-players, also members of the Orchestre National, are not quite so distinctive yet provide most sympathetic support.

Alfred Boskovsky's account, with members of the **Vienna Octet**, of the *Clarinet Quintet* is fresh but relaxed, glowing with Viennese warmth and with the intimacy of home music-making. The vivid 1954 mono sound has been well transferred by Testament, but it is a bit close.

Clarinet Quintet; Clarinet Quintet Fragment in B flat, K.516c; (i) Quintet Fragment in F for Clarinet in C, Basset Horn & String Trio, K.580b (both completed by Druce)

🎧 *** Amon Ra/Saydisc (ADD) CD-SAR 17. Hacker, Salomon Qt, (i) with Schatzberger

This is a superb recording by **Alan Hacker** with the **Salomon Quartet**, using original instruments. Hacker's gentle sound on his period instrument is displayed at its most ravishing in the *Larghetto*. Tempi are wonderfully apt and the rhythms of the finale are infectious, the music's sense of joy fully projected. The recording balance is near perfect. Hacker includes a fragment from an earlier projected *Quintet* and a similar sketch for a work featuring C clarinet and basset horn with string trio. Both are skilfully completed by Duncan Druce.

(i) Clarinet Quintet; (ii) Clarinet Trio (Kegelstatt)

*** Praga Compatible Surround Sound **SACD** PRD/DSD 250 200. Moraguès; with (i) Pražák Qt; (ii) Braley, V. Mendelssohn

The fine Czech clarinettist **Pascal Moraguès** subtly varies his timbre in this pair of performances, comparatively limpid in the *Quintet* – seductively so in the slow movement – and slightly more robust in the *Trio* to match the style of the excellent pianist, **Frank Braley**. Moreover, the *Quintet* has a subtlety of dynamic and a nicely judged variety of tempi that, together with a feeling of natural spontaneity, create what is a virtually ideal performance. The finale is especially enticing, with an infectious burst of bubbling bravura just before the coda. Moreover, the SACD transfer gives the players a natural presence within a most attractive acoustic, especially to those collectors with full surround-sound facilities, but sounding pretty impressive as a normal CD.

(i) Clarinet Quintet, K.581; (ii) Horn Quintet, K.407

**(*) MDG 304 1184-2. (i) Rodenhäuser; (ii) Vlatkovic; Ens. Villa Musica

The richness of **Ulf Rodenhäuser's** timbre in the *Clarinet Quintet* combines with beautifully blended string-playing to provide a result to captivate any listener, with sheer beauty of timbre and limpid phrasing. Tempi are consistently relaxed, and although in that respect there is perhaps not enough variety, the result never quite becomes bland. The performance of the *Horn Quintet* has similar finesse, but **Radovan Vlatkovic's** horn-playing is robust enough to create a contrast between the two performances.

(i) Clarinet Quintet; (ii) Horn Quintet; (iii) Oboe Quartet, K.370

*** Nim. NI 5487. (i) Leister; (ii) Seifert; (iii) Koch; Brandis Qt

Karl Leister provides an essentially light-hearted account of the *Clarinet Quintet*, with the slow movement tranquil and beautifully poised. **Gerd Seifert** is just as lively and sensitive in the work for horn, even if his tone is a little plump. **Lothar Koch** is equally personable in the *Oboe Quartet*, although perhaps just a trifle studied in sustaining the *Adagio* (so

beautifully opened by the **Brandis Quartet**). The recording, comparatively forward, is vividly present.

(i) Clarinet Quintet in A, K.581; (ii) Piano Quartets 1 in G min., K.478; 2 in E flat, K.493

BB (***) Naxos 8.111238. (i) Benny Goodman; (ii) Szell; Budapest Qt

These legendary records come from the days of shellac. **Benny Goodman's** set comes from 1938 (these were the days when popular musicians were musically educated) and the **Szell** set of the *Piano Quartets* was recorded in Hollywood in 1946. He was an elegant pianist although these performances did not enjoy wide currency in Britain or Europe. Curzon and the Amadeus came along on Decca a few years later and dominated the catalogue for some time afterwards. Readers can at last relish these classical and stylish performances in what is the best sound they have yet enjoyed.

(i) Clarinet Quintet; String Quartet 20 in D (Hoffmeister), K.499

Ⓜ **(*) Whitehall Associates MQCD 600l. (i) Brymer; Medici Qt

Jack Brymer has a benign influence in a fine, mellifluous performance of the *Clarinet Quintet*. He plays the *Adagio* as a sustained half-tone and conjures from the strings comparably soft playing. The finale is delightful; there is an attractive improvisational feeling in the lyrical variation before the main theme makes its joyful return. The recording is truthful, but the close balance is more noticeable in the coupled *Hoffmeister Quartet*, which is a lively, well-integrated performance.

(i) Clarinet Quintet; (ii) Violin Sonatas in F, K.376; E flat, K.481

🎧 Ⓜ *** HM Cal. 5628. (i) Zahradnik, Talich Qt; (ii) Messiereur, Bogunia

The *Clarinet Quintet* is exquisitely done. **Bohuslav Zahradnik's** contribution has much delicacy of feeling and colour; he is highly seductive in the slow movement, and even in the finale the effect is gentle in the most appealing way without any loss of vitality. The recording balance is exemplary. The two *Violin Sonatas* are also beautifully played in a simple, direct style that is wholly persuasive. The recording is clearly detailed and well balanced, if slightly more shallow.

Clarinet Trio (Kegelstatt); Piano & Wind Quintet, K.452

**(*) CPO 777 010-2. Consortium Classicum – BEETHOVEN: Piano & Wind Quintet **(*)

On CPO the usual coupling of the *Piano and Wind Quintets* of Mozart and Beethoven, while perhaps not a first choice for these works, is enhanced by a fine account of the *Clarinet Trio*, with an excellent clarinettist in **Dieter Klöcker**. But the star of the proceedings overall is the fine pianist, **Werner Genuit**, who ensures that all three performances are enjoyable, with both the *Larghetto* and finale of the *Quintet* played most appealingly. Good, well-balanced recording.

(i) Divertimento in E flat for String Trio, K.563; (ii) Duos for Violin & Viola 1–2, K.423/4; (i) 6 Preludes & Fugues for String Trio, K.404a; (iii) Sonata (String Trio) in B flat, K.266

⊕– Ⓑ **** Ph. Duo (ADD) 454 023-2 (2). (i) Grumiaux, Janzer, Szabo; (ii) Grumiaux, Pelliccia; (iii) ASMF Chamber Ens.

Grumiaux's 1967 recorded performance of the *Divertimento in E flat* remains unsurpassed; he is here joined by two players with a similarly refined and classical style. In the *Duos*, which are ravishingly played, the balance is excellent, and **Arrigo Pelliccia** proves a natural partner in these inspired and rewarding works. The *Sonata for String Trio* is well played by the **ASMF Chamber Ensemble** and it has a modern, digital recording.

Divertimento in E flat for String Trio, K.563; Duo for Violin and Viola in B flat, K.424

⊕– *** Hyp. CDA 67246. Leopold String Trio

Here is a completely natural performance of Mozart's *E flat Divertimento* and the first for some years that can come close to approaching the celebrated Grumiaux Trio version, which has served us so well for the past three decades. **Marianne Thorsen** and **Scott Dickinson** give a first-rate account of the *B flat Duo*, K.424. Very lifelike recording, totally at the service of Mozart and the musicians.

Flute Quartets 1 in D, K.285; 2 in G, K.285a; 3 in C, K.285b; 4 in A, K.298

⊕– **** EMI 5 56829-2. Pahud, Poppen, Schlicht, Queras

⊕– **** Avie AV 2108. Lisa & Pavlo Beznosiuk, Dunn & Tunnicliffe – BEETHOVEN: *Serenade, Op. 25* ***

(i) Flute Quartets 1–4; (ii) Andante for Flute & Orchestra in C, K.315

Ⓑ *** DHM (ADD) 05472 77442-2. B. Kuijken; (i) Coll. Aur. (members); (ii) La Petite Bande

Emmanuel Pahud gives inspired performances of the four Mozart *Flute Quartets*. These are all early works, generally lightweight, but with one movement of deep emotional feeling, the B minor *Adagio* of the *First Quartet*, K.285. In that songful piece Pahud finds new mystery through his subtly shaded phrasing. Otherwise this is a fun disc, full of youthful high spirits, charming and witty. Even more than his earlier disc of Mozart concertos for EMI, this signals the arrival of a new master flautist.

Playing period instruments with pleasing refinement, **Lisa Beznosiuk's** group find much charm and delicacy of feeling in these four enticing works; they couple them with Beethoven's equally delightful early *Serenade for flute, violin and viola*. Other versions may be more robust, but none are more cultivated.

Barthold Kuijken plays a beguilingly soft instrument from Dresden, made by August Grenser in 1789, and the effect has great charm. The playing of the three string instruments is also very smooth and accomplished, and the ensemble is beautifully recorded in a warm acoustic. The pitch is lower by a semitone, but few listeners will mind

this. The *Andante for Flute and Orchestra* makes an engaging encore.

Flute Quartets 1–4 (arr. for Recorder)

Ⓝ ** MVD OUR 6.220570. Petri, Widman, Ulijona, Sudraba

Michala Petri is a true star among recorder players, but even she cannot convince the listener that these *Quartets* can be effectively presented using a recorder. Although the group make a pleasingly homogeneous sound, the recorder is not able to achieve the subtlety of dynamic and range of colour possible on a transverse flute.

Horn Quintet in E flat, K.407

ⒷⒷ *** Warner Apex 8573 89080-2. Vlatkovic, Berlin Soloists –
   BEETHOVEN: *Septet* ***

Radovan Vlatkovic is a most musical soloist, and his companions provide a warmly affectionate backing, most naturally recorded. The *Andante* is beautifully phrased by soloist and string group alike and the finale is appropriately perky. Excellent value.

Horn Quintet, K.407; Oboe Quartet, K.370; Piano and Wind Quintet, K.452; Quintet Movement, K.580b

⊕– **** Hyp. CDA 67277. Gaudier Ens.

The **Gaudier Ensemble** here offers an ideal Mozart coupling of four wind-based chamber works. The oboist, **Douglas Boyd**, brings out the depth in the D minor slow movement of the *Oboe Quartet* as well as the fun of the outer movements, while **Jonathan Williams** is brilliant in the *Horn Quintet*, with the more ambitious *Piano and Wind Quintet*, in which **Susan Tomes** is the outstanding pianist, providing the anchor point. The rarity is the *Quintet Movement* for the unusual grouping of clarinet, basset horn and string trio, a magnificent piece, left unfinished at Mozart's death and here completed by Duncan Druce.

(i) Horn Quintet; String Quartet 19 in C (Dissonance), K.465; (ii) String Quintet 4 in G min., K.516

ⒷⒷ (***) Dutton mono CDBP 9717. (i) Brain; (ii) Gilbert (viola); Griller Qt

This further outstanding disc of Mozart chamber music from the **Griller Quartet** offered in the Dutton bargain series, superbly transferred, demonstrates again the strength and refinement of this leading quartet of the post-war period, largely neglected by record companies during the age of the LP. The *G minor Quintet* is outstanding, with excellent sound, while it is also good to have the *Horn Quintet* in another vintage performance with **Dennis Brain** as soloist.

Piano Quartets 1 in G min., K.478; 2 in E flat, K.493

⊕– *** ASV Gold GLD 4015. Nash Ens.

⊕– *** Hyp. CDA 67373. Lewis, Leopold String Trio

ⒷⒷ *** EMI Encore 5 75873-2. Zacharias, F. & T. Zimmermann, Wick

Ⓜ *** Sony 517 484-2 [SK 93071]. Ax, Stern, Laredo, Ma

ⓜ *** DG 477 6732. Bilson (fortepiano), Wilcock, Schlapp, Mason

Mozart's *Piano Quartets*, sharply contrasted with one another, are among the finest of all his chamber works. The **Nash Ensemble** bring out weight of feeling and insight, and the hero of the performance is the pianist, **Ian Brown**, who is a constant delight, bringing out the sparkling clarity of his part. He is partnered by an exceptionally strong trio of string-players – the violinist **Marianne Thorsen**, the outstanding viola-player **Lawrence Power**, and the long-established cellist, **Ian Watkins**.

The newest Hyperion coupling is equally recommendable, the performances a shade more intimate in style and texture, and refined in a most attractive way, with much that is felicitous from all concerned. **Paul Lewis** plays most nimbly and takes his colleagues with him. Most enjoyable in all respects, not least the natural recording with clear inner detail.

The performances on the EMI Encore disc are pleasing and warmly spontaneous, and the recording is first class to make this a strong budget CD.

The grouping of star names by Sony offers performances of keen imagination and insight. Speeds are beautifully chosen and in both works the performances consistently convey a sense of happy spontaneity. It is striking that **Emanuel Ax**, in the many passages in which the piano is set against the strings, establishes the sort of primacy required, pointing rhythms and moulding phrases persuasively. The recording, made in the Manhattan Center, New York, in 1994, is a degree drier than in many previous versions, suggesting a small rather than a reverberant hall.

The balance between the three stringed instruments and the keyboard is immediately altered when heard on period instruments. The playing of **Malcolm Bilson** and his colleagues is excellent and has both sparkle and grace. The recording too is outstandingly natural and lifelike, so if you are an aficionado of period performance this will be an obvious first choice.

Piano Quartet 1 in G min., K.478

*** Ph. 446 001-2. Brendel, Zehetmair, Zimmermann, Duven
    – SCHUBERT: *Trout Quintet* ***

Brendel's performance of the *G minor Piano Quartet* has vigour and sensitivity and, not surprisingly, an admirable sense of style. It is very well recorded too and, although most collectors will prefer a disc containing both *Piano Quartets*, this is a sizeable bonus for an outstanding account of Schubert's *Trout Quintet*.

Piano Trios 1 in B flat, K.254; 2 in G, K.496; 3 in B flat, K.502; 4 in E, K.542; 5 in C, K.548; 6 in G, K.564

ⒷⒷ **** Warner Apex 2564 62189-2 (2). Trio Fontenay

*** Chan. 8536/7 (2). Borodin Trio

ⓝ ⒷⒷ **(*) Naxos 8.570518 (1–3); 8.570519 (4–6, plus *Trio in D, K.442*, completed Stadler). Kungsbacka Piano Trio

Piano Trios 1–6; 3 Movements, K.442

*** MDG 303 0373-2 (2). Trio Parnassus

The **Trio Fontenay** have already given us excellent accounts of the Brahms and Dvořák *Piano Trios* and they are equally happy in the music of Mozart. As before, the splendid pianist **Wolf Harden** dominates the music-making by strength of personality, although the others are well in the picture, and the contribution of the cellist, **Niklas Schmidt**, is notable. The playing of this group is consistently fresh and spontaneous and has the advantage of modern digital recording and a very reasonable cost.

The **Parnassus** have another outstanding pianist in **Chia Chou** and the advantage of particularly natural and beautifully balanced recording. Moreover, MDG includes as a delightful bonus the three movements for the same instrumentation completed by Abbé Stadler and published in 1797. They are well worth having, with the finale acting as a sparkling encore, and their inclusion gives this set a strong claim on the collector, even though it is more expensive than the Trio Fontenay.

The **Borodin Trio** are slightly weightier in their approach and their tempi are generally more measured, very strikingly so in the *Allegretto* of the *G major*. All the same, there is, as usual with this group, much sensitive playing and every evidence of distinguished musicianship. The Chandos balance, recorded at The Maltings, Snape, produces a pleasingly integrated sound.

The performances on Naxos are also fresh and pleasing. They are dominated by the excellent pianist, **Simon Crawford-Phillips**, but the violin timbre of **Malin Broman** sounds comparatively small, because of the balance, although this is more noticeable on the first CD than on the second. Otherwise the recording is very good. The Naxos set also includes the extra work completed by Stadler.

Piano Trios 1 in B flat; 2 in G, K.496; 5 in C, K.548

*** Hyp. CDA 67609. Florestan Trio

With **Susan Tomes** leading, this first instalment from the **Florestan Trio** promises to provide a top recommendation when its companion arrives. The performances are as fresh as you would expect and the recording balance is excellent.

(i) Piano Trios 2 in G, K.496; 3 in B flat, K.502; 4 in E, K.542; 5 in C, K.458; 6 in G, K.564; (ii) Clarinet Trio (Kegelstatt)

ⓝ ⊶ **** EMI 3 44643-2 (2). Barenboim; (i) Znaider, Zlotnikov; (ii) Glander, Schwarz

Mozart composed piano trios as early as his set of six (K.10–15) but it is the present works, covering a period of two years when Mozart was also occupied with *Figaro* and *Don Giovanni*, which are representative of his mastery. **Barenboim's** partners, the Danish violinist **Nikolaj Znaider** and **Kyril Zlotnikov**, are a natural and most musical team and their playing radiates an infectious pleasure in music-making. The recordings are well balanced and have excellent clarity.

Piano Trios 3 in B flat, K.502; 4 in E, K.542; 6 in G, K.564 (DVD version)

(*) DG **DVD 073 4216. 5.0 Surround Sound. Previn, Mutter, Müller-Schott

As a distinctive Mozartian **Ann-Sophie Mutter** seems less at home in the *Piano Trios* than in the violin sonatas and concertos, and these well-recorded performances are less beguiling than they might be, partly because tempi in outer movements feel rather brisk, with **Previn** pressing on strongly. The other snag is the kaleidoscopic changes of camera angle which many will find unsettling. As in the rest of this series, the DVD includes a documentary of the making of the recordings.

Piano Trios 4 in E, K.542; 5 in C, K.548; 6 in G, K.564; Trio Movement in D, K.542

**(*) Lyrichord LEMS 8054. Queen's Chamber Trio

**(*) Signum SIGCD 081. Ambache Chamber Ens.

Mozart composed his last three symphonies and his final three piano trios in the same year. Lyrichord offer them played as the composer might have heard them, using a (very well-recorded) harpsichord instead of a fortepiano, which ensures great transparency of texture, although the balance favours the violin – not surprisingly, as **Robert Zubrycki** has such a firm, full timbre. The performances by the young members of the American **Queen's Chamber Trio** are fresh and pleasing and well integrated, although at times rhythmically rather precise.

Diana Ambache is a most musical pianist and an affectionately stylish Mozartian. She totally dominates these performances both in temperament and in sound, for neither the violinist, **Gabrielle Lester**, nor (especially) the cellist, **Judith Herbert**, are as strong in personality or timbre. Apart from this imbalance the recording is faithful, and one cannot but respond to the spontaneity of the playing.

Piano & Wind Quintet in E flat, K.452

*** CBC MCVD 1137. Kuerti, Campbell, Mason, Sommerville, McKay – MOZART; WITT: *Quintets* ***

The performance by this excellent group of leading Canadian instrumentalists is hardly less captivating. They share this wonderful music as a perfectly matched team. This is playing of great freshness and striking spontaneity, given a perfectly balanced recording of vividness and presence. Moreover, the CBC issue scores by including also the quintet of Friedrich Witt, closely modelled on the present work.

Piano & Wind Quintet in E flat, K.452; Adagio in C min., & Rondo in C (arr. for piano & wind), K.617

*** BIS CD 1132. Hough, Berlin Philharmonic Wind Quintet

The *Quintet for Piano and Wind* finds **Stephen Hough** and the **Berlin Philharmonic Wind Quintet** in splendid form. They have lightness and wit to commend them, as well as an impeccable feeling for style. This recording is as good as any in the catalogue and survives the most exalted comparisons. The coupling is made the more attractive by the inclusion of Michael Hasel's felicitous transcription of the *Adagio and Rondo for glass harmonica, flute, oboe, and cello* which sounds equally delectable. First-class recording too.

String quartets

String Quartets 2 in D; 3 in G; 4 in C; 5 in F; 6 in B flat; 7 in E flat; K.155/160 (Cal. CAL 5246)

String Quartets 3, K.156; 14, K.387; 15, K.421 (Cal. Approche (ADD) CAL 5241)

String Quartets 8–12, K.168–72 (Cal. Approche (ADD) CAL 5247)

(M) *** Talich Qt

String Quartets 16, K.428; 17 (Hunt), K.458

(M) *** Cal. Approche (ADD) CAL 5242. Talich Qt – HAYDN: *String Quartet 74* ***

The prize-winning recordings by the **Talich Quartet** are here reissued in their previous couplings. Their playing is immaculate in ensemble and they have a special kind of shared intimacy which yet is immediately communicative. They are the soul of finesse and make music with expressive simplicity, while bringing vitality to *Allegros* and conveying a consistent feeling of spontaneous vitality throughout. They are naturally balanced. The analogue recordings have not been further remastered and remain beautiful, very warm and smooth on top, slightly middle- and bass-orientated. There are few records of Mozart's *Quartets* to match these.

String Quartets 4 in C, K.157; 6 in B flat, K.159; 11 in E flat, K.171; 14 in G, K.387; 15 in D min., K.421; 16 in E flat, K.428; 20 in D (Hoffmeister), K.499; 21 in D, K.575; 22 in B flat, K.589

(N) (M) **(*) Nimbus NI 2508/10. American Qt

The recordings by the **American Quartet** use Stradivari instruments as far as possible, and certainly the tonal matching is remarkably smooth. The present three discs are Volume 1 of a forthcoming complete set. The quartets are immaculately played and naturally recorded. Perhaps at times one would have liked a little more idiosyncrasy in the music-making, but it is polished and thoroughly musical, and easy to live with.

String Quartet 14 in G, K.387

(B) *** EMI 3 66557-2. Formosa Qt – DEBUSSY: *String Quartet*; SCHUBERT: *Quartettsatz*; WOLF: *Italian Serenade* ***

The young **Formosa Quartet** from Taiwan give searchingly intense readings of all four works on their EMI Début disc. For young players to give such a stylish performance as this of K.387 is a remarkable achievement, not just pure and refined but beautifully shaded, with crisp attack, culminating in a dazzling account of the fugal finale.

String Quartets 14, K.387; 15, K.421; 16, K.428; 17 (Hunt), K.458; 18, K.464; 19 (Dissonance), K.465 (Haydn Quartets); 20 (Hoffmeister), K.499; 21, K.575; 22, K.589; 23, K.590 (Prussian Quartets 1–3)

⊶ (M) *** Teldec 4509 95495-2 (4). Alban Berg Qt

⊶ (BB) *** CRD (ADD) CRD 5005 (5). Chilingirian Qt

The Teldec recordings were made by the **Alban Berg** in the latter half of the 1970s; the performances have not since been surpassed, and now they make one of the most distinguished sets of Mozart's late quartets currently available. The playing is thoroughly stylish and deeply musical; it is entirely free from surface gloss and there are none of the expressive exaggerations of dynamics and phrasing that marred this group's later records for EMI. The *Haydn Quartets* are consistently successful; the *Hunt* (1979) is still possibly the finest on the market and the *Dissonance* too is first class, with a wonderfully expressive account of the slow movement.

The splendid **Chilingirian** recordings on modern instruments have long been praised by us and rank among the freshest and most spontaneous performances in the catalogue. They are still second to none among versions using modern instruments, and at budget price this well-documented box is very highly recommendable.

String Quartets 14–19 (Haydn Quartets)

◑— Ⓜ ******** Auvidis (14 & 15: E 8843; 16 & 17: E 8844; 18 & 19: E 8845). Mosaïques Qt

*** Hyp. CDS 44001/3 (3). Salomon Qt

(i) String Quartets 14–19 (Haydn Quartets); also 3, K.156; (ii) Violin Sonata 18 in G, K.301

◑— Ⓜ ******* HM Cal. 3241/3 (3). (i) Talich Qt; (ii) Messiereur, Bogunia (with HAYDN: *String Quartet 74 in G min., Op. 74/3* ****(*)**)

As with their previous award-winning performances of Haydn, **Mosaïques Quartet** offer playing of great distinction which provides new insights in every one of the six quartets. Phrasing is wonderfully musical, textures are elegantly blended, there is great transparency yet a full sonority, and this music-making unfolds freshly and naturally. Slow movements have great concentration, yet *Allegros* are alert and vital and finales are a joy. The recording is first class. The three CDs are packaged in a slip-case and now they are also available separately, most attractively packaged.

The playing of the **Salomon Quartet** is highly accomplished and has a real sense of style; they do not eschew vibrato, though their use of it is not liberal, and there is admirable clarity of texture and vitality of articulation. There is no want of subtlety and imagination in the slow movements. The recordings are admirably truthful and lifelike, and those who seek 'authenticity' in Mozart's chamber music will not be disappointed.

The performances by the **Talich Quartet** are immaculate in ensemble and they have a special kind of shared intimacy which is yet immediately communicative. The analogue recordings are beautiful, very smooth on top, the balance slightly middle- and bass-orientated. The set has now been issued complete on three mid-priced discs with a pair of bonuses. The *Violin Sonata* comes after the *Dissonance Quartet*; the Haydn quartet, Op. 74/3, after the *Hunt*, K.458, at a disconcertingly higher level. This too is a fine performance – but be prepared!

String Quartets 14–19 (Haydn Quartets); 20 (Hoffmeister); 21–3 (Prussian)

◑— Ⓜ ******** Warner Elatus (ADD) 2-CD 2564 60678-2 (2) (14–17 & 20); 2564 60809-2 (2) (18–19; 21–3). Alban Berg Qt

These splendid recorded performances derive from the set made by the **Alban Berg Quartet** in the latter half of the 1970s, available on four CDs and highly praised by us above. This pair of separate reissues is most welcome.

String Quartets 14–15

◑— ✾ Ⓑⓑ **(****)** Dutton mono CDBP 9702. Griller Qt – HAYDN: *String Quartet 39* ✾ ********

◑— ******** MDG 307 1035-2. Leipzig Qt

Ⓜ ****(*)** Telarc CD 80297. Cleveland Qt

Even more than the *Adagio and Fugue* (above) the playing of 14, K.387, and 15, K.421, by the **Grillers** reveals their supreme musicianship in Mozart, their warmth and above all the spontaneous feeling of their playing. Moreover, the miraculous Dutton transfers of these superb Decca ffrr recordings are so natural and beautiful that the sound is preferable to many modern digital recordings. Just sample their fizzing account of the *Molto allegro* finale of K.387 or the simple beauty of the *Andante* of K.421 to discover quartet playing of a very rare calibre indeed.

Those preferring first-class digital recordings played on modern instruments with greater tonal warmth than that afforded by the Smithson group will find the **Leipzig Quartet** second to none. As in their recordings of the last three quartets (see below), these performances also combine warmth and finesse with a natural spontaneity, and their music-making has much in common with the Grillers. They play repeats omitted on the earlier recordings. A lovely disc.

These are engagingly warm performances by the **Clevelanders**, richly recorded in a warm acoustic. The playing throughout is polished, beautifully blended and affectionate, but the effect is that, at times, textures are just a trifle suave. Yet both performances are rewarding, with finales a special joy. The *Molto allegro* of K.387 brings an infectiously spirited contrapuntal interplay, with the swinging secondary theme a joy, while in K.421 the *Allegretto* siciliano finale with its variations is elegantly graceful.

String Quartets 14 in G, K.387; 15 in D min., K.421; 16 in E flat, K.428; 17 in B flat (Hunt), K.458; 18 in A, K.464; 19 in C, K.465 (Dissonance) (DVD versions)

Ⓝ ******* EuroArt Unitel **DVD** 2072328 (2). Hagen Qt

These are beautifully alive and sensitively phrased performances that give much pleasure. They were recorded in 1998 in the elegant environment (and excellent acoustic) of the Grosser Saal of the Salzburg Mozarteum and visually are presented impeccably. A most satisfying issue, which can be recommended with enthusiasm.

String Quartets: 14 in G, K.387: 19 in C (Dissonance), K.465 (Haydn Quartets); 21 in D (Prussian I), K.575; (i) Serenade 13 (Eine kleine Nachtmusik) K.525 (DVD Recordings)

◑— ✾ ******** EuroArts **DVD** 2054578. Gewandhaus Qt; (i) with S. Adelmann (double bass) (Director: Hans Hadulla)

The **Gewandhaus Quartet** is a superb group; their impeccable intonation, perfection of blending and vitality of attack remind us of the Alban Berg group at their best for, while they play with a deep seriousness of purpose, intensity of feeling is combined with spontaneity, as if they were playing to a live audience. This is helped by a beautifully balanced recording of the utmost fidelity. They are also in sparkling form in *Eine kleine Nachtmusik*, which is strikingly fresh; the delicacy of the *Romance* and vivacity of the finale are delightful. The quartet is seen against the beautiful backcloth of the Barockschloss in Rammenau, Saxony, where the acoustic is not too dry and not too resonant, so that one can always hear all four players individually and watch as Mozart's inspired part-writing passes between them.

String Quartet 14; (i) String Quintet 4 in G min., K.516

⊕ **** ASV CDDCA 923. Lindsay Qt, (i) with Ireland

This is what chamber-music playing is about. The **Lindsays** radiate a delight in their music and judge the character of each piece of music exactly; and one has only to sample the finale of K.387, played with enormous vitality and sparkle, to sense immediately that the music-making is a world apart. The slow movement of the *G minor String Quintet* is very touching in its gentle intensity. These are among the finest modern recordings of either work. The disc must be recommended with enthusiasm.

String Quartets 15; 16; 18

(***) Testament mono/stereo SBT 1117. Smetana Qt

These are performances of a singular distinction, supremely classical in every way. The slow movement of K.428 has rarely sounded more affecting. This quartet appears in stereo for the first time. The A major, K.464, has not been issued before, and gives equal satisfaction. A very special record.

String Quartets 15, K.421; 17 (Hunt), K.428; 19 (Dissonance)

⊕ **** Praga **SACD** PRD/DSD 250 242. Pražák Qt

The sophistication of detail of the outstanding **Pražák Quartet** is matched by the warmth and penetration of their playing, to say nothing of its fresh spontaneity. There is vigour, grace and expressive depth here in equal measure, and the darker atmosphere at the opening of the so-called *Dissonance Quartet* is most subtly evoked. The recording is in the demonstration bracket, with the resonance adding to the hall effect, remarkably live when the full SACD facility is used.

String Quartets 16, K.428; 18, K.464

⊕ **** MDG 307 1160-2. Leipzig Qt

The **Leipzig** performances of the Mozart *Quartets* continue to be second to none, and they are beautifully recorded.

String Quartet 17 (Hunt); (i) String Quintet 3 in G min., K.516

(**) EMI Classic Archive mono **DVD** DVB 5996839. Amadeus Qt, (i) with Aronowitz – BEETHOVEN: *String Quartets 4 & 6;*

16: *Lento assai* (only). (Bonus: BRAHMS: *Clarinet Quintet*: 3rd movt: Andantino; BARTÓK: *Quartet 4: Allegretto Pizzicato*; SCHUBERT: *Quartet 14 (Death and the Maiden)*: 4th movt) (***)

The performance of the *G minor String Quintet* shows the **Amadeus** in good form in 1971 and is quite respectably recorded. Alas, the *Hunt Quartet* suffers from unacceptable harmonic distortion. There are also severe reservations about the two recordings of the Beethoven Op. 18 *Quartets*; the bonuses are the highlight of this DVD and are discussed under the Beethoven couplings.

String Quartets 17 (Hunt); 19 (Dissonance)

⊕ ✺ (BB) **** Warner Apex (ADD) 0927 40828-2. Alban Berg Qt

⊕ **** MDG 307 1107-2. Leipzig Qt

The **Alban Berg Quartet** recorded the *Hunt* in 1979 and it still ranks among the very finest accounts on disc. It has much greater polish and freshness even than the Italian Quartet, and well withstands all the competition that has come since. The *Dissonance* is of similar vintage. It, too, is first class, with a wonderfully expressive account of the slow movement with a sense of total dedication about these wholly excellent performances, which are recommended with enthusiasm.

The **Leipzig Quartet** continue their excellent performances of Mozart's 'Haydn' quartets by pairing the two most famous works. As with their equally fine coupling of 14 and 15, these are most musicianly performances, strikingly fresh and free from the slightest trace of affectation, and full of vital musical feeling. This series ranks alongside the finest modern-instrument performances, for the recording, although fairly close, is naturally balanced.

String Quartets 17 (Hunt); 19 (Dissonance); Adagio & Fugue in C min., K.456

(M) *** Somm SOMMCD 040. Coull Qt

The **Coull Quartet**, who have already given us a fine set of the Mendelssohn *Quartets*, are now embarking on a Mozart survey, and their splendid coupling of the *Hunt* (spick and span and full of sparkle) and the *Dissonance*, with its arrestingly atmospheric opening, bodes well for the series. Both slow movements combine depth with a warm, expressive feeling. They are generous with repeats so that the vivacious finale of the *Dissonance* plays for just over 11 minutes. The *Adagio and Fugue*, too, is full of concentration, yet not exaggerated in intensity. First-rate recording, crisply focused and transparent.

String Quartets 19 in C (Dissonance), K.465; 20 in D (Hoffmeister), K.499

*** EMI 3 44455-2. Belcea Qt

The **Belcea Quartet** have now established themselves as one of the finest groups now before the public, and these two performances offer confirmation of their warm and penetrating response to a pair of Mozart's finest works. The playing is full of vitality, and its spontaneity is striking. The recording is faithful, although the upper range is a trifle over-bright in *fortissimos*.

String Quartet 19 (Dissonance); (i) String Quintet 6 in E flat, K.614

☛—**** ASV CDDCA 1069. Lindsay Qt, (i) with Williams

The **Lindsays** continue their combined series of Mozart's *String Quartets* and *Quintets* with one of the finest discs in the series so far. The striking harmonic atmosphere at the opening of K.465 immediately registers why it was nicknamed 'Dissonance', yet the following *Allegro* is sunny and the *Andante* has both serenity and depth of feeling to make a foil for the delightful Minuet and light-hearted finale. The *Quintet* is hardly less successful, with its witty finale brought off in a true Haydnesque spirit. The recording is real and immediate.

String Quartets 20 (Hoffmeister); 21–3 (Prussian Quartets 1–3)

Ⓜ *** CRD (ADD) CRD 3427/8. Chilingirian Qt

The **Chilingirian Quartet** give very natural, unforced, well-played and sweet-toned accounts of the last four *Quartets*. They are very well recorded too, with cleanly focused lines and a warm, pleasing ambience; indeed, in this respect these two discs are second to none.

String Quartets 20 (Hoffmeister), K.499; 21 (Prussian 1); K.575; (ii) Violin Sonata 17, K.296

Ⓜ *** Cal. Approche CAL 5244. Talich Qt

String Quartets 22 in B flat (Prussian 2), K.589; 23 in F (Prussian 3), K.590; Adagio & Fugue in C min., K.546

Ⓜ *** Cal. Approche CAL 5245. Talich Qt

The **Talich** couplings of the *Hoffmeister* and *Prussian Quartets* are digital and the recording is brighter and more present than in the earlier *Quartets*. The playing has comparable sensibility and plenty of vitality.

String Quartets 20 (Hoffmeister), K.499; 22, K.589

ⒷⒷ *** Hyp. Helios CDH 55094. Salomon Qt

The **Salomon Quartet** have impeccable ensemble and a real sense of style; they use vibrato judiciously and with taste. There is no lack of finesse or vitality, and if you want period-instrument performances of these two works, the present inexpensive CD could be a good choice. The recording is real and shows the transparency of texture these instrumentalists achieve, while blending beautifully together.

String Quartets 21–3 (Prussian Quartets 1–3)

☛— Ⓑ **** MDG Double MDG 307 0936-2 (2). Leipzig Qt

String Quartets 21–2 (Prussian 1–2)

*** Nim. NI 5351. Franz Schubert Qt

ⒷⒷ *** Warner Apex 0927 49575-2. Lotus Qt

String Quartets 21; 23 (Prussian)

☛— **** Astrée E 8659. Mosaïques Qt

The **Leipzig** performances of Mozart's last three quartets are second to none and have all the spontaneity of live music-making. They fill up the rest of the space on the second CD by ingeniously creating a 'sampler' composite quartet. This combines the opening *Allegro* of Schubert's D.353 with the glorious *Lento assai* of Beethoven's Op. 135, followed by the Scherzo from Brahms's Op. 51/2 and the finale from Beethoven's Op. 59/3. In principle one would resist such an idea, but all four movements are played superbly, and the amalgam works astonishingly well.

The **Franz Schubert Quartet** play with refreshing lack of affectation and with great sweetness of tone. There is perhaps more sweetness than depth in the slow movements; but at the same time it must be said that there is nothing narcissistic about the playing, and the listener is held from start to finish. They are very well recorded too.

On Apex most enjoyable performances by the **Lotus Quartet**, polished, well paced, fresh, bright, clearly and naturally recorded. If you want to sample the Lotus Quartet's feeling for a Mozartian line, sample the opening of 22. Excellent value at Apex price.

Even those collectors who do not normally respond to period-instrument performances should be swayed by the warmth and finesse of the playing of the **Mosaïques Quartet** and by their lightness of touch in the finale of K.590. The closing *Allegretto* of K.575 is revealing in quite a different way, and both slow movements have a searching intensity; yet there is an underlying lyrical feeling which often brings the sun out from behind the clouds. The recording is extremely lifelike.

The New York-based **Shanghai Quartet**, who use modern instruments, have won glowing opinions from the American press and elsewhere, and no wonder. They create a beautifully blended sound, warm and refined. Slow movements have a natural expressive flow, and there is all the delicacy of articulation needed for the dancing finales. They are recorded most naturally in a pleasingly spacious ambience. (Delos DE 3192)

String quintets

Complete Quintets: String Quintets 1 in B flat, K.174; 2 in C min., K.406; 3 in C, K.515; 4 in G min., K.516; 5 in D, K.593; 6 in E flat, K.614

☛— ✹ Ⓜ **** HM Cal. (ADD) CAL 5231/33 (available separately). Talich Qt, Rehák, (i) *Clarinet Quintet* with Zahradnik

*** MDG 304 1031-2 (1 & 2); 304 1032-2 (2 & 3); 304 1106-2 (4 & 5). Ens. Villa Musica

String Quintets 1 (with original version of Trio of the Minuet & Finale); 2–6

ⒷⒷ **(*) Naxos 8.553103 (1–2); 8.553104 (3–4); 8.553105 (5–6). Eder Qt, with Fehérvári

(i) String Quintets 1–6; Divertimento for String Trio in E flat, K. 563

☛— Ⓑ **** Ph. Trio (ADD) 470 950-2 (3). Grumiaux Trio, (i) with Gérecz, Lesueur

The six Mozart *String Quintets* played by the **Talich Quartet** and **Karel Rehák** are available in a mid-priced box, together with a radiant account of the *Clarinet Quintet* (with **Bohyslav Zahradnik** the sensitive soloist), on three Calliope discs which cost approximately the same as the pair of Duos above. The Calliope set will in the long run prove a far better investment.

On the bargain-priced Trio, **Grumiaux's** distinguished (1973) set of the *String Quintets* is coupled with his unsurpassed (1967) version of the rather less well-known but equally inspired *Divertimento for String Trio* – an ideal linking. The remastering of these fine analogue recordings is outstandingly natural – a tribute to the Philips engineers, for the bloom on the original LPs remains on CD, yet detail is enhanced.

The augmented **Eder Quartet** also offer a complete set of the *String Quintets*, and the first disc displays their unexaggerated Mozartian style, a fine blend of tone and musicianship. While not a match for the Talich, these performances are eminently recommendable to those with limited budgets. The last two quintets come off very well indeed. The recording is close but very realistic.

Another fine modern-instrument set of the Mozart *Quintets* comes from the **Ensemble Villa Musica**, led by **Rainer Kussmaul**, each disc available separately. The first, with the *B flat* and *E flat Quintets*, is particularly fine; the third includes a very impressive account of the *G minor*. The recording is real and present, although the balance lets Kussmaul's principal violin rather dominate the proceedings. The older recordings by the Grumiaux ensemble and the Talich are not surpassed.

String Quintets 1 (with original version of Minuet & Finale); 4 in G min. K.515

**** CRD 3521. Chilingirian Qt, with Inoue

Since they made their outstanding recordings of the *String Quartets* the **Chilingirian** personnel have changed. But **Leon Chilingirian** remains the leader, and **Philip De Groote** is still the cellist. The newcomers blend and respond as impressively as their predecessors. So these are among the very finest performances available on modern instruments, and the recording is exemplary in balance and natural in timbre.

Violin sonatas

Violin Sonatas 17–28; 32–4; Sonatina in F, K.547 (DVD & CD versions)

🎧➔ ******* DG **DVD** 073 4213 (2) (V/D: Christian Kurt Weiss); CD 477 580-2 (4). Mutter, Orkis

Recorded live in Munich in 2006, **Mutter's** collection of the 16 mature violin sonatas of Mozart completes her triptch of recordings made for the 250th Mozartian Anniversary. She follows a neat line between modern-instrument practice and the demands of period performance, leaning towards the former with tautly controlled vibrato in slow music. Whether observed in recital on DVD or simply listened to on CD, these performances are characteristically fresh and spontaneous, for Mutter is a natural Mozartian and **Lambert Orkis**

matches his violinist-partner well, with lively accompaniments. As with the companion DVD of the *Violin Concertos*, the camera angles are restless, with swiftly changing close-ups, moving from violin to piano and back and then showing the artists together. This may be found disconcerting. But the sound is very well balanced and truthful in both formats, and the audience is amazingly quiet. The DVD set includes as a bonus a documentary on the making of the recordings.

Violin Sonatas 18–20 in C, K 301–3; 6 Variations on 'Hélas, j'ai perdu mon amant', K.360; 12 Variations on 'La Bergère Célimène', K.359

Ⓝ ******* Chan. 0755 Duo Amadè

Violin Sonatas 18–22, K.301–5; 32–4, K.454, 481 & 526

Ⓝ **BB** ****** Virgin 2CD 5 93218-2 (2). Schröder, Orkis (fortepiano)

Of these two discs, the Chandos is the more enjoyable. **Catherine Mackintosh** and **Geoffrey Govier** (fortepiano) form a most winning partnership and make an engaging case for playing these works on period instruments. The variations, too, are most enjoyable, and the recording is vivid and natural.

Jaap Schröder and **Lambert Orkis** also form a complementary partnership. However, Schröder's timbre has a certain amount of edge to it and Orkis's fortepiano timbre is rather hard and somewhat lacking in sonority. This set is for authenticists only.

Violin Sonatas 18–23, K.301–306 (DVD version)

🎧➔ ✹ ******** EuroArts **DVD** 2055188 (optional 5.1 Surround Sound). Gil & Orli Shaham (Director: Michael Beyer)

Gil Shaham and his equally talented younger sister **Orli** make a perfect partnership in these six *Sonatas* and provide one of the finest DVDs of instrumental music in the catalogue. Recorded without an audience in the Palais Daun-Kinsky, Vienna, in 2006, they play very beautifully indeed, with the subtlest control of phasing and the widest range of dynamic, often reducing their tone to a whisper. Each individually is a supreme Mozartian and yet they play together as one, in perfect symbiosis. The recording is totally natural and (for once) the camera, while following their playing as one would wish, does not dart about restlessly, so that one can just sit back and enjoy their totally compelling music-making.

Violin Sonatas 17–28; 32–4; Sonatina in F, K.547

🎧➔ Ⓑ ******* DG 463 749-2 (4). Perlman, Barenboim

🎧➔ Ⓑ ******* Decca (ADD) 448 526-2 (4). Goldberg, Lupu

Violin Sonatas 17–25; 12 Variations in G on 'La Bergère Célimène', K.359

Ⓑ ******* Ph. Duo (ADD) 462 1852 (2). Szeryng, Haebler

Violin Sonatas 17–20 (Naxos 8.553111)

Violin Sonatas 21–3; 25 (Naxos 8.553110)

Violin Sonatas 26–8 (Naxos 8.553112)

Violin Sonatas 32–3

(BB) **(*) Naxos 8.553590. Nishizaki, Jandó

Violin Sonatas 29–30; in B flat, K.570 (arr. for Violin & Piano); *Variations in G min. on 'Au bord d'une fontaine' (Hélas j'ai perdu mon amant)*

(BB) *** Naxos 8.557665 Nishizaki, Loeb

Perlman and **Barenboim** form a distinguished team, with alert, vital playing and a sense of spontaneous music-making which pervades their four CDs. There is much attention to detail (though never fussy-sounding) which makes these come over as strikingly fresh accounts. Those who invest in this set will not be disappointed, and the recordings are vividly realistic.

Radu Lupu plays with uncommon freshness and insight, while **Szymon Goldberg** brings a wisdom, born of long experience, to these sonatas which is almost unfailingly revealing. Lupu gives instinctive musical support to his partner and both artists bring humanity and imagination to their performances. In short, very distinguished playing from both artists, expertly balanced.

Ingrid Haebler brings an admirable vitality and robustness to her part. **Szeryng's** contribution is altogether masterly, and all these performances find both partners in complete rapport. The analogue recordings from the mid-1970s provide striking realism and truthfulness, and they have been transferred immaculately to CD. The *Variations* included in the set are managed with charm. The intimate atmosphere of these performances is particularly appealing.

The partnership of **Takako Nishizaki** and **Jenö Jandó** is very successful. In the earlier of the more mature sonatas, which date from 1778, the violin often takes a subsidiary role, and here the balance and Jandó's strong personality emphasize the effect. This is slightly less striking in K.379–80 (on the third disc) which are later (1781) and in which the part-writing is more equal. On the fourth CD of the series we move on to K.454 and K.481, which date from 1785 and 1786, respectively. The two instruments now form a much more equal partnership. Nishizaki's tone is small and at times a little thin and uncovered (rather like a period instrument) but seems perfectly scaled for Mozart; her playing is highly musical, and these artists strike a Mozartian symbiosis that is appealing in its fresh simplicity of approach.

Nishizaki's new partnership with **Benjamin Loeb** seems propitious: even the recording seems more flattering to her tone, and Loeb plays appealingly. A most enjoyable disc, especially the *Variations*. But then her whole series is rewarding.

MUSIC FOR CLAVICHORD

(i; iv) *Andante & Variations, K.501* (for 4 hands); (i) *Allegro, K.312; Minuetto, K.135;* (ii) *Adagio for Glass Harmonica, K.356; Andantino (after Gluck), K.236; March funèbre, K.453a; Pieces, K.33b & K.623; Rondo, K.494;* (iii) *Fantasia in D min., K.397* (with

coda); *Sonata in D, K.381; Theme & 2 Variations, K.460*

*** DHM/BMG 82876 83288-2. Hogwood, playing (i) Hass clavichord; (ii) Mozart's clavichord; (iii) Schiedmayer clavichord; (iv) with Adlam

Curiously named 'The Secret Mozart', this had been better given the adjective 'Intimate', for this was the instrument Mozart played at home (the actual clavichord is included here and was almost certainly used in four-handed duets with his sister Nannerl in the *Variations* which are listed first, but which come second in the programme). The principal interest here is the different sound of the three instruments whose intimate timbre was suitable only for a small room. So these recordings must be played back *very* gently, and then you will enjoy some of the composer's lesser known music, admirably played by **Hogwood**, with **Derek Adlam** in the *Variations*.

Piano duets

Adagio, K.546, & Fugue, K.426 (arr. Franz Beyer); *Allegro & Andante in G, K.357* (completed Julius André); *Larghetto & Allegro in E flat, K.Deenst; Sonata in D (for 2 pianos), K.448; Sonata in C, K.190*

🎹 *** Sony 82876 78363-2. Tal & Groethuysen

Andante & Variations in G, K.501; Fantasia in F min., K.608; Fugue, K.401; Sonatas: in B flat, K.358; F, K.497

🎹 *** Sony SK 93868. Tal & Groethuysen

Allegro & Andante, K.357; Pieces for Mechanical Organ in F min., K.594; Sonatas: in D, K.381; in C, K.521; Fragments in G, K.357 (completed Robert Levin)

🎹 *** Sony 82876 74654-2. Tal & Groethuysen

Yaara Tal and **Andreas Groethuysen** enjoy an enviable reputation, and it must be said that Mozart duo playing doesn't come much better than this. Apart from the vibrant intelligence and sensitivity of the playing, the sound is bright and well detailed. They are arguably the finest piano-duet/two-piano partnership now before the public. Like their Schubert CDs some years back, these performances are impeccably musical, fresh and sensitive. In every way superb.

Adagio & Rondo in C min./maj., K.617; Sonatas (for 2 pianos) in D, K.448; in B flat (realized Goldstone); in G (with 2nd piano part by Grieg), K.283; Overture: Die Zauberflöte (arr. Busoni)

*** Divine Art dda 25046. Goldstone & Clemmow

Goldstone and **Clemmow** open their collection with the *Magic Flute Overture*, surprisingly successful in Busoni's transcription. But **Anthony Goldstone's** own arrangements are very attractive too – the *Rondo*, K.617, is delightful, while Grieg's second piano part for K.283 is a fascinating novelty. The performances are excellent, as is the recording.

(i) *Andante with 5 Variations, K.501; Fugue in C min., K.426; Sonatas for Piano Duet: in C, K.19d; G, K.357; B flat, K.358; D, K.381; Sonata in D for 2 Pianos, K.448; F, K.497; C, K.521* (both for piano duet)

🎵– (BB) *** Warner Apex 2564 62037-2 (2). Güher & Süher Pekinel

This excellent duo are in their element in Mozart. Their playing is full of life and spirit, yet their vigour never rides roughshod over Mozart. The *Andante* of K.381 is beautifully poised, while the *molto allegro* of its D major companion (for two pianos) is memorably bold, rhythmic and infectious. The other works are hardly less compelling and the *Andante and Variations* make an engaging counterpart. Excellent, modern, digital recording makes this a first recommendation for this repertoire.

Andante with 5 Variations, K.501; Sonata in D, K.448

*** Chan. 9162. Lortie, Mercier – SCHUBERT: *Fantasia in F min.* ***

Andante & Variations in G, K.501 (for piano, 4 hands); Sonata in D, K.448; Fantasia for Mechanical Organ in F min., K.608 (arr. Busoni for 2 pianos)

🎵– 🟊 (M) **** Sony 517490-2. Perahia & Lupu – SCHUBERT: *Fantasia in D min.* ****

The partnership of two such individual artists as **Murray Perahia** and **Radu Lupu** produces magical results, particularly when it was set up in the context of the Aldeburgh Festival, playing at The Maltings concert hall. The *D Major Sonata*, like the Schubert *Fantasia*, was recorded live. For this reissue two more works have been added, recorded at Abbey Road in 1990. The performance of the *Andante and Variations* is full of felicity and charm, but the transcribed *Fantasia* is another matter. All thoughts of the original instrumentation disappear in this remarkably arresting performance with its powerfully motivated outer movements and delicate but never flimsy *Adagio*. Very good recording makes this a reissue not to be missed.

The **Louis Lortie–Hélène Mercier** partnership also gives one of the most sensitive accounts of the *D major Sonata*, K.448, currently available on disc, and their account of the *Andante and Variations* is equally fine. The Schubert coupling is also recommendable. Very good recording.

Sonatas: in F, K.497; in C, K.521; Pieces for mechanical organ: Adagio & Allegro in F min., K.594; Adagio & Allegro in F min., K.608

🟊 *** Ottavio OTR C129242. Cooper, Queffélec

Above all, these performances convey a sense of joy in the music. The *Sonatas* – both highly inspired – are framed by the two works for mechanical clock, which here sound both thoughtful and unusually commanding: the opening *Adagio* of K.594 is wonderfully serene. The first movement of the *C major Sonata* sets off with great spirit, yet detail is always imaginatively observed. The slow movement of K.497 is a

lovely, flowing melody, persuasively presented, while the finale has a most engaging lilt. Altogether this is playing of great distinction. Everything is marvellously fresh. Very strongly recommended.

Solo piano music

Piano Sonatas 1–18 (complete)

(B) *** EMI (ADD) 7 67294-2 (5). Barenboim

Piano Sonatas 1–18; Adagio, K.540; Allegro, K.312; Fantasias, K.396; K.397 & K.475; Gigue, K.574; Minuets, K.1 & K.355; Rondos, K.485 & K.511; Variations, K.264/5; 455; 573; K.Anh. 137

(B) (***) DG (mono) 477 5856 (6). Seemann

Piano Sonatas 1–18; Fantasia in C min., K.475; Variations, K.24–5; 54; 179–80; 264–5; 353–4; 398; 455; 500; 573; 613

(B) **(*) EMI 5 73915-2 (8). Barenboim

Piano Sonatas 1–18; Fantasia in C min., K.475

🟊 (B) Ph. 468 356-2 (5). Uchida

(B) *** Decca (ADD) 443 717-2 (5). Schiff

Piano Sonatas 1–17; Fantasias: in D min., K.397; in C min., K.475; Rondo in D, K.488

(B) *** Sony 82876 88808-2 (4). Kraus

Piano Sonatas 1–18; Fantasias: in D min., K.397; C min., K.475

*** DG (IMS) 431 760-2 (6). Pires

Piano Sonatas 1–18; Fantasias, K.457 & K.396; Variations, K.353; Variations, K.398 & K.460; Allegro, K.312; Minuet, K.355; Rondo, K.511; Adagio, K.540; Gigue, K.574

(M) (***) Music & Arts mono (ADD) CD-1001 (5). Kraus

Piano Sonatas 1–18; Fantasia in C min., K.475; Adagio in B min., K.540; Eine kleine Gigue, K.574; Fantasy Fragment in D min., K.397; Klavierstücke in F, K.33b; Kleiner Trauermarsch, K.453a; Modulation Prelude in F/E min., K.6 Deest; Overture, K.399; Prelude in C, K.284a; Prelude & Fugue in C, K.394; Rondos, K.485 & K.511; Variations, K.24; K.25; K.180; K.264; K.265; K.352; K.353; K.354; K.398; K.455; K.457; K.460; K.573; K.613

🎵– (BB) *** BIS CD 1633/36 (10). Brautigam (fortepiano)

Ronald Brautigam's set is bursting with life and intelligence. He uses a 1992 copy (made in his native Amsterdam) of a fortepiano by Anton Gabriel Walter from about 1795. It is a very good instrument and he is a very good player. Dip in anywhere in this set and you will be rewarded with playing of great imagination and sensitivity – not to mention sureness and agility of mind and fingers, and he is completely inside the Mozartian sensibility of the period. This series has given great pleasure, and it is beautifully recorded too. The ten discs are offered for the price of four and now come in a box with two booklets offering separate documentation for the *Sonatas* and for the *Variations* plus miscellaneous pieces.

Maria João Pires is a stylist and a fine Mozartian. She is always refined yet never wanting in classical feeling, and she has a vital imagination. She strikes an ideal balance between poise and expressive sensibility, conveying a sense of spontaneity in everything she does. Moreover, the DG recording is full, and the slight dryness to the timbre suits the interpretations, which are expressively fluid and calm, without a trace of self-consciousness. While Uchida's much-praised versions are full of personal intimacy, Pires's more direct style with its tranquil eloquence is no less satisfying.

Uchida's set of the Mozart *Sonatas*, with the *C minor Fantasia* thrown in for good measure, brings playing of consistently fine sense and sound musicianship. Every phrase is beautifully placed, every detail registers, and the early *Sonatas* are as revealing as the later ones. The piano recording is completely realistic, slightly distanced in a believable ambience.

Barenboim, while keeping his playing well within scale in its crisp articulation, refuses to adopt the Dresden china approach to Mozart's *Sonatas*. Even the little *C major*, K.545, designed for a young player, has its element of toughness, minimizing its 'eighteenth-century drawing-room' associations. Though – with the exception of the two minor-key *Sonatas* – these are relatively unambitious works, Barenboim's voyage of discovery brings out their consistent freshness, with the orchestral implications of some of the *Allegros* strongly established. The recording, with a pleasant ambience round the piano sound, confirms the apt scale.

EMI now also offer an alternative choice of a complete coverage of *all* the important solo piano music. The *Variations* were recorded – more forwardly – in Munich in 1991. As before, **Barenboim's** positive, direct approach brings all this music fully to life. But compared with the *Sonatas* the music is much more variable in interest, and this is a set to dip into with a degree of discretion, for Mozart occasionally seems almost on auto-pilot, writing for comparatively unsophisticated tastes.

Schiff, without exceeding the essential Mozartian sensibility, takes a somewhat more romantic and forward-looking view of the music. His fingerwork is precise yet mellow, and his sense of colour consistently excites admiration. He is slightly prone to self-indulgence in the handling of some phrases, but such is the inherent freshness and spontaneity of his playing that one accepts the idiosyncrasies as a natural product of live performance. The piano is set just a little further back than in the Philips/Uchida recordings, and the acoustic is marginally more open, which suits his slightly more expansive manner.

Lili Kraus, born in Budapest in 1905, recorded her earlier cycle of the Mozart *Sonatas*, as well as shorter pieces, in New York for the Haydn Society in 1954. Compared with her later recording, issued by Sony, the closeness of the sound allows one to appreciate more the diamond clarity of Kraus's play-

ing with its high dynamic contrasts, even if *pianissimos* are not as hushed as they might be. These earlier performances are not only more dramatic but more spontaneous-sounding too, with firmer technical control. The mono sound is well transferred to make it firm and vivid. In both recordings Kraus omits the composite *Sonata in F*, K.533/494, which Mozart created by adding to two late movements an earlier *Rondo* in less complex style.

Sony have now reissued **Lili Kraus's** later recordings, made in 1967/8. They have the distinct advantage of a recording with a wider dynamic range and more bloom on the piano sound, which is very naturally balanced. Indeed, this set is very enjoyable indeed, so consistently engaging is Kraus's Mozartian touch, and her phrasing is equally refreshing.

Carl Seemann's simplicity of approach and his refusal to let his interpretations be coloured by self-seeking or wilful eccentricity may mean that to some ears his playing seems too plain, even aloof. Yet his natural musicality, the way he can turn a phrase dispassionately but thoughtfully and with subtle feeling, has its own appeal in this repertoire. His playing is intuitively balanced and, in its unostentatiously quiet way, very rewarding, for it has a natural, unforced spontaneity.

Piano Sonatas 2 in F, K.280; 13 in B flat. K.333; 14 in C min., K.457; Fantasia in C min., K.475

🅑🅑 **(*)** Naxos 8.550 449. Jandó

Jenö Jandó's Mozartian collection shows him as a natural Mozartian, if perhaps not an inspired one. He opens with impressive accounts of both the *Fantasia* and the *C minor Sonata*, which are related, finding their drama, and playing the central *Andantino* of the *Fantasia* very appealingly. Indeed, each of the *Sonatas* is firmly characterized, with thoughtful accounts of slow movements (the *Andante cantabile* of K.333 and the *Adagio* of K.280 are most sensitive without being sentimentalized) and in each case the finales are pleasingly light-hearted. The recording, made in the Budapest Unitarian Church, is faithful and this collection is satisfyingly unostentatious and direct.

Piano Sonatas: 3 in B flat, K.281; 10 in C, K.330; 11 in A, K.331; 12 Variations on 'Ah, vous dirai-je, Maman', K.265

⏽— 🅑🅑 *** Regis RRC 1255. Tirimo

Piano Sonatas: 12 in F, K.332; 13 in B flat, K.333; 16 in C, K.545; in D, K.576

⏽— 🅑🅑 *** Regis RRC 1254. Tirimo

Martino Tirimo's Regis CDs are taken from a complete cycle of Mozart's piano music which he undertook for the Mozart Anniversary in 2006. If the rest are as good as these, the set will be a top recommendation. This is playing of distinction, essaying as wide a dynamic and expressive range as is appropriate for this repertoire, and full of joyful spontaneity. The very realistic recordings, which bring out his perceptive keyboard colouring, were made in the Mendelssohn Saal at the Leipzig Gewandhaus, which seems to have an ideal ambience for the piano. Highly recommended.

Piano Sonatas 3; 10; 13; Adagio, K.540; Rondo, K.485

☛ Ⓜ *** DG 445 517-2. Horowitz

Playing of such strong personality from so great an artist is self-recommending. With **Horowitz** there were astonishingly few reminders of the passage of time and the artistry and magnetism remain undiminished. The recordings were made in the pianist's last vintage period, between 1985 and 1989, in either a New York studio, the pianist's home, or an Italian studio in Milan (K.333). Remarkable playing, not always completely free from affectation; but for variety of articulation just sample the *Allegretto grazioso* finale of K.333 and, for simply expressed depth of feeling, the *Adagio*, K.540.

Piano Sonatas 4 in E flat, K.282; 14 in C min., K.457; Fantasia in C min., K.475; Suite in C, K.388 with Gigue, K.574; 10 Variations in G on the Aria 'Unser dummer Pöbel meint' from Gluck's 'Die Pilgrime von Mekka'

☛ Ⓑ *** HMX 2961815. Staier (fortepiano)

We know that **Andreas Staier** is an outstanding artist, but on this CD he has surpassed himself. The instrument is a copy of a fortepiano by the Viennese maker Anton Walter, very similar to an instrument he built for Mozart. It is perfect for the opening piece in the programme, a baroque-styled *Suite* that Mozart wrote in 1782 but left unfinished. Staier has completed the *Sarabande* and supplied as the missing closing movement Mozart's '*kleine Gigue*', K.574, which makes a witty ending. Apart from the *Overture*, very much in the style of Handel, there is an exquisite *Allemande*, which is played here very beautifully and with every bit as much colour as could be given by a modern piano.

Staier's performance of the *E flat Sonata* is no less appealing, and the engaging *Variations* were used by Tchaikovsky in his *Mozartiana Suite* and show again the fortepiano's rich lower sonority to fine effect. But the highlight of the recital is the masterly *C minor Fantasy*, which is superbly played and leaves an unforgettable impression.

Piano Sonatas 7–10, K.309–11 & K.331

☛ ❀ ⒷⒷ **** Regis (ADD) RRC 1207. Walter Klien

Walter Klien's set of the Mozart sonatas, dates from 1964. The discs were originally issued in Vox Boxes (three LPs at a time). But they eventually found their way individually onto the celebrated Turnabout label. Now they are reintroduced to the British catalogue on Regis. Klien's playing is fresh, strongly characterized and with constant sensitivity; he is determined to show that there are no favourites, just a succession of masterpieces. Even so in this sampler the exquisite *Andante cantabile* of the A minor (K.310) and the spirited opening *Allegro* of the D major (K.311) are particularly memorable. On CD the recording is clean and clear, a little dry perhaps, but these performances are special.

Piano Sonatas 8; 11; 13; 14; Adagio, K.540; Fantasia, K.475; Rondo, K.511; 9 Variations in D on a Minuet by Dupont, K.573

Ⓑ **(*) Ph. Duo (ADD/DDD) 454 244-2 (2). Brendel

The recordings of the *A major Sonata*, K.331, and the *B flat*, K.333, come from 1971 and 1975 respectively and they show **Brendel** at his very finest, while the *B minor Adagio* is also memorable. K.331, with its engaging opening theme and variations and justly famous *Alla turca* finale, is a joy. The analogue recording, too, is most realistic. However, the *A minor*, K.310, and the *C minor*, recorded digitally in the following decade, are more controversial. Brendel seems unwilling to seduce us by beauty of sound, and the result is self-conscious playing, immaculately recorded. Fortunately, he is back on form in the *Fantasia in C minor*, the *Rondo* and the *Variations*.

Piano Sonatas 8; 11; 15

☛ ✪ **** Sony SK 48233. Perahia

Such is **Murray Perahia's** artistry that one is never consciously aware of it. Nothing is beautified, nor does he shrink from conveying that hint of pain that fleetingly disturbs the symmetry of the slow movements. The Sony engineers provide excellent sound.

Piano Sonatas: 10 in C, K.330; 11 in A, K.331; 12 in F, K.332; Adagio in B min., K.540; Fantasias: in C min., K.475; D min., K.385; Rondos: in D, K.485; A min., K.511; 9 Variations on a Minuet by Dupont in D, K.573

☛ **** EMI 2-CD 3 36080-2 (2). Lars Vogt

Not surprisingly, this is playing of distinction, and **Vogt** is fortunately given an outstandingly realistic recording with a wide dynamic range. The remarkably thoughtful and introspective *B minor Adagio* which ends the recital and the two *Fantasias* perhaps show him at his most imaginative and poetic, but the exquisite opening *Andante grazioso* of the *A major Sonata* is no less memorable, with the closing *Alla Turca Rondo* bursting in on the listener to make a thrilling, bravura finale. The two *Rondos* and the engaging *Variations* show the composer in lighter mood; but even here Vogt brings personal insights to the music, while the other two sonatas show him balancing Mozart's three-part structures with complete spontaneity and capturing every facet of the music's inner feeling.

Piano Sonatas 10; 11; 16; Rondo, K.511

*** Ph. 462 903-2. Brendel

Although for the most part recorded 'live', **Brendel's** performances here have an appealingly thoughtful intimacy, as if he were hardly conscious of the audience. Yet one still has the sense of being in Brendel's presence. Interestingly, the studio recording of the *C major Sonata*, K.330, seems very slightly less spontaneous in feeling than the rest of the programme. But altogether this is playing of distinction. Audience noises are minimal (although applause is included), and the recording, although fairly closely observed, is very natural.

Piano Sonata 15 in F, K.533/494

*** Calico Classics CCCR 101. Crossland – BEETHOVEN:
    Sonatas 17 & 31 **(*)

Jill Crossland is a natural Mozartian and gives a delightful
performance of this *F major Sonata*, compiled from a *Rondo*,
K.494, and a separate *Allegro* and *Andante*, K.533, making it
seem a composite whole. She is very well recorded.

Piano Sonatas 15 in F, K.533/494; 16 in C, K.545; 17 in B flat, K.570; 18 in D, K.576

**(*) Avie AV 0025. Haefliger

Andreas Haefliger is an artist of calibre who gives splendidly
vital accounts of these sonatas. He does not bring the same
variety of keyboard colour and dynamic nuance or poetic
feeling as do the likes of Perahia or Pletnev, but he has sobriety and an undoubted sense of style and unfailing musicianship. However, these four works are not otherwise
available together on a single CD, and it remains a satisfying
collection and benefits from excellent recorded sound.

Piano Sonatas 15 in F, K.533/494; 17 in B flat, K.570; 18 in D, K.576; Gigue, K.574; Minuet in D, K.355/594a

(M) *** Atma ACD2 2249. Sémerjian (fortepiano)

Very stylish Mozart playing by **Ludwig Sémerjian**, using a
fortepiano by Nanette Streicher, made in 1802–5 and now in
the German National Museum in Nuremburg; in any event
he is a splendid player and is well recorded too. If you want
Mozart on an instrument of the period, this is an eminently
satisfactory choice.

Piano Sonata 17

(***) Testament mono SBT 1089. Gilels – CHOPIN: *Sonata 2*;
    SHOSTAKOVICH: *Preludes & Fugues 1, 5 & 24* (***)

The *B flat Sonata* was recorded in Paris at the Théâtre des
Champs-Elysées in March 1954. The sound is a little dry and
close, but the playing has a simplicity and poetry that completely transcend sonic limitations.

Complete Variations, plus: Adagio in B min., K.540; Allegro of a Sonata in G min., K.312; Allegro & Rondo (Allegretto) in F, Anhang K.135; Andante for a Waltz in a Chamber Organ, K.616; Capriccio in C, K395; Eine kleine Gigue, K.574; Fantasies: in C min., K.396; in D min., K.397; Fantasy & Fugue in C, K.394; Fugue in G min., K.401; Kleiner Trauermarsch, K.453a; Minuet in D, K.355; 6 Pieces from London Sketchbook; Rondos: in D, K.455; in A min., K.511; Sonata movement in B flat, K.400; Sonata movement & Minuet in B flat, Anhang K.130

✿ (B) **** (Regis) Musical Concepts MC 131 (3). Klien

Some of Mozart's earliest piano pieces, like the *Variations on
a Dutch Song by Graaf*, written when he was in Amsterdam
and barely ten years old, are of relatively slight musical interest, but the remarkable *C minor Fantasy* and the *G minor
Fugue* (the product of his intense interest in Bach) are works
of substance. **Walter Klien's** playing is totally spontaneous
and can only be described as being in exemplary taste: there

is nothing self-conscious about it, his phrasing is unfailingly
musical and every detail is beautifully placed without there
being the slightest suggestion of precocity. The recorded
sound was always good; in its remastered form it is very good
indeed, wholly natural, and this is a set not to be missed.

ORGAN MUSIC

Andante in F, K.616; Adagio & Allegro in F min., K.594; Fantasia in F min. (Adagio & Allegro), K.608 (all for musical clock); Allegro in G (Veronese), K.72a; Gigue in G, K.574; (i) Epistle Sonatas: in F, K.244; in C, K.328

(BB) ** Warner (ADD) 2564 69256-5. Tachezi (organ of Basilika
    Maria Treu, Vienna); (i) with Alice and Nikolaus
    Harnoncourt and Pfeiffer

Mozart is never really thought of as a composer for the
organ. Until now, the only 'organ works' we have had on
record have been the three pieces he wrote for Count Deym's
mechanical organ attached to a clock. Mozart had no opinion of the mechanism for which his music was commissioned and is known to have wished the pieces were
intended for a large instrument. To these **Herbert Tachezi**
adds a brief *Allegro* and an attractive *Gigue*, plus two of the
Epistle Sonatas, in which he is joined by the **Harnoncourt
Trio**. The performances overall are acceptable and well registered, but there is nothing distinctive about this record,
although the sound is excellent.

VOCAL MUSIC

51 Concert Arias

(B) *** Decca (ADD/DDD) 455 241-2 (5). Te Kanawa, Gruberová,
    Berganza, Laki, Hobarth, Winbergh; VCO, Fischer; or LSO,
    Pritchard; Fischer-Dieskau, V. Haydn O, Reinhard Peters;
    Corena, ROHCGO, Quadri

This very comprehensive coverage is based on a five-LP
Decca set of the complete concert arias for female voice, published in 1981, to which those for male voice have subsequently been added. **Berganza's** collection includes the most
demanding soprano aria of all, *Ch'io me scordi di te?*, recorded
(with **Pritchard** and the **LSO**) a decade earlier than the rest.
Te Kanawa opens the programme memorably. **Gruberová's**
contribution is hardly less brilliant and charming, her
singing full of sparkle and character, and superbly articulated. The others, **Elfrieda Hobarth** and **Krisztina Laki**,
less individual personalities but do not disappoint vocally.
Laki shows impressive coloratura in her opening aria, the
little-known *Fra cento affanni*, K.88, and she is equally impressive in the lyrical flow of *Non curo l'affetto*, which again
demands comparable bravura. Hobarth's style is more operatic and she becomes a veritable Queen of the Night in
tackling the fearsome upper tessitura of *Ma che vi fece, o stelle*,
K.368, and *Mia speranza adorata!*, K.416, both of which are accomplished with confident bravado.

The digital recordings by **Gösta Winbergh**, an exceptionally stylish Mozart tenor, were added later; he rises splendidly to the challenges of such splendid arias as *Per pietà non*

ricercate, K.420, and *Aura che intorno spiri*, K.431. **Fischer-Dieskau's** contribution was a separate undertaking, recorded in 1969, and it includes a beautiful aria from 1787, *Mentre ti lascio*, which reveals Mozart's inspiration at its keenest. The other items too bring their delights. **Fernando Corena's** *Alcandro, lo confesso … Non so d'onde viene*, K.512, and *Per questa bella mano*, K.612, are less than ideally stylish and in the latter not always absolutely secure in intonation. Yet he is at his very finest in the *buffo* aria, *Rivolcete a lui lo sguardo*, K.584, originally written for *Così fan tutte* and later cut because of its length. It is a superb piece and it suits Corena's voice well, so that the full power is brought out magnificently. The CD transfers throughout are of high quality, and full translations are included, but the accompanying essay by Kenneth Chalmers documents the music only sketchily, because of limited space.

Concert arias: *Ah! lo previdi … Ah, t'invola*, K.272; *Alma grande e nobil core*, K.578; *A questo seno … Or che il cielo*, K.374; *Bella mia fiamma … Resta, o cara*, K.528; *Betracht dies Herz und frage mich*, K.42; *Misera, dove son! … Ah! non son io che parlo*, K.369; *Vado, ma dove? o Dei!*, K.583

Ⓜ *** DG (ADD) 449 723-2. Janowitz, VSO, Boettcher

Gundula Janowitz's voice combines a glorious tonal beauty with a surprising degree of flexibility so that Mozart's cruelly difficult divisions – usually written deliberately to tax the original ladies involved – present no apparent difficulty, but there is no mistaking the singer's ability to shade and refine the tone at will. An excellent collection of delightful concert arias that are too often neglected nowadays, thanks to the vagaries of modern concert-planning.

(i; iii) Lieder: *Abendempfindung; Als Luise die Briefe; Die Alte; An Chloe; Dans un bois solitaire; Im Frühlingsanfang; Das Kinderspiel; Die kleine Spinnerin; Das Lied der Trennung; Oiseaux, si tous les ans; Ridente la calma; Sehnsucht nach dem Frühling; Das Trumbild; Das Veilchen; Der Zauberer; Die Zuhfriedenheit*; (ii; iii) *Piano and Wind Quintet in E Flat*, K.452

⊶ Ⓜ **** EMI mono 3 53226-2. Schwarzkopf, Gieseking, (iii) Philh. Wind. Ens.

Schwarzkopf's classic recital of the Mozart songs with **Gieseking** was recorded in 1955 and includes the famous *Das Veilchen*. With such inspired performances, one hardly worries about the mono sound. The coupling includes Gieseking's famous recording of the *Piano and Wind Quintet* which sounds remarkably fresh. Thankfully, full texts and translations are included in this mid-price release.

Concert aria: *Ch'io mi scordi di te?*, K.505

(***) Testament mono SBT 1178. Schwarzkopf, Anda, Philh. O, Ackermann – BACH: *Cantatas 199; 202* ***

This account of *Ch'io mi scordi di te?*, recorded in 1955 with **Géza Anda** playing the difficult piano obbligato, is uniquely fresh and urgent, with **Schwarzkopf's** vehement side given free rein. A splendid and valuable supplement to the Bach

recordings, which have also remained unissued for far too long.

Concert aria: *Ombra felice*, K.255; Opera arias: *Ascanio in Alba: Ah di si nobil alma; Mitridate: Venga pur, Gia dagli occhi*

⊶ *** Virgin 5 45365-2. Daniels, OAE, Bicket – GLUCK; HANDEL: *Arias* ***

Under the title '*Sento amor*', **David Daniels** offers one of the finest of counter-tenor recitals. In the arias from early Mozart operas, the brilliance of his singing is what stands out above all, giving beauty and energy to the florid writing, as well as a deeper expressiveness to the lyrical passages than one might expect. At once pure and warm, completely avoiding the usual counter-tenor hoot, placing his voice flawlessly, Daniels is exceptional even in an age which has produced many outstanding rivals.

Sacred Vocal Music

Ave Maria, K.555; Ave verum corpus, K.618; Litaniae Lauretanae, K.109; Masses: 10 (spatzenmesse), K.220; 16 (Coronation); Regina Coeli, K.276

*** Lyrichord LEMS 8059. Amor Artis Ch., Musica Antiqua Sankt Petersburg

Johannes Somary and his excellent **Amor Artis** choral group has joined up with the excellent **Musica Antiqua Sankt Petersburg** period-instrument group in New York for a highly enjoyable selection of Mozart's choral music. The opening motet, *Regina coeli*, is warmly sung, but throughout this programme the singing combines (unexaggerated) fervour with lyrical warmth. Tempi are usually well judged (perhaps the famous *Ave verum corpus*, which is sung accompanied, is a trifle leisurely, but not to ill effect). The singing throughout combines joy in the music with an easy-going spontaneity and, with good balance and recording, this is a most recommendable programme, particularly as it includes the comparatively rare *Litaniae Lauretanae*.

Ave verum corpus, K.618; Exsultate, jubilate, K.165; Kyrie in D min., K.341; Vesperae solennes de confessore in C, K.339

⊶ **** Ph. 412 873-2. Te Kanawa, Bainbridge, R. Davies, Howell, L. Symphony Ch., LSO, C. Davis

This disc could hardly present a more delightful collection of Mozart choral music, ranging from the early soprano cantata, *Exsultate, jubilate*, with its famous setting of *Alleluia*, to the equally popular *Ave verum*. **Kiri Te Kanawa** is the brilliant soloist in the cantata, and her radiant account of the lovely *Laudate Dominum* is one of the high spots of the *Solemn Vespers*, here given a fine, responsive performance. The 1971 recording has been remastered effectively, although the choral sound is not ideally focused.

(i–ii) Ave verum corpus, K.618; (iii–iv) Exsultate, jubilate, K.165; Masses Nos. (i–iii; v) 10 in C (Missa brevis): Spatzenmesse, K.220; (ii–iii; vi) 16 in C (Coronation), K.317

(M) *** DG (IMS) (ADD) 419 060-2. (i) Regensburg Cathedral Ch.; (ii) Bav. RSO, Kubelik; (iii) Mathis; (iv) Dresden State O, Klee; (v) Troyanos, Laubenthal, Engen; (vi) Procter, Grobe, Shirley-Quirk, Bav. R. Ch.

Kubelik draws a fine, vivid performance of the *Coronation Mass* from his Bavarian forces and is no less impressive in the earlier *Missa brevis*, with excellent soloists in both works. Then **Edith Mathis** gives a first-class account of the *Exsultate, jubilate* as an encore. The concert ends with **Bernard Klee** directing a serenely gentle account of the *Ave verum corpus* (recorded in 1979).

Davide penitente (Oratorio); Regina coeli, K.108

(N) (BB) *** Naxos 8.570231. Lund, Wahlin, Odinius, Immortal Bach Ens., Leipzig CO, Schuldt-Jensen

Mozart's remarkably effective oratorio, using quite a big orchestra, was commissioned by the Vienna Society of Artists in 1785. He drew on previous music but also added a pair of splendid new arias and, although the choruses are lively, it is the soprano arias (and especially a duet and terzetto featuring the two sopranos) that brings some radiant singing from the two fine soloists here, **Trine Wilsberg Lund** and **Kristina Wahlin**, while the tenor, **Lothar Odinius**, is also excellent. The brief *Regina coeli*, written 14 years earlier, also features the soprano voice memorably and makes an enjoyable bonus. With fine choral singing and excellent playing from the **Leipzig Chamber Orchestra** under **Morten Schuldt-Jensen**, this is refreshingly enjoyable, the more so for being little known. The recording is first class and there are full texts and translations.

Davide penitente, K.469; Exsultate, jubilate, K.165; Così fan tutte: Temerari! . . . Come scoglio; Ei perte . . . Per pietà, ben mio; Un uomini, in soldati; Le nozze di Figaro: E Susanna non vien! . . . Dove sono; Giuse alfin il momento . . . Al desio; Don Giovanni: Batti, batti, o bel Masetto; In quali eccessi . . . Mi tradi quall'alma ingrati

🔄 (M) *** Decca 475 7526. Bartoli, V. CO, G. Fischer

'*Mozart Portraits*' is a truly remarkable Mozartian collection, showing that **Cecilia Bartoli** not only has an astonishing range – vocal and dramatic – and dazzling coloratura (as in *Exsultate, jubilate* and elsewhere), but she is also an artist who can create real operatic human characters and express their feelings vividly and touchingly. Fiordiligi's *Come scoglio* is tempestuous, her *Per pietà* ravishingly tender. For Despina the voice is much lighter (although one could have done without the 'laugh'), and her *Un uomini, in soldati* charmingly displays that she has no illusions about mankind, for all her vivacious femininity; while Zerlina's *Batti, batti* is simply enchanting Mozartian lyricism. The Countess's *Dove sono* is heart-rending, but then Bartoli becomes Susanna in her supreme moments of happy expectation. The selection ends as it began, in an expression of true female ferocity from Donna Elvira, but she is still in love, and her tenderness then brings most beautiful singing on the disc. With splendid accompaniments from **György Fischer** and the **Vienna Chamber Orchestra** (the bravura horns in the *Così fan tutte*

aria are really something), this excellently recorded disc returns to the catalogue as one of Decca's Originals (with full texts and translations included).

(i) Exsultate, jubilate, K.165; (ii) Litaniae Lauretanae in D, K.195; Mass 16 (Coronation), K.317; (iii) Requiem Mass (No. 19) in D min., K.626

(B) **(*) Double Decca (ADD) 443 009-2 (2). (i) Spoorenberg; (ii; iii) Cotrubas, Watts, Tear, Shirley-Quirk; (ii) Oxford Schola Cantorum; (iii) ASMF Ch; (i-iii), ASMF, Marriner

Marriner's 1971 (Argo) recordings of the *Litaniae Lauretanae* and the *Coronation Mass* are welcome, back in the catalogue on this Double Decca set. The solo work is particularly good (notably **Ileana Cotrubas** in the two lovely *Agnus Dei* versions) and the **Academy Choir** is on its best form. **Erna Spoorenberg's** impressive *Exsultate, jubilate* was recorded earlier (1966). However, Marriner generates less electricity than usual in the coupled (1977) *Requiem Mass*. It is interesting to have a version which uses the Beyer Edition and a text which aims at removing the faults of Süssmayr's completion. Solo singing is good, and some of the choruses (the *Dies irae*, for instance) are vibrant, but at other times they are less alert and the tension slackens. The sound is excellent, well balanced and vivid.

Exsultate, jubilate, K.165 (Salzburg version); Motets: Ergo interest, K.143; Regina coeli (2 settings), K.108, K.127

*** Australian Decca Eloquence 476 7460. Kirkby, Westminster Cathedral Boys' Ch., AAM Ch. & O, Hogwood

The boyish, bell-like tones of **Emma Kirkby** (in 1983) are perfectly suited to the most famous of Mozart's early cantatas, *Exsultate, jubilate*, culminating in a dazzling account of *Alleluia*. With accompaniment on period instruments, this is aptly coupled with far rarer but equally fascinating examples of Mozart's early genius, superbly recorded. A refreshing and enjoyable collection.

Kyrie, K.341/K368a

(*) Profil Medien PH 6039. Stuart, Schone (organ), Dresden PO Children's Ch., State Opera Ch. & Children's Ch., Symphony Ch., Singakademie; Dresden State O, C. Davis – BERLIOZ: *Te Deum* *

As a supplement to the Berlioz in the same concert (recorded live at the Kreuzkirche, Dresden, in October 1998), **Davis** conducted music by his other favourite composer, Mozart, the *Kyrie* in D minor, K.341. What will be disconcerting to many listeners today is that he treats it almost as though it is by Berlioz, with all idea of an apt 18th-century scale abandoned in a massive celebration.

Masses: 2 (Missa brevis), K.65; 3 (Dominicus), K.66; 4 (Waisenhaus), K.139; 7 (Missa in honorem Ssmae Trinitatis); 10 (Spatzenmesse), K.220; 11 (Credo), K.257; 12 (Spaur), K.258; 13 (Organ Solo), K.259; 16 (Coronation Mass), K.317; 17 (Missa solemnis), K.337; 18 (Great), K.427; 19 (Requiem), K.626; Ave verum corpus, K.618

(BB) **(*) Virgin 2x1 5 61769-2 (5). Frimmer, Kwella, Monoyios, Montague, Schlick, Graf, Groenewold, Chance, Pfaff, Prégardien, Schäfer, Mertens, Selig, Cologne Chamber Ch., Coll. Cartusianum, Neumann

As can be seen from our comments about the Virgin Double of Masses 16–18 below, **Peter Neumann's** performances are fresh, stylish, warmly enjoyable and very well sung. Most importantly, these artists give a very fine, dramatic account of the *Requiem* (not included below), and the recording here is excellent, clear and vivid. The soloists are all very good throughout, and the other Masses, early and late, have plenty of character. The backward balance of the chorus is not enough of a problem to make this other than a worthwhile collection of some of Mozart's finest non-operatic vocal music.

Mass 3 in C (Dominicus), K.66; Vesperae de Domenica, K.321

⊕━ (M) *** Teldec 2292 46469-2. Margiono, Bonney, von Magnus, Heilmann, Cachemaille, Arnold Schoenberg Ch., V. Hofburgkapelle Ch. Scholars, VCM, Harnoncourt

Harnoncourt is at his finest in this splendidly lively Mass, which the thirteen-year-old Mozart wrote for a personal friend ten years his senior when he took holy orders, and the direct Harnoncourt style, with its strong accents and positive characterization, brings it vividly to life. The more ambitious *Vesperae de Domenica*, written a decade later, forms a neat and joyful *Missa brevis*, here refreshingly alive and brimful of variety of invention. Again the singing of chorus and soloists alike is highly stimulating, and Harnoncourt's affection brings a committed and vivacious approach which is entirely successful. The recording is first rate.

Masses (i–ii) 4 (Waisenhaus); (iii) 7 (Missa in honorem Ssmae Trinitatis); (i–ii) 11 (Credo); (ii; iv) 16 (Coronation); 17 (Missa solemnis)

(B) **(*) Double Decca (ADD) 455 032-2 (2). (i) Mentzer, Manca di Nissa, Mackie, Roberts; (ii) King's College, Cambridge, Ch., ECO, Cleobury; (iii) V. State Op. Ch., VPO, Münchinger; (iv) with Marshall, Murray, Covey-Crump, Wilson-Johnson

Mozart's early *C minor Mass* is notable both for its rich choral writing and for the fine *Benedictus*, a dialogue between soprano and chorus, with the trumpets entering resplendently for the *Amen*. It is presented here most effectively by **Stephen Cleobury** and his team. The *Missa Trinitas*, written in Salzburg five years later, is even more ambitious, using a big orchestra with copious brass (four trumpets and three trombones) as well as oboe, strings and organ. **Münchinger** offers a strong, direct account, but the disappointment of this 1974 recording, made in the Sofiensaal, is how little is made of the trumpets, which, even in the *Credo*, are backwardly balanced. The other recordings are digital and were made a decade later. Cleobury is perhaps at his finest in the *Credo Mass* and, with the help of his excellent soloists, gives a vividly exuberant performance of a work that shows its composer at his most sunnily high-spirited throughout. The *Missa solemnis in C major*, K.337, was the very last of the 15 set-

tings that Mozart wrote for Salzburg, another work that is just as inspired as the better-known *Coronation Mass*. Though Cleobury's direction here could be rhythmically more lively, both performances are of high quality, with excellent soloists and fresh choral singing.

Masses (i) 10 (Spatzenmesse), K.220; (ii) 18 (Great), K.427; (iii) 19 (Requiem), K.626

(B) **(*) DG Double (ADD/DDD) 459 409-2 (2). (i) Mathis, Troyanos, Laubenthal, Engen, Regensburg Cathedral Ch., Bav. RSO, Kubelik; (ii) Battle, Cuberli, Seiffert, Moll, V. State Op. Konzertvereinigung, VPO, Levine; (iii) Tomowa-Sintow, Baltsa, Krenn, van Dam, V. Singverein, VPO, Karajan

Kubelik's direct but lively account of the *Spatzenmesse* does not disappoint: his soloists, led by **Edith Mathis**, make a good team and the recording from the early 1970s is fresh and clear. (This is also available coupled with the *Ave verum corpus* and *Coronation Mass* – see above.) **Karajan's** 1975 analogue recording of the *Requiem* is outstandingly fine, deeply committed, with incisive playing and clean-focused singing from the chorus, not too large and set a little behind. The fine quartet of soloists too is beautifully blended. **Levine's** recording of the *C minor Mass* is digital and dates from 1987. There are reservations about the tremulous soprano line in the chorus, which otherwise sings powerfully. The soloists are individually impressive (**Kathleen Battle** shines in the *Laudamus te*), but the ensemble of the *Quoniam* is less than ideally polished, and the performance overall is a little rough round the edges. Yet the music's emotional power is never in doubt, for Levine's reading has a compelling, spontaneous vigour. The recording, too, is very live and vivid.

Mass 16 in C (Coronation), K.317

(M) **(*) DG (IMS) 445 543-2 (2). Battle, Schmidt, Winbergh, Furlanetto, V. Singverein, VPO, Karajan – BEETHOVEN: *Missa solemnis* **(*)

(B) **(*) DG Double (ADD) 453 016-2 (2). Tomowa-Sintow, Baltsa, Krenn, van Dam, V. Singverein, BPO, Karajan – BEETHOVEN: *Missa solemnis* ***

Karajan's 1985 recording of Mozart's *Coronation Mass* is certainly vibrant, with fine choral singing and good soloists. **Kathleen Battle** sings beautifully in the *Agnus Dei*, and the recording is bright, if not ideally expansive.

Karajan's earlier (1976) recording is a dramatic reading, lacking something in rhythmic resilience perhaps; but, with excellent solo singing as well as an incisive contribution from the chorus, there is no lack of strength and the score's lyrical elements are sensitively managed. The current remastering has further improved the sound.

Masses (i) 16 (Coronation); 17 (Missa solemnis); (ii) 18 (Great); Kyrie in D min., K.341

(BB) **(*) Virgin 2x1 3 91803-2 (2). Cologne Chamber Ch., Coll. Cartusianum, Neumann; with (i) Kwella, Groenewold, Prégardien, Selig; (ii) Schlick, Frimmer, Prégardien, Mertens

Neumann directs an enjoyable account of the *Coronation Mass*, as well as the much rarer *Missa solemnis*, which is on a similar scale and is also very well sung. The *C minor Mass* has much to commend it: fine soloists – with **Barbara Schlick** always fresh and captivating in the *Laudamus te* – spacious choral singing (if, again, somewhat backwardly balanced) and excellent playing from an authentic-sized orchestra on original instruments. The only caveat is that the chorus again lacks the bite to make the performance really gripping. A good super-bargain set (if without texts or translations), which has much to recommend it.

Masses (i) 16 in C (Coronation); (ii) 19 in D min. (Requiem); Ave verum corpus

(M) *** DG 477 7164 (without *Ave verum corpus*). Tomowa-Sintow, Baltsa, Krenn, van Dam, V. Singverein, BPO, Karajan

🎵 (M) *** Ph. 464 720-2. (i) M. Price, Schmidt, Araiza, Adam; (ii) Mathis, Rappé, Blochwitz, Quasthoff; Leipzig R. Ch., Dresden Staatskapelle, Schreier

Karajan's earlier (1975) *Coronation Mass* is a dramatic reading, lacking something in rhythmic resilience perhaps but, with excellent solo singing as well as an incisive contribution from the chorus, there is no lack of strength and the score's lyrical elements are sensitively managed. The current remastering has further improved the sound. The *Requiem*, recorded at the same time, is even finer, deeply committed with incisive playing and clean-focused singing from the chorus, not too large and set a little behind. The fine quartet of soloists is again beautifully blended and nothing is smoothed over and, with excellent sound, such a passage as the *Dies irae* has exceptional freshness and intensity.

Schreier's 1982 version of the *Requiem* is here supplemented by the *Coronation Mass* and *Ave verum corpus*, recorded a decade later with the same choir and orchestra. By latter-day standards the opening *Introitus* of the *Requiem* is rather heavy, but that is the exception in this intensely dramatic and purposeful reading, with **Dame Margaret Price** singing ravishingly. The quartet of soloists is impressive too in the *Coronation Mass*, and in both the **Leipzig Radio Choir** sings with superb attack, if occasionally resorting to an aspirated style. Full, well-refurbished sound.

Mass 16 in C (Coronation), K.317; Vesperae solennes de Confessore, K.339

(N) (M) ** Teldec/Warner 2564 69259-7. Rodgers, von Magnus, Protschka, Polgár, Arnold Schoenberg Ch., V. Hofburkapelle Choral Scholars, VCM, Harnoncourt

Harnoncourt is not entirely logical in using period instruments but also women rather than boy trebles in the choir. As usual, accents are strong, dynamic contrasts are exaggerated, and phrasing is somewhat eccentrically moulded, although **Joan Rodgers** is a fine soprano soloist in both works, her line eloquent and without exaggerations. The recording has plenty of atmosphere, but could be more clearly defined.

Coronation Mass: Agnus Dei; Exsultate jubilate; Regina coeli, K.108; Regina coeli, K.127; Sancta

Maria, Mater Dei; Solemn Vespers: Laudate Dominum from K.321 & K.339; Sub tuum praesidium

🎵 *** Hyp. CDA 67560. Sampson, King's Consort and Ch., King

Carolyn Sampson with her bright, pure soprano provides the focus of **Robert King's** well-compiled collection of Mozart choral works, most of them early. Sampson's singing of the showpiece, *Exsultate jubilate*, rivals Dame Kiri Te Kanawa's and Cecilia Bartoli's classic recordings in its freshness and brilliance, and her radiance in the two settings of *Laudate Dominum* is a delight too. King's Mozartian style, incisive and direct, gives vigour to even the less inspired of the early works.

Mass 18 in C min. (Great), K.427

🎵 **** DG 439 012-2. Hendricks, Perry, Schreier, Luxon, V. Singverein, BPO, Karajan

🎵 **** Ph. 420 210-2. McNair, Montague, Rolfe Johnson, Hauptmann, Monteverdi Ch., E. Bar. Sol., Gardiner

In his (1982) digital recording of the *C minor Mass* **Karajan** gives Handelian splendour to this greatest of Mozart's choral works and, though the scale is large, the beauty and intensity are hard to resist. Solo singing is first rate, particularly that of **Barbara Hendricks**, the dreamy beauty of her voice ravishingly caught. Woodwind is rather backward, yet the sound is both rich and vivid – though, as the opening shows, the internal balance is not always completely consistent.

John Eliot Gardiner, using period instruments, gives an outstandingly fresh performance of high dramatic contrasts, marked by excellent solo singing: both the sopranos pure and bright-toned and **Anthony Rolfe Johnson** in outstandingly sweet voice. With the recording giving an ample scale without inflation, this too can be warmly recommended.

Mass 18 in C min., K.427; Mass 19 (Requiem), K.626 (DVD version)

🎵 **** Ph. **DVD** 074 3121. Bonney, von Otter, Rolfe Johnson, Miles, Monteverdi Ch., E. Bar. Sol., Gardiner (V/D: Jonathan Fulford)

As one would expect of Gardiner, playing and singing are both brilliant and incisive, with shattering impact in the *Dies irae*, yet there is also a tenderness not always apparent in period performances. Gardiner uses the traditional completion of the Mass published in 1901 by Alois Schmitt, yet with corrections he himself has made in the *Credo*, with the string parts in the *Et incarnatus* rewritten in a truer Mozartian style. Jonathan Fulford's video direction nicely exploits the colourful qualities of the Palau de la Musica Catelana in Barcelona, where the performance was given in 1991.

Requiem Mass (19) in D min., K.626 (DVD versions)

🎵 **** DG **DVD** 073 4135. McLaughlin, Ewing, Hadley, Hauptman, Bav. R. Ch. & O, Bernstein (V/D: Humphrey Burton)

(*) TDK **DVD DVWW-COMREQ. Yakar, Wenkel, Equiluz, Holl, V. State Op. Konzertvereinigung, VCM, Harnoncourt (with BACH: *Cantata 161: Komm du süsse Todsstunde*)

Bernstein's is an unashamedly modern-instrument version with a large choir, and the result is warmly expansive, with a broad, expressive style in the slower sections and plenty of choral weight and vitality in the fast ones. But with four excellent soloists the interpretation flows seamlessly and holds the listener in its grip. At the close Bernstein allows the last chord to diminish in a long morendo and in the following silence can be heard the tolling bells of the old collegiate church outside. Humphrey Burton ensures that we are made fully part of this remarkable occasion. (At the close there is a bonus of a brief spoken introduction to the work by Bernstein himself.)

Harnoncourt uses much smaller forces, but he also has the advantage of first-class soloists, with the soprano **Rachel Yakar** and contralto **Ortrun Wenkel** especially fine. With the camera focused on him, Harnoncourt creates a very sombre atmosphere at the opening, but his modest-sized choir respond tellingly, and his period-instrument orchestra brings clean textures, although the violins are sweet rather than abrasive. Unlike his previous audio version, the choral and orchestral focus is clean so that the impact of this relatively modest account is the more telling. He offers a Bach cantata as a bonus, also well presented.

Mass 19 (Requiem) in D min., K.626 (CD versions)

🎧 Ⓑ**** LSO **SACD** LSO 0627. Arnet, Stéphany, Kennedy, Jeffrey, L. Symphony Ch., LSO, C. Davis

🎧 Ⓑ**** Virgin 5 62478-2. Kenny, Hodgson, Davies, Howell, L. Symphony Ch., N. Sinf. & Ch., Hickox

ⓃⓂ*** EMI (ADD) 2 12718-2. Armstrong, J. Baker, Gedda, Fischer-Dieskau, John Alldis Ch., ECO, Barenboim – BRUCKNER: *Te Deum* **(*)

ⒷⒷ *** RCA Navigator (ADD) 74321 29238-2. Equiluz, Eder, V. Boys' Ch., V. State Op. Ch. & O, Gillesberger – HAYDN: *Te Deum* ***

Ⓑ **(*) CfP (ADD) 3 75934-2. Mathis, Bumbry, Shirley, Rintzler, New Philh. Ch. & O, Frühbeck de Burgos (with *Masonic Funeral Music*; cond. Klemperer)

Mass 19 in D min. (Requiem) (ed. Maunder)

🎧 Ⓜ **(*) O-L 411 712-2. Kirkby, Watkinson, Rolfe Johnson, Thomas, Westminster Cathedral Boys' Ch., AAM Ch. and O, Hogwood

Mass 19 (Requiem); (i) Grabmusik, K.42: Beatracht dies Herz; Vesperae solennes de confessore, K.339: Laudate Dominum

🎧 **** DG 463 181-2. (i) Harnisch; Mattila, Mingardo, Schade, Terfel, Swedish R. Ch.; BPO, Abbado

Mass 19 (Requiem); (i) Exsultate jubilate

**(*) Lyrichord LEMS 8056. (i) A. Brown; Kidwell, Garner, Bara, Ama Deus Ens. Ch. & O, Radu

Mass 19 (Requiem); Kyrie, K.341

🎧 **** HM HMC 901620. Rubens, Markert, Bostridge, Müller-Brachmann, La Chapelle Royale Coll. Voc., O des Champs Elysées, Herreweghe

🎧 *** Ph. 420 197-2. Bonney, von Otter, Blochwitz, White, Monteverdi Ch., E. Bar. Sol., Gardiner

(i) Mass 19 (Requiem); Maurerische Trauermusik, K.477

Ⓑ *** Auvidis ES 9965. Soloists, La Capella Reial de Catalunya; Le Concert des Nations, Savall

Recorded live at the Barbican in the autumn of 2007, **Sir Colin Davis's** new recording tends to sweep the board, and as it is offered on SACD at bargain price, the absence of a coupling is not a drawback. In any case the performance is superb. It has all the power and spontaneity of live music-making and employs characteristic influences from period performance which Davis integrates fully, with the hard-nosed timpani quite electrifying in the glorious *Sanctus* and again in the closing *Domine Jesu*. The soloists are all excellent individually, and they sing movingly together as a team in the *Recordare* and *Domine Jesu*. The **London Symphony Chorus** sing with passion and are recorded with plenty of bite, and the **LSO** back them up by playing very impressively. The SACD surround sound is very realistic indeed, and the overall effect is most vivid, making a full impact without seeming too dry.

Recorded live in July 1999 in Salzburg Cathedral, **Abbado's** performance of the traditional score with the **Berlin Philharmonic** was given to commemorate the tenth anniversary of the death of Herbert von Karajan. The dedicated atmosphere of such an occasion is powerfully caught, with the DG engineers clarifying the sound to a remarkable degree, with fine detail as well as ample weight. With the brilliant **Swedish Radio Choir** singing with exceptionally clear focus, such choruses as the *Dies irae* are thrillingly intense, and the starry yet youthful line-up of soloists – none of whom Karajan would ever have heard – makes an outstanding team. In the two extra items, among Mozart's loveliest soprano solos, **Rachel Harnisch** sings with warmth and refinement. This can be recommended to those wanting a traditional, modern-instrument account of Mozart's choral masterpiece.

Barenboim's exuberance may raise a few eyebrows. Mozart's *Dies irae*, for instance, has such zest that one senses the chorus galloping towards the Day of Judgement with enthusiasm. Yet the underlying drama and musicality of the performance as a whole disarm criticism. The intensity of Barenboim's feeling comes over from the opening bar, and the *Kyrie eleison* is stirring indeed. The lyricism of the score is beautifully calculated and the operatic-styled quartet which closes the *Tuba mirum* is particularly lovely. So too is the closing section of the *Confutatis maledictis*, which creates a gentle mood for the opening of the *Lacrimosa*. Here Barenboim's emotional contrasts dramatize the words superbly. The *Sanctus* is gloriously forthright. With a good solo team and excellent choral singing, this is a splendidly alive performance, and the recording is excellent.

Herreweghe is arresting from the very dramatic opening bars, and in the work's central Sequenz (*Dies irae; Tuba mirum; Rex Tremendae; Recordare; Confutatis* and the moving *Lacrimosa*) he achieves a remarkable emotional thrust. The orchestra gives weighty support, and one is hardly aware that this is a period-instrument performance, with the horns and trumpets capping climaxes forcefully. The soloists make an excellent team, singing with individuality (especially **Ian Bostridge**) but also blending together. The sound is spacious, but there is no feeling that the choral impact is blunted.

At super-bargain price, **Richard Hickox's** excellent EMI version of the *Requiem Mass* on the HMV label matches almost any in the catalogue. With generally brisk speeds and light, resilient rhythms, it combines gravity with authentically clean, transparent textures in which the dark colourings of the orchestration, as with the basset horn, come out vividly. All four soloists are outstandingly fine, and the choral singing is fresh and incisive, with crisp attack. The voices, solo and choral, are placed rather backwardly; otherwise the recording is excellent, full and clean to match the performance.

John Eliot Gardiner with characteristic panache also gives one of the most powerful performances on record, for while the lighter sound of the period orchestra makes for greater transparency, the weight and bite are formidable. The soloists are an outstanding quartet, well matched but characterfully contrasted too, and the choral singing is as bright and luminous as one expects of Gardiner's **Monteverdi Choir**. The superb *Kyrie in D minor* makes a very welcome and generous fill-up, to seal a firm recommendation.

The performance by **La Capella Reial de Catalunya** and **Le Concert des Nations** directed by **Jordi Savall** is both gutsy and expressive; at times tempi have great urgency – witness the thrilling *Dies irae* and the strong accents of the opening of the *Confutatis*, then contrasted by the angelic soprano line, with **Montserrat Figueras** a blissfully serene soloist. The trombones make a remarkable contribution throughout, and especially in the *Benedictus* and *Agnus Dei*. The recording is absolutely first class and, certainly, no other version of the *Requiem* makes more impact on the listener. It is aptly introduced by the plangent timbres of the *Maurerische Trauermusik*.

Valentin Radu's performance on Lyrichord is enjoyably direct, with the **Alma Deus** choral group lyrically strong and characterful. The excellent team of soloists is led by **Andrea Brown**, who opens the disc with a memorable performance of the *Exsultate jubilate*. Tempi are very comparable to those chosen by Colin Davis, although Radu's account is less fiercely dramatic than the LSO version; but it is enjoyably full-blooded and committed, and very well recorded.

Hogwood's version uses the edition of Richard Maunder, which aims to eliminate Süssmayr's contribution to the version of Mozart's unfinished masterpiece that has held sway for two centuries. So the *Lacrimosa* is completely different, after the opening eight bars, and concludes with an elaborate *Amen*, for which Mozart's own sketches were recently discovered. This textual clean-out goes with authentic perform-

ances of Hogwood's customary abrasiveness, very fresh and lively to underline the impact of novelty.

The surprise version is **Gillesberger's**. Using treble and alto soloists from the **Vienna Boys' Choir**, who sing with confidence and no little eloquence, this performance also has the advantage of a dedicated contribution from **Kurt Equiluz**. Gillesberger's pacing is well judged and the effect is as fresh as it is strong and direct. The 1982 recording is excellent, vivid yet full, and the result is powerful but not too heavy.

The glory of **Rafael Frühbeck de Burgos's** performance is the singing of the **New Philharmonia Chorus**. This is unashamedly big-scale Mozart; Frühbeck does not have a very subtle Mozart style; as an interpretation its stands well in the middle of the road, not too romantic, not too self-consciously classical, and, quite apart from the choral singing, the soloists are all first rate and are recorded with body and a fine balance. **Klemperer's** weightily imposing *Masonic Funeral Music* is used as an opening sinfonia.

OPERA

Apollo et Hyacinthus (complete); *Die Schuldigkeit des Ersten Gebets* (complete)

*** DG **DVD** 073 4253 (2). Berchtold, Karg, Kiener, Schlosser, Schuster, Sonn, Tretjakova, Watanabe, Mozarteum University SO, Walling (Stage by John Dew)

The amazement of the first-night audience at Mozart's achievement will surely be reflected by anyone watching and listening to this very attractive pair of video recordings. In *Apollo and Hyacinthus* Mozart provided a series of recitatives and arias which are remarkably inventive and surprisingly mature-sounding. The action of the opera is here very stylized, but the finale involves the arrival of Apollo, who provides an ending to the story by turning Hyacinth into a flower, and this is charmingly portrayed by moving a stage hyacinth bush over her dead body. *Die Schuldigkeit* is involved, not just with the first commandment but with all ten, and the allegorical characters, Justice, Mercy, Worldliness, Christianity and Christ himself, vie with each other with their conflicting doctrines to assert control over the human character, Christian. This sounds academic, but there is action too, including the seductive offer of earthly pleasures by the devilish Worldliness, who is most persuasive and vividly costumed. Visually much is added to the music by these colourful performances, well sung and played, and most imaginatively produced. There is excellent documentation.

Ascanio in Alba (complete; CD version)

🎧 (BB) *** Naxos 8.660040/1 (2). Windsor, Chance, Feldman, Milner, Mannion, Paris Sorbonne University Ch., Budapest Concerto Armonico, Grimbert

The Naxos version easily outshines previous recordings with a lightly sprung, stylishly conducted performance featuring an outstanding cast. The counter-tenor, **Michael Chance**, sings flawlessly in the castrato role of Ascanio, son of Venus, even-toned and brilliantly flexible. The others are fresh-toned too. **Lorna Windsor**, bright and clear as Venus, is nicely contrasted with the girlish-sounding Silvia of **Jill Feldman**, who sings with fine assurance in one of the two extended arias. The other, even more extended and demanding, is given to Fauno, with **Rosa Mannion** arguably the most accomplished soloist of all. The excellent tenor taking the role of Aceste is **Howard Milner**. Well recorded with transparent textures, if with chorus backwardly balanced, this makes an outstanding bargain in every way, rare Mozart that for most will be a delightful discovery.

La clemenza di Tito (complete; DVD version)

*(**) Arthaus **DVD** 100 407. Langridge, Putnam, Montague, Mahe, Szmytka, Rose, Glyndebourne Festival Ch., LPO, A. Davis (Producer: Nicholas Hytner)

Recorded at Glyndebourne during the 1991 festival, this Arthaus DVD version of Mozart's last opera is superbly sung by an outstanding cast, with conducting by **Andrew Davis** that brings out the charm as well as the power of this *opera seria*. Among the soloists there is no weak link. The singing is consistently firm, clear and stylish, with **Philip Langridge** masterly in the title-role, **Ashley Putnam** superb as Vitellia and **Diana Montague** most moving as Sesto. In place of the usual recitatives (not by Mozart) new ones have been provided by Stephen Oliver, though some of them seem very long, notably the five-minute stretch immediately after the overture and before the first duet between Sesto and Vitellia. However, as so often with modern opera productions, Nicholas Hytner's staging, with stylized geometric sets by David Fielding, will not be to all tastes, and the flat backdrops, often decorated with torn wallpaper effects, have their bizarre side. The Roman costumes are relatively conventional, even if the long swirling skirts for male characters sung by women are very questionable. Excellent sound, but this can be recommended only with considerable visual reservations.

La clemenza di Tito (complete; CD version)

⊕┉ **** HM HMC 901923.24 (2). Padmore, Pendatchanska, Fink, Chappuis, Freiburg Bar. O, Jacobs

⊕┉ **** DG 477 5792 (2). Trost, Kozena, Martinpelto, Rice, SCO, Mackerras

**** DG 431 806-2 (2). Rolfe Johnson, von Otter, McNair, Varady, Robbin, Hauptmann, Monteverdi Ch., E. Bar. Sol., Gardiner

*** Teldec 4509 90857-2 (2). Langridge, Popp, Ziesak, Murray, Ziegler, Polgár, Zürich Op. Ch. & O, Harnoncourt

René Jacobs's version with the period instruments of the **Freiburg Baroque Orchestra** offers a performance of extraordinary clarity and immediacy, at once sharp in attack, yet intimate too. Here the drama is vividly conveyed, with words crystal clear. Period performance also highlights the impact of timpani and brass, again adding to the drama, never more powerfully conveyed than here, with ensembles tautly controlled. The cast of principals is excellent, with **Mark Padmore** at once mellifluous and commanding as the Emperor, always imaginative and animated; and the little-known Bulgarian, **Alexandrina Pendatchanska**, proves an

outstanding choice as Vitellia, characterful and imaginative, matched by the golden-toned **Bernarda Fink** as Sesto and **Marie-Claude Chappuis** radiant as Annio.

Sir Charles Mackerras and the **Scottish Chamber Orchestra** add impressively to their Mozart opera series with a warmly alert version of *La clemenza di Tito* that provides an ideal alternative to the Jacobs set. Modern instruments, used with concern for period-performance style, make for a weightier as well as a warmer performance, a degree more relaxed than Jacobs. **Rainer Trost** is an excellent, heroic Tito, even if he is not as imaginative as Mark Padmore, while the rest of the cast of principals is comparably starry, with **Magdalena Kozena** tough-sounding as Sesto, and **Hillevi Martinpelto** as Vitellia.

Again, with his vitality and bite, **Gardiner** turns the piece into a genuinely involving drama. **Anthony Rolfe Johnson** is outstanding in the title-role, matching the vivid characterization of both **Anne Sofie von Otter** as Sesto and **Julia Varady** as Vitellia. **Sylvia McNair** is an enchanting, pure-toned Servilia and **Catherine Robbin** a well-matched Annio, though the microphone catches an unevenness in the voice, as it does with **Cornelius Hauptmann** in the incidental role of Publio. More seriously, DG's vivid, immediate recording picks up a distracting amount of banging and bumping on stage in the Süssmayr recitatives.

Nikolaus Harnoncourt uses modern, not period, instruments. Even so, he has not forgotten his early devotion to period performance, making this a very viable account for anyone wanting a halfway approach. Though recorded in association with **Zürich Opera**, this is a studio, not a live recording like Gardiner's. It gains from not having stage noises in recitatives. **Ann Murray** is at her finest as Sesto, if not quite as firm or dominant as von Otter for Gardiner. **Philip Langridge** is a splendid Tito, and it is good to have **Lucia Popp** so affecting in her very last recording. **Ruth Ziesak** and **Delores Ziegler** complete a strong team which will not disappoint anyone, even if it cannot quite compare with Gardiner's, singer for singer.

Così fan tutte (complete; DVD versions)

⊕┉ **** Opus Arte **DVD** OA 0970 D (2). Persson, Vondung, Lehtipu, Pisaroni, Rivenq, Garmendia, Glyndebourne Ch., OAE, Fischer (Director: Nicholas Hytner, V/D: James Whitbourn)

⊕┉ **** TDK **DVD** DVWW-OPCFTSF (2). Marshall, Murray, Morris, Araiza, Battle, Bruscantini, V. State Op. Konzertvereinigung, VPO, Muti (V/D: Claus Viller)

Ⓝ **** Medici Arts **DVD** 207 2368 (2). Frittoli, Kirchschlager, Skovhus, Schade, Corbelli, Bacelli, V. State Op. Ch. & O, Muti (Diector: Roberto de Simone; V/D: Brian Large)

⊕┉ *** DG **DVD** 073 026-9 (2). Roocroft, Mannion, Gilfry, Trost, James, Nicolai, Monteverdi Ch., E. Bar. Sol., Gardiner (Dir: Gardiner/Medcalf, TV Director: Mumford)

*** Arthaus **DVD** 101081. Doese, Lindenstrand, Perriers, Allen, Glyndebourne Ch., LPO, Pritchard (V/D: Dave Heather)

(*) Opus Arte **DVD OA LS 3006. Dessi, Ziegler, Corbelli, Kundlak, Scarabelli, Desderi, La Scala Ch. and O, Muti (Dir: Michael Hampe, V/D: Ilio Catani)

(*) Decca **DVD 074 3165 (2). Martínez, Koch, Degout, Mathey, Donath, Allen, V. State Op. Konzertvereinigung, VPO, Honeck (V/D: Thomas Grimm)

The stage director Nicholas Hytner on Opus Arte succeeded on every front, bringing out the fine qualities of the whole cast, both vocally and dramatically, brilliantly supported by **Ivan Fischer** and the period **Orchestra of the Age of Enlightenment**. Starriest of all is **Miah Persson** as Fiordiligi, singing gloriously with pure, even tone, both in the fireworks of *Come scoglio* and in the tender phrasing in *Per pietà*. Her ornamentation and trills are models of style. Though **Anke Vondung** as Dorabella cannot match her in vocal beauty, it is a strong and characterful performance. **Topi Lehtipu** as Ferrando sings with heady beauty, well contrasted with the Guglielmo of **Luca Pisaroni**. The teamwork as ever at Glyndebourne is superb, with **Nicolas Rivenq** as Don Alfonso and **Synhoa Garmendia** as Despina both excellent, too. Hytner's sensitivity is wonderfully illustrated at the final curtain. Where so many modern productions leave the four lovers angry with each other – something which defies the music – Hytner has the girls initially still angry at the beginning of the finale until, as a final touch, on the last chord the two men tenderly put their hands on the girls' shoulders in the gentlest of indications of reconciliation.

Muti's fizzing (1983) Salzburg Festival recording is fully traditional and visually a delight, with elegant sets and costumes, and even a troop of soldiers and a sailing boat to take Guglielmo and Ferrando away convincingly, and leave the ladies and Don Alfonso gently to sing the famous *Soave sia il vento*. There is no weak link in the cast and the action is very effectively dominated by **Sesto Bruscantini's** relatively genial Don Alfonso. The singing is strong and eloquent, the effect dramatic rather than intimate. Fiordiligi's *Come scoglio* (**Margaret Marshall**) is very telling indeed, while **Ann Murray** is a charming Dorabella. It is good to watch a completely fresh performance that carries out Mozart's intentions visually as well as musically. The recording itself is very lively and open, the voices resonant.

It is a pleasure to welcome the Medici Arts 1996 version from the **Vienna State Opera**. Roberto de Simone is one of those rare stage directors who do not seek to impose their own personality over that of the composer. This is a most stylish production, with attractive costumes, and sets that are a viewing pleasure, especially the sea vista at Naples. When Guglielmo and Ferrando leave, they do so on a convincing backstage boat simulation, while the famous *Trio* which follows reveals Mozart's exquisite part-writing clearly, instead of smoothing it into vocal homogeneity. Throughout, the singing (and acting) cast is in every way excellent, with **Barbara Frittoli** as convincing a Fiordiligi as **Angelika Kirchschlager** is an engaging Dorabella, and both feistily resist the temptation to stray, until their would-be seducers spectacularly feign arsenic poisoning. **Monica Bacelli** is a knowingly vivacious and ever resourceful Despina (especially when disguised as the doctor) and she sings both her arias with real charm. **Alessandro Corbelli**, too, is a conniving Don Alfonso, yet not overplaying his role. **Muti's** conducting is splendidly alive and fresh. What more could you want?

The DVD version of **John Eliot Gardiner's** recording of *Così fan tutte* was recorded live simultaneously with the audio recording issued on CD. The staged production at the Théâtre du Châtelet in Paris was the work of Gardiner himself in collaboration with Stephen Medcalf, involving pretty sets and handsome costumes by Carlo Tomassi. The traditional approach to staging nicely matches the freshness and imagination of the period performance, with uniforms from the Napoleonic period and Ferrando and Guglielmo in disguise dressed identifiably as Albanians, even if as usual one wonders how Fiordiligi and Dorabella fail to recognize their lovers. Visually, the whole production consistently heightens the impact of the opera, with video direction by Peter Mumford. Though the performance spreads on to two discs, the only extras are promotional, including a survey of Gardiner's recordings of Mozart operas.

Recorded at the Glyndebourne Festival in 1975, Adrian Slack's production, with sets and costumes by Emanuele Luzzati, is intimate, apt enough for the old theatre at Glyndebourne. The singing is first rate and the acting good, and Slack's production brings out the fun of the piece. The conductor, **Sir John Pritchard**, is at his most animated and magnetic, though in some of the ensembles he rushes his singers and players. **Helene Doese** as Fiordiligi and **Sylvia Lindenstrand**, a tall, imperious Dorabella, are both ideally steady and clear, and Doese's *Come scoglio* is brilliantly articulated, even though her Act II aria, *Per pietà*, could be more moving. The youthful **Thomas Allen** is a superb Guglielmo, and the American tenor, **Anson Austin**, is a handsome, open-toned Ferrando, with **Frantz Petri** a splendid Alfonso and **Daniele Perriers** a light, agile Despina.

Recorded at La Scala in April 1989, **Muti's** later DVD is very well paced and generally well cast and offers an attractive traditional production by Michael Hampe, with costumes and designs involving baroque arches by Mauro Pagano. **Daniela Dessi** sings with freshness and clarity as Fiordiligi, and **Delores Ziegler** is a handsome, finely projected Dorabella. The men, rather mature for young lovers, sing well, with **Josef Kundlak** a finely controlled Ferrando and **Alessandro Corbelli** a strong Guglielmo. Best of all is the veteran **Claudio Desderi** as Don Alfonso, in splendid voice. On only a single disc, the sound is thinner than most, a little veiled on the orchestra.

In the Decca set, **Sir Thomas Allen** is a wonderfully wily Don Alfonso and **Anna María Martínez** (as Fiordiligi) and **Sophie Koch** (as Dorabella) sing with great charm. Their male lovers also have very pleasing voices and they sing and act with ardour. Needless to say, **Helen Donath** is an engaging Despina. The dress style is comparatively modern. The sets, however, are plain and economical, using folding screens as 'furniture', and there is also a huge, rock-like egg mid-stage whose symbolic purpose is elusive. One important interference with Lorenzo da Ponte's plot is that the two women are allowed to overhear their lovers hatch their plan of deception. But apparently this does not prevent them falling in love with their men in their new roles. In spite of the frugal sets, the performance is carried by the fine singing and acting and by **Honeck's** lively direction of the music. Most enjoyable, and well documented.

Così fan tutte (complete; CD versions)

🔊 ⚙ Ⓜ ******** EMI (ADD) 5 67382-2 (3). Schwarzkopf, Ludwig, Steffek, Kraus, Taddei, Berry, Philh. Ch. & O, Boehm

Ⓝ Ⓑ ******* EMI 2 08830-2 (3). Vaness, Ziegler, Aler, Duesing, Watson, Desderi, Glyndebourne Ch., LPO, Haitink

*** DG 437 829-2 (3). Roocroft, Mannion, Gilfry, Trost, James, Feller, E. Bar. Sol., Gardiner

*** Decca 444 174-2 (3). Fleming, von Otter, Lopardo, Bär, Scarabelli, Pertusi, COE, Solti

⚙ Ⓜ **(***)** EMI mono 5 67064-2 (3) [567138]. Schwarzkopf, Otto, Merriman, Simoneau, Panerai, Bruscantini, Philh. Ch. & O, Karajan

ⒷⒷ **(***)** Regis mono RRC 3020 (3). Schwarzkopf, Otto, Merriman, Simoneau, Panerai, Bruscantini, Philh. Ch. & O, Karajan (with **Arias from:** *Don Giovanni, Le nozze di Figaro, Idomeneo, Die Zauberflöte,* sung by Schwarzkopf)

Ⓑ ****(*)** Double Decca (ADD) 455 476-2 (2). della Casa, Ludwig, Loose, Dermota, Kunz, Schoeffler, V. State Op. Ch., VPO, Boehm

Ⓜ ****(*)** Erato (ADD) 4509 98494-2 (3). Te Kanawa, Stratas, von Stade, Rendall, Huttenlocher, Bastin, Rhine Op. Ch., Strasbourg PO, Lombard

Boehm's classic set has been splendidly remastered as one of EMI's 'Great Recordings of the Century' and remains a clear first choice, despite the attractions of the Gardiner version. Its glorious solo singing is headed by the incomparable Fiordiligi of **Schwarzkopf** and the equally moving Dorabella of **Christa Ludwig**; it remains a superb memento of Walter Legge's recording genius and remains unsurpassed by any other recordings made before or since. The documentation is generous and includes a full libretto and sessions photographs.

With speeds often more measured than usual, **Haitink's** EMI version still conveys the sparkle of a live performance at Glyndebourne. The excellent teamwork, consistently conveying humour, makes up for a cast-list rather less starry than on some rival versions. This is above all a sunny performance, sailing happily over any serious shoals beneath Da Ponte's comedy. **Claudio Desderi** as Alfonso helps to establish that Glyndebourne atmosphere, with recitatives superbly timed and coloured. If **Carol Vaness** and **Delores Ziegler** are rather too alike in timbre to be distinguished easily, the relationship becomes all the more sisterly when, quite apart from the similarity, they respond so beautifully to each other. **John Aler** makes a headily unrestrained Ferrando, beautifully free in the upper register, and **Lillian Watson** and **Dale Duesing** make up a strong team. The recording gives a fine bloom and impressive dynamic range to voices and orchestra alike.

On CD as well as DVD, the full flavour of *Così*, its effervescence as well as its deeper qualities, come over the more intensely with **Gardiner**. Though **Amanda Roocroft** and **Rosa Mannion** do not sound quite as sweet and even as they can, few tenors on disc can rival the German **Rainer Trost** in the heady beauty of his voice, above all in Ferrando's aria, *Una aura amorosa*. The poise and technical assurance of

all the singers, not least **Rodney Gilfry** as Guglielmo, put this among the finest versions of *Così*.

Solti takes a fast and light approach which yet has none of his old fierceness. Much is owed to the superb playing of the **Chamber Orchestra of Europe**. **Renée Fleming** as Fiordiligi, sings with a firm, full voice that is yet brilliant and flexible, ranging down to a satisfyingly strong chest register. **Frank Lopardo**, too, as Ferrando most sensitively uses his distinctive tenor over an unusually wide dynamic range. **Anne Sofie von Otter** predictably makes a characterful Dorabella, well contrasted with Fleming, and **Olaf Bär** a keenly intelligent Guglielmo, while two Italian singers, less well known but well chosen, **Adelina Scarabelli** and **Michele Pertusi**, complete the team in the manipulative roles of Despina and Alfonso. Altogether Solti's finest Mozart recording, outshining even his *Figaro*.

Commanding as **Schwarzkopf** is as Fiordiligi in the 1962 Boehm set, the extra ease and freshness of her singing in the earlier (1954) version under **Karajan** makes it even more compelling. **Nan Merriman** is a distinctive and characterful Dorabella, and the role of Ferrando has never been sung more mellifluously on record than by **Leopold Simoneau**. The young **Rolando Panerai** is an ideal Guglielmo, and **Lisa Otto** a pert Despina; while **Sesto Bruscantini** in his prime brings to the role of Don Alfonso the wisdom and artistry which made him so compelling at Glyndebourne. Karajan has never sparkled more naturally in Mozart than here, for the high polish has nothing self-conscious about it. There is also a set of bargain highlights (72') on Classics for Pleasure with a simple cued synopsis (CfP 393369-2).

The Regis super-budget transfer is also very well managed, with the recording settling down nicely after the Overture, to give plenty of bloom on the voices. It includes a cued synopsis and tends to trump the EMI sets by including seven extra arias which **Schwarzkopf** recorded with Pritchard in 1953, exquisitely sung, three each from *Don Giovanni* and *Le nozze di Figaro*, including *Voi che sapete*, and one from *Idomeneo*, plus two live recordings from 1952 – *Ach, ich fühls* from *Zauberflöte* and *In quali eccessi* from *Don Giovanni* – which are all equally well transferred.

Boehm's 1955 Decca stereo set is not as polished a performance as his later one for EMI, and the cutting of brief passages from the ends of arias may worry those who know the opera very well. But it remains a captivatingly spontaneous account of the frothiest of Mozart's comedies. **Lisa della Casa** is strong and sweet-toned, **Christa Ludwig** is admirably fresh-voiced, and the rest are sparklingly good, especially **Emmy Loose's** deliciously knowing portrayal of Despina. **Paul Schoeffler** in the role of Don Alfonso is most appealing.

On Erato, **Kiri Te Kanawa's** voice sounds radiant, rich and creamy of tone; she is commanding in *Come scoglio*, and tenderly affecting in *Per pietà*. **Lombard** is a sympathetic accompanist, if not always the most perceptive of Mozartians; some of his tempi are on the slow side, but his sextet of young singers make up a team that rivals almost any other, giving firm, appealing performances. With warm recording of high quality, this is most enjoyable and could be a choice for any who follow the singers in question.

Così fan tutte (excerpts)

(***) Testament mono SBT 1040. Jurinac, Thebom, Lewis, Kunz, Borriello, Glyndebourne Festival O, Busch; Noni, Philh. O, Susskind

This is a superb Testament transfer of excerpts from Così fan tutte in the 1950 Glyndebourne production. **Sena Jurinac** as Fiordiligi, clear and vibrant, provides the central glory, with both her two big arias included, as well as six of her ensemble numbers, and three substantial rehearsal 'takes'. **Blanche Thebom** too, as Dorabella, sings with clarity and freshness, and the others make a splendid team. **Alda Noni**, the Despina, was not recorded at the Glyndebourne sessions but later, at Abbey Road, with **Susskind** and the Philharmonia. The recording brings out a flutter in her voice, less steady than the others. As in pre-war days, a piano is used instead of harpsichord for recitatives.

Così fan tutte (complete; in English)

(N) (M) *** Chan. 3152 (3). Watson, Montague, Maltman, Spence, Garrett, T. Allen, Geoffrey Mitchell Ch., OAE, Mackerras

Mackerras's sparkling account of this delightful opera comes over surprisingly well in English, for the change of language does not impair the vocal lines, and in a comedy of this kind it is good not to have to look continually to the translated libretto for the swiftly changing text. It may seem a bit strange to marry a period-instrument performance with a colloquial language, but it works admirably, for the orchestra under Sir Charles Mackerras plays superbly. Perhaps **Janice Watson** (Fiordiligi) and **Diana Montague** (Dorabella) are not always as sweet-toned as their finest counterparts who sing in the language Mozart expected, but **Leslie Garrett** makes an excellent Despina and **Sir Thomas Allen** is naturally at home as Don Alfonso. Vocally, **Toby Spence**, as an attractively ardent Ferrando, is the star of the show, and **Christopher Maltman** partners him well as Guglielmo. The recording is excellent.

Don Giovanni (complete; DVD versions)

⊶ *** Arthaus DVD 101 087. Luxon, Dean, Branisteani, Yakar, Gale, Goeke, Rawnsley, Thau, Glyndebourne Ch. & O, Haitink (Producer: Peter Hall, V/D: Dave Heather)

**(*) TDK DVD DVW-OPDG. Alvarez, Pieczonka, Antonacci, Schade, d'Arcangelo, Kirchschlager, Regazzo, V. State Op. Ch. & O, Muti (V/D: Brian Large)

When in 1977 Peter Hall added Don Giovanni to his list of Mozart/Da Ponte productions the action was updated to the Regency period and John Bury's sets gave a picture of a dark and rainy Seville. Deliberately gloomy, it would be oppressive but for the imagination of Hall in his detailed direction, with the superb Leporello of **Stafford Dean** unusually positive, and the whole performance heightened by the Mozartian strength of **Bernard Haitink's** conducting. The weakness in the cast is the Donna Anna of **Horiana Branisteani**, tending to be squally in the upper register, though she gathers strength as the opera proceeds, and the big aria, Non mi dir, is well controlled. **Benjamin Luxon** as Don Giovanni was at his peak, darkly characterful and with

a wide tonal range down to a seductive half-tone. **Rachel Yakar**, bright and fresh as Donna Elvira, and **Elizabeth Gale**, sweetly charming, make up the team of women principals, with **Leo Goeke** unstrained as Ottavio and **John Rawnsley** exceptionally characterful as Masetto. Camerawork on the video is imaginative too in concentrating on individual characters at key moments.

On TDK, **Muti's** approach is traditional, except that his Allegros are often very fast, racing the singers off their feet, though **Carlos Alvarez**, splendid in the title-role, looking the perfect roué, masterfully defies the conductor's challenge in the hectic but finely articulated performance of the Champagne Aria. **Adrienne Pieczonka's** full, warm soprano makes her an impressive Donna Anna opposite the honey-toned Ottavio of **Michael Schade**, while **Angelika Kirchschlager** as Zerlina and **Lorenzo Regazzo** are both superb as the peasant pair, with **Ildebrando d'Arcangelo** as a loud but well-focused Leporello. In this company, **Anna Caterina Antonacci** makes a disappointing Donna Elvira, often squally. Roberto de Simone's production is remarkable for the frequency of the scene and costume changes, which become distracting when Zaira Vincentiis is so lavish in her many costume designs. A mixed success, however well the orchestra plays.

Don Giovanni (complete; CD versions)

⊶ (M) **** EMI 5 67869-2 (3) [567873]. Waechter, Schwarzkopf, Sutherland, Alva, Frick, Sciutti, Taddei, Philh. Ch. & O, Giulini

**** DG 445 870-2 (3). Gilfry, Organasova, Margiono, James, d'Arcangelo, Prégardien, Clarkson, Silvestrelli, Monteverdi Ch., E. Bar. Sol., Gardiner

❀ (M) *** Decca (ADD) 466 389-2 (3). della Casa, Danco, Siepi, Corena, Dermota, V. State Op. Ch., VPO, Krips

*** HM HMC 901 964/6; SACD 801 964/6 (3). Weisser, Regazzo, Pendatchanska, Pasichnyk, Tarver, Im, Borchev, Guerzoni, RIAS Ch., Freiburg Bar. O, Jacobs

*** DG (IMS) 419 179-2 (3). Ramey, Tomowa-Sintow, Baltsa, Battle, Winbergh, Furlanetto, Malta, Burchuladze, German Op. Ch., Berlin, BPO, Karajan

(M) *** EMI (ADD) 7 63841-2 (3). Ghiaurov, Watson, Ludwig, Freni, Gedda, Berry, Montarsolo, Crass, New Philh. Ch. & O, Klemperer

On CD the classic **Giulini** EMI set, lovingly remastered, sets the standard by which all other recordings have come to be judged. **Elisabeth Schwarzkopf**, as Elvira, emerges as a dominant figure to give a distinctive but totally apt slant to this endlessly invigorating drama. The young **Sutherland** may be relatively reticent as Anna but, with such technical ease and consistent beauty of tone, she makes a superb foil. **Taddei** is a delightful Leporello, and each member of the cast – including the young **Cappuccilli** as Masetto – combines fine singing with keen dramatic sense.

John Eliot Gardiner's performance culminates in one of the most thrilling accounts ever recorded of the final scene, when Giovanni is dragged down to hell. Sometimes lightness goes too far, as when **Charlotte Margiono** as Donna

Elvira sings *Ah fuggi il traditor* in a half-tone; but increasingly Gardiner encourages his soloists, particularly Anna and Elvira, to sing expansively. **Luba Organasova** is even more assured and characterful as Anna, and the agility of both is exemplary. **Rodney Gilfry** excels himself, on one side tough and purposeful, on the other a smooth seducer, with the clean-toned voice finely shaded. **Ildebrando d'Arcangelo** is suitably darker-toned as Leporello, lithe and young-sounding, hardly a *buffo*. **Julian Clarkson** makes a crotchety Masetto, and **Eirian James** a warmer, tougher Zerlina than usual, aptly so for her extra scene. The Commendatore of **Andrea Silvestrelli**, though recessed on the recording, is magnificently dark and firm, not least in the final confrontation. A recording that sets new standards for period performance and vies with the finest of traditional versions.

Krips's version, recorded in 1955 for the Mozart bicentenary, has remained at or near the top of the list of recommendations ever since. Freshly remastered, it sounds better than ever. Its intense, dramatic account of the Don's disappearance into hell has rarely been equalled, and never surpassed on CD, though there are many equally memorable sequences: the finale to Act I is also electrifying. As a bass Don, **Siepi** is marvellously convincing, but there is hardly a weak link in the rest of the cast. The early stereo recording is pretty age-defying, full and warm, with a lovely Viennese glow which is preferable to many modern recordings.

René Jacobs conducts a bitingly sharp account of *Don Giovanni*. The Overture sets the pattern, with *fortissimos* reinforced strongly by timpani in period style. The violin sound may predictably be thin and the cast list does not sound distinguished, yet they make a superb team with no weak link, and Jacobs's speeds are sensible rather than exaggerated. The soloists all have fresh, clear, firm voices and though the Anna and Elvira are rather alike, the results are always satisfying, with Elvira rather weightier than Anna. **Johannes Weisser** sings the Don clearly if with occasionally fluttery tone and **Lorenzo Regazzo** is a characterful Leporello. The sound is clear and well defined and the SACD adds to the atmosphere.

Even if ensemble is less than perfect at times in the **Karajan** set and the final scene of Giovanni's descent to hell goes off the boil a little, the end result has fitting intensity and power. Though Karajan was plainly thinking of a big auditorium in his pacing of recitatives, having Jeffrey Tate as continuo player helps to keep them moving and to bring out word-meaning. The starry line-up of soloists is a distinctive one. **Samuel Ramey** is a noble rather than a menacing Giovanni, consistently clear and firm.

Most of the slow tempi that **Klemperer** regularly adopts, far from flagging, add a welcome breadth to the music, for they must be set against the unusually brisk and dramatic interpretation of the recitatives between numbers. Added to that, **Ghiaurov** as the Don and **Berry** as Leporello make a marvellously characterful pair. In this version the male members of the cast are dominant and, with Klemperer's help, they make the dramatic experience a strongly masculine one. Nor is the ironic humour forgotten with Berry and Ghiaurov about, and the Klemperer spaciousness allows them extra time for pointing. Among the women, **Ludwig** is

a strong and convincing Elvira, **Freni** a sweet-toned but rather unsmiling Zerlina; only **Claire Watson** seriously disappoints, with obvious nervousness marring the big climax of *Non mi dir*.

Don Giovanni (complete; in English)

Ⓜ **(*) Chan. 3057 (3). Magee, Cullagh, Shore, Tierney, Plazas, Banks, Robinson, Bayley, Geoffrey Mitchell Ch., Philh. O, Parry

Vividly recorded, **David Parry's** well-paced reading breaks new ground in offering the masterpiece in English, and very successful it is, even though the casting is not as starry as in many versions. Parry, on the grounds of its greater cohesion, firmly opts for the original, Prague version of the score, which may disappoint some when Elvira's *Mi tradi* and Ottavio's *Dalla sua pace* are omitted. **Garry Magee** as the Don makes a believably virile lover, vigorous and youthful, articulating the *Champagne* aria cleanly at a crisp, well-chosen tempo. **Andrew Shore** also characterizes well as Leporello, bringing out the comedy but not guying it. **Clive Bayley** as the Commendatore, **Barry Banks** as Ottavio, more heroic than usual, and **Dean Robinson** complete a strong team of men. Among the women the most satisfying performance comes from **Mary Plazas** as Zerlina, less soubrettish than usual but charming. **Majella Cullagh** is a warm-toned Donna Anna, only occasionally gusty, and **Vivian Tierney** a clear, reliable Elvira, whose voice is not flattered by the microphone.

Die Entführung aus dem Serail (complete; DVD versions)

🎞 **** DG DVD 073020-9. Holtzmann, Araiza, Gruberová, Grist, Orth, Talvela, Bav. R. Ch. & O, Boehm (V/D: Karlheinz Hundorf)

🎞 **** Arthaus DVD 101 091. Davies, Masterson, Watson, White, Hoback, Glyndebourne Ch., LPO, Kuhn (Director: Peter Wood, V/D: Dave Heather)

*** TDK DVD DV-OPEADS. Mei, Ciofi, Trost, Montazeri, Rydl, Markus John, Maggio Musicale Fiorentino Ch. & O, Mehta (V/D: George Blume)

Karl Boehm conducted this beautifully paced account of *Entführung* at the Bavarian State Opera in April 1980, just over a year before he died. **Edita Gruberová** as Konstanze is at her freshest: clear and agile, tender in *Traurigkeit*, brilliant in *Martern aller Arten*. Though **Reri Grist** as Blonde has an edge on the voice, hers is a charming and characterful assumption, most of all when confronting the powerful Osmin of **Martti Talvela**, a giant of a figure with a voice to match. **Francisco Araiza** too is at his peak, with **Norbert Orth** exceptionally strong as Pedrillo. August Everding's stylized production, with smoothly sliding scenery by Max Bignens, sets each scene deftly and atmospherically in the Pasha's palace. The 1980 sound is exceptionally bright and clear for its age.

The Arthaus version offers a live recording of Peter Wood's atmospheric Glyndebourne production of 1980, with a vintage cast conducted by **Gustav Kuhn**. The different scenes are beautifully devised by William Dudley, with fretted oriental screens used to speed changes of scene. **Ryland**

Davies is a clear-toned Belmonte, with **Valerie Masterson** sweet, true and agile, singing at her peak, tender in *Traurigkeit* and brilliant in *Martern aller Arten*. **Lillian Watson** is charming as Blonde, pertly defying the will of the magnificent Osmin of **Willard White**, in glorious voice. There are no tricks in the staging, which is a model of traditional production at Glyndebourne, with the forces wonderfully polished, recorded in the middle of a long run of performances.

One does not associate **Zubin Mehta** with Mozart opera, but here he is at his finest, obviously deeply involved, directing with warmth and vitality, with the orchestra on top form and providing a constantly lively backing for the singers. **Eva Mei** does not quite look like a Konstanze, but she sings with heartfelt passion as well as eloquence, so that the famous *Martern aller Arten* is a real dramatic highlight. **Patrizia Ciofi** is a sparkling, often fiercely vehement Blonde, and if **Rainer Trost** does not project as a very heroic Belmonte, he sings attractively enough. But the star of the action (as so often) is Osmin. **Kurt Rydl** makes the characterization deeper, more ambivalent than usual, but he sings with such brio and presence that one is captivated every time he appears. Thank goodness that, for once, the director produces no silly tricks, and the sets are visually most appealing. A real winner and most enjoyable listening and watching.

Die Entführung aus dem Serail (complete; CD versions)

🅜 ⓜ **** DG (ADD) 429 868-2 (2). Augér, Grist, Schreier, Neukirch, Moll, Leipzig R. Ch., Dresden State O, Boehm

🅜 ⓜ *** DG 477 5593-2 (2). Organasova, Sieden, Olsen, Peper, Hauptman, Minetti, Monteverdi Ch., E Bar. Sol., Gardiner

ⓜ *** Oehms OCD 249 (2). Haberman, Ellen, Bezcala, Kalchmair, Ringelhahn, Linz Landestheater Ch., Linz Bruckner O, Sieghart

ⓜ *** EMI (ADD) 7 63263-2 (2). Rothenberger, Popp, Gedda, Unger, Frick, V. State Op. Ch., VPO, Krips

Boehm's is a delectable account, superbly cast and warmly recorded. **Arleen Augér** proves the most accomplished singer on record in the role of Konstanze, girlish and fresh, yet rich, tender and dramatic by turns, with brilliant, almost flawless coloratura. The others are also outstandingly good, notably **Kurt Moll**, whose powerful, finely focused bass makes him a superb Osmin, one who relishes the comedy too. The warm recording is beautifully transferred, to make this easily the most sympathetic version of the opera on CD, with the added attraction of being at mid-price.

Gardiner's *Entführung* immediately establishes the extra zest of the performance. So Konstanze's great heroic aria, *Martern aller Arten*, has tremendous swagger; thanks also to glorious singing from **Luba Organasova**, at once rich, pure and agile, the close is triumphant. As Belmonte, **Stanfor Olsen** for Gardiner is firm and agile, and though **Cornelius Hauptman**, Gardiner's Osmin, lacks a really dark bass, he too is firm and characterful. Altogether this now makes a fine mid-priced recommendation.

With an excellent cast of young singers the Oehms (originally Arte Nova) set offers an outstanding version of *Entführung* to rival almost any in the catalogue. **Ingrid Haberman** is a formidable Konstanze, fresh and clear, bright in coloratura yet creamy of tone in lower registers, undaunted by the demands of *Martern aller Arten*. The American **Donna Ellen** is a lively Blonde with clear, unstrained top register. The Polish tenor **Piotr Bezcala** is a stylish, honey-toned Belmonte, with power as well as lyric beauty. Best of all is the Osmin of **Franz Kalchmair**, whose firm, dark bass copes masterfully with every demand of the role, cleanly focused from top to bottom. Good sound, though the spoken dialogue (well edited) is not consistent. Now at mid-price, the set comes with full libretto, including English translation.

Recorded in 1966, the **Krips** EMI version brings an amiable and highly enjoyable performance with a formidable line-up of soloists. The team of **Popp**, **Gedda**, **Unger** and **Frick** could hardly have been bettered at the time, each of them singing beautifully and with vivid characterization. **Anneliese Rothenberger**, potentially the weak link as Konstanze, not only sounds amply powerful as recorded, but she sings with a purity and sweetness rarely caught on her discs. This is arguably her finest recording ever. The stereo sound is warm and well balanced, with spoken dialogue well presented.

The Abduction from the Seraglio (Die Entführung aus dem Serail; complete; in English)

🅜 ✺ ⓜ **** Chan. 3081 (2). Dobbs, Eddy, Gedda, Fryatt, Mangin, Kelsey, Amb. S., Bath Festival O, Y. Menuhin

Menuhin's set of *The Abduction from the Seraglio* in English makes the performance sparkle from first to last, favouring brisk, well-lifted *Allegros*, so that the fun of the piece comes over vividly. The acting of the principal singers is exceptionally fine too, with **Noel Mangin** superb as Osmin, commandingly comic yet believable too, not least when in duo with **John Fryatt**, an outstanding Pedrillo. **Nicolai Gedda**, brought in as an international star, fully lives up to expectation, giving one of his finest Mozart performances, poised and stylish, his English accent flawless. The American soprano, **Mattiwilda Dobbs**, similarly brought in as a star, uses her bright, agile coloratura brilliantly. **Jennifer Eddy** makes an enchanting Blonde, perfect as a defiant English girl. What completes this as wonderful entertainment is the quality of the 1967 recording, as full and vivid as if it was recorded yesterday, the sound-stage cleanly and atmospherically focused.

Idomeneo (complete; DVD versions)

🅜 *** Arthaus DVD 101 079. Lewis, Goeke, Betley, Barstow, Oliver, Fryatt, Wicks, Glyndebourne Ch., LPO, Pritchard (Director: John Cox, V/D: Dave Heather)

**(*) Warner DVD 5050467 3922-2-9. Kenny, Hadley, Vaness, Hemsley, Langridge, Roden, Kennedy, Glyndebourne Ch., LPO, Haitink (Dir: Trevor Nunn, V/D: Christopher Swann)

ⓝ **(*) Medici Arts DVD 2072448 (2). Mark Ainsley, Banse, Breslik, Dasch, Trost, Bav. State Op. Ch. & O, Nagano

ⓝ **(*) Decca DVD 074 3258 (2). Pears, Harper, Pashley, Woodland, Tear, E. Op. Ch., ECO, Britten. Introduced by John Warrack (Producer: Colin Graham; V/D: Brian Large)

Like **Pritchard** as conductor, **Richard Lewis** in the title-role was a veteran still in superb voice. John Cox's production of 1974 is brilliantly devised to bring out the limited dimensions of the stage in the old Glyndebourne opera house, with concentric circles framing the whole stage, giving a long perspective to highly atmospheric scenes at the end of the tunnel. It works beautifully, not least when the sea monster appears at the end of Act II. It is a beautifully crafted reading, with **Leo Goeke's** tenor as Idamante well contrasted with the fine Idomeneo of **Ryland Davies**. **Josephine Barstow** at her peak is a formidable Elettra and **Bozena Betley** a sweet Ilia. The incidental roles are very well taken by vintage Glyndebourne performers, **Alexander Oliver**, **John Fryatt** and **Dennis Wicks**.

Dating from 1983, the Warner DVD of *Idomeneo* from Glyndebourne offers a fine production by Trevor Nunn, with handsome, stylized sets and classical Greek costumes designed by John Napier. **Bernard Haitink** is a powerful Mozartian, directing an excellent cast. Even in 1983 Glyndebourne used the version with Idamante as a tenor rather than a mezzo, as Mozart originally conceived it. Even so, the young **Jerry Hadley** in that role offers a lightly stylish contrast with the darkly intense Idomeneo of **Philip Langridge**. First-rate contributions too from **Yvonne Kenny** as Ilia and **Carol Vaness** as Elettra.

The Nagano and Britten DVDs of Mozart's great *opera seria* have something in common. The live **Bavarian State Opera** version returns to the theatre where the opera was first performed by Mozart in 1781; the Britten performance used the English translation made for the first English staging in London in 1937, and which was to receive its British première at the Snape, Maltings, Concert Hall during the 1969 Aldeburgh Festival. Near to the sea as he was, Britten must have wondered whether the sea god, Neptune, disapproved, as three days before the first performance the hall was razed to the ground by fire, and the opera had to be re-staged, without sets and with borrowed costumes, at a local church. The planned BBC TV broadcast, from which this recording came, had to move to the BBC Opera Centre. The original quaint costume designs were retained, but new sets were created by David Myerscough-Jones, and very simple and effective they were, with large blue cloths used to suggest the sea, and a genuine working 'monster' for Act II. The cast, dominated by **Peter Pears's** superb Idomeneo, also brought fine singing from **Heather Harper** in a convincing assumption of Ilia; Idamante (originally a mezzo part) was engagingly sung by **Anne Pashley**, and **Rae Woodland** and **Robert Tear** were excellent as Elektra and Arbace respectively. The score was pruned and then conducted by Britten with a composer's understanding and much passion.

It must first be said that the Bavarian production is marvellously sung. **John Mark Ainsley** is an authoritative Idomeneo, but it is **Julianne Banse** one especially remembers for her lovely singing as Ilia, although her lover/husband-to-be, Idamante, (here a tenor) and incongruously dressed, also has a golden voice. **Annette Dasch** is a properly fiery Elektra, especially in her final scene when all her hopes of getting Idamante are dashed, and she is finally abducted by the Furies. **Kent Nagano** conducts the Bavarian

Chorus and Orchestra with plenty of spirit (the storm chorus is especially riveting). But not all the production is as effective as that. The opera opens with an unnecessary slaughter scene, and (apart from the lead females) the costumes, to say the least, are curiously unconvincing. Moreover, lots of stage business for the large cast seems superfluous and visually boring. Without the surtitles one couldn't manage at all. A pity, when musically the performance is splendid.

Idomeneo (complete; CD versions)

🔸 ******** EMI 5 57260-2 (3). Bostridge, Hunt Lieberson, Milne, Frittoli, Rolfe Johnson, SCO, Mackerras

*** DG 431 674-2 (3). Rolfe Johnson, Von Otter, McNair, Martinpelto, Robson, Hauptmann, Monteverdi Choir, E. Bar. Sol., Gardiner

*** DG 447 737-2 (3). Bartoli, Domingo, Vaness, Grant-Murphy, Hampson, Lopardo, Terfel, Met. Op. Ch. & O, Levine

Ian Bostridge with his ever-illuminating feeling for words brings the character vividly to life, with never a hint of strain. It is a magnetic performance, helped by the stylish and perceptive conducting of **Sir Charles Mackerras**, who gives a very full text. The result is a performance, strong, dramatic and expressive, which brings out the originality of instrumentation, a point that Mackerras highlights. The others in the cast are first rate, with **Lorraine Hunt Lieberson** a bright, strong Idamante and **Lisa Milne** a charming, sweet-voiced Ilia and **Barbara Frittoli** a powerful Elettra. It is good too to have **Anthony Rolfe Johnson**, who takes the title-role in the Gardiner version, singing very stylishly as Arbace, here given both his arias, often cut.

With its exhilarating vigour and fine singing, **Gardiner's** aim has been to include all the material Mozart wrote for the original (1781) production, and he recommends the use of the CD programming device for listeners to select the version they prefer. Gardiner's Mozartian style is well sprung and subtly moulded rather than severe. The principals sing beautifully, notably **Anne Sofie von Otter** as Idamante and **Sylvia McNair** as Ilia, while **Anthony Rolfe Johnson** as Idomeneo is well suited here, with words finely projected. The electrifying singing of the **Monteverdi Choir** adds to the dramatic bite.

From the very opening of the overture it is clear what tense dramatic control **James Levine** has over this masterpiece of an *opera seria*, his finest Mozart opera performance on disc. The cast is not just starry but stylish, with **Plácido Domingo** a commanding Idomeneo, giving a noble, finely controlled performance, which makes it a pity that the shorter version of his big aria, *Fuor del mar*, is preferred. **Carol Vaness** is a powerful, dramatic Elettra, well focused, and **Cecilia Bartoli** characterizes well as Idamante, wonderfully pure-toned in the Trio, while **Heidi Grant-Murphy** is a charmingly girlish Ilia with a light, bright soprano. Completing this team, you have **Thomas Hampson** as a superb Arbace and **Bryn Terfel** commanding in the brief solo given to the Oracle. The Met. chorus, like the orchestra, is incisively dramatic.

Idomeneo (sung in English)

(M) *** Chan. 3103 (2). Ford, Montague, Evans, Patterson, Davies, Gedda, Bayley, Opera N. Ch. & O, Parry

On Chandos, the performance of *Idomeneo* in English works surprisingly well, with the role of Idamante taken by a high voice, but with substantial cuts to allow the whole opera to be fitted on two very well-filled discs. Both of Arbace's arias disappear (a pity, when **Ryland Davies** is strongly cast as the High Priest) as well as one of Idamante's and one of Idomeneo's in Act III. In the title-role, **Bruce Ford's** distinctive tenor is powerfully expressive, even if his rapidly flickering vibrato does tend to obtrude in the more lyrical passages. The cast of women is outstanding, with **Rebecca Evans** as Ilia and **Diana Montague** as Idamante as mellifluous a duo as one could imagine, deeply expressive, too. **Susan Patterson** is well contrasted as Elettra, with her rather harder soprano suiting the aggressive side of the character. Having the veteran **Nicolai Gedda** in the cameo role of the Voice of Neptune is also a welcome plus-point. The vivid Chandos recording brings excellent balances between voices and orchestra, with words admirably clear. Mozart's score has never sounded fresher.

Lucio Silla (complete)

(N) *** Dacapo 8.226069/71 (3). Odinus, Nold, Hammarström, Bonde-Hansen, Elmark, Danish R. Sinf., Adám Fischer

Harnoncourt has a temptingly starry cast, but the opera is cut (see below). **Fischer** has a list of unfamiliar names, but they are young and clear-voiced and sing well. So until the Hager recording returns, this must be a clear first choice for an opera in which Mozart wrote a whole string of telling arias, well shared, dramatically and lyrically, between the main characters, **Simone Nold** (as the fiery heroine, Giunia) and her husband-to-be, Cecilio (**Kristina Hammarström** – originally a castrato part). The second couple, Cinna (**Henriette Bonde-Hansen**) and Celia (**Susanne Elmark**), are hardly less impressive. **Adám Fischer** directs the proceedings with plenty of vitality and the **Danish Radio Sinfonietta** are clearly kept on their toes. Like *Idomeneo*, *Lucio Silla* demonstrates what memorable music Mozart was writing for the operatic stage this early in his career.

Lucio Silla (slightly abridged)

*** Teldec 2292 44928-2 (2). Schreier, Gruberová, Bartoli, Kenny, Upshaw, Schoenberg Ch., VCM, Harnoncourt

What **Harnoncourt** has done is to record a text which fits on to two generously filled CDs, not just trimming down the recitatives but omitting no fewer than four arias, all of them valuable. Yet his sparkling direction of an outstanding, characterful team of soloists brings an exhilarating demonstration of the boy Mozart's genius, with such marvels as the extended finale to Act I left intact. **Schreier** is masterly in the title-role, still fresh in his voice, while **Dawn Upshaw** is warm and sweet as Celia, and **Cecilia Bartoli** is full and rich as Cecilio. The singing of **Edita Gruberová** as Giunia and **Yvonne Kenny** as Cinna is not quite so immaculate but is still confident and stylish. The **Concentus Musicus of**

Vienna has rarely given so bright and lightly sprung a performance on record. Excellent digital sound.

Mitridate re di Ponto (DVD version)

**** EuroArts DVD 2053609. Blake, Kenny, Putnam, Boozer, Rozario, Papis, Dubosc, Lyon Op. O, Guschlbauer (V/D: Bernard Maigrot)

Strongly cast, the 1986 Lyon Opera production of *Mitridate* makes a powerful case for Mozart's early opera, written when he was 14. Though modern instruments are used, **Theodor Guschlbauer** paces the music well. Not only does the tenor, **Rockwell Blake**, in the title-role cope splendidly with the enormous vocal range demanded, **Yvonne Kenny**, firm and agile, is magnetic in the role of Aspasia. **Ashley Putnam** is bright and clear as Sifare, and **Brenda Boozer's** rich mezzo is ideal for the role of Farnace. **Patricia Rozario** as Ismene and **Catherine Dubosc** as Arbate are first rate too, making one wish that Mozart had given them more to sing. The sets are simple and stylish, and the costumes are traditional in Arab style.

Mitridate, re di Ponto (complete; CD version)

**** Decca 460 772-2 (3). Bartoli, Dessay, Sabbatini, Asawa, Piau, Les Talens Lyriques, Rousset

Christophe Rousset conducts his period forces with panache, pointing rhythms infectiously. The cast is characterful, with **Cecilia Bartoli** outstanding as the hero, Sifare, in love with Aspasia. In that prima donna role, **Natalie Dessay** is both rich of tone and brilliantly agile in coloratura. The counter-tenor, **Brian Asawa**, is firm and characterful as the predatory Farnace, and though in the title-role **Giuseppe Sabbatini** is overstrenuous at times, his is a heroic performance, clean in attack. The softer-grained **Sandrine Piau** as Ismene is well contrasted with the others. Vivid, well-balanced sound. An excellent set, unlikely to be easily supplanted.

Le nozze di Figaro (complete; DVD versions)

(N) 🎧 **** Opus Arte DVD OA 0999o D. Schrott, Persson, Röschmann, Finley, Shaham, ROHCG Ch. & O, Pappano (Director: David McVicar; V/D Director: Ferenc van Damme)

🎧 (B) **** Warner NVC DVD 0630-14013-2. Finley, Hagley, Fleming, Schmidt, LPO, Haitink (Producer: Stephen Medcalf, V/D: Derek Bailey)

🎧 **** Arthaus DVD 101 089. Skram, Cotrubas, Te Kanawa, Luxon, Stade, Rintzler, Condo, Glyndebourne Ch., LPO, Pritchard (V/D: Dave Heather)

*** DG DVD 073 018-9. Terfel, Hagley, Gilfry, Martinpelto, Monteverdi Ch., E. Bar. Sol., Gardiner

An outstanding, new-style DVD *Figaro* from David McVicar to lead the top choices. It is set in the 1830s, which simply means that the costumes are brought forward a few decades but are still a pleasure to look at. The Count's palace is on a realistically impressive scale, with a huge staff, and its elegance contrasts with the scruffy room to be allotted to Figaro and Susanna after they are married, where the opera opens. **Erwin Schrott** is a lively, resourceful and above all very good-looking Figaro, but the delightful Susanna (**Miah Persson**), charmingly dressed, is his match and they both sing splendidly. **Gerald Finley** does too, even if he portrays a truly unattractive and permanently disgruntled, jealous Count, and one wonders what Rosina originally saw in him. But his anger gives a spice to the action, especially in Mozart's marvellous extended finale to Act II which, with wonderful music, keeps the viewer continually wondering what is coming next. The dignified Countess (**Dorothea Röschmann**) sings her pair of key arias beautifully and affectingly. While she conveys her deep unhappiness at her husband's unfaithful behaviour, she is appealingly spirited and stands her own ground, obviously enjoying Cherubino's attempts to win her favours. **Rinat Shaham** is very personable, and her singing of 'his' two arias in that role, is another of the highlights of the production. Altogether this is very recommendable indeed. The sets are appealing and the action moves forward with a swing, with the performance conducted with his usual flair by Antonio Pappano.

The Warner version must be one of the great bargains of DVD. At the time of writing it retails at £19.99, and you would not find it easy to get a CD version of any distinction at this price. And this *is* a performance of distinction, wonderfully conducted by **Bernard Haitink** and with four first-class principals. **Gerald Finley's** Figaro is expertly characterized and beautifully sung, and the same goes for both **Renée Fleming's** Countess and **Alison Hagley's** Susanna. The three hours nine minutes are contained on one double-sided DVD, which accommodates two Acts per side. The quality of the colour and the sharpness of focus are in the demonstration bracket and so, too, is the vivid, well-balanced sound. Musically a satisfying set and one of the handful of DVDs that should be in every serious collection.

Recorded in 1973, Sir Peter Hall's production of *Figaro* at Glyndebourne is a model of its kind. Here is a traditional production that, far from being unimaginative, brings endless new perceptions and illuminations of the complicated plot devised by Lorenzo da Ponte from the original Beaumarchais play. John Bury's designs are solidly realistic yet comparably imaginative in the way that each scene is set diagonally on stage, giving interesting perspectives. The musical performance is led by three stars in their early prime: **Ileana Cotrubas** as a sparkling Susanna, **Frederica von Stade** as a wonderfully boyish Cherubino and, above all, **Kiri Te Kanawa** as the Countess, commanding yet tenderly affecting in her vulnerability. They are matched by the lively Figaro of **Knut Skram**, **Benjamin Luxon** at his finest as the Count, **Marius Rintzler** as a dark, firm Bartolo and **John Fryatt** a brilliant, witty Basilio.

John Eliot Gardiner's DG DVD was recorded for video live, at the Théâtre du Châtelet in Paris, with economical but evocative sets. Simple screens illustrating each scene are dropped in front of a panoramic backcloth with trees and the Almaviva Palace in black silhouette against blue. Props as well as scenery are minimal but succeed in pointing the humour without distracting. The performance follows the splendid pattern of the CD version, with **Terfel** superb in the title-role, already at his peak in 1993, leading a young and consistently attractive cast, and this makes for an outstanding, consistently exhilarating presentation of the Mozart/Da Ponte masterpiece.

Le nozze di Figaro (complete; CD versions)

🎵→ ******** HM HMC90 1818/20. Gens, Ciofi, Kirchschlager, McLaughlin, Keenlyside, Regazzo, Ghent Coll. Voc., Concerto Köln, Jacobs

🎵→ ******* Decca 410 150-2 (3). Te Kanawa, Popp, von Stade, Ramey, Allen, Moll, Tear, LPO & Ch., Solti

🎵→ Ⓜ ******* EMI (ADD) 3 58602-2 (2). Schwarzkopf, Moffo, Cossotto, Taddei, Waechter, Vinco, Philh. Ch. & O, Giulini

Ⓜ ******** Decca (ADD) 466 369-2 (3). Gueden, Danco, della Casa, Dickie, Poell, Corena, Siepi, V. State Op. Ch., VPO, Kleiber

*** DG 439 871-2 (3). Terfel, Hagley, Martinpelto, Gilfry, Stephen, McCulloch, Feller, Egerton, Backes, Monterverdi Ch., E. Bar. Sol., Gardiner

*** Teldec 4509 90861-2 (3). Scharinger, Bonney, Margiono, Hampson, Lang, Moll, Langridge, Netherlands Op. Ch., Concg. O, Harnoncourt

Ⓜ ******* DG (ADD) 449 728-2 (3). Janowitz, Mathis, Troyanos, Fischer-Dieskau, Prey, Lagger, German Op. Ch. & O, Boehm

René Jacobs conducts one of the most refreshing versions of *Figaro* to be issued in many years, with its excellent cast a worthy winner of the *Gramophone* 'Record of the Year Award' in 2004. It all adds up to a winning result. **Véronique Gens** is one of the most distinguished of Countesses, and **Patrizia Ciofi** is a sparkling Susanna, while **Simon Keenlyside** is a superb Count, well contrasted with the strongly acted Figaro of **Lorenzo Regazzo**. **Angelika Kirchschlager** sings flawlessly as Cherubino, while having **Marie McLaughlin** as Marcellina represents luxury casting.

Solti opts for a fair proportion of extreme speeds, slow as well as fast, but they rarely if ever intrude on the quintessential happiness of the entertainment. **Samuel Ramey**, a firm-toned baritone, makes a virile Figaro, superbly matched to the most enchanting of Susannas on record, **Lucia Popp**, who gives a sparkling and radiant performance. **Thomas Allen's** Count is magnificent too, tough in tone and characterization but always beautiful on the ear. **Kurt Moll** as Dr Bartolo sings an unforgettable *La vendetta* with triplets very fast and agile 'on the breath'. **Frederica von Stade** is a most attractive Cherubino, even if *Voi che sapete* is too slow; but crowning all is the Countess of **Kiri Te Kanawa**, challenged by Solti's spacious tempi in the two big arias, but producing ravishing tone, flawless phrasing and elegant ornamentation throughout. With superb, vivid recording this now makes a clear choice for a much-recorded opera. However, in view of the strong competition, Decca should find a way of reducing its price.

Giulini's set remains a classic, with a cast assembled by Walter Legge that has rarely been matched, let alone surpassed. **Taddei** with his dark bass-baritone makes a provocative Figaro; opposite him, **Anna Moffo** is at her freshest and sweetest as Susanna. **Schwarzkopf** as ever is the noblest of Countesses, and it is good to hear the young **Fiorenza**

Cossotto as a full-toned Cherubino. **Eberhard Waechter** is a strong and stylish Count. On only two mid-priced discs it makes a superb bargain.

Erich Kleiber's famous set was one of Decca's Mozart bicentenary recordings of the mid-1950s. It remains a memorably strong performance with much fine singing. Few sets since have matched its constant stylishness. **Hilde Gueden's** Susanna might be criticized but her golden tones are certainly characterful and her voice blends with **Lisa della Casa's** enchantingly. **Suzanne Danco** and della Casa are both at their finest. A dark-toned Figaro in **Cesare Siepi** brings added contrast and, if the pace of the recitatives is rather slow, this is not inconsistent within the context of Kleiber's overall approach. The closing scene of Act II is marvellously done.

Gardiner's CD version was recorded live. In one instance the effect of the moment goes too far, when Cherubino (**Pamela Helen Stephen**) sings *Voi che sapete* for the Countess in a funny, nervous voice. That is very much the exception, for Gardiner's approach is lively and often brisk, with period manners made more genial and elegant. One of the most consistent and characterful of modern casts is led superbly by **Bryn Terfel** as Figaro, already a master in this role, with the enchanting, bright-eyed **Alison Hagley** as Susanna. **Rodney Gilfry** and **Hillevi Martinpelto** are fresh and firm as the Count and Countess, aptly younger-sounding than usual. **Carlos Feller** is a characterful *buffo* Bartolo, and **Francis Egerton** a wickedly funny Basilio.

Harnoncourt on Teldec makes the **Royal Concertgebouw Orchestra** produce fresh, light and transparent sounds, close to period style. The excellent cast has **Thomas Hampson** as a dominant Count, **Charlotte Margiono** as a tenderly sweet Countess, with **Barbara Bonney** a charmingly provocative Susanna and **Anton Scharinger** a winning Figaro, both tough and comic. Recitative at flexible speeds conveys the dramatic confrontations and complications vividly. A version that gets the best of both interpretative worlds, new and old. A generous budget Apex CD of highlights (76′) is also available (2564 61514-2).

Boehm's version of *Figaro* is also among the most consistently assured performances available. The women all sing most beautifully, with **Gundula Janowitz's** Countess, **Edith Mathis's** Susanna and **Tatiana Troyanos's** Cherubino all ravishing the ear in contrasted ways. **Hermann Prey** is an intelligent if not very jolly-sounding Figaro, and **Dietrich Fischer-Dieskau** gives his dark, sharply defined reading of the Count's role. All told, a great success, with fine playing and recording, here impressively remastered.

Le nozze di Figaro (complete; CD version). Symphonies 38 (Prague); 39

Ⓝ ☛– Ⓜ *** EMI (stereo/mono) 2 12681-2 (3). Bruscantini, Sciutti, Wallace, Sinclair, Stevens, Calabrese, Cuénod, Jurinac, Glyndebourne Festival O, Gui

Gui's effervescent 1955 Glyndebourne set is at last reissued complete for the first time on CD, one of EMI's 'Great Recordings of the Century' series, with two Mozart symphonies used to fill up the CDs (they are placed at the end of Acts I & II). It remains a classic set with a cast which has seldom been bettered. Just as **Sesto Bruscantini** is the archetypal Glyndebourne Figaro, **Sena Jurinac** is the perfect Countess, with **Graziella Sciutti** a delectable Susanna and **Risë Stevens** a well-contrasted Cherubino, vivacious in their scenes together. **Franco Calabrese** as the Count is firm and virile, if occasionally stressed on top, and the three character roles have never been cast more vividly, with **Ian Wallace** as Bartolo, **Monica Sinclair** as Marcellina and the incomparable **Hugues Cuénod** as Basilio. Cuénod's brilliant performance of Basilio's aria in Act IV has now been restored for the present reissue. It is a great pity that a libretto wasn't included, though an excellent essay by Richard Osborne is. The sound for the opera is mightily impressive for 1955 stereo, warm and superbly balanced, and pretty good too for the earlier symphonies (given stylish performances), albeit in 1953 mono.

The Marriage of Figaro (in English)

Ⓜ **(*) Chan. 3113 (3). Kenny, Evans, Montague, Purves, Dazeley, Geoffrey Mitchell Ch., Philh. O, Parry

Arguably, *Figaro* gains more from being heard in English than any other opera, with the fun of the piece heightened; **Parry's** timing of the comedy here is impeccable, helped by light, clean textures and imaginative continuo-playing in recitatives, using fortepiano. Most of the principals have had long experience of singing their roles on stage: **Rebecca Evans** as a golden-voiced Susanna for Welsh National Opera, **Yvonne Kenny** as a feisty, defiant Countess for Washington Opera (having graduated from the role of Susanna elsewhere), **Diana Montague** as a glowing Cherubino at Covent Garden, **Christopher Purves** as a powerful Figaro with Scottish Opera, and **John Graham-Hall** as a characterful Basilio at Glyndebourne. **William Dazeley** is the upstanding Count, and **Jonathan Veira** a rather young-sounding Bartolo.

Il re pastore (CD version)

Ⓝ Ⓜ ** Warner Maestro 2564 69259-9 (2). Saccà, Murray, Mei, Nielsen, Schaeffer, VCM, Harnoncourt

Harnoncourt, in his period-instrument recording, characteristically takes a tough, vigorous view of this unpretentious serenata, pressing home allegros vigorously, with the horn and trumpet parts brightly brought out and with timpani added. This means that he misses the tenderness of such numbers as Agemore's first aria, though he relaxes for the most celebrated aria, Aminta's *L'amero*, beautifully sung by **Ann Murray**, the most characterful singer in the cast. Neither **Robert Saccà** as Alessandro nor **Marcus Schaeffer** as Agemore is stylish or agile enough. With its reverberation the recording enhances the big-scale impression, with occasional audience noises intruding.

Die Zauberflöte (DVD versions)

**** DG **DVD** 073 4106. Popp, Araiza, Gruberová, W. Brendel, Sieber, Moll, Orth, Bav. State Op. Ch. & O, Sawallisch (Director: August Everding, V/D: Oeter Windgassen)

☛– *** TDK **DVD** DVWW-CLOPMF. Cotrubas, Schreier, Gruberová, Talvela, Boesch, Sieber, Hiestermann, V. State

Op. Konzertvereinigung, VPO, Levine (Stage Director: Jean-Pierre Ponnelle, V/D: Brian Large)

🎜 *** Arthaus DVD 101 085. Lott, Goeke, Sandoz, Luxon, Thomaschke, Glyndebourne Ch., LPO, Haitink (Producer: John Cox, V/D: Dave Heather)

**(*) TDK DVD DVWW OPMFP. Röschmann, Beczala, Rancatore, Roth, Le Roi, Salminen, Peper, Paris Nat. Op. Ch. & O, Iván Fischer (Director: Benno Besson, V/D: François Roussillon)

Sawallisch's 1983 Bavarian account of *Die Zauberflöte* is outstanding in every way and will be difficult to surpass. **Lucia Popp** sings radiantly as Pamina and **Francisco Araiza** (who joined the cast at the last minute) is an equally golden-voiced Tamino. **Edita Gruverová** is a splendidly malignant Queen of the Night and her *Der Hölle Rache* is breathtaking. The lanky, rugged **Wolfgang Brendel** makes an utterly believable Papageno. When she arrives, his Papagena (**Gudrun Sieber**) is the prettiest wife, and after they have sung their famous duet they wheel the little Papagenas and Papagenos (who have appeared to illustrate their words) away in a barrow. This is one of many production touches from August Everding and the designer Jürgen Rose that add to the success of this attractively staged performance, with Rose's costumes completing the picture. Monostatos (**Norbert Orth**) is a real black-faced villain, and his counterpart, Sarastro (the resonant **Kurt Moll**) sings and acts nobly. The Three Boys are engagingly knowing and the Three Ladies make a balancing (not impartial) counterpart. Their very opening scene, when they dispatch the monster by magic, is especially effective. The ordeal by fire and water is also simply staged, to make the opera's close very satisfying. Throughout, Sawallisch conducts with inspirationally relaxed timing and gives the performance a natural, spontaneous flow. Vivid recording completes a superb set.

Jean-Pierre Ponnelle's production of *Die Zauberflöte*, with his own charming toytown sets and costumes. With **James Levine** at his brilliant and most perceptive as conductor, it struck an ideal between the pantomime element and the weightier implications of the Masonic background to the story. It makes an ideal entertainment on film in this 1982 recording. The cast is excellent, with **Peter Schreier** in his prime as Tamino, **Ileana Cotrubas** a charming Pamina and **Edita Gruberová** a dazzling Queen of the Night. **Martti Talvela** is the most resonant Sarastro, backed up by the veteran, **Walter Berry**, as the Speaker. Most imaginative of all is the casting of **Christian Boesch** as Papageno, a singing actor rather than a regular opera-singer. Few have presented the role quite so engagingly, and his duets with Pamina have a rare tenderness. The chorus and others in the cast are first rate.

What dominates John Cox's lively 1978 production of *Die Zauberflöte* for Glyndebourne are the sets and designs of David Hockney. He was following up the success of his unique designs for *The Rake's Progress*, and the vision again is striking, with stylized scenery and landscapes in false perspective, with something of a toytown atmosphere, including a delightful dragon and oriental costumes for Sarastro's followers. That puts the production firmly on the side of

pantomime rather than serious drama, but the excellent casting and the powerful conducting of **Bernard Haitink** ensure that this is not just a trivial entertainment. Though **Leo Goeke** as Tamino has his roughness of voice, he sings *Dies Bildnis* beautifully, with the young **Felicity Lott** a charming Pamina. **Benjamin Luxon** is a strong and positive Papageno, with **May Sandoz** light, bright and agile as the Queen of the Night and **Thomas Thomashke** a well-focused Sarastro, and with the young **Willard White** as the Speaker. A memorable version.

Not surprisingly, the TDK Paris production is strong on spectacle, changing sets for each colourful scene and using the full stage facilities. The result is visually appealing though there are some curious eccentricities in the production. Papageno (**Detlef Roth**) is an engaging, fully feathered bird catcher, and as he sings about himself, three birds fly across the stage and into his cage. **Dorothea Röschmann**, an appealingly resourceful Pamina, creates a stronger role than usual; she sings beautifully yet adds an extra dimension by the strength of her character. **Désirée Rancatore** is an arresting Queen of the Night and projects her famous aria with vehemence. There are some nice individual touches. The Three Boys are conveyed in a very handsome balloon, and when Tamino entices the animals with his magic flute they arrive elegantly dressed (almost Beatrix Potter style). Later, when Papageno and the old woman have their proposal scene, the disguised Papagena looks very unattractive indeed, then almost instantaneously she is a very pretty wife. The singing throughout is of a very high standard, not least the priests, who nevertheless are strangely casual in dress. But Sarastro, whose two great arias are superbly sung by **Matti Salminen**, is given an elongated egg-head, quite out of character with his noble personage. But **Iván Fisher's** musical direction is flexible and spirited, and the whole opera goes with a swing; with such colourful sets and costumes, it makes a very enjoyable entertainment.

Die Zauberflöte (CD versions)

🎜 ⚙ **** DG 477 5789 (2). Röschmann, Miklósa, Strehl, Pape, Müller-Brachmann, Kleiter, Azesberger, Georg Zeppenfeld, Arnold Schoenberg Ch., Mahler CO, Abbado

*** DG 449 166-2 (2); Video VHS 072 447-3. Oelze, Schade, Sieden, Peeters, Finley, Backes, Monteverdi Ch., E. Bar. Sol., Gardiner

*** Erato 0630 12705-2 (2). Mannion, Blochwitz, Dessay, Hagen, Scharinger, Les Arts Florissants, Christie

🎜 ⚙ Ⓜ (***) DG mono 435 741-2 (2). Stader, Streich, Fischer-Dieskau, Greindl, Haefliger, Berlin RIAS Ch. & SO, Fricsay

Ⓜ *** EMI (ADD) 5 67388-2 (2). Janowitz, Putz, Popp, Gedda, Berry, Frick, Schwarzkopf, Ludwig, Hoffgen (3 Ladies), Philh. Ch. & O, Klemperer

Ⓜ (***) EMI mono 5 67071-2 (2). Seefried, Lipp, Loose, Dermota, Kunz, Weber, V. State Op. Ch., VPO, Karajan

*** Telarc CD-80302 (2). Hadley, Hendricks, Allen, Anderson, Lloyd, SCO & Ch., Mackerras

Ⓝ Ⓜ ** Decca (ADD) 478 0394. Lorengar, Deutekom,

Burrows, Fischer-Dieskau, Prey, Talvela, V. State Op. Ch., VPO, Solti

As DG's wording on the box makes clear, this is **Abbado's** very first *Magic Flute* on record and indeed – as they claim – it is a triumphant success. **René Pape's** magnificent Sarastro dominates the opera, just as intended. He and the superb chorus bring just the right touch of gravitas, so all the pantomime fun with Papageno and Papagena is nicely balanced. Moreover, **Erika Miklósa's** Queen of the Night's second aria, *Der Hölle Rache*, is quite as dazzling as Rita Streich's celebrated version, and it is slightly fuller in tone. **Dorothea Röschmann** and **Christoph Strehl** are a perfectly matched Pamina and Tamino, for both have lovely voices: Strehl is ardent, and Röschmann is infinitely touching. The smaller parts are also without flaw. **Kurt Azesberger** is a splendid Monostatos, and even the Speaker, **George Zeppenfeld**, has a honeyed voice. But most magical of all are the little vocal ensembles, wonderfully warm and refined, especially the numbers featuring the Three Ladies, who blend so delightfully but not suavely, and the Three Boys (from the Tölzer Knabenchor), who are just as memorable. Although the moments of drama are not lost, this is above all an affectionately relaxed performance, with **Abbado** continually revelling in the lyrical beauty of Mozart's wonderful score. It is, of course, a live performance, so it has the extra communicative tension that brings. There is also a first class (74') set of highlights with full texts and translations (DG 4776319).

John Eliot Gardiner rounds off his outstanding series for DG Archiv of Mozart's seven great mature operas with an electrifying account of *Zauberflöte*, even though the generally inspired casting is marred by the underpowered and uneven Sarastro of **Harry Peeters**. Gardiner is helped enormously by his choice of singer as Pamina, a young German soprano with a ravishingly pure and sweet voice, flawlessly controlled, **Christiane Oelze**. Also superb is the American soprano who takes the role of Queen of the Night, with a voice as full and silvery as it is flexible, **Cyndia Sieden**. The Tamino of **Michael Schade** has youthful freshness combined with keen imagination; though there are more characterful Papagenos than **Gerald Finley**, few sing as freshly and cleanly as he. With recording clear and well balanced, the set offers an incidental practical advantage in putting the spoken dialogue on separate tracks.

More than his rivals, Christie wears his period manners easily and amiably, with fast speeds crisp and light, and with some numbers – such as Papageno's first aria – relaxedly expansive. There is no weak link in the cast, with **Rosa Mannion** a warm, touching Pamina, able to bring out deeper feelings as in *Ach, ich fühl's*, and **Hans-Peter Blochwitz** is an imaginative, sweetly expressive Tamino, while **Natalie Dessay** as Queen of the Night is unusually warm-toned for the role, not so much a frigid figure as a fully rounded character, with the coloratura display dazzlingly clear. **Anton Scharinger** is a genial, rich-toned Papageno, and **Reinhard Hagen** a Sarastro satisfyingly clean of focus. Above all, the joyful vigour of Mozart's inspiration captures one from first to last.

Fricsay's recording has been treasured by us since the early days of LP. It is an outstandingly fresh and alert *Die Zauberflöte*, marked by generally clear, pure singing and well-sprung orchestral playing at generally rather fast speeds which yet never sound rushed. **Maria Stader** and **Dietrich Fischer-Dieskau** phrase most beautifully, but the most spectacular singing comes from **Rita Streich** as a dazzling Queen of the Night, and the relatively close balance of the voice gives it the necessary power such as Streich could convey less readily in the opera house. **Ernst Haefliger**, too, is at his most honeyed in tone as Tamino, and only the rather gritty Sarastro of **Josef Greindl** falls short – and even he sings with a satisfying dark resonance. This was the first version to spice the musical numbers with brief sprinklings of dialogue, just enough to prevent the work from sounding like an oratorio.

Klemperer's conducting of *The Magic Flute* is one of his finest achievements on record; indeed, he is inspired, making the dramatic music sound more like Beethoven in its breadth and strength. The dialogue is omitted, but he does not miss the humour and point of the Papageno passages, and he gets the best of both worlds to a surprising degree. The cast is outstanding – look at the distinction of the Three Ladies alone – but curiously it is that generally most reliable of all the singers, **Gottlob Frick** as Sarastro, who comes nearest to letting the side down. **Lucia Popp** is in excellent form, and **Gundula Janowitz** sings Pamina's part with a creamy beauty that is just breathtaking. **Nicolai Gedda** too is a firm-voiced Tamino.

The **Vienna State Opera** cast of **Karajan's** mono version of 1950 has not since been matched on record: **Irmgard Seefried** and **Anton Dermota** both sing with radiant beauty and great character, **Wilma Lipp** is a dazzling Queen of the Night, **Erich Kunz** as Papageno sings with an infectious smile in the voice, and **Ludwig Weber** is a commanding Sarastro. There is no spoken dialogue; but it is a Mozart treat not to be missed, with mono sound still amazingly vivid and full of presence.

Solti's reading is tough, strong and brilliant, but the almost total absence of charm is disconcerting. The drama may be consistently vital, but ultimately the full variety of Mozart's inspiration is not achieved. Among the men, **Stuart Burrows** is especially impressive, with stylish and rich-toned singing; **Martti Talvela** and **Fischer-Dieskau** as Sarastro and the Speaker respectively provide a stronger contrast than usual and **Hermann Prey** rounds out the character of Papageno with intelligent pointing of words. The cast of women is less consistent. **Pilar Lorengar's** Pamina is sweetly attractive so long as your ear is not worried by the intrusive vibrato, while **Cristina Deutekom's** Queen of the Night is marred by a curious warbling quality in the coloratura. The recording is brilliant and there is a full libretto, but this is far from a first choice.

The Magic Flute (complete; in English)

(M) *** Chan. 3121 (2). Evans, Vidal, Banks, Keenlyside, Tomlinson, Graham-Hall, Mitchell Ch., LPO, Mackerras

Sir Charles Mackerras regularly opts for brisk and flowing speeds, most strikingly in Pamina's great G minor aria, *Ach, ich fühl's* ('Now I know that love can vanish' in Jeremy Sams's translation). **Rebecca Evans** sings passionately, as Mackerras suggests, coping splendidly with the florid writing. So does the French coloratura, **Elisabeth Vidal**, in the Queen of the Night's two big arias, bright and agile. That she betrays a hint of a foreign accent in the spoken dialogue (well edited in helpful links) is only apt. Standing out is the masterly portrayal of Papageno by **Simon Keenlyside**, vividly acted and flawlessly sung, and **Barry Banks** as Tamino sings very well in the lyrical numbers. **John Tomlinson** as Sarastro gives necessary weight to the role, even if he is not always quite as steady as he once was, while **John Graham-Hall** sings and acts vividly as Monostatos, unfazed by Mackerras's hectic speed for his aria. Defying the fast speeds, the vocal ensembles are wonderfully crisp, as is the playing of the **LPO**. As well as the well-delivered dialogue, the vivid sound-effects regularly add to the dramatic impact.

RECITALS

'Tutto Mozart'. Arias from: *Bastien und Bastienne; Così fan tutte; Don Giovanni; Le nozze di Figaro; Die Zauberflöte.* **Concert arias:** *Un bacio di mano; Così dunque tradisci – Aspri rimorsi atroci; Männer suchen stetz zu naschen* (also included: JACQUIN: *Io ti lascio, o cara, addio;* SCHACK: *Nun, liebes Weibchen, ziehst mit mir*)

🔊 *** DG 477 5886. Terfel, Persson, Rice, SNO, Mackerras

The astonishing versatility of **Bryn Terfel** as a Mozart singer is brilliantly demonstrated on this recital disc of 19 Mozart items. Not only does Terfel take on the roles of both Don Giovanni and Leporello in *Don Giovanni*, but Guglielmo and Alfonso in *Così* and Figaro and the Count in *Figaro*, plus a sparkling Papageno, all of them clearly contrasted; and he adds a fascinating collection of rarities to set them in contrast. So you have a duet by Gottfried von Jacquin, orchestrated by Mozart, with the baritone answered by the soprano singing 'Miaow'. Terfel sings with clean, firm tone throughout, avoiding the roughness which has sometimes afflicted his singing. A delightful Mozart offering, beautifully conducted and recorded, with **Miah Persson** and **Christine Rice** admirable partners in various items.

Arias from: (i) *La clemenza di Tito;* (ii) *Così fan tutte; Don Giovanni;* (ii) *Lucio Silla; Mitridate, rè di Ponto;* (i) *Le nozze di Figaro; Zaïde; Die Zauberflöte*

🔊 Ⓑ *** CfP 585 9022. SCO, with (i) Murray; cond. Leppard; (ii) Allen; cond. Armstrong

Dating from 1984, when both singers were in their prime, this is one of the most delectable collections of Mozart arias ever assembled on a single disc. **Sir Thomas Allen** has the lion's share, and he is in superb form in the four *Figaro* arias and in Papageno's pair from *Die Zauberflöte*. His honeyed legato in *Deh vieni alla finestra* from *Don Giovanni* is matched by the sheer gusto of *Finch'han dal vino*. To conclude, there are two rarer excerpts from *Zaïde*, and the engaging *Un bacio di mano*, an insertion aria which Mozart wrote for Pasquale Anfossi's *Le gelosie fortunate* in 1788. **Ann Murray** then takes over for splendidly sung excerpts from *La clemenza di Tito* (*Parto parto*, with the clarinet obbligato

stylishly played by **Lewis Morrison**) and the spectacular *Lungi da te, mio bene* from *Mitridate, rè di Ponto*, with a fine horn obbligato from **Frank Lloyd**, who also stays around to contribute similarly to the Handelian encore, *Va tacito e nascosto* from Act I of *Giulio Cesare*, which is equally impressive. With stylish accompaniments from the **Scottish Chamber Orchestra** under **Sir Richard Armstrong** or **Raymond Leppard**, and warm, natural recording, which (because of the skill of the balance engineer, Stuart Eltham) is kind to both voices. At Classics for Pleasure price this is quite irresistible.

Arias: *La clemenza di Tito; Don Giovanni; Die Entführung aus dem Serail; Idomeneo; Le nozze di Figaro; Il re pastore.* **Concert Arias:** *Ah, conte, partite, K.418; Resta o cara, K.528; Vado, ma dove?, K.583*

Ⓜ *** RCA 82876 65841-2. Margaret Price, ECO or LPO, Lockgart

An impressive disc of display arias. **Margaret Price** shows her versatility by singing excerpts from all three soprano roles in *Figaro*, but her most impressive performances remain those which demand coloratura brilliance combined with dramatic power. Strong accompaniments and good recording.

Arias from: *La clemenza di Tito; Idomeneo; Lucio Silla; Le nozze di Figaro*

🔊 *** Erato 8573 85768-2. Graham, OAE, Bickett – GLUCK: *Aria* ***

This is a glorious recital of Mozart and Gluck, with **Susan Graham** radiant and characterful in arias she has sung on stage, highlighting the distinctive points of each character. So from *La clemenza di Tito* she contrasts Sesto's purposeful first aria with the far gentler second, producing a breathtaking *pianissimo* on the reprise. Cherubino's two arias from *Figaro* are made to sound new and intense, with the last and longest item, Cecilio's big, taxing number from *Lucio Silla, Il tenero momento*, providing the title of the whole recital, making a superb climax. Fine, sympathetic accompaniment and perfect sound.

Arias from: *La clemenza di Tito; Così fan tutte; Don Giovanni; Idomeneo; Lucio Silla; Mitridate; Le nozze di Figaro*

*** RCA 09026 68661-2. Kasarova, Dresden State O, C. Davis

Here in a formidable collection of Mozart arias, much enhanced by **Colin Davis's** accompaniment, **Kasarova** demonstrates not only her stylishness and technical prowess – with not a single intrusive aitch allowed – but her musical flair. At the very start, she launches into the recitative before Dorabella's aria in *Così fan tutte* with a vehemence that takes the breath away, and vehemence is a quality that draws many of these portrayals together, whether as Donna Elvira in *Don Giovanni* (giving way to tenderness when required), Vitellia in *Clemenza* or a whole range of trouser-roles, including those in the early *Mitridate* and *Lucio Silla*.

'Arie di Bravura' from: Didone abbandonata; Lucio Silla; Die Zauberflöte

*** Virgin 3 95250-2. Damrau, Le Cercle de L'Harmonie, Rhorer (with arias by RIGHINI) – SALIERI: Arias ***

For her début recital the brilliant coloratura soprano **Diana Damrau** has chosen to contrast Mozartian operatic repertoire with arias by Salieri and in the event his contemporary, Vincenzo Righini, whose music she discovered when preparing this programme. The two arias by this contemporary and colleague of Salieri are from *Il natal d'Apollo*; the first is a virtuoso piece with a violin obbligato, the second, *Ombra dolente*, is really affecting, a little like Gluck. In the Mozart arias Damrau really rises to the occasion, singing with a rich espressivo in the excerpts from *Lucio Silla* and the little-known Mozartian version of Dido's Lament, while characterizing a very angry Queen of the Night in a bravura account of *Der Hölle Rache* as thrillingly accurate as any on record.

Arias from: Don Giovanni; Die Entführung aus dem Serail; La finta giardiniera; Le nozze di Figaro; Il re pastore; Il sogno di Scipione; Zaïde; Die Zauberflöte. Concert aria: Nehmt meinen Dank

🎧– *** Decca 452 602-2. Fleming, O of St Luke's, Mackerras

Renée Fleming has rarely sounded quite so beautiful on disc as in this wide-ranging collection of Mozart arias, one of the finest available. If it is disappointing not to have her singing the role of the Countess in *Figaro*, the two Susanna items are both welcome – *Deh vieni* bringing out her most golden tone and the big alternative aria, *Al desio*, challenging her to her most brilliant singing. Her account of La Fortuna's aria from *Il sogno di Scipione* is commanding too, and her ornamentation is phenomenally crisp and brilliant throughout, not least in *Ach ich liebte* from *Entführung*. The only reservations come with the brisk treatment, period-style, of Pamina's *Ach, ich fühl's* and the lovely aria from *Zaïde*, both of which could be much more tenderly expressive. Excellent, stylish accompaniment and first-rate recording.

Arias from: Don Giovanni; Zaïde; Die Zauberflöte

Ⓑ *** EMI 3 68255-2. Yu, Prague Philharmonia, Sato – BACH: Arias ***

The Korean soprano **Hyunah Yu** is blessed with a gloriously creamy and firm voice, which she uses most expressively in these Mozart arias, notably in the three arias from the incomplete Singspiel, *Zaïde*, which she has performed on stage – not only the well-known *Ruhe sanft* but the equally lyrical *Trostlos schluchtzet* and the violent 'Tiger!' aria, attacking the evil Sultan. Pamina's great Act II aria, *Ach ich fühl's*, is wonderfully pure and poised, with Yu charming in Zerlina's *Vedrai carino* from *Don Giovanni*. Well coupled with impressive Bach arias in EMI's adventurous Debut series.

Arias: Don Giovanni; Die Entführung aus dem Serail; Idomeneo; Le nozze di Figaro; Die Zauberflöte

🎧– Ⓜ (***) EMI mono 4 76844-2. Schwarzkopf (with various conductors & orchestras, including Pritchard, Krips, Braithwaite, Karajan)

This famous **Schwarzkopf** mono recital is reissued as one of EMI's 'Great Recordings of the Century', with two extra items added (to make 14 in all), including *L'amerò sarò costante*, Aminto's Act II aria from *Il re pastore*. This is the earliest, along with the two from *Die Entführung*; and one of the curiosities is a lovely account of Pamina's *Ach, ich fühl's*, recorded in English in 1948. The majority, including those from *Figaro* – Susanna's and Cherubino's arias as well as the Countess's – are taken from a recital disc conducted by John Pritchard in 1953. Full translations are included.

MUFFAT, Georg (1653–1704)

Florilegium secundum: Suites 1–4

Ⓜ **(*) Decca O/L 475 9118. AAM, Hogwood

George Muffat was born in Megève, Savoy. The *Florilegium secundum* was published in 1698 at Passau, where he served at the court of the bishop. It is a set of eight orchestral suites, the first four of which are recorded here. They are formally more adventurous than the dance movements of such contemporaries as Fischer and Schmelzer, though not all of them are of equal interest. These 1981, originally L'Oiseau-Lyre, performances are on period instruments and those unresponsive to the razor-edged strings of that period will probably find the sound unpleasing. The playing is often a bit heavy-handed too, but those intrigued by this set have no current alternative and the recording is very good indeed.

Missa in labore requies

🎧– Ⓑ **** HM HMA 1951667. Soloists, Cantus Cölln, Concerto Palatino, Junghänel (with Antonio BERTALI: Sonata a 13; Sonata Sancti Placidi) – BIBER: Litaniae de Sancto Josepho; Sonatas ***

Georg Muffat and Heinrich Biber had much in common. Not only did they work cordially together in Salzburg between 1678 and 1690, when Muffat was court organist, but they died in the same year, 1704. Moreover, Muffat's settings for large forces, vocal and instrumental, followed very much Biber's Salzburg tradition. Little of his music survives, but the *Missa in labore requies* shows its very high quality, especially the closing *Agnus Dei*. The performance also interpolates Biber's *Sonata Fidicinium sacro-profanum* and two sonatas by another contemporary composer, Antonio Bertali (1605–69). The performance here is of the highest quality and the recording admirably spacious. Full texts and translations are included, plus good documentation, making this reissue a very real bargain.

MUNDY, William (c. 1529–c. 1591)

Vox Patris caelestis

🎧– Ⓜ *** Gimell (ADD) Gimse 401 Tallis Scholars, Phillips – ALLEGRI: Miserere; PALESTRINA: Missa Papae Marcelli ***

Mundy's *Vox Patris caelestis* was written during the short reign of Queen Mary (1553–8). The work is structured in nine sections in groups of three, the last of each group being climactic and featuring the whole choir, with solo embroidery. Yet the music flows continuously, like a great river, and the complex vocal writing creates the most spectacular effects, with the trebles soaring up and shining out over the underlying cantilena. The **Tallis Scholars** give an account which balances linear clarity with considerable power. The recording is first class and the digital remastering for CD improves the focus further.

MUSGRAVE, Thea (born 1928)

(i) *Concerto for Orchestra*; (ii) *Clarinet Concerto*; (iii) *Horn Concerto*; (iv; v) *Excursions: 8 Duets for piano, four hands*; (iv) *Monologue for piano solo*

*** Lyrita (ADD) SRCD 253. (i) SNO, Gibson; (ii) de Peyer, LSO, Del Mar; (iii) Tuckwell, SNO, composer; (iv) composer (piano); (v) with Williamson

An impressive collection to represent a major but neglected composer, Scottish-born but resident in the USA. The *Concerto for Orchestra* (its five sections impressively interlinked), like the *Horn Concerto*, is among Thea Musgrave's most vital and original works. The work for horn has a spatial concept as part of its construction. The orchestral brass form a concertante group within the orchestra, with the percussion spread round the back. At one stage the trumpets take up antiphonal positions on either side of the orchestra, while the orchestral horns move out into the hall, strategically placed so as to surround the soloist. All this is vividly captured by the recording engineers. The *Clarinet Concerto* is peripatetic, the soloist (for clear artistic and sonic reasons) moving about the orchestra from one group of instruments to another. The tonal results are superbly caught here in wide-spanning stereo, and **Gervase de Peyer**, the dedicated soloist, gives a stunning performance, helped by an excellent accompaniment from his former colleagues in the **LSO** under **Del Mar**. The *Monologue for solo piano*, an early 12-note experimental piece, could not be more different from the exuberantly witty *Excursions*, full of charm, with titles like *The Sunday Driver, The Drunken Driver, The Road Hog* and the final *Backseat Driver*. The performance from the **composer** and **Malcolm Williamson** is most infectiously winning.

MUSSORGSKY, Modest
(1839–81)

The Capture of Kars (Triumphal March); St John's Night on the Bare Mountain (original score); Scherzo in B flat; Khovanshchina: Prelude to Act I; (i) Introduction to Act IV; The Destruction of Sennacherib; (i; ii) Joshua; (i) Oedipus in Athens: Temple Chorus; Salammbô: Priestesses' Chorus (operatic excerpts all orch. Rimsky-Korsakov)

*** (M) *** RCA (ADD) 09026 61354-2. (i) L. Symphony Ch.; (ii) Zehava Gal; LSO, Abbado

It is particularly good to have so vital and pungent an account of the original version of *Night on the Bare Mountain*,

different in all but its basic material from the Rimsky-Korsakov arrangement. Mussorgsky's scoring is so original and imaginative that the ear is readily held. Best of all are the four choral pieces; even when they are early and atypical (*Oedipus in Athens*, for example), they are immediately attractive and very Russian in feeling, and they include such evocative pieces as the *Chorus of Priestesses* (intoning over a pedal bass) from a projected opera on Flaubert's novel. The recording is first rate, and this is one of the most attractive Mussorgsky records in the catalogue.

Night on the Bare Mountain; St John's Night on the Bare Mountain (original score); Pictures at an Exhibition (orch. Ravel); Khovanshchina: Golitsïn's Departure; Sorochinsky Fair: Gopak

*** (BB) **** Naxos 8.555924. Nat. SO of Ukraine, Kuchar

It was an imaginative idea to record both Mussorgsky's original score – *St John's Night on the Bare Mountain* – alongside Rimsky's finished orchestral tone-poem, for in most respects they are entirely different works. For **Theodor Kuchar**, the far more integrated Rimsky-Korsakov piece is the finer work overall. With a superbly rasping opening from the heavy brass, Kuchar demonstrates its malignant force, deftly amalgamating Rimsky's interpolated, very Russian, brass fanfares, then producing a serenely peaceful close, with lovely playing from the strings and woodwind. *St John's Night* begins in a comparable atmosphere of malevolence, but the witches' jamboree which follows is bizarrely grotesque rather than evil. Yet Kuchar sustains the tension through the composer's weird sequential repetitions before the brief, unearthly coda, which of course is without Rimsky's radiant apotheosis.

Mussorgsky's jolliest Russian dance, the *Sorochinsky 'Gopak'*, is engagingly spirited, to be followed by a moving performance of the darkly mournful orchestral description of Prince Golitsïn's exile from Khovanshchina. Ravel's incomparable orchestration of *Pictures at an Exhibition* then proves an excitingly vivid showpiece for this superb Russian orchestra. The percussion really make their mark in *The Hut on Fowls' Legs*, and the bass drum adds dramatic impact, both here and in the triumphant climax of the closing *Great Gate of Kiev*, which is thrillingly expansive, with **Kuchar** broadening the final statement of the great chorale to produce a frisson of weighty spectacle, helped by the demonstration sound-quality. An outstanding disc in every way which is strongly recommendable, quite irrespective of its modest price.

Night on the Bare Mountain (arr. Rimsky-Korsakov); Pictures at an Exhibition (orch. Ravel)

*** (M) **** RCA SACD (ADD) 82876 61394-2. Chicago SO, Reiner (with TCHAIKOVSKY: *Marche slave; Marche miniature;* BORODIN: *Polovstian March;* KABALEVSKY: *Colas Breugnon Overture;* GLINKA: *Ruslan and Ludmilla Overture ****)

Reiner's 1957 *Pictures* is another demonstration of vintage stereo using simple microphone techniques to achieve a natural concert-hall ambience. The sound-balance is full and atmospheric, and Reiner's approach is evocative to match.

The final climax of *The Great Gate of Kiev* is massively effective. The Chicago brass is again very telling in *Night on the Bare Mountain*, made two years later, a performance that is just as strongly characterized. The rest of the orchestral items go splendidly, with the sparkling *Colas Breugnon Overture* one of the highlights. The charming *Marche miniature* is played with much delicacy, and there is no lack of energy in the *Ruslan and Ludmilla Overture*, with its superbly pointed strings and crisp brass. Those with SACD playback facilities will find even greater warmth and spread of sound.

(i) *Night on the Bare Mountain* (arr. Rimsky-Korsakov); *Pictures at an Exhibition* (arr. Funtek); (ii) *Songs & Dances of Death* (arr. Aho)

*** BIS CD 325. (i) Finnish RSO, Segerstam; (ii) Järvi, with Talvela

This CD offers an orchestration by Leo Funtek, made in the same year as Ravel's (1922). The use of a cor anglais in *The Old Castle* mirrors Stokowski, while the soft-grained wind scoring makes the portrait of *Samuel Goldenberg and Schmuyle* more sympathetic, if also blander. The performances by the **Finnish Radio Orchestra** under **Leif Segerstam** both of this and of the familiar Rimsky *Night on the Bare Mountain* are spontaneously presented and very well recorded. The extra item is no less valuable: an intense, darkly Russian account of the *Songs and Dances of Death* from **Martti Talvela** with the orchestral accompaniment plangently scored by Kalevi Aho.

Night on the Bare Mountain; *Pictures at an Exhibition*; *Khovanshchina, Act IV: Entr'acte*; *Boris Godunov: Symphonic Synthesis* (all arr. and orch. Stokowski)

✿ BB *** Naxos 8.557645. Bournemouth SO, Serebrier (with STOKOWSKI: *Slavic Christmas Music*. TCHAIKOVSKY: *Solitude*; *Humoresque* ***)

This Naxos collection of Stokowski's flamboyant arrangements of Mussorgsky at budget price offers outstanding performances by the **Bournemouth Symphony Orchestra**, brilliantly recorded in sound if anything even more spectacular than on rival discs. Though Stokowski's arrangement of *Pictures at an Exhibition* is less refined than that of Ravel, with its weighty brass it is certainly more Russian. The most serious shortcoming is Stokowski's omission of two of the movements, *Tuileries* and *The Market Place at Limoges*, made on the grounds that they are too French. The atmospheric qualities of the *Boris Godunov* symphonic synthesis also come over superbly, starting with a hauntingly rarefied bassoon solo, even if the recording catches the clicking of the keys. The mystery of the chimes in the *Coronation Scene* as well as the *Death Scene* are most evocative, and in *Night on the Bare Mountain* the weight of the arrangement comes over well, and the *Khovanshchina Entr'acte*, too, has impressive weight and clarity. Among the extra items, the Tchaikovsky song, *Solitude*, explores an astonishingly wide emotional range within a tiny span, and the jolly *Humoresque* is a piano piece that Stravinsky memorably used in his ballet *The Fairy's Kiss*. The baldly effective *Slavic Christmas Music*, attributed to

Stokowski himself, is based not just on a Christmas hymn but on Ippolitov-Ivanov's *In a Manger*. Altogether a treasurable collection, well worth its modest cost.

Pictures at an Exhibition (orch. Ravel)

🎧 Ⓜ **** DG (ADD) 447 426-2. BPO, Karajan – DEBUSSY: *La Mer*; RAVEL: *Boléro* ****

🎧 Ⓑ **** Sony (ADD) SBK 48162. Cleveland O, Szell – KODÁLY: *Háry János Suite*; PROKOFIEV: *Lieutenant Kijé Suite* ****

🎧 Ⓜ **** RCA (ADD) 09026 61401-2. Chicago SO, Reiner – RESPIGHI: *Fountains of Rome*; *Pines of Rome* ✿ ****

*** DG Gold 439 013-2. BPO, Karajan – RAVEL: *Boléro*, etc. ***

(**(*)) BBC mono BBCL 4023-2. Philh. O, Giulini – TCHAIKOVSKY: *Symphony 6* (**(*))

Pictures at an Exhibition (orch. Ravel); *Khovanshchina: Prelude*

Ⓜ **(*) Van. (ADD) Surround Sound **SACD** ATMCD 1504. New Philh. O, Mackerras

Among the many fine versions of Mussorgsky's *Pictures* on CD, **Karajan's** 1966 record stands out. It is undoubtedly a great performance, tingling with electricity from the opening *Promenade* to the spaciously conceived finale, *The Great Gate of Kiev*, which has real splendour. The remastered analogue recording still sounds marvellous, and this reissue, in DG's 'Originals' series of legendary recordings, includes a uniquely evocative performance of Debussy's *La Mer* as well as a very exciting account of Ravel's *Boléro*.

Szell's 1963 Cleveland performance also remains among the greatest of all recordings of Ravel's vividly inspired orchestration. Even if the recording has a somewhat less expansive dynamic-range, the character of each portrait is firmly drawn with vivid strokes of orchestral colour. The portrayal of *Goldenberg and Schmuyle* brings superbly full articulation from the lower strings, and *Baba-Yaga* makes the most incisive impact. Whether in the cheeping and chattering of the unhatched chicks, the bravura swirl of the *Limoges Market*, or the dignified grandiloquence of that final great gateway of Kiev, the controlled brilliance of the recording projects everything with extraordinary vividness.

With the advantage of the rich acoustics of Symphony Hall, the RCA sound-balance of **Reiner's** 1957 Chicago performance is highly atmospheric, if less sharply focused. The finale climax of *The Great Gate of Kiev* shows the concentration of the playing. The remastering is fully worthy, and there is excellent documentation.

Karajan's 1986 recording is one of the most impressive of DG's digital recordings. The tangibility of the sound is remarkable, with the opening brass *Promenade* and the massed strings in *Samuel Goldenberg and Schmuyle* notable in their naturalness of sonority. With superb **Berlin Philharmonic** playing and the weight of the climaxes contrasting with the wit of *Tuileries* and the exhilaration of *The Market at Limoges*, this is certainly now among the top recommendations.

The 1973 Vanguard recording was made on eight tracks

in Surround Sound, but it is possible to balance the sound to get a forward orchestral placement with the percussion behind, including a spectacular bass drum which can make you jump. Many will enjoy being enveloped by the orchestra, and **Mackerras** certainly paints a characteristically vivid set of pictures, obviously enhanced by the new technology. The orchestral playing does not bring the ultimate in refinement but has ample verve and colour, and the remaining pictures produce some very dramatic brass playing, even if the final climax is not as overwhelming as in the very finest versions. The *Khovanshchina Prelude* is well played but is not as evocative as the versions with Szell or Abbado.

Above all, **Ozawa** shows his feeling for orchestral colour in his undoubtedly successful version. Moreover, the orchestra is on top form; yet the virtuosity is always put to the service of the music's pictorialism and atmosphere. Ozawa does not force the pace or make unnecessary underlining; he lets the work unfold naturally, though with excellent incidental detail, and the climax of *The Great Gate of Kiev* has all the spectacle you could want. The current transfer is first class and the 1967 recording has plenty of atmosphere and a natural focus.

Though the initial impact of the dry mono sound of 1961 is disconcerting in **Giulini's** characterful BBC version, the bite and impact is intensified, so that in such a movement as *The Hut on Fowl's Legs* one even begins to think of this as a precursor of the *Rite of Spring*. The fast, light articulation of *Limoges* is very exciting, and the *Catacombs* brass fiercely sepulchral. Solo playing is immaculate too, despite the lack of bloom, and the closing *Great Gate of Kiev* makes a spectacularly spacious impact, with a fine contribution from the tam-tam. A generous coupling.

Pictures at an Exhibition (incomplete; orch. Ravel)

(BB) (**(*)) Naxos mono 8. 110105. Boston SO, Koussevitzky – BARTÓK: *Concerto for Orchestra* (***)

Koussevitzky's 1943 performance challenges his players to the very limit, as in the hectic account of the *Tuileries* movement, though, sadly, Koussevitzky omits the two most evocative movements, the *Old Castle* and *Bydlo* (the Polish ox-cart), together with the *Promenades* that frame them.

(i) Pictures at an Exhibition (arr. Leonard for piano and orchestra); 3 Pictures from the Crimea (orch. Goehr); A Night on the Bare Mountain (arr. & orch. Rimsky-Korsakov); Scherzo in B flat (orch. Rimsky-Korsakov); From my Tears (orch. Kindler); Khovanshchina: Prelude (orch. Rimsky-Korsakov); Golitsin's Journey (orch. Stokowski); Sorochinsky Fair: Gopak (orch. Liadov)

(M) *** Cala CACD 1030. (i) Ungár; Philh. O, Simon

Lawrence Leonard's arrangement of Mussorgsky's *Pictures* for piano and orchestra is remarkably effective and very entertaining. The concertante format works admirably, especially powerful in *Gnomus* and *The Hut on Fowl's Legs*, charmingly depicting the *Unhatched Chicks* (a piquant mixture of keyboard and woodwind, spiced with xylophone). There are many added touches of colour. The other pieces

are all well worth having, notably Rimsky's chimerical scoring (following the composer's orchestral sketch) of the *Scherzo in B flat*. The three *Pictures from the Crimea* are darkly nostalgic, and the lively *Gopak*, like the *Khovanshchina* excerpts (Stokowski's arrangement of *Golitsin's Journey* is sombrely characterful), is very welcome. All **Geoffrey Simon's** performances have plenty of life, and **Tamás Ungár** makes an exciting contribution and is fully equal to all the technical demands of the revised piano-part. The recording is warm, full and expansive, but not always sharply defined.

Pictures at an Exhibition (orch. Ellison; Gorchakov; Goehr; Naoumoff; Van Keulen; Ashkenazy; Simpson; Cailliet; Wood; Leonard; Funtek; Boyd; Ravel; Stokowski; Gamley)

*** Warner 2564 61954-2. BBC SO & Ch., Slatkin – RESPIGHI: *Pines of Rome* **(*)

This is the most original orchestral version of Mussorgsky's picture gallery on record. **Leonard Slatkin** conceived the idea of performing the work at the Proms using orchestrations by 15 different composers, reserving *Cum mortis in lingua mortua* for Ravel's own dramatic scoring. Byrwec Ellison opens with tolling bells, unpredictable percussion and a galaxy of colours, following (in microcosm) the style of Britten's *Young Person's Guide to the Orchestra*. Sergey Gorchakov's *Gnomus* is starkly primitive, and Goehr's following *Promenade* is contrastingly gentle, leading to Emile Naoumoff's melancholy minstrel's song outside *The Old Castle*, unexpectedly given a piano obbligato, while Cailliet's *Unhatched Chicks* trill vociferously. From there on the scoring becomes more and more exotic and extrovert, and none more so than Ashkenazy's larger-than-life *Bydlo*, using full-throated unison horns, and Henry Wood's *Goldenberg and Schmuyle*, with a surprise flourish at the latter's appearance, followed by guttural, protesting trombones. Lawrence Leonard's following *Promenade* (omitted by Ravel) is in piano concertante format. We are already familiar with the outrageous hyperbole of Stokowski's *Baba-Yaga*, and its spectacle prepares the way for Douglas Gamley's over-the-top, very Russian *Great Gate of Kiev*, using full chorus and bells and, finally, the thundering Albert Hall organ. The result, expanded by the hall's resonant acoustics, is quite overwhelming.

(i) Pictures at an Exhibition (orch. Ravel); (ii) Pictures at an Exhibition (original piano version)

⊕– (M) *** Sony SMK 89615. (i) BPO, Giulini; (ii) Bronfman

(N) *** Danacord DACOCD 656. (i) Odense SO, Jan Wagner; (ii) Marshev

Giulini's account of the orchestral score can be considered among the best accounts of the 1990s. Recorded in the Jesus-Christus-Kirche, Berlin, the sound is rich and spacious, the orchestral playing superb. The reading has a pervading sense of nostalgia which haunts the delicate portrayal of *The Old Castle* and even makes the wheedling interchange between the two Polish Jews more sympathetic than usual. In the lighter pieces the scherzando element brings a sparkling contrast, with the unhatched chicks cheeping piquantly, and there is sonorous solemnity for the *Catacombs* sequence. A powerful and weighty *Baba-Yaga*, yet with the bizarre element retained in the subtle rhythmic pointing in the middle section, leads naturally to a majestic finale, with the Berlin brass full-bloodedly resplendent and the tam-tam flashing vividly at the climax.

Yefim Bronfman's account of the original piano score then matches **Giulini's** approach surprisingly closely. *The Old Castle*, beautifully graduated, is most poignant, there is strong characterization throughout and plenty of picaresque detail. Bronfman finds an added sense of fantasy in *Baba-Yaga* and the massive closing spectacle of *The Great Gate at Kiev* is viscerally thrilling, to give a genuine frisson when the piano recording is so full-bodied, and the playing so grand and powerful.

Very well recorded, this coupling of Mussorgsky's original piano version alongside the masterly Ravel orchestration is highly recommendable. **Oleg Marshev** is meticulous in following Mussorgsky's markings, as in *Bydlo*, the *Polish Ox Cart*, which is loud all the way through until the final diminuendo on the very last bars. It is no exaggeration to say that the subtlety of Ravel's markings greatly improves the work, making it more effective; and the **Odense Symphony Orchestra** are on their toes throughout the orchestral performance.

Night on the Bare Mountain (trans. Tchernov for piano)

🔊 ✹ *** Teldec 4509 96516-2. Berezovsky – BALAKIREV: *Islamey* ✹ ***

This remarkable transcription by Konstantin Tchernov sounds hardly less dazzling in **Berezovsky's** hands than the outstanding *Islamey* with which it is coupled. The engineers capture very good piano sound.

Pictures at an Exhibition (original piano version)

🔊 ✹ (BB) **** Virgin 2 x 1 4 82055-2 (2). Pletnev – TCHAIKOVSKY: *The Seasons; Sleeping Beauty: Suite; Pieces* ✹ ****

Pictures at an Exhibition (piano version, ed. Horowitz)

🔊 (B) (***) RCA 2-CD mono 74321 84594-2 (2). Horowitz – (with CLEMENTI: *Sonatas, Op. 14/3; Op. 34/2; Op. 47/2: Rondo* (***)) – SCRIABIN: *Etudes; Preludes; Sonatas* (***)

There are remarkable effects of colour and of pedalling in **Pletnev's** performance, which is easily the most commanding to have appeared since Richter's and, one is tempted to say, a re-creation rather than a performance. Pletnev does not hesitate to modify the odd letter of the score in order to come closer to its spirit. *The Ballet of the Unhatched Chicks* has great wit and *The Great Gate of Kiev* is extraordinarily rich in colour. With its new couplings this is a truly outstanding reissue.

Horowitz's famous (1951) recording, made at a live performance at Carnegie Hall, is as thrilling as it is perceptive. Mussorgsky's darker colours are admirably caught and the lighter, scherzando evocations are dazzlingly articulated. In *The Great Gate of Kiev* Horowitz embellishes the texture to make the result even more spectacular. The performances of the Clementi *Sonatas*, also from the 1950s, are hardly less electrifying, and though the piano-sound is again shallow, the quality is a great improvement on their previous vinyl transfers.

VOCAL MUSIC

Songs

Song-cycles: (i) *The Nursery*; (ii) *Songs and Dances of Death*; (i) *Sunless Songs: Darling Savishna; Hopak; King Saul; Lullaby*; (ii) *Mephistopheles' Song of the Flea*; (i) *Where are you, little star?; The wild winds blow*

🔊 (M) (***) EMI mono 5 67993-2. Christoff, with (i) Labinsky; (ii) Fr. R. & TV O, Tzipine

Between 1955 and 1957 the great Bulgarian bass, **Boris Christoff**, recorded for EMI a pioneering set of the complete Mussorgsky songs, 63 of them. This well-filled disc in EMI's 'Great Recordings of the Century' series offers a very well-chosen selection, including the three great Mussorgsky song-cycles: *The Nursery* (with Christoff, amazingly for a bass, imitating the sound of a child singing), *Sunless* and, greatest of all, the *Songs and Dances of Death*, using the orchestral arrangement of the accompaniment by Glazunov and Rimsky-Korsakov. The selection starts with the earliest of Mussorgsky's songs, *Where are you, little star?*, and includes the lovely *Lullaby* to words by Ostrovsky (with Christoff producing a seamless legato), the setting of Byron in translation, *King Saul*, and the most popular of all Mussorgsky songs, *The Song of the Flea*, also in orchestral form. Christoff is in superb voice throughout, with his dark bass perfectly focused and steady as a rock. The orchestral sound is thinner than that of the rest, but what matters is the vividness of the voice.

Songs and Dances of Death

*** EMI **DVD** DVA 4901209. Vishnevskaya, Rostropovich – PROKOFIEV: *Sinfonia concertante*; SHOSTAKOVICH: *Cello Concerto 1* ***

Vishnevskaya's classic performance with her husband at the piano was filmed in 1970, and it comes as a bonus for a stunning DVD of **Rostropovich** playing key cello works by Prokofiev and Shostakovich which were specially written for him.

Songs and Dances of Death (orch. Shostakovich)

*** Warner 2564 62050-2. Hvorostovsky, St Petersburg PO, Temirkanov – RACHMANINOV: *Symphonic Dances* ***

Recorded live in the Albert Hall, **Hvorostovsky's** powerful and moving performances of these dark (but not depressing) songs, with their mixture of irony and grief, now clearly lead the field. **Temirkanov's** accompaniments are idiomatic and supportive, and the recording is both atmospheric and well balanced.

OPERA

Boris Godunov (complete DVD versions)

🎧 **** Ph. **DVD** 075 089-9 (2). Lloyd, Borodina, Steblianko, Leiferkus, Kirov Op. Ch. & O, Gergiev (Producer: Andrei Tarkovsky, V/D: Humphrey Burton)

🎧 *** Ph. **DVD** 075 099-9 (6). As above – BORODIN: *Prince Igor*; GLINKA: *Ruslan & Ludmilla*

*** Warner **DVD** 51011 1851-2. Nesterenko, Pyavko, Sinyavskaya, Kudryashov, Eizen, Bolshoi Theatre Ch. & O, Lazarev (Stage & Video Director: Irina Morozova)

In 1990 the Covent Garden production of *Boris Godunov*, directed by the Russian, Andre Tarkovsky, and rehearsed by Stephen Lawless, was adopted by the Mariinsky Theatre in St Petersburg. This two-disc DVD offers the resulting film, originally shown on BBC Television, a magnificent presentation of the opera in the edition prepared by David Lloyd-Jones using the original (1872) version of the score. **Valery Gergiev** conducts an outstanding **Kirov Opera** cast, joined in the title-role by **Robert Lloyd** from Covent Garden, giving one of his greatest performances ever, strong and resonant and movingly acted. It is astonishing how the different incidental parts are cast from strength with star singers, each rising superbly to the challenge of a major scene – Pimen, Varlaam, Rangoni and the Simpleton (who sings his pathetic solo twice – in the first scene of Act IV and at the end). **Olga Borodina** is magnificent as Marina in the Polish scenes opposite the powerful Grigory of **Alexei Steblianko**, and even such a small part as Feodor, Boris's young son, is taken with passionate intensity by a then-rising star, **Larissa Diadkova**. Musically it would be hard to imagine a finer performance, even though the recording balance sometimes has voices too distant and unrelated to close-up pictures. Visually it is superb too, with the complex, episodic story told with extraordinary clarity, set on a simple but very grand stage, with a floor in false perspective adding to the grandeur. Costumes are authentic and often colourful, with Tarkovsky's often stylized production bringing unforgettable moments, as when Rangoni comes and sits centre-stage at the end of the love scene between Marina and Grigory, and turns to give the most sinister stare as the curtain falls. This DVD set is now included in an attractive package with two other classic productions (presumably at an attractive discount) to mark Valery Gergiev's 25th anniversary at the Kirov, and those who do not have these performances should take advantage of this. All three performances are outstanding.

Until the late 1960s, in the days of Christoff, the only *Boris* to be recorded (or to be seen at Covent Garden) was the edition by Rimsky-Korsakov. In recent years it has been driven from the stage in favour of Mussorgsky's original. As learned an authority as Professor Gerald Abraham was at pains to point out that the Rimsky version, recorded here, is also a masterpiece, and it is good to have it again in this 1987 staging. **Nesterenko** was one of the commanding exponents of the role and it is thrilling to see and hear his magisterial account. The other major roles, **Vladislav Pyavko's** Grigory, **Tamara Sinyavskaya's** Marina, **Vladimir Kudryashov's** Prince Shuisky and **Arthur Eizen's** Varlaam are pretty im-

pressive, too. Nor are we let down by the orchestral playing under **Alexander Lazarev**. Of course Gergiev remains supreme, both in the DVD version of the Tarkovsky production and in the five-CD set of the 1869 and 1872 versions. However, this version of the alternative Rimsky-Korsakov score should be added to them. No booklet or notes.

Boris Godunov ((i) 1869 & (ii) 1872 versions) (CD version)

🎧 Ⓜ **** Ph. 462 230-2 (5). (i) Putilin, Lutsuk, (ii) Borodina; Vaneev, Galusin; (i; ii) Ohotnikov, Kuznetsov, Trifonova, Bulycheva, Pluzhnikov, Akimov, Kirov Op. Ch. & O, Gergiev

It makes a fascinating contrast on CD in **Gergiev's** St Petersburg set (five discs for the price of three) to have the original (1869) version of seven scenes set against the 1872 revision with its amplification in the extra Polish Act and elsewhere. Gergiev's incisive, keenly dramatic readings bring out the differences very effectively, and the casting of Boris in each heightens that. In 1869 the character is more direct, more of a villain, less of a victim – reflected in **Nikolai Putilin's** virile and firm singing – where in the expanded (1872) portrait the character is more equivocal, more self-searching, clearly verging on madness, and there you have **Vladimir Vaneev** bringing out the element of thoughtfulness and mystery over a wider expressive range. The role of Grigory, the Pretender, brings alternative casting too, but it is only in the 1872 version that the character plays a full part, very well taken by the ringing and clear, very Russian-sounding tenor, **Vladimir Galusin**. The others make a first-rate team, individually strong and idiomatic, and all enhancing the drama, obviously experienced on stage. Outstanding are **Olga Borodina** as Marina and **Konstantin Pluzhnikov** as a sinister Shuisky. The sound is fresh and forward, with voices set in front of the orchestra, more powerful in wind and brass than in the strings. The Abbado set on Sony (see below) offers a more starry cast and a more spacious reading, often more warmly expressive, but the practical advantages of the Gergiev set make it even more recommendable.

Boris Godunov (original version; complete)

*** Sony S3K 58977 (3). Kotcherga, Leiferkus, Larin, Lipovšek, Ramey, Nikolsky, Langridge, Slovak Philharmonic Ch., Bratislava, Tölz Boys' Ch., Berlin RSO, Abbado

Ⓜ **(*) EMI (ADD) 0 90178-2 (3). Talvela, Gedda, Mróz, Kinasz, Haugland, Polish R. Ch. & Nat. RSO, Semkow

Claudio Abbado recorded *Boris Godunov* in its original version with speeds that regularly press ahead, and the urgency of the composer's inspiration is conveyed without reducing the epic scale of the work or its ominously dark colouring. Abbado inserts the beautiful scene in front of St Basil's at the start of Act IV, but then omits from the final Kromy Forest scene the episode about the Simpleton losing his kopek. Vocally, the performance centres on the glorious singing of **Anatoly Kotcherga** as Boris. Rarely has this music been sung with such firmness and beauty as here. Kotcherga may not have a weighty voice, but the darkly meditative depth of the performance is enhanced without loss of power. The other principal basses, **Samuel Ramey** as the monk, Pimen, and **Gleb Nikolsky** as Varlaam, are well contrasted, even if Ramey's voice sounds un-Slavonic. The tenor, **Sergei Larin**, sings with beauty and clarity up to the highest register as the Pretender, not least in the Polish Act, while **Marjana Lipovšek** is a formidably characterful Marina, if not quite as well focused as usual. Having **Philip Langridge** as Shuisky and **Sergei Leiferkus** as Rangoni reinforces the starry strength of the team. The sound is spacious, more atmospheric than usual in recordings made in the Philharmonie in Berlin, and allowing high dynamic contrasts, with the choral ensembles – so vital in this work – full and glowing.

The EMI version offers an analogue recording of 1977, but its warmth and richness go with a forward balance and a high transfer level. The voices have an extra bite, not least the firm, weighty bass of **Martti Talvela** as Boris or of **Aage Haugland**, magnificent as Varlaam. **Nicolai Gedda** is excellent as the Pretender, if not as free on top as Larin in the Abbado set. The other soloists, as well as the chorus, make up a formidable Polish team, with hardly a weak link. **Bozena Kinasz** as Marina is particularly impressive. **Jerzy Semkow** may not convey as much bite and beauty as Abbado, but in his rugged, measured way he conveys a full intensity at moments of high drama, helped by the firm, full sound. This now returns to the catalogue at mid-price, neatly packaged with booklet and synopsis. The full libretto and translation is available from www.theoperaseries.com at www.emiclassics.com

Boris Godunov (arr. Rimsky-Korsakov)

Ⓜ *** Decca 475 7718 (3). Ghiaurov, Vishnevskaya, Spiess, Maslennikov, Talvela, V. Boys' Ch., Sofia R. Ch., V. State Op. Ch., VPO, Karajan

Ⓜ ** EMI 5 67877-2 (3) [567881-2]. Christoff, Lear, Lanigan, Alexieva, Sofia Nat. Op. Ch., Paris Conservatoire O, Cluytens

ⒷⒷ (***) Naxos mono 8.1102424. Christoff, Gedda, Zareska, Bielecki, Borg, Lebedeva, Romanova, Pasternak, Russian Ch. of Paris; French Nat. R. O, Dobrowen

With **Ghiaurov** in the title-role, **Karajan's** superbly controlled Decca version, technically outstanding, came far nearer than previous recordings to conveying the rugged greatness of Mussorgsky's masterpiece. Only the Coronation Scene lacked something of the weight and momentum one ideally wants. **Vishnevskaya** was far less appealing than the lovely non-Slavonic Marina of Evelyn Lear on EMI, but overall this Decca set had much more to offer. This reissue, as one of Decca's Originals, comes with full text and translation.

The EMI set is chiefly valuable for the resonant contribution of **Boris Christoff**, for a generation unmatched in the role of Boris. Here he takes the part not only of the Tsar but of Pimen and Varlaam, relishing the contrast of those other, highly colourful bass roles. It is good that his glorious voice is so vividly caught on CD, but sadly the overall performance under **Cluytens** does not add up to the sum of its parts as the earlier, mono recording did.

It is good to welcome back the pioneering (1952) mono *Boris* in which the celebrated **Christoff** sang not only Boris himself but Varlaam and Pimen. He skilfully varies his colour in these roles, but also gives a commanding account of Boris which is a triumph in every respect, as is **Dobrowen's** direction – as vital and idiomatic as any version since. The youthful **Nicolai Gedda** is a magnificent Grigory and **Eugenia Zareska** is an unforgettable Marina. **Kim Borg** doubles as Shchelkalov and Rangoni. And there is more duplication of roles with **Andrzej Bielecki** as Prince Shuisky, Missail and Krushchov. The choral singing is very good and the **French Radio Orchestra** under Dobrowen sound as if they are all from Moscow. The set appeared briefly on EMI Références, but Mark Obert-Thorn's transfer is equally fine – if not finer.

Boris Godunov (original, 1869 version): excerpts: Coronation Scene; Varlaam's Song; Apartment Scene; St Basil Scene; Death Scene (sung in English)

☛ ✿ Ⓜ *** Chan. 3007. Tomlinson, Kale, Bayley, Rodgers, Best, Opera N. Ch., E. N. Philh. O, Daniel

This generous, 75-minute selection of excerpts from *Boris Godunov* is highly recommendable even when compared with current Russian versions of Mussorgsky's masterpiece. **John Tomlinson** has never been in finer voice on disc than here, with his dark bass-baritone perfectly focused. This is an exceptionally lyrical view of the self-tortured tsar, both dramatically powerful and warmly expressive, letting one appreciate the beauty of Mussorgsky's melodies. Tomlinson is helped by **Paul Daniel's** inspired direction and opulent recorded sound, with excellent support from singers in the vintage Opera North production, including **Stuart Kale** as Prince Shuisky, **Clive Bayley** as Varlaam, **Joan Rodgers** as Xenia and **Matthew Best** as Pimen. Anyone who supports the idea of opera sung in English should not miss this highly compelling disc.

Boris Godunov: Selected Scenes

Ⓜ (***) Cala mono CACD 0535. Rossi-Lemeni, San Francisco Ch. and SO, Stokowski – WAGNER: *Parsifal: Good Friday Spell; Symphonic Synthesis of Act 3* ***

In December 1952 in San Francisco, **Stokowski** conducted a series of concert performances of highlights from *Boris Godnov* in the Rimsky-Korsakov version, and promptly recorded for RCA the same brilliantly chosen group of favourite passages. The result is spectacular, as Cala's superb CD transfer demonstrates. The sound is so full, vivid and immediate, with an impressive spread – not least in the Coronation Scene with its bells – that it is hard to believe it is in mono. Matching this, Stokowski's conducting inspires performances of the highest voltage, electrifying from first to last. Both the chorus and orchestra are incandescent, and the Russian-Italian bass, **Nicola Rossi-Lemeni** – then at the beginning of his career – sings with a firmness of focus that later deserted him, at least on disc. He is wonderfully characterful, not just as Boris, but in a wildly exciting account of *Varlaam's Song*. Well-coupled with selections from Act III of *Parsifal*, another opera specially dear to Stokowski.

Khovanshchina: Prelude

*** BBC (ADD) BBCL 4123-2. Philh. O, Giulini – BRUCKNER:
  Symphony 7; FALLA: *Three-Cornered Hat* (excerpts) ***

In his live recording **Giulini** draws refined, evocative playing
from the **Philharmonia**, an atmospheric supplement to the
Bruckner *Symphony*, the main work.

Khovanshchina (complete; DVD versions)

🎤 **** Arthaus DVD 100 310 (2). Ghiaurov, Atlantov,
  Marusin, Shaklovity; Burchuladze, Shemchuk, Slovak Phil.
  Ch., V. Boys' Ch.; V. State Op. Ch. & O, Abbado
  (Stage/Video Dir: Kirchner)

*** Opus Arte DVD OA 0989 D (2). Ognovenko, Galouzine,
  Brubaker, Putilin, Vaneev, Zaremba, Ch. & O of Gran
  Teatre del Liceu, Boder

Khovanshchina (complete; CD versions)

🎤 **** DG 429 758-2 (3). Lîpovšek, Burchuladze, Atlantov,
  Haugland, Borowska, Kotcherga, Popov, V. State Op. Ch. &
  O, Abbado

(BB) (***) Naxos 8.111124/26. Boris Freidkov, Ivan Nechayev,
  Mark Reizen, Vladimir Ulyanov, Sofya Preobrazhenskaya,
  Nina Serval, Kirov Ch. & O, Khaikin

This DVD recording was made at the same time as the DG
three-CD set, namely in September 1989. There are some
differences in cast: to name the most important, the late
Aage Haugland who was Ivan Khovansky is sung (wonderfully, too) by **Nicolai Ghiaurov**, **Vladimir Popov's** Prince
Golitsin is replaced by **Yuri Marusin** and the Marfa of
Marjana Lipovšek by **Ludmila Shemchuk**. Otherwise the
performance does not differ from the rightly admired CD
set. **Abbado's** version is essentially the Shostakovich version
(based on Pavel Lamm's 1929 edition) though he lightens
some of the scoring and discards the triumphant ending in
Act V with the return of the *Preobrazhensky March* in favour
of the finale prepared by Stravinsky. Rimsky-Korsakov's marvellous orchestration is rejected as too sumptuous these
days, and his corrections of Mussorgsky's harmony are seen
as too academically correct. And with the beautiful, tragic
music of Abbado's ending the strength and dignity of the
Old Believers is reinforced. However, Abbado, who has for
so long been Mussorgsky's most eloquent champion among
Western conductors of his generation, is electrifying. There
is an intensity here, and a mastery both of pace and of climax. The playing of the Vienna orchestra is exquisite in the
quieter episodes and sumptuous in tone throughout. The
recording for Abbado, too, is superbly balanced and defined.
Visually the production is good to look at, and the camera is
expertly directed and always where the viewer wants it. This
is a mandatory choice for all lovers of Russian opera.

The recent Liceu DVD version of the Shostakovich score
also has a great deal going for it. First of all, **Vladimir
Ognovenko** as Prince Ivan Khovansky and **Vladimir
Galouzine** as his son are both impressive actor-singers and
Vladimir Vaneev's Dosifey almost steals the show. What is
particularly striking (and perhaps surprisingly so) is the
choral singing, which is not lacking in the black tone and
strength of Slavonic rivals. Stein Winge's production is in-

telligent and unobtrusive and the camera-work is excellent:
the eye is always where the ear wants it to be. **Elena
Zaremba's** finely characterized Marfa is a little tarnished by
a Slav wobble and the Galitzin of **Robert Brubaker** does not
have quite the authority the role calls for.

Abbado's live CD recording also brings the most vivid
account of this epic Russian opera yet on CD. **Lipovšek's** glorious singing as Marfa, the Old Believer with whom one
most closely identifies, sets the seal on the whole performance. **Aage Haugland** is a rock-like Ivan Khovansky and,
though **Burchuladze** is no longer as steady of tone as he was,
he makes a noble Dosifey. Stage noises sometimes intrude
and voices are sometimes set back, but this remains a magnificent achievement.

You won't hear anything as remarkable as this Naxos
Khovanshchina again. First of all, we have the Rimsky-
Korsakov version. Secondly, we have an incomparable cast,
with **Mark Reizen's** Dosifey and **Sofya Preobrazhenskaya** as
Marfa. The 1946 recording sounds surprisingly good in Ward
Marston's remarkable transfer and the third CD has room
for 13 songs, some from the old Mussorgsky Song Society,
with Vladimir Rosing. Do not hesitate.

NICOLAI, Carl Otto (1810–49)

The Merry Wives of Windsor

(N) **(*) CPO 777 317-2 (2). Banse, Korondi, Markert,
  Bothmer, Schmitt, Eiche, Reiter, Bav. R. Ch., Munich R. O,
  Schirmer

There is so much to enjoy in the way of felicitous touches
in Nicolai's score, it would be good to have a really recommendable recording. However, until Kubelik's Decca version returns to the catalogue, this will have to do. Recorded
live from two performances in 2007 (with dialogue merci-
fully abridged), the cast is generally very good, with sopranos **Juliane Banse** and **Anna Korondi** both displaying
excellent technique as well as personality. **Alfred Reiter** is
equally characterful in the role of Falstaff, even if his voice
does lack consistent beauty of tone. The chorus sing lustily
and the sound is theatrical and vivid; and **Schirmer** conducts very well indeed. Curiously, the audience applause is
heard after the overture and during the performance, but
not at the end of the Acts, and this is a little disconcerting.
Only a German libretto is printed, but a good synopsis in
English is included.

NIELSEN, Carl (1865–1931)

(i) Aladdin Suite, Op. 54; (ii) 3 Motets, Op. 55; (i–iii) Springtime in Fünen

(BB) *** Regis RRC 1134. (i) Odense SO, Vetö; (ii) Klint Little
  Muko University Ch., St Klemens School Children's Ch.;
  (iii) with Nielsen, von Binzer

Regis offers a well-played account of the engaging *Aladdin
Suite* by the **Odense Symphony Orchestra** under **Tamás Vetö**,
and the choral *Springtime in Fünen*, which is one of those enchanting pieces to which everyone responds when they hear

it yet which is hardly ever performed outside Denmark. To make up the playing time Regis have now added the *Three Motets*, Op. 55. This disc is well worth its modest cost.

Clarinet Concerto, Op. 57

🎧 *** BIS SACD 1463. Fröst, Lahti SO, Vänskä – AHO: *Clarinet Concerto* ***

*** Chan. 8618. Hilton, SNO, Bamert (with COPLAND: *Concerto*; LUTOSŁAWSKI: *Dance Preludes* ***)

Martin Fröst's account of Nielsen's fine *Concerto*, which has the advantage of optional surround sound, is probably the finest now available, given outstanding support by **Osma Vänskä**, as he successfully responds to the work's changing moods and colours. The coupling is a spectacularly unpredictable concerto by Aho, which is similarly given an outstanding performance and recording.

Janet Hilton gives a highly sympathetic account of the Nielsen *Concerto*, but it is characteristically soft-centred and mellower in its response to the work's more disturbing emotional undercurrents than Olle Schill's splendid account on BIS – see below. The Chandos recording is first class.

(i) Clarinet Concerto; (ii) Flute Concerto; (iii) Violin Concerto, Op. 33

*** Chan. 8894. (i) Thomsen; (ii) Christiansen; (iii) Sjøgren; Danish RSO, Schønwandt

Niels Thomsen's powerfully intense account of the late *Clarinet Concerto* is completely gripping. **Michael Schønwandt** gives sensitive and imaginative support, both here and in the two companion works. **Toke Lund Christiansen** is hardly less successful in the *Flute Concerto*. **Kim Sjøgren** and Schønwandt give a penetrating and thoughtful account of the *Violin Concerto*; there is real depth here, thanks in no small measure to Schønwandt. The recording is first class.

(i) Clarinet Concerto; (ii) Flute Concerto; (iii) Violin Concerto. An Imaginary Journey to the Faeroe Islands; Helios Overture; Pan and Syrinx, Op. 49; Saga-drøm, Op. 39; Symphonic Rhapsody

*** EMI Gemini (ADD) 3 81503-2 (2). (i) Stevennson; (ii) Lemmser; (iii) Tellefsen; Danish RSO, Blomstedt

Arve Tellefsen is a first-class soloist in the *Violin Concerto* and **Kjell-Inge Stevennson** is pretty stunning in the *Clarinet Concerto*. The charm and subtleties of the *Flute Concerto* are hardly less well realized by **Franz Lemmser's** nimble and sensitive account. Moreover, since the orchestra is Danish, the other works (such as the marvellous *Pan and Syrinx* and the atmospheric *Helios Overture*) are played with authentic accents. The collection also includes a novelty in the *Symphonic Rhapsody*, composed before the *First Symphony*. Throughout, the EMI engineers secure a natural sound-balance.

(i) Clarinet Concerto; (ii) Flute Concerto; (iii) Wind Quintet

**** EMI 5 94421-2. (i) Meyer; (ii) Pahud; (i–ii) BPO, Rattle; (iii) Meyer, Pahud, Schweigert, Kelly, Baborák

Wonderfully elegant and masterly playing from all concerned in these live accounts. Technically immaculate and in terms of artistry highly intelligent and satisfying. If you want this collection of works, this is unsurpassed.

(i) Clarinet Concerto; (ii; iii) Violin Concerto; (ii; iv) Little Suite for Strings, Op. 1

🅱🅱 *** Warner Apex 0927 48311-2. (i) Kojo, Finnish RSO, Sarasate; (ii) Norwegian R. O, (iii) with Hannisdal, cond. Mikkelsen; (iv) cond. Rasilainen

A fine performance of the *Clarinet Concerto* from **Kullervo Kojo**, whose timbre has plenty of colour. He responds to the sudden bursts of bravura with aplomb and does not miss the work's gently musing, improvisatory quality, while **Tim Feerce** keeps the dramatic percussive interruptions in proportion, helped by a good balance. **Henrik Hannisdal** is equally at home in the *Violin Concerto*, and **Ari Rasilainen's** account of the *Little Suite* is most persuasive, and this inexpensive Apex disc is thoroughly recommendable.

(i) Clarinet Concerto; (ii) Symphony 3 (Sinfonia espansiva); Maskarade Overture

🎧 **** BIS CD 321. (i) Schill; (ii) Raanoja, Skram; Gothenburg SO, Chung

Olle Schill too brings brilliance and insight to what is one of the most disturbing and masterly of all modern concertos. The young Korean conductor secures playing of great fire and enthusiasm from the Gothenburgers in the *Third Symphony* and he has vision and breadth – and at the same time no want of momentum. Two soloists singing a wordless vocal are called for in the pastoral slow movement, and their contribution is admirable. **Myung-Whun Chung** also gives a high-spirited and sparkling account of the *Overture* to Nielsen's comic opera, *Maskarade*. The BIS recording is marvellous, even by the high standards of this small company.

(i) Flute Concerto; Symphony 1; Rhapsody Overture (An Imaginary Journey to the Faeroe Islands)

🎧 **** BIS CD 454. (i) Gallois; Gothenburg SO, Chung

The *Flute Concerto* is given a marvellous performance by **Patrick Gallois**, and **Myung-Whun Chung** and the **Gothenburg Symphony Orchestra** have an instinctive feeling for Nielsen. They play with commendable enthusiasm and warmth, and Chung shapes the *Symphony* with great sensitivity to detail and a convincing sense of the whole. The *Rhapsody Overture (An Imaginary Journey to the Faeroe Islands)* is not the composer at his strongest, but it has a highly imaginative opening.

(i) Flute Concerto; Symphony 5, Op. 50; Aladdin: Entrance March

Ⓜ *** Hallé CDHLL 7502. Hallé O, Elder; (i) with Nicholson

Mark Elder has a good feeling for this glorious repertoire and brings to the *Fifth Symphony* the epic sweep this great score needs. **Anthony Nicholson**, too, proves an eloquent soloist in the *Flute Concerto*, and the **Hallé** respond in both scores with enthusiasm and discipline, and offer the *Entrance March* from *Aladdin* as a nice little bonus. Good sound.

Violin Concerto, Op. 33

⊕→ 🏵 Ⓜ ******** Sony SMK 89748. Lin, Swedish RSO, Salonen – SIBELIUS: *Violin Concerto* 🏵 ********

(i) Violin Concerto; Symphony 5

*** BIS CD 370. (i) Kang; Gothenburg SO, Chung

Cho-Liang Lin brings as much authority to Nielsen's *Concerto* as he does to the Sibelius and he handles the numerous technical hurdles with breathtaking assurance. **Salonen** is supportive here and gets good playing from the **Swedish Radio Symphony Orchestra**.

Dong-Suk Kang too is more than equal to the technical demands of this concerto and is fully attuned to the Nordic sensibility. The *Fifth Symphony* is hardly less successful and is certainly one of the best-recorded versions now available. **Myung-Whun Chung** has a natural feeling for Nielsen's language and the first movement has real breadth.

Helios Overture, Op. 17; Pan and Syrinx, Op. 49; Rhapsody Overture: An Imaginary Journey to the Færoe Islands; Amor and the Poet; Maskarade: Overture & Dance of the Cockerels; Master Oluf Rides; Saul and David: Prelude; Snefrid; Willemoes: Prelude, Act III

*** Dacapo SACD 6 220518. Danish Nat. RSO, Dausgaard

Thomas Dausgaard gets exemplary results from the Copenhagen orchestra and deserves all the acclaim which greeted this issue. There are some treasurable rarities here, such as *Pan and Syrinx* and the late *Rhapsody Overture*, along with the more often heard *Helios* and *Maskarade Overtures*.

Little Suite for Strings, Op. 1

🏵 ******* Warner Apex 0927 43075-2. Norwegian R. O, Rasilainen – GRIEG: *Holberg Suite*; STENHAMMAR: *Serenade* 🏵 *******

An unaffected, well-played account of Nielsen's Op. 1 from **Ari Rasilainen** and the **Norwegian Radio Orchestra**, also available above coupled with the *Clarinet* and *Violin Concertos*, is here an attractive bonus for the Stenhammar *Serenade*.

Symphonies: 1, Op. 7; 2 (Four Temperaments), Op. 16; 3 (Espansiva), Op. 27; 4 (Inextinguishable), Op. 29; 5, Op. 50; 6 (Sinfonia semplice) (DVD version)

⊕→ ******* Dacapo DVD 2.110403-05. Danish Nat. RSO, Schønwandt

These are the same performances as those discussed below on CD, but this time with vision attached! The camera-work is tactful and restrained and it enhances our enjoyment of what are excellent performances, arguably the best since Blomstedt's San Francisco set – and perhaps even finer. There is a bonus CD in the form of a film by Karl Aage Rasmussen on Nielsen's life and music called *The Light and the Darkness*, which is well worth having.

Symphonies 1–6; (ii) Violin Concerto; (iii) Clarinet Concerto; (iv) Flute Concerto; (v) Rhapsody Overture, An Imaginary Journey to the Faeroe Islands; Little Suite, Op. 1; Maskarade: Overture; Prelude, Act II; Dance of the Cockerels; Pan and Syrinx; Sagadrøm;

The Mother: Prelude; Saul and David: Prelude Act II; Aladdin Suite; Springtime on Fünen; (vi) 3 Motets

🅱🅱 ******* Regis RRC 6002 (6). (i) LSO, Schmidt; (ii) Matsuyama, Odense SO, Wagner; (iii) McCaw, New Philh. O, Leppard; (iv) Stinton, SCO, Bedford; (v–vi) Odense SO, Vetö; (vi) Inga Nielsen, Von Binzer, Klint, Odense SO Ch.; University Ch., Woldike

This bargain-price collection presents the first accounts of all six symphonies to be recorded in stereo. They have long been out of circulation but are now also available separately (Nos. 1–3 & 6 on RRC 2046; 4 & 5 on RRC 1036) and as a separate set (RRC 3002), and have much going for them. Of the concertos (also available on RRC 1208), that for the *Flute* played by **Jennifer Stinton** and *Clarinet* by **John McCaw** have been newly and successfully remastered. The *Violin Concerto* with **Saeka Matsuyama** as soloist is remarkably fine, blending virtuosity and insight with refined musicianship. The Overtures, tone-poems and orchestral pieces were recorded by the **Odense Orchestra** under **Tamás Vetö** in 1988 and the performances are refreshingly idiomatic (RRC 1166). The Odense account of the adorable *Springtime on Fünen* and the *Aladdin Suite* comes off equally well. **Mogens Wöldike** brings special authority to the three late *a cappella Motets* whose première he conducted soon after their composition (RRC 1134). This is a most valuable set and although its six CDs are offered at a bargain price, they are also available separately.

Symphonies (i) 1–2; (i; ii) 3; (iii) 4; (i) 5; (iii) 6; (i; iv) Clarinet Concerto; (i; v) Flute Concerto; (i; vi) Violin Concerto

Ⓜ ******* BIS CD 614/6 (4). Gothenburg SO; (i) Chung; (ii) with Raanoja, Skram; (iii) Järvi; (iv) with Schill; (v) Gallois; (vi) Kang

Symphonies 1–2; (i) 3; (ii) Aladdin (suite); Maskarade Overture

⊕→ Ⓑ ******** Double Decca 460 985-2 (2). San Francisco SO, Blomstedt; (i) with Kromm, McMillan; (ii) San Francisco SO Ch.

(i) Symphonies 4–6; (ii) Little Suite; (ii; iii) Hymnus amoris, Op. 12

⊕→ Ⓑ ******** Double Decca 460 988-2 (2). (i) San Francisco SO, Blomstedt; (ii) Danish Nat. RSO, Schirmer; (iii) with Bonney, Pedersen, Mark Ainsley, M. & B. Hansen, Danish Nat. R. Ch., Copenhagen Boys' Ch.

Symphonies 1–6

Ⓑ ******* RCA 74321 20290-2 (3). Royal Danish O, Berglund (with soloists in 3)

🅱🅱 ****(*)** Regis (ADD) RRC 3002 (3). LSO, Schmidt

Herbert Blomstedt's complete Decca set of the symphonies is pretty well self-recommending. All six performances are among the finest available. The fill-ups are also very recommendable. Blomstedt is an eminently reliable guide to the *Aladdin Suite*. **Ulf Schirmer**, too, shows a natural affinity for Nielsen. On the second of the two Doubles, he gives us

Nielsen's early cantata, *Hymnus amoris*, one of his warmest and most open-hearted scores, and there is also a persuasive account of Nielsen's first published opus, the endearing *Little Suite for Strings*. To put it briefly, this remains the best all-round modern set of the symphonies and can be purchased with confidence.

Myung-Whun Chung's accounts of the *First* and *Second Symphonies* can also hold their own against the best, and his version of the *Sinfonia espansiva* is one of the *very* best – and can be recommended alongside Blomstedt. The concertos are all excellent – some may even prefer them to the rival collection on Chandos. The package as a whole with four records for the price of three is eminently competitive.

Berglund's set with the **Royal Danish Orchestra** was recorded between 1987 and 1989. The ever-fresh *First Symphony* is given a thoroughly straightforward account and the *Sinfonia espansiva* (No. 3) is perhaps the finest of his cycle. His two soloists, though unnamed, are very good and the general architecture of the work is well conveyed. The *Fourth* (*Inextinguishable*) is more problematic. Berglund tends to be impatient to move things on, particularly in the closing paragraphs. The *Fifth* opens with a strong sense of atmosphere and the second movement's complex structure is well controlled and satisfyingly resolved. In the *Sinfonia semplice* (No. 6) Berglund again proves a perceptive guide. Here as elsewhere, the playing of the Royal Danish Orchestra is beautifully prepared and full of vitality and the RCA engineers produce a recording of splendid body and presence.

Symphonies 1 in G min., Op. 7; 2 in B min. (Four Temperaments), Op. 16

*** Chan. 8880. RSNO, Thomson

Strong, vigorous accounts of both symphonies from the **Royal Scottish Orchestra** under **Bryden Thomson**, with a particularly well-characterized reading of *The Four Temperaments*. The second movement is perhaps a shade too brisk, but in most respects these performances are difficult to fault.

Symphonies 1; 6 (Sinfonia semplice)

*** Dacapo 8.224169. Danish Nat. RSO, Schønwandt

*** BIS CD 1079. BBC Scottish SO, Vänskä

(BB) *** Naxos 8.550826. Nat. SO of Ireland, Leaper

Michael Schønwandt's account of the *Sixth Symphony* shows a good grasp of structure, and in the inspired first movement he is particularly successful in conveying its atmosphere and sense of mystery. The *First* is sound and well proportioned, but does not carry all before it on an irresistible forward current. The *First* is noteworthy, but the *Sixth* is now a first recommendation.

Osmo Vänskä's *First Symphony* comes up fresh, though some expressive point-making does inhibit the onward flow in the first movement. The slow movement, perhaps, also needs to move forward a little more. The *Sixth Symphony*, in intensity and freshness of approach, makes a real challenge to Schønwandt. The **BBC Scottish Symphony Orchestra** give keenly responsive playing in all departments.

Very good performances indeed of Nielsen's first and last

symphonies from **Adrian Leaper** and the **National Symphony Orchestra of Ireland**. The sound is exceptionally well balanced, with exemplary detail and good perspective. The playing is well prepared, full of vitality, phrasing is always intelligent and the Naxos disc remains very good value for money.

Symphony 2 (Four Temperaments); Aladdin Suite

⊕→ *** BIS CD 247. Gothenburg SO, Chung

Symphonies 2 (Four Temperaments); (i) 3 (Sinfonia espansiva)

(BB) *** Naxos 8.550825. Nat. SO of Ireland, Leaper

*** Dacapo 8.224126. Danish Nat. SO, Schønwandt; (i) with Elming

Symphonies 2 (Four Temperaments); 5

*** Classico CD296. RLPO, Bostock

Myung-Whun Chung's account of the *Second Symphony* is among the best, while the *Aladdin Suite* is particularly successful. The **Gothenburg Symphony Orchestra** prove a spirited and responsive body of players. The recording is impressive, too, and can be recommended with enthusiasm.

Adrian Leaper gets vibrant and involved playing from the Dublin orchestra in *The Four Temperaments*, which is as good as any in the catalogue (save for the Jensen), and the *Espansiva* is well paced, with tempi well judged throughout. Not necessarily a first choice but highly competitive.

Schønwandt gets very cultured playing from his fine orchestra, and judges tempi to excellent effect. There is breadth and nobility in *The Four Temperaments* and his account of the *Espansiva* is equally well paced. Its attractions are greatly enhanced by the fine singing of both soloists. This can hold its own with the best.

Bostock's account of *The Four Temperaments* has tremendous character. In the *Fifth*, he really inspires his players, who convey enthusiasm and freshness and, though the playing has some rough edges, it more than compensates in fire and intensity.

(i) Symphonies 3 (Sinfonia espansiva); (ii) 5

⊕→ *** Chan. 9067. (i) Bott, Roberts; RSO, Thomson

Bryden Thomson's chosen tempi in the *Sinfonia espansiva* are just right, particularly in the finale. In the slow movement **Catherine Bott** and **Stephen Roberts** are excellent, and the performance has a refreshing directness that is most likeable. The *Fifth Symphony* is equally committed and satisfying. The recordings are very good indeed.

Symphony 4 (Inextinguishable); Pan and Syrinx

(B) *** EMI 5 03428-2. CBSO, Rattle – SIBELIUS: *Symphony 5* ***

Symphony 4 (Inextinguishable); Amor og digteren (Cupid and the Poet): extracts; Symphonic Rhapsody; (i) Genrebillede (Genre Picture), Op. 6/1; Ariel's Song; Hjemlige Jul

*** Classico CD298. RLPO, Bostock; (i) Lund

Simon Rattle's version of the *Inextinguishable* dates from 1981 and is very fine indeed; it deserves a strong recommendation, particularly given that it comes with an altogether outstanding account of *Pan and Syrinx*, and the recording is very good too.

In the *Fourth Symphony* **Douglas Bostock's** reading has tremendous character. Bostock includes the early *Symphonic Rhapsody* (1888), as well as various songs, the *Overture* and four new excerpts from the incidental music to *Amor og digteren*. The orchestral version of the *Genrebillede* (*Genre Picture*) is also new to the catalogue. Although the *Fourth Symphony* is not a first recommendation, it is certainly among the most fiery and committed accounts to have appeared in recent times. Good, though not outstanding sound.

Symphony 5, Op. 50

(**(*)) BBC Legends mono BBCL 4191-2. NPO, Horenstein
  (with ROSSINI: *Semiramide Overture*) – MAHLER: *Symphony 6* **(*)

Horenstein had a close relationship with the *Fifth Symphony*. He prepared the orchestra for the very first performance outside Denmark, in Frankfurt under Furtwängler. The broadcast was made only a year before his death and, after Jensen, ranks among the finest on record.

Symphony 6 (*Sinfonia semplice*)

*** BBC mono BBCL 4059-2. NPO, Stokowski – GABRIELI:
  Sonata pian e forte; LISZT: *Mephisto Waltz 1*; TIPPETT:
  Concerto for Double String Orchestra ***

Although **Leopold Stokowski** conducted the *Sixth Symphony* in Copenhagen, he never recorded any of the symphonies commercially. The first movement comes off marvellously, not that its companions fare less well. Meticulous playing, expertly prepared and thought through, which leaves one regretting that Stokowski never recorded the *Fifth*. The sound is very good and balanced beautifully.

CHAMBER MUSIC

(i) Canto serioso for Horn & Piano; Fantasy Piece for Clarinet & Piano (1881); Fantasy Pieces for Oboe & Piano; Moderen: excerpts; (ii) Piano Trio, Op. 2; (i) Serenata in Vano; Wind Quintet, Op. 43

*** Dacapo 8.226064. (i) Diamant Ensemblet; (ii) Trio Ondine

This anthology of wind music includes two rarities, the *Fantasy Piece for Clarinet and Piano* and the *Piano Trio in G major*, both very early pieces. The *Wind Quintet* will be the main attraction however, and this expert performance is as well characterized as anything in the catalogue, and the recording is very lifelike and immediate.

String Quartets 1 in G min., Op. 13; 2 in F min., Op. 5

(BB) *** Naxos 8.553908. Oslo Qt

String Quartets 3 in E flat, Op. 14; 4 in F, Op. 44

(BB) *** Naxos 8.553907. Oslo Qt

String Quartets 1 in G min., Op. 13; 4 in F, Op. 44; (i) String Quintet in G

*** Dacapo SACD 6.220521. Young Danish String Qt, (i) with Frederiksen

String Quartets 1–4; (i) String Quintet in G (1888); (ii) Andante lamentoso (At the Bier of a Young Artist) (1910)

*** BIS CD 503/4. Kontra Qt; (i) Naegele; (ii) Johansson

String Quartets 1–4; 5 Quartet Movements, FS2

*** Kontrapunkt 32150-1(2). Danish Qt

The *G major String Quintet* with second viola is an early work. The *F major Quartet* comes from 1906. These are all delightful pieces and it is astonishing that they have not entered the repertoire of international quartets. Good playing from the **Young Danish String Quartet**, and most realistic SACD recording.

The performances by the **Oslo Quartet** are spirited, sensitive and very alive. There is a touch of fierceness in the recording quality (they are rather closely balanced) but artistically they are a first recommendation. They also enjoy a hefty price advantage over their Danish rivals.

The **Danish Quartet** are sensitive to the shape of the phrase, they produce a wide dynamic range, including really soft *pianissimo* tone when required. They are not always the last word in polish, but everything they do is musical, which makes one forgive the occasional rough edge and the somewhat dry quality and rather close balance of the recording. The set also includes five short movements that Nielsen wrote in his late teens and early twenties.

There is an ardour and temperament to the playing by the **Kontra Quartet**, which most listeners will find very persuasive. In addition we are given the finest account yet recorded of the *G major String Quintet*, where they are joined by the American violist **Philipp Naegele**, and the only current account of the *Andante lamentoso* (*At the Bier of a Young Artist*) in its chamber form. The BIS recordings, made in the Malmö Concert Hall, have plenty of presence and clarity, and are rather forwardly (but not unpleasingly) balanced.

String Quintet in G (1888), FS5

*** Chan. 9258. ASMF Ens. – SVENDSEN: *Octet* ***

The *String Quintet in G major* is very well fashioned and owes more to Svendsen, under whose baton the composer was to play, than to his teacher, Gade. It makes both an agreeable and an appropriate companion for Svendsen's early and delightful *Octet*. It receives a three-star performance and recording.

Wind Quintet, Op. 43

*** Nim. NI 5728. V. Quintet – HINDEMITH: *Kleine Kammermusik*; LIGETI: *6 Bagatelles* ***

The **Vienna Quintet** give us a totally fresh and delightful account of the Nielsen, which proves, as do its two companions, a delight from start to finish. Beautifully cultured playing which reveals their affection for this piece. The recording, made in the Wiener Konzerthaus, is first class.

PIANO MUSIC

Complete piano music: Chaconne, Op. 32; Humoresque-Bagatelles, Op. 11; Piano music for Young and Old, Op. 53; 3 Piano Pieces, Op. 59; 5 Pieces, Op. 3; Symphonic Suite, Op. 8; Theme and Variations, Op. 40; Suite, Op. 45

(N) 🎧 *** Hyp. CDA 67591/2 (2). Roscoe

Apart from Grieg, no Scandinavian composer has written for the piano with more individuality or understanding than Nielsen. Even though the early Op. 3 *Pieces* are Schumannesque, they speak with distinctive and touching personal accents, and all five are strong on both humour and character. Nielsen's greatest piano music is clustered into a period of four years (1916–20) with his final thoughts in the medium, the *Three Pieces*, Op. 59, of 1928 being composed in the immediate wake of the *Clarinet Concerto*, music that already breathes the air of other planets. The *Suite* is not only Nielsen's greatest keyboard work but arguably the mightiest ever written in Scandinavia. **Martin Roscoe** is right inside this music and guides us through its marvels with great subtlety and authority. Hyperion give him vivid and natural recorded sound and there are outstanding notes by Daniel Grimley.

Chaconne; Humoresque-bagatelles, Op. 11; Luciferian Suite; 5 Pieces, Op. 3; 3 Pieces, Op. 59

(B) *** Virgin 2x1 3 49913-2 (2). Andsnes – JANÁČEK: *Sonata, etc.* ***

Nielsen's piano music is unmissable! The early pieces have great charm, and the later *Suite* and the *Three Pieces*, Op. 59, have great substance. **Leif Ove Andsnes** has a natural feeling for and understanding of this music, while the recorded sound is vivid and lifelike.

VOCAL MUSIC

Songs, Op. 4; 6; 10; Bow Down Your Head Now; Bright are the Leaves in the Woods Now; Flower; Italian Pastoral Aria; Maskerade: Duet; Nature Study; Oft am I Glad; Oh, Strange Evening Breezes

*** Dacapo 8.224218. Dam-Jensen, Lassen, Stærk

Nielsen's songs are strophic and fresh, touching and heart-warming. **Inger Dam-Jensen** captures their special character splendidly, and she has excellent support from the pianist **Ulrich Stærk**. Her choice ranges over the whole of Nielsen's career, from the Opp. 4 and 6 collections of 1891 through to the *Italian Pastoral* of 1931. There is also a short duet from the opera *Maskerade* in which she is partnered by **Morten Ernst Lassen**. Strongly recommended.

(i) Hymnus amoris; (ii) 3 Motets, Op. 55; The Sleep, Op. 18; (iii) Springtime in Fünen, Op. 43

🎧 *** Chan. 8853. Soloists; (i) Copenhagen Boys' Ch.; (ii–iii) Danish Nat. R. Ch.; (iii) Skt. Annai Gymnasium Children's Ch., Danish Nat. RSO; (i; iii) Segerstam; (ii) Parkman

Hymnus amoris is full of glorious music whose polyphony has a naturalness and freshness that it is difficult to resist, and which is generally well sung. The harsh dissonances of the middle *Nightmare* section of *Søvnen* ('The Sleep') still generate a powerful effect. **Segerstam** gets very good results in the enchanting *Springtime in Fünen*, and the solo singing is good. The *Three Motets* actually contain a Palestrina quotation. Generally excellent performances and fine recorded sound.

STAGE WORKS

Aladdin (complete incidental music), Op. 34

*** Chan. 9135. Ejsing, Paevatalu, Danish R. Chamber Ch. & SO, Rozhdestvensky

Until now the *Aladdin* music has been known only from the 20-minute, seven-movement suite, but the complete score runs to four times its length. Some numbers are choral, and there are songs and a short piece for solo flute. Thirteen of the movements are designed to accompany spoken dialogue and, although not all of it is of equal musical interest and substance, most of it is characteristically Nielsenesque, and much of it is delightful. The two soloists, **Mette Ejsing** and **Guido Paevatalu**, are very good and the Danish Radio forces respond keenly to **Rozhdestvensky's** baton. This is not top-drawer Nielsen but, given such a persuasive performance and excellent recording, one is almost lulled into the belief that it is.

OPERA

Maskarade (complete)

*** Dacapo (ADD) **SACD** 6.220507/8 (2). Hansen, Plesner, Landy, Johansen, Serensen, Bastian, Brodersen, Haugland, Danish R. Ch. & SO, Frandsen

Nielsen's second and last opera now comes realistically re-mastered on SACD and must be considered a triumphant success in its new format, with the rear speakers (used discreetly) adding to the atmospheric feeling. But it still sounds admirable through a normal stereo set-up. **Frandsen's** performance is distinguished by good – sometimes very good – singing and alert orchestral support. Above all, the sound is musical, the images are well located and firm, and the overall presentation is vivid. But the deleted Decca set remains first choice.

Saul and David (complete)

❀ **** Chan. 8911/12. Haugland, Lindroos, Kiberg, Westi, Ch. & Danish Nat. RSO, Järvi

Nielsen's first opera is here sung in the original language, which is as important with Nielsen as it is with Janáček, and it has the merit of an outstanding Saul in **Aage Haugland**. The remainder of the cast is very strong and the powerful choral writing is well served by the **Danish Radio Chorus**. The opera abounds in wonderful and noble music, the ideas are fresh and full of originality. It convinces here in a way that it rarely has before, and the action is borne along on an almost symphonic current that disarms criticism. A marvellous set.

NØRGÅRD, Per (born 1932)

Symphonies 3 & 7

(N) *** Dacapo 6.220547. Danish Nat. Ch., R. SO, Dausgaard

Per Nørgård is the leading Danish composer of his generation. He was a pupil of Vagn Holmboe and made a name for himself with his *First Symphony (Sinfonia austera)*. Although Holmboe's influence can be felt in his early twenties, he has developed a distinctive and arresting voice. The *Third Symphony* comes from 1972–5 and includes a setting of the *Ave Maris stella*, and lines from the Sonnets to Orpheus of Rilke. The *Seventh Symphony* (2004–6) was commissioned for the inauguration of the new Danish Radio Concert Hall in 2009. The performances here are very persuasive and the recording gives no possible cause for complaint.

NOVÁK, Vitězslav (1870–1949)

(i) Symphonic poems: About the Eternal Longing, Op. 33; In the Tatra Mountains, Op. 26; (ii) Moravian-Slovak Suite, Op. 32

(M) **(*) Sup. (ADD) 11 0682-2. (i) Czech PO; (ii) Brno State PO; Sejna

In the Tatras (1902), an opulent Straussian tone-poem, and *About the Eternal Longing* (1903–4) were inspired by unrequited love for a beautiful young pupil, Růžna. The *Slovak Suite* is a heavenly score. *In the Church*, the opening movement, has something in common with Mozart's *Ave verum corpus*, though more obviously romantic, and the closing *At Night* is beguilingly atmospheric. All three works here are also persuasively played on Supraphon. The recording of the two symphonic poems is atmospheric and clear but a bit pale in the more expansive tuttis; the suite has slightly more body and colour.

De profundis, Op. 67; Overture: Lady Godiva, Op. 41; Toman and the Wood Nymph, Op. 40

⊶ **** Chan. 9821. BBC PO, Pešek

De profundis, Op. 67; Overture: Lady Godiva, Op. 41; South Bohemian Suite, Op. 64

(***) Sup. mono 11 1873-2 011. Brno State PO, Vogel

There is a lot of Dvořák in these pieces and a considerable debt to both Strauss and Mahler, plus an obvious awareness of French musical culture. *Lady Godiva* has something of the opulence of Strauss or the Elgar of *In the South*. It is full of dramatic fire, and its ideas are bold and orchestrated marvellously. *Toman and the Wood Nymph* has a lush orchestral palette and rich harmonic language. The dark and anguished *De profundis* was written in 1941 for a large orchestra with piano and organ. Stunning recorded sound from Chandos and admirably vivid and idiomatic playing from the **BBC Philharmonic** under **Libor Pešek**.

The classic Supraphon performances all come from 1960, except for the *De profundis*, which **Jaroslav Vogel** recorded two years later. The recordings still sound very good for their period and the performances are very fine. What attractive music it is, too.

Pan (symphonic poem), Op. 43

⊶ *** Marco Polo 8.223325. Slovak PO, Bílek

Novák's five-movement symphonic poem, *Pan*, has some lovely music in it, and there is a pantheistic sensibility here. It is beautifully played by the **Slovak Philharmonic** under **Zdenek Bílek**, and no less beautifully recorded.

Cello Sonata, Op. 68

**** Sup. SU 3515-2. Barta, Cech – KODÁLY: *Cello Sonatas* ***

As a powerful supplement to Kodály's two cello masterpieces, **Jiří Barta** and **Jan Cech** offer one of Vitězslav Novák's late works, written in 1941 during the Nazi occupation of Czechoslovakia. Though it may not quite match the two Kodály works in emotional power, the darkness and intensity of the writing over the closely argued single movement – bringing together elements of a multi-movement sonata structure – are most impressive, particularly in a performance as commanding as this.

Trio quasi una balata

*** Sup. SU 3810. Smetana Trio – SMETANA: *Piano Trio*; SUK: *Elégie*; *Piano Trio* ***

Novák described his *Trio quasi una balata* as a work of blackest Baudelairean pessimism, and though its themes may not be as striking as those in the other works on the disc, all but one of them darkly elegiac, it is most skilfully argued, completing an excellent programme, superbly played and very well recorded.

The Storm, Op. 42

⊶ (M) **** Sup. (ADD) SU 3088-2 211. Soloists, Czech PO Ch. & O, Košler

The Storm is a work of great beauty and imagination, scored with consummate mastery and showing a lyrical gift of a high order. It has warmth and genuine individuality; the idiom owes something to Richard Strauss as well as to the Czech tradition, and there is an impressive command of both melody and structure. The performance is fully worthy and has splendid dramatic feeling, helped by good soloists and a fine chorus. The recording, too, is admirably balanced, and there is depth, and plenty of weight, even if the soloists are rather too forward.

OBRECHT, Jacob (1457–1505)

Benedictus in Laude; Plainchant: Sub tuum Praesidium; Missa sub tuum Praesidium; Beata est Maria; Factor orbis; Mille quingentis; Salva crux; Salve Regina a 3

*** ASV Gaudeamus CDGAU 341. Clerks' Group, Wickham

This splendidly sung and recorded collection gives an excellent survey of both Obrecht's compositional skills and his restrained but profound religious conviction.

Laudes Christo; Missa Malheur me bat

🎵 *** ASV Gaudeamus CDGAU 171. Clerks' Group, Wickham
– MARTINI: *Motets & Magnificat* ***

The Dutch composer, Jacob Obrecht, was one of the pioneers in developing a new, more closely organized polyphonic style, notably in his use of segmentation. This is well illustrated in this fine *Mass*, with the theme on which the work is based successively fragmented. There is a sublime summation at the end when the theme is restored to its original form, radiantly performed by the **Clerks' Group**, and with warmly atmospheric sound. The coupling is apt – Obrecht ended up as *Maestro di capella* at the court of Ferrara, where Martini had spent his career.

Missa Caput; Salve Regina: in 4 parts; in 6 parts; Venit ad Petrum

(BB) *** Naxos 8.553210. Oxford Camerata, Summerly

Both of the *Salve Regina* settings are based on plainchant melody and are *alternatim* settings, the music alternating between a polyphonic treatment of the chant and the unadorned chant itself. **Jeremy Summerly** and his **Oxford Camerata**, recorded in the Chapel of Hertford College, Oxford, give expert and committed accounts of this music and they are accorded first-class sound.

OCKEGHEM, Johannes
(c. 1410–97)

Alma redemptoris Mater; Ave Maria; Credo fors seulement; Fors seulement; Intemerata Dei Mater (2 versions); Masses: Au trail suis; Celeste beneficum; Cuiusvis toni; De plus en plus; Ecce ancilla Domini; L'Homme armé; Mi-mi; Prolationum; Quinti toni; Sine nomine (2 settings: à 3 & à 5); Requiem; Salve Regina; S'elle m'amera/Petite camusette

🎵 (B) **** ASV Gaudeamus CDGAU 550 (5). Clerks' Group, Wickham

This admirable bargain box collects together the survey by **Edward Wickham's Clerks' Group** of Ockeghem's major religious works (including 11 Mass settings and the *Requiem*), all discussed in detail below, but omitting the chansons and *Missa caput*. A treasure chest.

Alma redemptoris Mater; Missa Mi-Mi; Salve Regina

*** ASV Gaudeamus CDGAU 139. Clerks' Group, Wickham
(with motets by BUSNOIS, ISAAC and OBRECHT)

Ockeghem's *Salve Regina*, the motet *Alma redemptoris Mater* and the *Missa Mi-Mi* are contrasted here with motets by three of his contemporaries. The *Missa Mi-Mi* is so named because of the recurring descending fifth, named 'mi' in both the natural and soft hexachords. These performances have a refreshing enthusiasm and the approach to rhythm is remarkably free. An outstanding disc.

Ave Maria; Intemerata Dei Mater; Missa ecce ancilla Domina

*** ASV Gaudeamus CDGAU 223. Clerks' Group, Wickham
(with OBRECHT: *Salve Regina*; JOSQUIN DESPREZ: *Déploration sur la mort de Ockeghem* ***)

Ecce ancilla Domina is a middle-period Mass (c. 1470), but its polyphonic richness and unpredictable rhythmic impetus make for compelling listening in a performance so aptly paced and involvingly spontaneous. The *Ave Maria* is relatively familiar (see below), but *Intemerata Dei Mater* (from the 1480s) has a poignant atmosphere all its own which matches the expressive power of Obrecht's six-part *Salve Regina* from the same period. Josquin's valedictory musical farewell in the plaintive Phrygian mode also has links to Ockeghem's moving supplication to the mother of God. This beautifully recorded disc is well up to the high standard of ASV's admirable series.

Missa caput; Ma maistresse; Missa Ma maistresse: Kyrie & Gloria

*** ASV Gaudeamus CDGAU 186. Clerks' Group, Wickham
(with ANON.: Hymn: *O solis ortus cardine*; Motets: *O sidus Hispanie*; *Gaude Marie*; SARUM CHANT: Antiphon: *Venit ad Petrum*)

Only two movements survive of the *Missa Ma maistresse*, but very fine they are, bright and extrovert in feeling, making ingenious use of the song material. The cantus firmus of the *Missa caput* is derived from the long melisma on the word 'caput' which we have already heard at the end of the Sarum Antiphon, *Venit ad Petrum*. It is perhaps an awkward basis for a mass, but Ockeghem's polyphony rises to the challenge, and the work is both texturally and aurally intriguing, yet moves forward on a seemingly inevitable course, in spite of Ockeghem's frequent use of cadences. The two anonymous motets can be found in the same manuscript which is the earliest source of this mass and it is possible that *O sidus Hispanie*, a eulogy for St Anthony of Padua, was written by Du Fay, who greatly admired this saint. All the performances here are of the highest order and the recording is first class too.

Missa de plus en plus; Missa Fors seulement

*** Lyrichord LEMS 8029. Schola Discantus, Moll

This Lyrichord disc joins the beautiful middle-period four-part *Missa de plus en plus* with a later five-part work, *Missa Fors seulement*, based on one of the composer's own chansons, which is unfortunately not included here as it is on Edward Wickham's ASV disc (see below). However, the performances are finely sung and blended and have an appealing simplicity. **Ken Moll's** varied pacing is convincing. The *Missa Fors seulement* (which only consists of *Kyrie*, *Gloria* and *Credo*) is especially notable for its use of two basses, which darkens the texture very strikingly, although Moll takes care not to provide an exaggerated balance.

Missa L'Homme armé; Alma redemptoris Mater; Ave Maria

🎵 ✴ (BB) *** Naxos 8.554297. Oxford Camerata, Summerly
(with JOSQUIN DESPREZ: *Memor esto verbi tui* ***)

Missa L'Homme armé; Missa Sine nomine; Salve Regina (probably by Philippe Basiron)

*** Gaudeamus CDGAU 204. Clerks' Group, Wickham (with MORTON (attrib.): *Rondeau: Il sera pour vous (L'Homme armé)* ***)

On Naxos the soaring opening *Ave Maria*, gloriously sung, immediately sets the seal on the inspirational power of Ockeghem's music. It is followed by the plainchant, *Alma redemptoris Mater*, and then its polyphonic setting, simple and flowing and harmonically rich. The robust ballad, *L'Homme armé*, follows ('The armed man must be feared'), sounding vigorously jolly, like a carol. It must have been hugely popular in its day since so many composers used it as a basis for a Mass. While the polyphony in the *Gloria* and *Credo* moves onward inventively, the work's dramatic and emotional peak is readily found in the extended *Sanctus* (by far the longest section) and resolved in the sublime melancholy of the *Agnus Dei*. In short, this is a work of striking individuality and beauty, and it is sung superbly here, and marvellously paced. Josquin's setting of sixteen verses from Psalm 119, *Memor esto verbi tui*, with its expressively fertile imitative devices, makes an eloquent postlude, and the recording, made in the Chapel of Hertford College, Oxford, could hardly be bettered. It dates from February 1997, thus aptly celebrating the 500th anniversary of Ockeghem's death.

Ockeghem's striking *L'Homme armé* mass is always easy to follow as its cantus firmus is so characterful. On ASV it is quoted first in a rondeau, attributed to Ockeghem's contemporary, Robert Morton, where it is used mockingly; it is surprising that no translation is given, although it is provided for the other music. Both the *Missa Sine nomine* and the *Salve Regina* are dubiously attributed to Ockeghem, but he would surely have been glad to acknowledge the rich polyphony of the latter.

The *Sine nomine mass* for three voices, however, is much less characteristic, although to our ears its flowing lines are very attractive. The performances here are well up to the standard of this excellent group, but the Naxos recording of the *Missa L'Homme armé* by the Oxford Camerata is even more attractively coupled.

Missa Prolationum; Requiem; Intemerata Dei Mater

(BB) **(*) Naxos 8.554260. Musica Ficta, Holten

Ockeghem was a mathematician as well as a composer, and his *Missa Prolationum* is famous for its intellectually complex polyphony based on double canons, while the rhythmic discipline is also carefully calculated. To all but the most analytical listener this will not matter too much, for the resulting music has a seemingly effortless flow, although the eight-voiced **Clerks' Group**, without losing melismatic sonority, certainly do not miss the special rhythmic relationships. They support the Mass with five diverse motets by Ockeghem's contemporaries (nearly all set to Marian texts), to make a stimulating introduction to other Franco-Netherlands composers of this period. Excellent recording.

Masses for 3 voices: Missa Sine nomine; Missa Quinti toni

*** Lyrichord LEMS 8010. Schola Discantus, Moll

The very austerity of Ockeghem's part-writing, with its serenely flowing polyphony, adds to the potency of his music for modern ears. It is very beautifully sung by a vocal quartet of high quality whose tonal matching and fine tuning are ideal. The recording, too, is clear yet has a perfectly judged ambience.

Requiem; Motet and Missa Fors seulement

🎧 **** ASV Gaudeamus CDGAU 168. Clerks' Group, Wickham

Ockeghem's *Requiem* remains one of the riddles of medieval liturgical music. Its various surviving movements are very different in style, notation and part-writing, and (rather like the Du Fay *St Anthony Mass*) it was long thought that the manuscript might be a collection of fragments from a number of different works. Even so the *Requiem* holds together with a convincing unity.

Certainly every bar of the music is memorable in such a dedicated performance as we have from the **Clerks' Group** under **Edward Wickham**. In addition we are offered the *Kyrie*, *Gloria* and *Credo* of the *Missa Fors seulement*, plus the rondeau on which it is based, and further arrangements of the latter by Pierre de la Rue and Antoine Brumel, which offer more splendid music to intrigue the inquisitive ear.

OFFENBACH, Jacques
(1819–80)

(i) Cello Concerto (Concerto militaire); Les Fées du Rhin: Overture, ballet & Grande Valse; Orphée aux Enfers: Overture; Le Voyage dans la Lune: Ballet des Flocons de Neige

🎧 *** DG 477 6403. Les Musiciens du Louvre, Minkowski, (i) with Pernoo

Long before he scored his big success as a composer of operettas with *Orpheus in the Underworld*, Offenbach was renowned as the 'Liszt of the cello', an outstanding virtuoso. This 45-minute *Concerto militaire* is the most important of his compositions from that period, here recorded complete for the first time. Both the first movement and the finale introduce military themes, with timpani prominent in both, and with the main theme of the finale anticipating the style of Offenbach's operettas. That finale, 20 minutes long, offers a wide range of themes, including a funeral procession episode. The sound, recorded live in Grenoble, tends to be plummy, but there is ample detail to bring out the fine quality of the performance both by the soloist, **Jerome Pernoo**, and of the orchestra of period instruments under **Marc Minkowski**. The sparkling fill-ups add to the attractions of the disc, with the ballet from *Les Fées du Rhin* offering the first version of what later became the *Barcarolle* in the *Tales of Hoffmann*.

Concerto militaire; Concerto rondo; 4 Impressions: (ii) Deux âmes au ciel – Elégie; (iii) Introduction et valse mélancolique; Rêverie au bord de la mer; (ii) La Course en traîneau

*** CPO 777 069-2. Schiefen, WDR R. O, Köln, with (i) Froschauer; (ii) Villiers; (iii) Oskamp

Ofra Harnoy's deleted RCA recording made Offenbach's delightful *Concerto rondo* a famous novelty. **Guido Schiefen's** performance offers greater exuberance, but Harnoy offered greater elegance. However, Schiefen gives us the longer *Concerto militaire*, where there is plenty of sparkle throughout, especially in the irrepressibly catchy finale. The *Four Impressions* find Offenbach in more reflective mood and are lightly sentimental works of much charm, written for the instrument that he adored. Although Schiefen's timbre is not always as ideally rounded as it might be, there is nothing to deter Offenbachians. Accompaniments are well managed under three different conductors, and the recording is well balanced.

Gaîté parisienne (ballet, arr. Rosenthal; complete)

🎵 ✹ (M) **** RCA SACD 82876 66419-2. Boston Pops O, Fiedler – ROSSINI/RESPIGHI: *Boutique fantasque* ***

*** Decca Eloquence (ADD) 476 2724. ROHCG O, Solti – GOUNOD: *Faust: ballet music* ***; RESPIGHI: *Rossiniana* **(*)

Fiedler's *Gaîté parisienne* is irresistible – one of his very finest records. The orchestra are kept exhilaratingly on their toes throughout and are obviously enjoying themselves, not least in the elegantly tuneful waltzes and in the closing *Barcarolle*, which Fiedler prepares beautifully and to which the generous acoustic of Symphony Hall affords a pleasing warmth without in any way blunting or coarsening the brilliance. The percussion, including bass drum in the exuberant *Can-can*, adds an appropriate condiment and John Pfeiffer's superb SACD transfer makes the recording sound remarkably fresh and full.

Solti's 1959 *Gaîté parisienne* is the most brilliant version committed to disc. While some listeners may feel that the music-making is just that bit too hard-driven to be a top choice, there is no doubting the sheer virtuosity of the orchestra, and their bravura is hard to resist. Exciting music-making, and vintage Decca sound.

Overtures: Barbe-bleue; La Belle Hélène; La Grande Duchesse de Gérolstein; Le Mariage aux lanternes; Orfée aux Enfers

🎵 ✹ (****) Australian Decca Eloquence mono 476 2757. LPO, Martinon (with ADAM: *Si j'étais roi*; BOIELDIEU: *Le Calife de Bagdad; La Dame blanche*; HEROLD: *Zampa* (***))

Under **Martinon** these overtures explode like a suddenly shaken bottle of ice-cold champagne. The **LPO** strings play with polish as well as fizz, so the can-can finales of *Orfée* and *La Grande Duchesse* are both elegant and sparkling. While no one captures the whirlwind Offenbach impetus quite as Martinon does, one relishes this collection also for the charm of the playing. But nowhere is Martinon's rhythmic vitality and lift more apparent than in the deliciously crisp closing section of the rare *Le Mariage aux lanternes*; here one understands why Rossini dubbed Offenbach 'the Mozart of the Champs-Elysées'. Among the other delights here is the delicate oboe tune in *La Belle Hélène*, enchantingly played,

while during the lilting waltz theme you can understand how Offenbach once beat Johann Strauss in a waltz-writing competition!

Australian Decca have coupled the Offenbach items with Martinon's accounts of other French overtures which we described in the original Penguin review as 'four French soufflés served up by a conductor who obviously relishes every moment and the orchestra giving of their very best'. *La Dame blanche* is especially enjoyable, with the bravura bassoon accompaniment to the second subject as perky as can be. The early 1950s sound is certainly vivid, although still a shade too bright. A unique disc and well worth any effort to obtain.

Overtures: La Belle Hélène; Bluebeard; La Grande Duchesse de Gérolstein; Orpheus in the Underworld; Vert-vert; Barcarolle from Contes d'Hoffmann

**(*) DG 400 044-2. BPO, Karajan

Other hands besides Offenbach's helped to shape his overtures. Most are on a pot-pourri basis, but the tunes and scoring are so engagingly witty as to confound criticism. **Karajan's** performances racily evoke the theatre pit. The Berlin playing is very polished and, with so much to entice the ear, this cannot fail to be entertaining. However, the compact disc emphasizes the dryness of the orchestral sound; the effect is rather clinical, with the strings lacking bloom.

Overture: La Belle Hélène (arr. Haensch); (i) Les Contes d'Hoffmann: Entr'acte et Barcarolle

🎵 **** Chan. 9765. (i) RLPO Ch.; BBC PO, Y. P. Tortelier (with Concert: *French bonbons.* ***)

Haensch's *Overture La Belle Hélène* is a far better piece than the more famous overture to *Orpheus in the Underworld*. A stylish pot-pourri, it includes two of the opera's best tunes, the disarmingly seductive waltz, and a delightfully songful siciliano given to the oboe; it then ends with a brief, infectious can-can. **Tortelier** has its full measure, shaping it with great style and affection, and reminding us of Martinon's justly famous LPO mono Decca version. The *Barcarolle*, too, is very seductive, and both are given state-of-the-art recording. This is part of an unmissable concert of 'French bonbons'.

Le Papillon (ballet; complete)

(B) *** Decca (ADD) 444 827-2 (2). Nat. PO, Bonynge – TCHAIKOVSKY: *Nutcracker* ***

Le Papillon is Offenbach's only full-length ballet and it dates from 1860. The quality of invention is high and the music sparkles from beginning to end. In such a sympathetic performance, vividly recorded (in 1972 in the Kingsway Hall), it cannot fail to give pleasure.

Cello Duos, Op. 54: Suites 1–2

(B) *** HMA 1901043. Pidoux, Péclard

Offenbach was himself a very accomplished cellist, and these two works are tuneful and imaginatively laid out to exploit the tonal possibilities of such a duo. Offenbach's natural wit is especially apparent in the *First Suite in E major*. The performances are excellent and so is the recording.

PIANO MUSIC

Bella notte (Barcarola); Décaméron dramatique (Album du Théâtre français); Dernier souvenir (Valse de Zimmer); Les Roses du Bengale (6 Valses sentimentales)

*** CPO 777 079-2. Sollini

Offenbach's piano music is essentially salon music, tuneful and undemanding, and not terribly pianistic. Not all of it shows Offenbach in the best light, but there are some moments of charm, and his effervescent spirit certainly comes through. Excellent performances and recording, and guaranteed to bring a sentimental tear when the *Waltz* appears.

OPERA

La Belle Hélène (complete; DVD version)

(N) *** Arthaus DVD 107 100. Lott, Beuron, Sénéchal, Le Roux, Naouri, Todorovitch Ch. & Musiciens du Louvre, Minkowski (Stage Director: Laurent Pelly; V/D : Ross MacGibbon)

The new production staged by Laurent Pelly, with costumes by Chantal Thomas, retains all the mythological characters, but they appear to Helen as in a dream – of being the most beautiful woman in the world, and falling in love with the virile young Paris. Her double bed, to which she retires at the beginning, becomes the focus of the action until Act III, which takes place on the beach at Naples, from which she finally sails away with Paris. The whole production fizzes and has touches of romantic naughtiness which only the French can bring off with real style. Favouring brisk speeds and light textures **Mark Minkowski** gives a winning sparkle to this delectable send-up of the classical story. He also has the benefit of offering a more complete, more authentic text than any predecessor. It was recorded after the highly successful stage production at the Châtelet Théâtre in Paris, when **Felicity Lott** was hailed as an outstanding star in the role of Hélène. That is true, even if vocally there are moments when her voice is not at its sweetest, not as rounded as it might be; but her feeling for the idiom and her characterization are unerring. Outstanding in the cast is the seductively honey-toned tenor **Yan Beuron** as Paris. An excellent supporting cast including such stalwarts of the repertory as **Michel Sénéchal** and **François Le Roux**. And there is no doubt the DVD version adds an extra dimension to Offenbach's scintillating score.

Highlights from: (i) La Belle Hélène; (ii) Orpheus in the Underworld; (iii) La Vie parisienne (all sung in English)

🔊 ✺ (B) **** CfP (ADD) 5 75999-2 (2). (i) Blackham, Fryatt; (i; ii) Miller; (ii) Crofoot; (ii; iii) Bronhill, Shilling, Weaving; (iii) Steele, Sadler's Wells Op. Ch. & O, cond. (i; ii) Faris; (iii) Pollack, Matheson

These sparkling recordings of Sadler's Wells Offenbach productions from the early 1960s remain among the most convincing examples of operetta (or opera) sung in English on record. The English versions by Geoffrey Dunn are excellent examples of how French operetta can be brought to an English audience without losing the Gallic wit of the orginals. *La Belle Hélène* is a highly infectious performance, catching the comedy without overdoing things.

With a single reservation, *Orpheus in the Underworld* is the most successful of the three. Without visual help the recording manages to convey the high spirits and genuine gaiety of the piece, plus – and this is an achievement for a non-Parisian company – the sense of French poise and precision. One's only complaint is that **Alan Crofoot's** *King of Boeotians* number at the opening of Act III is needlesssly cruel vocally.

In *La Vie parisienne* the vocal standards may sound thinner on record than they did on stage – even **Anna Pollack** sounds over-parted – but the production is as imaginative as ever, and it is the Sadler's Wells teamwork that matters, so much of the effervescence of this Second Empire romp comes over well. Throughout, the CD remastering shows how vivid and clear were the original recordings, projecting the words admirably against a warm theatrical acoustic, even though the recordings were made at Abbey Road.

Les Contes d'Hoffmann (The Tales of Hoffmann; complete) (DVD versions)

🔊 *** Warner DVD 0630 19392-2. Domingo, Serra, Baltsa, Cotrubas, Evans, Nimsgern, Ghiuselev, Lloyd, ROHCG Ch. & O, Prêtre (V/D: Brian Large)

**(*) Opus Arte DVD OA0968 D (2). Machado, Gorny, Goeldner, Bayo, Kutzarove, Poblador, Bilbao Op. Ch., Bilbao SO, Guingal (Dir: Giancarlo del Monaco, V/D: Angel Ramirez)

The Warner DVD offers a 1981 performance at Covent Garden with **Plácido Domingo** ideally cast in the name-part, singing and acting superbly in John Schlesinger's production, here imaginatively directed for video by Brian Large. **Georges Prêtre** conducts an idiomatic performance, using the traditional score, with the climactic sextet as part of the Venice Act, which comes second in the sequence, leaving the Antonia Act till last and making the epilogue the briefest of afterthoughts.

Like the production, sets and costumes, the casting is lavish. **Luciana Serra** is bright and agile as the doll, Olympia, though edgy as recorded, while **Agnes Baltsa** is an imperious Giulietta in the Venice Act, tough and characterful with her tangy mezzo, and **Ileana Cotrubas** is charming and touching as Antonia. Among those outstanding in the character roles are **Geraint Evans** as Coppelius, **Robert Tear** as Spalanzani, and **Nicola Ghiuselev** as Dr Miracle. The sound is a little dry and is distracting in the context.

Filmed live in the handsome new opera house in Bilbao in 2006, the Opus Arte DVD offers a strong and colourful reading of Offenbach's last masterpiece with the tragic Antonia story left till last. The climactic *Septet* is included in the conventional place in the Venice scene. The conductor **Alain Guingal** does at least compensate by bringing the chorus and whole cast together at the end to provide a ringing conclusion. The production is set at the time of composition, towards the end of the 19th century, with good costumes but stylized, chunky sets, involving staircases and the use of drapes instead of a gondola in the Venice scene, but effective enough. As to the casting, **Aquiles Machado** sings powerfully and well-projected but, built to Pavarotti proportions, he is a totally unromantic figure. The Nicklaus of **Katharine Goeldner**, firm and true, and the Lindorf of **Konstantin Gorny**, who ably takes the bass parts through the opera, are both excellent. His *Scintille diamant* as Dappertutto makes a powerful climax. Sadly, the Olympia of **Milagros Poblador** is shrill and wobbly, not an attractive doll, though the glamorous **Valentina Kutzarove** as Giulietta and the touching Olympia of **Maria Bayo** (good, though not in her sweetest voice) are far preferable. **Marco Moncloa** is also memorable as an insect-like Schlemil in the Venice scene.

Les Contes d'Hoffmann (The Tales of Hoffmann; complete) (CD versions)

⊶ ❀ ******** Decca (ADD) 417 363-2 (2). Sutherland, Domingo, Tourangeau, Bacquier, R. Suisse Romande & Lausanne Pro Arte Ch., SRO, Bonynge

Ⓜ ****(*)** EMI 3 58613-2 (3). Shicoff, Murray, Serra, Plowright, Norman, Van Dam, Tear, Op. Nat. du Théâtre Royal de la Monnaie, Brussels Ch. & O, Cambreling

On Decca **Joan Sutherland** gives a virtuoso performance in four heroine roles, not only as Olympia, Giulietta and Antonia but also as Stella in the *Epilogue*. **Bonynge** opts for spoken dialogue, and puts the Antonia scene last, as being the more substantial. His direction is unfailingly sympathetic, while Sutherland is impressive in each role, notably as the doll Olympia and in the pathos of the Antonia scene. As Giulietta she hardly sounds like a *femme fatale*, but still produces beautiful singing. **Domingo** gives one of his finest performances on record, and so does **Gabriel Bacquier**. It is a memorable set, in every way, much more than the sum of its parts.

Cambreling's version broke new ground in opting for the complete text of Fritz Oser's edition, putting together nearly all the material which Offenbach failed to sort out before his untimely death. Here the expansions in the Venetian scene are attractive when the Giulietta is **Jessye Norman** and **Rosalind Plowright** brings extra – and satisfying – power to the Antonia episode without losing charm, and **Lucia Serra** is a bright, clear Olympia. **Neil Shicoff** as Hoffmann makes a confident Domingo-substitute (often sounding very like that model). **Ann Murray** is, as ever, a favourite Nicklaus, though the voice regularly loses focus above the stave. **José van Dam** sings with splendid firmness in the four villainous roles, if too nobly, while **Robert Tear** is excellent in the four character-tenor roles. EMI certainly does not sell anyone short, with no less than 214 minutes on the three discs and fine recording, but the Decca set manages with only two. There is a cued synopsis with a separate list of tracks.

Les Contes d'Hoffmann: highlights

⊶ Ⓜ ******* Decca (ADD) 458 234-2 (from above set, cond. Bonynge)

The Decca highlights disc is one of the finest sets of excerpts of its kind from any opera. With about 70 minutes of music, it offers a superbly managed distillation of nearly all the finest items and is edited most skilfully, including both the vocal and orchestral versions of the famous *Barcarolle*.

The Tales of Hoffmann (fairly complete; sung in English)

⊶ Ⓜ **(***)** Somm Beecham mono 13-2 (2). (Recording made for the soundtrack of the Michael Powell and Emeric Pressburger film) Rounseville, Bond, Grandi, Ayars, Dargavel, Sinclair, Brannigan, Clifford, Sadler's Wells Ch., RPO, Beecham (Includes Beecham at the piano, playing and singing through the score)

Somm have acquired the rights, not just to the Decca recording of the opera, but also to excerpts from **Beecham's** fascinating private introduction of the music to Michael Powell and Emeric Pressburger before the film was made.

None of the singers chosen by Beecham were famous, but all justified his confidence in them, and this new transfer brings plenty of bloom to their voices. **Robert Rounseville** is a warmly lyrical Hoffmann and, as one would expect, **Monica Sinclair** a superb Nicklaus, while **Dorothy Bond** makes a charmingly petite Olympia. **Margherita Grandi** may be a bit over the top in her sultry portrayal of Giulietta, but **Ann Ayars** is fully equal to the role of Antonia in the demanding final Act. The smaller parts are all characterfully sung, with **Grahame Clifford** excellent as both Spalanzani and Franz, and **Owen Brannigan** ready to change roles as Schlemil, Crespel and Hermann. But the surprise choice was Beecham's own discovery, **Bruce Dargavel**. He takes the three villanous roles, Coppelius, Dappertutto and Dr Miracle, and his richly resonant bass-baritone is wonderfully caught by the microphone in the celebrated *So Gleam with Desire* and of course in the finale. Franz's sole aria, *Day and Night I am Always Slaving*, included here, was cut from the film when the last Act was in danger of longueurs. In short this is very enjoyable indeed, for the words are crystal clear.

Les Fées du Rhin (opera; complete in German)

*** Accord 472 920-2 (3). Schörg, Gubisch, Beczala, Jenis, Klaveness, Pepper, R. Letton Ch., Montpellier Nat. O, Layer

Into *Les Fées du Rhin*, or *Die Rheinnixen*, Offenbach poured everything that embodied German romanticism: from ruined castles at midnight, to soldiers, hunters, village maidens, the Rhine, of course, with its water-sprites, pixies and elves, and even psychic shock is included! Add to this elements of French and Italian grand opera, and just about everything else you can think of, and the result is a Weber-cum-Offenbach mélange, and the opera includes plenty of splendid ensembles and vibrant choruses, as well as a delightful ballet and *grande valse*. The cast in this live 2002 recording is generally very good: the heroine, Armgard, sung by **Regina Schörg**, copes well with the coloratura passages. The hero, Franz, a light tenor, sung by **Piotr Beczala**, has an attractive voice, coping reasonably well in the high passages and singing with sensitivity when called for; he is well contrasted with the baritone of **Dalibor Jenis**, his rival, in splendid, full-blooded voice. Armgard's mother, Hedwig, sung by **Nora Gubisch**, is a fine mezzo, and the rest of the cast is good. That the whole thing works is a tribute to **Friedemann**

Layer, who draws an excellent response from his orchestra. The sound is very good, with very little noise from the audience, and full texts and translations are provided.

Orphée aux enfers (complete; 1858 version) (DVD version)

(*) Arthaus DVD 100 402. Badea, Vidal, Duesing, Macias, Jung, Quaille, Callatat, Théâtre de la Monnaie Ch. & O, Davin (Producer: Herbert Wernicke)

Although the Arthaus DVD performance, recorded in the Brussels Théâtre de la Monnaie in 1997, has been updated to the 20th century, the setting of Mount Olympus in the famous *fin-de-siècle* café La Mort Subite, with the gods wearing evening dress, ensures that there is less of a visual jolt of the kind which often affects modern productions of Offenbach. There are a few curiosities here which may irritate the DVD collector, notably the use of a honky-tonk piano in the finale of the Act I *Can-can*. However, the ensuing journey down to Hell, conveyed spectacularly by a steam train plummeting through the surface of Heaven into the Underworld, with great whooshes of steam, is considerable compensation.

The cast is a good one: **Alexandru Badea** is a younger, more ardent Orpheus than might be expected, but his well-focused tenor and convincing acting is certainly engaging, whilst his coquettish wife, Eurydice, is well characterized by **Elizabeth Vidal**, though her voice is less well caught by the microphones and is a little harsh at times. Both **Dale Duesing** and **Reinaldo Macias** in the roguish roles of Jupiter and Pluto sing with plenty of character. **André Jung's** drunken John Styx is amusing to watch – though it would be less of a pleasure just to hear – and most of the incidental parts are well done. The conducting is efficient rather than inspired. However, there is plenty to enjoy here and a good deal more so than in many recent productions of this work.

Orphée aux enfers (complete; 1858 version) (CD version)

**⊕─ **(*) EMI 5 56725-2 (2). Dessay, Beuron, Naouri, Fouchécourt, Lyons Nat. Op. O, Grenoble CO, Minkowski

The **Minkowski** version of Offenbach's first great success is based on the original 1858 version, with additions from the expanded 1874 score, including much of the delightful ballet music. Both the 'earthly' leads are superb: **Natalie Dessay's** secure, clear coloratura is well employed as the nagging wife, Eurydice, and one genuinely feels sorry for her hapless husband, Orphée, amiably characterized by **Yann Beuron**. **Jean Paul Fouchécourt** as Pluto oozes deceptive charm in his pastoral aria, though his true devilish character is revealed in some grotesque falsetto at the end, and Cupid's kissing song is charmingly sung by **Patricia Petibon**. From the opening bars, Minkowski's approach is apparent in the sparkling, crystal-clear textures, and he propels the opera along at a tremendous pace and with a bouncing rhythmic bite, matched by the exceptionally lively cast. The recording is superbly vivid and clear and adds to the immediacy of the drama.

La Périchole (complete)

⊕─ (M)*** Erato (ADD) 2292 45686-2 (2). Crespin, Vanzo, Bastin, Friedmann, Trigeau, Rhine Op. Ch., Strasbourg PO, Lombard

Though both **Régine Crespin** in the title-role and **Alain Vanzo** as her partner, Piquillo, were past their peak at that time, their vocal control is a model in this music, with character strongly portrayed but without any hint of vulgar underlining. Crespin is fresh and Vanzo produces heady tone in his varied arias, some of them brilliant. **Jules Bastin** is characterful too in the subsidiary role of Don Andres, Viceroy of Peru. **Lombard** secures excellent precision of ensemble from his Strasbourg forces, only occasionally pressing too hard. The recorded sound is vivid and immediate. A set of highlights is available at budget price (Apex 2564 61500-2).

Robinson Crusoe (sung in English)

⊕─ *** Opera Rara ORC 7 (3). Brecknock, Kenny, Kennedy, Hartle, Hill Smith, Oliver, Browne, Geoffrey Mitchell Ch., RPO, Francis

More ambitious than Offenbach's operettas, *Robinson Crusoe* offers a sequence of fresh and tuneful numbers with many striking ensembles. The plot is derived less from Daniel Defoe than from the British pantomime tradition. Characterization is strong and amusing, with a secondary couple shadowing Crusoe and his beloved Edwige. The casting is also from strength, with **John Brecknock** and **Yvonne Kenny** outstanding as Crusoe and Edwige, while Man Friday, as in the original Paris production, is sung by a mezzo, **Sandra Browne**. On the three discs are three hours of music, covering numbers which the composer cut even from the original production. The witty English translation, very freely adapted from the French text, with some changes of plot, is by Don White, and words are admirably clear.

La vie parisienne (complete; DVD version)

(N)** Virgin DVD 5193019. Bou, Callahan, Wesseling, Naouri, Canniccioni, Devellereau, Garcia, Lyon Nat. Op. Ch. & O, Rouland (V/D: François Roussillon; Dir: Laurent Pelly)

The problem with updating productions of Offenbach, such as here in *La vie parisienne*, is that it is like drinking champagne out of a plastic cup – the champagne makes its presence felt, but the taste has something odd about it. But the key factor is that the champagne comes through, and in this updated production to modern times, the zest and spirit of Offenbach are alive and well. **Jean-Sébastien Bou** and **Marc Callahan** make an entertaining Raoul de Gardefeu and Bobinet, and **Maria Riccarda Wesseling** as Métella is as commanding and sparkling. Her great bitter-sweet waltz aria was one of the best tunes Offenbach ever wrote. She comments on 'youth enjoying itself, singing at the top of its voice' and continues 'is it pleasure or is it fury . . . and when they no longer can, they'll keep silent, gaiety vanishes little by little . . . and that's how the party ends!' and it is as relevant today as it was in 1866. **Marie Devellereau** makes a delightful Gabrielle – a really nice character performance, and **Jesus Garcia** is wonderfully vulgar as the Brazilian, while all the smaller roles are very well done. Acts III and IV end in a suitable hedonistic whirl of intoxication. The orchestra plays with wit and style and one (almost) forgives the modern production, which, it has to be admitted, is very well done. There are little tableaux between the Acts which are quite amusing too, and we are even given a reprise of the can-can after the curtain calls – delightful.

Arias from: *Barbe-Blue; La Belle Hélène; Les Contes d'Hoffmann; La Grande-Duchesse de Gérolstein; Orphée aux Enfers; La Périchole; Pomme d'Api*

(N) **(*) Sony 8869 7234552. Kasarova, Bav. R. O, Schirmer

This is a decent enough collection of some of Offenbach's most famous arias and is well played and sung. In the last analysis, it lacks the last ounce of sparkle that makes Offenbach go with a swing, and excellent though **Vesselina Kasarova** is, she just misses being completely at home. There is plenty to enjoy, though. She is excellent in the *La Périchole*, not overdoing the drunken aria, 'Ah! Quel diner', which often happens. The result is much funnier when it is sung 'straight', as here. The *Overtures* to *La Grande-Duchesse* and *Barbe-Blue* are included and are well played, the former work offering one of Offenbach's most sparkling arias, 'Ah! Que j'aime les militaries', the latter some delightful rarities. The finale can-can from *Orphée aux Enfers* is certainly lively enough and Offenbachians will derive much pleasure from this recording. A pity texts were not included.

'The World of Offenbach': Overtures: (i; ii) *La Belle Hélène*; (iii; iv) *La Fille du tambour-major*; (i; ii) *Orpheus in the Underworld*; (iii; iv) *Le Papillon: Pas de deux* (excerpt); *Valse des rayons*; *Les Contes d'Hoffmann*: (v; i; iv) *Ballad of Kleinzach*; *O Dieu! De quelle ivresse*; (vi; i; iv) *Doll song*; (vi; vii; i; iv) *Barcarolle* (2 versions); *La Grande Duchesse de Gérolstein*: (viii–x) *Portez armes ... J'aime les militaires*; *La Périchole*: (viii; i; x) *O mon cher amant (Air de lettre)*; *Ah! quel dîner*; (vi; i; iv) *Robinson Crusoé: Conduisez-moi vers celui que j'adore (Waltz Song)*; (xi; iv) *Valse tyrolienne*

☛ ✹ (M) **** Decca ADD/DDD 452 942-2. (i) SRO; (ii) Ansermet; (iii) LSO; (iv) Bonynge; (v) Domingo; (vi) Sutherland; (vii) Tourangeau; (viii) Crespin; (ix) V. Volksopernorchester; (x) Lombard; (xi) Jo, ECO

This 'lucky-bag' of Offenbachian goodies which Decca have expanded for CD from the original LP selection is bursting with lollipops to make a marvellously entertaining 74 minutes. The programme now opens and closes with the *Barcarolle*. **Ansermet** and **Bonynge** offer much character in the overtures; even if the former takes the famous can-can which closes the *Orpheus* overture more slowly than usual, he invests it with much rhythmic vigour. Bonynge has another scintillating can-can to offer in *La Fille du tambour-major*, which opens with an arresting side-drum, and he now also includes two items from Offenbach's only ballet, *Le Papillon*. The various excerpts from Bonynge's complete *Contes d'Hoffmann* are matched by **Régine Crespin's** delightful contribution as *La Périchole*, and **Sutherland** returns to

sing the *Waltz Song* from *Robinson Crusoé*. The other additional item is **Sumi Jo's** sparkling *Valse tyrolienne*. With splendidly vivid recording this is an unmissable sampler, to match and even surpass 'The World of Borodin'.

ONSLOW, Georges (1784–1853)

Symphonies 1 – 4

(N) *** (1 & 3) CPO 999 747, N German R. Philh.; (2 & 4) CPO 999 738-2, Hannover PO; Goritzki (available separately)

Georges Onslow (a gifted pianist) originally came from an aristocratic English family who emigrated to the Auvergne in France, then, at the time of the French revolution, moved on to Hamburg, where the budding young musician studied with Dussek. In 1800 George moved safely back to the Auvergne where his desire to compose reasserted itself, and he studied under Antonin Reicha and, thus influenced, remained loyal to classicism for the rest of his career. He wrote four symphonies between 1831 and 1846, showing a natural melodic gift: they are never lacking in good ideas in all their four movements. While they are hardly profound works, they are thoroughly entertaining, and well worth investigating by anyone interested in rare symphonies. The performances and recordings are excellent.

Piano Trios, Op. 3/2; Op. 83

(N) *** CPO 777 231-2. Trio Cascades

String Quintets: in A min., Op. 34; G, Op. 35

(N) *** MDG 603 1253-2. Quintett Momento Musicale

Georges Onslow was one of the few French composers of his generation who wrote a substantial amount of chamber music. His quintets (and quartets) were published in his lifetime and reached a wide audience in their day. The disc of *Piano Trios* makes an admirable entry into his attractive musical world. The opening movement of Opus 83 has a particularly striking main theme; the movement (at 12 minutes 23 seconds) is impressively wrought and doesn't outlast its welcome, and there is a fine expressive *Adagio* to follow. The earlier Opus 3 *Quintet* is more lightweight, but each work offers four traditional classical movements, well crafted. With the excellent pianist **Thomas Palm** leading, the playing of the **Trio Cascades** is spontaneously appealing throughout.

The *String Quintets*, too, emerge as fresh, well-constructed pieces, unfailingly enjoyable. The *Adagio* movements are beautifully poised, while the lively outer movements have plenty of life – the *Presto* of Opus 35 is especially winning. The **Quintett Momento Musicale** have this music under their belts and their playing is seductive. Both CDs are very well recorded.

OPHICLEIDE

'Back from Oblivion' (Collection) includes:
PROCTOR: *Ophicleide Concerto: Adagio.*
DEMERSSEMAN: **Introduction & Polonaise.** ELGAR:

Romance, Op. 62. KUMMER: *5 Variations.*
RACHMANINOV: *Vocalise.* HANDEL: *O ruddier than the cherry.* GRIEG: *Ich liebe dich.* KLOSÉ: *Air Varié.*
PIAZZOLA: *Back from Oblivion*

(N) **** Melba MR 301111. Nick Byrne, David Miller (available from Melba Foundation, PO Box 415, Elwood, Victoria, Australia 3184; www.melbafoundation.org)

Yes, you are correct, Ophicleide is not the name of a composer, but of an 'obsolete' instrument. Berlioz and other composers scored for it, but it is best known (although now seldom used) to represent Bottom in Mendelssohn's *Midsummer Night's Dream Overture.* However, we attended a performance of Mendelssohn's *Elijah* recently in Berkhamsted, Herts, where a member of the orchestra played it to great effect.

It is a curious hybrid instrument, made of brass, but with keys on it, as on a bassoon or clarinet. Richard Bonynge has commented that it has 'a wonderfully plangent quality which stays with one and touches the heart'. Indeed, its uniquely fruity tone and rich bass notes in no way prevent it being played poetically, as is shown here by **Nick Byrne** (trombonist from the Sydney Symphony Orchestra) in the pieces by Grieg and Rachmaninov. The obvious demonstration item is Handel's '*O ruddier than the cherry*', for the ophicleide takes the role of Polyphemus with genial flair. Most impressive of all is the atmospheric *Back from Oblivion*, a memorable piece by Piazzola, which ends the recital. The CD comes beautifully packaged within a handsome stiff-covered booklet, including full documentation and colour photographs of the instrument being played.

ORFF, Carl (1895–1982)

O Fortuna! (film, by Tony Palmer)

Isolde Films **DVD** TP-DVD 118. Jones, Chilcott, Johnston, Hermann, Bav. RSO & Ch., Runnicles (Dir: Tony Palmer)

Tony Palmer's film about Carl Orff is typically revelatory. Not only does he demonstrate that Orff's work involved far more than *Carmina Burana* (much his most popular work), but that his relationship with the Nazi party was far more complex than has generally been thought. Orff accepted the need to go along with the Nazis, and actually accepted a monthly stipend of 1,000 marks in 1942. You could argue that anyone under a totalitarian regime has to play along with the system just to survive, but Orff would quite happily have accepted the role of Reichminister of music had he been offered it. Another aspect of his career that Palmer brings out vividly is the sequence of four wives he had, each related to an aspect of his composing career. One of the principal contributors to the film is Orff's daughter, Godela, who gives a fascinating insight into his household, emphasizing how daring it was for him to set a work in Latin, only to be triumphantly justified by the instant success of *Carmina Burana.* The film also emphasizes the positive work that Orff did for children, not only in *Schulwerk*, much valued by the Nazis for the Hitler Youth, but in his fascination with puppets. That Orff was justified in writing *Schulwerk* has been confirmed by its success outside Germany as an educational tool, and his sequence of operas, each related to one of his wives, makes up a substantial area of his achievement. A fascinating and moving portrait.

Carmina Burana (DVD version)

*** RCA **DVD** 74321 852859. Popp, Van Kesteren, Prey, Bavarian R. Ch., Munich R. O, Eichhorn (Video Producer: Jean-Pierre Ponnelle)

This fine RCA recording of *Carmina Burana*, conducted by **Kurt Eichhorn** with outstanding soloists in 1975, has been issued previously on CD, and here is treated to an imaginative staging for DVD by Jean-Pierre Ponnelle. The main background set is a ruined church against which the singers are seen in medieval costume, with action, sometimes surreal, invented to illustrate each section of the work, a technique which seems to anticipate the virtual reality of our digital age. So the roasted swan episode is introduced by a drunken monk, with a large swan in the background actually being roasted on a spit, and **Lucia Popp** in a medieval wimple looking and sounding enchanting. **Hermann Prey** is a superb baritone soloist, taking the main burden, and the choir is bright and lively. As a supplementary item comes a long interview with Orff himself – in German with English subtitles – in which he talks animatedly about key childhood experiences and how he came to write *Carmina Burana.*

Carmina Burana (CD versions)

🔊 (M) **** Ph. 464 725-2. Gruberová, Aler, Hampson, Shinyukai Ch., Knaben des Staats & Berlin Cathedral Ch., BPO, Ozawa

🔊 **** EMI (ADD) 5 66899-2. Armstrong, English, Allen, St Clement Danes Grammar School Boys' Ch., L. Symphony Ch., LSO, Previn

(N) 🔊 **** Chan. **SACD** CHSA 5067. Claycomb, Banks, Maltman, Tiffin Boys' Ch., L. Symphony Ch., LSO, Hickox

🔊 ✲ (BB) **** Sony (ADD) SBK 47668. Harsanyi, Petrak, Presnell, Rutgers University Ch., Phd. O, Ormandy

🔊 (BB) **** Naxos 8.570033. Rutter, Randle, Eiche, Bournemouth SO Ch., Youth Ch. and O, Alsop

(BB) *** Regis RRC 1136. Walmsley-Clark, Graham-Hall, Maxwell, Southend Boys' Ch., LSO Ch., LSO, Hickox

(B) *** RCA 09026 63981-2. Hendricks, Aler, Hagegård, St Paul's Cathedral Boys' Ch., L. Symphony Ch., LSO, Mata

Ozawa's recording of Orff's justly popular cantata carries all the freshness and spontaneity of his earlier successful Boston version. The *Cours d'amours* sequence is the highlight of his reading, with the soprano, **Edita Gruberová**, highly seductive; **Thomas Hampson's** contribution is also impressive. Ozawa's infectious rubato in *Oh, oh, oh, I am Bursting Out all Over*, interchanged between male and treble chorus towards the end of the work, is wonderfully bright and zestful, with the contrast of the big *Ave formossima* climax which follows made to sound spaciously grand. Taken overall, this Philips version holds its position near the top of the list alongside Ormandy, and it has the additional advantage of spectacular, demonstration-worthy, digital recording.

Previn's 1975 analogue version, vividly recorded, is even more sharply detailed than Ozawa's. It is strong on humour and rhythmic point. The chorus sings vigorously, the men often using an aptly rough tone; and the resilience of Previn's rhythms, finely sprung, brings out a strain not just of geniality but of real wit. Among the soloists, **Thomas Allen's** contribution is one of the glories of the music-making, and in their lesser roles the soprano and tenor are equally stylish. The digital remastering is wholly successful. This is now included among EMI's 'Great Recordings of the Century'.

There are many outstanding versions of *Carmina Burana*, but this live Chandos recording, directed with great flair by **Richard Hickox**, must go near the top of the list for its exhilaratingly spectacular, surround-sound recording, with the wide dynamic range making the very most of the Barbican acoustics. Hickox's pacing cannot be faulted, and there are many subtle dynamic touches; and the choral singing has such vigour and spontaneity that it is difficult to resist. The soloists are very good too, although **Christopher Maltman's** dusky baritone does not quite match Thomas Hampson's contribution to Ozawa's version or Thomas Allen's to Previn's. While **Laura Claycomb** sings tenderly in her soprano solo, she has a slightly intrusive vibrato when she makes her leap of submission. The **Tiffin Boys' Choir**, although very enthusiastic, does not quite match the eager knowing exuberance the boy trebles bring either to Previn's version or to Hickox's earlier recording with the Southern Boys' Choir. Nevertheless the impact of the Chandos recording is unforgettable.

Ormandy and his Philadelphians have just the right panache to bring off this wildly exuberant picture of the Middle Ages by the anonymous poets of former days, and there is no more enjoyable analogue version. It has tremendous vigour, warmth and colour and a genial, spontaneous enthusiasm from the **Rutgers University Chorus**, men and boys alike, that is irresistible. The soloists are excellent, but it is the chorus and orchestra who steal the show; the richness and eloquence of the choral tone is a joy in itself. This is quite splendid, one of Ormandy's most inspired recordings.

Marin Alsop also conducts a fine, distinctive reading of Carl Orff's most popular work, brilliantly recorded. The recording heightens the impact of the reading with its exceptionally wide dynamic range, so that *pianissimos* are hushed and intimate, set against great choral outbursts, with the **Bournemouth Chorus** and the **Youth Choirs** providing a powerful mainstay to the whole performance. Much the most important of the soloists is the baritone, here the dark, cleanly focused **Markus Eiche**, a great strength, while the tenor, **Tom Randle,** gives a delightful characterization in falsetto for the roast swan sequence, and **Claire Rutter** sings with perfect purity in the radiant soprano solos in the final section. A top bargain recommendation.

Richard Hickox, on his brilliantly recorded Regis CD, uses the **London Symphony Chorus** but adds the **Southend Boys' Choir**, which makes sure we know all about sexual abandon – their *Oh, oh, oh, I am Bursting Out all Over* is a joy. **Penelope Walmsley-Clark**, too, makes a rapturous contribu-

tion: her account of the girl in the red dress is equally delectable. The other soloists are good if less individual, but the chorus rises marvellously to climaxes, and the sharp articulation when the singers hiss out the words of *O Fortuna* in the closing section is a highlight. The documentation provides a vernacular narrative for each band, which works well enough when there is no translation. A most successful disc in every way.

Mata's splendid 1980 digital recording now comes at super-bargain price and is highly recommendable on all counts. It is a joyously alive and volatile reading, not as metrical in its rhythms as most; this means that at times the **London Symphony Chorus** is not as clean in ensemble as it is for Previn. The choristers of St Paul's Cathedral sing with purity and enthusiasm but are perhaps not boyish enough, though the soloists are first rate (with **John Aler** coping splendidly, in high, refined tones, with the Roast Swan episode). There is fine warmth of atmosphere and no lack in the lower range; indeed in almost every respect the sound is superb. This is unbeatable value for those wanting a bargain-priced version.

Carmina Burana; Catulli Carmina

Ⓑ *** Sony (ADD) 516026-2 (2). Soloists, Ch., Phd. O, Ormandy

If you want both the fine **Ormandy** performances, they are available together on this two-CD set, costing slightly less than the individual discs but including less music.

Catulli Carmina

Ⓑ **(*) Sony (ADD) SBK 61703. Blegen, Kness, Temple University Ch., Phd. O, Ormandy – STRAVINSKY: *Symphony of Psalms* ***

The exotic colours and rhythmic ostinatos are well brought out by the **Temple University Choir**, and **Ormandy's** vigorous performance produces an altogether rougher experience than Welser-Möst's version, for all the virtuosity of the players and singers. But the bluff humour of the piece comes out boldly. The 1967 recording is generally good, a little thin by modern standards, particularly at the top end, but nothing too serious. An undoubted CD bargain with the excellent Stravinsky coupling.

OPERA

(i) Die Kluge; (ii) Der Mond

Ⓜ *** EMI (ADD) 7 63712-2 (2). (i) Cordes, Frick, Schwarzkopf, Wieter, Christ, Kusche; (ii) Christ, Schmitt-Walter, Graml, Kuen, Lagger, Hotter; Philh. Ch. & O, Sawallisch

Sawallisch's pioneering Orff recordings of the mid-1950s are vivid and immediate on CD, with such effects as the thunderbolt in *Der Mond* impressive still. **Elisabeth Schwarzkopf** is characterful and dominant as the clever young woman of the title in *Die Kluge*. It is good too to hear such vintage singers as **Gottlob Frick** and **Hans Hotter** in unexpected roles. Musically, these may not be at all searching works, but both short operas provide easy, colourful entertainment, with Sawallisch drawing superb playing from the **Philharmonia**. Full texts are provided, and the discs are very generously banded.

PACHELBEL, Johann
(1653–1706)

Canon and Gigue in D; Partita (Suite) 6 in B flat; Suite in G

(BB) ** Warner Apex 0927 49980-2. Paillard CO, Paillard –
FASCH: *Concerto; Symphonies* **(*)

Pachelbel's famous baroque lollipop is given a warm, nicely paced performance, which brings out its noble progress admirably, but the pair of suites (containing the usual introduction – here brief – plus groups of dances) offers writing that is amiable but no more than that, although two *Sarabandes* are agreeably expressive. Good playing and pleasing sound, but this is not memorable music like the *Canon*.

Aria tertia (with 6 variations); Chorale Partita: Was Gott tut, das ist wohlgeten; 6 Chorale Preludes; Ciacona in F min.; Fugues: in C & D min.; Magnificat octavi toni; Prelude in D min.; Ricerars in C & C min.; 2 Toccatas in C

⊙– **** Oehms SACD OC 613. Kelemen (organs of St Petri, Erfurt- Büssleben & Klosterkirche, Pappenheim)

Every year the remarkably fine organist **Joseph Kelemen** sets off on an instrumental pilgrimage to discover new organs and, where possible, the associated composers. He then makes a CD for his record company, now Oehms, and phones us, later following up with the CD itself. Again this year he has been able to make his recording in surround sound, and the result is thrillingly realistic. This recording could not be more authentic, and in the robust opening *Prelude in D minor*, the fine *Ciacona in F minor*, the *Aria tertia and variations* and the impressive closing *Toccata in F* Kelemen demonstrates the organ's range of colour and power. When playing the CD through, the ear registers the difference as we move from the end of the *Chorale Partita* (track 25) to the reedy *Chorale Prelude* (on track 26) as Kelemen moves from Pappenheim to Büssleben.

PACINI, Giovanni (1796–1867)

Alessandro nelle India (complete)

*** Opera Rara ORC 35. Ford, Larmore, Claycomb, Mitchell Ch., LPO, Parry

Pacini, born in 1796, lived until 1867; but this, like most of his operas, dates from early in his career, a work built on strong material, here beautifully performed by a first-rate cast under **David Parry**. The team of women is particularly strong, with **Jennifer Larmore** radiant. Only the tenor **Bruce Ford** falls below the beauty and mellifluousness of the women singers, with a slightly gritty delivery. Excellent sound.

Maria, Regina d'Inghilterra (complete)

*** Opera Rara ORC 15. Miricioiu, Ford, Fardilha, Plazas, Miles, Bickley, Geoffrey Mitchell Ch., Philh. O, Parry

With an outstanding cast, full, well-balanced recording and powerful, well-paced conducting, this long-neglected opera about Mary Tudor emerges as a surprisingly strong and enjoyable piece, far finer than most conventional Ottocento operas from the contemporaries of Donizetti and Bellini. The admittedly improbable story is loosely based on a Victor Hugo play, centring on the love of Mary for Fenimoore (high tenor), her scheming favourite, also loved by Clotilde, who in turn is loved and protected by Ernesto (baritone). Add to that the Chancellor (bass), who is determined to unmask Fenimoore's evil-doing, and you have an operatic plot that gives ample scope for confrontation in duets and ensembles, skilfully and imaginatively exploited by Pacini.

Nelly Miricioiu sings with warmth and character as the suffering Queen, not least in her final agonized aria on Fenimoore's execution. She is well contrasted with the lighter **Mary Plazas** as Clotilde, with **José Fardilha** as Ernesto, distinctive with his flickering vibrato. **Alastair Miles** sings powerfully as the Chancellor, but it is the prowess of **Bruce Ford** in the demanding role of Fenimoore that more than anything holds the piece together, from his first evocative off-stage entry in Act I. **David Parry** draws strong, idiomatic playing from the Philharmonia, with the **Geoffrey Mitchell Choir** intensifying the big ensembles.

PACIUS, Fredrik (1809–91)

The Princess of Cyprus

*** BIS CD-1340. Wentzel, Åman, Eichenholz, Rantanen, Storgård, Jubilate Ch., Tapiola Sinf., Söderblom

Pacius is 'the father of Finnish music'. Even Sibelius paid tribute: 'Everything we musicians do here now is based on the life's work of Fredrik Pacius.' *The Princess of Cyprus* has been variously described as a Singspiel and sometimes even as an opera, but it is more accurately billed here as 'incidental music to Topelius's play'. In this version the plot is summarized and spoken by a narrator. For all his undoubted importance as a pioneering and inspiring force in Finland's musical life, Pacius's music is not in the least Finnish or Nordic in character, nor is the idiom particularly individual. The musical language is indebted to Weber, Spohr and Mendelssohn, and the texture is beautifully transparent. But what it lacks in individuality, it makes up for in charm, and both performance and recording are excellent.

PAER, Ferdinando (1771–1839)

Sofonisba (highlights)

*** Opera Rara ORR 237. Larmore, Evans, Nilon, Palazzi, Lee, Geoffrey Mitchell Ch., Philh. O, Guidarini

In their search for rare 19th-century operas, Opera Rara have lighted on some operas which seem best suited to 'highlight' recordings. This collection illustrates the point, with a complete libretto provided as well as comprehensive notes to let the listener place each selected item. Paer, a close contemporary of Beethoven, is here represented by *Sofonisba*, an opera first heard in Bologna in 1805. It was inspired by Roman history, involving the Consul, Scipione, as well as Siface and his wife Sofonisba and her former lover, Massinissa. As in other issues in this admirable series the clear mezzo of **Jennifer Larmore**, most impressive in her opening martial aria with chorus, is well contrasted with the glowing soprano of **Rebecca Evans**, fresh, pure and agile, an artist whose voice is ideally suited to recording. She is represented here not only by a fine aria, but also in the impressive series of big ensembles, all of them richly justifying Opera Rara's advocacy. Well-balanced sound.

PAGANINI, Niccolò (1782–1840)

Violin Concertos 1–6; 24 Caprices, Op. 1; Duo merveille; Introduction & Variations on 'Di tanti palpiti' from Rossini's Tancredi; Introduction & Variations on 'Nel cor più non mi sento' from Paisiello's La molinara; Maestoso sonata sentimentale; Perpetuela; La primavera; Sonata with Variations on a Theme by Joseph Weigl; Sonata Napoleone; Le streghe (Variations on a Theme by Süssmayr), Op. 8; Variations on 'God Save the King'; Variations on 'Non più mesta' from Rossini's La Cenerentola

(B) **** DG 463 754-2 (6). Accardo, LPO, Dutoit

(B) *** DG 437 210-2 (Violin Concertos 1–6 only)

A self-recommending set. The **Accardo/Dutoit** Paganini cycle remains a secure first choice: the *Concertos* are brilliantly and imaginatively played and well recorded. Indeed, these accounts do not fall down in any department. The individual discs are contained in an excellently packaged DG bargain box. There is also a 3-CD set with just the six concertos.

Violin Concerto 1 in D, Op. 6

⊕ (M) **** EMI (ADD) 5 62594-2. Perlman, RPO, Foster – SARASATE: *Carmen Fantasy*, etc. ****

⊕ **** DG 429 786-2. Shaham, NYPO, Sinopoli – SAINT-SAËNS: *Concerto 3* ***

*** DG 477 6232. Hahn, Swedish RSO, Oue – SPOHR: *Violin Concerto 8* ***

*** Decca Australian Eloquence 476 748-8. Belkin, Israel PO, Mehta (with TCHAIKOVSKY: *Valse-Scherzo*) – R. STRAUSS: *Violin Concerto* **(*)

(M) **(*) Warner Elatus 2564 60013-2. Vengerov, Israel PO, Mehta – SAINT-SAËNS: *Havanaise; Introduction & Rondo Capriccioso* ***; WAXMAN: *Carmen Fantasy* **(*)

Perlman's famous 1971 recording returns at mid-price in the 'Perlman Edition', with two extra Sarasate items added. Provided one does not feel strongly about the traditional cuts in the Paganini, this performance remains unsurpassed. He demonstrates a fabulously clean and assured technique

and, with the help of the EMI engineers, he produces a gleamingly rich tone, free from all scratchiness. **Lawrence Foster** matches the soloist's warmth with an alive and buoyant orchestral accompaniment.

Gil Shaham's technical ease in the histrionics of Paganini's stratospheric tessitura, harmonics and all, is breathtaking, and he can phrase an Italianate lyrical melody – and there are some good ones in this *Concerto* – with disarming charm and ravishing timbre.

A fine new account from **Hilary Hahn**, who revels unostentatiously but with easy brilliance in the work's bravura, yet tickles the ear with the first movement's beguiling lyrical melody.

Boris Belkin recorded the *Concerto* without cuts in 1977 and played it splendidly. He has a marvellous command of his instrument, plus a sweet and appealing tone, and he plays with much aplomb. The Decca recording is spectacular, one of the finest made in the Mann Auditorium in Tel Aviv.

Maxim Vengerov gives a strongly extrovert account, egged on by **Mehta**, whose fast opening tutti sets the scene without poise. In spite of this, however, the solo contribution has much warmth and some infectious fireworks in the finale.

Violin Concertos 1; 2 in B min. (La campanella), Op. 7

⊕ (BB) **** Naxos 8.550649. Kaler, Polish Nat. RSO, Gunzenhauser

Ilya Kaler is fully equal to Paganini's once-devilish technical demands and the phrasing of warm Italianate melody. In every respect his technique is commandingly secure.

Violin Concertos 1; 4 in D min.

⊕ **** Pentatone Surround Sound SACD PTC 5186178. Szeryng, LSO, Gibson

A famous coupling from 1973, originally recorded in quadraphony, emerges here sounding remarkably real and vivid. No. 1 is somewhat cut (as was common at the time). **Szeryng** plays with his accustomed brilliance and mastery, and in both concertos **Alexander Gibson** (without the 'Sir' on the original CD credits) is a sympathetic accompanist.

Violin Concertos 3 in E; 4 in D min.

(BB) **(*) Naxos 8.554396. Rózsa, Slovak RSO, Dittrich

Ernö Rózsa is a first-class soloist, fully equal to all Paganini's pyrotechnical demands, and on his bow the characteristic cantabile tunes (often over pizzicato accompaniments) sing out very winningly. He also plays his own cadenzas, which are perhaps rather too much of a good thing when these two *Concertos* are quite long enough already!

CHAMBER MUSIC

Allegro di concert (Moto perpetuo) in C, Op. 11; Cantabile in D, Op. 17; Centone si sonate: in D; in A, Op. 64/2 & 4; Guitar & Violin Sonatas: in A; A min.; E min., Op. 3/1, 4 & 6; Grand Sonata for Violin &

Guitar in A, Op. posth.; Sonata concertata in A, Op. 61; Sonata a preghiera (arr. Hannibal)

🎵— *** DG 437 837-2. Shaham, Söllscher

The atmosphere of much of this repertoire is comparatively intimate, something these artists readily appreciate, and their playing is immaculate and amiably easy-going. Perhaps at times here the style of performance could with advantage have been more extrovert, but the present hour-long recital will make attractive late-evening entertainment (not taken all at once, of course). The recording has a realistic balance and fine presence.

24 Caprices, Op. 1

🎵— Ⓜ **** EMI 5 67237-2 [567257]. Perlman

Ⓜ *** EMI 5 67986-2 [567998]. Rabin

Ⓝ Ⓜ *** Decca 477 7560. Mintz

🅱🅱 *** Naxos 8.550717. Kaler

*** Telarc CD 80398. Ehnes

Perlman's superbly played 1972 set now returns to the catalogue at mid-price as one of EMI's 'Great Recordings of the Century'. The transfer is immaculate, the violin image very real and vivid, and this can now be recommended without reservation.

Michael Rabin's consistent and astonishing dexterity is heard at its most electrifying in *No. 5 in A minor*, his sure sense of rhythmic style in *No. 9 in E major* and his delicious glissandi in *No. 13*, while he plays the most famous closing number with assured panache. His impeccable technique informs the whole set, and he is most vividly recorded.

There are many breathtaking things to admire in **Shlomo Mintz's** 1982 version, and plenty of colour and life in the set as a whole. He is recorded with admirable clarity and definition, though the overall effect is not as warm as Perlman's account which, if anything, is more dazzling. *No. 17 in E flat* is one example when one could wish that he had not been in quite so much of a hurry. On the other hand others, such as the *F major, No. 22*, could hardly be improved on.

Those looking for a bargain will surely not be disappointed with the Russian fiddler, **Ilya Kaler**, on Naxos. A pupil of Leonid Kogan, his playing is technically very assured, the lyrical bowing vibrant in a Slavic way, and he projects a strong profile. The 1992 Naxos recording is truthful and real.

James Ehnes is Juilliard-trained and has technique to burn. He tosses off these pieces with great bravura and aplomb. His playing has real personality, even if others have managed to find greater subtlety and delicacy. All the same, there is much to relish in his youthful ardour and the splendid sound the Telarc engineers give us.

Caprice 24, Op. 1/24; Grand Sonata in A

🅱🅱 *** Sony (ADD) SBK 62425. Williams (guitar) – GIULIANI: *Variations on a Theme by Handel*; D. SCARLATTI: *Sonatas*; VILLA-LOBOS: *5 Preludes* ***

John Williams is in excellent form in the *Grand Sonata*, with its charming central *Romanza* and ingenuous closing

Andantino variato (originally a duo for guitar and violin), and the famous *Caprice*, for violin solo, both arranged by Williams. The recording is only marginally balanced too forwardly and is otherwise truthful. Most enjoyable.

PALESTRINA, Giovanni Pierluigi da (1525–94)

Ad Dominum cum tribularer; Ad te levavi oculos meos; Alma redemptoris; Dum complerentur; Magnificat & Nunc dimittis; Recordare; Stabat Mater; Veni sancte spiritus; Victimae paschali

🎵— Ⓜ **** CRD (ADD) CRD 3519. New College, Oxford, Ch., Higginbottom

A particularly satisfying and beautiful collection of motets and canticles from the **New College Choir** singing with glorious, yet restrained feeling under **Edward Higginbottom**. The programme is arranged to give the kind of contrast that Palestrina himself achieves between the paired Vespers and Compline canticles, *Magnificat* and *Nunc dimittis*. Higginbottom and his choir achieve their contrasts in sound without attempting extreme left–right effects, and their recording engineer, Mike Clements, has produced a full, relatively homogeneous, yet detailed sound picture in the Chapel, which is very telling when all these works are texturally so rich and often radiant, as at the opening of *Ad te levavi oculos meos*.

Ardens est cor meum; Congratulamini mihi omnes; Crucem santam subiit; Crux fidelis; Fratres, ego enim accepi; Dominus Jesus; Haec Dies a 6; Improperium; Magnificat terti toni a 6 (with Plainsong: Et respicientes); Popule meus; Pueri Hebraeorum (with introductory Plainsong: Hosanna filio David); O Domine, Jesu Christe a 6; Stabat Mater a 8; Terra tremuit; Victimae paschali laudes a 6

🎵— **** ASV Gaudeamus CDGAU 333. Cardinall's Musick, Carwood

Beautifully recorded in the Fitzalan Chapel of Arundel Castle, this outstanding collection is yet another example of the sublime singing of the **Cardinall's Musick**, directed by **Andrew Carwood**, in this case a well-planned programme of Palestrina's beautiful music for Holy Week.

Mass & Motet: Assumpta est Maria; Motets: Ave Maria; Beata es, Virgo Maria; Hodie gloriosa semper Virgo Maria; Regina coeli; Magnificat septimi toni

Ⓝ 🅱🅱 *** EMI Encore 2 08120-2. Clare College, Cambridge, Ch., Timothy Brown

This an exceptionally well-chosen bargain collection, mainly of shorter works, but also including the splendid *Missa Assumpta est Maria*. The programme ends with an equally fine *Magnificat* setting. We are familiar with the excellent **Clare College Choir** and their rich sound (partly achieved by using women's voices) from earlier recordings directed by John Rutter. The EMI début CD introduces a new conductor, **Timothy Brown**, and the choir responds expressively to his melismatic direction in the beautiful opening motet with which the Mass is associated. The choir is beautifully recorded, and the only minor criticism is the relatively restricted dynamic range, which may partly be caused by the microphone placing, but which certainly reduces the dynamic contrast of the singing. But this remains a thoroughly worthwhile bargain disc, although it is a pity that the documentation has so little to say about the music.

Missa Ave Maria in 6 parts; Missa Brevis; Missa Hodie Christus natus est; Missa Papae Marcelli; Motets: Ave Maria; Canita tuba; Hodie Christus natus est; Jubilate Deo; O magnum mysterium; Tui sunt caeli

(N) (BB) **(*) EMI Gemini 2 17655 (2). King's College, Cambridge, Ch., Ledger; Willcocks

Palestrina wrote two *Ave Maria Masses*, neither of which was published in his lifetime: the present work did not appear in the original book of six-part Masses of 1594 but was included two years later. The merit of the recording here is in the inclusion of the plainchant of the *Introit, Gradual* and so on, that lends perspective to this Mass. The chant is sung with impressive restraint and a sense of space, and the acoustic is heard to good advantage, the recording superbly atmospheric, but with splendid clarity of texture too. **Philip Ledger** also directs colourful, dramatic readings of both Palestrina's magnificent eight-part *Missa Hodie Christus natus est* and six motets, including the one directly related to the Mass. With two choirs set in contrast and cross-rhythms sharply brought out, the joyfulness of Palestrina's inspiration is irresistibly conveyed. The *Missa Papae Marcelli*, with its apparent simplicity of line and serene beauty which disguises an underlying fervour, is not a work which lends itself readily to performers with an Anglican background. This and the *Missa brevis* receive smooth, limpid performances, well recorded. The singing style is direct and unmannered; but although the control of dynamic is impressive the inner mystery of the music is not readily conveyed.

Canticum canticorum Salomonis (Book 4 of motets for 5 voices from the Song of Songs)

⊕–ヿ (BB) *** Hyp. Helios CDH 55095. Pro Cantione Antiqua, Turner

The *Canticum canticorum Salomonis* is one of Palestrina's most sublime and expressive works, possibly wider in its range than anything else he composed, and certainly as deeply felt. The ten members of the **Pro Cantione Antiqua** under **Turner** bring an appropriate eloquence and ardour, tempered by restraint. They are accorded an excellently balanced and natural-sounding recording.

Lamentations of Jeremiah, Book 3 (complete)

⊕–ヿ **** Hyp. CDA 67610. Westminster Cathedral Ch., Baker
*** Chan. 0652. Musica Contexta, Ravens (with Vexilla regis)

This is the third Book of Palestrina's settings for Maundy Thursday, Good Friday and Holy Saturday, very beautifully

sung at Westminster Cathedral and superbly recorded. The variety of the music is much wider than one might have expected, and in Lectio III for Good Friday (*Adeph. Ego vir videns paupertatem meam*) the trebles soar up into the heavens ecstatically.

Simon Ravens and his **Musica Contexta** draw on both existing manuscripts with scholarly and eminently musical understanding. At the end of the service, the hymn *Vexilla regis* marked the recession from the Sistine Chapel, and it is used to close the performance here.

Lamentations and Responsories for Holy Saturday, Book 3, 1–3; Benedictus for Holy Week; Sicut cervus; Stabat Mater

*** Chan. 0679. Musica Contexta, Ravens

In his perceptive note **Simon Ravens** points out that Holy Saturday has inevitably tended to be overshadowed in the church calendar by the days immediately before and after, Good Friday and Easter Day. Yet in this fine collection, superbly performed by his group, **Musica Contexta**, and vividy recorded, he demonstrates what inspired music Palestrina wrote for this in-between occasion. More than usual, Palestrina's polyphony here has a biting edge, beautifully achieved in this performance. The *Stabat Mater* for double choir, one of Palestrina's best-loved works, follows up in its dedication, leading to the *Benedictus for Easter Saturday* and finally to the motet *Sicut cervus*, which prepares the way as a concluding liturgical act for the celebrations of the following day.

Lamentations of Jeremiah, Book 4 (complete)

⊕–ヿ (BB) *** Regis RRC 1038. Pro Cantione Antiqua, Turner

Many composers have set the Lamentation Lessons for the Tenebrae services on Maundy Thursday, Good Friday and Holy Saturday but, remarkably, Palestrina did so on five different occasions. The music has a serene but poignant simplicity, which **Bruno Turner** captures admirably with spacious tempi. The concentration is obvious and the quality of the singing from a group of eight (including several famous names) is of a high order. So is the recording, which is very well balanced in the warm acoustic of St Alban's Church, Brook Street, London.

MASSES

'The Essential Palestrina': Missa Assumpta est Maria (with Plainchant: Assumpta est Maria). Motet: Assumpta est Maria. Missa brevis; Missa Papae Marcelli; Missa Sicut lilium inter spinas. Motet: Sicut lilium inter spinas

⊕–ヿ (B) **** Gimell (ADD/DDD) CDGIM 204 (2). Tallis Scholars, Phillips

This highly recommendable and well-documented box joins together two CDs recorded by the **Tallis Scholars** between 1981 and 1989. As is their practice, this group records the *Masses* together with the motets on which they are based, even if they are by other composers. Their account of the most famous of Palestrina's works, the *Missa Papae Marcelli*, brings a characteristically eloquent performance.

Missa Assumpta est Maria (including Gregorian Chant Proper for the Feast of the Assumption); Missa Papae Marcelli

🎵 **(BB)** **** Regis RRC 1025. Pro Cantione Antiqua, M. Brown

Mark Brown and his **Pro Cantione Antiqua** give accounts of these celebrated pieces that aspire to total authenticity in that the forces used are those Palestrina himself would have known: no boys' voices, no women and just one-to-a-part, with the mass sections interspersed with plainchant. The Pro Cantione Antiqua sing with eloquence and power against the background of a resonant acoustic. The mid-1980s recording is splendidly balanced. Whatever other versions you might have of either work, this has special claims, and its outward severity does not preclude depth of feeling – rather the reverse.

Missa de Beata Virgine I (1567)

(BB) *** Naxos 8.553313. Soloists of the Cappella Musicale di S. Petronio di Bologna, Vartolo

Sergio Vartolo, the director of the **Cappella Musicale di S. Petronio di Bologna**, has sought to place the *Mass* within a liturgical sequence recalling early performance traditions. Thus it opens with the plainchant introit *Gaudeamus omnes in Domino* (intended for a major feast of the Virgin Mary) and after the *Gloria* comes a Gradual and an organ paraphrase of the hymn *Ave maris stella* (by Girolamo Cavazzoni), very well played by Vartolo himself. Then comes the plainchant *Alleluia* and, following the *Credo*, the Gregorian Offertory, *Beata ex Virgo Maria*, which leads on to the *Sanctus*; the communion verse precedes Palestrina's very beautiful double *Agnus Dei*. The performance has striking character and powerful devotional feeling and is very well recorded in the Church of St Zeno, Cavalo, Verona.

Missa: Benedicta es (with Plainchant)

🎵 **(B)** *** Gimell GIMSE (DDD/AAD) 402. Tallis Scholars, Phillips (with JOSQUIN DESPREZ: *Motet Benedicta es*)

It would seem that this Mass was the immediate predecessor of the *Missa Papae Marcelli* and was composed while the music of *Benedictus* was still at the forefront of the composer's mind. Palestrina's *Missa Benedicta es*, coupled with the Josquin motet, *Benedicta es*, on which it is based, is here a bargain reissue to celebrate the 25th anniversary of the formation of the **Tallis Scholars**, with the *Missa Nasce la gioia mia* included as a special bonus. The performances are exemplary, and full documentation is included to make this a genuine bargain.

Missa dum complerentur. Motet: Dum complerentur. Magnificat sexti toni; Spiritus Sanctus replevit totam domum; Veni Creator Spiritus: Veni Sancte Spiritus (Alleluia, Sequence & Motet)

🎵 *** Hyp. CDA 67353. Westminster Cathedral Ch., Baker

Baker here reinforces his reputation and that of the choir

in fresh, energetic accounts of music by Palestrina celebrating Pentecost. The disc starts with the magnificent motet *Dum complerentur*, with its vivid portrayal of the rushing of winds. The magnificent parody *Mass* based on that motet, which Palestrina wrote some 30 years later, follows naturally, and so do three brilliant motets in eight voices, as well as the glorious *Magnificat sexti toni* with its graphic illustrations of the Virgin's prayer.

Missa Ecce ego Johannes; Cantantibus organis; Laudate pueri; Magnificat quarti toni; Peccantem me quotidie; Tribulationes civitatum; Tu es Petrus

🎵 **** Hyp. CDA 67099. Westminster Cathedral Ch., O'Donnell

Even among the **Westminster Cathedral Choir's** superb records this disc stands out. Perfect chording and ensemble, natural and musical phrasing, spot-on intonation and a glorious tonal blend, make this issue one to treasure. The recording serves the choir well and there are scholarly notes by Ivan Moody.

Missa Hodie Christus natus est. Motet: Hodie Christus natus est. Stabat Mater

🎵 **(BB)** **** Naxos 8.550836. Oxford Schola Cantorum, Summerly – LASSUS: *Missa Bell' Amfitrit' alterna* ***

Where in their account of Palestrina's *Missa Aeterna Christi munera* **Summerly's** group are restrained in their devotional manner, this celebrated Mass for Christmas has them joyful and exuberant. The choir, over 30 strong, brings out both the beauty and the drama of the writing, and equally so in the brief motet setting the Christmas words. The magnificent *Stabat Mater* is wisely given to a smaller group of 16 singers, two to a part, with added clarity in the complex polyphony. Well coupled with one of Lassus's best-loved Masses, Palestrina's close contemporary from Flanders, this CD represents the work of two supreme polyphonic masters who died in the same year.

Missa Hodie Christus natus est. Motets: Alma redemptoris mater; Canite tube; Deus tu converses; Christus, redemptor omnium; Hodie Christus natus est; Magnificat Primi toni; O admirabile commercium; O magnum mysterium; Tui sunt coeli

🎵 **** Hyp. CDA 67396. Westminster Cathedral Ch., Baker

Vividly set against the cathedral acoustic, warm but clear, this performance of the Christmas music brings out better than most rival versions the exuberance of the cries of 'Noe' (Noel) that dramatically punctuate the piece, reflecting individual joy in welcoming the birth of Christ. The eight other items, all relating to Advent and Christmas, culminate in the *Magnificat Primi toni* with its rich textures, framed before and after by the plainsong antiphon, *Hodie Christus natus est*.

Missa: Nasce la gioia mia; Missa brevis (with PRIMAVERA: Madrigal: Nasce la gioia mia)

*** Gimell CDGIM 008. Tallis Scholars, Phillips

The *Missa: Nasce la gioia mia* is a parody Mass, modelled on the madrigal, *Nasce la gioia mia* by Giovan Leonardo Primavera. The **Tallis Scholars** and **Peter Phillips** give expressive, finely shaped accounts of both the *Missa brevis* and the *Mass*, which they preface by the madrigal itself. A most rewarding disc: no grumbles about the recording.

Missa: Nigra sum (with Motets on Nigra sum by L'HERITIER; VICTORIA; DE SILVA)

⊕┐ *** Gimell CDGIM 003. Tallis Scholars, Phillips

Palestrina's *Missa: Nigra sum* is another parody Mass, based on a motet by Jean L'Heritier, and follows its model quite closely; its text comes from the Song of Solomon. On this record, the plainchant and the L'Heritier motet precede Palestrina's *Mass*, plus motets by Victoria and Andreas de Silva, a relatively little-known Flemish singer and composer who served in the Papal chapel and later in Mantua. The music is inspiring and the performances exemplary. This is a most beautiful record and the acoustic of Merton College, Oxford, is ideal.

Missa Papae Marcelli; Alma redemptoris Mater; Magnificat 1 toni; Nunc dimittis; Stabat Mater; Surge illuminare

(*) Gimell CDGIM 994-2. Tallis Scholars; Phillips (with ALLEGRI: *Miserere* *)

Missa Papae Marcelli; Missa brevis

⊕┐ *** Hyp. CDA 66266. Westminster Cathedral Ch., Hill

Missa Papae Marcelli; Stabat Mater; Tu es Petrus

**** Gimell CDGIM 041. Tallis Scholars, Phillips – ALLEGRI: *Miserere* ***

David Hill and the **Westminster Cathedral Choir** give an imposing and eloquent *Missa Papae Marcelli* that many collectors may prefer to the finely sung Gimell issue from the Tallis Scholars. They, too, have the advantage of a spacious acoustic and excellent recording.

For their second, digital recording, the **Tallis Scholars** were recorded in the Basilica of Maria Maggiore in Rome, where Palestrina was a choirboy and, later, master of the choristers. The most celebrated of Palestrina's Masses, *Missa Papae Marcelli*, receives as eloquent a performance as any in the catalogue. The Tallis Scholars have wonderful fluidity and the sense of movement never flags in this finely tuned, well-paced reading. Much the same goes for the remaining motets here and, of course, for the Allegri *Miserere*, which had a unique association with the Sistine Chapel. As the recording was made before an audience, there is applause, which is quite inappropriate and very tiresome. In every other respect this is a first-class issue and can be warmly recommended.

For their third (2006) recording of the *Missa Papae Marcelli*, the **Tallis Scholars** have returned to England and Merton College, Oxford. These pieces are beautifully sung, but the Rome performance is even more inspired.

Missa Veni sponsa Christi (with Motet)

Ⓑ **(*) CfP 575 5602. St John's College, Cambridge, Ch.,

Guest – ALLEGRI: *Miserere*; LASSUS: *Missa super Bell' Amfitrit' altera'* **(*)

Every section of the *Veni sponsa Christi Mass* is introduced by the same idea with much subtle variation, and this impressive work ends with two *Agnus Dei* settings, the second with an additional tenor part. It receives an eloquent, imaginatively detailed and finely shaped performance here, and the relative restraint of the Anglican choral tradition suits Palestrina's flowing counterpoint better than it does the Lassus Venetian coupling.

COLLECTIONS

Hodie Beata Virgo; Litaniae de Beata Virgine Maria in 8 parts; Magnificat in 8 parts (Primi toni); Senex puerum portabat; Stabat Mater

Ⓜ *** Decca (ADD) 466 373-2. King's College Ch., Willcocks – ALLEGRI: *Miserere* ***

The flowing melodic lines and serene beauty which are the unique features of Palestrina's music are apparent throughout this programme, and there is no question about the dedication and accomplishment of the performance. The recording is no less successful, sounding radiantly fresh and clear as remastered for Decca's Legend series.

25 Offertoria (Rome 1593)

*** Chan. 0732. Trinity College, Cambridge, Ch., Marlow

Here are 25 of the 68 pieces Palestrina published in 1593 for all Sundays and festivals of the church year. The offertory is that part of the Eucharist when the bread and wine are placed on the altar, and in Rome it is one of the main points in the service at which short motets would be performed. The collection here shows the full scope of these motets, which vary from *Ave Maria* and *Jubilate Deo* to *Laudate Dominum* and *Benedicti*. None of the pieces exceeds three minutes. **Richard Marlow's** choir is mixed, but it produces much of the purity of sound that is to be found in other traditionally male Oxbridge colleges and recorded in the best Chandos fashion and very rewarding.

PANUFNIK, Andrzej (1914–91)

Cello Concerto

⊕┐ *** NMC Single D 0105. Rostropovich, LSO, Wolff

Panufnik's *Cello Concerto* was his very last work, completed only days before his death in September 1991. The recording is even more successful at conveying the purposefulness of the writing than the first performance, bringing out the tautness of the palindromic structure, with the two movements, each in arch form, a mirror-image of the other, slow then fast. The result is not a drily schematic work, as one might expect, but a piece that in its warmth reflects the player who inspired it, strong and eventful with a more open lyricism than in many previous Panufnik compositions.

(i) Piano Concerto; Symphony 9 (Sinfonia della speranza)

Ⓜ *** RCA 82876 64280-2. (i) Poblocka; LSO, composer

In a massive single movement of 41 minutes Panufnik's *Ninth Symphony* brings a formidable example of the composer's fascination with translating geometric concepts into notes. The visual analogy here is with light travelling through a prism, and the accompanying booklet provides a diagram illustrating how this formula works, using a three-note cell refracted in various ways. The result has similarities with a gigantic passacaglia and there is no denying the music's strength.

Panufnik's *Piano Concerto* is not so extended, but it carries comparable weight. The opening *Entrada* has a neoclassical flavour in its ostinatos for the solo instrument, leading to a bald, spare, central slow movement. The mood is rather like that of some of Bartók's night music. By contrast the finale is violently rhythmic, with jazzy syncopations. Though the piano writing gives the soloist relatively little chance for conventional keyboard display, her playing adds to the power of the composer's purposeful interpretation. The piano tone is a degree too clangy, but otherwise the recording is spacious and full.

Sinfonia di sfere; Sinfonia mistica (5 & 6)

Ⓜ *** Explore (ADD) EXP 0014. LSO, Atherton

The *Sinfonia di sfere* consists of three movements in ternary form, representing a journey through three concentric spheres. The *Sinfonia mistica* takes the number '6' as its root in a single movement of six sections, with each parameter dominated by that division into sixths. Though the cerebration of the scheme sometimes has one questioning the intensity of emotion conveyed, the idiom is not difficult, and the structural firmness adds very plainly to the immediate sense of conviction in each sharp contrast as it develops. Excellent performances and fine (originally Decca) recording.

(i) Sinfonia rustica (No. 1); Sinfonia sacra (No. 3); (ii) Sinfonia concertante for flute, harp & strings (No. 4)

ⒷⒷ *** EMI (ADD) 3 52289-2. (i) Monte Carlo Opera O; (ii) Nicolet, Ellis, Menuhin Festival O; all cond. composer

The *Sinfonia rustica* is a highly individual piece and has plenty of character. The *Sinfonia sacra* is based on 'the earliest known hymn in the Polish language', which in the Middle Ages was used as both a prayer and an invocation before battle. The work is in three *Visions* – the first a brass fanfare to introduce the more expressive and poignant writing which follows, while the hymn is expanded in the fourth-movement finale, which is as long as the other three movements put together, and draws on the fanfare material at its close.

The *Sinfonia concertante* contrasts two movements, *Molto cantabile* and *Molto ritmico*, with the soloists well integrated to add colour and atmosphere to the texture, and it ends with a poignantly lyrical *Postscriptum*. All the performances here are directed by the composer, who also provides the notes in the accompanying booklet. The playing of the **Monte Carlo Orchestra** is both spirited and expressive (even if the orchestra itself is not in the top flight) but the **Menuhin Festival Orchestra**, with its two celebrated

soloists, plays with great finesse and understanding. The recording is excellent.

Symphony 8 (Sinfonia votiva)

ⒷⒷ *** Hyp. Helios CDH 55100. Boston SO, Ozawa – SESSIONS: *Concerto for Orchestra* ***

The *Sinfonia votiva* has a strongly formalistic structure, but its message is primarily emotional. Though Panufnik's melodic writing may as a rule reflect the formalism of his thought rather than tapping a vein of natural lyricism, the result is most impressive, particularly in a performance of such sharp clarity and definition as **Ozawa's**. Very well recorded, and excellent value.

PARKER, Clifton (1905–89)

Film music from: The Blue Lagoon: Rhapsody for Orchestra; Blue Pullman; Night of the Demon: Theme; Sea of Sand: March; Sink the Bismarck!: March; The Sword and the Rose; Treasure Island: Suite; Virgin Island: A Caribbean Rhapsody; Western Approaches: Seascapes

*** Chan. 10279. BBC Concert O, Gamba.

This Chandos CD shows just what a good film music composer Clifton Parker was. His bold, swashbuckling style was well suited to sea-subjects, and the music from *Treasure Island* (1949) is bold and briny. *Seascapes* (from the 1944 film, *Western Approaches*) is an effective and more restrained piece of descriptive writing, and both *The Blue Lagoon* (1948) and *A Caribbean Rhapsody* offer a touch of the exotic in Parker's picturesque writing. *Blue Pullman* is a British Transport Film about a new passenger express; it starts rather broodily before it gets into its stride. Both the *Night of the Demon* (1957) and *Sink the Bismarck!* (1960) excerpts are entertaining and very atmospheric. The former is a classic 'horror' film which can still send shivers down the spine 50 years after it was made. Excellent performances and sound.

PARRY, Hubert (1848–1918)

(i) The Birds: Bridal March; (ii) English Suite; Lady Radnor's Suite (both for strings); Overture to an Unwritten Tragedy; Symphonic Variations

🎵 **** Lyrita SRCD 220 [id.]. (i) LPO; (ii) LSO; Boult

The *Bridal March* comes from Parry's equivalent to Vaughan Williams's *Wasps*, a suite of incidental music for *The Birds*, also by Aristophanes. Here the rich, *nobilmente* string melody asserts itself strongly over any minor contributions from the woodwind aviary. The two *Suites* of dances for strings have some charming genre music and the *Overture* is very strongly constructed. But best of all is the set of variations, with its echoes of Brahms's *St Anthony* set and its foretastes of *Enigma*: a big work in a small compass. **Boult's** advocacy is irresistible and the CD transfer demonstrates the intrinsic excellence of the analogue recordings, with gloriously full string-sound.

Piano Concerto in F sharp min.

*** Hyp. CDA 66820. Lane, BBC Scottish SO, Brabbins –
   STANFORD: *Piano Concerto* ***

The *Piano Concerto in F sharp minor* may at first seem rather
naïve in the way it embraces a grand manner but, written in
1880, it is a relatively early work which appeals openly with
its directness and lyricism. The Brahmsian echoes are supplemented in the finale by clear if momentary echoes of
Bizet's *Carmen*, then a very new work. **Piers Lane** plays with
feeling and brilliance, helped by beautiful sound.

Concertstück in G min.; Elegy for Brahms; From Death to Life; Symphonic Variations

―― Ⓜ *** Chan. 6610. LPO, Bamert

The eloquent *Concertstück*, literally a 'concert piece' without
a soloist and with a strong Wagnerian flavour, is the least
known work here. The *Elegy for Brahms* conveys grief, but its
vigour rises above passive mourning into an expression of
what might almost be anger. *From Death to Life* consists of
two connected movements – hardly Lisztian as the title implies but exuberantly melodic, with a theme in the second
that echoes Sibelius's *Karelia* and is at the same time Elgarian
in its sweep. But the finest work of all is the *Symphonic
Variations*, with its echoes of Brahms's *St Anthony* set and its
foretastes of *Enigma*. Shorter than either, it does not waste a
note: a big work in a small compass. The performances could
hardly be more sympathetic, and the Chandos sound is suitably rich and clear.

Lady Radnor's Suite

*** Nim. NI 5068. E. String O, Boughton – BRIDGE: *Suite*;
   BUTTERWORTH: *Banks of Green Willow*, etc. ***

Parry's charming set of pastiche dances, now given an extra
period charm through their Victorian flavour, makes an attractive item in an excellent and generous English collection,
one of Nimbus's bestsellers. Warm, atmospheric recording,
with refined playing set against an ample acoustic.

Symphonies 1–5; Symphonic Variations in E min.

―― **** Chan. 9120-22 (3). LPO, Bamert

Bamert takes us convincingly through the symphonic terrain of a highly influential composer about whom Elgar
declared, 'He is our leader – no cloud of formality can dim
the healthy sympathy and broad influence he exerts upon
us. Amidst all the outpourings of modern English music
the work of Parry remains supreme.' Bamert's set, discussed
in detail below, is offered here complete on three CDs and
includes also Parry's best-known orchestral work, the
Symphonic Variations.

Cello Sonata in A

Ⓜ *** Dutton CDLX 7102. Fuller, Dussek – HARTY:
   Butterflies; Romance & Scherzo, Op. 8; Wood-Stillness;
   HURLSTONE: *Cello Sonata in D* ***

Parry's *Cello Sonata* is finely wrought, though it does not wear
its debt to Brahms lightly – understandably, perhaps, since
it is a fairly early piece dating from 1879. It is designed on an

almost symphonic scale – particularly the sinewy *Allegro* first
movement. A splendid performance and recording.

Nonet in B flat

―― ⒝⒝ *** Hyp. Helios CDH 55061. Capricorn – STANFORD:
   Serenade (Nonet) ***

Parry's *Nonet* is for flute, oboe, cor anglais and two each of
clarinets, bassoons and horns. Although the finale is perhaps
a little lightweight, it is a delight from beginning to end. If
one did not know what it was, one would think of early
Strauss, for it is music of enormous accomplishment and
culture as well as freshness. An excellent performance and
recording, the more attractive at bargain price.

(i) Piano Quartet in A flat; Piano Trio 1 in E min.

**(*) Mer. CDE 84248. Deakin Piano Trio; (i) with Inoue

The *E minor Piano Trio* is both shorter and more direct than
the *Piano Quartet*, which is more ambitious, with a darkly
meditative slow introduction echoing late Beethoven.
Though the performance on the disc is not as polished as
one would like, Parry's melodic writing is more than distinctive enough to rebut the charge of mere imitation, with
such a movement as the dashing tarantella-like Scherzo of
the *Piano Quartet* very effective indeed. The recording balances the piano rather behind the rest, which is a pity when
Catherine Dubois so often takes the lead.

Piano Trios 2 in B min.; 3 in G

*** Mer. CDE 84255. Deakin Piano Trio

In the two *Piano Trios* the English element in Parry's invention is more clearly identifiable, with some themes bringing
anticipations of Elgar. Equally, the healthy outdoor feel of
the triple-time main themes of the finales of both *Trios* has
a hint of English folk music. Both works are richly enjoyable, with the warm, open lyricism of the slow movement
of *No. 2* particularly attractive. The players of the **Deakin
Piano Trio** seem more happily adjusted to the rigours of
recording than in the first volume, with rather better
matching and intonation.

Violin Sonata in D, Op. 103; Fantaisie-sonata in B, Op. 75; 12 Short Pieces

⒝⒝ *** Hyp. Helios CDH 55266. Gruenberg, Vignoles

The *Fantaisie-sonata* provides a fascinating example of cyclic
sonata form, earlier than most but also echoing Schumann.
The three-movement *Sonata in D* is another compact, meaty
piece, the strongest work on the disc. The *Twelve Short Pieces*,
less demanding technically, are delightful miniatures.
Gruenberg and **Vignoles** prove persuasive advocates, and
the recording is first rate.

ORGAN MUSIC

Choral Fantasies on: 'When I survey the wondrous cross'; The Old Hundredth; 7 Chorale Preludes, Sets I & II; Elégie; Elegy; Fantasia & Fugue in G (2

versions); *Toccata & Fugue (The Wanderer). A Little Organ Book in Memory of Sir Hubert Parry*

**(*) Priory PRCD 682 AB (2). Lancelot (organ of Durham Cathedral)

Although Parry is not now remembered for his organ music, he was fascinated by the instrument. Like Bach, he loved to try out every organ he came into contact with, and he had a fine knowledge of their strengths and weaknesses. His two versions of the *G major Fantasia and Fugue*, which frame the programme here, demonstrate the confident, traditional style of his writing. But his two sets of *Chorale Preludes* make full use of the changing colours and contrasting registrations. The spectacular *Toccata and Fugue (The Wanderer* – the composer's yacht, stirringly seaborne) offers plentiful opportunities for bravura, as do the opening and closing sections of his *Fantasia on the Old Hundredth*, where Parry really lets himself go. But the most admired work here, the *Fantasia on 'When I survey the wondrous cross'*, deeply expressive, was highly praised by Gerald Finzi. For the Appendix, **James Lancelot** has added an engaging series of miniatures written in the composer's memory. James Lancelot is thoroughly at home in all this repertoire and plays with flair and understanding. The organ of Durham Cathedral seems well chosen, although, as with many English cathedrals, the resonance prevents absolute internal clarity in the recording.

VOCAL MUSIC

(i) *Blest Pair of Sirens; I was Glad* (anthems); (ii) *Invocation to Music (An Ode in Honour of Purcell)*; (iii) *The Lotus Eaters*; (iv) *The Soul's Ransom*

⊕– Ⓑ **** Chan. 2 for 1 241-31 (2). (i) L. Symphony Ch., LSO, Hickox; (ii) Dawson, Davies, Rayner Cook; (iii) (iv) Jones; (iv) Wilson Johnson; (ii–iv) LPO Ch., LPO, Bamert

Here is an outstanding collection of some of Parry's finest choral music, with two of his most popular anthems, admirably directed by **Richard Hickox**, used on the second disc to frame what is perhaps his most influential and powerful vocal work, the *Invocation to Music*, a superb setting of Robert Bridges's *Ode in Honour of Purcell*. Parry's inspiration was at its peak, and the flowing, richly melodic lyrical style was to anticipate the Elgar of the *Coronation Ode* and even *Gerontius*. The soloists here are splendid, with the passionate central soprano and tenor duet, *Love to Love calleth*, followed by the magnificent bass *Dirge*, and the very Elgarian chorus *Man, born of desire*, later to be capped by the glorious closing apotheosis, *O Queen of sinless grace*, which **Matthias Bamert** moves on arrestingly to its final climax.

The first disc pairs *The Lotus Eaters*, a setting for soprano, chorus and orchestra of eight stanzas from Tennyson's choric song of that name, with *The Soul's Ransom*, using a biblical text. This is subtitled *Sinfonia sacra* and forms a broadly symphonic four-movement structure with references back not only to Brahms and the 19th century, but to much earlier choral composers, notably Schütz. **Della Jones** is the characterful soloist in both works, to be joined by **David Wilson Johnson** in the latter piece. The singing of the

London Philharmonic Chorus throughout is first class, warmly sympathetic, as is the orchestral playing, and Matthias Bamert is in his element in this repertoire, as is the Chandos recording team.

The Chivalry of the Sea

Ⓜ *** Dutton CDLX 7172. BBC Ch. & SO, Lloyd-Jones (with KELLY: *Elegy (In Memoriam Rupert Brooke)*; ELKINGTON: *Out of the Mist* (***)) – ELGAR: *The Spirit of England*; GURNEY: *War Elegy* ***

Parry wrote this cantata in 1916 to commemorate the loss of HMS *Invincible* when it exploded, with many victims, at the battle of Jutland. The piece, which has many fine qualities, is saddled with a very poor poem, full of oddly archaic language, by the then Poet Laureate, Robert Bridges. Nevertheless, what matters is the quality of Parry's writing, not just elegiac but including vigorous passages and one sequence in sea-shanty rhythm. It comes on a fascinating disc offering first recordings of five war-inspired works.

Evening Service in D (Great): Magnificat; Nunc Dimittis. Hear My Words, ye People; I Was Glad when They Said Unto Me; Jerusalem; Songs of Farewell

⊕– *** Hyp. CDA 66273. St George's Chapel, Windsor, Ch., Robinson; Judd (organ)

Everyone knows *Jerusalem*, which highlights this collection resplendently. In the *Songs of Farewell* trebles are used and the effect is less robust than in Marlow's version, but undoubtedly very affecting. Perhaps the stirring coronation anthem, *I Was Glad*, needs the greater weight of an adult choir, but it is still telling here. The excerpts from the *Great Service in D* are well worth having on record, as is the anthem, *Hear My Words, ye People*. Excellent recording, the chapel ambience colouring the music without blunting the words.

I Was Glad (from *Psalm 122*)

Ⓜ **(*) EMI (ADD/DDD) 5 85148-2. Cambridge University Musical Soc., King's College, Cambridge, Ch., New Philh. O, Ledger – ELGAR: *Coronation Ode* etc. ***

This expansive version of Parry's most popular church anthem, very well recorded in 1977, makes an excellent bonus on this splendid Elgar disc.

Job (oratorio)

**(*) Hyp. CDA 67025. Coleman-Wright, Spence, Davies, Hitchcock, Guildford Choral Soc., RPO, Davan Wetton

Though Parry, as a Victorian, sidesteps the problem of conveying the pain and bitterness in the story of Job, this is a warm, beautifully written oratorio which is most welcome on disc, very English and optimistic. It would be even better, had **Hilary Davan Wetton** drawn a more biting response from the chorus and had **Peter Coleman-Wright** in the title role, clear and direct as he is, sounded less respectful. The other soloists are first-rate, notably **Toby Spence** in the tenor part of Satan, and the recording is warm and atmospheric, though with the chorus rather backwardly placed. For all its limitations a highly enjoyable curiosity.

Ode on the Nativity

*** Lyrita (ADD) SRCD 270. Cahill, Bach Ch., Royal College of Music Ch., LPO, Willcocks – HOLST: *The Mystic Trumpeter*; VAUGHAN WILLIAMS: *Sons of Light* ***

Parry's *Ode* is an elaborate, often highly contrapuntal setting of a poem of William Dunbar. Each of its six stanzas ends with the Latin line, *Et nobis Puer natus est*, which each time inspired Parry to a moment of dedicated intensity. The thematic material may not be as memorable as some of Parry's finest works (it was written in 1912, only five years before his death), but in a performance as committed as this, beautifully recorded, it makes a welcome rarity on record, and the couplings are equally rare.

PARSONS, Robert (1535–72)

First Great Service; Responds for the Dead

(BB) *** Naxos 8.570451. Voces Cantabiles, Barnaby Smith

Robert Parsons was a Gentleman of the Chapel Royal from 1563 until his death in 1572. Not only was his *Great Service* revolutionary in setting the English texts but it was also one of the first settings to attempt a musical unification between the different movements. As this disc shows, he was a master of polyphony and his *First Great Service* was probably the model for both Byrd and Tomkins. The Liturgy, interspersed with items from the *Responds for the Dead*, is very English in flavour, freshly and euphoniously so, making this yet another Naxos issue to expand our range of repertory. **Barnaby Smith** and his **Voces Cantabiles** make a strong case for this little-known master, and their expert recording team do them full justice. Excellent sound. Strongly recommended.

PÄRT, Arvo (born 1935)

(i) Arbos (2 performances); (ii) Pari Intervallo; (iii) An den Wassern zu Babel; De Profundis; (iv; v) Es sang vor langen Jahren; (iii) Summa; (iii; v; vi) Stabat Mater

*** ECM 831 959-2. (i) Brass Ens., Stuttgart State O, Davies; (ii) Bowers-Broadbent; (iii) Hilliard Ens., Hillier; (iv) Bickley; (v) Kremer, Mendelssohn; (vi) Demenga

All the music recorded here gives a good picture of Pärt's musical make-up with all its strengths and limitations. *Arbos*, which is heard in two different versions, 'seeks to create the image of a tree or family tree'. It does not modulate and has no development, though pitch and tempi are in proportional relationships. The *Stabat Mater* (1985) for soprano, counter-tenor, tenor and string trio is distinguished by extreme simplicity of utterance and is almost totally static. This music relies for its effect on minimal means and invites one to succumb to a kind of mystical, hypnotic repetition rather than a musical argument. The artists performing here do so with total commitment and are excellently recorded.

Bogoróditse Djévo; Dopo la vittoria; I Am the True Vine; Kanon pokajanen (Ode); Nunc dimittis;

Tribute to Caesar; Triodin; The Woman with the Alabaster Box

(BB) *** Naxos 8.570239. Elora Festival Singers, Edison

It is good to have an inexpensive collection to emphasize the strength of Arvo Pärt's choral writing. All this music has a ready appeal, particularly *I Am the True Vine* and *The Woman with the Alabaster Box*, set to unexpected texts, while the sparer *Nunc dimittis* reminds the listener of the individuality of the composer's ecclesiastical music. Excellent performances and very good recording.

(i) Cantus in Memory of Benjamin Britten; (ii) Festina lente; (i) Fratres (for string orchestra & percussion); Summa (for string orchestra); (iii) Fratres; Spiegel im Spiegel (both for violin & piano); (iv) The Beatitudes for Choir & Organ; Magnificat; (v) 7 Magnificat Antiphons; Summa

🔄 (B) **** CfP 585 9142. (i) Estonian Nat. SO, Järvi; (ii) Bournemouth Sinf., Studt; (iii) Little, Roscoe; (iv) King's College, Cambridge, Ch., Cleobury; (v) Varsai Singers, Backhouse

An admirable and enterprising compilation. In the two works for violin and piano, **Tasmin Little** holds the listener's attention by the intensity of her commitment and the powerful projection of her playing. *Summa* is heard in two versions, the choral one being a fresh and carol-like setting of the Creed, and this leads naturally into the brief but concentrated *Magnificat Antiphons*, with the seventh the longest and most telling. Pärt's comparatively static *Magnificat* relies on intensity of sonority rather than movement; his better-known *Beatitudes*, gentle and rippling, is regularly pierced by dissonance, with the organ entering briefly and unexpectedly at the end to add a florid postlude and then disappear into infinity. Fine, idiomatic performances throughout and excellent recording.

(i) Cantus in Memory of Benjamin Britten; Festina lente (for string orchestra & harp); Summa (for string orchestra); (ii; iii) Fratres; Spiegel im Spiegel (both for violin & piano); (iv; v) The Beatitudes (for choir & organ); (iv) Summa (for choir); (i; ii; v; vi) Tabula rasa (for 2 violins, string orchestra & prepared piano)

*** Telarc CD 80387. Manning, Springuel, Gleizes, I Fiamminghi, Werthen

Cantus in memoriam Benjamin Britten; Fratres (6 versions)

(BB) *** Naxos 8.553750 Hungarian State Op. O, Benedek

For all the repetitions involved in Pärt's minimalist progressions there are no more hypnotic examples of his curiously compelling, ritualistic writing than this sequence of six settings of a very simple monastic chorale which he calls *Fratres*. We hear it first slowly swelling up from a *piano-pianissimo* on strings, with unobtrusive decorative percussion, then sinking away again. Then follow variants and finally rustling on the cello with the piano tolling a bell-like accompaniment until a closing climax builds and abates. The Britten tribute and *Festina lente for Strings and Harp ad libitum* are used as interludes. The playing here has great atmosphere and concentration, while Telarc's glowing sound adds to the sensuous physical beauty.

However the Naxos Hungarian performance is also very fine, splendidly played and richly recorded. *Festina lente* is omitted; instead the *Cantus* is used as a powerful apotheosis to end the disc with a thrilling climax.

CHORAL MUSIC

And One of the Pharisees; (i) The Beatitudes; Cantate Domino (Psalm 95); (ii) De profundis (Psalm 129); Magnificat; 7 Magnificat Antiphons; Missa Syllabica; Solfeggio; Summa (Credo)

*** HM HMU 907182. Theatre of Voices, Hillier; (i) with Bowers-Broadbent (organ); Kennedy (percussion)

This 76-minute collection covers a very wide range of Pärt's choral output, from the short *Solfeggio* of 1964, which seems to float in space, to *The Beatitudes* (1990) of which this is the recording première. *De Profundis* again uses an organ pedal to underpin the climax. The *Missa Syllabica* (1977), heard here in a slightly revised version, is a fine example of Pärt's use of the simplest means to communicate his expression of the liturgical text, the repetitions within the 'Credo' a characteristic example. *And One of the Pharisees* is a setting for three voices of a text from Chapter 7 of St Luke's Gospel and its powerful medieval atmosphere, including solo chants, reminds us of the link which Pärt's liturgical music has with the distant past. The performances here could hardly be more powerful or atmospheric, yet they are firmly controlled. They are magnificently recorded.

St John Passion

🔗 (BB) **** Naxos 8.555860. Macdonald, Anderson, Tonus Peregrinus, Pitts

*** ECM 837 109-2. George, Potter, Hilliard Ens., Western Wind Chamber Ch. (Instrumental group), Hillier

Since it appeared in the late 1980s, the spare ritual of Arvo Pärt's setting of the *Passion According to St John* has established itself far more widely than could ever have been predicted, reflecting the hypnotic quality of this characteristic example of spiritual minimalism in music. **Antony Pitts** draws a magnetic performance from his newly founded choir, **Tonus Peregrinus**, and the soloists taking the roles of Christ and Pilate, and they are atmospherically recorded in bright, clear sound. It helps to sustain tension that the performance at just over an hour is some ten minutes shorter than its previous rival though that too is a dedicated performance, impeccably recorded.

PATTERSON, Paul (born 1947)

Missa brevis

(B) *** EMI 5 05921-2. LPO Ch., Arwel Hughes – Michael
BERKELEY: *Or shall we die?* **(*)

The *Missa brevis* uses a seemingly simple style boldly and

freshly. It must be as grateful for the singers as it is for the listener, with moments of pure poetry as in the *Benedictus*. The performance is first class.

PENDERECKI, Krzysztof (born 1933)

(i) Anaklasis; (ii; iii) Capriccio for Violin & Orchestra; (iii; iv) Cello Concerto; (iii) De natura sonoris I & II; The Dream of Jacob; Emanationen for String Orchestras; Fonogrammi; (iii; v) Partita for Harpsichord & Orchestra; (iii) Threnody for the Victims of Hiroshima; (i) Symphony; (vi) Canticum canticorum Salomonis

🔗 (BB) **** EMI Gemini (ADD) 3 81508-2 (2). (i) LSO;
(ii) Wilkomirska; (iii) Polish Nat. RSO; (iv) Palm;
(v) Blumenthal; (vi) Krakow Philh. Ch.; all cond. composer

For those who admire such athematic music this inexpensive anthology in authoritative performances under the composer's own direction makes a splendid introduction to Penderecki's music. *Anaklasis* is an inventive piece for strings and percussion, and *De natura sonoris* is also brilliant in its use of contrasts. **Wilkomirska** proves a superb soloist in the *Capriccio* and so does **Palm** in the *Cello Concerto*. The beautiful and touching *Threnody for 52 Strings* is the composer's best-known piece, and it is here given a magnificent performance. *The Dream of Jacob* of 1974 is as inventive as the rest, but sparer. Penderecki's music relies for its appeal on the resourceful use of sonorities, and his sound-world is undoubtedly imaginative, albeit limited. The choral work is a setting of a text from the *Song of Solomon* for large orchestra and 16 solo voices. But the *Symphony* is the most ambitious work here. With such a committed performance it is certainly memorable. The 1970s recordings are excellent, and this EMI Gemini is an undoubted bargain.

(i) Concerto grosso 1 for 3 Cellos & Orchestra. Largo for Cello & Orchestra; Sonata for Cello & Orchestra

(N) (BB) **(*) Naxos 8.5709509. Monighetti, (i) Noras, Kwaitkowski; Warsaw Nat. PO, Wit

The most interesting and most enjoyable work here is the *Concerto grosso*, in which the concertino is made of three cellos, often used to create a sumptuously rich amalgam of tone or comparable polyphony. The work is in six contrasted sections, alternating vigorous and slow music and with orchestral tuttis pulsatingly complex, even Straussian – indeed, the central *Allegro giocoso* brings a hint of *Till Eulenspiegel*. There is a good deal of dissonance, although the closing *Adagio* brings a certain calm. The *Largo for Cello and Orchestra* (in fact a 28-minute triptych of three, mainly slow, movements) is even more vigorously strident at its climaxes and, to be frank, hard going at times! The aggressiveness persists in the two-movement *Sonata*, which also has moments of feigned irony and is scored for a large orchestra, including two bongos, three wood blocks, whip, clave and tam-tam for good measure. All three performances are of high quality, played with total, even frenzied conviction and spectacularly recorded. But this is not a disc for faint-hearts.

CHORAL MUSIC

Benedictus; Benedictus Domine; Magnificat: Sicut locutus est; Polish Requiem: Agnus Dei; Saint Luke's Passion: Stabat Mater; In pulverem mortis; Miserere; Veni creator; Song of Cherubim

🎵 (BB) **** Warner Apex 8573 88433-2. Tapiola Chamber Ch., Kulvanen

This superbly sung collection inexpensively monitors Penderecki's changing style of vocal writing beginning with the excerpts from the *St Luke's Passion* (1962) for three mixed choruses, using dramatic spoken utterance as well as powerfully sustained block choral sonorities. The *Sicut locutus est* from the *Magnificat* (1974) works in a similar way. Then with the lovely, plaintive *Agnus Dei* (for eight-part mixed chorus) of 1981 there is much more movement, and a surge of romantic feeling, with a dissonant climax of real angst. The new, freer romantic style reaches its peak in the powerful and often seraphic *Song of Cherubim* (1986) with its gentle closing Alleluias, the finest work here. But the remarkable setting of *Veni creator* (1987) returns to the spoken murmurings and interjections, while climaxing with a passionate affirmation, before the ethereality of the closing Amen. By 1992 the *Benedictus Domine* for five-part male choir is looking back to organum, and the closing *Benedictus*, based on the text of the medieval *Sanctus* trope is linked to liturgical chant, yet romanticized and brought into our own time. The **Tapiola Choir** sings passionately, with fine blending and a bright firm line in an atmospheric but never blurring acoustic. With texts and translations included, this is a real bargain.

Symphony 7 (Seven Gates of Jerusalem)

🎵 (BB) **** Naxos 8.557766. Pasychniyk, Mikolaij, Marciniec, Tesarowicz, Carmel, Warsaw Nat. Ch. & PO, Wit

This is a massive cantata in seven movements, setting Psalms in Hebrew, with Penderecki handling colossal forces with thrilling mastery. The sequence of movements brings together the choral and symphonic elements in his work very effectively. The figure '7' is used obsessively, not least in seven-note themes. The very opening is shattering in its impact, setting *Psalm 48*, while the longest of the seven movements is the fifth, *Lauda Zion*, setting *Psalm 147*, a Scherzo introduced by timpani and percussion. With striking and immediately attractive themes, it brings a colossal climax as powerful as anything Penderecki has written. At its peak it is interrupted by the sixth movement, setting a declamation of words from the *Book of Ezekiel*, representing the word of God, reinforced by a distinctive bass trumpet solo. The seventh movement then rounds the work off with a triumphant setting of *Psalm 48*. Performances under **Antoni Wit** are superb, strong and intense, with an excellent chorus and team of soloists.

OPERA

Der Teufel von Loudun (complete; DVD version)

*** Arthaus DVD 101 279. Troyanos, Hiolski, Ladysz, Sotin, Gerdesmann, Hamburg State Op. Ch., Hamburg

Philharmonic State O, Janowski (Dir: Rolf Liebermann, V/D: Joachim Hess)

Krzysztof Penderecki adapted his opera, *Der Teufel von Loudon*, writing his own libretto from the John Whiting play drawn from Aldous Huxley's *Evils of Loudun*. From beginning to end it is wonderfully effective, with sinister scenery and costumes in period and **Liebermann's** inspired production all adding to the impact. The persecution of the priest Urbain Grandier and his burning at the stake in 1634, the victim of political intrigue, is a historical fact. Round this Huxley, Whiting and Penderecki have woven an effective web of characters, some of them satirically portrayed (the persecutors) but including a group of nuns. Leading them is **Tatiana Troyanos**, at her powerful peak, well supported by **Cvetka Ahlin, Ursula Boese** and **Helga Thieme** as her flock, as well as the young nun, Philippe, with **Ingeborg Kruger** scaling stratospheric heights. **Andrzej Hiolski** is excellent as Urbain himself, as is **Bernard Ladysz** in the role of Father Barre. A historic film, well directed to attract many who would not normally respond to a modern opera.

PERGOLESI, Giovanni
(1710–36)

Confitebor tibi Domine

🎵 ✹ (M) *** DHM/BMG 82876 60145-2. Monoyios, Landauer, Balthazar-Neumann Ch., Freiburg Bar. O, Hengelbrock – DURANTE: *Magnificat in B flat*; D'ASTORGA: *Stabat Mater.* ✹ ***

Pergolesi's little-known setting of *Psalm 110* immediately arrests the attention with its richly eloquent choral opening, but later it depends upon the solo soprano, who has a dialogue with the chorus in the *Confessio*, and the solo alto, whose *Sanctum et terrible* and *Intellectus bonus* create the work's expressive climax. Both **Ann Monoyios** and **Bernhard Landauer** rise to the occasion here, as does the chorus in the closing *Gloria Patri* and *Sicut erat*. The excellent period-instrument **Freiburg Baroque Orchestra** are notable for their characterful contribution to the *Sanctum*. In short, this performance, directed with life and spirit by **Thomas Hengelbrock**, is first class in every way, and so is the recording. Highly recommended.

(i) Magnificat in C; (ii) Stabat Mater

(B) **(*) Double Decca 443 868-2 (2). (i) Vaughan, J. Baker, Partridge, Keyte, King's College Ch., ASMF, Willcocks; (ii) Palmer, Hodgson, St John's College, Cambridge, Ch., Argo CO, Guest – BONONCINI: *Stabat Mater*; D. SCARLATTI: *Stabat Mater*; A. SCARLATTI: *Domine, refugium factus es nobis; O magnum mysterium*; CALDARA: *Crucifixus*; LOTTI: *Crucifixus* ***

This well-planned Double Decca collection centres on three different settings of the *Stabat Mater dolorosa*. Pergolesi's version dates from 1735 and, subsequently, settings were made by many other composers, including Vivaldi and Haydn. Pergolesi conceived a work which has secular and even theatrical overtones, and its devotional nature is unexaggerated. **George Guest** directs a sensible, unaffected performance, simple and expressive, with relaxed tempi, not overladen with romantic sentiment. The *Magnificat* – doubtfully attributed, like so much that goes under this composer's name – is a comparatively lightweight piece, notable for its rhythmic vitality. The **King's College Choir** under **Willcocks** gives a sensitive and vital performance, and the recording matches it in intensity of atmosphere.

Stabat Mater (DVD version)

Ⓝ *** Medici Arts **DVD** 2072378. Ricciarelli, Terrani, La Scala, Milan, O, Abbado (V/D: Hugo Käch) (with VIVALDI: *Concertos: in C 'per la solennita di S. Lorenzo' RV 556; in G min., 'per l'orchestra di Dresda', RV 777* ***)

Ⓝ *** EMI **DVD** 5 99404-9. Frittoli, Antonacci, La Scala Filharmonica, Muti (V/D: Xarlo Assalimi)

Both **Abbado's** and **Muti's** performances have two first-class soloists, who make a fine partnership in their expressive vocal exchanges and (more importantly) matching their vibratos. Both performances are beautifully sung; each conductor chooses spacious tempi, and the use of modern instruments and the resonant acoustic of each venue ensures a warm and beautiful sound from the comparatively modest-sized orchestral groups. The soloists are clearly focused and well balanced in relation to the overall visual imagery. The Medici Arts video uses the glorious baroque church of Stiftskirche, Ossiach, while the backcloth of the EMI version features the beautiful Cupola Frescoes of Gaudenzio Ferrari, on which the camera frequently dwells to poignant effect, to illustrate the crucifixion and the image of Mary standing at the foot of the Cross. The EMI bonuses include a long and intellectual exposition by Muti of the historical development of Italian music, and a whimsical commentary, 'Pergolesi and his Double', confirming that a great deal of music attributed to Pergolesi (but not the *Stabat Mater*) was written by others, hoping to take advantage of his reputation. The Medici Arts DVD, however, includes two of Vivaldi's finest *concerti con multi istrumenti*, superbly played and most effectively photographed, which are surely more enticing than the spoken alternative!

Stabat Mater (CD versions)

⊕ ✹ Ⓜ **** Naïve OP 30441. Bertagnolli, Mingardo, Concerto Italiano, Alessandrini – A. SCARLATTI: *Stabat Mater* ****

*** DG 415 103-2. Marshall, Terrani, LSO, Abbado

(i; ii) Stabat Mater; (ii) In coelestibus regnis; (i) Salve Regina in A

*** Hyp. CDA 66294. (i) Fisher; (ii) Chance; King's Consort, King

(i; ii) Stabat Mater; (ii) Salve Regina in A min.; (i) Salve Regina in F min.

*** Virgin 3 63340-2. (i) Röschmann; (ii) Daniels; Europa Galante, Biondi

*** Decca 466 134-2. (i) Scholl; (ii) Bonney, Les Talens Lyriques, Rousset

Both the soprano, **Gemma Bertagnolli**, and the contralto,

Sara Mingardo (with her remarkably resonant lower register) have extraordinarily colourful voices, which blend beautifully at the work's sustained opening, but which only display their full richness in their solos, notably *Cujus animam gementem* and *Fac ut portem Christi mortem*. This is a totally Italianate performance of both high drama and moving pathos. The closing *Quando corpus morietur*, in which both singers join in sustained legato, is very moving indeed, followed by a passionately final affirmation of faith. **Alessandrini's** instrumental support could not be more telling and the recording is made in an ideal acoustic.

Abbado's account brings great intensity and ardour to this piece, and he secures marvellously alive playing from the **LSO** – this without diminishing religious sentiment. The DG recording has warmth and good presence and the perspective is thoroughly acceptable. But there is no coupling.

The voices of **Dorothea Röschmann** and **David Daniels** blend perfectly together, and their performance of the *Stabat Mater* is movingly expressive, with **Biondi** and **Europa Galante** providing persuasive instrumental backing. Then each singer is given a different setting of *Salve Regina*, which they also sing with some distinction. Excellent recording, but not a first choice for the *Stabat Mater*.

The combination of **Andreas Scholl's** alto and **Barbara Bonney's** soprano makes a well-matched and certainly individual tonal blend and they often sing exquisitely, both solo and in tandem. Both settings of the *Salve Regina* are authentic: Andreas Scholl sings the *A minor*, Barbara Bonney the *F minor*. Throughout, **Christophe Rousset's** period-instrument accompaniments are outstandingly fine and full of life, and the Decca recording is splendidly real.

The Hyperion recording also makes a very good case for authenticity in this work. The combination of soprano and male alto blends well together yet offers considerable variety of colour. **Gillian Fisher's** *Salve Regina* is quite a considerable piece in four sections, whereas Michael Chance's motet is brief but makes an engaging postlude. Excellent sound.

PEROTINUS, Magister
(c. 1160–1225)

Organa: Alleluya, Nativitas; Sederunt principes

*** Lyrichord (ADD) LEMS 8002. Oberlin, Bressler, Perry, Barab – LEONIN: *Organa*

Perotinus extended the simple polyphony of Leonin from two to three and four parts, and the ear is very aware of the intervals which characterize the organum: unison, octave, fourths and fifths. This music is more florid, freer than the coupled works written several decades before. The performances here are totally compelling and the recording excellent.

Beata viscera; Sederunt principes; Viderunt omnes (with Plainchant)

⊕ ⑱ *** Naxos 8.557340. Tonus Peregrinus (with ANON.: *Vetus abit littera. Clausulae Motet on Dominus; Non nobis Domine*) – LEONIN: *Viderunt omnes* ***

The Naxos disc opens with a monophonic conductus, freely flowing and soaring, which reminds one of the music of Hildegard. But later in the collection we are offered *Viderunt omnes* as a four-part organum for male voices, a darkly powerful setting. Later, *Sederunt principes* brings in female voices over a drone effect; to conclude the disc, we are offered a four-part conductus for mixed voices, joyfully rhythmic in the way of a dance. The performances are first rate and the echoing acoustic is just right. If you have never heard organum with its bare intervals (octave, fourths and fifths), you will find this disc aurally fascinating.

PERRY, William (born 1930)

Mark Twain Film Scores: *Adventures of Huckleberry Finn; Innocents Abroad; Life on the Mississippi; (i) The Mysterious Stranger; The Private History of a Campaign that Failed; Pudd'nhead Wilson*

(BB) **** Naxos 8.570200. Various orchestras, composer;
  (i) with V. Boys' Ch.

William Perry wrote his Mark Twain film scores between 1980 and 1986, still golden years for Hollywood film music. The brilliant orchestrations were by **Richard Hayman** (who also plays the harmonica in the sessions) and three other musician-arrangers, besides the composer himself. Perry was not only a natural tunesmith, he had a feeling for the folksy American atmosphere essential for this repertoire. He could create a memorable Hollywoodian sweep too, as in the opening music for *Adventures of Huckleberry Finn*, where the ten vignettes are like a miniature suite, full of ear-tickling invention and glowing orchestral colour. But the other scores here are hardly less inventive. In *Life on the Mississippi* the hero's girl-friend Emmeline is given a charming waltz for her courtship, and *Innocents Abroad* brings orchestral vignettes of Paris, Venice and Genoa. The title music of *The Private History* is equally ear-catching and, to round things off, Perry employs the **Vienna Boys' Choir** for *The Mysterious Stranger*. The performances here, by three different orchestras, conducted by the composer, could not be more persuasive, and Hayman's harmonica interludes add to the rustic feeling. Excellently sumptuous and vivid recording increases the pleasures of this entertaining disc.

PERSICHETTI, Vincent (1915–87)

Divertimento for Band, Op. 42; Chorale Prelude, O God Unseen, Op. 160; Masquerade, Op. 102; O Cool is the Valley, Op. 118; Pageant, Op. 59; Parable, Op. 121; Psalm, Op. 53

(BB) *** Naxos 8.570123. LSO Winds, Amos

Persichetti was an inventive and powerful symphonist who followed the traditions of Piston, Roy Harris and William Schuman. He was a particularly distinguished composer for wind ensemble, and these inventive and vital works are well

worth exploring. The playing of the **LSO Winds** under **David Amos** is virtuosic and infectious.

PETTERSSON, Allan (1911–80)

Violin Concerto 2

*** CPO 777 199-2. Van Keulen, Swedish RSO, Dausgaard

Symphonies 1–15

(B) *** CPO 777 247-2 (12). BBC Scottish SO; Saarbrücken RSO, Francis; Berlin Deutsche SO, Francis, Trojahn or Ruzicka; Hamburg PO, Albrecht; Berlin RSO, Thomas Sandering or Arnell; NDR SO, Francis; Swedish R. Ch. & SO, Honeck

CPO have made something of a speciality of recording the music of Allan Pettersson. A pupil of René Leibowitz in Paris, Pettersson soon turned his back on twelve-note music. The Swedish public had been force-fed on serial and post-serial music and understandably turned to his tonal music with relief. The *Second Violin Concerto* comes from the late 1970s, in the last years of his life. The revision is blessed with the most dedicated and brilliant advocate in **Isabelle van Keulen**, who is expertly partnered by the same orchestra under **Thomas Dausgaard**. There is an unappealing vein of self-pity in Pettersson's music and none of the concentration and distinction of mind you find in such Nordic contemporaries as Rosenberg, Holmboe or Tubin. But Pettersson's many admirers can rest assured that the playing could hardly be bettered, and the recording is natural and lifelike.

All 15 of his *Symphonies* plus the *Symphonic Movement* have been recorded on the CPO label (CPO 777 247-2) and there are separate recordings on the BIS label of *Nos. 5*, coupled with the amorphous *Viola concerto* (BIS CD 480), 7 and 11 (BIS CD 580); and 8 and 10 (BIS CD 880). This music has a strong emotional appeal for some music lovers. Much of it (the *Seventh*, for instance) wears an anguished visage and packs a strong emotional punch. But in musical substance these works are less weighty than appears to be the case on first acquaintance. Often invention flags and (as in the *Fifth Symphony*) the brooding, expectant atmosphere and powerful ostinatos arouse more promise of development than fulfilment. In the *Eighth Symphony* the music is often static and wanting symphonic coherence. The *Ninth Symphony* was composed in the valley of the shadow of death. Life being short and sweet, one can only say that the 70 minutes which it takes to unfold seem an eternity. The *Tenth* is shorter, but is still essentially empty: the music of gesture, not substance.

PHILIPS, Peter (1560–1628)

Music for Clavichord, Harpsichord, Organ and Virginal

*** MDG 341 1257-2. Rampe (various keyboard instruments)

This disc is part of a Dabringhaus und Grimm series planning a complete survey of Peter Philips's keyboard works. But for most collectors this single disc will serve as an admirable introduction, as **Siegbert Rampe** is not only an expert keyboard player, but is also very knowledgeable about the repertoire. He uses two different organs to introduce and end his programme, and as a centrepiece plays on two different clavichords, a virginal and a Ruckers harpsichord. Moreover, the variety of the music (which all springs vividly to life) is increased by the Italian influence on Philips's compositions after he had fled to Rome in 1582 to escape persecution in England as a Catholic. Also much of his keyboard writing takes the form of intabulations of Italian vocal works – by Lassus, among others. There are seven such arrangements here. The performances are admirable, and so is the recording.

14 Motets

☛ (BB) *** Hyp. Helios CDH 55254. Winchester Cathedral Ch., Parley of Instruments, Hill

Peter Philips is the least known of the 'Elizabethan' composers and, as this splendid collection of his vocal music readily demonstrates, this is not because his compositions are of poor quality. Indeed their invention overflows with vitality and expressive conviction. His music is spirited and full of expressive fervour and joy, and this comes out splendidly in these eloquent performances by **David Hill** and his **Winchester Cathedral Choir**, accompanied by the **Parley of Instruments**, who in this instance use a continuo of lute, theorbo, double harp and chamber organs.

PHILLIPS, Montague
(1885–1969)

Arabesque; Moorland Idyll; The Rebel Maid: 4 Dances; Revelry Overture; A Shakespearean Scherzo (Titania and her Elvish Court); Sinfonietta; A Surrey Suite; Symphony in C min.

(M) *** Dutton CDLX 7140. BBC Concert O, Sutherland

Montague Phillips's collection gets off to an exhilarating start with the *Revelry Overture* of 1937, a lively six-minute piece encompassing many attractive ideas, all brightly orchestrated. The *Four Dances* from his comic-opera *The Rebel Maid* are very much in the vein of Edward German and Sullivan – and none the worse for that – with their rustic atmosphere also pervading other numbers, including the pleasing *Moorland Idyll*, which has a lilting middle section in the manner of Dvořák. The two movements which make up the *C minor Symphony* (first heard in 1912) include *A Summer Nocturne*, showing the composer in a rather deeper emotional mood, while *A Spring Rondo* is in a more characteristic and lighter vein (the other two movements of the *Symphony* have yet to be reconstructed). The *Arabesque* of 1927 has an appealing Russian flavour, while the *Shakespearean Scherzo*, a lively and inventive mini tone-poem, is very enjoyable too. Although written during wartime Britain in 1943, the *Sinfonietta* is stiff-upper-lip heroic music rather than reflecting the horrors of war, and the slow movement is agreeably nostalgic. The work ends triumphantly. Excellent performances as usual from Gavin Sutherland, well known

from his ASV recordings, but here on one of Dutton's discs, superbly engineered.

Charles II Overture; Empire March; Festival Overture (In Praise of my Country); Hampton Court; In May Time; In Old Verona: A Serenade for Strings; Hillside Melody; (i) Phantasy for Violin & Orchestra, Op. 16

*** Dutton CDLX 7158. BBC Concert O, Sutherland, (i) with Trusler

This second volume of Montague Phillips's orchestral music is every bit as good as the first. All this is 'light' music of the highest order, of the sort that rarely, if ever, gets played nowadays. Excellent performances and recording.

PIAZZOLA, Astor (1921–92)

Milonga del Angel; 3 Movimientos tanguisticos portenos; Sinfonietta; Tangazo

*** Chan. 10049. Württemberg Philharmonie Reutlingen, Castagno

Those who know Piazzola's music from popular arrangements of his tangos will be intrigued by this collection of more ambitious works, all of which demonstrate his vivid imagination in devising distinctive melody and harmonies, colourfully orchestrated. The strongly committed performances are very well recorded.

PIERNÉ, Gabriel (1863–1937)

(i) Andante; Berceuse; Canzonetta; Chamber Sonata; La Danseuse espagnole; Fantaisie impromptu; Violin Sonata; (ii) Giration (ballet); Sérénade; Pastorale variée; (ii; iii) Nuit divine; (ii) Pastorale for Wind Quintet; Pièce for Oboe & Piano; Piano Quintet; Préludio e fughetta; Solo de concert

☛ *** Timpani 2C 1110 (2). (i) Koch & Ivaldi; (ii) Instrumental Soloists of Luxembourg PO, Ivaldi; (iii) with Rémy Franck (narrator)

Those readers remembering the 78-r.p.m. era may recall Gabriel Pierné's once famous novelty, the *Parade of the Little Lead Soldiers*. He made his initial reputation with orchestral morceaux of this kind. With the arrival of the *Violin Sonata* at the turn of the century he began to write music of more depth. It is a work of feeling, the lyrical inspiration of the first movement is appealing, and the dreamy, folksy *Andante tranquillo* is hardly less endearing. Influences of Pierné's mentor, César Franck, are plain. But the work is impressive in its own terms, especially when played with such warmth and conviction as it is by **Philippe Koch** and **Christian Ivaldi**, and vividly recorded. The *Piano Quintet* of 1916/17 is also strongly influenced by the comparable Franck work. The performers play throughout with great conviction. However, with the wind music on the second disc, the ear is endlessly diverted. The pieces for plangent oboe, or bubbling bassoon (with piano) are delightful, as is the *Pastorale variée* for wind septet (including trumpet), while the *Giration ballet* (of 1933) is whimsically inventive and engagingly scored. These works are all played with pleasing elegance and are beautifully recorded. At times one is reminded of the music of Françaix. However, the last, rather sentimental item on the disc, *Nuit divine*, includes the recitation of a poem by d'Albert Samain for which no translation is provided! Otherwise presentation and documentation are impeccable.

Cello Sonata in F sharp min., Op. 46

*** Hyp. CDA 66979. Lidström, Forsberg – KOECHLIN: *Cello Sonata*; etc. ***

Pierné was an interesting and cultured composer. His sonata is finely wrought with touches of real individuality, and well worth getting to know. **Mats Lidström** and **Bengt Forsberg** play with great intelligence and refinement and are well served by the engineers.

PIGGOTT, Patrick (1915–90)

Fantasia quasi una sonata (No. 1); Sonata 2; 8 Preludes and a Postlude (3rd Set)

*** British Music Soc. BMS 430CD. Malcolm Binns

Born in Dover, Patrick Piggott developed first as a brilliant pianist. The *Fantasia quasi una sonata* is one of the few works from his earlier years that he acknowledged. Not surprisingly, for his complex individual musical language is firmly stamped upon it. The *Second Sonata* and *Third Set of Preludes* date from his later years; both were dedicated to **Malcolm Binns**. The *Preludes* unpredictably contrast fast and slow tempi (and sections) and, while the central *Presto Commodio* and following *Con Moto* both demand considerable bravura, the repose of the intervening sections makes for a satisfying emotional sequence; and the work ends with a dignified, contemplative *Postlude – In Tempo di Corteo*. The mature *Second Sonata* sums up Piggott's musical language, with its complex, all but obsessive figurations and its ambiguity of mode, though not easy to get to grips with, it undoubtedly blossoms with repeated listening. It is played persuasively and expertly by an artist who really understands its inherent ruminative intricacies, and very naturally recorded.

PINTO, George Frederick (1785–1806)

Fantasia & Sonata in C min. (completed Joseph Woelfl); Grand Sonatas 1 in E flat; 2 in A, Op. 3/1–2; in C min.; Minuetto in A flat; Rondo in E flat; Rondo on an Irish Air, 'Cory Owen'

🎧 *** Chan. 9798. O'Rorke (piano)

This unmissable Chandos collection reveals another forgotten composer of distinction, who might have become a very considerable figure had he not died prematurely at the age of 21. His first two *Grand Sonatas* were published in 1801 when Pinto was 16 and already a very accomplished composer indeed, with a distinct individuality, yet writing in a

forward-looking lyrical style, that sometimes reminds us of the young Schubert. The *C minor Sonata*, however, is dedicated to John Field and delightfully identifies with that composer's melodic simplicity. But most striking of all is the *Fantasia and Sonata in C minor*, left unfinished at the composer's death, the opening quite worthy of Mozart, with a following *Adagio–Fugato* which has all the serenity of Bach, followed by a Beethovenian finale, which yet still has a personality of its own. **Míceál O'Rorke** plays all this music very persuasively indeed and is beautifully recorded.

PISENDEL, Johann Georg (1687–1755)

Sonata in C min. for 2 Oboes & Strings; (i) Violin Concerto in D

Ⓑ *** DHM 05472 77339-2. (i) von der Goltz; Freiburg Bar. O, von der Goltz – ZELENKA: *Concertos* ***

Pisendel, also the leader/concert master of the Dresden Court Orchestra, was a famous solo violin virtuoso in his day, and a friend of Vivaldi. Compared with Zelenka, with whom he is paired on this disc, his music is more conventional, much less capricious, but the *Violin Concerto* is laced with virtuoso interludes for the soloist of which **Gottfried von der Goltz** takes full advantage. This is the **Freiburg Baroque Orchestra** of 1994, but it is already a very impressive ensemble.

5 Violin Sonatas

*** CPO 999 982-2. Steck, Rieger

Johann Pisendel wrote his *Violin Sonatas* after studying with Vivaldi in Italy, but these works have a distinct personality of their own, with plenty of dazzling bravura reflecting the composer's own virtuosity. The performances here by **Anton Steck** and **Christian Rieger** (harpsichord) revel in the bravura, but are also sensitively expressive. The recording is very good and this collection certainly brings its composer's music to life.

PISTON, Walter (1894–1976)

(i) Capriccio for Harp & String Orchestra; 3 New England Sketches; Serenata; Symphony 4

🎧 ✦ Ⓑ **** Naxos 8.559162. Seattle SO, Schwarz, with (i) Wunrow

The *Fourth* is Piston's most radiant and appealing symphony, one of the masterpieces of American – and not only American – symphonic writing. This and the three *New England Sketches* are among the composer's strongest and most attractive scores, and they come here in outstanding performances under **Gerald Schwarz**, originally issued on the Delos label, and here made doubly attractive at super-bargain price. The four movements of the *Symphony* are all strongly characterized, with the gentle *piacevole* opening of the first movement leading to tough counterpoint, strongly syncopated, and the second movement *Ballando* rather like a hoe-down, vigorous open-air music, with the evocative slow movement leading to a jaggedly rhythmic finale. The *New England Sketches* are more specifically evocative, set in contrast like a symphony, with a delicate picture of a *Summer Evening* placed between the opening picture of the seaside and the final rugged picture of *Mountains*. Even so, the musical argument is cogent, and although the *Capriccio* is less tautly constructed, it has an element of fantasy beautifully realized here by the excellent harpist, **Therese Elder Wunrow**. First-rate sound.

Violin Concertos 1–2; Fantasia for Violin & Orchestra

🎵 ✪ **BB** ******** Naxos 8.559003. Boswell, Ukraine Nat. SO, Kuchar

It is quite extraordinary that a work as inspired as Piston's *First Violin Concerto* (1939) should not already be in the standard repertoire alongside the Barber, with which it has much in common, including a comparable profusion of individual, lyrical melody. The second subject of the first movement persists in the memory until, most engagingly, it is rhythmically transformed to become the secondary theme of the riotous Rondo finale. The *Second Concerto* is more elusive, but its opening is no less haunting. The first movement is a two-part structure, developing two ideas, one sinuously 'expressible', the other pungently rhythmic and angular. The extended *Adagio* introduces a calm and very beautiful theme which is later to form a canonic duet with the flute. The *Fantasia* is a late work, first performed in 1973. Ruminative and searching, its language is more dissonant. It may seem remarkable that these works should be given their CD début by a Ukrainian orchestra, but they play the music with security, splendid commitment and feeling. **James Boswell**, who studied at Juilliard, is a superbly accomplished, dedicated and spontaneous soloist, and the recording is first class.

Symphonies 2; 6

🎵 **BB** ******** Naxos 8.559161. Seattle SO, Schwarz

Make no mistake, these are superb works and they are interpreted here with total dedication and eloquence. This competitively priced coupling makes as good an entry point into Piston's musical world as any – almost as good as the *Fourth*. On its original Delos release an additional work, the *Sinfonietta*, was included but is omitted here.

Symphonies 5; (i) 7 & 8

** Albany AR 011. Louisville O, Whitney; (i) Mester

The *Fifth Symphony* has a sureness of purpose and feeling for organic growth that are the hallmark of the true symphonist. The *Seventh* and *Eighth Symphonies*, though not quite the equal of the finest Piston, are powerful and rewarding works which will speak to those who are more concerned with substance than with surface appeal. The Louisville performances are thoroughly committed and good, without being outstanding. The recordings sound better than they did on LP.

Flute Quartet; Piano Quartet; Piano Quintet; String Sextet

BB ******* Naxos 8.559071. Shylayeva, Gurt, Munrow, Buswell, Walsh, Hall, Gault, Kuchar, Kelly, Glyde, Ou

The *Piano Quintet* is not only one of his finest works but one of the great quintets of the twentieth century, with a master's understanding of the medium and the musical material most effective and natural to it. It is a gripping and powerful piece, and the *Flute Quartet* and *Piano Quartet* are also well worth getting to know when the performances here are so sympathetic and the recording very good.

PIZZETTI, Ildebrando
(1880–1968)

Clitennestra: Preludio. Concerto dell'estate; La festa delle Panatenee: 3 pezzi per orchestra. Tre preludii Sinfonici per L'Edipo Re di Sofocle

Ⓝ **BB** ****(*)** Naxos 8.572013. Thessaloniki SO, Michailidis

The *Concerto dell'estate* has not been recorded since the days of LP, when it was very successfully performed by Lamberto Gardelli for Decca. It is a work of inventive skill and resource, and has no lack of charm, as have its companions on this disc. The performances from Thessalonika under **Myron Michailidis** are good without being top-drawer.

Concerto de l'estate; La pisanella: Suite

(*) Decca Australian Eloquence (ADD) 476 9766. SRO, Gardelli – RESPIGHI: *Trittico Botticelliano* *****; ROTA: *Concerto for Strings* *******

The best music here is contained in the *La pisanella* excerpts, where the colourful score is redolent of Respighi and full of lush orchestral sonorities. The *Concerto de l'estate* is a later work, dating from 1929, and does not wear quite so well. It may strike one as being as hollow as an Eastman-color epic, if you are not in the right mood, and its pentatonic opening soon becomes tiresome. However, if you are in the mood, **Gardelli's** direction is very positive, even if the **Suisse Romande Orchestra** is not the most virtuosic. The Decca sound is impressive for its age. Good couplings.

L'Edipo Re di Sofocle; La pisanella; Preludio a un altro giorno; Rondò veneziano

Ⓝ **BB** ******* Hyp. Helios CDH55329. BBC Scottish SO, Vänskä

Pizzetti's *La pisanella* is a delight and was one of his few works to make it into the 78-r.p.m. catalogue. But Pizzetti is, like Respighi, a master of the orchestra and richly inventive. **Osmo Vänskä** conducts with authority and flair, and obviously believes in these all-too-rarely performed scores.

La pisanella; Preludio a un altra giorno; 3 Symphonic Preludes (from L'Edipo Re); Rondò veneziano

Ⓝ ******* Hyp. CDA 67084. BBC Scottish SO, Vänskä

This well-filled programme makes an excellent introduction to Pizzetti. The *Rondò veneziano* of 1929 was first performed by Toscanini; the three *Preludes* from the opera *L'Edipo Re di Sofocle* are full of interest, and *La pisanella* is a sunny and glorious work. **Osmo Vänskä** plays all these pieces with appropriate feeling, but the string sound lacks real body and richness, particularly at the bass end of the spectrum.

Messa di requiem; De profundis

☾ 🌸 **** Hyp. CDA 67017. Westminster Cathedral Ch., O'Donnell – MARTIN: *Mass for Double Choir*, etc. 🌸 ****

Messa di Requiem; 2 composizioni corali: Il giardino dia Afrodite; Piena sorgeva la luna; 3 composizioni corali: Cade la sera; Ululate; Recordare, Domine

**(*) Chan. 8964. Danish Nat. R. Chamber Ch., Parkman

Pizzetti's 'serene and lyrical Requiem' (as his biographer, Guido Gatti puts it) is a work of surpassing beauty which will be a revelation to those who have not encountered it before, particularly in this fervent and inspired performance. It comes with the *De profundis* he composed in 1937 to mark the healing of his breach with Malipiero. Fine though the performance by the **Danish Radio Chamber Choir** under **Stephen Parkman** is, coupled with other Pizzetti choral pieces, this **Westminster Cathedral** version completely supplants it.

Assassinio nella Cattedrale (opera; complete)

Ⓝ 🌸 **** Decca DVD 0743253. Raimondi, Cordella, Valleggi, De Gobbi, Fabbian , Marrocu, Zarmella, Soloists & Ch. of the Conservatorio Piccinni di Bari, O Sinf. della Provincia di Bari, Morandi

Assassinio nella Cattedrale (1958) is the only Pizzetti opera to have been professionally staged in England. It is based on Alberto Castelli's translation of T. S. Eliot's play, which Pizzetti shortened and adapted: he omits the knights' justification of the murder of the archbishop in Eliot's epilogue. This performance, recorded in Basilica di San Nicola in Bari, should do much to put this wonderful score back on the map. **Ruggero Raimondi** has tremendous presence as the Archbishop and is in magnificent voice (he must now be in his mid-sixties) and acts majestically. The remainder of the cast is hardly less inspired, and the production is visually sumptuous. The opera is short, but it is totally compelling, both musically and dramatically. The musical flow is dignified and stately as befits the subject matter and the orchestral palette subtle in its colouring. There are moments when its melodic lines suggest that the lessons of Mussorgsky and Pelléas have been observed as well as late Verdi, and the choral writing has an almost symphonic sweep. *Assassinio nella Cattedrale* has been absurdly neglected on the stage (as indeed has Pizzetti generally) but this superbly paced and intensely felt reading brings home the beauty and nobility of this score. Recommended with enthusiasm.

PLEYEL, Ignaz (1757–1831)

Clarinet Concertos 1–2 in B flat; (i) Sinfonia concertante in B flat for 2 Clarinets & Orchestra

Ⓝ *** CPO 777 241-2. Klöcker; (i) Arnold; SW Deutsches CO, Pforzheim, Tewinkel

The name of Ignaz Pleyel is famous as a French manufacturer of pianos but, around the time that Haydn was visiting London for the Salomon concerts, Pleyel was far better known as a composer and his easily tuneful music was enormously popular. His writing is a bit like Boccherini without the pathos. Here the two *Clarinet Concertos* with their debt to Mozart (and others) have plenty of surface charm, especially in the jocular finales. The *Sinfonia concertante* is rare, not only in featuring a pair of clarinets, but also in using them a great deal in close duet, often playing in thirds – so the effect is more like a double concerto. Again the music is pleasing and it is very well played and recorded.

Violin Concerto in D; Symphonies concertantes: (i) in A; (ii) in B flat

Ⓝ ⒝⒝ *** Naxos 8.570320. Perry; (i) Lippi (violin); (ii) Chiang (viola); Baltimore CO, Thakar

As can be seen from the listing, the *B flat Sinfonie Concertante* features the viola as its second solo instrument. It has only two movements, the first characteristically expansive; but it is the *A major* that is the more striking work with its opening tutti sounding very like Mozart. It has a brief but memorable *Adagio* and closes with a delightful 'tic-toc' rondo that might almost have been by Paganini. The solo *Violin Concerto* has another fine *Cantabile* slow movement and a catchy finale (composed several years after the first two movements). Excellent solo playing, especially from the nimble **David Perry**, a stylish modern-instrument accompaniment from the **Baltimore Chamber Orchestra** and excellently balanced recording.

'Prussian Quartets': 7 in D; 8 in F; 9 in G min.

Ⓝ *** CPO 777 315-2. Pleyel Qt Köln

In 1776 Pleyel completed his studies with Haydn, with whom he had learned much about the string quartet medium. Even so, he preferred a three-movement format, and wrote 57 works in this form. It is not clear when the 12 *Prussian Quartets* were written, but they became the most popular of Pleyel's output. Mozart admired them and had commented earlier to his father, 'it will be a lucky day for music if later on Pleyel should be able to replace Haydn'. Certainly the three quartets here show a natural aptitude for the medium. The *D major* work has a fine *Amoroso* slow movement; the *F major* has only two movements because the second is extended, a set of variations on an engaging siciliano-type melody. It is the *G minor*, which has the most striking finale, a busy moto perpetuo frames a central *Menuetto cantabile*. All three works are excellently played and recorded.

PLUMMER, John (died c. 1487)

Missa Sine nomine

*** Signum SIGCD 015. Clerks' Group, Wickham (with BEDYNGHAM: *Myn hertis lust; Fortune alas; Mi verry joy;* ANON.: *Kyrie; Song; Pryncesse of youthe* ***) – FRYE: *Missa Flos regalis*, etc. ***

We know very little about the English composer, John

Plummer, whose *Mass* only survives in a Brussels manuscript. His setting is rather bare and primitive in its part-writing, less inspired than its coupling by Walter Frye, but it makes a fascinating aural glimpse into an unfamiliar period of English polyphony. The coupled songs by Bedyngham are delightful and this whole collection, beautifully sung and recorded, is treasurable.

PONCE, Manuel (1882–1948)

Concierto del sur

🔑 *** Warner 2564 60296-2. Isbin, NYPO, Serebrier – RODRIGO: *Concierto de Aranjuez*; VILLA-LÔBOS: *Guitar Concerto* ***

As **Sharon Isbin** suggests in her notes to this CD, Ponce has 'a magical gift of lyricism, counterpoint and colour', and this is a delightful, lightweight concerto, scored with a delicate palette and engaging transparency. Throughout, the guitar, in free fantasia, embroiders the glowing orchestral texture. The themes are gentle but soon insinuate themselves into the listener's consciousness, while Isbin's subtle guitar frescos and roulades captivate the ear. She plays marvellously and is accompanied by **Serebrier** with great skill.

Folia de España (Theme & Variations with Fugue)

🔑 (BB) *** Sony (ADD) SBK 47669. Williams (guitar) – BARRIOS: *Collection* ***

Ponce's *Variations on 'Folia de España'* are subtle and haunting, and their surface charm often conceals a vein of richer, darker feeling. The performance is first rate and the sound admirably clean and finely detailed, yet at the same time warm.

PONCHIELLI, Amilcare (1834–86)

La Gioconda (complete; DVD version)

(*) TDK **DVD DVWW OPGIOC (2). Voigt, Fiorillo, Columbara, Podles, Margison, Guelfi, Liceu Theatre Ch. & O, Callegari (Dir: Pier Luigi Pizzi, V/D: Pietro d'Agonistino)

Recorded in Barcelona at the Liceu Theatre in 2005, this DVD offers a powerful reading of Ponchielli's most celebrated opera, led by the formidable **Deborah Voigt** in the title-role, powerfully intense, not least in her *Suicidio*. Opposite her in the tenor role of Enzo is **Richard Margison**, strong and lusty rather than subtle in his big aria, *Cielo el mar*. Visually, neither is a romantic figure, nor is **Elisabetta Fiorillo** as Laura, but **Carlo Columbara** as Alvise is strong and handsome. Impressive too is the fruity-toned contralto, **Eva Podles**, as La Cieca, adding to the melodrama. In the Pizzi production the melodrama is sometimes overdone, as when La Gioconda stabs herself; but, with traditional costumes set against stylized sets involving a sequence of staircases, the production does not get in the way of the story-telling. **Daniele Callegari** is a lively conductor, drawing crisp playing from the orchestra in the celebrated *Dance of the Hours*.

La Gioconda (complete)

🔑 *** EMI 5 57451-2 (3). Urmana, Domingo, d'Intino, Fiorillo, Scandiuzi, Ataneli, Bavarian R. Ch., Munich R. O, Viotti

🔑 (M) *** EMI (ADD) 5 56291-2 (3) also 3 81854-2 (2). Callas, Cossotto, Ferraro, Vinco, Cappuccilli, Companeez, La Scala, Milan, Ch. & O, Votto

(M) *** Decca 475 6670 (3). Caballé, Baltsa, Pavarotti, Milnes, Ghiaurov, Hodgson, L. Op. Ch., Nat. PO, Bartolletti

(M) (***) Fonit mono 3984 29355-2 (3). Callas, Barbieri, Amadini, Silveri, Neri, Poggi, Turin R. Ch. & O, Votto

Though **Plácido Domingo** was 61 by the time of the sessions, you would never know that from his singing, which is full and rounded with no hint of strain, rising to a performance of the big tenor aria, *Cielo e mar*, that is beautiful, deeply felt and finely shaded. He is well matched by the soprano, formerly a mezzo, **Violeta Urmana**, in the title-role of La Gioconda. She may not have the temperament of such leading rivals on disc as Maria Callas and Montserrat Caballé, but the firm, rich focus of her voice is consistently satisfying. She brings out the musical qualities of Ponchielli's writing, with the big Act IV aria, *Suicidio*, offering a formidable range of tone and expression. Similarly, others in the generally excellent cast, such as **Luciana d'Intino** as Laura, **Elisabetta Fiorillo** as La Cieca and **Lado Ataneli** as the scheming Barnaba, may not be as characterful as some on the finest rival sets (none recent), but they tackle the vocal problems of this demanding score most satisfyingly. A clear choice among digital versions.

Maria Callas gave one of her most vibrant, most compelling, most totally inspired performances on record in the title-role of *La Gioconda*, with flaws very much subdued. The challenge she presented to those around her is reflected in the soloists – **Cossotto** and **Cappuccilli** both at the very beginning of distinguished careers – as well as the distinctive tenor **Ferraro** and the conductor **Votto**, who has never done anything finer on record. The recording still sounds well, though it dates from 1959. This a mid-priced set with a synopsis.

The casting of Decca's 1980 *La Gioconda* could hardly have been bettered in its day, with **Caballé** just a little overstressed in the title-role but producing glorious sounds. **Pavarotti**, for long immaculate in the aria *Cielo e mar*, here expands into the complete role with equally impressive control and heroic tone. **Bartolletti** proves a vigorous and understanding conductor, presenting the blood-and-thunder with total commitment but finding the proper charm in the most famous passage, the *Dance of the Hours*. Full texts and translation are included in this mid-priced Classic Opera release.

Like the companion **Callas** set of *La Traviata*, this Fonit set was recorded (for Cetra in 1952) very early in the diva's career. She was to re-record the opera in 1959, again **Votto**, but, as in the remake, the present set shows her dramatic powers at their peak and the voice fresher than ever. Votto conducts with understanding, maintaining a spontaneous dramatic flow and the remastering of the old mono recording is surprisingly good.

La Gioconda: Dance of the Hours

*** Testament (ADD) SBT 1327. Philh. O, Mackerras – VERDI:
Overtures and ballet music; WOLF-FERRARI: *Overtures,
Intermezzi & Dances* (***)

With the Philharmonia Orchestra in superb form,
Mackerras brings refinement and point to his performance
without loss of sparkle.

PORTER, Quincy (1897–1966)

String Quartets 1–4

(BB) *** Naxos 8.559305. Ives Qt

Quincy Porter comes from Connecticut and belongs to the
generation of Roy Harris, Howard Hanson and Roger
Sessions. The first four quartets, accommodated on this disc,
were composed over the period 1922–31 and are highly civilized, beautifully crafted pieces, though there is quite a lot
of Bloch in them. There is, as one might expect, a Gallic feel
to much of it, but the listener is held throughout and the
composer has a fine sense of line, and the contrapuntal writing and the texture are always transparent and full of interest. A very enjoyable disc, which whets one's appetite for the
remaining five quartets.

POTTS, Francis (born 1957)

Christus (Passion Symphony for solo organ)

(N) **** Signum SIGCD 062 (2). Filsell (organ of St Peter's
Church, Eaton Square, London)

Francis Potts is a virtuoso performer on both piano and
organ, and is Head of Composition and Research
Development at the London College of Music. It is perhaps
surprising he chose not to record *Christus* himself; but in
the event **Jeremy Filsell** was an expert choice, and the magnificent new organ at St Peter's, Eaton Square, proves ideal
for the music itself. In the composer's own words, '*Christus*
owes little to the French tradition of organ symphony', and
he further acknowledges the great influence of Carl Nielsen
on his music. The five movements of *Christus* trace the
'Coming of Christ', the 'Deposition', 'Gethsemane', the
'Tomb' and finally 'the Resurrection', portrayed as 'a vast
struggle towards ultimate triumph'. The music is fundamentally tonal, but the work's first four notes provide a continual motivic presence throughout. That *Christus* is
astonishingly original goes without saying and yet it is
wholly accessible. The composer has provided an extremely
detailed note about the music's progress which it is possible
to follow while listening, although one regrets that it is not
closely cued to the 45 bands offered on the pair of CDs.

POULENC, Francis (1899–1963)

ORCHESTRAL MUSIC

(i) *Les Animaux modèles*; (ii; iii) *Les Biches* (ballet;
complete); (ii) *Bucolique*; (i; iv) *Concert champêtre*

(for harpsichord & orchestra); (i; v) *Double Piano
Concerto in D min.*; (vi) 2 *Marches et un intermède
(for Chamber Orchestra)*; *Les Mariés de la Tour
Eiffel (La Baigneuse de Trouville; Discours du
général)*; (ii) *Matelote provençale*; *Pastourelle*;
(vi) *Sinfonietta*; *Suite française*

⊕–(B) **** EMI Rouge et Noir (ADD/DDD) 5 69446-2 (2).
(i) Paris Conservatoire O; (ii) Philh. O; (iii) Amb. S.; (iv) van
der Wiele; (v) composer; Février; (vi) O de Paris; all cond.
Prêtre

Les Biches comes here in its complete form, with the choral
additions that Poulenc made optional when he came to re-
work the score. The music is a delight, and so too is the
group of captivating short pieces, digitally recorded at the
same time (1980): *Bucolique*, *Pastourelle* and *Matelote
provençale*. High-spirited, fresh, elegant playing and sumptuous recorded sound enhance the claims of all this music.
The *Suite française* is another highlight. It is well played and
recorded in a pleasing, open acoustic. **Poulenc** himself was
a pianist of limited accomplishment, but his interpretation
with **Jacques Février** of his own skittish *Double Concerto* is
infectiously jolly. In the imitation pastoral concerto for
harpsichord, **Aimée van der Wiele** is a nimble soloist, but
here **Prêtre's** inflexibility as a conductor comes out the
more, even though the finale has plenty of high spirits.
With nearly 156 minutes' playing time, these CDs are well
worth exploring.

*Aubade; Concert champêtre; Piano Concerto; Double
Piano Concerto in D min.; Organ Concerto in G
min.; Sinfonietta*

(N) (BB) *** Virgin 2CD 2 522045-2 (2). Pommier, Cole,
Queffélec, Weir, City of L. Sinf., Hickox

Jean-Bernard Pommier gives a thoroughly idiomatic and incisive account of the *Aubade*, and both he and **Anne
Queffélec** play the *Concerto for Two Pianos* to the manner
born. They have the measure of the pastiche Mozart slow
movement and the quasi-Gamelan first. Pommier seems less
at home in the *Piano Concerto* and misses the *gamin*-like
charm of the opening. The instrument is also a bit laid back
and has a slightly resonant halo. The *Concert champêtre* is
charming, though the perspective is not good. However,
Gillian Weir is splendidly idiomatic in the *Organ Concerto*
and **Hickox** gives an affectionate and charming account of
the *Sinfonietta*. So, all in all this set is a good bargain.

*Aubade; Piano Concerto; (i) Double Piano Concerto
in D min.*

⊕– **** RCA 82876 60308-2. Le Sage, Liège PO, Denève;
(i) with Braley

⊕– (BB) **** Warner Apex 2564 62552-2. Duchable, Rotterdam
PO, Conlon; (i) with Collard

After the ambivalent mood of the opening *Toccata*, Poulenc's
Aubade ('an allegory of women and feminine solitude') is a
series of brief vignettes, witty, audacious and melancholy by
turns. The easy-going charm of the opening of the *Piano
Concerto* is also admirably caught, the *Andante* wistfully romantic and the skittish finale making a perfect foil. Both are

played with style and panache by **Eric le Sage**, persuasively accompanied by **Stéphane Denève**.

Frank Braley enthusiastically joins the team for the *Double Piano Concerto*, which opens at high speed, with exhilarating, almost reckless dash, so the contrast of the gentle quasi-Mozartian pastiche of the *Larghetto* is the more enticing. More fireworks in the finale, which brings virtuosic precision of articulation from the soloists, yet keeps its élan. All in all, a very successful, consistently diverting triptych, very well (if resonantly) recorded.

This Apex CD is one of the most attractive of all the issues in this enterprising series. The *Aubade* is an exhilarating work of great charm; the *Piano Concerto* evokes the faded charms of Paris in the 1930s. The performance of these two solo works by **François-René Duchable** and the **Rotterdam Orchestra** has a certain panache and flair that is most winning.

(i) *Aubade. Sinfonietta*

(BB) *** Hyp. Helios CDH 55167. New L. O, Corp – HAHN: *Le Bal de Béatrice d'Este.* ***

The *Sinfonietta* is a fluent and effortless piece, full of resource and imagination, and **Ronald Corp** and the **New London Orchestra** do it proud. **Julian Evans** is an alert soloist in the *Aubade*: his is a performance of real character and his account can hold its own artistically with the competition.

Les Biches (ballet; suite)

⊕ **** Chan. 9023. Ulster O, Y. P. Tortelier – IBERT: *Divertissement*; MILHAUD: *Le Bœuf; La Création* ****

(***) Testament mono SBT 1294. Paris Conservatoire O, Desormière (with DELIBES: *Coppélia & Sylvia Suites* (***))

Yan Pascal Tortelier and the **Ulster Orchestra** give an entirely winning account of Poulenc's ballet suite. Here the opening has delightfully keen rhythmic wit, and the playing is equally polished and crisply articulated in the gay *Rag-Mazurka* and infectious *Finale*. The lovely *Adagietto* is introduced with tender delicacy, yet reaches a suitably plangent climax. Top-drawer Chandos sound and splendid couplings ensure the overall success of this admirable compilation.

Desormière's pioneering 1951 mono set of the orchestral numbers from *Les Biches* has been out of circulation for almost four decades, but in terms of style and character it has never been surpassed and the present restoration makes it sound very good indeed.

(i; ii) *Concert champêtre*; (iii; iv) *Organ Concerto*; (ii; iii) *Piano Concerto*; (ii; iii; v) *Double Piano Concerto*; (i) *Animaux modèles – Suite d'après La Fontaine*; (i; ii) *Aubade*; (i) *La Baigneuse de Trouville; Les Biches: Suite; Bucolique; Discours du Général; Fanfare; 2 Marches et un Intermède; Matelote provençale; Pastourelle; Pièce brève sur le nom d'Albert Roussel; 2 Préludes posthumes et une Gnossienne; Sinfonietta; Suite française; 3 Mouvements perpétuels; Valse;* (i; vi) *Le Bal masqué; Le Bestiare ou Le Cortège d'Orphée; Cocardes;* (i; vi; vii) *Le Gendarme incompris (Comédie-bouffe);* (i; viii) *Gloria;* (ix) *Litanies à la Vierge noire;* (i; vi) 4

Poèmes de Max Jacob; Rapsodie nègre; (i; viii) *Stabat Mater*

⊕ (B) *** Decca 475 8454 (5). Dutoit, with (i) O Nat. de France; (ii) Rogé; (iii) Philh. O; (iv) Hurford; (v) Deferne; (vi) Le Roux; (vii) Visse, Wilson; (viii) Pollet, R. France Ch.; (ix) Maîtrise de R. France

This Decca set makes an ideal choice for those wanting the main orchestral and choral works of Poulenc. The *Aubade* is particularly delightful, and the richly orchestral arrangement of Satie's *Gnossiennes* ends the third disc magnetically. **Dutoit** readily catches in *Les Biches* the music's languid warmth and veiled eroticism, notable in the beautiful *Adagietto*, but the opening *Rondeau*, with its pert, jazzy trumpet solo, might have had more bite, partly the fault of the warm resonance of the recording. The major works on the second disc are the *Sinfonietta*, which comes off marvellously, and the *Concert champêtre*, where **Pascal Rogé** proved as fine a clavecinist as pianist and his account, equally strong on charm and elegance, ranks very highly indeed. He is equally captivating in the *Piano Concerto*, readily catching its moments of tenderness and gamin-like *joie de vivre*. In the D *minor Concerto for two pianos* he is partnered by **Silvia Deferne**, and both artists are completely attuned to the sensibility and spirit of this still underrated master. **Hurford** is hardly less successful in the *Organ Concerto* and the **Philharmonia Orchestra** produces a cultivated sound for Dutoit, marginally less characterful and idiomatic perhaps than the French orchestra on the companion discs, but warmly elegant. The fourth CD offers *Le Gendarme incompris* ('The misunderstood policeman'), a spoken entertainment. The rest of the CD comprises mainly early pieces, and they are offered together with the later, better-known and always captivating *Le Bal masqué*. Such was the popularity of the *Trois Mouvements perpétuels* that Poulenc orchestrated them in 1925 and made a second arrangement for nine instruments, as offered here. *Le Bestiare* is recorded in its original form, for baritone and a small instrumental ensemble without piano. The fifth disc offers the large-scale choral works: the opening of the *Gloria* is a bit heavy but is otherwise satisfactory, and there is much warmth and beauty found in the *Stabat Mater*. All in all, highly recommendable, and texts and translations are included.

Concerto in G min. for Organ, Strings & Timpani

⊕ (BB) *** Warner Apex 2564 61912-2. Alain, Bamberg SO, Kantorow – ALAIN: *Sarabande for Organ, String Quintet & Timpani;* DURUFLÉ: *3 Dances; Prélude et Fugue* ***

*** Ondine ODE 1094-5. Latry, Phd. O, Eschenbach – SAINT-SAENS: *Symphony 3;* BARBER: *Toccata Festiva* ***

(*) Chan. 9271. Tracey (organ of Liverpool Cathedral), BBC PO, Tortelier – GUILMANT: *Symphony 1;* WIDOR: *Symphony 5* *

Marie-Claire Alain's 1997 **Bamberg** recording is second to none. The unnamed organ in the Sinfonie an der Regnitz is eminently suitable, and she plays with her usual flair. **Kantorow** accompanies her with comparable élan, and the recording is excellent. The couplings too are highly desirable.

On Ondine the strikingly full and vivid (if rather dry) sound instantly commands attention. **Eschenbach** goes all out for drama, but the superb playing and beauty of the lyrical passages are equally impressive. This exciting version has something fresh to say about this marvellous work, and it is thoroughly recommended.

The wide reverberation period of Liverpool Cathedral produces gloriously plush textures (the orchestral strings are radiantly rich in colour) but little plangent bite, and some may feel that the effect is too overwhelmingly sumptuous for Poulenc's *Concerto*. Yet it is easy to wallow in the gloriously full sounds, and the performance itself, spacious to allow for the resonance, is certainly enjoyable.

'Francis Poulenc and Friends': (i) Double Piano Concerto in D min.; (ii) Concerto in G min. for organ, timpani & strings; (iii) Dialogues des Carmélites; La voix humaine; Les Mamelles de Tirésias; La Courte Paille; (iv) Flute Sonata; (v) Pastourelle; Toccata; (vi) 3 Mouvements perpétuells; (vii) Banalités; Chansons villageoises; Chansons gaillardes; (viii) Sarabande (DVD versions)

●—*** EMI **DVD** DVB 3102009. Composer, with (i) Février, O Nat. de l'ORTF, Prêtre; (ii) Grunewald, PO de l'ORTF, Prêtre; (iii) Duval; (iv) Rampal, Veyron-Lacroix; (v) Tacchino; (vi) Février; (vii) Bacquier, Février; (viii) Gendron, Ivadli

An indispensable item for admirers of this inspiriting and life-loving composer. Much of this DVD derives from a concert in the Salle Gaveau to mark Poulenc's sixtieth birthday, where he is seen in conversation with Bernard Gavoty. (He is as entertaining a speaker as he is witty a composer.) The two *Concertos* come from 1962 and 1968 respectively, the former at about the time when these artists recorded it commercially. Poulenc's score is both witty and at times profound, though he is by no means as elegant or polished at the keyboard as, say, Britten or for that matter his partner here, **Jacques Février**. It is good to see and hear the delightful **Denise Duval**, who sings with great artistry; small wonder that Poulenc adored her so much. The picture quality is variable but acceptable and, though the camerawork in the first movement of the *D minor Concerto* is a bit fussy, it is otherwise exemplary both in the other movements and elsewhere in this compilation.

The Story of Babar the Elephant (orch. Jean Françaix)

●— ⚙ (BB) **** Naxos 8.554170. Humphries, Melbourne SO, Lanchbery – BRITTEN: *Young Person's Guide to the Orchestra*; PROKOFIEV: *Peter and the Wolf*****

Barry Humphries adopts an engagingly cultivated male persona to tell *The Story of Babar* with an elegance and a sense of innocence which make the narrative seem completely believable, within a children's world where elephants can assume human vanities and aspirations. He is genial, gently touching and animated by turns, but always stylish; and so is **Lanchbery's** matching orchestral accompaniment, which catches the moments of nostalgia and joy with equal sensitivity and flair.

CHAMBER MUSIC

Complete chamber music: Cello Sonata; Clarinet Sonata; Sonata for 2 Clarinets; Sonata for Clarinet & Bassoon; Elégie for Horn & Piano (in Memory of Dennis Brain); Flute Sonata; Oboe Sonata; Sarabande for Guitar; Sextet for Piano, Flute, Oboe, Clarinet, Bassoon & Horn; Sonata for Horn, Trumpet & Trombone; Trio for Piano, Oboe & Bassoon; Villanelle for Piccolo (pipe) & Piano; Violin Sonata

●—*** Hyp. CDA 67255/6. Nash Ens., with I. Brown (piano)

Poulenc's delightful chamber music has done well in recent years: the set by various British artists on Cala has strong claims on the collector (see below). Poulenc is quintessential **Nash Ensemble** territory and their Hyperion survey is of predictable excellence. Common to most of these works is the pianist **Ian Brown**, a stylist if ever there was one, whose playing lends such character to the proceedings. There are few performances that fail to delight and fewer that are surpassed elsewhere. Very good recorded sound makes this an excellent recommendation.

Clarinet Sonata, Op. 184

●—*** EMI 3 79787-2. Meyer, Maisenberg – MILHAUD: *Scaramouche*; DEVIENNE; SAINT-SAËNS: *Sonatas* ***

Sabine Meyer and **Oleg Maisenberg** give a captivating account of the delightful Poulenc *Sonata*, with *tristamente* and *très calmé* dominating the mood of the first two movements, but with plenty of high spirits in the *Allegro con fuoco* finale (*très animé* – taken more than literally!).

(i) L'Invitation au château (for Clarinet, Violin & Piano); (i; ii; iv–vii) Mouvements perpétuels for Flute, Oboe, Clarinet, Bassoon, Horn, Violin, Viola, Cello & Bass; (i; ix; x) Rapsodie nègre for Flute, Clarinet, String Quartet, Baritone & Piano; (i; iv–vii; xi) Sextet for Flute, Oboe, Clarinet, Bassoon, Horn & Piano; (i; vi) Sonata for Clarinet; Sonata for Clarinet & Bassoon; (i) Sonata for 2 Clarinets; (iv; ix) Sonata for Flute & Piano; (v; x) Oboe Sonata; (iv; v; x) Trio for Oboe, Bassoon & Piano; (iv–ix) Villanelle for Piccolo & Piano

●— (B) **** Cala CACD 1018 (2). (i) Campbell; (ii) Carter; (iii) York; (iv) Bennett; (v) Daniel; (vi) Gough; (vii) Watkins; (viii) Tapping, Schrecker, West; (ix) Allegri Qt, Sidhom; (x) Drake; (xi) Benson – RAVEL: *Introduction & Allegro*, etc. ***

These Cala discs are a terrific bargain. The Poulenc accounts for the bulk of the two CDs (two hours' music in fact), all of it full of sparkle and freshness of invention. The discs comprise the complete chamber music for woodwind by Ravel and Poulenc, with the exception of works written primarily for the voice. The performances have great elegance and finesse. Poulenc has the rare gift of being able to move from the most flippant high spirits to the deepest poignancy, as in the *Oboe Sonata*, expressively played by **Nicholas Daniel**. His pianist, **Julius Drake**, is highly sensitive, though the piano is not always ideally focused in the excessively resonant acoustic. Elsewhere, in the captivating incidental music to a play by Jean Cocteau and Raymond Radiguet, *L'Invitation au château*, the playing is expert, tasteful and stylish. The *Mouvements perpétuels*, the *Sextet* and the various wind sonatas are beautifully played with great relish and spirit.

Sextet (for Piano and Wind)

*** Chan. 10420. Vovka Ashkenazy, Reykjavik Wind Qt (with FRANÇAIX: *L'Heure du berger*; D'INDY: *Sarabande et Menuet, Op. 72*; SAINT-SAËNS: *Caprice sur des air danois et russes, Op. 79*) – RIMSKY-KORSAKOV: *Piano Quintet* ***

Ⓜ *** Chan. 6543. I. Brown, Athena Ens. – GOUNOD: *Petite Symphonie in B flat*; IBERT: *3 Pièces brèves* ***

From **Ian Brown** and the **Athena Ensemble** a bravura and responsive performance of Poulenc's many-faceted *Sextet*, catching its high spirits as well as its wit, and the gentle melancholy which intervenes at the close of the boisterous finale. The recording is excellent, slightly dry, yet with a nice ambience. Even though the programme is short measure, every minute is enjoyable.

The alternative Chandos disc is equally attractive, bringing an enterprising programme from the **Reykjavik Wind Quintet** and **Vovka Ashkenazy**. The *Sextet for piano and wind* is a winner, full of charm, and beautifully done by these artists – and excellently recorded too.

Sextet for Piano & Wind; Trio for Piano, Oboe & Bassoon; (i) Le Bal masqué; Le Bestiaire

🎵 Ⓜ *** CRD CRD 3437. (i) Allen; Nash Ens., Friend

Thomas Allen is in excellent voice and gives a splendid account of both *Le Bal masqué* and *Le Bestiaire*. The **Nash Ensemble** play both the *Trio* and the *Sextet* with superb zest and character. The wit of this playing and the enormous resource, good humour and charm of Poulenc's music are well served by a recording of exemplary quality and definition. Not to be missed.

PIANO MUSIC

Piano duet

Capriccio; Elégie; L'Embarquement pour Cythère; Sonata for Piano, 4 Hands; Sonata for 2 Pianos

🎵 *** Chan. 8519. Tanyel, J. Brown

These two artists have a very close rapport and dispatch this repertoire with both character and sensitivity. The Chandos recording is excellent, very vivid and present.

Solo piano music

Complete Solo Piano Music: Badinage; Les Biches: 3 excerpts, including Adagietto; Bourrée, au pavillon d'Auvergne; Caprice; Feuillets d'album; Française; Humoresque; 5 Impromptus; 15 Improvisations; Intermède; Intermezzi 1–3; Mélancolie; Mouvements perpetuels; Napoli (Suite); Nocturnes Nos. 1–8; 3 Novelettes; Pastourelle; 3

Pièces; Pièce brève sur le nom d'Albert Roussel; Presto in B flat; Promenades; La Soirée de Nazelles (Suite); Suite; Suite française; Thème varié; Valse; Valse impromptu sur le nom de Bach; Villageoises

Ⓜ *** Chan. 10014 (3). Parkin

Eric Parkin is a much underrated artist who has never really received his due. He is a stylist and plays this music with elegance and taste, and is to be preferred to Eric le Sage's RCA set, which has great clarity and intelligence but, good as it is, is sometimes a bit short on charm.

Badinage; Bourrée, au pavillon d'Auvergne; Humoresque; Suite Française d'après Claude Gervaise; 15 Improvisations; 5 Impromptus; Intermède en ré mineur; 3 Intermezzi; Pastourelle; Presto en si bémol; Mélancolie; 3 Mouvements perpétuels; Napoli (suite); 8 Nocturnes; 3 Novelettes; 3 Pièces; Les Soirées de Nazelles; Suite; Suite française; Valse; Valse improvisation sur le nom de Bach

Ⓑ *** RCA 2 CD 74321 84603-2 (2). Le Sage

Eric le Sage is a virtuoso of a high order, as he immediately demonstrates in the opening *Presto en si bémol* (marked by Poulenc to be played as fast as possible), and later with the most precisely delicate articulation in *Les Soirées de Nazelles*, and in the second disc the amazingly varied *Improvisations* and the *Impromptus*, which are presented with great élan. Sometimes his tempi seem a fraction fast, as in the most famous of the *Mouvements perpétuels*, but he can readily please the ear. In short, the playing here is full of character and certainly does not lack spontaneity or variety of style and timbre. The closing group of *Nocturnes* are exquisite. The recording is very real and vivid.

CHORAL MUSIC

Sacred Music: Ave verum corpus; Exultate Deo; Laudes de Saint Antoine de Padoue; (i) Litanies à la vierge noire; 4 Motets pour un temps de Noël; 4 Motets pour un temps de Pénitence; Salve Regina; Secular Music: Chanson à boire; 7 Chansons (1936); 8 Chansons françaises (1945); Figure humaine; Un Soir de neige

ⒷⒷ **(*) EMI Gemini 5 85776-2 (2). Groupe Vocal de France, Alldis; (i) with Alain (organ)

Recognizing the need for a French chamber choir to match the great international choirs, the **Groupe Vocal de France** was formed in 1976. The result was these two recorded collections: the sacred, recorded in 1981 in L'Eglise Saint Germain, and the secular, recorded six years later in the Salle Wagram. This is all music that ideally needs French voices, and **John Alldis** has trained his French group splendidly so that they combine precision and fervour with a natural feeling for the words.

(i; ii) Gloria; Ave verum corpus; Exultate Deo; (ii) Litanies à la Vierge Noire; 4 Motets pour le temps

de Noël; 4 Motets pour un temps de pénitence; Salve Regina

☐─ (M) *** Coll. CSCD 506. (i) Deam, Cambridge Singers; (ii) City of L. Sinfonia, Rutter

A generous selection of Poulenc's choral music, much of it of great beauty and simplicity, in very fresh-sounding performances and well-focused sound. The performance of the *Gloria* is particularly fine and this disc is now offered at mid-price.

(i) *Gloria;* (ii) *Stabat Mater*

*** Australian Decca Eloquence 476 2947. (i) Greenberg, Lausanne Pro Arte Ch., Swiss R. Ch., SRO, López-Cobos; (ii) Pollet, R. France Ch. & O, Dutoit – BIZET: *Te Deum* **(*)

López-Cobos's account of the *Gloria* is here coupled with an equally fine performance of the *Stabat Mater*, where **Dutoit** brings out both its lyrical and its dramatic qualities with characteristic flair. In his hands it is a work full of character and memorable ideas, much helped by the atmospheric recording. The choir is excellent, as is the soloist.

Mass in G

(B) *** CfP 3 75906-2. Harris, Winchester Cathedral Ch., Neary (with DURUFLÉ: *Tu es Petrus; Tantum ergo*) – FAURÉ: *Requiem; Messe basse* ***

Martin Neary gets another fine perfomance from the **Winchester Cathedral Choir** and his fine treble soloist, **Mark Harris**. The recording is excellent, with well-defined detail and firm definition.

(i) *Mass in G; Exultate Deo;* (ii) *Litanies à la Vierge Noire; Salve Regina*

☐─ (B) *** Double Decca (ADD) 436 486-2 (2). St John's College, Cambridge, Ch., Guest; (i) with Bond; (ii) Cleobury – FAURÉ; DURUFLÉ: *Requiems* ***

As an extraordinarily generous bonus for the two great *Requiems* of Fauré and Duruflé, this Double Decca set offers the Poulenc *Mass in G* together with two motets, *Exultate Deo* and *Salve Regina*, finely wrought pieces in performances of great finish. Then, together with **Stephen Cleobury**, they give us the cool, gently dissonant *Litanies à la Vierge Noire*, a dialogue between voices and organ in which the voices eventually take dominance. It is beautifully done and the **St John's College** forces cope with the delicacy and sweetness of Poulenc's chromatic harmony throughout. The (originally Argo) recording is eminently realistic and truthful.

4 Motets pour le temps de Noël

(B) *** CfP 586 172-2 (2). Winchester Cathedral Ch., ECO, Neary – BERLIOZ: *L'enfance du Christ* **(*); HONEGGER: *Une Cantate de Noël* ***

Martin Neary gets excellent results from the **Winchester Cathedral Choir** in the delightful *Christmas Motets*, and the EMI recording is also first rate. The couplings are apt, and this is a very worthwhile CfP Double.

MÉLODIES

Mélodies (complete)

(M) *** Decca 475 9085 (4). Lott, Dubosc, Kryger, Le Roux, Cachemaille, Rogé

At mid-price, this collection repackages Decca's four CDs of Poulenc songs, accompanied by the ever-sensitive **Pascal Rogé**. For those who insist on fine modern recording, this provides consistently refined and idiomatic performances. **Felicity Lott** is a stylist par excellence and her sympathy for and affinity with the songs of Poulenc is long-standing. Her recordings centre on the theme of childhood, and range from *La courte paille* – written for Denise Duval, Poulenc's favourite soprano, to sing to her young son – to the *Cinq poèmes de Max Jacob*, which evoke the childhood memories of Brittany. Dame Felicity is in excellent form throughout and brings the right blend of feeling and style to everything here. *Hier*, the third of the *Trois poèmes de Louise Lalanne*, is marvellously characterized and quite haunting. **Catherine Dubosc** is thoroughly at home in the Poulenc idiom. Like her fellow artist, the baritone **Gilles Cachemaille**, she is rather forwardly balanced. **Francois Le Roux**, a high baritone who can cope with the demanding tessitura of the songs written for the composer's friend, Pierre Bernac, takes on the major share of his disc, notably the fine cycle *Tel jour, telle nuit*. He also sings superbly the three extra songs for *Le bestiaire*. On the fourth CD, Gilles Cachemaille, a warmer but less versatile baritone, and **Urszula Kryger** provide contrast in an equally varied selection. Throughout this series Pascal Rogé is the intensely poetic accompanist.

Banalités; 2 Mélodies de Guillaume Apollinaire

*** Virgin 5 45360-2. Gens, Vignoles – DEBUSSY, FAURÉ: *Mélodies* ***

Véronique Gens possesses a delightful voice of much beauty, and is very much at home in Poulenc's world. As with the Debussy, she is both imaginative and characterful. She receives sensitive support from **Roger Vignoles**, and Virgin give her excellent and natural sound.

Mélodies including Banalités; 4 Chansons pour enfants; Métamorphoses; 2 Poèmes de Louis Aragon; 3 Poèmes de Louise Lalanne

*** Hyp. CDA 66147. Songmakers' Almanac: Lott, Rolfe Johnson, Murray, Jackson

Felicity Lott sings the great majority of the songs here, joyful and tender, comic and tragic by turns. The other soloists have one song apiece, done with comparable magnetism, and **Richard Jackson** joins Felicity Lott (one stanza each) in Poulenc's solitary 'song for two voices', *Colloque*. First-rate recording, though Lott's soprano is not always as sweetly caught as it can be.

OPERA

Dialogue des Carmélites (complete; DVD versions)

☐─ ⊛ **** Arthaus DVD 100 004. Schmidt, Fassbender,

Petibon, Henry, Dale, Chœurs de l'Opéra du Rhin, Strasbourg PO, Latham-Koenig

(N) *** TDK **DVD** 01442 248601. Dever, Schellenberger, Silja, Aikin, Robertson, La Scala, Milan, Ch. & O, Muti (Dir: Robert Carson)

Poulenc set great store by this opera and this DVD is a remarkably gripping and wholly convincing production which may well serve to persuade those who have not seen the light about this piece. In **Anne-Sophie Schmidt** it has a Blanche who looks as good as she sounds, and a cast which has no weak member. The production conveys the period to striking effect and the claustrophobic atmosphere of the nunnery. The camerawork is imaginative without ever being intrusive and the production so well managed that the *longueurs* that normally afflict the closing scene in the opera house pass unnoticed. Of the other roles **Hedwig Fassbender** (Mère Marie de l'Incarnation), **Patricia Petibon** (Sœur Constance), **Didier Henry** (Le Marquis de la Force) and **Laurence Dale** (as the Chevalier de la Force) are exemplary both as singers and as interpreters.

Poulenc composed the *Dialogue des Carmelites* for La Scala, although in the event this 2004 production was staged in the smaller Teatro degli Arcimboldi. Nothing is lost as the stage is bare of elaborate sets, and this places the action, including the horrifying closing death scene (which is well handled), against a literal, unatmospheric background. The singing is generally of quality, with Blanche (**Dagmar Schellenberger**) and **Barbara Dever** (Mère Marie) standing out, although **Anja Silja** (Madame de Croissy) is rather less impressive. **Muti** conducts vividly, although the overall sound-picture in the Strasbourg production on Arthaus (perhaps not surprisingly) has more of a French feel, partly a matter of orchestral texture. The latter performance is a first choice for its added intensity, but this Italian version still has much to offer, it is well recorded, and the cameras are in the right place.

(i) *Dialogue des Carmelites*. (ii) PUCCINI: *Manon Lescaut*. **(iii)** DONIZETTI: *Don Pasquale* **(complete; DVD versions)**

(N) (M) *** TDK Gold **DVD** DVWW GOLDBOX3 (3). La Scala, Milan, Ch. & O, Muti, with (i) Dever, Schellenberger, Aikin, Silja; (ii) Guleghina, Cura, Gallo; (iii) Furlanetto, Focile, Gallo, Kunde

These three highly contrasted operas (all reviewed separately within these pages) come in a gold box at mid-price.

The Carmelites (sung in English)

(M) **(*) Chan. 314 (2). Wyn-Davies, Palmer, Barstow, Boylan, Powell, Gibbons, Davies, Wedd, Holland, ENO Op. Ch. & O, Daniel

The success of the English language version of Poulenc's masterly opera, one of Peter Moores's long series, is largely due to the fact that it was recorded soon after a series of live performances by the **ENO**, with a similar cast at the Coliseum. **Catrin Wyn-Davies** sings touchingly as Sister Blanche, and the other principal soloists, **Felicity Palmer**, **Josephine Barstow** and **Orla Boylan**, are characterfully con-

trasted, even if their voices have some unevenness of production. Excellent, atmospheric sound, bringing a harrowing account of the final guillotine scene.

La Voix humaine

🎧 (M) *** Warner Elatus 2564 60680-2. Migenes, O Nat. de France, Prêtre

Julia Migenes's dramatic and moving performance of Poulenc's theatrical telephone monologue, *La Voix humaine*, is the finest modern version on record. It is linked with the cantata, *Figure humaine*, and with some *a cappella* motets, but this separate issue is most welcome.

PRAETORIUS, Michael
(1571–1621)

Dances from Terpsichore

🎧 *** Hyp. CDA 67240. Parley of Instruments, Renaissance Violin Band, Holman

Terpsichore is a huge collection of some 300 dance tunes used by the French-court dance bands of Henri IV. They were enthusiastically assembled by the German composer, Michael Praetorius, who also harmonized them and arranged them in four to six parts; however, any selection is conjectural in the matter of orchestration. This 70-minute collection from Peter Holman and his various instrumental groups must be regarded as the most authentic and comprehensive now available. Praetorius makes it clear in the preface to *Terpsichore* that he regards these as French dances, and Holman convincingly suggests that they were intended primarily for performances on a French-style violin band, or a lute combination (a group of four lutes play together here), and that is the instrumentation that he very refreshingly offers.

Advent and Christmas Music

🎧 *** CPO 777 327-2. Bremer Bar. Cons., Cordes

These performances of some of Praetorius's most attractive Christmas music (many of the tunes familiar) are played and sung by a small vocal consort and chamber-sized instrumental group, using recorders, violas da gamba, harp and chamber organ. The textures are delightfully intimate: the arrangements of *In dulci jubilo, Puer natus in Bethlehem* and especially the combination of *Resonet in laudibus* and *Joseph, lieber, Joseph mein* are all especially memorable. Recommended.

Christmas music: *Polyhymnia caduceatrix et panegyrica 9–10, 12 & 17; Puericinium 2, 4 & 5; Musae Sionae VI, 53: Es ist ein Ros' entsprungen; Terpsichore: Dances 1; 283–5; 310*

*** Hyp. CDA 66200. Westminster Cathedral Ch., Parley of Instruments, Hill

Praetorius was much influenced by the polychoral style of the Gabrielis; these pieces reflect this interest. The music is simple in style and readily accessible, and its performance on this atmospheric Hyperion record is both spirited and sensitive.

Lutheran Mass for Christmas Morning (1620)

*** DG 439 250-2. Soloists, Boys' Ch. and Congregational Ch. of Roskilde Cathedral, Gabrieli Consort & Players, McCreesh

Following on after **Paul McCreesh's** hypothetical re-creation of Schütz's *Christmas Day Vespers* of 1664 (see below), this is an even more stimulating and enjoyable liturgical Feast-day celebration. It is also a most attractive way to present a great deal of Praetorius's music within a Lutheran Mass, as it might have been heard at one of the churches in central Germany around 1620.

Opening with a choral processional to a simply harmonized Lutheran melody, we pass straight into the *Introit, Puer natus in Bethlehem*, for three soloists and three choirs; and after the *Alleluia* comes a spectacularly fast choral entry, *Singet jubiliret triumphiret*. The *Kyrie* follows, set for pairs of soloists, and then the brilliantly florid *Gloria*, where the singers (solo and choral) are again joined by brass and organ.

This alternation sets the pattern for much that is to follow. The congregation participates richly in the *Gradual* hymn, *Vom Himmel hoch*, and as the *Mass* proceeds, there are also organ interludes and even a five-part brass sonata by Schein. After the jaunty closing hymn, *Puer nobus nascitur*, the *Mass* ends with the thrillingly exultant setting of *In dulci jubilo* for five choirs, including organ, six trumpets and drums. Here, magnificently sung and played in the echoing acoustic of Denmark's Roskilde Cathedral, the effect is most spectacular.

Renaissance Christmas Music

*** BIS CD 1035. Viva Voce

In collecting and arranging his litugical music, Praetorius indicated the part-writing in his manuscripts, but the choice of voices to be used and the continuo instruments (if any are indicated) is left to the performers. In this wholly delightful collection of Christmas music **Viva Voce** have solved this problem arbitrarily but convincingly. The basic group employs six voices, lute and organ; but the performances often vary the number of singers between different verses of a hymn or motet. The results, freshly sung and with tasteful accompaniments, could not be more appealing, less robust than some Praetorius presentations, but very effectively so. The recording is first class, and full texts and translations are included.

PREVIN, André (born 1929)

The Kindness of Strangers (Profile of the conductor and musician)

(N) *** Isolde Films TP **DVD** 153. Fleming, Gilfry, San Francisco Opera Ch. & O, Previn

This profile of **André Previn**, bringing out the astonishing range of his achievements, was made in 1998 at the time of the first production of Previn's opera, *A Streetcar Named*

Desire, based on the Tennessee Williams play. Now Bernstein has left us, no one today begins to match Previn as a musical polymath in so many fields, not just in conducting and composing, but in playing jazz and writing film music, winning his four Oscars before boldly giving up Hollywood and seeking to conquer the classical world, both as pianist and conductor. The profile is based not only on the opera, with extensive clips of **Renée Fleming** singing in a role created for her, but covers his many activities, giving a fair idea of his career, from his birth in Berlin into a prosperous Jewish family, with his father teaching him to sight-read music and keep up to speed, a valuable asset, to his career in MGM in Hollywood, writing his first score for a film starring Lassie and Jeanette Macdonald. But before that, when still at school, he was scoring the music of other Hollywood composers, being used a great deal, because, as he says, 'I was cheap.' The survey of his conducting career is necessarily limited, as is the survey of his many marriages. He remains a close friend of his last partner, the violinist **Anne Sophie Mutter**, despite being divorced. The clips of *Streetcar* include Renée Fleming's moving last monologue and the plaudits of the audience. Earlier clips include **Kiri Te Kanawa** singing to his accompaniment and his performance of jazz with bassist **Ray Brown**, all most illuminating. Over everything is Previn's own commentary, full of wit as well as graphic information. The interview with **Tennessee Williams** is particularly valuable. **Tony Palmer** has excelled himself in the range and depth of this profile, a masterpiece of a film.

PROKOFIEV, Serge (1891–1953)

Andante for Strings, Op. 50 bis; Autumnal (symphonic sketch), Op. 8; Lieutenant Kijé: Suite, Op. 60; The Stone Flower: Suite, Op. 118; Wedding Suite, Op. 126

*** Chan. 8806. SNO, Järvi

The *Andante* is a transcription for full strings of the slow movement of the *First String Quartet*, and its eloquence is more telling in this more expansive format. *Autumnal*, on the other hand, is an early piece, much influenced by Rachmaninov and full of imaginative touches. **Järvi** takes it at a fairly brisk tempo but it remains appropriately atmospheric. The *Wedding Suite* is drawn from *The Stone Flower* and complements the Op. 118 suite from Prokofiev's last full-length ballet. The performances and recording are in the best traditions of the house.

Autumnal, Op. 8; Egyptian Nights, Op. 61; Hamlet (incidental music), Op. 77; (i) Flourish, Mighty Land, Op. 114; Hail to Stalin, Op. 85

*** Chan. 10056. Russian State SO, Polyansky

The *Egyptian Nights* comes from incidental music composed in 1934, soon after Prokofiev's return to the Soviet Union, and the suite was made four years later, the year in which he also wrote a score for Sergei Radiov's production of *Hamlet*. Prokofiev at second best is better than most of his contemporaries on top form. Despite its naïve touches, the *Stalin*

Cantata is far from negligible. An interesting disc, well performed and recorded.

Boris Godunov, Op. 70 bis: Fountain Scene; Polonaise; Dreams, Op. 6; Eugene Onegin, Op. 71: Minuet, Polka, Mazurka; 2 Pushkin Waltzes, Op. 120; Romeo and Juliet (ballet): Suite 2, Op. 64

*** Chan. 8472. SNO, Järvi

Järvi's second suite from *Romeo and Juliet* has sensitivity, abundant atmosphere, a sense of the theatre, and is refreshingly unmannered. A fuller selection of the music Prokofiev wrote for a production of *Eugene Onegin* is available, but what is offered here, plus the *Two Pushkin Waltzes*, are rather engaging lighter pieces. The performances are predictably expert, the balance finely judged and detail is in exactly the right perspective.

Chout (ballet; complete), Op. 21

🎵– *** CPO 999 975-2. WDR SO, Cologne, Jurowski

Chout ('The Buffoon'), which Diaghilev mounted in 1921, did not enjoy the success its score deserved, though the music was not slow to reach the gramophone. It is a deliciously scored and inventive work with relatively few longueurs. Jurowski and his team maintain the high standards that he achieved in *The Stone Flower*. The **NordWestDeutscher Rundfunk** recording is to a very high standard in terms of clarity and definition.

Chout (ballet): Suite, Op. 21a; The Love for Three Oranges: Suite, Op. 33a; Le Pas d'acier: Suite, Op. 41a

*** Chan. 8729. SNO, Järvi

Järvi has a natural affinity for this repertoire and gets splendid results from the **SNO**; and the recording is pretty spectacular.

Cinderella (ballet; complete), Op. 87

🅑🅑 **** Double Decca 455 349-2 (2). Cleveland O, Ashkenazy –
GLAZUNOV: *The Seasons* ***

Cinderella (ballet: complete); Symphony 1 in D (Classical), Op. 25

🅑 *** EMI Gemini (DDD/ADD) 4 76945-2 (2). LSO, Previn

Artistic honours are very evenly divided between the **Ashkenazy** and **Previn** recordings. Some dances come off better in Previn's EMI version and there is an element of swings and roundabouts in comparing the two. Ashkenazy gets excellent results from the **Cleveland Orchestra**. On CD, the recording's fine definition is enhanced, yet not at the expense of atmosphere, and the bright, vivid image is given striking projection. The appeal of the Double Decca is greatly increased by the inclusion of Ashkenazy's splendid account of Glazunov's finest ballet score. However, the EMI engineers have a more spacious acoustic within which to work and yet lose no detail. Moreover the CD reissue adds a splendid account of the *Classical Symphony*, sunlit and vivacious and hardly less well recorded five years previously.

Cinderella: Suite 1, Op. 107; Lieutenant Kijé (suite); The Love for Three Oranges: March; Scherzo; The Prince and Princess. Romeo and Juliet: Madrigal; Dance of the Girls with Lilies

🎵– 🅑🅑 *** Naxos 8.550381. Slovak State PO, (Košice), Mogrelia

The calibre of this excellent **Slovak Orchestra** is well demonstrated here, and its perceptive conductor, **Andrew Mogrelia**, is at his finest in his gently humorous portrait of *Lieutenant Kijé*, the three 'best bits' from *The Love for Three Oranges* and the charming items from *Romeo and Juliet*. Excellent recording.

Cinderella: Suite. The Love for Three Oranges: March & Scherzo. The Prodigal Son: Suite. Romeo and Juliet: Suite. Scythian Suite

Ⓝ **(*) Australian Decca Eloquence (ADD) 480 0830 (2). SRO, Ansermet

A well-chosen anthology of some of Prokofiev's finest ballet scores, characterfully played by **Ansermet**. The *Scythian Suite* is one of the composer's most powerful and imaginative scores. *The Prodigal Son* is related to his *Fourth Symphony*, and the composer thought so highly of it that he made the *Suite* recorded here. He was right to do so, for this lyrical, inventive work must rank among his finest ballets. In both the more famous *Cinderella* and *Romeo and Juliet Suites*, Ansermet never forgets that this is ballet music, with extremes of tempo eschewed in favour of characterful and atmospheric performances. True, the **Suisse Romande Orchestra** is not the most precise orchestra in the world, but they make up for it in their distinctive and characteristic way, and none of these scores is wanting in drama. The early 1960s sound throughout this set is both warm and vivid.

Cinderella (ballet; excerpts)

🅑 *** CfP (ADD/DDD) 3 93233-2. LSO, Previn –
TCHAIKOVSKY: *Nutcracker (complete); 1812; Marche slave* ***

Previn and the **LSO** offer seven short excerpts (about a quarter of an hour of music) from their fine, complete recording of *Cinderella* as a bonus for a highly recommendable Tchaikovsky collection.

Concertino in G min. for Cello & Orchestra (original version); Cello Concerto in E min., Op. 58

*** Chan. 9890. Ivashkin, Russian State SO, Polyanski

This Chandos disc is called 'The Unknown Prokofiev' and offers the *Cello Concerto* in its original form, before Prokofiev reworked it for Rostropovich. These performances are very good indeed and splendidly recorded. There is much to be said for the original version of this piece: Prokofiev's second thoughts were not in every case improvements and he cut some inventive ideas.

(i) Concertino in G min. for Cello & Orchestra, Op. 132 (completed orch. Kabalevsky & Rostropovich); (ii) Piano Concertos 1–5; (iii) Violin

Concertos 1–2; (i) Sinfonia concertante for Cello & Orchestra, Op. 125

⊶ Ⓜ *** Decca Trio (ADD/DDD) 473 259-2 (3). (i) Harrell, RPO, Ashkenazy; (ii) Ashkenazy (piano), LSO, Previn; (iii) Bell, Montreal SO, Dutoit

The *Cello Concertino*, inspired by Prokofiev's collaboration with Rostropovich in Op. 125, is a comparatively slight piece, but it is very well played by **Lynn Harrell**. He gives an even more impressive account of the *Sinfonia concertante* and he sounds as if he is relishing the numerous challenges to his virtuosity that this score poses. His playing of the cadenza in the middle movement (fig. 18 in the score and the ensuing paragraphs) is pretty stunning and **Ashkenazy** draws strongly characterized playing from the **RPO**. Turning to the keyboard, Ashkenazy then offers vintage, authoritative accounts of the five *Piano Concertos*, which have been much praised by us. (These are also available separately – see below.)

Employing a measure of emotional restraint and an exceptionally pure tone, **Joshua Bell** completes this outstanding anthology with ravishingly beautiful accounts of both *Violin Concertos*, heightening the light and shade in the great lyrical passages to contrast with the formidable bravura writing, which finds him at his most commanding.

Concertino in G min. for Cello & Orchestra; Symphony-Concerto in E min. for Cello & Orchestra, Op. 125; 2 Pushkin Waltzes, Op. 120

ⒷⒷ *** Naxos 8.553624. Rudin, Ukraine Nat. SO, Kuchar

The Russian cellist, **Alexander Rudin**, proves a powerful interpreter of these two concertante works. Rudin can match and even outshine most other rivals, not least in the beauty of his half-tones, as in the slow movements of both works. He and the conductor, **Theodore Kuchar**, inspire the **Ukraine Orchestra** to play with similar incisiveness, helped by vivid, immediate sound. The two charming Pushkin-based *Waltzes* make an attractive fill-up, winningly pointed.

Piano Concertos 1–5

⊶ Ⓑ **** Double Decca (ADD) 452 588-2 (2). Ashkenazy, LSO, Previn

Ⓝ Ⓜ *** Chan. 10522 (2). Berman (in 1, 4 & 5); Gutiérrez (in 2 & 3), Concg. O, Järvi

ⒷⒷ **(*) Warner Apex 2564 61694-2 (2). Krainev, Frankfurt RSO, Kitaenko

Piano Concertos 1 in D flat, Op. 10; 3 in C, Op. 26; 4 in B flat, Op. 53

⊶ ⒷⒷ **** Naxos 8.550566. Paik, Polish Nat. RSO (Katowice), Wit

Piano Concertos 2 in G min., Op. 16; 5 in G, Op. 55

⊶ ⒷⒷ **** Naxos 8.550565. Paik, Polish Nat. RSO (Katowice), Wit

(i) Piano Concertos 1–5; (ii) Overture on Hebrew Themes; Visions fugitives, Op. 22

ⒷⒷ **(*) EMI Gemini 5 17629-2 (2). Béroff; (i) with Leipzig GO, Masur; (ii) with Portal, Parrenin Qt

Ashkenazy is a commanding soloist in both the *First* and *Second Concertos*, and his virtuosity in the *First* is quite dazzling. If he is curiously wayward in the opening of the *Second*, there is no question that this too is a masterly performance. The *Third Concerto* is keen-edged and crisply articulated, and the only reservation here concerns the slow movement which at times is uncharacteristically mannered. Ashkenazy is authoritative in *No. 4* and gives an admirable account of *No. 5*: every detail of phrasing and articulation is well thought out, and yet there is no want of spontaneity or any hint of calculation. Throughout, **Previn** and the **LSO** accompany sympathetically. Berman plays with panache in Nos. 1, 4 and 5, and has the nervous energy and ebullience the music needs. **Gutiérrez** gives vital and brilliant accounts of the solo parts of the remaining two *Concertos* (2 and 3) and is keenly responsive to the shifting moods and extreme dynamics of Prokofiev's writing. The **Concertgebouw Orchestra** under **Neeme Järvi** play magnificently throughout. As a package, their claims are strong, both artistically and in terms of recording quality.

Gutiérrez gives vital and brilliant accounts of the solo parts of the remaining two *Concertos* (2 and 3) and is keenly responsive to the shifting moods and extreme dynamics of Prokofiev's writing. The **Concertgebouw Orchestra** under **Neeme Järvi** play magnificently throughout. As a package, their claims are strong, both artistically and in terms of recording quality.

Kun Woo Paik's playing throughout these five concertos has exhilarating bravura. Tempi are dangerously fast at times and occasionally he has the orchestra almost scampering to keep up with him, but they do, and the result is often electrifying. The famous theme and variations central movement of the *Third Concerto* is played with great diversity of mood and style and the darkly expressive *Larghetto* of *No. 5* is very finely done. The *First Concerto*, which comes last on the first CD has great freshness and compares well with almost any version on disc. In short, with vivid recording in the Concert Hall of Polish Radio, which has plenty of ambience, this set is enormously stimulating and a remarkable bargain. It has far better sound than the remastered Decca recording for Ashkenazy.

Vladimir Krainev and the **Frankfurt Radio Orchestra** under **Dmitri Kitaenko** are also formidable contenders in their Apex Double format. The recordings were made in 1992 and offer sound of considerable warmth and naturalness.

A satisfying Rouge et Noir set from **Michel Béroff**, who plays masterfully and is a pianist of genuine insight where Prokofiev is concerned; **Masur** gives him excellent support. Béroff is free from some of the agogic mannerisms that distinguish Ashkenazy in the slow movement of the *Third*, and he has great poetry.

(i) Piano Concertos 1–5; (ii) Violin Concerto 1 in D, Op. 19

**(*) Testament (ADD) SBT2 1376. Boston SO, Leinsdorf with (i) Browning; (ii) Friedman

Browning gives pretty magisterial accounts of all five Prokofiev concertos, but his *Second* is particularly imposing in its breadth and grandeur, and he is very persuasive in the enigmatic but rewarding *Fourth* for the left hand alone. The *First Violin Concerto* inhabits a totally different world from the first two piano concertos. There is poetry, great tenderness and a fairy-tale quality that on **Erick Friedman's** bow immediately draws the listener into its world.

Piano Concerto 1 in D flat

Ⓝ *** Naïve V 5053. Lise de la Salle, Gulbenkian Foundation O, Lisbon, Foster – LISZT: *Concerto 1*; SHOSTAKOVICH: *Concerto 1* ***

Lise de la Salle sails off with captivating aplomb and dash, yet her slow movement (as with the Liszt coupling) captures the music's special romantic allure. This is a brilliantly commanding début, with **Lawrence Foster** providing an admirable partnership.

(i) Piano Concerto 1; Symphony 1 (Classical) (DVD version)

⊶ ✿ *** TDK **DVD** DVWW-COMARG. (i) Argerich; Flanders SO, Rabinovitch-Barakovsky (V/D: Frédéric le Clair) – BEETHOVEN: *Triple Concerto*; SCHUMANN: *Violin Sonata 1* ***

Alexander Rabinovitch-Barakovsky's account of the *Classical Symphony* with the excellent **Flanders Symphony Orchestra** is in every way first class, polished, witty and genial, but our Rosette is for **Martha Argerich's** dazzlingly passionate account of the *First Piano Concerto*. In the *Symphony* the camera angles change too readily, but in the *Concerto* the video director focuses a great deal on his sparkling soloist and often on her breathtaking digital dexterity, which makes the performance even more vividly communicative. The recording, resonant and vivid, but not absolutely refined, has the piano balanced forwardly, but the orchestra is well in the picture. This is a thrilling example of DVD at its most electrifying.

Piano Concerto 1 in D flat; Suggestion diabolique, Op. 4/4

⊶ ⒷⒷ **** EMI Encore 5 86881-2. Gavrilov, LSO, Rattle – BALAKIREV: *Islamey*; TCHAIKOVSKY: *Piano Concerto 1* etc. ****

A dazzling account of the *First Concerto* from **Andrei Gavrilov**. This version is second to none for virtuosity and sensitivity. Apart from its brilliance, it scores on other fronts too. **Simon Rattle** provides excellent orchestral support and the EMI engineers offer the most vivid recording, while the *Suggestion diabolique* makes a hardly less brilliant encore after the *Concerto*.

Piano Concertos 1; 3

⊶ *** DG 439 898-2. Kissin, BPO, Abbado

Ⓜ **(*) EMI 228531-2. Argerich, Montreal SO, Dutoit – BARTÓK: *Piano Concerto 3* **(*)

(i) Piano Concertos 1; 3; Piano Sonata 7 in B flat, Op. 83

*** ASV CDDCA 786. Kodama; (i) with Philh. O, Nagano

Yevgeni Kissin gives a virtuosic, dashing account of both concertos and is given highly sensitive and responsive support from the **Berlin Philharmonic** under **Abbado**. It is unfailingly brilliant, aristocratic in feeling and wonderfully controlled pianism, and the recording is very good. It is a pity that DG did not offer a fill-up, as this CD offers only 42 minutes 27 seconds of playing time.

Mari Kodama is a vital and imaginative player and the performances are wonderfully alert and fresh-eyed; there is splendid rapport between soloist and conductor (not surprisingly since they are husband and wife) and they benefit from first-class recording.

Argerich is pretty dazzling in the *First Concerto*, though there is perhaps more grace than fire. Indeed some will find it just a shade underpowered. The *Third*, too, has many felicitous touches and great refinement though it does not supersede the earlier version she made in Berlin for DG with Abbado (see below).

Piano Concertos 1; 4 for the Left Hand; 5

*(*) Hyp. CDA 67029. Demidenko, LPO, Lazarev

Nikolai Demidenko possesses formidable technical address but his musical personality is too intrusive for this to be the kind of recommendation his virtuosity should ensure. Tone above *forte* is not always beautiful, *pianissimo* markings are not always observed, and though there is much to admire, it is the pianist rather than the composer to whom one's attention is too often drawn.

Piano Concerto 2 in G min., Op. 16

*** DG 477 6593. Yundi Li, BPO, Ozawa – RAVEL: *Piano Concerto in G* **(*)

Yundi Li makes a bold choice with the Prokofiev *Second Concerto*, for which he professes a special affection and admiration. Prokofiev himself played it when he was in his early twenties (the same age as the present soloist) and it is difficult to think of him surpassing this. **Ozawa** and the **Berlin Philharmonic** give him excellent support.

Piano Concerto 3 in C, Op. 26 (DVD version)

(***) EMI mono **DVD** DVB 3 101989. Janis, O. Nat. de l'ORTF, Paray (with bonus: BRAHMS: *Piano Sonata 2 in F sharp min., Op. 2*; *Hungarian Dances 4 & 5* – Julius Katchen) – RACHMANINOV: *Rhapsody on a Theme by Paganini* (***)

Byron Janis was recorded by French Radio in 1963 in a black-and-white film, and the mono sound ought to be better than this. But if the violins sound thin and pinched, the piano tone is acceptable and, not surprisingly, Janis's virtuosity is dazzling. He is fascinating to watch, while the *Concerto's* full lyricism is caught in the orchestra, thanks to **Paray**: it just gets dehydrated by the inadequate microphones. The Brahms works are played commandingly by **Katchen**, and here the 1968 sound is much better.

Piano Concerto 3 in C, Op. 26

⊶ Ⓜ **** DG (ADD) 447 438-2. Argerich, BPO, Abbado – RAVEL: *Piano Concerto in G*; etc. ****

Ⓜ **(*) RCA **SACD** (ADD) 82876 67894-2. Van Cliburn, Chicago SO, Hendl – RACHMANINOV: *Piano Concerto 3* **(*)

(**(*)) Testament mono SBT 1300. Katchen, SRO, Ansermet – BARTÓK: *Piano Concerto 3*, etc. **(*)

ⒷⒷ (***) Naxos mono 8.110673. Kapell, Dallas SO, Dorati – KHACHATURIAN: *Piano Concerto* (***); SHOSTAKOVICH: *3 Preludes; Piano Concerto 3* (***)

(i) *Piano Concerto 3; Conte de la vieille grand-mère, Op. 31/2–3; Etude, Op. 52; Gavotte, Op. 32/3; Paysage, Op. 59/2; Sonata 4, Op. 29: Andante assai; Sonatine pastorale, Op. 59/3; Suggestion diabolique, Op. 4/4; Visions fugitives, Op. 22/3, 5–6, 9, 10–11, 16–18*

ⒷⒷ (***) Naxos mono 8.110670. Composer; (i) with LSO, Coppola

Martha Argerich made her outstanding record of the Prokofiev *Third Concerto* in 1967, while still in her twenties. There is nothing ladylike about the playing, but it displays countless indications of sensuous feminine perception and subtlety, and **Abbado's** direction underlines that from the very first, with a warmly romantic account of the ethereal opening phrases on the high violins. This is a much more individual performance of the Prokofiev than almost any other available and brings its own special insights. The 1967 recording, always excellent, sounds even more present in this new transfer.

Van Cliburn plays the work not only with astonishing digital brilliance but also with much sympathetic warmth. With a forward balance for the piano, the bold projection of both orchestra and soloist is undoubtedly telling, and especially so in the sharply characterized slow movement. But then the new compatible SACD transfer brings out the background Chicago ambience and the result is more flattering, less brittle than the original LP, even if the piano timbre is less than ideally sonorous.

In the 1930s and 1940s the *Third Piano Concerto* was represented in the catalogue solely by Prokofiev's own records on 78s, and **Katchen's** 1953 account was the first LP version to be issued in Britain. The 1955 edition of the *Record Guide* called his playing 'immaculate, deliciously fanciful but never merely superficial', and even now, half-a-century later, it sounds fresh and spontaneous. The transfer by Paul Baily is also immaculate.

Kapell's fabulously played and electrifying account of the Prokofiev concerto is a *must*. He outstrips even the composer himself – and most others who came after him. Not to be missed.

(i) *Piano concerto 3;* (ii) *Symphony 5*

ⒷⒷ (***) Dutton Lab mono CDBP 9706. (i) Composer, LSO, Coppola; (ii) Boston SO, Koussevitzky

Two classic performances from the days of shellac, **Prokofiev's** own pioneering and exhilarating account of his then relatively new *Third Piano Concerto* from 1932 coupled with the superb 1946 **Boston** version of the *Fifth Symphony*

under **Koussevitzky**. Both are indispensable and both have never sounded better.

(i) *Piano Concerto 5; Piano Sonata 8 in B flat, Op. 84; Visions fugitives, Op. 22/3, 6 & 9*

🎧 Ⓜ *** DG (ADD) 449 744-2. Richter; (i) with Warsaw PO, Rowicki

Richter's account of the *Fifth Piano Concerto* is a classic. It was recorded in 1959, yet the sound of this excellent CD transfer belies the age of the original in its clarity, detail and vividness of colour. Richter then plays the *Eighth Sonata* and the excerpts from the *Visions fugitives* with comparable mastery, the latter deriving from a live recital. In both cases the recording is surprisingly good.

Violin Concerto 1 in D, Op. 19 (DVD version)

Ⓝ *** Medici Arts **DVD** 3085228. Perlman, BBC SO, Rozhdestvensky (with SAINT-SAËNS: *Intro & Rondo capriccioso*) – ELGAR: *Violin Concerto* ***

An elegant account of the magical *D major Concerto* from **Perlman** and the **BBC Symphony Orchestra**, recorded at the orchestra's 50th anniversary concert in October 1980. There is a bonne-bouche in the form of the Saint-Saëns concerto, recorded ten years earlier (29 October 1970) at the London Coliseum with the **Sadler's Wells Orchestra** and **Charles Mackerras**.

Violin Concerto 1 in D, Op. 19 (CD versions)

🎧 **** Pentatone **SACD** PTC 5186 059. Fischer, Russian Nat. O, Kreizberg – GLAZUNOV: *Violin Concerto*; KHACHATURIAN: *Violin Concerto****

🌑 ⒷⒷ (***) Naxos mono 8.110973. Szigeti, LPO, Beecham – BARTÓK: *Portrait*; BLOCH: *Violin Concerto*. 🌑 (***)

Ⓜ *** Warner Elatus 0927 49014-2. Mutter, Nat. SO, Rostropovich – GLAZUNOV: *Violin Concerto, Op. 82*; SHCHEDRIN: *Stihira* ***

On Pentatone the unique triptych of three warmly compelling concertos from this brilliant young German virtuoso, **Julia Fischer**, superbly recorded in full, bright, clear sound, could hardly be bettered. Central to her choice is her love of the Khachaturian, but her approach to the Prokofiev is just as warm. With fine shading, she takes a thoughtful, meditative view of the yearning melodies, the element in the work that, as she says, most attracts her, but her bravura playing is just as impressive.

Szigeti's pioneering version of the Prokofiev *D major Concerto* with **Sir Thomas Beecham** and the **LPO** captures the bitter-sweet intensity of this magical score to perfection. The demonic brilliance of the Scherzo has never been surpassed, even by such great soloists as Oistrakh and Milstein, and the sense of character throughout is superb. Szigeti was a strongly individual artist, and the partnership with Sir Thomas and the LPO brings altogether special results.

As in the Glazunov, **Anne-Sophie Mutter** gives a warmly sympathetic account, responding to the inspirational direction of **Rostropovich**. The great melodies of the outer movements are tenderly expressive and the central Scherzo delightfully witty. The Washington recording, airy and spacious, has the soloist forwardly balanced.

Violin Concertos 1, Op. 19; 2, Op. 63

Ⓜ **** Decca (ADD) 425 003-2. Chung, LSO, Previn –
STRAVINSKY: *Concerto* ****

⊶ Ⓜ *** Warner Elatus 0927 49567-2. Vengerov, LSO,
Rostropovich – GLAZUNOV: *Concerto* ***

ⒷⒷ *** Virgin 2x1 5 61633-2 (2). Sitkovetsky, LSO, C. Davis –
SHOSTAKOVICH: *Concertos* ***

*** Chan. 8709. Mordkovitch, RSNO, Järvi

Kyung-Wha Chung's performances emphasize the lyrical quality of these concertos with playing that is both warm and strong, tender and full of fantasy. **Previn's** accompaniments are deeply understanding, while the Decca sound has lost only a little of its fullness in the digital remastering, and the soloist is now made very present. The Stravinsky coupling is equally stimulating.

Vengerov's account of the *First Concerto* was originally coupled with the Shostakovich *First* and as such not only won the *Gramophone* Concerto Award in 1995 but was also voted 'Record of the Year'. Now it reappears at mid-price, joined to a hardly less fine account of the *Second Concerto*. Vengerov's magnetism in both is in no doubt: his playing is full of life and spontaneous feeling, helped by **Rostropovich's** highly supportive accompaniments. In the *Second Concerto* Vengerov opens the *Andante* magically on a thread of tone, and the playing and orchestral backing are quite ravishing. The finale has splendid vigour and bite. This now becomes the primary recommendation, and the Glazunov is no less remarkable.

The Virgin two-for-one Double makes an amazing bargain in offering first-class versions of both the paired concertos of Prokofiev and Shostakovich. **Dmitri Sitkovetsky** conveys the demonic side of the *First Concerto* more effectively than any other player, without losing sight of its lyricism or sense of line. His version of the Scherzo touches an ironic, almost malignant nerve, while he has the measure of the ice-maiden fairy-tale element at the opening. He has a sympathetic collaborator in **Sir Colin Davis** and the *Second Concerto* is hardly less powerful, and the internal orchestral balance is very natural.

Lydia Mordkovitch gives readings of strong personality and character. She is well supported by the **RSNO** and **Järvi**, and more than holds her own with rival versions. There are some splendidly malignant sounds in the Scherzo of *No. 1*, and both performances make a very satisfying alternative and have first-class sound.

(i) Violin Concertos 1–2; (ii) Sonata for 2 Violins, Op. 56

Ⓝ ⒷⒷ *** EMI Encore 2 08118-2. Perlman; (i) BBC SO,
Rozhdestvensky; (ii) Zukerman

Perlman's 1980 performances bring virtuosity of such strength and command, one is reminded of the supremacy of Heifetz. Though the EMI recording has warmth and plenty of bloom, the balance of the soloist is unnaturally close, which has the effect of obscuring important melodic

ideas in the orchestra behind mere passagework from the soloist, as in the second subject of the *First Concerto's* finale. Nevertheless, in their slightly detached way these performances are impossible to resist as, excluding the balance, the recording is excellent. The *Double Violin Sonata* dates from 1932 when Prokofiev was still living in Paris and is lyrical in feeling, offering both depth and charm. The playing is excellent – as one has every right to expect from this partnership.

(i) Violin Concertos 1–2; (ii) Violin Sonatas 1–2; 5 Mélodies, Op. 35 bis

⊶ Ⓑ **** Decca 475 6712 (2). Bell; (i) Montreal SO, Dutoit;
(ii) Mustonen – SHOSTAKOVICH; *Piano Trio 2* ***

Joshua Bell gives a ravishingly beautiful account of both concertos, heightening in the great lyrical passages the light and shade contrasts with the formidable bravura writing, which finds him at his most commanding. Others like Chung may find darker emotions here but, with recording outstanding even by Decca's Montreal standard, these performances are made the more attractive by their coupling on a Double with the *Violin Sonatas* and the charming *Cinq Mélodies*. They give a highly intelligent reading of all three works.

Violin Concertos (i) 1; (ii) 2; (iii) Violin Sonata 2 in D, Op. 94

⊶ Ⓜ (***) EMI mono/stereo 5 62888-2. Oistrakh, with
(i) LSO, Matačić; (ii) Philh. O, Galliera; (iii) Yampolsky

These famous **Oistrakh** performances from the 1950s fully deserve their classic accolade. The *First*, with **Lovro von Matačić** and the **LSO**, is from the mid-1950s (like the *D major Sonata*), and only the *Second* (with **Galliera** and the **Philharmonia**) of 1958 is in stereo. But this is incomparable playing, and the transfers by Andrew Walter are immaculate.

Violin Concerto 2 in G min., Op. 63

⊶ ⒷⒷ *** EMI Gemini (ADD) 3 81487-2 (2). D. Oistrakh,
Philh. O, Galliera – BEETHOVEN: *Triple Concerto for Violin, Cello & Piano*; BRAHMS: *Double Concerto*; MOZART: *Violin Concerto 3* ***

Ⓜ *** RCA (ADD) **SACD** 82876 66372-2. Heifetz, Boston SO,
Munch – GLAZUNOV, SIBELIUS: *Concertos* ***

Ⓜ *** Warner Elatus 2564 61572-2. Perlman, Chicago SO,
Barenboim – STRAVINSKY: *Violin Concerto* ***

(***) Testament mono SBT 1224. Kogan, LSO, Cameron –
TCHAIKOVSKY: *Violin Concerto*, etc. (***)

David Oistrakh's is a beautifully balanced reading which lays stress on the lyricism of the *Concerto*, and the orchestral support he receives could hardly be improved on. The 1958 recording is admirably spacious and atmospheric, with finely focused detail and great warmth. The CD transfer is immaculate. An altogether marvellous performance, and the Gemini compilation of four very distinguished recordings is extraordinary value for money.

In the *arioso*-like slow movement, **Heifetz** chooses a faster speed than is usual, but there is nothing unresponsive about his playing, for his expressive rubato has an unfailing inevitability. In the spiky finale he is superb, and indeed his playing is glorious throughout. The recording is improved on SACD, and it has been made firmer in the current RCA remastering. No one is going to be prevented from enjoying this ethereal performance because the technical quality is dated.

Though **Perlman's** coupling of Prokofiev's *Second Concerto* and the Stravinsky is ungenerous, this performance, recorded live, is more compelling than his earlier studio recording, with **Barenboim** adding to the urgency and energy.

Leonid Kogan's mono recording from 1955 has never been reissued on CD and its reappearance here gives us a welcome chance to reassess it. No doubt some will find it cooler than Oistrakh, but Kogan is very aristocratic and has tremendous grip and energy. **Basil Cameron** proves how supportive an accompanist he could be.

Divertimento, Op. 43; Sinfonietta, Op. 5/48; (i) Sinfonia concertante, Op. 125

Ⓜ *** Chan. 10312X. SNO, Järvi; (i) with Wallfisch

The engaging *Divertimento* now comes additionally recoupled with the *Sinfonia concertante*, in which **Wallfisch** has the measure of the leisurely first movement and gives a thoroughly committed account of the Scherzo and the Theme and Variations which follow. **Neeme Järvi** lends him every support. The early *Sinfonietta* is offered as a highly attractive bonus (what a sunny and charming piece it is), and the recording throughout has great range, with no complaints about the balance elsewhere.

The Gambler: 4 Portraits, Op. 49; Semyon Kotko: Symphonic Suite, Op. 81 bis

*** Chan. 8803. RSNO, Järvi

Prokofiev's *Four Portraits* enshrine the best of the opera and are exhilarating and inventive. *Semyon Kotko*, though not top-drawer Prokofiev, is still thoroughly enjoyable. **Järvi** gives a thoroughly sympathetic reading in vivid and present sound.

Ivan the Terrible (Complete ballet, arr. Tchulaki; DVD version)

*** Arthaus **DVD** 101 107. Bolshoi Ballet & Theatre O, Zhuraitis (V/D: Motoko Sakaguchi)

The composer Mikhail Tchulaki was asked by the Bolshoi company to adapt the film score that Prokofiev wrote for the Eisenstein film, *Ivan the Terrible*, into a two-act ballet. Cunningly, he used not only 377 fragments from the original score, but also various extracts from other works of Prokofiev, including *Symphony No. 3* and the *Alexander Nevsky Cantata*. In the lavish **Bolshoi** production it works well, with spectacular dancing, atmospheric sets and costumes, a welcome addition to the list of the composer's ballets, well conducted here by **Algis Zhuraitis**.

Lieutenant Kijé (incidental music): Suite, Op. 60

◉━◉ Ⓑ **** Sony (ADD) SBK 48162. Cleveland O, Szell – KODÁLY: *Háry János Suite*; MUSSORGSKY: *Pictures at an Exhibition* ****

Szell is on his highest form. Seldom on record has the *Lieutenant Kijé* music been projected with such drama and substance, and Szell is wonderfully warm in the *Romance* without a suggestion of sentimentality. The recording, like the couplings, is balanced too closely, but the orchestral playing is so stunning one hardly minds, for the opening and closing trumpet-calls are properly distanced.

The Love for Three Oranges: Suite, Op. 33

*** BBC (ADD) BBCL 4056-2. BBC SO, Kempe – BEETHOVEN: *Overture: Leonore 3*; DVOŘÁK: *Symphony 9* ◉ ***

The Prokofiev suite, strikingly intense, finds **Kempe** at home in a sharply characterized performance full of grotesquerie. With well-defined contrasts of light and shade, bite and tenderness, it becomes more than a sequence of genre pieces. Vivid transfer of the 1975 radio recording, with high dynamic contrasts.

On the Dnieper, Op. 51 (ballet); (i) Songs of Our Days, Op. 76

*** Chan. 10044. Russian State SO, Polyansky with (i) Smolnikova, Tarasov, Russian State Symphonic Cappella

On the Dnieper or *Sur le Borysthène* was composed immediately after *The Prodigal Son* and though its invention is not as strong as *The Prodigal Son* nor is it as imaginative as *Chout*, it is well worth hearing. *Songs of Our Days* comes from 1937 and is simple in language and patriotic in sentiment. It is an attractively naïve and enjoyable piece splendidly sung by the soloists and chorus. Good playing from **Valéry Polyansky** and his Moscow forces and very musically balanced recorded sound.

The Prodigal Son, Op. 46; Le Pas d'acier, Op. 41 (ballets; complete)

*** CPO 999 974-2. West German RSO, Cologne, Jurowski

The Prodigal Son, on which Prokofiev drew for the *Fourth Symphony*, is a fine work. *Le Pas d'acier* is a little earlier and is as inventive and characterful, so this well-played and recorded newcomer deserves a welcome.

Peter and the Wolf (animated DVD version)

◉━◉ ◉ **** Arthaus **DVD** 101 804. Philh. O, Stephenson (adapted and directed by Suzie Templeton)

This DVD film of *Peter and the Wolf* is a treasure. Adults enjoy it immensely and it would be a perfect gift for children. **Suzie Templeton** tells the story entirely without narration (one finds oneself whispering it at times), using very realistic puppets who behave and move very believably indeed, using stop-frame model animation. Peter and his grandfather live in a cottage in the wilds. There is snow all around and the weather is singularly inclement. We first meet the characters involved, a bird who because of wing damage cannot fly without the aid of a balloon, a winsome, long-necked duck and a particularly noxious cat. The wolf is very formidable indeed. Peter proves very resourceful in setting out while his grandfather is asleep and the story continues as Prokofiev planned it until the close. Then Peter defeats the incompetent hunters, and lets the wolf escape. Alas, the duck remains unrescued. The music is admirably played by the

Philharmonia under **Mark Stephenson**, and this is altogether enchanting. A bonus takes us into the world of stop-frame model animation and shows us how the film was made.

Peter and the Wolf, Op. 67 (CD versions)

🎧 ⟼ (BB) ******** Naxos 8.554170. Dame Edna Everage, Melbourne SO, Lanchbery – BRITTEN: *Young Person's Guide* ********; POULENC: *The Story of Babar* 🏵 *******

(BB) (*******)Naxos mono 8,111437. Eleanor Roosevelt, Boston SO, Koussevitzky – SIBELIUS: *Symphony 2* (*******)

(B) ****(*)** CfP 586 1752. Rushton, LPO, Edwards (with DEBUSSY: *Children's Corner: 3 Pieces*) – BRITTEN: *Young Person's Guide* *******; RAVEL: *Ma Mère l'Oye* ******

(B) ****(*)** CfP (ADD) 3 82230-2. Richard Baker, New Philh. O, Leppard – BRITTEN: *The Young Person's Guide to the Orchestra*; RAWSTHORNE: *Practical Cats* ****(*)**

(i) Peter and the Wolf; (ii) Lieutenant Kijé: Suite

(M) ****(*)** Decca Phase Four (ADD) 444 104-2. (i) Connery (nar.), RPO; (ii) Netherlands R. PO; Doráti – BRITTEN: *Young Person's Guide* ****(*)**

If you react adversely to **Dame Edna Everage's** exuberantly eccentric persona, the Naxos version cannot be recommended. But for those willing to be included among her possums it is a highly entertaining and very dramatic narrative, with the orchestral accompaniment splendidly paced to match the gripping onward flow of the story. The couplings are equally splendid.

Although the narrative and orchestral commentary were recorded separately on the CfP disc, it is remarkable how well the two fit together. But the flair and professionalism of **Sian Edwards** meant that **William Rushton** was able to add his story-telling to a vividly colourful orchestral tapestry which had its momentum already established. He is a personable narrator, adding touches of his own like 'a vast grey wolf' and 'nothing to report' from the bird, and, overall this is a fine, sparkling presentation, brightly and realistically recorded, which cannot fail to entertain.

Naxos also offers **Koussevitzky's** second recording of *Peter and the Wolf*, with a former First Lady, **Eleanor Roosevelt**, as narrator. His account is supremely natural and should provide a model for young conductors. It comes with a powerful and unforgettable account of Sibelius's *Second Symphony* in which the mono sound may be regarded as historic.

Richard Baker, balanced well forward in a different acoustic from the orchestra, provides an extra introductory paragraph. But, conveniently, this is banded separately, as is each section of the story, and he enters into the spirit of the story and is only occasionally a little coy. **Raymond Leppard** provides an excellent accompaniment, the recording is vivid, and overall the presentation has a certain charm.

Sean Connery uses a modern script by Gabrielle Hilton which brings a certain colloquial friendliness to the narrative and invites a relaxed style, to which the actor readily responds. If you can accept such extensions as 'dumb duck' and a pussy cat who is 'smooth, but greedy and vain', you will not be disappointed with Connery's participation in the

climax of the tale, where **Doráti** supports him admirably. Both *Peter and the Wolf* and *The Young Person's Guide to the Orchestra* start with the orchestra tuning up, to create an anticipatory atmosphere, and the introductory matter is entirely fresh and informal. In *Lieutenant Kijé* Doráti is characteristically direct, with everything boldly characterized, and he secures excellent playing from the **Netherlands orchestra**. As with *Peter and the Wolf*, the extremely vivid Decca Phase Four recording (not unnaturally balanced but ensuring every detail is clear) gives the performance a strong projection.

Romeo and Juliet (ballet; complete; choreography and staging by Rudolf Nureyev; DVD version)

🎧 ⟼ ******* Warner NVC Arts **DVD** 0630 15154-2. Legris, Loudières, Jude, Delanoe, Carbonnel, Martinez, Paris Opéra O, Pähn. (Dir: Alexandre Tarta; Producers: François Duplet and Damien Mathieu)

David Garforth conducts the **La Scala Orchestra** with a passionate commitment to Prokofiev's inspired score, yet he shows a wonderful ear for detail, making the music totally at one with the stage action. The recording is first class, and watching and listening to this superb DVD is a truly memorable experience.

Rudolf Nureyev famously created the role of Romeo for the Royal Ballet in 1965 with Margot Fonteyn as Juliet. In 1977 he revised the choreography for his own London Festival Ballet production, and in 1984 reworked the entire ballet for the Paris Opéra Ballet. The present live performance dates from 1995, with **Manuel Legris** dancing the role of Romeo with great distinction and **Monique Loudières** a delightful, elegantly graceful and passionate Juliet. Their love scenes together, at first romantic and finally erotically ardent, are among the ballet's highlights. But so too are the scenes with Tybalt (**Charles Jude**) and Mercutio (**Lionel Delanoe**) on whom Nureyev's choreography places special emphasis as 'champions' of the younger generation of the two rival families.

The orchestra plays Prokofiev's infinitely inspired score very well indeed, and the recording, too, is very good (it seems to gain range and impact as the ballet proceeds). But it is not up to the superb demonstration quality provided by Decca for Ashkenazy's RPO audio recording (see below), which is surely an essential supplement to the DVD.

Romeo and Juliet, Op. 64 (ballet; complete)

🎧 ⟼ (M) ******** Decca 436 078-2 (2). RPO, Ashkenazy

(M) ******* Double Decca (ADD) 452 970-2 (2). Cleveland O, Maazel

(B) ******* EMI Gemini (ADD) 5 86254-2 (2). LSO, Previn

Vladimir Ashkenazy's outstanding version of *Romeo and Juliet* was recorded as long ago as early 1991 yet did not appear until 2003. That delay is all the more a mystery, when this version sets new standards: it is a full and rich digital recording of a reading that at once combines brilliance, warmth and a feeling of fantasy, with crisply sprung rhythms at speeds that are fresh and alert. The result is lighter and more idiomatic than the much earlier Decca analogue version from Lorin Maazel, and more sparkling than the Gergiev version on Philips.

Previn and the **LSO** made their recording in conjunction with live performances at the Royal Festival Hall, and the result reflects the humour and warmth which went with those live occasions. Previn's pointing of rhythm is consciously seductive, whether in fast, jaunty numbers or in the soaring lyricism of the love music. The Kingsway Hall recording quality is full and immediate, yet atmospheric too.

Maazel by contrast will please those who believe that this score should above all be bitingly incisive. The rhythms are more consciously metrical, the tempi generally faster, and the precision of ensemble of the **Cleveland Orchestra** is little short of miraculous. The recording is one of Decca's most spectacular, searingly detailed, but atmospheric too.

Romeo and Juliet, Op. 64 (ballet; highlights)

🎵 ⓑⓑ ******** Sony SBK 89740. BPO, Salonen

With magnificent playing from the **Berlin Philharmonic Orchestra**, **Esa-Pekka Salonen's** set of excerpts – now reissued at bargain price – is probably a 'best-buy' for those wanting an inexpensive single disc of highlights from Prokofiev's masterly score. The orchestral playing has an enormous intensity and a refined felicity in the score's more delicate evocations. One is touched and deeply moved by this music-making, while the selection admirably parallels the ballet's narrative. The recording, made in the Philharmonie, matches sumptuousness with a potent clarity of projection, and the dynamic range is dramatically wide.

Romeo and Juliet (ballet): Suites 1–3

🎵 ✹ ******** BIS Surround Sound **SACD** 1301. Bergen PO, Litton

Romeo and Juliet (ballet; excerpts including Suite 2)

🎵 Ⓜ ******* Classic fM 75605 57047. RPO, Gatti – TCHAIKOVSKY: *Romeo and Juliet (Fantasy Overture)* *******

Romeo and Juliet: Suites 1 & 2 (ballet; excerpts)

🎵 Ⓜ ******* Telarc CD 80089. Cleveland O, Levi

Litton offers the composer's three suites (74 minutes), but he presents the music in the order in which it appears in the ballet. He does not always press the music forward, as in concert performances, but follows ballet tempi, taking his time to relish the score's magical delicacy, with no loss of tension; and, with the recording providing the widest dynamic range, the **Bergen Philharmonic's** *pianissmo* playing is ravishing. The recording is in the demonstration bracket – and especially so played back in Surround Sound.

After a bitingly pungent opening (*Montagues and Capulets*), **Daniele Gatti's** 50-minute selection effectively encapsulates the ballet's dramatic narrative in nine key numbers. The **RPO** characterizes very strongly indeed and, with generally brisk tempi, the strongest contrast is made between the bold, pungent rhythms of the more vigorous dances and the exquisite delicacy of the gentler, romantic evocation with its wonderfully translucent orchestral colour-

ing. The portrait of *Friar Laurence* is touchingly gentle, but the ballet's passionate climax could not be more heart-rendingly plangent. The recording is superb, very much in the demonstration bracket, and the coupling with Tchaikovsky's *Fantasy Overture* is made the more apt by Gatti's highly romantic approach to that quite different response to Shakespeare's tragedy.

Yoel Levi also seems to have a special affinity with Prokofiev's score, for pacing is unerringly apt and characterization is strong. There are some wonderfully serene moments, as in the ethereal introduction of the flute melody in the first piece (*Montagues and Capulets*). The quicker movements have an engaging feeling of the dance and the light, graceful articulation in *The Child Juliet* is a delight; but the highlights of the performance are the *Romeo and Juliet Love Scene* and *Romeo at Juliet's before Parting*, bringing playing of great intensity, with a ravishing response from the **Cleveland strings**. The rich Telarc recording is in the demonstration class, and if this offers less music than several of its competitors it is now at medium price.

Romeo and Juliet (excerpts); Lieutenant Kijé: Suite, Op. 60

Ⓜ ****(*)** Sony stereo/mono 82876 78761-2. NYPO, Mitropoulos (with MUSSORGSKY: *Night on the Bare Mountain*)

**(*) Testament SBT 1394. Boston SO, Leinsdorf

Mitropoulos's splendid record comes from 1958 but, considering its date, the recording is remarkably good; it is very brightly lit but responds to the controls. The playing of the **NYPO** is electrifying. Prokofiev's score can seldom have received more passionate advocacy over the years, yet there are gentle moments too, for Mitropoulos can be tender as well as pungent. Even though the drama of the narrative is thrillingly projected, there is no feeling of aggressiveness here in either performance. A disc to be snapped up by admirers of this underrated conductor.

Leinsdorf devised from the ballet a suite of his own, which continues uninterrupted, making a chronological sequence that conveys the dramatic narrative of Prokofiev's masterpiece. This he recorded in Boston in 1967, together with a fine account of *Lieutenant Kijé*. He is not perhaps as subtle as some of his rivals, but there is plenty of dramatic tension and atmosphere here and very good recorded sound.

Romeo and Juliet: Suite 2

ⓑⓑ **(***)** Dutton mono CDBP 9754. Moscow State PO, composer – GLAZUNOV: *The Seasons* **(***)**

Prokofiev's own 1943 recording of music from his *Romeo and Juliet* ballet – at that time not yet recognized as a masterpiece – brings some rough ensemble in playing, not helped by the dry acoustic. Yet the warmth and energy of the playing under the composer make this a valuable document, with the Dutton transfer greatly improving the original 78-r.p.m. sound. It is a pity that in the notes so little information is given on the backgrounds, either to this or to the Glazunov.

Russian Overture, Op. 72; Summer Night: (suite from *The Duenna*), *Op. 123; War and Peace* (suite, arr. Palmer)

*** Chan. 9096. Philh. O, Järvi

The *Russian Overture* is determinedly popular in appeal, and it teems with ideas, both lyrical and grotesque, and has plenty of vitality. The *Summer Night Suite* is notable for its delicate *Serenade* and a charmingly romantic movement called *Dreams*. But the finest music here is Christopher Palmer's suite of interludes from *War and Peace*, full of splendid ideas. It ends triumphantly with the magnificent patriotic tune associated with Marshal Kutuzov, the architect of the Russian victory. **Järvi** and the **Philharmonia Orchestra** are thoroughly at home in these scores, and the Chandos recording is characteristically spectacular.

Scythian Suite, Op. 20 (with rehearsal; DVD version)

🔑 *** Arthaus **DVD** 100 314. Rotterdam PO, Gergiev (with DEBUSSY: *Le Martyre de Saint-Sébastien*). (Dir: Rob van der Berg, V/D: Peter Rump) – STRAVINSKY: *Piano Concerto*, etc. ***

Apart from performing it, **Gergiev** here discusses the *Scythian Suite* and its composer, championing the score with much eloquence. There are few pieces in 20th-century music that are as imaginative as its third movement, *Night*, or as inventive as the first, *The Adoration of Vélèss and Ala*, with its extraordinary lush contrasting group. Gergiev's performance has great fervour and eloquence. This includes some valuable archive material of Prokofiev himself and a contribution from his second son, the painter Oleg (who is also now no longer with us). The camera-work is unobtrusive and intelligent, though – as so often – one could do without some of the aerial shots of the orchestra. The *Scythian Suite* is difficult to balance, and some of the detail emerges in greater prominence than the main lines; but for the most part the sound balance is vivid and very present. The Debussy excerpts from *Le Martyre de Saint-Sébastien* are also most impressively played and recorded. This is an outstanding and invaluable DVD that is hugely enjoyable.

Sinfonia concertante for Cello & Orchestra, Op. 125 (DVD version) – see also under *Divertimento and Concertino*

🔑 ✿ **** EMI **DVD** DVA 4901209. Rostropovich, Monte Carlo Nat. Op. O, Kamu – SHOSTAKOVICH: *Cello Concerto 1*. Bonus: MUSSORGSKY: *Songs and Dances of Death* ***

The Prokofiev *Sinfonia concertante*, which reputedly inspired the coupled Shostakovich concerto, is an altogether more romantic, essentially lyrical work. But it has an extraordinarily manic Scherzo which **Rostropovich** plays with such breathtaking virtuosity that the audience breaks into applause at the end of the movement. The work then moves back to warm lyricism and on to a characteristic *Allegro marcato* theme, which the cellist shares joyfully with the orchestra, glancing towards other orchestral soloists when they take up the theme from him. Throughout both works the camera frequently focuses closely on the solo cello, which makes Rostropovich's playing intensely involving. The live communication between soloists and orchestra, projected out to the watcher/listener, is marked, with the work's close leaving one with the feeling that there is no more to be said. This is a DVD that is a historical treasure and also offers a performance that in its own right can surely never be surpassed and is here caught on the wing. The very dry Monte Carlo acoustic does not help the orchestra, but one soon adjusts to the unexpansive orchestral sound when the solo playing is so electrifying.

Sinfonia concertante in E min., Op. 125 (CD versions)

🔑 ✿ **** EMI 3 80013-2. Rostropovich, RPO, Sargent – MIASKOVSKY: *Cello Concerto in C min.*; RACHMANINOV: *Vocalise* ***

*** Avie AV 2090. Harrell, RLPO, Schwarz – SHOSTAKOVICH: *Cello Concerto 2* ***

This well-nigh definitive account of Prokofiev's reworking of material from his pre-war *Cello Concerto* is a classic. The composer and soloist worked together on the piece (originally billed as *Symphony-Concerto*) and **Rostropovich** gave the very first performance with a youth orchestra conducted by Sviatoslav Richter.

Lynn Harrell here is captured live with the excellent **Liverpool Orchestra** under **Gerard Schwarz** to impressive effect. The performance has great ardour and intelligence and those who do not possess the earlier account should invest in this, not only for its artistic quality but for the valuable coupling which Harrell has not given us before.

(i) *Sinfonia concertante for Cello & Orchestra, Op. 125*; (ii) *Cello Sonata in C, Op. 119*

🔑 (BB) *** EMI Encore 208119-2. Han-Na Chang, with (i) LSO, Pappano; (ii) Pappano (piano)

Han-Na Chang, in warm partnership with **Pappano** and the **LSO**, gives a rich, heartfelt, urgently impulsive reading of the *Sinfonia concertante*, powerful as well as polished, with the element of fantasy brought out in the central *Allegro giusto*, and the pawky humour nicely pointed. The late *Cello Sonata* makes an ideal coupling. Chang again brings youthful ardour and vigour to her performance, with Pappano at the piano proving a warmly sympathetic partner, even though the instrument is placed well behind the cello. A splendid, modestly priced reissue.

The Stone Flower (ballet; complete)

🔑 *** Chan. 10058 (2). BBC PO, Noseda

(M) *** CPO 999 385-2 (3). Hanover R. PO, Jurowski

Conceived in 1948, during Stalin's worst artistic crackdown, but not staged until 1954, after the composer's death, *The Stone Flower* is a massive ballet built on folk stories in 46 numbers lasting two and a half hours. The freshness of invention, with one striking idea after another, demonstrates Prokofiev's astonishing ability to work under the most severe mental stress and yet remain his highly individual self. As in other late works, he eked out his ideas with material drawn from earlier pieces, but a warm, colourful performance, brilliantly recorded, such as this from the **BBC Philharmonic** under **Gianandrea Noseda**, makes one appreciate that this deserves to be in the ballet-theatre repertory. The variety of mood is a delight, with incidental divertissements developing naturally in the telling of the story of the hero, Danilo, in search of the stone flower – symbolic, no doubt, of the artist's search for an otherworldly goal. The chain of numbers over four acts ends in a triumphant *Adagio* in characteristically flamboyant ballet style; then follows a bold epilogue with a touch of Hollywood in it, all vividly presented in this opulent Chandos recording.

The version from Hanover under **Mikhail Jurowski** has a lot going for it. The orchestral playing is polished and characterful, and the CPO recording is fresh and well detailed, though it is expensive on three mid-price discs.

SYMPHONIES

Symphonies 1, Op. 25 (Classical); 2, Op. 40; 3, Op. 44; 4, Opp. 47 & Op. 112 (rev. 1947); 5, Op. 100; 6, Op. 111; 7, Op. 131

Ⓝ ⊶ *** Chan. 10500X (4). RSNO, Järvi

These Chandos recordings from the mid-1980s are of the highest quality. They have been shorn of their couplings in this box, the only important loss being the delightful *Sinfonietta*. Both versions of the *Fourth Symphony* are included: the 1947 revision appears with the *Classical* on the first disc, while the 1930 original is coupled with the *Third*. Nos. 2 and 6 are on the third disc, and 5 and 7 on the last, so no side-breaks are involved. As performances, these are the equal of the best.

Symphony 1 in D (Classical), Op. 25 (DVD version)

⊶ *** TDK **DVD** DV-VPOVG. VPO, Gergiev (includes Gergiev talking on Prokofiev and Stravinsky) (V/D: Brian Large) – SCHNITTKE: *Viola Concerto*; STRAVINSKY: *Firebird Complete Ballet* ***

As the opening scenic view discloses, **Gergiev's** splendid performance, admirably paced and very well played, was recorded at the 2000 Salzburg Festival. The orchestra is perceptively photographed (the video director is **Brian Large**), although curiously, among the many effective instrumental spotlights, the camera misses the bassoon's genial solo in the first movement. Gergiev, although he looks as if he might need a shave, is always fascinating to watch; facial communication and hand movements equally expressive. Excellent sound, too.

Symphonies 1 (Classical); 4 in C, Op. 112 (revised, 1947 version)

*** Chan. 8400. RSNO, Järvi

Järvi succeeds in making out a more eloquent case for the revision of the *Fourth Symphony* than many of his predecessors. He also gives an exhilarating account of the *Classical Symphony*, one of the best on record. The slow movement has real douceur and the finale is wonderfully high-spirited. On CD in the *Fourth Symphony* the upper range is a little fierce in some of the more forceful climaxes.

Symphonies 1 (Classical); 5, Op. 100

ⒷⒷ **(*) Naxos 8.550237. Slovak PO, Gunzenhauser

The Naxos coupling is very good value indeed. The recording is altogether first class: there is splendid detail and definition, and the balance is extremely well judged. Moreover the American conductor, **Stephen Gunzenhauser**, gets very good playing from the excellent **Slovak Philharmonic** and the performances have the merit of being straightforward and unaffected.

Symphonies (i; ii) 1 (Classical); (ii) 5; 6

Ⓝ *(**) Australian Decca Eloquence mono/stereo 480 0834 (2). (i) Paris Conservatoire; (ii) SRO; cond. Ansermet

This two-CD set includes both of **Ansermet's** performances of the *Classical Symphony*, the earlier, mono recording with the **Paris Conservatoire Orchestra** dating from 1953, and the later, stereo re-make with the **Suisse Romande Orchestra** from 1961. The difference in sound quality is a tribute to how quickly Decca's recording technology transformed the vivid but rather over-bright mono sound to rich, warm and superbly vivid stereo sound. The performances are remarkably similar, though the sound of the earlier, Paris performance makes it particularly distinctive. Ansermet chooses quite slow tempi for the *Classical Symphony*, yet both are elegantly enjoyable performances. The *Fifth*, also caught in vivid stereo, was one of Ansermet's finest performances, straight and unaffected, and the playing of the SRO, though not the last word in virtuosity, is eminently spirited: the pointing and the crispness of the strings in the finale is one joy of this performance. The *Sixth Symphony* – a rare recording – has perhaps over-bright but vivid mono sound, and dates from 1951. If the first movement is a bit cool, the second is warm and passionate and the last sharply pointed and strongly characterized.

Symphonies 1 (Classical); 7, Op. 131; The Love for 3 Oranges: Suite

⊶ Ⓑ *** CfP 3 82229-2. Philh. O, Malko – TCHAIKOVSKY: *Nutcracker Suite* ***

All the performances on CfP are quite excellent and the *Seventh Symphony*, of which **Malko** conducted the UK première, is freshly conceived and finely shaped. What is so striking is the range and refinement of the 1955 stereo recording: the excellence of the balance and the body of the sound are remarkable. Moreover, the reissue comes with a fine account of Tchaikovsky's *Nutcracker Suite* from the same year which was among the very first of EMI's stereo recordings.

Symphony 2 in D min., Op. 40; Romeo and Juliet (ballet): Suite 1

*** Chan. 8368. RSNO, Järvi

The *Second Symphony* reflects Prokofiev's avowed intention of writing a work 'made of iron and steel'. **Neeme Järvi** produces altogether excellent results from the **Scottish National Orchestra** and the Chandos recording is impressively detailed and vivid. The *Romeo and Juliet* suite comes off well; the SNO play with real character.

Symphonies 2; 6 in E flat min., Op. 111

*** Testament (ADD) SBT 1395. Boston SO, Leinsdorf

The **Boston Symphony** had a close relationship with Prokofiev. And so it was natural that in the 1960s they should have embarked on (though never completed) a Prokofiev cycle. The *Second* has a layout similar to that of Beethoven's *C minor Sonata*, Op. 111, a powerful, concentrated sonata-form movement followed by a theme and variations, and it is in the latter that its most inspired invention is to be found. The quality of its invention and its fantasy and poetic feeling make its neglect hard to explain. The *Sixth* is the darkest and most concentrated, and **Leinsdorf** gives a powerful reading that (for its day) has an outstanding recorded sound. It still sounds very impressive.

Symphonies 3; 4 in C, Op. 47 (original, 1930 version)

*** Chan. 8401. RSNO, Järvi

Neeme Järvi's account of the *Third* is extremely successful. In many ways the original of the *Fourth Symphony* seems more like a ballet suite than a symphony: its insufficient tonal contrast tells – yet the Scherzo, drawn from the music for the Temptress in *The Prodigal Son* ballet, is particularly felicitous.

Symphonies 3, Op. 44; 5 in B flat, Op. 100

**(*) Testament (ADD) SBT 1396. Boston SO, Leinsdorf

Leinsdorf's account of the *Third* gets a strong atmosphere and a fine sonority from the **Boston Orchestra** in this highly imaginative score. The *Fifth* is a well-shaped account, though not everyone will care for the ritenuto Leinsdorf makes between the Trio section and the return of the Scherzo in the second movement. All the same, these performances make one regret that Leinsdorf never went on to complete his Prokofiev cycle. Exemplary transfers.

Symphony 4 in C (revised, 1947 version), Op. 112; The Prodigal Son (ballet; complete), Op. 46

⊕ 🅱🅱 *** Naxos 8.553055. Ukraine NSO, Kuchar

It makes an ideal coupling having the *Symphony No. 4* alongside the ballet score from which Prokofiev drew most of the material. The 1947 revision of the symphony, now generally preferred, is richer in both structure and instrumentation. **Kuchar's** readings are both powerful and idiomatic, with crisply disciplined playing from the **Ukraine Orchestra** bringing home the weight and violence of much of the writing. These are performances to match and even outshine current rivals at whatever price; the Naxos recording is satisfyingly full-bodied, not least in vivid brass and percussion sounds, with the piano both clear and well integrated in the *Symphony*.

Symphony 5 in B flat, Op. 100

⊕ Ⓜ **** DG (ADD) 463 613-2. BPO, Karajan –
STRAVINSKY: *Rite of Spring* **(*)

Ⓝ (***) Orfeo mono 427041. VPO, Mitropoulos –
SCHUMANN: *Symphony 2 in C* (***)

Symphony 5; Lieutenant Kijé: Suite

*** Telarc CD80683. Cincinnati SO, Järvi

Symphony 5; Romeo and Juliet: Death of Tybalt

*** BBC (ADD) BBCL 4184-2. Leningrad PO, Rozhdestvensky –
BRITTEN: *Young Person's Guide* ***

Symphony 5; Waltz Suite, Op. 110

*** Chan. 8450. RSNO, Järvi

Karajan's reading of the *Fifth Symphony* is outstanding in every way. It is a totally unaffected, beautifully played account, with the **Berlin Philharmonic** on top form, and the DG engineers at their best. The recording is a model of its kind, allowing all the subtleties of the orchestral colouring to register without any distortion of perspective. It has splendid range and fidelity and is wholly free from any artificial balance. It is here paired with his highly individual version of *The Rite of Spring* to make an intriguing coupling in DG's Originals series.

Mitropoulos was an outstanding conductor, and anything he did was special. Prokofiev's *Fifth* was recorded with the Vienna Philharmonic at the 1954 Salzburg Festival and the sound is light years removed from Telarc's Järvi. Moreover, the ORF (Austrian Radio) balance is not ideal either. However, there is only one word for the performance: electrifying. Readers should hear this powerful reading for themselves.

Rozhdestvensky's *Fifth Symphony* was recorded in September 1971 at the Royal Albert Hall, and the *Death of Tybalt* from *Romeo and Juliet* was an encore at an Edinburgh Festival concert during their 1960 tour when the **Leningrad Orchestra** brought the *Fourth Symphony* to the West for the first time. The *Fifth* was acclaimed by the late lamented Joan Chissell in *The Times*: 'this conductor relishes theatrical strokes, grotesquerie, the boldness and high voltage' . . . and 'his own high spirits burst out of every note'. The virtuosity of the orchestra is well captured by the BBC engineers.

Järvi's direction is unhurried, fluent and authoritative. His feeling for the music is unfailingly natural. The three *Waltzes* which derive from various sources are all elegantly played. The Chandos recording is set just a shade further back than some of its companions in the series, yet at the same time every detail is clear.

The **Cincinnati Orchestra** give a very well-prepared and polished account (without the rough edges in, for example, the Scherzo that are part of its character) and the Telarc recording reveals every strand in the texture. Very good playing, then, and an altogether excellent *Lieutenant Kijé*, although the first recommendations remain unchallenged.

Symphony 5; Ode to the End of the War

*** Pentatone **SACD** PTC 5186 083. Russian Nat. O, Jurowski
(with RIMSKY-KORSAKOV: *Russian Easter Festival Overture* ***) – RACHMANINOV: *Symphony 1* ***

Vladimir Jurowski and the **Russian National Orchestra** give a performance of strong personality and striking character. He conveys the asperity of the Scherzo and the incisiveness of the finale to excellent effect; everything is alive and immediate, and he does justice to the breadth and lyricism of the slow movement. The unusual (to put it mildly) orchestration of the coupled *Ode to the End of the War* (eight harps, four pianos, wind ensemble with no strings, only double-basses) makes for a startling and spectacular aural experience. Although it comes from 1945, Prokofiev draws on several passages from the 1936 cantata, *October*. This is an important and competitive issue, with good, well balanced sound.

Symphonies (i) 5 in B flat, Op. 100; (ii) 6, Op. 111

*** Praga PR 250 079. (i) Czech PO, Baudo; (ii) Leningrad PO, Mravinsky

Two Prokofiev symphonies recorded in the Smetana Hall, Prague. **Serge Baudo's** excellent account of the *Fifth* comes from 1976; **Mravinsky's** account of the *Sixth* with his visiting **Leningrad Philharmonic Orchestra** is from 1967, the year before the Soviet invasion, and is a great performance, taut, dramatic and intense. Very acceptable sound.

Symphony 6; Waltz Suite, Op. 110/1, 5 & 6

⊕┐ *** Chan. 8359. RSNO, Järvi

The *Sixth Symphony* goes much deeper than any of its companions; indeed it is perhaps the greatest of the Prokofiev cycle. **Neeme Järvi** shapes its detail as skilfully as he does its architecture as a whole. These artists have the measure of the music's tragic poignancy more than almost any of their predecessors on record. The fill-up is a set of waltzes, drawn and adapted from various stage works.

Symphony 7 in C sharp min., Op. 131; Sinfonietta in A, Op. 5/48

*** Chan. 8442. RSNO, Järvi

Neeme Järvi's account of the *Seventh Symphony* is hardly less successful than the other issues in this cycle. He draws very good playing from the **SNO** and has the full measure of this repertoire. The early *Sinfonietta* is a highly attractive coupling (what a sunny and charming piece it is!). The digital recording has great range and is excellently balanced.

Visions Fugitives (arr. Barshai)

**** Warner ONYX 4017. Moscow Soloists, Bashmet – STRAVINSKY: *Apollo; Concerto in D* ****

*** Australian Decca Eloquence (ADD) 442 8414. ASMF, Marriner – BARTÓK: *Divertimento*; HINDEMITH: *5 Pieces*; VIVALDI: *Concertos* ***

Rudolf Barshai made these brilliant string arrangements of Prokofiev's piano pieces for his Moscow Chamber Orchestra, so the superb new performance by the **Moscow Soloists** under **Yuri Bashmet** is especially welcome. Virtuosity and perfect ensemble are matched by expressive commitment, and the characterization of each vision is very striking. First-class recording too, and an apt coupling.

The **Saint Martin's Academy** equally relish the ingenuity of the transcription, which makes this sound like original string music. Fine, atmospheric recording and worthwhile couplings.

CHAMBER MUSIC

Music for cello and piano: *Adagio (Cinderella), Op. 976; Ballade in C min., Op. 15; Cello Sonata Op. 119; Solo Cello Sonata, Op. 134; 5 Mélodies, Op. 35 bis (arr. Wallfisch); The Love for Three Oranges: March; The Tale of the Stone Flower: Waltz*

⊕┐ **** Black Box Music BBM 1027. Wallfisch, York

Adagio (Cinderella); Ballade, Op. 15; Cello Sonata, Op. 119

*** HM Chant du Monde LDC 2781112. Hoffman, Bianconi – SHOSTAKOVICH: *Cello Sonata; Moderato* **(*)

Cello Sonata in C, Op. 119

⊕┐ ⑱ **** Double Decca 473 807-2 (2). Harrell, Ashkenazy – RACHMANINOV: *Cello Sonata, etc.*; SHOSTAKOVICH: *Cello Sonata, etc.* ****

*** Virgin 2x1 4 82067-2 (2). Mørk, Vogt – MIASKOVSKY, RACHMANINOV, SHOSTAKOVICH: *Cello Sonatas*; STRAVINSKY: *Suite italienne* ***

Ⓜ *** Somm CD 029. Walton, Grimwood – KABALEVSKY, MIASKOVSKY: *Cello Sonatas* ***

*** Chan. 8340. Turovsky, L. Edlina – SHOSTAKOVICH: *Sonata* ***

*** Berlin Classics 0017832BC. Bohorquez, Groh – BRITTEN, DEBUSSY: *Cello Sonatas* ***

Prokofiev's *Cello Sonata* is the product of his last years and, like the *Sinfonia concertante*, was inspired by the playing of the young Rostropovich. The excellent account from 1988 on Double Decca remains one of the top recommendations; readers will find **Lynn Harrell** and **Vladimir Ashkenazy** wholly satisfying on all accounts. The rest of the programme is equally fine.

In addition to the *Cello Sonata* **Raphael Wallfisch** and **John York** on Black Box give us the early *Ballade*, Op. 15, as well as Wallfisch's own transcription of the enchanting *Cinq mélodies*, Op. 35, and the *Solo Sonata* which Prokofiev began just before his death and whose first movement Vladimir Blok put into shape some years later. Wallfisch plays with superb golden tone and with great expressive eloquence. John York is a sensitive and intelligent partner. Their account can rank with the best.

Truls Mørk and **Lars Vogt** give a perceptive and thoughtful account of the *Sonata*, are expertly recorded in the Eidsvoll Church, Norway. In addition to the Shostakovich the set has the advantage of equally fine couplings of the Miaskovsky and Rachmaninov *Sonatas* and the Stravinsky *Suite italienne*.

Jamie Walton and **Daniel Grimwood** are new to the artists' catalogue, and their intelligently planned programme is a splendid visiting card. The Prokofiev *Sonata* is given with great character and musicality, and can hold its own with most of the competition. Moreover, the coupling with the Miaskovsky *Sonata* is a considerable plus point. Good recording, too.

Gary Hoffman and **Philippe Bianconi** are hardly less fine than their distinguished rivals and are every bit as well recorded. Indeed, there is more air round the aural image in their recital. They opt for the more traditional Shostakovich coupling but do offer the early *Ballade*.

Yuli Turovsky and **Luba Edlina** are also eloquent advocates of this *Sonata* and the balance is particularly lifelike.

Claudio Bohorquez, with a fine fellow artist at the piano, brings out the power of the first movement, measured until the final *animato* section. His account of the central *Moderato* movement is built on high contrasts between the wit of the opening and the lyricism of the later passages, while power again dominates in his weighty reading of the strongly rhythmic *Allegro* finale.

Flute Sonata in D, Op. 94

⊕—➤ ******** EMI 5 56982-2. Pahud, Kovacevich – DEBUSSY:*Syrinx; Bilitis*, etc.; RAVEL: *Chansons madécasses* *******

Ⓜ ******* RCA (ADD) 09026 61615-2. Galway, Argerich – FRANCK, REINECKE: *Sonatas* *******

Prokofiev's *Flute Sonata* (1943) is one of his sunniest and most serene wartime compositions. Played as it is on EMI, it is quite captivating. **Emmanuel Pahud** and **Stephen Kovacevich** set ideal tempi in each movement and their characterization is perfect as a result. The familiar ideas sound completely fresh and novel. Easily a first recommendation. A perfectly balanced recording.

With its combination of effortless virtuosity and spontaneity of feeling, every detail of the **Galway/Argerich** version falls naturally into place. The RCA recording is most sympathetic.

(i) String Quartets 1–2; (ii) Cello Sonata

ⒷⒷ ******* Naxos 8.553136. (i) Aurora Qt; (ii) Grebanier, Guggenheim

The **Aurora Quartet** give thoroughly straightforward, unaffected accounts of both *Quartets*. They are recorded in a warm, resonant acoustic. The *Cello Sonata* is a thoroughly musical account, not perhaps as strongly characterized as some, but eminently satisfying, and well recorded.

String Quartet 2 in F, Op. 92

✹ (*******) Testament mono SBT 1052. Hollywood Qt – HINDEMITH: *Quartet 3*; WALTON: *Quartet in A min.* ✹ *******

The pioneering **Hollywood Quartet** version of the *Second Quartet* is a stunning performance which has an extraordinary precision and intensity (as well as repose when this is required). The transfer sounds excellent.

Violin Sonata (for solo violin), Op. 115

*** Claudio CB 5256-2. Jin – LALO: *Symphonie espagnole*; SARASATE: *Carmen Fantasy, Op. 25* ******* (with KROLL: *Banjo and Fiddle*, orch. Bradbury; TARREGA: *Recuerdos de la Alhambra*, arr. Ricci ****(*)**)

Violin Sonata (for solo violin), Op. 115; Sonata for 2 Violins

*** Chan. 8988. Mordkovitch, Young – SCHNITTKE: *Prelude*; SHOSTAKOVICH: *Violin Sonata* *******

Violin Sonatas (i; ii) 1 in F min., Op. 80; (iii; iv) 2 in D, Op. 94; (i; iii) Sonata for 2 Violins, Op. 56

ⒷⒷ ******* Warner Apex 2564 60623-2. (i) Jaakko; Kuusisto; (ii) Paananen; (iii) Pekka Kuusisto; (iv) Kerppo

Violin Sonatas: 1; 2. 5 Melodies, Op. 35; March, Op. 12/1; Love for 3 Oranges: March. Romeo & Juliet: Masks (all trans. Heifetz)

Ⓑ ******* Artemis Vanguard CD 1555 (2). Gil & Orli Shaham

Sonata for 2 Violins, Op. 56

*** Hyp. CDA 66473. Osostowicz, Kovacic – MARTINŮ: *Violin Sonata*; MILHAUD: *Violin Duo*, etc. ****(*)**

The solo *Violin Sonata in D*, Op. 115, is a crisply characteristic piece in three short movements. The *Sonata in C for Two Violins*, written much earlier, is just as effective. The warmth of **Lydia Mordkovitch** is well matched by her partner, **Emma Young**.

Min Jin's disarmingly direct approach to the *Solo Sonata* is most appealing, crisply so in the opening *Moderato*, seductively simple in the *Tema con variazioni*, buoyantly rhythmic and certainly *Con brio* in the closing *Allegro precipitato*, where she brings out the lyrical underlay. She is truthfully recorded and not balanced too closely. An unexpected but welcome coupling for an equally fresh approach to Lalo's *Symphonie espagnole*.

Both **Jaakko** and **Pekka Kuusisto** produce playing with a youthful ardour and vitality that is refreshing. This (originally Finlandia) Apex reissue ranks among the best, yet it is now very inexpensive. Anyone investing in it is unlikely to be disappointed.

Gil and **Orli Shaham** (*frère* and *soeur*) form a mutually understanding partnership to present Prokofiev's three key works for violin and piano, interlaced with a trio of transcriptions by Heifetz. The major works are strongly characterized and are played with a nice balance between ardent boldness and lyrical delicacy. The *Five Melodies* are made strikingly diverse, and the account of the *Second, D major, Sonata* is particularly compelling. Clear, forward, if slightly dry recording, but a good balance, with the violin dominating, but the piano well in the picture.

The *Sonata for Two Violins* gives the impression of being vintage Prokofiev, as performed by **Krysia Osostowicz** and **Ernst Kovacic**. The slow movement is played with exceptional imagination and poetry.

Violin Sonata 1 in F min., Op. 80

*** Orfeo (ADD) C489981B. Oistrakh, Richter – BRAHMS: *Sonata 2* *******

(*) Avie AV0023. Gleusteen, Ordronneau – JANÁČEK: *Violin Sonata*; SHOSTAKOVICH: *19 Preludes from Op. 34* **(*)**

This Orfeo disc records the **Oistrakh–Richter** partnership in a live concert at the 1972 Salzburg Festival at the very top of their form. The playing, as one might expect, silences criticism and the recording from ORF (Austrian Radio) is perfectly serviceable.

Even more than in the Janáček and Shostakovich works,

Kai Gleusteen is in his element, and so is **Catherine Ordronneau**, bringing out the often violent contrasts in the writing, as well as the fantasy of the *Andante* third movement and the power and ebullience of the two fast movements, the second and the finale. The recording, one of a series made in Crear on the west coast of Scotland, is on the reverberant side, thanks to the large, bare studio in which it was made, but there is no lack of detail.

Violin Sonata 2 in D, Op. 94a

🎵 *** New Note Quartz QTZ 2002. Liebeck, Apekisheva –
   CHAUSSON: *Poème*; SAINT-SAENS: *Sonata 1*; YSAYE:
   Sonata 3 ***

Jack Liebeck's performance of the *D major Sonata*, admirably partnered by **Katya Apekisheva**, is second to none among modern recordings. The opening is exquisitely played, and the Scherzo crackles with rhythmic vitality. The wry, wistful quality of the *Andante* is perfectly caught and is followed by a gutsy, irresistibly spirited finale. The recording is vividly real, with the violin perhaps a little too close, and the couplings are equally good.

PIANO MUSIC

Cinderella: 3 Pieces, Op. 95; 3 Pieces, Op. 97; Romeo and Juliet: 10 Pieces, Op. 75; War and Peace: 3 Pieces, Op. 96

(BB) *** HM HCX 3957150. Chiu

Prokofiev's transcriptions of the ballet music from *Romeo and Juliet* are better known than *Cinderella* or the three pieces from the opera *War and Peace* (which include the delectable *Grand Waltz*). **Frederic Chiu**, who has already given us a first class set of the sonatas, plays with vivid colouring, often dazzling with his bravura. He is rather closely balanced, but the bright piano image is real enough, and this can be strongly recommended. Excellent value for money.

Piano Sonatas 1–9 (complete); Lieutenant Kijé (suite, transcribed Chiu)

🎵 **** Chan. (as listed below). Berman

Piano Sonata 1 in F min., Op. 1; 4 Pieces, Op. 4; Prelude & Fugue in D min. (Buxtehude, arr. Prokofiev); 2 Sonatinas, Op. 54; Gavotte (Hamlet, Op. 77 bis); 3 Pieces, Op. 96 (Chan. 9017)

Piano Sonata 2 in D min., Op. 14; Cinderella: 3 Pieces, Op. 102; Dumka; 3 Pieces, Op. 69; Waltzes (Schubert, arr. Prokofiev) (Chan. 9119)

Piano Sonata 3 in A min., Op. 28; Cinderella: 6 Pieces, Op. 95; 10 Pieces, Op. 12; Thoughts, Op. 62 (Chan. 9069)

Piano Sonata 4, Op. 29; Music for Children, Op. 65; 6 Pieces, Op. 52 (Chan. 8926).

Piano Sonata 5 in C, Op. 38/135; 4 Pieces, Op. 32; The Love for Three Oranges: Scherzo & March. Romeo and Juliet: 10 Pieces, Op. 75 (Chan. 8851)

Piano Sonatas 5 in C, Op. 38; 6 in A, Op. 82; 10 in E min., Op. 137 (fragment); Gavotte (from Classical Symphony, Op. 25); Juvenilia; Toccata, Op. 11 (Chan. 9361)

Piano Sonata 7; Sarcasms, Op. 17; Tales of an Old Grandmother, Op. 31; Visions fugitives, Op. 22 (Chan. 8881)

Piano Sonata 8; Cinderella: 10 Pieces, Op. 97; 4 Pieces, Op. 3 (Chan. 8976)

Piano Sonata 9; Choses en soi, Op. 45; Divertissement, Op. 43 bis; 4 Etudes, Op. 2 (Chan. 9211)

Boris Berman always plays with tremendous concentration and control. He commands a finely articulated and vital rhythmic sense as well as a wide range of keyboard colour. In the *Second Sonata in D minor* Berman is quite magnificent and full of panache. The *Third* remains one of the most desirable of the set. The *Fourth Sonata*, like its predecessor, takes its inspiration from Prokofiev's earlier notebooks. The Op. 52 *Pieces* are transcriptions of movements from other works. Berman plays them incisively, with marvellous articulation and wit. He plays the post-war revision of the *Fifth Sonata*, and its crisp, brittle inner movement is heard to splendid advantage. The other works are presented with equal perception.

With the *Sixth Sonata* Berman is traversing hotly contested ground. Yet his cooler and more collected reading remains eminently recommendable. He then gives us the original (1923) version of the *Fifth Sonata* (generally to be preferred to the revision) but also the minute or so that survives of a *Tenth Sonata*. Berman is completely inside the astringent idiom and subtle character of the *Seventh Sonata*, and his playing in the *Sarcasms* could scarcely be bettered.

In the expansive *Eighth Sonata*, there is pianistic refinement in Berman's account, though it is in the ten numbers from *Cinderella* and the Op. 3 *Pieces* that Berman's command of atmosphere and character tells most.

Berman plays the *Ninth Sonata* with tremendous concentration and control. The *Choses en soi* (*Things in Themselves*) comes from the period of the *Third Symphony*, though there is a momentary hint of *The Prodigal Son*. The *Divertissement* is a delightful piece in Prokofiev's most acerbic manner which derived from the ballet, *Trapeze*. Berman couples them with the brilliant Op. 2 *Etudes* of 1909. First class recording throughout.

Piano Sonatas 1; 6–7; Toccata in C, Op. 11

*** BIS CD 1260. Kempf

Freddy Kempf's Prokofiev finds him totally inside the idiom. He has all the technical address, flair and temperament this music needs. At present the sonatas are uncommonly well served on record. Kempf doesn't displace any of them, but his playing is satisfying and his admirers need not hesitate.

Piano Sonatas 4; 6; 10 Pieces from 'Romeo and Juliet', Op. 75

⊶ **** Warner 2564 61255-2. Lugansky

Dazzling playing from **Nikolai Lugansky**, performances that stand out even in exalted company. The *Sixth Sonata* is the most exciting and authoritative now before the public and supersedes the likes of Pogorelich and Kissin in musical insight and virtuosity. The *Romeo and Juliet Pieces* have equal mastery and fascination. Remarkable Prokofiev playing, wonderful in terms of characterization and effortless virtuosity.

Piano Sonatas 6; 8

⊶ *** Naive V 4898. Guy

Prokofiev's wartime trilogy of piano sonatas comprises *Nos. 6* through to *8*, and it is a pity that the present disc does not include *No. 7*. Be that as it may, these are electrifying performances of virtuosity and great musical intelligence.

Piano Sonatas 7; 8; Romeo and Juliet: Romeo and Juliet before Parting; Masks

Ⓜ *** Decca (ADD) 468 497-2. Ashkenazy – LISZT: *Impromptu (Nocturne); Mephisto Waltz 1* ***

Ashkenazy's commanding performances of these two sonatas, recorded in 1967, have great authority and conviction and the present recordings are rather special. The rhapsodical excerpts from *Romeo and Juliet* are also memorable and the Liszt couplings are hardly less impressive, the *Mephisto Waltz* is predictably dazzling.

Piano Sonatas 7–9

*** ASV CDDCA 755. Lill

This disc, coupling the last three *Sonatas*, offers good value, and the excellent ASV recording was made in Henry Wood Hall. All three performances are of high quality, and **John Lill** is never less than a thoughtful and intelligent guide in this repertoire.

Piano Sonata 8 in B flat, Op. 84

*** MDG 604 1141-2. Eckardstein – JANÁČEK: *Sonata 1.X.1905*; MESSIAEN: *La Rousserolle effarvatte* ***

Severin von Eckardstein won a special commendation at the Leeds Piano Competition for his advocacy of 20th-century music. His performance of the *Eighth Sonata* is beautifully shaped and expertly controlled. A fine début CD.

VOCAL MUSIC

Alexander Nevsky (cantata), Op. 78 (in English)

⊶ ✪ Ⓜ **** RCA (ADD) 09026 63708-2. Elias, Chicago SO & Ch., Reiner – KHACHATURIAN: *Violin Concerto* ****

Alexander Nevsky (cantata), Op. 78 (in Russian)

Ⓝ Ⓜ *** Medici Arts (ADD) MM 028-2. Van Sante,

Netherlands R. Ch. & R. PO, Stokowski (with RAVEL: *Fanfare: L'Eventail de Jeanne* ***) – FRANCK: *Symphony* **(*)

Ⓜ **(*) Sup. (ADD) SU 3696-2. Soukupová, Prague Philh. Ch., Czech PO, Ančerl – *Symphony-Concerto for Cello* **

Even now these early stereo Chicago recordings can astonish the listener, while **Reiner's** performance is among the most exciting accounts available, with the music for the Teutonic invaders as sinister as the *Battle on the Ice* is thrilling. No less effective is the scherzando-like middle section of the battle music, which Reiner points in the most sparkling manner. The fervour of the choral singing is matched by the eloquence of **Rosalind Elias's***Lament*.

Stokowski's broadcast recording has the advantage of the superb acoustics of the De Doelen concert hall in Rotterdam, which provides spectacular detail, colour and warmth for chorus and orchestra alike. **Sophie van Sante** gives a very touching performance of the *Lament for the Dead*; but it is the magnificent singing of the Netherlands Radio Chorus (uncredited in the listing!) that dominates the performance, although the orchestral textures also glitter tellingly. The sung text is available at www.mediciarts.co.uk

The strength of the Supraphon performance lies in the magnificent singing of the **Prague Philharmonic Choir**, richly resonant and clear. The closing chorus for Alexander's entry into Pskov is thrilling, sung in Russian (like the rest of the work), which adds much to its character. **Vera Soukupová** gives her elegiac tribute to the dead on the field of battle very movingly, if without the passion of a traditional Russian reading. **Ančerl** conducts a reading which is lyrically strong. Even if he misses much of the sinister quality of those menacing Teutonic Knights in Eisenstein's great film, the *Battle on the Ice* is still powerful, helped by the spectacular Supraphon recording, which sounds newly minted here. It is a pity that the coupling, although well played, is not more appropriate.

(i) Alexander Nevsky, Op. 78; Hamlet (incidental music), Op. 77: The Ghost of Hamlet's Father. Ivan the Terrible: Dance of the Oprichniks, Op. 116. Pushkiniana (ed. Rozhdestvensky)

ⒷⒷ *** Naxos 8.555710. (i) Gelahova, Stanislavsky Ch.; Russian State SO, Yablonsky

(i) Alexander Nevsky, Op. 78; (ii) Lieutenant Kijé, Op. 60; Scythian Suite, Op. 20

⊶ Ⓜ **** DG (ADD) 447 419-2. (i) Obraztsova; L. Symphony Ch., LSO; (ii) Chicago SO; Abbado

(i) Alexander Nevsky, Op. 78; Scythian Suite, Op. 20

⊶ **** Chan. 8584. (i) Finnie, RSNO Ch.; RSNO, Järvi

Abbado's performance of *Alexander Nevsky* culminates in a deeply moving account of the tragic lament after the battle (here very beautifully sung by **Obraztsova**), made the more telling when the battle itself is so fine an example of orchestral virtuosity. The chorus is as incisive as the orchestra. A fine account of *Lieutenant Kijé* and what is among the best versions of the *Scythian Suite* to appear in recent years make this a very desirable reissue.

The bitter chill of the Russian winter can be felt in the orchestra at the very opening of **Järvi's** reading and the melancholy of the choral entry has real Slavic feeling. His climactic point is the enormously spectacular *Battle on the Ice*, with the recording giving great pungency to the bizarre orchestral effects and the choral shouts riveting in their force and fervour. **Linda Finnie** sings the final lament eloquently and Järvi's apotheosis is very affecting. As coupling, Järvi also chooses the *Scythian Suite*.

Dmitri Yablonsky gives a strongly atmospheric account of *Alexander Nevsky*, with plenty of dramatic feeling and fire. The short movements from *Onegin* included in *Pushkiniana*, which Rozhdestvensky scored in the 1960s, and the excerpts from *Hamlet* are very well played. Good recording, too, and no one opting for this Naxos CD will be disappointed.

Cantata for the 20th Anniversary of the October Revolution, Op. 74; Stone Flower Suite

*** Chan. 9095. Rozhdestvensky (speaker), Philh. Ch. & O, Järvi

Even Prokofiev rarely wrote so wild and totally original a piece as this cantata. The key movement, centrally placed and the longest, uses such exotic percussion as rattles and sirens, with shouting from the chorus, in a graphic description of the revolution in St Petersburg. **Järvi**, here with his fellow-conductor **Gennadi Rozhdestvensky** as narrator, has made a first complete recording with the **Philharmonia Chorus and Orchestra**. As a valuable fill-up comes a suite of excerpts from the folk-tale ballet of 1948, *The Stone Flower*.

Ivan the Terrible (complete filmscore)

⊕− *** Ph. 475 7778-2. Sokolova, Putilin, Kirov Op. Ch., Rotterdam PO, Gergiev

Prokofiev's vividly colourful music for the Eisenstein film of *Ivan the Terrible* has never sounded quite so bitingly dramatic on disc as under **Gergiev** – as electrifying as any of his opera recordings with the Kirov Company. Here he has the advantage of excellent sound, recorded in the Rotterdam hall, De Doelen, with his 'other' orchestra, thrustful and earthy. Like competing versions, this one is based on Abram Stassevich's editing of the music into an 'oratorio', but without the spoken narration – hardly necessary on disc, when notes and text are provided. The two soloists, **Liubov Sokolova** and **Nikolai Putilin**, vibrantly Slavonic, add to the drama, as do the **Kirov Chorus**.

On Guard for Peace; Queen of Spade (Suites)

Ⓝ *** Chan 10619. Tchistjakova, Docherty, RSNO Ch. & O, Järvi

These two Prokofiev rarities make a worthwhile coupling. *On Guard for Peace* is a cantata from the Soviet period; in many ways it echoes the *Alexander Nevsky* cantata, though with less memorable material. It makes a powerful impact nonetheless with its massed choral forces which include children's voices as well as a treble soloist, **Neil Docherty**. Here, as in *Nevsky*, there is a mezzo solo over a Lullaby. The

orchestration adds consistently to the work's impact. The *Suite* from the *Queen of Spades* music is taken from an unrealized film score, with Michael Berkeley arranging and elaborating the sketches which have been found relatively recently. There is a fine *Adagio* and a jolly dance with a delightful pay-off. Not great music but well worth hearing in a performance as fine as this. First-rate, atmospheric sound.

OPERA

L'Amour des trois oranges (The Love for Three Oranges; sung in French; DVD version)

⊕− *** Arthaus DVD 100 404. Bacquier, Viala, Perraguin, Le Texier, Gautier, Henry, Reinhart, Lagrange, Caroli, Fournier, Dubosc, Bastin, Uria-Monzon, Lyon Opéra Ch. & O, Nagano (Producer: Erlo, V/P: Jung)

Although it contains some of Prokofiev's most popular orchestral interludes, the opera is in some ways less successful than its companions. As in *The Gambler* and *The Fiery Angel*, there are no set-pieces for the singers and there is scant thematic development. Indeed, the familiar orchestral March and Scherzo are practically the only elements that reappear. There is, however, no want of invention and exuberance, and the opera is ideal for DVD as it is very visual. The cast here is excellent, and so is the video recording. It offers subtitles in English, German, Italian, Spanish and the French in which it is sung. Recommended.

The Love for Three Oranges (complete; in Russian)

⊕− *** Ph. 462 913-2 (2). Akimov, Kit, Diadkova, Morozov, Pluzhnikov, Gerello, Shevchenko, soloists, Kirov Op. Ch. & O, Gergiev

Gergiev adds to his formidable Kirov series of Russian opera recordings with a brilliant reading of this fantasy fairy-tale. Using the Russian text this is earthier, tougher and more biting than the smoother French version offered on Virgin by Kent Nagano and his Lyon Opera team. The satirical element of the piece with its wry humour comes over the more sharply, with more sparkle, and though not all the Kirov cast can quite match their Lyon counterparts in vocal beauty, they are on balance more characterful, notably the formidable mezzo, **Larissa Diadkova**, as Princess Clarissa.

The Love for 3 Oranges (CD version; in English)

*** Chan. 10347 (2). Humble, MacMaster, Tahu Rhodes, Arthur, Whitehouse, Op. Australia Ch., Australian Op. & Ballet O, Hickox

There is every advantage in having this opera in English, particularly when the deft translation by Tom Stoppard is used. Recorded live, the humour comes over naturally, helped by the crispness of ensemble, even in the most complex passages. **Richard Hickox** proves the liveliest interpreter, securing excellent playing from the orchestra, brilliantly recorded, with crisp and incisive singing from the chorus. The singing of the principals is consistently strong and positive, even if the voices are not specially distinctive, with **Teddy Tahu Rhodes** as Leandro, **William Ferguson** as Truffaldino, **John MacMaster** as the Prince, and **Elizabeth**

Whitehouse as Fata Morgana all first rate. The set also scores over its rivals in the full, atmospheric, well-focused sound.

The Fiery Angel (complete; DVD version)

**** Arthaus **DVD** 100 390; CD Ph. 446 078-2 (2). Gorchakova, Leiferkus, Pluzhnikov, Ognovanko, soloists; Kirov Op. Ch. & O, Gergiev

The presence of vision in the finely directed DVD serves to underline an implicit ambiguity in the opera – whether Madiel and the spirits conjured up in Act II are real or are just Renata's paranoid delusions. Here the use of mimed figures, unseen by the protagonists but perceived by the audience, was a brilliant solution. The frenetic, highly charged atmosphere of the final Convent scene benefits by vision particularly in this splendid production. The sound has marvellous presence and detail.

The Fiery Angel (CD versions)

(M) ******** Ph. 446 078-2 (2). Gorchakova, Leiferkus, Pluzhnikov, Ognovanko, Kirov Op. Ch. & O, Gergiev

(M) ******* DG 477 5596 (2). Secunde, Lorenz, Zednik, Moll, Gothenburg SO, Järvi

Impressive as was Neeme Järvi's 1990 recording for DG of this elusive but powerful opera, **Gergiev's** with **Kirov** forces is even finer. From the very outset the style is declamatory in a way that recalls Mussorgsky. The vocal line is largely heightened speech, but Prokofiev does provide a series of leitmotivs which are identified with characters or situations in the opera. This Philips live recording, with full, forward sound, avoids most of the snags of a recorded stage-performance. Above all, it offers in the singing and acting of **Galina Gorchakova** in the central role of Renata, the hysterical woman obsessed by demons, one of the most compelling operatic performances in years, with the timbre of the voice often sensuously beautiful, even when stretched to the limit. **Sergei Leiferkus** as Ruprecht with his clear, firm baritone is also ideally cast; the remainder of the cast, from the Landlady of **Evgenia Perlasova** to the resonant Inquisitor of **Vladimir Ognovanko**, are absolutely first class, while the Kirov team provides outstanding, always idiomatic and individual performances in smaller roles. Gergiev proves an inspired conductor who secures orchestral playing of great dramatic eloquence. There are the inevitable stage noises, but any snag is quickly forgotten.

With **Järvi**, the final scene with the Inquisitor (**Kurt Moll**, ever sinister) and chattering nuns does not quite rise to the expected climax. **Nadine Secunde** sings passionately as Renata and she is well supported by **Siegfried Lorenz** as Ruprecht. With such warm advocacy once can fully appreciate the work's mastery, even if the reasons for its failure to get into the repertory remain very clear.

Ivan the Terrible, Parts I and II (complete; DVD version)

(***) Eureka **DVD** EKA 40018 (2). Cherkassov, Tselikovskaya, Birman (Dir: Sergei Eisenstein)

The subject of Ivan the Terrible equally inspired Prokofiev to write a powerful and distinctive score, which can stand on its own as a concert work. Yet over two films (94 and 85 minutes respectively) the result is necessarily more diffuse. **Eisenstein's** astonishingly striking and beautiful images in black and white have remarkable impact on DVD, based on an excellent copy of the original film, but sadly, the soundtrack is depressingly crumbly and ill-focused. Though it makes it hard to enjoy Prokofiev's music, its power is still very clear, enhancing the heavyweight treatment of history. It is a pity that it was not possible to superimpose a modern recording of the music, as has been effectively done in live concert-showings of the film.

Semyon Kotko (complete)

(M) **(***)** Chan. mono 10053 (3). Gres, Gelovani, Yanko, Troitsky, Penchekhin, USSR R. Ch. & O, Zhukov

Semyon Kotko (slightly abridged)

*** Ph. 464 605-2 (2). Lutsiuk, Pavlovskaya, Savoya, Bezzubenkov, Nikitin, Chernomortsev, Solovieva, Markova-Mikhailenko, Karasev, Akimov, Kirov Ch. & O, Gergiev

Semyon Kotko was the fifth of Prokofiev's eight operas and the first on a Soviet theme. It is a story of love and heroism in the Ukraine during the disturbed period after the 1917 Revolution. As for the music, it demonstrates once again that even when he was saddled with a propagandist Soviet theme, Prokofiev's fluent originality could not be submerged. The only disappointment is that it lacks the big surging melodies that make Prokofiev's masterpiece, *War and Peace*, so memorable, though some of the choruses come close.

This first really complete recording on Chandos stems from a studio performance for Moscow Radio in 1960, which in mono sound captures the voices vividly, with words exceptionally clear. It has the authority of being conducted by **Mikhail Zhukov** who was responsible for the 1940 première and would have known Prokofiev's intentions. It scores surprisingly well alongside the 1999 Philips version with Kirov soloists in concert conducted by Valery Gergiev, containing some 45 minutes more of music omitted from that later set. The Moscow cast is strong too, with Slavonic wobblers excluded. The tenor, **N. Gres**, in particular is magnificent in the title-role, firmer and more heroic than his opposite number on Philips. While most collectors will opt for the modern stereo version, this earlier recording is by no means outclassed.

On Philips **Viktor Lutsiuk** as Semyon and **Tatiana Pavlovskaya** as his fiancée Sofya are both first class; however, the real hero is **Gergiev** who phrases sensitively and paces the music with all his dramatic expertise and gets an enthusiastic response from his Kirov forces. The recording is excellent.

The Story of a Real Man (opera; complete)

(M) ******* Chan. (ADD) 10002(2). Kibkalo, Deomidova, Leonova, Pankov, Rezhetin, Maslennikov, Bolshoi Ch. & O, Ermler

Prokofiev's last opera, *The Story of a Real Man*, written just after the Second World War, was based on a novel by Boris Polevoy that, reflecting a true story, tells of a Soviet pilot,

Alexei, who is shot down behind the German lines and who, for 18 days, crawls to find safety. This first CD version brings a transfer of the 1961 Soviet recording based on that first stage production at the Bolshoi, and the sound is astonishingly full and vivid, with the voices clear and immediate. Central to the success of this recorded performance is not just the inspired conducting of **Mark Ermler**, but also the brilliant singing of **Yevgeny Kibkalo** as Alexei, satisfyingly firm and dark, and rising to the challenge of the arioso passages of heightened lyricism, notably when his rehabilitation monologue leads to a duet with the great Russian bass, **Mark Rezhetin**, as the head surgeon. Other Bolshoi basses in the cast are splendid too, as is the tenor, **Alexei Maslennikov**, as a pilot colleague, though **Glafira Deomidova** in the surprisingly small role of the heroine, Olga, is disappointingly edgy.

War and Peace (DVD versions)

*** Arthaus **DVD** 100 370-9. Gergalov, Prokina, Volkova, Sonya, Kanunnikova, Alexashkin, Gregoriam, Borodina, Bezukhova, Marusin, Morozov, Kit, Okhotnikov, Gerello, Kirov Ch. and O, Gergiev (Dir: Graham Vick; V/D: Humphrey Burton)

*** TDK **DVD** DV OPWP (2). Guryakova, Gunn, Brubaker, Kotcherga, Obraztsova, Gerello, Zaremba, Margita, Poretsky, Paris Nat. Op. Ch. & O, Bertini (Dir: Zambello, Hugues R. Gall)

We now have two versions of Prokofiev's monumental opera to choose between on DVD. **Bertini's** account was recorded at the Opéra Bastille in March 2000 and was the opera's first (and much heralded) staging in France. It has plenty in its favour, including a good cast, with an excellent Natasha in **Olga Guryakova**. There is a fine Bolkonsky in **Nathan Gunn** and an ideal Pierre Bezhukov (**Robert Brubaker**), who both looks and sounds exactly right. Perhaps **Anatoli Kotcherga** is not quite as memorable a Kutuzov as Nikolai Okhotnikov on the Kirov set, but he is commanding nevertheless. Gary Bertini conducts his fine chorus and orchestra well and, generally speaking, there are few serious weaknesses. In addition to the 210 minutes of the opera itself, the Paris recording includes two features on the production, running to 79 minutes or so. No one investing in the set is likely to be greatly disappointed, for the viewer is held from start to finish.

The alternative 1991 Kirov production was directed by **Graham Vick** with simple – but, on the whole, effective – designs and costumes. The Bolkonsky (**Alexandr Gergalov**), Pierre (**Gegam Gregoriam**) and Kutuzov (**Nikolai Okhotnikov**) are impressive, though the production, particularly in the first half, is not as distinguished as everyone said it was. However, it is the quality of **Gergiev's** conducting – War and Peace was the first opera he conducted, a quarter of a century ago – and the magnificent choral forces he has at his command that would probably in the end tip the scales in favour of the St Petersburg set, were we forced to choose. However, we would be happy with either.

War and Peace (CD versions)

○─┐ **** Chan. 9855 (4). Morozova, Williams, Lavender, Balashov, Dupont, Stephen, Ionova, Ewing, Opie, Russian State Symphonic Cappella, Spoleto Fest. O, Hickox

Ⓜ *** Erato (ADD) 2292 45331-2 (4). Vishnevskaya, Miller, Ciesinski, Tumagian, Ochman, Ghiuselev, Smith, Paunova, Petkov, Toczyska, Zakai, Gedda, Fr. R. Ch. & Nat. O, Rostropovich

Recorded live at the 1999 Spoleto Festival in full and open Chandos sound, **Richard Hickox's** formidable version of Prokofiev's epic opera offers a strong, thrustful performance with a cast more consistent than those on rival sets. With a warm understanding of the idiom, helped by a substantial Russian element among the singers, not least the chorus, Hickox keeps the 13 scenes moving well at speeds often on the fast side. Pointing the dramatic contrast between personal tragedy and great public events, the surging lyricism of Prokofiev's inspiration is sharply set against bitingly rhythmic writing, whether in the party scenes of the first part or the wartime scenes of the second half. The glorious tunefulness of the patriotic numbers has just the gulp-in-throat quality needed, whether General Kutuzov's big aria, nobly sung by **Alan Ewing**, or the big choruses fervently sung by the **Russian** choir.

Ekaterina Morozova is a moving Natasha, Slavonic in timbre, weighty but still girlish enough, with an edge to the voice that rarely turns squally. She is well matched in the beautiful opening scene by **Pamela Helen Stephen** as her cousin, Sonya, while **Roderick Williams** is a fresh, virile Andrei, and **Justin Lavender** a vulnerable-sounding Pierre, who convincingly erupts in anger.

Alan Opie is a characterful Napoleon, with the battle scene of Borodino thrillingly vivid, not least in shattering cannon shots. Other versions may have starrier individual contributions, but this one has no weak link, and the recording is not just full and brilliant, but, beautifully balanced, captures the sweetness of the **Spoleto** strings very persuasively. The four-disc layout (for the price of three) means breaks come at the ends of scenes.

In **Rostropovich's** powerful reading one revels – thanks also to the lively Erato recording – in the vividness of the atmosphere, both in the evocative love scenes and ball scenes of the first half (Peace) and in the high tensions of the battle scenes in the second (War). The opera culminates in a great patriotic chorus, using the most haunting tune of all, earlier sung by General Kutuzov after the Council of Fili, and the emotional thrust is overwhelming. The **French Radio Choir** sings that chorus with real Russian fervour. It was natural that Rostropovich's wife, **Galina Vishnevskaya**, should sing the central role of Natasha, as she did in the earlier, much-cut, Bolshoi recording. It is extraordinary how convincingly this mature soprano in her early sixties characterizes a young girl; there may be raw moments, but she is completely inside the role. The Hungarian baritone, **Lajos Miller**, not flawless either, is a clear-voiced Andrei, and **Wieslaw Ochman** is a first-rate Pierre, with the veteran, **Nicolai Gedda**, brought in as Kuragin. **Katherine Ciesinski** is a warm-toned Sonya, but **Dimiter Petkov** is disappointingly unsteady as Natasha's father, Count Rostov. The small role of Napoleon is strongly taken by **Eduard Tumagian**, while **Nicola Ghiuselev** is a noble Kutuzov, in some ways the most impressive of all. The libretto contains French and English translations, but no Russian transliteration, only the Cyrillic text in a separate section.

PUCCINI, Giacomo (1858–1924)

Capriccio sinfonico; Crisantemi; Minuets 1–3; Preludio sinfonico; Edgar: Preludes, Acts I & III; Manon Lescaut: Intermezzo, Act III; Le Villi: Prelude. La Tregenda (Act II)

Ⓜ *** Decca 475 7722. Berlin RSO, Chailly

In a highly attractive collection of Puccinian juvenilia and rarities, **Chailly** draws opulent and atmospheric playing from the **Berlin Radio Symphony Orchestra**, helped by outstandingly rich and full recording. The *Capriccio sinfonico* of 1876 brings the first characteristically Puccinian idea in what later became the opening Bohemian motif of *La Bohème*. There are other identifiable fingerprints here, even if the big melodies suggest Mascagni rather than full-blown Puccini. *Crisantemi* (with the original string quartet version expanded for full string orchestra) provided material for *Manon Lescaut*, as did the three little *Minuets*, pastiche 18th-century music.

Crisantemi for String Quartet

Ⓜ *** CRD (ADD) CRD 3366. Alberni Qt – DONIZETTI: *Quartet 13*; VERDI: *Quartet* ***

Crisantemi is given a warm, finely controlled performance by the **Alberni Quartet** and makes a valuable makeweight for the two full-scale *Quartets* by fellow opera-composers. The sound is excellent.

Crisantemi; Fugues 1–3; Minuets 1–3; Scherzo in A min.; String Quartet in D

*** ASV CDDCA 909. Puccini Qt – CATALANI: *String Quartet in A*, etc. ***

The *Minuets* are hardly identifiable as by Puccini. Then suddenly the full Puccini emerges in the beautiful *Crisantemi* of 1890. It is strange that though Puccini's musical personality began to emerge early in his choral and orchestral works, this sparer genre found him more anonymous, even in his melodies. Nonetheless, a delightful disc, warmly played and atmospherically recorded.

(i) Messa di gloria; (ii) Preludio sinfonico; Crisantemi

Ⓑ **** EMI 3 56519-2. (i) Alagna, Hampson, LSO Ch. LSO, Pappano

ⒷⒷ *** Warner Apex (DDD/ADD) 0927 48692-2. (i) Carreras, Prey, Amb. S., Philh. O; (ii) Monte Carlo Op. O; Scimone

Messa di gloria; Crisantemi; Preludio sinfonico

ⒷⒷ *** Naxos 8.555304. Palombi, Lundberg, Hungarian R. Ch. & Op. O, Morandi

Puccini's *Messa di gloria* is by far the most ambitious of his early works. He even uses material from the *Agnus Dei* in *Manon Lescaut*, yet the piece has been unfairly neglected on disc, when particularly the extended setting of the *Gloria* is so memorable, starting with a swaggering march such as Rossini might have put into a religious work.

Antonio Pappano easily outshines his rivals on disc, enhancing the operatic element, including obvious echoes not just of the Verdi *Requiem*, but of *Otello*. Ideal soloists in **Alagna** and **Hampson**, with the **London Symphony Chorus** and **LSO** in incandescent form. The two bonuses are welcome, aptly chosen and very well played.

The return of **Scimone's** second (1983) digital version on the super-bargain Apex label makes this version much more attractive, particularly as he includes the same two orchestral pieces as Pappano as makeweights. Excellent, atmospheric sound.

The Naxos recording from Budapest brings bright, urgent singing and playing under **Pier Morandi**. The early orchestral works make an attractive bonus.

OPERA

Collection: Renata Tebaldi: 'The Classic Puccini Recordings': La Bohème; Madama Butterfly; Turandot; La Fanciulla del West (with soloists, Ch. & O of Rome Santa Cecilia Academy)

Ⓑ (**(*)) Decca mono/stereo (ADD) 475 9385 (15)

Here are the LP sets that not only revealed **Renata Tebaldi** as one of the supreme 20th-century sopranos, at her very finest in Puccini, but that also helped to establish Decca as a major source of opera recordings. Listening through these remarkable recordings not only gives pleasure but also excites nostalgia for a period of recording history when the long playing record (and later stereo) transformed the operatic medium for home-listening. The operas are all available separately.

La Bohème (with Prandelli, Gueden, Inghilleri, Corena, Arié; cond. Erede)

Ⓑ Decca 440 233-2 (2)

The recording of *La Bohème* dates from 1951 and is still a lovely performance, more than fifty years later. **Gueden** is a most characterful Musetta, if not always in style vocally; **Prandelli** is a light-voiced but ardent and likeable Rodolfo; and **Inghilleri** is old-sounding but still interesting as Marcello. The main weakness lies in **Erede's** conducting, which is not terribly inspired. But even that is no serious drawback when the singing is so consistently compelling. The balance is still remarkably realistic, and the thin, edgy violins (for which early Decca LPs became notorious) have been satisfactorily contained in this vivid new transfer.

Madama Butterfly (with Campora, Rankin, Inghilleri; cond. Erede)

Ⓑ Decca 440 236-2 (2)

Madama Butterfly was also recorded in 1951, and astonishingly this set was made before Tebaldi ever sang the part in the opera house. Once again, the orchestral strings now offer little to worry the ear and generally sound much more full-bodied than previously.

Turandot (with Borkh, del Monaco; cond. Erede)

(B) Decca 452 964-2 (2)

Turandot, recorded a year later in 1955, proved to be the one near-failure of the series. The recording has a glitter and brilliance to match even the fabulous court of the emperor of China, yet somehow the performance lacks atmosphere and sheer vitality. **Tebaldi** opted for the part of Liù and sings beautifully, but **Inge Borkh** proved not the most biting of princesses, and the recording is not kind to her upper register, bringing out its unevenness. **Monaco** is his own loud-voiced self as the stranger prince, but **Erede's** conducting seems too careful in passages that should have the most barefaced oriental panache.

La Fanciulla del West (with del Monaco, MacNeil, Tozzi; cond. Capuana)

(B) Decca 421 595-2 (2)

Such was the success of *La Fanciulla del West*, made three years later in the summer of 1958, that it has remained unsurpassed until this day. It is discussed more fully below. Sufficient to say that both **Tebaldi** and **del Monaco** were at their finest, and **Tozzi** as Jake Wallace proved another outstanding asset. The Decca producers, James Walker and Christopher Raeburn, again demonstrated Decca's imaginative production values at their most impressive.

Other Recordings

(i) La Bohème; (ii) Madama Butterfly; (iii) Tosca (complete; DVD Versions)

(M) ***(*) DG DVD 073 4417 (3). (i) Freni, Martino, Raimondi, La Scala Ch. & O, Karajan; (ii) Freni, Ludwig, Domingo, VPO, Karajan; (iii) Kabaivanska, Domingo, Milnes, New Philh. O, Bartoletti

These three splendidly traditional filmed productions with starry casts are very highly recommendable and are discussed below. Two feature **Mirelli Freni**, two are with **Domingo** (both on top form), and two are conducted by **Karajan** and the third equally magnetically by **Bartoletti**; altogether they make a wonderful mid-priced package. This is what filmed opera should be about; and here it is, with backgrounds and productions which follow the composer's intentions. The wide-ranging photography is very well handled and the miming is not too distracting. The packaging is minimal but there is a good accompanying booklet.

'The Great Decca Puccini recordings': (i–iv) La Bohème; (i; ii; v) Madama Butterfly; (i; ii; vi) Manon Lescaut; (i; ii; vii) Tosca; (i; iii; viii) Turandot

(N) (B) *** Decca 475 9409 (11). (i) Pavarotti; (ii) Freni; (iii) Ghiaurov; (iv) Harwood, BPO, Karajan; (v) Ludwig, Kerns, VPO, Karajan; (vi) Met. Op. Ch. & O, Levine; (vii) Milnes, Nat. PO, Rescigno; (viii) Sutherland, Caballé, Krause, Alldis Ch., LPO, Mehta

'The EMI Operas':

La Bohème (Freni, Gedda, Adani, Sereni, Basiola, Mazzoli, Rome Op. Ch. & O, Schippers)

La Fanciulla del West (Nilsson, Gibin, Mongelli, La Scala, Milan, Ch. & O, Matačić)

Tosca (Callas, Bergonzi, Gobbi, Paris Op. Ch. & Conservatoire O, Prêtre)

Madama Butterfly (De los Angeles, Björling, Pirazzini, Rome Op. Ch. & O, Santini)

La Rondine (Gheorghiu, Alagna, L. Voices, LSO, Pappano)

Il trittico (*Il tabarro; Suor Angelica; Gianni Schicchi*) (Guelfi, Guleghina, Shicoff, Gallardo-Domas, Manca di Nissa, L. Voices, LSO, Tiffin Boys' Ch., Philh., Pappano; Gobbi, De los Angeles, Rome Op. O, Santini)

Turandot (Nilsson, Corelli, Scotto, Rome Op. Ch. & O, Molinari-Pradelli)

(N) (B) **(*) EMI 2 15460-2 (17)

The Complete Callas Studio Recordings

La Bohème (with Di Stefano, Panerei, Moffo, La Scala, Milan, Ch. & O, Votto)

Madama Butterfly (with Gedda, Danieli, La Scala, Milan, Ch. & O, Karajan)

Manon Lescaut (with Di Stefano, Fioravanti, La Scala, Milan, Ch. & O, Serafin)

Tosca (with di Stefano, La Scala, Milan, Ch. & O, De Sabata)

Tosca (with Cioni, Gobbi, ROHCG Ch. & O, Cillario)

Turandot (with Schwarzkopf, Fernandi, La Scala, Milan, Ch. & O, Serafin)

Arias (1954) (with Philh. O, Serafin)

(N) (B) (***) EMI mono/stereo 2 15894-2 (15)

To celebrate the 150th anniversary of Puccini's birth, at the end of 2008 Decca and EMI both made available their key recordings gathered together as sets. They are economically priced and suitable for those wanting to replace their collections in a way that reduces storage space but still makes the individual recordings easily accessible.

La Bohème (complete; DVD versions)

(⚙) **** DG DVD 073 4025. Scotto, Pavarotti, Niska,

Wixell, Monk, Plishka, Tajo, Met. Op. Ch. & O, Levine; Introduction: Tony Randall (Dir: Kirk Browning)

Ⓝ 🔑 ❀ **** EMI **DVD** 2 17417-9. Gheorghiu, Vargas, Arteta, Tézier, Gradus, Kelsey, Plishka, Met. Op. Ch. & O, Luisotti (Producer: Franco Zeffirelli)

(*) DG **DVD 073-4071. Freni, Martino, Raimondi, Panerai, La Scala Ch. & O, Karajan (Dir: Franco Zeffirelli)

(*) Warner **DVD 4509 99222-2. Cotrubas, Shicoff, Allen, Zschau, Howell, Rawnsley, ROHCG Ch. & O, Gardelli (Producer: John Copley, V/D: Brian Large)

(*) Arthaus **DVD 100 046. Freni, Pavarotti, Pacetti, Quilico, Ghiaurov, San Francisco Ch. & O, Severini (V/D: Brian Large)

(*) TDK **DVD DV-OPBOH. Gallardo-Domas, Hong, Alvarez, Servile, Carolis, Parodi, La Scala Ch. & O, Bartoletti (V/D: Carlo Battistoni)

This is the *Bohème* we have been waiting for, the 1972 Chicago Lyric Opera production, the first to be filmed in colour at the New York Met., in 1977. Three decades ago **Pavarotti** was in his prime, and he makes an ideal Rodolfo, not only singing with his usual vocal charisma, but acting movingly, particularly in the final scene. **Renata Scotto's** Mimì very nearly steals the show. She is plainly dressed, but her face lights up with a wonderful smile when she declares her feelings for Rodolfo. **Ingvar Wixell's** Marcello, with his rich baritone, is as passionately warm-hearted as you could wish, and **Maralin Niska** is a wilfully attractive and resourceful Musetta. Among the smaller parts **Italo Tajo's** Benoit stands out, and of course **Allan Monk's** Schaunard and **Paul Plishka's** Colline add much to the boisterous antics of the male quartet which frames the opera. **James Levine** conducts with wonderful flexibility, especially when accompanying Scotto, and the orchestra responds warmly, even if the recording does not do its opulence full justice. Never mind, to watch this (with subtitles) makes a wonderful evening's entertainment.

Zeffirelli's extraordinary set especially built for the Met. production of *La Bohème* has already been used for over 300 performances, over the years. It is still unsurpassed and visitors walking in the Act II street scene have felt they were actually in Paris itself! The opera opens and closes just as seductively in the house-top garret, while the snow in Act III is astonishingly tangible. One wishes opera settings could always be like this, instead of following producers' crazily eccentric whims, with no connection to the music. **Gheorghiu's** return to the Met. for this production was rightly celebrated. She sings gloriously, of course, but her portrayal of Mimì has matured, notably so in her acting in the opening scene, her first meeting with Rudolfo (**Ramón Vargas**), also singing ardently. Clearly this lovers' meeting is not quite as innocent as it seems, although Rudolfo is equally complicit in hiding the key. But what a shame that the surtitles (although otherwise admirable) have abandoned the familiar words 'Your tiny hand is frozen – let me warm it into life.' Before that, the horseplay between the four bohemians has been tingling with zest. Then the Café Momus scene of Act II is dazzling, with the interplay of a huge animated cast dominated by **Ainhoa Arteta's** sparklingly unpredictable Musetta. Marcello (**Ludovic Tézier**) joins Act III in the snow to sing in the memorable quartet, and the opera's closing scene could not be more moving. Throughout, **Nicola Luisotti** conducts Puccini's greatest score with passion and much tenderness, and the recording projects the voices and orchestra with admirable realism. A triumph, and wonderfully enjoyable to watch and listen to.

Based on Zeffirelli's spectacular 1963 production at La Scala, Milan, this **Karajan** DVD version of *La Bohème* gives no idea of stage limitations. Indeed by completely avoiding shots of the full stage, Acts II and III give the illusion of being out of doors. One snag is that with the singers miming to recorded voices, often distant, there is sometimes little relationship between what one hears and what one sees in close-up. Nonetheless, with Karajan second to none as a Puccini interpreter, pointing the great emotional climaxes unerringly, and with **Freni** a meltingly beautiful Mimì, the combination of vividly atmospheric settings and a high-powered performance have one forgiving any discrepancies. **Gianni Raimondi** is a forthright Rodolfo with his ringing, unstrained tenor, while **Panerai** is an outstanding Marcello, and **Adriana Martino** a spunky Musetta.

Recorded for television in February 1982 with Brian Large directing, the alternative Warner DVD gives a vivid idea of John Copley's classic production of *La Bohème* at Covent Garden when it was new, with its evocative sets by Julia Trevelyan Oman. Though **Lamberto Gardelli's** conducting is relatively relaxed, veering towards expansive speeds, the results are keenly idiomatic with an excellent cast of soloists. **Neil Shicoff** may be too loud at times, but this is yet a warmly sympathetic portrayal, never coarse, and **Ileana Cotrubas** at the peak of her career makes a charming Mimì, if at times with a beat in her voice. **Thomas Allen**, at his full maturity, is superb as Marcello, commanding in every way, but, for all her vivacity, the Musetta of **Marilyn Zschau**, suffering from a very slow speed in the *Waltz Song*, is often too tremulous.

Recorded in 1988, the **San Francisco Opera** production with **Pavarotti** and **Freni** offers a traditional production by Francesca Zambello, with the great tenor at his peak as Rodolfo and Freni still a tenderly moving Mimì, even though the voice is not as pure and even as it had been. She rises splendidly to the challenge of her big moments, such as Mimì's Farewell, like Pavarotti happily sustaining the lusciously measured speeds often allowed by the conductor, **Tiziano Severini**. **Sandra Pacetti** as Musetta is bright and characterful, and **Gino Quilico** as Marcello and **Nicolai Ghiaurov** as Colline are both excellent. The recording generally wears well, though the balance of voices in this live recording is sometimes odd.

Franco Zeffirelli's production of *La Bohème* for La Scala, Milan, was first seen in 1963 and was used by Karajan (see above). It here is filmed in a 2003 revival, celebrating its fortieth anniversary. In an interview, Zeffirelli marvels at its longevity, noting that many in the excellent team of singers had not even been born when the production was new. **Marcelo Alvarez** proves an outstanding Rodolfo from the younger generation, opposite the fresh and girlish Mimì of

Cristina Gallardo-Domas. Hei-Kyung Hong is a charmingly petite Musetta with a surprisingly strong character, and **Roberto Servile** as Marcello is powerful if rough at times. **Bruno Bartoletti** conducts a warm, well-paced and well-recorded reading, but it is the spectacle of Zeffirelli's lavish production that commands first attention.

La Bohème (complete; CD versions)

Ⓝ 🔑 ✿ **** DG 477 6600 (2). Netrebko, Villazón, Cabell, Daniel, Children's Ch. & Bav. R. Ch. & SO, De Billy

Ⓝ **** DG 477 7949 (2). Soundtrack recording with cast as above (includes bonus interviews with the principal singers)

**** EMI 3 58650-2 (2). Vaduva, Alagna, Swenson, Hampson, Keenlyside, Ramey, L. Voices, boys from L. Oratory School, Philh. O, Pappano

**** Decca (ADD) 478 0254 (2). Freni, Pavarotti, Harwood, Panerai, Ghiaurov, German Op. Ch., Berlin, BPO, Karajan

*** Decca 466 070-2 (2). Gheorghiu, Alagna, Scano, Keenlyside, D'Arcangelo, La Scala, Milan, Verdi Ch. & O, Chailly

🔑 Ⓑ **** Double Decca (ADD) 448 725-2 (2). Tebaldi, Bergonzi, Bastianini, Siepi, Corena, D'Angelo, St Cecilia Ac. Ch. & O, Serafin

Ⓜ *** RCA (ADD) 82876 82621-2 (2). Moffo, Tucker, Merrill, Costa, Rome Op. Ch. & O, Leinsdorf

(***) EMI mono 5 56295-2 (2). Callas, di Stefano, Moffo, Panerai, La Scala, Milan, Ch. & O, Votto

This new DG recording is surely the *La Bohème* for our time, and we are glad to see that the distinguished vocal critic of the *Gramophone*, John Steane, has given the set his enthusiastic imprimatur and has commented that the the singing of its two stars, the glorious-voiced **Anna Netrebko** and the thrilling **Rolando Villazón**, is 'as finely performed as in any recording known to me'. One need say little more, except that **Nicole Cabell** as Musetta and **Boaz Daniel** as Marcello are equally memorable, as is the vividly alive and expressive orchestral playing under **Betrand De Billy**. The recording also has splendid reality and projection. The set comes in a handsome box with libretto; an alternative jewel-case package offers a film soundtrack plus bonus material, including interviews with the principal artists. No doubt a DVD is in preparation which will be worth waiting for.

Pappano's CD recording of *Bohème* is conducted with ever-fresh imagination, bringing out not just subtle emotions alongside high passion, but also the fun of the piece in lightly sprung rhythms. Yet the exchanges when Mimì arrives have the most moving intimacy at the gentlest *pianissimo*, with the singers given full expressive freedom within a purposeful frame. The great set-piece numbers at the end of Act I, then have the freshness of genuine emotion swelling in a radiant, towering crescendo. **Alagna's** tenor may not be velvety, but it has a fine tonal range with a heroic ring and Adriva is similarly characterful rather than just sweet. The others make a superb team, virtually incomparable today – **Ruth Swenson** using her dramatic timbres most delicately even in the outburst of the waltz song, **Thomas Hampson** a swaggering Marcello, with **Samuel Ramey** and **Simon Keenlyside** characterfully contrasted as the other two Bohemians, all relishing the fun.

On Decca, **Karajan** takes a characteristically spacious view of *La Bohème*, but there is an electric intensity which holds the whole score together as in a live performance. **Pavarotti** is an inspired Rodolfo, with comic flair and expressive passion, while **Freni** is just as seductive as Mimì. **Elizabeth Harwood** is a charming Musetta. Fine singing throughout the set. The reverberant Berlin acoustic is glowing and brilliant in superb Decca recording, with the clean placing of voices enhancing the performance's dramatic warmth. The set is now beautifully re-packaged with lots of session photographs.

The husband-and-wife partnership of **Gheorghiu** and **Alagna** is formidably demonstrated in Decca's more recent recording, though with **Chailly** in taut control and speeds consistently on the fast side, this is a performance that misses some of the tenderness in the score, as well as some of the fun. Gheorghiu's glorious singing is powerfully matched by the heroic tones of Alagna, culminating in a deeply moving death scene. The notable casting among the rest is that of **Simon Keenlyside**, promoted to Marcello this time from Schaunard in the EMI set, again consistently responsive and alert. **Elisabetta Scano** is a light, bright Musetta, strongly contrasted with Gheorghiu, if a little shrill on top. **Roberto di Candia** makes a positive Schaunard, but **Ildebrando d'Arcangelo** as Colline is not helped by the close vocal balance, with a flutter emerging in the Act IV Coat Song.

Tebaldi's Decca set with **Bergonzi** dominated the catalogue in the early days of stereo, and it still sounds astonishingly vivid, with a very convincing theatrical atmosphere. Vocally the performance achieves a consistently high standard, with Tebaldi as Mimì the most affecting. Carlo Bergonzi is a fine Rodolfo; **Bastianini** and **Siepi** are both superb as Marcello and Colline, and even the small parts of Benoit and Alcindoro (as usual taken by a single artist) have the benefit of **Corena's** magnificent voice. The veteran **Serafin** was more vital here than on some of his records. The set comes with a perfectly adequate cued synopsis, for *La Bohème* is an exceptionally easy opera to follow.

Though **Anna Moffo's** singing career ended disappointingly, in her prime she was one of the great strengths of the company of the Met. in New York. Here in this vividly engineered set in the Living Stereo series, she sings magnetically as Mimì opposite **Richard Tucker** as an excellent Rodolfo and **Robert Merrill** typically strong and characterful as Marcello and **Mary Costa** as Musetta. **Leinsdorf** in this **Rome Opera House** recording is more sympathetic than he often was on disc at this period.

Callas, flashing-eyed and formidable, may seem even less suited to the role of Mimì than to that of Butterfly, but characteristically her insights make for a vibrantly involving performance. Though **Giuseppe di Stefano** is not the subtlest of Rodolfos, he is in excellent voice here, and **Moffo** and **Panerai** make a strong partnership as the second pair of lovers. **Votto** occasionally coarsens Puccini's score but he directs with energy.

The justly famous **Beecham** mono set with **Victoria de los Angeles** and **Jussi Björling** remains as a reminder of past glories (EMI mono 5 67750-2), while Naxos offer an admirable alternative transfer. This adds, at super-bargain price, an earlier recording of the whole of Act IV made by Beecham in 1936 at Abbey Road with **Heddle Nash** and **Dora Labette** singing memorably as Rodolfo and Mimì; also included is Labette's exquisite performance of *D'onde lieta uscì* from Act III (Naxos mono 8.111249/50). Regis too offer a very acceptable transfer at a comparable cost, and their bonus is seven key Puccini arias sung by Björling (RRC 2057).

La Bohème (complete; in English)

*** Chan. 3008 (2). Haymon, O'Neill, McLaughlin, Miles, Dazeley, Geoffrey Mitchell Ch., Peter Kay Children's Ch., Philh. O, Parry

The magic mixture of humour and pathos in this unsinkable masterpiece is brought all the closer for having it in translation, even if the occasional line may ring false. **Dennis O'Neill** reinforces his high reputation as the regular tenor in the series, despite some intrusive vibrato under pressure, and **Cynthia Haymon** as a touching Mimì has never sounded more beautiful on disc, with the widest range of expression and tone. **Marie McLaughlin** is a warm-toned Musetta, temperamental rather than just flighty, and the other three Bohemians are ideally cast. Voices are vividly caught in the atmospheric recording, with the crowd scenes of Act II beautifully clarified. Highest praise too for **David Parry** who knows how to relax in tenderness, as well as when to press home hard. Warm, refined playing from the **Philharmonia**. Highly recommended to all who enjoy opera in English.

Edgar (complete)

🎧 *** Naïve V4957 (2). Varady, McCormick, Tanner, Jenis, Cigni, R. France Ch. & O, Levi

Ⓜ ** Sony (ADD) M2K 79213 (2). Scotto, Bergonzi, Sardinero, Killibrew, NY Schola Cantorum and Op. O, Queler

Edgar has an elaborate story, with absurd developments that no composer could make convincing. However, the score of *Edgar* brings important developments in Puccini's technique as a composer, through-composed, merging arias and ensembles. The recording of *Edgar* scores in the refinement of the sound. **Julia Varady** as Fidelia and **Carl Tanner** in the title-role of Edgar are both outstanding, allowed a range of expression largely denied to their rivals on Queler's Sony version, which suffers from aggressively close-up sound. **Mary Ann McCormick** as Tigrana is well contrasted with Varady, with her firm, clear mezzo finely controlled. Clean-cut singing too from **Dalibor Jenis** as Frank and **Carlo Cigni** as Gualtiero, with excellent choral work from the **Choir of Radio France**, whose choirmaster is the great Norbert Balasch. **Yoel Levi** proves a warmly understanding Puccinian, pointing rhythms and phrases with natural sympathy.

There is much to enjoy in the alternative Sony version. The melodies are not quite vintage Puccini, but **Scotto** as Fidelia, **Killibrew** as Tigrana and **Bergonzi** as Edgar give

them compelling warmth. **Eve Queler** proves a variably convincing conductor, with Act III in need of more rehearsal. But this set, edited from live performances at Carnegie Hall, and commendably well recorded, makes a welcome alternative.

La Fanciulla del West (DVD versions)

🎧 **** DG DVD 073 4023. Daniels, Domingo, Milnes, Yannissis, Metropolitan Op. Ch. & O, Slatkin (V/D: Brian Large)

🎧 **** Warner DVD 5050466-8356-2-8. Neblett, Domingo, Carroli, Lloyd, Howell, ROHCG Ch. & O, Santi (V/D: John Vernon)

*** Opus Arte DVD OA LS 3004. Zampieri, Domingo, Pons, Roni, Salvadori, La Scala Ch. and O, Maazel (Executive producer: Hans Petri)

Leonard Slatkin conducts a bitingly dramatic account of Puccini's American opera with an outstanding cast in Giancarlo del Monaco's ultra-realistic production for the Met. in New York. In 1992 **Sherrill Milnes** was still an outstanding Rance, at once handsome and sinister, while **Plácido Domingo** is just as warmly expressive, both lyrical and heroic, as he is in the Covent Garden DVD of nine years earlier. As Minnie, the pretty and buxom **Barbara Daniels** with her bright, big soprano gives a characterful performance, even if her cheating in the poker game of Act II is no more convincing than usual. As Jake Wallace, the camp minstrel, **Yanni Yannissis** in his Act I solo is strong if a little tremulous. Bright, clear recording, bringing out the emotional tug behind Slatkin's reading, powerfully so at the very end.

Recorded live at Covent Garden in 1983, Piero Faggioni's production with realistic sets by Ken Adam offers a similar cast to that on the vintage DG audio recording made in the studio, except that **Silvano Carroli** replaces Sherrill Milnes as Rance and **Nello Santi** replaces Zubin Mehta as conductor. **Plácido Domingo** is in superb voice as Dick Johnson, the reformed bandit who falls in love with Minnie, Girl of the Golden West; and **Carol Neblett** as the Girl sings freshly with an appealing directness, untroubled by the formidable demands of the role. Carroli makes an aptly sinister Rance, with **Robert Lloyd** forthright as Ashby and **Gwynne Howell** as the Minstrel shining in his brief appearance at the start of Act I. Faggioni's production has its symbolic moments, as when Minnie concedes her very first kiss to Dick and the door of her hut flails wildly back and forth.

Jonathan Miller's production for La Scala, Milan, was recorded in 1991 with costumes by Sue Blane and sets by Stefanos Lazaridis half-stylized, half-realistic. What matters is that the singing cast is strong, and **Lorin Maazel's** conducting is persuasive, despite a tendency to dawdle in grand moments. As at Covent Garden eight years earlier, **Plácido Domingo** makes a heroic Dick Johnson, and though **Mara Zampieri** cannot match Kiri Te Kanawa in glamour of voice or presence, with occasionally hooty tone, it is a strong, positive performance, as is **Juan Pons** as Rance. Domingo is in superb voice and rightly wins ovations for each of his big solos. Juan Pons too is wonderfully firm and dark of tone as

Jack Rance, and Mara Zampieri as Minnie sings with fine, clear focus with no suspicion of a wobble.

La Fanciulla del West (The Girl of the Golden West; CD versions)

⊕—※ (M) **** Decca (ADD) 421 595-2 (2). Tebaldi, Del Monaco, MacNeil, Tozzi, St Cecilia Ac., Rome, Ch. & O, Capuana

(M) *** DG (ADD) 474 840-2 (2). Neblett, Domingo, Milnes, Howell, ROHCG Ch. & O, Mehta

(N) (***) Regis mono RRC 2080 (2). Steber, Guelfi, Del Monaco, De Palma, Tozzi, Maggio Musicale Fiorentino Ch. & O, Mitropoulos

Tebaldi here gives one of her most warm-hearted and understanding performances on record, and **Mario del Monaco** displays the wonderfully heroic quality of his voice to great – if sometimes tiring – effect. **Cornell MacNeil** as the villain, Sheriff Rance, sings with great precision and attack, but unfortunately has not a villainous-sounding voice to convey the character fully. Jake Wallace's entry and the song *Che faranno i viecchi miei* is one of the high spots of the recording, with **Tozzi** singing beautifully. **Capuana's** expansive reading is matched by the imagination of the production, with the closing scene wonderfully effective in spectacular sound.

On DG, **Mehta's** manner – as he makes clear at the very start – is on the brisk side, even refusing to let the first great melody, the nostalgic *Che faranno i viecchi*, linger into sentimentality. **Sherrill Milnes** as Jack Rance makes that villain into far more than a small-town Scarpia, giving nobility and understanding to the Act I arioso. **Domingo**, as in the theatre, sings heroically, disappointing only in his reluctance to produce soft tone in the great aria, *Ch'ella mi creda*. The rest of the team is excellent, not least **Gwynne Howell** as the minstrel who sings *Che faranno i viecchi miei*; but the crowning glory of a masterly set is the singing of **Carol Neblett** as the Girl of the Golden West herself, gloriously rich and true, with formidable attack on the exposed high notes. Full, atmospheric recording to match.

Regis have come up trumps with this early (1954) live Florence recording of *La Fanciulla del West*, thrillingly conducted by the underrated **Dimitri Mitropoulos**, with **Eleanor Steber** (as Minnie), **Mario del Monaco** (in his finest role) as Dick Johnson and **Gian Giacomo Guelfi** a splendidly ardent Jack Rance. Incidentally, **Giorgio Tozzi** features in the smaller part of Jake Wallace, who sings the ballad *Che faranno i viecchi miei* offstage. The sound is not of the finest but is more than acceptable when the performance is so thrilling.

Gianni Schicchi (DVD version)

⊕— *** Opus Arte DVD OA 0918 D. Corbelli, Matthews, Giordano, Palmer, McLaughlin, LPO, Jurowski (V/D: Francesca Kemp)

Puccini's comic masterpiece comes in a production by Annabel Arden that determinedly underlines the black side of this sparkling farce. The conductor, **Vladimir Jurowski**, also emphasizes that point, suggesting that Puccini's construction anticipates that of the modern film in its timing and cutting of scenes. The claustrophobic side of the piece is underlined by the heavily enclosed set of Vicki Mortimer, backing up the updating of the story from medieval to Edwardian times and largely eliminating the uplifting background of Florence. **Alessandro Corbelli** proves a masterly Schicchi, at once characterful, funny and sinister, and the two lovers are well taken by the tenor, **Massimo Giordano**, and the young soprano, **Sally Matthews**, with her fresh, flickering vibrato. Interviews with Jurowski, Arden and Corbelli come as extras.

Gianni Schicchi (CD versions)

⊕— (M) *** RCA 74321 25285-2. Panerai, Donath, Seiffert, Bav. R. Ch., Munich R. O, Patanè

The RCA (formerly Eurodisc) recording of *Gianni Schicchi* brings a co-production with **Bavarian Radio**, and the recording is vivid and well balanced. Central to the performance's success is the vintage Schicchi of **Rolando Panerai**, still rich and firm. He confidently characterizes the Florentine trickster in every phrase, building a superb portrait, finely timed. **Peter Seiffert** as Rinuccio gives a dashing performance, consistently clean and firm of tone, making light of the high tessitura and rising splendidly to the challenge of the big central aria. **Helen Donath** would have sounded even sweeter a few years earlier, but she gives a tender, appealing portrait of Lauretta, pretty and demure in *O mio babbino caro*. Though Italian voices are in the minority, it is a confident team.

Madama Butterfly (complete; DVD version)

(N) ⊕— *** Warner NVC Arts DVD 4509 99290-2. Kabaivanska, Antinori, Jankovic, Saccomani, Ferrara, Verona Ch. & O, Arena (Producer: Giulio Chazzalettes, V/D: Brian Large)

**(*) Decca DVD DG 073 4037. Freni, Ludwig, Domingo, Kerns, Sénéchal, VPO, Karajan (Dir: Jean-Pierre Ponnelle)

The Warner NVC Arts *Madama Butterfly* from Verona has no obvious starry names in the cast, but it has an unforgettably moving performance from **Raina Kabaivanska** as Butterfly herself. From the moment she comes demurely on stage she identifies completely with her role: she looks like Butterfly, she sings as Butterfly (*One fine day* is a real highlight), indeed she is Butterfly, and as her tragedy unfolds in Act II the result is increasingly moving. **Nazzareno Antinori** sings ardently as a convincingly unthinking Pinkerton, and **Eleonora Jankovic** is a touchingly sympathetic Suzuki. **Lorenzo Saccomani** takes the thankless role of Sharpless warmly. The Verona set may give Butterfly a larger house than would be realistic but, like the costumes, it is authentically designed, and the surrounding gardens provide an attractive setting for much of the action. **Mario Ferrara** is an appropriately wily marriage-broker, and the little boy who subsequently appears as Cio-Cio-San's son is charmingly portrayed. **Maurizio Arena** conducts Puccini's marvellous score with rich feeling, and if the recording is at times a little overbright, it has fine clarity and depth. Highly recommended: if you watch it at home, there won't be a dry eye in the house!

Recorded for television in 1974 in the same period as he recorded the opera for audio disc, **Karajan's** DVD of *Butterfly* is similarly magical in its evocation of Puccini's most atmospheric score. As on CD the title-role is taken by **Mirella Freni**, as tenderly appealing to see as to hear, but where for audio the role of Pinkerton was taken by Luciano Pavarotti, here you have the much more telegenic **Plácido Domingo**, singing with similar fervour, responding to the inspired stage direction of **Jean-Pierre Ponnelle** to make this cad of a hero more complex than usual. Otherwise the setting is conventional and effective, with a comic portrait of Goro given by **Michel Sénéchal**, politically incorrect in its Japanese send-up, and the Bonze rather like a caricature from *Turandot*. The sound is full and atmospheric, though there is a curious pitch-problem in the middle of the *Flower Duet*, one of the few flaws in a fine issue.

(i) *Madama Butterfly;* (ii) *Tosca;* (iii) *Turandot* (complete; DVD versions)

Ⓝ Ⓑ *** Warner **DVD** 50-51442-8637-2-7 (3). Verona productions, with (i) Kabaivanska, cond. Arena; (ii) Marton, cond. Oren; (iii) Dimitrova, cond. Arena (see below)

These three outstanding Verona productions make a tempting bargain box, with both *Madama Butterfly* and *Turandot* among the finest available versions. The documentation is minimal, but adequate.

Madama Butterfly (CD versions)

🎵— **** Decca (ADD) 417 577-2 (3). Freni, Ludwig, Pavarotti, Kerns, V. State Op. Ch., VPO, Karajan

*** DG 423 567-2 (3). Freni, Carreras, Berganza, Pons, Amb. Op. Ch., Philh. O, Sinopoli

Ⓑ *** Double Decca (ADD) 452 594-2 (2). Tebaldi, Bergonzi, Cossotto, Sordello, St Cecilia Ac., Rome, Ch. & O, Serafin

Ⓜ *** EMI (ADD) 5 67885-2 [567888] (2). Scotto, Bergonzi, di Stasio, Panerai, de Palma, Rome Op. Ch. & O, Barbirolli

Ⓝ Ⓑ Ⓑ (***) Naxos mono 8.111291/2. De los Angeles, Di Stefano, Gobbi, Canali, Rome Op. Ch. & O, Gavazzeni

Ⓑ Ⓑ (***) Regis mono RRC 2070 (2). De los Angeles, Di Stefano, Gobbi, Canali, Rome Op. Ch. & O, Gavazzeni

Ⓝ Ⓜ *** EMI mono ADD 2 12711-2 (2). Callas, Gedda, Danieli, Borriello, La Scala, Milan, Ch. & O, Karajan

Karajan's Decca CD set is extravagantly laid out on three discs instead of two as for most of the rival sets – slow speeds partly responsible. However, he inspires singers and orchestra to a radiant performance which brings out all the beauty and intensity of Puccini's score, sweet but not sentimental, powerfully dramatic but not vulgar. **Freni** is an enchanting Butterfly, consistently growing in stature from the young girl to the victim of tragedy, sweeter of voice than any rival on record. **Pavarotti** is an intensely imaginative Pinkerton, actually inspiring understanding for this thoughtless character, while **Christa Ludwig** is a splendid Suzuki. The recording is one of Decca's most resplendent, with the **Vienna** strings producing glowing tone.

However expansive his speeds, **Sinopoli** is never sentimental or self-indulgent. Puccini's honeyed moments are given, not sloppily, but with rapt intensity, through to the final aria, tough and intense. As she was for Karajan in his

classic Decca set, **Freni** is a model Butterfly; though the voice is no longer so girlish, she projects the tragedy even more weightily than before. **José Carreras** is similarly presented as a large-scale Pinkerton. **Juan Pons** is a virile Sharpless and **Teresa Berganza** an equally positive, unfruity Suzuki.

Serafin's sensitive and beautifully paced reading finds **Tebaldi** at her most radiant. Though she was never the most deft of Butterflies dramatically, her singing is consistently rich and beautiful. The excellence of the Decca engineering in 1958 is amply proved in the CD transfer.

Under **Sir John Barbirolli**, players and singers perform consistently with a dedication and intensity rare in opera recordings made in Italy, and the whole score glows more freshly than ever. There is hardly a weak link in the cast. **Bergonzi's** Pinkerton and **Panerai's** Sharpless are both sensitively and beautifully sung; **Anna di Stasio's** Suzuki is more than adequate, and **Renata Scotto's** Butterfly has a subtlety and perceptiveness in its characterization that more than make up for any shortcoming in the basic beauty of tone-colour. (There is a rather meagre set of highlights (54') on CfP 393370-2 with an equally meagre cued synopsis!)

Victoria de los Angeles's first recording of *Madama Butterfly*, a role which for a decade or more she made her own, was done in mono in 1954. The performance has many advantages over the later, stereo version. De los Angeles's tone is even more beautiful, **Di Stefano** is a more ardent Pinkerton, and **Tito Gobbi**, unexpectedly cast as a rugged Sharpless, uses that small role to point some of the set's most memorable moments, notably the Act I toasting duet with Pinkerton and the Act II confrontation with Butterfly. The Regis mono transfer is kind to the voices, which are given a full presence, and if the orchestra sounds a bit dry it still makes a vivid backcloth. There is a cued synopsis and good documentation.

The Naxos set is expertly restored by Mark Obert-Thorn and also comes with an excellent keyed synopsis.

Callas's view, aided by superbly imaginative and spacious conducting from **Karajan**, gives extra dimension to the Puccinian little woman, and with some keenly intelligent singing too from **Gedda** as Pinkerton this is a set which has a special compulsion. The performance projects the more vividly on CD, even though the lack of stereo in so atmospheric an opera is a serious disadvantage, and the new transfer is full and fairly spacious. It is now at mid-price as one of EMI's 'Great Recordings of the Century'.

Madam Butterfly (complete; in English)

Ⓜ **(*) Chan. 3070 (2). Barker, Clarke, Rigby, Yurisich, Kale, Geoffrey Mitchell Ch., Philh. O, Abel

With **Cheryl Barker** a warm, fresh heroine, bringing out the girlish shyness at the beginning, and singing with radiant tone, this set of *Butterfly* in English, sponsored by the Peter Moores Foundation, fills an important gap (as do many other operas in English). Cheryl Barker is helped by the expressive conducting of **Yves Abel** which consistently brings out the beauty of Puccini's orchestration, helped by full-bodied Chandos sound. As Pinkerton, the tenor, **Paul Charles Clarke**, is a disappointment with his gritty, tight tone, penetrating and un-Italianate, but he characterizes sensitively, and **Gregory Yurisich** is a splendid Sharpless and **Jean Rigby** a fine Suzuki. The old Elkins translation is used with a few necessary modifications.

Manon Lescaut (complete; DVD Versions)

(N) ⊕— ******** EMI DVD 2 17420 9. Mattila, Giordani, Croft, Travis, Met. Opera Ch. & O, Levine (Stage Director: Gina Lapinsky, V/D: Brian Large)

⊕— ******** Warner DVD 5050466-7174-2-9. Domingo, Te Kanawa, Allen, ROHCG Ch. & O, Sinopoli (V/D: Humphrey Burton)

(N) ******* TDK DVD DVWW-OPMLES. Guleghina, Cura, Roni, Gallo, La Scala, Milan, Ch. & O, Muti (Stage Director & V/D: Liliana Cavani)

**(*) NVC Arts DVD 50-0489-2-6. Nitescu, Denniston, De Candia, Palombi, Glyndebourne Ch., LPO, Gardiner (V/D: Humphrey Burton)

(N) ****** Arthaus DVD 101 319. Weber, Zurabishvili, Trinsinger, Räsänen, Chemnitz Opera Ch. & Robert Schumann Philharmonie, Beermann (Dir: Patrick Buttmann)

Whether in the very realistic opening Amiens inn scene or in Geronte's sumptuous apartment in Act II, the Met. production is characteristically spectacular, with superb costumes to match the sets, while the deportation in Act III is frighteningly realistic. The only let-down is the closing scene in the American wasteland of Act IV, which always seems an unrealistic ending, but that is Puccini's miscalculation, not the Met's. **Karita Mattila** is a beautiful Manon, but we see her age as the opera progresses. She sings very affectingly indeed and is matched by the ardent Des Grieux of **Marcello Giordani**, with a tenor voice of comparably rich quality. **Dale Travis** makes a splendidly unlikeable Geronte. **James Levine** conducts with a flowing, passionate lyricism; indeed the performance of the famous *Intermezzo* is an unforgettably passionate highlight. Very good sound completes a production which can be recommended alongside the Sinopoli Covent Garden version, which it equals; indeed, choice between them is difficult, while the TDK version below is also very competitive.

Götz Friedrich's production with solidly realistic sets by Gunther Schneider Siemssen was filmed at Covent Garden in 1983 with an ideal cast of principals and passionate, idiomatic conducting by **Giuseppe Sinopoli**. With voices well forward of the orchestra, the glorious singing of **Plácido Domingo** as Des Grieux comes over heroically, and **Kiri Te Kanawa** as Manon is both girlish and provocative, carefully modifying her tone between the open freshness of *In quelle trine morbide* in Act II and the darkened tone for her despairing final monologue in Act IV, *Sola, perduta, abbandonata*. **Thomas Allen** is equally strong and characterful as Lescaut, and the rest of the cast has no weak links. For a realistic presentation it would be hard to find any rival. No booklet is provided, with the full cast list given only on the film itself.

The 1998 La Scala production is less ambitious than the spectacle the Met. can provide, but it is still impressive, with the opening inn scene colourful and teeming with choral vitality, and Geronte's apartment certainly not lacking lux-ury. Moreover the harbour scene in Act III is strikingly realistic, and only the closing sequence 'in the wilderness outside New Orleans' with rocks all over the stage, is unconvincing. How did they get there? Costumes, too, are in period and the whole atmosphere is authentically French. The principals, too, are excellent. Although (as nearly always) Manon (**Maria Guleghina**) looks too old in Act I, she sings gloriously, and her love scene with her similarly ardent and warm-voiced Des Grieux (**José Cura**) in a splendidly staged Act II is suitably passionate. **Muti**, as always, directs with a happy combination of Puccinian lyricism and energy.

In this NVC **Glyndebourne** production, the two principal singers, **Patrick Denniston** (as Chevalier des Grieux) and **Adina Nitescu's** Manon, are only partly successful in managing the last Act, not helped visually by a set which is a flat plain with tiny 'boulders' scattered on it. The stage sets throughout are bare. Fortunately the costumes bring plenty of colour and the dance scene in Geronte's house in Act II is effectively staged, as is the climax of Act III, when Des Grieux is finally allowed to accompany Manon to America. Although he seems too old for a student part, Denniston sings ardently throughout, and Nitescu is a sympathetic Manon and sings her key numbers well. One of the other plus points of the performance is the vividly lively direction of the opera by **John Elliot Gardiner**. But overall this is not a match for the Domingo/Te Kanawa Warner version.

Although it is well sung, especially by **Astrid Weber**, a charmingly pretty, if initially too sophisticated and not strikingly young Manon, and by the fervent **Zurab Zurabishvili** as Des Grieux, this Arthaus production cannot be recommended for a number of reasons. The Stage Director Ansgar Weigner has decided to revise the plot-line to fit his own conception of the opera's characters (and their motivations). It is in modern dress, which places its atmosphere immediately out of period, and the characterization of Geronte (**Kouta Räsänen**) is lacking in elegance. But most importantly, the plot is altered in Act III when Manon succeeds in fleeing with Des Grieux and staying in Paris, instead of being deported. In Act IV she perishes in what is described as an 'underground dead-end' under the city. With **Frank Beermann** directing the orchestra vividly, the narrative is certainly alive, but hardly what Puccini intended.

Manon Lescaut (complete; CD Versions)

⊕— ******** Decca 440 200-2 (2). Freni, Pavarotti, Croft, Taddei, Vargas, Bartoli, NY Met. Op. Ch. & O, Levine

⊕— **(M)** ******** DG 477 6354 (2). Freni, Domingo, Bruson, ROHCG Ch., Philh. O, Sinopoli

(B) ******* Double Decca 460 750-2 (2). Te Kanawa, Carreras, Coni, Tajo, Matteuzzi, Ch. & O of Teatro Comunale di Bologna, Chailly

(BB) ******* Naxos 8.660019/20 (2). Gauci, Sardinero, Kaludov, BRT Philh. Ch. & O, Rahbari

(***) EMI mono 5 56301-2 (2). Callas, Di Stefano, Fioravanti, La Scala, Milan, Ch. & O, Serafin

(BB) **(***)** Naxos mono 8.111030/1 (2). Albanese, Bjoerling, Merrill, Calabrese, Rome Op. Ch. & O, Perlea (with Arias from BOITO: *Mefistofele*; CATALANI: *La Wally*;

CHARPENTIER: *Louise*; CILEA: *Adriana Lecouvreur*; VILLA-LÔBOS: *Bachianas Brasileiras 5*)

(BB) (***) Regis Alto mono ALC 2001 (2). Albanese, Bjoerling, Merrill, Calabrese, Rome Opera Ch. & O, Perlea (with Arias from *Madama Butterfly, La Bohème & Gianni Schicchi*)

With **Luciano Pavarotti** as a powerful Des Grieux, **James Levine** conducts a comparably big-boned performance of *Manon Lescaut*, bringing out the red-blooded drama of Puccini's first big success, while not ignoring its warmth and tender poetry. Pavarotti tackles his little opening aria, *Tra voi belle*, with a beefy bravado that misses the subtlety and point of Domingo, for example. But then he characteristically points word-meaning with a bright-eyed intensity that compels attention, and there is little harm in having so passionate a portrait of Des Grieux as Pavarotti's. The rest of the cast is strong too, with **Dwayne Croft** a magnificent Lescaut who brings out the character's wry humour. The veteran **Giuseppe Taddei** is superbly cast as Geronte, very characterful and still full-throated, while **Cecilia Bartoli** makes the unnamed singer in the Act II entertainment into far more than a cipher.

Plácido Domingo's portrait of Des Grieux on DG is far subtler and more detailed, with finer contrasts of tone and dynamic, than in his earlier, EMI recording opposite Caballé. **Freni** proves an outstanding choice: her girlish tones in Act I rebut any idea that she might be too mature. Of the others, a first-rate team, **Renato Bruson** nicely brings out the ironic side of Lescaut's character, and having **Brigitte Fassbaender** just to sing the *Madrigal* adds to the feeling of luxury, as does **John Tomlinson's** darkly intense moment of drama as the ship's captain.

The digital **Chailly** set dates from as recently as 1988. **Dame Kiri** gives an affecting characterization of Manon, at times rather heavily underlined but passionately convincing in the development from innocent girl to fallen woman. The playing from Chailly's **Bologna Orchestra** cannot quite match that of the Philharmonia for Sinopoli, yet Chailly is a degree more idiomatic in his pacing. **Carreras** is in good form, but sounds a little strained at times. The Decca sound, with the voices well forward is characteristically vivid.

On the Naxos issue, **Miriam Gauci** gives one of the most sensitive performances of this role on any set. The young Bulgarian, **Kaludi Kaludov**, is a clean-cut, virile Des Grieux, opening up impressively in his big moments. **Vincente Sardinero** makes a powerful Lescaut, and **Rahbari** is a red-blooded interpreter of Italian opera, generally pacing well, even if at the very start he is disconcertingly hectic.

It is typical of **Callas** that she turns the final scene into the most compelling part of the opera. **Serafin**, who could be a lethargic recording conductor, is here electrifying, and **Di Stefano** too is inspired to one of his finest complete opera recordings. The cast-list even includes the young **Fiorenza Cossotto**, impressive as the singer in the Act II *Madrigal*. The recording – still in mono, not a stereo transcription – minimizes the original boxiness and gives good detail.

With **Bjoerling** as Des Grieux giving one of his very finest performances on disc and with **Robert Merrill** in glorious voice as Lescaut, the Romanian conductor **Jonel Perlea** conducts one of the most passionate performances of this

opera ever recorded. Timing is masterly, and, though **Licia Albanese** no longer sounded girlish in 1954, she has the deepest understanding of the role of Manon. The transfer is bright and clear, with an edge that can readily be tamed. This was one of the very first complete operas recorded by RCA in Italy, and the thrust and enthusiasm of the whole company reflect that. As a bonus comes a valuable collection of Albanese's solo recordings, including most of the arias for which she was especially famous. Also the celebrated *Aria* from Villa-Lobos's *Bachianas brasileiras No. 5* with **Leopold Stokowski** conducting.

The Regis Alto transfer is bright and clean, and here the bonus features an all-Puccini programme with **Albanese** joined by **Jan Peerce**, and **Di Stefano** in his best voice in *Bohème*. The sound is impressive.

La Rondine (complete; DVD versions)

(N) *** Arthaus **DVD** 101 329. Cedolins, Portari, Pastrana, Giannino, Antonucci, Teatro La Fenice, Venice, Ch. & O, Rizzi (V/D & Dir: Tiziano Mancini)

(N) (B) ** Naxos **DVD** 2.110266. Vassileva, Sartori, Dashuk, Giannino, Giossi, Nice Puccini Festival Ch. & O, Veronesi (Dir: Lorenzo Amato, V/D: Matteo Ricchetti)

Puccini was never quite satisfied with *La Rondine* and revised it several times. The Nice version takes in some of his final revisions, whereas La Fenice uses the published score. The opera is very visual and the staging requires a special balance between sophistication and light-hearted delicacy, especially in the opening scene where the famous 'Che il bel sogno di Doretto' is a highlight. It is this lightly evoked atmosphere that Graham Vick, the director of the Venice production, captures admirably, alongside its growing warmth of passion as the two couples become more and more intertwined. The casting too in Venice is very successful with **Fiorenza Cedolins** an appealing Magda, and **Fernando Portari** a memorably warm-voiced, passionate Ruggero. **Sandra Pastrana** is a practical Lisette, a character not unlike Despina in *Così fan tutte*, although not so whimsical, and she pairs up well with her fake-poet, Prunier (**Emanuele Giannino**), who is excellent and is common to both DVDs. The production in Venice is very colourful, especially the spectacular scene at Bulliers (with a sparkling dancing sequence), which climaxes with the splendidly sung quartet, featuring the four lovers. **Carlo Rizzi** secures very polished orchestral playing and finds all the wistful delicacy in Puccini's lovely score.

In the Naxos version the story is well characterized and well sung by the four principals, although **Svelta Vassileva's** high tessitura (and Magda's part lies very high at times) is affected by her tight vibrato. But overall the performance misses the full Puccinian charm (especially in the opening scene) and the sets are less enticing than on Arthaus, though the central Act is lively enough. One curious feature is a pair of ballet dancers, all but naked, who dance a passionate pas de deux in each Act. Although this version has obvious merits, the Venice version is far preferable.

(i–iii) *La Rondine* (complete); (i; iii) *Le Villi*: Prelude, L'abbandono; La tregenda; Ecco la casa ... Torna al felice; (i; iv) Song: Morire!

⊕—**** EMI 5 56338-2 (2). (i) Alagna; (ii) Gheorghiu, Mula-Tchako, Matteuzzi, Rinaldi; (iii) L. Voices, LSO, Pappano; (iv) Pappano (piano)

Pappano on this EMI issue transforms the work, revealing it to be another masterpiece. He is aided by the partnership of **Angela Gheorghiu**, most moving in the Violetta-like role of the heroine, Magda, and of **Alagna** as the ardent young student she falls in love with. Consistently Gheorghiu makes you share the courtesan's wild dream of finding her young student. As Ruggero, the hero, Alagna winningly characterizes in his freshest voice. What will specially delight Puccinians in this set is that he is given an extra aria about Paris, *Parigi e un citta*, which transforms his otherwise minimal contribution to Act I. The role of the poet, Prunier, is also transformed thanks to the casting of the clear-toned **William Matteuzzi** in what is normally a comprimario role. **Inva Mula-Tchako** is equally well cast in the soubrette role of Lisette, bright, clear and vivacious, with **Alberto Rinaldi** making the sugar-daddy, Rambaldo, the dull dog intended. The excerpts from *Le Villi*, warm and dramatic, include two orchestral showpieces. Alagna also gives a ringing account of Roberto's aria, as he does of the song, *Morire!* – with Pappano at the piano – the source of the extra aria for Ruggero included in the main opera.

Suor Angelica (complete; CD version)

Ⓜ **(*) RCA (ADD) 74321 40575-2. Popp, Lipovšek, Schiml, Jennings, Bav. R. Ch., Munich R. O, Patanè

Ⓝ ⒷⒷ (**(*)) Regis mono RRC 1306. De los Angeles, Barbieri, Doro, Marimpietri, Rome Op. Ch. & O, Serafin (includes 3 excerpts from *La Bohème*)

Patanè's performance is idiomatic and consistently well placed. Neither **Lucia Popp** as Angelica nor **Marjana Lipovšek** as the vindictive Zia Principessa is ideally cast – the one overstressed, the other sounding too young – but these are both fine artists who sing with consistent imagination, and the recording is pleasingly atmospheric. There is a libretto/translation provided, and the only snag is the lack of cueing: only two tracks are indicated, one 28 minutes into the opera and the second 12 minutes later.

It is good to have a separate issue of **Victoria de los Angeles's** famous 1957 mono recording of *Suor Angelica*. The Regis transfer is warm and the voices are clear. No doubt we shall have a superior Naxos transfer in due course, but this is very acceptable, and includes three excerpts from Beecham's *La Bohème*, recorded a year earlier.

Il tabarro (complete; CD version)

Ⓝ ⒷⒷ (***) Naxos mono 8.111307. Gobbi, Prandelli, Mas, Rome Op. Ch. & O, Bellezza (with Gobbi: Arias from: *La Fanciulla del West*. MOZART: *Don Giovanni; Le nozze di Figaro*. ROSSINI: *Il barbiere di Siviglia*. VERDI: *La forza del destino; Otello*)

There is little to choose between the Naxos and Regis transfers, although Mark Obert-Thorn's on Naxos is marginally preferable. Choice may depend on the different bonuses offered by Naxos and Regis. However, the Naxos disc does offer a preferable keyed synopsis.

(i) *Il Tabarro* (complete); (ii) Excerpts from *La Bohème; Gianni Schicchi; Manon Lescaut; Tosca*

ⒷⒷ (***) Regis mono RRC 1263. (i) Gobbi, Prandelli, Mas; Welitsch; Tucker; Olivero; Sayao; Rome Op. Ch. & O, Bellezza

Good for Regis in making a perfectly good transfer of this famous pioneering mono recording of *Il Tabarro*. The central role of the cuckolded bargemaster, Michele, inspired **Gobbi** to one of his finest performances on record and, although the voices are rather forward, the mono recording has fair atmosphere. As a bonus we are offered some other key Puccini items. **Ljuba Welitsch** sings *Vissi d'arte* from *Tosca* and then is joined by **Richard Tucker** in the Act I Love Duet. **Magda Olivero** sings *Donde lieta usci* from *Bohème* and the two key arias from *Manon Lescaut*, and – an unexpected but welcome choice – **Bidú Sayao** closes the selection with the delightful *O mio babbino caro* from *Gianni Schicchi*.

Tosca (complete; DVD versions)

⊕—**** DG **DVD** 073 4038. Kabaivanska, Domingo, Milnes, Ch. & New Philh. O, Bartoletti (Dir: Gianfranco De Bosio, V/D: Harald Gericke)

*** TDK **DVD** DV-OPTOS. Guleghina, Licitra, Nucci, Parodi, Mariotti, La Scala Milan Ch. & O, Muti (V/D: Pierre Cavasillas)

*** Opus Arte **DVD** OA 0883 D. Gheorghiu, Alagna, Raimondi, ROHCG O, Pappano (Dir: Benoit Jacquot)

*** NVC Arts **DVD** 4509 99219-2. Marton, Aragall, Wixell, Ch. & O, of the Verona Arena, Oren (V/D: Brian Large)

Ⓝ *(*) Phoenix **DVD** 801. Michael, Todorovich, Saks, Bregenzer Festival Ch., VPO, Schirmer (Producer: Philipp Himmelmann)

Filmed on location in Rome with real-life backgrounds and recorded in Walthamstow (with Surround Sound), this DG set is unsurpassed. The singers mime to their parts and the lip-sync. is generally impressive (especially **Raina Kabaivanska's** thrillingly sung Tosca), although at the opening **Domingo** is obviously miming the part of Cavaradossi. But he sings so magnificently that one soon adjusts. **Sherrill Milnes**, whose vocal contribution is hardly less powerful, is an equally memorable Scarpia, patently evil, yet so smooth and commanding in his scenes with Tosca that it is not surprising that she is taken in. At the opening, the film cameras are outside the castle, so we see the escaping Angelotti arrive, search for the key, and find his way into the very beautiful church which is so ideal for the later spectacle of the *Te Deum* and Scarpia's brooding monologue. We then move to his lavish apartment for Act II, with its dramatically vivid torture scene, attempted rape and murder. For the finale we are taken to the battlements of the castle, and Puccini's closing vision of Tosca hurling herself off the battlements is fully maintained. With superb singing and fine acting from all concerned, and equally impressive conducting from **Bartoletti**, who has the **New Philharmonia** on top form, this is all pretty irresistible.

Muti knows unerringly how to pace his singers, letting them phrase expansively where needed, yet holding the structure firmly together. **Maria Guleghina** makes a formidable Tosca, at her finest in the great scene with Scarpia in Act II, leading up to a radiant account of *Vissi d'arte* and a chilling murder. The veteran **Leo Nucci**, tall, thin and mean, is most compelling as the police chief, at times a smiling villain, though the voice has its occasional roughness. As Cavaradossi **Salvatore Licitra** may be an unromantic figure, and he is heavy-handed at the start in *Recondita armonia*, but he develops from there and in Act III sings superbly, with fine shading of tone. The production, directed by **Luca Ronconi**, consistently heightens the dramatic conflicts. In period it is updated by roughly half a century from the Napoleonic era, with handsome costumes by Vera Marzot, though the sets of Margherita Palli bring a surreal contradiction between realism and fantasy. That makes the battlements of the Castell Sant'Angelo look like a bomb-site, which Tosca has to climb to fling herself to her death.

Using the outstanding EMI recording of *Tosca* conducted by **Antonio Pappano** for a soundtrack, the French film director **Benoit Jacquot** has created what he describes as a mixture of fiction and documentary. Clips of the recording sessions at Abbey Road in black and white punctuate elaborate stagings of the opera in full colour, filmed on location and with the singers miming to the music. In places – as when Scarpia voices his own thoughts while in conversation with Tosca – you hear **Ruggero Raimondi** singing without his lips moving. With shots of the action regularly taken from imaginative angles, and with **Angela Gheorghiu** the most masterful actress – herself very near the character, as Jacquot suggests – and Raimondi the most believably sinister of Scarpias, the mix works well, though reproduction of the EMI recording is not always perfect. Though **Roberto Alagna** as Cavaradossi is not at his most lyrical, the visuals certainly reinforce the judgement that this is the finest among recent versions of the opera, electrifyingly conducted by Antonio Pappano, who, along with Gheorghiu and Jacquot, contributes an interview.

The producer, Sylvano Busotti and designer, Fiorenzo Giorgi, have made the most of the spectacular natural Verona backcloth, a dramatic setting to all three acts, and with a fine acoustic for the solo voices, chorus and orchestra, so that the big *Te deum* scene at the close of Act I is very effective indeed. **Eva Marton** is perhaps not as glamorous a Tosca as Gheorghiu, but she is a handsome woman with fine presence. She and **Giacomo Aragall** are a well-matched pair of lovers, both in strong, unstrained vocal form, and the only drawback is that the key arias (very well sung) bring extended ovations from the audience which interrupt the continuity. However their presence undoubtedly adds to the tension. **Wixell** is a superb Scarpia, dignified as well as evil, and he sings magnificently throughout Act II. The murder scene with Tosca and the close of the opera itself are handled powerfully but without melodrama. Throughout **Daniel Oren** conducts his excellent chorus and orchestra with fine lyrical Puccinian ardour.

Johannes Leiacker, the stage designer of the Phoenix *Tosca*, created his own analysis of the opera's scenario, dominated by Scarpia, chief of the secret police, by having as a backcloth to the stage a huge eye, fifty metres wide and thirty

metres high – a 'visual symbol of the surveillance state'. There are other eccentricities too, including occasionally sub-dividing the video imagery into four different quarters of the screen, while the basic set at the opening is more like a construction site than any part of a church. Scarpia still has his torture chamber, but at the close of the opera Cavaradossi's dead body disappears into the river and Tosca's suicidal leap follows him. The singing of the main characters is impressive, **Nadja Michael's** *Vissi d'arte* and **Zoran Todorovich's** *Elucevan e stele* do not disappoint, and Scarpia's performance exudes sinister villainy. The chorus and orchestra, directed by **Ulf Schirmer**, are strongly supportive. But unless you are a fan of weird opera productions, this is not generally recommendable.

Tosca (complete; CD versions)

⊗— ❀ Ⓜ **** EMI mono 5 62890-2 (2). Callas, Di Stefano, Gobbi, Calabrese, La Scala, Milan, Ch. & O, De Sabata

⊗— ⒝⒝ **** EMI mono 5 85644–2 (2). Callas, Di Stefano, Gobbi, Calabrese, Mercuriali, La Scala, Milan, Ch. & O, De Sabata

⊗— **** EMI 5 57173-2 (2). Gheorghiu, Alagna, Raimondi, ROHCG Ch. & O, Pappano

⊗— Ⓜ **** Decca 475 7522 (2). Price, Di Stefano, Taddei, V. State Op. Ch., VPO, Karajan

⊗— ❀ Ⓑ **** Pentatone Surround Sound SACD 5186 147 (2). Caballé, Carreras, Wixell, ROHCG Ch. & O, C. Davis

Ⓜ *** RCA 82876 70783-2 (2). L. Price, Domingo, Milnes, Plishka, Alldis Ch., Wandsworth School Boys' Ch., New Philh. O, Mehta

Ⓜ (**(*)) ROH mono ROHS 005 (2). Milanov, Corelli, Guelfi, ROHCG Ch. & O, Gibson

**(*) Decca 414 597-2 (2). Te Kanawa, Aragall, Nucci, Welsh Nat. Op. Ch., Nat. PO, Solti

Ⓜ **(*) EMI CfP 2 08827-2 (2). Scotto, Domingo, Bruson, Amb. Op. Ch., St Clement Danes School Boys' Ch., Philh. O, Levine

There has never been a finer recorded performance of *Tosca* than **Callas's** first, with **Victor de Sabata** conducting and **Tito Gobbi** as Scarpia. Gobbi makes the unbelievably villainous police chief into a genuinely three-dimensional character, and **Di Stefano**, as the hero Cavaradossi, was at his finest. The conducting of De Sabata is spaciously lyrical as well as sharply dramatic, and the mono recording is superbly balanced in Walter Legge's fine production. The recording now rightly takes its place as one of EMI's 'Great Recordings of the Century' and the new transfer brings enhanced sound that could almost be stereo, with the voices caught gloriously, and the mid-priced set includes a full libretto and translation.

EMI's super-bargain transfer of the classic **Callas–Gobbi** set with **De Sabata** conducting is designed to outclass the rival set from Naxos. As well as being packaged much more attractively, it brings a transfer which, taken from the original tapes, has the voices brighter and more immediate than on the Naxos set. Though painstakingly transferred from a series of different LPs, with minor imperfections ironed out, the Naxos set brings few advantages (8.110256/7). The immediate impact of the voices on EMI will for most be the deciding factor. Neither set has a libretto, but both helpfully provide a detailed synopsis linked to the index points on the disc.

With all three principals the clarity of words adds to the power of this **Pappano** performance, most strikingly with **Gheorghiu**, who constantly sheds new light on one phrase after another. When Cavaradossi attempts to explain the black eyes of the Madonna he is painting, Gheorghiu, responding in the half-tone phrase 'Ah, quegli occhi' ('Ah, those eyes'), conveys her doubt with heart-stopping intensity. In Act II, when Scarpia is all-dominant, Gheorghiu, instead of being defiant from the outset is plainly frightened out of her wits, so that we then movingly witness the build-up of resolve that will lead to murder, punctuated by an account of the aria Vissi d'arte of velvet beauty. Gheorghiu's is a great performance, significantly expanding on what we already know of her, as magnetic as Callas's, rich and beautiful as well as dramatic. The EMI sound is superb, full, clear and atmospheric, making this a classic among the many versions of this opera.

Karajan's 1962 Vienna Tosca is now reissued as one of Decca's Originals, so it still includes a full libretto and translation. It remains one of the finest versions, with **Leontyne Price** at the peak of her form and **Di Stefano** singing most sensitively. But Karajan deserves equal credit with the principal singers, and the sound is first class.

Pacing the music naturally and sympathetically, **Sir Colin Davis** proves a superb Puccinian, one who not only presents Puccini's drama with richness and force but gives the score the musical strength of a great symphony. In this the quality of the singing from a cast of unusual consistency plays an important part. **Caballé** may not be as sharply jealous a heroine as her keenest rivals, but with the purity of Vissi d'arte coming as a key element in her interpretation, she still presents Tosca as a formidable siren-figure ('Mia sirena' being Cavaradossi's expression of endearment). **Carreras** reinforces his reputation as a tenor of unusual artistry as well as of superb vocal powers. Though **Wixell** is not ideally well focused as Scarpia, not at all Italianate of tone, he presents a completely credible lover-figure, not just the lusting ogre of convention. The 1976 analogue recording is full as well as refined, bringing out the beauties of Puccini's scoring, and now sounds very spectacular indeed, remasked in four channel sound by Pentatone.

Leontyne Price made her second complete recording of Tosca (for RCA) ten years after the first under Karajan, and the interpretation remained remarkably consistent, a shade tougher in the chest register – the great entry in Act III a magnificent moment – and a little more clipped of phrase. That last modification may reflect the relative manners of the two conductors – Karajan more individual in his refined expansiveness, **Mehta** more thrustful. On balance, taking Price alone, the preference is for the earlier set, but Mehta's version also boasts a fine cast, with the team of **Domingo** and **Milnes** at its most impressive. The recording, too, is admirable, even if it yields to the Decca in atmosphere and richness.

The spectacular qualities of the classic Tosca production with Callas and Gobbi have tended to put this other impressive presentation of the opera in the shade. Yet with good, bright, mono sound the performances of **Zinka Milanov** and **Franco Corelli** are both commanding, Corelli making his début at Covent Garden. He exaggerates boldly in his opening aria – but understandably so when, in 1957 at the time of this recording, he was little known. **Gian Giacomo Guelfi** is impressive as Scarpia, if not as commanding as Tito Gobbi, and **Alexander Gibson** demonstrates what a powerful opera conductor he was at this period.

Rarely has **Solti** phrased Italian melody so consistently con amore, his fiercer side subdued but with plenty of power when required. Even so, the timing is not always quite spontaneous-sounding, with transitions occasionally rushed. But the principal raison d'être of the set must be the casting of **Dame Kiri** as the jealous opera-singer. Her admirers will relish the glorious sounds, but the jealous side of Tosca's character is rather muted.

Levine directs a red-blooded performance which underlines the melodrama. **Domingo** here reinforces his claim to be the finest Cavaradossi today, while the clean-cut, incisive singing of **Renato Bruson** presents a powerful if rather young-sounding Scarpia. **Renata Scotto's** voice is in many ways ideally suited to the role of Tosca, certainly in its timbre and colouring; as caught on record, however, the upper register is often squally. The digital recording is full and forward. The set now comes with a full libretto.

Tosca (complete; in English)

🎵 Ⓜ *** Chan. 3000 (2). Eaglen, O'Neill, Yurisich, Mitchell Ch., Kay Children's Ch., Philh. O, Parry

David Parry with **Jane Eaglen**, in one of her finest performances on disc, directs a gripping account of Puccini's red-blooded drama, sung in English. What above all seals the success of the set is the power and command of Jane Eaglen as Tosca. The confident sureness with which she attacks every top note is a delight, so that in Act I she expresses her jealousy with the vehemence of a Wagnerian, while singing with warm, rounded tone. She is well matched by **Dennis O'Neill** as Cavaradossi, aptly Italianate, and **Gregory Yurisich** makes a powerful Scarpia, younger-sounding than most and therefore a plausible lover. The others are well cast too, notably **Peter Rose** as a fresh-voiced Angelotti. The **Geoffrey Mitchell Choir** and children's choir are superb in the crowd scenes of Act I. Highlights are available on CHAN 3066.

Il Trittico: (i) Il Tabarro; (ii) Suor Angelica; (iii) Gianni Schicchi (complete; DVD versions)

🎵 *** Warner DVD 5050467 0943-2. (i) Cappuccilli, Sass, Martinucci, Bertocchi, Bramante, Jankovic; (ii) Plowright, Vejzovic, Allegri, Verri, Santelli, Spezia, d'Amico; (iii) Pons, Gasdia, Marusin, Jankovik, Poggi; La Scala, Milan, Ch. & O, Gavazzeni (V/D: Brian Large)

*** TDK DVD DVWW-OPTRIT. Nizza; (i; iii) Mastromarino; (i) Pelizzari; (ii–iii) Chiuri; (iii) Giovannini; Modena Coro Lirico Amadeus, O della Fondazione Arturo Toscanini, Reynolds (Dir: Cristina Pezzoli, V/D: Loreena Kaufmann)

This **La Scala** production brings a fairly traditional approach and it will do very well, as the casting does not disappoint either. **Piero Cappuccilli** as the bargemaster is well supported by the believably hard-voiced **Sylvia Sass** as Giorgetta, and the melodrama is brought off effectively. In the title-role of *Suor Angelica*, **Rosalind Plowright** is at her finest, both vocally and in commanding our sympathy; **Dunja Vejzovic's** Princess is not as intimidating as she should be, but she sings well enough. The set for *Gianni Schicchi* is unrealistically spacious but **Cecilia Gasdia** is a rich-voiced Lauretta and, at the centre of the story, **Juan Pons** is a firm and believable Schicchi, although the staging of his final solo as a devil from hell is totally misguided in just the way that producers refuse to let well alone. But the veteran **Gianandrea Gavazzeni** conducts throughout with vitality and warmth, and altogether this has much to offer.

However, the live performances recorded at Modena are also very enjoyable indeed. There are no stars in the cast, but **Amarilli Nizza** is excellent in all three key roles and is especially moving as Suor Angelica, where **Annamaria Chiuri** is most commanding as La Zia Principessa. **Alberto Mastromarino** also makes a fine transformation between the two key male roles, the bargemaster and Gianni Schicchi, and the supporting cast are excellent too. The chorus is splendid, especially in *Suor Angelica*, which is very moving, musically as well as visually. It has a splendidly solid yet versatile set which moves to accommodate each scene. But all three sets are admirably realistic and the costumes too are well chosen with real grotesquerie in *Gianni Schicchi*.

Il Trittico: (i) *Il Tabarro*; (ii) *Suor Angelica*; (iii) *Gianni Schicchi* (CD versions)

🎵 ******** EMI 5 56587-2 (3) (i; iii) Gheorghiu, Alagna; (i) Guelfi, Guleghina, Shicoff; (ii) Gallardo-Domâs, Manca di Nissa; (ii; iii) Palmer; (iii) Van Dam, Roni; (i; ii) L. Voices; (ii) Tiffin School Boys' Ch., LSO or Philh. O, Pappano

Ⓝ Ⓜ ******* EMI stereo/mono 2 171402 (3). (i; iii) Gobbi; (i) Prandelli, Mas; (ii; iii) De los Angeles; (ii) Barbieri; (iii) Canali, Del Monte, Montarsolo; Rome Op. Ch. & O; (i) Bellezza; (ii) Seafin; (iii) Santini

Ⓝ Ⓜ *(*) Decca 478 0341 (3). (i–iii) Freni; (i) Pons; Giacomini; (ii) Souliotis; (iii) Nucci, Alagna; Ch. & O of Maggio Musicale Fiorentino, Bartoletti

No previous recordings of the three one-acters in Puccini's triptych bring quite such warmth or beauty or so powerful a drawing of the contrasts between each – in turn Grand Guignol melodrama, pure sentiment and high comedy. Pacing each opera masterfully, **Pappano** heightens emotions fearlessly to produce at key moments the authentic gulp-in-throat, whether for the cuckolded bargemaster, Michele, for Sister Angelica in her agonized suicide and heavenly absolution, or for the resolution of young love at the end of *Gianni Schicchi*.

Angela Gheorghiu and **Roberto Alagna**, as well as making a tiny cameo appearance in *Il Tabarro* as the off-stage departing lovers, sing radiantly as Lauretta and Rinuccio in *Gianni Schicchi*, with the happy ending most tenderly done. **Maria Guleghina**, well known for her fine Tosca, makes a

warm, vibrant Giorgetta, and the touch of acid at the top of the voice adds character. Even more remarkable is the singing of the young Chilean soprano, **Cristina Gallardo-Domâs** as Sister Angelica. This is a younger, more tender, more vulnerable Angelica than usual, the dynamic shading brings *pianissimos* of breathtaking delicacy, not least in floated top-notes. The casting in the middle opera is as near flawless as could be. The Zia Principessa is sung with chilling power by **Bernadette Manca di Nissa**, her tone firm and even throughout. **Felicity Palmer** with her tangy mezzo tone is well contrasted as the Abbess, and she is just as characterful as the crabby Zita in *Gianni Schicchi*. Among the men, **Carlo Guelfi** makes a superb Michele in *Il Tabarro*, incisive, dark and virile. **Neil Shicoff** makes a fine Luigi, his nervy tenor tone adding character. As Gianni Schicchi, **José van Dam** is in fine voice, with his clean focus bringing out the sardonic side of Schicchi, and his top Gs wonderfully strong and steady still. The recording is comfortingly sumptuous and atmospheric, very wide in its dynamic range, with magical off-stage effects.

The classic set of *Il Trittico*, which now returns as one of EMI's 'Great Recordings of the Century', has dominated the catalogue since the earliest days of LP, with **Tito Gobbi** giving two of his ripest characterizations. The central role of the cuckolded bargemaster, Michele, in the mono *Il Tabarro* inspired him to give his very best, both as actor and as singer. The central leaf of the triptych, *Suor Angelica*, brings a glowing performance from **Victoria de los Angeles**, giving a most affecting portrayal of Angelica, with **Fedora Barbieri** formidable as her unfeeling aunt, the Zia Principessa. De los Angeles reappears, charmingly girlish, as Lauretta, in *Gianni Schicchi*, where the high comedy fizzes deliciously. Though Gobbi's incomparable baritone is not by nature comic-sounding, he is unequalled as Schicchi. Only the last opera is in genuine and excellent stereo; *Il Tabarro* (1955) and *Suor Angelica* (1957) are mono, but the latest EMI transfers are expert, clear and convincingly balanced. A libretto comes with the reissued set.

It is a pity that **Mirella Freni** did not record *Il Trittico* earlier. It is taxing for any soprano to tackle three such contrasted roles as Giorgetta, Angelica and Lauretta, and in her 1991 Decca recording the only performance which sounds in character is the first of the three, with the portrait of the bargemaster's wife bright and detailed. The tenor, **Giuseppe Giacomini**, gives a weightier performance as Luigi than usual, his voice strong and baritonal. That makes **Juan Pons's** portrait of the cuckolded bargemaster, Michele, sound too light. The big aria, *Nulla, silenzio*, is cleanly sung, but with no bite of venom and **Bartoletti's** conducting in all three operas lacks the tension needed in such colourful, atmospheric pieces. Freni's soprano too often sounds strained in the role of Angelica, spreading uncomfortably at the top under pressure, and missing the beauty and poise, while, characterful though she is, **Elena Souliotis** is vocally idiosyncratic as the Zia Principessa. The high comedy of *Gianni Schicchi* suffers most of all from Bartoletti's limpness, and Freni is not remotely young-sounding in *O mio babbino caro*. **Roberto Alagna**, then very much a rising tenor, gives a clean, trumpet-toned performance as Rinuccio and, though **Leo Nucci** sings well enough in the title-role, he conveys nothing of the ironic humour behind this magic manipulator.

Turandot (complete; DVD versions)

**** TDK **DVD** DVWW-CLOPTUR. Marton, Carreras, Ricciarelli, Bogart, V. Sängerknaben, V. State Op. Ch. & O, Maazel (Dir: Harold Prince, V/D: Rodney Greenberg)

(N) *** Warner **DVD** 50 51442 8585 2. Dimitrova, Martinucci, Gasdia, Vinco, Verona Arena Ch. & O, Arena (Producer: Giuliano Montaldo, V/D: Brian Large)

(*) Arthaus **DVD 100 088. Marton, Sylver, Mazzaria, Langan, San Francisco Op. Ch. & O, Runnicles (Production/Design: David Hockney, Dir: Peter McClintock, V/D: Brian Large)

Maazel's spectacular 1983 **Vienna State Opera** version, recorded live, is outstanding in every way and is unlikely to be surpassed by more modern versions. The production, with splendidly vivid oriental costumes, using masks on the chorus and most of the principal characters, is exotically telling, with the set equally theatrical, its central staircase ideal for the enormously compelling scene where Turandot (**Eva Marton**) asks the three questions and **José Carreras** replies, with just the right degree of hesitation to keep the tension high. Eva Marton was surely born to take the part of the heroine, singing with great power, and conveying her final change of heart most believably. Carreras also sings gloriously, creating the role of Calaf as both heroic and warmly sympathetic. **Katia Ricciarelli** is a very touching Liù, her voice creamily beautiful, and Ping, Pang and Pong (again exotically costumed and masked) bring almost a Gilbertian touch to their bizarre characterization. The Vienna State Opera Chorus sing gloriously in the big scenes and the orchestra play with the utmost vividness under Maazel's thrilling direction. Very highly recommended.

The Verona Arena is ideal for *Turandot*; the spectacle of the big scenes is breathtaking, with a huge chorus. The title-role is superbly taken by the Bulgarian soprano **Ghena Dimitrova** and her big, powerful voice rides over the set-piece arias gloriously. She almost upstages her Calaf, but **Nicola Martinucci** too sings resoundingly and his *Nessun dorma* does not disappoint. But it is Dimitrova as Turandot who dominates, and her key riddle scene in Act II is vocally thrilling. The scene with the well-cast Ping, Pang and Pong is neatly contrasted. **Cecilia Gasdia** is a delightful, pure-voiced Liù, singing radiantly, and **Ivo Vinco** is a sympathetic Timur, who handles Liù's suicide very touchingly. **Maurizio Arena** conducts with flair and vigour, and the choral scenes are truly magnificent, to make a most satisfying musical and visual experience.

The Arthaus DVD comes from a 1994 San Francisco production and has **Eva Marton** in the title-role. Hers is a big, dramatic voice, but with far too little expressive variation in tone and she is content to sing loudly and leave it at that. However, there are other things in its favour: a decent Calaf in **Michael Sylver**, a good Ping (**Theodore Baerg**), Pang (**Dennis Peterson**) and Pong (**Craig Estep**). We have heard more moving accounts of Liù than **Lucia Mazzaria's**, but generally speaking the cast are more than acceptable. The orchestral and choral forces are very well harnessed by

Donald Runnicles, who fires on all cylinders and visually the designs by **David Hockney** are vivid and bold (some might think them garish, and they have had a dismissive press) but they will strike most readers as effective. The sound is rather forward and bright, and although there are more subtle Turandots to be found than Marton, the performance is thoroughly gripping.

Turandot (complete; CD versions)

♪— **** Decca (ADD) 414 274-2 (2). Sutherland, Pavarotti, Caballé, Pears, Ghiaurov, Alldis Ch., Wandsworth School Boys' Ch., LPO, Mehta

♪— (M) *** RCA (ADD) 82876 82624-2 (2). Nilsson, Tebaldi, Bjoerling, Tozzi, Rome Op. Ch. & O, Leinsdorf

♪— (M) *** EMI (ADD) 7 69327-2 (2). Nilsson, Corelli, Scotto, Mercuriali, Giaiotti, Rome Op. Ch. & O, Molinari-Pradelli

*** DG 423 855-2 (2). Ricciarelli, Domingo, Hendricks, Raimondi, V. State Op. Ch., V. Boys' Ch., VPO, Karajan

(M) (***) EMI mono 5 09683-2 (2). Callas, Fernandi, Schwarzkopf, Zaccaria, La Scala, Milan, Ch. & O, Serafin

(N) (BB) (**(*)) Regis mono RRC 2082 (2). Callas, Fernandi, Schwarzkopf, Zaccaria, La Scala, Milan, Ch. & O, Serafin

Joan Sutherland gives an intensely revealing and appealing interpretation, making the icy princess far more human and sympathetic than ever before, while **Pavarotti** gives a performance equally imaginative, beautiful in sound, strong on detail. To set **Caballé** against Sutherland was a daring idea, and it works superbly well; **Pears** as the Emperor is another imaginative choice. **Mehta** directs a gloriously rich and dramatic performance, superlatively recorded, still the best-sounding *Turandot* on CD, while the reading also remains supreme.

Recorded as long ago as 1959, the *Turandot* set, with **Birgit Nilsson**, **Renata Tebaldi** and **Jussi Bjoerling** an exceptionally strong team of principals and with the two distinguished sopranos perfectly contrasted, remains one of the finest, most powerful versions of the opera ever recorded. **Leinsdorf** is at his finest, thrusting and intense, and the new digital transfer in Living Stereo is admirably vivid.

The EMI set brings **Nilsson's** second assumption on record of the role of Puccini's formidable princess. As an interpretation it is very similar to the earlier, RCA performance, but its impact is immediate, thanks to the conducting of **Molinari-Pradelli**. **Corelli** may not be the most sensitive prince in the world, but the voice is in glorious condition. **Scotto's** Liù is very beautiful and characterful too. With vividly remastered sound, this makes an excellent mid-priced recommendation, though the documentation, as yet, does not include an English translation.

In **Karajan's** set, **Hendricks** is almost a sex-kitten with her seductively golden tone, and one wonders how Calaf could ever have overlooked her. This is very different from the usual picture of a chaste slave-girl. **Ricciarelli** is a far more vulnerable figure than one expects of the icy princess, and the very fact that the part strains her beyond reasonable vocal limits adds to the dramatic point, even if it subtracts from the musical joys. By contrast, **Plácido Domingo** is vocally superb, a commanding prince; and the rest of the cast present star names even in small roles.

With **Callas**, the character seems so much more believably complex than with others, and this 1957 recording is one of her most thrillingly magnetic performances on disc. **Schwarzkopf** provides a comparably characterful and distinctive portrait as Liù, far more than a Puccinian 'little woman', sweet and wilting. **Eugenio Fernandi** sounds relatively uncharacterful as Calaf, but his timbre is pleasing enough. By contrast, **Serafin's** masterly conducting exactly matches the characterfulness of Callas and Schwarzkopf, with colour, atmosphere and dramatic point all commandingly presented. With such a vivid performance, the 1957 mono sound is much more expansive in the new transfer.

The Regis set includes Callas's 1954 recordings of *Signore ascolta* and *Tu che di gel sei cinta* as a bonus. The Regis transfer is acceptable, but the spectacular choruses are not sharply focused.

Turandot (complete; sung in English)

🎵 *** Chan. 3086 (2). Eaglen, O'Neill, Plazas, Bayley, Gedda, George Mitchell Ch., Philh. O., Parry

The glory of the Chandos set of *Turandot* is not just the spectacular, wide-ranging sound, bringing out details never heard before, but the singing of **Jane Eaglen** in the title-role and here the voice is recorded with a satisfying firmness and precision apt for the icy princess. The total absence of strain, even in the most taxing passages above the stave, and the magnetic sense of purpose reflect Eaglen's experience singing this role at Covent Garden (in Italian), while the gentler moments point forward to the resolution when, against all the odds, the icy princess is made to melt in the face of love, normally an unconvincing transformation (as Puccini himself evidently felt), but here in total conviction. As Calaf **Dennis O'Neill** (who also appeared with Eaglen at Covent Garden) is strong and positive, even if the voice is no longer fresh and shows signs of strain. **Mary Plazas** is a charming, tender Liù and **Clive Bayley** a superb Timur, while **Nicolai Gedda**, sounding aptly old, takes on the cameo role of the ancient emperor. **David Parry**, as in his previous recordings for this Opera in English series, brings out the red-blooded thrust of the score, with the orchestral detail revealed as never before.

Turandot (highlights)

Ⓜ *** Decca (ADD) 458 202-2 (from above complete recording, with Sutherland, Pavarotti; cond. Mehta)

A generous and shrewdly chosen 70-minute collection of excerpts from the glorious full-priced Decca set of *Turandot*. *Nessun dorma*, with **Pavarotti** at his finest, is here given a closing cadence for neatness. The vintage Decca sound is outstandingly full and vivid. The reissue in Decca's Opera Gala series is neatly packaged in a slipcase and includes a full translation.

Le Villi (complete)

🎵 *** Naïve V4958. Diener, Machado, Tézier, David, French R. PO, Guidarini

Puccini wrote his first opera, *Le Villi*, using a story similar to that of Adam's ballet, *Giselle*: the faithless lover finally destroyed by the ghostly spirit of the beloved who has died of a broken heart. This **French Radio** recording scores impressively over Maazel's deleted Sony version in the refinement of the sound, which in turn brings out the subtleties of the fine singing from all the principals. The new set has a woman, **Sylvie David**, lighter and more conversational. **Marco Guidarini** proves a very convincing Puccinian, bringing out the dramatic bite of the orchestral showpieces, as well as moulding the big melodies affectionately. Equally **Ludovic Tézier** is clear and direct as Anna's father Guglielmo.

COLLECTIONS

(i) Crisantemi; Minuets 1–3; Quartet in A min.: Allegro moderato; Scherzo in A min.; (ii) Foglio d'album; Piccolo tango; (iii; ii) Songs: Avanti Urania; E l'uccellino; Inno a Diana; Menti all'avviso; Morire!; Salve regina; Sole e amore; Storiella d'amore; Terra e mare

*** Etcetera KTC 1050. (i) Raphael Qt; (ii) Crone; (iii) Alexander

It is fascinating to find among early, rather untypical songs like *Storiella d'amore* and *Menti all'avviso* a charming little song, *Sole e amore*, written jokingly for a journal, *Paganini*, in 1888, which provided, bar for bar, the main idea of the Act III quartet in *La Bohème* of eight years later. The two piano pieces are simple album-leaves; among the six quartet pieces, *Crisantemi* is already well known; the rest are student pieces, including a delightful fragment of a Scherzo. Performances are good, though **Roberta Alexander's** soprano is not ideally Italianate. The recorded sound is vivid and immediate against a lively hall ambience.

Scenes and Arias from: La Bohème; Madama Butterfly; Tosca; Il Trittico; Turandot

Ⓝ Ⓑ **** Decca 2-CD (ADD/DDD) 478 0368 (2). Freni, Pavarotti; with Ludwig, Milnes, VPO; or BPO, Karajan; Met. Op. O, Levine

A splendid collection centring on the partnership of **Freni** and **Pavarotti** (with **Karajan** and **Levine**) in the key Puccini roles, although Freni takes the part of Liù in *Turandot*, singing only one excerpt. Nevertheless with 152 minutes of excerpts this is a very impressive anthology.

Arias: La Bohème: Quando m'en vo' soletta; Gianni Schicchi: O mio babbino caro; Madama Butterfly: Un bel dì; Manon Lescaut: In quelle trine morbide; La Rondine: Chi il bel sogno di Doretta; Ora dolci e divine; Tosca: Vissi d'arte; Le Villi: Se come voi piccina

🎵 Ⓜ *** Sony (ADD) SMK 60975. Te Kanawa, LPO, Pritchard, or LSO, Maazel – VERDI: Arias. *** (with MOZART: *Don Giovanni: Ah! fuggi il traditor; In quali eccessi … Mi tradì;* HUMPERDINCK: *Der kleine Sandmann bin ich;* DURUFLÉ: *Requiem: Pie Jesu* ***)

In a recital recorded in 1981 the creamy beauty of **Kiri Te Kanawa's** voice is ideally suited to these seven lyrical Puccini arias including the little waltz-like song from *Le Villi*. The other excerpt from this opera comes from the complete set made around the same time. Throughout, expressive sweetness is more remarkable than characterization, but in such music it is difficult to complain. Kiri was also in top form in her 1978 assumption of the role of Elvira in Mozart's *Don Giovanni* (again with **Maazel**), and the delightful Sandman aria from *Hänsel und Gretel* and Duruflé's beautiful, serene *Pie Jesu* again show the voice at its most appealing.

Arias: (i) *La Bohème:* **Sì mi chiamano Mimì; Donde lieta uscì; Gianni Schicchi: O mio babbino caro; Madama Butterfly: Un bel dì; Con onor muore; Manon Lescaut: In quelle trine morbide; Sola perduta; Suor Angelica: Senza mamma; Turandot: Signore ascolta!; In questa reggia; Tu che del sei cinta. Duets: (ii; iii)** *La Bohème:* **O soave fanciulla; (ii; iv)** *Madama Butterfly:* **Vogliateme bene; (ii; v)** *Tosca: Non la sospiri.* **Aria: Vissi d'arte**

⊕—Ⓜ(***) EMI mono/stereo 5 62794-2. Callas; with (i) Philh. O, Serafin; (ii) La Scala, Milan O; (iii) Votto; with Di Stefano; (iv) cond. Karajan, with Gedda; (v) De Sabata; with Di Stefano

The first 11 items here formed **Callas's** first EMI recital, recorded in mono in Watford Town Hall in September 1954. She was vocally at her peak. Even when her concept of a Puccinian 'little woman' has eyes controversially flashing and fierce, the results are unforgettable, never for a moment relaxing on the easy course, always finding new revelation, whether as Turandot or Liù, as Manon, Mimì or Butterfly. The other items, mostly duets, come from her complete sets, including her famous and indispensable portrayal of Tosca, conducted by **Victor de Sabata**. The transfers are excellent, well balanced but with the voice always vividly projected. (The solo items are also available well transferred on Regis RRC 1234.)

Arias: Madama Butterfly: Un bel dì; Tu? tu? piccolo Iddio! (Death of Butterfly); La Rondine: Che il bel sogno di Doretta; Tosca: Vissi d'arte; Turandot: Signore ascolta; Tu che di gel sei cinta

Ⓜ **(*) RCA (ADD) **SACD** 82876 61395-2. Price, Rome Op. O, De Fabritiis or Basile – VERDI: *Arias* ***

There is some glorious singing in this recital from the beginning of the 1960s. Perhaps **Leontyne Price** does not always get right inside each heroine at this stage in her career, but *Un bel dì* is thrilling, with a sharp contrast of tone between the incisiveness of the opening and the delicacy of *Chi sarà, chi sarà.* In *Vissi d'arte* she forces a little too hard so that her vibrato becomes a wobble, but the two *Turandot* arias are very beautiful. Most welcome of all is Magda's aria from *La Rondine*, sweet, charming and lyrical. The recording was always very good indeed, and it sounds even more vivid in this SACD transfer.

PUCCINI, Giacomo Sr (1712–81)

Messa di Requiem; Overtures: Lucio Giunio Bruto; Marzio Coriolano

BB *** Arte Nova 74321 98497-2. Morgan, Kenny, Cornwell, Thomas, Kantorei Saarlouis, Ens. UnaVolta, Fontaine

The celebrated Giacomo Puccini was the last in a line of composers, starting with another Giacomo, born in 1712, his great-great-grandfather. As this fine setting of the *Requiem* demonstrates, he was a notable figure in 18th-century Italian music, one who (like his descendant) was not afraid to cherry-pick his ideas. Here his elaborate contrapuntal writing for double choir harks back to an earlier generation, with clashing discords based on suspensions, such as one finds in Purcell's choral music, and chromatic sequences refreshing to the modern ear, all set against elegant baroque solos, well sung by the stylish quartet of British-based soloists. The two overtures, too, written for the secular oratorios celebrating the city of Lucca's annual elections, are lively and refreshing, with vigorous performances, cleanly recorded.

PURCELL, Henry (1659–95)

'England, my England' (film by Tony Palmer)

Ⓝ *** Isolde Films TP **DVD** 151. Callow, Ball, Redgrave, Shrapnel, Graham, Varcoe, Dawson, Argenta, Monteverdi Ch., E. Bar. Sol., Gardiner

When little is known about the life of Henry Purcell except the date of his death and burial in Westminster Abbey, **Tony Palmer** has created a fantasy not just about the period but about its many great figures, from Milton and Locke to Pepys, Newton and Wren. The Great Plague and the Fire of London figure prominently, but over everything is the figure of Simon Callow, not just as Charles II but as himself, both tackling Shaw's play, *In Good King Charles's Golden Days*, at the Royal Court Theatre and quoting the jaundiced comments of John Osborne, co-author of the script, likening the 1680s to the 1880s. **Michael Ball** plays the part of the composer himself.

The musical side is splendidly presented, with **John Eliot Gardiner** directing his **Monteverdi Choir** and **English Baroque Soloists** and with a starry line-up of soloists. The result is a kaleidoscope of impressions, carefully put together, which add up to a most moving whole. The film ends with the finale of Benjamin Britten's *Variations and Fugue on a Theme of Purcell, The Young Person's Guide*, reflecting Palmer's own career. Not surprisingly, the film, first shown on Christmas Day 1995 on Channel 4, became an instant prize-winner.

CHAMBER MUSIC

Fantasias 1–3 in 3 Parts; 4–12 in 4 Parts; in 5 Parts in F 'upon one note'; in 6 Parts in G min. (In nomine); in 7 Parts in G min. (In nomine)

BB **(*) Virgin 2x1 4 82097-2 (2). L. Bar. – CORELLI: *Ciacona* etc. **(*)

The Purcell *Fantasias* are among the most searching and profound works in all music and the **London Baroque** do them fair justice. They are a very accomplished group and their intonation and blend are impeccable. The resonance of the recording, made in London's Temple Church in 1983, may trouble some collectors, but we did not find the halo round the aural image unpleasing. At the same time, it is possible to feel that in music so highly charged with feeling and so richly imbued with melancholy, the constraints exercised by these artists result in playing that at times is close to understatement.

Sonatas of 3 Parts: 1–12; 4 Parts: 1–10; Chacony; 3 Pavans; 3 Parts on a Ground

(N) *** Chan. 0572/3. Purcell Qt

Sonatas of 3 Parts, 1–12

(N) (M) *** Decca O/L 478 0027. Beznosiuk, Podger, Coin, Hogwood

10 Sonatas of Four Parts, 1–10

(N) ** Linn CKD 332. Retrospect Trio, Halls

In these *Sonatas* Purcell turns to a new, concerted style which had been developed in Italy. Interspersed among the *Sonatas* are three earlier and highly chromatic *Pavans* and the famous *Chacony in G minor*. The **Purcell Quartet** give a first-class account of themselves: their playing is authoritative and idiomatic, and the artists are firmly focused in a warm but not excessively reverberant acoustic.

The reissued Oiseau-Lyre recording includes all the three-part works on a single, mid-priced CD, and again the performances are of the highest standard and very well recorded.

The **Retrospect Trio** under **Matthew Halls** (successors to the King's Consort) in general give lively and resilient performances of the *Four-Part Sonatas*, very well recorded. The snag is that Halls falls seriously short over the greatest of all these sonatas, *No. 6 in G minor*, a massive *Chaconne* movement lasting a full seven minutes. Halls fails to keep up the momentum, and the result stagnates before the end, with no sense of climax, such as it must have. A pity.

KEYBOARD MUSIC

Harpsichord Suites 1–4, Z.660/663 (with alternative Preludes for Suites 1 & 4); Suites 5–8, Z.666/669; Transcriptions: A New Ground in E min., ZT.682; Theatre Music: Abdelazar: Round O, Z.684; Bonduca: Overture in C, Z.574/1; The Fairy Queen: Overture in D, ZT.692; King Arthur: Overture in D min., Z.628/2; Timon of Athens: Chaconne in G min., ZT.680; The Virtuous Wife: Overture in gamut flat, ZT.693

(BB) *** Naxos 8.553982. Charlston (harpsichord)

This is both an enjoyable and a valuable collection, which not only includes the eight *Harpsichord Suites* deriving from Purcell's *Choice Collection of Lessons for the Harpsichord* but also some of the transcriptions of popular pieces from the the-atre music. The *Suites* are usually in four short movements, featuring a *Prelude, Almand, Corant* and *Sarabande* or *Hornpipe*. The Transcriptions were thought to have been made by others, but modern scholarship suggests that they were possibly made by the composer himself, and each is used as a closing encore for one of the *Suites*, including the piece from *Abdelazar* made famous by Britten. **Terence Charlston**, who is thoroughly musical and consistently spontaneous, gives first-class performances, with apt tempi. He uses a modern harpsichord made by Bruce Kennedy in 1993: it seems ideal for the scale of the music and is perfectly recorded in a warm but not too resonant acoustic. Highly recommended.

VOCAL MUSIC

Anthems & Services, Vols 1–11 (complete)

⊟ (M) *** Hyp. CDS 44141/51 (11). Soloists, King's Cons., King

Anthems & Services, Vol. 1 (*** Hyp. CDA 66585.); Anthems & Services, Vol. 2 (*** Hyp. CDA 66609.); Anthems & Services, Vol. 3 (*** Hyp. CDA 66623.); Anthems & Services, Vol. 4 (*** Hyp. CDA 66644.); Anthems & Services, Vol. 5 (*** Hyp. CDA 66656.); Anthems & Services, Vol. 6 (*** Hyp. CDA 66663.); Anthems & Services, Vol. 7 (*** Hyp. CDA 66677.); Anthems & Services, Vol. 8 (*** Hyp. CDA 66686.); Anthems & Services, Vol. 9 (*** Hyp. CDA 66693.); Anthems & Services, Vol. 10 (*** Hyp. CDA 66707.); Anthems & Services, Vol. 11 (*** Hyp. CDA 66716.)

The different categories of work here, Services, Verse Anthems, Motets (or Full Anthems) and devotional songs, cover the widest range of style and expression, with **Robert King's** own helpful and scholarly notes setting each one in context. Generally the most adventurous in style are the Full Anthems, with elaborate counterpoint often bringing amazingly advanced harmonic progressions. Yet the Verse Anthems too include some which similarly demonstrate Purcell's extraordinary imagination in contrapuntal writing. So though Volume 6 is confined to Verse Anthems and devotional songs, they too offer passages of chromatic writing which defy the idea of these categories as plain and straightforward. As the title suggests, the devotional song, *Plung'd in the Confines of Despair*, is a particularly fine example. Although all the earlier volumes are full of good things, Volume 7 is the one to recommend first to anyone simply wanting to sample Purcell's church music. Not only does it contain the *Music for the Funeral of Queen Mary* in 1695, with drum processionals, the solemn *March* and *Canzona for Brass* and *Funeral Sentences*, it has the *B flat Morning Service*, two settings of the Coronation anthem, *I Was Glad* (one of them previously unrecorded), a magnificent Full Anthem, three Verse Anthems and two splendid devotional songs. Volume 8, too, is full of fine music. The opening Verse Anthem, *In Thee, O Lord, Do I Put my Trust*, opens with a very striking, slightly melancholy *Sinfonia*, with a six-note figure rising up from a ground bass, which sets the expressive mood. The closing anthem, so appropriate from an island composer, *They that Go Down to the Sea in Ships*, is characteristically diverse, with Purcell helping the Lord 'maketh the storm to cease' and at the end providing a joyful chorus of praise. King's notes and documentation closely identify each item, adding to one's illumination.

There are plenty of key items in the final three volumes including (in Volume 9), *In Guilty Night*, the dialogue cantata *Saul and the Witch of Endor*, with Susan Gritton, Rogers Covey-Crump and Michael George. An outstanding series, full of treasures, with King varying the scale of forces he uses for each item. Often he uses one voice per part, but he regularly expands the ensemble with the **King's Consort Choir** or turns to the full **New College Choir**, which includes trebles. Those who want to dive in at the deep end should invest in the complete set, with all eleven CDs neatly packaged in cardboard sleeves in a box with a booklet containing excellent extended documentation and full texts taken from the individual discs, which are, of course, all available separately.

Anthems: *Blow up the trumpet in Zion; My heart is inditing; O God, Thou art my God; O God, Thou has cast me out; Remember not, Lord, our offences; Rejoice in the Lord alway. Chaconne in G min. for 2 Violins & Continuo*

🎵 **(BB)** *** Warner Apex (ADD) 2564 60821-2. Bowman, Rogers, Van Egmond, King's College, Cambridge, Ch., Leonhardt Consort, Leonhardt

An attractive collection from the late 1960s, which happily blends scholarship and spontaneity. The instrumental ensemble uses period instruments and playing style, and the character of the sound is very distinctive. Not all the anthems have instrumental accompaniments – Purcell sometimes uses the organ, at others bass continuo – but they are all very well sung, with the characteristic **King's** penchant for tonal breadth and beauty. Excellent recording.

Anthems: *Man that is born of woman; O God, thou has cast us out; Lord, how long wilt thou be angry?; O God, thou art my God; O Lord God of hosts; Remember not, Lord, our offences; Thou knowest, Lord, the secrets of our hearts.* Verse Anthems: *My beloved spake; My heart is inditing; O sing unto the Lord; Praise the Lord, O Jerusalem; They that go down to the sea in ships; Morning Service in B flat: Benedicite omnia opera; Cantate Domino; Deus miscreatur; Magnificat; Nunc dimittis; Evening service in G min.: Magnificat; Nunc dimittis; Latin Psalm: Jehovah, quam multi sunt hostes mei; Te Deum & Jubilate in D.*

🎵 **(B)** *** DG Double (ADD) 459 487-2 (2). Thomas, Christ Church Cathedral, Oxford, Ch., E. Concert, Preston

Recorded in the Henry Wood Hall in 1980, this admirable collection of Purcell's church music is self-recommending. Apart from **David Thomas's** fine contribution (in the verse anthems) the soloists come from the choir, and very good they are too, especially the trebles. The performances are full of character, vigorous, yet with the widest range of colour and feeling, well projected in a recording which is both spacious and detailed. The sound is excellent in its current transfer, and as a DG Archiv Double this is even more attractive.

Odes & Welcome Songs Vols. 1–8 (complete)

🎵 **** Hyp. CDS 44031/8.

Odes & Welcome Songs, Vol. 1 (*** Hyp. CDA 66314.); Odes & Welcome Songs, Vol. 2 (*** Hyp. CDA 66349.); Odes & Welcome Songs, Vol. 3 (*** Hyp. CDA 66412.); Odes & Welcome Songs, Vol. 4 (*** Hyp. CDA 66456.); Odes & Welcome Songs, Vol. 5 (*** Hyp. CDA 66476.); Odes & Welcome Songs, Vol. 6 (*** Hyp. CDA 66494.); Odes & Welcome Songs, Vol. 7 (*** Hyp. CDA 66587.); Odes & Welcome Songs, Vol. 8 (*** Hyp. CDA 66598.)

Just what a wealth of inspiration Purcell brought to the occasional music he wrote for his royal and noble masters comes out again and again in **Robert King's** splendid collection of the odes and welcome songs. It is sad that for three centuries this fine music has been largely buried, with just a few of the odes achieving popularity. In those, King's performances do not always outshine the finest of previous versions, but with an outstanding team of soloists as well as his **King's Consort** the performances achieve a consistently high standard, with nothing falling seriously short. Being able to hear previously unrecorded rarities alongside the well-known works sets Purcell's achievement vividly in context, helped by informative notes in each volume, written by King himself. Volume 1 includes the shorter of the two *St Cecilia Odes* and immediately – among the fine team of soloists – it is a delight to hear such superb artists as the counter-tenors **James Bowman** and **Michael Chance** in duet. Volume 3 with the 1693 *Birthday Ode* and Volume 7 with the fascinating *Yorkshire Feast Song* are two more CDs that would make good samplers. First-rate sound throughout.

Gardiner Purcell Edition

(i) Disc 1: *Come, Ye Sons of Art Away; Funeral Music for Queen Mary (1695).* (ii) Disc 2: *Ode on St Cecilia's Day (Hail! Bright Cecilia).* (iii) Disc 3: *The Indian Queen (incidental music).* (iv) Disc 4: *The Tempest (incidental music)*

🎵 **(M)** *** Erato 5046 68281-2 (4). (i) Lott, Brett, Williams, Allen, Equale Brass Ens.; (ii) Gordon, Elliott; (ii; iii) Stafford; (ii; iii; iv) Jennifer Smith, Varcoe, Elwes, Thomas; (iii) Fisher, Hill; (iii; iv) Hardy; (iv) Hall, Earle; (i–iv) Monteverdi Ch. & O, Gardiner

Originally issued to commemorate the tercentenary of Purcell's death, **Gardiner's** distinguished early series of Erato recordings from the 1970s and 1980s now reappears as a four-disc set, each disc packaged separately in its jewel-case (the choral works with texts) and presented together in a slip-case. The individual CDs are not now available separately.

Gardiner's characteristic vigour and alertness in Purcell come out superbly in the delightful record of the 1692 *St Cecilia Ode* – not as well known as some of the other odes he wrote, but a masterpiece. Soloists and chorus are outstanding.

The Indian Queen is fully cast and uses an authentic accompanying baroque instrumental group. The choral singing is especially fine, with the close of the work movingly expressive. John Eliot Gardiner's choice of tempi is apt and the soloists are all good, although the men are more strongly characterful than the ladies; nevertheless the lyrical music comes off well. Highlights are available on a budget Apex CD (2564 61501-2).

Whether or not Purcell wrote this music for *The Tempest* (the scholarly arguments are still unresolved), Gardiner demonstrates how delightful it is, a masterly collection, in performances both polished and stylish and with excellent solo and choral singing. At least the overture is clearly Purcell's, and that sets a pattern for a very varied collection of numbers, including three *da capo* arias and a full-length masque celebrating Neptune for Act V. Throughout, the recordings are full and atmospheric; the words are beautifully clear, and the transfer to CD is admirably natural.

Pinnock Purcell Collection

(i) *Ode for the Birthday of Queen Mary* (1694): *Come, Ye Sons of Art Away; Ode for St Cecilia's Day: Welcome to All the Pleasures; Of Old when Heroes Thought it Base (The Yorkshire Feast Song);* (ii) *Dido and Aeneas* (complete); (iii) *Dioclesian* (masque); (iv) *King Arthur* (complete); (v) *Timon of Athens* (masque)

(B) *** DG 474 672-2 (5). (i) J. Smith, Chance, Wilson, Richardson, Mark Ainsley, George; (ii) Von Otter, Dawson, Varcoe, Rogers; (iii) Monoyios, Agnew, Edgar-Wilson, Gadd, Birchall, Wallington, Foster; (iii; iv) Argenta, Bannatyne-Scott; (iv) Perillo, Gooding, MacDougall, Tucker, Finley; E. Concert & Ch., Pinnock

Pinnock's is a somewhat arbitrary collection, but the standard of performance and recording is very high and this set represents excellent value. He directs exuberant performances of Purcell's two most celebrated odes; the weight and brightness of the choral sound go with infectiously lifted rhythms, making the music dance. The soloists are all outstanding, with the counter-tenor duetting of **Michael Chance** and **Timothy Wilson** in *Sound the Trumpet* delectably pointed. The coupling, the neglected *Yorkshire Feast Song*, is full of wonderful inspirations, like the tenor and counter-tenor duet, *And Now When the Renown'd Nassau* – a reference to the new king, William III.

The performance of *Dido and Aeneas* is more controversial, but though the reading is not as inspired as many that Pinnock has given us, the scale is attractive. Both **Anne Sofie von Otter** and **Lynne Dawson** have voices that are at once warm and aptly pure for authentic performance. Von Otter as Dido, both fresh and mature-sounding, sings her two big arias with a combination of weight, gravity and expressive warmth which is yet completely in scale. The final

lament, while faster than in traditional performances, still conveys the full tragic intensity of this epic in microcosm. Much more questionable is the casting on the male side, and that includes a tenor taking the role of the Sorceress. **Nigel Rogers**, not in his sweetest voice, takes that role as well as that of the Sailor. Confusingly, almost immediately after the Sailor's jolly song at the start of Act III, Rogers reappears as the Sorceress in a quite different mood, making much too quick a change. **Stephen Varcoe** is a rather unheroic-sounding Aeneas, but the chorus of the **English Concert** produces fresh, alert singing. Instead of a repetition of the final chorus, Pinnock opts for an instrumental reprise to provide an epilogue.

Dioclesian and *Timon of Athens*, both sets of theatre music including masques, were recorded in tandem. Pinnock presents both works on a slightly larger (but not inflated) scale and often adopts broader speeds, which allow him to spring rhythms the more infectiously, more clearly introducing an element of sparkle and humour. He includes the extra song in Act III of *Dioclesian*, 'When I First Saw', and certainly here the effervescence of Purcell's inspiration is consistently compelling.

King Arthur follows on after *Dido and Aeneas*, opening with the *Chaconne* and making a break between CDs at the end of Act I. **Linda Perillo** makes a charming Philidel; **Brian Bannatyne-Scott** and **Nancy Argenta** are equally memorable, and the chorus and orchestra sing and play throughout with consistent vitality.

Odes for the Birthday of Queen Mary (1692 & 1694); *Music for the Funeral of Queen Mary* (1695); *Funeral Anthem; Funeral Sentences; Praise the Lord, O Jerusalem*

&— *** EMI 3 44438-2. Soloists, King's College, Cambridge, Ch., AAM, Cleobury

Purcell composed some of his very finest vocal works for these royal celebrations, and the joyful Odes, *Come ye sons of Art* and *Love's Godess sure*, are among them. By contrast, the *Funeral Music* is infinitely touching in a quite different way. The performances here are authentic, superbly sung and played, full of life, and very well recorded. A disc to treasure.

Ode for Queen Mary's birthday; Come, ye sons of Art away; Funeral Music for Queen Mary (1695)

&— (BB) *** Warner Apex 0927 48593-2. Soloists, Monteverdi Ch. & O, Equale Brass Ens., Gardiner

Come, ye Sons of Art is splendidly paired here with the unforgettable funeral music he wrote on the death of the same monarch. With the **Monteverdi Choir** at its most incisive and understanding the performances are exemplary, and the recording, though balanced in favour of the instruments, is clear and refined. Among the soloists **Thomas Allen** is outstanding, while the two counter-tenors give a charming performance of the duet, *Sound the trumpet*. The *Funeral Music* includes the well-known *Solemn March* for trumpets and drums, a *Canzona* and simple anthem given at the funeral, and two of Purcell's most magnificent anthems setting the *Funeral Sentences*. Recording made in 1976 in Rosslyn Hill

Chapel, London. These works now come, coupled very economically together, on an Apex disc.

Funeral Music for Queen Mary (with (i) Queen's epicedium); March & Canzona on the Death of Queen Mary. Funeral sentences: Man that is born of a woman; In the midst of life are we in death; Thou knowest, Lord, the secrets of our hearts. Anthems: Hear my prayer; Jehovah quam multi sunt. (ii) 3 (Organ) Voluntaries: in D min.; in G; in C

⊖–↴ (BB) **** Naxos 8.553129. Oxford Camerata, Summerly; with (i) Lane; (ii) Cummings

On the Naxos CD this glorious, darkly intense funeral music is given an outstandingly fresh and clear rendition, vividly recorded, matching even the finest rival versions. The sharpness of focus in the sound means that Purcell's adventurous harmonies with their clashing intervals are given extra dramatic bite in these dedicated performances, marked by fresh, clear soprano tone in place of boy trebles. The choice of extra items – full anthems with their inspired counterpoint rather than verse anthems – is first rate. Aptly, the extended solo song for soprano (with simple organ accompaniment), The Queen's epicedium, is also included with the funeral music, sung with boyish tone by **Carys-Ann Lane**.

The Complete Secular Solo Songs

Volumes 1–3 (complete)

⊖–↴ (M) *** Hyp. CDS 44161/3 (3). Bonney, Gritton, Bowman, Covey-Crump, Daniels, George, King's Consort, King

Originally issued on three separate CDs, this boxed collection brings obvious advantages, not least in the alphabetical index provided of the 87 songs. It is good, for example, to be able instantly to compare the three different settings of Music for a while, each on a different disc. The second and best-known version is a revision of the first (both for tenor, elegantly sung here by **Rogers Covey-Crump**), whereas the third is quite different, a free-ranging arioso setting of the same text by Henry Heveningham, taking the first line from Shakespeare's Twelfth Night. **Barbara Bonney** sings it exquisitely, and all the soloists here are excellent, with **Robert King** with his **Consort**, notably on bass viols and theorbo, providing most sympathetic accompaniment. Not included are Purcell's bawdy songs and catches, usually for multiple voices.

Airs & Duets

⊖–↴ ❀ *** Lyrichord LEMS 8024. Dooley, Crook, Instrumental Ens., Brewer (harpsichord)

Jeffrey Dooley (counter-tenor), a pupil and protégé of the late Alfred Deller, has a truly beautiful voice and takes naturally to this repertoire. Among his solo items Be welcome, then,°great sir and the Divine Hymn (Lord, what is man) are quite ravishing, while Hark! the ech'ing air is delectably sprightly. Particularly engaging is One charming night from The Fairy Queen, with a pair of recorders. The tenor **Howard Crook** also has a disarmingly personable vocal line, and his solos, including Beauty, thou scene of love and the sombre

Here let my life, are hardly less memorable, with the famous If music be the food of love splendidly sung. But it is when these two voices join together in duet that one's senses are truly ravished, from the opening Let the fifes and the clarions and the similarly light-hearted Sacharissa's grown old to Many, many such days (with its bassoon obbligato), and not forgetting Sound the trumpet. The celebration of the queen, Hail, gracious Gloriana, hail!, makes a well-chosen finale. The simple instrumental accompaniments are managed most stylishly, and this concert cannot be too highly recommended.

Songs Duets for Counter-tenor

⊖–↴ **** Hyp. CDA 66253. Bowman, Chance, King's Cons., King – BLOW: Ode, etc. ***

A sparkling collection of solos and duets which show both the composer and these fine artists in inspirational form. The performances are joyous, witty and ravishing in their Purcellian melancholy, with often subtle response to word meanings, and King's accompaniments have plenty of character in their own right. Excellent recording.

Songs, Dialogues Theatre Music

⊖–↴ (BB) **** Hyp. Helios CDH 55065. Kirkby, Thomas, Rooley

This nicely planned Hyperion collection has one solo apiece for each of the singers, but otherwise consists of duets, five of them from dramatic works. These near-ideal performances, beautifully sung and sensitively accompanied on the lute, make a delightful record, helped by excellent sound.

Other Collections

Songs: An Evening Hymn; The bashful Thames; The Blessed Virgin's Expostulation; Fairest isle; The fatal hour; Epithalamion (Thrice happy lovers); From silent shades; I attempt from Love's sickness to fly in vain; If love's a sweet passion; If music be the food of love; Man is for the woman made; Music for a while; Now the night is chas'd away; Oh! fair Cedaria; O solitude; The Plaint; Sweeter than roses; They tell us that you mighty powers above; When first Amintas sued for a kiss

⊖–↴ ❀ **** BIS SACD 1536. Sampson, Cummings, Kenny, Lasla, Ens.

This disc (entitled 'Victorious Love') is arguably the finest collection of Purcell songs in the catalogue. Moreover, the layout of the recital could hardly be better managed: every song is set off by what has come before and what follows. The opening sequence shows this readily: the atmospheric Sweeter than roses is followed by The fatal hour, then the lively When first Amintas sued for a kiss and the very touching The Plaint. Other highlights are Man is for the woman made, Music for a while (of course) and, later, Fairest isle and the peaceful O solitude. The disc ends with An Evening Hymn, gloriously sung, and one wants to go back and start all over again! Splendid accompaniments from the varied instrumental team led by **Laurence Cummings** (harpsichord and spinet), beautifully recorded and (if you have SACD facilities) the most judicious use of Surround Sound, to give the voice added presence within a gently glowing acoustic.

(i) *Abdelazar: Suite*; (i; ii) *Cibell for Trumpet & Strings*; (i) *Dioclesian: Dances from the Masque*; Overtures: in D min.; G min.; (i; ii) *Sonata for Trumpet & Strings*; (i) *Staircase Overture*; *Suite in G, Z.770*; *Timon of Athens: Curtain Tune.* Keyboard works: (iii) *New Irish Tune*; *New Scotch Tune*; *Sefauchi's Farewell*; *Suite 6 in D.* Songs: (iv; i) *Hark How All Things*; *If Love's Sweet Passion*; (iv; iii) *If Music Be the Food of Love*; *Lord What is Man (Divine Hymn)*; (iv; i) *See, Even Night Herself is Here*; *Thus the Ever Grateful Spring*

⊕── **** Chan. 0571. (i) Purcell Qt; (ii) Bennett; (iii) Woolley; (iv) Bott

Catherine Bott opens this 72-minute concert with a glorious account of one of Purcell's most famous Shakespearean settings, most artfully decorated: *If Music Be the Food of Love*; if anything, the later song, *See, Even Night Herself is Here*, is even more ravishing, given an ethereal introduction by the string group. The instrumental items are most rewarding, notably the attractive unpublished suite of dances in G, while the three overtures are full of plangent character. **Robert Woolley's** harpsichord contribution is most infectious (the *New Irish Tune*, incidentally, is *Lilliburlero*) and he is beautifully recorded, the harpsichord set back in an intimate acoustic and perfectly in scale. There are few better Purcell anthologies than this, and overall the CD gives an ideal introduction to the music of one of the very greatest English composers. The Chandos recording is first class, well up to the standards of the house.

STAGE WORKS AND THEATRE MUSIC

Dido and Aeneas (complete; DVD version)

Ⓝ *** NVC Arts DVD BBC 30 51442 882223. Ewing, Evans, Daymond, Burgess, McDougall, Coll. Mus. 90, Hickox (Photography: Joss Barratt)

Purcell's great opera makes its DVD début in this satisfying BBC performance, filmed in believable sets and traditional-style costumes in 1995 at the Hampton Court Palace. **Maria Ewing** proves a highly dramatic Dido and sings her closing lament very movingly. **Karl Daymond** makes a good foil as Aeneas and **Rebecca Evans** is a touchingly sympathetic Belinda. The witches don't overdo their sorcery and **Jamie McDougall** calls the mariners back to their ship resonantly while they are still enjoying the erotic favours of the women they are now to leave behind. An excellent response from chorus and orchestra, with sympathetic and lively direction from **Hickox**.

Dido and Aeneas (complete; CD version)

⊕── ✱ Ⓜ **** Decca (ADD) 466 387-2. Baker, Herincx, Clark, Sinclair, St Anthony Singers, ECO, Lewis

Ⓝ **** Chan. 0757. Connolly, Finley, Crowe, Bardon, Ainsley, Purefoy, OAE, Kenny, Devine

**** Erato 4509-98477-2. Gens, Berg, Marin-Degor, Brua, Fouchécourt, Les Arts Florissants, Christie

BB *** Teldec 4509 91191-2. D. Jones, Harvey, Dean; Bickley, Murgatroyd, St James's Singers & Bar. Players, Bolton

*** Chan. 0586. Ewing, Daymond, MacDougall, Evans, Burgess, Bowman, Coll. Mus. 90, Hickox

*** Ph. 416 299-2. Norman, McLaughlin, Kern, Allen, Power, ECO and Ch., Leppard

Ⓜ (***) EMI mono 5 09690-2. Flagstad, Schwarzkopf, Hemsley, Mermaid Theatre Singers & O, Geraint Jones (with earlier (1948) recording of *Dido's Lament*)

BB (***) Naxos mono 8.111264. Flagstad, Schwarzkopf, Hemsley, Mermaid Theatre Singers & O, Geraint Jones (with 1948 *Lament*, and arias by Bach and Handel)

Janet Baker's 1962 recording of *Dido* is a truly great performance. The radiant beauty of the voice is obvious enough, but the opening phrase of *When I Am Laid in Earth* and its repeat a few bars later is a model of graduated *mezza voce*. Then with the words 'Remember Me!', delivered in a monotone, she subdues the natural vibrato to produce a white tone of hushed, aching intensity. **Anthony Lewis** and the **ECO** (**Thurston Dart** a model continuo player) produce the crispest and lightest of playing, which never sounds rushed. **Herincx** is a rather gruff Aeneas, but the only serious blemish is **Monica Sinclair's** Sorceress. She overcharacterizes in a way that is quite out of keeping with the rest of the production. Like most vintage Oiseau-Lyre recordings, this was beautifully engineered, and it is a welcome reissue on the Decca Legends label.

The outstanding mezzo **Sarah Connolly** is central to the success of this fine new Chandos version of Purcell's operatic masterpiece, with the period instrumentalists of the OAE accompanying, led by the violinist **Margaret Faultless** and with **Elizabeth Kenny** and **Steven Devine** directing. Connolly's characterization is deeply moving, with fine tonal contrasts in *Dido's Lament*. **Gerald Finley** too makes the most of the limited role of Aeneas with highly expressive singing. One young singer to note is **Lucy Crowe** as Belinda, with **John Mark Ainsley** as the Sailor, making up a cast with no weak link. First-rate recording, finely balanced to an apt scale.

On the Erato the scale is intimate, with one instrument per part, and one voice per part in choruses, yet **Christie** cunningly varies the pace to intensify the drama. Though speeds are generally fast, he points an extreme contrast in Dido's two big arias, giving them full expressiveness at measured speeds. In the final exchanges between Dido and Aeneas the hastening speed of the recitative directly reflects the mounting tensions. What then sets this above other period performances is the tragic depth conveyed by **Veronique Gens** in Dido's great *Lament*, taken very slowly, with the voice drained and agonized in a way that Janet Baker supremely achieved. The young Canadian baritone, **Nathan Berg**, dark and heroic of tone, is outstanding as Aeneas.

Ivor Bolton and the **St James's Singers and Players** present another period performance, intimately scaled, which avoids the snags of earlier versions, with **Della Jones**

as Dido giving one of her finest recorded performances yet. She has a weightier mezzo than her rivals in other periods performances, yet her Dido's lament is the more moving when she is restrained over expressive gestures, keeping a tender simplicity. There is no weak link, with **Peter Harvey** as Aeneas, **Susan Bickley** as a clear-toned Sorceress, **Donna Dean** as a characterful Belinda, and **Andrew Murgatroyd** as the Sailor, a tenor who plays no stylistic tricks. Setting the seal on the performance's success, the choir is among the freshest and liveliest, and the use of the guitar continuo, as well as brief guitar interludes (suggested by the original libretto), enhances the happy intimacy of the presentation. Moreover, this reissue is very reasonably priced.

Richard Hickox's version was linked to a striking television presentation revolving round the magnetically characterful portrayal of the central role by **Maria Ewing**. In the event her performance, as recorded, is both distinctive and stylish. Combined with Hickox's lively direction, unmarred by intrusive reallocation of voices, it makes an impressive version, with **Karl Daymond** making Aeneas a more complex character than usual, with **Rebecca Evans** a radiant Belinda, matching Ewing in emotional intensity, and with **Sally Burgess** a characterful, unexaggerated Sorceress. Add the excellent contributions of **James Bowman** and **Jamie MacDougall**, and it makes a strong contender, certainly for admirers of Maria Ewing.

The classic (1952) EMI recording now arrives as one of EMI's 'Great Recordings of the Century', given a new transfer which, while not bringing stereo, gives a clear and refined yet full sound to voices and orchestra alike, and EMI have added as a bonus Flagstad's earlier (1948) recording of *Dido's Lament*. The recording also emerges with striking freshness in Mark Obert-Thorn's new Naxos transfer, if not sounding quite as fine as in the latest EMI remastering. **Flagstad's** magnificent portrayal of Dido ranks alongside that of Janet Baker, and she scales her voice down superbly in her noble reading which brings beautiful shading and masterly control of breath and tone, so that the famous *Lament* touches the listener deeply. **Schwarzkopf** is brightly characterful as Belinda, and though **Thomas Hemsley** is not ideally sweet-toned as Aeneas, he sings very intelligently. For a bonus we are offered three extra items from Flagstad: her earlier (1948) recording of *Dido's Lament*, Handel's *Ombra mai fu* and *Erbarme dich* from the *St Matthew Passion*. This must be recommended alongside the EMI version, for it is more than worth its modest cost.

Authenticists should keep away, but the security and dark intensity of **Jessye Norman's** singing make for a memorable performance, heightened in the recitatives by the equally commanding singing of **Thomas Allen** as Aeneas. The range of expression is very wide – with Norman producing an agonized whisper in the recitative just before *Dido's Lament*. **Marie McLaughlin** is a pure-toned Belinda, **Patrick Power** a heady-toned Sailor, singing his song in a West Country accent, while **Patricia Kern's** performance as the Sorceress uses conventionally sinister expression. **Leppard's** direction is relatively plain and direct, with some slow speeds for choruses. Excellent recording.

(i) Dido and Aeneas (complete); A Midsummer Night's Dream: Suite. Chaconne

*** Lyrichord LEMS 8057. Baird, Bentch, Lauren Brown, Ama Deus Bar. Ens., Radu

Julianne Baird's voice is just right for Dido and she sings movingly, with fine support from the chorus. Her supporting cast is excellent. **Timothy Bentch** is an appealingly warm Aeneas, **Andrea Lauren Brown** a fresh-voiced, pert Belinda, **Tatyana Rashkovsky** a vivid Witch (though with a wide vibrato) and **Dennis Kalup** a personably nautical Sailor. The **Ama Deus Baroque Ensemble** is here a string quintet plus continuo, so the whole performance is in scale, and they accompany very stylishly. This is not a first choice, but it is a considerable one and the bonus is a generous suite from *A Midsummer Night's Dream* (9 movements) plus the famous *Chaconne*, taken briskly to make a suitable close after the *Hornpipe* and *Dance of the Fairies*. Good, well-balanced recording.

(i) Dido and Aeneas (arr. Britten/I. Holst); (ii) The Fairy Queen (adapted Britten)

Ⓑ *** Double Decca (ADD) 468 561-2 (2). (i) Baker, Pears, Burrowes, Reynolds, Lott, Palmer, Hodgson, Tear, L. Op. Ch., Aldeburgh Fest. Strings, Bedford; (ii) Vyvyan, Bowman, Pears, Wells, Partridge, Shirley-Quirk, Brannigan, Amb. Op. Ch., ECO, Britten, Ledger (harpsichord)

Dame **Janet Baker's** 1975 portrait of Dido is even richer than before, with more daring tonal colouring, and challengingly slow tempi for the two big arias. Many will prefer the heartfelt spontaneity of her youthful performance under Anthony Lewis, but the richer, more modern Kingsway Hall recording adds to the vividness of the experience. With **Norma Burrowes** a touchingly youthful Belinda, with **Peter Pears** using Lieder style in the unexpected role (for him) of Aeneas, with **Anna Reynolds** an admirable Sorceress, there is hardly a weak link.

Britten's edition of *The Fairy Queen* grouped Purcell's music into four sections, *Oberon's Birthday*, *Night and Silence*, *The Sweet Passion* and *Epithalamium*. This version is beautifully conveyed in the playing, the singing and the recording. **Philip Ledger's** imaginative harpsichord continuo is placed too far to one side, but otherwise the sound can hardly be faulted. The cast is consistently satisfying, with Peter Pears and **Jennifer Vyvyan** surviving from an earlier 'complete' mono recording directed by Anthony Lewis. At Double Decca price this is well worth exploring.

Dioclesian; Timon of Athens (masque)

*** Chan. 0569/70. Pierard, Bowman, Ainsley, George, Coll. Mus. 90, Hickox

Dioclesian; Timon of Athens (masques only)

*** Chan. 0568. (as above)

Richard Hickox on Chandos offers the apt coupling of *Dioclesian* and *Timon of Athens*, both sets of theatre music involving masques. Hickox takes a light view, at times detached, often adopting fast speeds and using on balance a consistent team of soloists, including in smaller roles such outstanding younger singers as **Ian Bostridge** and **Nathan Berg**. On the other hand, he does not include the overture to *Timon*. The single Chandos CD contains the masque music only.

Dioclesian: Overture excerpts

🎵— Ⓜ *** DHM/BMG 82876 60157-2. Argenta, Chance, Freiburg Bar. O, Von der Goltz – HANDEL: *Concerto grosso, Op. 6/6* etc. ***

Those not wanting the entire masque shold be well satisfied with this overture and set of songs and dances, presented with great zest by the superb **Freiburg Baroque Orchestra**, with excellent soloists in **Michael Chance** and **Nancy Argenta**. The *Chaconne* is beautfully played and the *Second Music*, which ends the selection, is particularly lively. Excellent couplings and first-class recording make this a highly recommendable reissue.

The Fairy Queen (complete; DVD version)

*** Arthaus DVD 100 200. Kenny, Randle, Rice, Van Allan, ENO Ch. & O, Kok (Dir: David Pountney)

Recorded live at the Coliseum in London in 1995, this DVD **ENO** production of *The Fairy Queen*, conducted by **Nicholas Kok**, turns an entertainment which can, under modern conditions, seem cumbersome into a sparkling fantasy, thanks to the brilliant stage direction of **David Pountney** and choreography of Quinny Sacks. The sequence of masques is treated as a series of circus turns, and thanks also to the fantastic costumes of Dunya Ramicova the atmosphere of the circus is never far away, helping to hold together an episodic sequence of scenes, originally designed to back up a garbled version of Shakespeare's *A Midsummer Night's Dream*.

The result is as much a surreal ballet as an opera, with Nicholas Kok drawing stylish playing from the ENO Orchestra, echoing period practice, using a realization prepared by Clifford Bartlett. So the scene of the Drunken Poet proves genuinely funny, with **Jonathan Best** (identified only in the final credits on film) doing a jolly imitation of a 1950s poet with scruffy sports jacket and pullover.

By contrast Titania – **Yvonne Kenny** at her finest – and Oberon – the exotic **Thomas Randle** – stand out the more sharply as otherworldly figures thanks to their glamorous costumes. More equivocal is the presentation of Puck by **Simon Rice**, lively as he is. A fun entertainment, as unstuffy a presentation of Purcell's problematic masterpiece as could be, vividly filmed and recorded.

The Fairy Queen (complete; CD versions)

🎵— Ⓜ **** DG Al Fresco 477 6733 (2). Harrhy, J. Smith, Nelson, Priday, Penrose, Stafford, Evans, Hill, Varcoe, Thomas, Monteverdi Ch., E. Bar. Sol., Gardiner

*** HM HMC 901308/9. Argenta, Dawson, Daniels, Loonen, Correas, Les Arts Florissants, Christie

ⒷⒷ *** Naxos 8.550660-1 (2). Atherton, Amps, Davidson & Soloists, Scholars Bar. Ens., Van Asch

Gardiner's CD performance is a delight from beginning to end, for, though authenticity and completeness reign, scholarship is worn lightly and the result is consistently exhilarating, with no longueurs whatever. The fresh-toned soloists are first rate, while Gardiner's regular choir and orchestra excel themselves, with Purcell's sense of fantasy brought out in each succeeding number. Beautifully clear and well-balanced recording. Reissued at mid-price on DG's Al Fresco label.

William Christie uses a far bigger team of both singers and instrumentalists than Gardiner, allowing a wider range of colours. The bite of the performance is increased by the relative dryness of the recorded sound. Among Christie's soloists, **Nancy Argenta** and **Lynne Dawson** are outstanding, and the whole team is a strong one. The number of singers in solo roles allows them to be used together as chorus too – an authentic 17th-century practice. This makes a vigorous and refreshing alternative to the fine Gardiner set; but the Harmonia Mundi booklet is inadequate.

For Naxos at bargain price the **Scholars Baroque Ensemble** offer an outstanding version, stylishly presented with a refreshing vigour in its scholarly approach. The recording too is exceptionally bright and immediate, regularly giving the illusion of a dramatic entertainment on stage. Logically this version, unlike previous ones, presents the purely instrumental numbers designed as interludes for *A Midsummer Night's Dream* as an appendix. The humour of the scene of the Drunken Poet is touched on delightfully without exaggeration, thanks to **David van Asch**, as is the Dialogue between Corydon and Mopsa, though the countertenor, **Angus Davidson**, has a flutter in the voice that the recording exaggerates. Outstanding among the sopranos are **Diane Atherton**, singing most beautifully in the Night solo of Act II, and **Kym Amps**, not only bright and agile in *Hark! The Ech'ing Air* but making the plaint, *O Ever Let Me Weep*, of Act V into the emotional high-point of the whole performance. Instrumental playing on period instruments is first rate, and the chorus sings consistently with bright, incisive attack.

The Indian Queen (complete; with Daniel Purcell (c. 1661–1717): The Masque of Hymen)

Ⓜ *** Decca 475 052-2. Kirkby, Bott, Ainsley, D. Thomas, Finley, Williams, AAM Ch. & O, Hogwood

Hogwood's recording of Purcell's fourth and last semi-opera, left incomplete at his death, was the first to include the Wedding cantata which the composer's brother, Daniel, wrote to round off the entertainment. It makes an attractive if inconsistent addition to a score which contains vintage Purcell inspirations, notably the solo with chorus, *All Dismal Sounds*, which was the last part of the work completed by Purcell himself. The elaborate chromatics in that confirm the continuing vigour of Purcell's genius to the end. With **John Mark Ainsley**, **Emma Kirkby** and **Catherine Bott** all making outstanding solo contributions, and with clean-cut period playing from the orchestra, this performance on a relatively grand scale is consistently convincing, by turns lively and moving.

King Arthur (complete)

🔑 **** Erato 4509 98535-2 (2). Gens, McFadden, Padmore, Best, Salomaa, Les Arts Florissants, Christie

Ⓜ *** Erato 4509 96552-2 (2). J. Smith, Fischer, Priday, Ross, Stafford, Elliot, Varcoe, Monteverdi Ch., E. Bar. Sol., Gardiner

Christie brings out the jollity behind much of the piece. Even the pomposo manner of some of the Act Tunes (or interludes) has fun in it, with the panoply of the ceremonial music swaggering along genially. Few will resist the jollity of *Your Hay it is Mow'd* when the chorus even includes 'gentlemen of the orchestra' in the last verse. Christie's soloists are generally warmer and weightier than Pinnock's, notably **Véronique Gens** as Venus, sustaining Christie's exceptionally slow speed for *Fairest Isle*. Otherwise speeds are generally on the fast side, with *Shepherd, Shepherd, Cease Decoying* deliciously light and brisk. The vigour of Purcell's inspiration in this semi-opera has never been more winningly conveyed in a period performance on disc.

Gardiner's solutions to the textual problems carry complete conviction, as for example his placing of the superb *Chaconne in F* at the end instead of the start. Solo singing for the most part is excellent, with **Stephen Varcoe** outstanding among the men. *Fairest Isle* is treated very gently, with **Gill Ross**, boyish of tone, reserved just for that number. Throughout, the chorus is characteristically fresh and vigorous, and the instrumentalists beautifully marry authentic technique to pure, unabrasive sounds.

Theatre Music (collection)

Disc 1: *Abdelazar: Overture & Suite; Distressed Innocence: Overture & Suite; The Gordian Knot Untied: Overture & Suite; The Married Beau: Overture & Suite; Sir Anthony Love: Overture & Suite*

Disc 2: *Bonduca: Overture & Suite; Circe: Suite; The Old Bachelor: Overture & Suite; The Virtuous Wife: Overture & Suite*

Disc 3: *Amphitryon: Overture & Suite; Overture in G min.; Don Quixote: Suite*

Disc 4: *Overture in G min; The Double Dealer: Overture & Suite; Henry II, King of England: In Vain, 'Gainst Love, in Vain I Strove; The Richmond Heiress: Behold the Man; The Rival Sisters: Overture; 3 Songs; Tyrannic Love: Hark my Damilcar!* (duet); *Ah! How Sweet it is to Love; Theodosius* (excerpts)

Disc 5: *Overture in D min; The Wives' Excuse* (excerpts and other excerpts)

Disc 6: *Chacony; Pavans 1-5; Trio Sonata for Violin, Viola de Gamba & Organ* (and other extracts)

Ⓑ *** Decca 475 529-2 (6). Kirkby, Nelson, Lane, Roberts, Lloyd, Bowman, Hill, Covey-Crump, Elliott, Byers, Bamber, Pike, Thomas, Keyte, Shaw, George, Taverner Ch., AAM, Hogwood

Most of the music Purcell wrote for the theatre is relatively little heard and much of the music comes up with striking freshness in these performances using authentic instruments. As well as the charming dances and more ambitious overtures, as the series proceeds we are offered more extended scenas with soloists and chorus, of which the nine excerpts from *Theodosius*, an early score (1680), are a particularly entertaining example. Before that, on Disc 3 we have already had the highly inventive *Overture and Incidental Music* for *Don Quixote*, with much enchanting singing from both the soprano soloists, **Emma Kirkby** and **Judith Nelson**. Disc 4 also includes a delightful duet from *The Richmond Heiress*, representing a flirtation in music. There are other attractive duets elsewhere, for instance the nautical *Blow, Blow, Boreas, Blow* from *Sir Barnaby Whigg*, which could fit admirably into *HMS Pinafore* (**Rogers Covey-Crump** and **David Thomas**) and the jovial *As Soon as the Chaos* from *The Marriage-hater Match'd*. In *Ah Me! to Many Deaths* from *Regulus*, Judith Nelson is at her most eloquent while, earlier on Disc 5, she sings charmingly the familiar *Nymphs and Shepherds*, which comes from *The Libertine*, a particularly fine score with imaginative use of the brass. The equally famous *Music for a While*, beautifully sung by **James Bowman**, derives from *Oedipus*. The last disc also includes a splendidly boisterous *Quartet* from *The Canterbury Guests*. The collection is appropriately rounded off by members of the **Academy** giving first-class performances of some of Purcell's instrumental music, ending with the famous *Chacony*. The discs are re-released at bargain price, but the set is let down by the absence of texts.

Theatre Music, Vol. 1: from *Amphitryon or The Two Sosias; Circe; The Gordian Knot Unty'd; Sir Barnaby Whigg: Blow, Boreas, Blow*

Ⓝ ⒷⒷ *** Naxos 8.570149. Soloists, Aradia Ens., Mallon

Naxos are now beginning their own series of collections of Purcell's theatre music – instrumental pieces, songs and choruses that would either have been incorporated into the action of a play or performed as preludes or interludes. The exception here is the jolly sea-song from *Sir Barnaby Whigg* for tenor and bass, the only single piece in the score! We are comparatively familiar with *The Gordian Knot Unty'd*, and the excerpts here are the highlight of the disc, but the suites from *Amphitryon* (25 minutes) and *Circe* (13 minutes) are little known, and are most welcome. The featured soloists are excellent, and so is the playing of the **Aradia Ensemble** under **Kevin Mallon**.

QUILTER, Roger (1877–1953)

A Children's Overture; Country Pieces; 3 English Dances; As You Like It: Suite; The Rake: Suite; Where the Rainbow Ends: Suite

**(*) Marco 8.223444. Slovak RSO (Bratislava), Leaper

Adrian Leaper plays the enchanting *Children's Overture* with the lightest touch, and the transparency of the recording ensures that all the woodwind detail comes through nicely, even if his performance could ideally have had a shade more momentum. One might also have wished for a bigger band with a more opulent string sheen, but the texture here well suits the suites of incidental music, an agreeable mixture of the styles of Edward German (especially the *Country Dance* from *As You Like It*), Eric Coates and sub-Elgar of the *Nursery Suites*. All this nicely scored and amiably tuneful music is freshly and spontaneously presented and the recording is nicely resonant.

RACHMANINOV, Sergei
(1873–1943)

'The Harvest of Sorrow': Portrait of the composer by Tony Palmer, with commentary spoken by Sir John Gielgud

*** Warner DVD 2564-69883 (Producer Mike Bluett)

The **Mariinsky Orchestra** under **Valery Gergiev** play excerpts from two of the operas, *Aleko* and *The Miserly Knight*, along with the *First Symphony* and *Isle of the Dead*. Splendid though they are, it is the archival material of Rachmaninov in the 1930s in his home in Switzerland that makes this an indispensable acquisition, as is **Mikhail Pletnev** playing some of the *Corelli Variations* on Rachmaninov's own piano at Senar, his Swiss villa. Eminently dispensable is the pedestrian, charactererless playing of the glamorous-looking **Valentina Igoshina** in three of the best-known preludes. Rachmaninov's grandson Alexander is a memorable and dignified participant, who brings the composer closer to us. The overall effect is moving.

Caprice bohémien, Op. 12; The Isle of the Dead, Op. 29; Prince Rostislav; The Rock, Op. 7; Scherzo in D min.

*** Chan. 10104. Russian State SO, Polyansky

The tone-poem, *Prince Rostislav*, is a rarity. The *Scherzo* is Rachmaninov's earliest orchestral score, dating from 1888, when he was 15, while *The Isle of the Dead* is one of his greatest. In the last **Polyansky** is certainly competitive and has this music in his blood. The recording is perhaps a bit too reverberant, but no reader wanting this repertoire should be put off, for the performances are all vivid.

Piano Concertos: (i; ii) 1 in F sharp min., Op. 1; (i; iii) 2 in C min., Op. 18 (2 versions); (i; ii) 3 in D min., Op. 30; 4 in G min., Op. 40; (i; iii) Rhapsody on a Theme of Paganini, Op. 43; (iv) Isle of the Dead, Op. 29; Symphony 3 in A min., Op. 44; Vocalise, Op. 34/14; (v) piano (4 hands) Polka Italienne; (solo piano) Barcarolle, Op. 10/2; Daisies (song transcription); Etudes-tableaux, Op. 33/2 & 7; Op. 39/6; Humoresque, Op. 10/3; Lilacs (song transcription; 2 versions); Mélodie, Op. 3/3; Moment musical, Op. 16/2; Oriental Sketch; Polichinelle, Op. 3/4; Polka de W. R. (3 versions); Preludes: in C sharp min., Op. 3/2 (3 versions); in G

min.; in G flat, Op. 23/5 & 10; in E, G, F min., F, G sharp, Op. 32/3, 5–7, 12; Serenade, Op. 3/5 (2 versions)

Other Performances: (vi) BEETHOVEN: *Violin Sonata 8, Op. 30/3.* SCHUBERT: *Violin Sonata in A, D.574.* GRIEG: *Violin Sonata, Op. 45.* BACH: *Partita 4, BWV 828: Sarabande.* BEETHOVEN: *32 Variations in C min.* BORODIN: *Scherzo in A flat.* CHOPIN: *Ballade 3; Mazurkas, Op. 63/3; Op. 68/2; Nocturnes, Op. 9/2; Op. 15/2; Scherzo 3; Sonata 2 (Funeral March); Waltzes, Op. 18; Op. 34/3; Op. 42; Op. 64/1 (2 versions); Op. 64/2; Op. 64/3 (2 versions); Op. 60/2; Op. 70/1; in E min., Op. posth.; Ballade 3.* DAQUIN: *Le coucou.* DEBUSSY: *Children's Corner: Dr Gradus ad Parnassam; Golliwog's Cakewalk.* DOHNÁNYI: *Etude, Op. 28/6.* GLUCK: *Orfeo ed Euridice: Mélodie.* GRIEG: *Lyric Pieces: Waltz; Elfin Dance.* HANDEL: *Suite 5: Air & Variations (Harmonious Blacksmith).* HENSELT: *Etude (Si oiseau étais), Op. 2/6.* LISZT: *Concert Paraphrases: Chopin: Polish Songs (Return home; The maiden's wish); Schubert: Das Wandern; Serenade; Concert Study: Gnomenreigen; Hungarian Rhapsody 3.* MENDELSSOHN: *Song without Words: Spinning Song, Op. 67 (2 versions); Etudes, 104b/2–3.* MOSZKOWSKI: *Etude (La jongleuse), Op. 52/4.* MOZART: *Sonata in A, K.331: Theme and Variations; Rondo alla Turca.* PADEREWSKI: *Minuet, Op. 14/1.* SAINT-SAËNS: *Le Cygne (arr. Siloti).* D. SCARLATTI: *Pastorale (arr. Tausig).* SCRIABIN: *Prelude, Op. 11/8.* SCHUBERT: *Impromptu in A flat, Op. 90/4.* SCHUMANN: *Carnaval, Op. 9; Der Kontrabandiste (arr. Tausig).* JOHANN STRAUSS JR: *One Lives but Once (arr. Tausig).* TCHAIKOVSKY: *Humoresque, Op. 10/2; The Seasons: November: Troika (2 versions); Waltz, Op. 40/8.* Piano Transcriptions: BACH (Violin) *Partita 3, BWV 1003: Preludio; Gavotte & Gigue.* BEETHOVEN: *Ruins of Athens: Turkish March.* BIZET: *L'Arlésienne: Minuet.* KREISLER: *Liebesfreud (3 versions).* MENDELSSOHN: *A Midsummer Night's Dream: Scherzo.* MUSSORGSKY: *Gopak.* RIMSKY-KORSAKOV: *Flight of the Bumblebee.* SCHUBERT: *Wohin?* TCHAIKOVSKY: *Lullaby, Op. 16/1.* **(viii)** TRAD.: *Powder and Paint*

⊕–✿–Ⓑ **** RCA mono 82876 67892-2 (10). Composer; (i) with Phd. O; (ii) Ormandy; (iii) Stokowski; (iv) cond. composer; with (v) Natalie Rachmaninov; (vi) Kreisler; (vii) Nadejda Plevotskaya

This reissued RCA collection originally appeared for the 50th anniversary of the composer's death, and it encompasses all the recordings Rachmaninov made from 1919, the time he arrived in America, until 1942, the year before his death. These include all four of his *Piano Concertos* (3 irritatingly cut) as well as the *Paganini Rhapsody*, the *Third Symphony* and the tone-poem, *The Isle of the Dead* (also with cuts). The recordings were of high quality, the piano tone is firm and the orchestral sound full, if acoustically dry. You will not be disappointed with **Stokowski's** Philadelphia strings in the famous 18th variation of the *Rhapsody*. The *Symphony* too, unsurpassed as a performance, sounds splendid, the **Philadelphia** strings again covering themselves with glory.

When one turns to the solo performances, the acoustic recordings made between 1920 and 1925 are on balance the most cherishable of all, with the sound again astonishingly full and the readings sparkling and vivid. That is true even of the 1924 recording of *Piano Concerto 2*, here for the very first time issued complete. As in the classic electrical recording of five years later, he is partnered by Stokowski and the **Philadelphia Orchestra**, but the earlier one had a more volatile quality, with the fingerwork remarkably clear.

Interpreting Chopin, Rachmaninov was also at his freshest and most imaginative in the early recordings, yet many of the items here bear witness to the claim often made that he was the greatest Golden Age pianist of all. The delicacy of his playing in Daquin's little piece, *Le coucou*, shows how he was able to scale down his block-busting virtuosity, and though in Beethoven's 32 *Variations in C minor* he omitted half a dozen variations so as to fit the piece on two 78 sides, it is full of flair.

There is magic too in the collaboration with **Fritz Kreisler**, not just in Beethoven, but also in the Grieg and Schumann *Sonatas*, and in the private recordings, when he accompanies a gypsy singer in a traditional Russian song or plays a piano duet, the *Polka Italienne*, with his wife Natalie. Transfers are commendably clean and truthful, and the ten discs come in a box with good documentation.

Piano Concertos 1–4

☞ (B) **** Double Decca (ADD) 444 839-2 (2). Ashkenazy, LSO, Previn

(BB) *** EMI 5 73765-2 (3). Rudy, St Petersburg PO, Jansons – TCHAIKOVSKY: *Piano Concerto 1* ***

Piano Concertos (i) 1 in F sharp min.; (ii) 2 in C min.; (iii) 3 in D min.; (i) 4 in G min.; (ii) Rhapsody on a Theme of Paganini, Op. 43

☞ ***(*) Hyp. CDA 67501/2 (2). Hough, Dallas SO, Litton (*Concertos 2 and 3* are available separately on CDA 67649)

(M) *** Chan. 7114 (2) Wild, RPO, Horenstein

(i) Piano Concertos 1–4; Rhapsody on a Theme of Paganini; Variations on a Theme of Chopin; Variations on a theme of Corelli

☞ ✿ (B) **** Warner 2564 63675-2 (3) Lugansky (i) with CBSO, Oramo

It is not easy to think of any recent CDs of these marvellous concertos that surpass these by **Nicolai Lugansky** except those by Stephen Hough. Lugansky's account of the *First* is the finest since Pletnev's Virgin CD from the early 1990s, and the *Third* is even more impressive than his earlier version, coupled with the *Fourth* (Vanguard 99091). The *Second*, too, ranks alongside Ashkenazy's outstanding version. The *Variations* are hardly less impressive. A superb bargain set.

The Double Decca set of the four Concertos is admirable, fully capturing the Kingsway Hall ambient warmth yet not lacking brilliance and clarity, and with the *Third Concerto* better focused than when it first appeared on LP. The vintage 1972 performances, with their understanding partnership between **Ashkenazy** and **Previn**, have achieved classic status. The *Second Concerto's* slow movement is particularly beautiful; it is almost matched by the close of the first movement of the *Third* and the restrained passion of the opening of the following *Adagio*. The individuality and imagination of the solo playing throughout, combined with the poetic feeling of Previn's accompaniments and the ever-persuasive response of the **LSO**, provide special rewards. An outstanding bargain in every way.

Recorded live in Dallas, **Stephen Hough's** prize-winning Rachmaninov concertos set offers magnetic performances that reflect the thoughtfulness and care with which this masterly pianist approaches even the most frequently performed works. So the opening of the *Second Concerto*, taken much faster than usual but at a very steady pace, is quite different from most interpretations, firmly based on indications in the score rather than performing tradition, and that is typical of Hough's refreshing approach to each of these works. With **Andrew Litton** equally a devotee of the composer, these are unique readings, marred only slightly by rather clangorous piano-tone and orchestral textures that are far less detailed than in many rival versions.

Mikhail Rudy and the **St Petersburg Philharmonic** under **Mariss Jansons** consistently demonstrate that poetry and refinement can offer exceptionally rewarding results in works which emerge here as far more than conventional warhorses. There is plenty to admire and relish. The results are fresh and unhackneyed from first to last, with Rudy's light, clean articulation adding sparkle. Not that he lacks weight, and the strong support of Jansons and the St Petersburg Philharmonic intensifies the idiomatic warmth, with mystery alongside passion in Rachmaninov's writing. This account of the *Fourth Concerto* is especially valuable in offering the original, uncut version of the finale, as well as the usual revised text.

The **Earl Wild** set with **Horenstein** was recorded at the Kingsway Hall in 1965. They worked marvellously together, with Horenstein producing an unexpected degree of romantic ardour from the orchestra. Earl Wild's technique is prodigious and sometimes (as in the first movement of the *Fourth Concerto*) he almost lets it run away with him. In terms of bravura, the *Third Concerto* is in the Horowitz class. However, he makes the three cuts Rachmaninov sanctioned, one in the second movement and two in the third, a total of 55 bars. All in all, this is a first-class and very rewarding set, and the sumptuousness of the sound belies the age of the recording.

(i) Piano Concertos 1–4; Rhapsody on a Theme of Paganini, Op. 43; (ii) (Music for 2 pianos): Suites 1–2, Opp. 5 & 17; Russian Rhapsody; Symphonic Dances, Op. 45. Solo piano: Etudes-tableaux, Opp. 33 & 39; 24 Preludes (complete); Piano Sonata 2 in B flat min., Op. 36; Variations on a Theme by Corelli, Op. 42

☞ (B) *** Decca (ADD/DDD) 455 234-2 (6). Ashkenazy; (i) LSO, Previn; (ii) with Previn (piano)

(i) Piano Concertos 1–4; Rhapsody on a Theme of Paganini; Piano Sonata 2 in B flat, Op. 36; Variations on a Theme of Corelli, Op. 42

⊟ Ⓜ **** Decca Trio (ADD) 473 251-2 (3). Ashkenazy, (i) with LSO, Previn

All these performances are very distinguished indeed. The vintage Decca recordings (made over a decade and a half between 1971 and 1986, mostly in the Kingsway Hall, but also at Walthamstow and All Saints', Petersham) are fully worthy of the quality of the music-making. **Ashkenazy's** readings, with **Previn** an admirable partner (whether conducting or at the keyboard), are unsurpassed on CD, except by the composer's own historic versions.

Piano Concertos 1 in F sharp, Op. 1; 2 in C min., Op. 16

⊟ **** DG 459 6432. Zimerman, Boston SO, Ozawa
Ⓜ **** EMI 518184-2. Andsnes, BPO, Pappano

Krystian Zimerman is an aristocrat among aristocrats of the piano and his playing is never less than awesome. Of course, like everything Zimerman does, they are touched by distinction, but for all the admiration they inspire, there is just a trace of self-possession about them: one would welcome greater emotional abandon. But this is playing at an exalted level and many readers may not respond in this way – and most critics we have read certainly have not. Good orchestral support from **Ozawa** and the **Boston Orchestra**, and very vivid and present recording.

Commanding and sensitive accounts of both concertos which find the great Norwegian pianist at his subtle best. **Pappano** and the **Berlin Philharmonic** have plenty of fire. Very good sound, too. A bargain.

Piano Concertos (i) 1; (ii; iii) 2; (ii; iv) Rhapsody on a Theme of Paganini

ⒷⒷ (***) Naxos mono 8.110676. Moiseiwitsch; with (i) Philh. O, Sargent; (ii) RLPO; cond. (iii) Goehr; or (iv) Cameron

Rachmaninov used to say that his friend **Moiseiwitsch** was an even finer interpreter of some of his works than himself, and from this vintage collection one can understand why. Moiseiwitsch recorded 2 in 1937 for HMV on four budget-label 78s, undercutting the composer's classic version by half in price, yet the performance is if anything more electrifying. The sound is limited, with the piano close, but in Ward Marston's masterly transfer one quickly forgets the limitations, as one does in the other pre-war recording of the *Rhapsody on a Theme of Paganini*, a sparkling performance, again urgent in its expression, with the celebrated eighteenth variation all the warmer for going at a flowing speed. The rarity is the post-war, 1948 account of 1, in which the sound is full and clear with Moiseiwitsch still at the peak of his form, both passionate and sparkling, powerful and poetic.

Piano Concertos 1; 3

Ⓝ *** RCA 7279722. Douglas, Russian State SO, Svetlanov

These are fine performances. **Barry Douglas** elicits an impressive amount of detail in these scores; he never hurries and his articulation is stupendous. He is helped by first-rate

support from both the conductor and orchestra – and by the RCA engineers with the bright and clear, but vivid sound. These are undoubtedly exciting, fresh performances, almost – but not quite – an absolute top recommendation.

Piano Concertos 1; 4 in G min.; Rhapsody on a Theme of Paganini

⊟ ⒷⒷ *** Naxos 8.550809. Glemser, Polish Nat. RSO, Wit

Bernd Glemser has a boldly impetuous way with Rachmaninov and, with excellent support from the **Polish National Radio Orchestra** under **Antoni Wit**, he generates plenty of excitement and expressive fervour in all three works here. Glemser is by no means unimaginative or wanting in poetic feeling, and he gives a very enjoyable account of the more elusive *Fourth Concerto*.

Piano Concerto 2 in C min., Op. 18

⊟ **** Häns. CD 98.932. Ohlsson, ASMF, Marriner – TCHAIKOVSKY: *Piano Concerto 1* ***

Ⓜ *** DG (ADD) 447 4202. S. Richter, Warsaw PO, Wislocki – TCHAIKOVSKY: *Piano Concerto 1* (**)

Ohlsson and **Marriner** combine to give a satisfyingly romantic account of this favourite concerto. The climax of the first movement is broad and very powerful, and the finale, while not lacking brilliance, makes the very most of Rachmaninov's great secondary melody with a gorgeously expansive final presentation. The *Adagio* is equally persuasive with the reprise tenderly beautiful, rapt in its gentle concentration. The recording is full-bodied and natural and is admirably balanced. If you want a modern, digital recording of this coupling, this Hänssler CD is hard to beat.

With **Richter** the long opening melody of the first movement is taken abnormally slowly, and it is only the sense of mastery that he conveys in every note which prevents one from complaining. The slow movement too is spacious – with complete justification this time – and the opening of the finale lets the floodgates open the other way, for Richter chooses a hair-raisingly fast *Allegro*, so this is a reading of vivid contrasts. The sound is very good.

Piano Concertos (i) 2; (ii) 3 (transfers use alternative takes)

⊟ (***) Biddulph mono LHW 036. (i) Composer, Phd. O, Stokowski; (ii) Horowitz, LSO, Coates

Two classics of the Rachmaninov discography: the 1929 account of the *C minor Concerto* the composer recorded with the **Philadelphia Orchestra**, coupled with the first (and in some ways most exciting) of Horowitz's recordings of the *Third*, made in London the following year with **Albert Coates** conducting. An electrifying performance. The Biddulph transfers made by Mark Obert Thorn are first-rate and in the *C minor*, use is made of alternative takes made at the original sessions. An invaluable supplement to RCA's Complete Rachmaninov Edition.

(i) Piano Concerto 2; (ii) Rhapsody on a Theme of Paganini

⊟ ⒷⒷ **** Naxos 8.550117. Jandó, Budapest SO, Lehel

(i) Piano Concerto 2 in C min., Op. 18; (ii) Rhapsody on a Theme of Paganini, Op. 43; Prelude in C sharp min., Op. 3/2

(BB) (***) Naxos mono 8.110692. Kapell, Robin Hood Dell O, Philadelphia; (i) Steinberg or (ii) Reiner

Jandó has the full measure of the ebb and flow of Rachmaninov's musical thinking, and the slow movement is romantically expansive and the finale has plenty of dash and ripe, lyrical feeling. The *Rhapsody* is as good as almost any around. The digital recording is satisfyingly balanced, with a bold piano image and a full, resonant orchestral tapestry.

Kapell's are exceptionally urgent readings, notably in 2, where the first movement gets you off to an electrifying start, pressing on at a far faster speed than usual. Yet there is nothing perfunctory about Kapell's fast speeds, just a demonstration of mastery, both in the *Concerto* and in the *Variations*. The Ward Marston transfers are vivid and full, both in the *Concerto* (1950) and in the *Rhapsody* (1951). The *Prelude*, recorded in 1945, is dimmer.

(i) Piano Concertos 2–3; Rhapsody on a Theme of Paganini. Preludes: in C sharp min., Op. 3/2; in B flat & G min., Op. 23/2 & 5; in B min. & D flat, Op. 32/10 & 13; Etudes-tableaux, Op. 39/1, 2 & 5

(B) *** Double Decca (ADD) 436 386-2 (2). Ashkenazy, (i) LSO, Previn

This pair of Decca CDs includes outstanding performances of Rachmaninov's three greatest concertante works for piano and orchestra, plus five favourite *Preludes* and three of the Op. 39 *Etudes-tableaux*. This is very highly recommendable.

Piano Concerto 3 in D min., Op. 30

**** Ph. 446 673-2. Argerich, Berlin RSO, Chailly – TCHAIKOVSKY: *Piano Concerto 1* ****

(M) **(*) RCA SACD (ADD) 82876 67894-2. Van Cliburn, Chicago SO, Hendl – PROKOFIEV: *Piano Concerto 3* **(*)

(BB) (***) Naxos mono 8.110696. Horowitz, LSO, Coates – Recital: CHOPIN, DEBUSSY, LISZT, SCARLATTI

(B) (****) RCA mono 82876 56052-2 (2). Horowitz, RCA Victor SO, Reiner – TCHAIKOVSKY: *Piano Concerto 1*; Recital: 'Legendary Recordings' (***)

(BB) (***) Naxos mono 8.110787. Horowitz, RCA Victor SO, Reiner – BEETHOVEN: *Piano Concerto 5* (***)

(M) **** EMI (ADD) 3 45819-2. Gilels, Paris Conservatoire O, Cluytens – SAINT-SAËNS: *Piano Concerto 2*; SHOSTAKOVICH: *Preludes & Fugues* ***

(i) Piano Concerto 3; Elegy, Op. 3/1; Polichinelle; Preludes: in C sharp min., Op. 3/2; in B flat; G min.; E flat, Op. 23/2, 5 & 6; in G; G sharp min., Op. 32/5 & 12

✸ **** Elan CD 82412. Rodriguez; (i) with Lake Forest SO, McRae

(i) Piano Concerto 3; Piano Sonata 2, Op. 36

(M) *** RCA (ADD) 82876 59411-2. Horowitz; (i) NYPO, Ormandy

(i) Piano Concerto 3; (ii) Suite for 2 Pianos 2, Op. 17

(M) *** Ph. 464 7322. Argerich; (i) Berlin RSO, Chailly; (ii) Freire

Santiago Rodriguez is Cuban by birth but like Bolet has made his home in the United States. There is no doubt from the opening bars of the *Third Concerto* that he is a Rachmaninov interpreter of outstanding calibre, whose playing withstands the most exalted comparisons. Indeed, as one plays this disc, one's thoughts turn only to the greatest exponents of this repertoire – Horowitz, Rachmaninov himself and William Kapell. Rodriguez, too, has dazzling virtuosity at his command and also fine musicianship and a rare keyboard authority. He plays the first-movement cadenza (and how!) that Rachmaninov himself favoured rather than the alternative one that came into fashion with Vladimir Ashkenazy. The eight remaining pieces are of the same exalted standard. A most exciting issue.

There are few finer examples of live recording than **Martha Argerich's** electrifying performance of Rachmaninov's *Third Concerto*, recorded in Berlin in 1982. Her volatility and dash are entirely at one with the romantic spirit of this music, and her interpretation is so commanding that individual eccentricities seem a natural part of the musical flow. Moreover she plays with great tenderness (well supported by **Chailly**) in the *Adagio* and the lyrical theme of the finale. The overall sound-picture satisfyingly demonstrates the skill of the Philips engineering team.

Those not wanting the coupling with Tchaikovsky will find the performance of the *Second Suite* for two pianos equally exciting. **Argerich** and **Nelson Freire** give it a dazzling virtuoso account, rushing the waltzes off their feet (the movement is marked *presto* but they play it *prestissimo*). They are as fresh, idiomatic and thoughtful as their Decca rivals (Ashkenazy and Previn – see below) and their performance is thoroughly exhilarating and well recorded too.

The first of the three commercial recordings **Horowitz** made with Albert Coates of the *D minor Concerto* comes from 1929 (the others were with Fritz Reiner in 1951 and Ormandy in 1978), and for many collectors it is the finest. (Actually, one is tempted to say that of whichever was the last one you have heard.) However, it is still tremendously impressive and sounds better than ever in this new transfer.

Horowitz's 1951 RCA account with **Reiner** now reappears, coupled with his earlier (1941) version of the Tchaikovsky *First Concerto* with Toscanini. The Rachmaninov performance is full of poetry yet, like the Tchaikovsky, it is electrifying in its excitement. In spite of its dated sound its magic comes over, and it is to be preferred to his later performance with Ormandy. The recital added to make a two-disc bargain double is assembled from various individual mono records mainly from the same era, but with a few items from the 1970s and 1980s.

Gilels's 1955 performance of the *Third Concerto* (miraculously recorded in very satisfactory stereo) can readily be placed alongside Horowitz. Like Horowitz, Gilels plays the simpler first cadenza, yet he still dazzles the ear with his virtuosity, as he does in the thrilling finale, where the climax (with **Cluytens** moved to an unexpected degree of passion) is overwhelmingly intense. Truly a great performance, and a very acceptable and certainly vivid transfer to CD.

In this remarkable 1958 live Carnegie Hall recording, which is new to CD, **Van Cliburn** gives one of the very finest accounts of the *D minor Concerto* on record, and it has much in common with Horowitz's classic 1941 mono version with Reiner. There is the same balance between delicate lyricism and power, the slow movement is ravishingly played, and the peroration has never sounded more exciting in its growth and full flowering at the climax. Alas, the recording leaves much to be desired. The balance is dry and close and the piano *fortissimos* unflattering.

On Naxos comes the second account **Horowitz** made of the *D minor Concerto* and, like its coupling, it remains one of the classics of the gramophone. Horowitz was unrivalled in this concerto. It is among the most classical of readings and Reiner is a totally like-minded partner. Good new transfers.

In 1978 **Horowitz** re-recorded the *D minor Piano Concerto* in stereo with **Ormandy** and the **New York Philharmonic Orchestra**, this time at a live concert in Carnegie Hall, but certain portions of the work were remade following the concert. The result is that the sound is not completely stable; at times it seems to recede. The *Sonata* comes from two live recitals in 1980 and is also pretty electrifying.

(i) Piano Concerto 3 in D min; (ii) The Isle of the Dead; Symphonic Dances; (iii) Symphony 2 in E min.

Ⓝ Ⓑ *** EMI 2-CD 2 37616-2. (i) Andsnes, Oslo PO, Berglund; (ii) LSO, Previn; (iii) St Petersburg PO, Jansons

Leif Ove Andsnes offers cultivated playing in the *D minor Concerto*, bringing finesse and a refined musicianship to the work, and **Berglund** is very supportive. **Previn's** accounts of *The Isle of the Dead* and the *Symphonic Dances* with the **LSO** have stood the test of time and are still among the strongest and most atmospheric versions. **Jansons's** 1993 account of the *E minor Symphony* is also both exciting and lyrically gripping. Altogether a rewarding compilation, all very well recorded.

Piano Concerto 4 in G min., Op. 40

☞ ✿ Ⓜ **** EMI (ADD) 5 67238-2. Michelangeli, Philh. O, Gracis – RAVEL: *Piano Concerto in G* ****✿

There are few records in the catalogue more worthy of being described as a 'Great Recording of the Century' than **Michelangeli's** superb coupling of Rachmaninov and Ravel. It has been with us for more than four decades and time has not diminished its unique appeal from the commanding opening onwards. The current remastering has been expertly managed and at mid-price it should be included in even the most modest collection.

The Isle of the Dead, Op. 29

*** BBC 4226-2. USSR State SO, Svetlanov – SHOSTAKOVICH: *Symphony 5* ***

Ⓝ (**(*)) Australian Decca Eloquence mono 480 0044 (2).Paris Conservatoire O, Ansermet – SIBELIUS: *Symphonies 2 & 4* **(*)

The great Russian conductor made an impressive recording

of Rachmaninov's masterpiece for Melodiya in the 1960s, but the present mesmeric and powerful account comes from 1968, the year when **Svetlanov** brought his orchestra to the Proms. It comes with a similarly high-powered account of the Shostakovich *Fifth Symphony*.

Rachmaninov's masterful *The Isle of the Dead* is used as a rather curious coupling for Sibelius. This mono account, with the **Paris Conservatoire Orchestra**, is full of personality and character, the mono sound warm and detailed so that it almost gives the effect of being a stereo recording.

The Isle of the Dead, Op. 29; Symphonic Dances, Op. 45

☞ Ⓜ *** Decca 430 733-2. Concg. O, Ashkenazy

Ashkenazy's is a superb coupling, rich and powerful in playing and interpretation, *The Isle of the Dead* relentless in its ominous build-up, while the *Symphonic Dances* have extra darkness and intensity too. The splendid digital recording highlights both the passion and the fine precision of the playing.

Rhapsody on a Theme of Paganini (DVD version)

(***) EMI mono **DVD** DVB 3 101989. Janis, O Philharmonique de l'ORTF, Froment – PROKOFIEV: *Piano Concerto 3* (***)

From **Byron Janis**, we hear and see (in black and white) playing of a very special order, and not just virtuosity either (although there is plenty of that). But Janis and **Froment** between them reveal much detail that often passes by unnoticed, and they do not fall short in the passionate 18th variation either. The snag is that the string-tone is thin and meagre: it is curious to watch a large orchestra produce tone which is entirely lacking in voluptuousness. But the recording of the piano is fully acceptable.

Rhapsody on a Theme of Paganini (CD versions)

☞ Ⓜ *** RCA (ADD) 09026 68886-2. Rubinstein, Chicago SO, Reiner – CHOPIN: *Andante spianato & Grand polonaise*; FALLA: *Nights in the Gardens of Spain* ***

Rubinstein's playing is dazzling and it continually delights with its poetic sensibility and flair. **Reiner** is with him in every bar, orchestral detail persuasively delineated, and the warm Chicago acoustic ensures a glorious blossoming of string-tone at the *Eighteenth*. The recording, with the piano forward but not unattractively so, sounds little short of ideal in Richard Mohr's otherwise splendid new remastering.

Symphonic Dances, Op. 45

*** Warner 2564 62050-2. St Petersburg PO, Temirkanov – MUSSORGSKY: *Songs & Dances of Death* ***

Temirkanov is at his best in front of an audience, and he characterizes the *Symphonic Dances* colourfully and idiomatically, securing fine playing from his **St Petersburg Orchestra**, especially in the engaging central waltz. The three-part third dance is less easily held together, but if he does not quite manage the forward impetus of Jurowski (see above), he explores the music's detail and has the closing pages firmly in his grip. The live recording, balanced by Mike Hatch, is excellent.

SYMPHONIES

Symphonies 1–3

- ⊕ Ⓜ *** Virgin 5 62037-2 (2). RPO, Litton
- ⊕ Ⓜ *** Double Decca 448 116-2 (2). Concg. O, Ashkenazy

Symphonies (i) 1; (ii) 2–3

Ⓝ *** Australian Decca Eloquence (ADD) 480 0824 (2). Weller, with (i) SRO; (ii) LPO

Symphonies 1–3; Caprice bohémien, Op. 12; Isle of the Dead, Op. 29; Scherzo in D min.; The Rock, Op. 7

**** Warner 5101 12235-2 (3). Russian Federation SO, Svetlanov

Symphonies 1–3; Isle of the Dead; Scherzo in D min.; Vocalise

Ⓑ *** EMI 5 00885-2 (3). St Petersburg PO, Jansons

Symphonies 1–3; The Isle of the Dead, Op. 29; Symphonic Dances, Op. 45; Vocalise, Op. 34/14; Aleko: Intermezzo & Women's Dance

Ⓜ *** EMI (ADD) 7 64530-2 (3). LSO, Previn

Symphonies 1–3; The Isle of the Dead; Symphonic Dances; (i) The Bells, Op. 35

- ⊕ Ⓑ *** Decca 455 798-2 (3). Concg. O, Ashkenazy; (i) with Troitskaya, Karczykowski; Concg. Ch.

Symphonies 1–3; Vocalise, Op. 34/14

- ⊕ ⒷⒷ **** Sony SB2K 63257 (2). Phd. O, Ormandy

Ormandy pioneered the recording of the three Rachmaninov symphonies in stereo, and in many ways his performances remain unsurpassed. Certainly they have never sounded as good as they do in these splendid new transfers. The *Second Symphony* has great intensity of feeling and passion. The *First Symphony* was the work's first stereo version, an exceptionally strong performance it is too. Ormandy's thrustful view of the outer movements is supported by superbly committed **Philadelphia** playing, with the orchestra on top form. The balance has woodwind solos spotlighted, but the spacious acoustic of Philadelphia Town Hall provides the necessary ambient warmth. In some ways the *Third Symphony* is even more distinguished and now that the artificial brilliance of the old LP has been tamed one can at last appreciate the body of tone this great orchestra commanded in its heyday. The playing itself is marvellous, and this warmth of feeling carries over into the touchingly shaped *Vocalise* which acts as a final encore.

Svetlanov's celebrated recordings of the Rachmaninov *Symphonies* with the USSR State Symphony Orchestra were one of the triumphs of the HMV Melodiya catalogue in the days of LP. This new survey, made during the course of a week in October 1995 at the Moscow Radio studios, has every bit as much sweep and passion as the earlier discs and it benefits from better sound.

Jansons and the **St Petersburg** musicians give a totally committed and finely shaped account of the *First Symphony*, and the performance of the *Second* is equally strong, with climaxes thrust home powerfully. In Russian fashion the clarinet in the slow movement sounds like an organ stop, but this exciting reading still stands among the best modern versions. Jansons's account of the *Third* is arguably the finest of the three, and with a highly atmospheric *Isle of the Dead*, a masterly set of the *Symphonic Dances*, and the *Vocalise* beautifully done, this is a highly recommendable set, as all the recordings offer first-class recorded sound.

Andrew Litton's mid-priced box is highly competitive. In 1, Litton is most persuasive in his free use of rubato and his performance combines power and ripeness of romantic feeling with tenderness, bringing out the refinement of Rachmaninov's scoring. In the *Second Symphony* he readily sustains the observance of the exposition repeat in the first movement, making it a very long movement indeed at just over 23 minutes. But the moments of special magic are those where, as in his lightly pointed account of the Scherzo or, most of all, the lovely clarinet melody of the slow movement, subtlety of expression gives Rachmaninov's romanticism an extra poignancy. In the *Third Symphony*, the gentleness of his treatment of the great second subject melody means that the transparent beauty of Rachmaninov's scoring is brought out luminously, and though the opening of the finale may not sound urgent enough, it is crisply pointed and leads on to a superbly brisk, tense conclusion.

The **Ashkenazy** digital set of the three symphonies now comes either as a Double Decca or in a bargain box of three discs, one symphony to each CD and coupled respectively with *The Isle of the Dead*, *Symphonic Dances* and the dramatic cantata, *The Bells*, outstanding in every way. The performances of the symphonies, passionate and volatile, are intensely Russian; the only possible reservation concerns the slow movement of the *Second*, where the clarinet solo is less ripe than in some versions. Elsewhere there is drama, energy and drive, balanced by much delicacy of feeling, while the **Concertgebouw** strings produce great ardour for Rachmaninov's long-breathed melodies. The vivid Decca sound within the glowing Concertgebouw ambience is ideal for the music.

Weller's Rachmaninov symphony cycle is hugely underrated. Splendidly recorded, it is undoubtedly one of the best of the stereo era. In the *First Symphony*, Weller has a fine feeling for the music's atmosphere (both inner movements show this readily). The *Second Symphony* is perhaps more restrained than in Previn's classic account, but is genuinely symphonic in stature, with a dreamy poetic quality in the slow movement. In the *Third*, although there may be some slight sacrifice of detail to atmosphere, the beautiful sound the orchestra consistently yields deserves this kind of richness and sense of space. The reading is essentially a lyrical one, showing great delicacy of feeling, notably in the preparation of the first movement's memorable second subject, but also in the sense of stillness that pervades the opening of the *Adagio* to make an absolute contrast with the *scherzando* middle section. The finale too responds to such spacious treatment, though its basic tempo has no lack of urgency. The playing of the **LPO** in *Symphonies* 2 and 3 is even finer than that of the **SRO** (1) but the sound is consistently brilliant throughout.

Previn's LSO set at mid-price offers some alternative couplings. His 1973 account of the *Second Symphony* – a passionately committed performance, with a glorious response from the LSO strings – has been remastered for CD again, with great improvement in the body of the string timbre. 1 is a forthright, clean-cut performance, beautifully played and very well recorded. Previn's account of the *Third* is outstanding: the LSO's playing again has enormous bravura and ardour, and the performances of the two shorter works have plenty of atmosphere and grip.

Symphony 1

*** BBCL 4233. BBC SO, Rozhdestvensky (with RIMSKY-
  KORSAKOV: *Russian Easter Festival Overture* ***) –
  PROKOFIEV: *Ode to the End of the War* ***

Symphony 1; 5 Etudes-tableaux (orch. Respighi)

*** Chan. 9822. Russian State SO, Polyansky

Symphony 1; Symphony in D min. (Youth) 1891; The Isle of the Dead

(N) **(*) Chan. 10475. BBC PO, Noseda

Symphony 1; The Isle of the Dead

🔊 ❀ **** DG 463 075-2. Russian Nat. O, Pletnev

In the *First Symphony* **Mikhail Pletnev** produces a range of sonority and clarity of articulation that we recognize from his keyboard playing, and there is poetic vision alongside a splendid command of architecture. The symphony is quite outstanding in his hands and so is *The Isle of the Dead* which has the sense of inevitability and forward movement that recall Rachmaninov himself, Koussevitzky and Reiner.

Rozhdestvensky's well-paced and expertly prepared account of the *First* dates from a 1979 Prom, during his period with the **BBC Symphony Orchestra**. They respond well to him, both here and in the Rimsky *Overture* from the same season. Very good sound, and the Prokofiev rarity from the 1978 Festival Hall season makes an attractive bonus.

Good playing and particularly good recording make **Polyansky's** Chandos CD a competitive issue. A worthwhile addition to the catalogue, particularly in view of the Respighi transcription of the *Etudes-tableaux*.

Noseda brings a superbly controlled account of Rachmaninov's *First Symphony*, with a particularly beautiful account of the slow movement, the highlight. If it doesn't quite have the character and adrenalin of the finest versions on CD (notably Ashkenazy and Pletnev), it is still very fine indeed. The *Isle of the Dead* is similarly beautifully played and moulded, if again lacking the white-hot intensity which the finest accounts offer. The inclusion of the enjoyably concise 'Youth' *Symphony* makes a good bonus.

Symphony 2 E min.; (i) The Bells; Symphonic Dances (DVD versions)

***(*) Arthaus **DVD** 101439 (2). (i) Pavlovskaya, Akimov, Vaneev, Legis Artis Ch., Cologne R. Ch.; Cologne RSO, Bychkov

These are performances of stature that can be recommended with great enthusiasm. The playing of the **Cologne Radio Orchestra** is of high quality and worthy of the most exalted comparisons. The performances come with documentaries by Enrique Sánchez Lansch which are less satisfying; they comprise bits of the rehearsals, some background material about Rachmaninov's life, with interesting footage intercut by interviews with members of the orchestra mostly saying how young they were when they joined and how old their colleagues seemed, and now they are not so young – and other rather obvious remarks. Anyway, the set is mandatory viewing for the sake of these impressive performances.

Symphony 2 in E min., Op. 27 (CD version)

🔊 (BB) *** Regis RRC 1210. LSO, Rozhdestvensky

Symphony 2; The Rock (CD version)

**(*) DG 439 8882. Russian Nat. O, Pletnev

Symphony 2; (i) Vocalise (CD version)

*** Channel Classics **SACD** CCS SA 21698. Budapest Festival O, Fischer

Rozhdestvensky gives a very Tchaikovskian reading of Rachmaninov's *E minor Symphony*. There is plenty of vitality but, with the big string melodies blossoming voluptuously, the slow movement, after a beguiling opening clarinet solo from **Andrew Marriner**, has a climax of spacious intensity, its power almost overwhelming. The finale is flamboyantly broadened at the end, and the feeling of apotheosis is very much in the Tchaikovsky mould. With the **LSO** responding superbly, this is a most satisfying account, and the richness, brilliance and weight of the recording add to the compulsion of the music-making.

A red-blooded account of the *Second Symphony* from **Iván Fischer** and the fine **Budapest Festival Orchestra** has much to commend it. It has splendid breadth and sweep, and Fischer generates admirable excitement. While it does not necessarily displace the finest alternatives, it may well be considered alongside them.

Pletnev brings a fresh mind to this symphony, with his approach very much controlled, giving a strong sense of onward current and producing none of the heart-on-sleeve emotion in the slow movement. The clarity and lightness of articulation that distinguish his piano playing seem to be in ample evidence and, throughout the work, feeling is held in perfect control. It is a performance of quality, though the recording, while good, could be cleaner-detailed in the lower end of the range. Ensemble is endangered by some frenetically fast speeds – as in the finale. *The Rock* makes a generous coupling.

Symphony 3; Symphony in D min. (Youth); Vocalise

*** BIS CD 1299. RSNO, Arwel Hughes

Symphony 3; Symphonic Dances

(M) *** Chan. 10234X. LSO, Järvi

(i) Symphony 3; (i-iii) Spring (cantata), Op. 20; (iii) 3 Unaccompanied Choruses

⊝— *** Chan. 9802. (i) Russian State SO; (ii) Martyrosyan; (iii) Russian State Symphonic Capella; Polyansky

A splendid, very Russian account of the *Third Symphony* from **Polyansky**, volatile but convincingly so, with some glorious playing from the strings, especially in the lovely, nostalgic secondary theme of the first movement which is so very Slavic in feeling. The choral works too are superbly done, with the widest range of dynamic in the masterly unaccompanied choruses, while **Tigram Martyrosyan** is a richly resonant bass soloist in the cantata.

Järvi in his weighty, purposeful way misses some of the subtleties of this symphony (although not the *Symphonic Dances*), but with superb playing from the **LSO** – linking back to André Previn's unsurpassed reading with them – the intensity is magnetic. The *Dances* too are superbly done, with the changes of tempo and mood in the third section both subtle and passionate. Outstanding recording too.

Owain Arwel Hughes draws from the **Scottish National Orchestra** a very well-played account of the *Third*, brilliantly recorded with textures exceptionally clear. Speeds are on the broad side in a reading less red-bloodedly emotional than most, with the BIS sound again slightly distanced. The degree of restraint brings advantages. That is especially so in the central *Adagio*, where the lovely horn solo at the start and the sweet solo violin entry at a full *pianissimo* have a tenderness that is most moving.

CHAMBER MUSIC

Cello Sonata in G min., Op. 19

Ⓜ *** Somm SOMMCD 026. Walton, Owen – CHOPIN: *Cello Sonata* ***

Ⓑ *** EMI (ADD) 5 74333-2 (2). P. Tortelier, Ciccolini – CHOPIN; FAURÉ; MENDELSSOHN: *Cello Sonatas* ***

Cello Sonata in G min.; Lied; Melody on a Theme by Rachmaninov (arr. Altschuler/Hayroudinoff); 2 Pieces, Op. 2; Prelude, Op. 23/10; Vocalise

**(*) Chan. 10095. Ivashkin, Hayroudinoff

Cello Sonata in G min.; Lied (Romance) in F min.; Mélodie in D; 2 Pieces, Op. 2; Romance in F, Op. 4/3; Vocalise

⊝— ⒷⒷ *** Naxos 8.550987. Grebanier, Guggenheim

Cello Sonata in G min.; 2 Pieces, Op. 2; Vocalise, Op. 34/14

ⒷⒷ *** Virgin 2x1 4 82067-2 (2). Mørk, Thibaudet – MIASKOVSKY; PROKOFIEV; SHOSTAKOVICH: *Cello Sonatas*; STRAVINSKY: *Suite Italienne* ***

Cello Sonata in G min.; 5 Pieces for Cello & Piano: Oriental Dance, Op. 2/2; Prelude, Op. 2/1; Romance; Vocalise, Op. 34/14 (with ALTSCHULER: Mélodie)

⊝— ⒷⒷ **** Double Decca 473 807-2 (2). Harrell, Ashkenazy –

PROKOFIEV: *Cello Sonata*; SHOSTAKOVICH: *Cello Sonata*, etc. ***

Lynn Harrell and **Vladimir Ashkenazy** give an impassioned, full-throated account of the glorious *Cello Sonata* and they capture its melancholy perfectly. They are very well attuned to its sensibility and to the affecting drama of the smaller pieces. The Decca recording is in the high traditions of the house; the balance and perspective are completely natural.

Michael Grebanier too gives it a powerful, richly expressive reading, with **Janet Guggenheim** an incisive partner, very clearly focused if not always as warm. The slow movement is most moving, the headlong finale thrilling in its clarity. The shorter pieces make up an excellent bargain disc to match rivals at premium price.

A first-class account from **Jamie Walton** and **Charles Owen** – warm, passionate and refined, with fine lyrical impetus in the finale. A good recording balance too, although the otherwise attractive acoustic does not offer the clearest separation.

The gifted Norwegian cellist **Truls Mørk** plays with a restrained eloquence that is totally compelling. The demanding (and commanding) piano part is given with authority and conviction by **Thibaudet**, and they handle the companion pieces excellently. This set is a remarkable bargain.

Alexander Ivashkin and **Rustem Hayroudinoff** give us the complete works for cello and piano, though it is only the *Sonata* that really counts. The *Two Pieces* of Op. 2 (a *Prelude* and *Danse orientale*) are very appealing, as is the slightly earlier *Lied*, written when Rachmaninov was seventeen. But the remainder are arrangements. Ivashkin produces a beautifully burnished, lustrous tone, and the playing of this duo is highly cultured. One would at times welcome more abandon in the second movement. It is all thoroughly enjoyable and well (if forwardly) recorded.

Trio élégiaque 1 in G min., Op. 8

⊝— *** BIS CD 1302. Kempf Trio – TCHAIKOVSKY: *Piano Trio* ***

Rachmaninov's first *Trio élégiaque*, Op. 8, was written in 1892. Its mood is tinged with melancholy throughout, surging to moments of ardour less extrovert than with Tchaikovsky, but with a characteristic Rachmaninovian ebb and flow of feeling, which is captured most spontaneously by these players. **Kempf** and his colleagues are by no means second best and are very well recorded.

Trios élégiaques 1 in G min., Op. 8; 2 in D min., Op. 9

*** Tavros EPT 4516. Koo, Sakharova, Arnadóttir

The *Trios* are both imbued with lyrical fervour and draw from the rich vein of melancholy so characteristic of Rachmaninov. Korean pianist **Yung Wook Koo**, Russian violinist **Julia Sakharova**, with the warm-toned Icelandic cellist, **Margrét Arnadóttir**, make a fine team and give performances that are as passionate as they are lyrically spontaneous. The recording is vividly up front but the performances are so committedly vivid and alive that this début CD must be welcomed with enthusiasm. (The disc is available from Tavros Records, 1187 Coast Village Road, 1-288, Santa Barbara, California 93108, USA. Fax: 00-1-805-969-5749. E-mail: info@tavrosrecords.com)

Trios élégiaques 1 & 2, Opp. 8–9; 2 Pieces for Cello & Piano, Op. 2; 2 Pieces for Violin & Piano, Op. 6.

⊛– ******** Hyp. CDA 67178. Moscow Rachmaninov Trio

Apart from two incomplete string quartets and the *Cello Sonata*, Op. 19, the four works here comprise Rachmaninov's complete chamber output. The **Moscow Rachmaninov Trio** (**Viktor Yampolsky**, **Mikhail Tsinman** and **Natalia Savinova**) are superb artists and play this music with feeling and sensitivity.

PIANO MUSIC

Piano duet

Music for 2 Pianos: Suites 1 & 2, Opp. 5 & 17; Symphonic Dances, Op. 43

BB ******* Naxos 8.557062. Roscoe & Donohoe

First-class playing from **Martin Roscoe** and **Peter Donohoe** in all three works.

Music for 2 pianos: (i) Suites 1–2, Opp. 5 & 17; Symphonic Dances, Op. 45; Russian Rhapsody. For solo piano: Etudes-tableaux, Op. 33; Variations on a Theme by Corelli, Op. 42

⊛– **(B)** ******** Double Decca (ADD) 444 845-2 (2). Ashkenazy, (i) with Previn

The colour and flair of Rachmaninov's writing in the two *Suites* (as inspired and tuneful as his concertos) are captured with wonderful imagination on Double Decca. The two-piano version of the *Symphonic Dances* is masterly and dazzling, and they are hardly less persuasive in the early *Russian Rhapsody*. **Ashkenazy's** superb solo performances of the *Etudes-tableaux* and the *Corelli Variations* (a rarity and a very fine work) cap the appeal of this bargain. The recording throughout is superb, with a natural presence and a most attractive ambience.

Suite 2, Op. 17

(M) ******* Ph. 475 8520. Argerich & Freire – LUTOSŁAWSKI: *Paganini Variations*; RAVEL: *La valse* *******

Argerich and **Freire** give a dazzling, virtuoso account of the *Second Suite*, rushing the waltzes off their feet (the movement is marked *presto* but they play it *prestissimo*). They are as fresh, idiomatic and thoughtful as their Decca rivals and their performance is thoroughly exhilarating.

Solo piano music

Andante ma non troppo in D min.; Canon in E min.; Fragments (1917); Fughetta; Lento in D min. (Song Without Words; 1866–7); Moment musical, Op. 16/2 (rev. version, 1940); Morceau de fantaisie in G min.; Oriental Sketch (1917); Prelude in F (1891); Variations on a Theme of Chopin, Op. 22

BB ******* Naxos 8.554426. Biret

Idil Biret's Rachmaninov recital here brings a powerful yet poetic reading of the *Chopin Variations*, one of Rachmaninov's finest piano works, coupled with miniatures and rarities including many rare early pieces. Excellent sound to bring out the subtleties of Biret's tonal shading.

Etudes-tableaux, Opp. 33 & 39; Fragments; Fughetta in F; Mélodie in E; Moments musicaux; Morceaux de fantaisie; Morceaux de salon; 3 Nocturnes; Oriental sketch; 4 Pieces; Piece in D min.; 25 Preludes (complete); Sonatas 1–3 (including original & revised versions of 2); Song Without Words; Transcriptions (complete); Variations: On a Theme of Chopin; On a Theme of Corelli

⊛– **(M)** ******* Hyp. DDD/ADD CDS 44041/8 (8). Shelley

Hyperion have collected **Howard Shelley's** exemplary survey of Rachmaninov into a mid-price, eight-CD set, and very good it is, too. Shelley can hold his own against most rivals not only in terms of poetic feeling but in keyboard authority and virtuosity. Some of these discs are all available seperately.

Etudes-tableaux, Opp. 33 & 39

*** Chan. 10391. Hayroudinoff

Rustem Hayroudinoff adds to the series of superb recordings he has made for Chandos with this outstanding disc of the two sets of Rachmaninov's *Etudes-Tableaux*. In magnetic playing his feeling for rubato is faultless, and his observance of the composer's dynamic indications, often very dramatic, is meticulous. First-rate sound.

Etudes-tableaux, Opp. 33 & 39; 6 Preludes, Op. 23/1–2, 4–5, 7–8; 7 Preludes, Op. 32/1–2, 6–7, 9–10, 12

⊛– **BB** ******* Regis (DDD/ADD) RRC 1022. Richter

Although he played them in public, **Sviatoslav Richter** did not record all the *Preludes*, only the ones he liked best. Those here were recorded in 1971 but the *Etudes-tableaux* are later digital recordings. The playing is of a rare order of mastery and leaves strong and powerful resonances. Richter's conception goes far beyond the abundant virtuosity this music calls for and the characterization is very strong and searching. The sound quality is less than ideal, a bit hard and two-dimensional, but fully acceptable when the playing is so riveting. This reissue (of the original Olympia CD) is unique and not to be missed.

Moments musicaux, Op. 16; Preludes, Op. 3/2; Op. 23/1–10

⊛– ******* Erato 8573 85770-2. Lugansky

Nikolai Lugansky belongs to the same generation as Andsnes and Kissin, and those who acquired his Chopin *Etudes* on Erato will know that he is an artist of impeccable technique and taste. As impressive an account of this repertoire as we have had since Ashkenazy and Shelley, and warmly recommended.

Morceaux de fantaisie, Op. 3; Sonata 2 in B flat min., Op. 36 (revised, 1931 version); Variations on a Theme of Corelli, Op. 42

*** Danacord DACOCD 525. Marshev

Oleg Marshev possesses the grand manner, and has won golden opinions for his Russian repertoire. Listening to his Rachmaninov, one can see why, for, apart from flawless technical address and sensitivity, he has an innate feeling for this repertoire. His account of all three pieces belongs up there with the finest. The dryish recording, if not ideal, is perfectly serviceable and should not deter readers from investigating some superbly idiomatic Rachmaninov playing.

Morceaux de fantaisie, Op. 3; Sonata 2 in B flat min., Op. 36; Variations on a Theme of Chopin, Op. 22

☷ ✿ **** Elan 82248. Rodriguez

Préludes, Op. 32/1–13; Sonata 1 in D min., Op. 28

☷ ✿ **** Elan 82244. Rodriguez

This is some Rachmaninov playing! **Santiago Rodriguez** is the real thing. For a moment one imagines that Rachmaninov himself is at the keyboard. Rodriguez has something of Pletnev about him: wonderful authority and immaculate technical control, tremendous electricity as well as great poetic feeling. Outstanding in every way.

24 Preludes (complete)

☷ Ⓜ **** Decca (ADD) 475 8238. Ashkenazy

24 Preludes, Op. 23/1–10; Op. 32/1–13; in D min. Mélodie; 6 Moments musicaux, Op. 16; Morceaux de fantaisie, Op. 3; Oriental Sketch; Song Transcriptions: Daisies; Lilacs

Ⓑ *** Virgin 2x1 5 61624 (2). Alexeev

There is superb flair and panache about **Ashkenazy's** playing and his poetic feeling is second to none. For its Originals reissue the whole set has been accommodated on a single mid-priced CD playing for just over 80 minutes, and as such sweeps the board, for the new transfer offers a most realistic piano image.

Dmitri Alexeev's 1989 two-CD set of the *Preludes* and various other works brings us formidable and powerful pianism. His mastery is evident throughout, and although there are occasions, such as in the *B minor Prelude*, Op. 32, No. 10, where one misses the depth and poetic feeling of some rivals, the recital is a satisfying one and value for money.

Piano Sonatas 1 in D min., Op. 28; 2 in B flat min., Op. 36 (revised 1931)

☷ *** Hyp. (ADD) CDA 66047. Shelley

Piano Sonata 2 in B flat min., Op. 36 (original version); Fragments in A flat; Fughetta in F; Gavotte in D; Mélodie in E; Morceau de fantaisie in G min.; Nocturnes 1–3; Oriental Sketch in B flat;

Piece in D min.; 4 Pieces; Prelude in E flat min.; Romance in F sharp min.; Song Without Words in D min.

☷ *** Hyp. (ADD) CDA 66198. Shelley

Piano Sonata 2, Op. 36 (original version); Etudes-tableaux, Op. 39; (trans. of KREISLER: Liebesleid)

☷ **** BIS CD-1042. Kempf

Piano Sonata 2, Op. 36; Etudes-tableaux, Op. 39/2, 6 & 9; Fugue; Preludes, Op. 23/5; Op. 32/12; Suite D min.

Ⓝ *** RCA 88697 15591-2. Denis Matsuev

Piano Sonata 2 in B flat min., Op. 36 (original version); Etudes-tableaux, Op. 33/1, 39/4; 7 Morceaux de fantaisie, Op. 3/3 & 5; Preludes, Op. 23/1 & 7; 32/2, 6, 9 & 10

☷ Ⓜ **** Ph. 475 7779. Zoltán Kocsis

Now reissued as one of Philips's Originals, this is one of the finest of all Rachmaninov recital discs. Be it in the smaller, reflective pieces or in the bigger-boned *B flat minor Sonata*, **Zoltán Kocsis's** piano speaks with totally idiomatic accents, effortless virtuosity and a keen poetic feeling. This is a most distinguished offering and it is once more recommended with enthusiasm. Excellent recording.

On CDA 66047, **Howard Shelley** offers the 1931 version of the *B flat minor Sonata*. He has plenty of sweep and grandeur and an appealing freshness, ardour and, when required, tenderness. He is accorded an excellent balance by the engineers.

Shelley then on CDA 66198 gives us the original version of Op. 36 and his performances here show unfailing sensitivity, intelligence and good taste. This is available special order in Hyperion's Archive Service.

Freddy Kempf has a real feeling for this composer, and the authority and technical prowess to go with it. He is also a narrative pianist – from the very beginning he has you in the palm of his hand. The *Second Sonata* in the original, 1913 version is as good as any now before the public, and the *Etudes-tableaux* come off equally well. Vivid, realistic piano sound.

A pianist in the grand tradition. **Denis Matsuev** has all the command and bravura this repertoire calls for. But the competition is strong and this collection would not be an obvious first choice.

Piano Sonata 2, Op. 36 (rev. 1931); Preludes, Op. 3/2; Op. 23/1–2, 4–5, 10; Op. 32/2, 12; Siren, Op. 21/5; Margaritiki, Op. 38/3. Transcriptions: Scherzo from 'A Midsummer Night's Dream' (MENDELSSOHN); Flight of the Bumblebee (RIMSKY-KORSAKOV); Lullaby (TCHAIKOVSKY)

☷ ✿ **** EMI 5 57943-2. Trpčeski

Simon Trpčeski's dazzling Rachmaninov recital reaffirms the arrival on the piano scene of a young keyboard master. His is an exciting talent, and this is wonderful Rachmaninov playing, expertly recorded in Potton Hall, Suffolk.

Recitals

A Window in Time: Barcarolle, Op.10/3; Elégie; Mélodie, Op. 3/3; Etudes-tableau, Op. 39/4 & 6; Humoresque, Op. 10/6; Polinchinelle; Polka de V. R.; Preludes, Op. 3/2 & 4; Op. 23/5; Lilacs.
Transcriptions: RIMSKY-KORSAKOV: *Flight of the Bumblebee.* KREISLER: *Liebesfreud; Liebeslied.* SCHUBERT: *Wohin?* BIZET: *L'arlésienne: Minuet.* MUSSORGSKY: *Sorochinsky Fair: Hopak.* TRAD.: *Star-Spangled Banner*

🔊 🌣 ******** Telarc CD 80489. Rachmaninov

Wayne Stahnke has recreated these recordings made by **Rachmaninov** between 1919 and 1929, using Ampico music rolls, only he has used modern computer technology via a Bösendorfer piano, then re-recorded digitally. The realism and sense of the composer's presence is amazing. There is no problem here about catching the most varied and subtle rubato or variations of dynamic, and in a transcription like the *Flight of the Bumblebee* the bravura is electrifying. *Lilacs* is captivating in its nuances of colour and Bizet's *Minuet* delicately entrancing. The freedom of style in the two Kreisler transcriptions, and indeed the famous *Prelude in C sharp minor*, which opens the programme dramatically, is remarkable. Needless to say the sound of the piano itself is very real and three-dimensional. Even after reading these comments we guarantee a suprise when you hear the disc itself!

VOCAL MUSIC

Songs

*** Chan. 9451. Rodgers, Popescu, Naoumenko, Leiferkus, Shelley

Fluent in Russian, **Joan Rodgers** with her richly expressive voice makes a perfect interpreter of Rachmaninov songs, ideally partnered by the pianist, **Howard Shelley**. This generous selection of those for soprano ranges through the whole of the composer's songwriting career up to his exile from Russia in 1917, when in rejection of his roots he stopped completely. Loveliest of the songs is the extended wordless *Vocalise*, here set against its neighbour in Op. 34, the dramatic song, *Dissonance*. Most distinctive are the six forward-looking songs, Op. 38, to words by symbolist poets.

The Bells, Op. 35

🔊 🌣 ******* DG 471 029-2. Mescheriakov, Larin, Chernov, Moscow State Ch., Russian Nat. O, Pletnev – TANEYEV: *John of Damascus* *******

Ⓜ ******* Telarc CD 80363. Fleming, Dent, Ledbetter, Atlanta Ch. & SO, Shaw – ADAMS: *Harmonium* *******

From **Pletnev** comes a performance and recording that shows *The Bells* in an entirely new light. He has his finger on the composer's pulse and always has special insights to bring to his music. He goes beyond the music's vivid colours and lush sonorities, and without in any way indulging in over-characterization gets singing and playing of impressive quality, much subtlety and intensity. The recording is first class.

The late **Robert Shaw** conducts a colourfully expansive performance of Rachmaninov's cantata. All three soloists are impressive and if **Renée Fleming**, who sings beautifully, is not especially Slavonic, in the closing Lento lugubre the baritone, **Victor Ledbetter**, catches the darkly expressive mood admirably.

6 Choruses for Women's Voices, Op. 15

*** Chan. 10311. Russian State Symphony Cappella & SO, Polyansky – SCRIABIN: *Symphony 1* *******

The *Choruses* for children's or women's voices are as appealing as they are demanding, the most haunting being the Lermontov setting, *The pine tree*, and *Dreaming waves*, both of which cast a distinct spell. Collectors attracted to this CD need not hesitate.

Liturgy of St John Chrysostom, Op. 31

Ⓝ Ⓑ ******* Hyp. Helios CDH 55318. Corydon Singers, Best

Rachmaninov's *Liturgy of St John Chrysostom*, written in 1910, is an even fuller setting than Tchaikovsky's of 1878, and one can be in no doubt that the work's powerful expressive feeling has an underlying deep spirituality. The fine Hyperion account is immensely stimulating, and very well recorded and documented. However, the **Corydons** curiously omit the prayer dialogue which is the centrepiece of the *Cherubic Hymn*. If you have already succumbed to the *Vespers*, you won't be disappointed with *St John Chrysostom Liturgy*.

3 Russian Songs, Op. 41

*** Warner 2564 61992-2. Latvian Ch., Nordic SO, Tali – SIBELIUS: *The Wood-Nymph*; TUUR: *Zeitraum; Action, Passion, Illusion* *******

These glorious songs were composed for Stokowski and the Philadelphia Orchestra, who gave the first performance in 1928. They are sung by these Baltic forces with feeling, though memories of Kondrashin's full-blooded, intoxicating account from the mid-1960s are not banished. But we are not spoilt for choice in this repertoire, and the enterprising coupling is well worth the money.

Vespers, Op. 37

🔊 🌣 Ⓜ ******* HM Chant du Monde RUS 788050. St Petersburg Capella, Chernuchenko

Ⓑ ******* Virgin 3 91375-2. Swedish R. Ch., Kaljuste

*(*) Hyp. CDA 66460. Corydon Singers, Best

**(*) EMI 5 56752-2. King's College Ch., Cleobury

Rachmaninov's *Vespers* – more correctly the '*All-night Vigil*' – rank not only among his most soulful and intensely powerful music but are also the finest of all Russian choral works. The **St Petersburg Capella** offers singing of an extraordinarily rapt intensity. The dynamic range is enormous, the perfection of ensemble and blend and the sheer beauty of tone such as to exhaust superlatives. The recording does them justice and is made in a suitably atmospheric acoustic.

Under **Tönu Kaljuste** the **Swedish Radio Choir's** account of the *Vespers* shows that they have lost nothing of their sensitivity and command of sonority. They can produce a wonderful range of colour, from the darkest to the most luminous. Their Russian sounds totally authentic too.

Though **Matthew Best's** British choir, the **Corydon Singers**, lacks the dark timbres associated with Russian choruses and though the result could be weightier and more biting, theirs is still a most beautiful performance, very well sung and recorded in an atmospheric, reverberant setting.

It also makes a moving experience having the Anglican tradition, as ideally represented by the choir of **King's College, Cambridge**, meeting the Russian Orthodox tradition. Against the warm acoustic of King's College Chapel, beauty and refinement are the keynotes.

OPERA

(i) *Aleko*; (ii) *Francesca da Rimini*; (iii) *The Miserly Knight*

⊶ Ⓑ *** DG Trio 477 041-2 (3). Levitsky, Kotscherga, von Otter; (i; ii) Guleghina, Leiferkus; (ii; iii) Larin, Aleksashkin; (iii) Chernov, Caley, Gothenburg SO, Järvi

Aleko (based on Pushkin) is rather like a Russian-flavoured *Cavalleria rusticana*, with the hero murdering his unfaithful sweetheart and her lover, but musically it brings echoes of Borodin, notably in evocative choruses like Polovtsian dances. Distinctive Rachmaninov fingerprints are few, but the result is most attractive, particularly in a performance like this, ideally cast, with **Sergei Leiferkus** a commanding Aleko and **Neeme Järvi** a warmly persuasive conductor.

Francesca da Rimini is encumbered by an unsatisfactory libretto by Modest Tchaikovsky, but there is some glorious music and some fine singing from **Maria Guleghina** as Francesca and **Sergei Leiferkus** as Lanciotto Malatesta, the jealous husband. **Sergei Larin** makes a convincing Paolo, and the **Gothenburg Orchestra** and **Chorus** again respond magnificently to Neeme Järvi. The recording quality is quite outstanding.

The Miserly Knight, to a Pushkin text, contrasts the old knight, whose devotion to gold is total, and his son, who eyes his father's fortune enviously. The famous soliloquy, arguably Rachmaninov's finest dramatic scena, is powerfully done by **Sergei Aleksashkin**, who succeeds in winning us over to the Knight. **Sergei Larin** is hardly less convincing as his son, Albert. The outstanding recording and the fine orchestral playing make this a most desirable set, apart from the lack of texts and translations.

The Miserly Knight (DVD version)

⊶ ✪ **** Opus Arte **DVD** oA 0919D. Leiferkus, Berkeley-Steele, Mikhailov, Voynarowsky, Schagidullin, LPO, Jurowski (Producer: Annabel Arden; V/D: James Whitbourn)

Visually this DVD of *The Miserly Knight* is sumptuous, musically it is superlative. Composed in 1906 for Chaliapin, this production has a magnificent successor in **Sergei Leiferkus**, who dominates the stage. Apart from his magnificent voice and compelling acting, he has tremendous presence. It is difficult to find any flaw with the other members of the cast either, and **Vladimir Jurowksi** gets a thoroughly idiomatic

sonority from the **London Philharmonic**. The production is a fine one, and the camera direction is equally distinguished. There is an illustrated synopsis on the disc as well as interviews with those taking part in the production. Recommended with enthusiasm.

(i) *Monna Vanna* (incomplete opera: Act I, orch. Buketoff); (ii) *Piano Concerto 4* (original version)

**(*) Chan. 8987. (i) Milnes, McCoy, Walker, Karoustos, Thorsteinsson, Blythe; (ii) Black; Iceland SO, Buketoff

Monna Vanna is the fragment of an opera based on Maeterlinck. **Igor Buketoff**, who knew the composer, has rescued this Act I score and orchestrated it very sensitively to make an interesting curiosity. In its ripely romantic manner the writing has lyrical warmth and flows freely, thrusting home climactic moments. Buketoff's performance with the **Iceland Symphony** is warmly convincing, but the singing is flawed, with **Sherrill Milnes**, as Monna Vanna's jealous husband, standing out from an indifferent team, otherwise thintoned and often wobbly. Buketoff's resurrection of the original score of the *Fourth Piano Concerto* is rather more expansive than the text we know. **William Black** is the powerful soloist, though the piano sound, unlike that of the orchestra, lacks weight.

RAMEAU, Jean Philippe
(1683–1764)

Anacréon: Suite; Daphnis et Eglé: Suite

ⒷⒷ *** Naxos 8.553746. Capella Savaria, Térey-Smith

The *Suite* from *Anacréon* is essentially lighthearted music, particularly vivid in its scoring, piquantly using sopranino recorders, notably in the *Premier et deuxième air vif*, the infectious *Premier et deuxième tambourin*, but even more strikingly in the penultimate *Bacchanales*. The *Suite* from *Daphnis et Eglé* is much longer and more varied including a gracious *Sarabande très tendre*, a *Gigue*, a *Gavotte*, a touching *Musette* and a sprightly *Contredanse très vive* to end. The **Capella Savaria**, using period instruments with fair panache, play all this music with considerable finesse and much spirit, and they are very well recorded.

Les Boréades (suite of dances); *Le Naissance d'Osiris: Suite*

ⒷⒷ **(*) Naxos 8.553388. Capella Savaria, Térey-Smith

The two suites on the second disc from **Capella Savaria** are also inventive, but, with a few exceptions, the various dances and interludes are less ear-tickling than those on the companion CD. The playing is lively and robust, with plenty of colour (including the use of horns in *Les Boréades*).

Dardanus (orchestral suite); *Platée* (orchestral suite)

Ⓜ *** RCA 74321 93580-2. Philh. Bar. O, McGegan

McGegan offers rather less music from *Dardanus* than Gardiner on his deleted Erato CD, but this makes room for the more extended suite from *Platée*, a *'ballet bouffon'* dating from 1745, written as an entertainment at a royal wedding. McGegan and his period-instrument orchestra are if anything more crisply resilient than Gardiner and not a whit less graceful. The music for *Platée* has plenty of character and charm and, like *Dardanus*, ends with a memorable *Chaconne* for which – as it is interrupted in the ballet – McGegan provides a concert ending.

Dardanus: Suite; Les Indes galantes: Suite

(BB) *** DHM/BMG 05472 77420-2. Coll. Aur.

Any abrasiveness here deriving from the use of original instruments is countered by the generous acoustics of the Cedernsaal in Schloss Kirchheim. But the playing has both life and elegance and the sound, though warm and full, is by no means bland: the flutes and oboes (and trumpets in *Les Indes galantes*) bring plenty of added colour. The selection from *Les Indes galantes* is shorter than that provided by McGegan, but many will welcome the coupling with *Dardanus*. At super-bargain price this is very recommendable.

Ballet music: Les Fêtes d'Hébé; Hippolyte et Aricie

⊕ *** Erato 3984 26129-2. Les Arts Florissants, Christie – M.-A. CHARPENTIER: *La Descente d'Orphée aux Enfers*, etc. ***

This is all delightfully fresh and inventive music and Rameau's scoring is ever-resourceful and as presented here constantly sparkling and ear-tickling. Most entertaining and beautifully recorded.

Hippolyte et Aricie (orchestral suites)

(B) *** DHM/BMG 74321 935542. La Petite Bande, Sigiswald Kuijken

All the orchestral music from *Hippolyte et Aricie* is here, with a long introductory Prologue and a section for each of the five Acts. The melodic invention is fresh and its orchestral presentation ingenious. **Sigiswald Kuijken** draws delightful results from his ensemble.

Les Indes galantes (orchestral suites)

(B) *** HM (ADD) HMA 1951130. Chapelle Royale O, Herreweghe

Besides the harpsichord arrangements listed below, Rameau also arranged his four 'concerts' of music from *Les Indes galantes* for orchestra. The result makes nearly three-quarters of an hour of agreeable listening, especially when played so elegantly – and painlessly – on original instruments, and very well recorded (in 1984) by Harmonia Mundi.

Naïs; Le Temple de la gloire (orchestral suites)

⊕ **** HM HMU 907121. Philh. Bar. O, McGegan

There is much delightful music here and the playing by the **Philharmonia Baroque Orchestra** has ravishing finesse, showing original instruments at their most persuasively delicate, textures always transparent; the ear is continually beguiled by this warm and polished playing, beautifully recorded. A quite lovely disc.

Pygmalion (Acte de ballet); Le Temple de la Gloire (excerpts); Air gay. Grands Motets: Deus noster refugium; In convertendo, Dominus; Quam dilecta tabernacula

(N) (BB) *** Virgin 2CD 5 22027-2 (2). Soloists, including, Fouchécourt, Piau, Gens, Le Concert Spirituel, Niquet

Pygmalion falls in love with a female statue he has sculpted. The statue is then (by courtesy of Venus) brought to life by that very love – a moment of sheer orchestral magic in Rameau's delightful score. The Virgin version is robustly operatic, immediately obvious in the Overture, with its boldly repeated notes, superbly articulated which may (or may not) have been intended by Rameau to simulate the sculptor's chisel. **Jean-Paul Fouchécourt** gives a strong characterization of Pygmalion and, apart from **Sandrine Piau** as the statue, her two female colleagues are suitably histrionic. The excerpts from *Le Temple de la Gloire* are quite brief (about 8 minutes). For the reissue, the coupling is three of Rameau's most impressive Grands Motets, beautifully sung with refined accompaniments. *Deus noster refugium* is a colourful setting of Psalm 46 while *Quam dilecta tabernacula* opens with a particularly lovely soprano solo, pure yet sensuous, followed by an impressive fugue. *In convertendo, Dominus* is an even more complex setting of Psalm 126 with great variety between the movements and an interpolation from Psalm 69 as the fifth movement.

Une Symphonie imaginaire

*** DG **SACD** 477 557-8; CD 474 514-2. Les Musiciens du Louvre, Minkowski

This 'imaginary' symphony is based on Rameau's theatre music; the result is a highly entertaining suite of dance movements, rather in the tradition of Beecham's Handel suites, but with somewhat more authentic orchestrations! Minkowski has selected some obvious highlights, including an orchestrated version of the famous *La Poule* , plus many of the dance numbers which we have enjoyed from complete opera recordings. No less impressive is the beauty of many of the slow numbers – the *Air gracieux* from *La Naissance d'Osiris* and the *Air Tendre* from *Les Fêtes d'Hébé* are hauntingly beautiful, Minkowski directs this delightful Rameau concoction with Gallic brilliance and elegance, all caught in exceptionally vivid sound.

CHAMBER MUSIC

Pièces de clavecin en concert 1–5

(B) **** HM Musique d'abord HMA 195 1418. Rousset, Terakado, Uemura

The instrumental *Pièces de clavecin* usually include a flute, but they are equally valid in the alternative format on Harmonia Mundi with baroque violin and viola da gamba. The playing is attractively spirited and rhythmically buoyant; the effect with period instruments brings a slightly abrasive edge at times, but not disagreeably so. The star here is **Christophe Rousset**, whose very imaginative contribution lights up this music-making. The recording is realistic and the balance excellent. At bargain price, well worth considering.

KEYBOARD MUSIC

Music for Harpsichord: Book I (1706); Pièces de clavecin (1724); Nouvelles Suites de pièces de clavecin (c. 1728); 5 Pièces (1741); La Dauphine (1747)

(M) *** CRD 35112 (2). Pinnock (harpsichord)

Trevor Pinnock chose a mellow instrument here, making his stylish, crisply rhythmic performances even more attractive. The second disc includes *La Dauphine*, the last keyboard piece which Rameau wrote, brilliantly performed. Pinnock is restrained in the matter of ornamentation, but his direct manner is both eloquent and stylish. The harpsichord is of the French type and is excellently recorded.

Pièces de clavecin, Book I: Suite in A min. (1706); Suites in E min.; D min. (1724, rev. 1731)

*** Chan. 0659. Yates (harpsichord)

Sophie Yates gives us Book I complete and plays it very appealingly indeed. Her ornamentation has flair and she is especially winning in the named pieces (notably the delightful *Vénétienne* in the *A minor suite* and the cascading *La Joyeuse* in the *D minor*). She uses a copy by Andrew Garlick of a 1749 Goujon harpsichord which has a most attractive palette, and she is very well recorded.

Pièces de clavecin: Suites in A min.; E min.; G min.

**** Hyp. CDA 67597. Hewitt (piano)

Angela Hewitt here moves forward from Bach to Rameau and plays as engagingly and spontaneously as ever. Her performances are stylish but totally pianistic, and her full, rich palette of colour is made apparent by the warmth of the hall acoustic which some ears may resist as being a shade too opulent.

Pièces de clavecin: Suite in E min.; Nouvelles Suites de Pièces de clavecin (1738): Suite in A min.; La Poule; L'Enharmonique; L'Egyptienne

⊕— **** Avie AV 2056. Trevor Pinnock (harpsichord)

Pinnock has already recorded three discs of Rameau's harpsichord suites for CRD. But this generous (80-minute) collection is played on a particularly attractive, authentic, two-manual instrument, built in Paris in 1764 and modified by Taskin 20 years later. Pinnock opens with a dazzling bravura piece called *Les Cyclopes* which gives the disc its title. The recital closes with the famous clucking *La Poule* and the hardly less characterful *L'Enharmonique* and *L'Egyptienne*, all from the *Nouvelles Pièces*. Altogether a most refreshing collection, and the recording gives the harpsichord splendid presence.

Suite de clavecin in E min. (1724)

(BB) *** HM Solo HMS 926018. Christie (harpsichord)

Rameau's *E minor Suite* is one of his most inventive from the bursting birdsong of *Le Rappel des oiseaux* to the charming

portrait of *La Villageoise*, while the penultimate movement, a tender *Musette en rondeau*, is splendidly contrasted with the rumbustious closing *Tambourin*. **William Christie** plays the whole suite with infectious spontaneity and in fine style, and his Goujon-Swanen harpsichord is vividly recorded.

In Convertendo (motet; DVD version) (with Pièces de clavecin en concert)

*** Opus Arte **DVD** OA 0956D. Nicolas Rivenq, Sophie Daneman, Jeffrey Thompson, Olga Pitarch, Les Arts Florissants, William Christie

In Convertendo is an early motet, written in 1718 and a setting of Psalm CXXVI. Its finest numbers are the first, an eloquent counter-tenor solo, and the poignant chorus *Neuntes et flebant*, full of restrained emotion and arguably the finest movement in all Rameau's church music. Also included here are the *Pièces de clavecin en concert*: *La Timide*, *La Pouplinière* and *La Rameau*, as well as an illuminating documentary in which **William Christie** takes a leading part, together with **John Eliot Gardiner** and some distinguished French scholars, **Sylvie Boissou** and **Andrei Serban**. (The only tiresome device is the dramatic representation of Diderot and Rameau's nephew.) Strongly recommended.

OPERA-BALLET AND OPERA

Les Boréades (complete)

⊕— (M) *** Erato (ADD) 2292 45572-2 (3). Smith, Rodde, Langridge, Aler, Lafont, Monteverdi Ch., E. Bar. Sol. Gardiner

Though the story – involving the followers of Boreas, the storm god – is highly artificial, the music, involving many crisp and brief dances and arias, is as vital and alive as anything Rameau ever wrote. **Gardiner** here directs an electrifying performance with generally first-rate singing, except that **Jennifer Smith's** upper register, in the central role of Alphise, Queen of Baltria, is not sweet. Chorus and orchestra are outstanding and the recording excellent. The synopsis is not cued. However, the set is very welcome.

Castor et Pollux (complete)

⊕— *** HM HMC 901435/7. Crook, Corréas, Mellon, Gens, Schirrer, Brua, Piau, Les Arts Florissants Ch. & O, Christie

Christie's performance consistently benefits from the dramatic timing, not least in the fluently alert and idiomatic exchanges in recitative, as well as in the broad, expressive treatment of set numbers like Telaire's lament, *Tristes apprets*, beautifully sung by **Agnès Mellon**. With such fine sopranos as **Véronique Gens** and **Sandrine Piau** in relatively small roles, the cast has no weakness. **Howard Crook** has the clear tenor needed for the role of Castor (who appears very late in the drama), with **Jérôme Corréas** a stylish Pollux. The sound is fresh and immediate and has plenty of body, with military percussion beautifully caught.

Dardanus (complete)

(M) **(*) Erato (ADD) 4509 95312-2 (2). Gautier, Eda-Pierre, von

Stade, Devlin, Teucer, Soyer, van Dam, Paris Op. Ch. & O, Leppard

Though the French chorus and orchestra (using modern instruments) here fail to perform with quite the rhythmic resilience that **Leppard** usually achieves on record, the results are refreshing and illuminating, helped by generally fine solo singing and naturally balanced (if not brilliant) 1980 analogue recording, smoothly transferred to CD, with the choral sound quite vivid. **José van Dam** as Ismenor copes superbly with the high tessitura, and **Christiane Eda-Pierre** is a radiant Venus. Well documented and well worth exploring.

La Guirlande; Zéphyre

*** Erato 8573 85774-2 (2). Daneman, Méchaly, Agnew, Bazola, Ockende, Decaudaveine, WDR Capella Coloniensis, Les Arts Florissants Ch. & O, Christie

La Guirlande appeared in 1751, but *Zéphyre*, telling the story of the Wind God, infatuated with the wood nymph Cloris, seems never to have been performed in Rameau's lifetime. Though it is more limited in scale, in having only soprano soloists, it is even more inventive musically, with a sequence of striking numbers, as when the goddess, Diana, briefly appears at the denouement, accompanied by braying horn-fanfares.

The duet which follows, with the voices of Zephyr and Cloris interweaving, is also one of the loveliest in this double bill. Not that *La Guirlande* is at all lacking in invention, with extended monologues and dialogues punctuated by brief set numbers not just for the soloists but for the chorus. In all this **Christie** and his team are at their most inspired, consistently fresh and lively; this is a delightful set, giving new perspectives on the composer.

Hippolyte et Aricie (complete)

🎵 *** Erato (ADD) 0630 15517-2 (3). Padmore, Panzarella, Hunt, Naouri, James, Les Arts Florissants, Christie

Christie bounces rhythms infectiously and allows himself flexible phrasing without undermining the classical purity of style. Though **Anna-Maria Panzarella** as Aricie is not golden in tone, she is fresh and bright, responding immediately to Christie's timing which consistently seems geared to stage presentation, with a conversational quality given to passages of recitative. **Mark Padmore** is an ardent Hippolyte and **Lorraine Hunt** a deeply tragic Phèdre, with **Eirian James** a warm Diana. The Erato sound is warm and immediate.

Les Indes Galantes (DVD version)

🎵 **** Opus Arte DVD OA 0923 D (2). Panzarella, Agnew, Berg, Croft, Petibon, Les Arts Florissants Ch. & O, Christie (V/D: Thomas Grimm)

Described as an Opera-Ballet in four Acts, *Les Indes Galantes* was Rameau's biggest stage success in his own lifetime, and one can understand why from this spectacular production, with the sort of lavish effects and movement that would have delighted 18th-century audiences. Act II, set in Peru at the time of the Incas, brings the most striking spectacle with the eruption of a volcano – cue for the backcloth of Andean

peaks to wobble and sway amid fiery lighting – for which Rameau devises vividly descriptive music. His inspiration is at white heat throughout, with **William Christie** and a large and stylish team of singers and players revelling in each number. Outstanding among the soloists are **Nathan Berg** as Huascar (crushed by a boulder from the sky after his Act II aria), **Anna Maria Panzarella** as Emilie and **Paul Agnew** as Valere, with **Joao Fernandez** memorably in drag as Bellone. Extras include a feature about Rameau with Christie, Serban and the choreographer, Bianca Li, among those interviewed.

Zoroastre (complete; DVD Version)

*** Opus Arte DVD OA04230 (2). Dahlin, Alexiev, Bundgaard, Panzarella, Drottningholm Court Ch. & O, Les Talens Lyriques, Rousset (Director: Pierre Audi)

After so many opera productions updated to modern dress, it is refreshing to have a thoroughly traditional production, set in the beautifully restored Drottningholm Court Theatre. First heard in 1749 and drastically reviewed in 1756, *Zoroastre*, like *The Magic Flute*, presents the conflict of good and evil, with good represented by Zoroastre and evil by Abramante and Amelite. Casting in this production is first rate, with clean, firm voices the rule and with the dances, so important in Rameau operas, perfectly integrated. **Christophe Rousset** is the stylish conductor. A first-class set in every way.

Zoroastre (complete; CD version)

🎵 *** Erato 0927 43182-2 (3). Padmore, Berg, Mechaly, Panzarella, Les Arts Florissants, Christie

Zoroastre is described as one of the composer's most uncompromising music-dramas. Although the central character is the ancient Persian philosopher and founder of the Magian religion, the themes are the very human ones of love, jealousy and vengeance. Christie directs a lively, beautifully paced performance, helped by a first-rate team of soloists. Standing out is **Mark Padmore** in the title-role, with his natural high tenor totally unstrained and perfectly contrasted with the darkly sinister Abramante of **Nathan Berg**. **Gaelle Mechaly** is ideally bright and agile as Amelite, and although **Anna Maria Panzarella** too often characterizes the malicious Erinice by attacking notes from below, her voice, too, is bright and agile. The third disc gives as a supplement the eight dances and one *Ariette* omitted in the main performance. First-rate sound.

RAMIREZ, Ariel (born 1921)

Missa Criolla; Navidad Nuestra; Missa Luba

🎵 (BB) *** Naxos 8.557542. Rheams, Melendez, Sacin, Talamante, Washington Choral Arts Soc. Chamber Ch. & Ens., Holt (with Father Guido HAAZEN: *Missa Luba*)

The *Missa Criolla* draws on Argentinian folk tunes and idioms, but in most respects is wholly original. The Mass is written for tenor celebrant, chorus, percussion, Andean instruments, including a notched flute or *quena*, a *charango* (small guitar), double bass and percussion, with a pair of tom-toms in the *Credo*. This is genuine crossover music of real quality.

The *Navidad Nuestra* ('Our Nativity') is a Creole tableau in six episodes (with a Spanish text by Félix Luna), telling the Christian Nativity story from the annunciation to the birth of Jesus, the venue relocated to northern Argentina, and ending with the family's flight. Ramirez again bases his music on dances and songs from the Argentinian folk tradition, this time even more unashamedly popular: the second part of the work, *La Peregrinación* ('The Pilgrimage'), has become famous on the hit parade.

The music of the *Missa Luba* comes from the Belgian Congo, and was arranged by a missionary, Father Guido Haazen, from the improvisations of the local singers and musicians, so the accompaniment consists entirely of local percussion sounds which create the rhythmic framework for the poplar melodies.

RATHAUS, Karol (1895–1954)

Symphonies 1; 2, Op. 7; 3, Op. 50

*** CPO 777 031-2. Brandenburgisches Staats O, Frankfurt, Yinon

The Polish-born Karol Rathaus enjoyed a short-lived success in Germany during the 1920s. The *First Symphony* was included in Decca's 'Entartete Music' series and now comes with its two companions of 1933 and 1943 in dedicated performances by the Frankfurt orchestra. Rathaus remained something of a name in the immediate post-war years but he was rarely played or recorded. Like Ernst Toch, he ended his days revered as a distinguished teacher rather than as an eminent composer. The idiom is far from 'atonal' as the anti-Semitic 1930s press had maintained: there are hints of his teacher Schreker and of Mahler, but the overall impression is of a highly gifted and inventive composer unafraid of dissonance but working well within the discipline of classical tonality. Music very much of its time, like a Teutonic Honegger, perhaps, whose argument carries you along with conviction. It is powerful and often disturbing music, which is well worth investigating, particularly in these dedicated performances. Good sound.

RAUTAVAARA, Einojuhani
(born 1928)

Adagio Celeste (for string orchestra); Book of Visions; Symphony 1

8—, **** Ondine SACD ODE 1064-5. Belgian Nat. O, Franck

This is recorded in spacious four-channel SACD, which admirably suits Rautavaara's rich orchestral textures, and immediately so in the sumptuously powerful string cantilena which opens the *First Symphony*, written in two movements in 1955, but with a third added in 2003. Rautavaara acknowledged his debt to Shostakovich in this work, partly because of its string writing, but also because of the 'grotesque and ironic' Scherzo which closes the work.

The *Adagio Celeste* then follows. Inspired by a poem by Lassi Nummi which begins, 'Then, that night, when you want to love me in the deep of night, wake me', it makes an ecstatic interlude between the *Symphony* and the imaginatively scored four chapters of the *Book of Visions*, each telling a *Tale*: darkly of *Night*, feverishly of *Fire*, warmly and sensuously of *Love*, and dramatic and apprehensive in *Fate*. The performances throughout are superbly played by this fine orchestra and, whether using two or four speakers, the sound is richly opulent, and in the demonstration bracket for its superb recording of the strings.

Anadyomene (Adoration of Aphrodite); (i) Flute Concerto; Op. 63; (ii) On the Last Frontier

*** Ondine ODE 921-2. Helsinki PO, Segerstam; with (i) Gallois; (ii) Finnish Philharmonic Ch.

Anadyomene or the *Adoration of Aphrodite* comes from 1969, and is highly atmospheric and compelling. The *Flute Concerto*, subtitled *Dances with the Winds*, employs bass flute, alto flute and piccolo. It is one of Rautavaara's most imaginative and resourceful scores, and its many hurdles are effortlessly cleared by the distinguished French soloist. *On the Last Frontier*, a fantasy for chorus and orchestra, is inspired by Edgar Allan Poe's description of Antarctica, at the end of *The Narrative of Arthur Gordon Pym*. Vaughan Williams occasionally comes to mind in its pages. All three pieces are expertly performed by these Helsinki forces under **Leif Segerstam** and superbly recorded.

Angels and Visitations; (i) Violin Concerto. Isle of Bliss

8—, ✿ **** Ondine ODE 881-2. (i) Oliveira; Helsinki PO, Segerstam

Rautavaara's wholly original *Violin Concerto* is hauntingly accessible and grips the listener completely. It moves from an ethereal opening cantilena, through a series of colourful events and experiences until, after a final burst of incandescent energy, it makes a sudden but positive homecoming. The lively opening of the *Isle of Bliss* is deceptive, for the music centres on a dreamy, sensual romanticism and creates a rich orchestral tapestry with a sense of yearning ecstasy, yet overall it has a surprisingly coherent orchestral structure. *Angels and Visitations* is close to the visions of William Blake and (as the composer tells us) brings a sense of 'holy dread'. The extraordinary opening evokes a rustling of angels' wings, which is then malignantly transformed, becoming a ferocious multitude of bumblebees. It is a passage of real imaginative power, in some ways comparable to the storm sequence in Sibelius's *Tapiola*. **Elmar Oliveira** is the inspired soloist in the *Violin Concerto*, floating his line magically and serenely in the opening *Tranquillo* and readily encompassing the work's adventurous shifts of colour and substance. **Segerstam** provides a shimmering backing and directs a committed and persuasively spontaneous orchestral response throughout all three works. The recording is superbly balanced, spacious and vivid in detail.

Angels and Visitations; Symphony 7 (Angel of Light)

(BB) *** Naxos 8.555814. RSNO, Koivula

The **Royal Scottish National Orchestra** under **Hannu Koivula** are vividly recorded and have impressive body and refinement, and, while this does not displace the BIS version of *Angels and Visitations*, which offers two couplings, for those unwilling to make the outlay, this Naxos performance offers a very desirable three-star alternative, including a fine performance of the *Seventh Symphony*.

Cantus arcticus (Concerto for Birds & Orchestra), Op. 61; (i) Piano Concerto, Op. 45; Symphony 3, Op. 20

⊕ (BB) *** Naxos 8.554147. (i) Mikkola; RSNO, Lintu

The *Cantus arcticus* (1972) uses taped Arctic bird-cries against an evocative orchestral background. The *Third Symphony* (1959–60) has genuine breadth and space. Rautavaara speaks of it as being 'freely constructed and emphatically tonal'. It has a strong feeling for nature. The later *Piano Concerto 1* (1969) has a certain neo-romantic feel to it. **Laura Mikkola** is a fervent exponent of it, and the **Royal Scottish National Orchestra** under **Hannu Lintu** play with real commitment and are well recorded.

(i) Harp Concerto; Symphony 8

⊕ **** Ondine ODE 978-2. (i) Nordmann; Helsinki PO, Segerstam

The *Concerto* (2001) is predominantly reflective and highly imaginative in its use of texture. In addition to the soloist, Rautavaara adds two harps in the orchestra in order, as he puts it, to create 'a really full and lush harp sound when needed'. The French soloist, **Marielle Nordmann**, a pupil of Lily Laskine, gives a performance of great distinction and subtlety of the *Eighth Symphony*. Rautavaara speaks of the musical growth of the *Eighth Symphony* as characterized by slow transformation, a strong narrative element and 'the generation of new, different aspects and perspectives from the same premises, the transformation of light and colour'. As always with this composer there is a strong feeling for nature. Perhaps the most haunting movement is the third, whose quiet radiance stays with the listener. Excellent playing from the **Helsinki Philharmonic** under **Leif Segerstam** and state-of-the-art recording.

Piano Concerto 3 (Gift of Dreams); Autumn Gardens

**** Ondine ODE 950-2. Ashkenazy, Helsinki PO

The *Third Piano Concerto* is predominantly meditative and unconcerned with conventional bravura. It gets its subtitle from a Baudelaire setting, *La Mort des pauvres*, which Rautavaara made in the late 1970s and in which the words '*le don des rêves*' appear. *Autumn Gardens*, from 1999, also has a dreamlike feel to it. The performances are exemplary and the recording is in the demonstration class. The disc also includes a conversation between Rautavaara and **Vladimir Ashkenazy**.

Symphonies 1–3

*** Ondine ODE 740-2. Leipzig RSO, Pommer

Einojuhani Rautavaara is a symphonist to be reckoned with. Ideas never outstay their welcome and there is a sense of inevitability about their development. Those with a taste for Shostakovich or Simpson should find these pieces congenial. Good performances by the **Leipzig Radio Orchestra** under **Max Pommer** and very decent recorded sound too.

Symphony 6 (Vincentiana); (i) Cello Concerto, Op. 41

*** Ondine ODE 819-2. (i) Ylönen; Helsinki PO, Pommer

The *Sixth Symphony* draws on material from the opera, *Vincent* (1985–7), based on the life of Van Gogh. There is, appropriately enough, no lack of colour, though the score tends to be both eclectic and amorphous. The orchestral scoring itself is quite sumptuous and there is no lack of incident. It comes with a much earlier and more cogently argued piece, the *Cello Concerto* of 1968, which is expertly played by **Marko Ylönen**. The recording is very impressive, well detailed and present, and is in the demonstration bracket.

Symphony 7 (Angel of Light); (i) Annunciations

*** Ondine ODE 869-2. (i) Jussila; Helsinki PO, Segerstam

Symphony 7; Cantus arcticus; (i) Dances with the Winds (Concerto for Flutes & Orchestra)

⊕ **** BIS CD 1038. (i) Alanko; Lahti SO, Vänskä

The *Seventh Symphony* is both powerful and atmospheric. There is a good deal of Sibelius in its first movement and there is a pervasive sense of nature. Rautavaara betrays some affinities with the minimalists but offers greater musical substance. *Annunciations* for organ, brass quintet, winds and percussion, written in 1976–7, strikes a more dissonant note but it is brilliant and well thought out. **Kari Jussila** is the virtuoso soloist, and the **Helsinki orchestra** under **Segerstam** are eminently well served by the Ondine engineers.

The BIS version of the *Seventh Symphony* is every bit as good as its Ondine competitor, both artistically and as a recording. The sound is pretty state-of-the-art, though its rival has the deeper perspective. But **Vänskä's** performance has impressive power and atmosphere; he keeps the music moving and casts the stronger spell. Both shorter pieces, the familiar *Cantus arcticus* and the *Dances with the Winds*, a concerto in which the solo flautist plays four members of the flute family, are from the 1970s, and these fine performances have appeared before in other couplings.

PIANO MUSIC

Etudes, Op. 42; Icons, Op. 6; Partita, Op. 34; Preludes, Op. 7; Piano Sonatas 1 (Christus und die Fischer), Op. 50; 2 (The Fire Sermon), Op. 64

⊕ (BB) *** Naxos 8.554292. Mikkola

These admirably lucid performances by **Laura Mikkola** fill an important gap. The *First Sonata* (*Christus und die Fischer*) comes from 1969, the same year as the *First Piano Concerto*, which this artist has also recorded with such success, and the *Second* (1970) is also most convincingly done. She is given first-class recorded sound.

VOCAL MUSIC

Ave Maria; Magnificat; Canticum Mariae Virginis; Missa Duodecanonica

*** Ondine ODE 935-2. Finnish R. Chamber Ch, Nuoranne

The *Ave Maria* (1957) for male voices and the *Missa Duodecanonica* (1963) for female voices are both serialist, albeit in much the same way as was Frank Martin at one time. The *Magnificat* of 1979, the first Finnish setting of the text, has dignity and eloquence. The singing of the **Finnish Radio Chamber Choir** under **Timo Nuoranne** has security of pitch, subtle colouring and purity of tone. Expert, well-balanced recording.

(i) Canción de nuestro tiempo; (ii) In the Shade of the Willow; (i; iii) True and False Unicorn

*** Ondine ODE 1020-2. (i) Kortekangas, Rissanen, Salomaa; (ii) Huhta; Finnish R. Chamber Ch.; (iii) with SO, Nuoranne

The setting of James Broughton's *True and False Unicorn* is a 45-minute work, often inventive and imaginative, and nearly always compelling, though the *Horn and Hounds* section with its quotations including 'God save the Queen' does not really come off. However, the writing is always effective and the Holstian opening of *Mon seul désir*, the closing section of the piece, is rather haunting. The other two pieces are for voices alone and exhibit much command of vocal resource and colour. The *Canción de nuestro tiempo*, to three Lorca poems, is highly inventive, and the Aleksis Kivi settings, *In the Shade of the Willow*, prove admirable vehicles for the virtuosity of the **Finnish Radio Chamber Choir** and their soloists.

Hymnus; Independence Fanfare; Octet for Winds; Playgrounds for Angels; A Requiem in our Time, Op. 3; A Soldier's Mass; Tarantara

*** Ondine ODE 957-2. Soloists, Finnish Brass Symphony, Lintu

A Requiem in our Time for brass and percussion put Rautavaara on the map. Rautavaara speaks of *A Soldier's Mass* (1968) as 'a companion work', although the forces involved are larger (it demands a full wind section) and the mood lighter. The *Octet for Winds* (1962) is mildly serial, but in no way inaccessible. Both the *Requiem* and the ingenious *Playgrounds for Angels*, the virtuoso piece written for the Philip Jones Brass Ensemble, are also available in a stunning BIS anthology by the German group, Brass Partout (BIS CD 1054) which is not easily eclipsed. The rest of the programme is not otherwise available: *Hymnus*, for trumpet and organ was written recently for the Wagner scholar and critic, Barry Millington; *Tarantara* is for solo trumpet and played brilliantly by **Pasi Pirinen**, as for that matter is the rest of the programme. The recording is of demonstration quality.

RAVEL, Maurice (1875–1937)

Alborada del gracioso; Une barque sur l'océan; Boléro; (i) Daphnis et Chloé (complete ballet);

L'Eventail de Jeanne: Fanfare; (ii) Introduction & Allegro for Harp, Flute, Clarinet & String Orchestra; Ma Mère l'Oye (complete ballet); Menuet antique; Pavane pour une infante défunte; Shéhérazade: Ouverture de féerie; Le Tombeau de Couperin; Trio in A min. (orch. Tortelier); Tzigane (for violin and orchestra); La Valse; Valses nobles et sentimentales; Song-cycles: (iii) Don Quichotte à Dulcinée; (iv) Shéhérazade

Ⓜ **(*) Chan. 10251X (4). Ulster O, Tortelier; with (i) Renaissance Singers, Belfast Philharmonic Soc.; (ii) Masters; (iii) Roberts; (iv) Finnie; (v) Tortelier (violin)

Tortelier's *Daphnis et Chloé* soon puts you under its spell: he conveys much of the sense of ecstasy and magic of this score and colours so richly hued and vivid that they belong to the world of the imagination rather than reality. Phrasing is sensitive, and there are some gorgeous sounds throughout.

Ma Mère l'Oye has a more balletic feel than usual, bringing out the affinities with *Daphnis et Chloé*. The exotic orchestration associated with *Laideronnette, Empress of the Pagodas* glitters vividly, while the lovely closing *Jardin féerique*, begins serenely before moving to a joyous climax. Tortelier's *Rapsodie espagnole* is not quite as gripping as some celebrated accounts, but it is highly atmospheric all the same.

Whether or not Ravel approved of full strings, the *Introduction and Allegro* loses some of its ethereal quality when given in this form, although the playing of the harpist, **Rachel Masters**, is impeccable. In Tortelier's own transcription of the *Piano Trio* although Tortelier's skill and musicianship are not in question, this transcription is not one to which many will want to return. Tortelier directs the *Tzigane* from the bow, as it were, and plays very well, and this and the performances of *Le Tombeau de Couperin*, *La Valse* and *Valses nobles* have plenty of appeal.

The *Ouverture de féerie* is impressive, as is **Linda Finnie's** account of the *Shéhérazade* song-cycle. No grumbles about **Stephen Roberts's** fine singing in the *Don Quichotte* songs, but overall this set has uneven appeal and will best suit those for whom outstanding recorded quality is paramount.

Alborada del gracioso; Une barque sur l'océan; Boléro; Daphnis et Chloé (Suite 2); L'Eventail de Jeanne: Fanfare; Menuet antique; Ma Mère l'Oye (complete); Pavane pour une enfante défunte; Rapsodie espagnole; Le Tombeau de Couperin; La Valse; Valses nobles et sentimentales

🔊 💠 **** Double Decca 460 214-2 (2). Montreal SO, Dutoit

Anyone beginning a Ravel collection, or coming fresh to most of this repertoire and willing to duplicate, will find this Double Decca unbeatable value, including as it does all the key orchestral works, though not the piano concertos. The orchestral playing is wonderfully sympathetic and the recording ideally combines atmospheric evocation with vividness. The balance is most musically judged and very realistic; indeed the sound remains in the demonstration class.

Alborada del gracioso; Une barque sur l'océan; Boléro; (i) Daphnis et Chloé (complete); Ma Mère

l'Oye (complete); *Menuet antique; Ouverture de féerie; Pavane pour une infante défunte; Rapsodie espagnole; Le Tombeau de Couperin; La Valse; Valses nobles et sentimentales*

🔑 (B) **** EMI (ADD) 5 00892-2 (3). O de Paris, Martinon; (i) with Paris Op. Ch.

Like his version of *Daphnis et Chloé*, **Martinon's** *Ma Mère l'Oye* is exquisite, among the finest ever put on record. Although the *Valses nobles et sentimentales* and *La Valse* do not eclipse the 1961 Cluytens versions (see below) and the present *La Valse* has a rather harsh climax, there is much ravishing delicacy of orchestral playing, notably in *Le Tombeau de Couperin* and the rare *Ouverture de féerie* (*Shéhérazade*). The sound is warm and luminously coloured and the refined virtuosity of the **Orchestre de Paris** is a constant source of delight. Excellent value.

(i) *Alborada de gracioso; Boléro;* (i–ii) *Piano Concerto in G;* (i–ii or iii) *Piano Concerto for the left hand* (2 versions); (i) *Daphnis et Chloé* (complete ballet); *Fanfare pour 'L'Éventail de Jeanne'; Ma Mère l'Oye;* also excerpt: (iv) *Le jardin féerique;* (i–ii) *Miroirs: La vallée des cloches* (orch. Grainger); *La valse;* (i; v) *Shéhérazade* (song cycle)

(BB) *** EMI (ADD/DDD) 5 14565-2 (5). (i) CBSO; (ii) with Ousset; (iii) Gavrilov, LSO; (iv) BPO; (v) Ewing; all cond. Rattle – DEBUSSY: *La Boîte à joujoux; Images; Jeux etc.* ***

There are few collections which offer two different versions of the same work, but here there are two performances of the *Left-hand Piano Concerto*: a fine account by **Cécile Ousset** (with the **CBSO**) and a dazzling one from **Gavrilov** (with the **LSO**), playing with effortless virtuosity and, when required, great sensitivity. Ousset, although combining vigour with delicacy, is rather less memorable in the *G major Concerto*. The shorter orchestral works, however, are nearly all distinctive and the CBSO has the advantage of outstandingly spacious recording. **Rattle** captures the lambent allure of Percy Grainger's orchestration of the last of the *Miroirs* and gives an equally glowing account of *Ma Mère l'Oye*, with delicately refined textures and the more exotic detail glittering amid the orchestral warmth. The lovely finale is then heard again, magically played by the **Berlin Philharmonic Orchestra**. *La valse* returns to the CBSO and sounds gorgeous too. At the beginning of the programme, **Maria Ewing's** *Shéhérazade* immediately follows Ravel's vivid *Fanfare*. The first song, *Asie*, is a performance of unbridled passion, matched in voluptuous intensity by Rattle and his players, so that *L'indifférent* ravishes in a more subtle manner, with the intensity simmering below the surface. But it is essentially a dramatic performance, and the shimmering *Alborada del gracioso* is well placed to follow on afterwards.

(i; ii) *Alborado del gracioso;* (i; iii) *Boléro;* (iv) *Piano Concerto in G;* (ii; v) *Daphnis et Chloé: Suite No. 2;* (vi) *Ma Mère l'Oye: Suite;* (ii; vii) *Pavane pour une infante défunte;* (vi) *La Valse;* (viii) *Introduction and Allegro;* (ix) *Gaspard de la nuit;* (x) *Shéhérazade*

(N) (BB) *** EMI (ADD) 237671-2 (2). (i) Karajan; (ii) O de Paris; (iii) BPO; (iv) Michelangeli, Philh. O, Gracis; (v) Munch; (vi) Toulouse O, Plasson; (vii) Martinon; (viii) Melos Ens.; (ix) Gavrilov; (x) Baker, New Philh. O, Barbirolli

Michelangeli's classic account of the *Piano Concerto in G* remains one of the top choices in this repertoire. The exquisite playing in the slow movement makes up for any deficiencies of dimensional balance. The **Melos Ensemble** give us a highly sensitive account of the *Introduction and Allegro*, almost as magical as their earlier Oiseau-Lyre version, while **Janet Baker** inspired **Barbirolli** to one of his most glowing performances in the atmospherically scored *Shéhérazade*. Few recordings have conveyed as much natural intensity as this, and the recording is warm to match. **Munch** is predictably impressive in the *Daphnis Suite*, and if **Plasson's** performances are not equally memorable, they are well played and idiomatic, while **Gavrilov** is on top form in *Gaspard*. **Karajan's** *Alborada* is a bit slow but full of atmosphere, and his *Boléro* is marvellously controlled and full of tension. **Martinon's** contribution of the *Pavane pour une infante défunte* is memorably poetic.

Alborada del gracioso; Boléro; Rapsodie espagnole; Le Tombeau de Couperin; La Valse

🔑 (M) **** EMI (ADD) 4 76859-2 [4 76860-2]. O de Paris (or, in *Boléro*, BPO), Karajan

🔑 (BB) *** RCA 74321 68015-2. Dallas SO, Mata

These are superb performances. The **Orchestre de Paris** responds splendidly to the conductor's sensuous approach to these scores, and only the saxophone-like quality of the French horns gives cause for doubt. The dynamic range is extremely wide and the acoustic resonant. There is no doubt about the mastery of *La Valse*, which is extremely fine, or the *Rapsodie espagnole*, the best account since Reiner's. The *Alborada* is a bit too slow; doubtless the reverberant acoustic prompted this and also brought a degree of mistiness in *pianissimo* detail (noticeably at the opening of *La Valse*). But the overall focus is impressive, and the climaxes expand excitingly. *Boléro* is superbly done.

In the late 1970s **Eduarda Mata** helped to build the **Dallas Orchestra** into a splendid band, and their excellence and his stylish conducting (helped by the splendid acoustics of the Dallas auditorium) was demonstrated by a series of outstanding Ravel recordings made in the early 1980s. The *Alborada* flashes, the *Rapsodie espagnole* shimmers and there is a balmy underlying patina of sensuous colour. Mata and his players are at their most impressive in *Le Tombeau de Couperin*, which has pleasing elegance and finesse and the expansive climaxes of *Boléro* and *La Valse* are very compelling. The recording has the most spectacular dynamic range and at bargain price this collection is most recommendable, standing up well to all the competition.

(i) *Alborado del gracioso; Boléro; Rapsodie espagnole; Le Tombeau de Couperin;* (ii) *Valses nobles et sentimentales*

(BB) **(*) Sony (ADD) SBK 48163. Phd; O, (i) Ormandy; (ii) Munch

Ormandy was a first-class Ravel conductor. These performances are eminently well worth the money at bargain price, even if the recording is not three-star by present-day standards.

Alborada del gracioso; (i) Daphnis et Chloé: Suites 1 & 2; Une barque sur l'océan; Menuet antique

(**(*)) Testament mono SBT 1238. French Nat. R. O, Cluytens; (i) with ch. – BIZET: La Jolie fille de Perth **(*); ROUSSEL: Le Festin de l'araignée ***

Cluytens's recording of these Ravel pieces is thoroughly idiomatic even if his later stereo versions sound better and are arguably superior artistically. The earlier versions come from 1953 and the Daphnis suites are unusual for that period in including the chorus. Une barque sur l'océan sounds eminently fresh though the later Conservatoire Orchestra version has the benefit of stereo. The coupling brings Le Festin de l'araignée, a magical account of Roussel's inspired score which has never been surpassed.

Alborada del gracioso; Daphnis et Chloé: Suite 2

➻—✿ (M) **** EMI 5 62746-2. Philh. O, Giulini – DEBUSSY: La Mer; Nocturnes. ****✿

Giulini's 1959 accounts of these two key works are not only among the most polished Ravel performances on record, but they are also richly sensuous, with the most refined detail and an exquisite feeling for atmosphere. The Alborada has great rhythmic flair and the sumptuous Kingsway Hall recordings reveal remarkable inner clarity as well as giving the orchestra a glowing overall bloom, which the CD transfer captures perfectly. The Debussy couplings are no less distinguished.

Alborada del gracioso; Daphnis et Chloé; Ma Mère l'Oye: Suite; Pavane pour une infante défunte; Rapsodie espagnole; Le Tombeau de Couperin; Valses nobles et sentimentales

(N)(***) Australian Decca Eloquence mono 442 8321 (2). SRO, Ansermet

Australian Decca have chosen to release **Ansermet's** much rarer mono recordings of Ravel's orchestral music which are, if anything, finer than the brilliantly recorded stereo remakes; for one thing, the orchestra is generally in better shape. The Rapsodie espagnole opens with haunting atmosphere as well as poetry, while, as ever, his rhythmic pulse brings out Ravel's subtle rhythmic fluctuations. The Alborada del gracioso is similarly possessed of much inner vitality, and if the following Pavane pour une infante défunte is perhaps a bit cool (there was some curious 'crackle' in our reproduction of this work, perhaps a faulty CD) the Valses nobles et sentimentales finds the conductor on top form, with a sensuous vitality which is commanding. The following Ma Mère l'Oye is given an enchanting performance, with the most shapely phrasing of the strings in the opening Prélude. Ansermet's account of the complete Daphnis et Chloé isn't quite in the Munch/Monteux league, but it is very good all the same. In the Bacchanale (Danse générale) there is a gripping tension and sensuality using a fairly slow and unyielding tempo. Ansermet never forgot that this music was written for dance.

From the very opening he creates a superb atmosphere (even if the nasal quality of the oboe does occasionally jar in this work). This second CD is followed by a stylish account of Le Tombeau de Couperin – with Ansermet in his element.

Alborada del gracioso; Pavane pour une infante défunte; Rapsodie espagnole; Le Tombeau de Couperin; Valses nobles et sentimentales

(BB) **(*) EMI Encore 5 85078-2. RPO, Previn

Opening with a provocatively languorous account of Valses nobles et sentimentales, lazy of tempo and affectionately indulgent, **Previn's** whole 1986 collection is imbued with sentient warmth. It even pervades Le Tombeau de Couperin, although, with some delectable oboe playing, this retains its neoclassical lightness of character. The Rapsodie espagnole is unashamedly sultry and the effect throughout is helped by the glowing EMI recording.

Alborada del gracioso; Pavane pour une infante défunte; Rapsodie espagnole; Valses nobles et sentimentales

➻—✿ (B) **** RCA 74321 88692-2 (2). Chicago SO, Reiner – DEBUSSY: Images: Ibéria. La Mer ✿ ****; MUSSORGSKY: Pictures **(*)

These performances are in an altogether special class. In the Rapsodie espagnole the Prélude à la nuit is heavy with fragrance and atmosphere; never have the colours in the Féria glowed more luminously, while the Malagueña glitters with iridescence. In the years since it first appeared on LP, this is the recording we have turned to whenever we wanted to hear the work for pleasure. No one captures its sensuous atmosphere so completely as did **Reiner**, and the recorded sound, with its natural concert-hall balance, still sounds pretty amazing. The recording is improved in terms of clarity and definition, even if with the digital remastering the fortissimo upper range of the violins has become sharper and less natural in focus.

Boléro

(M) *** DG (ADD) 447 426-2. BPO, Karajan – DEBUSSY: La Mer; MUSSORGSKY: Pictures ***

Boléro; Daphnis et Chloé: Suite 2

➻—✿ (M) *** DG (ADD) 477 716-1. BPO, Karajan – DEBUSSY: La Mer; Prélude ***

Karajan's 1964 Boléro is a hypnotically gripping performance, with the **Berlin Philharmonic** at the top of its form. The couplings on both discs show Karajan at his very finest.

(i) Boléro; (ii) Daphnis et Chloé Suites 1 & 2; Ma Mère l'Oye (complete)

(N) *** Pentatone PTC SACD 5186 167. (i) Rotterdam PO, De Waart; (ii) Concg. O, Haitink

Haitink's 1971 Ravel performances, with beautifully focused detail, make this CD a very attractive proposition. The performance of Ma Mère l'Oye is very special indeed, with wonderfully refined orchestral playing and a magical atmosphere. The Daphnis et Chloé Suites emerge here with greater sparkle than they did on LP and the *Danse générale* is very exciting indeed. **De Waart's** account of the *Boléro* is straightforward, somewhat unyielding, but not low in tension, and again very well recorded. The SACD sound simply amazes in its richness, warmth and detail.

Boléro; Daphnis et Chloé: Suite 2; Ma Mère l'Oye: suite; Pavane pour une infante défunte; La Valse

🎵⟶ ******** Telarc CD 80601. Cincinnati SO, Järvi

An outstanding collection in every way, gloriously recorded in the rich ambience of Cincinnati's Music Hall. **Paavo Järvi** secures performances which are beautifully played, affectionately detailed, warmly sensuous and radiantly textured (especially *Ma Mère l'Oye*, which is more romantic than usual). The brightly paced *Boléro* and the expansive but equally magnetic *La Valse* both move to thrilling climaxes, the former with a characteristically spectacular bass drum. The wide dynamic range increases the drama of the interpretations – and indeed the spectacle of the demonstration-standard sound. Highly recommended.

(i) Boléro; Daphnis et Chloé: Suite 2; Ma Mère l'Oye: Suite; (ii) Rapsodie espagnole; La Valse

**(*) Australian Decca Eloquence ADD 466 667-2. (i) LAPO, Mehta; (ii) LSO, Monteux

Mehta's Ravel is very high powered, but the visceral excitement he produces is most compelling. *La Valse* is full of tension, and the *Daphnis Suite* builds up to a splendid climax. *Ma Mère l'Oye* is brilliantly played too, although here the music's sense of gentle rapture is less fully realized. Not surprisingly, *Boléro* is a great success. Throughout, one marvels at the vivid Decca sound and the brilliance of the playing of the **Los Angeles orchestra**, and one feels that this period (late 1960s and 1970s) was Mehta's golden recording era. **Monteux's LSO** account of the *Rapsodie espagnole* is justly famous; it is a memorably glowing account, drenched in atmosphere, and, despite some tape hiss, it still sparkles.

Boléro; (i) Daphnis et Chloé: Suite 2; Ma Mère l'Oye (suite); Valses nobles et sentimentales

🅑🅑 ******** Naxos 8.550173. (i) Slovak Philharmonic Ch.; Slovak RSO (Bratislava), Jean

The **Slovak Radio Orchestra**, which is a fine body and is superbly recorded, respond warmly to **Kenneth Jean**. At the price, this is very good value indeed; the *Ma Mère l'Oye* can hold its own alongside all but the most distinguished competition: indeed *Les Entretiens de la belle et de la bête* is as keenly characterized as Dutoit at mid-price, and *Le Jardin féerique* is enchanting.

Boléro; Daphnis et Chloé: Suite 2; Rapsodie espagnole

Ⓜ ******* EMI (ADD) 5 67595-2. O de Paris, Munch – HONEGGER: *Symphony 2* *******

Munch recorded these Ravel pieces in 1968, shortly before his death on tour with the newly founded **Orchestre de Paris**. They bear the hallmark of his personality, intensity of expression and wonderful finesse. Excellent sound.

Boléro; Ma Mère l'Oye; Rapsodie espagnole

🅑🅑 **(**)** Naxos mono 8.110154. Boston SO, Koussevitzky – MUSSORGSKY: *Pictures at an Exhibition* **(**(*))**

Koussevitzky's feeling for Ravel is second to none. There is a certain want of enchantment in the first two movements of *Ma Mère l'Oye*, but for the most part criticism is silenced.

Boléro; Rapsodie espagnole; La Valse

Ⓜ ****(*)** RCA (ADD) **SACD** 82876 66374-2. Boston SO, Munch – DEBUSSY: *Images* *******

Munch's recordings originally appeared together on a single LP which was reviewed by us in the very first *Stereo Record Guide* in 1960. We found the sound in *Boléro* 'full-blooded yet well separated, the harp beautifully balanced in the opening music and the side-drum clear as a bell at the beginning and dominating the climax. The **Boston** trombone soloist does not slur his tune with glissandi (as on the recording which the composer himself supervises). Munch used the *Rapsodie* to show the orchestra's prowess in the many sparkling coloured effects it contains, with the percussion section marvellously captured and the string glissandi also. The Spanish condiment is not missing and the whole thing is highly entertaining.' We were much less happy with Munch's *La Valse* and thought it 'an unsubtle performance, for he presses the music to a frenzy in its final climax'.

Piano Concerto in G

🎵⟶ ✸ Ⓜ ******** EMI (ADD) 5 67238-2. Michelangeli, Philh. O, Gracis – RACHMANINOV: *Piano Concerto 4.* ******** ✸

(*) Sup. SU 3714- 2 031. Moravec, Prague Philh., Bělohlávek – BEETHOVEN: *Piano Concerto 4*; FRANCK: *Symphonic Variations* *****

(*) DG 477 659-3. Yundi Li, BPO, Ozawa – PROKOFIEV: *Piano Concerto 2* *****

Michelangeli's slow movement is ravishing, and the sparkle of the outer movements is underpinned by a refined Ravelian sensitivity. The remastering of the early stereo master (1957) is wholly beneficial, the sound full yet remarkably transparent in revealing detail.

Playing of great delicacy and effortless virtuosity from **Yundi Li. Ozawa** gives sympathetic support.

The lightness and clarity typical of the veteran Czech pianist **Ivan Moravec** brings out the neoclassical element in the Ravel *G major Concerto*, with **Bělohlávek** colourfully touching in the jazz influences. The slow movement is at once poised, rapt and poetic, the more moving for the degree of understatement, and Moravec characteristically manages a velvety legato with only the lightest use of the pedal. In the extrovert finale Bělohlávek more than ever relishes the jazz element, while Moravec brings his usual clarity to the rushing figuration.

Piano Concerto in G; Piano Concerto in D for the Left Hand

🅑🅑 ******* Warner Apex (ADD) 8573 89232-2. Queffélec, Strasbourg PO, Lombard – DEBUSSY: *Fantaisie for Piano & Orchestra* *******

*** Australian Decca Eloquence (ADD) 476 235-2. de Larrocha, LPO, Foster – FAURÉ: *Fantasie for Piano & Orchestra* ***; FRANCK: *Symphonic Variations* ***

(*) Chan. 8773. Lortie, LSO, Frühbeck de Burgos – FAURÉ: *Ballade* *

(i) *Piano Concerto in G; Piano Concerto for the Left Hand;* (ii) *Tzigane*

(N) *(*) Australian Decca Eloquence (ADD) 480 0070. SRO, Ansermet; with (i) Blancard; (ii) Ricci

(i; ii) *Piano Concerto in G; Piano Concerto for the Left Hand;* (ii) *La Valse;* (i) *Valses nobles et sentimentales* (for piano)

(B) *** CfP (ADD) 587 029-2. (i) Fowke; (ii) LPO, Baudo

(i; ii) *Piano Concerto in G;* (i; iii) *Piano Concerto for the Left Hand;* (ii) *Valses nobles et sentimentales*

●—❀ **** DG 449 213-2. (i) Zimerman; (ii) Cleveland O; (iii) LSO; Boulez

(i) *Piano Concerto in G; Gaspard de la nuit*

●—(M) *** DG (ADD) 447 438-2. Argerich; (i) BPO, Abbado – PROKOFIEV: *Piano Concerto 3* ***

Zimerman's *G major Concerto*, the *Valses nobles et sentimentales* and the *Left-hand Concerto* are well nigh perfect in every respect. **Boulez's** account of the *Valses nobles* is quite wonderfully atmospheric, indeed magical, and in the concertos the delicacy and finesse of Krystian Zimerman's pianism is dazzling, his refinement of nuance and clarity of articulation a source of wonder. Beautifully balanced and finely detailed recording.

Argerich's half-tones and clear fingerwork give the *G major Concerto* unusual delicacy, but its urgent virility – with jazz an important element – comes over the more forcefully by contrast. The compromise between coolness and expressiveness in the slow Minuet of the middle movement is tantalizingly sensual. Her *Gaspard de la nuit* abounds in character and colour. The remastered recordings sound first class.

Anne Queffélec's accounts of both Ravel concertos are thoughtful and imaginative and often bringing an enticing languor, yet without loss of sparkle in the outer movements of the *G major*. She is a thorough musician with a considerable technique and no mean sense of poetry and her approach is refreshing. The excellent **Strasbourg Orchestra** under **Alain Lombard** give her admirable support, and the recording is well balanced in a warm acoustic.

The performances of both the *Concertos* by **Philip Fowke** with **Baudo** and the **LPO** are particularly attractive in the way they bring out the jazzy side of Ravel's inspiration with winning results. In the slow movement of the *G major Concerto* the Spanish overtones also come out strongly, and Fowke's solo playing in the *Valses nobles et sentimentales* is clean, bright and rhythmic in a muscular way, without ever becoming brutal or unfeeling; nor does he lack poetry. Baudo and the orchestra also give a strongly characterized

reading of *La Valse*. Excellent 1988 recording – irresistible at bargain price.

Alicia de Larrocha's 1972 recordings of the Ravel piano concertos have been somewhat elusive on CD, making this Australian release very welcome indeed. The performances are excellent, with de Larrocha, in her distinctive way, finding plenty of colour and sparkle in these wonderful concertos; and she is very well supported by **Lawrence Foster** and the Decca recording. The couplings are excellent too.

Louis Lortie's account of the two *Concertos* on Chandos has the advantage of altogether outstanding recording. In the *G major* he is often highly personal without becoming unduly idiosyncratic, with a fastidious sense of colour at his command. In the *Left-hand Concerto* he really takes his time over the cadenzas and his agogic hesitations are sometimes over-indulgent. Immaculate playing as such, and superb recording.

In the darker *Piano Concerto for the Left Hand*, **Ansermet** commands an impressive grip on the movement's structure, allowing plenty of detail to emerge. But the piano sounds thin, even if it is quite well-balanced. **Blancard** was the first pianist to record this concerto (this was her second attempt) and though she is not the most inspired pianist on record, she is thoroughly inside the music. The quality at the opening of the *G major concerto* is initially disconcertingly dry and forward; but the performance makes one almost forget such limitations, with the slow movement richly poised and the finale with an enjoyable elegance. The soloist's articulation is impressively clear. **Ricci's** brilliantly played and recorded stereo version of the *Tzigane* is well known and always thoroughly enjoyable.

Daphnis et Chloé (ballet; complete)

●—❀ (M) **** RCA (ADD) **SACD** 82876 61388-2. New England Conservatory & Alumni Ch., Boston SO, Munch

Daphnis et Chloé (complete); *Pavane pour une infante défunte; Rapsodie espagnole*

●—(M) **** Decca 475 7525. LSO, Monteux

Charles Munch's Boston account is one of the great glories of the 1950s. The playing in all departments of the **Boston Orchestra** is simply electrifying. The sound here may not be as sumptuous as the Dutoit on Decca, but the richness of colour lies in the playing, and there is a heady sense of intoxication that at times sweeps you off your feet, and the integration of the chorus is impressively managed. Try the *Danse de supplication de Chloé* and the ensuing scene in which the pirates are put to flight, and you will get a good idea of how dazzling this is, with the ballet ending in tumultuous orchestral virtuosity. The SACD transfer offers a little more ambience than the CD and the effect is quite glorious.

Monteux conducted the first performance of *Daphnis et Chloé* in 1912 and it is a matter for gratitude that his poetic and subtly shaded reading should have been recorded in such astonishingly realistic sound which hardly sounds dated even now. It was made in the Kingsway Hall in 1959, with John Culshaw the producer. The *Pavane* and *Rapsodie espagnole* came two years later, in 1961, with Erik Smith in charge. The **LSO** again play superbly for Monteux and he achieves a balance and a contrast between a mood of quiet introspection for the opening of the *Rapsodie* and a vivid, flashing brilliance for the *Féria*. The *Pavane* is wonderfully poised, and is played most beautifully. An ideal choice for Decca's Originals label.

Daphnis et Chloé: Suite 2 (DVD version)

Ⓝ **** Sony **DVD** 88697202449. BPO, Karajan – DEBUSSY: *La mer; Prélude á l'après-midi d'un faune* ****

A magical account of *Daphnis*. Perhaps **Karajan's** DG recording on LP during the mid-1960s was even more sumptuous, but this superbly controlled and beautifully recorded performance still captivates, and it is expertly directed for the cameras. It was recorded at the Philharmonie in 1987, two years before his death.

Daphnis et Chloé: Suite 2 (CD version)

**(*) BBC (ADD) BBCL 4039-2. Philh. O, Boult – BIZET: *Jeux d'enfants*; SCHUBERT: *Symphony 8 (Unfinished)*; SIBELIUS: *Symphony 7* **(*)

RL recalls hearing Sir Adrian conduct *Daphnis* in the early 1950s and being astonished by his slow tempo in *Lever du jour*. He subsequently learnt that Boult had adopted Ravel's tempo, after Boult had heard the composer conduct the piece in the 1920s. It really feels too slow all the same, but his account has a finely controlled sensuousness that is very persuasive. Excellent sound.

Daphnis et Chloé: Suite 2; Pavane pour une infante défunte

🎧 Ⓜ *** Häns. CD 93013. Stuttgart SW RSO, Prêtre – BIZET: *Symphony in C* ***

(***) Testament mono SBT 1017. Philh. O, Cantelli – CASELLA: *Paganiniana*; DUKAS: *L'Apprenti sorcier*; FALLA: *Three-Cornered Hat* (***)

Prêtre shapes the opening of *Daybreak* with an ecstatic richness of line, the **Stuttgart** strings gloriously expansive. There is some radiant woodwind playing too in the *Pantomime* and the principal flute of this fine orchestra plays his famous solo with scintillating brilliance leading on to a thrillingly zestful *Danse générale*. *La Valse* rises out of the mists and Prêtre's string phrasing is again passionately seductive, the final climax thrillingly impulsive yet still controlled. This is 'live' music-making at its finest, and the warm ambience of the digital recording is just right for it.

Cantelli's account of *Daphnis* was among his last – and finest – records. It sounds remarkably good in this splendid transfer and has classic status.

Daphnis et Chloé: Suite 2

*** Sony 88869 7123632. Bav. RSO, Jansons – BARTÓK: *Concerto for Orchestra; Miraculous Mandarin: Suite* **(*)

The **Bavarian Radio Orchestra** is magnificent, with particularly lush string-tone. Collectors who recall **Jansons's** performance with the Oslo Philharmonic will know how seductive his Ravel is. This is among the best of the most recent *Daphnises*.

Daphnis et Chloé: Suite 2; Rapsodie espagnole

**** DG 477 7175. NYPO, Maazel – STRAVINSKY: *Chant du rossignol; Firebird Suite* ***

Not only are these two of the finest recordings ever to be made in the Avery Fisher Hall, but **Maazel's** performances are full of life and spontaneity, and the **NYPO** plays superbly. The opening *Daybreak* from *Daphnis* is gloriously evoked, with lustrous string phrasing and with the birds twittering in the dawn light. The same exotic atmosphere permeates the *Rapsodie espagnole*, which is richly atmospheric throughout, with rhythms nudged seductively, and the finales of both works are thrillingly played.

Ma Mère l'Oye (suite)

Ⓑ **(*) CfP 586 1752. LPO, Edwards (with DEBUSSY: *Children's Corner: 3 Pieces*) – BRITTEN: *Young Person's Guide* ***; PROKOFIEV: *Peter and the Wolf* **(*)

Warm and beautiful playing from the **LPO** under **Sian Edwards**, but Ravel's magical score does not yield all its secrets here; its sense of gentle, innocent ecstasy is missing. But the recording is excellent.

Ma Mère l'Oye (suite; with narration)

ⒷⒷ *** Naxos 8.554463. Morris (nar.), Slovak RSO, Jean – DUKAS: *L'Apprenti sorcier*; SAINT-SAËNS: *Carnival of the Animals* **(*)

Ma Mère l'Oye is exquisite music and it is most beautifully played by the **Slovak Orchestra** under **Kenneth Jean**. **Johnny Morris** provides a friendly spoken introduction for each fairy-tale number which has been admirably and concisely written by Keith and Anthony Anderson. To link them with Ravel's music is surely a marvellous way of familiarizing younger children with the music.

Ma Mère l'Oye: Suite; La Valse

*** MDG **SACD** 9371099-2; CD 337 1099-2. Orchester der Beethovenhalle, Bonn, Soustrot – DEBUSSY: *Le Martyre de Saint-Sébastien* ***

Soustrot gives a simple, dedicated reading of *Ma Mère l'Oye*, with the tender delicacy of Ravel's score glowingly revealed by the warm sensitivity of the players. The opening of *La Valse*, too, has an almost ethereal quality, but there is no lack of drama later. Indeed, Soustrot's approach, with careful attention to detail, allows the dramatic elements of the score to emerge without the exaggerated point-making one sometimes encounters in this score. The recording is beautifully balanced, with the natural concert-hall acoustic combining clarity with a warm ambience. On SACD it sounds even more beautiful.

Menuet antique; Pavane pour une infante défunte; Le Tombeau de Couperin; (i) Shéhérazade

*** DG 471 614-2. Cleveland O, Boulez; (i) with von Otter – DEBUSSY: *Danses; Le Jet d'eau; 3 Ballades de François Villon* ***

Even those who do not always admire **Boulez** tend to respond to his Ravel, and there is no reason not to do so in this well-planned release. The delicacy and elegance of *Le Tombeau* are well conveyed, and **Anne Sofie von Otter** gives a beautiful account of the magical *Shéhérazade*, one of the best to appear in recent years. The recorded sound and the balance are first class.

Rapsodie espagnole

*(**) BBCL (ADD) 4205-2. New Philh. O, Stokowski (with: KLEMPERER: *Merry Waltz*; NOVÁČEK: *Perpetuum mobile*) – BRAHMS: *Symphony 4* *(**); VAUGHAN WILLIAMS: *Tallis Fantasia* **(*)

Atmosphere is a vital ingredient in a performance of the *Rapsodie espanole*, and **Stokowski** provides it here in plenty. Despite the odd audience distraction, this is a compelling reading, with the *pianissimos* especially spine-tingling. Acceptable 1974 sound.

Tzigane (for violin and orchestra)

⊶ (M) *** EMI (ADD) 5 62599-2. Perlman, O de Paris, Martinon (with MASSENET: *Thaïs: Méditation*) – CHAUSSON: *Poème*; SAINT-SAËNS: *Havanaise*, etc. ***

(M) *** DG 447 445-2. Perlman, NYPO, Mehta – BERG; STRAVINSKY: *Concertos* ***

Perlman's classic (1974) account of Ravel's *Tzigane* for EMI is marvellously played; the added projection of the CD puts the soloist believably at the end of the living-room and the orchestral sound retains its atmosphere.

Perlman's later digital version is very fine and the recording is obviously modern. But the earlier, EMI performance has just that bit more charisma.

La valse; Valses nobles et sentimentales

(N) (***) VAI mono DVD 4226. Chicago SO, Munch (with BERLIOZ: *Royal Hunt and Storm*; RAMEAU, arr. D'INDY: *Dardanus suite*; cond. Monteux: BEETHOVEN: *Symphony 8*; BERLIOZ: *Carnaval romain*; WAGNER: *Die Meistersinger: Prelude to Act III*)

The *Valses nobles* is arguably the finest account of the piece we have heard. The sound on this black-and-white telecast of 1963 is far from ideal, but the performance has immense charm and character. The *Valses nobles* is perfectly paced, much more relaxed than we hear nowadays and with plenty of time for the artists to breathe. This is a model of Ravel style and, watching **Munch**, one realizes how naturally his charm captivates his players. The DVD is self-recommending, as it includes some fine Berlioz from both Munch and **Monteux** (recorded in 1961) and a splendidly characteristic Beethoven *Eighth* from the latter.

CHAMBER MUSIC

Berceuse; Pièce en forme de habanera; Tzigane

*** DG 445 880-2. Dumay, Pires – DEBUSSY; FRANCK: *Violin Sonatas* ***

Polished and elegant performances of these Ravel pieces. No complaints about the recording quality.

Introduction & Allegro for Harp, Flute, Clarinet & String Quartet

(***) Testament mono SBT 1053. Gleghorn, Lurie, Stockton, Hollywood Qt – CRESTON: *Quartet*; DEBUSSY: *Danse sacrée*, etc.; TURINA: *La oración del torero*; VILLA-LOBOS: *Quartet 6* (***)

(i) Introduction & Allegro; (ii) Pièce en forme de habanera

⊶ (B) *** Cala CACD 1018 (2). Campbell; (i) Bennett, Jones, Allegri Qt; (ii) York – POULENC: *L'Invitation au château*, etc. ***

The Cala performances are recommendable in their own right, but they come in a particularly valuable two-CD set for the price of one, which includes over two hours of music for wind instruments by Poulenc. It is sheer delight from start to finish and cannot be too strongly recommended.

The **Hollywood Quartet's** version of the *Introduction and Allegro* gives us an example of the exquisite flute playing of **Arthur Gleghorn** as well as the artistry of **Mitchell Lurie** and **Ann Mason Stockton**. A fine performance, sounding remarkably fresh for a 1951 recording.

Introduction & Allegro for Harp, Flute, Clarinet & String Quartet; String Quartet in G min.

⊶ (B) **** CfP (ADD) 3 82231-2. (i) Klinko, Soloists of Paris Bastille Op. O; (ii) Chilingirian Qt – DEBUSSY: *String Quartet* ****

Markus Klinko and his colleagues from the **Orchestre de l'Opéra de Paris Bastille** give one of the most satisfying accounts of Ravel's *Introduction and Allegro* to have appeared in recent years. It is beautifully played, finely balanced and is done with impeccable taste. In the *String Quartet* the **Chilingirians** have plenty of body and also the benefit of a warm acoustic. They give a thoroughly committed account, with well-judged tempi and very musical phrasing. The Scherzo is vital and spirited and there is no want of poetry in the slow movement. At bargain price this is very good value indeed.

Piano Trio in A min.

⊶ **** Hyp. CDA 67114. Florestan Trio – DEBUSSY; FAURÉ: *Piano Trios* ****

*** HMC 1951967. Trio Wanderer – CHAUSSON: *Trio* ***

*** Chan. 8458. Borodin Trio – DEBUSSY: *Violin & Cello Sonatas* ***

(BB) **(*) Naxos 8.550934. Joachim Trio – DEBUSSY: *Piano Trio in G*; SCHMITT: *Piano Trio: Très lent* **(*)

Led by the masterly pianist **Susan Tomes**, the **Florestan Trio** give an outstanding account of the Ravel masterpiece. They generally adopt speeds on the fast side, but with no feeling of haste, thanks to playing at once highly polished and flexibly expressive. The couplings are unique and apt, with each composer represented at a different period of his career. Vivid sound.

The **Borodin Trio** are excellently recorded and their playing has great warmth and is full of colour. Some may find them too hot-blooded by the side of the Florestan Trio.

The Naxos version by the **Joachim Trio** is worth any collector's notice. They play with sensitive musicianship and finesse. Their performance is imaginative and beautifully recorded.

Piano Trio in A min.; Violin Sonata in G; Violin Sonata posth.; Sonata for Violin & Cello

*** Virgin 5 45492-2. R. & G. Capuçon, Braley

Both the **Capuçon** brothers, are first-rate players, and the pianist, too, is excellent – very sensitive in *pianissimos*, though once or twice a little too overpowering in louder passages. However, this does not detract from what are by any standards first-class readings, splendidly characterized and imaginative performances from all three artists, which can hold their own with any in the current catalogue. This is brilliantly thought out and executed playing, and readers wanting all these pieces, including the rare *Sonata posthume*, on one CD will not be disappointed.

Piano Trio in A min.; Sonata for Violin & Cello; (i) Chansons madécasses; 3 Poèmes de Stéphane Mallarmé (song-cycle)

(BB) **(*) Virgin 2x1 5 61427-2 (2). Nash Ens. (members); (i) with Walker – DEBUSSY: *Chamber music* **

The *Sonata for Violin and Cello* is expertly played by **Marcia Crayford** and **Christopher van Kampen** – as good an account as any – and in the *Piano Trio* **Ian Brown** joins them in a performance of real stature and eloquence. In the *Chansons madécasses* and the exquisite *Trois poèmes de Stéphane Mallarmé* **Sarah Walker** is *prima inter pares* rather than a soloist, though she is not balanced as reticently by Andrew Keener's team as is **Delphine Seyrig** in the Debussy *Chansons de Bilitis*. This is a pity, but it is not an insuperable obstacle to an apt and inexpensive Ravel collection.

(i) Pièce en forme de habanera; (ii–iii) Violin Sonata; (iv; i) Violin Sonata (Posthume); (iv–v) Sonata for Violin & Cello; (ii–iii) Tzigane

(BB) *** Praga (ADD) PR 54016. (i) Hála; (ii) Oistrakh; (iii) Bauer; (iv) Suk; (v) Navarra

The *Sonata posthume*, which **Suk** and **Hála** recorded in 1979 for Prague Radio, is a beguiling piece, and Suk fully conveys its charms. **Oistrakh** recorded the *Violin Sonata* with **Frida Bauer** a few years later. The *Tzigane*, recorded in 1957, still sounds wonderfully persuasive. The 1967 *Sonata for Violin and Cello* with Suk and **Navarra** is pretty magisterial. This is not generously represented in the catalogue, so it enhances the undoubted value of this competitively priced reissue.

String Quartet in F

**** Sup. SU 3855-2. Panocha Qt – SUK: *Quartet 1*; etc. ****

⊶ (B) **** EMI Début 5 74020-2. Belcea Qt – DEBUSSY: *String Quartet in G min*; DUTILLEUX: *Ainsi la nuit* ***

*** HM HMI 987072. Casals Qt – TOLDRA: *Vistes al mar*; TURINA: *El Oracion del Torero* ***

(M) *** Ph. 464 6992. Italian Qt – DEBUSSY: *Quartet* ***

(BB) *** Naxos 8.554722. Ad Libitum Qt – FAURÉ: *Quartet* ***❀

(B) *** Calliope (ADD) CAL 5893. Talich Qt – DEBUSSY: *String Quartet* **(*)

(*) ASV CDDCA 930. Lindsay Qt – DEBUSSY: *String Quartet* **(*); STRAVINSKY: *3 Pieces* *

(**(*)) BBC mono BBCL 4063-2. Borodin Qt – BORODIN: *Quartet 2* (**(*)); SHOSTAKOVICH: *Quartet 8* **(*)

(M) **(*) EMI 5 67550-2. Alban Berg Qt – DEBUSSY: *String Quartet* **(*); STRAVINSKY: *Concertino; Double Canon; 3 Pieces* ***

String Quartet in F; (i) Introduction & Allegro for Harp, Flute, Clarinet & String Quartet

(BB) *** Naxos 8.550249. Kodály Qt; (i) with Maros, Gyöngyössy, Kovács – DEBUSSY: *Quartet* **(*)

There are many fine recordings of the Ravel *Quartet*, but the newest version from the **Panocha Quartet** is not only unsurpassed in terms of passion, subtlety and delicacy, as well as warmth of feeling, but it has an attractively unusual Suk coupling. It is outstandingly well recorded.

The **Belcea Quartet** sounds as if it is completely inside the music, but its responses are still fresh and felt keenly. As in the Debussy, it is scrupulous in detail and tempi could not be judged better. A performance of real finesse that can be recommended along with the best; at budget price it also enjoys a strong competitive edge.

Winner of the first prize in the 2000 London International Quartet Competition, the **Cuarteto Casals** here gives a sparkling account of the Ravel *Quartet*, covering a wide expressive range, from the bite of the Scherzo to the meditative depth of the slow movement. It is well coupled with two rarer quartet works from Spain.

For many years the **Italian Quartet** held pride of place in this coupling. Their playing is perfect in ensemble, attack and beauty of tone, and their performance remains highly recommendable, one of the most satisfying chamber-music records in the catalogue.

The ensemble and intonation of the Romanian **Ad Libitum Quartet** are perfect, and their tone is silken. They couple the quartet with the late *E minor Quartet* by Ravel's teacher, Gabriel Fauré, one of the most persuasive and most haunting accounts in the catalogue and given a Rosette by us. Their Ravel is also refined and sophisticated (some may find it just a shade over-characterized), but all the same, this is most distinguished playing and can be confidently recommended given the excellence of the recorded sound, which is natural and lifelike, and the appeal of the coupling.

The **Talich** recorded their Debussy–Ravel coupling in 1984, the Debussy in the studio and the Ravel at a public concert. It goes without saying that they are distinguished by refinement, perfect ensemble and warmth. The tempi are well judged, and the playing is completely free from idiosyncratic or egocentric touches. The recording is not in the first flight but is very acceptable.

The **Kodály** version can more than hold its own. Artistically and technically this is a satisfying performance which has the feel of real live music-making. The *Introduction and Allegro* is not as magical an account, but it is still thoroughly enjoyable.

A highly accomplished and finely etched performance from the **Lindsays**, who play with their usual aplomb and panache. There are splendid things here, notably the youthful fire of the opening movement and the vivid finale. They do not always match the poetic feeling and the *douceur* which some rivals find, but this is not a neglible account, and it is well recorded.

The sheer tonal finesse and subtlety of colouring that the **Borodin Quartet** bring to the score in their BBC version serve to make it a performance to remember. It is not quite as polished as their later studio version, but it is eminently fresh and the 1962 sound is well balanced.

Superb, indeed incomparable playing from the **Alban Berg Quartet**, and splendidly full and sonorous recording from the EMI engineers. Yet while this is marvellously polished and has such excellence in terms of ensemble and tonal blend, there is a want of spontaneity that ultimately weighs against it, so that one is unable to forget the physical aspects of the music-making and become totally absorbed in the music itself.

Violin Sonata in G

🔊 ****** Erato 0630 15110-2. Repin, Berezovsky – MEDTNER: *Sonata 3 (Sonata epica)* ***

🔊 ****** EMI 5 57679-2. Chang, Vogt – FRANCK; SAINT-SAENS: *Violin Sonatas* ***

(M) ****** DG 477 544-8 (2). Mintz, Bronfman (with Recital of encores by ALBÉNIZ; COUPERIN; GLAZUNOV; GRANADOS; KREISLER; WEBER; WIENIAWSKI) – DEBUSSY; FAURÉ; FRANCK: *Violin Sonatas* ***

Vadim Repin and **Boris Berezovsky** on Erato offer an unusual coupling. These two artists command a wide range of colour and dynamics, infuse every phrase with life, and have the full measure of the 'Blues' movement. Repin plays the Guarneri with which Isaac Stern delighted us for almost half a century and it sounds magnificently responsive in his hands. Very good and completely natural recording.

Sarah Chang and **Lars Vogt** give a brilliant and finely characterized account of the *Sonata* and in particular its blue movement. This has strong claims on the allegiance of the collector and is a splendid bargain if the couplings are suitable. Good recorded sound, too.

Shlomo Mintz and **Yefim Bronfman's** account offers highly polished playing, even if it is perhaps not so completely inside Ravel's world in the slow movement. The glorious sounds both artists produce are a source of unfailing delight, and they are beautifully recorded. At mid-price and coupled with fine performances of three other French violin sonatas, plus an enticing programme of encores, this is very recommendable.

Violin Sonata (1897); Tzigane

🔊 ****** Avie AV 2059. Graffin, Désert – DEBUSSY: *Violin Sonata; Nocturne et Scherzo*; ENESCU: *Impressions d'enfance* ***

Philippe Graffin and **Claire Désert** give an entirely delightful account of the early *Sonata posthume*, playing with much delicacy and subtlety to make it sound like mature Ravel. Their *Tzigane*, too, is played with refinement as well as sparkle: it has plenty of gypsy feeling but is not treated as just a virtuoso display piece.

Tzigane (for violin and piano)

(BB) (****) Dutton mono CDBP 9710. G. & J. Neveau – BRAHMS: *Violin Concerto; 4 Pieces*; SUK: *Encores* ***

Ginette Neveu's account of the *Tzigane* is full of gypsy temperament and fire, with some dazzling pyrotechnics at the close. She dominates the proceedings, although her brother, Jean, accompanies supportively. Also offered are some delectable encores including Chopin's *Nocturne in C sharp minor*, its cantilena sounding for all the world like a violin piece, and dazzling versions of Falla's *Spanish Dance* from *La vida breve* and Dinicu's gutsy *Hora Staccato*. The transfers of these 1946 Abbey Road sessions are vividly realistic.

PIANO MUSIC

Music for Piano Duet and Two Pianos

Boléro; Introduction & Allegro; Ma Mère l'Oye; Rapsodie espagnole; La Valse

🔊 ⚜ ******* Chan. 8905. Lortie, Mercier

Louis Lortie's recital for piano (four hands and two pianos) with his Canadian partner, **Hélène Mercier**, is quite magical; these artists command an exceptionally wide range of colour and dynamic nuance. The acoustic is that of The Maltings, Snape, and the result is quite outstanding sonically: you feel that you have only to stretch out and you can touch the instruments. Ravel's transcriptions are stunningly effective in their hands, even, surprisingly, *Boléro*.

(i) Boléro; Ma Mère l'Oye (Suite); Menuet antique; Prélude; Pavane pour une infante défunte; Rapsodie espagnole

****** KML 1111. Katia & Marielle Labèque (piano, 4 hands); (i) with Gustavo Gimeno (percussionist) (www.kmlrecordings.com)

This first disc from the **Labèques** on their new label proves to be a winner. The *Rapsodie espagnole*, which opens the recital, is richly evocative and the piano colouring of *Ma Mère l'Oye* is luminous. The transcribed *Pavane*, too, is most elegant. But the recital ends with a thrilling account of *Boléro* in which the duo are joined by **Gustavo Gimeno** playing various Basque percussion instruments. The recording is vividly real but rather too close, or this might have had four stars.

Entre cloches; (i) Frontispiece; Introduction and Allegro; Ma Mère l'Oye; Rapsodie espagnole; Shéhérazade: Ouverture de féerie; La Valse

(M) ****** Somm SOMMCD 025. Micallef, Inanga; (i) with Sterling

The young, prize-winning duo of **Micallef** and **Inanga** are warmly responsive, naturally in sympathy with the idiom. Their subtle and persuasive use of rubato comes out very clearly, as in the *Malagueña* from *Rapsodie espagnole*, a piece written earlier than the other three movements. *Frontispiece*, written in 1918 as the introduction to a collection of war poems brings some extraordinary polytonal writing, totally un-Ravelian. The other major item, *Shéhérazade*, with hard keyboard textures, is less evocative than tough, sounding more modern than the orchestral version. Best of all is *La Valse*, a brilliant transcription already a favourite with two-piano duos.

La valse

Ⓜ *** Ph. 475 8520. Argerich & Freire – LUTOSŁAWSKI: *Paganini Variations*; RACHMANINOV: *Suite 2* ***

The transcription is Ravel's own and was first heard in this form played by the composer himself and Alfredo Casella in 1920. Brilliant, atmospheric playing and very good recording.

Solo piano music

A la manière de Borodine; A la manière de Chabrier; Gaspard de la nuit; Jeux d'eau; Menuet antique; Menuet sur le nom de Haydn; Miroirs; Pavane pour une infante défunte; Prélude; Sérénade grotesque; Sonatine; Le Tombeau de Couperin; Valses nobles et sentimentales

⊕ **** Hyp. CDA 67341/2. Hewitt

⊕ ⒝⒝ **** EMI Gemini (ADD) 5 86061-2 (2). Collard

⊕ **** Decca 433 515-2 (2). Thibaudet

Ⓜ *** Chan. 10142X (2). Lortie

Ⓜ *** CRD CRD 3383/4 Crossley

⒝⒝ **(*) Virgin 5 62363-2 (4). Queffélec – SATIE: *Collection* ***

⊕ Ⓑ (***) EMI mono 5 74793-2 (2). Gieseking (without *Sérénade grotesque*)

Ravel's solo piano music has been well served in the last couple of decades but this newcomer from Hyperion is second to none and will now probably be a first choice for most collectors. We associate **Angela Hewitt** with Bach, but the clarity she brought to that repertoire serves to illuminate Ravel's textures without ever entailing any loss of atmosphere. Her performances are characteristically full of the searchingly imaginative approach she takes to everything she plays. The playing is impeccable, in both technique and taste. Altogether this is a fascinating new look at these inspired pieces, so perfect in their detail, and one continually has the sense of coming to this music afresh.

Jean-Philippe Collard is a stylist and a master, and Ravel playing doesn't come much better than this. What a beautiful sense of line he achieves in *Ondine*, the first of the *Gaspard de la nuit*, though it must be admitted that the right-hand ostinato is far from the *pianopianissimo* that Ravel marks. For the most part, however, this playing silences criticism. The recording, made in the Salle Wagram, is not wholly sympa-

thetic: there is a glassy, shallow quality, particularly on the upper part of the spectrum.

Jean-Yves Thibaudet's collected Ravel is quite outstanding playing on all counts; Thibaudet exhibits flawless technique, perfect control, refinement of touch and exemplary taste. The recording is of real distinction too.

The fine Canadian pianist **Louis Lortie** made a strong impression with the two Ravel *Concertos* and with this survey of the piano music when it first appeared in the 1980s. The recordings, made at The Maltings, Snape, have great clarity and presence, and the performances have proved very persuasive over the years.

Paul Crossley's accounts of all these works are aristocratic, with an admirable feeling for tone-colour and line, and rarely mannered. His version of *Le Tombeau de Couperin* has a classical refinement and delicacy that is refreshing. The CRD recording is very good indeed.

No quarrels with **Anne Queffélec's** playing. There are some masterly and enjoyable interpretations here, but it is all far too closely observed, as if one were in the front row of the concert hall; as a result not all the atmosphere registers to full effect, once the dynamics rise above *mf*.

Gieseking's classic recordings were made in 1954, with Walter Legge and Geraint Jones acting as producers. Gieseking's special affinity for this repertoire shines through, and no one with a serious interest in the French master should neglect these readings. Here is a pianist with a limpid, translucent tone playing a piano with apparently no hammers.

A la manière de Borodine; A la manière de Chabrier; Menuet antique; Prélude; Le Tombeau de Couperin; Valses nobles et sentimentales

**(*) Nim. (ADD) NI 5011. Perlemuter

Gaspard de la nuit; Jeux d'eau; Miroirs; Pavane

**(*) Nim. (ADD) NI 5005. Perlemuter

Though **Perlemuter's** technical command is not as complete as it had been, he gives delightful, deeply sympathetic readings; the sense of spontaneity is a joy. There may be Ravel recordings which bring more dazzling virtuoso displays, but none more persuasive. Nimbus's ample room acoustic makes the result naturally atmospheric on CD.

Gaspard de la nuit

⊕ (***) BBC mono BBCL 4064-2. Michelangeli – BEETHOVEN: *Sonatas 4 & 12*; DEBUSSY: *Hommage à Rameau* (**(*))

Michelangeli's *Gaspard* comes from a recital given in the Concert Hall of Broadcasting House in 1959, and those who were fortunate enough to be there were electrified by Michelangeli's playing. The mono sound is strikingly well transferred and infinitely better than earlier, unauthorized LP versions that have been in currency.

Miroirs

*** Wigmore Hall Live WHL 018. Cooper (with DEBUSSY: *La terrasse des audiences du clair de lune*; MOZART: *Sonata in A min., K.310*) – BEETHOVEN: *Sonata 28* ***

Given the quality of this recital, one wonders why **Imogen Cooper** has been so neglected by the record companies. It is good to have this Wigmore Hall recital which she gave in February 2007. Her account of the *Miroirs* is highly imaginative and expert and can hold its own among the finest available. The remainder of the programme is hardly less impressive, offering some highly distinguished and satisfying music-making.

Valses nobles et sentimentales (complete); Le Tombeau de Couperin; Forlane; Miroirs; La Vallée des cloches

●— (B) *** RCA 2CD (ADD) 74321 846062. Rubinstein –
CHABRIER: *Pièces Pittoresques: Scherzo-Valse;* DEBUSSY: *Estampes*, etc.; FAURÉ: *Nocturne 3;* FRANCK: *Symphonic Variations for Piano and Orchestra; Prélude choral et fugue;* SAINT-SAËNS: *Piano Concerto 2* ***

These pieces (including the Fauré and Chabrier) appear to derive from an LP called *'A French Programme'* which appeared in mono in the mid-1960s, and later in stereo. The playing is eminently aristocratic, and the sound greatly improved in these new transfers. Rubinstein could be a magician in French music just as he was in Chopin.

VOCAL MUSIC

Chansons madécasses

●— *** EMI 5 56982-2. Karnéus, Pahud, Mørk, Kovacevich –
DEBUSSY: *Syrinx; Bilitis*, etc.; PROKOFIEV: *Flute Sonata, Op. 94* ***

This EMI version of *Chansons madécasses* is primarily a vehicle for the virtuosity – or rather artistry – of **Emmanuel Pahud**, for there is no egotism in his playing, the virtuosity is merely by the by. He and **Kovacevich** are joined by **Katerina Karnéus** and **Truls Mørk**. Great sensitivity, powerful atmosphere, lucidity of diction and clarity of texture. This is an outstanding recital.

Don Quichotte à Dulcinée (song-cycle)

●— (***) Testament mono SBT 1312. Souzay, Paris Conservatoire O, Lindenberg – CHAUSSON: *Mélodies;* DEBUSSY: *Trois Ballades;* DUPARC: *12 Songs* (***)

Souzay's 1951 record of *Don Quichotte à Dulcinée* with the **Paris Conservatoire Orchestra** is part of an outstanding recital. This recording, however, is just a bit too closely balanced: the orchestra is very much in the background. Nevertheless, this Testament reissue remains indispensable.

Histoires naturelles

●— (***) Testament mono SBT 1311. Souzay, Bonneau –
FALLA: *7 canciones populares españolas;* FAURÉ: *Après un rêve*, etc. ***✿

Souzay made this record of the *Histoires naturelles* in 1951, only half a dozen years after his début in Paris, and it still remains arguably the finest recorded account of Ravel's imaginative cycle. Magnificently transferred, the sound belies its age and comes with some Fauré songs that are among the classics of the gramophone.

Shéhérazade (song-cycle)

●— ✿ (M) **** Decca 475 7712. Crespin, SRO, Ansermet (with Recital of French Songs (***)) – BERLIOZ: *Nuits d'été* ****

*** Warner 2564 61938-2. Graham, BBC SO, Tortelier –
CHAUSSON: *Poème de l'amour et de la mer;* DEBUSSY: *Poèmes de Charles Baudelaire* ***

Crespin is right inside these songs and Ravel's magically sensuous music emerges with striking spontaneity. She is superbly supported by **Ansermet** who, aided by the Decca engineers, weaves a fine tonal web round the voice. Her style has distinct echoes of the opera house; but the richness of the singer's tone does not detract from the delicate languor of *The Enchanted Flute*, in which the slave-girl listens to the distant sound of her lover's flute playing while her master sleeps. The new transfer of the 1963 recording adds to the allure of the remarkably rich and translucent Decca sound. The remastered reissue is now elevated to 'Originals' status and includes full documentation.

Susan Graham chooses wide contrasts for her performance of Ravel's inspired triptych, boldly operatic in line for *Asie*, tenderly languorous in the lovely *La Flûte enchantée* (with sensuous flute playing to match) and finding a delicate melancholy for *L'Indifférent*. **Yan Pascal Tortelier's** accompaniments are expressively ardent, and the recording is first class.

OPERA

L'Enfant et les sortilèges

●— ✿ (****) Testament mono SBT 1044. Sautereau, Vessières, Michel, Scharley, Le Marc'Hadour, Peyron, Angelici, French Nat. R. Ch. & O, Bour

There is a magic about this 1947 performance that completely captivates the listener. Each part, from **Nadine Sautereau's** Child, **Yvon Le Marc'Hadour's** Tom-Cat and Clock, and **Solange Michel's** touching Squirrel, to **Denise Scharley** as the Dragonfly and the Mother, could not be improved upon in character, subtlety and style. The singing and playing of the **French Radio** forces are vital and imaginative. Ravel's exquisite score is heard to best advantage in this extraordinary transfer with voices firm and immediate. With no stars but with no weak link, the singers make an outstanding team, helped by sound which, with background hiss eliminated, has astonishing presence. No other version casts quite such a strong spell.

(i) L'Enfant et les sortilèges; Ma Mère l'Oye (ballet; complete)

●— *** DG 457 589-2. (i) Stephen, Owens, Lascarro, Johnson, Soloists New L. Children's Ch., LSO Ch.; L. Symphony, Previn

(N) *** EMI 2 64197-2. BPO & Ch., Rattle, with (i) Koženà, Massis, Stutzman, Koch, van Dam, Le Roux, Fouchécourt, Erdman, Berlin R. Ch.

With opulent recording heightening the sumptuousness of Ravel's orchestration, and with **Previn** infectiously pointing rhythms at generally spacious speeds, this evocative one-acter could not be more persuasive, with the atmospheric magic beautifully captured. The apt and substantial fill-up, the complete *Mother Goose* ballet, also beautifully done, makes a welcome bonus.

EMI and **Rattle** offer a sumptuously recorded account of Ravel's masterpiece which boasts a distinguished cast and, of course, the wonderful sonority of the **Berlin Philharmonic**. **Magdalena Kožená** is strong and positive as the naughty child of the title, a superb actress as well as a glorious singer, and the other soloists are comparably well cast. One of the great advantages of this set is not only having the complete libretto (essential for full appreciation) but also the casting and the identification of each character. It is a magical score, as for that matter is the *Mother Goose* ballet. There is some expressive point-making that is a little exaggerated, but this is not too serious. As a final attraction, the design of the sleeve matches the music in its charm. However, in *L'enfant*, Previn's account and Maazel's DG version coupled with *L'Heure espagnole* remain the ones to have.

(i) *L'Enfant et les sortilèges*; (ii) *L'Heure espagnole* (both complete)

🎵—Ⓜ *** DG (ADD) 449 769-2 (2). (i) Ogéas, Collard, Berbié, Sénéchal, Gilma, Herzog, Rehfuss, Maurane, RTF Ch. & Boys' Ch., RTF Nat. O; (ii) Berbié, Sénéchal, Giraudeau, Bacquier, van Dam, Paris Opera O; Maazel – RIMSKY-KORSAKOV: *Capriccio espagnol*; STRAVINSKY: *Le Chant du rossignol*. *** 🎵 🎵

Maazel's recordings of Ravel's two one-act operas were made in the early 1960s and, though the solo voices in *L'Enfant* are balanced rather closely, the remastered sound in both operas is wonderfully vivid and atmospheric and each performance is splendidly stylish. The singing is delightful: neoclassical crispness of articulation goes with refined textures that convey the ripe humour of one piece, the tender poetry of the other. The inclusion of Maazel's superb early stereo accounts of Rimsky's *Capriccio* (with the **Berlin Philharmonic**) and *Le Chant du rossignol* glitteringly played by the **Berlin Radio Orchestra**, two classics of the gramophone, is particularly welcome.

(i; ii; iii) *L'enfant et les sortilèges*; (i; ii; iv) *L'Heure espagnole*; (i; ii;) 2 mélodies hébraïques; Shéhérazade; 3 poèmes de Stéphane Mallarmé; (v) Boléro; La Valse

Ⓝ **(*) Australian Decca Eloquence 480 0124 (2). Ansermet, with (i) SRO; (ii) Danco; (iii) Cuénod; Lovano; Migliette; Bisel, Wend, Bobillier; (iv) Rehfuss, Hamel, Derenne, Vessieres; (v) Paris Conservatoire O

Australian Decca have coupled Ravel's two operas with a host of other rare **Ansermet** performances. *L'enfant et les sortilèges* along with *L'Heure espagnole* were among his pioneering early LPs, while *L'enfant et les sortilèges* was one of Decca's first stereo recordings (October 1954) and its vividness still amazes. The performance is idiomatic, with artists like **Suzanne Danco** and **Hugues Cuénod** full of character, and the fresh, bright singing of **Flore Wend** as the Child still captures the ear. Ansermet's orchestral detail is vivid.

L'Heure espagnole was recorded a year earlier and the mono sound is obviously not so opulent. But the cast was quite a strong one, with Suzanne Danco as the provocative wife, with a slight flicker in the voice adding to its distinctively French timbre. **Heinz Rehfuss** sings with incisive clarity as the muleteer. Alas, the occasionally sour woodwinds and rather thin violins prevented these recordings from become top recommendations. Suzanne Danco's similarly idiomatic accounts of Ravel's *Shéhérazade, Deux melodies hébraïques* and *Trois poèmes de Stéphane Mallarmé* also project vividly. The finely etched orchestral writing is clearly brought out in the *Trois poèmes de Stéphane Mallarmé*. Ansermet's Paris recordings of *Boléro* (early stereo) and *La Valse* are not as exciting as his stereo, Suisse Romande accounts but viable enough.

RAWSTHORNE, Alan (1905–71)

(i) *Concertante pastorale for Flute, Horn & Strings*; *Concerto for String Orchestra*; *Divertimento for Chamber Orchestra*; *Elegiac Rhapsody for String Orchestra*; *Light Music for Strings* (based on Catalan tunes); (ii) *Suite for Recorder & String Orchestra* (orch. McCabe)

🎵— ⒷⒷ *** Naxos 8.553567. Northern CO, Lloyd-Jones; with (i) Marshall, Goldberg; (ii) Turner

Though the melodic writing is rarely as memorable as that of, say, Walton, all the works here are beautifully crafted, not least the *Concerto for String Orchestra*, with two dark movements followed by lightness and open intervals. The *Concertante* is most evocative with beautiful solos for flute and horn. The neoclassical *Recorder Suite* has been deftly arranged by John McCabe from an original with piano. Finest of all is the *Elegiac Rhapsody*, written in memory of the poet Louis MacNeice, touching a deeper vein, erupting from lamentation into anger. Outstanding performances, vividly recorded.

(i) *Cello Concerto*; (ii) *Oboe Concerto*; *Symphonic Studies*

🎵— ⒷⒷ *** Naxos 8.554763. RSNO, Lloyd-Jones; (i) with Baillie; (ii) Rancourt

The post-war *Oboe Concerto* is full of good things. **Alexander Baillie** gives a masterly account of the *Cello Concerto*, and **Stéphane Rancourt** is hardly less persuasive in its companion. First-class orchestral playing under **David Lloyd-Jones** and excellently balanced and vividly present recording. The *Symphonic Studies* is arguably Rawsthorne's masterpiece and one of the most ingenious works of its period. All Rawsthorne's music is crafted superbly and highly personal, so that the idiom is immediately recognizable as his.

Clarinet Concerto

ⒷⒷ *** Hyp. Helios CDH 55069. King, Northwest CO of Seattle, Francis – COOKE: *Concerto*; JACOB: *Mini-Concerto* ***

Though the *Clarinet Concerto* is an early work of Rawsthorne's it already establishes the authentic flavour of his writing, the more obviously so in a performance as persuasive as this from soloist and orchestra alike. Excellent recording, and very good value.

Piano Concertos 1–2; (i) Double Piano Concerto

Ⓜ *** Chan. 10339X. Tozer, LPO, Bamert; (i) with Cislowski

(i) Piano Concertos 1–2; Improvisations on a Theme of Constant Lambert

⊕— ⒷⒷ *** Naxos 8.555959. Donohoe, Ulster O, Yuasa

(i) Piano Concertos 1–2; (ii) Overture Street Corner; Symphonic Studies

⊕— **** Lyrita (ADD) SRCD 255. (i) Binns, LSO, Braithwaite; (ii) LPO, Pritchard

Both of Rawsthorne's concertos are among the most memorable written by British composers, providing a Prokofiev-like contrast between jagged figuration and lyrical warmth. Without losing the necssary edge in the writing, **Malcolm Binns** brings out the expressiveness of the music, particularly in the *First Concerto* with its hushed slow movement and interlude in the middle of the final *Tarantella*. There is plenty of vigour in both dance finales (the second has its quota of Latin American rhythms). The *Street Corner Overture* is one of Rawsthorne's once familiar shorter pieces, but it is not often heard now. The *Symphonic Studies* is by general consent Rawsthorne's most original and masterly composition and it well withstands the test of time. The **LPO** under **John Pritchard** plays with evident enjoyment, and the 1977 recording has a fine sense of space and splendid detail. An outstanding reissue in every way.

In the new Naxos recording **Peter Donohoe's** brilliant solo contribution has all the sparkle you could want. In the *Second Concerto* the opening surge of ardour, from soloist and orchestra alike, carries the music forward, while again there is some delightful woodwind detail. In the finale Rawsthorne almost immediately introduces his catchy main theme, which is in a two-four/three-eight metre, and the movement as a whole is played with gusto and wit, producing a blaze of virtuosity at the close. The orchestral *Improvisations* which come as a bonus, are based on a seven-note theme from Lambert's last ballet, *Tiresias*. They are widely varied and listener-friendly and easy to follow. With excellent recording, this can be strongly recommended on all counts.

Geoffrey Tozer also gives a good account of the concertos. The opening of 1 is a bit rushed; **Tamara-Anna Cislowski** is an excellent partner in the 1968 concerto. **Matthias Bamert** and the **LPO** are very supportive and the recording is in the best traditions of the house.

(i) Violin Concertos 1–2; Fantasy Overture: Cortèges

ⒷⒷ **** Naxos 8.554240. (i) Hirsch; BBC Scottish SO, Friend

The Naxos recording brings the accomplished **Rebecca Hirsch** as soloist, with excellent orchestral support from the **BBC Scottish Symphony** under **Lionel Friend**. Her performances hold their own, and the value of the disc is enhanced

by Rawsthorne's *Cortèges*. It is an imaginative and at times haunting piece, very well played and recorded here.

Cortèges (Fantasy Overture)

*** Lyrita SRCD 318. RPO, Wordsworth (with PIERSON: *Macbeth*; MORGAN: *Contrasts*) – ARNOLD: *Beckus the Dandipratt*; CHAGRIN: *Helter Skelter*; WARLOCK: *Serenade for Strings* ***

Cortèges, one of Rawsthorne's finest works, is a duality of processions, the first bringing a noble Mahlerian *Adagio*, the second a brilliant rondo/tarantella, with the two themes combined together in a climactic tour de force, and the work ending wistfully and movingly. **Barry Wordsworth's** performance is very fine indeed, as is the Lyrita recording.

Divertimento for Chamber Orchestra

*** Lyrita (ADD) SRCD 257. ECO, Del Mar – ARNOLD; L. BERKELEY; BRITTEN: *Sinfoniettas*; TIPPETT: *Divertimento* ***

Brief as Rawsthorne's *Divertimento* is, its spare textures and bony argument give it genuine seriousness, most attractively in the songfulness of the central lullaby movement. It is splendidly performed and recorded.

Film music: Burma Victory (suite); The Captive Heart (suite; both arr. Gerard Schurmann); The Cruel Sea: Main Titles & Nocturne; The Dancing Fleece: 3 Dances (both scores arr. & orch. Philip Lane); Lease of Life: Main Titles & Emergency; Saraband for Dead Lovers: Saraband & Carnival (both arr. Schurmann); Uncle Silas: Main Titles & Opening Scene; Valse Caprice; End Titles; West of Zanzibar: Main Titles; Where No Vultures Fly: Introduction; Main Titles & Opening Scene; Surveying the Game (all arr. & orch. Philip Lane)

*** Chan. 9749. BBC PO, Gamba

Between 1937 and 1964 Rawsthorne wrote music for 27 British films. He was not a ready melodist like Malcolm Arnold, but he could write memorable paragraphs, imaginatively and powerfully scored. Gerard Schurmann had worked with the composer in preparing the original scores, and Philip Lane demonstrates his skills of reconstruction using the original soundtracks when the manuscripts are missing. The music is splendidly played and given Chandos's top-quality sound.

Coronation Overture; Madame Chrysanthème: Ballet Suite; Street Corner Overture; Theme, Variations & Finale; (i) Medieval Diptych for baritone & orchestra; (ii) Practical Cats: An entertainment for speaker and orchestra

Ⓜ *** Dutton CDLX 7203. RLPO, Lloyd-Jones; with (i) Huw Williams; (ii) Callow

A superb modern collection of Alan Rawsthorne's most famous music. Both the *Street Corner Overture* and the *Madame Chrysanthème* ballet suite are given bright and breezy performances to match the tuneful nature of the music. The *Coronation Overture* (a première recording), though it has quite a brooding middle section, is essentially festive in spirit and is certainly enjoyable. The *Theme, Variations and Finale* – another première, dating from 1967 – is quite a knotty work, though the finale is rather more lyrical, and it ends in bright C major. The opening of the *Medieval Diptych* is powerfully brooding and atmospheric, and the atmosphere is maintained throughout the work's 14-minute duration. **Jeremy Huw Williams**, a light baritone, sings with evident conviction. **Simon Callow** adopts exactly the right tone in his narration for *Practical Cats*, one of the composer's most entertaining scores. Superb recording, and **David Lloyd-Jones's** direction cannot be faulted.

Practical Cats

Ⓑ **(*) CfP (ADD) 3 82230-2. Robert Donat, Philh. O, composer – BRITTEN: *The Young Person's Guide*; PROKOFIEV: *Peter and the Wolf* **(*)

Rawsthorne's own 1957 recording of his setting of seven of T. S. Eliot's highly engaging poems is a valuable addition to the catalogue, especially as the reissue includes a note by the composer himself. One feels that these musical illustrations will interest older rather than younger children, and will certainly appeal to those who enjoy the original poems. Bright, clear recording.

Symphonies (i) 1; (ii) 2 (A Pastoral Symphony); (iii) 3

ⒷⒷ *** Naxos 8.557480. (i) Ellett; Bournemouth SO, Lloyd-Jones

*** Lyrita (ADD/DDD) SRCD 291. (i–ii) LPO; (i) Pritchard; (ii) Chadwell, cond. Braithwaite; (iii) BBC SO, Del Mar

The *First Symphony* (1950) is a haunting and powerfully wrought piece, which grows in stature on every hearing. The *Second* comes from 1959, and its finale includes a setting of Henry Howard, Earl of Surrey, in praise of summer, with a soprano soloist. **Charlotte Ellett** proves an excellent soloist. The impressive *Third* (1964) is well served here by **David Lloyd-Jones** and his **Bournemouth** forces. This conductor directs all three works with total conviction and real imagination. Powerful music then, splendidly played and vividly recorded, and all for a modest outlay. All three works receive fine performances on Lyrita but, they are displaced by the Naxos newcomer.

Clarinet Quartet

*** Lyrita SRCD 256. King, Aeolian Qt (members) – BERKELEY: *Sextet; Sonatina*; BUSH: *Concert Studies*, etc. **(*)

*** Redcliffe RR 010. Cox, Redcliffe Ens. – BLISS; ROUTH: *Clarinet Quintets* ***

Rawsthorne dispenses with the second violin and opts for the more compressed form of the clarinet quartet. This balances the ensemble clearly in favour of the wind instrument, but on Lyrita **Thea King**, one of the most sensitive of clarinettists, responds to the position of prominence with intensely imaginative playing, drawing out the lyricism which reveals Rawsthorne's deep understanding of the instrument.

Rawsthorne's *Clarinet Quartet* is more ambivalent in feeling than the Bliss *Quintet*, but its quirky opening movement is appealing and the darker *Poco lento* hardly less striking.

With **Nicholas Cox** a most winning soloist, the performance here could hardly be improved upon, and the recording is first class. Choice between this and Thea King will depend on couplings.

String Quartets 1–3; Theme and Variations for 2 Violins

⮕ ⒷⒷ **** Naxos 8.570136. Maggini Quartet

The **Maggini** continue their survey of British quartets. What links all these works is Rawsthorne's obsession with variation form, very clearly demonstrated in that early Duet. The *First Quartet* of 1939 similarly consists of a Theme and Variations, while the *Second Quartet* of 1954 concludes with a variation movement, and the *Third Quartet* of 1965 has a Chaconne as its darkest and most intense movement. Those last two works increasingly demonstrate the influence of Bartók without disturbing the distinctive clarity of Rawsthorne's musical idiom. Ideal performances, vividly recorded.

(ii) Violin Sonata; (iii) Theme & Variations for 2 Violins

*** Metier MSV CD 92029. Skaerved; (i) Honma; (ii) Sohn – MCCABE: *Maze Dances*, etc. ***

Alan Rawsthorne's *Theme and Variations for Two Violins*, one of his earliest works, stands among the finest pieces ever written for this daunting medium, with the interplay between the two instruments bringing a kaleidoscopic sequence of ideas, sharply defined. The *Violin Sonata* of over 20 years later is tougher in its idiom with the four movements tautly argued within a compressed span, not a note wasted. **Peter Sheppard Skaerved** gives flawless performances, very well matched by **Christine Sohn** in the *Variations* and **Tamami Honma** in the *Sonata*. Clear, immediate sound.

READE, Paul (1943–97)

Hobson's Choice (ballet; complete; orchestrated by Lawrence Ashmore; devised and choreographed by David Bintley from the play by Harold Brighouse Dir: Tom Gutteridge)

⮕ 🏵 **** Arthaus DVD 100 442. Karen Donovan, Michael O'Hare, Desmond Kelly, Sandra Madgwick, Chenca Williams, Joseph Cipolla, Stephen Wicks; Birmingham Royal Ballet O, Wordsworth

David Bintley's ballet *Hobson's Choice* was created in 1989 for Sadler's Wells Royal Ballet in London, and it quickly became a box-office hit. However, it was first (at the turn of the century) a famous Lancashire play, then a book, and finally a film; and Bintley has obviously drawn on all three for his scenario for a story which popularized an old phrase in the English language.

The dancing itself is a delight, the choreography, like Paul Reade's brilliant and tuneful score, endlessly witty and inventive. Willie's engaging Dance with the Shoes at the end of Act I evokes Chaplin, and the solo Clog Dance which follows is a bravura highlight; and there is an ensemble clog encore in the park in Act II. With splendid sets and fine continuity, this is a wonderfully warm and repeatable entertainment, and the music, full of melody and attractive orchestral effects and cleverly drawing on popular folk themes, is a pleasure in itself, for the composer's ideas never flag. Surely Harold Brighouse would have been delighted with it.

REED, W. H. (1875–1942)

Andante con moto; Andante tranquillo; 2 Chinese Impressions; Fantaisie brillante; The Gentle Dove (Welsh Folksong); Lento and Prelude; Luddi Dance; On Waterford Quay (An Irish Impression); Punjabi Song; Reverie; Rhapsody for Viola and Piano; Rhapsody in E min. for Violin and Piano; Spanish Dance (Fragment); Toccata

(M) *** Dutton CDLX 7135. Gibbs, Mei-Loc Wu

Reed was a great friend of Elgar as well as being his musical colleague and adviser. Many of these pieces are romantic vignettes, which have something in common with Kreisler's miniatures, if without being quite so sharply memorable. But they include a pair of more ambitious *Rhapsodies* and a lighthearted, dancing *Andante tranquillo*, all of which display an easy-going fluency and genuine musical craftsmanship. The more extended *Fantaisie brillante*, with its agreeable central *Andante* and virtuoso moto perpetuo finale, was dedicated to Reed's teacher, Emile Sauret.

The advocacy here of the sweet-toned **Robert Gibbs**, partnered by **Mary Mei-Loc Wu** (who is much more than an accompanist), is very persuasive throughout this programme. Excellent recording too, natural and very well balanced.

REGER, Max (1873–1916)

Ballet Suite, Op. 130; 4 Böcklin Tone-Pictures, Op. 128; Variations & Fugue on a Theme by Beethoven, Op. 86

*** BIS CD 601. Norrköping SO, Segerstam

Segerstam gets a very good response from the **Norrköping Orchestra** and obviously cares for this music and makes the most of it without succumbing to the expressive exaggeration which spoils some of his other work. Both the *Ballet Suite* and the *Beethoven Variations* are well served, and very well recorded.

4 Böcklin Tone-Poems, Op. 128; Variations on a Theme by Hiller, Op. 100

☛ **** Chan. 8794. Concg. O, Järvi

Of the four *Tone Poems* on Chandos, textures in *Der geigende Eremit* ('Hermit playing the violin') are unexpectedly transparent, and *Im Spiel der Wellen* has something of the sparkle of the *Jeu de vagues* movement of *La Mer* photographed in sepia; while the *Isle of the Dead* is a lovely and often very touching piece. The *Hiller Variations* are gloriously inventive. These works are beautifully recorded and **Neeme Järvi's** perform-

ances have the combination of sensitivity and virtuosity that this composer needs.

Symphonic Prologue to a Tragedy; Variations & Fugue on a Theme of Mozart

*** BIS CD 771. Norrköping SO, Segerstam

Segerstam's obvious dedication to the spirit and the letter of these scores rises to their challenge admirably. The BIS recording is of demonstration standard.

Variations & Fugue on a Theme of Beethoven, Op. 86

(M) *** Chan. 7080 (2). LPO, Järvi – BRUCKNER: *Symphony 8* **(*)

Terminally ill, in his last years Reger concentrated on composition, here orchestrating eight of the 12 variations of a work he originally scored for two pianos. The result is a brilliant, sharply characterized piece with obvious echoes of Brahms, a fine companion for Reger's two better-known sets of variations on themes of Mozart and Hiller, and an attractive coupling for **Järvi's** warm-hearted reading of the Bruckner, now at mid-price. Rich 1986 Chandos sound.

CHAMBER MUSIC

(i) Cello Sonatas 1, Op. 5; 2, Op. 28; 3, Op. 78; 4, Op. 116; 3 (Unaccompanied) Cello Suites, Op. 131c

(M) *** Hyp. CDA 67581 (2). Gerhardt; (i) with Becker

Reger's first two *Cello Sonatas* are warmly Brahmsian, while having ample vitality. In the last two *Sonatas* (from 1904 and 1910) Reger has found a style of his own and 3 has the composer's trademark, a set of variations. The *Cello Suites* have an obvious allegiance to Bach; although they are not just a collection of baroque dances. The performances are excellent, vibrant, with plenty of bravura from the pianist, **Markus Becker**, and with a warmly persuasive style from the cellist, **Alban Gerhardt**. Good, but not quite state-of-the-art recording.

(i) Clarinet Quintet in A, Op. 146; String Quartets in G min. & A, Op. 54/1–2; D min., Op. 74; E flat, Op. 109; F sharp min., Op. 121

☛ (M) *** DG Trio 477 5518 (3). Drolc Qt; (i) with Leister

As these fine *Quartets* show, the melodic invention is more often than not distinguished and there is much that is both individual and beautiful. A good place to start is the Op. 109 *Quartet*, which is full of wonderful ideas. The *Clarinet Quintet* is one of his finest works and **Karl Leister** plays it with his usual artistry and eloquence. A real bargain.

(i) Clarinet Quintet in A, Op. 146; String Quartet in E flat, Op. 109

*** Nim. NI 5644. (i) Leister; Vogler Qt

Karl Leister's artistry and eloquence are very persuasive, as indeed are those of the wonderful **Vogler Quartet**. The Nimbus engineers place us rather too close to the artists and we would welcome rather more space round the sound, but there is no doubt that these are very distinguished perform-ances that call for a strong recommendation.

Piano Trios in B min., Op. 2; E minor, Op. 102

*** MDG 303 0751-2. Trio Parnassus

The *B minor Trio* is for piano, violin and viola and is very de-rivative. There are faint hints of things to come, but for the most part Brahms is the pervasive influence. The *E minor Trio* is another matter: there are some striking harmonic sleights of hand and a reminder of the first of the *Böcklin Portraits*, which bear a slightly later opus number. Fine per-formances, very well recorded too, and well worth taking the trouble to hear.

Violin Sonata 8 in E min., Op. 122; Suite, Op. 103a

*** CPO 777 296. Wallin, Pöntinen

Critics at the time complained that the melodic invention was not strong enough to sustain its length, but this per-formance from **Ulf Wallin** and **Roland Pöntinen** makes out the best possible case for it. Many will find it overlong, but admirers of the composer will find many rewards. In the earlier *Suite* the artistry of these players is again much in ev-idence and the German Radio engineers produce an exem-plary balance.

ORGAN WORKS

Aus tiefer Not schrei ich zu dir, Op. 67/3; Intermezzo in F min., Op. 129/7; Introduction & Passacaglia in D min., Op. posth.; Prelude in D min., Op. 65/7

*** Chan. 9097. Kee – HINDEMITH: *Organ Sonatas* ***

The Müller organ of St Bavo in Haarlem seems ideally suited to this repertoire, as is the slightly reverberant acoustic which rather softens the textures and contours of the Hindemith. **Piet Kee** plays with his customary authority and distinction. A rewarding and satisfying issue.

Chorale fantasia on Straff' mich nicht in deinem Zorn, Op. 40/2; Chorale Preludes, Op. 67/4, 13, 28, 40, 48; Introduction, Passacaglia & Fugue in E min., Op. 127

*** Hyp. CDA 66223. Barber (Klais organ of Limburg Cathedral)

The *Introduction, Passacaglia and Fugue* is bold in conception and vision and is played superbly on this excellently engi-neered Hyperion disc by **Graham Barber**. The five *Chorale Preludes* give him an admirable opportunity to show the va-riety and richness of tone-colours of this instrument.

PIANO MUSIC

5 Humoresques, Op. 20; Improvisations, Op. 18; In der nacht; Träume am Kamin, Op. 143

(BB) *** Naxos 8.553331. Pawlik

Markus Pawlik is a most musical and sensitive player who captures the intimacy of the *Träume am Kamin* to perfection. They are predominantly poetic and gentle pieces, but else-where in the *Humoresques* he shows formidable virtuosity. Very acceptable sound – and those with a taste for music off the beaten track will find this well rewards the modest outlay.

5 Humoresques; Variations & Fugue on a Theme of Johann Sebastian Bach, Op. 81; Variations & Fugue on a Theme of Georg Philipp Telemann, Op. 134

**** Hyp. CDA 66996. Hamelin

Variations & Fugue on a Theme of Bach, Op. 81

(M) *** Warner Elatus 2564 61762-2. Schiff (piano) – HANDEL: *Keyboard Suite in B flat (HWV 434)*; BRAHMS: *Variations & Fugue on a Theme of Handel* ***

(BB) **(*) Naxos 8.550469. Harden – SCHUMANN: *Humoreske* **(*)

Like Brahms, Reger was one of the greatest masters of the variation form. The Bach and Telemann sets are generally acknowledged to be among his finest keyboard works, and **Marc-André Hamelin's** playing has enormous eloquence and imagination as well as a wide range both of dynamics and tonal colour. This has an elegance and refinement that never calls attention to itself. Superbly natural recorded sound too.

Wolf Harden's account of the Reger *Variations and Fugue on a Theme of Bach*, Op. 81, is also very fine. The piano sounds much drier here than in the Schumann coupling. Yet the compelling quality of his playing is in no doubt.

Schiff's performance is splendidly equal to all Reger's demands, yet it never overwhelms the listener with rhetoric, and the linked Brahms and Handel couplings make this live recital, excellently recorded in the Concertgebouw in 1994, very recommendable.

VOCAL MUSIC

3 geistliche Gesänge, Op. 110; 3 Gesänge, Op. 39

*** Chan. 9298. Danish Nat. R. Ch., Parkman

Stefan Parkman and the **Danish National Radio Choir** are the most persuasive advocates of Reger's *a cappella* music. The chromaticism and dense polyphony hold no fears for them and their finely blended tone is in itself a source of pleasure. The Op. 110 *Motets* can be heavy-going but not in these clearly delineated and eloquent performances. Those who are intimidated by Reger's reputation should try this excellently recorded disc.

REICH, Steve (born 1936)

'Works': Disc 1: *It's gonna Rain* (1965); *Come out* (1966); *Piano Phase*: (i) *Double Edge* (1967); (ii) *4 Organs* (1970)

Disc 2: *Drumming* (1971)

Disc 3: (iii) *Clapping Music* (1972); *Music for Mallet Instruments, Voices and Organ* (1973); (iv) *6 Marimbas* (1973–86)

Disc 4: *Music for 18 Musicians* (1976)

Disc 5: (v) *8 Lines* (Octet) (1976); (vi) *Tehillim for Voices and Ensemble* (1981)

Disc 6: (vii) *The Desert Music* (1984)

Disc 7: (viii) *New York Counterpoint;* (ix) *Sextet* (1985); (x; xi) *The 4 Sections: Strings* (with Winds and Brass); *Percussion; Winds and Brass* (with Strings); *Full Orchestra* (1987)

Disc 8: (xi) *3 Movements* (1986); (xii) *Electric Counterpoint* (1987); (xiii) *Different Trains* (1988)

Disc 9: (xiv; xv; xvi) *The Cave* (excerpts) (1993)

Disc 10: (xv; xvii) *City Life;* (xviii) *Nagoya Marimbas* (1994); (xv; xvi; xix) *Proverb* (1995)

🔊 Ⓜ **** Nonesuch 7559 79451-2 (10). Steve Reich & his musicians; with (i) Nurit Tiles & Edmund Niman (pianos); (ii) Michael Gordon, Lisa Moore, Mark Stewart, Evan Ziporyn; James Preiss (percussion); (iii) Russell Hartenberger & composer; (iv) Marimba Quartet; (v) Ens., cond. Bradley Lubman; (vi) Schoenberg Ens., Hague Percussion Group, Reinbert de Leeuw; (vii) Members of Brooklyn Philharmonic & Chorus, Tilson-Thomas; (viii) Evan Ziporyn (clarinets); (ix) Nexus; (x) Edward Niemann & Nuril Tillis (pianos); (xi) Percussion Soloists, LSO, Tilson Thomas; (xii) Paul Metheny (guitar); (xiii) Kronos Quartet; (xiv) Rowe, Beckenstein, Bassi, Mundau; (xv) Steve Reich Ens.; (xvi) cond. Paul Hillier; (xvii) cond. Bradley Lubman; (xviii) Bob Becker, James Preiss; (xix) Theatre of Voices

This invaluable Nonesuch 10-disc anthology traces the steady development of Reich's writing over three decades, beginning with the pure rhythm of the spoken voice alone, with the seemingly interminable repeated word-phrases, 'It's gonna rain' and 'Come out', which by an electronic phasing process overlap and echo ('It's gonna/it's gonna, rain rain'). This led him logically to musical equivalents, a repeated four-note *Piano Phase* and a single chord, reiterated continually on *Four Organs. Clapping Music* speaks for itself, while *Drumming*, Reich's best-known piece, which involves tuned drums, is here heard in a revised version, lasting just under an hour. The *Six Marimbas* follow a similar pattern of repetition. *Music for 18 Musicians* and *Tehillim* mark a further exploration, with an extension of the key rhythmic pattern, and with voices adding depth of colour to the latter piece.

Scored for just clarinets, *New York Counterpoint* (one of the composer's most genial later works) is in three sections, of which the finale is a piquantly witty jazz riff. But Reich returns to tuned percussion in the *Sextet*, extending its dimensions to five movements, with even more complex variation of timbres and rhythms.

But is is with *Desert Music* that we experience a marked expansion of the composer's minimalist horizons. It is set to a philosophical text by William Carlos Williams, and voices are now a major part of the texture; moreover,

rhythms change between the three movements, harmonies are flexible, and there is a strong melodic element: the result is intriguing and attractive.

In *Three Movements* and *Four Sections* (1986/7) Reich turns to the resources of a full orchestra (though still, for the most part, used sectionally) and the second of the three movements develops a motif very like a folk tune, which is taken on into the finale.

Different Trains brings an excursion into descriptive evocation, opening with an obvious pulsing railway rhythm. Intoned dialogue forms a backing to the variety of imagery from the **Kronos Quartet** who, in the second movement (*Europe during the war*), even provide an impressive simulation of an air-raid siren.

The Cave is a unique kind of opera/oratorio, and easily Reich's most ambitious achievement. With the narrative based on Genesis, it tells the story of Abraham, God's refusal of the sacrificial offering of Isaac, and the equally dramatic rescue in the desert of Ishmail, Abraham's other son, born to him by his slave, Hagar. The Cave was the family burial place. The narrative is given a political significance by being laced with questions and comments from a cast of Israeli, Palestinian and American interviewees who, through their genealogy, feel themselves linked to these distant events.

The final disc sums up Reich's achievement, first with his vivid picture of *City Life* in New York, then with a nostalgic look back to his beloved marimbas, and finally the lovely *Proverb*, a floating vocal melisma. Beautifully sung by the **Theatre of Voices**, this somehow takes Reich into the mainstream of late-20th-century music, the world of Arvo Pärt and John Tavener.

(i; ii) *City Life;* (i; iii) *8 Lines for Octet;* (iv) *New York Counterpoint* (for clarinets); (v) *Violin Phase*

🔊 *** RCA 74321 66459-2. (i) Ens. Modern; (ii) Rundel; or (iii) Lubman; (iv) Diry; (v) Mistry

For his portrait of *City Life* Steve Reich took his tape recorder out on the streets of New York to record its background noises, from subway trains, alarm systems set off in parked cars, human heartbeats and various spoken street dialogues.

New York Counterpoint is scored for nine B flat clarinets and three bass clarinets, in which the soloist himself plays, using his own pre-recordings of the other 11 parts gently throbbing and with see-saw figurations. *Violin Phase* also brings four separate, amalgamated parts played by a single fiddler in the same way, and is even more naggingly repetitive.

The original version of *Eight Lines*, the most celebrated piece here, was scored for two pianists, string quartet and two woodwind players (who had to switch quickly between a variety of instruments). The revised version still uses the eight lines of the title, but now the strings underpin the counterpoint, in which the harmonic changes are as minimal as the ideas. The performances are expert.

(i) *Daniel Variations;* (ii) *Variations for Vibes, Piano & Strings*

Ⓝ *** Nonesuch 7559 79949-4. (i) Los Angeles Master Chorale, Gershon; (ii) L. Sinf., Pierson

With these works, following in the footsteps of John Adams, Steve Reich is moving further away from his basic, bare-faced minimalism. Inspired by the murder of an American reporter in 2002, the *Daniel Variations* combine biblical quotations with secular comments. The *Variations for Piano, Vibes, Piano and Strings* is in three sections and is genially full of spontaneous vitality, drawing on canonic interplay to move contrapuntally to a telling apotheosis. Impressive!

(i) *Different Trains*; (ii) *Piano Phase*

🎧 **** Black Box BBM 1007. (i) Duke Qt; (ii) Russo, Mellits – MELLITS: *String Quartet 2* ***

This is the most successful performance of *Different Trains* so far put on disc. The American train sequence is particularly haunting, with the spoken voices atmospherically interpolated; but throughout all three movements the train rhythms are insistently evocative. *Piano Phase* is minimalism pure and simple: over 19 minutes very little happens, while one waits for the basic remorseless rhythmic pattern to get out of phase. It is hypnotically played and the Black Box recording is first class in both works. A key Reich CD, and the coupling shows his influence on another talented composer.

Different Trains; Duet; Triple Quartet

*** Signum SIGCD 004. Smith Qt; composer

Different Trains is in three sections, evoking (but not describing) three different railway networks and their sounds – *America before the war, Europe during the war*, and *After the war*. The train rhythms and siren sounds are created by a string quartet, over which are superimposed speaking voices constantly repeating phrases.

Duet and the three-movement *Triple Quartet* use quartet sonorities alone, but they expand the sounds available by using pre-recorded tapes so that three and sometimes four groups can be heard playing together. The haunting central movement of the *Triple Quartet* is lyrical, even elegiac; the outer movements are abrasive and incisive. The effect in these performances is both spontaneous and original.

Drumming (original version)

Ⓑ *** DG (ADD) 474 323-2 (2). composer and musicians

Written between 1970 and 1971, *Drumming* was one of **Reich's** key early works, firmly establishing the basic style of minimalism. This four-part work, played without a break, in this intance lasts for about an hour and a half and features only one basic rhythmic pattern throughout.

For the aficionado, the result induces an increasing musical hypnosis; for the uninitiated, nothing very important appears to change. The present performance under the composer's direction was faithfully recorded in 1974 and is seemingly spontaneous.

Drumming (new version)

*** Cantaloupe CA 21026. So Percussion

This version of *Drumming* by **So Percussion** (with **Rebecca Armstrong** and **Jay Clayton**, vocals and whistling, and **Eric Lesser**, piccolo) lasts 73 minutes and is certainly hypnotic,

but we would not like to say that it is more or less effective than the performance under the composer.

8 Lines

🎧 Ⓜ **** Virgin 3 63308-2. LCO, Warren-Green – ADAMS: *Shaker Loops* *** 🏵; GLASS: *Company*, etc. ***; HEATH: *Frontier* ***

Steve Reich's *8 Lines* is minimalism in its most basic form, and, although the writing is full of good-humoured vitality, the listener without a score could be forgiven for sometimes thinking that the music was on an endless loop. The performance is expert.

(i) *Eight Lines*; (ii) *Four Organs*; (iii) *New York Counterpoint*; (iv) *Vermont Counterpoint*

Ⓝ Ⓜ *** EMI 2 06624-2. (i) Solisti New York; (ii) Tilson Thomas; (iii) Damiens; (iv) Wilson – GLASS: *Company; Façades* ***

Vermont Counterpoint is aurally fascinating, with its flute-dominated textures – **Random Wilson** here soloist as well as musical director – and the longer *Eight Lines* is also ingeniously scored. But this is minimalist music with a vengeance, with the textural alterations relatively significant over a fairly long time-span. *New York Counterpoint* brings **Alain Damiens's** clarinet multiplied by the use of tape. However, the harmony of *Four Organs* does not change throughout; instead there is a lengthening of the opening chord. The performances are all admirable and the hypnotic effect of much of this music is undeniable.

Music for 18 Musicians

🎧 **** RCA 09026 68672-2. Ens. Modern

Dating from 1974–6, *Music for 18 Musicians* derives from and returns to a pulsing 11-chord cyclic 'theme', framing 12 connected sections, which have comparatively simple additional material superimposed upon them, as the music proceeds. As the recording is cued into 14 separate tracks, the listener can readily isolate the changes within the basic structure. This is a hypnotic performance of a key work in Reich's continuing odyssey in musical minimalism.

(i) *Music for Mallet Instruments, Voices and Organ*; (ii) *Variations for Winds Strings and Keyboards*; (iii) *6 Pianos*

🎧 Ⓜ **** DG 471 591-2. (i) Instrumental & Vocal Ens., directed composer; (ii) San Francisco SO, de Waart; (iii) Chambers, Preiss, Hartenberger, Becker, Velez, composer

Easily the most attractive work here is the *Variations*, which was commissioned by the **San Francisco Symphony Orchestra** but is underpinned by the keyboard instruments (two pianos and three electric organs). The orchestral strings are used to double the harmony played by the organs, and the more active keyboard music is doubled by the woodwind. Only the brass act independently in the first and third of the work's three sections. Much more happens here than is usual with this composer, for that ostinato theme has a constantly varying chaconne bass, except that, as the composer suggests, the 'bass is in the middle register'. For the patient listener this work is well worth exploring.

Music for Mallet Instruments, Voices and Organ (1973) deals with two simultaneous, interrelated rhythmic processes, which purposely get out of sync (or 'phase' as the composer describes the process). *Six Pianos* opens with three of the six players sharing the same eight-beat rhythmic pattern, but with different notes for each pianist. The others then join in, again to produce a complicated rhythmic texture as the instruments get out of phase, substituting rests for notes. Both these works bring the seemingly endless repetitions for which Reich is famous, but the performance here cannot be faulted, neither can the recording, and there is excellent documentation.

Tehillim

🎵 ******** ECM 827 411-2. composer & musicians, Manahan

Steve Reich is listed among the percussion players in *Tehillim*, with **George Manahan** conducting. The central focus, in this Hebrew setting of Psalms 19 and 18 (in that order), is on the vocal ensemble of four voices. The result – with clapping and drumming punctuating the singing – has an element of charm rare in minimalist music. With jazzy syncopations and Cuban rhythms, the first of the two movements sounds like Bernstein's *Chichester Psalms* caught in a groove. The second starts slowly but speeds up for the verses of praise to the Lord and the final *Hallelujahs*. Clear, forward, analogue recording.

Variations for Wind, Strings & Keyboards

Ⓜ ******* Ph. 475 7551. San Francisco SO, Edo de Waart – ADAMS: *Shaker Loops* *******

The *Variations*, written for the **San Francisco orchestra** in 1980, marked a new departure in Reich's writing, using a large orchestra instead of a small chamber scale. The repetitions and ostinatos which gradually get out of phase (like *Drumming*) are used most skilfully to produce a kind of hypnotic poetry, soothing rather than compelling.

REICHA, Antonín (1770–1836)

(i) Sinfonia concertante in G for Flute, Violin & Orchestra; Symphony in E flat, Op. 41; Overture in D

*** MDG 335 0661-2. (i) Bieler, Gérard; Wuppertal SO, Gülke

The first movement of Reicha's *Sinfonia concertante* brings engaging textures but is otherwise relatively conventional. The galant *Andante*, however, brings a charming little violin melody over a tick-tock flute accompaniment; later the two instruments change roles. The *Overture in D minor* is, remarkably, in 5/8 time and its nagging ostinato main theme is at first quite catching. The snag is that, despite its variety of colour, it is a shade over-long. The *Symphony* is a different matter. Its main *Allegro* is very confidently constructed. The *Andante un poco adagio* doesn't disappoint, while in the lively finale the composer keeps a card or two up his sleeve until

the very end. A real discovery, which invites repeated hearings. The orchestra is a fine ensemble and, with two first-class soloists here, offers a rewarding collection, well recorded.

Flute Quartets 1 in E min.; 2 in A; 3 in D, Op. 98/1–3

🎵 ******* MDG 311 0630-2. Hünteler, R. & J. Küssmaul, Dietiens

In the opening *Quartet*, a particularly fine piece, one thinks often of Mozart, and Reicha's invention is seldom inferior. The piquant opening of the *Second Quartet* has a charming insouciance, and in the *Third Quartet* the quaint little tune, marching along slowly and elegantly is again Bohemian in spirit. Throughout all three works the solo flute part demands, and receives, the utmost virtuosity from its performer, here **Konrad Hünteler**, who either dominates or blends with his colleagues, all excellent players. The vivid recording completes the listener's pleasure.

Oboe Quintet in F, Op. 107

ⒷⒷ ******* Hyp. Helios CDH 55015. Francis, Allegri Qt – CRUSELL: *Divertimento* (with R. KREUTZER: *Grand Quintet*) ****(*)**

Antonín Reicha's *F major Quintet* is unmemorable but always amiable. The present performance is of high quality and very well recorded.

Wind Quintets: in F (1811); in E flat; in B flat, Op. 88/2 & 5; in D; in A, Op. 91/3 & 5

🎵 Ⓑ ******** Hyp. Dyad CDD 22006 (2). Academia Wind Quintet of Prague

Czech wind-playing in Czech wind music has a deservedly high entertainment rating, and the present performances are no exception. The music itself has great charm and geniality; it is ingenuous yet cultivated, with some delightful, smiling writing for the bassoon. The players are clearly enjoying themselves, yet they play and blend expertly. The sound too is admirable.

Wind Quintets in B flat, Op. 88/5; C, Op. 99/1

🎵 ⒷⒷ ******* Naxos 8 554227. Michael Thompson Wind Quintet

The **Michael Thompson Wind Quintet** give expert accounts of these attractive pieces. Their playing is very fresh and alive, and Reicha can be both rewarding and interesting – it is finely wrought and pleasing. Very good sound.

Wind Quintets in C & A min., Op. 91/1–2 (Crystal CD 264)

Wind Quintets in A & C min., Op. 91/5–6 (Crystal CD 266)

Wind Quintets in E flat & E min., Op. 100/3 & 4

*** Crystal CD 271. Westwood Wind Quintet

The **American Westwood Quintet** are an excellent group and are recording all Reicha's *Woodwind Quintets*. Their performances so far of these works, all considerable pieces, are excellent and well recorded. This is music of much facility and charm.

REINECKE, Carl (1824–1910)

Harp Concerto in E min., Op. 182

🎵 Ⓜ *** DG (ADD) 463 648-2. Zöller, Zabaleta, BPO, Märzendorfer – MOZART: *Flute & Harp Concerto in C, K. 299* ***; RODRIGO: *Concierto serenata* *** ❀

This is an attractive work, **Zabaleta's** performance is an outstanding one, and it is truthfully recorded. If the couplings are suitable this is a highly recommendable disc.

Symphonies 2 in C min., Op. 134; 3 in G min., Op. 227

🎵 **** Chan. 9893. Tasmanian SO, Shelley

Few forgotten 19th-century composers so richly deserve revival as Carl Reinecke, in his time a leading teacher as well as a successful composer. Almost 10 years older than his friend Brahms, he lived on until 1910, prolific into his eighties. His style is conservative but never bland, like a cross between Mendelssohn and Brahms, with memorable themes strongly developed, and with refined orchestration regularly revealing his Brahmsian love of the horn and oboe. You could hardly find more persuasive advocates than **Howard Shelley** and the brilliant **Tasmanian Symphony Orchestra**, vividly recorded.

Flute Sonata (Undine), Op. 167

Ⓜ *** RCA (ADD) 09026 61615-2. Galway, Argerich – FRANCK; PROKOFIEV: *Sonatas* ***

Some of Reinecke's invention here is quite striking (as in the *Sonata's* first movement). His writing, which has sudden florid bursts, makes an engaging vehicle for an artist of **Galway's** calibre, and this makes a fine bonus for the coupling of two masterly works by Prokofiev and Franck.

String Trio in C min., Op. 249

*** MDG 634 0841-2. Belcanto Strings – FUCHS: *Trio in A, Op. 94* ***

This *C minor Trio* comes from around 1898 and is conservative in style, finely crafted and cultured music, superbly played and recorded.

REIZENSTEIN, Franz (1911–68)

Piano Music: Impromptu Op. 14; Legend, Op. 24; Scherzo fantastique. Op. 26; Scherzo in A, Op. 21; Sonata, Op. 19

Ⓝ Ⓜ *** Lyrita mono REAM 2105. composer – BOWEN: *10 Preludes, Op. 102, etc.* (***)

This is a real rarity. Reizenstein has fallen completely out of the repertoire and we cannot recall seeing any of his works billed in the concert hall or on BBC Radio 3 since the 1950s. Like his contemporary, Arnold Cooke, he never completely escaped from the influence of Hindemith, with whom they both studied. But his finest music such as *Voices of Night* has real substance and vision. He was obviously a formidable pi-

anist, judging from the playing here in 1958, and the music itself is of unfailing interest.

RESPIGHI, Ottorino (1879–1936)

Adagio con variazioni (for cello & orchestra)

Ⓜ *** Sup. (ADD) SU 3667-2. Navarra, Czech PO, Ančerl – BLOCH: *Schelomo*; SCHUMANN: *Cello Concerto* **(*)

Respighi's short but charming set of variations shows the composer on top form. It is an Italianate equivalent of Tchaikovsky's *Rococo Variations* and has a burst of almost Russian romantic expressiveness to make a sunset-like ending. **Navarra** plays it very beautifully, and both his timbre and the orchestra are greatly enhanced by the current remastering.

(i) Adagio con variazioni (for cello & orchestra); The Birds; 3 Botticelli Pictures; (ii) Il tramonto

🎵 *** Chan. 8913. (i) Wallfisch; (ii) Finnie; Bournemouth Sinf., Vásáry

Raphael Wallfisch is very persuasive in Respighi's *Adagio*. *The Birds* brings lovely playing and the luminous recording gives much pleasure. The lambent Italianate evocation of the *Three Botticelli Pictures* is also aurally bewitching. But what caps the success of this Chandos Respighi anthology is **Linda Finnie's** ravishing account of *Il tramonto*. Again very responsive orchestral playing and the recording is in the demonstration class throughout this CD.

(i) Ancient Airs and Dances: Suites 1–3; The Birds (Gli Uccelli): Suite; (ii) Feste Romane; The Pines of Rome

🎵 Ⓑ **** Artemis Vanguard ATM-CD 1227 (2). (i) Australian CO, Lyndon-Gee; (ii) Baltimore SO, Comissiona

Ancient Airs & Dances: Suites 1–3; 3 Botticelli Pictures (Trittico botticelliano)

*** Telarc CD 80309. Lausanne CO, López-Cobos

Christopher Lyndon-Gee's performance of *The Birds* is a complete delight, opening and closing vigorously, yet providing the most refined portraits of the dove, nightingale and cuckoo, with particularly lovely oboe playing in *The Dove*. The opening of the first suite of *Ancient Airs and Dances* has a comparable grace and delicacy of feeling; throughout, Lyndon-Gee's response to Respighi's imaginative orchestration is wonderfully fresh, with the oboe (again) and bassoon distinguishing themselves among the many fine wind solos. The strings produce lovely, translucent textures at the beginning of the *Third Suite*; yet, when a robust approach is called for, the players respond admirably. The digital recording, made at the ABC Studios at Chatsworth, Sydney, is first class.

Feste Romane and *The Pines of Rome* were recorded a decade earlier in Washington DC's National Presbyterian Church and they take full advantage of the building's expansive acoustics. The splendid **Baltimore Orchestra** plays superbly and **Comissiona** generates plenty of adrenalin in the

Epiphany finale of *The Pines* and in the spectacle of the Roman legions marching down the Appian Way. The only snag is that *The Pines* has been assembled in the wrong order, with the finale second and the opening number third! However, one can easily reprogramme to have the movements in the correct order, and the descriptive notes make it plain which is which.

Opening brightly and comparatively robustly, the **Lausanne** performance of the *Ancient Airs* yet has both warmth and finesse. The rhythmic pulse is lively without being heavy, and there is much engaging woodwind detail; at the graceful beginning of the *Third Suite* textures are agreeably light and transparent. The Telarc recording is first rate and even more impressive in the *Botticelli Pictures*, with *La primavera* burgeoning with the extravagantly exotic spring blossoming, and *The Birth of Venus* rapt in its radiantly expansive ecstasy.

Ancient Airs & Dances: Suite 3 for Strings; The Fountains of Rome; The Pines of Rome

⊕ Ⓜ **** DG (ADD) 449 724-2. BPO, Karajan (with BOCCHERINI: *Quintettino*; ALBINONI: *Adagio in G min.* (arr. Giazotto) ***)

In the symphonic poems **Karajan** is in his element, and the playing of the **Berlin Philharmonic** is wonderfully refined as well as exciting. The opening of the *Ancient Airs* brings ravishing tone from the strings, and they sound even more lavish in Giazotto's famous arrangement of Albinoni's *Adagio*, while Boccherini's *Quintettino* makes an engaging additional lollipop.

Le astuzie di Colombina; La pentola magica; Sèvres de la vieille France

*** Marco 8.223346. Slovak RSO (Bratislava), Adriano

Sèvres de la vieille France is based on 17th- and 18th-century airs, scored with great elegance and charm; *La pentola magica* makes use of Russian models. *Le astuzie di Colombina*, described as a 'Scherzo Veneziano', uses popular Venetian melodies among other things. The scores contain some winning and delightful numbers. Decent performances and good recording.

Ballata delle Gnomidi; (i) Concerto gregoriano; Poema autunnale

⊕ *** Chan. 9232. (i) Mordkovitch; BBC PO, Downes

The *Concerto gregoriano* is a meditative, lyrical outpouring making free use of Gregorian modes. Apart from some moments of brilliant display, the slightly later *Poema autunnale* for violin and orchestra is also predominantly lyrical and has moments of a Delius-like mysticism. **Lydia Mordkovitch** gives most affecting accounts of both pieces and is very well supported by **Downes** and the **BBC Philharmonic**. The *Ballata delle Gnomidi* (1920) finds Respighi in his most exotic *Roman Trilogy* mode: it is a dazzling exercise in colour and orchestration.

Belfagor Overture; 3 Corali; (i) Fantasia slava for Piano & Orchestra; Toccata for Piano & Orchestra

*** Chan. 9311. (i) Tozer; BBC PO, Downes

The best thing here is the *Toccata for Piano and Orchestra*. It is better argued and structured, more inventive and novel, as well as more musically rewarding, than either of the piano concertos, and **Tozer** plays it with considerable bravura and panache and the **BBC Philharmonic** under **Sir Edward Downes** are admirably supportive. The *Fantasia slava* is shorter and less interesting, and the same goes for the three chorale arrangements. The *Belfagor* is a re-composition based on themes from his opera, and not the curtain-raiser heard in the theatre. Excellent in every way, and with recording of first-class quality.

Belkis, Queen of Sheba: Suite; Metamorphosen Modi XII

⊕ **** Chan. 8405. Philh. O, Simon

The ballet-suite *Belkis, Queen of Sheba*, is a score that set the pattern for later Hollywood biblical film music; but *Metamorphosen* is a taut and sympathetic set of variations. It has been ingeniously based on a medieval theme, and though a group of cadenza variations relaxes the tension of argument in the middle, the brilliance and variety of the writing have much in common with Elgar's *Enigma*. Superb playing from the Philharmonia, treated to one of the finest recordings that even Chandos has produced, outstanding in every way.

(i) The Birds (Gli uccelli); 3 Botticelli Pictures; (ii) Feste Romane; The Fountains of Rome; The Pines of Rome; (iii) La sensitiva; (iv) Il tramonto

Ⓝ Ⓑ *** EMI 2 37676-2 (2). (i) ASMF, Marriner; (ii) Phd. O, Muti; (iii) J. Baker, City of L. Sinf., Hickox; (iv) Rice, Santa Cecilia Acc. O, Pappano

Some excellent performances here. **Muti** gives warmly red-blooded performances of Respighi's Roman trilogy, captivatingly Italianate in their inflections. With brilliant playing from the **Philadelphia Orchestra** and warmly atmospheric recording, they sound far better than the quality EMI engineers generally produced in Philadelphia, and they are exceptional for their strength of characterization. They are preceded on CD 1 by an excellent account of the composer's glorious *Il tramonto* ('the Sunset'), very well performed by **Pappano**, even if **Christine Rice** is perhaps a shade too closely miked and has less warmth than Janet Baker on the companion disc. The setting of Shelley's poem, *La sensitiva* (in Italian translation), is a most beautiful piece which **Janet Baker** and **Richard Hickox** treat to a glowing recording. The vocal line, mainly declamatory, is sweetly sympathetic and the orchestration is both rich and subtle. Marriner offers delightful performances of *The Birds* and is beautifully recorded. The *Three Botticelli Pictures* are less well known, but they are delicately scored and, with presentation of this standard, they are certainly enjoyable.

The Birds (Gli uccelli); Church Windows (Vetrate di chiesa)

Ⓑ **(*) Sony (ADD) SBK 60311. Phd. O, Ormandy – SCARLATTI: *The Good-Humoured Ladies* **(*)

In *Church Windows* the picture of the baby Jesus in *The Flight into Egypt* has a Latin intensity of feeling which suits **Ormandy** and the rich-textured **Philadelphia** sound, while the following evocation of St Michael, sword in hand, is spectacularly painted with broad strokes of the orchestral brush. The finale, a papal blessing scene, is on the largest scale. Ormandy rises to the occasion and the spectacular recording is a match for the Philadelphia big guns – although subtlety is not the keynote here and the listener is all but overwhelmed. *The Birds* is slighter, but the playing is full of charm, especially the delicate tracery of the final cuckoo evocation.

3 Botticelli Pictures

*** Decca Australian Eloquence (ADD) 476 9766. L. Chamber Ch., Argo CO, Heltay – ROTA: *Concerto for Strings* ***; PIZZETTI: *Concerto de l'estate; La Pisanella: Suite* **(*)

The *Three Botticelli Pictures* are delicate and affecting, fastidiously scored, showing the composer's great skill in the handling of pastel colours. These excellent (Argo) recordings from 1978 have stood the test of time and find themselves on a disc of rare Pizzetti and a short and pleasing Rota work. Good, warm transfers.

Brazilian Impressions; Church Windows (Vetrate di chiesa)

*** Chan. 8317. Philh. O, Simon

Geoffrey Simon is sympathetic and he secures very fine playing from the **Philharmonia**. On CD, the wide dynamic range and a striking depth of perspective create the most spectacular effects.

Brazilian Impressions; Church Windows; Rossiniana

ⒷⒷ *** Naxos 8.557711. Buffalo PO, Falletta

Brazilian Impressions stemmed from a visit that the composer himself made to Brazil. But the longest and most ambitious of the three works here is *Church Windows*, with suitable paintings chosen to go with each piece – *The Flight into Egypt* for the gentle opening movement, *St Michael the Archangel* for the vigorous second, *The Matins of St Clare* for the third, and *St Gregory the Great* for the grandest of the four, rounding off the work with a glorious display, like a papal coronation in sound. This Naxos issue now upstages the Chandos disc above, which does not include *Rossiniana* of 1925, which was Respighi's attempt to follow up the enormous success of *La Boutique fantasque*, this time using some of Rossini's trifling piano pieces, *Les Riens*; but, colourful as these pieces are, they hardly rival those in the earlier suite. The **Buffalo Philharmonic** under its music director, **JoAnn Falletta**, is treated to warm and spectacular recording, apt for such exotic pieces.

Burlesca; 5 Études-Tableaux (Rachmaninov, orch. Respighi); Preludio, Corale e Fuga; Rossiniana

⊕ **** Chan. 10388. BBC PO, Noseda

Not for nothing was Respighi a pupil of Rimsky-Korsakov, for the orchestration is of remarkable brilliance and sub-

tlety. This splendid disc offers two important examples of his arrangements, not just the score he concocted from Rossinian fragments but, most impressive of all, the total re-creation of five of Rachmaninov's *Etudes-Tableaux*, turning them into totally new works, at times barely recognizable against the piano originals. Of the Rachmaninov arrangements there can be no reservations whatever, leaving one open-mouthed at Respighi's ingenuity and imagination. The other two works date from much earlier, with the *Burlesca* ripe with horn-writing, and the *Prelude, Chorale and Fugue* even more remarkable. Performances of all four works are outstanding, with the Chandos sound bringing out the full richness of Respighi's writing.

Piano Concerto in A min.; Fantasia slava; Toccata for Piano & Orchestra

⊕ ⒷⒷ *** Naxos 8.553207. Scherbakov, Slovak RSO (Bratislava), Griffiths

Concerto in modo misolidio; (i) Concerto a cinque

⊕ ⒷⒷ *** Naxos 8.553366. Scherbakov, Slovak RSO, Griffiths; (i) Capella Istropolitana, Danel

The first Naxos CD misses out the *Concerto in modo misolidio* and includes instead the much finer if rather extended *Toccata* and the concise and rather engaging *Fantasia slava*. The Russian pianist, **Konstantin Scherbakov**, is a persuasive and at times dazzlingly brilliant soloist and he is accompanied persuasively by the **Slovak Radio Symphony Orchestra** (**Bratislava**) under **Howard Griffiths**. The recording is excellent and this disc is well worth its modest cost.

Scherbakov's account of the *Concerto in modo misolidio* is superior in every way (except recorded quality) to Tozer's on Chandos – and a third of the price. The *Concerto a cinque* makes a delightful and inventive makeweight.

Feste romane; The Fountains of Rome; The Pines of Rome (symphonic poems)

⊕ Ⓜ **** RCA 82876 60869-2. Santa Cecilia Ac., Gatti

ⒷⒷ **(*) Sony (ADD) SBK 48267. Phd. O, Ormandy

Feste Romane; The Fountains of Rome; The Pines of Rome; (i) Il Tramonto

⊕ **** EMI 394429-2. Santa Cecilia Ac. O, Pappano; (i) with Christine Rice

The Fountains of Rome

(***) Testament mono SBT 1108. St Cecilia Ac., Rome, O, de Sabata – DEBUSSY: *La Mer; Jeux; Nuages; Fêtes* (***)

The Fountains of Rome; The Pines of Rome

⊕ ✿ Ⓜ **** RCA (ADD) 09026 61401-2. Chicago SO, Reiner – MUSSORGSKY: *Pictures at an Exhibition* *** ✿

⊕ Ⓜ **** RCA (ADD) **SACD** 82876 71614-2. Chicago SO, Reiner – DEBUSSY: *La Mer* ****

The Pines of Rome

*** BBC (ADD) BBCL 1007-2. Bournemouth SO, Silvestri – TCHAIKOVSKY: *Manfred Symphony* **(*)

What more appropriate orchestra to record the three Roman colour-scapes of Respighi than Rome's greatest orchestra, the **Accademia di Santa Cecilia**, under its music director, **Antonio Pappano**. As in Italian opera, Pappano has a natural feeling for flexible phrasing without exaggeration, while the fine EMI recording offers clean separation and a wide dynamic range to match even the brilliant RCA versions of Reiner and Gatti. It adds to the attractions of the disc that as a bonus Pappano offers the lovely setting of Shelley in translation for mezzo and strings, *Il Tramonto* ('The Sunset'), beautifully sung with clear, firm tone by **Christine Rice**.

Reiner's legendary recordings of *The Pines* and *Fountains of Rome* were made in Symphony Hall, Chicago, on 24 October 1959, and the extraordinarily atmospheric performances have never been surpassed since for their sultry Italian warmth. Yet the turning on of the Triton fountain brings an unforced cascade of orchestral brilliance. Reiner's classic recording has now been given RCA's SACD facelift and sounds more vividly brilliant than ever. It is presumably still to remain available, alternatively coupled with Mussorgsky's *Pictures at an Exhibition*, but Reiner's account of *La Mer* on the present disc is also pretty riveting.

Daniele Gatti brings something special to all three works: a rapt intensity and an extraordinary feeling for atmosphere and a total dedication to Respighi's glowing, richly coloured scoring that is completely involving. The **Santa Cecilia Orchestra** plays wonderfully for him, and the RCA recording challenges the very best of the competition and is very well detailed.

Ormandy's Sony *Feste romane* has great electricity and enormous surface excitement, and it is a pity that the sound-quality is fiercely brilliant. In the other two works the effect is more opulent, and the **Philadelphia** playing is fabulous, while the recording has come up astonishingly well. This is still a very exciting example of the Ormandy/Philadelphia regime at its most spectacularly compelling.

Victor de Sabata's 1947 account of *The Fountains of Rome* was the earliest post-war set and superseded Albert Coates's early 1930s version with the LSO, also on HMV. It is a magical performance with many touches that, though different from Reiner, are of comparable subtlety and atmosphere.

The Fountains of Rome; The Pines of Rome; Metamorphosen modi XII: Theme & Variations for Orchestra

**** Telarc CD 80505. Cincinnati SO, López-Cobos

This impressive Telarc disc springs a surprise in making a new pairing with the *Theme and Variations for Orchestra*. This suffers from the somewhat ungainly title of *Metamorphosen modi XII*, but it is a marvellously inventive and resourceful score. Expert and sympathetic playing by the excellent **Cincinnati Orchestra** under **Jesús López-Cobos** and (not unexpectedly from Telarc) altogether excellent recording which is spectacular, but also both natural in perspective and impressively detailed, with splendid range.

La Pentola Mafixa; (i) Aretusa; La Sensitiva

*** CPO 777 071-2. O of Teatro Massimo, Palermo; (i) with Pinti

The ballet *La Pentola Mafixa* does for Russian composers (Arensky, Gretchaninov, Rebikov and Anton Rubinstein) what *Rossiniana* did for Rossini. *La Sensitiva* is a setting of Shelley and a beautiful piece. Less familiar is *Aretusa*, another Shelley setting, in which **Damiana Pinti** is again the engaging soloist. The more one investigates him, the more interesting and rewarding Respighi becomes.

La Pentola magica (ballet); arr. of BACH: Prelude and Fugue in D; ROSSINI: La Boutique fantasque ***

☋— **** Chan. 10081. BBC PO, Noseda

Ottorino Respighi's sparkling arrangements of Rossini's late inspirations, the 'Sins of Old Age', which make up the ballet *La Boutique fantasque*, have long been popular, here inspiring an exhilarating performance from **Gianandrea Noseda** and the **BBC Philharmonic**, richly recorded. *La Pentola magica* ('The Magic Pot'), is a ballet score which remained unpublished until after the composer's death, drawing on rare Russian sources in a gentle sequence of ten brief movements, again beautifully orchestrated. The *Prelude and Fugue in D*, the most spectacular item, is an exuberant realization of Bach's organ original, which, far from imitating the organ, pulls out all the orchestral stops in a resounding display.

Rossiniana (arr. Respighi)

(*) Australian Decca Eloquence (ADD) 476 2724. SRO, Ansermet – OFFENBACH: *Gaîté parisienne*; GOUNOD: *Faust: ballet music* *

It is perhaps curious that this work is usually catalogued under Respighi, whereas *La boutique fantasque*, which Respighi also based on Rossini's music, is more often found under Rossini. **Ansermet's** performances are the very opposite of the Solti items on this CD, and it is the delicate colour and balance of these scores (rather than immaculate orchestral playing) that Ansermet fans will most admire. The final *Tarantella* is especially enjoyable here. Vintage Decca sound.

Sinfonia drammatica

*** Chan. 9213. BBC PO, Downes

Respighi's *Sinfonia drammatica* (1914) is a work of ambitious proportions: epic in scale, it lasts just over an hour, the first movement alone taking 25 minutes. Yet it proves rich in incident and lavish in its orchestral colours and virtuosity; even if it is not organic in conception or symphonic in the classical sense, it is an immensely worthwhile addition to the catalogue. If you enjoy the *Alpine Symphony*, you should try this. An excellent performance and outstanding recording.

CHAMBER MUSIC

String Quartet in D; Quartetto dorico; (i) Il tramonto (The Sunset)

☋— 🏵 Ⓜ **** Van. 99216. Brodsky Qt; (i) with von Otter

Ⓝ *** BISCD1454. New Hellenic Qt, (i) with Doufexis

Il tramonto, a setting of Shelley, is relatively familiar: a number of great singers have recorded it. **Anne Sofie von Otter** is a match for any of them. However, the little-known early *Quartet in D major* and the *Quartetto dorico* are quite a find. Respighi was in his late twenties when he wrote the *D major*. There is the occasional whiff of Brahms and even Debussy and at the beginning of the slow movement a fleeting suggestion of late Strauss, and there are moments of serene beauty throughout. The *Quartetto dorico*, which is hardly less rewarding, comes from the 1920s, when Respighi was at the height of his enthusiasm for Gregorian melody. Sensitive playing, finely blended tone and a magisterial authority distinguish the playing, and the recording team deserve congratulations on its truthfully balanced and natural sound.

The **New Hellenic** is reputedly the finest quartet in Greece, and their accounts of these two Respighi rarities are certainly accomplished. *Il tramonto* ('The Sunset'), a setting of Shelley, is more familiar in its orchestral form but **Stella Doufexis** blends in with the more intimate texture to good effect. The recording is in the high standards of the house.

PIANO MUSIC

Ancient Airs & Dances; 6 Pieces; 3 Preludi sopra melodie gregoriane; Sonata in F min.

🎵 **(BB)** *** Naxos 8.553704. Scherbakov

Respighi followed his famous orchestral set of *Antiche danze ed arie* (transcriptions from lute tablature), with some for the piano. He also transcribed others: the first by the Genovese, Simone Molinaro, *Balletto detto il Conte Orlando* bears a strong resemblance to the first movement of *The Birds*, as does the *Gagliarda* by Vincenzo Galileo (father of the famous scientist). Of the other pieces, the *Notturno* from the *Six Pieces* has a distinctly Rachmaninovian feel. The *F minor Sonata* (1897–8) is a rarity. **Konstantin Scherbakov** is a pianist of quality, combining the highest musicianship with sensitivity and refinement. He is excellently recorded too.

VOCAL MUSIC

La sensitiva

🎵 **(BB)** **** Virgin 2x1 5 61469-2 (2). J. Baker, City of L. Sinf., Hickox – BERLIOZ: *Les Nuits d'été*, etc.; BRAHMS: *Alto Rhapsody*, etc.; MENDELSSOHN: *Infelice*, etc. ***

Tautly structured over its span of more than half an hour, Respighi's setting of Shelley's poem, *The Sensitive Plant* (in Italian translation), is a most beautiful piece which **Janet Baker** and **Richard Hickox** treat to a glowing first recording.

Il tramonto

🎵 *** Hyp. CDA 66290. Madalin, ECO, Bonavera –
   MARTUCCI: *Le canzone dei ricordi; Notturno* ***

Respighi's *Il tramonto* (*The Sunset*) is a glorious work which at times calls to mind the world of late Strauss. A most lovely record. Recommended with all possible enthusiasm.

REVUELTAS, Silvestre
(1899–1940)

La Coronela (ballet; orch. Moncada; arr. Limantour); La noche de los Mayas (arr. Limantour); Sensemayá

🎵 **(BB)** *** Naxos 8.555917. Aguascalientes SO, Mexico, Barrios

The Mexican composer and violinist Silvestre Revueltas is essentially remembered for his colourful tone-poems, which are strongly influenced by Mexican folk music. His music is approachable: rhythmic, vibrant, even gaudily orchestrated, often with strong elements of popular Hispanic–American cultures in scores which also have strands of Stravinsky, Prokofiev and Chavez. Vibrant recording to match the performances.

REZNIČEK, Emil von
(1860–1945)

Raskolnikov (Phantasy Overture); (i) Schlemihl (A Symphonic Life Story)

*** CPO 999 795-2. WDR SO, Cologne, Jurowski; (i) with Yamamasu

It is good to have more music from the composer of the brilliant *Donna Diana Overture*, and it is immediately striking to hear the Richard Strauss parallels in *Schlemihl*, *A Symphonic Life Story*, first performed in 1912. It is loosely autobiographical, and the sleeve-note writer at one point suggests it might be entitled 'Not a Hero's Life'. It makes for very enjoyable listening, especially Rezniček's gift for bright orchestrations. This committed performance makes a fair case for this work, though **Nobuaki Yamamasu** is a little unsteady in his short solo. The 22-minute *Raskolnikov Overture* (1932) is, once again, very much in the vein of Richard Strauss (if without the genius), and has some fine passages in it, but in its meandering way it does not always sustain interest. Good recording.

Der Sieger (symphonic poem)

*** CPO 999898-2. Koepp, West German RSO and Ch. of Cologne, Jurowski

First heard in December 1913, *Der Sieger* ('The Victor') is a massive symphonic poem in three movements, involving an enormous orchestra with quadruple woodwind, as well as chorus and soloist. In its own right it stands as a formidable work, rich in ideas, closely argued, with orchestral effects brilliantly handled to have maximum impact, a point superbly realized by **Jurowski's** performance with the **Cologne Radio Orchestra**. Though it was praised at the time, it was a work which failed to stay even in the German repertory in the post-war period of economy in music. This disc, spectacularly recorded, fills an important gap.

OPERA

Donna Diana (complete)

🎵 *** CPO 999 991-2 (2). Uhl, Sadnik, Wittlieb, Pauly, Schluter, Wittges Kiel Op. Ch. and O, Windfuhr

This live recording of a comic opera known till now only from its sparkling overture fills an intriguing gap. The overture is one of the most scintillating in the whole repertory, and the rest of the piece is written just as skilfully, with many ensembles in compound time, inevitably echoing the music we know. The story involves a lovesick prince, Don Cesar, who despairs when his beloved princess, Donna Diana, daughter of the ruling Count of Barcelona, remains cold, repelling all suitors. Needless to say, after many complications, Cesar finally wins Diana's love, with two other pairs also happily coupled. The score moves swiftly, with few set numbers of any length, and arias are generally avoided in favour of duets and ensembles. This recording from the **Kiel Opera** brings lively performances from everyone, with the tenor **Roman Sadnik** excellent as Don Cesar. The casting of **Manuela Uhl** in the title-role is more problematic, when in Act I the beat in her rich soprano is very obtrusive. Happily, in Acts II and III the voice comes into firm focus with clarity, power and warmth, with exposed top notes satisfyingly steady, and subtle shading of *pianissimos*. Warm, atmospheric recording.

RHEINBERGER, Joseph
(1839–1901)

Organ Concerto 1 in F, Op. 137

*** Telarc CD 80136. Murray, RPO, Ling – DUPRÉ: *Symphony* ***

Rheinberger's *Concerto* is well made, its invention is attractive and it has suitable moments of spectacle that render it admirable for a coupling with the Dupré *Symphony*, with its use of the massive Albert Hall organ. The performance here is first rate. A fine demonstration disc.

Organ Music (complete) including Sonatas 1–20; 12 Characteristic Pieces (Meditations), Op. 167; Monologue (12 Pieces), Op. 152; 12 Organ Pieces, Op. 174; Trios Opp. 49 & 189; & miscellaneous works

*** MDG 317 891 (Vol. 1); 317 892 (Vol. 2); 317 893 (Vol. 3); 317 894 (Vol. 4); 317 895 (Vol. 5); 317 896 (Vol. 6); 317 897 (Vol. 7); 317 898 (Vol. 8); 317 899 (Vol. 9); 317 900 (Vol. 10); 317 901 (Vol. 11); 317 902 (Vol. 12). Innig (Kuhn organs at Stadtkirche, St Anton, Zürich; Neumünster, Zürich; St Johann Schaffhausen; & in Winterthur & Zürich's new Cathedral organ)

Organ Sonatas 1–13; 10 Trios, Op. 49; 5 Trios, Op. 189/1–5; 7 Trios, Op. 189/6–12

(BB) **(*) Naxos 8.554212 (Sonatas 1–4); 8.554213 (Sonatas 5–7); 8.554549 (Sonatas 8–9 & Trios, Op. 49); 8.554809 (Sonatas 10–11 & Trios, Op. 189/1–5); 8.557184 (Sonatas 12–13 & Trios, Op. 189/6–12). Rübsam (organ of Fulda Cathedral, Germany)

Rheinberger's 20 *Organ Sonatas*, in as many keys, are the province of the organ fraternity rather than the general collector. But this excellent Naxos survey on a fine organ persuasively shows the variety of their invention. Most have a

Fugue but also include movements described as *Prelude, Canzona, Fantasia, Intermezzo, Pastoral, Toccata*, even *Marcia religiosa*, while other *Sonatas* are simple three-movement works, *Allegro–Andante–Finale*, with the first movement often having a free sonata-form structure and with thematic motives common to more than one movement. The *Trios* are brief, single-movement pieces, occasionally in ternary form, sometimes using canonic devices, and always exploiting the full possibilities of organ registration.

Wolfgang Rübsam's credentials have been established by his Bach recordings, and his survey has so far reached Volume 13, maintaining a high standard of performance and recording on a suitable organ throughout. However, this music is for organ aficionados; other listeners may find much of it rather heavy going!

Rudolf Innig's survey is complete. He uses state-of-the-art organs, notably the instrument at St Anton, Zürich, originally built in 1914, and all restored by the Kuhn Organ Building Company to a standard, which in his view 'represents in authentic manner the late romantic sound ideal of the organ music of the late nineteenth and early twentieth centuries'. His performances are remarkable in their power and colour. Their authority is unassailable and represents a remarkable overall achievement, for the MDG recording is also outstanding in its realism.

6 Pieces for Violin & Organ, Op. 150; (i) Suite for Organ, Violin & Cello, Op. 149

(BB) *** Hyp. Helios CDH 55211. Barritt; (i) Lester; Herrick (organ of All Saints, Kingston-upon-Thames)

6 Pieces for Violin & Organ, Op. 150; Suite for Violin & Organ, Op. 166

(BB) *** Naxos 8.557383. Most, Zeiner (organ of St David's Church, Copenhagen)

Paul Barritt, **Richard Lester** and **Christopher Herrick** make a good case for these slight but charming pieces. Not great music perhaps, but showing Rheinberger at his most winning, tuneful and diverting, and very well and affectionately played, with the recording excellently balanced to give an intimate chamber-music feeling.

The alternative Naxos partnership of **Line Most** and **Marie Zeiner** chooses the four-movement *Suite for Violin and Organ* for their coupling, which is equally agreeable. They seek a rather larger scale, with a more resonant Danish organ. Yet again the balance is adroitly managed and the performances are just as persuasive as those on Hyperion.

Masses: in E flat (Cantus missae), Op. 109; in G min., for Female Voices & Organ, Op. 187; in F for Male Voices & Organ, Op. 190; Hymn: Tribulationes. Motets: Anima nostra; Laudate Dominum; Meditabor

**(*) Paraclete Press Gloria Dei Cantores GDCD 108. Gloria Dei Cantores, Patterson

Having given us a stimulating collection of the music of William Mathias, the Cape Cod-based choir **Gloria Dei Cantores** turn their attention to Rheinberger, best known for his oratorio, *The Star of Bethlehem*. But he composed his first Latin Mass in 1847, when he was just eight years old.

The finest work here is the *E flat Cantus missae* for double chorus, dating from 1878. It is eloquently performed, with the sequence of *Credo, Sanctus Bendictus* and *Agnus Dei* inspiring the singers to considerable expressive fervour. Among the motets the Offertory for Lent in D minor, *Meditabor*, is the most appealing.

The divided choirs seem slightly less confident, although the men are on the whole impressive in the *F major Mass*, with the rather sombre *Credo* the highlight. The women, however, have occasional moments of insecurity in the *G minor* work (dedicated to Brahms) although they still convey its linear beauty. Excellent recording (made in 1994) and an enterprising programme that deserves support. (Your supplier can obtain the disc via: www.paraclete-press.com.)

RICHTER, Franz Xaver
(1709–89)

12 Grandes Symphonies: Set 1/1–6; Set 2/7–12

(N) (BB) *** Naxos 8.557818 (Set 1); 8. 570597 (Set 2). Helsinki Bar. O, Häkkinen

Franz Xaver Richter was one of the leading composers of the Mannheim School, the group who in the first half of the 18th century developed the (then new) form of the symphony. The two sets each of *6 Grandes Symphonies* were published separately, the second group in Paris in 1744. The principal characteristics of these works include a driving intensity in outer movements, while slow movements are rich in harmonic interest and texture. Richter's ideas are imaginative and these works all make enjoyably spontaneous listening. The performances by the youthful **Helsinki Baroque Orchestra** under their conductor **Aapo Häkkinen** are both spirited and expressive, and the use of period instruments does not prevent the central *Andantes* of these (usually three-movement) works from being warmly expressive. They are excellently recorded.

Symphonies 29 in G min. (with fugue); 43 in F min.; 52 in D; 53 in D (Trumpet Symphony)

𝄞⌐ *** Chan. 10386. LMP, Bamert

The vigour and colour of the writing in the five symphonies chosen here is consistently winning, starting brilliantly on this disc with the so-called *Trumpet Symphony*. Also impressive is *Symphony 29* with its powerful fugal writing. Richter is consistently inventive, not least in the three symphonies in minor keys, with the central slow movements staying in the minor, and with the *F minor*, *43*, ending not with a dashing *Allegro* or *Presto* but with a minuet, predicting the future. Excellent, lively performances from the **London Mozart Players**, beautifully recorded.

RIDOUT, Alan (1934–96)

(i; ii) Cello Concerto 1 for Cello, Strings and Percussion; (i; iii) 2: Concerto for Cello and Voices; (i;

ii) 3: The Prisoner (for cello solo & 8 cellos); (iv) The Emperor and the Bird of Paradise

𝄞⌐ *** Black Box BBM 1037. (i) Leclerk; (ii) ECO, Barlow; (iii) Laudibus; (iv) Lumley, Edmund-Davies

Alan Ridout is another fine English composer whose concert music has fallen by the wayside, unheard during the last few decades. The *First Cello Concerto* is a work of distinction, richly lyrical and valedictory in feeling, especially in the third and final movements; the latter is very movingly played here. The *Second Concerto for Cello and Voices* is another valedictory work in three movements (*Threnody, Estampie* and a touching *Sarabande*) associated in the composer's mind with Hiroshima (which he recalls hearing about as a 10-year-old). Some may feel that the use of voices instead of an orchestra gives a gimmicky feel to the piece, but Ridout's sincerity is in no doubt, and the work certainly communicates readily again, ending nobly and in tranquil mood. In the *Third Concerto* the setting of a solo cello against 'an orchestra of cellos' provides a depth and darkness of texture that is used to mirror Ridout's conception of the stress suffered by a political prisoner. But the music reflects also the suffering and final release of Christ: 'The captive world awakened and found the prisoner loose, the jailer bound.' The performances are persuasively dedicated. Just occasionally the intonation of the solo cellist, **Gérard Leclerk**, is a little insecure in its highest range, but he plays with such warmth of lyrical feeling and finds such bravura for the scherzando passages, that this seems a minor flaw.

As a gentle postscript, the tale of *The Emperor and the Bird of Paradise*, told simply by **Joanna Lumley**, is also about a caged prisoner being freed. As the narrator clearly recognizes, the piece has much in common with *Peter and the Wolf*, but here the flute obbligato, which serves for the accompaniment, is simple and unpretentious. It is very well played by **Paul Edmund-Davies**.

RIES, Ferdinand (1784–1838)

Piano Concerto, Op. 132; Grand Variations on 'Rule Britannia', Op. 116; Introduction et Variations Brillantes, Op. 170

(N) (BB) **** Naxos 8.570440. Hinterhuber, RLPO, Grodd

These three works are associated with Ferdinand Ries's successful period of living in England, from 1813 until the early 1820s. Beethoven's influence in this 35-minute piano concerto is obvious and it is a thoroughly entertaining work, subtitled as his 'Farewell to England'. Written in 1823, it is very much in the same vein as Hummel's concertos of the period: very tuneful, with melodic classicism tempered with more dramatic overtones. The finale is a toe-tapping delight. It would be wonderful to hear such music in the concert hall, but we suspect that all we shall ever get is this recording, which luckily is first rate. The *Grand Variations on 'Rule Britannia'* is an absolute hoot, with its bold introduction leading up to its famous theme, which is treated to some brilliant variations. The *Introduction et Variations Brillantes* is a similarly brilliant treatment of 'Soldier, soldier, will you marry me?' Sparkling performances to match the music, and the recording is first-rate.

RIGEL, Henri-Joseph (1741–99)

Symphonies 4, 7, 8, 10 & 14

(N) *** Berlin Classics 0016432BC. Concerto Köln

Henri-Joseph Rigel, born in Germany, made his career in Paris, becoming a key figure at the French court, and later, after the Revolution, in the newly formed Academy of Music. He has been almost totally forgotten, so this disc, as is claimed, rescues him from oblivion. Rightly so, when his writing is always lively, notably in the vigorous outer movements of these three-movement symphonies, products of his early career. Happily, he survived the Revolution among such figures as Méhul, writing works apt for the time like his *Hymn to Liberty*, written three years before his death in 1799. The performances by **Concerto Köln** are superb, lively and understanding and very well recorded.

RIHM, Wolfgang (born 1952)

Gesungene Zeit (Time Chant)

*** DG 437 093-2. Mutter, Chicago SO, Levine – BERG: *Violin Concerto* ***

Under the title *Gesungene Zeit* ('Time Chant'), Rihm has written what is in effect an extended lyrical meditation for the soloist, heightened and illustrated by the orchestra in the most discreet way. As in the Berg, **Mutter** is inspired, playing with an inner hush that only rarely marks her recordings.

RILEY, Terry (born 1935)

The Heavenly Ladder, Book 7; The Walrus in memoriam

⊶ (M) *** Telarc CD 80513. Cheng-Cochran – ADAMS: *China Gates; Phrygian Gates* ***

The five pieces which make up *The Heavenly Ladder* were written in 1994 and represent the composer's move away from an aleatory improvisational style into written 'paper music'. The jazz element remains and is never more effectively interpolated than in the third piece, the polyphonic *Ragtempus fugatum*. *Venus in '94* is a bizarre waltz-scherzo and the *Fandango on the Heavenly Ladder* (the most extended movement) intriguingly combines melancholy with energy. Its three themes are then gently re-explored in the closing *Simone's Lullaby*, a set of variations marked *pianissimo* throughout, and dedicated to the composer's newly arrived granddaughter. *The Walrus in memoriam* is a witty ragtime encore piece ending more reflectively, as it is intended as a memorial to John Lennon. The performances here are persuasive: **Gloria Cheng-Cochran** is very sensitive to the composer's eclectic but very personal pianistic excursions, and with the stimulating Adams couplings (dating from the late 1970s) this is an important issue for those interested in the way mimimalism is developing.

In C

*** Ars Nova 8.226049. Copenhagen, Percurama Percussion Ens., Hillier

Terry Riley's *In C* brings a repeated 'C' as a hypnotic basis for various instrumental permutations. In this new version (which surely has an Adams influence) vocal contributions are added with coloristic advantage, swelling out to form various climaxes. This extension is clearly intended by the composer to increase the music's appeal, and the performance is authentic. But many may feel that the original version is more potent.

RIMSKY-KORSAKOV, Nikolay (1844–1908)

Capriccio espagnol, Op. 34

⊶ (M) **** RCA (ADD) 09026 63302-2. RCA Victor SO, Kondrashin – KABALEVSKY: *The Comedians Suite*; KHACHATURIAN: *Masquerade Suite*; TCHAIKOVSKY: *Capriccio italien* **** ❀

⊶ (M) *** DG (IMS) (ADD) 449 769-2 (2). BPO, Maazel – RAVEL: *L'Heure espagnole; L'Enfant et les sortiléges* ***; STRAVINSKY: *Le Chant du rossignol* *** ❀

Kondrashin's 1958 performance is among the finest ever recorded, ranking alongside Maazel's famous Berlin Philharmonic account, but with the advantage of slightly more sumptuous string textures. Like the coupled Tchaikovsky *Capriccio* it has great flair and excitement, with glittering colour and detail in the variations and the *Scena e canto gitana*. The orchestral zest is exhilarating, yet there is warmth too and the resonant recording still sounds very good indeed.

Maazel's 1960 recording of the *Capriccio espagnol* is memorable in every way, and remains one of his finest recorded performances. With gorgeous string and horn playing and a debonair, relaxed virtuosity in the *Scena e canto gitano*, leading to remarkable bravura in the closing sequence, every note in place, this is unforgettable.

Capriccio espagnol; Christmas Eve: Suite. Dubinushka; May Night: Overture. Russian Easter Festival Overture; Sadko; The Snow Maiden: Suite. Symphony 2 (Antar); The Tale of Tsar Saltan: Suite

(N) ❀ *** Australian Decca Eloquence stereo/mono 480 0827 (2). SRO, Ansermet

This two-CD Rimsky-Korsakov set surely shows **Ansermet** at his very finest. The opening of the *Christmas Eve Suite* has a chilled, icy, magical atmosphere, and this colourful tone-poem builds up to a magnificent polonaise – an adrenalin-inducing moment – where Ansermet's rhythmic bite is at its best. The *Snow Maiden Suite* is similarly colourful, with Ansermet bringing out all the brilliance of the woodwind and percussion in particular. Neither the *Russian Easter Festival Overture* nor *Capriccio espagnol* performances are as inspired as this, though the rhythmic point in *Capriccio espagnol* (the only mono recording on this CD) is unfailingly enjoyable. The opening of *Dubinushka* is delightfully and jauntily pointed, with the bass drum (as always from this source, beautifully captured) adding to the piquant effect. *Sadko* has marvellous atmosphere and intensity – as well as drama – and there is plenty of felicitous music, as well as playing, in this score. *May Night*, with its vibrant strings, comes off well, as does all the brilliance in the *Tale of Tsar Saltan Suite* – again, the sparkle of the recording amazes. Even if Ansermet's bee in the *Flight of the Bumblebee* is a rather leisurely creature, it is invested with plenty of buzz from all departments of the orchestra. The longest work in this collection is the still rare *Antar* which Ansermet helped to pioneer on LP – he recorded its first stereo release in astonishingly early stereo, dating from June 1954, yet sounding amazingly full, if not as expansive as the later, stereo recordings on this CD.

Capriccio espagnol; Legend, Op. 29; Neapolitan Song; Overtures: Ivan the Terrible: The Tsar's Bride; The Maid of Pskov; Sinfonietta on Russian Themes

**** Chan. 10424. BBC PO, Sinaisky

A first-class new collection with some unfamiliar items, but plenty of fine Rimskyan invention. The *Overtures* are brightly hued and vivacious, with strong Russian themes. The *Sinfonietta* has a set of variations for its slow movement, but is missing its finale (which the composer abandoned) yet is just as vividly scored. The programme of the *Legend* is unclear, but it is in four parts, with moments of melodrama and much of the exotic colouring of *Scheherazade*, if not quite as inspired. The *Neapolitan Song* is a fun piece, a brilliant tarantella variant of Denza's *Funiculi, funicula*. The best-known work, the *Capriccio espagnol*, is comparatively relaxed, with **Sinaisky** and the **BBC Philharmonic Orchestra** revelling in its kaleidoscopic Mediterranean colours. It certainly glitters, especially the exhilarating closing *Fandango*. Top-quality Chandos recording makes this a very enticing disc.

Christmas Eve: Suite; Le Coq d'or: Suite; Legend of the Invisible City of Kitezh: Suite; May Night: Overture; Mlada: Suite; The Snow Maiden: Suite; The Tale of Tsar Saltan: 3 Musical Pictures; The Flight of the Bumblebee

🎵 Ⓜ *** Chan. 10369X (2). SNO, Järvi

Originally on three full-priced discs, this selection is now offered on a pair of mid-priced CDs, a remarkable saving. **Neeme Järvi** draws the most seductive response from the **SNO**; he continually creates orchestral textures which are diaphanously sinuous. Yet the moments when the brass blazes or the horns ring out sumptuously are caught just as strikingly, and the listener is assured that here is music which survives repetition very well.

Christmas Eve: Suite; Le Coq d'or: Suite; The Tale of Tsar Saltan: Suite; Flight of the Bumblebee

🎵 *** ASV CDDCA 772. Armenian PO, Tjeknavorian

Tjeknavorian and his fine **Armenian Orchestra** are completely at home in Rimsky's sinuous orientalism, with its glittering, iridescent wind-colouring. The racy vigour and

sparkle of the playing brings a jet-setting bumblebee and the carolling horns and bold brass add to the vividness.

Christmas Eve: Suite; Overture on Russian Themes, Op. 28; Pan Voyevoda: Suite; The Snow Maiden: Suite; The Tsar's Bride: Overture

🎵 **** BIS CD 1577. Malaysian PO, Bakels

A superb collection even more seductive than Järvi's compilation, above, and including several novelties. *The Tsar's Bride Overture* ought to be better known, while the *Pan Voyevoda Suite* is very rare and yet also includes some of Rimsky's most colourful ideas. The more familar *Christmas Eve Suite* (a favourite of Ansermet's) opens with a glowing horn solo, and the three central dances of the stars and comets are played with much delicacy, while the following *Polonaise* has splendid rhythmic lift. The *Overture on Russian Themes* is also most imaginatively presented. Here and in *The Snow Maiden Suite* Rimsky's orchestral palette glitters and glows iridescently, the *Dance of the Birds* is delightful, and the famous closing *Dance of the Clowns* has real rhythmic panache. The BIS recording is very much in the demonstration bracket.

Christmas Eve: Polonaise; Mlada: Procession of the Nobles; Snow Maiden: Dance of the Tumblers; Tsar Saltan: Farewell of the Tsar

Ⓑ *** Sony (ADD) 517482-2. Phd., Ormandy – TCHAIKOVSKY: *Nutcracker Suite* **

These four Rimsky lollipops are marvellously played and brightly recorded, with exhilarating brass in the closing excerpt from *Tsar Saltan*.

Concert Fantasy on Russian Themes for Violin & Orchestra in B min., Op. 33

**(*) Globe GLO 5174. Lubotsky, Estonian Nat. SO, Volmer – ARENSKY; TCHAIKOVSKY: *Violin Concertos* **(*)

The *Concert Fantasy in B minor on Two Russian Themes* is a slight but colourful piece, and it is persuasively performed here. It makes an admirable fill-up to Arensky's endearing *Violin Concerto* and the Tchaikovsky which inspired it. Good orchestral playing under **Arvo Volmer** and naturally balanced sound.

Piano Concerto in C sharp min., Op. 30

Ⓝ Ⓑ *** Naxos 8.557794. Liù, RPO, Yablonsky – KABALEVSKY: *Piano Concerto 3, etc.* ***

*** Hyp. CDA 66640. Binns, E. N. Philh. O, Lloyd-Jones – BALAKIREV: *Concertos 1–2* ***

Rimsky-Korsakov's *Piano Concerto* is surprisingly under-represented on CD and is almost totally unknown in the concert hall, no doubt because of its short duration (just over 14 minutes long). Yet it is a thoroughly entertaining piece, with its appealing Russian folk-song motive, and all the colour for which the composer is famous. This inexpensive but excellent Naxos performance and recording makes a welcome addition to the catalogue.

Malcolm Binns also proves a sensitive and intelligent exponent in the Rimsky-Korsakov *Concerto*, which comes aptly coupled with Balakirev's two essays in the form. The

Northern Philharmonia under David Lloyd-Jones give excellent support and the Hyperion recording is first class.

Le Coq d'or: Suite

(***) BBC Legends mono BBCL 4084-2. RPO, Beecham – BALAKIREV: *Symphony 1*; BORODIN: *Polovtsian Dances* (***)

This live broadcast performance has all the swagger and panache that one would expect of **Beecham** in this music, compensating for the lack of stereo. A welcome fill-up for the outstanding account of the Balakirev *Symphony 1*.

Le Coq d'or; The Maid of Pskov; Pan Voyevoda: suites

⊕– 🌣 **** Kontrapunct 32247. Odense SO, Serov

Serov is complete master of the repertoire, and the playing of the **Odense Orchestra** is glorious, the glowing woodwind palette matched by the most seductive and transparent string textures. Serov's performance of *Le Coq d'or* is every bit as fine as Maazel's, and the recording here is even more luxuriant. In *The Maid of Pskov* suite *The Tsar Hunting in the Wood and Tempest* has much of the imaginative pictorial evocation and imagery of Berlioz's *Royal Hunt and Storm*. Again it is superbly presented, as is the hardly less attractive *Pan Voyevoda* which opens with a pastoral evocation rather like Wagner's *Forest Murmurs*, and includes three brilliantly scored *Russian Dances*.

(i) Le Coq d'or: Suite; (ii) Scheherazade (Symphonic Suite), Op. 35

Ⓝ (*(**)) Australian Decca Eloquence mono/stereo 480 0081. Ansermet, with (i) SRO; (ii) Paris Conservatoire O

For *Scheherazade* Australian Decca have used **Ansermet's** rare 1954 performance with the **Paris Conservatoire Orchestra**. This is generally more lively than his later, albeit more brilliantly recorded, version with the Suisse Romande Orchestra, and jolly good it is too. It offers more subtlety than you might expect, with Richard Osborne noting (of the third movement) in his 1979 BBC Radio 3 *Building a Library* survey of this work, that Ansermet observed 'repeated arpeggios on wind and strings which should be nothing more than delicate veils of sound, like the quiet murmurings of an Aeolian harp caressed by a summer's breeze'. With the exception of slight tubbiness in the bass, the sound is astonishingly good, and many will appreciate the distinctive 'French' timbres of the orchestra. It is coupled with the (new to CD) mono version of *Le Coq d'or Suite*. Here the effect is rather shrill, but not unbearably so. Ansermet, typically, brings out all the music's colour, with the opening hauntingly mysterious and the *Marriage Feast* and *Lamentable End of King Dodan* excitingly done, with Ansermet's strong rhythmic grip keeping the tension racked up.

Scheherazade (ballet; complete; with choreography by Michael Fokine and costumes and sets adapted from the original Ballets Russes production by Anatoly and Anna Nezhny; DVD version)

⊕– 🌣 **** Decca DVD 079 322-9. Ilze Liepa, Andris Liepa, Victor Yeremenko, Bolshoi State Academic Theatre O, Chistiakov (Dir.: Andris Liepa) – STRAVINSKY: *Petrushka; The Firebird* ****

This indispensable DVD offers recreations of three key Diaghilev productions from the peak era of the Ballets Russes, with choreography, décor and costumes as near as possible to the original staging. In its day *Scheherazade* (with the heroine renamed Zabeida) was something of a *coup de théâtre*, because its climax was a bacchanalian orgy, with Zabeida and her Golden Slave lover caught *in flagrante delicto* by the sudden return of her master, Sultan Shakhriar, from a supposed hunting expedition.

All this happens to edited sections of the first movement of Rimsky's suite. Then the slow movement is played in its entirety for the vividly sensuous *pas de deux* of Zabeida and her lover, which becomes increasingly erotic. With the opening of the finale the whole company has joined them, and the dancing becomes riotously orgiastic. Zabeida and her lover become more and more abandoned. The Sultan and his friend have no doubt as to what is going on, and with their armed entourage they promptly slaughter all the slaves. But Zabeida steals his knife and stabs herself to death. The Shah is left devastated as Rimsky's closing bars act as a threnody rather than the peaceful, much happier ending the composer intended. But what makes this melodramatic ballet so enjoyable is the luxurious décor and costumes, and the excitement and overt eroticism of the dancing itself. The **Bolshoi State Academic Theatre Orchestra** plays voluptuously and excitingly throughout under **Andrey Chistiakov** and the recording is vividly wide-ranging and full-blooded, if not entirely refined. Moreover, this DVD also includes *The Firebird* and *Petrushka*.

Scheherazade, Op. 35 (DVD version)

Ⓝ **** Medici Arts DVD 2072276. Phd. O, Ormandy (with GLINKA: *Ruslan and Ludmilla Overture*; HANDEL: *Concerto in D, HWV 335a*; WOLF-FERRARI: *Il segreto di Susanna Overture*; R. STRAUSS: *Der Rosenkavalier suite*)

Now here is something rather special. **Eugene Ormandy** recorded at the Academy of Music, Philadelphia, in 1977–8. This great American partnership, stretching over many years, produced a unique sonority, flair and virtuosity. Just listen to the gorgeous lower strings in the second subject of the *Ruslan and Ludmilla Overture*. But the most cherishable piece is a performance of *Scheherazade* which is perfect in every way, with a superb violin soloist in **Norman Carol**. There is some wonderfully beautiful string-playing too in the *Rosenkavalier Suite*, although the closing climax is less than refined (not the orchestra's fault but the arrangement), and the old-fashioned account of the Handel *Concerto*, richtextured and with unashamedly dignified tempi, is a joy. The visual side of things is as expertly managed as the sound. Not to be missed.

Scheherazade (symphonic suite), Op. 35 (CD versions)

⊕– 🌣 Ⓜ **** RCA SACD 82876 66377-2. Chicago SO, Reiner – STRAVINSKY: *Song of the Nightingale* ***

🔑 **** Ph. **SACD** 470 618-2; CD 470 840-2. Kirov O, Gergiev – BORODIN: *In the Steppes of Central Asia;* BALAKIREV: *Islamey* ***

🔑 (M) **** EMI 5 66983-2. RPO, Beecham (with BORODIN: *Polovtsian Dances* ****)

🔑 (M) *** Cala (ADD) CACD 0536. LSO, Stokowski (with rehearsal sequence) – TCHAIKOVSKY: *Marche slave* **(*)

*** DG 437 818-2. O de l'Opéra Bastille, Chung – STRAVINSKY: *Firebird Suite* ***

(i) *Scheherazade;* (ii) *Capriccio espagnol, Op. 34.*

🔑 *** Telarc CD 80208. LSO, Mackerras

(i–ii) *Scheherazade;* (iii–iv) *Capriccio espagnol;* (i; iv) *Russian Easter Festival Overture, Op. 36*

🔑 (M) *** Ph. (ADD) 442 643-2. (i) Concg. O; (ii) Kondrashin; (iii) LSO; (iv) Markevitch

(i) *Scheherazade;* (ii) *Fairy Tale (Skazka)*

(BB) (**) Dutton mono CDBP 9712. (i) Paris Conservatoire O, Ansermet; (ii) Philh. O, Lambert (with BORODIN: *Polovtsian Dances* arr. Rimsky-Korsakov (**))

Scheherazade; Fairy Tale (Skazka), Op. 29; Sadko, Op. 5; Song of India, from Sadko (arr. Tjeknavorian)

*** ASV CDDCA 771. Armenian PO, Tjeknavorian

Scheherazade; Mlada: Procession of the Nobles

*** BBC (ADD) BBCL 4121-2. Georgiadis, LSO, Svetlanov – SCRIABIN: *Poème de l'extase* ***

Scheherazade; Russian Easter Festival Overture; The Maid of Pskov: Hunt and Storm

(M) (***) Biddulph mono WHL 010. Phd. O, Stokowski

Scheherazade; Tsar Saltan: Orchestral Suite

(BB) *** Naxos 8.550726. Philh. O, Bátiz

Reiner's magnificent (1956) *Scheherazade* stands out among the many superb RCA recordings made in Chicago in the 1950s. In the new SACD transfer the feeling of sitting in the concert hall is uncannily real, and the recording itself has extraordinary lustre. Reiner's first movement opens richly and dramatically and has a strong forward impulse. **Sidney Harth**, the orchestral leader, naturally balanced, plays most seductively. Reiner's affectionate individual touches in the gloriously played slow movement have much in common with Beecham's version and they sound similarly spontaneous. The finale, brilliant and exciting, was recorded in a single take and has a climax of resounding power and amplitude, and the acoustics throughout provide the orchestra with plenty of body and arresting brass sonorities. The new Stravinsky coupling also shows the conductor and his orchestra at their finest, and this is a disc that should find a place in every collection.

Gergiev's Kirov performance is the most exciting, most red-blooded account of Rimsky-Korsakov's orchestral warhorse in many years, electrifying from beginning to end, with sound of a fullness and brilliance never before heard in Russian recordings. The two shorter pieces, the atmospheric Borodin tone poem and Lyapounov's brilliant orchestration of Balakirev's virtuoso piano piece, *Islamey*, are welcome makeweights.

Mackerras's reading combines gripping drama with romantic ardour, subtlety of colour with voluptuousness; he is helped by a wonderfully beguiling portrait of Scheherazade herself, provided by his orchestral leader, in this case **Kees Hulsmann**. Mackerras then delivers a thrilling bravura account of *Capriccio espagnol*, lushly opulent in the variations, glittering in the exotic *Scena e canto gitano*, and carrying all before it in the impetus of the closing *Fandango asturiano*. Telarc's digital recording is very much in the demonstration class.

Kondrashin's version of *Scheherazade* with the **Concertgebouw Orchestra** has the advantage of splendidly glowing (1980) analogue recorded sound. **Markevitch** gives an excellent account of the *Russian Easter Festival Overture* with the same orchestra; the *Capriccio espagnol*, too, is brilliantly played by the **LSO**, and in both the sound also has considerable allure, with the present CD transfer much more vivid than the original LP.

Beecham's 1957 *Scheherazade* is a performance of extraordinary drama and charisma. Alongside the violin contribution of **Stephen Staryk**, all the solo playing has great distinction; in the second movement Beecham gives the woodwind complete metrical freedom. The sumptuousness and glamour of the slow movement are very apparent and the finale has an explosive excitement, rising to an electrifying climax. This could well be first choice for some collectors, although the *fortissimo* massed strings in the first movement are on the thin side and show the age of the recording.

The BBC disc brings a welcome reminder of the highly charged and intense playing that **Svetlanov** could achieve in the concert hall. These pieces find the **LSO** responding with enthusiasm and virtuosity to his direction.

On his visits to England in the 1960s, **Leopold Stokowski** was still at the height of his powers, and the result is even more thrillingly high-powered than the multiple versions he had already put on disc and the one which (11 years later) he was to make for RCA. This Cala version comes with fascinating couplings: the thrilling live performance of Tchaikovsky's *Marche slave* that Stokowski conducted as an encore at his ninetieth birthday concert in London, with a spoken introduction by himself, and, fascinatingly, four substantial clips from the rehearsals the conductor took in the Phase Four sessions on *Scheherazade*.

On ASV a refreshing and totally gripping *Scheherazade* from Eastern Russia. **Tjeknavorian** shows great imaginative flair in the two shorter folk tales and also offers his own gently luscious arrangement of the *Chant hindue*, which caresses the ear beguilingly. The brilliant recording has great vividness and projection, but relatively little sumptuousness.

There is a certain freshness about the Paris account under **Myung-Whun Chung**; nothing is routine and the playing has a certain enthusiasm. Very fast and effective tempo in the finale. The sound has warmth and perspective, though the timpani resonate perhaps a bit too much. All the same, a very enjoyable newcomer.

Bátiz's reputation for spontaneity in the recording studio is demonstrated at its most telling. His performance is impulsive, full of momentum and seductively volatile. The colourful *Tsar Saltan Suite* is comparably dramatic and vivid. In short, with first-class recording, both clear in detail and full-bodied, at super-bargain price this is hard to beat.

The collection of **Leopold Stokowski's** recordings of Rimsky-Korsakov on Biddulph centres on the first of his five versions of *Scheherazade*. Made in 1927, it is wilder and more passionate than later ones; fascinatingly, an alternative version of the first movement, never issued before, is included as a supplement. Equally impressive is Stokowski's intense, volatile account of the *Russian Easter Festival Overture*, dating from 1929, while the *Hunt and Storm* sequence from the *The Maid of Pskov* comes from ten years later. The Biddulph transfers are excellent, with plenty of body.

Ansermet's 1948 recording with its lighter manner has an attractively balletic quality, building up gradually rather than packing a punch. The usual reservations need mentioning about the playing of the Paris orchestra – with brass vibrato and a sugary solo violin among them. As transferred, this is not one of the most vivid of early Decca mono ffrr recordings. The rarity, *Skazka*, conducted by **Constant Lambert**, is taken from a 1946 EMI recording, with **Gregor Fitelberg's** reading of the *Polovtsian Dances* a welcome bonus.

Symphonies 1, Op. 1; 2 (Antar), Op. 9; 3, Op. 32; Capriccio espagnol; Russian Easter Festival Overture

(M) *** DG 459 512-2 (2). Gothenburg SO, Järvi

Symphonies 1 in E min., Op. 1; 2 (Antar), Op. 9; 3 in C, Op. 32; Capriccio espagnol, Op. 36; (i) Piano Concerto in C sharp min., Op. 30; Russian Easter Festival Overture, Op. 36; Sadko, Op. 5

(M) **(*) Chan. 6613 (2). (i) Tozer; Bergen PO, Kitaienko

Whatever Rimsky-Korsakov's symphonies may lack in symphonic coherence they make up for in colour and charm. *Antar* is not quite as strong as some of its protagonists would have us believe, but it should surely have a stronger presence in the concert and recorded repertoire than it has. The performances under **Neeme Järvi** have considerable merit and the **Gothenburg Orchestra** is excellently recorded; moreover, the addition of the *Capriccio* and *Russian Easter Festival Overture* make the DG set a very attractive proposition. A clear first choice.

Kitaienko draws very good playing from the **Bergen Philharmonic** throughout and the first two symphonies are generally successful. In the *Third Symphony* the lustrous colours of the secondary material glow appealingly, but the Scherzo lacks sparkle. He gets very lively results in the *Capriccio espagnol*, but *Sadko* takes a while to warm up, although it has a spectacular close. With **Tozer** at the keyboard

he shares a warmly lyrical view of the *Piano Concerto* but, partly because of the resonant sound, the finale again lacks something in sparkle, and Malcolm Binns on Hyperion (see above) is preferable.

Symphonies: 1, Op. 1; 3, Op. 32; Fantasia on Serbian Themes

꒐ *** BIS CD 1477. Malaysian PO, Bakels

Here, in the two less well-known symphonies of Rimsky-Korsakov, **Bakels** offers performances of admirable point and refinement, particularly in the strings, with the slow movement of 3, for example, tender in its delicate phrasing, and with the 5/4 rhythms of the Scherzo delectably pointed. The *Fantasia on Serbian Themes* makes an attractive supplement. Clear, well-balanced recording, with air round the sound.

Symphony 2 (Antar); Russian Easter Festival Overture

꒐ (BB) *** Hyp. Helios CDH 55137. Philh. O, Svetlanov

It goes without saying that the **Philharmonia Orchestra** under **Svetlanov** produce an excellent account of Rimsky-Korsakov's colourful score and there is no want of atmosphere or spirit in their playing. Moreover, they are given excellent recorded sound by the Hyperion team.

Piano & Wind Quintet in B flat

(BB) *** Hyp. Helios CDH 55173. Capricorn – GLINKA: *Grand Sextet in E flat* ***

*** CRD (ADD) 3409. Brown, Nash Ens. – ARENSKY: *Piano Trio 1* ***

Capricorn's sparkling account of Rimsky's youthful *Quintet* for piano, flute, clarinet, horn and bassoon is all the more welcome at budget price, particularly as it is very well recorded.

The **Nash Ensemble** also give a spirited and delightful account of it on CRD that can be warmly recommended for its dash and sparkle and full, naturally balanced sound.

OPERA

The Legend of the Invisible City of Kitezh (complete; CD version)

*** Ph. 462 225-2 (2). Gorchakova, Galuzin, Putilin, Ohotnikov, Marusin, Minjilkiev, Ognovienko, Kirov Opera Ch. & O, Gergiev

Recorded live at the Mariinsky Theatre in St Peterburg, this long fairy-tale piece (lasting almost three hours) relies above all on the cadences of Russian folk song. As usual with Russian folk-tales the plot brings a curious mixture of jollity and bitterness. Though the Prince dies in battle in the middle of Act III – illustrated in an interlude – he is resurrected in Act IV, when the disappearing City of Kitezh is magically transformed into Paradise, with hero and heroine united in life after death. What adds spice to the plot is the equivocal character of the drunkard, Grishka, comic only in part, who initially is prompted to attack Fevroniya, but who later is befriended by her. **Galina Gorchakova** sings powerfully as Fevroniya and **Yuri Marusin** is a strong, idiomatic Prince, whose distinctive tenor is well contrasted with that of **Vladimir Galuzin** as an incisive Grishka, characterizing splendidly. Despite moments of strain, the rest of the **Kirov** cast make an excellent team. Live recording inevitably brings intrusive stage noises and odd balances, but this is another warmly recommendable set in **Gergiev's** excellent Philips series.

Mlada (complete; DVD version)

🎬 **★★★★** Teldec DVD 6 & 4509-92052-3. Nina Ananiashvili (dancer), Oleg Kulko, Maria Gavrilova, Gleb Nikolsky. Galina Borisova, Mikhail Maslov, Lyudmila Nam, Olga Velichko, Vladimir Kudriashov, Bolshoi Ballet, Bolshoi Ch. & O, Lazarev (Stage/Video Director: Boris Pokrovsky)

Mlada is a curious hybrid, half choral ballet and half opera with dancing. The score is full of colour, and so is this **Bolshoi** production, expertly directed by **Boris Pokrovsky**. It is best known to most music lovers for the *Procession of the Nobles*. The scoring is lavish even by Rimsky's own standards: the wind, brass and percussion are all expanded, and there are three harps and an organ. On stage there is a stage band in Act III which includes two pan-pipes (ancient Slavonic instruments) and eight lyres. The plot is flimsy, but it was the elaborate scoring which held up the production. A wonderful performance from **Nina Ananiashvili**, dancing the role of Princess Mlada, and impressive singing from the imposing cast. A highly enjoyable rarity which we can strongly recommend.

The Tsar's Bride (complete; CD version)

🎬 **★★★★** Ph. 462 618-2 (2). Bezzuenkov, Shaguch, Hvorostovsky, Alexashkin, Akimov, Borodina, Kirov Ch. & O, Gergiev

Gergiev firmly establishes *The Tsar's Bride* as a most richly enjoyable opera, full of outstanding set numbers, such as the banqueting song in the party scene of Act I, which uses the Tsar's Hymn in opulent counterpoint. The story itself, set at the time of Ivan the Terrible, is a curious mixture of darkness and light, of fairy-tale fantasy and melodramatic realism. Jealousy is the dominant emotion, when the sinister adventurer, Gryaznoy, and the scheming Lyubasha take priority over even the hero and heroine. In the casting here, that priority is a great source of strength, when **Dmitri Hvorostovsky** as Gryaznoy and **Olga Borodina** as Lyubasha give superb performances, not just singing with rich, firm tone but characterizing powerfully. **Marina Shaguch** is fresh and clear as Marfa the heroine, if edgy under pressure, and **Evgeny Akimov** with his typically Slavonic tenor sings idiomatically if with forced tone. In Act IV, with the plot turning sour, Rimsky is prompted to round the work off with a sequence of remarkable numbers, including a splendid quintet with chorus, when Gryaznoy stabs Lyubasha to death, and a mad-scene for Marfa. A rich offering, strongly recommended.

ROBINSON, Thomas
(fl. 1589–1609)

Lute pieces: *Bonny Sweet Boy; A Galliard; A Gigue; Go from My Window; A Toy*. Lute duets: (i) *A Fantasy for 2 Lutes; Pazzamezzo Galliard; A Plaine Song for 2 Lutes; The Queen's Goodnight; A Toy for 2 Lutes; 20 Ways upon the Bells*

BB **★★★** Naxos 8.553974. Wilson (lute); (i) with Rumsey –
HOLBORNE: *Lute Pieces* **★★**(★)

Thomas Robinson taught the future Queen Anne in Denmark before she married King James. He liked to write and play duets with his pupils and the '*Goodnight*' here is obviously addressed to her. All the duets here are delightful, particularly *Twenty Ways upon the Bells* with its two players ingeniously ringing the changes. The solo pieces, too, are full of character, notably the melancholy solo *Toy*, worthy of Dowland. But Robinson has a personality in his own right and it is good to have his music rediscovered. **Christopher Wilson** and his pupil **Shirley Rumsey** play everything intimately and spontaneously, readily conveying their pleasure in the music. They are truthfully recorded (not too close) in a pleasant acoustic.

ROCHBERG, George
(1918–2005)

Symphony 5; Black Sounds; Transcendental Variations

🎬 ✹ BB **★★★★** Naxos 8.559115. Saarbrücken RSO, Lyndon-Gee

George Rochberg was born in New Jersey, became an accomplished pianist and worked his way through college playing in jazz bands. After the war he studied at the Curtis Institute in Philadelphia, and, like many of his generation, he began composing as a serialist, eventually returning to tonality.

His magnificent *Fifth Symphony* (1984–5) is expressive yet never indulgent; passionate yet stringently argued. Opening boldly and assertively, it is continuous and in seven major sections. The music is both hard-driven and evocatively lyrical while the otherworldly finale brings a dreamily withdrawn cello solo, until in the closing section reality takes over.

The formidable *Black Sounds* (1965) is based on an earlier composition, *Apocalyptica*, for large wind ensemble, piano and percussion, whose score is headed by a Shakespeare quotation, calling up the tempest from *King Lear*. Stark and emotionally spare, it makes a powerful statement about human violence. After the climax, the epilogue closes the work gently in muted cries of anguish.

But it is with the masterly *Transcendental Variations* for string orchestra that the newcomer to Rochberg's music should begin any exploration. Written in 1975, it was the composer's first work to embrace tonality without reserve, and it is derived from his *Third String Quartet*, written three years earlier.

All three performances here are marvellously played by the **Saarbrücken Radio Orchestra** under **Christopher Lyndon-Gee**, who seems to find a total affinity with the composer. The recording is first class, too, and this is a record not to be missed by anyone who cares about *real* 20th-century music.

RODGERS, Richard (1902–79)

Ballet Scores: *Ghost Town; On Your Toes: La Princess Zenobia; Slaughter on Tenth Avenue*

*** TER CDTER 1114. O, Mauceri

Richard Rodgers often wrote quite extensive ballets for his Broadway output, the best known being *Slaughter on Tenth Avenue*, first heard in the 1936 musical *On Your Toes*, which also presented *La Princess Zenobia* for the first time. However, *Ghost Town*, an American folk ballet about the Gold Rush, was commissioned by the Ballet Russe de Monte Carlo in 1939 and produced at the Metropolitan Opera that year. All three ballets have their fair share of good tunes – *Slaughter on Tenth Avenue*, easily the best of them, has three superb melodies (among Rodgers's finest) – and there is no doubting that the colourful orchestrations of Hans Spialek go a large way towards making these scores as sparkling as they are. The performances under **John Mauceri** are first rate, as is the vivid and bright recording, which admirably catches the Hollywoodesque orchestrations. The fine orchestra is presumably a pick-up ensemble as, curiously, it is not credited with a name.

Carousel (film musical)

⊕ *** EMI (ADD) 5 27352-2. Film soundtrack recording with MacRae, Jones, Mitchell, Ruick, Turner, Rounseville, Christie, 20th Century Fox Ch. & O, Newman

The King and I (film musical)

⊕ *** EMI (ADD) 5 27351-2. Film soundtrack recording with Nixon/Kerr, Brynner, Gordon/Moreno, Saunders, Fuentes/Rivas, 20th Century Fox Ch. & O, Newman

Oklahoma! (film musical)

⊕ *** EMI (ADD) 5 27350-2. Film soundtrack recording with MacRae, Jones, Greenwood, Grahame, Nelson, Steiger, 20th Century Fox Ch. & O, Newman

In these days when so many composers of so-called 'serious' music and opera seem unwilling, or unable, to write hummable melodies, it seems worth while to celebrate again the achievement of three great Rodgers and Hammerstein musicals of the 1940s and early 1950s. The sheer tunefulness of the music is of the kind which, once lodged in the memory, is impossible to erase. And Richard Rodgers had the good fortune to collaborate with a librettist who showed not only a natural feeling for a melodic line, but also an inspired ear for the vernacular. The Rodgers and Hammerstein love songs communicate directly and universally.

In short, these are masterly scores, with masterly lyrics and, as the recent outstanding National Theatre revival of *Oklahoma!* demonstrated, this is a work of classic stature, with much greater depth of characterization than had been hitherto realized.

The dubbing of Deborah Kerr's songs in *The King and I* by the sweet-voiced **Marni Nixon**, and Tuptim's 'We kiss in the shadow' by the sultry **Leonora Gordon** (originally undisclosed), is now part of the current documentation, although **Rita Moreno** herself narrates the highly dramatic ballet sequence, *The Small House of Uncle Tom*. In *Carousel* and *Oklahoma!* **Gordon MacRae** and **Shirley Jones** make a delightfully fresh-voiced pair of lovers, and the smaller parts are all full of character. Much that was previously omitted has now been restored, including items which did not appear in the final edited films. This means that there is a good deal of repetition and reprises. Never mind, these three discs are very enjoyable, and you may even find yourself humming along. The documentation is excellent.

'*Rodgers & Hammerstein Songs*' from: *Allegro; Carousel; The King and I; Me and Juliet; Oklahoma!; The Sound of Music; South Pacific; State Fair*

*** DG 449 163-2. Terfel, Opera North Ch., E. N. Philh., Daniel

Bryn Terfel masterfully embraces the Broadway idiom, projecting his magnetic personality in the widest range of songs, using a remarkable range of tone, from a whispered head voice (as he does magically at the end of 'Some enchanted evening') to a tough, almost gravelly *fortissimo* at climaxes, from the biting toughness of 'Nothing like a dame' or Billy Bigelow's big soliloquy in *Carousel* (using a very convincing American accent) to the warmth of 'If I loved you' and 'You'll never walk alone' (with chorus). Specially welcome are the rarities, including one number from *Me and Juliet* and four from the stylized and underprized *Allegro*, including the powerfully emotional 'Come home'. With excellent sound and fine playing from **Opera North** forces under **Paul Daniel**, this is a wide-ranging survey.

RODRIGO, Joaquín (1901–99)

Orchestral Works, Vol. 1: *Soleriana* (ballet, arr. from Soler's keyboard music); *5 Piezas infantiles; Zarabanda lejana y Vallancico*

(BB) **(*) Naxos 8.555844. Asturias SO, Valdés

Rodrigo's delightfully imagined 18th-century picture of Spain is the essence of *Soleriana*, which is based on the keyboard works of Antonio Soler and consists of eight dances, lasting some 40 minutes in all. The *Pastoral* has a lovely melancholy beauty, though most of the movements are relatively lively and portray a picturesque, rococo image of the local scene in music, which displays both charm and piquancy. The *Zarabanda lejana* ('Distant Sarabande') is a haunting work, its two movements displaying some lovely string-writing, and the highly engaging *Cinco piezas infantiles* are characteristically brightly coloured. The performances are good; the massed strings sound a bit thin above the stave, but the overall sound-picture is very acceptable.

Orchestral Works, Vol. 2: (i) *Concierto Andaluz for 4 Guitars and Orchestra*; (ii) *Concierto de Aranjuez*; *Fantasía para un gentilhombre*

(BB) **(*) Naxos 8.555841. Asturias SO, Valdés; with (i) EntreQuatre Guitar Qt; (ii) Gallén

The popular *Concierto de Aranjuez* and *Fantasia para un gentilhombre* are given very decent performances, but they lack the last ounce of polish and, in terms of recording and performance, cannot match the very best versions, such as Bonell–Dutoit on Decca. The *Concierto Andaluz*, with its *Tempo di boléro* opening movement and use of Andalusian folk tunes, makes an enjoyable companion-piece.

Orchestral Works, Vol. 3: (i) *Concerto in modo galante* (for cello & orchestra); *Concierto como un divertimento* (for cello & orchestra); (ii) *Concierto de estío* (for violin & orchestra); *Cançoneta* (for violin & string orchestra)

(BB) *** Naxos 8.555840. Castile and León SO, Darman; with (i) Polo; (ii) Ovrutsky

Volume 3 plunges into rarer Rodrigo: in the jolly *Concierto in modo galante*, written in 1949 for cellist Cassadó, Rodrigo's easy-going manner has an 18th-century Spanish spirit. The *Concierto como un divertimento*, written in 1981, is another agreeable cello concerto, peppered with all sorts of Spanishry. Rodrigo looked to Vivaldi (in structural form, at least) in his *Concierto de estío* for violin and orchestra: the two lively outer movements are separated by an especially attractive central Siciliana *adagio*. The *Cançoneta for Violin and String Orchestra* is short and pleasurable.

Orchestral Works, Vol. 4: (i) *Concierto para piano y orquesta* (rev. Achúcarro); *Homenaje a la tempranica*; *Juglares*; *Música para un jardín*; *Preludio para un poema a la Alhambra*

(BB) **(*) Naxos 8.557101. Castile and León SO, Darman; (i) with Ferrandiz

Starting dramatically, the *Concierto para piano y orquesta* soon enters familiar Rodrigo territory, with some attractive episodes, but not really having enough inspired music to sustain its 30 minutes. The *Música para un jardín*, written in 1935, depicts the growth of a garden throughout the year. It's a slight work, with one or two nice touches, but hardly another *Nights in the Gardens of Spain*. More successful and more deeply reminiscent of Falla is the *Preludio para un poema a la Alhambra*, a mini tone-poem: 'At twilight, the guitar sighs, and beyond, almost within the Alhambra, rings out the rhythms which drive the dance.' It was first performed in 1930. Similarly, the *Homenaje a la tempranica* and *Juglares* find the composer at his best in short, undemanding movements. Lively performances and good sound.

Orchestral Works, Vol. 5: *Concierto Madrigal*; *Concierto para una fiesta*

(BB) **(*) Naxos 8.555842. Gallén, Clerch, Asturias SO, Valdés

The *Concierto Madrigal*, a suite of movements with the common link of the Renaissance madrigal *O felici ocche*, is one of the composer's finest compositions, with a real piquancy. It

has been recorded several times of course, and this performance is a good, warmly relaxed one, though other versions, such as the Yepes on DG, are livelier, with more character and flair. The *Concierto para una fiesta* has a slow movement not unlike that of the *Concierto de Aranjuez*, if not so inspired. The outer movements are predictably tuneful and undemanding. The orchestral playing and the recordings are both up to standard.

Other Recordings

(i; iv) *Concierto Andaluz* (for 4 guitars); (ii; iv) *Concierto de Aranjuez* (for guitar); (ii–iv) *Concierto madrigal* (for 2 guitars); (ii; iv) *Concierto para una fiesta*; *Fantasia para un gentilhombre*; *Sones en la Giralda*; (v) *Concierto serenata* (for harp)

⊕— (B) **** Ph. Duo (ADD) 462 296-2 (2). (i) Los Romeros; (ii) P. Romero; (iii) A. Romero; (iv) ASMF, Marriner; (v) Michel, Monte Carlo Op. O, Almeida

This Duo includes all Rodrigo's splendid concertante guitar works, plus the *Concierto serenata* for harp and orchestra, a delectable and unaccountably neglected work in which **Catherine Michel** is a seductive soloist, neatly accompanied by **Almeida**. La Giralda, the ancient tower of Seville Cathedral, obviously stimulated Rodrigo's imagination so that the first of its two sections is eerily atmospheric; then the clouds clear away and the finale sparkles with the flamenco dance rhythms of the *Sevillanas*. **Pepe Romero** and **Marriner** show an immediate response to its evocation and spirit, and the result is memorable, helped by the first-class recording which pertains throughout these two generously filled CDs.

Concierto de Aranjuez (for guitar & orchestra)

⊕— **** Warner 2564 60296-2. Isbin, NYPO, Serebrier – PONCE: *Concierto del sur*; VILLA-LOBOS: *Guitar Concerto* ***

*** Guild GMCD 7176. Jiménez, Bournemouth Sinf., Frazor – ANGULO: *Guitar Concerto 2 (El Alevín)*; VILLA-LOBOS: *Guitar Concerto* ***

(BB) *** Naxos 8.550729. Kraft, N. CO, Ward – CASTELNUOVO-TEDESCO: *Concerto* ***; VILLA-LOBOS: *Concerto* **(*)

(i) *Concierto de Aranjuez* (for guitar); (ii) *Concierto de estio* (for violin); (iii) *Concierto en modo galante* (for cello); (iv) *Concierto heroico* (for piano); (v) *Concierto pastoral* (for flute); (vi) *Concierto serenata* (for harp); *Zarabanda lejana y villancico*

(N) (B) **(*) EMI 5099923768123 (2). (i) Moreno; (ii) Ara; (iii) Cohen; (iv) Osorio; (v) Hansen; (vi) Allen; LSO or RPO, Batiz

(i) *Concierto de Aranjuez*; (ii) *Fantasia para un gentilhombre*

⊕— (B) **** Decca 448 243-2. Bonell, Montreal SO, Dutoit – ALBÉNIZ: *Rapsodia española*; TURINA: *Rapsodia sinfónica* ***

(BB) *** Virgin 2x1 5 61627-2 (2). Isbin, Lausanne CO, Foster –
SCHWANTER: *From Afar* (fantasy) **; Recital: '*Latin
Romances*' ***

(BB) **(*) Sony (ADD) SBK 61716. Williams; (i) Philadelphia O,
Ormandy; (ii) ECO, Groves – DODGSON: *Concerto*, etc **(*)

(i) *Concierto de Aranjuez*; (ii) *Fantasia para un gentilhombre*; *En los trigales*; *Invocation & Dance (Hommage à Manuel de Falla)*; *3 Piezas españolas*

☞ (M) **** RCA 82876 60870-2. Bream; (i) COE, Gardiner;
(ii) RCA Victor CO, Brouwer

The **Bonell/Dutoit** *Concierto* was originally paired with the
Fantasia para un gentilhombre. In the *Fantasia*, the balance be-
tween warmly gracious lyricism and sprightly rhythmic re-
silience is most engaging. The generous coupling on Decca's
Eclipse bargain label is well worth considering, as the
Albéniz and Turina concertante works for piano are also
given dazzling, sultry performances by de Larrocha and
Frühbeck de Burgos.

Sharon Isbin is an ideal exponent of this concerto. A
quite exceptional guitarist, she has the gift of creating a musing, improvisatory feeling which is seemingly totally spontaneous and is heard at its most magical in the famous slow
movement. In a chamber-styled performance **Serebrier** accompanies with comparable delicacy, ensuring that the orchestral detail is vividly realized, but always in scale with the
soloist. Yet the climax is full of yearning passion. The recording is outstanding and perfectly balanced.

The differences between **Bream's** two earlier RCA readings of the *Concierto*, the first (analogue) with Colin Davis in
1963 (now deleted), the second (digital) with **Gardiner** in 1982,
are almost too subtle to analyse and perhaps depend as
much on the personalities of the two conductors as on that
of the soloist. The Gardiner version has a little extra dash
and, for those who prefer an all-Rodrigo programme, this
could be a good choice and the famous *Adagio* is played in a
very free, improvisatory way, with some highly atmospheric
wind solos in the orchestra. In the *Fantasia para un gentilhombre* **Leo Brouwer**, himself a guitarist, brings plenty of
orchestral vitality to the later sections of the score. The *Tres
piezas españolas* add to the value of the disc, and both this
and the *Homage to Falla* show Bream at his most inspirationally spontaneous.

Sharon Isbin's alternative recording of Rodrigo's two
most popular works with the **Lausanne Chamber Orchestra**
under **Lawrence Foster** received the imprimatur of the composer before he died, and justly so. They are both played with
flair and the orchestral detail could not be more vivid, while
the famous slow movement of the *Concierto* is most atmospherically done. The recording is in the demonstration
bracket. The snag is that the Schwanter coupling is a good
deal less tangible. However her recording of the *Concierto*
with Serebrier has no such problem.

Rafael Jiménez and the **Bournemouth Sinfonietta** under
Terence Frazor make a fine partnership. The slow movement brings an appealing, ruminative intimacy to contrast
with its bold, passionate climax, and the finale also has a
neat delicacy of touch from the soloist, with buoyant rhyth-

mic pointing from the orchestra. The recording is very
good too.

Norbert Kraft is a soloist of personality and he receives
spirited, sensitive accompaniments from the **Northern
Chamber Orchestra** under **Nicholas Ward**. Indeed the work
sounds remarkably fresh using a smaller-sized orchestral
group. The recording is very well balanced, with the guitar
given a most convincing relationship with the orchestra and
the sound itself vividly realistic.

With **Ormandy** providing a rich orchestral tapestry
Williams's earlier version is a distinctly romantic reading
of the *Concierto*. If the later recording (currently withdrawn)
is maturer and has greater subtlety of detail, this performance, taken a little bit faster, remains fresh and enjoyable.
Groves and the **ECO** take over for the *Fantasia*, and once
again, the interpretation is a shade brisker than the later,
digital version.

The group of EMI recordings are from the early 1980s
and are of very good quality, although the early digital technique often brings an overlit sound to the treble. The *Summer
Concerto* for violin ('conceived in the manner of Vivaldi') was
the composer's own favourite and **Augustin Leo Ara** catches
its neo-classical vitality admirably. The *Cello Concerto* is given
a masterly performance by **Robert Cohen**; the *Concierto serenata* (for harp) has both piquancy and charm. **Nancy Allen**
consistently beguiles the ear with her gentleness. The spiky
opening of the *Concierto pastoral* is far from pastoral in feeling, but the composer's fragmented melodies soon insinuate
themselves into the consciousness. The *Piano Concerto* has a
bolder programmatic content, with the four movements
written 'under the sign of the Sword, the Spur, the Cross
and the Laurel'. **Alfonso Moreno's** account of the *Concierto
de Aranjuez*, though bright and sympathetic, is in no way outstanding. The *Zarabanda lejana* was Rodrigo's first work for
guitar, the *villancico* was added later to combine elegiac and
dancing sections. Altogether a rewarding if lightweight collection, all vividly presented.

Concierto pastoral

☞ **** BIS-SACD 1559. Bezaly, São Paulo SO, Neschling
(with BORNE: *Carmen Fantasy*) – IBERT: *Flute Concerto* ***

Rodrigo's *Concierto pastoral* is undeservedly less well known
than his other works for guitar, yet its delicately textured
opening captivates with its chirping until a simple, more
dominating, lyrical theme arrives. The *Andante's* haunting
minor-key song without words has a distinctly Spanish
tinge: the flute ruminates gently, leading to an extended solo
cadenza to introduce the delighful return of the decorated
main theme. The catchy rhythmic ostinato of the rondo
finale then rollicks effervescently, but once again there is a
pastoral lyrical core. Throughout, **Bezaly** catches the work's
beguiling charm and **Neschling** supports her admirably, as
does the splendid BIS recording. A most winning disc in
every way.

Concierto serenata (for harp & orchestra)

☞ ✹ (M) **** DG (ADD) 463 648-2. Zöller, Zabaleta, BPO,
Märzendorfer – MOZART: *Flute & Harp Concerto in C,
K.299*; REINECKE: *Harp Concerto* ***

We have always had a special regard for **Zabaleta's** pioneering version of Rodrigo's *Concierto serenata*, which has an unforgettable piquancy and charm both in its invention and in its felicity of scoring. The performance has great virtuosity and flair, and our Rosette is carried over from the original LP. It is excellently recorded, with the delicate yet colourful orchestral palette tickling the ear in charming contrast to the beautifully-focused timbre of the harp.

Soleriana (ballet, arr. from Soler's keyboard music); *5 Piezas infantiles; Zarabanda lejana y villancico*

(BB) **(*) Naxos 8.555844. Asturias SO, Valdés

Valdés includes Rodrigo's delightful 18th-century picture of Spain in his ballet *Soleriana*. The *Pastoral* has a lovely melancholy beauty, though most of the movements are relatively lively and well portray a picturesque, rococo image of 18th-century Spain in music of great charm and piquancy. The *Zarabanda lejana* ('Distant Sarabande') is a haunting work, its two movements displaying some lovely string writing, and the highly engaging *Cinco piezas infantiles* are characteristically brightly coloured. The performances are good, if perhaps not quite so imaginative as Bátiz on EMI (see above), who also benefited from more vivid sound. Here, the massed strings sound a bit thin above the stave (especially noticeable in the *Zarabanda lejana*), but the overall sound-picture is very acceptable, and this disc is well worth its modest price.

SOLO GUITAR MUSIC

Bajando de la Meseta; Elegio de la guitarra; En los trigales; En tierras de Jerez; Invocaciòn y danza (Homenaje a Manuel de Falla); Junto al Generalife; 3 Piezas españolas

◑— **** MDG 305 0834-2. Bungarten

Frank Bungarten, born in Cologne in 1958, was awarded the first prize at the International Guitar Competition in Granada when Segovia was president of the jury, so his credentials for this repertoire are impeccable. His brusque chords at the opening *Fandango* of the *Three Spanish Pieces* contrast with a thoughtful account of the noble central *Passacaglia*, and in *En tierras de Jerez* and the atmospheric *Bajando de la Meseta* his playing is masterly. The *Junto al Generalife*, the *Homenaje a Manuel de Falla* and the deliciously nuanced *Zarabanda lejana* are most all highly evocative. He is given a fine, natural presence here, and this collection will be hard to beat.

(i) *Fandango del ventorrillo* (arr. Pepe Romero); *Tonadilla* (for 2 guitars); *Por los campos de España; 3 Piezas españolas; Sonata giocosa*

(BB) *** Naxos 8.570286. Jouve; (i) with Perroy (guitars)

The best-known work here is the *Tres piezas españolas*, of which the closing *Zapateado* is the most familiar. The young French guitarist **Jérémy Jouve** plays it brilliantly, although he is not a show-off artist, preferring musical values, which

he displays in the sensitive account of the *Andante moderato* slow movement of the *Sonata giocosa*, yet finding plenty of life and sparkle in the outer movements, especially the boisterous finale. He is at his finest in *Por los campos de España* ('In the Spanish Countryside'), a group of five miniature pictures, which he plays very evocatively. The duet works are also very well played, but are not as individual as the solo pieces.

PIANO MUSIC

Music for 2 pianos: (i) *5 Piezas infantiles* (piano, 4 hands): *Atardecer; Gran marcha de los subsecretarios; Sonatina para dos Muñecas.* **Solo piano:** *Air de ballet sur le nom d'une jeune fille; Album de Cecilia; A l'ombre de Torre Bermeja; Bagatela; Berceuse d'automne; Berceuse de printemps; Danza de la Amapola; 3 Danzas de España; 4 Estampas andaluzas; 3 Evocaciones; Pastorale; 4 Piezas (Caleseras: Homenaje a Chueca; Fandango del Ventorrillo; Plegaria de la Infanta de Castilla; Danza Valenciana); Preludio de Añoranza; Preludio al gallo mañanero; Serenata española; Sonada de adiós (Hommage à Paul Dukas); 5 Sonatas de Castilla, con toccata a modo de Pregón: 1–2 in F sharp min.; 3 in D; 4 in B min. (como un tiento); 5 in A.* **Suite:** *Zarabanda lejana*

◑— ✿ **** Bridge BCD 9027 A/B. Allen; (i) with Nel

Air de ballet sur le nom d'une jeune fille; Album de Cecilia; A l'ombre de Torre Bermeja; Bagatela; 2 Berceuses; Canción y danza; Danza de la Amapola; 3 Danzas de España; 4 Estampas Andaluzas; 3 Evocaciones; Pastoral; 4 Piezas; 5 Piezas del sieglo XVI; Preludio de Añoranza; Preludio al gallo mañanero; Serenata española; Sonata de adiós (Homage to Paul Dukas); 5 Sonatas de Castilla con Toccata a modo de Pregón; Suite; Zarabanda Lejana

◑— *** Sony S2K 89828 (2). Marianovich

Rodrigo's keyboard music is all but unknown and, as this first-class and comprehensive survey shows, for all its eclecticism it is well worth exploring. In his earliest piano work, the *Suite* of 1923, with its sprightly *Prelude*, cool *Sicilienne* and Satie-ish *Minuet*, the link with the French idiom is obvious, while the glittering brilliance of the *Preludio al gallo mañanero* is unmistakably Debussian. The *Cinco sonatas de Castilla* look back further in time and draw continually on the keyboard writing of Scarlatti. But they are spiced with piquant dissonances which the Italian composer would have disowned. The *Serenata española* marks Rodrigo's positive adoption of an overtly Andalusian style, while the *Cuatro piezas* and the *Cuatro estampas andaluzas* are as sharply Spanish in character as any of the similarly picaresque miniatures of Granados or Albéniz. The darker side of Rodrigo's nature, sometimes brooding, sometimes nostalgic, is at its most expressive in the nocturne, *Atardecer*, an ambitious piece for two players; but it also colours some of the miniatures, not least the austere yet deeply felt *Plegaria de la Infanta de Castilla* from the *Cuatro piezas*. The recording is uncommonly real and has great presence. In the duo works **Gregory Allen** is admirably partnered by **Anton Nel**.

Sara Marianovich knew Rodrigo personally and played for him, learning a great deal, so that her performances received his imprimatur. The music is attractively arranged, as far as possible in order of composition, and ends nostalgically with Rodrigo's last piano work, the *Preludio de Añoranza* of 1987. But besides her ready bravura and feeling for the Spanish as well as the French pianistic palette, Sara Marianovich is also at her finest in the simpler pieces, the charming early *Suite*, the *Pastoral* (a captivating siciliana), the pair of *Berceuses*, the touching 'Adios' to Paul Dukas, the children's album, written for the composer's daughter, Cecilia, and the *Five Pieces from the Sixteenth Century* – transcriptions of Spanish renaissance miniatures. Also included is an impressive first recording of the rare *Canción y danza* of 1925 which opens musingly, but slowly becomes more passionate. This does not appear in the coverage of this repertoire by Gregory Allen. However, joined by Anton Nel, he *does* include the repertoire for two pianos, which the Sony set omits. So that probably remains a primary choice. But Sara Marianovich's playing is so compellingly persuasive that her new set must also receive the strongest possible advocacy. She is vividly and truthfully recorded, and this highly rewarding music is undeservedly neglected.

Air de ballet sur le nom d'une jeune fille; A l'ombre de Torre Bermeja; Bagatella; 2 Berceuses; 4 Estampas andaluzas; Fantasía que contrahace la harpa de Ludovico; Pastorale; 4 Piezas; Préludio de añoranza; Serenata española; Sonata de adiós; Zarabanda lejana; 5 Piezas del siglo XVI

⊕ (BB) **** Naxos 8.557272. Pizarro

For most collectors, this excellent single-CD budget-priced collection from the highly sympathetic **Artur Pizarro** will prove an admirable introduction to Rodrigo's piano music. From the brilliant opening *A l'ombre de Torre Bermeja* onwards he brings out the music's ready associations with the guitar. Pizarro plays spontaneously and perceptively and proves very much at home in this repertoire; he is vividly recorded, and there is an excellent commentary on the music by Graham Wade.

Album de Cecilia; Cancion y danza; Danza de la amapola; 3 Danzas de España; 3 Evocations; Prelude of the Dawn Cockerel; Sonatas de Castilla with Toccata in the Style of a Proclamation; Suite for Piano

(BB) **** Naxos 8.557923. Pizarro

Opening with the engaging *Dance of the Poppy*, **Artur Pizarro** continues his survey of Rodrigo's sadly underrated piano music; he shows a natural feeling for the instrument which is so full of diversity and listener appeal. There is so much to savour here. The recording is first class and this is highly recommended alongside its companion. If you dip into either of them you will surely want to continue listening.

ROOTHAM, Cyril (1875–1938)

Symphony 1

*** Lyrita (ADD) SRCD 269. Philh. O, Braithwaite – BANTOCK: *Overture to a Greek Tragedy; Oedipus at Colonus*; HOLBROOKE: *The Birds of Rhiannon* ***

Cyril Rootham, who was born in Bristol, spent the bulk of his life at Cambridge, where his pupils included Arthur Bliss. The first of his two symphonies was composed in 1932 and leaves no doubt as to his expertise and powers of craftsmanship. Rootham was a dedicated and serious musician, though it must be said that his is not a distinctive voice in English music. His orchestration is very fine, and it is reproduced here in sound of quite remarkable realism. Readers might investigate this CD for themselves, for there is much to admire, both here and in the couplings, even if few would claim that the symphony is a powerfully original work.

RORE, Cipriano da (c. 1515–65)

Missa Praeter rerum seriem. Motets: Ave regina; Descendit in hortum meum; Infelix ego; Parce mihi

⊕ *** Gimell CDGIM 029. Tallis Scholars, Phillips (with JOSQUIN DESPREZ: Motet: *Praeter rerum seriem* ***)

Cipriano da Rore was Josquin's successor at the Italian Court of the Este at Ferrara. His *Missa Praeter rerum seriem* is appropriately preceded by the richly textured six-part Josquin motet based on the same melodic sequence. Rore's piece was intended as a tribute to his illustrious predecessor and is a worthy accolade, lyrically powerful, contrapuntally fascinating, spiritually serene and beautifully sung by these highly experienced singers, whose director knows just how to pace and inflect its linear detail and shape its overall structure. The four motets are hardly less impressive, and Gimell's recording, as ever, is virtually flawless.

ROREM, Ned (born 1923)

(i) Flute Concerto; (ii) Violin Concerto; Pilgrims

⊕ (BB) *** Naxos 8.559278. (i) Khaner; (ii) Quint; RLPO, Serebrier

Each of the two *Concertos* is programmatic, the work for flute offering a series of vignettes with often virtuosic embroidery. It is superbly played by **Jeffrey Khaner**. The arresting opening drum-command introduces the haunting five-note motif on which the six movements all draw. So the work is almost a set of variations, ending with a catchy *False Waltz* and on to the refined mood of the closing *Résumé and Prayer*. The result is highly imaginative and full of variety, if perhaps a little over-extended.

The *Violin Concerto* opens dramatically and ardently and is a true interplay between soloist and accompaniment, its second movement an unlikely *Toccata-Chaconne* built over a jagged timpani rhythm. But the heart of the work is lyrically heart-warming in its gentle beauty, first a simple *Romance without Words*, followed by the serene *Midnight*, 'a microsonic variation'. **Philippe Quint** is a deeply responsive soloist, playing with silvery timbre: the composer could not have asked for better, and throughout **Serebrier** directs the accompanying **RLPO** most sympathetically. First-class recording.

(i) Double Concerto for Violin & Cello; After Reading Shakespeare

BB *** Naxos 8.559316. Robinson; (i) with Laredo, IRIS CO, Stern

Ned Rorem's *Concerto for Violin and Cello* has a sobriquet for each of its attractively diverse movements. After the introductory, slightly pungent 'Morning', 'Looking' centres on the solo violin alternating with the brass. 'Conversation at Midnight', the centrepiece, frames a concertante dialogue plus a string chorale with a livelier central section, and the finale takes off brilliantly and briefly into 'Flight'. The nine sections of *After Reading Shakespeare* for solo cello are indeed Shakespearean, all named after famous characters in the Bard's plays. *Lear* is perhaps the most important, as he gets two sections, while *Iago* and *Othello* have to share, if not in the most friendly fashion. It's all very ingenious and very well played, but not as memorable as the concerto.

Songs

*** Erato 8573 80222-2. Graham, Martineau

Ned Rorem spent many of his formative years in Paris during the 1950s, when he came to know Poulenc and Auric, but he never lost the American flavour that makes his style so distinctive. This recital, encompassing settings of English, American and French verse, gives a good idea of his melodic resource and feeling for words. His songs, such as the *Santa Fé* series and the setting of Tennyson's *Now sleeps the crimson petal*, bear witness to a rich imagination and a marvellous feel for both the voice and the piano. **Susan Graham** does them all proud, and **Malcolm Martineau** gives impeccable support.

ROSE, Pierre (1774–1830)

Violin Concertos 7 in A min., Op. 9; 10 in B min., Op. 19; 13 in F sharp min., Op. posth.

N **BB** *** Naxos 8.570469. Eichhorn, SW German R. O, Kaiserslautern, Pasquet

Virtually unknown today, except by students of his instrument, Pierre Rose was a famous violinist in early 19th-century Paris, though his concertos, despite the advocacy of Paganini (in 7), have fallen from the repertoire. The three on this CD are all agreeably tuneful works – and even if they are not strikingly distinctive, they offer plenty of rewards, notably in their enjoyably bubbling finales. First rate performances.

ROSSETER, Philip (1567–1623)

Lute Pieces: Almayne; Fantasia; Galliard; 3rd Galliard for the Countess of Sussex; Pavin; Pavin by Rosseter; Prelude. Lute Songs: And would you see

my Mistress' face; If she forsake me; Kind in unkindness; No grave for woe; Reprove not love; Shall I come if I swim?; Sweet come again; Though far from joy; What heart's content; What then is love but mourning?; When Laura smiles; Whether men do laugh or weep

**(*) Avie AV 2074. Gilchrist, Wadsworth (lute)

James Gilchrist has just the right warm vocal timbre for these songs and he sings them eloquently, and **Matthew Wadsworth** plays the lute pieces as interludes. They are beautifully recorded and the opening *Sweet come again* is quite lovely. But this is a collection to dip into rather than to play all at once, for Rosseter's songs (and, to a lesser extent, his instrumental writing) bring a pervading melancholy, so that one is very glad to welcome lively numbers like *When Laura smiles* or *If she forsake me*.

ROSSINI, Gioachino (1792–1868)

La Boutique fantasque (ballet; complete; arr. Respighi)

⊕ ✱ **M** (****) Somm mono SOMMCD 027. LSO, Ansermet – STRAVINSKY: *Petrushka*. (***)

⊕ **** Chan. 10081. BBC PO, Noseda – RESPIGHI: *La Pentola magica*, etc. ***

Ansermet's classic 'complete' version (there are some fairly minor cuts) of *La Boutique fantasque* was outstanding among early LPs. It was recorded in the Kingsway Hall in 1950, which lends its ambient richness to the proceedings, and was one of the rare occasions on which Ansermet conducted the **LSO**. They play wonderfully for him, especially the woodwind, and in particular the distinguished principal oboe, whose phrasing and tone are exquisite. The whole orchestra are clearly on their toes and the exhilarating can-can and brilliantly executed finale have tremendous vivacity. But the disc is especially famous for its magical opening which has an extraordinary aura, with the gentle pizzicatos of the lower strings answered by glowing horn chords. Fortunately, David Henning's digital remastering miraculously reflects the outstanding quality of those early Decca LXTs. As it now stands the sound has fine range and bloom, almost like stereo at times. This is one of Ansermet's finest ballet records, if not the finest of all. What a pity he made so few recordings with the London orchestra.

Noseda's sparkling account of the famous Rossini/Respighi ballet is complete and is splendidly recorded. It is discussed under Respighi above, where it is combined with other spectacular Respighi arrangements.

La Boutique fantasque (extended suite)

⊕ **M** **** RCA (ADD) **SACD** 82876 66419-2. Boston Pops O, Fiedler – OFFENBACH: *Gaîté parisienne* **** ✱

M **(*) Chan. 6503. SNO, Gibson – DUKAS: *L'Apprenti sorcier*; SAINT-SAËNS: *Danse macabre* **(*)

Fiedler offers nearly half an hour of the ballet, not missing out much of importance. The performance sparkles, the playing has warmth and finesse and the Boston acoustics add the necessary atmosphere at the magically evocative opening. Mark Donahue's remastering of this 1956 recording for SACD leaves little to be desired and the coupling is indispensable.

Gibson's version of the suite is strikingly atmospheric. Helped by the glowing acoustics of Glasgow's City Hall, the opening has much evocation. The orchestra is on its toes and plays with warmth and zest, and the 1973 recording has transferred vividly to CD.

Introduction, Theme & Variations in C min. (for clarinet & orchestra)

*** ASV CDDCA 559. Johnson, ECO, Groves – CRUSELL: *Concerto 2* *** ✺; BAERMANN: *Adagio* ***; WEBER: *Concertino* ***

Introduction, Theme & Variations in B flat; Variations in C (for clarinet & orchestra)

*** Sup. SU 3554-2. Peterkova, Prague Philh., Bělohlávek – BRUCH: *Double Concerto*; MENDELSSOHN: 2 *Concert Pieces* ***

The Czech clarinettist **Ludmila Peterkova** is an artist who is not only warmly expressive, but sparkles in everything she plays, bringing out the pure fun of the two sets of Rossini variations, warmly accompanied by **Bělohlávek** and the **Prague Philharmonia**. A delightful fill-up for an outstanding disc of rare clarinet pieces.

As in all her recordings, **Emma Johnson's** lilting timbre and sensitive control of dynamic bring imaginative light and shade to the melodic line. Brilliance for its own sake is not the keynote, but her relaxed pacing is made to sound exactly right. Vivid recording.

String Sonatas 1–6 (complete)

⊕– (BB) **** Double Decca (ADD) 443 838-2 (2). ASMF, Marriner (with CHERUBINI: *Etude 2 for French Horn & Strings* (with Tuckwell); BELLINI: *Oboe Concerto in E flat* (with Lord) ***) – DONIZETTI: *String Quartet* ***

String Sonatas 4–6; (i) Variations in C (for violin & small orchestra)

*** ASV (ADD) CDDCA 767. Serenata of L. (members)

(BB) *** Hyp. Helios CDH 55200. OAE (members): Wallfisch, Marcus, Tunnicliffe, Nwanoku

We have a very soft spot for the sparkle, elegance and wit of these **ASMF** performances of the Rossini *String Sonatas*, amazingly accomplished products for a 12-year-old. **Marriner** offers them on full orchestral strings but with such finesse and precision of ensemble that the result is all gain. The 1966 recording still sounds remarkably full and natural, and the current CD transfer adds to the feeling of presence. The new Double Decca format has other music added. Apart from the Donizetti *Quartet*, which has an appropriately Rossinian flavour, the two minor concertante works are well worth having, with both **Barry Tuckwell** (in what is in essence a three-movement horn concertino) and **Roger Lord** in excellent form.

The **Serenata of London**, working as a string quartet, and a comparably sized group from the **Orchestra of the Age of Enlightenment**, playing period instruments, each manage to include all six of the *String Sonatas* on one CD. As might be expected, the Serenata, playing modern instruments and led by the easily brilliant **Barry Wilde**, give the warmer, more sunny bouquet to Rossini's string textures; their competitors, led by the dazzling **Elizabeth Wallfisch**, offer a slightly drier vintage, though their approach is by no means unsmiling. On both discs the recording is truthful and naturally balanced. However, the OAE members' performance now reissued on Helios has a distinct price advantage.

PIANO MUSIC

Péchés de vieillesse, Volume VI: Album pour les enfants dégourdis

(N) *** Chan. 10520. Sollini

These delightful pieces, written when Rossini was long retired from opera, are what he described as an 'Album for Bright Young People', his so-called *Sins of Old Age*. Rossini is here writing very much with his tongue in his cheek, pointing each idea with wit, beautifully caught by the pianist, **Marco Sollini**, pointing each phrase to bring out the humour and sparkle. That he uses a slightly twangy fortepiano adds to the charm, bringing a decorative quality to the music. The most striking of this group of 12 is the longest, '*Un petit train de plaisir comico-imitatif*' a programme piece representing a train journey. This is complete with the engine's whistle and surging ideas in waltz-time, which sadly ends on the second journey in a train crash, soon rectified. Other pieces have ironic funeral marches, which no one can take seriously, with the final piece a haunting *Polka Mazurka*. First-rate sound.

Péchés de vieillesse (Sins of Old Age), Volume VII: Album de chaumière (The Cottage Album; complete); Volume IX (excerpts)

(BB) **(*) Naxos 8.570590/1. Marangoni (piano)

Rossini retired (absolutely) from composing operas at the age of 37 and spent his final years in writing numerous piano pieces (not always so short – several here are over ten minutes in length). He called them *Péchés de vieillesse* ('Sins of Old Age') and arranged them in 14 volumes. Each of the pieces has a neat sobriquet; one of the most charming here is the *Petite polka chinoise*; others are *Une pensée à Florence* and the well-named *Petite valse de boudoir*. Many start with a bold, commanding introduction and then lapse into a simple melody. *Une Cauchemar* is like an impromptu, while *Gymnastique d'écartement* certainly requires delicate exertion from its performer, and *Un réveil en sursant* is crisp and pointed. There is even a fugue (*Prélude fugassé*). Although lightweight, Rossini displays a continuing fund of invention, and these pieces are well worth exploring. **Alessandro Marangoni** plays them persuasively, although he might at times display just a little lighter touch; but the piano (although truthfully recorded) is closely balanced, and that does not help him.

VOCAL MUSIC

Messa di gloria

◑ (M) **** Ph. 475 7781. Jo, Murray, Giménez, Araiza, Ramey, Ch. & ASMF, Marriner

This is a surprisingly neglected work, considering its excellence. Rossini's *Messa di gloria* is in nine movements, offering appropriately ambitious but never heavy settings of the *Kyrie*, deeply expressive, and a jauntily operatic *Gloria*, products of Rossini's first full maturity at a time (1820) when he was otherwise totally occupied with writing operas. There are links between the tenor duet which starts the *Christe* (beautifully sung by **Giménez** and **Araiza**) and Mathilde's aria in *William Tell*, but the delight is that so much unknown Rossini contains so much new to charm us, including the beautiful *Gratias*, with its obbligato cor anglais. **Marriner's** account replaces Handt's earlier version, good though that was, for he has a starry team of soloists, **Sumi Jo** notably fresh-voiced and Giménez equally memorable. The **St Martin's Chorus** predictably matches the **ASMF** in excellence, rising exultantly to the closing contrapuntal *Cum sancto spirito*, which incidentally may not have been wholly Rossini's work. First-class recording.

Missa di Milano; Petite messe solennelle (1867 orchestral version)

◑ (B) *** Ph. Duo 475 230-2 (2). Mentzer, Giménez, Bostridge, Alaimo, Ch. & ASMF, Marriner

This reissued 1995 recording of Rossini's *Missa di Milano* is a real find. It is not really a complete Mass but the assembly of a *Kyrie*, *Gloria* and *Credo* probably composed independently before 1808. They are three separate manuscripts held in the Milan Conservatory (hence the title) but they fit together convincingly. They are well sprinkled with the musical fingerprints of the youthful, zestful Rossini, notably the crescendo in the *Gloria in excelsis Deo*, the nimble *Laudamus*, the lighthearted *Domine Deus*, and the *Qui tollis* with violin obbligato, very well sung here by **Susanne Mentzer**. The closing repeated *Amen* has an irresistible exuberance. The performance could hardly be better, full of jubilation, with the chorus singing lustily and the excellent soloists, including an early recorded contribution by **Ian Bostridge**, whose vocal personality comes over more robustly than we expect now.

Comparable praise applies to **Marriner's** account of the orchestral version of the *Petite messe solennelle*, which may not be as winningly coloured as the original score for two pianos and harmonium, but is very enjoyable in its own right. Marriner strikes a happy balance between the swingingly exuberant *Cum sancto spiritus*, and the more serious mood of the closing *Agnus Dei* – beautifully sung here. Excellent recording makes this a reissue to cherish.

Petite messe solennelle

(M) **(*) Decca 444 134-2 (2). Dessì, Scalchi, Sabbatini, Pertusi, Bologna Teatro Comunale Ch. & O, Chailly

Chailly chooses Rossini's orchestral version (made in 1867), although Rossini himself preferred his original, as do we. Nevertheless, with a fine solo team, **Daniella Dessì** and

Gloria Scalchi both singing beautifully (and ravishing in their *Qui tollis* duet), and with the bass rising to the occasion in the *Quoniam tu solus sanctus*, this is a very considerable account. The **Bologna Chorus** are not helped by a somewhat backward balance which, within the warmly resonant acoustic, does not provide an ideal sharpness of focus. But they sing with much ardour, especially in the *Gloria* and *Credo*, and Chailly ensures that the *Et resurrexit* caps the performance ebulliently. Apart from the choral balance (and that is not a real problem when the performers are so committed), the recording is glowing and vivid.

Soirées musicales (excerpts); La partenza; La pesca; La promessa; La regatta veneziana

◑ *** BBC (ADD) BBCB 8001-2. Harper, Baker, Britten – BRAHMS: *Liebeslieder Waltzes, Op. 52*; TCHAIKOVSKY: *4 Duets* ***

Both the tongue-in-cheek humour and the outright fun (as in the gondolier race of *La regatta veneziana*) are vividly caught in this BBC recording from the 1971 Aldeburgh Festival. **Heather Harper** and **Janet Baker** match beautifully, while remaining characterfully distinct, yet **Britten** at the piano remains master of ceremonies in family music-making idealized.

Stabat Mater

◑ ✹ **** Chan. 8780. Field, D. Jones, A. Davies, Earle, L. Symphony Ch., City of L. Sinfonia, Hickox

Richard Hickox rightly presents Rossini's *Stabat Mater* warmly and with gutsy strength. All four soloists here are first rate, not Italianate of tone but full and warm, and the **London Symphony Chorus** sings with fine attack as well as producing the most refined *pianissimos* in the unaccompanied quartet, here as usual given to the full chorus rather than to the soloists. Full-bodied and atmospheric sound.

OVERTURES

Overtures: Armida; Il barbiere di Siviglia; Bianca e Faliero; La cambiale di matrimonio; La Cenerentola; Demetrio e Poblibio; Edipo a Colono; Edoardo e Cristina; (i) Ermione; La gazza ladra; L'inganno felice; L'Italiana in Algeri; Maometto II; Otello; (ii) Ricciardo e Zoraide; La scala di seta; Semiramide; Le siège de Corinthe; Il Signor Bruschino; Tancredi; Il Turco in Italia; Torvaldo e Dorliska; Il viaggio a Reims; William Tell; Sinfonia al Conventello; Sinfonia di Bologna

◑ (M) **** Ph. Trio (ADD) 473 967-2 (3). ASMF, Marriner; (i) with Amb. S.

Marriner's reissued Trio spans all Rossini's overtures, but one must remember that the early Neapolitan operas, with the exception of *Ricciardo e Zoraide* and *Ermione*, make do with a simple Prelude, leading into the opening chorus. *Ricciardo e Zoraide*, however, is an extended piece (12 minutes 25 seconds), with the choral entry indicating that the introduction is at an end. *Maometto II* is on a comparable scale, while the more succinct *Armida* is an example of Rossini's picturesque evocation, almost like a miniature tone-poem. Twenty-four overtures plus two sinfonias make a delightful package in such sparkling performances, which eruditely use original orchestrations. Full, bright and atmospheric recording, spaciously reverberant, with no artificial brilliance.

Overtures: *Il barbiere di Siviglia; La cambiale di matrimonio; La Cenerentola; La gazza ladra; L'Italiana in Algeri; La scala di seta; Semiramide; Il Turco in Italia; William Tell*

Ⓜ *** Classic fM 75605 57031-2. Sinfonia Varsovia, Menuhin

Menuhin and his Polish group, the **Sinfonia Varsovia**, present a stylishly enjoyable collection of nine favourite Rossini overtures. There is a nice balance between wit and finesse, geniality and grace. Tempi are often brisk, but when there is a surge of vivacity there is no loss of poise. The wind solos are elegantly done and the string phrasing combines neatness with graceful warmth. Above all there is spontaneity here, and even at times a Beechamesque twinkle. The recording, made in the No. 1 Studio of Polish Radio in Warsaw, is full and resonant but not excessively so.

Overtures: *Il barbiere di Siviglia; La cambiale di matrimonio; La gazza ladra; L'Italiana in Algeri; Otello; La scala di seta; Semiramide; Le Siège de Corinthe; Il signor Bruschino; Tancredi; Torvaldo e Dorliska; Il Turco in Italia; Il viaggio a Reims; William Tell*

Ⓑ *** Double Decca 443 850-2 (2). Nat. PO, Chailly

In 1981 **Chailly** and the **National Philharmonic** made the first compact disc of Rossini overtures and these performances are here combined with their further compilation, recorded in 1984, to make a desirable bargain double. At times on the first disc there is a degree of digital edge on tuttis, but the bustle from the cellos is particularly engaging. The solo playing is fully worthy of such clear presentation demonstrating that this is an orchestra of London's finest musicians. Under Chailly the spirit of the music-making conveys spontaneous enjoyment too. Incidentally, *Il viaggio a Reims* had no overture at its first performance, but one was cobbled together later, drawing on the ballet music from *Le Siège de Corinthe*. The other novelties, *Otello* – played with great dash – and *Torvaldo e Dorliska*, with its witty interchanges between woodwind and strings, are among the highlights, and overall the performances are undoubtedly as infectious as they are stylish.

Overtures: *Il barbiere di Siviglia; La Cenerentola; La gazza ladra; La scala di seta; Il Signor Bruschino; William Tell*

🎞 Ⓜ *** RCA (ADD) 82876 65844-2. Chicago SO, Reiner

Reiner's classic collection from 1958 here emerges as sparkling and vivacious as ever. A fine set of performances, with *La Cenerentola* in particular offering superb orchestral bravura. The recording has good range, and the acoustic of the Chicago Hall casts a pleasing bloom. Everything sounds fresh, and after lovely, refined cello playing at the opening

of *William Tell*, the blaze of brass tone announcing the galop reminds us that the **Chicago Orchestra** was always famous in this department.

Overtures: *Il Barbiere di Siviglia; La Cenerentola; L'Italiana in Algeri; La scala di seta; Semiramide; Il Signor Bruschino; The Thieving Magpie; William Tell*

Ⓝ Ⓑ *** CfP 2 28281-2. Philh. O, Giulini

Giulini's performances combine refinement of detail with sophisticated **Philharmonia** playing from this orchestra's peak period during the early 1960s. *La scala di seta* has an almost ridiculously fast introduction, but *William Tell* has a natural flair. The recording is of EMI's best quality from this period.

Overtures: *Il barbiere di Siviglia; La gazza ladra; L'Italiana in Algeri; La scala di seta; Semiramide; William Tell*

Ⓑ **(*) DG (ADD) 415 377-2. BPO, Karajan

Karajan's virtuoso performances are polished like fine silver. The main *Allegro* of *La scala di seta* abandons all decorum when played as fast as this, and elsewhere bravura often takes precedence over poise. However, with the **Berlin Philharmonic** on sparkling form, there is wit as well as excitement; but the remastering casts very bright lighting on the upper range, which makes sonic brilliance approach aggressiveness in some climaxes.

Overtures: *Elisabetta, Regina d'Inghilterra; La scala di seta; Semiramide; Tancredi; Il Turco in Italia; William Tell*

🔁 ⒷⒷ *** RCA 74321 68012-2. LSO, Abbado – VERDI: *Overtures* ***

The *Overture Elisabetta, Regina d'Inghilterra* is in fact our familiar friend, *The Barber of Seville Overture*, and is listed as such on this reissued CD. But there is a subtle change here which surely implies the use of the proper title – a triplet in the first theme of the *Allegro* which is repeated each time the theme reappears. This adds a touch of novelty to these zestful performances from **Abbado**, with exhilaratingly fast tempi, the **LSO** players kept constantly on their toes and obviously enjoying themselves. The exuberance comes to the fore especially in *Tancredi* – there is even a brief clarinet glissando – heard in a revised version by Philip Gosset. But some might feel that *La scala di seta* would be more effective if a fraction more relaxed and poised. *William Tell* opens with elegant cellos, then offers an unashamedly over-the-top storm sequence and a final galop taken at breakneck speed. The remastered recording is vividly bright, but it matches Abbado's approach and has plenty of supporting weight and a concert hall ambience.

Overtures: *La gazza ladra; L'Italiana in Algeri; Semiramide; Il Signor Bruschino; William Tell*

*** BBC (ADD) BBCL 4159-2 (2). Philh. O, Giulini – DVOŘÁK: *Symphony 8* (**(*)); BRUCKNER: *Symphony 8* ***

A sparkling bonus from **Giulini** for impressive performances of Dvořák's and Bruckner's *Eighth Symphonies*.

Semiramide: Overture

(***) Testament mono SBT 1015. BBC SO, Toscanini –
BRAHMS: *Symphony 2* (***); MENDELSSOHN: *Midsummer Night's Dream* (excerpt) (**)

Toscanini's famous concerts with the **BBC Symphony Orchestra** were obviously very special. This overture from a 1935 concert has one on the edge of one's seat. Quite electrifying. The sound calls for tolerance – but what playing!

OPERA

Adelaide di Borgogna (complete; CD version)

🔘– *** Opera Rara ORC32 (2). Cullogh, Larmore, Ford, Scottish CO & Ch., Carella

Unlike most Opera Rara recordings of operatic rarities, this one was recorded live at the Edinburgh Festival in 2005. It was the last session supervised by the indefatigable founder of the label, Patric Schmid, and proves a triumphant success, with one superb number after another. It delves into an obscure tale from German history, when the Emperor Otto (a castrato role, here superbly sung by **Jennifer Larmore**) rescued a damsel in distress (**Majella Cullogh** in the title-role). Both of them negotiate florid arias of formidable difficulty, as well as the many tautly written ensemble numbers. The tenor **Bruce Ford** is also impressive as Adelberto, the bad guy in the story, and the opera is sparklingly directed by **Carella**.

Il barbiere di Siviglia (complete; DVD version)

(N) 🔘– **** Warner NVC Arts **DVD** 4509 99223-2. Ewing, Rawnsley, Cosotti, Desderi, Furlanetto, Glyndebourne Ch., LPO, Cambreling (Producer: John Cox; V/D: Dave Heather)

(*) Arthaus **DVD 100 090. Bartoli, Quilico, Kuebler, Feller, Lloyd, Cologne City Op. Ch., Stuttgart RSO, Ferro. (Dir: Michael Hampe.)

This is the finest recording of *Il barbiere* since the famous Callas/Gobbi and Bartoli/Nucci sets on CD; moreover it has the inestimable advantage of video, which greatly enhances the humour. **Maria Ewing** is an absolutely delightful Rosina, matching her prettiness with coquettish charm and superb vocal bravura. **John Rawnsley's** ebulliently self-assured Figaro dominates the proceedings as he should, and **Max-René Cosotti's** golden-toned Almaviva completes the vocal cast with distinction, although as Basilio **Ferruccio Furlanetto's** *La calunnia* is also a joy. **Claudio Desderi** is an old hand at *opera buffa*, and his Bartolo is as vocally fluent as his demeanour is amusingly angry. All told, a marvellous cast, superb singing and sparklingly stylish orchestral playing under **Cambreling** make this 1981 Glyndebourne recording a set to treasure.

Recorded live at the Schwetzingen Festival in a very pretty theatre in 1988, this Arthaus DVD version of *Il barbiere* centres around the superb performances of the two principals, **Cecilia Bartoli**, already dominant, with voice and tech

nique fully developed even before she became a superstar, and **Gino Quilico** as Figaro, wonderfully winning in his acting with voice magnificently firm.

David Kuebler with his rather gritty tenor is far from winning as the Count, **Robert Lloyd** is an imposing Basilio and **Carlos Feller** a characterful Bartolo. **Gabriele Ferro** springs the rhythms persuasively, and **Michael Hampe's** production works well using realistic sets by Ezio Frigerio and costumes by Mauro Pagano. Excellent, cleanly separated sound.

(i) Il barbiere di Siviglia; (ii) La Cenerentola; (iii) Le Comte Ory (DVD versions; complete)

(N) (M) *** Warner NVC Arts **DVD** 50-51442-7848-2-4 (3). Glyndebourne productions, LPO, with (i) Ewing, Rawnsley, Cosotti; cond. Cambreling; (ii) Kuhlmann, Dale, Desderi, Rinaldo; cond. Renzetti; (iii) Laho, Woodman, Tézier, Massis; cond. A. Davis

This is another outstanding triptych: three of Rossini's finest operas in excellent Glyndebourne performances – a true bargain; although the documentation is relatively sparse, it is more than adequate.

Il barbiere di Siviglia (complete; CD versions)

🔘– **** Decca 425 520-2 (3). Bartoli, Nucci, Matteuzzi, Fissore, Burchuladze, Ch. & O of Teatro Comunale di Bologna, Patanè

🔘– (M) **** EMI 3 92046-2 (2). Callas, Gobbi, Alva, Ollendorff, Philh. Ch. & O, Galliera

🔘– (BB) *** Warner 9031 74885-2 (2). Hagegård, Larmore, Giménez, Corbelli, Ramey, Lausanne CO, López-Cobos

(M) **** EMI 5 67762-2 (2). de los Angeles, Alva, Cava, Wallace, Bruscantini, Glyndebourne Festival Ch., RPO, Gui

(***) Testament mono SBT 2166 (2). de los Angeles, Monti, Bechi, Rossi-Lemeni, Milan Ch. & SO, Serafin

(BB) *** Naxos 8.660027/29 (3) Ganassi, Serville, Vargas, Romero, De Grandis, Hungaria R. Ch., Failoni CO, Budapest, Humburg

On CD, **Cecilia Bartoli's** rich, vibrant voice not only copes brilliantly with the technical demands but she also gives a winningly provocative characterization. Like the conductor, Bartoli is wonderful at bringing out the fun. So is **Leo Nucci**, and he gives a beautifully rounded portrait of the wily barber. **Burchuladze**, unidiomatic next to the others, still gives a monumentally lugubrious portrait of Basilio, and the Bartolo of **Enrico Fissore** is outstanding, with the patter song wonderfully articulated at **Patanè's** sensible speed. The snag is that this Decca set is on three CDs; other recommended versions manage with two.

Gobbi and **Callas** were here at their most inspired and, with the recording quality nicely refurbished, the EMI is an outstanding set, not absolutely complete in its text, but so crisp and sparkling it can be confidently recommended. Callas remains supreme as a minx-like Rosina, summing up the character superbly in *Una voce poco fa*. The early stereo sound comes up very acceptably in this fine new transfer, clarified, fuller and more atmospheric, presenting a uniquely characterful performance with new freshness and immediacy.

López-Cobos directs a scintillating performance, helped by brilliant enssembles, generally taken at high speed, with rhythms sprung delectably. Though **Håkan Hagegård** is a dry-toned Figaro, the recording sets him in a helpful ambience, which equally helps to enhance the comic atmosphere, with the interplay of characters well managed. There are few more stylish Rossini tenors today than **Raúl Giménez**, and though his voice is not as youthful as some, his musical imagination goes with fine flexibility and point. As for **Jennifer Larmore**, she is is an enchanting Rosina, both firm and rich of tone. Crisply consistent, this makes a strong contender among modern digital versions, even next to the delectable Decca set featuring Cecilia Bartoli. An excellent collection of highlights is available on a budget Apex disc, playing for 76 minutes (2564 61502-2).

Gui's 1962 Glydebourne production has been remastered for EMI's 'Great Recordings of the Century', and the bloom on voices and orchestra is even more apparent. The charm of **de los Angeles's** Rosina matches the unforced geniality of the production as a whole, strongly cast and easy to enjoy. Good documentation too. Not perhaps a first choice against competition but a good mid-priced recommendation.

The Testament issue, superbly transferred, brings out of EMI's archive the long-buried set which **Victoria de los Angeles** recorded with **Serafin** in mono in 1952, when her voice was at its fullest and most golden. Though the orchestral playing is often rough, and Serafin is relaxed rather than sparkling, the performance of de los Angeles could not be more seductive. Not as light as her later account with Gui in stereo, this is even sunnier and more glowing. **Gino Bechi** is a strong if gruff Figaro, **Nicola Monti** a heady-toned Almaviva and **Nicola Rossi-Lemeni** a characterful Basilio.

Though the cast is not as starry as with most full-price rivals, the Naxos set makes a first-rate bargain. The singing is hardly less stylish, with **Sonia Ganassi** a rich-toned Rosina, controlling vibrato well, and with **Ramon Vargas** an agile and attractively youthful-sounding Almaviva. **Roberto Serville** as Figaro conveys the fun of the role brilliantly. The *buffo* characters are strongly cast too, with Basilio's *La calunnia* (**Franco de Grandis**) delightfully enlivened by comments from Bartolo (**Angelo Romero**), both very much involved in their roles. **Will Humburg's** often brisk speeds, with crisp recitative matched by dazzling ensembles, never prevent the music (and the singers) from breathing.

The Barber of Seville (in English)

(M) ****(*)** Chan. 3025 (2). Jones, Ford, Opie, Rose, Shore, ENO Ch. & O, Bellini

Chandos here offers at mid-price this *Barber* in English, using the bright translation of Amanda and Anthony Holden. Strongly cast, it is a genial performance, very well played and recorded. The only reservation is over the relaxed conducting of **Gabriele Bellini** which lacks dramatic bite. Compensating for that, the principal singers not only characterize vividly but together form a lively ensemble. **Alan Opie** is a strong, positive Figaro, while **Della Jones** as Rosina

both exploits her rich mezzo tones and brings sparkle to the coloratura. It is good too to have so accomplished a Rossini tenor as **Bruce Ford** singing Almaviva. **Peter Rose** as Basilio and **Andrew Shore** as Dr Bartolo, both young-sounding for these roles, are fresh and firm too. Excellent documentation includes a full English libretto.

La Cenerentola (DVD versions)

🎞→ ******** Decca **DVD** 071 444-9. Bartoli, Dara, Giménez, Corbelli, Pertusi, Houston Grand Op. Ch. & Symphony, Campanella. (V/D: Brian Large.)

*** Arthaus **DVD** 100 214. Murray, Berry, Araiza, Quilico, Schöne, V. State Op. Ch., VPO, Chailly. (Dir: Michael Hampe. V/D: Claus Viller.)

(N) ****(*)** Warner NVC Arts **DVD** 5050467-0940-2-4. Kuhlmann, Dale, Desderi, Rinaldi, Taddei, Zannini, Kennedy, Glyndebourne Ch., LPO, Renzetti

Few Rossini operas have such fizz as Decca's **Houston Opera** production of *La Cenerentola*, a part **Cecilia Bartoli** was born to play. The rest of the cast is the same as the CD set, except that **Raúl Giménez** takes the part of Don Ramiro. **Bruno Campanella** conducts very spiritedly. Visually the production could not be more winning, and the camera placing is a great credit to **Brian Large**.

Riccardo Chailly (who directed the Decca CDs) conducts the alternative version, which comes from the 1982 Salzburg Festival, and had the Bartoli set not been available it would have been a very strong recommendation, for **Ann Murray** is delightful in the principal role and the rest of the cast is excellent. If in Act I Don Magnifico's castle looks run down and needing a coat of paint, the glamour of the palace more than compensates. The recording is bright and sparking but has plenty of bloom and the camerawork is always well managed. Most enjoyable, with a dazzling *Non più mesta* and a particularly infectious finale. But Chailly is at his finest throughout and so are the chorus and orchestra.

Rossini's *La Cenerentola* is quite long at 151 minutes, and the plot is simpler than the story we are used to, with no glass slippers (a bracelet belonging to Cinderella substitutes) and Alidoro, the Prince's philosopher/tutor (given excellent presence here by **Roderick Kennedy**), substitutes for a fairy godmother. The ugly sisters remain to torment the heroine until the prince finally finds her at the end, and the wedding banquet is spiced by her famous *Non più mesta*. The Glyndebourne version has a pleasing Cinderella in **Kathleen Kuhlmann**, who sings well, although she is no Bartoli, and one of her two ugly sisters is prettier than she is (though not nicer!). Her Prince (**Laurence Dale**) isn't very dashing, and Alidoro has more presence. Both **Alberto Rinaldi** as Dandini and (especially) the veteran **Claudio Desderi**, as her father, Don Magnifico, are strongly characterized. The many buffo ensembles go well enough and are enjoyably sung, with spirit and remarkable diction, but one feels that the conductor **Donato Renzetti** could have achieved rather more sparkle overall.

La Cenerentola (CD versions)

🎞→ ******** Decca 436 902-2 (2). Bartoli, Matteuzzi, Corbelli,

Dara, Costa, Banditelli, Pertusi, Ch. & O of Teatro Comunale di Bologna Ch. & O, Chailly

Ⓜ **** Teldec 4509 94553-2 (2). Larmore, Giménez, Quilico, Corbelli, Scarabelli, ROHCG Ch. & O, Rizzi

Ⓑ ** DG Double (ADD) 477 5659 (2). Berganza, Alva, Montarsolo, Capecchi, Scottish Op., Ch., LSO, Abbado

On the Decca CDs **Cecilia Bartoli** again makes an inspired Cenerentola. Her tone-colours are not just more sensuous than those of her rivals: her imagination and feeling for detail add enormously to her vivid characterization, culminating in a stunning account of the final rondo, *Non più mesta*. **William Matteuzzi** is an engaging prince, sweeter of tone and more stylish than his direct rivals, while the contrasting of the bass and baritone roles is ideal between **Alessandro Corbelli** as Dandini, **Michele Pertusi** as the tutor, Alidoro, and **Enzo Dara** as Don Magnifico. Few Rossini opera-sets have such fizz as this, and the recording is one of Decca's most vivid.

In **Carlo Rizzi's** mid-priced Teldec version, **Jennifer Larmore** makes an enchanting heroine, with her creamily beautiful mezzo both tenderly expressive in cantilena and flawlessly controlled through the most elaborate coloratura passages. This is a more smiling character, not least in the final exuberant rondo, *Non più mesta*, which sparkles deliciously, more relaxed than with Bartoli. As Ramiro, **Raúl Giménez** sings with a commanding sense of style, less youthful but more assured than his rival, while **Alessandro Corbelli** is far more aptly cast here as Don Magnifico than as Dandini in the Decca set. Here the Dandini of Gino Quilico is youthful and debonair, and **Alastair Miles** is a magnificent Alidoro. Though the **Covent Garden** forces cannot quite match the close-knit Bologna team in underlining the comedy as in a live performance, as directed by Carlo Rizzi they are consistently more refined, with more light and shade, bringing out the musical sparkle all the more. Excellent, well-balanced sound. A generous highlights disc (75 minutes) is available on a budget Apex CD (2564 61503-2).

Abbado's 1971 DG set lacks the extrovert bravura and sparkle of an ideal performance. The atmosphere in places is almost of a concert performance, helped by fine analogue recording. **Berganza**, agile in the coloratura, seems too mature, even matronly, for the fairy-tale role of Cinderella. **Alva** sings well enough but is somewhat self-conscious in the florid writing. Abbado, although hardly witty in his direction, inspires delicate playing throughout. The CD transfer is admirably fresh. The reissue includes a track-by-track synopsis.

Le Comte Ory (complete; DVD version)

**** Warner DVD 0630 18646-2. Laho, Massis, Montague, Shaulis, Tezier, Robbins, Glyndebourne Ch., LPO, A. Davis (V/D: Brian Large)

Le Comte Ory, written for Paris in 1828, was Rossini's very last comic opera, and one which prompted a classic Glyndebourne production in 1997 by Jerome Savary. With colourful sets and costumes by Ezio Toffolutti, the fun is just as exuberant. That is so both in Act I, when the predatory Count Ory disguises himself as a hermit, intent on waylaying

the Countess Adele in her castle while her brother is away at the Crusades, and in Act II when Ory and his followers disguise themselves as nuns and inveigle their way into the castle. Their drinking chorus – punctuated by pretended devotions when approached by strangers – is a delight, and the comic bed-scene when Ory thinks he is fondling the Countess when in fact it is the page, Isolier, is brilliantly handled. The cast, led by **Marc Laho** as Ory, **Annick Massis** as the Countess and **Diana Montague** as Isolier, has no weak link, with ensembles delectably timed and pointed by the conductor, **Andrew Davis**.

Le Comte Ory (CD version)

**** DG 477 5020 (2). Flórez, Miles, Bonfadelli, Todorovitch, De Liso, Pratico, Prague Ch., Bologna Theatre O, López-Cobos

This is one of the most delectable of all Rossini's comic operas, an essay in French that set a new pattern for the composer. **Jesus López-Cobos**, the most skilled of Rossini conductors, even matches in rhythmic lift and comic timing the magic example of Vittorio Gui in the classic Glyndebourne recording of the 1950s. The big ensemble that ends Act I is taken even faster than with Gui, yet it is just as effervescent. The presence of an audience plainly helps, and the performance gains enormously too from the brilliant characterization of the central character of the predatory Count himself by **Juan Diego Flórez**, tackling the most formidable florid passages with ease and imagination. As the object of his desires, the Countess Adele, whose husband is away at the crusades, **Stefania Bonfadelli** sings with equal fluency, a coloratura soprano with a mezzo-ish tinge in the lower register who can reach a top E flat with ease. **Alastair Miles** as the Count's tutor sings strongly, making him rather a severe character, with **Marina De Liso** light and sparkling as the page, Isolier. The closely focused recording is full and firm, if not always kind to the orchestra, with the voices very well caught, and vociferous applause at the end of each Act adding to the sense of presence.

La donna del lago (complete; DVD version)

**(*) Opus Arte DVD OA LS 3009 D. Anderson, Blake, Merritt, La Scala Ch. & O, Muti (Dir: Werner Herzog; V/D: Ilio Catani)

La donna del lago (*The Lady of the Lake*) with lavish sets by Maurizio Balo, evocative and realistic, it establishes the period atmosphere well; but it is Muti's evident enthusiasm for the piece in his taut and exciting conducting that above all brings out the drama of conflict in 16th-century Scotland, with the melancholy Elena, the heroine, caught between rival forces. **June Anderson** in that role sings very reliably, but it is hardly a characterful performance, and it is left to the two principal tenors, both with an impressive upper range so necessary in Rossini, to make the most striking vocal contributions, **Rockwell Blake** as Giacomo V (James V) of Scotland and **Chris Merritt** as Rodrigo di Dhu. Though Merritt has the weightier voice, he produces astounding top notes out of the blue, while Blake with sweeter tone is amazingly agile, relishing the most taxing divisions. The others make a strong, consistent team. A complete libretto is provided and a good synopsis of the plot, but no information on the opera's history.

La donna del lago (complete; CD version)

(BB) *** Naxos 8.660235/6. Ganassi, Pizzolato, Mironov, Bothmer, Gierlach, Prague Chamber Ch., Tübingen Festival Band, SWR R. O, Kaiserslautern, Zedda

Until Pollini's Sony set returns, this new Naxos live recording reigns supreme for this opera, freely adapted from Scott's novel *The Lady of the Lake*, and even if it were not in the budget range it would still be fully competitive. **Zedda** conducts with élan and his young cast make a splendid team. **Sonia Ganassi** is excellent in the title-role of Elena, and the pair of tenors, **Maxim Mironov** as Uberto and **Ferdinand von Bothmer** as Rodrigo, are both most convincing. The duet between Uberto and Elena in Act I, *Quali accenti! . . . Ma son sorpreso* is one of the opera's highlights; later, the duets between Elena and Malcolm (**Marianna Pizzolato**) are equally telling, as is Pizzolato's spectacular earlier aria (*Mura felici*). The chorus and orchestra are first class, and there is some spectacular horn playing in the opera's opening scene. The set comes with a good synopsis and is far preferable to Muti's reissued Philips version (473 307-20), where the ensemble of chorus and orchestra, so successful with Zedda, is rough, and the principals coarse by comparison. The Naxos set is enjoyable on all counts, not least the excellent recording.

Elisabetta, Regina d'Inghilterra (complete; CD version)

⊕▬ *** Opera Rara ORC 22 (3). Larmore, Ford, Cullagh, LPO, Carella

Elisabetta d'Inghilterra, produced in 1815, like Walter Scott's novel, *Kenilworth*, of five years later, deals with the love of Queen Elizabeth for Leicester, but with the added gloss that Mary Queen of Scots had given birth during her captivity to two unacknowledged children by the Duke of Norfolk, one of whom married Leicester. The overture is the one that Rossini re-used in the *Barber of Seville*, and Elisabetta's first aria brings material later developed in the *Barber* as Rosina's *Una voce poco fa*. What matters is the vigour of the writing and many marvellous ensembles, beautifully performed on Opera Rara by a strong cast led by **Jennifer Larmore**, **Bruce Ford** and **Majella Cullagh**, with **Giuliano Carella** the idiomatic conductor. This can be strongly recommended.

L'equivoco stravagante (complete)

(BB) **(*) Naxos 8.660087/8 (2). Petrova, Felice, Vinco, Schmunck, Minarelli, Santamaria, Czech Chamber Ch. & Chamber Soloists, Zedda

L'equivoco stravagante ('The Bizarre Deception'), is one of Rossini's earliest operas, written when he was only 19. Already the Rossini fingerprints are firmly in place, with the music regularly sparkling from the Overture, with its brilliant horn triplets, onwards. The story of this *dramma giocoso*

involves a scheming servant, Frontino, who deceives the stupid suitor, Buralichio, into believing that the girl he is wooing, the heroine, Ernestina, is in fact male and whose nouveau riche father, Gamberotto, has had 'him' castrated so that he could become a high-earning opera-singer. The complications are many, until Ernestina is safely united with Ermanno, the impecunious tutor whom she loves. After three performances in 1811 the piece was banned for being too licentious. Rossini cut his losses, using material from it in his subsequent operas. It makes an attractive rarity, generally well sung and very well conducted in this live recording by the Rossini scholar **Alberto Zedda** – if unhelpfully punctuated by tepid applause.

Ermione (complete; DVD version)

⊕▬ *** Warner DVD 0630 1012-2. Antonacci, Montague, Ford, Lopez-Janez, Austin Kelly, Howell, Glyndebourne Ch., LPO, A. Davis (Dir: Graham Vick; V/D: Humphrey Burton)

Recorded live in the new Glyndebourne Opera House in 1995, the Warner disc updates the action – in a plot based on Racine's tragedy, *Andromaque* – to the early 20th century, with colourful military uniforms to the fore. Fascinatingly, the set represents sections of an 18th-century theatre with its galleries and boxes, a device that works flexibly enough. As usual in an *opera seria* of Rossini, the mixture of jolly music may seem incongruous, bringing unexpected lurches of mood, but it is always lively and it offers the three principal tenors some spectacular vocal challenges. **Bruce Ford** as Oreste sings powerfully, producing penetrating top notes out of the blue, while **Jorge Lopez-Janez** as Pyrrhus sings more gently and with a sweeter tone, also coping well with the high tessitura. Oddly, this adaptation of *Andromaque* slants the story away from her – superbly played here by **Diana Montague** – towards Ermione, whose Act II aria provides an emotional high point in the piece. Excellent contributions too from the third tenor, **Paul Austin Kelly**, as Pilade and from **Gwynne Howell** as Phoenix. **Andrew Davis**, Glyndebourne music director at the time, draws fresh, incisive performances from chorus and orchestra. As so often with Warner DVDs, there is no booklet, only a synopsis and a list of chapters – a pity when such a rarity really requires some background information.

La gazza ladra (complete; DVD version)

⊕▬ **** Arthaus DVD 102 203. Feller, Condo, Kuebler, Contrabus, Cologne Op. Ch., Gürzenich O, Cologne, Bartoletti (TV Dir: José Montes-Baquer)

Recorded live at the **Cologne Opera** in 1987, this sparkling performance is a winner. One forgets the improbabilities of the plot, so agreeably enjoyable is the performance, with **Contrabus** as a charming Ninetta; and her suitor, Giannetto, sung by **David Kuebler**, is ardent but tender when he needs to be. All the roles are done with character and obvious enjoyment, including the ensembles and choruses. The orchestra is lively and alert, with Rossini's tuneful invention a constant source of delight. The production is the crowning glory of this performance, with beautiful sets and costumes, all brightly and sympathetically lit; this lesser-known Rossini opera is well worth watching.

The Thieving Magpie (complete; in English)

⊕ (M) *** Chan. 3097 (2). Cullagh, Banks, Bickley, White, Smythe, Purves, Geoffrey Mitchell Ch., Philh. O, Parry

David Parry draws sparkling performances from his excellent cast of singers, as well as from the **Philharmonia Orchestra**. Using a lively translation by Jeremy Sams, the performance makes light of the improbabilities of the plot, which has its unpleasantly dark element when the heroine is threatened with death after being accused of stealing one of her mistress's silver spoons. The culprit is of course the magpie of the opera's title, and all turns out well in the end. The set gains enormously from having been made in the wake of a stage production at Garsington Manor in 2002, also conducted by Parry. As he points out in a note, the full score is unmanageably long, which has entailed some cutting. As Parry claims, the arias that are dramatically less essential tend to be those least interesting musically. As it is, the piece moves swiftly along, with the Irish soprano **Majella Cullagh** as the heroine, Ninetta, and **Christopher Purves** as the Mayor, her employer, outstanding both musically and dramatically with cleanly focused singing. It helps no doubt that they both took part in the Garsington production, but the others are first rate too, with the tenor **Barry Banks** as the hero, Giannetto, **Susan Bickley** as the Mayor's wife Lucia, **Russell Smythe** as Ninetta's father and **John Graham-Hall** as the pedlar, Isacco. Full, well-balanced sound, recorded in the Blackheath Concert Halls.

Guglielmo Tell (complete; CD version in Italian)

⊕ (M) **** Decca (ADD) 475 7723 (4). Pavarotti, Freni, Milnes, Ghiaurov, Amb. Op. Ch., Nat. PO, Chailly

This now arrives at last at mid-price as one of Decca's Originals, with **Milnes** a heroic Tell, and, although **Pavarotti** has his moments of coarseness, he sings the role of Arnoldo glowingly. **Mirella Freni** as the heroine, Matilde, provides strength as well as sweetness, and **Chailly** controls this massive opera puposefully, with the many ensembles particularly impressive, especially when the Decca analogue recording is so fine.

Guillaume Tell (William Tell; in French)

⊕ (M) **** EMI (ADD) 7 69951-2 (4). Bacquier, Caballé, Gedda, Mesplé, Amb. Op. Ch., RPO, Gardelli

The interest of the 1973 EMI set is that it is sung in the original French. **Gardelli** proves an imaginative Rossini interpreter, allying his formidable team to vigorous and sensitive performances. **Bacquier** makes an impressive Tell, developing the character as the story progresses; **Gedda** is a model of taste, and **Montserrat Caballé** copes ravishingly with the coloratura problems of Mathilde's role. While Chailly's full-price Decca set puts forward a strong case for using Italian with its open vowels, this remains a fully worthwhile alternative, with excellent CD sound. Indeed the current remastering is first class in every way and the choral passages,

incisively sung, are among the most impressive; moreover the set now comes with full translation.

L'Italiana in Algeri (complete; DVD versions)

⊕ **** DG DVD 073 4261. Horne, Montarsolo, Ahlstedt, Merritt, Kesling, Milas, Met. Op. Ch. & O, Levine (V/D: Brian Large)

**(*) TDK DVD DVWW-OPITAL. Larmore, Alaimo, Fischer, Trullu, Smith, Ford, Op. Nat. de Paris, Campanella (Dir: Andrei Serban; V/D: André Flédérick)

Marilyn Horne is the great star focus of the 1986 production from the **Met**. She had a great affinity with the role of Isabella: 'I don't know where she leaves off and I begin: the character comes too easily to me,' she comments. She is predictably brilliant in the coloratura passages, with her commanding presence not getting in the way of a sense of fun. Her lover, Lindoro, is more than capably sung by **Douglas Ahlstedt**, though his tone is not consistently beautiful (some high-lying passages are a bit strained). Mustafâ, sung by the veteran, **Paolo Montarsolo**, has a bit of wobble in his voice, but he has the relish of an old pro who knows his role inside out. His wife Elvira is charmingly sung by **Myra Merritt**. All the various comic roles are well done, especially with such seasoned singers as **Spiro Milas** in the role of Haly, the captain of the Algerian pirates. The production by Jean-Pierre Ponnelle is brightly attractive, and the direction is at the service of the performance. **Levine** conducts with characteristic energy, though his style is more suited to Verdi than to the charm of Rossini. The bonuses include an interview with Marilyn Horne, talking about Rossini, plus a couple of extra arias from *Samson et Dalila* and *The Ghosts of Versailles*.

The TDK version, with its stylized modern production, initially takes a bit of getting used to, especially with the opening chorus of the eunuchs in rather grotesque costumes. However, the production grows on you, and it is not without its clever touches. The performance is excellent from the word go, with **Campanella** finding Rossini's sparkle more readily than Levine's super-charged Verdi-esque conducting. **Bruce Ford** is superb in the role of Lindoro, coping with all his vocal fireworks evenly and smoothly. **Simone Alaimo** as Mustafâ offers a lively and stylish reading, working wonderfully well with Ford in the first Act I duet. **Jennifer Larmore** is a bright and forthright Isabella, singing with remarkable precision and energy. Mustafâ's long-suffering wife Elvira, sung by **Jeannette Fischer**, has bags of character and is very enjoyable to watch; the whole cast works well as a team. Good sound and excellent picture quality.

L'Italiana in Algeri (complete; CD versions)

⊕ **** Teldec 0630 17130-2 (2). Larmore, Giménez, Del Carlo, Corbelli, Grand Theatre Ch., Lausanne CO, López-Cobos

⊕ ✹ **** DG (ADD) 427 331-2 (2). Baltsa, Raimondi, Dara, Lopardo, V. State Op. Konzertvereinigung, VPO, Abbado

(M) *** Erato 2292 45404-2 (2). Horne, Palacio, Ramey, Trimarchi, Battle, Zaccaria, Prague Ch., I Sol. Ven., Scimone

Ⓜ *** Decca (ADD) 475 8275 (2). Berganza, Alva, Corena, Panerai, Maggio Musicale Fiorentino Ch. & O, Varviso

The Teldec recording offers a near-ideal account, superbly sung, sparklingly conducted and brilliantly recorded. **Jennifer Larmore** in the title-role is both youthfully seductive and ripely characterful, with her firm, fresh voice beautifully caught, at once easily flexible on top and rich in the chest register. Her big Rondo in Act II is one of the high spots of the set, stylishly ornamented. **Raúl Giménez** as Lindoro makes a perfect counterpart, establishing his comparable brilliance in his elaborate Act I aria and investing everything he sings with character and a sense of fun, not just singing the notes. He is wonderfully fluent in the brilliant patter duet with Mustafa, Bey of Algiers, characterfully sung by **John Del Carlo**. **Alexander Corbelli** too makes the most of the humour in the role of the put-upon servant, Taddeo. In a fascinating appendix, Giménez also sings Lindoro's alternative aria in Act II with its clarinet obbligato. A clear first choice among CD versions.

Abbado's brilliant version was recorded in conjunction with a new staging by the **Vienna State Opera**, with timing and pointing all geared for wit on stage to make this one of the most captivating of all recordings of the opera. **Agnes Baltsa** is a real fire-eater in the title-role, and **Ruggero Raimondi** with his massively sepulchral bass gives weight to his part without undermining the comedy. The American tenor, **Frank Lopardo**, proves the most stylish Rossinian, singing with heady clarity in superbly articulated divisions, while both *buffo* baritones are excellent too. This uses the authentic score, published by the Fondazione Rossini in Pesaro.

Scimone's highly enjoyable version is beautifully played and recorded with as stylish a team of soloists as one can expect nowadays. The text is complete and alternative versions of certain arias are given as an appendix. **Marilyn Horne** makes a dazzling, positive Isabella, and **Samuel Ramey** is splendidly firm as Mustafa. **Domenico Trimarchi** is a delightful Taddeo and **Ernesto Palacio** an agile Lindoro, not coarse, though the recording does not always catch his tenor timbre well. Nevertheless the sound is generally very good indeed.

Under **Varviso** the opera has Rossinian sparkle in abundance and the music blossoms readily. **Teresa Berganza** makes an enchanting Italian Girl and the three principal men are all characterful. The recording is vintage Decca, vividly remastered, and adds greatly to the sparkle of the whole proceedings. The reissue includes a libretto with translation, and this makes a fine bargain, even if many will still opt for the later and more complete Scimone version.

The Italian Girl in Algiers (Highlights; in English)

Ⓝ Ⓜ *** Chan. 3160. Larmore, Tynan, Miles, Opie, Banks, Philh., Cohen

The Opera in English series promoted by Sir Peter Moores is now offering recordings of generous highlights, such as this selection from Rossini's *The Italian Girl in Algiers* in a translation by David Parry (who, for once, is not the conductor here, handing over to the capable **Brad Cohen**). The high-

lights centre round the outstanding American mezzo, **Jennifer Larmore**, who gives a wonderful performance, with every note of the elaborate coloratura cleanly in place and with no suspicion of any unwanted aspiration. Her final display aria, backed up by the **Geoffrey Mitchell Choir**, crowns a superb performance. The rest of the cast is comparably strong, with **Alastair Miles** an aptly comic Mustafa, capturing the humour as well as singing flawlessly, again with no aspiration on coloratura. **Alan Opie** is also a masterly comic actor in the role of Taddeo, Isabella's companion, with **Barry Banks** as Lindoro, Mustafa's favourite slave.

Maometto II (complete)

Ⓑ *** Ph. Trio 475 5092-2 (3). Anderson, Zimmermann, Palacio, Ramey, Dale, Amb. Op. Ch., Philh. O, Scimone

Claudio Scimone's account of *Maometto II* has **Samuel Ramey** magnificently focusing the whole story in his portrait of the Muslim invader in love with the heroine. The other singing is less sharply characterized but is generally stylish, with **Margarita Zimmermann** in the *travesti* role of Calbo and **June Anderson** singing sweetly as Anna. **Laurence Dale** is excellent in two smaller roles, while **Ernesto Palacio** mars some fresh-toned singing with his intrusive aitches. Excellently recorded, this is well worth exploring at bargain price, even though only a synopsis is included.

Matilde de Shabran (complete; CD version)

**(*) Decca 475 7688 (3). Massis, Flórez, Halevy, de Simone, Bonfatti, Cucci (fortepiano), Prague Ch., Galicia SO, Frizza

Matilde de Shabran was the penultimate opera that Rossini wrote for Italy, before taking up residence in Paris. It was written for the Roman Carnival of 1821, with some of the numbers provided by Pacini. By the time Rossini had prepared the score for performance in Naples that autumn, he replaced the Pacini items with his own work. The result is a strong, characterful opera, with impressive ensembles, that yet lacks the really striking melodies which make Rossini's masterpieces so memorable. Nevertheless it is most welcome on disc in a lively performance with the masterly **Juan Diego Flórez** in the principal tenor role of Corradino Cuor de ferro (Ironheart), free and flexible. In the title-role, **Annick Massis** is less even in her production, but with a strong supporting cast it makes an excellent issue, filling in an important gap in the Rossini repertory.

Mosè in Egitto (complete; CD version)

Ⓝ Ⓜ *** Ph. (ADD) 478 0149 (2). Raimondi, Nimsgern, Anderson, Palacio, Gal, Lewis, Fischella, Amb. Op. Ch., Philh. O, Scimone

Ⓑ *** Naxos 8.660220/1. Regazzo, Amou, Gierlach, Bevacqua, Adami, Trucco, San Pietro Conservatory Ch., Wildbad Wind Band, Württemberg PO, Fogliani

Scimone on Philips justifies his claim that the 1819 version is dramatically more effective than either the earlier Italian one or the later Paris one. Rossini's score brings much fine music, and among the soloists **Raimondi** relishes not only the solemn moments like the great invocation in Act I and the soaring prayer of Act III, but also the rage aria in Act II, almost like Handel updated, if with disconcerting foretastes of Dr Malatesta in Donizetti's *Don Pasquale*. The writing for the soprano and tenor lovers (the latter the son of Pharaoh and in effect the villain of the piece) is relatively conventional, though the military flavour of their Act I cabaletta is refreshingly different. **Ernesto Palacio** and **June Anderson** make a strong pair, and the mezzo, **Zehava Gal**, is another welcome singer as Pharaoh's wife. **Siegmund Nimsgern** makes a fine Pharaoh, **Salvatore Fischella** an adequate Arone (Aaron). The well-balanced recording emerges most vividly.

Antonio Fogliani's new Naxos version, recorded live during the 'Rossini in Wildbad' Festival offers genuine competition to Scimone's fine Philips set. **Lorenzo Regazzo's** Mosè may not quite match Raimondi's account in richness of sonority, but he rises to his big moments and the closing *Prayer* sequence is splendidly sung. Akie Amou (as Elcia) also rises to the occasion in her big aria at the end of Act I, and even more so in *Porgi la destra amata* at the close of Act II. The tenor **Filippo Adami** is an ardent Osiride, even if sometimes showing strain in his upper range. The rest of the cast are sound, but what make this set so enjoyable is the fine singing of the grouped soloists in the various ensembles and the chorus in the big scenes, which are tinglingly directed by **Fogliani**. The recording is clear and full-bodied and, as usual with Naxos, the set comes with a good synopsis, and this is well worth its modest cost.

Otello (complete)

&— *** Opera Rara ORC 18 (3). Ford, Futral, Matteuzzi, D'Arcangelo, Lopera, Philh. O, Parry

&— (B) *** Ph. Duo (ADD) 475 448-2 (2). Carreras, von Stade, Condò, Pastine, Fischella, Ramey, Amb. S., Philh. O, López-Cobos

Justifiably overshadowed by Verdi's masterpiece, this early opera of Rossini, written in 1816 for Naples, is a piece very much of its time. Rossini is inspired by a serious subject to produce a striking series of arias and ensembles, which culminate in what was then a revolutionary course in Italian opera, a tragic ending. Significantly, later, in 1820 and pressured by the authorities, Rossini provided a happy ending, when Otello is finally convinced of Desdemona's innocence. That alternative close is the first of three important appendices included in this very well-documented Opera Rara set. Where the previous Philips recording, more starrily cast, provided a badly cut text on two CDs merely, this one stretches to three very well-filled discs.

It is a credit to Opera Rara that three formidable Rossini tenors are here involved, not just **Bruce Ford** in the title role, strong and stylish if a little gritty as recorded, but also **Juan José Lopera**, impressive as Iago, and, singing even more sweetly, **William Matteuzzi** as Rodrigo, here given a relatively big role. **Elizabeth Futral** is a strong, dramatic heroine, rising superbly to the challenge of the final Act, which, coming closer to Shakespeare, brings the most memorable music, including a lovely *Willow Song*. **Enkeljda Shkosa** sings most beautifully as Emilia, as she does too in the alternative Malibran version of the Act II duet, in which she sings Otello, transformed into a breeches-role. **David Parry** excels

himself in drawing powerful, sensitive playing from the Philharmonia, dramatically paced, with some outstanding solo work from the wind. Vivid, well-balanced sound.

It is some tribute to the Philips performance, superbly recorded and brightly and stylishly conducted by **López-Cobos**, that the line-up of tenors is turned into an asset, with three nicely contrasted soloists. **Carreras** here is at his finest – most affecting in his recitative before the murder, while **Fisichella** copes splendidly with the high tessitura of Rodrigo's role, and **Pastine** has a distinct timbre to identify him as the villain. **Frederica von Stade** pours forth a glorious flow of beautiful tone, well matched by **Nucci Condò** as Emilia. **Samuel Ramey** is excellent too in the bass role of Elmiro. It makes an undoubted bargain at its new price; its cost, alas, precluding the possibility of including text and translation.

La scala di seta (complete)

&— *** Claves 50-9219/20. Corbelli, Ringholz, Vargas, De Carolis, Provvisionato, Massa, ECO, Viotti

The *Overture* is among the best known of all that Rossini wrote, and here **Viotti** establishes his individuality with an unusually expansive slow introduction leading to a brisk and well-sprung *Allegro*, scintillatingly played by the ECO. The cast here is strong vocally, with **Teresa Ringholz** delightful as the heroine, Giulia, warm and agile, shading her voice seductively. She and the *buffo*, sung by **Alessandro Corbelli**, have the biggest share of the solo work, and he is also first rate. The tenor **Ramon Vargas** sings without strain – rare in this series – and the mezzo, **Francesca Provvisionato**, sings vivaciously as the heroine's cousin, with a little aria in military rhythm a special delight. Warm sound with good bloom on the voices.

Semiramide (complete, but with traditional cuts; DVD version)

&— **** Arthaus DVD 100 222 (2). Anderson, Horne, Olsen, Ramey, Met. Op. O and Ch., Conlon. (Dir: John Copley; TV Dir: Brian Large.)

Grand opera presented unapologetically on a monumental scale in traditional style typifies this 1990 production of *Semiramide* at the **Met** in New York. The casting is very strong, centring as much around the commanding Arsace of Marilyn Horne as the powerful but less characterful **June Anderson** in the title role, both of them wonderfully agile in coloratura. Yet on DVD, with **Brian Large** as video director, it is the fine production of **John Copley**, using very grand sets by John Conklin and sumptuous costumes by Michael Stennett, that stands out. The tenor, **Stanford Olsen**, is impressive as Idreno, and **Samuel Ramey** is handsome of voice and presence as Assur, setting the seal on this supremely confident presentation of a difficult opera, purposefully conducted by **James Conlon**.

Semiramide (complete; CD version)

&— (M) **** Decca (ADD) 475 7918-2 (3). Sutherland, Horne, Rouleau, Malas, Serge, Amb. Op. Ch., LSO, Bonynge

Rossini concentrates on the love of Queen Semiramide for

Prince Arsace (a mezzo-soprano), and musically the result is a series of fine duets, superbly performed here by **Sutherland** and **Horne** (in the mid-1960s when they were both at the top of their form). In Sutherland's interpretation, Semiramide is not so much a Lady Macbeth as a passionate, sympathetic woman and, with dramatic music predominating over languorous cantilena, one has her best, bright manner. Horne is well contrasted, direct and masculine in style, and **Spiro Malas** makes a firm, clear contribution in a minor role. **Rouleau** and **Serge** are variable but more than adequate, and **Bonynge** keeps the whole opera together with his alert, rhythmic control of tension and pacing. A full libretto is included.

Il Signor Bruschino (complete; CD versions)

🔑 (M) **** DG 477 5668. Battle, Ramey, Lopardo, Desderi, Larmore, ECO, Ion Marin

(BB) *** Naxos 8.660128. Codeluppi, Leoni, Rossi, Giorgelè, Marani, Giangaspero, Barbolini, Martino, I Virtuosi Italiani, Desderi

You could hardly devise a starrier cast for this 'comic farce in one act' than that assembled by DG, with even the tiny role of the maid, Marianna, taken by **Jennifer Lamore. Ion Marin** springs rhythms very persuasively, with the first *Cavatina* of Gaudenzio, the tutor, so delectably pointed in the introduction that one registers the character even before **Samuel Ramey** enters. **Kathleen Battle** makes a provocative heroine, and the tenor **Frank Lopardo** sings sweetly and freshly as Sofia's lover, Florville. He is delightfully agile in the platter duet with Filiberto, the innkeeper, taken by **Michele Pertusi**. Excellent, well-balanced sound. The single disc come with a particularly well-produced cued synopsis.

As this lively alternative Naxos account demonstrates, vigorously conducted by the former baritone **Claudio Desderi**, Rossini's style was already fully developed in such characteristic numbers as the patter-duet between the hero, Florville, and the guardian of his beloved, Gaudenzio. The involved plot is typical of the genre, with the Naxos booklet providing a detailed synopsis as well as a full libretto in Italian. The singing is stylish, led by **Alessandro Codeluppi** as Florville, and with **Elena Rossi** as the heroine, Sofia, bright and agile if rather unvaried in tone. An outstanding bargain.

Tancredi (complete; DVD version)

🔑 **** TDK **DVD** DVWW OPTANC. Barcellons, Takova, Giménez, Spotti, Maggio Musicale Fiorentino, Frizza (V/D: Andrea Bevilacqua)

Tancredi (1813) was Rossini's first mature opera, and it secured his popularity at home and abroad as the leading composer of Italian opera. Recordings have already revealed it to be a score of some power, but now we have a superb performance on DVD. The cast is terrific, with **Raúl Giménez** (tenor) coping with Rossini's florid and high-flying writing, and **Marco Spotti's** bass, firm and rich. The women are equally impressive: **Darina Takova** (soprano) is agile and she gets round her fiendishly difficult writing with aplomb. She is sweetly affecting in her yearning numbers and looks marvellous on the stage. **Daniela Barcellons,** in the trouser role of Tancredi, is very fine indeed, providing appropriate contrast to Takova. **Riccardo Frizza's** conducting is ideal and he maintains the forward impulse of the rather complicated story with both musical spontaneity and theatrical drama. One's admiration for this Rossini opera is enhanced too: apart from the impressive arias and duets, the exciting rum-ti-tum choruses and grand finales are irresistible: no wonder he became so popular! The (alas!) sad ending is touchingly and exquisitely done. The production, by Pier Luigi Pizzi, is unfussy and effective, with the greys and blacks of the stylish set sympathetically lit to provide an excellent backdrop to the drama. Simple costumes but, again, very effective. The production works for the opera, the music and the singers. Decent sound. Thoroughly recommended.

Tancredi (complete; CD versions)

🔑 (BB) **** Naxos 8.660037/8. Podles, Jo, Olsen, Spagnoli, Di Micco, Lendi, Capella Brugensis, Brugense Coll. Instrumentale, Zedda

(M) *** Warner Fonit (ADD) 5050466-1814-2-8 (3). Cossotto, Cuberli, Hollweg, Ghiuselev, WDR Ch. Cologne, Cappella Coloniensis of WDR, Ferro

Tancredi, which was based on Tasso's epic poem *Gerusalemme Liberata* and was first heard in 1813, is most widely remembered for its overture, but this excellent Naxos set makes a strong case for the piece. It completely displaces the previous versions from Sony and RCA, and the eminent Rossini scholar and conductor, **Alberto Zedda**, proves a far more resilient, generally brisker and lighter Rossini interpreter than his predecessors. **Sumi Jo** is superb as the heroine, Amenaide, in dazzlingly clear coloratura, as well as imaginative pointing of phrase, rhythm and words. The mezzo, **Ewa Podles**, is less characterful, yet the voice is firm and rich as well as flexible; but it is the tenor, **Stanford Olsen**, previously heard as Belmonte on John Eliot Gardiner's recording of *Entführung*, who offers some of the freshest, most stylish and sweetly tuned singing from a Rossini tenor in recent years. The recording is a little lacking in body, but that partly reflects the use of a small orchestra, and the voices come over well. An Italian libretto is provided but no translation. Instead, a helpful synopsis is geared to the different tracks on the discs; had there been a libretto, this could well have received a Rosette.

The (1979) Warner Fonit version is a formidable competitor for the excellent Naxos set, generally using weightier voices and with an excellent orchestra of period instruments, whereas on Naxos there are modern instruments played in period style. **Fiorenza Cossotto** sings powerfully in the breeches role of Tancredi, and **Lella Cuberli**, then at her peak, is a most winning Amenaide, full and pure of tone as well as wonderfully agile. **Werner Hollweg's** headily light tenor is very apt for the role of Argirio, and **Nicola Ghiuselev** is a weighty Orbazzano. Though not digital, the recording is full and well balanced, with the scholar **Gabriele Ferro** drawing fresh, stylish playing from his period orchestra. As on Naxos, an Italian libretto is provided but no translation; unlike Naxos, there is no English synopsis. The three-disc format contrasts with the two of Naxos, but that brings only one break in Act II instead of two.

Torvaldo e Dorliska (*Dramma semiserio*; complete; DVD version)

*** Dynamic **DVD** 33 528 (2). Takova, Pertusi, Meli, Pratico, Fischer, Alberghini, Prague Chamber Ch., Bolzano e Trento Haydn O, Pérez

This rare opera in an excellent live recording from the 2006 Rossini Opera Festival in Pesaro is quite a find. *Torvaldo e Dorliska* can be placed somewhere between a *dramma serioso* and the usual *opera buffa* for which Rossini was celebrated. It has a potentially serious plot, with shades of both *Fidelio* and *Tosca*, and the German name for this kind of stage work was *Rettungsstück* ('Rescue opera'). The tormented villain, the Duke of Ordow, intends to seduce Dorliska, the young wife of the hero, Torvaldo, after having her husband assassinated, while Dorliska, first trusting the Duke, seeks refuge in his castle. However, what makes the piece naturally Rossinian is that the key figure in the plot, the castle warden Giorgio, is a *buffo* (who sings most resonantly here), helped by his mezzo sister, Carlotta. Rescue in the nick of time comes from the summoned Governor and his armed men who, together with the revolting peasants, make a spectacular closing scene, retrieving Torvaldo from his cage cell and replacing him with the Duke!

Darina Takova and **Francesco Meli** make an appealing pair of loving spouses, and the villain, **Michele Pertusi**, is sufficiently grim and sinister to be convincing, even though Giorgio (**Bruno Pratico**) defies him splendidly in a *buffo* style which one can't take quite seriously. Excellent singing from all concerned, especially in the lively ensembles, and traditional costumes and sets – rather dark, to make clear this is a serious drama. **Victor Pérez** directs the music vibrantly and makes the most of the bravura sparkle too, and altogether this is most enjoyable.

Il Turco in Italia (complete; CD versions)

&⟶ (M) **** Decca 475 8249 (2). Sumi Jo, Alaimo, Fissore, Giménez, Mentzler, Corbelli, Bronder, Amb. Op. Ch., ASMF, Marriner

&⟶ **** Decca 458 924-2 (2). Bartoli, Corbelli, Pertusi, Vargas, Ch. & O. of La Scala, Milan, Chailly

&⟶ ❀ (M)(***) EMI mono 3 58662-2 (2). Rossi-Lemeni, Callas, Gedda, Stabile, Ch. & O of La Scala, Milan, Gavazzeni

On Decca, **Sumi Jo** as Fiorilla, the sharp-tongued heroine, unhappily married to old Don Geronio, is no fire-eater, as Callas was in her vintage recording, but she sparkles delightfully, a most believable young wife. What seals the success of the Philips version is the playing of the **St Martin's Academy** under **Sir Neville Marriner**, consistently crisp and light, wittily bringing out the light and shade in Rossini's score and offering a full text. The big snag with the old Callas set was that it was severely cut by half an hour and more of music. As for the rest of the Philips cast, **Simone Alaimo** as the visiting Turkish Prince Selim, may lack sardonic weight, but it is a fine voice; and the *buffo* role of Geronio finds **Enrico**

Fissore agile and characterful in his patter numbers. **Raúl Giménez** is the stylish tenor in the relatively small role of Narciso, which happily acquires an extra aria. Altogether most recommendable and welcome back as one of Decca's 'Originals'.

Chailly's Decca version centres round the brilliantly characterful singing of **Cecilia Bartoli** as a fire-eating Fiorilla. The tessitura is high for a mezzo, but she copes with sparkling confidence. Chailly paces the many ensembles most effectively, with a first-rate team of soloists to back up Bartoli, agile and sparkling.

Callas was at her peak when she recorded this rare Rossini opera in the mid-1950s. As ever, there are lumpy moments vocally, but she gives a sharply characterful performance as the capricious Fiorilla, married to an elderly, jealous husband and bored with it. **Nicola Rossi-Lemeni** as the Turk of the title is characterful too, but the voice is ill-focused, and it is left to **Nicolai Gedda** as the young lover and **Franco Calabrese** as the jealous husband to match Callas in stylishness. It is good too to have the veteran **Mariano Stabile** singing the role of the poet in search of a plot. Walter Legge's production has plainly added to the sparkle. It is a vintage Callas reissue, her first uniquely cherishable essay in operatic comedy.

Il viaggio a Reims (complete; DVD version)

&⟶ **** Opus Arte **DVD** OA 0967 D. Belyaeva, Ouspenki, Shtoda, Tsanga, Mariinsky Theatre Academy, Mariinsky Theatre O, Gergiev (Dir: Alain Maratrat; V/D: Vincent Bataillon)

In a co-production with the Théâtre Châtelet in Paris, the singing team and orchestra from the **Mariinsky Theatre** in St Petersburg offer a sparkling account of Rossini's festival opera under their director, **Valery Gergiev**. Originally written for a one-off celebration, *Il Viaggio a Reims* was almost entirely forgotten until recent years; it proves to be a delight from beginning to end, with a feast of fine numbers. Some of these were quickly used by Rossini in one of his earliest Paris operas, *Le Comte Ory*, but there is much more besides. **Maratrat's** production updates the action to the 1930s, with the men in the cast wearing trilbies. That includes Gergiev himself, who conducts his orchestra on stage. With such a well-coordinated team it is hard to pick out individual stars among the young singers, but **Vladislav Ouspenski** as Baron von Trombonon, **Anastasi Belyaeva** as Madame Cortese, **Daniil Shtoda** as Count Libenskof and **Edouard Tsanga** as Lord Sindey all give memorable performances.

Il viaggio a Reims (complete; CD version)

(N) &⟶ ❀ (M) **** DG 477 7435 (2). Ricciarelli, Terrani, Cuberli, Gasdia, Araiza, Giménez, Nucci, Raimondi, Ramey, Dara, Prague Philh. Ch., COE, Abbado

This DG set is one of the most sparkling and totally successful live opera recordings available, with **Claudio Abbado** in particular freer and more spontaneous-sounding than he generally is on disc, relishing the sparkle of the comedy, and the line-up of soloists here could hardly be more impressive, with no weak link. Apart from the established stars the set introduces two formidable newcomers in principal roles, **Cecilia Gasdia** as a self-important poetess and, even finer, **Lella Cuberli** as a young fashion-crazed widow. Abbado's brilliance and sympathy draw the musical threads compellingly together with the help of superb, totally committed playing from the young members of the **Chamber Orchestra of Europe**.

Zelmira (complete)

**(*) Opera Rara ORC 27 (3). Futral, Ford, Custer, Siragusa, Scottish Ch. & CO, Benini

Zelmira was recorded live at a concert performance given at the Edinburgh Festival in 2003. **Maurizio Benini** directs a lively, well-sprung performance, and the singing is consistently stylish and often brilliant. The wild applause for the astonishing Act I aria of Ilo, Zelmira's returning husband, and of the comparably challenging Act II aria of Zelmira's handmaid, Emma, is well deserved, for **Antonino Siragusa** as Ilo has both flexibility and an astonishing upper range, and **Manuela Custer** as Emma has fine vocal control, with crisp ornamentation and flawless trills. So too has the excellent **Elizabeth Futral** in the title-role, while **Bruce Ford** as the usurping Antenore, with a baritonal quality in his tenor tone, is well contrasted with the higher, lighter Ilo of Siragusa. The set takes up three discs, but it brings a full text.

COLLECTIONS

Arias from: Armida; L'assedio di Corinto; La donna del lago; Otello; Stabat Mater; Tancredi

(M) *** RCA (ADD) 82876 62309-2 (2). Caballé, RCA Italiana Op. Ch. & O, Cillario – DONIZETTI; VERDI: *Arias* ***

Originally entitled 'Rossini Rarities', much of the music here, taken from a 1967 LP, is not over-familiar even today. It does, however, show **Caballé** displaying some of her finest qualities; indeed, there is tonal beauty and brilliance in equal measure. If the Italian orchestra is not the most refined in the world, **Cillario** achieves lively results, and the sound is suitably theatrical. The recording has transferred well to CD – full and vivid – and texts and translations are included.

'Rossini Gala', arias from: Armida; Aureliano in Palmira; Bianca e Falliero; Elisabetta, Regina d'Inghilterra; Mosè in Egitto; Semiramide; Vallace; Zelmira

*** Opera Rara ORR 211. Miricioiu, Ford, Magee, Banks, ASMF, Parry

Nelly Miricioiu, Romanian-born and British-based, is a soprano who deserves to be recorded far more. This wide-ranging, imaginatively devised recital of rare Rossini arias admirably fills a gap with Miricioiu strongly supported by a range of singers, including the Rossini tenors **Bruce Ford** and **Barry Banks**. Miricioiu's is a warm, characterful voice, which she uses with a fine feeling for dramatic point, bringing to life even the most conventional of operatic numbers. She also has the merit, very necessary in Rossini, of coloratura flexibility, which she relishes brilliantly in the ca-

balettas to arias. Strong support from **David Parry** and the **Academy**, with full, brilliant recording.

'Serious Rossini', excerpts from: Armida; Mosé in Egitto; Otello; Ricciardo e Zoraide; Ugo Re d'Italia

*** Opera Rara ORR 218 Ford, Miricioiu, Matteuzzi, Kelly, Soloists, Geoffrey Mitchell Ch., Phil. O or ASMF, Parry

Here is a further glorious recital of Rossini excerpts, this time centring on the excellent tenor **Bruce Ford**, but including many memorable ensemble items. All are vividly projected by this outstanding cast of singers. Highlights include the duet of Agorante and Ricciardo (**William Matteuzzi**) in *Ricciardo e Zoraide*, and the quintet from the finale of Act I. The trio *In quale aspetto imbello* (from *Armida*) and the quartet *Mi manca la voce* (from *Mosè in Egitto*) also stand out, as does the supremely dramatic finale of *Otello*, where **Bruce Ford** is powerfully partnered by **Nelly Miricioiu**. **David Parry** keeps the tension high and the chorus and orchestra give admirable support. The recording is splendidly vivid.

Arias from: Il barbiere di Siviglia; La Cenerentola; La donna del lago; La gazza ladra; L'Italiana in Algeri; Otello; Semiramide; Zelmira

*** Decca 470 024-2. Flórez, Verdi O Sinfonica di Milano, Chailly

Even in a generation that has thrown up some remarkable Rossini tenors, the Peruvian, **Juan Diego Flórez**, stands out with his clean-cut, wonderfully flexible voice, with not a suspicion of an intrusive aitch in the extraordinarily elaborate divisions of these challenging arias and with top Cs thrown off with consistent ease. The authority is never in doubt, and it is good to have such brilliant performances mainly of little-known arias, yet one hopes that Flórez will develop a gentler touch in hushed passages, with half-tones and a diamond bright timbre regularly dominating. Yet there are few recent discs of Rossini's tenor arias that begin to match this in excitement, with **Chailly** and the **Milan Orchestra** the most understanding partners. Full, clear sound.

Arias from: Il barbiere di Siviglia; La Cenerentola; La donna del lago; L'Italiana in Algeri; Maometto II; Semiramide; Tancredi

(BB) **** Naxos 8.553543. Podles, Hungarian State Op. Ch. & O, Morandi

The Hungarian mezzo, **Ewa Podles**, earlier the star singer in the complete set of Rossini's *Tancredi* on Naxos, is here even more impressive in one of the finest Rossini recitals in years. Hers is a rich and even voice which is not only weighty throughout its range but is also extraordinarily agile, dazzling in the elaborate divisions in all these coloratura numbers. She may find it hard to convey the fun and sparkle in Rossini, but the bright-eyed intensity provides fair compensation even with Cinderella or Rosina, and the cabaletta of Cinderella's final aria is breathtaking in its bravura at a formidably fast tempo. By contrast, this great voice is an ideal vehicle for the *opera seria* arias here, with the male characters very well characterized. First-rate accompaniment too.

Arias: *La Cenerentola: Non più mesta; La donna del lago: Mura felici ... Elena! O tu, che chiamo; L'Italiana in Algeri: Cruda sorte! Amor tiranno! Pronti abbiamo ... Pensa all patria. Otello: Deh! calma, o ciel; La Pietra del Paragone: Se l'Italie contrade ... Se per voi lo care io torno; Tancredi: Di tanti palpiti; Stabat Mater: Fac ut portem*

⏚ *** Decca 425 430-2. Bartoli, A. Schoenberg Ch., V. Volksoper O, Patanè

Cecilia Bartoli's first recital of Rossini showpieces brings a formidable demonstration not only of Bartoli's remarkable voice but of her personality and artistry, bringing natural warmth and imagination to each item without ever quite making you smile with delight. Yet there are not many Rossini recitals of any vintage to match this. Vocally, the one controversial point to note is the way that Bartoli articulates her coloratura with a half-aspirate, closer to the Supervia 'rattle' than anything else, but rather obtrusive. Accompaniments are exemplary, and Decca provided the luxury of a chorus in some of the items, with hints of staging. Full, vivid recording. Recommended.

'Rossini Heroines', arias from: *La donna del lago; Elisabetta, Regina d'Inghilterra; Maometto II; Le nozze di Teti e Peleo; Semiramide; Zelmira*

⏚ *** Decca 436 075-2. Bartoli, Ch. & O of Teatro la Fenice, Marin

Cecilia Bartoli follows up the success of her earlier Rossini recital-disc with this second brilliant collection of arias, mostly rarities. The tangy, distinctive timbre of her mezzo goes with a magnetic projection of personality to bring to life even formal passage-work, with all the elaborate coloratura bright and sparkling. The rarest item of all is an aria for the goddess Ceres from the classically based entertainment, *Le nozze di Teti e Peleo*, making a splendid showpiece. The collection is crowned by a formidably high-powered reading of *Bel raggio* from *Semiramide*, with Bartoli excitingly braving every danger.

ROTA, Nino (1911–79)

(i) *Castel del Monte* **(ballad for horn & orchestra); (ii)** *Bassoon Concerto;* **(iii)** *Harp Concerto;* **(iv)** *Trombone Concerto*

⏚ **** Chan. 9954 (i) Corti; (ii) Carlini; (iii) Prandina; (iv) A. Conti; I Virtuosi Italiani, M. Conti

This is a delightful disc in every way, a collection of three concertos and one concertante work for horn demonstrating the unforced mastery of Rota, a composer remembered almost entirely for his film scores. Both in the *Harp Concerto* of 1947 and the three other works from much later in his career the outer movements regularly display a sparkle more often associated with French composers of the inter-war period, with chattering ostinato rhythms supporting jaunty melodies, and slow movements striking deeper, darker moods. In each Rota gives important solos to rival instruments, varying textures. This is fun music in the best sense,

regularly concealing the ingenuity of the writing in the overall light-heartedness. The *Trombone Concerto* – the only one of the four works to have been recorded before – has exuberant outer movements framing a much longer Lento movement with a powerful climax. The *Bassoon Concerto* is the most original in structure, while the *Ballad for Horn and Orchestra, Castel del Monte* (a title taken from a medieval castle built by the Emperor Frederick II) builds up passionately over sharply contrasted sections. With brilliant playing from all the Italian soloists as well as the orchestra this is a celebratory disc to parade the gifts of a long-neglected but warmly approachable composer, helped by full, well-balanced sound.

ROUSE, Christopher (born 1949)

(i) *Clarinet Concerto. Iscariot (for Chamber Orchestra); Symphony 1*

Ⓝ *** BISCD 1386. (i) Fröst; R. Stockholm PO, Gilbert

Christopher Rouse made his name by writing successful concertos for flute and clarinet. Alas, the *Clarinet Concerto*, brilliantly played by **Martin Fröst**, is less memorable, except as a non-friendly experience. Almost incredibly fragmented, with its composition accompanied by the composer's dice throwing to determine the music's course, it is not a work to endear itself to the lover of an instrument which Mozart made his own. *Iscariot*, inspired by the Bible betrayer, promises more, opening (and closing) with a bang, followed by drenchingly intense writing for strings, then delicate scoring for celesta and ruminative writing for woodwind. The climax brings a cacophonous percussion break, no doubt symbolizing the treachery, but there is a positive ending based on the chorale *Es ist genug*. The First Symphony also has a 'programme', only heroic in the sense that its struggle against adversity would inevitably end in failure and oblivion. The composer draws on a theme from the *Adagio* of Bruckner's *Seventh Symphony* played by the deep brass, which is much corrupted in the course of the work's single slow movement, while the hero's defeat is represented by a triple-note rhythmic ostinato. The work ends in elegiac darkness. It is rather remarkable and very atmospheric, and both here and in *Iscariot* the conductor and his orchestra sustain the *pianissimo* tension of the string playing with remarkable concentration. Fine, truthful, atmospheric BIS recording.

(i) *Flute Concerto; Phaeton; Symphony 2*

⏚ **** Telarc CD 80452. (i) Wincenc; Houston SO, Eschenbach

The remarkable five-movement *Flute Concerto*, commissioned by the present soloist, followed two years after Rouse's *Trombone Concerto*. The beautiful first and last movements, with their serene, soaring solo line, are connected thematically, and share the Gaelic title *Anhran* ('Song'). They frame two faster, much more dissonant and rhythmically unpredictable movements. The kernel of the work is the gripping central *Elegia*, written in response to the terrible murder of the two-year-old James Bulger by two ten-year-old schoolboys. Rouse introduces a rich, Bach-like chorale, which moves with a wake-like solemnity towards a central explosion of passionate despair. Throughout, the solo writing demands great bravura and intense emotional commitment from the flautist, which is certainly forthcoming here.

The *Second Symphony* is a three-part structure, with the outer movements again using identical material to frame the anguished central slow movement. In the composer's words that forms a 'prism' through which the mercurial opening material is 'refracted' to yield the angry, tempestuous finale. The desperately grieving *Adagio* is another threnody for a personal friend and colleague, Stephen Albert, killed in a car accident in 1992. *Phaeton* is a savage, explosive early work (1986), which could hardly be more different from the tone poem of Saint-Saëns. Helios's sun chariot, immediately out of his son's control, charges its way across the heavens with horns roistering, and is very quickly blown out of the sky by Zeus's thunderbolt. Performances here are excellent, very well played and recorded, and the *Flute Concerto* is unforgettable.

(i) *Violin Concerto*; (ii) *Der Gerettete Alberich (Fantasy for Solo Percussion and Orchestra)*; *Rapture*

**(*) Ondine ODE 1016-2. (i) Lin; (ii) Glennie; Helsinki PO, Segerstam

If not offering the visual spectacle of James MacMillan's *Veni, veni, Emmanuel*, and not to be taken too seriously, Rouse eagerly laminates Glennie's virtuosity into a spectacular biographical backcloth, with Alberich portrayed as a tragic figure in the central 'tableau' and a frenzied finale suggesting his physical and mental collapse, which unleashes a wild virtuoso percussion cadenza-break. *Rapture* begins in a glow of pastoral euphoria, but the mood becomes increasingly ecstatic, with a gradual increase of tempo used to create another big climax. Rouse's ambitious *Violin Concerto*, which comes last on the disc, then immediately confronts the listener with the diminutive solo voice of the violin singing a gentle barcarolle, but soon enveloped in a hugely dramatic, very loud, percussion-laced orchestral tutti. This contrast is the more disconcerting as **Cho-Liang Lin's** solo timbre as recorded here is so small, though his playing is tonally exquisite. The *Toccata* second movement is a Rondo demanding great solo bravura (and orchestral virtuosity too). Here the scoring is more economical, but the orchestral outbursts, boldly rhythmic, regularly return and, after a brief return to the elegiac mood of the barcarolle, it is the orchestra which has the last word. The performances are obviously expert and powerfully dedicated, and the recording is wide-ranging and spacious, but this is not a collection for aural fainthearts.

ROUSSEAU, Jean-Jacques
(1712–78)

Le Devin du village (complete)

╾(B) *** EMI 5 75266-2 (2). Micheau, Gedda, Roux, Ch. Raymond St-Paul, Louis de Froment CO, Froment – GRÉTRY: *Richard Coeur-de-Lion* **(*)

The one-act Intermezzo, *Le Devin du village (The Village Soothsayer)*, is Rousseau's most celebrated musical work, written in 1752, an unpretentious piece in what he conceived as the Italian style of the day, which he vigorously supported against the French, even though he here uses a French text. Starting with an overture in the Italian style, fast-slow-fast, it is charming in a plain and straightforward style, hardly original, and the baldness of the writing is rather underlined in this performance with continuo in bare chords. The 25 sections, mostly very short indeed, last well under an hour, offering a simple story of the soothsayer reconciling the estranged lovers, for a price. All three soloists are first rate, with **Micheau** at her most seductive, and the young **Gedda** heady-toned. This now returns to the EMI label coupled with Grétry but with no texts provided.

ROUSSEL, Albert (1869–1937)

Aeneas; Bacchus et Ariane, Op. 43: Suites 1 & 2

╾ ✸ (M) **** Erato (ADD) 2564 60576-2. ORTF Nat. O, Martinon

Erato have at long last released **Martinon's** classic 1969 version of *Bacchus et Ariane* (1930) on CD. It's a thrilling performance, and comparing it to Dutoit's version on the same label, one finds the latter sounding tame by comparison. Martinon's energy and drive do not smudge the Roussel dense orchestration, and there is both inner life and outer drive here, and the quiet passages are held with both tension and atmosphere. Splendid remastered sound, too, much better than it ever was on LP. The coupling of *Aeneas* – a much rarer work – is equally compelling and undeniably powerful. It is full of Roussel's characteristic rich textures and orchestrations, with the chorus playing an important role. There is no lack of vigorous imagination, both rhythmically and harmonically, during its 40 minutes, ending with a triumphant hymn 'to his glory and the glory of Rome'. The only reservation is that *Aeneas* has only one cue.

Bacchus et Ariane (ballet; complete), *Op. 43; Le Festin de l'araignée (The Spider's Feast), Op. 17*

╾ ✸ **** Chan. 9494. BBC PO, Tortelier

Tortelier offers the best *Bacchus et Ariane* yet – and what a marvellously inventive and resourceful score it is. The **BBC Philharmonic** play with tremendous zest and give a sensitive and atmospheric account of *Le Festin de l'araignée*. They offer us the complete banquet, not just the chosen dishes on the set menu! Splendid recording and performances of rewarding and colourful music that deserve to be more widely heard.

(i) *Bacchus et Ariane* (ballet; complete); *Le Festin de l'araignée, Op. 17*; (ii) *Sinfonietta*; *Symphonies*: (iii) 2; (ii) 3–4

(BB) *** EMI Gemini (DDD/ADD) 3714872 (2). (i) O Nat. de Fr., Prêtre; (ii) Paris Conservatoire O, Cluytens; (iii) Colonne O, Dervaux

The exhilarating 1931 score for *Bacchus et Ariane* teems with life and is full of rhythmic vitality, even if it has perhaps less poetic feeling than *Le Festin de l'araignée*. **Prêtre** obtains an excellent response from the **Orchestre National de France** in both scores and, while the recording is a shade too reverberant at times, no detail is masked. The performances of the symphonies are slightly more uneven. 2 is given a persuasive enough performance by the **Colonne Orchestra** under **Pierre Dervaux**, but **Cluytens** has a splendid grasp of the energy and character of 3 and 4. They are recorded in too reverberant an acoustic, but detail again emerges clearly.

Le Festin de l'araignée (The Spider's Feast), Op. 17

🎵—*** Testament (ADD) SBT 1238. Paris Conservatoire O, Cluytens – BIZET: *La Jolie Fille de Perth*; RAVEL: *Daphnis*, etc. **(*)

Cluytens's 1963 recording of *Le Festin de l'araignée* remains in a class of its own: it has never been surpassed. There is tremendous atmosphere and delicacy of feeling. The recording was made in the rather reverberant Salle Wagram, but every strand is beautifully transparent and the orchestral texture expertly balanced with a lifelike perspective. This magical score strikes a strong spell, and this is one of Cluytens's finest recordings.

Suite in F, Op. 33

Ⓜ *** Mercury (ADD) 434 303-2. Detroit SO, Paray – CHABRIER: *Bourée fantasque*, etc. ***

The Mercury recording dates from 1957. With **Paray** on top form, the music generates plenty of adrenalin, with the closing *Gigue* especially lively and exciting. The new transfer brings the benefit of greater warmth, and undoubtedly the sound overall is enhanced.

Symphonies 1 (Le Poème de la forêt); 4, Op. 35

**(*) Ondine ODE 1092-2. O de Paris, Eschenbach

Christoph Eschenbach's CD is extremely well played and recorded. But there is just a hint of the earth-bound about the works. Other accounts have greater lightness and animation, as well as sheer excitement in the vigorous passages (especially in the marvellous *Fourth Symphony*). The notes are all here, but not quite all the spirit.

Symphony 2 in B flat, Op. 23; Le Festin de l'araignée, Op. 17

🎵—Ⓜ *** Erato (ADD) 2564 60577-2. ORTF Nat. O, Martinon

Martinon fully captures the brooding atmosphere of the slow sections of Roussel's *Second Symphony*, and from the opening bars the listener's attention is caught. This is one of the finest accounts available, with the richness of the score fully realized and an inner vitality ensuring total conviction. The lighter score to the magical *Le Festin de l'araignée* provides the perfect contrast, and it receives a similarly superb performance, with all the subtleties and nuances vividly caught. The remastered sound is very good for its date (1969).

Symphony 2 in B flat, Op. 23; Bacchus et Ariane: Suites 1 & 2, Op. 43

*** Ondine ODE1065-2. O de Paris, Eschenbach

Christoph Eschenbach's new record with the **Orchestre de Paris** is another welcome addition to the Roussel discography and, in addition to the symphony, also brings well-prepared and vital accounts of the *Bacchus et Ariane* ballet. Not only does Eschenbach show obvious sympathy with this repertoire, but he gets absolutely first-class recorded sound, too. The *Second Symphony* is a powerful score and we must hope that this recording will make many new friends for it.

Symphony 2; Pour une fête de printemps; Suite in F

🎵—ⒷⒷ *** Naxos 8.570529. RSNO, Denève

Stéphane Denève, Music Director of the **Royal Scottish National Orchestra**, draws strong contrasts between the three movements, returning at the end to the introspective mood of the beginning. The plaintive feeling of the opening of the similarly arch-structured *Pour une fête de printemps* is well caught, and the work's climax makes a pungent centrepiece before once again the composer returns to more peaceful nostalgia. The *Suite* is much more extrovert, its opening rumbustious, the central *Sarabande* bitter-sweet, and final *Gigue* again pungently boisterous. The RSNO play as if they have really lived with these scores, and the Naxos recording is excellent. A good disc for those new to the composer to find their way into his plangent harmonic world.

Symphony 3 in G min., Op. 42; Bacchus et Ariane (ballet; complete)

🎵—ⒷⒷ *** Naxos 8.570245. RSNO, Denève

Stéphane Denève's performances are lively and invigorating, with all the sensuous elements brought out fully in the ballet as well as its rhythmic drive. The dense textures of Roussel's scores can be tricky to capture on CD, but the recordings offers excellent detail within a warm and nicely reverberant acoustic. Listening again to the masterful *Third Symphony*, one wonders why it is so scandalously neglected in the concert hall.

Symphony 3, Op. 42; Le Festin de l'araignée (ballet; complete), Op. 17

Ⓝ *** Ondine ODE 1107-2. O de Paris, Eschenbach

What **Christoph Eschenbach's** performances lack in sheer guts, they make up for in meticulous attention to detail, first-class orchestral playing and superb modern sound, pinpointing the strands in Roussel's often thick textures. The *Third Symphony* is a powerful, exciting work, and this performance has its full measure. *Le Festin de l'araignée* is beautifully performed, and its leisurely tempi give it an especially haunting beauty.

Symphonies 3 in G min.; 4 in A

Ⓜ **(*) Warner Elatus 0927 46730-2. LOP, Munch

Another Erato disc from the LP era that makes a most welcome return to the catalogue, here on CD for the first time. **Munch's** coupling with the **Lamoureux Orchestra** dates from 1965 and had the benefit of infinitely better orchestral playing and greater commitment than its earlier Decca rival (Ansermet and the SRO, made in the earliest days of stereo). These are invigorating performances, well worth the money, and although the recording is not as rich or as refined as the finest modern discs, it is perfectly acceptable at mid-price.

Symphonies 3; 4 in A, Op. 53; Bacchus et Ariane: Suite 2; Sinfonietta for String Orchestra, Op. 52

(M) **(*) Chan. 10217X. Detroit SO, Järvi

Neeme Järvi's account of the *Third Symphony* has an engaging vitality and character, and the playing of the **Detroit Orchestra** is highly responsive. In the slow movement he indulges in a rather steep accelerando after the fugal section. Likewise his finale feels too fast. But it is a committed performance. Some may find the acoustic a shade too resonant, but the overall balance is very natural and pleasing and this is certainly very recommendable, given the superior sound and Järvi's obvious enthusiasm for this repertoire.

CHAMBER MUSIC

Le Marchand de sable qui passe (Incidental music): Suite, Op. 13; Divertissement for Piano Quintet, Op. 6; Sérénade for Flute, Harp, & String Trio; Trio for Flute, Viola & Cello, Op. 40; Impromptu for Harp, Op. 21; Duo for Bassoon & Double-Bass

🔗 🌼 **** Praga PRD 350018. Czech Nonet, with Englichová (harp), Wiesner (piano)

This is an enchanting disc, revealing another side to Roussel in the elegance and refinement of his writing for small instrumental groups. The incidental music for *Le Marchand de sable qui passe*, scored for string quintet, harp, flute, clarinet and horn, is hauntingly atmospheric, recalling Ravel's *Introduction and allegro*. Although the textures and colouring are quite individual, the ethereal melody of the *Scène finale* has a magic comparable with the closing scene of Ravel's *Ma Mère l'Oye*. The piquant *Sérénade* and *Flute Trio* are hardly less delicate in feeling; both have subtly restless slow movements, the latter closing with whimsically capricious high spirits. The *Duo for Bassoon and Double-Bass* (written for Serge Koussevitzky) brings an interlude of bucolic humour, and the miniature *Divertissement* for piano quintet is also capriciously light-hearted and worthy of Jean Françaix, although still Rousselian. The performances have an Elysian charm and sophistication of feeling and are beautifully recorded.

ROUTH, Francis (born 1927)

Clarinet Quintet

*** Redcliffe RR 010. Redcliffe Ens. – BLISS: *Clarinet Quintet*; RAWSTHORNE: *Clarinet Quartet* ***

Routh's *Quintet* was written for **Nicholas Cox**, who plays it with great skill and understanding. Its variety of mood makes up for the melodic fragmentation, and its invention is lively throughout. Excellent recording.

ROWLEY, Alec (1892–1958)

Piano Concerto in D, Op. 49 (for strings & percussion)

(BB) *** Naxos 8.557290. Donohoe, Northern Sinfonia – DARNTON; GERHARD; FERGUSON: *Piano Concertos* ***

Alec Rowley, best known for his educational music, also wrote more ambitious works, including this miniature *Concerto for Piano, Strings and Optional Percussion*. The writing is fluent and attractive, with sharp harmonies and cluster chords and a fanfare motif in the first movement, leading to open-air freshness in the slow movement and a jocular, easygoing finale. The addition of percussion adds piquancy to the writing. A welcome and rare addition to **Peter Donohoe's** imaginatively conceived collection of British piano concertos, brilliantly played and recorded.

ROYER, Joseph-Nicolas-Pancrace (c. 1705–55)

Pièces de clavecin

🔗 (B) *** HM Musique d'abord HMA 1951037. Christie (harpsichord)

Royer's *Pièces de clavecin*, his only collection to appear in print, had their origins in his stage works but, unlike Rameau, who transcribed instrumental pieces for the keyboard, Royer drew on arias and choral pieces as well. **William Christie's** Harmonia Mundi recording, made in the 1980s, is very fine and, at bargain price, deserves an enthusiastic recommendation.

RÓZSA, Miklós (1907–94)

(i) Cello Concerto, Op. 32; (ii) Violin Concerto, Op. 24; (i; ii) Theme & Variations for Violin, Cello & Orchestra, Op. 29a

🔗 *** Telarc CD 80518. Atlanta SO, Levi; with (i) Harrell; (ii) McDuffie

These are splendid new recordings of Rózsa's highly romantic *Violin* and *Cello Concertos*, plus an enjoyable set of *Variations* in which both soloists join. The performances are superb and the recording is warm and detailed. Recommendable in every way.

Film scores: (i) Ben Hur; (ii) Quo Vadis (extended excerpts)

🔗 (M) *** Dutton (ADD) CDLK 4332 (2). (i) Nat. PO; (ii) RPO; composer

Rósza's scores for both *Ben Hur* and *Quo Vadis* are a potent mixture of orchestral spectacle and choral kitsch. In *Ben Hur* there is an appealing lyrical theme for the love story, an exciting sequence for the galley slaves rowing into battle, and a stirring *Parade* for the famous chariot race. Towards the end, the religiosity, with its lavish panoply of chorus and orchestra, overwhelms the listener in an ocean of sumptuous vulgarity. *Quo Vadis* is no less full-blooded in its go-for-it, pumped-up exotica, and again the dramatic sequences are tempered by more gentle passages, such as the attractive *Marcus and Lygia* music. Both these scores were recorded by Decca in the late 1970s and the multi-channelled Phase Four recording techniques work well with this music. The British orchestras play with total enthusiasm and these outrageous scores emerge freshly in Dutton's new transfer.

Hungarian Serenade; 3 Hungarian Sketches; Overture to a Symphony Concert; Tripartita

(N) **** Chan. 10488. BBC PO, Gamba

Rózsa wrote a substantial amount of orchestral music, most of which is unrelated to his film scores. His style remained as appealing in his orchestral writing, however, and this disc begins appropriately with his entertaining *Overture to a Symphony Concert*. It is an imaginative, optimistic piece, with the composer's Hungarian roots emerging in this work conceived during the hopeful days of the abortive 1956 Hungarian revolution, when the composer was living in exile. The *Hungarian Serenade* is a delightfully tuneful and light work, piquant in its orchestral and harmonic colourings. *Tripartita* shows the composer experimenting with a more gritty style in 1971/2, with its finale reminiscent of Walton; it is nevertheless exciting and accessible music. The earlier *3 Hungarian Sketches* comprise three descriptive movements which are vibrant with local colour and melody. **Rumon Gamba** and the **BBC Philharmonic** play all this music with brilliance and the Chandos sound is quite superlative.

(i) *String Quartets 1, Op. 22; 2, Op. 38;* (ii) *Sonata for 2 Violins, Op. 15a*

*** ASV CDDCA 1105. (i) Flesch Qt; (ii) Ibbotson, Gibbs

The *First String Quartet* was written in the late 1940s and revised and shortened in 1950. It is dedicated to Peter Ustinov, who was playing Nero in the film *Quo Vadis* for which Rósza composed the score. It is a rewarding score, finely wrought and civilized, which improves as you get to know it better. There are reminders of Rózsa's kinship with Bartók and with Debussy in the slow movement. The *Second Quartet* is much later, completed in 1981, again the product of a cultured musical mind. Perhaps not as distinctively individual as, say, the Kodály *Second Quartet* but again eminently well worth getting to know. The *Sonata for Two Violins* is an early piece from 1933, which Rósza overhauled in 1973 and which the leader and violist of the **Flesch** play with spirit. Altogether an interesting and worthwhile issue, very well played and well if perhaps forwardly recorded.

RUBBRA, Edmund (1901–86)

(i) *Viola Concerto, Op 75; Meditations on a Byzantine Hymn*

*** Hyp. CDA 67587. Power; (i) with BBC Scottish SO, Volkov –
  WALTON: *Viola Concerto* ***

The two Rubbra items make an unusual but attractive cou-

pling for the Walton. The *Viola Concerto* was commissioned by William Primrose. Though the melodic material cannot compare with Walton's in memorability, it suits the ideas, with a similar reliance on warm lyricism. **Lawrence Power** again gives a magisterial performance which has both eloquence and virtuosity, again brilliantly supported by **Ilan Volkov** and the **BBC Scottish Orchestra**. The *Meditations on a Byzantine Hymn*, here given its first recording in the version for unaccompanied viola solo, make an apt extra, particularly when the finale of the *Concerto* is similarly based on Rubbra's distinctive brand of sectional writing which he dubbed 'Meditations'. In this, related sections merge and match but do not actually quote one another.

(i) *Violin Concerto, Op. 103; Improvisation for Violin & Orchestra, Op. 89; Improvisations on virginal pieces by Giles Farnaby, Op. 50*

(BB) **** Naxos 8.557591. (i) Osostowicz; Ulster O, Yuasa

The *Improvisation for Violin and Orchestra* (1956), commissioned by the Louisville Orchestra, no doubt stimulated Rubbra's interest in the idea of a full-blown concerto. It unfolds with a seeming inevitability and naturalness and, above all, an eloquence which speaks directly to the listener. **Krysia Osostowicz** and the **Ulster Orchestra** really get to its heart. Her noble account of the *Violin Concerto* is hardly less persuasive. And the satisfaction this concerto gives resides primarily in the subtlety with which its lines evolve and grow. Osostowicz engages with the score at the deepest level. Some music lovers are worried by Rubbra's opaque orchestral textures, but in **Takuo Yuasa's** hands they are sensitively laid out and the reading finely paced. The *Farnaby Improvisations*, at one time a regular feature of BBC programmes, has never sounded better. As always with Rubbra, there is little surface glamour but great musical substance.

(i) *Sinfonia concertante, Op. 38; A Tribute, Op. 56;* (ii) *The Morning Watch;* (iii) *Ode to the Queen, Op. 55*

**** Chan. 9966. BBC Nat. O of Wales, Hickox; with
  (i) Shelley; (ii) BBC Nat. Ch. of Wales; (iii) Bickley

The form in which we know the *Sinfonia concertante* is the revision Rubbra made in the 1940s. Its beautiful opening almost anticipates the *Piano Concerto in G major*, but it is the searching and thoughtful finale, a prelude and fugue, which makes the strongest impression. **Howard Shelley** is a superb advocate and it is difficult to imagine a better performance. *The Morning Watch* is Rubbra at his most inspired. The text comes from the seventeenth-century metaphysical poet Henry Vaughan, and the music matches its profundity and eloquence.

The *Tribute* is to Vaughan Williams, and the *Ode to the Queen* was commissioned by the BBC to celebrate the Coronation of the present Queen and is Rubbra's only song-cycle with full orchestra.

Symphonies 1–8 (Hommage à Teilhard de Chardin); (i) *9 (Sinfonia Sacra); 10–11*

**** Chan. 9944 (5). BBC Nat. O of Wales, Hickox; (i) with
  Dawson, D. Jones, Roberts, BBC Nat. Ch. of Wales

As can be seen, Chandos have collected all 11 Rubbra *Symphonies* in a box of five CDs offered for the price of four, which can be strongly recommended to those collectors who have not already begun investing in the individual records.

Symphony 1, Op. 44; (i) Sinfonia concertante for Piano & Orchestra, Op. 38; A Tribute, Op. 56

*** Chan. 9538. BBC Nat. O of Wales, Hickox; (i) with Shelley

The first movement of the symphony is fiercely turbulent; a French dance tune, a *Perigourdine*, forms the basis of the middle movement, but the pensive, inward-looking finale, which is as long as the first two movements put together, is the most powerful and haunting of the three. The *Sinfonia concertante* is no less symphonic in character and substance. The opening *Fantasia* begins with a reflective *Lento* passage which anticipates the tranquillity of the *G major Piano Concerto*, though it is the final *Prelude and Fugue*, composed in memory of his teacher, Gustav Holst, which lingers longest in the memory. **Howard Shelley** is an inspired soloist and the sometimes thick textures of the symphony sound remarkably lucid in **Richard Hickox's** hands. The **BBC National Orchestra of Wales** play splendidly and the Chandos sound is in the best traditions of the house.

Symphonies 2 in D, Op. 45; 6, Op. 80

*** Chan. 9481. BBC Nat. O of Wales, Hickox

Richard Hickox and his fine players do make the score of the *Second Symphony* more lucid than Handley's Lyrita recording from the 1970s. The performance is meticulously prepared and yet flows effortlessly, and the slow movement speaks with great eloquence. The heart of the *Sixth Symphony* is the serene *Canto* movement which is not dissimilar in character to the *Missa in honorem Sancti Dominici*. It is arguably the finest of the cycle after 9, and Hickox and his fine players do it proud. So, too, do the Chandos engineers.

Symphonies (i) 2 in D, Op. 45; (ii) 7 in C, Op. 88; (i) Festival Overture, Op. 62

*** Lyrita SRCD 235. (i) New Philh. O, Handley; (ii) LPO, Boult

Good performances from **Handley** of both the symphony and the overture, which bears an adjacent opus number to the *Fifth*. The *Seventh Symphony* is also a very considerable piece. The first movement brings a cogent argument based on a simple four-note motif, and the second a rhythmic Scherzo that leads to a more lyrical, noble climax. **Boult's** performance is outstandingly successful and the 1970 recording, like that of the *Second* (made eight years later), is up to the high standards of realism one expects from this label. A thoroughly worthwhile and generous coupling (78 minutes).

Symphonies 3, Op. 49; 4, Op. 53; Resurgam Overture, Op. 149; A Tribute, Op. 56

*** Lyrita SRCD 202. Philh. O, Del Mar

The opening of the *Fourth Symphony* is of quite exceptional beauty and has a serenity and quietude; there is a consistent elevation of feeling and continuity of musical thought. Rubbra's music is steeped in English polyphony and it could

not come from any time other than our own. Unquestionably both symphonies have a nobility and spirituality that is rare in any age. The fine *Resurgam Overture* is a late work.

Symphonies 3; 7 in C, Op. 88

⊕— 🌑 **** Chan. 9634. BBC Nat. O of Wales, Hickox

The *Third Symphony* (1939) has a pastoral character and a certain Sibelian feel to it (woodwind in thirds), though Rubbra is always himself. In the final movement there is even a hint of Elgar in the fourth variation. **Hickox's** is a more eloquent and ultimately more convincing account than the older Philharmonia version under Norman Del Mar on Lyrita.

The *Seventh Symphony* (1956) receives a performance of real power from Hickox and his Welsh orchestra. This is music that speaks of deep and serious things and its opening paragraphs are among the most inspired that Rubbra ever penned. Noble performances and excellent recorded sound.

Symphonies 4; 10 (Sinfonia da camera), Op. 145; 11, Op. 153

*** Chan. 9401. BBC Nat. O of Wales, Hickox

Richard Hickox offers a particularly imaginative account of the *Eleventh Symphony* in one movement (1979). Like so much of Rubbra's music, it has an organic continuity and inner logic that are immediately striking, and in common with the *Tenth Symphony*, also in one movement, its textures are spare and limpid. Hickox's account of the *Fourth Symphony* is totally convincing. The Chandos recording is excellent in every respect, with plenty of warmth and transparency of detail.

Symphony 5 in B flat, Op. 63

Ⓜ **(*) Chan. 6576. Melbourne SO, Schönzeler – BLISS: *Checkmate* ***; TIPPETT: *Little Music* **(*)

Symphonies 5; 8 (Hommage à Teilhard de Chardin), Op. 132; (i) Ode to the Queen, Op. 83

⊕— *** Chan. 9714. BBC Nat. O of Wales, Hickox; (i) with Bickley

Richard Hickox's reading of the *Fifth Symphony* is easily the finest and most penetrating; the slow movement has depth and, thanks to a magnificent recording, a greater clarity than either of its predecessors. Tempi are unerringly judged and he brings great breadth and gravitas to the very opening of the work. He gives, too, a more intense account of the *Eighth* (*Hommage à Teilhard de Chardin*) than we have had before. *Ode to the Queen*, is a setting of three poems, variously by Richard Crashaw, Sir William d'Avenant and Thomas Campion, for mezzo-soprano and full orchestra and is strong in inspiration. Excellent performances and outstanding recorded sound from the Chandos/BBC team.

Although the **Melbourne orchestra** is not in the very top division, they play this music for all they are worth, and the strings have a genuine intensity and lyrical fervour that compensate for the opaque effect of the octave doublings. Altogether, though, this is an imposing performance which reflects credit on all concerned. The recording is well balanced and lifelike; but the ear perceives that the upper range is rather restricted.

(i) Symphonies 6, Op. 80; 8 (Hommage à Teilhard de Chardin), Op. 132; (ii) Soliloquy for Cello & Orchestra, Op. 57

**** Lyrita SRCD 234. (i) Philh. O, Del Mar; (ii) de Saram, LSO, Handley

The *Sixth* is one of the most admired of Rubbra's symphonies and its slow movement is arguably the most beautiful single movement in all of Rubbra's output. The *Eighth* pays tribute to Teilhard de Chardin, a Jesuit and palaeontologist (1881–1955) who fell out with the Church over his approach to evolution. It has something of the mystical intensity that finds its most visionary outlet in the *Ninth Symphony*. In **Norman Del Mar's** hands Rubbra's music speaks here with directness and without artifice; the **Philharmonia** play marvellously and the composer's soundworld is very well served by the recording balance. The *Soliloquy* has been described by Ronald Stevenson as 'a saraband, symphonically developed in flexible tempo . . . a meditation with flashes of interior drama', and its grave beauty exerts a strong appeal. **Rohan de Saram** plays with a restrained eloquence that is impressive and he has excellent support from the **LSO** under **Vernon Handley**.

(i) Symphony 9 (Sinfonia sacra), Op. 140; The Morning Watch for Chorus & Orchestra, Op. 55

⊕ ❀ **** Chan. 9441. (i) Dawson, Jones, Roberts; BBC Nat. Ch. & O of Wales, Hickox

The *Ninth Symphony*, arguably Rubbra's greatest work, is an unqualified masterpiece. Subtitled *The Resurrection*, it was inspired by a painting of Donato Bramante and has something of the character of the Passion, which the three soloists relate in moving fashion. *The Morning Watch*, a setting of Henry Vaughan for chorus and orchestra, which was originally to have formed part of a choral fifth symphony, is another score of great nobility, which has taken even longer (half a century) to be recorded. Both works are superbly served here by all these fine musicians, and the Chandos recording is no less magnificent.

Symphony 10 (Sinfonia da camera), Op. 145; Improvisations on Virginal Pieces by Giles Farnaby, Op. 50; A Tribute to Vaughan Williams on his 70th Birthday (Introduction & Danza alla fuga), Op. 56

Ⓜ *** Chan. 6599. Bournemouth Sinf., Schönzeler

Rubbra's *Tenth Symphony* is a short, one-movement work, whose opening has a Sibelian seriousness and a strong atmosphere that grip one immediately. **Schönzeler** is scrupulously attentive to dynamic nuance and internal balance, while keeping a firm grip on the architecture as a whole. The 1977 recording has been impressively remastered. It has a warm acoustic and reproduces natural, well-placed orchestral tone. The upper range is crisply defined. The *Farnaby Variations* is a pre-war work whose charm Schönzeler uncovers effectively, revealing its textures to best advantage. *Loth to Depart*, the best-known movement,

has gentleness and vision in this performance. Strongly recommended. Even though this CD plays for only 40 minutes, it remains indispensable.

CHAMBER MUSIC

The Buddha (incidental music; suite, arr. Croft); Duo for Cor Anglais & Piano, Op. 156; Meditazioni sopra 'coeurs désolés', Op. 67b; Phantasy for 2 Violins & Piano; Oboe Sonata in C, Op. 100; Piano Trios 1, Op. 68 (one movement); 2, Op. 138

Ⓜ *** Dutton Lab. CDLX 7106. Endymion Ens. (members)

Rubbra had a lifelong interest in the East, and his incidental music for Clifford Bax's radio play on the life of the Buddha makes a strong impression. The *Duo for Cor Anglais and Piano* is a late work, written in 1980 after the *Eleventh Symphony*, with a deeply felt, elegiac and valedictory character. The *Meditazioni sopra 'coeurs désolés'* (1949), originally for recorder and harpsichord, is a set of variations on Josquin's chanson. The wonderful *Oboe Sonata*, written in 1958 for Evelyn Rothwell (Lady Barbirolli), is the best known of the seven pieces on this disc, and **Melinda Maxwell** and **Michael Dussek** successfully capture its nobility of spirit. The *Phantasy for Two Violins and Piano* (1927) was Rubbra's first published work and is finely wrought in every way. The *First Piano Trio* was written in 1950 and has the quiet seriousness of late Fauré and the same naturalness of speech; there is no trace of rhetoric or expressive emphasis, qualities which hold true of this dignified and selfless performance. 2 was composed 20 years later and is sparer than its predecessor. A thoroughly recommendable anthology, admirably recorded.

(i) Cello Sonata in G min.; String Quartets 1 in F min., Op. 35; 3, Op. 112; Improvisation for Unaccompanied Cello

⊕ *** Dutton CDLX 7123. Dante Qt (members); with (i) Dussek

String Quartets 2 in E flat, Op. 73; 4, Op. 150; (i) Lyric Movement for String Quartet and Piano, Op. 24; Meditations on a Byzantime Hymn 'O Quando in Cruce', Op. 117a

⊕ *** Dutton CDLX 7114. Dante Qt; with (i) Dussek

The *G minor Cello Sonata* of 1946 is one of Rubbra's finest chamber works, and it is beautifully played here, but it is the inclusion of the four *String Quartets* that is particularly valuable. The first version of the *F minor Quartet* comes from 1933, before the *First Symphony*, while the *Fourth* dates from 1977. The *First* pays homage to Vaughan Williams, 'whose persistent interest' in the original 1933 version led to a complete revision of the piece in 1946, while the *Fourth* is dedicated to Robert Simpson. There is a nobility and breadth of line that make these pieces resonate in the memory. The *Third*, written in 1963, moves with a tremendous sense of purpose and expressive substance, as does the elegiac *Fourth*. Dutton deserves many congratulations in making them available in such excellent performances together with other chamber pieces, some of which, such as *Lyric Movement for Piano Quintet* and the *Meditations on a Byzantine Hymn* for two violas, will be new to most collectors. Recommended with enthusiasm.

Oboe Sonata in C, Op. 100

(BB) *** Hyp Helios CDH 55008. Francis, Dickinson – BOUGHTON: *Pastoral*; HARTY: *3 Pieces*; HOWELLS: *Sonata* ***

Rubbra's *Oboe Sonata in C, Op. 100* has a songful, rhapsodic opening movement, which leads naturally into the soulful central *Elegie*; the fluent finale is a rondo with a semi-oriented melodic line. The performance here is of quality, but these artists are not helped by the forward balance and the background resonance. It is important not to have the volume level set too high.

(i) Violin Sonatas 1, Op. 11; 2, Op. 31; 3, Op. 133; 4 Pieces, Op. 29; Variations on a Phrygian Theme for Solo Violin, Op. 105

⊶ (M) *** Dutton Lab. CDLX 7101. Osostowicz; (i) with Dussek

The *Second Violin Sonata*, with Albert Sammons and Gerald Moore, was the first Rubbra work to reach the gramophone. **Krysia Osostowicz** and **Michael Dussek** are worth waiting for, since not only the recording but also, surprisingly, the performance eclipses its distinguished predecessors. The *First Sonata*, Op. 11, from the 1920s, is heavily indebted to Debussy and Rubbra's teacher, Gustav Holst. The *Third* is a sinewy work from 1963, formidably argued and finely laid out for the medium. The Op. 29 *Pieces* are really teaching material, as is the set of *Variations* for violin alone.

PIANO MUSIC

Fantasy Fugue, Op. 161; Fukagawa (Deep River); Introduction & Fugue, Op. 19; Introduction, Aria & Fugue, Op. 104; Invention on the Name of Haydn, Op. 160; Nemo Fugue; Prelude & Fugue on a Theme of Cyril Scott, Op. 69; 8 Preludes, Op. 131; 4 Studies, Op. 139; (i) 9 Teaching Pieces, Op. 74

(M) *** Dutton CDLX 7112. M. Dussek; (i) with R. Dussek

Considering that he was an outstanding pianist, Rubbra wrote relatively little for his instrument. Apart from the seraphic *Piano Concerto in G major*, of which we badly need a new recording, and the *Sinfonia concertante* the present disc contains the lot. Although all these pieces do exist in various other versions, **Michael Dussek's** fine survey is undoubtedly the one to have. Artistic matters apart, it also has the benefit of vivid and truthful recorded sound.

VOCAL MUSIC

(i) Advent Cantata: Natum Maria Virgine, Op. 136; Inscape, Op. 122; (i) 4 Mediaeval Latin Lyrics, Op. 32; Song of the Soul, Op. 78; Veni, creator spiritus, Op. 130

⊶ ❀ *** Chan. 9847. ASMF Ch., City of L. Sinf., Hickox; (i) with Varcoe

Having put us in their debt with their survey of the symphonies, **Richard Hickox** and Chandos now turn to the choral music. Three of the pieces here are first recordings. *Natum Maria Virgine* comes from the late 1960s when Rubbra was working on the *Sinfonia sacra*. As with all his vocal music it is beautifully crafted, its polyphony growing effortlessly and inevitably. *Song of the Soul* comes from 1951, the year of the *Second String Quartet*, and has dipped under the horizon as far as both concert and recorded performances are concerned, as has the *Veni, creator spiritus*, another late and inspiring piece. The *Four Mediæval Latin Lyrics* with **Stephen Varcoe** and Hickox are equally fine. The Abelard setting, the fourth of the *Mediævel Latin Lyrics*, sounds particularly beautiful. *Inscape*, which is set to the words of Gerard Manley Hopkins, has a quiet eloquence and depth that puts it among Rubbra's most memorable works in any genre. Hickox has real feeling for the mystical side of Rubbra and conveys his elevation of feeling. The recording has amplitude yet clarity and is expertly and naturally balanced. A very special disc.

The Beatitudes, Op. 109; 4 Carols; Lauda Sion, Op. 110; 5 Madrigals, Op. 51; 2 Madrigals, Op. 52; Mass in Honour of St Teresa of Avila; Missa a 3 voci, Op. 98; 5 Motets, Op. 37

*** ASV CDDCA 1093. Voces Sacrae, Martin

This CD is devoted to Rubbra's *a cappella* music and ranges from the early Motets of 1934, settings of Herrick, Donne and Vaughan, through to his last Mass, the *Mass in Honour of St Teresa of Avila*, which was composed in 1981, five years before his death. It also includes the spare and austere *Missa a 3 voci* from the early 1960s; both these Masses have a sense of the eternal verities. The most important work here is the *Mass in Honour of St Teresa of Avila*, a work of haunting beauty and directness. The *Lauda Sion* (1960) is another work that leaves one feeling cleansed. **Judy Martin** and **Voces Sacrae** give sympathetic and idiomatic accounts of all these pieces, and the sound is natural and present.

Songs: (i; ii) A Hymn to the Virgin; The Jade Mountain; Jesukin; Mystery; Orpheus with his Lute; Rosa mundi. Instrumental pieces: (ii; iii) Discourse, Op. 127; (iii) Fukagawa; Improvisation, Op. 124; (ii) Harp pieces: Pezzo ostinato, Op. 102; Transformations, Op. 141

*** ASV CDDCA 1036. (i) Chadwell; (ii) Perrett; (iii) Gill (with L. BERKELEY: *Nocturne for Harp*; HOWELLS: *Prelude* ***)

The CD reflects Rubbra's lifelong interest in the Orient from the early *Fukagawa* (1929), an arrangement of a Japanese melody, to *The Jade Mountain* songs (1962). The two pieces for harp, the *Pezzo ostinato* and the *Transformations*, both reflect the fascination that Indian music exercised. They are both impressive – indeed, exalted is the word that springs to mind. Some of the very early pieces reflect the spell cast by Holst and Cyril Scott but the bulk of the music here finds him at his most individual. **Tracy Chadwell** sings ethereally though there is perhaps a little too much echo round her voice, but the harp pieces are both exquisitely played and could hardly be more authoritative. A most rewarding and recommendable issue.

Magnificat & Nunc Dimittis, Op. 65; Missa Cantuariensis, Op. 59; Missa in honorem Sancti Dominici; Tenebrae Motets, Op. 72: Nocturns 1–3; (i) (Organ) Meditation, Op. 79; Prelude & Fugue, Op. 69

⊛ (BB) **** Naxos 8.555255. Ch. of St John's College, Cambridge, Robinson; (i) Houssart

The present inexpensive recording by **Christopher Robinson** and the **Choir of St John's College**, Cambridge, makes an excellent entry point into Rubbra's sacred music. The *Missa Cantuariensis* was composed for Canterbury Cathedral, whereas the *Missa in honorem Sancti Dominici* (1948) was written for the Catholic Rite. Both are crafted beautifully and elevated in feeling. The first *Nocturn* (which comprises three motets) of the *Tenebrae* was written in 1951, and a further two *Nocturns* followed ten years later. They are anguished and eloquent expressions of faith. This deeply satisfying recording is completed by the *Meditation* for organ, which was written for James Dalton, and Bernard Rose's transcription of the *Prelude and Fugue on a Theme of Cyril Scott*, a seventieth-birthday tribute to Rubbra's first teacher. The performances are quite outstanding and well recorded.

(i) Magnificat & Nunc Dimittis in A flat, Op. 65; Missa in honorem Sancti Dominici, Op. 66; 3 Hymn Tunes, Op. 114; 3 Motets, Op. 78

*** ASV CDDCA 881. Ch. of Gonville & Caius College, Cambridge, Webber; (i) Phillips (organ) – HADLEY: *Lenten cantata*, etc. ***

The most important work here is the *Missa in honorem Sancti Dominici* (1948), written at about the time of the *Fifth Symphony* and one of the most beautiful of 20th-century *a cappella* choral pieces written in this or any other country. None of the other works on the disc is its equal. The performance by the **Choir of Gonville & Caius College**, Cambridge, under **Geoffrey Webber** is dedicated and sensitive. Excellent balance, though the organ is obtrusive, particularly so in the first of the Op. 78 *Motets*.

RUBINSTEIN, Anton (1829–94)

Piano Sonatas 1 in E min., Op. 12; 2 in C min., Op. 20; 3 in F, Op. 41; 4 in A min., Op. 100

⊛ (B) *** Hyp. Dyad CCD 22007 (2). Howard

Leslie Howard proves highly persuasive in all four works. The 1981 recordings sound excellent, and this set is more enticing as a Dyad, with two discs offered for the price of one. Returning to these works, one is surprised to find how enjoyable the music is, with some good lyrical ideas, phrased romantically, to balance the arrestingly flamboyant rhetoric which Leslie Howard obviously relishes.

RUTTER, John (born 1945)

(i; ii) Suite antique (for flute and orchestra); (iii) 5 Childhood Lyrics (for unaccompanied choir); (ii; iii) Fancies; When Icicles Hang (for choir and orchestra)

*** Coll. COLCD 117. (i) Dobing, Marshall; (ii) City of L. Sinfonia; (iii) Soloists, Cambridge Singers; Composer

This whole collection is imbued with Rutter's easy melodic style and the touches of offbeat rhythm which he uses to give a lift to his lively settings. The *Antique Suite* (for flute, harpsichord and strings) opens with a serene *Prelude*, but includes a typically catchy *Ostinato*, a gay *Waltz* and a chirpy closing *Rondeau*. *Fancies* has a delightful *Urchins' Dance*, after the fairy style of Mendelssohn, and its *Riddle Song* has a most appealing lyrical melody. But the mood darkens for the closing *Bellman's Song*. Among the *Childhood Lyrics*, the settings of Edward Lear's *Owl and the Pussy-cat* and *Sing a Song of Sixpence* are particularly endearing.

The evocative *When Icicles Hang* brings characteristically winning scoring for the orchestral woodwind (Rutter loves flutes) and another fine melody in *Blow, Blow Thou Winter Wind*. The work ends happily in folksy style. Splendid performances throughout. Rutter is currently the most performed (by amateur choirs) of any living English composer, and no wonder. The performances here are excellent and so is the recording.

Christmas carols: Angels' Carol; Candelight Carol; Carol of the Children; Christmas Lullaby; Donkey Carol; Dormi Jesu; Jesus Child; Love Came Down at Christmas; Mary's Lullaby; Nativity Carol; Sans Day Carol; Second Amen; Shepherd's Pipe Carol; Star Carol; There is a Flower; The Very Best Time of Year; What Sweeter Music; Wild Wood Carol. Arrangements: Angel Tidings; Away in a Manger; I Wonder as I Wander; Silent Night

⊛ **** Hyp. CDA 67245. Polyphony, City of L. Sinfonia, Layton

John Rutter's delightful carols will always be especially remembered. 'They were my calling cards,' he says. 'You have to remember that the Christmas carol is one of the very few musical forms which allows classically trained musicians to feel it's permissible to write tunes!' And, as is shown again and again here, Rutter never had difficulty in coming up with a memorable melodic line, whether it be the *Shepherd's Pipe Carol*, with its characteristic flute writing, which opens the programme, or the deliciously perky *Donkey Carol*, with its catchy 5/8 syncopated rhythm, which closes it.

The 22 carols included here were composed in a steady stream over a period of three decades, with the charming *Dormi Jesu* dating from as recently as 1999. Rutter's writing is notable not only for its tunefulness and winning use of choral textures, but also for its always engaging orchestrations.

(i; ii) The Falcon; (ii) 2 Festival Anthems: O praise the Lord in Heaven; Behold, the Tabernacle of God; (ii; iii) Magnificat

*** Coll. COLCD 114. (i) St Paul's Cathedral Choristers; (ii) Cambridge Singers, City of L. Sinfonia; (iii) with Forbes; all cond. composer

The Falcon was **Rutter's** first large-scale choral work. Its inspiration was a medieval poem, which is linked to the Crucifixion story, but the core of the piece is the mystical central *Lento*. The *Magnificat* has the usual Rutter stylistic touches, with a syncopated treatment of the opening *Magnificat anima mea*, and a joyous closing *Gloria Patri*. The two anthems are characteristically expansive and resplendent with brass. Fine performances and recording in the best Collegium tradition.

Gloria; Magnificat; Psalm 150

⊕━ **** EMI 5 57952-2. Treble soloists from the Choirs of King's College & Gonville and Caius College, Cambridge, CBSO, composer; T. Winpenny or A. Grote (organ)

John Rutter's choral music is the most widely performed of any contemporary English composer, not only in England and the Commonweath, but in North America too; listening to the *Gloria*, one can understand why. With its Waltonesque opening and thrilling use of the brass, it communicates immdiately and directly; the central section is touchingly elegiac, and the closing *Amens* are exultant. It makes you feel good.

In the *Magnificat* setting, Rutter characteristically uses a recognizable four-note motif to fit the word itself, and the lovely second movement, *Of a Rose, a lovely rose*, is memorable enough to be extracted for separate performance. Some might feel that, for a *Magnificat*, the setting is a little soft-centred, as both the *Misericordia* and the *Esurientes* are gently lyrical, each featuring a diminutive solo treble, but the closing *Gloria Patri* is triumphant.

The closing *Psalm 150*, where the words actually invite an instrumental response, brings sounding brass, organ, full choir and percussion, and again it is spectacular, with the *Laudate Dominum* giving contrast by using a distanced group of singers. But the closing *Alleluia . . . Amen* is Rutter at his most extravagantly exuberant. The performances here are quite splendid in every respect, with the King's acoustic adding a glowing aura to the music-making.

(i) Mass of the Children; A Clare Benediction; I will sing with the Spirit; Look at the World; To Every thing there is a Season; Wings of the Morning; A cappella settings: Come down O Love Divine; I my Best Beloved's Am; Musica Dei dominum

*** Coll. CSCD 129. (i) Lunn, Williams, Cantatas Youth Ch., Cambridge Singers, City of L. Sinfonia, composer

John Rutter's *Mass of the Children* has a characteristic simplicity of style and it immediately establishes his identity with the easily flexible musical phrase he has devised for the repetitions of the words 'Kyrie eleison'. The light-hearted *Gloria* similarly is well conceived for a work designed for children's participation alongside adults, and in the finale, in which each soloist interpolates a sung medieval prayer, children and adults again join together for the *Dona nobis*

pacem. It is a work of genuine charm, yet not lacking substance, designed for wide popularity.

The other songs all have the immediacy of melodic flow and skilful orchestral colour we expect from Rutter's carols. The three *a cappella* items also show the composer at his most rewarding, notably the lovely *Musica Dei Dominum* with its flute obbligato and *Come down O Love Divine* for double choir, a richly harmonized setting of 15th-century English text. Not surprisingly, performances are of the highest quality and the recording is finely balanced in a warm acoustic.

(i–iv; vii) Mass of the Children; (ii; v) Shadows (Song-cycle with Guitar); (iii; v; vi) Wedding Canticle

(BB) **(*) Naxos 8.557922. (i) Gruffydd-Jones; (ii) Huw Williams; (iii) Clare College, Cambridge, Ch.; (iv) Farnham Youth Ch., Clare Chamber Ens.; (v) French (guitar); (vi) Pailthorpe (flute); (vii) McVinnie (organ), T. Brown

The brief *Wedding Canticle* is written serenely for mixed choir, flute and guitar, and is directly and beautifully presented here as a closing bonus. But it did not seem an ideal choice to include on this CD Rutter's song-cycle, *Shadows*, which apparently attempts to recreate the tradition of the melancholy lute songs of the Elizabethan era. They are sung simply and often mournfully by **Jeremy Huw Williams**, accompanied most delicately by **Stewart French** on the guitar. But it is the lively songs, like *Gather ye rosebuds* and *In a goodly night*, which come off best.

3 Musical Fables: (i) Brother Heinrich's Christmas; (ii) The Reluctant Dragon; The Wind in the Willows

**(*) Coll. COLCD 115; City of L. Sinfonia; with (i) Kay, Cambridge Singers, composer; (ii) R. Baker, King's Singers, Hickox

Brother Heinrich's Christmas is a musical narrative with choir, telling the story of how one of the most famous of all carols was introduced late at night by the angels to Brother Heinrich, just in time for it to be included in the monks' Christmas Day service. It is all highly ingenuous but engagingly presented, and should appeal to young listeners who have enjoyed Howard Blake's *The Snowman*. The settings of the two famous Kenneth Grahame stories are no less tunefully communicative and include simulations of pop music of the 1940s (among other derivations), notably a Rodgers-style ballad which sentimentalizes the end of *The Wind in the Willows* episode, after Toad's escape from prison. All the music is expertly sung and played and blends well with the warmly involving narrative, splendidly done by **Richard Baker**.

Gloria; As the Bridegroom to His Chosen; Clare Benediction; Come Down, O Love Divine; Go Forth into this World; I My Best-beloved's Am; Lord Make Me an Instrument of Thy Peace; Psalmfest: I Will Lift Up Mine Eyes; The Lord is My Light and My Salvation; Praise the Lord O My Soul; Te Deum; To Everything There Is a Season

⊕━ **** Hyp. CDA 67259. Polyphony, Wallace Collection, City of L. Sinfonia, Layton

Framed by superb accounts of the *Gloria* and *Te Deum*, each with a magnificent brass contribution from the **Wallace Collection**, and given demonstration-standard sound quality, this is one of the most attractive Rutter collections yet. Brass is used again to introduce the first of the three psalm settings taken from the nine-movement, *Psalmfest*, followed by *I Will Lift Up My Eyes* introduced serenely by woodwind, which has much in common with Vaughan Williams's *Serenade to Music*. The third, *The Lord is My Light and My Salvation*, opens with a clarinet solo and has one of Rutter's most beguiling melodies. But everywhere here there is melody. **Polyphony** sing rapturously, with lovely blended tone, and the warmly persuasive accompaniments are ideally balanced within a pleasingly resonant but not blurring acoustic.

(i–iv) *Requiem*. Anthems: (i; iv) *Arise, shine*; (i) *Come Down, O Love Divine*; (ii; v) *Musica Dei dominum*; (i; iv) *2 Blessings for Choir & Organ*. Organ Pieces: (iv) *Toccata in 7*; (iv; vi) *Variations on an Easter Theme for Organ Duet*

⊛ **(BB)** **** Naxos 8.557130. (i) Clare College, Cambridge, Ch.; (ii) L. Sinfonia; (iii) with Thomas; (iv) Rimmer (organ); (v) Jones; all cond. Brown; (vi) with Collon

(i) *Requiem*; (ii) *Magnificat*

Ⓜ *** Coll. CSCD 504. (i) Ashton, Dean; (ii) Forbes; Cambridge Singers, City of L. Sinfonia, composer

(i) *Requiem*; *Cantata Domino*; (ii) *Cantus; Hymn to the Creator of light*; *Veni sancte spiritus*; *What Sweeter Music*; (ii)*Te Deum*

*** EMI 5 56605-2. King's College, Cambridge, Ch., Cleobury; with (i) Saklatvala, Harries, City of L. Sinfonia; (ii) The Wallace Collection

(i) *Requiem*; *Cantata Domino*; *Choral Fanfare*; *Draw on Sweet Night*; (ii) *Gaelic Blessing*; *God Be In My Head*; *Hymn to the Creator of Light*; *My True Love Hath My Heart*; (ii) *The Lord Bless You and Keep You*; *Open Thou Mine Eyes*; *A Prayer for Saint Patrick*

*** Hyp. CDA 66947. Polyphony, Layton; with (i) Manion; (ii) Bournemouth Sinf.

John Rutter's melodic gift, so well illustrated in his carols, is used in the simplest and most direct way to create a small-scale *Requiem* that is as beautiful and satisfying in its English way as the works of Fauré and Duruflé. The penultimate movement, a ripe setting of *The Lord is my Shepherd* with a lovely oboe obbligato, sounds almost like an anglicized *Song of the Auvergne*.

The newest Naxos recording of the *Requiem* tends to trump all previous versions, even the composer's own very fine account. Recorded in the expansive acoustic of Douai Abbey, Berkshire, it is very beautifully sung indeed, joyful in the *Sanctus* and darkly dramatic in the *Agnus Dei* with its steady drum beat. **Elin Manahan Thomas** is an ideal soloist singing the *Pie Jesu* with touching simplicity, and rising up

celestially in the *Lux aeterna*. **Christopher Hooker's** oboe obbligato in *The Lord is my Shepherd* is comparably sensitive. The extra items are equally successful. The *Two Blessings*, with their easy melodic flow, are rather like Rutter's carols, and the pair of thematically linked organ voluntaries, the first immediately rhythmically catchy, the duet *Variations*, sonorous and unpredictable, round off the programme most satisfyingly. Both are very well played, indeed, and the recording is first class.

On Collegium **Caroline Ashton's** performance of the delightful *Pie Jesu* is wonderfully warm and spontaneous, most beautifully recorded on CD, with the equally glorious *Magnificat* setting (see above) making a superb bonus on this mid-priced reissue.

Both the EMI and Hyperion recordings are of high quality and both bring first-class digital sound. On EMI there is something special about hearing this music within the **King's** acoustic, and using boy trebles in the choir as well as for the two solos. At times there is an ethereal resonance here, although climaxes emerge strongly.

Polyphony uses women's voices (as does Rutter himself) in a choir of 25 voices. The balance is slightly more forward, and the result brings a radiant richness of sound which is hardly less enjoyable. Both Polyphony and King's complete their programmes with some of Rutter's shorter choral works.

COLLECTION

'The Gift of Music', Sacred: *All things bright and beautiful; Be Thou my vision; A Clare Benediction; For the beauty of the earth; Hymn to the Creator of Light; Look at the world; The Lord bless you and keep you; Lord, make me an instrument of Thy Peace; Magnificat; Of a Rose, a lovely Rose; Requiem: Pie Jesu; Sanctus.* arr. Rutter: Spiritual: (i) *Deep River.* Shaker Song: *Lord of the Dance.* TRAD.: *Gaelic Blessing.* Secular: (ii) *The Gift of Music; Mary's Lullaby.* Arrangements: *Golden slumbers; I know where I'm going; The keel row; O waly waly; Sans Day Carol; Willow Song*

⊛ Ⓜ **** Universal 476 3068. Cambridge Singers, City of L. Sinfonia (or BBC Concert O), composer; (ii) with Melanie Marshall

Universal have had the bright idea of asking Rutter to choose an anthology of some of the many original compositions and arrangements which he has recorded on his own Collegium label with the excellent **Clare College Choir**. The result is a generous, 78-minute cornucopia of musical delights, opening with a happy *Look at the world* and going on immediately to *Of a rose, a lovely rose*, which is the second movement of his *Magnificat*, and the characteristic flowing melody of *For the beauty of the earth*, liltingly decorated with Rutter's familiar flute cascades. But then comes the masterly *Hymn to the Creator of Light*, with its thrilling dissonances, which out-Taveners Tavener. There are some attractive arrangements included, too, from the Shaker song, *The Lord of the Dance*, to a group of English folksongs, including *O* *waly waly* (very different from Britten's setting), *The keel row* and the haunting *I know where I'm going*. Finally there are two of Rutter's delectable carols (his speciality): the traditional Cornish *Sans Day* (with more decorative flutes) and Rutter's own enchantingly simple *Mary's Lullaby*. Superb singing and first-class recording.

RYBA, Jakob Jan (1765–1815)

Czech Christmas Mass; Missa pastoralis

🎵 (BB) **** Naxos 8.554428. Soloists, Czech Madrigalists Ch. & O, Thuri

The Czech composer, Jakob Jan Ryba, contemporary with Mozart, wrote these *Christmas Masses* – one long, one short – as seasonal cantatas. With only token references to the liturgy, obvious enough in the *Gloria*, they relate the story of the shepherds visiting the baby Jesus to the various sections of the Mass. Understandably, with their simple folk-like tunes and harmonies, they have long been part of traditional Czech celebrations at Christmas, and they here receive winningly fresh and direct performances, atmospherically recorded.

SÆVERUD, Harald (1897–1992)

Symphony 6 (Sinfonia dolorosa), Op. 19; Galdreslåtten, Op. 20; Kjæmpevise-slåtten, Op. 22; Peer Gynt Suites 1 & 2

**** BIS CD 762. Stavanger SO, Dmitriev

The *Sixth Symphony* (*Sinfonia dolorosa*) is a short but intense piece from the war years, dedicated to a close friend who perished in the resistance, and the *Kjæmpevise-slåtten* ('Ballad of Revolt') comes from the same years. It is an inspiriting work, an outraged, combative reaction to the sight of the Nazi occupation barracks near his Bergen home. The *Peer Gynt* music, written for a post-war production of Ibsen's play, could not be further removed from Grieg's celebrated score. It is earthy and rambunctious and makes Grieg sound positively genteel. So, too, does the delightful, inventive and wholly original *Galdreslåtten*. Eminently satisfactory performances from the **Stavanger Orchestra** under **Alexander Dmitriev**, brought vividly to life by the BIS recording team.

Symphony 7 (Salme), Op. 27; (i) Bassoon Concerto, Op. 44; Lucretia (suite), Op. 10

**** BIS CD 822 (i) Rønnes; Stavanger SO, Dmitriev

The one-movement *Seventh* (1945) is a deeply felt work, a hymn of thanksgiving for peace. The *Lucretia Suite* derives from the incidental music Sæverud wrote in 1936 for André Obey's play. Much of it is highly imaginative (the evocation of night in the fourth movement, for example), and the charming middle movement, *Lucretia Sleeping*. The *Bassoon Concerto* (1965) was revised towards the end of his long life in collaboration with **Robert Rønnes**, the soloist here. Absolutely first-class performances and recordings.

Symphony 8 (Minnesota), Op. 40; (i) Cello Concerto, Op. 7

**** BIS CD 972. (i) Mørk; Stavanger SO, Ruud

The *Eighth Symphony* is full of imaginative things, particularly the mysterious opening pages, and the invention often takes you by surprise. Its four movements all have their rewards though the whole is ultimately less than the sum of its parts. Nevertheless, this is a world well worth exploring and to which you will want to return. In the concerto **Truls Mørk** is masterly and plays with a glorious tone, and the **Stavanger Orchestra** does well throughout. The recording is superb.

The *Cello Concerto* was first performed in April 1999 and although Sæverud had intended to revise it he never got round to finishing it. The present score has been prepared by Robert Rønnes. Although Sæverud writes gratefully for the cello, the invention is less memorable or imaginative than in the *Lucretia* or *Peer Gynt* suites.

Symphony 9, Op. 45; (i) Piano Concerto, Op. 31; Fanfare & Hymn, Op. 48

**** BIS CD 962. Stavanger SO, Dmitriev (i) with Ogawa

Alexander Dmitriev and the **Stavanger Orchestra** are very persuasive in the *Ninth Symphony*. There is a strong sense of the Norwegian landscape here and the BIS recording conveys it all with striking clarity and presence. The *Piano Concerto* of 1950 is a delightful piece, full of quirky, robust humour. It is a work that haunts and fascinates, and the farmyard noises of the finale together with the strongly atmospheric slow movement linger in the memory. **Norika Ogawa** is an alert, sensitive player who has the measure of this piece, and Alexander Dmitriev and the Stavanger Orchestra are eminently supportive. The short *Fanfare and Hymn* was commissioned by the City of Bergen to celebrate its 900th anniversary. The sound is in the demonstration bracket.

SAINT-SAËNS, Camille (1835–1921)

Carnival of the Animals (with narration)

(BB) **(*) Naxos 8.554463. Morris (nar.), Slovak RSO, Lenárd – DUKAS: L'Apprenti sorcier **(*); RAVEL: Ma Mère l'Oye ***

This Naxos collection is clearly aimed at younger children, and many adults could find **Johnny Morris's** very personal (and often eccentric) descriptions and rhymes, which adorn this performance, too much to take. But the playing of the **Slovak Orchestra**, with a persuasively spontaneous contribution from the two anonymous pianists, is most attractive.

(i) Carnival of the Animals; (ii) Le Cygne; Piano Concertos; (iii) 2; (iv) 4 in C min., Op. 44; (v) Violin Concerto 3; (vi) Danse macabre; (v) Introduction & rondo capriccioso; (vii) Symphony 3 in C min. (Organ)

(B) **(*) Ph. Duo (ADD) 442 608-2 (2). (i) Villa, Jennings, Pittsburgh SO, Previn; (ii) Gendron, Gallion; (iii)

Davidovich, Concg. O, Järvi; (iv) Campanella, Monte Carlo Op. O, Ceccato; (v) Szeryng, Monte Carlo Op. O, Remoortel; (vi) Concg. O, Haitink; (vii) Chorzempa, Rotterdam PO, de Waart

Notable here is **Previn's** 1980 *Carnival of the Animals*, as fine as almost any available. (Philips have also included a second performance of *Le Cygne* by the inestimable **Maurice Gendron**.) **Bella Davidovich** gives a most sympathetic account of the *G minor Piano Concerto* and draws pleasing tone-quality from the instrument. She has the advantage of excellent orchestral support from the **Concertgebouw Orchestra**, who also give a lively account of the *Danse macabre* under **Haitink**. In the *C minor Concerto* (which is analogue) the effect is harder, partly because **Michele Campanella** is a more boldly extrovert soloist; but this account has undoubted vitality and no lack of *espressivo*. **Henryk Szeryng** gives clean, immaculate performances of the *B minor Violin Concerto* and the *Introduction and Rondo capriccioso*. **Edo de Waart's** 1976 recording of the *Organ Symphony* is not among the most exciting versions available but it is certainly enjoyable.

Cello Concertos 1 in A min., Op. 33; 2 in D min., Op. 119; Allegro appassionato in B min., Op. 43; Suite in D min., Op. 16; Carnival of the Animals: The Swan (orch. Vidal)

(BB) **(*) Naxos 8.553039. Kliegel, Bournemouth Sinf., Monnard

Maria Kliegel proves a most sympathetic soloist, technically immaculate, undeterred even by the relatively ungrateful writing for the cello in the *Second Concerto*, so much less striking a work than 1. It is good to have the early *Suite*, a colourful collection of genre pieces, and the dashing *Allegro appassionato*, both originally with piano accompaniment and here arranged by the composer himself.

Cello Concertos (i; ii) 1, Op. 33; (i; iii) 2, Op. 119; Piano Concertos (iv; v; vi;) 1 in D, Op. 17; (iv; v; vii) 2 in G min., Op. 22; (iv; v; viii) 3 in E flat, Op. 29; (iv; v; vi) 4 in C min., Op. 44; (iv; v; vii) 5 in F, Op. 103; Violin Concertos; (v; ix; x) 1 in A, Op. 20; (ix; xi; xii) 3 in B min., Op. 61; (v; ix; vii) Havanaise; Introduction et Rondo capriccioso; (v; xiii) Carnival of the Animals; (v; vi) Danse macabre; La Jeunesse d'Hercule; Marche héroïque; Phaéton; Le Rouet d'Omphale; (v; x; xiv) Symphony 3 (Organ) in C min., Op. 78

(B) **** Decca (ADD/DDD) 475 465-2 (5). (i) Harrell; (ii) Cleveland O, Marriner; (iii) German RSO, Chailly; (iv) Rogé; (v) Dutoit; (vi) Philh. O; (vii) RPO; (viii) LPO; (ix) Kyung Wha Chung; (x) Montreal SO; (xi) LSO; (xii) Foster; (xiii) L. Sinf.; (xiv) Hurford

Exceptional value here, with quantity and quality, and with myriad orchestras involved to make this a Saint-Saëns feast. **Pascal Rogé** brings delicacy, virtuosity and sparkle to the *Piano Concertos*. **Chung** presents the short *First Violin Concerto* delightfully and gets similarly admirable accompaniments from **Dutoit**. She gives a passionate account of the *B minor*

Concerto, so intense that even a sceptical listener will find it hard not to be convinced that this is a great work, with excellent support from **Foster**. Both the *Havanaise* and *Introduction and Rondo capriccioso* have beauty and bravura in plenty, and they come up as fresh as paint. **Harrell's** account of the *First Cello Concerto* is an extrovert reading, and one which makes light of any idea that this composer always worked on a small scale. The *Second Cello Concerto* is beautifully played and recorded: at its close, Harrell refines his timbre to an exquisite half-tone and the effect is ravishing, with a gently muted horn decoration. In Dutoit's collection of tone-poems, the works are beautifully played and recorded, with the 1979 Kingway Hall sound giving it all an appropriate atmosphere. The *Organ Symphony* was one of the first demonstration digital recordings (1982).

(i) Cello Concertos 1; 2; (ii) Cello Sonata 1; Le Cygne

⟐ *** Quartz QTZ 2039. Walton; with (i) Philh. O, Briger; (ii) Grimwood

Shrewdly, the talented young British cellist, **Jamie Walton**, offers a coupling of Saint-Saëns cello works that is near ideal. It says much for Walton that in every way his readings stand the closest comparison with those of Isserlis (see below), both in expressive imagination and in virtuosity. Helped by rather fuller recording, the Walton performances are even a shade warmer than those of Isserlis, notably in slow movements, and though the cello is balanced well forward the playing of the **Philharmonia** under **Alex Briger** has an impact to enhance Walton's playing, as at the sharply rhythmic opening of *Concerto* 2. The disc also reminds us of the comparable power of the *First Cello Sonata* from the striking, vigorous opening onwards, in every way a work of comparable stature. **Daniel Grimwood** proves an excellent partner for Walton.

Cello Concerto 1 in A min., Op. 33 (DVD version)

*** EMI **DVD** 3 58232-9. Rostropovich, LPO, Giulini (Dir: Suvi Raj Grubb; V/D: Hugo Käch) – DVOŘÁK: *Cello Concerto 1* **(*)

Rostropovich's 1977 DVD serves as a pairing for an intensely involving account of the Dvořák concerto. It is a reading of considerable rhetorical intensity, as is shown by the very opening flourish, but it also has warmth (and moments of great delicacy too). The performance, which is warmly and atmospherically recorded in the Henry Wood Hall, is also available as one of EMI's 'Great Recordings of the Century' (5 67593-2). The video, well directed by Hugo Käch, exploits the handsome background of the Henry Wood Hall. Full sound, if on the dry side.

Cello Concerto 1 in A min., Op. 33 (CD Versions)

⟐ **** EMI 5 56126-2. Han-Na Chang, LSO, Rostropovich – BRUCH: *Kol Nidrei* ****; FAURÉ: *Elégie* ****; TCHAIKOVSKY *Rococo Variations* **** ⬤

*** Teldec 8573-85340-2. du Pré, Phd. O, Barenboim – DVOŘÁK: *Cello Concerto* ***

*** ASV CDDCA 867. Rolland, BBC PO, Varga – LALO: *Cello Concerto in D min.*; MASSENET: *Fantaisie* ***

Ⓜ *** DG (ADD) 457 761-2. Fournier, LOP, Martinon –
BLOCH: *Schelomo*; BRUCH: *Kol Nidrei*; LALO: *Cello
Concerto* ***

(***) BBC mono BBCL 4198-2. Rostropovich, LSO,
Rozhdestvensky – ELGAR: *Cello Concerto*; HAYDN: *Cello
Concerto in C* (***)

(i) *Cello Concerto 1, Op. 33*; (ii) *The Swan*; (iii) *Allegro appassionato, Op. 43*; *Cello Sonata 1, Op. 32*; *Chant saphique, Op. 91*; *Gavotte, Op. posth.*; *Romances 1 in F, Op. 36*; *2 in D, Op. 51*; (iv) *Prière (for cello & organ)*

🎵 **** RCA 09026 61678-2. Isserlis; (i) LSO, Tilson-Thomas;
(ii) Tilson-Thomas, Moore; (iii) Devoyon; (iv) Grier

Steven Isserlis's account of the *Cello Concerto in A minor* is
among the best on record. Of particular interest too is the
Cello Sonata 1 in C minor, composed in the same year, in which
he is accompanied with elegance and finesse by **Pascal
Devoyon**. Isserlis himself plays with the musicianship and
virtuosity one has come to expect from him. Most of the remaining pieces are both worthwhile and entertaining, particularly the *Allegro appassionato*. The *Prière*, Op. 159, for cello
and organ, is a small but affecting addition to the Saint-
Saëns discography. The recorded sound is very good indeed.

The Saint-Saëns, recorded live in Philadelphia in 1971,
makes a good coupling for **du Pré's** warmly expressive account of the Dvořák with Celibidache. Though this came
right at the end of du Pré's playing career, before the onset
of multiple sclerosis, the performance is typically magnetic
in its high-powered intensity, full of manic energy, faster
and wilder than her studio account, if not quite so cleanly
recorded.

Sophie Rolland takes its technical hurdles in her effort-
less stride and is very well supported by the **BBC
Philharmonic** under **Gilbert Varga**. The excellence of the
BBC/ASV recording makes for a strong recommendation.

Fournier brings his customary nobility to the concerto,
and is well supported by **Martinon**, who provides stylish support with the **Lamoureux Orchestra**. The recording from
1960 has never sounded better than on this new DG
Originals transfer, and the collection is excellent in every
way.

This 1965 BBC Legends account of the Saint-Saëns *First
Concerto* brings a passionate performance from
Rostropovich, powerful and incisive, one of the epic series
he performed in a live sequence at that time. It comes in a
generous and revealing package with the Elgar and Haydn
Concerto in C. Mono recording only, but very acceptable.

(i) *Cello Concerto 1*; (ii) *Piano Concerto 2*; (iii) *Violin Concerto 3*

🎵 💿 Ⓜ **** Sony SMK 89873. (i) Ma, O Nat. de France,
Maazel; (ii) Licad, LPO, Previn; (iii) Lin, Philh. O, Tilson-
Thomas

Three outstanding performances from the early 1980s are
admirably linked together in this highly desirable CBS mid-
price reissue. **Yo-Yo Ma's** performance of the *Cello Concerto*
is distinguished by fine sensitivity and beautiful tone, while

Cécile Licad and the **LPO** under **Previn** turn in an eminently
satisfactory reading of the *G minor Piano Concerto* that has
the requisite delicacy in the Scherzo and seriousness elsewhere. **Cho-Liang Lin's** account of the *B minor Violin Concerto*
with the **Philharmonia Orchestra** and **Michael Tilson-
Thomas** is exhilarating and thrilling.

Piano Concertos 1 in D, Op. 17; 2 in G min., Op. 22; 3 in E flat, Op. 29; 4 in C min., Op. 44; 5 in F (Egyptian), Op. 103

Ⓑ *** Double Decca (ADD) 443 865-2 (2). Rogé, Philh. O, RPO
or LPO, Dutoit

Piano Concertos 1–5; Africa Fantaisie, Op. 89; Wedding-Cake Caprice-valse, Op. 76 (both for piano and orchestra)

🎵 ⚙ **** Hyp. CDA 67331/2 (2). Hough, CBSO, Oramo
(with *Allegro appassionato*; *Rapsodie d'Auvergne*)

Ⓑ *** EMI Gemini 5 86245-2 (2). Collard, RPO, Previn

Marvellous performances from **Stephen Hough**, full of joy,
vigour and sparkle, with **Oramo** and the **CBSO** accompanying spiritedly and with the lightest touch. The recording is
in the demonstration bracket, and this Hyperion set includes no fewer than four encores. An easy first choice.

Pascal Rogé brings delicacy, virtuosity and sparkle to the
piano part and he receives expert support from the various
London orchestras under **Dutoit**. Altogether delicious playing and excellent piano-sound from Decca, who secure a
most realistic balance. A fine bargain alternative to Hough.

As always with **Collard** there is splendid character and a
dazzling technique. He brings panache and virtuosity to
these concertos, as well as impressive poetic feeling. At one
point in the *Fifth (Egyptian) Concerto* Collard exploits Saint-
Saëns's genius in manipulating the piano to suggest Eastern
sonorities and makes his instrument sound exactly like an
Arab *qunan* or zither. Throughout, **Previn** and the **Royal
Philharmonic Orchestra** are sensitive accompanists. The
digital sound is very good too, but there is a distinct touch
of hardness on top.

(ii) *Piano Concertos 1 in D, Op. 17; 2 in G min., Op. 22*; (i) *Orchestral Suite in D, Op. 49*

*** BIS CD 1040. (i) Tapiola Sinf., Kantorow; (ii) with Ogawa

BIS couples the *First* and *Second Piano Concertos*, which are
played with great charm and grace by **Norika Ogawa** and the
Tapiola Sinfonietta under **Jean-Jacques Kantorow**. As a
makeweight it has added the *Suite in D major*, Op. 49, which
was originally conceived for the harmonium and later
arranged for orchestra. It is all attractive and engaging and
excellently recorded too.

Piano Concerto 2 in G min., Op. 22

🎵 Ⓜ *** EMI (ADD) 3 45819-2. Gilels, Paris Conservatoire
O, Cluytens – RACHMANINOV: *Piano Concerto 3*;
SHOSTAKOVICH: *Preludes & Fugues* ***

ⒷⒷ (***) Naxos mono 8.110683. Moiseiwitsch, LPO, Cameron
– GRIEG: *Piano Concerto* (***); LISZT: *Fantasia on
Hungarian Folk Themes* (***)

With **Gilels**, Saint-Saëns's most popular piano concerto becomes a bigger, more commanding work than usual. The opening movement is remarkably serious, with genuine depth of feeling to balance the sparkling Scherzo and even more dazzling finale. **Cluytens** is a splendid partner, investing the orchestral accompaniment with both gravitas and bravura as needed, and the 1954 recording sounds remarkably good in its new transfer.

On Naxos, a neat-fingered and characterful account of this popular concerto and a welcome reminder of **Moiseiwitsch's** art. Good transfer.

Piano Concertos 2 in G min.; 5 in F (Egyptian)

**** Decca 475 8764. Thibaudet, SRO, Dutoit – FRANCK: *Variations symphoniques* ****

Once the G *minor Concerto* was a regular part of the concert repertoire, but now – like so much of Saint-Saëns's output – it seldom turns up. **Thibaudet** plays both concertos with a great sense of style and much charm, and **Dutoit** and the Geneva orchestra give him excellent support. The recording is very fine indeed. Recommended.

Violin Concertos 1–3

⌕ **** Hyp. CDA 67074. Graffin, BBC Scottish SO, Brabbins

Violin Concertos (i) 1; (ii) 3; (iii) Havanaise; Introduction & rondo capriccioso

⌕ Ⓜ **** Decca (ADD) 460 008-2. Chung; (i) Montreal SO, Dutoit; (ii) LSO, Lawrence Foster; (iii) RPO, Dutoit

Violin Concerto 1; Havanaise in E, Op. 83; Introduction & rondo capriccioso, Op. 28; Morceau de concert, Op. 62; Romance in C, Op. 48; Sarabande, Op. 93/1

**** BIS CD 860. Kantorow, Tapiola Sinf.

Though Saint-Saëns's *Third Concerto* is relatively well known, with its charming central *Andantino* set between two bravura movements, and the *First Concerto*, in a single movement, has not been neglected either, the *Second Concerto* is the earliest and longest, yet arguably the most memorable – full of the youthful exuberance of a 23-year-old. The French violinist **Philippe Graffin**, with rich, firm tone, gives performances full of temperament, warmly supported by **Martyn Brabbins** and the **BBC Scottish Symphony Orchestra**, and the recording cannot be faulted.

Kyung Wha Chung presents Saint-Saëns's *First Violin Concerto* delightfully and receives admirable support from **Dutoit**. She gives a passionate account of the *B minor Concerto*, so intense that even a sceptical listener will find it hard not to be convinced that this is a great work. Such music needs this kind of advocacy, and Miss Chung is splendidly backed up by the **LSO** under **Lawrence Foster**.

It is a pleasure also to welcome this fine BIS collection which brings the short and early *First Violin Concerto* with such rightly popular display pieces as the *Introduction and Rondo capriccioso* and the *Havanaise*. Everything is expertly played and **Kantorow** has the right blend of panache and

spontaneity. First-class sound, as one expects from this source.

Violin Concerto 3 in B min., Op. 61

*** Australian Ph. Eloquence (ADD) 442 8561. Grumiaux, LOP, Rosenthal – VIEUXTEMPS: *Violin Concertos 4 & 5* ***

Stylish and warm playing from **Arthur Grumiaux**, with equally stylish playing from the Paris **Lamoureux Orchestra** in this attractive reissue. The distinctive sound of the orchestra gives the performances a theatrical edge, by no means unattractive. Decent 1963 sound.

Violin Concerto 3 in B min., Op. 61; Caprice andalous in G, Op. 122; Introduction & rondo capriccioso in A min., Op. 28; Morceau de concert in G, Op. 62

🅑🅑 **(*) Naxos 8.550752. Kang, Polish Nat. RSO, Wit

Dong-Suk Kang brings out the delicate lyricism in Saint-Saëns's most popular violin concerto. The coupling of concertante works brings similar charm, and it is good to have the rarer *Caprice andalous* included, a 10-minute piece with many typical Saint-Saëns felicities.

(i; ii) Violin Concerto 3, Op. 61; Caprice andalous; Caprice d'après l'Etude en form de valse; (ii) Le déluge: Introduction; (iii; ii) Allegro appassionato; Wedding Cake Caprice

⌕ **** BIS CD 1470. (i) Kantorow; (ii) Tapiola Sinf., Bakels; (iii) Kärkkaïnen

The *Third Concerto* represents Saint-Saëns at his most endearing, and the soaring lyricism of the first movement is perfectly caught by **Kantorow**, who then phrases the delightful siciliana *Andantino* to perfection, with the orchestral woodwind joining him with exquisite sensitivity. The introduction of the finale is crisply articulated, and Kantorow bounces off into the main theme with great élan. Throughout the disc there is a true partnership between each soloist with **Kees Bakels** and the **Tapiola Sinfonietta**, and with first-class BIS sound and a most convincing balance this collection is very recommendable indeed, and certainly a first choice among current recordings of the *B minor Violin Concerto*.

Danse macabre, Op. 40; (i) Havanaise; Introduction & rondo capriccioso; La Jeunesse d'Hercule, Op. 50; Marche héroïque, Op. 34; Phaéton, Op. 39; Le Rouet d'Omphale, Op. 31

⌕ Ⓜ **** Decca (ADD) 425 021-2. (i) Kyung Wha Chung, RPO; Philh. O; Dutoit

The symphonic poems are beautifully played, and the 1979 Kingsway Hall recording lends the appropriate atmosphere. Decca have now added **Kyung Wha Chung's** equally charismatic and individual 1977 accounts of what are perhaps the two most inspired short display-pieces for violin and orchestra in the repertoire.

Havanaise, Op. 83

⌕ Ⓜ (***) RCA mono 09026 61753-2. Heifetz, RCA Victor

SO, Steinberg – CHAUSSON: *Poème* **(*); LALO: *Symphonie espagnole* (**(*)); SARASATE: *Zigeunerweisen* (***)

**(*) EMI 5 55026-2. Chang, Phd. O, Sawallisch – PAGANINI: *Violin Concerto 1* **(*)

The **Heifetz** performances have quite extraordinary panache: his bowing in the coda of the *Havanaise* is utterly captivating. Indeed, this dazzling playing is unsurpassed on record and the 1951 mono recording, if closely balanced, is very faithful. Even if you have these works in more modern versions, this marvellous disc should not be passed by.

Although she misses some of the sultry seductiveness in the *Havanaise*, the twelve-year-old **Sarah Chang** still captures the gleaming Spanish sunshine. She is well supported by **Sawallisch** but is not flattered by the close recording-balance.

Havanaise, Op. 83; Introduction & Rondo Capriccioso, Op. 28

🎵– Ⓜ *** EMI (ADD) 5 62599-2. Perlman, O de Paris, Martinon (with MASSENET: *Thaïs: Méditation*) – CHAUSSON: *Poème*; RAVEL: *Tzigane* ***

Ⓜ **(*) Warner Elatus 2564 60013-2. Vengerov, Israel PO, Mehta – PAGANINI: *Violin Concerto 1* **(*); WAXMAN: *Carmen Fantasy* ***

Perlman plays these Saint-Saëns warhorses with special panache. The digital remastering brings Perlman's gorgeous fiddling right into the room, at the expense of a touch of aggressiveness when the orchestra lets rip, but the concert-hall ambience prevents this from being a problem.

Maxim Vengerov really show his mettle in these Saint-Saëns *morceaux de concert*. He plays with much finesse and dazzles with his easy fireworks, the *Havanaise* in particular producing ravishing tone, yet no over-indulgence. **Mehta** stands back and gives his young soloist his head.

Henry VIII (ballet music)

ⒷⒷ *** Naxos 8.553338/9. Razumovsky Sinfonia, Mogrelia – DELIBES: *Sylvia* ***

This ballet-divertissement, described as a '*fête populaire*', comes in Act II of the opera, and in the outer movements Saint-Saëns wittily introduces first a Scottish reel then an Irish jig with Gallic insouciance. But all six numbers, which are enjoyably tuneful, unashamedly incorporate a great many airs from both countries, and **Mogrelia** presents them affectionately and vividly. With excellent recording, this is a genuine bonus to a pleasing account of Delibes's *Sylvia*.

Le rouet d'Omphale

🎵– Ⓜ *** EMI (ADD) 3 79986-2. RPO Beecham – BIZET: *Carmen Suite 1*, etc.; CHABRIER: *España*, etc.; FAURÉ: *Dolly* ***

The delicacy of string textures and wind playing (notably the flute) is utterly beguiling in **Beecham's** unsurpassed version of *Le rouet d'Omphale*, with its exquisite closing section, part of an unmissable concert of French lollipops.

Suite algérienne, Op. 60

*** Talent **SACD** DOM 2929 106. Nice PO, Guidarini (with G.

CHARPENTIER: *Impressions d'Italie* ***) – MASSENET: *Scènes alsaciennes* ***

This is part of an attractive triptych of modestly impressionistic pictorial writing, of which the *Italian Impressions* of Gustave Charpentier are the most poetically evocative. Massenet's *Scènes alsaciennes* are full of charm, and Saint-Saëns's picture postcards are both colourful and tuneful. *Rêverie du soir* is a delicate highlight, but the trump card is the closing *Marche militaire français* which in its central trio has one of the catchiest tunes the composer ever wrote, bouncing along irresistibly. Splendid playing and fine recording.

Symphonies: in A; in F (Urbs Roma); Symphonies 1–3

Ⓑ *** EMI (ADD) 5 85186-2 (2). French Nat. RO, Martinon (with Gavoty, organ of the Église Saint-Louis des Invalides in 3)

The *A* and *F major* works were totally unknown and unpublished at the time of their recording and have never been dignified with numbers. Yet the *A major*, written when the composer was only 15, is a delight and may reasonably be compared with Bizet's youthful work in the same genre. More obviously mature, the *Urbs Roma Symphony* is perhaps a shade more self-conscious, and more ambitious too, showing striking imagination in such movements as the darkly vigorous Scherzo and the variation movement at the end.

The first of the numbered symphonies is a well-fashioned and genial piece, again much indebted to Mendelssohn and Schumann, but with much delightfully fresh invention. The *Second* is full of excellent ideas. **Martinon** directs splendid performances of the whole set, well prepared and lively. The account of the *Third* ranks with the best: freshly spontaneous in the opening movement, and the threads knitted powerfully together at the end of the finale. Here the recording could do with rather more sumptuousness. Elsewhere the quality is bright and fresh, with no lack of body.

Symphony in F (Urbs Roma); Symphony 2 in A min., Op. 55; (i) Africa (for Piano & Orchestra), Op. 89

*** BIS CD 790. (i) Mikkola; Tapiola Sinfonietta, Kantorow

The *F major 'Urbs Roma' Symphony* and the delightful *Second Symphony in A minor* are played with great spirit and zest by the **Tapiola Sinfonietta** and **Jean-Jacques Kantorow**. If the coupling is suitable, these intelligent and well-recorded performances can be recommended.

Symphony 2; Phaéton, Op. 39; Suite algérienne, Op. 60

*** ASV CDDCA 599. LSO, Butt

Symphonies 2; (i) 3 in C min., Op. 78

*** Chan. 8822. Ulster O, Tortelier; (i) with Weir

If you want the *Second Symphony*, it is particularly well played by the **LSO** under **Yondani Butt**, with the freshness of a major orchestra discovering something unfamiliar and enjoying themselves.

Yan Pascal Tortelier's performance of the *Second* is also very attractive and very well recorded; but Butt's account of this work has greater freshness, and the slightly less reverberant ASV recording contributes to this. If, however, your main interest lies with the *Third Symphony*, this extra resonance proves no disadvantage and the Tortelier version is a 'best buy', both for the appeal of the performance overall and for the state-of-the-art Chandos recording.

Symphony 3 in C min., Op. 78

**** Ondine ODE 1094-5. Latry, Phd. O, Eschenbach –
POULENC: *Organ Concerto*; BARBER: *Toccata Festiva* ***

*** DG 419 6172. Preston, BPO, Levine – DUKAS: *L'Apprenti sorcier* ***

Ⓜ *** Decca 475 7728. (i) Hurford, Montreal SO, Dutoit (with POULENC: *Organ Concerto* (***))

(i) Symphony 3; (ii; iv) Carnival of the Animals; (iii; iv) Danse macabre

🅱🅱 **(*) Regis RRC 1262. (i) Rawsthorne, RLPO, Tjeknavorian; (ii) Salvador (Sr & Jr), Mexico City PO; (iii) Mexico State SO; (iv) Bátiz

(i) Symphony 3; (ii) Danse macabre; Le Déluge: Prelude, Op. 48; Samson et Dalila: Bacchanale

Ⓜ *** DG (ADD) 474 612-2. (i) Litaize, Chicago SO; (ii) O de Paris., Barenboim

A brilliantly virtuoso live performance from **Eschenbach**, with dazzling playing from **Olivier Latry**. Equally impressive is the superb playing of the **Philadelphia Orchestra**, with the strings wonderfully warm and glowing, coping with the often fast tempi set by Eschenbach. The couplings are equally spectacular.

With the **Berlin Philharmonic** in cracking form, **Levine's** is a grippingly dramatic reading, full of imaginative detail. The great thrust of the performance does not stem from fast pacing: rather it is the result of incisive articulation, while the clarity of the digital recording allows the pianistic detail to register crisply. The thunderous organ entry in the finale makes a magnificent effect, and the tension is held at white heat throughout the movement.

Tjeknavorian's recording of the *Symphony* made in Liverpool Cathedral is perhaps the most sumptuous and spectacular so far, with an overwhelming climax at the close of the finale, organ pedals effectively underpinning the spacious orchestral tutti. The *Carnival of the Animals* (with a robust father-and-son pianistic partnership) and *Danse macabre* have plenty of geniality under **Bátiz** but the playing of the **Mexican Orchestra** is less strong on finesse.

Dutoit brings to the symphony his usual gifts of freshness and a natural sympathy for Saint-Saëns's attractive score. There is a ready spontaneity here. The recording is very bright, with luminous strings given a thrilling brilliance above the stave, perhaps a shade too much at times, but there is a balancing weight, and the reading effectively combines lyricism with passion.

Barenboim's inspirational 1976 performance of the *Symphony* glows with warmth and vitality from beginning to end. However, although the remastering has brought an excitingly vivid impact, especially in the finale of the *Symphony*, the effect is not entirely advantageous. While detail is sharper, the massed violins sound thinner and less natural at *fortissimo* level.

CHAMBER MUSIC

Bassoon Sonata, Op. 168; Clarinet Sonata, Op. 167; Caprice on Danish & Russian Airs for Flute, Oboe, Clarinet & Piano, Op. 79; Feuillet d'album, Op. 81 (arr. Taffanel); Oboe Sonata, Op. 166; Odelette for Flute & Piano, Op. 162; Romance in D flat for Flute & Piano, Op. 37; Tarantelle for Flute, Clarinet & Piano, Op. 6

🎵 Ⓑ *** Cala CACD 1017 (2). Bennett, Daniel, Campbell, Gough & Ens. – DEBUSSY: *Chamber Music* ***

The *Sonatas for Clarinet, for Oboe* and *for Bassoon* are elegantly finished but surprising pieces, with an unaccustomed depth of feeling. The *Caprice* is a diverting kind of pot-pourri, inspired by the composer's visit to Russia in 1876. Paul Taffanel's arrangement of the *Feuillet d'album*, Op. 81, for flute, oboe and two each of clarinets, bassoons and horns, is a first recording and, like almost everything on this record, refreshing and elegant. That goes for the performances too, which are well recorded, though the piano is occasionally overpowering. Strongly recommended – and outstanding value.

Cello Sonatas 1 in C min., Op. 32; 2 in F, Op. 123; Le Cygne (trans. Godowski)

🎵 *** Hyp. CDA 67095. Lidström, Forsberg

Written 30 years apart, the two *Cello Sonatas* have an abundant and fluent invention, and are captivating when played with such fervour and polish. These artists radiate total conviction and a life-enhancing vitality and sensitivity.

Clarinet Sonata, Op. 167

*** EMI 3 79787-2. Meyer, Maisenberg – MILHAUD: *Scaramouche*; DEVIENNE; POULENC: *Sonatas* ***

Sabine Meyer and **Oleg Maisenberg** open this diverting collection of French sonatas with Saint-Saëns, as melodically appealing as ever, but more thoughtfully nostalgic in mood than usual – perhaps because it is a late work, written in the composer's last year – until the sparkling closing *Molto allegro*, when the playing really takes off. Excellent recording, and the Milhaud and Poulenc works are even more entertaining.

Piano Quartet in B flat, Op. 41

Ⓜ *** Virgin 4 82061-2 (2). Kandinsky Qt – CASTILLON; CHAUSSON; LEKEU: *Piano Quartets* ***

The *B flat major Piano Quartet* comes from 1875, and is a masterly piece. There is a Mendelssohnian feel to it in places, and the score is characterized by lucidity of texture and the grace and fluency of the writing. Good playing and recording, and thoroughly rewarding couplings.

Piano Trio 1 in F, Op. 18

(*) Ara. Z 6643. Golub-Kaplan-Carr Trio – DEBUSSY; FAURÉ: *Trios* ***

Piano Trios 1 in F, Op. 18; 2 in E min., Op. 92

⊕– **** Hyp. CDA 67538. Florestan Trio

ⒷⒷ *** Naxos 8.550935. Joachim Trio

These are such captivating performances on Hyperion that they must take preference even over those listed below. They radiate a vital intelligence that shows both scores to best effect. All three players are superb, and **Susan Tomes's** pianism is particularly rewarding and virtuosic. The recording serves them excellently.

No quarrels with the playing of the **Joachim Trio** (**Rebecca Hirsch**, **Caroline Dearnley** and **John Lenehan**). The pianist in particular has elegance and charm. This is delightful and inventive music, well recorded – and well worth the money.

David Golub, **Mark Kaplan** and **Colin Carr** also give a very good account of themselves in the *Piano Trio in F major*. They are intelligent and imaginative. The piano dominates in the right way, and David Golub makes a particularly strong and vital impression. They are very well recorded too.

(i) String Quartets 1 in E min., Op. 112; 2 in G, Op. 153; (ii) Violin Sonatas 1 in D min., Op. 75; 2 in E flat, Op. 102; Berceuse, Op. 38; Elégies Op. 143 & 160; Romance, Op. 37

ⒷⒷ **(*)** Warner Apex 2564 61426-2 (2). (i) Viotti Qt; (ii) Charlier, Hubeau

Saint-Saëns was 64 years old when he wrote the *First Quartet*, and 84 when he composed its successor! Although neither finds him at his most inspired, a lifetime's experience and an effortless mastery are evident. As a glance at the opus numbers will show, the two *Violin Sonatas* are relatively late, the *First* coming from 1885 and the *Second* a decade later. Nevertheless, they are fresh and inventive and full of the composer's usual charm and fluency. **Olivier Charlier** makes a persuasive case for them.

Violin Sonata 1 in D min., Op. 75

Ⓝ ⊕– ⒷⒷ *** EMI Encore 208122-2. Chang, Vogt – FRANCK: *Violin Sonata*; RAVEL: *Violin Sonata* ***

Ⓝ *** Chan. 10510. Rimonda, Canziana – MASSENET: *Méditation from 'Thaïs'*; DANCLA: *Petite Ecole de la mélodie*, *Op. 123* ***

*** New Note Quartz QTZ 2002. Liebeck, Apekisheva – CHAUSSON: *Poème*; PROKOFIEV; YSAŸE: *Violin Sonatas* ***

*** Essex (ADD) CDS 6044. Accardo, Canio – CHAUSSON: *Concert* ***

Sarah Chang and **Lars Vogt** make a winning partnership and give an infectiously vivacious account of this engaging sonata. Together with the Franck and the Ravel *G major Sonata* it makes for a strong contender in each work. Good recorded sound too.

The Saint-Saëns *D minor Sonata*, the finer of the two he wrote, is also given a winning performance on Chandos, with

the characteristic structure of four movements in pairs cleanly brought out and the contrasts well established. At just under an hour of music this may not be a generous disc but it is an exceptionally attractive one.

Jack Liebeck and **Katya Apekisheva** find all Saint-Saëns's wistful charm, especially in the *Adagio*, while the Scherzo has the lightest rhythmic touch and the exhilarating finale is busy as a bee. The sound is good, although the violin's upper range can sometimes seem a little undernourished.

The performance of the *D minor Sonata* by **Accardo** and **Canio** is also marvellously played, selfless and dedicated. The recording too is very good, and this can be recommended strongly, if the coupling is suitable.

Violin Sonatas 1 in D min., Op. 75; 2 in E flat, Op. 102; Berceuse in B flat, Op. 38; Elégie, Op. 143; Triptyque, Op. 136

⊕– **** Hyp. CDA 67100. Graffin, Devoyon

Violin Sonatas 1; 2 in E flat, Op. 102; Berceuse, Op. 38; Introduction & rondo capriccioso, Op. 28 (arr. Bizet)

(*) ASV CDDCA 892. Xue Wei, Lenehan

Of Saint-Saëns's two *Violin Sonatas* the second is especially appealing with its simple *Andante* and closing *Allegro grazioso*, in which **Xue Wei** seems thoroughly at home. He is also delightfully nimble in the Scherzo (as is his fine partner, **John Lenehan**) and he manages the *moto perpetuo* finale of the *First Sonata* with equal facility. Before that comes the lovely *Berceuse*, which shows Xue Wei's tone at its most appealing, but in the opening *Introduction and Rondo capriccioso*, played with real sparkle, the close microphones are unflattering to the violin's upper range.

However Hyperion score over its competitors, not only in the up-to-date and beautifully balanced recorded sound but also artistically. **Pascal Devoyon** is the most imaginative pianist and like his Korean colleague **Philippe Graffin** has both style and charm. This is an enjoyable disc in every way and more generous than the ASV collection.

ORGAN MUSIC

Bénédiction nuptial, Op. 9; Cyprès et Lauriers, Op. 156; Élévation, ou Communion, Op. 13; Fantaisies 1–3; 7 Improvisations; Marche religieuse, Op. 107; Offertoire in E; O salutaris hostia; 9 Pièces for Organ or Harmonium; Prédication aux oiseaux; Préludes in C, C min. & F; 6 Préludes & Fugues, Opp. 99 & 109; 3 Rhapsodies (on Breton folksongs), Op. 7; Thème, Variations et Choral de Dies irae

*** Arte Nova 74321 35088-2 (4). Bleichen (organ of Church of St Johann, Schaffhausen)

We already have an outstanding SACD of some of Saint-Saëns's organ music on Capriccio, but if you want everything he wrote, then this Arte Nova set will do nicely. **Stefan Bleichen** has a fine organ at his disposal and he plays this music, all of it attractive and much admired in its day, very persuasively. The *Preludes and Fugues* are very diverse, and the *Theme, Variations et Choral de Dies irae*, which the composer never finished, is worthy of Liszt; and it is Liszt's music which inspired the *Prédication aux oiseaux de St François d'Assise*. Fine recording, but not as spectacular as the Capriccio disc.

Organ music: *Bénédiction nuptiale, Op. 9; Cyprès; Fantaisie, Op. 101; Fantaisie (1857); Marche religieuse; Préludes et Fugues, Op. 99/1–3*

(N) *** Hyp. CDA 7713. Smith

Saint-Saëns's organ music is very tuneful and attractive. This disc begins with one of the more flamboyant *Préludes et Fugues* and ends with the very appealing *Fantaisie* of 1857. There is much to delight the ear here and much writing of great charm. The *Bénédiction nuptiale* is particularly touching. In fact, much of this repertoire is more intimate than extrovert, with the composer impressing more by his rich harmonies, such as in the rather haunting *Cyprès*, than by showy writing. The closely miked organ of La Madeleine, Paris, is richly detailed and warm-sounding, and the performances by **Andrew-John Smith** are excellent.

Bénédiction nuptiale, Op. 9; Elévation ou Communion; Fantaisies: in E flat; in D, Op. 101; 2 Improvisations, Op. 150/1 & 7; Prélude & Fugue in E flat, Op. 99/3

⊕–●**** Capriccio Surround Sound **SACD** 71 046. Dorfmüller (Doms Klais organ, Altenburg Cathedral)

In spite of the celebrated *Third Symphony*, one does not think of Saint-Saëns first and foremost as a composer of organ music; yet in 1853 he became the resident at the church at Sainte-Merry (an appropriate name) and four years later was appointed to play the Cavaillé-Coll instrument at Sainte-Madeleine, where he continued until 1877. This CD offers a representative survey of his organ music, and very enjoyable it is. **Joachim Dorfmüller** is completely at one with the composer, and his performances on this ideal organ are spontaneous and totally involving, especially when the surround sound gives the listener the impression of sitting in the cathedral itself.

VOCAL MUSIC

Choral songs: *Calme des nuits; Des pas dans l'allée; Les Fleurs et les arbres*

⊕–*** Ph. 438 149-2. Monteverdi Ch., ORR, Gardiner – FAURÉ: *Requiem*; DEBUSSY; RAVEL: *Choral Works* ***

Three charming examples of Saint-Saëns's skill and finesse in drawing inspiration from early sources in a way remarkable at the time he was writing. **Gardiner** and his team give ideal performances, adding to the valuable list of rarities that he provides as coupling for the Fauré *Requiem*.

Mass, Op. 4

(BB) *** Warner Apex 8573 89235-2. Lausanne Vocal Ens., Corboz; Alain; Fuchs (organ) – GOUNOD: *Mass Chorale* ***

The Op. 4 *Mass* of Saint-Saens, like its Gounod coupling, is an early work (1855) but although it still draws on the alter-

nation tradition of the French organ mass, the addition of soloists and orchestral accompaniment makes for a more modern larger-scale work, with only the organ preserving the plainsong tradition. Here the *Mass* is performed with the orchestral music transcribed for a second organ by Léon Rogues, which is less than ideal. Nevertheless this is generally a fine performance. Even if the soloists are not as impressive as the chorus, the choral alternation with the main organ (magnificently played by **Marie-Claire Alain**) in the *Sanctus* is very impressive, while the *O Salutaris* brings a memorable floating choral line against a gently pointed organ accompaniment, leading to a romantically seraphic *Agnus Dei*. At its modest cost this disc is well worth having.

OPERA

Hélène (opera; complete); *Nuit persane, Op. 26 bis*

(N) *** Melba MR 301114-2. Illing, Davislim, McKendree-Wright, Mouellic (narrator), Belle Epoque Ch. & O, Victoria, Tourniaire (Melba, PO Box 415, Elwood, Victoria, Australia 3184; www.melbafoundation.org)

Saint-Saëns's one-act opera *Hélène* is based on the story of Helen of Troy. The composer wrote it with Nellie Melba in mind, so the name of the recording company is apt. The plot centres on the love between the heroine and Paris, which does not please Menelaus, her husband, a bit. Just the same, the pair of lovers set off for Troy as the opera closes. The work is modestly tuneful, well worth hearing, and felicitously conducted by **Guillaume Tourniaire**, with the Melba substitute **Rosmunde Illing** singing, if not voluptuously, clearly and brightly; but she is upstaged by the ardent Paris, tenor **Steve Davislim**. It is he who sings the bonus songcycle, *Nuit persane*, in duet with the mezzo, **Zan McKendree-Wright**, which is introduced by the narrator, **Amanda Mouellic**. Altogether a novelty worth exploring, as it is excellently recorded and lavishly packaged.

Samson et Dalila (opera; complete; DVD version)

⊕–**** Arthaus **DVD** 100 202. Domingo, Verrett, Wolfgang Brendel, San Francisco Opera Ch. & O, Rudel. (Dir: Nicolas Joel; V/D: Kirk Browning.)

Recorded in 1981 at the **San Francisco Opera** House, this DVD of Saint-Saëns's biblical opera offers a heavily traditional production with realistic sets and costumes like those in a Hollywood epic. Sporting a vast bouffant wig like a teacosy (ripe for Dalila's shears in Act II), **Plácido Domingo** is in magnificent, heroic voice, with **Shirley Verrett** also at her peak as Dalila, at once seductive and sinister. Other principals are first-rate too, and the chorus, so vital in this opera, sings with incandescent tone in a riproaring performance under Julius Rudel, culminating in a spectacular presentation of the fall of the Temple of Dagon. Most enjoyable.

Samson et Dalila (opera; complete; CD versions)

⊕–**** EMI 5 09185-2 (2). Domingo, Meier, Fondary, Courtis, L'Opéra-Bastille Ch. & O, Myung-Whun Chung

(M) **(*) DG (ADD) 477 560-2 (2). Obraztsova, Domingo, Bruson, Lloyd, Thau, Ch. & O de Paris, Barenboim

Ⓜ **(*) Ph. 475 8706 (2). Carreras, Baltsa, Estes, Burchuladze, Bav. R. CH. & RSO, C. Davis

In the EMI CD set, **Domingo** with **Chung** gives a deeper, more thoughtful performance than on DG, broader, with greater repose and a sense of power in reserve. When the big melody appears in Dalila's seduction aria, *Mon cœur s'ouvre*, Chung's idiomatic conducting encourages a tender restraint, where others produce a full-throated roar. **Meier** may not have an ideally sensuous voice for the role, with some unwanted harshness in her expressive account of Dalila's first monologue, but her feeling for words is strong and the characterization vivid. Generally Chung's speeds are on the fast side, yet the performance does not lack weight, with some first-rate singing in the incidental roles from **Alain Fondary**, **Samuel Ramey** and **Jean-Philippe Courtis**. Apart from backwardly placed choral sound, the recording is warm and well focused.

Barenboim proves as passionately dedicated an interpreter of Saint-Saëns here as he did in the *Third Symphony*, sweeping away any Victorian cobwebs. It is important, too, that the choral passages, so vital in this work, be sung with this sort of freshness, and **Domingo** has rarely sounded happier in French music, the bite as well as the heroic richness of the voice well caught. **Renato Bruson** and **Robert Lloyd** are both admirable too; sadly, however, the key role of Dalila is given an unpersuasive, unsensuous performance by **Obraztsova**, with her vibrato often verging on a wobble. The recording is as ripe as the music deserves.

When the role of Samson is not one naturally suited to **Carreras**, it is amazing how strong and effective his performance is, even if top notes under stress grow uneven. Even the very strain seems to add to the intensity of communication, above all the great aria in the last Act, when Samson, blinded, is turning the mill. Unevenness of production is more serious, with **Agnes Baltsa** as Dalila. The microphone often brings out her vibrato, turning it into a judder, hers is hardly the seductive portrait required in this role, and it is a shortcoming that, like the rest of the cast, she is not a native French-speaker. Both **Burchuladze** as the Old Hebrew and **Simon Estes** as Abimelech equally seem intent on misusing once fine voices, but **Jonathan Summers** as the High Priest of Dagon is far more persuasive.

SAINT-COLOMBE
(died c. 1700)

Concerts à deux violes, Volume IV (Rougeville): Concerts 51–67

🎵 **** ATMA ACD2 2278 (2). Napper & Little

In spite of the film mentioned below, Saint-Colombe's life is shrouded in mystery. The latest research suggests that he was born in about 1630, and that he lived in Paris as a famous virtuoso and teacher; but nothing is certain about his last years. Undoubtedly his music was very influential indeed. The manuscript of the 67 *Concerts à deux violes* was discovered at the end of the 1960s. Each of the four volumes is given

the title of the first piece, in this instance *Rougeville*, which is the longest of the concerts here and is in the form of a very free chaconne, sometimes with the two soloists echoing each other. All the pieces are titled, often wittily. However, much of the music is sober and solemn and quite seriously expressive. **Susie Napper** and **Margaret Little** give really excellent performances, and they are well recorded. But be warned: two bass viols playing togther creates a limited tonal range and is an acquired taste; not everyone will find this repertoire easy listening.

Concerts for 2 Bass Violas da gamba: III (Le Tendre); VIII (La Conférence); XLII (Dalain); LI (La Rougeville); LXVII (Le Figure)

**(*) Naïve Astrée ES 9933. Savall, W. Kuijken

Le Retour; Tombeau 'les regrets'

🎵 BB *** Naxos 8.550750. Spectre de la Rose – MARAIS: *Tombeau pour M. de Saint-Colombe* etc. ***

The success of the film (*Tous les matins du monde*) about this reclusive composer and his relationship with his pupil, Marin Marais, has led to the soundtrack becoming a bestseller. However, this enterprising and inexpensive Naxos recital includes the 'hits' from the film. The two Saint-Colombe works included are austerely but certainly touchingly played by a fresh-sounding 'authentic' group led by **Alison Crum** (viola da gamba) and **Marie Knight** (baroque violin). The Naxos recording is vivid, but its forward balance means that for a realistic effect a modest setting of the volume control should be chosen.

Saint-Colombe's music is certainly austere and uncompromising, but if you want to hear it without frills then the combination of **Jordi Savall** and **Wieland Kuijken** is as authentic and responsive as you will get, and they are recorded vividly.

SALIERI, Antonio (1750–1825)

Overtures: Angiolina, ossia Il matrimonio per sussurro; Cublai, gran kan de'Tartari; Falstaff, ossia Le tre burle; La locandiera. Sinfonia Il giorno onomastico; Sinfonia Veneziana; 26 Variations on La follia di Spagna

🎵 **** Chan. 9877. LMP, Bamert

The music here brings a profusion of ear-tickling ideas and the secondary themes for his concise and lively overtures are most engaging. Tuttis, with trumpets, are invariably bright and rather grand, but the lighter scoring shows a nice feeling for woodwind colour and there is much elegant phrasing for the violins. Perhaps the most striking work is the kaleidoscopic set of *26 Variations on 'La follia'* which occupies eighteen minutes, continually changing colour and mood, often dramatically, sometimes bizarrely, but usually entertainingly (although there is an element of repetition). The **London Mozart Players** play all this music most winningly, with vigour, polish and charm and the Chandos recording is state of the art.

Double Concerto in C for Flute & Oboe

🎧— *** Chan. 9051. Milan, Theodore, City of L. Sinf., Hickox –
 MOZART: *Flute & Harp Concerto; Oboe Concerto* ***

Salieri's innocently insubstantial *Double concerto* is quite
transformed by the charisma and sheer style of the solo
playing from **Susan Milan** and **David Theodore**. The exquisite playing of Theodore in the simple melody of the
Largo and the perfect blending of the two soloists turn
it into a really memorable slow movement, and the flute
and oboe chase each other round engagingly in their winning decorations of the nicely poised Minuet finale.
Hickox's accompaniment is both polished and genial,
and the recording casts a pleasing glow over the whole
proceedings.

Fortepiano Concertos: in B flat and C

🎧— Ⓜ *** Warner Elatus 0927 49556-2. Staier, Concerto Köln
 – STEFFAN: *Fortepiano Concerto* ***

These two attractive works show Salieri as quite a dab hand
at a keyboard concerto, with a distinct personality of his own.
Overall the performances could hardly be more persuasive,
with the bold, slightly abrasive tuttis from the **Concerto Köln**
adding to the strength of characterization. The recording is
first class.

Falstaff, or The 3 Tricks (complete)

*** Chan. 9613 (2). Franceschetto, Myeounghee, De Filippo,
 Chialli, Luis Ciuffo, Bettoschi, Valli, Milan Madrigalists &
 Guido Cantelli, O, Veronesi

Like Verdi, Salieri and his librettist ignore the Falstaff of the
histories. They tell the story within the framework of the
conventional two-act opera of the period with crisp and brief
numbers leading to extended finales. Though Fenton and
Anne (Nannetta) are omitted, Mistress Page (here renamed
Slender) is given her husband. Though it never comes near
to matching Mozart, it is all great fun, particularly in performances as fresh and lively as these.

'Arie di bravura' from: Cublai gran Khan del Tartari; L'Europa riconosciuta; La finta scena; Der Rauchfangekehrer; Semiramide

*** Virgin 3 95250-2. Damrau, Le Cercle de l'Harmonie,
 Rhorer (with RIGHINI: *Arias*) – MOZART: *Arias* ***

Diana Damrau planned her début recital to juxtapose arias
of Mozart alongside those of Salieri, and the result is fascinating; while confirming that Mozart was by far the greater
composer, Salieri's own musical skills are well demonstrated. He is very dependent on brilliant, ear-catching coloratura, which Damrau despatches with thrilling ease. And
what are especially striking here are Salieri's orchestral introductions for the arias from *Semiramide*, and *L'Europa ri-
conosciuta*, which feature seductive orchestral woodwind
writing in the first, and an engaging oboe solo to introduce
the second. Throughout, the orchestral playing is excellent
and gives admirable support to Damrau's constant spectacular bursts of virtuoso fioritura and her sensitive lyrical
singing. A memorable disc.

SALLINEN, Aulis (born 1935)

(i; ii) Cello Concerto, Op. 44; (iii) Chamber Music I, Op. 38; (i; iii) Chamber Music III, Op. 58; (iii) Some Aspects of Peltoniemi Hintrik's Funeral March; (iv) Sunrise Serenade (for 2 trumpets and chamber orchestra), Op. 63; (ii) Shadows, Op. 52; Symphonies 4, Op. 49; 5 (Washington Mosaics), Op. 57

Ⓑ *** Finlandia 4509 99966-2 (2). (i) Noras; (ii) Helsinki PO,
 or (iii) Finland Sinfonietta, Kamu; (iv) Harjanne, Välimäki,
 Avanti CO

This Finlandia Double brings an extensive survey of
Sallinen's music and provides an inexpensive entry into the
composer's world. Apart from the symphonies, the *Cello
Concerto* of 1976 is the most commanding piece here.
Sallinen's ideas resonate in the mind. **Artos Noras** has its
measure and plays with masterly eloquence. The performances, under **Okko Kamu**, are very impressive and the
recording quite exemplary. Overall, excellent value.

(i) Symphonies 1, 3; (ii) Chorali; (iii) Cadenze for Solo Violin; (iv) Elegy for Sebastian Knight; (v) String Quartet 3

*** BIS (ADD) CD 41. (i) Finnish RSO, Kamu; (ii) Helsinki PO,
 Berglund; (iii) Paavo Pohjola; (iv) Frans Helmerson;
 (v) Voces Intimae Qt

The *First Symphony*, in one movement, is diatonic and full of
atmosphere, as indeed is the *Third*, a powerful, imaginative
piece which appears to be haunted by the sounds and smells
of nature. The performances under **Okko Kamu** are excellent. The recordings are from the 1970s and are all very well
balanced. Highly recommended.

Symphonies 2 (Symphonic Dialogue for Solo Percussion Player & Orchestra), Op. 29; 6 (From a New Zealand Diary), Op. 65; Sunrise Serenade, Op. 63

*** BIS CD 511. Malmö SO, Okko Kamu

The *Second Symphony*, like the *First*, is a one-movement
affair lasting a quarter of an hour. Its sub-title, *Symphonic
Dialogue for Solo Percussion Player and Orchestra*, gives an accurate idea of its character, pitting the fine soloist, **Gerd
Mortensen**, against the remaining orchestral forces. The
main work is the ambitious *Sixth Symphony*. Like the *Third
Symphony*, it is powerfully evocative of natural landscape;
indeed, it is one of the strongest and most imaginative of
all Sallinen's symphonies. **Okko Kamu** gets very responsive
playing from the **Malmö Symphony Orchestra** in both
symphonies and in the slight but effective *Sunrise Serenade*.
The recording is excellent.

Symphonies 4, Op. 49; 5 (Washington Mosaics), Op. 57; Shadows (Prelude for Orchestra), Op. 52

*** BIS CD 607. Malmö SO, James DePreist

Suffice it to say that these performances by the **Malmö
Symphony Orchestra** under **James DePreist** are every bit as
good as the Helsinki rivals listed above; if anything, the
recording has more impressive range and definition.

Kullervo (opera)

*** Ondine ODE 780-3T. Hynninen, Sallinen, Jakobsson, Silvasti, Vihavainen, Finnish Nat. Op. Ch. & O, Söderblom

Although the theme will be familiar from Sibelius's early symphony of the same name, Sallinen has based his *Kullervo* on the play by Aleksis Kivi and he wrote the libretto himself. The plot emerges from a mixture of narration, in which the chorus plays a central role, and dreams. The opera is a compelling musical drama. There is impressive variety of pace and atmosphere, and the black voices of the **Finnish Opera Chorus** resonate in the memory. So, too, do the impressive performances of **Jorma Hynninen** as Kullervo and **Anna-Lisa Jakobsson** as the smith's young wife and, indeed, the remainder of the cast and the **Finnish National Opera Orchestra** under **Ulf Söderblom**. While *Kullervo* may not be a great opera, it is gripping and effective musical theatre, and the Ondine recording has excellent presence and detail.

SAMMARTINI, Giovanni
(1700/1–75)

Aventura in D, JC 14; Overturas in C min., JC 9; F, JC 33, 36 & 37; Sinfonias in D, JC 15; G, JC 39; Sonatas in C, JC 7; in A, JC 65; Del Sigr. Baptista St Martino a 4 Stromenti

*** Dynamic CDS 460. Milan Classica CO, Gini

Sammartini composed at a time when the sinfonia was in a state of flux in Italy. He wrote some 20 three-movement works, calling them by different names, although the *Sinfonia in G*, JC 39, had an additional Minuet with variations. They are scored for strings except for the *Overtura a 6 in F*, JC 33, which includes a couple of braying horns in the outer movements. The allegros are in baroque style, slow movements are gently elegant or nostalgic (as in the *Sinfonia in D*, JC 15), occasionally quite touching, as is the *Largo* of the *Sonata in A*, JC 65. They are essentially slight but certainly enjoyable when played as stylishly and affectionately as they are here. The recording is excellent too, in a pleasing acoustic, and the disc's presentation is handsome with good notes.

SARASATE, Pablo (1844–1908)

Carmen Fantasy, Op. 25; Introduction et Tarantelle, Op. 43; Zigeunerweisen

⊕— Ⓜ **** EMI (ADD/DDD) 5 62594-2. Perlman, Abbey Road Ens., Foster – PAGANINI: *Violin Concerto 1* ****

Perlman's *Carmen Fantasy* makes a dazzling encore for his unsurpassed account of the Paganini *Concerto*, and for this reissue in the 'Perlman Edition' EMI have added more dazzling accounts of two other showpieces, the *Introduction et Tarantelle* and *Zigeunerweisen*, recorded digitally in 1995, in which Perlman's tone is even more luscious.

Carmen Fantasy, Op. 25

*** Claudio CB 5256-2. Jin, LSO, Wordsworth – LALO:

Symphonie espagnole; PROKOFIEV: *Solo Violin Sonata*. *** (with KROLL: *Banjo and Fiddle*, orch. Bradbury; TARREGA: *Recuerdos de la Alhambra*, arr. Ricci **(*))

Min Jin does not quite have Perlman's flamboyant panache in Sarasate's brilliant arrangement of Bizet, but her airily fragile approach is equally spontaneous and refreshingly different. Against a strong backing from **Barry Wordsworth** and the **LSO**, the solo playing is still dazzling, but never uses effect for its own sake. Very good recording, much more naturally balanced than Perlman.

Carmen Fantasy, Op. 25; Zigeunerweisen, Op. 20

*** Ph. 464 531-2. Suwanai, Budapest Fest O, Iván Fischer – DVOŘÁK: *Violin Concerto; Masurek* ***

Suwanai's virtuoso flair comes out not just in bold bravura playing, but in the daring range of dynamic, with Suwanai communing with herself in extreme, hushed pianissimos. An unexpected if attractive coupling for the Dvořák concerto, very well recorded.

Zigeunerweisen, Op. 20

⊕— *** DG 431 815-2. Shaham, LSO, Foster – WIENIAWSKI: *Violin Concertos 1 & 2, etc.* ***

⊕— Ⓜ (***) RCA mono 09026 61753-2. Heifetz, RCA Victor SO, Steinberg – CHAUSSON: *Poème* **(*); LALO: *Symphony espagnole* (**(*)); SAINT-SAËNS: *Havanaise, etc.* (***)

Ⓜ (***) EMI mono 7 64251-2. Heifetz, LPO, Barbirolli – SAINT-SAËNS: *Havanaise, etc.*; VIEUXTEMPS: *Concerto 4*; WIENIAWSKI: *Concerto 2* (***)

Gil Shaham plays Sarasate's sultry and dashing gypsy confection with rich timbre, languorous ardour and a dazzling display of fireworks at the close.

What can one say about the **Heifetz** performances except that they are unsurpassed: they are dazzling in the fireworks and with the most luscious tone and sophisticated colouring in the lyrical melody. The recording is dry but faithful. This is a marvellous disc.

Navarra (for violin and piano)

*** Warner 0927 45664-2. Hanslip, Ovrutsky – BRUCH: *Violin Concertos 1 & 3* ***

The Sarasate showpiece with its jaunty Spanish dance-rhythms makes a sparkling extra on **Chloë Hanslip's** fine recording of the Bruch *Violin Concertos 1 and 3*. Here she is sensitively accompanied by **Mikhail Ovrutsky**.

SARUM CHANT

Missa in gallicantu; Hymns: A solis ortus cardine; Christe Redemptor omnium; Salvator mundi; Domine; Veni Redemptor omnium

*** Gimell CDGIM 017. Tallis Scholars, Phillips

Filling in our knowledge of early church music, the **Tallis Scholars** under **Peter Phillips** here present a whole disc of chant according to the Salisbury rite – in other words *Sarum Chant* – which, rather than the regular Gregorian style, was what churchgoers of the Tudor period and earlier in England heard at their devotions. The greater part of the record is given over to the setting of the First Mass of Christmas, intriguingly entitled *Missa in gallicantu* or *Mass at Cock-Crow*. Though this is simply monophonic (the men's voices alone are used), it is surprising what antiphonal variety there is. The record is completed with four hymns from the Divine Offices of Christmas Day. The record is warmly atmospheric in the characteristic Gimell manner.

SATIE, Erik (1866–1925)

Gymnopédies 1 & 3 (orch. Debussy); Relâche (ballet); Parade (ballet); Gnossienne 3 (orch. Poulenc); La belle excentrique; 5 Grimaces pour le songe d'une nuit d'été (orch. Milhaud)

(BB) **(*) EMI Encore 3 41444-2. Toulouse Capitole O, Plasson

Plasson gets sensitive and lively performances from the **Toulouse orchestra**, though in *Parade* they do not have quite the same circus spirit and abandon as did the LSO for Dorati in the 1960s. However, few collectors will quarrel with these performances at this modest cost, and the music has much gamin-like charm. Moreover, this is better than many recent recordings from the Salle-aux-Grains in Toulouse; detail is more transparent and the textures somewhat better observed.

PIANO MUSIC

Piano, 4 Hands: (i) La Belle excentrique; 3 Morceaux en forme de poire. Solo piano: Avant-dernières pensées; Caresse; Chapitres tournés en tous sens; Croquis et agaceries d'un gros bonhomme en bois; Danse de travers; Descriptions automatiques; Embryons desséchés; 6 Gnossiennes; 3 Gymnopédies; Heures séculaires et instantanées; Je te veux; 2 Oeuvres de jeunesse: Valse ballet; Fantaisie valse. Passacaille; Les pantins dansant; Le Piccadilly (Marche); Première Pensée Rose + Croix; Petite ouverture à danser; Pièces froides I: Airs à faire fuir; II: Danse de travers. Poudre d'or; Prélude de la porte héroïque du ciel; Prélude et tapisserie; Sonatine bureaucratique; 3 Valses distinguées du précieux dégoûté

(N) 〄 (BB) *** Virgin 5 22050-2 (2). Queffélec; (i) with Collard

Although we think Pascal Rogé is very special in this repertoire, **Anne Queffélec** has strong claims too. She can be quirky, as in the opening *Croquis et agaceries d'un gros bonhomme en bois* or, more particularly, the satirical *Valse ballet*. In the *Trois morceaux en forme de poire* and the lively *La Belle excentrique* she is partnered by the late lamented **Catherine Collard**, and how brilliantly they end the first CD with that final quartet of sparkling vignettes, opening with the dazzling *Grande ritournelle* and ending with the irrepressible *Can-can 'grand-mondain'*.

The second disc includes the celebrated *Gnossiennes* and *Gymnopédies*, beautifully evoked, and fills out the collection

to make it one of the most comprehensive in the catalogue. Throughout, her playing has much subtlety and character, and the music is dispatched with great character and style. Nor does she possess less charm than Pascal Rogé. The piano sound is excellent: it is firm, clean and fresh, with a splendid tonal bloom. This is very recommendable.

Piano, 4 hands: (i) La Belle excentrique; 3 Morceaux en forme de poire. Solo piano: Descriptions automatiques; Embryons desséchés; 3 Gnossiennes; 3 Gymnopédies; 2 Valses

(B) *** Virgin 3 63296-2. Queffélec; (i) with Collard

This bargain reissue also includes solo items from the earlier recital above, dating from 1988, notably the celebrated *Gymnopédies* and *Gnossiennes*. All the music here is dispatched with great character and style, and these artists are exceptionally well served by the engineers.

Music for Piano, 4 hands: (i) La Belle excentrique; 3 Morceaux en forme de poire. Solo piano: Avant-dernières pensées; Embryons desséchés; 6 Gnossiennes; Croquis et agaceries d'un gros bonhomme en bois; 3 Gymnopédies; 5 Nocturnes; Sonatine bureaucratique; Véritables préludes flasques (pour un chien)

(M) *** EMI 5 67239-2. Ciccolini; (i) with Tacchino

Aldo Ciccolini recorded this selection during the 1980s and he is completely in sympathy with their style. He is totally inside this music and makes the most of its (not particularly wide) contrasts of mood and atmosphere. The recorded sound, harder in outline and not as rich as afforded to Pascal Rogé in his complete survey on Decca, is still very good. And some may feel that the slight edge given to the sharply articulated pieces (the *Embryons desséchés* and the *Sonatine bureaucratique* for instance) adds to their witty vitality. **Gabriel Tacchino** joins his colleague for the four-handed pieces. In many ways this is one of the most distinctive Satie collections in the catalogue.

Avant-dernières pensées; Chapitres tournés en tous sens; Gnossiennes 1–5; 5 Grimaces; 3 Gymnopédies; Je te veux (Valse); Nocturnes 1, 3 & 5; Passacaglia; Pièces froides (Airs à faire fuir 1–3); Le piège de Méduse; Ragtime Parade; Rêverie du pauvre; Sonatine bureaucratique; Sports et divertissements; Valse-ballet

〄 (BB) *** Regis (ADD) RRC 1327. McCabe

This attractive and generous (77 minutes) anthology draws on a pair of Saga records which have been much praised by us over the years. **John McCabe** has the full measure of Satie's understated melancholy and lyrical nostalgia, and he also has insights of his own to offer. His style might be described as gently cool: the three *Gymnopédies*, for instance, are played a little slower than usual, and the *Gnossiennes* are very delicately evoked. His programme ranges from the simple, almost Chopinesque *Valse-ballet*, Satie's first published piano piece, to the three *Nocturnes* of 1919–20, which are exquisitely played. The *Ragtime Parade* is a transcription from his ballet

Parade, in which his collaborators were none other than Diaghilev, Massine and Picasso, but its style is not unlike Gottschalk. The intelligent planning of this recital and the penetrating response of the pianism place this inexpensive CD among the most desirable Satie collections, and the recording, though not vividly present like the Virgin Queffélec recital, is natural and intimate, within a highly appropriate ambience.

Chapitres tournés en tous sens; Croquis et agaceries d'un gros bonhomme en bois; Le Fils des étoiles; Gymnopédies; Je te veux (valse); Prélude et tapisserie; Le Piccadilly; Pièces froides; Le Piège de Méduse; Poudre d'or; Sonatine bureaucratique; Sports et divertissements; Véritables préludes flasques (pour un chien); Vexations

(M) **** RCA 09026 63976-2. Dickinson

Peter Dickinson has made Satie's music a centrepoint of his repertoire, and his thoughtful approach to this highly rewarding music is all his own, often more withdrawn than usual. By his side Ciccolini sounds almost brittle. The Trois Gymnopédies, taken very slowly, have a grave dignity, and Dickinson finds a captivating delicacy of feeling for the Chapitres tournés en tous sens. The Sonatine bureaucratique is playful rather than ironic, its Andante most delicate, while the Pièces froides have a distinct air of nostalgia.

Piccadilly is as perky as ever, and the charming rhythmic diversity of the dance vignettes which make up Le Piège de Méduse is matched by the Sports et divertissements, which have a much wider range of character and feeling here than in most performances. Throughout, Dickinson's variety of articulation and colour is fully at the service of the composer, and he departs in an air of mystery with his gentle account of the enigmatic Vexations. The recording is very real indeed.

Embryons desséchés; 6 Gnossiennes; 3 Gymnopédies; Heures séculaires et instantanées; Nocturnes 1–5; Sonatine bureaucratique; Sports et divertissements

(BB) *** Hyp. Helios CDH 55176. Seow

The Singapore-born pianist **Yitkin Seow** is a good stylist; his approach is fresh and his playing crisp and marked by consistent beauty of sound. His playing has a quiet reticence that is well suited to this repertoire. The recording is eminently truthful.

Embryons desséchés; 6 Gnossiennes; 3 Gymnopédies; Je te veux; Nocturne 4; Le Piccadilly; 4 Préludes flasques; Prélude et tapisserie; Sonatine bureaucratique; Vieux sequins et vieilles cuirasses

⌐ (M) **** Decca 475 7527. Rogé

Pascal Rogé gave Satie his compact disc debut with this fine recital which is splendidly caught by the microphones. So this is a perfect candidate for Decca's series of Originals. Rogé has a real feeling for this repertoire and he conveys its bitter-sweet quality and its grave melancholy as well as he does its lighter qualities. He produces, as usual, consistent beauty of tone, and this is well projected by the recording.

SAUER, Emil von (1862–1942)

Piano Concerto 1 in E min.

⌐ *** Hyp. CDA 66790. Hough, CBSO, Foster –
   SCHARWENKA: Piano Concerto 4 ***

As a greatly admired virtuoso, Emil von Sauer was an able exponent of the Scharwenka concerto; and his own work, although lighter in feeling, makes comparable demands on the dexterity of the soloist. Its delightful melodic vein and style have much in common with Saint-Saëns. **Stephen Hough** sparkles his way through its glittering upper tessitura. Altogether this makes a perfect foil for the more ambitious concerto with which it is paired. Splendid recording, with a nice sense of scale.

SAUGUET, Henri (1901–89)

Mélodie concertante for Cello & Orchestra

*** Russian Disc (ADD) RDCD 11108. Rostropovich, USSR SO,
   composer – BRITTEN: Cello Symphony **(*)

Sauguet belongs at the heart of the Gallic tradition, and the opening of his Mélodie concertante has a dream-like pastoral. Its source of inspiration was an old, persistent memory of a young cellist from Bordeaux. It is an extended improvisation, based on a haunting, introspective theme heard at the beginning of the piece. The performance is, of course, authoritative in every way, and the 1964 analogue recording sounds every bit as good as it did in its fine LP format.

SCARLATTI, Alessandro (1660–1725)

(i) Cello Sonata 2 in C min.; (ii) Toccata in A; (iii) La concettione della Beata Vergine (Oratorio); Euridice dall'Inferno (Cantata)

(N) (BB) *** Naxos 8.570950. (i), Sills, Savino; (ii) Dirst ; (iii)
   Givens, Ars Lyrica, Houston

A well-planned collection showing all sides of Scarlatti's output, with the Cello Sonata persuasively played on a baroque instrument and featured with the inventive harpsichord Toccata as an interlude between the solo cantata, Euridice in the Underworld and the more substantial (31-minute) oratorio celebrating the conception of the Virgin Mary. All this music is highly expressive and the members of **Ars Lyrica** respond admirably, with the pure-toned soprano **Melissa Givens** standing out from the other soloists. Excellent recording and full translations add to the listener's pleasure.

Sonatas for Recorder, 2 Violins & Continuo in A min. & F. Cantatas: Bella Dama di nome Santa; Perchè tacete, regolati concenti?

**(*) MDG 309 0632-2. Wessel, Musica Alta Ripa (with
   FRANCESCO SCARLATTI: Cantata in un'ostante) –
   DOMENICO SCARLATTI: Cantata: Doppo lungo servire **(*)

A well-planned record in that it not only includes music by

Domenico Scarlatti, but also a charming pastoral cantata by Alessandro's brother, Francesco. The works by Alessandro include a pair of lively *Trio Sonatas* and two *Cantatas*, each with an instrumental obbligato to tickle the ear; *Bella Dama* uses a flute and *Perchè tacete* a solo violin. **Musica Alta Ripa's** instrumental contribution is first class, and **Kai Wessel** sings with espressivo and style. The only possible reservation is that his male alto timbre, which is slightly 'hooty', may not appeal to all listeners.

Cantatas

(i; ii) *Cantatas: Correa nel seno amato; Già lusingato appieno;* (ii) *Variations on 'La Follia'*

⊕→ ⒝⒝ **** Hyp. Helios CDH 55233. (i; ii) Dawson, Purcell Qt; (ii) Woolley (harpsichord)

A delightful juxtaposition of two pastoral cantatas, the first picturing the traditional lovelorn shepherd, the second telling of an English hero who is about to cross the sea to claim his throne and must leave behind him his much loved queenly wife and son. Both are ravishingly sung by **Lynne Dawson** and tastefully accompanied by the **Purcell Quartet** while, in between, **Robert Woolley**, as an interlude, winningly plays an inventive set of *Variations* on the famous 'La Follia'. Splendid recording and full texts and translations. Not to be missed.

Cantata per la Notte di Natale: Abramo, il tuo sembiante (Christmas Eve cantata)

⊕→ **** Naïve OP 30-156. Bertini, Fedi, Cavina, Naglia, Foresti, Concerto Italiano, Alessandrini – CORELLI: *Christmas concerto grosso in G min., Op. 6/8* ***

This delightful semi-operatic cantata presents the Nativity through the eyes of five figures from the Old Testament, Abraham (bass), Ezekiel (soprano), Isaiah (tenor), Jeremiah (alto) and Daniel (soprano), who are all together in Limbo, where they await the Messiah. There is splendid music for all the soloists, and especially the excellent male alto, **Claudio Cavina**, who, as Jeremiah, foresees and laments the coming suffering and death of Christ. The whole performance bursts with life under **Rinaldo Alessandrini**, and makes a fine entertainment, touching, but never solemn. Corelli's most famous *concerto grosso*, with its *Pastorale* closing movement, is used as a vivacious introduction. The recording sparkles and this is very highly recommended.

Motets: *Domine, refugium factus es nobis; O magnum mysterium*

⒝ *** Double Decca (ADD) 443 868-2 (2). Schütz Ch. of L., Roger Norrington – BONONCINI: *Stabat Mater* ***; PERGOLESI: *Magnificat in C; Stabat Mater* **(*); DOMENICO SCARLATTI: *Stabat Mater;* CALDARA: *Crucifixus;* LOTTI: *Crucifixus* ***

These two motets are fine pieces that show how enduring the Palestrina tradition was in 17th-century Italy. They are noble in conception and are beautifully performed here and, given first-class sound, make a fine bonus for this enterprising Double Decca collection of Italian baroque choral music.

La Giuditta (Oratorio)

Ⓝ *** Dynamic CDS 596. Landy, Pichon, Ghazarossian, Nice Bar. Ens., Bezzina

It appears that Scarlatti twice set the story of Judith from Bethulia (which is under siege by the Assyrians) and Holofernes, their leader, who is hoping to seduce her. The version which has survived and which is recorded here is known as the 'Cambridge' *Giuditta*, as its manuscript is held in the Rowe Music Library of King's College. There is no chorus, and three soloists carry the oratorio between them, Giuditta (soprano), Holofernes (tenor) and the Nurse (contralto) who has some of the finest music, including the sleep aria in Part II, *Dormi o fulmine di guerra*. The score consists of short recitatives and compressed arias and a few duets, which to some extent limits its lyrical expansiveness. The climax, when the Nurse sings the inebriated Holofernes to sleep so that Judith can take his sword and successfully cut off his head, lacks the kind of melodramatic drama one would expect. Even so, the scene works well lyrically, and the close of the oratorio, when Judith bravely returns to her people with Holofernes's head held high (!) is accompanied with her longest aria. *La Giuditta* is a fascinating discovery, and it is impressively performed here, with the essential full translation provided.

Oratorio per la Santissima Trinità

⊕→ **** Virgin 5 45666-2. Invernizzi, Gens, Genaux, Agnew, Abbondanza, Europa Galante Ens., Biondi

When, in 1715 in Naples, Alessandro Scarlatti wrote this, one of the last of his 40 oratorios, his music was coming to be regarded as out of date. It did not help that, unlike most of his religious oratorios, based on biblical sources, the subject was undramatic, a theological discussion on the doctrine of the Trinity, personalized in the allegorical figures of Faith, Divine Love, Theology, Time and Infidelity, that last improbably a tenor role, excellently taken here by **Paul Agnew**. What this fresh account of the oratorio under **Fabio Biondi** demonstrates throughout is the liveliness of Scarlatti's inspiration. The 49 sections last a little over an hour, with brief recitatives punctuating dozens of tiny arias and duets, almost all brisk. Outstanding in a first-rate team of soloists is the ravishing **Véronique Gens** as Divine Love.

(i) *Salve Regina;* (i; ii) *Stabat Mater;* (iii) Motet: *Quae est ista*

**(*) Virgin 5 45366-2. (i) Lesne; (ii) Piau; (i–iii) Novelli; Il Seminario Musicale

Gérard Lesne is heard at his finest in Scarlatti's eloquent A minor setting (one of five) of the *Salve Regina*, expressive and dramatic by turns. But when he joins with **Sandrine Piau** for the *Stabat Mater* the combination of voices is characterful in its contrast rather than a vocal symbiosis. Sandrine Piau's singing is pure, and tenderly touching, Lesne is more dramatic and brings a wider range of vocal colour, but his contribution is less moving. The two singers are successfully joined by the tenor **Jean-François Novelli** for the attractive closing motet, *Quae est ista*, which is widely varied in style; but again it is the soprano who stands out. **Il Seminario** give pleasing authentic support and this is a stimulating collection, but collectors primarily interested in the *Stabat Mater* will find that the performance by Gemma Bertagnolli and Sara Mingardo with the Concerto Italiano remains unsurpassed (see below).

Stabat Mater

❋— (B) **** Naïve OPS 30406. Bertagnolli, Mingardo, Concerto Italiano, Alessandrini – PERGOLESI: *Stabat Mater* *** ❋

If somewhat less theatrical than Pergolesi's setting, Scarlatti's music brings continual bursts of vitality to contrast with the rich flowing polyphonic lines when the soprano and alto voices are combined. There are memorably expressive solos for both singers and, as in the companion work, they combine touchingly for the work's closing benediction before the tension lifts at the coda. Once again both the radiant soprano, **Gemma Bertagnolli**, and the dark-voiced contralto, **Sara Mingardo**, rise fully to the challenge of this remarkable music, and **Alessandrini's** instrumental support could not be more persuasive or authentic.

SCARLATTI, Domenico
(1685–1757)

The Good-humoured Ladies (ballet suite; arr. Tommasini)

(***) Testament mono SBT 1309. Paris Conservatoire O, Désormière (with IPPOLITOV-IVANOV: *Caucasian Sketches, Op. 10*; TCHAIKOVSKY: *Sleeping Beauty: Suite* (***))

(BB) **(*) Sony (ADD) SBK 60311. Cleveland O, Lane – RESPIGHI: *The Birds; Church Windows* **(*)

The Good-humoured Ladies was a Diaghilev commission which enjoyed much success in its day; it draws on Scarlatti in much the same way as Stravinsky drew on Pergolesi in *Pulchinella*. Tommasini scores with great wit and **Roger Désormière** directs with unerring style and character. This 1951 performance, originally coupled with *Les biches*, is unlikely to be surpassed except in recording quality. It was produced (like the rest of the programme) by John Culshaw, and readers should snap it up.

Scarlatti's music in Tommasini's witty arrangement chatters along very like a group of dear old ladies gossiping over tea. **Louis Lane** directs freshly an enjoyable account of this delightfully light-hearted music, so wittily scored. The **Clevelanders** respond with style and delicacy, and the 1970 Severance Hall recording is warm and pleasing, even if ideally it could be a little more transparent. However, the so-called '*Cats' Fugue*' is neatly and clearly articulated, and Lane scores a bonus point by including the *Overture*.

Keyboard Sonatas (complete)

Vol. 1. Venice I & II (1752): *Essercizi per gravicembalo, Kk.1–30: Sonatas Kk.49; 98; 99; 129; 148–201* (Nim. 1725 (6))

Vol. 2. Venice III & IV (1753): *Sonatas Kk.206–95* (Nim. 1726 (6))

Vol. 3. Venice VI–VIII (1753–4): *Sonatas Kk.296–355; 358–87* (Nim. 1727 (6))

Vol. 4. Venice IX–XI (1754–6): *Sonatas Kk.388–451; 454–6; 388–451; 454–83* (Nim. 1728 (6))

Vol. 5. Venice XII–XIII (1756–7) *Sonatas Kk.484–543.* **(i)** *Continuo Sonatas, Kk.78; 81; 88–91* (with treble or descant recorders) (with HANDEL: *Sonata in F, HWV 405.* A. SCARLATTI: *Sinfonia in C min.* (both for treble recorders)) (Nim. 1729 (5))

Vol. 6. Venice XIV (1742): *Sonatas Kk.3; 10–12; 17; 31; 36–38; 43–77; 79–80; 82–87; 92–93.* **Venice XV** (1749): *Kk.96; 98–138* (Nim. 1730 (6))

Vol. 7. Appendices & Diversities: 23 *Sonatas* from existing and unpublished manuscripts, including *Kk.95; 97; 141–6*; Other Sources: Roseingrave: *Kk.31–42*. Parma: *Kk.202–3; 204a & b; 205; 356–7; 544–5*. Münster: *Kk.452/3* (Nim. 1731 (3) with Richard Lester (harpsichord or organ); and Lester and N. Evans (recorders))

48 'Favourite' Sonatas (selected from above)

(BB) **** Nim. 5822/3. Lester

Richard Lester's coverage of the complete Scarlatti keyboard sonatas is very impressive indeed; it has the great advantage both of economy and of being made available in seven separate boxes, so that the collector can dip into the collection and make a survey box at a time. Lester's credentials are impeccable but, more importantly, he is obviously very enthusiastic about this repertoire and his spontaneous playing conveys that dedication. His style is admirably flexible and altogether most winning. He uses three different harpsichords (copies of an impressive Portuguese instrument by José Jochim Antones, an English two-manual harpsichord, and a Ruckers single-manual instrument). The fortepiano is a copy of a 1795 instrument by Anton Walter.

The six *Continuo Sonatas* are not written for specific instruments and Lester has chosen to feature a pair of recorders, well played by **Elizabeth Lester** and **Nerys Evans**, and they throw in two of contemporary works by Handel and Alessandro Scarlatti for good measure. But this choice of instruments represents a slight miscalculation, for the result is somewhat bland, and it would have been wiser to use string instruments in some of the sonatas to offer more variety of timbre. In that way the Scott Ross Erato set scores. However, the Nimbus recording is of the highest quality, beautifully focused within an attractive acoustic – not too resonant. This set is well documented and can be highly recommended. At the very least, readers are urged to try the two-CD sampler, which opens with some brilliant displays of sparkling solo virtuosity.

Keyboard Sonatas (complete), plus Sonatas for Violin & Continuo; Violin and Oboe

(BB) *** Erato 2564 62092-2 (34). Scott Ross (harpsichord & organ), Huggett, Coin, Henry, Vallon

The outstanding integral recording of Scarlatti's 555 *Keyboard Sonatas* (originally issued for the composer's tercentenary) has reappeared, complete with the accompanying 200-page book at less than half the original price. They include works for violin and continuo, and for the unlikely combination of violin and oboe in unison. **Scott Ross** at the keyboard (harpsichord and organ) is joined by **Monica Huggett**, **Christophe Coin** and others and this excellently recorded set provides an endless source of interest and satisfaction.

Keyboard Sonatas, Kk.1; 20; 98; 159; 450; 487 (DVD version)

&— *** DG **DVD** 073 4045. Pogorelich (piano) (Director: Humphrey Burton) – BACH: *English Suites* 2 & 3 **(*); BEETHOVEN: *Piano Sonata* 11 **(*)

Ivo Pogorelich is at his most dazzling in these brilliant accounts of a well-chosen clutch of sonatas, crisply articulated on the piano. His tempi are brisk but never sound hurried. This is not the only way to play Scarlatti, but it is certainly involving, especially the well-known *C major* piece, Kk.159, which ends the recital infectiously. The camera watches his hands as well as taking overall shots, and the changes are not distracting. Good, clean, bright sound.

Keyboard Sonatas, Kk.1; 9; 14; 27; 38; 103; 114; 141; 208; 213; 296–9; 380; 490–92; 555

(M) **(*) Warner Elatus 2564 60030-2. Ross (harpsichord)

This is a well-chosen selection from **Scott Ross's** complete coverage of the *keyboard sonatas*, made in 1984–5. He plays freshly, perhaps a little didactically at times, but always very musically, and he is very well recorded. The harpsichord is not named.

Keyboard Sonatas, Kk.1; 3; 8–9; 11; 17; 24–5; 27; 29; 87; 96; 113; 141; 146; 173; 213–14; 247; 259; 268; 283–4; 380; 386–7; 404; 443; 519–20; 523

&— **** Virgin 5 61961-2 (2). Pletnev (piano)

This carefully chosen selection of some of Scarlatti's finest and most adventurous sonatas, stretches over two CDs, giving the fullest opportunity to demonstrate the extraordinary range of this music in a recital-length programme playing for 140 minutes. In the opening *D major Sonata*, Kk.443, **Pletnev** establishes a firm pianistic approach, yet the staccato articulation reminds us that the world of the harpsichord is not so far away. However, in the *G major Sonata*, Kk.283, and in the following Kk.284 his fuller piano sonority transforms the effect of the writing. The second CD opens with the almost orchestral Kk.96 *in D*, with its resonant horn calls, and later the lovely, flowing *C minor Sonata* and the even more expressive Kk.11 *in F sharp minor* bring a reflective poetic feeling, which could not have been matched in colour by the plucked instrument. The performances throughout are in the very front rank.

Keyboard Sonatas, Kk.1; 8–9; 11; 13; 20; 87; 98; 119; 135; 159; 380; 450; 487 & 529

&— **** DG 435 855-2. Pogorelich (piano)

Pogorelich plays with captivating simplicity and convinces the listener that this is music which sounds far more enjoyable on the piano than on the harpsichord. His dazzling execution, using the lightest touch, consistently enchants the ear with its subtle tonal colouring, and the music emerges ever sparkling and fresh. The hour-long programme is admirably chosen to provide maximum variety.

Keyboard Sonatas, Kk.9; 13 & 430

(M) **(*) Sony (ADD) SMK 87753. Gould (piano) – BACH: *Aria variata*; C. P. E. BACH: *Sonata* **(*)

Glenn Gould's precise articulation suits Scarlatti and these three varied *Sonatas* are full of life. Good, clear (if rather dry) recording to match.

Keyboard Sonatas, Kk.9; 27; 33; 69; 87; 96; 159; 193; 247; 427; 492; 531; Fugue in G min.; Kk.30

&— **(BB)** *** Warner Apex (ADD) 0927 44353-2. Queffélec (piano)

Anne Queffélec employs a modern Steinway with great character and aplomb. She immediately captures the listener in the dashing opening of the *D major Sonata*, Kk.96, with its lively fanfares and, in the gentler *B minor*, Kk.27, her rippling passage-work is Bach-like in its simplicity. She alternates reflective works with those sonatas calling for sparkling bravura and her choice is unerringly effective: the recital closes with the *Fugue*, which unfolds with calm inevitability. The 1970 recording is first class; the piano is naturally focused and has plenty of space without any resonant blurring.

Keyboard Sonatas; Kk. 11; 27; 159 & 322 (DVD Version)

&— *** Opus Arte **DVD** OA 0939D. Michelangeli – BEETHOVEN: *Piano Sonatas* 3 & 32; GALUPPI: *Sonata* ***

Recorded at a recital in Turin in 1962, these are a model of delicacy and refinement. **Michelangeli** always played Scarlatti with a special distinction that only Horowitz, Queffélec and Pletnev have matched in recent times. Very good sound.

Keyboard Sonatas, Kk. 20; 24; 27; 30; 87; 197; 365; 426; 427; 429; 435; 448; 455; 466; 487; 492; 545; in G min.

&— **** BIS-CD 1508. Sudbin (piano)

Yevgeny Sudbin finds, besides much to charm the ear, an infinite expressive depth in many of the minor key works, which are played here with appealing expressive freedom. (Sample Kk.87 or Kk.197 in B minor or the delicacy of Kk.466 in F minor.) From the very opening B flat major work we are aware that this is a modern piano, but how well it suits these innovative and infinitely diverse *Sonatas*. There is sparkle and brilliance here too, and Sudbin can be both strong and delectably light-fingered. He is splendidly recorded, and this can be placed among the finest and most generous of recent single-disc Scarlatti collections (76 minutes).

Keyboard Sonatas: Kk.20; 32; 39; 79; 109; 124–5; 128; 342; 381; 394; 425; 454; 470; 491; 495; 547; 551

🎧 **BB** ******** EMI Encore 5 74968-2. Tipo (piano)

Maria Tipo's 18 Scarlatti *Sonatas* first appeared in 1989 and sound every bit as good now as they did then. Tipo has not gained the wider recognition for which her artistry entitles her, but this recital shows her in the best possible light. Her range of keyboard colour is wide and her sense of dynamic contrast strong, but she never uses them simply to make effect. This record is an unmissable bargain.

Keyboard Sonatas, Kk.25; 33; 39; 52; 54; 96; 146; 162; 197–8; 201; 260; 303; 319; 466; 474; 481; 491; 525; 547

(B) ****(*)** Sony (ADD) 517487-2. Horowitz (piano)

Provided you are prepared to accept sometimes less than flattering and often rather dry recorded sound, this is marvellous playing, which sweeps away any purist notions about Scarlatti having to be played on the harpsichord. The 20 sonatas were chosen by **Horowitz** after he had recorded nearly twice as many throughout 1964.

Keyboard Sonatas, Kk.32; 64; 69; 87; 133; 146; 160; 198; 208; 213; 380; 429; 466; 481; 511; 517; Toccata in D min.

(B) ****(*)** Cal. CAL 6670. Södergren (piano)

Inger Södergren gives an appealing recital of 16 well-contrasted *Sonatas* plus a brilliant account of the highly individual *Toccata in D minor*. Some might feel that her gentle, almost wistful treatment of the lyrical sonatas errs towards being too romantic, but her keen sensitivity and crisp articulation in the lively pieces are unimpeachable, and she is very well recorded.

Keyboard Sonatas, Kk.46; 87; 99; 124; 201; 204a; 490–2; 513; 520–1

(M) ******* CRD (ADD) CRD 3368. Pinnock (harpsichord)

No need to say much about this: the playing is first rate and the recording outstanding in its presence and clarity. There are few better harpsichord anthologies of Scarlatti in the catalogue, although the measure is not particularly generous.

Keyboard Sonatas: Kk. 64; 87; 96; 108; 118–19; 132–3; 141; 175; 198; 202–3; 213–14; 263–4; 277–8; 420–1; 454–5; 460–1; 490–2; 501–2; 516–19

🎧 **(B)** ******** DHM 82876 67375-2 (2). Staier (harpsichord)

We welcomed **Andreas Staier's** Haydn sonata collection with much enthusiasm. He seems equally at home with the music of Scarlatti, and he characterizes each of these *Sonatas* vividly and with real imagination. This pair of CDs (originally published in 1991/2) may well have been planned to be part of an integral collection which was never completed. In any event the choice of repertoire is fruitful; playing (and record-

ing) of this quality has no need to fear even the most exalted competition. A strongly recommended reissue.

Keyboard Sonatas, Kk.159; 175; 208; 213; 322 & 380 (arr. for guitar)

BB ******* Sony (ADD) SBK 62425. Williams (guitar) – GIULIANI: *Variations on a Theme by Handel*; PAGANINI: *Caprice*; *Grand Sonata*; VILLA-LOBOS: *5 Preludes* *******

Guitar arrangements of Scarlatti *Sonatas* have their charms when played by an artist as imaginative as **John Williams**. He manages by percussive plucking to sound at times almost like a harpsichord, while his gentle playing is always beguiling, especially in the delightful *D major Sonata*, Kk.159. The recording is faithful, somewhat close and larger than life, but never unacceptably so. This diverse and well-planned recital (76 minutes) is very enjoyable indeed.

VOCAL MUSIC

Cantatas: Che vidi, oh Ciel, che vidi; O qual mecco Nice; Pur nel sonno almen tal'ora. Sinfonia

**(*) Astrée Naïve E 8673. Gerstenberger, Musique des Lumières, Frisch

Although these cantatas were written for the castrato voice, they suit a high soprano very well. Each is quite extended, but it is *Pur nel sonno almen tal'ora* ('Even in slumber, the lady of my heart appears to comfort me in my sorrow') with its flute obbligato which is especially delightful. The other two works are more theatrical, and **Cyrille Gerstenberger** sings them vividly, with plenty of temperament. However, Scarlatti's writing is often richly expressive too and her cantabile line is always affecting. The accompaniments, on period instruments, are at times curiously abrasive. Full texts and translations are provided.

Cantata: Doppo lungo servire

**(*) MDG 309 0632-2. Wessel, Musica Alta Ripa (with
    FRANCESCO SCARLATTI: *Cantata in un'ostante*) –
    ALESSANDRO SCARLATTI: *Sonatas & Cantatas* ****(*)**

Scarlatti's pastoral cantata is about the troubles of Filenus, who cannot persuade the fickle Phyllis to respond to his advances, and it ends with his melancholy siciliana. It is very well performed, but not all will take to **Kai Wessel's** male alto timbre. The documentation is first class.

Salve Regina

🎧 ******** Analekta FL 2 3171. Lemieux, Tafelmusik, Lamon (with
    AVISON: *Concerto grossi after Scarlatti 7*) – VIVALDI: *Stabat Mater*, etc. *******

Domenico Scarlatti's beautiful setting of the *Salve Regina* is gloriously sung here and is paired with an equally fine performance of Vivaldi's *Stabat Mater*, plus some attractive Vivaldi string concertos to make up a balanced concert. The inclusion of one of Avison's concertos transcribed from Scarlatti sonatas seems rather appropriate.

Stabat Mater

(B) ******* Double Decca (ADD) 443 868-2 (2). Schütz Ch. of L.,

Norrington – BONONCINI: *Stabat Mater* ***; PERGOLESI: *Magnificat in C; Stabat Mater* **(*); A. SCARLATTI: *Domine, refugium factus es nobis; O magnum mysterium;* CALDARA: *Crucifixus;* LOTTI: *Crucifixus* ***

Norrington's performance is admirable, though not always impeccable in matters of tonal balance; and the recording is very good. Overall this well-designed Double Decca set combines three fine *Stabat Mater* settings with other comparable baroque choral music, all well performed and impressively recorded.

Stabat Mater; Cibavit nos Dominus; Magnificat; Missa breve (La Stella); Te Deum

Ⓑ *** Naxos 8.570382. Immortal Bach Ens., Schuldt-Jensen

Stabat Mater; Laetatus sum (Psalm 121); Magnificat; Te Deum; Miserere in E min.

Ⓝ Ⓑ *** EMI Encore 2 35735-2. King's College, Cambridge, Ch., Cleobury

Stabat Mater; Miserere; Salve Regina; Te Deum Laudamus; Organ Sonatas, Kk.87 & Kk 417

*** Ricercar RIC 258. Vox Luminis

Both the Naxos and Ricercar performances feature less than a dozen singers, accompanied by a continuo including a chamber organ, which on the Ricercar disc plays two of the composer's keyboard *Sonatas* as a bonus, and very well too. The **Immortal Bach Ensemble** sing warmly and sensitively, and offer equally fine accounts of the enterprising bonuses. However, the Dutch **Vox Luminis**, who appear to sing without a conductor, are finer still, richly expressive, sonorous, and very touching in the four-part *Miserere* and two-part *Salve Regina*.

On EMI, **King's College Choir** also offer a fine representative collection of Scarlatti's church music, freshly and atmospherically performed in the reverberant acoustic of King's Chapel. The most ambitious piece here is the *Stabat Mater*, described as being in ten parts (though the full ten are reserved for special moments); and the work which most impressively demonstrates Scarlatti's skill with polyphony is the *Magnificat* in four parts, with its superb climax in the *Gloria*. The other works are also given dedicated performances and are all very well recorded.

SCHARWENKA, Franz Xaver (1850–1924)

Piano Concertos 2 in C min., Op. 56; 3 in C sharp min., Op. 80

*** Hyp. CDA 67365. Tanyel, Hanover R. Philharmonie des NDR, Strugala

These two *Concertos* bristle with technical challenges of which **Seta Tanyel** makes light. She is fully equal to their technical demands and takes them comfortably in her stride. The *Second Concerto* comes from 1880, and the debt to both

Chopin and Hummel can be clearly discerned. He gave the first performance of the *Third* in Berlin in 1899 to much acclaim – understandably so, given the quality of the central *Adagio*. Tanyel not only copes with the virtuoso demands of Scharwenka's writing but is a very musical player. Excellent support from **Tadeusz Strugala** and the **Hanover Radio Orchestra**, and a first-class (1996) recording.

Piano Concerto 4 in F min., Op. 82

🎧 *** Hyp. CDA 66790. Hough, CBSO, Foster – SAUER: *Piano Concerto 1* ***

Scharwenka wrote four piano concertos; this, his finest, was very famous in its time. It is ambitiously flamboyant and on the largest scale. Its invention, which manages a potent mix of bravura and lyricism, readily holds the attention, with plenty of interest in the bold orchestral tuttis. The second-movement *Allegretto* has much charm and is very deftly scored; a full flood of romanticism blossoms in the *Lento* slow movement. The stormy *con fuoco* finale combines a touch of wit and more robust geniality with glittering brilliance and power; and all four movements make prodigious technical and artistic demands on the soloist, to which **Stephen Hough** rises with great technical aplomb and consistent panache; he also plays with fine poetic sensibility. He is given vigorously committed support by **Lawrence Foster** and the **CBSO** and a first-class Hyperion recording.

SCHIERBECK, Poul
(1888–1949)

The Chinese Flute, Op. 10

(**(*)) Bluebell mono ABCD 075. Nilsson, Swedish Radio O, Mann – BARTÓK: *Bluebeard's Castle* (**(*))

The Chinese Flute, Op. 10; Queen Dagmar; The Tinder-Box, Op. 61

🎧 *** dacapo 224104. Dam-Jensen, Dolberg, Larsen, Van Hal, Dreyer, Odense SO, Bellincampi

Schierbeck belongs to the generation midway between Nielsen and Vagn Holmboe. Until recently he was unrepresented in the catalogue, now no fewer than three versions of his charming songs *The Chinese Flute*, to poems by Hans Bethge, which inspired many composers, not least Mahler in *Das Lied*, are available and the present issue also brings the cantata *Dronning Dagmar* ('Queen Dagmar'). The melodrama *Fyrtøjet* ('The Tinder-Box'), based on Hans Andersen, is both inventive and imaginative. This is an excellent introduction to a gifted minor master. **Inger Dam-Jensen** is excellent in the Bethge settings, and the orchestral playing and recording are first class.

Nilsson's first recording was in 1946 of an aria from Berwald's *Estrella di Soria*, and this recording of *The Chinese Flute* comes from a Swedish Radio broadcast two years later. What a voice! It comes with a haunting but unaccountably cut *Bluebeard's Castle* under Fricsay.

SCHMIDT, Franz (1874–1939)

Symphonies 1–4

⊕ (M) **** Chan. 9568 (4). Detroit SO, Järvi

Chandos have now boxed their individual releases of the symphonies into a four-CD set, discarding the fill-ups. The *First Symphony* was composed during Schmidt's early to mid-20s and, as one might expect, is derivative, even if his orchestration is masterly. Right from the start, one is left in no doubt that Schmidt is a born symphonic composer with a real feeling for the long-breathed line and the natural growth flow of ideas. He began work on the *Second Symphony* on leaving the Vienna Philharmonic in 1911 and finished two years later. The *Third* (1927–8) is a richly imaginative score in the romantic tradition, though it yields pride of place among the symphonies to the elegiac, valedictory *Fourth* (1933–4), whose nobility and depth of feeling shine through every bar. The **Detroit Symphony Orchestra** under **Neeme Järvi** play with a freshness and enthusiasm that is totally persuasive. They almost sound Viennese and the recordings are very good indeed.

Clarinet Quintet 2 in A (for clarinet, piano & strings)

⊕ *** Marco 8.223414. Jánoska, Mucha, Lakatos, Slávik, Ruso

The *Quintet in A major for Clarinet, Piano and Strings* is unusual: it begins like some mysterious other-worldly scherzo which immediately introduces a pastoral idea of beguiling charm. The second movement is a piano piece in ternary form; there is a longish Scherzo, full of fantasy and wit, and there is an affecting trio, tinged with the melancholy of late Brahms. The fourth movement sets out as if it, too, is going to be a long, meditative piano piece, but its nobility and depth almost put one in mind of the Elgar *Quintet*. The fifth is a set of variations on a theme of Josef Labor, and is sometimes played on its own. The recording has freshness and bloom, though it could benefit from a bigger recording venue. This is a glorious work.

Piano Quintet in G (arr. Wührer)

*** Australian Decca Eloquence (ADD) 476 2455. Mrasek, VPO Qt – BRUCKNER: *String Quartet in F* ***

Franz Schmidt's *Piano Quintet in G* is rewarding music, full of unexpected touches; it is also possessed of genuine nobility, as one would expect from the composer of the *Fourth Symphony*. The performance is elegant and beautifully recorded in the Sofiensaal in 1974.

Das Buch mit sieben Siegeln (The Book with 7 Seals)

⊕ **** Chan. **SACD** CHSA 5061 (2). Chum, Holl, Trattnigg, Breedt, Schukoff, Hemm, Wiener Singverein, Tonkünstler-Orchester Niederösterreich, K. Järvi

(BB) *** EMI Gemini 5 85782-2 (2). Oelze, Kallisch, Andersen, Odinius, Pape, Reiter, Bav. R. Ch. & SO, Welser-Möst; Winklhofer (organ)

The latest recording of Franz Schmidt's masterpiece is recorded in the Vienna Musikverein and is a live performance. The tenor **Johannes Chum** is a fine St John and **Robert Holl** a no less impressive Voice of the Lord. Although memories of Mitropoulos's account with Anton Dermota and Fritz Wunderlich are not wholly eclipsed, this newcomer, recorded in 2005, must claim pride of place, not only for the excellence of the recorded sound, but for the fervour and dedication of the performance.

This EMI bargain version of Schmidt's *Book with Seven Seals* was recorded live in the Herculessaal in 1997 and is played by the magnificent **Bavarian Radio Orchestra** with the **Bavarian Radio Chorus** under **Franz Welser-Möst**, who shows great sympathy for the score. The soloists are excellent. However, no texts are included.

SCHMITT, Florent (1870–1958)

Symphony 2, Op. 137; La Danse d'Abisag, Op. 75; (i) Habeyssée (suite for violin and orchestra), Op. 110; Rêves, Op. 65

*** Marco 8.223689. (i) Segerstam; Rheinland-Pfalz PO, Segerstam

La Danse d'Abisag, like the much earlier *Tragédie de Salomé*, has a biblical theme: unlike Salome, Abisag, despite her erotic dancing, fails to arouse the ageing monarch (King David). *Symphony 2* was no mean achievement for a composer in his 88th year! In terms of orchestral expertise and flair, it is second to none, and the opulence of its palette and its imaginative vitality are remarkable. *Rêves* is an early piece, inspired by a poem by Léon-Paul Fargue and appropriately atmospheric; and *Habeyssée*, said to be inspired by an Islamic legend, is a three-movement suite for violin and orchestra. This is a rewarding issue which offers some good playing from the **Rheinland-Pfalz Orchestra** under **Segerstam**, who excels in this repertoire. Good recording too.

La tragédie de Salomé (ballet; Suite); (i) Psalm 47, Op. 38

(BB) *** Warner Apex 2564 62764-2. (i) Sweet, Fr. R. Ch.; Gill, Fr. R. Philh. O, Janowski

Schmitt's setting of *Psalm 47* dates from his last year as a Prix de Rome scholar at the Villa Medici, and is a stirring and imposing piece which contrasts two aspects of the great books of exaltation and jubilation: the tenderness and voluptuousness of the *Song of Songs*. Good performances from the **Orchestre Philharmonique de Radio France** under **Marek Janowski**. Eminently recommendable – save for **Sharon Sweet's** wide and ugly vibrato.

Piano trio: Très lent

(BB) **(*) Naxos 8.550934. Joachim Trio – DEBUSSY; RAVEL: *Piano Trios* **(*)

This three-minute fragment, about which the notes are uninformative, is rather haunting and, like the rest of the programme, beautifully played and recorded.

SCHNITTKE, Alfred (1934–98)

Viola Concerto (DVD version)

*** TDK **DVD** DV-VPOVG. Bashmet, VPO, Gergiev (includes Bashmet talking about Schnittke; Gergiev talking on Prokofiev and Stravinsky). Director and VD: Brian Large – PROKOFIEV: *Symphony 1 (Classical), Op. 25*; STRAVINSKY: *Firebird Complete Ballet* ***

Schnittke's *Viola Concerto* is made up of two *Largos* surrounding a fast, often violent, central movement, the mood swinging between a pensive brooding and frenetic activity. It is certainly written well for the viola, and **Yuri Bashmet** plays it with great intensity and dedication. Whether one warms to the music or not, it communicates very directly here to the viewer/listener. The orchestral tuttis are sometimes wildly explosive, and **Gergiev's** face registers their demonic force as he directs the orchestra with enormous conviction. The documentary is a considerable bonus, but it is for the fine performance of *The Firebird* that most collectors will seek out this DVD.

Violin Concertos 1–2

*** BIS CD 487. Lubotsky, Malmö SO, Klas

The *First Violin Concerto* inhabits a post-romantic era. Its lyricism is profoundly at variance with its successor of 1966, commissioned by **Mark Lubotsky**, the soloist on this record. Here the central concept is what Schnittke calls 'a certain drama of tone colours', and there is no doubt that much of it is vividly imagined and strongly individual. The double-bass is assigned a special role of a caricatured 'anti-soloist'. There is recourse to the once fashionable aleatoric technique, but this is all within carefully controlled parameters. The **Malmö Orchestra** under **Eri Klas** play with evident feeling in both works and are very well recorded. This is an altogether highly satisfactory coupling.

(i) Gogol Suite (compiled Rozhdestvensky); Labyrinths

*** BIS CD 557. Malmö SO, Markiz; (i) with Kontra

There is a surrealistic quality to the *Gogol Suite* reminiscent of Gogol's own words quoted in Jürgen Köchel's note: 'The world hears my laughter; my tears it does not see nor recognize.' *Labyrinths* is a ballet score composed in 1971, thin in development and musical ideas but sufficiently strong in atmosphere to survive the transition from stage to concert hall. The **Malmö Orchestra** under **Lev Markiz** play very well and the recording is in the demonstration class.

Symphony 1

*** Chan. 9417. Russian State SO, Rozhdestvensky

Schnittke's *First Symphony* is a huge radical canvas lasting some 68 minutes. It is essentially a musical gesture, a tirade rather than a symphony of protest and anger which sounds pretty thin now. **Rozhdestvensky's** performance is committed, and the recording, made at a public performance in the Moscow Conservatoire in 1988, is well detailed. There is more rhetoric than substance here. The three stars are allotted for the performance and recording; for the composition the stars can be aleatoric!

(i) Symphony 4; (ii) 3 Sacred Hymns

*** Chan. 9463. (i) Zdorov, Pianov; (i–ii) Russian State Symphonic Cappella; (i) Russian State SO; Polyansky

The *Fourth Symphony* draws on Christian (Catholic, Lutheran and Russian Orthodox) and Jewish chant and is avowedly religious in programme, reflecting episodes in the life of the Virgin Mary. It is scored for two singers, one a counter-tenor, chorus and orchestra; it also makes inventive and colourful use of keyboard sonorities. Both the performance and the recording are of high quality, but the piece seems too concerned with gesture and is essentially empty of musical substance. The *Three Sacred Hymns* for *a cappella* choir from 1983 are both eloquent and beautiful.

Symphony 8; The Census List: Suite

🎵 **** Chan. 9885. Russian State SO, Polyansky; with (i) Butenin (nar.)

Symphony 8; (i) Concerto Grosso 6

*** Chan. 9359. Stockholm RSO, G. Rozhdestvensky, with (i) S. Rozhdestvensky; Postnikova

Symphony 8 is one of the most moving of Schnittke's later works. In it he develops a sparer style, often angular but warmly lyrical, reflecting his inspiration over a five-movement structure in the sections of the Mass. Earlier works were similarly inspired from spiritual sources, but this most clearly of all, with a rising scale figure a symbolic element. **Polyansky** directs a warmly expressive performance, opulently recorded, with the generous coupling providing a delightful contrast. The incidental music to a play drawn from Gogol, *The Census List*, dates from 1978; it is pastiche writing designed as a cheeky thrust at Soviet authority, with witty parodies over the eight movements. The fifth involves a narrator, **Lev Butenin**, reciting a satirical poem about Ferdinand VIII.

Rozhdestvensky and the **Stockholm Orchestra** give a powerful, warmly committed performance, if not quite so sharply focused as Polyansky's, also on Chandos. The fill-up is less generous but arguably more apt: written in 1993 for the Rozhdestvensky family in Schnittke's neo-classical manner, it is much drier than the *Symphony* and again is very well played by the dedicatees.

Cello Sonata

*** BIS CD 336. Thedéen, Pöntinen – STRAVINSKY: *Suite italienne*; SHOSTAKOVICH: *Sonata* ***

The *Cello Sonata* is a powerfully expressive piece, its avant-garde surface enshrining a neo-romantic soul. **Torleif Thedéen** is a refined and intelligent player who gives a thoroughly committed account of this piece with his countryman, **Roland Pöntinen**.

Piano Quintet

🎵 Ⓑ🅱 **** Naxos 8.554830-2. Berman, Vermeer Qt – SHOSTAKOVICH: *Piano Quintet* ***

*** ECM 461 815-2. Lubimov, Keller Qt – SHOSTAKOVICH: *String Quartet 15* ***

Like the Shostakovich *Piano Quintet*, with which it is aptly coupled, the Schnittke *Piano Quintet* of 1972–5 is one of the composer's most poignant and haunting works. Dedicated to the memory of his mother, and darkly elegiac, it was finished in the year of Shostakovich's death. Its mood of gloom, unrelieved except for a painfully plaintive waltz in the second of the five movements, inspires **Berman** and the **Vermeers** to a performance as powerfully concentrated as that of the Shostakovich; if the CBC studios in Toronto do not always flatter their tone, this a real bargain.

The anguished *Piano Quintet* is also deeply felt and powerful in the hands of **Lubimov** and the **Keller Quartet**. Good recording too.

Piano Trio

🎧 *** Nim. NI 5572. V. Piano Trio – SHOSTAKOVICH: *Trios, Opp. 8 & 67* ***

Schnittke's *Piano Trio* has its origins in a string trio written in 1985. In 1987 it was transcribed as the *Trio Sonata for Chamber Orchestra* and then in 1992 put into its present form. The **Vienna Piano Trio** give as convincing a performance as you are ever likely to hear, and they certainly get superb recorded sound.

Prelude in Memoriam Shostakovich (for 2 solo violins)

*** Chan. 8988. Mordkovitch, Young – PROKOFIEV; SHOSTAKOVICH: *Violin Sonatas* ***

The Schnittke *Prelude* for two solo violins is the shortest of the works on **Lydia Mordkovitch's** excellent disc of Soviet violin music, but it is among the most moving in its intense, elegiac way. She is well matched by her partner, **Emma Young**.

Violin Sonata 1; Sonata in the Olden Style

*** Chan. 8343. Dubinsky, Edlina – SHOSTAKOVICH: *Violin Sonata* ***

Schnittke's *First Sonata* is a well-argued piece that seems to unify his awareness of the post-serial musical world with the tradition of Shostakovich. On this version it is linked with a pastiche of less interest, dating from 1977. Excellent playing from both artists, and very good recording too.

Piano Sonata

🎧 *** Chan. 8962. Berman – STRAVINSKY: *Serenade*, etc. ***

Berman gives as persuasive an account of Schnittke's *Piano Sonata* as it is possible to imagine. He is very well recorded, too, and the three Stravinsky pieces with which it comes are also given with great pianistic elegance.

SCHOECK, Othmar (1886–1957)

(i) Concerto for cello & strings, Op. 62. Cello Sonata; Six Song transcriptions

Ⓝ 🎧 *** BIS-CD–1597. Poltéra, Drake, (i) with Malmö SO, Ollila

Although best known for his songs, some 300 in number, plus the remarkable cycle, *Lebendigbegraben*, and several operas, the Swiss composer Othmar Schoeck composed concertos for violin, horn, and in the last decade of his life, the *Cello Concerto*, which Pierre Fournier premièred in 1948. This has a strong vein of melancholy and a poignant eloquence redolent of the previous century. It is a work characterized by great lyrical intensity and depth of feeling, beautifully conveyed here by his countryman, **Christian Poltéra**, with the Swedish **Malmö Orchestra**. Poltéra also gives us the three-movement *Cello Sonata* which the composer left incomplete on his death. Deeply satisfying music, impeccably played and equally impeccably recorded.

Elegie (song cycle), Op. 36

🎧 ✪ Ⓜ **** CPO 999 472-2. Schmidt, Winterthur Music Collegium, Albert

The *Elegie*, Op. 36, has been described as 'a narrative of a dying love' and to some extent charts the turbulent course of the composer's affair with the pianist Mary de Senger. The cycle comprises twenty-four short but concentrated settings of poems by Lenau and Eichendorff, and is for baritone and a small instrumental ensemble, used with great subtlety and resource. The songs are powerfully evocative and beautifully fashioned; each one immediately establishes its own atmosphere within a bar or two, and draws the listener completely into its world. Almost any would serve as an example but particularly potent is the third, *Stille Sicherheit*, which is extraordinarily concentrated in feeling, or the wonderfully haunting *Vesper*, with its tolling bells and almost tangible half lights. This is deeply felt music with a wonderful sense of line, and **Andreas Schmidt** sings with tremendous conviction. **Werner Andreas Albert** gets very sensitive and supportive playing from the **Winterthur ensemble** and the CPO recording is first class.

OPERA

Venus (complete)

*** MGB Musikszene Schweiz CD 6112 (2). Lang, Popp, O'Neal, Fassbaender, Skovhus, Alföldi, Heidelberg Kammer Ch., Basle Boys' Ch., Swiss Youth PO, Venzago

Venus is based on a libretto by Schoeck's school-friend, Armin Rüeger, and comes from Ovid, though Rüeger sets the action in a country castle in the south of France. **Venzago's** conducting radiates total dedication, and so does the playing of the young **Swiss Orchestra**. The opening scene almost prompts one's thoughts to turn to the Strauss of *Ariadne*, but as the opera unfolds Venzago's view of the work as partly 'an enormous orchestral poem (exposition, development, Scherzo and recapitulation) with obbligato voices' seems more and more valid. The sheer quality of the invention is notable and many of the ideas, particularly the Venus motive, have great tenderness and delicacy. Good and atmospheric recording.

SCHOENBERG, Arnold
(1874–1951)

Chamber Symphonies: (i; ii) 1, Op. 9; (ii) 2, Op. 38; (iii) 5 Orchestral Pieces, Op. 16; Variations for Orchestra, Op. 31; (iv) Verklaerte Nacht, Op. 4; (v) Ewartung

(N) (BB) *** EMI 2 CD 2 06785-2 (2). (i) Birmingham
Contemporary Music Group, Rattle; (ii) ECO, Tate;
(iii; v) CBSO, Rattle; (iv) Artemis Qt (augmented);
(v) Bryn-Julson

In *Chamber Symphony 1* **Rattle**, with fifteen players from the **Birmingham Contemporary Music Group**, springs rhythms infectiously, yet relaxedly bringing out the thrust of the argument. The playing may not be as bitingly crisp as in some rival versions, but there is no question of missing the heart behind the composer's severe intellectual writing, which is given far more character than usual, thanks to both conductor and players. **Jeffrey Tate's** approach to 2 is persuasive in his own way, presenting the music with heartfelt warmth, while the rich **ECO** ensemble, well presented in radiant EMI sound, gives it the necessary weight combined with ample clarity of detail. In the *Five Orchestral Pieces* Rattle is again at his finest, bringing out the music's red-blooded strength, neither too austere nor too plushy, helped by sound of demonstration standard. By contrast, he is daringly expansive in the *Variations* of 1928, even more so than Karajan on his classic recording with the Berlin Philharmonic. The Birmingham players may not always be as refined as the Berliners, but they play with even greater emotional thrust and with a keener sense of mystery, while heightened dynamic contrasts add to the dramatic bite. Equally, in Schoenberg's taxing atonal vocal lines, **Phyllis Bryn-Julson** sings with a clarity and definition to coax the ear instead of assaulting it, giving a more vulnerable portrait than usual, tender and compelling. The chamber performance of *Verklaerte Nacht* by the augmented **Artemis Quartet** is equally telling in its passionate feeling and powerful atmosphere.

Chamber Symphonies 1–2, Opp. 9 & 38; Verklaerte Nacht, Op. 4

⌐ (BB) **** Warner Apex 0927 44399-2. COE, Holliger

Schoenberg's *Chamber Symphonies* are superbly performed by the **COE**, played with both warmth and thrust, with complex textual problems masterfully solved. *Verklaerte Nacht* in its orchestral version receives one of its most passionate performances on disc, reflecting 'the glow of inmost warmth' in the Richard Dehmel poem which inspired it. This new coupling makes an excellent bargain on the Apex label, and the sound is first-rate.

(i) Chamber Symphony 1; (ii) Verklaerte Nacht; (i–iii) Gurrelider

⌐ (B) **** Double Decca 473 728-2 (2). (i) Concg. O;
(ii) Berlin RSO; (iii) Jerusalem, Dunn, Fassbaender, Brecht,
Haage, Hotter, St Hedwig's Cathedral Ch., Berlin,
Düsseldorf State Musikverein; all cond. Chailly

Chailly's magnificent (1985) recording of Schoenberg's massive *Gurrelieder* is among the finest of modern versions and, if that weren't enough, for this Double Decca reissue the considerable bonus of *Verklaerte Nacht* and *Chamber Symphony 1* have been added. If these performances are not in the same league as the *Gurrelieder*, they are still very worthwhile. The **Berlin** recording of *Gurrelieder* is full and rich, well detailed and balanced, and conveys a natural dramatic tension not easy to find in studio conditions. **Siegfried Jerusalem** as Waldemar is not only warmer and firmer of tone than most of his rivals but more imaginative too. **Susan Dunn** makes a sweet, touchingly vulnerable Tove, while **Brigitte Fassbaender** gives darkly baleful intensity to the message of the Wood-dove. **Hans Hotter** is a characterful Speaker in the final section. The impact of the performance is the more telling with sound both atmospheric and immediate, bringing a fine sense of presence, not least in the final choral outburst. Texts and translations are included, and this is an undoubted bargain.

(i) Piano concerto, Op. 42; Pieces, Op. 11 & 19

⌐ **** Ph. 468 033-2. Uchida; (i) Cleveland O, Boulez –
BERG: *Piano Sonata*; WEBERN: *Variations* ***

Mitsuko Uchida is logically coupled, and she and **Boulez** and the **Cleveland Orchestra** give us a keenly articulate account of the *Piano Concerto* that may well reach home to a wider audience than before. There is both delicacy and lyrical feeling. She is also very persuasive in the Opp. 11 and 19 *Klavierstücke*. The Philips recording has both clarity and warmth. Those who have not responded even to the Brendel account should try this beautifully recorded piece.

Concerto for String Quartet & Orchestra after Handel's Concerto Grosso, Op. 6/7

(BB) *** Warner Apex 7559 79675-2. American Qt., NYCO,
Schwarz – R. STRAUSS: *Divertimento (after Couperin)* ***

*** Ara. Z 6723. San Francisco Ballet O, Lark Qt, Le Roux –
HANDEL: *Concerto grosso in B flat, Op. 6/7*; ELGAR:
Introduction & Allegro for Strings; SPOHR: *Concerto for
String Quartet & Orchestra* ***

Schoenberg virtually recomposed Handel's Op. 6/7 for string quartet and orchestra, offering a rich spicing of dissonance. The result, inflated to nearly twice the size of the original, is at times grotesque, but always aurally fascinating and entertaining. The performance by the excellent **American Quartet** with the **New York Chamber Orchestra** under **Gerard Schwarz** is spirited and given bright, lively sound. The coupling too is particularly desirable, and the price will surely tempt the collector to explore this excellent CD.

The **San Francisco** performance also has plenty of edge, vitality and colour and it was a bright idea to include Handel's original (in a performance for full modern strings) so the listener can switch back and forth between the two utterly different sound-worlds.

Pelleas und Melisande; Verklaerte Nacht

⌐ (M) **** DG 457 721-2. BPO, Karajan

The Straussian opulence of Schoenberg's early symphonic poem has never been as ravishingly presented as by **Karajan** and the **Berlin Philharmonic** in this splendidly recorded version. The gorgeous tapestry of sound is both rich and full of refinement and detail, while the thrust of argument is powerfully conveyed. These are superb performances which present the emotional element at full power but give unequalled precision and refinement. They make an ideal candidate for separate reissue in DG's series of Originals.

5 Orchestral Pieces (DVD version)

*** Ideale-Audience **DVD** 3. Netherlands R. PO, Gielen –
STRAVINSKY: 'The Final Chorale' – a documentary about the Symphony of Wind Instruments ***

This is a most illuminating feature by Frank Scheffer that follows the genesis and musical development of the Five Orchestral Pieces of Schoenberg. **Michael Gielen** rehearses and performs this revolutionary piece, and there are contributions from **Carl Schorske** and **Charles Rosen**, as well as some archival footage. A fascinating study (available from www.ideale-audience.dot.com.) that will deepen your understanding of this strange and disturbing music.

(i) Suite in G for String Orchestra; (ii) String Quartet 2, Op. 10; (iii) 6 a cappella Mixed Choruses

(BB) *** Naxos 8.557521. (i) Twentieth Century Classics Ens.; (ii) Fred Sherry Qt, with Welch-Babbage; (iii) Simon Joly Singers; Craft

Schoenberg famously said that there is plenty of music still to be written in C major, and here in his six *a cappella Choruses* he deliberately relaxes in setting 16th-century German folksongs, harmonizing them in his own distinctive way. Three were written in 1948, not long before he died, following up the three he had composed 20 years earlier, all superbly sung here by the **Simon Joly Singers**. The *String Quartet 2* is distinctive in having a vocal part in the last two of the four movements, with **Jennifer Welch-Babbage** ideally cast, her fresh, clear soprano as precise as any instrument. The texts of the poems by Stefan George are provided, as are the words for the six *a cappella Choruses*. The *Suite in G* of 1934, less demanding, makes an apt coupling. The vocal pieces were recorded in London, the instrumental in New York, both in superb sound.

Variations for Orchestra, Op. 31

🔗 (M) **** DG (ADD) 457 760-2. BPO, Karajan – BERG: Lyric Suite, etc.; WEBERN: Passacaglia ***

Karajan's version of the *Variations* is altogether magical and very much in a class of its own. There is a tremendous intensity and variety of tone and colour: the palette that the strings of the **Berlin Philharmonic** have at their command is altogether extraordinarily wide-ranging.

Verklaerte Nacht

(BB) **** Virgin 2x1 4 82112-2 (2). Sinfonia Varsovia, Y. Menuhin – MOZART: Divertimento 1, etc.; WAGNER: Siegfried Idyll; WOLF: Italian Serenade ****

**** Chan. 9616. Norwegian CO, I. Brown – SCHUBERT: String Quartet 14 (Death and the Maiden), arr. Mahler **(*)

In a passionately volatile performance **Menuhin** encom-

passes the changing moods of Schoenberg's masterpiece with wonderful spontaneity and ardour. The fourth section, *Sehr breit und langsam*, is particularly eloquent, but the closing *Sehr ruhig* is also deeply felt, with superbly responsive playing from members of the **Sinfonia Varsovia**, and the work closes in a mood of gently sensuous nostalgia. Textures are rich yet they never clot, a tribute to the unnamed Virgin balance engineer.

An eloquent and impressive *Verklaerte Nacht* from the splendid **Norwegian Chamber Orchestra** and **Iona Brown**. It comes with Mahler's transcription of *Death and the Maiden*, made when opportunities to hear Schubert's masterpiece were rare. Those who want to hear it need have no doubts as to the excellence of the playing or of the Chandos recording.

CHAMBER MUSIC

Chamber Symphony 1 (arr. Webern for piano quintet); (i) Concerto for String Quartet and Orchestra (after Handel's Concerto grosso, Op. 6/7); (ii) Ode to Napoleon, Op. 41; Phantasy for Violin and Piano, Op. 47; String Quartet in D; String Quartets 1–4; String Trio, Op. 45; Wind Quintet, Op. 26; 6 Little Piano Pieces, Op. 19 (both arr. Guittart for strings); Verklaerte Nacht

*** Chan. 9939 (5). Schoenberg Qt with Narucki, Grotenhuis; (i) Arnhem PO, Benzi; (ii) Grandage

This ambitious five-disc set brilliantly brings together all of Schoenberg's chamber music for strings, including several arrangements. What is so persuasive is the expressive warmth of the **Schoenberg Quartet**. Even when the atonal Schoenberg is at his most abrasively intellectual, as in the *String Trio* of 1946, one is made to appreciate that this is music with an emotional core. So it is, too, in the four *String Quartets*, which form a central core to the collection, a splendid cycle stretching from the post-romantic 1 of 1904–5 through the mould-breaking 2 of 1907–8 with its evocative use of a soprano soloist in the third and fourth movements to the severity of 3 and 4, both commissioned by Mrs Sprague Coolidge, a great musical patron. The portrait of the composer is made all the more persuasive by having such a wide range of works including not just the early *Verklaerte Nacht*, wonderfully evocative, but the unnumbered string quartet of 1897. It is good, too, to find him relaxing in the *Concerto for String Quartet and Orchestra* of 1933, which he freely transcribed from Handel's *Concerto grosso* Op. 6, No. 7, which he wrote in France as a relaxation immediately after fleeing from Germany in 1933. One also welcomes the inclusion of the *Napoleon Buonaparte Ode* in its version for reciter and piano quintet. The recordings made in Holland are first-rate, warm and atmospheric.

(i) Chamber Symphony 2, Op. 38; (ii) Wind Quintet, Op. 26; (i; iii) Die glückliche Hand, Op. 18

(BB) *** Naxos 8.557526. (i) Philh. O, Craft; (ii) New York Woodwind Quintet; (iii) with Beesley, Simon Joly Ch.

Robert Craft continues his excellent and dedicated series of key 20th-century works with this expertly played and sung Schoenberg collection. The complex second movement of the *Second Chamber Symphony* is vital, richly textured and carefully balanced, The weird *Die glückliche Hand* is dramatic and hauntingly atmospheric. It is well sung by **Mark Beesley**, while the chorus are extraordinarily vivid, and the **Philharmonia Orchestra** give a virtuoso account of the orchestral score, held in a firm grip by Craft. The *Wind Quintet*, dating from 1923/4, requires even more virtuosity, and it is only recently that it has been found possible to play the work up to tempo (the first performance by members of the Vienna Philharmonic Orchestra in 1924 took an hour against the present 38 minutes). The **New York Woodwind Quintet** take it in their stride. Although at first hearing it does not sound it, the work is written traditionally, the first movement in sonata form with a repeated exposition, followed by a witty Scherzo, melancholy *Adagio*, and Rondo finale. The recording throughout is very clear and well balanced, and there are (very necessary) excellent notes by Robert Craft himself.

String Trio, Op. 45

⏻ *** Hyp. CDA 67429. Leopold String Trio – DOHNÁNYI: *Serenade in C*; MARTINŮ: *Trio 2* ***

Many critics have hailed the *String Trio* as Schoenberg's masterpiece. It is certainly one of his most intensely felt works, composed in the wake of a severe heart attack and the experience of being snatched back from the grave. The dreadful breathlessness of an asthmatic attack, the stopping of his heart, the injection into the heart itself that saved him, even the personalities of his nurses are said to be recorded in this music. (Calum MacDonald reproduces his masterly account of the piece in the excellent note.) The **Leopold Trio** play the work with consummate mastery and are superbly recorded. If you want this piece, you can't really do better than this.

String Quartets 1 in D min., Op. 7; (i) 2 in F sharp min., Op. 10. 3, Op. 30; 4, Op. 37

(***) Archiphon ARC mono 103/4. Kolisch Qt; (i) with Gifford

String Quartet (1897); String Quartet 1, Op. 7

**** MDG 307 0919-2. Leipzig Qt

String Quartets Nos. (i) 2, Op. 10; 4, Op. 37

**** MDG 307 0935-2. (i) Oelze; Leipzig Qt

No quartet has ever been more closely associated with these pieces than the **Kolisch**, and the present recordings were made at the turn of 1936–7. It is well worth putting up with surface noise for the sake of *real* music-making. Indeed, given phrasing of this quality there is more to the rigorously disciplined *Third* and *Fourth Quartets* than most later ensembles have found; and never have the two earlier *Quartets* sounded so eloquent. The set contains a short speech of thanks by Schoenberg.

MDG and the **Leipzig Quartet** do go in for extravagant layout. Their Schoenberg runs to three CDs – 3 is coupled with *Verklaerte Nacht* on a third disc which we have not heard. It is difficult to fault them in the two early quartets or for

that matter in the *Second*, Op. 10, in which **Christiane Oelze** sings beautifully. They phrase with great naturalness, their ensemble is perfect and they have great warmth, richness and tonal beauty, though nothing is overstated or projected. If any ensemble or recording could win doubting listeners over to this repertoire, this is it. The recording balance is perfect.

Verklaerte Nacht, Op. 4 (string sextet version)

(***) Testament mono SBT 1031. Hollywood Qt, with Dinkin, Reher – SCHUBERT: *String Quintet* (***) ❀

*** Hyp. CDA 66425. Raphael Ens. – KORNGOLD: *Sextet* ***

*** Nim. NI 5614. Brandis Qt, with Küssner, Schwalke – R. STRAUSS: *Metamorphosen; Capriccio: Prelude* ***

The 1950 **Hollywood** account was the first version of *Verklaerte Nacht* in its original sextet form ever to appear on records, and arguably it remains unsurpassed and possibly unequalled. This almost flawless performance enjoyed the imprimatur of Schoenberg himself, who supplied the sleevenote for it (reproduced in the excellent booklet), the only time he ever did so. The sound is remarkably good and very musical. Recommended with enthusiasm.

For those wanting a modern, digital version, the **Raphael Ensemble** have the advantage of very good recorded sound and give a fine account of Schoenberg's score. They also have the advantage of a rarity in their coupling, the youthful *Sextet* of Korngold.

The **Brandis Quartet** with two colleagues from the Berlin Philharmonic are in excellent form. They possess an unforced eloquence and expressive beauty that is impressive. The Nimbus recording is well balanced and very lifelike and can be recommended alongside the Raphael version.

Piano music: 3 Pieces, Op. 11; 6 Little Pieces, Op. 19; 5 Pieces, Op. 23; 2 Pieces, Op. 33a & b; Suite, Op. 25

Ⓑ *** Naxos 8.553870. Hill – BERG: *Piano Sonata*; WEBERN: *Variations, Op. 27* ***

Peter Hill may not challenge Pollini's magisterial survey of the Schoenberg canon (DG 423 249-2) but his is highly intelligent, thoughtful playing, acutely sensitive to dynamic and tonal shading. In some ways he is more persuasive than Pollini in that one feels more completely drawn into this musical world. In any event, given the low price tag and the high quality of the recorded sound, this is self-recommending.

VOCAL MUSIC

Gurrelieder – see also under Chamber Symphony 1

⏻ **** EMI 5 57303-2 (2). Mattila, von Otter, Moser, Langridge, Quasthoff, Berlin R. Ch., Leipzig R. Ch., Ernest Senff Ch., BPO, Rattle

*** Teldec 4509-98424-2 (2). Moser, Voigt, Larmore, Weikl, Riegel, Brandauer, Saxon State Op. Ch., Dresden, Leipzig R. Ch., Prague Male Ch., Dresden State O, Sinopoli

Ⓑ *** Naxos 8.557518/9. O'Mara, Diener, Lane, Wilson-

Johnson, Hill, Haefliger (speaker), Simon Joly Ch., Philh. O, Craft

Ⓜ *** Ph. 475 7782 (2). McCracken, Norman, Troyanos, Tanglewood Festival Ch., Boston SO, Ozawa

Drawn from live performances given in the Philharmonie in Berlin in September 2001, **Rattle's** version of Schoenberg's opulent score is the most refined yet in its beauty, warmly spontaneous from first to last, sweeping you away with its richness and magnetism up to the final choral climax. The soloists and massed choruses are all first-rate, with **Karita Mattila** as Tove consistently warm and tenderly responsive, opposite **Thomas Moser** in the key role of Waldemar, here more firmly focused than usual, stronger than on Sinopoli's Teldec version. As in Abbado's Vienna version on DG, **Philip Langridge** is outstanding as Klaus-Narr, and though **Anne Sofie von Otter** sings with grainy tone in the *Song of the Wood Dove*, her performance is both dramatic and moving, while **Thomas Quasthoff** is superb both as the Woodsman (Bauer) and in the difficult role of the Speaker in the melodrama of the final section, sounding younger and fresher than immediate rivals.

In his highly compelling live recording, **Sinopoli** conducts a most sensuous reading of *Gurrelieder*, bringing out all its high romantic voluptuousness. Speeds are spacious, thanks in part to his expressive freedom, and anyone who has ever thought of Schoenberg as cold should certainly hear this, magnetic from first to last, helped by rich, immediate sound. The soloists are excellent, even if **Thomas Moser** as Waldemar is gritty at times in a Wagnerian way.

Craft directs a performance which brings out the work's warmly romantic qualities rather than its foretastes of later Schoenberg. He is helped by an outstanding team of soloists, headed by the clear, strong tenor, **Stephen O'Mara**, as Waldemar and the radiant, fresh **Natalie Diener** as Tove, with **Jennifer Lane** firm and cleanly focused in the *Song of the Woodbird*. **David Wilson-Johnson** as the Peasant and **Martyn Hill** as Klaus-Narr both characterize well, and the veteran tenor, now retired from singing, **Ernst Haefliger**, copes with the sing-speech of the Speaker's role in a high-pitched way that Schoenberg himself evidently wanted. The **Philharmonia** plays with passionate conviction throughout, with textures consistently refined, and the **Simon Joly Chorale** provides a glorious choral conclusion.

Ozawa's gloriously opulent live performance of *Gurrelieder*, with a ravishing contribution from **Jessye Norman**, which won the *Gramophone* Choral Award in 1979, now returns to the catalogue as one of Philips's Originals, with text and translation included.

Die Jakobsleiter; Friede auf Erden, Op. 13 (Instrumental Prelude & a cappella Choral Postlude)

**** HM **SACD** 801821. Henschel, Kammer, Meier, Kaufmann, Rügamer, Azesberger, Volle, Johnson, Berlin R. Ch., Berlin SO, Nagano

Like the later opera, *Moses und Aron*, this oratorio, *Jacob's Ladder*, another work devoted to the composer's thoughts on God, remained unfinished at his death, closing on the sound of the Soul (a soprano) and heavenly woman's voices. The baritone, **Dietrich Henschel**, is superb in the central role of Gabriel, with the **Berlin Radio Choir** bringing out the warmth as well as the power of the choral writing. It remains an enigmatic work, inspired as it was, not just by the Bible, but by the philosophy of Swedenborg and by Balzac's novel, *Seraphita*. *Friede auf Erden*, 'Joy on Earth', provides a prelude in its orchestral form (sounding surprisingly consonant) and a postlude in the original *a cappella* choral version. Brilliant performances and exceptionally full and vivid recording.

Pierrot lunaire, Op. 21

🔊 Ⓜ **** Chan. 6534. Manning, Nash Ens., Rattle – WEBERN: *Concerto* ***

(i) Pierrot lunaire; Herzgewächse, Op. 20; (ii) Ode to Napoleon Buonaparte

*** DG 457 630-2. (i) Schäfer; (ii) Pittman-Jennings; Soloists of Ensemble InterContemporain, Boulez

Jane Manning is outstanding among singers who have tackled this most taxing of works, steering a masterful course between the twin perils of, on the one hand, actually singing and, on the other, simply speaking; her sing-speech brings out the element of irony and darkly pointed wit that is essential. **Rattle** draws strong, committed performances from the members of the **Nash Ensemble** and, apart from some intermittently odd balances, the sound is excellent.

For *Pierrot lunaire*, **Boulez** imaginatively chooses a sweet-toned soprano and the result is the more revealing, in an element of beauty and mystery usually missing while the dramatic point of this cabaret-like sequence is never underplayed. Balance is excellent, with the **Ensemble InterContemporain** playing with warmth and brilliance, as they do in the brief *Herzgewächse* (**Schäfer** again radiant) and in the *Ode to Napoleon*. **David Pittman-Jennings** takes an idiosyncratic view of the narration, reciting in a stylized way as though English is a foreign language, but it is good to have this neglected work so well played and recorded.

OPERA

Moses und Aron (complete; DVD version)

(*) Arthaus **DVD 101 259. Grundheber, T. Moser, Slovak Philh. Ch., V. State Op. Ch. & O, Gatti (Dir: Reto Nickler; V/D: Claus Viller)

Recorded at the Vienna State Opera in 2006, the Arthaus version of Schoenberg's powerful masterpiece offers a production by **Reto Nickler** which seeks to relate the plight of Moses and the Jews enslaved in Egypt with the period of the Holocaust under the Nazis. The costumes are uniformly drab with each of the large chorus carrying suitcases, like refugees herded into concentration camps. Though there are some good individual contributions, the success of the whole performance rests on the contrast between the gruff and rugged Moses of **Franz Grundheber**, powerful in his rendering of sing-speech, and the Aron of **Thomas Moser** in vocal lines that are surprisingly clear and mellifluous, making a striking contrast. The vital element of the choral writing is vividly brought out by **Daniele Gatti**, and though the updating brings some oddities of production the result is most moving. Grundheber is superb above all in the tragic final lines of Act II, establishing it as a satisfying conclusion even in the absence of the projected third act. Details of that are offered as an extra on the DVD.

Moses and Aaron (CD version)

🎵—Ⓜ **** Decca 475 8678 (2). Mazura, Langridge, Bonney, Haugland, Chicago SO & Ch., Solti

Solti gives Schoenberg's masterly score a dynamism and warmth which sets it firmly – if perhaps surprisingly – in the grand romantic tradition, yet finds an element of fantasy and, in places – as in the *Golden Calf* episode – a sparkle such as you would never expect from Schoenberg. The Moses of **Franz Mazura** may not be as specific in his sing-speech as was Gunter Reich in the two previous versions – far less sing than speech – but the characterization of an Old Testament patriarch is the more convincing. As Aaron, **Philip Langridge** is lighter and more lyrical, as well as more accurate, than his predecessor with Boulez, Richard Cassily. **Aage Haugland** with his firm, dark bass makes his mark in the small role of the Priest; **Barbara Bonney** too is excellent as the Young Girl. Above all, the brilliant singing of the **Chicago Symphony Chorus** matches the playing of the orchestra in virtuosity. More than ever the question mark concluding Act II makes a pointful close, with no feeling of a work unfinished. The brilliant recording emerges with its focus as sharp as ever on the Originals reissue.

SCHREKER, Franz (1878–1934)

Ekkehard (Symphonic Overture), Op. 12; Fantastic Overture, Op. 15; Interlude from Der Schatzgräber; Nächtstuck (from Der ferne Klang); Prelude to a Drama; Valse lente

🎵—*** Chan. 9797. BBC PO, Sinaisky

This sequence of six pieces presents a good cross-section of his output, demonstrating Schreker's development from the *Symphonic Overture, Ekkehard*, and the charmingly unpretentious *Valse lente*, to the later works, which remain sumptuously late-romantic but which were regarded as daringly modern by early audiences. Both the *Nachtstück* from *Der ferne Klang* (1909) and the *Prelude to a Drama* (1913) – the drama in question being the opera *Die Gezeichneten* – are powerfully imaginative. Perhaps the most seductive piece is the *Valse lente*. Schreker had a wonderful sense of fantasy, a feeling for colour, and impressive mastery of the orchestra. The textures are lush and overheated. **Sinaisky** draws seductively beautiful playing from the **BBC Philharmonic**, heightened by gloriously rich Chandos sound, and the whole disc serves to advance Schreker's cause.

Prelude to a Grand Opera; Prelude to Das Spielwerk; Romantic Suite, Op. 14; (i) 5 Gesäng

**** Chan. 9951 (i) Katarina Karnéus; BBC PO, Sinaisky

The *Romantic Suite* comes from 1903, when Schreker was in his mid-twenties, though its third movement began life independently as an *Intermezzo for Strings* a year earlier. It is a rather beautiful piece as, for that matter, is the opening *Idylle*, written at much the same time as he was making the first sketches for *Der ferne Klang*. There is a lot of Strauss here and in the mercurial Scherzo, Reger – the latter is a highly inventive movement. Only the finale, *Tanz*, is routine. The *Five Songs*, imaginatively sung by the Swedish mezzo, **Katarina Karnéus**, have plenty of atmosphere and mystery, and are well worth getting to know. The disc covers the whole of Schreker's career: the Prelude to *Das Spielwerk* is a wartime piece while the *Vorspiel zu einer grosen Oper* comes from the last months of his life. It is darker than his earlier pieces but despite its expert orchestration remains somewhat overblown. The playing of the **BBC Philharmonic** under **Sinaisky** is superb and the recording is in the demonstration class. Intelligent liner notes.

Der ferne Klang (opera; complete)

Ⓑ *** Naxos 8.660074/5 (2). Grigorescu, Harper, Haller, Hagen Op. Ch. & PO, Halász

Der ferne Klang's central character is an ambitious young dramatist, Fritz, who pursues his creative ambitions and his search for *Der ferne Klang* ('the distant sound') at the expense of his love for Grete, whom he abandons and who turns to prostitution. Schreker scores with chamber-like delicacy and has a Puccini-like finesse in the handling of colour, and great imagination in his handling of harmonic resource. The score is quite gripping, its sound world at times astringent in its harmonies, at others lush and intoxicating. Good soloists, though it is a pity that the voices are rather prominently balanced in this 1989 recording and that the subtlety of Schreker's lavish scoring is not always heard to best advantage. Strongly recommended.

Die Gezeichneten (opera; complete; DVD version)

*** EuroArts DVD 20555298. Brubaker, Schwanewilms, Volle, Hale, Schöne, V. Statsopernchor, Deutsches SO, Berlin, Nagano (Producer: Nikolaus Lehnhoff)

Die Gezeichneten ('The Branded' or 'The Marked One') now enters the DVD market in the Salzburg Festival production of 2005. The *New York Times* hailed it as the 'rediscovery of the year' and the score's riches will delight those coming to it anew. It is sumptuously orchestrated: its colours and textures intoxicated its first audiences and still dazzle today. Best summed up as a blend of post-*Salomé* luxuriance and exoticism with a pretty heady mixture of Scriabin, Szymanowski, Korngold and Puccini, it was Schreker's fourth and arguably most powerful opera, and it enjoyed immediate success when it first appeared in 1918. The cast is very good, though **Robert Brubaker's** Alviano does not displace memories of Kenneth Riegel in the 1984 Salzburg set under Gerd Albrecht. But there is a fine sense of dramatic momentum and sensitive orchestral playing under **Kent Nagano**, who generates a strong sense of atmosphere. **Nikolaus Lehnhoff** translates this extraordinary work into a compelling and effective stage experience.

Der Schatzgräber (opera; complete)

**(*) Cap. 60010-2 (2). Protschka, Schnaut, Stamm, Haage, Hamburg State O, Albrecht

The attractions of Schreker's sweet-sour treatment of a curious morality fairy story are fairly well conveyed in this first recording, made live at the Hamburg State Opera in 1989. **Josef Protschka** sings powerfully as Elis, hardly ever over-strenuous, but **Gabriele Schnaut** finds it hard to scale down her very bright and powerful soprano and seems happiest when she is scything your ears with loud and often unsteady top notes; yet she is certainly dramatic in this equivocal role. Outstanding among the others is **Peter Haage** as the court jester. *Der Schatzgräber* may be hokum, but it is enjoyable hokum, and, with **Albrecht** drawing committed performances from the whole company, this well-made recording is most welcome.

SCHUBERT, Franz (1797–1828)

ORCHESTRAL MUSIC

Concerto Movement for Violin and Orchestra in D, D.345

(M) *** CRD (ADD) CRD 3369. Thomas, Bournemouth SO –
BEETHOVEN: *Romances 1–2*; MENDELSSOHN: *Violin Concerto* ***

Schubert's *Konzertstück* is slight, but **Ronald Thomas's** refreshing playing and direction make it well worth having on disc, along with the excellent Beethoven and Mendelssohn. The recording is first class.

Overtures: Fierrabras; Overture in D; Overture in E min., D.648; Overtures in the Italian Style in D, D.590 & D.591. Rosamunde; Die Verschworenen; Die Zwillingsbrüder

(N) (BB) **(*) Naxos 8.570329. Prague Sinf., Benda

Schubert's early Rossiniesque overtures are delightfully tuneful and enjoyable, as is the more dramatic and rarely heard *Overture in E minor*. The opera overtures – even the rare ones such as *Die Verschworenen* ('The Conspirators') – offer much delightful colour and invention and make one wonder at their neglect. The most famous work here, the *Rosamunde Overture*, is sympathetically played, even if the performance, as in the other overtures, lacks the last ounce of character. Good playing and decent recording throughout.

Rondo in A for Violin & Strings, D.438

*** EMI 7 49663-2. Kennedy, ECO, Tate – BRUCH; MENDELSSOHN: *Concertos* ***

The ideas in Schubert's *Rondo* flow very sweetly with **Kennedy**, making this an attractive bonus to the usual Bruch–Mendelssohn coupling.

Symphonies 1–6; 8–9

(B) **** RCA 82876 60392-2 (4). Dresden State O, Davis
(BB) **** Warner Apex 2564 60532-2 (5). Sinfonia Varsovia, Y.

Menuhin (disc 5 includes conversation in German: Menuhin/Jurgen Seeger)

(BB) **(*) Brilliant 99587 (4). Hanover Band, Goodman
(B) **(*) DG (ADD) 471 307-2 (4). BPO, Boehm

Symphonies 1–6; 8 (Unfinished); 9 (Great); 2 Overtures in the Italian Style

(B) **(*) Warner 2564 62323-2 (4). Concg. O, Harnoncourt

Sir Colin Davis's Dresden cycle (on four bargain discs), despite observing all repeats, makes a glowing tribute that regularly reveals Davis drawing magnetic and intense playing from the **Dresden Orchestra**, with the polish of the ensemble adding to the impact, never making the results sound self-conscious. This is a most distinguished cycle, helped by glowing sound.

Menuhin's more recent (1997) IMG set of the Schubert *Symphonies*, now reissued on Apex, offers performances electrically tense, generally at brisk speeds, with an easy feeling for Schubertian lyricism, helped by alert, warmly responsive playing from this leading Polish chamber orchestra and full, immediate recording. The disappointment is that the supplementary conversation is in German only.

Boehm does not smile as often as Schubert's music demands – especially by the side of Beecham in 3 and 5 – but he is always sympathetic. Certainly the Berlin wind are a joy to listen to, and it is only in the early symphonies that he does not quite capture the youthful sparkle of these delightful scores. Boehm's warmly graceful account of 5 and the glowing performance of 6, coupled together, show Boehm at his best, taking an easy-going view, with relaxed tempi that never grow heavy. Boehm capped his series with an outstanding account of the *Unfinished Symphony* and one of the finest of all recorded performances of the *Great C major*, to make an excellent coupling.

Harnoncourt takes a relatively severe view and, significantly, he is at his finest in the darkness of the *Tragic Symphony*. There is little of Schubertian charm here, with his eccentrically slow tempo for the finale of 6 in its lumbering gait missing the pure sunlight of the piece which Beecham displayed so well. Harnoncourt's preference for short phrasing also tends to make slow movements less songful, though equally it adds to the bite and intensity of other movements, notably Scherzos with their sharp cross-rhythms. However, there is a lighter touch in the *Italian Overtures* and even moments of charm, with the introductions (especially the quote from *Rosamunde*) affectionately done. Harnoncourt has used specially prepared texts.

Goodman draws lively, beautifully sprung performances from the players of the **Hanover Band**. For anyone wanting an inexpensive set of period performances of these symphonies, they can be warmly recommended with the reservation that the (originally Nimbus) sound balance is very reverberant. However, this Brilliant reissue is in the lowest possible price range, although documentation is non-existent.

Symphonies 1–3; 4 (Tragic); 5–7; 8 (Unfinished); 9 (Great); 10 in D, D.936a; Symphonic Fragments: in D, D.615 and D.708a (completed & orch. Newbold)

(B) *** Ph. 470 886-2 (6). ASMF, Marriner

Marriner's excellent set gathers together not only the eight symphonies of the regular canon, but two more symphonies now 'realized', thanks to the work of Brian Newbold of Hull University. For full measure, half a dozen fragments of other symphonic movements are included, orchestrated by Professor Newbold. The set brings sparkling examples of the **Academy's** work at its finest, while the bigger challenges of the *Unfinished* (here completed with Schubert's Scherzo filled out and the *Rosamunde B minor Entr'acte* used as finale) and the *Great C major* are splendidly taken. These are fresh, direct readings, making up in rhythmic vitality for any lack of weight. The recordings, all digital, present consistent refinement and undistractingly good balance. Now reissued as a bargain box, this set is well worth any collector's attention.

Symphonies 1–4; Rosamunde: Ballet music 1 & 2

(BB) **(*) EMI Gemini (ADD) 5 86064-2 (2). BPO, Karajan (with WEBER: *Der Freischütz Overture* (***))

Symphonies 5–6; 8 (Unfinished); 9 (Great); Rosamunde: Overture

(BB) **(*) EMI Gemini (ADD) 5 86067-2 (2). BPO, Karajan

Karajan presents a most polished and beautiful set of Schubert symphonies, reissued on a pair of Gemini CD doubles at budget price. The point and elegance of the **Berliners'** playing in the early symphonies is most persuasive, yet the results are never mannered. The *Unfinished*, dating from 1975, brings characteristic Berlin refinement. The first movement is the original first take restored; there were technical problems with it and so Karajan re-recorded the movement a month later. Those problems have now been solved by the current re-mix, with excellent results. The *Great C major* (1977) is also compelling. The overtures and ballet music make a fine bonus (the Weber, notable for its dramatic opening, is digital).

EMI Collector's Edition

Symphonies 1–6; 8–9; 2 Overtures: Alfonso and Estrella; In the Italian Style, D.590/1; Die Zwillingsbrüder (Munich Festival O, Yehudi Menuhin). Chamber Music: *Arpeggione Sonata for Viola & Piano* (Caussé, Duchable); *Flute Quartet* (arr. of *Matiegka's Notturno*) (Debost, Ghiglia, Pasquier, Boulfli); *Introduction, Theme & Variations for flute & piano on 'Trockne Blumen' from 'Die schöne Müllerin'* (Rampal, Veyron-Lacroix); *Octet, D.803* (Melos Ens.). *Piano Quintet (Trout)* (Pludermacher, French String Trio, with Cazauran); *Piano Trios 1–2; Sonata (Duo) for Violin & Piano, D.574; Notturno, D.897; Sonatensatz, D.28* (Collard, Dumay, Lodéon). *Adagio and Rondo concertante for Piano, Violin & Strings, D.487* (with Domus); *Fantasy, D.934; Rondo brillant, D.895; Sonatinas 1–3* (all for Violin & Piano) (all with Hoelscher, Engel); *String Quartets, D.94; D 804; D. 810 (Death and the Maiden); D.887* (Hungarian

Quartet). *String Quartets, D.87; D.94; D.112; D.173; D.353; Quartettsatz* (Heutling Qt). *String Quintet in C, D.956* (Hungarian Qt, with Varga). Music for piano 4 hands: *Divertissement à la hongroise; Fantasy in F min., Rondo in A; Variations on an Original Theme* (Février & Tacchino). *Allegro in A min. (Lebensstürme); Divertissement à la française in E min.; Grand Duo Sonata, in C; 6 Grandes marches; Grande marche funèbre; Grande marche héroïque in A min.; Kindermarsch in G; Marches caractéristiques; Marches militaires* (Eschenbach & Frantz). Solo piano music: *Albumblatt* (Rudy); *Allegretto in C min., D.915; Cotillon in E flat; 12 Deutsche Ländler; Galop in G; 2 Ecossaises* (Katsaris); *Fantasia in C (Wanderer)* (Rudy); *8 Impromptus, D.899 & D.935* (Ciccolini); *13 Lieder (Concert paraphrases, arr Liszt)* (Setrak, piano). *6 Moments Musicaux* (Naoumoff); *Piano Sonatas: 4 in A min., D.537; 14 in A min., D.784; 2 Scherzos, D.593* (Rudy); *Sonatas: 13 in A, D.664; 21 in B flat, D.960* (Ciccolini); *7 in E flat, D.568; 9 in B flat, D.575; 16 in A min., D.845; 17 in D, D.850; 18 in G, D.894; 19 in C min., D.958; 20 in A, D.959* (Zacharias); *34 Valses sentimentales, D.779; 12 Waltzes, D.145; 20 Waltzes, D.146; 12 Gräzer Waltzes, D.924; Valses nobles, D.969* (Bordoni). Choral music: *Deutsche Mass, D.872; Gesang der Geister über den Wassem; Nachtgesang im Walde* (both for men's chorus) (St Hedwig's Cathedral Ch., BPO, Forster). *Lazarus (Cantata), D.869; Magnificat in C, D.486; Masses: 1 in F, D.105; 4 in C, D.452; 5 in A flat, D.678; Missas brevis in G, D.167; in B flat, D.324; Stabat Mater in F, D.383* (Soloists, Bav. R. Ch. & O, Sawallisch); *6 in E flat, D.950* (Soloists, St Hedwig's Cathedral Ch., BPO, Leinsdorf); *7 Gesang* (for male voices) (Hilliard Ens.); *7 Gesang* (Laki, Stuttgart Chamber Ch., Bernius, with Rothkopf, piano); *26 Part songs for chorus* (Soloists, Capella Bavariae, Sawallisch); *Ständchen* (Bav. State Op. Ch., Baumgart); *Rosamunde: Incidental music* (complete) (Rothenberger, Bav. R. Ch. & O, Hager). *Auf der Strom* (with Arom, horn); *Der Hirt auf dem Felsen* (with Lancelot, clarinet); *Mitleiden; Viola* (Retchitzka, Barbier); *5 Lieder* (Fassbaender, Werba); *8 Lieder* (Popp, Gage); *14 Lieder* (J. Baker, Moore or Parsons); *14 Lieder* (Fischer-Dieskau, Moore); *17 Lieder* (Hendricks, Lupu). Song-cycles: *Die schöne Müllerin; Schwanengesang* (Bär, Parsons); *Winterreise* (Vickers, Parsons)

(BB) **(*) EMI (ADD) 3 85853-2 (50)

Another extraordinary, super-bargain cornucopia from EMI. **Menuhin's** set of the *Symphonies*, **Sawallisch's** *Mass* recordings and *Lazarus*, and much other rare choral music, the **Lieder** recitals from **Janet Baker**, **Fischer-Dieskau** and **Olaf Bär** among others, are all first class, and most of the chamber music is eminently desirable. Indeed there is little here which is not of a fairly high standard, and the possibilities for exploration are endless. There are no texts or translations, and the booklet merely offers a list of titles and the artists concerned, but this is still remarkable value for money.

Symphonies 1 in D, D.82; 2 in B flat, D.125

(BB) **(*) Naxos 8.553093. Failoni O of Budapest, Halász

Michael Halász and the **Failoni Orchestra** are affectionately easy-going rather than overtly dramatic, but they play both these works most winningly. The recording too is full and naturally balanced, although the resonance of the Italian Institute in Budapest makes the tuttis spread and lose some of the sharpness of focus.

Symphonies 1–2; 8 in B min. (Unfinished)

(M) (**(*)) Sony mono SMK 87876. RPO, Beecham

Beecham's versions of the first two Schubert *Symphonies* remain second to none, and the finale of the *Second Symphony* has rarely been given with greater vivacity or lightness of touch. However, the 1953 recording sounds less transparent and fresh than many LPs of the period. The *Unfinished* is quite special, however, and among the best things **Sir Thomas** did in the early 1950s.

Symphonies 1 in D, D.82; 4 in C min. (Tragic)

(BB) **(*) Warner Apex 2564 60527-2. Sinfonia Varsovia, Y. Menuhin

Menuhin's *First Symphony* opens weightily (partly the effect of the resonant recording), but the *Allegro*, fast and resilient, is graceful as well as lively, and the *Andante* has characteristic warmth. As throughout the cycle, the Minuet is briskly characterful and the finale captivates with energetic lightness of articulation from the strings. The *Tragic Symphony* opens powerfully, yet again the main *Allegro*, like the finale, is resilient as well as boldly forward-looking, and the slow movement nobly expressive. The Trio of the Minuet is most engagingly done. The sound is full-bodied, with tuttis not completely transparent, but this is certainly very recommendable in the budget range.

Symphonies 2 in B flat; 6 in C

⊙— (BB) **** Warner Apex 2564 60529-2. Sinfonia Varsovia, Y. Menuhin

Menuhin's coupling is outstanding in every way, with first-movement *Allegros* swiftly paced and fizzing with vitality. Both *Andantes* are beautifully played, each elegant and poised. With vigorous Scherzi (winning Trios) and jaunty finales, these performances are hard to beat, full of Schubertian character. The orchestral playing is first class, glowing and vivacious, and the recording is both full and transparent.

Symphonies 3 in D; 5 in B flat; 8 in B min. (Unfinished)

⊙— (BB) **** Warner Apex 2564 60530-2. Sinfonia Varsovia, Y. Menuhin

A truly outstanding triptych from **Menuhin** at his most inspired. 3 is bold, strong and forward-looking. 5, too, has both

strength and grace. The *Unfinished* then emerges as the most powerful, most romantic of the cycle, superb playing from the **Sinfonia Varsovia** and first-rate recording.

Symphonies 3; 4 (Tragic)

⊙— **** DG 423 653-2. COE, Abbado

Crisp, fast and light, 3 is given a delectable performance by Abbado. In 4, the *Tragic*, **Abbado** makes the slow C minor introduction bitingly mysterious before a clean, elegant *Allegro*, and with this conductor the other movements are also elegant and polished as well as strong. Textually, 4 eliminates the extra bars in the slow movement, which had been inserted originally by Brahms. The slow movement is outstandingly beautiful, with the oboe solo – presumably **COE's Douglas Boyd** – most tenderly expressive.

Symphonies 3; 5; 6

⊙— ✲ (M) **** EMI (ADD) 5 66984-2. RPO, Beecham

Beecham's are magical performances in which every phrase breathes. There is no substitute for imaginative phrasing and each line is shaped with affection and spirit. The *Allegretto* of the *Third Symphony* is an absolute delight. The delicacy of the opening of the *Fifth* is matched by the simple lyrical beauty of the *Andante*, while few conductors have been as persuasive as Beecham in the *Sixth* 'little' C major *Symphony*. The sound is generally faithful and spacious.

Symphonies 3 in D, D.200; 6 in C, D.589

⊙— (BB) *** Naxos 8.553094. Failoni O of Budapest, Halász

These are delightful performances, fully capturing the innocent charm of these youthful symphonies. **Michael Halász** is most sensitive, and his style is Beechamesque in its affectionate elegance.

Symphony 4 in C min. (Tragic), D.417

⊙— *** BBC (ADD) BBCL 4093-2 (2). New Philh. O, Giulini – BEETHOVEN: *Missa solemnis* **(*)

Recorded at the Edinburgh Festival in 1968, **Giulini's** reading of Schubert's *Tragic Symphony* brings a bitingly intense reading, more than usually making this early work live up to its nickname. It makes an attractive fill-up to Giulini's monumental reading of Beethoven's *Missa solemnis* recorded earlier in that year.

Symphony 4 (Tragic); Grand Duo in C, D.812 (orch. Joachim)

(BB) **(*) Naxos 8.553095. Failoni O of Budapest, Halász

Halász presents the *Tragic Symphony* sympathetically and, though this is not a strongly dramatic reading, the resonant acoustic adds a certain weight, and the *Andante* is warmly and expressively played. This inexpensive disc is valuable for its coupling, the orchestration of the large-scale *Grand Duo* for piano duet by Joachim. The work is convincingly played, with gravitas and freshness nicely balanced. The warm resonancy of the Budapest Italian Institute suits this work very well.

(i) Symphonies 4 in C min.; 5 in B flat; (ii) 8 in B min. (Unfinished); (i) 9 in C (Great); Rosamunde: Entr'acte 3 & ballet music, 1 & 2

(B) *** RCA (ADD/DDD) 74321 84607-2 (2). (i) N. German RSO, Wand; (ii) Chicago SO, Reiner

The freshness and robust, spirited vigour of **Günter Wand's** Schubert shines through all of his performances and cannot fail to give pleasure. The recordings are excellent (the *Fourth* is analogue; 5 and 9, plus the engaging *Rosamunde* excerpts, are digital). **Reiner's** *Unfinished*, however, dates from the early days of stereo but hardly betrays its age. The performance is atmospheric and dramatic, especially so in the impulsive first movement, the second is richly lyrical. Good value if the programme suits.

Symphony 5 in B flat, D.485

ⓑ (BB) *** DG (ADD) 447 433-2. VPO, Boehm – BEETHOVEN: *Symphony 6* ***

**(*) BBC (ADD) BBCL 4003-2. BBC SO, Kempe – BRAHMS: *Symphony 4* **(*)

(BB) (***) Dutton Lab. mono CDK 1208. Concg. O, van Beinum (with BEETHOVEN: *Creatures of Prometheus: Overture* (LPO)) – BERLIOZ: *Symphonie fantastique, Op. 14* (***)

Boehm's VPO recording of the *Fifth Symphony* dates from the very end of his career. In his eighties he preferred a tauter, more incisive view than he had given in his 1967 Berlin performance, weightier, but still with a light rhythmic touch, while the slow movement is not lacking grace. The finale is strong and purposeful and this is Boehm at his finest, with superbly polished and responsive VPO playing in repertoire they know and love. The 1980 recording is full and warm, a live performance.

Kempe's *Fifth Symphony* comes as a makeweight to an excellent 1974 concert performance of the Brahms *Fourth*. The Schubert was recorded at a Promenade Concert three years earlier, and is a delight from start to finish. Very musicianly, enjoyable, natural and full of life. Very decent sound too.

From **Eduard van Beinum** and the **Concertgebouw Orchestra** come cultured playing and well-balanced sound. An enjoyable reminder of the fine results Eduard van Beinum achieved in Amsterdam.

Symphonies 5 in B flat; 6 in C

ⓑ **** DG 423 654-2. COE, Abbado

Abbado brings out the happy songfulness of the slow movements in these works, as well as the rhythmic resilience of the *Allegros*. As in 4, so also in 6 Abbado eliminates the extra bars added by Brahms in his original Schubert edition. Excellent recording, with fine bloom and good, natural contrasts.

Symphonies 5 in B flat; 8 (Unfinished)

ⓑ (M) *** Sony 82876 78741-2. NYPO, Walter (with BEETHOVEN: *Overture Leonora 3* (***))

(***) BBC stereo/mono BBCL 4120-2. Hallé O, Barbirolli – MOZART: *Symphony 40* (***)

Bruno Walter brings special qualities of warmth and lyri-

cism to the *Unfinished*. Affection, gentleness and humanity are the keynotes of this performance; while the first movement of the *Fifth* is a shade too measured, there is much loving attention to detail in the *Andante*. The recording remains fully acceptable, and the return of this famous (1961) coupling to the catalogue is most welcome.

Barbirolli conducts a light, beautifully sprung reading of the *Fifth Symphony*, well paced, leading up to an exhilarating account of the finale. There is no exposition repeat in the first movement, and in the **Unfinished** Barbirolli after a slow, deliberate first phrase offers a performance which combines warmly expressive phrasing and steady speeds, with magic in such passages as the big crescendo in the first-movement development.

Symphonies 5; 8 (Unfinished); 9 in C (Great)

ⓑ (B) **** Double Decca 448 927-2 (2). VPO, Solti

Symphonies 5; 8 in B min. (completed by Brian Newbould); 9 in C (Great); Rosamunde (Ballet Music), D.797: 2 in G

(B) *** Virgin 2x1 5 61806-2 (2). OAE, Mackerras

This Double Decca coupling of three favourite Schubert *Symphonies* is one of the most attractive of all **Solti's** many reissues on the Decca label. There have been more charming versions of 5 but few that so beautifully combine freshness with refined polish. The *Unfinished* has Solti adopting measured speeds but with his refined manner keeping total concentration. The *Great C major Symphony* is an outstanding version, among the very finest, beautifully paced and sprung in all four movements, and superbly played. It has drama as well as lyrical feeling, but above all it has a natural sense of spontaneity and freshness. The recordings all confirm the Vienna Sofiensaal as an ideal recording location, and the glowing detail, especially in 9, is a source of consistent pleasure.

Mackerras was the first to use period instruments in Schubert's *Ninth*. The characterful rasp on the period brass instruments and the crisp attack of timpani are much more striking than any thinness of string-tone. It is a performance of outstanding freshness and resilience. The *Fifth* is not quite as magnetic as the *Ninth*, but still has comparable qualities. The special claim of this second disc is the inclusion of the *Unfinished Symphony* heard here as 'finished' by Brian Newbould. Mackerras opens in the mysterious depths with the darkest *pianopianissimo*, and the plangent period timbres bring a real sense of *Sturm und Drang*, with powerful contrasts and strong, forceful accents in the second movement. The recording is excellent throughout.

Symphony 8 in B min. (Unfinished), D.759 (CD versions)

**(*) BBC (ADD) BBCL 4039-2. Philh. O, Boult – BIZET: *Jeux d'enfants*; RAVEL: *Daphnis et Chloé: Suite 2*; SIBELIUS: *Symphony 7* **(*)

(B) **(*) DG (ADD/DDD) 477 5324. VPO, C. Kleiber – BRAHMS: *Symphony 4*; WAGNER: *Tristan und Isolde: Act III: excerpts* ***

Symphony 8 (Unfinished); Grand Duo (orch. Joachim)

**** DG 423 655-2. COE, Abbado

Abbado's outstandingly refined and sensitive version comes with a valuable coupling. The second subject in the *Unfinished* brings some slightly obtrusive agogic hesitations at the beginning of each phrase; but with such responsive playing they quickly sound fresh and natural.

Showmanship and flamboyance were alien to **Sir Adrian's** personality, which is perhaps why he remains under-represented on CD and underrated by the wider public. This recording serves as a reminder of his stature and the quiet, natural dignity that informed his music-making. The Bizet, Schubert and Ravel come from a Promenade Concert in 1964 and the Sibelius from a Festival Hall concert given the preceding year. In the *Unfinished* there is the unforced eloquence that distinguished his famous *Great C major*.

Carlos Kleiber's account of the *Unfinished* was more compelling than the *Third Symphony* with which it was originally coupled; but here there is an unease in the first movement where first and second subjects are not fully coordinated, the contrasts sounding a little forced. Still, this is undoubtedly a performance of some stature which many will find compelling. The 1978 analogue recording brings out the brass well and is wide-ranging.

Symphony 8 (Unfinished); String Quartet in D min. (Death and the Maiden) (orch. Stein)

Ⓝ ⒝⒝ ** Naxos 8.572051. Buffalo PO, Falletta

The arrangement of the *Death and the Maiden Quartet* for an expanded Schubertian orchestra by Andy Stein, well played as it is, simply doesn't work. The use of woodwind and four horns gives the music added colour, but robs it of its plangent bite, character, and intensity. Indeed it becomes an entirely different work – not the fault of the playing of the **Buffalo Philharmonic Orchestra** under **JoAnne Falletta**, who give an excellent account of themselves in the *Unfinished Symphony*.

'Ultimate Schubert': Disc 1: Symphony 8 (Unfinished) (Concg. O, Haitink). Rosamunde (Overture & Incidental Music) with Heynis, Netherlands R. Ch. Disc 2: Symphonies 5 & 9 (Great) (VPO, Kertesz). Disc 3: Piano Quintet in A (Trout) (Pressler); String Quartet 14 (Death and the Maiden) (Beaux Arts Trio augmented). Disc 4: String Quintet; Quartettsatz (Weller Qt, augmented). Disc 5: Piano Sonata 17 in D, D.850; Impromptus in G flat & A flat, D.899/3-4; Moments musicaux 1–6 (Curzon)

⒝⒝ *** Decca 475 8542 (5)

The only real (and surprising) disappointment here is **Haitink's** account of the *Unfinished Symphony*, which is disappointingly dull. Yet his *Rosamunde* ballet music shows him at his very finest, beautifully played, with a simple eloquence. The vocal items, with **Aafjé Heynis** in fine voice, are especially memorable. So too is **Kertész's** account of the *Great C*

major Symphony, strong, flexible and direct, and still among the finest versions. The **Beaux Arts** performances of the *Trout Quintet* and the *Death and the Maiden Quartet* are well up to standard and self-recommending, but the **Weller** account of the *String Quintet*, although finely played, is a trifle sweet and suave. Needless to say, **Clifford Curzon's** performances are in every way outstanding; but one can only lament that space could not have been found for Schubert's last and greatest piano *Sonata in B flat*.

Symphonies: (i) 8 (Unfinished); (ii) 9 in C (Great) (DVD versions)

☞—☀ **** TDK **DVD** DVWW-COWAND6. NDR SO, Wand (V/D: Hugo Käch)

Recorded live, **Günter Wand's** performances of the two greatest Schubert *Symphonies* have the same concentration and visionary atmosphere as his equally memorable Berlin Philharmonic CD of the *Ninth*. But to have his magically evocative and ravishingly played account of the *Unfinished* as well as the *Great C major* on a single DVD makes for an unforgettable listening and watching experience. The cameras continually and perceptively follow the performance detail, showing Wand as a direct, unostentatious conductor, often achieving remarkable results with the minimum of gesture. The interpretation of the *Ninth*, as on CD, solves the work's problems of tempo changes by achieving a warmly natural musical flow, expanding spontaneously to high drama at key moments. The sound in the Musik-und-Kongresshalle, Lübeck, is first class too, and this must be counted among the finest orchestral DVDs yet to appear.

Symphonies 8 (Unfinished); 9 in C (Great)

*** RCA **SACD** (ADD) 88697 04603-2. Boston SO, Munch

*** Telarc CD 80502. Sc CO, Mackerras

Ⓑ **(*) Sony (ADD) SBK 48268. Cleveland O, Szell

Ⓑ *** CfP (ADD) 574 8852. LPO, Pritchard

Ⓜ **(*) EMI (ADD) 4 76895-2. BPO Karajan

Munch gives a magnificent performance of the *Great C major Symphony*. In sheer dramatic tension he even outshines Toscanini. This is very much the Toscanini approach – the introduction and *Allegro* of the first movement even faster than his – but one must emphasize that it is far from being an unsympathetic or rough-riding account of the kind we sometimes get from the other side of the Atlantic. The remastered 1958 recording still has plenty of edge, yet in the impressive new SACD transfer the sound is filled out by the warm resonance of the Boston acoustic. This is even more striking in the expansive lower strings at the opening of the *Unfinished*, recorded three years earlier. Here Munch's performance has a fine, lyrical impulse, with sensitive wind-playing in the second movement; but there is a certain heaviness in his approach which is quite different from his reading of the *Ninth Symphony*.

Szell's, too, is a splendid performance of the *Unfinished*. Phrasing and general discipline are immaculate, but Szell never lacks warmth here, and drama and beauty walk hand in hand in the second movement. Apart from the lack of a real *pianissimo*, the 1960 recording is very good for its time. The *Ninth* dates from the previous year. Szell's control of tempo in the first movement brings a convincing onward flow, and the performance is notable for the alertness and rhythmic energy of the playing, yet there is no lack of resilience in the *Andante*. In the brilliant finale few rivals can match the precision of the hectic triplet rhythms.

Pritchard's reading of the *Unfinished* is magnetic, unusually direct, even in the melting lyricism of the incomparable second subject. The *Great C major* is as vital as it is refreshing. Pritchard observed repeats more than anyone else on record. Only the exposition repeat in the finale is omitted. Both recordings have the advantage of a warm ambience (Watford Town Hall) and are naturally balanced.

Karajan's EMI *Unfinished*, which dates from 1975, finds Berlin refinement at its most ethereal. The performance has an other-worldly quality, rapt and concentrated. The *Great C major* is also compelling, but here some may find the reverberant acoustic gives the impression of too much weightiness.

Symphony 9 in C (Great), D.944 (DVD version)

*** EuroArts **DVD** 2072168. Bav. RSO, Bernstein (with SCHUMANN: *Manfred Overture* (with VPO ***))

It is good to have **Bernstein's** fine (1987) recording of the *Great C major* on DVD, with the extra zest of live performance. He negotiates all the changes of pace and thrust to the manner born, and makes the work flow easily and spontaneously. The slow movement is played most beautifully. He then moves from the Munich Kongresssaal to the Musikvereinssaal for a similarly impressive account of Schumann's *Manfred Overture* with the **VPO**, a work not otherwise available on DVD. Recommended.

Symphony 9 in C (Great), D.944 (CD versions)

⟿ Ⓜ **** RCA 82876 59425-2. BPO, Wand

⟿ ✿ Ⓜ **** Decca Legends (ADD) 460 311-2. VPO, Solti – WAGNER: *Siegfried Idyll* ****

⟿ ⒝⒝ *** EMI Encore 5 09022-2. BPO, Tennstedt – MENDELSSOHN: *Symphony 4 (Italian)* **(*)

Ⓝ Ⓜ **** Signum SIGCD 133. Philh. O, Mackerras

**** EMI 2 28533-2. BPO, Rattle

Ⓜ *** EMI (ADD) 5 62791-2. LPO, Boult – BRAHMS: *Alto Rhapsody; Academic Festival Overture* ***

⒝⒝ *** Warner Apex 2564 60531-2. Sinfonia Varsovia, Y. Menuhin

Ⓜ *** BBC Legends BBCL 4140. LPO, Giulini – BRITTEN: *The Building of the House Overture*; WEBER: *Der Freischütz: Overture* ***

(*) Tudor **SACD Surround Sound 7144. Bamberg SO, Nott

Symphony 9 in C (Great); Rosamunde: Overture (Die Zauberharfe), D.644

*** DG 423 656-2. COE, Abbado

*** Häns. CD 93.044. Stuttgart RSO, Norrington

Günter Wand offers a visionary account of Schubert's *Great*

C major Symphony, taken from superbly played, live, **Berlin** performances, glowingly recorded. Consistently he makes the playing sound spontaneous, even in the tricky problems of speed changes inherent in this work. In the manner of his generation, he does not observe exposition repeats in the outher movements or second-half repeats in the Scherzo, but this is a beautifully coordinated, strong and warm reading.

Solti's superb recording with the **VPO** (one of his finest records) is also available as part of a Double Decca, which includes 5 and 8 (see above). Decca have rightly chosen it for reissue in their Legends series, coupled with Wagner's *Siegfried Idyll*. Both performances have comparable distinction and show that Solti could relax in music which he loved without sacrificing concentration and drama.

Tennstedt's 1983 EMI recording ranks alongside those of both Wand and Solti, and some may find his account even more satisfying. It is an incandescent reading that brings home afresh how Schubert, even in this last and grandest of his symphonies is still youthfully energetic. With superb playing from the **Berlin Philharmonic Orchestra** in sound of natural warmth, this is certainly among the very finest versions available.

Sir Charles Mackerras offers a strikingly vital account of the *Great C major Symphony* with the **Philharmonia Orchestra**, showing distinct influences of period-instrumental practice, absorbed but not too overwhelming. Light, clear textures, speeds brisk but not over-driven, detail clear, with the Philharmonia string-playing responsive and polished. Repeats are generous: both outer-movement expositions are repeated and the Scherzo moves from section to section with plenty of rhythmic lift. The tempo fluctuations in the first movement are seamlessly resolved and the warmly lyrical secondary theme in the slow movement is affectionately contrasted. The finale races forward with a strong, bold impetus to make a satisfying close, and the result overall is refreshingly vigorous and spontaneous. The recording, made in the Queen Elizabeth Hall, is perhaps a little dry but is admirably clear, not lacking weight or body, and this now replaces his earlier, Telarc version.

Though the **COE** is by definition an orchestra of chamber scale, the weight of **Abbado's** version, taken from his complete cycle, is ample, while allowing extra detail to be heard, thanks also to the orchestra's outstandingly crisp ensemble. Speeds are very well chosen, and the expressive detail is consistently made to sound natural. The *Rosamunde* *(Zauberharfe) Overture* makes a valuable and generous fill-up.

When **Sir Simon Rattle** over the years has regularly conducted orchestras of period instruments, it may come as a surprise that with his own **Berlin Philharmonic** he takes a relatively free and romantic view of this massive symphony, perhaps reflecting in part the fact that this is a live recording. His moulding of phrases too seems to reflect the older traditions of this great orchestra rather than those of his predecessor as music director, Herbert von Karajan. What emerges from this relatively relaxed approach is an extra sense of joy in Schubert's inspiration, with rhythms lifted infectiously. Not that the playing lacks bite or precision, far from it, with many counter-motifs brought out that are too often hidden by the main melodies. The recording also has an admirably wide range, down to magical *pianissimos* from the strings.

Older readers will welcome back to the catalogue this splendidly wise and magisterial account from the doyen of British conductors. There is not a whit of hyperbole; indeed, **Sir Adrian's** tendency to understate is evident in the slow movement, just as his feeling for the overall design is undiminished. The **LPO** respond with playing of high quality and the 1972 Kingsway Hall recording (like the Brahms coupling) is transferred admirably to CD.

In some ways **Jonathan Nott's** account of the Schubert *Ninth* has much in common with the Boult version. The **Bamberg Symphony Orchestra** play very enticingly, and create a warm, Schubertian atmosphere. Nott's reading, too, is relaxed, spontaneous in an unforced way, yet with the concentration maintained throughout. The surround sound (the first this work has received) is gloriously warm and yet vivid in detail.

Most listeners will surely do an aural double-take at the astonishing speed of the opening horn solo of **Menuhin's** highly individual and original interpretation. Yet the movement moves forward in a single thrust, gathering power, energy and momentum to its thrilling coda. The *Andante con moto* is also brisker than usual, but it comes naturally within Menuhin's conception, and the Scherzo rollicks forcefully and genially before the closing *Allegro vivace* sweeps all before it, the trombones helping to drive the music onwards. The sheer exuberance of this performance all but negates the idea of a work of 'heavenly' length and, with such vigour and zest, it is impossible to be bored for a moment, even if you resist the conception. Marvellous playing and splendid recording, leaving the listener on a high.

Roger Norrington's second recording of the *Great C major Symphony* was taken live by **Stuttgart Radio** engineers, with modern instruments using period techniques. The first two movements are marginally faster even than Norrington's earlier EMI recording with the London Classical Players. The interpretation is very similar, with rhythms lightly sprung. The *Die Zauberharfe Overture* (usually known as *Rosamunde*) makes a welcome extra, with a powerful introduction and a fast, light *Allegro*.

CHAMBER MUSIC

Arpeggione Sonata, D.821 (arr. for cello)

*** Ph. 412 230-2. Maisky, Argerich – SCHUMANN: *Fantasiestücke* etc. ***

(BB) *** Naxos 8.550654. Kliegel, Merscher – SCHUMANN: *Adagio & Allegro*, etc. ***

(B) **(*) Cal. (ADD) CAL 3614. Navarra, d'Arco – DVOŘÁK: *Humoresque*, etc.; SCHUMANN: *Adagio & Allegro*, etc. **(*)

Mischa Maisky and **Martha Argerich** make much more of the *Arpeggione Sonata* than any of their rivals. Their approach may be relaxed, but they bring much pleasure through their variety of colour and sensitivity. The Philips recording is in the very best traditions of the house.

At super-bargain price, **Maria Kliegel** and **Kristin Merscher** are highly competitive. The performances are well shaped and sensitive, though perhaps lacking the last ounce of character. All the same, neither the Schubert nor the Schumann coupling will disappoint at this price, given the general high standard of playing and recording.

A warm-hearted, rather old-fashioned performance from **Navarra**, rather discreetly accompanied by **Annie d'Arco**. The cello itself is richly caught, the piano truthful but a little backward.

Arpeggione Sonata; Cello Sonatinas 1–3, D.384–5 & D.408

*** Channel Classics CCS 9696. Wispelwey, Giacometti

The highly musical **Pieter Wispelwey** has the full measure of Schubert's innocent lyricism, and the pianist's light touch in the finale is especially persuasive. **Paolo Giacometti** makes a most convincing case for the use of the fortepiano in Schubert, and the restored instrument has a remarkable range of colour. Pieter Wispelwey's tone, using gut strings, always sings and, even using a minimum of vibrato, he constantly cajoles the ear, while his phrasing has an appealing simplicity. Thus the three violin *Sonatinas* are made to sound convincing in these cello transcriptions, especially the G minor, D.408, in which the *Andante* and finale are endearing. The recording is forwardly but truthfully balanced. Recommended.

Arpeggione Sonata, D.821 (arr. in G min. for clarinet & piano)

*** Chan. 8506. de Peyer, Pryor – SCHUMANN: *Fantasiestücke*; *3 Romances*; WEBER: *Silvana Variations* ***

So persuasive is the performance of **Gervase de Peyer** and **Gwenneth Pryor** that the listener is all but persuaded that the work was actually written for this combination.

(i) Arpeggione Sonata; (ii) Duo in A, D. 574; Fantaisie in C, D. 943; Violin Sonatinas 1–3, D. 384-5 & D. 408

⊶ (B) *** Double Decca stereo/mono (ADD) 466 748-2 (2).
  (i) Gendron, Françaix; (ii) Goldberg, Lupu

Szymon Goldberg and **Radu Lupu** give us the complete violin and piano music (except for one small piece) in beautifully played and well-recorded performances, which have an unaffected Schubertian feeling. Indeed, Goldberg's account of the *Fantasy* is particularly intimate and appealing. The presence of Lupu ensures that these performances give pleasure, and his playing has a vitality and inner life that are undoubtedly rewarding. These recordings date from the end of the 1970s, but the *Arpeggione Sonata*, which has a comparable intimacy and Schubertian affinity, is hardly less appealing even though the recording is mono (but very truthful mono) and dates from 1954.

(i) Fantasy in C, D.934; (i; ii) Piano Trio 2 in E flat, D.929; (iii) String Quartets 8 in B flat, D.112 (Op. 168); 14 in D min. (Death and the Maiden), D.810; 15 in G, D.887 (Op. 161)

(B) (***) HM Pearl mono GEMMCDS 9141 (2). (i) Adolf Busch, Serkin; (iii) with Hermann Busch; (iii) Busch Qt

Some have spoken of the **Busch Quartet's** Schubert as the greatest ever committed to disc. Certainly the *G major Quartet* has never had so searching and powerful a reading, and the early *B flat Quartet*, which used to be known as Op. 168, sounds every bit as captivating as one remembers it from the days of shellac. The *E flat Trio* and the *C major Fantasy* are also in the highest class, and the Pearl transfers are very good indeed. These two CDs, packed economically in one jewel-case, encompass three LPs and are really excellent value for money. A lovely set.

Octet in F, D.803

🔊 **** Onyx ONYX4006. Mullova, Moraguès, Postinghel, Cori, Chamorro, Krüger, M. Fischer-Dieskau, Stall

🔊 ✿ (M) **** Decca (ADD) 466 580-2. Vienna Octet – SPOHR: *Octet in E* ***

(BB) **** HM Classical Express HCX 3957049. Music from Aston Magna

*** Chan. 8585. ASMF Chamber Ens.

*** ASV CDDCA 694. Gaudier Ens.

(BB) *** EMI Gemini (ADD) 3 50864-2 (2). Melos Ens. of L. – BEETHOVEN: *Octet*, etc.; MENDELSSOHN: *Octet* **

Octet in F, D. 803; Wind Octet, in F, D.72

(BB) **(*) Naxos 8.550389. Budapest Schubert Ens.

This newest version of the *Octet* from Onyx is not only the best since the celebrated 1957 Vienna Octet version on Decca, it actually surpasses it. These artists find a greater depth than their predecessors in a work that we all think we know well. There is not only grace, pathos and tenderness here, but also a thoughtful attention to details of phrasing and internal balance. Tempi are generally on the slow side, but the listener's attention is compelled throughout. Musically, a most satisfying and revealing account – and a moving one too. Very fine recording.

The **Vienna Octet's** 1958 recording of the Schubert *Octet* has stood the test of time. It has a magical glow with the group at its peak under the leadership of **Willi Boskovsky**. The horn has a Viennese fruitiness which helps to make the performance more authentic, and these fine players never put a foot wrong throughout. The recording only betrays its age in the upper registers, but is basically full and modern sounding. The delightful and unusual Spohr coupling makes this a fine addition to Decca's Legends series.

A wholly delightful account from the **Aston Magna** American group using period instruments with great finesse and affectionate warmth. Indeed, the music-making is pervaded with an American-styled geniality throughout, although the *Allegro* of the first movement, like the jocular finale, is agreeably brisk and vivacious. All the playing is very personable, but the star of the occasion is the clarinettist, **Eric Hoeprich**, whose timbre is utterly seductive. He uses a pair of instruments, including a C clarinet in the fourth movement *Andante con variazioni*. The recording is first class and this is a real bargain.

The Chandos version brings a performance just as delightful as the earlier one by the **ASMF**, less classical in style, a degree freer in expression, with Viennese overtones brought out in Schubert's sunny invention. It has the benefit of excellent modern digital sound, cleaner on detail than before.

The **Gaudier Ensemble** on ASV give an entirely winning account of the *Octet*, essentially spontaneous yet very relaxed and catching all the ingenuous Schubertian charm. Excellent sound, vivid yet well balanced within a pleasing acoustic which gives a feeling of intimacy. An ideal record for a warm summer evening.

Another very fine account comes from the **Melos** group. Although made in the late 1960s, this is still one of the best versions available, and is especially welcome at budget price. The playing is fresh and spontaneous, yet polished, with excellent ensemble. The recording is splendidly detailed and truthful. It is a pity that the couplings are not caught as sweetly by the engineers.

A vivacious enough account from the **Schubert Ensemble** on Naxos provides a more than viable super-bargain version, particularly as the bonus, a little *Wind Octet* in the same key, has a winning finale. Good playing and lively recording ensure that this disc gives much pleasure.

Octet; (i) Der Hirt aus dem Felsen

*** Wigmore Live WH Live 0017. Michael Collins and Friends, (i) with Tynan, Martineau

This is an intensely enjoyable account of Schubert's *Octet*. It is a work lasting an hour, which with its many repeats can easily outstay its welcome despite the freshness of Schubert's invention. But here **Michael Collins** and a brilliant group of friends – not just from Britain but from Europe too – give a performance wonderfully resilient and imaginative. In the lovely song with clarinet obbligato, *Der Hirt auf dem Felsen*, 'The Shepherd on the Rock', **Malcolm Martineau** is the sensitive pianist accompanying the bright, fresh soprano, **Alison Tynan**. It would be hard to devise a more distinguished group, and that is reflected in the freshness and resilience of the playing.

Piano Quintet in A (Trout) (DVD version)

*** Opus Arte DVD OA CN 0903. D. Barenboim, Perlman, Zukerman, du Pré, Mehta. 'The Trout': Documentary and performance; The Greatest Love and the Greatest Sorrow – Documentary (V/D: Christopher Nupen)

(i) Piano Quintet in A (Trout), D.667; Quartettsatz in C min., D.703 (DVD version)

🔊 *** Testament DVD SBDVD1001 (i) Clifford Curzon; Amadeus Qt – BRITTEN: *String Quartet 2* ***

The performance telerecorded in Aldeburgh was part of a week-long celebration of Schubert and Britten staged in September 1977. It was recorded by a team that included John Culshaw, previously of Decca but by then Head of Music at BBC Television. It is superbly and simply directed, with totally unobtrusive camerawork and expertly balanced sound, with the legendary Jimmy Burnett in charge. **Curzon** is wonderfully natural yet patrician in the *Trout Quintet* and the playing throughout gives unalloyed pleasure.

Christopher Nupen, defying convention, in 1969 made his classic film, 'The Trout', combining documentary with musical performance. The performers, all emerging into international stardom, still in their twenties, provide an effervescent picture of musical preparation behind the scenes. Waiting for the performance at the newly opened Queen Elizabeth Hall in London, they simply have fun, with **Jacqueline du Pré** jazzing up the Mendelssohn *Violin Concerto* while pretending to be Pablo Casals, **Zubin Mehta** bowing **Perlman's** violin as he fingers the opening of that same work, and Perlman playing the *Flight of the Bumblebee* on the cello. Part of the challenge – realized in the exhilarating performance which follows – was that **Pinchas Zukerman** was playing the viola instead of the violin and the conductor, Zubin Mehta, was returning to his old instrument, the double-bass, just for the occasion, while another conductor, Lawrence Foster, turned the pages for **Daniel Barenboim**. Much more sombre, but moving too, is the other film on the disc, a survey of the remaining months of Schubert's short life after the death of Beethoven, when he wrote a sequence of supreme masterpieces.

Piano Quintet in A (Trout), D.667 (CD versions)

☛ ******** EMI 5 57664-2. Adès, Belcea Qt. (members) with C. Long – ADÈS: *Piano Quintet* *******

☛ ******** BBC (ADD) BBCL 4009-2 (2). Curzon, Amadeus Qt, Merret – BRAHMS: *Piano Quintet in F min., Op. 34* *******

*** Ph. 446 001-2. Brendel, Zehetmair, Zimmermann, Duven, Riegelbauer – MOZART: *Piano Quartet 1* *******

Piano Quintet in A (Trout); Piano Trio 1 in B flat

*** ASV Gold GLD 4000. W. Howard & Schubert Ens.

(i) Piano Quintet in A (Trout); (ii) String Quartet 14 (Death and the Maiden)

(M) ******* DG Entrée 471 740-2. (i) Levine, Hetzel, Christ, Faust, Posch; (ii) Hagen Qt

(M) ****(*)** DG (ADD) 449 746-2. Amadeus Qt; with (i) Gilels, Zepperitz

(i) Piano Quintet in A (Trout); Moments musicaux, D.780

☛ (M) ******** Decca 458 608-2. Schiff; (i) Hagen Qt

András Schiff and the **Hagen Quartet** give a delectably fresh and youthful reading of the *Trout Quintet*, full of the joys of spring, but one which is also remarkable for hushed concentration, as in the exceptionally dark and intense account of the opening of the first movement. The Scherzo brings a light, quick and bouncing performance, and there is extra lightness too in the other middle movements. Alongside Brendel's (and Berezovsky's), this version observes the exposition repeat in the finale, and with such a joyful, brightly pointed performance one welcomes that. The *Moments musicaux* are also beautifully played and recorded, and make a considerable bonus.

The performance from **Thomas Adès** and the **Belcea Quartet** is in every way distinctive and, not surprisingly, full of fresh insights. Opening dramatically, tempi are brisk throughout, with the Scherzo making a vibrant centrepiece. The performance is generous on repeats and this brings its own sense of spaciousness. The recording was made at the Maltings so has the expected bloom.

Like the Brahms *Quintet*, with which it is coupled on a bonus disc, **Curzon's** live BBC recording of the *Trout Quintet* with the augmented **Amadeus Quartet**, made at the Royal Festival Hall in 1971, amply compensates in warmth and power for what it may lack in high studio polish, with all five artists at their most spontaneous. The *Trout Variations* may be on the slow side, but the rhythmic pointing is a delight. Good radio sound, smoother on top than Curzon's famous Decca version.

ASV's paired performances from the **Schubert Ensemble** are vibrant accounts, full of life but not lacking charm, with the excellent pianist, **William Howard**, dominating artistically (although the piano is not unnaturally balanced). Both accounts are seemingly spontaneous and if you want this coupling, the disc can receive a firm recommendation.

On a first-class DG Entrée reissue from the early 1990s **James Levine** leads a highly spontaneous performance of the *Trout*, full of vigour, but also striking for its delicacy of lyrical feeling in the delightful account of the famous theme and variations, which contrasts so well with the vibrant Scherzo and crisply animated finale. Excellent, modern recording, with the piano dominating in the right way. The **Hagen Quartet** then give a vital, well-shaped and sensitive account of *Death and the Maiden*, and produce consistent beauty of sound. They are fully alive to the darker side of the work, and even if they rather overdo the *pianissimo* markings, reducing them to the faintest whisper in the slow movement, this remains one of the best modern accounts of the work, and they are very well recorded.

The **Brendel** performance is superbly recorded, the imagery rich and tangible, especially the piano, with **Thomas Zehetmair's** violin sweetly caught and the string bass gently resounding at the bottom. It lacks something in traditional Viennese charm, but has a compensating warmth and weight and certainly plenty of natural impetus, with Brendel consistently persuasive.

In the 1975 DG recording of the *Trout* there is a masterly contribution from **Gilels**, and the **Amadeus** play with considerable freshness. The approach is very positive, not as sunny and spring-like as in some versions, but rewarding in its seriousness of purpose. The Amadeus's account of the *Death and the Maiden Quartet* was their first analogue recording of this work in 1959. The unanimity of ensemble is remarkable. The early DG stereo, too, is very good.

Piano Trio 1 in B flat (DVD version)

(*) EMI DVD 4904519. Y. & H. Menuhin, Gendron – BARTÓK: *Contrasts*, etc.; ENESCU: *Sonata 3*; FRANCK: *Violin Sonata in A* **(***)

Recorded in rather grainy black-and-white at the Bath Festival in 1964, this is still a rewarding account, thanks to the rapport between the players. It serves as a reminder not only of the two **Menuhins** but of the wonderful artistry of **Maurice Gendron**. For all the frailty of the sound, this is a thoroughly enjoyable experience.

Piano Trios 1 in B flat, D.898; 2 in E flat

🎧 *** Praga **SACD** PRD/DSD 250 201. Guarneri Trio, Prague

*** Pentatone **SACD** PTC 5186050. Storioni Trio

Piano Trios 1–2; Adagio in E flat (Notturno) (for piano trio), D.897; Sonata in B flat (for piano trio), D.28

🎧 *** EMI 365476-2. Renaud & Gautier Capuçon, Braley

🎧 **** MDG 342 1166-2 (*Trio 1*); 342 1167-2 (*Trio 2; Notturno; Sonata*). V. Piano Trio

*** HMC 902002-03. Trio Wanderer

(i–iii) Piano Trios 1–2; Notturno in E flat, D.897; Sonata Movement, D.28; (i, ii) Grand Duo in A, D.574

🅱🅱 **(*) EMI Gemini 3 65295-2 (2). (i) Collard; (ii) Dumay; (iii) Lodéon

(i) Piano trios 1–2; Notturno, D.897; Sonata in B flat, D.28; (ii) String Trios: in B flat (in one movement), D.471; in B flat, D.581

Ⓜ *** Ph. 475 7571 (2). Beaux Arts Trio

We are rather spoiled for choice in this repertoire, and readers can't go far wrong with any of the top recommendations currently in circulation. Among them this newcomer from **Renaud** and **Gautier Capuçon**, and **Frank Braley**, recorded in the autumn of 2006 at the Maison de la Culture in Grenoble, must be numbered. They offer warm and characterful readings of Schubert's four works for *Piano Trio*, not only the two big, numbered masterpieces, but also the early *Sonata Movement* and the *Notturno*. They are a vital and sensitive partnership. An issue to be warmly welcomed, even in a hotly competitive field, for its individual and spontaneous-sounding readings, very well recorded.

The set of the *Piano Trios* from the **Vienna Piano Trio** on MDG is outstanding in every way. Their playing is wonderfully fresh and spring-like, and the contribution of the pianist, **Stefan Mendl**, is ear-catchingly crisp. This is true chamber music-making by a beautifully matched team, dramatic and expressive by turns, with remarkable ongoing spontaneity, yet full of incidental subtleties. The recording is in the demonstration class, perfectly balanced. The two CDs are available separately; the first includes the alternative version of the finale, which Schubert composed first, as an appendix.

The much-praised **Beaux Arts** performances are an obvious choice for Philips's Originals label. The performances combine impeccable ensemble with simple dedication.

Czech musicians often display a special feeling for Schubert; the **Guarneri** players are no exception. They set off into the *B flat Trio* with an attractive jauntiness of spirit and then find a nice delicacy for the opening of the lovely *Andante*. After the jolly Scherzo there is a comparably light-

ness of touch for the finale. The *E flat Trio* has a similar vivacious impetus, and the *Andante* with its gentle bouncing underlay is delightfully done; and the same rhythmic lift brings added joy to the rondo finale. In short these are wholly delightful accounts, with a true Schubertian spirit. They are truthfully recorded, although, surprisingly for a SACD, the upper range is a little dry, which affects the violin timbre. But both the performances are memorable.

The young members of the **Storioni Trio** of Amsterdam, founded in 1995, here give exceptionally light and sparkling accounts of both of Schubert's *Trios*. The players take their name from the violin made in Cremona in 1794 by Laorentius Storioni, which is played by the violinist, **Wouter Vossen**. These two *Trios* may be among the deepest of Schubert's chamber works, but they are still well served by such an approach, giving the music light and air. Speeds tend to be on the fast side, except in the two slow movements, which are slowish and very steady. What is a delight in the *B flat Trio*, D.898, is the springing of rhythms, most strikingly in the finale with dotted rhythms exaggerated.

On Harmonia Mundi intelligent and vital accounts from the **Trio Wanderer** which benefit from recorded sound of great clarity and finesse.

Jean-Philippe Collard, **Augustin Dumay** and **Frédéric Lodéon**, all splendid performers in their own right, create a fully integrated ensemble that sounds as if the players enjoy chamber music at home. All these performances sparkle, and there is a true Schubertian spirit in the *Grand Duo*. The recordings were made in a concert-hall acoustic (the Salle Wagram, Paris), and the early digital sound is bright and clearly focused, if a touch dry.

Piano Trio 1 in B flat, D.898

🅱🅱 *** Warner Apex (ADD) 2564 60164-2. Suk Trio (with *Notturno, D. 897*)

🅱🅱 (***) Naxos mono 8.110188. Thibaud, Casals, Cortot – BEETHOVEN: *Variations on 'Ich bin der Schneider Kakadu'*; HAYDN: *Piano Trio 39 in G* (***)

The performances of the **Suk Trio** (**Josef Suk** and **Joseph Chuchra**, with **Jan Panenka**, piano) are appealingly warm and intimate, truly Schubertian; and the truthful 1970 recording ensures that this inexpensive disc will give much pleasure.

The **Thibaud–Casals–Cortot** partnership made their famous recording of the Schubert *B flat Trio* in 1926, and it was long one of the classics of the gramophone. It still has a rich humanity and warmth that explain its reputation. The Ward Marston transfer is very good indeed, even if the sound now seems very dated and two-dimensional.

Piano Trio 1 in B flat, D.898; Sonata in B flat (for piano trio), D.28; Notturno, D.897

🎧 **** Hyp. CDA 67273. Florestan Trio

Piano Trio 2 in E flat, D.929 (includes both first and second versions of finale)

🎧 **** Hyp. CDA 67347. Florestan Trio

The **Florestan Trio** are among the latest to tackle the

Schubert *Piano Trios* and are among the finest on disc. This is highly musical playing, whose value is enhanced by the contributions of that fine pianist **Susan Tomes**. They have the benefit of excellent recording. As a bonus we are additionally offered Schubert's original finale of the *Second Trio*, nearly two minutes longer without the two cuts in the development made by the composer, totalling 98 bars.

Rondo in B min. (for violin & piano), D.895

(B) *** EMI Debut 5 74017-2 Batiashvili, Chernyavska – BACH: *Partita 1*; BRAHMS: *Violin Sonata 1 in G*

A pupil of Mark Lubotsky, the Georgian-born **Elisabeth Batiashvili** makes her EMI début with a mixed programme. She gives a vital and lyrical account of this Schubert piece and is expertly partnered by **Milana Chernyavska**.

String Quartets

String Quartets 1–15

*** Cascavelle VEL 3115 (5). Quatuor Sine Nomine

String Quartets 1–15; Quartet Movement in C min., D.103

(B) **(*) DG (ADD) 463 151-2 (6). Melos Qt of Stuttgart

String Quartets 1; 13; Overture in B flat, D.470 (MDG 307 0602-2)

String Quartets 2; 11; Overture in C min. (for quintet), D.8; Fragment, D. 87a (MDG 307 0609-2)

String Quartets 3; 8; in B flat (fragment), D.470 (MDG 307 0606-5)

String Quartets 4; 5 (including 1st & 2nd versions of Allegro maestoso); 2 Ländler for 2 Violins in D, D.354 (MDG 307 0608-2)

String Quartets 6; 10; in C min. (fragment), D.103 (MDG 307 0605-5)

String Quartets 7; 9; Quartet movement in C min., D. 703 (MDG 307 0607-2)

String Quartet 14 (Death and the Maiden); Minuet, D.86; Minuets & German Dances, D.89 (MDG 307 0604-2)

String Quartet 15; Fragment, D.2c; String Trio, D.472

*** MDG 307 0601-2. New Leipzig Qt

(i) String Quintet in C, D.956. Fragment, D.3; Overture, D.8a

*** MDG 307 0603-2. (i) Sanderling; New Leipzig Qt

The **New Leipzig Quartet** offer an ideal approach. They have great sweetness of tone, yet they are not sugary; they give us a wide dynamic range without drawing attention to themselves, and they seem totally inside the Schubert tradition. They have much greater warmth than the Melos Quartet of Stuttgart on DG and are far removed from the overpowering jet-setting quartet-machines. Theirs is humane music-making which conveys some sense of period and naturalness of expression. The *Quintet* may not be as intense as some versions but it is still very rewarding. The recordings are very good and the set has the merit of including various less familiar fragments. A thoroughly musical and well-recorded series.

The Lausanne-based **Quatuor Sine Nomine** was founded in the mid-1970s and made their breakthrough at the Concours d'Evian in 1985. They recorded the present cycle between 1989 and 1994, though their records did not gain wide currency in Britain. It proves to be eminently serviceable and worthy of their mentors, the Melos Quartet of Stuttgart. They give sensitive and vital performances and, apart from 1, 2, 6 and 10 (which were recorded in Paris), have the benefit of the fine acoustic of the Salle de Chatoneyre, Corseaux in Switzerland.

The **Melos Quartet** give us an inexpensive survey. The early works have a disarming grace and innocence and some of their ideas are most touching (witness the *Adagio* introduction of *4 in C*). The Melos Quartet give impressive, unmannered accounts of all these works, finding the drama as well as the music's inner tensions. They are, however, let down by the recording, which, although faithful, is rather too closely balanced. The remastering provides good presence, and conveys a wide dynamic range, but *fortissimos* can be a little fierce. Nevertheless, this well-documented set is value for money and worth considering when the full-priced competition costs more than twice as much.

String Quartets 1, D.18; 4, D.46; 8, D.112

🎧 (BB) *** Naxos 8.555921. Kodály Qt

The **Kodály Quartet** are embarking with distinction on a complete Schubert cycle. Their playing has the same simplicity of style that they brought to early Haydn, yet the Schubertian colouring emerges immediately at the opening of the very *First Quartet*. This astonishingly confident work was written as early as 1810–11, yet it has a delightful, Ländler-like Minuet which calls for mutes, a graceful *Andante* and a busy, sparkling finale. *4*, written two years later, opens with a grave echo of Mozart's *Dissonance Quartet* and has a delicate slow movement in siciliano rhythm, while the cheerful finale returns to the mood of a rustic Austrian dance. *8* has a G minor slow movement, again obviously influenced by Mozart, which lightens its mood later, but it never shakes off its seriousness entirely until the Haydnesque dancing Minuet and energetic finale. Altogether a splendid beginning, very naturally recorded.

String Quartets 3, D.36; 7, D.94; 9, D.173

🎧 (BB) **** Naxos 8.550592. Kodály Qt

Schubert's *Third Quartet* was written in 1812–13. It is a cheerful work, with a dominating motif in the first movement to remind us of Haydn's *Fifths Quartet*. *7* in D major, written a year earlier, has a disarming opening movement, the effect astonishingly mature, and the *Andante* is comparably serene. The **Kodály Quartet** play this work marvellously and make it the highlight of the disc. *9 in G minor* opens very positively, its argument both dramatic and serious, but the *Andantino* (though still Haydnesque) has a Schubertian theme. The Minuet then reminds us dramatically of the comparable movement in Mozart's *Symphony 40*, and the engaging finale echoes and quickens that same idea. Once again the playing is splendid, and the recording most naturally balanced throughout.

String Quartet 5, D.68; 12 (Quartettsatz); 5 Minuets & 6 Trios, D.89; Overture in C min. for String Quintet, D.8 (ed. Hess); String Trio (movement) in B flat, D.471

⊛–. **(BB)** *** Naxos 8.557126. Kodály Qt (augmented)

For the final volume in their splendid cycle, the **Kodály Quartet** open with the familiar *Quartettsatz*, then set off with spirit and élan into the engaging two-movement *B flat Quartet, D.68* (written when Schubert was 16) and continue with various novelties, including an *Overture* for string quintet written two years before the early quartet. Playing and recording are well up to the high standard of this illustrious series.

String Quartet 8 in B flat, D.112

Ⓜ (***) EMI mono 5 65308-2 (4). Busch Qt (with
MENDELSSOHN: *Capriccio in E min.*) – BEETHOVEN: *String Quartets.* *** ❀

The excellence and lightness of spirit the Busch communicate in this quartet is exhilarating.

String Quartets 8; 13 in A min., D.804

⊛–. **** ASV CDDCA 593. Lindsay Qt

In the glorious *A minor* the **Lindsays** lead the field. It would be difficult to fault their judgement in both these works on tempi and expression, and dynamics are always the result of keen musical thinking. Excellent recording.

String Quartets 10 (7); 13, D.804

⊛–. ❀ **** Astrée E 8580. Mosaïques Qt
⊛–. **(BB)** **** Naxos 8.550591. Kodály Qt
Ⓝ **(BB)** *** EMI Encore 2 35738-2. Belcea Qt

Above all, these Mosaïques period-instrument performances, so notable for their points of closely observed detail, are highly spontaneous. The very opening of the *E flat Quartet* (published posthumously as 10) is warmly inviting, and the players have the full measure of the songful serenity of its lovely *Adagio*. The profundities of the *A minor* are fully understood by this highly sensitive group, and the recapitulation is particularly memorable. There is dramatic intensity as well as charm in the famous (*Rosamunde*) *Andante*, with the finale following gracefully: the delicacy of the shading of the playing here is a marvel. A superb disc, beautifully recorded.

What strikes one immediately at the opening of the **Kodály's** account of the great *A minor Quartet, D.804*, is the

guileless simplicity of their approach. There is drama too, but the innocent, lyrical feeling persists, and it enhances the lovely *Andante* with its *Rosamunde* theme. The earlier *E flat major Quartet* is presented with comparable geniality and again the ensemble is immaculate, with some delightful interchanges in the vigorous finale with its wistful secondary theme. Once again excellent recording.

The **Belcea** made a strong impression with their début recordings of Debussy and Ravel, and they follow up here with another of the best Schubert quartet discs to have appeared recently. Tempi are expertly judged and they command both feeling and concentration. Competition is strong for this coupling, but at budget price this is very attractive.

String Quartets 10, D.87; 14 (Death and the Maiden)

⊛–. Ⓜ **** Cal. Approche CAL 5234. Talich Qt

The **Talich Quartet** do not wear their hearts on their sleeves: the intensity of their performance of *Death and the Maiden* comes from within. There is a profundity in the theme and variations of the *Andante* which, together with the richness of texture that they create, is wonderfully heart-warming. The performance of the earlier *D major Quartet* is hardly less fine: more volatile, with the spirited finale concluding the disc unforgettably. Superb recording; string quartet discs do not come any better than this.

String Quartet 12 (Quartettsatz), D.703

Ⓑ *** EMI 3 66557-2. Formosa Qt – DEBUSSY: *String Quartet*;
MOZART: *String Quartet 14*; WOLF: *Italian Serenade* ***

As a fill-up to their EMI Debut disc of Mozart and Debussy, the brilliant prize-winning **Formosa Quartet** give a brisk, fluent, finely shaded and intense reading of this tricky *Quartet Movement*, making one want to hear them in more Schubert.

String Quartets 12 (Quartettsatz); 13; 14 (Death and the Maiden); 15, D.887

⊛–. Ⓑ *** Ph. (ADD) Duo 446 163-2 (2). Italian Qt

String Quartets 12–15; (i) String Quintet in C, D.956

⊛–. Ⓜ *** Nim. NI 1770. Brandis Qt; (i) with Yang
Ⓑ **(*) DG Trio 477 045-2 (3). Emerson Qt; with (i)
Rostropovich

The **Brandis Quartet**, a fine Central European group, have warmth and they bring a natural eloquence to all these quartets, which are all the more potent for being free of interpretative point-making. In the great *C major Quintet*, with beautiful matching, they again convey spontaneous expressiveness, and they are not afraid to linger a little over the first movement's lovely second-subject melody. Their slow movement, played freely, has rapt tension but, again, also conveys warmth, rather an ethereal, withdrawn atmosphere which communicates in a quite individual way. They are very naturally recorded.

The **Italian Quartet's** 1965 coupling of the *Quartettsatz* and the *Death and the Maiden Quartet* was counted the finest available in its day. These players' understanding of Schubert is equally reflected in their performance of the *A minor*

Quartet, recorded a decade later. The familiar 'Rosamunde' slow movement is beautifully paced, with an impressive command of feeling. The 1976 sound, too, is first class. The G major Quartet is, if anything, even finer. And the recording is extremely vivid, making this one of the most thought-provoking accounts of the Quartet ever.

The **Emersons** certainly have an amazing technical address and are among the finest quartets playing now. Their attack and ensemble are impeccable; their tonal blend and finesse disarm criticism. Their approach is distinctly late twentieth-century Manhattan, rather than early nineteenth-century Europe with its gentler colours. Yet they spring from a different culture and have no want of intelligence and insight. There is tenderness at times and, in the C major Quintet with **Rostropovich** as second cello, an abundant eloquence. Good recording.

String Quartets 12 (Quartettsatz); 14 (Death and the Maiden)

🎵 **** ASV CDDCA 560. Lindsay Qt

(BB) *** Naxos 8.550590. Kodály Qt

The **Lindsays'** intense, volatile account of the Death and the Maiden Quartet is played with considerable metrical freedom and the widest range of dynamic, and the Quartettsatz, which acts as the usual filler, is unusually poetic and spontaneous in feeling. The recording is excellent.

The **Kodály** players are not renowned for wearing their hearts on their bow-arms, and their performance of the first movement of the Death and the Maiden, though not lacking in point and responsive intensity, is not as sharply extrovert in its associations with mortality as some. They find the heart of the work in the slow movement variations, which they open very intimately and they play with their usual humanity and feeling, if without quite the potency of the Lindsays. This is certainly a performance to live with, even if it does not dwell on the tragedy of Schubert's inspiration and the playing in the Quartettsatz, agitated and lilting by turns, is also very fine. The recording, which has a natural presence, is well up to the high standard of this fine series.

String Quartet 14 in D min. (Death and the Maiden) (DVD version)

*** EMI **DVD** 0946 3 38446 9 2. Alban Berg Qt (with documentary by Bruno Monsaigeon)

A very well-thought-out reading of Death and the Maiden by the **Alban Berg Quartet**, recorded in 1995 in the Mozartsaal, Vienna, and played with their usual mastery. Bruno Monsaigeon's documentary is very largely a masterclass by the members of the quartet with the Artemis Quartet. The celebrated Lied on which the slow movement is based is sung by **Julia Varady**, with her husband, **Dietrich Fischer-Dieskau**, as pianist.

String Quartets 14 (Death and the Maiden); 15 in G

(M) (***) EMI mono 3 61588-2. Busch Qt

The **Busch Quartet's** account is more than 50 years old, but it brings us closer to the heart of this music than almost any

other. The slow movement of the Death and the Maiden Quartet is a revelation, and the same must be said of the G major, which has great depth and humanity. For its age, the sound is still amazing.

String Quartet 14 (Death and the Maiden) (arr. for string orchestra by Mahler)

(*) Chan. 9616. Norwegian CO, I. Brown – SCHOENBERG: Verklaerte Nacht **

Mahler made his transcription of Death and the Maiden when opportunities to hear Schubert's masterpiece were few and far between. In the days of its ready accessibility on records and in the concert hall, the idea of recording it seems a false reverence (just as recording piano-duet versions of Glazunov symphonies would be). Its character is naturally changed in the orchestral medium, but those who want this transcription will find the playing of the **Norwegian Chamber Orchestra** and the Chandos recording both first class.

String Quartet 15 in G, D.887

🎵 (BB) **** Naxos 8.557125. Kodály Qt

(M) (**(*)) Orfeo mono C604031B. Hungarian Qt – BARTÓK: Quartet 5 (**(*))

A truly outstanding performance of Schubert's last and probably greatest String Quartet from the **Kodály** group, who open dramatically and encompass all the work's magical changing moods with consistent concentration and deep feeling. Spontaneity informs every bar: the Andante has an unforgettable atmosphere of gentle melancholy, yet there is a joyful simplicity in the dancing finale, which is brilliantly played. Indeed, this is one of the group's very finest records, for the infectious German Dances make a most engaging bonus, the closing Laendler particularly winning. First-class recording.

This Orfeo performance comes from a concert given at the Salzburg Mozarteum in August 1961, some seven years before the **Hungarian Quartet's** commercial recording at the Salle Wagram. The live occasion prompts playing of tremendous intensity and heartfelt feeling. This has a higher emotional temperature than the latter; the mono sound is perfectly acceptable.

String Quintet in C, D.956 (DVD version)

🎵 *** Testament **DVD** SBDVD1002. Amadeus Qt, Pleeth – BRITTEN: String Quartet 3 ***

Many listeners find **Norbert Brainin's** sound a little oversweet, but this performance is in many respects superior to the earlier commercial versions (and certainly to the DG set): the whole concert is rewarding to listen to and follow on screen. It comes with an authoritative version of Benjamin Britten's Third Quartet, composed for the **Amadeus Quartet** in the last months of his life. As with its companion, the camerawork is unobtrusive and never attracts attention to itself.

String Quintet in C, D.956

🎵 ❀ (BB) *** Regis (ADD) RRC 1278. Aeolian Qt (with MOZART: Divertimento in D, K.136 ***)

🎵 (M) *** EMI 5 66890-2. Alban Berg Qt with Schiff

🔊⟶ (***) Testament mono SBT 1031 Hollywood Qt, Reher –
SCHOENBERG: *Verklaerte Nacht.* (***) ✹

Ⓜ *** DG (ADD) 477 6357. Melos Qt, with Rostropovich

*** Nim. NI 5313. Brandis Qt, Yang

*** Channel Classics CCS 6794. Orpheus Qt, Wispelwey

(***) Biddulph mono LAB 093. Pro Arte Qt, Pini – BRAHMS:
String Sextet 1. (***)

String Quintet in C; String Quartet 14 (Death and the Maiden); Quartettsatz, D. 703

🔊⟶ ✹ Ⓜ **** ASV CDDCS 243 (2). Lindsay Qt

String Quintet in C; String Trio in B flat, D.471

ⒷⒷ *** Hyp. Helios CDH 55305. Raphael Ens.

String Quintet in C; String Trio in B flat, D.581

ⒷⒷ *** Naxos 8.550388. Villa Musica Ens.

The **Lindsay** version gives the impression that one is eavesdropping on music-making in the intimacy of a private concert. They observe the first-movement exposition repeat and the effortlessness of their approach does not preclude intellectual strength. In the ethereal *Adagio* they effectively convey the sense of it appearing motionless, suspended, as it were, between reality and dream, yet at the same time they never allow it to become static. Their reading must rank at the top of the list; it is very well recorded. It now comes coupled at mid-price with an equally memorable version of the *Death and the Maiden Quartet* – a virtually unbeatable pairing, with the *Quartettsatz* thrown in for good measure.

The **Aeolian Quartet** also give an altogether outstanding performance that some may feel is even finer than the Lindsays' account. Even if the recording is not as modern, in its latest remastering it is crystal clear and has great presence. The playing is strong and virile, direct and with no mannerisms whatsoever. It might seem bald, were it not for the depth of concentration in every bar. The finale, for example, is fresh and rustic-sounding, not because of pointing of the rhythm, but because of the very simplicity of utterance. But the heart of the performance lies in the slow movement, where the Aeolians daringly adopt the slowest possible *Adagio*, and the result might have seemed static but for the 'inner' tension which holds one breathless through hushed *pianissimos* of the most intense beauty. The Mozart *String Divertimento* makes an engaging lightweight encore.

Few ensembles offer timbre as full-bodied or as richly burnished as that produced by the **Alban Berg** and **Heinrich Schiff**, whose recording has impressive sonority, although there is just a touch of digital fierceness on top. However, unlike the Lindsays, they do not observe the first movement exposition repeat.

The **Hollywood Quartet's** 1951 version of the *Quintet* with **Kurt Reher** as second cello stands apart. Over 50 years on, its qualities of freshness and poetry, as well as an impeccably confident technical address, still impress as deeply as ever. This is the product of consummate artistry and remains very special indeed.

Rostropovich plays as second cello in the **Melos** per-

formance, and no doubt his influence from the centre of the string texture contributes to the eloquence of the famous *Adagio* which, like the performance as a whole, is strongly, even dramatically characterized. However in the opening and closing sections of the slow movement, the performance in the last analysis is less persuasive than the Lindsays' or Aeolian versions. The DG recording is live and immediate.

The **Brandis Quartet** with **Wen-Sin Yang** (cello) give a very satisfying account which is also available coupled with *Quartets 12–15* (see above).

The **Raphael Ensemble** couple the great *C major Quintet* with the miniature *String Trio*, which is played most winningly. This is one of the most gripping versions available, and the recording is well up to Hyperion house standards. A real bargain.

The **Villa Musica** players tackle the great *C major Quintet* with a freshness and concentration that are consistently compelling, even if the finale is neat and clean rather than urgently dramatic. The little *String Trio* makes an attractive and generous fill-up, another assured and stylish performance. With clear, well-balanced recording this super-budget issue makes an outstanding bargain.

The **Orpheus Quintet** offer a performance of communicated warmth and feeling, both in the slow movement and in the remarkable *Andante* central section of the Scherzo. The playing is fresh and feels alive, and the recording has striking body and realism.

The **Pro Arte Quartet's** 1935 account of the Schubert *Quintet*, with **Anthony Pini** as second cello, dominated the pre-war catalogues. Its humanity and warmth still tell, particularly in the slow movement. It comes with a fine account of the Brahms *B flat Sextet*, made in the same year. Needless to say, some allowance has to be made for the recording, eminently well transferred though it is.

(i) String Quintet in C, D.956; (ii) Symphony 5 in B flat

Ⓜ (***) Sony 82876 78759-2. (i) Stern, Schneider, Katims, Casals, Tortelier; (ii) Prades Festival O, Casals

Everything **Casals** did on record was touched with distinction and although the recordings are dated, both these performances are very special.

(i) String Quintet in C; (ii) Lieder: An die Musik; An Sylvia; Ave Maria; Gretchen am Spinnrade; Heldenroslein; Auf dem Wasser zu singen; Die Forelle; Der Tod und das Mädchen

Ⓝ Ⓑ **** CfP 2 28282-2 . (i) Chilingirian Qt; (ii) Janet Baker, Parsons or Moore (Ave Maria)

Vividly recorded in 1980, with clear placing of instruments in a smallish but not dry acoustic (in fact a chapel), the Chilingirians present a most compelling account, totally unmannered and direct in style but full of concentration and spontaneity. One has the consistent sense of live performance, and the great melody of the first movement's second subject emerges without any intrusive nudging or overexpressiveness. The slow movement too has natural intensity, though the closeness of the recording prevents one from registering a really soft *pianissimo*. Throughout, the string timbres and blending are most natural, so if you fancy the couplings of favourite Lieder, admirably sung by Janet Baker, this is a real bargain.

Violin Sonatinas 1–3, D.384–5 & D.408; Duo in A, D.574

⊶ Ⓜ *** Explore (ADD) EXP 015. Schröder, Hogwood

The Explore reissue label offers the only available performances of the *Duo* and *Sonatinas* on period instruments, and it makes most rewarding listening, particularly in the sympathetic hands of these artists. **Jaap Schröder** uses a Stradivarius and **Christopher Hogwood** a piano from 1825 by Georg Hascha, which he plays with exemplary skill and artistry. If it does not produce the range of nuance and tonal subtlety of which the modern piano is capable, its lightness of colour has a special charm. Schröder also plays with characteristic authority and artistry, and both are very well recorded; indeed, the CD transfer is very fine and realistically balanced.

(Violin Sonatina) Duo in A, D.574; Fantasia in C, D.934; Rondo brillant, D.895

Ⓑ **** EMI 3 63303-2. Renaud Capuçon, Ducros

The *Duo* and the *Fantasia* (plus the *Rondo*) are a decade apart. The *Duo* of 1817 has a charm, spontaneity and easy naturalness typical of early Schubert, the *Fantasia* (1827), one of the composer's very last works, was in Alfred Einstein's opinion 'a substitute for the violin concerto which Schubert never wrote'. Its centrepiece is an inspired set of variations of great variety and felicity. The *Rondo brillant* (1826) is a skilful, virtuosic piece of rather less interest. All three works are played splendidly here by **Renaud Capuçon** and **Jérôme Ducros** and they show the range of Schubert's invention to diverting effect without seeking profundity. A thoroughly worthwhile reissue.

PIANO MUSIC

PIANO DUET

Piano music for 4 hands

Allegro in A min. (Lebensstürme), D.947; Divertissement à la française in E min., D.823; Divertissement à la hongroise in G min., D.818; Fantasia in F min., D.940; Grand duo in C, D.812; 4 Ländler, D.814

ⓑⓑ *** EMI Gemini (ADD) 3 65326-2 (2). Eschenbach, Frantz

German Dance in G min., D.818; Grande marche funèbre, D.859; Grande marche héroïque, D.885; 6 Grandes marches et trios, D.819; Grand rondeau (allegretto quasi andantino), D.951; Kindermarsch in G min., D.928; 2 Ländler in E, D.618; 2 Marches caractéristiques, D.886; 2 Marches héroïques, D.602; 3 Marches militaires, D.733

ⓑⓑ *** EMI Gemini (ADD) 3 65321-2 (2). Eschenbach, Frantz

Christoph Eschenbach and **Justus Frantz** made their extensive survey of Schubert's four-handed piano music in 1978 and 1979, and the Abbey Road recording was of high quality. The opening of the *F minor Fantasia* here may suggest that the performance is too reticent, but that is deceptive and this is as powerful a reading as any available with its rhythms well sprung; and the same comment applies to the *Grand Duo*, while the wide range of mood in the *Lebensstürme* is encompassed impressively. The delicate interplay between the two pianists is a constant delight, whether in the simple *Ländler*, the charming central *Andantino varié* of the *Divertissement à la française* or the cimbalom imitations in the companion Hungarian-style *Divertissement*, both extended three-movement works showing the composer at his most felicitously inventive and presented here joyfully.

Most remarkable of all are the *Grande marche funèbre* and the *Grande marche héroïque*. The closing *Grand rondeau*, most touchingly played, was written in June 1828, only five months before the composer's death at the age of thirty-one. Overall Eschenbach and Frantz score in sheer freshness, but the EMI sound at times has a bright edge.

Music for piano, 4 hands: Allegro in A min., D.947; Fantasy in F min., D.940; Marche caractéristique 1 in C, D.968b; Marche militaire 1 in D, D.733; Sonata in C (Grand Duo), D.812

⊶ **** RCA 82876 69283-2 (2). Kissin, Levine

This set provides a record of the recital that **Evgeny Kissin** and **James Levine** gave in Carnegie Hall on 1 May 2005. Their programme draws on Schubert's work for piano, four hands, or, in the case of the *Grand Duo*, two keyboards. For the sake of both comfort and sonority, they use two pianos throughout. All this music comes from the late 1820s and it is difficult to find fault with this distinguished partnership, in terms of either spontaneity or sensitivity.

Allegro moderato & Andante, D.968; Fantasy in G min., D.9; 3 Marches militaires D.733; 4 Polonaises, D.599; Variations on 'Marie' by Hérold

ⓑⓑ **(*) Naxos 8.553441. Jandó, Kollar

This disc of some of Schubert's lesser works for piano duet begins most temptingly with the most famous of his *Marches militaires*, played by the Hungarian duo with crispness and vigour. Ranging from the very early *Fantasy* to the late *Allegro & Andante*, this well-recorded collection may be a little short on charm, but is winningly fresh throughout.

Duo, D.947; Fantasia in F min., D.940; 6 Polonaises, D.824; Variations on an Original Theme, D.813

⊶ ⓑⓑ *** Warner Apex (ADD) 0927 49812-2. Queffélec, Cooper

The playing of **Anne Queffélec** and **Imogen Cooper** is hardly less eloquent than any of their rivals', and they also offer a commanding account of the *Fantasia in F minor*. The slighter pieces also come off well: the *Variations* are beautifully played and have an engaging innocence, while the six *Polonaises* are also worth having on disc when played so brightly and spontaneously. The 1978 analogue recording is well balanced, clear and natural, the acoustic neither over-reverberant nor too confined.

Fantasia in F min., D.940

⊕– **** Sony 517490-2. Perahia, Lupu – MOZART: *Double Piano Sonata* ****

*** Chan. 9162. Lortie, Mercier – MOZART: *Andante with Variations*, etc. ***

Ⓜ *** DG (ADD) 463 652-2. Emil & Elena Gilels – MOZART: *Piano Concerto 27; Double Piano Concerto* *** ❀

Recorded live at The Maltings, the performance of **Lupu** and **Perahia** is full of haunting poetry, with each of these highly individual artists challenging the other in imagination. Warmly atmospheric recording.

The **Louis Lortie–Hélène Mercier** partnership is as impressive here as it is elsewhere. The Schubert holds its own even against such illustrious competition as the Lupu–Perahia recording on Sony, also coupled with Mozart. Very good recording.

On DG an apt and finely played bonus for a treasurable Mozart coupling.

Fantasia in F min., D.940; German Dance & 2 Ländler, D.618; 3 Marches héroïques, D.602; Overture in F; Variations on an Original Theme, D.968a

ⒷⒷ *** Naxos 8.554513. Jandó, Kollar

The Hungarian pianist **Jenö Jandó** with his colleague **Zsuzsa Kollar** gives a magnetic reading of what by any reckoning is the greatest of all piano duets, Schubert's haunting *F minor Fantasia*, with its inspired telescoping of a four-movement structure. With Jandó and partner, nothing distracts one from the beauty of Schubert's writing, and the lesser pieces, including the dramatic *Overture in F* and some delectable dances and marches, have comparable freshness, cleanly recorded.

Fantasia in F min.; Grand Duo; Variations, D.813

⊕– Ⓜ *** Decca (ADD) 466 822-2. Richter, Britten

As these electrically intense performances demonstrate, **Richter** and **Britten** favoured fast speeds, which yet allowed crisply sprung rhythms and warmly lyrical phrasing, with phenomenally crisp articulation from both players. The two major works were recorded in 1965 in Jubilee Hall, Aldeburgh, the *Variations* in the Parish Church a year earlier, both with clear, immediate stereo-sound balanced for radio by BBC engineers.

Grand Duo in C, D.812; 2 Grandes Marches, D.819/2–3; 4 Ländler, D.814; 8 Variations on an Original Theme, D.813

Ⓝ ⒷⒷ *** Naxos 8.570354. Schiller, Humphreys

Excellent performances from the four-handed partnership of **Allan Schiller** and **John Humphreys** of some of the rarer of Schubert's pieces for piano, four hands, although the re-markable *Grand Duo* does not fit that description. They are most realistically recorded.

Solo piano music

Fantasia in C (Wanderer), D.760 (DVD version)

*** EMI **DVD** (ADD) 4 901229. Katchen – BEETHOVEN: *Piano Sonata 29* ***

Like his celebrated recording of the Ravel *Left-hand Concerto*, this was made in the shadows of the illness that claimed **Katchen** some months later. It is a poignant and impressive reading, and its appearance here is a cause for celebration for all his admirers.

Fantasia in C (Wanderer), D.760 (CD versions)

⊕– Ⓜ **** EMI 5 66895-2. Richter – DVOŘÁK: *Piano Concerto* ****

Ⓜ *** DG (ADD) 447 451-2. Pollini – SCHUMANN: *Fantasia, Op. 17* ***

Richter's 1963 performance is masterly in every way. The piano timbre is real and the remastering for EMI's 'Great Recordings of the Century' gives the pianist a compelling presence.

Pollini's account is outstanding and, though he is not ideally recorded and the piano timbre is shallow, the playing still shows remarkable insights. Moreover the Schumann coupling is equally fine.

Fantasia in C (Wanderer), D.760; Piano Sonata 21 in B flat, D.960; Impromptus D 899/3–4

❀ Ⓜ **** RCA 09026 63054-2. Rubinstein

Rubinstein plays the *Wanderer fantasia* with sure magnificence. The extended structure needs a master to hold it together and, particularly in the variations section, Rubinstein is electrifying. He compels attention as though he is improvising the work himself, but even so avoids any sentimentality. The 1965 recording sounds surprisingly full, and it is even better in the two *Impromptus*, played with the most subtle shading of colour and delectable control of rubato, and in the superb account of the *Sonata*. Unaccountably, this has never been issued before, yet it shows Rubinstein as a magically persuasive Schubertian.

Impromptus 1–4, D. 899; 5–8, D.935

⊕– **** Sony SK 94732. Perahia (with LISZT: *Concert paraphrases of Schubert Lieder: Auf dem Wasser zu singen; Erlkönig; Ständchen – Leise flehen meine Lieder* (***))

Ⓜ *** Decca 460 975-2. Lupu

Perahia's account of the *Impromptus* is very special indeed. Directness of utterance and purity of spirit are of the essence here, with articulation of sparkling clarity. The CBS recording is very good and truthful in timbre. Perahia's set of *Impromptus* remains at the top of the recommended list (see our main volume) and now has three Liszt/Schubert song transcriptions as a tempting bonus, played equally perceptively.

Lupu's *Impromptus* are of the same calibre as the **Brendel**

analogue versions (see below), and he is most beautifully recorded on CD. Indeed, in terms of natural sound this is a most believable image.

4 Impromptus 1–4, D.899; 5–8, D.935; Moments musicaux, D.780; Piano Sonatas 13 in A, D.664; 21 in B flat, D.960

⊕–⌐ (M) **** DG (ADD) 459 412-2 (2). Kempff

Kempff always had something special to say in Schubert. The *Impromptus* are beautifully done, especially the D.899 set, and in his hands the *Moments musicaux* range so much further than one expects. Kempff characteristically gives intimate performances. His *Allegros* are never very fast and the results sing in the most relaxed way. The *B flat Sonata* is the highlight of the collection, and it is a tribute to Kempff's artistry that, with the most relaxed tempi, he conveys such consistent, compulsive intensity. Rightly, Kempff repeats the first-movement exposition with the important nine bars of lead-back, and though the overall manner is less obviously dramatic than is common, the range of tone colour is magical, with sharp terracing of dynamics to plot the geography of each movement. Though very much a personal utterance, this interpretation is no less great for that. It belongs to a tradition of pianism that has almost disappeared, and we must be eternally grateful that its expression has been so glowingly captured on this reissue.

Impromptus 1–8; 3 Klavierstücke, D.946; 6 Moments musicaux, D.780

(B) *** Virgin 2x1 5 62233-2 (2). Tan (fortepiano) –
BEETHOVEN: *Allegretto*, etc. ***

Melvyn Tan's playing is refreshingly unmannered and for the most part very persuasive: he is at pains to avoid any sentimentality, yet he succeeds in conveying the music's tenderness. He has the measure of the scale of the *F minor Impromptu*, D.935/1, and brings both dramatic fire and poetic feeling to it. In the *Moments musicaux* he has remarkable feeling for colour and never approaches the music with any excess of that judicious reverence which distinguishes some musicians using period instruments. His Schubert is consistently spirited and fresh and, throughout, this stimulating and lively playing casts new light on the composer. The recording is excellent.

Impromptus 1–8; 3 Klavierstücke, D.946; Moments musicaux 1–6, D.780; Allegretto in C min., D.915; 6 German Dances, D.820; Grazer Galopp, D.925; Hungarian Melody in B min., D.817; 12 Ländler, D.790

(B) *** Double Decca 458 139-2 (2). Schiff

Impromptus 1–8; 3 Klavierstücke (Impromptus), D.946; 6 Moments musicaux, D.780; 12 German Dances, D.790; 16 German Dances, D.783

⊕–⌐ ❀ (B) **** Ph. (ADD) Duo 456 061-2 (2). Brendel

Brendel's analogue set of the *Impromptus* is magical, and the *Moments musicaux* are among the most poetic in the catalogue. The *Klavierstücke* are searching, and in his hands the

German Dances, although retaining their underlying charm, sound anything but trivial. The recordings offer Philips's very finest analogue quality.

András Schiff's playing is idiomatic, intelligent and humane, and the recording is more than acceptable. It is impossible to recommend his *Impromptus* in preference to those of Brendel, but no one will be disappointed with them. Schiff has the advantage of very natural digital recording, the effect lighter-textured than with Brendel.

Impromptus 1–8; Moments musicaux, D.780/3–6

(BB) *** Regis (ADD) RRC 1019. Brendel

Brendel's playing has an unaffected simplicity that is utterly disarming, and the lightness of his articulation is a pleasure in itself. The fresh, natural eloquence is also very striking in the four favourite *Moments musicaux*, which are offered here as a bonus (the disc has a playing time of 71 minutes). The recording, too, is surprisingly good.

Impromptus 1–4, D.899; Piano Sonata 21 in B flat, D.960

*** Cal. CAL 6689. Södergren

Inger Södergren's account of the first four *Impromptus* belongs in exalted company, and the *B flat Sonata* is hardly less fine. Her playing is marked throughout by sensitivity and a selfless and unostentatious dedication to Schubert. The recording is acceptable rather than outstanding.

3 Klavierstücke, D.946

(M) (***) BBC mono BBCL 4125. Claudio Arrau – BRAHMS: *Piano Concerto 2* (***)

Arrau's magisterial artistry is captured here in the BBC's Maida Vale Studios in 1959. These are searching accounts, which should be eagerly snapped up by admirers of Arrau.

Moments musicaux 1–6, D.780; 3 Klavierstücke, D.946; Allegretto in C min., D.915

(BB) **(*) Naxos 8.550259. Jandó

Jandó is much better recorded here than he often has been. He proves a thoroughly sympathetic and sensitive Schubertian, but he is still too upfront. The opening of the *Drei Klavierstücke* is a shade too fast (Jandó does not completely convey its dark, disturbing overtones) but the middle section is beautifully judged. Thoughtful and intelligent music-making, acceptably recorded, and very good value for money.

Piano sonatas

Piano Sonatas 1 in E, D.157; 2 in C, D.279; 3 in E, D.459; 4 in A min., D.537; 5 in A flat, D.557; 6 in E min., D.566; 7 in E flat, D.568; 9 in B, D.575; 11 in F min., D.625; 12 in F min, D.625; 13 in A, D.664; 14 in A min., D.784; 15 in C, D.840 (Relique); 16 in A min., D.845; 17 in D, D.850; 18 in G, D.894; 19 in C min., D.958; 20 in A, D.959; 21 in B flat, D.960

(B) **** DG 463 766-2 (7). Kempff

Wilhelm Kempff's cycle was recorded over a four-year period

(1965–9) and has been much admired over the years. These are among the most consistently satisfying accounts of the *Sonatas*, with a wisdom that puts them in a category of their own. Indeed their insights are very special indeed. The recording has a touch of shallowness, but is generally excellent. All seven CDs are now available in a convenient, inexpensive bargain box, and represent exceptional value.

Piano Sonatas 14–21; German Dances; Impromptus; Moments musicaux; Wanderer fantasia

*** Ph. 426 128-2 (7). Brendel

Piano Sonatas 16 in A min., D.845; 3 Impromptus, D.946

*** Ph. 422 075-2. Brendel

Piano Sonatas 19 in C min., D.958; Moments musicaux 1–6, D.780

*** Ph. 422 076-2. Brendel

Piano Sonatas 20 in A, D.959; Allegretto in C min., D.915; 16 German dances, D.783; Hungarian Melody in B min., D.817

**(*) Ph. 422 229-2. Brendel

Piano Sonata 21 in B flat, D.960; Wanderer fantasia, D.760

*** Ph. 422 062-2. Brendel

Brendel's later digital set is more intense than his earlier cycle of recordings for Philips, though there was a touching freshness in the earlier set, and he has the benefit of clean, well-focused sound. These are warm performances, strongly delineated and powerfully characterized, which occupy a commanding place in the catalogue. They are separately available, and all of them can be confidently recommended to Brendel's admirers.

'The Last Six Years, 1823–1828': Vol. 1: Piano Sonatas 14 in A min., D.784; 18 in G, D.894; 12 German Dances (Ländler), D.790 (Priory/Ottavo OTR C68608)

Vol. 2: Piano Sonatas 15 in C, D.840; 20 in C, D.959; 11 Ecossaises, D.781 (Priory/Ottavo OTR C58714)

Vol. 3: Piano Sonata 16 in A min., D.845; 4 Impromptus, D.935 (Priory/Ottavo OTR C88817)

Vol. 4: Piano Sonata 17 in D, D.850; 6 Moments musicaux, D.780 (Priory/Ottavo OTR C128715)

Vol. 5: Piano Sonata 21 in B flat, D.960; Allegretto in C min., D.915; 3 Impromptus (Klavierstücke), D.946 (Priory/Ottavo OTR C88821)

Vol. 6: Piano Sonata 19 in C min., D. 958; 4 Impromptus, D.899 (Priory/Ottavo OTR C78923)

⌐ **** Cooper

Imogen Cooper, in her outstanding set on the Dutch Ottavo label, has a true Schubertian sensibility; her feeling for this composer's special lyricism is second to none, yet her playing has both strength and a complete understanding of the music's architecture. The recordings were made in the Henry Wood Hall, London, over a period of three years, between June 1986 and July 1989, using a Steinway for the first three volumes and a fine-sounding Yamaha for the later records. The balance is admirable and the sound full, with a convincing natural resonance. The playing has the spontaneity of live music-making, and the warm colouring and fine shading of timbre are as pleasing to the ear as the many subtle nuances of phrasing, which are essentially based on a strong melodic line. With their fine, modern, digital recording these CDs will give much delight and refreshment.

Piano Sonatas 4, D.537; 7, D.568; 9, D.575; 13, D.664; 14, D.784; 15 (Relique), D.840; 16, D.845; 17, D.850; 18, D.894; 19, D.958; 20, D.959; 21, D. 960; German Dances, D.790 & 820; 8 Impromptus, D.899 & 935; 3 Klavierstücke, D.946; Moments musicaux, D.70

ⓑ **(*) Ph. 475 6282 (8). Uchida

Mitsuko Uchida began her Schubert survey in 1997 and continued until 2002, then leaving the cycle incomplete. As can be seen from the separate reviews below, she did not have quite the same degree of success here that she did with the sonatas of Mozart. This is distinctive playing, sensitive and eloquent; moreover the Philips recording is exceptionally truthful. Certain sonatas, the *Relique* for instance, are outstanding in every way and the great *B flat Sonata, D. 960* shows her at her very finest. But at other times she does not always leave the composer to speak for himself and Schubert's special quality of innocence all but eludes her.

Piano Sonata 7 in E flat, D.568; Moments musicaux, D.780

*** Ph. 470 164-2. Uchida

As piano playing this is consummate, though some may feel that she tends to beautify further what is already beautiful, and the innocence of Schubert succumbs to over-sophistication. The recording is wonderfully realistic, indeed state-of-the-art sound.

Piano Sonatas 9; 11; 13; Moment musical, D.780/1

*** BBC (ADD) BBCL 4010-2. Richter

This disc comprises a Schubert recital **Richter** gave at the Royal Festival Hall in 1979, and the dryish sound is perfectly acceptable. As always, his playing is magisterial and eloquent. Thoroughly recommendable.

Piano Sonatas 9 in B, D.575; 18 in G, D.894; 20 in A, D.959; 21 in B flat, D.960

**(*) Ph. 456 573-2 (2). Brendel

Though **Brendel's** approach to Schubert remains broadly the same as in his 1971 series of late sonatas and the more individual digital versions of the late 1980s, there is an extra magnetism in these live accounts of 2001, intensifying the depth of what he has to say. He is more freely expressive than before, with speeds more flexible, and with rhythms given an extra lift. At times he seems improvisational in his flights of fantasy, while the depth of concentration conveyed in pianissimos is consistently greater than in his studio performances.

Three of the four last and greatest *Sonatas* are included, with the early *B major Sonata* of 1817 as a supplement, a sonata not previously recorded by Brendel and one that, as he sees it, points forward to the late works. The opening of the great *B flat Sonata* is marred by intrusive coughing from a woman in the Festival Hall audience, but otherwise the sound is excellent, bright and full-toned, with acoustic differences between four different venues ironed out – the Alte Oper in Frankfurt, the Concertgebouw in Amsterdam, the Snape Maltings and the Royal Festival Hall.

Piano Sonatas 13, D.664; 21 in B flat

&— *** Decca 440 295-2. Lupu

Radu Lupu's is one of the most searching of all his Schubert recordings and finds this masterly pianist at his most eloquent and thoughtful.

Piano Sonatas 15 (Relique); 18, D.894

&— **** Ph. 454 453-2. Uchida

The unfinished torso of the *Relique Sonata* is given an eloquent, inward-looking reading of great tonal beauty. The *G major Sonata* is masterly, combining careful thought with emotional depth. Another of the best Schubert sonata discs. The Philips recording is excellent in every way.

Piano Sonatas 15 in C, D.840; 19 in C min., D.958; 16 German Dances, D.783

(N) (BB) *** Regis Alto (ADD) ALC 1040. Brendel

This recording comes from the Vanguard Catalogue. Brendel was at his finest and most spontaneous in the 1960s. The *C minor Sonata* is particularly fine, with a thoughtful improvisatory feeling in the slow movement which is consistently illuminating. The two-movement *C major Sonata* also has a memorable *Andante*, and the *German Dances* are an endless delight. The recording is full and bold.

Piano Sonatas 15 in C (Relique), D.840; 21 in B flat, D.960

(M) **(*) Sony mono/stereo 512874-2. Serkin

Although he opens the *B flat major Sonata* persuasively, **Rudolf Serkin's** rugged, less lyrical manner in Schubert will not be to all tastes, but it is undeniably strong in impact. The slow movement is squarer and less flowing than usual, and the interpretation registers the mature, uncompromising response of an artist intent on reading his Schubert directly, and less intent on beguiling his audience. But there is no question of the patrician character of both these readings. The two-movement *C major Sonata* was recorded (in mono) in 1955, 20 years before the *B flat major*, and with very much the same positive manner, although the *Andante* has an appealing simplicity. In both, the recording is close, strikingly present, but rather hard.

Piano Sonatas 16 in A min., D.845; 17 in D, D.850; 20 in A, D.959; 11 Ecossaises, D.781; 3 Klavierstücke, D.946

(N) (B) **** Avie/BBC Radio 3 AV 2156 (2). Cooper

It looks as though **Imogen Cooper** is about to undertake a new survey of the Schubert *Sonatas* for Avie, taken from live broadcasts. She is a natural Schubertian, as you can discover by playing the delectably pointed finale of D.850. Her performances admirably combine style and spontaneity, and the recordings, made in the Queen Elizabeth Hall, London, have a natural balance and fine presence.

Sonatas 17 in D, D.850; 19 C min., D.858; 20 in A, D.959; 21 in B flat, D.960

&— (B) **** EMI Classics 5 16448-2 (2). Andsnes

In their first incarnation these magisterial accounts by **Leif Ove Andsnes** appeared in harness with Schubert songs with Ian Bostridge. It makes better sense to assemble them on two bargain-priced CDs, for they are superb readings, insightful and humane and they have the full measure of this extraordinary music. Not to be missed.

Piano Sonata 19; Moments musicaux, D.780

&— (M) *** Decca 417 785-2. Lupu

Lupu's performance has a simple eloquence that is most moving. His *Moments musicaux* are very fine indeed. The Decca recording is very natural and, at mid-price, this is extremely competitive.

Piano Sonata 19 in C min., D.958; (i) Gesänge des Harfners, D.478; Totengräbers Heimweh, D.842 (Fragments)

&— **** EMI 3 84321-2. Andsnes; (i) with Bostridge

Leif Ove Andsnes follows his impressive account of the (see below) with the powerful *C minor*, of which he gives a penetrating and revealing account. It comes with the much earlier *Gesänge des Harfners* and a selection of songs and fragments both for voice and for piano solo, little jewels usually overlooked. There is a degree of freedom in his spontaneous-sounding readings, and he is well matched by the tenor, **Ian Bostridge**, in glowing voice. The three Harper songs, inspired by Goethe's *Mignon*, are a special delight.

Piano Sonatas 19–21; Allegretto in C min., D.915; 3 Klavierstücke, D.944

&— (M) *** DG 474 613-2 (2). Pollini

Piano Sonatas 19–21; 4 Impromptus, D.899/1–4

&— (B) *** Double Decca 475 184-2 (2). Schiff

Piano Sonatas 19–21; 3 Klavierstücke, D. 946/1–3

(B) **(*) Ph. Duo (ADD) 438 703-2 (2). Brendel

In his note **András Schiff** calls Schubert's last three *Sonatas* 'among the most sublime compositions written for the instrument' – and he plays them as if they are too. There is formidable competition, but admirers of the present fine artist can rest assured that the finesse and insight of his playing are undiminished. The bold drama of the *C minor* work is set in contrast with the more ruminative approach to the *B flat Sonata*. Excellent, truthful recording.

Brendel's analogue recording of the *A major* suffers from rather more agogic changes than is desirable. Some listeners may find these interferences with the flow of the musical argument a little too personal. The *C minor Sonata* is not free from this charge, but it remains an impressive performance. Brendel's account of the *B flat Sonata* is characteristically imposing and full of insight, as one would expect; moreover he is at his very finest in the *Klavierstücke*. This is eloquent and profoundly musical playing. Throughout, the recording is well up to Philips's high standard of realism.

In **Pollini's** hands the three last *Sonatas* emerge as strongly structured and powerful, yet he is far from unresponsive to the voices from the other world with which these pieces resonate. However with his perfect pianism he does not always convey a sense of human vulnerability, as have some of the greatest Schubert interpreters.

Sonata 20 in A, D.959

(N) *** BBC Legends (ADD) BBCL 4254-2. Cherkassky (with MENDELSSOHN: *Andante & Rondo capriccioso*) – SCHUMANN: *Carnaval* ***

When the textures of Schubert's piano writing are often thick, it is astonishing how Cherkassky in this live performance lightens the result and gives a revelatory transparency to the music. The tonal variety too in this recital, recorded at the Queen Elizabeth Hall in November 1970, is a model of its kind, with the poignancy of the minor-key variations of the slow movement movingly conveyed, and the free-flowing lyricism of the rest a regular delight. It would be hard to find a more sparkling account of the *Rondo capriccioso* than this, making this as light as Mendelssohn's *Scherzo* for the *Midsummer Night's Dream* music. It goes with equally inspired accounts of the Mendelssohn and Schumann items, the more compelling for being recorded in a live recital. Good sound.

Piano Sonata 20 in A, D.959; 4 Impromptus, D.935/1–4

(M) **(*) Sony (ADD) 512873-2. Serkin

A much-praised performance in its day (1966), **Rudolf Serkin's** account of Schubert's *A major Sonata* seems somewhat less sensitive than one remembers and expects from an artist of this stature, although it has some moments of appealing lyricism. His command of the structure of the work is impressive enough, but the *fortissimos* are rather hard (partly the fault of the recording) and one would have liked more finesse in the phrasing. The *Impromptus*, recorded 13 years later, are a different matter, undoubtedly distinguished, and the recording, if slightly dry, is truthful and sounds even better in its new transfer.

Piano Sonatas 20 in A, D.959; 21 in B flat, D.960

🎧 **** HM HMC 901800. Lewis

Paul Lewis's performances of both these late masterpieces are completely individual and deeply felt, using the widest range of colour and dynamic and great variety of articulation. At one moment his playing is touchingly gentle, thoughtful and introspective, at others intensely dramatic; yet the result sounds totally spontaneous, as at a live recital. These are among the most stimulating and thoughtful Schubert performances of the last few years, and they are very well recorded. A disc to seek out, even if you already have this repertoire.

Piano Sonata 21 in B flat, D.960; Allegretto in C min., D.915; 6 Moments musicaux, D.780

🎧 ✲ (M) **** EMI 5 03423-2. Kovacevich

Piano Sonata 21; 3 Klavierstücke, D.946

*** Ph. 456 572-2. Uchida

Piano Sonata 21 in B flat, D.960; (i) Lieder: Abschied von der Erde; Viola; Der Winterabend

**** EMI 5 57901-2. Andsnes; (i) with Bostridge

Stephen Kovacevich made a memorable recording of the great *B flat major Sonata* for Hyperion which (in our 1988 edition) we called 'one of the most eloquent accounts on record of this sublime sonata'. One could well say the same of the later (1994) EMI version though, if anything, it explores an even deeper vein of feeling than its predecessor. Indeed, it is a most searching and penetrating account of the work to have appeared in recent years and, given the excellence and truthfulness of the recording, must carry the strongest and most enthusiastic recommendation. For this reissue EMI have added the six *Moments musicaux* which he recorded six months later, also at Abbey Road, and which have comparable insights.

EMI continue their Schubert series combining the sonatas played by **Leif Ove Andsnes** with a few songs in which he accompanies **Ian Bostridge**. The *Sonata* is impressive in its range and depth of emotion and fine musical discipline. Richard Wigmore's excellent sleeve-note speaks of the ethereal tranquillity of the first two movements, and Andsnes conveys this with simplicity and artistry.

Mitsuko Uchida couples the last *Sonata* with the *Drei Klavierstücke*. Hers is a performance of considerable stature; she allows Schubert to speak for himself. There is a rapt concentration and an almost other-worldly quality about her playing that will repay the attentive listener. Some may feel that she lingers a little too long in the slow movement and allows the onward flow of the music to stagnate. In any event there is no doubt whatever as to the excellence of the Philips recording.

Complete Waltzes: 36 Dances (Erste Walzer), D.365; Scherzos, D.593; 12 Valses nobles, D.969; 34 Valses sentimentales, D.779; 2 Waltzes, D.980; 12 Waltzes, D.145; 12 (Graz) Waltzes, D.924; 20 Waltzes (Letzte Walzer); Waltzes with Trios in E flat, D.146; F, D.146

(BB) *** EMI Gemini (ADD) 3 50894-2 (2). Bordoni

A first look at this two-disc Gemini set brings an astonished double-take, for it contains no fewer than 132 waltzes (or pieces in waltz format). How could such a collection hold the interest? But it does – partly because Schubert was a master of the form (very popular in his day), and partly because **Paolo Bordoni** is such a sympathetic exponent, and he is very well recorded. Of course we are not suggesting they should all be played at once, but in groups. That is what Schubert planned; if you heed our advice, you will find that they follow each other very pleasingly – then suddenly there is a Schubertian jewel.

VOCAL MUSIC

Dietrich Fischer-Dieskau: The EMI Recordings

The First Recital (1951): *Der Atlas; Ihr Bild; Fischermädchen; Die Stadt; Am Meer; Der Doppelgänger; Erlkönig; Nacht und Träume; Du bist die Ruh; Ständchen*

Vol. I (1955); Vol. II (1957); Vol. IIIa (1958); Vol. IIIb (1958)

(all with Gerald Moore)

Vol. IV (1959); Vol. V (1959); Vol. VIa (1959); Vol. VIb (1959)

(Vols. IV–VIb with Karl Engel)

Vol. VII (1962); Vol. VIII (1965); Vol. IX (1965)

☞ Ⓜ *** EMI mono/stereo 5 65670-2 (6). Fischer-Dieskau, Moore or Engel

This HMV set makes an admirable survey of **Fischer-Dieskau's** Schubert recordings for EMI over a decade and a half before he moved to Deutsche Grammophon to make the extensive survey listed below. It is particularly interesting to compare the earliest recordings (the first in mono), with the voice and manner still youthfully fresh, to the second generation, again with **Gerald Moore** but also with **Karl Engel**. The contrast is fascinating, with the voice still younger than on DG. The transfers are superbly managed and full translations are provided to make this an indispensable supplement to the DG sets.

DG Fischer-Dieskau Schubert Lieder Edition with Gerald Moore

Song-cycles: *Die schöne Müllerin; Winterreise; Schwanengesang* (complete) & *405 key Lieder*

☞ Ⓑ **** DG 477 5765 (21). Fischer-Dieskau, Moore

Fischer-Dieskau's monumental survey of all the Schubert songs suitable for a man's voice (some of the longer ones excepted) was made over a relatively brief span, with the last 300 songs concentrated in a period of only two months in 1969; yet there is not a hint of routine. No fewer than 405 songs are included here, plus the three song-cycles, which were also new recordings, made in 1971/2. If anything, these performances – notably that of the darkest and greatest of the cycles, *Winterreise* – are even more searching than before, with **Moore** matching the concentration of the singer in some of the most remarkable playing that even he has put

on record. As in the miscellaneous songs (which we do not have space to list), Fischer-Dieskau is in wonderfully fresh voice, and the transfers to CD have been managed very naturally. The documentation includes full texts and translations and an essay by André Tubeuf. The one serious omission is an alphabetical list of titles. This makes it unnecessarily hard to find a particular song – much the most likely way of using so compendious a collection.

Song Cycles: *Die schöne Müllerin; Schwanengesang; Winterreise*

Ⓝ ☞ Ⓜ **** DG (ADD) 477 7956 (3). Fischer-Dieskau, Moore

Fischer-Dieskau and **Moore** had each recorded these great cycles of Schubert several times already before they embarked on this set in 1971/2. It was no mere repeat of earlier triumphs. If anything, these performances – notably that of the darkest and greatest of the cycles, *Winterreise* – are even more searching than before, with Moore matching the hushed concentration of the singer in some of the most remarkable playing that even he had ever put on record. Fischer-Dieskau is in wonderfully fresh voice, and the transfers to CD have been managed very naturally.

The Graham Johnson Schubert Lieder Edition

☞ Ⓑ **** Hyp. CDS 44201/40 (40). 60 soloists, including Ian Bostridge singing *Die schöne Müllerin* and Matthias Goerne singing *Winterreise*

Hyperion's complete coverage of Schubert's *Lieder* is a monumental achievement. The individal discs are still all available separately but now come in a box presented in chronological order of composition. Three bonus CDs now complete the survey by adding 81 further songs by Schubert's friends and contemporaries. There is a handsome book, including complete texts and translations, which is also available separately (BKS 44201/40).

When it comes to background information, Graham Johnson's Schubert Lieder Edition for Hyperion using some of the greatest singers of the day is unmatchable. With each disc devoted to a group of songs on a particular theme, Johnson provides notes that add enormously to the enjoyment, heightening the experience of hearing even the most familiar songs.

Throughout the whole series Johnson in his inspired accompaniments consistently revels in Schubert's joyfully original piano writing, and his carefully detailed revelatory notes provide constant illumination. Few series of recordings so richly repay detailed study and all are a pleasure to return to, when the sound and balance too are consistently of such high quality. All collectors should dip into this remarkable anthology, and be encouraged to return again and again.

Miscellaneous vocal recitals

'A Schubert Evening'

☞ ✸ ⒷⒷ **** EMI Gemini (ADD) 5 86251-2 (2). Baker, with Moore or Parsons

This very generous collection combines a pair of recitals recorded by **Dame Janet Baker** at two different stages in her career, in 1970 and a decade later. The first collection ranges wide in an imaginative *Liederabend* of Schubert songs that includes a number of comparative rarities. They move from the delectably comic *Epistel* to the ominous darkness of *Die junge Nonne.* With **Gerald Moore** (who returned to the studio out of retirement especially for the occasion) still at his finest, this is a rarely satisfying collection. A very high proportion of favourite Schubert songs is included in the 1980 group. With a great singer treating each with loving, detailed care, the result is a charmer of a recital. The very first item, Dame Janet's strongly characterized reading of *Die Forelle,* makes it a fun song, and similarly **Parsons's** naughty, springing accompaniment to *An Sylvia* (echoed later by the singer) gives a twinkle to a song that can easily be treated too seriously. One also remembers the ravishing *subito piano* for the second stanza of *An die Musik.* The later recording is of fine EMI vintage and catches the more mature voice naturally and with rather more presence than a decade earlier. It is a pity that, because the set is so economically priced, there are no texts, but this remains an unmissable reissue.

Lieder, Vol. 1

🔑 (M) **** EMI 4 76851-2. Bostridge, Drake

Few discs of favourite Schubert songs match this for sheer beauty. **Ian Bostridge** here not only sings with ravishing tenor tone but, with German words heightened, offers fresh revelation in even the best-known songs, with **Julius Drake** matching him in insight.

Lieder, Vol. II: Goethe Lieder

🔑 (M) **** EMI 5 03424-2. Bostridge, Drake

This second volume of Schubert songs from **Ian Bostridge** and **Julius Drake** is divided neatly between songs to poems by Goethe and Mayerhofer, and miscellaneous songs, many less well known. In this wide-ranging selection Bostridge reveals his expanding mastery in the widest variety of expression, with the subtlest range of tone, and with a deliberate hardening of the characteristically sweet voice in some of the more dramatic songs, effectively so when the sense of strain adds to the intensity. In all this Drake is the perfect partner, ranging wide in his tonal palette too. Natural, beautifully balanced sound. Full texts and translations are included.

Lieder: *An die Musik; An Sylvia; Auf dem Wasser zu singen; Ave Maria; Du bist die Ruh'; Die Forelle; Ganymed; Gretchen am Spinnrade; Heidenröslein; Im Frühling; Die junge Nonne; Litanei; Mignon und der Harfner; Der Musensohn; Nacht und Träume; Sei mir gegrüsst; Seligkeit*

(BB) *** Regis RRC 1052. Lott, Johnson

At budget price, **Felicity Lott's** collection brings an ideal choice of songs for the general collector. With **Graham Johnson** the most imaginative accompanist, even the best-known songs emerge fresh and new, and gentle songs like *Litanei* are raptly beautiful.

Lieder: (i) *An die Musik; An Sylvia; Auf dem Wasser zu singen; Ganymed; Gretchen am Spinnrade; Im Frühling; Die junge Nonne; Das Lied im Grünen; Der Musensohn; Nachtviolen; Nähe des Geliebten; Wehmut;* (ii) *Der Einsame; Die Forelle; Heidenröslein; Der Jüngling an der Quelle; Liebe schwärmt auf allen Wegen; Liebhaber in allen Gestalten; Seligkeit; Litanei; Ungeduld; Die Vögel;* (iii) *An mein Klavier; Erlkönig*

🔑 ❀ (M) (****) EMI mono/stereo 5 62754-2 [5 62773-2]. Schwarzkopf; with (i) Fischer; (ii) Moore; (iii) Parsons

Elisabeth Schwarzkopf had her doubts about taking many of the Schubert songs into her repertoire, most of which she felt were more suitable for the male voice; but the present survey includes some of those for which she felt a strong personal identification, including *Gretchen am Spinnrade* and the passionate *Die junge Nonne.* The main group here is drawn from an Elysian selection she put on disc at the beginning of her recording career in partnership with **Edwin Fischer**, who was at the end of his. In spite of her reservations about lack of experience in this repertoire (in the early 1950s), she and Fischer create a magical partnership, full of intimate intercommunication, with even the simplest of songs inspiring intensely subtle expression from singer and pianist alike. Among the items accompanied by **Gerald Moore**, *Die Vögel* and *Liebhaber in allen Gestalten* date from 1948, *Litanei* and *Ungeduld* from 1954, and the others from 1965/6, including the two final songs accompanied by **Geoffrey Parsons**, of which *Erlkönig* was one of her favourites.

Lieder: (i) *An die Musik; An Sylvia; Auf dem Wasser zu singen; Ganymed; Gretchen am Spinnrade; Im Frühling; Die junge Nonne; Das Lied im Grunen; Der Musensohn; Nachtviolen; Nähe des Geliebten; Wehmut;* (ii) *Litanei auf das Fest Allerseelen; Ungeduld*

(N) 🔑 (BB) (****) Naxos 8.111287. Schwarzkopf; (i) Fischer; (ii) Moore – BEETHOVEN: *Ah perfido!* (***)

In 1952 **Schwarzkopf**, at the beginning of her recording career, and **Edwin Fischer** at the end of his made a magical partnership, with even the simplest of songs inspiring intensely subtle expression from singer and pianist alike. Though Fischer's playing is not immaculate, he left few records more endearing than this, and Schwarzkopf's colouring of word and tone is masterly. For this carefully remastered Naxos reissue, Mark Obert-Thorn has added two extra recordings, with **Gerald Moore** accompanying, made two years later, and an equally valuable Beethoven bonus.

Goethe Lieder

(M) *** DG (ADD) 457 747-2. Fischer-Dieskau, Demus or Moore

This reissued collection draws on three sets of recordings: **Fischer-Dieskau's** first stereo DG Goethe LP, recorded with **Joerg Demus** in 1960, and two subsequent groups with **Gerald Moore** dating from a decade later. Some of the very finest Goethe settings are here and Fischer-Dieskau is on top of his form, but the partnership with Demus is less than ideal. He proves a capable but not highly imaginative accompanist, although his artistry is not to be denied. But as for the singing, the spectrum of emotion takes on a new glow as each song begins. The two settings of *Wandrers Nachtlied* are particularly fine, as are the joyous *Der Musensohn* and the fiery *An schwager Kronos*. Needless to say the partnership with Gerald Moore is much more of a symbiosis, and these later performances are outstanding in every way. The recording, too, is warmer and has a more pleasing ambience. A treasurable disc, just the same.

Lieder

Ⓜ *** CRD CRD 3464. Walker, Vignoles

Sarah Walker's début Lieder recital was made not long before she joined Graham Johnson for her contribution to Hyperion's Schubert Lieder Edition. Here she is accompanied by **Roger Vignoles** on a period piano of 1864. The attractive selection of songs, with many favourites, consistently draws warm, easily confident singing from her, full of charm, yet she is dramatic when required, as in *Erlkönig*. There she is not helped by the balance with the piano, which slightly favours the accompanist, masking the full intensity of her characterization, with power kept in reserve until the end. That contrasts beautifully with her easy-going lightness in such a song as *Der Einsame* and the poise of *Nacht und Träume*, with phrases sustained on a mere thread of sound. Despite the balance, words are clear thanks to the singer's fine diction and feeling for word-meaning. Roger Vignoles accompanies persuasively, full translations are included.

Lieder: (i) *An die Freunde; Auf der Donau; Aus Heliopolis; Fischerweise; Freiwilliges Versinken; Gruppe aus dem Tartarus;* (ii) *Der Hirt auf dem Felsen;* (i) *Prometheus; Der Strom; Der Wanderer; Der Wanderer an den Mond*

•─ Ⓑ **** BBC (ADD) BBCB 8011-2. (i) Fischer-Dieskau; (ii) Harper, King; Britten – WOLF: 3 *Christmas Songs; 3 Michelangelo Lieder* ***

Fischer-Dieskau has rarely if ever been more inspired in his recordings of Schubert than here, in live performances given with **Britten** at the Snape Maltings in 1972 – the last year Britten was able to take an active part in the Aldeburgh Festival. The great baritone, then at his peak, was plainly inspired by the quality of his accompanist's playing, and the selection of songs, well contrasted, brings together an attractive mixture of rare and well known. Similarly, in the *Shepherd on the Rock*, with **Thea King** producing honeyed tone in the clarinet obbligato, the magnetism is irresistible. The Wolf songs from **Pears** and **Shirley-Quirk** make an attractive bonus.

23 Favourite Lieder

Ⓜ *** DG 477 6358-2. Terfel, Martineau

Bryn Terfel's DG disc of Schubert was one of his first recordings to confirm his exceptional gift of projecting his magnetic personality with keen intensity, in Lieder, not just in opera. Terfel emerges as a positive artist, giving strikingly individual and imaginative readings of these 23 favourite

songs. As you immediately realize in three favourite songs, *Heidenröslein, An Sylvia* and *Du bist die Ruh,* Terfel is daring in confronting you face to face, very much as the young Fischer-Dieskau did, using the widest range of dynamic and tone. Full, firm sound.

Lieder

•─ Ⓜ *** DG (ADD) 449 747-2. Wunderlich, Giesen – BEETHOVEN: *Lieder;* SCHUMANN: *Dichterliebe* ***

Few tenors have matched the young **Wunderlich** in the freshness and golden bloom of the voice. The open manner could not be more appealing here in glowing performances, well coupled with other fine examples of this sadly short-lived artist's work.

Goethe Lieder

•─ Ⓜ **** DG Entrée (ADD) 474 173-2. Fischer-Dieskau, Moore

This superb collection makes the perfect entrée into the world of Schubertian song. Twenty-two items (67 minutes) with nine Goethe settings (including an unforgettable *Erlkönig*) and many lovely performances of top favourites: *Lachen und Weinen,* two different *Serenades, The Trout* and none more beautifully sung than *Der Lindenbaum.* The recordings come from 1969 and 1970 and throughout **Gerald Moore** is a superb partner. Texts and translations are included.

'Favourite Lieder'

•─ Ⓑ *** CfP 585 6182. Keenlyside, Martineau

The velvety beauty of **Simon Keenlyside's** cleanly focused baritone goes with fresh, thoughtful readings of 20 favourite songs, perfectly judged, with ever-sensitive accompaniment from **Malcolm Martineau.** Now at bargain price, this disc makes another outstanding Schubert Lieder recommendation, which includes one or two unusual songs among many favourites.

Lieder

•─ Ⓜ *** Warner Elatus 0927 46741-2. Bonney, Parsons; (i) with Kam

Barbara Bonney here is at her freshest, and who better to accompany her than **Geoffrey Parsons?** The generous programme (well over an hour) includes many firm favourites, and Bonney not only sings with much beauty of tone and a flowing Schubertian line but with keen concern for word-meanings. Songs like *Die Forelle, Auf dem Wasser zu singen* and the lovely *So lasst mich scheinen* sound especially fresh; and it is always good to have *Der Hirt auf dem Felsen* ('The shepherd on the rock') with its fluid obbligato clarinet (here the persuasive **Sharon Kam**). Spontaneous-sounding expressiveness in a natural partnership between fine artists.

Lieder

Ⓑ **(*) CfP (ADD) 575 7732 (2) M. Price, Lockhart; (i) with Brymer – LISZT; TCHAIKOVSKY: *Songs* ***; SCHUMANN: *Frauenliebe und Leben* **(*)

Dame Margaret Price was in fine voice when she made this record in 1971. Her singing of Schubert is full-throated in style, although she successfully fines down the tone for a song like *Du bist die Ruh'*. The opening recitative of *Auf der Riesenkoppe* takes us straight into the opera house; *La pastorella* (a charming song) reminds us of Rossini, and in *The Shepherd on the rock* the sheer breadth of the singing tends to dwarf even **Jack Brymer's** beguiling clarinet obbligato. **James Lockhart** accompanies most sensitively but, maybe because of the recording balance, like Brymer he tends to be dwarfed by the voice. No translations are provided, but the notes give a synopsis of each song. This now comes on a two-disc set, coupled with Schumann's *Frauenliebe und Leben* and two well-chosen groups of songs by Tchaikovsky and Liszt, recorded two years later.

Auf dem Strom

(BB) *** Naxos 8.557471. Kuhmeier, Tomboeck, Inui –
BEETHOVEN: *Horn Sonata*; BRAHMS: *Horn Trio*;
SCHUMANN: *Adagio and Allegro* ***

The Schubert song, *Auf dem Strom* ('Upon the River'), with its horn obbligato is parallel with another late song, *The Shepherd on the Rock*, with its clarinet obbligato. The pure, fresh-toned soprano, **Genia Kuhmeier**, matches the ripe-toned horn-player, **Wolfgang Tomboeck**, in the warmth and imagination of her phrasing. A valuable supplement to the instrumental works illustrating the Vienna horn.

Lieder

●—(M) **** EMI (ADD) 5 62896-2. Ludwig, Parsons or Moore;
(i) with de Peyer

Most of these songs, including some of Schubert's most justly popular, come from a 1959 recital with **Geoffrey Parsons**, who accompanies with great tact and sensitivity, although **Gerald Moore** takes his place sympathetically in *Die Allmacht* and *Fischerweise*. **Christa Ludwig** presents them with disarming dedication and to hear the hackneyed *Ave Maria* sung like this is to realize afresh the beauty which all too often is jellied over with sentiment. **Gervase de Peyer** provides an engaging clarinet obbligato in *The Shepherd and the Rock* and in *Musensohn*, most exuberant of Schubert songs, the bouncing jollity is unbounded.

Song cycles

Song cycles: *Die schöne Müllerin; Schwanengesang; Winterreise*

●—(M) **** DG (ADD) 437 235-2 (3). Fischer-Dieskau, Moore
●—(B) **** EMI 5 00934-2 (3). Bär, Parsons

Fischer-Dieskau and **Moore** had each recorded these great cycles of Schubert several times already before they embarked on this set in 1971-2 as part of DG's Schubert song series. It was no mere repeat of earlier triumphs. If anything, these performances – notably that of the darkest and greatest of the cycles, *Winterreise* – are even more searching than before, with Moore matching the hushed concentration of the singer in some of the most remarkable playing that even he has put on record. As in the extensive recitals listed above, Fischer-Dieskau is in wonderfully fresh voice.

Die schöne Müllerin was the first of the cycles **Olaf Bär** recorded, in 1986, in Dresden, with the voice fresher and more velvety than later. The tone is better suited to this young man's cycle, even more so when contrasted with Fischer-Dieskau's EMI version, especially when the digital recording is so flattering to Bär's warmly beautiful lyrical flow. In *Winterreise*, recorded two years later, once more with **Geoffrey Parsons** a masterful accompanist, Bär again finds a winning beauty of line and tone in singing that is deeply reflective and strongly dramatic. If without quite the power of Fischer-Dieskau, this is a truly memorable set, most welcome back to the catalogue (and a first choice for I.M.). At this price, even if you have other recordings of these cycles, Bär's is not to be missed. However, there are no texts and translations – a sad omission.

Die schöne Müllerin (complete; DVD version)

(N) ●—**** Medici Arts **DVD** 2057308 (with bonus:
Schwanengesang; Liebesbotschaft; Aufenthalt; Die Taubenpost) DVD Producer: Wolf Seesemann (CD:
Challenge Classics: CC 72292) Prégardien; Gees

*** TDK **DVD** DV-CODSM. Fischer-Dieskau, Schiff (V/D: Fritz Jurmann)

Recorded in the Liederhalle, Mozartsaal, Stuttgart, in August 2008, **Christoph Prégardien's** memorable live performance of *Die schöne Müllerin* with **Michael Gees** has already achieved classic status. Prégardien's honey-toned tenor with its moments of darker baritonal colouring is ideal to express the sadness of this moving journey in song. As Prégardien himself comments, 'the youth never speaks to the girl, and never tells the woman he loves that he loves her', but Schubert 'was drawn to texts that tend in the direction of melancholy', which he expresses so exquisitely. Yet the performance is full of subtly graded variety of feeling and when there is a moment of illusory happiness, the ever-sensitive pianist also makes the very most of it. The extended closing lullaby has great pathos and simple beauty, and leaves the listener feeling sad but not dejected. But the partnership has chosen three encores from *Schwanengesang*, and the final cheerful *Die Taubenpost* sends us away lifted up. The recording is resonant but beautifully balanced and truthful. (There is a bonus talk by the singer on Schubert's setting of his text.)

Dietrich Fischer-Dieskau was filmed by Austrian Radio singing *Die schöne Müllerin* in 1991. He was 66, yet the voice is still in remarkable shape, and he compensates for any lack of bloom by dramatizing the cycle with facial expression and body language. With a superb partnership established with **András Schiff**, the performance has great concentration and spontaneity, leading invitably on to the closing three songs, which are most movingly sung. As a bonus there is a short portrait of the singer, filmed at the 1985 Schubertiade, in which we learn a great deal about him and his approach to interpretation.

Die schöne Müllerin (song-cycle), D.795 (*see also* above, under Graham Johnson Schubert Lieder Edition, Vol. 25)

●—**** DG (ADD) 415 186-2. Fischer-Dieskau, Moore

(B) *** CfP (ADD) 586 1812 (2). Ian & Jennifer Partridge –
SCHUMANN: *Dichterliebe; Liederkreis* ***

Fischer-Dieskau's classic 1972 version on DG remains among the very finest ever recorded, combining as it does his developed sense of drama and story-telling, his mature feeling for detail and yet spontaneity too, helped by the searching accompaniment of **Gerald Moore**. It is a performance with premonitions of *Winterreise*.

Ian Partridge's is an exceptionally fresh and urgent account. Rarely has the dynamic quality of the cycle been so effectively conveyed, rising to an emotional climax at the end of the first half with the song *Mein'*, expressing the poet's ill-founded joy, welling up infectiously. Partridge's subtle and beautiful range of tone is a constant delight, and he is most imaginatively accompanied by his sister, **Jennifer**. An outstanding bargain coupling that should win many new friends for Lieder, although there are no texts and translations.

Schwanengesang, D.957

*** Amphion/Priory (ADD) PHI CD157. Hemsley, Wilde

Schwanengesang, D.957; Lieder

🎵 (M) (***) EMI mono 5 65196-2. Hotter, Moore

As in his darkly searching account of *Winterreise*, also recorded in mono with **Gerald Moore** in the 1950s, this Schubert collection coupling *Schwanengesang* with other favourite songs reveals **Hotter** at his peak. The voice as recorded may not always be beautiful, but the gravity and intensity of the singing reveal a master Lieder-singer, as commanding here as in his Wagner interpretations.

Thomas Hemsley spent much of his career in opera houses in Germany and made few commercial Lieder records. This *Schwanengesang* from 1976 derives from live performances with **David Wilde** and serves as a welcome reminder of the artistry of this master singer.

Winterreise (song-cycle), D.911 (DVD versions)

*** Warner NVC Arts **DVD** 8573 83780-2. Bostridge, Drake. (Producer: Gordon Baskerville. V/D: David Alden.)

(*) Arthaus **DVD 100 258. Hynninen, Gothoni. (V/D: Julie Didier.)

These two admirably sung DVD recordings of Schubert's *Winterreise* demonstrate only too well the difficulties of 'staging' an extended song-cycle, however imaginative the producer and director. **Ian Bostridge's** account of *Winterreise*, with a hardly less fine partner in **Julius Drake**, brings great imaginative detail. The performance also has an extraordinarily powerful atmosphere – it is imbued with an air of desolation which we can see in his gaunt face as well as hear in his voice. **David Alden's** setting is an empty room, within which Bostridge, in his dark coat, can freely move about. There are occasional bursts of visual histrionics, which not all will take to, but on the whole the production works well, and the performance itself is gripping throughout, especially as the recording is so vivid. An additional documentary, rather facetiously titled 'Over the Top with Franz',

details the background to the recording and filming and the artistic conflicts generated.

Jorma Hynninen and **Ralf Gothoni** recorded their fine account of *Winterreise* in 1994 at the Särestöniemi Museum in Finnish Lapland. The artist Reidar Särestöniemi (1925–81) designed the building so that he could draw inspiration in both winter and summer from the beauties of the Finnish countryside. The performance takes place before a small audience, and apart from the two artists themselves, we see some of Särestöniemi's impressions of the Finnish landscape as well as nature itself. The visual side of the production is handled with both taste and imagination, and the musical balance is well focused and natural. Hynninen and his admirable partner convey the poignancy of this music to splendid effect, although some may well find that the pauses between each song could have been fractionally longer.

Winterreise (song-cycle), D.911 (CD versions)

🎵 **** DG 415 187-2. Fischer-Dieskau, Moore

🎵 **** Ph. 464 739-2. Fischer-Dieskau, Brendel

🎵 (M) *** EMI (ADD) 5 62784-2. Fischer-Dieskau, Moore

🎵 ✿ (M) **** Decca (ADD) 466 382-2. Pears, Britten

**** EMI 5 57790-2. Bostridge, Andsnes

(M) (***) EMI mono 5 66985-2 [5 67002]. Hotter, Moore

In the early 1970s **Dietrich Fischer-Dieskau's** voice was still at its freshest, yet the singer had deepened and intensified his understanding of this greatest of song-cycles to a degree where his finely detailed and thoughtful interpretation sounded totally spontaneous, and this DG version is now freshened on CD. However on Philips, the collaboration of Fischer-Dieskau with one of today's great Schubert pianists, **Alfred Brendel**, brings endless illumination in the interplay and challenge between singer and pianist, magnetic from first to last. With incidental flaws, this may not be the definitive Fischer-Dieskau reading, but in many ways it is the deepest and most moving he has ever given.

For their reissue in the 'Great Artists of the Century' series EMI have chosen **Dietrich Fischer-Dieskau's** 1962 *Winterreise*, which combines direct power of expression with rich vocal power. A great performance which has the virtue of striking freshness from singer and pianist alike. The recording scarcely shows its age. A full text and translation are included.

What is so striking about **Pears's** performance is its intensity. One continually has the sense of a live occasion and, next to it, even Fischer-Dieskau's beautifully wrought singing sounds too easy. As for **Britten**, he recreates the music, sometimes with a fair freedom from Schubert's markings, but always with scrupulous concern for the overall musical shaping and sense of atmosphere. The sprung rhythm of *Gefror'ne Tränen* is magical in creating the impression of frozen teardrops falling, and almost every song brings similar magic. The recording and the CD transfer are exceptionally successful in bringing a sense of presence and realism.

In some ways **Ian Bostridge's** latest (2004) account of

Winterreise does not quite match his earlier DVD account in conveying the full underlying desolation of Schubert's masterly cycle. Here Bostridge, though no less sensitive, is more direct, more positive in projection, less bleak in feeling. Yet even so, it is a highly involving performance and is continually lifted by **Leif Ove Andsnes's** imaginative and atmospheric accompaniments. The delightful lilt at the opening of *Frülingstraume*, the galloping *Post*, and the very touching presentation of *Das Wirthaus* are matched by the simplicity of the penultimate *Die Nebensonnen*, and the delicate portrayal of *Der Leiermann*, to which Bostridge responds so tenderly. The recording is beautifully balanced, and this remains an unforgettable performance.

Hans Hotter's 1954 mono recording of *Winterreise* brings an exceptionally dark, even sepulchral performance, lightened by the imagination of **Gerald Moore's** accompaniment. Hotter scales down his great Wagnerian baritone so that only occasionally is the tone gritty. His concern for detail brings many moments of illumination, but the lack of animation makes this an unrelievedly depressing view.

Church music

Auguste jam coelestium, D.488; 6 Antiphonen zu Palmsonntag, D.696; Deutsche Messe, D.872; Graduale in C, D.184; Hymnus an den heiligen Geist, D.964; Kyries: in D min., D.31; B flat, D.45; D min., D.49; F, D.66; Lazarus, D.689; Magnificat in D, D.486; Masses: 1 in F, D.105; 2 in G, D.167; 3 in B flat, D.324; 4 in C, D.452; 5 in A flat, D.678; 6 in E flat, D.950; Offertoriums: (Salve Regina) in F, D.223; (Salve Regina) in A, D.676; (Totus in corde) in C, D.136; (Tres sunt) in A min., D.181; in B flat, D.963; Psalms: 23, D.706; 92, D.953; Salve Reginas: in B flat, D.106, D.379 & D.386; in A, D.676; Stabat Maters: in G min., D.175; in F, D.383; Tantum ergos: in C, D.461; D.462; D.739 & D.811; in D, D.750; in E flat, D.962

⊕—ᴛ **(BB)** **** EMI (ADD/DDD) 5 86011-2 (7). Popp, Donath, Rüggerberg, Venuti, Hautermann, Falk, Fassbaender, Greindle-Rosner, Dallapozza, Araiza, Protschka, Tear, Lika, Fischer-Dieskau, Schreier, Capella Bavariae, Bav. R. Ch. & SO, Sawallisch

Sawallisch's highly distinguished survey of Schubert's church music – one of the most impressive gramophone achievements of this composer's music – was recorded in the late 1970s and early 1980s, and is now available in one bargain-box set for the first time. The performances of the *Masses* are warm and understanding, even if, in his masterpiece in this form, the *Mass in E flat*, the chorus isn't always flawless. The earlier *Mass* settings bring superb, lively inspiration, not to mention the separate *Kyries* and *Salve Reginas*. Much of this glorious music is rare, but little or none of it is inconsequential. Even some of the shortest items – such as the six tiny *Antiphons*, allegedly written in half an hour – have magic and originality in them. Plainer, but still glowing with Schubertian joy, is the so-called *Deutsche Messe*. The *Magnificat*, too, is a strongly characterized setting, and even

the settings of St Thomas Aquinas's *Tantum ergo* have their charm. There are many other surprises. The lovely setting of the *Offertorium in C (Totus in corde)* is for soprano, clarinet and orchestra, with the vocal and instrumental lines intertwining delectably, while the no less appealing *Auguste jam coelestium* is a soprano–tenor duet. The *Salve Regina in C*, D.811, is written for four male voices, *a cappella*, and they again contribute to the performance of *Psalm 23*, where Sawallisch provides a piano accompaniment. Schubert left the religious drama *Lazarus* unfinished and, though no more dramatic than his operas, it contains much delightful music. Some of it is as touching as the finest Schubert, while other sections are little short of inspired; there are some thoroughly characteristic harmonic colourings and some powerful writing for trombones. With **Robert Tear** in the name-role, **Helen Donath** as Maria, **Lucia Popp** as Jemima, **Maria Venuti** as Martha, **Joseph Protschka** as Nathanael and **Fischer-Dieskau** as Simon, it is very strongly cast, and the performance is splendid; indeed, the singing throughout this set is outstanding from chorus and soloists alike, and the recordings, made in the Munich Hercules Hall, are warm and well balanced, adding to one's pleasure. An outstanding bargain.

Magnificat, D.486; Offertorium in B flat, D.963 (Intende voci)

*** Teldec 3984 26094-2. Oelze, von Magnus, Lippert, Finley, Arnold Schoenberg Ch., VCM, Harnoncourt – HAYDN: *Mass 13 in B flat: Schöpfungsmesse* ***

Harnoncourt's period performances, set in a warm church acoustic, were recorded live, like the Haydn Mass with which they are coupled, sounding similarly fresh and new. The *Magnificat* is relatively well known, with **Christiane Oelze** ravishingly beautiful in the central *Deposuit* section. By contrast the offertorium *Intende voci* for tenor soloist, choir and orchestra, written in 1828 within weeks of the composer's death, is surprisingly a rarity. Though the formalized style harks back to Haydn and Mozart, the gravity of the inspiration is clear. The recording is warmly atmospheric, even if the balance of the choir, slightly backward, prevents it from having quite the impact its incisive singing deserves. An unexpected coupling, but an illuminating one.

Masses 5 in A flat, D.678; 6 in E flat, D.950

⊕—ᴛ **(B)** **** Ph. Duo (ADD) 473 892-2 (2). Donath, Springer, Schreier, Rotzsch, Adam, Leipzig R. Ch., Dresden State O, Sawallisch

Sawallisch's glorious Philips recordings from 1971 have remained submerged in the catalogue by his EMI versions, which were made in the 1980s. Yet the earlier Dresden sound is first class: spacious, with plenty of depth and a very good overall balance. The conductor has chosen a superb team of soloists, as is immediately apparent in their contribution to the exultant *Gloria* of the *A flat Mass*, after the radiantly serene opening *Kyrie*. The **Leipzig Radio Chorus** too makes a thrillingly ardent contribution in the *Sanctus* and the soloists return in the celestial *Benedictus* and *Agnus Dei*, where they are led by **Helen Donath** who sings very beautifully. The choral singing in the *Gloria* of the *E flat Mass* is even more incisive, and equally impressive here is the dramatic contribution of the three orchestral trombones. The *Sanctus* is as resplendent as in the earlier work, but the *Benedictus* is graver, and the brass return to lead the powerfully solemn and extended *Agnus Dei*, which is so forward-looking in its style and ends the work so movingly. The body of sound in these performances, the use of women's voices and the gloriously full-textured **Dresden Staatskapellen** do not mean that detail is obscured or that there is a lack of freshness, and undoubtedly Sawallisch is at his most inspired throughout.

Masses: (i–iv) 4 in C, D.452; (ii; iv; vi) 5; 6; (iii; vii) Offertorium, D.963; (i–iii; iv; vii) Tantum ergo, D.962

🎵 **BB** *** EMI Gemini 3 81519-2 (2). (i) Popp; (ii) Fassbaender; (iii) Dallapozza; (iv) Fischer-Dieskau; (v) Donath; (vi) Araiza; (vii) Schreier; Bav. R. Ch. & SO, Sawallisch

This inexpensive reissue from **Sawallisch's** excellent choral series combines three settings of the *Mass*, including the two finest, the one in *A flat* and the masterly work in *E flat*, while the *Tantum ergo* (in *C*) also undoubtedly has its charm. These performances have stood the test of time, containing some outstanding singing from soloists and chorus, although the latter is not flawless in D.950. Sawallisch proves to be a warmly understanding Schubertian, and the recordings are both vivid and atmospheric.

Mass 6 in E flat, D.950

**** Chan. 0750. Gritton, Stephen, Padmore, Gilchrist, Rose, Coll. Mus. 90, Hickox

*** BBC (ADD) BBCL 4029-2 (2). Scottish Festival Ch., New Philh. O, Giulini – VERDI: *Requiem* ***

Richard Hickox offers an inspired account of Schubert's imposing last *Mass*, bringing out the work's expressive qualities as well as its dramatic ones. His period band offers sharply defined playing, with the work's textures amazingly clear, and he is helped by a superb collection of soloists and a rich, full-blooded recording.

Schubert's last and most ambitious setting of the *Mass* makes a generous coupling for **Giulini's** inspired account of the Verdi *Requiem*. It was recorded at the Edinburgh Festival in 1968 with radio sound remarkably free and full for a performance in the Usher Hall. As in the Verdi, Giulini directs a dedicated performance, again with incandescent choral singing from the **Scottish Festival Chorus**.

Mass 6 in E flat, D.950; Stabat Mater in G min., D.175

BB *** Naxos 8.570381. Immortal Bach Ens., Leipzig CO, Schuldt-Jensen

Schuldt-Jensen's is an extrovert account of Schubert's *Mass* in *E flat*, some six minutes quicker than the rival, Hickox version. That makes for a more obviously dramatic performance in the fast, exciting passages, though this high level of tension is sustained throughout. While it lacks the sharply

defined recording of the Chandos version, it is still an impressive, well-balanced sound, with an excellent chorus and orchestra. Moreover, it is available at bargain price, with an attractive 6-minute bonus in the form of his *Stabat Mater in G minor*.

OPERA AND INCIDENTAL MUSIC

Alfonso und Estrella (complete)

🎵 *** Berlin Classics BC2156-2 (3). Schreier, Mathis, Prey, Adam, Fischer-Dieskau, Berlin R. Ch. & State Op. O, Suitner

It is strange that Schubert, whose feeling for words in lyric poetry drew out emotions which have natural drama in them, had little or no feeling for the stage. Had his operas been produced, no doubt he would have learnt how to use music more positively; as it is, this tale of royal intrigue in medieval times never quite captures the listener as an opera should. Even so, it contains a stream of delightful music, Schubert at his most open and refreshing; under **Suitner's** direction it here receives a sparkling performance, excellently cast. **Edith Mathis** makes a sweet heroine, and **Peter Schreier** sings radiantly, as if in an orchestrated *Schöne Müllerin*. The reconciliation of the two principal male characters, Froila and Mauregato, is most touching as sung by **Fischer-Dieskau** and **Prey**. The recording is richly atmospheric and is splendidly transferred to CD. A full translation is included.

Rosamunde Overture (Die Zauberharfe, D.644) & Incidental Music, D.797 (complete)

🎵 *** DG 431 655-2. von Otter, Ernst Senff Ch., COE, Abbado

🎵 *** Australian Decca Eloquence (ADD) 466 677-2. Yachmi, Vienna State O Ch., VPO, Münchinger

Abbado and the **COE** give joyful performances of this magical incidental music. It is a revelation to hear the most popular of the entr'actes played so gently: it is like a whispered meditation. Even with a slow speed and affectionate phrasing, it yet avoids any feeling of being mannered. Glowing recording to match. **Anne Sofie von Otter** is an ideal soloist.

Münchinger's performance of the delightful *Rosamunde* music glows with an affectionate warmth and understanding which places this as one of his very best records. Its unavailability on CD until this Australian disc appeared is unaccountable: there is an unforced spontaneity, as well as strength here, and the 1970s recording is rich and naturally balanced. The vocal numbers are superbly done, and the **VPO** is at its magnificent best.

SCHULHOFF, Ervin
(1894–1942)

String Sextet

Ⓝ Ⓑ *** Hyp. Helios. CDH 55321. Raphael Ens. – MARTINŮ: *String Sextet; 3 Madrigals* ***

Like Martinů, Schulhoff was born in Bohemia and studied

in Prague. He studied briefly with Reger and Debussy, no less, and was highly prolific (there are eight symphonies though the last two were not completed). The *Sextet* of 1924 is an effective piece, with traces of Mahler and early Schoenberg. Its première at Donaueschingen in 1924 took place in the same week as Schoenberg's *Serenade*. Schulhoff lived in Germany during the interwar years, returning to Prague at the time of the Nazi invasion. A man of the Left, he had taken Soviet citizenship, which afforded him protection until Hitler invaded Russia. As a Jew, he was arrested and died in the notorious Würzburg concentration camp.

6 Ironies (for piano, 4 hands), Op. 34; 8 Jazz Improvisations (for 2 pianos). Piano Sonatas 1 & 3; 5 Burlesques, Op. 23; 5 Grotesques, Op. 21; 6 Ironies, Op. 34; 5 Picturesques, Op. 31

Ⓝ **** Phoenix 181. Babinsky, with (i) Lettberg; (ii) Wykydal

The titles of these engaging pieces are not misleading. The *Six Ironies* are 'dedicated to all cholerically', and much of the writing here is whimsical and witty. All of it creates a highly individual style peculiar to a period of the composer's life between 1917 and 1919, when he devoted himself to writing *Grotesques* and *Burlesques*, full of genial harmonic volatility and melodic quirkiness, as if he was satirizing everything the world's bourgeoisie took for granted. He was the first important German composer to dabble in American ragtime and its derivations. The *Sonatas* are more forward-looking. He had already written atonally in the *Ironies*, but in the *First Sonata* (dedicated to Thomas Mann) he turned partly back to classical forms, and the slow movement is a chromatic *Passacaglia* and the finale a perpetuum mobile. But the important aspect of all this music is that it is appealingly melodic, communicative and entertaining, very well played indeed, and excellently recorded.

SCHUMAN, William
(1910–92)

Piano Concerto

(**(*)) VAI mono VAIA 1124. Tureck, Saidenberg Little Symphony, Daniel Saidenberg – DALLAPICCOLA: *2 Studies for Violin & Piano* (**); DIAMOND: *Piano Sonata* (***)

William Schuman's *Piano Concerto*, written in 1938, but revised in 1942, is worthy of a modern recording, and we hope Naxos will soon oblige in their American series. There is no doubt about the power, expressive commitment and virtuosity of **Rosalyn Tureck's** première performance, recorded in New York's Town Hall in 1943, and the orchestra for the most part plays well enough, especially in the fine central slow movement, in which Tureck certainly observes the composer's marking, 'Deliberately'. Her virtuosity in the brilliant, glitteringly rhythmic finale is hardly less impressive. But the piano is placed well forward, and the dry recording is very unflattering to all concerned, especially the orchestral brass, while in the accompanied piano passages the strings are distant and ill-focused.

(i) Violin Concerto; New England Triptych

⏵ BB **** Naxos 8.559083. (i) Quint; Bournemouth SO, Serebrier – IVES: *Variations on America* ***

Schuman's powerfully expressive *Violin Concerto* (1959) underwent more than one transformation in its gestation, with the original three movements becoming two. After a strong, rhythmically angular opening (with the soloist immediately introducing the work's dominating motif) the first movement soon slips into a magically lyrical *molto tranquillo*. Later there is a sparkling scherzando section and an extended cadenza before the brilliant conclusion. Lyrical feeling also seeps through the finale, although there is plenty of vigour and spectacle too, and a fugue, before the bravura *moto perpetuo* display of the closing section. Altogether a splendidly rewarding work, given a first-rate performance here by **Philip Quint** and the strongly involved **Bournemouth** players under **Serebrier**.

They are no less persuasive in the *New England Triptych*, a folksy, immediately communicative work. First-class recording in an attractively spacious acoustic. The coupling, which Schuman orchestrated, could not be more apt.

Violin Concerto

Ⓝ Ⓜ *** EMI 2 06611-2. McDuffie, St Louis SO, Slatkin – BERNSTEIN: *Serenade* ***

Schuman's *Violin Concerto* is also given a highly sensitive performance by **McDuffie** and **Slatkin**.

In Praise of Shahn (Canticle for Orchestra); (i) To Thee Old Cause (Evocation for Oboe, Brass, Timpani, Piano & Strings)

Ⓜ *** Sony (ADD) 516235-2 [SK 90390]. (i) Gomberg (oboe); NYPO, Bernstein – BARBER: *Adagio for Strings; Violin Concerto* ***

Both of these works are commemorative. *To Thee Old Cause* is dedicated to the memory of Dr Martin Luther King, and the score quotes from Walt Whitman ('Thou peerless, passionate, good cause, Thou stern, remorseless, sweet idea'). It features an oboe obbligato within its string textures which are reinforced by brass sonorities. In a single movement, its *Larghissimo* opening is intense and evocative, although poignant lyrical feeling predominates. *In Praise of* (Ben) *Shahn* remembers the New York artist. It is in two sections, both (drawing on Eastern European Jewish folk material) include dynamic and expressive writing. This is music which in its atmosphere and use of dissonance often looks back to Charles Ives, although Schuman's own individual voice is never submerged. **Bernstein** is in his element and neither piece could receive more passionate advocacy. The (1970) Avery Fisher Hall recording is very immediate but has plenty of atmosphere too.

Symphonies 4 & 9 (Le Fosse Ardeatine)

⏵ BB **** Naxos 8.559254. Seattle SO, Schwarz

Symphonies 7 & 10 (The American Muse)

⏵ BB **** Naxos 8.559255. Seattle SO, Schwarz

Gerard Schwarz and the Seattle Orchestra give finely pre-pared and totally committed accounts of the present four symphonies. Schuman is said to have composed early in the morning and then turned to musical education and admin-istration for the rest of the day. The *Fourth Symphony* followed its famous predecessor within a few months, and its pre-mière was conducted by Koussevitzky. The *Ninth* was written in 1967, when Schuman had visited Rome and seen the me-morial *Le Fosse Ardeatine* that commemorates a random mas-sacre by Nazi forces. It is a dark and powerful score. The *Seventh* (1960) marks Schuman's return to the symphony after a gap of 11 years, while the *Tenth* was commissioned for the bicentennial celebrations of 1975. No one investigating these works will be disappointed.

String Quartet 3

*** Testament SBT 1374. Juilliard Qt – BERG: *Lyric Suite*;
   CARTER: *Quartet 2* ***

It was William Schuman who, when he became President of the Juilliard School, made plans for a resident quartet, and he who hailed their début concert: 'I'll never forget it if I live to be a thousand, it was greater than anything I'd ever dreamed of.' They recorded Schuman's own *Quartet* (1940) in 1958 and play it with consistent fervour and the deep un-derstanding that they show in the companion works. The *Third* is a powerful and strongly original piece which alone is worth the price of this record.

SCHUMANN, Clara (1819–96)

Piano Trio in G min., Op. 17

Ⓑ *** Helios CDH 55078. Dartington Piano Trio – FANNY
   MENDELSSOHN: *Trio* ***

Clara's *Piano Trio* moves within the Mendelssohn–Schumann tradition with apparently effortless ease and, when played as persuasively as it is here by the **Dartington Trio**, makes a pleasing impression. If it does not command the depth of Robert, it has a great deal of charm to commend it. Excellent recording.

3 Romances, Op. 22

*** Avie AV 2075. Khaner, Abramovic – BRAHMS: *Clarinet
   Sonatas 1–2*; ROBERT SCHUMANN: *Romances* ***

Though Clara Schumann's charming *Romances* were origi-nally written for violin, they make an apt and attractive fill-up to the flute transcriptions of the other works on the disc, rarities that deserve to be heard more often, here most sen-sitively performed.

6 Lieder from Jucunde, Op. 23; 6 Lieder, Op. 13; Lieder, Op. 12. Lieder.

Ⓑ *** Hyp. Helios CDH 55275. Gritton, Loges, Asti

Clara Schumann wrote almost all her songs during her marriage to Robert, often inspired by special occasions such as birthdays and Christmases. When he died she wrote no more, which is greatly to be regretted when these charm-ing inspirations have so many delightful qualities, generally light-hearted and lyrical. Her Rückert setting, *Liebst du um Schönheit*, in its folk-like innocence contrasts nicely with the well-known Mahler setting of the same words. Another of her early songs, *Der Wanderer in der Sägemühle* ('The wan-derer at the sawmill'), has unexpected harmonic twists, rather in the manner of Schubert, as do many of her songs. **Susan Gritton** is a charming soloist in the *Jucunde* songs. She and **Stephan Loges** are the excellent soloists in the whole programme, given inspired accompaniment by **Eugene Asti**.

4 Songs, Op. 12

*** Philadelphia Orchestral Association POA 2003 (3).
   Hampson, Sawallisch – ROBERT SCHUMANN: *Violin
   Concerto; Symphonies 1–4*, etc. **(*)

The songs by Clara Schumann find **Thomas Hampson** in superb form, communicating vividly with every word, flaw-lessly supported by **Wolfgang Sawallisch** on the piano.

SCHUMANN, Robert (1810–56)

(i; ii) Adagio and Allegro brillante; (ii) Carnaval (excerpts orch. Ravel); (i; ii) Piano Concerto in A min.; (i) Kinderszenen; Of Foreign Lands and People; (ii) Symphony 4 in D min., Op. 20 (DVD version)

🎬 *** EuroArts **DVD** 2055498. (i) Argerich; (ii) Leipzig GO,
   Chailly (Dir: Michael Beyer)

Any doubts about the music here are silenced by the charisma of the performances. Certainly the opening *Adagio and Allegro* is brilliant, but little else, and Ravel's scoring of four movements from *Carnaval* was his one misguided or-chestral transcription, for their distinction and poetry evap-orate in orchestral dress. The *Piano Concerto* is a different matter, and **Martha Argerich** plays it with cascading bril-liance, yet finding much delicate charm for the central *Intermezzo*. Some might feel that her exuberance elsewhere occasionally carries her away, but such sparkling bravura is difficult to resist. She then plays the miniature from *Kinderszenen* as a gentle encore. **Chailly** gives the *Fourth Symphony* its full head, and it is magnificently played by the **Leipzig Gewandhaus Orchestra**. The transition to the excit-ing finale is superbly graduated to its Wagnerian climax, and the brilliant, wide-ranging recording lets us discover that the acoustics of the Gewandhaus are ideal; it is a magnificent venue which the camera lets us appreciate.

Carnaval (arr. various composers)

Ⓝ *** Australian Decca Eloquence 480 038 (2). SRO,
   Ansermet – GLAZUNOV: *The Seasons*, etc; GLINKA: *Ruslan
   and Ludmilla*, etc; LIADOV: *Baba-Yaga*, etc ***

Carnaval, orchestrated by Glazunov, Rimsky-Korsakov, Liadov and Tcherepnin, gives Schumann a distinctly Russian flavour. But the orchestrations are done with such flair that any reservations about transcribing Schumann's piano music are dispelled and it offers 25 or so pleasing minutes. An imaginative inclusion in this disc of colourful Russian show pieces. This is another of Ansermet's most rewarding reissues.

Cello Concerto in A min., Op. 129 (DVD version)

☦– ******** DG **DVD** 073 4351. Maisky, VPO, Bernstein – HAYDN: *Cello Concertos*, etc. ******** (Dir: Humphrey Burton)

Maisky and **Bernstein** make a splendid partnership in Schumann's *Cello Concerto*, ardent and commanding, with a warmly expressive slow movement. Visually this could hardly be better managed, and the recording too is first class. With its coupling of both Haydn *Cello Concertos* and transcribed concertante music for violin, this is a very attractive compilation.

Cello Concerto in A min., Op. 129

☦– ******* BIS CD 486. Thedéen, Malmö SO, Markiz – ELGAR: *Concerto* *******

☦– ⒝⒝ ******* Naxos 8.550938. Kliegel, Nat. SO of Ireland, Constantine – BRAHMS: *Double Concerto* *******

Ⓜ ****(*)** EMI (ADD) 5 62803-2. du Pré, New Philh. O, Barenboim – DVOŘÁK: *Cello Concerto* ****(*)**

Ⓜ ****(*)** Sup. (ADD) SU 3667-2. Navarra, Czech PO, Ančerl – BLOCH: *Schelomo* ****(*)**; RESPIGHI: *Adagio con variazioni* *******

The young Swedish virtuoso, **Torleif Thedéen**, is splendidly recorded on BIS, and the **Malmö Orchestra** give him sympathetic support. He plays with a refreshing ardour, tempered by nobility and a reticence that is strongly appealing. He couples it with an account of the Elgar that is every bit as attuned to the latter's sensibility as any in the catalogue. Strongly recommended.

The Schumann *Cello Concerto* comes on Naxos in a warmly spontaneous-sounding performance, very well recorded. **Kliegel** takes a spacious, lyrical view of the first movement, using a soft-grained tone at the start, with wide vibrato. The simple, dedicated approach to the central *Langsam* also brings dedicated playing, while the finale is wittily pointed, not least in the second subject.

Jacqueline du Pré's spontaneous style is well suited to this most recalcitrant of concertos and the slow movement is particularly beautiful. As in the coupling, the partnership with **Daniel Barenboim** is very successful, and the remastered 1968 recording has brought a firmer orchestral focus to match the realistic cello timbre.

André Navarra on his day is one of the most commanding of cellists and his performance here has real personality, rivalling some versions on dearer labels. The Supraphon sound has been made more vivid by the remastering, with the cello focus real and present, and the orchestra caught warmly and naturally.

(i; iii) Cello Concerto; (ii; iii) Piano Concerto; (ii) Etudes symphoniques, Op. 13

☦– Ⓜ ******* Sony SMK 89716. (i) Ma; (ii) Perahia; (iii) Bav. RSO, C. Davis

In the *Cello Concerto* **Yo-Yo Ma's** playing is characteristically refined, but keenly affectionate too, although at times he car-

ries tonal sophistication to excess and suddenly drops into *sotto voce* tone and near inaudibility. But both he and **Sir Colin Davis** are thoroughly attuned to the sensibility of this composer and the recording balance is excellent. Similarly Davis makes a fine partner for **Perahia**, who in the *Piano Concerto* enjoys displaying his ardour and virtuosity, as well as his ability to invest a phrase with poetry and magic. The recording is live, but is full and spacious. The *Symphonic Etudes* are equally fine although here the balance is rather close.

(i) Cello Concerto; (ii) 3 Fantasiestücke, Op. 73; 3 Romanzen, Op. 94

(***) Testament mono SBT 1310. Gendron, SRO; (i) Ansermet (ii) Françaix – TCHAIKOVSKY: *Variations on a Rococo Theme* (***)

Maurice Gendron was rather overshadowed by his countrymen and contemporaries, Pierre Fournier and Paul Tortelier, but he was no less eloquent an artist and had much of the former's aristocratic finesse and the latter's intensity. His playing was quite personal and his tonal burnish reflects his admiration for Feuermann. Gendron's remains an impressive account, well worth reviving. It makes its first appearance on CD. The Opp. 73 and 94 pieces, recorded in 1952, serve as a reminder of the refined musicianship of the elegant composer-pianist, **Jean Françaix**.

(i) Piano Concerto in A min., Op. 54. Carnaval, Op. 9 (DVD versions)

☦– ******* EMI **DVD** DBV4 928399. Arrau, (i) LPO, Hurst (with BEETHOVEN: *Piano Sonata 32 in C min., Op. 111*). (Also *Piano Sonata 23 in F min. (Appassionata), Op. 57* played by Solomon)

Claudio Arrau's *A minor Concerto* was filmed in a dryish BBC Studio in London in June 1963 and *Carnaval* two years earlier, both produced by the legendary Walter Todds. His account of Beethoven's *C minor Sonata* comes from a Paris studio recital from 1970, and of these three works it best captures the distinctive Arrau sonority. Fine though his *Carnaval* is, it is Op. 111 that brings the wonderful range of tone and colour that readers who heard him in the concert hall will remember. In the *Piano Concerto* it is good to be reminded of the excellence of the underrated **George Hurst's** accompanying. Some of the footage is grainy in the *Concerto*, but the camera-work is always unobtrusive. One of the most exciting things here is the so-called bonus which offers an altogether electrifying performance of the *Appassionata* by **Solomon**, recorded in January 1956 not long before he suffered the stroke that immobilized him. An indispensable issue.

Piano Concerto in A min., Op. 56 (DVD version with Documentary by Wulf Konold and others)

Ⓝ ******** EuroArts **DVD** 2056068. Argerich, Leipzig GO, Chailly (Performance directed by Michael Beyer; Documentary directed by Angelika Stiehler)

This DVD derives from a concert at the Leipzig Gewandhaus in June 2006 and offers one of the finest accounts of the Schumann *Piano Concerto* ever recorded.

Martha Argerich is consistently imaginative, her magical sharing of the melody with the woodwind in the first movement is matched by the interplay between her and the strings in the *Intermezzo*. The whole performance is a wonderful amalgam of brilliance and romantic sensitivity, a delight to hear and see – the scintillating passagework in the finale radiates joy. One can also get the whole concert on EuroArts DVD (2055498), where Chailly is also impressive in the *Fourth Symphony* and rare arrangements by Ravel and Tchaikovsky of excerpts from *Carnaval* and the *Etudes symphoniques*. But many will prefer the half-hour documentary on the present disc, planned by Wulf Konoldt, which analyses the music fascinatingly and explains why the work is such a masterpiece, besides giving a revealing picture of the lives of the composer and his wife.

Piano Concerto in A min., Op. 54

⊕—⊛ Ⓜ ******** EMI 5 03419-2. Andsnes, BPO, Jansons – GRIEG: *Piano Concerto* ********⊛

⊕—Ⓜ ******** Ph. (ADD) 475 7773. Kovacevich, BBC SO, C. Davis – GRIEG: *Concerto* ********

⊕—******* EMI 5 57773-2. Argerich, Svizzera-Italiana O, Rabinovitch-Barakovsky – BEETHOVEN: *Triple Concerto* *******

⊕—******* EMI 7 54746-2. Vogt, CBSO, Rattle – GRIEG: *Concerto* *******

⊕—******* Sony 518810-2 [SK 92736]. Perahia, Bav. RSO, C. Davis – GRIEG: *Concerto* *******

Ⓜ ******* Decca (ADD) 458 628-2. Ashkenazy, LSO, Segal – TCHAIKOVSKY: *Concerto* 1 ****(*)**

Ⓜ ******* Decca (ADD) 466 383-2. Lupu, LSO, Previn – GRIEG: *Piano Concerto* *******

Ⓜ ******* Warner Elatus 0927 49617-2. Grimaud, Berlin Deutsche SO, Zinman – BEETHOVEN: *Piano Concerto 4* *******

Ⓝ Ⓑ ******* CfP 2 28368-2. Devoyon, LPO, Maksymiuk – GRIEG: *Piano Concerto* *******

Ⓜ **(***)** DG mono 474 024-2 (5). Kempff, LSO, Krips – BEETHOVEN: *Piano Concertos 1–5*; BRAHMS: *Piano Concerto 1*; MOZART: *Piano Concertos 9 & 15*; LISZT: *Piano Concertos 1 and 2* **(***)**

ⒷⒷ **(***)** Dutton CDBP 9719. Lipatti, Philh. O, Karajan – GRIEG: *Concerto* **(***)**

ⒷⒷ **(***)** Naxos mono 8.110612. Cortot, LPO, Ronald – CHOPIN: *Piano Concerto 2 in F min., Op. 21*

Piano Concerto in A min.; Concert-allegro with Introduction in D min., Op. 134; Introduction & Allegro appassionato, Op. 92

**(*) MDG 340 1033-2. Zacharias, Lausanne Chamber O

Andsnes's Schumann is a performance of the highest poetic feeling and distinction. Like the Grieg, it brings glorious playing from both soloist and the orchestra under **Jansons**, a performance similarly combining spontaneity and concentration, dedication and poetry, with no hint of self-consciousness or routine. The pianistic virtuosity is commanding but never overrides tenderness. A performance of both authority and nobility, recorded in particularly lifelike and well-balanced sound. A classic version for our time.

Although Pires should not be forgotten (coupled with the *Piano Quartet*), our primary recommendation for this favourite Romantic *Concerto* remains with the successful symbiosis of **Stephen Kovacevich** and **Sir Colin Davis**, who give an interpretation which is both fresh and poetic, unexaggerated but powerful in its directness and clarity, and the spring-like element of the outer movements is finely presented by orchestra and soloist alike.

EMI's live recording of the Schumann, made at the Lugano Festival, has a rare vitality, thanks to the vividly characterful playing of **Martha Argerich**. This account may not be as polished as Argerich's studio version, when impulsively she keeps taking her conductor by surprise, but the magnetism of her playing is here irresistible, with high dramatic contrasts between sparkling virtuosity and yearning lyricism. With the Beethoven *Triple Concerto*, similarly animated, as an unusual coupling, this makes an attractive recommendation.

Lars Vogt's sensitivity, an innate sense of style and a keen imagination are strongly in evidence in this account of the Schumann, in which he is well supported by **Simon Rattle** and the **CBSO**. There is stiff competition, of course, but among modern recordings Vogt acquits himself with honour.

Perahia's 1988 version also benefits from having the guiding hand of **Sir Colin Davis** directing the orchestra. The recording is live. Perahia is never merely showy, but here he enjoys displaying his ardour and virtuosity as well as his ability to invest a phrase with poetry and magic. With its full and spacious sound, the Perahia is among the finest current versions of this favourite coupling, and it now comes at mid-price with the finale of the Mendelssohn *Second Concerto* as a bonus.

Ashkenazy's performance, balancing the demands of drama against poetry, comes down rather more in favour of the former than one might expect, but it is a refined reading as well as a powerful one, with the finale rather more spacious than usual. The recording, from the late 70s, is of vintage quality and has been remastered most successfully. However, Ashkenazy is less obviously attuned to the rhetoric of the Tchaikovsky coupling.

The **Lupu–Previn** performance suits the music admirably, with the piano lucidly and truthfully caught against a natural orchestral backcloth. Lupu's clean boldness of approach in the outer movements is appealingly fresh, while the finale brilliant yet unforced, while the *Intermezzo* has both warmth and the necessary tender delicacy.

A most enjoyably spontaneous performance from **Hélène Grimaud** in a very successful coupling with Beethoven's *G major Concerto*. **David Zinman** proves a sympathetic partner and, while the opening movement has a flexible, romantic flamboyance, its delicate moments are thoughtfully poetic, as is the gentle account of the *Intermezzo*, to be followed by an exhilarating finale. The spaciously resonant recording has an attractive concert-hall ambience.

Coupled with an excellent account of the Grieg *Concerto*, **Pascal Devoyon's** performance brings natural musicianship, technical brilliance and artistry in equal measure, and he receives excellent support from **Maksymiuk**. A fine budget coupling, well recorded too.

Kempff's first recording of the Schumann, made for Decca in 1953, is unique in its magic, sparklingly transparent in its textures, delicately pointed and consistently poetic. No pianist with such light pedalling could play with a smoother legato, making the melodies sing. This mono recording, unavailable for 40 years and more, is a wonderful addition to Kempff's legacy on disc, helped by sparklingly clear sound, engineered by the legendary Kenneth Wilkinson.

Dinu Lipatti's classic version of the Schumann *Concerto*, a staple of the catalogue from when it was recorded in the late 1940s, now comes in this Dutton bargain issue with the sound fuller and clearer than ever before, and superior to the newest EMI transfer.

Zacharias, with chamber forces, offers a comparatively small-scale approach, with textures exceptionally transparent, and with his crisp articulation consistently adding sparkle in the most elaborate passage-work. But both in the finale and in the two rarer concertante works he takes a broad view, avoiding pomposity in the rhetorical gestures of Op. 134, and springing rhythms lightly, never letting the music drag, the effect carefree if lacking flamboyance. With exceptionally clear recording, it makes a refreshing and distinctive view, certainly poetic.

There is something quite special about **Cortot**. There is lyrical warmth, poetic feeling and a wonderful freshness and individuality. Mark Obert-Thorn gets a very good sound from the shellac originals.

(i) *Piano Concerto in A min.; (ii) Violin Concerto in D*

(N) (M) ** Warner Maestro 2564 69868-5. (i) Argerich; (ii) Kremer; COE, Harnoncourt

Martha Argerich, recorded live, gives a vividly compelling, characteristically volatile reading of the *Piano Concerto*, at once poetic and full of fancy, powerful and often wildly individual, culminating in an account of the finale so daring one wants to cheer at the end, so freely does the adrenalin flow. Though the orchestra is hard pressed to keep up with her at her fast basic speed, there is a splendid swing to the rhythm and no sense of haste. However, this is not as inspired an account as her EMI DVD (see above). **Kremer's** performance of the *Violin Concerto* is similarly disappointing by comparison with the warmth and bravura of his earlier, EMI version with Muti. In neither concerto is the recorded sound ideally warm or full-bodied, with tuttis rather muddy in texture.

(i) *Piano Concerto in A min; Symphony 1*

(M) **(*) Warner Elatus 0927 49568-2. (i) Argerich; COE, Harnoncourt

In her live recording of the *Piano Concerto* **Martha Argerich** gives a vividly compelling, characteristically volatile reading, at once poetic and full of fancy, powerful and often wildly individual. The orchestra is hard pressed to keep up with her at her fast basic speed, and the first movement takes

some time to settle down (the woodwind ensemble at the start is a bit rough). **Harnoncourt's** account of the *Symphony* is very well played but is much less individual and it lacks the spontaneous thrust of the *Concerto*.

(i) *Piano Concerto in A min., Op. 54; (ii) Piano Quintet in E flat, Op. 44*

⊕— (M) *** RCA 82876 65830-2. Alicia de Larrocha; (i) LSO, C. Davis; (ii) Tokyo Qt

Alicia de Larrocha made the rare coupling with the *Piano Quintet*, and she is very successful. With **Sir Colin Davis** as partner, it is not surprising that the *Concerto* strikes a perfect balance between poetic feeling and drama, and the LSO players respond sensitively to both pianist and conductor. The Abbey Road recording is first class. Similarly, the *Quintet* brings a truly responsive performance, full of warmth, the engaging *In modo d'una marcia* making a perfect contrast to the joyously vigorous Scherzo. Here the recording is close but, with piano and strings well balanced, makes a fine mid-priced version.

Piano Concerto in A min., Op. 54; (i) Carnaval, Op. 9; Waldszenen: Vogel als Prophet (only)

(BB) (***) Naxos mono 8.110604. Hess; (i) O, Goehr

Dame Myra Hess was admired particularly for her Schumann, which was both authoritative and sensitive. Nothing is ever overstated, and she is completely inside Schumann's poetic world. Virtuosity and display are by-products of her dedication to the letter and spirit of the score. Her rubato seems completely right and tempi are judged perfectly. The recording of the *Piano Concerto* (in the 78 era, the preferred choice of most collectors) is a little dry, but the performance is fresher than her mono account with Rudolf Schwarz and the Philharmonia. Decent transfers.

Violin Concerto in D min.

⊕— (B) *** Decca 475 6703 (2). Bell, Cleveland O, Dohnányi – BRAHMS; TCHAIKOVSKY; WIENIAWSKI: *Violin Concertos* ***

⊕— (BB) *** Warner Apex 0927 49517-2. Zehetmair, Philh. O, Eschenbach – DVOŘÁK: *Violin Concerto; Romance* **(*)

*** Virgin 5 45663-2. Capuçon, Mahler CO, Harding – MENDELSSOHN: *Violin Concerto* ***

With **Christoph von Dohnányi** adding to the weight of the drama, **Jamie Bell**, in a commanding performance defies the old idea of this concerto as an impossibly flawed piece, bringing out the charm as well as the power. The central slow movement has a rapt intensity rarely matched, and the dance-rhythms of the finale have fantasy as well as jauntiness and jollity. With full-bodied, well-balanced recording this is a Double which offers three equally recommendable couplings, with the Brahms concerto among the very finest in the catalogue.

Thomas Zehetmair is perfectly cast for the Schumann *Concerto*. He understands the central European tradition and makes the very most of the comparatively weak first movement. The *Langsam* slow movement is glorious (Schumann seemingly at his most inspired) and even the erratic finale is made to sound jolly and not too disjointed. **Eschenbach** accompanies sympathetically, the recording is excellent, and this performance is outstanding in every way.

Renaud Capuçon's performance of Schumann's still under-appreciated *Violin Concerto* is marked by lightness and transparency, not least in the chamber-scale orchestral accompaniment, with bright, crisp attack and a tender account of the second subject. With free, open sound, recorded in the Jugendstill theatre in Vienna, this makes an outstanding version of an apt and rare coupling.

Fantasy for Violin & Orchestra, Op. 131

(BB) *** Warner Apex 0927 4959-2. Zehetmair, Cleveland O, Dohnányi – BRAHMS: *Violin Concerto* **

Schumann's rarely heard *Fantasy* was presented to his wife for Clara's 34th birthday. The violin dominates reflectively throughout and has many solo passages which are improvisational in character. It is not a masterpiece, but its lyrical inspiration is strong and its loose structure surprisingly convincing. Both **Zehetmair** and **Dohnányi** are in total sympathy with the music and the recording is excellent.

SYMPHONIES

Symphony in G min. (Zwickau); Symphonies 1–3 (Rhenish), Op. 97; Symphony 4 (original 1841 version revised 1851 version); (i) Konzertstück for 4 Horns & Orchestra in F, Op. 86

**** DG 457 591-2 (3). ORR, Gardiner

With his brilliant orchestra of period instruments **Gardiner** offers not just the four regular *Symphonies* but a complete survey of Schumann as symphonist. He seeks specifically to explode the myth that Schumann was a poor orchestrator, pointing out how quick he was to learn from his own mistakes. Gardiner makes an exception over the 1851 revision of the *Fourth Symphony*, in which Schumann thickened the woodwind writing with much doubling. Illuminatingly, both versions of that symphony are included, with the contrasts well brought out. Gardiner himself, like Brahms, prefers the slimmer, more transparent first version, suggesting that the 1851 changes made it safer and less original. Yet, paradoxically, in performance Gardiner is even more inspired in the later version, which here emerges as bitingly dramatic, working up to a thrilling coda. Like other cycles, this one offers the *Overture, Scherzo and Finale* of 1841 as a necessary extra, but still more fascinating is the *Konzertstück* of 1849 for four horns, with the ORR soloists breathtaking in their virtuosity on nineteenth-century instruments. Also included is the early, incomplete *Symphony in G minor* of 1832 (named after Schumann's home town of Zwickau). Under Gardiner the two completed movements emerge as highly original in their own right.

Symphonies 1–4 (DVD versions)

(N) ☱–✿ **** DG DVD 073 4512. VPO, Bernstein

Bernstein's outstanding complete DVD set of the Schumann symphonies (on a single disc) shows him at his very finest – electrifying in controlling tension, spirited and genial in bringing out Schumann's rich lyricism, powerful in creating the music's drama. John Rockwell of the *New York Times* suggested that in these later Schumann performances 'the orchestral playing is surer and more idiomatic . . . warm, full and Germanic'. 'Bernstein,' he concludes, 'catches the romantic secret of this music in a way that most conductors have not.' Throughout the set he achieves glorious orchestral textures from the **VPO** that completely negate any suggestion that the composer's scoring is thick and unwieldy; indeed, he always uses the original scores, and the *First Symphony* sounds wonderfully fresh and spring-like, the performance joyously light-hearted. In the *Second* Bernstein obviously identifies completely with the *Adagio*, playing it with great tenderness, and then the orchestra jubilantly explodes into the closing *molto vivace*. In the *Third* the very opening is exuberant and the brass produces remarkable sonority in the fourth movement's opening evocation of Cologne Cathedral. Most remarkable of all is the *Fourth*, played with enormous zest, and in the extraordinary 'Wagnerian' transition, from Scherzo to finale, Bernstein out-Furtwänglers Furtwängler in bringing a feeling of actual creative growth, as the brass, with unforgettable power, makes its way remorselessly to the main allegro, which then dashes off bitingly and exhilaratingly, and accelerates spontaneously into the unstoppable coda. Throughout, the Vienna Philharmonic give their all, and watching Bernstein enjoying himself doing the same is an experience in itself. Fortunately Humphrey Burton's video direction is worthy of the occasion, and the Audio Producer, John McClure, can take similar credit for the superbly balanced sound in the Musikverein.

Symphonies 1–4 (CD versions)

☱–(BB) *** Arte Nova 8287657743-2 (2). Zürich Tonhalle O, Zinman

Symphonies 1–4; Scherzo in G min. (ed. Draheim)

☱–(M) *** DG 429 672-2 (2). BPO, Karajan

(B) **(*) DG Double 453 049-2 (2). VPO, Bernstein

Symphonies 1–4: Manfred Overture, Op. 115

(B) **(*) Sony (ADD) 516027-2 (2). Cleveland O, Szell

Symphonies 1 in B flat (Spring), Op. 38; 2 in C, Op. 61

(B) *** Sony (ADD) SBK 48269. Bav. RSO, Kubelik

Symphonies 3 in E flat (Rhenish), Op. 97; 4 in D min., Op. 120; Overture Manfred, Op. 115

(B) *** Sony (ADD) SBK 48270. Bav. RSO, Kubelik

Symphonies 1–4; Overture, Scherzo & Finale, Op. 52

(M) *** EMI 567768-2 (2). Dresden State O, Sawallisch

Symphonies 1–4; Overtures: The Bride of Messina; Hermann und Dorothea

(BB) **(*) EMI Gemini (ADD) 3 71497-2 (2). Philh. O or (4) New Philh. O, Muti

Symphonies 1–4; Overture: Julius Caesar, Op. 128; Overture, Scherzo & Finale, Op. 52

(B) **(*) Double Decca (ADD) 448 930-2 (2). VPO, Solti

Symphonies 1–2 in C; Genoveva Overture

**(*) Australian DG Eloquence 463 200-2. BPO, Kubelik

Symphonies 3–4; Manfred Overture

**(*) Australian DG Eloquence 463 201-2. BPO, Kubelik

Karajan's interpretations of the Schumann *Symphonies* stand above all other recordings on modern instruments. 1 is a beautifully shaped performance, with orchestral playing of the highest distinction; 2 is among the most powerful ever recorded, combining poetic intensity and intellectual strength in equal proportions; and 3 is also among the most impressive versions ever committed to disc: its famous fourth-movement evocation of Cologne Cathedral is superbly spacious and eloquent, with quite magnificent brass playing. 4 can be classed alongside Furtwängler's famous record, with Karajan similarly inspirational, yet a shade more self-disciplined than his illustrious predecessor.

The Dresden CDs of the Schumann *Symphonies* under **Sawallisch** are as deeply musical as they are carefully considered; the orchestral playing combines superb discipline with refreshing naturalness and spontaneity. Sawallisch catches all Schumann's varying moods, and his direction has splendid vigour. Although the reverberant acoustic brought a degree of edge to the upper strings, the sound-picture has the essential fullness which the Karajan transfers lack, and the remastering has cleaned up the upper range to a considerable extent.

As in his outstanding cycle of the Beethoven symphonies, **David Zinman** with the **Tonhalle Orchestra** offers modern-instrument performances which have taken on board the lessons learned from period-instrument performances. With speeds on the fast side, these are all readings which, with excellent sound, are at once fresh, resilient and transparent, defying the old idea of Schumann's thickness of orchestration.

Kubelik's fine Sony set also remains fully competitive. The recording was made in the Hercules-Saal, Munich, in 1979, and the advantages of that glowing acoustic can be felt throughout. The orchestral playing is generally very fine (if not quite as polished as the Berlin Philharmonic) and is especially eloquent in the spacious slow movements. These are strongly characterized readings with plenty of vitality which display the same bright and alert sensitivity to Schumann's style as did his earlier set for DG. But the Sony recording is obviously more modern, and the latest CD transfer brings plenty of body to the sound and a better focus to the violins than in the Sawallisch set.

2, with which **Szell** began his cycle in October 1958, proves to be a thrilling performance of great power and strong forward thrust, yet the eloquent *Adagio* expands gloriously and brings the most ardent response from the Cleveland strings. Szell is at his most incisive and the orchestra are at their warmest in 1. The account of the *Rhenish* is even finer, marvellously full of life. The playing is breath-taking, with the horns gloriously full-blooded. 4 is strong and dramatic, not as weighty as some, but equally convincing. Szell proves himself an outstanding exponent of Schumann, able to stand alongside the finest interpreters of his day, and, were it not for the reduced range of dynamic, this set would have been even more recommended.

Kubelik's earlier accounts of the symphonies are beautifully played and well recorded. The readings have not the drive of Karajan, notably in 4, but they undoubtedly have both eloquence and warmth. They are straightforward and unmannered and recorded in a spacious acoustic with good CD transfers. Kubelik's ear for balance removes all suspicions of heaviness in the orchestration, and the recordings, dating from the mid-1960s, still sound good. Two enjoyable *Overtures* are offered as a bonus.

Bernstein's VPO recordings from 1984–5 have the extra voltage which comes with live music-making at its most compulsive, though he seems reluctant to let the music speak for itself. With splendid orchestral playing and much engaging detail, there is a great deal to admire throughout these performances, and the resonant acoustic of the Grossersaal of the Musikverein gives the music-making a robust immediacy.

Solti's Schumann interpretations are full of his personal brand of lyrical intensity. The most compelling performance of the cycle is the *Second Symphony*, with its passionate slow movement. And with a feeling of spontaneous lyricism paramount, this is a most compellingly individual reading. The *Julius Caesar Overture* is no masterpiece, but makes an enjoyable bonus and the *Overture, Scherzo and Finale* is very successful. The late 1960s recordings are slightly dry, bright and forward, but one cannot complain that Schumann's scoring sounds too thick!

Muti is a spirited and warm-hearted interpreter of Schumann, and all four *Symphonies* are most enjoyable, as are the rare overtures. But the very opening of the *First Symphony* brings what is probably the most controversial speed in the whole set, so hectic that the spring-like freshness is rather missed. Though the **Philharmonic** strings are not always as polished as they have since become, both playing and the late-1970s recording are warm and ripe, making this a very acceptable budget set.

Symphony 1 in B flat (Spring), Op. 38

⊕—(M) **** DG (ADD) 447 408-2. BPO, Karajan – BRAHMS: *Symphony 1* ****

Karajan is totally attuned to Schumann's sensibility and he provides a strong yet beautifully shaped performance of the *Spring Symphony*. The very opening is electrifying, with the **Berlin Philharmonic** giving of their finest. The sound is an obvious improvement on the previous CD incarnation of this well-balanced analogue recording from the early 1970s, adding body and weight to the clear, fresh detail.

Symphonies 1 in B flat (Spring), Op. 38; 4 in D min., Op. 120; Konzertstück for 4 Horns & Orchestra in F, Op. 86

(M) *** DG 474 551-2. ORR, Gardiner

This mid-price release gives us the familiar (1851) version of the *Fourth*, less bold than the original version, but still striking in this vivid performance. The *Spring Symphony*, too, is fresh and dynamic, and full of energy. But perhaps the most fascinating work here is the 1841 *Konzertstück for four horns*, virtually unplayable in Schumann's own time, but presented here with extraordinary panache, with the **ORR** soloists breathtaking in their virtuosity.

Symphony 1 in B flat (Spring), Op 38; Overture, Scherzo & Finale, Op. 52; Overture to Schiller's 'Bride of Messina', Op. 100; Overture, Genoveva, Op. 81; Zwickau Symphony (first movement)

*** BIS **SACD** 1560. Swedish CO, Dausgaard

Thomas Dausgaard and the **Swedish Chamber Orchestra** give us an interesting anthology, including the *Spring Symphony* of 1841. The *Overtures* apart, the rarity here is the opening movement of an early *G minor Symphony* premièred in Zwickau in 1832. Dausgaard shows how much less of a hapless forerunner of the mature symphonies the piece is. All these performances benefit from the clarity of sound that this 38-man band and the excellent acoustic of the Örebro Concert Hall can offer on atmospheric SACD. Dausgaard is an excellent conductor and the BIS team do him and the orchestra proud.

Symphony 1 (Spring) in B flat, Op. 38; 2 in C, Op. 61

(N) **(*) Pentatone **SACD** PTC 5186 326. Czech PO, Foster.

Lawrence Foster offers very decent performances of Schumann's *Symphonies* 1 and 2, recorded live in Dvořák Hall in 2007. That the orchestra (and conductor) love this music is in no doubt – the loving way the slow movements are played is very telling. This is rich-orchestral-sound Schumann, yet the fast movements are both lively and well articulated. These performance have neither the originality that Gardiner or Dausgaard have bought to this repertoire, and they fall just short of the distinction which Karajan and Sawallisch, for example, achieved. However, on their own terms, they are eminently satisfying, and well recorded in the ample acoustic.

Symphony 2 in C

🎧— *** Testament (ADD) SBT 1378. BPO, Szell (with
BRAHMS: *Tragic Overture*; RICHARD STRAUSS: *Don Juan*)

(N) (***) Orfeo mono 427041. VPO, Mitropoulos –
PROKOFIEV: *Symphony 5* (***)

Szell's account of the *Second Symphony* is among the finest in the current catalogue. The performance comes from a concert given at the Philharmonie in June 1969 and, apart from the immaculate control which distinguished all his music making, has a powerful sense of line and in the slow movement great lyrical feeling and humanity. The Deutschland Radio recording is very faithful and communicates the sense of occasion. The other works on the programme, and in particular the *Don Juan*, are likewise performances of stature. Strongly recommended.

Mitropoulos was an artist of the strongest personality and integrity. Schumann's greatest symphony, together with

Prokofiev's *Fifth*, comprised his début with the **Vienna Philharmonic** at the 1954 Salzburg Festival, and he brings great intensity to its heavenly slow movement. The Austrian Radio balance is not ideal but, given the quality of this electrifying performance, sound is of lesser importance.

Symphonies 2; 4 (original version); Overture: Julius Caesar; Prelude: Scenes from Goethe's Faust

(*) BIS **SACD 1519. Swedish CO, Dausgaard

With sharp accents and dynamic contrasts, **Dausgaard** is determined to extract as much drama out of these scores as possible. He achieves admirably clear textures, bringing out much fresh detail. The original version of the *Fourth Symphony* is lighter in texture than in the later version, and Dausgaard balances the internal dialogue of the instruments to telling effect. These are undoubtedly fresh performances, which offer something new. Good sound and unexpected couplings.

Symphony 3 (Rhenish); (i) Des Sängers Fluch, Op. 139

🎧— *** Chan. 9760. Danish Nat. RSO, Schonwandt; (i) with Fischer, Rorholm, Wagenführer, Henschel, Hansen, Danish Nat. R. Ch.

Schonwandt lifts rhythms infectiously in a performance full of light and shade, giving rapt intensity to the inner meditation of the Cologne Cathedral movement. The playing of the fine **Copenhagen Orchestra** is unfailingly cultured. A strongly competitive and compelling account, beautifully recorded by the Danish Radio engineers. The rare and generous coupling is most welcome, the 40-minute long choral ballad *The Minstrel's Curse*. A late work, it comes from 1852 and is a setting of Ludwig Uhland's ballad, which Schumann's collaborator Richard Pohl interspersed with other Uhland poems. Not all the soloists are ideally steady, but the chorus is outstanding. First-rate sound.

Symphonies 3 (Rhenish); 4. Overtures: Hermann und Dorothea; Manfred

(N) *** BIS **SACD** 1619. Swedish CO, Dausgaard

As in **Dausgaard's** other Schumann recordings, this latest is fresh, bracing and impressive. The *Rhenish* sets off at a brisk pace, and if initially it feels as though this is a lightweight performance, with its relatively small orchestra (38 musicians) Dausgaard's overall conception is soon apparent and the symphony's splendour vividly emerges. There is a chamber-like intimacy in the third movement which is very appealing, though the fourth movement doesn't quite evoke the greatness of Cologne Cathedral as some other performances have. The dramatic qualities of the *Fourth Symphony* are impressively brought out, but there is real repose in the slow movement. The Scherzo goes with a bounce and the finale, though perhaps over-emphatic in its clipped point-making, is most exciting. The masterful *Manfred Overture* receives a superb performance, and the rarely heard *Hermann und Dorothea* overture, with its prominent use of the *Marseillaise*, is thoroughly entertaining. Superb sound, as always, from this source.

Symphonies 3 in E flat (Rhenish); 4 in D min., Op. 120

(BB) **(*) Virgin 2x1 3 49983-2 (2). LCP, Norrington –
MENDELSSOHN: *Symphonies 3; 4* ***

With Schumann's orchestration usually accused of being too thick, there is much to be said for period performances like this. **Norrington** not only clarifies textures, with natural horns in particular standing out dramatically, but, at unexaggerated speeds for the outer movements – even a little too slow for the first movement of 3 – the results are often almost Mendelssohnian, to make a clear link with the coupling. Middle movements in both *Symphonies* are unusually brisk, turning slow movements into lyrical interludes. Warm, atmospheric recording.

Symphony 4 (DVD version)

⊙— 🌼 *** EuroArts **DVD** 2072118 (with rehearsal of *Andante*). VSO, Karajan – BEETHOVEN: *Symphony 5* (with rehearsal) ***

Apart from the comparatively brief Beethoven coupling, this is the only visual record (in excellent black-and-white imagery) of **Karajan** rehearsing a major *Symphony*. Moreover, it is the final hour-long rehearsal for the recording which is to follow. Obviously much has already been achieved in earlier rehearsals, yet detail has still to be refined in each of the four movements. It is a relatively young Karajan who is working with the **Vienna Symphoniker** in 1965, a fine orchestra but not the Berlin Philharmonic, and there is a good deal that he has to rectify: phrasing, accents, dynamics, the use of fermata, and much else besides. As one listens to him and watches him working on this great romantic symphony, the insights and subtle perceptions which he conveys to the orchestra are revealed to the listener too, and one's conception of the work's stature steadily expands. One cannot help but learn much from this experience, and the documentary value of this DVD confirms the view that in German repertoire Karajan was one of the greatest conductors of the 20th century. The rehearsal is followed by an electrifying performance of the symphony itself, perhaps without all the lyrical warmth of tone he has tried to instil in the orchestra, but with playing of remarkable virtuosity, particularly in the thrilling coda. The recording of the rehearsal is very bright and top-heavy, but the performance itself is better balanced and is certainly vivid.

Symphony 4 in D min., Op. 120

🌼 **(M)** (****) DG mono 474 988-2. BPO, Furtwängler –
HAYDN: *Symphony 88* (****)🌼

*** Orfeo (ADD) C 522 991 B. VPO, Boehm – MAHLER: *Lieder eines fahrenden Gesellen*; BEETHOVEN: *Symphony 4* ***

*** BBC (ADD) BBCL4058-2. BBC SO, Monteux – BRAHMS: *Symphony 3* *** (with ROSSINI: *L'italiana in Algeri Overture* **(*))

Furtwängler's famous, uniquely inspired version has now been reunited with its original coupling (in a facsimile of the original LP sleeve), Furtwängler's inspired account of Haydn's *Symphony 88*.

Boehm was rarely so fiery as here, with biting attack and strong rhythmic emphasis from the **Vienna Philharmonic** in superb form. The second-movement *Romanze* is set in sharp contrast: the deeply meditative opening theme gives way to lightness and transparency. Good radio sound, if with some edge on high violins.

By comparison, **Monteux** produces a lighter, more transparent sound, given the constraints of Schumann's much criticized scoring. Rhythmic accents are lighter and there is a sense of drama without any histrionics. A valuable memento of Monteux in repertoire that is not associated with him.

CHAMBER MUSIC

Abendlied, Op. 85/2; Adagio & Allegro in A flat, Op. 70; Fantasiestücke, Op. 73; 3 Romances, Op. 94; 3 Pieces in Folk Style, Op. 102/2–4

⊙— **(M)** *** Ph. (ADD) 426 386-2. Holliger, Brendel

Adagio & Allegro in A flat, Op. 70

⊙— **(BB)** *** Naxos 8.557471. Tomboeck, Inui – BEETHOVEN: *Horn Sonata*; BRAHMS: *Horn Trio*; SCHUBERT: *Auf dem Strom* ***

Adagio & Allegro, Op. 70; Fantasiestücke, Op. 73; 5 Stücke im Volkston, Op. 102

⊙— **(BB)** *** Naxos 8.550654. Kliegel, Merscher – SCHUBERT: *Arpeggione Sonata* ***

Adagio & Allegro in A flat, Op. 70; Fantasiestücke, Op. 73; 5 Stücke im Volkston, Op. 102 (all for cello & piano)

**(*) BIS CD 1076. Thedéen, Pöntinen – CHOPIN: *Cello Sonata* **(*)

Adagio & Allegro, Op. 70; 5 Pieces in Popular Style

(B) **(*) Cal. (ADD) CAL 3614. Navarra, Annie d'Arco –
DVOŘÁK: *Humoresque*, etc.; SCHUBERT: *Arpeggione Sonata* **(*)

In the *Adagio and Allegro*, Op. 70, the distinctively fruity sound of the Vienna horn is wonderfully caught on the superb Naxos disc. Like the other works, the Schumann is warmly done, with **Wolfgang Tomboeck** producing the ripest tones and the hunting-horn rhythms of the *Allegro* have an infectious brilliance and swagger. The three *Romances* are specifically for oboe, but **Holliger** suggests that the others too are suitable for oboe, since the composer himself gave different options. One misses something by not having a horn in the *Adagio and Allegro*, a cello in the folkstyle pieces, or a clarinet in the *Fantasiestücke* (the oboe d'amore is used here); but Holliger has never sounded more magical on record and, with superbly real recording and deeply imaginative accompaniment, the result is an unexpected revelation.

Maria Kliegel and **Kristin Merscher** couple these charming Schumann miniatures with the Schubert *Arpeggione* and turn in fresh and musical performances and are recorded in very clean and well-focused sound.

Navarra plays the *Adagio* very romantically and then finds ready bravura for the *Allegro*. But it is the five miniatures in which he is most eloquent, playing them very appealingly.

Torleif Thedéen and **Roland Pöntinen** are sympathetic exponents of this repertoire even if in the *Fünf Stücke im Volkston* they are just a bit too earnest and lacking in charm.

Adagio & Allegro, Op. 70; 3 Fantasiestücke, Op. 73; 3 Romanzen; Märchenbilder; (i) Märchenerzählungen, Op. 132

🎵— *** Zig-Zag Territoires ZZT 010401. Beranger, Gastaldi; (i) with Heau

Schumann was always accommodating about the instrumentation of these pieces, with the viola regularly interchanged with the clarinet. This has no doubt led Beranger to also take on the *Fantasiestücke* and the *Romanzen*, where Schumann suggests clarinet and violin as options but not the viola. The *Adagio and Allegro*, originally with horn or cello, works beautifully here, and the two later 'fairy-tale' works, *Märchenbilder* and *Märchenerzählungen*, are among the glories of the viola repertoire. It is only in the latter work that the clarinettist **Florent Heau** appears, another sensitive artist.

Fantasiestücke; 5 Stücke in Volkston

*** Ph. 412 230-2. Maisky, Argerich – SCHUBERT: *Arpeggione Sonata* ***

Mischa Maisky on cello and **Martha Argerich** give relaxed, leisurely accounts of these pieces that some collectors will find a bit self-indulgent. Others will luxuriate in the refinement and sensitivity of their playing.

Märchenbilder, Op. 113

**(*) Chan. 8550. Imai, Vignoles – BRAHMS: *Viola Sonatas* **(*)

The *Märchenbilder* are also persuasively played here by **Nobuko Imai** and **Roger Vignoles**. The recording acoustic is not ideal, but this does not seriously detract from the value of this coupling.

Piano Quartet in E flat, Op. 47; Piano Quintet in E flat, Op. 44

Ⓜ **(*) Berlin Classics (ADD) 0094032BC. Rösel, Gewandhaus Qt

**(*) Chan. 0698. Michelangelo Piano Qt; with (i) De Secondi

Ⓜ **(*) CRD (ADD) CRD 3324. Rajna, members of the Alberni Qt

The playing of **Peter Rösel** and the **Gewandhaus Quartet** is keenly alive and very musical. Tempi are fairly brisk but phrasing is affectionate and sensitive. This is playing of quality and good value at mid-price.

Recorded in Florence in 2000, the **Michelangelo Piano Quartet** gives stylish pioneer versions of these works on period instruments. The fortepiano, a fine 1830 instrument from Vienna, cannot sustain legato lines as a modern piano

would (notably in the warmly lyrical slow movement of the *Piano Quartet*), but the extra clarity of articulation is a delight, while the stilling of vibrato by the strings intensifies the mood of dedication in slow passages, with splendidly crisp attack in *Allegros*.

Though not flawlessly polished in their playing, **Thomas Rajna** and the **Alberni** give performances that in their way are urgent and enjoyable. The recording is brighter and crisper, which gives an extra (and not unlikeable) edge to the performances.

(i) Piano Quartet, Op. 47; Piano Quintet, Op. 44; Piano Trios 1 in D min., Op. 63; 2 in F, Op. 80; 3 in G min., Op. 110

🎵— Ⓑ *** Ph. Duo (ADD) 456 323-2 (2). Beaux Arts Trio; (i) with Bettelheim and Rhodes

Once again Philips have compiled a particularly generous measure for this Duo of **Beaux Arts** Schumann performances from the 1970s. This illustrious **Trio** (with associates) give splendid readings of the *Piano Quartet* and *Quintet*. The vitality of inspiration is brought out consistently, and with that goes their characteristic concern for fine ensemble and refined textures. They are also probably the safest bet for the three *Piano Trios*.

Piano Quintet in E flat, Op. 44

🎵— *** Virgin 3 95143-2. Andsnes, Artemis Qt – BRAHMS: *Piano Quintet* ***

Ⓑ🅑 *** Naxos 8.550406. Jandó, Kodály Qt – BRAHMS: *Piano Quintet* ***

(***) Testament mono SBT 3063. Aller, Hollywood Qt – BRAHMS: *Piano Quartets*, etc. (***)

Leif Ove Andsnes and the **Artemis Quartet** are totally attuned to Schumann's sensibility and have the benefit of very natural and vivid recording. A first recommendation.

A strongly characterized performance of Schumann's fine *Quintet* from **Jenö Jandó** and the **Kodály Quartet**. This is robust music-making, romantic in spirit, and its spontaneity is well projected by a vivid recording, made in an attractively resonant acoustic. An excellent bargain.

Exhilarating and masterly, the **Hollywood Quartet** and **Victor Aller** on Testament come from the compilation of Brahms chamber music, recorded in the mid-1950s. A performance of some stature which transcends sonic limitations.

(i) Piano Quintet in E flat, Op. 44; String Quartets 1–3, Op. 41/1–3

Ⓑ🅑 **(*) EMI Gemini 3 50819-2 (2). (i) Zacharias; Cherubini Qt

The account of the *Piano Quintet* is first class in every way, with **Christian Zacharias** dominating and taking the string players with him. It has splendid vigour and spirit, with the *In modo d'una Marcia* very characterfully done. The recording is excellent. The three *String Quartets* were recorded in a different venue, and both performances and sound are slightly drier. Without Zacharias, the **Cherubini Quartet** seem slightly more inhibited, less spontaneous, though they still play very well indeed.

Piano Quintet, Op. 44; Andante & Variations for 2 Pianos, 2 Cellos & Horn, Op. 46; Fantasiestücke for Cello and Piano, Op. 73; Märchenbilder for Viola & Piano, Op. 113

⌑ᷓ *** EMI 5 57308-2. Argerich, Rabinovitch, Hall, Imai, Gutman, Maisky, Neunecker

A very distinguished line-up. We have already highly praised the performance of the *Piano Quintet*, recorded at the Concertgebouw, Nijmegen, in 1994. We also note the informality of the music-making, which had 'the enthusiasm and intimate inspiration of a house-party'. The other items are also finely done.

(i; ii) Piano Quintet in E flat, Op. 44; (ii) String Quartet 1 in A min., Op. 41/1; (i) Arabeske, Op. 18; Blumenstück, Op. 19

*** Linn CKD132. (i) d'Ascoli; (ii) Schidlof Qt

In the *Piano Quintet* it is **d'Ascoli** who leads the ensemble, maybe controversially in the first movement, when he unashamedly encourages marked changes of tempo – persuasively so, thanks to the feeling of spontaneity. There are similar qualities in d'Ascoli's performances of the *Arabeske* and *Blumenstück*, with textures fresh and clean. The *String Quartet* brings another refined performance with plenty of light and shade. The recording, made in the Blackheath Concert Halls, is finely focused within a helpful acoustic.

Piano Trio 1 in D min., Op. 63; Bilder aus Osten, Op. 66; Phantasiestücke, Op. 88

⌑ᷓ *** MDG 303 0921-2. Trio Parnassus

Piano Trios 2 in F, Op. 80; 3 in G min., Op. 110; 6 Pieces in the Form of a Canon, Op. 56

⌑ᷓ *** MDG 303 0922-2. Trio Parnassus

Piano Trio 1 in D min., Op. 63

Ⓜ **(*) CRD (ADD) CRD 3433. Israel Piano Trio – BRAHMS: *Piano Trio 2* **(*)

ⒷⒷ (***) Naxos mono 8.110185. Cortot, Thibaud, Casals – MENDELSSOHN: *Piano Trio 1* (***)

Piano Trios 2 in F, Op. 80; 3 in G min., Op. 110; Fantasiestücke, Op. 88

Ⓜ **(*) CRD (ADD) CRD 3458. Israel Piano Trio

Piano Trios 1, Op. 63; 2, Op. 80

ⒷⒷ *** Naxos 8.553836. Vienna Brahms Trio

The **Trio Parnassus** are a very good ensemble and give characterful and sensitive accounts of the three *Piano Trios* and the other repertoire included here. The MDG recording is very natural and well focused.

The **Israel Piano Trio** give a powerfully projected account of the *D minor Trio*; the pianist is at times rather carried away, as if he were playing a Brahms concerto. There are, however, some sensitive and intelligent touches, and the recording is first class. 2 and 3 are much the same: lively, articulate playing with a sometimes over-forceful pianist.

The **Vienna Brahms Trio** give eminently musical ac-

counts of both scores and are satisfactorily recorded. The Beaux Arts Trio on Philips, however, are every bit as competitive (see above).

The partnership of **Jacques Thibaud**, **Pablo Casals** and **Alfred Cortot** made their recording of the *D minor Piano Trio* in 1928, so the sound is wanting the body and colour of later recordings. Coming to this set afresh one wonders if it has ever been surpassed in musical insight. They are immaculate, wonderfully singing in their phrasing, and their apparent spontaneity of feeling is born of a firm musical grip. Ward Marston's transfer is first rate.

Piano Trio 3 in G min.; Piano Quartet in E flat, Op. 47; Fantasiestücke, Op. 88

⌑ᷓ *** Hyp. CDA 67175. Florestan Trio (augmented)

The **Florestan Trio** is first rate in every way and gives thoughtful and spirited accounts of all three of these Schumann pieces. It is joined effectively in the *E flat Piano Quartet* by the violist **Thomas Riebl**.

3 Romances Op. 95

*** Avie AV 2075. Khaner, Abramovic – BRAHMS: *Clarinet Sonatas 1–2*; CLARA SCHUMANN: *3 Romances* ***

When Schumann gave the option of playing these pieces on violin or clarinet in place of the oboe, which he originally had in mind, there is a strong case for welcoming **Jeffrey Khaner's** arrangements for flute, ideal fill-ups for his transcriptions of the two Brahms *Clarinet Sonatas*, the main works on the disc. As in the other items, Khaner's performances could not be more sensitive.

String Quartets 1–3, Op. 41/1–3

⌑ᷓ ⒷⒷ *** Naxos 8.570151. Fine Arts Qt

*** HM HMU 907270. Eroica Qt

Ⓜ *** CRD 2-CD CRD 2414 (2). Alberni Qt – MENDELSSOHN: *Quartet 2* ***

Having all three of Schumann's Opus 41 *Quartets* on a single Naxos disc makes a superb bargain. These fine works, notably the last and most impressive, 3, are the products of Schumann's extraordinary year of chamber inspirations, 1842, which also saw the composition of the *Piano Quintet* and *Piano Quartet*. The **Fine Arts Quartet**, founded as long ago as 1946, remains a magnificent interpreter, here vividly recorded in sessions in Holland in 2006.

The **Eroica** is the second ensemble so far to have squeezed all three Schumann quartets on to a single CD. Schumann's writing benefits from the transparency of tone produced by the group's early instruments. Tempi are judged well, and the overall impression is fresh and enjoyable.

The well-recorded and sympathetic performances by the **Alberni Quartet** have plenty of finesse and charm and are guided throughout by sound musical instinct. The Mendelssohn coupling is equally attractive.

Violin Sonata 1 (DVD version)

*** TDK **DVD** DVWW-COMARG. Argerich & Gautier Capuçon (V/D: Frédéric Le Clair) – BEETHOVEN: *Triple Concerto*; PROKOFIEV: *Piano Concerto 1; Symphony 1* ***

A wholly satisfying performance from **Argerich** and **Gautier Capuçon**, persuasively presented on DVD. A fine bonus for Argerich's electrifying Prokofiev concerto.

Violin Sonata 1 in A min., Op. 105

(***) Biddulph mono LAB 165. Busch and Serkin – BRAHMS: *String Quartets 1–2* (**(*)) (with REGER: *Violin Sonata 5, Op. 84: Allegretto* (***))

The Biddulph sleeve-note hails the 1937 **Busch–Serkin** account of the *A minor Sonata*, Op. 105, erroneously billed as 2 on both the label and sleeve, as 'never having been equalled for its intensity and romantic ardour'. This is absolutely right. The disc throws in the only Reger that Busch recorded, the *Allegretto* from the *F sharp minor Sonata*, Op. 84.

Violin Sonata 2 in D min., Op. 121

BB (***) Naxos mono 8.119771. Yehudi & Hephzibah Menuhin – BRAHMS: *Sonatas 1 & 3* (***)

This recording was made in Paris in 1934 when **Yehudi** was 18 and his sister just 14. It was the première recording of the piece, and in **Hephzibah's** hands the piano writing has enormous freshness. More persuasive than many subsequent recordings.

PIANO MUSIC

'Abegg' Variations, Op. 1; Arabeske, Op. 18; Blumenstück, Op. 19; Bunte Blätter, Op. 99; Carnaval, Op. 9; Davidsbündlertänze, Op. 6; Etudes symphoniques, Op. 13; Fantasie, Op. 17; Fantasiestücke, Op. 12; Faschingsschwank aus Wien, Op. 26; Humoreske, Op. 20; Kinderszenen, Op. 15; Kreisleriana, Op. 16; Nachtstücke; Novellette, Op. 21/1, 2 & 8; Papillons, Op. 2; 3 Romanzen, Op. 28; Sonatas 1–2; Waldszenen, Op. 82

☷ (B) *** Decca 470 915-2 (7). Ashkenazy

Vladimir Ashkenazy's survey of the Schumann piano music comes from the late 1980s through to the mid-1990s. Of course there are individual performances that have been surpassed by other artists (Perahia's *C major Fantasy* has perhaps the greater poetic intensity and spontaneity, and Lupu's unforgettable accounts of the *Humoreske* and *Kreisleriana* are performances of real distinction). But this is not to minimize the achievement of these thoughtful and intuitive performances or the artistry and excellence which Ashkenazy brings to bear on a composer for whom he obviously has great feeling. The recordings are generally very natural, and readers wanting a complete Schumann coverage will find much to reward them here.

Abegg Variations, Op. 1; Davidsbündlertänze, Op. 6

☷ *** Ottavio OTRC 39027. Cooper – BRAHMS: *Fantasias, Op. 116* ***

Imogen Cooper plays the *Abegg Variations* with a rare combination of iridescent brilliance and poetic feeling, and she characterizes the *Davidsbündlertänze* with consistent imagi-

nation and colour. Her playing is spontaneous from first to last, and the recording most realistic.

Albumblätter, Op. 99; Arabeske, Op. 18; Etudes symphoniques, Op. 13

☷ **BB** *** Naxos 8.550144. Vladar

Stefan Vladar intersperses the additional studies that Schumann published as an appendix into the *Etudes symphoniques*. His account is quite simply superb in every respect and deserves recording of comparable excellence. The *Albumblätter* is hardly less masterly. Artistically this rates three stars, with the compelling quality of the playing transcending the sonic limitations of the recording.

Allegro in B min., Op. 8; Carnaval, Op. 9; Fantasie in C, Op. 17; Faschingsschwank aus Wien; Kreisleriana; Novellette 8 in F sharp, Op. 21; Romance 2 in F sharp, Op. 28/2

(*) Australian Decca Eloquence (ADD/DDD) 476 9910 (2). de Larrocha

Alicia de Larrocha's performance of *Kreisleriana* is notable for its blend of thoughtfulness and romanticism, the control of rubato and generally unaffected musicality. The style in the shorter pieces is bolder, to match their character. *Carnaval*, and also the *Fantasie in C*, are both strongly characterized. But hers is a committed personal view which demands attention.

Allegro in B min., Op. 8; Concerto without Orchestra, Op. 14; Davidsbündlertänze, Op. 6; Gesänge der Frühe, Op. 133; Kreisleriana, Op. 16

☷ (B) *** DG 471 3682 (2). Pollini

This Schumann reissue finds **Maurizio Pollini** on his best form, with something of the spontaneity and freshness he showed when he first emerged on the scene in the early 1960s tempered with the wisdom of advancing years. Indeed, this *Kreisleriana* is among the very finest. Pollini is wonderfully satisfying and is beautifully recorded; the only reservation to be made is that both discs offer short measure at 48 minutes. However as a Double the set remains good value.

Arabeske, Op. 18; Blumenstücke, Op. 19; Davidsbündlertänze; Etudes symphoniques, Op. 13

☷ (M) *** Warner Elatus 0927 49612-2. Schiff

András Schiff opts for the original (1837) *Davidsbündlertänze*, rather than the more usual 1851 revision. Each of the pieces is strongly characterized and played with appropriate ardour. In the *Etudes symphoniques* he chooses the generally used late version of 1852 (posthumously revised to restore two rejected earlier numbers). The *Arabeske* and the *Blumenstücke* complete a satisfying and competitively priced recital.

Arabeske, Op. 18; Carnaval, Op. 9; Davidsbündlertänze, Op. 6; Fantasie in C, Op. 17; Humoreske, Op. 20; Kinderszenen; Kreisleriana, Op. 16; Nachtstücke, Op. 23; Novellette, Op. 99/9; Papillons, Op. 2; 3 Romances, Op. 28; Sonata 2 in G

min., Op. 22; Symphonic Studies, Op. 13; Waldszenen, Op. 21

⟜ Ⓑ *** DG (ADD) 471 312-2 (4). Kempff

Kempff is in his element in pieces like the *Arabeske*, the relatively little-known first and third *Romances*, and the *Novelette*, where he inspires an element of fantasy, of spontaneous recreation, and he is also at his most inspirational in the *Fantasie in C major. Davidsbündlertänze*, the *Nachtstücke* and *Papillons* are all extremely fine.

On the other hand the comparatively extrovert style of *Carnaval* suits him less well. Kempff's thoughtful, intimate readings of two of the *Etudes symphoniques* and *Kreisleriana* are marvellously persuasive, giving a clear illusion of live performances, spontaneously caught and again well recorded. Similarly if the sharper contrasts of the *Humoreske* are toned down by charm and geniality, the *Waldszenen* are glowingly relaxed and both are comparably personal and individual.

Arabeske, Op. 18; Carnaval, Op. 9; Humoreske, Op. 20; Toccata in C, Op. 7

⟜ *** BIS CD-960. Kempf

A début recital from **Freddy Kempf**. His Schumann blends the right amount of intelligence and intuitive feeling. He is at his best in the reflective and inward moments and his *Humoreske* is particularly successful. He has remarkable technical prowess and refined musicianship. The recorded sound is very lively and natural, and the disc as a whole gives much satisfaction.

Arabeske, Op. 18; Fantasy in C, Op. 17; Kreisleriana, Op. 16

*** EMI 3 65391-2. Biss

Schumann playing of real quality. **Jonathan Biss** is a young American pianist and his artistry is evident throughout this recital. An impressive début which can be recommended along with the very best. Good recorded sound too.

Carnaval, Op. 9

⟜ (***) BBC Legends mono BBCL 4201-2. Hess – BACH: *English Suite 2* (**(*)); HAYDN: *Keyboard Sonata 62* (**)

Dame Myra Hess was long noted for her performances of Schumann's *Carnaval*, and here in a BBC recording of 1950 the result could hardly be more persuasive, so spontaneous-sounding it feels as though she is improvising over the long sequence of contrasted pieces. Well coupled with lyrical Bach and a Haydn *Sonata*, recorded at the very end of her career. Mono recording very acceptable.

Carnaval, Op.9; Der Kontrabandiste (arr. Tausig)

Ⓝ *** BBC Legends (ADD) BBCL 4254-2 . Cherkassky (with MENDELSSOHN: *Andante & Rondo capriccioso*) – SCHUBERT: *Sonata 20 in A* ***

Ⓝ ⒷⒷ (***) Naxos mono 8.112020. Rachmaninov – CHOPIN: *Piano Sonata 2* (***)

Schumann's *Carnaval* is ideally suited to the volatile qualities in **Shura Cherkassky's** playing. The varied textures of the piece are delightfully conveyed, not only the lightness of many sections but the firmness and power of such passages as the very opening, even if the playing is not always finger-perfect. Rhythms are consistently lifted infectiously, adding to the delights. The Tausig arrangement of the song, *Der Kontrabandiste*, makes the lightest of encores, rounding the recital off delectably.

Rachmaninov's *Carnaval* comes from 1929. Ward Marston produces very fine results in his transfers and brings presence to these unique performances.

Davidsbündlertänze, Op. 6

Ⓑ **(*) EMI Debut 5 85894-2. Biss – BEETHOVEN: *Piano Sonata 23; Fantasy in G min.* **(*)

Jonathan Biss commands superb technical address and a keen dramatic sense, though his temperament seems more attuned to the impulsive side of Schumann's sensibility rather than the inward-looking and poetic. Compelling playing all the same, without being totally satisfying. The recording captures the timbre and colour of the piano most truthfully.

Davidsbündlertänze, Op. 6; Fantasiestücke, Op. 12; Papillons, Op. 2

⟜ Ⓜ *** Sony (ADD) SMK 89714. Perahia

Perahia has a magic touch and his electric spontaneity is naturally caught in the studio. In the works of Schumann, which can splinter apart, this quality of concentration is enormously valuable, and the results could hardly be more powerfully convincing, despite recording quality which lacks something in bloom and refinement. The *Papillons*, added for this reissue, are unlikely to be surpassed, and it is a pity that the close balance robs the piano timbre of some of its allure.

Davidsbündlertänze, Op. 6; Sonata 2 in G min., Op. 22; Toccata, Op. 7

⟜ ⒷⒷ *** Warner Apex 0927 40834-2. Berezovsky

Boris Berezovsky is a keyboard lion of the first order. Everything we have so far heard of his has been of exceptional artistry and great finesse. His formidable musicianship is allied to a technique of magisterial calibre, and this coupling is very impressive indeed. These performances are of the highest calibre. The *Davidsbündlertänze* is particularly charismatic and this bargain reissue cannot be too strongly recommended.

Etudes symphoniques, Op. 13; Fantasia in C, Op. 1

Ⓝ ⒷⒷ **(*) Regis Alto ALC 1046. Brendel

Brendel's opening phrase of the *Symphonic studies* is immediately individual, and yet in essence these are not wayward performances, even though they are strongly personalized. Brendel's reputation is as a player in the mainstream of the classical tradition, and it is the strength of that tradition which gives these performances their character and power. There are other ways of approaching Schumann (Kempff's for instance) but in Brendel's hands the music's structure emerges anew and has the emotional grip one associates with Beethoven. Excellent 1966 (originally Vanguard) recording.

Fantasia in C, Op. 17

⊕—Ⓜ️ *** DG (ADD) 447 451-2. Pollini – SCHUBERT: *Wanderer fantasia* ***

*** Chan. 9793. Lortie – LISZT: *Concert Paraphrases of Beethoven's An die ferne Geliebte; Mignon; Schumann Lieder* ***

Pollini's playing throughout has a command and authority on the one hand and deep poetic feeling on the other that hold the listener spellbound. The recording is good but not outstanding. A welcome mid-priced reissue in DG's series of 'Originals'.

Lortie is an unfailingly thoughtful and thought-provoking artist of compelling utterance, who always has something new to say – and whose expressive eloquence is always at the service of the composer. This newcomer ranks alongside the finest and most satisfying versions of the C major Fantasia now around. And it is *very* well recorded.

Fantasiestücke, Op. 12; Kinderszenen, Op. 15; Kreisleriana, Op. 16

⊕—Ⓜ️ *** Ph. 434 732-2. Brendel

Fantasiestücke is strong as well as poetic. The *Kinderszenen* is also one of the finest performances of the 1980s and is touched with real distinction. **Brendel's** *Kreisleriana* is intelligent and finely characterized. He is better recorded (in 1981–2) than most of his rivals and the overall impression is highly persuasive.

Humoreske in B flat, Op. 20

*** Hyp. CDA67618. Hewitt (with Piano Sonata 1)

ⒷⒷ **(*) Naxos 8.550469. Harden – REGER: *Variations* **(*)

Although she does not displace Andsnes in the *First Sonata* (see above), **Angela Hewitt** gives a most impressive account of the work and a no less commanding performance of the *Humoreske*. The sound-quality is admirable: she is recorded in the Grand Hotel, Dobbiaco, in Italy and her engineers do her justice.

Wolf Harden's performance of the Schumann *Humoreske* is highly imaginative, idiomatic and full of sensitive touches. There is plenty of air around the aural image.

Humoreske, Op. 20; Kinderszenen, Op. 15; Kreisleriana, Op. 16

⊕—*** Decca 440 496-2. Lupu

Lupu is one of the artists whose understanding of the composer can be measured alongside that of Murray Perahia. His account of the *Humoreske*, Op. 20, is both poetic and hardly less magical than the *Kreisleriana*. This is playing of great poetry and authority. The recording is excellent, albeit resonant.

Humoreske, Op. 20; Nachtstücke, Op. 23; 8 Novelletten, Op. 21; Sonata in F sharp min., Op. 14

⊕—*** ECM 472 119-2 (2). Schiff

András Schiff's playing is refreshingly light-textured with much delicacy of colour plus a natural response to the music's mood swings. This especially applies to the eight *Novelletten*, by no means easy works to bring off, for they can easily seem inflated. The *Sonata* too is finely played, never hectoring, and imaginatively detailed, the *Variations on Clara's Andantino* especially so, followed by a brilliantly articulated finale. The closing encore, the *Nachtstücke*, is quite magical. The recording is excellent, the piano image clear and realistic.

Kinderszenen, Op. 15

⊕—ⒷⒷ *** Naxos 8.550885. Biret – DEBUSSY: *Children's Corner Suite* **(*); TCHAIKOVSKY: *Album for the Young* ***

Idil Biret was a pupil of Kempff and is completely at home in the delightful children's pieces of Schumann. The characterization is strong, sensitive and often touching, as in *Träumerei* and the lovely closing movement, *The Poet Speaks*. The piano recording, made in the Clara Wieck Auditorium, is forward but realistic.

VOCAL MUSIC

Lieder from Album für die Jugend, Op. 79; Gedichte der Königen Maria Stuart, Op. 135; Myrthen Lieder, Op. 25 (excerpts); Abends am Strand; Die Kartenlegerin; Ständchen; Stille Tränen; Verratene Liebe

⊕—Ⓜ️ *** CRD (ADD) CRD 3401. Walker, Vignoles

Sarah Walker's 1982 Schumann collection is most cherishable, notably the five Mary Stuart songs which, in their brooding darkness, are among Schumann's most memorable. With superb accompaniment and splendid recording, this is an outstanding issue.

Andersen Lieder, Op. 40; Eichendorff Liederkreis, Op. 39; Der Einsiedler; Harpers' Songs, Op. 98a; Mélancholie, Op. 74/6; 6 Poems, Op. 36; Tief im Herzen

*** RCA 88697 1681/72. Gerhaher, Huber

Centring on the Opus 39 *Liederkreis* setting of Eichendorff poems **Christian Gerhaher** has assembled a most satisfying collection of songs on the related theme of *Melancholy*, the title of the first song. The *Six Songs*, Op. 36, setting poems by Reineck, may not quite match Opus 39 in depth of expressiveness, but they are valuable nonetheless, as are the settings of Hans Andersen poems. Gerhaher's tone is unfailingly beautiful, ranging over the widest tonal range, with words perfectly clear, and he is most sensitively accompanied by his regular partner, **Gerold Huber**.

2 Balladen, Op. 122; Dichterliebe, Op. 48; 6 fruhe Lieder, Op. posth; Excerpts from: 3 Gedichte, Op. 30; 4 Gedichte aus Ruckers Liebesfruhlinge, Op 37; 6 Gedichte aus dem Liederbuch eines Malers, Op. 36; 12 Gedichte, Op. 35; 3 Gedichte, Op. 119; 3 Gesange, Op. 31; 3 Gesange, Op. 83; 5 heitere Gesang, Op. 125; 4 Husarenlieder Op. 117; 5 Lieder, Op. 40; 4 Gesange, Op. 142; Lieder und Gesang, Op. 127/51

& 77 ; *Liederalbum für die Jungende, Op. 79;*
Liederkreis, Opp. 24 & 39; Myrthen, Op. 25;
Romanzen und Balladen, Opp. 45; 49 & 64;
Spanische Liebeslieder, Op. 138; Spanisches
Liederspiel, Op. 74

(N) (M) *** DG 477 7957 (6). Fischer-Dieskau, Eschenbach

The recordings of the three cycles, *Dichterliebe* and two sets
of *Liederkreis* with **Christoph Eschenbach** were made in 1974,
1975 and 1976 and are most impressive when considered in
detail against other versions of these much-recorded works.
Eschenbach's accompaniments are superb, consistently
imaginative. The collection has now been expanded to six
CDs with the other recordings, made between 1961 and 1979,
spanning the early to middle years of the singer's career. As
it developed, his readings acquired a sharper edge, with the
darkness and irony in some of the songs more specifically
contrasted against the poetry and expressive warmth. The
recording is excellent and this new collection includes full
texts and translations.

Dichterliebe, Op. 48 (with four songs intended for the cycle, but discarded); 12 *Lieder*

(N) **** Hyp. CDA 67676. Finley, Drake

Gerald Finley, making a symbiotic partnership with **Julius
Drake**, sings Schumann's great song-cycle with much tonal
beauty and feeling, above all capturing the deep disillusion
of Schumann's inspiration, capped by the bold resignation
expressed in the powerfully cutting final song, *Die alten,
bösen Lieder* ('The bad old songs, the bad and bitter dreams.
Let us now bury them'). He also fascinatingly includes four
Lieder intended for the cycle, but in the end not included.
The remaining songs are imaginatively chosen. Beginning
with *Tragedy* and the melancholy tale of *The two grenadiers*
returning home to discover the army defeated, they continue
the theme of human unhappiness in love, and then change
the mood with three lovely, happy flower songs. The recording is truthful but rather reverberant.

Dichterliebe, Op. 48; Liederkreis, Op. 39

(B) *** CfP (ADD) 586 1812 (2). Ian & Jennifer Partridge –
SCHUBERT: *Die schöne Müllerin* ***

As in the excellent Schubert coupling, **Ian Partridge** here
shows himself a deeply sensitive Lieder singer, blessed
with a radiant light voice. In both cycles his thoughtfulness
illuminates every line, helped by superbly matched accompaniment from his sister and well-balanced, truthful
recording.

Dichterliebe, Op. 48; 12 Gedichte, Op. 35 (Kerner Lieder); Liederkreis, Op. 24 & Op. 39; Myrthen, Op. 25: Aus dem östlichen Rosen; Aus dem Schenkenbuch im Divan I & II; Du bist wie eine Blume; Freisinn; Die Lotusblume; Der Nussbaum; Was will die einsame Träne; Venetianisches Lied I & II; Widmung; Zum Schluss. Other Lieder; Tragödie (I; II)

(●) *** Australian Ph. Eloquence 476 9974 (2). Holzmair,
Cooper

Holzmair with his light, tenorish baritone proves a perfect
poet in *Dichterliebe* and **Imogen Cooper** is an inspired accompanist. That cycle to poems by Heine is then perfectly
complemented by Schumann's other, more disparate and
varied Heine cycle, the *Liederkreis* (recorded 1999), as well as
other Heine and Rückert items. Here, too, Holzmair proves
a masterly interpreter, alert and intense but finely controlled. The 12 settings of Kerner, among other items, were
taken from a later recording (2002) and the performances
are just as impressive and have one eager to listen on from
one item to the next. The sound throughout is impressive.

Frauenliebe und Leben, Op. 42

(●) (✹) (BB) *** Regis (ADD) RRC 1225. J. Baker, Isepp – Vocal
Recital, including Brahms & Schubert *Songs* ***

(B) **(*) CfP 2-CD (ADD) 575 7732 (2). M. Price, Lockhart;
(i) with Brymer (with LISZT: *Es muss ein Wunderbares sein;
Kling leise, mein Lied; O lieb', so lang du lieben kännst; Die
Lorelei; Die stille Wasserrose;* TCHAIKOVSKY: *None but the
lonely heart; Do not believe my friend; At the Ball* ***) –
SCHUBERT: *Lieder* **(*)

(BB) (**(*)) Naxos mono 8.11009. Ferrier, Newmark – BRAHMS:
Alto Rhapsody, etc. (**(*))

Dame Janet Baker's famous early (1966) Saga recording of
Schumann's great song-cycle at last re-emerges on another
budget label, Regis, carefully remastered and sounding remarkably real and vivid. As we said in our original review,
her range of expression runs the whole gamut, from a
joyful golden tone-colour in the exhilaration of *Ich kann's
nicht fassen*, through an ecstatic half-tone in *Süsser Freund*
(the fulfilment of the line 'Du geliebter Mann' wonderfully
conveyed), to the dead, vibratoless agony at the bereavement
in the final song. A performance that should be in every
collection.

Margaret Price's performance of the famous *Frauenliebe*
cycle brings most affecting and dedicated singing, particularly in the touching closing song, and the voice seems well
suited to three of Tchaikovsky's best-known songs, and even
more so to the equally well-chosen Liszt group, of which *O
lieb', so lang du lieben kännst* is a setting of words to the composer's most famous piano piece, *Liebesträume*.

Ferrier was a deeply impressive Lieder singer, but there
are more tender, more loving emotions in Schumann's cycle
than she was able to convey at that stage of her career (1950).
She is not helped by the limited accompaniment of **John
Newmark**. Nevertheless, who will fail to be moved by her
touching singing of the closing song, *Nun hast du mir den er-
sten Schmerz getan*, and the Brahms couplings make this reissue indispensable.

Frauenliebe und Leben, Op. 42; Liederkreis, Op. 39

(B) ** Ph. ADD 475 6374 (2). Norman, Gage – BRAHMS: *Lieder*
**(*)

The richness and power of **Jessye Norman's** voice are well
caught in this 1975 recital, but in *Frauenliebe* she is not quite
at her happiest or most spontaneous. It has its quota of
mawkish words, and Norman does not seem naturally to
identify. Richer in poetry, the Eichendorff *Liederkreis* is more

sympathetic to her; but other versions are even more sensitive. Accompaniments and recordings are most refined.

Frauenliebe und Leben, Op. 42; Lieder

🎵–**** DG 445 881-2. von Otter, Forsberg

Anne Sofie von Otter characterizes the contrasting songs in *Frauenliebe* with exceptional intensity, presenting a character, as in an opera, developing from youthful, eager girl to bereaved widow, but that strengthens the cycle, minimizing the sentimentality of the poems. This is an exceptionally generous recital (79 minutes) and other songs on the disc are characterized commandingly, with dramatic contrasts heightened. Excellent sound and fine accompaniment from **Forsberg**. Highly recommended.

Frauenliebe und Leben, Op. 42; Liederkreis, Op. 39; Aus den östlichen Rosen; Kennst du das Land; Meine Rose; Der Nussbaum; Requiem; Die Soldatenbraut; Widmung

(BB) *** Regis RRC 1051. Lott, Johnson

Felicity Lott is a connoisseur's artist, far greater than many more illustrious and publicized rivals, and she sings here with great poise and a completely unaffected artistry. The recording comes from 1990 and is not new, but the finesse and musicianship of this partnership, as well as the intelligence which guides everything they do, make it treasurable. The sound, too, is very good indeed.

Liederkreis, Op. 39; 12 Kerner Lieder, Op. 35

🎵–(BB) *** Hyp. Helios CDH 55011. Price, Johnson

A superb Schumann disc, coupling the sequence of 12 *Settings of Justinus Kerner*, Op. 35, with the Eichendorff *Liederkreis*, Op. 39. The singer's presence, magnetism and weight of expression are superbly caught, and the tonal beauty and immaculate sense of line go with detailed imagination in word-pointing. The lesser-known *Kerner Lieder* also contain many treasures. First-rate sound. Full notes and texts with translations are included in this bargain reissue.

(i; ii) Mass, Op. 147; (ii–vi) Requiem für Mignon; (ii; iv–viii) Requiem, Op. 148; (ii; v; vii; x; xi) Der Rose Pilgerfahrt

🎵–(BB) *** EMI Gemini 3 50900-2 (2). (i) Shirai, Seiffert, Rootering, BPO, Sawallisch; (ii) Ch. of the State Musikvereins, Düsseldorf; (iii) Lindner, Andonian, Georg, Welchhold; (iv) Fischer-Dieskau; (v) Düsseldorf SO; (vi) Klee; (vii) Donath; (viii) Soffel; (vix) Gedda; (x) Lövaas, Hamarl, Altmeyer, Pola; (xi) de Burgos

Sawallisch's dedicated performance of Schumann's long-neglected and under-prized setting of the *Mass* was recorded live in Düsseldorf in September 1987. Of the soloists, only the soprano has much to sing (the delectable **Mitsuko Shirai**, sensuously beautiful in the *Offertorium* solo) and the weight of the work rests on the chorus, a fine body here, warmly rather than clinically recorded.

Like Mozart, Schumann was unable to shake off the conviction that the *Requiem* was for himself. The opening *Requiem aeternam* is affecting and dignified, and the final *Benedictus* has a haunting eloquence. **Bernhard Klee** extracts a very sympathetic response from his distinguished team of soloists and the fine **Düsseldorf** chorus and orchestra. They also give an attentive and committed account of the 1849 *Requiem for Mignon*, and the attractive cantata, *Der Rose Pilgerfahrt*, is equally successful. The EMI recording is natural and well balanced.

Mass in C min., Op. 147; Requiem for Mignon, Op. 98b

🎵–(BB) *** Warner Apex 0927 49977-2. Michael, Bizimeche-Eisinger, Silveira, Schaeffer, Brodard, Lisbon Gulbenkian Foundation Ch. & O, Corboz

Schumann's *Mass in C minor* is a powerful work in which the chorus is all-important. The **Lisbon** singers rise to the challenge eloquently under **Corboz**, who is a persuasive exponent. He has good soloists, and **Audrey Michael** is particularly touching in the *Offertorium*, where she sings with treble-like purity. The *Sanctus* which follows is also very fine. The less ambitious *Requiem für Mignon* is also very attractively done, with the matching of the female solo voices particularly pleasing, and the documentation about the music has been restored for this inexpensive reissue.

Das Paradies und die Peri, Op. 50

(N) *** RCA 88697 27155-2 (2). Röschmann, Fink, Strehl, Gerhaher, Bav. R Ch. & SO, Harnoncourt

(i) Das Paradies und die Peri, Op. 50; (ii) Requiem für Mignon, Op. 98b; Nachtlied (for chorus & orchestra), Op. 108

🎵–*** DG 457 660-2 (2). (i) Bonney, Coku, Fink, Prégardien, Archer, Finley, Hauptman; (ii) Dazeley; Monteverdi Ch., ORR, Gardiner

It takes a conductor as perceptive and persuasive as **Sir John Eliot Gardiner** to transform *Das Paradies und die Peri* into something like a masterpiece. That he does with his period forces in this fine version on DG Archiv. For good measure he adds two other much shorter neglected works and similarly presents them in their full originality. With **William Dazeley** as soloist, and with four trebles from the **Hanover Boys Choir** in key solo roles, the *Requiem für Mignon* is also most atmospherically done with wonderfully varied textures. To words by Hebbel, the *Nachtlied*, too, is revealed as more buried treasure. Refined, beautifully balanced recording made at the Watford Colosseum.

Harnoncourt's account with **Bavarian Radio** forces makes an attractive alternative to the Gardiner version. **Dorothea Röschmann** is a more intense Peri than Barbara Bonney for Gardiner, while, on the minus side, undoubtedly the golden-voiced **Christoph Prégardien** is more winning than Harnoncourt's **Christoph Strehl**. Yet the latter is very impressive too; the contralto angel, **Bernarda Fink**, also makes a telling contribution, and the **Bavarian Chorus** is outstandingly vivid. The recording, made in the Herkulessaal, is spacious yet clear, and the lithe orchestral playing has obvious influences from Harnoncourt's period-instrument ventures. Overall this new RCA set does Schumann's remarkable oratorio much justice.

Der Rose Pilgerfahrt, Op. 112

*** Chan. 9350. Nielsen, van der Walt, Møller, Paevatalu, Danish Nat. R. Ch. and SO, Kuhn

Schumann wrote his cantata, *Der Rose Pilgerfahrt* ('The Pilgrimage of the Rose') in 1851, towards the end of his career. The idiom, as well as recalling Schubert, often suggests the folk-based writing of Humperdinck in *Hänsel und Gretel*, similarly innocent-seeming, but in fact subtle. **Gustav Kuhn** conducts an aptly bright and atmospheric performance, very well recorded, with **Inga Nielsen** and **Deon van der Walt** in the two principal roles. The chorus and orchestra are first rate and the recording, sponsored by Danish Radio, is full-bodied and atmospheric. A valuable rarity. Sadly, the booklet contains no translation alongside the German text, though Richard Wigmore's note and summary are very helpful.

OPERA

Genoveva (complete; DVD version)

(N)**(*) Arthaus DVD 101 327. Banse, Kallisch, Mathey, Gantner, Muff, Zürich Op. Ch. & O, Harnoncourt (Stage Director: Martin Kušej; V/D: Felix Breisach)

It is to **Harnoncourt** that we owe the stage revival of Schumann's only opera, *Genoveva*, with its heroine an almost mystical image of beauty and chaste faithfulness. The double villains are Goro, who wants to seduce her while her husband Siegfried is away at the Crusades, and Margaretha his nurse, who stirs up Goro's desires for her own reasons. They are in league, either to achieve the seduction or to persuade Siegfried that his wife has been unfaithful. In the end they are unsuccessful when Siegfried discovers the truth at the last minute, and Genoveva is spared a violent death. Schumann wrote in a parlando, forward-looking style and the music is of quality, with fine arias for all the principals, and some excellent choruses for the servants and retainers. The plot may be convoluted, but it works well enough, although the opera at 146 minutes could do with a little pruning. The other snags are the various production eccentricities. The Set Designer, Rolf Glittenberg, has the bare stage dominated by a bloodstained white backcloth; the Costume Designer, Heidl Hackl, has chosen modern dress suits for the men (although Genoveva looks beautiful and chaste enough), and half-blackened make-up for the cast, none of which helps to make the action convincing. Nevertheless, Harnoncourt directs with spirit, and the singing is excellent, especially **Juliane Banse** as a glorious Genoveva, **Cornelia Kallisch**, a suitably wild Margaretha, and **Shawn Mathey** a strongly characterized Goro.

SCHÜTZ, Heinrich (1585–1672)

Die Auferstehung unseres Herren Jesu Christi; (i) Meine Seele erhebt den Herren

**** HM HMC 90 1310. Concerto Vocale, Jacobs; (i) with Kiehr

Schütz's *Resurrection* has a purity of feeling and a depth that cleanses the spirit, and **René Jacobs's** wonderfully paced and unhurried account of the Passion story has the listener (or at least this listener) completely under his spell. The quality and imaginative playing of the instrumentalists are no less impressive than the vocal contributions, especially that of **Maria Cristina Kiehr**. The recording is very well balanced and real.

Christmas Day Vespers 1664 (including: Christmas Story; Magnificat with Christmas Interpolations; O bone Jesu, fili Mariae (Sacred Concerto); Warum toben die Heiden)

*** DG 463 046-2. (i) Daniels, Boys Ch. & Congregational Ch. of Roskilde Cathedral, Gabrieli Consort and Players, McCreesh

As in his earlier hypothetical recreation of Vespers, at St Mark's, Venice, **Paul McCreesh** here celebrates *Christmas Vespers* as it might have been heard at the Dresden Court in 1664. The result is an immensely varied vocal and instrumental tapestry, ranging from congregational hymns, to Schütz's glorious *Magnificat* setting, including such familiar Christmas interpolations as the chorales *Lobt Gott, ihr Christen all zugleich* and *In dulci jubilo*, and ending with a burst of magnificence in the organ postlude, *Benedicamus Domino* by Samuel Scheidt. The centrepiece is a very fine performance of Schütz's *Christmas Story* with **Charles Daniels** a lyrical rather than a dramatic Evangelist. Other soloists are drawn from the **Gabrieli Consort** and the instrumental groups include wind instruments, cornetts and sackbuts, strings and a widely varied palette of continuo. The cathedral ambience adds to the sense of occasion, and the variety of the music here is matched by the colourful and dedicated response of the performers. A remarkable achievement.

Christmas Story (Weihnachtshistorie); 3 Cantiones sacrae (1625); Psalm 100

(BB) *** Naxos 8.553514. Agnew, Crookes, MacCarthy, Oxford Camerata, Summerly

On Naxos **Summerly** with his talented group of ten singers – two of them doubling as soloists – give a compelling reading of Schütz's vivid and compact telling of the *Christmas Story*. Aptly austere in its overall manner, with clear instrumental accompaniment, it yet brings out the beauty and vigour of the numbers depicting the different groups, in turn the angels, the shepherds and the wise men. The scholarly credentials are impeccable, with excellent notes provided, and the recording, made in Hertford College, Oxford, is full and vivid. The motets and the psalm-setting make a welcome fill-up.

Lukas Passion

(N)**(*) DaCapo 8.226019. Linderoth, Jesperson, Ars Nova Copenhagen, Hillier

The *Lukas Passion* was composed for the Dresden Court, which by tradition used no instruments during Holy Week. So, after a brief choral introduction, the work is dominated by the Evangelist's narrative with Jesus' participation. This means that, apart from very occasional and brief choral contributions from the Disciples, the work consists largely of recitative in German. A text and translation are provided, but with no solo commentary the musical appeal of the *Passion* is limited.

Motets

⊕ (BB) *** Regis (ADD) RRC 1168. Esswood, Keven Smith, Elliott, Griffet, Partridge, Etheridge, George, Pro Cantione Antiqua, L. Cornet & Sackbut Ens., Restoration Ac., Fleet

An eminently useful and well-recorded super-bargain anthology of Schütz motets that offers such masterpieces as *Fili mi Absolon* (for bass voice, five sackbuts, organ and violone continuo) and the glorious *Selig sind die Todten* in well-thought-out and carefully prepared performances under **Edgar Fleet**. These accounts have a dignity and warmth that make them distinctive. Moreover, the CD sound is excellently managed, rich and clear.

Musicalische Vesper

⊕ *** MDG 332 1170-2. Kölner Kammerchor, Coll. Cartusianum, Neumann

Taking Monteverdi's great 1610 set of *Vespers* as a model, **Peter Neumann** with his talented **Cologne** period group has here devised a thrilling German equivalent to Monteverdi's masterpiece, using appropriate Psalm settings and antiphons from Schütz's principal collections. The German sequence gains greatly in cohesion from being relatively compact, at just over an hour, ending with a glorious setting of the *Magnificat*. The Psalm settings leading up to that are drawn from such collections as the composer's *Psalms of David* and *Symphoniae Sacrae*, some items already well known on disc, but others not otherwise available. Peter Neumann draws singing and playing from his Cologne forces of spectacular precision and clarity, and he gains greatly from the brilliant engineering of the record company, MDG, which, using only two channels, yet gives a vivid illusion of surround sound.

O bone Jesu, fili Mariae

⊕ (M) *** DG 447 298-2. Monteverdi Ch., E. Bar. Soloists, Gardiner – BUXTEHUDE: *Membra Jesu nostri* ***

A wonderfully eloquent performance of this *Spiritual Concerto* by one of the greatest of baroque masters. Schütz juxtaposes stanzas of a poem ascribed to St Bernard of Clairvaux with prose passages of Latin devotional literature, treating the latter as recitative and the former set homophonically, and ending the cantata in *concertato* style. Beautifully recorded.

Der Schwanengesang (reconstructed Wolfram Steude)

(BB) **(*) Virgin 2x1 4 82100-2 (2). Hanover Boys' Ch., Hilliard Ens., L. Bar., Hillier – BACH: *Motets* ***

Schütz's *opus ultimum* is a setting of Psalm 119 (the longest psalm in the psalter), which he divides into 11 sections. He finishes off this 13-part motet cycle with the final setting of Psalm 100, which he had originally composed in 1662, and the *Deutsches Magnificat*. Wolfram Steude's note recounts the history of the work, parts of which disappeared after Schütz's death; and his reconstruction of two of the vocal parts is obviously a labour of love. The performance is a completely dedicated one, with excellent singing from all concerned and good instrumental playing, and the conductor, **Heinz Hennig**, secures warm and responsive singing from the **Hannover Knabenchor**. The acoustic is spacious and warm and the recording balance well focused. The sound is firm, clear, and spacious.

Sinfoniae Sacrae, Op. 6/2–13, 15, 17–19, SWV 258–69, 271, & 273–5

⊕ (BB) *** Warner Apex 2564 61143-2. Dietschy, Bellamy, Lurens, Zaepfel, Elwes, Guy de Mey, Fabre-Garrus, Les Saqueboutiers de Toulouse

Schütz's 20 *Sinfoniae Sacrae* of 1629 (of which 16 are included here) are the result of the Dresden composer's second visit to Italy in 1628, when he was strongly influenced by Monteverdi and the Italian *concertato* style. These pieces fascinatingly combine voices and instruments in a single texture, usually with an interweaving interplay, and rarely with the instruments acting just as an obbligato. The performances are eminently stylish and freshly spontaneous, and the instrumentalists are expert – and, moreover, they play in tune. The balance is beautifully judged, with voices and instruments within the same perspective, and the recording is wholly realistic.

St John Passion; 8 Passion Motets

(N) *(**) Christophorus CHE 0142-2. Coll. Mus. Plagense

The excellent performance of Schütz's crisp and dramatic *St John Passion* is undermined by poor presentation, with the 33-minute work transferred on a single track with no clue over the development of the Passion story except in the German-only text. The Passion motets are more easily appreciated, with the **Collegium Musicum Plagense** giving first-rate performances, well recorded.

SCOTT, Cyril (1879–1970)

Aubade, Op. 77; (i) Violin Concerto; (ii) Festival Overture; 3 Symphonic Dances

**** Chan. 10407. BBC PO, Brabbins; with (i) Charlier; (ii) Sheffield Philharmonic Ch.

These are all most persuasive performances, given Chandos's top-quality recording which makes the *Three Symphonic Dances* glow with colour and all but lose their capacity to seem over-long. The *Festival Overture* is more of an atmospheric evocation than an occasional piece, lustrously orchestrated, with the finale suddenly reinforced by organ and chorus. The *Violin Concerto* is a one-movement, rhapsodical work, elusive structurally, but lyrically appealing. It has a distinctly improvisatory character, which **Olivier Charlier** and **Brabbins** catch with admirable spontaneity. But easily the best work here is the *Aubade*, richly sensuous in its scoring and voluptuous in its manipulation of texture. It is superbly played.

(i) Cello Concerto. Symphony 1

**** Chan. 10452. BBC PO, Brabbins; (i) with Watkins

This is in some ways the most revealing of the issues in **Brabbins's** Cyril Scott series for Chandos, with works from opposite ends of his long career, *Symphony 1* of 1899 and the *Cello Concerto* of 1937. The *Symphony* is more traditional than Scott's later symphonies, with its clean-cut thematic material, and the result is very attractive. The *Cello Concerto*, beautifully played, with **Paul Watkins** as soloist, is in a conventional three movements, with the fast outer movements separated by a reflective *Pastoral* for unaccompanied cello, before the jolly, sparkling finale. Watkins rises to its challenges and Martyn Brabbins and the **BBC Philharmonic** give admirable support. As usual from this Manchester team, there is excellent recorded sound.

Piano Concertos 1 in C; 2; Early One Morning (poem for piano & orchestra)

🎵 ******** Lyrita (ADD) SRCD 251. Ogdon, LPO, Herrmann

Cyril Scott's lush *First Piano Concerto* dates from 1913 and its extravagant style belongs to the pre-war era. Those for whom Scott's name conjures memories of a piece called *Lotus Land* might feel that its atmosphere is well expressed by that title. **Ogdon** and **Herrmann** make a coherent whole out of Scott's essentially rhapsodical piece. The *Second Concerto* dates from Scott's later years, and although it has undoubted atmosphere, its shifting moods and rhapsodic chromaticism may not suit all tastes. The spirit of Delius is certainly evoked in this work, and it is even more apparent in the poem, *Early One Morning*. But for all one's reservations, Scott's music has a haunting quality that makes one want to return to it. The composer is splendidly served by his performers here, who create a feeling of spontaneity even when the music itself eddies gently with comparatively little forward movement. The recording from the mid-1970s is quite excellent in its CD format.

(i) Piano Concerto 1; 'Early One Morning' (for Piano & Orchestra); Symphony 4

*** Chan. 10376. BBC PO, Brabbins; (i) with Shelley

Scott's *First Piano Concerto* is not a work offering a traditional dialogue between piano and orchestra, the music changing from mood to mood; yet there is a chromatic lusciousness about the texture that is appealing, especially in the slow movement. The *Fourth Symphony* is similarly exotic, flowing forward with a tidal surge and a chromatic impressionistic atmosphere to make up for the structural ambiguity. After all this fluidity, the concertante *Variations on 'Early One Morning'* are joyfully explicit, though still never predictable. Excellent performances throughout.

(i) Piano Concerto 2; Neptune (Poem of the Sea); (ii) Symphony 3 (The Muses)

*** Chan. 10211. BBC PO, Brabbins; with (i) Shelley; (ii) Huddersfield Ch. Soc.

The *Piano Concerto* performance by **Howard Shelley** is every bit as convincing as Ogdon's and is certainly compelling. *Symphony 3*, subtitled *The Muses*, has four clearly defined movements, devoted to 'Epic Poetry and Tragedy', 'Comedy and Merry Verse', 'Love and Poetry' and, finally, the 'Muse of

Dance and Song'. Although it opens gently on four muted violins, it soon expands into a vast and complex score, with distinct reminders not only of Debussy's *La Mer* but also of Ravel's *Daphnis et Chloé*.

Undoubtedly the most successful work here is *Neptune* (*Poem of the Sea*). Here the constantly changing moods and tempi certainly evoke the restless ocean. It still depicts a central storm sequence and the work ends with an elegiac lament, creating a mood of twilight brooding.

The performances are very fine, Chandos has provided its most spectacular sound and, for all its diffuseness of ideas, Scott's music undoubtedly has a haunting quality which makes one want to return to it.

Piano Music Vol. 1: 2 Alpine Sketches, Op. 54/4; Autumn Idyll; Cherry Ripe; 3 Dances, Op. 20; Deuxième Suite, Op. 75; Handelian Rhapsody, Op. 17; Indian Suite; Miniatures; 3 Little Waltzes, Op. 58; Notturno, Op. 54/5; 3 Old Country Dances; A Pageant: 3 Dances; 3 Pastorals; Pastoral Suite; Requiescat; Sphinx, Op. 63; Soirée Japonnaise, Op. 67/4; Twilight-tide; Valse caprice, Op. 74/7; Vesperale, Op. 40/2; Vistas (includes bonus tracks of Cyril Scott playing his own music)

(B) ******* Dutton CDLX 7150 (2). De'Ath

Piano Music, Vol. 2: Piano Sonatas: in D, Op. 17; 1 (Original Version), Op. 66; 2–3

(M) ******* Dutton CDLX 7155. De'Ath

Piano Music, Vol. 3: (i) Piano Duet: Andante in F; 3 Danses; Diversion in F; Gigue in G; 2 Impressions from 'The Jungle Book'; Russian Fair; Sarabande in A; 3 Symphonic Dances (arr. Grainger); Theme and Variations; Gigue & Fugue in G & 3 Preludes & Fugues of J. S. Bach; Concert Pieces & Ballet Scores for Solo Piano

(B) ******* Dutton CDLX 7166 (2). De'Ath; (i) with Alexeyev

Piano Music, Vol. 4: Piano works published up to 1910, including: Summerland; 3 Frivolous Pieces, Op. 2; 2 Sketches, Op. 57; Suite in the Old Style, Op. 71/1; 3 Danses tristes. Piano works published after 1910, including: Impressions from 'The Jungle Book'; Over the Prairie; A Little Russian Suite; Old China Suite

(B) ******* Dutton CDLX 7183 (2). De'Ath

Cyril Scott's piano music is distinct from all others – varied and difficult to pin down exactly, yet not to be dismissed as derivative. Of particular interest and individuality is the *Deuxième Suite* of 1910. In addition to **De'Ath's** own sympathetic performances, there is an additional attraction in that Scott's own recordings (he was a formidable pianist) from 1928–30 are included as an appendix on the first disc.

The four *Sonatas* on the second CD were written over half a century. The sonata which Scott called 1, written in 1908, is a confident, interwoven four-movement work, with a characteristic slow movement, full of Scott's flowing, voluptuous English romanticism, yet also Straussian. The *Second Sonata* of 1933 is a single-movement work, textually and harmonically rich, somewhat after the exotic manner of Scriabin, but with a touch of impressionism. The *Third Sonata*, published in 1956, is marginally sparer in atmosphere; it has three distinct movements but remains harmonically oblique, yet its invention, like the earlier works, is both individual and quite haunting.

We are inclined to think that these miniatures for piano often brought out the best in their composer by their very compact format, consistently stimulating new ideas. The last volume includes a good deal of attractive music for piano duet which ought to be better known, including the *Theme and Variations* and Bach pastiches, while Percy Grainger made an effective transcription of the *Three Symphonic Dances*. Incidentally, *Russian Fair* quotes the same Russian folksong Tchaikovsky used in the finale of his *String Serenade*. With continually persuasive performances from **Leslie De'Ath**, joined by **Anya Alexeyev** in the piano duets, these discs offer much to divert the listener, for they are very well recorded.

Piano Music, Vol. 5: An English Waltz; Arabesque; Barcarolle; Ballade; Britain's War March; British Melodies; Caprice chinois; Carillon; Cavatina; (i) Concerto in C; Danse nègre. Diatonic Study; 2 Etudes; First Bagatelle; Impromptu; (i) Lotus Land. Mazurka; Miss Remington; Moods (1922); My Heart Is Ever Faithful; Pastoral Ode; 2 Piano Pieces; 2 Pierrot Pieces; Pierrette; Poems (1912); Prelude solennel; Rainbow Trout; Russian Dance; Sea-Marge: Meditation. Ode héroïque; Solitude; Tarantula; Valse sentimentale; Water-wagtail

Ⓝ Ⓜ *** Dutton CDLX 7224 (2). De'Ath, (i) with Alexeyev

This fifth volume contains Scott's most famous piano piece, *Lotus Land*, heard here as a solo piano and also for two pianos. Its popularity is easy to understand – it is a beautifully haunting piece of music, and receives first-rate performances here. The rest of the pieces in this fifth volume show that the composer's inspiration in his piano music was consistently high. There are many delights on this volume. The *Valse sentimentale* has a lovely nostalgic quality, a trait which runs through much of this music, especially in such numbers as *An English Waltz*. The local colour in the *Russian Dance*, *Caprice chinois* and *Danse nègre*, the last heard in solo form and for two pianos, is enchanting, and the longer works, such as the late *Pastoral Ode*, hold the listener's attention through a concentration of atmosphere and musical argument. **Leslie De'Ath**, as in the other volumes in this series, has the full measure of this music and the Dutton sound is superb: richly full yet atmospheric too. Two CDs are available for the price of one.

SCRIABIN, Alexander
(1872–1915)

(i) Piano Concerto in F sharp min., Op. 20; (ii) Prometheus (The Poem of Fire), Op. 60; Rêverie; (iii) Le Poème de l'extase, Op. 54; Symphonies 1 in

E, Op. 26; 2 in C min., Op. 29; 3 (The Divine Poem). Op. 43

Ⓜ *** BIS CD 1669-70 (3). (i) Pöntinen; (ii) Derwinger; (iii) Blom, Magnusson; (ii–iii) Stockholm Ph. Ch.; all with Royal Stockholm PO, Segerstam

(i) Piano Concerto in F sharp min., Op. 20; Poème de l'extase, Op. 54; (i; ii) Prometheus (Le Poème du feu), Op. 60; Rêverie, Op. 24; Symphonies Nos. (ii; iii) 1, Op. 26; 2; 3 (Le Divin Poème)

Ⓜ **(*) Decca Trio 473 971-2 (3). Deutsches SO, Berlin, Ashkenazy; with (i) Jablonski; (ii) Berlin R. Ch.; (iii) Balleys, Larin

(i) Piano Concerto; (i; ii) Prometheus; (i) Preludes, Op. 11/6, 10, 15, & 17; Fragilité, Op. 51/1; Sonata 1, Op. 6: Marche funèbre (orch. Rogal-Levitsky)

Ⓑ🅱️ *** Naxos 8.550818. (i) Scherbakov; (ii) Russian State TV and R. Ch.; Moscow SO, Golovschin

Segerstam is very much at home in this repertoire and he gets very good results from this fine orchestra. Both **Love Derwinger** in *Prometheus* and **Pöntinen** in the *F sharp minor Concerto* are equally intuitive interpreters of the art nouveau Russian master. BIS offer this as three CDs for the price of two. The recordings come from 1989–91 and enjoy the excellent acoustic of the Stockholm Konserthus.

Ashkenazy's set of the Scriabin *Symphonies* is available on a Double Decca, together with his highly charged **Berlin Radio** version of the *Poème de l'extase* (460 299-2). They are beautifully recorded; the performances shimmer with sensuality, but are lacking in the last degree of dramatic intensity. The same comments apply here to the *Piano Concerto*, in which **Jablonski** is a sympathetic if rather self-effacing soloist (he is not very forwardly balanced). Nevertheless he and Ashkenazy find plenty of romantic poetry in the music, especially in the slow movement, and with such good sound this is certainly enjoyable.

On Naxos **Konstantin Scherbakov** gives a most poetic account of the Chopinesque *F sharp minor Concerto*. The improvisatory musings of the slow movement come over beautifully, and *Prometheus* is no less characterful. Of course, the **Moscow Symphony** are not in the same league as the Cleveland Orchestra, but they play with ardour and the sound is very natural without being in the demonstration category.

Le Poème de l'extase, Op. 54

Ⓓ *** BBC (ADD) BBCL 4121-2. USSR State SO, Svetlanov – RIMSKY-KORSAKOV: *Scheherazade; Procession of the Nobles* ***

Ⓓ *** BBC (ADD) BBCL 4018-2. New Philh. O, Stokowski (and conversation with Deryck Cooke) – BERLIOZ: *Symphonie fantastique* **(*)

*** Naïve V 4946. O Nat. de France, Svetlanov – DEBUSSY: *La Mer* ***

*** Australian Decca Eloquence (ADD) 466 904-2. LAPO, Mehta – NIELSEN: *Symphony 4* **

Svetlanov's powerful and enormously authoritative account was recorded with his own orchestra at a BBC Prom in the expansive acoustics of the Royal Albert Hall in August 1968. His reading is one of the most compelling accounts of Scriabin's extraordinary score that one is likely to encounter and is second to none (not even Stokowski). The performance has much subtle light and shade but is underpinned by a Slavonic, extrovert passion that is very compelling indeed, leading to a tremendously exciting climax, with strings and horns at their absolute zenith, before the lush close. Like the coupling, the recording is more brilliant and has greater range than one expects from this source.

Stokowski conducted the American première of *Le Poème de l'extase* in 1917, a performance of great luminosity and energy. This account comes from a 1968 Festival Hall concert with the **New Philharmonia Orchestra**. Orgiastic, no holds barred, totally abandoned and wonderfully dedicated playing. However, the BBC sound is less than ideally transparent in its handling of detail.

An impressive memento on Naïve of **Svetlanov's** last visit to Paris. He seems to have established an excellent rapport with this great French orchestra, and he casts a powerful spell. A fine account, which comes with a no less atmospheric *La Mer*. Very good recorded sound.

This is **Mehta** on top form in his vintage Decca years. Recorded in the mid-1960s, it is still sonically very impressive, with the engineers doing ample justice to the complexity and opulence of this lavishly self-intoxicated and orgasmic score. It remains one of the most gripping performances available today, but is coupled with an extrovert and less recommendable account of Nielsen's *Fourth Symphony*.

Prometheus (The Poem of Fire), Op. 60

🎵 *** Ph. 446 715-2. Toradze, Kirov Op. Ch. & O, Gergiev –
STRAVINSKY: *Firebird* (complete ballet) ***

On Philips an *echt*-Russian account of *Prometheus*, with a suitably inflammable pianist in the person of **Alexander Toradze**. This is the only current recording by a Russian orchestra, and under **Gergiev's** masterly direction they give an outstanding account of this voluptuous and gloriously decadent score. The recording, too, is in the demonstration class even if the pianist is perhaps slightly too forwardly placed in the aural picture. It comes with an appropriately incandescent *Firebird*, marvellously played and recorded.

Symphonies 1–3; Le Poème de l'extase

Ⓜ **(*) Decca 460 299-2 (2). Deutsches SO, Berlin, or Berlin RSO, Ashkenazy

This Decca **Ashkenazy** set is an alternative to that listed above for those not requiring the *Piano Concerto* and the symphonic poems.

Symphonies 1–3; Le Poème de l'extase; (i) Prometheus

🎵 Ⓜ *** EMI ADD 5 67720-2 (3). Toczyska, Myers, Westminster Ch. (in 1), Phd. O, Muti; (i) with Alexeev

(i) Symphonies 2; (ii) 3 (Le Divin Poème); (iii) Le Poème de l'extase; (i) Rêverie, Op. 24

🎵 Ⓑ *** Chan. 2-for-1 241-5 (2). (i) RSNO; (ii) Danish Nat. RSO; (iii) Chicago SO; Järvi

Muti's complete set of the Scriabin *Symphonies* can be recommended almost without reservation; overall the sound is as vivid and richly coloured as the performances. With the two later symphonies-cum-symphonic poems (*Le Poème de l'extase* white-hot with passionate intensity, yet masterfully controlled) now added, this is an impressive achievement.

The splendid account of the *Second Symphony* from **Järvi**, with its richly detailed recording, can also be recommended strongly. There is something refreshingly unforced and natural about Järvi's version of the *Third*, which puts this score in a far better light than those conductors who play it for all they are worth. Järvi's version of *Le Poème de l'extase*, played superbly and recorded vividly and resonantly in Chicago's Orchestral Hall, emphasizes Scriabin's primary colours, with the trumpet solo penetrating boldly through the voluptuous texture and skirting vulgarity by a small margin. There have been more subtle performances, but this one certainly makes a strong impact.

Symphony 1 in E, Op. 26

*** Chan. 10311. Kostyuk, Dolgov, Russian State SO, Polyansky
– RACHMANINOV: *Six Choruses* ***

Scriabin's 50-minute *First Symphony* in six movements was his first major work not written for the piano. It is a diffuse work with some inspired episodes. It needs a conductor with a very firm grip on its generally rhapsodic discourse. **Polyansky** proves a sympathetic guide, though Muti exercises an even stronger hold over its architecture. All the same, this account is very persuasive, the soloists in the last movement eminently acceptable and the sound warm and well defined.

PIANO MUSIC

Complete Recording

Allegro appassionato & miscellaneous works; Piano Sonatas 1–10; Etudes; Impromptus; Mazurkas; Poèmes; Preludes; Waltzes; Poèmes

Ⓜ *** Capriccio AH 193 (8). Lettberg (plus **DVD** Documentary)

The present set encompasses Scriabin's complete piano output, recorded in collaboration with Deutschlandradio Kultur between 2004 and 2007. **Lettberg** can withstand comparison with the most exalted company. She is completely attuned to the hyper-refined sensibility and ecstatic rapture of Scriabin's world and, whether it be in the Chopinesque foothills of the *Preludes* or the mesmeric power of the late *Sonatas*, she characterizes this repertoire to something like perfection. In addition to the eight CDs there is a DVD entitled '*Alexander Scriabin: Mysterium*' which includes paintings and animations by Andrea Schmidt and interviews which examine the composer's musical beliefs and his mysticism. Strongly recommended.

Allegro Appassionato, Op. 4; Canon in D min.; Etude in D sharp min.; Fugue in E min.; Mazurkas in: B min. & F; Nocturnes in F sharp min., Op. 5/1; A, Op. 5/2; D flat, Op. 9/2; A flat; Prelude in C sharp min., Op. 9/1; Sonata in E flat min.; Sonate-fantaisie; Variations on a Theme by Mlle Egorova; Waltz in F min., Op. 1; Waltzes in G sharp min. & D flat

*** Hyp. CDA 67149. Coombs

Stephen Coombs concentrates on Scriabin's early period, when he had yet to escape from Chopin's magnetic field, which has received less attention than the late sonatas. The earliest piece here, a *Canon in D minor*, was written when he was only 11 years old, but many of these Chopinesque pieces are of real quality and do not deserve to be so completely overshadowed. Coombs has a genuine feel for this repertoire and is very well served by the recording team.

Études, Opp. 2 & 8/12; Nuances, Op. 56; 4 Mazurkas, Op. 3/1, 3, 4 & 6; Poème, Op. 59; Piano Sonatas 2 (Sonate-Fantaisie), Op. 19; 5, Op. 53; 9 (Black Mass), Op. 68; Valse, Op. 38

**** BIS **SACD** 1568. Sudbin

Yevgeny Sudbin's recording début with Scarlatti sonatas enjoyed a spectacular success and announced the arrival of a major pianistic talent. Successive records have only confirmed this, and the present Scriabin recital is arguably his most exciting record to date. He seems totally bound up in this seductive music and plays it with demonic fire. BIS's recording, made at the Västerås Concert Hall, is (as usual with this company) in the demonstration category.

Etudes, Op. 8/7 & 12; Op. 42/5; Preludes, Op. 11/1, 3, 9–10, 13–14, 16; Op. 13/6; Op. 15/2; Op. 16/1 & 4; Op. 27/1; Op. 48/3; Op. 51/2; Op. 59/2; Op. 67/1; Sonatas 3, Op. 23; 5, Op. 53; 9 (Black Mass), Op. 68

Ⓑ (***) RCA 2-CD mono 74321 84594-2 (2). Horowitz – CLEMENTI: *Sonatas, Op. 14/3; Op. 34/2; Op. 47/2: Rondo* (***); MUSSORGSKY: *Pictures at an Exhibition* (***)

The engineers have done wonders to these recordings from the 1950s, though some of the original shallowness and clatter remains. The *Preludes* and the legendary accounts of the *Third* and *Ninth Sonatas* come from 1956, the *Fifth* is much later, coming from 1976, and has more bloom. The performances form an essential part of any good **Horowitz** collection, and the Mussorgsky and Clementi couplings are equally indispensable.

10 Mazurkas, Op. 3; 9 Mazurkas, Op. 25; 2 Mazurkas, Op. 40

*** ASV CDDCA 1066. Fergus-Thompson

An impressive instalment of Scriabin's piano music from **Gordon Fergus-Thompson**, a masterly and underrated artist. Even when put alongside native Russian pianists he can hold his own.

Preludes: Op. 2/2; Prelude for the Left Hand, Op. 9/1; 24 Preludes, Op. 11; 6 Preludes, Op. 13; 5

Preludes, Op. 15; 5 Preludes, Op. 16; 7 Preludes, Op. 17; 4 Preludes, Op. 22; 2 Preludes, Op. 27; 4 Preludes, Op. 31; 4 Preludes, Op. 33; 3 Preludes, Op. 35; 4 Preludes, Op. 37; 4 Preludes, Op. 39; Op. 45/3; 4 Preludes, Op. 48; Preludes, Op. 49/2; Op. 51/2; Op. 56/1; Op. 59/2; 2 Preludes, Op. 67; 5 Preludes, Op. 74

*** Hyp. CDA 67057/8. Lane

Piers Lane has the measure of Scriabin's idiom and seems completely attuned to his musical language and sensibility. These preludes range from his formative Chopinesque years, around 1889, through to 1914, and Lane traverses them with flair.

5 Preludes, Op. 15; Sonata 3, Op. 23

🎧 *** RCA 82876 65390-2. Evgeny Kissin – MEDTNER: *Sonata-Reminiscenza* **(*); STRAVINSKY: *Movements from 'Petrushka'* ***

Kissin is in his element in Scriabin. He is attuned to the pianistic flair and keen narcissism of the composer and surmounts the formidable difficulties of the big-boned *Third Sonata* with great aplomb.

Piano Sonatas 1–10; Sonate-fantaisie in G sharp min.

🎧 **** Hyp. CDA 67131/2. Hamelin

Piano Sonatas 1–10; Etude in C sharp min., Op. 2/1; Feuillet d'album, Op. 58; 2 Morceaux, Op. 57; 2 Poèmes, Op. 63; 4 Preludes, Op. 48; 5 Preludes, Op. 64; 2 Preludes, Op. 67; Vers la flamme, Op. 72

ⒷⒷ *** EMI (ADD) Gemini 3 65332-2 (2). Ogdon

Piano Sonatas 1–10; 2 Danses, Op. 73; 4 Morceaux, Op. 51; 4 Morceaux, Op. 56; 2 Poèmes, Op. 32

Ⓑ *** Double Decca ADD/DDD 452 961-2 (2). Ashkenazy

Marc-André Hamelin commands the feverish intensity, the manic vision, wide dynamic range and fastidious pedalling that Scriabin must have. There are other fine Scriabin cycles and, of course, celebrated accounts of single sonatas from Richter and others, but of newer cycles Hamelin's must now be a first recommendation.

Ogdon is nothing if not persuasive, and the only reservation one need feel about his playing is an occasional tendency to be less than scrupulous in observing dynamic indications and a certain lack of finish. His account of the *Tenth Sonata*, however, is particularly fine. The shorter pieces are particularly appealing (the richly coloured *Etude in C sharp minor* which opens the first disc should tempt anyone to explore further). The piano is very well recorded throughout (at Abbey Road in 1971).

Ashkenazy's Scriabin set was made over a decade between 1972 and 1984, but the sound is remarkably consistent. Ashkenazy is clearly attuned to this repertoire: he is as thoroughly at home in the *Miniatures* as in the *Sonatas*, readily finding their special atmosphere and colour.

Piano Sonatas 2 in G sharp min., Op. 19; 5 in F sharp, Op. 53; 6 in G, Op. 63; 7 in F sharp (White

Mass), Op. 64; 9 in F (Black Mass), Op. 68; Fantaisie in B min., Op. 28

(BB) *** Naxos 8.553158. Glemser

Piano Sonatas 3 in F sharp min., Op. 23; 10 in C, Op. 70; in E flat (1890); Poème nocturne, Op. 61; Vers la flamme, Op. 72

(BB) *** Naxos 8.555468. Glemser

These performances are very good indeed. **Bernd Glemser** has an excellent feel for the Scriabin world. He commands a keen imagination, a wide range of keyboard colour and he possesses an impressive technical address.

Piano Sonata 3 in F sharp min., Op. 23; 2 Poèmes, Op. 32; Vers la flamme, Op. 72

**(*) Kingdom KCLCD 2001. Fergus-Thompson – BALAKIREV: *Piano Sonata* **(*)

Gordon Fergus-Thompson gives a splendid account of Scriabin's overheated *F sharp minor Sonata* and sensitive, atmospheric performances of the other pieces here. A reverberant but good recording.

SCULTHORPE, Peter
(born 1929)

Piano Concerto

**(*) Australian ABC Eloquence 426 483-2. Fogg, Melbourne SO, Fredman – EDWARDS: *Piano Concerto*; WILLIAMSON: *Concerto for 2 Pianos* **(*)

In many ways, Sculthorpe's *Piano Concerto* is the most difficult of the three works to get to grips with on this Australian Eloquence CD. Written during a very sad time in the composer's life, its mood reflects that. It is not a virtuosic showpiece for the pianist, but stands as an interesting modern concerto that repays listening. The performance here is excellent and the recording acceptable.

SEARLE, Humphrey (1915–82)

Symphonies 1–5; Night Music; Overture to a Drama

*** CPO 777 131-2 (2). BBC Scottish SO, Francis

Searle's *First Symphony* was championed by Sir Adrian Boult and the LPO, the *Second* by Josef Krips; but his later symphonies have not enjoyed the exposure they deserve either in the concert hall or on CD. This two-CD set makes handsome amends: Searle's music is concentrated and powerful and it rewards study and attention. It is an unlikely candidate for popularity but, like Fricker's, is a strong contender for revaluation.

Symphony 2, Op. 33

(N) *** Lyrita (ADD) SRCD 285. LPO, Krips – STILL: *Symphonies 3 & 4* ***

Josef Krips, in one of his last recording sessions, conducted a superbly expressive performance of Searle's *Second*

Symphony. Like its predecessor it follows the composer's characteristic brand of twelve-note serialism, but even more than the earlier work it shows Searle following the central English tradition. If Walton had ever written a serial symphony, it might sound very much like this. The performance and sound (from 1975) are both excellent, and the couplings of Still's symphonies are superb.

SEIBER, Mátyás (1905–60)

Clarinet Concertino

⊕ (BB) *** Hyp. Helios CDH 55068. King, ECO, Litton – BLAKE: *Clarinet Concerto* ***; LUTOSŁAWSKI: *Dance Preludes* ***

Mátyás Seiber's highly engaging *Concertino* was sketched during a train journey in 1926 (before the days of seamless rails) and certainly the opening *Toccata* has the jumpy, rhythmic feeling of railway line joints and points. Yet the haunting slow movement has a touch of the ethereal, while the Scherzo has a witty jazz element. **Thea King** has the measure of the piece; she is accompanied well by **Andrew Litton**, and very well recorded.

SERLY, Tibor (1901–78)

Rhapsody for Viola & Orchestra

(BB) *** Naxos 8.554183. Xiao, Budapest PO, Kovacs – BARTÓK: *Viola Concerto* (2 versions; ed. Bartók & ed. Serly); *Two Pictures* ***

Tibor Serly, friend of Bartók and first editor of the unfinished *Viola Concerto*, here offers a closely related work, less individual than Bartók's own, but well worth hearing. Beautifully played by the Chinese viola-player, **Hong-Mei Xiao**, it provides a good makeweight for the disc containing both editions of the Bartók *Concerto*.

SÉVERAC, Déodat de (1872–1921)

Piano, 4 hands: L'Album pour les enfants petits et grands: Le Soldat de plomb (Histoire vraie en trois récits). Solo piano: Baigneuses au soleil (Souvenir de Banyul-sur-mer); Cerdaña (5 Etudes pittoresques); Le Chant de la terre (poème géorgique); En Languedoc (suite); En vacances (petites pièces romantiques); Les Naïades et le faune indiscret; Pipperment-get (Valse brillante de concert); Premier Recueil (Au château et dans le parc); Deuxième Recueil (inachevé); Sous les lauriers roses ou Soir de Carnaval sur la Côte Catalane; Stances à Madame de Pompadour; Valse romantique

(B) **(*) EMI (ADD)5 72372-2 (3). Ciccolini

Déodat de Séverac came from the Pays d'Oc and always retained his roots in the region. He first studied law at Toulouse before deciding on music and becoming a pupil of Magnard and then d'Indy. He was a friend of Ravel, to whom his musical language is much indebted. All the music on these CDs is civilized and has great charm. The recordings were made between 1968 and 1977 and are serviceable rather than distinguished. But the set will give much pleasure.

Cerdaña (5 Etudes pittoresques pour le piano); En Languedoc

☞─ **(BB)** *** Naxos 8.555855. Masó

Aldo Ciccolini's set of Déodat de Séverac's music has much to commend it, but three CDs may be too many for some collectors. **Jordi Masó's** lucid and sensitive accounts will make an excellent introduction to this delightful composer. His playing is finely characterized and there is a subtle use of keyboard colour. Good sound, too.

SHCHEDRIN, Rodion
(born 1932)

☞─ *** DG 471 136-2. Russian Nat. O, Pletnev

(i) Carmen (ballet; arr. from Bizet): Suite; Humoresque; In Imitation of Albéniz; Stalin Cocktail

*** Chan. 9288. I Musici de Montréal, Turovski; (i) with Ens. Répercussion – TURINA: La oración del torero ***

The Chandos version by **I Musici de Montréal** is very much in the demonstration bracket, with glittering percussion effects (marimba and vibraphone particularly well caught) and dramatic use of sidedrum snares. The pastiche, *In Imitation of Albéniz*, and the grotesque, Shostakovich-like *Humoresque* are offset by a malignant parody-evocation of Stalin, full of creepy special effects and with a shout of horror at the end. They are very well presented here, but one would not want to return to them very often.

Stihira

(M) *** Warner Elatus 0927 49014-2. Nat. SO, Rostropovich – GLAZUNOV: *Violin Concerto in A min., Op. 82*; PROKOFIEV: *Violin Concerto 1 in D, Op. 19* ***

Shchedrin here celebrates the millennium of the introduction of Christianity into Russia with a measured passacaglia-like piece based on Russian Orthodox chant, which builds up to a central climax of Mussorgskian splendour. The recording, made in the Kennedy Center, Washington, is more airy and spacious than many from this venue.

Piano Concerto 2

*** Hyp. **SACD**: SACDA 67425; CD: CDA 67425. Hamelin, BBC Scottish SO, Litton – SHOSTAKOVICH: *Piano Concertos 1–2* ****

In the *Second Concerto* in 1966, Shchedrin experimented with 12-note technique and jazz. Shchedrin himself recorded it with Svetlanov in the late 1970s, but this newcomer supersedes it in sheer virtuosity and panache, not to mention the clarity and presence of the Hyperion recording.

Balalaika; Echo Sonata for Solo Violin

☞─ *** EMI 5 57384-2. Vengerov – BACH: *Toccata & Fugue in D min.*; YSAŸE: *Solo Violin Sonatas 2, 3, 4 & 6* ***

Shchedrin's party-piece encore, *Balalaika*, has **Vengerov** the perfect showman in this live recording of a solo recital, playing pizzicato throughout with the violin held like a balalaika, to the great amusement of the audience. The *Echo Sonata* is far more formidable, again with Vengerov an intense communicator, always spontaneous.

SHEPPARD, John (c. 1515–c. 1559)

Aeterne rex altissime; Audivi vocem de coelo; Beata nobis gaudia; Dum transisset Sabbatum (1st & 2nd settings); In manus tuas (2nd & 3rd settings); Gaude, gaude, gaude Maria; Hostis Herodes impie; Impetum fecerunt unanimes; In manus tuas (3rd setting); Libera nos, salva nos (2nd setting); Sacris solemniis; Sancte Dei pretiose; Spiritus sanctus procedens (2nd setting). Second Service: Magnificat; Nunc dimittis; Te Deum laudamus. Western Wynde Mass

(B) **** Hyp. Dyad CDD 22022 (2). The Sixteen, Christophers

Ave maris stella; Cantate Mass. Motets: Deus tuorum militum (1st setting); Filiae Hierusalem venite; Haec dies; In manus tuas Domine (1st setting); In pacem in idipsum; Jesu salvator saeculi, redemptis; Jesu salvator saeculi verbum; Justi in perpetuum vivent; Laudem dicite Deo; Libera nos, salva nos (1st setting); Paschal Kyrie; Regis Tharsis et insulae; Salvator mundi, Domine; Spiritus sanctus procedens (1st setting); Verbum caro factus est

☞─ 🏵 **(B)** **** Hyp. Dyad CDD 22021 (2). The Sixteen, Christophers

The first collection listed (CD 22022) is especially attractive as it includes Sheppard's *Western Wynde Mass*. However, this is a less elaborate setting of this famous theme than some others, notably that of John Taverner, for until the closing *Agnus Dei* Sheppard consistently places the melodic line on top, whereas Taverner moves the tune about within the lower parts. Nevertheless, Sheppard's setting has an appealingly simple beauty, while the extended *Te Deum laudamus* is even richer in its harmonic progressions.

However, we have given our Rosette to the companion set (CDD 22021), for it includes Sheppard's glorious six-voiced *Cantate Mass*, much more complex than *Western Wynde* and, with its glowingly textured polyphony, surely among his most inspired works. **The Sixteen** consistently convey the rapturous beauty of Sheppard's writing, above all in the ethereal passages in the highest register, very characteristic of him. There are not many more beautiful examples of Tudor polyphony than this.

Christe redemptor omnium; In manus tuas; Media vita; Reges Tharsis; Sacris solemniis; Verbum caro; Western Wind Mass

(N) ▷—(B) **** Gimell CDGIM 210 (2). Tallis Scholars,
Phillips – TALLIS; WHITE: *Motets*

All the music here is based on chant, and much of it is for
the six-part choir, which produces a particularly striking
sonority. The *Media vita* ('In the midst of life we are in death')
is a piece of astonishing beauty, and it is sung with remarkable purity of tone by the **Tallis Scholars** under **Peter
Phillips**. Glorious and little-known music: the recording
could hardly be improved on. The *Western Wind Mass* has
been added for this reissue.

SHIELD, William (1748–1829)

Rosina

▷— *** ABC Classics (ADD) 461 922-2. Elkins, Harwood,
Sinclair, Tear, Macdonald, Ambrosian Singers, LSO,
Bonynge – ELGAR: *Sea Pictures* **(*)

Shield's rustic comedy *Rosina* is a delight from beginning to
end. First heard at Covent Garden in 1782, it is crammed full
of delights. Even the *Overture*, with its witty interjections
from the woodwind, threatens to upstage the main work.
The performance is lively and fun, with **Bonynge** allowing
the singers to embellish their vocal lines while the orchestra
provides a stylish and vivid accompaniment. **Margreta
Elkins** is superb as Rosina, and she is matched by the rest of
the team; whether they be joyful rustic arias, or sentimental
ballads, each is characterized beautifully. The full English
text is provided in the lavishly illustrated booklet, and with
vintage Decca sound (1966) this CD is a winner. The unexpected couplings are well worth having too.

SHOSTAKOVICH, Dmitri
(1906–75)

Testimony (Film, directed by Tony Palmer)

(N) *** TP **DVD** 145. Kingsley, Shrapnel, Rigby, Shirley-Quirk,
Golden Age Singers, Chilingirian Qt, Shelley, LPO, Barshai

Described by *Films and Filming* as 'the best British film of
the year', Tony Palmer's study of Shostakovich is typically
revelatory. Palmer follows the line presented by the unauthorized biography, *Testimony*, that the composer was hostile
to the Soviet regime, whatever compromises he had to make.
Ben Kingsley movingly presents the composer with great
sympathy, highlighting Shostakovich's experiences in the
300-day siege of Leningrad, when human flesh was eaten so
as to avoid starvation, though Shostakovich himself did not
have to endure that. The snarling of Zhdanov, artistic chief,
and the boasting of Stalin are equally well conveyed by **John
Shrapnel** and **Terence Rigby** respectively. The musical side
could hardly be finer, with **Rudolf Barshai** drawing dramatic
playing from the **LPO**, backed up by the **Chilingirian
Quartet** in *String Quartet 8*. Six of the symphonies are quoted,
notably the *Leningrad Symphony* with its portrayal of the Nazi
invasion in the nagging ostinato of the first movement. Also
very effective are the vocal contributions of **John Shirley-
Quirk** and the **Golden Age Singers** in the quotations from

Symphony 13 with its setting of Yevtushenko. A great film, one
of the finest that even Tony Palmer has made.

**(i; ii) *Alone: Suite, Op 26*; (i; iii) *The Bolt: Suite, Op.
27a* (1934 version); (iv) *The Bolt: Suite, Op. 27a*
(1931 version); (v) *Chamber Symphony (String Qt 4),
Op. 83a*; *Chamber Symphony (String Quartet 8), Op.
110a*; (vi) *Cello Concertos 1–2*; *Piano Concertos*: (i; ii;
vii) *1 in C min. for Trumpet & Strings*; (viii; ix) *2 in
F, Op. 102*; *Violin Concertos*: (x) *1 in E min., Op. 99*;
(xi) *2 in C sharp min., Op. 129*; (i; ii) *The
Counterplan: Suite*; (viii) *Festive Overture, Op. 96*; *5
Fragments, Op. 42*; *Funeral and Triumphal Prelude*;
(i; iii) *The Gadfly* (excerpts); (iv) *The Golden Age:
Suite, Op. 22*; (i; ii) *The Great Citizen: Funeral
March*; (iv) *Hamlet: Suite, Op. 32a*; (i; ii) *Hamlet*
(excerpts), *Op. 116*; *Jazz Suites 1 & 2*; (i; iii)
Moscow-Cheryomushki: Suite, Op. 105; (viii)
October, Op. 131; (ii; xii) *Overture on Russian and
Kirghiz Folk Themes, Op. 115*; (i; ii) *Pirogov: Scherzo
& Finale*; *Sofia Perovskaya: Waltz*; (v) *Symphony for
Strings, Op. 118a*; *Symphony for Strings and
Woodwinds, Op. 73a*; (i; ii) *Tahiti Trot (Tea for Two)*;
The Tale of the Silly Little Mouse (arr. Cornall), *Op.
56*; (xiii) *The Execution of Stepan Razin*; (viii; xiv)
*The Song of the Forests***

(B) *** Decca 475 7431 (9). (i) Chailly; (ii) Concg. O; (iii) Philh.
O; (iv) Gothenberg SO, Järvi; (v) COE, Barshai; (vi) Schiff,
Bav. RSO, Maxim Shostakovich; (vii) Brautigam, Masseurs;
(viii) RPO, Ashkenazy; (ix) Ortiz; (x) Mullova, RPO, Previn;
(xi) Kremer, Boston SO, Ozawa; (xii) Haitink; (xiii) Vogel,
Leipzig Ch. & RSO, Kegel; (xiv) Kotliarov, Storojev, New
London Children's Ch., Brighton Festival Ch.

This feast of Shostakovich includes **Chailly's** three famous
CDs of ballet and film suites and the supremely delightful
Jazz Suites – some of the most appealing music Shostakovich
ever wrote. All sorts of intriguing repertoire is here, and
Shostakovich's ready fund of melody and his exotic orchestral palette, spiced with touches of wit, make for a kaleidoscope of memorable vignettes. The *Romance* from *The Gadfly*
is included (in its original orchestration). *Hamlet* (there are
two versions of the music here) brings music of more pungency and dramatic power, while the composer's instanta-
neous and irresistible arrangement of Youmans's 'Tea for
Two', the *Tahiti Trot*, almost upstages everything. One of the
most substantial film scores, *Alone*, brings a wide range of
picaresque and touching evocations. Other highlights include the opening number from *Moscow-Cheryomushki*,
which has great energy and élan, and the luscious violins in
the *Tango* from *The Bolt* are a joy. Chailly plays this repertoire
superbly and receives magnificent orchestral playing from
both the **Concertgebouw** and **Philadelphia** orchestras, with
Decca sound to match.

   In the concertos, the *Cello Concertos* with **Schiff** are superbly recorded and the *First* can hold its own with the finest.
The *Second* is a haunting piece, essentially lyrical; it is gently
discursive, sadly whimsical at times, and tinged with smiling
melancholy that hides deeper troubles. The recording
(Philips) is enormously impressive. There's a perfectly

enjoyable account of the *Piano and Trumpet Concerto* from **Brautigam** and his excellent trumpet partner, **Peter Masseurs**, vividly accompanied by Chailly. The *Second Piano Concerto* with **Ortiz** is very successful: she gives a sparkling account of the jaunty first movement and brings out the fun and wit in the finale with fluent, finely pointed playing. The *First Violin Concerto* is disappointing, although it is all very expert, the performance is ultimately routine and wanting in atmosphere. **Gidon Kremer's** DG account of the *Second Violin Concerto* is played with his customary aplomb, but the recording is not really in the demonstration bracket.

The *Chamber Symphony* is an arrangement for full strings of the *Eighth Quartet* and the *Symphony for Strings* is a similar transcription of the *Tenth*. These are strong performances and are excellently recorded (DG). With two substantial choral rarities – **Ashkenazy's** *The Song of the Forests* (a freshly tuneful and enjoyable work that would have pleased the Soviet authorities) and **Kegel's** dramatic 1972 recording of the red-blooded *The Execution of Stepan Razin* – this bargain set is well worth considering. Texts and translations included.

Film Music: *Suites from: 5 Days and 5 Nights; Hamlet;* (i) *The Unforgettable Year 1919; The Young Guard*

🎵 *** Chan. 10361. BBC PO, Sinaisky; (i) with Roscoe

Throughout his career, Shostakovich was a regular contributor to Soviet films, offering colourful and evocative music such as you find in this collection of four examples. *Five Days and Five Nights* commemorates the destruction of Dresden in the Second World War, while this *Hamlet* music must be distinguished from the suite which Shostakovich also wrote for a staged production of the play. This suite has eight brief movements, illustrating various scenes in the story, ending with the Duel and Death of Hamlet. *The Unforgettable Year 1919* features the wildly romantic pseudo-piano concerto, *The Assault on Krasbaya Gorka*, which almost outdoes the *Warsaw Concerto* in its cinematic sweep. Brilliant and full Chandos sound reinforces the impact of **Sinaisky's** idiomatic performances.

'The Film Album': *Alone, Op. 26* (extended excerpts); *The Counterplan, Op. 33* (excerpts). *The Gadfly: Romance; The Great Citizen, Op. 55: Funeral March. Hamlet, Op. 116* (excerpts); *Pirogov, Op. 76a: Scherzo & Finale; Sofia Perovskaya, Op. 132: Waltz; The Tale of the Silly Little Mouse, Op. 56* (arr. **Andrew Cornhall**)

🎵 **** Decca 460 792-2. Concg. O, Chailly

Shostakovich's ready fund of melody and exotic orchestral palette spiced with touches of wit make here for a kaleidoscope of memorable vignettes. First-rate **Concertgebouw** playing and the most vivid Decca recording ensure the success of this entertaining collection.

Ballet Suites 1–5; Festive Overture, Op. 96; Katerina Ismailova: Suite

🎵 **** Chan. 7000/1. RSNO, Järvi

This highly entertaining set again represents Shostakovich in light-hearted, often ironic mood, throwing out *bonnes-bouches* like fireworks and with a sparkling vividness of orchestral colour. The *Ballet Suites* reuse material from earlier works: the *Fifth Suite* draws entirely on music from the 1931 ballet, *The Bolt* (see below). This is the most extended of the five suites, and typical of the young Shostakovich. The recording is spectacular and resonantly wide-ranging in the Chandos manner.

The Bolt (ballet; complete recording)

*** Chan. 9343/4 (2). Stockholm PO, Stockholm Transport Band, Rozhdestvensky

The Bolt dates from 1931 and in its original form sank without trace, largely thanks to the feeble, cumbersome propagandist libretto. Yet the dances are so sharp and colourful in their inspiration that over the years suites of movements have been heard, and now, in this vivid, full-blooded recording, **Rozhdestvensky** resurrects the complete score of 43 movements, lasting two and a half hours. Rozhdestvensky plainly believes passionately in this score, and he draws an electrifying performance from the Swedish orchestra. Demonstration sound.

'The Dance Album': *The Bolt: Ballet Suite, Op. 27a* (1934 version); *The Gadfly* (extended excerpts from the film score), *Op. 97* (original orchestration); *Moscow-Cheryomushki* (suite from the operetta), *Op. 105*

🎵 **** Decca 452 597-2. Phd. O, Chailly

Chailly offers 13 items from *The Gadfly* and reveals it to be far finer music than hitherto suspected, partly by using the original scoring. For all his sophistication of detail and expressive expansiveness, Chailly does not miss out on the witty audacity. The opening number of *Moscow-Cheryomushki, A Spin through Moscow* (when the chauffeur borrows the boss's car), has great energy and élan, the *Polka* from *The Bolt* combines wit with narrowly avoided vulgarity, and the boisterous opening of the following *Variations* will disappoint nobody. But, apart from the tunefulness, what one remembers most here is the superb playing of the **Philadelphia Orchestra**: the sonorous brass and vivid woodwind, while the strings have not sounded like this in decades.

The Bolt: Suite; Jazz Suites 1 & 2; Tahiti Trot

🅑🅑 **(*) Naxos 8.555949. Russian State SO, Yablonsky

The *Jazz Suites* show a light-hearted Shostakovich at his witty best, with some delightful melodies, colourfully orchestrated, with the composer's ironic tang adding a piquant spice. Likewise, the dances from *The Bolt*, not quite so inconsequential, but just as enjoyable, have an edge, which makes Shostakovich in popular mode so enticing. **Yablonsky** directs enjoyable, straightforward accounts of these works.

(i) *Chamber Symphonies: in D, Op. 83a; in C min., Op. 110a* (arr. of *String Quartets 4 & 8*);

Symphonies: for Strings & Woodwind, Op. 73a; for Strings, Op.118a (arr. of String Quartets 3 & 8) (all orch. Barshai); (ii) Symphony 15 in A, Op. 141bis (arr. for violin, cello, piano, celesta & percussion by Viktor Derevianko)

⊕ Ⓜ *** DG 2-CD 477 5442 (2). (i) COE, Barshai; (ii) Kremerata (with ALFRED SCHNITTKE: *Prelude in memory of Shostakovich*)

This DG Double usefully gathers together **Rudolf Barshai's** distinguished arrangements for orchestra of four of Shostakovich's *String Quartets*. The players of the **Chamber Orchestra of Europe** excel themselves in the tonal beauty, refinement and responsiveness of their playing. The added weight of sound gives greater impact to such movements as the *Allegro molto* of Op. 110a. These are strong performances of real eloquence and power, very well recorded. Viktor Derevianko's remarkably successful transcription of the *15th Symphony* for a chamber quintet (essentially a piano trio plus percussion) makes a surprise bonus. The sound is again first class. Alfred Schnittke's *Prelude* (for two violins, with **Gidon Kremer** playing with his own pre-recorded tape, as the composer directed) makes a strikingly stark *In memoriam*, being placed between Op. 73a and the *Symphony*.

Chamber Symphony, Op. 83a (String Quartet 4; orch. Barshai); Symphony for Strings & Woodwinds (String Quartet 3; orch. Barshai)

*** BIS CD 1180. Tapiola Sinf., Kantorow

⊕ *** Praga PRSD 250 232. Prague CO, Hradil – BARBER: *Adagio* **(*)

Shostakovich did authorize the transcription for full strings of the *Eighth* and *Tenth Quartets* and did apparently give Rudolf Barshai permission to arrange some of the other quartets for larger forces. Those willing to try these powerful works in this form will not be disappointed by the playing of the **Tapiola Sinfonietta**, who are superbly recorded by BIS.

However, the superbly played performances from **Antonín Hradil** and the **Prague Chamber Orchestra** are as fine as any, intense in feeling and bringing out the music's strong emotional contrasts. Their playing makes a link with Samuel Barber's music with their coupling of a performance of the famous *Adagio*, which has a comparable valedictory atmosphere.

Chamber Symphony 1, Op. 110a; Symphony for Strings, Op. 118a (both arr. Barshai); (i) From Jewish folk poetry

Ⓜ *** Chan. 6617. I Musici de Montréal, Turovsky; (i) with Pelle, Hart, Nolan

A fine record. The performances have plenty of bite and intensity and top-quality Chandos sound. The 11 vignettes, which Shostakovich based on Jewish folk music, have the widest diversity of mood and are splendidly sung here, the dialogue songs especially idiomatic. They are surprisingly upbeat, with the final concerted number, *Happiness*, ending the cycle robustly. **Turovsky's** framing accompaniments, too, are colourful and vividly caught by the engineers.

Chamber Symphony 1, Op. 110a; Symphony for Strings, Op. 118a; (i) Suite on Finnish Themes

*** BIS CD 1256. (i) Komsi, Nyman; Ostrobothian CO, Kangas

The *Suite on Finnish Themes* was written in 1939 in the immediate wake of the *Sixth Symphony*. It is slight (lasting less than 12 minutes) and yet often very characteristic, and it is scored for soprano, tenor, flute, oboe, clarinet, trumpet, triangle, tambourine, side-drum, piano and strings. For some reason it was never performed at the time (Shostakovich did not add the words himself) and the score has only recently come to light in a private collection in St Petersburg. Dedicated playing and exemplary recording.

Cello Concerto 1 in E flat, Op. 107 (DVD version)

⊕ ✿ *** EMI **DVD** DVA 4901209. Rostropovich, Monte Carlo Nat. Op. O, Kamu – PROKOFIEV: *Sinfonia Concertante*. Bonus: MUSSORGSKY: *Songs and Dances of Death* ***

When he came to befriend Shostakovich in the 1950s, **Rostropovich** obviously wanted to ask him for a cello concerto, but prudently withheld a request. Here is the result, and Rostropovich recorded it in London two years later. It is tersely scored for quite a small orchestra, double woodwind, celesta, but just one horn (here the splendid **Barry Tuckwell**) with whom the solo cello often duets. As with the Prokofiev coupling, one watches engrossed at the way Rostropovich shares the work with his orchestral colleagues; but the camera, rightly, often centres on the cellist and gives him great presence. The filming is in black and white, but the 1961 recording of the orchestra is better than the dry Monte Carlo sound, although acceptable rather than outstanding. Fortunately there are no complaints about the recording of the great cellist himself, who often seems to come right into the listener/watcher's room.

Cello Concerto 1 in E flat, Op. 107 (CD versions)

⊕ *** Chan. 8322. Wallfisch, ECO, Simon – BARBER: *Cello Concerto* ***

⊕ (***) BBC Legends mono BBCL 4143-2. Rostropovich, Leningrad PO, Rozhdestvensky – TCHAIKOVSKY: *Symphony 4* (***)

Wallfisch handles the first movement splendidly and he gives a sensitive account of the slow movement and has thoughtful and responsive support from the **ECO**. The Chandos recording is outstandingly fine.

William Mann is quoted by the notes as saying about **Rostropovich's** BBC recording that 'Rostropovich's tone has to be heard to be believed, so mighty is its strength, so richly varied its colour, and so beautiful its quality throughout its range, and the virtuosity and tonal homogeneity of the **Leningrad Philharmonic** is astonishing'. An exceptionally compelling musical document, matching the DVD version.

(i) Cello Concerto 1; Piano Concertos Nos. (ii) 1, Op. 35; (iii) 2, Op. 102

⊕ Ⓜ *** Sony (DDD/ADD) SMK 89752. (i) Ma, Phd. O, Ormandy; (ii) Previn, Vacchiano, NYPO, Bernstein; (iii) Bernstein (piano & cond.), NYPO

Yo-Yo Ma plays with an intensity that compels the listener, the **Philadelphia Orchestra** give eloquent support, and the digital recording is excellent. This couples aptly with the shrewd, much earlier pairing of Bernstein's radiant account of the *Second Piano Concerto* with **Previn's** equally striking reading of 1. If these recordings are far from recent they are transferred most vividly.

(i) *Cello Concerto 1*; (ii) *Piano Concerto 2*; (iii) *Violin Concerto 1*; (iv) *Jazz Suite 1*; *Tahiti Trot (Tea for Two)*; (v) *Symphony 1*; (vi) *String Quartet 8*

(N) (B) *** EMI 2-CD 2 37686-2 (2). (i) Han-Na Chang, LSO, Pappano; (ii) Ogdon, RPO, Foster; (iii) Sarah Chang, BPO, Rattle; (iv) Phd. O, Jansons; (v) BPO, Jansons; (vi) St Lawrence Qt

An impressive cross-section of Shostakovich's concertante works, all in fine performances and excellent recordings, with the single proviso that **Jansons's** version of the *First Symphony* with the **Berlin Philharmonic Orchestra**, although wonderfully played, is a little studied, a little wanting in spontaneity.

(i) *Cello Concerto 1*; (ii) *Violin Concerto 1 in A min.*, *Op. 99*

☛ 🏵 (M) (***) Sony stereo/mono MHK 63327. (i) Rostropovich, Phd. O, Ormandy; (ii) D. Oistrakh, NYPO, Mitropoulos

Rostropovich's studio recording première of the Shostakovich *First Cello Concerto* was made in 1959 and has for long enjoyed legendary status. It has probably not been surpassed, even by Rostropovich himself in subsequent recordings. **David Oistrakh's** mono recording of the *Violin Concerto* with **Mitropoulos** conducting the **New York Philharmonic** still sounds stunning.

Cello Concerto 1 in E flat, Op. 107; (i) *Cello Sonata in D min., Op. 40*

*** EMI 3 33242-2. Han-Na Chang, LSO, Pappano; (i) with Pappano (piano)

A highly impressive account of the *First Concerto* from **Han-Na Chang**, which can hold its own in the most exalted company. The same can be said of the *Sonata*, in which **Pappano** abandons the baton for the keyboard. He is a very fine pianist and gives Han-Na Chang excellent support.

Cello Concertos 1; 2 in G, Op. 126

☛ (M) **** Ph. 475 7575. Schiff, Bav. RSO, Maxim Shostakovich

(BB) *** Naxos 8.550813. Kliegel, Polish Nat. RSO (Katowice), Wit

(M) *** BIS CD 300626. Thedéen, Malmö SO, DePreist

(BB) *** Warner Apex 0927 40604-2. Noras, Norwegian RO, Rasilainen (with RICHARD STRAUSS: *Romanze ***)

Heinrich Schiff was the first cellist to couple these two *Concertos*. The *Second Concerto* is the more elusive of the two. A haunting piece, essentially lyrical, it is gently discursive, sadly whimsical at times and tinged with a smiling melan-

choly that hides deeper troubles. Schiff has its full measure, as indeed he has of the more direct *First Concerto*, and this has long been a favourite coupling of ours. The recording is enormously impressive.

Maria Kliegel and the **Polish National Radio Orchestra** at Katowice under **Antoni Wit** also give a very good account of both concertos that can be confidently recommended at this price, and on all counts is well worth considering.

The fine Swedish cellist, **Torleif Thedéen**, has a lot going for him, and his passionately committed performances would honour any collection. He has the advantage of excellent engineering, which gives a very alive sound, plus good orchestral support from the **Malmö Orchestra** under **James DePreist**.

Arto Noras is an aristocratic artist with a beautiful tone, and his playing is wonderfully flexible with intelligent phrasing and an instinctive feel for this repertoire. He never plays to the gallery, and his performances are all the more effective as a result.

Cello Concerto 2, Op. 126

☛ *** Avie AV 2090. Harrell, RLPO, Schwarz— PROKOFIEV: *Sinfonia concertante ***

(**(*)) BBC mono BBCL 4073-2. Rostropovich, LSO, Hurst (with KHACHATURIAN: *Concerto Rhapsody*; TCHAIKOVSKY: *Rococo Variations **(*))

(N) *(*) Signum Classics SIGCD137. Walton, Philh. O, Briger— BRITTEN: *Cello Symphony *(*)

Avie offer a strong coupling and a welcome addition to the catalogue. **Lynn Harrell** is captured live in performances from May 2005, and he gives (as one would expect) a masterly account of this elusive score and one which has all the electricity of live music-making. And what good results **Gerard Schwarz** gets from the **Liverpool Orchestra**. Very acceptable recording quality.

The BBC recording of the Shostakovich *Second Cello Concerto* was made at the Festival Hall in October 1966, not long after its Soviet première in Moscow, with **Colin Davis** conducting. The sound has the intensity of a première performance and the consequent excitement. The Khachaturian *Concerto Rhapsody* of 1963 is also captured at its première with the **LSO** and **George Hurst**, and the 1964 *Rococo Variations*, again with Colin Davis but at the Albert Hall, is a performance of no mean mastery. All in all, well worth having as a document of both the master cellist and two new works to which he is so deeply committed.

An intelligent coupling with an excellent soloist in **Jamie Walton**, but the sound is not satisfactory or well balanced. Whether played on a simple straightforward set-up or on highly sophisticated equipment, it still sounds unpleasing.

Piano Concerto 1 for Piano, Trumpet & Strings, *Op. 35*

(N) *** Naïve V 5053. Lise de la Salle, Boldoczki, Gulbenkian Foundation O, Lisbon, Foster — LISZT; PROKOFIEV: *Piano Concerto 1 ***

(***) British Music Society mono BMS 101 CDH. Mewton-Wood, Sevenstern, Concert Hall O, Goehr — BLISS:

Concerto (***)💿; STRAVINSKY: *Concerto for Piano and Wind* (***)

Lise de la Salle, with her trumpeter **Gabor Boldoczki**, finds plenty of sparkle and wit in a performance that dazzles, measuring up to those by more famous names, including Argerich. If you want the three works on this CD, de la Salle will give every satisfaction, and she is very well recorded.

The Shostakovich concerto was the last commercial recording made by **Noel Mewton-Wood**, in 1953, and the sound is the finest of the three concertos reissued on this British Music Society CD, the orchestral strings lustrous in the delicately romantic *Largo*, warm and full in the *Moderato* and with plenty of bite in the outer movements, with **Harry Sevenstern's** crisply articulated trumpet-playing cleanly caught. The performance is full of wit, gently ironic in the first movement, sharply brilliant in the dazzlingly played finale.

(i) *Piano Concerto 1, Op. 35*; (ii) *Piano Quintet, Op. 57*; (iii) *Concertino, Op. 94*

*** EMI 5 04504-2. Argerich; with (i) Nakariakov, O della Svizerra Italiana, Verdernikov; (ii) Renaud Capuçon, Margulis, Chen, Maisky; (iii) Zilberstein

An exhilarating and thought-provoking account of the *Concerto for Piano, Trumpet and Strings* which makes a very strong impact, not only for the extraordinary **Argerich** but also the amazing **Sergei Nakariakov**. It is the finest version of the *Concerto* yet – and very well recorded too. The *Piano Quintet* is also in a league of its own, though we would not wish to part with Richter and the Borodins.

Piano Concertos: (i) 1 for Piano, Trumpet & Strings in C min., Op. 35; 2 in F, Op. 102

➤ **** Hyp. **SACD**: SACDA 67425; CD: CDA 67425. Hamelin; (i) O'Keeffe; BBC Scottish SO, Litton – SHCHEDRIN: *Piano Concerto 2* ***

(i) *Piano Concertos 1–2; Piano Sonata 2 in B min., Op. 61*

(BB) *** Warner Apex 8573 89092-2. Leonskaya; (i) Saint Paul CO, Wolf

Marc-André Hamelin gives a vibrant, superbly articulate and dazzling account of both *Concertos*. These are stunning performances, which fully deserve the plaudits that have been showered on them. The listener is on the edge of the seat throughout, with both poetic insights and the right kind of excitement. Both works are splendidly characterized, though the trumpeter really rather overdoes things in the 'Poor Jenny is a Weeping' section of the finale. The recording, made in the Caird Hall, Dundee, is in the demonstration class. There is no better version of the two *Piano Concertos* coupled together on the market.

We know from her fine Tchaikovsky recordings that **Elisabeth Leonskaya** is thoroughly at home in Russian music, and so it proves in her sparkling and wittily pointed accounts of these two *Concertos*. The **Saint Paul Chamber Orchestra**, too, provide admirable backing. The strings play

with striking beauty in both slow movements, the *Andante* of 2 is ravishing, and the solo trumpeter, **Gary Borden**, brings a nice sense of humour to his solos in the finale of 1. What makes this disc doubly attractive is Leonskaya's distinctive account of the *B minor Piano Sonata*, with thoughtful playing not only in the slow movement but in the finale, which is in essence a set of variations. Vivid recording, with a touch of hardness on the piano tone, which does not come amiss in this repertoire.

Piano Concerto 2 in F, Op. 102

(BB) *** EMI Encore (ADD) 5 574991-2. Ogdon, RPO, Foster – BARTÓK: *Piano Concerto 3*, etc. **(*)

John Ogdon, at the height of his powers, gives a splendidly idiomatic account of this concerto written originally for Shostakovich's son, Maxim. The playing is full of character, the outer movements striking for their wit and dash, and the beautiful slow movement richly romantic without being sentimentalized. This remains one of the finest versions available, and the 1971 sound is excellent.

Violin Concerto 1 in A min., Op. 99

➤ *** Sony SK 68338. Midori, BPO, Abbado – TCHAIKOVSKY: *Violin Concerto* ***

**(*) Simax PSC 1159. Tellefsen, RPO, Berglund – BACH: *Violin Concerto 2* **(*)

Having the Tchaikovsky *Concerto* together with this 20th-century Russian masterpiece brings out the parallels between the two, a point enhanced by **Midori's** readings, recorded live, with rhythm and phrasing freely expressive. At the start of the *Moderato* first movement of the Shostakovich her tone is so withdrawn that one has to prick the ears, and in the *Passacaglia* third movement she also conveys an ethereal poignancy in her *pianissimo* playing. **Abbado** is a powerful and sympathetic, yet discreet accompanist, with recording that is both warm and well detailed.

Arve Tellefsen gives a fine account of the *concerto* and brings fine musicianship and no lack of passion to it. **Berglund** proves a supportive accompanist and the **RPO** play well for him. Moreover the sound is very well balanced. But this is not a first choice.

(i) *Violin Concerto 1 in A min., Op. 99*; (ii) *3 Violin Duets*

(M) **(*) EMI (DDD/ADD) 5 62593-2. Perlman; with (i) Israel PO, Mehta; (ii) Pinchas Zukerman – GLAZUNOV: *Violin Concerto* **(*)

Perlman and **Mehta** put the work in the light of day and, in the two fast movements and the cadenza, that brings tremendous dividends. Yet some of the mystery and fantasy which Russian interpreters have found – from David Oistrakh onwards – is missing, and the close balance of the solo instrument, characteristic of Perlman's concerto recordings, undermines hushed intensity. The three *Violin Duets* which act as an encore are entertaining trifles (there is a salon piece, a gavotte and some waltzes), all betraying some measure of wit. They are, of course, marvellously played.

Violin Concertos 1; 2 in C sharp min., Op. 129

⊛⟶ Ⓜ **** Warner Elatus 0927 46742-2. Vengerov, LSO, Rostropovich

*** Naïve V5025. Kachaturyan, O Nat. de France, Masur

*** Warner 2564 62546-2 Hope, BBC SO, M. Shostakovich

ⒷⒷ *** Virgin 2x1 5 61633-2. Sitkovetsky, BBC SO, Davis

*** Chan. 8820. Mordkovitch, SNO, Järvi

ⒷⒷ *** Naxos 8.550814. Kaler, Polish Nat. RSO (Katowice), Wit

**(*) BBC (ADD) BBCL 4060. D. Oistrakh; (i) Philh. O, Rozhdestvensky; (ii) USSR State O, Svetlanov – YSAŸE: Amitié **(*)

Vengerov comes into direct competition with Sitkovetsky on Virgin, yet his playing can dazzle the ear equally tellingly; he also really gets under the skin of both *Concertos* and finds an added depth of poetic feeling, while fully retaining the music's thrust and spontaneity. The haunting intensity, both at the opening of the *Second Concerto* and in its *Adagio* slow movement, is totally memorable. **Rostropovich** and the **LSO** give splendid support, and this mid-priced Warner Elatus disc now becomes a first recommendation.

Sergey Kachaturyan is a most impressive and persuasive artist who enjoys a supportive and idiomatic response from the **Orchestre National de France** under **Kurt Masur**. They are clean, lightish readings, making a worthwhile contrast with the weightier, more intense Lydia Mordkovitch, whose vintage, prize-winning reading on Chandos still remains among the most moving. Kachaturyan's performances have much eloquence to commend them and, among recent couplings of these masterly concertos, have strong claims on the collector. A very well-balanced recording, too. Many will find their naturalness of expression preferable to the Vengerov–Rostropovich set.

Daniel Hope is a brilliant and thoughtful soloist in both the familiar *First Concerto* and its underrated successor. **Maxim Shostakovich** gets good results from the **BBC Symphony Orchestra**, and the recording team offer excellent and natural sound. This is as good as almost any rival coupling on the market.

Virgin's coupling by **Sitkovetsky** and the **BBC Symphony Orchestra** under **Andrew Davis** is impressive and intense; there is no doubt as to its excellence, it has tremendous bite. It is splendidly recorded, and also takes its place at the top of the list.

Mordkovitch's concentrated reading of 2 is matched by **Järvi** and the orchestra in their total commitment. She even outshines the work's dedicatee and first interpreter, David Oistrakh, in the dark reflectiveness of her playing, even if she cannot quite match him in bravura passages. In the better-known *Concerto (1)* the meditative intensity is magnetic, with a fullness and warmth of tone that have not always marked her playing on record before.

Ilya Kaler's technique is flawless, with playing that is not only brilliant but consistently beautiful tonally. The *Second Violin Concerto*, the more wayward, more problematic work, is particularly fine and Kaler relishes the key role given to the cadenzas. If in the better-known *First Concerto* Kaler's performance does not quite have the same intensity, that is partly a question of the marginally less taut orchestral accompaniment and of the recording balance.

David Oistrakh's recording of the *First Violin Concerto* comes from the Edinburgh Festival of 1962 and the *Second* from a Prom in 1968. Both are performances to cherish, there is the electricity of a live occasion that gives something extra, and the first movement (*Nocturne*) of the *First* has an atmosphere that is as powerful as it was under Mitropoulos. The sound is very good.

The Girlfriends; Salute to Spain; Rule, Britannia!; Symphonic Movement (1945)

Ⓝ ⒷⒷ Naxos 8.572138. Camerata Silesia, Polish Nat. RSO, FitzGerald

The music to *The Girlfriends* comes from the score for a film made just before the *Pravda* attack on the composer put him in disgrace. 'The Girlfriends' are three young women who help in the 1917 Revolution, featuring some ingenious counterpoint and plenty of military fanfares, also a movement for theremin attempting to perform the communist anthem, the *Internationale*. *Salute to Spain* is a propaganda work in support of the Republican cause in the Spanish Civil War. *Rule Britannia!* takes its name from a boat moored in a Western harbour, this time leading to a thrilling account of the *Internationale* with full chorus. The *Symphonic Movement* of 1945 was the composer's first idea for a ninth symphony, brashly militaristic, quickly rejected for a far lighter piece. None of this may be great music, but it offers a fascinating portrait of the composer in one of his most prolific periods.

The Golden Age (ballet; complete)

**(*) Chan. 9251/2. Stockholm PO, Rozhdestvensky

The Chandos was the first complete recording of Shostakovich's first ballet, with its extraordinary plot of Soviet and capitalist sportsmen and women. The famous *Polka* is meant to satirize a disarmament meeting in Geneva. The music as a whole is remarkably potent and full of succulent ideas (even *Tea for Two* arrives during Act II), and the big set-pieces are expansively and sometimes darkly symphonic. The score is well played in Stockholm, but the warm orchestral style does not always readily bring out the music's plangent character and moments of barbed wit.

Hamlet (1932 production; complete incidental music), Op. 32; (1954 production; incidental music); King Lear (1941 production; complete incidental music), Op. 58a

Ⓜ *** Cala CACD 1021. Winter, Wilson-Johnson, CBSO, Elder

This is not top-drawer Shostakovich, but congratulations are in order for Cala's enterprise in recording all this and to the **City of Birmingham Orchestra** under **Mark Elder** for the vital and alert performances. The recording too is expertly and tastefully balanced.

New Babylon (film score); (i) From Jewish Folk Poetry (song-cycle)

*** Chan. 9600. Russian State SO, Polyansky; with (i) Sharova, Kuznetsova, Martynov

It makes an unusual and revealing coupling having Shostakovich's long-buried music for the satirical silent film, *New Babylon*, paired with the moving sequence of Jewish song-settings. **Polyansky** and an excellent trio of soloists bring out the expressive depth of these deceptively simple, lyrical songs, regularly reflecting the composer's sympathy with the suffering of the Jews. *New Babylon* was the composer's very first film score, with sharp parodies, 1920s-style, of French models reflecting the Parisian background of the story. Colourful, atmospheric orchestration beautifully caught in full-bodied, well-balanced sound.

SYMPHONIES

Symphonies 1–12; (i) 13; (ii) 14; 15; (iii) (iv) *The Execution of Stepan Razin*, Op. 119; *The Sun Shines on our Motherland*, Op. 90

Ⓑ *** Melodiya MELCD 10 01065 (11). Moscow PO, Kondrashin; with (i) Eisen, RSFSR Ac. Ch.; (ii) Tselovalnik, Nestorenko; (iii) D. Oistrakh; (iv) Gromadsky

Symphonies 1–2; (i) 3; 4–13 (*Babi Yar*); (i; ii) 14; (iii) 15

Ⓑ *** Cap. **SACD** 71029 (12). (i) Prague Ph. Ch.; (iii) Shaguch; (ii; iii) Kotchinian; Gürzenich O, Cologne, Kitajenko

Symphonies (i) 1 in F min., Op. 10; (i; iv) 2 (*To October*), Op. 14; (i;v) 3 (*1st of May*), Op. 20; (iii) 4, Op. 43; (i) 5 in D min., Op. 47; 6 in B min., Op. 54; (ii) 7 (*Leningrad*), Op. 60; (i) 8 in C min., Op. 65; 9 in E flat, Op. 70; 10 in E min., Op. 93; (ii) 11 (*The Year 1905*), Op. 103; (i) 12 (*The Year 1917*), Op. 112; (iii; vi) 13 (*Babi Yar*), Op. 113; (iii; vi; vii) 14, Op. 135; (i) 15, Op. 141; (i) Festival Overture, Op. 96; October, Op. 131; (i; iv; viii) Song of the Forests, Op. 81; (i) 5 Fragments, Op. 42; Funeral & Triumphal Prelude, Op. 130; Chamber Symphony, Op. 110a (trans. of String Quartet 8 by Rudolf Barshai

Ⓑ *** Decca 475 8748 (12). (i) RPO; (ii) St Petersburg PO; (iii) NHK SO; (iv) Brighton Festival Ch.; (v) Bach Ch.; (vi) Koptchak; (vii) Rodgers; (viii) Kotliarov, Storojev; cond. Ashkenazy

Symphonies 1–15; (i; ii) From *Jewish Folk Poetry*; (ii) 6 Poems of Marina Tsvetaeva

Ⓑ *** Decca DDD/ADD 475 7413 (11). Varady, Fischer-Dieskau, Rintzler; (i) Söderström, Karczykowski; (ii) Wenkel; Ch. of LPO or Concg. O; LPO or Concg. O, Haitink

An outstanding compilation from **Ashkenazy** to supplement the **Haitink** Decca cycle. In addition to the symphonies, this new box offers a number of other rarities which fill out our picture of the symphonist. Most of these recordings have appeared before but 7 and 11 with the **St Petersburg Orchestra** and 4, 13 and 14 with the **NHK Orchestra**, Tokyo,

are new. They are very fine indeed and are performed by Vladimir Ashkenazy with fidelity to both the letter and the spirit of the score. The earliest recording (apart from a few spoken words from Shostakovich himself, recorded at the time of the siege of Leningrad) comes from 1987; of the newcomers 4, 7, 11, 13 and 14 are all 2007 recordings. The Decca engineers offer us sound that is worthy of the house.

Our last encounter with **Kondrashin's** cycle was on 12 boxed LPs, and it remains mandatory listening. The *Fourth*, its première recording, has wonderful intensity, as indeed does the *Eighth*, though we prefer Mravinsky's 1960 broadcast on BBC Legends. (The first movement of the *Sixth* still strikes us as a bit fast.) But on balance this all has the ring of authenticity one expects from a conductor who was so closely associated with the composer and who gave the premières of *Symphonies* 4 and 13.

Alternatively there is a competitively priced survey of the Shostakovich canon from **Dmitri Kitajenko** and the **Cologne Gürzenich Orchestra**. 1, 4, 7, 8, 11 and 15 were recorded at live concerts at the Cologne Philharmonic in 2003–4 and the remaining nine at the Stolberger Straße Studios. Kitajenko has the measure not only of the tauter works such as 1 and 9, but also of the epic canvases of 8 and 11. His *Tenth* has the tragic power and concentration that this great symphony calls for. Readers needing a complete survey, recorded in magnificent and finely detailed sound, with performances that rarely fall short of distinction, can invest in this set with confidence.

No one artist or set of performances holds all the insights into this remarkable symphonic canon, but what can be said of **Haitink's** set is that the playing of both the **London Philharmonic** and the **Concertgebouw** orchestras is of the highest calibre and is very responsive; moreover the Decca recordings, whether analogue or digital, are consistently of this company's highest standard, outstandingly brilliant and full. If without the temperament of a Mravinsky, Haitink proves a reliable guide to this repertoire, often much more than that, and sometimes inspired. All in all, a considerable achievement. The 11 discs are now offered together at bargain price.

(i) *Symphony 1 in F min.*, Op. 10; (ii) *Festive Overture*. Collection: *The Age of Gold: Polka; Ballet Suite 1: Galop; Music-box Waltz; Dance; Ballet Suite 2: Polka; Galop; The Gadfly: Introduction; Barrel Organ Waltz; Nocturne; Folk Festival; Galop; Moscow-Cheryomushki: Overture Waltz; Galop

🡒 ✹ Ⓑ **** Sony (ADD) SBK 62642. (i) Phd. O, Ormandy; (ii) Columbia SO, Kostelanetz

Ormandy and the **Philadelphia Orchestra** recorded this version of the *First Symphony* in the presence of the composer in 1959. It is a beautifully proportioned, tense and vivid account. The sound, too, is excellent. Still, after 40 years, a front-runner in spite of some excellent successors. The coupling could not have been better chosen: a suite of Shostakovichian orchestral lollipops selected by Kostelanetz, a dab hand at this kind of audacious light music. **Kostelanetz** plays this music for all it is worth, and if again the recording is brash, this time it fits the music like a glove.

Symphony 1 in F min. (complete; DVD version, plus rehearsal)

(N) 🎬.*,**** Medici Arts DVD 2072158. Schleswig-Holstein Music Festival O, Bernstein

As **Bernstein** says before he begins the rehearsal which goes with this performance, Shostakovich's *First Symphony* is a quirky, unpredictable piece which pokes fun at authority with an 'Up yours' attitude, yet which begins to falter as its young composer suddenly finds himself being taken over by the expressive power of the music he is writing. So this is no ordinary rehearsal. The orchestral players learn much more than they expected about what the composer is trying to convey, and so do we. The performance of the symphony itself has extraordinary power, a palette of colour and revelation of detail far beyond what we hear during an ordinary account. It is also thrilling, marvellously played and very vividly recorded. Bernstein has such a friendly spirit of communication as he unlocks the music's secrets that, by watching and listening to this DVD, it is possible to get inside this very remarkable and original work that was its composer's symphonic début.

Symphonies (i) 1; (ii) 5

(M) **(*) LPO **SACD** LPO 0001. LPO, Masur

(N) (B) ** CfP (ADD 2 28283-2. (i) Philh., Kurtz; (ii) Chicago SO, Previn

These live recordings from the first batch of the **LPO's** own-label discs demonstrate the orchestra at its finest. The crispness and point of the ensemble and the refined beauty of the strings are most impressive, recorded in full, forward sound at Royal Festival Hall concerts early in 2004. **Masur** as the orchestra's music director has perfect control, even if his reading of the *First Symphony* is more remarkable for its brilliance than for its wit; for all the beauty, refinement and precision of the *Fifth*, it remains a little straight-faced, contemplative in the first and third movements, and genuinely jubilant in the rumbustious finale, ignoring the element of irony.

Kurtz's account of 1 has the distinction of being one of EMI's first stereo recordings – and very good it still sounds, as does the excellent performance with the **Philharmonia Orchestra** on top form. Unfortunately, **Previn's** account of the *Fifth Symphony*, which is also extremely well played and recorded, is disappointing by comparison, for the reading has little sense of freshness or urgency.

Symphonies 1; 5 in D min., Op. 47; (i) 7 (Leningrad); Prelude 14 in E flat min., Op. 34 (arr. Stokowski)

(***) Pearl GEMM CDS 9044 (2). Phd. O; (i) NBC SO, Stokowski

Stokowski's *First Symphony* was recorded in 1934, less than a decade after its première under Malko. The sound is dryish, but there is tremendous atmosphere and concentration, and the transfers are excellent. Stokowski's (1939) pioneering *Fifth* is an electrifying performance, impeccably played and splendidly transferred. The slow movement has a gripping intensity that is quite exceptional. The famous transcription of the *E flat minor Prelude*, Op. 34, has a brooding, Mussorgskian

menace all its own, while Stokowski's *Leningrad Symphony* is hardly less gripping. This *Leningrad* for all its sonic defects makes for exciting listening.

Symphonies 1; 6 in B min., Op. 54

*** Chan. 8411. SNO, Järvi

Järvi's account of the *First Symphony* is more volatile than Haitink's in the outer movements – there is no lack of quirkiness in the finale, while the *Largo* is intense and passionate. The *Sixth* has comparable intensity, with an element of starkness in the austerity of the first movement. The *Scherzo* is skittish at first but, like the finale, has no lack of pungent force.

Symphonies 1 & 7 (Leningrad)

(N) (B) ** DG 477 7587 (2). Chicago SO, Bernstein

A two-disc set for these two symphonies is extravagant, but **Bernstein's** expansive treatment of both works demands it. The **Chicago Symphony Orchestra** plays superbly for him, but the full bite and ruthlessness of the *Leningrad Symphony* are largely missing, with the celebrated ostinato of the first movement dragging at a slow speed. The soft-grained quality extends to Bernstein's Chicago view of 1, which does not match the performance on DVD, although the manically energetic sequences of the second and fourth movements spark him to performances of characteristically high voltage. Full-bodied sound.

Symphonies 1, Op. 10; 9 in E flat, Op. 70

🎬 (M) *** Warner Elatus 2564 60121-2. Nat. SO of Washington, Rostropovich

In **Rostropovich's** hands the youthful *First Symphony* begins very promisingly and continues well. Indeed, there is plenty of fulfilment. The reading is free from exaggeration, even if the Scherzo is rushed off its feet. The *Ninth*, too, is well served: the slow movement is shapely, and there is only one moment of agogic exaggeration. Rostropovich is also given a decently balanced recording, and this can certainly be recommended to those looking for this particular coupling.

Symphonies 2, Op. 14 (To October); (i) 12 in D min., Op. 112 (The Year 1917)

🎬 *** EMI 3 35994-2. Bav. RSO; (i) & Ch., Jansons

By general consent the *Twelfth* is the emptiest and weakest of the Shostakovich symphonies, yet in the hands of a Mravinsky it can exert a strange and compelling fascination. **Mariss Jansons** and the wonderful, rich-toned **Bayerisches Rundfunk Orchestra** do their very best for the piece and for the *Second*, also inspired by the October revolution. The latter never really lives up to the promise of its opening, but there is no question that Jansons secures first-class performances of both and that the recording quality does full justice to the Munich players.

Symphonies (i) 2 (October); (ii) 14, Op 135

(M) **(*) Warner Elatus 2564 61374-2. (i) London Voices, LSO; (ii) Vishnevskaya, Reshetin, Moscow Ac. SO (members); Rostropovich

The two **Rostropovich** performances were recorded 20 years apart, 2 in London in 1993 and 14 much earlier in Moscow. In 2 the **LSO** respond to his direction with real fervour, everything is well prepared and well thought out. The performance of *No. 14* is dark and intense, with expressive detail sometimes underlined. **Vishnevskaya** will not be to all tastes (she is thin and shrill above the stave at the top of her register), but **Reshetin** is most impressive. The soloists are balanced a little too close, but otherwise the sound has fine presence and definition in both recordings.

Symphony 4 in C min., Op. 43 (DVD Version)

(N) *** Medici Arts DVD 3085276. BBC SO, Rozhdestvensky (with RIMSKY-KORSAKOV: *Russian Easter Festival Overture*; RACHMANINOV: *Piano Concerto 1* ***)

The *Fourth* gets an intensely felt and highly imaginative performance from the **BBC Symphony Orchestra**, even if memories of Kyril Kondrashin's pioneering 1961 recording are not banished. This telecast has good sound and has the benefit of discreetly directed camerawork, even if the images have lost some of their freshness. It comes from a 1978 Prom, while its companions, the *Russian Easter Festival Overture* of Rimsky-Korsakov and Rachmaninov's *First Piano Concerto* with **Victoria Postnikova** (Rozhdestvensky's wife) as the brilliant soloist, are taken from a 1979 Prom. There is no programme note. Recommendable nonetheless.

Symphony 4 in C min., Op. 43 (CD versions)

*** Avie AV 2114. WDR SO, Cologne, Bychkov

🎵 *** EMI 5 57824-2 Bav. RSO, Jansons

*** Chan. 8640. SNO, Järvi

Semyon Bychkov has recorded the *Fifth*, *Eighth* and *Eleventh Symphonies* with the Berlin Philharmonic for Philips, on which we reported in earlier editions. The present account comes from 2005 and has great concentration and power; indeed this is probably the most intense reading since Kondrashin's pioneering 1961 record.

The **Bavarian Radio Orchestra** is one of the finest in Europe and under **Mariss Jansons** it produces a wonderful range of sonorities and finely blended tone. The EMI recording is very detailed and present, and Jansons is completely inside the work and conveys his intentions in masterly fashion.

Järvi draws from the **SNO** playing which is both rugged and expressive, consistently conveying the emotional thrust of the piece and making the enigmatic ending, with its ticking rhythm, warmer than usual, as though bitterness is finally evaporating. He is helped by exceptionally rich, full recording.

'The War Symphonies' (Documentary on Symphonies 4–9 by Larry Weinstein; Prod: Niv Fichman; DVD version)

🎵 *** Ph. DVD 074 3117. Kirov O or Rotterdam PO, Gergiev

Don't be put off by the tabloid-like title 'Shostakovich against Stalin', for there is nothing glib or crude about this remarkable and searching documentary. Anyone who cares about the Shostakovich *Symphonies* should lose no time in getting

this DVD. It includes contributions from Shostakovich's circle of family, including his daughter Galina, friends and colleagues. They and the widow of the composer Shebalin all bear witness to what life was like during the terrible Stalinist years. The programme has a unique authority – as one would expect, given the participation of **Gergiev**, whose brainchild it was, and the collaboration of Elizabeth Wilson, daughter of a former British Ambassador to Moscow and author of an excellent biography of the composer. There is even an appearance by Khrennikov, who launched the attack on 'formalism' during the 1948 Congress of Soviet Composers presided over by Zhdanov. There is a great deal of rare archive material.

Symphony 5 in D min., Op. 47 – see also Cello Concerto 1

🎵 **** BBC (ADD) BBCL 4165-2. LSO, Stokowski – VAUGHAN WILLIAMS: *Symphony 8* ***

(***) BBC Legends mono BBCL 4193-2. Hallé O, Barbirolli – BEETHOVEN: *Symphony 5* (***)

(i) Symphony 5 in D min., Op. 47; (ii) Chamber Symphony in C min. (arr. of String Quartet 8)

🎵 (M) *** Sony SK 94733. (i) NYPO, Bernstein; (ii) MITD SO, Barshai

(i) Symphony 5; (ii) Hamlet (film incidental music), Suite, Op. 116

🎵 (M) **** RCA (ADD/DDD) 82876 55493-2. (i) LSO, Previn; (ii) Belgian RSO, Serebrier

Previn's RCA version, dating from early in his recording career (1965), remains among the top of the list for this much-recorded symphony, sounding excellent in this new transfer. This is one of the most concentrated and intense readings ever, superbly played by the LSO at their peak. In the third movement, Previn sustains a slower speed than anyone else, making it deeply meditative in its dark intensity, while the build-up in the central development section brings playing of white heat. The bite and urgency of the second and fourth movements are also irresistible. Only in the slight lack of opulence in the violins does the sound fall short of the finest modern recordings, but it is more immediate than most. The playing of the **Belgian Radio Orchestra** under **Serebrier** on the *Hamlet Suite* is eminently serviceable without being really distinguished but, with an atmospheric recording, this 28-minute suite makes a considerable bonus.

Stokowski's performance, recorded live in the Royal Albert Hall in the 1964 Prom season, vividly demonstrates that even in his eighties he had few rivals in inspiring performances of the highest voltage. The Shostakovich *Fifth Symphony* was his favourite, and here the biting tensions of the opening are masterfully contrasted with the pure, sinuous lines of the second subject in a performance of exceptional refinement and dedication, with each movement bringing fresh revelations, fully faithful to the score. Excellent stereo sound, remarkably vivid for a radio broadcast of the period. Very well coupled with another revelatory performance of Vaughan Williams's *Symphony 8*.

Though in 1966, when **Barbirolli** made this live recording, Shostakovich was a composer he rarely conducted, the insights here are many, with Barbirolli typically adopting steady, measured speeds, with ample expressiveness in the phrasing but relatively little use of rubato. That makes the long first movement seem exceptionally spacious, but the equivalent slow movement then crowns the performance emotionally, with playing of keen concentration, leading to a thrustful account of the rumbustious finale. A fine, revealing coupling.

Unashamedly, **Bernstein** treats the work as a romantic *Symphony*. The very opening makes a strong impact and then, exceptionally, in the cool and beautiful second-subject melody Bernstein takes a slightly detached view, though as soon as that same melody comes up for development after the exposition the result is altogether more warmly expressive. Yet the movement's central climax, with its emphasis on the deep brass, injects a powerful element of menace, and the coda communicates a strongly Russian melancholy, which is perhaps why the composer admired Bernstein above other American interpreters of his music. The *Allegretto* becomes a burlesque, but here its Mahlerian roots are strongly conveyed. The slow movement is raptly beautiful (marvellously sustained *pianissimo* playing from the **New York** strings) and the finale is brilliant and extrovert, with the first part dazzlingly fast and the conclusion one of unalloyed triumph, even if its very vehemence suggests a hollow victory. The performance of the *Chamber Symphony* under **Barshai** is no less intense and deeply expressive in its essential melancholy, but more austere in texture and refined in feeling. It is superbly played and recorded.

(i) *Symphony 5 in D min., Op. 47;* (ii) *7 Romances on Poems of Alexander Blok, Op. 127*

(N) *(**) Ondine **SACD** ODE 1109-5. (i) Phd. O, Eschenbach; (ii) Naef, Kang, Hai-Ye Ni, Eschenbach (piano)

The **Philadelphia Orchestra**, and especially the strings, always have something special to contribute to the *Fifth Symphony*, but here **Eschenbach's** interpretation is muted and certainly lacking in the passionate thrust that Stokowski brought to this work. Moreover, the coda curiously hangs fire. The recording is spectacular, especially on SACD. The *Seven Romances* are given an intense performance by **Yvonne Naef**, at times very histrionic, at others touchingly gentle.

Symphonies (i) *5;* (ii) *6 in B min., Op. 54*

(M) *** Warner Elatus 0927 46732-2. (i) Leningrad PO, Mravinsky; (ii) Nat. SO of Washington, Rostropovich

(BB) *** Regis RRC 1075. Cologne RSO, Barshai

Mravinsky conducted the première of the *Fifth Symphony* in 1937 and so brings a special authority to this work. This Erato Elatus account emanates from a concert performance almost half a century later (in 1984); but there is still evidence of a commanding personality and, even though the recording itself is not in the luxury bracket, this performance must figure high on any list. It comes coupled with **Rostropovich's** *Sixth*, recorded ten years later in the Washington Kennedy

Center. In his spacious account of the opening *Largo*, Rostropovich does not wear his heart on his sleeve, and the burlesque Scherzo which follows is pointed with nice ironic geniality, while the following finale bursts with witty high spirits. Excellent orchestral playing and fine recording make this a coupling to reckon with.

Rudolf Barshai's coupling comes from concert performances in the **Cologne Philharmonie** in 1995–6. Barshai's credentials in this repertoire are well known. He conducted the first recording of the *Fourteenth Symphony* and has, of course, arranged the *Fourth, Eighth* and *Tenth Quartets* for full strings with the composer's blessing. These are very well-prepared and expertly played accounts, which are finely shaped and felt.

Symphonies 5 in D min.; 9 in E flat, Op. 70

(BB) **** Naxos 8.550427. Belgian R. & TV O, Rahbari

Both in the hushed intensity of the lyrical passages and in the vigour and bite of Shostakovich's violent *Allegros* **Rahbari's** reading is most convincing, with dramatic tensions finely controlled in a spontaneous-sounding way. In *9* Rahbari opts for a controversially slow *Moderato* second movement but sustains it well, and the outer movements are deliciously witty in their pointing. The playing of all sections is first rate, and the sound is full and brilliant.

Symphonies 6 in B min.; 9 in E flat (DVD version)

🎬 *** DG **DVD** 073 4170. VPO, Bernstein

The *Ninth Symphony* was recorded in October 1985 and the *Sixth* 12 months later. The first movement of the *Sixth* is deeply felt, as indeed is the slow movement of the *Ninth*. Bernstein enjoyed a very strong rapport with the **Vienna Philharmonic Orchestra** and Humphrey Burton's direction is appropriately unobtrusive. Bernstein introduces both works with his customary lucidity.

Symphony 7 in C (Leningrad), Op. 60

🎬 **** MDG **Surround Sound SACD** 937 1203-6. Beethoven O, Bonn, Kofman

*** Chan. 8623. SNO, Järvi

*** Naïve V 5971. O. Nat. de France, Masur

(BB) *** Regis RRC 1074. Cologne RSO, Barshai

(BB) **(*) Sony (ADD) SBK 89904. NYPO, Bernstein

This superbly realistic and spectacular new recording from the unlikely source of the **Beethoven Orchestra**, Bonn, rather sweeps the board. **Roman Kofman** has the full measure of this remarkable *Symphony*. He builds the famous first-movement ostinato with unremitting concentration into an overwhelming climax, and his reading creates a satisfying combination of passion and irony in the work as a whole, with raptly beautiful playing and great intensity from the strings in the *Adagio* and jubilant triumph at the work's close. The recording is very much in the demonstration bracket, whether using two speakers or four.

Järvi's is a strong, intense reading, beautifully played and recorded, which brings out the full drama of this *Symphony* in a performance that consistently gives the illusion of spontaneity in a live performance, as in the hushed tension of the slow, expansive passages.

Masur and his fine Paris Orchestra recorded the *Seventh* at the Théâtre des Champs-Elysées in May 2006, before bringing it to the BBC Proms a couple of months later. There is nothing over- or under-stated about this convincing and thoughtful performance, which can be rated among the best. Good sound.

Barshai's recording comes from a concert performance in the **Cologne Philharmonie** in 1992. There is no bombast, yet the understatement does not entail loss of character and impact, and the sound quality is very good indeed, thanks to the excellent Cologne acoustic.

Bernstein brings a certain panache and fervour to his reading, particularly in the inspired slow movement, so that one is tempted to look indulgently at its occasional over-statements.

Symphony 8 in C min., Op. 65

**** BBC (ADD) BBCL4002-2. Leningrad PO, Mravinsky – MOZART: *Symphony 33 in B flat, K.319* ******

(BB) ******* Regis RRC 1250. Leningrad PO, Mravinsky

(BB) ******* EMI Encore (ADD) 5 09024-2. LSO, Previn

(B) ******* CfP 587 034-2. Bournemouth SO, Barshai

Mravinsky's BBC recording comes from the Festival Hall Concert given on the Leningrad Orchestra tour in 1960 at which Shostakovich himself was present. This transfer reproduces the occasion with great realism and a wide dynamic range. This reading has tremendous intensity and authenticity of feeling. It comes with a bonus – the first half of the concert, which was given over to an elegant performance of Mozart's *Symphony 33*. Even among modern recordings this more than holds its own and the sound is very good indeed. Mandatory listening.

The Regis reissue is of a live performance given in 1982, but not, it seems, the account which appeared on Philips and which has been strongly recommended by us in the past. It would be easy to think it was, for **Mravinsky's** pacing is very similar. However, this alternative account is marginally less concentrated than the Philips version and takes fractionally longer overall. Even so, this Regis version can still be strongly recommended at its modest price, for Mravinsky's interpretation of this work is very special and the recording sounds impressive as remastered here.

With **Previn**, the opening slow movement emerges not only as involving but also cogent in symphonic terms. The sharp predictability of the remaining movements, alternately cajoling and battering the listener, shows Shostakovich at his most inspired. The **LSO** is prompted by Previn to playing that is both intense and brilliant, while the 1973 Abbey Road recording is outstandingly rich and vivid for its time.

Barshai holds up surprisingly well against the competition. The noble symphonic *Adagio* which opens the work is marvellously sustained, and the playing of the **Bournemouth Orchestra** is extremely fine in all departments. This is a finely paced and powerful reading which, particularly in the first movement, has a wonderful brooding intensity and eloquence. The *Passacaglia* has a real epic sweep. As far as sound

quality is concerned, the balance of this 1985 recording could hardly be improved upon, and the excellent acoustic is used to splendid and thrilling effect.

Symphony 9 in E flat, Op. 70 (DVD version)

⊕→ ******* Arthaus **DVD** 100 302. Bav. RSO, Solti (V/D: Klaus Lindemann) – TCHAIKOVSKY: *Symphony 6* ****(*)**

Solti's performance of the *Ninth Symphony* (filmed in 1990) is admirable. He catches its wit and humour readily (one responds to the occasional half-smile on his face) and, with his economical, purposive gestures, he is a pleasure to watch. The **Bavarian Radio Orchestra** plays marvellously and obviously are enjoying themselves too, appreciating the yearning lyricism of the second movement as well as the humour. The camera observes everything without moving about excessively.

Symphony 9 in E flat, Op. 70; Festive Overture, Op. 96; Katerina Ismailova (Lady Macbeth of Mtsensk): 5 Entr'actes; Tahiti Trot (arr. of Youmans's Tea for Two), Op. 16

⊕→ ******* Chan. 8587. SNO, Järvi

Järvi's version of the *Ninth* brings a warmly expressive, strongly characterized reading in superb, wide-ranging sound and the fill-up items are well worth having too.

Symphony 10 in E min., Op. 93

⊕→ (M) ******** DG 477 5909. BPO, Karajan

(M) ****(*)** Warner Elatus 2564 60660-2 Leningrad PO, Mravinsky (with WAGNER: *Tristan: Prelude and Liebestod* ****(*)**)

(N) (M) ****(*)** LPO LPO 0034. LPO, Haitink

Symphony 10 in E min., Op. 93; Ballet Suite 4

*** Chan. 8630. SNO, Järvi

Already in his 1967 recording **Karajan** had shown that he had the measure of this symphony; this newer version is, if anything, even finer. In the first movement he distils an atmosphere as concentrated as before, bleak and unremitting, while in the *Allegro* the **Berlin Philharmonic** leave no doubts as to their peerless virtuosity. Everything is marvellously shaped and proportioned, and the early (1981) digital sound is made firmer by this 'original-image' bit re-processing.

Mravinsky conducted the work's première. This Elatus recording was made at a 1976 concert performance and it has no want of intensity or power. The recording is less than ideal, but this is a performance to reckon with, and the Wagner bonus (recorded live, two years later) also rises to a passionate climax.

Järvi, too, conducts an outstandingly strong and purposeful reading in superb sound, full and atmospheric, and the *Ballet Suite* makes an attractive bonus.

Haitink's recording dates from 1986 and comes from the BBC archives. It has more flair than his Decca studio version, and the live occasion ensures that the adrenalin flows readily enough, especially in the violent Scherzo. The opening movement, however, has a certain spacious dignity. The

Royal Albert Hall acoustic ensures richly full-bodied textures and, while not a first choice, this is still a very considerable performance.

(i) *Symphony 10 in E min., Op. 93* (arr. for piano duet); (ii) *4 Preludes from Op. 34* (arr. for violin & piano)

Ⓜ (***) Revelation mono RV 70002. Composer; with (i) Vainberg; (ii) Kogan

The recording may be primitive but this is of great documentary interest, capturing Shostakovich and his fellow composer **Moisei Vainberg** playing the *Tenth Symphony* in a piano-duet arrangement only a few months after its completion and not long before Mravinsky made the première recording. They play with great fervour and strain the instrument to the limit. The performance is surprisingly brisk (47 minutes as opposed to the usual 50) and completely involving. The transcriptions of the *Preludes* are wonderfully played by **Kogan** and the composer, and there are also a few bars from *The Gadfly* too.

Symphony 11 *(The Year 1905), Op. 103*

🎙 *** Testament SBT 1099. French R.O., Cluytens

Ⓝ ⒝⒝ *** Naxos 8.572082. RLPO, Petrenko

Cluytens's performance was recorded in Paris in the presence of the composer. It appears now in stereo for the very first time and sounds quite astonishing. Indeed, it stands up to modern competition very well. Shostakovich called the *Eleventh* his 'most Mussorgskian work' and it was clear to Soviet audiences that its 'subtext' was not so much the abortive February rebellion of the title as the events in Budapest, where the Soviet Union had just suppressed the Hungarian uprising.

Although our allegiance to the pioneering French Radio performance under André Cluytens remains unshaken, this newcomer on Naxos is certainly a strong competitor. The performance has great intensity of spirit and much atmosphere and, at its bargain price, is likely to attract many collectors. It augurs well for the promised cycle of which this is the first instalment.

Symphony 13 in B flat min. *(Babi-Yar)*

🎙 *** EMI 5 57902-2. Aleksashkin, Bav. R. Ch. & SO, Jansons

*** Sup. SU 0160-2 231. Mikuláš, Prague Philharmonic Ch., Prague SO, M. Shostakovich

With the superb Russian bass **Sergi Aleksashkin** dominating the performance, so that the **Bavarian Radio Chorus** too are encouraged to sing with intense Slavonic fervour, **Jansons's** new EMI recording is very powerful indeed. The work's dark, forceful irony is well caught in the *Allegretto* second movement, yet it is in the third movement that the performance reaches its merciless climax which is so well resolved in the epilogue-like finale, strangely uplifting with its celestial flutes. Jansons secures splendid playing from the **Bavarian Orchestra**. The EMI recording has great vividness and atmosphere.

Maxim Shostakovich's Supraphon version, with sound so vivid you hear some alien noises, is menacingly atmos-

pheric, one of the finest of his recordings of his father's symphonies. Helped by the immediate sound, he sustains each movement with fine concentration, with each movement heightened by characterful singing from the superb Czech bass **Peter Mikuláš**.

Symphonies Nos. (i) 13 *(Babi Yar), Op. 113;* (ii) 14, *Op. 135. 15, Op. 141*

Ⓜ **(*) DG 474 469-2 (2). Gothenburg SO, Järvi; with (i) Kotscherga, Estonian Nat. Male Ch.; (ii) Kazarnovskaya, Leiferkus

Järvi has a good feeling for Shostakovich and this two-CD DG reissue offers a generally recommendable set of performances with impressive soloists. In *Babi Yar*, **Anatoly Kotscherga** proves resonantly theatrical and the **Estonian Choir** sing confidently and idiomatically. Throughout all three *Symphonies*, the recording is impressively spacious and, as full texts and translations are included, this set is well worth considering.

Symphony 14 in G min., Op. 135

🎙 ⒝⒝ *** Naxos 8.550631. Hajóssyová, Mikuláš, Slovak RSO (Bratislava), Slovák

**(*) BBC (ADD) BBCB 8013-2. Vishnevskaya, Rezhetin, ECO, Britten – BRITTEN: *Nocturne* **(*)

Slovák's account of 14 is one of the finest, strongly characterized in each of the 11 contrasted movements with the help of two superb soloists. **Mikuláš** is just as strong and individual as in 13, and **Hajóssyová**, with her firm, Slavonic mezzo, is equally idiomatic. The booklet gives a summary of each poem, but no texts or translations. Full, immediate sound.

This was the symphony which Shostakovich dedicated to **Britten**, and this Snape Maltings performance of 1970 with the **ECO** conducted by Britten was the very first outside Russia. **Galina Vishnevskaya's** sharply distinctive soprano has rarely sounded so rich or firmly focused on disc, and the bass, **Mark Rezhetin**, firm and dark, sings gloriously too. The tensions of a live performance add to the drama, poignantly so, when both Britten and Shostakovich were facing terminal illness.

CHAMBER MUSIC

Adagio and Allegretto for String Quartet; (i) *Piano Quintet, Op. 57;* (ii) *2 Pieces for String Octet, Op. 1/1;* (i) *5 Pieces for 2 Violins and Piano* (arr. Atovmian)

🎙 **** Challenge CC 72093. Brodsky Qt (members); with (i) Blackshaw; (ii) Shave, Theaker, Atkins, Baillie; (available from www.challengeclassics.com)

A superb collection. Like the **Brodsky's** equally recommended coupling of *String Quartets* by Britten and Tchaikovsky, the sense of spontaneous, live music-making inhabits every bar here. The range of mood is remarkably wide. The early *Pieces for String Octet*, Op. 1 are as wild and uninhibited as the delightful *Pieces for Two Violins and Piano* are elegantly tuneful. The deeply expressive *Adagio* and quirky *Allegretto* are arrangements of Katerina's aria from *Lady Macbeth of the Mtsensk District* and the famously witty *Polka* from *The Golden Age* ballet. But the key work here is the *Piano Quintet*, a marvellously concentrated performance. The second movement *Fugue-Adagio* and the *Intermezzo* both open with a rapt *pianissimo* framing the bold, jaunty central *Scherzo* and leading on to the puissant finale. Excellent recording throughout, although some might think the acoustic for the *Quintet* gives the piano a rather too resonant image.

Cello Sonata in D min., Op. 40

⊕⊶ (BB) *** Virgin 2x1 4 82067-2 (2)-2. Mørk, Vogt –
MIASKOVKY; RACHMANINOV; PROKOFIEV: *Cello Sonatas*;
STRAVINSKY: *Suite italienne* ***

*** Chan. 8340. Turovsky, Edlina – PROKOFIEV: *Sonata* ***

*** BIS CD 336. Thedéen, Pöntinen – SCHNITTKE: *Sonata*;
STRAVINSKY: *Suite italienne* ***

Truls Mørk and **Lars Vogt** can more than hold their own with the best. The performances are very vital and intelligent, and eminently well recorded and the couplings are astonishingly generous.

Yuli Turovsky and **Luba Edlina** play the *Cello Sonata* with great panache and eloquence, if in the finale they almost succumb at times to exaggeration in their handling of its humour – no understatement here.

The Swedish cellist **Torleif Thedéen** has a real feeling for its structure and the vein of bitter melancholy under its ironic surface. **Roland Pöntinen** gives him excellent support and the BIS recording does justice to this partnership.

(i) Cello Sonata in D min., Op. 40; Moderato for cello & piano; (ii) Piano Quintet; (iii) 2 Pieces

⊕⊶ (BB) *** Double Decca 473 807-2 (2). (i) Harrell;
(i; ii) Ashkenazy; (ii) Fitzwilliam Qt – PROKOFIEV: *Cello Sonata*; RACHMANINOV: *Cello Sonata*, etc. ***

Lynn Harrell and **Vladimir Ashkenazy** give a convincing account of the *Cello Sonata*, though they slow down rather a lot for the second group of the first movement. All the same, their brisk tempo and their freedom from affectation are refreshing. The short *Moderato* for cello and piano was discovered in the Moscow State Archives only in the 1980s. The *Piano Quintet*, with Ashkenazy and the **Fitzwilliam Quartet**, cannot be seriously faulted and withstands comparison with the illustrious Richter and Borodin Quartet version, and the recording is superb. With the highly attractive *Two Pieces* – the first mysteriously haunting, the second delightfully quirky – also included, this set, with its excellent couplings, is an undoubted bargain.

(i; ii) Cello Sonata; (iii) Violin Sonata; (iv) The Gadfly: Romance; Nocturne

⊕⊶ (BB) *** Naxos 8.557722. (i) Yablonsky; (ii) Saranseva;
(iii) Fedotov, Petrova; (iv) Russian PO

The *Cello Sonata* is a relatively early work, dating from 1934, but the Shostakovich idiom is already clearly established, not only in the sharply rhythmic writing of the fast movements, but also in the darkness and hushed intensity of the

third-movement Largo, beautifully brought out by the cellist **Dmitry Yablonsky**. The *Violin Sonata* dates from much later in the composer's career (1968), a work inspired by David Oistrakh. It is a masterly work, ending with the last of the *Passacaglias* which he wrote, an extended, spare and dark piece evoking a mood of disquieting calm in music of high contrasts. Again the performance is masterly, with **Maxim Fedotov** as violinist. The concertante piece taken from the music to *The Gadfly* is here just as effective on the cello as in the original version with violin.

Piano Quintet in G min., Op. 57

⊕⊶ (M) *** Warner Elatus 2564 60813-2. Leonskaja, Borodin Qt

⊕⊶ (BB) *** Naxos 8.554830-2. Berman, Vermeer Qt –
SCHNITTKE: *Piano Quintet* ***

(***) Testament mono SBT 1077. Aller, Hollywood Qt –
FRANCK: *Piano Quintet* (***)

(M) **(*) CRD (ADD) CRD 3351. Benson, Alberni Qt –
BRITTEN: *Quartet 1* ***

Piano Quintet in G min., Op. 57; Piano Trio 2 in E min., Op. 67

**(*) Chan. 8342. Borodin Trio, Zweig, Horner

Piano Quintet in G min., Op. 57; Piano Trio 2 in E min., Op. 67; 4 Waltzes for Flute, Clarinet & Piano

⊕⊶ (BB) *** Virgin 2x1 5 61760-2 (2). Nash Ens. –
SCHOENBERG: *Chamber Symphony, Op. 9, etc.* **(*)

The **Nash Ensemble** on Virgin offer the ideal coupling – plus an interesting makeweight – of two of Shostakovich's key chamber works, written before his quartet series developed, when he had completed only the first, relatively trivial work. The *Piano Trio* is a particularly painful and anguished work, dedicated to the memory of a close friend, Ivan Sollertinsky, who died in the year of its composition. The **Nash** players bring out the dedicated intensity in this very personal writing, with refined readings which can be warmly recommended, and the new pairing with Schoenberg makes for a highly intriguing collection, well worth its modest cost. But the Shostakovich items are also available separately on 3 91337-2.

It is luxury casting to have on the Naxos budget label the **Vermeer Quartet**, one of the finest in America, in partnership with another star artist, **Boris Berman**. This is a dedicated performance, recorded for Canadian radio, which with fearlessly extreme dynamic contrasts brings out the full greatness of the piece. The Schnittke *Piano Quintet* of 1972–5 makes an apt and unusual coupling, similarly one of the composer's finest chamber works. The CBC studio recording is acceptable, and if the sound is somewhat wanting in warmth and bloom this is a still a formidable bargain.

With **Leonskaja** leading, yet still very much a partner, these Teldec performances of the *Piano Quintet* and *Second Trio* are very fine indeed, with inspired playing from all concerned. The very wide range of dynamic and string timbre of the *Fugue*, with the music initially sustained on a thread of tone, moving to a climax and back, has enormous concentration, and the spikier humour of the *Scherzo* is splendidly pointed. After the poignant *Intermezzo*, the close of the finale is most subtly managed. Similarly, the valedictory *E minor Piano Trio* opens with an exquisitely withdrawn pianissimo, and the robust *Scherzo* has vehement bite.

On Testament is a magisterial account of the *Piano Quintet* if ever there was one. This belongs among the finest of interpretations. Its praises were sung by the authors of *The Record Guide* in the mid-1950s when they spoke of it in their down-to-earth manner as 'a dazzling performance and their tone, though often extremely delicate, is never skinny'. Readers who care about Shostakovich should find it an indispensable issue and need make few allowances for the 1952 sound.

The Chandos version is bold in character and concentrated in feeling. Alternatively, there is a vigorous and finely conceived account from **Clifford Benson** and the **Alberni Quartet**, vividly recorded; if the Britten coupling is wanted, this will be found fully satisfactory.

Piano Trios 1, Op. 8; 2, Op. 67

🎵—*** Simax PSC 1147. Grieg Trio – BLOCH: *3 Nocturnes*;
  MARTIN: *Piano Trio on Irish Folktunes* ***

🎵—*** Nim. NI 5572. V. Piano Trio – SCHNITTKE: *Trio* ***

The first of the Shostakovich *Piano Trios* remained in the obscurity of manuscript, until one of Shostakovich's students, the composer Boris Tischenko, put it into performable shape (20 bars had gone missing). The **Grieg Trio** play it with vital feeling and sensitivity; its dreamy opening, a kind of impressionistic Schumann, sounds exceptionally convincing in their hands. Moreover, they give as fine an account of the wartime *Piano Trio in E minor* as any now before the public. The couplings further enhance the value of this issue.

The **Vienna Piano Trio** on Nimbus also give cogently argued and finely paced accounts of both the Shostakovich trios. The Vienna are among the best and are naturally and vividly recorded. If the 1985 Schnittke *Trio* appeals as a coupling, this is an eminently desirable recommendation.

Piano Trio 2 in E min., Op. 67

Ⓑ *** Decca 475 6712 (2). Bell, Mustonen, Isserlis –
  PROKOFIEV: *Violin Concertos & Sonatas* ***

ⒷⒷ **(*) Regis Alto ALC 1005. Tirimo, Sayevich, Veis –
  TCHAIKOVSKY: *Piano Trio* **(*)

The Decca is a marvellously telling and perceptive account of Shostakovich's masterpiece and is very truthfully balanced. The only snag is the very wide dynamic range of the recording. The opening *piano/pianissimo* has ethereal concentration, but registers so quietly that the listener is tempted to turn up the volume. If one does, the *fortissimos* are not quite comfortable, for the microphones are fairly close. But it is possible to get it right and the rewards of the playing are very considerable

A first-class account from **Tirimo** and his colleagues, recorded in Prague in 2005. The playing is expert, crisp and intense, with the Scherzo engagingly witty. The recording is a bit too close, but vivid and truthful. Coupled with an ex-

cellent version of the great Tchaikovsky *Trio*, this budget disc is worth anyone's money.

2 Pieces for String Octet, Op. 11

*** Chan. 9131. ASMF Chamber Ens. – ENESCU: *Octet in C*;
  RICHARD STRAUSS: *Capriccio: Sextet* ***

The **Academy of St Martin-in-the-Fields Chamber Ensemble** play splendidly and with conviction; they are beautifully recorded and also offer a highly recommendable version of the Enescu *Octet*.

String Quartets

String Quartets 1–15; (i) Piano Quintet; (ii) 2 Pieces for String Octet, Op. 11

🎵—Ⓑ *** Melodiya (ADD) 100177 (6). Borodin Qt; with (i) S.
  Richter; (ii) Prokofiev Qt

First issued on EMI, then on BMG, the **Borodin Quartet's** second recording of the *String Quartets* now reverts to Melodiya and, on six CDs, including the *Piano Quintet* and the *Two Pieces for String Octet*, makes a very economical investment when purchased complete. The present recordings are made in a generally drier acoustic than their predecessors, and 3 and 5 suffer noticeably in this respect. However, the transfers are clean and faithful, and the ears quickly adjust when the performances can only be described as masterly. The Borodins possess enormous refinement, an altogether sumptuous tone and a perfection of technical address that is almost in a class of its own – and what wonderful intonation. The *Piano Quintet* was recorded at a concert at the Moscow Conservatory, and it goes without saying that with Richter at the helm the account is powerful, although the quality of the sound here is noticeably dry and forward. The *Two Pieces for String Octet* are now added to the second CD.

String Quartets 1–15

🎵—Ⓑ *** Fuga Libera FUG512. Danel Qt

String Quartets 1–15; (i) Piano Quintet

*** Chan. 10398 (6). Sorrel Qt; (i) with Roscoe

String Quartets 1–15; 3 Pieces for String Quartet, Op. 36

🎵— ⒷⒷ *** Regis (ADD) 5001 (5). Shostakovich Qt

String Quartets 1 in C, Op. 49; 2 in A, Op. 68; 3 in F, Op. 73; 4 in D, Op. 83; 5 in B flat, Op. 92; 7 in F sharp min., Op. 108; 2 Pieces, Op. 36 (Regis (ADD) 2028 (2))

String Quartets 6 in G, Op. 101; 8 in C min., Op. 110; 9 in E flat, Op. 117; 10 in A flat, Op. 118; 11 in F min., Op. 122; 15 in E flat min., Op. 144 (Regis (ADD) 2029 (2))

String Quartets 12 in D flat, Op. 133; 13 in B flat min., Op. 138; 14 in F sharp min., Op. 142 (Regis (ADD) 1024)

ⒷⒷ *** Shostakovich Qt

String Quartets 1–15; Adagio (Elegy after Katerina's Aria from Scene 3 of Lady Macbeth of the Mtsensk District); Allegretto (after Polka from The Age of Gold ballet, Op. 22)

**(*) DG 463 284-2 (5). Emerson Qt

The eponymous **Shostakovich Quartet** recorded a cycle over the period 1978 to 1985 and bring a special intensity to this repertoire as well as effortless technical address, and a tonal blend that gives their readings a strong claim on the collector's allegiance.

The **Danel Quartet's** survey, recorded by Bayerisches Rundfunk over the period 2001–5 is of the highest quality, thoughtful and inward. The recordings too are very good, though in some instances there is not quite enough air round the sound. But this is a distinguished cycle, offered with exemplary presentation and at budget price.

The **Sorrel Quartet** are sound and reliable guides in this cycle, and indeed they are often touched with distinction. Given the good recording and competitive price, this offers a useful alternative choice.

If sheer brilliance and virtuosity were all that mattered, the **Emerson Quartet** would lead the field. Their playing is technically immaculate, with spot-on intonation, accuracy and unanimity of ensemble, but they bring an unrelieved intensity to everything they touch and offer little real repose, when that is called for.

String Quartets 1; 4; 9

**** HM HMC 891865 Jerusalem Qt

Although we are well served in this repertoire, this version by the **Jerusalem Quartet** is arguably the finest to appear since the days of the Borodin and Fitzwilliam sets in the 1970s. This young group brings tremendous concentration and commitment to the three *Quartets* recorded here, and even if you have either of the classic sets mentioned above – or indeed the eponymous group on Regis – you should try to hear this illuminating and brilliantly recorded newcomer.

String Quartets 1; 8 & 9 (Naxos 8.550973)

String Quartets 2 in A, Op. 68; 12 in D flat, Op. 133 (Naxos 8.550975)

(BB) *** Eder Qt

String Quartets 4; 6–7 (Naxos 8.550972)

(BB) *** Eder Qt

The **Eder Quartet** is a very distinguished ensemble and have a very good feeling for this repertoire, and those for whom economy is a primary concern should consider this.

String Quartets 2; 3; 7; 8; 12

(BB) *** Virgin 5 61630-2 (2). Borodin Qt

The third series of **Borodin** accounts now on a Virgin Double have the benefit of far better and more refined recording than their earlier, Melodiya versions. The sound is richer, cleaner and has a pleasing bloom, as one would expect from the Snape Maltings. As far as the performances are concerned, some things come off better than others so

that on balance there is little to choose between the earlier and newer sets; those who have the former need not make a change. This is one of the greatest quartets now before the public and they are completely inside this music.

String Quartets 3 in F, Op. 73; 7 in F sharp min., Op. 108; 8 in C min., Op. 110

**** DG 477 6146. Hagen Qt

*** EMI 3 59956-2. St Lawrence Qt

*** BIS CD 913. Yggdrasil Qt

Three identical couplings. The **Hagens'** present coupling is recorded in a sympathetic acoustic (the Grosse Universitäts Aula, Salzburg) and finds them on top form. The *Eighth* has splendid intensity and they invest the post-war *Third* (1946) with much feeling.

Generally speaking, the Hagen Quartet are marginally to be preferred to the **St Lawrence Quartet**, though this ensemble, new to the catalogue, play with great freshness and fervour; their disc will not in any way disappoint those who invest in it.

The **Yggdrasil Quartet** are a young Swedish group who are now embarking on a Shostakovich cycle. This first issue is an auspicious start with a bold and searching account of the autobiographical *Eighth*, and intelligent and satisfying readings of its companions.

String Quartets 4; 8 & 11

*** ASV CDDCA 631. Coull Qt

The *Fourth Quartet* is a work of exceptional beauty and lucidity, one of the most haunting of the cycle; the *Eleventh Quartet* is a puzzling, almost cryptic work in seven short movements. The **Coull Quartet** are among the most gifted of the younger British quartets and give eminently creditable accounts of all three pieces. Good if slightly overlit recording.

String Quartet 8, Op. 110

(M) *** Classic fM 75605 57027-2. Chilingirian Qt – BORODIN: *Quartet 2*; DVOŘÁK: *Quartet in F, Op. 96* ***

On Classic fM the **Chilingirians** also give a tautly controlled performance, not as flexible as some but with the power enhanced by the rich, immediate digital recording.

String Quartet 15

*** ECM 461 815-2. Keller Qt. – SCHNITTKE: *Piano Quintet* ***

Sorrow drained to the bitterest dregs is how one eminent critic described the *Fifteenth Quartet*. The **Keller Quartet** make out a strong case for the work, and they are superbly recorded.

Violin Sonata, Op. 134

*** Chan. 8988. Mordkovitch, Benson – PROKOFIEV: *Sonatas*; SCHNITTKE: *In Memoriam* ***

(*) Chan. 8343. Dubinsky, Edlina – SCHNITTKE: *Sonata 1*; etc. *

The *Violin Sonata* can seem a dry piece, but **Mordkovitch's** natural intensity, her ability to convey depth of feeling without sentimentality, transforms it. **Clifford Benson** is the understanding pianist. In first-rate sound it makes a fine central offering for Mordkovitch's well-planned disc of Soviet violin music.

Rostislav Dubinsky's account is also undoubtedly eloquent, and **Luba Edlina** makes a fine partner. The recording is excellent too, although it is balanced a shade closely.

PIANO MUSIC

Aphorisms, Op. 13; 3 Fantastic Dances, Op. 5; Piano Sonata 1; 24 Preludes, Op. 34

⊕ (BB) *** Naxos 8.555781. Scherbakov

Beautifully recorded at Potton Hall in Suffolk, **Konstantin Scherbakov** gives thought-provoking and wonderfully controlled accounts of the Op. 34 *Preludes*. By comparison with Nikolayeva he is at times a little too sophisticated in matters of tonal finesse, and dynamic markings are a shade exaggerated; but this has such imaginative and masterly pianism that readers can afford to overlook the occasional affectation. He plays the whole recital with the keyboard mastery we associate with him. Strongly recommended.

24 Preludes, Op. 34; Prelude & Fugue in D min., Op. 87/24; Piano Sonatas 1, Op. 12; 2 in B min., Op. 61

⊕ *** Athene ATH CD 18. Clarke

24 Preludes; Piano Sonata 2, Op. 61; 3 Fantastic Dances, Op. 5

⊕ *** Hyp. CDA 66620. Nikolayeva

Raymond Clarke generously couples the two *Sonatas* with the aphoristic and witty *Preludes*, Op. 34, and these new performances are a viable first-choice for anyone coming to this repertoire afresh.

Tatiana Nikolayeva is very well recorded indeed. She is one of the authentic advocates of Shostakovich, and her CD will be a must for most collectors. Recommended alongside Clarke.

24 Preludes and fugues, Op. 87 (DVD version)

(N) *** Medici Arts **DVD** 3085248. Nikolayeva

During the Bach bicentenary year in 1950, Shostakovich heard the *Forty-Eight* played by the young **Tatiana Nikolayeva** with such admiration that he composed his own *Preludes and Fugues* for her. Some 40 years on, she recorded them in Scotland for BBC Television, and her mastery still shines through. Authoritative performances, well recorded and with discreet, intelligent camerawork, this is a set to cherish. There is a short but admirable feature by the artist, setting out the circumstances of their composition.

24 Preludes & Fugues, Op. 87 (CD version)

⊕ ✹ (BB) *** Regis RRC 3005 (3). Nikolayeva

In this repertoire, the first choice must inevitably be **Tatiana Nikolayeva**, 'the onlie begetter', as it were, of the *Preludes and Fugues*. Her reading has enormous concentration and a natural authority that is majestic. There is wisdom and human-

ity here, and she finds depths in this music that have eluded most other pianists who have offered samples.

Preludes & Fugues, Op. 87/5 & 24

⊕ (M) *** EMI (ADD) 3 45819-2. Gilels – RACHMANINOV: *Piano Concerto 3*; SAINT-SAËNS: *Piano Concerto 2* ***

These two *Preludes and Fugues* make a fine contrasting encore for **Gilels's** Rachmaninov and Saint-Saëns *Concertos*; the *Second*, the last of the 24, brings a tremendous crescendo and is very commanding indeed. Good recording too.

VOCAL MUSIC

The Execution of Stepan Razin, Op. 119; October: 5 fragments

(BB) *** Naxos 8.557812. Charles Robert Austin, Seattle Ch. & SO, Schwarz

The Execution of Stepan Razin is a setting of Yevtushenko and comes two years after the *Thirteenth Symphony*. It does not have the concentration or emotional intensity of the symphony, but it is well worth hearing. Kondrashin's pioneering recording of 1969 is no longer in circulation; until it returns, this well-played and expertly recorded version will serve well.

Songs: (i) 2 Fables of Krylov; From Jewish Folk Poetry, Op. 79a; 6 Poèmes d'Alexandre Blok, Op. 127; 6 Poems of Marina Tsvetayeva, Op. 143; 3 Romances on Poems by Pushkin, Op. 46; 6 Romances, Op. 62/140; 6 Romances on Texts by Japanese Poets, Op. 21; Suite of Verses of Michelangelo Buonarroti, Op. 145a; 4 Verses of Captain Lebyadkin; (ii) Lady Macbeth of Mtsensk District (opera; complete)

⊕ **** (B) Decca 475 7441 (5). (i) Leiferkus, Orgonosova, Levinsky, Zaremba, Fischer-Dieskau, Söderström, Shirley-Quirk, with Ashkenazy (piano) or Gothenburg SO, Järvi; (ii) Ewing, Haugland, Langridge, Larin, Ciesinski, Zednik, Bastille Op. Ch. & O, Chung

An outstanding compilation of Shostakovich's songs, as well as **Myung-Whun Chung's** superb version of *Lady Macbeth of Mtsensk*. Shostakovich's songs brim with character and nuance: the first two CDs are with **Neeme Järvi** and the **Gothenburg Orchestra**, and the accompaniments are of as much interest and importance as the vocal lines themselves. Järvi coaxes playing which is both atmospheric and sensitive and this is very much one of the main joys of these recordings. The soloists are characterful and distinguished. **Ashkenazy** provides excellent accompaniments for both the **Fischer-Dieskau** and **John Shirley-Quirk** items on the third CD and the **Söderström** recordings, with violin, cello and piano, are quite superb, with haunting, spine-tingling atmosphere in the quiet numbers and plenty of drama in the lively ones. Myung-Whun Chung's performance of *Lady Macbeth of Mtsensk* is very successful too and the most moving account on disc. **Maria Ewing** gives a vulnerable portrayal of her character in this 1992, (originally) DG recording with moods and responses subtly varied. As a heroine, she is insinuatingly seductive in singing that is far more sensuous, with the beauty of tone and hushed *pianissimos* most tenderly affecting. **Sergei Larin** as Katerina's labourer-lover equally gains by sounding more aptly youthful, with his tenor sounding both firm and clear yet Slavic-sounding. **Aage Haugland** is magnificent as Boris, Katerina's father-in-law, and **Philip Langridge** sings sensitively as her husband, Zinovi, while **Kurt Moll** as the Old Convict provides emotional focus in his important solo at the start of the last Act. The recording is atmospheric. Texts and translations are provided in this handsome bargain set.

OPERA

The Gamblers

Ⓝ *** AVIE 2121 (2). RLPO, Petrenko

Based on a play of Gogol, Shostakovich wrote this fragment of an opera during the war, but failed to complete it. What we have here is very promising, with sharp focus in the typical hard-edged themes. **Petrenko** proves a powerful advocate with the **RLPO**.

Lady Macbeth of Mtsensk (DVD version)

⌕ *** Opus Arte **DVD** OA 0965 D (2). Westbrook, Ventris, Wilson, Vaneev, Ludha, Netherlands Op. Ch., Concg. O, Jansons (Dir: Martin Kušej; V/D: Ferenc van Damme)

Mariss Jansons, an inspired interpreter of Shostakovich, conducts a searingly dramatic performance of *Lady Macbeth of Mtsensk* (the violent original score, not the rewrite, *Katerina Ismaelova*) with the glorious sounds of the **Royal Concertgebouw Orchestra** bringing beauty as well as power. The casting is strong, with **Eva-Maria Westbrook** in the title-role bringing out the poignancy of her situation, as her love for the workman, Sergei, turns sour and finally tragic, a role well sung and acted by **Christopher Ventris**. Outstanding too is the dark and sinister bass, **Vladimir Vaneev**, as the evil father-in-law, Boris. As her husband, Zinovy, the character tenor **Ludovico Ludha** is ideally cast, as is the Chief of Police, sung by **Nikita Storajev**. The production is updated, generally effectively, but with various oddities resulting.

Lady Macbeth of Mtsensk (complete; CD Version)

⌕ ❀ Ⓜ **** EMI (ADD) 5 67776-2 (2). Vishnevskaya, Gedda, Petkov, Finnilä, Krenn, Tear, Malta, Valjakka, Amb. Op. Ch., LPO, Rostropovich

Rostropovich, in his finest recording ever, proves with thrilling conviction that this first version of Shostakovich's greatest work for the stage is among the most original operas of the century. **Vishnevskaya** is inspired to give an outstanding performance and provides moments of great beauty alongside aptly coarser singing; **Gedda** matches her well, totally idiomatic. As the sadistic father-in-law, **Petkov** is magnificent, particularly in his ghostly return, and there are fine contributions from **Robert Tear**, **Werner Krenn**, **Birgit Finnilä** and **Alexander Malta**.

The Nose

Ⓝ *** Mariinsky 0501 (2). Sulimsky, Tanovitski, Semishkur, Skorokhodov, Mariinsky O & Ch., Gergiev

With a cast drawn entirely from the Mariinsky company under its long-time Music Director, **Valeri Gergiev**, this first issue on the Mariinsky's own label is a resounding success. Though the recording, directed by James Mallinson, was made in the company's concert hall, the performance of this satirical opera based on Gogol plainly reflects the company's experience in the opera-house, very important when timing is so vital. This is an early work of the composer, with percussion very prominent along with the typical motor rhythms of early Shostakovich. The pay-off in Act III brings a powerful swipe on the bass drum, vividly caught.

SIBELIUS, Jean (1865–1957)

Andante festivo (for strings & timpani); The Bard; (i) Violin Concerto, Op. 47; En Saga (revised 1902); (ii) Karelia Suite (includes Ballade); Kuolema: Valse triste; The Oceanides; Pohjola's Daughter; Porilaisen Marssi (arr. Sibelius); Tapiola; The Wood Nymph

Ⓜ *** BIS CD 1557/8. Lahti SO, Vänskä; with (i) Kavakos; (ii) Laukka

This is the third collection of Sibelius's shorter orchestral works from **Osmo Vänskä**, plus of course the mature *Violin Concerto* of 1905, which he and **Kavakos** have already recorded successfully, coupled to the earlier, 1903/4 version. Some of the other works here are also duplicated on the earlier discs, including *En Saga, The Oceanides, Pohjola's Daughter, Tapiola*, and *The Wood Nymph. The March of the Pori Regiment* is orchestrated from a traditional melody used by the Finnish armed forces for their parades. *Karelia* comes with a sung version of the *Ballade* by **Raimo Laukka**. While not all these performances are first choices (notably *The Oceanides*), Vänskä and his fine orchestra are thoroughly at home in this repertoire, and the recording is first class. If you want this particular group of works, this set is excellent value.

Andante festivo; The Bard; Canzonetta, Op. 62a; En Saga; Finlandia; Karelia Suite; King Christian II (Suite), Op. 27; Kuolema: Valse triste; Scene with Cranes, Op. 44/1–2; 4 Legends, Op. 22; (i) Luonnotar, Op. 70; Night Ride and Sunrise, Op. 55; 4 Legends, Op. 22; The Oceanides, Op. 73; Pohjola's Daughter; Spring Song, Op. 16; Tapiola, Op. 112; Valse romantique, Op. 62b

⌕ Ⓑ **** DG Trio 477 5522 (3). Gothenberg SO, Järvi; (i) with Isokoski

This impeccably recorded, bargain-priced Trio groups together three separate CD collections of Sibelius's orchestral works, each of which has been highly praised by us. It includes one of the best accounts of *The Oceanides* we have had since the celebrated Beecham version, and a first-class *Luonnotar. The Bard* is brooding and mysterious, the *Canzonetta* for strings and *Valse triste* have great poetry, and the *Scene with Cranes* is full of atmosphere. **Järvi** gives a passionate and atmospheric reading of the first *Legend*, and his account of *The Swan of Tuonela* is altogether magical, one of the best in the catalogue. He takes a broader view of *Lemminkäinen in Tuonela* than many of his rivals and builds up an appropriately black and powerful atmosphere. The disappointment is *Lemminkäinen's Homeward Journey*, which lacks the possessed, manic quality of Beecham's very first record (see below), which sounded as if a thousand demons were in pursuit. However, *Tapiola* is a great success: Järvi produces a performance of commanding power, and the unhurried (and all the more terrifying) storm is judged excellently. *En Saga*, on the other hand, fares less well and at times seems almost matter of fact, although the introspective, quieter sections in the middle and closing paragraphs are evocative. *Spring Song* also borders on the routine – but then so does the music. Certainly overall this is an estimable survey, and the modern digital sound and truthful balance are equally commendable.

(i) *Andante festivo;* (ii) *En Saga;* (iii) *Pohjola's Daughter;* (iv) *Rakastava; Impromptu*

(***) Ondine mono/stereo ODE 992-2. (i) Finnish RSO, Composer; (ii) Swedish RSO, Franck; (iii) Tampere PO, Ollila; (iv) Virtuosi di Kuhmo, Czaba – KAJANUS: Aino ***

Though, unlike Svendsen and Nielsen, Sibelius was not a conductor by profession, he was a highly effective interpreter of his own music. The *Andante festivo* is the only surviving recording of him conducting and he draws playing of great intensity. (An earlier account attributed to him was in fact a recording of a rehearsal under Tauno Hannikainen.) **Mikko Franck's** version of *En Saga* is both concentrated and atmospheric. There is a more than serviceable account of *Pohjola's Daughter* and an affecting *Rakastava*, while the *Impromptu* is an arrangement for strings of two early piano pieces, Op. 5. The bonus is a rarity, the 1991 recording under **Jorma Panula** of *Aino* by Sibelius's great champion, Robert Kajanus, which was the spark that kindled the flame that led to Sibelius's *Kullervo Symphony*.

Autrefois (Scène pastorale), Op. 96b; The Bard, Op. 64; Presto in D for Strings; Spring Song, Op. 16; Suite caractéristique, Op. 100; Suite champêtre, Op. 98b; Suite mignonne, Op. 98a; Valse chevaleresque, Op. 96c; Valse lyrique, Op. 96a

*** BIS CD 384. Gothenburg SO, Järvi

A mixed bag. *The Bard* is Sibelius at his greatest and most powerful, and it finds **Järvi** at his best. The remaining pieces are all light: some of the movements of the *Suite mignonne* and *Suite champêtre* could come straight out of a Tchaikovsky ballet, and Järvi does them with great charm. The last thing that the *Suite*, Op. 100, can be called is *caractéristique*, while the three pieces, Op. 96, find Sibelius in Viennese waltz mood. The rarity is *Autrefois*, which has a beguiling charm and is by far the most haunting of these pastiches. Sibelius introduces two sopranos and their *vocalise* is altogether captivating. The *Presto in D major for Strings* is a transcription – and a highly effective one – of the third movement of the *B flat Quartet*, Op. 4. Excellent recording.

BIS Sibelius Edition, Volume 1: Tone-Poems: *The Bard; The Dryad; En Saga; Finlandia* (with

preliminary version: *Finland Awakes*); 4 *Lemminkäinen Legends* (original & final versions); *Luonnotar* (with Helena Juntunen); *Night Ride & Sunrise; The Oceanides; Tapiola; Pohjola's Daughter; The Wood Nymph; Cassione; Dance Intermezzo* (with preliminary version); *In Memoriam; Scènes historiques I & II; Spring Song* (with preliminary version)

Ⓑ *** BIS-CD 1900/02 (5). Lahti SO, Vänskä; or Gothenburg SO, Neeme Järvi

This set collects together the major orchestral works in thoroughly recommendable performances, given first-class BIS recordings and offered at a very reasonable price.

The Bard, Op. 64; En Saga, Op. 9; Finlandia, Op. 26; Legend: Lemminkäinen's Return, Op. 22; Symphony 4 in A min., Op. 63

⊘ ⒷⒷ (***) Naxos mono 8.110867. LPO, Beecham

The merits of these classic recordings are too well known to require further exegesis. The transfers by Mark Obert-Thorn are very good indeed (though so were the earlier, HMV issues by Anthony Griffith) and can be confidently recommended.

Belshazzar's Feast, Op. 51: Suite. Canzonetta, Op. 62a; Kuolema: Scene with Cranes; Valse triste, Op. 44/1–2. Night Ride and Sunrise, Op. 55; Pan and Echo, Op. 53; 2 Pieces, Op.45; Valse romantique, Op. 62b

Ⓝ ⒷⒷ *** Naxos 8.570763. New Zealand SO, Inkinen

This is the Finnish conductor **Pietari Inkinen's** second Sibelius anthology with the excellent **New Zealand Symphony Orchestra**, and for the most part he again stays off the beaten path. The *Canzonetta* and *Valse romantique* are little more than salon pieces, but his delicacy of feeling gives them status. *Pan and Echo* and the engaging *Suite* from *Belshazzar's Feast* are more substantial and, like the masterly *Night Ride and Sunrise*, are played with splendid idiomatic feeling. The favourite *Valse triste* once again, in its charm, shows just why it is a favourite. First-class recording completes the listener's pleasure in an anthology that is worth every penny of its modest cost.

Belshazzar's Feast (suite), Op. 54; *Dance Intermezzo, Op. 45/2; The Dryad, Op. 45/1; Pan and Echo, Op. 53; Swanwhite, Op. 54*

⊘ **** BIS CD 359. Gothenburg SO, Järvi

Belshazzar's Feast, a beautifully atmospheric piece of orientalism, and the incidental music for Strindberg's *Swanwhite* may not be Sibelius at his most powerful, but both include wonderful things. **Neeme Järvi's** collection with the **Gothenburg Orchestra** is first class in every way.

The Breaking of the Ice on the Oulo River; Press Celebrations Music; Song of the Athenians

*** BIS CD 1115. Lahti SO, Vänskä

A recording which will be of compelling interest for all Sibelians. It contains the music Sibelius composed for a pageant in 1899, the so-called *Press Celebrations Music*, from which he later fashioned the first set of *Historic Scenes* and *Finlandia*. In all there is some 40 minutes of music. Here we have Sibelius's original thoughts, as well as a *Prelude for Wind Instruments* and two movements which he left in manuscript. Not all of it is top-drawer Sibelius, but the fifth tableau is powerful and atmospheric, and it is surprising that he made no effort to reshape it and include it with the other *Historic Scenes*. The third tableau is the original version of the *Boléro*, which Sibelius revised in 1900 and then again in 1911 as *Festivo*. There are other rarities from the same period, including *The Breaking of the Ice on the Oulo River*, all worth hearing and given an excellent performance by **Osmo Vänskä** and the **Lahti Symphony Orchestra** and first-rate recorded sound.

Cassazione, Op. 6 (first version); Coronation March; Cortège; Morceau romantique sur un motif de Monsieur Jakob de Julin; Musik zu einer Scene; The Oceanides, Op. 73 (final and Yale versions). Spring Song. Trad.: March of the People of Pori (arr. Sibelius)

*** BIS CD 1445. Lahti SO, Vänskä

Osmo Vänskä and the **Lahti Symphony Orchestra** add to their outstanding Sibelius series with this fascinating collection of rarities, centring on *The Oceanides*, the only item here that has been recorded before. The original MS eventually found its way into the Yale University Library and, although its existence has long been known to scholars, it makes its début on record. So, too, do two further MS pieces which Sibelius himself called 'Fragments for a Suite for Orchestra/Predecessor of *The Oceanides*'.

The Oceanides is one of Sibelius's greatest tone-poems and the Yale MS gives a fascinating glimpse of its gestation. Originally called *Rondo of the Waves*, it presents the material in an unexpected order, with what became the main theme set nearer the middle and with the stormy climax even more of a culmination than in the final version, making the result more dramatic.

Otherwise, the most substantial work here is the *Cassazione*, which in this original version of 1904 uses a bigger orchestra than what became Op. 6. The first version contains a quite ethereal episode for wind. The tiny *Morceau romantique*, written for a charity concert, whose opening bars sound almost like Rachmaninov, becomes a jolly waltz movement. The *Coronation March* of 1896, which comes from the music Sibelius composed for Tsar Nicholas II, is unlike any coronation march you have ever heard. *Spring Song* of 1895 is uninhibitedly melodic, and *Cortège* in a polonaise rhythm is rather like the *Karelia Suite*. Trivial or not, it makes compelling listening, helped by masterly performances and beautifully balanced recording. This is a most interesting and rewarding issue, excellently annotated.

Cassazione, Op. 6; Preludio; The Tempest: Prelude & Suites 1–2, Op. 109; Tiera

&— *** BIS CD 448. Gothenburg SO, Järvi

Järvi's recording of Sibelius's incidental music to *The Tempest*

is among the most atmospheric since Beecham and, though it does not surpass the latter in pieces like *The Oak-Tree* or the *Chorus of the Winds*, it is still very good. The *Cassazione* resembles the *King Christian II* music in character, but it is well worth having on disc. Neither *Tiera* nor the *Preludio*, both from the 1890s, is of great interest or particularly characteristic.

Violin Concerto in D min. (1903–4 version); Violin Concerto in D min., Op. 47 (1905; published version)

&— Ⓜ *** BIS CD 300500. Kavakos, Lahti SO, Vänskä

The first performance of the *Violin Concerto* left Sibelius dissatisfied, and he immediately withdrew it for revision. This CD presents Sibelius's initial thoughts so that for the first time we can see the familiar final version struggling to emerge from the chrysalis. Comparison of the two Concertos makes a fascinating study: the middle movement is the least affected by change, but the outer movements are both longer in the original score, and the whole piece takes almost 40 minutes. The Greek violinist **Leonidis Kavakos** proves more than capable of handling the hair-raising difficulties of the 1904 version and is an idiomatic exponent of the definitive concerto. The **Lahti Orchestra** under **Osmo Vänskä** give excellent support and the balance is natural and realistic. An issue of exceptional interest and value.

Violin Concerto in D min., Op. 47 (CD versions)

&— ✸ Ⓜ **** Sony SMK 89748. Lin, Philh. O, Salonen – NIELSEN: *Violin Concerto* *** ✸

&— **** HM Naïve V 4959. Sergey Khachaturian, Sinfonia Varsovia, Krivine – KHACHATURIAN: *Violin Concerto* ***

&— Ⓜ **** Decca 475 7734. Chung, LSO, Previn – TCHAIKOVSKY: *Violin Concerto* ***

&— Ⓜ *** RCA (ADD) 82876 66372-2. Heifetz, Chicago SO, Hendl – GLAZUNOV: *Concerto*; PROKOFIEV: *Concerto 2* ***

*** EMI 5 56418-2. Chang, BPO, Jansons – MENDELSSOHN: *Violin Concerto in E min* ***

Ⓜ *** Ph. 464 741-2. Mullova, Boston SO, Ozawa – TCHAIKOVSKY: *Violin Concerto* **(*)

Ⓜ *** EMI (ADD) 5 62590-2. Perlman, Pittsburgh SO, Previn – KORNGOLD: *Concerto*; SINDING: *Suite* ***

*** EMI 7 54559-2. Kennedy, CBSO, Rattle – TCHAIKOVSKY: *Concerto* **(*)

*** Erato 4509-98537-2. Repin, LSO, Krivine – TCHAIKOVSKY: *Violin Concerto* ****

Ⓜ (***) EMI mono 4 76830-2. Neveu, Philh. O, Susskind – BRAHMS: *Violin Concerto* (***)

BB *** Naxos 8.550329. Kang, Slovak (Bratislava) RSO, Leaper – HALVORSEN: *Air norvégien*, etc.; SINDING: *Légende* ***; SVENSSEN: *Romance* ***

BB (**(*)) Naxos mono 8.110938. Heifetz, LPO, Beecham – TCHAIKOVSKY: *Violin Concerto*; WIENIAWSKI: *Violin Concerto 2 in D min.* (***)

Ⓜ **(*) Warner Elatus 0927 46743-2. Vengerov, Chicago SO, Barenboim – TCHAIKOVSKY: *Violin Concerto* ****

Violin Concerto; 2 Serenades, Op. 69; Humoresque 1 in D min., Op. 87/1

*** DG 447 895-2. Mutter, Dresden State O, Previn

Violin Concerto; Serenade 2 in G min.

(BB) **(*) Naxos 8.557266. Kraggerud, Bournemouth SO, Engeset – SINDING: *Violin Concerto*, etc. ***

(i) Violin Concerto; The Tempest: Prelude; Suites 1 & 2, Op. 109

*** Häns. 98353. (i) Sitkovetsky; ASMF, Marriner

Cho-Liang Lin's playing is distinguished not only by flawless intonation and an apparently effortless virtuosity but also by great artistry. He produces a glorious sonority at the opening and the slow movement has tenderness, warmth and yet restraint with not a hint of over-heated emotions. Lin encompasses the extrovert brilliance of the finale and the bravura of the cadenza with real mastery. The **Philharmonia Orchestra** rise to the occasion under **Esa-Pekka Salonen**, and the recording is first class.

Sergey Khachaturian comes from a famous Armenian musical family and in 2000 he won first prize in the Jean Sibelius competition in Helsinki. His account of the *Concerto*, although opening ethereally, is full of Slavic feeling, with the slow movement passionately intense. It is a powerfully spontaneous performance, very well accompanied by the excellent Polish **Sinfonia Varsovia**, and excellently recorded. The coupling is an outstanding account of the (underrated) Khachaturian *Violin Concerto*.

Kyung-Wha Chung's feeling for the Sibelius *Concerto* is second to none, and **Previn's** accompanying cannot be praised too highly: it is poetic when required, restrained and full of controlled vitality and well-defined detail. The Kingsway Hall recording is superbly balanced.

Heifetz's stereo performance of the Sibelius *Concerto* with the **Chicago Symphony Orchestra** under **Walter Hendl** set the standard by which others have come to be judged. It is one of his finest recordings; in remastered SACD form the sound is vivid, the Chicago ambience making an apt setting for the finely focused violin line.

In her live recording, made at a concert in the Philharmonie, **Sarah Chang** gives an astonishingly mature reading of the Sibelius. She may not be as passionate as her fellow-Korean, Kyung-Wha Chung, but with sweet, refined tone the thoughtfulness and spontaneous poetry of the playing make her comparably magnetic. Warm, atmospheric sound.

Viktoria Mullova's account of the *Concerto* is very successful, capturing its magical element right from the very opening, while the slow movement has a cool dignity that is impressive. What this concerto needs above all else is finesse and a certain aristocratic feeling, as well as warmth, which is free of the *Zigeuner* element, and Mullova meets these combined needs admirably. The recording is excellent.

Where most violinists treat the opening as a deep meditation, **Mutter** makes it tougher than usual, less beautiful, using momentarily a vibratoless, slightly steely tone. Not that her reading lacks inner qualities for, despite the close balance, the opening of the slow movement finds Mutter playing in rapt meditation on a half-tone. In the finale, taken fast, power is again the keynote. **Previn** draws a committed performance from an orchestra not noted for playing Sibelius. In the two *Serenades*, Mutter, at her most inspired, beautifully captures the wayward, quasi-improvisatory quality of these pieces.

Perlman plays the work as a full-blooded virtuoso showpiece, and the **Pittsburgh Orchestra** under **Previn** support him to the last man and woman. In the first movement his tempo is broader than that of **Heifetz**, and in the rest of the work he is more expansive than he was on the earlier record. Perlman is at his stunning best in the first cadenza and he makes light of the fiendish difficulties with which the solo part abounds. He takes a conventional view of the slow movement, underlining its passion, and he gives an exhilarating finale. As usual with this artist, the balance places him rather forward, but the sound is marvellously alive, the CD transfer making the forward balance even more apparent.

Sitkovetsky's is a fine reading, positive, powerful and direct, with no suspicion of self-indulgence. With **Marriner** and the **Academy** in fresh, clear partnership, this is a performance that, warmly expressive as it is, keeps tempi steadier and less volatile than most. In terms of length, the incidental music for *The Tempest*, with 18 brief movements, is the major item here. Thanks to the vividness of the recording, the originality of this late Sibelius inspiration comes over even more strikingly than usual. Marriner reveals the charm of the dance rhythms in such colourful genre movements as *Caliban's Songs* in Suite 1 and the *Dance of the Nymphs* in *Suite 2*

Throughout, **Nigel Kennedy's** intonation is true and he takes all the technical hurdles of this concerto in his stride. There is a touch of the *zigeuner* throb in the slow movement, but on the whole he plays with real spirit and panache. This can be confidently recommended if the coupling with the Tchaikovsky, a rather more indulgent performance, is suitable. The playing of the **Birmingham Orchestra** is excellent throughout as, indeed, is the EMI recording.

The purity and refinement of **Vadim Repin's** playing are what strike one first in his earlier recording with **Krivine**. The withdrawn darkness at the very start quickly opens out thrillingly to reveal his total command, the tautness of his control, with tone sharply focused. Here is a young artist who, for all the brilliance of his virtuosity, regularly keeps a degree of emotion in reserve, his very restraint adding to the intensity. The speed in the finale is thrillingly fast, yet Repin with light attack brings out the scherzando element as well as the passion.

Ginette Neveu's celebrated performance – her first concerto recording, from 1945 – is magnetic from the opening phrase onwards.

Heifetz made his first historic recording of the Sibelius *Violin Concerto* with **Beecham** in 1935, a reading that set standards in virtuosity for generations to come. Next to many later recordings, it may be short on mystery, but the passion as well as the brilliance of the playing is very clear, with Beecham a challenging partner. The Naxos transfer is well balanced but the surface hiss is intrusive at times. But despite Sir Thomas's direction, Heifetz gave the more powerful account of it in his later, Chicago, recording with **Walter Hendl** in the early days of stereo. (The reverse was the case with the Glazunov.)

Dong-Suk Kang chooses some popular Scandinavian repertoire pieces, such as the charming Svendsen *Romance in G*, as makeweights. His version of the *Concerto* is very fine, though the slow movement could do with more tenderness as opposed to passion. There is splendid virtuosity and authoritative playing in the outer movements. The orchestral playing is very acceptable too.

Henning Kraggerud also gives a powerful, red-blooded reading of the Sibelius *Violin Concerto*, treating it as a work very much in the great Romantic tradition. He may lack some of the deeper, more inward qualities that the very finest versions possess, but, with an unusual and very attractive coupling, it stands out among the bargain recommendations. The poignant *G minor Serenade* is also well served.

Maxim Vengerov's Chicago account is dazzling and brilliant. He is much and rightly admired, but here he seems insensitive to the special atmosphere of this work. It is all too glib and flashy. **Barenboim** draws good playing from the **Chicago Orchestra**, and the recording is very full-bodied and pleasant. The Tchaikovsky coupling is a different matter – inspired in every way.

(i) *En Saga, Op. 9; Finlandia;* (ii) *Karelia Suite;* (i) *Legend: The Swan of Tuonela, Op. 22/2; Tapiola, Op. 112*

Ⓜ **(*)** EMI ADD/DDD EMI 4 76846 [476847]. BPO, Karajan

Karajan's *En Saga* is more concerned with narrative than with atmosphere to start with; the climax is very exciting and the *lento assai* section and the coda are quite magical. *Tapiola* is broader and more expansive than the first DG version; at the storm section the more spacious tempo is vindicated, and the climax is electrifying. *The Swan of Tuonela* is most persuasively done. These recordings date from 1977. The later, digital recording of *Karelia* has been added for the current reissue.

En Saga; Karelia Suite; Kuolema: Valse triste; Pohjola's Daughter; Tapiola

**** Australian Ph. Eloquence (ADD) 476 2817. Boston SO, Colin Davis

Beautifully refined and imaginative performances from the **Boston Orchestra**, with a particularly distinguished account of *Pohjola's Daughter*; indeed, it ranks with the very finest ever recorded; **Sir Colin Davis's** maiden has real allure, Väinämöinen's struggles with his various tasks have never been more heroic. The relaxed pace of the *Karelia Suite* works very well, the *Intermezzo* delightful with its unforced yet genuine rhythmic lift which carries one along. There is tremendous atmosphere in these recordings; *Tapiola* is full of mystery and power and, like the rest of the programme, is superbly done. Colin Davis is a born Sibelian and the Boston orchestra play magnificently for him. A very welcome return to the catalogue.

En Saga; Scènes historiques, Opp. 25, 66

*** BIS CD 295. Gothenburg SO, Järvi

Järvi has the advantage of modern digital sound and the **Gothenburg Orchestra** is fully inside the idiom of this music and plays very well indeed. *En Saga* is exciting and well paced.

Finlandia; Kuolema: Valse triste; Legend: The Swan of Tuonela, Op. 22/2

*** DG 439 010-2. BPO, Karajan – GRIEG: *Holberg Suite*, etc. *******

Coupled with Grieg, this is **Karajan** at his very finest in the early 1980s, and the remastered digital recording is impressively real and present, particularly in the languorous *Valse triste* and in *The Swan*, Karajan's third and final account on record, powerful in its brooding atmosphere. There is a touch of brashness in the brass in *Finlandia*, but generally this **Berlin**–Karajan partnership has never been surpassed.

Finlandia, Op. 26; Kuolema, Op. 44: Valse triste; Legend: The Swan of Tuonela, Op. 22/2; Pelléas et Mélisande: Suite, Op. 46; Tapiola, Op. 112

☀ Ⓑ ******** DG (ADD/DDD) 2-CD 474 269-2 (2). BPO, Karajan – GRIEG: *Holberg Suite*, etc. ********

Karajan's *Pelléas* can compare with the classic Beecham version. Indeed, in certain movements, *By the spring in the park* and the *Pastorale*, it not only matches Sir Thomas but almost surpasses him. The *Pastorale* is altogether magical and there is plenty of mystery in the third movement, *At the seashore*, omitted by Beecham. The recording here is in the demonstration bracket and this bargain coupling with Grieg cannot be recommended too highly.

(i) *Humoresque, Op. 87/1* (1st version); *In memoriam* (2 versions); *Legend: Lemminkäinen in Tuonela, Op. 22/3* (reconstructed 1896 version); *3 Pieces, Op. 96; Presto for Strings;* (ii) *2 Serious Melodies, Op. 77*

*** BIS-CD 1485. (i) Kuusisto; (ii) Ylönen; Lahti SO, Vänskä

The first ideas of *In memoriam* date from 1905, but Sibelius did not return to it until late in 1909. Even then he was seized with doubts, particularly concerning the orchestration, and the two versions offer an illuminating study in his compositional processes. In the original suite, *Lemminkäinen in Tuonela* was placed before *The Swan of Tuonela* (hence the numbering), the order being reversed for the 1897 revision. When **Vänskä** recorded the *Suite* in 1999 he included as an appendix the original versions of the first and fourth *Legends* as well as a brief excerpt from *Lemminkäinen in Tuonela*. Now enough of the score and parts have come to light to enable the reconstruction of the complete original, and Sibelians will be able to compare Sibelius's first thoughts (or something closely approaching them) with his final 1939 revision. Impressive playing and recording.

(i) *Six Humoresques, Op. 87 & 89; 2 Serenades, Op. 69; 2 Serious Melodies, Op. 79; Ballet Scene (1891); Overture in E (1891)*

**** BIS CD 472. (i) Kang, Gothenburg SO, Järvi

The *Humoresques* are among Sibelius's most inspired smaller pieces. They are poignant as well as virtuosic and have a lightness of touch, a freshness and a sparkle. The two *Serenades* have great poetic feeling and a keen Nordic melancholy. They are wonderfully played by this distinguished Korean artist, who is beautifully accompanied. The two orchestral works are juvenilia, which predate the *Kullervo Symphony*. There are some characteristic touches, but Sibelius himself did not think well enough of them to permit their publication. All the violin pieces, however, are to be treasured, and the recording is top class.

King Christian II (suite); Pelléas et Mélisande (suite), Op. 46; Swanwhite (suite; excerpts), Op. 54

🎵– *** Chan. 9158. Iceland SO, Sakari

The *King Christian II* music is a winner and full of the most musical touches. It also includes a previously unrecorded *Minuet* and the *Fool's Song*, excellently sung by **Sauli Tiilikainen**. Although the *Pelléas et Mélisande* suite does not displace either Beecham or Karajan, it makes a useful alternative to either – and that is praise indeed! It has plenty of atmosphere and, though tempi are on the slow side, there is always plenty of inner life. The *Swanwhite* (five movements only) is attentive to refinements of phrasing and dynamics and at the same time free from the slightest trace of narcissism. Beautifully natural recording, warm and well balanced.

King Christian II Suite, Op. 27; Scènes historiques: 1, Op. 25; 2, Op. 66

(BB) *** Naxos 8.570068. New Zealand SO, Inkinen

The first set of *Scènes historiques* was drawn from the patriotic pageant mounted in 1899 that included the celebrated *Finlandia* which served to put Sibelius firmly on the map. The second is much later and includes the poetic vignette, *At the drawbridge* and *The Chase*. All of them show Sibelius at his most characteristic. The incidental music for *King Christian II*, a play by his friend Adolf Paul, also comes from the late 1890s. The **New Zealanders** are thoroughly in sympathy with Sibelius's world and play with enthusiasm for their Finnish conductor.

Four Legends from the Kalevala (Lemminkäinen suite), Op. 22; Lemminkäinen and the Maidens of Saari; Lemminkäinen's Homeward Journey (1896 versions); Second ending of Lemminkäinen's Homeward Journey (1897 version); Excerpt from Lemminkäinen in Tuonela (1896 version)

*** BIS. CD 1015. Lahti SO, Vänskä

BIS continues its exploration of the first version of Sibelius's orchestral scores by bringing us the 1896 version of the former and also the first, much longer score of *Lemminkäinen's Homeward Journey*. This is very nearly twice as long as the definitive version and considerably less effective. The first *Legend* underwent a particularly fascinating transformation. The disc also offers the alternative 1897 ending of *Lemminkäinen's Homeward Journey* and an excerpt from *Lemminkäinen in Tuonela*, which Sibelius excised. The

finished work is played in exemplary fashion by **Osmo Vänskä** and his **Lahti Orchestra** and superbly recorded. *The Swan of Tuonela* is highly evocative and way up there among the best.

Four Legends, Op. 22

*** BIS CD 294. Gothenburg SO, Neeme Järvi

Four Legends; The Bard; (i) Luonnotar

(M) *** Chan. (ADD) 6586. SNO, Gibson; (i) with Bryn-Johnson

Four Legends; Tapiola

🎵– **** Ondine ODE 852-2. Helsinki PO, Segerstam

Although **Segerstam** perversely ignores Sibelius's instructions about the order of the *Legends* (so, for that matter, did Salonen), this is of little moment, given the fact that collectors can easily reprogramme the disc. The performances of both the *Legends* and *Tapiola* are first class and are infinitely preferable to the symphony cycle Segerstam recorded in Copenhagen for Chandos. This is now a first recommendation for the *Legends*, while *Tapiola* is one of the best since Karajan.

Neeme Järvi has the advantage of fine, modern digital sound and a wonderfully truthful balance. He gives a passionate and atmospheric reading of the first *Legend*, and his account of *The Swan of Tuonela* is altogether magical, one of the best in the catalogue. He takes a broader view of *Lemminkäinen in Tuonela* than many of his rivals and builds up an appropriately black and powerful atmosphere. The disappointment is *Lemminkäinen's Homeward Journey*, which lacks the possessed, manic quality of Beecham's very first record.

Gibson comes at mid-price and offers sensitive performances of *The Bard* and *Luonnotar*, where the soprano voice is made to seem like another orchestral instrument. The **Scottish Orchestra** play freshly and with much commitment. *The Swan of Tuonela* has a darkly brooding primeval quality, and there is an electric degree of tension in the third piece, *Lemminkäinen in Tuonela*. The two outer *Legends* have ardent rhythmic feeling, and altogether this is highly successful. The recorded sound is excellent.

Rakastava (suite), Op. 14; Scènes historiques, Opp. 25, 66; Valse lyrique, Op. 96/1

🎵– (M) **** Chan. 6591. RSNO, Gibson

Derived from music for a patriotic pageant, the first set of *Scènes historiques* are vintage Sibelius. In the *Love Song* **Gibson** strikes the right blend of depth and reticence, while elsewhere he conveys a fine sense of controlled power. Convincing and eloquent performances that have a natural feeling for the music. Gibson's *Rakastava* is beautifully unforced and natural, save for the last movement, which is a shade too slow. The *Valse lyrique* is not good Sibelius, but everything else certainly is. Gibson plays this repertoire with real commitment, and the recorded sound is excellent, with the orchestral layout, slightly distanced, most believable.

Scaramouche, Op. 71; The Language of the Birds: Wedding March

⊕ *** BIS CD 502. Gothenburg SO, Järvi

Scaramouche, Sibelius's only ballet, is scored for relatively small forces, including piano (not unlike Strauss's music for *Le Bourgeois Gentilhomme*), and at its best it reminds one of the luminous colourings of the *Humoresques* of five years later. A wistful, gentle and haunting score, often inspired though slightly let down by its uneventful second act. Sibelius did not think highly enough of the *Wedding March* to Adolf Paul's play, *The Language of the Birds*, to give it an opus number, but it is in fact quite an attractive miniature. The playing of the **Gothenburg Orchestra** under **Neeme Järvi** is altogether excellent and so, too, is the BIS recording.

SYMPHONIES

Symphonies 1–7; Finlandia, Op. 26; Karelia Suite, Op. 11; Kuolema: Valse triste, Op. 44/1. Rakastava, Op. 16; The Swan of Tuonela, Op. 22/2; Tapiola, Op. 112

Ⓝ **** Exton OVCL-00279 (*Symphonies 1 & 3; Rakastava*); OVCL 00292 (*Symphony 2; Swan of Tuonela; Tapiola*); OVCL 00282 (*Symphonies 4 & 5; Finlandia*); OVCL 00293 (*Symphonies 6 & 7; Karelia Suite; Valse triste*) (available separately) Royal Stockholm PO, Ashkenazy

These performances come from a cycle **Vladimir Ashkenazy** gave in Stockholm in 2006–7, and very impressive they are. Ashkenazy has a pretty unerring feeling for the inner pulse of Sibelius. The *Third* marks a major turning point in his creative development, an affirmation of his oft-quoted remark that classicism is the way of the future. Here is a symphony, if ever there was one, *contra torrentem*. (Think of the opulence of the *First Symphony* only eight years before: nothing could be further removed from its tonal and orchestral palette than the lithe and muscular *Third*.) The *Fourth*, too, is an intense and powerful reading which casts a powerful spell. Occasionally one's thoughts turn to the leaner, chamber-like sonorities of Beecham, but the desolate closing paragraphs of the finale with the repeated oboe phrase (which Sibelius once told his son-in-law, the conductor Jüssi Jalas, represented Peter's thrice denial of Christ) are portrayed with real eloquence. The *Fifth* has the sense of mystery and the majestic breadth required and he handles the transition into the Scherzo section of the first movement with impressive control. The *Sixth* and *Seventh* are hardly less masterly. *Rakastava* occupies a very special place in all Sibelius for its purity and sense of innocence, and Ashkenazy does it with great feeling and restraint. For many collectors the extremely vivid and natural sound of this Stockholm recording will be a decisive factor: it has great presence and realism. But Ashkenazy and his orchestra penetrate the spirit of these wonderful scores.

Symphonies 1–7; (i) Kullervo; The Bard, Op. 22; Finlandia, Op. 26; Karelia Suite, Op. 11; Kuolema: Valse triste; 4 Legends, Op. 22; Night Ride and

Sunrise, Op. 55; The Oceanides, Op. 73; Pohjola's Daughter, Op. 49; Rakastava Tapiola, Op. 112

⊕ ❀ Ⓑ**** **** RCA 82876 55706-2 (7). LSO, C. Davis; (i) with Martinpelto, Fredriksson, LSO Ch.

Symphonies 1–7

⊕ **** DG **SACD**/CD (compatible) 477 5688 (3). Gothenburg SO, Neeme Järvi

Ⓜ **(*) Chan. 6559 (3). SNO, Gibson

Symphonies 1 in E min., Op. 39; 2 in D, Op. 43; 4 in A min., Op. 63; 5 in E flat, Op. 82

Ⓑ *** Ph. Duo (ADD) 446 157-2 (2). Boston SO, Davis

Symphonies 3 in C, Op. 52; 6 in D min., Op. 104; 7 in C, Op. 105; (i) Violin Concerto; Finlandia; Legend: The Swan of Tuonela; Tapiola

Ⓑ *** Ph. Duo (ADD) 446 160-2 (2). (i) Accardo; Boston SO, Davis

Symphonies 1–7; Finlandia; Karelia Suite, Op. 11; Kuolema: Valse triste; Legends: The Swan of Tuonela; Lemminkäinen's Return; Pelléas et Mélisande: Suite; Pohjola's Daughter; Rakastava; Romance for Strings in C, Op. 42; Scènes historiques: All'overtura; The Hunt; Scena

Ⓜ **(*) EMI (ADD) 5 67299-2 (5). Hallé O, Barbirolli

(i) Symphonies 1–7; Karelia Overture; (ii) Karelia Suite; (i) Night Ride and Sunrise; Pelléas et Mélisande: excerpts

⊕ (***) Australian Decca Eloquence 442 9490 (2) (*Symphonies 1–4*); 442 9493 (2) (*Symphonies 5–7 & Orchestral Music*). (i) LSO, Collins; (ii) Danish RSO, Jensen

Sir Colin Davis's RCA set of the *Symphonies* has now been reissued together with his other major **LSO** recordings of the principal orchestral works on 7 CDs. The excellence of the LSO playing is matched by the consistently fine RCA recordings, made in the Blackheath Concert Halls, Watford Town Hall or Walthamstow, between 1992 and 2000. It is a totally authoritative survey, and nearly all the symphonic poems are of a similar calibre, with the magical account of *The Bard*, *Night Ride and Sunrise*, *The Oceanides* and a riveting *Tapiola* standing out. This box should be at the centre of any representative Sibelius collection, especially at its new budget price.

Sir Colin Davis's earlier Boston set of the symphonies, recorded during the second half of the 1970s, includes three tone-poems and an estimable account of the *Violin Concerto* thrown in for good measure. Indeed **Accardo's** performance of the latter is very high on the recommended list. *Tapiola*, too, is atmospheric and superbly played. The idiomatic playing Davis secures from the **Boston Orchestra** is immediately apparent, though the recording is not quite as fine as Ashkenazy's on Decca. In the *Third* Davis judges the tempi in all three movements to perfection; no conductor has captured the elusive spirit of the slow movement or the power of the finale more effectively. The *Fourth* is arguably the finest of the cycle; there is a powerful sense of mystery, and the slow movement in particular conveys the feeling of communication with nature that lies at the heart of its inspiration. The *Fifth* is no match for Karajan, the *Seventh* is not as fine as with Rattle. The *Sixth* is altogether more impressive and much more vivid as sound.

Sir John Barbirolli favoured spacious tempi, but almost always held the listener in his spell. All seven symphonies were recorded in the Kingsway Hall. The first two date from 1966, but in 1 in the present remastering string *fortissimos* are made fierce. No. 2 is in every way more successful. The **Hallé** play particularly well and give a warm-hearted account, romantic in approach. In 3, tempi are well judged, but the inner tension is less well maintained than in 2. Even so, there is some very fine wind-playing in the *Andante* and the transition to the finale is very convincingly managed. In Barbirolli's account of 4 the Hallé strings produce an admirably chilling quality, far removed from the well-nourished string sound in Karajan's Berlin Philharmonic versions. Unfortunately, things come adrift in the development of the first movement where the wind and strings are out of step for quite a few bars. The *Fifth*, like the *Second*, is one of the finest of the series and has great breadth and nobility. Sir John draws playing of high quality from the orchestra, who are on top form throughout. Barbirolli included the *Sixth Symphony* in the last concert he conducted in Manchester on 3 May 1970, and he recorded it three weeks later, only two months before he died. It is easy to sense an elegiac feeling in the performance, which remains most compelling, especially in the beautiful closing passage for the strings, given the benefit of radiant sound. The *Seventh* makes a fine culmination for the cycle, bringing a feeling of power and a sense of inevitability which increases as the work progresses. The build-up to its climax is well paced. The recording is very fine.

The suite from *Pelléas et Mélisande* is powerfully atmospheric, as is *The Swan of Tuonela*, but here Sir John's rather endearing vocalizations are clearly audible. *Pohjola's Daughter* is very strongly characterized, as are the *Scènes historiques*. *Rakastava*, and especially the touching *Romance for Strings*, are much rarer, originally having a short catalogue life. They are very well played and recorded. All in all, this is a cherishable box, attractively illustrated with some of the original LP sleeve pictures.

Sir Alexander Gibson's Sibelius cycle is impressive, both musically and from an engineering point of view; there are no weak spots anywhere. The performances are eminently sane, sound and reliable, and no one investing in the set is likely to be at all disappointed. Taken individually, none would be an absolute first choice.

Anthony Collins (1893–1963) is remembered these days almost solely for these Decca recordings. His was the first integral set of the symphonies to appear in this country. Collins has an instinctive feeling for pace, with the sole exception of the second movement of the *Third Symphony*, which is far too fast. In terms of sheer electricity, his 1952 account of the *First Symphony* remains pretty well unsurpassed, even by the likes of Karajan, Sir Colin Davis or Bernstein. It is taut and concentrated, yet full of feeling and wonderfully paced.

Collin's accounts of *Night Ride and Sunrise* and *Pohjola's Daughter* are hardly less impressive: the former can hold its own alongside the Jochum and Davis versions. Collins was in some ways the ideal recording conductor, for he could combine an unerring sense of style with a natural gift for spontaneity. It is good to see these authoritative accounts returning to circulation at bargain price, for they have a prized and special place in the Sibelius discography and still sound remarkably vivid. The set also includes **Jensen's** mono recording of the *Karelia Suite* with the **Danish Radio Symphony Orchestra**, as Collins only included the *Overture* in his series of recordings.

(i) *Symphonies 1–7; Andante festivo; The Bard*; (i; ii) *Violin Concerto*; (i) *En Saga; Finlandia*; (iii; iv) 6 *Humoresques* (for Violin & Orchestra); (i) *Karelia Suite; King Christian II Suite*; (i; v) *Kullervo Symphony*; (i) 4 *Legends*; (i; vi) *Luonnatar*; (i) *The Ocanides*; (v) *The Origin of Fire*; (i) *Pelleas and Melisande Suite; Pohjola's Daughter; Rakastava; Scènes historiques*; (vii; i) 2 *Serious Melodies* (for Cello & Orchestra); (iii; iv) *Serenades* (for Violin & Orchestra); (viii; ix; i) *Snöfrid* (for recitation, chorus & orchestra); (i) *Tapiola; The Tempest* (incidental music) *Suite; The Wood Nymph*. Chamber Music: (x) *Allegro appassionato*; (xi) *Piano Trio in D (Korpo); Piano Quintet in G min.; La pompeuse March d'Asis* (for piano trio); (x) *String Quartets: in A min.; D min. (Voces intimae)*; (xi) *Andante cantabile in E flat for Piano & Harmonium; Andante cantabile in G* (for Violin & Piano); 2 *Danses Champêtres* (for Violin & Piano); *Malinconia* (for Cello & Piano); 4 *Pieces* (for Violin & Piano); *Violin Sonatina; Violin Sonata in F; Water Drops* (for violin & cello). Piano music: (xii) *Florestan; Impromptu in B min.*; (xiii) *Kyllikki; Romance in D flat; Scène romantique; The Solitary Fir Tree*; (xi) *Sonata in F*; (xii) *Sonatinas: in B min.; E; F sharp min.; The Spruce; The Village Church*. (v; ix; xiv) Choral music *(a cappella)* for Male Choir & Mixed Choir; (xv) Songs including *The Watersprite* (melodrama)

(BB) **** BIS (DDD/ADD) CD 1697/1700 (15). (i) Lahti SO, Vänskä; (ii) with Kavakos; (iii) with Dong-Suk Kang; (iv) Gothenburg SO, Järvi; (v) Helsinki University Ch.; (vi) Juntunen; (vii) Ylönen; (viii) Ekblad, (ix) Jubilate Ch.; (x) Tempera Qt; (xi) various instrumentalists; (xii) Gräsbeck; (xiii) Tawaststiera; (xiv) Orphei Drängar; various conductors; (xiv) von Otter or Hynninen, with Fosberg or Gothenburg SO, Panula; Häggander, Panula; Groop, Derwinger

BIS have called this generous budget-priced anthology (15 CDs for the cost of four) 'The Essential Sibelius', and it is surely as wide-ranging as any collector could wish, even including as a bonus a première recording of the little melodrama *Näcken* (*The Watersprite*). There is little need for further comment. **Osmo Vänskä**, who conducts most of the orchestral music, including the *Symphonies* and **Leonidas Kavakos's** fine account of the *Violin Concerto*, is an instinctive Sibelian: his pacing and structural command are virtually without flaw, and all these performancs have striking concentration and spontaneity. Perhaps not all the instrumental and vocal music is 'essential', but all of it is worth exploring and the songs are splendidly sung. The recordings are consistently up to the high standards of BIS and the documentation cannot be faulted. A set to be strongly recommended.

Symphonies 1–3; 5; Belshazzar's Feast (incidental music); Karelia Suite; Pohjola's Daughter; Tapiola

⊕—(M)(***) Finlandia mono 4509 95882-2 (3). LSO, Kajanus

When the Finnish government sponsored recordings of the first two *Symphonies* in 1930, Sibelius insisted on having **Kajanus** as the most authentic interpreter. These performances were all made in 1930 and 1932 and sound amazingly good for the period. The celebrated storm in *Tapiola*, taken at a much slower and more effective tempo than is now usual, still has the power to terrify, despite the inevitable sonic limitations, and no conductor has ever given a more spell-binding and atmospheric account of the suite from *Belshazzar's Feast*. The broader, more leisurely view Kajanus takes of the *Third Symphony* comes as a refreshing corrective to the later, more hurried accounts by Anthony Collins and Lorin Maazel. No performer, save Davis, Beecham and Karajan, came closer to Sibelius's intentions. Essential listening for all Sibelians.

Symphonies 1 in E min.; 3 in C, Op. 52

(N)(M)*** Hallé CDHLL75514. Hallé O, Elder

(***) Testament mono SBT 1049. Philh. O, Kletzki

(BB)**(*) Naxos 8.554102. Iceland SO, Sakari

The **Hallé** have followed the example of the LSO, LPO and Concertgebouw Orchestras by publishing their own recordings rather than waiting for the ministrations of EMI or other commercial companies. **Sir Mark Elder** has been collecting golden opinions for his work with the Hallé Orchestra, which has flourished under his direction, and this offers excellent testimony to his efforts. More to the point, however, he is a sensitive and authoritative Sibelian, as these accounts of the *First* and *Third* symphonies clearly show. If he and the Hallé continue and complete the cycle to the present level of distinction, it should be strongly competitive.

Kletzki is tauter than the traditional Kajanus school yet far less headlong (or headstrong) than Collins. In both scores he and the **Philharmonia Orchestra** strike the right balance between the romantic legacy of the 19th century and the more severe climate of the 20th. The recordings are beautifully balanced and have great warmth, and they come up splendidly in these transfers.

Petri Sakari proves a sound and straightforward interpreter. The playing of the **Iceland Orchestra** in both *Symphonies* is spirited and vital, even if they do not command the virtuosity and polish of the major international ensembles. The *Third Symphony* is very well paced indeed and the playing has conviction. The recording, too, is natural and

vivid, with a good balance between the various sections of the orchestra. In any event, good value for money.

Symphonies 1; 4 in A min., Op. 63

⊕—**** BIS BIS CD 861. Lahti SO, Vänskä

Symphonies 1 in E min., Op. 39; 4 in A min., Op. 63

(N)(M)*** LSO Live **SACD** LSO0601. LSO C. Davis

In the *First Symphony* the Finnish conductor **Vänskä** secures a marvellously controlled and splendidly executed performance from his dedicated players. There is that sense of inevitability and of an irresistible forward movement throughout, though never at the expense of incidental beauty. The Scherzo is among the most exciting on disc, very fast and full of controlled abandon. The *Fourth Symphony* receives a perceptive and deeply intelligent reading. The **Lahti Orchestra** play with keen concentration and intensity and though tempi are very slow (perhaps too much so in the case of the slow movement), the performance is marvellously sustained. The recording is natural and eminently well balanced. A distinguished issue.

Colin Davis's accounts of the *First* and *Fourth Symphonies* come from 2006 and 2008 and were recorded at the Barbican Centre. Sir Colin has always been a particularly thoughtful interpreter of the *Fourth*, and we recall hearing him conducting it with great natural authority when he was with the BBC Scottish Orchestra in the 1960s. His reading has deepened over the years and is much broader in tempo and more profound in feeling. The present reading of the *Fourth* runs to a little under 40 minutes and has an even greater sense of breadth than his 1994 account on RCA. Sir Colin allows himself more space but there is even more imaginative and poetic depth. He takes us completely inside this world; we become enveloped by it and feel we inhabit it. The *First Symphony*, too, has all the ardour and excitement of his earlier recordings. In short, Sibelius conducting of real stature, to which the **LSO** respond wholeheartedly. James Mallinson succeeds in getting consistently good results from the Barbican acoustic.

Symphony 2 in D, Op. 43

⊕—(M)*** Concg. O RCO 05005. Concg. O, Jansons

⊕—(***) BBC mono BBCL 4154-2. BBC SO, Beecham –
DVOŘÁK: *Symphony 8* (***)

(***) BBC mono BBCL 4115-2. BBC SO, Stokowski (with
BEETHOVEN: *Overture Egmont* ***) – TCHAIKOVSKY:
Sleeping Beauty: Suite (***)

Symphony 2 in D, Op. 43; En Saga, Op. 9

⊕—(BB)**** EMI Encore 3 41441-2. BPO, Karajan

(i) Symphony 2; (ii) Karelia Suite; (i) Legend: The Swan of Tuonela

(BB)**(*) Regis RRC 1220. (i) LSO; (ii) RPO, Mackerras

Symphony 2; Romance in C

*** BIS CD 252. Gothenburg SO, Järvi

Mariss Jansons is a totally committed and authoritative Sibelian and throughout the performance he holds the listener totally in his grip. It is a joy to hear this wonderful orchestra in all its tonal opulence and splendour. Jansons's reading is splendidly fresh and at times makes you feel that you are listening to this familiar music for the first time. At its modest price, a fraction of the cost of a concert ticket, this disc, one of the first on the **Concertgebouw's** own label, is well worth adding to your collection, even if rival versions offer couplings.

Karajan's 1980 digital version of the *Second Symphony* with the **Berlin Philharmonic** is more spacious than his earlier reading with the Philharmonia. Tempi in all four movements are fractionally broader; nevertheless, the first movement is still a genuine *Allegretto* basically in the brisker tradition of Kajanus. Throughout all four movements there is a splendour and nobility here – and some glorious sounds from the Berlin strings and brass. This is a performance of stature, and is well recorded, too. In *En Saga* Karajan is a brisk story-teller, more concerned with narrative than with atmosphere at the beginning, but the *lento assai* section and the coda are quite magical. The EMI recording has plenty of body and presence. A remarkable bargain.

Sir Thomas Beecham's famous broadcast account of the *Second Symphony* comes from a BBC Symphony concert on the occasion of the composer's 89th birthday on 8 December 1954 and relayed to Finland. The knowledge that Sibelius was listening lent an added frisson to the occasion, for the playing is very intent and exciting. The microphones picked up various whoops and other vocal exhortations from Sir Thomas, and the playing is of pretty high voltage. The playing has an electricity and immediacy of impact that are quite special.

Throughout, **Järvi** has an unerring sense of purpose and direction and the BIS performance is concentrated in feeling and thoroughly convincing. The *Romance for Strings* is attractively done.

Surprisingly, **Stokowski's** 1964 Sibelius *Second* is a mono recording, but the warmth of the Royal Albert Hall acoustic adds ambience and sonority so that one does not miss the stereo too much (though the bronchial afflictions of the audience are a deterrent). It is a widely contrasted reading, using constantly flexible tempi as only Stokowski can, without loss of tension. He thought of the *Symphony* as 'free and rhapsodic' but kept the horizon always in view. The *Andante* generates a grave melancholy towards the close, then the eruption of energy (though not of volume) at the *vivacissimo* makes a dynamic contrast. The great tune of the finale is superbly prepared, and Stokowski builds steadily towards the expansive final peroration (often slowing down on the way without the slightest loss of concentration). A remarkable if unpredictable reading of a masterly symphony (which the conductor very unfashionably thought 'more inspired than the Seventh').

Sir Charles Mackerras gives an eminently well-judged account of the *Second Symphony*. The tempo of the first movement is apt, a real *Allegretto*, fast but without going to extremes. There is no lack of tenderness and he shapes phrases with sensitivity. *The Swan of Tuonela* too has no lack of at-

mosphere. The 1988 recording (originally from the Pickwick label) was made in the EMI Abbey Road studio and is bright and clean. The lively **RPO** account of *Karelia* was made five years later.

Symphonies 2; 3 in C, Op. 52

**(*) BIS CD 862. Lahti SO, Vänskä

Osmo Vänskä's accounts of the *Second* and *Third Symphonies* are as thought-provoking as his remarkable pairing of 1 and 4, though they are not quite deserving of the same star rating. The dynamic markings are sometimes a little too extreme, the second theme of the slow movement marked *piano/pianissimo* is almost whispered rather than played, and to readers playing the disc at less than full-room volume, it will be barely audible. It is just a shade self-conscious. Everything is carefully thought out, and the general effect is impressive. The *Third Symphony* is generally well paced and has the right atmosphere.

Symphonies 2 & 4; Tapiola

(N) **(*) Australian Decca Eloquence 480 0044 (2). SRO, Ansermet – RACHMANINOV: *The Isle of the Dead* **(*)

Ansermet's Sibelius, like his performances of the German repertoire, holds a certain fascination. Certainly, in the *Second Symphony* Ansermet could not be accused of going overboard with romantic gestures. Indeed, this reading is entirely free from over-emphasis, yet the effect is cumulatively powerful. There's a sense of real logic with, again, some striking moments of textual clarity. The *Fourth Symphony* is impressive in many ways, though perhaps here Ansermet lets the tension sag a little in the slow movement. The use of tubular bells (instead of the composer's intended glockenspiel) gives the finale a unique and fascinating colouring. Colin Anderson remarks in his excellent sleeve-notes that 'Ansermet is one of the few musicians who take seriously Sibelius's tacit instructions to do nothing as the symphony reaches its end; by not slowing it, the music stops rather than ends – and the effect is chillingly mournful: surely what Sibelius intended'. Anderson also beautifully sums up the performance of Sibelius's last great work, *Tapiola*: 'Ansermet and his varnish-free orchestra give an urgent, taut and raw account, absolutely at one with the music.'

Symphonies 2; 5 in E flat, Op. 82

**** Testament SBT1418. (i) RPO; (ii) Hallé O; Barbirolli

(M) *** Chan. (ADD) 6556. SNO, Gibson

(M) **(*) EMI (ADD) 4 76882-2. Philh. O, Karajan

Barbirolli's RPO *Second Symphony* was recorded in 1962 at Walthamstow with Charles Gerhardt as producer and Kenneth Wilkinson as the balance engineer. It was originally issued in collaboration with *Reader's Digest* and was rightly hailed as a triumph. The composer Robert Simpson called it the best Sibelius he had heard from Barbirolli, much superior to the versions he had made with the Hallé Orchestra. The *Fifth*, no less impressive, comes from a 1968 Prom performance and so is not to be confused with the commercial set he made with the **Hallé** for HMV. A really outstanding coupling in every respect.

The *Second* is among the best of **Gibson's** cycle and scores highly, thanks to the impressive clarity, fullness and impact of the 1982 digital recording. Gibson's reading is honest and straightforward, free of bombast in the finale. Tempi are well judged: the first movement is neither too taut nor too relaxed – it is well shaped and feels right. Overall this is most satisfying, as is the *Fifth*, which has similar virtues. At no time is there any attempt to interpose the personality of the interpreter, and the finale has genuine weight and power.

With **Karajan's** coupling, in spite of the superb playing from the **Philharmonia** (especially the strings), the problem is one of concentration in the earlier movements. While his long-drawn paragraphs, dramatic and solemn, strong and personal, are particularly suitable for Sibelius's idiom, at times the concentration slips. Even so, he brings off the slower-than-usual tempo for the finale of the *Second* because of the sheer intensity of the orchestral response. The *Fifth Symphony*, too, has a superbly graduated finale: the first appearance of the swinging horn tune is a glorious moment. Excellent sound, well transferred.

Symphonies 2; 6 in D min., Op. 104

🎵 *** RCA 09026 68218-2. LSO, C. Davis

The *Sixth* is a work for which **Colin Davis** has always shown a special affinity and understanding. Sir Colin's earlier recording with the Boston orchestra (see above) was one of the best in that magisterial cycle, and this newcomer is if anything even finer. There is 'nothing of the circus' (to quote the composer's own words apropos the *Fourth Symphony*) in his reading of the *Second* and no playing to the gallery. There is a grandeur and a natural distinction about the playing.

Symphony 3; King Kristian II (suite)

🎵 **** BIS CD 228. Gothenburg SO, Järvi

With the *Third Symphony* there is a sense of the epic in **Järvi's** hands, and it can hold its own with any in the catalogue. In Gothenburg, the slow movement is first class and the leisurely tempo adopted here by the Estonian conductor is just right. Järvi's coupling is the incidental music to *King Kristian II*. This is very beautifully played and recorded.

Symphonies 3; 6; 7

🎵 (M) *** Chan. (ADD) 6557. SNO, Gibson

With three *Symphonies* offered, some 74 minutes overall, this is a fine bargain and an excellent way to experience **Gibson's** special feeling for this composer. The SNO is in very good form. The first movement of the *Third* has real momentum. The *Andantino* is fast, faster than the composer's marking. But there is more here to admire than to cavil at. The *Sixth* is impressive too, with plenty of atmosphere and some radiant playing from the Scottish violin section; the *Seventh* has a rather relaxed feeling throughout, but it does not lack warmth and, as in 1, Gibson draws the threads together at the close with satisfying breadth.

Symphonies 4 in A min.; 5 in E flat

(B) **(*) CfP (ADD) 5 21872-2. BPO, Karajan

(BB) *** Naxos 8.554377. Iceland SO, Sakari

Karajan's 1976 recording of the *Fourth Symphony* must in some ways be counted controversial. He gives broadly spacious and highly atmospheric accounts of the first and third movements, a good deal slower than in his earlier, DG version. He conveys eloquently the other-worldly quality of the landscape in the third movement. The first movement undoubtedly has great mystery and power, and the recording still sounds remarkably good. Similarly in the *Fifth* the first movement is broader and more spacious than on DG, and Karajan achieves a remarkable sense of the work's power and majesty. The variety of tone-colours and, above all, the weight of sonority that the **Berlin Philharmonic** had at their command in the mid-1970s is astonishing, and the bassoon lament in the development section finds the Berlin strings reduced to the merest whisper. Both the slow movement and the finale are glorious and have real vision; and the recording, made at the same time as the *Fourth*, is again excellent.

Had one heard either of **Sakari's** performances in the concert hall, one would have left feeling very satisfied. Both grip the listener. They are straightforward and unaffected, dedicated and selfless, and free from interpretative point-making. Tempi are for the most part uncommonly well judged, and you feel that Sakari really sees the works as a whole, rather than as a sequence of wonderful episodes. The first movement of the *Fifth* has splendid breadth, and the transition into the Scherzo section is expertly handled. The **Iceland Orchestra** may not be in the luxury league but their responses are keen and alert. Moreover, the sound is truthfully balanced and well detailed.

Symphonies 4 in A min., Op. 63; 6 in D min., Op. 104

🎵 (***) Somm-Beecham mono 16. (i) BBC SO; (ii) RPO; Beecham

The performances are immaculately prepared and the orchestra play as if their very lives depend on it. Beecham's recording of the *Sixth* has all the vision and authority that his commercial discs had, and the sound (apart from a problem with the level at the very outset) is eminently acceptable. The closing section of the finale has great feeling and poignancy. The recording is transferred from acetates and shows some signs of wear, particularly in the *Fourth Symphony*. However, it is good to have these performances, whatever their sonic limitations.

Symphonies 4; 7; Pelléas et Mélisande Suite; Swanwhite; Tapiola; The Tempest (incidental music): Dance of the Nymphs

🎵 (***) BBC mono BBCL 4041-2 (2). RPO, Beecham (with British and Finnish National anthems, and speeches by Beecham, including Beecham on Sibelius)

Beecham never re-recorded the *Fourth Symphony* commercially after his 1938 recording but, judging from this 1955 performance, his basic approach remained little changed. He also never recorded the *Swanwhite* suite. Here he omits only *The Prince Alone*. He did make stereo versions of the *Pelléas et Mélisande* music (without the brief *By the Seashore* movement) and *Tapiola* a few days on either side of the birthday concert. He also recorded the *Seventh* commercially at the same time, but this performance comes from a Royal Albert Hall concert of the previous year and is slightly higher in voltage than his Abbey Road recording. There is a tremendous sense of occasion here, which is supplemented by his famous talk describing his long friendship with Sibelius and recounting his hilarious visit to his home the previous year.

Symphony 5 (1915 version); En Saga (1892 version)

*** BIS CD 800. Lahti SO, Vänskä

Symphony 5 (1915 version & definitive 1919 version)

*** BIS CD 863. Lahti SO, Vänskä

Not long after Sibelius's death, the orchestral material for the first version of the *Fifth Symphony* was discovered in the attic at Ainola. To reconstruct the actual score was a simple matter. The work is in four (not three) movements, the opening horn-call is yet to be discovered; and there are no final hammer-blow chords. But there is much else that is different, and to study these differences offers an endless source of fascination. The *En Saga* we know comes from 1901, when it was extensively revised for Busoni to conduct in Berlin. There are some Brucknerian touches in one or two places, and the orchestration is less expert. Totally dedicated performances. An essential disc for all Sibelians, and magnificently recorded into the bargain.

BIS have also recoupled the original 1915 four-movement version of the *Fifth Symphony* with the definitive 1919 version, as part of their ongoing cycle from **Osmo Vänskä** and the **Lahti Orchestra**. Vänskä has a great feeling for the general architecture of the piece and paces it superbly. Our only reservation is his penchant for extreme *pianissimos* – the development section in the finale drops beyond a whisper to virtual inaudibility.

Symphonies 5; 6; Legend: The Swan of Tuonela

⌐ (BB) **** LSO Live LSO 0037. LSO, C. Davis

Sir Colin Davis's performances come from 2002–3 and, like the cycle he recorded with the **LSO** in the 1990s, are at bargain price. The first movement of the *Fifth* has a magnificent breadth and a powerful atmosphere, and he handles the transition into the Scherzo section, always a crucial test, with masterly control. Tempi feel just right, and both the symphonic architecture and the musical atmosphere emerge to eloquent effect. The final chords are splendidly paced and powerfully delivered. The opening of the *Sixth* seems slightly more relaxed than before, and the strange, other-worldly atmosphere of the second movement registers perfectly. Very good sound.

Symphonies 6; 7; Tapiola

*** BIS CD 864. Lahti SO, Vänskä

Symphony 6–7; The Tempest: Suite 2, Op. 109/3

(BB) *** Naxos 8.554387. Iceland SO, Sakari

Osmo Vänskä's account of the *Sixth* and *Seventh Symphonies* brings his cycle to a fitting climax. The *Sixth* is serene yet

taut, and the *Seventh* particularly fine, both in pacing and character. Vänskä's reading of *Tapiola* has a thrilling intensity and if it is not the equal of Karajan or Beecham, it is certainly among the very best of the others. The **Lahti Orchestra** always plays with enthusiasm and fire, and the BIS recording is first class.

Petri Sakari's *Sixth Symphony* is thoughtful, well prepared and dedicated, and even if the **Iceland Orchestra** is not in the same league as the Vienna Philharmonic or the Concertgebouw, they are a very good ensemble. The *Seventh* is powerful and has breadth and majesty; not the equal of Colin Davis, perhaps, but eminently satisfying all the same. The second suite from *The Tempest* is magnificent (the *Chorus of the Winds* sounds quite magical) and full of mystery and atmosphere, and the well-balanced sound does credit to all concerned.

Symphony 7 in C, Op. 150

**(*) BBC (ADD) BBCL 4039-2. Philih. O, Boult – BIZET: *Jeux d'enfants*; RAVEL: *Daphnis et Chloé: Suite 2.* SCHUBERT: *Symphony 8 (Unfinished)* **(*)

Symphony 7 in C; Canzonetta, Op. 62a; Kuolema: Valse triste; Scene with Cranes; Night Ride and Sunrise; Valse romantique, Op. 62b

*** BIS CD 311. Gothenburg SO, Järvi

(i) Symphony 7 in C, Op. 105; (ii) Pohjola's Daughter; Swanwhite: The Maiden with the Roses; Tapiola

⌐ (BB) (***) Naxos mono 8.110168. (i) BBC SO; (ii) Boston SO; Koussevitzky (with GRIEG: *The Last Spring* (***))

Koussevitzky's pioneering (1933) recording of the *Seventh Symphony* with the then newly formed **BBC Symphony Orchestra** has rarely been challenged and never surpassed and, together with his *Pohjola's Daughter* and *Tapiola* from 1936 and 1939 respectively, is among the classics of recorded music.

Neeme Järvi and the **Gothenburg Orchestra** bring great energy and concentration to the *Seventh Symphony*. The only disappointment is the final climax, which is perhaps less intense than the best versions. However, it is a fine performance, and the music to *Kuolema* is splendidly atmospheric; *Night Ride* is strongly characterized. The recording exhibits the usual characteristics of the Gothenburg Concert Hall and has plenty of body and presence.

Anyone who remembers **Sir Adrian Boult's** set of the Sibelius tone-poems on Pye Records from the 1950s or his broadcasts from the 1940s and 1950s will have high expectations of his *Seventh Symphony* and will not be disappointed. It is finely shaped and superbly paced. A Festival Hall performance from 1963, it is well worth rescuing from oblivion. Good sound too.

The Wood Nymph (tone-poem), Op. 15; (i) The Wood Nymph (melodrama) (1895); A Lonely Ski-trail; Swanwhite, Op. 54

⌐ **** BIS CD 815. (i) Pöysti; Lahti SO, Vänskä

Sibelius composed *The Wood Nymph* in 1894–5, when the four

Lemminkäinen Legends were taking shape in his mind. It is stirring stuff and begins with echoes of the *Karelia* music and in places comes close to both the first of the *Legends* and *Lemminkäinen's Homeward Journey*. It improves with every hearing: its main ideas haunt the listener and are difficult to dislodge from the brain! *A Lonely Ski-trail* is slight, but *The Wood Nymph* melodrama is imaginative and highly unusual. The original music to *Swanwhite* has some poetic ideas that did not find their way into the suite, though for the most part there is not a great deal that is unfamiliar. Superb playing from the **Lahti Orchestra** under **Osmo Vänskä**, and spacious, impeccably balanced recording.

The Wood Nymph (melodrama), Op. 15

*** Warner 2564 61992-2 Pöysti, Nordic SO,Tali –
  RACHMANINOV: *3 Russian Songs*; TUUR: *Zeitraum; Action, Passion, Illusion* ***

This *Wood Nymph* is not the tone-poem for full orchestra that Osmo Vänskä recorded (see above) but the thematically related melodrama of 1894 to the Rydberg text and scored for narrator, two horns, piano and strings. The speaker on this CD is **Lasse Pöysti**, who also took part in the earlier, rather more atmospheric 1996 BIS recording above.

CHAMBER MUSIC

BIS Sibelius Edition,Volume 2: Chamber Music I: String Quartets 1-4 (including preliminary ending of Voces intimae). Movements for String Quartet: Adagio in D min.; Allegro in G min.; Andante festivo; Andantino in C; Andante – Allegro molto in D; Andante molto sostenuto in B min.; Allegrettos in B flat & D; Moderato – Allegro appassionato in C sharp min.; Fuga for Martin Wegelius; Molto moderato (Scherzo); 4 Themes; 3 Pieces; 33 Small Pieces; Scherzo in B min.; Theme and Variations in C sharp min. (both completed Aho); Piano Quartets in C min.; D min.; Piano (4 Hands) Quartet (Ljunga Wirginia) & Scherzo in E min.; Quartet in G min. (for harmonium, violin, cello & piano); Andante cantabile in E flat (for piano & harmonium); Piano Trios: in A min.; in A min. (Hafträsk); in D (Korpo); in C (Lovisa). Movements for Piano Trio: Andante – Adagio – Allegro maestoso; Allegrettos in A flat & E flat; Allegros in C; D; D min.; Andantinos in A & G min.; Minuets in D min. & F; Moderato in A min.; La pompeuse March d'Asis; String Trio in G

Ⓑ *** BIS-CD 1903/5 (6). Tempera Qt; Kuusisto,Vänskä, Ylönen, Turunen, Gräsbeck, Lönnqvist, Vitanen

Much of this music is of specialist interest, but many of these miniatures will make fascinating listening for the serious Sibelian, and they are all finely played by dedicated musicians, and very well recorded. The box is inexpensive too.

(i) Adagio in D min.; (ii, iii) Duo in C for Violin & Viola; (i) Fugue for Martin Wegelius; (iii, iv, v) Piano

Trio in C (Lovisa); (vi, vii) Suite in E for Violin & Piano; (iii, iv) Water Drops for Violin & Cello

*** Ondine ODE 850-2. (i) Sibelius Qt; (ii) Hirvikangas;
  (iii) Kimangen; (iv) Arai; (v) Lagerspetz; (vi) Kuusisto;
  (vii) Kerppo

These are all slight pieces from Sibelius's youth and student years: *Water Drops* was written when he was ten and is of no artistic interest. The *Fugue* for his teacher, Martin Wegelius, of 1888 was originally intended as the finale for his *A minor Quartet*, just as the *Adagio in D minor* (1890) was probably to have formed part of the *B flat Quartet*, Op. 4. This is the most individual of the pieces on this well-played and well-recorded set. With the exception of the *Lovisa Trio* of 1888, these are all first recordings.

Allegretto in B flat; Moderato – Allegro Appassionato in C sharp min.; 3 Pieces; Fugue; String Quartet in A min.

*** BIS CD 1476. Tempera Qt

All this music was written between 1888 and 1889 and is mostly new to CD. Perhaps it is too reverential to record the fugue the composer wrote as a student exercise for his teacher, Martin Wegelius. The all-female **Tempera Quartet** play the *A minor Quartet* and the remaining pieces splendidly.

Piano Quartets: in C min. for 2 violins, cello & piano; in D min. for 2 violins, cello & piano; in G min. for violin, cello, piano & harmonium; (i) Andante Cantabile in E flat (for piano & harmonium). Scherzo in E min. (for violin, cello & piano, four hands); Ljunga Wirginia (for violin, cello & piano, four hands)

**(*) BIS CD 1182. Kuusisto, Satu Vänskä, Turunen, Gräsbeck, Lönnqvist; (i) Viitanen

The various works and fragments recorded here come from 1884–91, when Sibelius was yet to find his voice. None is written for the combination of instruments one would expect (string trio and piano) and only one, the eight-minute *C minor Quartet*, has been recorded before (see below). There are unusual ensembles: violin, cello, piano and harmonium in the *G minor quartet* of 1887. The fragments for violin, cello and piano four hands (*Ljunga Wirginia*), intended for a projected dramatic venture Sibelius planned with his friend Walter von Konow, are completely new, if unimportant. Indeed, it would be idle to pretend that any of these slight pieces gives us the slightest glimpse of the real Sibelius; but the performances and the recorded sound are excellent.

(i) Piano Quintet in G min.; Piano Trio in C (Lovisa); String Quartet in E flat

*** Finlandia 4509 95858-2. Sibelius Ac. Qt, (i) with Tawaststjerna

(i) Piano Quintet in G min.; String Quartet in D min. (Voces intimae), Op. 56

*** Chan. 8742. (i) Goldstone; Gabrieli Qt

The *Piano Quintet* is a long and far from characteristic piece in five movements. **Anthony Goldstone** and the **Gabrielis** reverse the order of the second and third movements so as to maximize contrast. The first movement is probably the finest, and Goldstone, an impressive player by any standards, makes the most of Sibelius's piano writing to produce a very committed performance. The *Voces intimae Quartet* is given a reflective, intelligent reading, perhaps at times wanting in momentum but finely shaped. Good recording.

The early *Quartet in E flat* is Haydnesque and insignificant, and the *Lovisa Trio*, so called because it was written in that small town in the summer of 1888, offers only sporadic glimpses of things to come. The *Piano Quintet* is given a fine performance on Finlandia, and there is little to choose between it and the more expansive Goldstone/Gabrieli account on Chandos.

Piano Trios in A min.; in A min. (Hafträsk); in G for 2 Violins & Piano; Piano Trio movements: Allegro in C; Andantino in A; Allegro in D; Andante – Adagio – Allegro maestoso; Minuet in D min.; Minuet in F for 2 Violins & Piano; Moderato in A min.

*** BIS CD 1282. Kuusisto, Vänskä, Ylönen. Gräsbeck

In all his correspondence with the Sibelius Museum in Turku (Åbo), the composer was at pains to emphasize that these chamber works were *neither to be published nor performed – even after his death!* The earliest work is the *G major Trio* for two violins and piano, a fluent and attractive piece, which reflects Sibelius's own youthful experience as a player. Perhaps the most striking work is the *A minor Trio* of 1884, whose provenance **Folke Gräsbeck** explores in his well-researched notes. It owes something to Haydn in its layout, and its *Trio* has distinctly rustic accents. The *Andantino in A major* of 1886 is a rather lovely piece, too. No one would make exaggerated claims for these pieces, some of which have scant merit but the performances are alert and intelligent and the recording exemplary and wonderfully present.

Piano Trios in D (Korpo) (1887); in C, (Lovisa); Alla Marcia in C; Andantino in G min.; Allegretto in A flat; Allegro in D min. (completed Aho); Allegretto in E flat (completed Kuusisto)

*** BIS CD 1292. Kuusisto, Ylönen, Gräsbeck

The '*Lovisa* 'Trio, so called because it was written in the family summer home in Lovisa, is available in two alternative versions, but otherwise this music is all new. The '*Korpo*' Trio (1887) is by far the most substantial piece here, running to over 35 minutes. Few coming to it with innocent ears would guess the identity of the composer but it evinces a natural feeling for form. There are other rarities too, some of which are in fragmentary form. The most engaging is the *March in C major*, which almost calls to mind the Saint-Saëns of the *Carnival of the Animals!* Expert performances.

String Quartets in E flat (1885); A min. (1889); B flat, Op. 4 (1890); D min. (Voces intimae), Op. 56

⊶ Ⓜ **** Finlandia (ADD/DDD) 4509 95851-2 (2). Sibelius Academy Qt

The *E flat Quartet* is an exercise, modelled on the Viennese classics, and shows that Sibelius knew his Haydn. The *A minor* (1889) is another matter, and it is highly inventive. Sibelius first thought well enough of it to list it as Op. 2, though he later had second thoughts and never published it. The *B flat Quartet* (1891) is a fine piece whose slow movement bears a resemblance to one of the themes from *Rakastava*, which was to follow in 1894. The Scherzo of the *A minor Quartet* is wonderfully exhilarating. The performances are first rate and are generally well served by the engineers. There is only one mature Sibelius *Quartet*, *Voces intimae* (1909), and this performance is arguably still the finest now available. An outstanding bargain, and strongly recommended.

String Quartet in D min. (Voces intimae), Op. 56

*** Australian Decca Eloquence (ADD) 442 9486. (i) Fitzwilliam Qt – DELIUS: *String Quartet*, etc. **(*)

(***) Biddulph mono LAB 098. Budapest Qt – GRIEG: *Quartet*; WOLF: *Italian Serenade*. (***)

The **Fitzwilliams** give a deeply felt and no less deeply considered account of the Sibelius *Quartet*. In their hands the work becomes bigger in scale and more symphonic in feeling. There is a wide range of sonority and a scrupulous regard for dynamic graduations. The opening is very much *con amore*, but it is evident from the cello entry (bar 18) that this is going to be a big-boned account that declares its proximity to the *Fourth Symphony*. The generally measured tempo is justified on the original LP sleeve-note by **Alan George**, the violist of the quartet, who bases their choice of tempi on metronome markings that the composer himself gave to the Griller Quartet. This is a thought-provoking and impressive recording which makes a welcome return to the catalogue – and the 1978 sound is superb.

A welcome transfer – the first on CD – of the 1933 pioneering **Budapest** *Voces intimae*, still unbeaten. It briefly appeared on LP (on the World Record label) and is newly (and well) transferred here by Ward Marston. Sibelians will need no reminders of its excellence – and the same goes for the couplings.

Music for violin and piano

Sibelius Edition, Volume 6: Complete Music for Violin and Piano: Concerto in D min., Op. 47 (Original & Final Version); Sonata in A min.; Sonatina in E, Op. 80; Danses champêtres, Op. 106; Pieces, Opp. 77–79, 81, 115–16; Student works; Late Works

Ⓝ *** BIS CD 1915/7 (5). Kuusisto, Sato, Spark, Gräsbeck, Sparf, Forsberg

Like the other boxes in this series, this is excellent value: five CDs are offered for the price of three, and this is highly recommendable for those collecting this BIS series.

Adagio in D min.; Allegretto in C; 2 Pieces; 3 Pieces; Sonata Exposition: Allegro in A min.; Grave (Fragment) in D min.; Largamento (Fragments) in E min.; in D min.; Sonata in F; Suite in E; Tempo di valse in A. Music for solo violin: Allegretto in A; Etude in D; A Happy Musician; Romance in G

*** BIS CD 1023. Kuusisto, Gräsbeck

All the material recorded here is completely new. The *A minor Sonata* has echoes of early Beethoven and comes from his school years; the *Suite in D minor* (1887–8) shows that his writing for the violin was naturally fluent and idiomatic even then. It seems that the composer was sufficiently taken with it to show it to his first biographer, Erik Furujhelm.

Andante grazioso in D major (1884–5); 5 Pieces (1886–7); Violin Sonata in A minor (1884); Sonata Movement (1885); Sonata Fragment in B minor (1887); Suite in D minor (1887–8); Various short movements and fragments

*** BIS CD 1022. Kuusisto, Gräsbeck

The *A minor Sonata* of 1884, from his school years, is redolent of the early Beethoven sonatas: it is highly accomplished but totally derivative. There are a number of short movements, some mere fragments, and not all of them are worth committing to disc. The *Suite in D minor* (1887–8) is another matter and shows just how good his writing for the instrument was. Very good playing from **Jaakko Kuusisto** and **Folke Gräsbeck**, as well as good and scholarly sleeve notes from the latter. Excellent sound.

5 Danses champêtres, Op. 106; Novellette, Op. 102; 5 Pieces, Op. 81; 4 Pieces, Op. 115; 3 Pieces, Op. 116

*** BIS CD 625. Sparf, Forsberg

Many of the items here, such as the delightful *Rondino* from Op. 81, are little more than salon music, but some of the others are rewarding pieces. Indeed the first of the *Danses champêtres* almost suggests the music to *The Tempest*, written at much the same time. Both the Opp. 115 and 116 pieces contain music of quality. As in the companion disc, **Nils-Erik Sparf** and **Bengt Forsberg** prove as imaginative as they are accomplished.

2 Pieces, Op. 2 (2 versions); Scaramouche: Scène d'amour; 2 Serious melodies, Op. 77; 4 Pieces, Op. 78; 6 Pieces, Op. 79; Sonatina in E, Op. 80

*** BIS CD 525. Sparf, Forsberg

This CD offers the first recording of the 1888 versions of the *Grave* and the *Perpetuum mobile*, the two pieces which Sibelius assigned to Op. 2, together with the 1911 versions, in which the former was revised as *Romance in B minor* and the latter overhauled as *Epilogue*. The former bears a certain affinity to the slow movement of the *Violin Concerto* and the prevalence of the tritone in the latter acts as a reminder that it was re-worked in the wake of the *Fourth Symphony*. Exemplary performances of the later pieces, including *Laetare anima mea* and the 1915 *Sonatina*, Op. 80.

PIANO MUSIC

Sibelius Edition, Volume 4: Piano Music: Complete Youthful Productions & Student Compositions of Music for Piano (including *A Catalogue of Themes* (50 Short Pieces) (1885–93). *10 Bagatelles*, Op. 34; *The Dryad*, Op. 45/1 (arr. 1910); *Finlandia* (rev. arr. 1900); *Finnish Folk Songs*, (arr. for piano, 1902/3); *6 Impromptus*, Op. 5; *Karelia Suite*: excerpts (arr. 1897); *King Kristian II* (4 Pieces), Op. 27; *Kyllikki*, Op. 41; *10 Pensées lyriques*, Op. 40; *Preliminary Sketch for slow movement of Symphony 1*; *Sonata in F*, Op. 12 (1893); *21 Miscellaneous Pieces* (1894–1914); *10 Pieces*, Op. 24; *Valse triste*, Op. 44/1 (2 versions, 1903/4)

(N) (B) *** BIS CD 1909/11. Folke Gräsbeck (piano)

As with the previous boxes in this well-packaged and -documented coverage, the discs are inexpensive – five CDs for the price of three.

Andante in E flat; Aubade in A flat; Au crépuscule; A Catalogue of Themes, 50 Short Pieces; Con moto, sempre una corda; 3 Pieces; Scherzo in E & Trio in E min.; 3 Short Pieces; 5 Short Pieces; Trio in E min. (arr. for piano); Trånaden (Yearning); 11 Variations on a Harmonic Formula (BIS CD 1067)

Complete Youthful Production of Music for the Piano I (BIS CD 1067)

Complete Youthful Production of Music for the Piano II (BIS CD 1202)

*** Folke Gräsbeck

As part of its ambitious scheme to record every note that Sibelius ever wrote, BIS has turned its attention to the early piano pieces Sibelius composed in his study years. All these are unpublished and give no hint of what was to come. Perhaps the most imaginative is *Trånaden* to accompany a recitation of Stagnelius's poem.

Some of the pieces, such as the *Moderato – Presto in D minor* (1888) are worth hearing, but none can be said to be remotely characteristic. All, with the exception of the *Florestan Suite* of 1889, are first recordings. **Folke Gräsbeck** plays them with fluent grace, and the BIS recording and documentation are exemplary.

10 Bagatelles, Op. 34; The Cavalier; Dance Intermezzo; 6 Finnish Folk Songs; Kyllikki (3 Lyric Pieces), Op. 41; Mandolinato; Morceau romantique; Pensées lyriques, Op. 40; Spagnuolo; To Longing

(B) (BB) *** Naxos 8.554808. Gimse

The Norwegian pianist **Håvard Gimse** here includes two important sets of the piano pieces, Opp. 34 and 40, and the *6 Finnish Folk Songs*, the fifth of which, *Fratricide*, is slightly Bartókian. Sibelius's contemporary and countryman Selim Palmgren put it perfectly when he wrote that 'even in what for him were alien regions, [Sibelius] moves with an unfailing responsiveness to tone colour', and Gimse brings finesse and distinction to this repertoire. This and the companion disc are first recommendations.

6 Bagatelles, Op. 97; 5 Characteristic Impressions, Op. 103; 8 Little Pieces, Op. 99; 5 Romantic Pieces, Op. 101; 5 Sketches, Op. 114

⊙— (BB) *** Naxos 8.555853. Gimse

All the pieces recorded here come from the 1920s, the period of the *Sixth* and *Seventh Symphonies*, and are rarities. Among the finest are the *Five Sketches*, which come from the very end of the decade and are among Sibelius's last published works. *The Village Church* from Op. 103 has overtones of the *Andante festivo* for strings, and *The Oarsman* seems to ruminate on ideas in the *Seventh Symphony*. But pieces like *In Mournful Mood* and *Landscape* from Op. 114 are curiously haunting. So is the rest of the Op. 114 set, and its neglect has been our loss.

5 Characteristic Pieces, Op. 103; 5 Sketches, Op. 114; 5 Pieces (The Trees), Op. 75; 5 Pieces (The Flowers), Op. 85; 5 Romantic Pieces, Op. 101

*** Chan. 9833. Tabe

Kyoko Tabe makes the most of these miniatures without making too much of them. Opp. 75 and 85 come from the period 1914–15 and the remainder from the 1920s. She conveys some of their charm and individuality with expertise and is recorded with a lifelike and natural sound.

6 Impromptus, Op. 5; Sonata in F, Op. 12; 10 Pieces, Op. 24

⊙— (BB) **** Naxos 8.553899. Gimse

The *Sonata* and *Impromptus* come from the year in which the first version of *En Saga* was composed. The *Sonata* has a genuine sense of forward movement and some of its ideas are appealing. The Op. 24 *Pieces* were written at various times between 1894 and 1903. The Norwegian pianist **Håvard Gimse** has consistent tonal beauty and unfailing musicianship. This is distinguished playing and a strong recommendation at any price level.

3 Lyric Pieces, Op. 41; 5 Characteristic Impressions, Op. 103; 6 Impromptus, Op. 5; 5 Pieces, Op. 75; 5 Pieces, Op. 85; Finlandia (arr. composer)

(BB) *** Naxos 8.553661. Lauriala

Perfectly good playing and decent recording make this a useful alternative to the complete survey by Gimse, and it also enjoys the benefit of decent recorded sound.

4 Lyric Pieces, Op. 74; 5 Pieces (The Flowers), Op. 35; 5 Pieces (The Trees), Op. 75; 6 Pieces, Op. 94; 13 Pieces, Op. 76

⊙— (BB) **** Naxos 8.555363. Gimse

10 Pieces, Op. 58; 2 Rondinos, Op. 68; 3 Sonatinas, Op. 67

⊙— (BB) **** Naxos 8.554814. Gimse

The *Ten Pieces* of Op. 58 date from 1909, the year of the *String Quartet (Voces intimae)*. They are delightful and by no means

just trivial. Each has its own sobriquet and shows real keyboard character. The final rather solemn *Summer Song* is memorable, as is the wistful mood of the first of the *Two Rondinos*, written two years later; the second sparkles most pianistically. The three *Sonatinas*, written together in the summer of 1912, are also full of charming ideas, giving the impression of a composer relaxing in holiday mood. **Håvard Gimse** plays all this music freshly, and finds its simple beauty. He is very well recorded and this Naxos disc more than bears out the promise of its companions.

ORGAN MUSIC

Intrada, Op. 111a; Masonic Music, Op. 113/1 & 10; Surusoitto, Op. 111b

*** BIS CD 1101. Ericsson – DVOŘÁK: *Preludes & Fugues* **(*); GLAZUNOV: *Preludes & Fugues*, etc. ***

After the death of Sibelius's old friend and drinking companion, the artist Akseli Gallen-Kalela, the composer was forced to compose something at short notice for the ceremony. *Surusoitto* was the result. In the late 1960s the composer Joonas Kokkonen put forward the theory that given the pressure of time, Sibelius might have drawn on material from the *Eighth Symphony*, on which he was working throughout 1931. Aino Sibelius, the composer's widow, also thought this likely. The *Intrada* (1925) is powerful, but the *Funeral March* from the *Masonic Music* (1927) betrays its proximity to the *Tempest* music. Superb playing from **Hans-Ola Ericsson** on a magnificently powerful instrument.

THEATRE MUSIC

Sibelius Edition, Volume 5: Theatre Music: Original Theatre Music: Jedermann, Op. 83 (1916). Belshazzar's Feast, Concert Suite, Op. 51 (1906/7); King Christian I, Op. 27 (1898). Kuolema (1903); The Language of the Bird: Wedding March (1911); Pelleas and Melisande, Op. 46: Concert Suite (1905); Scaramouche, Op. 71 (1913); Swanwhite, Concert Suite, Op. 54 (1908); The Tempest: Prelude; Suites 1–2 (1927); Twelfth Night, Op. 60 (1909)

(N) *** BIS-CD 1912/4. Soloists, Lahti SO, Vänskä; Gothenburg SO, Neeme Järvi

This set covers performances from the original manuscripts of Sibelius's theatre music and the concert suites and revised versions which followed. Offered at six CDs for the price of three, it is a very real bargain, with full documentation included.

VOCAL MUSIC

Academic March; Finlandia (arr. composer); Har du mod?, Op. 31/2; March of the Finnish Jaeger Battalion, Op. 91/1; (i) The Origin of Fire, Op. 32; Sandels, Op. 28; Song of the Athenians, Op. 31/3

**(*) BIS CD 314. (i) Tiilikainen, Laulun Ystävät Male Ch.; Gothenburg SO, Järvi

The Origin of Fire is by far the most important work on this record. **Sauli Tiilikainen** is very impressive indeed, and the playing of the **Gothenburg Symphony Orchestra** under **Neeme Järvi** has plenty of feeling and atmosphere. None of the other pieces is essential Sibelius. The singing of the **Laulun Ystävät Choir** is good rather than outstanding, and the fine recording in the best BIS traditions.

(i) *Belshazzar's Feast* (complete score), Op. 51; *The Countess's Portrait (Grefvinnans konterfej)*; (ii) *Jedermann (Everyman)* (incidental music), Op. 83

➻ **** BIS CD 737. (i) Passikivi; Lahti SO, Vänskä; (ii) with Lehto, Tiilikainen, Pietiläinen, Lahti Chamber Ch.

The incidental music to Hugo von Hofmannsthal's morality play *Everyman* is fragmentary, wisps of sound; all of it is atmospheric and the best of it (the *Largo* section from track 12 onwards) finds Sibelius at his most inspired. The complete score for Hjalmar Procopé's *Belshazzar's Feast* brings us some seven minutes of extra music. The scoring is different from and less effective than the concert suite. *Grefvinnans konterfej* (*The Countess's Portrait*) is a short, wistful piece for strings which comes from 1906. Dedicated, sensitive performances from the **Lahti Symphony Orchestra** and excellent recording. An indispensable disc for all Sibelians.

The Captive Queen; Have you courage, Op. 31/2 (2nd & 4th versions); *March of the Jäger Battalion*, Op. 91a; (i) *The Origin of Fire*, Op. 32 (2 versions). *Rapids-Rider's Brides*; (ii) *Rakastava; Sandels*, Op. 28 (2 versions)

*** BIS CD 1525. YL Male Ch., Lahti SO, Vänskä; with (i) Hakala; (ii) Nyman

Here we have not only the revised 1910 version of *The Origin of Fire* but Sibelius's first thoughts from 1902; and similarly the first (1898) version of *Sandels*, preceding the *First Symphony*, together with its revision of 1915, by which time he was working on the *Fifth*. A fascinating issue in authoritative performances under **Osmo Vänskä** and equally authoritative notes by Andrew Barnett.

(i) *Karelia* (complete incidental music); (ii) *Kuolema*, Op. 44; *Valse triste* (1904 version)

➻ **** BIS CD 915. (i) Laitinen, Hoffgren; (i; ii) Laukka; (ii) Tiilhonen; Lahti SO, Vänskä

The *Karelia Suite* is familiar enough, but few readers will have heard the complete score. Some things are disconcerting: the familiar cor anglais melody in the *Ballade* is given to a tenor, and the movement is far too long. But there is much of interest here. The incidental music to *Kuolema* ('Death'), written ten years later, was revised the following year (1904) and re-scored. The original second section, *Paavali's Song*, is quite inspired, though Sibelius was quite right to add wind to represent the bird cries in the following scene (he conflated scenes 3 and 4 to form *Scene with Cranes*). The disc also affords an opportunity to contrast the 1903 and 1904 versions of *Valse triste*; the differences will bring you up with a start. Superb playing and recording.

(i) *Karelia Suite*, Op. 11 (original scoring); (ii) *King Christian II*, Op. 27 (complete original score); (iii) *Pelléas et Mélisande* (original scoring)

*** BIS CD 918. (i; ii) Laukka; (iii) Jakobsson; Lahti SO, Vänskä

Sibelius re-scored all three works for larger forces when he made his *King Christian* concert suite the following year, his first orchestral work to be published. It is particularly good to hear the *Musette* from that suite in such a characterful form, just for wind. The changes in the score Sibelius composed for Bertel Gripenberg's Swedish translation of Maeterlinck's *Pelléas et Mélisande* are less extensive but we do have an additional section that has never been published. The *Karelia Suite* is drawn from BIS CD 915. A highly successful issue of great interest to all Sibelians.

Kullervo Symphony, Op. 7

➻ (BB) **** LSO Live 0074. Groop, Mattei, L. Symphony Ch., LSO, C. Davis

➻ **** BIS CD 1215. Paasikivi, Laukka, Helsinki University Ch., Lahti SO, Vänskä

Sir Colin's first movement is spacious – certainly broader than the 1958 performance by Sibelius's son-in-law, Jussi Jalas, which brought this piece alive again after its long slumber. The slow movement, *Kullervo's Youth*, is powerfully characterized, as indeed is the central *Kullervo and his Sister* movement. Sir Colin is a Sibelian of commanding stature, and the **LSO** and **London Symphony Chorus** give of their finest. Both soloists **Monica Groop** and **Peter Mattei** are in fine voice here. Good recording, though the acoustic is just a little dry, thanks to the full house. This is arguably the finest *Kullervo* now before the public.

Having completed an impressive cycle of the symphonies **Osmo Vänskä** and the **Lahti Orchestra** give us a finely paced reading of Sibelius's groundbreaking work, with plenty of dramatic intensity and a strong atmosphere. There is the same sense of grip and epic sweep that distinguishes Sir Colin Davis's LSO recording. Apart from two fine soloists, Vänskä has the advantage of a Finnish male choir. Incidentally, some small errors in the published score have been corrected. For many this BIS CD will be a first choice.

Cantatas: *Laulu Lemminkäiselle (Song to Lemminkäinen)*, Op. 31/1; *Maan virsi (Hymn to the earth)*, Op. 95; *Oma Maa (Our native land)*, Op. 92; *Sandels*, Op. 28; *Snöfrid*, Op. 29; *Väinön virsi (Väinö's Song)*, Op. 110; *Finlandia*, Op. 26

*** Virgin 5 45589-2. Ellerhein Girls' Ch., Estonian Nat. Male Ch. & SO, Järvi

Three of these *Cantatas* come from Sibelius's last period: *Our native land*, probably the best known of these pieces, comes from 1918. *Hymn to the earth* from 1919 is also conventional and, although *Väinö's Song* is a neighbour of *The Tempest* and *Tapiola*, it betrays nothing of their vision or mastery. *Our native land* certainly sounds stronger and more appealing in this performance than in any other version on disc. **Paavo Järvi** makes the most of Sibelius's evocative description of the aurora borealis and the white nights of the Nordic summer. These *Cantatas* are well worth hearing and Järvi gives a totally committed account of them and has a fine body of singers. Excellent sound.

(i; ii) Snöfrid, Op. 29; (i) Coronation Cantata, JS104; Oma maa, Op. 92; Andante festivo, JS34b; Overture in A min., JS144; Rakastava, Op. 14

*** BIS CD 1265. Lahti SO, Vänskä; with (i) Jubilate Ch.; (ii) Stina Ekblad (narr.)

Snöfrid is an 'improvisation' for narrator, mixed choir and orchestra, dating from 1900, and it accompanies lines from Rydberg's poem of that name. It is characteristic of early Sibelius, often powerful and consistent in quality. The Overture was written at high speed two years later to fill out the programme which included the première of the Second Symphony, and is a rewarding piece. It looks forward to the period of the Voces intimae Quartet, which one of its themes actually anticipates. Tavaststjerna is pretty routine stuff. Oma maa ('My own Land') is an altogether different matter. The 1912 transcription of the early choral suite Rakastava ('The Lover') for strings and percussion is Sibelius at his most inspired and poignant. Fine performances and recording.

The Tempest (incidental music), Op. 109 (complete)

*** BIS CD 581. Tiihonen, Passikivi, Hirvonen, Kerola, Heinonen, Lahti Opera Ch. & SO, Vänskä

**(*) Ondine ODE 813-2. Groop, Viljakainen, Hynninen, Silvasti, Tiilikainen, Op. Festival Ch., Finnish RSO, Saraste

The Tempest: Prelude. Suites 1 & 2

(N) *** Reference Recordings RR115. Kansas City SO, Stern – SULLIVAN: The Tempest ***

Sibelius's score, commissioned for a 1926 Copenhagen production, was his last major work and one of his most visionary. It is one of the four masterpieces (the others being the Sixth and Seventh Symphonies and Tapiola) that crowned his creative career. The BIS and Ondine CDs both have the advantage of singers, and in fact the vocal writing is often highly imaginative and the singers on the BIS CD are especially good. The atmosphere is strong too and puts one completely under its spell.

Michael Stern is a thoroughly idiomatic interpreter and, judging by this Tempest, a Sibelian of rare insight. We have not heard a more imaginative account of this music since the celebrated Beecham version of the 1950s. Indeed, the Intrada and Berceuse from the Second Suite even surpass the latter! The Kansas City Orchestra respond with enthusiasm – perhaps the strings could at times have a weightier sonority but, given the overall quality of this reading, reservations are silent. The recording is well balanced and natural: Anthony Hodgson's notes are predictably insightful and authoritative.

If clarity and definition are a first priority, the Ondine version under Saraste is the one to go for. There is good singing here, too, from Monica Groop, Jorma Hynninen and the rest of the cast. The performance is given in Danish (as it would have been in the 1926 version, rather than the Finnish text used by BIS). However, Saraste is nowhere near as sensitive as Vänskä and does not have his sense of mystery or atmosphere. His Prospero is too fast, almost routine by comparison with Vänskä, who draws the listener more completely into Sibelius's and Shakespeare's world. Both accounts are recommendable and either is to be acquired rather than none. But the BIS makes a clear first choice.

Songs

18 Songs

(N) (M) (**(*)) DG mono/stereo 477 6612. Borg, Werba

When this collection was first issued in 1958, our own Robert Layton reviewed the mono LP as a 'pinnacle of the Sibelius song discography'. Now it returns in a handy reduction of the original sleeve (LPEM 19113) adjusted to CD size. However, apart from the untranslated titles, and a brief note about Kim Borg, the documentation is non-existent. The collection now includes, beside the original 16 songs, which are well chosen, Borg's stereo remake of two of them, Lastu lainchilla and Illalle, plus three more by another Finnish composer, Kilpinen. It is a pity about the absence of documentation and translations, but this disc is certainly collectable by those who admire the repertoire.

Songs: Arioso; The Jewish Maiden's Song; Belshazzar's Feast; Autumn Evening; Luonnotar; Sancta Maria The Maiden in the Tower; And I questioned her no further; Sunrise; The Spring is Flying

⊕ *** Warner 8573 8.0243-2. Mattila, CBSO, Oramo – GRIEG: Songs (***)

Karita Mattila is in powerful, expressive form. She has a splendid breadth in the Arioso, a much later song than its early opus number would indicate, and her Luonnotar is second to none. These are marvellous songs and Mattila deserves much credit for including an aria from the early (and unsuccessful) opera, The Maiden in the Tower, which the composer subsequently withdrew. Sakari Oramo and the Birmingham Orchestra give splendid support throughout, and the recording has great naturalness and presence.

Arioso, Op. 3; Narcissus; Pelléas et Mélisande: The Three Blind Sisters; 7 Songs, Op. 17; 6 Songs, Op. 36; 5 Songs, Op. 37; 6 Songs, Op. 88; Souda, souda, sinisorsa

⊕ *** BIS CD 457. von Otter, Forsberg

Sophie von Otter always makes a beautiful sound, but she has a highly developed sense of line and brings great interpretative insight to such songs as 'My bird is long in homing' and 'Tennis at Trianon', which has even greater finesse than Söderström's. And what a good accompanist Bengt Forsberg is. The recording is good if a bit reverberant.

Songs with orchestra: Arioso; Autumn evening; Come away, Death!; The diamond on the March snow; The fool's song of the spider; Luonnotar, Op. 70; On a balcony by the sea; The rapids-rider's

brides; Serenade; Since then I have questioned no further; Spring flies hastily; Sunrise

🎵 **** BIS CD 270. Hynninen, Häggander, Gothenburg SO, Panula

Jorma Hynninen is a fine interpreter of this repertoire: his singing can only be called glorious. **Mari-Anne Häggander** manages the demanding tessitura of *Arioso* and *Luonnotar* with much artistry, and her *Luonnotar* is certainly to be preferred to Söderström's. **Jorma Panula** proves a sensitive accompanist and secures fine playing from the **Gothenburg Orchestra**. In any event, this is indispensable.

Belshazzar's Feast; The Jewish Girl's Song; 6 Songs, Op. 36; Black Roses; But my Bird is Long in Homing; Tennis at Trianon; Sigh, Sedges, Sigh; The March Snow; The Diamond on the March Snow; 5 Songs, Op. 37: The First Kiss; Little Lasse; Sunrise; Was it a dream?; The Tryst; 6 Songs, Op. 50: Spring Song; Loneliness; In the Field a Maiden Sings; From anxious heart; The Silent Town; Rose Song; To Evening; I am a Tree; The Watersprite or The Elf King; Beneath the Fir Trees; Spring is Flying; The North; Who Brought you Here?

🎵 **** Hyp. CDA 67318. Karnéus, Drake

The only Finnish song here is *Illale* ('To Evening'), among the most lyrical and affecting of his songs. **Katarina Karnéus** offers the Opp. 36 and 37 sets, which include some of the best loved (and best) songs like *Säv, säv susa* and *Men min fågel märks dock icke*, and one of the subtlest, *Bollspelet vid Trianon*. She also includes the German settings, Op. 50, written in 1906. (Sibelius spoke little French or English). Two of them, *Im Feld ein Mädchen* ('In the Field a Maiden Sings') and *Die stille Stadt* ('The Silent Town') are among his greatest songs. Karnéus possesses a glorious voice and sings with real interpretative insight, and in these inspired performances she and **Julius Drake** find new dimensions in these jewels of songs, performances that sharply bring out the contrasts of mood, the range of emotion and the sense of drama, as in the overpowering tragic climax of *The Tryst*. The eerie originality of such a song as *Näcken* ('The Watersprite') is perfectly caught. It is a magical partnership, giving fresh insights in every item. Those who have yet to explore Sibelius's songs should start right here.

7 Songs, Op. 13; 6 Songs, Op. 50; 6 Songs, Op. 90; Resemblance; A song; Serenade; The wood-nymph; The Jewish girl's song; (i) The Thought

🎵 Ⓜ *** BIS CD 757. von Otter, Forsberg; (i) with Groop

The Opp. 13 and 90 songs are all settings of Runeberg, Sibelius's favourite poet, but there are rarities such as *Skogsrået* ('The Wood-nymph') – totally unrelated, by the way, to the melodrama and tone-poem of the same name which Sibelius wrote in the early 1890s, and never before recorded. Also new are the duet, *Tanken* ('The Thought'), *Resemblance* and *A song*. **Von Otter** and her partner characterize each song with the consummate artistry one expects from them, and the only possible reservation concerns the balance, which in some of the early songs favours the piano.

OPERA

The Maiden in the Tower (opera; complete); *Karelia Suite, Op. 11*

Ⓝ *** BIS CD 250. Häggander, Hynninen, Hagegård, Kruse, Gothenburg Ch. & SO, Järvi

The Maiden in the Tower (opera; complete); *Pelléas et Mélisande* (incidental music), Op. 46; *Kuolema: Valse triste*

Ⓝ ⒷⒷ *** Virgin 5 22055(2). (i) Kringelborn, Jonsson, Passikivi, Magee, Estonian Girls' Ch. & Nat. Male Ch., Estonian Nat. SO, Paavo Järvi (with 4 *Legends*, etc. ***)

The Maiden in the Tower falls into eight short scenes. The orchestral interlude between the first two scenes brings us the real Sibelius, and the second scene is undoubtedly impressive; there are echoes of Wagner, such as we find in some of the great orchestral songs of the following decade. All the same, it lack something we look for in all Sibelius's most characteristic music: quite simply a sense of mastery. Yet there are telling performances here from **Mari Anne Häggander** and **Jorma Hynninen** and the **Gothenburg Symphony Orchestra**. **Neeme Järvi's** account of the *Karelia Suite* is certainly original, with its *Intermezzo* too broad to make an effective contrast with the ensuing *Ballade*.

The Virgin Double reissue is more generously filled than the rival version from Gothenburg, and it comes with the *Pelléas Suite*, which was composed a decade later. Jorma Hynninen is an imposing villain in the Gothenburg version, and of the two heroines, Häggander is perhaps the more convincing. This a useful alternative to the BIS account, even if it does not completely replace it.

SIMPSON, Robert (1921–97)

Energy; Introduction & Allegro on a Theme by Max Reger; The Four Temperaments; Volcano; Vortex

*** Hyp. CDA 66449. Desford Colliery Caterpillar Band, Watson

The Four Temperaments is a four-movement, 22-minute symphony of great imaginative power, and ingeniously laid out for the band. The *Introduction and Allegro on a Theme by Max Reger* is awesome and impressive. Together with *Volcano* and his most recent piece, *Vortex*, it makes up his entire output in this medium. The **Desford Colliery Caterpillar Band** under **James Watson** play with all the expertise and virtuosity one expects, and the recording has admirable clarity and body, although the acoustic is on the dry side.

Symphonies: (i) 1; (ii) 2; (i) 3; (ii) 4; (i) 5; (iii) 6; 7; (i) 8; (ii) 9; (iii) 10; (iv) 11; Variations on a Theme by Nielsen

Ⓜ *** Hyp. CDS 44191/7. (i) RPO; (ii) Bournemouth SO; (iii) RLPO; all cond. Handley; (iv) City of L. SO, Taylor

For anyone interested in the progress of the symphony in England in the 20th century, this is a self-recommending set. All these recordings are available separately, but for those willing to jump in at the deep end this should prove an admirable investment.

Symphonies 1; 8

*** Hyp. CDA 66890. RPO, Handley

Robert Simpson's *First Symphony* holds up to the test of time remarkably well and better than much other music of the 1950s. One critic has pointed to the *Eighth* as seeming to embody some 'colossal inner rage' and, like the *Fifth*, it undoubtedly has a combative tumult that rarely passes into tranquillity. Handley makes out a strong case for both scores, and the sound is absolutely first class. An indispensable issue for anyone who cares about the post-war symphony in Britain.

Symphonies 2; 4

ꙮ *** Hyp. CDA 66505. Bournemouth SO, Handley

The *Second* is one of the very best; its opening is one of Simpson's most mysterious and inspired ideas, lean and sinuous but full of poetic vision. The variation slow movement is one of the most virtuosic and remarkable exercises in the palindrome, yet such is the quality of Simpson's artistry in concealing his ingenuity that no one coming to it innocently would be aware of this. The *Fourth Symphony* is the more extended piece. Powerful and inspiriting music in totally dedicated performances by **Vernon Handley**, and excellent recording quality.

Symphonies 3; 5

*** Hyp. CDA 66728. RPO, Handley

Vernon Handley brings us the première recording of the *Fifth Symphony* (1971), a work of striking power and range. It is combative and intense and enjoys at times an almost unbridled ferocity that enhances the admittedly few moments of repose, for it is music of a vital and forceful eloquence. Fine playing by the **RPO** under Handley, and exemplary recording.

Symphonies 6; 7

*** Hyp. CDA 66280. RLPO, Handley

The *Sixth* is inspired by the idea of growth: the development of a musical structure from initial melodic cells in much the same way as life emerges from a single fertilized cell in nature. The *Seventh*, scored for chamber orchestral forces, is hardly less powerful in its imaginative vision and sense of purpose. Both scores are bracingly Nordic in their inner landscape and exhilarating in aural experience. The playing of the **Liverpool Orchestra** under **Vernon Handley** could hardly be bettered, and the recording is altogether first class.

Symphony 9

ꙮ ✸ *** Hyp. CDA 66299. Bournemouth SO, Handley (with talk by the composer)

What can one say about the *Ninth* of Robert Simpson, except that its gestures are confident and its control of pace and its material are masterly? It is a one-movement work, but at no time in its 45 minutes does it falter – nor does the attention of the listener. The CD also includes a spoken introduction

to the piece that many listeners will probably find helpful. It is played superbly by the **Bournemouth Symphony Orchestra** under **Vernon Handley**, and is no less superbly recorded.

Symphony 10

*** Hyp. CDA 66510. RLPO, Handley

The *Tenth Symphony* (1988) will be a tough nut to crack for many collectors. Its musical argument is unfailingly concentrated. Like its predecessor, it has a Beethovenian strength and momentum. The *Symphony* lasts almost an hour and is not the ideal starting place from which to explore this composer's world. But make no mistake: it is a work of stature, and it is very well played and recorded here.

Symphony 11; Variations on a Theme by Nielsen

ꙮ *** Hyp. CDA 67500. City of L. Sinfonia, Taylor

The *Eleventh Symphony* comes from 1990 and is a two-movement work: an *Andante* followed by an *Allegro*. Scored for smaller forces than its two immediate predecessors, it has the powerful and uncompromising logic that shapes all the composer's best music; indeed, many may feel that it is his finest symphony. The *Variations on a Theme by Nielsen* was written in 1983 and includes some highly evocative and resourceful invention. An essential acquisition for anyone who cares about the modern British symphony, and very well-detailed sound indeed.

(i) Canzona for Brass; (i & ii) Media morte in vita sumus; (ii) Tempi; (iii) Eppur si muove

*** Hyp. CDA 67016. (i) Corydon Brass Ens.; (ii) Corydon Singers, Best; (iii) Quinn

The *Canzona for Brass* from 1957 has never sounded more impressive on CD. It has the dignity and grandeur of Gabrieli. The *Media morte in vita sumus* ('In the midst of death we are in life') is for voices and brass. It has a depth and eloquence completely at variance with so much contemporary music. *Tempi* (1988) is a setting for *a cappella* choir of various Italian tempo indications, written for a choral competition in the composer's adopted Eire. Such is its beauty that it makes one regret that it is Simpson's only contribution to the medium. *Eppur si muove* (1988) is an imposing 30-minute piece for organ, not dissimilar in scope and ambition to Nielsen's *Commotio*. It derives its title from Galileo's response when he was compelled by the Church to recant his view that the earth revolved round the sun: 'But it *does* move.' **Iain Quinn** plays it with consummate mastery on the organ of Winchester Cathedral. The brass playing is superb and the **Corydon Singers** cope with Simpson's demanding vocal writing admirably even if the sopranos are obviously taxed at times above the stave. State-of-the-art recording. Not to be missed.

(i) Clarinet Quintet; String Quartet 13; (ii) String Quintet 2

ꙮ *** Hyp. CDA 66905. (i) King; (ii) Van Kampen; Delmé Qt

The *Clarinet Quintet* is arguably the most searching example of the genre to have appeared since the war and not just in this country. From the opening, with the model of Beethoven's *C sharp minor Quartet*, Op. 131, not far from view, right to the ending, this is a subtle, concentrated and profoundly original – and profound – work. It is one of those pieces which is more than the sum of its parts and which resonates long in the memory. The *Thirteenth Quartet* is a concentrated piece and the **Delmé Quartet** are ideal exponents.

Horn Quartet (for horn, violin, cello & piano); Horn Trio (for horn, violin & piano)

🎜 *** Hyp. CDA 66695. Watkins, Lowbury, Armytage, Dearnley

The *Quartet for Horn, Violin, Cello and Piano* of 1976 is of unfailing quality and imagination, and its development is magnificently sustained. The composer's command of large-scale musical thinking is much in evidence – but so, too, is his feeling for sonority. He draws some extraordinary sounds from these four instruments. In some ways this is one of his most deeply original and compelling works. The later *Horn Trio* immediately pre-dates the *Ninth Symphony*. These are most impressive pieces, and the performances are completely dedicated and highly imaginative. Excellent recording too.

String Quartets 1; 4

*** Hyp. CDA 66419. Delmé Qt

The *First Quartet* opens in as innocent a fashion as the Haydn *Lark Quartet* or Nielsen's *E flat*, but the better one comes to know it the more it is obvious that Simpson is already his own man. The second movement is a palindrome (many modern composers do not know how to write forwards, let alone backwards as well) but its ingenuity is worn lightly. The *Fourth* is part of the trilogy which Simpson conceived as a kind of commentary on Beethoven's *Rasumovsky Quartets*, yet they live very much in their own right. Excellent performances from the **Delmé Quartet**, and fine recording too.

String Quartets 2; 5

*** Hyp. CDA 66386. Delmé Qt

The *Second Quartet* is thought-provoking and full of character. The *Fifth*, composed over 20 years later in 1974, is one of the three modelled on Beethoven's *Rasumovsky Quartets* – in this case, Op. 59, *No.* 2 – and even emulates the phrase structure of the Beethoven. It is a long and powerfully sustained piece, which receives expert advocacy from the **Delmé Quartet** and excellent Hyperion sound.

String Quartets 3 & 6; String Trio (prelude, adagio & fugue)

*** Hyp. CDA 66376. Delmé Qt

The *Third Quartet* is a two-movement piece. Its finale is a veritable power-house, with its unrelenting sense of onward movement which almost strains the medium. Its first movement is a deeply felt piece that has a powerful and haunting eloquence. The *Sixth* is further evidence of Simpson's remarkable musical mind. The *String Trio* is a marvellously

stimulating and thoughtful piece. Dedicated performances and excellent recording.

String Quartets 7 & 8

*** Hyp. CDA 66117. Delmé Qt

The *Seventh Quartet* has a real sense of vision and something of the stillness of the remote worlds it evokes, 'quiet and mysterious yet pulsating with energy'. The *Eighth* turns from the vastness of space to the microcosmic world of insect-life, but, as with so much of Simpson's music, there is a concern for musical continuity rather than beauty of incident. Excellent playing from the **Delmé Quartet**, and very good recorded sound, too.

String Quartet 9 (32 Variations & Fugue on a Theme of Haydn)

*** Hyp. CDA 66127. Delmé Qt

The *Ninth Quartet* is a set of 32 variations and a fugue on the Minuet of Haydn's *Symphony 47*. Like the Minuet itself, all the variations are in the form of a palindrome. It is a mighty and serious work, argued with all the resource and ingenuity one expects from this composer. A formidable achievement in any age, and a rarity in ours. The **Delmé Quartet** cope with its difficulties splendidly, and the performance carries the imprimatur of the composer.

String Quartets 10 (For Peace); 11

*** Hyp. CDA 66225. Coull Qt

The subtitle of 10, *For Peace*, refers to 'its generally pacific character' and aspires to define 'the condition of peace which excludes aggression but not strong feeling'. Listening to this *Quartet* is like hearing a quiet, cool voice of sanity that refreshes the troubled spirit after a long period in an alien, hostile world. The one-movement *Eleventh* draws on some of the inspiration of its predecessor. It is a work of enormous power and momentum. Excellent performances and recording.

String Quartet 12 (1987); (i) String Quintet (1987)

*** Hyp. CDA 66503. Coull Qt; (i) with Bigley

Robert Simpson's *Twelfth Quartet* is a masterly and absorbing score. His *String Quintet* is another work of sustained inventive power. We are unlikely to get another recording, so this is self-recommending; but it must be noted that the heroic demands this score makes on the players keep them fully stretched. The intonation and tone of the leader is not always impeccable, but the playing has commitment and intelligence.

String Quartets 14 & 15; (i) Quintet for Clarinet, Bass Clarinet & Strings

*** Hyp. CDA 66626. (i) Farrall, Cross; Vanbrugh Qt

The *Fourteenth Quartet* comes from 1990 and the *Fifteenth*, written when Simpson was 70 (in 1991), was his last. This is surely the greatest quartet cycle produced in the last half of the 20th century, and in terms of contrapuntal ingenuity and musical depth belongs with Bartók, Shostakovich and Holmboe. The *Clarinet Quintet* is not to be confused with the

1968 work listed above; it is an arrangement for clarinet, bass clarinet and string trio of a 1983 quintet intriguingly scored for clarinet, bass clarinet and three double basses. These are powerful Beethovenian scores whose stature and musical processes are easier to recognize than describe. Dedicated performances, superbly recorded.

Piano Sonata; Michael Tippett, his Mystery; Variations & Finale on a Theme by Beethoven; Variations & Finale on a Theme by Haydn

*** Hyp. CDA 66827. Clarke

The *Piano Sonata* is a concentrated, craggy, powerfully argued piece, not obviously pianistic but bristling with challenges and difficulties. The *Variations and Finale on a Theme of Haydn* (1948) evince Simpson's lifelong interest in the palindrome. The slow movement of the *Second Symphony* is a palindrome, and the theme he uses here (that of the Minuet of Haydn's *Symphony 47*) also forms the basis of the mighty variations which comprise the *Ninth String Quartet*. The short piece written for Tippett was a contribution to a birthday tribute. The *Variations and Finale on a Theme of Beethoven* are based on a little-known *Bagatelle*, WoO 61a, and were written for Charles Burney's granddaughter, and with the present pianist in mind. The performances are authoritative and, apart from a certain over-resonance, the recording is satisfactory.

SINDING, Christian (1856–1941)

Piano Concerto in D flat, Op. 6

*** Hyp. CDA 67555. Lane, Bergen PO, Litton – ALNÆS: *Piano Concerto in D* ***

Sinding has none of the national colouring of Grieg and Svendsen, and he showed little interest in the Norwegian folk tradition. The *Concerto* is an early work, coming from 1889, four years after the *Piano Quintet* which Busoni and the Brodsky Quartet had successfully championed in Germany. Sinding reworked the solo part in 1890 and again in 1901, and **Piers Lane** negotiates its difficulties with dazzling virtuosity and fine musicianship.

Violin Concerto 1 in A, Op. 45; Romance in D, Op. 100

ⒷⒷ *** Naxos 8.557266. Kraggerud, Bournemouth SO, Engeset – SIBELIUS: *Violin Concerto*, etc. **(*)

Henning Kraggerud's powerful reading of the Sibelius *Violin Concerto* comes here with an unusual and attractive coupling in another Scandinavian *Violin Concerto*, the first of the three written by the Norwegian Christian Sinding. Though the opening theme in this work is a barefaced crib from the finale of the Brahms *Violin Concerto*, Sinding's individual voice is quickly established in the full-blooded first movement, leading to a darkly intense slow movement and dance-like finale. The shorter piece nicely points the contrast of character between the two composers. Full, vivid sound.

Suite in A min., Op. 10

🔊–Ⓜ *** EMI (ADD) 5 62590-2. Perlman, Pittsburgh SO, Previn – KORNGOLD; SIBELIUS: *Concertos* ***

Heifetz recorded this dazzling piece in the 1950s, and it need only be said that **Perlman's** version (restored to the catalogue as part of the 'Perlman Edition') is not inferior. The blend of archaism and fantasy in Sinding's *Suite* sounds distinctly Scandinavian of the 1890s yet is altogether fresh and quite delightful. Such is the velocity of Perlman's first movement that one wonders whether the recording transfer is playing at the right speed. Stunning virtuosity and vivid recording.

Légende, Op. 46

ⒷⒷ *** Naxos 8.550329. Dong-Suk Kang, Slovak (Bratislava) RSO, Leaper – HALVORSEN: *Air norvégien*, etc.; SIBELIUS: *Violin Concerto*; SVENDSEN: *Romance* ***

Dong-Suk Kang plays Sinding's *Légende* with great conviction and an effortless, songful virtuosity. It is by no means as appealing as the Halvorsen and Svendsen pieces but makes a good makeweight for an excellent collection in the lowest price range.

Symphonies 1 in D min., Op. 21; 2 in D, Op. 83

*** CPO 999 502-2 Hanover NDR PO, Dausgaard

ⒷⒷ *** Warner Apex 0927 48310-2. Norwegian R.O, Rasilainen

Symphonies 3 in F, Op. 121; 4 (winter and spring), Op. 129

*** CPO 999 596-2. N. German R. PO, Porcelijn

*** Finlandia 8573 82356-2. Norwegian R. O, Rasilainen

Both the first two *Symphonies* are well crafted, though the scoring is often opaque. **Thomas Dausgaard** is a persuasive advocate and gets good playing from the excellent **Hanover Orchestra**. On balance, this is to be preferred to the rival **Norwegian Radio** accounts under **Ari Rasilainen**; however, readers wanting to explore the first two *Symphonies* will surely be tempted by the low price of the Apex disc.

Sinding's *Symphony 3* is his longest and most ambitious work. In a leaping 9/8 compound-time the first theme enters at once, with horns whooping exuberantly, leading to a second subject which echoes the Rhine motif in Wagner's *Ring* cycle, and though the slow movement with its gentle flow of themes is less striking, the skipping dance-rhythms of the Scherzo and the strong, *Meistersinger*-like tread of the celebratory finale again bring exhilaration. *Symphony 4*, like 3 warmly and colourfully performed under the Dutch conductor **David Porcelijn**, is structurally more adventurous, with its linked sequence of seven sections offering a satisfying one-movement symphonic structure. Amazingly, the piece was produced for Sinding's 80th birthday. Like the performances, the **North German Radio** recording is first rate, and it is again preferable to the alternative Finlandia coupling.

Violin Sonatas in C, Op. 12; in F, Op. 74; Suite in F, Op. 14

*** ASV CDDCA 1166. Rogliano, Paciariello

Like *Symphony 3*, the *C major Violin Sonata* starts with another surging theme, leaping in compound-time, while the *F major* work is warmly Brahmsian in its positive sequence of attractive ideas. The *Suite*, written at the same time as the *C major* work, is like a sonata with a shortened first movement. An amiable piece, like the *Sonatas* very well performed and recorded by the Italian duo of **Marco Rogliano** and **Maurizio Paciariello**.

SLAVICKY, Klement (1910–99)

Moravian Dance Fantasies; Rhapsodic Variations

Ⓜ (***) Sup. mono SU 3688-2. Czech PO, Ančerl – NOVÁK: *In the Tatras* (***)

Klement Slavicky was Moravian (his father had been a pupil of Janáček) and served until 1951 on the staff of the Czechoslovak Radio, ending up as its head of music. The *Moravian Dance Fantasies* come from 1951 and its companion here from 1953. **Ančerl** conducted the première the following year. They are both folkloric in feeling and are scored with great expertise and a feeling for colour. Well worth seeking out.

SMETANA, Bedřich (1824–84)

Festive Symphony in E, Op. 6; Festive Overture, Op. 4

Ⓜ (***) Sup. stereo/mono SU1914 011. Czech PO, Sejna – with DVOŘÁK: *Cunning Peasant Overture*; SKROUP: *The Tinker Overture* (**)

Smetana's *Festive* or *Triumphal Symphony* from 1853 is best known for its effervescent Scherzo, which is often performed on its own. It is also by far the best of the four movements. **Karel Sejna's** account was recorded in 1966, though the orchestral texture is so well balanced that it can hold its own with more modern recordings. The *Festive Overture*, Op. 4, recorded in 1955, is amazingly good for its period and the couplings are attractive.

Der Fischer, Rybár; Hakon Jarl; Jubel Overture; March for the Shakespeare Festival; Prague Carnival; Richard III; Venkovanka, the Peasant Woman; Wallenstein's Camp (symphonic poems)

✿ 🎧 **** Chan. 10413. BBC PO, Noseda

This is simply the finest compilation of Smetana's colourful symphonic poems ever put on disc. We have had a previous fine collection of the key works by the Bavarian Radio Orchestra under Kubelik, but that has now been reissued as a double-set, paired with a less attractive version of *Má Vlast* (DG 459 418-2). In any case, apart from **Gianandrea Noseda's** splendidly vivid and imaginative performances (especially the darkly atmospheric *Richard III*, the highly dramatic *Hakon Jarl* and the spectacularly military evocations of *Wallenstein's Camp*) the Chandos disc triumphs by its demonstration-quality, state-of-the-art recording. Not to be missed.

Má Vlast (complete; DVD version)

Ⓝ **(*) Medici Arts **DVD** 2072388. Bav. RSO, Kubelik (V/D Producer: Korbinian Mayer)

Recorded in 1984, this DVD version of *Má Vlast* is a disappointment. **Rafael Kubelik**, of course, is thoroughly at home in the score and the **Bavarian Radio Orchestra** play very well indeed, although there is not the special character of music-making one would experience with the Czech Philharmonic. Moreover, the performance itself cannot compare in vibrancy with the superb Supraphon 1990 account on CD listed below, even if the acoustic of the Munich Herkulessaal gives a fine, warm ambience to the sound. But the real problem is that the complete work runs to 82 minutes, and the experience of watching the conductor and various shots of the orchestra for this period of time without a real break, rather conventionally photographed, outlasts its welcome. It might have been an idea to have some colour imagery of Vyšehrad (which is still there!), the river Vltava, which runs right through Prague, and indeed Bohemia's woods and fields. This is a work that certainly offers the potential for illustration in that way if it can be imaginatively photographed.

Má Vlast (complete; CD versions)

🎧 **** Sup. 11 1208-2. Czech PO, Kubelik

🎧 ⒷⒷ **** Naxos 8.550931. Polish Nat. RSO (Katowice), Wit

🎧 **** Telarc CD 80265. Milwaukee SO, Macal

Ⓜ *** LSO Live **SACD** LSO 0516. LSO, C. Davis

Ⓝ Ⓑ *** Virgin 5 22129-2. RLPO, Pešek

*** Chan. 9366. Detroit SO, Järvi

Ⓜ *** Sup. SU 3672-2 901. Czech PO, Ančerl

*** Sup. SU 3465-2 031. Czech PO, Mackerras

ⒷⒷ (***) Naxos mono 8.111237. Czech PO, Talich

Rafael Kubelik's vibrant performance of *Má Vlast* is special, imbued with passionate national feeling, yet never letting the emotions boil over. At the bold opening of *Vyšehrad*, with the harp strongly profiled, the intensity of the music-making is immediately projected, and the trickling streams, which are the source of *Vltava*, have a delicacy almost of fantasy. *Sárka*, with its bloodthirsty tale of revenge and slaughter, is immensely dramatic, contrasting with the pastoral evocations of the following piece; the Slavonic lilt of the music's lighter moments brings the necessary contrast and release. The recording is vivid and full but not sumptuous, yet this suits the powerful impulse of Kubelik's overall view, with the build-up to the exultant close of *Blaník* producing a dénouement of great majesty.

Antoni Wit and his excellent **Polish National Radio Orchestra** give us a superbly played and consistently imaginative account. The spacious opening of *Vyšehrad*, marginally slower than usual, glows with romantic evocation; equally the flutes, trickling down from the sources of the *Vltava*, captivate the ear and the famous string-tune is unusually gracious and relaxed. The opening of *Sárka* brings tingling melodrama, which subsides naturally for the jaunty theme which follows. *From Bohemia's Woods and Fields* opens with opulent expansiveness, and later the ethereal high string entry is exquisitely made. *Tábor* develops great weight and gravitas. The warm resonance of the Concert Hall of Polish Radio in Katowice seems right for this very individual reading, full of fantasy, which goes automatically to the top of the list alongside Kubelik's distinguished, and justly renowned, 1990 Czech Philharmonic version on Supraphon, which is rather special.

Macal's Telarc version offers the finest recording of all; indeed it approaches the demonstration bracket. He provides a highly spontaneous and enjoyable performance, imaginatively conceived and convincingly paced. Other accounts, notably Kubelik's, have greater Slavic fire and find a more red-bloodedly patriotic feeling, but the excellent orchestral playing is responsive to his less histrionic view. *Sárka* has a folksy flavour, the melodrama good-humoured, while in *From Bohemia's Woods and Fields*, after the radiant high string passage, the horns steal in magically with their chorale. Throughout, the brass are full and sonorous, mitigating any rhetorical bombast in the last two symphonic poems; and Macal's Czech nationality ensures that the performance has idiomatic feeling.

Recorded live at the Barbican in May 2005, **Sir Colin Davis** offers a warm, incisive reading which brings out the drama as well as the poetry behind each portrait of Smetana's homeland, clearly integrating the final two symphonic poems, *Tábor* and *Blaník*, noisier than the rest and written rather as an afterthought. It is true that the limited Barbican acoustic does not make for the very finest sound, yet it is well detailed, and there are advantages of having a slightly more distanced sound in places, as in the evocative central section of *Vltava*.

Pešek's idiomatic reading does not miss the music's epic, patriotic feeling, yet never becomes bombastic. There is plenty of evocation, from the richly romantic opening of *Vyšehrad* to the more mysterious scene-setting in *Tábor*, while the climax of *Sárka*, with its potent anticipatory horn-call, is a gripping piece of melodrama. The two main sections of the work, *Vltava* and *From Bohemia's Woods and Fields*, are especially enjoyable for their vivid characterization, while at the very end of *Blaník* Pešek draws together the two key themes – the *Vyšehrad* motif and the Hussite chorale – very satisfyingly.

Järvi's, too, is an enjoyably vivid performance, and he has the double advantage of first-class playing from the highly committed **Detroit Orchestra** and the splendid acoustics of Symphony Hall. The romantic *Vyšehrad* is fresh and immediate, and the mountain streams of *Vltava* gleam brightly in the sunlight before the string tune arrives and moves on with plenty of lyrical impetus. *Sárka* is very dramatic indeed, with great melodramatic gusto and a heartfelt response from the strings. The opening of *Tábor* is tellingly ominous, and the weight of the Detroit brass makes a powerful contribution to both of the final two sections of the score.

The CD of **Karel Ančerl's** 1963 performance is something of a revelation, the quality now transformed by the CD transfer, full, warmly atmospheric yet still brilliant. The performance is full of character and the playing of the Czech Philharmonic is superb, with glowing woodwind detail and much beautiful string-playing.

Mackerras's affinity with Czech music is well known, and his version of *Má Vlast* ranks high. The sound has presence and body, and the warm, reverberant acoustic is pleasing yet allows plenty of detail to register.

Of the multiple recordings of *Má Vlast* made by the veteran Czech conductor, **Vaclav Talich**, this is the last, made in 1954, and the mono sound is very acceptable as transferred by Mark Obert-Thorn. The buoyancy of the rhythms and the warmth of the strings set against the typically rustic sound of the woodwind are exactly right for the music, ending with fiery accounts of the last two of the six symphonic poems, *Tabor* and *Blaník*.

Má Vlast: From Bohemia's Woods and Fields; Vltava; Vyšehrad. The Bartered Bride: Overture & Dances

(BB) *** DG 427 340-2. VPO, Levine

The three *Má Vlast* excerpts, taken from **Levine's** deleted complete set, are quite splendid, full of momentum and thrust, aptly paced, with much imaginative detail. The *Bartered Bride Overture* and *Dances* are highly infectious: Levine offers the usual numbers, plus the *Skocná*. The sound is full-blooded and vivid, with a wide amplitude and range to give the music plenty of atmosphere.

Má Vlast: Vltava

**(*) DG 439 009-2. VPO, Karajan – DVOŘÁK: *Symphony 9 (New World)* **(*)

(M) (***) EMI mono 5 62790-2. VPO, Furtwängler – RICHARD STRAUSS: *Death and Transfiguration, etc.* (***)

Karajan's VPO performance is characteristically well structured, and the recorded sound sounds quite expansive in this remastered format, even if the balance is not quite natural.

Furtwängler's recording of *Vltava* was made in the Musikvereinsaal in 1951 with Walter Legge producing, a guarantee of a finely balanced musical sound which does justice to the tonal finesse of the **Vienna orchestra**. It serves as an introduction and makeweight to three Strauss tone-poems that were given performances of commanding eloquence.

Má Vlast: Vltava; The Bartered Bride: Overture; Polka; Furiant

(M) *** Decca (ADD) 475 7730. (i) Israel PO; (ii) LSO; Kertész – DVOŘÁK: *Slavonic Dances; Symphonic Variations* ***

With **Kertész**, these pieces are exceptionally vivid. The separate entries in the *Overture* are beautifully positioned by the stereo, and the ambience makes the background rustle of all the strings weaving away at their fugato theme sound quite captivating.

CHAMBER MUSIC

Duo for Violin & Piano (From the Homeland)

🎻 *** Praga PRD 250 153. Remeš, Kayahara – DVOŘÁK: *Sonatina*; JANÁČEK; MARTINŮ: *Violin Sonatas* ***

Ⓜ *** Sup. SU 3772. Suk, Panenka – DVOŘÁK: *Romantic Pieces, Sonatina*; SUK: *Ballade; 4 Pieces* ***

Smetana's two-movement *Duo (From the Homeland)* is, not surprisingly, full of endearing Czech folk influences, with the dumka style hovering over the first movement. It is marvellously played by these two fine artists, who are thoroughly immersed in its local atmosphere. The recording is vividly live and present.

They are also admirably played by **Suk** and **Panenka**, who are just as idiomatic in feeling, and are most naturally recorded.

Piano Trio in G min., Op. 15

Ⓝ *** MDG 942 1512-2. V. Piano Trio – TCHAIKOVSKY: *Piano Trio* ***

*** Chan. 8445; Borodin Trio – DVOŘÁK: *Dumky Trio* ***

ⒷⒷ *** Warner Apex 7559 79679-2. Boston Symphony Chamber Players – DVOŘÁK: *String Sextet in A* ***

*** Sup. SU 3810. Smetana Trio – NOVAK: *Trio quasi una balata*; SUK: *Elegie; Piano Trio* ***

*** Ara. Z6661. Golub-Kaplan-Carr Trio – TCHAIKOVSKY: *Piano Trio* ***

**(*) MDG MDGL 3247. Trio Parnassus – ARENSKY: *Piano Trio in D min* **(*)

Writing the *G minor Trio* was the composer's cathartic act, following the death of his four-year-old daughter, so it is not surprising that it is a movingly expressive work. The newest version from Dabringhaus und Grimm measures up extremely well against its competitors. The pianist **Stefan Mendl** is able to dominate yet become a full member of the partnership throughout. All three movements are in the home key and are thematically linked, yet they are enticingly diverse, while in the hand of the **Vienna Piano Trio** the rondo finale bursts with vitality. All in all, a real winner of a disc that can be highly recommended on all counts.

The writing gives fine expressive opportunities for both the violin and cello, which are taken up eloquently on the Chandos recording by **Rostislav Dubinsky** and **Yuli Turovsky**, and the pianist, **Luba Edlina**, is also wonderfully sympathetic. In short, a superb account, given a most realistic recording balance. Highly recommended.

The 1983 **Boston** performance on Warner Apex brings a distinguished line-up, **Joseph Silverstein**, the cellist **Jules Eskine** and the pianist **Gilbert Kalisch**. This sensitive and vital account ranks among the most competitive of Smetana's *Piano Trio*, particularly given its price bracket.

Smetana's *Piano Trio* is given a strongly characterized, idiomatic and finely polished reading by the eponymous **Smetana Trio**, a re-formed group whose cellist, **Jan Paleníček**, is the son of Josef Paleníček, pianist in the original Smetana Trio, founded in the 1930s.

The Arabesque CD offers the kind of chamber-music playing to inspire confidence in the future: nothing overdriven, mechanized or attention-seeking.

The **Trio Parnassus** give a likeable and convincing performance, very alive and vivid. Their coupling, the Arensky *D minor Trio*, may well sway some readers in their favour.

String Quartet 1 in E min. (From My Life).

🎙–*** EMI 7 54215-2. Alban Berg Qt – DVOŘÁK: *String Quartet 12* ***

(***) Testament mono SBT 1072. Hollywood Qt – DVOŘÁK; KODÁLY: *Quartets* (***)

Ⓜ (***) BBC mono BBCL 4137-2. Smetana Qt – BEETHOVEN: *String Quartet 1* (**); MOZART: *String Quartet 20* (**(*))

There is much more to admire in the **Alban Berg's** reading than to cavil at: the first movement comes off well, and the EMI recording is very truthful and present.

This **Hollywood Quartet** recording is a performance of tremendous fire and passion, with an exhilarating rhythmic drive and a powerful sense of momentum. Yet everything sounds perfectly natural and not overdriven. Great quartet playing – and perfectly acceptable sound, given the mid-1950s date.

The **Smetana Quartet's** performance of the *E minor Quartet (From my Life)* comes from a BBC relay from the Royal Festival Hall in June 1965, and the mono sound is very acceptable indeed. Their playing here has polish, ardour and freshness.

String Quartet 1 (From My Life) (orchestral version by George Szell); The Bartered Bride: Overture & Dances

*** Chan. 8412. LSO, Simon

The Czech feeling of Szell's scoring is especially noticeable in the *Polka*, but overall there is no doubt that the fuller textures add a dimension to the music, though inevitably there are losses as well as gains. The recording is well up to the usual high Chandos standards.

String Quartets 1 in E min. (From my Life); 2 in D min. (plus documentary; DVD version)

(*) Sup. **DVD SU 7004-2. Smetana Qt – DVOŘÁK: *Sextet in A* **(*)

From the **Smetana Quartet**, straightforward performances and equally straightforward presentation for the camera. However, the documentary in which the members of the quartet look back over their career is curiously stiff and it is difficult to imagine oneself replaying it. Recommended for the performances, however.

String Quartets 1 (From My Life); 2 in D min.

🎙–*** ASV CDDCA 777. Lindsay Qt – DVOŘÁK: *Romance; Waltzes 1–2* ***

Ⓜ **(*) Telarc CD 80178. Cleveland Qt – BORODIN: *Quartet 1* **(*)

The **Lindsay Quartet** bring dramatic intensity to the *E minor Quartet* and play with great fire and vitality. Their recording is very good indeed, and readers wanting both the Smetana *Quartets* together need look no further.

The **Cleveland Quartet** play magnificently but, as in the coupled Borodin, their performance is a bit short on spontaneity. The recording is first class.

PIANO MUSIC

Czech Dances I & II; 8 Bagatelles and Impromptus

(BB) *** Regis RRC 1223. Kvapil

Radoslav Kvapil is entirely inside this music, even if his account of the *F major Polka* from the first book of *Czech Dances* does not eclipse memories of Firkušný's celebrated mono LP account, which had great exuberance and dash! All the same, Kvapil is a highly sensitive exponent of this repertoire. The recording is good, too. The disc also comes as part of a four-disc survey of Czech piano music (Regis RRC 4006).

OPERA

The Bartered Bride (complete in English)

⊘−⌐ (M) **** Chan. 3128 (2). Gritton, Clarke, Robinson, Rose, Davies, Montague, Moses, Bonner, Leggate, Hesketh-Harvey, ROHCG Ch., Philh. O, Mackerras

What makes this translated version so successful is not just the brilliant conducting of **Sir Charles Mackerras** and the scintillating playing of the **Philharmonia Orchestra**, with an exceptionally strong team of soloists working well together, but also the extra impact of the comedy made by a performance in the vernacular. The echoes of G & S, with double-rhymes given a jolly, Gilbertian ring, distracting in many operas, for once seem entirely appropriate, adding to the joy of the piece. Kecal, the marriage-broker, has so many patter numbers in which **Peter Rose** is wonderfully agile, characterfully establishing himself as the key figure in the story. Even the chorus has rapid tongue-twisters to cope with, crisply performed by the **Covent Garden Chorus**. Susan Gritton is a radiant heroine, producing golden tone and rising superbly to the challenge of the poignant numbers when it seems that Jeník has betrayed her. **Paul Charles Clarke** as Jeník is less successful when his tenor grows uneven under pressure, though his characterization is first rate. The two other tenor roles are both superbly taken by **Timothy Robinson** as the stuttering simpleton, Vašek, and **Robin Leggate** as the ringmaster in Act III. Strong casting too for Mařenka's parents, **Neal Davies** as Krušina and **Yvonne Howard** as Ludmila, clearly establishing their contrasted responses to the proposed marriage of Mařenka and Vašek.

The Bartered Bride: Overture

(M) *** RCA (ADD) **SACD** 82876 66376-2. Chicago SO, Reiner – DVOŘÁK: *Symphony 9 (New World)*; WEINBERGER: *Schwanda: Polka & Fugue* ***

The easy, bustling virtuosity of the **Chicago** strings makes this vivacious performance of Smetana's famous overture hard to beat, when the remastered recording is so full on SACD, while retaining its clear inner detail.

The Bartered Bride (complete; sung in German; CD version)

(M) *** EMI (ADD) 3 81872-2 (2). Lorengar, Wunderlich, Frick, Berlin RIAS Ch., Bamberg SO, Kempe

(M) (**) Somm Beecham mono 14-2. Konetzni, Tauber, Jarred, Tessmer, Ch., LPO, Beecham

The Bartered Bride sung in German seems an unlikely candidate for a recommendation, yet this vivacious **Bamberg** set is a remarkable success and is very enjoyable indeed. **Pilar Lorengar** is most appealing as Mařenka and **Fritz Wunderlich**, in one of his all too few complete-opera recordings, is outstanding as Jeník. **Gottlob Frick** gives a strong, earthy characterization of Kečal, the marriage-broker. The whole production is full of high spirits. The recording is bright and vivid, yet has plenty of depth. The reissue comes with a synopsis and separate list of items.

Here is the first of three performances of Smetana's masterpiece that **Sir Thomas Beecham** conducted at Covent Garden in his last pre-war opera season. It was recorded on 1 May 1939, only a few weeks after the Nazi annexation of Czechoslovakia, but they had to settle, ironically enough, on giving it in German. However, Beecham managed to assemble a pretty stellar line-up, including the glorious **Hilda Konetzni**, **Richard Tauber**, **Mary Jarred** and **Marko Rothmüller**. But there is an exhilarating sense of occasion, plenty of spirit and the glory of the singing comes across. The sound quality calls for a tolerance that is well worth extending.

The Brandenburgers in Bohemia (complete)

**(*) Sup. (ADD) 11 1804-2 (2). Zídek, Otava, Subrtová, Kalaš, Joran, Vich, Prague Nat. Theatre soloists, Ch. & O, Jan Hus Tich

Though much of the drama centres on the fate of the heroine, Liduše, abducted by a Prague burgher with the mercenary Germanic name of Tausendmark, the love interest which must sustain any romantic opera is sketched in only cursorily. The main duet between Liduše and her beloved, Junoš, is charming and jolly rather than heartfelt, an opportunity missed. Nevertheless there is much to enjoy in a performance as lively as this, with stirring patriotic choruses sung with a will, even if their melodic invention is hardly distinguished. A collector's item.

Dalibor (complete)

⊘−⌐ *** Sup. (ADD) 11 2185-2 (2). Přibyl, Kniplová, Jindrák, Svorc, Horáček, Prague Nat. Theatre Ch. & O, Krombholc

In the development of the plot, when the imprisoned hero's lover is disguised as the gaoler's assistant, *Dalibor* readily evokes associations with *Fidelio*, and the subject prompted Smetana to write some of his most inspired music. The confrontations between hero and heroine also inspire Smetana to some glorious writing, richly lyrical, most notably the love duet in the prison scene of Act II. This vintage set of 1967, sounding more vivid and full-blooded than many more recent recordings, features in those roles two of the most distinguished Czech singers of their time, both in their prime, the tenor **Vílém Přibyl** and the dramatic soprano **Nadezda Kniplová**. **Krombholc** proves a most persuasive advocate, consistently bringing out the red-blooded fervour of the writing. A full translation is provided.

Libuše

**(*) Sup. 11 1276-2 633 (3). Be ačková, Zítek, Svorc, Vodička, Děpoltová, Prague Nat. Theatre Ch. & O, Košler

Recorded live, with **Gabriela Beňačková-Cápová** as Libuše memorable in her prophetic aria in Act III. **Václav Zítek** as Přemysi, her consort, provides an attractive lyrical interlude in Act II, which, with its chorus of harvesters, has affinities with *The Bartered Bride*. **Košler** directs committedly; with the stage perspectives well caught; the recording is very satisfactory. The cues still provide poor internal access for an opera playing for not far short of three hours. Twelve extra index points have been added to the 14 bands – not nearly enough for a work of this kind.

The Two Widows (complete)

** Sup. (ADD) 11 2122-2 (2). Sormová, Machotková, Zahradníček, Horáček, Prague Nat. Theatre Ch. & O, Jílek

The Two Widows is a tale of country life in the big house rather than among the peasantry, with the plot centring on two cousins, both widows, and inconsequential confusions over which of them is going to marry the hero, Ladislav. Smetana offers much delightful music and there are some charming numbers in between, not least an aria for the hero, '*When Maytime arrives*', at the beginning of Act II. **Jiří Zahradníček** is at his best there, singing lustily, though in gentler moments Slavonic unsteadiness develops. **Jaroslav Horáček** is effective in the *buffo* bass role of Mumlal but, sadly, the casting of the two widows, both sopranos, involves the major role of Karolina going to the shrill and wobbly **Nada Sormová**, while **Marcela Machotková**, who is altogether sweeter and firmer, with a mezzo-ish quality, is consigned to the role of Anežka with far less to sing, even though it is she who gets the hero. Recorded in 1975, this lively performance under **Frantisek Jílek** is on the whole well transferred to CD, though in a dryish acoustic the **Prague Theatre** violins sound undernourished. The libretto includes a very necessary translation.

SMITH, Alice Mary (1839–84)

Symphonies in A min.; C min.; (i) Andante for Clarinet & Orchestra

🕭 ⚜ *** Chan. 10283. LMP, Shelley; (i) with Malsbury

Alice Mary Smith was the first British woman to have composed a symphony and had it performed. And what a fine work it is, attractively tuneful throughout and with a fine grasp of orchestration and form. It has a particularly delightful second-movement *Allegretto amorevole*, with a folksy principal melody of real memorability. The Scherzo opens with rollicking horns, and even the Victorian *maestoso* finale lightens up after a bit.

The *A minor Symphony* is immediately Mendelssohnian in its richly lyrical forward impetus, and the romantic *Andante* opens with the horns and then offers a flowing cantilena. The third movement is a little like a Laendler; the finale is boisterous and confident.

Her *Andante for Clarinet and Orchestra*, delicately scored and persuasively played here by **Angela Malsbury**, again demonstrates Smith's easy melodic gifts, very songlike and pleasing. **Howard Shelley** and the **London Mozart Players**

are admirable advocates throughout, and this CD is most enjoyable.

SMYTH, Ethel (1858–1944)

(i) *Concerto for Violin, Horn & Orchestra; Serenade in D*

🕭 *** Chan. 9449. (i) Langdon, Watkins; BBC PO, De la Martinez

The *Concerto for Violin, Horn and Orchestra* is a highly successful piece in every respect. The first movement begins with an ambitious string melody, then the soloists enter alternately with the endearing secondary idea (one of the composer's very best tunes), which is imaginatively developed in a free fantasia of flowing and dancing melody and varying moods; only at the recapitulation do the soloists share the opening theme. The romantic central *Elegy* brings a touchingly beautiful and nostalgic exchange between the two soloists.

The *Serenade in D major* might well be Brahms's. Not only does the rich string writing of the first movement have a glorious sweep, but the harmonic thinking and progressions are *echt*-Brahms. Yet Smyth's invention is of high quality, for all its eclecticism. With superb performances and warm, sumptuous recording, both these colourful and tuneful works will give great pleasure. This is easily the most impressive Smyth offering yet to have appeared on CD, and it is conducted with understanding and commitment.

The Wreckers: Overture

🕭 Ⓑ *** CfP (ADD) 3 52405-2. RSNO, Gibson – GERMAN: *Welsh Rhapsody*; HARTY: *With the Wild Geese*; MACCUNN: *Land of the Mountain and Flood* ***

Ethel Smyth's *Overture* for her opera, *The Wreckers*, is a strong, meaty piece, which shows the calibre of this remarkable woman's personality for, while the material itself is not memorable, it is put together most compellingly and orchestrated with real flair. The recording is full and the CD has refined detail.

SOLER, Antonio (1729–83)

Sonatas for Harpsichord (complete)

⚜ ⒷⒷ **** Naxos 8.553462/3/4/5 (Vols. 1–4); 8.554434 (Vol. 5); 8.554565/6 (Vols. 6–7); 8.555031/2 (Vols. 8–9); 8.557137 (Vol. 10); 8.557640 (Vol. 11); 8.557937 (Vol. 12); 8.570292 (Vol. 13) Rowland (harpsichord)

The Catalan composer Padre Antonio Soler was a monk who spent most of his life at the Escorial, a famous monastery near Madrid. There his duties included choir master, the provision of choral music for services and the writing of secular music for the royal family (who often visited the monastery). Yet he found time to compose 150 keyboard *Sonatas* (he apparently managed to survive on four hours' sleep each night, rising in time for early morning Mass). Between 1752 and 1757 he is reputed to have studied with Domenico Scarlatti, and most of his own sonatas show this influence. They are single-movement works in binary form (two sections), often exuberant, bravura pieces, some with dance rhythms; others are slow movements (some of these extended and marked *cantabile* and *espressivo*). But he also wrote more ambitious sonatas. 63 *in F* and 67 *in D* (in Volume 12) are three-movement works, each beginning with a slow movement, and are part of a group of six *Sonatas* dating from 1777, while 97–9 are part of a group of three *Sonatas* in four movements (Op. 8) written in 1783. The variety of Soler's invention is remarkable, sometimes drawing on local folk themes. The outstanding Scottish keyboard player **Gilbert Rowland** has recorded this repertoire over a long period, beginning in the late 1990s and concluding in 2005, playing with great vitality and variety of characterization, bringing every sonata fully to life. He is truthfully recorded, in a perfect acoustic, and you can dip into any one of these 13 discs (all available separately) and be sure of receiving musical refreshment. We have now spent some time with these works.

Keyboard Sonatas 17; 19; 20; 71–73; 77; 87; 115 & 118 (Numbering after Samuel Rubio)

(N) *** CPO 777 200-2. Hinrichs (piano)

While the extensive coverage of these attractive sonatas on the harpsichord by Gilbert Rowland is entirely valid, it seems likely that Soler's favourite instrument was the soft-voiced clavichord. However, **Marie-Luise Hinrichs** has decided to present her selection on a modern grand piano, and her performances are very appealing. Certainly the use of the modern instrument makes the music sound more forward-looking, although the link with Scarlatti remains. The choice of sonatas here is felicitous and Hinrichs plays them stylishly and with pleasing spontaneity. A most enjoyable disc.

SOMERVELL, Arthur
(1863–1937)

Violin Concerto in G

*** Hyp. CDA 67420. Marwood, BBC Scottish SO, Brabbins –
COLERIDGE-TAYLOR: *Violin Concerto* **(*)

Sir Arthur Somervell is best remembered for his settings of *A Shropshire Lad* and Tennyson's *Maud*. Like the Coleridge-Taylor concerto with which it is coupled, it was its composer's last work. In its easy late-romantic style, it makes a strong impression. The long first movement in traditional layout includes an opening orchestral tutti and a big cadenza, with a warmly Elgarian theme for second subject. The central *Adagio* is richly lyrical and beautifully orchestrated (a song-composer's inspiration), leading to a jaunty, brightly inventive finale rather like a pastoral dance. Superbly played and brilliantly recorded, it makes a most attractive rarity. **Anthony Marwood** is a fine soloist and no more committed than the orchestra under **Martyn Brabbins**. An interesting and worthwhile coupling.

Clarinet Quintet in G

(BB) *** Hyp. Helios (ADD) CDH 55110. King, Aeolian Qt –
JACOB: *Clarinet Quintet* ***

Sir Arthur Somervell's dominating musical influences came from the German school and in particular from Brahms, whose voice can be heard at the very opening of this rather lovely *Quintet*. The *grazioso* first movement and touching *Adagio (Lament)* are in contrast to the bubbling finale which is a special delight, with **Thea King** and the **Aeolian Quartet** at their most persuasive, helped by very good (1979) recording, well transferred to CD.

SORABJI, Khaikhosru
(1892–1988)

Fantaisie Espagnole; Fantasiettina sul nome illustre dell'egregio poeta Christopher Grieve ossia Hugh M'Diarmid (Tiny Little Fantasy on the Illustrious Name of the Distinguished Poet Christopher Grieve, i.e. Hugh M'Diarmid); Fragment for Harold Rutland; Gulistán (The Rose Garden): Nocturne for Piano; Introito and Preludio-Corale from Opus Clavicembalisticum; Le Jardin parfumé (Poem for Piano); Nocturne: Djâmî; 3 Pastiches: Chopin's Valse, Op. 64/1; Habanera from Bizet's Carmen; Hindu Merchant's Song (Rimsky-Korsakov). Piano Pieces: In the Hothouse; Prelude, Interlude & Fugue; Toccata; Quaere relique hujus materiei inter secretiora; St Bertrand de Comminges: 'He was Laughing in the Tower'; Valse Fantaisie (Hommage à J. Strauss)

⊷ *** British Music Society BMS 427-9 (3). Habermann –
HABERMANN: *A la manière de Sorabji: 'Au clair de la lune'*
***

Michael Habermann proves an extraordinarily persuasive advocate of this music: he has all the virtuosity it needs, as well as the musical and imaginative insight. When Sorabji played his *First Sonata* to Busoni in London in 1919, Busoni observed that it was like 'a tropical forest' and it is for its luxuriant, hothouse textures that it has gained a reputation. The *Fantaisie espagnole* (1918) is an extraordinarily fantastic evocation of the sights and sounds of Spain and *Le Jardin parfumé*, which earned Delius's admiration, has all the sensuous loveliness of the latter but with an added vivid luxuriance of texture and colour. Habermann's excellent notes are worth quoting for they sum the composer up well: 'The interaction of imaginative rhythms, melodies, harmonies and textures in his music is fascinating – perhaps even awe-inspiring. Moods are varied. The nocturnal pieces explore mystical trance states. The energetic pieces grab the listener by their sheer obstinacy and determination, and massive climaxes encompass the entire arsenal of the piano (and pianist).' Habermann is a splendid exponent of the pyrotechnical wizardry and the richness of imagination of these scores, and he gives us an admirable entry point into Sorabji's world. The recordings are eminently acceptable.

SPOHR, Ludwig (1784–1859)

Clarinet Concerto 1 in C min., Op. 26

(M) *** Classic fM 75605 57019-2. Lawson, Hanover Band, Goodman – WEBER: *Clarinet Concertos 1–2 etc.* ***

The first of Spohr's *Clarinet Concertos* provides a generous bonus on an outstanding disc. **Colin Lawson**, principal clarinet of the **Hanover Band**, plays most imaginatively with attractively reedy tone to match the period instruments of his colleagues. Full and vivid sound.

(i) Clarinet Concertos 1 in C min., Op. 26; 3 in F min., WoO19; (ii) Potpourri for Clarinet & Orchestra in F, Op. 80

🎧 (BB) *** Naxos 8.550688. Ottensamer; (i) Slovak State PO (Košice); (ii) Slovak RSO (Bratislava), Wildner

Clarinet Concertos: 1 in C min.; 2 in E flat; Potpourri in F; Variations in B flat

🎧 *** Hyp. CDA 67509. Collins, Swedish CO, O'Neill

Clarinet Concertos (i) 2 in E flat; (ii) 4 in E min.

*** EMI 379786-2. (i) Meyer; (ii) Bliss; ASMF, Sillito

Clarinet Concertos 2 in E flat, Op. 57; 4 in E min.; Fantasia & Variations on a Theme of Danzi, Op. 81

🎧 (BB) *** Naxos 8.550689. Ottensamer, Slovak RSO (Bratislava), Wildner

Clarinet Concertos 3 in F min.; 4 in E min.

*** Hyp. CDA 67561. Collins, Swedish CO, O'Neill

Spohr's four *Concertos* were written between 1808 and 1829 for the clarinettist Johann Simon Hermstedt, but although they are all in a traditional three-movement format, each work has a character of its own. The *Danzi Fantasia* opens very dramatically, but its basic theme is simple and ingenuous, its treatment histrionically operatic.

On EMI, each clarinettist is given one *Concerto* to play. Luckily for them, both *Concertos* are equally enjoyable, with lively, inventive first movements, delightful slow movements, and characterful finales, in the case of the *Second Concerto*, a *Rondo alla Polacca*, and in the *Fourth* a *Rondo al Espagnol*. Both offer extremely catchy tunes with a dash of 'local' colour. The *Fourth Concerto* is the more substantial work, with its long brooding introduction. It is also written for the clarinet in A, mellower than the more commonly used and brighter clarinet in B flat. Both soloists are superb and are well supported by the **Academy of St Martin-in-the-Fields** under **Kenneth Sillito**. Warm, expansive EMI recording.

Ernst Ottensamer is a most sensitive artist and a superb player with an appealingly warm, liquid tone. Apart from sailing through all Spohr's decorative roulades and technical extravagances with aplomb, he plays over the widest range of dynamic, often fining down his tone to a pianis-

simo to echo a phrase with magical effect. **Johann Wildner** provides lively, polished accompaniments, and the recording is first rate.

The six works on Hyperion are perfect vehicles for the dazzling virtuosity of **Michael Collins**, superbly accompanied by the **Swedish Chamber Orchestra** under **Robin O'Neill**. The treatment is always nicely pointed and inventive. The *Second Concerto* in particular is a delight, with jaunty martial rhythms in the outer movements. The *Potpourri* is a double set of variations on themes from a long-forgotten opera by Peter von Winter, and the *Variations in B flat* similarly use a theme from Spohr's own opera, *Alruna*. Spohr was still in his twenties when he wrote these works, and that is reflected in the consistent freshness of the writing. Full, immediate sound.

Concerto for String Quartet & Orchestra in A min., Op. 131

🎧 *** Ara. Z 6723. San Francisco Ballet O, Lark Qt, Le Roux – HANDEL: *Concerto grosso in B flat, Op. 6/7;* SCHOENBERG: *Concerto for String Quartet & Orchestra after Handel's Concerto grosso, Op. 4/7;* ELGAR: *Introduction & Allegro for Strings* ***

This is a consistently engaging work (Spohr's very last *Concerto*), inventive and tuneful – the slow movement is particularly fine – using the players in the solo quartet individually as well as in consort. It is very persuasively played, and with the proviso that the solo group are balanced rather forwardly, the recording is very good too. With imaginative couplings this is very much worth trying.

Violin Concertos 7 in E min., Op. 38; 12 in A min., Op. 79

(BB) **(*) Naxos 8.555101. Nishizaki, Bratislava Philharmonic CO, Pešek

The key of Spohr's *E minor Concerto* brings a certain Mendelssohnian affinity, especially in the passage work. Its lyrical ideas are attractive, especially the rather lovely *Adagio*, and the bouncing finale dances in a fast waltz tempo. The more rhapsodic *Twelfth Concerto*, written over a decade later (and actually designated a concertino), is in a single movement of three linked sections, with a closing *Polacca*. **Takako Nishizaki** plays both works affectionately and very stylishly, and she is warmly accompanied by **Pešek** and the **Bratislava orchestra**. The recording is pleasingly resonant.

Violin Concerto 8 (In modo di scena cantata)

*** DG 477 6232. Hahn, Swedish RSO, Oue – PAGANINI: *Violin Concerto 1* ***

Spohr's *Violin Concerto 8* is one of his best-proportioned and most classically conceived works, quite apart from its innovatory features, including recitative sections, well handled here. But it is a virtuoso piece too, with a winningly bravura finale, which **Hilary Hahn** despatches with aplomb. Fine accompaniments from the **Swedish Radio Orchestra** and excellent recording make this rather apt coupling with Paganini very tempting.

Symphonies 1 in E flat, Op. 20; 2 in D min., Op. 49; Grand Concert Overture in F

Ⓝ *** Hyp. CDA 7616. O della Svizzera Italiana, Shelley

It is good that Hyperion are embarking on the Symphonies of Louis Spohr. One can't help but think of the G&S line from the *Mikado*: 'Bach interwoven with Spohr and Beethoven', which gives an indication of Spohr's popularity in 19th-century London. Indeed, when the *Second Symphony* (recorded here) was first performed in London in 1820, it was a considerable success. The work launches with a fast introduction and leads to some quite stormy and dramatic writing, with the spirit of Beethoven hovering in the background. The *First Symphony*, written some nine years previously, is not quite so distinctive and is much more a work of the classical era, though there is a distinctly romantic Beethovenian spirit too. It is very pleasing and melodic and well worth an occasional hearing. The *Concert Overture* makes a fine bonus. Excellent performances and recording.

Symphonies 2 in D min., Op. 49; 8 in G, Op. 137; Concerto Overture (Im ernsten Stil)

Ⓝ *** CPO 777 178-2. N. German Radiophilharmonie, Griffiths

Griffiths offers a slightly less polished account of the *Second Symphony* than Shelley on Hyperion, yet this is equally and lustily enjoyable. The *Eighth Symphony* was written for, and first performed in, London in 1847. It didn't meet with the same success as the *Second*, being considered lacking in originality compared to Spohr's earlier symphonies. From a modern point of view, it is an attractive romantic symphony, eminently tuneful and appealing, with plenty of incidental delights (such as the slightly quirky solo woodwind and string writing in the Scherzo) and possessing lively writing and invention. The *Overture* makes a fine bonus. Excellent performances and recording.

Symphonies 3 in C min., Op. 78; 6 in G (Historical Symphony in the Style and Taste of Four Different Periods), Op. 116

🎗 *** Marco Polo 8.223349. Slovak State PO (Košice), Walter

The *Historical Symphony* is a fascinating pastiche, and the *C minor* is one of the finest of Spohr's early symphonies, inspiring **Walter** to give one of his most vigorous and committed performances. The *Larghetto* has genuine depth, but the most ambitious movement is the highly inventive finale, both life-enhancing and energetic, and with plenty of contrapuntal interest, including a full-scale central fugue. It is very well played indeed. The *Historical Symphony* is most endearing in its respect for the great masters. It opens with a solemn, full-orchestral treatment of the *C major fugue* from Book I of Bach's '48', and also introduces pastoral reminders of Handel's *Messiah*, including an allusion to 'He shall feed his flock'. The slow movement, richly scored, remembers both Mozart's *39th* and *Prague Symphonies*, and in the curiously lyrical Scherzo the timpani (rather too muted here) recall the Beethoven of the *Seventh Symphony*. The inappropriately but agreeably frivolous finale, 'the latest of the new', then bursts with energy, drawing on the vivacious

ideas of Adam and Auber, in particular the *Muette de Portici Overture*. Walter is a convincing exponent of this curiously balanced work, and his orchestra respond with enthusiasm.

Symphonies 4 in F (The Consecration of Sounds), Op. 86; 5 in C min., Op. 102; Overture: Das befreite Deutschland

Ⓝ *** Hyp. CDA 67622. O della Svizzera Italiana, Shelley

The imposingly named 'The Consecration of Sounds' *Fourth Symphony* derives its name from a volume of poems by Carl Pfeiffer which the composer originally intended to set as a cantata; but he thought the words unsuitable to set to music and used them instead as inspiration for a symphony. The result is a colourfully romantic work, premièred with success in 1832, after which it was performed for many years. The fourth movement is subtitled 'Funeral music. Consolation through tears', but it is a far from gloomy symphony. The previous movement, with its striking trumpet fanfares and marching theme, suitably evokes its title, 'Music of War'. The *Fifth Symphony* was premièred in Vienna in 1838, and is imbued with a certain melancholy which reflected personal sadnesses at the time of its composition. It is highly expressive, with a particularly fine slow movement. There are plenty of incidental delights, such as the horn writing in the bright Scherzo. Superb performances and recording, and with the entertaining Overture, *Das befreite Deutschland* ('Germany liberated') included, this makes another fine instalment in Hyperion's Spohr symphony survey.

CHAMBER MUSIC

Double Quartets 1 in D min., Op. 65; 2 in E flat, Op. 77; 3 in E min., Op. 87; 4 in G min., Op. 136

Ⓑ *** Hyp. Dyad CDD 22014 (2). ASMF Chamber Ens.

The opening of the first *Double Quartet* is inviting (as again is the rather solemn introduction of the *Third*, which then lightens, yet retains its nostalgic feeling). While this is all essentially amiable music, the standard of Spohr's invention is quite high throughout all four works, and the scoring cleverly makes the most of the antiphony between the two groups. So does the recording here, with a natural interplay within a pleasingly warm acoustic. The playing is predictably fluent and spontaneous-sounding, well blended and polished.

Nonet in F, Op. 31

(***) Testament mono SBT 1261. Augmented Vienna Octet – BEETHOVEN: *Septet* (***)

Nonet in F, Op. 31; Octet in E, Op. 32

🎗 *** Hyp. CDA 66699. Gaudier Ens.
🎗 Ⓜ *** CRD (ADD) CRD 3354. Nash Ens.

The **Gaudier Ensemble** give us a performance of the *Octet* as imaginative as it is spontaneous, and the work's finale with its lolloping main theme is joyously spirited. The *Nonet* is also very attractive. Spohr's invention is again at its freshest and his propensity for chromaticism is held reasonably in check. The Hyperion recording is fresh and warm, clearly detailed against a resonant acoustic.

The sound on the competing CRD disc is natural and lifelike. The **Nash Ensemble** play both works with much elegance and style, and these performances are very civilized and hardly less spontaneous.

It is good to see this 1952 Decca recording of Spohr's delightful *Nonet*. The playing here is superb, full of unforced charm, with a lovely Viennese glow. The transfers are excellent, the mono sound unbelievably warm and rich for the period.

Nonet in F, Op. 31; Septet, Op. 147

*** ASV Gold GLD 4026. Ens. 360

There are various permutations of these works available, but the **Ensemble 360** ranks with the finest. How delightfully they play the finale of the *Nonet*, and the *Pastorale* (Larghetto) of the *Septet* has equal charm. Fine intimate recording.

Octet in E, Op. 32

⌐– (M) **** Decca (ADD) 466 580-2. Vienna Octet – SCHUBERT: *Octet in F, D.803* ***

Spohr's *Octet* is a particularly charming work, and the variations on Handel's *Harmonious Blacksmith*, which forms one of the central movements, offer that kind of naivety which, when so stylishly done as here, makes for delicious listening. The playing is expert throughout, with the five strings blending perfectly with the two horns and clarinet, and altogether this is a winning performance. The 1960 recording is fresh and open and leaves little to be desired.

Piano Quintet in D min., Op. 130; Septet, Op. 147

⌐– **** MDG 304 0534-2. Villa Musica Ensemble

The *Piano Quintet* is a dashingly amiable work. The spirited MDG performance is most enjoyable and the much better-known *Septet* for piano and wind is played with comparable relish and warmth. Excellent, vividly present recording makes this a most enjoyable coupling.

Piano & Wind Quintet in C min., Op. 52; String Quintet 6, Op. 130; Septet, Op. 147; String Sextet, Op. 140

*** MDG 304 1263-2. Ens. Villa Musica

These are all attractive works, a little garrulous at times but always fluently melodic and well crafted. In the two works with piano, the pianist at times is called upon to play some hair-raising runs, which **Kalle Randalu** manages with aplomb. Both the *String Sextet* and *Quintet* have fine slow movements, and the *Piano and Wind Quintet* has a sparkling finale, with a particularly winning secondary theme. Fine performances throughout and natural recording, although rather resonant.

Piano Trios 1 in E min., Op. 119; 2 in F, Op. 123; 3 in A min., Op. 124; 4 in B flat, Op. 133; 5 in G min., Op. 142

(B) *** CPO 999 246-2 (3). Ravensburg Beethoven Trio

Spohr's five *Piano Trios* are among his freshest, most appeal-

ing chamber works, full of attractive ideas and fine craftsmanship. The **Ravensburg Trio** give fine performances, mellow, with slightly more gravitas than sparkle, although they too have an excellent pianist in **Inge-Susann Römchild**, whose touch is often pleasingly light. The CPO recording is warm and full to suit the playing. The five *Trios* are just too long to fit on a pair of CDs, and the third plays for only 31 minutes.

Piano & Wind Quintet in C min., Op. 52; Septet in A min. for Flute, Clarinet, Horn, Bassoon, Violin, Cello & Piano, Op. 147

(M) **** CRD (ADD) CRD 3399. Brown, Nash Ens.

These two pieces, the sparkling *Quintet* and the more substantial but still charmingly lighthearted *Septet*, are among Spohr's most delightful. **Ian Brown** at the piano leads the ensemble with flair and vigour, and the recording quality is outstandingly vivid.

String Quartets 1 in C; 2 in C min., Op. 4/1-2; 5 in D, Op. 15/2

*** Marco 8.223253. New Budapest Qt

String Quartets 7 in E flat; 8 in C, Op. 29/1-2

**(*) Marco 8.22355. New Budapest Qt

String Quartets 11 in E (Quatuor brillant), Op. 43; 12 in C, Op. 45/1

**(*) Marco 8.223257. New Budapest Qt

String Quartets 13 in E min.; 14 in F min., Op. 45/2–3

*** Marco 8.223258. New Budapest Qt

String Quartets 15 in E flat; 16 in A, Op. 58/1-2

*** Marco 8.23256. New Budapest Qt

String Quartets 20 in A min.; 21 in B flat, Op. 74/1-2

*** Marco 8.223259. New Budapest Qt

String Quartets 27 in D min.; 28 in A flat, Op. 84/1-2

**(*) Marco 8.223251. New Budapest Qt

String Quartets 29 in B min., Op. 84/3; 30 in A, Op. 93

**(*) Marco 8.223252. New Budapest Qt

If you enjoy the earlier and middle-period Haydn *Quartets*, you might well try Spohr. He seems also to have an almost inexhaustible fund of ideas and writes enjoyably smooth, well-crafted works, which every so often produce a movement which is quite memorable – like the gentle *Adagio* of his very first essay in the medium, strikingly fresh, written when the composer had just turned 20. The performances here are always persuasive and well recorded too: praise is due for the excellent documentation. The Op. 29 *Quartets* are associated with Johann Tost (dedicatee of Haydn's Opp. 54/5 and 65). Both are written in Spohr's friendly, accomplished style; the first ingeniously bases its opening movement on a two-note motto theme and has an outstanding set of variations for its slow movement. The tender *Adagio* of the *C major* is even finer, daring in its expressive chromaticism. Both performances are spontaneous and this is vibrant, felt quartet-playing, without artifice, and the recording is lively and present. The *Quatuor brillant* dates from 1817, and its subtitle is deceptive, for, as its engaging opening suggests, it is essentially a lyrical work, although the closing Minuet sparkles brightly enough. The Op. 45 *Quartets* are more romantic in feeling, suaver in texture, moving further away from the classical Haydn idiom. The **Budapest** players are at their very best in these fine works. The two Op. 58 *Quartets* written in 1821 show a new maturity, especially the noble *Adagio* of the *E flat major*, which reminds one of Mozart, after a cheerful first movement laced with effective pizzicatos. The light-hearted Scherzo with its Viennese, Ländler-influenced Trio has much charm, and the work is capped by a springy closing Rondo. A splendid disc in every way. The Op. 74 *Quartets*, dating from 1826, are further evidence of Spohr's increasingly deft integration of his ideas in finely argued first movements, essentially lyrical but not lacking dramatic elements. The players here again respond very sympathetically to these attractive quartets and capture their spirit admirably. These two works, written in 1831–2, exemplify Spohr's smooth, finely integrated quartet-writing at its most characteristic. The slow movement, sustaining a mood of serene simplicity, is the most memorable in each case, although the lyrical finale of the *A flat major Quartet* is also rather appealing. Good performances, lively enough, but capturing the suaveness of the idiom. In many ways 29 *in B minor* is the finest of the Op. 84 set, with its touch of melancholy in the first movement, a lively minuet and a pensive slow movement. Op. 93, written in 1835, is more extrovert in atmosphere in the first movement (after a sombre introduction), but it offers another thoughtfully intense slow movement and a very jolly finale. It brings out the best in these players – and there is plenty of bravura for the first violin – and, again, good tonal matching plus a smooth, warm recording combine effectively for this slightly suave music.

String Quartets 32 in C, Op. 141; 34 in E flat, Op. 152

**(*) Marco 8.225307. Moscow Philharmonic Concertino Qt

In continuing their string quartet cycle, Marco Polo appear to have left Budapest in favour of Moscow, not entirely to advantage. These are enjoyable performances, with the *Larghetto* and Scherzo of 32 standing out, alongside the perky Minuet of 34. But there is a touch of astringency on the leader's tone that is pretty certainly due to the microphones; the recording balance otherwise is good.

String Quintets 1 in E flat; 2 in G, Op. 3/1–2

⊕ 🅱🅱 *** Naxos 8.555965. Augmented Danubius Qt

Spohr's *String Quintets* feature a second viola, which gives them a characteristically full, slightly bland texture. But the suave opening theme of the *E flat major Quartet* is deceptive, for it is strong enough to influence the two following movements including the near-melancholy *Larghetto* and the at-

tractive Minuet and Trio. In the *G major* work a similarly mild opening theme is to dominate. Both *Quintets* are warmly and sympathetically played by the **Danubius Quartet**, augmented by **Sándor Papp**, and smoothly and pleasingly recorded.

String Quintets 3 in B min., Op. 69; 4 in A min., Op. 91

⊕ 🅱🅱 *** Naxos 8.555966. Augmented New Haydn Qt

These two minor-key works have much of the wistful mood for which the composer is noted, especially the *Adagio* of the *B minor*, which is rather memorable, while there is also a rocking barcarolle finale. The quality of Spohr's invention is well maintained throughout, and they are warmly played and pleasingly recorded.

String Quintets 5 in G min., Op. 106; 6 in E min., Op. 129

🅱🅱 **(*) Naxos 8.555967. Augmented Budapest Haydn Qt

The *G minor Quintet* has a disarmingly winsome opening movement, followed by a simple *Larghetto*, rich in texture. Then, after the vigorous Scherzo, the finale has a rustic character with a drone-like accompaniment for the main theme. The *E minor Quintet* brings a busy but blander opening movement, with an underlying melancholy lyricism, which is dispelled by the Mendelssohnian Scherzo, with the gracious Trio coming twice, but in different keys. These are two fine works, very persuasively played, even if the ensemble is not always absolutely immaculate. Good recording too.

String Quintet 7 in G min., Op. 144; Potpourri (for solo violin & string quartet), Op. 22; Sextet in C, Op. 140

⊕ 🅱🅱 *** Naxos 8.555968. Augmented New Haydn Qt

The three works are admirably contrasted, the *Quintet* uncertain in mood, often permeated with a feeling of unease, and the *Sextet* much sunnier, while the *Potpourri* combines a Russian folk tune with Mozart's *Là ci darem la mano* to form a showoff piece, suitable as an encore. Very good performances and first rate recording.

STAINER, John (1840–1901)

The Crucifixion

⊕ 🅱🅱 *** Naxos 8.557624. Gilchrist, Bailey, Clare College, Cambridge Ch., T. Brown; S. Farr (organ)

🅱 *** CfP (ADD) 575 7792 (2). Hughes, Lawrenson, Guildford Cathedral Ch., Rose; Williams – MAUNDER: *Olivet to Calvary* ***

It is good to have an outstanding digital recording of *The Crucifixion*, with excellent soloists (the tenor **James Gilchrist** outstandingly eloquent); and **Clare College Choir**, directed by **Timothy Brown**, sings very beautifully, catching the music's devotional simplicity movingly, without sentimentality. **Stephen Farr's** organ contribution is supportive but not intrusive. The recording, made in Guildford Cathedral, is first class. With the congregational hymns included, this must now take pride of place, although we still have a soft spot for the old St John's version with Owen Brannigan and Richard Lewis.

The Classics for Pleasure version (from the late 1960s) is of high quality and, although one of the congregational hymns is omitted, in every other respect this can be recommended. **John Lawrenson** makes a movingly eloquent solo contribution and the choral singing is excellent.

STAMITZ, Carl (1745–1801)

Cello Concertos 1 in G; 2 in A; 3 in C

🔊 (BB) **** Naxos 8.550865. Benda, Prague CO

These three delightful *Concertos* are admirably played by **Christian Benda**, who also directs his own accompaniments. He is a present member of a well-known family of Czech musicians, a dynasty which reaches back to the court of Frederick the Great. The *First G major Concerto* is particularly winning, and the spirited *Allegros* of the other two works are hardly less amiable and each has a slow movement with a yearning contour, with the closing *Rondo* of the *C major* work the most infectious of all. The recording is excellent, and if you enjoy *Cello concertos* this group is not to be missed.

Clarinet Concerto 1 in F; (i) Double Clarinet Concerto in B flat; (ii) Double Concerto for Clarinet & Bassoon in B flat

🔊 (BB) *** Naxos 8.553584. Berkes; with (i) Takashima; (ii) Okazaki; Nicholas Esterházy Sinfonia

The *F major* solo *Concerto* is a delightful work with a vigorous first movement leading to a lyrical minor-key *Andante* and a jig finale. The double concerto was a favourite form with Stamitz, with long opening tuttis in the slow movements as well as the first. Both works are linked to the sinfonia concertante format as well as to the earlier form of the concerto grosso with its strongly contrasted, lightly scored passages for the solo instruments. As soloist as well as director, **Berkes**, with his reedy clarinet tone, is well matched by his Japanese partners, helped by full, open recording.

Clarinet Concertos 7 in E flat; 8 in B flat (Darmstadt 1-2); 10 in B flat; 11 in E flat

🔊 (BB) *** Naxos 8.554339. Berkes, Nicholas Esterházy Sinfonia

Clarinet Concerto 10 in B flat

🔊 *** EMI 55155-2. Meyer, ASMF, Brown – MOZART: *Clarinet Concerto*, etc.; WEBER: *Clarinet Concerto 1* ***

Sabine Meyer's performances are highly musical and she is given characteristically polished and elegant accompaniments by **Iona Brown** and the **Academy**. However **Kálmán Berkes** on Naxos is by no means a lesser soloist. He finds a Bohemian sense of fun in the closing Rondos, which is less obvious with Meyer, although she still plays them lightheartedly and her collection remains very enjoyable. The accompaniments on Naxos are also warm and stylish and the recording is excellent.

Symphonies: in D (La Chasse); in C & G, Op. 13/16, 4 & 5; in F, Op. 24/3

*** Chan. 9358. LMP, Bamert

Carl Stamitz wrote over 50 symphonies and the present examples are most attractive examples of his three-movement 'Italian overture' style. His slow movements are Haydnesque and quite gracious; his finales are witty: that for the *F major* work is particularly catchy. *La Chasse* is the earliest work here and the outer movements have plenty of energy and whooping horn-calls, with a rather wistful *Andante* to separate them. Excellent performances, very well played and recorded.

STAMITZ, Johann (1717–57)

Trumpet Concerto in D (arr. Boustead)

(B) *** Ph. Duo 464 028-2 (2). Hardenberger, ASMF, Marriner – HAYDN; HERTEL; HUMMEL: *Concertos* **** (with concert: 'Famous Classical Trumpet Concertos' **** 🏅).

This *Concerto* was written either by Stamitz or by a composer called J. G. Holzbogen. The writing lies consistently up in the instrument's stratosphere and includes some awkward leaps. It is quite inventive, however, notably the finale, which is exhilarating on the lips of **Håken Hardenberger**. There is no lack of panache here and **Marriner** accompanies expertly. Good if reverberant recording, with the trumpet given great presence. This now comes as part of a Duo anthology, which is very highly recommendable.

Symphonies: in A; B flat; G (Mannheim); in D, Op. 3/2; in E flat, Op. 11/2; Orchestral Trio in E, Op. 5/3

🔊 (BB) *** Naxos 8.553194. New Zealand CO, Armstrong

The bold opening chords and immediately following crescendo of the *D major Symphony*, Op. 3/2 (from the early 1750s) immediately establish its Mannheim credentials, as do the elegantly sophisticated scoring of the *Andantino* and the effective use of horns in the *Minuet* and *Trio*. The *E flat Symphony*, one of the composer's last, follows a similar pattern, but the three earlier works (from the 1740s), which are actually designated as 'Mannheim' Symphonies are altogether simpler, each with only three movements.

The *E major Trio* is much more ambitious, with a searchingly expressive *Adagio*, all but worthy of Haydn. The excellent **New Zealand Chamber Orchestra** under **Donald Armstrong** play with finesse and vitality and are persuasive advocates of music which so far proves not especially adventurous.

(Orchestral) Trios, Op. 1/1-4

(BB) **(*) Naxos 8.553213. New Zealand CO, Armstrong

Although designated Op. 1, the six *Orchestral Trios* appear to be relatively late works (1755–6) and were designated by the composer to be performed optionally either as trios or by a fuller chamber orchestra, as here. They are each in four movements, elegant, simply constructed, with a divertimento-like character, but not trivial. The most striking is *4 in C minor*, which explores a wider range of expressive feeling than its companions, but the Siciliana-like *Larghetto* of the *F major* (3), followed by a rather striking *Minuet* and robust finale, also sets that work apart. They are very well played here, polished in ensemble with musical phrasing and good use of light and shade. The recording is very natural. But one cannot pretend this is anything but pleasing wallpaper music, although it must have been rewarding for talented amateurs to play.

STANFORD, Charles (1852–1924)

Clarinet Concerto in A min., Op. 80

(BB) *** Hyp. Helios CDH 55101. King, Philh. O, Francis – FINZI: *Concerto* ***

The Stanford *Clarinet Concerto* finds **Thea King** bringing a firm, sharp attack. In the finale too King is strong and forthright, but she is warmer and more flexible in the slow movement, and at bargain price the Helios reissue is very competitive.

(i) Clarinet Concerto, Op. 80. Symphony 1 in B flat

(N) (BB) *** Naxos 8.570356. Bournemouth SO, Lloyd-Jones, (i) with Plane

There is much to enjoy here, despite Stanford's lack of really memorable themes. The recording and playing are superb, and the *Scherzo – In Ländler Tempo* is particularly enjoyable. The much shorter *Clarinet Concerto* is superbly played and similarly well recorded, **Robert Plane** proving an expert and sympathetic soloist. The bold brass writing at the opening of the finale is particularly striking, and this leads to appealingly bold themes on the clarinet.

Piano Concerto 1 in G, Op. 59

⊕ *** Hyp. CDA 66820. Lane, BBC Scottish SO, Brabbins – PARRY: *Piano Concerto* ***

Written in 1894, the first of Stanford's two *Piano concertos* brings even clearer Brahmsian echoes than usual, but the finesse of the writing and the ravishing beauty of the slow movement make it almost as enjoyable as the second and better-known concerto, particularly in a performance by turns as brilliant and poetic as **Piers Lane's**. Full, warm sound.

(i) Piano Concerto 2, Op. 126; Down among the Dead Men, Op. 71; Irish Rhapsodies 1; 2 (The Lament for the Son of Ossian); (ii) 3 (for Cello & Orchestra); 4 (The Fisherman of Lough Neagh and What He Saw); 5; (iii) 6 (for Violin & Orchestra)

⊕ (M) *** Chan. X10116 (2). (i) Fingerhut; (ii) Wallfisch; (iii) Mordkovitch; Ulster O, Handley

Stanford's ambitious *Second Piano Concerto*, although in three rather than four movements, is a work on the largest scale, recalling Brahms's *B flat Concerto*. **Margaret Fingerhut** is a first-rate soloist, both here and in her apt and entertaining account of the *Down among the Dead Men Variations*, for Stanford was a dab hand at this format. The new coupling is with the six *Irish Rhapsodies* (two of them also concertante

pieces with highly responsive soloists), which are the more impressive when heard as a set. They too are splendidly played and recorded.

(i) Piano Concerto 2 in C min., Op. 126; (ii) Becket, Op. 48: The Martyrdom (Funeral March); (iii) The Fisherman of Lough Neagh and What He Saw (Irish Rhapsody 4), Op. 141

*** Lyrita SRCD 219. (i) Binns, LSO; (ii–iii) LPO; (i; iii) Braithwaite; (ii) Boult

The Lyrita recording is surely a demonstration of just how a *Piano Concerto* should be balanced. The *Funeral March* comes from incidental music commissioned at the request of Tennyson for Irving's production of his tragedy, *Becket*. It has an arresting opening but is otherwise a fairly straightforward piece, strongly melodic in a Stanfordian manner. Like the more familiar *Irish Rhapsody*, it is splendidly played and recorded.

Violin Concerto in D, Op. 74; Suite for Violin & Orchestra, Op. 132

⊕ *** Hyp. CDA 67208. Marwood, BBC Scottish SO, Brabbins

Starting magically with the violin entering over an impressionistic twitter on woodwind, the Stanford *Violin Concerto* provides an important link between the Brahms concerto of 1878 and the Elgar of 1909–10. After that poetic start, Stanford builds his expansive structure in a strong Brahmsian manner, using clear, positive themes. He ends with an Irish jig finale, the nationalistic equivalent of Brahms's Hungarian finale. **Anthony Marwood** gives a warm, clean-cut reading, as he also does in the *Suite*, an attractive if heavyweight example of 19th-century neoclassicism.

Irish Rhapsody 4: The Fisherman of Lough Neagh and What He Saw

(M) *** Chan. 10426X. Ulster O, Handley – BAX: *On the Sea-Shore*; BRIDGE: *The Sea*; BRITTEN: *Sea Interludes* ***

Stanford's folksy *Fourth Irish Rhapsody* is now added to this already attractive reissue as a bonus.

Symphonies 1–7

*** Chan. 9279/82 (4). Ulster O, Handley

Now available in a box of four CDs, with the fill-ups which accompanied the original CDs now put aside for separate reissue, this is obviously the most attractive way to approach this generally impressive if uneven British symphonic canon. **Handley** and his **Ulster Orchestra** are completely at home in this repertoire, and the Chandos recording is consistently of this company's best quality.

Symphonies 3 (Irish) in F min., Op. 28; 6 (In honour of the life-work of a great artist: George Frederick Watts) in E flat, Op. 94

(N) (BB) *** Naxos 8.570355. Bournemouth SO, Lloyd-Jones

Stanford's *Irish Symphony* is understandably one of his most popular works, with its attractive Irish melodies running though the score, such as the jaunty second-movement

Scherzo – very jig-like – and the haunting beauty of the slow movement, as well as the lovely folk melodies used in the finale. The less popular *Sixth Symphony*, written in response to the death of the Victorian artist George Frederick Watts, also comes off almost equally well here. The score is a bit rambling, but Lloyd-Jones holds it together with conviction on Chandos. Indeed, the richness of the playing is especially to be appreciated in the beautiful slow movement, and there are many pleasures to be found in this score and performance.

Symphonies 4 in F, Op. 31; 7 in D min., Op. 124

🎵 ⑱ *** Naxos 8.570285. Bournemouth SO, Lloyd-Jones

4, written in 1888, has many Brahmsian touches, particularly in the use of woodwind and horns, but the Irish flavour of the thematic material gives the piece a distinctive flavour, with the composer's acute control of structure sustaining tension well. 7, written in 1911, when Stanford had been overtaken among British composers, is a lighter, more compact work, with Mendelssohn and Schumann among the influences, and with the same taut control of structure and clear orchestration Lloyd-Jones's readings may not quite rival in warmth those of Vernon Handley and the Ulster Orchestra on the rival Chandos series, differently coupled, but he compensates in his extra tautness and urgency. Brilliant, clear sound.

CHAMBER MUSIC

(i) Piano Quintet in D min.; (ii) String Quintet 1

🎵 **** Hyp. CDA 65505. Vanbrugh Qt; with (i) Lane; (ii) Knox

The *Piano Quintet* comes from 1886, when Stanford was 33, and is an ambitious and powerfully argued score, beautifully laid out for the medium. Although Stanford's music may not possess the strong individuality of Fauré or any comparable contemporary, it is powerful music and its neglect unaccountable. The *First String Quintet* (1903), with second viola, is hardly less persuasive. The ideas are keenly lyrical and their quality distinguished, and the overall flow of the music is extraordinarily natural. Excellent music that will delight and give pleasure; and both the performances and recording, produced by Andrew Keener, are of real excellence.

Serenade (Nonet) in F, Op. 95

🎵 ⑱ *** Hyp. Helios CDH 55061. Capricorn – PARRY: *Nonet ***

Like the Parry *Nonet*, with which it is coupled, the *Serenade* is an inventive and delightful piece, its discourse civilized and the Scherzo full of charm. **Capricorn** play this piece with evident pleasure and convey this to the listener. The recording is very natural and truthfully balanced.

Violin Sonatas 1 in D, Op. 11; 2 in A, Op. 70; Irish Fantasy 1 (Caoine), Op. 54 1; 5 Characteristic Pieces, Op. 93

🎵 **** Hyp. CDA 67024. Barritt, Edwards

One expected these to be enjoyably well-crafted works but they are a great deal more than that, teeming with memo-

rable ideas, to make consistently delightful listing. **Paul Barritt** and **Catherine Edwards** play all this music with a spring-like freshness, and obviously enjoy every bar. They are beautifully recorded.

PIANO MUSIC

24 Preludes, Set 1, Op. 163; 6 Characteristic Pieces, Op. 132

*** Priory PRCD 449. Jacobs

The 24 *Preludes* are not bravura works like those of Chopin and Rachmaninov. Written in 1918, their chromatic key-sequence would suggest that they are more readily associated with Bach's *Well-tempered Clavier*. The variety of Stanford's invention brings a continuing freshness throughout the set, which can be enjoyed as a progression as well as by selecting individual items. The *Characteristic Pieces* were written six years earlier and are also of high quality, with the engaging *Rondel* (4) dedicated to the Schumann of *Kinderszenen*. **Peter Jacobs** almost never disappoints and his performances here are accomplished, stylish, spontaneous and thoroughly sympathetic, while the recording is first class.

VOCAL MUSIC

3 Motets, Op. 38: Beati quorum via; Cœlos ascendit; Justorum animae. Anthems: For lo, I raise up; Glorious and powerful God; How beautiful are their feet; If ye then be risen with Christ; The Lord is my Shepherd; Ye choirs of new Jerusalem; Ye holy angels bright. (Organ) Preludes & Fugues in B & C, Op. 193/2-3

🎵 Ⓜ **** CRD CRD 3497. New College, Oxford, Ch., Higginbottom; Plummer or Smith (organ)

All this music shows Stanford at his most confidently inspired, readily carrying the listener with him, when the performances are so secure and committed and superbly recorded in the Chapel of New College, Oxford.

Communion Service in C, Op. 115: Kyrie; Credo. Evening Service in G, Op. 81: Magnificat; Nunc dimittis. Evening Service in C, Op. 115: Magnificat; Nunc dimittis. Morning Service in C, Op. 115: Te deum and Benedictus. For lo, I raise up, Op. 145; 3 Latin Motets: Beati quorum via; Coelos ascendit hodie; Justorum animae. (Organ) (i) Postlude in D min.; Prelude in G min.

🎵 ⑱ **** Naxos 8.555794. St John's College Ch., Robinson; (i) Whitton

When Stanford tended to concentrate on setting the *Magnificat* and *Nunc dimittis* of the *Evening Service*, it is good to have two examples represented, the *G major* with its opening treble solo more intimate and less dramatic than the *C major*. Having the *C major Morning Service* (but without the *Jubilate*) as well as the *Communion Service* gives a broader perspective, with the traditional Cranmer words for the *Mass* ending with the *Gloria*, where nowadays Anglo-Catholics follow the Roman order in their devotions. The chapel acoustic is warmly atmospheric, while allowing lightness and transparency in the choral textures, with words commendably clear.

(i) *Requiem, Op. 63*; (ii) *The Veiled Prophet of Khorassan* (excerpts)

🎵 **(BB)** ******** Naxos 8.555201/2. (i) Lucy, McGahon, Kerr, Leeson-Williams, RTE Philharmonic Ch.; (ii) Kerr; Nat. SO of Ireland, cond. (i) Leaper; (ii) Pearce

Stanford's magnificent *Requiem* (1897) was composed in honour of the painter Lord Leighton, who died in 1896. The contrasts of the writing, from the ethereal opening of the *Kyrie* to the blazing *fortissimo* of the *Tuba mirum*, are superbly caught here, one of the best recordings we have had from Naxos and surely in the demonstration bracket. With fine solo singing to match the fervour of the chorus, **Adrian Leaper** can be congratulated on the great success of the first recording of a work that should surely be in the general choral repertoire. The exotic suite from Stanford's first opera, *The Veiled Prophet of Khorassan*, makes an agreeable if not distinctive encore.

The Revenge: A Ballad of the Fleet, Op. 24; Songs of the Fleet, Op. 117; Songs of the Sea, Op. 91

🎵 **✳** ******** Chan. **SACD** CHSA 5043. Finley, Welsh Nat. Ch. & BBC SO of Wales, Hickox

These inspired works are immediately memorable, with *The Old Superb* and *Drake's Drum* being real hits. There is much here that is genuinely touching, such as *Homeward Bound* from the *Songs of the Sea*; the more moody and brooding items from *The Songs of the Fleet* offer contrast to the extrovert numbers, but throughout, Stanford's briny inspiration always comes up as fresh as the sea air. *The Revenge* tells the story of Richard Grenville's heroic 1591 battle against the Spanish fleet, and it was a huge success at its 1886 première. It is just as entertaining as the more famous works on this CD. **Gerald Finley's** golden tone is superb and he rises to both the heroic and tender passages with total conviction. With equal dedication from the chorus – not to mention the orchestra, which offers both enthusiasm and sensitivity – this CD is an outstanding success. The Chandos recording is warm and detailed, offering plenty of spine-tingling atmosphere, which is even more impressive when played through an SACD system.

(i) *Stabat Mater, Op. 96; Te Deum* (from *Service in B flat, Op. 10*); (ii) *6 Bible Songs, Op. 113*

🎵 ******* Chan. 9548. (i) Attrot, Stephen, Robson; (i; ii) Varcoe; (ii) Watson; Leeds Philharmonic Ch., BBC PO, Hickox

Stanford, Irish to the core, here offers a Protestant setting of the deeply Catholic text of the *Stabat Mater*. In its directness and vigour, this relates to Stanford's healthily Anglican church music on the one hand and to his symphonic writing on the other. Like his *Requiem*, this is a piece, long-neglected, that richly deserves revival, and **Hickox** with his excellent forces directs a performance, atmospherically recorded, that demands its return to the repertory. The six settings of biblical texts for baritone and organ (warmly done by **Stephen Varcoe** and **Ian Watson**) are fresh and forthright, leading to the stirring *Te Deum in B flat*, one of the glories of English church music.

STEFAN, Joseph Anton (1726–97)

Fortepiano Concerto in B flat

Ⓜ ******* Warner Elatus 0927 49556-2. Staier, Concerto Köln – SALIERI: *Fortepiano Concertos* *******

The Bohemian-born Joseph Stefan's *Concerto* (from the 1780s) is fluent and musical, if slightly overlong, but with a rather fine slow movement; the concerto also opens with an extended and quite touching *Adagio in D minor*. **Staier's** performance is highly persuasive, and he is given alert and sympathetic support by the excellent **Concerto Köln**.

STEFFANI, Agostino (1654–1728)

Stabat Mater

Ⓑ ******* DHM/BMG 82876 60149-2. Alamanjo, Van der Sluis, Elwes, Padmore, Van der Kamp, Netherlands Bach Festival Ch. & O, Leonhardt – BIBER: *Requiem à 15 in A* *******

Agostino Steffani was diplomat and priest as well as a composer, but his music has a strongly individual character. His serene, melancholy *Stabat Mater* has moving and expressive content and much imaginative word-setting, while the *Cujus animam* and *Pro peccatis* are glorious in their expressively rich harmonies. The solo writing is imaginative and the layering of parts in the closing *Quando corpus*, which gathers pace as it proceeds, is very telling. The performance could hardly be bettered, with soloists and chorus equally dedicated. First-rate recording.

STENHAMMAR, Wilhelm (1871–1927)

(i) *Piano Concerto 1 in B flat min., Op. 1; Symphony 3* (fragment)

🎵 ******* Chan. 9074. (i) Widlund; Royal Stockholm PO, Rozhdestvensky

(i) *Piano Concerto 1*; (ii) *Florez och Blanzeflor, Op. 3*; (iii) *2 Sentimental Romances, Op. 28*

*** BIS CD 550. (i) Derwinger; (ii) Mattei; (iii) Wallin, Malmö SO, Järvi

Stenhammar's *First Piano Concerto* is full of beautiful ideas and the invention is fresh. **Love Derwinger** proves an impressive and sympathetic intepreter and gets good support from **Paavo Järvi**. The early *Florez och Blanzeflor* ('Flower and Whiteflower'), a ballad by Oscar Levertin, brings a certain Wagnerian flavour but has a charm that is sensitively sung by the young Swedish baritone **Peter Mattei**.

Chandos offer the less substantial coupling, a three-minute fragment from the *Third Symphony*. But in the *Concerto* **Mats Widlund** proves the more imaginative soloist and brings just that little bit more finesse to the solo part. **Rozhdestvensky** gives excellent support and the **Stockholm Orchestra** (and in particular their strings) have greater richness of sonority. The Chandos recording also has the edge on its BIS competitor in terms of depth and warmth.

Serenade for Orchestra, Op. 31

➥ ❀ (BB) **** Warner Apex 0927 43075-2. Royal Stockholm PO, A. Davis – GRIEG: *Holberg Suite* (Helsinki Strings, Szilvay); NIELSEN: *Little Suite* (Norwegian R.O, Rasilainen) ***

The Stenhammar was recorded in 1998 and originally coupled with the Brahms *D major Serenade*. We can only reiterate our wonder at this glorious work; its invention is rich and its harmonies subtle. Nothing more perfectly enshrines the spirit of the Swedish summer night than its *Notturno*, but throughout the level of inspiration is uniformly high. **Andrew Davis** shapes the score with scrupulous attention to detail and evident sensitivity and feeling. In this bargain-basement refurbishment it is coupled with fine performances of the Grieg *Holberg Suite* from Helsinki and the enchanting Nielsen *Little Suite* from Norway. A terrific bargain.

(i) Symphonies 1 in F; 2 in G min., Op. 34; Serenade for Orchestra, Op. 31 (with Reverenza movement); Excelsior Overture, Op. 13; The Song (Sången): Interlude, Op. 44; Lodolezzi Sings (Lodolezzi sjunger): suite; (ii) Piano Concertos 1; (iii) 2 in D min., Op. 23; (iv) Ballad: Florez och Blanzeflor; (v) 2 Sentimental Romances; (vi) Midwinter, Op. 24; Snöfrid, Op. 5

➥ (M) **** BIS (DDD/ADD) CD 714/716. (i) Gothenburg SO, Järvi; (ii) Derwinger; (iii) Ortiz; (iv) Matthei; (v) Wallin; (vi) Gothenburg Ch.; (ii–v) Malmö SO, P. Järvi

Paavo Järvi's performances are now repackaged at a distinctly advantageous price. The *First Piano Concerto* makes use of Stenhammar's own orchestration, which came to light only recently in America; and this is the most comprehensive compilation of Stenhammar's orchestral music now on the market. All the performances and recordings are of high quality, and the only serious criticism to make affects the first movement of the *Second Symphony*, which Järvi takes rather too briskly. In the *Second Piano Concerto* **Cristina Ortiz** is a good soloist.

Symphony 2 in G min., Op. 34

➥ **** Cap. (ADD)CAP 21151. Stockholm PO, Westerberg

Symphony 2; Overture, Excelsior!, Op. 13

(BB) **(*) Naxos 8.553888. RSNO, Sundkvist

This is a marvellous *Symphony*. It is direct in utterance; the melodic invention is fresh and abundant, and the generosity of spirit it radiates is heart-warming. The **Stockholm** **Philharmonic** under **Stig Westerberg** play with conviction and eloquence; the strings have warmth and body, and the wind are very fine too. The recording is vivid and full-bodied even by the digital standards of today: as sound, this record is absolutely first class.

Petter Sundkvist's account too is absolutely first class interpretatively, though it is rather let down by the quality of sound, which does not match that of his Stockholm rivals. It is a meticulous, dedicated account, which radiates an understanding of and love for this music. The **Royal Scottish National Orchestra** respond with enthusiasm.

CHAMBER MUSIC

String Quartets (i) 1 in C, Op. 2; (ii) 2 in C min., Op. 14; (iii) 3 in F, Op. 18; 4 in A min., Op. 25; (i) 5 in C (Serenade), Op. 29; (ii) 6 in D min., Op. 35

(M) *** Cap. (ADD) CAP 21536 (3). (i) Fresk Qt; (ii) Copenhagen Qt; (iii) Gotland Qt

The *First Quartet* shows Stenhammar steeped in the chamber music of Beethoven and Brahms, though there is a brief reminder of Grieg; the *Second* is far more individual. By the *Third* and *Fourth*, arguably the greatest of the six, the influence of Brahms and Dvořák is fully assimilated, and the *Fourth* reflects that gentle melancholy which lies at the heart of Stenhammar's sensibility. The *Fifth* is the shortest; the *Sixth* comes from the war years when the composer was feeling worn out and depressed, though there is little evidence of this in the music. Performances are generally excellent, as indeed is the recording, and it is good to have this thoroughly worthwhile set at mid-price.

PIANO MUSIC

Piano Sonatas in G min.; A flat, Op. 12; 3 Fantasies; Nights of Late Summer, Op. 33

(N) **** Hyp. CDA 67689. Sturfält

Stenhammar's *G minor Sonata* is an ambitious, romantic work with an unforgettable main theme dominating its first movement; in its youthful ardour, in many ways it is an equivalent of the Brahms F minor work. The *Three Fantasies*, Op. 11, of 1895 are Brahmsian in influence, the first again boldly passionate; but the composer's own personality come through, and notably so in the charming *Dolce scherzando* and the closing *Molto espressivo*. The five pieces which make up the *Nights of Late Summer* are not overtly descriptive: their feeling is personal, although the exception is the closing charming *Poco allegretto*, which has almost a tang of Grieg. But the late *A major Sonata* (composed in the same year) is a highly individual work, balancing serious lyricism with drama, and closing with a vibrant, unpredictable finale. **Martin Sturfält** suggests it has an affinity with Beethoven. He plays all this music with much feeling and understanding, and great spontaneity, as at a live recital; and the recording (produced by Andrew Keener) is very real indeed. This is a disc well worth exploring.

VOCAL MUSIC

30 Songs

*** MSVE (ADD) MSCD 623. von Otter, Hagegård, Forsberg, Schuback

These songs cover the whole of Stenhammar's career: the earliest, 'In the forest', was composed when he was 16, while the last, *Minnesang*, was written three years before his death. The songs are unpretentious and charming, fresh and idyllic, and nearly all are strophic. **Hagegård** sings the majority of them with his usual intelligence and artistry, though there is an occasional hardening of timbre. **Anne Sofie von Otter** is in wonderful voice and sings with great sensitivity and charm. **Bengt Forsberg** and **Thomas Schuback** accompany with great taste, and the recording is of the highest quality.

Lodolezzi Sings: suite, Op. 39; (i) Midwinter, Op. 24; (ii) Snöfrid, Op. 5; The Song (interlude)

*** BIS CD 438. (i; ii) Gothenburg Concert Hall Ch., (ii) with Ahlén, Nilsson, Zackrisson, Enoksson; Gothenburg SO, Järvi

Snöfrid is an early cantata. The young composer was completely under the spell of Wagner at this time and it offers only occasional glimpses of the mature Stenhammar. *Midwinter* is a kind of folk-music fantasy or potpourri on the lines of Alfvén's *Midsummer Vigil*, though not quite so appealing. *Lodolezzi Sings* has much innocent charm. None of this is great Stenhammar but it is well worth hearing; the performances under **Neeme Järvi** are very sympathetic, and the recording is natural and present.

(i) The Song (Sången), Op. 44; (ii) 2 Sentimental Romances, Op. 28; (iii) Ithaca, Op. 21

🎧 *** Cap. (ADD) CAP 21358. (i) Sörenson, von Otter, Dahlberg, Wahlgren, State Ac. Ch., Adolf Fredrik Music School Children's Ch.; (ii) Tellefsen; (iii) Hagegård, Swedish RSO; (i) Blomstedt; (ii) Westerberg; (iii) Ingelbretsen

The first half of *The Song* has been described as 'a great fantasy' and is Stenhammar at his best and most individual: the choral writing is imaginatively laid out and the contrapuntal ingenuity is always at the service of poetic ends: the second half is less individual. The solo and choral singing is superb and the whole performance has the total commitment one might expect from these forces. The superbly engineered recording does them full justice. The *Two Sentimental Romances* have great charm and are very well played, and **Hagegård** is in fine voice in another rarity, *Ithaca*.

Tirfing (opera; excerpts)

*** Sterling CDO 1033-2. Tobiasson, Morling, Taube, Stockholm Royal Op. O, Segerstam

Tirfing is a 'mystical saga-poem', based on the Hervarar Saga. It is all terribly Wagnerian, but even so, the music has the power and sweep of Stenhammar. There are characteristic modulations (one is reminded of *Excelsior!* among other things). Above all, even at its most Wagnerian, the music

grips the listener from start to finish. **Leif Segerstam** gets first-rate results from the **Royal Opera Orchestra** and the same from the three soloists, in particular **Ingrid Tobiasson** as Hervor. Good wide-ranging recording.

STERNDALE BENNETT, William (1816–75)

Piano Concertos 1 in D min., Op. 1; 3 in C min., Op. 9

✿ **** Lyrita SRCD 204. Binns, LPO, Braithwaite

Sterndale Bennett's *Concerto in D minor* is a work of extraordinary fluency and accomplishment. David Byers, who has edited the *Concertos*, speaks of Sterndale Bennett's 'gentle lyricism, the strength and energy of the orchestral tuttis'. No praise can be too high for the playing of **Malcolm Binns**, whose fleetness of finger and poetic sensibility are a constant source of delight, and for the admirable support he receives from **Nicholas Braithwaite** and the **LPO**. The engineers produce sound of the highest quality. A most enjoyable disc.

Piano Concertos 2 in E flat, Op. 4; 5 in F min.; Adagio

*** Lyrita SRCD 205. Binns, Philh. O, Braithwaite

The *Second Concerto* proves to be another work of great facility and charm. It takes as its model the concertos of Mozart and Mendelssohn, and the brilliance and delicacy of the keyboard writing make one understand why the composer was so highly regarded by his contemporaries. The *F minor Concerto* of 1836 is eminently civilized music with lots of charm; the *Adagio*, which completes the disc, is thought to be an alternative slow movement for Sterndale Bennett's *Third Concerto* (1837). Whether or not this is the case, it is certainly a lovely piece. **Malcolm Binns** plays with great artistry, and the accompaniment by the **Philharmonia Orchestra** and **Nicholas Braithwaite** is equally sensitive. First-class recording.

STEVENS, Bernard (1916–83)

(i) Cello Concerto; Symphony of Liberation

🎧 *** Mer. (ADD) CDE 84124. (i) Baillie, BBC PO, Downes

Bernard Stevens came to wider notice at the end of the war when his *Symphony of Liberation* won a *Daily Express* competition. What a fine work it proves to be, though the somewhat later *Cello Concerto* is even stronger. Dedicated performances from **Alexander Baillie** and the **BBC Philharmonic**. Good recording.

(i) Violin Concerto; Symphony 2

*** Mer. (ADD) CDE 84174. (i) Kovacic; BBC PO, Downes

The *Violin Concerto* is a good piece and well worth investigating. Stevens is a composer of real substance, and the *Second Symphony* (1964) is impressive in its sustained power and resource. **Ernst Kovacic** is persuasive in the *Concerto*, and **Downes** and the **BBC Philharmonic** play well. Good (but not spectacular) recording.

STEVENSON, Ronald
(born 1928)

Passacaglia on D-S-C-H

⊖ *** Divine Art 25013. McLachlan

Ronald Stevenson's *Passacaglia* is something of a tour de force. It is a mighty set of variations on the four-note motif D-S-C-H derived from Shostakovich's monogram, lasting without a break for some 80 minutes. Later on in the score Stevenson introduces another four-note anagram, B-A-C-H, perhaps a reference to Busoni's *Fantasia contrappuntistica*. The twelfth section cleverly alludes to the microtonal scale of the Highland bagpipes and incorporates a 17th-century Pibroch *Cumha ne Cloinne* ('Lament for the Children') and there is a formidable climactic triple fugue in which the *Dies irae* surfaces. In the 1960s Sir William Walton hailed the pieces as 'really tremendous – magnificent – I can't remember having been so excited by a new work for a very long time'. **Murray McLachlan** is an impressive exponent of this score and he is very well recorded. An earlier version by Raymond Clarke (Marco Polo 8.223545), though a formidable musical achievement, is rather let down by the boxy recording, and neither of the composer's own accounts is easily available.

STILL, Robert (1910–71)

Symphonies (i) 3; (ii) 4

Ⓝ *** Lyrita (ADD) SRCD 285. (i) LSO, Goossens; (ii) RPO, Fredman – SEARLE: *Symphony 2* ***

At last Robert Still's highly entertaining symphonies are making it on to CD. Still was a gifted composer and a very considerable musician. His *Third Symphony* is an expertly written piece (the opening sounds a bit Prokofievian and is undeniably attractive), and although it is fair to say that the slow movement lacks real depth, it is again very attractive. The *Fourth Symphony* is inspired by a psychological case-history and reflects the composer's interest and specialized knowledge of psychiatry. It is a hugely entertaining work – colourful and varied and often excitingly dramatic. Both symphonies receive superb performances and recordings (from the 1960s and '70s). Good coupling too.

STILL, William Grant (1895–1978)

Symphony 2 (Song of a New Race) in G min.

*** Chan. 9226. Detroit SO, Järvi – DAWSON: *Negro Folk Symphony*; ELLINGTON: *Harlem* ***

Stokowski conducted the première of this attractive piece in 1937, seven years after the composer's *First Symphony* had been the first work by an Afro-American composer to be played by a major orchestra (the NYPO). Still worked as an arranger, so he knew how to score, and he had a fund of tunes: the slow movement is haunting, the high-spirited Scherzo whistles along like someone out walking on a spring morning. The idiom is totally American and, if the score is more a suite than a symphony, it remains very personable. It is played most persuasively here and is given a richly expansive recording.

STOCKHAUSEN, Karlheinz
(1928–2006)

(i) *Mikrophonie 1; Mikrophonie 2;* (ii) *Klavierstücke 1–11*

Ⓜ *** Sony (ADD) S2K 53346 (2). (i) Members of W. German R. Ch. & Studio Ch. for New Music, Cologne, Kontarsky, Alings, Fritsch, Bojé, cond. Schernus; supervised by composer; (ii) Kontarsky (piano)

This reissue combines two important Stockhausen recordings from the mid-1960s. *Mikrophonie 1* is electronic music proper; *Mikrophonie 2* attempts a synthesis of electronic music and choral sounds, and it is the vocal work that is the more immediately intriguing. It may be in dispute just how valid performances like these are when the composer's score allows many variables, but at least it is the composer himself who is supervising the production. Outstanding recording-quality for its time – as, of course, it should be with so many musician-engineers around in the Cologne studios.

The *Klavierstücke* provide a stimulating coupling. **Aloys Kontarsky** plays these 11 pieces – arguably the purest expression yet of Stockhausen's musical imagination – with a dedication that can readily convince even the unconverted listener. Seven of the pieces are very brief epigrammatic utterances, each sharply defined. The sixth and tenth pieces (the latter placed separately on the second disc) are more extended, each taking over 20 minutes. The effect at the beginning of the ninth piece provides a clear indication of Stockhausen's aural imagination. The pianist repeats the same, not very interesting discord no fewer than 228 times, and one might dismiss that as merely pointless. What emerges from sympathetic listening is that the repetitions go nagging on so that the sound of the discord seems to vary, like a visual image shimmering in heat-haze. The other pieces, too, bring similar extensions of musical experience, and all this music is certainly communicative. Excellent if forward recording and extensive back-up notes. A good set on which to sharpen avant-garde teeth.

Stimmung (1968)

*** Hyp. CDA 66115. Singcircle, Rose

Gregory Rose with his talented vocal group directs an intensely beautiful account of Stockhausen's 70-minute minimalist meditation on six notes. Though the unsympathetic listener might still find the result boring, this explains admirably how Stockhausen's musical personality can hypnotize, with his variety of effect and response, even with the simplest of formulae. Excellent recording.

STORACE, Bernardo
(c. 1637–c. 1707)

Selve di varie compositioni d'intavolatura (for harpsichord and organ); **Harpsichord:** *Ciaccona; Passacaglia sopra f; Balletto; Follia; Passacaglia sopra c; Spagnaletta; Partite sopra il cinque passi;* **Organ:** *Toccatas in F & G; Romanesca; Ballo della Battaglia; Ruggiero; Recercer in e; Passacaglia sopra c*

Ⓝ *** CPO 777 444-2. Halubek (Italian harpsichord & organ)

The present collection is taken from Bernardo Storace's only manuscript of works for harpsichord and organ which has survived. The pieces are attractively varied and full of life. The well-known *Follia* is, of course, a source for variations, and the *Passacaglias* are similarly inventive. The writing is vivid and colourful for both instruments, with the organ *Ballo della Battaglia* particularly vivid. By using authentic period instruments and interspersing the pieces **Jörg Halubek** makes up an entertaining programme which he plays with flair, and he is very well recorded. A most rewarding disc.

STRADELLA, Alessandro
(1639–82)

Christmas Cantatas: (i) *Ah, ah, troppo è ver;* (ii) *Si apra al riso* (both *per Il Santissimo natale*)

🎧–⊙ ⒝⒝ *** DHM 05472 77463 2. (i) Bach, Ziesak, Prégardien; (i; ii) Wessel, Schopper; (ii) Schlick; La Stagione Frankfurt, Schneider

With a freshness and originality one expects from the composer of *San Giovanni Battista*, Stradella's Christmas cantata, *Ah, ah, troppo è ver*, is a great deal more than a serene pastorella. Lucifer (**Michael Schopper**) appears at the very opening, strenuously to interrupt the good-natured *Sinfonia*, to announce his determination to thwart the influence of the Christ child. Then come three scenas, in turn depicting the Annunciation, the Nativity and the Adoration of the Magi with the Angel and Mary (**Mechthild Bach**), followed by the Shepherd (**Ruth Ziesak**), each given beautiful narrative arias, all of which are sung ravishingly here. Joseph (**Christoph Prégardien**) then rounds off the story-telling, and the work closes with an engagingly happy madrigal in which all participate. *Si apra al riso* is less dramatic but musically just as inspired, with two duets and a madrigal trio interspersed among the solo numbers, here with **Barbara Schlick** standing out from her excellent colleagues. **Michael Schneider** paces the music admirably and the instrumental playing is first class. Vivid recording in a pleasing acoustic completes the listener's pleasure.

San Giovanni Battista (oratorio)

**(*) Hyp. CDA 67617. Herrmann, Fedi, Oro, Akselberg, Abete, Academia Montis Regalis, De Marchi

Stradella's oratorio on the biblical subject of John the Baptist and Salome is an amazing masterpiece and offers unashamedly sensuous treatment of the story. Insinuatingly chromatic melodic lines for Salome (here described simply as Herodias's daughter) are set against plainer, more forthright writing for the castrato role of the saint, showing the composer as a seventeenth-century equivalent of Richard Strauss. There is one amazing phrase for Salome, which starts well above the stave and ends after much twisting nearly two octaves below with a glorious chest-note, a hair-raising moment. Herod's anger arias bring reminders of both Purcell and Handel, and at the end Stradella ingeniously superimposes Salome's gloating music and Herod's expressions of regret, finally cutting off the duet in mid-air as Charles Ives might have done, bringing the whole work to an indeterminate close.

The new Hyperion version is very successful and enjoyable, well cast, well sung and impressively accompanied by a combination of concerto grosso and concertino, which usually alternate but sometimes play as one group. **Martin Oro**, bold and full-timbred, is an excellent John the Baptist. **Anke Herrmann**, although characterizing Salome very believably, does not equal the remarkable eloquence of Catherine Bott on Minkowski's deleted Warner Elatus version.

STRAUSS Family, The

Strauss, Johann Sr (1804–49)

Strauss, Johann Jr (1825–99)

Strauss, Josef (1827–70)

Strauss, Eduard (1835–1916)

(all music listed is by Johann Strauss Jr unless otherwise stated)

Johann Strauss Jr: The Complete Edition
All played by the CSSR State PO (Košice) unless indicated otherwise)

The Complete Edition of the music of Johann Strauss on Marco covers 53 CDs. This collection has great documentary value, but only some of the CDs can be recommended to the general collector: Volumes 17 (8.223217), 27, to which we gave a Rosette (8.223227), 34 (8.223234), 37 (8.223237), 46 (8.223246), 47 (8.223247), 50 (8.223276) and 51 (8.223279), which earned the series its second Rosette.

Boskovsky Decca Strauss Edition
Ⓑ **(*) Decca (ADD) 455 254-2 (6). VPO, Boskovsky

These six vintage CDs (offering 86 titles) span **Willi Boskovsky's** long (analogue) recording career for Decca, stretching over two decades from the late 1950s onwards. In 1979 he directed the first of the now famous VPO New Year Concerts (see below) and that recording tradition has continued until the present day. Boskovsky's achievement in this repertoire remains unique, both in its range – the output of Josef, particularly his polkas, is notably well covered – and the almost unfailing sparkle of the performances. Following a sequence begun by Decca in the days of mono LPs with Clemens Kraus, he showed a unique feeling for the Straussian lilt in the waltzes, while the playing he drew from the **Vienna Philharmonic Orchestra** was consistently persuasive. The Decca engineers rose to the occasion (notably so when special effects were required, as in the *Explosion* and *Thunder and Lightning Polkas*) and the Sofiensaal provided an ideal ambience, with plenty of warmth and bloom. The one snag is the thinness of violin-tone, especially on the earlier records – it is immediately noticeable here on *An der schönen blauen Donau*, which rightly opens the first disc. The present CD transfers are very vivid and immediate, and their brightness has also served to add a hint of coarseness to some of the lively music. The ear adjusts, however, when the music-making is so zestful and alive.

Boskovsky EMI recordings

(BB) **(*) EMI (ADD/DDD) 586019 (6). Johann Strauss O, Boskovsky

Willi Boskovsky's EMI recordings date from 1971 to 1985 and this is a pretty complete survey. By any standards, these are excellent performances, with many of the popular works (and just about all the popular works are here) showing Boskovsky at his best: from the very opening of the *Blue Danube*, the playing of Boskovsky's **Johann Strauss Orchestra** balances an evocative Viennese warmth with the right sort of vigour, and other major waltzes, such as *Morning Papers*, are very enjoyable too. All the various overtures are full of attractive tunes and are highly entertaining overall, it must be admitted the playing is not as uniformly memorable as his classic Decca accounts; just occasionally a hint of blandness creeps in here. But the resonant, warm EMI sound makes for enjoyable listening.

NEW YEAR CONCERTS

1963–79 New Year's Concerts; (excerpts DVD Versions); 1974 New Year Concert (complete): **Czárdás: Ritter Pásmán (1967) Einzugmarsch** from **'Zigeunerbaron' (1969); Galopp: Banditen (1972); Overture 'Die Fledermaus' (1972); Perpetuum mobile (1978). Polkas: Annen (1966); Auf der Jagd (1979); Bitte schön (1972); Leichtes Blut (1975); Unter Donner und Blitz (1967); Vergnügungszug (1970). Waltz: Kaiser (1975).** JOSEF STRAUSS: **Polkas: Auf Ferienreisen (1964); Eingesendet (1968); Feuerfest (1971); Jockey (1972); Waltzes: Dorfschwalben aus Osterreich (1963); Sphärenklänge (1964). 1974 Concert: Galopp: Wetrennen. Polkas: Explosions; Pizzicato (with Josef); Tritsch-Tratsch; Rasch in der Tat; Künstergruss. Waltzes: An der schönen blauen Donau; Freut euch des Lebens; Geschichten aus dem Wienerwald.** JOSEF STRAUSS: **Polkas: Frauenherz; Künstlergruss; Ohne Sorgen; Plappermälchen.** JOHANN STRAUSS SR: **Radetzky Marsch**

(***) DG **DVD** mono 073 4002 (2). VPO, Boskovsky (with Bonus: *Boskovsky Portrait*)

Willi Boskovsky took over the direction of the **Vienna Philharmonic's** traditional New Year's concert in 1955 and continued for 25 years. Apart from being the orchestra's leader, he was a superb solo fiddler and so he continued to direct the concerts in Strauss's own style, leading and con-

ducting from his violin bow and often participating, nowhere more impressively than in the *Ritter Pásmán Csárdás* (1967), when the VPO assumes a Hungarian mantle; nowhere more charmingly than in *Tales from the Vienna Woods* (1974), when in the introduction he plays an engaging little duet with the orchestra's concert master. Even in the *Pizzicato Polka* he opens the piece alongside his players.

The first of the two DVDs here gives us the complete 1974 Concert, a surprisingly mellow affair, not helped by the mono recording which (presumingly deriving from a telecast) has a restricted range of sound, although the acoustic of the Golden Hall of the Musikverein, so visually pleasing, brings plenty of warmth and atmosphere. The programme is relatively short by today's standards, but Boskovsky in his frock coat sustains his patrician image seductively with his Viennese charm and natural feeling for Straussian inflexion and rubato. Especially beguiling is the introduction to the two most famous waltzes, *The Blue Danube* and *Tales from the Vienna Woods*, where it is fascinating to watch the zither player in close-up, with his subtle finger-vibrato. The orchestra itself makes a robust vocal contribution in *Ohne Sorgen*. The camerawork is effective enough, although in the latter piece the producer misses picturing a horn solo by focusing on the wrong player!

The second DVD assembles 19 items from various other concerts of which seven are in black-and-white. If visually these are less attractive, musically they certainly are not, for in the earlier concerts the obviously younger Boskovsky is often at his most vivacious and, throughout, the sound (still mono) is much brighter and more vivid. There are many highlights here, not least the two great Josef Strauss waltzes, while the side-drummer in the percussion department enjoys himself with various jokes and explosive effects in *Unter Donner und Blitz*, the *Banditen Galop*, and notably *Auf der Jagd*, where he presents Boskovsky with the results of the shoot. But he amuses the audience most with his pair of anvils in *Feuerfest*. On both discs, every now and then the orchestral visuals are interrupted by dancing from members of the Vienna State Opera and Volksoper Ballets, but for the most part we watch the conductor and his players, all so obviously enjoying themselves.

'New Year's Day Concert in Vienna (1979)': **Polkas: Auf der Jagd (with encore); Bitte schön! Leichtes Blut; Pizzicato (with Josef); Tik-Tak. Waltzes: An der schönen blauen Donau; Bei uns zu Haus; Loreley-Rheine-Klänge; Wein, Weib und Gesang.** JOSEF STRAUSS: **Moulinet Polka; Die Emanzipierte Polka-Mazurka; Rudolfsheimer-Polka; Sphärenklänge Waltz.** JOHANN STRAUSS SR: **Radetzky March.** E. STRAUSS: **Ohne Bremse Polka.** ZIEHRER: **Herreinspaziert! Waltz.** SUPPÉ: **Die schöne Galathee Overture**

(M) *** Decca 468 489-2. VPO, Boskovsky

Decca chose to record **Boskovsky's** 1979 New Year's Day concert in Vienna for their very first digital issue on LP. The clarity, immediacy and natural separation of detail are very striking throughout, and the strings of the **Vienna Philharmonic** are brightly lit.

'1989 New Year Concert in Vienna' (DVD versions):
Overture: Die Fledermaus; Ritter Pásmán: Czárdás.
Polkas: *Bauern; Eljen a Magyar; Im Krapfenwald'l;*
Pizzicato (with Josef). **Waltzes:** *Accelerationen; An*
der schönen blauen Donau (Blue Danube); Bei uns
z'Haus; Frühlingsstimmen; Künstlerleben. JOSEF
STRAUSS: **Polkas:** *Jockey; Die Libelle; Moulinet;*
Plappemäulchen. JOHANN STRAUSS SR.: *Radetzky*
March

(*) DG **DVD** 073 024-9. VPO, C. Kleiber. (Prod: Horst Bosch;
V/D: Brian Large.)

Carlos Kleiber's pursuit of knife-edged precision prevents
the results here from sounding quite relaxed enough, although the advantage of the DVD is that being able to watch
his flexible and often graceful arm-movements makes his
rather precise style with Viennese rhythms easier to accept.
But in one or two numbers Kleiber really lets rip, as in the
Hungarian polka, *Eljen a Magyar*, and in the *Ritter Pásmán*
Czárdás. With well-judged camera work the viewer is made
to feel closely involved with the orchestra's music-making,
making this an enjoyably spontaneous concert. The recording is both vivid and warmly atmospheric, although the violin timbre is brightly lit to match Kleiber's style.

'New Year Concert 2002' (DVD and CD versions):
March: *Zivio!* **Overture** *Die Fledermaus*. **Polkas:**
Beliebte Annen; Elisen; Tik-Tak. **Waltzes:** *An der*
schönen blauen Donau; Carnevalsbotschafter;
Künsterleben; Wiener Blut. JOSEF STRAUSS: **Polkas:**
Aquarellen; Im Fluge; Die Libelle;
Plappermäulchen!; Die Schwäzerin; Vorwärts!
JOHANN STRAUSS SR: *Radetzky March* (with
HELLMESBERGER: *Danse diabolique*)

*** TDK **DVD** DV-WPNK02. VPO, Ozawa. (V/D: Brian Large.)

*** Ph. 468 999-2. VPO, Ozawa. (without *Arm in Arm; Beliebte*
Annen & Elisen Polkas; Perpetuum mobile;
Carnevalsbotschafter Waltz)

Ozawa's 2002 Concert was certainly a great success, and he
made a special feature of including no fewer than six memorable polkas by Josef Strauss. The background took the
form of a large sign over the organ pipes celebrating the arrival of the Euro on that very day. Among the special extras
on the DVD is a second performance of *Perpetuum mobile*,
with illustrations of the new currency being manufactured
and printed. Also among the 'specials' are the **Vienna State**
Opera Ballet dancing to the *Blue Danube* and the Spanish
Riding School demonstrating against the background of a
pair of polkas. These items are all included in the main concert, which **Brian Large** and his cameras follow with his
usual expertise. Ozawa proves a warmly flexible Straussian,
even without the aid of a baton, and his performances are
consistently enjoyable, if perhaps not as individual as those
of Harnoncourt. The end-of-concert joke is the New Year
greeting offered in a host of different languages by orchestral
members (who are not all Viennese), with Ozawa himself
contributing in Japanese and Chinese, and the German version coming from the orchestra en masse. Altogether a most
enjoyable occasion. The equivalent SACD, although it plays

for 79 minutes, omits five items, but it can certainly be recommended, if you fancy the programme.

'New Year Concert 2003' (DVD versions): *Kaiser*
Franz Joseph I: Rettungs-Jubel-Marsch. **Polkas:**
Bauern; Furioso; Hellenen; Leichtes Blut; Lob der
Frauen; Niko; Scherz; Secunden. **Waltzes:** *An der*
schönen blauen Donau; Kaiser; Krönungs-Lieder;
Schatz. JOSEF STRAUSS: *Delirien Waltz; Pélé-Méle*
Polka. JOHANN STRAUSS SR: *Chinese Galop;*
Radetzky March (with WEBER/BERLIOZ: *Invitation*
to the Dance; BRAHMS: *Hungarian Dance 5 & 6*)

****DVD Arthaus 107013. VPO, Harnoncourt. (V/D: Brian
Large.) (Bonus includes Soloists of V. St. Op. Ballet in the
Hellenen Polka; and Kirov Ballet in the *Krönungs-Lieder*
Waltz.)

Harnoncourt's 2003 DVD is really special – the most memorable New Year celebration since the famous 1987 occasion,
which saw the return of Karajan to the Musikverein. What is
so striking with Harnoncourt is the seductive combination
of relaxed warmth (with some leisurely tempi in the Polkas)
and the laid-back refinement of the orchestral playing. Even
the trombone raspberry in the *Scherz Polka* is delicately done.
Highlights include the beautifully played *Schatz* and *Emperor*
Waltzes, especially the gentle coda of the latter, and Josef's
sparkling *Pélé-Méle Polka*. The ravishing account of the
Weber/Berlioz *Invitation to the Dance* is equally memorable.

Harnoncourt himself is a joy to watch. Never more so
than when he comes back for the encores, and, with flashing
eyes, unleashes an extraordinary bravura performance of the
Furioso Polka. Then, after sailing on the *Blue Danube*, he has
the audience totally under control for the clapping in the
very theatrical account of the *Radetzky March*. Although the
camera does occasionally stray away from the musicians to
roam outside the concert hall, the ballet dancing and the
visit to the Chinese Chamber at the Schönbrunn Palace are
kept as special features at the end.

'New Year Concert, 2004' (DVD and CD versions):
JOHANN STRAUSS SR: **Galopps:** *Cachucha. Indiana;*
March: *Radetzky.* **Polkas:** *Beliebte-Sperl; Frederika.*
Waltz: *Philomelen.* JOHANN STRAUSS JR: *Czárdás*
(Die Fledermaus). **March:** *Es war so wunderschön.*
Overture: *Das Sitzentuch der Königin.* **Polkas:**
Champagne; Im Sturmschritt; Satanella. **Quadrille:**
Zigeunerin. **Waltzes:** *Accelerationen; An der schönen*
blauen Donau. JOSEF STRAUSS: **Polkas:** *Eislauf;*
Stiefmütterchen. **Waltz:** *Sphärenklänge.* EDUARD
STRAUSS: *Polka: Mit Vergnügen* (with LANNER:
Tarantel Galopp; Hofball-Tänze Waltz)

*** DG **DVD** 073 097-9. VPO, Muti (V/D Brian Large); CD
474 900-2 (2)

Riccardo Muti once again presents his programme with an
authentic Viennese glow. The concert in 2004 was designed
to celebrate the bicentenary of Johann Strauss Sr, father of
the waltz-king we most revere. Normally the final encore,
the *Radetzky March*, is his most notable contribution, but
here we have four rare pieces by him, including the delec-

table *Philomena Waltz*, leading to two seductive items by his contemporary Joseph Lanner, presented with an endearing, gentle touch of Viennese schmalz in the more modern Schrammeln style that we remember from the early recordings of the Boskovsky Ensemble.

Johann Strauss Jr and his siblings take over again in the second half, with more rarities and an ecstatic account of the *Sphärenklänge Waltz* to match an equally ravishing account of the *Accelerationen Waltz* in the first half, where the increase in tempo is managed most engagingly. While the *Champagne Polka* fizzes appropriately, it cannot be said that visually the 2004 concert is as electrifying as Harnoncourt's 2003 proceedings. Muti's visual image is dapper; curiously, his bespectacled countenance reminds one a little of Glenn Miller, though there is nothing jazzy about his affectionately cultivated conducting style. With **Brian Large** in command, the camera angles are almost always impeccable, and only very occasionally do we leave the auditorium. The sound is excellent. There are optional filmed sequences of the **Vienna State Opera Ballet** for *Accelerations* and the *Champagne Polka* and for Josef Strauss's *Eislauf Polka*, and we are offered a choice of figure-skating impressions. But it is much more rewarding to be caught up in the music-making itself.

'New Year Concert, 2005' (DVD versions): Marches: Indigo; Russische. Polkas: An der Jagd; Die Bajadere; Bauern; Ein Herz, ein Sinn; Fata Morgana; Haut-Volée; Klipp-Klapp; Nordseebilder; Pizzicato (with Josef); Vergnügungszug. Waltzes: An der schönen blauen Donau; Geschichten aus dem Wienerwald; 1001 Nacht. JOSEF STRAUSS: **Polkas: Die Emancipirte; Winterlust. Waltzes: Lustschwärmer.** EDUARD STRAUSS: *Electrisch Polka* (with SUPPÉ: *Overture 'Die schöne Galathee'*; JOSEPH HELLMESBERGER: *Auf Wiener Art*)

⚏— *** DG **DVD** 073 4020. VPO, Maazel (V/D: Brian Large)

It is fascinating how the New Year's Day concert in Vienna seems to mellow even the severest disciplinarians among conductors. **Lorin Maazel** has never been so warm as when conducting this event, yet throughout his face registers (and his body movements confirm) an extraordinary kaleidoscopic range of emotions, from relaxed geniality and a hint of a smile to the strongest forcefulness and determination, communicated directly to the players and, of course, to us (one of the fascinations of DVD). The discipline underlies every performance, the playing has consistently precise ensemble without a hint of stiffness, and there is always plenty of lift. Maazel zips through over a dozen polkas with consistent exhilaration but saves his greatest affection for waltzes, and also the opening of the Suppé overture – a truly *schöne* Galatea – with magical playing from the **Vienna** strings (and an engaging bouquet of roses appearing on the screen). As a superb violinist, he has already followed Boskovsky's example in joining the orchestra to lead the *Pizzicato Polka*, and in *Geschichten aus dem Wienerwald* he takes up the violin again to play the delightful gentle passage in the introduction normally given to the zither.

Because of the tsunami catastrophe only a few days before the concert, it was decided it would be inappropriate to end the concert with the *Radetzky March* so, after the speeches and multi-language 'Happy New Year', it was the *Blue Danube Waltz* which ended the concert, played quite gloriously and with infinite flexibility. Indeed, in the coda, Maazel manages an extra touch of indulgent rubato, quite impermissible, of course, but totally captivating in this instance because it was seemingly spontaneous on a very special occasion. **Brian Large**, as usual, supervised the visuals expertly, and allowed himself to take the camera outside the Musikverein into the Vienna Woods at the appropriate time to show how they mirror the beauty of Strauss's waltz. Otherwise, in three optional filmed sequences, the viewer can choose to watch the **Vienna State Opera Ballet**. But we prefer the orchestra. Excellent sound.

2006 New Year's Concert' (CD version): Auf's Korn!; Künstler Quadrille. Galopps: Banditen; Liebesbotschaft. Marches: Spanischer; Der Zigeunerbaron. Polkas: Diplomaten; Eljen a Magyar!; Furioso; Im Krapfenwald'l; Lob der Frauen; Neue Pizzicato. Waltzes: An der schönen, blauen Donau; Du und Du; Frühlingsstimmen; Künsterleben; Lagunen. EDUARD STRAUSS: **Polka: Telephon.** JOHANN STRAUSS SR: **Radetzky March.** JOSEF STRAUSS: **Polkas: Eingesendet; Ohne Sorgen!** (with MOZART: *Le nozze di Figaro;* LANNER: **Waltz: Die Mozartisten**)

⚏—Ⓜ *** DG 477 5566 (2). VPO, Jansons

After New Year's Concerts conducted by Harnoncourt and Muti, **Jansons** is altogether mellower.

'New Year's Eve Concert 2007' (DVD & CD versions): March: Zivio!. Overture Waldmeister. Polka: Stadt und Land. Waltzes: An der schönen blauen Donau; Wo die Zitronen blüh'n. EDUARD STRAUSS: **Ohne Bremse Polka.** JOSEF STRAUSS: **Polkas: Irenen; Matrosen. Waltzes: Dynamiden; Delirien; Flattereister.** JOHANN STRAUSS SR: **Galops: Einzugs; Furioso. Radetzky March; Der Karneval von Venedig (Fantasy)**

⚏—✿ **** DG **DVD** 073 4188; 2-CD 477 6225 (2). VPO, Mehta (with Joseph HELLMESBERGER: *Dance of the Elves; Leichtfüssig Polka*) (DVD includes optional filmed ballet sequence for *Dynamiden* and *An der schönen blauen Donau*)

Zubin Mehta returned to direct the annual New Year Concert in Vienna for the fourth time in 2007 – and very memorably, too. He has mellowed even further, and he directs the five major waltzes here very seductively indeed, taking alluring risks with the Viennese rubato, especially in those by Josef and Johann's *Wo di Zitronen blüh'n*, in which he conveys great warmth of affection. The rest of the programme includes plenty of agreeable novelties. Joseph Hellmesberger's *Leichtfüssig Polka* is irresistibly vivacious and the orchestra obviously enjoy playing it. Characteristically atmospheric recording and a generous programme make this a very desirable collection indeed, and **Brian Large's** video direction is superb: the cameras find the right angle every time. This is a very repeatable programme to watch and listen to.

'2009 New Year's Concert' (CD Version): Galop:
Zampa; Marches: Einzugs; Märchen aus dem
Orient; Overtures: Ein Nacht in Venedig; Der
Zigeunerbaron; Polkas: Annen; Alexandrinan; Elgen
a Magyär; Freikugein; Schnellpost; So ängstlich sind
wir nicht; Unter Donner und Blitz; Waltzes: An der
blauen Donau; Rosen aus dem Süden; Schatz; (with
JOSEF STRAUSS: *Sphären-Klänge.* HAYDN: *Symphony*
45 (Farewell): Finale. HELLMESSBERGER: *Spanish*
Waltz. JOHANN STRAUSS SR.: *Radezsky Marsch)*

(N) *** Decca 478 1133. VPO, Barenboim

For 2009 **Barenboim** makes a very successful début, including in his programme six New Year premières. His style is often relaxed, as is immediately shown in the *Annen Polka*, but the programme is a stimulating one and has plenty of life. He may be forgiven for indulging himself in the *Blue Danube*, as it is an encore, but for the most part he proves a natural Johann Straussian. Another entertaining concert, superbly played and recorded.

Other Strauss Recordings

Overture: Die Fledermaus; Emperor Waltz; Perpetuum mobile; Tritsch-Tratsch Polka

8— **** BBC (ADD) BBCL 4038. Hallé O, Barbirolli – HAYDN: *Symphony 83 in G min. (La Poule)*; LEHÁR: *Gold and Silver*; RICHARD STRAUSS: *Der Rosenkavalier Suite* ****

Barbirolli's performances exude the full communicative atmosphere of this 1969 Prom, and one can hear Sir John himself vocalizing in the overture. The performance of the *Emperor Waltz* is ravishing, and an outrageous fun performance of *Tritsch-Tratsch* follows, with sudden pauses to bring bursts of laughter from the promenaders.

Polka: Unter Donner und Blitz. Waltzes: An der schönen, blauen Donau; Kaiser; Morgenblätter; Rosen aus dem Süden; Treasure; Wiener blut. JOSEF STRAUSS: Dorfschwalben aus Osterreich

8— (M) *** RCA SACD 82876 671615-2. Chicago SO, Reiner – WEBER: *Invitation to the Dance*; RICHARD STRAUSS: *Der Rosenkavalier: Waltzes*

Reiner's collection was recorded in 1957 and 1960, but the new SACD transfer restores the voluptuousness to the sound. Although the *Thunder and Lightning Polka* has an unforgettable explosive exuberance, these performances are memorable for their Viennese lilt, especially the *Emperor Waltz* and Josef's *Village Swallows*. Reiner is especially persuasive in the introductory interchanges of Weber's *Invitation to the Waltz*, while the *Der Rosenkavalier Waltz* sequence brings a passionate surge of adrenalin.

OPERA AND OPERETTA

Die Fledermaus (complete; DVD version)

**(*) DG DVD 073 007-9. Coburn, Perry, Fassbaender, Waechter, Brendel, Hopferwieser, Bav. State Op. Ch. & O, C. Kleiber (Dir: Otto Schenk.)

Recorded live at the **Bavarian State Opera** in 1987, **Carlos Kleiber's** film version of *Die Fledermaus* is preferable to his audio recording, also for DG (457 765-2), in fair measure because of the superb assumption of the role of Prince Orlofsky by **Brigitte Fassbaender**, a fire-eater who makes the most positive host in the party scene of Act II, singing superbly, where the audio recording has a feeble falsettist. Though **Janet Perry's** soprano is shallow and bright, she has the agility and sparkle for the role of Adèle, with **Patricia Coburn** as a warm, positive Rosalinde, whooping away persuasively in the waltz numbers, and entering into the spirit of the party, despite a violently unconvincing red wig. **Eberhard Waechter** sounds too old and unsteady as Eisenstein, and **Josef Hopferwieser** is also unconvincingly old as the philandering tenor, Alfred, both shown up by the dark, firm **Wolfgang Brendel** as Falke. As on CD, Kleiber directs a taut performance, which yet has plenty of sparkle, helped by full-bodied sound.

Die Fledermaus (complete; CD versions)

8— (B) **** Ph. Duo 464 031-2 (2). Te Kanawa, Gruberová, Leech, W. Brendel, Bär, Fassbaender, Göttling, Krause, Wendler, Schenk, V. State Op. Ch., VPO, Previn

8— (BB) (****) Naxos mono 8.110180/181 (2). Gueden, Lipp, Patzak, Dermota, Poell, Wagner, Preger, Vienna State Op. Ch., VPO, Krauss

(M) (***) EMI mono 5 67074-2 [567153] (2). Schwarzkopf, Streich, Gedda, Krebs, Kunz, Christ, Philh. Ch. & O, Karajan

Die Fledermaus (Gala performance)

(M) **(*) Decca (ADD) 475 8319 (2). Gueden, Koth, Kmentt, Waechter, Berry, Zampieri, Resnik, V. State Op. Ch., VPO, Karajan (with guests: Tebaldi, Corena, Nilsson, Del Monaco, Berganza, Sutherland, Bjoerling, L. Price, Simionato, Bastianini, Welitsch)

Dame Kiri Te Kanawa's portrait of Rosalinde brings not only gloriously firm, golden sound but also vocal acting with star quality. **Brigitte Fassbaender** is the most dominant Prince Orlofsky on disc. Singing with a tangy richness and firmness, she emerges as the genuine focus of the party scene. **Edita Gruberová** is a sparkling, characterful and full-voiced Adèle; **Wolfgang Brendel** as Eisenstein and **Olaf Bär** as Dr Falke both sing very well indeed, though their voices sound too alike. **Richard Leech** as Alfred provides heady tone and a hint of parody. **Tom Krause** makes a splendid Frank, the more characterful for no longer sounding young. **Anton Wendler** as Dr Blind and **Otto Schenk** as Frosch the jailer give vintage Viennese performances, with Frosch's cavortings well tailored and not too extended. Vivaciously directed, this now goes to the top of the list of latterday *Fledermaus* recordings, though with one serious reservation: the Philips production in Act II adds a layer of crowd noise as background throughout the Party scene, even during Orlofsky's solos and in the lovely chorus, *Bruderlein und Schwesterlein*, yearningly done. Otherwise the recorded sound is superb. Like Kleiber on DG, **Previn** opts for the *Thunder and Lightning Polka* instead of the ballet. Its reissue at bargain price is welcome and retains all the qualities of the original (except texts and translations).

Clemens Krauss conducts an irresistibly sparkling account of the score with the starry cast forming a wonderfully coordinated ensemble. **Hilde Gueden** with her golden tones makes a deliciously minxish Rosalinde, with a naughty, provocative smile implied, and **Julius Patzak** as a tenor Eisenstein has never been surpassed, totally idiomatic, well contrasted with the equally fine Alfred of **Anton Dermota**. Add to that **Wilma Lipp's** bright, agile Adèle and the firm, clear if very feminine Orlofsky of **Sieglinde Wagner**. The original snag was the thin violin-timbre which became even more 'whistly' in the old Ace of Clubs reissue. In the latest Naxos transfer the voices are very well caught, set very much in front of the orchestra, and Davis Lennick's remastering tames the sound, even if the violins remain a little fizzy. This is a gramophone classic by any standards.

Karajan's 1960 Decca set was originally issued – very handsomely presented and with much blazing of publicity trumpets as a so-called 'Gala performance' – with various artists from the Decca roster turning up to do their party piece at the 'cabaret' included in the Orlovsky ball sequence. This was a famous tradition of performances of *Die Fledermaus* at the New York Met. in the early years of the last century. The party pieces now have a vintage appeal and even **Tebaldi's** *Viljalied* (rather heavy in style) invokes nostalgia for an earlier era. There is a breathtaking display of coloratura from **Joan Sutherland** in *Il Bacio*, a Basque folksong sung with delicious simplicity by **Teresa Berganza**, and **Leontyne Price** is wonderfully at home in Gershwin's *Summertime*. But the most famous item is **Simionato** and **Bastianini's** *Anything you can do I can do better*, sung with more punch than sophistication, but endearingly memorable, nearly half a century after it was recorded.

The performance of the opera itself has all the sparkle one could ask for, although the solo singing itself is variable. If anything, Karajan is even more brilliant than he was on the old EMI mono issue, and the Decca recording is scintillating in its clarity.

The mono recording of Karajan's 1955 EMI version has great freshness and clarity, along with the polish which for many will make it a first favourite. **Schwarzkopf** makes an enchanting Rosalinde, not just in the imagination and sparkle of her singing but also in the snatches of spoken dialogue (never too long) which leaven the entertainment. As Adèle, **Rita Streich** produces her most dazzling coloratura; **Nicolai Gedda** and **Helmut Krebs** are beautifully contrasted in their tenor tone, and **Erich Kunz** gives a vintage performance as Falke.

Die Fledermaus (complete; in English; DVD version)

☝ *** Arthaus **DVD** 100 134 (2). Gustafson, Howarth, Kowalski, Otey, Michaels-Moore, Bottone, ROHCG Ch. & O, Bonynge (Dir: John Cox)

Lasting well over three and a quarter hours, this version of *Die Fledermaus*, in an English version by John Mortimer, stretches to two DVDs, largely because in this gala performance at Covent Garden on New Year's Eve 1989/90 a half-hour of performances by the 'surprise guests' is included in the party scene: **Luciano Pavarotti**, **Marilyn Horne** and – making her farewell to the opera stage – **Dame Joan Sutherland**. For Sutherland devotees it is an essential item, with the two duets specially cherishable, the *Semiramide* duet with Horne and *Parigi o cara* from *La Traviata* with Pavarotti.

Under **Richard Bonynge's** light, beautifully sprung direction, the gala fizzes splendidly with a first-rate cast, even though at the start of Act II Falke (**Michaels-Moore**) unwittingly loses his monocle. The countertenor, **Jochen Kowalski**, makes a characterful, distinctive Orlofsky with baritone speaking voice contrasted with his singing. **Nancy Gustafson** is a warm Rosalinde and **Judith Howarth** a sweet Adèle, and the others all sing well, despite the pressure of the occasion.

Fürstin Ninetta (complete; CD version)

Ⓝ ⒝⒝ **(*) Naxos mono 8.660227/8 (2). Aberg, Rombo, Gröndahl, Taube, Strid, Eliasson, Jarrick, Ninetta Ch., Stockholm Strauss O, Csányi

It is good that Naxos are exploring the later and less well-known operettas of Johann Strauss. This one offers a zany plot revolving round a young couple staying in a Sorrento hotel whose wedding plans keep getting thwarted by bizarre turns of events. Of course it all ends happily and this excellent recording, recorded live in 2007, makes for thoroughly entertaining listening. The score is full of attractive dance-like music, such as the opening tarantella number, while the superb *Quintet* and a 'Hypnotic Duet' in Act II are highlights. The cast is generally very good – the men especially so – and so are the orchestra and chorus. It is possible to imagine a performance with greater zest from the conductor, but that is a small quibble, especially when the price of this set is so low.

Jabouka (complete)

⒝⒝ *** Naxos 8.660216/7 (2). Tischler, Veith, Schober, Groiss, Gaudeamus Ch., Brno, European Johann Strauss O, Pollack

Jabouka was the fourteenth of the operettas of the young Johann Strauss, written for Vienna's Apple Festival. Its weakness lies in the libretto, but this excellent Naxos recording, made in Brno, brings out its distinctive qualities, which suggest a similarity with the operetta-writing of Lehár, Strauss's successor. So the drinking sextet clearly anticipates the *Merry Widow*, as does the reliance above all on ensembles rather than arias. The chorus work on this set is not just incisive but often very delicate. Recommended.

A Night in Venice (Eine Nacht in Venedig) (complete)

⒝⒝ (***) Naxos mono 8.111254 (from recording, with Schwarzkopf, Gedda, Köth, Philh. Ch. & O, Ackermann)

A Night in Venice, in Erich Korngold's revision, is a superb example of Walter Legge's **Philharmonia** productions, honeyed and atmospheric. As a sampler, try the jaunty little waltz duet in Act I between **Schwarzkopf** as the heroine, Annina, and the baritone **Erich Kunz** as Caramello, normally a tenor role. **Nicolai Gedda** as the Duke then appropriates the most famous waltz song of all, the *Gondola Song*, but, with such a frothy production, purism would be out of place. This Naxos remastering of EMI's Kingsway Hall recording by Mark Obert-Thorn sounds remarkably good. The set comes with a cued synopsis. Recommended.

Wiener Blut (complete)

(M) **(*) EMI (ADD) 5 66176-2 (2). Rothenberger, Gedda, Holm, Hirte, Putz, Cologne Op. Ch., Philh. Hungarica, Boskovsky

The EMI set conducted by **Willi Boskovsky** makes a delightful entertainment, the performance authentic and with a strong singing cast. The recording is atmospherically reverberant, but there is no lack of sparkle. However, for some there will be too much German dialogue, which also involves two CDs.

Der Zigeunerbaron (arr. Harnoncourt; Linke; complete)

*(**) Teldec 4509 94555-2 (2). Coburn, Lippert, Schasching, Hamari, Holzmair, Oelze, von Magnus, Lazar, Arnold Schoenberg Ch., VSO, Harnoncourt

When *Der Zigeunerbaron*, second only to *Der Fledermaus* among Strauss operettas, has been so neglected on disc, this new Teldec set, offering a more expanded text than ever before, fills an important gap. **Harnoncourt**, as a Viennese and with a Viennese orchestra, ensures that the Strauss lilt is winningly and authentically observed from the pot-pourri overture onwards, and Harnoncourt's concern (as a period specialist) for clarity of texture gives the whole performance a sparkling freshness. Sadly, the casting is seriously flawed, when the central character of the gypsy princess, Saffi, is taken by a soprano, **Pamela Coburn**, who, as recorded, sounds strained and unsteady. The others are better, with **Rudolf Schasching** catching the fun behind the comic role of the pig-breeder, Zsupán, authentically but without exaggeration, and the light tenor, **Herbert Lippert**, is charming as the hero, Barinkay. Among the rest, the mezzo, **Elisabeth von Magnus**, sings in cabaret style in the supporting role of Mirabella, given a major point-number here, often omitted. **Christiane Oelze** as Arsena, the girl who does not get the hero, sings far more sweetly than Coburn, and **Julia Hamari** as Saffi's foster-mother, Czipra, sounds younger than her daughter. The recording is full and vivid, but many will feel that there is too much German dialogue – largely accounting for the extended length of two and a half hours.

Der Zigeunerbaron (original version; complete)

(N) (BB) (***) Naxos mono 8.11329/30. Schwarzkopf, Gedda, Kunz, Koth, Prey, Philh. Ch. & O, Ackermann (with excerpts from earlier recordings of *Der Zigeunerbaron* by Elisabeth Rethberg (1930); Lotte Lehman, Richard Tauber (1928); *Schatz Walz*: Berlin State Op. Ch. & O, Leo Blech (1929))

This superb **Philharmonia** version of *The Gypsy Baron* from the mid-1950s, now reappearing on Naxos, has never been matched in its rich stylishness and polish. **Schwarzkopf**, as the gipsy princess, sings radiantly, not least in the heavenly *Bullfinch Duet* (to the melody made famous by MGM as 'One day when we were young'). **Gedda**, still youthful, produces heady tone and **Erich Kunz** as the rough pig-breeder gives a vintage *echt*-Viennese performance of the irresistible *Ja das schhreiben und das lessen*. Mark Obert-Thorn's transfer is immaculate, and the bonus extra items are a pleasure in themselves.

Josef Strauss: The Complete Edition

As with Marco's Johann Strauss Edition, our coverage of the Josef Strauss Edition must be omitted for shortage of space. However, we must draw readers' attention to Volumes 9 (8.223569), 10 (8.223570), 12 (8.223572), 17 (8.223619), 18 (8.223619), 20 (8.223622) – a delightful collection, 22 (8.223624) (with four unknown waltzes), 24 (8.223626), 25 (8.223664) and 26 (8.223679) – all worthy of any collector's attention. A full review will be found in earlier editions of our Guide.

STRAUSS, Franz (1822–1905)

Horn Concerto in C min., Op. 8

(B) **(*) Double Decca (ADD) 460 296 (2). Tuckwell, LSO, Kertész – RICHARD STRAUSS: *Concertos* **(*)

Tuckwell's performance is responsive and secure, but fails to convince the listener that the work should not be put back in the attic where it rightly belongs.

STRAUSS, Richard (1864–1949)

Symphonic poems: An Alpine Symphony, Op. 64; Death and Transfiguration, Op. 24; Don Juan, Op. 20; Ein Heldenleben, Op. 40

(M) *** Chan. 7009/10. RSNO, Järvi

Symphonic poems: Also sprach Zarathustra, Op. 30; (i) Don Quixote, Op. 35; Macbeth, Op. 23; Symphonia domestica, Op. 53; Till Eulenspiegel, Op. 38

(M) *** Chan. 7011/12. RSNO, Järvi; (i) with Wallfisch

Järvi's generally distinguished survey of the Strauss symphonic poems was recorded in the sumptuous acoustics of the Caird Hall, Dundee, between 1986 and 1989. If occasionally the resonance prevents the sharpest internal clarity, the skilled Chandos engineering ensures that the orchestral layout is very believable, heard within a natural perspective. The account of *An Alpine Symphony* is ripely enjoyable, with the reverberant acoustic here very helpful. *Death and Transfiguration* shows the orchestra at its finest and here detail is revealed well, within a reading which has impressive control. *Don Juan* is portrayed as a bluff philanderer and the reading seeks sentience and amplitude rather than searing brilliance. *Ein Heldenleben* is strongly characterized and warmly sympathetic from first to last, marked by powerful, thrustful playing, lacking only the last degree of refinement in ensemble.

Järvi's *Symphonia domestica* is particularly successful, as indeed is his joyful portrait of *Till*. *Macbeth*, less than a masterpiece, is also presented very persuasively; few if any recorded performances make a better case for it. *Don Quixote* then takes a rather leisurely journey, although an amiable one. **Raphael Wallfisch**, the solo cellist, plays splendidly but, like the excellent violist, **John Harrington**, is very forwardly balanced, while inner orchestral detail is less than ideally clear. *Also sprach Zarathustra*, which closes the programme, is the least successful of the series.

An Alpine Symphony, Op. 64 (DVD versions with documentaries)

*** EuroArts DVD 2056 138. Dresden State O, Sinopoli (performance directed by Elisabeth Birke-Malzer; Documentary by Angelika Stiehler; DVD Producer: Tobias Möller)

**(*) Arthaus DVD 101437. Deutsche SO, Berlin, Nagano (performance directed by Ellen Fallman; Documentary by Oliver Becker; DVD Producer: Bernhard Fleischer)

It would have been tempting in making a DVD of *An Alpine Symphony* to follow the progress of the climber visually in the mountains, but neither of these recorded performances makes this mistake. Each includes a documentary analysing the music and its visual impressions; of the two, the EuroArts is by far the more perceptive, beginning with pictures of Strauss himself walking in the mountains, then providing the biographical background, and finally analysing the music, section by section, with illustrations. Of the two separate performances **Sinopoli's** stands out for the truly magnificent playing of the **Dresden Staatskapelle** and a recording which is rich and full-bodied, but remarkably clear, in a perfect acoustic. The camerawork follows the orchestral playing on the whole satisfactorily. On the Arthaus DVD the opening and closing photography is made misty, intending to create an evocative effect which many will find irritating, and later the camera movement is fairly continuous. The performance is also a fine one, and it scores with a positively apocalyptic account of the *Storm* sequence which many will enjoy for its spectacle. But overall Sinopoli's reading is more balanced and very involving indeed.

An Alpine Symphony, Op. 64

🎵 **(BB)** **** Naxos 8.557811. Weimar Staatskapelle, Wit

🎵 **** DG 439 017-2. BPO, Karajan

Wit's highly imaginative performance, with the remarkably fine **Weimar Orchestra**, is in the class of Kempe, having something in common with the analogue performances of Strauss by the Dresden Staatskapelle, both in the radiance of the orchestral sounds and the warm acoustic of the Weimarhalle (not unlike the Dresden Lukaskirche). Wit's tempi, too, are often unhurried; his overall performance takes 54 minutes against Welser-Möst's 45, but it gives the Weimar experience an extra spaciousness, and the panoramic sweep of the strings is rapturously beautiful in the opening *Night* and *Sunrise* sequences, and, most of all, the thrilling radiance *On the summit*. The storm on the way down is thunderingly real, and in the moments before it breaks Wit creates a subtle feeling of apprehension; then, as the descent nears safety, the orchestra mirrors a glorious sunset and evokes a sense of thankfulness for past excitement, and an elegiac contemplation of the natural wonders experienced. In that '*Ausklang*' the organ steals in gently and magically, and night falls in peace and tranquillity. Throughout, the Naxos recording is wonderfully vivid and spectacular, and the disc is a well-documented one, too.

This DG reissue in the **Karajan** Gold series is one of the most remarkable in its improvement of the sound over the original CD issue. Undoubtedly this performance is very distinguished, wonderfully spacious and beautifully shaped – the closing *Night* sequence is very touching – and played with the utmost virtuosity.

(i) An Alpine Symphony; (ii) Also sprach Zarathustra; Don Juan; (iii) Ein Heldenleben; (ii) Till Eulenspiegel

🎵 **(B)** *** Double Decca (ADD) 440 618-2 (2). (i) Bav. RSO; (ii) Chicago SO; (iii) VPO; Solti

The **Bavarian Radio Orchestra** recorded in the Herculessaal in Munich could hardly sound more opulent in the *Alpine Symphony* and the superb quality of the 1979 analogue recording tends to counterbalance **Solti's** generally fast tempi. The performances of *Also sprach Zarathustra*, *Don Juan* and *Till Eulenspiegel* come from analogue originals, made in Chicago a few years earlier. Solti is ripely expansive in *Zarathustra*, and throughout all three symphonic poems there is the most glorious playing from the **Chicago Orchestra** in peak form. For *Ein Heldenleben* Solti went (in 1977–8) to Vienna, and this is another fast-moving performance, tense to the point of fierceness in the opening tutti and elsewhere. It underlines the urgency rather than the opulence of the writing but Solti is at his finest in the final coda after the fulfilment theme, where in touching simplicity he finds complete relaxation at last, helped by the exquisite playing of the **Vienna Philharmonic** concertmaster, **Rainer Küchl**. The Decca recording is formidably wide-ranging to match this high-powered performance and, as with the rest of the programme, the transfers to CD are full-bodied and vividly detailed.

An Alpine Symphony; Don Juan

(N) (M) *** RCO Live RCO 8006. Concg. O, Jansons

Jansons directs a truly outstanding account of the *Alpine Symphony* with the **Concertgebouw Orchestra** providing extraordinarily vivid detail at every point of a journey, full of evocation; and after the spectacle of the storm and summit sequences, the closing section, with rich sonority from the deep brass as night falls, is most telling. *Don Juan* has splendid impetus and passion too, but he is portrayed as a romantic seducer rather than one carried away by physical passion. The eloquent strings are equally memorable, although the microphones are a shade close. Nevertheless a most impressive coupling.

An Alpine Symphony; Don Juan; Suite for 13 Wind Instruments, Op. 4; Symphonia domestica; Till Eulenspiegel

(BB) **(*) Virgin 2×1 5 61460-2 (2). Minnesota O, de Waart

An excellent and inexpensive anthology, very well played and recorded, over which there are only minor reservations.

An Alpine Symphony; Festival Prelude (Festliches Praeludium)

(BB) *** Arte Nova 74321 92779-2. Zürich Tonhalle O, Zinman

More than usual, **David Zinman** finds clarity and refinement in the *Alpine Symphony*. It has space as well as real poetic feeling and imagination. The effect may be less opulent than some versions, vividly recorded as it is, but there is no lack of passion or emotional thrust in presenting a score which is not just a musical picture postcard of a mountain-ascent, but a tautly conceived structure in which the spectacular orchestral effects are controlled with masterly finesse. The rarely heard *Festival Prelude*, written for Vienna in 1913, uses even bigger forces, an occasional piece which in this ripe performance makes a sumptuous fill-up.

(i) An Alpine Symphony; (ii) Macbeth; (iii) Parergon zur Symphonie Domestica for Piano (left hand); (i) Symphonia Domestica

(N) **(*) Australian Decca Eloquence (ADD) 480 0408 (2). (i) LAPO, Mehta; (ii) Detroit SO, Dorati; (iii) Graffman, VPO, Previn

Mehta's virtuoso account of the *Alpine Symphony* (1975) was among the best Strauss he gave us, and he is supported by recording quality that is wide in range and rich in detail. His account of the *Symphonia Domestica* is not quite so successful – it gives the impression that he has relocated Strauss's domestic household to a well-lit penthouse in downtown Manhattan. There is no doubting the quality of the orchestral playing, nor of the (1969) recording, both of which remain impressive. **Previn's** account of the rare *Parergon*, based on themes from the symphony, which was written for Paul Wittgenstein in 1924, is a complete success. Previn gives the **VPO** its head in repertoire that they know inside out, and **Gary Graffman** proves an eloquent soloist. The DG sound is first class. **Dorati's** digital *Macbeth* is very well played and brilliantly recorded, though other versions have offered sharper characterization.

Also sprach Zarathustra, Op. 30 (DVD version)

(⊖) *** Sony DVD SVD 46388. BPO, Karajan – MOZART: *Divertimento 17* **(*)

By the time **Karajan** conducted the concert celebrating the 750th anniversary of the founding of Berlin, he was already ailing, as one registers from his painful progress to the podium each time; once there, however, the electric intensity of his conducting never falters in passionate commitment to this great Strauss work, always a favourite of his. Though the hushed close makes this a subdued sort of celebration, Karajan's control is emphasized in the total silence at the end, until his subtle signal of release for the applause

to begin, at which the audience responds with fervour. It is a help that the DVD offers ample index points separating the sections. This DVD is short measure but is still indispensable.

Also sprach Zarathustra; Death and Transfiguration

(⊖) *** Telarc CD 80167. VPO, Previn (without *Don Juan*)

Previn draws magnificent playing from the **Vienna Philharmonic** in powerful, red-blooded readings of the symphonic poems, and the recording is among Telarc's finest. Strongly recommended for anyone wanting this particular coupling, and enjoying spectacularly voluptuous sound-quality.

Also sprach Zarathustra; Death and Transfiguration; Don Quixote; Ein Alpensinfonie; Ein Heldenleben, Op. 40; Metamorphosen; Sinfonia domestica

(N) *** Sony DVD 886971954469. BPO, Karajan

Karajan had a special way with this composer, as we are reminded in these DVD performances, sensitively handled by the video director and of course stunningly played. The *Metamorphosen* is moving, even if Karajan's pioneering set with the Vienna Philharmonic had even greater immediacy of feeling. *Death and Transfiguration* is also marvellously played and has genuine grandeur and nobility. These performances belong in any good collection. Unaccountably (and unforgivably) the two soloists in *Don Quixote* are not credited either in the skimpy booklet, on the sleeve, or on the screen.

Also sprach Zarathustra, Op. 30; Ein Heldenleben, Op. 40

(⊖) ✿ (M) **** RCA SACD (ADD) 82876 61389-2. Chicago SO, Reiner

(***) Testament mono SBT 1183. VPO, Krauss

These were the first stereo sessions the RCA engineers arranged with **Fritz Reiner**, after the company had taken over the **Chicago Orchestra's** recording contract from Mercury, and the series of records they made with Reiner and his players in Orchestra Hall remain a technical peak in the history of stereo recording and the impressive feeling of space it conveyed. Later reissues have improved on its definition but none has done so with the stunning success of the present transfer. *Ein Heldenleben* shows Reiner in equally splendid form. There have been more incisive, more spectacular and more romantic performances, but Reiner achieves an admirable balance and whatever he does is convincing. If anything, the recording sounds even better than *Also sprach* and the warm acoustics of Orchestra Hall help convey Reiner's humanity in the closing pages of the work.

Clemens Krauss brings the heroic sweep, the contrasts and delicacy of texture and the breadth of *Ein Heldenleben* before one's eyes. There is a nobility here (and, for that matter, in *Zarathustra* too) that not every Strauss conductor conveys.

Aus Italien, Op. 16; Don Juan, Op. 20

(N) (M) *** Oehms OC 631. V. RSO, De Billy

The **Vienna Radio Symphony Orchestra** (founded in 1969) is a first-class ensemble, with a rich, yet brilliant, string patina, and excellent wind soloists, and **Bertrand De Billy's** account of *Aus Italien* is full of warmth and colour, while the musical characterization is excellent. It is coupled with a splendidly vibrant performance of *Don Juan*, exhilarating in its vigour and compelling flow of adrenalin. The horns are passionately thrusting in the big climax, matched by the thrilling ardour of the strings. The recording is very good; but it is superior when played as a SACD, with the back speakers adding extra ambient lustre to the sound picture.

Aus Italien; Die Liebe der Danae (symphonic fragment); Der Rosenkavalier: Waltz sequence 2

(BB) *** Naxos 8.550342. Slovak PO, Košler

On Naxos, a very well-recorded and vividly detailed account of *Aus Italien* with an excellent sense of presence. The orchestra plays very well for **Zdenék Košler** both here and in the ten-minute symphonic fragment Clemens Krauss made from *Die Liebe der Danae* and in the *Rosenkavalier* waltz sequence. The **Slovak Philharmonic** is a highly responsive body, with cultured strings and wind departments and, given the quality of the recorded sound, this represents a real bargain.

Aus Italien, Op.16; Metamorphosen for 23 Solo Strings

☞ (M) **** Chan. 10218X. RSNO, Järvi

Aus Italien is early and does not do the composer the fullest justice. The orchestra seems at home in the score, giving the finale a certain Celtic lilt. *Metamorphosen* finds Järvi's account deeply felt and ardent, and the **Scottish** strings convey the underlying angst of the music with moving passion: they also play very well indeed. The recording is rich, expansive and natural. All in all, a great success and attractively priced.

Le Bourgeois Gentilhomme (Suite, Op. 60); Dance Suite (after Couperin)

☞ (BB) *** ASV COE CD COE 809. COE, Leinsdorf

Erich Leinsdorf is an unexpected conductor in this repertoire; although he has not quite the light touch of a Beecham, he enjoys the advantage of the superb wind soloists and ensemble of the **Chamber Orchestra of Europe**, whom he directs with genuine style and affection. The coupling is ideal, for Strauss's *Dance Suite*, arranged from keyboard pieces of Couperin, has much anachronistic charm. The suite from *Le Bourgeois Gentilhomme* has two numbers not included by Beecham, the *Courante* and the exquisitely played *Entry of Cleonte*. Altogether a most successful coupling, very well recorded.

(i) Le Bourgeois Gentilhomme (Suite, Op. 60); (i; ii) Don Quixote, Op. 35; (i) Ein Heldenleben; (iii) Metamorphosen

☞ (BB) (**(*)) EMI mono/stereo Gemini 3 71502-2 (2). (i) RPO, Beecham; (ii) with Paul Tortelier; (iii) New Philh. O, Barbirolli

Strauss's incidental music for *Le Bourgeois Gentilhomme*, with its pastiche poise and elegance, was surely custom-made for **Beecham**, whose performance is full of delightful touches, yet with plenty of energy when called for, as in the portrayal of *The Fencing Master*. The 1947/8 Abbey Road recording is clear and faithful, but rather dry, and the lack of stereo warmth and amplitude is even more noticeable in the climaxes of *Don Quixote* in the later part of the work. But this is again an inimitably detailed Beecham reading, made special by the tenderly refined contribution of **Paul Tortelier**. Beecham's 1961 *Ein Heldenleben* is in stereo, of course, and the performance is immensely vigorous yet tender and sensuous when the music calls for it. **Barbirolli's** *Metamorphosen*, too, is a fine one. The playing of the **New Philharmonia** strings is most eloquent, with a warm glow and an intense valedictory feeling. In both these works the advantages of stereo are obvious.

Le Bourgeois Gentilhomme (incidental music); (i) Ein Heldenleben

☞ **** EMI 3 39339-2. BPO, Rattle; (i) with Braunstein

It says much for **Sir Simon Rattle's** achievement in Berlin that the result in this live recording offers the keenest rivalry for the recordings of his great predecessor, Herbert von Karajan, for whom *Ein Heldenleben* was a favourite work. The heroic opening section already establishes the extra warmth and expressive flexibility of Rattle's approach. What remains a constant is the opulence of the **Berlin Philharmonic** sound, bringing out the subtlety of Rattle's control and the refinement of the orchestra's playing. *Le Bourgeois Gentilhomme* is a generous coupling, bringing the overall timing of the disc to an exceptional 82 minutes. The engineers, though working in the Philharmonie as in *Heldenleben*, have rightly balanced the microphones to give a much more intimate result with this chamber ensemble in a performance that delightfully captures the light-heartedness of this music.

Le Bourgeois Gentilhomme: Suite, Op. 60; Symphonia domestica, Op. 53

☞ (***) Testament mono SBT 1184. VPO, Krauss

Remarkably few allowances need be made for the 1951 recording of the *Symphonia domestica*. **Krauss** had given it its Viennese première in 1922, and this was its first (and for many years only) LP recording. This has a special authenticity of feeling and richness of response that disarm criticism. Krauss conducted many early performances of the suite from *Le Bourgeois Gentilhomme* and this unforgettable (1952) account has wonderful lightness of touch and delicacy of feeling. Its charm is quite irresistible.

Burleske for piano and orchestra

(M) *** Warner Elatus 0927 46768-2. Grimaud, Berlin State O, Kurt Sanderling – BRAHMS: *Piano Concerto 1 in D min.* ***

Hélène Grimaud is not only an impressive Brahms interpreter but a virtuoso of no mean order. She dispatches the Richard Strauss *Burleske* with great aplomb and, with the help of **Sanderling**, finds much character in the music. Good recording too.

(i) Capriccio: Sextet (arr. for strings); (ii) Don Quixote, Op. 35; (iii) Feuersnot: Love Scene. Die Frau ohne Schatten: Symphonic fantasy. Metamorphosen; (iv) Der Rosenkavalier: First & Second Suite of Waltzes; (iii) Salome: Dance of the Seven Veils; (iv) Till Eulenspiegel

(N) *** Australian DG Eloquence (ADD/DDD) 480 0478 (2).
  (i) Stuttgart CO, Münchinger; (ii) Machula, Concg. O, Haitink; (iii) Dresden State O, Sinopoli; (iv) Concg. O, Jochum

Sinopoli is an excellent Straussian and, in the mid-1990s, he achieved very impressive results with the **Dresden Orchestra** with very sensuous playing, not least in *Salome's Dance*, where ravishing string-tone is perfectly married to his moulded and flexible style. The *Love Scene* from Strauss's very first opera, *Feuersnot*, is drawn from the closing pages of the opera, a delectable passage that ought to be better known. The *Symphonic Fantasy* from *Die Frau ohne Schatten* was put together in 1946 at a time when complete performances of this favourite among his operas looked unlikely. Again Sinopoli's concentration and the fine playing of the orchestra, sumptuously recorded, give cohesion to an obviously sectional piece. The strings of the **Staatskapelle Dresden** also produce a magnificent sonority in *Metamorphosen*, and the DG engineers do them proud. There are some splendid things in **Haitink's** performance of *Don Quixote*. Although it does not match the heady, intoxicating flamboyance of either of the Karajan versions, the orchestral playing is still superb. **Machula** does not quite touch the depths of Fournier in the Don's dying peroration, but he has great dignity and beauty of tone. The 1974 recording remains impressive. **Jochum's** early (1960s) account of *Till Eulenspiegel* is excellently characterized, and the *Waltz* sequences from *Der Rosenkavalier* are stylishly enjoyable. **Münchinger's** richly recorded *Sextet* from *Capriccio* is very enjoyable too.

Horn Concertos 1 in E flat, Op. 11; 2 in E flat

⊕— 🌑 (M)(***) EMI mono 5 67782-2 [Angel 5 67783-2]. Brain, Philh. O, Sawallisch – HINDEMITH: *Horn Concerto; Concert Music* ***

(i) Horn Concertos 1; (ii) 2; (iii) Oboe Concerto; (iv) Duet Concertino for Clarinet & Bassoon

*** DG 453 483-2. (i) Janezic; (ii) Stransky; (iii) Gabriel; (iv) Schmidl, Werba; VPO, Previn

(i) Horn Concertos 1-2; (ii) Duet Concertino for Clarinet & Bassoon; Wind Serenade in E flat, Op. 11

⊕— (B) *** CfP 573 5132. (i) Pyatt; (ii) Farrall, Andrews; Britten Sinfonia, Cleobury

Dennis Brain's performances are incomparable. **Sawallisch** gives him admirable support, and fortunately the latest EMI CD transfer captures the full quality of the 1956 mono recording.

David Pyatt gives a ripely exuberant performance of the first of Strauss's two *Horn Concertos*. The more elusive first movement of the *Second Concerto* is shaped – often quite subtly – in an attractively rhapsodical style, while the finale brings heady, lightly tongued bravura. The outer movements of the gently rapturous *Duet Concertino* are presented with enticing delicacy of texture, and the slow movement again brings a most touchingly doleful opening solo, this time from the bassoonist, **Julie Andrews**. **Cleobury** and the **Britten Sinfonia** give sensitive support throughout, and the early *Serenade* is always fresh, never congealing, helped by the naturally balanced recording, made in the Henry Wood Hall, Southwark.

On DG some glorious music-making, relaxed, unforced and full of expressive delights. The virtuosity is at no time self-regarding and everybody appears to be enjoying themselves. The sound, too, is as natural as the music-making. A most welcome addition to the catalogue.

Oboe Concerto in D

⊕— (BB) *** ASV CD COE 808. Boyd, COE, Berglund – MOZART: *Oboe Concerto* ***

(N) (M)** Sup. SU 3955-2. Hanták, Brno PO, Vogel (with MOZART: *Oboe Concerto*) – MARTINŮ: *Oboe Concerto* **

Douglas Boyd winningly brings out the happy glow of Strauss's inspiration of old age, and the ebb-and-flow of his expression with its delicate touching in of the characteristic flourishes in the solo line sounds totally spontaneous. His warm oboe tone, less reedy than some, equally brings out the *Rosenkavalier* element in this lovely concerto. The coupling with Mozart is uniquely apt and, with warm, well-balanced recording, the gentle contrast of romantic and classical in this work is delectably conveyed.

In the Supraphon recording, **Hanták** is placed right on top of the microphone (as he is in the Mozart), which gives a certain 'squawkiness' to his tone. The orchestra too is on the fierce side, although these defects of balance are reasonably tameable on a flexible reproducer. The performance is vivid and forthright, not quite relaxed enough, but by no means insensitive.

Violin Concerto in D min., Op. 8

⊕— *** ASV CDDCA 780. Xue Wei, LPO, Glover – HEADINGTON: *Violin concerto* *** 🌑

With **Jane Glover** and the **LPO** warmly sympathetic accompanists, **Xue Wei** makes a very persuasive case for this very early work of Strauss, with its echoes of Mendelssohn and Bruch.

Death and Transfiguration; Don Juan; Till Eulenspiegel

(M)(***) EMI mono 5 62790-2. VPO, Furtwängler – SMETANA: *Vltava* ***

⊕— (***) Testament mono SBT 1383. Philh. O, Karajan – WAGNER: *Tannhäuser: Venusberg music* (***)

Don Juan and *Till Eulenspiegel* come from 1954, some months before the onset of deafness brought Furtwängler's career to an end, while *Death and Transfiguration* was recorded in Vienna in 1950. They are performances of commanding stature and have the glowing sonorities, naturalness of utterance and mastery of pace that characterized Furtwängler at his best. The EMI recordings still sound glorious despite their age, though climaxes in *Death and Transfiguration* are distinctly opaque.

Karajan's *Till* and the *Don* were recorded in the Kingsway Hall in 1951 with Walter Legge producing, and *Death and Transfiguration* followed 18 months later. Sound that is over half a century old can still convey a sense of freshness and sparkle. The Wagner makeweight (with the same venue and recording team) comes from 1954 and is of the same order of inspiration.

Death and Transfiguration; Metamorphosen for 23 Solo Strings

🅱—⚙ Ⓜ ******** DG 410 892-2. BPO, Karajan

Ⓜ ******* EMI (ADD) 3 80008-2. Philh. O, Klemperer – MAHLER: *Symphony 9* *******

Karajan's digital coupling of *Death and Transfiguration* and the *Metamorphosen* is one of his very finest records. This famous CD is now available at mid-price.

Both performances excite the greatest admiration. With Klemperer the work for strings has a ripeness that exactly fits Strauss's last essay for orchestra, while *Death and Transfiguration* is invested with a nobility too rarely heard in this work.

Death and Transfiguration; Ein Heldenleben; Salome: Dance of the 7 Veils

🅱—Ⓜ ******* EMI 5 67891-2. Dresden State O, Kempe

Kempe and the great **Dresden Orchestra** at their finest. *Death and Transfiguration* is marvellously characterized. Similarly *Salome's Dance* is sinuously compelling but less voluptuous than with some versions, while *Ein Heldenleben* glows with life, and the closing pages have a special kind of rapt intensity. The excellent recordings from the early 1970s, made in the Dresden Lukaskirche, have been splendidly remastered by Andrew Walter.

(i) Death and Transfiguration; Symphonia domestica; (ii) Salome's Dance of the Seven Veils

🅑 ******* Sony (ADD) SBK 53511. (i) Cleveland O, Szell; (ii) Phd. O, Ormandy

Szell's *Death and Transfiguration* has the most compelling atmosphere and the triumphant closing pages are the more effective for Szell's complete lack of indulgence. The recording has been vastly improved in the present transfer, with Cleveland's Masonic Temple providing a richly expansive ambience. The *Symphonia domestica*, recorded in 1964, is less naturally balanced but the performance brings such powerful orchestral playing, with glorious strings especially in the passionate *Adagio*, that criticism is disarmed: there is certainly no lack of body here. The programme ends with an extraordinarily voluptuous **Philadelphia** performance of *Salome's Dance*. **Ormandy** directs with licentious abandon, and the orchestra responds with tremendous virtuosity and ardour, unashamedly going over the top at the climax.

Divertimento (after Couperin) for Small Orchestra, Op. 86

🅑🅑 ******* Warner Apex 7559 79675-2. NYCO, Schwarz – SCHOENBERG: *Concerto for String Quartet & Orchestra after Handel* *******

Strauss's *Divertimento* draws on sixteen of the keyboard pieces of François Couperin and scores them for small orchestra. The result is expressive, witty and tangy by turns in this very spirited account by the **New York Chamber Orchestra** under **Gerard Schwarz**. With vivid recordings and an unexpectedly entertaining Schoenberg/Handel coupling, this is well worth exploring.

Don Juan (Rehearsal and Performance; DVD version)

Ⓝ ****(*)** EuroArts **DVD** 20172188. VPO, Boehm

It is good to see **Karl Boehm** on video. His rehearsal, however, is relatively without incident, mainly a painstaking concentration on detail. However, the performance, when it finally comes, is very impressive, not over the top, but full of vitality, missing nothing in the score and carrying complete spontaneity.

Don Juan, Op. 20

Ⓝ ******* Testament (ADD) SBT 1378. BPO, Szell – SCHUMANN: *Symphony 2* *******

Ⓜ ******* Decca 475 8225. V. State Op. Ch., VPO, Karajan – HOLST: *The Planets* *******

It is fascinating to hear **Szell's** live account of *Don Juan*, much warmer and less tightly controlled than his studio recordings, but with the same electricity and concern for clarity of texture. Recorded in the Phiharmonie in Berlin, the sound of the strings in the great love theme is ravishing, and so is the great horn climax in the middle of the piece, ripe beyond any rival. Excellent stereo radio sound.

Karajan's Decca recording of *Don Juan*, recorded in the Sofiensaal in 1960, is still among the finest versions. The sound of the **Vienna Philharmonic** is more leonine than that of the Berlin Philharmonic but does not lack either body or attack, and this *Don* has great zest and passion.

Don Juan, Op. 20; (i) Don Quixote, Op. 35

🅱—⚙ ******** RCA **SACD** (ADD) 88697 046042. Chicago SO, Reiner; (i) with Janigro

Reiner was a masterly Straussian, and *Don Juan* dates from the earliest days of stereo (1954); it is most famous for the sensuously erotic central section with its *coitus triste*, and for its superbly thrilling climax in which the great horn then leaps out unforgettably, thrustfully and opulently echoed by the strings. *Don Quixote* too is a top recommendation, and this 1959 version was one of the very finest of RCA's Chicago Symphony Hall recordings. **Antonio Janigro** plays stylishly and with assurance, and his touching contribution to the close of the work is distinguished. The new SACD transfer brings out the most refined detail; indeed, the inner clarity is astonishing, with the cello ideally balanced, though there is no loss of amplitude at climaxes.

Don Juan; Ein Heldenleben

(BB) (***) Dutton Lab. mono CDEA 5025. Concg. O, Mengelberg

(i) Don Juan; (ii) Ein Heldenleben; (iii) Till Eulenspiegel

⊕– (B) *** Sony (ADD) SBK 48272. (iii) Cleveland O, Szell; (ii) Phd. O, Ormandy

Don Juan, Op. 20; Feuersnot: Love Scene

(**(*)) Testament mono SBT 1255. VPO, Cluytens – WAGNER: Siegfried idyll, etc. (**(*))

Don Juan; Metamorphosen; Der Rosenkavalier: Waltzes; Till Eulenspiegel

⊕– (M) **** EMI 3 45826-2. Dresden State O, Kempe

Szell's Don Juan delights ear and senses by its forward surge of passionate lyricism, the whole interpretation founded on a bedrock of virtuosity from the remarkable Cleveland players. Till is irrepressibly cheeky and here the recording acoustic is almost perfect, with a warm glow on the tone of the players and every detail – and Szell makes sure one can hear every detail – crystal clear, without any loss of momentum or drama.

Ormandy's Ein Heldenleben is an engulfing performance, and the composite richness of tone and the fervour of the playing, from the Battle section onwards, bring the highest possible level of orchestral tension, finally relaxing most touchingly for the fulfilment sequence. The 1960 recording is more two-dimensional, less full, than the Cleveland recordings (which, surprisingly, were made as early as 1957) but is still appropriately spacious.

André Cluytens was rather taken for granted (at least on this side of La Manche) during the 1950s when these recordings were made. He took the Vienna Philharmonic on tour to the United States, making this inspiriting account of Don Juan with them in 1958. It was not released in Britain at that time (no doubt the catalogues were awash with alternatives), but it is well worth while catching up with it now, particularly in this splendid new transfer.

Willem Mengelberg and the Concertgebouw Orchestra were jointly the dedicatees of Richard Strauss's most ambitious orchestral work, Ein Heldenleben. They give a heartfelt performance, freely spontaneous and expansive, with old-fashioned string portamento intensifying the warmth. The splendid Dutton transfer is clear on detail with plenty of body and fair bloom on top. The Don Juan recording of 1938 is even more cleanly focused.

Don Quixote, Op. 35

⊕– (M) *** EMI (ADD) 5 66913-2. Rostropovich, BPO, Karajan (SCHUMANN: Cello Concerto)

*** EMI (ADD) 5 55528-2. du Pré, New Philh. O, Boult – LALO: Cello Concerto in D min ***

(i) Don Quixote; (ii) Horn Concerto 2

(M) *** DG (ADD) 457 725-2. (i) Fournier; (ii) Hauptmann; BPO, Karajan

(i) Don Quixote; Don Juan, Op. 20; Till Eulenspiegel, Op. 28

(***) Testament mono SBT 1185. (i) Fournier, Moraweg; VPO, Krauss

The Karajan/Rostropovich account of Don Quixote is predictably fine. This now comes recoupled with Schumann's Cello Concerto as one of EMI's 'Great Recordings of the Century' series, which the latter performance (with Bernstein) certainly is not. A sad mismatching! But the performance is also available below on a recommendable Double differently coupled.

Fournier's partnership with Karajan is also outstanding and so is the 1966 recording. It is of DG's very finest quality, with remarkable transparency, yet plenty of warmth and a believable perspective. The great cellist brings infinite subtlety and (when required) repose to his part, and Karajan's handling of the orchestral detail is quite splendid. The finale and Don Quixote's death are very moving. Norbert Hauptmann's account of the more florid of Strauss's two Horn Concertos is ripely assured with a most eloquent and touching Andante.

A magnificent Don Quixote from Clemens Krauss and his eminent soloist which encapsulates the essence of Strauss's score, and this performance with that aristocrat of cellists, Pierre Fournier, has a special nobility and authority. Both Don Juan and Till Eulenspiegel were recorded in 1950 (the Don Quixote in 1953) and are superbly characterized. In the latter, Krauss clearly does not regard this as just a conductor's showpiece but puts characterization before orchestral display.

Jacqueline du Pré's Don Quixote comes in a studio recording, dating from 1968, which has been lovingly pieced together from long-buried tapes. No doubt du Pré with more time would have sharpened up some of the bravura passages, but in its tenderness and poignancy this reading is unsurpassed. The lyrical dialogue between Sancho Panza and Quixote in the third variation has a heartfelt warmth, with Herbert Downes a fine partner on the viola. Above all, the final death scene is more yearningly tender than on any rival recording, a magical example of her art.

(i) Don Quixote; Ein Heldenleben; Symphonia domestica

⊕– (M) **** EMI (ADD) 4 76903-2 (2). BPO, Karajan; (i) with Rostropovich

Rostropovich dominates artistically. His Don is superbly characterized, and the expressiveness and richnss of tone he commands are a joy in themselves. Ein Heldenleben, superbly recorded a year earlier, again offers a performance which shows a remarkable consistency of approach on Karajan's part and an equal virtuosity of technique, and even greater sumptuousness of tone on the part of the Berlin Philharmonic compared with the earlier DG performances, while the playing is gloriously ardent. The Symphonia domestica is equally admirably served by a recording from one more year earlier. The playing is stunningly good and the sumptuous Berlin strings produce tone of great magnificence. Altogether a superb triptych for reissue in EMI's Karajan Collection, the only snag being that the *Symphonia domestica* involves a side-break immediately before the finale.

(i) *Don Quixote, Op. 35; Romance in F; (i) Cello Sonata in F, Op. 6*

*** RCA 74321 75398-2. (i) Isserlis, Bavarian Radio SO, Maazel; (ii) Hough, Maazel (piano)

Steven Isserlis on RCA is an ardent soloist and is even more impressive than he was in his earlier recording with Edo de Waart (Virgin). He makes a glorious sound and characterizes each variation with flair and is well partnered by an anonymous Sancho Panza, presumably the first violist of the **Bavarian Orchestra**. It is among the best of the recent *Dons* though it does not displace the likes of Rostropovich or Fournier (both with Karajan). One of the other attractions of the disc is a vibrant account of the early *Cello Sonata* with **Stephen Hough** as a splendid partner. Very good sound.

Duet Concertino (for clarinet & bassoon)

ⓑⓑ *** ASV COE CD COE 811. Hosford, Wilkie, COE, T. Fischer – COPLAND; MOZART: *Clarinet Concertos* ***

As with the Copland coupling, **Richard Hosford** and the strings of the **COE** open the *Duet Concertino* beguilingly, and the bassoonist **Matthew Wilkie** is equally seductive in his introductory solo in the *Andante*, while both soloists intertwine engagingly in the finale. **Thierry Fischer** and the COE provide a highly atmospheric backcloth and the recording is warm and beautifully balanced.

Ein Heldenleben, Op. 40 (DVD version)

ⓞ– **** RCO Live **DVD** RCO 04103, or Surround Sound **SACD** RCO 04005. Concg. O, Jansons; (DVD – V/D: Hans Hulscher – with Documentary *'The Sixth Maestro'* – introducing Mariss Jansons as the orchestra's conductor)

Jansons's magnificent **Concertgebouw** performance of *Ein Heldenleben* comes in a superb SACD recording in natural surround sound which, with four speakers, captures the richness of the Concertgebouw acoustic and gives the orchestra the most sumptuous and detailed presentation in a live performance which is unsurpassed in adrenalin flow, refinement of detail, and glorious playing. The DVD offers the special visual treat of the magnificent Concertgebouw as a backcloth for great music-making and at the same time provides first class sound (though not quite as opulent as the CD) plus a vivid pictorial survey of the performance, which is both rewarding and interesting in a score as diverse and detailed as *Ein Heldenleben*, as the camera follows the orchestra's involvement.

Ein Heldenleben, Op. 40 (CD versions)

ⓝ ✷ *** Testament SBT 1430. BPO, Karajan – BEETHOVEN: *Symphony 4 in B flat* ***

ⓑ *** EMI Gemini (ADD) 3 65285-2 (2). LSO, Barbirolli – MAHLER: *Symphony 6* **(*)

Ein Heldenleben; Feuersnot: Liebszene; Intermezzo: Träumerei am Kamin; Salome: Dance of the Seven Veils

(***) Testament mono SBT 11147. RPO, Beecham

Ein Heldenleben, Op. 40; Till Eulenspiegel

ⓝ *** Signum SIGCD 148. Philh. O, Dohnányi

ⓜ *** Warner Elatus 0927 49555-2. Chicago SO, Barenboim

(i) *Ein Heldenleben; (ii) Till Eulenspiegel; (iii) Salome: Dance of the Seven Veils*

ⓑⓑ (***) Dutton CDBP 9737. (i) Bav. State O; (ii) Berlin State Op. O; (iii) BPO; composer

This **Karajan** *Heldenleben* was recorded at the Royal Festival Hall when the **Berlin Philharmonic** came to London in April 1985. The performance can only be described in superlatives and the Testament sound is similarly impressive. In his sleeve-note Richard Osborne speaks of its wonderful sonority, 'lambent in its beauty, never cloying or opaque'. And that is spot on!

Dohnányi's *Ein Heldenleben* is richly evocative, and exceptionally well detailed, with **Radoslav Szulc** outstanding in his representation of the hero's wife as a delightfully capricious but seductive heroine/partner. Excellent live recording in the Royal Festival Hall, and the moment when the Hero ventures into battle brings some of the most viscerally thrilling side-drum playing on record. Yet the great melody of apotheosis offers a glorious, rapturous finality at the close. *Till Eulenspiegel* too is effectively portrayed as a sprightly, endearing rogue, with refined **Philharmonia** playing a particular pleasure.

Recorded in 1990, shortly before **Barenboim** took over the **Chicago Orchestra**, this Elatus reissue is an extremely worthwhile account, particularly at its bargain price. Barenboim propels the music onwards and never allows the tension to sag: the *Battle* is fast, almost Scherzo-like, and the whole performance is both splendidly conceived and brilliantly executed. A very well-balanced and richly detailed recorded sound, too.

Sir John Barbirolli recorded *Ein Heldenleben* at Abbey Road in 1969, not long before his death, and here he sets the seal on his Indian summer in the recording studio. All the tempi are slow, even by his latter-day standards. He luxuriates in every moment of this opulent score (his occasional groans of pleasure sometimes punctuating the score) and the **LSO**, in superb form, follows him with warmth and ardour through every expressive rallentando. The result has the inescapable electricity of a great occasion.

Strauss returned to DG to record this wonderfully humane account of *Ein Heldenleben* with the **Bavarian State Orchestra**. Siemens had developed a new recording process which extended the frequency range, and no previous transfer has ever reproduced its sound quite so vividly. The playing Strauss produces is characterized by such unforced virtuosity and naturalness of feeling that it is put quite in a class of its own. *The Dance of the Seven Veils* and *Till Eulenspiegel* both come from the late 1920s and are less revelatory.

Beecham's 1947 account remains a model of its kind: authoritative, marvellously paced and beautifully transparent in its textures. A glorious performance which long held sway until Karajan's 1959 account came along. The other Strauss excerpts were recorded in the late 1940s before the advent of the mono LP.

Joseph's Legende (complete ballet by John Neumeier; DVD version)

(*) DG **DVD 073 4315. Judith Jamison, Kevin Haigen, Karl Musil, Franz Wilhelm, V. State Op. Ballet, VPO, Hollreiser (Dir: John Neumeier)

The original version of *Joseph's Legende* for the Ballets Russes, choreographed by Fokine, was a 'costume ballet' in which there was very little dancing, so **John Neumeier** rethought the project, and this spectacularly exotic production, with costumes and set to match, is the result. The choreography is a mixture of traditional and new ideas which has been greatly acclaimed. Before the sinuous seduction of young Joseph by Potiphar's wife, he has a marvellously extended pas de deux with the Angel who at the end is to 'take him away and lead him to his destiny' and this (at least partly because of the radiant costuming) is the highlight of the evening. Potiphar's wife is sensuous enough and certainly convincing, but her choreography is less overwhelming. What must be said is that the dancing of the young **Kevin Haigen** as Joseph and of **Karl Musil** as the Angel is riveting, and the **Vienna Philharmonic** under **Hollreiser** gives a gloriously expansive account of Richard Strauss's score.

Josephslegende (ballet score; complete)

*** Channel Classics Surround Sound **SACD** CCS SA 24507. Budapest Festival O, I. Fischer

Strauss's extraordinary work is heard here for the first time complete on CD, gloriously played in sumptuous surround sound. The full score has much variety of colour and feeling and, although it is undoubtely inflated, it is also richly sensuous and spectacular. The scene when young Joseph, knowing nothing of what is to come that night, dances for Potiphar and his wife is most delicately scored. There are fascinating reminders here of Strauss's other works, from *An Alpine Symphony* to *Salome*, and when **Fischer's** performance is so powerfully involving, this is surely a remarkable addition to the catalogue, even if the music does go over the top at times.

Metamorphosen for 23 Solo Strings

🎧 **** Chan. 9708. Norwegian CO, I. Brown – TCHAIKOVSKY: *Souvenir de Florence* ****

*** EMI 5 56580-2 (2). VPO, Rattle – MAHLER: *Symphony 9* ***

*** Delos DE 3121. Seattle SO, Schwarz – HONEGGER: *Symphony 2*; WEBERN arr. SCHWARZ: *Langsamer satz* ***

Iona Brown's performance has a powerfully passionate impetus that is wholly spontaneous, with intense valedictory feeling in the shading down of the closing pages, which has wonderful concentration. The Chandos recording is outstandingly fine.

Rattle with the **Vienna Philharmonic**, producing string sounds of magical beauty, brings out the visionary intensity behind this late flowering of Strauss's genius, sustaining its long span masterfully. Warm, atmospheric sound. An excellent coupling for Mahler's *Ninth*.

Gerard Schwarz's account of Strauss's elegiac threnody is as deeply felt and dignified as it is unhurried, and it should be heard. The listener is completely drawn into its world and, although it does not supersede the Kempe or any of the the Karajan accounts except perhaps in terms of recorded realism, it deserves to be recommended alongside them. At 32 minutes it may be the slowest *Metamorphosen* on disc, but it is certainly one of the best.

Symphony 2 in F min.; (i) Romance in F (for cello & orchestra); (ii) 6 Lieder, Op. 68

Ⓜ *** Chan. 10236X. (i) Wallfisch; (ii) Hulse; RSNO, Järvi

This early symphony may give little idea of the mature composer's style, but the skill of the writing is astonishing, not least the instrumentation. **Järvi** paces the score with real mastery and gets very good playing from the **Royal Scottish National Orchestra**. The glorious Brentano *Lieder*, Op. 68, date from 1918 and Strauss transcribed them for orchestra in 1941. **Eileen Hulse** produces some beautiful tone and is sensitively supported throughout. The *Romance* was another early work which Strauss abridged when he scored it for orchestra. It is charmingly nostalgic, and most persuasively played here. Not core repertory this, but a disc for Straussians.

Till Eulenspiegel

Ⓑ (***) Dutton Lab. mono CDEA 5013. Boston SO, Koussevitzky – BERLIOZ: *Harold in Italy* (**(*))

Till Eulenspiegel, recorded in 1945, makes a spectacular fill-up to **Koussevitzky's** pioneering account of the Berlioz, another fizzing performance, both warm and brilliant, very well transferred in sound both full-bodied and airy.

CHAMBER MUSIC

Cello Sonata in F, Op. 6

Ⓝ (***) Testament (ADD) SBT 1419. Piatigorsky, Pennario (with CHOPIN: *Sonata in G min., Op. 65*; MENDELSSOHN: *Cello Sonata 2 in D, Op. 58*)

The *Cello Sonata* is early Strauss and does not find him in the first flow of inspiration. But **Piatigorsky** is so eloquent an advocate that you are almost persuaded that it is better music than it is. This Piatigorsky recital is altogether exceptional and beautifully transferred.

Piano Quartet in C min., Op. 13

*** Black Box BBX 1048. Lyric Piano Qt – TURINA: *Piano Quartet in A min., Op. 67* ***

By general consent the *Piano Quartet in C minor* is not great Strauss, but it is well played and recorded here and coupled with another rarity by Turina. A disc for those with a taste for offbeat repertoire.

Serenade for Wind; Sonatina 1 in F for Wind (From an Invalid's Workshop); Suite in B flat for 13 Wind Instruments; Symphony for Wind (The Happy Workshop)

🎶 *** Royal Academy RAM 034 (2). Ac. Symphonic Wind Ens., Bragg

Ⓑ *** Hyp. Dyad CDD 22015 (2). London Winds, Collins

These fresh, new performances from the Royal Academy of Music's **Symphonic Wind Ensemble** are superb in every way, spontaneously paced by **Keith Bragg**, and played by eager young musicians who are all expert instrumentalists and know how to blend as well as take solos. The recording is first class, both sonorous and clear. This is now a first choice for these endearing works which Strauss obviously wrote for pleasure.

The **London Winds** on Hyperion are fairly closely observed by the microphone-balance and the effect is clearly defined and dramatic. The playing has the strongest impulse, the autumnal feeling less apparent in the *Serenade*. But one cannot help being caught up by playing that is so vividly robust and vital, and by no means lacking in warmth and affection. Even if there is a touch of over-projection, inner detail is clear and many will like the extra bite on the sound.

Serenade in E flat, Op. 7; Sonatina in F (From an Invalid's Workshop); Suite in B flat, Op. 4.

*** MDG 304 1173 Ens. Villa Musica.

These civilised and genial pieces are a joy and splendidly played here by the **Villa Musica Ensemble**. One marvels afresh at the inventiveness, skill and culture of Strauss's writing for wind instruments. Demonstration sound.

String Quartet in A, Op. 2

Ⓑ**Ⓑ** **(*) Hyp. Helios CDH 55012. Delmé Qt – VERDI: *Quartet* **(*)

The Strauss *Quartet* is early and derivative, as one might expect from a 16-year-old, but it is amazingly assured and fluent. The **Delmé** version is well played; however, although the basic acoustic is pleasing, the sound-balance remains a little on the dry side.

(i) Metamorphosen (arr. for string septet); Capriccio: Prelude

*** Nim. NI 5614. Brandis Qt., with Küssner, Schwalke – SCHOENBERG: *Verklaerte Nacht* ***

Metamorphosen (arr. for string septet); Capriccio: Prelude; Piano Quartet, Op. 13

*** Hyp. CDA 67574. Nash Ens.

The first ideas for *Metamorphosen* came to Strauss as a string septet. In 1990, Strauss's pencil sketch came to light and, with the aid of that and the definitive score, Rudolf Leopold has carefully reconstructed the original. The **Brandis Quartet** and three Berlin colleagues play with magnificent artistry and eloquence, both here and in the opening sextet from *Capriccio*. The Nimbus sound is first class.

Metamorphosen loses little in its reduction for string septet in the hands of the **Nash Ensemble**: its sonorities are

full and vivid, its emotional eloquence very telling. The *Capriccio Prelude* is hardly less successful. But what makes this disc worth considering is the splendidly alive and vivacious account of the *Piano Quartet* (the Scherzo scintillates in the hands of **Ian Brown**) which emerges as a far finer work than hitherto suspected. Really first-class recording makes this collection very appealing.

Violin Sonata in E flat, Op. 18

🎶 **** Erato 8573-85769-2. Repin, Berezovsky – BARTÓK: *Romanian folk dances*; STRAVINSKY: *Divertimento* ****

The sheer sweep and intensity of the extraordinary **Repin–Berezovsky** partnership brings a captivating reading. It is arguably the best we have had since the days of Neveu and Heifetz.

Enoch Arden, Op. 38 (melodrama for narrator and piano)

**(*) VAI Audio (ADD) VAIA 1179-2 (2). Vickers, Hamelin

Jon Vickers, the narrator on VAIA, recommends (in English) how so 'soul-satisfying' a piece gives a powerful reminder of 'the timeless truths of Love, Patience, Fidelity and Steadfastness'. In his declamation he makes a persuasive case for the piece, but even **Marc-André Hamelin**, equally persuasive, cannot mask the fact that the piano-writing in its illustrative naivety has much in common with the accompaniments for silent films, which soon after became so popular. The live recording (with much applause beforehand) is aptly atmospheric.

CHORAL MUSIC

(i) An den Baum Daphne; (ii) Der Abend; Hymne, Op. 34/1–2; (iii) Deutsche Motette, Op. 62; (iv) Die Göttin im Putzzimer

*** Chan. 9223. (i) Lund, Lisdorf, Copenhagen Boys' Ch.; (iii) Kiberg, Stene, Henning-Jensen, Cold; (i-iv) Danish Nat. R. Ch., Parkman

This disc brings very good performances of some very beautiful and curiously little-known music. The engineers produce a realistic sound too.

VOCAL MUSIC

Lieder (complete songs for male voice)

🎶 Ⓜ **** EMI (ADD) 7 63995-2 (6). Fischer-Dieskau, Moore

Fischer-Dieskau and **Moore** made these recordings of the 134 Strauss songs suitable for a man's voice between 1967 and 1970, tackling them in roughly chronological order. With both artists at their very peak, the results are endlessly imaginative, and the transfers are full and immediate, giving fine presence to the voice.

4 Last Songs

(*(**)) Testament mono SBT 1410. Flagstad, Philh. O, Furtwängler – WAGNER: *Tristan: Prelude and Liebestod*, etc. *(**)

This historic recording of the world première of the *Four Last Songs*, at the Royal Albert Hall on 22 May 1950, is seriously flawed in the sound, with a scrunching background. Yet the drama of the occasion and the glorious, rock-steady sounds of **Flagstad's** voice are clearly identifiable in this excellent transfer of lacquer originals. The songs come in a different order from what is now usual, with *Beim Schlafengehen* performed first, not third. With the important Wagner excerpts recorded at the same concert, an important issue.

4 *Last Songs*; Orchestral Lieder

🔊 🌼 ******** EMI (ADD) 566908-2. Schwarzkopf, Berlin RSO or LSO, Szell

(i) *Four Last Songs. Orchestral Lieder*: (ii) *Das Bächlein*; (i) *Cäcilie; Freundliche Vision; Frühlingsfeier; Gesang der Apollopriesterin*; (ii) *Liebeshymnus; Morgen; Das Rosenband*; (i) *Verführung; Waldseligkeit*; (ii) *Wiegenlied*

Ⓝ ******* Australian DG Eloquence 480 0414. BPO, Abbado, with (i) Mattila; (ii) Schäfer

(i) 4 *Last Songs*; Orchestral Lieder: *Befreit; Cäcilie; Muttertändelei; Waldseligkeit; Wiegenlied. Der Rosenkavalier: suite*

Ⓜ ****(*)** RCA 82876 59408-2. (i) Fleming; Houston SO, Eschenbach

(i) 4 *Last Songs; Cäcilie; Morgen; Meinem Kinde; Ruhe, meine Seele!; Wiegenlied; Zueignung*; (ii) *Ach Lieb, ich muss nun scheiden; Allerseelen; Befreit; Du meines Herzens Krönelein; Einerlei; Heimliche Aufforderung; Ich trage meine Minne; Kling!; Lob des Leidens; Malven; Mit deinen blauen Augen; Die Nacht; Schlechtes Wetter; Seitdem dein Aug'; Ständchen; Stiller Gang; Traum durch die Dämmerung; Wir beide wollen springen; Wir sollten wir geheim sie halten; Die Zeitlose*

🔊 🌼 Ⓑ ******** Ph. 475 8507. Norman; with (i) Leipzig GO, Masur; (ii) Parsons

(i) 4 *Last Songs*; (ii) *Du meines Herzens Krönelein; Ruhe, meine Seele; Zueignung*

(*******) BBC mono BBCL 4107-2. (i) Jurinac; BBC SO, Sargent; (ii) Ludwig, Parsons (with BRAHMS: *Ständchen; Wiegenlied* *******) – MAHLER: *Lieder eines fahrenden Gesellen*, etc.

(i) 4 *Last Songs*; (ii) *Arabella* (opera; excerpts); (i) *Capriccio* (opera): *Closing Scene*

🔊 Ⓜ (*******) EMI mono 5 85825-2. Schwarzkopf (i) Philh. O, Ackermann; (ii) Metternich, Gedda, Philh. O, Von Matačic

4 *Last Songs*; (i) *Arabella* (excerpts); *Ariadne auf Naxos: Ariadne's Lament; Capriccio: Closing scene*

🔊 Ⓜ (*******) Decca mono 467 118-2. Lisa della Casa; (i) with Gueden, Schoeffler, Poell; VPO, Boehm, Moralt; Hollreiser

(i; ii) 4 *Last Songs (Vier letzte Lieder); Operatic Scenes & Arias*: (i; iii; iv) *Arabella: Er ist der Richtige nicht für mich . . . Aber der Richtige*; (i; iii; v) *Der Richtige so hab'ich still zu mir gesagt . . . So wie Sie sind . . . Und du wirst mein Geliebter sein*; (i; iii; vi) *Das war sehn gut, Mandryka*; (i; ii; iv; vi) *Ariadne auf Naxos: Ein schönes war; Es gibt ein Reich*; (vii) *Capriccio: Intermezzo & Closing Scene*

Ⓑ**Ⓑ** (***(**)**) Regis mono RRC 1192. Lisa della Casa; (i) VPO; (ii) Boehm; (iii) Moralt; (iv) Gueden; (v) Schoeffler; (vi) Poell; (vii) Elderling, O, cond. den Hertog.

Vier letzte Lieder; Capriccio: Interlude; Morgen mittag um elf; Salome: Ach, du wollst mich nicht deinen Mond küssen lassen.

*** EMI 3 78797-2 Stemme & soloists, ROHCGO, Pappano

Schwarzkopf's 1953 mono version of the *Four Last Songs* comes with both its original coupling, the closing scene from *Capriccio*, also recorded in 1953, and the four major excerpts from *Arabella* which she recorded two years later. The *Four Last Songs* are here less reflective, less sensuous, than in Schwarzkopf's later version with Szell, but the more flowing speeds and the extra tautness and freshness of voice bring equally illuminating performances. Fascinatingly, this separate account of the *Capriccio* scene is even more ravishing than the one in the complete set, and the sound is even fuller, astonishing for its period.

The power of **Jessye Norman's** singing the *Four Last Songs* reminds one of the first ever interpreter, Kirsten Flagstad. In concern for word detail Norman is outshone by Schwarzkopf (unique in conveying the poignancy of old age), but in the *Four Last Songs* and in the orchestral songs the stylistic as well as the vocal command is irresistible, with *Cäcilie* given operatic strength. In the 1985 recital with **Geoffrey Parsons**, Norman brings heartfelt, deeply committed performances, at times larger than life, which satisfyingly exploit the unique glory of her voice. The magnetism of the singer generally silences any reservations, and Geoffrey Parsons is the most understanding of accompanists, brilliant too. Excellent recording.

Lisa della Casa with her creamily beautiful soprano was a radiant Straussian, as these precious excerpts demonstrate. Her account of the *Four Last Songs* (given in the original order, not that usually adopted) has a commanding nobility. *Ariadne's Lament* also receives a heartfelt performance, soaring to a thrilling climax, and the *Arabella* duets with **Gueden**, **Schoeffler** and **Poell** are hauntingly tender. For this superb reissue the transfer has been vastly improved; both voice and orchestra and the ambience of the Grosser Saal in the Musikverein are faithfully caught, with no lack of bloom.

In the alternative Regis collection the transfers have smoothed the original Decca mono sound, although Decca's own remastering is preferable. The main interest of this CD is that the live (1953) *Capriccio* excerpts with **Anton Elderling** and conducted by **Johannes den Hertog** are new. Here the sound is more restricted, with thin, papery violins. An intriguing disc nevertheless, for the glorious voice comes over in its full richness. This collection is without texts and translations but is enticingly inexpensive.

This is very much a portrait of **Nina Stemme**, richly creamy vocally in partnership with **Pappano**, at times warmly moving as in the *Four last Songs* (*Frühling* is *especially* memorable) at others thrillingly, fiendishly dramatic as in the finale from Salome, which is almost over the top, or intense with inner feeling as in the *Capriccio* excerpt, which includes the Moonlit intermezzo. Comparison with other older, more celebrated versions, is not always to the advantage of this new compilation, but in its own right it is very rewarding, and superbly recorded.

Karita Mattila, with **Abbado** and the **Berlin PO** providing sensuously beautiful support, gives one of the most moving of all the many recordings of Strauss's *Four Last Songs*. She is at once youthfully ardent, yet poised and controlled, floating her loveliest, creamy tone in breathtaking *pianissimos*, as at the start of the final song, *Im Abendrot*. She touches the deeper emotions behind these valedictory pieces, using a wide tonal and dynamic range. Consistently she brings out their mystery in singing the more intense for being live. The fill-ups were recorded in the studio, bringing performances just as commanding. The original release, which offered only 50 minutes' playing time, has been impressively filled up by five extra songs, beautifully sung by **Christine Schäfer**.

Renée Fleming with her rich, mature soprano gives warmly sympathetic readings of the *Four Last Songs*, thrilling in climaxes as the voice is allowed to expand, and full of fine detail, even if these readings lack the variety of a Schwarzkopf. The five separate orchestral Lieder also bring a wide expressive range, with *Waldseligkeit* beautifully poised, and ending boldly on *Cäcilie*. The singer is not helped by the way that **Eschenbach** makes the accompaniments seem a little sluggish, polished though the playing is. Something of the same lack of thrust marks his account of Strauss's own arrangement of the *Rosenkavalier* excerpts, despite beautiful playing from the **Houston Orchestra**. How much more welcome would it have been to have had extra items from the singer.

Coupled with outstanding items from **Christa Ludwig**, **Sena Jurinac's** historic version of the *Four Last Songs* was recorded at a Prom in 1961 with **Sargent** conducting the **BBC Symphony Orchestra**. All four songs are faster than usual, even faster than in Jurinac's earlier live broadcast performance of ten years before, recorded in Stockholm and issued by EMI. Defying rather rough mono sound, the result is ardent and animated rather than meditative, almost operatic and not at all valedictory. The Strauss songs with Christa Ludwig accompanied by **Geoffrey Parsons** come from a Wigmore Hall recital of 1978, with the glorious voice flawless in legato. As a first encore, *Zueignung* wins storms of applause.

Lieder

☙ (B) *** CfP 585 9032. Keenlyside, Martineau

Simon Keenlyside follows up the success of his fine Schubert recital (now also reissued on CfP) with this excellent collection of Strauss Lieder, beautifully sung, again with **Malcolm Martineau** a most sensitive accompanist. Try the

highly distinctive, intimate reading of *Ständchen* ('Serenade'), with Keenlyside singing almost in a half-tone and with Martineau playing magically. The fine-spun legato of *Waldseligkeit* and the poise of *Meinem Kinde* are equally impressive. Keenlyside uses a head voice for the gentle top notes of *Allerseelen* ('All Saints' Day') but then finds plenty of power, sharply focused, in songs like *Befreit*. The sequence is rounded off with two exhilarating songs, *Cäcilie* and *Herr Lenz* (with its pun on the name Strauss – nosegay). No texts are provided in its Classics for Pleasure release.

Lieder

*** Hyp. CDA 67588. Schwanewilms, Vignoles

Anne Schwanewilms's soprano is sweet and pure, ideally suited to singing Strauss songs, particularly the early ones. This collection, devised by her accompanist, **Roger Vignoles**, is presented in chronological order, leading up to the creepily disturbing *Ophelia Songs*, with their wild use of key, almost atonal. As Vignoles explains, there are a number of favourites here, including *All' mein gedanken*, *Ruhe meine Seele* and *Waldseligkeit*, but other little-known ones are just as rewarding. An outstanding contribution to an important series.

OPERA

Die Aegyptische Helena (complete)

*** Telarc CD 80605 (2). Voigt, Tanner, Shafer, Grove, Robertson, NY Concert Chorale, American SO, Botstein

This Telarc version, made live in New York in 2002, is the finest yet. The role of Menelaus is arguably the finest he ever gave to a tenor, very well sung here by **Carl Tanner**. What the New York recording triumphantly brings out is the melodic sumptuousness of Strauss's score, wonderfully crafted throughout, with orchestral writing of a richness that even Strauss never surpassed. Where the conductor, **Leon Botstein**, scores is the extra warmth he finds in the score, helped by rich, digital sound. The new set also scores heavily in having **Deborah Voigt**, whose richness and command are a joy, with even the most challenging top notes firm and pure. She is well matched by **Celena Shafer** as Aithra, singing with consistent freshness and clarity. **Jill Grove** is the wonderfully resonant contralto in the improbable role of the Omniscient Seashell (adviser to Aithra), with **Christopher Robertson** as Altair, prince of the Atlas Mountains, and **Eric Cutler** as his son, Da-ud.

Arabella (complete DVD versions)

Ⓝ ☙ **** Decca DVD 074 3263. Fleming, Larsen, Kleiter, Weigel, Zürich Op. Ch. & O, Welser-Möst (Stage Director: Götz Friedrich; V/D: Felix Breitsch)

*** Warner DVD 0630-16912-2. Putnam, Brocheler, Rolandi, Sarfaty, Korn, Lewis, Bradley, LPO, Haitink (Dir.: John Cox; DVD Dir.: John Vernon)

*** DG DVD 073 005-9. Te Kanawa, Wolfgang Brendel, McLaughlin, Dessay, Kuebler, Dernesch, McIntyre, Met. Op. Ch. and O, Thielemann (Producer: Otto Schenk. V/D: Brian Large)

Renée Fleming truly makes an ideal Arabella, beautiful of person and voice, and with a natural freshness of characterization. One watches and listens avidly as she meets her 'Mr Right', equally impressively personified by a slightly gaunt but very convincing **Morten Frank Larsen**. **Julia Kleiter**, too, is perfectly cast as Zdenka; and when the opera has reached its happy ending and Fleming has sung her lovely closing scene, one is left with a warm romantic glow. Sets and costumes are admirably in period, and **Welser-Möst** directs the orchestra with proper Straussian romantic warmth, giving his excellent singers admirable support. Highly recommended.

The Warner DVD offers a live recording of a classic Glyndebourne production of *Arabella* with handsome, realistic sets by Julia Trevelyan Oman. In this 1984 performance **Bernard Haitink**, then music director at Glyndebourne, draws ravishing playing from the **LPO** in support of an outstanding cast with not a single flaw. **Ashley Putnam** makes a tall and imposing Arabella, at once pretty and girlishly eager, yet with a natural dignity and a vocal command that makes her performance magnetic, with the set-piece solos and duets deeply moving. Opposite her, **John Brocheler** is a formidable Mandryka, handsome and heavily bearded, with a clean-cut voice that has just a hint of grit in it, aptly so. As Zdenka **Gianna Rolandi** cuts a vivacious, eager figure, even if her tiny stature next to the imposing Putnam makes it unlikely that even the simple-minded Matteo (superbly sung by **Keith Lewis**) would mistake her for Arabella even in bed. **John Vernon's** video direction, using many helpful close-ups, adds to the impact. It is inadequate that only the briefest synopsis is given on the box, with no booklet provided.

One of the great strengths of this DG live production is the conducting of **Christian Thielemann**, who was then just emerging as a new star among Strauss conductors. He is at once thrustful and emotional, drawing ripe sounds from the orchestra. **Dame Kiri Te Kanawa** gives a convincing dramatic account of the title role and is in glorious voice, producing ravishing sounds in her big numbers, even more charming when observed in close-up. She obviously relishes the sumptuous production, which is as traditional as could be, with grandly realistic sets by Gunther Schneider-Siemssen. The stage direction is by **Otto Schenk**, who shows appropriate respect for Hofmannsthal and Strauss's wishes, and the intelligence of the public.

The Mandryka of **Wolfgang Brendel** carries conviction even if he looks somewhat older than he should (mid-thirties). His voice is strong, firm and unstrained in a rather intimidating yet ultimately vulnerable characterization, and **Marie McLaughlin** is poignantly convincing as Zdenka, the younger sister forced to adopt the role of boy. **Donald McIntyre** and **Helga Dernesch** are vividly characterful as Arabella's parents, and in the second act **Natalie Dessay** as the Fiakermilli is full of character, and she makes much of her brief appearance at the ball, bright and brilliant in her showpiece.

The balance favours the voices and not all the wealth of orchestral detail registers, but the recording is aptly rich and full-bodied. The visual side of the production is first rate. As usual **Brian Large's** camera is pointing exactly where one wants it to point. Strongly recommended.

Arabella (complete; CD version)

🎬 Ⓜ *** Decca 475 7731 (2) Della Casa, Gueden, London, VPO, Solti

Della Casa soars above the stave with the creamiest, most beautiful sounds and constantly charms one with her swiftly alternating moods of seriousness and gaiety. Perhaps **Solti** does not linger as he might over the waltz rhythms, and it may be Solti too who prevents **Edelmann** from making his first scene with Mandryka as genuinely humorous as it can be. Edelmann otherwise is superb, as fine a Count as he was an Ochs in the Karajan *Rosenkavalier*. **Gueden**, too, is ideally cast as Zdenka and, if anything, in Act I manages to steal our sympathies from Arabella, as a good Zdenka can. **George London** is on the ungainly side, but then Mandryka is a boorish fellow anyway. **Dermota** is a fine Matteo, and **Mimi Coertse** makes as much sense as anyone could of the ridiculously difficult part of Fiakermilli, the female yodeller. The sound is brilliant.

Ariadne auf Naxos (complete; DVD versions)

(*) TDK **DVD DVWW OPAAN. Magee, Mosuc, Saccà, Volle, Breedt, Zürich Op. O, Dohnányi (Stage Dir: Claus Guth, TV Dir: Thomas Grimm)

(***) Arthaus **DVD** 100 170. Anthony, Martinez, Koch, Villars, Junge, Adam, Semper Oper Ch., Dresden State O, C. Davis. (Producer: Marco Arturo Marelli. V/D: Felix Breisach.)

(*) DG **DVD 073 028-9. Norman, Battle, Troyanos, King, Netwig, Dickson, Laciura, Met. Op. Ch. & O, Levine (V/D: Brian Large)

In Zürich, **Claus Guth** presents the piece in modern dress, with the main opera after the Prologue set in a restaurant, with dozens of tables. It works reasonably well, even if the magic of Strauss's score is in no way mirrored in the visual presentation. Casting is first rate, with the Zerbinetta of **Elena Mosuc** stealing the limelight with an account of her big aria which prompts an ovation. **Emily Magee's** Ariadne is hardly less fine, ranging impressively and with full, creamy tone, and **Michelle Breedt** as the Composer in the Prologue sings movingly too. **Roberto Saccà** as Theseus has happily little of the gruffness of the Heldentenor, yet is amply powerful enough. **Christoph von Dohnányi** as conductor proves a passionate Straussian.

We are at odds about the Arthaus DVD *Ariadne auf Naxos*, recorded live at the **Semper Oper** in Dresden. R.L. feels that for most collectors it will be a complete turn-off. The setting is in a present-day museum of modern art whose visitors wander in and out of the gallery throughout the whole opera to mightily distracting effect. The performance is not particularly distinguished vocally either, save for **Sophie Koch's** Composer. The best of the others are **John Villars's** Bacchus and **Theo Adam's** Music Master, and the orchestra make a pretty sumptuous sound under **Sir Colin Davis**. The intrusive silliness of the production makes it difficult to sit through this performance once, let alone a second time!

E.G. on the other hand feels that Sir Colin Davis, at his most inspired, directs a glowing performance with a cast of young singers who respond superbly, both to the conducting and to the imaginative stage direction of **Marco Arturo Marelli**. The Prologue, updated to the 20th century, takes you behind the scenes of an impromptu theatre, with a piano centre-stage and with a washroom half visible behind. The costumes, also designed by Marelli, add to the atmosphere of fantasy. The Composer, characterfully sung by **Sophie Koch**, heartfelt in the final solo, rightly provides the central focus, with his new passion for Zerbinetta well established. The main opera follows without an interval. The scene is neatly changed before our eyes to a picture gallery during a private view.

Central to the performance's success is the radiant singing of **Susan Anthony** as Ariadne with her firm, creamily beautiful voice. The sparky Zerbinetta of **Iride Martinez**, vivaciously Spanish-looking, unashamedly shows off in her big aria, both vocally in her dazzling coloratura and in her acting. **Jon Villars** is a powerful, unstrained Bacchus in the final scene, with the commedia dell'arte characters all very well taken too.

Levine's DG recording of the opera (see below) had been made only a year earlier in Vienna with Anna Tomowa-Sintow as Ariadne, Agnes Baltsa as the Composer and **Kathleen Battle** as Zerbinetta. This is straight and unfussy in its staging, and the video production by **Brian Large** could not be more expert and unobtrusive (save for one or two close-ups of **Jessye Norman's** larynx). **Tatiana Troyanos's** Composer is quite superb, and neither Battle nor Norman can be faulted vocally, even if some will find the former's charm a bit overdone. No complaints about the men either, even if **James King's** Bacchus is a mite strained on some of his top notes. **James Levine** is a fine musician, but the orchestral playing has all too little of the finesse and subtlety of Kempe or Karajan and the orchestral textures are nowhere near as refined as they achieve.

Ariadne auf Naxos (complete; CD versions)

🔊 Ⓜ **** Ph. 475 6674 (2). J. Norman, Varady, Gruberová, Asmus, Bär, Frey, Leipzig GO, Masur.

🔊 ✹ Ⓜ (****) EMI mono 5 67077-2 (2) [5671562]. Schwarzkopf, Schock, Rita Streich, Dönch, Seefried, Cuénod, Philh. O, Karajan

🆑 *** Arte Nova 74321 77073-2 (2). Wachutka, Woodrow, Komlosi, Kutan, San Carlo, Naples O, Kuhn

Ⓝ Ⓜ *** EMI 2 08824-2 (2). Janowitz, Geszty, Zylis-Gara, King, Adam, Schreier, Dresden State O, Kempe

In the Philips CD version, **Jessye Norman's** is a commanding, noble, deeply felt performance, ranging extraordinarily wide; if she does not find the same raptness, the inner agony that still makes Elisabeth Schwarzkopf's performance unique, she yet provides the perfect focus for a near ideal cast. **Julia Varady** as the Composer brings out the vulnerability of the character as well as the ardour in radiant singing. The Zerbinetta of **Edita Gruberová** adds an extra dimension to previous recordings in the way she translates the panache of her stage performance into purely aural

terms for recording. It is a thrilling performance and, even if the voice is not always ideally sweet, the range of emotions Gruberová conveys, as in her duet with the Composer, is enchanting. **Paul Frey** is the sweetest-sounding Bacchus on record yet, while **Olaf Bär** as Harlekin and **Dietrich Fischer-Dieskau** in the vignette role of the Music-Master are typical of the fine team of artists here in the smaller character parts. **Masur** proves a masterly Straussian and he is helped by the typically warm Leipzig recording, with sound rich and mellow to cocoon the listener, yet finely balanced to allow you to hear the inter-weaving of the piano as never before in 20th century imitation of a continuo.

Elisabeth Schwarzkopf makes a radiant, deeply moving Ariadne, giving as bonus a delicious little portrait of the Prima Donna in the Prologue. **Rita Streich** was at her most dazzling in the coloratura of Zerbinetta's aria and, in partnership with the harlequinade characters, sparkles engagingly. But it is **Irmgard Seefried** who gives perhaps the supreme performance of all as the Composer, exceptionally beautiful of tone, conveying a depth and intensity rarely if ever matched. **Rudolf Schock** is a fine Bacchus, strained less than most, and the team of theatrical characters includes such stars as **Hugues Cuénod** as the Dancing Master. The fine pacing and delectably pointed ensemble add to the impact of a uniquely perceptive **Karajan** interpretation. Though in mono and with the orchestral sound a little dry, the voices come out superbly.

The modestly priced Arte Nova version can also be strongly recommended. The cast is a strong one, with **Elisabeth-Marie Wachutka** outstanding as Ariadne, sweet and pure over the widest range, and bringing girlish passion to the role, culminating in a heartwarming account of Ariadne's final solo in response to Bacchus, the excellent clear-voiced **Alan Woodrow**. **Aline Kutan** is a similarly impressive Zerbinetta, matching more starry rivals, brilliant in coloratura with a winning sparkle. Though the harlequinade characters are inevitably less polished in their ensembles than in a studio recording, the fun of the piece comes over well, as well as the atmospheric beauty of the Naiads' music. The one snag is the miscasting of **Ildiko Komlosi** as the Composer. It is a rich, warm contralto rather than a mezzo, satisfying enough vocally except under pressure, but too feminine for this trouser role. Yet the thrust of a live performance makes this a highly competitive version at super-budget price. The German libretto is included but, alas, no translation.

Kempe's relaxed, languishing performance of this most atmospheric of Strauss's operas is matched by opulent 1969 EMI recording. **Janowitz** sings with heavenly tone-colour (marred only when hard pressed at the climax of the Lament) and **Zylis-Gara** makes an ardent and understanding Composer. **Sylvia Geszty's** voice is a little heavy for the fantastic coloratura of Zerbinetta's part, but she sings with charm and assurance. **James King** sings the role of Bacchus with forthright tone and more taste than many tenors. Those who remembers Karajan's mono set with Schwarzkopf will not find this ideal, but there is warmth and atmosphere here in plenty. The reissue comes with full libretto.

(i) *Ariadne auf Naxos* (excerpts); Lieder: (ii) *Befreit; Einerlei; Hat gesagt; Morgen!; Schlechtes Wetter; Seit dem dein Aug'; Waldseligkeit*

⊕— *** Testament (ADD) SBT 1036. Lisa della Casa; with (i) Schock, BPO, Erede; (ii) Peschko

The 1959 stereo recording is full and immediate, bringing out the glories of **Lisa della Casa's** creamy soprano but failing to convey the full, atmospheric beauty of the music, notably in the echo chorus of Naiads. Della Casa had earlier recorded *Ariadne's Lament* for Decca, but this is even more powerful. The first excerpt is of the opening of the entertainment from the overture through to Ariadne's first solo. There follow her second solo, *Ein Schönes war*, and the *Lament*, while the last extended excerpt has the whole of the final scene from the entry of Bacchus. **Rudolf Schock**, as in the Karajan version, sings nobly, and **Erede** brings out the lyrical warmth of the writing. Della Casa is less imaginative in the Strauss Lieder but still sings very beautifully and persuasively. The faithful and full Testament transfers bring out the wide range of the recording, tending to emphasize sibilants in the singing.

Capriccio (complete; DVD versions)

⊕— **** Arthaus DVD 100 354. Te Kanawa, Hagegård, Troyanos, Braun, Kuebler, Keenlyside, Sénéchal, Travis, San Francisco Op. O, Runnicles (Dir: Lawless; DVD Dir: Maniura)

⊕— **** TDK DVD DVWW OPCAPR (2). Fleming, Henschel, Trost, Finley, von Otter, Hawlata, Tear, Banks, Paris Nat. Op. O, Schirmer (Dir: Robert Carsen, V/D: François Roussillon)

With evocative sets by Mauro Pagano and in-period 18th-century costumes by Thierry Bosquet, **Stephen Lawless's** production for the **San Francisco Opera** will delight traditionalists. In this live (1993) performance, **Donald Runnicles** is the deeply sympathetic conductor inspiring an outstanding cast with no weak link. **Kiri Te Kanawa** not only sings gloriously with a continuous flow of full, warm sound, she acts most movingly. **Håkan Hagegård** as the Count, her brother, is a big, burly figure, bumbling enough in his overacting to make the rehearsal scene with **Tatiana Troyanos** as a characterful Clairon both funny and believable. The rival duo of poet and composer is superbly taken by **David Kuebler** as Flamand and **Simon Keenlyside** as Olivier, vocally and visually handsome, with **Victor Braun** as La Roche, **Maria Fortuna** and **Craig Estep** as the Italian soprano and tenor ideally cast, and with even the role of the Major Domo very strongly sung by **Dale Travis**, and with the veteran **Michel Sénéchal** masterly in the cameo role of the prompter, Monsieur Taupe. For sheer Straussian beauty, evocatively presented, it would be hard to match the rendering here of the final scene. First-rate sound and excellent documentation in the accompanying booklet, as usual with Arthaus DVDs.

For **Robert Carsen's** production at the **Paris Opera** in 2004, **Renée Fleming** as the Countess is at her radiant peak, in golden voice, and the Count of **Dietrich Henschel** is vocally perfect and strongly characterized. The rivals, poet and composer Flamand and Olivier, are equally fine, with **Rainer** **Trost's** heady tenor set against **Gerald Finley's** perfectly focused baritone. **Anne-Sofie von Otter** as Clairon makes a wonderfully histrionic actress. In the cameo role of Monsieur Taupe, the Prompter, **Robert Tear** could not be more characterful, with **Franz Hawlata** as a formidable La Roche, the stage director, and **Barry Banks** doing an amusing parody as the Italian tenor. The updating to modern dress is generally undistracting. The final scene with its moonlight interlude makes a radiant conclusion, with Fleming even transcending what has gone before, singing with beauty, power and purity.

Capriccio (complete; CD versions)

⊕— 🌐 Ⓜ (****) EMI mono 5 67394-2(2) [567391-2]. Schwarzkopf, Waechter, Gedda, Fischer-Dieskau, Hotter, Ludwig, Moffo, Philh. O, Sawallisch

*** Forlane UCD 268052 (2). Lott, Allen, Kunde, Genz, von Kannen, Vermillion, SWR Stuttgart Vocal Ens. & Radio SO, Prêtre

**(*) Orfeo C 518 992 i (2). Tomowa-Sintow, Schöne, Büchner, Grundheber, Jungwirth, Schmidt, Ridder, Scarabelli, Ballo, Minth, VPO, Stein

In the role of the Countess in Strauss's last opera, **Elisabeth Schwarzkopf** has had no equals on CD. This recording, made in 1957 and 1958, brings a peerless performance from her, full of magical detail both in the pointing of words and in the presentation of the character in all its variety. Not only are the other singers ideal choices in each instance, they form a wonderfully coordinated team, beautifully held together by **Sawallisch's** sensitive conducting. As a performance this is never likely to be superseded. Excellent documentation and a full libretto.

Recorded at a series of concert performances in Mannheim in 1999, the Forlane set, with **Prêtre** an understanding Straussian, offers vivid, immediate sound, giving extra intensity to this inspired 'conversation-piece' on the subject of opera. Central to the set's success is the inspired portrayal of the Countess by **Dame Felicity Lott** in one of her great roles. Her feeling for the idiom is unerring, and though the closeness of the recording brings out the occasional unevenness under pressure, this will delight Dame Felicity's many admirers. With **Thomas Allen** ideally cast as the Count, with **Gregory Kunde** as the composer, Flamand, and **Stephan Genz** as the poet, Olivier, the supporting cast is first rate, with voices cleanly focused, and conversational exchanges beautifully timed. This team yields only to the even more sharply characterful one on EMI.

The Austrian Radio recording from Orfeo offers a warm, rich performance in satisfyingly full sound, made the more compelling for being taken live at a Salzburg Festival performance in August 1985. **Tomowa-Sintow** sings with poise and tenderness, with the rest of the cast making a strong team. Outstanding is **Trudeliese Schmidt** as the flamboyant actress Clairon, and **Horst Stein** is inspired by the beauty of the score to conduct with more passion than in studio recordings. No libretto is provided, only a detailed synopsis, a serious shortcoming in this of all operas with its complex interchanges.

Capriccio, Op. 85: String Sextet

*** Hyp. CDA 66704. Ens. – BRUCKNER: *String Quintet* ***

*** Chan. 9131. ASMF Chamber Ens. – ENESCU: *Octet in C*;
SHOSTAKOVICH: *2 Pieces for String Octet* ***

The opening sextet from Strauss's last opera, *Capriccio*, makes an excellent fill-up to the Bruckner *String Quintet* on Hyperion. Obviously readers are unlikely to buy the Bruckner for the sake of such a short work, even though it is of great beauty, but those who do will be rewarded by some fine music-making and recording.

The autumnal preface to *Capriccio* is also the expertly played fill-up to Enescu's remarkable *Octet*; very well recorded it is, too.

Daphne (complete; CD version)

⏵—**** Decca 475 6926 (2). Fleming, Botha, Schade, Youn, Larsson, WDR Ch. & O, Cologne, Bychkov

Daphne really requires a girlish-sounding soprano in the title-role, and **Renée Fleming** might in principle seem too mature-sounding a singer. In fact, she copes beautifully with the high tessitura of the role, and she produces her clearest, brightest tone, making this a very enjoyable version of an opera which exploits her acting powers in this Decca set, with bright, cleanly focused sound backing **Bychkov's** urgent and sensuous reading, the result is very convincing. **Johan Botha** as Apollo sings with a rather pinched sound, but the notes come over cleanly and powerfully enough, and he is well contrasted with the mellifluous tenor of **Michael Schade** as Leukippos, and the mezzo, **Anna Larsson**, brings out rich tones in the role of Gaea.

Elektra (complete; DVD versions)

⏵—**** Arthaus **DVD** 100 048. Marton, Fassbaender, Studer, King, Grundheber, V. St. Op. Ch. & O, Abbado

(*) TDK **DVD DVWW OPELEK. Johansson, Diener, Lipovšek, Muff, Schasching, Zürich Op. House Ch. & O, Dohnányi (Dir: Martin Kasej, V/D: Felix Breisach)

Eva Marton recorded *Elektra* with Wolfgang Sawallisch in 1990, but the present account comes from a Vienna performance of the preceding year with **Abbado** conducting. The performance has enormous intensity: both Marton's Elektra and **Fassbaender's** Klytemnestra stay long in the memory, and all the remaining characters are triumphantly realized, not least **Franz Grundheber's** blood-thirsty Orestes. Marton makes the most of the intent, obsessive, powerfully demonic Elektra and has enormous dramatic presence.

Harry Kupfer's production is gripping. The setting is dark though not quite as dismal as Götz Friedrich's 1981 production with Rysanek and Varnay under Boehm on a Decca LD. Musically, this is an exciting and concentrated account, and the camera is musically handled by **Brian Large**. He has an unerring feel for directing our attention where it needs to be, and many collectors will feel that this is an essential acquisition, alongside the Sinopoli CD set.

Recorded at the Zürich Opera House in December 2005, **Christoph Dohnányi's** powerful conducting and the singing of a fine cast make this TDK account of Strauss's *Elektra* mag-

netically compelling. **Eva Johansson** has a sharp cutting edge to her soprano, entirely apt for the role, well contrasted with the much sweeter Chrysothemis of **Melanie Diener**. In this modern-dress setting, Elektra with her wild blonde hair emerges as a terrifying drop-out, already at the start driven to near madness. She is clearly set against the much more feminine and controlled sister, Chrysothemis, and the formidably powerful and sinister Klytemnestra of **Marjana Lipovšek**. The only disappointment is in the casting of **Alfred Muff** as Orestes, with his fluttery baritone not mellifluous enough for the climactic moment of recognition by Elektra. At that point Johannson scales her voice down and in her emotional relief purifies her tone. In the small role of Aegisthus **Rudolf Schasching** makes his mark well. The set is like a modern prison, stylized and undistracting enough.

Elektra (complete; CD versions)

⏵—Ⓜ**** Decca (ADD) 475 8231 (2). Nilsson, Collier, Resnik, Stolze, Krause, V. State Op. Ch., VPO, Solti

Ⓜ**(*) EMI 5 09190-2 (2). Marton, Lipovšek, Studer, Winkler, Weikl, Bav. R. Ch. & O, Sawallisch

Nilsson is almost incomparable in the name-part, with the hard side of Elektra's character brutally dominant. Only when – as in the Recognition scene with Orestes – she tries to soften the naturally bright tone does she let out a suspect flat note or two. As a rule she is searingly accurate in approaching even the most formidable exposed top notes. One might draw a parallel with **Solti's** direction – sharply focused and brilliant in the savage music which predominates, but lacking the languorous warmth one really needs in the Recognition scene, if only for contrast. The brilliance of the 1967 Decca recording is brought out the more in the newest digital transfer, aptly so in this work. The fullness and clarity are amazing for the period.

Sawallisch may miss the full violence of Strauss's score which the fierce Solti so brilliantly captures in his vintage Decca version; but, with its warm, wide-ranging sound, his account conveys more light and shade, more mystery. **Eva Marton** in her characterization of the tormented heroine similarly finds more light and shade than Birgit Nilsson did for Solti, but the voice spreads distressingly under pressure. Notably disappointing is the failure of both singer and conductor to convey the full emotional thrust of Elektra's radiant solo after the great moment of recognition between her and her brother, Orestes (**Bernd Weikl** in fine, incisive voice). **Marjana Lipovšek's** Klytämnestra is among the finest on record, and **Cheryl Studer** as Chrysothemis, well contrasted in bright clarity, has wonderful moments, notably in her solo after the murders.

(i) Elektra: Soliloquy; Recognition scene; Finale. Salome: Dance of the seven veils; Finale

⏵—Ⓜ*** RCA **SACD** (ADD) 82876 67900-2. Borkh, Chicago SO, Reiner; with (i) Schoeffler, Yeend, Chicago Lyric Theatre Ch.

With **Borkh** singing superbly in the title-role alongside **Paul Schoeffler** and **Francis Yeend**, this is a real collector's piece. **Reiner** provides a superbly telling accompaniment; the performances of the Recognition scene and final duet are as ripely passionate as Beecham's old 78-r.p.m. excerpts and outstrip the complete versions. The orchestral sound is thrillingly rich, the brass superbly expansive. Reiner's full-blooded account of *Salome's Dance* is very exciting too, and Borkh is comparably memorable in the final scene. No Straussian should miss this disc.

Feuersnot (complete)

🎧–🅱 *** Arts 47546-2 (2). Varady, Weikl, Bergere-Tuna, Tölz Boys' Ch., Bav. R. Ch., Munich RO, Fricke

Feuersnot, Strauss's second opera, which was first given in 1901, is an allegory with an element of satire, set in medieval times. Like his first (*Guntram*) it is opulently scored, and in three compact Acts tells its story of Kunrad, a young sorcerer who, when rejected and ridiculed, puts a curse on the town, extinguishing all fire and light. The performance is a fine one, with **Bernd Weikl** as Kunrad and **Julia Varady** as Dimut, his beloved, the Mayor's daughter - both outstanding. **Heinz Fricke** directs a warmly expressive performance in well-balanced digital radio sound. Recommended.

Die Frau ohne Schatten (complete; DVD version)

*** TDK **DVD** DVWW OPFROS. Seiffert, DeVol, Titus, Martin, Lipovšek, Bav. State Op. Ch. & O, Sawallisch (Dir: Einosuko Ishikawa, V/D: Andreas Mazur)

Recorded in Nagoya in Japan, when the **Bavarian State Opera** was on tour in November 1992, the TDK DVD offers a striking production in which the Japanese director **Ishikawa** has translated this symbolic story of the empress who is seeking to obtain a shadow (symbol of fertility) into a Japanese and oriental setting. So the Emperor and Empress and the courtiers are presented in Japanese costume, while the Dyer and the Dyer's Wife are in Arab costume. The role of the Emperor, sung by the Heldentenor **Peter Seiffert**, and the Empress, sung by **Luana DeVol**, are both excellent in these very demanding roles, with **Marjana Lipovšek** superb in the sinister attendant role of the nurse. Equally effective are **Alan Titus** as Barak the Dyer, and **Janis Martin** as his wife. This is a difficult opera to sustain over its contorted plot, but **Wolfgang Sawallisch** is a master Straussian, shaping each phrase and building each climax unerringly, bringing out drama and atmosphere, with the magnificent choir and orchestra of Bavarian State Opera. The production ends with a charmingly symbolic setting of a Japanese bridge in gold, with the Emperor and Empress on top and the Dyer and his wife below. There may be overtones in the visual production of *Turandot* or even of *Mikado*, but the result is most compelling. The set's only snag is that no synopsis is included in the accompanying booklet.

Die Frau ohne Schatten (CD version)

🎧–⚙ **** Decca 436 243-2 (3). Behrens, Varady, Domingo, van Dam, Runkel, Jo, VPO, Solti

In the Heldentenor role of the Emperor, **Plácido Domingo**, the superstar tenor, gives a performance that is not only beautiful to the ear beyond previous recordings but which has an extra feeling for expressive detail, deeper than that

which was previously recorded. **Hildegard Behrens** as the Dyer's wife is also a huge success. Her very feminine vulnerability is here a positive strength, and the voice has rarely sounded so beautiful on record. **Julia Varady** as the Empress is equally imaginative, with a beautiful voice, and **José van Dam** with his clean, dark voice brings a warmth and depth of expression to the role of Barak, the Dyer, which goes with a satisfyingly firm focus. **Reinhild Runkel** in the key role of the Nurse is well in character, with her mature, fruity sound. **Eva Lind** is shrill in the tiny role of the Guardian of the Threshold, but there is compensation in having **Sumi Jo** as the Voice of the Falcon. With the **Vienna Philharmonic** surpassing themselves, and the big choral ensembles both well disciplined and warmly expressive, this superb recording is unlikely to be matched, let alone surpassed, for many years. **Solti** himself is inspired throughout.

Guntram (complete)

🅱🅱 ** Arte Nova 74321 61339-2 (2). Woodrow, Wachutka, Konsulov, Scheidegger, Marchigiana PO, Kuhn

Strauss's very first opera, set in the age of chivalry, is an opulent piece, unashamed in its high romanticism. On the Arte Nova label **Gustav Kuhn** conducts a warm, thrustful performance, recorded live at Garmisch-Partenkirchen, with the rich orchestral tapestries beautifully caught in open, refined sound, only occasionally disturbed by audience noises. **Alan Woodrow** makes a strong Guntram, with his firm Heldentenor tone only occasionally strained. **Elisabeth Wachutka** with her fruity soprano sounds too mature for the heroine, Freihild.

Intermezzo: Symphonic Interludes

*** Chan. 9357. Detroit SO, Järvi – SCHMIDT: *Symphony 1* ***

Neeme Järvi is an underrated Straussian and here he proves equal to the very best. He and his **Detroit** musicians give a thoroughly persuasive account of the interludes Strauss extracted from *Intermezzo*, and this comes as a generous fill-up to Schmidt's derivative but delightful *First Symphony*. Strongly recommended.

Intermezzo (complete; DVD version)

Ⓝ 🎧– **** Warner NVC Arts **DVD** 50-51442-8857-2-9. Lott, Pringle, Caley, Gale, Glyndebourne Festival Op. Ch., LPO, Kuhn (Stage Director: John Cox; V/D: David Buckton)

This is as perfect a realization of Strauss's conversation piece as one could possible imagine, and it is even more enjoyable for being performed in Andrew Porter's brilliant English translation. **Felicity Lott** looks ravishing and sings delightfully as Christine, **John Pringle** is perfectly cast as her husband, Robert, and **Ian Caley** makes a winningly ingenuous foil as the young baron. John Cox's 1920s sets and costumes are ideal (notably Felicity Lott's dresses) and the production values are what every stage director should seek, and few find. Moreover, the clever alignment with the composer's own domestic situation is neatly achieved. **Gustav Kuhn** directs the complex orchestral accompaniments with great skill and the **LPO** is in sparkling form. If only all opera productions were as beautifully realized as this!

Die Liebe der Danae (complete)

🎵—**** CPO 999 967-2 (3). Grundheber, Schöpflin, McNamara, Uhl, Zach, Chafin, Behle, Fleitmann, Kiel Op. Ch. & PO, Windfuhr

**(*) Telarc CD 80570 (3). Flanigan, Coleman-Wright, Smith, Lewis, Saffer, NY Concert Chorale, American SO, Botstein

Die Liebe der Danae is an ingenious conflation – originally suggested by Hugo von Hofmannsthal – of two myths involving gold, the legend of Midas and the golden touch, and Jupiter's seduction of Danae in the guise of golden rain. Where the account under **Ulrich Windfuhr** consistently scores is in the dramatic bite of the performance, with singers on stage conveying each confrontation of character more convincingly than is ever likely in a concert performance. Though Botstein is a formidable Straussian, Windfuhr is even more warmly idiomatic, conveying a surge of warmth at the big climaxes, and his singers too seem to understand the idiom far more clearly than their American counterparts. Standing out from an excellent cast is the magnificent Jupiter of **Franz Grundheber**, weightily Wagnerian like a latter-day Wotan; and **Robert Chafin** in the tenor role of Midas is also splendid. **Manuela Uhl** as Danae has a bright, clear soprano, which she shades down seductively in gentler passages such as the meeting with Midas, but she tends to sound inflexible under pressure. Her counterpart on Telarc is sweeter and easier on the ear. Though in precision of ensemble the chorus on stage cannot match the American chorus in concert, the singers regularly convey an extra warmth in compensation, adding to the impact of the big choral moments.

Leon Botstein, a dedicated advocate of the piece, conducts a loving performance with his excellent cast. As Danae, **Lauren Flanigan** has ample richness and power, yet remains girlish, while **Hugh Smith** makes an engaging Midas, fresh and unstrained, with **Peter Coleman-Wright** in the difficult role of Jupiter repeating his formidable Garsington interpretation. The quartet of queens – all of them, like Leda and Semele, seduced by Jupiter in their time – and the quartet of kings are beautifully integrated, and **Lisa Saffer** is outstanding as Xanthe, Danae's maid, who has just one ravishing and very demanding duet with her mistress in Act I. First-rate chorus work. Though the clean if rather dry recording fails to do justice to the sumptuous scoring, with voices to the fore, the result is still magnetic, although the CPO set is a clear first choice.

Der Rosenkavalier (complete; DVD versions)

🎵—🏵 **** DG **DVD** 073 4072 (2). Lott, von Otter, Bonney, Moll, Hornik, V. St. Op. Ch. & O, Carlos Kleiber. (Producer: Otto Schenck, V/D: Horant Hohlfeld)

🎵—**** EMI **DVD** 5 44258-9 (2). Nina Stemme, Kasarova, Hartelius, Muff, Zürich Op., Ch. & O, Welser-Möst. (Producer: Sven-Eric Bechtolf, V/D Dir: Chloé Perlemuter, Sets: Rolf Glittenberg)

**** TDK **DVD** DVWW-OPRC (2). Pieczonka, Kirchschlager, Persson, Hawlata, V. State Op. Konzertvereinigung, VPO, Bychkov (Dir: Robert Carsen, V/D: Brian Large)

Carlos Kleiber has spoken of **Felicity Lott** as his ideal Marschallin, and she is probably currently as unrivalled in this role as was Schwarzkopf in the 1950s. She does not wear her heart on her sleeve, and her reticence makes her all the more telling and memorable. The other roles are hardly less distinguished, with **Anne Sofie von Otter's** Octavian splendidly characterized and boyish, while **Barbara Bonney's** Sophie floats her top notes in the Presentation of the Rose scene with great poise and impressive accuracy. **Kurt Moll's** Ochs, a splendidly three-dimensional and subtle reading, is one of the highlights of the performance. **Otto Schenck's** production deserves the praises that have been lavished on it, and Rudolf Heinrich's sets are handsome. Carlos Kleiber gets some ravishing sounds from the **Vienna Philharmonic**, and his reading of the score is as Straussian and as perfect as you are likely to encounter in this world. The sound is very natural and lifelike, not too forward, and with a good perspective.

The competing **Zürich Opera** production, recorded a decade later, is also outstanding in every way. **Nina Stemme** is a superb Marschallin, a sophisticated portrayal, but with deep underlying feeling which is so affecting in the great closing trio. **Vesselina Kasarova's** Octavian has a most engaging boyish quality while her richly contrasted mezzo blends perfectly with **Malin Hartelius**, an enchanting Sophie, whose exquisite singing in the Silver Rose scene is unforgettable. **Alfred Muff** is a splendid three-dimensional **Baron Ochs**, clumsily oafish, yet believably real. Moreover he has a rich, deep bass voice.

But there are many other plus points. As a backcloth for Marianne Glittenberg's lavish costumes, Rolf Glittenberg's sets are a visual delight, from the Marschallin's elegant bedroom of Act I to the colourful following kitchen scene where the nervous Sophie hides in the cupboard until her Cavalier persuades her to step out, and in the ravishingly sung final trio, one is made well aware of the conflicting emotions of the Marschallin, and the two lovers, who cannot believe what is happening. **Franz Welser-Möst** conducts comparably elegantly, yet with ardour (the Waltz music is gorgeous), and the orchestral playing is richly responsive. But the opera's close is very moving indeed. Excellent sound and the all-essential subtitles are splendidly managed.

Der Rosenkavalier is a remarkably lucky opera on DVD, for the 2004 Salzburg Festival production, richly and sensitively conducted by **Semyon Bychkov**, is very fine indeed, and compares well with its illustrious predecessors. It is set a little forward in time from usual, in the early years of the 20th century, but costumes and settings are lavish and visually appealing. The cast has no weak link. **Adrianne Pieczonka** looks exactly right as the Marschallin and sings and acts very movingly throughout, especially in the closing scene. The very boyish **Angelika Kirchschlager** is perfectly cast as Octavian and, like the lovely Sophie (**Miah Persson**), sings very beautifully: the presentation of the silver rose scene is exquisite. **Franz Hawlata** as Baron Ochs is less of an oaf than usual, a believable characterization, self-important, self-indulgent, and at first supremely self-confident until he is spectacularly demolished. **Brian Large's** video direction is near-perfect (especially in the great Trio) and the orchestra plays gloriously throughout. Very enjoyable indeed.

Der Rosenkavalier (complete; CD versions)

- ⊶ ❀ Ⓜ **** EMI (ADD) 5 67605-2 (3). Schwarzkopf, Ludwig, Stich-Randall, Edelmann, Waechter, Philh. Ch. & O, Karajan

- ⊶ *** EMI 3 58618-2 (3). Te Kanawa, von Otter, Rydl, Grundheber, Hendricks, Dresden Op. Ch., Dresden Boys' Ch., Dresden State O, Haitink

- **(*) Decca (ADD) 417 493-2 (3). Crespin, Minton, Jungwirth, Donath, Wienr, V. State Op. Ch., VPO, Solti

- ⒃ (**(*)) Naxos mono 8.111011/13 (3) Reining, Jurinac, Gueden, Weber, Dermota, Vienna PO, and State Op. Ch, Erich Kleiber

- ⒃ (**) Regis mono RRC 3007 (3) Reining, Jurinac, Gueden, Weber, Dermota, Vienna PO, and State Op. Ch, Erich Kleiber

Karajan's 1956 version, one of the greatest of all opera recordings, is in a class of its own, with the patrician refinement of Karajan's spacious reading combining with an emotional intensity that he has rarely equalled, even in Strauss, of whose music he remains a supreme interpreter. Matching that achievement is the incomparable portrait of the Marschallin from **Schwarzkopf**, bringing out detail as no one else can, yet equally presenting the breadth and richness of the character, a woman still young and attractive. **Christa Ludwig** with her firm, clear mezzo tone makes an ideal, ardent Octavian and **Teresa Stich-Randall** a radiant Sophie, with **Otto Edelmann** a winningly characterful Ochs, who yet sings every note clearly.

Vocally the biggest triumph of **Haitink's** beautifully paced reading is the Octavian of **Anne Sofie von Otter**, not only beautifully sung but acted with a boyish animation to make most rivals sound very feminine by comparison. If the first great – and predictable – glory of **Dame Kiri's** assumption of the role of the Marschallin is the sheer beauty of the sound, the portrait she paints is an intense and individual one, totally convincing. The portrait of Sophie from **Barbara Hendricks** is a warm and moving one, but less completely satisfying, if only because her voice is not quite so pure as one needs for this young, innocent girl. **Kurt Rydl** with his warm and resonant bass makes a splendid Baron Ochs, not always ideally steady, but giving the character a magnificent scale and breadth. Whatever the detailed reservations over the singing, it is mainly due to **Bernard Haitink** that this is the most totally convincing and heartwarming CD version of *Rosenkavalier* since Karajan's 1956 set. This recording, unlike the Karajan, opens out the small stage cuts sanctioned by the composer.

The current remastering of the **Solti** *Der Rosenkavalier* from the late 1960s has brought the most striking improvement in the sound among all the Decca reissues of his Strauss opera series and there is now body and ambient warmth, so essential for this gloriously ripe score. The **VPO** strings have a lovely sheen, yet inner detail is glowingly clear. **Crespin** is here at her finest on record, with tone well focused; the slightly maternal maturity of her approach will

appear for many ideal. **Mandfred Jungwirth** makes a firm and virile, if not always imaginative Ochs, **Yvonne Minton** a finely projected Octavian and **Helen Donath** a sweet-toned Sophie. Solti's direction is fittingly honeyed, with tempi even slower than Karajan in the climactic moments. The one serious disappointment is that the great concluding Trio does not quite lift one to the tear-laden height one ideally wants. Even so this *Rosenkavalier* offers much to ravish the ear.

Decca's set conducted by **Eric Kleiber** was the first ever complete recording of *Rosenkavalier*, and it has long enjoyed cult status. **Sena Jurinac** is a charming Octavian, strong and sympathetic, and **Hilde Gueden** a sweetly characterful Sophie, not just a wilting innocent. **Ludwig Weber** characterizes deliciously in a very Viennese way as Ochs; but the disappointment is the Marschallin of **Maria Reining**, very plain and lacking intensity. She is not helped by Kleiber's refusal to linger; with the singers recorded close, the effect of age on what was once a fine voice is very clear, even in the opening solo of the culminating trio. And ensemble is not good, with even the prelude to Act I a muddle.

The Naxos transfer, meticulously made by Mark Obert-Thorn, irons out some of those inconsistencies as well as some electronic clicks and some distortion, and also offers full sound, a little more detailed but with some fizz occasionally and some veiling of voices in places.

The Regis version offers full, warm sound, less detailed and with a more noticeable surface-hiss, making it rather less recommendable. None of the three gives the strings of the **Vienna Philharmonic** their full bloom. Only the Decca Legends issue offers the libretto, with Naxos and Regis providing instead detailed synopses linked to the index points.

Der Rosenkavalier (abridged; highlights from early recordings)

- ⊶ ⒃ (***) Naxos mono 8.110191-2 (2). Lehmann, Olszewska, Schumann, Mayr, VPO, Heger

Mark Obert-Thorn's meticulous transfer of the original 78s of this classic opera set has the voices just as vivid as on EMI's own transfer, tending to bring out more clearly the variable balances and volume-levels which marked the original. The performance remains peerless, with all four principal soloists at their peak. That makes the substantial 43-minute appendix specially valuable, with alternative performances by **Lehmann** and **Richard Mayr** set against recordings by such rivals at the time as **Barbara Kemp** a superb Marschallin, **Alexander Kipnis** an Ochs even more powerful than Mayr, with **Richard Tauber** masterly in the tenor aria of Act I (omitted in the main set of excerpts) and **Conchita Supervia** a delectable Octavian opposite the Sophie of **Maria Ferraris** singing in Italian. The selection is rounded off with live recordings of the final trio and part of the duet made at the Theater der Unter den Linden in 1928 with **Barbara Kemp**, **Delia Reinhardt** and **Marion Claire** – a wonderful historic document.

Der Rosenkavalier (highlights)

- Ⓜ *** EMI 5 65571-2. Schwarzkopf, Ludwig, Stich-Randall, Edelmann, Waechter, Philh. Ch. & O, Karajan

(N) (B) *** CfP 3 93372-2 (from above set with Te Kanawa, von Otter, Hendricks, Dresden State Op., Haitink)

On EMI we are offered the Marschallin's monologue to the end of Act I (25 minutes); the Presentation of the silver rose and finale from Act II; and the Duet and Closing scene, with the Trio from Act III, flawlessly and gloriously sung and transferred most beautifully to CD. A superb disc in every way.

The set of highlights with **Te Kanawa** plays for 76 minutes, and many will count the disc good value as a sampler.

Der Rosenkavalier (highlights; in English)

(M) **(*) Chan. 3022. Kenny, Montague, Joshua, Tomlinson, Shore, Mitchell Ch., Kay Children's Ch., LPO, Parry

This generous 80-minute selection from *Der Rosenkavalier*, sung in English, reflects the strength of English National Opera's highly successful stage production. **David Parry** paces the score most persuasively, and the orchestral sound is aptly sumptuous, if a little clouded on detail. The selection of items, concentrating on the beginnings and endings of Acts, cannot be faulted, except that **John Tomlinson's** strongly characterized Baron Ochs – with nobility part of the mixture – is represented only by the end of Act II, with its great Waltz theme. One snag is, that the recording tends to exaggerate the singers' vibratos, intrusively so only with **Yvonne Kenny** as the Marschallin. She is strong but not very warm with such a noticeable flutter in the voice. On the other hand, **Diana Montague** is a winningly expressive Octavian, and **Rosemary Joshua** a sweet-toned Sophie. The booklet includes full text in the English version of Alfred Kalisch.

Der Rosenkavalier Suite

🔊 **** BBC (ADD) BBCL 4038. Hallé O, Barbirolli – HAYDN: *Symphony 83 in G min. (La Poule)*; LEHÁR: *Gold and Silver*; JOHANN STRAUSS JR: *Emperor Waltz*, etc. ****

A glorious performance from **Barbirolli** with the kind of affectionate attention to detail which all but disguises the fact that this is a musical patchwork. The **Hallé** horns and strings excel themselves in a performance that is full of uninhibited ardour, yet the *Presentation of the Rose* sequence is lovingly tender, and the final *Trio* full of bliss.

Salome (complete; DVD versions)

🔊 ✿ **** DG **DVD** 973 4339. Stratas, Beirer, Varnay, Stratas, Weikl, soloists, VPO, Boehm (Producer: Götz Friedrich)

(*) Warner NVC Arts **DVD 9031 73827-2. Malfitano, Estes, Rysanek, Hiestermann, Deutsche Op. Ch. and O, Sinopoli (Dir: Petr Weigl, V/D: Brian Large)

(N) ** TDK **DVD** DVWWOP-SALOME. Michael, Vermillion, Bronder, Struckmann, La Scala, Milan, O, Harding (Stage Director: Luc Bondy; V/D: Emanuele Garofalo)

(N) ** Opus Arte **DVD** OA 0996D. Michael, Schuster, Moser, Volle, ROHCG O, Jordan (Stage Director: David McVicar; V/D: Jonathan Haswell)

We have long treasured **Karl Boehm's** 1976 performance on LaserDisc (where it lacked English subtitles) and it is splendid that it now appears on so excellent a DVD transfer. Quite frankly it is the best *Salome* either on CD or DVD. **Teresa Stratas** really looks the part as well as singing it (she has been acclaimed as the finest singing-actress of the day) and the rest of the cast is superb. **Astrid Varnay's** depiction of Herodias is masterly, as is **Hans Beirer's** Herod. Above all, Götz Friedrich's production evokes the atmosphere and dramatic intensity of Strauss's opera, and one can only echo the New York critic who declared it 'one of the most successful musical-theatrical performances I have ever seen'. Friedrich serves the score to perfection: his production is miles removed from the 'dustbin on Mars' set favoured by so many directors nowadays. This eclipses all rivals.

Recorded in 1990 at the **Deutsche Opera** in Berlin, the Warner DVD offers a powerful and warmly expressive performance under **Giuseppe Sinopoli**, the counterpart of his outstanding CD recording. **Catherine Malfitano** is an abrasive Salome, confident from the start, knowing exactly what she wants, and not at all girlish as she snarls out her demands or curiously asks the age of the prophet imprisoned in the cistern below. **Simon Estes** in his prime is a powerful Jokanaan, noble and handsome as he stands tall. **Horst Hiestermann** characterizes well as Herod and sings accurately, even if his voice is never beautiful, while **Leonie Rysanek** – earlier a great Salome – here gives a classic performance as Herodias, searingly compelling in her imperious way. The others make a first-rate team, well directed against the stylized white sets like great blocks of concrete. Malfitano is seductive in the *Dance of the Seven Veils*, and grows obsessively lascivious when fondling the head of the Baptist, repulsively so.

Neither of the two new *Salomes*, with both, astonishingly, featuring the young, lithe **Nadia Michael** – a new star in the name-role – matches our current recommendations, so well directed by Karl Boehm and Sinopoli respectively. The Covent Garden producer Luc Bondy is concerned with animation and keeps the heroine on the move, not just in her famous dance routine. The costumes are not entirely convincing, but the singing is uniformly quite impressive, with Nadia Michael and **Peter Bronder's** Herod the more memorable. **Daniel Harding** conducts sensuously and the orchestra plays with Italianate warmth. The camerawork is acceptable but isn't very consistent.

Not surprisingly, David McVicar's Covent Garden production seeks to impress – and indeed horrify – with lots of blood and a near naked executioner. The colourful sets amplify the decadence, and Salome's dance is sensuously managed. Indeed, **Nadia Michael's** Salome can sing and dance with comparable flair and accuracy. **Thomas Moser's** Herod is genuinely moving and makes a good foil for his sensuously attractive Salome. The orchestra plays splendidly under **Philippe Jordan** and Jonathan Haswell's photography is more imaginative than the work of his colleague at La Scala.

Salome (complete)

🔊 **** DG. 431 810-2 (2). Studer, Rysanek, Terfel, Hiestermann, German Opera, Berlin, Ch. & O, Sinopoli

⊶ Ⓜ **** Decca 475 7528 (2). Nilsson, Hoffmann, Stolze, Waechter, VPO, Solti

⊶ *** Chan. 9611 (2). Nielsen, Hale, Goldberg, Silja, Danish National RSO, Schonwandt

Ⓜ *** EMI 567080-2 (2) [5671592]. Behrens, Bohme, Baltsa, van Dam, VPO, Karajan

ⒷⒷ (**(*)) Naxos mono 8.111014/5. Goltz, Kenny, Patzak, Dermota, Braun, VPO, Krauss

The glory of **Sinopoli's** DG version is the singing of **Cheryl Studer** as Salome, producing glorious sounds throughout. Her voice is both rich and finely controlled, with delicately spun *pianissimos* that chill you the more for their beauty, not least in Salome's attempted seduction of John the Baptist. Sinopoli's reading is often unconventional in its speeds, but it is always positive, thrusting and full of passion, the most opulent account on disc, matched by full, forward recording. As Jokanaan, **Bryn Terfel** makes a compelling recording début, strong and noble, though the prophet's voice as heard from the cistern sounds far too distant. Among modern sets this makes a clear first choice, though Solti's vintage Decca recording remains the most firmly focused, with the keenest sense of presence, especially in the newly remastered version.

Birgit Nilsson is splendid throughout; she is hardedged as usual but, on that account, more convincingly wicked: the determination and depravity are latent in the girl's character from the start. Of this score **Solti** is a master. He has rarely sounded so abandoned in a recorded performance. **Waechter** makes a clear, young-sounding Jokanaan. **Gerhardt Stolze** portrays the unbalance of Herod with frightening conviction, and **Grace Hoffman** does all she can in the comparatively ungrateful part of Herodias. The vivid CD projection makes the final scene, where Salome kisses the head of John the Baptist in delighted horror (*I have kissed thy mouth, Jokanaan!*), all the more spine-tingling, with a close-up effect of the voice whispering almost in one's ear. Full documentation.

With an outstanding cast, the Chandos version, superbly recorded in cooperation with the Danish Broadcasting Corporation, stands out among modern digital versions. **Inga Nielsen** is a superb Salome, pingingly precise in her vocal attack, with an apt hint of acid in the voice but always firm, with no shrillness. The result is a portrayal with all the strength needed, not least for the unrelenting malevolence at the end, but leaving one with the impression of a character still young. **Robert Hale** is a characterful and expressive, if at times gruff, Jokanaan, and the Heldentenor **Reiner Goldberg** and the veteran **Anja Silja**, make an exceptionally strong, well-characterized duo as Herod and Herodias. Smaller roles are also well cast.

Hildegard Behrens is also a triumphantly successful Salome. The sensuous beauty of tone is conveyed ravishingly, but the recording is not always fair to her fine projection of sound, occasionally masking the voice. All the same, the feeling of a live performance has been captured well, and the rest of the cast is of the finest Salzburg standard. In particular **José van Dam** makes a gloriously noble Jokanaan, and in the early scenes his offstage voice from

the cistern at once commands attention. **Karajan** – as so often in Strauss – is at his most commanding and sympathetic, with the orchestra, more forward than some will like, playing rapturously. This is a performance which, so far from making one recoil from perverted horrors, has one revelling in sensuousness.

However on Naxos Mark Obert-Thorn has made one of his miraculous transformations of the sound, somehow adding lustre and body to the strings, and without losing vividness of wind and brass detail, giving the whole recording, voices and orchestra alike, added ambient warmth. The set comes with a cued synopsis, costs less than the Decca, and is much preferable. It certainly demonstrates what a great conductor **Krauss** was. Moreover the set's bonus is an extra 53 minutes of four legendary historical recordings of music from *Salome* (from 1907–49).

Salome (sung in English)

Ⓝ *(*) Chan. 3157 (2). Bullock, Graham-Hall, Burgess, Wegner, Philh. O, Mackerras

Alas, this English-language version of *Salome* has little going for it as **Susan Bullock** is frankly inadequate in the key role, the voice neither sensuous nor beautiful enough, nor really commanding. The rest of the cast are adequate but little more than that, and by far the best feature of the recording is the rich orchestral tapestry provided by the **Philharmonia Orchestra** who play so dramatically and sensuously for **Mackerras**. Incidentally, the famous *Salome's Dance* is played for a second time, in its concert version, as an extra item.

Die schweigsame Frau (complete)

**(*) Orfeo C 516 992, (2). Böhme, Mödl, McDaniel, Kusche, Grobe, Grist, Schädle, Loulis, Peter, Proebstl, Bellgardt, Strauch, Horn, Schreiber, Bav. State Ch. and O, Sawallisch

Recorded live at the **Bavarian State Opera** in July 1971, the Orfeo performance consistently demonstrates the mastery of **Sawallisch** as a Strauss interpreter. The orchestral sound is atmospheric if rather thin, and stage noises are often intrusive, but one can still readily appreciate how perfectly Sawallisch paces the score. **Reri Grist** is a charming heroine, with the edge on her bright soprano making her the more compelling as a scold. **Kurt Böhme** right at the end of his long career sings most characterfully as the old man, Sir Morosus, with the supporting team consistently strong. An enjoyable alternative to Karl Boehm on DG. Disappointingly, no libretto is provided, only a synopsis.

COLLECTIONS

Arias from: (i) *Die Aegyptische Helena*; (ii) *Ariadne auf Naxos*; (i) *Die Frau ohne Schatten; Guntram; Der Rosenkavalier; Salome*. (iii) Lieder: *Allerseelen; Freundliche Vision; Schlangende hertzen; Wie Sollten wir geheim*

Ⓑ *** RCA 2-CD 74321 88687-2. L. Price; with (i) Boston SO or New Philh. O, Leinsdorf; (ii) LSO, Cleva; (iii) Garvey (piano) – PUCCINI: *Arias* ***

Leontyne Price, always at her finest in Strauss, here gives generous performances of an unusually rich collection of Strauss scenes and arias, strongly accompanied by Leinsdorf (or by Cleva in *Ariadne*). Recorded between 1965 and 1973, Price was still at her peak, even if occasionally the voice grows raw under stress in Strauss's heavier passages. It is particularly good to have rarities as well as such regular favourites as the Empress's awakening in *Die Frau ohne Schatten*, one of the finest of all the performances here. The four Lieder make an attractive encore, although no translations are provided, and the documentation is poor.

'Strauss's Heroines': Arabella, Act I: Duet. Capriccio: Moonlight Music and closing scene. Der Rosenkavalier, Act I: closing scene, Act III: Trio and finale

B⌐ *** Decca 466 314-2. Fleming, Bonney, Graham, VPO, Eschenbach

Under the title 'Strauss's heroines', this ravishing disc offers a generous collection of the most seductive scenes in the Strauss operas. In the end of Act I of *Rosenkavalier*, Renée Fleming and Susan Graham come near to matching the example of Elisabeth Schwarzkopf and Christa Ludwig as the Marschallin and Octavian. Then, sadly, the Act III Trio has Christoph Eschenbach opting for an absurdly sluggish speed, but the singing is superb, and so it is in the lovely duet between the sisters in *Arabella* and the magical closing scene of *Capriccio*, where Fleming is at her most moving. Opulent sound to match.

Arias and scenes from: Ariadne auf Naxos; Capriccio; Die Liebe der Danae; Salome

*** Orfeo C 511991A. Varady, Bamberg SO, Fischer-Dieskau

Recorded just before Julia Varady's retirement in 1999, still at the height of her powers, this wide-ranging collection of excerpts contains some of the most magnificent Strauss singing in years. The wonder is that any soprano can range so wide, while producing the most beautiful, full and even stream of sound, whether in the closing scene of *Salome*, in Ariadne's monologue and lament, in the heroine's big Act III solo from *Die Liebe der Danae* or as the Countess in the closing scene of *Capriccio*. Helped by the understanding conducting of her husband, Dietrich Fischer-Dieskau – who contributes a solitary line of singing as Major Domo at the end of *Capriccio* – she sings with consistent fervour. This Salome may not be as sinister as many in kissing the lips of John the Baptist – the sound is too beautiful for that – but the poise as well as the power and the detailed expressiveness are magnetic. Excellent sound to match.

STRAVINSKY, Igor (1882–1971)

The Stravinsky Edition: Vols. 1–7, Ballets, etc.: (i) *The Firebird;* (i) *Fireworks;* (iii) *Histoire du soldat;* (i) *Petrushka;* (iv, iii) *Renard the Fox;* (i) *The Rite of Spring;* (i) *Scherzo à la russe;* (ii) *Scherzo fantastique;* (v) *The Wedding* (Les Noces); (vi) *Agon;* (i) *Apollo;* (i) *Le Baiser de la fée;* (i) *Bluebird (pas de deux);* (vii) *Jeu*

de cartes; (viii) *Orphée;* (ix, i) *Pulcinella;* (ii) *Scènes de ballet.* Ballet suites: (i) *Firebird; Petrushka; Pulcinella*

Vols. 8/9, Symphonies: (i) *Symphony in E;* (ii) *Symphony in C;* (i) *Symphony in 3 movements;* (x, ii) *Symphony of Psalms;* (i) *Stravinsky in rehearsal: Apollo; Piano Concerto; Pulcinella; Sleeping Beauty; Symphony in C; 3 Souvenirs*

Vol. 10, Concertos: (xi, i) *Capriccio for Piano & Orchestra* (with Robert Craft); *Concerto for Piano & Wind;* (xii; i) *Movements for Piano & Orchestra;* (xiii; i) *Violin Concerto in D*

Vol. 11, Miniatures: (i) *Circus Polka; Concerto in D for String Orchestra; Concerto for Chamber Orchestra, 'Dumbarton Oaks';* (ii) *4 Etudes for Orchestra;* (i) *Greeting Prelude;* (ii) *8 Instrumental miniatures; 4 Norwegian moods; Suites 1–2 for Small Orchestra*

Vols. 12/13, Chamber music and historical recordings: (iii) *Concertino for 12 Instruments;* (xiv; xv) *Concerto for 2 solo Pianos;* (xv; xvi) *Duo concertante for Violin & Piano;* (xvii; xviii) *Ebony Concerto (for Clarinet & Big Band);* (iii) *Octet for Wind;* (xix; iii) *Pastorale for Violin & Wind Quartet;* (xv) *Piano Rag Music;* (xviii) *Preludium;* (xx; iii) *Ragtime (for 11 instruments);* (xv) *Serenade in A;* (iii) *Septet;* (xii) *Sonata for Piano;* (xxi) *Sonata for 2 Pianos;* (xviii) *Tango;* (xxii) *Wind Symphonies*

Vols. 14/15, Operas and songs: (xxiii; iii) *Cat's cradle songs;* (xxiii; xxiv) *Elegy for J. F. K.;* (xxv; ii) *Faun and shepherdess;* (xxvi; iii) *In memoriam Dylan Thomas;* (xxvii; iii) *3 Japanese Lyrics* (with Robert Craft); (xxvii; xxix) *The owl and the pussycat;* (xxvii; iii) *2 poems by K. Bal'mont;* (xxx; i) *2 poems of Paul Verlaine;* (xxiii; i) *Pribaoutki (peasant songs);* (xxiii; i) *Recollections of my childhood;* (xxviii; xxxi) *4 Russian songs;* (xxxvii) *4 Russian peasant songs;* (xxiii; iii) *3 songs from William Shakespeare;* (xxvii; i) *Tilim-Bom* (3 stories for children); (xxxii) *Mavra;* (xxxiii) *The Nightingale*

Vols. 16/17, (xxxiv) *The Rake's Progress*

Vols. 18/19, Oratorio and Melodrama: (xxxv; i) *The Flood* (with Robert Craft); (i) *Monumentum pro Gesualdo di Venosa* (3 madrigals recomposed for instruments); (vii) *Ode;* (xxxvi) *Oedipus Rex;* (xxxvii; xxxviii, i) *Perséphone*

Vols. 20/21, Sacred works: (x) *Anthem (the dove descending breaks the air);* (x) *Ave Maria;* (xxxix; x, i) *Babel;* (xxviii; xxvi; x, iii) *Cantata;* (xl) *Canticum sacrum;* (x; ii) *Credo;* (x, iii) *Introitus* (T. S. Eliot in

Memoriam); (xli) *Mass*; (x; i) *Pater noster*; (xlii; i) *A Sermon, a narrative & a prayer*; (xliii; i) *Threni*; (x, i) *Chorale*: Variations on: *Vom Himmel hoch, da komm ich her* (arr.); *Zvezdoliki*

Vols. 22, Robert Craft conducts: (xliv, i) *Abraham and Isaac*; (iii) *Danses concertantes*; (xlv) *Double Canon: Raoul Dufy in memoriam*; (xlvi) *Epitaphium*; (i) *Le Chant du rossignol* (symphonic poem); (i) *Orchestral Variations: Aldous Huxley in memoriam*; (xlvii) *Requiem Canticles*; (i) *Song of the Nightingale* (symphonic poem)

Complete Stravinsky Edition

🅱🅱 *** Sony 88697 103112 (22). (i) Columbia SO; (ii) CBC SO; (iii) Columbia CO; (iv) Shirley, Driscoll, Gramm, Koves; (v) Allen, Sarfaty, Driscoll, Barber, Copland, Foss, Sessions, American Chamber Ch., Hills, Columbia Percussion Ens.; (vi) Los Angeles Festival SO; (vii) Cleveland O; (viii) Chicago SO; (ix) Jordan, Shirley, Gramm; (x) Festival Singers of Toronto, Iseler; (xi) Entremont; (xii) Rosen; (xiii) Stern; (xiv) Soulima Stravinsky; (xv) Igor Stravinsky; (xvi) Szigeti; (xvii) Goodman; (xviii) Columbia Jazz Ens.; (xix) Baker; (xx) Koves; (xxi) Gold, Fizdale; (xxii) N. W. German RSO; (xxiii) Berberian; (xxiv) Howland, Kreiselman, Russo; (xxv) Simmons; (xxvi) Young; (xxvii) Lear; (xxviii) Albert; (xxix) Craft; (xxx) Gramm; (xxxi) Di Tullio, Remsen, Almeida; (xxxii) Belinck, Simmons, Rideout, Kolk; (xxxiii) Driscoll, Grist, Picassi, Smith, Beattie, Gramm, Kolk, Murphy, Kaiser, Bonazzi, Washington, D. C., Op. Society Ch. & O; (xxxiv) Young, Raskin, Reardon, Sarfaty, Miller, Manning, Garrard, Tracey, Tilney, Sadler's Wells Op. Ch., Baker, RPO; (xxxv) Harvey, Cabot, Lanchester, Reardon, Oliver, Tripp, Robinson, Columbia SO Ch., Smith; (xxxvi) Westbrook (nar.), Shirley, Verrett, Gramm, Reardon, Driscoll, Chester Watson Ch., Washington, D. C., Op. Society O; (xxxvii) Gregg Smith Singers, Smith; (xxxviii) Zorina, Molese, Ithaca College Concert Ch., Fort Worth Texas Boys' Ch.; (xxxix) Calicos (nar.); (xl) Robinson, Chitjian, Los Angeles Festival Ch. & SO; (xli) Baxter, Albert, Gregg Smith Singers, Columbia Symphony Winds & Brass; (xlii) Verrett, Driscoll, Hornton (nar.); (xliii) Beardslee, Krebs, Lewis, Wainner, Morgan, Oliver, Schola Cantorum, Ross; all cond. composer. (xliv) Frisch; (xlv) Baker, Igleman, Schonbach, Neikrug; (xlvi) Anderson, Bonazzi, Bressler, Gramm, Ithaca College Concert Ch., Gregg Smith; cond. Craft

On these 22 budget-price discs you have the unique archive of recordings which **Stravinsky** left of his own music. Almost all the performances are conducted by the composer, with a few at the very end of his career – like the magnificent *Requiem canticles* – left to **Robert Craft** to conduct, with the composer supervising. In addition there is a handful of recordings of works otherwise not covered, mainly chamber pieces. With some recordings of Stravinsky talking and in rehearsal (included in the box devoted to the symphonies) it makes a vivid portrait.

Of the major ballets, *Petrushka* and *The Firebird* are valuable, but *The Rite* is required listening: it has real savagery

and astonishing electricity. (It is also available in a separate issue – see below.) The link between *Jeu de cartes* from the mid-1930s and Stravinsky's post-war opera *The Rake's Progress* is striking, and Stravinsky's sharp-edged conducting style underlines it, while the *Scènes de ballet* certainly have their attractive moments. If *Orpheus* has a powerful atmosphere, *Apollo* is one of Stravinsky's most gravely beautiful scores, while *Agon* is one of the most stimulating of Stravinsky's later works, and here the orchestra respond with tremendous alertness and enthusiasm to Stravinsky's direction. The recording of *Le Baiser de la fée* is a typical CBS balance with forward woodwind. However the splendid performance overcomes such a technical drawback. Stravinsky's recording of *Pulcinella* includes the vocal numbers, while in the orchestra the clowning of the trombone and the humour generally is strikingly vivid and never too broad. Similarly with the chamber scoring of the suite from *The Soldier's Tale*, the crisp, clear reading brings out the underlying intense emotion of the music with its nagging, insistent little themes. There is a ruthlessness in the composer's own reading of *Les Noces* which exactly matches its primitive Russian feeling, and as the performance goes on so one senses the added alertness and enthusiasm of the performers. *Renard* is a curious work, a sophisticated fable which here receives too unrelenting a performance. The voices are very forward and tend to drown the instrumentalists.

In the early *Symphony in E flat*, Op. 1, the young Stravinsky's material may be comparatively conventional, but in this definitive performance the music springs to life. Each movement has its special delights to outweigh any shortcomings, while in the *Symphony in Three Movements* Stravinsky shows how, by vigorous, forthright treatment of the notes, the emotion implicit is made all the more compelling. The **Columbia Symphony** plays superbly and the recording is full and brilliant. Stravinsky never quite equalled the intensity of the pre-war 78-r.p.m. performance of the *Symphony of Psalms*, but the later, stereo version is still impressive. It is just that, with so vivid a work, it is a shade disappointing to find Stravinsky as interpreter at less than maximum voltage. Even so, the closing section of the work is very beautiful and compelling. The CD transfers of the American recordings are somewhat monochrome by modern standards but fully acceptable.

The iron-fingered touch of **Philippe Entremont** has something to be said for it in the *Capriccio for Piano and Wind*, but this performance conveys too little of the music's charm. The *Movements for Piano and Orchestra* with the composer conducting could hardly be more compelling. **Stern's** memorable account of the *Violin Concerto in D* adds a romantic perspective to the framework. But an expressive approach to Stravinsky works marvellously when the composer is there to provide the bedrock under the expressive cantilena.

The *Dumbarton Oaks Concerto* with its obvious echoes of Bach's *Brandenburgs* is one of the most warmly attractive of Stravinsky's neoclassical works, all beautifully played and acceptably recorded. The *Octet for Wind* of 1924 comes out with surprising freshness and if the *Ragtime* could be more lighthearted, Stravinsky gives the impression of knowing what he wants. The *Ebony Concerto*, in this version conducted by the composer, may have little of 'swung' rhythm, but it is completely faithful to Stravinsky's deadpan approach to jazz.

In *Le Rossignol* the singing is not always on a par with the conducting, but it is always perfectly adequate and the recording is brilliant and immediate. *Mavra* is sung in Russian and, as usual, the soloists – who are good – are too closely balanced, but the performance has punch and authority and on the whole the CD quality is fully acceptable. The songs represent a fascinating collection of trifles, chips from the master's workbench dating from the earliest years. There are many incidental delights, not least those in which the magnetic **Cathy Berberian** is featured.

The Rake's Progress has never since been surpassed. **Alexander Young's** assumption of the title-role is a marvellous achievement, sweet-toned, accurate and well characterized. In the choice of other principals, too, it is noticeable what store Stravinsky set by vocal precision. **Judith Raskin** makes an appealing Anne Trulove, **John Reardon** is remarkable more for vocal accuracy than for striking characterization, but **Regina Sarfaty's** Baba is marvellous on both counts. The **Sadler's Wells Chorus** sings with great drive under the composer, and the **Royal Philharmonic** play with warmth and a fittingly Mozartian sense of style to match Stravinsky's surprisingly lyrical approach to his score. The CDs offer excellent sound and are available separately.

The *Cantata* of 1952 is a transitional piece between Stravinsky's tonal and serial periods. However, of the two soloists, **Alexander Young** is much more impressive than **Adrienne Albert**, for her voice brings an unformed choirboy sound somehow married to wide vibrato. The *Canticum sacrum* includes music that some listeners might find tough (the strictly serial choral section). But the performance is a fine one and the tenor solo from **Richard Robinson** is very moving. The Bach *Chorale Variations* has a synthetic modernity that recalls the espresso bar, though one which still reveals underlying mastery. The *Epitaphium* and the *Double canon* are miniatures, dating from the composer's serial period, but the *Canon* is deliberately euphonious.

The *Mass* is a work of the greatest concentration, a quality that comes out strongly if one plays this performance immediately after *The Flood*, with its inevitably slack passages. As directed in the score, trebles are used here, and it is a pity that the engineers have not brought them further forward: their sweet, clear tone is sometimes lost among the lower strands. In *The Flood*, originally written for television, it is difficult to take the bald narrations seriously, particularly when **Laurence Harvey** sanctimoniously keeps talking of the will of 'Gud'. The performance of *Oedipus Rex*, too, is not one of the highlights of the set. *Perséphone*, however, is full of that cool lyricism that marks much of Stravinsky's music inspired by classical myths. As with many of these vocal recordings, the balance is too close, and various orchestral solos are highlighted.

Of the items recorded by **Robert Craft**, the *Requiem canticles* stands out, the one incontrovertible masterpiece among the composer's very last serial works and one of the most deeply moving works ever written in the serial idiom. Even more strikingly than in the *Mass* of 1948, Stravinsky

conveys his religious feelings with a searing intensity. The *Aldous Huxley Variations* are more difficult to comprehend but have similar intensity. Valuable, too, is the ballad *Abraham and Isaac*.

Agon; Apollo (complete ballets); Symphony in 3 Movements; The Firebird (ballet): Finale

Ⓝ(****) BBC mono BBCL 4253-2 BBC SO, composer

This is a recorded broadcast, made in the Royal Festival Hall on 10 December 1958, during the composer's visit to London. Stravinsky felt great trepidation about the event: 'two very difficult works never played by the BBC Orchestra which take much time to rehearse'. But the concert came up trumps, especially the very beautiful account of *Apollo*, one of the composer's most inspired later works. The more intractable serial work, *Agon*, not everybody's favourite, also came off well, as did the colourful and vibrant *Symphony in 3 Movements*. The recording is mono but very faithful to the BBC strings in *Apollo*.

Apollo (Apollon musagète); Le Baiser de la fée (complete; ballet & Divertimento); (i) Capriccio for Piano & Orchestra; Concerto for Piano & Wind Instruments; Le Chant du rossignol; Circus Polka; 4 Etudes; The Firebird (complete; ballet); Petrushka (1911 version; complete); Pulcinella (suite and (ii) complete ballet); Rite of Spring; Scherzo à la russe; Soldier's Tale (suite); Suites 1 & 2; Symphony in C; Symphony in 3 Movements; Symphonies of Wind Instruments; (iii) Les Noces (ballet-cantata); (iv) Symphony of Psalms; (v) Mavra; (vi) Renard

Ⓑ **(*) Decca (ADD) 467 818-2 (8) SRO, Ansermet; with
(i) Magaloff; (ii) Tyler, Franzini, Carmeli; (iii) Retchitzka, Devallier, Cuénod, Rehfuss, Diakoff, Geneva Motet Ch.;
(iv) Choeur des Jeunes & Ch. of R. Lausanne; (v) Carlyle, Watts, Sinclair, Macdonald; (vi) English, Mitchinson, Glossop, Rouleau

Having begun his Stravinsky recordings for Decca during the days of ffrr 78s, **Ansermet** finally undertook his major survey with the coming of stereo. *Apollon Musagète*, the complete *Firebird* ballet and the two *Piano Concertos* – with **Nikita Magaloff** in fine form – date from as early as 1955, yet the recording still sounds remarkably well, and if in the concertante works Ansermet's direction lacks some of the bite and sharp wit that this neoclassical music needs, they follow an authentic tradition from Parisian music-making between the wars.

The Firebird was highly praised by us for its clarity of detail when it first appeared, although we commented on the lack of body to the upper strings. Undoubtedly Ansermet's later Philharmonia recording (not included here) is finer still, better played and with richer sound, but this remains impressive for its time.

Le Chant du rossignol and the *Pulcinella Ballet Suite* followed in 1956, both showing Ansermet at his interpretative best. The recordings, too, were considered demonstration-worthy in their day, with *The Song of the Nightingale* showing how clearly and beautifully Decca could cope with a big

Stravinsky orchestra, while *Pulcinella* showed even more impressively how a small chamber group of instruments could be projected with vivid realism.

The 1957 *Petrushka* also set high standards of clarity and vividness, although the Swiss violins were not flattered by the close microphones and, fine as it was, Ansermet's performance did not quite match his earlier 78 version (available in a fine Dutton transfer – see below) in dramatic and emotional vividness. It was soon to be upstaged by Dorati's famous Mercury version. *The Rite of Spring*, however, recorded in the same year, was a performance of great integrity. Ansermet's scrupulous insistence on maintaining the score's natural balance brought an awe-inspiring relentlessness and a wild primitive beauty.

In 1960 came the *Symphony in C*, strongly played, and often incisive, but the companion *Symphony in Three Movements* lacks a feeling of strong rhythmic vitality, and is without the fullest impetus. However, the clean stylish account of *The Soldier's Tale*, given (1961) sound of tingling immediacy, is matched by the fine performance of the haunting *Symphonies for Wind Instruments*, where Ansermet's warmth more than compensates for any lack of tautness.

The *Quatre Etudes* (from 1962) have considerable subtlety, and the *Suites* are enjoyable in a spontaneous, extrovert way. Both show the lighter side of Stravinsky, and Ansermet plays them with spirit and style. However, there is something curiously heavy and lethargic about his account of the *Symphony of Psalms*, even though this account is better than the earlier version on 78s (see Dutton reissue below). Fortunately the well-projected recording adds sharpness to a reading which might otherwise have sounded flat.

In *Les Noces*, recorded that same year, Ansermet fails to capture the essential bite in Stravinsky's sharply etched portrait of a peasant wedding. The hammered rhythms must sound ruthless and here they are merely tame. This was followed with complete versions of *Le Baiser de la fée* (in 1963), and *Pulcinella* (with vocal numbers) in 1965, neither of which was as successful as the earlier recordings of the *Fairy's Kiss Divertimento* and the *Pulcinella Ballet Suite*, primarily because of moments of slackness and under-par orchestral playing. However, yet again Ansermet's warmth and the splendidly vivid recording help to project the music in spite of the inadequacies of the playing.

The series culminated in 1964 with *Mavra* and *Renard* (where one enjoys the clear English). Both were a great success, vividly performed and brilliantly recorded. Here more than usual Ansermet caught the sort of toughness one recognizes in the composer's own performances of his music, and the haunting yet light-hearted *Scherzo à la russe*, with its bouncing main theme, is a splendid bonus.

(i) *Apollo*; (ii) *The Firebird*; *Petrushka* (1911 score); *The Rite of Spring* (ballets; complete)

🔊 💥 (B) ***** Ph. Duo (ADD) 438 350-2 (2). (i) LSO, Markevitch; (ii) LPO, Haitink

Apollo (*Apollon musagète*) (1947 version); *Firebird: Suite* (1945 version); *Jeu de cartes*; *Petrushka* (1947 version); *The Rite of Spring*

(B) **(*) Double Decca 473 731-2 (2). Concg. O, or Cleveland O; Chailly

Apollo; *Orpheus* (ballets)

🔊 *** ASV CDDCA 618. O of St John's, Lubbock

The ASV issue offers an ideal coupling, with refined performances and excellent recording. The delicacy of the rhythmic pointing in *Apollo* gives special pleasure, and there is a first-rate solo violin contribution from **Richard Deakin**.

Markevitch's gravely beautiful reading of *Apollon musagète* here comes with **Haitink's** strikingly refined account of the other key ballets. In *The Firebird* the sheer savagery of *Katshchei's Dance* may be a little muted, but the sharpness of attack and clarity of detail make for a thrilling result, while the magic and poetry of the whole score are given a hypnotic beauty. In *Petrushka* the rhythmic feeling is strong, especially in the Second Tableau and the finale, where the fairground bustle is vivid. The natural, unforced quality of Haitink's *Rite* also brings real compulsion. Other versions may hammer the listener more powerfully, thrust him or her along more forcefully; but the bite and precision of the **LPO** playing here are most impressive, as throughout the set, while the recording's firm definition and the well-proportioned and truthful aural perspective make it a joy to listen to. Outstanding value.

The Double Decca anthology is rather more notable for Decca's demonstration-quality sound than for **Chailly's** interpretations, but the orchestral playing itself remains outstanding throughout. In this somewhat indulgent reading of *Apollo*, the score's refined neoclassicism is muted in favour of opulent warmth, and some of the ballet's rhythmic profile is lost, especially in the celebrated *Pas de deux*, which is far more voluptuous here than with Karajan. Chailly is more naturally at home revelling in the rich Rimskian colours of the extended 1945 *Firebird Suite*, which includes the delectable *Pantomimes*. The explosive entry of *Katshchei* is riveting and the expansive finale could not be more voluptuous.

Jeu de cartes, recorded in 1996, is released here for the first time. The performance is impressive. Chailly's *Petrushka* is vividly characterized, and he brings a genuine pathos to Petrushka's cell scene. The Decca engineers provide glittering detail, yet make full use of the warm **Concertgebouw** ambience. With speeds faster than usual – markedly so in Part Two – Chailly's taut and urgent reading of *The Rite of Spring* is gripping throughout, and bass-drum enthusiasts will find that it plays its part with a precision and resonance to startle the listener. If, with Chailly's urgent pacing in Part Two, there is less contrast than usual in the final *Sacrificial Dance*, there is no doubting the intrinsic power of the reading overall. Moreover, Decca have given it sufficient cueing points for the first time. For audiophiles, this collection is a real Stravinskian bargain: the second CD lasts over 81 minutes.

(i–ii) *Le Baiser de la fée* (ballet; complete); (i; iii) *Ode*; (iv) *Symphonies of Wind Instruments*; (i; ii) *Symphony in E flat, Op. 1*; (i; iii) *Symphony in C*; *Symphony in 3 Movements*

☞ ⓑ *** Chan. 2-for-1 ADD/DDD 241-8 (2). (i) RSNO; (ii) Järvi; (iii) Gibson; (iv) Nash Ens., Rattle

Le Baiser de la fée (divertimento)

☞ **** Pentatone **SACD** Surround Sound PTC 5186 061. Russian Nat. O, Jurowski – TCHAIKOVSKY: Suite 3 ***

(i) Le Baiser de la fée (divertimento); Le Chant du rossignol; (ii) Dumbarton Oaks Concerto; (iii) Petrushka (1911); The Rite of Spring

ⓑ **(*) RCA 2CD stereo/mono 74321 84609-2. (i) Chicago SO, Reiner; (ii) NDR SO, Wand; (iii) Boston SO, Monteux

On Chandos Strauss's deft scoring of Le Baiser de la fée is a constant delight, much of it on a chamber-music scale; and its delicacy, wit and occasional pungency are fully appreciated by **Järvi**, who secures a wholly admirable response from his Scottish Orchestra. The ambience seems exactly right, bringing out wind and brass colours vividly. As for the symphonies, even when compared with the composer's own versions, the performances by the **Royal Scottish Orchestra** – in excellent form under **Sir Alexander Gibson** – stand up well, with Järvi directing the early E flat work equally impressively. The vivid naturalness of the splendid 1982 digital recordings compensates for any slight lack of bite. The cool, almost whimsical beauty of the Andante of the Symphony in Three Movements is most subtly conveyed, and the inner movements of the Symphony in C are beautifully played. Moreover the **Nash Ensemble's** perceptive account of the Symphonies of Wind Instruments under **Rattle** does not let the side down. It is good to have also as a bonus the Ode in memory of Natalia Koussevitzky, which has an extrovert, rustic Scherzo section framed by short elegies.

The young Russian **Vladimir Jurowski** offers performances of both works that are as near ideal as one can imagine, electric in tension to give the illusion of live music-making. In the Stravinsky Divertimento, Jurowski steers a nice course between bringing out the romantic warmth of the Tchaikovsky sources from which Stravinsky took his material (songs and piano pieces) and the neoclassical element in his style of the 1920s. So the chugging rhythms on horns in the most memorable section of the second movement convey jollity in their springing step, while the pointing of contrasts in the final Pas de deux, the longest of the four movements, brings yearning warmth in the big lyrical moments and wit in the faster sections. Exceptionally vivid sound, recorded by Pentatone's Dutch engineers in Moscow, which sounds superb in surround sound.

Reiner's Chicago recordings of Le Baiser de la fée and Le Chant du rossignol are legendary. The latter is praised below, where it is coupled with Rimsky's Scheherazade; the equally delightful Fairy's Kiss Divertimento has character and life as well as much charm, with the Pas de deux beautifully done. The overall performance has great atmosphere, with distinguished woodwind and brass contributions, helped by the astonishingly vivid 1958 Chicago recording. Wand's hardly less engaging account of the Dumbarton Oaks Concerto, played with great geniality and finesse, is also most naturally recorded in an attractive acoustic.

For Petrushka and The Rite of Spring RCA have turned to **Monteux**, who conducted the première of the latter. But not to his Paris Conservatoire stereo performances. Instead they have chosen the alternative **Boston** versions, which are much better played. The Rite dates from 1951 and is mono, with a recording which harshens at climaxes. But the performance powerfully captures the wild intensity of the ballet's violent pagan ritual, and, just as tellingly, projects the hauntingly mysterious evocation of the opening of the second part.

The Boston recording of Petrushka is stereo and dates from 1959. There is still an edge to the sound at climaxes, but the Boston acoustic adds its ambient glow throughout, and the performance is extremely lively, with memorable solo contributions in the central tableaux and a particularly exciting and dramatic account of the final scene, all the bustle of the Shrovetide carnival brilliantly conveyed.

(i) Capriccio for piano and orchestra; Concerto for Piano and Orchestra; Movements for piano and orchestra. Piano Music: Les cinq doigts; 4 Études, Op. 7; 3 Movements from Petrushka; Piano-Rag Music; Scherzo; Serenade in A; Sonata for Piano (1924); Sonata in F sharp min.; Souvenir d'une marche boche; Tango; Valse pour les enfants.

☞ ⓑ **** EMI Gemini (ADD) 5 86073-2 (2) Michel Béroff; (i) Orchestre de Paris, Ozawa

This classic set comes from the 1970s when **Béroff** was astonishing the musical world with his dazzling virtuosity and musicianship. Although most of this repertoire is well represented on disc, this issue remains a highly satisfying and competitive one, still a first choice. The three Concertos (or rather two concertos and a capriccio) are also first rate and well accompanied by **Seiji Ozawa** and the **Orchestre de Paris**.

(i–ii) Capriccio for Piano & Orchestra; (iii) Jeu de cartes; (iv) Danses concertantes; (ii) Scènes de Ballet; (v) Variations

ⓑⓑ *** Naxos 8.557506. (i) Wait; (ii) O of St Luke's; (iii) Philh. O; (iv) 20th Century Classics Ens.; (v) LPO; all cond. Craft

The Jeu de cartes with the **Philharmonia Orchestra** is exhilarating and gives much pleasure. Probably the best thing on the disc is Scènes de Ballet, which has rarely been given with greater charm and wit. Very good sound.

Le Chant du rossignol (Song of the Nightingale) (symphonic poem – see also The Firebird)

☞ ✿ Ⓜ *** DG (ADD) 449 769-2 (2). Berlin RSO, Maazel – RAVEL: L'heure espagnole; L'enfant et les sortilèges; RIMSKY-KORSAKOV: Capriccio espagnol ***

☞ Ⓜ *** RCA SACD (ADD) 82876 66377-2. Chicago SO, Reiner – RIMSKY-KORSAKOV: Scheherazade *** ✿

Le Chant du rossignol, which Stravinsky made from the material of his opera, deserves a much more established place in the concert repertoire. **Maazel** is nothing if not dramatic, but above all he revels in the glittering orchestral detail and the marvellous atmosphere this score commands. The **Berlin Radio Orchestra** produces a feast of chimerical glowing colours, and the DG engineers of the time surpassed themselves. It is well coupled with Ravel's two delightful neoclassical operas and Maazel's superb Berlin Philharmonic version of Rimsky-Korsakov's *Capriccio espagnol* from the same period.

On its new SACD format **Reiner's** 1956 *Chant du rossignol* brings astonishingly vivid sound, full of presence, an excellent coupling for his strong and dramatic reading of *Scheherazade*. Where this transitional work – composed over two separate periods – can seem lacking something in thrust, Reiner's virile, sharply focused reading relates it more clearly to the *Rite of Spring*. The virtuosity of the playing and the clarity of the direction are arresting, while the glittering detail of the orchestral palette in the work's five titled (and here cued) closing sections is most evocative.

Le Chant du rossignol

(N) **(*) Häns. CD.93234. SW German RSO, Bour –
TCHAIKOVSKY: *Sleeping Beauty: Suite*, etc. **(*)

Le Chant du rossignol is drawn from Stravinsky's early opera, *Le Rossignol*, making an attractive filler for the Tchaikovsky suites. Excellent performances, with **Ernest Bour** making one of his last appearances before his death.

Le Chant du rossignol; Firebird Suite

*** DG 477 7175. NYPO, Maazel – RAVEL: *Daphnis et Chloé: Suite 2; Rapsodie espagnole* ***

Recorded live at the Avery Fisher Hall, this recording points the way to the future, as it comes from digital downloads taken from New York concerts. The sound is spectacular, *Le Chant du rossignol* very crisply detailed, if a littler close, but the *Firebird* is in the demonstration bracket, very naturally balanced indeed. It is a superb performance, dramatic and full of warmth and colour, with the finale beginning with a magical *pianissimo* and building to a magnificent climax.

(i) Concerto for Piano and Wind; Fireworks (DVD version)

⟿ *** Arthaus DVD 100 314. (i) Toradze; Rotterdam PO, Gergiev (with DEBUSSY – *Le Martyre de Saint-Sébastien* ***) (Dir: Rob van der Berg, V/D: Peter Rump) – PROKOFIEV: *Scythian Suite, Op. 20* (with Rehearsal) ***

Alexander Toradze is as impressive an exponent of Stravinsky as he was of the Prokofiev concertos he recorded with Gergiev and the Kirov Orchestra for Philips, and while the main interest of this DVD is the Prokofiev coupling, this well-planned concert is very rewarding throughout and stimulating to watch.

Concerto for Piano & Wind

(***) British Music Society mono BMS 101 CDH. Mewton-Wood, Hague Residentie O, Goehr – BLISS: *Concerto* ***; SHOSTAKOVICH: *Piano Concerto 1* (***)

Edward Sackville-West placed this record as one of two recordings that serve as the 'best memorial of his [**Mewton-Wood's**] style', and certainly the partnership here with **Walter Goehr** is very impressive indeed. It is the central *Largo* one especially remembers, wonderfully cool and beautiful, immediately offset by the brilliance of the finale. The recording

of the piano is very good, and the orchestra has more body than in the Bliss coupling.

Concerto for Strings in D

(M) *** DG (ADD) 447 435-2. BPO, Karajan – HONEGGER: *Symphonies 2–3* ***

Karajan's version of the *Concerto in D for Strings* – written within a few months of the Honegger *Symphonie Liturgique*, with which it is coupled – may strike some listeners as not quite acerbic or biting enough, but the finesse and lightness of touch of the Berlin strings and their rhythmic legerdemain are a delight. The recording is first class.

(i) Concerto in D for Strings; Danses concertantes; Dumbarton Oaks Concerto in E flat; 4 Etudes; (ii) 4 Norwegian Moods; (iii) Orchestral Suites 1–2. Chamber music: (iv) Concertino for 12 instruments; Epitaphium; L'Histoire du soldat (suite for violin, clarinet and piano); Octet; Ragtime; Pastorale; 3 Pieces for Solo Clarinet; Septet; (v) Concerto for 2 Pianos

⟿ (B) **** Double Decca (DDD/ADD) 473 810-2 (2). (i) Montreal SO, Dutoit; (ii) Cleveland O, Chailly; (iii) SRO, Ansermet; (iv) European Soloists Ens., Ashkenazy; (v) Ashkenazy & Gavrilov

Apart from the two *Suites for Orchestra*, which **Ansermet** recorded in 1961, these performances come from various times between 1987 and 1996 and, apart from their musical excellence, are superbly recorded. Of particular value is the *Concerto for Two Pianos*, written in the early 1930s, with **Ashkenazy** and **Gavrilov**. The **European Soloists** are a first-class group who give wonderfully alert and vital accounts of the *Octet* and the *Concertino for Twelve Instruments*. **Dutoit** and his Montreal players are on very good form, too, in the *Dumbarton Oaks Concerto* and the *Danse concertantes*. In every respect this collection cannot be recommended too highly.

Violin Concerto in D

⟿ (M) **** Decca (ADD) 425 003-2. Chung, LSO, Previn – PROKOFIEV: *Violin Concertos 1–2* ****

⟿ (M) **** Sony SMK 87996. Lin, LAPO, Salonen – PROKOFIEV: *Violin Concertos 1–2* ****

(M) *** Warner Elatus 2564 6572-2. Perlman, Chicago SO, Barenboim – PROKOFIEV: *Violin Concerto 2* ***

(M) *** DG 477 5376. Mutter, Philh., Paul Sacher – BARTÓK: *Violin Concerto 2* **(*); DUTILLEUX: *Sur le même accord* ***

(M) *** DG (ADD) 447 445-2. Perlman, Boston SO, Ozawa – BERG: *Concerto*; RAVEL: *Tzigane* ***

*** Sony SK 89649. Hahn, ASMF, Marriner – BRAHMS: *Violin Concerto* ***

Kyung-Wha Chung is at her most incisive in the spicily swaggering outer movements which, with **Previn's** help, are presented here in all their distinctiveness, tough and witty at the same time. In the two movements labelled *Aria*, Chung brings fantasy as well as lyricism, conveying an inner, brooding quality.

As in the two Prokofiev concertos, so in the Stravinsky

Cho-Liang Lin plays with power and warmth, while **Salonen** terraces the accompaniments dramatically, with woodwind and brass bold and full. The Prokofiev coupling is outstanding too.

Perlman's Warner performance, recorded live in 1994, is more compelling than his earlier studio recording, with **Barenboim** adding to the urgency and energy. Far more Stravinskian wit is conveyed in the outer movements, with rhythms more bouncy and with phrasing more seductively individual.

DG restore **Anne-Sophie Mutter's** brilliant 1988 account of the Stravinsky and her 1991 Bartók to circulation, coupling it with a new work by Dutilleux. The recording is spacious and well focused with Ms Mutter not too prominently placed in the aural picture. A very good performance and recommended alongside though not necessarily in preference to Kyung-Wha Chung, Cho-Liang Lin and Perlman.

Perlman's precision, remarkable in both concertos on the DG disc, underlines the neoclassical element in the outer movements of the Stravinsky, while the two *Aria* movements are more deeply felt and expressive. The balance favours the soloist, but no one will miss the commitment of the **Boston orchestra's** playing, vividly recorded. The Ravel *Tzigane* has now been added for good measure.

The opening of **Hilary Hahn's** reading of the Stravinsky *Concerto* is the more striking in its power because of the close balance of the violin, intensifying the impact of the very fast tempo she adopts. Her playing is phenomenal in its precision, but anyone used to more conventional readings such as Chung's will find it sounding very hectic. Hahn, needless to say, in the two arias brings out the full meditative depth of the music. The result is to underline the toughness of the work.

(i) *Violin Concerto; The Rite of Spring*

Ⓜ (**) Medici Masters mono MM020-2. (i) Grumiaux; Cologne RSO, Fricsay – BARTÓK: *Divertimento for Strings* (**)

These recordings on Medici Masters come from the early 1950s, so audiophiles should be warned. **Fricsay's** *Rite* and the **Bartók** *Divertimento* are somewhat special, very fresh and authentic in feeling, and, of course, **Grumiaux** was a marvellously aristocratic artist.

Dumbarton Oaks Concerto; 8 Instrumental Miniatures; (i) *Ebony Concerto*

Ⓜ *** DG (ADD) 447 405-2. (i) Arrignon; Ens. InterContemporain, Boulez – BERG: *Chamber Concerto* ***

The playing of the **Ensemble InterContemporain** is very brilliant indeed. There is much to enjoy in these performances, which are spiced with the right kind of wit and keenness of edge, and even those who do not normally respond to **Boulez's** conducting will be pleasantly surprised with the results he obtains here.

(i) *The Firebird;* (ii) *Orpheus;* (i) *Petrushka* (1947 version); *The Rite of Spring* (ballets; complete)

Ⓜ **(*) Ph. 464 744-2 (2) (i) Concg. O; (ii) LSO, C. Davis

An outstanding set. **Sir Colin Davis** directs a magically evocative account of the complete *Firebird,* helped not just by the playing of the **Concertgebouw Orchestra** (the strings outstandingly fine) but by the ambience of the hall, which allows inner clarity, yet gives a bloom to the sound, open and spacious, superbly coordinated. Similarly the Philips recording of *Petrushka* (although not so well balanced as *Firebird*) reveals details of the rich texture that are often obscured.

Davis has his idiosyncrasies in *The Rite of Spring* (one of them his strange hold-up on the last chord), but generally he takes a direct view and the result is strong, forthright and powerful. *Orpheus* is much less frequently heard and even Davis's excellent account cannot create a richness of colour to match its companions. The recording is warm and very natural, if not so lustrous at those made in the Concertgebouw, but that is partly the effect of the composer's scoring.

(i) *The Firebird* (ballet; complete; choreography: Mikhail Fokine); (ii) *Les Noces* (choreography: Bronislava Nijinska; (DVD versions)

🔑 ✿ **** Opus Arte **DVD** OA 0832 D. (i) Benjamin, Cope, Rosato, Drew; (ii) Yanowsky, Pickering and members of Royal Ballet; ROHCG O, or 4 Pianos, cond. Carewe. (V/D: Ross MacGibbon.)

A moving and well-directed visual record, totally free from attention-seeking camerawork, brings these two marvellous ballets in their original choreography back to life, as if one had the privilege of visiting Diaghilev's Ballets Russes. The dancing is of the highest standard, led by **Leanne Benjamin's** Firebird, and costumes and sets are visually equally memorable. There are two important bonuses, in addition to the rehearsal footage. Those who have treasured their TV recordings of Stravinsky's own appearance with the **New Philharmonia Orchestra** at the Royal Festival Hall in 1965 when he was 83 will cherish the DVD transfer, which has much-enhanced definition, both visually and aurally. Finally there is a hilarious description by **David Drew** of Nijinska's visit to Covent Garden to mount *Les noces* in the late 1960s.

The Firebird; Petrushka (ballets; complete with choreography by Michael Fokine and costumes and sets adapted from the original Ballets Russes production by Anatoly and Anna Nezhny; DVD versions)

🔑 ✿ **** Decca **DVD** 079 322-9. Nina Ananiashvili, Andris Liepa, Ekatrina Liepa, Victor Yeremenko, Tatiana Beltskaya, Gediminas Taranda Bolshoi, Sergey Petukhov, Vitaly Breusnko, State Academic Theatre O, Andrey Chistiakov (Dir: Andris Liepa) – RIMSKY-KORSAKOV: *Scheherazade* ***

Both the authentic **Bolshoi** productions of *The Firebird* and *Petrushka* are very spectacular indeed, as are the costumes and sets. The presentation is vividly and colourfully handled, and **Nina Ananiashvili** is a truly sparkling Firebird, dancing very gracefully. The handsome Prince Ivan, **Andris Liepa** (who later transforms himself into the puppet, Petrushka), has little to do but be resourcful and court his beautiful Princess. The entry of Katshchei (**Sergey Petukhov**) is truly demonic: the grotesque make-up and bizarre costumes create a gothically evil atmosphere, and he is a wonderfully malignant ogre. When the Prince finds the huge golden egg that contains Katshchei's soul and smashes it, all the stone images around become human again and can be the guests at Ivan's wedding to the most radiant tune of all.

In *Petrushka* the opening Shovetide Fair scene fills the huge Bolshoi stage with myriad different characters and vividly colourful events, all happening simultaneously; but at the centre is the Magician/Showman's stage, from which Petrushka, the Moor and the Ballerina emerge to dance into the audience. The drama of Petrushka's unrequited love for the Ballerina, who prefers the Moor, begins almost immediately and reaches its peak in Petrushka's cell. This is the one miscalculation of the production, for the cell scene is not nearly claustrophobic enough. However, Andris Liepa is a very touching Petrushka, and his murder (and the puppet substitution) is effectively managed, while the final ghost appearance is splendidly dramatic. Both ballets are entertaining to watch, but one continually reflects that Stravinsky's music is far, far greater and more imaginative than the choreography.

The Firebird (ballet; complete; DVD version)

*** TDK **DVD** DV-VPOVG. VPO, Gergiev (includes Gergiev talking on Prokofiev and Stravinsky) (Dir and V/D: Brian Large) – PROKOFIEV: *Symphony 1 (Classical), Op. 25*; SCHNITTKE: *Viola Concerto* ***

This is, of course, not the performed ballet as above, but an orchestral performance of Stravinsky's glittering score, filmed at the Salzburg Festival in 2000. **Gergiev** has an excellent rapport with his players and the performance is most impressive, both musically and, thanks to an excellent balance, aurally. The complete score is recorded here, and if there are times when one feels Gergiev could give his players just a little more time (the *Dance of the Princesses*), this is still a very fine reading, with superb playing from the Viennese. The performance is enhanced by the visual direction which, as so often with **Brian Large**, directs the listener's eyes where his ears want them to be. The sound itself is extremely vivid.

The Firebird (ballet; complete; CD versions)

⊕ *** Ph. 446 715-2. Kirov O, Gergiev – SCRIABIN: *Prometheus* ***

(*) Australian Decca Eloquence 476 2700. VPO, Dohnányi – BARTÓK: *Two Portraits, Op. 5.* *

The Firebird (ballet; complete); Le Chant du Rossignol; Fireworks; Scherzo à la russe; Tango

⊕ ✹ Ⓜ **** Mercury (ADD) 432 012-2. LSO, Dorati

Mercury's electrifying 1959 version of *The Firebird* is perhaps **Dorati's** finest recording, and one of the great recordings of all time. It sounds as fresh and as vivid as the day it was made; the brilliantly transparent detail and enormous impact suggest state of the art modern sound, rather than something

which is now 50 years old! Only the sound of the massed upper strings reveals the age of the original master, although this does not spoil the ravishing final climax: the bite of the brass and the transient edge of the percussion are thrilling. The performance sounds completely spontaneous and the **LSO** wind playing is especially sensitive. The recording of Stravinsky's glittering symphonic poem *The Song of the Nightingale* is hardly less compelling – urgent and finely pointed – and the shorter pieces come up in a blaze of colour and energy.

The complete *Firebird* (on Philips) played by Russian artists has, as one might expect, a strong sense both of atmosphere and theatre, and **Valery Gergiev** manages the transitions between sections, dramatic characterization and contrasts with consummate mastery. The orchestra play with effortless virtuosity and are recorded with remarkable realism and definition. The coupling, Scriabin's *Prometheus*, can hold its own alongside most rivals.

For a score as magical as *The Firebird* a recording can be too clear, and the digital sound in **Dohnányi's** version tends to be too analytical, separating the threads in a way which prevents the music from making its full evocative effect. That said, there are many good things in this performance, and those who enjoy sound for sound's sake will like it for that reason, for it is indeed impressive, and it is good to have it available again.

The Firebird (complete); 4 Etudes; Petrushka (1947 version; complete); Scherzo à la russe (2 versions: for jazz band; for orchestra); Symphony in 3 Movements

Ⓑ **(*) EMI Gemini 5 85538-2 (2). CBSO, Rattle

Strong, clean and well played, **Rattle's CBSO** version of *The Firebird* is forthright and positive rather than atmospheric, looking forward to the *Rite of Spring* rather than back to Russian nationalism. The recording is warm and full, but this is not one of Rattle's most inspired recordings. His reading of *Petrushka* brings out the sturdy jollity of the ballet, contrasting it with the poignancy of the puppet's own feelings. Rattle and his players benefit in clarity by their use of the 1947 scoring, finely detailed to bring out many points that are normally obscured. In the *Symphony in Three Movements*, done with comparable power, colour and robustness, Rattle brings out the syncopations and pop references with great panache. The two versions of the *Scherzo à la russe* then make a fascinating comparison – both given with Rattle's usual flair, infectiously bouncy. The *Four Studies* provide another light-hearted makeweight.

The Firebird; Petrushka (1947) (ballets; complete)

⊕ Ⓑ *** Naxos 8.557500 Philh. O, Craft

Vividly recorded and played with fire and warmth by the **Philharmonia**, **Robert Craft's** generous coupling of the complete *Firebird* and *Petrushka* ballets makes an outstanding bargain on the Naxos label. The clarity of sound brings out the extra transparency of *Petrushka* in the revised 1947 scoring, with well-sprung rhythms in the dance movements, and with the *Russian Dance* biting in its impact. The complete

Firebird of 1910 is advertised as the first recording of the original version, but the differences with the usual 1910 score amount to no more than the inclusion of two long valveless trumpets on stage playing a single note in places. Nonetheless, Craft inspires a taut performance which holds the structure together, while bringing out the atmospheric beauty of this warmest of Stravinsky's scores, while *Katshchei's Infernal Dance* has all the bite and weight you need. Helpfully, there are copious tracks to help identify the narrative, 22 in *Firebird* and 17 in *Petrushka*.

(i) *The Firebird* (complete); (ii) *The Rite of Spring* (complete)

🎧 ❀ Ⓜ️ **** Sony SMK 89875. Columbia SO, composer

Stravinsky's own (1961) version of *Firebird* is of far more than documentary interest, when the composer so tellingly relates it to his later work, refusing to treat it as merely atmospheric. What he brings out more than others is the element of grotesque fantasy, the quality he was about to develop in *Petrushka*, while the tense violence with which he presents such a passage as *Katshchei's Dance* clearly looks forward to *The Rite of Spring*. That said, he encourages warmly expressive rubato to a surprising degree, with the line of the music always held firm. But the revelatory performance here is *The Rite of Spring*, for Stravinsky's own (1960) reading has never been surpassed as an interpretation of this seminal 20th-century score. Over and over again, one finds passages which in the balancing and pacing (generally fast) give extra thrust and resilience, as well as extra light and shade. The digital transfer may be on the bright side, but brass and percussion have thrilling impact, sharply terraced and positioned in the stereo spectrum.

(i) *The Firebird* (original, 1910 version); (ii) *The Rite of Spring*; (i) *Symphonies of Wind Instruments*; (ii; iii) *Perséphone* (complete)

🎧 Ⓑ *** Virgin 2x1 4 82106-2 (2). (i) LSO; (ii) LPO; Nagano; (iii) with Anne Fournet (narrator), Rolfe Johnson, LPO Ch. & Tiffin School Boys' Ch.

Kent Nagano's vividly detailed **LSO** recording of the original *Firebird* score is a top recommendation, with its apt coupling of the original (1920) score of the *Symphonies of Wind Instruments*, divertingly cool, with sonorities and textures keenly balanced. Nagano's reading of *The Rite of Spring* has similar qualities. If it is less weightily barbaric than many, the springing of rhythm and the clarity and refinement of instrumental textures make it very compelling, with only the final *Danse sacrale* lacking something in dramatic bite.

The only rival for Nagano's *Perséphone* – with its spoken narration described by the librettist, André Gide, as 'a melodrama in three scenes' – is the composer's own version, and the contrasts are extreme. Where Stravinsky himself – at speeds consistently more measured – takes a rugged, square-cut view, Nagano, much lighter as well as more fleet, makes the work a far more atmospheric evocation of spring. The playing and singing are consistently more refined, and the modern digital recording gives a warm bloom, while the sung French sounds far more idiomatic

for everyone. The narration of **Anne Fournet** brings out all the beauty of Gide's words, with **Anthony Rolfe Johnson** free-toned in the taxing tenor solos. All in all, a highly recommendable Virgin double.

The Firebird (ballet; complete; 1910 version); *Symphonies of Wind Instruments* (1947 revision)

Ⓝ Ⓑ **(*) EMI 2-CD 5 20969-2 (2). LPO, Welser-Möst – *Oedipus Rex* ***

In *The Firebird* the **LPO** play very beautifully indeed, creating magically atmospheric textures, and they are superbly recorded too. The snag is a lack of sustained tension in the gentler music, although the climaxes are vivid enough. **Welser-Möst**, however, finds plenty of wit in the *Symphonies of Wind Instruments*, also splendidly played.

The Firebird: Suite (1919 version)

*** DG 437 818-2. O de l'Opéra Bastille, Chung – RIMSKY-KORSAKOV: *Scheherazade* ***

Ⓜ️ *** Telarc CD 80039. Atlanta Ch. & SO, Shaw – BORODIN: *Prince Igor: Overture; Polovtsian Dances* ***

Myung-Whun Chung gets very musical results from his players and there are many imaginative touches. The sound has great warmth and richness, but the perspective is absolutely right too.

Robert Shaw achieves a vivid and atmospheric reading of Stravinsky's famous suite. The *Round Dance of the Princesses* is played very gently to maximize the shock of the entry of Kastchei, and the very wide dynamic range of the recording achieves the most dramatic impact both here and in the closing pages of the finale. With its equally spectacular coupling, this disc is designed to please those wanting to show off their reproducer – and this it will certainly do.

Ballets: *The Firebird* (suite; 1919 version); *Jeu de cartes*; *Petrushka* (1911 version); (i) *Pulcinella* (1947 version); *The Rite of Spring*

🎧 Ⓑ *** DG Double (ADD) 453 085-2 (2). LSO, Abbado; (i) with Berganza, R. Davies, Shirley-Quirk

The highlight on this DG Double is *Petrushka*, while both the *Firebird Suite* and *Jeux de cartes* are given stunning performances. The **LSO** plays with superb virtuosity and spirit. The neoclassical score of *Pulcinella* is given a surprisingly high-powered reading, and not just the playing but the singers too are outstandingly fine. **Abbado's** feeling for atmosphere and colour is everywhere in evidence, heard against an excellently judged perspective. There is a degree of detachment in Abbado's reading of *The Rite of Spring*, although his observance of markings is meticulous and the orchestra obviously revels in the security given by the conductor's direction.

The Firebird Suite (1919 version); *Petrushka* (1947 version; complete); *Scherzo à la Russe*

🎧 **** Telarc CD 80587. Cincinnati SO, Järvi

Paavo Järvi's Telarc coupling of the *Firebird Suite* and *Petrushka* is outstanding in every way, with the **Cincinnati** orchestral playing superb throughout. The Telarc recording, balanced by Jack Renner, offers demonstration sound which can be enjoyed for its natural perspective as well as for its impressive amplitude and range of dynamic.

The Firebird Suite (1919 version); Petrushka; (i) Symphony of Psalms

(BB) (***) Dutton mono CDBP 9700. LPO, Ansermet; with (i) LPO Ch.

Here are three celebrated recordings which dominated the immediate post-war catalogue, restored in altogether outstanding transfers. The set of **Ansermet's** Petrushka was hailed by Alec Robertson (not Robinson, as given in the notes) as 'the most sensational advance in recording we have yet'. The Symphony of Psalms was the first recording since Stravinsky's own, somewhat primitive, Paris recording from the early 1930s and was again a revelation. Self-recommending.

(i) The Firebird (suite; 1919 score); (ii) The Rite of Spring

(B) **(*) Sony (ADD) 516240. (i) NYPO; (ii) LSO; Bernstein – PROKOFIEV: Scythian Suite (*)

Bernstein's Rite (1972) was recorded with quadraphonic 'surround sound' in mind. Although it does not have the pinpoint precision of some other versions, the electric intensity is never in doubt. The Firebird Suite (1957) is in most ways better recorded: more open, better defined and with rather greater depth.

Firebird Suite (1945 version); The Rite of Spring

(BB) **(*) Regis RRC 1276. RPO, Simonov

Yuri Simonov directs highly individual and certainly enjoyable performances of both ballets, which are warm and idiomatic rather than bitingly brilliant, bringing out the Russian elements and echoes of Rimsky-Korsakov, Stravinsky's teacher. The Rite of Spring is not barbaric, even though rhythms are sprung persuasively, and the playing is always alert. But the recording is superb, allowing one to hear inner textures. In the Firebird Simonov adopts daringly broad speeds for the closing section. The great horn solo is gloriously done.

Histoire du Soldat (Suite); Pastorale, Op. 5; Renard (Burlesque); Scherzo à la Russe; Song of the Volga Boatmen; 3 Pieces for Clarinet; Pour Picasso. Vocal Music: 2 Belmont Songs; Berceuses du Chat; 3 Japanese Lyrics; Pribaoutki

⟿ (BB) **** Naxos 8.557505. Instrumental & Vocal Soloists, O of St John's or Philh. O, Craft

The Pastorale (in the composer's arrangement for violin and woodwind) opens this collection with a gentle, wistful charm. Written originally as a vocal piece in 1908, it introduces **Robert Craft's** collection of early works dating from 1911 to 1918, the exception being the brazen arrangement of the Scherzo à la Russe which Stravinsky re-orchestrated for the Paul Whiteman Band in 1944. The most familiar work here is the Histoire du Soldat Suite, given an animated, boldly characterized performance, with splendid playing from the orchestral soloists. But Renard creates a similar

dynamic instrumental character, with the vividly histrionic vocal participation (Stravinsky wrote the libretto himself) impressively well sung and exuberantly full of ribald wit. It is presented at top speed with sharp accuracy and bravura by the present group, laced with bizarre barnyard effects from the orchestra. The Three Pieces for Clarinet are miniatures of sharp originality. The two Belmont Songs are lyrical and beautiful, and the Three Japanese Lyrics are sinuously seductive, all exquisitely sung by **Susan Narucki**. These are provided with translations, but the four Pribaoutki are not. Here **Catherine Ciesinski** brings out their bold Russian folk derivation, with the composer's scoring ever ear-tickling. The four Berceuses du chat are equally memorable, with stealthy clarinet colouring. The programme ends with the Song of the Volga Boatmen, boisterously scored, and played with enthusiasm by the **Philharmonia Orchestra**. All these performances offer first-class playing from a galaxy of artists and spirited, crisply detailed direction from Robert Craft, who also provides excellent notes. The recording cannot be faulted, except perhaps for a rather backward balance of the soloists in Renard.

(i) Les Noces; (ii) Oedipus Rex

(BB) **(*) Naxos 8.557499. (i) Wells, Bickley, Ewing, International Piano Qt., Tristan Fry Percussion Ens.; (ii) Lane, Cornwell, Wilson Johnson, Greenan, Fox (speaker); (i; ii) Simon Joly Ch., Philh. O, Craft

This first issue in the **Robert Craft** collection to be issued on Naxos provides an exceptionally generous coupling of two of Stravinsky's supreme masterpieces in excellent versions superbly recorded. Craft, the composer's amanuensis in his later years, began conducting as a loyal helper of Stravinsky, but here he reveals himself as much more, an inspired interpreter who can reveal the fire and freshness of these two works, in performances of high voltage superbly recorded. The distinctive timbre of Les noces with its four pianos and percussion is vividly caught, and the Western singers capture the Russian idiom well with a rustic tinge. Oedipus Rex is just as powerfully projected with **Edward Fox** as narrator in English and **Martyn Hill** in the title role dramatic if under strain at times, as is **Jennifer Lane** as Jocasta.

Petrushka (1911 score; complete; CD versions)

⟿ (****) Testament mono SBT 1139. Philh. O, Stokowski – RIMSKY-KORSAKOV: Scheherazade **

⟿ (M)(***) Somm mono SOMMCD 027. SRO, Ansermet – ROSSINI: La boutique fantasque *** ❀

(M)(***) RCA mono 09026 63303-2. Boston SO, Monteux – FRANCK: Symphony in D min. *** ❀

Stokowski's Petrushka with the **Philharmonia Orchestra** is superb. The orchestral playing is exciting and full of colour. It is almost as impressive as his famous pre-war set with the Philadelphia Orchestra – and that is saying something. It is coupled, however, with a somewhat idiosyncratic Scheherazade, but is still indispensable.

In November 1949, when **Ansermet's** ffrr Decca recording of Petrushka was made, the **Suisse Romande Orchestra** was in better shape than when he made his stereo Stravinsky discs in the later 1950s. Overall the performance, besides being better played, is more gutsy than Ansermet's later stereo version. Its strikingly vivid quality and sense of the dramatic is brought about by everything being sharply focused in strong primary colours, a tribute to the engineering as well as the performance, and it is only the inherent thinness in the upper range of the violins that gives cause for complaint.

As he conducted the ballet's première, it is good to have **Monteux's** 1931 **Boston** recording at last satisfactorily remastered, with the sound now vivid and the Boston ambience more of an advantage than a drawback. The performance has undoubted flair and is very well played.

Petrushka (1911 score; complete); The Rite of Spring (ballets; complete)

🔊 Ⓑ (***) Sanctuary Living Era mono AJC 8554. SRO, Ansermet

Older readers re-encountering **Ansermet's** famous pioneering 1946 version of *Petrushka* in this very faithful transfer will share our astonishment at the way this extraordinarily vivid performance and recording has remained in the memory in every detail. It is a true classic of the gramophone. Indeed, the sense of the drama inherent in the engineering and performance alike is unforgettable. Everything is sharply focused in strong primary colours in front of the listener, and more than half-a-century after the LP first appeared, the immediacy of the sound in this remarkable score remains unsurpassed, so that one soon puts aside the well remembered thin, 'whistly' edge on the *fortissimo* upper strings. The *Rite of Spring*, recorded a year later, still retains the stereoscopic detail, sense of drama and spontaneity for which the conductor was famous in the recording studio.

Petrushka (1947 score; complete)

**(*) Australian Decca Eloquence 476 2686. VPO, Dohnányi – BARTÓK: *The Miraculous Mandarin* **(*)

Dohnányi directs a genial and well-paced reading, slightly lacking in sparkle and imagination but revealing the **VPO** as a band very sympathetic to repertoire not normally associated with it. Though the piano and trumpet might with advantage have been placed closer, the (1977) sound is generally of Decca's best late analogue quality.

(i) Petrushka (1947 score); (ii) Pulcinella (suite)

🔊 Ⓜ **** Sony 82876 78749-2. NYPO, Bernstein (with talk by Bernstein)

**(*) Testament SBT 1156. (i) New Philh O; (ii) Philh. O; Klemperer

Leonard Bernstein's 1969 performance of *Petrushka* is among the most involving and warm-hearted on record. Bernstein goes to the emotional heart of the score, without violating Stravinsky's expressed markings except in a couple of minor instances. The panoply of the fair music, the inbred hysteria of the puppet's rage and, above all, the tragedy of the death are here conveyed with unrivalled intensity, and the vivid recording adds to the compulsion of the performance. Fortunately the coupling, recorded a year later, is equally distinctive, stylish and with playing of subtlety and precision fully worthy of Stravinsky's witty Pergolesian pastiche; and for good measure this reissue includes a talk by Bernstein discussing Stravinsky's approach to the score of *Petrushka*.

Following a concert performance in 1967, **Klemperer** insisted on recording *Petrushka*. EMI initially edited together a finished copy that was rejected. What Stewart Brown of Testament has done is to investigate the original tapes, and put together a recording drawn from the first day's sessions instead of the third – sharper and more intense. The result is a fascinating version, strong and symphonic rather than atmospheric, and magnetic from first to last. Vivid recording, full of presence. The *Pulcinella Suite* of four years earlier has already appeared on CD, an attractively fresh performance, not quite as biting as that of *Petrushka*.

(i) Pulcinella (complete); Danses concertantes

🔊 ⒷⒷ *** Naxos 8.553181. (i) James, Bostridge, Herford; Bournemouth Sinf., Sanderling

The Naxos complete *Pulcinella* ballet is fresh and alert and with the impact of the crisp, clean ensemble reinforced by full and immediate sound on an apt chamber scale. This was one of the very first recordings made (in 1993) by the tenor **Ian Bostridge**, and the heady beauty of his voice is superbly caught in such vocal numbers as the *Serenata*. The other soloists are also good. A full text and English translation are given, and it is good to have the far later *Danses concertantes* (1941–2) as a valuable makeweight, done with equal point and polish. Strongly recommended.

The Rite of Spring (ballet; complete)

Ⓜ **(*) DG (ADD) 463 613-2. BPO, Karajan – PROKOFIEV: *Symphony 5* ****

Ⓜ **(*) DG (ADD) 477 7160. BPO, Karajan – BARTÓK: *Concerto for Orchestra* **(*)

The Rite of Spring; Symphony of Psalms

Ⓜ **(*) Warner Elatus 2564 60120-2. Ch. & O de Paris, Barenboim

The Rite of Spring; Symphony in 3 Movements

🔊 **** Tudor SACD 7145. Bamberg SO, Nott

Outstanding new performances of both works. **Jonathan Nott** and the transformed **Bamberg Symphony Orchestra** are riding high at the moment in their superb surround sound recordings for Tudor. The music is very strongly characterized and full of personality, the *Rite* both magically evocative and rivetingly incisive, not as violent as some versions, but still very compelling indeed. The *Symphony in Three Movements* is mellower and has both warmth and spirit. The sound really is state-of-the-art even if reproduced on a normal CD player without rear speakers.

Barenboim's coupling of an exciting and atmospheric *Rite of Spring* and a bitingly eloquent *Symphony of Psalms* dates from 1987 but has only recently reappeared on Elatus. The resonant recording, if not sharply detailed, brings spectacular results in the ballet, including impressive contributions from the timpani and bass drum, and is even better focused and balanced in the *Symphony of Psalms*, where the **Paris Choir** sings powerfully and committedly, with the lovely closing *Hallelujahs* particularly telling. The orchestral contribution, too, with its French woodwind colouring, is full of character, and this fine performance can be considered alongside Bernstein's (see below), although the latter is still a preferable choice.

Karajan's approach may have excitement but, next to other more extrovert accounts, it sounds a bit too smooth and civilized. His attention to detail is striking, but at the expense of sheer elemental strength, though it is interesting to hear such a sophisticated reading of this score. The recording is technically outstanding, with its vivid projection countering the high degree of reverberation. Not a top recommendation, but an interesting performance with integrity, which will not disappoint Karajan admirers, and those coming new to it will certainly see the work in a different light.

The Soldier's Tale (L'histoire du soldat; complete)

🎵—Ⓜ️ *** Vanguard (ADD) **SACD** ATMSC 1559. Madeleine Milhaud, Aumont, Singer, Instrumental Ens., Stokowski

*** Chan. 9189. Haugland, SNO, Järvi

(i) The Soldier's Tale (complete); (ii) Dumbarton Oaks Concerto in E flat

🎵—ⒷⒷ *** Naxos 8.55366-2. D. Thomas, Soames, Keeble, & Instrumental Ens.; (ii) N. Ch. O; Ward

This surprisingly neglected score is heard here for the first time on CD as the composer intended. It might be questioned why Vanguard chose a woman as narrator, but Milhaud's wife had already acted in a similar role in a concert performance of Stravinsky's *Persephone* under the composer's direction, and she received his imprimatur. She was also able to record the piece in the original French as well as English, and her diction is both clear and histrionically involving, even reminding one a little of Dame Edith Sitwell in Walton's *Façade*. The rhyming libretto was the work of the Swiss writer Charles Ferdinand Ramuz, who had provided the French text for *Les Noces*. The two actors playing the Soldier (**Jean Pierre Aumont**) and the Devil (a dominating **Martial Singer**) are excellent; the latter produces a remarkable falsetto while in the guise of the old clothes woman. Whether the piece works or not only the listener can decide, but the performance is certainly first rate and full of life. Throughout, **Stokowski** magics Stravinsky's vivid score, making the most of its lyrical warmth as well as the more abrasive Devil's music, which has plenty of rhythmic bite. The septet of expert instrumentalists was recorded (in 1967) on three tracks – the narration separately, as it had to be bilingual. The solo violinist (**Charles Tarrack**) and the trumpeter (**Theodore Weis**) are fully up to the considerable demands placed on them (the *Tango*, *Waltz* and *Ragtime* are delightfully played), and here everything is expertly combined to make a most convincingly balanced SACD, with

each item of music separately cued. This may be an eccentric artistic amalgamation, but it includes the whole of Stravinsky's score, and is aurally fascinating. The sound is remarkably vivid and immediate.

With recording ideally balanced, intimate but not too dry, with fair bloom on voices and instruments, **Nicholas Ward** on Naxos offers a crisp and well-lifted account, with seven stylish players from the **Northern Chamber Orchestra**. Using the idiomatic English version of Michael Flanders and Kitty Black, the three actors characterize well without exaggeration. From the full chamber orchestra the *Dumbarton Oaks Concerto* makes a generous and apt coupling, similarly crisp and persuasive

Aage Haugland takes a forthright view, with the Devil given a crypto-French accent as a very oily character. Where the Chandos scores is in the sharp focus of the performance, generally brisk and taut at fast speeds, helped by a close recording which yet has plenty of air round the sound.

Symphony in 3 Movements; Symphony in C; (i) Symphony of Psalms

Ⓝ *** EMI 2 07630-0. BPO, Rattle; (i) with Berlin R. Ch.

Rattle is less strident in the *Symphony in 3 Movements* than Boulez, but more polished, more civilized, and without loss of bite. The *Symphony in C* is even finer – a performance of great intensity and urgency. The *Symphony of Psalms* is ideal, too, and beautifully sung. Altogether this is a very impressive triptych indeed and superbly recorded.

Symphony in 3 Movements; Symphonies of Wind Instruments; (i) Symphony of Psalms

**(*) DG 457 616-2. BPO, Pierre Boulez; (i) with Berlin R. Ch.

The *Symphony in Three Movements* brings a violent approach from **Boulez**, with the **Berliners** relishing the jazzy outbursts of the outer movements and the warmth of the central slow movement. An unexpected but revelatory disc. The results are refined rather than biting in the *Symphony of Psalms* and *Wind Symphonies*, where Boulez's restraint combined with beautifully moulded ensemble gives way to dramatic power only at key climaxes. The poignancy of the *Wind Symphonies* is reinforced, and the beauty of the *Symphony of Psalms* culminates in a glowing account of the final apotheosis, one of Stravinsky's most sublime inspirations.

'The Final Chorale' – a documentary about the Symphony of Wind Instruments (DVD version)

*** Ideale-Audience **DVD** 3. Netherlands Wind Ens., de Leeuw – SCHOENBERG: *5 Orchestral Pieces* ***

This is a most illuminating feature (available from www.ideale-audience.com.) that follows the musical development of the *Symphonies of Wind Instruments*, composed in 1920 in memory of Debussy, and explores what makes them so profoundly original. The exposition by Frank Scheffer has clarity and insight, and there is some archival material and a highly interesting interview with Robert Craft. Splendid playing, as one might expect, from the **Netherlands Wind Ensemble** under **Reinbert de Leeuw**.

CHAMBER MUSIC

Ballad; Chanson russe; Danse russe; Divertimento; Duo concertante; Pastorale; Suite italienne

🎵 *** Chan. 9756. Mordkovitch, Milford

Lydia Mordkovitch, truly Russian, defies the idea of Stravinsky as a cold composer, finding radiant intensity even in the neoclassical *Duo concertante*, notably in the lovely final *Dithyrambe*. This was a work Stravinsky wrote for himself to play with the violinist Samuel Dushkin, and the other pieces, all lighter, are arrangements he also made for their recitals, based on some of his most approachable works. So the ballets *Pulcinella* and *The Fairy's Kiss* prompted respectively the *Suite italienne* and the *Divertimento*, while the other shorter pieces culminate here in a fizzing account of the *Danse russe* from *Petrushka*.

Concertino; Double Canon; 3 Pieces for String Quartet

🎵 (M) *** EMI 5 67550-2. Alban Berg Qt – DEBUSSY; RAVEL: *String Quartets* **(*)

(BB) *** Naxos 8.554315. Goldner Qt – SZYMANOWSKI: *String Quartets 1–2* ***

(M) *** Wigmore Live WHLive 0012. Ysaÿe Qt – DEBUSSY; FAURÉ: *Quartets* ***

Stravinsky's original titles for the *Three Pieces* were *Danse, Excentrique* and *Cantique*, with the second an etching of the contortions of the famous clown Little Tich, and the third a Russian chant. The playing of the **Alban Berg Quartet** has tremendous bite and grip, and the music's spare lyricism and irony is indelibly caught, as is the rhythmic energy and bustle of the *Concertino*. The economic *Double Canon* is dedicated to the memory of the painter Raoul Dufy, and this short valediction is touchingly realized. First class, vividly present recording.

On Naxos Stravinsky's bright and brittle miniatures for *String Quartet*, with their compressed and cryptic arguments, make a striking contrast with the rich and exotic quartets of Szymanowski. The excellent **Goldner Quartet** play them with dramatic bite, underlining that contrast. Excellent sound.

As part of the Wigmore Hall recital by the **Ysaÿe Quartet**, these Stravinsky rarities, so interesting and diverting, also make an admirable foil for the two great French *Quartets*.

Divertimento

*** Erato 8573-85769-2. Repin, Berezovsky – BARTÓK: *Romanian folk dances*; STRAUSS: *Violin Sonata* ***

On Erato **Repin** and **Berezovsky** give a performance of immense character and elegance, and ideally balanced.

3 Pieces for String Quartet

🎵 *** ASV CDDCA 930. Lindsay Qt – DEBUSSY; RAVEL: *Quartets* **(*)

A vital, finely etched performance of these delightful pieces from the **Lindsays**. A good fill-up to thoughtful and vigorous accounts of the Debussy and Ravel *Quartets*. Good recordings.

Suite italienne for Cello & Piano

(BB) *** Virgin 2x1 4 82067-2. Mørk, Vogt – MIASKOVSKY; PROKOFIEV; RACHMANINOV: *Cello Sonata*; SHOSTAKOVICH: *Cello Sonata* ***

Suite italienne for Violin & Piano

*** BIS CD 336. Thedéen, Pöntinen – SCHNITTKE: *Sonata*; SHOSTAKOVICH: *Sonata* ***

Stravinsky made several transcriptions of movements from *Pulcinella*, including the *Suite italienne* for both cello and alternatively violin and piano. The performances by **Torleif Thedéen** and **Roland Pöntinen** are felicitous and spontaneous, and they are afforded strikingly natural recording.

Truls Mørk and **Lars Vogt** also give a very lively account. It is a welcome makeweight for their eloquent accounts of the Shostakovich, Miaskovky, Rachmaninov and Prokofiev *Sonatas*, and this budget reissue is very strongly recommended.

PIANO MUSIC

Concerto for 2 pianos; 3 Easy Pieces for piano 4 hands; 5 Easy Pieces for piano 4 hands; Ragtime; (i) From 5 fingers; Tango; Valse des fleurs

*** KML **DVD** 1112/3. Katia & (i) Marielle Labèque – DEBUSSY: *En blanc et noir*

This issue offers two discs, one a straightforward CD, the other a DVD, though the latter does not include *Ragtime*, the three movements from *The Five Fingers* or the *Valse des fleurs*. The *Concerto for two pianos* was one of Stravinsky's favourite compositions and **the Labèques** play it marvellously. Skip the gimmicky DVD, or throw it out.

Solo piano music

Circus Polka; 4 Etudes; Piano Rag Music; Ragtime; Scherzo; Serenade; Sonata; Sonata in F sharp min.; Tango; Valse pour les enfants. Piano transcriptions: Le Chant du rossignol (probably made by Arthur Lourié); 3 Movements from The Firebird (trans. Agosti); 3 Movements from Petrushka; Symphonies for Wind Instruments (arr. Arthur Lourié)

🎵 (B) *** Nim. NI 5519/20. Jones

The piano was Stravinsky's indispensable work-tool. He thought of it as 'a utility instrument which sounds right only as percussion', but Rubinstein convinced him otherwise, and it was for Rubinstein that he transcribed the *Three Movements from Petrushka*. **Martin Jones** plays them vividly, and is particularly evocative in the central *Chez Pétrouchka* (as he is in the *Firebird* finale). The other piano transcriptions, wanted for use at ballet rehearsals, were made by others. *Le Chant du rossignol* is very orchestral and prolix, but again Martin Jones finds atmospheric magic in the third and final tableau.

The earliest work here is the charming *Scherzo* with its rhythmic hoppity-jump, while Jones relishes the full-blooded Tchaikovskian romanticism of the *F sharp minor Sonata*, an entirely uncharacteristic but very enjoyable student work from 1903–4: its simple *Andante* is touching. The *Etudes* of 1908 move into the world of Scriabin and the *Valse pour les enfants* is rather like Poulenc, but the *Piano Rag Music* and the engaging *Ragtime* (1918–19) are harder-edged and more typical.

The *Sonata* (1924) with its cool, almost Ravelian *Adagietto* and the delightful *Serenade* (1925) are perhaps Stravinsky's two finest solo works, and ought to be much better known. The much later and beguiling *Tango* (1940) contrasts with the *Circus Polka* (1942), which, with its parody of Schubert's *Marche militaire*, brings an element of the bizarre. Martin Jones readily encompasses the wide range of these pieces.

Piano music: *Circus Polka; 4 Etudes, Op. 7; Piano Rag-Music; Scherzo; Serenade in A; Sonata (1924); Sonata in F sharp min.; Sonata (1924); Tango*

(N) (BB) ******** Naxos 8.570377. Sangiorgio

While the *Piano Rag-Music* and *Tango* have an undoubted quirky rhythmic vitality and charm, it would be difficult for the uninformed listener to pin down the composer of the two *Sonatas* with their attractive slow movements, or indeed the four flamboyant *Etudes*. **Victor Sangiorgio** plays everything here with great character and virtuosity, and in some pieces he is even more successful than any of his previous rivals. He also benefits from vivid and present recording (originally from Collins) and excellent notes. A truly indispensable record which is thoroughly rewarding.

3 Movements from Petrushka

*** RCA 82876 65390-2. Evgeny Kissin – MEDTNER: *Sonata-Reminiscenza* ****(*)**; SCRIABIN: *5 Preludes; Sonata 3* *******

Kissin is a wonderful pianist – of that there is no question. However, those who recall the celebrated Gilels recording of *Petrushka* may find some touches here just a shade self-regarding. Even so, this is pretty memorable.

Piano Sonata; Piano-rag Music; Serenade in A

*** Chan. 8962. Berman – SCHNITTKE: *Sonata* *******

Boris Berman is an artist of powerful intelligence who gives vivid and alertly characterized accounts of all these pieces. Excellent piano sound, too. Strongly recommended.

VOCAL MUSIC

(i) *Babel; Cantata; Mass; Symphony of Psalms; 3 Russian Sacred Choruses*

(BB) ******* Naxos 8.557504. Gregg Smith Singers, Simon Joly Chorale, Philharmonia O, Craft; (i) with Wilson-Johnson (narrator)

This was one of the first discs that **Robert Craft** recorded in his Stravinsky series, with the *Symphony of Psalms* as the centrepiece for a varied group of sacred choral pieces. Though it offers a clean, intense reading of the main work, it reaches full power only in the glorious final movement. The other works all come in clear, direct readings, with **David Wilson-**

Johnson the Narrator in the strange movement, **Babel**, that Stravinsky wrote on commission from the publisher Nathanial Shilkret, illustrating the Bible story of the Tower of Babel. The programme opens with three haunting *Russian Sacred Chorales* which are immediately appealing and as idiomatic as one can expect from non-Russian singers. The recordings were made over a decade, between 1992 and 2002. Full documentation by Craft, but no texts.

(i) *Cantata on Old English Texts; Mass;* (ii) *Les Noces*

**** HM HMC 801913. Sampson, Parry & soloists, RIAS Kammerchor, MusikFabrik, Reuss

Stravinsky, an ardent believer and a member of the Russian Orthodox Church, wrote the *Mass* for himself and for liturgical rather than concert use. It has an archaic feeling, but it is gloriously lyrical and inspired, the plangent harmonies giving it dramatic bite, especially in the thrilling *Sanctus*, while the *Agnus Dei* is raptly beautiful in the same way that the 'Alleluias' at the end of the *Symphony of Psalms* are so memorable.

The *Cantata*, too, opens unforgettably and is lyrically inspired throughout, using four verses from *A Lyke-Wake Dirge*, interspersed with polyphonic *Ricercari* allotted to solo voices and accompanied by celestial flutes, oboe, cor anglais and cello.

Les Noces simulates a folk wedding, and its special feature is exuberant rhythmic joy, which is just what this new Harmonia Mundi performance so exhilaratingly captures. Then, of course, there is that haunting tolling bell at the end, which somehow confirms that the ritual is archaic but eternal. The performance here is directed with superb exuberance by **Daniel Reuss**; when listening to it, you'll also discover where Orff's *Carmina Burana* came from. The *Cantata* and *Mass* are equally beautifully sung, with the glorious **Carolyn Sampson** standing out among the excellent soloists. The recording is in the demonstration class.

OPERA

Oedipus Rex (with narration in English)

**** CfP 585 0112. Dowd, Herincx, Blackburn, Johnson, Remedios, Richardson (nar.), Sadler's Wells Op. Ch. (men's voices), RPO, C. Davis

In 1960 the **Sadler's Wells Opera Company** (predecessor of the ENO) had one of its most spectacular successes when **Colin Davis** as Music Director conducted a revelatory production of *Oedipus Rex*, directed by the legendary Michel St Denis. What till then had generally been regarded as a dry, over-intellectual piece, not helped by using a Latin text, was triumphantly revealed as an overwhelming, vitally dramatic opera, defying convention. Davis and his team went into the recording studio the following year – with the opera company's orchestra replaced by the **RPO** – and this thrilling account of Stravinsky's score resulted. In full, immediate sound, vividly transferred to CD, there is a hit-you-between-the-eyes quality which reflects the original stage experience, with each member of the cast singing challenging music with heartfelt commitment. The involvement is intensified by the nobly formalized narrations of **Sir Ralph Richardson**, preparing one for the colourful, energetic performance. There is no more red-blooded version of this opera than this, with **Ronald Dowd** a powerful, cleanly focused Oedipus, deeply affecting in his two climactic solos, *Invidia fortunam odit*, and the final, agonized *Lux facta est* – all is revealed. **Patricia Johnson** is similarly firm as Jocasta, with a balefully dark chest register, and **Raimund Herincx** as Creon, **Harold Blackburn** as Tiresias and the young **Alberto Remedios** in the tiny role of the Shepherd all bear witness to the vocal and dramatic strengths of the company at that time. It is astonishing that this superb recording has been buried for many decades, making this vividly immediate CD transfer doubly welcome on the CfP label.

Oedipus Rex (with narration in French)

(N)(B) **(*) EMI 2-CD 520969-2 (2). Rolfe Johnson, Lipovšek, Tomlinson, Miles, LPO Ch., LPO, Welser-Möst – *Firebird* etc. **(*)

Franz Welser-Möst and the **London Philharmonic** take an expressive rather than a severe neo-classical view. The singing of the men of the **London Philharmonic Choir** is less incisive than that of their principal rivals, but is satisfyingly weighty, and the soloists are on balance among the most involvingly characterful of any, led by **Anthony Rolfe Johnson**, magnificent as Oedipus, weightily heroic but inflecting words meaningfully. **Marjana Lipovšek** brings mature warmth and substance to the role of Jocasta, while **John Tomlinson** as Creon and **John Mark Ainsley** as the Shepherd are outstanding too. Only the brisk, prosaic French narration of **Lambert Wilson** sells the listener short.

(i) *Oedipus Rex*; (ii) *Symphony of Psalms* (CD versions)

(M) **** Sony (ADD) 88697 00819. (i) Kollo, Krause, Troyanos, Harvard Glee Club, Boston SO; (ii) English Bach Festival Ch., LSO; all cond. Bernstein

Recorded in 1972, not long before **Bernstein** transferred allegiance from CBS to DG, these performances of the two supreme masterpieces of Stravinsky's inter-war years make a formidable coupling. In *Oedipus Rex*, with **Michael Wagner** an excellent narrator (naturally pronouncing it 'Eddipus' in the American way), the casting is exceptionally strong in what is a severely stylized opera, a work which increasingly reveals its emotional heart. The two principal soloists are outstandingly fine – **René Kollo** excitingly heroic as Oedipus and **Tatiana Troyanos** affecting as Jocasta – and there is no serious weakness among the others either, with the chorus shading the repetitions of the closing pages beautifully. Bernstein's view of the *Symphony of Psalms* is not as austere and ascetic as the composer's own; instead, there is a grandeur and a powerful sense of atmosphere, strong and intense, ending with a tender account of the final *Laudate Dominum*, one of the most beautiful inspirations in all Stravinsky. First-class singing and playing from the **Bach Festival Chorus** and the **LSO**. The recording too has both clarity and range.

(i) *Oedipus Rex* (with narration in French); *Symphony of Psalms*

(M) **(*) Sup. SU 3674-2 11. (i) Desailly (nar.), Zidek, Soukupová, Bermann, Haken, Kroupa; Prague Philharmonic Ch., Czech PO, Ančerl

Ančerl's account of the *Symphony of Psalms* is beautifully sung but suffers from rhythmic heaviness in all three movements, for he fails to sustain his rather slow tempi, notably in the finale. The phrasing is not as flexible as it might be but, with good choral recording, the result is still moving, especially at the close. *Oedipus Rex* is a different matter, and it understandably won a Grand Prix du Disque in 1968. There is a degree of expressiveness in the phrasing that might not please the composer himself but Ančerl has at his disposal a large group of virtuoso singers, and the result is sharp and committed: the precision of discipline is much more acute than in Stravinsky's performance. The Czech soloists too are not only movingly eloquent but bring a Slavonic timbre which is not at all inappropriate in this work with its lingering traces of Russian influence. The recording quality is very natural, and so is the CD transfer. There are two snags: the text is provided but no translation, and there are no internal cues to separate out the spoken narrative, only a single band between Acts I and II.

The Rake's Progress (complete; DVD versions)

🔲 *** Warner **DVD** 3984 22352-2. Fedderly, Hendricks, Hagegård, Asawa, Swedish R. Ch. & O, Salonen (V/D: Inger Aby)

** Opus Arte **DVD** OA 0991D (2). Claycomb, Kennedy, Shimell, Peckova, La Monnaie Ch. & SO, Ono (Dir: Robert Lepage)

The Warner DVD version offers not a regular staging but a filmed version, made in Sweden with a strong trio of principals. The tenor **Greg Fedderly** makes a handsome Tom, with a clean, well-focused voice, opposite the provocative soprano **Barbara Hendricks**, not quite the innocent maiden of an ideal casting, but vocally strong. **Håkan Hagegård** on his home territory is a formidable Nick Shadow, smooth and sinister. Exceptionally, the bearded lady, Baba the Turk, is played by a man, **Brian Asawa**, certainly characterful. The sound is bright and forward to reinforce the incisiveness of **Esa-Pekka Salonen's** conducting. Documentation is poor, with only a synopsis and a brief list of chapters.

Recorded live at La Monnaie in Brussels, **Robert Lepage's** production presents a bare, updated view of Stravinsky's memorable opera, with an excellent cast led by the Anne Trulove of **Laura Claycomb**, with **Andrew Kennedy** a clean-cut Rake and **William Shimell** a formidable Nick Shadow, arriving as a sinister motorcyclist. It works well, largely through the singing and the lively conducting of **Kazushi Ono**, though there are few if any overtones of Hogarth. It is the sort of production best experienced with one's eyes closed!

The Rake's Progress (complete; CD versions)

🔲 (M) **** Sony (ADD) SM2K 46299 (2). Young, Raskin, Reardon, Sarfaty, Miller, Manning, Sadler's Wells Op. Ch., RPO, composer

(N) (BB) *** Naxos 8.660272/3 (2). Garrison, West, Cheek, Woodley, White, Lowery, O of St Luke's, Craft

🎧 *** DG 459 648-2 (2). Bostridge, York, Terfel, Robson, Howells, von Otter, Monteverdi Ch., Gardiner

🎧 *** Erato 0630 12715-2 (2). Hadley, Upshaw, Lloyd, Ramey, Collins, Bumbry, Lyon Opéra Ch. & O, Nagano

(M) **(*) Decca 475 7005 (2). Langridge, Pope, Walker, Ramey, Dean, Dobson, L. Sinf. Ch. & O, Chailly

Stravinsky's own recording of *The Rake's Progress* has many elements of the original **Sadler's Wells** production. The casting is uniformly excellent with the Rake of **Alexander Young** dominating but **Judith Raskin** an attractive heroine. **Regina Sarfaty's** Baba is superbly characterized and her anger at being spurned just before the 'squelching' makes a riveting moment. The composer conducts with warmth as well as precision, both chorus and orchestra respond persuasively.

It was **Robert Craft**, Stravinsky's devoted amanuensis, who was behind the composer's own second recording of the *Rake*, made in London on his last visit with a largely Sadler's Wells cast. Here, in this 1993 recording made in New York, he follows what he has learned from the composer in an electrifying account, very well cast and recorded, making this an outstanding bargain. **Jon Garrison** is a clear, strong Rake with plenty of character in coping with the malicious help of the devilish Nick Shadow. 'This beggar shall ride,' he brazenly claims when first appreciating his new wealth. **John Cheek** as Nick is wonderfully sinister. As Anne Trulove **Jayne West** is not so characterful, but she sings with all the necessary combination of purity and power. First-rate performances from the other principals too, notably **Wendy White** as Baba the Turk, the Bearded Lady. **Arthur Woodley** as Father Trulove and **Melvin Lowery** as Sellem the auctioneer are not quite so characterful, but they sing well. Every word in Auden and Kallman's brilliant and ingenious libretto is crystal clear, also a tribute to the balance engineers, and the precise, staccato contributions of chorus and orchestra add to the impact of the whole performance.

Gardiner's incisive direction brings extra sparkle to the rhythmic neoclassical writing and conveys a hushed intensity in the many tender moments of this moral tale. **Ian Bostridge's** lyric tenor might seem light for the role of Tom but with fine pointing of words he underlines the Rake's vulnerability, the ease with which he gives way to temptation. **Bryn Terfel** makes a seductive **Nick Shadow**, strong and sardonic, singing superbly, and the young American **Deborah York** sings with golden tone and dazzling flexibility as Anne, untroubled by high tessitura. The rest of the team is equally strong, with **Anne Sofie von Otter** making Baba the Turk the most eloquent nagger. Well-balanced recording.

Kent Nagano, with his **Lyon Opera** forces and an outstanding cast of soloists, directs a fresh and crisp account. In the title-role **Jerry Hadley**, with his fresh, clear tone, is aptly youthful-sounding and brings out the pathos of the final scenes when struck insane by Nick Shadow. **Samuel Ramey** is powerful and sinister in that devilish role, as he was in the earlier, Chailly version, and **Dawn Upshaw** makes a tenderly affecting Anne Trulove, bringing out the heroine's vulnerability. **Robert Lloyd** as Trulove and **Anne Collins** as

Mother Goose are both very well cast, and the veteran **Grace Bumbry** makes a fruity Baba the Turk. Excellent ensemble from the Lyon Opera chorus, though the balance is a little backward. Otherwise first-rate sound.

Richard Chailly draws from the **London Sinfonietta** playing of a clarity and brightness to set the piece aptly on a chamber scale without reducing the power of this elaborately neoclassical work. **Philip Langridge** is excellent as the Rake himself, very moving when Tom is afflicted with madness. **Samuel Ramey** as Nick, **Stafford Dean** as Trulove, and **Sarah Walker** as Baba the Turk are all first rate, but **Cathryn Pope's** soprano as recorded is too soft-grained for Anne. Charming as the idea is of getting the veteran **Astrid Varnay** to sing Mother Goose the result is out of style. The recording is exceptionally full and vivid but the balances are sometimes odd: the orchestra recedes behind the singers and the chorus sounds congested, with little air round the sound.

Le Rossignol (complete; DVD version)

(*) Virgin Classics **DVD 5 44242. Dessay, Simcic, McLaughlin, Urmana, Grivnov, Scjagidulli, Naouri, Mikhailov, O & Ch. de l'Opéra de Paris, Conlon (a film by Christian Chaudet)

This is very much a film – and not a filmed performance of the opera. Christian Chaudet is inventive – perhaps too inventive, as he draws attention away from the music and towards the visual presentation. **Natalie Dessay** makes a splendid nightingale, and the remainder of the cast is very good, too. **James Conlon** gets a sensitive response from the fine **Orchestre de l'Opéra de Paris**. It can certainly be enjoyed without the distraction of vision, but we can imagine others preferring the wonderful post-war account by Janine Micheau, conducted by André Cluytens and available on Testament, which still sounds marvellous. Not even Stravinsky's own recording surpasses it.

SUK, Josef (1874–1935)

Asrael Symphony, Op. 27

(***) Sup. mono 11 1902-2 (2). Czech PO, Talich – DVOŘÁK: *Stabat Mater* (*)

Václav Talich's pioneering mono account from the early 1950s has great intensity of utterance and poignancy and provides a link with the composer himself. Talich knew him well and conducted many Suk premières. The sound is very acceptable for the period, and it is a pity that it comes harnessed to a less successful Dvořák *Stabat Mater*.

(i) Asrael Symphony in C min., Op. 27; (ii) A Fairy Tale, Op. 16; Praga, Op. 26; (i) The Ripening; (ii) A Summer's Tale, Op. 29; (i; iii) Epilogue

(B) *** Sup. SU 3864-2(4). Czech PO; with (i) Neumann; (ii) Pešek; (iii) Jehličková, Kusnjer, Galla, Prague Chamber Ch., Máti

This bargain set comprises Supraphon's digital recordings of Suk's orchestral music, recorded in the 1980s. **Neumann's** performance of the marvellous *Asrael Symphony* is a very fine one, as is his performance of the inventive tone-poem, *The Ripening*. *A Fairy Tale* is full of charm and originality and, although *Praga* is not in the same league, it is worth a hearing. The *Epilogue* is a large piece, taking some 40 minutes. Suk spoke of it as the last part of a cycle, beginning with *Asrael* and 'going through the whole of human life, into reflection on death and the dread of it', before the appearance of earthly love – all this leading up to the 'exhilarating song of liberated mankind'. An inexpensive way to acquire some of this composer's finest music. Good sound.

Asrael Symphony, Op. 27; Praga; Ripening (symphonic poems)

(N) (BB) ******** EMI 2-CD 2 06873 (2). RLPO, Pešek

Pešek's Liverpool version of the *Asrael Symphony* has altogether greater sensitivity and imagination than the earlier Supraphon account from Vaclav Neuman, and the sympathy of the Liverpool players is very apparent. This is well worth having in its own right. However, the EMI two-CD set is very competitively priced and also includes very fine performances of *Praga* and *Ripening*, as dedicated as one could possibly wish. Very good recorded sound too.

A Fairy-Tale; Praga, Op. 26

☛ **** Sup. 10 3389-2. Czech PO, Libor Pešek

It is persuasively played under **Pešek**. It is coupled with *Praga*, a patriotic tone-poem reflecting a more public, outgoing figure than *Asrael*, which was to follow it. Pešek secures an excellent response from the **Czech Philharmonic**; the recordings, which date from 1981–2, are reverberant but good.

Fantasy in G min. (for violin and orchestra), Op. 24

(M) **** Sup. (ADD) SU 1928-2 011. Suk, Czech PO, Ančerl – DVOŘÁK: *Violin Concerto*, etc. ****

Suk's playing is refreshing and the orchestral accompaniment under **Ančerl** is no less impressive. Good remastered 1960s sound.

Fantastic Scherzo, Op. 25

☛ **** Chan. 8897. Czech PO, Bělohlávek – MARTINŮ: *Symphony 6*; JANÁČEK: *Sinfonietta* ****

This captivating piece brings playing from the **Czech Philharmonic** under **Bělohlávek** which is even finer than any of the earlier performances and it cannot be too strongly recommended, particularly in view of the excellence of the couplings.

Fantastique Scherzo; Serenade for Strings

☛ **** Sup. SU 3882-2. Prague Philh., Hrusa – DVOŘÁK: *American Suite* ****

Like the Dvořák *American Suite*, with which they are coupled, these two works of Josef Suk are given fresh and inspired performances under the brilliant young Czech conductor **Jakob Hrusa**. Suk was still in his teens when in 1892 he completed his *Serenade for Strings*, and it remains one of his most

delightful works. The *Scherzo Fantastique* is altogether darker and more distinctive, with an emphasis on the adjective 'fantastic', very inventive in its contrasted sections. The Supraphon recording is full and vivid.

Serenade for Strings in E flat, Op. 6

☛ (BB) **** Virgin 2x1 5 61763-2 (2). LCO, Warren-Green – DVOŘÁK: *Serenade for Strings*; ELGAR: *Introduction & Allegro; Serenade;* TCHAIKOVSKY: *Serenade;* VAUGHAN WILLIAMS: *Fantasia on Greensleeves*, etc. ****

(BB) **** Naxos 8.550419. Capella Istropolitana, Krěchek – DVOŘÁK: *String Serenade* ****(*)

Warren-Green and his **LCO** give a wonderfully persuasive account of Suk's *Serenade*, making obvious that its inspiration is every bit as vivid as in the comparable work of Dvořák. The recording, made in All Saints', Petersham, is fresh, full and natural without blurring from the ecclesiastical acoustic.

On Naxos another entirely delightful account of Suk's *Serenade*. The innocent delicacy of the opening is perfectly caught and the *Adagio* is played most beautifully and then, with a burst of high spirits (and excellent ensemble), the finale bustles to its conclusion with exhilarating zest. The recording is first class, fresh yet full-textured, naturally balanced and transparent.

A Summer's Tale, Op. 29

☛ **** CPO 777 174-2. O of the Comic Opera, Berlin, Petrenko – LIADOV: *The Enchanted Lake*

Suk's *A Summer's Tale* is a 50-minute, five-movement symphonic poem which was composed in the immediate wake of Suk's grief-stricken *Asrael Symphony*. Its inspiration is of a high level and one of its early admirers was Mahler who, shortly before his death, had planned to conduct it. **Kirill Petrenko** offers a thoroughly idiomatic account and he rounds off the disc with a rapt account of Liadov's *Enchanted Lake*.

A Summer Tale, Op. 29; A Winter's Tale, Op. 9

(BB) ***(*) Naxos 8.553703. Slovak RSO, Mogrelia

Good, very musical performances, with fine sound to boot. The **Slovak Orchestra** are not the equal of the Czech Philharmonic but they produce eminently decent results. This is lovely music and the performances are enjoyable and well worth the modest outlay.

CHAMBER MUSIC

Ballade, Op. 30; 4 Pieces, Op. 17 (for violin & piano)

(M) *** Sup. SU 3772. Suk, Panenka – DVOŘÁK: *Romantic Pieces; Violin Sonatina;* SMETANA: *From the Homeland* ****

The *Four Pieces* are quite well known and very attractive, given the persuasive advocacy of these fine artists; the early *Ballade* is comparatively unmemorable, if by no means without interest. But this reissue is desirable for the highly idiomatic accounts of the Smetana pieces and the delightful Dvořák *Violin Sonatina*.

4 Pieces for Violin and Piano, Op. 17

*** Sup. SU 3884-2. Šporcl, Jiřikovský – DVOŘÁK: *Violin Sonata Op. 57,* etc.***

ⓑⓑ (***) Dutton mono CDBP 9710. G. Neveu, J. Neveu – BRAHMS: *Violin Concerto in D, Op. 77;* RAVEL: *Tzigane; Encores* (***)

The Suk *Pieces,* Opus 17, make an apt coupling for the Dvořák items, written in 1900 before the tragedy of the death of Dvořák's daughter and Suk's wife, which was such a blow to both of them. The second of the four is much the most popular, but all are most attractive, particularly when played as well as here by **Pavel Šporcl** and **Petr Jiřikovský**. First-rate sound, recorded in the Rudolfinum in Prague in July 2007.

Ginette Neveu's fiery temperament is shown at its most compelling in these lively genre pieces by Josef Suk with the closing moto perpetuo *Burleska* scintillating on her nimble bow. Her brother Jean accompanies attentively and the recording sounds most real and present in this first-class Dutton transfer.

Piano Quartet in A min., Op. 1

ⓑ *** Virgin 2x1 5 61904-2 (2). Domus – MARTINŮ: *Piano Quartet 1,* etc. DOHNÁNYI: *Serenade.* DVOŘÁK: *Bagatelles.* KODÁLY: *Intermezzo* ***

Suk's early *Piano Quartet* shows this master below his inspired best, but it is still worth having in so sympathetic a performance as **Domus** gives us. It is a well-filled set and well worth having in particular for the Martinů pieces which are not generously represented on disc.

Piano Trio; Elegie

☌ *** Sup. SU 3810. Smetana Trio – NOVAK: *Trio quasi una balata;* SMETANA: *Piano Trio* ***

Unlike the other items on this disc, which are darkly elegiac, Suk's *Piano Trio* is a miniature work, its three movements lasting less than a quarter of an hour; it stands as a delightful piece, full of light and shade, built on clear, memorable themes, with a wonderfully compact, sonata-form finale. Following that, the *Elegie* is a far deeper composition, opening with a violin melody which inspires **Jana Nováková** to playing of an other-worldly delicacy, rapt (like so much of the playing here), building into a passionate central climax.

String Quartets 1 in B flat, Op. 11; 2, Op. 31; Ballade; Barcarolle; Meditation on the Czech Choral, St Wenceslas, Op 35a; Minuet

☌ ✿ Ⓜ **** CRD CRD 3472. Suk Qt

The early *B flat Quartet* is essentially a sunny work, yet its *Adagio* has a remarkable potency of elegiac feeling, which is very affecting in a performance as ardently responsive as that by the eponymous **Suk Quartet** on CRD. The *Second Quartet* is far more concentrated than its predecessor, its thematic material is curiously haunting and in some ways its boldness and forward-looking writing suggest that Janáček's quartets are just around the corner. The performance here is not only deeply moving and seemingly spontaneous, it is wonderfully

full of observed detail. Of the other works here the simple *Meditation* is played very touchingly, while the *Barcarolle* is a charming piece of juvenilia, a real lollipop, to show the composer's ready melodic facility. CRD have never made a better record than this superb collection. The beauty and internal transparency of string texture is matched by the natural presence of the group itself.

PIANO MUSIC

About Mother, Op. 28; Lullabies, Op. 33; 4 Piano Pieces, Op. 7; Spring, Op. 22a; Summer, Op. 22b; Things Lived and Dreamed, Op. 30

*** Chan. 9026/7. Fingerhut

It is striking how the earliest works here have a carefree, sweetly lyrical character, gentler than Dvořák but typically Czech. Then, after the death in 1904 and 1905 of his mentor, Dvořák, and his wife (Dvořák's daughter), even these fragmentary inspirations, like the massive *Asrael Symphony,* become sharp, sometimes even abrasive. The second disc brings the finest and most ambitious of the suites in which Suk generally collected his genre pieces, *Things Lived and Dreamed.* **Margaret Fingerhut** proves a devoted advocate, playing with point and concentration, helped by full-ranging Chandos sound.

About Mother (O matince), Op. 28; Moods (Nálady), Op. 18; 6 Pieces, Op. 7

ⓑⓑ **(*) Naxos 8.553762. Lauriala

The Finnish pianist **Risto Lauriala** has a strong affinity with this music and gives a sympathetic account of the five pictures, Op. 28, *O matince (About Mother),* composed for Suk's son in 1907, two years after Otilie's death. The recording is generally well balanced if a little close, so that there is a touch of glare in *fortissimo* passages.

About Mother, Op. 28; Piano Pieces, Op. 7; Spring, Op. 22a; Summer Impressions, Op. 27b

☌ ⓑⓑ *** Regis RRC 1174. Kvapil

A most attractive anthology, beautifully played and well recorded. The disc also comes with three others devoted to Czech piano music, including music by Dvořák, Smetana and Janáček (Regis RRC 4005).

SULLIVAN, Arthur (1842–1900)

Pineapple Poll (ballet; arr. Mackerras)

☌ ⓑ *** Decca Double 473 653-2 (2). Philh. O, Mackerras – *Princess Ida* ***

☌ ⓑ *** CfP (ADD) 3 93231-2. LPO, Mackerras – VERDI: *Lady and the Fool* ***

On Decca **Mackerras** conducts with warmth as well as vivacity, and the elegantly polished playing of the **Philharmonia Orchestra** gives much pleasure. The record was made in the Kingsway Hall with its glowing ambience, and the CD transfer, though brightly vivid, has a pleasing bloom. Indeed the quality is in the demonstration bracket, with particularly natural string textures.

Mackerras's LPO version of the suite on CfP, made in the London Henry Wood Hall in 1977, is striking for its affection and vivacity. With an apt Verdi coupling, this is excellent value, very well transferred to CD.

Symphony in E (Irish); In memoriam Overture; The Tempest: Suite, Op. 1

⊙—*** Chan. 9859. BBC PO, Hickox

Richard Hickox makes a strong and persuasive case for these Sullivan pieces, notably the attractive *Irish Symphony*, which at last receives a first-class recording. The **BBC Philharmonic** respond with alert and sensitive playing. Sullivan wrote the *In memoriam Overture* in the space of ten days following the sudden death of his father. *The Tempest* music, composed when he was only 18, is not otherwise available. The recording is in the best traditions of the house.

The Tempest: Introduction; Prelude to Act 3; Banquet Dance; Overture to Act 4; Dance of Nymphs and Reapers; Prelude to Act 5; Postlude

Ⓝ*** Reference Recordings RR115. Kansas City SO, Stern – SIBELIUS: *The Tempest: suites* ***

Sullivan's *Tempest* music was his first major orchestral work, dating from 1861, when he was only 19 and still a student at Leipzig. He conducted it at a graduation concert in 1861, and later went on to write scores for *The Merchant of Venice*, *Macbeth* and *The Merry Wives of Windsor*. Mendelssohn is the predominant influence and the music throughout is touched by enchantment. The melodic invention is fresh and the scoring remarkably accomplished; indeed, at its best, it is little short of masterly. Very good playing and recording.

OPERA

DVD Collection: (i) Cox and Box; (ii) The Gondoliers; (iii) HMS Pinafore; (iv) Iolanthe; (v) The Mikado; (vi) Patience; (vii) The Pirates of Penzance; (viii) Princess Ida; (ix) Ruddigore; (x) The Sorcerer; (xi) Trial by Jury; (xii) The Yeomen of the Guard

Ⓜ*(**) Universal **DVD** 8228651-11 (10). Amb.Ch., LSO, Faris; with (i) Russell Smythe, Fryatt, Lawlor; (ii) Michell, Shilling, McDonnell, Egerton, Collins; (iii) Marshall, Frankie Howerd, Drower, Della Jones, Bulman, Watt; (iv) Stroud, van Allan, Oliver, Hemsley, Flowers, Mills, Collins; (v) Conrad, Revill, Collins, Stewart, Dean, Flowers; (vi) Hammond Stroud, Fryatt, Dugdale, Jenkins, Collins, Kennedy, Adams; (vii) Mitchell, Oliver, Knight, Kelly, Hudson; (viii) Gorshin, Christie, Dale, Collins, Dickenson, Powell, Jackson; (ix) Treleaven, Howard, Adams, Peters, Hudson; (x) Revill, Kerman, Oliver, Christie, Adams, Willis; (xi) Frankie Howard, Flowers, Ryland Davies, McDonell, Bryson, Donlan; (xii) Gale, Powell, Marks, Hillman, Bainbridge (V/D: Dave Heather)

Producer George Walker made this series of Gilbert and

Sullivan recordings for television in the early 1980s and they have now appeared on DVD for the first time. The critical reception was mixed – and remains so – but as a whole the series succeeds more than it fails. Firstly, it has the advantage of being filmed on a studio set which ensures that lighting and sound are of uniformly good quality. Secondly, producer Judith de Paul has provided attractive sets, with little of the gratuitous 'souping up' which often mars modern production. Thirdly, **Alexander Faris** paces the music well and has the support of the **LSO** and the **Ambrosian Chorus**, which ensures a good basis of quality. The casting of the smaller roles is usually more than adequate, but the controversy comes with some of the major casting: whilst **Frankie Howerd** is always a delight to see, his personality does not sit happily in *HMS Pinafore* as Sir Joseph Porter, though, if anything, **Peter Marshall** as Captain Corcoran is worse: an embarrassingly overacted caricature. These two leads diminish the otherwise attractive performance. Frankie Howerd is better in *Trial by Jury*, but again his personality is not really suited to the piece. On the other hand, the ballet which has been contrived before the opening of this work, set to the *Overture di Ballo*, is a delight. **Joel Grey** as Jack Point is an irritant that mars a decent *Yeomen of the Guard*, prompting one unkind critic to remark that his insensible collapse at the end comes as a relief for all the wrong reasons. The *Pirates of Penzance* is bright and breezy but the snag is **Peter Allen** camping it up as the Pirate King (not to mention his grating voice). The celebrity casting is much better in *Ruddigore*, which has **Vincent Price** as Sir Despard Murgatroyd who (almost) manages to make one forget his lack of singing ability through sheer personality. In *Princess Ida*, uniquely in the series, the original G & S conception is tampered with so that you have a play within a play; you may or may not like the idea, but why did they bother? The performance is quite a good one, though **Frank Gorshin** as King Gama is a big let down, with little flair for the idiom. The most successful performances – mainly the ones with fewer celeb castings – include *Patience*, *The Sorcerer*, *The Gondoliers* and *Iolanthe* (ideal for a television production to aid the supernatural qualities of the story) which offer generally unalloyed delight. *The Mikado*, too, is generally good, with television star **William Conrad** as the Mikado far more integrated into the performance than many of the other stars. *Cox and Box* (not a Gilbert libretto, by the way) is one of the set's gems, an exhilarating early one-acter from 1867, which brims with sparkling ideas and memorable tunes. The sound and picture quality have been dramatically improved on DVD and each disc comes with full texts. As on the videos – for better or worse – **Douglas Fairbanks Jr's** introductions are included though can be skipped. For all these annoying faults, there is still plenty to enjoy.

(i) Cox and Box; (ii) Trial by Jury (complete; CD versions)

⊙—*** Chan. 10321. (i;ii) Evans, Brook, Maxwell; (ii) Gilchrist, RMCM Chamber Ch.; BBC Nat. O of Wales, Hickox

Cox and Box, Sullivan's collaboration with F. C. Burnand, is here well-coupled with his first collaboration with W. S. Gilbert. Never on disc before has the sparkle of this preparatory piece been caught so brilliantly, bringing out the fact that this is already vintage Sullivan, superbly orchestrated. The text is fuller too, even though the *Gambling Duet* has had to be omitted for lack of space. The trio of soloists is first rate, with the resonant **Donald Maxwell** as the landlord, Bouncer, acting as narrator in the well-tailored spoken links, a crisp and effective alternative to the dialogue. **James Gilchrist** as Box and **Neal Davies** as Cox make an excellent duo, and the same three soloists are equally impressive in *Trial by Jury*, particularly Donald Maxwell who relishes the exhilarating speed set by **Hickox** for the *Judge's Song*, setting a brilliant pattern for patter-numbers in G. & S. to follow. **Rebecca Evans** makes a charming Plaintiff, and in both pieces the vividly atmospheric recording brings out the beauty and point of the writing.

Haddon Hall (complete; without dialogue)

& **✿** *** Divine Art 21201 (2). Timmons, Griffin, Lawson, Smart, Main, Borthwick, Boyd, Thomson, Edinburgh Prince Consort Ch. & O, Lyle

In 1892 Sullivan needed a new source of income, yet had fallen out with Gilbert. So he decided to collaborate with a different librettist, Sidney Grundy, with a considerable reputation in the field of light opera. The result was *Haddon Hall*, based on a true story about the elopement of Lady Dorothy Vernon with her Royalist lover, John Manners, from her ancestral home. But Grundy resourcefully predated the action so that he could use period costumes, and bring in a chorus of Puritans who in the last act, in true topsy-turvy fashion, renounce 'being thoroughly miserable' and instead plan to 'merry-make the livelong day'.

At the beginning of Act II Grundy also introduces an unforgettable Scottish character, The McCrankie, from the Isle of Rum, and he appears to an extraordinarily convincing orchestral evocation of bagpipes. *My name is McCrankie* is followed by his duet with Rupert, *There's no one by*, a wittily dour exposition of their Puritan creed ('We'd supervise the plants and flowers, prescribe them early-closing hours'). Then follows *Hoity-toity*, a delightful trio with Dorcas, the heroine's maid (who sings most engagingly in her own solos), to make three of the most delightful numbers in the whole opera.

Sir John Manners's servant, Oswald (the excellent **Alan Borthwick**), arrives disguised as travelling salesman and introduces himself with the engagingly lively *Come simples and gentles*, full of musical quotations, and this leads to a heavenly duet with Dorcas, *The sun's in the sky*. But it is Rupert, the heroine's Roundhead cousin, splendidly sung by **Ian Lawson**, who is the key humorous figure. He only wants Lady Dorothy's hand as it comes with the Haddon Hall estates, and his very winning *I've heard it said* is an inimitable patter style we all recognize; he also has a fine number with chorus, *When I was but a little lad*.

The performance by the semi-professional Prince Consort, from the Edinburgh Festival Fringe, but using a professional orchestra, may have its rough patches, but it is very well cast, with **Mary Timmons** a pleasing heroine, who blends appealingly with **Steven Griffin** as her lover, John Manners. He sings very strongly, especially when he domi-

nates the opera's spectacular finale, when everything is happily resolved. **Davis Lyle's** conducting is full of vigour and the opera comes vividly to life in this excellent recording, well balanced and with a fine, full theatrical ambience.

The Savoy Operas

The Savoy Operas: EMI recordings: (i) *The Gondoliers; Cello Concerto* (CFP 2 13428-2 (2)). **(ii)** *HMS Pinafore; Trial by Jury* (CFP 2 13433-2 (2)). **(iii)** *Iolanthe;* **(xi)** *Overture Di Ballo* (CFP 2 13439-2 (2)). **(iv)** *The Mikado* (CFP 2 13444-(2)). **(v)** *Patience;* **(xiii)** *Symphony in E, 'Irish'* (CFP 2 13449-2 (2)). **(vi)** *The Pirates of Penzance;* **(xi)** *Overtures Cox & Box; Princess Ida; The Sorcerer;* **(xii)** *In Memoriam* (CFP 2 13454-2 (2)). **(vii)** *Ruddigore;* **(xii)** *The Merchant of Venice: suite; The Tempest: suite* (CFP 2 13459-2 (2)). **(ix)** *The Yeomen of the Guard* (CFP 2 13465-2 (2))

& **(BB)** *** EMI (ADD/DDD) 5 74468-2 (16). (i) Graham; (i; vi) Milligan; (i; iii; v; ix) Young; (i; iv; ix) G. Evans; (i; ii; iv; vi–ix) Lewis; (i–iv; vi; viii; ix) Cameron; (i–ix) Brannigan, Morison; (i–vi; ix) Thomas; (i–vii; ix) Sinclair; (ii; iii; v–viii) G. Baker; (iii) Cantelo; (iii; vi) Harper; (iii; iv) Wallace; (v) Shaw, Anthony, Harwood, Harper; (vii) Blackburn, Bowden, Rouleau; (ix) Dowling; Glyndebourne Festival Ch., Pro Arte O, Sargent; (x) Lloyd Webber, LSO, Mackerras; (xi) Pro Arte O or BBC SO, Sargent; (xii) CBSO, Dunn; (xiii) RLPO, Groves

The distinguished **Sir Malcolm Sargent** EMI series of the Savoy Operas are now available separately on Classics for Pleasure, but this generously filled box is at super-budget price and is first-class value for money. The performances are uniformly notable for the quality of the soloists (and, indeed, the excellent chorus). Sargent was a long-experienced advocate and he conducts with consistent authority, if not always with the 'first-night' zest that Isidore Godfrey managed consistently to achieve in his D'Oyly Carte recordings.

The Gondoliers is a case in point. Sargent chose a curiously slow tempo for the *Cachucha*, while the long opening scene is rather relaxed and leisurely. At the entrance of the Duke of Plaza Toro (**Sir Geraint Evans**, no less) things wake up considerably and **Owen Brannigan**, whose larger-than-life vocal personality dominates the whole series, is a perfectly cast Don Alhambra. **Edna Graham** only sang in this one recording, but she is a charmingly small-voiced Casilda, and there is much else to enjoy.

It was to Owen Brannigan's credit that, little as he has to do in *HMS Pinafore* without the dialogue, he conveys the force of Dick Deadeye's personality so strongly. **George Baker** is splendid as Sir Joseph and **John Cameron**, **Richard Lewis** and (especially) **Monica Sinclair** as Buttercup make much of their songs. **Elsie Morison** is rather disappointing: she spoils the end of her lovely song in Act I by singing sharp. The whole of the final scene is musically quite ravishing, and if Sir Malcolm fails to find quite all the wit in the music he is never less than lively.

There is much to praise, too, in *Iolanthe*. The climax of Act I, the scene in which the Queen of the Fairies lays a curse on members of both Houses of Parliament, shows most excitingly what can be achieved with the 'full operatic treatment'. George Baker is an excellent Lord Chancellor: the famous *Nightmare Song* is very well and clearly sung; however, for some ears John Cameron's dark timbre may not readily evoke an Arcadian Shepherd. The two Earls and Private Willis are excellent, and all of Act II – except perhaps Iolanthe's recitative and ballad near the end (which is always a bit of a problem) – goes well. The famous Trio with the Lord Chancellor and the two Earls is a joy.

The Sargent set of *The Mikado* was the first to be recorded, in 1957, but it has been given remarkable vividness and presence by the digital remastering. The grand operatic style for the finales of both acts, the trio about the 'death' of Nanki-Poo, and the glee that follows are characteristic of the stylish singing, even if the humour is less readily caught than in the D'Oyly Carte version. Owen Brannigan makes a fine Mikado, but the star performance is that of Richard Lewis, who sings most engagingly throughout as Nanki-Poo. Elsie Morison is back on form as a charming Yum-Yum, and Monica Sinclair is a generally impressive Katisha, although she could sound more convinced when she sings 'These Arms shall Now Enfold You'. This set is available separately (7 64403-2).

Patience was one of the great successes of the Sargent cycle. It is a pity that there is no dialogue, which is so important to establish the character of Bunthorne, the 'fleshly poet'. But there is more business than usual from this EMI series and a convincing theatrical atmosphere. The chorus is a strong feature throughout, and Elsie Morison's Patience, George Baker's Bunthorne and John Cameron's Grosvenor are all admirably characterized, while the military men are also excellent.

Once again in *Pirates*, the EMI recording has more atmosphere than usual, and the performance is (for the most part) highly successful, stylish as well as lively, conveying both the fun of the words and the charm of the music. Undoubtedly the star of this piece is George Baker: he is a splendid Major-General, and Owen Brannigan is his inimitable self as the Sergeant of the Police. The performance takes a little time to warm up, and in 'Poor Wandering One', Mabel's opening cadenza, Elsie Morison is angular and overdramatic. However, elsewhere she is much more convincing, especially in the famous duet, 'Leave Me not to Pine Alone'. The choral contributions are pleasingly refined yet have no lack of vigour. 'Hail Poetry' is resplendent, while the choral finale is vigorously done and with a balance which allows the inner parts to emerge effectively.

In most respects *Ruddigore* crowned the EMI series. Sargent's essentially lyrical approach brings out the associations this lovely score has with Schubert. The performance is beautifully sung. Perhaps George Baker sounds a little old in voice for Robin Oakapple, but he manages his 'character' transformation later in the opera splendidly. **Pamela Bowden** is a first-class Mad Margaret, and her short Donizettian scene is superbly done. Equally Richard Lewis is an admirably bumptious Richard. Owen Brannigan's delicious Act II duet with Mad Margaret has irresistible gentility. The drama is well managed too; the scene in the

picture gallery (given a touch of added resonance by the recording) is effectively sombre. Altogether a superb set, probably unsurpassed on record.

Sargent's *Trial by Jury* (with George Baker as the Judge) is by general consent the best there is, splendidly spirited and very well sung and recorded; and *The Yeomen of the Guard* is also very fine. The trios and quartets with which this score abounds are most beautifully performed and skilfully balanced, and the ear is continually beguiled. Owen Brannigan's portrayal of Wilfred again comes up trumps, and Monica Sinclair is a memorable Dame Carruthers. The finales to both acts have striking breadth, and the delightfully sung trio of Elsie, Phoebe and the Dame in the finale of Act II is a charming example of the many felicities of this set. 'Strange Adventure', too, is beautifully done. There is very little feeling of humour, but the music triumphs and, as with the rest of the series, the sound is excellent, with fine presence and definition.

It might have been better had EMI not included the fillers which accompanied the individual issues of the operas. The most interesting and most disappointing is the *Cello Concerto*, written when Sullivan was 19, after he returned from study in Leipzig. It was given a few performances and then forgotten. In 1964 the one surviving score was destroyed in the fire at Chappell's publishing house; but the work was reconstructed in the late 1980s with the help of the solo cello part. Sadly, the end result hardly justifies such labours. Curiously proportioned, with the first movement too brief for any symphonic pretensions and with themes less than memorable, it is a lightweight divertissement, pleasant but undistinguished. However, **Julian Lloyd Webber** and **Mackerras**, very well recorded, do all they can to give the flimsy inspiration some bite.

The *Symphony* is a far better proposition, pleasingly lyrical, with echoes of Schumann as much as the more predictable Mendelssohn and Schubert. The jaunty *Allegretto* of the third movement with its 'Irish' tune on the oboe is nothing less than haunting. **Groves** and the **RLPO** give an affectionate performance, and the 1986 recording has emerged freshly on CD.

The pair of Shakespeare-inspired *Suites* are also well worth having. The longer selection from *The Tempest* dates from 1861, the same year as the *Cello Concerto*, but shows distinctive flair and orchestral confidence. The shorter *Merchant of Venice Suite* was composed five years later; almost immediately, the writing begins to anticipate the lively style which was so soon to find a happy marriage with Gilbert's words. The performance here is highly infectious and the sound is first class. Of the overtures, *Di ballo* is the most useful, well worth having in Sargent's performance, but *In Memoriam*, a somewhat inflated religious piece, written for the 1866 Norwich Festival, is for Sullivan aficionados only.

The Major Decca Analogue Stereo Sets

Complete Decca D'Oyly Carte Recordings: *Cox and Box; The Gondoliers; The Grand Duke; HMS Pinafore; Iolanthe; The Mikado; Patience; The Pirates of Penzance; Princess Ida; Ruddigore; The*

Sorcerer; Trial by Jury; Utopia Ltd; The Yeomen of the Guard; The Zoo; plus Overtures: Di Ballo; Macbeth; Marmion; Pineapple Poll (ballet, arr. Mackerras); excerpts: Henry VIII; Victoria and Merrie England

↦ Ⓑ *** Decca (ADD) 473 631-2 (24). Artists & orchestras listed below, cond. Godfrey; Nash; Sargent; Mackerras

(i) *Cox and Box* (libretto by F. C. Burnand) complete; (ii) *Ruddigore* (complete; without dialogue)

Ⓑ *** Double Decca (ADD) 473 656-2 (2). (i) Styler, Riordan, Adams; New SO of L.; (ii) Reed, Round, Sandford, Riley, Adams, Hindmarsh, Knight, Sansom, Allister, D'Oyly Carte Op. Ch., ROHCG O, Godfrey

The Gondoliers (complete; with dialogue)

Ⓑ *** Decca Double (ADD) 473 632-2 (2). Reed, Skitch, Sandford, Round, Styler, Knight, Toye, Sansom, Wright, D'Oyly Carte Op. Ch., New SO of L., Godfrey

(i; ii) *The Grand Duke*; (ii) *Henry VIII: March & Graceful Dance*; (iii) *Overture Di Ballo*

Ⓑ *** Double Decca (ADD) 473 635-2 (2). (i) Reed, Reid, Sandford, Rayner, Ayldon, Ellison, Conroy-Ward, Lilley, Holland, Goss, Metcalfe, D'Oyly Carte Op. Ch.; (ii) RPO, Nash; (iii) Philh. O, Mackerras

HMS Pinafore (complete; with dialogue)

↦ 🏵 Ⓑ **** Double Decca (ADD) 473 638-2. Reed, Skitch, Round, Adams, Hindmarsh, Wright, Knight, D'Oyly Carte Op. Ch., New SO of L., Godfrey

Iolanthe (complete; with dialogue)

Ⓑ *** Double Decca (ADD) 473 641-2 (2). Sansom, Reed, Adams, Round, Sandford, Styler, Knight, Newman, D'Oyly Carte Op. Ch., Grenadier Guards Band, New SO, Godfrey

The Mikado (complete; without dialogue)

↦ Ⓑ *** Double Decca (ADD) 473 644-2 (2). Ayldon, Wright, Reed, Sandford, Masterson, Holland, D'Oyly Carte Op. Ch., RPO, Nash

Patience (complete; with dialogue)

Ⓑ *** Double Decca (ADD) 473 647-2 (2). Sansom, Adams, Cartier, Potter, Reed, Sandford, Newman, Lloyd-Jones, Toye, Knight, D'Oyly Carte Op. Ch. & O, Godfrey

The Pirates of Penzance (complete; with dialogue)

↦ Ⓑ *** Double Decca (ADD) 473 650-2. Reed, Adams, Potter, Masterson, Palmer, Brannigan, D'Oyly Carte Op. Ch., RPO, Godfrey

(i) *Princess Ida* (complete; without dialogue); (ii) *Pineapple Poll* (ballet; arr. Mackerras)

Ⓑ *** Double Decca (ADD) 473 653-2 (2). (i) Sandford, Potter, Palmer, Skitch, Reed, Adams, Raffell, Cook, Harwood, Palmer, Hood, Masterson, D'Oyly Carte Op. Ch., RPO, Sargent; (ii) Philh. O, Mackerras

(i) *The Sorcerer* (complete; without dialogue); (ii) *The Zoo* (libretto by Bolton Rowe)

Ⓑ *** Double Decca (ADD) 473 659-2 (2). (i) Adams, D. Palmer, Styler, Reed, C. Palmer, Masterson; (ii) Reid, Sandford, Ayldon, Goss, Metcalfe; nar. Shovelton; (i; ii) D'Oyly Carte Op. Ch., RPO; (i) Godfrey; (ii) Nash

(i) *Utopia Ltd* (complete). Overtures: *Macbeth; Marmion; Victoria and Merrie England*

Ⓑ **(*) Double Decca (ADD) 473 662-2 (2). (i) Sandford, Reed, Ayldon, Ellison, Buchan, Conroy-Ward, Reid, Broad, Rayner, Wright, Porter, Field, Goss, Merri, Holland, Griffiths, D'Oyly Carte Op. Ch.; RPO, Nash

(i) *The Yeomen of the Guard* (complete; without dialogue); (ii) *Trial by Jury*

↦ Ⓑ *** Double Decca (ADD) 473 665-2. Hood, Reed, Sandford, Adams, Raffell; (i) Harwood, Knight; (ii) Round; D'Oyly Carte Op. Ch.; (i) RPO, Sargent; (ii) ROHCG O, Godfrey

Decca have now additionally provided their twelve major sets in a slip-case; and they have restored the splendid original artwork on each separate reissue, which are offered at a new lower price. The Decca series usually has the advantage (or disadvantage, according to taste) of including the dialogue. The **D'Oyly Carte** performances are splendid in every way, given recordings which, without sacrificing clarity, convey with perfect balance the stage atmosphere.

The Grand Duke was the 14th and last of the Savoy operas. The present recording, the only complete version, came after a successful concert presentation in 1975, and the recorded performance has both polish and vigour, although the chorus does not display the crispness of articulation of ready familiarity. The recording is characteristically brilliant. The bonuses are well worth having, with **Mackerras's** account of the *Overture Di Ballo* showing more delicacy of approach than usual, though certainly not lacking sparkle.

The 1960 **Godfrey** set of *HMS Pinafore* is in our view the finest of all the D'Oyly Carte analogue stereo recordings. **Donald Adams's** assumption of the role of Dick Deadeye on Decca (which does have the dialogue) is little short of inspired, and his larger-than-life characterization underpins the whole piece. The rest of the cast make a splendid team: **Jean Hindmarsh** is a totally convincing Josephine – she sings with great charm – and **John Reed's** Sir Joseph Porter is a delight.

In the D'Oyly Carte set of *The Gondoliers* the solo singing throughout is consistently good, the ensembles have plenty of spirit and the dialogue is for the most part well spoken. As a performance this is on the whole preferable to the Sargent account.

With *Iolanthe*, the 1960 Decca set was given added panache by the introduction of the **Grenadier Guards Band** into the *March of the Peers*. **Mary Sansom** is quite a convincing Phyllis, and if her singing has not the sense of style that Elsie

Morison brought to the part, she is completely at home with the dialogue. Also **Alan Styler** makes a vivid and charming personal identification with the role of Strephon, an Arcadian shepherd. **John Reed** is very good as the Lord Chancellor: dryly whimsical, and he provides an individual characterization. **Godfrey's** conducting is lighter and more infectious than Sargent's in the Act I finale, and there is much to delight the ear in the famous Trio of Act II with the Lord Chancellor and the two Earls.

The 1973 stereo remake of *The Mikado* by the D'Oyly Carte Company directed by **Royston Nash** is a complete success in every way and shows the Savoy tradition at its most attractive. It is a pity no dialogue is included, but the choral singing is first rate, and the glees are refreshingly done, polished and refined, yet with plenty of vitality. **John Reed** is a splendid Ko-Ko, **Kenneth Sandford** a vintage Pooh-Bah and **Valerie Masterson** a charming Yum-Yum. **John Ayldon** as the Mikado provides a laugh of terrifying bravura, and **Lyndsie Holland** is a formidable and commanding Katisha.

Owen Brannigan was surely born to play the Sergeant of Police in *The Pirates of Penzance*, and he does so unforgettably. On Decca there is a considerable advantage in the inclusion of the dialogue, and here theatrical spontaneity is well maintained. **Donald Adams** is a splendid Pirate King. **John Reed's** portrayal of the Major General is one of his strongest roles, while **Valerie Masterson** is an excellent Mabel. **Godfrey's** conducting is as affectionate as ever, and the dialogue undoubtedly adds an extra sense of the theatre.

Patience and *Ruddigore* were the two greatest successes of the Sargent series. However, the extra card in the D'Oyly Carte hand in *Patience* is the dialogue, so important in this opera above all, with its spoken poetry; if **Mary Sansom** does not give the strongest portrayal vocally of the main role, both Bunthorne and Grosvenor are well played, while the military numbers, led by **Donald Adams** in glorious voice, have an unforgettable vigour and presence.

The D'Oyly Carte *Ruddigore* comes up surprisingly freshly, in fact better than we had remembered it, though it is a pity the dialogue was omitted. The performance includes *The battle's roar is over*, which is (for whatever reason) traditionally omitted. There is much to enjoy here (especially **Gillian Knight** and **Donald Adams**, whose *Ghosts' high noon* song is a marvellous highlight). **Isidore Godfrey** is his inimitable sprightly self and the chorus and orchestra are excellent. A fine traditional D'Oyly Carte set, then, brightly recorded.

Princess Ida is fake feminism with a vengeance. **Elizabeth Harwood** in the name-part sings splendidly, and **John Reed's** irritably gruff portrayal of the irascible King Gama is memorable; he certainly is a properly 'disagreeable man'. The rest of the cast is no less strong and, with excellent teamwork from the company as a whole and a splendid recording, spacious and immediate, this has much to offer, even if Sullivan's invention is somewhat variable in quality. The CD transfer is outstanding and the 1965 recording has splendid depth and presence. As a bonus we are offered **Mackerras's** vivacious and polished 1982 digital recording of his scintillating ballet score, *Pineapple Poll*.

The Sorcerer is the Gilbert and Sullivan equivalent of *L'elisir d'amore*, only here a whole English village is affected, with hilarious results. **John Reed's** portrayal of the sorcerer himself is one of the finest of all his characterizations. The plot drew from Sullivan a great deal of music in his fey, pastoral vein. By 1966, when the set was made, Decca had stretched the recording budget to embrace the **RPO**, and the orchestral playing is especially fine, as is the singing of the **D'Oyly Carte Chorus**, at their peak. John Reed gives a truly virtuoso performance of his famous introductory song, while the spell-casting scene is equally compelling. The final sequence in Act II is also memorable. The sound is well up to Decca's usual high standard .

Both recordings of *The Yeomen of the Guard*, Decca's and EMI's sets, were conducted by **Sir Malcolm Sargent**. The later Decca account has marginally the finer recording and Sir Malcolm's breadth of approach is immediately apparent in the *Overture*. Both chorus and orchestra (the **RPO**) are superbly expansive and there is again consistently fine singing from all the principals (and especially from **Elizabeth Harwood** as Elsie). This Decca *Yeomen* is unreservedly a success, with its brilliant and atmospheric recording. In any case, the considerable bonus is the inclusion of Godfrey's immaculately stylish and affectionate *Trial by Jury* with **John Reed** as the Judge.

Utopia Ltd was revived for the D'Oyly Carte centenary London season in 1974, which led to this recording. Its complete neglect is unaccountable. **Royston Nash** shows plenty of skill in the matter of musical characterization, and the solo singing is consistently assured. When **Meston Reid** as Captain FitzBattleaxe sings 'You see I can't do myself justice' in *Oh, Zara*, he is far from speaking the truth – this is a performance of considerable bravura. The ensembles are not always as immaculately disciplined as one is used to from the D'Oyly Carte, and *Eagle high* is disappointingly focused: the intonation here is less than secure. However, the sparkle and spontaneity of the performance as a whole are irresistible.

The Zoo (with a libretto by Bolton Rowe, a pseudonym of B. C. Stevenson) dates from June 1875, only three months after the success of *Trial by Jury* – which it obviously seeks to imitate, as the music more than once reminds us. Although the libretto lacks the finesse and whimsicality of Gilbert, it is not without humour, and many of the situations presented by the plot (and indeed the actual combinations of words and music) are typical of the later Savoy Operas. As the piece has no spoken dialogue it is provided here with a stylized narration, well enough presented by **Geoffrey Shovelton**. The performance is first class, splendidly sung, fresh as paint and admirably recorded, and it fits very well alongside *The Sorcerer*. The CD transfer is more brightly lit than its companion, and the opera has animal noises to set the scene and close the opera.

Telarc Mackerras Series

HMS Pinafore

⊶ ✸ ******** Telarc CD 80374. Suart, Allen, Evans, Schade, Palmer, Adams, Ch. & O of Welsh Nat. Opera, Mackerras

The Mikado

🎭 ⚙ **** Telarc CD 80284. Adams, Rolfe Johnson, Suart, McLaughlin, Palmer, van Allan, Folwell, Ch. & O of Welsh Nat. Opera, Mackerras

The Pirates of Penzance

*** Telarc CD80353. Mark Ainsley, Evans, Suart, van Allan, Adams, Knight, Ch. & O of Welsh Nat. Opera, Mackerras

(i) The Yeomen of the Guard; (ii) Trial by Jury

*** Telarc 80404 (2). (i) Mellor, Archer, Palmer; (i; ii) Suart, Adams, Maxwell; (ii) Evans, Banks, Savidge; Ch. & O of Welsh Nat. Opera, Mackerras

HMS Pinafore; The Mikado; The Pirates of Penzance; Trial by Jury; The Yeomen of the Guard

🎭 ⚙ Ⓜ **** Telarc CD 80500 (5). Above five complete recordings; cond. Mackerras

As can be seen, the five Telarc operas also come together in a slip-case, with five CDs offered for the cost of three – in every way a superb bargain.

Sir Charles Mackerras here gives an exuberant reading of the first operetta of the cycle, *HMS Pinafore*. The lyricism and transparency of Sullivan's inspiration shine out with winning freshness. The casting is not just starry but inspired. Even such a jaunty number as the 'encore' trio, *Never mind the why and wherefore*, gains in point when so well sung and played as here, with **Allen** joined by **Rebecca Evans** as an appealing Josephine and **Richard Suart** as a dry Sir Joseph Porter. **Michael Schade** is heady-toned as the hero, Ralph Rackstraw, while among character roles **Felicity Palmer** is a marvellously fruity Little Buttercup, with **Richard van Allan** as Bill Bobstay and the veteran, **Donald Adams**, a lugubrious Dick Deadeye. As with the previous CDs of *Mikado* and *Pirates of Penzance*, Telarc squeezes the whole score on to a single CD, vividly recorded.

With the overture again omitted (not Sullivan's work) and one of the stanzas in Ko-Ko's 'little list' song (with words unpalatable today), the whole fizzing **Mackerras** performance of *The Mikado* is fitted on to a single, very well-filled disc. The cast has no weak link, and Mackerras is electrically sharp at brisk speeds, sounding totally idiomatic and giving this most popular of the G&S operettas an irresistible freshness at high voltage. The tingling vigour of Sullivan's invention is constantly brought out, with performances from the **WNO Chorus and Orchestra** at once powerful and refined. With that sharpness of focus Sullivan's parodies of grand opera become more than just witty imitations. So Katisha's aria at the end of Act II, with **Felicity Palmer** the delectable soloist, has a Verdian depth of feeling. It is good too to hear the veteran Savoyard, **Donald Adams**, as firm and resonant as he was in his D'Oyly Carte recording made no less than 33 years earlier.

The Pirates of Penzance is characteristic of the rest of this splendid Telarc series. **Mackerras's** exuberant direction often brings fast tempi (as in *How beautifully blue the sky*) but the underlying lyricism is as ardently conveyed as ever, especially by **John Mark Ainsley**, who is a really passionate Frederic. **Rebecca Evans** makes him a good partner and sings with great charm as Mabel. Needless to say, **Richard Suart** is a memorable Major General (his patter song is thrown off at great speed) and **Donald Adams** has not lost his touch. His vintage portrayal of the Pirate King is well matched by **Gillian Knight's** Ruth in their engaging 'Paradox' duet of Act II. While memories of Owen Brannigan are far from banished, **Richard van Allan** is a suitably bumptious Sergeant of the Police, and the **Welsh Opera Chorus** are splendidly fervent in *Hail poetry!* The recording has fine depth and realism and as a single-disc modern digital version this will be hard to beat.

The Yeomen of the Guard, the fourth Telarc issue of G&S, is very involving as a performance, conveying most exuberantly the sparkle as well as the emotional weight of this most serious of the canon. **Alwyn Mellor** makes an appealing heroine. Among the others, **Felicity Palmer** makes a delectably fire-snorting Dame Carruthers, and the veteran, **Donald Adams**, an incomparable Sergeant Meryll. (His cries of 'Ghastly, ghastly' when cornered by the Dame are wonderful.) **Richard Suart** as Jack Point characterizes vividly in authentic style, and the only weak link is the Fairfax of **Neil Archer**, who too often sounds strained. Even so, the final bringing-together of Fairfax and Elsie could not be more touching. The absence of spoken dialogue allows *Trial by Jury* to be included as a fill-up, with Suart even more aptly cast and Adams again incomparable as the Usher, while the **WNO Chorus** again sings with ideal clarity. Otherwise it involves different singers, with **Rebecca Evans** golden-toned as the Plaintiff and **Barry Banks** firm if light as the Defendant.

Other complete recordings

Cox and Box (original, full-length, 1866 version)

*** Divine Arts 2-4104. Berger, Kennedy, Francke, Barclay

This lively and enjoyable performance recreates the original version of *Cox and Box*, first heard at a private gathering at the librettist Burnand's own house in May 1866, with Sullivan himself improvising the accompaniment at the piano. The orchestration came a year later for the work's prèmiere at the Adelphi Theatre, and the *Overture* and the duet *Stay Bouncer stay* were also added subsequently.

The present account (based on a professional production for **London Chamber Opera**) is spirited and polished, and its considerable length (over an hour) serves to demonstrate the reasons for Sullivan's own shortened version in 1894. It was further truncated in 1921 to produce the concise version which remained in the **D'Oyly Carte Company's** repertoire until the late 1970s. However, the performance on the present disc is most enjoyable and does not outstay its welcome. **Donald Francke** is a splendidly rumbustious Bouncer. The charming original compound-time version of the *Bacon lullaby* is considerably different from the song known in the revised score. *Stay Bouncer stay* is added in for good measure. Of course, one misses the orchestra, but the piano accompaniment, using a suitable period instrument, is well managed. The words are admirably clear, a consideration which would surely have been just as important to Burnand as to Gilbert. It is good to see that the production is dedicated to the memory of the late Arthur Jacobs, biographer of Sullivan, at whose insistence this recording (sponsored by the Sullivan Society) was issued commercially.

(i) *Iolanthe*: highlights; (ii) *The Mikado* (complete; without dialogue)

🔊 ⓑ *** CfP (ADD) 575 9902 (2). (i) Shilling, Harwood, Moyle, Dowling, Begg, Bevan, Greene, Kern; (ii) Holmes, Revill, Wakefield, Studholme, Dowling, Allister, John Heddle Nash; Sadler's Wells Op. Ch. & O, Faris

The **Sadler's Wells** *Iolanthe* is stylistically superior to Sargent's earlier EMI recording and is often musically superior to the Decca/D'Oyly Carte versions. **Alexander Faris** often chooses untraditional tempi. *When I went to the bar* is very much faster than usual, with less dignity but with a compensating lightness of touch. **Eric Shilling** is excellent here, as he is also in the *Nightmare song*, which is really *sung*, much being made of the ham operatic recitative at the beginning. The lovers, **Elizabeth Harwood** as Phyllis and **Julian Moyle** as Strephon, make a charming duo, and the Peers are splendid. Their entry chorus is thrilling and their reaction to the Fairy Queen's curse is delightfully, emphatically horrified, while the whole Act I finale (the finest in any of the operas) goes with infectious stylishness. All the solo singing is of a high standard and **Leon Greene** sings the Sentry song well. But one has to single out for special praise **Patricia Kern's** really lovely singing of Iolanthe's aria at the end of the opera. The recording has splendid presence and realism.

The Sadler's Wells *Mikado* is traditional in the best sense, bringing a humorous sparkle to the proceedings which gives great delight. **Clive Revill** is a splendid Ko-Ko; **John Heddle Nash** is an outstanding Pish-Tush, and it is partly because of him that the *Chippy chopper* trio is so effective. **Denis Dowling** is a superb Pooh-Bah, and **Marion Studholme** a charming Yum-Yum. **Jean Allister's** Katisha is first rate in every way; listen to the venom she puts into the word '*bravado*' in the Act I finale. Even the chorus scores a new point by their stylized singing of *Mi-ya-sa-ma*, which sounds engagingly mock-Japanese. The one disappointment is **John Holmes** in the name-part. He sings well but conveys little of the mock-satanic quality. But this is a small point in an otherwise magnificent set, which has a vivacious new overture arranged by **Charles Mackerras**.

Collections

'The Best of Gilbert and Sullivan', highlights from: The Gondoliers; HMS Pinafore; Iolanthe; The Mikado; Patience; The Pirates of Penzance; Ruddigore; Trial by Jury; The Yeomen of the Guard

ⓑ *** EMI (ADD) 5 73869-2 (3). Morison, M. Sinclair, Thomas, G. Baker, Lewis, Brannigan, Young, Wallace, Cameron, Evans, Milligan, Glyndebourne Festival Ch., Pro Arte O, Sargent

This three-disc EMI set makes a good supplement for the comparable Double Decca collection (see above). The **Sir Malcolm Sargent** recordings are generally more grandly operatic in style and at times they are rather less fun. But, as one might expect from the starry cast list, there is some outstandingly fine solo and concerted singing from the principals in the lyrical numbers. Obviously with the film *Topsy-Turvy* in mind, the major selection is from *The Mikado* (some 20 items), and Sargent's expansive manner has much in common with **Carl Davis's** approach (especially in the Finale). With **Owen Brannigan** as The Mikado, **Monica Sinclair** as Katisha, **Richard Lewis** as Nanki-Poo, **Elsie Morison** as Yum-Yum and **Ian Wallace** as Pooh Bah, the results will surely please those who enjoyed the movie.

Princess Ida and *The Sorcerer* are not represented, but the other key operas (apart from the single Learned Judge's number from *Trial by Jury*) have from between five to eight items each, including the substantial and treasurable finales from *Iolanthe* and (to conclude the programme) *The Yeomen of the Guard*. Besides taking the role of the Judge in *Trial*, **George Baker** is a stalwart of the series and he delivers the famous patter songs with aplomb.

No less a figure than **Sir Geraint Evans** takes his place as the Duke of Plaza Toro (*Gondoliers*) and Jack Point (*Yeomen*). Owen Brannigan is an unforgettable Sergeant of Police (*Pirates*) and is hardly less memorable as Private Willis (*Iolanthe*) and Sir Despard (*Ruddigore*). The choral contribution is first class, and Sargent conducts freshly throughout, although not always with the sparkle that Godfrey commanded, as is instanced by his curiously measured *Cachucha* in *The Gondoliers*. But the selections from *Patience* and *Ruddigore* show him and this talented company (Elsie Morison especially) at their very finest.

Two recommendable separate collections from Sargent's recordings are available on Classics for Pleasure (3 52398-2 and 5 86655-2) each with approximately 72 minutes of excerpts.

Highlights from: (i; ii) HMS Pinafore; (iii; iv) The Mikado; (ii; iv; v) The Pirates of Penzance; (ii; vi) Trial by Jury; (vii) The Yeomen of the Guard

*** Telarc CD 80431. Suart; with (i) Allen, Palmer; (ii) Evans; (iii) Rolfe Johnson, McLaughlin, Howells, Watson; (iv) van Allan, Folwell; (v) Mark Ainsley, Gossage; (vi) Banks, Garrett, Savidge, Rhys Davies; (vii) Archer, Mellor, Stephen; Welsh Nat. Op. Ch. & O, Mackerras

Even with 76 minutes' playing time, this can be no more than a sampler of Mackerras's effervescent G. & S. series for Telarc, dominated by the dry-timbred **Richard Suart** in the key patrician roles. As can be seen, most of the other soloists change with each opera, but the standard remains extraordinarily high. The choice of excerpts is inevitably arbitrary, with about half a dozen items from each of the two-Act operas and three from *Trial by Jury*. If you buy this, you will inevitably be tempted to go on to one or other of the complete sets. Nevertheless it is a splendid collection in its own right. Characteristically first-class Telarc sound.

SUPPÉ, Franz von (1819–95)

Overtures: Beautiful Galathea; The Jolly Robbers (Banditenstreich); Light Cavalry; Morning, Noon and Night in Vienna; Pique Dame; Poet and Peasant

Ⓜ (**(*)) Archipel mono ARPCD 0373. Hallé O, Barbirolli – CHOPIN: *Piano Concerto 1* (***)

Sir John's vintage collection has tremendous spirit and the orchestral playing is crisply alert and sparkling, if not always completely refined. The (originally Pye) recordings have been most effectively remastered, which compensates for a certain overall brashness. The recording is somewhat dry, but has a convincing background acoustic. The extraordinary Chopin coupling, with **Rubinstein** the soloist, is listed as a 'bonus'. What a bonus!

Overtures: Die Frau Meisterin; Die Irrfahrt um's Glück; Light Cavalry; Morning, Noon and Night in Vienna; Pique Dame; Poet and Peasant; Tantalusqualen; Wiener-Jubel (Vienna Jubilee)

🎶 ✦ Ⓑ **** EMI 5 09029 2. ASMF, Marriner

Marriner's collection of Suppé *Overtures* has been out of the catalogue too long and now goes straight to the top of the list. The sound has opulence, bloom, a wide amplitude, realistic definition and a natural presence. The performances admirably combine exuberance, fine ensemble and style. At Encore price this is a reissue not to be missed on any account.

OPERETTA

Die schöne Galathee

🎶 *** CPO 999 726. Bogner, Rickenbacher, Heyn, Kupfer, Koblenz State Theatre Ch., Rhenish State Op. O, Eitler

Starting with the famous galumphing overture, Suppé's one-act operetta on a classical theme is a delight. Pygmalion may still fall in love with his statue of Galathea, when she comes to life – a marvellous moment for the bright, clear soprano, **Andrea Bogner** – but in this comic retelling she is just a provocative coquette, who much prefers the young Ganymed, taken here by another soprano, **Juliane Heyn**. First heard in Vienna in 1865, this starts like Offenbach in German, but turns into a precursor of Viennese operetta the moment that waltz-time is engaged. Based on a production in Koblenz on the Rhine, this is a sparkling, well-balanced recording, with the comic personas characterfully taken by **Hans-Jurg Rickenbacher** and **Michael Kupfer**. It might have been even more fun had a sprinkling of spoken dialogue been included. As it is, the single disc comes with libretto and translation in a cumbersome double-disc jewel-case.

SURINACH, Carlos (1915–97)

Piano Concerto

Ⓑ *** Decca Eloquence (ADD) 476 2971. Larrocha, RPO,

Burgos – ALBENIZ: *Rapsodia española*; MONTSALVATGE: *Concerto breve* ***; TURINA: *Rapsodia sinfónica* ***

Carlos Surinach's *Piano Concerto*, like its Montsalvatge companion on this disc, was written for **Alicia de Larrocha**, and, as with that work, she plays it with total conviction. If, once again, the writing is short on really memorable themes, it is made enjoyable through its colourful orchestration, plus a fine performance, backed up by first-class Decca (1977) sound. Anyone who enjoys a dash of Spanish colour in their music will enjoy this rare *Concerto*, and offered with imaginative couplings too.

SUSSMAYR, Franz (1766–1803)

Requiem

**(*) Avie AV 0047. Jette, Larmore, Taylor, Owens, St Olaf Ch, St Paul CO, Delfs – MOZART: *Requiem* **(*)

All credit to the recording producer, Malcolm Bruno, for searching out the long-forgotten *Requiem* of Franz Sussmayr, written about the time he made his completion of the Mozart *Requiem*. Though it is no masterpiece it is a fascinating curiosity, a setting in German written for one of the Austrian duchies which by a special papal dispensation were allowed to sing the Requiem in the vernacular. The choral writing is plain and direct in a simple homophonic idiom, influenced by the cadences of Austrian folk music. It is a style well-suited to this paraphrase of the usual Latin text. **Andreas Delfs's** direction, as in the Mozart with which it is coupled, is on the square side, but with fresh, alert singing by the **St Olaf Choir** under their director, Anton Armstrong, that matches the music well. Full, open sound.

SVENDSEN, Johann Severin (1840–1911)

Romance in G, Op. 26

ⒷⒷ *** Naxos 8.550329. Kang, Slovak (Bratislava) RSO, Leaper – HALVORSEN: *Air Norvégien etc.*; SIBELIUS: *Violin Concerto*; SINDING: *Légende* ***

Dong-Suk Kang plays Svendsen's once-popular *Romance in G* without sentimentality but with full-hearted lyricism. The balance places him a little too forward, but the recording is very satisfactory.

Symphonies 1 in D, Op. 4; 2 in B flat, Op. 15

ⒷⒷ *** Naxos 8.553898. Bournemouth SO, Engeset

ⒷⒷ **(*) Warner Apex 0927 40621-2. Norwegian R.O, Rasilainen

Symphonies 1 in D, Op. 4; 2 in B flat, Op. 23; Polonaise, Op. 28

*** Chan. 9932 Danish Nat. R. SO, Dausgaard

Symphonies 1-2; 2 Swedish Folk-Melodies, Op. 27

🎶 **** BIS CD 347. Gothenburg SO, Järvi

Svendsen's *D major Symphony* is a student work of astonishing assurance and freshness, in some ways even more remarkable than the *B flat*. **Neeme Järvi** gives first-class performances, sensitive and vital, and the excellent recordings earn them a strong recommendation.

Thomas Dausgaard and the **Danish Radio Orchestra** also capture the youthful exuberance of the one and the warmth and generosity of spirit of the other. This is captivating music and the Danes, among whom Svendsen spent so much of his life, respond with enthusiasm. Tempi are well judged though the Scherzo of the *D major* would benefit from being brisker. The *Polonaise* of 1881 is not the equal of the famous *Fest-Polonaise*. Recommended alongside though not necessarily in preference to Järvi.

Järvi's recording is also strongly challenged by **Bjarte Engeset** and the **Bournemouth Orchestra**. These players are obviously encountering this music with enthusiasm and they are well served by both the acoustic and the engineering.

There is nothing wrong with the Finlandia version from the **Norwegian Radio Orchestra** under **Ari Rasilainen** either, though the recording is not as good as BIS for Järvi.

(i) Octet in A, Op. 3; (i) Romance in G for Violin & Strings, Op. 26

🎵 *** Chan. 9258. ASMF Chamber Ens; (i) with Sillito –
NIELSEN: *String Quintet in G* ***

(i) Octet; String Quartet in A min., Op. 1

🎵 *** BIS CD753. Kontra Qt; with (i) Bjørnkjaer, Madsen, Rasmussen, Johansen

Svendsen's youthful *Octet*, Op. 3 is a product of his student years at Leipzig, and was obviously inspired by Mendelssohn. But it has a strong personality of its own and is full of lively and attractive invention. The Scherzo is particularly delightful. The **Kontra Quartet** and their colleagues give a spirited account of it, coupling it with another student work, the *A minor Quartet*, Op. 1. A good well-balanced sound.

However, those primarily wanting the *Octet* should turn to the **Academy of St Martin-in-the-Fields Chamber Ensemble** whose leader **Kenneth Sillito** plays the *G major Romance* as a fill-up. First-rate performances and recording.

String Quartet in A min., Op. 1; (i) String Quintet in C, Op. 5

🎵 *** CPO 999 858-2. Oslo String Qt; (i) with Graggerud

Two early works, composed while Svendsen was at the Leipzig Conservatoire. Both show a natural feeling for form and an unfailing sense of proportion. Svendsen thinks in long musical paragraphs, and his ideas have a strong, lyrical momentum as well as astonishing assurance and freshness. Op. 1 and Op. 5 were coupled together many years ago by the Hindar Quartet, but these Oslo players have much greater tonal blend and refinement, as well as unanimity of attack. Two delightful and rewarding scores that have been absurdly neglected, now very persuasively played and well recorded.

SWEELINCK, Jan (1562–1621)

KEYBOARD MUSIC

Allemand (Gratie); Est-ce Mars; Die flichtig Nimphae; Fantasia cromatica; Mein junges Leben hat ein End; Paduana Lachrymae; Pavana Philippi; Toccata a 3 G2; Toccata C2; Toccata Nono Toni; Toccata Primi Toni; Toccata Secundi Toni; Under der Linden grune; Von der Fortuna werd ich getrieben

Ⓝ **** Chan. 0758. Woolley

Robert Woolley, using two harpsichords, has produced a glorious CD of some of Sweelinck's most inspired keyboard music. There are all sorts of delights here, from the beautiful variations on *Mein junges Leben hat ein End*, to the substantial *Fantasia cromatica* which ends the recital – and what an impressive piece it is too. Sweelinck's music is full of imagination, taking influence from all over Europe and mixing them together to form an original voice. *Die flichtig Nimphae* is very charming indeed, but there is an unforced elegance about all the music on this CD which is quite captivating. The recital is superbly recorded and Robert Woolley is a masterful exponent of this repertoire.

Echo Fantasia in C; Fantasia cromatica; Fantasia primi toni a 4; Nun komm der Heiden Heiland; Passomezzo moderno a 4 Voc.; Pavana Lachrimae (arr. of Dowland); Pavana Philippi (Variatio); Praeludium (or Fantasia); Toccata in D min.; Variations on 'Allein Gott is der höh sei Her' Variations on 'Est-ce Mars'; Variations on 'Fortune my Foe'; Variations on 'Mein junges Leben hat ein End'

Ⓝ Ⓑ **** Naxos 8.570894. Glen Wilson (harpsichord)

Glen Wilson is also a splendid player and his less expensive recital is just as enticing as the Chandos collection. Items like the *Echo Fantasia*, and the *Variations on 'Fortune my Foe'* and *Pavana Philippi* are very diverting. But this whole recital, given demonstration recording, is first class.

ORGAN MUSIC

Allein Gott in der Höh sei Ehr; Ballo del granduca; Christe qui lux est et dies; Echo Fantasia (Ionian); Engelsche Foruyn; Erbarme dich mein; Est-ce Mars?; O Herre Gott; Fantasia (a-Phrygian); Fantasia Chromatica; Ich ruf zu dir, Herr Jesu Christ; Ick voer al over Rhijn; Ik heb den Heer lief (Psalm 116); Malle Sijmen; Mein junges Leben hat ein End; More palatino; Nun freut euch, lieben Christen gemein; Onder een linde groen; Ons is gheboren een kindekijn; Onse Vader hemelrijck; Pavana hispanica; Pavana Lachrimae; Pavana Philippi; Poolsche dans; Ricercar (Aeolian); Toccata (Ionian)

🎵 **** Hyp. CDA 67421/2 (2). Herrick (organ of the Norrfjärden Kyrka, Norrfjärden, Piteå, Sweden)

Sweelinck exerted enormous influence during his lifetime. **Christopher Herrick** has chosen the organ of the Norrfjärden Kyrka, Piteå, on the northeastern coast of Sweden. It is based on a reconstruction of the 1609–84 organ of the Tyskakyrkan in Stockholm, an instrument closely associated with one of Sweelinck's pupils. Herrick is completely attuned to the flavour and style of this repertoire and draws a consistently characterful sound from this lovely instrument and collectors should investigate this fine set of a composer who remains seriously underrated outside the Netherlands. The recording is in the best traditions of the house.

Ballo del granduca; Chorale variations: Erbarm dich mein, O Herr Gott; Mein junges Leben hat ein End'. Echo fantasia in A min.; Malle Sijmen; Onder een linde groen; Poolsche dans; Ricercar; Toccatas: in A min. & C

🅱🅱 **** Naxos 8.550904. Christie (C.B. Fisk organ, Houghton Chapel, Wellesley College, USA)

Those wanting a larger, more fully representative collection of Sweelinck's organ music can turn to Naxos, who do not usually let us down with their one-disc surveys. Certainly the Wellesley College organ sounds right, **James David Christie** is a persuasive exponent, and his pacing is convincing. The two *Toccatas* are the most commanding pieces here, the C *major* quite virtuosic. Sweelinck's chorale variations repeat the cantus firmus clearly with embellishments of increasing complexity. The secular variations are simpler. Those based on a Dutch song are derived from an English ballad, *All in a garden green*, and the jolly *Malle Sijmen* ('Simple Simon') is based on an old English dance-tune, and is piquantly registered. *Poolsche dans* ('Polish dance') is much more elaborate. It is in the middle section of the *Echo Fantasia* that the cuckoo-like echoes finally appear and the piece concludes like a toccata. Excellent recording.

Cantiones sacrae (1619)

🎧 **** Hyp. CDA 67103 (Nos. 1–21); CDA 67104 (Nos. 22–37). Trinity College Chapel Ch., Cambridge, Marlow

Sweelinck wrote a great deal of vocal music (though none in his own language), including French chansons and Psalm settings, and Italian madrigals. The 37 *Cantiones sacrae*, which date from 1691, are in Latin, for five-part choir, and surely represent him at a peak of inspiration. The range of texts is wide, but most pertain to major feasts of the liturgical year. This pair of Hyperion discs (each available separately) offers glorious music, gloriously sung. The simplicity and underlying vitality of the very first piece, *Non omnis qui dicit mihi, Domine*, captures the listener's ear, and the opening sequence of some half-a-dozen fairly serene settings is then interrupted by three exuberant motets of praise, *Ecce nunc benedicte Dominum, Cantate Domino* and the exultant *Venite exultemus Domino*. But the sequence which opens the second disc, beginning with *In illo tempore*, celebrating the naming of Jesus, is hardly less fine. The resonant acoustic is right for the music, but brings some distinct blurring of the upper focus. Nevertheless this is an outstanding set.

SZYMANOWSKI, Karol
(1882–1937)

(i; ii) Concert Overture, Op. 12; (iii; iv) Harnasie, Op. 55; Symphonies Nos. (i; ii) 2 in B flat, Op. 19; (i; iv–vi) 3 (Song of the Night), Op. 27; (i; v; vii) 4 (Symphonie concertante), Op. 60. (viii) 20 Mazurkas for Solo Piano, Op. 50/1 & 2; Theme & Variations for Solo Piano, Op. 3

🎧 🅱🅱 **(*) EMI Gemini (ADD) 585539-2 (2). (i) Polish R. Nat. SO; (ii) Kaspszyk; (iii) Bachleda, Kwasny, Polish R. O of Kraków, Wit; (iv) Polish R. Ch. of Kraków; (v) Semkow; (vi) Ochman; (vii) Paleczny; (viii) Blumenthal

This is an excellent and inexpensive way to explore this often marvellous composer. The *Second Symphony* is not as rewarding as the *Third*, but it is unusual in form: there are only two movements, the second being a set of variations, culminating in a fugue. The influences of Richard Strauss and Scriabin are clearly audible, if not altogether assimilated. The *Third Symphony* (*Song of the Night*), however, is one of the composer's most beautiful scores, with a heady, intoxicated – and intoxicating – atmosphere. These performances date from 1982, and they remain full and atmospheric, even if the quality of the orchestral playing, though good, has been superseded in more recent versions (the vibrato on the brass instruments will not be to all tastes). The gripping account of the ambitious *Concert Overture*, which sounds for all the world like an undiscovered symphonic poem by Richard Strauss, is highly enjoyable. In the *Symphonie concertante*, **Piotr Paleczny** is no mean artist and he has all the finesse and imagination as well as the requisite command of colour that this work calls for; **Wit** provides him with admirable support, and this 1979 account, as a whole, makes a stronger impression than the more recent Naxos version, similarly priced. *Harnasie* is also very successful; it reflects Szymanowski's discovery of the folk music of the Tatras. It calls for large forces, including a solo violinist as well as a tenor and full chorus, and poses obvious practical production problems. As always with this composer, there is a sense of rapture, the soaring, ecstatic lines and the intoxicating exoticism that distinguish the mature Szymanowski, and it comes across most tellingly here. The sound is spaciously wide-ranging and full, but it is a bit fierce on top. **Blumenthal's** accounts of the piano items are reasonably persuasive, though they are sound rather than inspired performances; however, they make a nice bonus.

(i) Violin Concertos 1–2; Concert Overture, Op. 12

*** Chan. 9496. (i) Mordkovitch; BBC PO, Sinaisky

Violin Concertos 1, Op. 35; 2, Op. 61; Nocturne; Tarantella

🅱🅱 *** Naxos 8.557981. Kaler, Warsaw PO, Wit

(i) Violin Concertos 1–2; (ii) Romance, Op. 23; 3 Paganini Caprices, Op. 40

(B) **** EMI 5 03429-2. Zehetmair; (i) CBSO, Rattle; (ii) Avenhaus

Thomas Zehetmair's deeply felt versions with **Rattle** and the **CBSO** conjure up the Szymanowskian sound-world with real flair, capturing the sensuous luminosity of the central movement; and Rattle unleashes the wildness of the finale with great vigour. The engineers deliver first-rate sound in both works and in the four violin and piano pieces, in which Zehetmair is well supported by the young German pianist, **Silke Avenhaus.**

Naxos offer an exceptionally clear recording of these four concertante works by Szymanowski, not just the two *Violin Concertos* but orchestrated versions of the *Nocturne* and *Tarantella*. **Ilya Kaler**, as on other Naxos discs, gives pure, clear readings, with flawless intonation and careful use of vibrato. Having a Polish conductor and orchestra as his accompanists adds to the idiomatic feel of each, with the magical orchestral sounds beautifully conjured up, particularly in *No. 1*, the more radical of the two works. This matches almost any current version at whatever price.

Lydia Mordkovitch is also admirably suited, full-toned and red-blooded, for these exotic concertos, helped by playing, richly recorded, from the **BBC Philharmonic** under **Vassily Sinaisky**. Both works are strongly contrasted with the early and extrovert *Concert Overture*, an illuminating coupling.

(i) Violin Concertos 1–2; Symphonies (ii) 3 (Song of the Night); (iii) 4 (Sinfonia concertante). (iv; v) Harnasie; (v; vi); Litany to the Virgin Mary; (v; vii) Love Songs of Hafiz; (v; viii) Songs of a Fairy-tale Princess; (v; vi; ix) Stabat Mater; (v; vi; x) King Roger, Op. 46

(B) *** EMI 5 14576-2 (4). CBSO, Rattle; with (i) Zehetmair; (ii) Garrison, Thomas; (iii) Andsnes; (iv) Robinson; (v) CBSO Ch.; (vi) Szmytka; (vii) Karnéus; (viii) Sóbotka; (ix) Quivar; (x) Hampson, Minkiewicz, Youth Ch.

A thoroughly worthwhile anthology from **Rattle** who, with his **CBSO** and **Chorus** is thoroughly at home in the music of Szymanowski, especially the symphonies. **Zehetmair** proves a highly sensitive soloist in the *Violin concertos*, and the *Sinfonia concertante* has greater lucidity of textures than any of its previous rivals and brings magical playing from **Andsnes**. The vocal soloists are highly idiomatic, **Timothy Robinson** in *Harnasie* (a so-called 'ballet-pantomime'), **Katarina Karnéus** in *Love Songs of Hafiz* and **Iwona Sóbotka** in *Songs of a Fairy-tale Princess*, and Rattle's accompaniments are always alluring.

King Roger, however, stands on the borderline between opera and music drama. The opening in Palermo Cathedral is of awesome opulence and, given such sounds as here, one hardly needs a stage representation. All the singers are first rate, **Thomas Hampson** has what one can only call magisterial presence and the Roksana is quite ethereal. Only **Ryszard Minkiwicz's** Shepherd is, perhaps, wanting in tonal bloom. Of course the opening of the third Act is inspired and atmospheric, and Rattle readily demonstrates his special feeling for the composer here. With first-rate

recording throughout, this set could make a cornerstone in any collection of Szymanowski's music.

(i) Violin Concertos 1–2. Symphonies (ii) 3 (Song of the Night); (iii) 4 (Symphonie concertante); (iv) Demeter; (v) Litany to the Virgin Mary; (vi) Stabat Mater

(N) (BB) *** EMI (ADD) 2CD 2 06870-2 (2). Polish R. Nat. SO, with (i) Kulka; cond. Maksymiuk; (ii) Ochman, Krakow R. Ch.; (iii) Paleczyny; both cond. Semkow; (iv) Rappé; (v) Gadulanka; (vi) Hiolski & Ch., cond. Wit

These committed performances are from the 1970s and early 1980s and are atmospheric and sensitive. **Kulka's** accounts of the two *Violin Concertos* are highly finished and convey much of the ecstasy, longing and sensuousness of these luminous scores. The pianist in the *Symphonie concertante*, **Piotr Paleczyny**, is no mean artist and has all the finesse and imagination as well as the requisite command of colour. *The Song of the Night* has great refinement and atmosphere, and the other vocal and choral works are similarly idiomatic. The sound generally is naturally recorded and balanced.

(i) Harnasie (ballet pantomime), Op. 55; (ii) Mandragora (pantomime), Op. 43; Etude for Orchestra in B flat min., Op. 3 (orch. Fitelberg)

(B—) (BB) *** Naxos 8.553686. Polish State PO (Katowice), Stryja; (i) with Grychnik, Polish State PO Ch.; Meus

Harnasie, like the Op. 50 *Mazurkas*, is the fruit of Szymanowski's encounter with the Polish folk music of the Góral mountains, and its heady exoticism is quite captivating. **Stryja's** recording is a good one and it is coupled with *Mandragora*, a harlequinade for chamber forces from 1920 – not Szymanowski at his most fully characteristic but a cultivated and intelligent score.

Symphonies 1 in F min., Op. 15; 2, Op. 19

(BB) *** Naxos 8.553683. Polish State PO (Katowice), Stryja

The two-movement *First Symphony* (1906–7) was first performed in 1909 and was received coolly. Alistair Wightman called it heavily overscored even by the standards of the period. The *Second* (1911) is heavily indebted to Reger, Scriabin and Strauss and contains original and memorable passages.

Symphony 2 in B flat, Op.19; Concert Overture, Op. 12; (i) Slopiewnie (Wordsong), Op. 46; Songs of the Infatuated Muezzin, Op. 42

*** Telarc CD 80567. LPO, Botstein; (i) with Kilanowicz

Neither of the orchestral pieces are quite *echt*-Szymanowski, the *Symphony* and *Overture* being still very much under the influence of Strauss and Reger. All the same, both are heard to best advantage in this finely detailed recording with highly persuasive performances. The two sets of songs are rarities; indeed, *Slopiewnie* is not otherwise available on disc in its orchestral form and the *Songs of the Infatuated Muezzin* – composed at the height of the composer's interest in the oriental and the exotic in 1918 (four of which he later scored in 1934) – are not generously represented on disc. **Zofia Kilanowicz** has just the right blend of purity and seductiveness and the orchestral playing under **Leon Botstein** is first class.

Symphonies 2; (i) 3 (Song of the Night)

Ⓝ ⒝Ⓑ *** Naxos 8.570721. (i) Minkiewicz ;Warsaw Philharmonic Ch. & O, Wit

These are notably warm and idiomatic performances, again showing **Antoni Wit** as a conductor to reckon with, creating orchestral colour and passion with equal intensity. The excellent clear-voiced tenor soloist, **Ryszard Minkiewicz**, and the chorus make a passionate impression during 3 and altogether this pair of performances could not be more idiomatic. The recording too is first class.

Symphonies 2; (i) 4 (Sinfonia concertante)

⟿ **** Chan. 9478. (i) Shelley; BBC PO, Sinaisky

The *Second* and *Fourth Symphonies* are two decades apart. The soft-focus Chandos recording of 2 presents an atmospheric aural picture. **Vassily Sinaisky** is a highly sympathetic interpreter of the piece, and this BBC version must be a prime recommendation. So, too, is the coupling, the *Sinfonia concertante* (1932). **Howard Shelley** produces a quality of sound that is luminous, refined and velvet-toned. The balance between piano and orchestra is particularly well managed, and the lush orchestral textures are more lucid than we have heard them elsewhere.

Symphonies (i) 3 (Song of the Night), Op. 27; (ii) 4, Concert Overture, Op. 12

⒝Ⓑ *** Naxos 8.553684. (i) Ochmann, Polish State Philharmonic Ch.; (ii) Zmudzinski; Polish State PO (Katowice), Stryja

Szymanowski has that fastidious ear for texture and heightened sense of vision that distinguish mystics, and nowhere is atmosphere more potent than in the *Third Symphony*, the *Song of the Night*.

Stryja's set of the *Song of the Night* and the *Fourth Symphony* offers a well-filled disc. He uses a tenor in the *Third Symphony* and **Tadeusz Zmudzinski** is an effective soloist in the *Fourth Symphony* or *Sinfonia concertante* for piano and orchestra. The performance of the Straussian and derivative *Concert Overture* is as persuasive as it can be. The sound in the *Third Symphony* is good, in the remaining pieces rather less impressive but still acceptable.

CHAMBER MUSIC

3 Mythes, Op. 30; Kurpian Folk Song; King Roger: Roxana's Aria (both arr. Kochanski)

⟿ ✿ Ⓜ **** DG (ADD) 477 590-3. Danczowska, Zimerman – FRANCK: *Violin Sonata* ****

Kaja Danczowska brings vision and poetry to the ecstatic, soaring lines of the opening movement of *Mythes*, *The Fountains of Arethusa*. Her intonation is impeccable, and she has the measure of these other-worldly, intoxicating scores. There is a sense of rapture here that is totally persuasive, and **Krystian Zimerman** plays with a virtuosity and imagination that silence criticism. An indispensable reissue.

String Quartets 1, Op. 37; 2, Op. 56

Ⓝ *** Hyp. CDA67684. Royal Qt (with RÓZYCKI: *Quartet in D min., Op. 49*)

⟿ ⒝Ⓑ *** Naxos 8.554315. Goldner Qt – STRAVINSKY: *Concertino; 3 Pieces; Double Canon* ***

The inspired *First Quartet* of 1915–16 comes from the period of the *First Violin Concerto* and the *Third Symphony* and shares their mystical harmonic sound-world. The *Second* (1927) comes from the years after the composition of *King Roger*, and is as fastidiously conceived as its predecessor. Both are masterpieces which should figure alongside Bartók in public esteem, and both are well served by this fine Polish ensemble. They include as a makeweight a quartet by Szymanowski's immediate contemporary but more conservative colleague, Ludomir Rózycki (1884–1953), well worth hearing but not in the same league as its companions.

The **Goldner Quartet** prove understanding, refined interpreters of both composers, playing with rapt intensity in the hushed slow movements of the Szymanowski works. Excellent sound. We would like to give an unreserved welcome to this disc for the sake of its highly interesting and satisfying repertoire. However the **Schoenberg Quartet** do not have the immaculate intonation and ensemble needed for this repertoire.

Violin Sonata; Mythes, Op. 30; Nocturne & Tarantella, Op. 28

**(*) Chan. 8747. Mordkovitch, Gusk-Grin

Lydia Mordkovitch is ideally attuned to this sensibility and plays both the *Sonata* and the later works beautifully, and she is sensitively partnered by **Marina Gusk-Grin**. This can be recommended, though this account of the *Mythes* does not displace Danczowska and Zimerman.

PIANO MUSIC

Complete piano music

Disc 1: 9 Preludes, Op. 1; Variations in B flat min., Op. 3; 4 Etudes, Op. 4; Sonata 1 in C min., Op. 8 (NI 5405)

Disc 2: Variations on a Polish Theme in B min., Op. 10; Fantasia in C min., Op. 14; Prelude & Fugue in C sharp min., (1909); Sonata 2 in A, Op. 21 (NI 5406)

Disc 3: Métopes (3 Poèmes), op. 29; 15 Etudes, Op. 34; Sonata 3, Op. 36 (NI 5435)

Disc 4: 20 Mazurkas, Op. 50; 2 Mazurkas, op. 62; 4 Polish Pieces (1926); Romantic Waltz (1925) (NI 5436)

*** Nim. NI 1750 (4). M. Jones

This complete Nimbus survey invites enthusiasm, particularly as the music is presented in historical sequence. The *Nine Preludes* of Op. 1, although published in 1906, were composed much earlier and are simple, romantic miniatures, with at times a flavour of Chopin. The two sets of *Variations* of Op. 3 and Op. 10, although appealingly inventive, are in the received German tradition; but the *Four Etudes* of Op. 4 and the opening movement of the impressive *First Sonata* already suggest Scriabin. The *Second Sonata* (1910/11) is much more complex in both its structure and use of chromaticism. The later pieces, *Masques* and *Métopes*, written at about the time of the *First Violin Concerto*, show Szymanowski responding to French influences and early Stravinsky, and evolving a sophisticated exoticism all his own. The beautiful and always imaginative *Etudes* (1916) draw on a whole range of styles from Ravel and Debussy, and even Bartók, but they are well assimilated. The *Third Sonata* (1917) is wholly impressionistic and **Martin Jones** manages its quixotic changes of mood and atmosphere most compellingly. The *Mazurkas*, from the 1920s, find Symanowski seeking to create an authentic Polish idiom in contemporary terms. The advantage of listening to this rewarding music in sequence means that one senses the composer gradually forging his own individuality. Martin Jones is a consistently persuasive advocate and he is naturally recorded. A most rewarding set.

Fantasy in F min.; Masques; 2 Mazurkas; 20 Mazurkas; Métopes; Piano Sonatas 1–3; 4 Polish Dances; 9 Preludes, Op. 1; Prelude and Fugue in C sharp min.; Prelude in C sharp min.; Romantic Waltz; 4 Studies; 12 Studies; Variations in B flat min.; Variations on a Polish Theme

*** Divine Art 21400 (4). Lee

Sinae Lee is a reliable guide in this interesting repertoire, handling the Chopinesque early period as confidently as the enigmatic late *Mazurkas*. Perhaps the refinement of such works as the *Masques* and *Métopes* eludes her.

4 Etudes, Op. 4; Fantasy, Op. 14; Masques, Op. 34; Métopes, Op. 29

⊶ **(BB)** **** Hyp. Helios CDH 55081. Lee

Dennis Lee not only encompasses the technical hurdles of *Masques* and *Métopes* with dazzling virtuosity but also provides the keenest artistic insights. He conveys the exoticism and hothouse atmosphere of these pieces; moreover he handles the early Chopinesque *Etudes* and the *Fantasy* with much the same feeling for characterization and artistry. The Hyperion sound is very good indeed. An excellent bargain.

4 Etudes, Op. 4; Mazurkas, Op. 50/1–4; Métopes, Op. 29; Piano sonata 2 in A, Op. 21

(BB) *** Naxos 8.553016-2. Roscoe

Fantasy in C, Op. 14; Masques, Op. 34; Mazurkas, Op. 50/5–12; Variations on a Polish theme, Op. 10

(BB) *** Naxos 8.553300. Roscoe

Martin Roscoe proves a perceptive and sensitive interpreter of Szymanowski and the first two discs augur well for this ongoing series. In the four *Mazurkas*, Op. 50, that open the first CD he shows real feeling and insight. He is equally persuasive in the early Chopinesque *Etudes*, Op. 4, and the

refined impressionism of *Métopes*. The *Second Sonata* is a problematic piece, full of virtuosic hurdles, romantic gestures and Regerian ingenuity. The second disc gives us the *C major Fantasy*, Op. 14, and the Op. 10 *Variations*, in which the debts to Scriabin and Chopin have yet to be fully discharged. A fine account of the *Masques*, too. This is playing of quality. As far as recording is concerned, Martin Roscoe is well served.

20 Mazurkas, Op. 50; 2 Mazurkas, Op. 62; 4 Polish Dances; Valse Romantique

⊶ **** Hyp. CDA 67399. Hamelin

The Szymanowski *Mazurkas* are late works and are among his best and certainly his most haunting piano pieces. They are without doubt the finest mazurkas after Chopin. Their inward qualities and their sense of mystery elude many pianists, but **Marc-André Hamelin** gives as perceptive and authoritative an account of these extraordinary pieces as any. In this music Szymanowski was entering new territory, and their significance in his development cannot be underestimated. Hyperion give Hamelin natural and truthfully balanced sound, and no readers interested in this once neglected but now rightly appreciated master should overlook this fine issue.

Piano Sonatas 1 in C min., Op. 8; 2 in A, op. 21; 3, Op. 35; Prelude & Fugue in C sharp min.

⊶ *** Athene ATHCD 19. Clark

Readers who want to explore just the three *Piano Sonatas* should consider this excellently played offering. No less than Martin Jones, **Raymond Clarke** has an intuitive grasp of – and affinity with – Szymanowski's sound-world. He is second to none in terms of sensibility and keyboard command. His version of the *First Sonata* is particularly convincing. Good recording, though not in the demonstration class.

Piano Sonata 3, Op. 36; Mazurkas, Op. 50/9–12; Op. 62/1–2; Masques, Op. 34; Métopes, Op. 29

(N) *** BIS-CD1137. Pöntinen

The Swedish pianist **Roland Pöntinen** is wholly attuned to the Szymanowskian sensibility. His account of the *Mazurkas* chosen here is highly sensitive and idiomatic. In *Masques* we retain a slight preference for Dennis Lee on Hyperion.

VOCAL MUSIC

(i) Stabat Mater, Op. 53; (ii) Demeter, Op. 37b; (iii) Litany to the Virgin Mary, Op. 59; (iv) Penthesilea, Op. 18; (v) Veni Creator, Op. 57

(N) ⊶ **(BB)** **** Naxos 8.570724. Warsaw Ch. & Philh. O, Wit; with (i; iii–v) Hossa; (i–ii) Marciniec; (i) Brek

Naxos have replaced the performers of their previous (identical) collection of Szymanowski's choral music with a new team, and in particular using fine soloists. The *Stabat Mater* is not only one of Szymanowski's greatest achievements but one of the greatest choral works of the 20th century. This new account has the advantage of highly sensitive conducting and an excellent response from the choir and orchestra.

The *Liturgy to the Virgin Mary* is another late work of great poignancy, but *Demeter* has exotic, almost hallucinatory textures. It is all heady and intoxicating stuff, and not to be missed by those with a taste for this wonderful composer. The recording is excellent.

(i) *3 Fragments of the Poems by Jan Kasprowicz;* (ii) *Love Songs of Hafiz;* (iii) *Songs of the Fairy-Tale Princess;* (iv) *Songs of the Infatuated Muezzin;* (v) *King Roger: Roxana's Song*

(BB) **(*) Naxos 8.553688. (i) Malewicz-Madej; (ii; iv) Ryszard Minkiewicz; (iii) Gadulanka; (v) Zagórzanka; Katowice Polish State PO, Stryja

In the *Songs of the Fairy-Tale Princess*, one feels that Szymanowski must have known Stravinsky's *Le Rossignol*. On Naxos, both the *Songs of the Infatuated Muezzin* and the *Love Songs of Hafiz* are sung by a tenor (**Ryszard Minkiewicz**) with impressive insight, but the 1989 recording is resonant and does not flatter him. **Jadwiga Gadulanka** is hardly less impressive in the extraordinary *Songs of the fairy-tale princess* and **Barbara Zagórzanka** sings the famous *Chant de Roxane* beautifully, and both she and **Anna Malewicz-Madej** in the Kasprowicz songs are very well balanced.

STAGE WORKS

King Roger, Op. 46 (complete)

*** Accord ACD 131-2. Drabowicz, Pasiecznik, Beczala, Tesarowicz, Toczyska, Szymt, 'Alla Polacca' Youth Ch., Ch., Polish Nat. Op. O, Kaspszyk

Jacek Kaspszyk's set is finer than any of the three earlier Polish versions. Indeed, it is possible to prefer it to Sir Simon Rattle's version which is available in 4-CD EMI box – see above. In the title-role **Wojtek Drabowicz** is every bit as authoritative as Thomas Hampson and arguably is better characterized, and in vocal quality the Roksana of **Olga Pasiecznik** sounds even purer than Rattle's Elzbieta Szmytka. Her famous aria is quite ravishing. Indeed, the whole performance is strong vocally and the choral singing is magnificent. Kaspszyk paces the work in masterly fashion: the opening in Palermo Cathedral is one of the most glowing and atmospheric in all Szymanowski, and its sense of mysticism is conveyed with authority. The recording, too, has impressive range and definition, and this new Polish set is very powerful and makes a highly competitive alternative.

TAKEMITSU, Toru (1930–96)

A Flock Descends into the Pentagonal Garden; (i) *Quatrain; Ring; Sacrifice; Stanza I; Valeria*

&— **** DG 477 5381. Boston SO, Ozawa; (i) with Tashi; (ii) Nagano with instrumentalists

In *Quatrain* Takemitsu contrasts his solo concertino of clarinet, violin, cello and piano with the full orchestra in a way that might suggest neoclassicism, except that Takemitsu's music is essentially sensuous and evocative; one might almost count him a Japanese Debussy. The other piece, which is purely orchestral, is overtly impressionistic. Both are superbly played; the outstanding **Tashi** group is ideally suited to *Quatrain*. The other pieces, earlier works from the 1960s, feature **Yonako Nagano** (mezzo) and an instrumental group including piccolo, flute, vibraphone, violin, cello, harp, guitar, lute and piano; and they offer more of Takemitsu's unique kind of seductive oriental impressionism.

Quotations of Dream (Day Signals from Heaven; How slow the wind; Twill by Twilight; Archipelago G; Dream Window; Night Signals from Heaven)

&— **** DG 453 4952. Crossley, Serkin, L. Sinf., Knussen

Takemitsu suggested that his music endeavoured 'to create a perspective of sound – music that forever strides the border between dream and reality'. The *Quotations of Dream* is extremely varied in scoring and in the size of the ensemble used, and is held together stylistically by the composer's 'enigmatic, murmuring, ever flowing currents of sound . . . drifting into being at the time of performance'. The five pieces are framed by *Day* and *Night Signals from Heaven*, each an antiphonal fanfare for brass, and the following segment, for two pianos and orchestra, which bears the title of the whole work, not only dominates but epitomizes the character of what is to follow. Its evocation of the sea subtly draws on wisps of Debussy's *La Mer*, and throughout the other sections the listener has the feeling that Takemitsu is haunted by memories of music from the recent past, which are woven into his textures. The other movements are *How slow the wind* (for chamber orchestra), the gently rocking *Twill by Twilight* for a larger orchestra, the antiphonal *Archipelago G* (for 21 wind players, including horn and trumpet), and *Dream Window*, with its Buddhist ambiguity. The performance (from **Oliver Knussen**, his two piano soloists, **Paul Crossley** and **Peter Serkin**, and members of the **London Sinfonietta**) is remarkably fine, and the recording, made in two different venues, is richly atmospheric. The *Gramophone*, giving the disc its Contemporary Award in 1999, suggested that 'this is the best single CD of Takemitsu's music so far issued', and it certainly has not been surpassed since.

Corona (London version for pianos, organ & harpsichord); *Far Away; Piano Distance; Undisturbed Rest*

(M) **(*) Explore EXP 0016. Woodward

Roger Woodward sympathetically draws out a seductive range of colours in *Corona* with its essentially improvisational feeling. The other music, despite its too easy reliance on texture, is still undeniably attractive, combining a flavour of Scriabin with the avant-garde. Excellent (originally Decca) recording.

TALLIS, Thomas (c. 1505–85)

The Complete Vocal and Instrumental Music of Tallis: Volumes 1–9

&— (M) *** Signum SIGCD 060 (10). Chapelle du Roi, Alistair Dixon, with Soloists, Instrumentalists and Charivari Agréable

Alistair Dixon and his Chapelle du Roi (plus other contributors) have now completed their distinguished integral coverage of the music of the great Elizabethan composer, Thomas Tallis. The complete series is currently available in a mid-priced box with full documentation, but the discs are all available separately and are praised individually below.

**** SIGCD 001. Vol. 1: *The Early Works*

**** SIGCD 002. Vol. 2: *Music at the Reformation*

**** SIGCD 003. Vol. 3: *Music for Queen Mary*

**** SIGCD 010. Vol. 4: *Music for the Divine Office – I*

**** SIGCD 016. Vol. 5: *Music for the Divine Office – II*

**** SIGCD 022. Vol. 6: *Music for a Reformed Church*

**** SIGCD 029. Vol. 7: *Music for Queen Elizabeth*

*** SIGCD 036. Vol. 8: *Lamentations & English Motets*

*** SIGCD 042 (with bonus CD). Vol. 9: *Instrumental Music & Songs*

Just looking at the titles of the individual volumes underlines the dramatic period of English history through which Tallis lived and composed, successfully moving from a Latin liturgy to English settings, then back again. Finally, during the reign of Elizabeth I in the best spirit of English compromise, he created new from the old in setting English words to music originally written to serve Latin texts. Even the famous *Spem in Alium* was heard anew as *Sing and glorify*, although generations later it reverted to its original Latin format.

The first disc augurs extremely well for the project. The programme is framed by three Marian votive antiphons, the first two comparatively immature and rather similar. *Salve intemerata*, however, is masterly in its concisely integrated part-writing (with some soaring treble solos, beautifully sung here). The *Mass* sharing its name uses much of the same material: the *Gloria* and *Sanctus* are particularly fine. The *Alleluia* and *Euge celi porta* are less ambitious, but still serenely beautiful, four-part plainchant settings used as part of the Ladymass.

Most, possibly all, of the music in Volume 2 dates from the 1540s and reflects the remarkable diversity of musical response that came directly from the profound change in reformed religious procedures that developed in England within a single decade. Much liturgical music was still sung in Latin, notably the splendid *Magnificat* and the deeply felt *Sancte Deus*, but already there are settings in English, including three fine early anthems, an extended English *Benedictus* and a remarkable five-part *Te Deum*, all very different from the music on Volume 1 of this series. The surprisingly homophonic setting of the Latin *Mass* is forward-looking, too, and very telling.

Volume 3 returns to the Latin rite and all the works here date from the reign of Mary Tudor (1553–8). The collection opens with the Psalm setting *Beati immaculati*, and includes also the glorious, large-scale votive antiphon *Gaude gloriosa*, magnificently sung. The key work, however, is the seven-part *Mass Puer natus est nobis*, which is incomplete. Here the *Gloria*, *Sanctus* and *Agnus Dei* are performed with the plainchant Propers for the third *Mass* of Christmas. As usual the

singing is splendid, but there is a good deal of monodic chant here, beautifully phrased certainly, but which will reduce the appeal of this volume for some collectors.

Volume 4 in this ever-rewarding series is the first to concentrate on music for the cycle of eight services, Matins, Lauds, Prime, Terce, Sext, None, Vespers and Compline, sung daily in Latin Christendom. The riches of the polyphony here are unending. *Dum transisset sabbatum* and the six-part *Videte miraculum* are particularly fine, while the seven-part *Loquebantur variis linguis* with its recurring *Alleluias* spins an even more complex contrapuntal web. Even the simplest of the settings here, *Quod chorus vatum*, is moving by its comparative austerity.

Volume 5 of Alistair Dixon's invaluable survey continues the music that Tallis wrote for the Divine Office begun in Volume 4. But the special interest of this CD is the inclusion of the organ music, simply written and based on plainchant melismas. Tallis generally used the organ as a substitute for voices, interchanging instrumental with sung text. In this aurally appealing alternation, the organist played the odd-numbered verses, usually providing – as in *Veni redemptor genitum* – a piquant introduction to contrast with the sonorous vocal entry. The organ used for the recordings, in the private chapel at Knole, is the oldest playable organ in England, so its choice seems admirable, and **Andrew Benson-Wilson's** contribution to the success of this CD is considerable, since all the organ music is most appealing.

Volume 6 is devoted to music which he composed for use in the reformed services promulgated by *The Booke of the Common Prayer*, which came into effect in 1549, here presented in the normal liturgical sequence. Much of the music is simple and homophonic, but it has an unadorned beauty of its own. The anthems are richer in the interplay of parts but are still brief, and the collection ends with the nine even briefer psalm-tune harmonizations which Tallis contributed to Archbishop Matthew Parker's *Psalter*, published in about 1567.

Elizabeth was the fourth monarch to sit on the throne in Tallis's lifetime, and Tallis was by then in his sixties. Both composer and monarch appear to have been determined that the new Elizabethan Latin motets should seek new expressive approaches, while drawing on the best of the past. Their success is confirmed by the fact that cathedral musicians fitted English words to much of Tallis's music. *Absterge Domine* therefore also becomes *Discomfort them O Lord*. The two Psalm settings included, *Domine, quis habitat* (Psalm 15) and the shorter but no less impressive *Laudate Dominum* (Psalm 117), are both memorable. The most celebrated of these motets is of course *Spem in Alium*, with its incredibly dense part-writing still able to astonish the ear. It is sung gloriously here, its ebb and flow and rich climaxes splendidly controlled.

Tallis's two richly expressive settings of the *Lamentations of Jeremiah* are given in Volume 8 in serene and dedicated performances, followed by what are known as *contrafacta*, English versions by the post-Reformation English Church of Latin motets rewritten by Tallis. The music itself, usually in five parts, seems to adapt very well to its linguistic transformation; the first piece here, *Wipe away my sins (Absterge*

Domine), described as 'A Prayer', is particularly beautiful. *With all our hearts and mouths* and the lovely *Arise, O Lord* both derive from Tallis's first setting of *Salvator mundi*, while *I call and cry to Thee (O sacrum convivium)*, very popular in its day, was to lay the basis for Tallis's English anthems.

The fascination of the final volume in Signum's comprehensive survey is the virtually unknown instrumental music, consisting of a small collection of works for viols and some fine pieces for keyboard, which we hear variously on virginals, harpsichord or organ. In his excellent notes, John Milsom suggests that while Tallis's official duties involved him only as a church musician, he may have written some of this music for the Tudor Court, and the keyboard pieces could conceivably have been written for Queen Elizabeth I, who was a celebrated amateur performer. Certainly they are attractive enough.

The consort manuscripts give no indication of the instrumentation, but viols (as used here) seem a likely choice, and Tallis's pair of *In nomines* are the first known examples of this form (settings using the *Gloria tibi Trinitas* as a basis). As far as is known, Tallis did not write for the lute, so the impressively complex work based on the plainsong '*Felix namque*' is almost certainly an arrangement by an unknown lutenist. This is heard alongside the less virtuosic keyboard version written two years earlier. *Mr Tallis's Lesson* (which we hear both on harpsichord and on organ) is a very agreeable pedagogic piece based on a decorated canon, and was no doubt intended as a study for the composer's choirboy pupils.

As for the songs, they make a wonderful closing section. The very touching *When shall my sorrowful sighing* might well have been composed by Dowland, and *Ye sacred music*, a tribute to Byrd, is fully worthy. They are sung most sympathetically by **Stephen Taylor** (counter-tenor), and the instrumental pieces from **Charivari Agréable**, **Laurence Cummings** (virginals and harpsichord) and **Andrew Benson-Wilson** (organ) are expertly played, while **Lynda Sayce** gives a virtuoso account of the arrangement of *Felix namque*.

The bonus disc includes a complete setting of the *Litany*, omitted from Volume 6, two brief organ Versets, and a further performance of the earlier, less complex version of *Felix Namque*. As with the other organ pieces, Benson-Wilson uses the organ at the private chapel in Knole in Kent (owned during Tallis's lifetime by both Archbishop Cranmer and Henry VIII). All in all, Volume 9 makes a fitting conclusion to a splendid project, admirably realized, and as before full texts and translations are included.

'Portrait': Anthems; Antiphons; Cantiones Sacrae; Lamentations of Jeremiah; Motets; Psalm Settings; Responsories

(BB) *** Regis Portrait PCL 2101 (2). Chapelle du Roi, Dixon

This well-chosen selection from the **Chapelle du Roi** survey opens with the characteristic early setting of *Ave dei patris filia* and explores the full range of Tallis's music, including, on the second disc, the *Lamentations of Jeremiah* and of course the famous 40-part motet, *Spem in alium*. Altogether a splendid and inexpensive sampler.

Anthems; Lamentations of Jeremiah I & II; Motets including Spem in alium (on GDGIM 006, 007 and 025)

🎧 (M) **** Gimell 2-CD CDGIM 203 (2). Tallis Scholars, Phillips

This collection from the eponymous **Tallis Scholars** directed by **Peter Phillips** now includes, on a pair of CDs, the music from three earlier issues (each still available separately). The performances are outstanding, wonderfully secure and very beautiful, recorded in an ideal acoustic. This mid-priced set has as its highlight a quite glorious account of the famous 40-part motet *Spem in alium*; so this would be an admirable basis for any collection, small or large.

Lamentations I & II; Audivi vocem de caelo

(M) *** CRD 3499 Clerks of New College, Oxford, Ch., Higginbottom – BYRD: *Lamentations; Mass for 4 Voices* ***

The performance by the **Clerks of New College, Oxford, Choir** (16 strong) directed by **Edward Higginbottom** is no less serenely beautiful and deeply felt. It is appropriately coupled with Byrd's only surviving setting of the *Lamentations* and an equally rewarding account of the Tallis responsory *Audivi vocem de caelo* with its interchange of polyphony and plainchant, which makes an admirable postlude. The recording is first class, with a richly appealing ambience.

9 Psalm Tunes for Archbishop Parker's Psalter

🎧 ✲ **** HM HMU 807463. Stile antico – BYRD: *Cantiones sacrae; Mass propers* ***

The opening of this disc immediately brings an aural double-take, for Tallis's Third Tune, *Why fum'th in fight*, does not mirror its text, but is the wonderfully serene melody Vaughan Williams chose for his inspired *Variations*. All of these Tunes (written for a metrical psalter in 1576) are as brief as they are memorable, and they are interwoven here by more complex polyphonic settings by Byrd, making a stimulating contrast. **Style antico** is a baker's dozen of mixed men's and women's voices, superbly blended, who sing with absolute precision, sensitive use of light and shade, and impeccable tuning. They also bring to the music just the right degree of expressive warmth for this repertoire and they are beautifully recorded.

Absterge Domine; Candidi facti sunt; Nazareri; Derelinquat impius; Dum transisset sabbatum; Gaude gloriosa Dei Mater; Magnificat & Nunc dimittis; Salvator mundi

(M) *** CRD (ADD) 3429. New College, Oxford, Ch., Higginbottom

The performances by the **Choir of New College, Oxford** – recorded in the splendid acoustic of the College Chapel – are very well prepared, with good internal balance, excellent intonation, ensemble and phrasing. The *Gaude gloriosa* is one of Tallis's most powerful and eloquent works.

Audivici vocem de caelo; Candidi facti sunt Nazarei eius a 5; Dum transisset sabbatus; Gaude gloriosa,

*Dei Mater; Hodie nobis celorum rex; Homo quidam
fecit cenam magnam; Honor, virtus et potestas; In
jejunio et fletu; In pace in idipsum; Lamentations of
Jeremiah I & II; Loquebantur variis linguis;
Miserere nostri; O nata lux de lumine; O sacrum
convivium; Salvator mundi I & II; Spem in alium;
Suscipe quaeso Domine; Te lucis ante terminum
(Procul recedante somnia) I; Videte miraculum*

(B) *** Virgin 2x1 5 62230-2 (2). Taverner Consort, Parrott

The **Taverner** style is brighter and more abrasive than we
are used to in this often ethereal music but, apart from the
scholarly justification, the polyphonic cohesion of the writing comes over the more tellingly. Our listing is in alphabetical order, but the programme – as presented here – was
planned as two separate collections, the first disc containing
Tallis's most elaborate and most celebrated choral piece,
the 40-part motet *Spem in alium*, as well as nine other magnificent responsories, some of them – like *Videte miraculum*
and *Dum transisset sabbatus* – almost as extended in argument. The second of the two discs has two magnificent
Lamentations of Jeremiah as well as an even more expansive
motet, which Tallis wrote early in his career, *Gaude, gloriosa,
Dei Mater*, and a number of the shorter *Cantiones sacrae*.
This reissue is warmly recommendable and very well
recorded.

Audivi vocem de Caelo; Honor virtus et postestas; O sacrum convivium; Salvator mundi; Sancte Deus

(M) *** CRD 3372, Ch. of New College, Oxford, Higginbottom
– TAVERNER: *Western Wynde* etc ***

This collection of votive antiphons, motets and responds
makes up an attractive group, and the **Choir of New College,
Oxford**, produces a clean and well-blended sound. Given the
attractions of the coupling this disc has a strong appeal.

Magnificat (4 vv); Mass Puer natus est nobis. Motets: Audivi vocem; Ave Dei patris filia

⊕ **** Gimell CDGIM 034-2. Tallis Scholars, Phillips

The performance by the **Tallis Scholars** of the reconstructed
Tallis Christmas *Mass* has an appealing directness and simplicity and is well up to the standard of its competitors. The
four-part *Magnificat* is an early work, but is again very impressively sung here, and the programme is completed with
two votive antiphons. *Ave Dei patris filia* is particularly appealing. It has a striking, soaring opening from the trebles
emphasizing the word 'Ave', which illuminates the music
throughout its seven stanzas. Excellent recording, but there
would have been room for more music here.

Mass for 4 Voices; Motets: Audivi vocem; In manus tuas Domine; Loquebantur variis linguis; O sacrum convivium; Salvator mundi; Sancte Deus; Te lucis ante terminum; Videte miraculum

⊕ (BB) *** Naxos 8.550576. Oxford Camerata, Summerly

The **Oxford Camerata** with their beautifully blended timbre
have their own way with Tallis. Lines are firm, the singing
has serenity but also a firm pulse. In the *Mass* (and particularly in the *Sanctus*) the expressive strength is quite strongly

communicated, while the *Benedictus* moves on sponta-
neously at the close. The motets respond particularly well to
Jeremy Summerly's degree of intensity. The opening
Loquebantur variis linguis has much passionate feeling, and
this (together with the *Audivi vocem* and, especially, the lovely
Sancte Deus) shows this choir of a dozen singers at their most
eloquent. The recording, made in the Chapel of Wellington
College, is very fine indeed. Excellent value.

Spem in alium (40 Part Motet); Salve intemerata (Mass & Motet); I call and cry to thee, O Lord; Discomfort them O Lord; With all our heart

⊕ (BB) *** Naxos 8.557770. Oxford Camerata, Summerly

Spem in alium is justly famous. In order to replicate the circular effect intended by the composer, the producer here,
Andrew Walton, and engineer, Mike Clements, recorded the
four choirs positioned in the form of four sides of a huge St
Chad Cross. The result (especially at the climax of *Spem in
alium*) is overwhelming. But the extended motet, *Salve intemerata*, and its associated *Mass* are superb too, while the
three English motets which complete the programme are
by no means an anticlimax. The performances here are beyond praise, as is the skill of the Naxos recording team, while
the acoustic of All Hallows, Gospel Oak, London, was ideally
chosen for this remarkable enterprise.

TANEYEV, Sergei (1856–1915)

(i) Piano Concerto in E flat; (ii) Allegro in E flat; Andantino semplice; (iii) The Composer's Birthday. 4 Improvisations (with Arensky, Glazunov & Rachmaninov); Lullaby; Repose; March in D min.; Prelude in F

**(*) Toccata Classics TOCC 0402. (i) Banowetz, Russian Philh.
O of Moscow, Thomas Sanderling; (ii) Wodnicki; (iii)
Ashkenazy (narr.)

Taneyev began his only *Piano Concerto* when he was 19, the
year after he had given the Moscow première of
Tchaikovsky's *B flat minor Concerto*. Not even the encouragement of Tchaikovsky could induce him to complete it.
Although the latter's influence is obvious, Taneyev is already
his own man – particularly in the short second movement
(orchestrated by Shebalin), and the writing is cultured and
dignified. The seven piano pieces, mostly from the 1870s, are
rewarding and already exhibit the fastidious craftsmanship
you find in his mature compositions. Most of these pieces
are new to the catalogue, including the light-hearted birthday tribute to Tchaikovsky in which **Ashkenazy** appears as
narrator. The performances are of quality. In the concerto,
the recording could perhaps be fresher and the orchestral
texture better ventilated; and the piano in the solo pieces
could also benefit with more air.

Suite de Concert, Op. 28

(N) *** Chan. 10491. Mordkovitch, RSNO, Järvi. (with
RIMSKY-KORSAKOV: *Fantasy on Russian Themes, Op. 33*
***)

M) *** EMI mono 3 61570-2. D. Oistrakh, Philh. O, Malko –
KHACHATURIAN: *Violin Concerto in D min.* (***)

Taneyev's *Suite de Concert* is now well served on CD, with
Oistrakh's classic account available alongside this excellent
new version on Chandos with **Lydia Mordkovitch**, which is
no less enjoyable. Lydia above all goes in for bringing out an
incredible range of colours from her instrument, and if her
intonation isn't always immaculate, her sheer intensity carries the day. The *Tarantella* finale is excitingly done. One at-
tracting feature of this release is the colourfully tuneful work
by Rimsky-Korsakov, where the composer's gift of conjuring
up a magical atmosphere is superbly realized by the soloist.
Järvi conducts both works with his usual expertise and the
Chandos recording is warm and richly detailed.

Taneyev's five-movement *Suite* has much charm when
played as beautifully and warmly as it is here by **David
Oistrakh**. Needless to say Oistrakh's lovely performance invites all the superlatives, and **Malko** accompanies most
persuasively. The 1956 Abbey Road recording is excellsent,
far smoother and more pleasing than the Khachaturian
coupling.

Symphonies 1 in E min; 3 in D min.

🎵 **** Chan. 10390.Russian State SO, Polyansky

BB **(*) Naxos 8.570336. Novosibirsk Ac. SO, Thomas
Sanderling

The *First Symphony* is a student work from 1873 when he was
16, and it was never performed or published in Taneyev's
lifetime. Immature though it is at times, the *symphony* still
shows real originality: the *Andantino* is captivating. The *Third*
is both masterly and compelling. David Brown once wrote
that Taneyev 'commanded a compositional skill unsurpassed
by any composer of his period', and this shows. His melodic
ideas may not be in the same league as those of Glazunov or
Arensky, but his arguments are always cogent and regularly
erupt in lyrical passages that smack of the tunesmith in him.
Polyansky's direction of the **Russian State Symphony
Orchestra** results in vivid and colourful performances, establishing Taneyev as a figure subtly different from his close
contemporaries, quite individual. Full, brilliant sound.
Recommended with enthusiasm.

Thomas Sanderling and the **Novosibirsk Orchestra** are
broader and more leisurely than Polyansky on Chandos and
the playing is a good deal less finished. All the same, there is
a genuine seriousness of purpose here which serves these
admirable symphonies well. Polyansky remains a first
choice.

Symphonies 2 in B flat; 4 in C min., Op. 12

*** Chan. 9998. Russian State SO, Polyansky

Symphony 4 in C min., Op. 12; Overture The Oresteia, Op. 6

*** Chan. 8953. Philh. O, Järvi

The *Fourth* is a long piece of over 40 minutes. The outer
movements were scored, but the central *Andante* was left in
short score, and the work was put into performable shape
by Vladimir Blok. But the *Fourth* has a particularly inventive

and delightful *Scherzo*, which shows his keenness of wit.
The Russian performances are very good, though Järvi's CD
of the *Fourth* with the **Philharmonia Orchestra** is not displaced. He gets very good playing from the Philharmonia
and similarly first-class recording.

(i) Piano Quartet in E, Op. 20; Piano Trio, Op. 22

M) *** Dutton CDSA 6882. Barbican Piano Trio; (i) with J.
Boyd

The **Barbican Trio** is a fine ensemble and excellently
recorded. Theirs is a well-shaped account of the Op. 22 *Trio*.
Their excellent pianist is highly musical. Their coupling is
the slightly earlier but equally rewarding E major *Piano
Quartet*. Taneyev's music is full of subtleties and surprises
and gives much delight.

Piano Quintet in G min., Op. 30

*** Ara. Z 6539. Lowenthal, Rosenthal, Kamei, Thompson,
Kates

Not only is the *Piano Quintet* well structured and its motivic
organization subtle, but its melodic ideas are strong and individual. It is arguably the greatest Russian chamber work
between Tchaikovsky and Shostakovich. The recording is
not in the demonstration bracket, but it is very good, and
the playing, particularly of the pianist **Jerome Lowenthal**, is
excellent. Strongly recommended but no coupling.

Piano Quintet, Op. 10; Piano Trio. Op.22

🎵 **** DG 477 5419. Pletnev, Repin, Gringolts, Imai, Harrell

The present DG disc (82 minutes) rather upstages the opposition. The *Piano Quintet* is a particularly strong and enjoyable work. **Pletnev** and his colleagues make it sound like a
true masterpiece, and they are nearly as convincing in the
Trio. Excellent recording, too.

String Quartets 1 in B flat Min., Op. 4; 2 in C, Op. 5

*** OCD 697. Krasni Qt

The *First Quartet*, written in 1890, is a distinctly individual
piece in five movements, alternating slow and fast tempi.
The beautiful *Largo* is searching, with an almost improvisatory feel, the *Scherzo* dances along spiritedly, and a delicately nostalgic *Intermezzo* intervenes before the
light-hearted *Giocoso* finale, which has a charming secondary theme. The *Second Quartet* (1895) has a pervading folksy
quality and is certainly Slavic in feeling, especially the
melody that forms the centrepiece of the *Scherzo*. The
Adagio espressivo is very intense, but also restless; the finale
(*vigorosamente*) resolves matters cheerfully, and halfway
through introduces a double fugue, gathering together the
work's principal ideas. These performances are first class,
and the recording is truthful (even if perhaps a little close).
Recommended.

String Trios in E flat, Op. 31; in B min.; in D

N) **** Hyp. CDA 67573. Leopold String Trio

If you enjoy the Tchaikovsky *Quartets*, you'll almost certainly enjoy these *Trios*, although there is no movement

quite as memorable as the Tchaikovsky *Andante cantabile*. The *Op. 31 Trio*, which opens the disc, is the finest, with consistently memorable invention. Taneyev, like Mendelssohn, is particularly good at scherzos and both scherzi, in Op. 31 and the *D major* work, are prime examples. The (reconstructed) two-movement *B minor Trio* opens rather lugubriously, but its second movement *Theme and variations* is quixotically inventive, yet is far from frivolous, with fine, expressive writing to balance the characteristic scherzando writing. The *D major Trio* was written three decades before the others: it has a friendly opening movement and a very touching *Adagio*. The **Leopold String Trio** are right inside all this music, play and balance impeccably, and they are very realistically recorded.

Cantata 2, Op. 36 (At the Reading of a Psalm)

⊕ **** PentaTone **SACD** PTC 5186 038. Semenina, Tarassova, Gubsky, Baturkin, St Petersburg State Ac. Ch., Glinka Choral College Boys' Ch., Russian Nat. O, Pletnev

In March 2005 **Pletnev** and the **Russian National Orchestra** broke a lance for Taneyev by bringing two of his big choral works and the *Fourth Symphony* to London's Barbican Hall – and to packed houses! This account of *At the Reading of a Psalm* is every bit as dedicated and committed as their London concert, and the choral singing is wonderfully full-blooded and rich in tone. This music speaks with a completely individual voice.

John of Damascus

*** DG 471 029-2. Mescheriakov, Larin, Chernov, Moscow State Ch. O, RNO, Mikhail Pletnev – RACHMANINOV: *The Bells.* ❀ ***

Taneyev's *John of Damascus* is his Op. 1 and a noble piece, whose long neglect on the gramophone is at last remedied. An earlier version from Valéry Polyansky on Chandos made a strong impression but was encumbered with a perfectly adequate but unwanted performance of Tchaikovsky's *Fourth Symphony*. In any event this is vastly superior in every way.

TANSMAN, Alexandre
(1897–1986)

Symphonies 2 & 3; Quatre Mouvements pour orchestre

Ⓝ *** Chan. 5065. Melbourne SO, Caetani

Tansman was born into a wealthy Jewish family in Łódź but settled in Paris when he was twenty where he became a protégé of Ravel. Koussevitzky premièred his *Second Symphony* in 1927 and the *Third* (*Symphonie concertante for piano quartet and orchestra*) was composed in 1931 when he was working with Gershwin on the orchestration of *An American in Paris*. It is inventive and entertaining music with a strong appeal. The *Quatre Mouvements* come from the mid-1960s and have a distinctive texture with the occasional hint of Szymanowski and some of Stravinsky's rhythmic fertility. They are well served by the **Melbourne Orchestra** and the recording team. Strongly recommended.

Symphonies 7 (Lyrique); 8 (Musique pour orchestre); 9

⊕ *** Chan. **SACD** CHSA 5054. Melbourne SO, Caetani

Tansman has been neglected by the gramophone, though the *Triptych* (see below) was recorded in the early days of LP, and his guitar music was given by such luminaries of that instrument as Segovia and John Williams. The *Seventh Symphony* has a Bartókian slow introduction, but the atmosphere is tinged with touches of Stravinsky and Milhaud. The *Eighth*, completed on his return to France in 1948, and its successor of ten years later are both rewarding scores, neoclassical in style but strongly atmospheric in feeling. This will be new repertoire for all but specialist collectors and should be a welcome discovery. In **Oleg Caetani** and the **Melbourne Symphony Orchestra** the *symphonies* have persuasive advocacy and the expansive Chandos SACD recording is admirable.

Musique for Clarinet Quintet; Musique à six for Clarinet Quintet & Piano; 3 Pièces for Clarinet, Harp & String Quartet; Triptyque for String Quartet

ⒷⒷ *** Naxos 8.570235. Fessard, Reyes, Pierre, Quatuor Elysée

With **Jean-Marc Fessard** the central performer in this collection, playing on bass clarinet as well as the regular instrument, this gives an attractive survey of Tansman's music, most of it written when he was in wartime exile in the United States. There is an obvious influence from Stravinsky, both in these works and in the much earlier *Triptyque* for *String Quartet* of 1930. First-rate sound.

TARTINI, Giuseppe (1692–1770)

(i; ii) Cello Concerto in A; (iii; ii) Violin Concertos in D min., D.45; (iv; ii) in E min., D.56; in G, D. 82; (iii; v) Violin sonatas (for violin & continuo): in A; in G min.; in F, Op. 1/1, 10 & 12; in C, Op. 2/2; in G min. (Devil's Trill)

⊕ ⒷⒷ **** Warner Apex 2564 61693-2 (2). (i) Zannerini; (ii) Sol. Ven.; (iii) Toso; (iv) Amoyal; (v) Farina

Here is a collection to make the listener understand why Tartini was so admired in his day. Spanning both halves of the 18th century as he did, he possesses the lyrical purity of Corelli and Vivaldi with a forward-looking sensibility that is highly expressive. Indeed, his invention is almost romantic at times and there are moments of vision which leave no doubt that he is underrated. The orchestral playing is committed, and the fresh, warm analogue recording from the 1970s is pleasingly transferred. Tartini's *Sonatas* take their virtuosity for granted; even the *Devil's Trill* does not flaunt its bravura until the finale with its extended trills – considered impossibly difficult in his day. These works call for playing of the greatest technical finesse and musicianship. Amoyal plays them superbly; he makes no attempt to adapt his style to period-instrument practice. Instead his performances have a sweetness of tone and expressive eloquence to commend them, and though he is forwardly placed, the (unimportant) harpsichord continuo just comes through to give support. The violin is beautifully recorded. A most desirable pair of CDs.

Cello Concerto in D

Ⓜ *** Warner Elatus 0927 49839-2. Rostropovich, St Paul CO, Wolff – C. P. E. BACH; VIVALDI: *Concertos* ***

Another commanding performance by **Rostropovich** of the Tartini *Concerto*, originally written for viola da gamba and transcribed for cello in the late 1920s by Rudolf Hindemith and revised here by **Hugh Wolff**. It is a mellifluous and beautiful work, played with great eloquence not only by the distinguished soloist, but also the fine **St Paul orchestra**. Excellent recorded sound.

Violin Concertos, Op. 1/1, 4–5 & 12; in C

🔲 **** Hyp. CDA 67345. Wallfisch, Raglan Bar. Players, Kraemer

Tartini's Op. 1 was published in Amsterdam in 1728, but only included Nos. 1, 4 & 5 of the present set. No matter what their provenance, they are all most engaging works in three movements, although the first includes an additional and modestly paced *Fugue à la brève*. The performances here are splendid. **Elizabeth Wallfisch** may be playing a period instrument, but her timbre is smooth and polished, with no edginess, and the *Adagio* or *Cantabile* slow movements could not be sweeter. She is splendidly athletic in *allegros* as are her alert accompanying group and they are very well balanced in recording. This disc can be specially ordered on Hyperion's Archive Service.

Violin Concertos in C, D.2; F, D.67; A, D.96; A min. (A Lunardo Venier), D.115; B min., D.125

🅑🅑 *** Warner Apex (ADD) 2564 60152-2. Toso, Sol. Ven., Scimone

Tartini is a much underrated composer, as the many beautiful slow movements of these *concertos* will readily show. **Pierre Toso** is consistently stylish and pleasing: the *Adagio* of the *A major* is most gracious, and the *Largo/Andante* finale (which has the inscription 'Flow bitter tears until my anguish is consumed') is movingly played. No less touching is the *Larghetto* of the *B minor* Concerto, which brings another inscription, '*Lascia ch'io dica addio*', while the *Andante cantabile* of the *F major* is a charming siciliano with the indication '*Misterio anima mea*'. **Scimone** and **I Solisti Veneti** accompany sympathetically and, while the balance tends to favour the solo violin a little, it otherwise produces excellent results.

Violin Concertos: in C, D.7; in D, D.28, D.31, D.33, & D.34; in F, D.65, D.68; in G, D.78; in A, D.102, D.103, & D.107 (Dynamic CDS 548/1-2)

Violin Concertos: D.19, D.20, D.22, D.83, D.94, D.95, D.96 & D.117 (Dynamic CDS 399/1-2.)

Violin Concertos: D.26, D.39, D.50, D.84, D.99, D.101, & D.105

Ⓝ *** Dynamic CDS 485/1-2. Carlo Lazari, or Federico Guglielmo, L'Arte dell' Arco, Guglielmo

This is a part of an ongoing series aiming to include all Tartini's authentic violin concertos. According to the editor, Nicola Reniero, much restoration had to be done, as passages were missing or mutilated, and the added sections were especially written in observance of the composer's formal, structural and harmonic straits. Cadenzas were added by the soloists, special care was given to ornamentation, and such procedures appear to have been successful. The performances are very well played, straightforward in the best sense, and appealingly spontaneous; they are on original instruments and the solo timbre is not edgy but silvery. The baroque orchestra provides crisp, supportive textures which are full of life and well judged expressive feeling. This is a considerable undertaking but a worthwhile one. Each issue covers a pair of CDs. We have only heard the fully listed selection on CDS 548/1-2, and the recordings are well balanced and of good quality.

(i) Violin Concertos: in C, D.12; in D min., D.45; in E, D.51; in B flat, D.117; (ii) Sonata in G min. (Devil's Trill), g.5

*** Regis RRC 1283. (i) Nikolitch, O d'Auvergne, Van Beek; (ii) Krylov, Lithuanian CO, Sondeckis

The performances by **Gordan Nikolitch** and the **Orchestre d'Auvergne** are played on modern instruments; they yet have an athletic quality that evokes period performance. Nikolitch is a most sensitive and virile soloist and the named slow movements of the *C major* (*Felice età dell'oro*) and *E major* (*Tortorella bacie*) are played very beautifully indeed. The recording is first class, bracing to suit the sparkle of the performances. What makes the disc unique is the inclusion of an orchestral transcription (rather plain, but effective enough) of the *Devil's Trill Sonata* by H. Kauder. This is played by **Sergei Krylov** with suitably abrasive but not startling trills.

Violin Concertos: in D, D.28; in E, D.50; in G, D.80; in G, D.96; in B min., D.125

🔲 🅑🅑 **** Naxos 8.570222. Daskalakis, Cologne CO, Müller-Brühl

The five *Violin Concertos* here have a fresh simplicity, which the excellent soloist **Ariadne Daskalakis** and the **Cologne Chamber Orchestra** directed spiritedly by **Helmut Müller-Brühl** capture to perfection, as they do the expressive appeal of the slow movements, notably that of the *G major*, D.80, and the *D major*, D.28; but the *B minor* is graceful too, and its *Larghetto* is given a title, *Lascia ch'io dica addio* ('Let me say goodbye'). The recording is first class and, for those who like modern-instrument performances, as do we, the disc is worth seeking out.

Violin Sonatas, Op. 1/ 2, 8, 10, 12 & 13; in A (sopra lo stile che suona il Prette dalla Chitarra Portoghese), A.4; in B flat, Bb.1 & Op. 5/6, Bb.12; in D, D.19; in G min. (Devil's Trill), g.5

Ⓑ *** Hyp. Dyad CDD 22061 (2). Locatelli Trio

Elizabeth Wallfisch is a suitably athletic soloist, and she plays slow movements expressively and unsentimentally. She is on her mettle in the *Devil's Trill*, but (unlike Manze) does not seek to emphasize its Devilish spectacle. But she makes the most of the *Sonata in A* ('in the style of the priest who plays the Portuguese guitar'). This combines lyricism with plenty of opportunities for bravura, plus a characterful folk influence, with harmonic clashes and a bold percussive element to simulate the strumming of the guitar. The recording places the violin well forward; **Paul Nicholson's** harpsichord is rather backward, but the **Trio** integrates well.

(Unaccompanied) Violin Sonatas: in A min., B:a3; in G min.; (Sonata de Diavolo), B:g5; L'arte del arco, B:f11; 14 Variations on the Gavotte from Corelli's Op. 5/10; Pastorale for violin in scordatura, B:a16

🎻 💠 ******** HM HMU 907213. Manze

Andrew Manze plays those genuinely fiendish trills in the finale of the *Devil's Trill Sonata* quite hair-raisingly. Manze calls the opening *Largo* an 'infernal siciliana' (yet presents it with great poise and refined espressivo), and the central movement (hardly less remarkable) becomes a 'demonic moto perpetuo'. Yet Corelli's gavotte is played with engaging delicacy, the bravura left for the variations. The *A minor Sonata* also includes a set of variations, which again offers an amazing range of musical and technical opportunities, as does the colourful hurdy-gurdy finale of the *Pastorale* which ends so hauntingly. Manze's playing is totally compelling and confirms that the music is 'complete' without a continuo. The recording is very real and immediate.

TAVENER, John (born 1944)

Beyond the Veil (A Portrait of John Tavener) (DVD version)

*** Warner **DVD** 3984 23931. Rozario, Westminster Abbey Ch., Camerata at the Megaron Athens (V/D: Bryan Izzard)

This DVD gives a graphic portrait of John Tavener as presented by **Melvyn Bragg** on ITV's *South Bank Show*. Illustrations include the *Song for Athene*, which made such an impact at the funeral of Princess Diana, and excerpts from *The Protecting Veil*, *The Akathist of Thanksgiving* (one of Tavener's finest works) and the *Bless Duet* from the opera, *Mary of Egypt*.

(i) Eternal Memory for Cello and Strings; (ii) The Hidden Treasure (for String Quartet); Svyati (O Holy One); for Cello & Chorus; (iv) Akhmatova Songs for Soprano & Cello; Chant for Solo Cello

🎻 Ⓜ ******* RCA 82876 64278-2. Isserlis, with (i) Moscow Virtuosi, Spivakov; (ii) Philips, Feeney, Phillips; (iii) Kiev Chamber Ch., Gobdych; (iv) Rosario

All this music is constructed simply (simplistically, some might say) and is based for the most part on a straightforward rising and falling scalic sequence, in the case of *Svyati* and *Eternal Memory* linked thematically. Their atmosphere is magnetic. *The Hidden Treasure* for string quartet still has a dominating cello role and might be described as a religious pilgrimage, closing with a mystical transformation. In the *Akhmatova Songs* the rising and falling sequence is floridly

ornamented, and the singer is required to soar up ecstatically to the top of her range, which **Patricia Rosario** manages confidently. *Svyati* returns to a simple but radiant dialogue, alternating cello soliloquy with a mystical choral response. **Steven Isserlis** gives the feeling of quiet improvisation (especially in his solo *Chant*); the singing and playing throughout capture the music's atmosphere superbly. The beautiful recording has a natural presence.

(i) The Protecting Veil; (ii) The Last Sleep of the Virgin (a Veneration for Strings & Handbells)

Ⓜ ****(*)** Telarc CD 80487. (i) Springuel; (ii) Willems; I Flamminghi, Werthen

(i) The Protecting Veil; (ii;iii) The Last Sleep of the Virgin; (iv;v) Angels; Annunciation; The Lament of the Mother of God; (iv;vi) Hymns of Paradise; God is with us (iii; iv;vi) Thunder entered her

Ⓝ Ⓑ ******* EMI 2-CD 2 37691-2. (i) Isserlis, LSO, Rozhdestvensky; (ii) Chilingirian Qt; (iii) Simcock (handbells); (iv) Winchester Cathedral Ch., Hill; (v) Kingelborg; (vi) Kendall

(i) The Protecting Veil; Thrinos

🎻 Ⓑ ******** Virgin 5 03430-2. Isserlis; (i) LSO, Rozhdestvensky – BRITTEN: *Cello Suite 3* *******

(i) The Protecting Veil; (ii) Wake up ... and die

*** Sony SK 62821. Ma; with (i) Baltimore SO; (ii) cellos of Baltimore SO; Zinman

(i) The Protecting Veil; (ii) In alium (for soprano, tape and orchestra)

🎻 ⒷⒷ ******* Naxos 8.554388. (i) Kliegel; (ii) Hulse; Ulster O, Yuasa

In the inspired performance of **Steven Isserlis**, dedicatedly accompanied by **Rozhdestvensky** and the **LSO**, *The Protecting Veil* has an instant magnetism, at once gentle and compelling. The 'protecting veil' of the title refers to the Orthodox Church's celebration of a 10th century vision, when in Constantinople the Virgin Mary appeared and cast her protecting veil over the Christians who were being attacked by the Saracen armies. Much is owed to the performance, with Isserlis a commanding soloist. He is just as compelling in the other two works on the disc, not just the Britten but also the simple lyrical lament, *Thrinos*, which Tavener wrote especially for him. Excellent recording.

Using a warm, wide vibrato, **Maria Kliegel** gives a dedicated performance. With **Yuasa** drawing superb playing from the **Ulster Orchestra**, this is an unusually spacious reading that sustains its length well. What makes it specially attractive is the coupling, *In Alium*, a piece for soprano, tape and orchestra which is at once devotional and sensuous. The layering of textures, with dramatic contasts, is vividly caught in the excellent Naxos recording. Warmly recommended.

Yo-Yo Ma, rather more withdrawn, is equally concentrated, daringly adopting an even slower tempo in the central section, *Lament of the Mother of God*. He is helped by the sympathetic accompaniment of **David Zinman** and the **Baltimore Orchestra**, with recording a degree more transparent than the original RCA. The fill-up is a new work, similarly visionary, commissioned from Tavener by Sony, in which, using a palindromic motif, the spacious cello solo is enhanced by cellos from the orchestra.

This EMI double joins **Steven Isserlis's** outstanding account of *The Protecting Veil* to a choral collection. **David Hill** conducts the **Winchester Cathedral Choir** with **David Dunnett** at the organ, all very atmospherically recorded. Though some of the longer and more meditative pieces rather outstay their welcome, each one presents a sharply definitive vision, culminating in a magnificent Christmas proclamation, *God is with us*. 'Quiet and intensely fragile' is Tavener's guide to performances of the bonus item here, *The Last sleep of the Virgin*.

The cello soloist in the Telarc version is relatively reticent emerging out of the orchestra, but the playing is beautiful in its gentle way. *The Last Sleep of the Virgin*, written originally for string quartet in memory of Dame Margot Fonteyn, makes an apt coupling in the conductor's enriched version for string orchestra.

(i) String Quartets: *The Hidden Treasure*; (ii) *The Last Sleep of the Virgin*; (iii) *Angels; Annunciation; God is with us; Hymns of Paradise; Lament of the Mother of God; Thunder entered her*

(N)(B) *** Virgin 2-CD 693233-2(2). (i) Chillingirian Qt (ii) with Ian Simcock (handbells) (ii) Winchester Cathedral Ch., Hill; David Dunnett (organ) (with PÄRT: *Summa; Fratres* ***)

The Last Sleep of the Virgin is a work which might be described as an ethereal suggestion, using the simplest means (string quartet and tolling bell) to convey both the reality and the implications of the death and burial of 'the Mother of God'. *The Hidden Treasure* in its seeking for Paradise offers more violent contrasts, (a brief cello cadenza-soliloquy a key factor) with cries of anguish interrupting the flow of the spiritual journey. Tavener's world is all his own and the artists have to create the music's logic with a hypnotic concentration which is certainly achieved here, using a suitable resonance of acoustic. The mystical close of *The Hidden Treasure* brings a shimmering *pianissimo-diminuendo* of remarkable intensity. '*Thunder entered her*' is the sobriquet given to the choral collection on the second disc, named after the longest and most striking piece of the six recorded here. With distant choirs set against the main body, and weighty organ accompaniment, this relates closely to the *akathist*, though Tavener resorts too readily to formula-like scale *ostinati* and oriental augmented intervals. The Pärt couplings are also both atmospheric works with a liturgical basis, using sparse basic material, which try to convey a sense of eternity. The performances here are obviously felt, but it must be admitted that, as music, they are less potent than the Tavener pieces.

Piano Music: *In Memory of Two Cats; Mandoodles; Palin; Pratirupa; Ypakë; Zodiacs*

(N)(BB) *** Naxos 8.570442. Ralph van Raat

Those familiar with Tavener's most famous, large-scale orchestral and choral music will be a bit surprised by the composer's harder-edge style of his piano music. Not that it is difficult music: much of it is really quite beautiful, with very appealing harmonies and unexpected rhythms. The longest work here, *Pratirupa* (meaning 'Reflections') is half an hour long, with the composer using various musical themes treated in a manner not dissimilar to that of Messiaen, and it holds remarkably well together, no doubt a tribute to the pianist, **Ralph van Raat**. Of course, the music is all tied up with the composer's spirituality and there is much that is reflective and haunting, but there is humour too, such as when the composer quotes some Chopin in *Mandoodles*. All in all, a varied collection of pieces which adds an interesting dimension to this very popular composer. Excellent sound too.

VOCAL MUSIC

(i) *Akhmatova Songs; Many Years; The World* (all for soprano and string quartet); *Diódia (String Quartet 3)*

⊕ **** Hyp. CDA 67217. (i) Rozario; Vanbrugh Qt

Tavener's six *Akhmatova Songs* here are rearranged even more tellingly, using a string quartet but still relying a great deal on a solo cello. **Patricia Rozario** is now completely at home in the soaring melisma and surpasses her earlier performance for RCA, with her account of the exotic melody of *The Muse*, sounding like a celestial Russian folksong. However, it is the hauntingly passionate closing evocation of *Death* which gains most from the new instrumentation. *The World* depends much on sustained high notes for the voice over a gentle pedal and 'should be performed at maximum intensity throughout', which it certainly is here.

But the most ambitious work here is the *Third String Quartet*, *Diódia*, which in a series of very similar episodes considers 'the posthumous states of being of the soul'. The performance has great concentration, achieving a remarkable closing *pianissimo* over a beating drum (perhaps a fading heartbeat). The recording is of Hyperion's best quality.

(i) *Angels*; (ii) *Collegium regale: Magnificat & Nunc Dimittis*; (i; iii) *God is with us (A Christmas Proclamation)*; (iv) *Funeral Ikos; 2 Hymns to the Mother of God; The Lamb*; (i) *Lament of the Mother of God*; (i) *Song for Athene*; (v) *The Protecting Veil* (excerpt; 1st section only).

(B) *** CfP 585 9152. (i) Winchester Cathedral Ch., Hill; (ii) King's College, Cambridge, Ch., Cleobury; (iii) with Kendall, Dunnet (organ); (iv) Vasari Singers, Backhouse; (v) Isserlis, LSO, Rozhdestvensky

Like the companion Classics for Pleasure introduction to the music of Arvo Pärt, this compilation draws on a number of similar sources, all of high quality, both musically and as recordings. The items from the **Vasari Singers** include Tavener's justly famous and haunting carol *The Lamb*. **Jeremy Backhouse** enhances his performance with an effective ritardando at the end of each verse, while he links the melancholy simplicity of the *Funeral Ikos* naturally to the ethereality of the *Two Hymns to the Mother of God*. The items from the **Winchester Choir** conducted by **David Hill** (with **David Dunnet** at the organ in *God is with us*) are all atmospherically recorded: each one presents a sharply distinctive vision, culminating in the magnificent Christmas proclamation, *God is with us*. The choir then closes the programme with the beautiful and intense *Song for Athene*, heard at the funeral of Princess Diana.

'Choral Ikons': Annunciation; As One who has Slept; The Hymn of the Unwaning Light; A Hymn to the Mother of God; The Lamb; The Lord's Prayer; Magnificat and Nunc Dimittis; A Parting Gift for Tom Farrow; Song for Athene; The Tyger (DVD version)

⊛–¬ **** BBC Opus Arte **DVD** OS 0854 D. The Choir, Whitbourn

Using virtual-reality techniques, the 14 singers, recorded in a Dutch television studio in Hilversum, are placed against the background of Hagia Sophia in Istanbul (what was in medieval times the church of St Sophia). With heavy reverberation added, some of the items suggest a far bigger choir, as in the longest item, *The Hymn of the Unwaning Light*, marred slightly by the wobbly contributions of the baritone soloist. The dedication behind all the pieces is very clear, each of them introduced visually by an ikon or an ikon-like illustration. A fine DVD première for Tavener's music. As supplementary items the disc offers a long and illuminating interview with the composer, who provides a spoken commentary on each piece (not the most convenient method of providing programme notes), and a Dutch expert talking about the sources of ikon painting.

Annunciation; 2 Hymns to the Mother of God; (i) Innocence; The Lamb; (ii) Little Requiem for Father Malachy Lynch; Song for Athene; The Tyger

*** Sony SK 66613. Westminster Abbey Ch., Neary; with (i) Rozario, Titus, A. Nixon, M. Neary, Baker; (ii) ECO

With **Martin Neary** drawing incandescent singing from the **Westminster Abbey Choir**, this CD offers a sequence of Tavener's best-known short works – such as the Blake settings, *The Lamb* and *The Tyger*, and the *Hymns to the Mother of God* – as well as longer pieces in which he movingly exploits spatial effects. *Innocence* encapsulates in its 25-minute ritual what many of his more expansive pieces have told us, with multi-layered elements atmospherically contrasted, near and far, starting with apocalyptic organ-sounds and ending with a surging climax. The Sony recording vividly captures the Abbey acoustic, with extreme dynamics used impressively to convey space and distance.

As one who has slept; Birthday Sleep; The Bridal Chamber; Butterfly Dreams; Exhortation and Kohima; Schuon Hymnen; Schûnya; The Second Coming

*** Hyp. CDA 67475. Polyphony, Layton

Stephen Layton's superb professional choir, **Polyphony**, does wonders in bringing variety to a sequence of Sir John Tavener's recent works for small chorus which might easily have seemed too persistently slow and meditative. Most impressive of the longer works is *Schuon Hymnen*, setting German words by the Sufi sheikh Frithjof Schuon, with verses and refrains bringing sharp contrasts between powerful unisons and distant choral comment, punctuated by mantra-like phrases for solo tenor. *Birthday Sleep*, setting a Vernon Watkins poem, brings attractively scrunching harmonies, and the eight tiny movements of *Butterfly Dreams* include one which delightfully captures the fluttering of a butterfly.

As one who has slept; Funeral Ikos; God is with us (Christmas Proclamation); 2 Hymns to the Mother of God; The Lamb; The Lord's Prayer; Love bade me welcome; Magnificat & Nunc dimittis; Song for Athene; (i) Svyati (O Holy One); The Tyger

⊛–¬ (BB) **** Naxos 8.555256. Choir of St John's College, Cambridge, Robinson; (i) with Hugh

The Christmas Proclamation, *God is with us* was inspired, like so many of Tavener's works, by Greek Orthodox liturgy, rising in thrilling crescendo and punctuated at the end by *fortissimo* organ chords. The *Song for Athene* is here presented as an anthem rather than a processional. The longest work, *Svyati*, with its cello solo magnetically played by **Tim Hugh**, echoes the example of Tavener's visionary cello work *The Protecting Veil*, while the shorter pieces include most of the favourite Tavener items. Superb singing throughout and vividly atmospheric sound.

(i) Eternity's Sunrise; (ii) Funeral Canticle; Petra; A Ritual Dream; (i; iv) Sappho: Lyrical Fragments; (i; v) Song of the Angel

*** HM HMU 907231. (i) Rozario; (ii) Mosely, AAM Ch.; (iv) Gooding; (v) Manze; with AAM, Goodwin

Eternity's Sunrise is an elegiac setting of words by Blake in Tavener's rapt and intense style, with the soprano, **Patricia Rozario**, both pure and sensuous in singing the soaring cantilena. The final work on the disc, *Funeral Canticle* for baritone and chorus, is related in being written in memory of the composer's father; 'calm and mesmeric' as **Paul Goodwin** says in his note. Of the rest, *Sappho* represents Tavener at an earlier period, grittier in expression, while *Petra* and the *Song of the Angel* bring ethereal violin solos from **Andrew Manze** set against the voices. Radiantly atmospheric sound to match.

Ex Maria Virgine (A Christmas Sequence for Choir and Orchestra)

Ⓝ (BB) **** Naxos 8.572168 Clare College Ch.,Cambridge, Timothy Brown; McVinnie or Jacobs (organ)

This is an ideal CD for those collectors who are unfamiliar with Tavener's music, for it covers the full range of his diverse choral writing, and indeed his imaginative organ effects. The title work, *Ex Maria Virgine*, was dedicated to Prince Charles and Camilla on their marriage. It has ten sections, displaying much choral variety, throbbing to

'Nowell! Out of your sleep', producing a chorale lullaby for 'Sweet was the song', vigorously extolling the 'King of the Angels' in *Ave Rex Angelorum*, then 'Ding-donging merrily on high', before gently 'Rocking' Mary's babe to sleep. *Unto us is born a son* is both peaceful and fiercely triumphant, while *Verbum caro* plangently rises to a glorious close. The other motets here picture the *Nativity*, move radiantly through *O Thou gentle light*, closing with a portrayal of the *Angels*, set among delicate organ filigree. Throughout, the singing of **Clare College Choir** under **Timothy Brown** rises richly (and falls meditatively) for every occasion, and the two organists, **James McVinnie** and **Simon Thomas Jacobs** make the very most of their many opportunities. Much of this music shows the composer at his most inspired, and the recording, produced by John Rutter in Norwich Cathedral is outstandingly fine.

Fall and Resurrection

*** Chan. 9800. Rozario, Chance, Hill, Richardson, Peacock, BBC Singers, St Paul's Cathedral Ch., City of L. Sinf., Hickox

In *Fall and Resurrection* Tavener's ambitious aim is to 'encompass in brief glimpses the events which have taken place since the beginning of time and before time'. So, after the slow emergence of the prelude out of silence, darkness and the representation of Chaos (with massive banks of timpani), the voice of Adam is heard against a chill flute solo, a simple dedicated vision. The first of the three parts is devoted to the fall of Adam and Eve, with the Serpent illustrated by a whining saxophone. The second section, representing prediction, leads from the fall to a quotation from Psalm 121, *I lift my eyes to the hills*, movingly sung by the countertenor, **Michael Chance**. The final part, *The Incarnation of the Logos*, in telegraphic brevity encompasses the birth of Jesus, the Crucifixion and finally the Resurrection in a Cosmic dance, when 'all is transfigured' underpinned by a heartfelt performance here under **Richard Hickox** with a superb team of choirs and soloists.

Lament for Jerusalem

(BB) *** Naxos 8.557826. Gryffydd Jones, Crawford, Ch. & O of L., Summerly

Lament for Jerusalem consists of seven cycles, each beginning with a quotation from Psalm 137, 'By the Waters of Babylon', and each following a similar layout, with an instrumental texture, solos for counter-tenor and soprano, and a final choral lament. **Summerly** draws incandescent singing from his choir of just over 30 singers, sounding far bigger than that thanks to the warmly atmospheric recording, made in the church of All Hallows, Gospel Oak. Outstanding solo singing too from **Angharad Gryffydd Jones** and **Peter Crawford**.

The Repentant Thief; To a Child Dancing in the Wind; Lamentation; A Mini-Song-Cycle for Gina; Melina

*** RCA 8869 7217612. Rozario, A. Marriner, LSO, Tilson Thomas

The Repentant Thief, written in 1990, was inspired by the image of the thief crucified with Christ, and it features the clarinet, beautifully played by **Andrew Marriner**, as the focus of the work – just as the cello is in *The Protecting Veil*. There are snatches of oriental-style music between the more meditative passages, with raucous woodwind and percussion, both in *The Repentant Thief* and in *To a Child Dancing*, which sets nine poems of W. B. Yeats. It is sweetly sung by **Patricia Rozario**, with the final number unaccompanied, fading away at the end. The *Mini-Song-Cycle* of 1984 sets more Yeats poems, with the composer accompanying Rozario at the piano. *Lamentation* of 1977 is for soprano and handbells, while *Melina* is a simple elegy for Melina Mercouri which Tavener wrote on hearing of her death. First-rate performances and well-balanced sound.

(i) Requiem for Father Malachy; (ii) Cantiones espanolas

(N) *** Lyrita (ADD) SRCD 311. Nash Ens., the Composer with (i) King's Singers; (ii) Bowman, Kevin Smith

The *Requiem*, written in memory of a priest who deeply influenced the composer, evoked a mood of dedication rare in new music by a composer as young as Tavener when it was written (in 1973). If in his earlier works there was sometimes a suspicion that the brilliant and memorable effects were actually more important than the argument, here the balance has clearly been righted. It is a work in which every sequence has one thinking afresh about the words of the liturgy, and this superb performance conveys total concentration. The fill-up could not be more welcome or attractive, a colourful and lightweight group of works based on early Spanish music, fizzing encore pieces. The 1976 (originally RCA) sound has transferred beautifully and vividly to CD.

Requiem, Eternal Memory; Mahashakti

(N) *** EMI 50999-2 35134-2. Palmer, Knight, Thomas, Kennedy, RLPO & Ch, Petrenko

John Tavener's second setting of the *Requiem*, commissioned to celebrate Liverpool as the European City of Culture in 2008, is the more moving when the composer had been told he was under sentence of death through persistent ill-health. He explains his theme, quoting the idea, 'Our glory lies where we cease to exist', thinking to write about the afterlife. The result is a characteristic example of Tavener's 'spiritual minimalism' with evocative choruses and repeated mantras for the soprano in *ostinato* above the choir. Various movements echo those in the traditional *Requiem*, the *Kyrie* following the opening movement *Primordial White Light* and *Kali's Dance* which is the equivalent to the traditional *Dies Irae* in its bite. The closing movement, *Ananda*, rounds the work off in a moving crescendo of choral sound, finally fading to nothing.

Mahashakti is for solo violin, tam-tam and strings, also highly evocative in its celebration of celestial feminine energy, and *Eternal Memory* is a deep meditation on the memory of death, including a brisk passage for solo strings. Excellent sound, though the chorus could be a little closer. Performances otherwise are first-rate from soloists, chorus and orchestra under the inspired direction of **Vasily Petrenko**.

We Shall See Him as He Is

*** Chan. 9128. Rozario, Ainsley, Murgatroyd, Britten Singers, Chester Festival Ch., Hickox

We Shall See Him as He Is is a sequence of what Tavener describes as musical ikons, setting brief, poetic texts based on the Epistle of St John, each inspired by a salient event in the life of Christ. Each ikon is punctuated by a choral refrain, setting the words of the work's title in Greek. Though at first the inspiration may seem painfully thin, the simple ritual becomes magnetic, with its structured, highly atmospheric use of large-scale choral forces progressing towards rapt contemplation of the Resurrection, the ultimate ikon. The recording was made live at a dedicated Prom performance. The tenor, **John Mark Ainsley**, in the central solo role of St John, sings with deep feeling, while **Patricia Rozario** makes her brief, wide-ranging solo a soaring climax.

The Veil of the Temple

*** RCA 82876 661154-2 (2). Rozario, Temple Church Ch., Holst Singers, Layton

Tavener describes *The Veil of the Temple* as an all-night vigil, which it literally is, when in its full form it lasts eight hours, a choral sequence in eight cycles. It represents a journey from darkness to light, from death to rebirth, ending on the eighth cycle, which represents a new week and a new creation. He has taken his inspiration not just from Greek Orthodox rituals (a regular source for him) but from Russian church music too, and more particularly from eastern sources, Sufi, Hindu, Tibetan and Sanskrit, a meeting of East and West. Yet with dedicated performances from all the forces, this disc, recorded live at two performances in the summer of 2003, makes for magnetic results over the span of two and a half hours, increasingly involving massive percussion sounds with gongs of different kinds and weighty choral interventions, is most compelling. The ending brings obsessive cries of 'Shantih', Peace, from the basses as the choir moves off. Spectacular recording, vividly capturing the atmosphere of the Temple Church.

TAVERNER, John (c. 1495–1545)

Missa Corona spinea. Motets: *Gaude plurium; In pace*

🔑 ✿ (BB) **** Hyp. Helios CDH 55051. The Sixteen, Christophers

Missa Corona spinea. Motet: *O Wilhelme, pastor bone*

**(*) ASV CDGAU 115. Christ Church Cathedral Ch., Grier

As with the *Missa Mater Christi sanctissima* (see below), we are offered a choice of performance style for the inspired *Missa Corona spinea*, perhaps the most thrilling of all the Taverner *Mass* settings. In the **Christ Church** performance **Francis Grier** has transposed the music up, and his choir, although always eloquent, have to try very hard to cope with the highest tessitura.

The Sixteen, using professional singers (and secure female trebles), have no such problems and they sing gloriously throughout. Taverner's inspiration is consistent and his flowing melismas are radiantly realized, with fine support from the lower voices; indeed, the balance and blend are nigh perfect. The two motets are no less beautifully sung, and the recording, made in St Jude's Church, Hampstead, is outstanding both in clarity and in its perfectly judged ambience. A superb disc and an astonishing bargain.

Missa Gloria tibi Trinitas; Audivi vocem (responsory); anon.: *Gloria tibi Trinitas*

🔑 (BB) **** Hyp. Helios CDH 55052. The Sixteen, Christophers

Missa Gloria tibi Trinitas; Dum transisset sabbatum; Kyrie a 4 (Leroy); Western Wynde Mass (with song: *Western Wynde*)

🔑 **** Gimell CDGIM 004. Tallis Scholars, Phillips

This six-voice setting of the *Gloria tibi Trinitas* Mass is richly varied in its invention (not least in rhythm) and expressive in a deeply personal way very rare for its period. **Harry Christophers** and **The Sixteen** underline the beauty with an exceptionally pure and clear account, superbly recorded and made the more brilliant by having the pitch a minor third higher than modern concert pitch.

Peter Phillips and the **Tallis Scholars** give an intensely involving performance of this glorious example of Tudor music. The recording may not be as clear as on the rival Hyperion version, but Phillips rejects all idea of reserve or cautiousness of expression; the result reflects the emotional basis of the inspiration the more compellingly. The motet *Dum transisset sabbatum* is then presented more reflectively, another rich inspiration. To make this reissue even more attractive, Gimell have now added first-class accounts of the famous *Western Wynde Mass* and the song on which it is based. This mass is also available differently coupled with music by Tye and others – see below.

(i) *Missa Mater Christi sanctissima; Hodie nobis coelorum rex; Magnificat a 4: Nesciene mater; Mater Christi sanctissima*; (ii) *In nomine a 4; Quemadmodum a 6*

(BB) *** Hyp. Helios CDH 55053. (i) The Sixteen, Christophers; (ii) Fretwork

Continuing their outstanding Taverner survey, **The Sixteen** here offer the *Missa Mater Christi sanctissima* plus the votive anthem on which it is based. **Christophers** presents the *Mass* as it stands, and the music itself is all sung a tone up, which certainly makes it sound brighter. His pacing is rather restrained, and that adds a touch of breadth. The Helios disc includes extra music, including the Christmas responsory *Hodie nobis*, a fine four-part *Magnificat* and, a surprise, two rather grave pieces for viols from **Fretwork** to frame the *Mass* itself. The recording is outstandingly fine, spacious yet clear.

Mass, O Michael; Dum transisset sabbatum; Kyrie a 4 (Leroy)

(BB) *** Hyp. Helios CDH 55054. The Sixteen, Christophers

The *Missa O Michael* is an ambitious six-part *Mass* lasting nearly 40 minutes which derives its name from the respond, *Archangeli Michaelis interventione*, which prefaces the performance. The chant on which the *Mass* is built appears no fewer than seven times during its course. The so-called Leroy *Kyrie* (the name thought to be a reference to *le roi* Henry) fittingly precedes it: the *Missa O Michael* has no Kyrie. The Easter motet, *Dum transisset sabbatum*, completes an impressive disc.

Missa Sancti Wilhelmi; Dum transisset Sabbatum; Ex eius tumba; O Wilhelme, pastor bone

⊶ **(BB)** **** Hyp. Helios CDH 55055. The Sixteen, Christophers

The *Missa Sancti Wilhelmi* (known as 'Small Devotion' in two sources and possibly a corruption of *S. Will devotio*) is prefaced by the antiphon, *O Wilhelme, pastor bone*, written in a largely syllabic, note-against-note texture, and the second of his two five-part settings of the Easter respond, *Dum transisset Sabbatum*, and washed down, as it were, by the Matins responds for the Feast of St Nicholas, *Ex eius tumba*, believed to be the only 16th-century setting of this text. The singing of **The Sixteen** under **Harry Christophers** is expressive and ethereal, and the recording impressively truthful. Recommended with confidence.

Mass: The Western Wynde; Mater Christi

(M) *** CRD CRD 3372, Ch. of New College, Oxford, Higginbottom – TALLIS: *Audivi vocem de Caelo* etc. ***

Mass: The Western Wynde; Alleluia, Veni, electa mea; O splendor gloria; Te Deum

⊶ **(BB)** **** Hyp. Helios CDH 55056. The Sixteen, Christophers

Western Wynde Mass is also beautifully sung and recorded by **Harry Christophers' Sixteen** in what must be regarded as an ideally paced and proportioned performance. But what makes this inexpensive Helios reissue doubly attractive is the collection of other works included. *O splendor gloria* carries the exulted mood inherent in its title (referring to Christ and the Trinity) and the *Alleluia* is equally jubilant. Most remarkable and individual of all is the masterly five-part *Te Deum*, a profoundly poignant setting, harmonically and polyphonically, even richer than the *Mass*, and using those momentary shafts of dissonance that can make music of this period sound so forward-looking. The recording is superb and this CD is obviously the place to start for those wanting to explore this excellent Helios series.

This CRD version of Taverner's *Mass* was the first to appear after the King's College, Cambridge, recording of 1961. Since then there have been others, but it was a worthy successor and the acoustic of **New College, Oxford**, is, if anything, superior to King's, producing greater clarity and definition. **Higginbottom's** choir sings with great feeling

but with restraint and splendid control, both of line and ensemble.

TCHAIKOVSKY, Peter
(1840–93)

Andante cantabile for Strings (arr. Serebrier); Capriccio italien; 1812 Overture; Elégie for Strings in G; Fatum, Op. 77; Marche slave

**** BIS CD 1283. Bamberg SO, Serebrier

In this, the third of **José Serebrier's** Tchaikovsky discs for BIS, the popular coupling of *Capriccio italien*, the *1812 Overture* and *Marche slave* brings a fresh, distinctive approach that underlines the purely musical qualities of works that are easily vulgarized. In the *1812* and *Marche slave*, it is a revelation to find the conductor's refining process bringing out beauties in the instrumentation that are normally plastered over. Although the cannon and bell effects at the end of *1812* are not identified as coming from anywhere but the orchestra, the excellent BIS recording gives them plenty of punch. *Marche slave* also gains clarity, even in the heaviest passages, with a swaggering spring given to the march rhythms.

The popular *Andante cantabile* is a degree more refined than before, as is the surprisingly neglected *Elégie*, a lovely late work written in a single day. *Fatum*, dates from 1868, soon after Tchaikovsky left the St Petersburg Conservatory, and it has a spontaneity and thrust that point forward to Tchaikovsky's later fate-obsessed works, making it a welcome addition to a well-contrasted collection.

(i) Andante cantabile; (i;ii) Violin Concerto; Symphonies: (i) 4 (iii) 5

(N) ⊶ ✿ **** DG **DVD** 073 4511 (i) NYPO; (ii) Belkin; (iii) Boston SO; Bernstein

This superb collection not only shows **Bernstein** at his most inspired, communicating his own great pleasure in the music, but also – in the manner of Stokowski – his ability so implant his own charismatic personality on *any* orchestra. Here there is virtually no difference between the electrifying results in Boston and New York. For instance, although the interpretations of the two symphonies are different, the *Fourth* relatively straightforward, the *Fifth* with Bernstein responding literally to Tchaikovky's marking, 'con alcuna licenza', the rich sweep of string tone is common to each venue. But especially so in the **Boston** *Fifth*, where the second subject of the first movement, and the glorious climax of the *Andante cantabile* are both almost overwhelming.

Each work too, has an electrifying coda, the kind that sends the audience and orchestra home thrilled and satisfied in equal measure, feeling again what wonderful symphonies these are, even if Tchaikovsky himself had nagging doubts about the uninhibited splendour of the closing peroration of the *Fifth*. Koussevitzky in Boston had felt his mission with Tchaikovsky was 'to open the gate of heaven and let the people experience ecstasy', and Bernstein followed his mentor's 'theme song'.

Boris Belkin joins the orchestra for a moving and beautifully played account of the *Violin Concerto*, where the laurels are shared equally by orchestra and soloist. But the lovely *Andante cantabile* is kept back for the final encore, ravishingly played and confirming that its composer was one of the greatest melodists of all time. All this is captured marvellously by Humphrey Burton's video direction, for Bernstein is always a joy to watch, and the result is one of the key recordings in the whole Tchaikovsky discography.

Andante cantabile, Op. 11; Nocturne, Op. 19/4; Pezzo capriccioso, Op. 62 (1887 version); 2 Songs: Legend; Was I not a little blade of grass; Variations on a Rococo Theme, Op. 33 (1876 version)

⏮ *** Chan. 8347. Wallfisch, ECO, Simon

Andante cantabile; Nocturne (both arr. for cello & orchestra); Pezzo capriccioso; Variations on a Rococo Theme (original versions)

ⓑⓑ *** Virgin 2x1 5 61490-2(2). Isserlis, COE, Gardiner –
BLOCH: *Schelomo*; ELGAR: *Cello Concerto*; KABALEVSKY: *Cello Concerto 2*; RICHARD STRAUSS: *Don Quixote* ***

The delightful Chandos record gathers together all of Tchaikovsky's music for cello and orchestra, including his arrangements of such items as the famous *Andante cantabile* and two songs. The major item is the original version of the *Rococo Variations* with an extra variation and the earlier variations put in a more effective order, as Tchaikovsky wanted. **Geoffrey Simon** draws lively and sympathetic playing from the **ECO**, with **Wallfisch** a vital if not quite flawless soloist. Excellent recording, with the CD providing fine presence and an excellent perspective.

On this bargain Virgin Double, not only are all the performances of high quality, but **Isserlis** also offers Tchaikovsky's original versions of both the *Pezzo capriccioso* and the *Rococo Variations*. The solo playing has at times a slight reserve, but also an elegant delicacy, most noticeable in the *Andante cantabile*. Throughout, **Gardiner** provides gracefully lightweight accompaniments and the Virgin recording is faithfully balanced, fresh in texture and warm in ambience.

Capriccio italien, Op. 45

⏮ ✹ Ⓜ **** RCA (ADD) 09026 63302-2. RCA Victor SO, Kondrashin – KABALEVSKY: *The Comedians Suite*; KHACHATURIAN: *Masquerade Suite*; RIMSKY-KORSAKOV: *Capriccio espagnol* ***

Kondrashin's 1958 recording of Tchaikovsky's *Capriccio italien* has never been surpassed. The arresting opening still surprises by its impact, the brass fanfares – first trumpets, then horns, then the full tutti – sonically riveting. The music is alive in every bar and a model of careful preparation, with the composer's dynamic markings meticulously terraced. Kondrashin's pacing throughout is absolutely right and the closing section is highly exhilarating. This is a stereo demonstration disc if ever there was one. And the couplings are pretty good too.

Capriccio italien; (i) 1812; Festival Coronation March; Marche slave; Eugene Onegin: Polonaise; Waltz; Mazeppa: Cossack Dance

**(*) Telarc CD 80541. Cincinnati Pops O, Kunzel; (i) with Kiev Symphony Ch., Cincinnati Children's Ch., Cannon & Cleveland carillon

The Telarc CD is aimed straight at audiophiles. But the snag is that the real cannon, spectacularly reproduced, the carillon and choruses singing the folktunes in *1812* very freshly cannot turn a good performance into a thrilling one, and here the adrenalin does not run as free as it should. *Marche slave*, however, is much more successful.

Capriccio italien, Op. 45; 1812 Overture, Op. 49; Fate, Op. 77; Festival Overture on the Danish National Anthem, Op. 15; Francesca da Rimini, Op. 32; Hamlet, Op. 67a; Manfred Symphony, Op. 58; Marche slave, Op. 31; Overture in F, Op. 67; Romeo and Juliet (Fantasy Overture); The Tempest, Op 18; The Voyevoda, Op. 87

⏮ ✹ Ⓑ **** DG Trio 477 053-2 (3). Russian Nat. O, Pletnev

Pletnev has a quite special feeling for Tchaikovsky's music, gauging its highly charged emotional content and dramatic flair to perfection, and never losing sight of the disciplined mind which oversaw the musical design. There is no shortage of great performances of *Romeo and Juliet* and *Francesca da Rimini*, and Pletnev's account with his **Russian National Orchestra** certainly ranks among them. But the special value of this set is that it offers rarities like *The Voyevoda* and the *F major Overture* in performances which are unlikely to be bettered for a very long time. When it first appeared, we placed his *Manfred* among the finest in the catalogue, and that judgement still holds. An essential purchase, particularly at so competitive a price.

Capriccio italien; 1812 Overture; Francesca da Rimini; Marche slave

*** Capriccio Surround Sound **SACD** 71 042. ASMF, Marriner

Marriner's performances are very fine, perhaps lacking the very last drop of adrenalin at the climaxes of *Capriccio* and *Francesca*, but still involvingly enjoyable for the polish and commitment of the orchestral response. The back speakers add just enough ambience to give a concert-hall illusion; the orchestra is naturally balanced and the effect vividly dramatic, while the cannon in *1812* are really spectacular, without dwarfing the orchestra.

Capriccio italien; 1812 Overture; Marche slave; Romeo and Juliet (fantasy overture)

⏮ ⓑⓑ **** Naxos 8.550500. RPO, Leaper

Adrian Leaper proves a natural Tchaikovskian: whether in the colourful extravagance of the composer's memento of his Italian holiday, the romantic ardour and passionate conflict of *Romeo and Juliet*, the sombre expansiveness of *Marche slave* with its surge of adrenalin at the close, or in the extrovert celebration of *1812*, he draws playing from the **RPO** that is spontaneously committed and exciting. The brilliantly spectacular recording, with plenty of weight for the brass, was made in Watford Town Hall, with realistic cannon and an impressively resonant imported carillon to add to the exciting climax of 1812.

Capriccio italien; 1812 Overture; Mazeppa: Cossack Dance

(*) Telarc **SACD 60646. Cincinnati SO, Kunzel – GERSHWIN: *American in Paris; Rhapsody in Blue* **(*)

The original compact disc of the Telarc performances gave due warning that the cannon in 1812 might damage speakers and windows if the disc was played at too high a level! So if you need a recording of cannon plus 1812, and your speakers can accommodate the dynamic range and amplitude, both impressively wide on SACD, this issue is for you. In the *Capriccio Italien* there are no cannon, so the engineers substitute the bass drum, which is very prominent. The orchestral contribution throughout is lively but not memorable, and the playing simply does not generate enough adenalin to compensate for the lack of projection of the orchestral tone. At the end of 1812, Tchaikovsky's carefully contrived climax, with its full-blooded scalic descent, lacks weight. The most enjoyable item is the sparkling *Cossack Dance*, a favourite item in the days of 78s.

Capriccio italien, Op. 45; 1812 Overture, Op. 49; Marche slave; Romeo and Juliet: Fantasy Overture; The Snow Maiden: Dance of the Tumblers

(BB) **** Naxos 8.555923. Nat. SO of Ukraine, Kuchar

Theodore Kuchar and the excellent **Ukraine Orchestra** follow up their highly recommendable Mussorgsky disc with an almost equally impressive Tchaikovsky collection. Once again the recording is spectacular, with striking depth and resonance. The orchestra is set slightly back, so you need to set the volume a little higher than usual. While there are other more distinctive versions of some of these pieces, this collection is very enjoyable overall and excellent value.

(i) Capriccio italien; (ii) Francesca da Ramini; (i) Nutcracker Suite; (ii) Serenade for Strings; (i) Eugene Onegin: Polonaise and Waltz

**(*) Australian Ph. Eloquence 442 8335 (2). Stokowski; with (i) LPO; (ii) LSO

It is good to have these **Stokowski** recordings, dating from 1973 and 1974, restored to circulation. *Capriccio italien* brings genuine panache, and the infectiously vigorous *Eugene Onegin* dances have characteristic flair. But in the *Nutcracker Suite* (which he played so beautifully for Disney in Fantasia), the *March* is rather hard-driven and the middle section sounds a bit gabbled. Then, after introducing the *Sugar Plum Fairy* with a string tremolando, his phrasing is so mannered (with repeated tenutos on the falling clarinet phrase) that few will find this comfortable to live with, even if, later, the *Waltz of the Flowers* is exhilarating. The 1974 account of *Francesca da Rimini*, although not as well controlled as his classic earlier version with the New York Stadium Orchestra, is very exciting indeed; there is no doubt about the temperament of the reading and Stokowski generates tremendous emotional thrust at the climax. The *String Serenade* is char-acteristically bold and romantic, with sumptuous tone from the **LSO** strings – a real 'Stokowski sound' – and after the characteristically luscious *Waltz*, the *Elégie* is ardent and the finale full of energy. One can forgive the idiosyncrasies for much else that is uniquely Stokowskian.

Concert Fantasy, Op. 56; Piano Concertos 1–3

(BB) **(*) EMI Gemini 5 85540-2 (2). Donohoe, Bournemouth SO, Barshai

Peter Donohoe's account of the *B flat minor Concerto*, although thoroughly sympathetic and spaciously conceived, lacks the thrust and indeed the electricity of the finest versions. The *Third Concerto* is altogether more successful, dramatic and lyrically persuasive, and held together well by **Barshai**. The *Concert Fantasia* is even more in need of interpretative cohesion. But what makes this inexpensive Gemini Double distinctive is the inclusion of Donohoe's much praised account of the *Second Concerto*. This superb recording of the full original score in every way justifies the work's length and the unusual format of the slow movement. Its extended solos for violin and cello are played with beguiling warmth by **Nigel Kennedy** and **Steven Isserlis**. The first movement goes with splendid impetus, and the performance of the finale is a delight from beginning to end. Donohoe plays with infectious bravura, and he is well supported by sparkling playing from the **Bournemouth orchestra** under Barshai.

Concert Fantasy in G, Op. 56; Piano Concertos 1–3; Andante & Finale, Op. 70 (orch. Taneyev)

(BB) **(*) Naxos 8.557257 (1 & 3; *Andante & Finale*); 8.557824 (2; *Concert Fantasy*) (available separately). Scherbakov, Russian PO, Yablonsky

Konstantin Scherbakov gives us all Tchaikovsky's concertante music for piano, including the *Andante and Finale*, Op. 79 (drawing on music for a discarded symphony) which Taneyev revised and scored after the composer's death. The performances are full of impulsive virtuosity, but the famous *B flat minor*, while not a barnstorming account, is satisfying for its overall balance, as well as for an exciting finale. The *Third Concerto* comes off very well indeed; the *Second Concerto* is played uncut and the slow movement and the brilliant finale are very successful. The highlight of the set is a superb, bravura account of the *Concert Fantasy*, lyrical and sparkling by turns. The recording is spacious, the piano boldly placed in front of the orchestra. The two discs are available separately.

(i; ii) Piano concertos 1–3; Concert Fantasy, Op. 56; (iii) Symphony 6 (Pathétique); Marche slave; (i) The Seasons; 6 Pieces, Op. 21; Sleeping Beauty (excerpts; arr. Pletnev).

(BB) **** Virgin 5 62358-2 (4). (i) Pletnev (piano); (ii) Philh. O, Fedoseyev; (iii) Russian Nat. O, cond. Pletnev

Mikhail Pletnev's masterful account of the *First Concerto* has all the qualities we associate with his remarkable pianism. This high-voltage account, together with that of the *Concert Fantasy*, is among the very finest of modern recordings in the catalogue. The *Second Concerto* brings comparably commanding playing from Pletnev, but it also brings a small but unnecessary cut in the slow movement. It would be difficult to improve on the *Third Concerto*, which is characterized strongly and interestingly. The recording is very good, but not in the demonstration bracket.

The way in which Pletnev launches us into the development of the first movement of the *Pathétique* in his earlier Virgin recording still takes one aback, even when one knows what to expect. His hand-picked orchestra is as virtuosic as Pletnev himself can be on the keyboard, with a challengingly fast tempo for the Scherzo. There is a stirring account of *Marche slave* too, and a very fine recording, perfectly balanced, although the effect is a little recessed.

In Tchaikovsky's 12 *Seasons* Pletnev shows exceptional feeling for Tchaikovsky. He grips one from first note to last, not only in *The Seasons* but also in the charming and touching *Six morceaux*, Op. 21. Fresh and natural recorded sound.

Piano Concerto 1 in B flat min., Op. 23 (DVD versions)

** Sony **DVD** SVD 45986. Kissin, BPO, Karajan (with PROKOFIEV: *Classical Symphony* **(*))

Both works on the Sony DVD were recorded at a New Year's Eve concert at the end of 1988, and the concerto was issued on DG 427 485-2 as well as on video. **Kissin** was 16 at the time of this performance, though he looks even younger, and the whole occasion must have been rather an awesome experience for him. His playing has great elegance and tremendous poise – his *pianissimo* tone is quite ravishing – but he tends not to let himself go, and there is just a slight feeling that he is playing safe, particularly in the finale. The performance as a whole, for all its finesse, lacks abandon. The strings in the DVD of Prokofiev's *Classical Symphony* have the characteristic Berlin sheen, and the slow movement has great tonal sweetness. The *Scherzo* is a bit heavy-handed, but it is offset by an altogether captivating finale, perfectly judged in pace and character. The camera work is unobtrusive, and although the piano is rather forward, the balance is well judged, though the overall sound is a shade dry.

Piano Concerto 1 in B flat min., Op. 23

**** Häns. CD 98.932. Ohlsson, ASMF, Marriner – RACHMANINOV: *Piano Concerto 2* ***

**** Ph. 446 673-2. Argerich, Bav. RSO, Kondrashin – RACHMANINOV: *Piano Concerto 3* ****

*** BIS **SACD**-1588. Sudbin, São Paolo SO, Neschling – MEDTNER: *Piano Concerto 1* ***

(BB) *** EMI 5 73765-2 (3). Rudy, St Petersburg PO, Jansons – RACHMANINOV: *Piano Concertos 1–3; Rhapsody on a Theme of Paganini* ***

*** Warner 2564 63074-2. Berezovsky, Ural PO, Liss – KHACHATURIAN: *Piano Concerto* ***

(*) DG **SACD 474 637-2; CD 474 291-2. Lang Lang, Chicago SO, Barenboim – MENDELSSOHN: *Piano Concerto 1* ***

(BB) (***) Naxos mono 8.110671. Horowitz, NBC O, Toscanini – BRAHMS: *Piano Concerto 2.* (**)

(M) (**) DG (ADD) 447 420-2. Richter, VSO, Karajan – RACHMANINOV: *Piano Concerto 2* ***

(i) Piano Concerto 1; (ii) Nutcracker Suite, Op. 71a (arr. Economou, for 2 pianos)

*** DG (ADD/DDD) 449 816-2. Argerich, (i) BPO, Abbado; (ii) with Economou

It is good to have a really splendid, modern coupling of these two most popular romantic *Concertos* from **Ohlsson** and **Marriner** that can measure up to the finest versions from the past, presented in naturally balanced, modern, digital recording of the very highest quality. The Tchaikovsky opens with a commanding melodic sweep, and the first-movement *Allegro* is as full of poetic detail as it is exciting, leading on to the cadenza in the most spontaneous way. The *Andante semplice* is charmingly light-hearted and, after the scintillating centrepiece, is very tender at its reprise. The dancing finale brings all the bravura you could ask for, with weight and power as well as excitement.

Argerich's 1994 live performance with the **Berlin Philharmonic** under **Abbado** is undoubtedly the finest of her three recordings. It has prodigious virtuosity, while in the first movement, after a richly commanding opening, conductor and pianist find a perfect balance between dynamism and magically gentle poetry. Even though Argerich's impetuosity is famous, on first hearing the listener will surely be astonished by her two tempestuous octave entries, where she carries all before her. And the cadenza, like the barnstorming closing pages of the finale, brings a thrilling, all-out bravura of the kind one normally only associates with Horowitz. Yet the *Andante semplice* has wonderful delicacy with the central *Prestissimo* glittering like a shower of meteorites. Economou's arrangement of the *Nutcracker Suite* for two pianos works well enough. The digital recording is good but rather dry. This CD, fine as it is, should have been reissued at mid-price.

Argerich's Philips issue comes from a live performance given in October 1980, full of animal excitement, with astonishingly fast speeds in the outer movements. The impetuous virtuosity is breathtaking, even if passage-work is not always cleanly articulated. The CD version clarifies and intensifies the already vivid sound, which is fuller than her DG version of nine years earlier (see below), and the new coupling with her even more sensational account of Rachmaninov's *Third Concerto* from earlier makes this a very desirable issue.

Yevgeny Sudbin's account of the *B flat minor Concerto* serves as a reminder that this familiar warhorse is always able to take one by surprise and make one wonder anew at its abundance of ideas and its originality. A rewarding issue, and of particular value in offering Medtner's *First Concerto*. Let us hope that BIS will follow this with the remaining two.

As always, **Rudy** exhibits much artistry and taste in this eloquent **St Petersburg** account, partnered by **Mariss Jansons**. His playing is not short on virtuosity and command, but never at the expense of poetic feeling; the warmly idiomatic orchestral playing under Jansons has great character and personality. Altogether it makes a refreshing alternative version, here offered in a bargain package with equally illuminating accounts of the Rachmaninov *Concertos*. Excellent sound, full and vivid.

Berezovsky's recording of the *B flat minor Concerto* is the very opposite of routine and is full of imaginative touches, seeking, rather like Ashkenazy's Decca version, to move away from a barnstorming approach and bring out the concerto's lyrical core. The opening is properly flamboyant and the *Allegro con spirito* sets off with fine impetus. But when the second-subject group arrives, both pianist and conductor combine to produce the utmost delicacy. The recording has a very wide dynamic range, and the result is that their joint image recedes and all but loses its tangibility. However, as the movement progresses, the performance gathers impetus and power, and the cadenza is most poetically done. The pizzicato opening of the slow movement brings another *pianissimo* from the orchestra which is only just audible; but the movement brings more refined delicacy from Berezvosky and a dazzling scherzando centrepiece. The finale then sets off in sparkling fashion, and **Liss** gives the secondary lyrical tune a lighter dancing rhythmic profile than usual. This remains at the climactic reprise, giving the end of the work an added freshness, without losing the pianistic bravura. In spite of the idiosyncrasies, this remains a real three-star performance, well worth hearing.

Lang Lang's performance tempos tend to be broader than usual, only occasionally sounding self-conscious, for in general he is masterly in his control of rubato. The opening instantly establishes this as a big-scale performance, strongly rhythmic and sharply accented, though – with the piano balanced close – the big melody on the first violins sounds surprisingly weak, hidden behind the pianist's monumental chords: the reason for our reservation, when this is one of the composer's most eloquent themes. The outer sections of the slow movement, like the lyrical passages of the first movement, are daringly broad, with **Barenboim** helping to sustain tension, while in the finale Lang Lang, again encouraged by Barenboim, himself a keyboard virtuoso, varies the tempo boldly, while sustaining a purposeful thrust. The Mendelssohn makes an unusual but attractive coupling.

Horowitz's famous wartime Carnegie Hall recording of the *B flat minor Concerto* has since remained the yardstick by which all subsequent versions have been judged. Somehow the alchemy of the occasion was unique and the result is unforgettable. In spite of the Carnegie Hall ambience, the recording is confined and lacking bass, but the Naxos transfer engineer, Mark Obert-Thorn, has achieved impressive results from a single post-war set of 78s in mint condition. Such is the magnetism of the playing, however, that the ear forgets the sonic limitations within moments. **Toscanini's** accompaniment is remarkable not only for matching the adrenalin of his soloist (particularly in the visceral thrill of the finale's climax), but for the tenderness he finds for the lyrical passages of the first movement and the *Andantino*, which is truly *semplice*, even when accompanying the coruscating pianistic fireworks of the central section. The finale carries all before it, with Horowitz's riveting octaves leading to a tremendously exciting statement of the big tune before storming off furiously to the coda.

The element of struggle for which this work is famous is all too clear in the **Richter/Karajan** performance; not surprisingly, these two musical giants do not always agree: each chooses a different tempo for the second subject of the finale and maintains it, despite the other. In both the dramatic opening and the closing pages of the work the approach is mannered and self-conscious, not easy to enjoy. The recording is full-blooded, with a firm piano image.

(i) *Piano Concerto 1*; (ii) *Violin Concerto in D, Op. 35*

🎧 **** Pentatone **SACD**/CD PTC 5186 022. (i) Lugansky; (ii) Tetzlaff; Russian Nat. O, Nagano

Nicolai Lugansky was a pupil of Tatiana Nikolaeva, and his is a far from barnstorming performance of the *B flat minor Concerto*. The famous opening is broad and weighty, and the vividly Russian first subject of the *Allegro* is given a bold, rhythmic character, yet it is not pressed too hard. In both the exposition and recapitulation the beauty of the lyrical secondary material is relished. The *Andantino*, introduced exquisitely by the flute, is played by Lugansky with comparable delicacy, followed by a scintillating central scherzando section. The finale then bursts forth with irrepressible impetus, and the coda would certainly bring the house down at a concert. In his warmly romantic but never sentimental account of the *Violin Concerto*, **Tetzlaff's** beguiling introduction of the two main themes is invested with a natural lyrical feeling. Not surprisingly, the orchestral colouring of the slow movement is very Russian, and this ripely nostalgic palette carries through to the contrasting woodwind interludes in the exuberant finale. Tetzlaff's bravura playing, almost unbelievably polished and secure, is thrilling in its sparkling virtuosity, the closing bars dazzling in their exuberance.

Piano Concerto 1 in B flat min.; Theme and Variations, Op. 19/6

🎧 (BB) *** EMI Encore 5 86881-2. Gavrilov – BALAKIREV: *Islamey*; PROKOFIEV: *Piano Concerto 1*, etc. ****

Gavrilov is stunning in the finale of the *Concerto*; however, the final statement of the big tune is broadened very positively so that one is not entirely convinced. Similarly in the first movement, contrasts of dynamic and tempo are extreme, and the element of self-consciousness is apparent. The *Andante* is full of tenderness and the *prestissimo* middle section goes like quicksilver, displaying the vein of spontaneous imagination that we recognize in Gavrilov's other records. The recording is full and sumptuous. In the *Variations*, Op. 19, Tchaikovsky's invention has great felicity. Gavrilov's playing is stylishly sympathetic here, and the Balakirev and Prokofiev couplings are dazzling.

(i) *Piano Concerto 1 in B flat min., Op. 23. Symphony 4 in F min., Op. 36*

*** Sony 82876777182. Bav. RSO, Jansons; (i) with Bronfman

Jansons, famous for his Tchaikovsky *Symphony* cycle on Chandos, delivers predictably superb results on this new live Sony recording from 2005. In the *Concerto*, **Bronfman** is dazzlingly brilliant but not in a merely showy way: the excitement here is generated from within the music-making. Jansons provides much animation with the orchestra, and the interplay between orchestra and soloist is one of the joys of the performance. The finale is superbly exciting. Perhaps the strings could have been placed more forward, but in general the sound is excellent. The opening 'fate' theme of the *Fourth Symphony* immediately makes this out as a performance of intensity, and if it cannot match the Chandos sound in terms of open expansiveness, it is certainly vivid enough.

Piano Concerto 2 in G, Op. 44; Concert Fantasy, Op. 56

>> (BB) ******** Naxos 8.550820. Glemser, Polish Nat. RSO, Wit

This Naxos coupling can be strongly recommended on all counts, quite irrespective of cost. **Bernd Glemser** and the **Polish National Radio Symphony Orchestra** give an outstanding account of Tchaikovsky's underrated *G major Concerto*, flamboyant and poetic by turns. The unnamed orchestral principal cellist introduces the *Andante* gently and tenderly and his two string colleagues join him with equal sensitivity. The finale has plenty of sparkle and gusto and the whole account is very enjoyable indeed.

The *Concert Fantasy* too, is treated as a large-scale work. Both pianist and orchestra play it with total conviction, and much virtuosity (the cadenza very impressive). The *Contrasts* of the second movement are most tellingly made, with the lyrical minor key *cantabile* touching, and the Russian dance element as vigorous as one could wish. Excellent, well-balanced, full-bodied recording.

Piano Concertos 2 in G, Op. 44; 3 in E flat, Op. 75

*** Ara. Z 6583. Lowenthal, LSO, Comissiona

(BB) ******* Warner Apex 2564 61913-2. Leonskaya, NYPO, Masur

In an attractive coupling of two unjustly neglected works, the energy and flair of **Lowenthal** and **Comissiona** combine to give highly spontaneous performances, well balanced and recorded. With very good sound, this is well worth investigating, as the account of the *Third Concerto* is comparably spontaneous.

Leonskaya is a splendid Tchaikovskian and she finds a sympathetic partner in **Kurt Masur**. Their account of the elusive *Second Piano Concerto* is very fine, weighty, expansive and compelling. The red-blooded orchestral tuttis are matched by Leonskaya's bold, forwardly balanced pianism, and if in the (uncut) slow movement she misses some of its delicacy, she is ardently lyrical. The finale is forceful in its exuberance, powerful and exciting, and the rich Leipzig recording matches the style of the performance. The *Third Concerto* follows on with equal success, and offers brilliant playing with plenty of zest and ardour from soloist and orchestra alike. Outstanding value.

Piano Concerto 3

(*) Chan. 9130. Tozer, LPO, Järvi – *Symphony 7* *****

It was a good idea to record the *Third Piano Concerto* alongside the *Seventh Symphony*, on whose first movement it is based (see below). **Geoffrey Tozer** is an excellent soloist and, as in his Medtner performances for Chandos, plays with sympathy

as well as powerful bravura. The playing of the **London Philharmonic** is not so consistent, with violin tone as recorded often thin, not opulent enough for big Tchaikovsky melodies.

Violin Concerto, Op. 35; Souvenir d'un lien cher (Méditation; Scherzo; Mélodie), Op. 42 (orch. Glazunov); Swan Lake, Act 2: Pas d'action; Act 3: Danse russe

(N) **>>** ******** Sony 88697214232. Baiba Skride, CBSO, Nelsons

Tchaikovsky composed his *Violin Concerto* in just eleven days during a short, but badly needed holiday in the Swiss village of Clarens – where Stravinsky was later to compose *The Rite of Spring* and *Pulcinella*. In a letter to his patroness, Nadezda von Meck, Tchaikovsky wrote at the time of this sudden outburst of creative activity 'composing doesn't seem like like work at all, its pure pleaure!'. This relaxed feeling of joy permeates **Baiba Skride's** wonderful performance, from the gently inviting introduction, created by **Andris Nelsons** and the **CBSO**, onwards to the very last bar.

Born in Riga, Baiba Skride was prizewinner at the Brussels Queen Elisabeth International Music Competition, especially for her interpretation of the Tchaikovsky Concerto, and no wonder! She has a most remarkable natural affinity for the work, choosing a very relaxed tempo for the opening movement, and so making a splendid contrast when the polacca rhythm arrives. Her warmly tender playing, which extends to the slow movement, is gently ravishing, and her performance of the cadenza has a uniquely spontaneous lyricism, making it an integral and magical part of the work's structure; then the finale bursts into a wonderful display of fireworks, with the jaunty folksy subsidiary theme sounding intrinsically Russian in its colouring. For coupling Baiba Skride has made the perfect choice of all three parts of the *Souvenir d'un lieu cher* plus two substantial concertante excerpts from *Swan Lake*, which are played with comparable beauty and sparkle. With recording in the demonstration bracket this now is an easy first choice among the many modern recordings of this repertoire.

Violin Concerto in D; Souvenir d'un lieu cher, Op. 42 (orch. Glazunov)

**** BIS SACD 1432. Gluzman, Bergen PO, Litton – GLAZUNOV: *Violin Concerto* ********

Violin Concerto in D, Op. 35

**** Ph. 473 343-2. Repin, Kirov O., Gergiev – MIASKOVSKY: *Violin Concerto.* ********

(M) ******** Warner Elatus 0927 46743-2. Vengerov, BPO, Abbado – SIBELIUS: *Violin Concerto* ****(*)**

*** Erato 4509 98537-2. Repin, LSO, Krivine – SIBELIUS: *Violin Concerto* *******

(M) ******** Decca 475 7734. Chung, LSO, Previn – SIBELIUS: *Violin Concerto* ********

(B) ******* Decca 475 6703. Bell, Cleveland O, Dohnányi – BRAHMS; SCHUMANN; WIENIAWSKI: *Violin Concertos* *******

*** DG **SACD** 474 874-2; CD 474 515-2. Mutter, VPO, Previn –
KORNGOLD: *Violin Concerto* ***

*** Sony SK 68338. Midori, BPO, Abbado – SHOSTAKOVICH:
Violin Concerto 1 ***

Ⓜ *** EMI 5 03433-2. Chang, LSO, C. Davis – BRAHMS:
Hungarian Dances ***

ⒷⒷ *** Naxos 8.550153. Nishizaki, Slovak PO, Jean –
MENDELSSOHN: *Concerto* ***

Ⓑ *** DG Double (ADD) 453 142-2 (2). Milstein, VPO, Abbado
– BEETHOVEN: *Concerto* *** ; BRAHMS: *Concerto* **(*) ;
MENDELSSOHN: *Concerto* ***

Ⓜ *** DG (ADD) 477 5914. Milstein, VPO, Abbado (with
'Encores' (with Georges Pludermacher, piano): GEMINIANI:
Sonata in A; SCHUBERT: *Rondo brilliant in B min.*;
MILSTEIN: *Paganiniana*; LISZT: *Consolation 3 in D flat*;
STRAVINSKY: *Chanson russe*; KODÁLY: *Il pleut dans la ville*;
MUSSORGSKY: *Hopak*)

ⒷⒷ (***) Naxos mono 8.110938. Heifetz, LPO, Barbirolli –
SIBELIUS: *Violin Concerto*; WIENIAWSKI: *Violin Concerto 2
in D min.* (***)

*** Sup. SU 3709-2. Sporcl, Czech PO, Bělohlávek– DVOŘÁK:
Violin Concerto in D. **(*)

ⒷⒷ (***) Naxos mono 8.110977. Milstein, Chicago SO, Stock –
BRUCH: *Violin Concerto 1*; MENDELSSOHN: *Violin Concerto.*
(***)

Ⓜ **(*) EMI (ADD) 5 62591-2. Perlman, Phd. O, Ormandy –
MENDELSSOHN: *Concerto.* ***

Ⓜ **(*) Ph. 464 741-2. Mullova, Boston SO, Ozawa –
SIBELIUS: *Violin Concerto* ***

**(*) Globe GLO 5174. Lubotsky, Estonian Nat. SO, Volmer –
ARENSKY: *Violin Concerto*; RIMSKY-KORSAKOV: *Concert
Fantasy* **(*)

Violin Concerto; Meditation; Swan Lake, Op. 20: Danse russe

*** Sony SH 94829. Bell, BPO, Tilson Thomas

Violin Concerto; Sérénade mélancolique; (i) Souvenirs d'un lieu cher; Valse-Scherzo

**** Pentatone **SACD** PTC 5186 095. Fischer, Russian Nat. O,
Kreizberg; (i) Kreizberg (piano)

Violin Concerto; Sérénade mélancolique; Souvenir d'un lieu cher; Valse-Scherzo

ⒷⒷ **(*) Naxos 8.557690. Kaler, Russian PO, Yablonsky

Violin Concerto in D; Sérénade mélancolique; String Serenade: Waltz

Ⓜ **(*) RCA (ADD) 09026 61743-2. Heifetz, Chicago SO,
Reiner – MENDELSSOHN: *Concerto* ***

(i) Violin Concerto in D; (ii) Méditation, Op. 42/1; (iii) Sérénade mélancolique, Op. 26

(***) Testament mono/stereo SBT 1224. Kogan; (i; ii) Paris
Conservatoire O; (i) Vandernoot; (ii) Silvestri; (iii) Philh. O,
Kondrashin – PROKOFIEV: *Violin Concerto 2* ***

Violin Concerto; Souvenir d'un lieu cher (arr. for violin & strings, Lascae)

Ⓝ **(*) Decca 478 0651 Jansen, Mahler CO, Harding

Of the many memorable recordings of the Tchaikovsky
Violin Concerto but few are finer than **Vadim Gluzman's** wonderfully warm and lyrical account, and certainly none has
such quite such a totally realistic recording, perfectly balanced. Listening in surround sound (with the back speakers
just adding ambience) gives one the feeling of actually sitting
in the Bergen Grieg Concert Hall with its spacious acoustic.
Gluzman's reading has a comparatively relaxed yet totally
spontaneous opening movement, and the *Andante* is wholly
seductive in its songful melodic flow; then in the finale
Gluzman is off with the wind, playing with dazzling virtuosity, yet relaxing again in the Russian woodwind interludes.
Throughout the performance the **Bergen Orchestra** is far
more than an accompaniment, and Litton's final tutti brings
the work to a thrilling close, as at a live concert. The engaging
three-section *Souvenir d'un lieu cher* is no less beautifully
played and the coupling with Glazunov is ideal, for again
Gluzman's warmly relaxed approach, with its flashes of
bravura, is captivating.

Vadim Repin's newest account of the Tchaikovsky
Concerto with the **Kirov Orchestra** under **Gergiev** has effortless virtuosity and a compelling dramatic fire and nobility
of feeling. His account would stand high in the lists even if
it were uncoupled but it has the additional attraction of a
masterly account of Miaskovsky's glorious 1939 *Violin
Concerto*, which is not to be missed.

Vengerov gives an inspired performance, with magic inspiration breathing new life into well-known music. For all
his power and his youthfully eager love of brilliance,
Vengerov is never reluctant to play really softly. The central
Canzonetta is full of Russian temperament, and the finale is
sparklingly light, with articulation breathtakingly clean to
match the transparency of the orchestral textures. What a
pity the original coupling was not retained for this reissue,
for the Sibelius *Concerto* is much less successful.

In his first recording with the **LSO** under **Krivine**,
Repin's withdrawn tone in moments of meditation and his
fondness for the gentlest *pianissimos* are as remarkable as his
purity and sharpness of focus in bravura. He brings many
moments of magic, such as the gentle lead-in to the second
subject and the whispered statement of the main theme in
the central *Canzonetta*, enhanced by the natural balance of
the soloist in a refined and well-detailed Erato recording,
making this a highly recommendable alternative.

Kyung-Wha Chung's earlier recording of the *Violin
Concerto* with **Previn** conducting now returns to the catalogue as one of Decca's Originals; it has remained one of the
strongest recommendations for a much-recorded work ever
since it was made, right at the beginning of her career. With
Previn a most sympathetic and responsive accompanist, this
has warmth, spontaneity and discipline, every detail is beautifully shaped and turned without a trace of sentimentality.
The recording is well balanced and detail is clean.

Joshua Bell plays with an expressive warmth which is on
Decca kept within a relatively steady pulse. The symphonic
strength of the work is brought out without any loss of ex-

citement rather than the opposite. Bell may not have quite the fantasy of a version like Chung's, but it is an outstanding account, nevertheless, very recommendable if the very generous couplings are suitable (all outstanding). In the finale of the Tchaikovsky, Bell does not open out the tiny cuts in the passage-work that until recently have been traditional. Brilliant recording, with the soloist well balanced.

Recorded in the **Berlin Philharmonie** in January 2005, **Joshua Bell's** Sony version is freer, more volatile and even more affectionate than his studio account of 1988 for Decca, yet he never indulges in excessive mannerism, giving an impression of improvisation more clearly than before. In the central *Canzonetta* Bell is this time even more tender and more individual in his phrasing, despite a more closely balanced sound, and, as before, he achieves a genuine *pianissimo* without using a mute. In the finale he opens up the brief traditional cuts that he allowed in his 1988 performance, an obvious advantage, and he adopts a marginally faster speed with more exciting results, particularly at the end, where the Berlin audience understandably responds with great enthusiasm. The coupling this time is not generous but is still valuable.

By happy coincidence, these two versions of the Tchaikovsky *Violin Concerto* by **Julia Fischer** and **Kaler** appeared simultaneously, each with the same coupling. The only difference is that where the Naxos version offers the three pieces of *Souvenir d'un lieu cher* in Glazunov's orchestration, the Pentatone has it with the original piano accompaniment, played by the conductor, **Jakov Kreizberg**. Interpretatively, the two versions offer a very distinct choice. Kaler's approach is fresh, clean and direct, by no means unfeeling, with flawless intonation and fine shading of dynamic. He is not helped by his rather close balance in an otherwise excellent recording.

Fischer is characterful in every phrase she plays, with sparkle and a sense of fantasy in virtuoso passages and with an inner intensity when playing the intimate lyrical sections, and she is greatly helped by the conducting of **Kreizberg** with the **Russian National Orchestra**, which is both taut and sympathetic, with an ideal balance of soloist, allowing the widest range of dynamic, and the SACD sound is impressively spacious and realistic.

When it comes to the fill-ups, it is specially relevant to have the *Méditation*, first of the pieces of *Souvenir d'un lieu cher*: this was the composer's first idea of a slow movement for the *Concerto*, later replaced by the *Canzonetta*. Here Kaler plays all three pieces with a folk-like freshness, where Fischer again goes deeper, as she does also in the *Sérénade mélancolique* in a similar contrast.

Mutter, accompanied by Previn in a live recording, gives a notably free, spontaneous-sounding performance. Some may find the results too extreme, but the natural warmth of the playing, enhanced by a phenomenal range of tone-colours (something which Mutter claims has developed over the years), makes the result magnetic. Like the majority of players, she observes the brief statutory cuts in the semiquaver passage-work of the finale.

In her live recording, **Midori**, with the solo instrument naturally balanced, gives a reading that makes its impact as much in hushed poetry as in virtuoso display, with rhythms and phrasing freely expressive. Though the central *Canzonetta* is taken dangerously slowly, the rapt intensity is most compelling. As in the Shostakovich, **Abbado** and the **Berlin Philharmonic** give warm and powerful support, very well recorded. Midori adopts the tiny traditional cuts in the finale.

Sarah Chang plays with exceptionally pure tone, avoiding heavy coloration, and her individual artistry does not demand the wayward pulling-about often found in this work. In that she is enormously helped by the fresh, bright and dramatic accompaniment provided by the **LSO** under **Sir Colin Davis**, always a sensitive and helpful concerto conductor, and here encouraging generally steady speeds. The snag is the ungenerous coupling, but Chang's performances of the four Brahms *Hungarian Dances* are delectable.

Kogan's account of the Tchaikovsky *Concerto* was made in Paris in 1956, three years before his better known (and generally speaking better) version with Constantin Silvestri conducting the same orchestra. However, any performance by this aristocrat of violinists is worth having and his effortless virtuosity and purity of tone is heard to excellent effect in this well-balanced mono recording. The *Sérénade mélancolique* and the *Méditation*, both recorded in 1959, are in stereo and among the finest performances of the pieces on disc.

There can be no real reservations about the sound of the present remastering of **Heifetz's** 1957 stereo recording, both full and brilliant. Heifetz is closely balanced, but the magic of his playing can be fully enjoyed. There is some gorgeous lyrical phrasing, and the slow movement marries deep feeling and tenderness in an ideal performance. The finale is dazzling but is never driven too hard. **Reiner** always accompanies understandingly, producing fierily positive tuttis. The Mendelssohn coupling is equally desirable, and the *Sérénade mélancolique* makes a splendid bonus.

Takako Nishizaki gives a warm and colourful reading, tender but purposeful and full of temperament. As in the Mendelssohn with which this is coupled, the central slow movement is on the measured side but flows sweetly, while the finale has all the necessary bravura, even at a speed that avoids breathlessness. Nishizaki opens out the little cuts which had become traditional. With excellent playing and recording, this makes a first-rate recommendation in the super-bargain bracket.

Milstein's fine (1973) version with **Abbado** now comes as part of a DG Double with three other *Concertos*. He plays beautifully, Abbado secures playing of genuine sensitivity and scale from the **VPO**, and the recording is first class. A 1984 collection of encores makes an unusual and attractive alternative coupling, with plenty of contrasting and thoroughly entertaining pieces: the Liszt is very effective when played so seductively and, if the Geminiani is not successful stylistically, Milstein comes into his own in his own arrangement of Paganini's most famous *Caprice* and the vivacious *Hopak* of Mussorgsky. Excellent 1975 sound.

Heifetz's first (mono) recording of the Tchaikovsky *Violin Concerto*, made in 1937, has tremendous virtuosity and warmth. The sound is opaque by modern standards but the ear quickly adjusts, and the performance is special even by

Heifetz's own standards. The Naxos transfer, too, is very good and, coming as it does with a classic account of the Glazunov and a fascinating Sibelius, this is a fine bargain.

The young Czech virtuoso **Pavel Sporcl** brings not only dashing virtuosity but tonal variety and tender expressiveness to the Tchaikovsky, with speed changes always sounding natural and spontaneous. The central *Canzonetta* has a hushed poignancy, with the recording beautifully capturing the subtlety of Sporcl's *pianissimo* playing. In the finale his clarity of articulation is a delight, with the coda irresistibly exciting.

Milstein first recorded the Tchaikovsky in Chicago in March 1940 with **Frederick Stock**, an underrated maestro. It is a more classical reading than his later versions, though the finale is a remarkably dashing tour de force on the part of soloist and orchestra. The recording is also very fine, for at this time American Columbia had begun to record on to 33⅓ rpm lacquer master discs. The recordings sound as well as 1950s early tape masters. This comes with two superb performances of the Bruch and Mendelssohn *Concertos*.

The expressive warmth of **Perlman's** 1978 recording goes with a very bold orchestral texture from **Ormandy** and the **Philadelphia Orchestra**. The focus of sound is not quite as clean as this work ideally needs, but Perlman's panache always carries the day.

Janine Jansen and **Daniel Harding** choose a spacious tempo for the first movement, but the solo playing is less charismatic, less moving than the finest versions, and when Harding goes into polonaise rhythm he doesn't achieve the same lift that illuminates (for instance) the CBSO under Andris Nelsons on our primary recommendation. There is still much to admire here, but the coupling is ungenerous, and this can hardly be among the top recommendations, even though the Decca recording is excellent.

Viktoria Mullova's performance is immaculate and finely controlled – as is the coupling – but she does not always succeed in achieving the combination of warmth and nobility that this score above all requires. However, her playing has an effortless virtuosity. **Ozawa** and the **Boston Orchestra** give excellent support and the recording is exemplary.

Mark Lubotsky's performance with **Arvo Volmer** and the fine **Estonian National Orchestra** is wonderfully musical and natural. Not perhaps as high-powered or flamboyant as many rivals, but everything unfolds naturally and effortlessly. It comes with enterprising couplings, including the endearing Arensky *Concerto*.

(i) 1812 Overture; Capriccio italien

⊶ 🏵 Ⓜ *** Mercury Philips (ADD) 475 8508. (i) Bronze French cannon, bells of Laura Spelman Rockefeller Memorial Carillon, Riverside Church, New York City; Minneapolis SO, Dorati (with separate descriptive commentary by Deems Taylor) – BEETHOVEN: *Wellington's Victory* *** 🏵

Just as in our listing of this famous Mercury record we have placed 1812 first, so in the credits the cannon and the glorious sounds of the Laura Spelman Carillon take precedence, for in the riveting climax of Tchaikovsky's most famous work

the effects completely upstage the orchestra. On this remastered CD the balance is managed spectacularly, with the 'shots' perfectly timed, while the **Minneapolis Orchestra** clearly enjoy themselves both in 1812 and in the brilliant account of *Capriccio italien*. **Deems Taylor** provides an avuncular commentary on the technical background to the original recording.

(i) 1812 Overture; Francesca da Rimini; Marche slave; Romeo and Juliet (Fantasy Overture); (ii) Eugene Onegin: Tatiana's Letter Scene

⊶ Ⓑ **** CfP 575 5672. (i) RLPO; (ii) LPO; Edwards; (ii) with Hannan

An outstanding reissue, which shows **Sian Edwards** as an instinctive Tchaikovskian. In *Romeo and Juliet* the love-theme is ushered in very naturally and blossoms with the fullest ardour, while the combination of the feud music with the Friar Lawrence theme reaches a very dramatic climax. *Marche slave*, resplendently high-spirited and exhilarating, makes a splendid foil. The emotional ebb and flow of *Francesca da Rimini* is persuasively managed, and this performance is the highlight of the disc. The inclusion of *Tatiana's Letter Scene* was a capital idea. This is freshly and dramatically sung in a convincingly girlish impersonation by the Australian **Eileen Hannan**. *1812*, which closes the concert, is also very enjoyable indeed.

1812 Overture; Francesca da Rimini; Romeo and Juliet; Eugene Onegin: Polonaise & Waltz

⊶ **** EMI 3 70065-2. Santa Cecilia Ch. & O, Pappano

What is very striking with **Pappano** is how refreshing 1812 is when played with such incisiveness and care for detail, with textures clearly defined. It starts with the chorus singing the opening hymn, expanding thrillingly. A women's chorus then comes in very effectively, twice over, for one of the folk-themes; and at the end the full chorus sings the 'Tsar's Hymn' amid the usual percussion and bells, though Pappano avoids extraneous effects. It is equally refreshing to have the *Waltz* from *Eugene Onegin* in the full vocal version from the opera, again wonderfully pointed, as is the *Polonaise* which follows. There have been many Tchaikovsky collections like this, but with well-balanced sound, outstandingly rich and ripe in the brass section, this is among the finest.

Fatum (Symphonic Poem). Dances and Overtures from Operas: Cherevichki ('The Slippers'): Cossack Dance; Russian Dance. The Enchantress: Introduction; Dance of the Histrions. The Maid of Orleans: Entr'acte between Acts I & II; Dance of the Bohemians; Dance of the Polichinelles and Histrions. Mazeppa: Gopak. The Oprichnik: Dances, Act IV; The Queen of Spades: Overture. The Voyevoda: Overture

⊶ BB **** Naxos 8.554845. Ukraine Nat. SO, Kuchar

A fascinating disc containing much unknown Tchaikovsky, opening with the histrionic *Overture* to *The Queen of Spades*, followed by the even more melodramatic early symphonic poem, *Fatum*, of 1868. What redeems both works is the undeniably Tchaikovskian lyrical inspiration, and the characteristic scoring. The same comments might apply to the *Voyevoda Overture*, written in the same year as *Fatum* and belonging to the one opera the composer destroyed. The other operas had greater or lesser success. *The Maid of Orleans* has now been recorded, and we know it contains some fine music. The excerpts here are attractive, as is the *Cossack Dance* from *Cherevichki* which, like the similar dance from *Mazeppa*, is the one familiar item. Performances are first class, full of Russian vitality, and the recording most vivid. An unmissable bargain for keen Tchaikovskians.

Festival Overture on the Danish National Anthem, Op. 15; (i) Hamlet: Overture & Incidental Music, Op. 67a

Ⓜ *** Chan. X10108. (i) Kelly, Hammond-Stroud; LSO, Simon

Tchaikovsky himself thought his *Danish Festival Overture* superior to the *1812*, and though one cannot agree with his judgement it is well worth hearing. The *Hamlet Incidental Music*, however, shows the composer's inspiration at its most memorable. The *Overture* is a shortened version of the *Hamlet Fantasy Overture*, but much of the rest of the incidental music is virtually unknown, and the engaging *Funeral March* and the two poignant string elegies show the composer at his finest. *Ophelia's Mad Scene* is partly sung and partly spoken, and **Janis Kelly's** performance is most sympathetic, while **Derek Hammond-Stroud** is suitably robust in the *Gravedigger's Song*. A translation of the vocal music is provided. It is sung in French (as in the original production of *Hamlet*, performed in St Petersburg). The digital recording has spectacular resonance and depth to balance its brilliance, and there are excellent notes by Noel Goodwin.

Francesca da Rimini

(**(*)) BBC Legends mono BBCL 4163-2. Leningrad PO, Rozhdestvensky – BERLIOZ: *Symphonie fantastique* (**(*))

It was in 1960 that the **Leningrad Philharmonic** first visited Britain, giving spectacular concerts, conducted by **Gennadi Rozhdestvensky**, then still in his twenties. Here, in an Edinburgh Festival performance at the Usher Hall, we can hear inspired playing of comparable fire and refinement in Tchaikovsky's *Francesca da Rimini*. This is a weighty and impulsive reading which holds this episodic piece tautly together, and the 1960 mono recording is surprisingly warm and full, if not ideally detailed.

Hamlet (Fantasy Overture); Romeo and Juliet (Fantasy Overture); The Tempest, Op. 18

☛ **** BIS CD 1073. Bamberg SO, Serebrier

It is typical of **Serebrier's** performance that he makes *The Tempest* sound so fresh and original. *Hamlet*, dating from much later, is treated to a similarly fresh and dramatic reading, with Serebrier bringing out the yearningly Russian flavour of the lovely oboe theme representing Ophelia. He may not quite match the thrusting power of his mentor, Stokowski, but he is not far short.

In *Romeo and Juliet* the central development section, built

on the conflict music, is rightly restrained, mainly *mezzo forte* but down to *pp* for the violins in places. Yet the playing of the **Bamberg Orchestra**, incisive as in the earlier BIS disc, both wonderfully drilled and warmly committed, with outstanding solos from wind and brass, ensures that there is no lack of power. It is good to welcome so refreshing a Tchaikovsky compilation.

Manfred Symphony, Op. 58

☛ ❀ **** Chan. 8535. Oslo PO, Jansons

☛ (***) Testament mono SBT 1048. Philh. O, Kletzki – BORODIN: *Symphony 2*. (***)

(i) Manfred Symphony, Op. 58; (ii) Elégie in G for Strings

*** Australian Decca Eloquence (ADD/DDD) 476 7415. (i) Philh. O; (ii) RPO; Ashkenazy

Manfred Symphony; The Tempest, Op. 18

☛ *** DG 439 891-2. Russian Nat. O, Pletnev

Manfred Symphony; The Voyevoda

Ⓝ ☛ ⒝⒝ **** Naxos 8.570568 RLPO, Petrenko

Except in a relatively relaxed view of the *vivace* second movement, **Jansons** favours speeds flowing faster than usual, bringing out the drama but subtly varying the tensions; his warmly expressive phrasing never sounds self-conscious when it is regularly given the freshness of folksong. The performance culminates in a thrilling account of the finale, leading up to the entry of the organ, gloriously resonant and supported by luxuriant string sound. The Chandos recording is among the finest in the Oslo series.

Vasily Petrenko, the brilliant young Russian conductor, is a new star in the firmament. Anyone who has been to his **Liverpool Philharmonic** concerts will have already discovered how he is transforming a very fine orchestra into a great one. His manner is simple, but he creates electrifying tension, and achieves striking refinement of detail, while the orchestra clearly likes and responds to his inspirational style. No better example than this memorable performance of Tchaikovsky's *Manfred Symphony*, an uneven work but one with magnificent moments, not least the riveting coda of the first movement. The slow movement is beautiful, but can produce longueurs, yet not here, when it is played so tenderly. Tchaikovsky was always good at scherzos and in this work uses one to create a sparkling waterfall, with a luscious central string melody to represent the Alpine Fairy, which Petrenko obviously relishes. The fury of the spectacular finale has its weaknesses, but they are forgotten here, and the work's close could not be better handled. The *Voyevoda* is not a masterpiece – Tchaikovsky tried to destroy his score; but it was reconstituted from the orchestral parts which he forgot about! Good to hear it (and its colourful orchestration), but it is *Manfred* that makes this bargain disc indispensable.

Under **Ashkenazy**, the atmosphere and power of the opening movement are fully realized, and the Scherzo has the most refined lyrical impulse, with wonderfully fresh string-playing and sparkling articulation in the outer sections. The *Andante* is even finer; indeed, in Ashkenazy's hands it is revealed as one of Tchaikovsky's most successful symphonic slow movements, full of lyrical fervour when the playing shows such strength of feeling, yet it is completely without exaggeration. The reading culminates in a stunning account of the finale, and the work's closing pages are given a satisfying feeling of apotheosis. The 1978 recording is immensely full-blooded and brilliant, yet natural in perspective.

Pletnev identifies with the ongoing sweep of the work, yet he can relax glowingly in the pastoral evocation of the slow movement. In *The Tempest* Pletnev again carries the piece through on a wave of passionate romantic feeling. The recording is first class and this is one of his finest Tchaikovsky records.

Though **Kletzki** makes cuts and one or two amendments of orchestration, this is another reading which, far more than usual, carries you warmly and thrustfully through music that can seem unduly episodic. As to the mid-1950s recording and transfer, the brass and wind have thrilling immediacy, and the dynamic range is astonishing for the time.

Marche slave

Ⓜ **(*) Cala (ADD) CACD 0536. LSO, Stokowski – RIMSKY-KORSAKOV: *Scheherazade*. (***)

This Cala version of **Stokowski's** Phase Four account of Rimsky-Korsakov's *Sheherazade* comes with this thrilling live performance of Tchaikovsky's *Marche slave*, given as an encore at his 90th birthday concert in 1972 in London, with a spoken introduction by himself. It even outshines his studio recording in high-voltage electricity.

Méditation, Op. 42/1

🎧 ✿ **** RCA 74321 87454-2. Znaider, Bav. RSO, Jansons – GLAZUNOV: *Violin Concerto*; PROKOFIEV: *Violin Concerto 2*. **** ✿

This piece comes from the *Souvenir d'un lieu cher* for violin and piano which Tchaikovsky composed while staying on the estate of his patroness, Madame von Meck. It had originally been planned as the slow movement of the *Violin Concerto*, and it fell to Glazunov to put it into orchestral form. It is beautifully played and comes here as a fill-up to **Nikolaj Znaider's** outstanding set of the Glazunov and Prokofiev *Concertos*.

(i) The Nutcracker, Op. 71; (ii) The Sleeping Beauty, Op. 66; (iii) Swan Lake, Op. 20 (ballets complete.)

Ⓑ **(*) Decca (ADD) 460 411-2 (6). Nat. PO, Bonynge

Ⓑ **(*) EMI (ADD) 5 73624-2 (6). LSO, Previn

Bonynge's Tchaikovsky performances are all recommendable. *Swan Lake* receives a red-blooded performance in which the forward impulse of the music-making is immediately striking. The 1975 recording is vivid and bright, though a little dry, producing a leonine string-tone sound rather than a feeling of sumptuousness. If the full romantic essence of this masterly score is not totally conveyed (partly as a result

of the recording), the commitment of the orchestral playing is never in doubt. *The Sleeping Beauty* was recorded a year later with similarly vivid sound. Bonynge secures brilliant and often elegant playing from the **National Philharmonic**, and his rhythmic pointing is always characterful. He is especially good at the close of Act II when, after the magical *Panorama*, the Princess is awakened – there is a frisson of tension here and the atmosphere is most evocative. Bonynge's *Nutcracker* is finely done too, with plenty of colour in the characteristic dances. The recording from 1974 is rich and brilliant. All are packed in one of Decca's space-saving 'Collector Boxes', and this set is undoubtedly a bargain.

Previn's 1972 *Nutcracker* is superbly played by the **LSO** – it is a wonderfully warm account which gets more involving as it goes along. If *The Sleeping Beauty* is not as vital as it could be (though never slack), it makes up for it with the superb playing of the orchestra: the *Panorama* is beautifully done. The recording (1974) could sparkle a little more though. *Swan Lake* (1976) is given a similarly warm performance, though the overall effect is at times just that bit too 'cosy' for such dramatic writing. The music never drags though, and the excellence of the orchestral playing does much to enhance one's pleasure. The choice between these two bargain boxes is a matter of personal taste: Bonynge offers the more vivid performances (thanks also to the sound), while Previn has more opulence. Both are equally enjoyable and well packaged.

The Nutcracker, Op. 71 (ballet; complete; DVD versions)

🎧 ✿ **** Warner NIVC Arts DVD 0630 19394-2. Collier, Dowell, Coleman, Rose, Niblett, Royal Ballet, ROHCG O, Rozhdestvensky (Producer: Peter Wright; V/D: John Vernon, in association with Peter Wright; Choreography: Lev Ivanov and Peter Wright)

🎧 ✿ **** BBC Opus Arts DVD OA 0827 D. Yoshida, Cope, Dowell, Cojocara, Putrov, Royal Ballet, ROHCG, Svetlanov (Producer: Peter Wright; V/D: Ross MacGibbon; Choreography: Lev Ivanov & Peter Wright)

*** Ph. DVD 070 173-2 (Choreography by Petipa, adapted Vasily Vainonen). Larissa Lezhnina, Victor Baranov, Piotr Russanov, Kirov Ballet at Mariinsky Theatre, St Petersburg, Kirov O, Victor Fedotov (Dir Oleg Vinogradov)

Here, side by side, we have two separate DVDs of **Sir Peter Wright's** outstanding production of Tchaikovsky's magical Christmas ballet. They are both wonderfully realized, and it is impossible to choose between them. In the first, from 1985, **Lesley Collier**, who has already enchanted us in *La fille mal gardée*, is ideally cast as the Sugar Plum Fairy. Her Prince is elegantly characterized and finely danced by **Anthony Dowell**, and her romantic partner in the earlier ballet, **Michael Coleman**, now takes a more dramatic and slightly sinister role as Herr Drosselmeyer.

In the later (1996) BBC Opus Arte version, **Anthony Dowell** takes over as the strangely benign Drosselmeyer (whose nephew has been transformed into a grotesque Nutcracker Doll). In Peter Wright's production Drosselmeyer is always at the background of the narrative to remind us that his aim is to break the spell (through Clara – a non-dancing role) and have his nephew return to human form. **Jonathan Cope**, who was the Mouse King in the earlier production, is now an elegant Prince. His new partner, **Miyako Yoshida**, is an enchanting Sugar Plum Fairy, and the Nutcracker is **Ivan Putrov**.

If anything, the transformation scene when the Christmas Tree grows to a huge height is even more spectacularly managed in the later set, and we have a very soft spot for the moment when Clara deftly comes to the Nutcracker's rescue by hitting the Mouse King over the head with her shoe. But in the earlier version the Christmas party scene is especially endearing in its detail. In both the sequence where Clara and the transformed Nutcracker journey together in a sleigh, through the Pine Forest and among the waltzing Snowflakes, to the Land of Snow – against a musical background of two of Tchaikovsky's finest melodic inspirations – and on to the Kingdom of Sweets is delightfully managed. Peter Wright's production is gloriously traditional, brilliantly choreographed, lavishly spectacular, while Julia Oman's costumes (especially for the battling Mice) are no less imaginative. The camera is always in the right place and Tchaikovsky's miraculouly inspired score, of which one never tires, is marvellously played by the **Covent Garden Orchestra**, whether conducted by **Rozhdestvensky** or by **Svetlanov**.

The **Kirov** *Nutcracker* is a delight, following the story simply, with wonderful sets and superb dancing. We see the guests for the party arriving through the snow (a huge number of them, but then it's a big stage) and meet Drosselmeyer (the excellent **Piotr Russanov**) at the very beginning, while the Mice make their appearance earlier than usual and frighten Clara (Masha in the Russian production) before the very well-staged battle. The production is traditional and no attempt is made to explain the background to the story, as in Peter Wright's Royal Ballet production. But that is unimportant when the dancing is of the highest quality, both from the principals and from the corps de ballet. The *Waltz of the Snowflakes* is a highlight, and the Russians know how to produce plenty of snow. In the final divertissement the costumes are unadventurous, but the Mirlitons, Chinese Dancers and Sugar Plum Fairy are enchanting; and the grand *Pas de deux* is really spectacular. The Kirov orchestra plays marvellously and the recording is first class. Altogether a wonderful entertainment.

The Nutcracker, Op. 71 (ballet; complete; CD versions)

🎬 **** Ph. 462 114-2. Kirov O & Ch., Gergiev

🎬 **** Telarc CD 80137 (2). L. Symphony Ch., LSO, Mackerras

The Nutcracker (ballet: complete); Suites Nos. 3 in G; 4 in G (Mozartiana)

Ⓝ ❀ **** Australian Decca Eloquence ADD 480 0557 (2). SRO, Ansermet

The Nutcracker (ballet; complete); 1812 Overture; Marche slave

Ⓑ *** CfP (ADD/DDD) 3 93233-2. LSO, Previn – PROKOFIEV: *Cinderella* (excerpts) ***

Ansermet's 1958 *Nutcracker* is simply one of the best performances of this score ever committed to disc. This was undoubtedly one of the finest things Ansermet did for Decca and the recording still sounds remarkably rich and vivid, with a freshness and sparkle to match the composer's approach. Ansermet's feeling for orchestral colour and detail tells throughout, and the short dances of Act 2 have much piquancy of characterization. Indeed, the whole performance feels as magical as the story itself and all lovers of this score should acquire this release. The two very appealing *Suites* which fill up this disc are not quite in this league of inspiration but they are affectionately played and well worth having, but the ❀ is for *The Nutcracker*.

Gergiev's complete CD recording is on a single disc (over 80 minutes) and it is magnificently played and recorded. Tchaikovsky's inspired score emerges pristine and fresh as one of his most perfect masterpieces. The great *Adagio* for the two principal dancers has a passionate Russian ardour; the lively characteristic dances are simply bursting with Slavonic fervour. If there is a certain want of magic and charm, Gergiev everywhere displays a keen ear for Tchaikovsky's vivid orchestral detail. There are no pauses between numbers in the *Divertissement*, and this may well be dictated by the single-disc format. But it also increases the feeling that the score overall is a composite whole, and this is emphasized by the sense of apotheosis in the finale. Unless you are looking for a more relaxed, spacious approach, this can be highly recommended.

Mackerras's Telarc set was recorded in Watford Town Hall, which adds glamour to the violins and a glowing warmth in the middle and lower range. When the magic spell begins, the spectacularly wide dynamic range and the extra amplitude make for a physical frisson in the climaxes, while the glorious climbing melody, as Clara and the Prince travel through the pine forest, sounds richly expansive. Before that, the battle has some real cannon-shots interpolated but is done good-humouredly, for this is a toy battle. The great *Pas de deux* brings the most sumptuous climax, with superb sonority from the brass. The Telarc presentation is ideal, with a detailed synopsis.

A remarkably attractive and generous bargain double. **Previn's** complete *Nutcracker*, recorded at Kingsway Hall in 1972, is affectionately and sumptuously played; the famous dances of Act II have much sophistication of detail, and the set can be recommended most warmly. Previn then takes a clear-headed, totally unsentimental view of the other three works and as a result the music emerges stronger in design (even *1812*) and no less exciting than usual, although here the Abbey Road sound is drier, concentrating on fidelity and balance.

Nutcracker Suite

Ⓑ *** CfP 3 82229-2. Philh. O, Malko – PROKOFIEV: *Symphonies 1 & 7*, etc. ***

(*) Telarc **SACD** 60650. Cleveland O, Maazel – BERLIOZ: *Symphonie fantastique* **

In 1955 **Malko's** *Nutcracker Suite* was one of EMI's very first (Kingsway Hall) stereo recordings. In the present transfer it sounds as if it was done yesterday and, with the **Philharmonia** on peak form, the playing is a joy. Malko's tempi are relaxed, but none the worse for that.

Nutcracker Suite; Romeo and Juliet (Fantasy Overture)

Ⓜ **(*) Telarc CD 80068. Cleveland O, Maazel

With vivid orchestral playing and bright, crisply focused recording within a natural ambience, **Maazel's** *Nutcracker Suite* is enjoyably colourful. His manner is affectionate (especially in the warmly lilting *Waltz of the Flowers*) and the only idiosyncrasy is the sudden accelerando at the close of the *Russian Dance*. *Romeo and Juliet* is given a spaciously romantic performance, reaching a climax of considerable passion. However, the almost overwhelming impact of the percussion in the undoubtedly exciting feud music is obviously designed for those who like to say 'Listen to that bass drum!'

Nutcracker; Sleeping Beauty; Swan Lake (ballets; excerpts)

**(*) Avie AV 2139. RLPO, Petrenko

The **Royal Liverpool Philharmonic Orchestra** plays very well indeed under its new conductor, **Vasily Petrenko**, as is immediately obvious from the beautifully played oboe solo at the opening of the *Swan Lake* selection, which comes first. There is much finesse and elegance elsewhere: the delicate trumpet in the *Danse napolitaine* is another instance, as is the *Blue bird pas de quatre* from the *Sleeping Beauty* selection. But why no *Panorama*, and why is the *Arab Dance* missing from the otherwise delightful *Nutcraker Suite*? No complaints about the recording, only the measure – just 58 minutes!

Nutcracker Suite; Sleeping Beauty: Suite; Swan Lake: Suite

⊶ ❀ Ⓜ **** DG (ADD) 449 726-2. BPO, Rostropovich
Ⓜ *** Decca (ADD) 466 379-2. VPO, Karajan

Rostropovich's triptych of Tchaikovsky ballet suites is very special. His account of the *Nutcracker Suite* is enchanting: the *Sugar Plum Fairy* is introduced with ethereal gentleness, the *Russian Dance* has marvellous zest and the *Waltz of the Flowers* combines warmth and elegance with an exhilarating vigour. The *Sleeping Beauty* and *Swan Lake* selections are hardly less distinguished, and in the former the *Panorama* is gloriously played. The CD remastering now approaches demonstration standard, combining bloom with enhanced detail. Sixty-nine minutes of sheer joy and at mid-price.

As reissued in Decca's Legend series, the **Karajan** recording is very impressive indeed; tuttis are well focused by the digital transfer, and the glowing ambience of the Sofiensaal flatters the strings and adds to the woodwind colourings, particularly in the *Nutcracker Suite*, which is less bland here than in Karajan's later re-recording with the BPO. Overall this disc offers very fine playing from the **VPO** and, although the atmosphere is generally relaxed (especially in *Sleeping Beauty*), there is a persuasive warmth.

Romeo and Juliet (Fantasy Overture)

⊶ Ⓜ *** Classic fM 75605 57047. RPO, Gatti – PROKOFIEV: *Romeo and Juliet* (ballet; excerpts) ***

(*) Pentatone **SACD PTC 5186 019. Netherlands PO, Kreizberg – DVOŘÁK: *Symphony 9 (From the New World)* **(*)

Daniele Gatti's performances could not be more highly charged romantically, and with a vividly passionate (if not always immaculate) response from the **RPO**, the climaxes are thrilling, with the horns and trumpets ringing out superbly at the climax of the duel sequence. The recording too is splendidly full and sumptuous, and the rare coupling with Prokofiev could not be more apt. This is one of Classic fM's finest issues so far.

A strong, incisive performance of Tchaikovsky's *Romeo and Juliet* from **Kreizberg** to match the Dvořák *Symphony*, very well played and brilliantly recorded.

The Seasons, Op. 37b; Chanson triste; Mazurka, Chant sans paroles; Danse russe, Op. 40/2, 4, 6 & 10; Rêverie interrompte (arr. for violin & orchestra by Breiner)

BB **(*) Naxos 8.553510. Nishizaki, Queensland SO, Breiner

If Tchaikovsky's 12 *Seasons* are to be arranged for violin, **Takako Nishizaki** is surely their ideal exponent, for she plays with delicacy and charm. If the fully scored items (the *February* 'Carnival' and the brassy picture of the *September* 'Hunt') are rather inflated by the resonant acoustic, these arrangements overall can be counted a modest success, alongside those of the piano pieces from Op. 40 (the *Danse russe* will be recognized from *Swan Lake*), while the closing *Rêverie* has a proper salon daintiness.

Sérénade mélancólique (for violin and orchestra), Op. 26

*** EMI 5 62607-2. Menuhin, RPO, Boult – BEETHOVEN: *Violin Concerto in D; Romance 1 in G* ***

Recorded in 1959 as a filler for a version of the Tchaikovsky *Violin Concerto* never completed, **Menuhin's** account of the *Sérénade mélancolique*, previously unpublished, conveys a gravity beyond its modest span. It is a welcome coupling for the superb Beethoven performances.

Serenade for Strings in C, Op. 48

⊶ BB *** Virgin 2x1 5 61763-2 (2). LCO, Warren-Green – DVOŘÁK: *Serenade for Strings in E, Op. 22*; ELGAR: *Introduction & allegro; Serenade*; SUK: *Serenade*; VAUGHAN WILLIAMS: *Fantasia on Greensleeves*, etc ***

⊶ Ⓜ *** Decca (ADD) 470 262-2. ASMF, Marriner – GRIEG: *Holberg Suite* *** ; (with DVOŘÁK: *Serenade* **(*))

Serenade for Strings; Souvenir de Florence. Op. 70

BB *** Naxos 8.550404. VCO, Entremont
BB **(*) Virgin 2x1 4 82103-2. City of L. Sinfonia, Hickox (with FAURÉ: *Pavane*) – BIZET: *Symphony in C*; IBERT: *Divertissement*; RAVEL: *Tombeau de Couperin* **(*)

Not surprisingly, **Christopher Warren-Green's** reading of

Tchaikovsky's *Serenade* with the excellent **London Chamber Orchestra** is full of individuality. The first movement's secondary idea has an appealing feathery lightness, and when the striding opening theme reappears at the end of the movement it brings a spontaneous-sounding burst of expressive intensity characteristic of this group. The *Waltz* lilts gently, with the tenutos nicely managed, the *Elégie* has delicacy as well as fervour, and the finale develops plenty of energy. Very well recorded, it is a performance to give pleasure for its freshness and natural impetus, and the couplings are amazingly generous and equally stimulating.

Marriner's classic 1968 version holds its place among the best. Although Tchaikovsky asked for as big a body of strings as possible in his delectable *Serenade*, there is much to be said, in these days of increased string resonance and clever microphone placing, for having a more modest band like the **Academy of St Martin's-in-the-Field**. However, one does notice the lack of sheer tonal weight that a larger group would afford. Marriner's performance compensates with expressive phrasing (most striking in the slow movement), imaginative and fresh playing from the Academy, and the finest pointing and precision of ensemble. The original coupling of the *Souvenir de Florence* now lives on a Double Decca CD with the *String Quartets* (452 614-2), but the couplings here are excellent. A fine transfer in this Legends reissue.

Philip Entremont's performances of Tchaikovsky's two major string works communicate above all a feeling of passionate thrust and energy. After the ardour of the *Elégie*, the finale steals in persuasively, with dance-rhythms bracing and strong. The *Souvenir de Florence* has comparable momentum and eagerness. The **VCO** are committed, persuasive advocates to make one wonder why the *Souvenir* does not have a more central place in the string repertoire.

Hickox's well-played performances are both vivacious and nicely detailed, with Tchaikovsky's contrasts of mood in the *Souvenir* well observed. The recording is full and resonant, with the upper range perhaps lacking the last touch of refinement. But overall this is a worthwhile bargain package.

The Sleeping Beauty, Op. 66 (ballet; complete; DVD versions)

🔊 ⚙ ******** Arthaus **DVD** 101 113 (Choreography: Marius Petipa; staged Yuri Grigorovich). Nina Semizorova, Aleksei Fadeyechev, Nina Speranskaya, Yuri Vetrov, Maria Bilova, Bolshoi Ballet & Theatre O, Aleksander Kopilov (V/D: Shuji Fujii)

🔊 ******** Arthaus **DVD** 100 312 (Choreography: Petipa, revised Konstantin Sergeyev). Lezhnina, Ruzimatov, Makhalina, Guliayev (Carabosse), Kirov Ballet Co. & O, Fedotov (V/D: Bernard Picard)

Of the three great Tchaikovsky ballets, in the view of the composer's biographer, David Brown, the greatest score of all is the *Sleeping Beauty*, if only for its sheer fecundity – well over two hours of continuous melodic inspiration – and incredibly imaginative scoring. Tchaikovsky, too, thought it was among his best works. 'The subject is so poetic and so well suited to music,' he wrote, and he was very disappointed

when, at its first performance, it received a lukewarm reception. But, of course, it has survived, although even today one of the problems of production is that **Petipa's** highly demanding choreography needs not just two or four but a whole group of leading dancers, with both Princess Aurora and the Lilac Fairy major female roles.

The story, histrionic as it is, occupies very little of the scenario – one of the weaknesses of the original 'libretto'. All three Acts have *Divertissements*, and both the outer Acts include variations for the key fairy attendants and solos for the Lilac Fairy. But in the extended third Act not only are there characteristic dances by Little Red Riding Hood and the Wolf, and by Puss-in-Boots and the White Cat (exquisitely danced here), but a big, demanding number for the Blue Bird, while the Prince and Princess (separately, and together) have a whole series of bravura dances, all to marvellous music.

The 1989 **Bolshoi** production offered here is as lavish as one could wish, and historically traditional in the sense that **Yuri Grigorovich** has rescued a very high proportion of Petipa's original choreography and scenario so that, as nearly as possible, we are seeing what Tchaikovsky envisaged, produced with a large cast in terms of the huge stage of the Bolshoi Theatre.

As for the dancing, not surpisingly it is quite fabulous, with the key characters matched in their virtuosity by the many ensemble dances for the corps de ballet, but with **Nina Semizorova** outstanding in the role of Princess Aurora, matched by the incredibly virile (and good-looking) Prince, **Aleksei Fadeyechev**. Nina Sperankaya is a delectably graceful Lilac Fairy, given another of Tchaikovsky's most memorable tunes whenever she appears. Even so, **Yuri Vetrov** as the grotesquely malignant Carabosse nearly steals the show in his two main appearances.

With traditional sets, one cannot think that we will see Tchaikovsky's and Petipa's masterpiece more effectively staged or better danced, and the cameras follow the dancers in close-up or long shot very perceptively. The lavish period costumes are based on the illustrations which accompanied the original story, reflecting the court of the Sun King, where Charles Perrault's fairytale was first heard.

The Arthaus DVD performance was recorded and filmed in June 1989 during the **Kirov's** guest appearance in Canada at the Place des Arts in Montreal. The dancing is pretty virtuosic and both the character dances and the main roles are flawless: the performance lingers in the memory long afterwards. The production, too, conveys an appropriate sense of magic, and the visual direction is well handled. The orchestral playing under **Viktor Fedotov** is first class (save for an unappealing clarinet quality) but the recording is inconsistent in balance, with a very prominent piano at one point. Things settle down, however, and the bulk of the last act is in good perspective. This does not detract from the overall satisfaction and sheer delight these dancers give.

The Sleeping Beauty, Op. 66 (ballet; complete; CD versions)

🔊 ⚙ ******** BBC (ADD) BBCL 4091-2 (2). BBC SO, Rozhdestvensky

☛─ **** DG 457 634-2 (2). Russian Nat. O, Pletnev

Ⓝ *** Australian Decca Eloquence (ADD) 480 0560 (2). OSR, Ansermet

ⒷⒷ *** Naxos 8.550490/2. Slovak State PO (Košice), Mogrelia

ⒷⒷ **(*) EMI Gemini (ADD) 5 85788-2 (2). LSO, Previn

Rozhdestvensky's recording, made in 1979, was part of the **BBC Symphony Orchestra's** 50th anniversary celebrations and is fully worthy of the occasion. The great Russian conductor (using the original Russian score which is absolutely complete) shows just how to hold Tchaikovsky's ballet together as a symphonic entity by creating a consistent narrative pulse. In Tchaikovsky's inspired series of characteristic dances the conductor's light rhythmic touch and delicacy of feeling draw a wonderfully refined yet vividly coloured response from the BBC players. The ballet ends majestically, and the BBC recording has plenty of amplitude, warm strings, glowing woodwind and a natural concert-hall balance.

Pletnev's is a performance of individuality and high quality. It is a strongly narrative and dramatic account that has tenderness and much the same virtuosity that Pletnev exhibits at the keyboard. It is now offered at mid-price for the first time.

Ansermet's 1959 *Sleeping Beauty* recording has been remastered with great success. The stereo conveys the attractive concert hall ambience splendidly, and the climaxes remain spectacular. The strings have clean outline and there is no lack of body. If the solo wind-playing sometimes lacks the last ounce of polish, the overall effect is alive and colourful. Indeed, the opening is highly dramatic, and a high tension is maintained throughout this performance, with Ansermet's rhythmic grip unfailingly impressive. The conductor is at his very best in the characteristic dances which show the composer at his most felicitous, especially in the later part of the score, and here the sparkle of the Decca recording tells again and again. A very welcome return to the catalogue.

Andrew Mogrelia conducts Tchaikovsky's score with a fine combination of warmth, grace and vitality. Moreover, the **Slovak State Philharmonic** prove to be an excellent orchestra for this repertoire, with good wind-players and equally impressive string principals for the important violin and cello solos. The Naxos digital recording is full and brilliant without being overlit, and the acoustics of the House of Arts in Košice bring a spacious ambience, with vivid orchestral colours. First class value.

With warm, polished orchestral playing and recording to match (though it expands at climaxes), **Previn** conveys his affection throughout; but too often – in the famous *Waltz*, for instance – there could be more sparkle. On the other hand, the *Panorama* shows Previn and the **LSO** at their very best, the tune floating over its rocking bass in the most magical way. There is also much delightful wind-playing but, with Previn's tempi sometimes indulgently relaxed, it has been impossible to get the complete recording on a pair of CDs and the penultimate number (29) in Act III (included in the original three-disc LP issue) has been cut.

Ballet Suites, selections from: (i) Sleeping Beauty (3 pieces orch. Stravinsky) (ii) Swan Lake

Ⓝ **(*) Hanssler CD.93234. SWR. SO, (i) Wakasugi; (ii) Ahronovich – STRAVINSKY: *Chant du Rossignol* ***

This mixed disc is issued to celebrate the Ballet Russe, founded by Diaghilev in 1909. *Swan Lake* comes in a suite of 8 movements, mainly the lesser-known ones, except for the *Waltz*. The three pieces from *Sleeping Beauty* are in an arrangement commissioned from Stravinsky, who echoes the example of Tchaikovsky but with even greater reliance on woodwind solos.

Sleeping Beauty: Aurora's Wedding (suite selected and edited by Diaghilev)

☛─ ❀ Ⓜ *** Cala CACD 0529 (ADD) Nat. PO, Stokowski (with 'Encores', all arr. Stokowski: DEBUSSY: *Clair de lune; Soirée dans Grenade;* ALBENIZ: *Ibéria: Fête-Dieu à Seville;* NOVÁČEK: *Perpetuum mobile;* SHOSTAKOVICH: *Prelude in E flat min;* RIMSKY-KORSAKOV: *Flight of the Bumble-bee;* TCHAIKOVSKY: *Humoresque in G, Op. 10/2;* CHOPIN: *Mazurka in B flat min.; Prélude in D min. Op.28/24* ***)

Diaghilev staged the first performance of Tchaikovsky's *Sleeping Beauty* outside Russia in a London season in 1921. The result was a financial disaster. The following year the great impresario devised a one-act version centring on the Act III *Divertissement*, framed by the Introduction and final *Apothéose*. **Stokowski** was attracted to the score and recorded it twice. His stereo version, made when he was 94, dates from 1976, yet, as with so many of the recordings he made during his 'Indian summer', the electricity crackles throughout, and his charisma is felt in every bar. The Sony recording is vividly brilliant, lacking sumptuousness in the violins, but otherwise very good.

It was an inspired idea of Edward Johnson of the Stokowski Society to link *Aurora* with his even more charismatic collection of encores, recorded three months later. Here the sound is even better, approaching demonstration quality.

Souvenir de Florence, Op. 70 (string orchestra version)

☛─ **** Channel Classics **SACD**: CCS SA 21504. Amsterdam Sinf., Thompson – VERDI: *String Quartet* ***

☛─ **** Chan. 9708. Norwegian CO, Brown – RICHARD STRAUSS: *Metamorphosen* ***

The **Amsterdam Sinfonietta**, formerly called the Nieuw Sinfonietta Amsterdam, here offers outstanding performances of two works originally written for solo strings which, played like this by a string orchestra, are if anything even more impressive, and the unanimity of the playing, the immaculate precision of ensemble, is phenomenal, yet it is never a cold precision. The resonance of the playing is exceptional too, involving a strikingly wide dynamic range and a meticulous observance of markings. The opulent recording helps, with a helpful ambience allowing ample detail, with the opportunity of 'surround sound' if you have the additional speakers.

Iona Brown and the **Norwegian Chamber Orchestra** give

us a splendid account of the full orchestral version of Tchaikovsky's invigorating and captivating *Souvenir de Florence*, bouncingly rhythmic in the opening movement, and buoyantly exuberant in the swinging secondary theme of the finale. There is both warmth and subtlety in the inner movements; and it is given one of Chandos's most brilliant and full-bodied recordings. The result is irresistible.

Souvenir d'un lieu cher, Op. 42; Valse scherzo in C, Op. 34 (orch. Glazunov)

(M) *** DG 457 064-2. Shaham, Russian Nat. O, Pletnev – GLAZUNOV; KABALEVSKY: *Concertos* ***

Eloquent and dazzling playing of these two Tchaikovsky pieces by **Gil Shaham** are an additional inducement to get this fine coupling of the Glazunov and Kabalevsky *Concertos*.

Suites 1 in D min., Op. 43; 2 in C; 3 in G, Op. 55; 4 in G, (Mozartiana), Op. 56

*** Chan. 9676 (2). Detroit SO, Järvi

(BB) *** Naxos 8.550644 (*Nos. 1–2*); **(*) 8.550728 (*Nos. 3–4*). Nat. SO of Ireland, Sanderling

Järvi generally adopts somewhat brisk tempi, especially in 1, but the **Detroit** orchestral response in both the two earliest suites is consistently winning. The performance of the *Fourth Suite* also has an agreeable warmth, aptly Tchaikovskian even more than it is elegantly Mozartian. In 3, the most ambitious of the set, Järvi continues to draw warmly expressive playing from his Detroit musicians even if his treatment here is a little heavy-handed (as it is just occasionally in 2). The performance is well characterized – not least in the colourfully diverse variations that make up the last and longest movement and that are given an ebullient finale – but lacks something in charm. In this the acoustic of the Detroit hall is not as helpful as it might be to high *fortissimo* violins.

On Naxos, **Stefan Sanderling** (son of Kurt) gives nicely turned performances of the first two suites, neatly characterized and with much charm and colour. The *Third* and *Fourth Suites* are slightly less successful. Sanderling shows much delicacy of feeling, both in the opening *Gigue* of *Mozartiana* and in the *Elégie*, the first movement of the *Third Suite*. In *Mozartiana* Sanderling is very romantic. The masterly *Theme and Variations* which end the *Third Suite* are splendidly done until the finale, which refuses to take off: Sanderling is that bit too grandiose and measured.

Suite 3 in G, Op. 55

⊕→ **** Pentatone **SACD** PTC 5186 061. Russian Nat. O, Jurowski – STRAVINSKY: *Le Baiser de la fée (divertimento)* ****

The *Third Suite* with its extended set of variations for finale can seem rather square under some conductors, but Jurowski, maybe influenced by his conducting of opera and ballet, brings out the surging lyricism of all four movements. So the opening *Elégie* is warmly moulded without ever sounding fussy, with phrasing that seems totally idiomatic. The rhythmic lightness of the second-movement *Waltz* leads to a dazzling account of the third-movement *Scherzo*, taken at a genuine *Presto*, yet with no feeling of breathlessness,

while the *Variations* have rarely seemed so attractive in their breadth of ideas, leading to a thrilling build-up and conclusion. Exceptionally vivid sound, recorded by Pentatone's Dutch engineers in Moscow, spectacular in surround sound.

Suites: (i) 3 in G, Op. 55; (ii) 4 (Mozartiana) in G, Op. 61

**(*) Australian Decca Eloquence (ADD) 476 2723. (i) VPO, Maazel; (ii) SRO, Ansermet

The first thing one notices about **Maazel's** 1977 recording of the underrated *Third Suite* with its superb closing set of variations is the ravishing playing of the **VPO**, with the strings sounding gloriously rich and glowing in the Decca sound, and with Maazel relaxed and unforced. The performance is not as strongly characterized as some, but it is far from bland, especially the woodwind detail, having a pleasing individuality of colour. All the things one expects from a classic Ansermet performance are here in the *Fourth (Mozartiana) Suite*: vivid sound (with a lovely, warm ambience), felicity of detail, especially in the pointing of the strings, but less than ideally polished orchestral playing for a work drawing on Mozart. However, it remains enjoyable for its distinct character and spontaneity.

Swan Lake (complete recording of original Mariinsky performing edition; CD version)

**(*) Decca 475 7669 (2). Mariinsky Theatre O, Gergiev

Swan Lake (highlights from the above)

*** Decca 475 9080

Here is the original **Mariinsky** performing edition of the score, which the composer never heard and which he did not plan himself. It is marvellously played under **Gergiev** and given a gorgeously sumptuous Decca recording. But the total timing of the two discs is just 107 minutes, so collectors will surely find the very enjoyable highlights disc (76 minutes) a better investment.

Swan Lake, Op. 20 (ballet; complete; DVD versions)

⊕→ ✿ ******DVD** 073 4044. Fonteyn, Nureyev, V. State Op. Ballet, VSO, Lanchbery (Chorography; Rudolf Nureyev; Dir: Truck Branss)

⊕→ **** Opus Arte **DVD** OA0966D. Fernandez, Letestu, Martinez, Paquette, Paris Opéra Ballet, Paris Opéra O, Vello Pähn (Choreography: Rudolf Nureyev)

*** Opus Arte **DVD** OA 0865 D. (Choreography: Peter Wright, after Petipa and Ivanov) Nordquist, Nordström, Kaila, Rambe, Ohman, Swedish Ballet School, Royal Swedish Op. O, Quéval (V/D: Kirsty Garland)

There is little one needs to say about the 1966 *Swan Lake* except that it is one of the great ballet films of all time and looks marvellous on DVD. Moreover, the sound is excellent, as is the photography, with the camera angles well judged so that there are frequent close-ups of the most famous ballet dance partnership of our time. Nureyev's choreography (based on Ivanov/Petipa), like the production, décor and costumes, is satifyingly traditional, which means it is what Tchaikovsky and Petipa envisaged, without spurious additions. The story is told simply and dramatically and, apart from the unforgettable and moving dancing of the two principals, the whole company give outstanding support in the many colourful individual dances. Highlights include the touching scene in Act II when Prince Siegfried, crossbow at the ready, is disconcerted to meet and fall in love with Odette, and the following *Danses des cygnes* (with some lovely, tender playing from the solo violin of the orchestra's principal violin). After the delightful *Divertissement*, Siegfried's great *pas de deux* of Act III, with Odile, is breathtaking, and the ballet's tragic end when, after parting from Odette, Siegfried sinks between the swirling waters of Rotbart's lake is most imaginatively achieved. **John Lanchbery** conducts the excellent **Vienna Symphony Orchestra** with great flair, and altogether this is unbeatable.

This Parisian *Swan Lake* offers the reworked choreography which Nureyev devised for his 1984 production of the ballet and which has remained a favoured revival ever since. In this production the roles of the Prince's tutor, Wolfgang, and Rothbart are taken – brilliantly – by **Karl Paquette**, and Wolfgang becomes an equivocal and manipulative character and the double of the ballet's evil genius, the magician Rothbart. The performance is compelling, indeed riveting, though we didn't find **Agnès Letestu** as warm as the sleeve-note proclaims; on the contrary, she is distinctly cool, un-smiling and wanting in charm. **José Fernandez** is lyrical and a musical artist, but the *corps de ballet* is stunning in its unanimity and character – the equal of any in the world. Readers used to traditional views of the ballet should see this gripping newcomer.

The **Royal Swedish Ballet's** *Swan Lake*, recorded on 24 May 2002, is elegant and sumptuous, inventively choreographed and beautifully staged by **Sir Peter Wright** and Galina Samsova, with particularly splendid sets and costumes. Peter Wright stages it as a Gothic tragedy concentrating on the role of the Prince and honouring the 1895 Petipa/Ivanov original. In **Nathalie Nordquist** and **Anders Nordström** it has a fine and expressive partnership, and the cast as a whole has no weaknesses. Indeed, one of the strengths of the performance is the excellence of the teamwork of the company. (It is tastefully and imaginatively lit, too, by Martin Säfström.) It is very well danced, though the Odette/Odile is not perhaps as strongly characterized as Steffi Scherzer in the Berlin performance under Daniel Barenboim, available on Arthaus.

Swan Lake, Op. 20 (ballet; complete; CD versions)

⊙~ *** Decca 436 212-2 (2). Montreal SO, Dutoit

Ⓑ *** CfP (ADD) 3 93243-2. LSO, Previn

Ⓜ *** Naxos 8.555873/4. Russian State SO, Yablonsky

Ⓑ **(*) DG Double 453 055-2 (2). Boston SO, Ozawa

ⒷⒷ **(*) EMI Gemini 5 85541-2 (2). Phd. O, Sawallisch

Dutoit offers the original score virtually complete. The **Montreal Orchestra** play it beautifully, rising to the plot's histrionic moments while not lacking the final apotheosis.

Dutoit's reading, while not lacking drama, emphasizes the warmth and grace of the music and its infinite variety.

Previn's mid-1970s set, like his recordings of the other Tchaikovsky ballets, offers extremely polished orchestral playing, with beautiful wind solos. **Ida Haendel's** solo contributions are first class, and there is much refined detail and no lack of drama when the music calls for it. Previn is at his finest in the Act II *Divertissement* with its variety of national dances, where the orchestral soloists all excel themselves. The remastered recording also sounds very fresh, with little loss of ambient warmth.

A very Russian performance of *Swan Lake* on Naxos, superbly recorded. The playing is idiomatic, polished and exciting, with the unnamed solo violinist making an excellent contribution; but the whole orchestra are on their toes. This is not a relaxed performance but one in which there is plenty of charm and character, and free-running adrenalin too. A real bargain.

Ozawa's version omits the Act III *Pas de deux* but otherwise plays the complete original score. His performance is alive and vigorous (as at the opening *Allegro giusto*), but it has not quite the verve of Lanchbery's EMI version; Ozawa's approach is more serious, less flexible. Yet with polished, sympathetic playing from the **Boston Orchestra** there are many impressive and enjoyable things here, with wind (and violin) solos always giving pleasure. The end result is a little faceless, in spite of a spectacular, wide-ranging analogue recording, as vivid as it is powerful.

Sawallisch directs Tchaikovsky's greatest ballet score with pleasing freshness, and the **Philadelphia Orchestra** play superbly. But, as so often in the past, they are let down by the choice of venue for the recording, in this instance the Memorial Hall, Fairmount Park, whose apparently intractible acoustics have led to close microphone placing, creating an unnatural effect. There is no lack of atmosphere, but very soon it becomes apparent that *fortissimos* are un-refined, with fierce cymbals, grainy violins, even an element of harshness. Yet there is much to enjoy, while the thrilling final climax (with gorgeously full horn-tone at the restatement of the famous *idée fixe*) makes an overwhelming apotheosis, even if the shrillness added to the violins, who play with enormous fervour, is not a plus factor.

Swan Lake (ballet: abridged); (i) Rococo Variations. Symphony 6 (Pathétique)

Ⓝ **(*) Australian Decca Eloquence (ADD) 480 0563 (2). SRO, Ansermet with (i) Gendron

Ansermet is best in the characteristic dances in *Act 3* in his vividly recorded fairly complete *Swan Lake*, dating from 1958. The *Entrée des invites (Fanfares)* are strikingly bright and crisp, and the *Danse espagnole* and *Danse napolitaine* are delightfully pointed. However, there is plenty of drama and feeling of theatre throughout this performance. **Gendron** plays the charming *Variations* with a sense of elegance and a fine, firm tone. Ansermet accompanies affectionately, and the mono sound is excellent, even if the orchestra is inclined to a touch of shrillness. As for the *Pathétique*, the first Penguin review said, 'Ansermet is Ansermet', and whilst the original reviewer felt he had little sympathy with this work, the present writer feels Ansermet fans will get much pleasure from his clear-headed interpretation. The introduction has a cool beauty to it, and the famous third movement is excitingly lively and energetic, if not immaculate in ensemble. But it is Ansermet's avoidance of excess which makes his performance so satisfying, and the 1956 recording amazes in its brilliance.

Swan Lake, Op. 20 (highlights)

✣ **** Australian Decca Eloquence (ADD) 442 9032. Concg. O, Fistoulari

Ⓜ (**(*)) Cala mono CACD0543. NBC SO, Stokowski – STRAUSS: Waltzes: *An der schönen blauen Donau; Geschichten aus den Wiener Wald;* BEETHOVEN: *Ruins of Athens: Turkish March;* MOZART: *Turkish March* (arr. Stokowski from *Piano Sonata 11: Alla Turca*)

Fistoulari was a great conductor of ballet music, and we have long admired this 1960 selection of highlights from *Swan Lake*, which at the time of its first issue was revelatory. It is a real collectors' item and this is its CD debut. It is essentially a relaxed reading, but the **Concertgebouw Orchestra** plays superbly and there is a wonderful sense of the theatre combined with spontaneous music-making. For its date, the recording is outstanding too. At only a little over 46 minutes' playing time, this is very much quality over quantity.

Stokowski's 1954/5 set of highlights from *Swan Lake* (more than an hour of music) was a recording première; hitherto only the suite had been readily available (although some extended excerpts of little-known passages from the score had been issued on four Columbia 78s in the 1940s). Most of the music here comes from Acts II and III, but the sequence is Stokowski's own, and includes one of the composer's piano pieces from Op. 72, orchestrated by Drigo and used in performances at that time.

The response of the **NBC Orchestra** has both panache and excitement, with fine woodwind playing. An enjoyable selection, then, and not at all predictable. The transfer to CD is remarkably good and this is well worth having, if not one of the maestro's very finest records from this era.

SYMPHONIES

Symphonies 1–6

Ⓑ *** DG (ADD) 429 675-2 (4). BPO, Karajan

**(*) DG 449 967-2 (5). Russian Nat. O, Pletnev

Symphonies 1–6; Capriccio italien; Manfred Symphony

☛ ✣ Ⓑ **** Chan. 10392 (6). Oslo PO, Jansons

Jansons's Tchaikovsky series, which includes *Manfred*, is self-recommending. The full romantic power of the music is consistently conveyed and, above all, the music-making is urgently spontaneous throughout, with the **Oslo Philharmonic Orchestra** always committed and fresh, helped by the richly atmospheric Chandos sound. A supreme bargain.

Having recorded the last three Tchaikovsky symphonies

three times over in little more than ten years, **Karajan** finally turned to the early symphonies; and there, in 1975/6, displaying the same superlative refined qualities, produced performances equally illuminating. It is typical that, though the opening *Allegro tranquillo* of the first movement of 1 is taken fast, there is no feeling of breathlessness, as there often is: it is a genuine *tranquillo*, though the rhythmic bite of the syncopated passages, so important in these early symphonies, could hardly be sharper. The high polish may give a hint of the ballroom to some of the dance movements, with the folk element underplayed, but no finer set of symphonies has been recorded since: it is commandingly consistent and vivid in sound, although (in the last three symphonies especially), it is not always richly resonant in the lower range.

Pletnev's readings have all the innate aristocratic feeling Tchaikovsky could ask for, but at no time does Pletnev wear his heart on his sleeve. Some may feel that the emphasis in the *First Symphony* is too much on the *rêveries* of the title, and Tchaikovsky's rhetoric might be handled more convincingly; but, for the most part, Pletnev's approach throughout the cycle is the reverse of overblown. Indeed, the highly charged, high-voltage sound which we associate with Mravinsky surfaces in the *Pathétique*, but otherwise he sets greater store by classicism, carefully balanced proportions and a masterly sense of line. DG have accorded the cycle very fine and well-detailed sound.

Symphonies 1–6; (i) Piano Concerto 1; (ii) Violin Concerto; Capriccio italien; Eugene Onegin: Polonaise & Waltz; Marche slave; The Nutcracker Suite; 1812 Overture; Romeo and Juliet (Fantasy Overture); Sleeping Beauty: Suite; String Serenade; Swan Lake: Suite; (iii) Variations on a Rococo Theme

Ⓑ **(*) DG (ADD) 463 774-2 (8). (i) Richter, VSO; (ii) Ferras; (iii) Rostropovich; BPO; all cond. Karajan

These **Berlin** performances of the *Symphonies* are fine in every way; perhaps a bit of over-refinement creeps in from time to time, but by any standards they are a magnificent achievement, especially the symphonies. The *Violin Concerto* is superbly shaped by **Karajan**, though some will find **Ferras's** tone lacking charm – his close vibrato in lyrical passages tends to emphasize schmaltz on the G string. **Richter** and Karajan are, to say the least, controversial in the *Piano Concerto*. In the first movement, both artists play havoc with any sense of forward tempo (though there are occasional bursts of real excitement). Clearly two major artists at work, but the result is none too convincing. The *Rococo Variations* with **Rostropovich** is a breath of fresh air after all that – lovely glowing accounts – and the orchestral music is generally fine, but not outstanding, and a hint of glossiness creeps in from time to time (though the *Sleeping Beauty* and *Swan Lake* suites are quite superb). The sound throughout the set is of a generally high standard.

Symphonies 1–6; Manfred Symphony; Capriccio italien; Romeo and Juliet (Fantasy Overture); Serenade for Strings; The Tempest; Eugene Onegin: Polonaise

(BB) *** Virgin 5 61893-2 (6). Bournemouth SO, Litton

Andrew Litton's set of the Tchaikovsky *Symphonies*, including *Manfred*, is in many ways his finest achievement on record, and this super-super-bargain Virgin box is very desirable indeed. The cycle gets off to a splendid start with the first two *Symphonies*, which are very successful. With warm and full recording, less distanced than many on this label, these urgently spontaneous performances rival any in the catalogue.

Again in the outer movements of *3* Litton challenges his players to the limit, setting fast speeds, but the clean, purposeful manner is very satisfying, even if some other versions spring rhythms more infectiously. Litton's finesse comes out impressively in the *Andante elegiaco*, where he chooses a flowing tempo needing no modification for the broad melody that follows, which is then nobly moulded. *4* is essentially spacious, both in choice of tempi and the rather backward balance of the orchestra. Ideally one needs a brighter focus in this symphony, yet Litton, with crisp ensemble, builds the structure of the first movement steadily and unerringly.

The first movement of the *Fifth* is surprisingly slow and steady, and here the reading lacks the high voltage of Litton's finest Tchaikovsky performances. But the slow movement brings a beautiful horn solo, and the *Waltz* is delightfully fresh and delicate. The finale is again on the broad side, warm rather than ominous, with very clean articulation in the playing. The *Pathétique* caps the cycle impressively: an outstanding performance, full of temperament, not just fiery but tender too, arguably the finest of the whole cycle. The Bournemouth playing has never been more clearly articulated.

Manfred is both individual and satisfying and throughout Litton controls the tension to bring out the narrative sequence and heighten the dramatic cohesion. The sound is clean cut and well balanced, with the organ entry at the end of the finale among the most dramatic on record.

The encores are substantial and add much to the attractions of the set. In the *Capriccio italien* both playing and recording display the dramatic contrasts of texture and dynamic to the full, while the *Eugene Onegin Polonaise* brings an even more infectiously rhythmic lift. On the other hand the *String Serenade* is warmly romantic, with the *Waltz* elegant and the *Elégie* expressively intense, and the finale bursts with energy. *The Tempest* is given an outstanding performance, while *Romeo and Juliet* is similarly fine. All in all, this is an astonishing bargain.

Symphonies 1-6; Manfred; Francesca da Rimini; Romeo and Juliet (Fantasy Overture)

(N) (B) *** EMI (ADD) 5 19443-2 (5). LPO, Rostropovich

Rostropovich recorded his Tchaikovsky cycle concurrently with live performances at the Royal Festival Hall, and though at certain points (as in some of the *fugato* development sections) the ensemble could be a shade crisper, the performances have not only passion and electricity but great charm and refinement too. The first three symphonies are superbly done in every way – Rostropovich manages to choose his tempi most persuasively, and his rhythmic pointing is consistently delectable – outshining here almost any opposition outside the complete sets. *Symphonies Nos. 4* to *6* are all characterised by relatively slow but well-pointed accounts of the first movements, and only in *No. 5* is there a suspicion of the argument dragging. Otherwise these are sensitive, deeply felt readings which should be easy to live with. *Manfred* too is most persuasively done, with a scherzo of Berliozian refinement, though the recording in that work is not quite so rich and atmospheric as in the rest of the cycle. However the pianissimo string tone is particularly beautiful.

The readings of *Francesca da Rimini* and *Romeo and Juliet* are intensely individual and full of poetic feeling, yet they are underpinned by the drama of the narrative. The ebb and flow of tension have the spontaneity of live performances and the listener is carried along by the expressive vitality of the orchestral playing. Rostropovich achieves an epic rather than a romantic approach to *Romeo and Juliet*, and *Francesca* has a similar sense of scale and high drama, with a breathtaking finale, yet touching delicacy in the work's central section with radiant sounds from the **LPO** woodwind. The recording is resonant and spacious, with great body and impact, altogether thrilling.

Symphonies 1–3; Capriccio italien; Marche slave

🎵 (M) **** DG 459 518-2 (2). BPO, Karajan

Having recorded the last three Tchaikovsky symphonies three times in little more than a decade, **Karajan** then, at the end of the 1970s, turned to the early *Symphonies* and brought to them the same superlative qualities. With his great orchestra finely honed in ensemble the playing throughout proved marvellous and the performances equally illuminating. It is typical that even though the opening *tranquillo* of *1* is taken fast there is no feeling of breathlessness, it is genuinely *tranquillo*, although the rhythmic bite of the syncopated passages, so important in these early symphonies, could hardly be sharper. In the *Little Russian Symphony* the tempo for the *Andante* is very nicely judged and the outer movements have plenty of drama and fire. In *3* Karajan even finds an affinity with Brahms in the second movement (which Tchaikovsky would not have acknowledged), yet the climax of the *Andante* is full of Tchaikovskian fervour and in the less tractable finale the articulation of the *Polacca* (which gave the symphony its sobriquet 'Polish') is both vigorous and joyful. The recording is bold, full-bodied, brilliant and clear.

Symphony 1 (Winter Daydreams); Francesca da Rimini; (i) Variations on a Rococo Theme for Cello & Orchestra (DVD versions)

🎵 ⚙ **** Arthaus **DVD** 102 121. Moscow RSO, Fedoseyev; (i) with Meneses

Fedoseyev has the full measure of the *Winter Daydreams Symphony*, catching the lyrical delicacy of the first movement, while the lovely *Adagio* blossoms in its touchingly nostalgic yet rich espressivo. The finale is very exciting without being over-driven. The account of *Francesca da Rimini* which follows is superb, easily matching Stokowski's famous early version both in colour and in passionate intensity, after creating a delightful portrait of Francesca herself. Then the whirlwinds of the inferno are taken to a tempestuous climax and Fedoseyev's accelerando in the coda has one on the edge of one's seat. As a closing highlight, **Antonio Meneses** joins the orchestra for an equally outstanding account of the delightful *Rococo Variations*, alternating sparkling bravura with touching warmth. The recording is first class, and this is among the finest of all Tchaikovsky DVDs. The camerawork cannot be faulted.

Symphony 1 in G min. (Winter Daydreams) (CD version)

⏻ **** Chan. 8402. Oslo PO, Jansons

Symphony 1; Hamlet (Fantasy Overture)

🅱🅱 *** Naxos 8.550517. Polish Nat. RSO, Leaper

Refreshingly direct in style, **Mariss Jansons** with his brilliant orchestra gives an electrically compelling performance of this earliest of the *Symphonies*. Structurally strong, the result tingles with excitement, most of all in the finale, faster than usual, with the challenge of the complex fugato passages taken superbly. The recording is highly successful.

   Adrian Leaper also conducts a taut and sympathetic reading of *Winter Daydreams*, with excellent playing from the **Polish Orchestra** enhanced by vivid recording, fresh and clear, with plenty of body and with refined *pianissimo* playing from the strings in the slow movement. This is among the finest Tchaikovsky recordings on the Naxos list, with all four movements sharply characterized. The overture too comes in a tautly dramatic reading. An outstanding bargain.

Symphonies 1, 5 & 6 (Pathétique); Romeo and Juliet Fantasy Overture; The Tempest

Ⓝ Ⓑ **(*)   Virgin 6 93238-2 (2). Bournemouth SO, Litton

Litton's performances are drawn from his complete cycle listed above. The three chosen symphonies are all impressively played, with the exception of the outer movements of the *Fifth* which lack something in forward thrust. But the *Pathétique* is very successful in every respect and so are the brilliant accounts of *Romeo and Juliet* and *The Tempest*. Excellent recording too.

Symphony 2 in C min. (Little Russian), Op. 17 (original (1872) score); Festive Overture on the Danish National Anthem, Op. 15; Serenade for Nikolai Rubinstein's Saint's Day; Mazeppa: Battle of Poltava; Cossack Dance

*** Chan. 9190. LSO, Simon

This was the first recording of Tchaikovsky's original score of the *Little Russian Symphony* and probably the first performance outside Russia. In 1879 Tchaikovsky retrieved the score and rewrote the first movement. He left the *Andante* virtually unaltered, touched up the scoring of the Scherzo, made minor excisions and added repeats, and made a huge cut of 150 bars (some two minutes of music) in the finale. He then destroyed the original. (The present performance has been possible because of the surviving orchestral parts.) Though

this first attempt cannot match the reworked first movement, and the finale – delightful though it is – needs no extra bars, it is fascinating to hear the composer's first thoughts, and this is an indispensable recording for all Tchaikovskians. **Geoffrey Simon** secures a committed response from the **LSO**, and the recording is striking in its inner orchestral detail and freshness. The music from *Mazeppa*, the *Danish Festival Overture* and the tribute to Rubinstein make engaging bonuses.

Symphony 2; Capriccio italien, Op. 45

*** Chan. 8460. Oslo PO, Jansons

Jansons prefers a fastish speed for the *Andantino* second movement, but what above all distinguishes this version is the joyful exuberance both of the bouncy Scherzo – fresh and folk-like in the Trio – and of the finale, and the final coda brings a surge of excitement, making most others seem stiff. The coupling is a fizzing performance of the *Capriccio italien*. With some edge on violin tone, this is not the finest of the Chandos **Oslo** recordings, but it is still fresh and atmospheric.

Symphony 2 (Little Russian); Serenade for Strings

🅱🅱 *** Regis RRC 1266. USSR State SO, Svetlanov

Svetlanov's 1967 account of the *Little Russian Symphony* is very strong in character and the whole reading is consistent. The immediate yet full-bodied recording suits the very positive style; Svetlanov takes the *Andantino* quite slowly, and this brings out the charm of the orchestration, but his approach to the finale again generates great energy, although perhaps less in the way of geniality. Yet detail is well revealed, the impetus is irresistible, and at the close, although the rhetoric is kept firmly under control, there is a most satisfying culmination. The *String Serenade* is equally distinguished. Following Tchaikovsky's wishes, Svetlanov uses a large body of strings which brings richly expressive eloquence to the *Elegia* slow movement, yet the bouncing secondary theme of the first movement is delightfully pointed. The *Waltz* is graceful and its lightness and delicacy bring a scherzando element, while the finale, opening nostalgically, then bustles with vigour. The upper range of the strings does show the age of the recording (1970), but they have plenty of body, and this is still a very recommendable coupling.

Symphonies 2 (Little Russian); 6 (Pathétique); Francesca da Rimini; Romeo and Juliet (Fantasy Overture)

⏻ 🅱🅱 **** EMI Gemini (ADD) 5 86531-2 (2). Philh. O, Giulini

Giulini's very distinguished recordings were made between 1956 and 1962 when the **Philharmonia** was at its peak and the conductor on top form. The *Little Russian Symphony* was the first version to appear on CD, and it still ranks among the finest. The performance is full of vitality, with brisk tempi throughout, except for the engagingly wistful little march of the *Andantino*, which makes a perfect foil. The *Pathétique* is comparatively spacious, and equally memorable. There is a degree of restraint in the way Giulini interprets the big melodies of the first and last movements, which are given an almost Elgarian nobility. Yet passionate intensity is conveyed by the purity and concentration of the playing, which equally builds up electric tension and excitement without hysteria. The performances of *Francesca da Rimini* and *Romeo and Juliet* are in a similar mould, full of impetus, colour and passion; in *Romeo*, Giulini brings out the dignity of the opening and closing pages, and the first appearance of the great love theme is superbly managed. The Kingsway Hall recordings are spectacular, but there is a degree of harshness and fierceness in tuttis, to show the age of the *Little Russian Symphony* (1956). The *Pathétique* sounds magnificent, as does *Romeo and Juliet*, and this set is a superb reminder of Giulini and the Philharmonia at their greatest.

Symphony 3 in D (Polish), Op. 29

&—, **** Chan. 8463. Oslo PO, Jansons

Tchaikovsky's *Third* is given a clear, refreshingly direct reading by **Jansons**, but it is the irresistible sweep of urgency with which he builds the development section of the first movement that sets his performance apart, with the basic tempo varied less than usual. The second movement is beautifully relaxed, the *Andante elegiaco* heartwarmingly expressive, tender and refined, and the Scherzo has a Mendelssohnian elfin quality; but it is the swaggering reading of the finale that sets the seal on the whole performance. Though the recording does not convey a genuinely hushed *pianissimo* for the strings, it brings full, rich and brilliant sound.

Symphonies 4 & 5

(N) ❀ Sony DVD 888579849. VPO, Karajan

The *Fourth* and *Fifth* were recorded in 1984 at the Grosser Musikvereinssaal with the **Vienna Philharmonic** at the time when **Karajan's** relationship with the Berlin Philharmonic was under some strain. The *Fourth* is one of the most commanding and compelling accounts of this great work we have heard and rivets the attention throughout. Karajan's famous 1950s account of the *Fourth* with the Philharmonia Orchestra bore witness to his special relationship with this music and this makes an equally strong impression. Excellent video presentation enhances its impact.

Symphonies 4–6 (Pathétique) (DVD versions)

*** DG DVD 073 4384. BPO, Karajan

As Richard Osborne reminds us, the Tchaikovsky symphonies were among the first that the young **Herbert von Karajan** took into his repertoire, the *Fifth* as early as 1929, when he was 20 and he recorded the *Sixth* only six months after Furtwängler had made his HMV set with the same orchestra, just before the war. Karajan was a masterly Tchaikovsky interpreter (his post-war *Fourth* with the Philharmonia was tremendous and created renewed enthusiasm for the work). These 1973 performances, recorded in the Philharmonie, are both eloquent and gripping. Strongly recommended for the performances and the imaginative use of the camera.

Symphonies 4–6 (Pathétique) (CD versions)

(B) *** DG Double (ADD) 453 088-2 (2). BPO, Karajan

(B) *** Double Decca (ADD) 443 844-2 (2). Philh. O, Ashkenazy

&—, **** EMI 3 53258-2 (2). St Cecilia O, Pappano

(BB) **(*) EMI Gemini (ADD) 3 81798-2 (2). BPO, Karajan

Karajan's 1977 analogue version of *4* (the most atmospherically recorded of the three) is more compelling than his previous recordings and also is preferable to the newer, digital, Vienna version. Similarly the 1976 reading of the *Fifth* stands out from his other recordings. The **Berlin Philharmonic** string-playing is peerless. Karajan had a special affinity with Tchaikovsky's *Pathétique Symphony*, and of his five stereo versions this one from 1977 is the finest. The digital remastering of the analogue recordings is first rate.

Ashkenazy's set makes a fine alternative bargain on Double Decca. Apart from the emotional power and strong Russian feeling of the readings, the special quality that Ashkenazy conveys is spontaneity. The freshness of his approach, his natural feeling for lyricism on the one hand and drama on the other is consistently compelling. The late-1970s Kingsway Hall recording quality is full and atmospheric.

It says much for **Pappano's** warmly dramatic approach to Tchaikovsky that these are performances which consistently have one wanting to hear more. The brilliant quality of the digital sound with clean separation adds to the impact of each performance, with the timpani exceptionally clear, and with the outstanding wind soloists of the **St Cecilia Orchestra** adding distinction to each work. So the rising figure of the second subject given to the clarinet in the *Fourth* has a cheeky persuasiveness, and the great horn solo in the slow movement of the *Fifth* is not just refined in its delicacy but intensely meditative. As in his conducting of Puccini, Pappano is consistently persuasive in his use of rubato, notably in the great melodies of the *Pathétique*, and his control of the all-important climaxes is unerring. These are performances that have one marvelling afresh at the composer's mastery as a symphonist, a quality not always appreciated.

The EMI Gemini set is a pretty good bargain. **Karajan's** 1971 EMI performances of these three *Symphonies* are a satisfying achievement, with fine orchestral playing and recording, made in the Berlin Jesus-Christus-Kirche, with plenty of body, even if the sound does produce a degree of edgy fierceness at moments of extreme pressure. Karajan's readings are in many ways similar to his earlier ones for DG, but both 5 and 6 have moments when the music-making is less completely spontaneous than in the DG versions. Nevertheless this is a fine set which will give considerable satisfaction, for Karajan was a great Tchaikovsky conductor and these performances are full of adrenalin and still rank high in the list of recommendations.

(i) Symphony 4; (ii) Francesca da Rimini (DVD versions)

&—, *** EMI DVD DVB 5 996899. (i) Leningrad PO, Rozhdestvensky (colour); (ii) Leningrad PO, Mravinsky (black and white) – see under Documentaries: 'Yevgeny

Mravinsky – Soviet Conductor, Russian Aristocrat'. A documentary by Dennis Marks

These memorable performances are a bonus for a splendid documentary about Mravinsky.

Symphony 4 in F min., Op. 36

(***) BBC Legends mono BBCL 4143-2. Leningrad PO, Rozhdestvensky – SHOSTAKOVICH: *Cello Concerto 1.* (***)

A particularly valuable reminder of the days when orchestras from the then Soviet Union were heard relatively rarely in the West. This high-voltage account of the *Fourth Symphony* was recorded at one of three Promenade Concerts this great orchestra gave in the 1971 season, and it has the compelling quality and excitement that live music-making generates. The BBC recording does justice to the rich sonority this great orchestra produced at that period.

Symphony 4 in F min., Op. 36

🎧 **** Decca **SACD** 475 6196. VPO, Gergiev

🎧 **** Chan. 8361. Oslo PO, Jansons

Symphony 4; Capriccio italien

*** HM HMU 90 7393 RPO, Gatti

Symphony 4; Francesca da Rimini

🎧 **** BIS CD 1273. Bamberg SO, Serebrier

Symphony 4 in F min.; Nutcracker Suite; Eugene Onegin: Waltz

Ⓑ (**(*)) EMI mono/stereo 3 80016-2. RPO, Beecham

Gergiev's account of 4 was recorded live in the orchestra's home, the Musikverein in Vienna, and the performance captures many of the vital qualities that made his earlier reading of 5 so magnetic. The opening fanfare motif calls us compellingly to attention; but then, after the slow introduction, the start of the main *Moderato con anima* with its lilting compound time is surprisingly relaxed, yet very convincing. Typically for Gergiev, the tension mounts magnetically, when the balletic waltz-rhythms develop into the movement's big climaxes. The **Vienna Philharmonic** playing is wonderfully taut in the pizzicato Scherzo, with the 'drunken peasant' passage wittily pointed, while the finale culminates in a subtle accelerando in the closing bars of the coda, with thrilling results. There is no applause at the end, suggesting, as is usual in 'live recordings' in the Musikverein, that a modest amount of patching was conceded.

Jansons conducts a dazzling performance, unusually fresh and natural in its expressiveness, yet with countless subtleties of expression, as in the balletic account of the second-subject group of the first movement. The *Andantino* flows lightly and persuasively, the Scherzo is very fast and lightly sprung, while the finale reinforces the impact of the whole performance: fast and exciting, but with no synthetic whipping-up of tempo. That is so until the very end of the coda, which finds Jansons pressing ahead just fractionally as he would in a concert, a thrilling conclusion made the

more so by the wide-ranging, brilliant and realistic recording.

On the Swedish BIS label the *Fourth Symphony* is superbly played and recorded. Consistently textures are clarified, helped by the thoughtful, finely judged reading of **José Serebrier**. The **Bamberg Orchestra** boasts an exceptional line-up of refined wind soloists, phrasing subtly. Not that in this concern for detail there is any lack of excitement, for the incisive attack and Serebrier's preference for steady speeds brings a structural strength too rarely achieved in Tchaikovsky. *Francesca da Rimini*, inspired by Dante, makes an apt coupling, a work written in very much the same period as the *Symphony*.

Gatti's interpretation, as in his memorable version of the *Fifth Symphony*, often favours tempi which press the music on more swiftly than usual. Yet Gatti's momentum is compulsive and he finds his contrast in the rocking string melody, played so beautifully by the **RPO** strings. The nostalgic second movement is also beautifully played, yet the melancholy oboe melody is again taken a little faster than usual. But here the vigorous middle section makes a spontaneous contrast, and the decorated reprise shows the RPO woodwind at their most sensitive. After the balalaika pizzicato Scherzo, the finale bursts in on the listener and, with the dramatic re-entry of the fatal fanfare, Gatti carries forward to a spectacular coda. His performance of the *Capriccio italien* is vigorously enjoyable, if not as distinctive as the *Symphony*. The Walthamstow recording is full-blooded and realistic, but could perhaps be more expansive.

After a dramatic opening, **Beecham** lets the tension of the first-movement *Allegretto* build up from within the music itself. The result is a steady increase of excitement; the overall structure of the movement is perfectly judged and the climax at the centre of the development is tremendous, while the recapitulation moves to the coda with a feeling of great strength and emotional power. The 1958 Kingsway Hall recording is good, clear and sonorous. Yet it is mono and is bright and a little light in the bass, and in the finale the lower brass do not tell as they do at a live concert. However, the *Nutcracker Suite* (also mono) sounds splendidly fresh and the sound is warmer; the *Eugene Onegin Waltz*, played with élan, is in stereo and makes a delectable encore.

Symphony 5 in E min., Op. 64

🎧 **** Warner **DVD** + CD 2564 62190-5. West-Eastern Divan Orchestra, Barenboim – SIBELIUS: *Valse triste*; VERDI: *La Forza del destino Overture* (***)

The **West-Eastern Divan Orchestra** – the name taken from Goethe – was the amazing inspiration of **Daniel Barenboim** and his Palestinian philosopher-friend, the late Edward Said. The idea was to bring together in direct collaboration young Arab musicians and young Israelis, for them to make music together, sharing at every level, so that each would more readily come to understand the other.

The result, inspired above all by Barenboim's dynamic leadership, has been an unqualified success musically. Their performance of the Tchaikovsky, recorded live in Geneva in 2004, is electrifying from beginning to end, remarkable not just for the weight of the string-tone but for its refinement in *pianissimos*. The finale is thrilling, and though on the CD applause has been eliminated, the DVD version brings out on video what an ecstatic reception the Geneva audience gave, ending with a prolonged standing ovation after the encore, Verdi's *Forza del destino Overture*, dazzlingly done. The DVD omits the other encore, Sibelius's *Valse triste*, but includes the symphony and overture complete, as well as the 75-minute conversation between Barenboim and Said, recorded in Weimar in 1999, and a documentary, 'Lessons in Harmony', vividly illustrating the orchestra's preparations in sessions in Seville and the way the young musicians work together. An inspiring issue.

Symphony 5 in E min., Op. 64

🎵 ⊛ **** Decca. 475 6718. VPO, Gergiev

*** Chan. 8351. Oslo PO, Jansons

Ⓜ **(*) Warner Elatus 2564 60035-2. Leningrad PO, Mravinsky

Symphony 5; Capriccio italien

🎵 Ⓜ **** Sony (ADD) 82876 78744-2. Cleveland O, Szell

Symphony 5; Romeo and Juliet (Fantasy Overture)

🎵 **** HM HMU 907381. RPO, Gatti

(i) Symphony 5; (ii) Variations on a Rococo Theme for Cello & Orchestra

🎵 Ⓑ **** CfP 586 1682. LPO; (i) Edwards; (ii) Del Mar

Ⓜ **(*) Sony SMK 89795. (i) Chicago SO, Abbado; (ii) Ma, Pittsburgh SO, Maazel

Symphony 5; Francesca da Rimini

Ⓝ ** DG 477 8022. Simón Bolivar Youth Orchestra of Venezuela, Dudamel

Valery Gergiev's account of the *Fifth Symphony* is really quite special. It is a performance of real stature, totally electrifying. No wonder the audience went wild at the end. It certainly belongs among the best *Fifths* on record. Some collectors will find full price a bit steep for 46 minutes, no matter how marvellous the performance and excellent the recording; but if you can put economy to one side, you will be rewarded with out-of-the-ordinary music-making.

If anything, **Szell's** 1959 performance of the *Fifth Symphony* is even finer than his *Fourth* for Decca (currently withdrawn, alas). Its sense of romantic urgency is finely judged, with a splendid surge and momentum in the outer movements. The recording has a resonant bass and treble but has been smoothed in the latest remastering so that an exciting effect can be achieved. The *Capriccio italien* too is played with great flair, and again it is one of the finest accounts in the catalogue.

The still much-underrated **Sian Edwards** is a natural Tchaikovskian, and on CfP she conducts an electrifying and warm-hearted reading of Tchaikovsky's *Fifth*. With refined playing from the **LPO** and brilliant recording, it matches any version in the catalogue. Her control of rubato is excep-

tionally persuasive, notably so in moulding the different sections of the first movement, while the great horn solo of the slow movement is played with exquisite delicacy by **Richard Bissell**. The *Waltz* third movement is tenderly done, as though for a ballet, while the finale brings a very fast and exciting allegro, challenging the orchestra to brilliant, incisive playing. By the side of Edwards's natural vitality, **Norman Del Mar's** warmly agreeable account of the *String Serenade* seems just a little bland, although it is well played and the 1978 recording is warm and pleasing.

Daniele Gatti often chooses tempi that are brisker than usual and that are closer to the composer's own metronome markings. The result in the first movement, with crisp rhythmic pointing, is an invigorating forward thrust from beginning to end, with the primary second subject theme on the violins romantic in its rubato, rather than impassioned, as with Gergiev. The elegiac melancholy of the slow movement, with its evocative horn solo most sensitively played by **Martin Owen**, brings climaxes which are spaciously affecting but not as passionately overwhelming as with Gergiev, the forceful interruptions of the motto theme less histrionic, and the movement brings a gently touching close. The *Waltz* is elegant and graceful, with neatly decorative violins, a contrasting interlude before the excitingly strong, direct finale. Here the brass is crisp and urgent, especially in the repeated reprise of the Fate theme, which is very sharply focused. Once again Gatti takes the movement forward in a single sweep, with free-running adrenalin, pausing only briefly to reflect Tchaikovsky's moment of self-doubt before pressing onwards to the triumphant coda with its blazing trumpets. Gatti offers in addition a superb account of *Romeo and Juliet*. The Abbey Road recording throughout both symphony and overture is excellent, full-bodied, with vivid, weightily sonorous bass.

In the first movement, **Jansons's** refusal to linger never sounds anything but warmly idiomatic, lacking only a little in charm. The slow movement again brings a steady tempo, with climaxes built strongly and patiently but with enormous power, the final culmination topping everything. In the finale, taken very fast, Jansons tightens the screw of the excitement without ever making it a scramble, following Tchaikovsky's notated slowings rather than allowing extra rallentandos. The sound is excellent, specific and well focused within a warmly reverberant acoustic, with digital recording on CD reinforcing any lightness of bass.

Abbado's Chicago *Fifth* is admirably fresh and superbly played. All Tchaikovsky's markings are scrupulously yet imaginatively observed and the reading is full of contrast. Other versions of the slow movement have more extrovert passion, but Abbado shows that the climaxes can be involving without being histrionic. After an elegant *Waltz*, with the orchestra in sparkling form, the finale has fine energy and momentum. If it does not have quite the gripping excitement of Jansons or Gergiev, the moment of the composer's self-doubt, before the *Poco più animato*, is the more effectively characterized. The recording is made in a convincingly resonant acoustic. As an encore **Yo-Yo Ma's** *Rococo Variations* are characteristically refined, and although his playing is at times just a little mannered (and one longs for the full-timbred Rostropovich approach), Ma always engages the listener's sympathy by his delicacy and grace. **Maazel's** less than inspired accompaniment does, however, diminish the appeal of the performance, which is again very well recorded.

Mravinsky's account of the *Fifth Symphony* on Elatus comes from a concert performance on 19 March 1983. It is his last recording of the symphony that survives and is perhaps less 'possessed' than his famous DG accounts issued in 1956 and 1961 or the subsequent deleted performances from 1965 and 1973 on Olympia and RCA/BMG. Yet it is hardly less compelling and if anything more human.

Dudamel's performance of the *Fifth Symphony* is a disappointment. It has little of the fizzing energy of his live performances. Indeed, the first movement has places where all tension is lost. The slow movement is beautiful and refined, but lacks the intensity which gives the horn's entry the frisson it ideally should have and even the finale lacks the excitement one expects from this source. *Francesca da Rimini* possess more of the conductor's characteristic energy and one admires the attention to detail, but here, as in the *Symphony*, the DG (live) recording is very average.

Symphony 6 in B min. (Pathétique), Op. 74 (DVD version)

(*) Arthaus **DVD 100 302. Bav. RSO, Solti (V/D: Klaus Lindemann) – SHOSTAKOVICH: *Symphony 9* ***

Solti's *Pathétique*, even with the extra involvement of visual communication, is not the overwhelming experience one might have expected. We watch him shape the opening movement and the arrival of the great second subject, which is played with real tenderness; and again we watch as he directs the Scherzo/march crisply and builds the big climax at the end, which is inevitably exciting but not overwhelming. Then the finale, although it is played very beautifully, is curiously low-key, and we are left without the lift that comes with a powerful communication of Tchaikovsky's deeply felt but resigned despair. The recording is excellent, and so is the camerawork. But there are many CD performances that are more moving than this.

Symphony 6 in B min. (Pathétique), Op. 74 (CD versions)

🎧 **** Chan. 8446. Oslo PO, Jansons

🎧 **** Decca **SACD** 475 6197. VPO, Gergiev

✿ Ⓑ (***) Naxos mono 8.110865. BPO, Furtwängler – WAGNER: *Tristan: Prelude & Liebestod* (***)

Ⓜ (***) Sup. mono SU 3828-2. Czech PO, Talich – WAGNER: *Tristan: Prelude & Liebestod* – Prague RSO (***)

(***) Biddulph mono WHL 046. Phd. O, Ormandy – MUSSORGSKY: *Pictures at an Exhibition* (orch Cailliet) (***)

Ⓜ *(**) RCA **SACD** (ADD) 82876 61397-2. Boston SO, Monteux

Symphony 6 (Pathétique); Capriccio italien; Eugene Onegin: Waltz & Polonaise

Ⓑ **(*) Sony (ADD) SBK 47657. Phd. O, Ormandy

Symphony 6 (Pathétique) in B min., Op. 74; Francesca da Rimini, Op. 32

Ⓜ **(*) Warner Elatus (ADD) 0927 46733-2. Leningrad PO, Mravinsky

(i) Symphony 6 (Pathétique); (ii) Romeo and Juliet (Fantasy Overture)

🎧 Ⓜ **** DG 471 742-2. Russian Nat. O, Pletnev

Ⓜ ** RCA 82876 62320-2. (i) St Petersburg PO; (ii) RPO; Temirkanov

Symphony 6, 'Pathetique'. Serenade for Strings

*** HM HMU90 7394 RPO, Gatti

Symphony 6 (Pathétique); The Storm: Overture

🅱🅱 *** Regis RRC 1214. LSO, Rozhdestvensky

(i) Symphony 6 (Pathétique); (ii) (Piano) Dumka, Op. 59

Ⓝ *(**) Ondine ODE 1131-5. (i) Phd. O, Eschenbach; (ii) Eschenbach (piano)

Pletnev's account of the *Pathétique* with the **Russian National Orchestra** comes from the complete cycle he recorded in November 1995, four years after the Virgin recording he made shortly after the orchestra's formation. This is no less impressive and its level of dramatic intensity and emotional concentration are even higher. The *Allegro* is a shade steadier perhaps but the March is every bit as breathtaking. The dark colourings of the finale and the soulful lyricism of the strings resonate in the memory. The *Romeo and Juliet* is both exciting and moving, and the DG recording is even more detailed, present and realistic than the Virgin version.

Valery Gergiev's *Pathétique* has a similar intensity and dramatic power to his *Fifth*. Some may find it hard-driven at times, but there is great excitement and firmness of grip. Gergiev is by no means as subtle – certainly in matters of dynamic nuance – as Pletnev. The recording on CD has impressive depth and resonance and in surround sound it is tremendously exciting, especially the climax of the headlong Scherzo. On SACD this is certainly the finest recording the *Symphony* has ever received, and the sense of ambience, of sitting in the hall, is uncanny. The performance, especially in the impulsively passionate finale, will not appeal to everyone, but it is I.M.'s first choice.

Mariss Jansons and the **Oslo Philharmonic** crown their magnetically compelling Tchaikovsky series with a superbly concentrated account of the last and greatest of the *Symphonies*. It is characteristic of Jansons that the great second-subject melody is at once warm and passionate yet totally unsentimental, with rubato barely noticeable. The very fast speed for the third-movement *March* stretches the players to the very limit, but the exhilaration is infectious, leading to the simple dedication of the slow finale, unexaggerated but deeply felt. Fine, warm recording as in the rest of the series.

Furtwängler's Berlin Philharmonic *Pathétique* was quite simply the finest recorded account of the whole 78 era. The reading showed him at his most inspirational, his control of tension in the first movement unerringly spontaneous, with its burst of excitement in the development section and its sombre close. Never before or since have the changing tempi of the Scherzo/March been more successfully graduated, with a superb final march reprise, which (as Mark Obert-Thorn's superb transfer demonstrates) was captured on the long 78-r.p.m. side without noticeable falling off in quality. The close of a finale without a hint of hysteria is both noble and grave. The Berlin Philharmonic play marvellously throughout, and the recording (for which no apologies whatsoever need be made) sounds exactly as we remember the original 78s. The *Tristan* excerpts are, understandably, equally marvellously played, and again the transfer loses nothing of the original sound.

Talich's legendary 1953 *Pathétique* was undoubtedly also a great performance. Its combination of spaciousness and concentration hold the listener consistently in its spell, and the first movement builds to a riveting climax. The *Allegro con grazia* is unusually rich in lyrical feeling and the Scherzo is unrushed, a true Scherzo, Talich tellingly holding back the apotheosis of the March until its final thrilling return. The finale is then powerfully moving, ending in a *pianissimo* of desolation. The recording has been cleaned up, although it is now a shade over-bright. The Wagner items are comparably richly spacious and gripping.

With **Daniele Gatti**, if the opening *Adagio* of the *Pathétique* seems rather staid, slow and very steady, a total transformation comes with the shattering *fortissimo* that opens the development section. From then on, through all four movements the performance is magnetic, with Gatti consistently conveying the white heat of Tchaikovsky's inspiration. The Harmonia Mundi recording, made at the Colosseum, Watford, offers the widest dynamic range and brings out the clarity of texture and of articulation that Gatti draws from his players. Gatti and the **RPO** also hold a trump card in their exceptionally generous coupling, a warmly persuasive reading of the *Serenade for Strings* which builds on the ripe resonance of the RPO string section, again with clear textures and articulation and a wide dynamic range.

This electrifying performance of the *Pathétique Symphony* on Biddulph, one of the fastest ever on disc, was **Ormandy's** first **Philadelphia** recording, begun in December of 1936 and completed the following month. So in the first movement Ormandy is more volatile than in his later recordings, tending to press on faster after setting a tempo. The result is very powerful and exciting, not at all sentimental. First-rate transfer.

Like **Mravinsky's** companion account of *Symphony 5* on Warner's Elatus label, the Russian conductor's approach to this repertoire has mellowed a little since his blazing DG recordings from the early 1960s, though this live 1982 account of the *Pathétique* is only marginally less emotionally tense and generates plenty of excitement. The audience is reasonably well behaved (although the coughs at the beginning of the second movement are a bit irritating), and the sound is generally very good, if a bit raucous in the climaxes. With the characteristic Leningrad brass, *Francesca da Rimini* (coming from the same concert as the *Pathétique*) sounds particularly Russian, and has white-hot emotional intensity. Considering its provenance, the sound is good, and one can put aside the imperfections of a live occasion listening to this immensely vivid and exciting music-making.

Ormandy's fine 1960 performance on Sony is a reading of impressive breadth, dignity and power, with no suggestion of routine in a single bar. The orchestra makes much of the first-movement climax and plays with considerable passion and impressive body of tone in both outer movements; yet there is an element of restraint in the finale which prevents any feeling of hysteria. In short, this is most satisfying, a performance to live with; the CD transfer, while brightly lit, avoids glare in the upper range. Ormandy's panache and gusto give the *Capriccio italien* plenty of life without driving too hard, and the dances are rhythmically infectious.

Rozhdestvensky's 1987 performance with the **LSO**, originally on Pickwick, now perceptively reissued by Regis, is generously coupled with a fine version of the comparatively little-known symphonic poem *The Storm*. His passionate reading of the *Symphony* fails to match the finest in precision of ensemble – the slow finale is warm rather than tense or tragic – but the sense of spontaneity is most compelling, and the digital recording is impressive still.

If the sound of **Monteux's** performance is not 'state of the art', it is still amazing for 1955; and it is well balanced, full in texture, with a decent amount of warmth for the strings. The performance, while not lacking in excitement, is essentially no-nonsense in approach, while in the 5/4 movement there is some lack of graciousness (especially with the increase in pace of the close). The brass come through vividly, and if their distinctive, rather French-sounding vibrato will not to be all tastes, the playing still has character. The Scherzo is crisply pointed; the finale is heart-felt and passionate.

Eschenbach's *Pathétique*, finely played and recorded as it is, is very far from a general recommendation. The reading is filtered through the conductor's more restrained sensibility, rather than closely reflecting the composer's own deeply moving darkness of feeling. The climax of the first movement, after a restrained second subject, certainly does not send shivers down the spine by its plangent intensity; instead it reflects the overall mood of the performance which is essentially elegiac. This is felt in the 5/4 movement too, and after an attractively spirited *molto vivace* (which is truly a scherzo) the symphony closes, not in abject despair, but in resigned melancholy. Even the following *Dumka*, which Eschenbach plays sensitively on the piano, misses the high spirits one might expect.

Variations on a Rococo Theme for Cello & Orchestra, Op. 33

⊶ 🌑 ******** EMI 5 56126-2. Chang, LSO, Rostropovich – BRUCH: *Kol Nidrei*; FAURÉ: *Elégie*; SAINT-SAËNS: *Cello Concerto 1* *******

⊶ Ⓜ ******** DG (ADD) 447 413-2. Rostropovich, BPO, Karajan – DVOŘÁK: *Cello Concerto* ******* 🌑

(***) Testament mono SBT 1310. Gendron, SRO, Ansermet – SCHUMANN: *Cello Concerto* etc. (***)

(M) **(*) Mercury SACD 475 6608. Starker, LSO, Dorati –
DVOŘÁK: *Cello Concerto*; BRUCH: *Kol Nidrei* **(*)

(B) **(*) Virgin 3 63287-2. Mørk, Oslo PO, Jansons – DVOŘÁK:
Cello Concerto **(*)

The phenomenally gifted 13-year-old Korean-born cellist
Han-Na Chang has the most ravishing tone and a wonderfully musical sense of line. **Rostropovich** as conductor sets
the scene with an affectionate elegance, and then Chang introduces Tchaikovsky's theme with disarming simplicity.
Andante grazioso, introduced very gently, is quite ethereal and
the finale has the expected dash, and the crispest articulation. The **LSO** are inspired by Chang to give a wonderfully
sensitive accompaniment, and the recording is in the
demonstration class.

Like Chang, **Rostropovich** uses the published score
rather than the original version which more accurately
reflects the composer's intentions. But this account, with
Karajan's glowing support, is so superbly structured in its
control of emotional light and shade that one is readily convinced that this is the work Tchaikovsky conceived. The
recording (made in the Jesus-Christus Kirche) is beautifully
balanced and is surely one of the most perfect examples of
DG's analogue techniques.

Although **Maurice Gendron** was rather overshadowed in
the 1950s and 1960s by Fournier and Tortelier, he was no less
eloquent an artist, who brought an aristocratic finesse and
tonal richness to everything he did. The virtuosity is effortless and his phrasing seamless; Gendron's artistry gives unalloyed pleasure. As always with this label, the transfer does
justice to the 1953 Decca recording.

Starker's relaxed, elegant performance may lack romantic urgency, but with **Dorati** accompanying sympathetically
it has a relaxed, ruminative quality which is endearing. It
never sounded more warmly persuasive than in this new
SACD remastering, which has quite transformed the recording, making it warmer and fuller, more flattering to the cello
timbre.

A fine performance from **Truls Mørk**, with plenty of energy and finesse, and the *Andante* of Variation 11 played with
an appealingly Slavonic, plaintive feeling. Very good recording too, but in sheer elegance and panache this is no match
for Rostropovich.

CHAMBER MUSIC

Piano Trio in A min., Op. 50

🎧 *** BIS CD 1302. Kempf Trio – RACHMANINOV: *Trio
élégiaque 1* ***

(N) *** Canary Classics CC05. Bronfman, Shaham, Mørk

(N) *** MDG 942 1512-6. Vienna Piano Trio – SMETANA: *Piano
Trio* ***

*** Ara. Z 6661. Golub–Kaplan–Carr Trio – SMETANA: *Piano
Trio* ***

(BB) **(*) Warner Apex 0927 48728-2. Amoyal, Lodeon, Rogé

(N) **(*) Sup. SU 3949-2. Smetana Piano Trio – DVOŘÁK:
Piano Trio 2 **(*)

(BB) **(*) Regis Alto ALC 1005. Tirimo, Sayevich, Veis –
SHOSTAKOVICH: *Piano Trio 2* **(*)

Freddy Kempf leads with great conviction, yet can pull back
whenever necessary; moreover he provides some dazzlingly
light-fingered playing during the kaleidoscopic variations
of the second movement, which are presented with sparkling
panache. The recording is very well balanced, although
under moments of passionate stress in the Tchaikovsky *trio*
it catches a touch of wiriness in the upper register of the violin. But the effect overall is convincingly realistic.

During 1908 three different new versions of
Tchaikovsky's masterly *Piano Trio* arrived within two months.
The Canary Classics recording is, dominated by the challenging playing of **Yerim Bronfman** and the performance is
in every way first class and the delightful *Variations* are given
kaleidoscopic variety. **Gil Shaham** and **Truls Mørk** are fully
in the picture. Yet the drawback to that disc was the absence
of any coupling. The alternative version from the **Vienna
Piano Trio** measures up extremely well against its competitor; moreover it is (like all chamber recordings from this
source) extremely well balanced. The pianist, **Stefan Mendl**
is able to lead the group, yet create a convincing partnership
throughout the almost concertante-style first movement.
The engaging second movement *Variations* open gently but
move spontaneously through Tchaikovsky's constantly varied invention, often with touching lyrical feeling.

The **Golub/Kaplan/Carr** account of the Smetana G minor
Piano Trio is well matched in the Tchaikovsky. The balance
places the listener rather too close to the players, but the
sound is perfectly pleasing and the performance refreshingly
unaffected. Nothing is overdriven, mechanized or attention-
seeking.

The Apex team give an eloquent performance which
finds **Pierre Amoyal** in impressive form. The same must be
said of **Pascal Rogé** whose account of the piano part is brilliant and sensitive. **Frédéric Lodeon** completes a fine team
and though the recording is a bit close, artistically these
dedicated French players give much satisfaction. A good
bargain.

The **Smetana** performance of the Tchaikovsky *Trio* is also
a fine one, rather more intimately balanced than its competitors and with its pianist, although well placed in the integrated overall sound picture, less dominant. The *Variations*
are given a strong forward pulse and plenty of character; certainly this Supraphon disc is very enjoyable throughout, but
not a first choice for the Tchaikovsky.

An excellent account from **Tirimo** and his colleagues,
recorded in Prague in 2005. The playing is full of life, with
the *Theme and Variations* strongly characterized. The recording is a bit too close, but vivid and truthful. Coupled with an
excellent version of the *Second* Shostakovich *Trio*, this inexpensive disc is excellent value.

(i) *Souvenir de Florence, Op. 70* (string sextet)

🎧 **** Hyp. CDA 66648. Raphael Ens. – ARENSKY: *String
Quartet in A min.* ***

🎧 **** Chan. 9878. ASMF Chamber Ens. – GLAZUNOV:
String Quintet ***

** Mer. CDE 84211. Arienski Ens. – ARENSKY: *String Quartet 2*
*** ; BORODIN: *Sextet movements* **

A first-rate performance from the **Raphael Ensemble**. They play with total unanimity of ensemble and richness of tone. Their coupling, the Arensky *Quartet with Two Cellos*, is magnificently played. The recording may be a snag for some collectors – it is all a bit too forward and we are very much in the front row – but there is no reason to withhold a third star given its artistry and authority.

From the **ASMF Chamber Ensemble**, a very sympathetic and well-recorded account which deserves a warm recommendation. Its coupling, which brings a Glazunov rarity, strengthens its claims.

A very good rather than a distinguished performance of Tchaikovsky's eloquent *Souvenir de Florence* on Meridian, very decently recorded. The strength of the issue lies in the interest of its coupling, an Arensky rarity, the *A minor Quartet*, from which the well-known *Variations on a Theme of Tchaikovsky* derive, and two Mendelssohnian movements from the Borodin *Sextet*.

String Quartet in B flat; String Quartets 1–3; (i) Souvenir de Florence

⊶ Ⓜ **** Warner Elatus 2564 61774-2 (2). Borodin Qt; (i) with Yurov, Milman

String Quartets 1–3; (i) Souvenir de Florence

*** Telarc CD 80685 (2). Ying Qt; (i) with Dunham & Katz

String Quartet Movement in B flat; String Quartets 1–3; 4 Early Pieces; (i) Souvenir de Florence

⊶ *** CRD CRD 3501 (1 & 2; *Movement*); CRD 3502 (3; *Early Pieces*; *Souvenir*). Endellion Qt; (i) with T. Boulton & R. Cohen

String Quartets 1 in D, Op. 11; 2 in F, Op. 22; 3 in E flat, Op. 30; Adagio molto for String Quartet & Harp; 5 Early Pieces for String Quartet; Souvenir de Florence: Adagio cantabile e con moto

ⓑⓑ **(*) Regis (ADD) RRC 2071 (2). Shostakovich Qt

String Quartets 1–3; (i) Souvenir de Florence, Op.70

Ⓑ **(*) Nim. NI 5711/2. Schubert Qt

The Elatus set, made in 1993 in the Berlin Teldec studios, is digital and the sound is a shade dry. It includes the early *B flat Movement* and is a superb, unassailable recommendation for a complete set.

The **Endellion Quartet** are completely at home in Tchaikovsky's special chamber-music idiom, and they give very persuasive and understanding performances of all this music. They are less vibrant, more intimate, than the Borodin or Brodsky Quartets, but their mellower approach brings its own rewards; their playing certainly does not lack vitality or spontaneity. But what makes this set especially desirable is the closing bonus of the four brief but characterful *Early Pieces*, and especially the gentle final *Andante molto*, which remains in the memory after the second disc has

faded into silence. Excellent recording: close, but full-bodied and real. The two CDs are available separately.

A fine new set of performances by the excellent **Ying Quartet**, who play with conviction and fine ensemble. Overall, these performances, if not quite as idiomatic as their Russian competitors, are consistently enjoyable, and the Telarc sound is very full and realistic.

The Nimbus set from the early 1990s has been issued as a two-for-the-price-of-one Double. The **Franz Schubert Quartet** are thoroughly sympathetic and produce smooth, beautifully balanced sound and good ensemble. Indeed, this is one of the best chamber-music recordings Nimbus have given us. All the same, the performances yield to the Borodin versions on Elatus made at about the same time.

These performances by the **Shostakovich Quartet**, which derive from Moscow Radio broadcasts in the 1970s, if not in the league of the Borodin or Brodsky Quartet, are value for money. The recordings sound a shade strident at the upper end of the spectrum, though this is easily tamed. Indeed, in the *Third Quartet* this is barely noticeable; the sound has warmth and presence. The *Adagio for String Quartet and Harp* is one of the few Tchaikovsky rarities that are not of real interest; but the early pieces, dating from the composer's student years at the St Petersburg Conservatory, are – though they are not masterpieces.

String Quartet 1 in D, Op. 11

⊶ ❁ *** Challenge Classics CC 72106. Brodsky Qt – BRITTEN: *String Quartet 1*; *Divertimenti* ***❁

⊶ Ⓜ *** Cal. 6202. Talich Qt – BORODIN: *Quartet 2* **(*)

(***) Testament mono SBT 1061. Hollywood Qt – GLAZUNOV: *5 Novelettes*; BORODIN: *String Quartet 2 in D* (***)

The **Brodsky Quartet** seem to find an affinity between the gently lyrical opening theme of Tchaikovsky's *D major Quartet* and the luminous magic at the beginning of the coupled Britten work in the same key; in both there is an elliptical reprise, but although Britten ends his movement hauntingly, Tchaikovsky characteristically provides a dashing coda. The Brodskys are completely at home in both works, and after a superb account of Tchaikovsky's opening movement, passionate yet full of dynamic contrast and delicately observed detail, they provide a ravishingly tender *Andante cantabile*. The performance has all the spontaneity of live music-making and the Brodskys are given a superb presence by the recording, made at The Maltings.

A glorious account of Tchaikovsky's best-loved quartet from the **Talich** group. They play the opening movement with an unassertive, lyrical feeling that is quite disarming, while the famous *Andante cantabile* has never sounded more beautiful on record, shaped with a combination of delicacy of feeling and warmth that is wholly persuasive. The Scherzo has plenty of verve, and the finale winningly balances the music's joyful vigour and its underlying hint of melancholy with a typical lightness of touch. The 1987 digital recording is beautifully balanced. Highly recommended.

The **Hollywood Quartet's** LP first appeared in 1953 and their fervent account has a persuasive eloquence that still puts one under its spell. The sound has been improved, and the addition of the Glazunov, which is new to the catalogue, enhances its value. The disc runs to one second short of 80 minutes, and the sleeve warns that some older CD players may have difficulty in tracking it.

String Quartet 1 in D; 2 in F, Op. 22

(BB) **(*) Naxos 8.550847. New Haydn Qt

Very well-played accounts of both *Quartets* from the **New Haydn Quartet**, which, taken on their own merits, have much to recommend them – warmth, intelligence and some finesse. In the slow movement of the *D major* the group has real eloquence, and in the finale it scores by observing the exposition repeat. However, it is not in the same league as the Brodsky (see above), which remains a strong first choice.

String Quartets 2 in F, Op. 22; 3 in E flat min., Op. 30.

⌐ **** Brodsky Records BRD 3500. Brodsky Qt

The **Brodsky Quartet** have already given us a superb account of Tchaikovsky's *First Quartet* – see above. Now they have followed up on their own label with an equally memorable coupling of the two remaining works. They fully understand and respond to the passionate ebb and flow of this music, and these are wonderfully ardent and compelling performances. Indeed, the first movement of the *E flat Quartet* has an enormous surge of lyrical impetus, and the *Andante funèbre* has comparable depth of intensity. The recording has great immediacy, which suits the performances.

PIANO DUET

Nutcracker; Sleeping Beauty; Swan Lake: Suites (arr. for 4 hands)

(BB) *** Naxos 8.570418. Aurora Duo

Considering how much it depends on orchestral colour, it is a astonishing how well Tchaikovsky's ballet music comes off in piano-duet form, if the players are sympathetic and stylish. And the members of the **Aurora Duo** (**Julia Severus** and **Alina Luschtschizkaja**) most certainly are both. In the *Sleeping Beauty* the cat duet is deliciously pictorialized and the gorgeous *Panorama* is beautifully poised over its gently rocking bass. The baby swans dance very daintily, and in the *Nutcracker* the duo's crisp articulation in the *Miniature Overture*, *Marche* and *Chinese Dance* is perfectly precise, while the *Sugar Plum Fairy* enters to a timbre very like a celeste. Very good, clear recording too. Most enjoyable.

PIANO MUSIC

Album for the Young, Op. 39

⌐ (BB) *** Naxos 8.550885. Biret – DEBUSSY: *Children's Corner Suite*; SCHUMANN: *Kinderszenen* ***

Album for the Young, Op. 39: (i) original piano version; (ii) trans. for string quartet by Dubinsky

*** Chan. 8365. (i) Edlina; (ii) augmented Borodin Trio

These 24 pieces are all miniatures, but they have great

charm; their invention is often memorable, with quotations from Russian folksongs and one French, plus a brief reminder of *Swan Lake*. Here they are presented twice, in their original piano versions, sympathetically played by **Luba Edlina**, and in effective string quartet transcriptions arranged by her husband, Rostislav Dubinsky. The **Borodin** group play them with both affection and finesse. The CD has plenty of presence.

Idil Biret's has the full measure of Tchaikovsky's two dozen vignettes and plays them all with affection and charm. They range from miniature portraits of *Maman*, *Dolly*, a *Lark* and even a witch (*Baba-Yaga*) to a *Toy Soldier's March* and an *Organ-grinder's Song*, as well as folksy pieces from Italy, France and Germany and Russia's own *Kamarinskaya*. The recording cannot be faulted.

Capriccioso in B flat, Op. 19/5; Chanson triste, Op. 40/2; L'Espiègle, Op. 72/12; Humoresque in G, Op. 10/2; Méditation, Op. 72/5; Menuetto-scherzoso, Op. 51/3; Nocturne in F, Op. 10/1; Rêverie du soir, Op. 19/1; Romances: in F min., Op. 5; in F, Op. 51/5; The Seasons: May (White Nights), June (Barcarolle), November (Troika), January (By the fireplace); Un poco di Chopin, Op. 72/15; Valse de salon, Op. 51/2; Waltz in A flat, Op. 40/8; Waltz-scherzo in A min., Op. 7

⌐ (BB) **** Regis (ADD) RRC 1093. Richter

It is good to hear **Richter** (recorded in 1983 by Ariola-Eurodisc) given first-class, modern sound and on top technical form, showing that he had lost none of his flair. These miniatures are invested with enormous character in playing of consistent poetry; there is never a whiff of the salon. They are all captivating, and the bolder *Menuetto-scherzoso* also shows Tchaikovsky at his most attractively inventive. With its very truthful sound-picture, this is a first recommendation for anyone wanting a single CD of Tchaikovsky's piano music.

The Seasons, Op. 37b; 6 Pieces, Op. 21; Sleeping Beauty (excerpts; arr. Pletnev)

⌐ ❀ (BB) *** Virgin 2x1 4 82055-2 (2). Pletnev – MUSSORGSKY: *Pictures at an Exhibition* ***❀

The Seasons; Aveu passioné; Berceuse, Op. 72/2; Méditation, Op. 72/5; Polka peu dansante, Op. 51/2; Tendres reproches, Op. 72/3

*** Decca 466 562-2. Ashkenazy

The Seasons; Piano Sonata in C sharp min., Op.80

(N) (BB) *** Naxos 8.570787. Ilya Rachkovsky

Tchaikovsky's 12 *Seasons* (they would have been better called 'Months') were written to a regular deadline for publication in a St Petersburg music magazine, *Nuvellist*. Like the Opus 72 *Pieces*, above, and the touching *Morceaux*, Op. 21, **Pletnev** reveals depths that are hidden to most interpreters and he grips one from first note to last. Then, in the present transcription, he gives us about 30 minutes of *The Sleeping Beauty* in a dazzling performance. In sheer clarity of articulation and virtuosity this is pretty remarkable – also in poetry and depth of feeling. An altogether outstanding reissue, very well recorded, and in every way a tour de force.

Vladimir Ashkenazy gives a poised and finely prepared account of *The Seasons* which is very well recorded. At the same time it does not match Pletnev in terms of poetic insight or tenderness. The charming numbers from the *Eighteen Pieces*, Op. 72, are beautifully done too.

The performances by **Ilya Rachkovsky** are sensitive and well recorded. If they are not quite on the exulted level of Ashkenazy and Pletnev, they are thoroughly musical, and spontaneous in feeling. The *Sonata* was a student work and is rather Schumanesque. But Tchaikovsky thought well of the Scherzo and used it again later in his *Winter Daydreams Symphony*.

VOCAL MUSIC

4 Duets: *Dawn; Evening; In the Garden by the River; Tears*

🎵– Ⓑ *** BBC (ADD) BBCB 8001-2. Harper, Baker, Britten – BRAHMS: *Liebeslieder Waltzes, Op. 52*; ROSSINI: *Soirées musicales* ***

Heather Harper and **Janet Baker**, recorded at the Aldeburgh Festival in 1971, make a dream duet partnership in these tenderly sentimental duets, sung in English. **Britten's** inspired accompaniment adds poetry to Tchaikovsky's distinctive piano writing. No texts are given, but James Bowman writes movingly of such 'family music-making' at Aldeburgh.

Liturgy of St John Chrysostom, Op. 41

🅱🅱 **(*) Naxos Dig 8.553854.2. Ovdiy, Mezhulin, Kiev Chamber Ch., Hobdych

Liturgy of St John Chrysostom; Anthem: An angel crying; 9 Sacred Pieces (for unaccompanied chorus)

🎵– **** Hyp. CDA 66948. Corydon Singers, Best

The *a cappella Liturgy of St John Chrysostom*, which dates from 1878, was not commissioned but written simply to reflect Tchaikovsky's devotion to the Russian Orthodox Church. **Best** and the **Corydon Singers** in their refined, dedicated performances bring out the freshness and energy in this inspired music, with basses cleanly focused down to subterranean depths, echoing authentic Russian examples. The disc also contains the sequence of *9 Sacred Choruses* which Tchaikovsky wrote five or six years after the *Liturgy*, even simpler in style, but showing his ready melodic gift, and a separate piece, a dramatic Easter Day anthem, *An angel crying*, which is a miniature masterpiece. Warm, clear sound.

In contrast with the rival version of this masterpiece of Russian Orthodox music, which offer substantial couplings, the Naxos issue presents a liturgical performance complete with the priests' solos, almost 70 minutes long. Not all collectors will want such a format for repeated listening, but for those who prefer such an authentic course, this Naxos disc can be warmly recommended, strongly and idiomatically performed with fine solos, and atmospherically recorded in a church in Kiev.

The Snow Maiden, Op. 12 (complete incidental music)

🎵– **** Chan. 9324. Mishura-Lekhman, Girshko, Michigan University Ch. Soc., Detroit SO, Järvi

Ⓜ *** Chant du Monde RUS 788090. Erasova, Arkipov, Vassiliev, Sveshnikov Russian State Ch., Bolshoi Theatre O, Chistiakov

🅱🅱 **(*) Naxos 8.553856. Okolysheva, Mishenkin, Moscow Capella, Moscow SO, Golovschin

Ostrovsky's play *The Snow Maiden*, based on a Russian folk-tale, prompted Tchaikovsky to compose incidental music, a cherishable rarity. Much of it is vintage material, very delightful, bringing reminders of *Eugene Onegin* in the peasant choruses and some of the folk-based songs, and of the later Tchaikovskian world of *The Nutcracker* in some of the dances. He himself thought so well of the music that he wanted to develop it into an opera, but was frustrated when Rimsky-Korsakov wrote one first. The consistent freshness and charm of invention comes out in **Järvi's** reading of the 19 numbers, lasting just under 80 minutes. It makes a delightful, undemanding cantata, very well played and sung, and is a clear first choice.

Chistiakov's fine 1994 performance, now reissued on Chant du Monde's mid-priced Russian label, is in every way recommendable at mid-price. The three excellent soloists are characterfully Slavonic, rather too forwardly balanced but well caught by the recording, and the fine singing of the chorus is given both sonority and plenty of bite. The orchestral playing is highly persuasive in a pleasingly atmospheric acoustic.

Tchaikovsky's engaging score also inspires **Golovschin** and his **Moscow** forces to a warmly idiomatic performance on Naxos, richly and colourfully recorded, if without quite the same degree of vividness. This may not match the Chant du Monde version in vitality, which at generally faster speeds sparkles more and offers crisper ensemble, but it is similarly persuasive. The conductor's affection is obvious. There are only two soloists to share the vocal music, but they are convincingly Slavonic and they are balanced slightly less forwardly. This Naxos disc is well worth its more modest cost.

Songs

Songs: *Amid the noise of the ball; Behind the window; The canary; Cradle song; The cuckoo; Does the day reign?; Do not believe; The fearful minute; If only I had known; It was in the early spring; Last night; Lullaby in a storm; The nightingale; None but the lonely heart; Not a word, O my friend; Serenade; Spring; To forget so soon; Was I not a little blade of grass?; Why?; Why did I dream of you?*

🎵– *** Hyp. Helios CDH 55331. Rodgers, Vignoles

The warmly distinctive timbre of **Joan Rodgers's** lovely soprano has been heard mainly in opera but she is equally compelling in this glowing disc of songs. Her fluency with

Russian texts as well as the golden colourings of her voice make this wide-ranging collection a delight from first to last. Though the voice is not quite at its richest in the most celebrated song of all, *None but the lonely heart*, the singer's subtle varying of mood and tone completely refutes the idea that Tchaikovsky as a song-composer was limited. One of the finest discs issued to mark the Tchaikovsky centenary in 1993.

OPERA

Eugene Onegin (complete; DVD versions)

🎦 **** Warner **DVD** 0630-14014-2. Prokina, Drabowicz, Thompson, Winter, Minton, Filatova, Olsen, LPO, A. Davis (Dir: Graham Vick; V/D: Humphrey Burton)

🎦 *** Decca **DVD** 071 124-9. Kubiak, Weikl, Burrows, Reynolds, Ghiaurov, Hamari, Hartle, Sénéchal, van Allan, Mason, John Alldis Ch., ROHCG O, Solti (V/Dir: Petr Weigl)

*** Decca **DVD** 074 3248 (2). Fleming, Hvorostovsky, Zaremba, Vargas, Volkova, Shevchenko, Met. Op. Ch., Ballet & O, Gergiev (V/D: Brian Large)

Ⓝ **(*) DG **DVD** 073 4434. Samuil, Mattei, Kaiser, Gubenova, Furlanello, Konzertvereinigung V. State Opera Ch., VPO, Barenboim (Stage Director: Andrea Breth; V/D Brian Large)

We are well served on both DVD and CD in this opera, but this recording of Graham Vick's acclaimed Glyndebourne production from 1994 is a welcome addition. Not only is the production convincing but the cast is, too. But it is **Elena Prokina's** magnificent portrayal of Tatiana that makes this so desirable. The video direction is admirably discreet, with no intrusive camerawork and with the eye being directed where one feels it ought to be. Among the Onegins now before the public, this ranks high.

In the DVD of **Solti's** the brilliant Czech director **Petr Weigl** has in his 1988 film illustrated the familiar Decca audio recording, conducted by Solti, with the most evocative visual realization of the narrative. Actors mime to the words in settings as nearly as possible those of the original Pushkin story, whether in the Russian countryside or in St Petersburg. The result is all the more moving, when the agonizing of the young Tatiana or of the disillusioned Onegin is presented by actors who so accurately look the part, as do all the authentically costumed cast. The contrast between the country ball of Act II with the grand ball of Act III set in a St Petersburg palace is brought out in a way that could never be achieved on stage, and the chill of the duel scene is all the more involving when the scene is of genuine snow in a genuine forest. Musically, the oddity is that the Prelude and first scene (the Tatiana–Olga duet) are presented in audio recording only, for Weigl starts his film most atmospherically with the peasants' chorus which opens the second scene of Act I, with the reapers observed from afar wending their way in the mist down a winding country path.

But because the action is filmed in various locations, including the open air, with actors miming the singers, the Kingsway Hall acoustic in which Decca recorded the original in the mid-1970s does not quite match up with what we see, and though the direction and the sets are always imaginative, the free-ranging camera does not (and cannot) match the evidence of the ear, so that the acoustic disparity is obvious.

The cast are handsome and mime for the most part successfully. But some collectors, like R.L., may be unable to sustain the suspension of disbelief, and will find the result here ultimately unconvincing. R.L. feels that here is a case where the collector is better served by the original CD set, which sounds splendid.

But both E.G. and I.M. find the DVD totally compelling and convincing, even though there are cuts in the music, and are only too delighted that the recording was made in such an attractive acoustic ambience, with the disparity soon forgotten. With the surtitles so easy to follow, the viewer/listener can be totally caught up in the action and at the same time enjoy not only the glorious singing, but also the inspired orchestral detail of Solti's accompaniment through which Tchaikovsky is conveying the emotions of the characters as one watches them. The sound itself is superb. So while R.L. has his doubts, for E.G. and I.M. this set is a triumph.

Musically, the Decca Metropolitan Opera *Eugene Onegin* is superb, with the two key roles, Tatiana (**Renée Fleming**) and Onegin (**Dmitri Hvorostovsky**), singing and acting magnetically, and **Valery Gergiev** (who is curious to watch, with his fluttering hand movements) phrasing Tchaikovsky's wonderful score with the warmest and most touching, lyrical and dramatic support for the singers. The famous letter scene is unforgettable and the dialogue/duet at the opening of Act I, between Madame Larina (**Svetlana Volkova**) and the old nurse, Filipyevna (**Larisa Shevchenko**), is very touching – about contented habit replacing happiness in old age. **Ramón Vargas** is an engagingly Schubertian Lensky, yet he sings ardently, and Olga (**Elena Zaremba**) makes a convincing partner, although her voice is not caught flatteringly by the microphones. But Fleming's certainly is, glorious throughout, and Hvorostovsky matches her, a convincingly strong and dignified characterization. **Sergei Aleksashkin's** Prince Gremin is excellent too, and he has one of the opera's other great hits.

The problem lies in the production. A large, bare stage is used, covered with leaves in Act I. It is too big and dwarfs the characters, and the total lack of background colour quite spoils the great waltz scene, although the bareness suits the duel sequence. Then, unbelievably, Onegin's seconds help him change clothes for the final Act during the *Polonaise*, which is not danced, and the scene at Gremin's palace immediately follows, even though it is supposed to be some years later. Presentation apart, this is a magnificent performance, but – except in the first Act – better heard than seen. The bonuses include a rehearsal sequence and 'Backstage at the Met.' with Beverly Sills.

It is a pity that so many modern stage directors are not willing to mount an opera following the composer's intentions. This new 2007 Salzburg Festival production offers consistently splendid singing, especially **Anna Samuil's** delightful Tatiana, **Peter Mattei's** ardent Onegin and **Ferrucio Furlanetto's** resonant Prince Gremin. But alas the production is moved forward to Russia of the 1980s and the costumes are modern. In spite of that, the Lensky/Onegin duel is fought with eighteenth-century pistols! And the famous *Polonaise* is not used as a dance. What would Tchaikovsky have thought of that? However such is the quality of the music and indeed **Barenboim's** direction, that after a while, reason is suspended, and one simply gets caught up in this extraordinary masterpiece, and forgets one's quibbles about the directorial eccentricities.

Eugene Onegin (complete; CD versions)

⊕—, ******** Decca (ADD) 417 413-2 (2). Kubiak, Weikl, Burrows, Reynolds, Ghiaurov, Hamari, Sénéchal, Alldis Ch., ROHCG O, Solti

**(*) DG 423 959-2 (2). Freni, Allen, von Otter, Shicoff, Burchuladze, Sénéchal, Leipzig R. Ch., Dresden State O, Levine

(BB) **(***)** Naxos mono 8.110216/17 (2). Nortsov, Kruglikova, Antonova, Kozlovsky, Mikhailov, Bolshoi Ch. & O, Melik-Pashaev, Orlov

Solti, characteristically crisp in attack, has plainly warmed to the score of Tchaikovsky's colourful opera, allowing his singers full rein in rallentando and rubato to a degree one might not have expected of him. The Tatiana of **Teresa Kubiak** is most moving – rather mature-sounding for the *ingénue* of Act I, but with her golden, vibrant voice rising most impressively to the final confrontation of Act III. The Onegin of **Bernd Weikl** may have too little variety of tone, but again this is firm singing that yet has authentic Slavonic tinges. The rest of the cast is excellent, with **Stuart Burrows** as Lensky giving one of his finest performances on record yet. Here, for the first time, the full range of expression in this most atmospheric of operas is superbly caught, with the Decca CDs vividly capturing every subtlety – including the wonderful off-stage effects.

The DG CD version brings a magnificent Onegin in **Thomas Allen**, the most satisfying account of the title-role yet recorded. It is matched by the Tatiana of **Mirella Freni**, even at a late stage in her career readily conveying girlish freshness in her voice. The other parts are also strongly taken. The tautened-nerves quality in the character of Lensky comes out vividly in the portrayal by **Neil Shicoff**, and **Anne Sofie von Otter** with her firm, clear mezzo believably makes Olga a younger sister, not too mature a character. **Paata Burchuladze** is a satisfyingly resonant Gremin and **Michel Sénéchal**, as on the Solti set, is an incomparable Monsieur Triquet. What welds all these fine components into a rich and exciting whole is the conducting of **James Levine**. The **Leipzig Radio Choir** sings superbly as well. The snag is that the DG recording is dry and studio-bound, with sound close and congested enough to undermine the bloom on both voices and instruments. In every way the more spacious acoustic in the Solti set is preferable.

Recorded in Moscow in 1937 on 40 short-playing 78 r.p.m. discs, this historic version of *Eugene Onegin* on Naxos was the first complete recording of the opera ever made, and it is remarkable not just for the idiomatic warmth of the conducting – with **Alexander Orlov** replacing **Alexander Melik-Pashaev** for some passages – but for the fine singing of the principals, with not a Slavonic wobbler among them. **Panteleimon Nortsov** in the title role sings with a firmness and clarity that is most moving, his tone rather darker than usual in this role. **Elena Kruglikova** is equally moving as Tatiana, even though the voice, generally warm and clear, acquires an edginess when under pressure at the top. **Elizaveta Antonova** sings with rich, velvet tone as Olga, and though **Ivan Kozlovsky** as Lensky has the nasal twang that is typical of many Russian tenors, his firmly focused expressiveness is equally compelling. The transfers of Ward Marston are astonishingly fine, firm and full bodied.

The Maid of Orleans (complete; DVD version)

**(*) Warner DVD 4509-94191-2. Rautio, Kulko, Gavrilova, Krutikov, Redkin, Nikolsky, Bolshoi Theatre Ch. & O, Lazarev (Dir: Boris Pokrovsky; V/D: Brian Large)

Tchaikovsky embarked on his own adaptation of Zhukovsky's translation of Schiller's *Jungfrau von Orleans* immediately after *Eugene Onegin*, with the intention of composing a score that would succeed on the Paris stage. Hence the crowd effects, coronation scene, and so on. Not only Meyerbeer but Gounod, whose scores he had been studying, were his models. The exception is Joan herself, where Tchaikovsky carried over identification with his heroine from *Onegin*. It is her music, and that of her beloved but ill-fated Lionel, that gives us the best music. And it is these roles that are the most memorable in this **Bolshoi** performance, recorded in 1993 without an audience present. This set is worth having for the sake of **Nina Rautio's** superb Joan – beautifully rounded in tone and finely shaped phrasing, and with excellent acting. The staging is somewhat stiff and traditional, and the orchestral response decent rather than distinguished. All the same, although this is not top-drawer Tchaikovsky it is well worth seeing, and there is after all Joan's narrative in Act II and other set pieces that are worthy of the master.

Mazeppa (complete; DVD version)

⊕—, ******** Ph. DVD 074 1949. Putilin, Loskutova, Alexashkin, Dyadkova, Lutsiuk, Kirov Op. Ch. & O, Gergiev

This performance was recorded live from performances at the Maryinsky Theatre, St Petersburg. The production is in the best spirit of the Maryinsky, sumptuous to look at and full of period atmosphere. No dustbins in the Gorbals, no T-shirts or pairs of holed jeans in sight but a faithful attempt to match what the composer might have expected to see on stage. **Putilin** scores in terms of range and is the more credible a tyrant. **Irina Loskutova's** Maria is less memorable in terms of tonal lustre or beauty of line, but she is more dramatically convincing. No complaints about the remainder of the cast and the wonderful, full-throated singing of the chorus and the magnificence of the **Kirov Orchestra** under **Gergiev**. This is a very distinguished production and a hugely enjoyable evening.

The Queen of Spades (Pique Dame) (complete; DVD versions)

**** Ph. **DVD** 070 434-9. Grigorian, Gulegina, Leiferkus, Gergalov, Filatova, Borodina, Kirov Op. Ch. & O, Gergiev (Producer: Temirkanov; V/D: Brian Large)

(*) Arthaus **DVD 100 272-2. Marusin, Gustafson, Leiferkus, Khartinov, Palmer, Todorovich, Glyndebourne Fest. Ch., LPO, A. Davis (Producer: Vick; V/D: Peter Maniura)

Pushkin's dark story of a gambler's growing obsession with discovering the secret that will bring him riches is taut and concentrated. It unfolds with a gripping psychological intensity, all the more powerful for its understatement. Though modest, Tchaikovsky's libretto differs in many respects from Pushkin's story.

Dating from 1992, the Philips DVD, with the conductor, **Valery Gergiev**, looking very young, is a live recording of the **Kirov Company's** grandly traditional production. It is handsome to look at and very well staged, a joy to watch as well as listen to. **Yuri Temirkanov** (Gergiev's predecessor at the Kirov) produces and does not lose sight of the rococo component in this wonderful opera. Yet it is a straightforward and clean-cut presentation, deftly using massive choruses to match the opulent costumes and scenery, and nearly all the cast is first-rate. Incidentally, this cast differs from the CDs, with Irina Arkhipova's Countess being replaced by **Ludmila Filatova** and Nikolai Putilin giving way to **Leiferkus** as Tomsky, who appeared in the Ozawa set on RCA and also in the Glyndebourne production reviewed below.

Gegam Grigorian's Herman makes an unromantic figure, a predator rather than an ardent lover. He is a little stiff to start with and rarely sings below *forte*, but he improves as the opera unfolds and his performance acquires intensity, the characterization deepens, and he sings powerfully and cleanly. **Maria Gulegina** is superb as the heroine, Lisa, impressively dramatic and vocally powerful. The others are first-rate with the sad exception of **Ludmila Filatova** as the Countess, with a voice that is too thin and tremulous even to be acceptable in that aged role. This shortcoming is serious in her big scenes, which should be the climax of the whole drama, though she is certainly affecting, and makes up for it in vocal characterization.

Leiferkus is the soul of elegance, both vocally and as an actor. Nor should **Olga Borodina's** outstanding Pauline go unmentioned. Above all the hero is Gergiev himself who paces this marvellous score with depth and passion, and **Brian Large's** visual direction is superb. The eyes are directed to where the action and sound naturally dictate. The video recording was made after the CD and without the audience.

After the Gergiev–Temirkanov DVD, **Graham Vick's Glyndebourne** production is a distinctly lesser pleasure, albeit a pleasure nonetheless. The smaller stage (this was recorded in 1992 before the renovation) naturally imposes constraints, and the set, a slanted black box whose walls are daubed with paint, is a self-imposed limitation. **Yuri Masurin's** Herman is if anything more impressive than Grigorian's; he is the part from beginning to end. **Nancy**

Gustafson is an expressive Lisa, who conveys her bewilderment and anguish with much artistry and the cast in general is first-rate. **Felicity Palmer's** Countess is particularly fine. **Andrew Davis** holds all the threads together magnificently and gets an impressive response from his singers and the **LPO**. Gergiev perhaps gets the greater sweep and depth of tone and has of course the most sumptuous and authentic staging.

The Queen of Spades (Pique Dame) (complete; CD versions)

**** Ph. 438 141-2 (3). Grigorian, Putilin, Chernov, Solodovnikov, Arkhipova, Gulegina, Borodina, Kirov Op. Ch. & O, Gergiev

(M) *** DG (ADD) 463 679-2 (3). Gougaloff, Vishnevskaya, Resnik, Schwarz, Weikl, Petkov, Popp, Tchaikovsky Ch. & O Nat. de France, Rostropovich

In the CD set **Gergiev** and his talented team from the **Kirov Opera** in St Petersburg have also produced a winner. The very opening, refined and purposeful, sets the pattern, with Gergiev controlling this episodic work with fine concern for atmosphere and dramatic impact, unafraid of extreme speeds and telling pauses. Though the engineers fail to give a supernatural aura to the voice of the Countess when she returns as a ghost, the recorded sound is consistently warm and clear. It is good to have the veteran **Irina Arkhipova** singing powerfully and bitingly in that key role, while the other international star, **Olga Borodina**, is unforgettable as Pauline, singing gloriously with keen temperament. Otherwise Gergiev's chosen team offers characterful Slavonic voices that are yet well focused and unstrained, specially important with the tenor hero, Herman, here dashingly sung by **Gegam Grigorian**. As the heroine, Lisa, **Maria Gulegina** sings with warm tone and well-controlled vibrato, slightly edgy under pressure.

This DG version is among the finest of the opera sets conducted by **Mstislav Rostropovich** and now emerges at mid-price in DG's series of vintage 'Originals'. With a strong cast which – with a stiffening of non-Russian stars – avoids the penalties of Slavonic wobblers, it is even a contender for first choice against Gergiev's Philips version with the Kirov Opera. In the mid-1970s **Galina Vishnevskaya** was still at her peak, here proving a strong and vibrant Lisa, not youngsounding but with plenty of temperament. The firm velvet tones of **Hanna Schwarz's** mezzo as her sister, Pauline, provide a fine contrast. Schwarz is also well-matched in the duet which is the high point of the Act II *Intermezzo*, with **Lucia Popp** as a starry soprano partner, a charming pastiche sequence. **Peter Gougaloff** is a characterful Herman, the key figure in this story based on Pushkin. His very Russian tenor lacks beauty, but it is firm and full toned, with words expressively brought out. As the Countess **Regina Resnik** gives an aptly over-the-top performance, biting and incisive, not only in her death scene but in the Countess's ghostly reappearance, atmospherically presented using an echo chamber. The rest of the large cast assembled in Paris includes such leading singers in incidental roles as **Bernd Weikl** and **Dimiter Petkov**.

Iolanta (complete)

🎞—**** Ph. 442 796-2 (2). Gorchakova, Alexashkin, Hvorostovsky, Grigorian, Kirov Op. Ch. & O, Gergiev

Gergiev and his outstanding Kirov team give a warm, id-iomatic reading of Tchaikovsky's charming fairy-tale opera of the blind princess. Bringing out the atmospheric beauty of the score, it completely outshines the deleted Rostropovich version on Erato. **Galina Gorchakova** gives the most moving portrait of the heroine, tender and vul-nerable, with words delicately touched in. As Vaudémont, the knight who falls in love with her, **Gegam Grigorian** sings with rather tight, very Russian tenor-tone, not always pleasing but with a fine feeling for the idiom and a natural ease in high tessitura. **Dmitri Hvorostovsky** sings nobly and heroically as Robert, his more vigorous friend and rival, while **Sergei Alexashkin** sings with dark, grainy – again very Russian – tone as King René, Iolanta's father. Above all, the exchanges between characters consistently convey the feeling of stage-experience. The recording, not ideally clear but well balanced, was made in the theatre but under studio conditions.

OPERA BALLET MUSIC

Opera Ballet music from: *Cherevichki; Eugene Onegin; The Maid of Orléans; Oprichnik; The Sorceress*

*** Australian Ph. Eloquence (ADD) 442 8933. ROHCG O, C. Davis

This is a supremely engaging collection of (in the main) rare Tchaikovsky dances, drawn from his operas, revealing no new masterpieces but again showing the composer's vigor-ous melodic resourcefulness and his brilliant use of orches-tral palette. The opening items from *Eugene Onegin* tend to overshadow what follows in their tuneful inspiration, espe-cially when they are played with such brio and commitment; but there are no disappointments in the rest of the pro-gramme. The lively, characterful playing from the **Royal Opera House, Covent Garden, Orchestra**, directed by **Sir Colin Davis**, is matched by lavishly sumptuous analogue sound.

TCHEREPNIN, Alexander
(1899–1977)

Piano Concertos 2, Op. 26; 4 (Fantaisie), Op. 78; Magna mater, Op. 41; Symphonic Prayer, Op. 93

*** BIS CD 1247. Ogawa, Singapore SO, Lan Shui

The *Piano Concerto 2* is 'European' in style, while the *Fourth Concerto*, written shortly before he emigrated to the USA, is full of Chinese influence. Neither *Concerto* is new to the cat-alogue but the present versions supersede their predeces-sors. Eminently serviceable recording.

Piano Concertos 2, Op. 26; 4 (Fantaisie), Op. 78; 6, Op. 99

🎞—(BB) *** Regis RRC 9110. McLachlan, Chetham's SO, Clayton

A most attractive disc, with brilliant playing from **Murray McLachlan** in all three works, while the young orchestra is highly responsive. The *Fourth Concerto* is exotically pro-grammatic (a bit like a Chinese opera). In McLachlan's hands the piano writing glitters and the Eastern influence is in no doubt, while the orchestral woodwind playing en-sures that the finale is charmingly pentatonic. The *Sixth Concerto* was written many years later, in 1965, and is more Prokofievian, with the opening movement bringing a long, unstoppable toccata before the lyrical material enters. The *Andantino* is simpler but still exotic, and soon leads to more brilliant playing from the soloist; while the finale, opening with the bass drum, brings greater weight, with a curious main theme, and later powerfully quoting the Russian folksong *Do not flood, my quiet Don*. The **Chetham's Orchestra** plays throughout with remarkably spontaneous brilliance, the players obviously enjoying themselves. Excellent recording, too.

(i) *Piano Concerto 5, Op. 96; Symphonies 1 in E, Op. 42; 2 in E flat, Op. 77*

*** BIS CD 1017. Singapore SO, Shui; (i) with Ogawa

(i) *Piano Concerto 6, Op. 99; Symphonies 3 in F sharp, Op. 83; 4 in E , Op. 91*

*** BIS CD 1018. Singapore SO, Shui; (i) with Ogawa

The *First Symphony* of 1927 caused a stir, not so much on ac-count of its radical musical language as the fact that its Scherzo was written for percussion only. It is inventive and stimulating and full of personality. The *Second Symphony* did not follow until the end of the 1939–45 war, and two succes-sors followed in the 1950s: the *Third* in 1952, and the *Fourth*, commissioned by Charles Munch and the Boston Symphony Orchestra, in 1958–9.

It is with the *Fourth* that the newcomer to Tcherepnin's music should start. Its invention is wonderfully alert and fresh, and the control of pace masterly. It is neoclassical in feeling with a great sense of wit and style. The two *Piano Concertos* are from the 1960s and are elegantly played by **Noriko Ogawa**. The **Singapore Orchestra** has greatly im-proved since its early Marco Polo records under Choo Hoey, and the Chinese conductor **Lan Shui** gets generally good re-sults from them.

Symphony 4; Romantic Overture, Op. 67; Russian Dances, Op. 50; Suite for Orchestra, Op. 87

🎞—**(*) Marco 8.223380. Czech-Slovak State PO (Košice), Yip

The *Fourth Symphony* is among Tcherepnin's finest works. The *Suite*, Op. 67, is less individual and in places recalls the Stravinsky of *Petrushka* and *Le Chant du rossignol*. Like the much earlier *Russian Dances*, it is uneven in quality but far from unattractive. The *Romantic Overture* was composed in wartime Paris. Generally good performances, decently recorded too under the young Chinese conductor **Wing-Sie Yip**, who draws a lively response from her players.

TCHEREPNIN, Nikolai
(1873–1945)

Narcisse et Echo, Op. 40

☙ *** Chan. 9670. Hague Chamber Ch., & Residentie O, Rozhdestvensky

This endearing and atmospheric choral ballet *Narcisse et Echo* for much of the time sounds more French than Russian, with fascinating anticipations of *Daphnis*, not least in obbligato choral passages. Other sections mirror what the young Stravinsky was writing, but toned down. There also is a lot of Rimsky-Korsakov in it, and if you respond to that Russian master as well as Scriabin and Ravel, you will like this. It is somewhat static and in the last part of the ballet Narcissus is simply absorbed in gazing at his own reflection. However, though it is emphatically not great music, there is much that enchants. **Rozhdestvensky** is the ideal advocate, helped by ripe Chandos sound.

Le Pavillon d'Armide (ballet; complete)

**(*) Marco 8.223779. Moscow SO, Shek

Le Pavillon d'Armide was the ballet with which Diaghilev opened his first *Ballets russes* season introducing Nijinsky. Its invention is fluent, owing much to Tcherepnin's teacher Rimsky-Korsakov and to Glazunov and Tchaikovsky. It runs to well over an hour and the inspiration is uneven. At its best, though, it has real charm, and the scoring is always full of colour. It is very well recorded.

TELEMANN, Georg (1681–1767)

Concertos: for 2 Chalumeaux in D min.; for Flute in D; for 3 Oboes, 3 Violins in B flat; for Recorder & Flute in E min.; for Trumpet in D; for Trumpet & Violin in D

☙ Ⓜ **** DG 419 633-2. Soloists, Col. Mus. Ant., Goebel

As **Reinhard Goebel** points out, Telemann 'displayed immense audacity in the imaginative and ingenious mixing of the colours from the palette of the baroque orchestra', and these are heard to excellent effect here. Those who know the vital *B flat Concerto* for three oboes and violins from earlier versions, will find the *Allegro* very fast indeed and the slow movement quite thought-provoking. The chalumeau is the precursor of the clarinet, and the concerto for two chalumeaux recorded here is full of unexpected delights. Marvellously alive and accomplished playing, even if one occasionally tires of the bulges and nudges on the first beats of bars.

Concerto for 2 Chalumeaux in D min.; Sonata for 2 Chalumeaux in F; in G; Viola Concerto in G; Overture des Nations anciennes et modernes in G; Völker Overture (Suite in B flat)

*** Chan. 0593. Lawson, Harris, Standage, Coll. Mus. 90

Colin Lawson and **Michael Harris** with their 'liquid' timbres find a delicate charm in the two works for chalumeax and

the *Sonata* has a rather touching *Grave*, which is played very serenely. **Standage** himself takes the solo part with distinction and pleasingly full timbre in the famous *Viola Concerto*, and his characterization of the *Ancient and Modern Overture* is alert and strong, finding dignity in *Les Allemands* and not overdoing the closing parody lament for *Les Vieilles Femmes*. He is equally positive in the so-called 'Folk' Overture, played vibrantly: its last five movements each draw on a different culture – Turkish, Russian and so on – but with their rhythms given a Western overlay.

Concertos: for 2 Corni da caccia in F, TWV 52:F3; for Violin & 3 Corni di caccia in D, TWV 54:D2. Overtures for 2 Corni di caccia in D. TWV 55:D17; for 2 Corni di caccia & 2 Oboes in F, TWV 55:F3

☙ **** MDG 605 1045-2. Deutsch Natural Horn Soloists, New Düsseldorf Hofmusik

The **Deutsch Natural Horn Soloists** are a superb group. They play here expertly using hand horns without valves and demonstrating the most thrilling bravura, whether in partnership with oboes, where the interplay of the *Réjouissance* in the *F major Overture* (or *Suite*) is a real hit number, or in the *Concerto in F*, which reminds one a little of Handel's *Water Music*. In the *Concerto* scored for three horns, the solo violin in the *Grave* slow movement gives expressive contrast before sharing the exuberant finale. With excellent recording, this is outstanding in every way, but not to be played all in one go!

Concertos, Overtures: (i) 5 Concertos for 2 Flutes, with Lute, Bassoon & Strings (10 284); (ii) Chamber Concerto for Alto Recorder in G min., TWV 43:G3; (iii) Double Concerto in E min. for Recorder & Flute; (iv) Concerto for 3 Trumpets & 2 Oboes in D; (ii) Sonata in A for Recorder, 2 Scordato Violins & Continuo, TWV 43:A7; (v) Tafelmusik II: Trio in E min. for Recorder, Oboe & Continuo (49 431); (vi) Overtures (Suites): in C, TWV 55:C3 (Hamburg Ebb and Flow) & C6; Overture in E min., TWV 55:C5 (10 625); Overtures: in D (connected with a Tragicomical Suite); in F (Alster Echo), TVW 55:F11; in D, TWV 55:D15 (49 428); (vii) Overtures (Suites): in D, TWV D18; TWV 55:D6 & D7; in F (49 429)

Ⓑ *** Cap. 49 426 (5). (i) Dresden Bar. Soloists, Haupt; (ii) Huntgeburth, Berlin Bar. Company; (iii) Höller, Hünteler, Capella Colonsiensis, G. Fischer; (iv) Friedrich & soloists, Budapest Strings; (v) Passin, Gütz, Leipzig Bach Coll.; (vi) Capella Colonsiensis, Linde; (vii) Deutsch Bach Soloists, Winschermann

If you want a representative collection of Telemann at his best, this Capriccio box (with the five CDs in a slip case) is hard to better. The *Concertos* for a pair of flutes are continually inventive and the two compilations of miscellaneous concertos and chamber music offer plenty of variety, not only in the music but also the performances, although all are authentic in the best possible way. The *Suites* (*Overtures*) are all among the composer's best, including the two most famous, both pictorial or progammatic, the *Alster Echo* and the *Hamburg Water Music*. The performances and recordings are excellent, as is the documentation. As far as we know, the discs are not currently available separately.

Flute Concerto in B min.; Double Concertos: in A min. for 2 Recorders; in E min. for Recorder & Flute; in C min., for Violin & Oboe; in D for 2 Oboes d'amore; Chamber Concerto in B flat for Oboe, Violin, 2 Flutes, 2 Violins & Continuo

(M) *** DHM/BMG 05472 77367-2. Camerata Köln

A very attractive collection of mostly *Double Concertos*, of which the *E minor Concerto for Recorder and Flute* is perhaps the most winning as it has a *Largo* slow movement which recalls Handel's *Where'er you walk* and a bustling finale using a drone bass. The closing *Chamber Concerto* for six soloists is also very diverting, but the whole programme offers playing and recording of high quality. However, the documentation is inadequate, with no TWV identification.

Flute Concertos: in B min.; C; D (2); E; E min.

*** VAI Audio VAIA 1166. Stallman, Phd. Concerto Soloists CO

Every one of these fine *Concertos*, *galant* and Italianate by turns, shows the composer's invention at its most fertile and imaginative. All but one is in four movements. The *E minor*, which is in five, is perhaps finest of all. **Robert Stallman** is a stylish and elegant player and he is given crisply sympathetic modern instrument accompaniments from the **Philadelphia Chamber Orchestra**. Excellent recording too.

Flute Concertos in D, TWV:51:D2; in G, TWV:51:G2. Concerto for 2 Flutes, Violone in A min., TWV:53:a; Concerto for Flute, Oboe d'amore & Viola d'amore in E, TWV:53:E; Tafelmusik: Concerto for Flute & Violin in A, TWV:53:A2

⊶ (M) **** EMI 5 03435-2. Pahud, Berlin Bar. Soloists, Kussmaul

An enchanting disc. Everything **Emmanuel Pahud** plays seems to turn to gold, and he has admirable support from his solo colleagues (including **Albrecht Meyer**, oboe d'amore and **Wolfram Christ**, viola d'amore). Throughout *Allegros* are wonderfully nimble and light-hearted. The **Berlin Baroque Soloists** directed by **Rainer Kussmaul** accompany with wonderful finesse and warmth and the recording is in the demonstration bracket.

(i) Flute Concerto in G, TWV 51:G1; (ii) Double Horn Concerto in D, TWV 52:D1; (i) Oboe Concerto in F, TWV 51:F1; (ii) Triple Concerto for 2 Oboes & Bassoon, TWV 53:D1; (ii) Recorder Concerto in C, TWV 51:C1

(N) **** CPO 777 267-2. Soloists, (i) Camerata Köln; (ii) La Stagione Frankfurt, Schneider

The **Camerata Köln** (of five players) and **La Stagione Frankfurt**, a full baroque orchestra (of 16), alternate in this particularly inventive collection of wind concertos of which the *Recorder Concerto* and *Flute Concerto* are the most ambitious, each with four movements. The former has an extended closing Minuet which requires much virtuosity, the latter is pastoral in feeling with a musette introduced in the finale. But the concertos featuring horns and oboes are also very pleasing, and altogether this is a most entertaining and varied collection, very well played indeed.

Horn Concerto in D

*** Ara. Z 6750. Rose, St Luke's Chamber Ens. – FORSTER; HAYDN; L. MOZART: *Horn Concertos* ***

Telemann's *D major Horn Concerto* (designated for the *corno di caccia* or hunting horn) is one of his best, and indeed one of the most attractive of all concertos for the instrument, other than those of Mozart. **Stewart Rose's** broad, open tone suits this robust music admirably and he plays with confident finesse; the crisply stylish accompaniment provides an excellent backcloth and the recording is excellent.

Concertos: in D for 2 Horns, TWV 52:D2; in E for Flute, TWV 51:E1; in D min. for Oboe, TWV 51:d1; in E min. for Recorder & Flute, TWV 52:e1; (i) Concerto da camera in G min. for Recorder & 2 Violins, TWV 43:g3

CPO 777 032-2. Camerata Köln; or (i) La Stagione Frankfurt, Schneider

Another clutch of inventive concertos, expertly and vivaciously played by members of the small-scale **Camerata Köln**. Indeed the robust hand horns project almost into the room as they duet spiritedly. The *Double Concerto for transverse flute and recorder* is also highly effective, the two instruments sometimes piping together in harmony, at others in imitation. The *Oboe concerto* is agreeable plaintive while the larger-scale *Concerto da camera*, as its name suggests is played by the much bigger **Frankfurt Stagione**. Both ensembles use period instruments very pleasingly.

Triple Horn Concerto in D; Alster (Overture) Suite; La Bouffonne Suite; Grillen-Symphonie

⊶ **** Chan. 0547. Coll. Mus. 90, Standage

The *Triple Horn Concerto* opens the programme with the hand-horns rasping boisterously. Then comes *La Bouffonne Suite*, with its elegant *Loure* and the extremely fetching *Rigaudon*, while the work ends with a touchingly delicate *Pastourelle*, beautifully played here. The *Grillen-Symphonie* ('cricket symphony') brings a piquant dialogue between upper wind and double-basses in the first movement, while the second has unexpected accents and lives up to its name *Tändelnd* ('flirtatious'). The horns (four of them) re-enter ambitiously at the colourful *Overture* of the *Alster Suite*, add to the fun in the *Echo* movement and help to simulate the Hamburg glockenspiel that follows. The entry of the Alster Shepherds brings a piquant drone effect, but best of all is the wailing *Concerto of Frogs and Crows*, with drooping bleats from the oboe and then the principal horn. **Standage** and his group make the very most of Telemann's remarkable orchestral palette and play with great vitality as well as finesse.

Oboe Concertos: in C min.; D min.; E min.; F min.

(BB) *** EMI Gemini (ADD) 3 50905-2 (2). de Vries (baroque oboe), Amsterdam Alma Musica, Van Dael – BACH; VIVALDI: *Oboe Concertos* ***

These four *Oboe Concertos* of Telemann are beautifully played by **Han de Vries** on a piquant baroque oboe; if their sprightly invention does not quite match that of Bach, the *C minor Concerto* is a piece of more than usual depth of imagination, and the wistful central *Largo* of the *E minor* work is quite memorable. Excellent recording, but with the oboe dominating the sound-picture.

Oboe Concerto in D min., TWV 51:d2; Violin Concerto in E, TWV51:E3; Double Violin Concerto in A, TWV 52:A2; Overture in C, TWV 55:c4; Sinfonia melodica for 2 Oboes & Strings; Sonata (Concerto ripieno) for Strings, TW 43:Es1

*** DG 477 5923. Berlin Barock Soloists, Kussmaul

Here is splendid example of a well-planned Telemann programme, played by a modern-instrument ensemble, yet whose conductor, **Rainer Kussmaul**, understands and accepts period-instrument style. The brief *Overture* here is a reconstruction and sets the concert off to a lively start, and all the *Concertos* are attractive in their various ways. The most interesting work is the *Sinfonia melodica*, which turns out to be a French Suite with a brilliant *Vivace* in place of the usual Overture, followed by a plaintive *Sarabande* and other dances, including a *Chaconnette*, and ending with a delightful, bouncing *Gigue en Canarie*. A most enjoyable disc, very well recorded.

Oboe Concertos: in C min. (2); D (Concerto grazioso); D min.; E; E flat; F; F min.; Oboe d'amore Concertos: E; E min.; G; (i) Triple Concerto for Oboe d'amore, Flute & Viola d'amore

ᵇ⁻ (BB) **** Regis RRC 2057 (2). Francis, L. Harpsichord Ens.; (i) with Mayer, Watson

Sarah Francis's survey of Telemann's *Oboe* and *Oboe d'amore Concertos* brings modern-instrument performances which are a model of style. The *G major Oboe d'amore Concerto* on the first disc is most gracious (with colouring dark-timbred like a cor anglais in the *soave* first movement). The *Concerto grazioso*, too, is aptly named. The *C minor Oboe Concerto* begins with a *Grave*, then the main *Allegro* brings a witty dialogue between soloist and violins, with the theme tossed backwards and forwards like a shuttlecock. But it is the works for oboe d'amore that are again so striking. The performances are full of joy and sparkle as well as expressive. They are beautifully recorded and make a very good case for playing this repertoire on modern instruments. Now reissued as a budget Double on Regis they are even more highly recommended.

(i) Oboe Concertos: in D min.; E min.; F min.; (ii) Sonatas: E min. (from Esercizi musici); in G (from Sonata metodiche, Op. 13/6); G min. (from Tafelmusik, Part III)

(BB) *** Virgin 2x1 5 61878-2 (2). de Vries; (i) Amsterdam Alma Musica, Van Asperen; (ii) Van Asperen, Möller – ALBINONI: Concerti a cinque, Op. 9. ***

Hans de Vries is a fine player and he produces an attractively full timbre on his baroque oboe. All three *Concertos* are char-

acteristically inventive, with alert and stylish accompaniments, but the three *Sonatas* are a delight, the work from the *Tafelmusik* particularly diverse. The slight snag is the very forward balance of the solo instrument, which reduces the overall range of dynamic, but apart from that the sound is vivid, and the harpsichord image in the *Sonatas* is pleasing. This comes as part of an inexpensive Double, but the present CD only plays for just over 40 minutes and one wonders what has happened to the fourth *Concerto in C minor* which was on the original CD.

Double Concertos: for 2 Oboes d'amore in A; for Recorder & Flute in E min.; Violin Concerto in B flat; Overtures (Suites): in F sharp min.; D

*** Chan. 0661 Holtslag, Brown, Robson, Eastaway, Coll. Mus 90, Standage

The title of this Chandos disc, 'Ouverture comique', refers to the last of the five Telemann works included in this delightful programme. It is a weirdly surreal musical portrait – 18th-century style – of a hypochondriac afflicted with gout. Over seven movements he, in turn, finds remedies in dancing – cue for inserted dance-fragments – in a coach-ride, and even a visit to a brothel. Telemann wrote this sparkling piece in his eighties with his imagination still working overtime. The other works, more conventional but just as inventive, include another overture/suite and three refreshing *Concertos*, all beautifully done.

Concerto in B flat for 3 Oboes & 3 Violins; Concerto in E for Flute, Oboe d'amore & Viola d'amore. Tafelmusik, Part I: Concerto in A for Flute, Violin & Cello; Part II: Concerto in F for 3 Violins

*** Chan. 0580. Soloists, Coll. Mus. 90, Standage

The triple *Concertos* here are among the composer's most colourful works and the period wind-instruments here are piquant in their mixed colours, the strings lithe, yet not abrasive. The opening of the *E major Concerto* (which comes last in the programme) tickles the ear engagingly with its opening *Andante*, and the third movement *Siciliano* is equally diverting. The lively opening movement of the *Tafelmusik Triple Violin Concerto* momentarily recalls Handel's *Queen of Sheba*, and it has a particularly eloquent *Largo*. First-class playing and recording throughout.

Concertos in B flat for 3 Oboes, 3 Violins & Continuo, TWV 44:43; F for Recorder, Bassoon & Strings; for 4 Violins in G, TWV 40:201. Overture in F for 2 Horns & Strings, TWV 44:7

ᵇ⁻ (BB) **** Warner Apex 2564 60523-2. Soloists, VCM, Harnoncourt

This 1966 collection remains one of the best Telemann discs in the catalogue with first class soloists, including Franz Brüggen (recorder), all with strong personalities. Excellent recording too.

Recorder Concerto in C, TWV 51:C1; Suite for Recorder in A min., TWV 55:a2; C (Hamburger Ebb und Flut), TWV 55:C3

*** HM HMC 901917. Maurice Steger, Akademie für Alte Musik, Berlin

This recording offers a triptych of three of Telemann's finest works, the well-known *Suite for Recorder and Strings in A minor*, played with virtuosity and élan by **Maurice Steger** (sample the *Réjouissance* for an astonishing example of his bravura) plus the *Concerto in C*, which has a similarly dazzling finale, and the celebrated *Hamburg Water Music*, in which all the movements are associated with mythology, except for the finale, which is a *Jolly Sailors' Dance*. A first-class collection, splendidly recorded.

Recorder Concertos: in C & E major; Double Concerto for Recorder & Flute; Suite in A min. for Recorder & Strings

⊕━ ⓑⓑ **** Naxos 8.554018. Rothert, Umbach, Cologne CO, Müller-Brühl

It is a pity that Naxos do not provide TWV identification as do EMI and DG Archiv, but the *Suite in A minor* is an irresistible masterpiece if ever there was one, and is easily identified. It is played here as winningly and stylishly as anywhere else on disc. The two named soloists share the *Double Concerto* (which has a delightful *Largo* that starts off like Handel's 'Where'er you walk'), but it is not clear who plays elsewhere. However it is of no moment; all the solo playing here is expert and personable, and there is some delicious virtuoso piping in the second movement of the *E major Concerto*. Indeed all four works show Telemann on top form, **Helmut Müller-Brühl's** accompaniments are polished and equally stylish, and the recording is first class.

(i) Recorder Concertos: in C; in F; (ii) Suite in A min. for Recorder & Strings; (i) Sinfonia in F

ⓑⓑ **(*) Hyp. Helios CDH 55091. (i) Holtslag, Parley of Instruments; (ii) cond. Goodman

The three solo *Concertos* here are a delight. **Peter Holtslag's** piping treble recorder is truthfully balanced, in proper scale with the authentic accompaniments, which are neat, polished, sympathetic and animated. The *Sinfonia* is curiously scored, for recorder, oboe, solo bass viol, strings, cornett, three trombones and an organ, with doubling of wind and string parts. Even with **Roy Goodman** balancing everything expertly the effect is slightly bizarre. About the great *Suite in A minor* there are some reservations: it is played with much nimble bravura and sympathy on the part of the soloist, but the orchestral texture sounds rather thin. However, at budget price this remains an attractive proposition.

(i–iii) Double Concerto in E min. for Recorder & Transverse Flute; (iv) Viola Concerto in G; (i; v) Suite in A min. for Flute & Strings; (iii) Overture des nations anciens et modernes in G

⊕━ ⓑⓑ **** Warner Apex (ADD) 0927 40843-2. (i) Brüggen; (ii) Vester; (iii) Amsterdam CO, Rieu; (iv) Doctor, Concerto Amsterdam, Brüggen; (v) Southwest German CO, Tilegant

All these works show Telemann as an original and often inspired craftsman. His use of contrasting timbres in the *Double Concerto* has considerable charm; the *Overture des nations anciens et modernes* is slighter but is consistently and agreeably inventive, and the *Suite in A minor*, one of his best-known works, is worthy of Handel or Bach. **Frans Brüggen** and **Franz Vester** are expert soloists and Brüggen shows himself equally impressive on the conductor's podium accompanying **Paul Doctor**, the rich-timbred soloist in the engaging *Viola Concerto*. The 1960s sound, splendidly remastered, is still superb, with excellent body and presence, and this Apex reissue is a fine bargain.

(i) Viola Concerto in G; (ii) Suite in A min. for Recorder & Strings; Tafelmusik, Part 2: (iii) Triple Violin Concerto in F; Part 3: (iv) Double Horn Concerto in E flat

⊕━ ✹ ⓑⓑ **** Naxos 8.550156. (i) Kyselak; (ii) Stivín; (iii) Hoelblingova, Hoelbling, Jablokov; (iv) Z. & B. Tylšar; Capella Istropolitana, Edlinger

It is difficult to conceive of a better Telemann programme for anyone encountering this versatile composer for the first time and coming fresh to this repertoire, having bought the inexpensive Naxos CD on impulse. **Ladislav Kyselak** is a fine violist and is thoroughly at home in Telemann's splendid four-movement *Concerto*; **Jiři Stivín** is an equally personable recorder soloist in the masterly *Suite in A minor*; his decoration is a special joy. The *Triple Violin Concerto* with its memorable *Vivace* finale and the *Double Horn Concerto* also show the finesse which these musicians readily display. **Richard Edlinger** provides polished and alert accompaniments throughout. The digital sound is first class.

Violin Concertos: in A; A min.; B min.; B flat; C; G; G min., TWV 51: a4; a2; h2; B1; C3; g1; G7

*** CPO 777 089-2. Wallfisch, Orfeo Bar. O

Violin Concertos: in C; D; E; E min.; F & G, TWV 51: C2; D9 & D10; E2; E3; F2; G8

⊕━ *** CPO 999 900-2. Wallfisch, Orfeo Bar. O.

These *Concertos* require a fair degree of virtuosity and, if less individually original than those of Vivaldi, their invention is consistently stimulating. The opening *Affetuoso* of the *C major* work here, with the oboe prominent in the orchestra, is particularly appealing, its melody almost Handelian. The other four-movement *Concertos* here are similarly inviting, the *D major* opening *Con contento* and the *E major* again marked *Affetuoso*. The three-movement *concertos* are more conventional, but Telemann's ideas never desert him. **Elizabeth Wallfisch** is a complete master of this repertoire, playing with plenty of authentic dash and an agreeable expressive lyricism, and at the same time directing vivacious accompaniments from her excellent **Baroque Orchestra**. The balance is just as it should be.

(i) Violin Concerto in A (Les Rainettes); Overtures (Suites) in B flat (Les Nations); in D TWV 55; in G (La Bizarre)

*** HM HMC 901744. (i) Seiler; Berlin Akademie for Alte Musik

The bluff good humour of Telemann and his fondness for a

musical joke are splendidly illustrated in this delightful disc of three of his *Overture/Suites* and a *Violin Concerto* equally spirited with its joky imitation of frogs ('rainettes' in French), which the note suggests might be a take-off of Vivaldi. The *B flat Overture* with its sequence of brief movements celebrating different nations is well enough known, but the jolliest work of all here is the one nicknamed *La Bizarre*, with its deliberate rule-breaking in the fugue of the opening movement. The players of the **Berlin Academy of Early Music** bring out the fun all the more effectively with the brilliance, precision and energy of their playing, vividly recorded.

(i) *Violin Concertos: in D; in E; in G; in G; in B flat;* (ii) *12 Fantasias for solo violin*

*** Australian Ph. Eloquence (ADD/DDD) 442 8291 (2). (i) Brown, ASMF; (ii) Grumiaux

Iona Brown's violin tone is pure and sweet, and these warmly vital readings of Telemann's *Violin Concertos* are most enjoyable. The **Academy of St Martin-in-the-Fields** offer their characteristic style and polish and the digital recording is first rate. The 12 *Fantasias* for solo violin were written a decade after Bach's *Partitas* and they are less ambitious and demanding. Yet there is much that is rewarding here, particularly given such artistry as **Grumiaux's**; Telemann's invention is fresh, though none of these short suites can claim depth.

Darmstadt Overtures (Suites): for 3 Oboes, Bassoon, & Strings: in C, TWV 55/C6; in D, TWV 55/D15; in G min., TWV 55/G4

(BB) *** Naxos 8.554244. Cologne CO, Müller-Brühl

The modern-instrument performances on Naxos are delightfully vivacious and elegant. This is a first-class chamber orchestra and **Müller-Brühl's** light rhythmic touch keeps the dance movements sparkling. The recording is excellent. A most entertaining collection.

Don Quixote (Suite burlesque in G); Concerto in D for 2 Violins & Bassoon; Overtures in B min.; G

*** Chan. 0700. Coll. Mus. 90, Standage

Don Quixote (Suite burlesque); Overtures (Suites) in F (Alster); in B flat (La Bourse)

⊕ **** Analekta Fleur de Lys FL2 3138. Tafelmusik, Lamon

The *Don Quixote Burlesque* is scored for strings without wind, but Telemann is as resourceful as ever and the portrayal of Sancho Panza is as striking as the gallop of Sancho's donkey. The lively *Windmills* sequence contrasts with the Don's gentle sighs for *Dulcinée*. Not surprisingly the performance of the *Alster Suite* by the superb **Tafelmusik** under **Jean Lamon** upstages all the competition, with superbly exuberant horn-playing and especially imaginative echo effects. With outstanding recording, this is one of the most winning of all Telemann orchestral discs.

The descriptive *Don Quixote* burlesque is well covered in the catalogue, but this account from **Collegium Musicum 90** is among the best; and the other two *Suites*, if not especially individual, are very well played too. The engaging little *Concerto in D* with its string–bassoon solo interplay is also played and recorded most elegantly.

Die Kleine Kammermusik, Orchestral Suites 1–6

*** CPO 999 994-2. La Stagione, Frankfurt, Schneider

Telemann had great success with the 6 *Partitas* which made up the second part of his *Kleine Kammermusik* which he published in 1716. So he decided to compose an orchestral version of the whole series, scored for two oboes, strings and continuo, although he omitted the woodwind in 2 and 3 of the set. During the reworking he added a newly composed French overture, lasting about six minutes, which altered the scale of the *Suites* altogether. They are most agreeable and entertaining works and, as played here by the excellent period-instrument **Frankfurt chamber orchestra**, make enjoyably elegant listening.

Overtures (Suites) in F (Alster); in F (La Chasse); in G min. (La Musette); in D (for the Jubilee of the Hamburg Admiralty); in D (Ouverture jointe d'une suite tragi-comique)

⊕ **** HM HMC 901654. Berlin Akademie für Alte Musik

The opening *Overture in D*, written for the Hamburg Admiralty's centenary celebration, is remarkably like Handel's *Fireworks Music* and makes a festive start to this very attractive Harmonia Mundi period-instrument collection. We have had the *Alster Suite* before, with all its pictorial effects. In the *Musette Suite* Telemann reuses a drone effect for his fifth movement (hence the sobriquet), but this is otherwise a collection of lively dance vignettes from various national sources, of which the most attractive are the Italian *Napolitaine* and *Harliquinade*. *La Chasse* is scored for wind instruments alone. There is engaging writing for oboes, and they echo the horns in the *Sarabande*. The Minuet closing movement, *Le Plaisir*, pictures the hunting party gathered for drinks when the chase is over. The atmosphere of the witty *Tragi-comique Suite* depicts human aches and pains, from the gout-stricken *Loure* to a hypochondriac, cured by being forced to dance in swiftly changing style and time-signature, while the brass dauntlessly depict the only general remedy available (apart from a suggested alternative visit to a brothel): *'souffrance héroïque'*. Excellent, lively playing and vivid recording.

Overtures (Suites): La Changeante; Les Nations anciens et modernes; in D

(BB) **(*) Naxos 8.553791. N. CO, Ward

These are agreeably mellow performances on modern instruments, which come into their own in the warmly Handelian lyrical melodies, like the *Avec douceur* from *La Changeante* and the *Plainte* from the *D major Suite for Strings and Horns* (which is the highlight of the disc), and in neatly making the contrasts between the *Ancient and Modern* pairs of movements, the first slow, the second more animated.

Tafelmusik (Productions 1–3; complete)

⊕ **** DG 427 619-2 (4). Col. Mus. Ant., Goebel

(BB) **(*) Naxos 8.553724/5 & 8.553731. O of the Golden Age

The playing of the **Cologne Musiqua Antiqua** is distinguished by dazzling virtuosity and unanimity of ensemble and musical thinking. They also have the advantage of very vivid and fresh recording quality; the balance is close and present without being too forward and there is a pleasing acoustic ambience.

The **Orchestra of the Golden Age** plays with a good sense of style, plenty of life and a convincing linear manner in expressive music. They represent one of Naxos's first excursions into period-instrument music-making and are very well recorded. While Reinhard Goebel's version has something special to offer in this music, this Naxos set is excellent value and will give considerable satisfaction.

Tafelmusik (excerpts): Production 2: Suite in D (for trumpet, oboe & strings); Production 3: Suite in B flat (for 2 oboes & strings)

(BB) *** Hyp. Helios CDH 55278. King's Consort, King

A happy juxtaposition of two contrasted *Suites*, the first pairing a trumpet and oboe very successfully in juxtaposition, the second using a pair of oboes with equal felicity. The *D major* is the more ambitious work, the *B flat* with its *Bergerie*, *Postillons*, *Bandidage* and *Furioso* conclusion is more lightweight. But both show the composer in good form and both are persuasively played and recorded here on a disc which offers not far off 70 minutes of diverting music for a modest cost.

Water Music (Hamburger Ebb' und Fluth)

⊕ *** Hyp. CDA 66967. King's Cons., King – HANDEL: *Water Music* ***

Telemann's *Water Music* is rightly one of his most popular works, and it is good to have a thoroughly recommendable period-instrument performance available and aptly coupled with Handel. The **King's Consort** performance is most enjoyable. There is exhilarating playing from the oboes in the *Overture* and the following Sarabande (with recorders) is seductive, as is the later Minuet (*Der angeneheme Zephir*). In short, this is excellent in every way and coupled with the *Water Music* of Handel.

CHAMBER MUSIC

6 Concertos & 6 Suites (1734) for Flute, Violin, Viola da gamba, or Cello & Harpsichord (Lute or Organ)

*** CPO 999 690-2 (3). Camerata Köln

This remarkable set of four-movement *Concertos* and seven- or eight-movement *Suites*, published by Telemann in Hamburg in 1734, was resourcefully written so that in each case the four parts could be played by a varying combination of instruments, which is what happens here, with sometimes only three instruments in use, sometimes four. This adds variety and freshness to music which constantly shows the composer's astonishing musical fertility. Throughout, the ear is always entertained, when the period-instrument playing is so expert, with the musicians clearly enjoying them-

selves. As an example, the *Airs* that conclude *Suite 1* are all ear-tickling, and, throughout, the more expansive concerto slow movements always have memorable expressive content. The recording is excellent.

Chamber Concertos: for 2 Violins & Viola in D, TWV 43:D4; in G min. for Recorder & 2 Violins, TWV 42:g9; Overture in F for 2 violas & continuo, TWV 55:F2; Sonatinas: for recorder in A min., TWV 41:a4; for Bassoon in C min., TWV 41:c2; Sonata corellisante in B min., TWV 42:h3

⊕ **** MDG 309 1314-2. Musica Alta Ripa

Once again, in this mixed bag of *Concertos*, *Sonatinas* (and even an *Overture* to give added variety of timbre), one is amazed at the fecundity of Telemann's invention, so well displayed here. Splendidly played and recorded, this programme balances an engaging combination of sprightly rhythms (as in the works for recorder and bassoon) with expressive string writing (as in the more extended, six-movement works: the *Overture in F* and the *Sonata*, which pays homage to Corelli). Performances and recording are first class and, such is the diversity of the music, the disc can be played through as a satisfying concert.

Fantasias for Solo Treble Recorder: in C; D min.; G min.; A min.; B flat, TWV 40/2, 4, 9, 11 & 12. Sonatas for Treble Recorder & Continuo: Esercizi musici. Sonatas in C, TWV 41:C5; D min., TWV 41:d4; Der getreue Music-Meister: Canonic Sonata in B flat, TWV 41:B3; Sonatas in C, TWV 41:C2; F, TWV 41:F2; F min., TWV 41:f1

(BB) *** Warner Apex 2564 60368-2. Brüggen, Bylsma, Leonhardt

The 12 solo *Fantasias* were actually written for transverse flute, but **Frans Brüggen** plays them very effectively on the treble recorder, transposing them up a minor third in order to do so. The *Sonatas for Treble Recorder and Continuo* are all most winning and well chosen to show the composer at his most inventive, and are played with breathtaking virtuosity and a marvellous sense of style. The sound is excellent.

12 Fantasias for Unaccompanied Violin

(M) *** Maya MCD 9302. Homburger

(N) (BB) *** Naxos 8.570563. Augustin Hadelich

Telemann's 12 *Fantasias* for solo violin are a decade later than Bach's *Partitas* and *Sonatas*, and they are less ambitious and less demanding. Each is in either three or four movements, usually opening with a *Largo* or *Grave*, alternating with *Allegros*. With striking invention, they make very enjoyable listening, especially when played with such life and style. **Maya Homburger** uses a baroque violin. This is cheerful music and it would be difficult to imagine these works being played more freshly or with a more sensitive espressivo.

They are also played here with plenty of flair by the excellent **Augustin Hadelich** using a modern instrument. Violinists should find them worth exploring, with a view to getting the music for their own use; others can enjoy their ready facility, for they do not outlast their welcome.

Kleine Cammermusic (6 Partitas for Violin, Flute or Oboe Continuo)

Ⓜ *** CPO 999 497-2. Camerata Köln

The six *Partitas* of the *Kleine Cammermusik*, published in 1716, were written – as was the composer's policy – to be playable by three alternative solo instruments with harpsichord. Each consists of an opening slow introduction, followed by a group of six *Arias* (or airs), varying in style and tempo. As ever, Telemann never seems to run out of attractive ideas and here the works are allotted in turn to oboe (1 and 3, both delightful, the latter with a lovely opening *Adagio*), flute (2, which opens *dolce* with a charming *Siciliana*, and is worthy of comparison with Bach), viola da gamba (4 and very well chosen), violin (5) and recorder (6, with organ continuo, and another of the most attractive). The performances here could hardly be bettered and they are beautifully balanced and recorded. The variety of instrumentation makes this one of the most enticing of all the Telemann chamber music CDs.

Overtures (Suites) for 2 Oboes, 2 Horns, Bassoon and Double Bass in F: (La Joie); in F (La Fortune); in F (La Chasse), TWV55:F5; F8; F9; in F, TWV55: F15 & F18

*** MDG 301 1109-2. Consortium Classicum

Telemann wrote many works for wind ensemble but only ten Overtures/Suites have survived, five of which are offered here. They are all essentially in the same pattern of five or six movements although the dances vary between them. One would have expected the work nicknamed *La Chasse* to have the most spectacular horn parts, but in the event *La Fortune* and *La Joie* are the most impressive in this respect and the two works without nicknames are just as inventive as those with a sobriquet, with TWV 55:F18 the most attractive of all. The playing here is expert and full of life, but with similar sonorities throughout and all the works in the key of F, this is a CD to dip into rather than play right through. Excellent recording.

Paris Flute Quartets 1–6 (1730) (for flute, violine, viola da gamba & continuo)

🎧 Ⓑ **** HM HMA 901787. Freiburg Bar. Cons.

The splendid **Freiburg Baroque Consort** (including the exceedingly nimble flautist **Karl Kaiser**), drawn from the excellent orchestra of that name, give first-class period-instrument performances of these delightful works, and the recording is excellent. An outstanding disc in every way.

6 Nouveaux Paris Flute Quartets (1738)

Ⓑ *** Virgin 2x1 5 61812-2 (2). Trio Sonnerie

In 1730 Telemann published in Hamburg a set of six *Quartets* for violin, flauto traverso, viola da gamba and bass continuo, and these were sufficiently popular to be pirated by the French publishing house Le Clerk, and reprinted in 1736 – without the composer's permission. Telemann learned by this experience: during a long and fruitful visit to Paris in 1737–8, by virtue of a Privilège du Roi, he was able himself to publish a new and even finer set, which he called *Nouveaux quatuors*.

The performances on Virgin are of a high calibre and are representative of modern practice, using original instruments and bringing lighter textures and greater delicacy of style. Thus, they have a different kind of charm. Tempi with this group are almost always brisker, with both losses and gains. The **Trio Sonnerie** are led by the expert **Monica Huggett**, and their timbre is clean and transparent. Certainly, the results on Virgin Veritas are refreshing, while the sound is truthful and again very well balanced.

Paris Quartets (Quadri) (1730) in D, TWV4: D1; in A, TWV 43: A1. Nouveaux Quatuors (1738) in A min., TWV 43: A2; in E min., TWV 43: E1

Ⓝ **** CPO 777 375-2. Holloway, Brunmayr, Duftschmid; Becker, Mortensen

As can be seen this is a somewhat arbitrary selection, with two of the works coming from the first set of *Paris Quartets* and two from the second. But they are all particularly attractive works and with a distinguished ensemble they are expertly played, with **Linde Brunmayr's** dominent transverse flute particularly rich-timbred for a period instrument, while the overall balance is very beguiling. Excellent documentation too. A fine disc.

Paris Quartets (1730): 2, Concerto secondo in D; 3, Sonata prima in A; 4, Sonata seconda in G min.; 5, Première suite in E min. Fantasias: 5 in A for (solo) Violin; 7 in D for (solo) Flute; 8 in G min. for Harpsichord

🎧 *** Channel Classics CCS 13598. Florilegium

Instead of providing a set, **Florilegium** have chosen four of the earlier *Quartets* and set them in the context of a concert, interspersed with solo *Fantasias*. They play with affectionate warmth, readily bringing out shades of melancholy in slow movements, to contrast with the busy allegros, played with real virtuosity, with the tone of **Ashley Solomon's** period flute particularly enticing. But the timbre and clean articulation of the two string players, **Rachel Podger** (violin) and **Daniel Yeadon** (viola da gamba), are hardly less appealing, and the overall blend of tone in a warm but intimate acoustic could not be more attractive. These players convey a deep expressive feeling.

6 Flute Quartets or Trios (Hamburg, 1733); Der Getreue Musikmeister: Cello Sonata (for cello and continuo) in D

**(*) Lyrichord LEMS 8028. Mélomanie

Telemann himself published his *Six quatuors ou trios*, ensuring their success by making them available for performance on various alternative combinations of flutes, violins, bassoon and cello, with a flexible continuo. This is their first complete recording. The collection divides into two groups. The first three works are three- or four-movement *Sonatas* in an elegant conversational style; the last three each open with a slow movement followed by three unpredictable 'Divertimenti', showing the composer imaginatively trying out different dance forms. The four-movement *Cello sonata* offered as bonus also shows the composer at his best. It is very well played, as are the Quartets (favouring two period flutes – not always absolutely immaculate in tuning – cello and harpsichord).

Quartets (Concertos) for Flute, Bassoon, Viola da gamba & Continuo: in B min., TWV 43:b3; in C, TWV 43:C2; Quartet in G for Flute, 2 Violas da gamba, TWV 43:G12; Trio Sonatas: in F for Violin, Viola da gamba & Continuo, TWV 42:F10; in G min., for Flute, Viola da gamba & Continuo, TWV42:G7 (from Darmstadt manuscripts)

*** Astrée Auvidis E 8632. Limoges Bar. Ens., Coin

All these manuscripts come from the Darmstadt Library, and the two most attractive *Quartets* (which include a bassoon) bear the additional title *Concerto*. All five works here are in the four-movement Italian *sonata di chiesa* form (slow-fast-slow-fast), although the *Trio Sonata in G minor* has additionally a characteristic opening *Siciliana*. Although the *Allegros* are lively enough, the pervading mood is often attractively dolorous, and the intimacy of the excellent performances enhances that impression. Very good recording.

Quadros (Quartets): in A min. for Recorder, Oboe, Violin & Continuo, TWV 43:a3; in G, for Recorder, Oboe, Violin & Continuo, TWV 43:g6; in G min. for Oboe, Violin, Viola da gamba & Continuo, TWV43:g92; in G min. for Recorder, Violin, Viola da gamba & Continuo, TWV43:g94. Esercizi musici: Trio Sonatas: in C min. for Recorder, Oboe & Continuo, TWV 42:c2; in F for Recorder, Viola da gamba & Continuo, TWV 42:f3. Trio Sonata in D min. for Recorder, Violin & Continuo, TWV 42:d10

♫⌐ **** Globe GLO 5154. Ens. Senario

These *Quadros* (or Quartets) are among Telemann's very finest chamber music, every bit as inventive and diverting as the more famous *Paris* quartets. Telemann writes parts of equal interest for all three of his solo instruments, and provides slow movements of considerable expressive intensity, framed by winningly virtuosic *Allegros*. Perhaps finest of all is the *G major Quartet*, with its solemn central *Grave*, but the *G minor Quartet* (TWV 43:g94), which opens the programme, is hardly less seductive. Telemann subtitles the *A minor* work 'Concerto', and indeed there is plenty of opportunity for virtuoso display here, and its four movements also include a pair of touching *Adagios*. The *Trio Sonatas*, slighter in texture, are also very enjoyable when presented so freshly. Indeed, the performances here could hardly be bettered. The brilliant recorder playing of **Saskia Coolen** is well matched by the oboist, **Peter Frankenberg**, and the group overall integrates splendidly. The balance and recording could hardly be improved on.

Quadros (Flute or Recorder Quartets) in B flat, for 2 Violins, Viola & Continuo, G 43:B2; in A min. for Recorder, Oboe, Violin & Continuo, TWV 43:a3; in D min. for Flute, Violin, Cello & Continuo, TWV 43:d3; in G min., for Recorder, Violin, Viola & Continuo, TWV 43:g4; in G, for Recorder, Oboe, Violin & Continuo, TWV 43:G6; in G, for Flute, 2

Violins & Continuo, TWV 43:G10; for Flute, Violin, Cello & Continuo, TWV 43:G11; for Flute, 2 Violins & Continuo, TWV 43:G12

*** DG 477 5379. Mus. Ant. Köln, Goebel

The playing here is expert and full of life, and the balance and recording are very realistic, so this is a very recommendable disc.

Recorder Sonatas: Esercizi musici: in C, TWV 41:C5; D min., TWV 41:D2. Der Getreue Musikmeister: in A/B flat TWV41:B3 (Canonic Sonata), TWV 41:A3; in C, TWV 41:C2; in F, TWV 41:F2; in F min., TWV 41:F1; Neue Sonatinen; in A min., TWV 41:A4; in C min., TWV 41:C2. Sonatina in F min., TWV41:D4

*** Cap. 67 070. Michael & Annette Schneider, Beuse, Imamura, Bauer

Both Capriccio and Globe offer what are described as Telemann's 'complete sonatas for recorder and continuo', two of which derive from the *Esercizi musici* and four from *Der Getreue Musikmeister*. Like the comparable Naxos collection of recorder concertos, there is the danger here of unvarying sameness of timbre. Both sets of performances are stylish and the recorder playing is nimble and highly musical. But on the whole we are inclined to give our vote to the Capriccio set, which features a bassoon in the excerpts from *Der Getreue Musikmeister* and employs a continuo using a lute and clavierorganum.

Sonatas for 2 Recorders 1–6; Duetto in B flat

*** BIS CD 334. Pehrsson, Laurin

Canon Sonatas 1–6; Duettos 1–6

*** BIS CD 335. Pehrsson, Laurin

All the *Duet Sonatas* are in four movements, the second being a fugue; the *Canon Sonatas* are for two flutes, violins or bass viols. Needless to say, listening to two recorders for longer than one piece at a time imposes a strain on one's powers of endurance, no matter how expert the playing – and expert it certainly is. The BIS versions can be recommended. However, although it is good to have the two treble recorders blending so well together, a clearer degree of separation would have helped in the imitative writing.

Sonata Metodiche 1–6 (1728); 7–12 (1732)

*** Accent ACC 94104/5D (2). B. and W. Kuijken, Kohnen

Telemann's *Methodical Sonatas* were written in two sets of six, the first designated 'for violin or flute', the second 'for flute or violin', which is a curious alternation of emphases, the more so as the second set sometimes uses keys that are less comfortable for the baroque flute. Not that this is apparent in these expert performances, lively and expressive by turns, and there is plenty of variety in the music itself. One of the purposes of these *Sonatas* was to instruct amateurs in the art of ornamentation, so Telemann wrote out ornaments in the French style for each first movement, while mixing French and Italian styles in the writing itself. A worthwhile addition to the catalogue, very well recorded.

6 Trios (1718): 1 (Oboe & Violin); 2 (Recorder & Violin); 3 (Flute & Violin); 4 (2 Violins); 5 (Violin & Viola da gamba); 6 (2 Violins), TWV:42:B1, a1, G1, D1, g1, & F1

*** CPO 999 957-2 Camerata Köln

Trio Sonatas 1–6, TWV43:G3, c1, A2, d2, e1, D4; Trio Sonata in B flat for Violin, Bassoon & Continuo, TWV42:B5; Bassoon Quartet in E min., TWV43:E3.

*** CPO 999 934-2. Parnassi Musici, with Azzolini

The two CPO collections above are linked, for the composition of the *6 Trios of 1718* served Telemann as a prototype for establishing the format of the *Trio Sonatas* which followed in the 1720s. Each work has a different instrumental combination, and Telemann resourcefully finds suitable ideas to match his lead instrument. All but two of the six are in the four-movement *sonata da chiesa* format, which brings an opportunity for extra variety. The three-movement *Trio* for the violin, cello and continuo brings a particularly stimulating dialogue between the two soloists in the opening movement, to anticipate the regular use of this combination by many composers. Performances are excellent.

Having experimented with various instrumentations, Telemann settled on the combination of two violins (or two flutes as a possible alternative) and wrote *Trio Sonatas* essentially derived from Corelli's Italian style (and advertised as such on publication). These *Sonatas* show Telemann at his finest. *Allegros* are full of bouncing vitality and the slow movements are often delicately charming. The performances are outstandingly fine, full of life and with a graceful elegance, and they are ideally recorded in a friendly but not too resonant acoustic. The only irritating feature of this latter disc is the absence of dividing bands for the individual movements (as indicated in the documentation).

6 Trio Sonatas in the Italian Style (Sonates en Trios dans le Goût Italien) TWV 42: g3; c1; a2; d2; e1; d4; Trio Sonata in G, TWV 42: g12

*** Lyrichord LEMS 8035. Moore, Myford, Fournier, Palumbo

Telemann had altogether greater success with his *Trio Sonatas in the Italian Style* than he did with his Corelli imitations. They are pleasingly lightweight, sunny works, played here with the second part authentically given to the violin rather than a flute. The *C minor* and *A major* works are particularly attractive, but the standard of invention is high, and particularly striking in the minor-key works. They are most felicitously played by this very musical period-instrument group, who know all about elegance, and very well balanced. **Tom Moore's** baroque flute has a most agreeably watery timbre that is wholly authentic.

Trio Sonatas for Recorder or Oboe, Violin & Continuo: TWV 42:d10; Esercizi Musici: Trio Sonatas A min.; in B flat; E flat; G min. Der Music-Meister: Sonata in D

🎧 **** Naïve Ambroisie AM 112. Amarillis

This is easily the most attractive of these collections of

Telemann's *Trio Sonatas*. **Amarillis** is a first-rate ensemble, led by **Héloïse Gaillard** (who alternates between baroque recorder and oboe) with **David Plantier** (violin), **Emmanuel Jacques** (cello) and **Violaine Cochard** (harpsichord), both of whom make attractive solo contributions, and **Laura Pustilnik** (archlute). The alternation of recorder and flute is most felicitous, and every one of the works here shows the composer at his most fluent, and the music is captivatingly full of attractive invention. The playing too is full of life and spontaneity, and the recording splendidly balanced. A disc not to be missed.

Music for Oboe & Continuo: (i) 'Dresden' Sonata for Oboe & Bassoon, TWV 41:g10. Esercizi musici: Sonatas in B flat, TWV 41:B6; E min., TWV 41:e6. Trio Sonata in E flat. Der getreue Musikmeister: Sonata in A min., TWV 41:a3. Tafelmusik: Sonata in G min. for Oboe & Bassoon, TWV 41:g6

🎧 (BB) **** Regis RRC 1240. Francis, Dodd, Powell, Jordan; (i) with Beach

Originally issued by Somm, this admirable collection in which **Sarah Francis** is the star performer draws on both the *Esercizi musici* and *Der getreue Musikmeister*, and includes an extra *Sonata*, found in a Dresden manuscript. The performances are first class in every way and the recording is very well balanced and this is even more recommendable on the Regis budget label.

Esercizi musici: Solo 2: Flute Sonata in D; Solo 4: Recorder Sonata in D min; Solo 5: Chalumeau Sonata in B flat; Solo 8: Flute Sonata in G. Der getreue Music-Meister: Bassoon Sonata in F min; Tafelmusik, Part III: Oboe Sonata in G min. Harpsichord Fantasias: in E min. & F, Set 1/4–5; Harpsichord Overture in G min.

🎧 *** Mer. CDE 84347. Badinage

This is an ideal way of assembling a concert of Telemann's chamber and instrumental music, not centring on a single instrument, but making a hand-picked selection of music (much of it from the *Solos* in the *Esercizi musici*) featuring a wide range of instrumental colour, from the dolorous bassoon and the piquantly watery timbre of the primitive chalumeaux to the brighter recorder and flute. All the soloists here are expert, and the fine harpsichordist provides interludes, lively and *dolce* at three strategic points in the programme. The recording is excellent.

3 Trietti metodici & 3 Scherzi

(N) *** CPO 777 301-2. Parnassi Musici

Telemann had written trio sonatas in the 1720s and in 1731 returned to the format by publishing a cycle of *Il Trietti metodici e Scherzi a 2 Flauti traversier overo 2 Violini con Fondamento*. The instrumentation of either flutes or violins as the melody instruments was to offer buyers a choice to fit their personal needs. However on the music itself the violins are named first. They are obviously linked to the *Methodical Sonatas* (see above) but with the *Trietti* ('Little Methodic Trios') Telemann also provided his clients with instruction on the art of ornamentation, in particular embellishment in the slow movements. All but two of the works are in three movements but one *Trietto* and one *Scherzo* are each extended to four, also using a quartet of four musicians featuring flute, violin, bassoon and continuo. These miniature works are both diverse and engaging. The first *Scherzo* is in an exotic syncopated Moravian hurdy-gurdy style, the first *Trio* opens with a fugue and ends with a busy bourée. The second *Trio* has an influence from Corelli, the third, uniquely in a minor key, has a *Siciliano* as its centrepiece and a virtuoso finale. All these works are persuasively presented and well recorded to show yet another side of this remarkably innovative composer.

KEYBOARD MUSIC

Organ music: *6 Chorale Preludes; Fantasia in D; Pasacaille in B min.; Sonata in D for 2 Manuals & Pedal; Concerto in G min. (trans. Bach as BWV 985); Concerto per la chiesa on G (trans. J. G. Walther)*

**(*) MDG 320 0078-2. Baumgratz (Bach organ, Bremer Dom)

This collection opens commandingly with the *Concerto in G minor*, attributed to Telemann, and transcribed by Bach. But it is such a magnificent tripartite piece that one is tempted to believe that there is more Bach in it than Telemann. The *Passacaglia* that follows, with its decoration increasingly florid, moves to a fair climax, and the four *Chorale Preludes* that come next (each in two sections) are agreeably managed, *Komm heiliger Geist* easily the most telling, especially the jaunty second part. However, the pair of chorales based on *Nun freut euch lieben Christen g'mein*, brief as they may be, show Telemann nearer to Bach in his manipulation of variations around a clear cantus firmus.

Wolfgang Baumgratz makes the most of all this music by registering brightly and imaginatively, and he is very well recorded. But this collection serves to confirm that Telemann's talent lay not with the organ, but with the baroque orchestra and in the world of chamber music.

VOCAL MUSIC

Ach Herr! Lehr uns Bedenken wohl, TWV 1:24; Der am Olberg zagende Jesus, TWV1: 364; Ich will den Kreuzweg gerne gehen, TWV1: 884; Jesus liegt in letzten Zügen TWV1: 983; Was gibst du denn o meine Seele, TWV11510 (Passion Cantatas)

(N)*** CPO 777 299-2. Klaus Mertens, Accademia, Daniel, Shalev Ad-El

From his early years Telemann was attracted to the drama of opera, but he also professed to a great love for church music 'above all else', so the two needs came together in his many religious cantatas, where he interweaves dramatic recitative with arias and often uses a chorale to introduce or conclude work, sometimes both, as in the Trinity cantata *Ach Herr! Lehr uns Bedenken wohl* ('Ah Lord teach us to consider well that someday we shall die'). It seems possible that two other things contributed to his many works in this form,

firstly that he was a more than competent baritone singer and secondly that he was able to write the cantata texts himself, and perhaps also perform them himself. It has been suggested that two of the works in the present collection are linked, namely *Jesus liegt in letzten Zügen* ('Jesus lies breathing his last') and *Der am Olberg zagende Jesus* ('Jesus on the Mount of Olives'). Whether that is so, they are both movingly expressive. **Klaus Mertens** proves a fine sympathetic soloist in all these cantatas and he receives excellent support from the **Accademia Daniel** playing on period instruments

Ach, Herr, straf mich nicht in deinem Zorn; Ach wie nichtig, ach wie flüchtig; Du aber, Daniel, gehe hin; Sei getreu bis in den Tod. (In Festo Penticost): Schaffe in mir, Gott, ein reines Herz (Trauer-Actus Cantatas)

*** HM HMC 901768. Koslowsky, Popien, Jochens, Mammel, Shreckenberger, Cantus Cölln, Junghänel

These *Cantatas* date from Telemann's earliest composing years (1697–1708), and although they are simple in style, they already show his remarkable skill and melodic talent. The *Adagio* close of the *Funeral cantata*, *Du aber, Daniel, gehe hin*, is introduced by flute and oboe, *Schlaft wohl, ihr seligen Gebeine* is wonderfully serene while in *Sei gettreu bis in den Tod*, the lovely alto aria *Dich lieb ich allein* is in no way immature. It is followed by a light-hearted soprano aria and another expressive aria for tenor. In the five-movement *Pentecost Cantata* a tenor aria and a touching soprano/alto duet are framed and interwoven by three simple choruses. The performances here are dedicated and the soloists are excellent, and this well-recorded and enterprising collection throws new light on a truly remarkable composer.

Die Auferstehung (The Resurrection): Easter Oratorio; Cantata: De Danske, Norske og Tydske Undersaaters Glaede (The Joy of the Danish, Norwegian and German Citizens)

*** CPO 999 634-2. Mields, Schwarz, Post, Mertens, Decker, Magdeburg Chamber Ch., Michaelstein Telemann CO, Rémy

Telemann's *Easter Oratorio* of 1761 has an appealing simplicity. It opens without preamble with a solo lament from the soprano, and only then does the chorus enter, joyfully asserting 'The Lord Has Risen'. The bass then tells of the angel arriving 'fast as a flash of lightning' (illustrated by a brilliant violin obbligato) and the narrative continues with the alto and chorus dramatically describing the despair of Hell, while the reappearance of the risen Christ is depicted in a lovely soprano aria (beautifully sung here by **Dorothee Mields**). The Resurrection is then further celebrated in fine expressive arias from tenor and bass, before the joyful closing chorus with trumpets.

The reconstructed *Cantata* celebrating the birthday of the Danish King Frederick V, written four years earlier, was a curious choice of coupling, but it is a happy work. Both performances here are first class, with a sensitive team of soloists and excellent support from the fine chorus and orchestra. The recording is very well balanced, spacious and natural.

Das befreit Israel (oratorio; complete); Der May (Eine musicalische Idylle); Overture in F min. for 2 Recorders, 2 Oboes, Bassoon & Strings, TWV 55:f1

*** CPO 999 673-2. Schmithüsen, Schubert, Crook, Mertens, Abele, Rheinisch Kantorei, Kleine Konzert, Max

Handel's *Israel in Egypt* was possibly the source of inspiration for Telemann's much briefer (27 minutes) and less complex, but cheerfully melodic and appealing oratorio, which was premièred in 1759. It is very well sung here and makes a fine contrast with the pastoral idyll *Der May*, in which the scoring for flutes, horns and bassoons is used very effectively to colour the text. It forms a charming series of arias and duets gently extolling the joys of spring. Phillis (the soprano **Ingrid Schmithüsen**) and Daphnis (the bass **Klaus Mertens**), who has already made a strong impression in the oratorio, both sing very pleasingly. In between the vocal works comes a fine performance of one of Telemann's most inventive *Suites* (*Overtures*). A most engaging disc, very well recorded.

Betrachtung der 9 Stunde an dem Todstage Jesu (Passion Oratorio); Cantatas: Ein Mensch is in seinem Leben wie Gras, TWV 4:18; Herr, ich habe lieb die Stätte deines Hauses, TWV 2:2

*** CPO 999 500-2. Zádori, Jochens, Wessel, Cordier, Wimmer, Schreckenberger, Van der Kamp, Rheinisch Kantorei, Kleine Konzert, Max

Telemann's *Passion Cantata, Reflection of the Ninth Hour on the Day of Jesus's Death* (with a text by Joachim Zimmerman) is an unusual conception, in that the figure who is involved in these personal reflections is not a biblical character but a poetic creation, who provides a reflective meditation on the events surrounding the Crucifixion. Telemann added three chorales to create a binding structure and the vocal observations are not centred on a single soloist but four, with tenor, alto and two basses together providing the introduction. If the musical result is less imaginative than the conception, the work is still well worth hearing, as are the pair of contrasted *Cantatas* with which it is coupled, which show Telemann's invention at its freshest. All three pieces are very well sung and accompanied, and the recording is well up to the high standard of this excellent CPO series.

Cantatas for the first Sunday of Advent: Saget den verzagten Herzen, TWV 1:1233; Saget der Tochter Zion, TWV 1: 1235. Cantatas for the first day of Christmas: Auf Zion! Und lass in geheiligten Hallen, TWV 1: 109; Kündlich gross ist das Gottselige Geheimnis, TWV 1: 1020

**** CPO 999 515-2. Mields, Schwarz, Jochens, Schmidt, Magdeburg Chamber Ch., Michaelstein Telemann CO, Rémy

This is marginally the finest of **Ludger Rémy's** series of Telemann's festive *Cantatas* so far. The opening of *Saget den verzagten Herzen* brings a splendid interchange between soloists and chorus, and the following alto aria (marked *Affettuoso*), *So komm den auch*, is touchingly eloquent, while the bass and tenor soloists both have lively arias to follow. The bravura bass aria, *Zerstreuet euch*, which opens *Saget der*

Tochter Zion, has even more brilliant trumpet parts, and the opening bass aria of *Auf Zion*, decorated with flutes, is equally memorable. The Christmas story is then told in a series of brief recitatives and choruses, much more atmospheric and dramatic than the so-called 'Christmas Oratorio' (see below). The second of the two Christmas Day *Cantatas, Kündlich gross ist das Gottselige Geheimnis*, is even more dramatic and has a remarkable soprano aria punctuated by trumpets and drums. The alto air *Göttlich Kind* is a Handelian alto and trumpet duet, and the trumpets stay for the bass aria. Rémy directs with flair, and with strikingly good male soloists, fine choral singing and first-rate playing from his period-instrument accompanying group, this is well worth seeking out. The documentation (as throughout the series) is impeccable, including full translations.

Christmas Oratorio: Die Hirten on der Krippe zu Bethlehem, TWV 1:797; Christmas Cantatas: Siehe, ich verkündige Euc (1761), TWV 1:1334; Der Herr hat offenbaret (1762): TWV 1: 262

**(*) CPO 999 419-2. Backes, George, Post, Mertens, Michaelstein Chamber Ch. & Telemann CO, Rémy

The so-called 'Christmas Oratorio' opens with the chorale we know as *In dulci jubilo*, fully scored with trumpets, to the words *O Jesu parvule* – and is simply structured and comparatively unambitious, with the chorus interleaving the arias with chorales. Flutes and trumpets are used to decorate the pastoral scenes. There is a fine bass aria welcoming the shepherds. But the *Cantatas* are much more ambitious. The 1761 work opens arrestingly with a brilliant soprano aria when the angel sings those famous words '*Behold I bring you glad tidings*' with trumpets blazing, and she is answered dramatically by the choral heavenly host, who return to praise God after fine contributions from both the tenor and bass. The 1762 *Cantata* opens and closes with a chorus, and the following arias for soprano and bass (again using trumpets and flutes) are both rather fine. Fortunately, the soloists here are again excellent and if the conductor of the small period-instrument ensemble is at times rhythmically a bit emphatic in the oratorio, he keeps the music alive and flowing. The recording is excellent.

Cornett cantatas: Cantata for the 2nd Sunday after Epiphany: Sehet an die Exempel der Alten, TWV 1: 1259; Cantata for Exaudi Sunday: Ich halte aber dafür, TWV 1: 840; Cantata for Rogation Sunday: Erhöre mich, wenn ich rufe, TWV 1: 459

*** CPO 999 542-2. Spägele, Vass, Jochens, Mertens, Leipzig Bläser Collegium, Michaelstein Telemann CO, Rémy

The rich textures Telemann creates are very much his own, not like Gabrieli, rather nearer to Schütz. In consequence, he does not demand a chorus, and the chorales are sung by the soloists, never more effectively than at the end of the *Epiphany Cantata*, following a fine soprano aria. Telemann uses his colourful ripieno imaginatively throughout, especially so in the *Rogation Cantata*, which is shared by tenor and bass. **Wilfried Jochens** and **Klaus Mertens** are in splendid form and make the most of all their opportunities, especially their fine penultimate duet, richly embroidered by the brass and wind, *Herr, auf dein Wort verlass ich mich*, which is again followed by the closing chorale. The *Cantata for Exaudi Sunday* opens with a spectacular polyphonic interplay, shared by singers and orchestra, and after an alto recitative the cornetti decorate the bass aria, while oboes are used later for the alto solo, and the work closes with a serene Martin Luther hymn. If the invention in these works is less dramatic than in the *Advent* and *Christmas Cantatas*, many of the individual numbers are lyrically very persuasive, especially when they are so well sung and so musically accompanied by this strikingly well-balanced period-instrument ensemble under the excellent **Ludger Rémy**.

(i) Fortsetzung des Harmonischen Gottesdienstes: Cantatas 5: Ein Jammerton, en schluchzend Ach, TWV1:424; 35: Ertrage nur das Joch des Mängel, TWV1:479; 42: Die Glut des Zorns, TWV1:331; 48: Da, Jesu, Deinen Ruhm zu mehren, TWV1:531:67; Mein Glaube ringt in letzten Zügen, TWV1:184; (ii) 20 Little Fugues for Organ, TWV30:6, 8, 20 & 30

*** CPO 999 764-2. (i) Ziesak, Camerata Köln; (ii) Bauer.

The *Harmonischen Gottesdienstes* ('Harmonous Divine Service') of 1731/2 consists of no fewer than 72 *Cantatas*, of which these five are typical examples, each consisting of two arias (usually one fast and the other slow) with a brief linking recitative (in effect a miniature vocalised sermon). The settings depend a great deal for their appeal on their use of obbligato solo instruments, in 5 flute and oboe, in 35 (very attractive) and 67 two flutes, in 48 (the most engaging of all) recorder and oboe. **Ruth Ziesak** sings throughout with true baroque freshness, matching her woodwind partners most expertly, and the accompaniments have plenty of life. One of Telemann's *Little Fugues for Organ*, also dating from 1731, is effectively used as a brief interlude between each *Cantata*. The recording is excellent, and full texts and translations are provided.

Hamburg Admiralitätsmusik (1723); Water Music (Hamburger Ebb' und Fluth)

🔊 *** CPO 999 373-2 (2). Van der Sluis, Pushee, Müller, Mertens, Thomas, Schopper, Alsfeder Vokalensemble, Bremen Baroque O, Helbich

As the main work here is set to a poem by Michael Richey in praise of Hamburg, the allegorical characters represented by the soloists are all associated with the city. The soprano (as Hammonia) embodies Hamburg itself and the principal bass (as Neptunus) symbolizes the North Sea, and he has a memorable lyrical aria celebrating Hamburg's prosperity. More remarkably, the two tenors, as Themis and Mercurius, represent the prospering economy, and the privileges and rights of the constitution.

One of the other two basses symbolizes Mars, and sings a dramatic aria of defiance of lightning and stormy blasts. The third bass as Albis (the Elbe) celebrates his flowing currents and then has a charming tête-à-tête with Hammonia. Not surprisingly, there is a chorus of Nymphs and Tritons and the finale, *Long live the Admiralty*, is almost worthy of Sullivan! The performance is full of life, and of high quality,

with no weak link in the cast, and with excellent recording, overall this is a delightful surprise.

Kapitänsmusik, 1724

**** CPO **SACD** 777 176-2. Podkoscielna, Post, Vieweg, Abele, Telemannisches Collegium Michaelstein, Rémy

In Hamburg, Telemann often had to compose celebratory occasional pieces called *Kapitänsmusik*, consisting of an oratorio and serenata. The one on this CD was first performed in 1724 and this is the first time it has been performed complete since that time. The oratorio part has sacred texts, whilst the serenata part has secular texts but both find the composer providing some extraordinarily good music. This music shows Telemann as his most flamboyantly creative, with some brilliantly florid, virtuosic writing, performed with comparable vigour by the soloists and the orchestra. The lively arias in both the oratorio and serenata are very exciting, and the opening of the serenata with its minor-keyed woodwinds is deliciously piquant and memorable, as is the aria which follows. One marvels time and time again with Telemann's inventive orchestration, especially in his use of woodwind colouring, and this whole CD is one of flamboyant invigoration. Superbly recorded in SACD surround sound, warm yet sharply vivid. Full texts and translations are provided.

THOMAS, Ambroise (1811–96)

Mignon; Overture & Gavotte

🔊 *** Chan. 9765. BBC PO, Y. P. Tortelier (with Concert: 'French bonbons' ***)

Thomas's opera *Mignon* has one of the most delectable of all French *Overtures*, with its opening woodwind and harp solos followed by a romantic horn tune. It is beautifully played and recorded on Chandos in this first-rate concert of French lollipops.

Mignon (complete)

🔊 (Ⓜ) *** Sony (ADD) SM3K 34590 (3). Horne, Vanzo, Welting, Zaccaria, von Stade, Méloni, Battedou, Hudson, Ambrosian Op. Ch., Philh. O, Almeida

Thomas's once-popular adaptation of Goethe has many vocal plums, and here a very full account of the score is given, with virtually all the alternatives that the composer devised for productions after the first, not least one at Drury Lane in London where recitatives were used (as here) instead of spoken dialogue; an extra aria was given to the soubrette Philine and other arias were expanded. The role of Frédéric was given to a mezzo-soprano instead of a tenor, and here the appropriately named **Frederica von Stade** is superb in that role, making one rather regret that she was not chosen as the heroine. However, **Marilyn Horne** is in fine voice and sings with great character and flair, even if she hardly sounds the frail figure of the ideal Mignon. Nonetheless, with **Alain Vanzo** a sensitive Wilhelm, **Ruth Welting** a charming Philine and colourful conducting from **Almeida**, this is an essential set for lovers of French opera. The 1977 recording has a pleasingly warm ambience and the voices are naturally caught in the present transfer.

THOMPSON, Randall
(1899–1984)

Alleluia; Choose something like a Star; The best of Rooms; The Eternal Dove; Felices ter

🎵 *** ASV CDDCA 1125. Harvard University Ch., Somerville; Johnson (organ) – BEACH: *Choral Music* ***

Commissioned by Koussevitzky in 1940 for the opening of the Tanglewood Music Center, Randall Thompson's *Alleluia* is for choral societies the American vocal equivalent of Barber's *Adagio* for string orchestras. Built on that single word it rises to a climax of comparable intensity, never losing its grip on the listener during its imaginative forward progress. *The Eternal Dove* and *Choose something like a Star* are much later works and in many ways equally fine and almost as memorable. Thompson is an individual writer, and all these works are very rewarding when so committedly sung.

THOMSON, Virgil (1896–1989)

(i) Autumn (Concertino for Harp, Strings, & Percussion); The Plow that broke the Plains; The River (Suite)

(N) (M) *** EMI 2 06612-2. (i) Mason; LAPO, Marriner

These pieces are often quite attractive even if none of them is really first-rate. *Autumn* has a cool yet distinctly American flavour, and many readers will find it highly attractive. The playing of the **Los Angeles Orchestra** is altogether excellent, and the recording has admirable space and realism.

Film music: *Louisiana Story: Arcadian Songs & Dances & Suite; The Plow that Broke the Plains: Suite; Power among Men: Fugues & Cantilenas*

**(*) Hyp. CDA 66576. New L.O, Corp

Apart from his opera *Four Saints in Three Acts* (available on two separate recordings in the USA), Virgil Thomson is best known for his film score to Flaherty's *Louisiana Story*. Here we are offered both the four-movement suite and a series of brief vignettes, called *Arcadian Songs and Dances*, of which the first (*Sadness*) and last (*The Squeeze Box*) are the most striking. The *Fugues and Cantilenas* from *Power among Men* are also not what one might expect from the titles, but are atmospheric and imaginatively scored. All this music is quite appealing, even if only very occasionally does one feel it is first rate. The performances by **Ronald Corp** and the **New London Orchestra**, are deft, evocatively played, and well recorded.

Film Scores: *The Plow that Broke The Plains; The River*

🎵 (BB) *** Naxos 8.559291. Post Classical Ens., Gil-Ordóñez

Virgil Thomson's scores for the two American documentary films, *The Plow that Broke the Plains* (evoking the American 'Dust Bowl') and *The River* (making a spectacular case for flood control), are among the most deservedly famous in film history, and this is the first time they have been recorded in their entirety. Each is constructed in a series of musical vignettes, quoting cowboy songs, popular and patriotic melodies, nursery tunes, folk music and even jazz; but composed music also intervenes to create atmosphere and accompanies the final scenes of both films, the drought in one, the flooding waters in the other, devastation in both. They are remarkable kalaidescopic scores and are presented here in sequence, rather than seamlessly, very well played and recorded. Excellent notes too.

TIPPETT, Michael (1905–98)

Concerto for Orchestra; (i) Triple Concerto

🎵 **** Chan. 93842. (i) Chilingirian, Rowland-Jones, De Groote; Bournemouth SO, Hickox

Hickox's coupling of these two major orchestral works is a fine supplement to his set of the four Tippett symphonies, also with the **Bournemouth orchestra**, warmly recorded in well-focused sound. **Levon Chilingirian** makes a powerful leader for the trio of soloists, heightening the sharp contrasts of the elliptical argument in Tippett's late return to lyricism. The *Concerto for Orchestra* is presented with similar concentration and concern for lyrical warmth.

(i) Concerto for Double String Orchestra; (ii) Piano Concerto; (iii) Fantasia concertante on a theme of Corelli

(BB) *** EMI (ADD) Encore 2 35744-2. (i) Moscow Chamber O & Bath Fest. O, Barshai; (ii) Ogdon, Philh. O., C. Davis; (iii) Menuhin, Masters, Simpson, Bath Fest. O, Composer

Tippett's eloquent string concerto is well served by **Barshai's** performance, which has both warmth and vitality. The recording is lively but a shade dry in the upper range. The string textures are clear but not ideally expansive. The *Fantasia concertante* is not as immediately striking as its predecessor, but with the composer in charge and **Menuhin** as principal soloist, its inventiveness and expressive feeling are never in doubt. The *Piano concerto* also represents Tippett's complex-textured and starkly conceived earlier style. **Ogdon** gives it a fine performance, although he does not rescue it from waywardness. However the recording now sounds clearer than originally.

(i) Concerto for Double String Orchestra; (ii–iv) Piano Concerto; (i) Fantasia concertante on a Theme of Corelli; Little Music for Strings; (v; iv) Praeludium for Brass, Bells & Percussion; Suite for the Birthday of Prince Charles; (vi; iii–iv) Triple Concerto for Violin, Viola, Cello & Orchestra; (vii) The Blue Guitar (sonata for solo guitar). Vocal music: (viii; ix) Bonny at morn (Northumbrian folksong for unison voices and 3 recorders); (viii) A Child of Our Time: 5 Negro Spirituals. (viii; x) Crown of the Year (cantata); (viii) Dance, Clarion Air (madrigal); (xi) Evening Canticles; (viii) Music (unison song);

Plebs Angelica (motet for double choir); *The Weeping Babe* (motet for soprano and choir). *The Midsummer Marriage:* (v; iv) *Ritual Dances*; (xii) *Sosostris's Aria*

Ⓑ️Ⓑ️ *** Nim. NI 1759 (4). (i) E. String O, Boughton; (ii) Tirimo; (iii) BBC PO; (iv) cond. composer; (v) E.N. Philh. O; (vi) Kovacic, Causé, Baillie; (vii) Ogden; (viii) Christ Church Cathedral Ch., Oxford (members), Darlington; (ix) Copley, Hodges, Nallen; (x) Medici Qt, with wind soloists, Jones (piano) and percussion; (xi) St John's College, Cambridge, Ch., Guest; (xii) Hodgson

This bargain collection of Tippett, is specially valuable for containing two discs of recordings made by **Tippett** himself. When he did them, he was already in his late eighties, and the performance of the *Ritual Dances* from *The Midsummer Marriage* is not as incisive as most other versions, but the warmth of expressiveness and the sense of occasion conveyed are most compelling, the more so in **Alfreda Hodgson's** rich and resonant performance of Sosostris's aria from the same opera, even though the voice is backwardly balanced. It is good too to have Tippett offering a rare example of his occasional music in the uncomplicated *Prince Charles Suite*. Even more valuable is the concerto disc, again more relaxed at more spacious speeds than rival versions, but with outstanding soloists revealing Tippett at his most warmly magnetic. **Martino Tirimo** is particularly impressive in the elaborate figuration of the *Piano Concerto*, which can easily sound empty. Broad speeds, well sustained, also mark **William Boughton's** readings of the string pieces on the fourth disc; the *Guitar Sonata*, tautly played by **Craig Ogden**, and *Evening Canticles* sung by the **St John's College Choir** under **George Guest** (for whom they were written) make a splendid supplement. The choral singing from **Christ Church Cathedral Choir** on the second disc is also excellent, with the school *Cantata, The Crown of the Year*, revealing the composer at his most open and least enigmatic. Warm, atmospheric sound, characteristic of Nimbus.

'Tippett Collection': (i) *Concerto for Orchestra*; (ii) *Concerto for Double String Orchestra*; (ii; iii) *Triple Concerto for Violin, Viola, Cello & Orchestra*; (i) *Fantasia Concertante on a Theme of Corelli*; (iv) *Fanfare for Brass*; (i) *Little Music for Strings*; (v) *Suite for the Birthday of Prince Charles*; *Symphonies* (i) 1–2; (i; vi) 3; (v) 4; (vii) *Sonata for 4 Horns*; (viii) *String Quartets 1–3*; (ix) *Piano Sonatas 1–3*; (x) *Midsummer Marriage; Ritual Dances*

Ⓑ *** Decca 475 6750 (6). (i) LSO, C. Davis; (ii) ASMF, Marriner; (iii) with Pauk, Imai, Kirshbaum; (iv) Philip Jones Brass Ens.; (v) Chicago SO, Solti; (vi) with Harper; (vii) Tuckwell Horn Qt; (viii) Lindsay Qt; (ix) Crossley; (x) ROHCG O, Pritchard

For those wanting to explore Tippett's music in depth, Decca provided, for the centenary of his birth, an even more extensive collection, which includes the four *Symphonies*, the first three conducted by **Sir Colin Davis** with the **LSO** fully committed, and the *Fourth* by **Sir George Solti**, who also offers the agreeable if less substantial *Suite for the Birthday of Prince Charles*.

Tippett himself described the *Third* as a hybrid symphony and he consciously follows the example of Beethoven's *Ninth* in the transition to the final vocal section, in which the soprano sings three blues numbers and **Heather Harper** almost manages to mute the comparative crudities of Tippett's text. Solti's brilliantly played account of the *Fourth Symphony* is comparably powerful, although there are depths and tenderness in this score yet to be uncovered. Certainly these recordings and performances have a special place in the catalogue, although (as Hickox has since shown) there are other dimensions to these scores which are not uncovered here.

(i) *Concerto for Double String Orchestra*; **(ii)** *Fanfare for Brass*; **(i)** *Fantasia Concertante on a Theme of Corelli*; *Little Music for String Orchestra*; **(iii)** *Suite in D for the birthday of Prince Charles*

✹ **** Australian Decca Eloquence (ADD) 476 7960. (i) ASMF, Marriner; (ii) Philip Jones Brass Ens.; (iii) LSO, C. Davis

A splendid Tippett anthology and an ideal introduction to this composer. Beginning with the striking *Fanfare for Brass*, it moves on to the charming *Suite in D for the Birthday of Prince Charles*, full of attractive ideas and a distinct 'Robin Hood' atmosphere – the subject of an early folksong opera Tippett composed, parts of it used in this score. Next comes **Marriner's** classic Argo recording featuring some of his most inspired and approachable music. On any count, the *Concerto for Double String Orchestra* is one of the most beautiful works for strings of the 20th century. The *Corelli Fantasia* is a similarly sumptuous work, and the *Little Music* is very appealing too. Superb 1970s recordings and altogether an outstanding compilation.

Concerto for Double String Orchestra

Ⓑ *** CfP 5 75978-2. LPO, Pritchard – BRITTEN: *Violin Concerto; Serenade* ***

(***) BBC BBCL mono 4059-2. LSO, Stokowski – GABRIELI: *Sonata pian'e forte*; LISZT: *Mephisto Waltz 1*; NIELSEN: *Symphony 6* ***

This Classics for Pleasure reissue is a first-rate bargain, well recorded, and coupling one of the warmest and most memorable string works of the 20th century with two key works of Britten. In **Handley's** fine performance no one could miss the passion behind the sharp, rhythmic inspirations of the outer movement and the glorious lyricism of the central slow movement.

As far as we know **Stokowski** did not conduct any other Tippett and this eloquent account of the *Double Concerto* is a 'must', particularly as it comes with another rarity, a studio performance of Nielsen's *Sixth Symphony*. Commanding accounts, recorded in vivid and well-balanced mono sound.

Concerto for Double String Orchestra; Divertimento on 'Sellinger's round'; Little Music for Strings; (i) *The Heart's Assurance* (orch. Meirion Bowen)

**(*) Chan. 9409. City of L. Sinf., Hickox; (i) with Mark Ainsley

Hickox draws warm and energetic performances from his chamber orchestra, opulently recorded with fine definition. The first movement of the *Concerto* may lack a little in bite, but the slow movement is ravishing and the finale fizzes with energy. The playing may not always be quite as polished as that of the Academy on the rival Decca disc, but the big bonus is the first recording of the song-cycle *The Heart's Assurance* in the orchestration prepared by Meirion Bowen with the composer's express approval. What with piano accompaniment can seem a gritty, uncompromising piece here emerges with warmth and beauty, thanks also to the fine singing of **John Mark Ainsley**.

Concerto for Double String Orchestra; Fantasia concertante on a Theme of Corelli; (i) The Midsummer Marriage: Ritual Dances

☕ 🌑 (BB) **** Warner Apex 8573 89098-2. BBC SO, A. Davis; (i) with BBC Symphony Ch.

This outstanding bargain disc offers superb performances from **Sir Andrew Davis** and the **BBC Symphony Orchestra**. The *Concerto* and *Fantasia* are warmly passionate, yet wonderfully detailed, helped by a spaciously resonant recording which is internally clear, yet has a wide dynamic range to match the dynamic contrasts of the playing. In the third of the *Ritual Dances*, *The air in spring*, the chimerical delicacy of the orchestral playing makes the bold entry of the **BBC Chorus**, near the close, the more arresting and thrilling. If you buy only one Tippett CD, this is the one to have; for apart from being ridiculously inexpensive, it makes an ideal introduction to his music and the sound could hardly be more vivid.

Concerto for Double String Orchestra; Little Music for Strings

(BB) *** ASV Resonance CD RSN 3057. E. Sinfonia, Farrer – VAUGHAN WILLIAMS: *Dives & Lazarus; Partita* ***

John Farrer conducts strong, athletic performances, very well played and recorded, with slow movements touching but not over-ripe. If you want the fine Vaughan Williams coupling, this is excellent value.

(i) Piano Concerto; Fantasia on a Theme of Handel; Piano Sonatas 1–4

**** Hyp. CDA 67461/2. Osborne; (i) BBC Scottish SO, Brabbins

The *Piano Concerto* represents Tippett's complex, rich-textured style. It is essentially a lyrical and inspired piece, and this fine new recording copes with it by making an overall blend between piano and orchestra. The *Fantasia* with its variations is an early work, slightly eclectic, based on a theme which mirrors that used also by Brahms. To quote the composer it is 'vigorous and gay', but it is also full-blooded and dramatic, very much a youthful piece. **Stephen Osborne** and the **BBC Scottish Orchestra** under **Brabbins** are fully at home here, and these performances are unsurpassed. Osborne is equally involved in the four *Sonatas*, matching Paul Crossley, who has been very much identified with them

(see below). They are not easy works to bring off, being often prolix, but Osborne's total conviction carries the day and he is splendidly recorded.

(i) Piano Concerto; Piano Sonatas 1 & 2

(B) **(*) EMI (ADD) 5 86586-2. Ogdon; (i) Philh. O, C. Davis

John Ogdon and **Sir Colin Davis** present the *Concerto* persuasively enough. But Ogdon is at his best in the *First Sonata*. It has great vitality of invention, is harmonically direct and well suited to Ogdon's forthright approach. He plays it superbly and is movingly simple in his presentation of the *Andante molto tranquillo*, yet he readily catches the lighter, syncopated mood of the *Rondo giocoso* finale. The single-movement *Second Sonata*, written nearly three decades later, is more intractable. Without being as uninhibited as he might be, John Ogdon displays his usual virtuosity.

Divertimento for Chamber Orchestra (Sellinger's Round)

*** Lyrita (ADD) SRCD 257. ECO, Del Mar – ARNOLD; BERKELEY; BRITTEN: *Sinfoniettas*; RAWSTHORNE: *Divertimentos* ***

A series of variations on the English folk-dance tune by different hands led Tippett to develop his variation into this lively work, diverting exactly as a divertimento should be. It comes in an excellent performance, beautifully recorded.

Little Music for String Orchestra

(M) **(*) Chan. 6576. Soloists of Australia, Thomas – BLISS: *Checkmate*; RUBBRA: *Symphony 5* ***

Tippett's *Little Music* was written in 1946 for the Jacques Orchestra. Its contrapuntal style is stimulating but the music is more inconsequential than the *Concerto for Double String Orchestra*. It receives a good if not distinctive performance here, truthfully recorded.

(i) The Rose Lake; (ii) The Vision of St Augustine

☕ 🌑 **** RCA 82876 64284-2. LSO; (i) C. Davis; (ii) with Shirley Quirk, L. Ch., composer

As **Sir Colin Davis's** superb recording with the **LSO** demonstrates from first to last, *The Rose Lake* is arguably the most beautiful of all Tippett's works. It was in 1990 on a visit to Senegal that the 85-year-old composer visited a lake, Le Lac Rose, where at midday the sun transformed its whitish-green colour to translucent pink. It led to this musical evocation of the lake from dawn to dusk, centred round the climactic mid-moment when the lake is in full song. The 12 sections, sharply delineated, form a musical arch, with the lake-song represented in five of them on soaring unison strings in free variation form.

That culminating masterpiece is well coupled with **Tippett's** own 1971 recording, never previously available on CD, of his *Cantata, The Vision of St Augustine*. First heard in 1965, it is a work which can now be recognized as the beginning of his adventurous Indian Summer. His reading is expansively atmospheric rather than tautly drawn, bringing out the mystery of the piece.

Symphonies 1–4; New Year Suite

🎵 Ⓜ **** Chan. 10330X (3). Robinson, Bournemouth SO, Hickox

Symphony 1; (i) Piano Concerto

🎵 **** Chan. 9333. (i) Shelley; Bournemouth SO, Hickox

Those who thought that Sir Colin Davis's pioneering recordings of the first three Tippett symphonies were definitive will find fresh revelation in **Richard Hickox's** readings, not least in the First Symphony. Hickox gives an extra spring to the chattering motor rhythms at the start, and from then on the **Bournemouth** performance is regularly warmer and more expressive, as in the distinctive trumpet melody in the slow movement. In the last two movements too, Hickox finds more fun and jollity in Tippett's wild inspirations. The Piano Concerto, with **Howard Shelley** a superb soloist, brings another revelatory performance, warm and affectionate but purposeful too, rebutting any idea that with their fluttering piano figurations these are meandering arguments. Warm, full, atmospheric sound, with the piano balanced within the orchestra instead of in front of it. This must now be a first recommendation, although all four symphonies are now available in a box at mid-price.

Symphony 2; New Year (opera): Suite

*** Chan. 9299. Bournemouth SO, Hickox

As in the First Symphony, **Hickox** brings out the joy behind Tippett's inspirations without ever losing a sense of purpose. This may be a less biting performance than Sir Colin Davis's was on Decca, but it is consistently warmer, with extra fun and wit in the third-movement Scherzo. The coupling is also valuable, when Tippett's own suite from his last opera, New Year, brings out the colour and wild energy of this inspiration of his mid-eighties. If anything, the music seems the more telling for being shorn of the composer's own problematic libretto. The obbligato instruments – saxophones, electric guitars and kit drums – are most evocatively balanced in the warm, atmospheric recording.

(i) Symphony 3; Praeludium for Brass, Bells & Percussion

*** Chan. 9276. Bournemouth SO, Hickox; (i) with Robinson

In two long movements, each lasting nearly half an hour, the Third Symphony is not easy to hold together and, though **Richard Hickox** and the **Bournemouth Orchestra** cannot match the original performers, Sir Colin Davis and the LSO, in power, they find more light and shade. Though **Faye Robinson's** voice in the blues sections of the second movement is not as warm or firm as Heather Harper's was, she is more closely in tune with the idiom, helping to build the sequence to a purposeful conclusion in the long final scene. The recording is full and warm to match. The Praeludium for Brass, Bells and Percussion was written in 1962 for the 40th anniversary of the BBC, a gruff, angular piece hardly suggesting celebration, but none the less welcome in a well-played performance.

Symphony 4; Fantasia concertante on a Theme of Corelli; (i) Fantasia on a Theme of Handel (for piano and orchestra)

*** Chan. 9233. (i) Shelley, Bournemouth SO, Hickox

In the Fourth Symphony, **Richard Hickox** and the **Bournemouth Symphony** are less weighty than the work's originators, but they are generally warmer and more atmospheric. The well-known Corelli Variations have never sounded quite as sumptuous and resonant as here, and the disc is generously rounded off with a welcome rarity: the early Handel Fantasia for Piano and Orchestra. **Howard Shelley** is most convincing in the weighty piano-writing, like his accompanists giving the music warmth. Full-blooded sound to match.

String Quartets 1–5

🎵 *** ASV (ADD/DDD) CDDCS 231 (2). Lindsay Qt

String Quartets 1, 2 & 4

Ⓝ ⒝⒝ **(*) Naxos 8.570496. Tippett Qt

String Quartet 4

*** ASV CDDCA 608. Lindsay Qt – BRITTEN: Quartet 3 ***

This set neatly brings together the première recordings of Tippett's last two Quartets with the recordings the same players made in the 1970s for L'Oiseau-Lyre of the first three Quartets in the series, long unavailable. The notes include the composer's own commentary on the first three Quartets, written for the original issue. The **Lindsays** give performances as near definitive as could be, making one realize why they inspired the composer so positively. The analogue sound for 1–3, as transferred, is brighter, with less body than the digital recordings for 4 and 5. As can be seen, the Fourth Quartet is also available separately, well coupled with Britten's Third.

The eponymous **Tippett Quartet** give perceptive performances of three of the Quartets, but they are not as penetrating as the Lindsays, nor are the recordings so fresh and open. There is no lack of dedication or feeling, yet one does not feel these performances are as completely inside the music as their competitors.

Piano Sonatas 1 (Fantasy-Sonata); 2–3

*** Chan. 9468. Unwin

Piano Sonatas 1 (Fantasy Sonata); 2–4

🎵 Ⓜ **** CRD CRD 34301 (2). Crossley

Paul Crossley has been strongly identified with the Tippett Sonatas; he recorded the first three for Philips in the mid-1970s: indeed, 3 was written for him. The Fourth and last (1983–4) started life as a set of five bagatelles. Crossley contributes an informative and illuminating note on the Sonata and its relationship with, among other things, Ravel's Miroirs; his performance has all the lucidity and subtlety one would expect from him. These masterly accounts are matched by truthful and immediate sound-quality.

Nicholas Unwin has an exceptionally wide range of

colour, though at times Crossley has more subtlety and delicacy when Tippett's fantasy takes wing. The Chandos recording is superb. Crossley's set takes two CDs but, if you happen not to need or want the *Fourth*, this is a viable alternative.

VOCAL MUSIC

Boyhood's End

**** Hyp. CDA 67459. Padmore, Vignoles – BRITTEN: *Who are these children?*; *6 Holderlin Fragments*; FINZI: *A Young Man's Exhortation* ***

Mark Padmore, in his first solo song-recital disc, makes an inspired choice, bringing together four cycles on the theme of youth and friendship. Warmly accompanied by **Roger Vignoles**, he sings with a heady beauty and deep understanding, not least in this unusual Tippett cycle. Asked by his friends Benjamin Britten and Peter Pears to write a piece for them when they returned from America in 1943, Tippett chose to set not verse but prose passages by W. H. Hudson. The result is very characteristic of his early style, with often craggy vocal lines, which Padmore copes with superbly, and awkwardly written piano accompaniment, which Vignoles equally masters with apparent ease.

A Child of Our Time (oratorio)

Ⓜ *** LSO Live SACD LSO 0670. Thomas, Fujimura, Davislim, Rose, LSO & Ch, Colin Davis

🔗 **** Chan. 9123. Haymon, Clarey, Evans, White, L. Symphony Ch., LSO, Hickox

ⒷⒷ *** Naxos 8.557570. Robinson, Walker, Garrison, Cheel, CBSO Ch. & O, composer

The outstanding quality in this SACD version of Tippett's oratorio is the richness and variety of the choral sound, a tribute not just to the singers but to the engineers. Davis recorded the work for Philips many years ago, but this LSO Live version completely supplants it, even though the line-up of soloists is not so starry.

'I have no money for my bread' sings the tenor representing the hero, and **Steve Davislim's** performance conveys that emotion naturally with no exaggeration. **Indra Thomas** is the vibrant soprano soloist, specially moving in her descants over some of the *Spirituals* which movingly take the place of chorales in the piece. **Mihoko Fujimura**, firmly focused, makes the most of her limited opportunities as mezzo soloist, and **Matthew Rose** is a powerful and sensitive bass soloist. Yet it is the crisply incisive singing of the chorus that above all makes this a totally compelling issue, ripely recorded in SACD surround sound.

Hickox's version of Tippett's oratorio *A Child of Our Time* establishes its place against severe competition largely through the exceptionally rich recording and its distinctive choice of soloists, a quartet of black singers. Not only do **Cynthia Haymon**, **Cynthia Clarey**, **Damon Evans** and **Willard White** make the transitions into the spirituals (used in the way Bach used chorales) seem all the more natural, their timbres all have a very sensuous quality. The **London Symphony Chorus**, though not at its most incisive, sings

well, responding to Hickox's warmly expressive style, often even more expansive than the composer himself on his recent recording.

Sir Michael Tippett in his mid-eighties may not secure the best-disciplined performance on record of the earliest of his oratorios, but it is undoubtedly very moving. The spirituals have a heart-easing expressiveness, warmly idiomatic, while the lightness and resilience of *Nobody knows* allows the syncopations to be pointed with winning jazziness. Next to Sir Colin Davis's taut, tough reading (now reissued on Decca) this may be relatively slack, taking a full five minutes longer overall, but the sound on the Naxos disc (originally Collins) is fuller and warmer than that on the Davis set. The soloists are placed well forward, an outstandingly characterful team of singers especially associated with Tippett's music. Although overall the Hickox version on Chandos must be counted first choice, at Naxos price the composer's own version can certainly be recommended alongside it.

OPERA

King Priam (complete; DVD version)

Ⓝ **(*) Arthaus DVD 102 087. Macann, Walker, Haskin, Mason, Janet Price, Jenkins, Ebrahim, Kent Opera Ch. & O, Norrington (Stage Director: Nicholas Hyntner; V/D: Robin Lough)

Tippett's *King Priam* is a work concerned with 'the psychological balance between the characters', and this is far from a conventional entertainment. **Rodney Macann** in the demanding title role, **Sarah Walker's** Andromache, **Neil Jenkins's** Achilles are all powerfully portrayed, but whether the opera communicates to the ordinary non-intellectual operagoer is another matter. Certainly this is a video to see, for Robin Lough's TV version is full of tension and **Roger Norrington** is at home with the music.

King Priam (complete; CD Version)

🔗 **** Chan. 9406/7 (2). Bailey, Harper, Allen, Palmer, Langridge, Minton, Tear, Roberts, L. Symphony Ch., LSO, Atherton

In *King Priam* the dry fragmentation of texture and choppy compression of the drama then seems at odds with an epic subject, particularly after the lyrical, expansive warmth of Tippett's preceding opera, *The Midsummer Marriage*. With an outstanding cast of the finest British singers of the time, **Atherton** in this 1980 recording brings out the sharp cogency of the writing, the composer's single-mindedness in pursuing his own individual line. The Wagnerian **Norman Bailey** sounds agedly noble in the title-role, with **Robert Tear** a shiningly heroic Achilles and **Thomas Allen** a commanding Hector, illuminating every word. The digital recording, originally made by Decca, comes out brilliantly on CD, with each Act fitted conveniently on a single disc.

The Midsummer Marriage (complete)

🔗 ✦ **** Lyrita (ADD) SRCD 2217 (2). Remedios, Carlyle, Burrows, Herinx, Harwood, Watts, Ch. & O of ROHCG, C. Davis

At long last this outstanding (originally Philips) 1970 recording of Tippett's masterpiece reappears on CD. It is a work that should be in the standard repertoire, alongside Britten's *Peter Grimes*, for the music consistently has that inspired melodic flow which distinguishes all great operas. There are few operas of any period which use the chorus to such glorious effect, often in haunting offstage passages, and, with **Sir Colin Davis** a burningly committed advocate and with a cast that was inspired by live performances in the opera house, this is a set hard to resist, even for those not normally fond of modern opera. The so-called 'difficulties' of the libretto, with its mystical philosophical references, fade when the sounds are so honeyed in texture and so consistently lyrical, while the story – for all its complications – preserves a clear sense of emotional involvement throughout. The singing is glorious, the playing magnificent and the recording outstandingly atmospheric, and the Lyrita transfer brings an extraordinary sense of realism, the feeling of sitting in the stalls inside an opera house with quite perfect acoustics – even though the recording was made in Wembley Town Hall.

TOCH, Ernst (1887–1964)

(i) Cello Concerto; Dance Suite

🎶 ⏻ (BB) *** Naxos 8.559282. Spectrum Concerts, Berlin; with (i) Poltera

The *Cello Concerto* in four movements has the solo cello, superbly played by **Christian Poltera**, well matched against a chamber group, with the soloist often playing without any accompaniment. The idiom in the first movement is less tonal than in the other three movements, demonstrating Toch's ability to bridge the gaps between the different modernist movements of the period. The work ends with a contrapuntal finale very close to the music of Toch's contemporary Hindemith. The *Dance Suite*, written at the same time as Bartók's *Dance Suite*, has six varied movements that are far from lightweight. The performances by a talented Berlin group are exemplary, very well recorded.

Symphonies 1, Op. 72; 2, Op. 73; 3, Op. 75; 4, Op. 80; 5, Op. 89 (Jephtha); 6, Op. 93; 7, Op. 95

*** CPO 777 191-2 (3). Berlin RSO, Francis

Toch's *First Symphony* was written at the age of 61 in 1948, not long after he had suffered a heart attack. The *Third Symphony* won a Pulitzer Prize and was recorded in the mid-1950s by William Steinberg and the Pittsburgh orchestra on Capitol. His later music was relatively ignored, though the ever-enterprising Louisville Orchestra recorded the *Fifth*. Toch certainly made up for his neglect of the symphony (a genre which came so naturally to him), for the last three were written in under a year and a half, shortly before his death from cancer in October 1964. It is amazing how, when we think there are no composers of the 20th century left to rediscover, an unfamiliar – and major – figure surfaces. Those investing in this set will be well rewarded.

(i) Symphony 5 (Jephtha); (ii) Cantata of the Bitter Herbs

🎶 ⏻ *** (BB) Naxos 8.559417. (i) Seattle SO; (ii) Bikel, Meyer, Shammash, Clement, Christopher, Prague Philharmonic Ch., Czech PO; Schwarz

What an interesting and rewarding composer Toch is! The *Cantata of the Bitter Herbs* for narrator, soloists, chorus and orchestra comes from 1938, four years after he had left Nazi Germany to settle in the United States. It is neo-romantic and at times even Straussian (he had, incidentally, gone with Strauss to Florence in 1934 to a musical conference). No doubt prompted by the death of his mother in Vienna, it is a work of much inventive resource and undoubted expressive eloquence. The *Fifth* of his seven *Symphonies* comes from 1962–3 and, like the *Cantata*, is based on Exodus. It is subtitled 'Rhapsodic Poem' and is altogether freer in style than 6 and 7, to which he turned in the last year of his life. Both works are of quality and are very well performed and recorded: at a fraction of the price of a concert ticket, this is a real bargain which will well repay curiosity.

Piano Quintet, Op. 64; 3 Impromptus for Cello, Op. 90c; Violin Sonata 2, Op. 44; (Piano) Burlesque, Op. 31

(N) (BB) *** Naxos 8 559324. Spectrum Concerts (Berlin)

As we have discovered from his symphonies Toch is a highly rewarding composer, inventive yet unpredictable, as his fine *Piano Quintet* readily shows, with the four movements bearing out their sub-titles, 'Lyrical', 'Whimsical', 'Contemplative' and 'Dramatic'. The three *Impromptus for Cello*, written for Piatigorsky in 1963, are essentially lyrical, but the *Second Violin Sonata* offers real contrasts, the outer music stormy and the centrepiece *grazioso*. Of the three-part piano *Burlesque*, the final *moto perpetuo*, 'Der Jongleur' became something of a hit in its day (1923). Excellent performances throughout make all this music truly communicative. The recording is rather close but truthful. Well worth investigating.

TOLDRA, Eduardo (1895–1962)

Viste al Mar

*** HM HMI 987072. Cuarteto Casals – RAVEL: *String Quartet*; TURINA: *El Oracion del Torero* ***

Here is a disc promoted by the Spanish department of Harmonia Mundi, designed to link the work of Ravel with that of two Catalan composers, Eduardo Toldra and Joaquin Turina. The players are the greatly talented young **Cuarteto Casals**, winners of the first prize in the 2000 London International Quartet Competition. *Viste al Mar* is the Catalan title of Toldra's 1921 String Quartet (in Spanish *Vista del Mar*, 'View of the Sea'). It was inspired by three poems by Joan Maragall. The composer's original idea was to have each movement prefaced by a recitation of the poem which inspired it, a device adopted on this disc. Though there are several recordings of the composer's orchestration of the piece for strings, this is unique in offering his first ideas for string quartet.

TOMKINS, Thomas (1572–1656)

Music for viols: *Almain in F* (for 4 viols); *Fantasias 1, 12 & 14* (for 3 viols); *Fantasia* (for 6 viols); *Galliard: Thomas Simpson* (5 viols & organ); *In Nomine II* (for 3 viols); *Pavane in A min.* (for 5 viols & organ); *Pavane in F; Ut re mi (Hexachord fantasia)* (both for 4 viols); *(Keyboard)* (i) *Fancy for two to play. Pavan & Galliard: Earl Strafford. (Organ) In nomine; Miserere; Voluntary; Verse anthems: Above the stars; O Lord, let me know mine end; Thou art my King*

⊕ ✹ (BB) **** Naxos 8.550602. Rose Consort of Viols, Red Byrd; Roberts; (i) with Bryan

This well-planned Naxos programme is carefully laid out in two parts, each of viol music interspersed with harpsichord and organ pieces and ending with an anthem. It gives collectors an admirable opportunity to sample, very inexpensively, the wider output of Thomas Tomkins, an outstandingly fine Elizabethan musician whose music is still too little known. Perhaps the most remarkable piece here is the *Hexachord fantasia*, where the scurrying part-writing ornaments a rising and falling six-note scale (hexachord). The two five-part verse anthems and *Above the stars*, which is in six parts, are accompanied by five viols, with a fine counter-tenor in *Above the stars* and a bass in *Thou art my King*.

KEYBOARD MUSIC

Music for harpsichord and virginals: *Barafostus Dreame; 2 Fancies; Fancy for 2 to Play; Fortune my Foe; Galliard of 3 Parts; Galliard Earl Strafford; 2 Grounds; In nomine; Lady Folliott's Galliard; Miserere; Pavan; Pavan Earl Strafford with its devision; Pavane of 3 parts; A Sad Pavane for these Distracted Times; Toy made at Poole Court; What if a Day; Worcester Brawls*

⊕ **** Metronome METCD 1049. Cerasi

Carole Cerasi offers here the finest available collection of the keyboard music of the last of the great English virginalists, Thomas Tomkins. Indeed, it is the repertoire played on the virginals that stands out, especially her exquisitely spontaneous performance of *A Sad Pavane for these Distracted Times*, and her equally sensitive response to the dolorous *Fortune my Foe* (the two most extended pieces here). In contrast, the charmingly good-humoured *Toy made at Poole Court* is given the lightest rhythmic lift. She uses a modern copy of an early 17th-century Ruckers and it could hardly be more realistically recorded. The harpsichord pieces (using a copy of an instrument by Bartolomeno Stephanini) are more robust and often have exuberant decoration, as in the disc's title piece *Barafostus Dreame*. *Earl Strafford's Galliard* is another splendid example of her exciting bravura on the latter

instrument and the closing *Ground* with extended variations is a tour de force. The recording venue has a pleasing ambience and the balance is ideal if you set the volume level carefully.

Fancy; Fancy (for Viols); Galliard; Ground; In Nomine, In Nomine Versions I–II; 4 Pavans; Prelude; Robin Hood; Toy – Made at Poole Court; Voluntary

*** MDG 607 0704-2. Klapprott (harpsichord or virginal)

Bernhard Klapprott is well attuned to Tomkins with his often measured tread, especially in the *Pavans*, which are given a noble dignity. Yet he also seems outgoing, and in the single *Galliard* included here he obviously revels in the fast passage-work. *The Toy – Made at Poole Court* is a most engaging little tune, while the *Robin Hood* variations, using a memorable basic theme, suggest a horse-riding hero. Both this and the closing *Ground* are similarly lively. Excellent recording, not too close and not too resonant.

The Great Service (No. 3); Anthems: Know you not; Oh, that the Salvation; O Lord, let me know mine end; (i) Organ Voluntaries: in A; C; G

⊕ (M) **** CRD CRD 3467. New College, Oxford, Ch., Higginbottom; (i) Burchell

The Great Service (No. 3); When David Heard; Then David Mourned; Almighty God, the Fountain of All Wisdom; Woe is Me; Be Strong and of a Good Courage; O Sing unto the Lord a New Song; O God, the Proud are then Risen Against Me

⊕ **** Gimell CDGIM 024. Tallis Scholars, Phillips

The *Great Service*, in no fewer than ten parts, sets the four canticles – *Te Deum, Jubilate, Magnificat* and *Nunc dimittis* – with a grandeur rarely matched, using the most complex polyphony. The following motets bring comparable examples of his mastery. These complex pieces bring the flawless matching and even tone for which the **Tallis Scholars** are celebrated, and with recording to match.

Many will prefer the more direct and throatier style of the **Choir of New College, Oxford**; even if the choral sound (recorded in the chapel of New College) is less sharply defined, the effect is very satisfying and real. The service is given added variety by the inclusion of three organ voluntaries, well played by **David Burchell**. What makes this record especially attractive is the inclusion of three of Tomkins's most beautiful anthems. The treble solos in *Know you not* and *Oh, that the Salvation* are ravishingly done, and the alto soloist in *O Lord, let me know mine end* is hardly less impressive.

ANTHEMS AND MOTETS

Above the stars my Saviour dwells; Almighty God, the fountain of all wisdom; Arise O Lord, lift up thine hand; Behold the hour cometh and now is; Funeral Sentences; Great and marvellous are Thy works; My Shepherd is the living Lord; O sing unto

the Lord a new song; A Sad Psalm; Then David mourned; When David heard; Fifth Service: Magnificat and Nunc dimittis; (i) Organ Voluntary in D; Pavan & Galliard

∩– (BB) ******** Naxos 8.553794. Oxford Camerata, Summerly; (i) L. Cummings (organ)

Not surprisingly, **Jeremy Summerly** and his **Oxford Camerata** give us an outstanding collection of Tomkins's sacred vocal music, very well laid out. Among the highlights are the beautiful *Funeral Sentences*, and the following glorious *Above the stars my Saviour dwells*, the group which begins with *When David heard that Absolom was slain* and ends with the serene *Almighty God, the fountain of all wisdom* and the glowing *O sing unto the Lord a new Song*. Laurence Cummings adds *A Sad Pavan for these distracted times* to this melancholy sequence, but elsewhere he plays a cheerful *Pavan and Galliard* as another interlude. The choir (with fine soloists) are vividly recorded, with the acoustic resonance of Hertford College Chapel well controlled so that words are clear. An outstanding disc in every way.

Songs of 3, 4, 5 & 6 Parts (1622)

*** Chan. 0680. I Fagiolini, Hollingworth

This enterprising Chandos disc introduces us to a side of Tomkins which, for the most part, is very different from his sacred music. Certainly this collection includes a few deeply religious settings, such as the meltingly beautiful *Woe is me! that I am constrained* (from Psalm 120) and its companion *Turn unto the Lord our God*. But many of these songs are madrigals concerned with more earthly love, even though they remain just as richly expressive, like *Weep no more thou sorry boy*. Others are jolly: *Oyez! Has any found a lad* and the delightful *To the shady woods now wend we*, with its 'fa-la-la-la-las' not as innocent as they seem. The charming, lightweight *See, see the Shepherds' Queen* is a glee which might almost have been written by Sullivan. **I Fagiolini** sing this nicely varied prograame expertly, with a neat rhythmic touch and an attractive blending of voices. They are beautifully recorded.

TOMLINSON, Ernest
(born 1924)

Aladdin: 3 Dances (Birdcage Dance; Cushion Dance; Belly Dance); Comedy Overture; Cumberland Square; English Folk-Dance Suite 1; Light Music Suite; Passepied; (i) Rhapsody & Rondo for Horn & Orchestra. Brigadoon; Shenandoah (arrangement)

*** Marco 8.223513. (i) Watkins; Slovak RSO (Bratislava), composer

The opening *Comedy Overture* is racily vivacious, and there are many charming vignettes here, delectably tuneful and neatly scored, and the pastiche dance movements are nicely elegant. The *Pizzicato humoresque* (from the *Light Music Suite*) is every bit as winning as other, more famous pizzicato movements, and in the *Rhapsody and Rondo* for horn Tomlinson quotes wittily from both Mozart and Britten. The

composer finally lets his hair down in the rather vulgar *Belly Dance*, but the concert ends well with the charming *Georgian Miniature*. The playing is elegant and polished, its scale perfectly judged, and the recording is first class.

An English Overture; 3 Gaelic Sketches: Gaelic Lullaby; Kielder Water; Little Serenade; Lyrical Suite: Nocturne; Nautical Interlude; 3 Pastoral Dances: Hornpipe; Silverthorne Suite; 2nd Suite of English Folk Dances; Sweet and Dainty; arr. of Coates: The Fairy Coach; Cinderella Waltz

*** Marco 8.223413. Slovak RSO (Bratislava), composer

Ernest Tomlinson's orchestral pieces charm by the frothy lightness of the scoring. The winningly delicate *Little Serenade*, which opens the disc, is the most famous, but the gentle, evocative *Kielder Water*, the captivating *Canzonet* from the *Silverthorne Suite* and the *Nocturne* are hardly less appealing. *Love-in-a-mist* is as intangible as it sounds, with the most fragile of oboe solos, and it is not surprising that *Sweet and Dainty* has been used for a TV commercial. There is robust writing, too, in the *Folk Dance Suite* – but not too robust, although the jolly *English Overture* begins with *Here's a Health unto His Majesty* and certainly does not lack vitality. The music is played with much grace and the lightest possible touch by the remarkably versatile **Slovak Radio Orchestra** under the composer, and the vivid recording has delightfully transparent textures, so vital in this repertoire.

TORCH, Sidney (1908–90)

All Strings and Fancy Free; Barbecue; Bicycle Belles; Comic Cuts; Concerto Incognito; Cresta Run; Duel for Drummers; Going for a Ride; London Transport Suite; Mexican Fiesta; On a Spring Note; Petite Valse; Samba Sud; Shooting Star; Shortcake Walk; Slavonic Rhapsody; Trapeze Waltz

*** Marco 8.223443. BBC Concert O, Wordsworth

Sydney Torch worked frequently with the **BBC Concert Orchestra** (the orchestra on this CD), and for many he is remembered for his weekly broadcasts 'Friday Night is Music Night'. The *London Transport Suite* was commissioned by the BBC for their Light Music festival of 1957 and was inspired by the withdrawal of the 'Brighton Belle' on the London-to-Brighton railway service. All the music here is tuneful, at times wistful and nostalgic, at others bright and breezy – *All Strings and Fancy Free* is both. *Barbecue* sounds like a Scottish snap, while the *Trapeze Waltz* is reminiscent of the circus music of Satie. The *Concerto Incognito* is very much in the *Warsaw Concerto* mould, and the *Petite Valse* (also with piano) is more robust than its title suggests. The *Mexican Fiesta* and *Samba Sud* produce some fine local colour and are very jolly, while the *Slavonic Rhapsody* (with two pianos) is a fun work, drawing on the music of Rimsky-Korsakov, Tchaikovsky, Knipper, Borodin and Khachaturian, to form an entertaining if outrageous pastiche. The longest work is the *Duel for Drummers*, which, as its title suggests, is a tour de force for the percussion department; it has some ideas which are reminiscent of Eric Coates and a few surprises, including a cock-erel crowing, and a desert-island storm in the central movement. It ends with a lively *galop*. **Barry Wordsworth** conducts with flair, and the recording is excellent.

TORELLI, Giuseppe (1658–1709)

Concerti musicali, Op. 6/1-12 ; Sonata a 4 in A min.

(N) **** Signum SIGCD 157. Charivari Agréable, Kah-Ming Ng

This set is given the sobriquet 'the original Brandenburg concertos'. Up to a point that is acceptable, but Bach's Margrave of Brandenburg was a different person from Torelli's employer, the Margrave of Brandenburg-Ansbach. However Torelli did dedicate his *Concerti musicale* to Sophie Charlotte, Electress of Brandenburg, although nothing came of the dedication. But the *Concerti musicali* are a real discovery and they are most attractively presented here. Originally intended for strings alone, the Charivari have included oboes, recorders and bassoon and a continuo featuring chamber organ as well as theorbo and harpsichord. The result is most enjoyable: allegros are jolly and slow movements expressive and appealing, and **Kah Ming Ng** brings the music to life vividly and spontaneously, helped by lively, truthful recording

(i) Violin Concertos, Op. 8/8, 9 & 11; (i; ii) Double Violin Concertos, Op. 8/2, 4, 5, 6; (iii) Sinfonias for Trumpet in D (G 8); (iii; iv) for 2 Trumpets, (G 23).

🎧 **** Chan. 0716. (i) Standage; (ii) Weiss; (iii) Steele-Perkins; (ii) Blackadder; Coll. Mus. 90

While Torelli's earlier *Concertos* remain in the world of the concerto grosso, by the time he came to write Op. 8 (published in 1709), he had moved away to give his soloists independence. The lustrous, busy opening of Op. 8/2 is immediatiay enticing, but these are all attractive works, particularly 4 (where the pointed theme of the finale reminds one of 'All we like sheep') and 6, with its *Largo e staccato* central movement anticipating Vivaldi. The solo *Concerto in E minor*, Op. 8/11, is also a particularly fine work. Not surprisingly, the period performances here are first class. The rather more conventional *Trumpet Concertos* are also in confident hands, and throughout the accompaniments are characteristically stylish and the Chandos recording first rate.

TORMIS, Veljo (born 1930)

Autumn Landscapes; 3 Estonian Folk Songs; 4 Estonian Lullabies; Livonian Heritage; Singing aboard ship; 3 Songs from the epic 'Kalev's Son'; 2 Songs to Words by Ernst Enno

🎧 *** Hyp. CDA 67601. Holst Singers, Layton

Internationally, Arvo Pärt is the most familiar name among Estonian composers, but Veljo Tormis, five years older, and once his teacher, is the composer most loved in his own country. One has only to start this programme with his set-

ting of *Two Songs* by Ernst Enno, *Early Summer* and *Soundlessly somewhere murmurings homeward*, to discover the harmonic richness and evocative atmosphere, to say nothing of the originality and passionate unpredictability of his music. In *Waking the Birds* from the *Livonian Heritage* he writes hypnotically over a quiet sustained pedal; in *Shrovetide* he alternates men's and women's voices in different rhythms; while in *Singing aboard ship* the women sing the poem while the men wordlessly create the rocking waves. Contrastingly, *Wee winkie mouse* is a delightfully gentle lullaby. The variety of style and feeling continues through the seven-part *Autumn Landscapes*, and the programme climaxes with the strongly felt *Childhood memory* (*Herding Calls*). All the music is melodically rich, and it is all sung gloriously by the **Holst Singers** under **Stephen Layton**, who obviously identifies completely with the composer's muse. Splendid recording too, clear yet with a warm ambience.

TÓRROBA, Federico (1891–1982)

Luisa Fernanda (complete; DVD and CD versions)

*** Opus Arte **DVD** OA 0969 D.; CD 0028947658252 Domingo, Herrera, Bros, Cantarero, Teatro Madrid Ch. & O, López-Cobos (Dir: Emilio Sagi, V/D: Angel Luis Ramirez)

Plácido Domingo has been a lifelong advocate of the zarzuela, the Spanish genre of operetta. Here he takes the lead in one of the most celebrated, full of attractive tunes, not least the *Romanza di Vidal*. Vidal's rival in love for his beloved Luisa, well taken by the soprano **Nancy Herrera**, is another tenor, who offers vocal as well as dramatic rivalry to Domingo, **José Bros** as Javier, though he is no match for Domingo as an actor. Among the jewels here are a number of ensemble numbers, including the martial finale to Act II and a ballet in Mazurka rhythm. The staging is generally traditional and effective, a co-production between Madrid and the opera companies of Washington and Los Angeles. Full, bright sound.

The CD version includes full documentation including a libretto.

TOURNEMIRE, Charles (1870–1939)

L'Orgue mystique, Op. 56: Volumes 1 & 2

*** Priory PRCD 669 AB. Dufourcet (organs of Sainte-Trinité, Paris, & Basilique du Sacré-Coeur de Montmartre, Paris)

L'Orgue mystique (of which these are only the first two volumes) was designed for use within the *Masses* on Sundays and Feast Days, being useful for organists who have not the skill to improvise their own voluntaries. Tournemire uses no fewer than 300 different chants throughout his work, providing spectacular *Postludes* for the exit music. But the centrepieces of each of these two volumes include *Paraphrases*, *Fantaisies* and four or five *Chorale Alleluias*. The music is diverse and often powerful, but some of the intricate passagework tends to get lost in the reverberation, an effect that must be intended, as the recording is obviously truthful. **Marie-Bernadette Dufourcet** is a splendid advocate, using the Sainte-Trinité organ throughout, except for the *Fantasie for Epiphany* in Volume 1 and the closing *Fantaisie on the Te Deum* in Volume 2, where she chooses the organ at Sacré-Coeur.

Choral-improvisation on the Victimae paschali laudes; Lento; Suite évocatrice, Op. 74; Office: Domenica Resurrectionis: 5 Petites fleurs musicales, Op. 66; Postludes pour les Antiennes de Magnificat: Amen & Postlude; L'Orgue mystique: Volume 17, Op. 56 (excerpts); Toccata, Op. 19/3

*** ATMA ACD2 2470. Boucher (Casavant organ at L'Eglise des Saints-Anges-Gardiens, Lachine, Quebec)

This collection is a much more enjoyable way of discovering the variety of Tournemire's output than *L'Orgue mystique*. **Vincent Boucher** opens dramatically with a *Choral-improvisation* and follows with a rather beautiful, brief *Lento* that immediately reveals Tournemire as able to compose a slow movement without sentimentality, far more appealing than a comparable Widor piece. The *Suite évocatrice* is made up of five neatly registered miniatures, of which the closing *Caprice* is engagingly playful, and the *Petites fleurs musicales* offer comparable diversity. The *Amen* and *Postlude* each last barely a minute, yet again make their mark with gentle colouring, and the closing five movements from *L'Orgue mystique* show this work at its most impressive. The Quebec organ has a fine weight of sonority, but also in the hands of the excellent Boucher a rich palette of colour.

TOVEY, Donald (1875–1940)

Piano Concerto in A, Op. 15

*** Hyp. CDA 67023. Osborne, BBC Scottish SO, Brabbins –
  MACKENZIE: *Scottish Concerto* ***

Hyperion in its imaginative series of Romantic *Piano Concertos* here offers two Scottish works. Sir Donald Tovey is best known for his analytical essays, and his *Concerto*, if less distinctively Scottish, is the grander work, with weighty textures and a strongly controlled structure. The young Scottish pianist **Steven Osborne** is a brilliant advocate.

TREDICI, David Del (b. 1937)

Final Alice

(N) **** Australian Decca Eloquence 442 9955. Hendricks, Chicago SO, Solti

Improbably commissioned to celebrate the bicentennial of the United States in 1976, this instalment of Del Tredici's sequence of Lewis Carroll settings has much to fascinate the ear, particularly in a virtuoso performance like this. Familiar texts are neatly assembled, with a minimum of violence to the original, to present a dramatic cantata for just one voice and orchestra. **Barbara Hendricks** proves a characterful and urgent guide, a vibrant narrator as well as a fine singer. **Solti**

and his superb orchestra plainly enjoy the fun from first to last: it is good to welcome an extended work which sustains its length without pomposity and with immediate warmth of communication. The recording is outstandingly brilliant and its premiere release on CD is enormously welcomed.

TUBIN, Eduard (1905–82)

(i) Balalaika Concerto; Music for Strings; Symphony 1

🎧 *** BIS CD 351. (i) Sheynkman; Swedish RSO, Järvi

The opening of the *First Symphony* has a Sibelian breadth, but for the most part it is a symphony apart from its fellows. The quality of the musical substance is high; its presentation is astonishingly assured for a young man still in his twenties, and the scoring is masterly. **Emanuil Sheynkman's** account of the *Balalaika Concerto* with **Neeme Järvi** is first class, both taut and concentrated. Excellent recording.

(i) Ballade for Violin & Orchestra; (ii) Double-bass Concerto; (i) Violin Concerto 2; Estonian Dance Suite; Valse triste

🎧 *** BIS CD 337. (i) Garcia; (ii) Ehren; Gothenburg SO, Järvi

Tubin's highly imaginative *Double-bass Concerto* has an unflagging sense of momentum and is ideally proportioned; the ideas never outstay their welcome and one's attention is always held. The *Second Violin Concerto* has an appealing lyricism, is well proportioned and has a strong sense of forward movement. The *Ballade* is a work of gravity and eloquence. *Valse triste* is a short and rather charming piece, while the *Dance Suite* is the Estonian equivalent of the *Dances of Galánta*. Splendid performances from both soloists in the *Concertos* and from the orchestra under **Järvi** throughout, and excellent recording.

Symphonies (i) 1 in C min.; 2 (The Legendary); 3 in D min.; (ii) 4 in A (Sinfonia lirica); (iii) 5 in B min.; (ii) 6; (iv) 7; (ii) 8; (iv) 9 (Sinfonia semplice); 10; (ii) Suite from the ballet, Kratt; (iv) Toccata for Orchestra

🎧 ✹ (M) **** BIS CD 1402/06 (5). (i) Swedish RSO; (ii) Bergen PO; (iii) Bamberg SO; (iv) Gothenburg SO; Järvi

Neeme Järvi's survey of the Tubin *Symphonies* is here packaged shorn of some of its couplings and presented in an attractive and competitive format (five CDs for the price of three). These are marvellous works, rich in invention and with the real breadth of the symphonist about them. Anyone who is attuned to the symphonies of Sibelius or Prokofiev will find themselves at home in this world. The opening of the *Second Symphony* is magical: there are soft, luminous string chords that evoke a strong atmosphere of wide vistas and white summer nights, but the music soon gathers power and reveals a genuine feeling for proportion and of organic growth. If there is a Sibelian strength in the *Second Symphony*, the *Sixth*, written after Tubin had settled in Sweden, has obvious resonances of Prokofiev – even down to instrumentation – and yet Tubin's rhythmic vitality and melodic invention are quietly distinctive. The first two movements of the wartime *Third Symphony* are vintage Tubin, but the heroic finale approaches bombast. The *Eighth* is his masterpiece; its opening movement has a sense of vision and mystery, and the atmosphere stays with you. This is the darkest of the symphonies and the most intense in feeling, music of great substance. The first two movements of the wartime *Third Symphony* are vintage Tubin, but the heroic finale approaches bombast. The *Eighth* is his masterpiece; its opening movement has a sense of vision and mystery, and the atmosphere stays with you. This is the darkest of the symphonies and the most intense in feeling, music of great substance. The *Fourth* is a highly attractive piece, immediately accessible, the music well argued and expertly crafted. The opening has a Sibelian feel to it but, the closer one comes to it, the more individual it seems. The *Ninth Symphony* is in two movements: its mood is elegiac and a restrained melancholy permeates the slower sections. Its musical language is direct, tonal and, once one gets to grips with it, quite personal. If its spiritual world is clearly Nordic, the textures are transparent and luminous, and its argument unfolds naturally and cogently. The *Fifth* makes as good a starting point as any to investigate the Tubin canon. Written after he had settled in Sweden, it finds him at his most neoclassical; the music is finely paced and full of energy and invention. The *Seventh* is a marvellous work and it receives a concentrated and impressive reading. As always with Tubin, you are never in doubt that this is a real *Symphony*, which sets out purposefully and reaches its goal. The ideas could not be by anyone else and the music unfolds with a powerful logic and inevitability. The *Tenth Symphony* is a one-movement piece that begins with a sombre string idea, which is soon interrupted by a periodically recurring horn call – and which resonates in the mind long afterwards. The recordings are absolutely first class.

(i; iii) *Ballade; Capricci 1 & 2; The Cock's Dance; Meditation; 3 Pieces; Prelude;* (i) *Sonata for Unaccompanied Violin;* (i; iii) *Violin Sonatas 1 & 2; Suite of Estonian Dance Tunes; Suite on Estonian Dances;* (ii; iii) *Viola Sonata; Viola Sonata* (arr. of *Alto Saxophone Sonata*)

★★★ BIS CD 541/542 (2). (i) Leibur; (ii) Vahle; (iii) Rumessen

Although the smaller pieces are finely wrought, Tubin seems to come into his own on a larger canvas. Particularly impressive are the *Second Violin Sonata* (*In the Phrygian Mode*), the visionary *Second Piano Sonata*, and the two sonatas for viola, one a transcription of the *Alto Saxophone Sonata* with its foretaste of the *Sixth Symphony* (1954) in which that instrument plays a prominent, almost soloistic role, and the later *Viola Sonata* (1965). Highly accomplished performances from **Arvo Leibur** and **Petra Vahle**, and exceptionally thorough documentation from the pianist **Vardo Rumessen**, with over 40 music-type examples. The recording is truthful, but the acoustic lends a shade too much resonance to the piano, which is often bottom-heavy.

Complete piano music: *Album leaf; Ballad on a Theme by Maat Saar; 3 Estonian folk-dances; 4 Folksongs from my Country; A Little March for*

Rana; Lullaby; 3 Pieces for Children; Prelude 1; 7 Preludes; Sonatas 1-2; Sonatina in D min.; Suite on Estonian Shepherd Melodies; Variations on an Estonian folk-tune

★★★ BIS CD 414/6. Rumessen

Tubin's first works for piano inhabit a world in which Scriabin, Ravel and Eller were clearly dominant influences but in which an individual sensibility is also to be discerned. The resourceful *Variations on an Estonian folk-tune* is a lovely work that deserves a place in the repertoire, as does the *Sonatina in D minor*, where the ideas and sense of momentum are on a larger scale than one would expect in a sonatina. The *Second Sonata* is a key work in Tubin's development. It opens with a shimmering figure in free rhythm, inspired by the play of the aurora borealis, and is much more concentrated than his earlier piano works. **Vardo Rumessen** makes an excellent case for it and it is impressive stuff. The performances are consistently fine, full of understanding and flair, and the recording is very natural.

OPERA

Barbara von Tisenhusen

★★★ Ondine ODE776-2 (2). Raamat, Sild, Kuusk, Puurabar, Kollo, Estonian Op. Company & O, Lilje

Tubin's opera with its theme of illicit passion is not long, consisting of three acts of roughly 30 minutes each. It has pace and a variety of dramatic incident and musical textures, and the main roles in the action are vividly characterized. The musical substance of the opera is largely based on a chaconne-like figure of nine notes heard at the very outset, yet the theme changes subtly and skilfully to meet the constantly shifting dramatic environment so that the casual listener will probably not be consciously aware of the musical means Tubin is employing. All the singers are dedicated and serve the composer well and, though the orchestra is not first class, it too plays with spirit and enthusiasm under **Peeter Lilje**. The recording produces a sound comparable to that of a broadcast relay rather than the opulent sound one can expect from a commercial studio recording. A strong recommendation.

The Parson of Reigi; (i) *Requiem for Fallen Soldiers*

★★★ Ondine ODE783-2 (2). Maiste, Eensalu, Tõnuri, Kuusk, Estonian Op. Company & O, Mägi; (i) Tauts; Deksnis, Leiten; Tiido, Roos, Estonian Nat. Male Ch., Klas

After the success of *Barbara von Tisenhusen*, the **Estonian Opera** immediately commissioned Tubin to compose *The Parson of Reigi*, and it, too, concerns an illicit relationship. Tubin's music powerfully evokes the claustrophobic milieu of a small, closely knit fishing community and is particularly successful in conveying atmosphere. The dawn scene, where the parson, Lampelius, blesses the departing fishermen, is particularly imaginative, as is the evocation of the white summer nights in the garden scene, where the heroine confesses her illicit passion. As in *Barbara von Tisenhusen*, Tubin's powers of characterization of both the major and supporting roles are striking, and there is a compelling sense of dramatic narrative as well as variety of pace. The performance of the three principal singers is very good – especially the parson, splendidly sung by the baritone **Teo Maiste** – and the only let-down is in the quality of the orchestral playing, which is little more than passable.

The coupled *Requiem for Fallen Soldiers* is generally to be preferred to the rival account on BIS coupled with the *Tenth Symphony* (see above). The Estonian singers produce better focused and darker tone than their Swedish colleagues, though the BIS recording has some amazingly lyrical playing by Håkan Hardenberger. The Estonian player, **Urmas Leiten**, is very eloquent too. Strongly recommended.

TURINA, Joaquin (1882–1949)

Danzas fantásticas, Op. 22; La Procesión del Rocio, Op. 9; Sinfonia sevillana, Op. 23

⊶ (M) **** Telarc CD 80574. Cincinnati SO, López-Cobos –
   DEBUSSY: *Ibéria* ***

As we have already discovered with his earlier Decca recording of the *Danzas fantásticas*, **Jesús López-Cobos** is at his finest in these alluring and exotically orchestrated pieces. The **Cincinnati Orchestra** play throughout with voluptuous brilliance and are especially exciting in the closing *Orgía* of the *Danzas fantásticas*. The recording is of Telarc's finest quality, a rich, glittering tapestry of sound.

(i) *Danzas fantásticas*; (ii) *La Oración del Torero, Op. 34; La Procesión del Rocio, Op. 9;* (i; iii) *Rapsodia sinfonica*; (i) *Sinfonia Sevilla*

(N) (BB) *** Regis RRC 1299. Bátiz with (i) LPO; (ii) Mexico City PO; (iii) Wibaut

The three **LPO** items were recorded in 1983 and originally released on HMV. The three *Danzas fantásticas* are understandably better known than the other two works included on the original LP. The *Sinfonia* is a programmatic triptych, with an attractive nocturnal slow movement, the scoring of the outer movements (as in the *Danzas*) is gaudy but effective. The *Rapsodia* is a pleasant if not especially memorable piece for piano and orchestra. **Bátiz** is a sympathetic exponent of this repertoire and, with the LPO, he brings out the Latin colours and atmosphere. Two further colourful pieces have been added to this bargain release, with the **Mexico City Philharmonic**, also conducted by Bátiz. They are similarly well played and well recorded. An undoubted bargain.

La oración del torero (version for string orchestra)

*** Chan. 9288. I Musici di Montréal, Turovsky – SHCHEDRIN: *Carmen ballet suite* etc ***

The composer's string-orchestral version of the haunting *Oración del torero* is warmly and sensitively played and very well recorded here, and if the quartet version is even more subtle (see below) this makes an enjoyable foil for Shchedrin's brilliant arrangement of music from Bizet's *Carmen*.

Rapsodia sinfónica (arr. Halffter)

⊶ (B) *** Decca 448 243-2. de Larrocha, LPO, Frühbeck de Burgos – ALBÉNIZ: *Rapsodia española*; RODRIGO: *Concierto de Aranjuez*, etc ***

*** Australian Decca Eloquence 476 2971. de Larrocha, LPO, Burgos – ALBÉNIZ: *Rapsodia española*; MONTSALVATGE: *Concerto breve*; SURINACH: *Piano Concerto* ***

(BB) *** Warner Apex 8573 89223-2 Heisser, Lausanne CO, López-Cobos – ALBÉNIZ: *Concierto fantástico; Rapsodia española*; FALLA: *Nights in the Gardens of Spain* ***

Turina's *Rapsodia sinfónica* has been recorded by others, but in the hands of **Alicia de Larrocha** it is played with such éclat that it becomes memorable and thoroughly entertaining. This performance is also available on an Australian Decca reissue, coupled to rare concertos by other lesser-known composers.

The performance by **Jean-François Heisser** (with **López-Cobos** a brilliantly idiomatic partner) is also first class in every way, combining seductive poetic feeling, brilliant colouring and excitement. The digital recording is vividly balanced and the couplings are no less attractive.

CHAMBER MUSIC

La oración del torero

*** HM HMI 987072. Casals Qt – RAVEL: *String Quartet*; TOLDRA: *Viste al Mar* ***

(***) Testament mono SBT 1053. Hollywood Qt – CRESTON: *Quartet*; DEBUSSY: *Danses sacrée*; RAVEL: *Introduction & Allegro*; VILLA-LOBOS: *Quartet 6*. (***)

The idea of the bullfighter's prayer inspires Turina to a warmly lyrical piece which nicely complements the Ravel and Toldra works under the title *Influencias*. Well recorded by Spanish Harmonia Mundi.

It is difficult to imagine Turina's famous piece being played with greater expressive eloquence or more perfect ensemble than by the incomparable **Hollywood Quartet**, and it comes as part of a valuable and beautifully transferred anthology.

Piano Quartet in A min., Op. 67

*** Black Box BBX 1048. Lyric Piano Qt – STRAUSS: *Piano Quartet in C min.*, Op. 13 ***

Turina's *Piano Quartet in A minor* comes from 1931, and though it is not great music it is far from negligible. It is well played and recorded here, and the coupling is equally rare.

Contes d'espagne, Series I & II, Opp. 20 & 47; Silhouettes, Op. 70; Souvenirs de l'Ancienne Espagne, Op. 48

(N) (BB) *** Naxos 8.570370 Jordi Masú

The two volumes of the *Contes d'espagne* established Turina's keyboard reputation. The first series (1918) offers seven impressionistic 'perceptions', but not picture postcards, of various areas in Spain, with themes that recur cyclically in each movement. The second series offers impressionistic vignettes, evocative but in no way pictorial. The *Silhouettes* are more tangibly evocative of famous landmarks including Segovia's Roman Aqueduct and the Lighthouse at Cádiz, while the *Souvenirs* recreate famous Spanish characters including Carmen (though not reflecting Bizet's opera) and Don Juan as drawn from José Zorrilla's play. **Jordi Masú** plays with a nice balance between virtuosity and an evocative colour palette, and he is well recorded.

TURNAGE, Mark-Anthony
(born 1960)

Blood on the Floor (DVD version)

*** Arthaus **DVD** 100 430. Ens. Modern, Rundel (Dir: Doris Götzl; V/D Dir: Barrie Gavin)

With **Peter Rundel** conducting a group of German musicians, *Blood on the Floor* is a powerful piece inspired by a painting of Francis Bacon. A complete performance is here introduced by a feature film. Characteristically the idiom is abrasive with a jazz element important, making it attractive despite the unpleasantness of the subject with its element of drug addiction. It would be hard to imagine a better performance, very well played and recorded.

CHAMBER MUSIC

An Invention on Solitude; Cortège for Chris; 2 Elegies Framing a Shout; 3 Farewells; 2 Memorials; Sleep On; True Life Stories: Tune for Toru

⊕– **** Black Box BBM 1065. Nash Ens. (members)

Anyone coming new to Turnage could not do better than start here, for all this music is intensely expressive and instantly communicative. Its overriding character is thoughtful and contemplative, although *An Invention of Solitude* is the exception, for while inspired by the Brahms *Clarinet Quintet*, the writing, for the same combination, 'fluctuates between stillness and violence'. The *Cortège for Chris* (Christopher Van Kempen, the **Nash Ensemble's** cellist who died in 1998) features both cello and clarinet, as well as a ruminative piano, while the *Two Memorials* are commemorated with haunting soliloquizing from the solo saxophone.

The *Three Farewells* are strangely obsessive: each has a hidden text, the second, *Music to Hear*, for viola and muted cello, a Shakespeare sonnet. The finale, *All will be well*, was written as a wedding piece, and the composer observes ironically 'the marriage didn't last'. Not surprisingly, some of the most peaceful and serene writing comes in *Sleep On*, for cello and piano, a triptych framed by a lovely *Berceuse*, and a restful *Lullaby*. The solo saxophone returns for the first of the *Two Elegies* and after being exuberantly interrupted by the *Shout* – a spiky and restlessly energetic boogie – the piano (with the saxophone) 'searches for and finds repose'.

The reflective closing *Tune for Toru* (a gentle piano piece) was written in response to the death of the Japanese composer Toru Takemitsu and readily finds the stillness the composer was searching for in his *Invention on Solitude*. Superbly responsive performances throughout and vividly real recording, within an attractively spacious acoustic.

Greek (opera; complete; DVD version)

*** Arthaus **DVD** 102 105. Hayes, Kimm, Suart, Charnock, Almeida Ens., Bernas (V/D: Dennis Marks)

Mark-Anthony Turnage's *Greek*, based on a libretto by Steven Berkoff, is an opera of violence, a retelling of the Oedipus myth. It is an abrasive piece but is nevertheless most approachable. This BBC production introduces the work as well as presenting the opera complete. It is a memorable work well worth investigating, very well performed and recorded.

TVEITT, Geirr (1908–81)

Piano Concertos (i) 1, Op. 1; (ii) 4 (Northern Lights), Op. 130; (iii) The Turtle

*** BIS CD 1397. Stavanger SO, Ruud; with (i) Bjelland; (ii) Austbø; (iii) Kosmo

The *First Piano Concerto*, written in his early twenties, has a natural fluency and a certain Gallic charm. The opening of *The Turtle*, a setting of a passage from Steinbeck's *The Grapes of Wrath*, once again leaves no doubt as to the vividness of his orchestral imagination. Like our own Robert Simpson, Tveitt was a keen amateur astronomer, and the *Fourth Concerto*, inspired by the Aurora Borealis, shows his strong fascination with the heavens. It is imaginative if diffuse and wanting in concentration; but there are flashes of colour and inspiration that really reward investigation. Exceptionally wide-ranging recorded sound.

Piano Concertos 1 in F, Op. 1; 5, Op. 156.

BB *** Naxos 8.555077. Gimse, RSNO, Engeset

Geirr Tveitt (pronounced with a soft 'G' and surname as in 'Tate') was obviously an accomplished pianist as, when he gave the first performance of the *Fifth Piano Concerto* in 1954 in Paris under Jean Martinon, he also played the *B flat minor Concerto* of Tchaikovsky and Brahms's *D minor Concerto*! **Håvard Gimse** is an artist of quality and well supported by the **Royal Scottish National Orchestra** under **Bjarte Engeset**.

Piano Concerto 4 (Aurora borealis), Op. 130; (i) Variations on a Folksong from Hardanger for 2 Pianos & Orchestra

BB *** Naxos 8.555761. Gimse, RSNO, Engeset; with (i) Süssmann

Geirr Tveitt's *Fourth Piano Concerto* of 1947 is highly original and, as its subtitle suggests, evokes the extraordinary display and movement of the *Northern Lights*. It is superbly played by **Håvard Gimse** and the **Scottish Orchestra** under **Bjarte Engeset**. The *Variations*, in which Gimse is joined by **Gunilla Süssmann**, are also full of character and colour, even if they somewhat outstay their welcome. Strongly recommended.

A Hundred Hardanger Tunes, Op. 151: Suites 1, 1–15; 4 (Nuptials) 46–60.

(BB) *** Naxos 8.555078. RSNO, Engeset

A Hundred Hardanger Tunes: Suites 2: 15 Mountain Songs (Nos. 16–30); 5: Troll Tunes (61–75)

(BB) *** Naxos 8.555770. RSNO, Engeset

Try 'So stilt dei ror på glitre-fjord' (*How silently they row on the glittering fjord*), and you will understand why Tveitt enjoyed such an enviable reputation as an orchestrator. His sound world is highly original and imaginative, and unfailingly inventive. Each of these suites comprises fifteen numbers, which some may find too much of a good thing, and there is something to be said for making one's own shorter compilations. The **Royal Scottish National Orchestra** play with evident enthusiasm for **Bjarte Engeset**, who has collated the various different sources in preparing his edition. Nearly all these pieces are delightful and many are quite captivating. The second selection is every bit as imaginative and colourful as the earlier sets. Something of a find.

TYE, Christopher (c. 1505–c. 1572)

Complete instrumental music: *Amavit a 5; Christus Resurgens a 5; Dum Transisset a 5 (4 versions); In Nomines a 4, a 5, a 6 (21 settings); Lawdes Deo a 5; Sit fast a 3*

(M) **(*) Astrée ES 9939. Hespèrion XX, Savall

Tye's consort music is unjustly neglected. The present collection includes all of his surviving instrumental pieces. Virtually all the music is slow and expressive; many of the *In nomine* pieces have biblical allusions in their simple titles. The performances here make a very strong impression; the viol timbre unexpectedly full-bodied. Indeed, the playing of **Hespèrion XX** has been criticized for being too rich in timbre for the period. We have no quarrel with the sound, but would have liked greater dynamic contrast in the playing. Excellent recording.

Euge bone; Kyrie: Orbis factor; Motets: Miserere mei, Deus; Omnes gentes, plaudite minibus; Peccavimus cum patribus nostris; Quaesumus omnipotens Deus

⊕– (BB) *** Hyp. Helios CDH 55079. Winchester Cathedral Ch., Hill

Masses: *Euge bone; Peterhouse; Western Wind*

⊕– (M) **** ASV CDGAU 190 (2). Ely Cathedral Ch., Trepte

Christopher Tye spent most of his musical life in Cambridge and Ely and became master of the chorus and organist at Ely Cathedral in 1543; he retired to take holy orders in 1560 but remained living near Ely. So the soaring acoustics of Ely Cathedral and performances by its present-day choir could not be more apt for his three greatest *Masses*, of which the large-scale *Euge bone* is the most splendid. The passionate singing on ASV is fully worthy, the choral sound glorious. With a playing time of 83 minutes, the three works would

not fit onto a single CD, but the two discs are offered for the price of one.

The performance from the splendid **Winchester Cathedral Choir** under **David Hill** is no less eloquent; the contrast between the *Gloria*, pressed on ardently, and the serene *Sanctus* is particularly telling. Moreover, the four accompanying motets are also very fine, especially the exuberant *Omnes gentes* (a setting of Psalm 46 from the Vulgate), and the extended and very beautiful supplication, *Peccavimus cum patribus nostris*, which soars up to the heavens. Fine atmospheric recording makes this bargain reissue particularly tempting.

VAET, Jacobus (c. 1529–1567)

Antevenis virides; Miss Ego flos campi.Ecce apparebit Dominus; Filiae Jerusalem; Magnificat octavi toni;.Miserere mei, Deus; Musica Dei donum; Spiritus Domini; Salve regina

(N) *** Hyp. CDA 67733. Cinquecento (augmented) (with CLEMENS NON PAPA: *Ego flos campi ***)

Jacobus Vaet is an unfamiliar name today but in the mid-1550s he had become Kapellmeister to the Archduke Maximilian, the nephew of the emperor, Charles V. His output was considerable (9 mass settings and 66 motets!) Jacob Clemens non Papa was the obvious influence on him and it is he who provides the motet on which the mass, *Ego flos camip* is built, immediately drawing its opening material. Vaet moves between six and four voices although the *Agnus Dei* is expanded to eight. His use of imitation flows pleasingly, yet his word-setting is often vivid and this applies also to the motets. The *Magnificat* also has plenty of variety in this respect, and the *Salve regina* is again imaginatively set. The performances by **Cinquecento** are very persuasive and beautifully recorded.

VAINBERG, Moishei (See also under Weinberg) (1919–96)

Violin Concerto

⊕– (BB) *** Naxos 8.557194. Grubert, Russian PO, Yablonsky – MIASKOVSKY: *Violin Concerto ***

The Lithuanian violinist **Ilya Grubert** on Naxos couples Miaskovsky's glorious *Concerto* with the relatively little known *Concerto* of Mieczyslaw (or Moishei) Vainberg, composed in 1958 for Leonid Kogan. The concerto owes a lot to Shostakovich, but an individual voice can be discerned as one comes closer to it.

Sinfonietta 1, Op. 41; Symphony 5, Op. 76

*** Chan. 10128. Polish Nat. RSO, Chmura

All the *Symphonies* we have heard betray a debt to Shostakovich, without being entirely overwhelmed by him. The *Fifth* is a long piece dating from 1962, and it holds the listener even when it doesn't wholly satisfy him or her. The slow movement is a little too long, given the quality of its ideas, but generally speaking the work has considerable power and eloquence. It has thoroughly committed players in **Gabriel Chmura** and his fine **Polish Orchestra** – and superb Chandos recording. The *Sinfonietta 1* (1948) makes use of Jewish melodies, which Vainberg fashions in a style influenced by Bartók. Well worth investigating.

VALEN, Fartein (1887–1962)

An Die Hoffnung; Epithalamion; Nenia; Symphonies 2–3

Ⓝ *** BIS CD 1632. Stavanger SO, Eggen

Fartein Valen enjoyed cult status in the late 1940s but has rather disappeared from view in recent years. Brought up in Madagascar where his father was a missionary, Valen studied philology in Oslo, becoming the University librarian in the 1920s. A reclusive and isolated figure he was to become the first dodecaphonic composer in northern Europe.

The three non-symphonic works on this CD were all composed in the space of over a year and express the composer's interest in classical antiquity and in Rome, where he visited in 1922. These works are atmospheric, rather than descriptive tone poems and one enjoys the richness of the work's textures rather than any lively, descriptive writing. The *Second Symphony's* four movements each uses all twelve notes of the scale to make up its principle themes. It is a 'pure' music symphony, although the composer's biographer, Olav Gurvin, claims there to be a Christmas feeling in the first movement, which the present writer finds hard to detect. The rather ambiguous mood of the *Second Symphony* is also carried over to the *Third*, though that has a rather more dramatic third movement. None of this is particularly easy music, but the sound world is often quite haunting and the sincerity of the composer and the cogency of the musical argument is never in doubt. First class performances and recording, and helpful notes by the conductor are included.

(i) *Piano Concerto, Op. 44. The Churchyard by the Sea; Ode to Solitude; The Silent Island; Symphony 4, Op. 43*

Ⓝ *** BIS CD1642. Stavanger SO, Christian Eggen with (i) Smebye

Valen's elegiac *Violin Concerto* (not included here, but promised on a future disc) is a haunting and poignant work which, like Berg's, commemorates the death of a young person. However the evocative tone-poems which are recorded here are most impressive. They are quite unlike any other Norwegian music and have no touch of folk nationalism. The shortish (ten-minute) piano concerto is not so memorable as its companions, but like everything on this disc, it is well played and eminently well recorded. We look forward to further issues in this series.

VALLS, Francisco (1665–1747)

Missa Scala Aretina

ⒷⒷ **(*) DHM 05472 77842-2. Piau, Van der Sluis, Lettinga,

Elwes, Van der Kamp, Netherlands Bach Fest. Bar. O, Leonhardt – BIBER: *Requiem in F min* **(*)

Francisco Valls, another name to spring suddenly out of the past, was choirmaster at Barcelona Cathedral, and the *Missa Scala Aretina* (1702) is the only one of his ten *Masses* to have gained any kind of fame outside Spain. It is a powerfully expressive piece, not always with conventional harmony. It is laid out for four separate groups of performers, containing, respectively, the soloists, instrumentalists (including harp in the continuo) and two choral ensembles. **Leonhardt** delivers a committed spontaneous performance, but the choral singing does not convey the impression that the Netherlanders are thoroughly at home in the Spanish idiom nor is it ideally crisp in ensemble. Nevertheless, with rich recording, this is by no means unimpressive and it is certainly not dull.

VAŇHAL, Jan (1739–1813)

Violin Concertos in G, GI & GII; in B flat, Bb1

☁ ⒷⒷ *** Naxos 8.557815. Nishizaki, Cologne CO, Müller-Brühl

Naxos follows up its series of Vaňhal symphonies with this excellent disc of three of his 17 *Violin Concertos*. The most celebrated of these unpretentious works is the *B flat Concerto*, which Mozart is recorded as having played, alongside his own K.216. The writing involves little virtuosity, but it never flags in its easy energy, with opening movements relaxed rather than thrusting and lively music restricted to the finales. **Takako Nishizaki** gives a modern-instrument performance with fresh, clean intonation, very well accompanied by the **Cologne Chamber Orchestra** under **Müller-Brühl**. First-rate sound.

Symphonies in A, Bryan A9; in C, Bryan C3; in C, Bryan C11; in D, Bryan D17

☁ ⒷⒷ **** Naxos 8.554341. Esterházy Sinfonia, Grodd

Symphonies in B flat, Bryan 3; in D min., Bryan d2; in G, Bryan G11

☁ ⒷⒷ **** Naxos 8.554138. City of L. Sinfonia, Watkinson

Among the many new discs of forgotten music by Mozart's contemporaries this Naxos issue stands out. These compact *Symphonies* are all winningly colourful and inventive, often bringing surprises that defy the conventions of the time. The **Esterházy Sinfonia** under **Uwe Grodd** give attractively lively performances with some stylish solo work, vividly recorded.

The *B flat Symphony* (from the early 1760s) reminds the listener of both Haydn and Mozart. The *D minor Symphony* in only three movements, written a decade later, is scored for five horns, yet the main string theme of the first movement is quite haunting. The *G major* work (1775) also has an endearingly gracious first movement, although horns are still prominent in the scoring. Excellent, polished performances from the **City of London Sinfonia** under **Andrew Watkinson** and very good recording.

Symphonies in C min., Bryan Cm2; in D, Bryan D4; in G min., Bryan Gm2

🎵—**** Chan. 9607. LMP, Bamert

The *G minor Symphony*, the second of Vaňhal's symphonies in that key, is an absolute delight, full of good ideas and comparable with the *Sturm und Drang* of Haydn's 39 or Mozart's 25 in the same key. The *C minor Symphony* (1770) is also a work of originality with an occasional foreshadowing of Beethoven. **Matthias Bamert** and the **London Mozart Players** give an excellent account of themselves, and are recorded with great clarity and warmth.

Missa pastoralis in G; Missa solemnis in C

🎵—(BB) *** Naxos 8.555080. Haines, Ainsworth, Pitkanen, Tower Voices, New Zealand Arcadia Ens., Grodd

Va hal's *Pastoral Mass* has a delightfully lyrical *cantabile* feeling, which gives the music a warmth and Arcadian simplicity that is very beguiling. Not all the solo contributions are absolutely secure, especially when two female voices are combined, but the choral response is very persuasive and the result is most rewarding. The *Missa solemnis* is rather more conventional, but Vaňhal's setting is still richly enjoyable with the *Bendictus* and *Agnus Dei* particularly lovely. And he always makes the most of his 'Amens'. The spacious recording adds to one's enjoyment, and any minor reservations are swept aside when the disc is so inexpensive.

VARÈSE, Edgar (1883–1965)

Tuning Up; Amériques (original version); Arcana; Dance for Burgesses; (i) Density 21.5; Déserts; (ii) Ecuatorial; (iii; iv) Un grand sommeil noir (original version); (iii) Un grand sommeil noir (orch. Beaumont); Hyperprism; Intégrales; Ionisation; (v; vi) Nocturnal; Octandre; (v) Offrandes; Poème électronique

🎵—✹ (M) **** Decca 460 208-2 (2) Concg. O or ASKO Ens., Chailly; with (i) Zoon; (ii) Deas; (iii; iv) Delunsch; (iv) Kardoncuff; (v) Leonard; (vi) Prague Philharmonic Male Ch.

This comprehensive coverage of the music of Varèse was given the 1999 *Gramophone* Award for 20th-Century Music. He first came to public notice in the 1930s when Percy Scholes chose him to represent the last word in zany modernity in his 'Columbia History of Music', but his mockery backfired. *Octandre* (one movement then recorded) sounds as quirkily original now as it did then (it is played marvellously here). The witty opening *Tuning Up* sets the mood for writing which is ever ready to take its own course regardless of tradition and set new musical paths. *Amériques*, which follows, is heard in its original (1921) version, lavishly scored, with reminiscences of music by others, not least the Stravinsky of *The Rite of Spring*. It makes fascinating listening. *Ionisation*, less ear-catching, stands as a historic pointer towards developments in percussion writing. *Poème*

électronique originated at the 1958 Brussels World Fair, where it was played through more than 400 loudspeakers inside the Philips pavilion. The montage of familiar and electronic sounds (machine noises, sonorous bells, etc.) comes from the composer's own original four-track tape. The vocal pieces are among the most fascinating aurally, not least *Ecuatorial*, a setting in Spanish with bass soloist of a Maya prayer, brightly coloured and sharp with brass, percussion, organ, piano and ondes martenot. *Un Grand Sommeil noir* is a rare surviving early song, lyrically Ravelian in feeling, heard here in both the original version with piano, and in an orchestration by Antony Beaumont. *Nocturnal*, Varèse's haunting last piece, was left unfinished. Completed by Professor Chou, it is as extravagant and uninhibited as ever, featuring male chorus and a solo soprano voice, used melodically to evoke a mysterious dream-world. All the performances here are superbly definitive and this set will be hard to surpass. The recording acoustic, too, is open, yet everything is clear.

Tuning Up; Amériques (original version); Dance for Burgess; Density; Ecuatorial; Un grand Sommeil noir; Hyperism; Ionisation

(N) (BB) *** Naxos 8.557882 Watts, Gruchowska, Bloch, Camerata Silesia Men's Voices, Polish Nat. RSO, Lydon-Gee (piano & conductor)

Amériques (revised version); Arcana; (i) Densité; Déserts; Hyperprism; Intégrales; Ionisation; Octandre; (ii) Ecuatorial; (iii; iv) Nocturnal; (iii) Offrandes

🎵—(BB) *** Warner Apex 2564 62087-2. O de France, Nagano; with (i) Philippe Pierlot; (ii) Isherwood; (iii) Bryn-Julson; (iv) Male Ch. of R. France

Anyone wanting an inexpensive voyage through Varèse's extraordinary sound-world can turn to **Nagano** and his team on Apex. The Erato recording is both strikingly vivid and atmospheric. The Stravinsky associations (and in one instance a virtual quotation) in *Arcana* and *Amériques* come over dramatically and with plenty of vitality. The latter gains from its revision: more concise and orchestrally hardly less luscious. *Ionisation* (for percussion) is surprisingly listener-friendly, and *Octandre* even has an element of wit. Both soloists are excellent, **Nicholas Isherwood** in *Ecuatorial*, with its weirdly exotic jungle background including two ondes martenot and organ, all but out-Loboses Villa-Lobos, and **Phyllis Bryn-Julson** is engagingly refined, especially in *Offrandes*; while the choral contribution to *Nocturnal* is quite extraordinary. *Déserts* ends the programme even more spectacularly. What Nagano achieves here (helped by the excellent performances and often sensational sound) is to make this music seem just as audaciously new and uncompromisingly avant garde as when it first astonished the musical public. And no one could say, when it is presented so vitally and spontaneously, that it is not stimulating – though not heard all at once!

The Naxos performances (and recording) are also vividly full of life and the recording has striking clarity and presence. Although the offering is not as generous as the Warner Apex collection it remains very enticing, if for bargain-hunters **Nagano's** disc is an obvious first choice.

VAUGHAN WILLIAMS, Ralph (1872–1958)

The Life of Vaughan Williams: 'O Thou Transcendent'

✿ **** Isolde Films **DVD** TPDVD 106. Ursula Vaughan Williams, Kennedy (Dir: Tony Palmer)

Even among Tony Palmer's many documentaries of musicians, this study of Vaughan Williams, lasting some two and a half hours, gives the most illuminating picture of the composer and his music, with an astonishing line-up of contributors, led by the composer's widow and his biographer, **Michael Kennedy**. The whole film brings home what an astonishingly wide range the composer's music covered, starting with the English pastoral style; then, after the composer's traumatic experience in the First World War, his style grew much tougher and abrasive. The revelations are many, as for example that Ursula Vaughan Williams had an abortion in the 1930s, before VW's first wife died, and that the American composer, John Adams, was profoundly influenced by the *Tallis Fantasia*, the very first orchestral music he heard live as a child. The result is both moving and beautiful, fulfilling in every way, demonstrating what a passionate personality VW was.

(i) Concerto accademico; Fantasia on Greensleeves; 5 Variants of Dives and Lazarus; 2 Hymn-Tune Preludes; (i) The Lark Ascending; (ii) Oboe Concerto; Old King Cole (ballet); The Poisoned Kiss: Overture; 49th Parallel: Prelude; Prelude on an Old Carol Tune; 2 Preludes on Welsh Hymn Tunes; The Running Set; Sea Songs: Quick march. Serenade to Music (orchestral version); (ii) 5 Mystical Songs

Ⓑ *** EMI 5 73986-2 (2). (i) Creswick; (ii) Wingfield; (iii) Roberts; E. N. Sinfonia, Hickox

This disc comprises the bulk of three LPs **Richard Hickox** made in the mid-1980s. It includes some rarities and occasional pieces written for particular events or projects, such as the *Prelude* to the film, *49th Parallel*. The ballet music for *Old King Cole* is lively and full of charm, as is the tuneful overture to the sadly neglected opera, *The Poisoned Kiss*. **Bradley Creswick's** account of the *Concerto accademico* is one of the finest available, with the complex mood of the *Adagio*, both ethereal and ecstatic, caught on the wing, and he seems equally at home in *The Lark Ascending*. **Roger Wingfield** is hardly less engaging in the *Oboe Concerto*, his timbre full of pastoral colour, while he displays a deliciously light touch in the finale. *Greensleeves* is taken spaciously, but Hickox brings out the breadth as well as the lyrical beauty of the melody. *Dives and Lazarus*, rich in sonority, and the two *Hymn-Tune Preludes* have their elegiac mood judged perfectly. The *Five Mystical Songs* are sensitively done, though **Stephen Roberts** displays a rather gritty vi-

brato. All in all, an excellent bargain collection, very well recorded. The *Serenade to Music*, however, loses a dimension in its orchestral version.

(i) Concerto accademico for Violin; Concerto grosso for Strings; (ii) Oboe Concerto; (iii) Piano Concerto in C; (iv) Tuba Concerto. 2 Hymn-Tune Preludes; (v) The Lark Ascending; Partita for Double String Orchestra; (vi) Towards the Unknown Region

*** Chan. 9262/3. (i) Sillito; (ii) Theodore; (iii) Shelley; (iv) Harrild; (v) M. Davis; (vi) L. Symphony Ch.; LSO, Thomson

With immaculate **LSO** string ensemble, the *Concerto grosso* under **Thomson's** persuasive direction shows how in glowing sound its easy, unforced inspiration brings it close to the world of the *Tallis Fantasia*. While many performances of the *Concerto accademico* make the composer's neoclassical manner sound like Stravinsky with an English accent, Thomson and **Sillito** find a rustic jollity in the outer movements very characteristic of Vaughan Williams. **David Theodore's** plangent tones in the *Oboe Concerto* effectively bring out the equivocal character of this highly original work, making it far more than just another pastoral piece. **Howard Shelley** addresses the neglected *Piano Concerto* with flair and brilliance, making light of the disconcerting cragginess of the piano writing and consistently bringing out both the wit and the underlying emotional power. The bluff good humour of the *Tuba Concerto* is beautifully caught in **Patrick Harrild's** rumbustious account, and this outstanding tuba soloist plays with wit and panache. **Michael Davis** makes a rich-toned soloist in *The Lark Ascending*, presenting it as more than a pastoral evocation. The *Hymn-Tune Preludes* are unashamedly pastoral in tone; then the *Partita* finds the composer in more abrasive mood, less easily sympathetic. *Towards the Unknown Region* is the only relative disappointment – a setting of Whitman that antedates the *Sea Symphony*. The choral sound is beautiful, but this early work really needs tauter treatment.

(i) Concerto grosso for Strings; (i; ii) Oboe Concerto; (i) English Folksongs Suite (trans. Gordon Jacob); Fantasia on Greensleeves (arr. GREAVES); (iii) Fantasia on a Theme by Thomas Tallis; (i; iv) The Lark Ascending; (iii) 5 Variants of Dives and Lazarus; In the Fen Country; Norfolk Rhapsody 1; (v) Partita for Double String Orchestra; (i; vi) Romance for Harmonica, Strings & Piano

Ⓑ **(*) Double Decca ADD/DDD 460 357-2 (2). (i) ASMF, Marriner; (ii) Nicklin; (iii) New Queen's Hall O, Wordsworth; (iv) Brown; (v) LPO, Boult; (vi) Reilly

This Double Decca offers a fascinating comparison in that the first disc brings modern-instrument recordings (from **Marriner** and his **Academy**) and the second a special kind of period-instrument performance, although it is **Boult** and the **LPO** who give us the *Partita*. With the ASMF, **Celia Nicklin** gives a most persuasive account of the elusive *Oboe Concerto*, while the *Concerto grosso* is lively and polished. The atmospheric *Romance*, although not one of the composer's most inspired works, is still worth having, and the

Folksongs could hardly be presented more breezily; *The Lark Ascending* is superbly balanced and refined, with **Iona Brown** an inspirational soloist. The performances on the second disc are given by the re-formed **New Queen's Hall Orchestra** playing instruments in use at the turn of the century. *Portamento* is featured in the string style but here it is applied very judiciously, and for the most part the ear notices the fuller, warmer sonority of the violins, the treble less brilliant in attack. In works like the *Tallis Fantasia* and *Dives and Lazarus* one can readily wallow in the richly refined textures, but **Wordsworth's** performance of *Tallis* misses the final degree of intensity at the climax, and the opening of *Dives and Lazarus* is also rather relaxed, even indulgent in relishing the sheer breadth of sonority achieved, though the closing pages are ethereally lovely. The performers are at their finest in the evocative opening of the *Norfolk Rhapsody*, while *In the Fen Country* has a fine idyllic ardour, with some very sensitive playing from wind and brass in the coda. The Wordsworth recording, made in Walthamstow Assembly Hall, is splendidly expansive and natural.

Concerto grosso; English Folksongs Suite; Fantasia on a Theme by Thomas Tallis; Fantasia on Greensleeves; 5 Variants of Dives and Lazarus; In the Fen Country; Norfolk Rhapsody 1 in E min.; (i) Romance for Harmonica & Strings; Variations for Orchestra (orch. Jacob); The Wasps: Overture (with English folk songs arrangements: The British Grenadiers; Early one morning; I will give my love an apple; John Peel; The jolly miller; The keeper; The oak and the ash; Summer is a'coming; The turtle dove)

*** Australian Decca Eloquence (ADD/DDD) 442 8341 (2). ASMF, Marriner; (i) with Reilly

This two-CD compilation combines **Marriner's** digital 1995 Vaughan Williams collection with his vintage Argo ones from the 1970s. The former offers a bright and brisk account of the *Wasps Overture* and the rare *Variations*, written as a brass test-piece in 1957 and skilfully orchestrated by Gordon Jacob. It is not a masterpiece but is well worth having on disc. The *Tallis* is beautifully played, though it lacks the last degree of ethereal beauty. Marriner makes up for this with the climax of *Dives and Lazarus*, which is really expansive, and he and the **ASMF** are at their finest in the gentle, evocative opening and closing sections of the *First Norfolk Rhapsody*. *In the Fen Country* brings more fine playing, and the digital recording is good rather than outstanding. The rest of the items are classic accounts in every way. Highlights include the breezy performance of the delightful *English Folksongs Suite* and the lively and polished *Concerto grosso*. The Vaughan Williams items are almost upstaged by the outstanding 30-minute collection of folk-songs arrangements by Leslie Pearson and Chris Hazell. These very enjoyable folk tunes, from the rousing *British Grenadiers* to the haunting melody of *The oak and the ash*, have been superbly orchestrated, full of apposite and piquant colour, very well played and recorded in the best Decca/Argo tradition.

Concerto grosso; Fantasia on Greensleeves; Fantasia on a Theme of Thomas Tallis; In the Fen Country; Norfolk Rhapsody 1

(BB) **(*) Naxos 8.555867. New Zealand SO, Judd

A sequence of recordings by this orchestra has demonstrated what a fine body it has become, and there are outstanding solo contributions from the leading string-players in the *Tallis Fantasia*. The folk-based writing of the *Norfolk Rhapsody* and the impressionistic study *In the Fen Country* are given a satisfying firmness of purpose, with climaxes surging passionately. The *Greensleeves Fantasia* is treated with a degree of reserve, avoiding all sentimentality, and although the *Concerto grosso*, with its contrasted groups of players is a degree less polished in ensemble, the warmth and impulsiveness make ample amends, helped by the full-bodied sound.

(i; ii) Concerto grosso; (iii; iv) Fantasia on a Theme by Thomas Tallis; (i; ii; v) The Lark Ascending; (i; ii) Partita; (vi; iv) Romance in D flat; (i; ii; vii; viii) Dona nobis pacem; (i; ii; vii; ix) Fantasia on the Old 104th Psalm Tune; (x) Magnificat; (i; ii; vii; viii) Towards the Unknown Region

(B) **(*) EMI mono/stereo 5 74782-2 (2). (i) LPO; (ii) Boult; (iii) Philh. O; (iv) Sargent; (v) with Pougnet; (vi) Adler, Gritton, BBC SO; (vii) LPO Ch.; (viii) Armstrong, Carol Case; (ix) Katin; (x) Watts, Amb. S., O Nova of London, Davies

This self-recommending Vaughan Williams anthology includes some unexpected items, notably the atmospheric *Romance*, beautifully performed by **Larry Adler**, its dedicatee, in 1952. **Boult's** affinity with this composer is well known, and it is good to hear again just how well he presents the powerful and sustained climax in the *Dona nobis pacem*. As for the *Fantasia on the Old 104th* (for piano, chorus and orchestra) – far from the composer's greatest work – Boult's team (with **Peter Katin** as the pianist) makes it sound better than it really is. The *Partita* and *Concerto grosso* are beautifully done, and *Towards the Unknown Region* is similarly impressive. The *Lark Ascending* is the only Boult item not dating from the 1970s: it was recorded (in mono) with **Jean Pougnet** as the soloist in 1952 and made its CD début here. It's a good performance, though some allowances have to be made for the sound. Also, it was a pity that Boult's 1970s version of the *Tallis Fantasia* was not chosen; **Sargent** doesn't quite produce the spiritual quality this work ideally needs, despite the beautiful playing and good 1959 sound. The Holstian *Magnificat* is performed with sympathy and imagination by **Meredith Davies's** team, and the 1970 recording has transferred well. This set is well worth considering, even though no texts are offered.

(i; ii) Oboe Concerto; (i; iii) Tuba Concerto; (iv) Fantasia on Greensleeves; 5 Variants of Dives and Lazarus; Sinfonia Antartica (No. 7); The Wasps: Overture

(M) (***) EMI mono 5 66543-2 (2). (i) LSO; with (ii) Rothwell; (iii) Catelinet; (iv) Hallé O, Barbirolli – ELGAR: *Cockaigne; Introduction & Allegro; Serenade* (***)

Vividly transferred, this double-disc collection brings together **Barbirolli's** superb readings of Vaughan Williams and Elgar from the early 1950s. Strong and warmly expressive, these performances reflect the quality of the **Hallé** in the early 1950s, with the **LSO** equally responsive in the *Concertos*. Central to the collection is the première recording of the *Sinfonia Antartica*, made only five months after Barbirolli had conducted the first performance in January 1953. The thrust and power have never been surpassed, and the clear, immediate recording brings out the originality of the orchestration. **Evelyn Rothwell**, Lady Barbirolli, plays the *Oboe Concerto* with heartfelt warmth and understanding, while the *Tuba Concerto* is superbly characterized, bluff in the outer movements, tender in the slow movement. With the coupled Elgar items, an outstanding reissue.

'Portrait of Vaughan Williams': (i–iii) *Oboe Concerto;* **(i; ii)** *Fantasia on Greensleeves; Fantasia on a Theme by Thomas Tallis; 5 Variants of Dives and Lazarus;* **(i; ii; iv)** *The Lark Ascending;* **(i; ii)** *The Wasps Overture;* **(v; vi)** *Phantasy Quintet;* **(v)** *String Quartets 1–2;* **(vii; viii; i)** *Flos campi;* **(vii)** *Mass in G min.;* **(vii; i)** *O, clap your hands; The Old Hundredth Psalm Tune;* **(viii; i; ix)** *An Oxford Elegy;* **(vii)** *3 Shakespeare Songs.* **Sacred and secular songs:** *Blessed Son of God; Lord, Thou hast been our refuge; No sad thought his soul affright; O taste and see; Valiant for truth;* **(vii; i)** *Te Deum*

⊛⇥ Ⓑ Ⓑ ******** Nim. NI 1754 (4). (i) English String O; (ii) Boughton; (iii) with Bourge; (iv) with Bochman; (v) Medici Qt; (vi) with Rowland-Jones; (vii) Christ Church Cathedral Ch., Oxford, Darlington; (viii) with Best; (ix) with May (narrator)

This super-budget Nimbus boxed set offers a wonderfully illuminating cross-section of Vaughan Williams's music, showing its consistent inspiration, and both its diversity and its linkages. The orchestral and concertante music included here is all very familiar, but is most sympathetically played under **William Boughton** (with sensitive soloists) and presented amply and atmospherically, and with a rich amplitude of string tone. The chamber music shows a more intimate side of the composer: the special atmosphere of these works, with moments of haunting delicacy, is warmly and idiomatically caught, but with no lack of concentration and intensity. The **Medici players** were recorded in The Maltings, which means a sympathetic ambience, but also that the microphones are rather close. The glorious sonorities of the unaccompanied *Mass in G minor*, with its double choir and four soloists, draw an immediate vocal parallel with the *Tallis Fantasia*. The *Mass* opens with a *Kyrie* which looks back to the Elizabethan era and beyond, and then blossoms polyphonically in the *Gloria* and swaying *Sanctus* before the beautiful closing *Agnus Dei*. The *Oxford Elegy* brings more fine music, but the narrative, confidently and clearly delivered here by **Jack May**, remains as intrusive as ever (its inclusion was not one of the composer's best ideas). With **Roger Best** a fine viola soloist, *Flos campi* is particularly successful, as are the *Te Deum* and the shorter unaccompanied choral songs, especially the three imaginative Shakespeare settings. All in all this is a cornucopia of musical joys, worth

getting, even if you already have recordings of the better-known orchestral pieces.

(i) *Oboe Concerto; Fantasia on Greensleeves; Fantasia on a Theme of Thomas Tallis; 5 Variants of Dives and Lazarus;* **(ii)** *The Lark Ascending; The Wasps: Overture*

⊛⇥ Ⓜ ******* Nim. NI 7013. (i) Bourgue; (ii) Bochmann; E. String O or SO, Boughton

Opening with an exuberant account of *The Wasps Overture*, this is a very attractive and generous 70-minute collection of favourite Vaughan Williams orchestral pieces, taken from the anthology above.

(i; ii; iii) *Oboe Concerto;* **(ii; iv)** *Fantasia on a theme by Thomas Tallis;* **Symphonies: (v; iii)** *4 in F min.;* **(v; vi)** *5 in D;* **(ii; iii)** *6 in E min;* **(ii; iv)** *The Wasps Overture*

Ⓝ Ⓑ ****(*)** EMI ADD/DDD 2 16146-2 (2). (i) Williams; (ii) Bournemouth SO; (iii) Berglund; (iv) Silvestri; (v) RPO; (vi) Gibson

This anthology draws on the HMV back catalogue with recordings of varying interest dating from between 1967 and 1982. The delightful *Oboe Concerto* is beautifully played by the principal oboist of the **Bournemouth Orchestra**. Silvestri then gives a brilliant reading of the *Tallis Fantasia*, less expansive than some, but bringing remarkable tension to the opening and closing pages. The central climax of the work is tremendously passionate, in a tighter more direct way than with Barbirolli. His account of *The Wasps Overture* also makes the most of the *brio*, with crisp, fast tempi and the expansiveness of the great tune in the middle not allowed to interfere with the forward momentum. In both works the vivacity of the playing and the vivid recording adds to the listener's enjoyment. **Berglund** directs a rugged, purposeful account of the *Fourth Symphony*, following the composer in preferring an unusually fast speed in the first movement, while the second is superbly sustained at a very slow tempo. He then brings out the Sibelian undertones in the *Sixth Symphony* in a strong, direct performance, very well recorded, and with the long unrelieved *pianissimo* finale sustaining a hushed concentration to hold the listener in its spell. **Gibson's** account of the beautiful *Fifth Symphony* is attractively flowing and direct, but other versions get closer to the heart of the music with more refinement and more power at climaxes.

Piano Concerto in C

⊛⇥ ******* Lyrita SRCD 211 [id.]. Shelley, RPO, Handley –
FOULDS: *Dynamic Triptych* *******

⊛⇥ Ⓑ ******* CFP 575 9832. Lane, RLPO, Handley – DELIUS: *Piano Concerto;* FINZI: *Eclogue* *******

This Lyrita version was the first recording of the *Concerto* in solo form, not quite as originally written, because the definitive score, published not too long before this record was made and giving the alternatives of one or two pianos, opts for ending with a serene coda instead of the original brief dispatching coda of ten bars. That is certainly an improvement, and the wonder is that, though the solo piano writing is hardly pianistic, the very challenge to as fine an exponent as **Howard Shelley** brings out an extra intensity to a highly individual work. Since this record was made, Shelley has re-recorded the piece digitally for Chandos (see below), but that is coupled with the *Ninth Symphony*, and many may find the stimulating Foulds coupling on Lyrita even more enticing. The 1984 recording is very impressive in its remastered form.

Piers Lane defies the old idea of this as a grittily un-pianistic work, giving it a powerful, refreshing reading, helped by fine playing from the **RLPO** under **Handley**, always a sympathetic Vaughan Williams interpreter, while the apt and unusual coupling can be warmly recommended.

(i) *Piano Concerto; Symphony 9 in E min.*

*** Chan. 8941. (i) Shelley, LPO, Thomson

In his Chandos version **Howard Shelley** addresses the concerto with flair and brilliance. He makes light of the disconcerting cragginess of the piano writing and consistently brings out both the wit and the underlying emotional power. **Bryden Thomson** conducts a powerful performance of the last of Vaughan Williams's symphonies. Though the playing may not be ideally incisive, it brings out an extra warmth of expression. Both performances are greatly helped by the richness and weight of the Chandos sound, warmly atmospheric but with ample detail and fine presence.

'Essential Vaughan Williams': *English Folk Songs Suite* (orch. Jacob); *Fantasia on Greensleeves; Fantasia on a Theme by Thomas Tallis; Five Variants of Dives & Lazarus; The Lark Ascending; Rhosymedre; The Wasps Overture; Serenade to Music.* Excerpts from: *Hodie; Job; Sinfonia antartica; Mass in G min.; On Wenlock Edge.* Songs include: *The Call; The Lamb; Linden Lea; Orpheus with his lute; Silent Noon; The Vagabond.* Hymns & Folk Song Arrangements. *The Old Hundredth*

(N) (BB) *** EMI 2 07992-2 (2). Artists include: LSO or LPO, Boult; L. Sinf., Barbirolli; Jacques O, Willcocks; Bean(vln), New Philh., Boult; ASMF, Marriner; King's College Cambridge Ch., Cleobury; Shirley-Quirk; Janet Baker; Ian Bostridge; Ian Partridge; Rolfe Johnson; David Daniels

While much is omitted, including the symphonies, many favourites are here from *The Lark Ascending* and **Barbirolli's** *Tallis Fantasia*, to **Janet Baker's** *Linden Lea* and *The Old Hundredth* from King's College. All-in-all a superb collection, even if duplication is involved.

English Folksongs Suite; Flourish for Wind Band; Toccata marziale

*** Chan. 9697. Royal N. College of Music Wind O, Reynish – HOLST: *Hammersmith*, etc. ***

Vaughan Williams's music for wind band is less inspired than that of Holst, but the jaunty *English Folksongs Suite* certainly sounds more vivid in its original scoring than it does in the orchestral version. It could hardly be played more

breezily than it is here, and the other two pieces also come off splendidly. Demonstration sound.

Fantasia on Greensleeves; (i) *Fantasia on a Theme of Thomas Tallis*

⊕–⚫ ⚙ (M) **** EMI (ADD) 5 67240-2. Sinfonia of L.; (i) with Allegri Qt; Barbirolli – ELGAR: *Introduction & Allegro for Strings*, etc. **** ⚙

(i) *Fantasia on Greensleeves; Fantasia on a Theme of Tallis;* (ii) *The Lark Ascending*

⊕– (BB) *** Virgin 2x1 5 61763-2 (2). (i) LCO, Warren-Green; (ii) with Warren-Green (violin) – DVOŘÁK: *Serenade for Strings;* ELGAR: *Introduction & Allegro; Serenade;* SUK: *Serenade;* TCHAIKOVSKY: *Serenade* ***

⊕– (B) *** Sony (ADD) SBK 62645. (i) Phd. O, Ormandy; (ii) Druian, Cleveland Sinf., Lane – DELIUS: *Brigg Fair*, etc. ***

Barbirolli's inspirational performance of the *Tallis Fantasia* now rightly takes its place among EMI's 'Great Recordings of the Century'. His ardour combined with the magically quiet playing of the second orchestra is unforgettable. The recording has magnificent definition and sonority, achieving dramatic contrasts between the main orchestra and the distanced solo group, which sounds wonderfully ethereal.

Christopher Warren-Green and his **London Chamber Orchestra** give a radiant account of *The Lark Ascending*, in which Warren-Green makes a charismatic solo contribution, very free and soaring in its flight and with beautifully sustained true *pianissimo* playing at the opening and close. For the *Tallis Fantasia*, the second orchestra (2.2.2.2.1) contrasts with the main group (5.4.2.2.1) and here, though the effect is beautifully serene, Warren-Green does not quite match the ethereal, otherworldly *pianissimo* that made Barbirolli's reading unforgettable. The performance overall has great ardour and breadth, almost to match the coupled *Introduction and Allegro* of Elgar in its intensity. The recording, made at All Saints' Church, Petersham, has resonant warmth and atmosphere yet sharp definition.

The excellent performances from 1963 on Sony demonstrate the special feeling American musicians can find for English music. In the *Tallis Fantasia* **Ormandy** (like Barbirolli) characteristically underlines the drama of a work that is often regarded as delicate and atmospheric. The recording of *The Lark Ascending* was made during the period when **Louis Lane** was a colleague of **George Szell** at Cleveland and the orchestra was at the peak of its form. **Rafael Druian** is the intensely poetic violin soloist, producing the most delicate sustained *pianissimos*, even though the balance is close. The orchestral playing is both polished and characterful. The CD transfers have expanded the original sound most strikingly. With expressive Delius performances as coupling, this is one of the most desirable of Sony's 'Essential Classics'.

(i) *Fantasia on Greensleeves;* (ii) *Fantasia on a Theme by Thomas Tallis; 5 Variants on Dives and Lazarus; In the Fen Country;* (i; iii) *The Lark Ascending;* (ii) *Norfolk Rhapsody 1*

*** Chan. 9775. (i) LSO; (ii) LPO; Thomson; (iii) with M. Davis

It is good to have *In the Fen Country* and the *First Norfolk Rhapsody* in such beautiful modern digital sound and played so sympathetically. Indeed, **Bryden Thomson** is a most persuasive guide in all this repertoire, although in the *Tallis Fantasia* he is rather more concerned with sonority, beauty and contrasts of texture than with subtlety. **Michael Davis** makes a rich-toned soloist in *The Lark Ascending*, presenting it as more than a gentle pastoral invocation. Although these recordings are now nearly a decade old, the generous measure (79 minutes) almost compensates for the continued premium price.

Fantasia on Greensleeves; Fantasia on a Theme of Thomas Tallis; The Wasps: Overture

(B) *** EMI (ADD) 3 82157-2. LSO, Previn (with
BUTTERWORTH: *Banks of Green Willow*) – ELGAR: *Enigma Variations* ***

Coupled with Elgar's most popular orchestral work, **Previn's** performances of the *Tallis Fantasia* and the *Wasps Overture* are warmly persuasive. The wasps' music buzzes with point and energy, while the *Tallis Fantasia*, after a restrained opening, builds up finally with great conviction into a blazing climax, with no inhibition over stringendo. Warm, opulent recording to match.

Fantasia on a Theme of Thomas Tallis

⊶ ✿ (B) (***) EMI mono 4 76880-2. Philh. O, Karajan (with
HANDEL (arr. Harty): *Water Music Suite*) – BRITTEN:
Variations on a Theme of Frank Bridge *** ✿

⊶ (BB) *** Warner Apex 2564 61437-2. RPO, Warren-Green –
BRITTEN: *Simple Symphony*; BUTTERWORTH: *Banks of Green Willow*; ELGAR: *String Serenade*; HOLST: *St Paul's Suite* ***

*(**) BBCL (ADD) 4205-2. New Philh. O, Stokowski (with:
KLEMPERER: *Merry Waltz*; NOVAČEK: *Perpetuum mobile*
(*(**))) – BRAHMS: *Symphony 4* ***; RAVEL: *Rapsodie espagnole* *(**)

Karajan's version of the *Tallis Fantasia*, coupled with Britten's *Variations on a Theme of Frank Bridge*, is one of his greatest records, sounding as fresh and sonorous today as it did in the 1950s, when it first appeared. Sonically it is little short of amazing, and artistically it is no less impressive. The playing of the **Philharmonia** strings for Karajan is altogether superlative, and the *Tallis Fantasia* sounds both idiomatic and vivid, rather like a newly cleaned painting. Recordings of this work are legion, and stereo undoubtedly brings an added dimension, but this mono version ranks among the best. The *Water Music* is an unexpected but welcome bonus, also superbly played.

Christopher Warren-Green's rich-textured **RPO** performance is even finer than his earlier, Virgin version in creating the necessary dynamic contrast between the opposing string goups, with the tension in *pianissimos* raptly sustained and climaxes richly expansive. This is part of an outstanding anthology of English music, all excellently played and recorded.

On the BBC disc a wonderfully warm account of the *Tallis Fantasia* from a live Royal Albert Hall performance in 1974. The **New Philharmonia** strings ooze **Stokowski** magic and this account is compelling and highly distinctive in every way: the *pianissimos* are simply ravishing!

Fantasia on a Theme of Thomas Tallis; 5 Variants of Dives and Lazarus; In the Fen Country; Norfolk Rhapsody

*** Chan. 8502. LPO, Thomson

Fantasia on a Theme of Thomas Tallis; In the Fen Country; (i) The Lark Ascending; Norfolk Rhapsody 1; (ii) On Wenlock Edge

(M) **(*) EMI 5 85151-2. LPO, Haitink; with (i) Chang; (ii)
Bostridge

Bryden Thomson is a most persuasive guide in all this repertoire and more than holds his own with most of the opposition.

Haitink's way with the *Tallis Fantasia*, where the straight rhythmic manners sound somewhat unidiomatic, is certainly powerful in its monumental directness, especially with the wide-ranging recording. In the *Norfolk Rhapsody* there is also a direct quality which is certainly appealing, especially with the beautiful playing of the **LPO**; the same comments apply to *In the Fen Country*. **Sarah Chang** proves an intensely poetic soloist in *The Lark Ascending* magnetically concentrated throughout. **Ian Bostridge** is the sensitive, honey-toned soloist in the Housman song-cycle, *On Wenlock Edge*, which ends this disc.

Fantasia on a Theme of Thomas Tallis; Symphony 5 in D; (i) Serenade to Music

⊶ **** Telarc CD 80676. Atlanta SO, Spano; (i) with Rivera,
O'Connor, Studebaker, Ford, Atlanta Chamber Ch. –
TALLIS: *Psalm Tune: Why fum'th in fight?*

Tallis's hauntingly simple psalm tune makes a perfect prelude to create the atmosphere for a very fine performance of the Vaughan Williams work, in which the playing of the second, smaller string group is memorably ethereal, and beautifully balanced and recorded. Then follows a superb account of the *D major Symphony*, passionate and moving, with the opening and closing horn motive particularly evocative. As if that was not enough, the performance of the *Serenade to Music*, in the composer's alternative version for four soloists and choir, is equally understanding, with **Jessica Rivera** a fine, ardent soprano soloist leading the team spiritedly as well as lyrically. Throughout, the recording is of Telarc's demonstration quality. Altogether a splendid disc, and a great credit to the conductor **Robert Spano**, readily showing that American performers can find a real identification with the music of Vaughan Williams.

Film Music: Coastal Command (suite); Elizabeth of England: Three Portraits; 49th Parallel: Prelude; The Story of a Flemish Farm (suite)

**(*) Marco 8.223665. RTE Concert O, Dublin, Penny

Vaughan Williams's wartime film music was of the highest quality. The Powell/Pressburger movie *49th Parallel* (1941), made in the early years of the war, inspired a *Prelude* with a nostalgic patriotic feeling. *Coastal Command* (1942) was a dramatized documentary which centred on the romantic profiles of the Catalina flying-boats, resulting in warmly evocative music, with echoes from the composer's symphonic writing. The even more imaginative (1943) score for *The Story of a Flemish Farm* (a true story about personal sacrifice which enabled a wartime escape to England) brings similar resonances. *Elizabeth of England* (1955–7), another documentary, narrated by **Alec Clunes**, has a haunting *Poet* sequence which introduces a magically gentle tune, also used in the *Sea Symphony*. **Andrew Penny** is a splendid advocate in performances eloquent in their mood-painting. The recording is bright and full, if rather two-dimensional.

Film Music: *Coastal Command; The People's Land; Scott of the Antarctic*

*** Chan. 10007. Gamba, Sheffield Philh. Ch., BBC PO, Gamba

When, in 1947, Vaughan Williams was asked to write the music for Michael Balcon's film *Scott of the Antarctic*, he was so enthusiastic about the idea that he composed a great deal of the score before he had even seen the script. This 40-minute suite brings together virtually all the music he wrote, including much striking material not used in either the film or the symphony. Helped by vividly atmospheric sound, **Rumon Gamba** draws superb playing from the **BBC Philharmonic**, and there are haunting vocal effects from **Merryn Gamba** and the **Sheffield Philharmonic Choir**. Suites from two other characterful film scores make a colourful supplement.

Film Music: *The Dim Little Island; Elizabeth of England; 49th Parallel* (all ed. Stephen Hogger)

*** Chan. 10244. Soloists, Chetham's Chamber Ch., BBC PO, Gamba

The magnetic *nobilmente* theme for the title and closing sequence of *49th Parallel* is totally memorable, to match the outstanding film it illustrated, and much of the rest of this score shows the composer at his most pictorially imaginative. For the ten-minute short, *The Dim Little Island*, however, VW effectively reworked his *Variants on Dives and Lazarus*. The documentary *Elizabeth of England*, with its generous folksong and folk-dance influences, shows how he felt completely at home in the musical world of Tudor England. Splendidly restored by Stephen Hogger, the music is superbly played, sung and recorded.

5 Variants on Dives and Lazarus; Partita for Double String Orchestra

(BB) *** ASV Resonance CD RSN 3057. E. Sinfonia, Farrer – TIPPETT: *Concerto for Double String Orchestra, etc.* ***

John Farrer conducts a particularly fine account of *Dives and Lazarus*, opening delicately and finding plenty of contrast between the five variants, leading to a richly eloquent conclusion. The underrated *Partita* too is very persuasively played, again opening seductively, providing a brilliant *Scherzo ostinato* and finale, athletic yet full of lyrical fervour.

5 Variants of Dives and Lazarus; (i) The Songs of Light; Toward the Unknown Region; The Voice out of the Whirlwind; (ii) Willow Wood

(BB) **** Naxos 8.557798. (i) RLPO Ch.; RLPO, Lloyd-Jones; (ii) with Williams

Toward the Unknown Region, like the glorious *Dives and Lazarus*, is comparatively well known, but *The Songs of Light* less so. It is a setting of three poems about the creation by Vaughan Williams's wife, Ursula. *The Voice out of the Whirlwind* draws on the magical *Galliard for the Songs of the Morning* from *Job*. But the real novelty here is *Willow Wood*, which lasts about a quarter of an hour and is a setting of Rossetti for baritone, optional female chorus and orchestra; and it is really rather beautiful. Altogether an unexpectedly attractive disc, very well sung and played and recorded.

Job (A Masque for Dancing)

(BB) *** Warner Apex 0927 443 394-2. BBC SO, A. Davis – WALTON: *Belshazzar's Feast* ***

Job (A Masque for Dancing); Fantasia on a Theme by Thomas Tallis; 5 Variants on Dives and Lazarus

(B) **** CfP (ADD/DDD) 5 75314-2. LPO, Handley

Job (A Masque for Dancing); (i) The Lark Ascending

(BB) **** Naxos 8.553955. E. N. Philh., Lloyd-Jones; (i) with Greed

David Lloyd-Jones – at super-budget price on Naxos – upstages all competition. He gives a performance tingling with drama, yet with great delicacy. The opening scene is particularly atmospheric and the *Saraband of the Sons of God* brings a noble dignity, especially when it returns expansively on the full brass. There is much fine orchestral playing. The big climaxes bring a superb brass contribution, almost submerging the organ at the vision of Satan. The Epilogue is touchingly ethereal. The recording, made in Leeds Town Hall, has an ideal spaciousness, yet combines vivid detail with glowing textures. For an encore the orchestral leader, **David Greed**, provides an exquisitely delicate portrayal of *The Lark Ascending*, with a beautifully sustained closing *pianissimo*.

Handley's performance of *Job* too is outstandingly fine. His dedicated approach shows the composer's inspiration at its most deeply characteristic and most consistently noble. The breadth of dynamic of the EMI analogue recording is used to enormous effect to increase the drama: the organ entry representing Satan enthroned in heaven has great presence and is overwhelming in impact. Comparably the ravishingly luminous espressivo playing in the work's quieter lyrical pages is movingly beautiful, with the music's evocative feeling memorably captured. The other works also show Handley at his best, especially *Dives and Lazarus*.

The **BBC Symphony Orchestra** plays *Job* splendidly, and the recording is spacious. As in Davis's other Vaughan Williams records, the orchestra is set back and some of their power is lost. However, no one could say that the spectacular organ entry (recorded earlier by Andrew Davis in King's College Chapel, Cambridge, and effectively dubbed in) does not make a huge impact, while Job's comforters are strongly characterized and the serene closing music, including the lovely *Pavane of the Sons of the Morning*, is radiantly presented.

The Lark Ascending

⊶ (M) *** EMI 5 03417-2. Kennedy, CBSO, Rattle – ELGAR: *Violin Concerto* ***

⊶ (M) *** EMI 5 62813-2. Kennedy, CBSO, Rattle – WALTON: *Viola Concerto; Violin Concerto* ***

*** DG 476 6198. Benedetti, LPO, Litton – TAVENER: *Song for Athene; Dhyana; Lalishri* ***

Nigel Kennedy provides a valuable and welcome fill-up to his fine remake of the Elgar *Concerto* in this spacious and inspirational account of Vaughan Williams's evocative piece.

Vaughan Williams's piece also makes a fine bonus for the two Walton *Concertos* chosen to represent Nigel among EMI's 'Great Artists of the Century'. It is beautifully recorded.

The Lark Ascending, voted in a Classic fM poll the country's most popular work, also makes a good fill-up for **Nicola Benedetti's** Tavener pieces. It comes in a spacious performance, not just reflective and pure-toned but powerful too in the tuttis, thanks to the weighty accompaniment from **Andrew Litton** and the **LPO**.

(i) Old King Cole (ballet); (ii) On Wenlock Edge; (iii) Serenade to Music; (i; iv) Song of Thanksgiving

✿ (****) Regis Alto (mono) ALC 1025. (i) LPO, Boult; (ii) Maran, L. String Qt, Newton; (iii) 16 soloists, BBC SO, Sir Henry Wood; (iv) with Speight (nar.), Betty Dilmore, Luton Girl's Ch.

Boult's spirited, early (1954) recording of *Old King Cole* reveals it as a first-class work, boisterously tuneful and of immediate appeal. Then follows **George Maran's** moving performance of *A Shropshire Lad*, with *Is my Team Ploughing?* especially dramatic and moving, but with the whole cycle memorably sung and played. **Robert Speight's** commanding RP narration and **Boult's** stirring conducting ensures that *The Song of Thanksgiving* is more than just an occasional piece. But the highlight of the disc is the remastered recording of **Sir Henry Wood's** inspired original performance of the *Serenade to Music*, with the 16 soloists, including **Elsie Suddaby, Margaret Balfour, Muriel Brunskill, Heddle Nash, Parry Jones, Roy Henderson, Harold Williams, Stiles-Allen, Eva Turner, Astra Desmond, Mary Jarred, Walter Widdop, Frank Titterton, Robert Easton** and **Norman Allin**, and with **Isobel Baillie** soaring radiantly up into the heavens. Apart from the solo contributions, how well they blend together! Excellent transfers bring all these mono recordings vividly to life.

Preludes on 3 Welsh Hymn Tunes

(BB) **(*) Hyp. Helios CDH 55070. L. Brass Virtuosi, Honeyball – ELGAR: *Severn Suite*; IRELAND: *Comedy Overture* **(*)

The three hymn tunes which Vaughan Williams favours and which are united here are Ebenezer, Calfaria and Hyfrydol, and the result is quite short and very effective, if not memorable, on a brass group.

SYMPHONIES

Symphonies 1–9

⊶ ✿ (B) (***) Decca mono 473 241-2 (5). LPO, Boult, with I. Baillie, Cameron, Ritchie, Gielgud, LPO Ch. in No. 1

In some ways **Boult's** mono set of the Vaughan Williams symphonies (8 is in stereo) is unsurpassed and the recording still sounds amazingly realistic, especially in the *Sea Symphony*, a demonstration LP in its day. The composer was present at the recording sessions, and the orchestral playing was notable for its inspirational intensity. The five discs come in a strong cardboard box. A set which is as indispensable as it is inexpensive. Boult's first recording of 9 is an Everest recording.

(i) Symphonies 1–9; (ii) Concerto accademico in D min.; (iii) Tuba Concerto in F min.; 3 Portraits from Elizabeth of England; The Wasps: Overture

⊶ ✿ (B) **** RCA 82876 55708-2 (6). LSO, Previn; with (i) Harper, Shirley-Quirk, Amb. S., L. Symphony Ch., R. Richardson (speaker); (ii) J. O. Buswell; (iii) J. Fletcher

Symphonies 1–9; Oboe Concerto; English Folksongs Suite; Fantasia on Greensleeves; Fantasia on a Theme by Thomas Tallis; 5 Variants on Dives and Lazarus; Flos Campi; Job; Partita for String Orchestra; Serenade to Music

⊶ (B) *** CfP (DDD/ADD) 575 7602 (7). Soloists, incl. Christopher Balmer, RLPO Ch. & O, Handley

Symphonies 1–9; (i) Double Piano Concerto; English Folk Song Suite; Fantasia on Greensleeves; Fantasia on a Theme by Thomas Tallis; In the Fen Country; Job; (ii) The Lark Ascending; Norfolk Rhapsody; The Wasps: Overture & Suite; (iii) Serenade to Music

(B) *** EMI 5 73924-2 (8). (i) Vronsky & Babin; (ii) Bean; (iii) 16 Vocal Soloists; LPO Ch., LPO, New Philh. O, or LSO Boult.

Symphonies: 1–9; Flos Campi; Norfolk Rhpsody; The Wasps Overture

(N) (BB) **(*) Naxos 8.506017 (6). Soloists & Ch., Bournemouth SO, Kees Bakels; Paul Daniel

Previn recorded the Vaughan Williams *Symphonies* over a five-year span from 1968 to 1972, and his achievement in this repertoire represented a peak in his recording career at that time. Here the nine *Symphonies* plus their original fill-ups have been neatly compressed on to six CDs. The most striking performances are those which were recorded last, *2, 3* and *5*; for these Previn achieves an extra depth of understanding, an extra intensity, whether in the purity of *pianissimo* or the outpouring of emotional resolution. For the rest there is only one performance that can be counted at all disappointing, and that is of the *Symphony* one might have expected Previn to interpret best, the taut and dramatic *Fourth*. Even that is an impressive account, if less intense than the rest. Otherwise, the great landscape of the whole cycle is presented with richness and detail in totally refreshing interpretations, brilliantly recorded and impressively transferred to CD. The extra items are worth having too, notably the two *Concertos* with responsive soloists.

For its reissue, **Handley's** set has been expanded to seven bargain CDs to include more of the extra works he recorded so sympathetically. It will especially suit those requiring modern digital sound, for only the *Sinfonia Antartica* is analogue – and that is still a fine, modern recording, offering also the orchestral version of the *Serenade to Music* as a fill-up. In all his Vaughan Williams recordings Handley shows a natural understanding for expressive rubato and is totally sympathetic. Many of his performances are first or near first choices. *5* is also outstanding in every way and was given a Rosette by us on its first appearance. Its original coupling, a very successful account of *Flos campi*, is also included here, as is his memorable version of *Job*.

Boult's late 1960s vintage stereo performances remain very satisfying indeed. Boult's approach to Vaughan Williams was firmly symphonic rather than evocative, and many lovers of the composer will like them for their warmly consistent view, patiently studied and broadly presented. If at times the playing is not so electrically urgent as with, for instance, Previn, the maturity of Vaughan Williams's vision has never been more convincingly presented. This newest collection includes also the shorter pieces originally included as fill-ups on LP, plus some extra and important bonuses including the 2-*Piano Concerto* and *Job*, a work dedicated to Boult and for which he had a special affinity, and which is superbly recorded. But overall the sound is full-bodied and well-focused, and this set presents a comprehensive portrait of the composer, unmatched by any other single issue.

The Naxos cycle was recorded between 1992 and 2003 and to high standards of fidelity and realism. The performances are mostly of quality and the **Bournemouth Orchestra** plays with zest and enthusiasm with **Kees Bakels** taking over from **Paul Daniel** after the *Sea Symphony*. He draws lovely playing throughout, and especially in the *Pastoral* and *Fifth Symphonies*. The visionary beauty of the *Ninth Symphony* is well caught and the *Sinfonia antartica* is very impressive both as a performance and a recording (with the superscriptions, read by **David Timson**, separately cued) and an atmospheric vocal contribution from **Lynda Russell**. *8* is strongly characterised too, although in *6* Bakels misses much of the menance if not the intensity of the slow movement. The six discs are available separately and are coupled as listed below: *A Sea Symphony* (Naxos 8.557059 with Rodgers, Maltman, Bournemouth Ch., Daniel). *Symphony 2; The Wasps Overture* (Naxos 8.550734). *Symphonies 3 & 6* (Naxos 8.550733 both Bournemouth SO, Bakels). *Symphony 4; Norfolk Rhapsody;* (i) *Flos Campi* (Naxos 8.550734 Bournemouth SO, Daniel with (i) Paul Silverthorne, Bournemouth Symphony Ch). *Symphonies 5 & 9* (Naxos 550738). *Symphonies 7 & 8* (Naxos 8.550737 both Bournemouth SO, Kees Bakels).

A Sea Symphony (1)

🔊— Ⓑ **** CfP 575 3082. Rodgers, Shimell, RLPO & Ch., Handley

🔊— ⒷⒷ (***) Belart mono 450 144-2. Baillie, Cameron, LPO Ch. & O, Boult

Ⓜ *** EMI 7 64016-2. Armstrong, Carol Case, LPO Ch., LPO, Boult

A Sea Symphony; The Wasps: Overture

🔊— **** Chan. **SACD** CHSA 5047. Gritton, Finlay, L. Symphony Ch., LSO, Hickox

Vernon Handley conducts a warmly idiomatic performance, which sustains relatively slow speeds masterfully. The reading is crowned by Handley's rapt account of the slow movement, *On the Beach at Night Alone*, as well as by the long duet in the finale, leading on through the exciting final ensemble, *Sail Forth*, to a deeply satisfying culmination in *O my Brave Soul!* **Joan Rodgers** makes an outstandingly beautiful soprano soloist, with **William Shimell** drier-toned but expressive. The recording, full and warm, has an extreme dynamic range, placing the two soloists rather distantly.

As a performance, **Boult's** (early 1952) Decca mono recording with outstanding soloists and incisive and sympathetic singing from the **LPO Choir** has never been surpassed. This conveys the urgency of a live performance, with the dramatic opening astonishingly vivid and real in the vintage sound. Boult was at his most inspired. This Belart CD makes the very most of the master tape, and only the lack of body of the massed upper strings betrays the age of the original. The choral sound is full and well focused and the Kingsway Hall acoustic spacious and warm; the closing section, *Away O soul*, is particularly beautiful.

Hickox's version of Vaughan Williams's first and most ambitious symphonic venture comes in vivid sound on surround sound SACD, with more bloom and atmosphere than usual in this venue and with clean, natural separation. The performance gains greatly from being recorded live, with the **LSO** and **London Symphony Chorus** in superb form, backing up the two excellent soloists (**Susan Gritton** sweet and pure, **Gerald Finlay** dark and firm) over the widest dynamic range – as in the meditative second movement, *On the Beach at Night, Alone*. Where studio versions of this massive work tend to tail off a degree in the long final movement, *The Explorers*, even the excellent CfP version from Handley, Hickox's offers mounting excitement as in the concert hall. A splendid addition to Hickox's RVW series.

Boult's stereo version demonstrates his affectionate style, drawing consistently expressive but never sentimental phrasing from his singers and players. **John Carol Case's** baritone does not sound well on disc with his rather plaintive tone-colour, but his style is right, and **Sheila Armstrong** sings most beautifully. The set has been remastered with outstanding success.

A London Symphony (2) (original 1913 version)

🔊— ✿ **** Chan. 9902. LSO, Hickox– G. BUTTERWORTH: *The Banks of Green Willow.* (***)

A London Symphony was Vaughan Williams's own favourite among his symphonies (and I. M.'s too). It was the one he revised most often, first between 1918 and 1920, and later even more radically in the 1930s, with the definitive score finally published in 1936. What this revelatory recording demonstrates is that the 20 minutes or so of music that were excised include many passages that represent the composer at his most magically poetic. Vaughan Williams undoubtedly made the work structurally tauter, but discursiveness in a symphony is no longer regarded as a necessary fault.

Hickox draws ravishing sounds throughout from the **LSO**, with an unerring feeling for idiomatic rubato and a powerful control of massive dynamic contrasts. In this first version the first movement is no different, but each of the other movements here includes substantial sections completely eliminated later, some of them echoing the Ravel of *Daphnis and Chloé*, including an extended one in the Scherzo. The sumptuous Chandos sound, with an extraordinarily wide dynamic range, adds to the impact of the performance, which comes with a short but valuable and beautifully played fill-up.

A London Symphony (2) (1920 version)

(***) Biddulph mono WHL 016. Cincinnati SO, Goossens –
    WALTON: *Violin Concerto* (***) (with Concert (***))

This is the only recording ever made of the 1920 version of Vaughan Williams's *London Symphony*. That involves three minutes of intensely poetic music, later excised in RVW's definitive 1936 edition. The sessions immediately followed the first recording of the Walton *Violin Concerto* with Heifetz in 1941 in which **Eugene Goossens** and the **Cincinnati Orchestra** provided the accompaniment. The coupling (together with other British music) is among the most valuable of all the reissues in the Biddulph catalogue, with excellent CD transfers.

A London Symphony; The Wasps: Overture

(BB) *** Naxos 8.550734. Bournemouth SO, Bakels

The Naxos version of Vaughan Williams's *London Symphony*, coupled with the *Wasps Overture*, is powerful and dedicated. **Kees Bakels** draws ravishing sounds from the **Bournemouth Symphony Orchestra**, notably the strings, with the Scherzo cleanly pointed and the slow movement both warm-hearted and refined, and with *pianissimos* that have you catching the breath. The problem is the extreme range of dynamic in the recording. A thrilling experience nonetheless.

(i) A London Symphony (2); Fantasia on Greensleeves; The Wasps: Overture. (ii) Serenade to Music

(BB) (***) Dutton Lab. mono CDBP 9707. (i) Queen's Hall O; (ii)
    Baillie, Stiles-Allen, Suddaby, Turner, Balfour, Desmond,
    Brunskill, Jarred, Nash, Widdop, Jones, Titterton,
    Henderson, Easton, Williams, Allin, BBC SO; Wood

The historic Decca recording of Vaughan Williams's *London Symphony*, with the specially assembled group of musicians designated as the '**Queen's Hall Orchestra**', conducted by **Sir Henry Wood**, brings a most striking discrepancy of pace with modern performances. The first movement alone takes over three minutes less than in most latter-day recordings. The not-so-slow introduction may lack mystery but there has never been a more passionate account of the work than this on record, and even with limited dynamic range – no true *pianissimo* is caught – the hushed intensity of the slow

movement is tellingly conveyed. The *Symphony* comes coupled with shorter Vaughan Williams works: *The Wasps Overture, Greensleeves* and, best of all, the original (1938) Columbia recording of the *Serenade to Music*, with the 16 soloists specified in the score, a stellar group. The gently soaring phrase 'of sweet harmony' has never sounded so sweetly angelic as when sung here by **Isobel Baillie**. The Dutton Laboratory transfers are outstandingly true to the originals.

Symphonies 2 (London); 6 in E min.; (i) Prelude & Fugue in C min.

(B) *** EMI (ADD) 5 86592-2 (2). LPO, Handley; (i) with
    Bell

These recordings of Vaughan Williams's *Second* and *Sixth* were made by **Vernon Handley** and the **London Philharmonic** in the late 1970s. When Handley went on to record a complete cycle of the nine Vaughan Williams *Symphonies* for CfP in digital sound, these earlier versions were put to one side and largely forgotten. Yet they stand up extraordinarily well, and in some ways are even preferable to the rightly praised CfP versions. That is especially so of the wonderfully rich and evocative *London Symphony*, which benefits from the fuller-bodied, analogue recording, here transferred more immediately and at a higher level. Though the interpretation is very little different, there is more mystery and hushed intensity in this earlier account. The advantages of late analogue sound over early digital are not so great in the *Sixth Symphony*. As fill-up, the rare *Prelude and Fugue in C minor*, originally written for organ in 1921 and orchestrated a decade later, makes a relatively brief but worthwhile supplement, pointing forward to the later symphonies.

A London Symphony (2); Symphony 8 in E min.

(B) *** CfP 575 3092. RLPO, Handley

Vernon Handley gives a beautifully paced and well-sprung reading of the *London Symphony*, although not as crisp in ensemble as some and with sound diffused rather than sharply focused. The result is warmly sympathetic and can be strongly recommended if the generous coupling of the *Eighth Symphony*, an underestimated work, is preferred.

A Pastoral Symphony (3); Norfolk Rhapsodies 1 in E min.; 2 in D min.; The Running Set

**** Chan. 10001. LSO, Hickox; (i) with Evans

The *Pastoral Symphony*, inspired not by the English countryside as much as by the composer's experiences on the Western Front in the First World War, is among his most elusive works, yet here, with **Rebecca Evans** a radiant soprano soloist in the melismatic writing of the finale, the magnetism of Vaughan Williams's spacious inspirations is irresistible. The three folk-based works make an apt coupling. The *Norfolk Rhapsody 1* has remained in the regular repertory over the years, but the *Norfolk Rhapsody 2*, just as warmly attractive in its use of folk material, was here receiving its first performance since 1914, with two missing pages of the score judiciously reconstructed by Stephen Hogger.

(i) A Pastoral Symphony (3); Symphonies 4 in F min.; 5 in D; 6 in E min.

⊕–ᵀ Ⓑ *** RCA (ADD) 74321 88680-2 (2). LSO, Previn; (i) with Harper

The most striking of **Previn's** performances is the *Fifth Symphony*, and the only performance that can be accounted at all disappointing is the dramatic *Fourth*. This work is the tautest and most dramatic of the cycle, but the somewhat ponderous tempo he adopts for the first movement lets it down. Nevertheless, on the whole it is a powerful reading and is vividly recorded.

Previn draws an outstandingly beautiful and refined performance from the **LSO** of the *Pastoral Symphony*, the bare textures sounding austere but never thin and the few climaxes emerging at full force with purity undiminished. In the third movement the final coda – the only really fast music in the whole work – brings a magic tracery of *pianissimo* in this performance, lighter, faster and even clearer than achieved by Boult.

The *Sixth Symphony*, with its moments of darkness and brutality contrasted against the warmth of the second subject or the hushed intensity of the final, otherworldly, slow movement, is a work for which Previn has an innate affinity. In the first three movements his performance is superbly dramatic, clear-headed and direct, with natural understanding. His account of the mystic final movement with its endless *pianissimo* is not, however, on the same level, for – whether on not the fault of the recording – the playing is not quite hushed enough and the tempo is just a little too fast.

In the *Fifth* Previn refuses to be lured into pastoral by-ways. His tempi may – rather surprisingly – be consistently on the slow side, but the purity of tone he draws from the LSO strings, the precise shading of dynamic and phasing and the sustaining of tension through the longest, most hushed passages produce results that will persuade many not normally convinced of the greatness of this music. In the first movement Previn builds the great climaxes of the second subject with much warmth, but he reserves for the climax of the slow movement his culminating thrust of emotion, a moment of visionary sublimity, after which the gentle urgency of the *Passacaglia* finale and the stillness of the *Epilogue* seem a perfect happy conclusion. Special tribute must also be paid to the uncredited remastering engineer and to the producer of this reissue, Lionel Falleur, for the sound really is superb throughout the set.

(i) A Pastoral Symphony (3); (ii) Symphony 5 in D

Ⓜ *** EMI (ADD) 7 64018-2. (i) M. Price, New Philh. O; (ii) LPO; Boult

ⒷⒷ (***) Belart mono 461 118-2. (i) Ritchie; LPO, Boult

On EMI, in the *Pastoral Symphony* **Boult** is not entirely successful in controlling the tension of the short but elusive first movement, although it is beautifully played. The opening of the *Lento moderato*, however, is very fine, and its close is sustained with a perfect blend of restraint and intensity. In a generous coupling Boult gives a loving and gentle performance of *5*, easier and more flowing than most rivals', and some may prefer it for that reason, but the emotional

involvement is a degree less intense, particularly in the slow movement. Both recordings have been very successfully remastered.

It is good to have **Boult's** earlier, Kingsway Hall recordings back in the catalogue although some allowances have to be made for the lack of amplitude in the upper string climaxes, the CD transfer is impressively full and the recording luminous. The translucent textures Boult creates in the *Pastoral Symphony*, with its ethereal opening, and his delicacy later are balanced by his intensity in the *Fifth*, where the climax of the first movement has wonderful breadth and passion. The **LPO** of the time play with great sympathy and warmth.

Symphony 4 in F min.

Ⓝ *** BBC (ADD) BBCL 4237-2. BBC SO, Sargent – SIBELIUS: *Symphony 4* ***

Ⓜ (***) Cala mono CACD 0528. NBC SO, Stokowski – ANTHEIL: *Symphony 4* (***); BUTTERWORTH: *Shropshire Lad* (**)

Symphony 4; Norfolk Rhapsody 1; (i) Flos campi

⊕–ᵀ ⒷⒷ *** Naxos 8.557276. Bournemouth SO, Daniel; (i) with Silverthorne, Bournemouth SO Ch.

Symphony 4 in F min.; (i) Mass in G min.; (ii) Six Choral Songs to be Sung in Time of War

⊕–ᵀ ✿ **** Chan. 9984. (i) Hickox Singers; (ii) L. Symphony Ch.; LSO, Hickox

Richard Hickox's searing reading of the *Fourth Symphony* matches, and even outshines in its fury, the première recording conducted by the composer in 1937. Hickox even manages to match the very fast speed RVW set, angry to the very last bar. The intensity of the **LSO's** playing, brilliant from first to last, has one magnetized in all four movements, chill in the slow movement with its eerie polytonal writing, and unrelenting even in the skipping rhythms of the Scherzo and the oompah sequences of the finale. The *Mass in G minor* makes a fine and unusual coupling, here given sharper focus than usual, with dramatic contrasts underlined, and with the precision of ensemble compensating for having women's rather than boy's voices in the upper parts. The six unison *Songs to be Sung in Time of War*, which come as a unique supplement, were written at the outbreak of war in 1939 to texts by Shelley, miniatures that in their natural lyrical intensity rise beyond the limits of scale. Superb Chandos sound in both the symphony and the choral works.

Vaughan Williams's abrasive *Fourth Symphony* emerges in **Paul Daniel's** powerful performance as one of the most vital of Vaughan Williams's works, at once chilling and lyrical in its forward thrust. The impact of the opening has never been sharper than here, helped by the weighty and atmospheric recording. The *Symphony* is superbly contrasted with a masterpiece from the 1920, the visionary piece, *Flos campi*, for viola and orchestra, inspired over its six sections by the Song of Solomon, with **Paul Silverthorne** a superb soloist. Covering the full range of Vaughan Williams's achievement, the disc also includes the *Norfolk*

Rhapsody 1 of 1906, representing the composer's early pastoral style at its most attractive.

Sargent performed Vaughan Williams *Fourth Symphony* with impressive directness, with the strong emotions of this work compellingly brought out. The slow movement is particularly impressive for its warmth, and if the *Scherzo* lacks the sheer bite that others have bought to it, the finale is excitingly done, generating real electricity. The 1963 stereo recording, from a live Albert Hall performance, is surprisingly vivid and warm.

The only time that **Stokowski** ever conducted Vaughan Williams's provocative *Fourth Symphony* was in March 1943, when this high-powered, red-blooded reading was recorded, the first to be made outside Britain, and throughout the performance one marvels that Stokowski could draw sounds from the **NBC Orchestra** so different from those the same players produced under Toscanini. The chill and poignancy of the slow movement and the bluff humour of the Scherzo, each strongly characterized, lead to a comparably positive account of the finale. The sound, limited in range, is yet satisfyingly full-bodied.

Symphony 5 in D; (i) Oboe Concerto; (ii) Flos campi

☞— Ⓑ **** CfP 575 3112. (i) Small; (ii) Balmer, RLPO Ch.; RLPO, Handley

Symphony 5 in D; Hymn-Tune Prelude; Prelude & Fugue in C min.; (i) The Pilgrim Pavement; Psalm 23; Valiant for Truth.

☞— ✸ **** Chan. 9666. (i) Hickox Singers; LSO, Hickox

Hickox with the **LSO** captures a visionary fervour in this most characteristic of the series. Hickox's style is warmly expressive, moulding phrases and tempo affectionately, always sounding spontaneous, building climaxes with shattering power. The LSO respond with playing both rich and refined, helped by the wide-ranging Chandos sound. Equally, the rarities on the disc are most persuasively done, three of them première recordings. *The Pilgrim Pavement* is a touchingly direct devotional motet written for the Church of St John the Divine in New York, and the setting of *Psalm 23* for soprano is adapted from his opera *The Pilgrim's Progress*, while the *Prelude and Fugue* is an amplification of an organ work of 1930, which anticipates the abrasive Vaughan Williams of *Job*.

Vernon Handley's disc is also outstanding in every way, a spacious yet concentrated reading, superbly played and recorded, which masterfully holds the broad structure of this *Symphony* together, building to massive climaxes. The warmth and poetry of the work are also beautifully caught. The rare and evocative *Flos campi*, inspired by the Song of Solomon, makes a generous and attractive coupling, equally well played if rather closely balanced. The sound is outstandingly full, giving fine clarity of texture. For this reissue **Jonathan Small** adds a delectable account of the charmingly lyrical *Oboe Concerto*.

(i) Symphony 5; (ii) Dona nobis pacem

(***) Somm mono SOMMCD 071. (i) LPO; (ii) Flynn, Henderson, BBC Ch. & SO; composer

Transferred from LP acetate originals, this recording of the *Fifth Symphony* derives from a 1952 Promenade Concert with the composer at the helm. What an occasion it must have been! **Vaughan Williams** creates real tension in a reading that is as noble and inspirational as it is spacious, increasing in spontaneous feeling as it proceeds. The coupling comes from the BBC – the première broadcast of *Dona nobis pacem*, with fine, ardent soloists and a comparable response from the **BBC Chorus** and **Symphony Orchestra**. The sound is less than ideal, but this is a coupling not to be missed by any VW aficionado.

Symphonies 5 in D; 9 in E min.

🅱🅱 *** Naxos 8.550738. Bournemouth SO, Bakels

Kees Bakels and the **Bournemouth Symphony** follow up their earlier issues with a superb coupling of 5, arguably the peak of the series, and the very last *Symphony*, long underestimated. Drawing the most refined playing from the Bournemouth orchestra, not least the strings, he finds in a relatively direct reading an extra purity and nobility, pointing the big emotional climaxes of the first and third movements most tellingly. Speeds are on the fast side, but the visionary beauty is perfectly caught. 9, with its original structure flouting convention, emerges strong and fresh, with the *Andante tranquillo* finale bringing echoes of the comparable movement of 6. Clear, refined recording to match.

Symphony 6 in E min

(**(*)) Cala mono CACD 0537. NYPO, Stokowski –
TCHAIKOVSKY: *Romeo and Juliet* (abridged version);
MOZART: *Symphony 35 (Haffner)*; SCOTT: *From the Sacred Harp*; WEINBERGER: *Schwanda the Bagpiper: Polka & Fugue* (**)

Symphony 6; Fantasia on a Theme of Thomas Tallis

Ⓝ *** BBC Legends BBCL 4256-2. New Philh. O, Boult (with
BAX: *Mediterranean*; HADLEY: *One Morning in Spring*;
BERG: *Lyric Suite* ***)

Symphony 6 in E min.; Fantasia on a Theme of Thomas Tallis; (i) The Lark Ascending

☞— 🅱🅱 *** Warner Apex 0927 49584-2. (i) Little; BBC SO, A. Davis

Andrew Davis's reading of the *Sixth* is taut and urgent, with emotions kept under firm control. The two shorter works which come as supplement are given more warmly expressive, exceptionally beautiful performances, with **Tasmin Little** an immaculate soloist in *The Lark Ascending*. Warner Apex's wide-ranging sound, setting the orchestra at a slight distance, blunts the impact of the *Symphony* in the first three movements, but then works beautifully in the chill of the hushed *pianissimo* meditation of the finale, as it does too in the fill-ups.

It was **Boult** who in 1948 conducted the first performance of this apocalyptic work, and he has recorded it in the studio several times since, but this live account from the Vaughan Williams Centenary concert in Cheltenham Town Hall in July 1972 far outshines any of them, reflecting the atmos-

1180 VAUGHAN WILLIAMS, Ralph

phere of a special occasion. The BBC recording splendidly captures the weight of sound in the *tuttis* and the other-worldly calm of the *pianissimo* finale. One admires afresh the way that the jaunty second subject in the first movement is transformed into the richly lyrical melody in the coda, also the ominous interruptions in *crescendo* in the second movement and the haunting saxophone theme in the central section of the *Scherzo*. The extra items add to the value of the disc.

The Cala performance has a riveting foward impetus and, characteristically, **Stokowski** relishes the big tune on the strings in the first movement; but the slow movement is controversially fast. The *Haffner* is Stokowski's only recording of any Mozart *Symphony*: it is certainly lively and has a beautifully pointed *Andante* and a sparkling finale. But it suffers badly from audience noises. *Romeo and Juliet* is well played but hardly riveting, and the recording lacks range. Moreover, Stokowski substitutes a quiet ending for the composer's dramatic final chords, doubtfully claiming that such an alteration had Tchaikovsky's sanction. Thomas Jefferson Scott's folksy *From the Sacred Harp* is hardly one of the conductor's major discoveries, but the Weinberger *Polka and Fugue* is certainly successful, and the only time Stokowski conducted any music by this composer. Good transfers, but not really a satisfying collection.

(i) *Symphony 6 in E min.; (ii; iii) The Lark Ascending; (iii; iv) A Song of Thanksgiving*

(BB) (***) Dutton Lab. mono CDBP 9703. (i) LSO; (ii) Pougnet; (ii, iii) LPO; (iii) with Dolemore, Speight, Luton Choral Soc. & Girls' Ch.; Boult

Boult's pioneer 1949 recording of the *Sixth Symphony* with the **LSO**, vividly transferred from 78s, has the original, heavily scored version of the Scherzo included as a supplement. It remains among the finest ever versions of this bitingly dramatic work. The total chill of the slow finale has never been more tellingly conveyed, even though the relatively close-up sound cannot convey an extreme *pianissimo*. **Jean Pougnet**, then leader of the **LPO**, proves a most understanding soloist in *The Lark Ascending*, with *A Song of Thanksgiving* providing an attractive makeweight, a piece with narrator, soprano soloist and chorus, written to celebrate victory in the Second World War.

Symphonies 6 in E min.; 8 in D min.; (i) Nocturne

🎵 *** Chan. **SACD** CHSA 5016; CD Chan. 10103. LSO, Hickox; (i) with Roderick Williams

Richard Hickox is particularly fine in the dedicated slow finale of *6* with its visionary overtones; yet in the first three movements of that darkly intense work the abrasiveness of the writing is a little muted, thanks to the mellow recording acoustic of All Saints', Tooting. It does not help either that the transfer level is on the low side, so that the heavy brass passages, for all their weight, lack something in bite. In *8* the acoustic is less of a problem, even if the Scherzo for wind alone could be even more jaunty. The slow movement for strings brings tender refinement and the rumbustious finale a swaggering conclusion. The *Nocturne* for baritone and or-

chestra makes a most valuable supplement and demonstrates here what mastery he already had over orchestral colour, giving forecasts of *A London Symphony*.

Symphonies 6 in E min.; 9 in E min.; Fantasia on Greensleeves

🎵 (B) *** CfP 575 3122-2. RLPO, Handley

Next to Previn's now withdrawn recording in the same coupling, **Handley** lacks some of the darker, sharper qualities implied. Though his speeds are consistently faster, his is a more comfortable reading, and the recording adds to that impression. Handley's approach is a valid one as the slow *pianissimo* finale, here presented as mysterious rather than desolate, was inspired not by a world laid waste by nuclear war (as was once thought), but by Prospero's 'cloud-capp'd towers' in Shakespeare's *The Tempest*. The *Greensleeves Fantasia* is now added as a contrasting encore.

Sinfonia Antartica (7) (CD versions)

🎵 (BB) *** RCA Navigator (ADD) 74321 29248-2. Harper, Richardson, L. Symphony Ch., LSO, Previn – WALTON: *Cello Concerto* ***

(i) *Sinfonia Antartica (7); (ii) Serenade to Music (choral version); Partita for Double String Orchestra*

🎵 (B) *** CfP (ADD) 575 3132. (i) Hargan; (ii) RLPO Ch.; RLPO, Handley

(i) *Sinfonia Antartica (7); The Wasps (incidental music): Overture & Suite*

(M) **(*) EMI (ADD) 7 64020-2. (i) Armstrong; LPO, Boult

Previn's interpretation concentrates on atmosphere rather than drama in a performance that is sensitive and literal. Because of the recessed effect of the sound, the portrayal of the ice-fall (represented by the sudden entry of the organ) has a good deal less impact than in **Vernon Handley's** version. Before each movement **Sir Ralph Richardson** speaks the superscript written by the composer on his score. As can be seen, Previn's *Sinfonia Antartica* is coupled with Walton's *Cello Concerto*.

Handley shows a natural feeling for expressive rubato and draws refined playing from the **Liverpool Orchestra**. At the end of the epilogue **Alison Hargan** makes a notable first appearance on disc, a soprano with an exceptionally sweet and pure voice. In well-balanced digital sound it makes an outstanding bargain, particularly when it offers an excellent fill-up, the *Serenade to Music* (though in this lovely score a chorus never sounds as characterful as a group of well-chosen soloists). Also added for this latest reissue is the rare *Partita*, very well-played and sonorously recorded.

Sir Adrian Boult gives a stirring account and is well served by the EMI engineers. The inclusion of Vaughan Williams's Aristophanic suite, *The Wasps*, with its endearing participation of the kitchen utensils plus its tuneful *Overture*, is a bonus, although in the *Overture* the upper strings sound a bit thin.

(i) Sinfonia Antartica (7); Symphony 8 in D min.

- 🎵 (BB) *** Belart mono/stereo 461 116-2. LPO, Boult; (i) with Ritchie, LPO Ch. (superscriptions spoken by Gielgud)
- 🎵 (BB) *** Naxos 8.550737. Bournemouth SO, Bakels; (i) with Russell, Waynflete Singers (superscriptions read by Timson)

Boult's 1953 mono performance of the *Sinfonia Antartica* has never been surpassed; the atmospheric recording, with its translucent icy vistas and **Margaret Ritchie's** floating, wordless soprano voice sounding ethereal, remains a model of balancing. Boult and the **LPO** achieve keen concentration throughout, and the evocation of the frozen landscapes and the shifting ice-floes is as compelling as his control of the structure of a work that is never easy to hold together. **Sir John Gielgud's** superscriptions (from the score) act as moving preludes. The recording of the *Eighth Symphony* is early stereo (1956). The LPO plays beautifully, and the Decca engineers have relished the challenge of balancing the exotic sounds of glissando tubular bells, tuned gongs, vibraphone and xylophone. The string-tone sounds far fuller than it did when this recording last appeared.

Kees Bakels's *Antartica* is particularly impressive, helped by vividly atmospheric recording that, with superb separation, clarifies textures – not least the percussion and wind-machine – and beautifully captures the ethereal sound of **Lynda Russell** singing off-stage. Bakels's fast speed for the opening movement tautly draws together a structure which can seem dangerously episodic, and the thrust is maintained through the other movements. Sensibly, the superscriptions are included on separate tracks at the end of the disc. 8 is excellently done too, with an element of wildness brought out in the sharp contrasts of the first movement, bouncing humour in the Scherzo and refinement in the slow movement and finale.

Symphony 8 in D min. (DVD version)

- 🎵 *** EMI **DVD** DVB 3884569o. LPO, Boult – BEETHOVEN: *Violin Concerto* ***

Filmed at a Royal Festival Hall concert in October 1972, this offers **Boult's** telling reading of Vaughan Williams's least-performed *Symphony*, a work which the conductor opens magically and then brings out its rich vein of lyricism – the tender expression of the slow movement alongside the colourful wind scoring in the Scherzo and the percussive detail in the finale – without exaggeration. Fine playing, well-detailed recording, and what a pleasure to watch Boult's economy of gesture as he holds the work's structure firmly together.

Symphony 9 in E min.

(***) Cala mono CACD 0539. O, Stokowski – RIEGGER: *New Dance*; HOVHANESS: *Symphony 2*; CRESTON: *Toccata, Op. 68* (***)

Stokowski was a fervent advocate of Vaughan Williams; the *Symphony* is given with great dedication and authority and is a reading that is second to none despite some slight tape imperfection at the beginning of the first movement. Percy

Grainger, who was in the audience, wrote of its beauty and cosmic quality, and the 76-year-old Stokowski certainly conveyed its power and nobility. The American works have comparable authority and vitality, and there need be no reservations concerning the quality of the mono sound, given the period.

CHAMBER MUSIC

Piano Quintet in C min.; Quintet in D for Clarinet, Horn, Violin, Cello & Piano; String Quartet; Nocturne & Scherzo; 3 Preludes on Welsh Hymn Tunes; Romance; Romance & Pastorale; Scherzo; Suite de Ballet

- 🎵 *** Hyp. CDA 67381/2 (2). Nash Ens.

On the first of the two discs the *Piano Quintet* of 1903 opens strikingly with sharp discords and then whirls you into a vigorous movement with French overtones. The *String Quartet* of 1898, with its folk-like pentatonic writing, sounds more like the RVW we know, and again his mastery in handling a difficult medium is perfectly clear, as it is even more strikingly in the *Quintet* for the difficult and unusual combination of piano, clarinet, horn, violin and cello. The *Nocturne and Scherzo* (1906) for string quintet clearly anticipate the song-cycle *On Wenlock Edge*, and other shorter works for various combinations from later in his career help to fill out the musical portrait of a composer whose music seems to grow in vitality with the years, largely thanks to brilliant performances like these. The recording is well up to house standards.

Piano Quintet; Romance and Pastorale; (i) On Wenlock Edge (song-cycle)

*** Chan.10465. Schubert Ens.; (i) with Padmore

Mark Padmore proves a passionate interpreter of Vaughan Williams's cycle of settings from Housman's *The Shropshire Lad*, with accompaniment for piano quintet. The result is thrillingly dramatic with high dynamic contrasts, notably in the eerie song, *Is my Team Ploughing?*, with the ghostly ploughman eliciting powerful responses from his live companion. The build-up there is thrilling, but all these songs have maximum impact and the rare coupling makes the disc especially attractive. The *Piano Quintet* is hardly typical of the mature composer, but various lyrical passages point forward, even if the melodic writing is more repetitious than in the later VW. The *Romance and Pastorale* also dates from before the First World War, a charming miniature dedicated to a friend's wife.

6 Studies in English Folksong for Clarinet & Piano

*** Chan. 8683. Hilton, Swallow – BAX: *Sonata* **(*); BLISS: *Quintet* ***

These *Folksong Studies*, which Vaughan Williams published in arrangements for the viola and cello, come from the mid-1920s and are very beautiful, most sensitively played by **Janet Hilton** and **Keith Swallow**.

String Quartets 1 in G min.; 2 in A min.; (i) Phantasy Quintet

➡─ 🏵 BB **** Naxos 8.555300. Maggini Qt; with (i) Jackson

The **Magginis** find a rare clarity and warmth in both quartets. The *First* was written soon after Vaughan Williams's studies with Ravel in Paris, with obvious echoes not just of Ravel but of the Debussy *Quartet*. The *Second Quartet* dates from 1942 to 1943, written in the crucial gap between the lyrical *Symphony 5* and the abrasive 6. Most revelatory of all is the Maggini performance of the *Phantasy Quintet* of 1912, a masterpiece long neglected, weighty and compressed. A slow prelude as intense as that of a Purcell Fantasy leads to three comparably strong and sharply characterized sections.

VOCAL MUSIC

Benedicite; Let Us Now Praise Famous Men; O Clap Your Hands; Old Hundreth Psalm; O Taste and See; Toward the Unknown Region

**(*) Australian Decca Eloquence 467 613-2. Byram-Wigfield, Winchester Cathedral Ch., Waynefleet Singers, Bournemouth SO, Hill – WALTON: *Coronation March & Te Deum*, etc. **(*)

Enthusiastic performances, set in a reverberant acoustic and well recorded. They may not be the most polished available but the infectious quality of the music-making is very involving. The *Benedicite*, a strong 16-minute work, which is too often overlooked, is hugely enjoyable. Well worth considering.

(i; ii) Dona nobis pacem; (i; iii) Fantasia (quasi variations) on the Old 104th Psalm Tune; (iv) Magnificat; (i) Toward the Unknown Region

B *** EMI (ADD) 5 74782-2 (2). (i) LPO Ch., LPO, Boult; (ii) with Armstrong, Carol Case; (iii) Katin; (iv) Watts, Amb. S., O Nova, Davies – *Concerto grosso*, etc. **(*)

Dona nobis pacem, which appeared in 1936 as a direct response to the dark uneasy peace of the 1930s, is a work that was obviously relevant but is still elusive. The central setting of a Whitman poem, 'Dirge for Two Veterans' presents a strong and sustained climax, while the more austere settings of biblical texts have a dark simplicity that is most compelling. The *Magnificat* shows Vaughan Williams in his most Holstian vein. It dates from the early 1930s and has strong suggestions of *Flos campi*. Its inspiration is of high quality, and it is performed here with sympathy and imagination. The *Psalm Tune Fantasia*, however, is not one of the composer's most successful works, although these artists do their best for it. The early setting of Whitman, *Toward the Unknown Region*, is much more rewarding and is finely sung.

Dona nobis pacem; 4 Hymns; Lord, Thou hast been our refuge (Psalm 90); O clap your hands (Psalm 47); Toward the Unknown Region

*** Hyp. CDA 66655. Howarth, Ainsley, Allen, Corydon Singers & O, Best

(i; ii) Dona nobis pacem; (ii; iii) Sancta civitas

➡─ **** EMI 7 54788-2. (i) Kenny; (ii) Terfel; (iii) Langridge, St Paul's Cathedral Choristers; L. Symphony Ch., LSO, Hickox

These two visionary masterpieces, both seriously neglected, both with Latin titles and both dating from the interwar period, make an ideal and generous coupling on EMI. Drawing passionate performances from his choir and soloists (notably from **Bryn Terfel** in both works), **Hickox** brings out not only the visionary intensity and atmospheric beauty – as in the offstage trumpets and 'Alleluias' near the start of *Sancta civitas* – but also the dramatic power. Both these works may be predominantly meditative, but they have moments of violence which relate directly to the dark side of VW, as expressed in the *Fourth Symphony*, such as the chorus *Beat! Beat! Drums!*, the second section of *Dona nobis pacem*. Hickox is a degree broader in his speeds than previous interpreters on disc, but is all the warmer for it.

Using a relatively small choir and orchestra, **Best** takes an intimate view of *Dona nobis pacem* but one which, as a result, is even sharper in focus, capturing the dramatic contrasts as a big performance would, with words unusually clear. The sweet-toned **Judith Howarth** and the warmly expressive **Thomas Allen** are ideal soloists. *Toward the Unknown Region* was VW's first big choral work, not as distinctive as his later music but with many typical fingerprints. Best brings out the beauty of the choral writing, as he does in the even rarer *Four Hymns* for tenor, viola and strings, which the composer intended as a counterpart to the *Five Mystical Songs*. **Ainsley** is the clear tenor soloist, though strained a little at the top. The setting of *Psalm 90* is the more effective here for having, instead of a semi-chorus, the optional baritone soloist, with Allen again singing with deep dedication.

5 English Folk Songs; An acre of Land; Bushes and Briars; Ca' the Yowes; Early in the Spring; Greensleeves; John Dory; Loch Lomond; The Seeds of Love; The Turtle Dove; The Unquiet Grave; Ward the Pirate

N B *** EMI (ADD) 2 16155-2. L. Madrigal Singers, Bishop – HOLST: *Choral music* ***

Using a choir of hand-picked singers **Christopher Bishop** provides here a delightful collection of part songs, far more varied than one might expect, each one showing subtly the distinction of Vaughan Williams's mind, never falling into mere routine. The singing of the **London Madrigal Singers** is admirably lithe and sensitive and this is altogether a most rewarding disc, beautifully engineered.

(i) Arrangements of Folk Songs from East Anglia; France; Herefordshire Carols; Newfoundland; Wessex; (ii) 3 Arrangements with Violin; (iii) 6 Studies in English Folk-Song

N B *** EMI (ADD) 2 16156-2. (i) Tear, Ledger; (ii) with Hugh Bean; (iii) Jean Stewart, Daphne Ibbott

Robert Tear, who earlier made a delightful record of Benjamin Britten's folksong settings here turns to the very different, more innocent settings of Vaughan Williams and conveys comparable intensity, not least in those songs where the singer has a stanza or so unaccompanied. The selection could hardly be more attractive or more varied in mood and expression. Stylish accompaniments. **Hugh Bean's** sensitive violin *obbligati* in the three closing songs of the recital are a highlight. For this reissue **Jean Stewart** adds the engaging *Six Studies in English Folk Song*.

Fantasia on Christmas Carols; The First Nowell; On Christmas Night (Masque)

*** Chan. 10385. Fox, Williams, Joyful Company of Singers, L. Sinf. Ch. & O, Hickox

Vaughan Williams's love of Christmas and carols has long been familiar from his *Fantasia*, here premièred in a version for baritone soloist (the warm-voiced **Roderick Williams**), chorus, strings and organ, a performance unsurpassed on record. But his masque *On Christmas Night* (adapted from *A Christmas Carol*) is an attractive surprise, showing the composer at his most winningly inventive, closely following the Dickens narrative. *The First Nowell* (centring on a favourite carol featured in all three works) is described as a nativity play, but is an entirely musical setting, featuring more traditional melodies handled with loving expertise. **Richard Hickox** has said how much he and his singers and players enjoyed making these recordings, and their pleasure comes over in these moving and exhilarating performances, superbly sung, played and recorded. A splendid Christmas gift for anyone.

(i) Fantasia on Christmas Carols; (ii) Flos campi; (i) 5 Mystical Songs; (iii) Serenade to Music

⊕— ⒝ **** Hyp. Helios CDH55004. (i) Allen; (ii) Imai & Corydon Singers; (iii) 16 soloists; ECO, Best

This radiant record centres round the *Serenade to Music* and, as in the original performance, sixteen star soloists are here lined up; though the team of women does not quite match the stars of 1938, the men are generally fresher and clearer. Above all, thanks largely to fuller, modern recording, the result is much more sensuous than the original, with ensemble better matched and with **Matthew Best** drawing glowing sounds from the **English Chamber Orchestra**. The other items are superbly done too, with **Nobuko Imai** a powerful viola soloist in the mystical cantata *Flos campi*, another Vaughan Williams masterpiece. **Thomas Allen** is the characterful soloist in the *Five Mystical Songs*. Warmly atmospheric sound to match the performances.

(i) Flos campi; Household Music (3 Preludes on Welsh Hymn Tunes)

*** Chan. 9392. (i) Dukes; N. Sinfonia, Hickox – *Riders to the Sea* ***

Philip Dukes proves a rich and eloquent viola soloist in *Flos campi*, in which the **Northern Sinfonia Chorus** is balanced more forwardly and powerfully than usual, and this is a remarkably successful performance on all counts. The *Household Music*, never recorded before, offers three delightful miniatures, written in 1941 as a wartime exercise, intended for amateur musicians as well as professionals.

(i) Hodie (Christmas Cantata); (ii) Fantasia on Christmas Carols

⊕— Ⓜ *** EMI (ADD) 5 67427-2. (i) Baker, Lewis, Shirley-Quirk, Bach Ch., Westminster Abbey Ch., LSO, Willcocks; (ii) Barrow, Guildford Cathedral Ch. & String O, Rose

⒝ *** Naxos 8.570439. Watson, Hoare, Gadd, Guildford Ch. Soc., RPO, Davan Wetton

Hodie is, above all, bluff and jolly, not very subtle in its effects, but full of open-hearted humanity. Those qualities are splendidly realized in this fine performance, not just by the choir, but most of all by the excellent trio of soloists, with **Dame Janet Baker** as ever giving heartfelt intensity to Vaughan Williams's broad melodic lines. The *Fantasia on Christmas Carols*, easy and approachable, makes a generous and apt coupling. The transfers of both recordings are newly done and give an excellent example of mid-1960s EMI sound.

In *Hodie* there is an attractive medieval flavour to these settings of Christmas texts, with sharp cross-rhythms, which is well brought out on Naxos – with **Janice Watson** an excellent, creamy-toned soprano. The main vocal items are linked by narration in recitative, with the recording bringing excellent separation of the different elements, including the organ. The brassy *March of the Three Kings* brings a colourful oriental flavour. The much better-known *Fantasia on Christmas Carols*, dedicated to the leading folk-songs collector, Cecil Sharp, makes an ideal coupling, similarly well performed, making this Naxos disc a fine alternative to the EMI pairing.

22 Hymns

Ⓝ *** Griffin GCCD 4063 Cardiff Fest. Ch., Arwel Hughes

Vaughan Williams harmonised or adapted tunes for all the hymns for a new edition of *The English Hymnal*, it took him two years to complete, and he did so in his own individual way. For instance *He who would valiant be* uses the folk tune 'Our captain calls'. All his original tunes are included here, of which *All the Saints* is the most famous (to the tune which he named *Sine Nomine*, a quite arbitrary choice). He said afterwards: 'I know that two years of close association with some of the best (as well as some of the worst) tunes in the world was a better musical education than any amount of sonatas and fugues'. Here they all are, splendidly sung by the **Cardiff Festival Choir**, with **Owain Arwel Hughes** making the most of dynamic contrast to give the simple melodies variety of presentation.

The House of Life (6 sonnets); Songs of Travel; 4 Poems by Fredegond Shove; 4 Last Songs: 2, Tired; Songs: In the spring; Linden Lea

**(*) Chan. 8475. Luxon, Williams

Though **Benjamin Luxon's** vibrato is distractingly wide, the warmth and clarity of the recording help to make his well-chosen collection of Vaughan Williams songs very attractive, including as it does not only the well-known Stevenson travel cycle but the Rossetti cycle, *The House of Life* (including *The water mill*), as well as the most famous song of all, *Linden Lea*.

Lord Thou hast been our refuge; Prayer to the Father of Heaven; A Vision of Aeroplanes

*** Chan. 9019. Finzi Singers, Spicer – HOWELLS: *Requiem, etc.* ***

These three choral pieces make an apt coupling for the Howells choral works on the Finzi Singers' disc. *A Vision of Aeroplanes* improbably but most imaginatively uses a text from Ezekiel.

SONGS

'*The Sky Shall be our Roof*' (Opera Songs)

Ⓝ *** Albion ALB 001. Fox, Pochin, Staples, Williams, Burnside

The 19 songs on this attractive disc, sponsored by the Vaughan Williams Society, are drawn from three of Vaughan Williams's operas: ten from *Hugh the Drover*, two from *Sir John in Love* (including *Greensleeves*), and seven from *The Pilgrim's Progress*. The most varied group are those from *Hugh the Drover* with vigorous songs like Hugh's *Song of the Road*, beautifully sung in a light tenor by **Andrew Staples** and two charming duets for Hugh and Mary with Staples joined by the soprano, **Sarah Fox**. Also a lively song for the Showman sung by the baritone, **Roderick Williams**. Helpfully, complete texts are provided. The whole collection has been masterminded by **Iain Burnside** who winningly accompanies at the piano. Well-balanced sound.

'*Kissing her Hair*': 20 Early Songs

Ⓝ *** Albion ALBCD 002. Fox, Staples, Williams, Burnside

This second disc sponsored by the Vaughan Williams Society is again masterminded by the fine accompanist, **Iain Burnside** with similar singers. This time the excellent baritone, **Roderick Williams** has the biggest share of the choice, with *Linden Lea*, by far the most popular of Vaughan Williams's songs sung by Williams in a fair attempt at an authentic Dorset accent. The atmosphere of Thomas Hardy country is reflected in a fair proportion of the songs, with a delightful duet '*If I were queen*' sung by **Sarah Fox**, with a second stanza, '*If I were king*' sung by the tenor, **Andrew Staples**.

For variety there are several songs in French and *The Sky Above the Roof* which is a translation of Verlaine's 'Le ciel est par dessus le toit' by the wife of Percy Dearmer, which she wanted for a play. It was a commission which Vaughan Williams did not want so he wrote it in double quick time. There is also a sensitive setting of Tennyson's *The Splendour Falls*, which yet can hardly compare with Britten's inspired setting in his *Serenade*. As an exception to early songs there are three Walt Whitman settings from 1925. Detailed notes are provided on each song in turn as well as texts.

Choral Songs (for mixed chorus): '*Where Hope is Shining*'

Ⓝ *** Albion ALBCD 006 Joyful Company of Singers, Alistair Young (piano), Peter Broadbent.

These 23 Songs for Mixed Chorus span the widest repertory. The most ambitious piece is a group of four, *Sun, Moon, Stars and Man*, ending triumphantly on *The Song of the Sons of Light*, Vaughan Williams at his most exhilarating. There are a number of Shakespeare settings as well as folk-song settings, an arrangement of Vaughan Williams's own *Linden Lea* by Arthur Somervell, and an ingenious arrangement of *Loch Lomond*. Most of the songs are unaccompanied, but piano accompaniment adds to the power of *Sun, Moon, Stars and Man*, as well as *The Mermaid* and the *Turtle Dove*. Immaculate performances by the **Joyful Company of Singers** under **Peter Broadbent**. As a charming bonus to this issue, sponsored by the Vaughan Williams Society the cover has an infectious portrait of the composer with his second wife, Ursula.

5 Mystical Songs; O Clap Your Hands

Ⓜ *** EMI (ADD) 5 65588-2. Shirley-Quirk, King's College, Cambridge, Ch., ECO, Willcocks – FINZI: *Dies natalis*; HOLST: *Choral Fantasia; Psalm 86* ***

In the *Five Mystical Songs* to words by George Herbert, **John Shirley-Quirk** sings admirably, and the motet *O Clap Your Hands* makes a fine bonus for a recommendable triptych of English vocal works.

(i) *5 Mystical Songs*; (i; ii) *5 Tudor Portraits*

ⒷⒷ **(*) Hyp. Helios CDH 55004. (i) Herford; (ii) Walker; Guildford Ch. Soc., Philh. O, Davan Wetton

The contrast of the religious pastoralism of the *Five Mystical Songs* and the rumbustious vigour of the *Tudor Portraits* is well understood by **Hilary Davan Wetton**. **Henry Herford** is the rather restrained but sympathetic soloist in the former (an early work, concurrent with the *Sea Symphony*); his vocal style is less well suited to the portrait of *Pretty Bess* in the latter, written a quarter of a century later. **Sarah Walker** touchingly sings her *Lament* for her pet sparrow (the victim of her cat). She also paints a robust picture of *The Tunning of Elinor Rumming*. The chorus are boldly enthusiastic both here and in the burlesque *Epitaph on John Jayberd of Diss*. The recording is truthful, although the chorus could have been given more bite, for the words are not ideally clear. Otherwise an enjoyable and recommendable bargain coupling, which supplies full texts and even a brief glossary of unfamiliar Elizabethan terms.

Mass in G min.; Silence and Music

Ⓝ *** Hänssler **SACD** 93.250. SWR Vocal Ens, Marcus Creed

Vaughan Williams wrote his *Mass in G minor* for his friend Gustav Holst to be given at the festival he organised. It is one of Vaughan Williams gentler works, beautifully crafted, echoing traditional examples. *Silence and Music* is a lovely setting of words by Vaughan Williams's second wife, Ursula Wood.

(i) *On Wenlock Edge*; (ii) *Songs of Travel* (song-cycles)

🔗 Ⓜ **** EMI 7 64731-2. (i) Tear; (ii) Allen; CBSO, Rattle – BUTTERWORTH; ELGAR: *Songs* ***

Vaughan Williams's own orchestration of his Housman song-cycle, made in the early 1920s, has been curiously neglected. It lacks something of the apt, ghostly quality of the version for piano and string quartet, but some will prefer the bigger scale. The orchestral version brings home the aptness of treating the nine songs as a cycle, particularly when the soloist is as characterful and understanding a singer as **Thomas Allen**. The Housman settings in the other cycle are far better known, and **Robert Tear**, as in his earlier recording with Vernon Handley, proves a deeply perceptive soloist. Warm, understanding conducting and playing, and excellent sound.

(ii) *The Pilgrim's Journey* (arr. Roy Douglas); (i) *Serenade to Music*

Ⓝ (***) Albion mono ALBCD 009 (2). (i) Allen, Baillie, Mitchell, Suddaby, Brunskill, Desmond, Jarred, Ripley, Herbert, Lewis, Manton, Nash, Allin, Easton, Henderson, Williams, Liverpool PO, Composer; (ii) Plymouth Church of the Pilgrims, Pfohl

The Pilgrim's Journey is made up of items from the opera, *The Pilgrim's Progress*, selected by Roy Douglas and Christopher Morris. It makes a delightful work well sung by the **Choir of the Plymouth Church of the Pilgrims in Brooklyn New York** with **Henry Pfohl**, recorded in April 1965. A valuable extra item comes on a bonus disc with the composer giving a half-hour of comments on his musical education with Parry, Stanford and others, recorded in November 1955. His voice is wonderfully characterful and expressive. There is also an excerpt from the composer's funeral service in September 1958 included. But the really valuable item in this live recording from the Royal Festival Hall in 1951, is the *Serenade to Music* conducted by **Vaughan Williams** himself with 11 of the original soloists taking part, including all four of the basses. The sound is scrubby in reproducing the instrumental accompaniment, but the voices are well caught, and the magic of the occasion is superbly conveyed, a most moving performance of one of the composer's most magical works.

The Pilgrim's Progress (incidental music, ed. Palmer)

🔑 *** Hyp. CDA 66511. Gielgud, Pasco, Howells, Corydon Singers, City of L. Sinfonia, Best

Vaughan Williams had a lifelong devotion to Bunyan's great allegory, which fired his inspiration to write incidental music for a BBC radio adaptation of the complete *Pilgrim's Progress*. Much of the material, but not all, then found a place in the opera. Christopher Palmer has here devised a sequence of 12 movements, which – overlapping with the opera and the *Fifth Symphony* – throws up long-buried treasure. **Matthew Best** draws warmly sympathetic performances from his singers and players, in support of the masterly contributions of **Sir John Gielgud**, taking the role of Pilgrim as he did on radio in 1942, and **Richard Pasco** as the Evangelist.

The Shepherds of the Delectable Mountains; 3 Choral Hymns; Magnificat; A Song of Thanksgiving; Psalm 100

🔑 *** Hyp. CDA 66569. Gielgud, Dawson, Kitchen, Wyn-Rogers, Mark Ainsley, Bowen, Thompson, Opie, Terfel, Best, Corydon Singers, L. Oratory Junior Ch., City of L. Sinfonia, Best

With **Sir John Gielgud** as narrator and **Lynne Dawson** as the sweet-toned soprano soloist, **Best** gives *A Song of Thanksgiving* a tautness and sense of drama, bringing out the originality of the writing, simple and stirring in its grandeur, not for a moment pompous. The *Magnificat* brings more buried treasure, a massive setting designed not for liturgical but for concert use. With its haunting ostinatos it is closer to Holst's choral music than most Vaughan Williams. The *Three Hymns* and the setting of *Psalm 100* are comparably distinctive in their contrasted ways, and it is good to have a recording of the Bunyan setting, *The Shepherds of the Delectable Mountains*. Most of the solo singing is excellent, and the chorus is superb, helped by warmly atmospheric recording.

The Sons of Light

*** Lyrita (ADD) SRCD 270. Royal College of Music Ch., LPO, Willcocks – HOLST: *The Mystic Trumpeter*; PARRY: *Ode on the Nativity* ***

Composed for the Schools Music Association in 1951 and given its first performance at the Royal Albert Hall by massed school choirs under Sir Adrian Boult, *The Sons of Light* has been unfairly neglected. Its three sections set words by Ursula Vaughan Williams graphically and colourfully, starting with trumpet calls. Only marginally did the composer modify the tangy bluffness of his late idiom for young performers. In a strong and committed performance, it makes a valuable coupling for the Holst and Parry works.

The Wasps (complete recording of Aristophanes' play with *Overture and incidental music*; English translation by David Pountney)

🔑 Ⓜ **** Hallé HLD 7510 (2). Goodman (nar.), Hallé Ch. & O, Elder

Vaughan Williams composed his score for Aristophanes' satirical comedy *The Wasps* for a production of the play in Greek at Cambridge University in 1909. Since then the justly famous *Overture* and a 1912 suite (admittedly containing almost all the best music) is all that has been heard of the score. But the choral writing itself is splendid, and the most ambitious part of the score is the *Parabasis* (a diatribe on human behaviour, drawing a parallel with the conduct of wasps, sung directly by the chorus to the audience).

The original play had three characters, but David Pountney's translation reduces the text to a narration from just one, Procleon, a 'curmudgeonly old codger, an old soldier, and a bigot', a part which **Henry Goodman** takes with relish. A full text is included, but if you do not want to repeat the dialogue it is cued separately; you can programme your player accordingly and just enjoy the superb singing and playing of the **Hallé Chorus and Orchestra**, vividly directed by **Mark Elder**, and excellently recorded. A major scoop for the Orchestra's own record label.

OPERA

A Cotswold Romance (adapted by Maurice Jacobson in collaboration with the composer from *Hugh the Drover*); *Death of Tintagiles*

*** Chan. 9646. Mannion, Randle, Brook, LPO Ch., LSO, Hickox

This makes a splendid supplement to **Hickox's** outstanding recording of Vaughan Williams's last opera, *The Pilgrim's Progress*. Saddened towards the end of his life that his tuneful ballad opera, *Hugh the Drover*, was seriously neglected, he adapted some of the most winning sequences to produce this cantata, *A Cotswold Romance*, never recorded before. Even though some striking items from the opera are omitted, it helps that the role of the chorus is expanded, with the colour and vigour of the original enhanced. *The Death of Tintagiles*, even more neglected, is drawn from Vaughan Williams's incidental music for a Maeterlinck play, six dark and spare fragments anticipating later Vaughan Williams works.

Hugh the Drover (complete)

⊶ Ⓑ *** Hyp. Dyad CDD 22049 (2). Bottone, Evans, Walker, Van Allan, Opie, New L. Children's Ch., Corydon Singers & O, Best

Described as a ballad opera, *Hugh the Drover* uses folk-themes with full-throated Puccinian warmth. The Hyperion version in atmospheric digital sound offers a fresh, light view, resilient and urgent in the first act, hauntingly tender in the second. **Rebecca Evans** is superb as the heroine, Mary, with **Bonaventura Bottone** an amiable Hugh, only occasionally strained, well supported by a cast of generally fresh young singers.

The Poisoned Kiss (complete)

⊶ *** Chan. **SACD** 5020 (2); CD 10120 (2). Watson, Gilchrist, Helen Stephen, Williams, N. Davies, Collins, Adrian Partington Singers, BBC Nat. O of Wales, Hickox

Vaughan Williams began writing *The Poisoned Kiss* in 1927 yet it has been consistently neglected, not just in performance but on disc too, for this is its very first complete recording. It centres round a beautiful princess who lives on poison.

This recording helps towards rehabilitating the opera by eliminating virtually all the spoken dialogue, including it merely in the libretto, printed in shaded sections. Despite the irritations of the libretto, repeated hearings bring out how rich this score is in vintage Vaughan Williams inspiration. The inspiration never flags, charm predominating, with tenderly beautiful melodies like that in the Act I duet of Amaryllis and Tormentilla, *Blue Larkspur in a Garden*, and a surgingly emotional climax in the ensemble which crowns Act II, when their love leads passionately to the poisoned kiss and the threat of death to Amaryllus.

Janice Watson as Tormentilla sings with sweetness and warmth, while giving point to the literally poisonous side of the character, and **James Gilchrist** makes an ardent Amaryllus, with **Pamela Helen Stephen** as Angelica and **Roderick Williams** totally affecting in their love music, given many of the most charming moments of all. **Neal Davies** is firm and strong as the magician, Dipsacus, and, though the Empress does not arrive until Act III, she then dominates things, following the G&S tradition of formidable contraltos: in that role the veteran Anne Collins is aptly larger than life.

The incidental trios of Hobgoblins and Mediums are also cast from strength with leading singers, the chorus is fresh and bright, and the **BBC National Orchestra of Wales** plays throughout with winning warmth. Outstandingly atmospheric recording, especially on SACD.

The Pilgrim's Progress (complete)

⊶ ✿ Ⓑ **** Chan. 9625 (2). Finley, and soloists, ROHCG Ch. & O, Hickox

Richard Hickox not only brings out the visionary intensity of much of the writing – notably in the ideas drawn from the *Fifth Symphony* – but also the passion and urgency, pacing the music to bring out the underlying drama in heightened contrasts. As in his recording of that symphony, Hickox is masterly in moulding phrases to magnetize the ear, always a warm interpreter, reflected in the unfailing ardour of the **Covent Garden Chorus and Orchestra**. The big cast is a strong one, mainly of young singers, led by **Gerald Finley** as a firm, fresh-voiced Pilgrim, and with **Peter Coleman-Wright** introducing the opera strongly as John Bunyan. The Chandos recording is superb, spacious and atmospheric, with the many offstage effects beautifully balanced, yet with words always clear.

Riders to the Sea (DVD version)

Ⓝ *** NVC Arts **DVD** 50-51442 9784-2-1 Walker, Brennan, Tynan, Mackey, R & TV Eireann Ch. & O, Thomson (with M. Murphy as J.M. Synge) (Director: Louis Lentin)

J.M. Synge lived on the Aran Islands, and was an onlooker for some of the tragic events on which his play is based. So it was appropriate for the opening of the present production of Vaughan Williams's opera to be introduced with a brief spoken scene featuring the author. The opera itself is short (44 minutes), succinct and emotionally harrowing. **Sarah Walker's** performance as the mother who has lost her husband and entire family of six sons to the sea is powerfully telling, dramatically and vocally and she receives fine support from the excellent cast. The music, including the closing lament, anticipates Vaughan Williams's later writing especially that for *Scott of the Antarctic*. The video presentation is simple with an excellent set, and **Bryden Thomson's** musical direction is thoroughly sympathetic.

Riders to the Sea (complete; CD version)

*** Chan. 9392. Finnie, Daymond, Dawson, Attrot, Stephen, N. Sinfonia, Hickox – *Flos campi*, etc. ***

As in other Vaughan Williams works, **Hickox** takes a broad, warmly idiomatic view, less urgent than the previous EMI recording, more timeless and mysterious, helped by opulently atmospheric recording. He is helped too by an excellent cast. Even if **Linda Finnie** as the old woman, Maurya, who loses all her sons to the sea, cannot quite match Helen Watts on the original recording, her final monologue of lament and resignation provides a moving, deeply expressive culmination. Among the others, **Karl Daymond** as Bartley, the last son to drown, is a newcomer to note, as impressive here as he was in Hickox's recording of Purcell's *Dido*. The generous coupling adds to the disc's attractions.

Sir John in Love (complete)

✇ *** Chan. 9928 (2). Maxwell, Gritton, Claycomb, Connolly, Owens, Padmore, Thompson, Best, Williams, Varcoe, Sinfonia Ch., Northern Sinf., Hickox

Ⓜ *** EMI (ADD) 5 66123-2 (2). Herincx, Bainbridge, Watts, English, Eathorne, Tear, John Alldis Ch., New Philh. O, M. Davies

As an opera this may not match Verdi's *Falstaff* in polish or sophistication, but in its more relaxed, more lyrical way it offers a comparably individual slant on Shakespeare, with the title, *Sir John in Love*, clearly indicating a different emphasis on the character of Falstaff.

In the casting the central strength of the Chandos set is the Falstaff of **Donald Maxwell**, with his full, dark bass fatter-sounding than that of **Raimund Herincx**. **Susan Gritton** is also outstanding as Anne, rich and golden, relishing the glorious duet she sings with Fenton in the very first scene, with **Mark Padmore** fresh and youthful too. Not all the others are as characterful as their predecessors, good as they are, as for example **Laura Claycomb** as Mistress Page. Yet the very large cast works together splendidly, with clear differentiation of the many extra characters that Vaughan Williams includes.

In the EMI set **Meredith Davies** relishes the colourfulness of the score. **Raimund Herincx** is a positive and sympathetic Falstaff, and **Helen Watts** as Mrs Quickly and **Elizabeth Bainbridge** as Mrs Ford rise ripely to the occasion. **Wendy Eathorne** as Anne Page and **Robert Tear** as Fenton make a delightful pair of lovers, and such singers as **Gerald English** as Dr Caius add to the stylishness. The 1974 Abbey Road recording is vivid and warmly atmospheric and beautifully balanced, and this is still very much worth considering at mid-price.

VEALE, John (born 1922)

Violin Concerto

✇ *** Chan. 9910. Mordkovitch, BBC SO, Hickox –
  BRITTEN: *Violin Concerto* ***

Surgingly lyrical in a melodic idiom echoing Mahler on the one hand and Walton on the other, John Veale's *Violin Concerto* of 1984 makes an unusual, highly enjoyable coupling for **Lydia Mordkovitch's** searching account of the Britten. His development was strongly influenced by his consultations with Walton, and the vigorous finale of this concerto with its swinging Cuban rhythms directly echoes not only Walton but Lambert too. That prompts Mordkovitch to a dazzling performance, with Hickox drawing brilliant, vigorous playing from the **BBC orchestra**.

Yet the first two movements, both more expansive, are the ones that bear the main emotional weight, with Mordkovitch's passionate intensity heightening the impact. The central slow movement is entitled *Lament*, but the mood is sensuous rather than elegiac, with ecstatic outpouring of melody high above the stave from the soloist at the beginning and end, and with a passionate climax in the middle. A most rewarding coupling for the Britten for anyone who en-

joys post-romantic writing, superbly recorded in the richest Chandos sound.

VECCHI, Orazio (1550–1605)

L'amfiparnaso (commedia harmonica)

✇ ⒷⒷ *** Naxos 8.553312. Cappella Musicale di Petronio di Bologna, Vartolo

Unlike Lassus, Vecchi, although earning his living as a *maestro di capella* in the church, leaned in his own music towards the secular. Described as a 'madrigal comedy', *L'amfiparnaso*, first performed in 1594, fascinatingly points forward to the development of opera as a new genre in the following decade. The text in a Prologue and three brief acts develops a comic plot stocked with *commedia dell'arte* characters, but, instead of solo voices representing different characters, here each scene is set as a madrigal for a small group of voices. Each madrigal, three in the first act, five in both the other two, is preceded by a brief spoken summary, the whole making up a taut entertainment that still sounds fresh and charming after 400 years. Much is owed to the liveliness of the Naxos performance, using a first-rate ensemble from Bologna under **Sergio Vartolo**. With splendidly crisp ensemble the singers consistently bring out the sharply rhythmic quality of Vecchi's writing, with clear, well-balanced sound. Full texts and an English translation are provided.

VERACINI, Francesco Maria (1690–1768)

Violin Concertos: a cinque in A & D; a otto stromenti in D; Aria schiavona in B flat for Orchestra (attrib.); Overture 5 in B flat

✇ ⒷⒷ *** Naxos 8.553413. Accademia I Filarmonici (Verona), Martini

Veracini's *Violin Concerto a otto stromenti* is endearingly ambitious in its scoring, and the brilliant opening, with its two trumpets and oboes, must have made quite an impression when it was first heard in Venice in 1712. Tartini's influence is apparent. The decorative figurations in the outer movements rise and fall in scalic sequence. Some solo passages are left to the soloist to fill in and the unusual minor-key slow movement is very improvisatory in feeling.

The two earlier *Concerti a cinque* are more modest, closer to Vivaldi, although Veracini's own presence is very apparent at times and especially in the finale of the *A major* work. The *Overture in B flat* is one of the finest of the complete set discussed below, and the *Aria schiavona* is an engaging minuet lollipop, very gallant in feeling and almost certainly not by Veracini at all. First-class performances throughout with fine solo contributions, presumably from **Alberto Martini**, the leader of the **Accademia I Filarmonici**, which claims to have no conductor. The recording is excellent.

Overtures (Suites) 1–6

✇ ⒷⒷ *** Naxos 8.553412. Accademia I Filarmonici (Verona), Martini

These overtures were composed for the Dresden court orchestra, probably around 1716. Their character brings a curious amalgam of Italian volatility and German weight, and they have something in common with the orchestral suites of Telemann. Yet Telemann loved instrumental light and shade, whereas Veracini favoured tutti scoring. The music is strong in personality and there is no shortage of ideas, but energy is more important than expressive lyricism, with usually a single brief sarabande to provide contrast as the centrepiece of up to half-a-dozen dance movements.

The **Accademia I Filarmonici** claim to use the original manuscripts, but they play on modern instruments, and their bright, gleaming sound is full of Italian sunshine. The performances are Italianate and they play the *Sarabandes* of 1 and 2 with an attractive air of relaxed graciousness, while the sparkling opening movement of 6 is made to seem almost a tarantella. So at Naxos price this could well be an attractive introduction to this composer.

12 *Sonate accademiche, Op. 2*

🎵 Ⓜ️ *** Hyp. CDS 44241/3 (3). Locatelli Trio

The 12 *Sonate accademiche* are much more Italianate than the overtures, though German influence remains strong. The writing has a rhapsodic exuberance and drive, and, as with the overtures, dance movements predominate. But there are touching lyrical interludes and some lovely slow movements. The last *Sonata* is masterly, opening with a descending minor scalic theme, which is first used for a *Passacaglia*, then for a *Capriccio cromatico*, and finally provides the basis for an ambitious closing *Ciaccona*. The **Locatelli Trio**, led by **Elizabeth Wallfisch**, are a first-class group, and their authentic style, strongly etched, is full of joy in the music's vitality, while the composer's lyrical side is most persuasively revealed. **Paul Nicholson's** continuo is very much a part of the picture, especially in the works using an organ, which is very pleasingly balanced. The recording is vivid and immediate.

VERDI, Giuseppe (1813–1901)

The Lady and the Fool (ballet suite; arr. Mackerras)

Ⓑ *** CfP 3 93231-2. LPO, Mackerras – SULLIVAN: *Pineapple Poll* ***

The Lady and the Fool (ballet; arr. Mackerras); Overtures: *Alzira; La forza del destino; Nabucco.*

(***) Testament mono/stereo SBT 1326. Philh. O, Mackerras

Three of Verdi's finest overtures come in a coupling with the ballet score, *The Lady and the Fool*, which **Mackerras** drew from the lesser-known operas of Verdi. To choreography by John Cranko. Mackerras's aim was to follow up the brilliant success of his earlier ballet score, *Pineapple Poll*, which in a very similar way uses material drawn from Sullivan's operettas and other works. This is the only complete recording ever made, demonstrating what a superb sequel it is. Not only has Mackerras drawn on dozens of delectable Verdian ideas, he has woven them into a scintillating tapestry. The orchestration too is far more adventurous than the originals,

while remaining broadly faithful to Verdi's distinctive timbre. Though the recording is in mono only, the sense of presence is most impressive, at least as vivid as in the stereo recordings of the three overtures which come as bonus to the 50-minute ballet, all of them combining brilliance and expressive warmth.

Those content with the *Ballet Suite* only can choose **Mackerras's** later stereo recording which is equally vivacious and appropriately coupled with *Pineapple Poll.*

Ballet Music from: (i) *Il trovatore; I vespri siciliani;* (ii) *Otello;* (i) Overture: *Luisa Miller*

(***) Testament (ADD) SBT 1327. Mackerras with (i) Philh. O; (ii) ROHCG O – PONCHIELLI: *La Gioconda: Dance of the Hours* ***; WOLF-FERRARI: *Overtures, Intermezzi and Dances* (***)

This mixed bag of **Mackerras's** recordings from the mid-1950s has as its centrepiece his brilliant recordings of the *Luisa Miller Overture* and three examples of the ballet music which Verdi provided for Paris productions of his operas. It is striking, even in the *Otello* ballet music with its orientalism, how Verdi regularly harks back to a much earlier, less sophisticated style than he uses in the main body of the opera in question, perhaps a reflection on Parisian taste. The results may have their banalities – even the more ambitious *Four Seasons*, written for the original production of *Les Vêpres siciliennes* – but Mackerras's springing of rhythm and the sparkle of the **Philharmonia** playing fully bring out their unassuming delights. He is helped by the finely balanced stereo sound in all but the *Otello* music, which curiously seems only ever to have been issued on a 45-r.p.m. EP.

Complete Overtures, Preludes and Ballet Music

Vol. 1: Overtures and Preludes: *Alzira* (overture); *Attila* (prelude); *La battaglia di Legnano* (overture); *Il corsaro; I due Foscari; Ernani* (preludes); *Un giorno di regno (Il finto Stanislao); Giovanna d'Arco* (overtures); *Macbeth* (prelude with ballet music); *I Masnadieri* (prelude); *Nabucco; Oberto* (overtures) (Chan. 9510)

Vol. 2: *Jérusalem* (overture and ballet music); *Luisa Miller* (overture); *Rigoletto* (prelude); *Il trovatore* (ballet music) (Chan. 9594)

Vol. 3: *Un ballo in maschera* (prelude); *Simon Boccanegra* (prelude: 1st version, 1857); *La traviata* (preludes to Acts I & III); *Les Vêpres siciliennes: Ballet of the 4 Seasons* (Chan. 9696)

Vol. 4: *Aida* (prelude for Cairo première, 1871; Overture for Italian première, 1872; 2 Dances & Act II ballet music); *Don Carlos* (prelude to Act III and ballet music: *La peregrina); La forza del destino* (prelude, 1862); *Otello* (ballet music, Act III) (Chan. 9788)

*** BBC PO, Downes

Preludes, Overtures and Ballet Music (as above)

*** Chan. 9787 (4). BBC PO, Downes

Overtures and Preludes: *Aida; Alzira; Aroldo; Un ballo in maschera; La battaglia di Legnano; Il corsaro; Ernani; La forza del destino; Un giorno di regno; Giovanna d'Arco; Luisa Miller; Macbeth; I Masnadieri; Nabucco; Oberto; Rigoletto; La traviata; I vespri siciliani*

(M) *** DG 453 058-2 (2) BPO, Karajan

Karajan's 1975 complete set of Overtures and Preludes was one of the best analogue recordings made in the Philharmonie and the performances have an electricity, refinement and authority that sweep the board. The best known overtures are given with tremendous panache and virtuosity without the slightest suggestion of routine.

Overtures and Preludes: *Aida* (prelude); *Alzira* (sinfonia); *Aroldo* (sinfonia); *Attila* (prelude); *Un ballo in maschera* (prelude); *Il corsaro* (prelude); *Luisa Miller* (sinfonia); *Oberto, Conte di San Bonifacio* (sinfonia); *La traviata* (preludes to Acts I & III); *I vespri siciliani* (sinfonia)

(BB) **(*) Naxos 8.553018. Hungarian State Op. O, Morandi

Overtures: *Aida* (reconstructed and arr. Spada); *La forza del destino; I vespri siciliani*

(BB) *** RCA 74321 68012-2. LSO, Abbado – ROSSINI: *Overtures* ***

Overtures and Preludes: *La battaglia di Legnano* (sinfonia); *Don Carlos* (prelude to Act III); *I due Foscari* (prelude); *Ernani* (prelude); *La forza del destino* (sinfonia); *Un giorno di regno* (sinfonia); *Giovanna d'Arco* (sinfonia); *Macbeth* (sinfonia); *I Masnadieri* (prelude); *Nabucco* (overture); *Rigoletto* (prelude)

(BB) **(*) Naxos 8.553089. Hungarian State Op. O, Morandi

Edward Downes's Verdi survey covers virtually all the overtures, preludes and ballet music, the latter full of charm when so elegantly played and beautifully recorded. Original versions are chosen where available, so we get the first 1857 score of the *Prelude* to *Simon Boccanegra* and the brief 1862 *Overture* to *La forza del destino*, rather than the familiar expanded, 1869 version. The outstanding novelty is Verdi's extended 1872 overture written for the Italian première of *Aida*. The shorter Prelude heard at the opera's Cairo première was substituted at the last moment. The 1872 piece was never heard of again. The ballet music was, of course, an essential requirement if a work was to be performed at the Paris Opéra. Verdi often rises to the occasion and produces charming, tuneful music, felicitously scored. In the suite from *Il trovatore* (an unlikely subject for a balletic diversion), the delightful third section, *La Bohémienne*, is worthy of Delibes in its use of the graceful violins and piquant woodwind. Not surprisingly Edward Downes has the full measure of this music. The finer Overtures are played with bold characterization and dramatic fire, *Nabucco*, with its

dignified sonority, and *Giovanna d'Arco* both show the **BBC Philharmonic** brass at their finest in quite different ways, and *Luisa Miller* is another very strong performance. The strings play most beautifully in the *Traviata Preludes*. With such richly expansive recording, showing Chandos engineering at its most spectacular, the effect is less bitingly leonine than in Karajan's electrifying two-disc survey. But even if not all of this music is top-class Verdi, the Chandos set offers much to enjoy, and the spontaneity and elegance of the music-making are never in doubt.

Morandi has served his time conducting at La Scala and he gives ripely robust accounts of these colourful *Overtures* and sinfonias, with excellent playing from his **Hungarian** musicians, notably from the strings in the *Traviata* and *Aida Preludes* and from the brass in *Nabucco*. *La forza del destino* ends the second disc strongly. Full-bloodedly resonant sound (with the second collection at times marginally sharper in definition) makes this an excellent bargain, even if the readings are not as individual as those of Downes and Karajan.

Abbado also included the *Overture* which Verdi originally wrote for the first Italian performance of *Aida*. It is a considerably extended piece in Spada's reconstruction and one can hear why the composer decided against anticipating effects in instrumental terms far more telling in the full operatic setting. But heard independently it is most entertaining and deftly scored. Together with the other two familiar *Overtures* it is given a strong and brilliant performance with the conductor's magnetism felt not only in the *pianissimo* string playing but especially in the exciting account of *La forza del destino*. The sound is bright, but has supporting weight and a concert-hall resonance.

String Quartet in E min.

(⌐) (M) *** CRD 3366. Alberni Qt – DONIZETTI: *Quartet 13*; PUCCINI: *Crisantemi* ***

(M) **(*) HM HMA 1951671. Melos Qt – SIBELIUS: *String Quartet in D min.* **(*)

(BB) **(*) Hyp. Helios CDH 55012. Delmé Qt – RICHARD STRAUSS: *Quartet* **(*)

The **Alberni Quartet's** performance is strong and compelling, and it is most imaginatively and attractively coupled with the Puccini and Donizetti pieces.

The distinguished **Melos** ensemble give a suitably well-turned-out performance of the Verdi, though they tend to underplay its pure lyricism. We are not so well served in this repertoire at present that new Verdi *Quartets* can be lightly passed over. The recording is truthful but with the *Voces intimae* as its sole companion, the 50 minutes or so of this issue makes for relatively short measure.

The **Delmé** are not a 'high-powered', jet-setting ensemble and they give a very natural performance of the Verdi, which will give much pleasure: there is the sense of music-making in the home among intimate friends, refreshingly unforced, even if the sound is on the dry side.

String Quartet in E min. (arr. for string orchestra)

*** Channel Classics **SACD** CCS SA 21504. Amsterdam Sinf., Thompson – TCHAIKOVSKY: *Souvenir de Florence* ***

The **Amsterdam Sinfonietta**, recording for the first time under its new name and with its new leader/conductor **Candida Thompson**, plays with phenomenal unanimity, demonstrating what gains there are in having a full string orchestra performing the Verdi *String Quartet*. As in the Tchaikovsky *Souvenir de Florence*, with which it is aptly coupled, speeds are ideally chosen, with the second movement clearly an *Andantino*, light and elegant, and the chattering quavers of the fugal finale shaped more clearly. The thrust and warmth of the performance is enhanced by the wide dynamic range of the playing, well caught in the opulent recording (with the option of surround sound).

CHORAL MUSIC

Messa per Rossini (includes VERDI's *Libera me*) (DVD version) (other composers contributing: BUZZOLA, BAZZINI, PEDROTTI, CAGNONI, RICCI, NINI, BOUCHERON, COCCIA, GASPARI, PLATANIA, ROSSI, MABELLINI)

*** Warner **DVD** 50-510ll 7396-2-0. Benačkova, Quivar, Wagner, Agache, Haugland, Stuttart Gächinger Kantorei, Prague Philharmonic Ch., Stuttgart RSO, Rilling

When Rossini died in 1868, Verdi conceived the idea of promoting a composite requiem in his memory, to which he would (and did) contribute the closing *Libera me*. But the rest was to be written by 'the best composers in Italy'. This splendid performance, recorded live in 1988 in Württemberg, shows how successfully he chose his colleagues, for, if none of the contributions matches his, all are impressively written in a winningly communicative Italianate, operatic style. Melodically fluent, with the choruses all stirring (Pietro Platania's lovely *Sanctus* particularly fine), the work stands up well, and this performance is very enjoyable indeed. While **Helmuth Rilling** takes much credit for directing his forces so powerfully and spontaneously, the soloists too make a fine team, with no weak link. **Gabriella Benačkova** (especially) and **Florence Quivar** are outstanding, singing together especially beautifully in Antonio Cagnoni's *Quid sum miser*, while the tenor **James Wagner** is very stirring in Alessandro Nini's *Ingemisco*. Each of the 13 composers wrote substantially, so the total timing is about two and a half hours! But the work is most rewarding to watch and to listen to, and Rilling makes sure that Verdi's finale is overwhelming.

Requiem Mass (DVD versions)

🎵 **** EMI **DVD** DVB4 92693-9. Gheorghiu, Barcellona, Alagna, Konstantinov, Swedish Radio Ch., Eric Ericson Chamber Ch., BPO, Abbado

🎵 *** DG **DVD** 730 055. L. Price, Cossotto, Pavarotti, Ghiaurov, La Scala, Milan, Ch. & O, Karajan

(*) Arthaus **DVD 100 146. Price, Norman, Carreras, Raimondi, Edinburgh Fest. Ch., LSO, Abbado

The EMI DVD offers the video version, very well presented, of **Abbado's** superb live recording of the Verdi *Requiem* made at the Philharmonie in Berlin in January 2001 to commemorate the 100th anniversary of the composer's death. The visual element adds significantly to the impact with the chorus full-toned and weighty, and with the four soloists an outstanding team of singers, all still young. The power and beauty of **Gheorghiu's** singing are even more striking when one can see as well as hear the vibrant intensity with which she attacks her key solos.

Karajan, for his performance at **La Scala** in 1967, chose the starriest possible quartet of soloists, and all four are at their peak, even the still-young **Luciano Pavarotti**, who, beardless, is barely recognizable visually, even if the voice is already glowingly distinctive. The firmness and focus of all four is a joy to the ear, and the 1967 recording is surprisingly full and bright, which makes it marginally more recommendable than Abbado's Edinburgh Festival recording, below. The great French film director **Henri-Georges Clouzot** is relatively conservative in his camerawork but regularly uses his shots for beautifully stylized pattern-making, with the members of the chorus and the orchestra often symmetrically placed.

As a performance, **Abbado's** earlier live DVD recording, made for television at the Edinburgh Festival in 1982, outshines his regular audio recordings of the *Requiem*, not least thanks to the extraordinary line-up of soloists, with **Jessye Norman** taking the mezzo role against **Margaret Price** as the soprano. All four soloists are in superb voice, with **Ruggiero Raimondi** almost sinister in *Mors stupebit* when viewed in close-up, his villainous expressions projected, quite apart from the power and precision of his singing. Similarly, **José Carreras** has never sounded more powerful, with the big solo *Ingemisco* flawlessly delivered. Jessye Norman sings gloriously too, in such solos as the *Liber scriptus* and the *Recordare*, and she makes a fine match with Margaret Price in their duetting, equally firm and secure, distinct yet blended.

Yet it is Margaret Price who crowns the whole performance in the final *Libera me*, deeply moving and keenly dramatic, the more so when seen in close-up. The **Edinburgh Festival Chorus** sing as though possessed, and Abbado draws passionate playing from the **LSO**, with none of the coolness that can mark this conductor's work in the studio. The sound cannot match the finest modern recordings, and it is not helped by the dryness of the Usher Hall, where the performance was recorded, but, as transferred to DVD, the result is still full and vivid, with powerful impact.

Requiem Mass (CD versions)

🎵 **** Chan. 9490. Crider, Hatziano, Sade, Lloyd, L. Symphony Ch., LSO, Hickox

🎵 Ⓜ (***) DG mono 447 442-2. Stader, Radev, Krebs, Borg, St Hedwig's Cathedral Ch., Berlin RIAS O, Fricsay

**(*) Ph. 468 079-2 (2). Fleming, Borodina, Bocelli, d'Arcangelo, Kirov Ch. & O, Gergiev

Ⓜ **(*) RCA 82876 62318-2 (2). L. Price, J. Baker, Luchetti, van Dam, Chicago Symphony Ch. & O, Solti

(i) *Requiem Mass;* (ii) *4 Sacred Pieces*

🎵 **** Ph. 442 142-2 (2). (i) Orgonasova, von Otter, Canonici, Miles; (ii) D. Brown; Monteverdi Ch., ORR, Gardiner

Ⓜ *** Decca (ADD) 475 7735 (2). (i) Sutherland, Horne, Pavarotti, Talvela; VPO, Solti

Ⓜ **(*) EMI 5 67560-2. (i) Schwarzkopf, Ludwig, Gedda, Ghiaurov; (ii) J. Baker; Philh. Ch. & O, Giulini

Ⓑ **(*) Decca (ADD) 467 119-2 (2). (i) L. Price, Elias, Björling, Tozzi, V. Musikverein, VPO, Reiner; (ii) Minton, Los Angeles Master Ch., LAPO, Mehta

Requiem Mass. La forza del destino: Overture

(**(*)) BBC Legends mono BBCL 4144-2 (2). (i) Ligabue, Bumbry, Kónya, Arié, Philh. Ch.; Philh. O, Giulini (also Interview: Giulini in Conversation wih Michael Oliver)

(i) *Requiem Mass.* Choruses from: *Aida; Don Carlo; Macbeth; Nabucco; Otello*

🎜— *** Telarc CD 80152 (2). (i) Dunn, Curry, Hadley, Plishka; Atlanta Ch. & SO, Shaw

It says much for **Richard Hickox's** recording for Chandos with the **LSO** and **London Symphony Chorus** that in important ways – not just practically as the only modern single-disc version – it marked the first of a new generation of readings of Verdi's choral masterpiece. His pacing flows more freely than has become the rule in latterday performances, yet there is never a feeling of haste, simply of heightened intensity when his control of rubato and phrase is so warmly idiomatic. These are very much the speeds which made the vintage Serafin recording of 1939 so compelling, but with singing from the London Symphony Chorus infinitely finer than that of Serafin's Italian chorus. In their fire they rival Giulini's classic Philharmonia set, even outshining that in luminosity, thanks in part to the spacious and full recording which, in a reverberant church acoustic, yet reveals ample detail. The warm-toned soprano, **Michele Crider**, has a glorious chest register, and the mezzo, **Markella Hatziano**, is equally warm and characterful, while the tenor, **Gabriel Sade**, sings with clear, heady beauty, not least in a radiant *Ingemisco*, and **Robert Lloyd** gives one of his noblest, most commanding performances. A winning set in every way.

Gardiner, using period forces, is searingly dramatic and superbly recorded, with fine detail, combining transparent textures, weight and atmospheric bloom. It can still be recommended as a fine alternative among modern digital recordings even to collectors not drawn to period performance. The soloists make a characterful quartet, with the vibrant **Orgonasova** set against the rock-steady **Von Otter**, and with **Canonici** bringing welcome Italianate colourings to the tenor role. The *Four Sacred Pieces* are equally revealing. The longest and most complex, the final *Te Deum*, is the most successful of all, marked by thrillingly dramatic contrasts, as in the *fortissimo* cries of '*Sanctus*'.

Giulini's performances of the Verdi *Requiem* in the early 1960s have become legendary, electrifying occasions that led to a benchmark studio recording of 1964. Here the BBC Legends series puts an important gloss on that in offering a Prom recording of 1963, even more dramatically involving for the extra spontaneity of a live performance. The stereo sound is first-rate, and though the British soloists may not

be such stars as their studio counterparts, they sing beautifully, with firm, clear tone. The Schubert *Mass*, recorded at the Edinburgh Festival of 1968, makes a welcome and generous coupling (BBCL 4029-3).

Six months later **Giulini** performed the *Requiem* once more, again with **Philharmonia** forces, but this time at the Royal Festival Hall and with a starrier international quartet of soloists. This second live recording comes as a valuable supplement, though it hardly replaces the earlier BBC version. Sadly, it comes in mono only, with the dry Festival Hall acoustic unhelpful, not nearly as warm or atmospheric as the stereo recording from the Prom. The biting drama of Giulini's performance comes over thrillingly, but with some harshness in such passages as the *Dies irae*, and, though the singing of the international quartet is more strongly characterized than that of the fine British one at the Prom, they are no more imaginative. The *Overture* makes a good supplement, and Michael Oliver's interview with Giulini on the subject of recording is more valuable still (how easy to create a 'beautiful corpse' in the studio, he says), but the extras on the rival BBC version are much more generous.

Robert Shaw, in the finest of his Atlanta recordings, may not have quite the same searing electricity as Toscanini's classic NBC recording (for which he trained the chorus), but it regularly echoes it in power and the well-calculated pacing. In the *Dies irae*, for example, like Toscanini he gains in thrust and power from a speed marginally slower than usual. With sound of spectacular quality, beautifully balanced and clear, the many felicities of the performance, not least the electricity of the choral singing and the consistency of the solo singing, add up to an exceptionally satisfying reading. The fill-up of five Verdi opera choruses is colourful, and again brings superb choral singing.

Fricsay's superb earlier mono studio recording of Verdi's *Requiem* caused a sensation when it first appeared on LP in 1954. This makes a worthy reissue in DG's 'Legendary Recordings' series, with the full, spacious mono recording already showing that the DG engineers, using mono techniques, could achieve a combination of clarity and atmosphere. The solo team is first class with the contribution of **Kim Borg** standing out, as in the live performance.

Recorded during the **Kirov Company's** visit to Covent Garden in 2000, **Gergiev's** reading is one of high contrasts. Though the chorus often sounds misty and distant in hushed passages, the fervour of the singing is never in doubt in the big dramatic moments, as in the opening of the *Dies irae*. Yet what above all makes a powerful impact is the orchestra recorded close, so that the instrumental fire of the *Dies irae* has rarely come over so vividly, complete with shattering bass drum. **Renée Fleming** and **Olga Borodina** could hardly be bettered as the two women soloists, both characterful and well-contrasted, yet with a fine blend in their duets. **Andrea Bocelli** produces a fine flow of sweet tenor-tone controlling the *Ingemisco* well, if at times with excessive portamento, but **Ildebrando d'Arcangelo** sounds rather underpowered in the bass role.

What **Giulini** on EMI proved was that refinement added to power can provide an even more intense experience than the traditional Italian approach. The array of soloists could hardly be bettered. **Schwarzkopf** caresses each phrase, and the exactness of her voice matches the firm mezzo of **Christa Ludwig** in their difficult octave passages. **Gedda** is at his most reliable, and **Ghiaurov** with his really dark bass actually manages to sing the almost impossible *Mors stupebit* in tune without a suspicion of wobble. Giulini's set also finds space to include the *Four Sacred Pieces* in polished and dramatic performances which bring out the element of greatness in often uneven works. This has been carefully remastered as one of EMI's 'Great Recordings of the Century' but the otherwise excellent new transfer of the 1963/4 recording still reveals roughness in heavy climaxes of the *Dies irae* in the *Requiem*.

Reiner's opening of the *Requiem* is very slow and atmospheric. He takes the music at something like half the speed of Toscanini and shapes everything very carefully. Yet as the work proceeds the performance soon sparks into life, and there is some superb and memorable singing from a distinguished team of soloists. The recording has a spectacularly wide dynamic range, and, with the chorus singing fervently, the *Dies irae* is overwhelming. **Mehta's** performance of the *Sacred Pieces* is enhanced by brilliant, sharply focused recording.

Solti's Decca performance, now reissued as one of Universal's series of Originals, is not really a rival to any other. He plays up the dramatic side of the work at the expense of the spiritual, his conception very operatic. The team of soloists is strong, so if you want an extrovert performance with spectacular recording, you could hardly do better.

On RCA, with an unusually sensitive and pure-toned quartet of soloists – **Luchetti** perhaps not as characterful as the others, **Leontyne Price** occasionally showing strain – and with superb choral singing and orchestral playing, **Solti's** 1977 **Chicago** version has all the ingredients for success. The set is well worth having for **Dame Janet Baker's** deeply sensitive singing, but the remastered recording – less than ideally balanced – tends to be fierce on climaxes; and in other ways too, Solti's earlier Decca/Vienna set is preferable.

Te Deum (from Quattro pezzi sacri)

(BB) *** Warner Apex 8573 89128-2. Soloists, Bielefeld Musikvereins Ch., Philh. Hungarica, Stephani –
BRUCKNER: *Te Deum* ***

Although Verdi's *Te Deum* was published as the last of the *Four Sacred Pieces*, Verdi did not expect them to be performed as a group, and the *Te Deum* for double chorus makes a fine independent work. The choral singing is first class, the brass resplendent and the conductor, **Martin Stephani**, keeps everyone on their toes. The recording has a warmly resonant acoustic against which the singing projects thrillingly. Aptly coupled with Bruckner's much more devotional setting, this can be strongly recommended, especially at such a modest cost. Text and translation are included.

OPERA

Aida (complete; DVD versions)

🎬– *** DG DVD 073 001-9. Millo, Domingo, Zajick, Milnes, Burchuladze, Kavrakos, Met. Op. Ch. & O, Levine

🎬– 🌐 **** NVC Arts **DVD** 0630 198389-2. Chiara, Cossotto, Martinucci, Scandola, Zanazzo, Ch., O & Corps de Ballet of Verona Arena, Guadagno (Producer: Giancarlo Sbragia, V/D: Brian Large)

Recorded live at the **Metropolitan** in New York in October 1988, **James Levine's** powerful and starrily cast DVD of *Aida* brings a grandly traditional staging. The sets and costumes are so lavish that the unveiling of the same scene in Act II prompts enthusiastic applause. In that same scene **Plácido Domingo** is encumbered not only with his golden armour but with a ridiculously tall egg-shaped headdress. Yet he still manages to sing superbly throughout, a believable hero, and though **Aprile Millo** has her edgy moments, her poise as well as her power are impressive, not least in the Nile Scene. **Dolora Zajick** is a vibrant, powerful Amneris, and **Sherrill Milnes**, only just past his peak, is a magnificent Amonasro. Luxury casting brings **Paata Burchuladze** in as Ramfis, though **Dimitri Kavrakos** is less impressive as the King. Levine is in his element, drawing warm and dramatic playing and singing from his formidable team at the Met. Good, bright sound.

Recorded in the **Verona Arena**, from which we have already had a splendid *Tosca*, the spectacle of *Aida* with its dignified Triumphal March (with a surprise at the climax) is ideal for the spaciousness available, and Vittorio Rossi has designed a wonderful set, geometrically based round a pyramid to provide a satisfying backcloth. But the singing is superb. **Maria Chiara** sings gloriously in the title-role and never more affectingly than in the great closing duet. **Fiorenza Cossotto** is a memorable foil as Amneris, **Nicola Martinucci** is a properly heroic Radames, with a strong voice to match a striking presence, and the others complete a fine team, with Amonasro (**Giuseppe Scandola**) standing out. **Brian Large** deals with the huge set by varying between long shots and intimate close-ups for the main solos and duets. **Anton Guadagno** conducts with consistent vitality, the ballet is visually pleasing, and the huge chorus is very impressive indeed. The excellent stereo brings out the antiphonal trumpets in the March, yet strangely the camera fails to do so. Nevertheless, this is both vocally and visually a feast, and the applause is fully acceptable in the context of a live performance so powerful and finely sung by all concerned.

Aida (complete; CD versions)

🎬– (B) **** EMI (ADD) 3 81877-2 (3). Freni, Carreras, Baltsa, Cappuccilli, Raimondi, van Dam, V. State Op. Ch., VPO, Karajan

🎬– (BB) (***) Naxos mono 8.111240/1 (2). Callas, Barbieri, Tucker, Gobbi, La Scala, Milan, Ch. & O, Serafin

🎬– (BB) (***) Regis mono RRC 1074 (2). Callas, Barbieri, Tucker, Gobbi, La Scala, Milan, Ch. & O, Serafin

🎬– (B) *** Double Decca (ADD) 460 765-2 (2). L. Price, Gorr, Vickers, Merrill, Tozzi, Rome Op. Ch. & O, Solti

🎬– (M) *** Decca (ADD) 475 8240 (3). Tebaldi, Simionato, Bergonzi, MacNeil, van Mill, Corena, V. Singverein, VPO, Karajan

(***) Testament (mono) SBT2 1355 (2). Callas, Baum, Simionato, Walters, Neri, ROHCG Ch. & O, Barbirolli

(BB) (***) Naxos 8.110156/7. Caniglia, Gigli, Tajo, Stignani, Bechi, Pasero, Rome Op. Ch. & O, Serafin

(M) (**) EMI mono 5 56316-2 (2). Callas, Tucker, Barbieri, Gobbi, La Scala, Milan, Ch. & O, Serafin

On EMI, **Karajan's** is a performance of *Aida* full of splendour and pageantry, which is yet fundamentally lyrical. On disc there is no feeling of **Freni** lacking power even in a role normally given to a larger voice, and there is ample gain in the tender beauty of her singing. **Carreras** makes a fresh, sensitive Radames, **Raimondi** a darkly intense Ramfis and **van Dam** a cleanly focused King, his relative lightness no drawback. **Cappuccilli** gives a finely detailed performance as Amonasro, while **Baltsa** as Amneris crowns the whole performance with her fine, incisive singing. Despite some overbrightness on cymbals and trumpet, the **Vienna Orchestra's** sound for Karajan, as transferred to CD, is richly atmospheric, both in the intimate scenes and, most strikingly, in the scenes of pageant, reflecting the Salzburg Festival production which was linked to the recording. The set has been attractively re-packaged and remains a first choice, irrespective of price.

Leontyne Price is an outstandingly assured Aida on Decca, rich, accurate and imaginative, while **Solti's** direction is superbly dramatic, notably in the Nile Scene. **Merrill** is a richly secure Amonasro, **Rita Gorr** a characterful Amneris, and **Jon Vickers** is splendidly heroic as Radames. Though the digital transfer betrays the age of the recording (1962), making the result fierce at times to match the reading, Solti's version otherwise brings full, spacious sound, finer, more open and with greater sense of presence than most versions since. As a Double Decca reissue this is a formidable bargain, and the new-style cued synopsis with 'listening guide' is a fair substitute for a full libretto.

On Decca, as on EMI, **Karajan** was helped by having a **Viennese Orchestra and Chorus**; but most important of all is the musical teamwork of his soloists. **Bergonzi** in particular emerges here as a model among tenors, with a rare feeling for the shaping of phrases and attention to detail. **Cornell MacNeil** too is splendid. **Tebaldi's** creamy tone-colour rides beautifully over the phrases and she too acquires a new depth of imagination. Among the other soloists **Arnold van Mill** and **Fernando Corena** are both superb, and **Simionato** provides one of the finest portrayals of Amneris. The recording has long been famous for its technical bravura and flair. It has now been impressively remastered for Decca's current Legend series, and remains a remarkable technical achievement.

This is arguably the finest commercial recording of an opera that **Maria Callas** ever made. With her portrayal of the Ethiopian princess wonderfully intense, opposite the masterfully dramatic **Tito Gobbi** as her father, Amonasro, this readily matches their similar partnership in Puccini's *Tosca*. Their duet at the climax of the Nile Scene, following on Aida's big aria, *O patria mia*, has never been matched, and though Callas's top notes are not quite as firm as they had been in her live Covent Garden recording of two years

earlier under Barbirolli (Testament), few will resist. Though **Richard Tucker** as Radames is not the subtlest of tenors, his is a fine, heroic performance, and **Fedora Barbieri** is an impressive Amneris. The mono sound is clear and generally well balanced in Mark Obert-Thorn's excellent transfer. But the Regis transfer (by Tony Watts) is pretty sophisticated too. In the first Act it sounds remarkably full, with the solo voices splendidly caught (especially Callas's) and, while *Gloria all'Egitto* remains two-dimensional, overall there is no lack of atmospheric warmth. Both sets include cued libretti and you could be happy with either. But one or other is essential.

It was in 1953, during the Coronation season at Covent Garden, that **Callas** took the title-role in Verdi's Aida, with **John Barbirolli** conducting; as this CD set of the live broadcast vividly demonstrates, it was in many ways a performance that outshines almost all her studio recordings, with the stage atmosphere well caught. Barbirolli too is a winningly warm and sympathetic Verdian. The Czech tenor **Kurt Baum**, as Radames, may not have an Italianate voice, but he sings clearly, without strain or exaggeration, and **Giulietta Simionato** is a superb Amneris, searingly powerful. As Amonasro, the American baritone **Jess Walters** sings firmly and incisively, with **Giulio Neri** as Ramfis and **Michael Langdon** as the King both excellent. As a curiosity, the tiny role of the Priestess who sings off-stage at the start of the second scene is taken by the young **Joan Sutherland**, sounding very distant but perfectly identifiable.

Serafin's 78-r.p.m. version was recorded in July 1948, the last of the complete opera sets from HMV that featured **Beniamino Gigli** as the hero. It is an electrifying performance, with Serafin at his most magnetic leading an outstanding cast of principals, all with voices firm and true. Heralded by trumpets that vividly leap out of the speakers, Gigli launches into *Celeste Aida* at the start with a clarity and bravura that mark his whole performance. **Maria Caniglia** in the title role is at her very finest, using the widest range of expression, a fire-eater who knows tenderness too, while **Gino Bechi** is a superbly sinister Amonasro with a natural snarl in the voice. The others characterize strongly too, with the close balance of the voices and relative dryness of acoustic vividly bringing out words and expression. The transfers by Ward Marston are outstanding, making this one of the very finest of the impressive Naxos historic opera series.

The Nile Scene has never been performed more powerfully and characterfully on record than in this vintage **La Scala** set. Though **Callas** is not a sweet-toned Aida, her detailed imagination is irresistible, and she is matched by **Tito Gobbi** at the very height of his powers. **Tucker** gives one of his very finest performances on record, and **Barbieri** is a commanding Amneris. The mono sound is greatly improved in the latest transfer, but this remains at full price.

Aida (highlights)

(N) *** Australian Decca Eloquence (ADD) 480 1283. Price, Gorr, Clabassi, Vickers, Merrill, Rome Op. Ch. & O, Solti

This is an expanded highlights CD from Solti's superb *Aida* from the early 1960s. All excerpts have been chosen with care and this classic recording is self-recommending. The remastering for this Australian Decca release is superb, bringing out all the dramatic qualities of both the performance and recordings very vividly indeed.

Aida (complete; in English)

Ⓜ **(*) Chan. 3074 (2). Eaglen, Plowright, O'Neill, Yurisich, Rose, Alistair, Miles, Geoffrey Mitchell Ch., Philh. O, Parry

Central to the Chandos set's success is the formidable assumption of the title role by **Jane Eaglen**, here sounding more comfortable singing in English than she often has in international original-language recordings. The voice is rich and warm, better focused than it often has been, with fearless attack above the stave, and fine poise in reflective moments. After his strenuous start **O'Neill** sings most sensitively, so that even by the end of his first aria he achieves a quiet top B flat such as Verdi wanted, and sustains it impressively using a head-voice. **Rosalind Plowright**, gravitating down to the mezzo register, makes a suitably fruity and vehement Amneris, not quite steady enough, with **Gregory Yurisich** an incisive Amonasro, and **Peter Rose** and **Alastair Miles** strongly cast as Pharaoh and Ramfis respectively. Though **David Parry** does not always keep dramatic tensions as taut as they might be, the rich and vividly atmospheric Chandos sound regularly compensates.

Alzira (complete)

** Orfeo (ADD) CO 57832 (2). Cotrubas, Araiza, Bruson, Rootering, Bav. R. Ch., Munich RO, Gardelli

Alzira, dating from 1845, is at once the least cherished and the most compact of Verdi's operas, yet on disc, when brevity is often an asset, it emerges as far from perfunctory. Indeed, it can stand comparison with any of the other operas Verdi wrote in his years 'in the galleys'. **Gardelli** recorded the piece for Orfeo with an excellent cast, helped by warm and well-balanced recording supervised by Munich Radio engineers, with **Cotrubas** flexible in coloratura, **Francisco Araiza** as the Inca hero, Zamoro, and **Renato Bruson** as Gusmano, Governor of Peru. Though the Orfeo recording is excellent, the earlier, deleted Philips set was finer on all counts.

Attila (complete; DVD version)

▸ **** Opus Arte DVD 09478 03010. Ramey, Zancanaro, Studer, Kaludov, Gavazzi, Luperi, La Scala, Milan, Ch. and O, Muti

The 1991 production of *Attila* from La Scala with **Riccardo Muti** taut and incisive in this strong, compact piece is outstandingly dramatic. It helps that the chorus takes a vital part, rather as it does in the even earlier *Nabucco*. There are also anticipations of later Verdi operas like *Rigoletto*, notably in the storm scene. The relative brevity of the piece, with one key number following promptly on another, makes a strong impact on DVD, in a production with traditional costumes and using minimal but atmospheric sets. **Samuel Ramey** in the title-role and and **Giorgio Zancanaro** as the Roman general, Ezio, both at their peak, in their nicely contrasted ways firm and dark, are ideally cast, with **Cheryl Studer** also outstanding as Odabella.

Attila (complete)

▸ Ⓜ **** Ph. (ADD) 475 6766-2 (2). Raimondi, Deutekom, Bergonzi, Milnes, Amb. S., Finchley Children's Music Group, RPO, Gardelli

With its dramatic anticipations of *Macbeth* and musical ones of *Rigoletto*, and the compression which (on record if not on the stage) becomes a positive merit, *Attila*, in a fine performance under **Gardelli** on this Philips set, is an intensely enjoyable experience. **Deutekom**, not a sweet-toned soprano, has never sung better on record, and the rest of the cast is outstandingly good. The 1973 recording is well balanced and atmospheric, and this reissue in the Classic Opera series comes with a full libretto.

Un ballo in maschera (complete; DVD version)

▸ **** Decca DVD 074 3227 (2). Pavarotti, Ricciarelli, Quilico, Blegen, Berini, Met. Op. Ch. & O, Patanè (Producer: Elijah Moshinsky, V/D: Brian Large)

▸ **** EuroArts DVD 2055 108. Pisapia, Vassallo, Talgi, Chiuri, You, Leipzig Op. Ch. & ballet, Leipzig GO, Chailly (Dir: Ermanno Olmi, V/D: Don Kent)

This 1980 live performance is another of the productions from the New York Met. to show **Pavarotti** at his very finest, both as singer and actor. (His dying scene of forgiveness is especially telling.) He is in splendid voice as Riccardo and is partnered by **Katia Ricciarelli** as Amelia, also at her finest, and looking ravishing. Their great love-duet in Act II is gloriously sung and **Patanè** rises to the occasion and creates a richly romantic orchestral outburst, all but anticipating Puccini. Among the others in this superb cast, **Judith Blegen** is a delightful Oscar, with sparkling coloratura, and **Bianca Berini** an unforgettable fortune-teller (Ulrica) virtually stealing the scenes in which she appears (with her eyes as well as her voice). **Louis Quilico** make an effectively agonized Renato, Amelia's unfortunate husband. The costumes are traditional, the sets practical. Patanè conducts throughout with flair and **Brian Large's** video direction could hardly be bettered. Highly recommended.

Ermanno Olmi's production offers traditional costumes and stylized sets, though visually the tenor, **Massimilliano Pisapia**, taking the role of Riccardo, is not helped by an unbecoming high collar in Act I which exaggerates his absence of neck. What matters is that he has a cleanly focused, agile voice, revealing few signs of strain, and bringing out the fun in the role. **Chiara Talgi** as Amelia has a pure, warm soprano, finely controlled in her legato singing, and **Franco Vassallo** sings magnificently, making his defying aria, *Eri tu*, a powerful climax, helped by **Riccardo Chailly's** inspired conducting. **Ein Yee You** is brilliant in the trouser role of Oscar the page; and as the witch, Ulrica, **Anna-Maria Chiuri** sings with a tough, throaty contralto, characterful but not quite steady. The **Leipzig Opera Ballet** adds effectively to the final Ball Scene.

Un ballo in maschera (complete; CD versions)

▸ Ⓑ *** DG Double 453 148-2 (2). Ricciarelli, Domingo, Bruson, Obraztsova, Gruberová, Raimondi, La Scala, Milan, Ch. & O, Abbado

⊶ (M) *** DG 477 5641 (2). Domingo, Barstow, Nucci, Quivar, Jo, V. State Op. Konzertvereinigung, VPO, Karajan

⊶ (BB) (***) Naxos mono 8.111278/9. Callas, Di Stefano, Gobbi, Ratti, Barbieri, La Scala, Milan, Ch. & O, Votto

⊶ (***) EMI mono 5 56320-2 (2). Callas, di Stefano, Gobbi, Ratti, Barbieri, La Scala, Milan, Ch. & O, Votto

(M) **(*) Decca (ADD) 475 8278 (2). Bergonzi, MacNeil, Nilsson, Simionato, Krause, Corena, Santa Cecilia Ch. & O, Solti

(B) **(*) Double Decca (IMS) (ADD) 460 762-2 (2). Tebaldi, Pavarotti, Milnes, Resnik, Donath, St Cecilia Academy, Rome, Ch. & O, Bartoletti

(N) (**(*)) ROH Heritage mono ROHS 009 (2). Vickers, Shuard, Bastianini, Resnik, Carlyle, ROHCG Ch. & O, Downes

Abbado's powerful reading, admirably paced and with a splendid feeling for the sparkle of the comedy, remains highly recommendable at bargain price. The cast is very strong, with **Ricciarelli** at her very finest and **Domingo** sweeter of tone and more deft of characterization than on the Muti set of five years earlier. **Bruson** as the wronged husband Renato (a role he also takes for Solti) sings magnificently, and only **Obraztsova** as Ulrica and **Gruberová** as Oscar are less consistently convincing. The analogue recording clearly separates the voices and instruments in different acoustics, which, though distracting at first, brings the drama closer.

Recorded in Vienna early in 1989, *Un ballo in maschera* was **Karajan's** last opera recording. Standing out vocally is the Gustave of **Plácido Domingo**, strong and imaginative, dominating the whole cast. **Josephine Barstow** as Amelia certainly makes for a striking and characterful performance, even if it is flawed vocally, with the tone growing raw under pressure. Nevertheless, this is Barstow's finest achievement on record, and she is most compelling dramatically. **Leo Nucci**, though not as rough in tone as in some of his other recent recordings, is over-emphatic, with poor legato in his great solo, *Eri tu*. **Sumi Jo**, a Karajan discovery, gives a delicious performance as Oscar, the page, coping splendidly with Karajan's slow speed for her Act I solo. **Florence Quivar** produces satisfyingly rich tone as Ulrica. Though the sound is not as cleanly focused as in the Decca recording for Solti, it is warm and full.

Votto's 1956 mono recording, with voices set close but with a fair amount of space round them, is among the best of the sets with **Callas** from **La Scala**, and the CD focuses its qualities the more sharply. Cast from strength, with all the principals – notably **Gobbi** and **Giuseppe di Stefano** – on top form, this is indispensable for Callas's admirers.

However, Mark Obert-Thorn's transfer for Naxos immaculately preserves the recording with plenty of bloom on the voices, and there seems no reason to prefer the EMI set which is still at full price, especially when the Naxos documentation is excellent.

The *Guide* has always been rather rude about the 1961 Decca performance, but listening to it again calls for re-assessment. There are far too many good points, not least in terms of sheer voice – where would you find singers like this today? **Birgit Nilsson** may not sound totally idiomatic in Verdi, but the voice is glorious and she is far from the cold performer which she has sometimes been accused of being. **Simionato** is full of character, **MacNeil** is warmly impressive, and all the smaller parts have been cast with excellent singers, notably **Fernando Corena** and **Tom Krause**. **Carlo Bergonzi** is a stylish Verdian as always. **Solti's** lively conducting suits the vivid and theatrical Decca recording. Texts and translations included.

The main interest in the earlier Decca set rests in the pairing of **Tebaldi** and **Pavorotti**. The latter was in young, vibrant voice but Tebaldi made her recording in the full maturity of her career. She gives a commanding performance, but there is no mistaking that her voice here is not as even as it once was. The supporting cast is strong, not only **Milnes** as Renato and **Donath** as Oscar, but **Resnik** a dark-voiced Ulrica. **Bartoletti** directs the proceedings dramatically, and the (1970) Decca recording remains strikingly vivid and atmospheric. Now reissued as a Double Decca with new-style cued synopsis, this makes a good bargain recommendation.

Jon Vickers is unquestionably the star of this 1962 Covent Garden performance. **Amy Shuard** is unmemorable and **Bastianini** fails to meet full expectations. Overall not as exciting as expected; and why was a 1962 performance not recorded in stereo?

La battaglia di Legnano (complete; CD version)

(M) *** Ph. (ADD) 475 8694 (2). Ricciarelli, Carreras, Manuguerra, Ghiuselev, Austrian R. Ch. & O, Gardelli

La battaglia di Legnano is a compact, sharply conceived piece, made the more intense by the subject's obvious relationship with the situation in Verdi's own time. One weakness is that the villainy is not effectively personalized, but the juxtaposition of the individual drama of supposed infidelity against a patriotic theme brings most effective musical contrasts. **Gardelli** directs a fine performance, helped by a strong cast of principals, with **Carreras, Ricciarelli** and **Manuguerra** all at their finest. Excellent recording.

Il Corsaro (complete)

⊶ (M) *** Ph. 475 6769 (2). Norman, Caballé, Carreras, Grant, Mastromei, Noble, Amb. S., New Philh. O, Gardelli

In *Il Corsaro*, although the characterization is rudimentary, the contrast between the two heroines is effective, with Gulnara, the Pasha's slave, carrying conviction in the *coup de foudre* which has her promptly worshipping the Corsair, an early example of the Rudolph Valentino figure. The rival heroines are splendidly taken here, with **Jessye Norman** as the faithful wife, Medora, actually upstaging **Montserrat Caballé** as Gulnara. **Gardelli** directs a vivid performance, with fine singing from the hero, portrayed by **José Carreras**. **Gian-Piero Mastromei**, not rich in tone, still rises to the challenge of the Pasha's music. Excellent, firmly focused and well-balanced, mid-1970s Philips sound, well transferred in this mid-priced reissue, with full libretto included.

Don Carlos (complete; DVD versions)

🎛—******** Warner **DVD** 0630 16318-2. Alagna, Hampson, van Dam, Mattila, Meier, Halfvarson, Théâtre du Châtelet Ch., O de Paris, Pappano

TDK **DVD** DVWW OPCARLOS. Miles, Vargas, Skovhus, Tamar, Michael, V. State Op. Ch. & O, De Billy (Dir: Peter Kowitschny, V/D: Anton Reizenstein)

This fine Warner issue provides one of the clearest instances where DVD scores on almost every level over the equivalent CD set. Here you have a full three and half hours of music on a single disc, as against the three-CD set from EMI. The sound on DVD may be marginally less full than on CD, but it would take someone with an exceptional ear to feel short-changed. The chorus is rather less crisply disciplined in places, but rises splendidly to the big challenge of the *Auto da fé* scene of Act III. And where too many DVDs skimp on the number of index points, this one follows the normal CD practice of having them at every crucial point.

All that plus the advantage of having a visual presentation of Luc Bondy's production. Though the sets are simple and stylized, the production never gets in the way of the music, with the costumes of Moidele Bickel (coloured black, white or crimson) close enough to 17th-century fashion not to distract from the drama. The score is tautly and warmly presented, as on CD, by **Antonio Pappano** and the principals are as fine a team as have ever been assembled for this opera on disc – here using the original French text and the full five-act score complete with Fontainebleau scene. **Karita Mattila** gives the most masterly performance as the Queen, with one inspired passage after another culminating in a supreme account of her Act V aria. **Roberto Alagna** is in superb voice too, firm and heroic, well-matched against **Thomas Hampson**, noble as Rodrigo. **José van Dam** may not have the deep bass normal for the role of Philip II, but having a more lyrical voice brings compensating assets, and he contrasts well with the Grand Inquisitor of **Eric Halfvarson**. An outstanding issue.

While **Bertrand De Billy** conducts his **Viennese** forces with conviction and the singing on the TDK set is often impressive, the cast is a good deal more than adequate; sample the famous duet between Don Carlos and King Philip (**Ramón Vargas** and **Alastair Miles**). But the production is a travesty, mirroring modern political chicanery, with secret police wearing dark glasses and hitting out with clubs; and the unpleasant action comes right out into the theatre. The set is white and square, the costumes are mixed, both ancient and modern, and there is much else besides that has no connection with Verdi. There is even booing from the audience – and rightly so. How can stage directors get away with such rubbish! Keep away.

Don Carlos (complete; CD versions)

🎛—******** EMI 5 56152-2 (3). Alagna, van Dam, Hampson, Mattila, Meier, Ch. de Théâtre du Châtelet, O de Paris, Pappano

🎛—Ⓜ ******** EMI (ADD) 7 69304-2 (3). Carreras, Freni, Ghiaurov, Baltsa, Cappuccilli, Raimondi, German Op. Ch., Berlin, BPO, Karajan

Ⓜ ******* EMI 5 67401-2 (3) [567397]. Domingo, Caballé, Raimondi, Verrett, Milnes, Amb. Op. Ch., ROHCG O, Giulini

Ⓝ Ⓜ ******* Decca (ADD) 478 0345 (3). Tebaldi, Bergonzi, Bumbry, Fischer-Dieskau, Ghiaurov, ROHCG Ch. & O, Solti

**(*) DG 415 316-2 (4). Ricciarelli, Domingo, Valentini Terrani, Nucci, Raimondi, Ghiaurov, La Scala, Milan, Ch. & O, Abbado

Ⓜ **(***)** ROH mono RPHS 003 (3). Vickers, Brouwenstijn, Barbieri, Gobbi, Christoff, ROHCG Ch. & O, Giulini

Ⓜ ****(*)** EMI 3 58631-2 (3). Pavarotti, Conti, Ramey, Dessi, D'Intino, Anisimov, La Scala, Milan, Ch. & O, Muti

ⒷⒷ **(**(*))** Naxos mono 8111132/4 (3). Filippeschi, Stella, Nicolai, Gobbi, Christoff, Rome Opera Ch. & O, Santini (with bonus: historical duets and arias from *Don Carlo* from Bjorling & Merrill, Pinza, Marian Anderson, Battistini & Seinmeyer)

ⒷⒷ **(**(*))** Regis mono RRC 3011 (3). Filippeschi, Stella, Nicolai, Gobbi, Christoff, Rome Opera Ch. & O, Santini (with bonus: excerpts from *Don Carlo* (Bjoerling & Merrill); *I vespri siciliani*; *Ernani* (Christoff); *Forza del destino*; *Un ballo in maschera*; *Otello* (Gobbi))

ⒷⒷ ****(*)** Naxos 8.660096/8. Cleveman, Ryhänen, Mattei, Rundgren, Martinpelto, Tobiasson, Sörensen, Hedlund, Wallén, Leidland, Royal Swedish Op. Ch. & O, Hold-Garrido

In the five-act CD version **Pappano** may not include as much of the extra and optional material as Abbado has on his four-disc DG La Scala set (the only rival in French), but his judgement on the text is good, with one or two variants included. The whole performance sounds more idiomatic, helped by a cast more fluent in French than Abbado's. Regularly Pappano conveys the dramatic thrust more intensely. Naturally impetuous as well as expressive, he inspires his players as well as his singers, an exceptionally strong team. **Waltraud Meier** is not caught at her best as Eboli, but relishes the drama of *O don fatale*. As the Grand Inquisitor, **Eric Halfvarson** is not quite steady enough, even if (thanks to Pappano) the confrontation with the King is thrilling. The live recording brings some odd balances, with the sound transferred at a lowish level, but the opera-house atmosphere, vividly caught, amply compensates for any shortcoming.

Karajan opts for the four-act version of the opera, merely opening out the cuts he adopted on stage. The *Auto da fé* scene is here superb, while Karajan's characteristic choice of singers for refinement of voice rather than sheer size consistently pays off. Both **Carreras** and **Freni** are most moving. **Baltsa** is a superlative Eboli and **Cappuccilli** an affecting Rodrigo. **Raimondi** and **Ghiaurov** as the Grand Inquisitor and Philip II provide the most powerful confrontation. The sound is both rich and atmospheric and is made to seem even firmer and more vivid in its current remastering, giving great power to Karajan's uniquely taut account, full of panache.

Yet it is **Giulini's** 1971 set that EMI have chosen as one of their 'Great Recordings of the Century'. He uses the full, five-act text. Generally the cast is strong; the only vocal disappointment among the principals lies in **Caballé's** account of the big aria *Tu che le vanità* in the final act. The CD transfer of the analogue recording brings astonishing vividness and realism, a tribute to the original engineering of Christopher Parker. Even in the big ensembles the focus is very precise, yet atmospheric too, not just analytic. Excellent documentation and a full libretto and translation.

Unlike earlier 'complete' recordings, which used the four-act revision, the Decca version included the important passages excised, notably the Fontainebleau scene, and that may underline the one major deficiency of the set, that the dramatic temperature fails to rise as it should until the duet between Philip and Rodrigo at the end of Act II (Act I in the four-act version). Till then **Solti** tends to be somewhat rigid, but once the right mood is established he does marvellously with his own Covent Garden forces, and the result is that the *Auto da fé* scene is very fine. **Tebaldi** too in this most exacting Verdian role warms up well, and gives a magnificent account of *Tu che la vanità*. **Bumbry** and **Bergonzi** both sing splendidly, and after some rather gritty singing early on **Fischer-Dieskau** rises fittingly to Rodrigo's great death scene. **Ghiaurov** as Philip brings a nobility, a sense of stoic pride to his characterisation, that is most compelling. The recording is one of Decca's best and this is welcome back to the catalogue as one of Decca's 'Originals' with a full libretto.

Abbado's set was the first recording to use the language which Verdi originally set, French, in the full five-act text. The first disappointment lies in the variable quality of the sound, with odd balances, yet the cast is a strong one. **Domingo** easily outshines his earlier recording with Giulini (in Italian), while **Katia Ricciarelli** as the Queen gives a tenderly moving performance, if not quite commanding enough in the Act V aria. **Ruggero Raimondi** is a finely focused Philip II, nicely contrasted with **Nicolai Ghiaurov** as the Grand Inquisitor in the other black-toned bass role. **Lucia Valentini Terrani** as Eboli is warm-toned if not very characterful, and **Leo Nucci** makes a noble Posa.

The immediate impact of Luchino Visconti's production of *Don Carlos* in 1958, then a relatively little-known Verdi opera, comes over vividly in this live recording, made in bright mono sound. **Carlo-Maria Giulini** was making his Covent Garden debut, and the power and intensity of his conducting match the strength of an outstanding cast. **Jon Vickers** in the name-part was at his formidable peak, and the sweet-toned Dutch soprano, **Gre Brouwenstijn**, is most impressive in the placement of the voice, rising superbly to the challenge of *Tu che le vanità* in the final Act. **Tito Gobbi** sings magnificently as Rodrigo, not least in his death scene, and **Boris Christoff** is most moving as King Philip, bringing rare tenderness to his big aria, *Ella gimmai m'amo*. Hearing this, one cannot be surprised that this Visconti–Giulini production became one of the classics at Covent Garden over many years.

The EMI set with **Muti** was recorded at **La Scala** in the run of performances in 1992 which followed **Pavarotti's** first appearance as Don Carlo, and his magnetism and sensitive control of word-meaning provide a fine focus, even though

he is inclined to rush his fences, rarely singing gently. Even so, in the final duet he makes amends; Muti, uncomfortably taut for much of the opera and pressing ahead with fast, unsprung tempi, finds more relaxation and a more lyrical style by the close. **Daniela Dessi** is a positive, characterful Elisabetta, though often gutsy in production. **Ramey** is a sympathetic Philip II, though the voice is not quite dark or firm enough, and **Paolo Conti** is a strong if not very imaginative Rodrigo. **Luciana D'Intino** is a fine Eboli. The sound is dry in the La Scala manner, with voices placed forward, though some bloom remains. The recording returns to the catalogue at mid-price with a cued synopsis.

The 1954 EMI recording of *Don Carlos* is chiefly memorable for the incomparable contributions of **Tito Gobbi** and **Boris Christoff**, but **Santini** conducts a strong performance, well transferred in both these reissues, the Naxos the more vivid, the Regis smoother but with rather less range. It is a seriously cut version of the four-Act score, but it is still an indispensable set and well worth having at budget price, with performances from Gobbi as Rodrigo and Christoff as Philip which have never been matched since. Gobbi's singing in the Death Scene is arguably the finest recorded performance that even this glorious artist ever made, with a wonderful range of tone and feeling for words. The bitingly dark tone of Christoff as the King also goes with intense feeling for the dramatic situation, making his big monologue one of the peaks of the performance. **Antonietta Stella**, never a very distinctive artist, gives one of her finest recorded performances as Elisabetta, only occasionally squally. As Eboli, **Elena Nicolai** controls her fruity mezzo well, even if the vibrato becomes obtrusive; and the most serious blot is the singing of the tenor, **Mario Filippeschi**, and even that is not as coarse as we have often had latterly. Choice might rest on the supplementary historic recordings offered on each alternative set, with the Naxos selection of recordings from *Don Carlos* marginally the more interesting: it includes **Bjoerling** and **Merrill** in the *Oath Duet*, **Pinza** in Philip II's aria, **Marian Anderson** as Eboli, **Battistini** in 1913 as Rodrigo, and **Seinemeyer** as Elisabetta in her Act IV aria. The Regis reissue includes a number of key Verdi performances by the principal artists here, including also the big *Don Carlos* duet scene from Bjoerling and Merrill, plus six other solo contributions from Christoff and Gobbi.

Edited together from three live performances, the Naxos Swedish set offers a lively, incisive account of the five-act version of *Don Carlos*, with the **Swedish Opera's** Spanish music-director, **Alberto Hold-Garrido**, drawing out the formidable talents of his company in a warmly idiomatic reading. It is the more impressive that this is a repertory performance without imported stars. **Hillevi Martinpelto**, commanding as Elisabetta, and **Peter Mattei**, the powerful Rodrigo.

In the title-role, **Lars Cleveman** may not be a match for such a star as Plácido Domingo in imagination, but this is a fresh, gripping performance which in Carlo's duets with Rodrigo can live up to almost any comparison. As Philip II, **Jaakko Ryhänen** sings magnificently, movingly so in his monologue, carrying on the Finnish tradition of Martti Talvela, while **Ingrid Tobiasson** makes a feisty Eboli. As usual with this opera the text is an amalgam, mainly drawn from the 1886 Modena version. An outstanding bargain issue that even includes the full Italian libretto.

(i) *Don Carlo*, Act III, Scene 2; (ii) *Simon Boccanegra*, Act I, Scene 2

⊕—Ⓜ *** EMI 5 62777-2. Gobbi, (i) Filippesci; (ii) de los Angeles; (i) Rome Op. O, Santini – PUCCINI: *Gianni Schicchi* ***

Rodrigo in *Don Carlo* and his golden-voiced *Simon Boccanegra* were two of **Tito Gobbi's** most famous roles, and they are well celebrated in this dramatic pair of excerpts, with honeyed support from **de los Angeles** as Amelia and **Mario Filippesci** as Don Carlo. Texts and translations are included.

Ernani (complete; DVD versions)

⊕—**** Decca DVD 074 3228. Pavarotti, Mitchell, Milnes, Raimondi, Met. Op. Ch. & O, Levine (Dir: Kirk Browning)

⊕—**** Warner DVD 4509 99213-2. Domingo, Freni, Bruson, Ghiaurov, La Scala, Milan, Ch. & O, Muti

This live (1983) recording from the **Met.** is magnificent. Like *Trovatore*, it needs four great singers, and here it has **Pavarotti** (in magnificent form), **Leona Mitchell** (in splendid voice), **Sherrill Milnes** (a commanding Don Carlo) and **Ruggero Raimondi** (a memorably powerful Don Ruy Gomez de Silva). While all four solo performances are superb, one has only to sample the finale to Act I to discover what an electrifying team they make, while the close of Act II, led by Pavarotti, is equally thrilling. If Pavarotti dominates by the sheer ardour of his singing, overall this is a totally gripping performance, unlikely to be surpassed on DVD. Fortunately, costumes and sets are colourful and traditional. Throughout, **James Levine** conducts with consistent zest and Verdian vitality, and the choruses are a joy. The camerawork is well managed too. Not to be missed.

Although the cast is starry, it is **Muti** who ensures that this live **La Scala**, Milan, production of *Ernani* is so gripping, as we know from the CD set. Even if **Mirella Freni** at the opening sounds strained, it is still a powerful, rich-voiced performance, and **Bruson** is here on better form than on the CD set and he makes a superb contribution as Don Carlo, while **Ghiaurov**, as on CD, is a characterful Silva. But it is **Domingo's** set and he sings magnificently, while the staging is traditional, thank goodness, though not unimaginative. Good camera angles, too.

Ernani (complete; CD versions)

⊕—Ⓜ **** Decca 475 7008 (2). Pavarotti, Sutherland, Nucci, Burchuladze, Welsh Nat. Op. Ch. & O, Bonynge

⊕—Ⓜ *** RCA (ADD) GD 86503 (2). L. Price, Bergonzi, Sereni, Flagello, RCA Italiana Op. Ch. & O, Schippers

Bonynge's celebrated Decca (late 1990s) recording now returns to the catalogue at mid-price (with libretto included). **Sutherland** gives a commanding account of the role of Elvira, and though the beat in her voice betrays her age, the challenging aria, *Ernani involami*, brings not just power but all the old flexibility. Helped by the sympathetic conducting

of her husband, she endearingly throws caution to the winds. **Pavarotti** too, balanced rather close, gives a vividly characterful portrait of Ernani himself, always ready to shade down his tone, characteristically bringing out the word-meaning. **Leo Nucci** as Don Carlo, the King, his rival in love, is also firmer and more characterful than others on disc, and **Paata Burchuladze** as the vengeful de Silva was caught here at the brief peak of his career, his dark, sinister bass well controlled. On sound terms, this reissue easily outshines its CD rivals.

Leontyne Price may take the most celebrated aria, *Ernani involami*, rather cautiously, but the voice is gloriously firm and rich, and **Bergonzi** is comparably strong and vivid, though **Mario Sereni**, vocally reliable, is dull, and **Ezio Flagello** gritty-toned. With Schippers drawing the team powerfully together, it remains a highly enjoyable set, with the digital transfer making voices and orchestra sound full and vivid.

Ernani (complete; in English)

⊕—Ⓜ *** Chan. 3052 (2). Gavin, Patterson, Opie, Wedd, Rose, ENO Ch. & O, Parry

In a lively, vibrant performance like this, recorded soon after the **ENO** production in 2000, it is in some ways even more vital than a performance in Italian. The principals are first rate, with **Susan Patterson** a formidable Elvira, tackling her big aria in Act I firmly and confidently, at once rich-toned and agile with a perfect trill. The Australian tenor **Julian Gavin** is also well cast in the title role, with a cleanly focused voice and clear diction, while **Alan Opie** gives a vintage performance in the baritone role of the King. Full, vivid recording. A welcome if unexpected addition to the Peter Moores/Chandos Opera in English series.

Falstaff (complete; DVD versions)

⊕—**** Warner DVD 50-51442-0494-2-8. Bruson, Ricciarelli, Nucci, Hendricks, Gonzales, Valentini-Terrani, ROHCG Ch. & O, Giulini

**(*) BBC Opus Arte DVD OA 0812D. Terfel, Frittoli, Rancatore, Manca di Nissa, Montague, Frontali, Tarver, Leggate, Howell, ROHCG Ch. & O, Haitink

(**(*)) Arthaus DVD mono 101 083. Gramm, Luxon, Griffel, Gale, Cosotti, Condo, Fryatt, Dickerson, Trama, Glyndebourne Ch., Philh. O, Pritchard (V/D: Dave Heather)

On Warner a very similar cast to the Philips Los Angeles CD version, also conducted by **Giulini** spaciously, but with comparable flair. **Renato Bruson** emerges here visually as well as vocally as an ideal Falstaff and his comic timing cannot be faulted. **Barbara Hendricks** is again a charmer as Nanetta and **Dalmacio Gonzales** is a most appealing Fenton. **Leo Nucci** is an excellent Ford, the rest of the cast come up trumps and the whole opera moves with a lively swing. The production is both dramatic and civilized in that costumes and set would not disappoint the composer. Recommended alongside the Muti version.

Graham Vick's provocative DVD production with crudely-coloured toy-town sets by Paul Brown is powerfully conducted by **Bernard Haitink**. The production's principal asset is the strong, characterful Falstaff of **Bryn Terfel**, musically and dramatically most satisfying despite his grotesquely exaggerated costume and pot-belly. In the tradition of the finest Falstaffs, he is at once comic and dignified and ultimately moving, while the voice is in splendid form. **Barbara Frittoli** also makes an excellent Alice, and the rest of the cast is consistently fine. The problem lies in the sets with their aggressive primary colours and simplistic lines, though the false perspectives have a vaguely medieval look. The costumes, although equally garish, are in Elizabethan style, and Vick allows Falstaff to be tipped into the Thames in a genuine laundry basket, but he removes all magic from the final Windsor Forest scene, with a tower of bodies (intrepid members of the chorus) taking the place of Herne's Oak. Unlike many operas on DVD this one has ample index points, with 31 chapters or tracks.

Donald Gramm's Falstaff is well (if not memorably) sung and elegantly characterized and with a proper touch of dignity; and he gets excellent support from a fine cast, notably from **Benjamin Luxon** as Ford and **Kay Griffel's** bright-eyed portrayal of Alice. **Elizabeth Gale's** fresh Nannetta and **Max-René Cosotti's** very eligible Fenton make a delightful pair of lovers, silhouetted behind sheets in Act I, an example of Jean-Pierre Ponnelle's engaging production, typical of Glyndebourne at its finest in 1976. The lesser characters, **John Fryatt's** Dr Caius, **Bernard Dickerson's** Bardolph and **Ugo Trama's** Pistol, are all well observed, and there are nice touches of humour. **Pritchard** keeps the action sparkling and the cameras seem always to be in the right place. The sound is mono, but very acceptable.

Falstaff (complete; CD versions)

🎵 **** DG 471 194-2 (2). Terfel, Pieczonka, Diadkova, Hampson, Röschmann, Shtoda, Berlin R. Ch., BPO, Abbado

🎵 Ⓜ **** EMI 3 77349-2 (2). Gobbi, Schwarzkopf, Zaccaria, Moffo, Panerai, Philh. Ch. & O, Karajan

🎵 ⒷⒷ **** LSO Live 0055 (2). Pertusi, Alvarez, Ibarra, Domashenko, Henschel, L. Symphony Ch., LSO, C. Davis

🎵 Ⓜ *** Decca (ADD) 475 6677 (2). G. Evans, Ligabue, Freni, Kraus, Elias, Simionato, RCA Italiana Op. Ch. & O, Solti

Ⓜ **(*) Sony (ADD) SM2K 91181 (2). Fischer-Dieskau, Panerai, Ligabue, Sciutti, Oncina, Resnik, Rössl-Majdan, V. State Op. Ch., VPO, Bernstein

ⒷⒷ (***) Naxos mono 8.110198/9 (2). Rimini, Tassinari, Tellini, Buades, D'Alessio, Monticone, Ghirardini, La Scala Ch. & O, Molajoli (with arias by MASCAGNI, MASSENET, MOZART, PUCCINI, WAGNER(***))

Bryn Terfel gives a vital, three-dimensional reading as one might expect, but uses tone-colours that do not generally have you picturing a fat character, a point that also applies to the classic portrayal by Tito Gobbi in the first Karajan recording on EMI. The darkness of Falstaff's Act III monologue after his ducking is as intense as you will ever hear it, while the final fugue at a very fast tempo is thrillingly precise, thanks to a team of leading singers who respond brilliantly to Abbado's strong, thoughtful direction. **Adrianna**

Pieczonka is a superb Alice, full-toned and characterful, and **Dorothea Röschmann** a charming Nannetta, with **Larissa Diadkova** a fruity Mrs Quickly. The male characters are well contrasted too, and though **Thomas Hampson's** velvety baritone hardly conveys the meanness of Ford, the sensitive detail in his characterization is magnetic. For most collectors this will now be the primary recommendation.

The earlier (1956) **Karajan** recording presents not only the most pointed account orchestrally of Verdi's comic masterpiece (the **Philharmonia Orchestra** at its very peak) but the most vividly characterful cast ever gathered for a recording. If you relish the idea of **Tito Gobbi** as Falstaff (his many-coloured voice, not quite fat-sounding in humour, presents a sharper character than usual), then this is clearly the best choice. The rest of the cast too is a delight, with **Schwarzkopf** a tinglingly masterful Mistress Ford, **Anna Moffo** sweet as Nannetta and **Rolando Panerai** a formidable Ford. On CD the digital transfer is sharply focused.

Davis springs rhythms infectiously, bringing out the sparkle and wit in this magical score. The recording helps, with voices cleanly separated so that, though this was taken from concert performances, the sense of live drama is irresistible. **Pertusi** is brilliant in the title-role, bluff and powerful, with voice cleanly focused over the widest expressive range. **Carlos Alvarez** as Ford is nicely contrasted, his dark anger coming over powerfully in his Act II monologue, while **Ana Ibarra** as Alice Ford leads a superb team of women soloists, phenomenally precise in their chattering ensembles, with **Jane Henschel** a wonderfully fruity Mistress Quickly. **Maria José Moreno** as Nannetta and **Bülent Bezdüz** as Fenton make a winning pair of lovers. Above all, the liveness of the experience adds to the electricity, as it does in the classic Toscanini version. Like all **LSO** Live issues, this one comes at budget price, making it an astonishing bargain, with libretto and translation included in the booklet, as well as a thoughtful essay by Rodney Milnes.

Sir Geraint Evans's 1963 assumption of the role of Verdi's Falstaff in partnership with **Sir George Solti** was originally issued by RCA, and here it returns to the catalogue in Decca's Classic Opera series, in a mid-priced box (with libretto) as sparkling as ever. There is an energy, a sense of fun and vivacity that outshines most rival versions, outstanding though they may be. Evans never sounded better on record, and the rest of the cast live up to his example admirably. Solti drives hard, but it is an exciting and well-pointed performance, and the rest of the cast is well contrasted.

Bernstein's mid-1960s set, with **Fischer-Dieskau** in the title-role, is flawed by Sony's inept presentation. The *Allegros* may be consistently faster than Toscanini's, but they never sound rushed, and always Bernstein conveys a sense of fun, while in relaxed passages, helped by warm Viennese sensitivity, he allows a full rotundity of phrasing, at least as much as any rival. Fischer-Dieskau does wonders in pointing the humour. In his scene with Mistress Quickly arranging an assignation with Alice, he can inflect a simple '*Ebben?*' to make it intensely funny, but he finally suffers from having a voice one inevitably associates with baritonal solemnity. The others are first rate – **Panerai** singing superbly as Ford, **Ilva Ligabue** as Mistress Ford, **Regina Resnik** as Mistress

Quickly, and **Graziella Sciutti** and **Juan Oncina** as the young lovers. Excellent engineering (by a Decca recording team) together with effective remastering have produced a very satisfactory sound-balance. But this set is let down by its inadequate documentation.

Recorded in 1930 for Italian Columbia, the **La Scala** version of *Falstaff* in Naxos's historical series was the first ever made and is here superbly restored on CD by Ward Marston. **Giacomo Rimini**, with his firm, dark voice, not only articulates well but also conveys the humour of the fat knight, and **Pia Tassinari**, then not quite 30 years old, is a fresh, characterful Alice. **Aurora Buades** is a fruity Mrs Quickly with a formidable chest register, and the casting of the rest is also near-ideal. The first two acts are contained complete on the first disc, leaving room for a 35-minute supplement on the second, gathering together arias and ensembles with **Pia Tassinari**, mostly dating from 1941–3 when her voice was weightier but still fresh and pure. A cherishable supplement, with Tassinari's husband, **Ferruccio Tagliavini**, joining her in the concluding quartet from Act III of Puccini's *La Bohème*.

Falstaff (complete; in English)

☦ Ⓜ ******** Chan. 3079 (2). Shore, Kenny, Gritton, Holland, Banks, Kale, De Pont, Davies, Coote, ENO Ch. & O, Daniel

Paul Daniel's brilliant version of *Falstaff* is among the finest of the Opera in English series sponsored by the Peter Moores Foundation. The role of Falstaff is a speciality of **Andrew Shore**, and he delivers a vivid portrait, at once comic and weighty, but with lightness and sparkle part of the mixture, and with the Act III monologue of disillusion after his ducking ('*Your world is crumbling*' in the excellent translation of Amanda Holden) a high point. The voice grows rough in places, but Shore is unfazed by the high-lying passages, which come over well. There is no weak link in the rest of the cast, with **Yvonne Kenny** as Alice and **Susan Gritton** as Nannetta both outstanding. Yet above all, it is the taut and finely paced conducting of Paul Daniel and the playing of the orchestra, superbly recorded, which make this set musically competitive with the finest versions in Italian. As they sing in the final fugue, '*Life is a burst of laughter*'.

La forza del destino (1862 version; complete; DVD version)

☦ ******** Arthaus **DVD** 100 078. Gorchakova, Putilin, Grigorian, Tarasova, Kirov Ch. & O, Gergiev. (Producer: Elijah Moshinsky, V/D: Brian Large.)

Ⓝ ****(*)** TDK **DVD** DVWW-OPFORZA. Urmana, Guelfi, Giordani, Dal Monte, Giordani, Gertseva, Scandiuzzi, Maggio Musicale Fiorentino, Ch. & O, Mehta (Stage Director: Nicolas Joël; V/D Andrea Bevilacque)

Gegam Grigorian is an impressively confident Alvaro, and **Nikolai Putilin's** Don Carlo is every bit as good as on CD. **Tarasova's** Preziosilla does not disappoint, and **Sergei Alexashin's** Guardiano is better focused than Mikhail Kit in the 1996 CD. The opera looks very good – and sounds very good: the audio balance is first class. **Brian Large's** video direction is first class, too, and although Moshinsky's direction is busy, it is for the most part effective.

The DVD production of the 1862 version of *La forza* comes from St Petersburg, where the opera had its première. In 1862 the overture was replaced by a short prelude, but otherwise the changes concern the final scenes of Act III, where the duo between Don Alvaro and Don Carlo follows rather than precedes the encampment scene. The finale is also different: the Alvaro–Carlo duel takes place on stage and Alvaro does not survive, but takes his own life. Of particular interest is the fact that the **Kirov** reproduce the original sets, which look quite handsome, even if the staging is at times a bit hyperactive.

The performance is much stronger than in the version that the Kirov brought to Covent Garden in the summer of 2001, and **Valéry Gergiev** here proves a more idiomatic Verdi conductor than he was during the London season. The cast is strong, with **Gorchakova** in good form as Leonora, singing with great dramatic eloquence.

This Florentine *Forza del destino* is enjoyable but not really distinctive. All the soloists sing to quite a high standard (with vibratos well in evidence). **Violeta Urmana** is an impressive and often moving Leonora, and she sings her most famous aria quite memorably, and **Carlo Guelfi** as Don Carlo and **Marcello Giordani** as Don Alvaro are all generally vocally strong, but are not always individually memorable. **Bruno De Simone** as Fra Melitone and **Julia Gertseva** as Preziosilla are excellent, but the opera doesn't stand or fall by them. The chorus sings well enough, but the big scenes, though vocally impressive, are visually static. **Mehta** conducts the orchestra vividly and keeps the tension quite high. The sets are quite acceptable but the costumes are a something of a compromise between ancient and modern.

La forza del destino (1862 version; complete; CD versions)

☦ Ⓜ ******** RCA (ADD) 74321 39502-2 (3). L. Price, Domingo, Milnes, Cossotto, Giaiotti, Bacquier, Alldis Ch., LSO, Levine

Ⓜ ******* DG 477 5621 (3). Plowright, Carreras, Bruson, Burchuladze, Baltsa, Amb. Op. Ch., Philh. O, Sinopoli

Ⓜ ****** Decca (ADD) 475 8681 (3). Tebaldi, Del Monaco, Bastianini, Siepi, Simionato, Corena, Maionica, St Cecilia Ac., Rome, Ch. & O, Molinari-Pradelli

Leontyne Price recorded the role of Leonora in an earlier RCA version made in Rome in 1956, but the years hardly touched her voice. The roles of Don Alvaro and Don Carlo are ideally suited to the team of **Plácido Domingo** and **Sherrill Milnes** so that their confrontations are the cornerstones of the dramatic structure. **Fiorenza Cossotto** makes a formidable rather than a jolly Preziosilla, while on the male side the line-up of **Bonaldo Giaiotti**, **Gabriel Bacquier**, **Kurt Moll** and **Michel Sénéchal** is far stronger than on rival sets. In a vivid transfer of the mid-1970s sound, this is a strong, well-paced version with an exceptionally good and consistent cast.

Sinopoli's performance is notable for the creamy soprano of **Rosalind Plowright**, **Agnes Baltsa's** splendidly assured Preziosilla and **Paata Burchuladze's** resonant portrayal of the Padre Guardiano. Sinopoli draws out phrases lovingly, sustaining pauses to the limit, putting extra strain on the singers. Happily, the whole cast thrives on the challenge, and the spaciousness of the recording acoustic not only makes the dramatic interchanges the more realistic, it brings out the bloom on all the voices. Though **José Carreras** is sometimes too conventionally histrionic, even strained, it is a strong, involved performance. **Renato Bruson** is a thoughtful Carlo, while some of the finest singing of all comes from Agnes Baltsa as Preziosilla.

The 1955 Decca set with **Renata Tebaldi** on top form is now reissued as one of Decca's Originals, and the recording is outstanding for its time. Tebaldi, as always, makes some lovely sounds and the mezza voce in the soaring theme (first heard in the overture) in *Madre madre pietosa Vergine* is exquisite. **Mario del Monaco** never really matches this. He sings straight through his part – often with the most heroic-sounding noises – with little attention to the finer points of shading that Verdi expects. That the whole performance does not add up the sum of its parts is largely the fault of the conductor, **Molinari-Pradelli**. He can be exciting, but his control of ensemble is weak at times.

La forza del destino (slightly abridged)

☯ (ⒷⒷ) (***) Naxos 8.111322/4. Callas, Tucker, Tagliabue, Nicolai, Rossi-Lemeni, Capecchi, La Scala, Milan, Ch. & O, Serafin (with *Forza del destino* (highlights): Milanov, Peerce, Warren, Moscona, Shaw Chorale, RCA Victor O, Perlea)

☯ (***) EMI mono 5 56323-2 (3). Callas, Tucker, Tagliabue, Nicolai, Rossi-Lemeni, Capecchi, La Scala, Milan, Ch. & O, Serafin

Though there are classic examples of **Callas's** raw tone on top notes, they are insignificant next to the wealth of phrasing which sets a totally new and individual stamp on even the most familiar passages. Apart from his tendency to disturb his phrasing with sobs, **Richard Tucker** sings superbly; but not even he – and certainly none of the others (including the baritone **Carlo Tagliabue**, well past his prime) – begin to rival the dominance of Callas. **Serafin's** direction is crisp, dramatic and well paced, again drawing the threads together. The 1955 mono sound is less aggressive than many La Scala recordings of this vintage and has been freshened by EMI on CD.

However, Mark Obert-Thorn's newest transfer is splendid, beautifully smooth and clean, seemingly even fresher than the full-priced original. But what makes this Naxos set indispensable is the coupling, a generous set of highlights from a vintage set of the opera with **Zinka Milanov** on top form and a splendid supporting cast. Her glorious *Madre, pietosa Vergine* and *La Vergine degli angeli* with chorus are alone worth the cost of the set!

Un giorno di regno (complete)

☯ (ⒷⒷ) **** Ph 475 6772 (2). Cossotto, Norman, Carreras, Wixell, Sardinero, Ganzarolli, Amb. S., RPO, Gardelli

Un giorno di regno may not be the greatest comic opera of the period, but this scintillating performance under **Gardelli** clearly reveals the young Verdi as more than an imitator of Rossini and Donizetti, and there are striking passages that clearly give a foretaste of such numbers as the duet *Si vendetta* from *Rigoletto*. Despite the absurd plot, this is as light and frothy an entertainment as anyone could want. Excellent singing from a fine team, with **Jessye Norman** and **José Carreras** outstanding. The recorded sound is vivid, and the Philips reissue includes full libretto.

Giovanna d'Arco (complete)

☯ (Ⓜ) **(*) EMI (ADD) 7 63226-2 (2). Caballé, Domingo, Milnes, Amb. Ch., LSO, Levine

The seventh of Verdi's operas, based very loosely indeed on Schiller's drama, is typical of the works which the master was writing during his 'years in the galleys', exuberantly melodic. **James Levine**, a youthful whirlwind in his very first opera recording, presses on too hard in fast music, with the rum-ti-tum hammered home, but is warmly sympathetic in melodic writing, particularly when **Caballé** is singing. What had become a standard trio of principals for the 1970s here gives far more than a routine performance. With fine recording there is much to enjoy, even when the plot – involving merely Joan, her father (who betrays her) and the King – is so naive.

I Lombardi (complete)

☯ **** Decca 455 287-2 (2). Pavarotti, Anderson, Leech, Ramey, Met. Opera Ch. and O, Levine

(Ⓜ) **(*) Ph. (ADD) 475 8700 (2). Deutekom, Domingo, Raimondi, Amb. S., RPO, Gardelli

With the help of brilliant Decca recording, **Levine** consistently brings out this early work's adventurousness, its striking anticipations of *La forza del destino*. Based on the staging of the opera at the **Met.** in New York, the chief glory of the set is the casting of **Pavarotti** as the hero, Oronte. As Oronte does not appear until Act II and dies at the end of Act III (signal for the *Great Trio*, much the finest number in the opera), it is not a role one would have expected Pavarotti to take on at this stage of his career. He does it masterfully, on the whole. Unfortunately, the visionary appearance of the dead hero in Act IV (*Benedetto del cielo*) has the singer placed far too close, a very corporeal ghost. **Samuel Ramey** sings strongly in the baritone role of the evil brother, Pagano (who appears later as a Hermit). **June Anderson** as the heroine, Giselda, is both sweet and sympathetic.

I Lombardi reaches its apotheosis in the famous *Trio*, well known from 78-r.p.m. recordings. By those standards **Cristina Deutekom** is not an ideal Verdi singer: her tone is sometimes hard and her voice is not always perfectly under control. However, **Domingo** as Oronte is in superb voice, and the villain, Pagano, is well characterized by **Raimondi**. Impressive singing too from **Stafford Dean** and **Clifford Grant**. **Gardelli** conducts dramatically, heightening the impact of the plot. However, Levine's Decca set is the one to go for.

Luisa Miller (complete; DVD version)

☯ **** DG **DVD** 073 4027. Scotto, Domingo, Milnes, Morris, Giaiotti, Met. Ch. & O, Levine (Dir: Nathaniel Merrill, V/D: Roland Ott)

Recorded at the **Met.** in New York in 1979, **James Levine's** version of *Luisa Miller* consistently demonstrates his Verdian mastery, and not just in the best-known masterpieces. This production is superbly cast, with **Renata Scotto** agile, bright and characterful in the title-role, with **Plácido Domingo** singing gloriously as the enamoured Rodolfo and **Sherill Milnes** comparably fine as Luisa's father. This opera is unusual in not having the principal baritone as the villain, but here **James Morris** as Wurm and **Bonaldo Giaiotti** as Count Walter provide the necessary bite. Not only in Levine's conducting but also in the sets and costumes of Nathanial Merrill's production the attractive rustic element of the piece is effectively brought out.

Luisa Miller (complete; CD versions)

&—**(M)** *** Decca 475 8496-2 (2). Caballé, Pavarotti, Milnes, Reynolds, L. Op. Ch., Nat. PO, Maag

(B) *** DG Double (ADD) 459 481-2 (2). Ricciarelli, Obraztsova, Domingo, Bruson, Howell, ROHCG Ch. & O, Maazel

On Decca, **Caballé**, though not flawless vocally, gives a splendidly dramatic portrait of the heroine, and **Pavarotti's** performance is full of creative, detailed imagination. As Federica, **Anna Reynolds** underlines the light and shade, consistently bringing out atmospheric qualities. Vividly transferred to CD. This is now reissued at mid-price, neatly repackaged in Decca's Compact Opera Collection, with a cued synopsis and the libretto obtainable via a CD-ROM, which is provided with the set.

Maazel's 1979 Covent Garden set returns to the catalogue as a DG Double and would have been very competitive indeed had it included a full libretto and translation instead of just a synopsis. Though taut in his control, Maazel uses his stage experience of working with these soloists to draw them out to their finest, most sympathetic form. **Ricciarelli** gives one of her tenderest and most beautiful performances on record, **Domingo** is in glorious voice, and **Bruson** as Luisa's father sings with a velvet tone. **Gwynne Howell** is impressive as the Conte di Walter, and **Wladimiro Ganzarolli's** vocal roughness is apt for the character of Wurm. The snag is the abrasive Countess Federica of **Elena Obraztsova**.

Macbeth (1847 version; complete)

&— **** Opera Rara ORCV 301 (2). Glossop, Hunter, Tomlinson, Collins, BBC Singers & Concert O, Matheson

What till now have been seriously neglected on disc have been Verdi's first thoughts, the versions of operas which he went on to revise, none more radically than his first Shakespearean venture, *Macbeth*. This fascinating recording of the original version will be a revelation to most Verdians. Taken from a BBC studio broadcast of 1979, masterminded by the Verdi scholar Julian Budden, it demonstrates very clearly how many of the most strikingly original passages were already there in Verdi's first version. Lady Macbeth's great sleepwalking scene of Act IV, one of the most memorable passages of all, is already fully developed. Yet the revisions, involving almost a third of the score, are radical, the more strikingly so as the opera progresses. So in Act II, instead of the dramatic aria, *La luce langue*, Lady Macbeth

sings a more conventional display piece which, like her Brindisi later in the act, involves a jolly oompah rhythm, while in Act III, the scene of Macbeth's hallucinations is quite different. Act IV is what Verdi changed most. Here it opens with a bold chorus involving a big tune sung in unison on the lines of *Va pensiero*, the chorus of Hebrew Slaves from *Nabucco*. Like almost all of Verdi's other first thoughts, it is not as refined musically as the magnificent chorus of lamentation with which it was replaced in 1865, but stylistically it is more consistent with the rest of the opera. The final scene too is quite different in this first version. A sequence of fanfares instead of a fugato represents the battle, with the whole opera ending on a death scene for Macbeth instead of a victory chorus.

This set is the more cherishable when the performance, incisively conducted by **John Matheson**, is so strongly cast. In this version the central roles of Macbeth and Lady Macbeth are vocally even more demanding than in Verdi's revision, and the baritone, **Peter Glossop**, here gives a searingly powerful performance as Macbeth. **Rita Hunter** is equally commanding as Lady Macbeth, as for her massive soprano, Wagnerian in scale, is surprisingly flexible in coloratura, with a perfectly controlled trill. The young **John Tomlinson** is magnificent as Banquo, and the tenor **Kenneth Collins** makes a fine Macduff.

Macbeth (complete; DVD versions)

*** TDK **DVD** DVWW-OPMACPA. Nucci, Valayre, Iori, Iuliano, Pascoli, Parma Teatro Regio Ch. & O, Bartoletti (Dir: Liliana Cavani, V/D: Andrea Amodio)

(N) *** EMI **DVD** 206304-9 (2). Luči , Guleghina, Relyea, Renault, Pittas, Met. Ch. Ballet & Opera O, Levine (Director: Gary Halvorsen)

*** Opus Arte **DVD** OA 0922 D (2). Alvarez, Guleghina, Scandiuzzu, Berti, Liceu Ch. & O, Campanella (Dir: Phyllida Lloyd, V/D: Toni Bargallo)

(*) Arthaus **DVD 100 140. Bruson, Zampieri, Morris, O'Neill, Deutsche Op. Ch. & O, Sinopoli. (Dir: Luca Ronconi.)

(*) Arthaus **DVD 101 895. Paskalis, Barstow, Morris, Erwin, Glyndebourne Ch., LPO, Pritchard (V/D: Dave Heather)

This 2006 live **Parma** production goes to the top of the list because **Leo Nucci's** unforgettably powerful portrayal of Macbeth is a tower of strength. **Sylvie Valayre** as Lady Macbeth, if not Callas, is physically attractive and resourcefully seductive in dominating her husband in their joint Machiavellian plotting. Her voice has a certain amount of intrusive vibrato but is strong and clear, and her acting is vivid yet not overtly melodramatic. Her sleepwalking scene (seemingly filmed separately) is most tellingly done and very well sung. **Roberto Iuliano** is an excellent Macduff. The rest of the cast gives good support, especially the Chorus, who sing superbly throughout, with **Bartoletti** preventing the closing sequence (with both principal characters dead) from being an anticlimax. The production is acceptable, although having the audience visible on either side of the stage is disconcerting. Moreover, the witches' scenes are extraordinarily conceived, with the witches apparently doing their laundry, so that when Macbeth arrives he has to push his way through the washing on the line outside! However, even with these distractions, this is all very compelling, especially the banquet scene in Act II, when Macbeth loses his reason; here both the two principal characters are at their finest.

The Met Production is characteristically lavish, with a big chorus, singing really splendidly, and a whole bevy of witches, malignant enough, but dressed in simple peasant costumes, which do not set any positive period for the narrative. The sets are realistic, with generally dark lighting to amplify the generally sinister atmosphere, and there's plenty of blood about! Željco Lučić as a murderous Macbeth, singing strongly, is determined enough, but Maria Guleghina is even more so; she is a powerful Lady Macbeth, with a big voice, but a wide vibrato under pressure. She does the sleepwalking scene impressively. The rest of the male cast make a good team. As for the effects: the appearance of Macbeth's vision in a kind of bubble is not very convincing and frankly, the Birnam Wood advance of the British troops is poorly handled. Moreover, they are carrying modern weapons, which doesn't fit in with the production as a whole. Levine conducts dramatically and the production gains from its spectacle, and with a powerfully sung close, many will feel that this should be a primary choice.

Extravagantly spread over two DVDs, the production from the Liceu in Barcelona offers a striking version, set on a bare stage with stylized geometric squares taking the place of scenery. It works surprisingly well, with the opening chorus of witches – a large contingent – singing powerfully, dressed in black with vermilion turbans. Otherwise costumes are relatively conventional. The drama of the piece is intensified by the sharp attack and crisp ensemble secured by the conductor, Bruno Campanella, though the dryness of the Liceu acoustic is no help for the atmospheric moments. Even more than Carlos Alvarez as a fine Macbeth, Maria Guleghina dominates the performance as Lady Macbeth, singing with a generous vibrato, well controlled, and staring hypnotically with wide, madly obsessed eyes. She rises well to the challenge of her sleepwalking scene, even if her final top note develops into a scream. Roberto Scandiuzzi is first rate as Banquo, but Marco Berti makes a coarse if confident Macduff.

In his second recording, on DVD, made at the Deutsche Oper in Berlin in 1987, Giuseppe Sinopoli conducts a dramatic reading of Macbeth, dominated by the fine Macbeth of Renato Bruson, his self-searching the more compelling in close-up on DVD, and the powerful, if sometimes hooty, Lady Macbeth of Mara Zampieri, perfectly looking the part, young and handsome still. She points the drinking-song well, and although she avoids the final top note of the sleep walking scene, it is still a magnetic performance. The rest of the cast is strong too, with Dennis O'Neill as Macduff and James Morris as Banquo. The chorus sings splendidly, with a line-up of dozens of witches in the opening scene, gathered behind the long table that dominates a fair proportion of scenes in Luca Ronconi's bare production, with sets and costumes by Luciano Damiani. Excellent, well-separated sound.

It was at Glyndebourne in the 1930s that Verdi's Macbeth was first produced in Britain, and the 1972 television recording demonstrates what power the piece has when presented in an intimate setting. Dominating the performance is the young Josephine Barstow as Lady Macbeth, singing powerfully and acting with venom and malice mixed with humour. Hers is hardly a beautiful voice as recorded, but the bite and edge add greatly to the impact. As Macbeth, Paskalis sings powerfully too, presenting in Michael Hadjimischev's production a worryingly equivocal character. The young James Morris as Banquo focuses his voice cleanly and incisively, and Keith Erwin as Macduff provides a refreshing contrast. Strong choral work and atmospheric sets by Emanuele Luzzati.

Macbeth (complete; CD versions)

Ⓜ *** Ph 475 8393 (3). Bruson, Zampieri, Shicoff, Lloyd, Deutsche Oper, Berlin, Ch. & O, Sinopoli

⊶ Ⓜ *** DG (ADD) 449 732-2 (2). Cappuccilli, Verrett, Ghiaurov, Domingo, La Scala, Milan, Ch. & O, Abbado

Ⓜ (*(**)) EMI mono 5 66447-2 (2). Callas, Mascherini, Tajo, Penno, Della Pergola, La Scala, Milan, Ch. & O, de Sabata

Even more than his finest rivals, Sinopoli presents this opera as a searing Shakespearean inspiration, scarcely more uneven than much of the work of the Bard himself. In the Banqueting Scene, for example, Sinopoli creates extra dramatic intensity by his concern for detail and his preference for extreme dynamics, and Renato Bruson and Mara Zampieri respond vividly. Zampieri's voice may be biting rather than beautiful, occasionally threatening to come off the rails; but, with musical precision an asset, she matches exactly Verdi's request for the voice of a she-devil. Neil Shicoff as Macduff and Robert Lloyd as Banquo make up the excellent quartet of principals, while the high voltage of the whole performance clearly reflects Sinopoli's experience with the same chorus and orchestra at the Deutsche Oper in Berlin. The recording is vivid, well balanced and focused, but atmospheric.

At times Abbado's tempi are unconventional, but with slow speeds he springs the rhythm so infectiously that the results are most compelling. Together making a fine team, each of the principals is meticulous about observing Verdi's detailed markings, above all those for pianissimo and sotto voce. Verrett, powerful above the stave, makes a virtue out of necessity in floating glorious half-tones, and with so firm and characterful a voice she makes a highly individual Lady Macbeth. Cappuccilli has never sung with a finer range of tone or more imagination on record than here, and Plácido Domingo makes a real, sensitive character out of the small role of Macduff. Excellent recording, splendidly remastered and now at mid-price on two discs.

The role of Lady Macbeth could hardly have been more perfectly suited to Maria Callas, and though there are serious flaws in this live recording of 1952 – evidently taken off a radio relay – the commanding presence, the magnetic musical imagination and the abrasive tones make this a unique experience. In 1952 the vocal flaws that beset Callas were largely in the future, and there is a thrilling sound in every register. Also Victor de Sabata, despite some odd misjudgements like his brisk tempo for the sleepwalking scene, is comparably incisive. Sadly, nothing else in the performance matches such mastery, with **Enzo Mascherini** a dull, uncharacterful Macbeth and only the resonant **Italo Tajo** as Banquo otherwise commanding attention. Scrubby, limited sound, which most ears will still accommodate for the sake of such a performance.

I Masnadieri (complete; CD version)

(M) *** Ph. (ADD) 475 8703 (2). Caballé, Bergonzi, Raimondi, Cappuccilli, Amb. S., New Philh. O, Gardelli

Few will seriously identify with the hero-turned-brigand of *I Masnadieri*, who stabs his beloved rather than lead her into a life of shame; but on record, flaws of motivation are of far less moment than on stage. The melodies may only fitfully be of Verdi's more memorable quality, but the musical structure and argument often look forward to a much later period, with hints of *Forza*, *Don Carlo*, and even *Otello*. With **Gardelli** as ever an urgently sympathetic Verdian, and a team of four excellent principals, splendidly recorded, this set can be warmly welcomed back to the catalogue.

Nabucco (complete; DVD versions)

⊙ **** NVC Arts **DVD** 0630 19390-2. Bruson, Dimitrova, D'Artegna, Petkov, Baglioni, Garaventa, Ch. & O of Verona Arena, Maurizio Arena (Producer: Renzo Giacchieri, V/D: Brian Large)

*** Decca **DVD** 074 3245. Nucci, Colombara, Guleghina, Sartori, Surguladze, Striulli, Verona Arena Ch. & O, Oren (Dir: Denis Krief, V/D: Tiziano Mancini)

*** EuroArts **DVD** 2056228. Morosow, Yang, Morigi, Ribeiro, Kulman, Monarcha, Arad State Philharmonic Ch., Europa SO, Märzendorfer (Dir: Robert Herzi, V/D: Rudi Dolezal & Hannes Rossacher)

*** TDK **DVD** DVWW OPNAB. Nucci, Dvorský, Prestia, Guleghina, Domashenko, V. Op. Ch. & O, Luisi (Dir: Gunter Kraker, V/D: Anton Reitzenstein)

In some ways Verdi's *Nabucco*, dealing as it does with the conflict between a pagan religion and Christianity, is half-opera, half histrionic-oratorio, and **Renzo Giacchieri's** somewhat stylized production – the clashes between the rival groups of soldiers are symbolic rather than realistic – against a comparatively primitive rocky set is highly effective, with the costumes providing plenty of colour. Yet the two 'miracles', when Nabucco is struck down by a thunderbolt and, later, the destruction of the statue of Baal, are simply and effectively managed. The opera is cast from strength, with **Renato Bruson's** Nabucco dominating the action powerfully and the High Priest (**Ellero D'Artegna**) singing nobly. Dimitrova is hardly less commanding as Abigaille; her big Act II aria and her scene with Nabucco in Act III are equally memorable. But, above all, *Nabucco* grips its audience with its big choruses, and they are splendidly sung here. The orchestra too plays vibrantly under the appropriately named **Maurizio Arena**, and altogether this is visually and vocally first class.

Leo Nucci has already given us outstanding portrayals of Macbeth and Rigoletto, and now in a 2007 Verona production he is equally commanding as an unforgettable Nabucco. **Maria Guleghina** does not quite match him, but she is vocally strong as Abigaille, if not without an intrusive vibrato. Nevertheless, she sings her closing aria, as she dies, very movingly. **Fabio Sartori**, an ardent Ismaele, and the very attractive Fenena of **Nino Surguladze**, curiously modern-looking and not a strong acting personality, make a personable pair of lovers and **Carlo Colombara** is a fine Zaccaria. So the performance overall works well, even though it is hampered by a set which consists mainly of scaffolding which, though presumably representing the Hebrews' prison, is visually unappealing. However, the special effects work well enough, and the whole performance is well held together by **Daniel Oren** and the magnificent singing of the **Verona Chorus**.

The emphasis of the EuroArts version is the sheer spectacle of this 2007 production from the St Margareten Opera Festival. It really goes over the top, with Nabucco making his entry on a huge siege machine, belching fire from the gold dragon-mouth at its summit. Everywhere else there are plenty of flames and light, and (incongruously) searchlights occasionally light up the background. However, **Igor Morosow**, if not as individual as Nucci in the name-role, makes a strong characterization of Nabucco. **Gabriella Morigi** is a properly histrionic Abigaille, though her voice is not always perfectly focused and at times her vibrato is intrusive. But apart from Nabucco, the performance is dominated by **Simon Yang's** splendid, memorable portrayal of Zaccaria, his rich voice and resonant bass notes a vocal joy. **Elisabeth Kulman** is a very self-possessed Fenena, and her lover, **Bruno Ribeiro**, is a very believable and youthfully impetuous Ismaele. Once again, it is the superb singing of the chorus which is the most thrilling part of the opera, with the performance excellently directed by Ernst Märzendorfer.

Recorded at the Vienna State Opera in 2001, the TDK disc offers a spectacular production, which makes full use of the very large stage. At the opening, the enormous chorus instantly establishes the dominance of choral music in this work, not just the ever-popular *Chorus of Hebrew Slaves* but in key numbers throughout the piece. This biblical story is updated to the 1940s, bringing out the parallels with the plight of the Jewish people in Europe at that time. The costumes are drab and dark, with the men in trilbies or bowler hats, with Abigaille providing a contrast in her elaborate costumes, reflecting her association with Nabucco and the Babylonian court. **Maria Guleghina** sings compellingly; but it is the two bass roles that provide the key to any performance and, though **Giacomo Prestia** is not always ideally steady, his is a powerful performance, a good match for the strong Nabucco of **Leo Nucci**. **Marina Domashenko** as Fenena and **Miroslav Dvorský** as Ismaele are well cast, too; but it is the chorus that dominates, with **Fabio Luisi** securing splendid ensemble. Sadly, there is no synopsis of the plot, but instead a good essay about the background to this first of Verdi's big successes.

Nabucco (complete; CD versions)

⊙ **** DG 413 321-2 (2). Cappuccilli, Dimitrova, Nesterenko, Domingo, Ch. & O of German Op., Berlin, Sinopoli

⊙ **** Decca (ADD) 417 407-2 (2). Gobbi, Souliotis, Cava, Previdi, V. State Op. Ch. & O, Gardelli

With **Sinopoli** one keeps hearing details normally obscured. Even the thrill of the great chorus *Va, pensiero* is the greater when the melody first emerges at a hushed *pianissimo*, as marked. **Dimitrova** is superb in Abigaille's big Act II aria, noble in her evil, as is **Cappuccilli** as Nabucco, less intense than Gobbi was on Gardelli's classic set for Decca, but stylistically pure. The rest of the cast is strong too, including **Domingo** in the unusually small tenor role and **Nesterenko** superb as the High Priest, Zaccaria. Bright and forward digital sound, less atmospheric than the 1965 Decca set with Gobbi and Souliotis, conducted by Gardelli.

On Decca, the Viennese chorus lacks bite in *Va, pensiero*; but in every other way this is a masterly performance, with dramatically intense and deeply imaginative contributions from **Tito Gobbi** as Nabucco and **Elena Souliotis** as the evil Abigaille. Souliotis made this the one totally satisfying performance of an all-too-brief recording career, wild in places but no more than is dramatically necessary. Though **Carlo Cava** as Zaccaria is not ideally rich of tone, it is a strong performance, and **Gardelli**, as in his later Verdi recordings for both Decca and Philips, showed what a Verdian master he is, whether in pointing individual phrases or whole scenes, simply and naturally. Vivid and atmospheric 1965 Decca recording.

Nabucco (highlights)

Ⓜ *** Decca (ADD) 458 246-2 (from above recording, with Souliotis, Gobbi; cond. Gardelli)

Ⓑ ** CfP (ADD) 393374-2 (from complete recording, with Manuguerra, Scotto, Luchetti, Obraztsova, Ghiaurov, Amb. Op. Ch., Philh. O, Muti)

Souliotis's impressive contribution is well represented on the Decca highlights disc, and there are fine contributions too from **Gobbi**. Needless to say the chorus *Va, pensiero* is given its place of honour and the reissued selection now runs for 69 minutes. As in other Opera Gala reissues, a full translation is now included.

Muti's 1978 set has a cast as impressive as could be assembled at the time, with **Matteo Manuguerra** an imaginative choice as Nabucco. He proves strong and reliable but lacks something in flair, and overall the singing fails to equal the three-dimensional characterizations of its competitors. **Renata Scotto** sings well but is not entirely inside her role. The complete set is still available (EMI 7 47488-8) but the above 65 minutes of bargain highlights would seem a better investment for those interested in the cast.

Nabucco (complete; sung in English)

⟿ Ⓜ *** Chan. 3136 (2). Opie, Capalho, Miles, Patterson, Irwin, Op. N. Ch. & O, Parry

Based on the staged production of **Opera North**, the version of *Nabucco* in English is one of the best in the long series promoted by Sir Peter Moores. **Alan Opie** is at his finest in the title-role, commanding and characterful, well contrasted with **Alastair Miles** as Zachariah, the High priest. Other principals are first rate, even if **Jane Irwin** as Fenena, the king's daughter, is less weighty than most mezzos in that role. The chorus – so important in this work – are outstanding, with

David Parry drawing crisp, incisive performances from singers and orchestra, while the Chandos sound is weighty and well balanced.

Otello (complete; DVD versions)

**** Opus Arte **DVD** OAR3102D. Domingo, Te Kanawa, Leiferkus, ROHCG Ch. & O, Solti (Dir: Elijah Moshinsky, VD: Brian Large)

⟿ **** DG **DVD** 0734040. Vickers, Freni, Glossop, Malagu, Bottion, Deutsche Oper Ch., BPO, Karajan (Dir: Karajan, V/D: Georges Wakhevitch)

**** NVC Arts **DVD** 4509 99214-2. Te Kanawa, Atlantov, Cappuccilli, Bevacqua, Schiavon, Rafanelli, Ch. & O of Verona Arena, Peskó (Producer: Gianfranco de Bosio; V/D: Preben Montell)

⟿ **** DG **DVD** 073 092-9. Domingo, Fleming, Morris, Bunnell, Croft, Anthony, Metropolitan Ch. & O, Levine (Producer: Louisa Briccetti, V/D: Brian Large)

*** TDK **DVD** DV-OPOTEL. Domingo, Frittoli, Nucci, Catani, Ceron, La Scala, Milan, Children's Ch., Ch. & O, Muti (V/D: Carlo Battistoni)

Filmed in 1992, Moshinsky's traditional **Covent Garden** production with lavish costumes and sets makes an ideal DVD with an almost unmatchable cast of principals. **Plácido Domingo** was at his peak as Otello, powerful and heroic, while **Dame Kiri Te Kanawa** as Desdemona sings ravishingly, fining her tone down to a mere whisper at times. **Sergei Leiferkus** too was at his finest as Iago, and **Sir Georg Solti** conducts his Covent Garden forces with characteristic high drama. Well recorded, it is an outstanding DVD.

Filmed in Munich and Salzburg in 1972/3, **Karajan's** disc offers a vivid production, taken from the Salzburg Festival and superbly cast. **Jon Vickers** sings gloriously in the title-role, a heroic tenor who sings cleanly and accurately and with great passion, totally unstrained. Though **Mirella Freni's** soprano might seem a little lightweight for Desdemona, it is sweetly beautiful, a totally charming portrayal of the wronged heroine, with **Peter Glossop** at his peak as the most sinister Iago, again totally unstrained. The coordination that Karajan obtains from his fine team, not just soloists but chorus and orchestra too, is a model for any rival, with **Wakhevitch** adding to the impact in the visual element, often set in the open air with a spectacular stormy seascape at the start (where the singers mime their parts) and architectural sets. The film was made in conjunction with an audio recording, and the only slight snag is that there is a minor cut in the big central ensemble of Act III.

The Verona producer **Gianfranco de Bosio** and designer Vittorio Rossi have chosen a very plain set, yet they used the full resources of Verona for the one big scene at the end of Act III, which is magnificently staged. **Vladimir Atlantov** is a very real, believable Otello, often grim-faced yet obviously melted in Act I by Desdemona's love. **Kiri Te Kanawa** is at her glorious best as Desdemona, ravishingly clear-voiced and true, and her final Willow Song is infinitely touching before the opera's terrible close. **Piero Cappuccilli** is an obsequiously wily Iago. As we discover in his Creed, his voice is less strong than Atlanov's powerful Otello, but his false-friendly *Era la notte* is superbly characterized, and in the big duet with Otello at the end of Act II the two voices are naturally blended. In short there are no flaws here, and the video direction centres on the principal characters very vividly, while **Zoltan Peskó** keeps the tension at a high level. Another Verona triumph, which is very compelling.

It is good to have so telling a reminder on DVD of **Plácido Domingo's** masterly assumption of the role of Otello: commanding in every way, particularly when at the **Met.** in New York in 1996 he was singing opposite **Renée Fleming** as Desdemona, then at her freshest and purest, yet also with power, looking and sounding girlish. **James Levine's** direction is high-powered from beginning to end, matching the singing of his principals, controlling the massive forces provided in this lavish production directed by Elijah Moshinsky with sets by Michael Yeargan and costumes by Peter J. Hall. Though **James Morris** is not the most sinister of Iagos, his singing is clean and firm, well varied in the two big monologues of Act II. Excellent singing too from **Jane Bunnell** as a very positive Emilia and **Richard Croft** as Cassio, a tenor well contrasted with Domingo. The only bonuses on DVD are a picture gallery and trailer.

Imaginatively overseen by Graham Vick, who never seems to let his personal conception override Verdi's intentions, and with an imaginative set and traditional costumes, this *La Scala Otello* is very recommendable, with **Domingo** and **Frittoli** always singing and acting movingly, to create a real-life situation of passion and tenderness ruined by unthinking jealousy. By their side, **Leo Nucci's** Iago is disappointingly low-key, and **Cesare Catani's** Cassio is not memorable either. But **Muti** directs with his usual brio and the video presentation is admirable. Even with the disappointing Iago, this still projects Verdi's great opera very powerfully, for the sound is first class.

Otello (complete; CD versions)

⬥—**** DG 439 805-2 (2). Domingo, Studer, Leiferkus, Ch. & O of Bastille Opera, Chung

⬥—Ⓜ**** RCA (ADD) 74321 39501-2 (2). Domingo, Scotto, Milnes, Amb. Op. Ch., Nat. PO, Levine

*** Decca 433 669-2 (2). Pavarotti, Te Kanawa, Nucci, Rolfe Johnson, Chicago SO & Ch., Solti

Ⓜ*** EMI 7 69308-2 (2). Vickers, Freni, Glossop, Ch. of German Op., Berlin, BPO, Karajan

Ⓑ**(*) HM Music & Arts CD 1043 (2). Domingo, Freni, Cappuccilli, Ciannella, Raffanti, La Scala, Milan, Ch. & O, C. Kleiber

✿ Ⓜ*** EMI 3 58670 (2). Domingo, Ricciarelli, Diaz, Zaharia, La Scala, Milan, Ch. & O, Maazel

Ⓜ**(*) Decca 411 618-2 (2). Del Monaco, Tebaldi, Protti, V. State Ch., VPO, Karajan

On CD, **Plácido Domingo's** third recording of *Otello* proves to be more freely expressive, even more involved than his previous ones; the baritonal quality of his tenor has here developed to bring extra darkness, with the final solo, *Niun mi tema*, poignantly tender. **Cheryl Studer** gives one of her finest performances as Desdemona, the tone both full and pure,

while **Sergei Leiferkus** makes a chillingly evil Iago, the more so when his voice is the opposite of Italianate, verging on the gritty, which not everyone will like. With plenty of light and shade, **Myung-Whun Chung** is an urgent Verdian, adopting free-flowing speeds yet allowing Domingo full expansiveness in the death scene. The **Chorus and Orchestra of the Bastille Opera** excel themselves, setting new standards for an opera recording from Paris, and the sound is first rate.

On RCA, **Domingo** as Otello combines glorious heroic tone with lyrical tenderness. **Scotto** is not always sweettoned in the upper register, and the big ensemble at the end of Act III brings obvious strain; nevertheless, it is a deeply felt performance which culminates in a most affecting account of the all-important Act IV solos, the *Willow Song* and *Ave Maria*. **Milnes** makes a powerful Iago, a handsome, virile creature beset by the biggest of chips on the shoulder. In the transfer of the 1977 analogue original the voices are caught vividly and immediately, and the orchestral sound too is fuller and cleaner than in many more recent versions.

In the Decca Chicago set the key element is the singing of **Pavarotti**, new to his role of Otello, as was **Nucci** as Iago. In obedience to **Solti**, Pavarotti often adopts faster speeds than usual. Whatever the detailed reservations, this is a memorable reading, heightened by Pavarotti's keen feeling for the words and consistently golden tone. With a close microphone-balance, like the others he is prevented from achieving genuine *pianissimos*; but above all he offers a vital, animated Otello, always individual. **Dame Kiri Te Kanawa** produces consistently sumptuous tone; the *Willow Song* is glorious. The impact of the whole is greatly enhanced by the splendid singing of the **Chicago Symphony Chorus**, helped by digital sound that is fuller and more vivid than on any rival set.

On EMI, **Karajan** directs a big, bold and brilliant account, for the most part splendidly sung and with all the dramatic contrasts strongly underlined. There are several tiny, but irritating, statutory cuts, but otherwise on two midprice CDs this is well worth considering. **Freni's** Desdemona is delightful, delicate and beautiful, while **Vickers** and **Glossop** are both positive and characterful, only occasionally forcing their tone and losing focus. The recording is clarified on CD.

Carlos Kleiber demonstrates the high voltage electricity he can produce on a big occasion, here matching the searing intensity of Toscanini in this work. **Plácido Domingo**, having just completed a series of performances in Hamburg and Paris, is in superb form, with the voice at its finest, and his personal magnetism as an actor is heightened by the conductor's challenge. **Mirella Freni** as Desdemona is at her freshest, sweet and vulnerable, while **Cappuccilli** sings with keen incisiveness as Iago, not always sinister-sounding but musically superb. Stage noises are endlessly intrusive, but the atmosphere of a great occasion is vividly caught.

Maazel's 1986 version, used as a soundtrack for the Zeffirelli film but with the text uncut (unlike that of the film), brings another fine performance from **Domingo** and generally taut, subtle control from Maazel, particularly good in the spacious, tenderly emotional treatment of the final scene but with a disappointingly negative, un-sinister

Iago in **Justino Diaz**, the result often loses in dramatic bite, and Maazel's direction occasionally sags, as in the closing pages of Act II at the end of the oath duet. **Ricciarelli**, though not an ideal Desdemona, sings most affectingly, with *pianissimos* beautifully caught in the *Willow Song* and *Ave Maria*. One snag is the sound, which is curiously recessed, with the voices often not quite in focus and with little sense of presence.

Karajan's 1961 version, flawed in its casting, yet brings remarkably fine sound to match any version since – a tribute to the artistry of the producer, John Culshaw, and the skill of his team of Decca engineers. Its main flaw is the casting of **Aldo Protti** whose Iago is undercharacterized. He is always reliable but never imaginative or even sinister – a very obvious drawback in an opera whose plot hinges on Iago's machinations. **Mario Del Monaco** is hardly a subtle Otello, but his voice is gloriously heroic, and this is one of his finest collaborations with **Renata Tebaldi** on disc. There is much to enjoy in the conducting of Karajan – even more so on this latest release, as it now includes the tuneful ballet music for the first time.

Otello (complete; in English)

(M) ****(*)** Chan. 3068 (2). Craig, Plowright, Howlett, Bottone, ENO Ch. & O, Elder

The **ENO** version of *Otello* is flawed both vocally and in the sound with the level of stage noise, the thud and ramble of wandering feet all the more noticeable on CD. The performance itself is most enjoyable, with dramatic tension building up compellingly. **Charles Craig's** Otello is most moving, the character's inner pain brought out vividly, though top notes are fallible. **Neil Howlett** as Iago may not have the most distinctive baritone, but finely controlled vocal colouring adds to a deeply perceptive performance. **Rosalind Plowright** makes a superb Desdemona, singing with rich, dramatic weight but also with poise and purity. The death scene reveals her at her finest, radiant of tone, with flawless attack.

Rigoletto (complete; DVD versions)

⊕─ ******** Decca **DVD** 074 3220. Wixell, Pavarotti, Furlanetto, V. State Op. Konzertvereinigung, VPO, Chailly

⊕─ ******** TDK **DVD** DV-OPRIGM. Nucci, Mula, Machado, Luperi, Ch., O & Corps de Ballet of Verona Arena, Viotti (Dir: Charles Roubaud, V/D: Pierre Cavassilas & Resina Stefanini)

*** Arthaus **DVD** 101 285. Nucci, Mosuc, Beczala, Polgár, Zürich Op. Ch. & O, Santi

(*) TDK **DVD DVWW-OPRIGL. C. Alvarez, Mula, M. Álvarez, Konstaninov, O & Ch. Gran Teatre del Liceu, López-Cobos (Dir: Graham Vick, V/D: Xavi Bové)

(*) BBC Opus Arte **DVD OA 0829D. Gavanelli, Schäfer, Alvarez, Halfvarson, ROHCG Ch. & O, Downes (Director: David McVicar)

Chailly's *Rigoletto* was filmed on location in Italy in 1982 with the cast miming to a recording made in Vienna the year before. It is truly memorable, with **Pavarotti** a Bacchus-like figure in the orgy scene of Act I, which is both spectacular and very dramatic. He acts the part of the Count as believably as if the latter's philosophy was his very own, and he sings gloriously throughout. But **Ingvar Wixell's** magnificently powerful Rigoletto still dominates the narrative, while **Edita Gruberová** is in exquisitely fresh voice as a vulnerable Gilda. The production is traditional in the best sense; costumes are colourful, sets believable. The abduction of Gilda is especially well managed and the closing scene, with Wixell at his most moving, is very telling indeed. Chailly keeps the action flowing splendidly and the recording is vivid and spacious. A clear first choice.

Verona productions seldom disappoint, and this 2001 traditional *Rigoletto* is in every way outstanding. As it so happens, the Gilda, **Inva Mula** acts splendidly in both this and the other TDK version, but in Verona she is three years younger, her voice at its lovely peak. Moreover, she has the superb **Leo Nucci** as Rigoletto, and his is a great performance, gathering strength and power as the opera proceeds. Their closing duet in Act II, *Sì vendetta, tremenda vendetta*, makes the hair stand on end in its passion, and rightly brings the house down. **Aquiles Machado** isn't a very romantic figure as the Duke, but he sings ardently, even getting an encore for his stylish *La donna è mobile*. But the other star of the occasion is the conductor **Marcello Viotti**, who creates consistent tension, especially at that riveting end of the second Act and at the close of the opera; his orchestra is recorded with great vividness, surging out at climaxes. The Verona stage is huge, of course, and lends itself to the spectacle of the first Act, ballet included, and the choral scenes are excellent. But it is the interchanges between the principal characters that matter, and Nucci dominates the opera, and the camera often dwells on his face in close-up, revealing the agony of his despair.

Nucci's characterization of Rigoletto is justly famous (as we know from the Verona version above) both for his vividly memorable acting and for his singing. He could well treasure his daughter in **Elena Mosuc's** portrayal of her as a simple soul with the sweetest way of remembering her lover in *Caro nome*. **Piotr Beczala's** Duke is splendidly ardent and self-centred, to complete a strong trio of principals. The stage director rightly chooses an authentic period setting, but the costumes are of a later period; never mind, he maintains a period flavour and there are no directorial excrescences. Excellent, vivid conducting from **Nello Santi**, but it is Rigoletto's haunted, staring eyes one remembers most.

Graham Vick's competing TDK production has an ingeniously designed revolve at the centre of the set, around which the Duke's past female conquests are paraded in tableau at the opening, and which later makes for quick, dramatically effective scene-changes. The performance is strongly conducted by **Jesus López-Cobos**, and **Inva Mula** again makes a memorable and moving Gilda, with her voice still appealing and her acting poignantly dramatic. **Carlos Alvarez**, too, is a powerful and dominating Rigoletto, although his vibrato may not please all ears. The one flaw in the production is at the close, when Rigoletto props up the dying Gilda on the bare stage, and on to a (comparatively) modern armchair.

David McVicar's Covent Garden production of *Rigoletto*

was one of the offerings leading towards the Verdi centenary in January 2001, strongly cast with **Paolo Gavanelli** firm and powerful in the title-role. McVicar points out that the opera dates from the period of Marx and the Communist Manifesto, though the menace in the production has as much to do with sado-masochistic violence as with politics, helped by Tanya McCallin's costumes (with a leather clown costume making Rigoletto into a gnome-like figure and the Duke's leather outfit when he meets Gilda underlining his role as predator). The setting is rough too in what looks like an old junk-yard with much wire-netting and corrugated-iron sheets. However, this twentieth-century touch hardly gets in the way of the drama, with the costumes broadly traditional in period.

The casting is first rate, with Gavanelli well matched by the girlish Gilda of **Christine Schäfer** (not previously known as a coloratura but admirably flexible) and the menacingly seductive Duke of **Marcelo Alvarez**. **Edward Downes** as ever is a masterly Verdi interpreter, pacing the drama strongly and purposefully. The extra features include a BBC documentary celebrating the Verdi centenary, with atmospheric shots of Busseto, doing for Verdi what Salzburg has done for Mozart.

Rigoletto (complete; CD versions)

☞ (B) **** Ph. Duo 462 158-2 (2). Bruson, Gruberová, Shicoff, Fassbaender, Lloyd, St Cecilia Ac., Rome, Ch. & O, Sinopoli

☞ *** Decca (ADD) 414 269-2 (2). Milnes, Sutherland, Pavarotti, Talvela, Tourangeau, Amb. Op. Ch., LSO, Bonynge

☞ **** DG 447 064-2 (2). Chernov, Pavarotti, Studer, Scandiuzzi, Graves, Met. Op. Ch. & O, Levine

☞ (BB) **** Naxos mono 8.111242/3 (2). Callas, Gobbi, Di Stefano, Lazzarini, Zaccaria, La Scala, Milan, Ch. & O, Serafin

☞ **** EMI mono 5 56327-2 (2). Gobbi, Callas, di Stefano, La Scala, Milan, Ch. & O, Serafin

(BB) (***) Regis mono RRC 2076 (2). Gobbi, Callas, di Stefano, La Scala, Milan, Ch. & O, Serafin (with *Forza del destino: Madre, pietosa Vergine* and *Pace, pace, mio Dio* – 1954 recording)

(M) *** RCA SACD (ADD) 82876 82623-2 (2). Merrill, Moffo, Kraus, Flagello, Elias, RCA Italiana Op. Ch. & O, Solti

(N) (BB) (**) Naxos mono 8-111276/7 Merrill, Bjoerling, Peters, Tozzi, Rome Opera Ch. & O, Perlea

Edita Gruberová might have been considered an unexpected choice for Gilda, remarkable for her brilliant coloratura rather than for deeper expression, yet here she makes the heroine a tender, feeling creature, emotionally vulnerable yet vocally immaculate. Similarly, **Renato Bruson** as Rigoletto does far more than produce a stream of velvety tone, detailed and intense, responding to the conductor and combining beauty with dramatic bite. Even more remarkable is the brilliant success of **Neil Shicoff** as the Duke, more than a match for his most distinguished rivals. Here the *Quartet* becomes a genuine climax. **Brigitte Fassbaender** as

Maddalena is sharply unconventional but vocally most satisfying. **Sinopoli's** speeds, too, are unconventional at times, but the fresh look he provides is most exciting, helped by full and vivid recording, consistently well balanced.

Just over ten years after her first recording of this opera, **Sutherland** appeared in it again, this time with **Pavarotti**, who is an intensely characterful Duke: an unmistakable rogue but a charmer, too. Thanks to him and to **Bonynge** above all, the *Quartet*, as on the Sinopoli set, becomes a genuine musical climax. Sutherland's voice has acquired a hint of a beat, but there is little of the mooning manner that disfigured her earlier assumption, and the result is glowingly beautiful as well as supremely assured technically. **Milnes** makes a strong Rigoletto, vocally masterful rather than strongly characterful. The digital transfer is exceptionally vivid and atmospheric.

With an excellent cast **James Levine** conducts a thrustful, exceptionally high-powered reading of *Rigoletto*, vividly dramatic. The sound is full and immediate, with the solo voices in sharp focus, enhancing the power. **Vladimir Chernov** is a firm, clear, virile Rigoletto, not as searchingly characterful as some, but maybe because he sings with no hint of strain, with the beauty and accuracy of the singing consistently satisfying. **Cheryl Studer** is a tenderly affecting Gilda, singing with a bright, girlish tone, at once youthful and mature, defying age. **Pavarotti** was fresher in his earlier recording with Bonynge, but heard in close-up his is a thrillingly involving performance still, and the rest of the cast are first-rate too. Not a first choice perhaps, but a strong and sound one.

With her fiery temperament one would not naturally have thought of **Callas** as an apt choice for the innocent Gilda, yet her singing freshly conveys just that quality, while her voice was still at its peak, with none of the flaws that later came to mar her vocal production. Her command in her big aria, *Caro nome*, is complete, yet the set is even more remarkable for the magnificent assumption of the title-role by Tito Gobbi, dark, intense and deeply moving in his portrayal of the hunchback jester, which has never been surpassed on disc. **Giuseppe di Stefano**, also at his peak, completes a trio of principals that became a watchword of excellence in these recordings masterminded by Walter Legge. The EMI set remains at full price, but there is full-bodied sound in Mark Obert-Thorn's Naxos transfer which is first rate.

The Regis reissue also costs much less than the EMI version and, apart from a tiny blip at the very opening of the *Prelude*, the transfer is smooth and clean, with voices vivid, although we marginally prefer the Naxos version. However, on the Regis set there is a bonus of two key **Callas** arias from *La forza del destino*, the 1954 recording.

Robert Merrill sang Rigoletto in a very early RCA LP version of the opera (see below) but this reissued set is more impressive, with its rich flow of tone and clean-styled musical strength. The Gilda of **Anna Moffo** is enchanting and, aided by the rest of the production, gives a firm interpretation. Admittedly she is not always helped by **Solti's** conducting, for he seems determined to rush everyone on, and his beat is often too stiff for middle-period Verdi. But that is a comparatively small drawback, for the briskness brings a consistent intensity to the interpretation, and there are only the barest 'statutory' cuts. The recording too, now on SACD, like the rest of this series, is very good for its period.

Naxos have made an excellent transfer of one of the earliest mono LP recordings of *Rigoletto* dating from June 1956. The set is mainly of interest for **Jussi Bjoerling's** contribution, although not one of his outstanding opera sets. It opens well and generally the conducting of **Jonel Perlea** controls the music effectively. But he is hampered by **Robert Merrill's** rather hammy Rigoletto and the fact that **Roberta Peters**, although she sings very nicely, does not project the character of Gilda at all. Indeed the whole atmosphere of the set is of a concert performance, and the close of the opera degenerates into melodrama.

Rigoletto (complete; in English)

🔊 Ⓜ *** Chan. 3030 (2). Rawnsley, Field, A. Davies, Tomlinson, ENO Ch. & O, Elder

The flair of the original **English National Opera** production, setting *Rigoletto* in the Little Italy area of New York in the 1950s and making the Mafia boss the 'Duke', is superbly carried through to this originally EMI studio recording. The intensity and fine pacing of the stage performances are splendidly caught, thanks to **Mark Elder's** keenly rhythmic conducting, making this one of the most successful of the ENO's Verdi sets. Outstanding vocally is the heady-toned Duke of **Arthur Davies**, and though neither **John Rawnsley** as Rigoletto nor **Helen Field** as Gilda has a voice so naturally beautiful, they too sing both powerfully and stylishly. Excellent recording, clean and full, and the production of the opening scene includes an effective crowd ambience of the kind pioneered by Decca.

Simon Boccanegra (1857 version; complete)

**(*) Opera Rara ORCV 302 (2). Bruscantini, Ligi, Turp, Elvin, Howell, Hudson, BBC Singers, BBC Concert O, Matheson

The revision of *Simon Boccanegra* which, prompted by Boito's rewriting of the libretto, Verdi produced in 1881 has now firmly been accepted as one of the composer's supreme masterpieces, defying the old idea that it could never be popular. This valuable Opera Rara issue, like that company's recording of the original version of Verdi's *Macbeth*, is taken from a BBC recording made in 1976. The sound is satisfyingly vivid and well balanced, and the performance under **John Matheson** is warmly idiomatic, with the **BBC Concert Orchestra** rivalling the work of the other BBC orchestras. Casting is strong, with **Sesto Bruscantini** (towards the end of his career) as characterful as ever, with the voice still lyrical, set in striking contrast against the powerful Fiesco of the bass, **Gwynne Howell**, singing magnificently. **Josella Ligi**, little known on disc, makes an appealing Amelia, with the Canadian tenor **André Turp** singing strongly as Gabriele. Even so, the set is rather of specialist than of general interest, when this first version is disappointingly conventional. So even the great Recognition scene fails in its timing and structure to have the overwhelming impact of the revised version, and the scene which was later replaced by the great Council Chamber scene seems astonishingly flat and perfunctory by comparison.

Simon Boccanegra (complete; DVD versions)

🔊 **** TDK **DVD** DVWW OPSIBOW. Hampson, Gallardo-Domas, Furlanetto, Dvorsky, Daniel, V. State Op. Ch. & O, Gatti (Dir: Peter Stein, V/D: Anton Reitzenstein)

Ⓝ *** DG **DVD** 073 4403. Milnes, Tomowa-Sintow, Moldoveanu, Plishka, Met. Opera Ch. & O, Levine (Producer: Tito Capobianco; V/D: Brian Large)

Ⓝ **(*) Arthaus **DVD** 101 307. Frontali, Giannattasio, Prestia, Gipali, Teatro Comunale di Bolgna, Mariotti (Director: Giorgio Gallione; V/D: Francesca Nesler)

It is rare that you have a quintet of principals who sing with such clear and rock-steady tone as those chosen for **Peter Stein's Vienna State Opera** production of *Simon Boccanegra* in 2002. **Thomas Hampson** as Boccanegra is at his peak, singing and acting magnificently. He is deeply moving opposite **Cristina Gallardo-Domas** as Maria in their great Recognition scene, one of the most touching moments in all Verdi. Hampson is well matched by **Ferruccio Furlanetto** with his dark, finely controlled bass as Fiesco, his adversary, and by **Boaz Daniel** as Paolo. The great Council Chamber scene is not only sung superbly, with Hampson in his address, *Plebe, Patrizi,* **Chailly** builds up to the 'gulp' moment unerringly. At this point the set is less minimally stylized and more realistic than in other scenes of this great opera, setting the seal on a fine version, well recorded.

Not surprisingly, **Sherrill Milnes's** Boccanegra is totally memorable, sung and acted completely within a believable human characterisation. He is well partnered by the not quite as memorable, but still impressive Amelia of **Anna Tomowa-Sintow**. **Paul Plishka** is a commanding Jacobo Fiesco and the cast is completed by the excellent **Vasile Moldoveanu**. Add to this the characteristic Met production values, with a superb chorus and more than excellent orchestra under the inimitable and always reliable **James Levine**. 'Live from the Met' usually means something special, and it does here.

The Bologna production is enjoyable too but not quite on this level. The Amelia, **Carmen Giannattasio**, is genuinely moving and **Roberto Fontali** sings strongly and characterises well, but he is not as three-dimensional as Milnes. The rest of the Bologna cast provides a good professional team. **Michele Mariotti** conducts with considerable flair, and this is an enjoyable realisation of Verdi's masterly opera. But the production values are dwarfed by what the Met can and does provide.

Simon Boccanegra (complete; CD versions)

🔊 ✺ Ⓜ **** DG (ADD) 449 752-2 (2). Freni, Cappuccilli, Ghiaurov, van Dam, Carreras, La Scala, Milan, Ch. and O, Abbado

ⒷⒷ (***) Naxos mono 8.110119-20. Gobbi, Christoff, de los Angeles, Campora, Rome Opera House Ch. & O., Santini

ⒷⒷ (***) Regis mono RRC 2083 (2). Gobbi, Christoff, de los Angeles, Campora, Rome Opera House Ch. & O., Santini

Ⓜ ** Decca 475 7011 (2). Nucci, Te Kanawa, Burchuladze, Aragall, Coni, La Scala, Milan, Ch. & O, Solti

Abbado's 1977 recording of *Simon Boccanegra* is one of the most beautiful Verdi sets ever made. The playing of the orchestra is brilliantly incisive as well as refined, so that the drama is underlined by extra sharpness of focus. The cursing of Paolo after the great Council Chamber scene makes the scalp prickle, with the chorus muttering in horror and the bass clarinet adding a sinister comment, here beautifully moulded. **Cappuccilli**, always intelligent, gives a far more intense and illuminating performance than the one he recorded for RCA earlier in his career; and **Ghiaurov** as Fiesco sings beautifully too. **Freni** as Maria Boccanegra sings with freshness and clarity, while **van Dam** is an impressive Paolo. With electrically intense choral singing as well, this is a set to outshine even Abbado's superb *Macbeth*, and it is superbly transferred to CD. The set is now all the more desirable at mid-price.

An enthusiastic welcome to this classic recording, now over half-a-century old, which is admirably brought back to life by Mark Obert-Thorne on Naxos and Tony Watts and Hilton Grove on Regis. The set preserves two outstanding interpretations, **Gobbi's** Boccanegra and **Christoff's** Fiesco, the brothers-in-law who rival each other in dramatic conviction. Gobbi's superb diction and subtle gradations of tone magisterially portray the Doge's changes of character. He is matched by Christoff's masterly and commanding performance as Fiesco which musicians will relish. **Los Angeles's** tone is exquisite and the performance is expertly characterised. **Gabrieli Santini's** conducting and the playing of the **Rome Opera Orchestra** fall short, perhaps, of the ideal but no collectors interested in great recordings of Verdi operas will want to miss this – in spite of the small cuts that are made. Both transfers are excellent: there is little to choose between them in terms of the vocal projection, but we were struck by the body of sound achieved in the orchestra on Regis.

The glory of **Solti's** reissued set from the late 1980s is the singing of **Kiri Te Kanawa** as Amelia, a beautiful, touching performance. The freedom and absence of strain in the voice go with an almost Straussian quality in her characterization, with the widest dynamic and expressive range. **Giacomo Aragall** makes a strong, unforced Gabriele, but the others are less distinguished. **Leo Nucci** is most disappointing, the voice showing signs of wear, not nearly steady enough. He sings powerfully, but Boccanegra's solo in the great Council Chamber scene finds the voice spreading. **Burchuladze** also is surprisingly less steady than usual, and **Paolo Coni** is capable but undistinguished. What also makes this a less compelling reading compared with the DG is Solti's obsession with observing the metronome markings in the score very precisely – laudable in theory, but often questionable in practice; so the great Recognition scene lacks tenderness and fails to convey the joy of recognition which Abbado finds so movingly.

Stiffelio (complete; DVD version)

(*) DG **DVD 073 4288. Domingo, Sweet, Chernov, Riberi, Plishka, Met. Op. Ch. & O, Levine (Dir: Giancarlo Del Monaco, V/D: Brian Large)

This was something of a historical coup for the Met., being in 1993 the first authentic production since the opera's début.

(The score was thought to have been lost, but in 1992 Verdi's original manuscript came to light, to form the basis for the **Met**. performances.) The story concerns a pastor who preaches forgiveness yet finds it difficult to forgive his own wife for adultery. It was **Plácido Domingo** who initiated the project and he is clearly the star of the performance in the name-role. Otherwise the cast is mixed, with **Vladimir Chernov's** excellent performance as Count Stankar not balanced by **Sharon Sweet's** Lina (his daughter and Stiffelio's errant wife), who is neither vocally or dramatically well cast opposite Domingo. Nevertheless, because of Domingo's powerful performance the opera is really gripping; it is well staged and costumed without eccentricity, and **Levine's** conducting is well up to form.

Stiffelio (complete; CD version)

⊕—(M) *** Ph. 475 6775-2 (2). Carreras, Sass, Manuguerra, Ganzarolli, Austrian R. Ch. & SO, Gardelli

Coming just before the great trio of masterpieces, *Rigoletto*, *Il trovatore* and *La traviata*, *Stiffelio* is still a sharply telling work, largely because of the originality of the relationships and the superb final scene in which Stiffelio reads from the pulpit the parable of the woman taken in adultery. **Gardelli** directs a fresh performance with consistent singing, notably from **Carreras** and **Manuguerra**. First-rate recording from Philips, typical of this fine series, and including a full libretto.

La traviata (complete; DVD versions)

⊕—✿ **** Decca **DVD** 071 431-9. Gheorghiu, Lopardo, Nucci, ROHCG Ch. & O, Solti. (Dir: Richard Eyre, V/D: Humphrey Burton & Peter Maniura)

⊕—**** Decca **DVD** 074 3215 Fleming, Villazón, Bruson, Los Angeles Op. Ch. & O, Conlon (Dir: Marta Domingo, V/D: Brian Large)

⊕—**** DG **DVD** 073 4189. Netrebko, Villazón, Hampson, V. State Op. Konzertvereinigung, VPO, Rizzi (Producer: Willy Decker, V/D: Brian Large)

(N) *** Arthaus **DVD** 101 343 (or Blu-ray 101 344). Gheorghiu, Vargas, Frontali, La Scala Milan Ch. & O., Maazel (Stage Director: Liliana Cavani; V/D: Paola Longobardo)

*** DG **DVD** 073 4364. Stratas, Domingo, Met. Op. Ch. & O, Levine (Dir: Franco Zeffirelli)

*** Arthaus **DVD** 100 112. McLaughlin, MacNeil, Ellis, LPO & Glyndebourne Ch., Haitink. (Dir & V/D. Dir: Peter Hall)

*** Warner NVC **DVD** 4509 92409-2. Gruberová, Shicoff, Zancanaro, La Fenice Ch. & O, Rizzi

As the DVD rightly claims, this famous **Solti** performance of *La traviata* captures one of the most sensational debuts in recent operatic history. Singing Violetta for the first time, **Angela Gheorghiu** made the part entirely her own. But the DVD can also claim a special plaudit for the magical opening, when the camera focuses closely on Solti while he conducts the *Prelude*, with every movement of his hands and the concentration in his eyes creating the music in front of us. He holds the tension at the highest level throughout, with the strings playing marvellously, and recorded with absolute realism. Then the curtain goes up and Bob Crowley's superb stage spectacle spreads out in front of our eyes. The singing is glorious, and this is one of the DVDs that should be a cornerstone in any collection.

Defying the problems of recording opera live at **Covent Garden**, the Decca engineers here offer one of the most vivid and involving versions ever of *La traviata*. As on stage, Gheorghiu brings heartfelt revelations, using her rich and vibrant, finely shaded soprano with consistent subtlety. Youthfully vivacious in Act I, dazzling in her coloratura, she already reveals the depths of feeling which compel her later self-sacrifice. In Act II she finds ample power for the great outburst of *Amami, Alfredo*, and in Act III almost uniquely uses the second stanza of *Addio del passato* (often omitted) to heighten the intensity of the heroine's emotions. **Frank Lopardo** emerges as a fresh, lyrical Alfredo with a distinctive timbre, passionate and youthful-sounding too. **Leo Nucci**, a favourite baritone with Solti, provides a sharp contrast as a stolid but convincing Germont.

As we could guess from her Tatiana in *Eugene Onegin*, **Renée Fleming** is an ideal Violetta, singing radiantly, and **Rolando Villazón** is both ardent and rich-toned, never coarse. Their two personalities strike sparks off each other, yet their voices blend rapturously. **Renato Bruson**, too, is splendid, making a dignified and strong character of Germont Senior, splendidly costumed (so important), and his scene with Violetta in Act II is very telling. The sumptuous set for the opening is visually spectacular to make the party very much an occasion. Overall, **Conlon** paces the score spaciously and holds the tension well in the very moving closing scene. **Brian Large**, as usual, covers the action with his cameras very perceptively, and the only slight drawback is the frequent, understandably enthusiastic applause.

Remarkably, the 2005 Salzburg Festival saw yet another sensational debut from **Anna Netrebko**, also making the role of Violetta totally her own, which understandably prompted huge ovations, not seen in Salzburg since Karajan's heyday. This is an astonishingly successful modern production, staged by **Willy Decker** and passionately conducted by **Carlo Rizzi** with the **Vienna State Opera Konzertvereinigung** and **VPO** contributing magnificently. Throughout the opera Netrebko sings gloriously, her tone pure, the lyrical line effortless, with exquisite controlled *pianissimos*. Moreover, she is partnered by the equally charismatic and equally glorious-voiced **Rolando Villazón**, who makes a perfect partner for her as Alfredo, their acting as well as their singing consistently real and spontaneous. **Thomas Hampson**, too, is a quite unforgettable Germont père. He is dressed plainly and soberly to preserve the character of the unrelenting father figure, holding completely to the original characterization and giving the story its period reality, even when Violetta, in her seductive red dress, brings the narrative into our time. The bright, spacious modern set is dominated by a huge clock which Violetta desperately tries to turn back in Act I; but it remains to dominate the final, infinitely touching scene of her death, with the doctor standing as a gaunt warning figure throughout the Act. In short, this is a production, full of imagination. The DVD comes with an additional disc with a documentary 'Behind the Scenes', excerpts from rehearsals, and an introduction by Rolando Villazón himself.

Angela Gheorghiu as both golden-toned singer and actress doesn't disappoint in her alternative recording with **Ramón Vargas** and father, Giorgio (**Roberto Frontali**). The two men do almost all that is needed in their roles, and both sing with feeling and ardour if with no special imagination. The stage spectacle, as one would expect from this source, is full of colour too and the production overall is satisfying. **Lorin Maazel** directs his **La Scala** forces with vitality and warmth and there is excellent camera control. From the beginning to the close, one is caught up in the tragedy of the characters who sadly cannot manage their lives more successfully. While the earlier Decca version must be a primary recommendation this Arthaus alternative is still rewarding. As can be seen there is an enhanced Blu-ray version for which you need special reproducing equipment.

It is **Zeffirelli** who dominates the filmed **Met.** production, which can move out and about as well as providing the most lavish interiors. But that does not detract from the passion or the tragedy. **Teresa Stratas** may not quite match Fleming, say, in sheer liquid beauty, but she totally identifies with Violetta and movingly carries us with her through all her reversals of fortune. **Domingo** is Domingo, and he sings with the fullest, boldest ardour. **Cornell MacNeil** is a less cultured Germont than usual, and this is reflected not only in his singing and manner but also, once more, in his costume. But **Levine** puts plenty of life into the performance, and overall this is a very telling production; and its spectacle is visually distinctly appealing. There are some small cuts, but none is vital.

Sir Peter Hall's production of *La traviata* for **Glyndebourne** in 1988, powerfully directed for television by Sir Peter himself, makes a very satisfying DVD version. The camera is used to disguise the relative smallness of the stage in the old Glyndebourne, with the necessary grandeur of the two party scenes, both at the start and at the end of Act II, vividly conveyed. At the same time, the intimacy of the drama of the dying Violetta is made the more affecting in close-up. **Marie McLaughlin** sings beautifully, yet too often fails to convey her deepest emotions in facial expressions, although arguably understatement is a fault on the right side. Only in the coloratura at the end of Act I does she have moments of vocal uncertainty, for this was a role that drew out her finest qualities. One is glad to have both verses of the *Addio del passato*. **Walter MacNeil** is a winningly lyrical Alfredo, and **Brent Ellis** is a strong, if slightly gruff Germont. **Bernard Haitink** is refreshingly direct in bringing out the drama of Verdi's score. The video direction is the more effective when this was recorded on stage but not in a live performance.

The alternative Warner DVD offers a moving performance, well cast and with sympathetic conducting from **Carlo Rizzi**, despite an excessively slow opening prelude. Though **Neil Shicoff** as Alfredo is made to look like a Victorian bank-clerk, hardly a romantic figure in metal-framed spectacles, the production is traditional, with colourful costumes and evocative sets. Romantic or not, Shicoff is in splendid voice, phrasing and shaping his big set-pieces sensitively, and **Edita Gruberová** makes a moving Violetta, jolly and vivacious in Act I, taking to the coloratura like a bird before gradually transforming into the haggard tragic figure of Act IV, crowning her performance with the most tender singing. Just as **Giorgio Zancanaro** as a strong, forthright Germont sings both verses of *Di Provenza al mar* in Act II, Gruberová sings both verses of the *Addio del passato*, surpassing herself in the whispered half-tone, perfectly controlled, of the second stanza.

La traviata (complete; CD versions)

🅞—🌼 ******** Decca 448 119-2 (2). Gheorghiu, Lopardo, Nucci, ROHCG Ch. & O, Solti

🅞— ******** Decca 430 491-2 (2). Sutherland, Pavarotti, Manuguerra, L. Op. Ch., Nat. PO, Bonynge

Ⓜ ****(*)** EMI 7 47538-8 (2). Scotto, Kraus, Bruson, Amb. Op. Ch., Philh. O, Muti

🅞— Ⓜ ******* RCA (ADD) 82876 82623 (2). Moffo, Tucker, Merrill, Rome Op. Ch. & O, Previtali

(***) Testament mono SBT2 1369 (2). Carteri, Valletti, Warren, Rome Op. Ch. & O, Monteux

Ⓜ ****(*)** DG **SACD** 477 0772 or CD 415 132-2 (2). Cotrubas, Domingo, Milnes, Bav. State Op. Ch. & O, C. Kleiber

Ⓑ ****(*)** Decca (ADD) 460 759-2 (2). Sutherland, Bergonzi, Merrill, Ch. & O of Maggio Musicale Fiorentino, Pritchard

Ⓑ ****(*)** DG (ADD) 4775665-2 (2). Scotto, Raimondi, Bastianini, La Scala, Milan, Ch. & O, Votto

ⒷⒷ **(***)** Naxos mono 8.110115/6 (2). Steber, di Stefano, Merrill, Met Ch. & O, Antonicelli (with Steber Recital (***))

Ⓜ **(**)** Fonit mono 3984 29354-2 (2). Callas, Albanese, Savarese, Turin R. Ch. & O, Santini

ⒷⒷ ****(*)** Naxos mono 8.110300/01. Callas, Albanese, Savarese, Turin R. Ch. & O, Santini

Ⓜ ***(**)** EMI mono 5 66450-2 (2). Callas, di Stefano, Bastianini, La Scala Ch. & O, Giulini

Sutherland's second recording of the role of Violetta has a breadth and exuberance beyond her achievement in the earlier version of 1963, conducted by **John Pritchard**, and the richness and command of the singing put this among the very finest of her later recordings. **Pavarotti** too, though he overemphasizes *Di miei bollenti spiriti*, sings with splendid panache as Alfredo. **Manuguerra** as Germont lacks something in authority, but the firmness and clarity are splendid. **Bonynge's** conducting is finely sprung, the style direct, the speeds often spacious in lyrical music, generally undistracting. The digital recording is outstandingly vivid and beautifully balanced but the CD booklet includes a libretto.

Muti has no concern for tradition; at the start of the Act I party music, he is even faster than Toscanini, but the result is dazzling; and when he needs to give sympathetic support to his soloists, above all in the great Act II duet between Violetta and Germont, there is no lack of tenderness. Overall, it is an intensely compelling account, using the complete text (like Bonynge), and it gains from having three Italy-based principals. **Scotto** and **Kraus** have long been among

the most sensitive and perceptive interpreters of these roles, and so they are here; with bright digital recording, however, it is obvious that these voices are no longer young, with Scotto's soprano spreading above the stave and Kraus's tenor often sounding thin. **Bruson** makes a fine, forthright Germont, though it does not add to dramatic conviction that his is the youngest voice. Small parts are well taken, and the stage picture is projected clearly on CD in a pleasantly reverberant acoustic.

It is good to be reminded in this vividly remastered set how sensitive and powerful **Anna Moffo's** singing was in her prime. Her coloratura is impeccable in Act I of *La traviata*, yet consistently she conveys a girlish freshness apt for the character. She is particularly remarkable, when she goes on to produce beautiful lyric singing in Act II, opposite the powerful **Robert Merrill** as Germont père, while her dramatic singing in the *Addio del passato* in Act III is deeply moving, though, sadly, only one of the two verses is included, a regular cut at the **Met**. in 1960.

In 1956 one of the first recordings made by RCA in Rome, this version of *La traviata* on Testament brings together three principals better known at the Met. in New York than in Europe, notably the American baritone, by then a legendary figure, **Leonard Warren**, who here sings the role of Germont père with deep feeling. As Alfredo, **Cesare Valletti** sings most sensitively, colouring each phrase individually, with no hint of strain in his mellifluous tenor. **Rosanna Carteri** in the title-role sings with poise and tenderness, as well as brilliance in the coloratura of Act I, if with some edge. Her legato in her *Addio del passato* and Violetta's final solo in Act II are exquisite. Yet perhaps the principal reason for valuing this vintage set lies in the conducting of the octogenarian, **Pierre Monteux**. He brings together lyrical warmth and vigour with a rhythmic lift that is amazing in an ageing conductor. The mono sound is nicely balanced.

Cotrubas makes an ideal heroine in this opera, for her characterization combines strength with vulnerability. But **Kleiber's** direction is controversial, with more than a hint of Toscanini-like rigidity in the party music, and an occasional uncomfortable insistence on discipline. The characteristic contributions of **Domingo** and **Milnes**, both highly commendable, hardly alter the issue. However, played back in surround sound, the sense of presence in a three-dimensional acoustic is very impressive, particularly in the party scenes where the 'offstage' orchestra is cunningly repositioned, as indeed is Domingo. There is still spotlighting of soloists, but Cotrubas projects very realistically and vividly. While the balance still underlines the fierce side of Kleiber's conducting, which contrasts strongly with his ripely romantic side, the overall effect is highly involving, indeed thrilling, and this reissue must be counted an outstanding success.

In **Sutherland's** 1963 recording of *La traviata*, it is true that her diction is poor, but it is also true that she has rarely sung on record with such deep feeling as in the final scene. The *Addio del passato* (both stanzas included and sung with an unexpected lilt) merely provides a beginning, for the duet with **Bergonzi** is most winning, and the final death scene, *Se una pudica vergine*, is overwhelmingly beautiful. This is not a sparkling Violetta, but it is vocally close to perfection. Bergonzi is an attractive Alfredo and **Merrill** a clean-cut Germont. This is excellent value as a Double Decca, although now the libretto has been replaced with Decca's cued synopsis and 'listening guide'.

It is worth having the 1962 DG **La Scala** set for the moving and deeply considered singing of **Renata Scotto** as Violetta, fresher in voice than in her later, HMV set. In a role which has usually eluded the efforts of prima donnas on record, she gives one of the most complete portraits, with thrilling coloratura in Act I and with the closing scene unforgettably moving. It is sad that the rest of the cast is largely undistinguished. **Gianni Raimondi** as Alfredo is stirring if not refined, and **Bastianini** is a coarse Germont *père*. The conductor, **Antonino Votto**, gives routine direction but keeps the music alive. The usual stage cuts are observed. The recording is vividly atmospheric, a fair bargain. There are good notes and a well-cued synopsis.

Few singers on disc can match **Eleanor Steber** as Violetta in the historic live recording of *La traviata*, made at the **Met**; in New York on New Year's Day 1949, and now reissued on Naxos. The beauty and precision as well as the power of Steber's singing are phenomenal, with each note clearly defined down to ornamentation of diamond clarity. With the eager and youthful **Giuseppe di Stefano** as Alfredo, and **Robert Merrill** as a rock-steady, intense Germont, the emotional thrust of the drama comes over at full force, with **Giuseppe Antonicelli** drawing playing and singing from his Met. forces to match even a Toscanini. Limited radio sound clearly transferred. As a very welcome supplement come a series of Steber's commercial recordings of different arias, showing her versatility, from Verdi, Rossini and Puccini to Romberg and Richard Rodgers.

Like the companion Cetra set of *La gioconda*, this Fonit set was made by **Callas** very early in her career (in 1952) and in the present transfer the overall effect is quite open. Callas's characterization of Violetta had not fully reached maturity, but the fresh youthfulness of the voice more than compensates. All the singing is very characteristic (including an odd mistake in the vocal flurries before *Sempre libera* – otherwise an excitingly brilliant account). **Francesco Albanese** is a sympathetic Alfredo, especially in the closing act, but **Ugo Savarese** as Germont *père* is no more distinguished than Bastianini in the later La Scala set. However, Callas admirers will surely find this reissue worth having alone for Callas's very moving closing scene. The Italian libretto, though, is without a translation. However, Naxos have now made available a superior transfer by Ward Marston, still shrill at the opening but catching the voices well. The documentation includes a cued synopsis and this is a super-bargain issue.

Callas's version with **Giulini** was recorded in 1955. There is no more vividly dramatic a performance on record than this, unmatchable in conveying Violetta's agony; sadly, the sound, always limited, grows crumbly towards the end. It is sad too that **Bastianini** sings so lumpishly as Germont *père*, even in the great duet of Act II, while **di Stefano** also fails to match his partner in the supreme test of the final scene. The transfer is fair.

La traviata (complete; in English)

(M) *** Chan. 3023 (2). Masterson, Brecknock, Du Plessis, E. Nat. Op. Ch. & O, Mackerras

Mackerras directs a vigorous, colourful reading which brings out the drama, and **Valerie Masterson** is given the chance on record she has so long deserved. The voice is caught beautifully, if not always very characterfully, and **John Brecknock** makes a fine Alfredo, most effective in the final scene. **Christian Du Plessis's** baritone is less suitable for recording. The conviction of the whole enterprise is infectious.

Il trovatore (complete; DVD versions)

⏤ **** TDK **DVD** DV-CLOPIT. Kabaivanska, Domingo, Cappuccilli, Cossotto, van Dam, V. State Op. Ch. & O, Karajan (V/D: Günther Schneider-Siemssen)

(*) NVC Arts **DVD 4509 99215-2. Plowright, Cossotto, Bonisolli, Zancanaro, Ch. & O of Verona Arena, Giovaninetti (Video Producer: Robin Scott, V/D: Brian Large)

(*) Arthaus **DVD 100 276. Sutherland, Collins, Summers, Elms, Shanks, Australian Op. Ch., Elizabethan Sydney O., Bonynge (Dir: Elijah Moshinsky.)

Domingo joined the production only at the last moment and so ensured that this 1978 *Il trovatore* was all but ideally cast and with **Karajan** returning to the **Vienna State Opera** to direct an undoubtedly great performance. How lucky we are that the cameras were there and that the staging was traditional, with no silly quirks, indeed nothing to mar an evening of glorious singing, with **Cappuccilli** in first-class voice as Count de Luna matching his famous troubador adversary. As for **Fiorenza Cossotto's** Azucena, it is surely unsurpassable in our own time. And **José van Dam** is there too, to sing one of Verdi's finest arias at the opening of the opera. Perhaps **Raina Kabaivanska** does no quite match the others in sheer beauty of voice, but dramatically she is a very convincing Leonora indeed. Fortunately, **Günther Schneider-Siemssen's** video direction is very well managed, and the sound is first class.

At the opening of the Verona *Il trovatore*, the camera focuses on the audience, then moves forward and turns to show the Count de Luna's soldiers with their siege machine and the wooden set which is obviously connected with the planned attack in Act III. Thereafter **Brian Large** ensures that we are drawn closely into the interplay of the characters. However, this opera (as Caruso told us) is concerned with great voices, and one welcomes in the opening scene the richness of Ferrando's timbre as he relates to the soldiers the grim tale on which the opera is based. The three principal characters soon arrive, the fine Leonora of **Rosalind Plowright** clear and true, the richly dramatic baritone of the Count di Luna (**Giorgio Zancanaro**) and the bold but less distinctive tenor of Manrico (**Franco Bonisolli**) who, later in Act III, almost shouts *Di quella pira*. If Leonora were to choose her lover on vocal power alone, it would have to be the Count, unattractive though his character may be. **Fiorenza Cossotto** is the ever reliable, intensely dramatic Azucena, and the chorus are splendidly drilled in their crisply dotted numbers. Under the baton of **Reynald**

Giovaninetti the whole opera goes foward with a vibrant propulsion, with the various duets and unforgettable trios splendidly gutsy. All in all, a most enjoyable DVD, very well recorded, but not the finest performance on record.

Recorded live in July 1983, the **Australian Opera** DVD presentation of *Il trovatore* offers a bravura display from **Dame Joan Sutherland** as Leonora, bringing the rarest combination of weight and flexibility to the role, surpassing in mastery her Decca studio recording of six years earlier, gloriously free over the widest range. Though the rest of the cast may not be so starry, they all sing with firmness and clarity to make it an exceptionally satisfying performance, with **Richard Bonynge** persuasively idiomatic in his conducting. **Kenneth Collins** is far more sensitive than many more celebrated Manricos – even though he is made to look like a Sicilian bandit – and **Jonathan Summers** is a strong, handsome di Luna, with **Lauris Elms** as Azucena making one wonder why she was never used as she should have been in recordings. **Elijah Moshinsky's** production updates the story to the time of Verdi, with characterful backcloths by Sydney Nolan, colourful if not always helpful to the story. The sound on DVD has an edge to it that does not help the voices, but the magnetism of the occasion has one forgetting that.

Il trovatore (complete; CD versions)

🎵 **** EMI 5 57360-2 (2). Gheorghiu, Alagna, Hampson, Diadkova, d'Arcangelo, L. Voices, LSO, Pappano

🎵 ❀ (M) **** RCA (ADD) 74321 39504-2 (2). L. Price, Domingo, Milnes, Cossotto, Amb. Op. Ch., New Philh. O, Mehta

🎵 (M) **** DG 477 5915 (2). Plowright, Domingo, Fassbaender, Zancanaro, Nesterenko, Ch. & O of St Cecilia Ac., Rome, Giulini

🎵 (BB) (***) Naxos mono 8.110240/1 (2) Milanov, Bjorling, Warren, Barbieri, Robert Shaw Ch., RCA Victor O, Cellini (with *6 Songs of Yugoslavia*; Milanov, with piano & violin)

🎵 (BB) (***) Regis mono RRC 2060 (2). Milanov, Björling, Warren, Barbieri, Moscona, Robert Shaw Ch., RCA Victor O, Cellini

🎵 (M) (***) EMI mono 5 62898-2 (2). Callas, Barbieri, di Stefano, Panerai, La Scala, Milan, Ch. & O, Karajan

🎵 (BB) (***) Naxos mono 8.111280/1. Callas, Barbieri, di Stefano, Panerai, La Scala, Milan, Ch. & O, Karajan

(N) (***) ROHCG mono ROHS 011 (2). Previdi, G. Jones, Glossop, Simionato, ROHCG Ch. & O, Giulini

(B) *** DG Double (ADD) 477 5662 (2). Stella, Bergonzi, Cossotto, Bastianini, La Scala, Milan, Ch. & O, Serafin

(BB) (***) Regis Alto mono ALC 2004 (2). Callas, Barbieri, di Stefano, Panerai, La Scala, Milan, Ch. & O, Karajan

The problem for the two principals on EMI CD, **Angela Gheorghiu** and **Roberto Alagna**, is rather greater than in their previous recordings with **Pappano**, when their lyric voices might not seem weighty enough for the roles of Leonora and of Manrico. Gheorghiu characteristically capitalizes on the problem, bringing a rare tenderness to her big arias, floating her top notes ravishingly, and exploiting her formidable coloratura powers in cabalettas, always stylish in ornamentation. Only in the bravura aria *Tu vedrai che amore in terra* and the final scenes does she press the voice, so that it flickers in emotion. Though in the heroic outburst of *Di quella pira* Alagna tends to force his tone, holding on provocatively to his final top C, that is rather the exception, and generally this is a performance marked, like Gheorghiu's, by individual phrasing to bring out the warmth of emotion along with the meaning of the words. **Thomas Hampson** as di Luna is at once sinister and ardently sincere in his love for Leonora, giving a warmly involved performance, while **Larissa Diadkova** with a Slavonic tang in her mezzo tone is a formidable and moving Azucena. Ripely atmospheric recording beautifully balanced, with fine playing and singing from the **LSO** and **London Voices**. This is now a pretty clear first choice, though the mid-priced RCA set is still very strongly recommendable, and will still be first choice for some collectors.

The soaring curve of **Leontyne Price's** rich vocal line is immediately thrilling in her famous Act I aria, and it sets the style of the RCA performance, full-bodied and with dramatic tension consistently high. The choral contribution is superb; the famous *Soldiers'* and *Anvil Choruses* are marvellously fresh and dramatic. When *Di quella pira* comes, the orchestra opens with great gusto and **Domingo** sings with a ringing, heroic quality worthy of Caruso himself. There are many dramatic felicities, and **Sherrill Milnes** is in fine voice throughout; but perhaps the highlight of the set is the opening section of Act III, when Azucena finds her way to Conte di Luna's camp. The ensuing scene with **Fiorenza Cossotto** is vocally and dramatically electrifying.

As it so happens, DG have also re-released, as one of their Originals, Domingo's later (1984) portrayal of Manrico on CD, perhaps even more heroic and only very occasionally showing signs of vocal strain. **Giorgio Zancanaro** matches him with a firmly resonant Count, but the special joy of this set is **Rosalind Plowright's** Leonora, the singing not just having sweetness and purity (one can imagine her ending up in a convent) but with spirited and brilliantly flexible coloratura. **Giulini's** tempi are measured, but the intensity of concentration is in no doubt, and the recording is both naturally balanced and vivid.

The classic RCA recording of 1952, with four of the reigning stars of the **Metropolitan Opera** at their peak, remains among the very finest recorded versions. The transfers by Mark Obert-Thorn bring out the full beauty and character of all four principals very vividly and are particularly valuable when **Zinka Milanov**, always an iconic figure at the Met., is here recorded with a purity and firmness that transcends many of her later, all-too-rare recordings. **Bjorling** is, as ever, superb in his heroic projection, though in a performance with the usual cuts he is allowed only one stanza of *Di quella pira*. **Leonard Warren** and **Fedora Barbieri** are also perfectly focused, with **Renato Cellini** drawing lively playing and singing from the **RCA Victor Orchestra** and the hand-picked **Robert Shaw Chorale**. A recording to treasure and not to be missed at Naxos price. The bonus items of six songs from Milanov's native Yugoslavia, recorded in New York in 1944, give a different perspective on the voice: closer and earthier if just as characterful.

The new Regis transfer seems to us to give the voices marginally more presence, although there is not a great deal in it, and the Naxos sound is a little more rounded. Both sets are very enjoyable indeed, so choice can be made by considering whether or not you require the Naxos bonus of six Yugoslavian folksongs sung by Milanov. Incidentally, we omitted to mention the superb contribution of **Nicola Moscona** as Ferrando in the opera's first scene.

The combination of **Karajan** and **Callas** is formidably impressive. There is toughness and dramatic determination in Callas's singing, whether in the coloratura or in the dramatic passages, and this gives the heroine an unsuspected depth of character which culminates in Callas's fine singing of an aria that used often to be cut entirely – *Tu vedrai che amore in terra*, here with its first stanza alone included. **Barbieri** is a magnificent Azucena, **Panerai** is a strong, incisive Count, and **di Stefano** is at his finest as Manrico. On CD the 1956 mono sound, now greatly improved, is one of the more vivid from **La Scala** at that period. The set is now available fully documented at mid price as one of EMI's 'Great Recordings of the Century'.

The Naxos transfer is well up to Mark Obert-Thorn's usual high standard, and one is struck by the wide dynamic range of the recording. The Regis Alto transfer is clear and clean, but the upper range is sharper and the orchestral strings thinner. The voices however are well caught and this is certainly worth its modest cost.

Gwyneth Jones was at her peak in 1964 (substituting for Leontyne Price) when this set was recorded live in 1964. **Peter Glossop** as Il Conte di Luna also sung splendidly, warm-toned and full-bodied. **Simionato**, however, was past her best as Azucena, but **Bruno Previdi's** Manrico certainly had its thrills. **Giulini** conducts with real electricity although without pressurising the singers, and altogether this is worth its relatively modest cost. But again we ask: why was it not recorded in stereo?

Serafin's splendidly red-blooded **La Scala** version on a DG Double is most enjoyable, with the contributions of **Cossotto** as Azucena and **Carlo Bergonzi**, splendid as Manrico, matching almost any rival. **Stella** and **Bastianini** give flawed performances, but they have many impressive moments; as Leonora's opening aria readily demonstrates, Stella is in full voice and identifies strongly with the heroine. The conducting of Serafin is crisp and stylish, and the 1963 recording is vividly transferred to CD with plenty of atmosphere.

Il trovatore (highlights)

(B) **(*) CfP 3 93375-2 (from complete recording, with Corelli, Tucci, Merrill, Simionato, Mazzoni, Rome Op. Ch. & O, Schippers)

The 1964 EMI **Rome** set of *Il Trovatore* is a long way short of ideal, but **Merrill's** Conte di Luna is characterful and firmly sung, if sometimes ungainly. **Simionato** is an excellent Azucena; **Tucci**, though less assured than her colleagues, sings beautifully. **Corelli** is at his powerful best as Manrico, a really heroic tenor, if not always subtle. His *Di quella pira*

displays rather crude histrionics, but its gutsiness is welcome when **Schippers's** conducting is inclined to be rigid; however, his incisiveness is also compelling. The highlights disc comprises over 70 minutes and would seem a good recommendation.

I vespri siciliani (complete; DVD version)

☞ **** Opus Arte **DVD** OALS 3008D. Studer, Zancanaro, Mritt, Furlanetto, La Scala, Milan, Ch. & O, Muti (V/D: Preben Montell)

As with *Ernani*, we have had this production already on CD and it is **Muti** who, conducting tautly, ensures that this live performance carries high drama, with the orchestra too playing splendidly. **Cheryl Studer** sings gloriously as Elena and **Chris Merritt** (as Arrigo) is in even better form here than on the CD set. They get excellent support from **Giorgio Zancanaro** as Montfort, the Governor of Sicily who also turns out to be Arrigo's father – while **Ferruccio Furlanetto**, who is vocally less strong than his colleagues, still cuts a convincing figure as Procida. As with *Ernani*, the production is straightforward, with no crazy impositions from a self-conscious stage director. The ballet is included, but it is presented effectively and danced well, and the music is tuneful enough. Excellent sound, too.

I vespri siciliani (CD version)

(***) Testament mono SBT 21416 (2). Callas, Christoff, Kokolios Bardi, Mascherini, Maggio Musicale Fiorentino Ch. & O, Erich Kleiber

This Testament reissue derives from a live recording which Walter Legge made on tape when **Callas** sang in Florence at the very beginning of her career in 1951. She is already magnetic, the voice at its freshest. She is partnered by the Greek tenor, **Giorgio Kokolios Bardi** who, while no Caruso, is very acceptable. Remarkably, **Boris Christoff** stars as a melancholy Procida, and **Enzo Mascherini** is a telling Montfort (not a grateful part to sing). The sound has been again remastered and, though very variable, is certainly acceptable.

Les Vêpres siciliennes (original; French version)

☞ *** Opera Rara ORCV 303 (3). Brumaire, Bonhomme, Taylor, Baran, BBC Concert O, Rossi (or Lawrence in ballet)

Musically, the differences between this and *I vespri siciliani* are relatively small, but the use of French does alter the feel of Verdi's big melodies, even in the famous bass aria for the rebel, Procida, *Et toi, Palerme*, instead of 'O tu Palermo', well sung by **Ayhan Baran**, if with some flutter. As the hero, Henri, **Jean Bonhomme** is ideally cast with his very French-sounding tenor and stylish phrasing. As the Duchess Hélène, **Jacqueline Brumaire** sounds equally French with her warm, vibrant and agile soprano, and **Neilson Taylor** is excellent in the baritone role of the Sicilian Governor, Guy de Montfort. **Mario Rossi** conducts a lively, very well-paced reading of the score, totally idiomatic – though, oddly, the Act III ballet is conducted not by him but by Ashley Lawrence.

COLLECTIONS

'Verdi Heroines'; Arias from: *Aida; Un ballo in maschera; Ernani; La forza del destino; Macbeth* (sleepwalking scene); *Otello; La traviata; Il trovatore*

⊶ Ⓜ ******** RCA (ADD) 82876 7629-2. Leontyne Price (with various orchestras and conductors)

A famous collection from the 1960s, issued without additions. However, **Leontyne Price**, peerless in her generation, is here at her finest in virtually all these arias, recorded between 1959 and 1967, at the peak of her career, with the glorious voice well caught in the transfers. Full texts and translations included.

Arias from: (i) *Aida;* **(ii & iii)** *Don Carlo;* **(ii)** *Ernani; Macbeth;* **(i)** *Otello;* **(ii)** *Nabucco* (with bonus DVD: **1965 Paris recital, arias by Massenet; Bellini; Puccini)**

⊶ Ⓜ ******** EMI Legends (ADD) 5 57760-2. Callas; with (i) Paris Conservatoire O; (ii) Philh. O; Rescigno

The **Philharmonia** recordings, made in 1958, marked **Callas's** only visit to record at Abbey Studios. Much of the content shows the great diva at her very finest. Dismiss the top-note wobbles from your mind, and the rest has you enthralled by the vividness of characterization as well as musical imagination. It is sad that Callas did not record the role of Lady Macbeth complete. Here *La luce langue* is not as intense as the Act I aria and sleepwalking scene, which are both unforgettable, while she holds the tension masterfully in the long *Don Carlos* scene. Abigaille, Elvira and Elisabetta all come out as real figures, sharply individual. Finely balanced recordings, sounding good in their Legends transfer. The **Paris** recordings (with the orchestra's distinctive timbre) are exciting too, with the Desdemona from *Otello* commandingly taken, Aida's *Ritorna vincitor* vehemently done, and *O don fatale* as theatrical as you might expect. With the bonus DVD of arias filmed in 1965 with the **Orchestre National de l'ORTF** under **Prêtre**, this is one of the most tempting Callas collections about, though no texts are included.

Arias from: *Aida; Ernani; La forza del destino; Otello; Il trovatore; I vespri siciliani*

⊶ ⒷⒷ (*******) Naxos mono 8.110728. Ponselle (with various partners & accompanists including Martinelli, Pinza & Stracciari)

This splendid disc celebrating the glories of **Rosa Ponselle's** unique voice and interpretative powers brings excellent CD transfers of her most celebrated electrical recordings made for RCA in 1928, including the heroine's big aria from *Ernani*, spectacularly well done, and the sequence of *Forza* recordings with **Martinelli** and **Pinza** – as well as Columbia recordings from the pre-electric period, made between 1918 and 1924 – all chosen by Ward Marston as being the finest Ponselle versions of each item. The result is a wonderful gallery of perfection, beautifully transferred with the voice vividly caught.

Arias from: *Aida: Ritorna vincitor!; Qui Radamès verrà! O patria mia. Il trovatore: Che più t'arresti; Tacea la notte;* **(i)** *Di tale amor. Timor di me?; D'amor sull'ali rosee*

⊶ Ⓜ ******* RCA SACD 82876 61395-2. L. Price, Rome Op. O, De Fabritiis or Basile; (i) with Londi – PUCCINI: *Arias* ******(*)

This 1959 recital, known as the 'blue album' (the colour of the original LP is reproduced on the CD), has justly become a collectors' item – the glorious flow of tone makes one understand why, even if tension is lower than in **Price's** performances of the complete operas. The SACD brings added bloom to the excellent recording.

Arias from: (i) *Alzira;* **(ii)** *Aroldo; Attila; I corsaro; I due Foscari; Un giorno di regno; I Lombardi*

⊶ Ⓜ ******* RCA (ADD) 82876 62309-2 (2). Caballé, RCA Italian Op. Ch. & O, with (i) Sunara; (ii) Kozma – ROSSINI; DONIZETTI: *Arias* *******

As in the Rossini and Donizetti arias, recorded around the same time (1967), these Verdi items (originally called 'Verdi Rarities') find **Caballé** at her finest. Re-listening to these performances, one can understand why Caballé's career really took off, when around this time she also had enormous stage success in America. Her bel canto has a fine-spun purity, and in these excerpts of Verdi's early genius she conveys the melodic freshness, against the conventional rum-ti-tum accompaniments: there is both brilliance and beauty in plenty here. Good accompaniments from the Italian orchestra, and vivid sound. Texts and translations – not to be taken for granted these days – are included.

Arias: *Don Carlos: Tu che la vanità. La traviata: Ah fors è lui. Il trovatore: Timor di me*

Ⓜ ******* Sony SMK 60975. Te Kanawa, LPO, Pritchard, or LSO, Maazel – PUCCINI: *Arias* ******* (with MOZART: *Don Giovanni: Ah! Fuggi il traditor; In quali eccessi ... Mi tradì;* HUMPERDINCK: *Der kleine Sandmann bin ich;* DURUFLÉ: *Requiem: Pie Jesu* *******)

The Verdi part of **Kiri Te Kanawa's** Verdi–Puccini recital brings three substantial items, less obviously apt for the singer, but in each the singing is felt as well as beautiful. The coloratura of the *Traviata* and *Trovatore* items is admirably clean, and it is a special joy to hear Elisabetta's big aria from *Don Carlos* sung with such truth and precision. Good recording, enhanced on CD.

Choruses: *Requiem excerpts: Dies irae; Tuba mirum; Sanctus.* **Choruses from:** *Aida; Un ballo in maschera; Don Carlo; Ernani; I Lombardi; Macbeth; Nabucco; Otello; Simon Boccanegra; Il trovatore*

⊶ Ⓜ ******* DG (IMS) (ADD) 463 655-2. Ch. & O of La Scala Milan, Abbado

The basic collection here, of nine opera choruses, was welcomed by us with enthusiasm when it was first issued in 1975. The combination of precision and tension is riveting and the analogue recording is of DG's highest standard, offering a wide dynamic range, fine detail in the *pianissimos*, and splendid weight in the moments of spectacle. The *diminuendo* at the end of the *Anvil Chorus* is most subtly managed, while the fine rhythmic bounce of *Si, redesti* (from *Ernani*) is matched by the expansive brilliance of the excerpts from *Aida* (lovely fruity trumpets) and *Don Carlo*, and by the atmospheric power of *Patria oppressa* from *Macbeth*.

For the reissue, as one of their 'Originals', DG have expanded the contents to a more realistic 68 minutes, by adding some more items from **Abbado's** complete recordings, including *Un ballo in maschera* and *Simon Boccanegra*. The snag is that the collection ends with three excerpts from Abbado's 1980 set of the *Requiem*, where, compared with what has gone before, there is a degree of slackness and lack of bite. In the *Dies irae* the chorus sounds too small and there is little excitement. However, the recording is excellent and the rest of the programme remains highly desirable.

Choruses from: Aida; La battaglia di Legnano; Don Carlo; Ernani; La forza del destino; Macbeth; Nabucco; Otello; La traviata; Il trovatore

🎵 (BB) *** Naxos 8.550241. Slovak Philharmonic Ch. & RSO, Dohnányi

Under **Oliver Dohnányi's** lively direction the chorus sings with fervour. The collection ends resplendently with the triumphal scene from *Aida*, omitting the ballet but with the fanfare trumpets blazing out on either side most tellingly. With a playing time of 56 minutes this is an excellent bargain, with naturally balanced recording from the Bratislava Radio Concert Hall.

Choruses from: (i) Aida; (ii) I due foscari; Ernani; I Lombardi; Luisa Miller; Macbeth; Nabucco; Il trovatore; I vespri siciliani. (iii) Overtures: La forza del destino; Nabucco; I vespri siciliani

(B) *** CfP (ADD) 5 87035-2. (i) ROHCG Ch. & O, Muti; (ii) Welsh Nat. Op. Ch. & O, Armstrong; (iii) New Philh. O, Muti

The **Welsh National Opera** made its reputation by the strength of its chorus work, and these performances are for the most part vivid and lusty, with plenty of character and rhythmic feeling, even if *Va, pensiero* from *Nabucco*, though effective, is not as memorable as one might have expected. The witches in *Macbeth*, however, are rather quaintly characterized to make a moment of light relief, and the recording is full and clear. **Muti**, at **Covent Garden**, gives us the closing *Triumphal March* scene from *Aida* and also directs the three *Overtures*, which are played with great spirit and character. A good bargain collection overall.

VICTORIA, Tomás Luis de
(c. 1548–1611)

Ascendens Christus (motet); Missa Ascendis Christus in altum; O Magnum mysterium (motet); Missa O Magnum mysterium

🎵 **** Hyp. CDA 66190. Westminster Cathedral Ch., Hill

Missa Ave maris stella; O quam gloriosum est regnum (motet); Missa O quam gloriosum

🎵 ✹ **** Hyp. CDA 66114. Westminster Cathedral Ch., Hill

The Latin fervour of the singing is very involving; some listeners may initially be surprised at the volatile way **David Hill** moves the music on, with the trebles eloquently soaring aloft on the line of the music. The spontaneous ebb and flow of the pacing is at the heart of David Hill's understanding of this superb music. *Ave maris stella* is particularly fine. Hill's mastery of the overall structure produces a cumulative effect as the choir moves towards the magnificent closing *Agnus Dei*.

On the companion disc, the spirited presentation of the motet, *Missa Ascendis Christus in altum* prepares the way for a performance of the *Mass* that is similarly invigorating. The recording balance is perfectly judged, with the **Westminster** acoustic adding resonance (in both senses of the word) to singing of the highest calibre, combining a sense of timelessness and mystery with real expressive power.

Ave Maria; Ave Maris stella (hymn); Missa Vidi speciosam; Ne timeas, Maria; Sancta Maria, succurre miseris; Vidi speciosam (motets)

🎵 **** Hyp. CDA 66129. Westminster Cathedral Ch., Hill

An outstanding collection of some of Victoria's most beautiful music celebrating the Virgin Mary. The four-part *Ave Maria* may not be authentic, but the composer would surely not be reluctant to own it. The **Westminster Choir** again show their flexibly volatile response to this music with that special amalgam of fervour and serenity that Victoria's writing demands. This CD is withdrawn but is available to special order on Hyperion's Archive Service.

Missa Ave Regina caelorum (with motet: Ave Regina caelorum for 8 voices); Ave Maria (for 4 voices); Ave Maria (for 8 voices); Dixit Dominus; Laetatus sum; Laudate Dominum omnes gentes; Laudate pueri Dominum; Magnificat septimi toni; Nisi Dominus

🎵 **** Hyp. CDA 67479. Westminster Cathedral Ch., Martin Baker

Although it does not have the advantage of 'surround sound' like the account of the *Officium defunctorum* by The Sixteen (see below), this Hyperion collection also stands out among recordings of Victoria's music. Under the direction of **Martin Baker** the **Westminster** style is volatile and strikingly passionate (their account of the *Dixit Dominus* arrestingly so), yet there is serenity too in the lovely *Missa Ave Regina caelorum*, a parody *Mass* based on Victoria's two motet settings of which the eight-part version is used here to introduce the *Mass*. But it is the shorter works that stand out even more strikingly, especially the joyous *Laetatus sum* for 12 voices and the richly blended eight-part setting of *Ave Maria*, which closes the concert. The recording, made in the Cathedral, is not crystal clear, but otherwise is in every way first class.

Canta Beata Virginis: Ave Maria a 4; Ave Regina caelorum; Gaude, Maria virgo a 5; Magnificat primi toni; Ne timeas, O magnum mysterium a 4; Maria a 4; Sancta Maria, succurre miseris a 4; Trahe me post te; Salve Regina a 8; Vidi speciosam sicut columbam; (Instrumental) Senex, Puerum portabat a 4

🎵— *** Astrée Naive ES 9975. La Capella Reial de Catalunya, Hespèrion XX, Savall

This admirable collection of some of Victoria's most beautiful, and often celestially serene, Marian motets has as its highlights two eight-part works for double choir – the memorable antiphon, *Salve Regina*, and the glorious *Magnificat primi toni*, the *Canticle of the Blessed Virgin*, sung at the end of Vespers. But the four-part settings are hardly less memorable in these spontaneous, deeply felt and impressively blended performances, where the brass of **Hespèrion XX** are well integrated into the vocal textures, and indeed have the sombre *Senex, Puerum portabat* to themselves. The resonance casts a lovely aura over the sound, but it does blur inner definition and the words. However, full texts and translations are included.

Missa Gaudeamus; Missa Pro Victoria. Motets: Cum beatus Ignatius; Descendit Angelus Domini; Doctor bonus, amicus Dei Andreas; Ecce sacerdos magnus; Estote fortes in bello; Hic vir despiciens mundum; O decus apostolicum; Tu es Petrus; Vieni sponsa Christis

🎵— ⚙ **** ASV CDGAU 198. Cardinall's Musick, Carwood

Happily the name of the opening *Missa Gaudeamus*, for six voices, celebrates the label on which it is issued. It is a relatively serene 'backward-looking' work, yet with the closing *Sanctus* and *Agnus Dei* richly memorable. The shorter *Missa Pro Victoria* is even finer, indeed one of Victoria's most powerful and expressive utterances, and unique in being based on a secular chanson, *La guerre, escoutez lous gentilz* by Janequin. **Andrew Carwood's** performance moves forward with true Latin passion and grips the listener from first to last. Among the nine very varied additional motets, *Tu es Petrus* and *O decus apostolicum* and the remarkable *Descendit Angelus Domini* stand out. The recording is of the very highest quality.

Mass and motet: O magnum mysterium. Mass and motet: O quam gloriosum; Ardens est cor meum; Ave Maria

🎵— ⒷⒷ *** Naxos 8.550575. Oxford Camerata, Summerly – A. LOBO: *Versa est in luctum* ***

Like David Hill, **Jeremy Summerly** moves the music of each *Mass* on fairly briskly until the *Sanctus* and *Agnus Dei*, when the spacious *espressivo* of the singing makes a poignant contrast. The two motets on which the *Masses* are based are sung as postludes, and very beautiful they are, especially the idyllic *O magnum mysterium*. Finally, the short *Versa est in luctum* (a setting of a section of the *Requiem Mass*) by Alonso Lôbo, a Spanish contemporary, ends the concert serenely. The recording is excellent and this is a fine bargain.

Officium defunctorum (Requiem, 1605)

*** Hyp. CDA 66250. Westminster Cathedral Ch., Hill

Officium defunctorum (Requiem, 1605); Motet: Versa est in luctum

🎵— Ⓑ *** Gimell CDGIM 205 (2). Tallis Scholars, Phillips – CARDOSO: *Requiem*; D. LÔBO: *Requiem*; A. LÔBO: *Motets* ***

The *Officium defunctorum* is a work of great serenity and beauty. Honours are fairly evenly divided between the **Westminster Cathedral Choir** on Hyperion and the **Tallis Scholars** under **Peter Phillips**. The Westminster Choir has the advantage of boys' voices and larger forces; they are recorded in a warmer, more spacious acoustic. By comparison with the Gimell recording, the sound seems a little less well focused, but on its own terms it is thoroughly convincing. They permit themselves greater expressiveness, too. Moreover the *Requiem* is set in the wider liturgical context by the use of some chants.

The Tallis Scholars achieve great clarity of texture in this masterly work; they are 12 in number and, as a result, the polyphony is clearer and so are the words. They embrace also the motet, *Versa est in luctum*, which Victoria included as an appendix to his score. This outstanding performance of the *Requiem* is also available on a single disc with Alonso Lôbo's setting of the same motet text, but the present two-CD set includes Duarte Lôbo's *Requiem* as well as more motets by Alonso.

Officium defunctorum (Requiem), including Taedet animam meam vitae meae. Ave Regina caelorum a 8; Nigra sum; Quam pulchri sunt; Salve Regina; Trahe me post te

🎵— ⚙ **** Coro Surround Sound **SACD** CORSACD 16033. The Sixteen. Christophers

Harry Christophers and his **Sixteen** give a gloriously expressive performance of Victoria's *Requiem*, his supreme masterpiece, written in 1605 for the Dowager Empress Maria of Austria, and they have every advantage over their competitors above in the superb recording made in the Church of St Silas the Martyr, London, engineered in 'surround sound' by Mike Hatch. This compatible SACD is pretty impressive heard in the normal CD format, but when the rear speakers are brought into use and carefully balanced, the effect is of sitting in the Church itself; moreover not only is the sound more expansive but the range of dynamic is increased. The performance is prefaced by *Taedet animam meam vitae*, a Lesson from Matins setting a bleak text from the Book of Job, and the performance closes with the funeral motet *Versa est in luctum* and the responsory *Libera me*. The music of the Mass is supplemented by the proper plainsong intonations and verses (monody, beautifully sung by the sopranos). Before the *Mass* we are offered six other shorter works in which the eight-voice *Ave Regina* and *Salve Regina* both stand out. Altogether this is the most impressive of recent issues in the Victoria discography and it is strongly recommended.

Responsories for Tenebrae

🎵 *** Hyp. CDA 66304. Westminster Cathedral Ch., Hill

Ⓜ *** Virgin 5 61221-2. The Sixteen, Christophers

The *Tenebrae responsories* are so called because of the tradition of performing them in the evening in increasing darkness as the candles are extinguished one by one. The **Westminster Cathedral Choir** under **David Hill** on Hyperion find atmosphere in this music and bring a sense of spontaneous feeling to their performance. Of recent versions, this can be welcomed without reservation.

Harry Christophers and **The Sixteen** too are fully in sympathy with Victoria's *Tenebrae responsories*, combining serenity, beautiful blending of timbres and a willingness to be volatile when the music demands it. Excellent recording in a suitably warm acoustic.

VIERNE, Louis (1870–1937)

Piano Quintet in C minor

🎵 *** Hyp. CDA 67258. Coombs, Chilingirian Qt. – HAHN: *Piano Quintet in F sharp minor* ***

Vierne composed his *Piano Quintet* in 1917 after the death of his second son, killed in action at only 17 during the Great War. It is finely structured and its slow movement is particularly searching and thoughtful. The sleeve note draws a parallel with Frank Bridge, and its dark chromaticism is bleak and its world altogether harsher than the more familiar organ. Its centrepiece is the haunting and powerful *Andante*, the emotional core of the work. **Stephen Coombs** and the **Chilingirians** play with conviction and character, and are given the benefit of excellently vivid recorded sound. If you enjoy the Franck *F minor Piano Quintet* or the Chausson *Concert*, you will feel very much at home here.

Suite 3, Op. 54: Carillon de Westminster

🎵 *** DG 413 438-2. Preston (organ of Westminster Abbey) – WIDOR: *Symphony 5* ***

The Vierne *Carillon de Westminster* is splendidly played by **Simon Preston** and sounds appropriately atmospheric in this spacious acoustic and well-judged recording. It makes an attractive makeweight to the Widor *Fifth Symphony*.

ORGAN SYMPHONIES

Symphonies 1 in D min., Op. 14; 2 in E min., Op. 20; 3 in F sharp min., Op. 28; 4 in G min., Op. 32; 5 in A min., Op. 47; 6 in B min., Op. 59

🎵 ✿ **** MDG 316 0732-2 (3). van Oosten (Cavaillé-Coll organs in Saint-François-de-Sales, Lyons (*Symphonies 1 & 4*); Saint-Ouen, Rouen (*Symphonies 2 & 6*); Basilica Saint-Sernin, Toulouse (*Symphonies 3 & 5*))

Symphonies 1 in D min., Op. 14; 2 in E min., Op. 20; 3 in F sharp min., Op. 28; 4 in G min., Op. 32; 5 in A min., Op. 47; 6 in B min., Op. 59

*** Signum SIGCD 063 (3). Filsell (Cavaillé-Coll organ of Saint-Ouen de Rouen)

Symphonies 3 & 6

🎵 ⒝⒝ *** Naxos 8.553524. Mathieu (Dalstein-Haerpfer organ of Eglise Saint-Sébastien de Nancy)

Widor's *Symphonies* certainly have their impressive moments, but Vierne's are far more consistent in quality, and if you have not already explored them, this new survey from **Ben van Oosten**, superbly recorded on three different Cavaillé-Coll organs, provides an admirable opportunity to do so.

Ben van Oosten's performances cannot be too highly praised. He is deeply committed, has a wonderful ear for sonority and detail (witness his uniquely grotesque playing in the *Scherzo* of *6*), and every performance creates the thrill and spontaneity of live music-making, while the recording of all three organs is magnificent.

Jeremy Filsell also plays these works splendidly and he has a fine organ in Rouen. Listen to the finale of the *First Symphony* to discover how thrilling it can be. But its sound, as recorded, spreads more than the MDG recording of van Osten's performances and detail is sometimes blurred. However, this is still a fine set which gives much satisfaction.

The Naxos pairing is also more than worth its modest price. **Bruno Mathieu** chooses the 'historic' organ at Nancy, which still has mechanical traction, and provides a very characterful baroque palette of its own, richly displayed in the *Cantilène* of *3*. But the pedals are very telling, too, and the finale of *6* is powerfully spectacular; yet overall, inner detail is remarkably clear. The only small disappointment is the *Scherzo* of *6*, where the diabolic rhythmic figure is not as ironically piquant as with van Oosten.

On Priory, both **Colin Walsh** at Lincoln Cathedral, and **Ian Simcocks** at Westminster (the more suitable organ of the two) show their mettle and understanding of this repertoire, and Vierne's music is projected powerfully and colourfully. But the Vierne *Symphonies* gain much from being recorded on Cavaillé-Coll instruments, so these discs must take second place to the others.

Messe solennelle

🎵 *** Priory PRDC 597. Mark Lee (organ), Gloucester Cathedral Ch., David Briggs – LANGLAIS: *Organ Pieces* & *Messe solennelle* ***

Vierne's setting of the *Messe solennelle* is less dependent on dramatically turbulent organ contrasts with the choir than the coupled work of Langlais, with the organ's role here more fully integrated. But it is still a *Mass* setting which is both thrilling and full of cantabile melody, and the *Sanctus* builds richly and climactically to the closing *Hosanna*. The *Benedictus* is full of gentle radiance, while the *Agnus Dei* brings a moving tranquillity, the *Dona nobis pacem* quite magical. The performance here could not be more sympathetic and is not in the least Anglican-sounding. It is remarkable that an English cathedral choir and organist should be able to capture the music's essence so movingly.

Congratulations to all concerned, including the recording producer, Caroline Paschalides.

VIEUXTEMPS, Henri
(1820–81)

(i) Violin Concertos 1 in E, Op. 10; (ii) 4 in D min., Op. 31

✇ⓑⓑ *** Naxos 8.554506. Keylin; (i) Janáček PO, Burkh; (ii) Arnhem PO, Yuasa

Misha Keylin couples the unfamiliar *First* with the much better-known *D minor Concerto*, which we are told he plays on a famous Stradivarius violin. Certainly its *Andante religioso* brings a generous-toned romanticism. But the solo timbre in the *E major* work is sweet and full, and he plays the dazzling lightweight finale with charm as well as sparkle. This is an excellent coupling, very well recorded, and both accompanying groups, Czech and Dutch respectively, are very supportive indeed.

Violin Concertos 2 in F sharp min., Op. 19; 3 in A, Op. 25

✇ⓑⓑ *** Naxos 8.554114. Keylin, Janáček PO, Burkh

2 and 3 are by no means inferior to the better known 4 and 5. They are full of good tunes, both slow movements are warmly touching, and the finales have lyrical as well as histrionic appeal. **Misha Keylin** gives highly persuasive performances that constantly tickle the ear in their subtlety of bowing and colour, easy rubato and imaginative dynamic shading. **Dennis Burkh** provides the strongest backing: his spirited introductions for both works (and especially the *Third*, with its throbbing drama) are arresting, and the orchestral playing, somewhat leonine in timbre, is excellent. So too is the recording, made in the Janáček Concert Hall, Ostrava.

Violin Concertos 4, Op.31; 5 in A min., Op. 37

✇ *** Australian Philips Eloquence (ADD) 442 8561. Grumiaux, LOP, Rosenthal – SAINT-SAËNS: *Violin Concerto 3* ***

✇ⓑⓑ (***) Naxos mono 8.110943. Heifetz; (i) LPO, Barbirolli; (ii) LSO, Sargent – SAINT-SAËNS: *Introduction & Rondo capriccioso; Havanaise;* SARASATE: *Zigeunerweisen* (with LPO or LSO, Barbirolli); WAXMAN: *'Carmen' Fantasy* (with RCA Victor SO, Voorhees) (***)

Violin Concerto 4 in D min., Op. 31

✇Ⓜ(***) EMI mono 7 64251-2. Heifetz, LPO, Barbirolli – SAINT-SAËNS: *Havanaise* etc.; SARASATE: *Zigeunerweisen;* WIENIAWSKI: *Concerto 2* (***)

Heifetz was the first leading violinist to revive the long-neglected concertos of the 19th-century Belgian violinist-composer, Henri Vieuxtemps, recording 4 in 1935 and 5 in 1947. Both are compact works, rhapsodic in structure, which brilliantly exploit violin technique, making an attractive

centrepiece for this disc of showpieces. The two Saint-Saëns pieces inspire Heifetz to much witty pointing and seductive phrasing, as do the Sarasate firework piece and the *Fantasy on Themes from Bizet's Carmen*, written for the film *Intermezzo* by the Hollywood composer, Franz Waxman. Each has remarkably good recorded sound for the period, well transferred, if with some surface hiss.

However, Viextemps's *Fourth* and *Fifth Concertos* are worthy of modern stereo, and the *Fourth* in particular is well worth hearing in as eloquent and persuasive reading as **Grumiaux** gives. The eloquent introduction operatically builds up very effectively to the soloist's entry, the theatrical effect heightened by the distinctive sound of the **Lamoureux Orchestra**. The melodic invention of both *Concertos* is most beguiling and their brilliance exciting (the finale of 4 especially so) and it is good to welcome these distinctive performances back to the catalogue.

Violin Concerto 5 in A min., Op. 37

✇ **** EMI 5 55292-2. Chang, Philh. O, Dutoit – LALO: *Symphonie espagnole* ***

✇Ⓜ **** DG (IMS) 457 896-2. Mintz, Israel PO, Mehta – LALO: *Symphonie espagnole;* SAINT-SAËNS: *Introduction & Rondo capriccioso* ***

✇Ⓜ *** RCA (ADD) 09026 61745-2. Heifetz, New SO of L, Sargent – BRUCH: *Violin Concerto, 1* etc ***

ⓑⓑ **(*) Sony (ADD) SBK 48274. Zukerman, LSO, Mackerras – BRUCH: *Concerto 1;* LALO: *Symphonie espagnole* **(*)

Sarah Chang's recording, coupling a scintillating account of the Lalo *Symphonie espagnole*, goes readily to the top of the list. It is beautifully recorded, with a perfect balance, in an agreeably warm acoustic. Chang's vitality is matched by **Dutoit** and her playing has a magically gentle tenderness in presenting the engaging lyrical themes of the first movement and the *Adagio*. The brief finale has splendid élan.

Mintz's performance has enormous dash and also real lyrical magic. **Mehta**, obviously caught up in the inspiration of the solo playing, provides an excellent accompaniment. This is another example of a memorable live performance 'recorded on the wing' and, if the acoustic is not very flattering, the sound is truthful and well balanced.

The quicksilver of **Heifetz** is well suited to the modest but attractive *Fifth Concerto* of Vieuxtemps, and **Sir Malcolm** again provides a musical and well-recorded accompaniment. The balance of the soloist is rather close, but the digital remastering is successful, and the couplings are both attractive and generous.

Zukerman provides here an enjoyable bonus to his dazzling accounts of the Bruch and Lalo works. There is comparable dash for Vieuxtemps, yet he coaxes the *Adagio* tenderly. Again a very forward balance, but the ear adjusts.

Violin Concertos (i) 5, Op. 37; 6 in G, Op. 47; (ii) 7 in A min., Op. 49

✇ⓑⓑ *** Naxos 8.557016. Keylin, (i) Slovak RSO, Mogrelia; (ii) Arnhem PO, Yuasa

Misha Keylin here completes his valuable set of the

Vieuxtemps *Concertos* with a fine, fully competitive version of the popular 5, and he also gives première recordings of 6 and 7. They belong to the last year of the composer's life and show no diminution of his melodic facility. The *G major* is in four movements and, in addition to the lovely *Pastoral* slow movement, has a charming *Intermezzo siciliano* before the sparkling *Allegretto* Rondo finale. Keylin is a very persuasive advocate, equally at home and accomplished in the *A minor Concerto*, with its *Mélancholie* central movement and dashing closing *Allegro vivo*. He plays a 1715 Stradivarius, and his elegantly warm lyricism shows its timbre off to seductive effect. The recording is very good, too.

Violin Concertos 6–7; *Salut à l'Amérique, Op. 56*

*** Audivis Valois V 4797. Poulet, Liège R. PO, Bartholomée

Gérard Poulet has a small tone, but his playing is polished and warmly cultivated, and it suits these charmingly elegant works admirably. He is well accompanied, and is recorded in a pleasing acoustic. The novelty here is the engaging concertante fantasy, *Greeting to America*, written by Vieuxtemps for his first tour of the USA in 1844. It opens genially, featuring the American National Anthem intimately rather than flamboyantly. Poulet has its full measure, as he has the variations on 'Yankee doodle dandy' which follow.

Viola Sonata in B flat, *Op. 36*; Elégie, *Op. 30*; Morceaux, *Op. 61*.

*** Chan. 8873. Imai, Vignoles – FRANCK: *Viola Sonata in A* ***

*** Simax PSC 1126. Tomter, Gimse – FRANCK: *Viola Sonata in A* ***

The Vieuxtemps *Sonata* is expertly crafted and well laid out for the instruments but it is no masterpiece. **Nobuko Imai** and **Roger Vignoles** give an exemplary account of it and are given expert recording from the Chandos engineers.

The Norwegian, **Lars Anders Tomter**, is hardly less accomplished and every bit as eloquent a player as his celebrated rival and countryman, **Håvard Gimse**, is a first-rate pianist. There is absolutely nothing to choose between them, and both couple the Vieuxtemps with the Franck *Sonata* arranged for viola.

VILLA-LOBOS, Heitor
(1887–1959)

Amazonas; *Dawn in a Tropical Forest*; Erosão; Gênesis

*** Marco Polo 8.223357. Czecho-Slovak RSO (Bratislava), Duarte

These are imaginative scores with tropical colouring and exotic textures, all sounding rather similar in their luxuriance – but who cares! *Amazonas* is the earliest and most astonishing score, dating from the First World War, and in its vivid sonorities affirms Villa-Lobos's contention that his first harmony book was the map of Brazil. The **Bratislava**

strings could be more opulent, but the performances under a Brazilian conductor are very good indeed, as is the recording.

Bachianas brasileiras (i) 1; 2; (ii) 3–4; (iii) 5; (iv) 6–9

(BB) *** Naxos 8.557460/2 (3). (ii) Feghali, (iii) Lamosa, (iv) Gratton; Nashville SO; (i) Mogrelia; (ii–iv) Schermerhorn

The present issue makes an excellent introduction to the composer, and its three CDs assemble the nine *Bachianas brasileiras* he composed between 1930 and 1945. They were conceived as homage to Bach and range from instrumental and chamber pieces (like the *First* for an orchestra of cellos, the *Fifth* for voice and eight cellos, and the *Sixth* for flute and bassoon) to larger orchestral forces (the *Ninth* for strings and the *Third* for piano and orchestra and 7 and 8 for orchestra). They are all highly original and mostly colourful, and they are very well played. **José Feghali** is an excellent soloist in the *Third*, as is **Rosana Lamosa** in the well-known *Fifth*. The **Nashville Orchestra** respond with enthusiasm to **Kenneth Schermerhorn** who, alas, died before he could complete all nine pieces, and the *First*, which had been left to last, was conducted by **Andrew Mogrelia**.

(i) Bachianas brasileiras *1–9*; (ii) Guitar Concerto; (iii) Mômoprecóce *(fantasy for piano & orchestra)*

(B) *** EMI 5 00843-2 (3). (i) Hendricks, Osorio, RPO, Bátiz; (ii) Romero, LPO, López-Cobos; (iii) Ortiz, New Philh. O, Ashkenazy

The **Bátiz** set of *Bachianas* dates from 1985/7. There is abundant spirit here and the performances are thoroughly persuasive; the popular last movement of 2, *The little train of the Caipira*, moves on its track with evident zest. **Jorge Federico Osorio** is an excellent piano soloist in 3, **Lisa Hansen** (flute) and **Susan Bell** (bassoon) contribute expertly to 6 – and it goes without saying that **Barbara Hendricks** is her appealing self in 5. The *Guitar Concerto*, written for Segovia, is not Villa-Lobos at his best: an amiable but inconsequential work, but **Angel Romero** makes the most of it, bringing out its Latin feeling. The *Mômoprecóce* began life in 1920 as a solo piano piece and was reworked in its concertante form later. The score is rowdy and colourful. **Cristina Ortiz**, herself Brazilian, is a natural choice for this repertoire, and she plays with appropriate vigour, reflective feeling and colour, and **Ashkenazy** gives splendid support. The late 1970s recording is excellent, although there is a degree of edge on high violins. Otherwise the sound is very good.

Bachianas brasileiras (iii) 1; (i; iii) 5; (i; ii) *Suite for Voice & Violin.* (iii) Arr. of BACH: *The Well-Tempered Clavier: Prelude in D min., BWV 583; Fugue in B flat, BWV 846; Prelude in G min., BWV 867; Fugue in D, BWV 874*

(B) *** Hyp. Helios CDH 55316. (i) Gomez; (ii) Manning; (iii) Pleeth Cello Octet

Jill Gomez is outstanding in the popular *Bachianas brasileiras* 5 and with the violinist, **Peter Manning**, in the *Suite* (1923). Villa-Lobos's favourite 'orchestra of cellos' produce sumptuous sounds in both the *Bachianas brasileiras*, and an added point of interest is the effective transcriptions for cellos of unrelated Bach preludes and fugues.

Bachianas brasileiras 5 for Soprano & Cellos

(B) *** Double Decca 444 995-2 (2). Te Kanawa, Harrell and instrumental ens. – CANTELOUBE: *Songs of the Auvergne* ***

The Villa-Lobos piece makes an apt fill-up for the Canteloube songs, completing **Kiri Te Kanawa's** recording of all five books. It is, if anything, even more sensuously done, well sustained at a speed far slower than one would normally expect. Rich recording to match.

(i) Chôros 1; (ii) Chôros 4 for 3 horns and trombone; (iii) Choros 6, 8 & 9

(N) **** BIS CD1450 (i) Zanon; (ii) Venque, Arantes, Hamzem, Coleman Milling; (iii) São Paulo SO, John Neschling

The series of *Chôros* on which Villa-Lobos embarked in the 1920s, employ various instrumental combinations. The *First* (1920) is for solo guitar, and the *Fourth* (1926) for three horns and bass trombone. The *Sixth* (also 1926) is the first for orchestra, and both the *Eighth* (1925) and *Ninth* (1929) employ Brazilian percussion instruments and the resulting sonorities, such as the caracaxa (children's rattle) have great exotic appeal. Villa-Lobos absorbed into his system much of the contemporary music of the day, Debussy, *The Rite of Spring, Le boeuf sur le toit* and other works of Les Six. Yet it is the richly textured exoticism evoking the sounds of the Brazilian forest, the boundless vitality of the dance, which resonates in the memory. Villa-Lobos creates his own sound world and there is an infectious life and atmosphere here. **John Neschling**, born in Rio de Janeiro, and a pupil of Swarowsky and Bernstein, gets an enthusiastic response from his fine **São Paolo** players and the BIS recording team does them proud. A good entry point into this composer's world.

Chôros 5, 'Alma Brasileira', for piano; 7, 'Settimino', for winds, violin & cello; 11 for piano & orchestra

*** BIS CD 1440. Ortiz, São Paulo SO, Neschling

When he discussed the *Chôros* towards the end of his life, Villa-Lobos spoke of it as 'a genre, even if an ill-defined one'. The *Fifth* (1925) is a five-minute pieces for solo piano (perhaps the nearest word to approximate to *Chôros* is 'serenade') and the *Seventh*, for winds, violin and cello, is a strikingly original piece and the last of the *Chôros* composed for chamber forces. The *Eleventh* (1928) was written for Rubinstein and is a work of exceptional size and grandeur. The Finnish scholar Eero Tarasti called it the most remarkable of all his works. It is an inflated concerto grosso, turned into a truly romantic concerto for piano and a large orchestra, and it runs to over an hour (its last movement alone is 26 minutes long). **Cristina Ortiz** plays all this music with relish and the **São Paulo Symphony Orchestra** and **John Neschling** provide excellent support. A valuable addition to the Villa-Lobos discography.

Chôros 8; 9

🎵– (BB) *** Naxos 8.555241. Hong Kong PO, Schermerhorn

The *Chôros 8* (1925) is what we think of as quintessential Villa-Lobos, exotic, full of colour and superbly evocative insect, bird and forest sounds, all effectively conveyed by the **Hong Kong orchestra** under **Kenneth Schermerhorn**. Villa-Lobos himself spoke of the *Chôros* as 'representing a new form of musical composition synthesizing different kinds of Brazilian Indian and folk-music, having as their principal elements rhythm and all kinds of typical folk melody that appear accidentally from time to time, always transformed by the personality of the composer'. Like *8*, the *Chôros 9* (1929) calls for a huge orchestra, including Brazilian percussion instruments. There is an exuberance, exoticism and an abundance of musical ideas clamouring for attention. The recordings were made in the 1980s and are very good indeed.

Guitar Concerto

🎵– *** Warner 2564 60296-2. Isbin, NYPO, Serebrier – PONCE: *Concierto del sur*; RODRIGO: *Concierto de Aranjuez* ***

(BB) *** Naxos 8.550729. Kraft, N. CO, Ward – CASTELNUOVO-TEDESCO: *Concerto*; RODRIGO: *Concierto de Aranjuez* ***

*** Guild GMCD 7176. Jiménez, Bournemouth Sinf., Frazor – ANGULO: *Guitar Concerto 2 (El Alevín)*; RODRIGO: *Concierto de Aranjuez* ***

(i) Guitar Concerto; 12 Etudes; 5 Preludes

🎵– (M) *** RCA (ADD) 09026 61604-2. Bream; (i) LSO, Previn

From the very opening, **Serebrier** spins a web of vividly colourful sounds from the orchestra, which **Sharon Isbin** gently dominates. The lyrical secondary theme floats enticingly by, but the effect in the opening movment is of a free fantasia in which guitar and orchestra find true serendipity. The *Andantino* is charmingly romantic, the finale with its playful touches from the bassoon is zestful but rhythmically graceful. The recording is first class and beautifully balanced.

A highly distinguished account of the *Guitar Concerto* from **Bream**, magnetic and full of atmosphere in the slow movement and finale. **Previn** accompanies sympathetically and with spirit. The rest of the programme also shows Bream in inspirational form. He engages the listener's attention from the opening of the first study and holds it to the last. The recording has a nice intimacy in the *Concerto* and the solo items have fine presence against an attractive ambience.

An excellent account from **Norbert Kraft**, spontaneous and catching well the music's colour and atmosphere. If it is not quite as individual as Bream's version, it has the advantage of vivid, well-balanced, modern, digital recording and excellent couplings. Another genuine Naxos bargain.

Rafael Jiménez also proves a natural soloist for Villa-Lobos's intimate *Concerto*, and **Terence Frazor** and the **Bournemouth Sinfonietta** make the very most of the orchestral colouring, which sounds more vivid than usual. Yet the balance integrates the soloist appealingly within the orchestral texture.

Piano Concertos 1–5

⊕—Ⓑ *** Double Decca 452 617-2 (2). Ortiz, RPO, Gómez-Martínez

What emerges from the series of *Concertos*, as played here by **Cristina Ortiz**, is that the first two are the most immediately identifiable as Brazilian in their warm colouring and sense of atmosphere, even though the eclectic borrowings are often more unashamed than later, with many passages suggesting Rachmaninov with a Brazilian accent. 3, the work Villa-Lobos found it hard to complete, tends to sound bitty in its changes of direction. 4, more crisply conceived, has one or two splendid tunes, but it is in 5 that Villa-Lobos becomes most warmly convincing again, returning unashamedly to more echoes of Rachmaninov. With Ortiz articulating crisply, there is much to enjoy from such colourful, undemanding music, brilliantly recorded and sympathetically performed.

Symphony 2 (Ascenção); New York Skyline Melody

*** CPO 999 785. Stuttgart RSO, St Clair

The *Second Symphony* comes from 1917, at a time when the composer was much influenced by Vincent d'Indy. There are five *Symphonies* from the period 1916–20, the *Sixth* appearing in 1944. 2 was probably left in an incomplete state, since it did not receive a performance until 1944, when Villa-Lobos conducted it in Rio and then in Los Angeles. It is a long piece of 50 minutes' duration, with an opening allegro of nearly 18 minutes! By contrast, the *New York Skyline Melody* takes less than three. The *Symphony* is for 'completists' and, for all its abundant vitality, is wanting in symphonic concentration. **Carl St Clair** and his **Stuttgart Orchestra** play very persuasively and the studio recording is first class.

Symphony 10 (Amerindia)

*** HM 987041. Tenerife SO & Ch., Victor Pablo Perez

Amerindia was written in 1952 for the 400th anniversary of the city of São Paulo; it celebrates the example of St José de Anchieta, who called the cabin which served him as church, school, home and hospital, São Paulo. Anchieta was sent to Brazil by the Jesuits, and here he created small village communities which protected the local tribes from the savage Portuguese colonizers and slave traders. It is Father Anchieta's story and his poem in praise of the Virgin Mary that inspire the *Tenth Symphony*. It is a huge work some 70 minutes in length and is full of the sprawling invention and lush vegetation characteristic of the composer. Each of the movements has lots of character and each rather outstays its welcome. The fourth movement is the longest at 27 minutes. There are simple melodies in the native Indian style, syncopated rhythms of the Afro-Brazilian people, plus birdsong, and traditional percussion instruments mixed with the huge orchestra. The canvas may be too large and overcrowded with detail but there is a vitality here that makes it worth investigating.

GUITAR MUSIC

Chôros 1 (Typico); 12 Etudes; 5 Préludes; Suite populaire brésilienne

⊕—ⒷⒷ **** Naxos 8.553987. Kraft

Norbert Kraft show his absolute mastery of his instrument in his dazzling account of the *Twelve Etudes*, which have contrasting moments of reflection. He plays the *Five Préludes* beautifully, too, with a fine control of atmosphere and rubato. The *Chôros* and *Suite populaire brésilienne* are marginally less spontaneous-sounding, and the latter is not as colourfully idiomatic as in the hands of Julian Bream. But this inexpensive disc gathers together all the composer's important music for solo guitar, and by any standards this is fine playing. The recording is naturally balanced and has a vivid but not exaggerated presence.

5 Preludes for Guitar

⊕—ⒷⒷ **** Sony (ADD) SBK 62425. Williams (guitar) –
GIULIANI: *Variations on a Theme by Handel*; PAGANINI: *Caprice 24*; *Grand Sonata*; D. SCARLATTI: *Sonatas* ***

Although **John Williams** is balanced a shade too closely, he is very well recorded; his playing, improvisationally spontaneous and full of magical evocation, is of the highest level of mastery. A lower-level setting compensates for the balance and enables this artist's playing to register effectively. These are as perfect and as finely turned as any performances in the catalogue.

CHAMBER MUSIC

Assobio a jato (for flute & cello); Bachianas brasileiras 6 (for flute & bassoon); Canço do amor (for flute & guitar); Chôros 2 (for flute & clarinet); Modinha; Distribuição do flores (both for flute & guitar); Quinteto en forma e chôros (for wind); Trio for Oboe, Clarinet & Bassoon

⊕—ⒷⒷ **** Hyp. Helios CDH 55057. Bennett, Tunnell, O'Neill, Wynberg, King, Black, Knight

There are few more inviting introductions to the exotic colours and indelible invention that this Brazilian composer has made his own. With the superb flautist **William Bennett** at the centre of the group, the performances could hardly be more enticing, or indeed more polished. For the engaging Parisian *Quinteto en forma de chôros* of 1928, with its vivid mood changes, it is equally expert playing from **Thea King** (clarinet), **Neil Black** (oboe), **Robin O'Neill** (bassoon) and **Janice Knight** (cor anglais). Among the various duos in the improvisatory duet style of Rio's street musicians (to which **Charles Tunnell**, guitar, also contributes) the romantic *Modinha*, the lovely *Distribution of Flowers*, the *Song of Love* and the chirping flute and fluid cello lines of the *Jet Whistle*, with its touching centrepiece, contrast with the witty *Chôros 2*. The most ambitious Brazilian piece is the unpredictable *Trio* with its raw jungle voicings, dextrous rhythms and syncopations and lyrical *Languisamente*. This slow central section and the *Vivo* finale are faintly Stravinskyan, but with an added touch of witty geniality. First-class recording, present but not too close. Not to be missed.

PIANO MUSIC

Alma brasileira, Bachianas brasileiras 4; Ciclo brasileiro; Chôros 5; Valsa da dor (Waltz of Sorrows)

*** ASV CDDCA 607. Petchersky

Alma Petchersky's style is romantic, and some might find her thoughtful deliberation in the *Preludio* of the *Bachianas brasileiras 4* overdone. Her very free rubato is immediately apparent in the *Valsa da dor*, which opens the recital. Yet she clearly feels all this music deeply, and the playing is strong in personality and her timbre is often richly coloured. She is at her finest in the *Brazilian Cycle*. The recording is excellent.

As três Marias; Bachianas brasileiras 4: Preludio. Prole do bèbe (The Child's Doll): Suite; Rudepoema

(BB) **(*) Warner Apex (ADD 0927 40837-2). Freire

Excellent playing and eminently satisfactory recording of some delightfully colourful piano music. But at 40 minutes the measure is short, even at Apex price.

Cirandas; Rudepoema

⊖→ *** ASV CDDCA 957. Petchersky

Not only is the playing here first class, but the music itself is of much interest. *Rudepoema* (1921–6) is a musical portrait of Artur Rubinstein and is full of temperament and virtuosity. **Alma Petchersky** rises to its innumerable challenges with great spirit and panache. The *Cirandas* (1926), which make formidable technical demands on the pianist, are despatched with great brilliance and poetic feeling. Alma Petchersky is very well recorded and, if the standards of this series are maintained, future issues will be self-recommending.

VINTER, Gilbert (1909–69)

Hunter's Moon

*** Lyrita SRCD 316. Pyatt, LPO, Braithwaite – ARNOLD; BOWEN; GIPPS; JACOBS: *Horn Concertos* ***

Gilbert Vinter's *Hunter's Moon* is all but a mini-concerto for the horn, engagingly combining lyricism with bravura. A favourite encore with Dennis Brain, it is superbly played here by the estimable **David Pyatt**, part of the most enjoyable collection of British horn concertos in the catalogue.

VIOTTI, Giovanni Battista (1755–1824)

3 Nocturnes for Flute & Piano; 6 Serenades for Flute & Piano

(N) *** Dynamic CDS 620/1-2 (2) Carbotta, Balzaretti

Viotti was primarily – both as composer and performer – devoted to the violin, but he also transcribed a good deal of his own music for the flute (or delegated arrangements to others). His three *Nocturnes*, published in 1820 (arranged by the French flautist Berbiguier) derive from his *Trois divertissements for cello and piano*, the *Six Serenades*, Op. 23 originate as works for two violins, and were apparently adapted by other composers too, as works for various combinations of instruments. This was obviously because Viotti was a natural melodist. So while the three *Nocturnes* are comparatively simple, the *Serenades* each have five or seven diverse, very inventive movements and, eight sections in the case of the last of the set. The tunes are catchy (some of them obvious 'hits' in the manner of their time), and varying from meditative feeling, in the case of the *Nocturnes*, to cantabile *Andantes* (sometimes with 'tricky technical passages'), *Pastorales* or *Variations*. The *Allegrettos* are usually bright and lively, but occasionally make a surprise move into the minor key. The piano reinforces the music's character, but also at times plays alone. Altogether these are most rewarding pieces and they are played with skill and spontaneity by **Mario Carbotta** (flute) and **Carlo Balzaretti** (piano).

VISÉE, Robert de (c.1660–before 1732)

Pièces de théorbe in D min.; G; A min.; Suite of arrangements for theorbo of music by Lully

(N) **** Metronome METCD 1072. Fred Jacobs (French theorbo)

We usually hear the theorbo as part of a continuo, but here are three suites of original music for this divertingly intimate instrument, plus some attractive arrangements of theatre music by Lully. There are seven or eight *Pièces* in each collection, in the usual dance forms, although the D minor collection ends with a *Passacaille* and the G major a *Musette*. The penultimate movement of the A minor set is the famous *Les Folies d'Espagne*, and its finale is a sombre elegiac lament for the death of his wife and daughters. But most of this music is cheerful. It is splendidly played, but with appropriate delicacy by **Fred Jacobs** on a large French theorbo built in the second half of the seventeenth century, and truthfully recorded in a pleasing acoustic.

VIVALDI, Antonio (1678–1741)

'Masterworks': Sonatas for 2 Violins, Op. 1/1–12; Violin Sonatas, Op. 2/1–12; L'estro armonico (12 Concertos), Op. 3; La Stravaganza (12 Concertos), Op. 4; 6 Sonatas for 1 or 2 Violins, Op. 5; 6 Violin Concertos, Op. 6; 12 Concertos for Oboe or Violin, Op. 7; Il Cimento dell'Armonia e dell'invenzione (12 Violin Concertos), Op. 8 (including The Four Seasons, Op. 8/1–4); La Cetra (12 Concertos), Op. 9; 6 Flute Concertos, Op. 10; 6 Violin Concertos, Op. 11; 6 Violin Concertos, Op. 12 (Artists include Accardo (Opp. 1, 2, 5, 7, 8, 11 & 12); Michelucci (Op. 3); I Musici (Op. 3, 4, 6 & 12); Carmirelli (Op. 6); Holliger (Op. 7); Gazzeloni (Op. 10) & others.) 7

Trio Sonatas (for flute, violin & continuo) *(Musique des Lumières). Concertos: for Guitar* (after *Trio Sonata, Op. 14/3); Lute, RV 93; Mandolin, RV 425; 2 Mandolins, RV 532* (Lagoya, Presti, Munich Pro Arte O, Redel); *Double Trumpet Concerto in C, RV 537* (with André, Lagorce); *Concertos à quatre for Flute, Oboe, Cello & Harpsichord, RV 100 & 106; Concertos for 2 Horns, RV 538 & 539; Cello Sonata, Op. 15/5; Oboe Sonata, RV 53* (all with Paris Coll. Mus.). *Concertos: for Bassoon, RV 484; 2 Cellos, RV 130; Oboe & Violin, RV 548; Strings, RV 158; Viola d'amore, RV 540. Concertos: for flautino (Piccolo), RV 444 & 445; for Violin, RV 326; for 2 Violins, RV 514; for 3 Violins, RV 551* (all with soloists, Sarre CO, Ristenpart). *Concerto (La Pastorella) RV 95. Concertos for 2 Oboes, RV 536; for Violin & Cello, RV 544; for Violin & Organ, RV 542; for Viola d'amore, RV 397; Cello Sonata, RV 41; Trio Sonata for Recorder, Bassoon & Continuo, RV 86* (I Musici). *Concertos: for Flute, Oboe, Violin, Bassoon & Harpsichord (La Pastorella), RV 95; for Flute, Oboe & Bassoon, RV 103* (Paris Baroque Ens. including Rampal, Pierlot, Gendre, Hongne). J. S. BACH: *Transcriptions of Concertos for Harpsichord, BWV 972/3; 975/6; 978; 980* (Luciano Sgrizzi); *for Organ, BWV 593/4; 595; 596* (Jean Guillou). *Choral Music: Beatus vir* (2 settings), *RV 597 & 598; Canto in prato, RV 623; Confitebor, RV 696; Crediti propter quod, RV 605; Credos, RV 591 & 592; Deus tuorum militum, RV 612; Introduction al Dixit, RV 636 & 635; Dixit Dominus* (2 settings), *RV 594 & 595; Domine ad adiuvandum me, RV 593; In exitu Israel, RV 604; Introductions al Gloria, RV 639 & 642; Gaude Mater Ecclesia, RV 613; Glorias, RV 588 & 589; In fuore, RV 626; Kyrie, RV 587; Laetatus sum, RV 607; Laudate Dominum, RV 606; Laudate Pueri* (3 settings), *RV 600, 601 & 602; Magnificats, RV 610 & 611; Nisi Dominus, RV 608; Nulla in mundo pax, RV 630; O qui coeli, RV 631; Regina coeli, RV 615; Sacrum, RV 686; Salve Reginas, RV 616, 617 & 618; Sanctorum meritis, RV 620; Stabat Mater, RV 621* (Soloists, John Alldis Ch., ECO or Concg. CO, Negri). *Cantatas for alto, RV 674, 677, 683 & 684* (Lesne, Il Seminario Musicale) *Juditha Triumphans* (Oratorio), *RV 644* (soloists, Ch. & Berlin CO, Negri). *La Senna Festeggiante* (complete) (soloists, La Parlement de Musique, Gester)

(BB) **(*) Decca/ Ph. (ADD/DDD) 442 9337 (40)

Although this super-bargain box has a Decca logo, these recordings (made between 1959 – one of the first stereo recordings of *The Four Seasons* – and 1991) almost all derive from the Philips catalogue, although a few come from the French branch of Universal Classics – who provide the only period-instrument recordings from **Musique des Lumières**. Everything else is recorded on modern instruments and, with artists of the calibre of **Accardo**, **Carmirelli**, **Holliger** and **Gazzeloni**, their excellence can be taken for granted.

Most of the performances have been praised by us over the years (especially **Vittorio Negri's** pioneering series of the major choral works). Among the novelties are the *Cantatas for alto*, (admirably sung by **Gérard Lesne** with **Il Seminario Musicale**), the oratorio *Juditha Triumphans* and the virtually unknown *La Senna Festeggiante*. The recordings cannot be faulted; however, although music and performers are listed in detail in the booklet, there is no other documentation. Nevertheless this is a supreme Vivaldi bargain set.

Concertos & Sonatas, Opp. 1–12: *Sonatas for 2 Violins, Op. 1/1–12; Violin Sonatas, Op. 2/1–12; L'estro armonico, Op. 3; La Stravaganza, Op. 4; 6 Sonatas for 1 or 2 Violins, Op. 5; 6 Violin Concertos, Op. 6; 12 Concertos for Violin or Oboe, Op. 7; Il Cimento dell'armonia e dell'invenzione, Op. 8 (including The Four Seasons); La Cetra, Op. 9* (with Toso, Rybin, Pierlot & soloists); *6 Concertos for Flute, Op. 10* (with Rampal); *6 Concertos for Violin or Oboe, Op. 11* (with Toso, Rybin & Pierlot); *6 Violin Concertos, Op. 12* (with Toso, Rybin & Carmignola; all with Sol. Ven., Scimone). NICOLAS CHÉDEVILLE **(attrib. Vivaldi):** *Il Pastor Fido* **(6 Sonatas for Flute & Harpsichord)** (Rampal & Veyron-Lacroix); *6 Cello Sonatas, RV 40/46* (Tortelier & Veyron-Lacroix)

(B) **(*) Warner (ADD/DDD) 2564 64320-2 (18)

These Erato recordings were made between 1965 and 1988, with **I Solisti Veneti** under **Scimone**. They now come more handsomely boxed than the Decca set; moreover, they include proper documentation (and also *Il Pastor Fido*, which is worth having, even if only a Vivaldian pastiche by Nicolas Chédeville).

It has to be said that, side by side with the finest analogue versions of the time, the Erato sets of Opp. 3, 4 and 8, for all the intelligence and sensitivity of Scimone's readings, are lacking something in individuality. They are energetic and enjoyable in their way, with **Toso** an excellent soloist, positively mercurial in his eccentric but imaginative account of the *Four Seasons*. The recording is nicely balanced, but the backward placing of the continuo and sparseness of ornamentation do not help. However, *La Cetra* stands out as the finest of these sets of the *Concertos*, intimate and stylish, with the excellent **Juan Carlos Rybin** joining **Toso** as soloist. Many too will welcome the appearance of **Rampal** and **Tortelier** in the *Cello* and *Flute Sonatas*, particularly as they are partnered by **Veyron-Lacroix** on the harpsichord. All the recordings still sound well, and undoubtedly offer much enjoyment.

L'estro armonico (12 Concertos), Op. 3

🎧 **** Analekta AN 2 9835 (2). Wallfisch, Tafelmusik Bar. O, Lamon (with bonus DVD: '*Four Seasons Mosaic*', including *Spring & Autumn*) (Dir: Ann Shin, V/D: Chris Romeike)

🎧 **** Chan. 0689 (2). Guglielmo & soloists, L'Arte dell'Arco, Hogwood

🎧 (M) *** Virgin 5 45315-2 (2). Biondi, Longo, Casazza, Negri, Naddeo, Europa Galante

L'estro armonico, Op. 3; (i) *Bassoon Concerto in A min., RV 498;* (ii) *Flute Concerto in C min., RV 441;* (iii) *Oboe Concerto in F, RV 456;* (i; iii; iv) *Concerto in F for 2 Oboes, Bassoon, 2 Horns & Violin, RV 574*

🎵 ⓑ **** Double Decca (ADD) 443 476-2 (2). ASMF, Marriner; with (i) Gatt; (ii) Bennett; (iii) Black; (iv) Nicklin, T. Brown, Davis, I. Brown

(i) *L'estro armonico, Op. 3;* (ii) *6 Flute Concertos, Op. 10*

🎵 ⓑ *** DG 477 5421 (2). (i) Standage & soloists, E. Concert, Pinnock; (ii) with Beznosiuk

Wallfisch is an ideal soloist, fresh and appealing, and the transparent textures of Tafelmusik are most engaging. There is much subtlety of light and shade; vitality is balanced by expressive warmth and there is also a rare sense of fantasy. The recording is in the demonstration bracket. The set comes with a bonus DVD, 'The Four Seasons Mosaic', a 'cross-cultural performing arts documentary including musical traditions from around the world'. Filmed in India, China, the Canadian Arctic and Toronto, it features, besides Jeanne Lamon and Tafelmusik, sarangi player **Aruna Narayan**, pipa player **Wen Zhao**, and a duo of throat singers, **Aqsamiit**. Fascinating! But it comes free with the set anyway.

Using a new edition, based on the earliest printed manuscripts, **Christopher Hogwood** has returned to *L'estro armonico*, using a group of Italian musicians and, in particular, their *maestro al violino*, **Federico Guglielmo**. The fruitful results are borne out here in a glowing performance, with one instrument to a part, combining (unexaggerated) vitality with gleaming Italian expressive warmth. The quality of sonority is nearer to the ASMF style than some of the abrasive sounds we hear from some 'authentic' performances.

Pinnock's *l'Estro armonico* (with one instrument to a part) brings together the best features from past versions: there is as much sparkle and liveliness as with Hogwood, for rhythms are consistently resilient, the ensemble crisp and vigorous. In the *Flute Concertos* Lisa Beznosiuk is a superb soloist and the sound is first class throughout.

Fabio Biondi and **Europa Galante** start with 2, whose arresting opening *Adagio e spiccato* is very dramatic. Indeed, these performances are tremendously alert, crisply rhythmic and marvellously played, with the lyrical writing always winningly expressive. Biondi and **Isabella Longo** make a captivating partnership in the *Double Violin Concerto, RV 519* (7). Period-instrument playing of Vivaldi has clearly matured and, with first-class modern recording, this offers a strong challenge to both Pinnock and Hogwood.

Marriner directs the **Academy** in radiant and imaginative performances of baroque music and yet observes scholarly good manners. The delightful use of continuo – lute and organ as well as harpsichord – the sharing of solo honours and the consistently resilient string playing of the ensemble make for compelling listening. The 1972 recording, made in St John's, Smith Square, is immaculately transferred, and as a bonus come four of Vivaldi's most inventive *Concertos*, each with its own special effects.

(i) *L'estro armonico, Op. 3* (complete); (ii) *6 Flute Concertos, Op. 10.* Miscellaneous concertos:

CD 1: *Double Mandolin Concerto, RG 532; Oboe Concertos, RV 548 & 461; Concerto for Strings (alla rustica), RV 151; Con molti stromenti, RV 558; Double Violin Concerto, RV 516*

CD 2: *Concertos for Bassoon, RV 484; for Flute, RV 436; for Oboe & Bassoon, RV 545; for Strings, RV 159; for Viola d'amore & Lute, RV 540; for Violin (L'amoroso), RV 271*

ⓑ *** DG 471 317-2 (5). (i) Standage, Wilcock, Golding, Comberti, Jaap ter Linden; (ii) Beznosiuk; soloists, E. Concert, Pinnock

Pinnock's performances of *L'estro armonico* and the Op. 10 *Flute Concertos* with **Lisa Beznosiuk** are among our top recommendations. The two separate single-CD collections, one entitled *Alla rustica* the other *L'amoroso*, offer lively, communicative performances, using period instruments in the most enticing way. The sheer variety of Vivaldi is constantly established, totally contradicting the old idea that he wrote one concerto hundreds of times over. The documentation is excellent.

L'estro armonico, Op. 3/1, 2, 4, 7, 8 & 10–11

ⓑⓑ *** Naxos 8.550160. Capella Istropolitana, Kopelman

Jozef Kopelman and the **Capella Istropolitana** are robustly competitive with their bargain disc. The performances are lively, and the recording has warmth and presence. Good value for money.

L'estro armonico: Violin Concertos in B min. & D min., Op. 3/10 & 11

*** Australian Decca Eloquence (ADD) 442 8414. Barshai, Moscow CO, Barshai – HINDEMITH: *5 Pieces*; PROKOFIEV: *Visions Fugitives* ***

The playing of **Barshai** and the **Moscow Chamber Orchestra** is fresh and brilliant (technically it is impeccable), and if the original review thought that 'the lift is sometimes achieved at the expense of limpidity and warmth of phrasing', it sounds large-scale and warm by the 'authentic' styles of today. The bright (1962) recording is admirably warm and clear and lets the harpsichord continuo through adequately.

La stravaganza (12 concertos), *Op. 4* (complete)

🎵 **** Channel Classics **SACD** CCS SA 19503 (2). Podger, Arte Dei Suonatori

🎵 ⚙ ⓑ **** Double Decca 444 821-2 (2). Soloists, ASMF, Marriner

Podger's solo playing is full of vitality and imaginative, expressive feeling, and the orchestra and continuo players all combine to give her a richly persuasive and detailed backcloth. Whether played using only the front speakers or also the third channel at the back (the fourth is silent) the recording has a spacious realism. While Rachel Podger's gleaming timbre dominates, the other soloists, drawn from the orchestra, are all excellent, as is the ensemble, apparently achieved without a conductor. The continuo too – archlute, guitar, theorbo, harpsichord and organ – comes through believably.

Marriner's performances make the music irresistible. The solo playing of **Carmel Kaine** and **Alan Loveday** is superb and, when the **Academy's** rhythms have such splendid buoyancy and lift, it is easy enough to accept Marriner's preference for a relatively sweet style in the often heavenly slow movements. The contribution of an imaginatively varied continuo (which includes cello and bassoon, in addition to harpsichord, theorbo and organ) adds much to the colour of Vivaldi's score.

The Trial between Harmony and Invention (12 Concertos), Op. 8; (i) 1–4: The Four Seasons; (ii) 5–12 (complete); (ii; iii) Double Violin Concerto in D, RV 513.

🔑 ✿ (BB) (***) Naxos mono 8.110297/8. Kaufman; (i) Concert Hall CO, Swoboda; (ii) Winterthur SO, Dahinden; (iii) with Rybar

This is a very special *Four Seasons*. Recorded in Carnegie Hall in December 1947 by **Louis Kaufman**, a soloist of distinction, very famous in America in his day, and the **Concert Hall Chamber Orchestra** directed by **Henry Swoboda**, it was the work's recording première. Some 3,000 sets were pressed – and so too was re-established the reputation of Antonio Vivaldi. Kaufman went on to record the other eight *Concertos* of Op. 8 on Zürich in 1950 with the **Winterthur Symphony Orchestra** conducted by **Clemens Dahinden**, who was a natural Vivaldian and supported him well.

Kaufman was thus a key pioneer in promoting the Vivaldi revival, which came with the long-playing record. What is astonishing is how like modern-day performances these are, with apt tempi and a style which is athletic and expressive by turns. Indeed, all this music sounds as fresh as ever and, with excellent transfers, the sound too is astonishingly good, the *Four Seasons* limited in range but well balanced (with even a hint of the continuo now and then) and aurally pleasing.

The Trial between Harmony and Invention (12 Concertos), Op. 8

🔑 (M) **** Virgin 5 61980-2 (2) Biondi, Europa Galante

The Trial between Harmony and Invention (12 Concertos), Op. 8; (i) Double Concertos: for Violin, Cello & Strings in A, RV 546; for 2 Violins in G, RV 516

(BB) *** Virgin 2x1 5 61668-2 (2). Huggett, Raglan Bar. Players, Kraemer; (i) with E. Wallfisch & Mason (cello)

Fabio Biondi and **Europa Galante** have already recorded the *Four Seasons* and their period-instrument performance is highly praised below. The new version, within the complete Op. 8, is just as fresh and certainly as vibrant, with some dazzling solo playing full of dynamic subtlety.

Kraemer's complete Op. 8 *Concertos* with **Monica Huggett** make a fine alternative bargain recommendation in its new Virgin 2x1 format. In the *Four Seasons*, a lovely spontaneous feeling emerges: the light textures and dancing tempo of the finale of *Spring* are matched by the sense of fantasy in the central movement of *Summer*, while the rumbustious energy of the latter's last movement is gloriously invigorating. With two other enjoyable concertos thrown in for good measure, this is very highly recommendable.

The Four Seasons, Op. 8/1–4 (DVD versions)

🔑 **** DG **DVD** 073 4415. Kremer, ECO (Dir: Christopher Nupen)

🔑 **** BBC Opus Arte **DVD** OA 0818D. Fischer, ASMF, Sillito. (Producer: Gethin Scourfield, V/D: Ferenc van Damme.)

(N) *(**) Warner NVC Arts **DVD** 50-51442-7865-2-1 Il Giardino Armonico, Antonini

Recorded against the attractive backcloth of the Abbey Library near Munich in 1981, **Kremer's** performance finds an almost ideal balance between virtuosity in outer movements and sensitivity in slow ones – where the orchestral group matches the soloist with textures of striking delicacy, and **Philip Ledger's** harpsichord contribution comes through gently. The direction by **Christopher Nupen** is quite imaginative and those who want no visuals except the musicians themselves playing will find this admirably satisfying. The modern-instrument sound from the **ECO** strings is pleasingly full and the balance excellent.

It seems rather appropriate that, as with LP and CD, one of the first really outstanding DVDs of *The Four Seasons* should come from the **Academy of St Martin-in-the-Fields**, this time directed and led vivaciously by **Kenneth Sillito**, and with a brilliant young soloist in **Julia Fischer**. She plays with remarkable freshness, obviously inspiring the Academy players also to give of their very best. The result is remarkably spontaneous, and one feels one is hearing this baroque masterpiece anew. The recording was made in the dome of the National Botanic Gardens of Wales, which has surprisingly good acoustics. All four of the *Seasons* were recorded separately. So the viewer watches the musicians in close-up or enjoys the pictorial splendour of the changing Welsh countryside, lakeland and glowing sunsets. There are 'director's cut' and 'performance edit' options and the bonuses include a series of brief interviews with the soloist.

This is a visualisation of Vivaldi's *Four Seasons*, taking the viewer on a tour of Venice during the four seasons of the year. The pictorialisation every so often fits with the music, as when a host of pigeons dramatically fly away, but at other times it is contrived. Mostly it is a series of vignettes of the thriving city, with its regular inhabitants, tourist visitors and craftsmen. It is certainly beautifully and vividly photographed, although at the very beginning there is no attempt to picture the shepherd's dog barking, so explicitly described in Vivaldi's music. However the package also includes a digital CD audio version, so you can listen to that alone, and the performance by **Il Giardino Armonico** is full of vitality, and delicate evocation, although the tempi of allegros are very brisk indeed: the *Allegro non molto* of 'Winter', for instance, is much too fast. The recording is first class.

The Four Seasons, Op. 8/1–4 (CD version)

(N) 🔊— 🌼 ******** Sony/BMG 88697 11013-2 Joshua Bell, ASMF

(i) The Four Seasons, Op. 8/1–4; (ii) Bassoon Concerto in A min., RV 498; (iii) Double Concerto for 2 Oboes in D min., RV 535; (iv) Piccolo Concerto in C, RV 443

🔊— (M) ******* Decca 475 7531. ASMF, Marriner; with (i) Loveday; (ii) Gatt; (iii) Black, Nicklin; (iv) Bennett

The Four Seasons; Cello Concerto in B min., RV 424; Double Oboe Concerto in D min., RV 535; Concerto for Strings in G (Alla Rustica), RV 151; (i) Double Trumpet Concerto in C, RV 337

🔊— (M) ******** Sony SMK 89987. Lamon, Tafelmusik; (i) with Steele-Perkins, Thiessen

(i) The Four Seasons; (ii) Oboe Concertos: in D min., Op. 8/9 (RV 454); in A min., RV 461.

🔊— (M) ******** Warner Elatus 0927 46726-2. (i) Manze; (ii) Ponselle; Amsterdam Bar. O, Koopman

The Four Seasons, Op. 8/1–4; Double Violin Concerto in G, RV 516; Double Concerto for Violin & Oboe in F, RV 548

(M) ******* DG 474 616-2. Standage, E. Concert, Pinnock

The Four Seasons, Op. 8/1–4; Triple Violin Concerto in F, RV 551; Quadruple Violin Concerto in B min., RV 580

🔊— 🌼 (M) ******** Ph. 422 065-2. Accardo & I Solisti di Napoli

The Four Seasons; Violin Concerto in D, RV 171; Concerto for Strings in B flat (Concha), RV 163

🔊— ******** Naïve 111 OPS 569120. Biondi, Europa Galante

The Four Seasons; Violin Concertos: in E flat (La tempesta di mare), RV 253; in C (Il piacere), RV 108, Op. 8/5–6

🔊— ******* DHM/BMG 82876 60158-2. von der Goltz, Freiburg Bar. O & Harp Consort (with Vivaldi's Four Descriptive Sonnets in Italian and English)

(BB) ******* Warner Apex 8573 89097-2. Blankestijn, COE

The Four Seasons, Op. 8/1–4; Violin Concertos: in D, RV 211; in E flat, RV 257; in B flat, RV 276

*** Sony SK 51352. Carmignola, Venice Bar. O, Marcon

It seems that *The Four Seasons* is inevitably linked on record with the **Academy of St Martin-in-the-Fields**. They participated in the first outstanding LP/CD version (still a top choice), and in one of the finest DVDs with Julia Fischer, see above. Now they offer a truly outstanding new performance and recording in an inspired partnership with **Joshua Bell** directing from the bow. The solo playing is matchless, lithe and beautiful, full of expressive vitality, evocative of Vivaldi's descriptive intentions and ideally paced to catch the score's

vivid detail. Moreover the bonus is an equally electrifying account of Tartini's *'Devil's Trill' Sonata*. The recording is in the demonstration bracket.

Marriner's 1969 recording of *The Four Seasons* with **Alan Loveday** has been our top recommendation for nearly four decades and is still unsurpassed. Its stylish success on modern instruments makes one wonder what all the fuss about period performance is all about. It now comes back into the catalogue with three bonus *Concertos* which are hardly less enjoyable.

Salvatore Accardo's is a version with a difference. Recorded in live performances at the 1987 Cremona Festival, it is of particular interest in that Accardo uses a different Stradivarius for each of the four *Concertos* – period instruments with a difference! Thanks to this aristocrat of violinists, the sounds are of exceptional beauty, both here and also in the two multiple *Concertos* which are added as a bonus.

Tafelmusik offers another superbly imaginative version, but on period instruments. The playing is at once full of fantasy and yet has a robust gusto that is irresistible. The Sony recording is first class, with most refined detail.

Not surprisingly, **Andrew Manze's** bravura performance is hugely dramatic, fiercely energetic and full of individuality. In *Spring*, the shepherd's dog really means to be heard; in *Summer* the storms must be the worst for more than a decade, yet *Autumn*, while opening boldly, has a lusciously sensuous *Adagio*, followed by a very boisterous hunting party. The slow movement of *Winter* is similarly seductive, with very gentle raindrops, and the finale opens in a temperate, improvisatory mood, before dashing away impetuously to its riotous conclusion. **Koopman** matches Manze's virtuosity and feeling for atmosphere throughout and provides many subtle touches in the continuo (on harpsichord and organ). The bonus of two of Vivaldi's finest *Oboe Concertos* is the more winning for the sunny geniality of **Marcel Ponselle's** playing on a baroque oboe with a particularly attractive timbre. First-class recording.

Fabio Biondi and his similarly excellent period-instrument group, **Europa Galante**, have already given us an outstanding set of *L'estro armonico*, and their account of *The Four Seasons* is equally fresh. There is not a hint of routine anywhere, the solo playing is often exquisite; and even if the soloist nearly gets blown away by the gusto of the summer winds, the central reverie in *Autumn* is hauntingly gentle and serene. The bonuses are imaginative and include another of Vivaldi's most individual *Violin Concertos* and the *Concerto for Strings* given the nickname *Concha* because it is supposed to simulate a primitive instrument made from a seashell, notably in the central *Andante* with its echoing fifth (B flat and F).

Gottfried von der Golz is a highly sensitive soloist on DHM, but it is the sheer personality of the justly renowned **Freiburg Baroque Orchestra** that dominates this music-making. It is a performance of contrasts – indeed of extremes, with great energy in *Allegros* and very measured tempi in slow movements. In *Spring* the continuo at times suggests a hurdy-gurdy, while the shepherd's dog barks to a crisp abrasive staccato, and there is a similar sharpness of attack in the orchestral *Presto* at the centre of the slow movement of *Summer*, and again in the *impetuoso* finale. In the *Adagio* of *Autumn* the violin soloist floats delicately and languorously over an ethereal accompaniment with a delicate continuo; and *Winter* has similar evocative contrasts. The two additional *Concertos* are equally vibrant, their central *Largos* again ravishing in gentle espressivo. At the close we hear the four sonnets Vivaldi appended to his score, delightfully read in fluid yet theatrical Italian, but with a translation provided.

Trevor Pinnock directs his 1981 Archiv version from the keyboard, with **Simon Standage** leading the **English Concert**. Although a relatively intimate sound is produced, their approach is certainly not without drama, while the solo contributions have impressive flair and bravura.

The Sony version, with **Giuliano Carmignola** the breathtakingly brilliant soloist, is another period performance with no holds barred. Incredibly fast tempi for *Allegros* contrast with gently lyrical, highly atmospheric slow movements in which one is given the feeling almost of ruminative improvisation. Certainly the performances are full of imagination and there are many new touches (witness the *sotto voce* opening of *Winter*). Carmignola offers as his bonus similarly dazzling accounts of what are described as première recordings of three more *Violin Concertos*, all very attractive. The brilliant yet transparent recording matches the performances admirably. The CD offers texts and translations of the poems with which the works are associated.

For those still preferring the fuller texture of modern instruments, the Apex version with the **COE** provides the perfect alternative and at super-bargain price too. The chimerical solo playing of **Marieke Blankestijn** is a delight and her clean style shows that she has learned from authentic manners.

'Ultimate Vivaldi': Disc 1: *The Four Seasons; Triple Violin Concrto in F, RV 551; Quadruple Violin Concerto in B min., RV 580* (Accardo & soloists, I Solisti di Napoli). Disc 2: *Concertos for Bassoon, RV 498* (Gatt); *Flute, RV 441* (Bennett); *Oboe, RV 456* (Black); *2 Oboes, RV 535* (with Nicklin); *2 Oboes, Bassoon, 2 Horns & Violin, RV 574* (as above, with T. & I. Brown; Davis); *Piccolo Concerto in C, RV 443* (Bennett). Disc 3: *Cello Concertos, RV 401; 411; 412; 413; 418; 424* (Schiff, ASMF, Marriner). Disc 4: *Concertos for Guitar, RV 93; 356; 425; for 2 Guitars, RV 532; for 4 Guitars, RV 356* (Los Romeros (members), ASMF, I. Brown). Disc 5: *Double Concerto for Guitar & Viola d'amore*, arr. Malipiero (Fernández, Blume, ECO, Malcolm). *2 Glorias in D, RV 588 & 589* (soloists, St John's College, Cambridge, Ch., Wren O, Guest)

(BB) *** Decca (ADD) 475 8536 (5)

This is undoubtedly the highlight of Decca's super-budget 'Ultimate' composer series. There is no better Vivaldi collection in the catalogue, led by **Salvatore Accardo's** outstanding version of *The Four Seasons* and including a superb collection of miscellaneous *Concertos* with outstanding wind soloists from **Marriner's Academy** (plus the excellent **Heinrich Schiff** in the *Cello Concertos*), and members of **Los**

Romeros (originally by Philips) in the works for guitar (originally for mandolin, lute or violins). The selection is capped by splendid accounts from **St John's** of the two *Glorias*, including the more famous – RV 589. But it is a pity there are no accompanying liner notes.

The Four Seasons, Op. 8/1–4 (arr. for flute and strings)

(M) *** RCA (ADD) GD 60748. Galway, Zagreb Soloists

James Galway's sensitive transcription is so convincing that at times one is tempted to believe that the work was conceived in this form. The playing is marvellous, full of detail and imagination, and the recording is excellent, even if the flute is given a forward balance, the more striking on CD.

(i) The Four Seasons, Op. 8/1–4 (arr. for recorder and strings); Recorder Concertos in G & C min., RV 437 and 441; Concerto for Strings in D, RV 124

(*) BIS **SACD 1605. (i) Laurin; Arte Dei Suonatori

Dan Laurin plays the *Four Seasons* with an almost whimsical virtuosity, so that one is tempted to smile at times at his piquancy. However, it is the pair of *Recorder Concertos* that show him at his best, as Vivaldi knew just what he was about when he wrote them so freshly and wittily. The *Concerto in D for Strings* is also in some ways playful, and especially so in the finale, when Vivaldi creates a winning fugato out of a descending scale. The recording is very realistic, especially when the back speakers are used to add ambience.

La cetra (12 Violin Concertos), Op. 9

⊶ (BB) **** Virgin 2x1 5 61594-2 (2). Huggett, Raglan Bar. Players, Kraemer

(i) La cetra; (ii) Double Oboe Concerto in D min., RV 535; (iii) Piccolo Concerto in C, RV 443

⊶ ⊛ (B) **** Double Decca 448 110-2 (2). (i) I. Brown, ASMF; (ii) Black; (iii) Nicklin; both with ASMF, Marriner

Iona Brown here acts as director in the place of **Sir Neville Marriner**. So resilient and imaginative are the results that one detects no difference from the immaculate and stylish Vivaldi playing in earlier Academy Vivaldi sets. There is some wonderful music here; the later *Concertos* are every bit the equal of anything in *The Trial between Harmony and Invention*, and they are played gloriously. The recording too is outstandingly rich and vivid, even by earlier Argo standards with this group. For the Double Decca reissue, two of Vivaldi's most engaging *Wind Concertos* have been added, winningly played by two fine Academy soloists.

Monica Huggett and the **Raglan Baroque Players** offer performances so accomplished and in such good style that they are unlikely to be surpassed in authentic-instrument versions of *La cetra*. The Raglan Baroque Players are of the same size as the **Academy of Ancient Music** and some players are common to both groups. First-class recording.

Bassoon Concertos: in C, RV 466; in C, RV 467; in C, RV 469; in C, RV 470; in C, RV 471; in C, RV 472; in C, RV 473; in C, RV 474; in C, RV 475; in C,

RV 476; in C, RV 477; in C, RV 478; in C, RV 479; in C min., RV 480; in D min., RV 481; in E flat, RV 483; in E min., RV 484; in F, RV 485; in F, RV 486; in F, RV 487; in F, RV 488; in F, RV 489; in F, RV 490; in F, RV 491; in G, RV 492; in G, RV 493; in G, RV 494; in G min., RV 495; in G min., RV 496; in A min., RV 497; in A min., RV 498; in A min., RV 499; in A min., RV 500; in B flat (La notte), RV 501; in B flat, RV 502; in B flat, RV 503; in B flat, RV 504

(M) *** ASV CDDCS 552 (5). Smith; ECO, Ledger; or Zagreb Soloists, Ninić

The bassoon brought out a generous fund of inspiration in Vivaldi, for few of his 37 *Concertos* for that instrument are in any way routine. **Daniel Smith** plays with constant freshness and enthusiasm. His woody tone is very attractive and he is very well caught by the engineers. This set can be welcomed almost without reservation and, dipped into, the various recordings will always give pleasure. Even if some of the more complicated roulades are not executed with exact precision, Smith's playing has undoubted flair. For the last three CDs of the series the **Zagreb Soloists** take over the accompaniments and offer alert, vivacious playing that adds to the pleasure of these warm, affectionate performances. Daniel Smith, too, responds with vigour and polish.

Bassoon Concertos: in C, RV 469–70, 472 & 474; in D min., RV 481; in F, RV 486 & 488 (from above complete set)

(BB) *** Regis RRC 1277. Smith, ECO, Ledger

This collection is taken from the earlier of **Daniel Smith's** recordings in which he is freshly accompanied by the **ECO** under **Philip Ledger**. Although the playing here is not quite as refined as that of Thunemann on Pentatone, it is always spirited and full of life. Moreover, the Regis disc offers seven *Concertos* at budget price against only four on Pentatone.

Bassoon Concertos, RV 471/473; 481/2; 484; 491/497; 499/500; 503/4

⊶ (B) **** Ph. Duo 475 233-2 (2). Thunemann, I Musici

Apart from the complete cycle by Daniel Smith on ASV, which has some rough edges, this is the most impressive survey of Vivaldi's bassoon concertos on CD. Moreover, **Klaus Thunemann** makes every work seem a masterpiece. **I Musici** are on their finest form, and all the slow movements here are touchingly expressive, with Thunemann's ease of execution adding to the enjoyment. With the Philips recording in the demonstration bracket, this reissue demonstrates just how well Vivaldi's music can sound on modern instruments.

Bassoon Concertos: in E min., RV 484; in F, RV 489; in A min., RV 498; in B flat, RV 502

** Pentatone **SACD** Surround Sound PTC 5186. Thunemann, I Musici – TARTINI: *Flute Concerto in G* – Gazzelloni

These recordings were originally made quadraphonically and the surround sound on SACD is very impressive. However, compared with the original Duo above, this Pentatone CD, offering only four *Concertos*, is very short

measure, and the Tartini bonus, although attractive, does not compensate, even though the surround sound is first class.

Complete Bassoon Concertos, Vol. 1: RV 471; 476; 480; 487; 493; 498; 503

(BB) *** Naxos 8.555937. Benkócs, Nicolaus Esterházy Sinf., Drahos

Complete Bassoon Concertos, Vol. 2: RV 467; 475; 486; 488 (La notte); 501; 504

(BB) *** Naxos 8.555938. Benkócs, Nicolaus Esterházy Sinf., Drahos

Complete Bassoon Concertos, Vol. 3: RV 472; 474; 483; 495; 500; 502

(BB) *** Naxos 8.557556. Benkócs, Nicolaus Esterházy Sinfonia, Drahos

Complete Bassoon Concertos, Vol. 4: RV 470; 477; 481; 485; 494; 499

(BB) *** Naxos 8.557829. Benkócs, Nicolaus Esterházy Sinfonia, Drahos

This excellent new Naxos survey seems set eventually to upstage Daniel Smith on ASV, and certainly to match the excellent recordings of Klaus Thunemann on Philips. **Tamás Benkócs** is a splendid, personable bassoonist, his expressive colouring matching his easy but sometimes remarkable bravura. Moreover, **Béla Drahos** supports him with accompaniments that are warmly phrased in slow movements and full of vitality in *Allegros*. If anything, the second collection (which includes the solo version of *La notte*) is more stimulating and lively than the first, and both make a good case for playing Vivaldi on modern instruments. The recording too is resonantly full without clouding detail; the balance, with the bassoon given a real presence, is very satisfactory.

Bassoon Concertos in A min., RV 497; D min., RV 481

(N) (***) Australian Decca Eloquence stereo/mono 480 0833. Helaerts, SRO, Ansermet – MARCELLO: *Oboe Concerto in C min.* (***); HANDEL: *Organ Concertos* ***

These two Vivaldi concertos start one of Ansermet's most unlikely recordings, comprising five baroque concertos. The first, in *A minor*, RV 497, was recorded in rich (1968) stereo sound, the second, in *D minor*, RV 481, in rather bright, upfront (1952) mono sound (almost 'authentic' sounding) – both offer surprisingly warmly stylish playing from both the orchestra (of a fair size) and the soloist, **Henri Helaerts**.

6 Flute Concertos, Op. 10; Flute Concertos: in A min., RV 108; in D, RV 429; in G, RV 438; in A min., RV 440; in C min., RV 441; (i) Double Flute Concerto in C, RV 533; Piccolo Concerto in A min., RV 445

⊶ (B) *** Ph. Duo (ADD) 454 256-2 (2). Gazzelloni, I Musici; (i) with Steinberg

A Duo collection entirely made up of concertante works for flute might be thought a rather daunting prospect, but **Gazzelloni** is an artist of such quality and poetry that such doubts are banished. And it must be added that these *Concertos* all show Vivaldi in the best light, not only in the best known, *La tempesta di mare* and *Il gardellino*, from Op. 10, but in many of the miscellaneous *Concertos*, too: witness the delicate slow movement of the *A minor*, RV 440, the touching *Largo* of the *C minor*, RV 441, or the lively opening movements of the *D major*, RV 429, and *A minor*, RV 108. In these modern-instrument performances Gazzelloni's tone is admirably fresh and clean, with **I Musici** giving him splendid support. The analogue recordings (from the 1960s and 1970s) are first rate.

6 Flute Concertos, Op. 10

Ⓝ *** MDG 311 0640-2 Konrad Hünteler, 18th Century Camerata

ⒷⒷ **(*) Naxos 8.553101. Drahos, Nicolaus Esterházy Sinf.

Konrad Hünteler plays an 18th century wooden flute and gives admirable period performances of this fine set of concertos, persuasively accompanied by the appropriately named **Camerata of the 18th Century**. *Il Gardellino* and *La Notte* are among the highlights of the collection, most naturally recorded. But, this disc is short measure at 47 minutes, and Emmanuel Pahud is even finer – see below – and he offers two extra concertos.

Béla Drahos is an excellent soloist, and he phrases very musically: the *Siciliana* slow movement of *Il gardellino* is beautifully played. He gets lively support from the **Nicolaus Esterházy Sinfonia**, who are also suitably gentle and evocative in the dream world of *La notte*. The *C minor Concerto* makes a welcome bonus, for in the finale the Goldfinch of *Il gardellino* appears to have flown back in through the window.

(i) Flute Concertos, Op. 10/1–6; (ii) L'estro armonico: Triple Violin Concerto in D min., RV 565; Quadruple Violin Concerto in B min., RV 58, Op. 3/10–11

ⒷⒷ **(*) Regis RRC 1243. (i) Hall, Divertimenti of L., Barritt; (ii) Laredo & soloists, SCO

Judith Hall's set of the Op. 10 *Flute Concertos* is fresh and brightly recorded. She plays with considerable virtuosity and a great deal of taste. The **Divertimento of London** is a modern-instrument group and the players are both sensitive and alert, and this is most enjoyable on all counts. The two accompanying *Violin Concertos* from *L'estro armonico*, for three and four violins respectively (although this is not made clear on the disc's packaging), are among Vivaldi's finest; they receive vigorous, spontaneous performances from the **Scottish Chamber Orchestra**, led from the bow by **Jaime Laredo**. At Regis price, a fair bargain.

Flute Concertos: Op. 10/1-6; in G, RV 414; in D, RV 427.

ⒷⒷ **(*) Warner Apex 2564 60373-2. Rampal, Sol. Ven., Scimone

Jean-Pierre Rampal was an aristocrat among flautists and it is surprising that his set of Op. 10, dating from 1966, has not resurfaced until now. His performances of the enigmatic *Fantasmi* of *La notte*, the delightful *Cantabile siciliana* of *Il gardellino*, the charmingly elegant opening movement of the *F major Concerto* (5), and the rollicking and echoing finale of the last *Concerto* of the set show him at his masterly best. His playing in the two additional *Concertos* offered as a bonus is no less delectable. **Scimone** and **I Solisti Veneti** provide more than acceptable accompaniments, and the sound is good, if not as transparent as we would expect today.

Flute Concertos, Op. 10/1–6; Flute Concertos in D, RV 429; A min., RV 440

☗⌐ **** EMI 3 47212-2. Pahud, Australian CO, Tognetti

Needless to say, the virtuosity of **Emmanuel Pahud** is dazzling in the first *Concerto* of Opus 10, *La tempesta di mare*, while the two *Largo* movements of *La notte* show his legato tone at its most beguiling. The **Australian Chamber Orchestra** accompany spiritedly, and they come into their own in the bustle of the finale, and Pahud chirrups with the best in the finale of *Il gardellino*, after a delicious *Siciliano Cantabile* central movement. Strangely, the sleeve-note mentions another track, a slow movement from RV 226, which does not appear to be on the disc at all. Truthful recording.

(i; ii) Flute Concertos; Op. 10: 1 in F (La tempesta di mare), RV 433; 2 in G min. (La notte), RV 439; 3 in D (Il gardellino), RV 428; (i; iii) 5 in F, RV 434. Flute Concerto in A min., RV 108s; Sopranino Recorder (Piccolo) Concertos: in C, RV 553.

ⒷⒷ *** Naxos 8.554053. Soloists; (i) Capella Istropolitana; (ii) Krechek; (iii) Dohnányi; (iv) City of L. Sinfonia, Kraemer

An attractive regrouping of recordings (78 minutes) brings a particularly generous clutch of modern-instrument performances that will especially suit those who want only the most famous named *Concertos* from Op. 10. They are most persuasively played and the recording is excellent throughout.

Complete cello concertos

Cello Concertos: in C, RV 398 & 399; in C, RV 400; in C min., RV 401/402; in D, RV 403/404; in D min., RV 405/406/407; in E flat, RV 408; in F, RV 410/411/412; in G, RV 413/414; in G min., RV 416/417; in A min., RV 418/419/420/421/422; in B flat, RV 423; in B min., RV 424; Concerto Movement in D min., RV 438; Double Cello Concerto in G min., RV 531; (i) Double Concerto in E min., for Cello & Bassoon, RV 409; (ii) Double Concertos: in B flat for Violin & Cello (Il Proteo o sia il mondo al rovesco), RV 544; RV 547

☗⌐ ⒷⒷ **** Naxos 8.550907 (RV 398–9; 404; 406; 410; 412; 419); 8.550908 (RV 400–1; 408; 413; 422; 531, with Keith Harvey); 8.550909 (RV 402–3; 407; 409, with Joanna Graham); 418; 423–4); 8.550910 (RV 405; 411; 414; 416–17; 420–21) (available separately). Wallfisch, City of L. Sinfonia, Kraemer (without RV 544; 547)

🎙—ⓑ ✱✱✱ RCA 82876 67886-2 (4) (without *RV 398, 400, 421, 531*). Harnoy, Toronto CO, Robinson; with (i) MacKay; (ii) Oistrakh

Vivaldi liked to write for instruments playing in the middle and lower register, favouring both the bassoon and cello (the latter a relatively new instrument in his time, having taken the place of the viola da gamba as a favoured solo instrument). Here are two highly recommendable recordings of Vivaldi's 'complete' *Cello Concertos*; neither is quite complete, but if it is the 27 solo *Concertos* you are most concerned with, then **Raphael Wallfisch** offers them all, including the sole *Double Cello Concerto, RV 531* (which **Ofra Harnoy** omits), and the *Concerto for Cello and Bassoon, RV 409*. Harnoy, however, includes the pair of *Double Concertos with Violin* (which the Naxos set omits). Here she achieves an excellent partnership with **Igor Oistrakh**, and in the work with the subtitle '*Il Proteo*' the *Adagio* is particularly touching. Hers are traditional performances with modern instruments; she plays with style, impeccable technique and eloquence. In short, she is a first-rate artist with a good lyrical sense. Her strength lies not so much in her tone, which is not big, but in her selfless approach to this repertoire. She is given good support from the **Toronto Chamber Orchestra** and is very well recorded.

The Naxos series is part of a planned overall survey, and in the solo *Concertos* the choice of Raphael Wallfisch could hardly have been bettered. He forms an admirable partnership with the **City of London Sinfonia**, directed from the harpsichord or chamber organ by **Nicholas Kraemer**, so that, although not using period instruments, the effect is as authentic as you could want. Kraemer's use of the organ continuo, both in tutti and to underpin the solo cello line (in *RV 419*, for instance), is most effective, while in *Allegros* the alert, resilient orchestral strings are a pleasure in themselves. Wallfisch plays with a restrained use of vibrato and a nicely judged expressive feeling, and in the *Double Concerto* (which he shares with **Keith Harvey**), there is much bustling interchange in the outer novements, with the soloists answering each other eloquently in the *Largo*.

Volume 3 (8.550909) is a particularly fine collection, including the *E minor Double Concerto, RV 409*, where the cello is joined by a subservient and somewhat doleful solo bassoon; but Volume 4 brings a further batch of *Concertos* notable for their vitality and the vigorous bravura demanded from the soloist. Throughout these four Naxos discs there is never a hint of routine; the recording is vividly realistic and the balance very well judged indeed.

Cello Concertos: in C min., RV 401; in F, RV 410; in G, RV 413; in A min., RV 418; in B min., RV 424; in A min. (trans. from Violin Concerto, RV 356); The Four Seasons: Winter

✱✱✱ RCA 88697 131692. Gabetta, Sonatori De la Gioiosa Marca

Sol Gabetta gives comparatively intimate performances with the small baroque group, just as Vivaldi planned. They are stylish and pleasing, their moments of gentle melancholy are touching, and if her solo personality is less strong than that of Rafael Wallfisch, she is still a fine, sensitive player

who understands the repertoire. But why transcribe two works for violin when there are so many Vivaldi *Concertos* for cello?

Cello Concerto in D min., RV 406.

Ⓜ ✱✱✱ Warner Elatus 0927 49839-2. Rostropovich, St Paul CO, Wolff – C. P. E. BACH; TARTINI: *Concertos* ✱✱✱

Who says that modern chamber orchestras cannot achieve the same transparency as period ensembles? Admittedly the **St Paul Chamber Orchestra** have had the advantage of Christopher Hogwood's presence, but the sound they produce blends transparency of texture with warmth and subtlety of colouring. **Rostropovich** is as masterly and eloquent as one could imagine, and he is accorded excellently balanced sound.

Flute concertos, Vol. 1: Chamber Concertos: in C, for Flute, Oboe, Violin, Bassoon & Continuo, RV 88; in D, for Flute & 2 Violins, RV 89; in D, for Flute, Violin, Bassoon & Continuo (Il gardellino), RV 90; in D, RV 91; in D min., RV 96 (both for Flute, Violin, Bassoon & Continuo); in F, RV 99; in G min., RV 107 (both for Flute, Oboe, Violin, Bassoon & Continuo)

ⒷⒷ ✱✱✱ Naxos 8.553365. Drahos and soloists, Nicolaus Esterházy Sinf.

This Naxos disc collects multiple *Concertos*, but with a continuo instead of an orchestra. Although not to be played at a single sitting, these works offer a great deal of pleasure, stemming from their rich textural interplay with plenty of imitation among the soloists. The quality of invention is astonishingly high. *Il gardellino* (which opens the programme) is justly famous, but the *G minor* work, *RV 107*, is also remarkable, with a touching *Siciliano* slow movement; it ends with a chaconne which maintains the minor key. *RV 88* has a strikingly cheerful opening movement, then gives prominence to the flute both in its central *Largo cantabile* and in another chirping finale. *RV 89* effectively brings a change of colour in the use of a pair of violins in juxtaposition to the flute. The performances here are admirable and the recording is most effectively balanced.

Flute Concertos: in A min., RV 108; in F, RV 434; Double Flute Concerto in C, RV 533; Sopranino Recorder Concertos: in C, RV 443 & RV 444; in A min., RV 445

ⒷⒷ ✱✱✱ Naxos 8.550385. Jálek, Novotny, Stivin, Capella Istropolitana, Dohnányi

The **Capella Istropolitana**, who are drawn from the excellent Slovak Philharmonic, play with vitality and sensitivity for **Oliver Dohnányi** and the soloists show appropriate virtuosity and flair. As always, there are rewards and surprises in this music. The sound is very good indeed, and so is the balance.

Flute Concertos: in D, RV 427 & RV 429; in E min., RV 431 & RV 432; in G, RV 436; RV 438 & RV 438 bis; in A min., RV 440; in C, RV 533.

⊕, *** Naïve OP 30298. Kuijken, Academia Montis Regale

If Jean-Pierre Rampal was the patrician among flautists of the 1950s and 1960s, it was **Barthold Kuijken** who took his place in the 1960s and 1970s, after discovering and mastering an original baroque instrument. For the present recordings he plays a copy of a Belgian transverse flute of 1735, while the **Academia Montis Regale** accompany him smoothly, proficiently and spiritedly on comparable period instruments. For the programme here he turned to a collection of manuscripts in the Turin Library, from which the *A minor Concerto*, RV 440, stands out, while Vivaldi's sole *Concerto for Two Flutes*, RV 533, is made doubly charming by the use of a bassoon continuo throughout. The *Concerto in G major*, K. 438, also features the bassoon in duet with the flute in the *Andante*, and the *Largo* of RV 436 proves to be rather similar, but with a cello in place of a bassoon. The other *Concertos* here are all elegant and attractive works. None is as spectacular as the Op. 10 set, but their simplicity is also their virtue. The performances could hardly be more authentic, and the recording is excellent.

Lute Concerto in D, RV 93; Mandolin Concerto in C, RV 425; (i) Double Mandolin Concerto, RV 432; (ii) Double Concerto in D min. for Viola d'amore and Lute, RV 540; (i) Sonata in G min., RV 42; Trio Sonata in C, RV 82

(N) **** Nimbus NI 2515 Eliot Fisk, O of St Lukes; (i) F. Hand; (ii) L. Schulman (with BACH: *Concerto in D, RV 972 (arr. for 2 Mandolins)* ***)

Among various collections featuring the lute and mandolin this Nimbus collection stands out. The modern instrument performances are full of character. The *Lute Concerto*, D.93 stands out for its strength of personality, but both *Double Concertos* are very successful too and the inclusion of the Bach transcription is a real bonus – a most attractive little work. Outstanding playing from everyone concerned, and excellent recording.

Mandolin Concertos in D, RV 93; C, RV 425; (i) Double Mandolin Concerto in G, RV 332; Concerto for 2 Flutes, 2 Chalumeaux, 2 Violins ('In tromba marina'), 2 Mandolins, 2 Theorbos & Cello in C, RV 558

⊕ **(BB)** *** Warner Apex 2564 61264-2. Orlandi; (i) Frati; soloists, Sol. Ven., Scimone

It is good to have a budget CD with excellent performances of the two solo *Mandolin Concertos* and the *Double Mandolin Concerto*, presented with style and delicacy and with the colourful *Concerto con molti istromenti* thrown in for good measure. The recording is very good indeed.

Mandolin Concerto, RV 435; (i) Double Mandolin Concert, RV 533; Double Concerto for Viola d'amore & Lute, RV 540; Concerto for Lute & 2 Violins; Trio Sonatas for Violin, Lute & Continuo, RV82 & 85

⊕ ***(*) Naïve OP 30429. Rolf Lislevand; (i) Murphy; Kapsberger Ens.

A superb disc, gathering Vivaldi's mandolin and lute music

neatly together with dazzling bravura from the key soloist, **Rolf Lislevand**, with **Stephen Murphy** joining him in a sparkling account of the *Double Concerto*. Some might find that the continuo (with extra plucking) is a bit over the top, and it can't be what Vivaldi had in mind. But the rest of the programme is delightfully planned, and it is good to hear the softer lute timbre in contrast. Apart from that continuo, this is highly recommendable.

Mandolin Concerto in C, RV 425; Double Mandolin Concerto in G, RV 532; (Soprano) Lute Concerto in D, RV 93; Double Concerto in D min. for Viola d'amore & Lute, RV 540. Trios: in C, RV 82; in G min., RV 85

*** Hyp. CDA 66160. Jeffrey, O'Dette, Parley of Instruments, Goodman & Holman

These are chamber performances, with one instrument to each part, providing an ideal balance for the *Mandolin Concertos*. An organ continuo replaces the usual harpsichord, and very effective it is; in the *Trios* and the *Lute Concerto* (but not in the *Double Concerto*, RV 540) **Paul O'Dette** uses a gut-strung soprano lute. The delightful sounds here, with all players using period instruments, are very convincing. The recording is realistically balanced within an attractively spacious acoustic.

(i) Mandolin Concerto in C, RV 425; (i, ii) Double Concerto for 2 Mandolins in G, RV 532; Concerti con molti strumenti: Concerto for Violin & 2 Flutes diritti; 3 Oboes & Bassoon (dedicated to a Sua Altezza Reale di Sassonia), RV 576; Concerto for 2 Violins in tromba marina, 2 Flutes diritti, 2 Mandolins, 2 Salmoe, 2 Theorbos & Cello, RV 558; Concerto for Violin solo, 2 Oboes & Bassoon (dedicated to S. Pisandel) (Dresden version), RV 319; Concerto for 2 Violins & 2 Cellos in D, RV 564; Concerto in C for 3 Violins, Oboe & 2 Flutes diritti; 2 Viole all'inglese, Salmoe, 2 Cellos, 2 Harpsichords & 2 Violins in tromba marina, RV 555

⊕ **** Virgin 5 45527-2. (i) Scaramuzzino; (ii) Maurer; soloists, Europa Galante, Biondi

Another excellent disc from **Fabio Biondi** and his outstanding period instrument group. The two simple *Mandolin Concerti* are played intimately and are perfectly balanced. The *Concertos con molti strumenti* offer an extraordinary range of tone colour, especially the extravagantly scored *C major Concerto*, RV 555. In the *Largo* of this work the violin plays an obbligato line to the two solo harpsichords, which are given alternating arpeggios in a pendulum style, embroidering them *a piacimento* ('as they please'). Toussaint Loviko, who provides the excellent notes, tells us that Vivaldi's girl musicians were hidden by grilles curtained with black gauze, so they were able to exchange instruments at will and were thus able to surprise their listeners.

Oboe Concertos in C, RV 447 & RV 451; in F, RV 455 & RV 457; in A min., RV 461 & RV 463

⊕ **(BB)** *** Naxos 8.550860. Schilli, Budapest Failoni CO, Nagy

Oboe Concertos in C, RV 450 & RV 452; in D, RV 453; in D min., RV 454; (i) Double Oboe Concertos in C, RV 534; D min., RV 535; A min., RV 536

🎵➔ (BB) *** Naxos 8.550859. Schilli; (i) with Jonas; Budapest Failoni CO, Nagy

Excellent playing from these **Budapest** musicians. The second of these two discs offers the three *Double Concertos*, and the two CDs between them include half the solo works. They are often surprisingly florid, requiring considerable bravura from the soloist. A good example is the Minuet finale of RV 447, which is a cross between a Rondo and a theme and variations. Vivaldi is never entirely predictable, except that his invention never seems to flag, and many of the simple *Grave*, *Larghetto* and *Largo* slow movements are very pleasing indeed.

Oboe Concertos in C, RV 178 & RV 450; in D, RV 453; in D min ., RV 454; in F, RV 456; in A min., RV 461; in B flat, RV 465

(BB) **(*) EMI Gemini (ADD) 3 50905-2 (2). de Vries, I Solisti di Zagreb – BACH; TELEMANN: *Oboe Concertos* ***

Han de Vries, playing a modern instrument, here offers no fewer than seven of Vivaldi's *Oboe Concertos*, and their variety of invention completely contradicts Stravinsky's famous remark that Vivaldi 'wrote the same concerto six hundred times'. The central group here are particularly varied, even though many of the slow movements are played with a delicate organ continuo. The outer movements of the *C major Concerto*, RV 450, are strikingly prolix, demanding (and here receiving) considerable virtuosity from the soloist; the *D major* and *D minor* works are more robust, but with pensive central *Largos*. All the performances are first class, spirited and expressive by turns, freshly accompanied by the **Zagreb players**, and the recording is excellent, with the soloist dominating the sound-picture.

Recorder Concertos: for Treble Recorder, RV 441 & 442; for Sopranino Recorder, RV 443, 444 & 445; Chamber Concerto for Recorder, Bassoon, Oboe, Cello, & Violin Continuo (La pastorella), RV 95

(BB) *** Naxos 8.553829. Kecskeméti, Czidra & Soloists, Nicolaus Esterházy Sinfonia, Zalay.

The performances from **László Kecskeméti** of the three works for the sopranino instrument are dazzling (though not to be played in a row); then follow the two fine works for treble recorder, the first of which is played by **László Czidra** with equal skill. Kecskeméti then takes over for the rest of the programme, which ends with the chamber concerto, *La Pastorella*. This is the highlight of the *Collection*, one of the composer's masterpieces, delightful in its range of colour and imitative echo effects, and indeed its *Siciliano* slow movement and ingenious fugal finale. Splendid contributions from the players of the **Nicolaus Esterházy Sinfonia** throughout, and excellent recording.

Concertos for Strings, Vol. 1: Paris Concertos 1 in G min. (with woodwind), RV 157; 2 in E min., RV 133; 3 in C min., RV 119; 4 in F, RV 136; 5 in C (with woodwind), RV 114; 6 in G min., RV 154; 7 in A, RV 160; 8 in D min., RV 127; 9 in B flat, RV 164; 10 in D, RV 121; 11 in G (with woodwind), RV 150; 12 in A, RV 159

🎵➔ **** Chan. 0647. Col. Mus. 90, Standage

Concertos for Strings, Vol. 2: in C, RV 109; in C (with flutes), RV 112; in C (with flutes), RV 117; in C min., RV 120; in D, RV 124; in D min., RV 128; in F min., RV 143; in G min. (Concerto ripieno; with woodwind), RV 152; in G min., RV 153; in B flat (with woodwind), RV 162; Conca, RV 163; in B min., RV 168.

**** Chan. 0668. Col. Mus. 90, Standage

Concertos for Strings, Vol. 3: in C, RV 110; in C (Concerto ripieno; with woodwind), RV 115; in C min. (with woodwind), RV 118; in D min. (Concerto madrigalesco), RV 129; in E min., RV 134; in F, RV 142; in G, RV 145; in G(Concerto alla rustica), RV 151; in G min., RV 156; in C (Concerto ripieno), RV 158; in A min., RV 161; in B flat, RV 166; in B flat, RV 167.

*** Chan. 0687. Col. Mus. 90, Standage

Vivaldi wrote over forty *concerti a quattro* for strings alone, without a soloist, and the present group were gathered together in a single manuscript, written in the hand of Vivaldi's father, and have been preserved in the Paris Conservatoire Library ever since. They are all freshly inventive and played here with springing rhythms and plenty of vitality. In three *Concertos*, though not specified by the composer, woodwind have been added to give extra colour. The touch of abrasiveness on the string sound is aurally bracing, and slow movements have a nicely ruminative improvisatory feel. The recording is first class.

Volumes 2 and 3 continue to demonstrate the amazing variety of invention in these *Concertos* for strings, some of which have added woodwind, with the pair using additional flutes. In Volume 2, RV 112 and RV 117 are particularly attractive.

The performances from Standage and his **Collegium Musicum 90** are full of life and expressively penetrating throughout both discs; the recording is as fine as ever.

Concertos for Strings, RV 111a; 114; 119; 121; 127; 146; 152; 156; 157; 163; 167 & 168

🎵➔ **** DG 474 5092. Venice Bar. O, Marcon

The **Venice Baroque Orchestra** now join the Concerto Italiano in offering competition to Standage's ongoing Chandos series. The performances are full of lyrical intensity, with slow movements seductively expressive, the continuo coming through nicely. Really excellent sound, too. Distinctly recommendable.

Concertos for Strings, RV 156; 413; 522; 531; 553; 565; 580

*** Avie 8553060. Berlin Bar. Soloists, Kussmaul

The **Berlin Baroque Soloists** are admirably stylish and vital but more robust than the Italians. Enjoyable performances, but less distinctive.

Concertos for Strings in C, RV 115; in C min., RV 120; in D, RV 121 & 123; in D min., RV 129; in F, RV 141; in F min., RV 143; in G min., RV 153, 154 & 156; in A, RV 158 & 159

🎵—**** Naïve OP 30377. Concerto Italiano, Alessandrini

Rinaldo Alessandrini and his **Concerto Italiano** offer 12 *Concertos* played with great brio and expressive sensibility, and you have only to sample the first or the last of the *Concertos* here, RV 159 and RV 123 respectively, to hear how deeply expressive are the brief slow movements, and how infectious are the *Allegros*. First-class recording ensures that this new series gets the strongest recommendation.

Concertos for Strings in D, Op. 12/3, RV 124; in D min. (Madrigalesco), RV 129; Sinfonia and Sonata al Santo Sepolcro, RV 130; (i) In furore iustissimae irae, RV 626; Laudate pueri Dominum, RV 601.

🎵—Ⓜ *** Chan. 0714X. (i) Bott; Augmented Purcell Qt

Framed by the *Sonata a quattro* and *Sinfonia al Santo Sepolcro*, which are among Vivaldi's most dramatically intense and poignant string works, this collection includes also two of his most original *Concertos*, including the 'Madrigalesco' (which draws its material from his sacred vocal works) and the harmonically abrasive *Concerto a quattro*, which closes with a passionate fugue. The playing here is fully worthy of this remarkable music, uniting rigour with expressive fervour. But this is **Catherine Bott's** record, and she gives a superb performance of the motet, *In furore iustissimae irae*, moving from fiery vocal bravura in expressing heaven's righteous anger to the limpid beauty of the lament, *Tunc meus fletus*. Her performance of *Laudate pueri Dominum*, Vivaldi's third setting of the Vesper Psalm (112) is equally memorable, dramatic and ravishing by turns, especially in her touching duet with the solo flute (**Stephen Preston**) in the *Gloria Patri*.

Concertos for Strings in D min. (Concerto madrigalesco), RV 129; in G (Alla rustica), RV 151; in G min., RV 157. (i) Motet: In turbato mare irato, RV 627; Cantata: Lungi dal vago volto, RV 680. Magnificat, RV 610

🎵—ⒷⒷ *** Hyp. Helios CDH 55190. (i) Kirkby; Leblanc, Forget, Cunningham, Ingram, Tafelmusik Ch. & Bar. O, Lamon

Mingling vocal and instrumental items, and works both well-known and unfamiliar, **Jean Lamon** provides a delightful collection, with **Emma Kirkby** a sparkling, pure-toned soloist in two items never recorded before: the motet, *In turbato mare irato*, and the chamber cantata, *Lungi dal vago volto*. The performance is lively, with fresh choral sound. The **Tafelmusik** performers come from Canada, and though the use of period instruments has some roughness, their vigour and alertness amply make up for that. Good, clear recorded sound.

Viola d'amore Concertos in D, RV 392; in D min., RV 393, RV 394 & RV 395; in A, RV 396; in D min., RV 397

ⒷⒷ **(*) Hyp. Helios CDH 55178. Mackintosh, OAE.

The viola d'amore was greatly admired in Vivaldi's time for its tone, apparently sweeter than that of the contemporary violin. Yet to today's ears its character is more plangent, and that especially applies to performance style on a baroque instrument. As can be seen, Vivaldi favoured the key of D minor above others for his *Concertos* for that instrument, which are generally less striking than most of his violin concertos. **Catherine Mackintosh** gives expert performances with the **Orchestra of the Age of Enlightenment**, using rather astringent tone.

Violin concertos

(i) Violin Concertos: RV 171–2; 186; 199; 205; 208; 213; 228; 230; 232; 237; 249; 254; 260; 265; 271; 302; 310; 319; 328; 340; 356; 370; 582. String Symphonies: 1, RV 159; 12, RV 164; 13, RV 134; 14, RV 136; 19, RV 127; 20, RV 119; 22, RV 160; 30, RV 121; 36, RV 150; 43, RV 133; 44, RV 114

🎵—Ⓑ **** Nim. NI 2500/4 (5). (i) Mintz (violin), Israel CO, Mintz

An extraordinary achievement from **Shlomo Mintz**, who plays all these *Violin Concertos* freshly, vitally and lyrically, without a suspicion of routine, and then goes on to discover 11 of Vivaldi's previously unknown *String Symphonies* (essentially Italian Overtures). Each is an engaging, individual three-movement work, with plenty of variety of lively invention, from imitation to a fugato, and each with a gentle, expressive slow movement, often quite haunting. The polished playing of the modern-instrument **Israel Chamber Orchestra**, directed by Mintz, is warm and elegant, and everything has an appealing lightness of touch. The recording too is truthful and in perfect scale.

Volume II: 6 Violin Concertos, Op. 6/1-6; Coucou, RV 325; 6 Violin Concertos, Op. 11/1-5; Riposo, RV 275; 6 Concertos, RV 189; 197; 215; 241; 321; 329 (1729); 12 Violin Concertos for Anna Maria

Ⓝ Ⓜ **** Nimbus NI 2523/7 (5). Mintz (Violin), Israel CO

Vivaldi composed almost countless violin concertos (we know of 220!), and during his service as Maestro di violino at the Pio Ospidale dalla Pietà, many of these works were intended for use by students to perform at the public concerts. One of the foremost was a brilliantly talented young violinist called Anna Maria, and Vivaldi composed twelve concertos allotted with her name. The remaining 12 *Concertos* of *Opp.* 6 and 11 cannot be dated exactly, but were published during the 1720s, along with the six separately listed concertos among the mature works. Yet, taken individually, they are all attractive 3-movement concertos, a few have sobriquets, and their quality of invention is usually especially high. **Shlomo Mintz** follows up his first Vivaldi volume by retaining his freshness of approach in the further collection: his silvery timbre seems just right for the music and the **Israel**

Chamber Orchestra continues to provide very persuasive accompaniments. The recording remains truthful and in perfect scale.

'Dresden Violin Concertos', Vol. 1: Violin Concertos: in C, RV 170; in G, RV 314a; in G min., RV 319; in A, RV 341; in B flat (Il carbonelli), RV 366; in B flat, RV 383

🎵 (BB) *** Naxos 8.553792. Martini, with Accademia I Filarmonici

This series concentrates on *Concertos* which survive in manuscript in the Dresden Saxony Landesbibliothek, and which may be connected with Vivaldi's association with an influential group of Dresden musicians, most notably the violinist, Johanne Pisendel. The quality of these works is often remarkably high, reflecting the calibre of the orchestra and indeed Pisendel's virtuosity and musicianship. They sound extremely well in these excellent modern-instrument performances. **Alberto Martini** directs bright, resilient performances, aptly paced, and he also proves a splendid soloist. There is nothing routine about any of these six works, as is demonstrated by the haunting *Largo* of the *A major*, RV 341, where the soloist plays over a gentle quasi-tremolando; the result is exquisite.

'Dresden Violin Concertos', Vol. 2: Violin Concertos: in C, RV 184; in D min., RV 241; in E, RV 267; in F, RV 292; in G min., RV 329; in B flat (Posthorn), RV 363

🎵 (BB) *** Naxos 8.553793. Baraldi, Accademia I Filarmonici, Martini

The concertos on the second disc are full of surprises, and **Roberto Baraldi** gives them the strongest profile. He is a very positive soloist, with a bolder sound image than Martini, which is not to say he is in the least insensitive. His strength of purpose is especially telling in the *Posthorn Concerto*, which features octave rhythmic figures on *B flat*, and also just right for the *D minor Concerto*, RV 241. Again excellent sound.

'Dresden Violin Concertos', Vol. 3: Violin Concertos in D, RV 228; in D min., RV 245; in E flat, RV 262; in F, RV 285; in G min., RV 323; in B min., RV 384

🎵 (BB) *** Naxos 8. 553860. Fornaciari, Accademia I Filarmonici, Martini

One is struck by the vigour of the *Allegros* in Volume 3, emphasized by **Marco Fornaciari's** extrovert style and very open timbre. Yet in slow movements he fines down his tone most beautifully.

'Dresden Violin Concertos', Vol. 4: Violin Concertos in D, RV 213; in D, RV 219; in D, RV 224; in D min., RV 240; in E flat, RV 260; in A, RV 344; in B min., RV 388

🎵 (BB) *** Naxos 8. 554310. Rossi, Accademia I Filarmonici, Martini

The use of a different soloist for each of these Naxos Dresden collections adds to their variety and interest. **Cristiano Rossi's** style is more intimate than that of Marco Fornaciari,

yet his playing is by no means without personality and rhythmic flair. *Allegros* bustle with life in the orchestra, and Vivaldi's slow movements never fail to bring textural interest, apart from their melodic appeal.

Violin Concertos in C, RV 177 & RV 191; D, RV 222; E min., RV 273; F, RV 295; B flat, RV 375

🎵 *** Sony SK 89362. Carmignola, Venice Bar. O, Marcon

Violin Concertos in D min., RV 235; E flat, RV. 251 & RV 256; F, RV 296; B min., RV 386; B min., RV 389

🎵 *** Sony SK 87733. Carmignola, Venice Bar. O, Marcon

New Italian string groups choose to play on period instruments not in a thin, colourless manner, but creating full, gleaming timbres, which still retain an overall transparency. The excellent **Venice Baroque Orchestra**, directed by **Andrea Marcon**, demonstrate this new stylistic development in these two very enjoyable compilations of 'late' *Violin Concertos* by Vivaldi. The playing combines resilience and unashamed beauty of line with lyrical finesse and the widest range of dynamic. Slow movements can often be exquisitely gentle, so that the continuo, often using lute or theorbo, comes through engagingly. **Giuliano Carmignola** is a superbly assured and imaginative soloist throughout, and the recording is first class.

Violin Concertos: in C, RV 187; in D (Grosso Mogul), RV 208; in D (L'inquietudine), RV 234; (Il favorito), RV 277. L'estro armonico: (i) Concerto for 4 Violins & cello in B min., Op. 3/10, RV 580

*** Onyx 4001. Mullova, Il Giardino Armonico, Antonini; (i) with Barneschi, Bianchi, Minasi

First-rate playing from **Viktoria Mullova** throughout, at her finest in the slow movement of *Il favorito*. The accompaniments from **Il Giardino Armonico** attack *Allegros* turbulently, especially in the fiery opening movement of *Grosso Mogul* and the furious *Allegro molto* of *L'inquietudine* ('Restlessness'). Indeed, the period-instrument style here is far removed from the mellow I Musici manners, emphasized by the vividly forward recording. It cannot really be faulted, yet charm isn't the strong point of these performances.

Violin Concertos in C, RV 187; in D, RV 209

(BB) *** RCA 74321 68002-2. Zukerman, ECO – BACH: *Violin Concertos, BWV 1041–2, BWV 1056; Double Violin Concerto* ***

Two of Vivaldi's most attractive *Concertos* played with great vitality and warmth, make a splendid coupling for Bach, particularly as the finale of the *C major* recalls the *Third Brandenburg Concerto*. Excellently vivid sound too.

'Violin Concertos for the Emperor': 2 in C, RV 189; 3 in C min., RV 202; 4 in F, RV 286; 7 in C, RV 183; 10 (L'amoroso) in E, RV 271; 11 (Il favorito) in E min., RV 277

🎵 ✹ **** HM HMU 907332. Manze, E. Concert

This CD brings together (in some cases reconstructed from

the original manuscript) six of the *Violin Concertos* which Vivaldi presented to the Holy Roman Emperor, Charles VI, in 1728. One assumes they were among the composer's most valued works (because he was hoping for a position at court) and several are otherwise well known. *Il favorito* has a memorable central *Andante*, but the other works are generally more robust, though their central movements are played with comparable sensitivity. In the *Largo* of the F major, RV 286 (also known as the *Concerto per la Solennità di San Lorenzo*), and in the finale of the opening C major work, RV 189, **Andrew Manze** improvises his own cadenzas. His playing throughout is of the very highest quality, with memorably characterful accompaniments from the **English Concert**, of which Manze was musical director. The recording is very truthful, and this is a very distinguished CD indeed.

'Music for the Chapel of the Pietà': (i) Violin Concerto fatto per la Solennità della S. Antonio in Padova, RV 212; Violin Concerto in F, RV 292; (i; ii; iii) Concerto for Violin, Cello, Organ & Continuo, RV 554a; (i; iii) Concerto for Violin & Organ in F, RV 542; (iv) Laudate pueri Dominum, RV 600; (iv; i) Salve Regina, RV 617.

♬—*** Avie AV 2063. (i) Chandler; (ii) McMahon; (iii) Howarth; (iv) Lawson; La Serenissima

The most strikingly original work here is the *Violin Concerto fatto per la Solennità della S. Antonio in Padova*, RV 212, which, like the F major *Concerto*, RV 292, with its multi-tempo opening movement, survives in Dresden. The former is a remarkable work, with a gutsy first movement and a dark, freely expressive *Grave*, where the soloist seems almost to be meditating; then the mood becomes buoyant for the virtuosic finale, including an extraordinary cadenza in which the soloist is taken up to the highest point of the normal violin register and then back down again. In the two *Concertos* featuring the organ, the violin dominates throughout, although the organ contibution (nicely played and balanced here) adds an extra palette of colour.

The *Laudate pueri Dominum* of 1713 is also a superior work and is eloquently and even dramatically sung by **Mhairi Lawson**, whose vocal line is clear and true. Yet she is even finer in the *Salve Regina* (which, unusually, has a violin obbligato), singing the lovely closing *Et Jesum benedictum* blissfully. Throughout, **La Serenissima** provide strongly characterized accompaniments under their excellent violinist/conductor, and the recording has splendid presence and detail.

Violin Concertos (for Anna Maria) in D, RV 229; in D min., RV 248; in A, RV 343 & RV 349; in B flat, RV 366 & RV 387

*** CPO SACD 777 078-2. Guglielmo, L'Arte dell'Arco

Anna Maria was the most brilliant of all Vivaldi's pupils, and Vivaldi wrote a great deal of music especially for her to play. A volume still exists with her name on it, listing some of these works, but including only the violin solo parts. However, research has provided the orchestral accompaniments, which were found in libraries either in Turin or Dresden. They are all bravura works, attesting to her virtu-

osity, but expressive too, and they are played most impressively here.

(i) Violin Concertos in D, RV 230; in A min., RV 356. (i; ii) Double Concerto for Oboe & Violin in B flat, RV 548; (i; iii) Double Violin Concertos in A, RV 519; in C, RV 507. (i; iii; iv) Triple Concerto for 2 Violins & Cello in G min., RV 578. (iv; v) Violin Sonata 2 in D min., RV 12

*** EMI 5 57859-2. Kennedy; (i) BPO (members); (ii) Mayer; (iii) Stabrawa; (iv) Maninger; (v) Mayerson, Takeuchi

Nigel Kennedy is back in the studio to play Vivaldi. As one immediately discovers from the opening *Double Violin Concerto in A major*, performances are rhythmically sharpedged and full of zest, yet lyrically free, and his partnership with his colleague on the violin, **Daniel Stabrawa**, is beautifully matched, whereas the oboist, **Albrecht Mayer**, is more delicately balanced. There is a particularly lovely oboe solo in the central *Largo* of RV 548, which Kennedy decorates ethereally. When the cellist, **Olaf Maninger**, joins them in the *Triple Concerto*, which opens with commanding spiccato chords, they play most subtly as a group, and the dynamic contrast inherent in the playing is most sensitive throughout. Altogether a most stimulating collection.

Violin Concertos in D (L'inquietudine), RV 234; E min., RV 273; E flat (La tempesta di mare), Op. 8/5; Double Violin Concerto in D min., Op. 3/11; Double Violin Sonata in D min., (La Folia) RV 63 (i) Aria 'Sovvente il sole' from Andromeda liberate

Ⓝ *** DG 477 7463. Hope, COE with (i) Otter

Some exhilarating playing here. This collection begins with a dynamic account of the '*L'inquietudine*', where the brilliance of the virtuosic writing is tempered with a timbre of both warmth and beauty. The opening of the E minor Concerto sounds darkly imposing whilst *La tempesta di mare* is as exciting as it gets. **Anne Sofie von Otter** sings her aria with great beauty (and what a meltingly haunting aria it is too!). The CD ends with a vibrantly stylish account of the *Double Concerto in D minor*, from *L'Estro armonico*. Superb recording and top productions standards from DG.

Violin Concerto in D (per Pisandel), RV 242

Ⓜ *** EuroArts Invitation DVD 2050746. Onofri, Il Giardino Armonica, Antonini (V/D: Karina Fibich) – C. P. E. BACH: *Sinfonia in G* ***; J. S. BACH: *Double Clavier Concerto 2; Triple Clavier Concerto* **(*)

This *Violin Concerto* is a most agreeable work, if not one of Vivaldi's finest, and it is very well played by **Enrico Onofri**, being placed after the C. P. E. Bach *Sinfonia* and before the closing Bach *Triple Keyboard Concerto*, the highlight of this well-planned concert.

COLLECTIONS

Bassoon Concerto in E min., RV 484; Flute Concerto in G min. (La notte), Op. 10/2, RV 439; Double Mandolin Concerto in G, RV 532; Concerto con molti

strumenti in C, RV 558; Double Concerto for Oboe & Violin in B flat, RV 548; Concerto for Strings (Alla rustica), RV 151; Concerto for 2 Violins & 2 Cellos in G, RV 575; L'estro armonico: Concerto for 4 Violins in D, Op. 3/1, RV 549

🎵 Ⓜ *** DG (IMS) 447 301-2. Soloists, E. Concert, Pinnock

This generous 72-minute collection of varied works is very enticing, showing **Pinnock** and the **English Concert** at their liveliest and most refreshing, although not always so strong on charm. The *Concerto for Four Violins* is very lithe, and throughout the concert the solo playing is most expert. The orchestral concerto, RV 558, involves an astonishing array of instruments.

Bassoon Concertos in A min., RV 497; in B flat (La notte), RV 501; Double Mandolin Concerto in G, RV 532; Piccolo Concerto in C, RV 443; Viola d'amore Concerto in D min., RV 394; Double Violin Concerto for Violin & Violin per eco lontano in A, RV 552

Ⓜ *** Vernay PV 730052. Soloists, Paul Kuentz CO, Kuentz

Although described as 'six rare concertos', this most enjoyable, 71-minute collection is made up entirely of favourites, all played with much character. The two mandolinists, **Takashi** and **Sylvia Ochi**, are as personable as the sprightly bassoonist, **Fernand Corbillon**, with his woody French timbre, while the *Echo Violin Concerto* (the echoes feature in the ripieno as well as the solo writing) comes off to great effect. Fine accompaniments from **Kuentz** and first-rate digital sound, naturally balanced.

Bassoon Concerto in B flat, RV 502; Cello Concerto in C min., RV 501; Oboe Concerto in C, RV 447; Double Trumpet Concerto in C, RV 537; L'estro armonico: Double Violin Concerto in A min., RV 522; Quadruple Violin Concerto in B min., RV 580; Triple Violin Concerto in F, RV 551

🎵 ⒷⒷ **** Virgin 4 82136-2. Soloists, LCO, Warren-Green

The opening *Double Trumpet Concerto* is brightly arresting, and in the works for oboe and bassoon both soloists (**Gordon Hunt** and **Merrick Alexander**, respectively) play with much character and elegance and, in the latter, also a touch of humour. The lovely slow movement of the *C minor Cello Concerto* is warmly sympathetic on **André Schulman's** bow. For some reason, a continuo is used only in the two woodwind *Concertos*. The excerpts from *L'estro armonico* are gleamingly strong and expressive, and one senses an added energy, possibly deriving from the musicians standing while they play. Excellent recording with the resonance never becoming oppressive.

Concerti 'con molti strumenti': Concerto funèbre in B flat for Oboe, Chalumeau, Violin, 3 Viole all'inglese, RV 579; Concerto in C for 2 Recorders, Oboe, Chalumeau, Violin, 2 Viole all'inglese, 2 Violins 'in tromba marina', 2 Harpsichords, RV 555; Concerto in D min. for 2 Oboes, Bassoon, 2 Violins, RV 566; Double Trumpet Concerto in D, RV 781; Concerto in F for Viola d'amore, 2 Horns, 2 Oboes & Bassoon,

RV 97; Concerto in F for Violin, 2 Oboes, Bassoon, 2 Horns, RV 574; Concerto in D for Violin, 2 Oboes, 2 Horns, RV 562

🎵 **** Hyp. CDA 67073. Soloists, King's Consort, King

This is one of the most attractive of all the CD groupings of Vivaldi's often extraordinarily scored multiple *Concertos*, in which the period-instrument playing is not only expert, but constantly tweaks the ear. The braying horns often dominate. The oboes are used to decorate the *Grave* of the latter, and elegantly open the finale of the former, before a bravura violin sends sparks flying. The *Concerto funèbre*, not surprisingly, opens with a *Largo* and combines the remarkable solo combination of muted oboe, tenor chalumeau, a trio of viole all'inglese accompanied by muted strings. Then (in RV 555) comes the most remarkable array of all. Vivaldi even throws in a pair of harpsichords for good measure, and they are given some most attractive solo passages and used to provide a gentle rocking background for a most engaging violin soliloquy in the central *Largo*. Throughout, the solo playing is wonderfully stylish and appealing, and **Robert King** maintains a fine vigour in *Allegros* and an often gentle espressivo in slow movements. The recording is first class. Very highly recommended.

Concerto funèbre con molti istromenti for muted Oboes, Chalumeaux (Salmoè), Violin & Viola da gamba; Double Concertos: for Violin & Cello in F (Il Proteo o sia il mondo al rovescio); for Violin & Viola da gamba in A, RV 546; Triple Concertos for 2 Violins & Viola da gamba: in D min., RV 565; in G min., RV 578; Concerto for 4 Violins & Cello in B Min. RV 580

🎵 *** Alia Vox AV 9835. Savall & soloists, Le Concert des Nations

This splendid collection centres on the vibrant presence of **Jordi Savall**, who contributes instrumentally to half the *Concertos* included here, and directs them all. The highly original *Funeral Concerto* (based on a *Sinfonia* from the opera *Tito Manlio*) creates most colourful sonorities by including muted oboes, tenor chalumeaux, and three viole' all'inglese. The *'Il Proteo'* (upside-down) *Concerto* is written with the violin solos written in the bass clef while the cello reads from the treble clef. This is a joke aimed at the players, for it makes no difference to the resulting sound. These are all aurally fascinating works, and they are superbly played and recorded, with characteristic Savall gusto in *Allegros* and warmly lyrical slow movements.

'Concerti con molti istromenti': Concerto in G min. for Oboe solo, Violin solo, 2 Flutes & 2 Oboes, RV 576; Concerto in G min. for Oboe solo, Violin solo, 2 Flutes & 2 Oboes, RV 577; Concerto in F for Violin, 2 Oboes & 2 Horns, RV 574; Concerto in F for Violin, 2 Oboes & 2 Horns, RV 569; Sinfonia for Strings in C, RV 192

🎵 **** Naïve OP 30283. Soloists, Freiburg Bar. O, von der Goltz

We know of the excellence of **Gottfried von der Goltz's**

period instrument **Freiburg Baroque Orchestra** from their outstanding DVD of the Bach *Brandenburg Concertos*. They are no less stimulating in these Vivaldi *Concertos*, written for Dresden, to which they bring a remarkable range of instrumental colour and dynamic, much vitality and expressive finesse. Slow movements, usually played gently, are always memorable, as in the *Grave* of RV 569 or the *Larghetto* of RV 576, and the excellence of their horn players is demonstrated vigorously in RV 574. A splendid collection, vividly recorded.

Double Cello Concerto in G min., RV 531; Concerto for Flute, Oboe, Bassoon & Violin in F (La tempesta di mare), RV 570; Concerto funèbre in B flat for Violin, Oboe, Salmoé & 3 Viole all'inglese, RV 579; Flute Concerto in G min. (La notte), RV 439; Violin Concertos in D (L'inquietudine), RV 234; in E (Il riposo – per il Natale), RV 270; in A (Per eco in lontano), RV 552

🎵 **** Virgin 5 45424-2. Europa Galante, Biondi

This collection of some of Vivaldi's most imaginative *Concertos*, played on period instruments, is just as attractive as its looks. All the special effects, from the ghost and sleep evocations in *La notte* to the echoing second violin in RV 552, are neatly managed, and the atmosphere of the *Concerto funèbre* is well sustained. This *Concerto* features a theme taken from *Tito Manlio* where it was used as part of a procession to execution, and the scoring is very telling (see above). **Fabio Biondi** leads an excellent team of soloists and directs sparkling accompaniments, with a touch of vintage dryness to the bouquet of string timbre. Excellent recording.

Double Cello Concerto in G min., RV 531; Lute (Guitar) Concerto in D, RV 93; Oboe Concerto in F, F.VII, 2 (RV 455); Double Concerto for Oboe & Violin; Trumpet Concerto in D (trans. Jean Thilde); Violin Concerto in G min., Op. 12/1, RV 317.

*** Naxos 8.550384. Capella Istropolitana, Kreček

This is a recommendable disc from which to set out to explore Vivaldi *Concertos*, especially if you are beginning a collection. **Gabriela Krcková** makes a sensitive contribution to the delightful *Oboe Concerto in F major* F.VII, No. 2 (R. 455), and the other soloists are pretty good too.

Double Concertos for 2 Cellos in G min., RV 531; for Violin, Cello & Strings in F (Il Proteo ò sia il mondo rovescio), RV 544; for 2 Violins in A (per eco in lontano), RV 552. Triple Concertos for 3 Violins in F, RV 551; for Violin & 2 Cellos in C, RV 561. Quadruple Concerto for 2 Violins & 2 Cellos in C, RV 561; in D, RV 564.

🎵 **** Teldec 4509 94552-2. Coin and soloists, Il Giardino Armonico, Antonini

An exceptionally rewarding collection of *Concertos* for multiple, stringed instruments. **Christophe Coin** leads an excellent team of soloists and the imaginative continuo (organ, harpsichord and archlute) adds to the colour of performances which are full of life, yet which also reveal the music's more subtle touches and are remarkably free from the exaggerated stylistic devices often associated with period instruments. The recording is excellent.

Double Concertos for 2 Cellos in G min., RV 531; for 2 Oboes in D min., RV 523; for 2 Violins in C, RV 505; in D, RV 511. Triple Concerto for Oboe & 2 Violins, RV 554

*** Chan. 0528. Coe, Warkin, Robson, Latham, Standage, Comberti, Coll. Mus. 90, Standage

Period-instrument performances are increasingly identified with the style of their performing groups, and that of **Simon Standage's Collegium Musicum 90** is most invigorating, stylish with no lack of expressive feeling. The rhythmic crispness and buoyancy and the plangent string-sound make for characterful performances. The ripe sound of the baroque oboes and the crunchy cello timbre are particularly attractive, although the tingling astringency characteristic of the accompanying group is even more strongly focused in the solo playing for the *Concertos* for two violins, and especially in the busy finale of RV 511. Outstanding Chandos sound.

Double Concertos for 2 Flutes in C, RV 533; for 2 Horns in F, RV 538 & RV 539; for 2 Trumpets in C, RV 537; for Oboe & Bassoon in G, RV 545. Concerto (Sinfonia in D) for Strings, RV 122; Quadruple Concerto for 2 Oboes & 2 Clarinets, RV 560

🅑🅑 *** Naxos 8.553204. Soloists, City of L. Sinfonia, Kraemer

The opening *Double Concertos* for two horns, RV 539, two flutes, RV 533, and two trumpets, RV 537, all go well enough and offer expert solo contributions, but then at the arrival of the *Quadruple Concerto for Two Oboes and Two Clarinets* the playing suddenly sparks into extra exuberance, and one senses the musicians' enjoyment of one of Vivaldi's most imaginatively scored multiple works. The *Concerto for Two Horns* which follows (RV 538) has a similar ebullience, and the concert is rounded off by a captivating account of RV 545, where both the oboe and bassoon clearly relish every bar of their engaging dialogue. **Kraemer's** accompaniments are polished and spirited.

Double Violin Concertos in C min., RV 509; D, RV 512; G, RV 516; D min., RV 514; A min., RV 523; B flat, RV 524

Ⓝ **** DG 477 7466. Mullova, Carmignola, Venice Baroque O, Marcon

A fresh, bracing collection of Vivaldi's *Double Violin Concertos*. Vivaldi gives each soloist an equal share, and **Viktoria Mullova** and **Giuliano Carmignola** play in total rapport with one other. Apart from their stylish contribution, what makes this disc so appealing is the vibrant support they receive from the orchestra, sharply pointed and dramatic in the lively *Allegros*, but also beautifully relaxed in Vivaldi's often magical slow movements (the *largo* in RV 511 is especially delightful). The finales bounce along in a most infectious manner – just sample the finale to *C minor Concerto*, RV 509, to see what we mean. The DG recording is both vivid and warm and this CD is strongly recommended.

Fourteen concertos: Disc 1: (i; ii) *Lute Concerto in D, RV 93; Double Concerto for 2 Mandolins in G, RV 532; (i; iii) Recorder Concertos in A min., RV 108; in G min. (La notte); (iv) Violin Concerto in D (Grosso Mogull), RV 208. Disc 2: (v) Double Concertos for 2 Cellos in G min., RV 531; for 2 Flutes in C, RV 533; for 2 Trumpets in C, RV 443. Concertos for Strings in D min. (Madrigalesco), RV 129; in G (Alla rustica), RV 151; in G min., RV 153. Quadruple Concerto for 2 Violins & 2 Cellos in D, RV 564; L'estro armonico: Quadruple Violin Concerto in B min., Op. 3/10, RV 580*

Ⓑ *** O-L Double (DDD/ADD) 455 703-2 (2). (i) New L. Cons., Pickett; with (ii) Finucane; (iii) Pickett; (iv) Ritchie, Bach Ens., Rifkin; (v) Soloists, AAM, Hogwood

The 14 *Concertos* on this Oiseau-Lyre Double readily demonstrate the extraordinary diversity of Vivaldi's musical ideas, and in many cases his originality too. None more so than the remarkable *Violin Concerto*, RV 208 (written about 1710), nicknamed – probably not by the composer – 'Grosso Mogull'. The outer movements with their *moto perpetuo* arpeggios demand great virtuosity from the soloist, and the slow movement is a long recitativo, more like an improvisation. The remarkable seven-minute finale, perhaps the longest in any Vivaldi *Concerto*, has a central cadenza which demands and is given a performance of dazzling virtuosity by the soloist here, **Stanley Ritchie**. The concertos for lute, mandolins and recorder are also expertly and pleasingly played by **Philip Pickett** and his group, whose brand of authenticity is rather less abrasive than Hogwood's. The digital sound is first class. For the reissue, three extra works have been added, most notably the famous *Quadruple Violin Concerto* from *L'estro armonico*, taken from the Academy's splendid complete set, with **John Holloway, Monica Huggett, Catherine Mackintosh** and **Elizabeth Wilcock** the excellent soloists.

CHAMBER MUSIC

Cello Sonatas 1–9, RV 39/47

Ⓑ *** CRD CRD 34401 (2). L'Ecole d'Orphée

Cello Sonatas in E flat, RV 39; in E min., RV 40; in F, RV 41; in G min., RV 42; in A min., RV 43 & 44

☛ Ⓜ *** DHM/BMG 74321 93561-2. Bylsma, Suzuki, Ogg

Cello Sonatas in E flat, RV 39; in E min., RV 40; in F, RV 41; in G min., RV 42; in A min., RV 43 & 44; in B flat, RV 45, 46 & 47

**(*) TDK DVD TDK-AD 012 (2). Suzuki, Zipperling, Palviainen

Vivaldi wrote ten *Sonatas* for cello and continuo, of which one is lost. These recordings use an edition published in Budapest in 1995. Their four-movement format probably derives from the *sonate da chiese*, but they were surely designed for concert performance for they afford the soloist both expressive and bravura opportunities, although they are not virtuoso works.

All nine *Sonatas* are given highly musical performances on CRD; they do not set out to impress by grand gestures but succeed in doing so by their dedication and sensitivity. **Susan Sheppard** is a thoughtful player and is well supported by her continuo team, **Lucy Carolan** and **Jane Coe**. The CRD recording is well focused with fine presence.

Hidemi Suzuki also offers them all, but **Anner Bylsma** and her companions content themselves with six of the best, and there is no question that the Deutsche Harmonia Mundi performances are preferable. Bylsma's tone is firm and full, with eloquent phrasing, and the continuo group is well balanced; although Suzuki plays very musically, his performances have a less strong profile and are rather less spontaneously enjoyable.

Chamber Concertos in D, RV 84; (Sonata) in A, RV 86; in D, RV 94; in D (La pastorella), RV 95; in F, RV 99; in G min., RV 103 & 105

Ⓑ *** HM Classical Express HCX 3957046. Verbruggen, Goodwin, Holloway, Godburn, Toll, Comberti

Vivaldi was at his most imaginatively inventive in his *Chamber Concertos*. The spicy, chirping opening of *La pastorella* (RV 95) is scored for recorder, oboe and bassoon to depict a shepherd piping. RV 94 opens with a simulated hurdy-gurdy effect, and RV 99 depicts a hunt (without horns!) and has a very rustic central *Largo*, while the slow movement of RV 105 is an almost bucolic duet for recorder and bassoon, with oboe added spiritedly in the finale. RV 84 was written for performance by the Dresden Orchestra and includes the composer's chromatic 'Sleep' motif in its finale, though it is not in the least somnambulant. Most delectable.

Chamber Concertos: in D for Flute, Violin & Bassoon, RV 91; in D for Lute & 2 Violins RV 93; in D for Recorder, Oboe, Violin, & Bassoon, RV 94; for Recorder, Violin & Bassoon, RV 106; for Viola d'amore, 2 Oboes, 2 Corni di Caccia, RV 97. Sonatina in A min., for Recorder & Bassoon, RV 86

Ⓝ **(*) Warner 2564 69260-8. Soloists, Il Giardino Armonico, Antonini

The concertos included here remained unpublished, after Vivaldi had decided that his works were too often being copied to make pirated editions. In his chamber concertos, curious mixtures of instruments occur, with 'intimate conversations' between them. The interplay did not always work smoothly. For instance the opening multi-instrument concerto, RV 97 is framed within robust movements for the two horns, with more astringent writing for the viola d'amore in between. Similarly the three works which try to combine recorder or flute, oboe, violin and bassoon are often at colouristic cross purposes. The *Sonatina for recorder and bassoon* and the more familiar *Lute Concerto* blend more readily, although the relatively plangent period instrument texture provided by **Il Giardino Armonico** is the opposite of mellow, even in the simple work for lute. Performances are virtuosic and vivid but this is not easy listening, but rather fascinating explorations of sounds possible.

Chamber Concertos for Recorder: in C, with Oboe, 2 Violins, Cello, with Harpsichord Continuo, RV 87; in D, with Violin & Cello Continuo, RV 92; in D, with Oboe, Violin & Bassoon, RV 94; in G, with Oboe, Violin & Bassoon, with Cello & Harpsichord Continuo, RV 101; in G min., with Oboe, Bassoon & Harpsichord, RV 103; in G, with Oboe, Violin & Bassoon, with Cello Continuo, RV 105; in A min., with 2 Violins, with Cello & Harpsichord Continuo, RV 108

(BB) *** Naxos 8.557215. Kecskeméti, Hadady, Falvay, Párkányi, Olajos, Kertész, Dobosy

These excellent Hungarian soloists offer a group of chamber works for various instruments, all dominated by the recorder, here **László Kecskeméti**, a brilliant player, matched by an impressive number of his colleagues. They play with great freshness and rhythmic zest, with the *Largo* central movements pleasingly expressive. It is the range of contrasting woodwind colour that makes these works so ear-tickling, especially those featuring the bassoon. Excellently balanced recording.

Chamber Concertos in C for Recorder, Oboe, 2 Violins, Cello, Harpsichord & Lute, RV 87; in D for Flute, Violin, & Cello, RV 92; in G min. for Flute, Oboe, Bassoon, Cello, Organ & Lute, RV 107; in D min. for Solo Organ & Flute, 2 Violins, Viola, Cello, Violone & Lute, RV 541; in F for Organ & Violin solo, 2 Violins, Viola, Cello, Violone & Lute, RV 542. Trio Sonata in D min. (La folia), RV 65

⊕—**** Channel Classics CCS 8495. Florilegium

These *Concertos* could hardly be played more persuasively (one instrument to each part) than they are by **Florilegium**, an outstanding period-instrument ensemble. The *Concertos*, which include a solo organ, are enchanting in their piquant colouring, and are full of splendid ideas. The finale of RV 107, for instance, is a kaleidoscopic chaconne, in effect a chimerical set of variations. But every work here is inspired and aurally stimulating, and they could hardly be better played. The programme ends with Vivaldi's extensive variations on *La follia* in the form of a *Trio Sonata*, which is presented with bravura, a wide range of dynamic and a sense of fantasy. The group, led by **Ashley Solomon** (flute/recorder), are all masters of their instruments and play infectiously together as a team. The recording is ideally balanced, within an acoustic with just the right feeling of ambient space.

Chamber Concertos for Treble Recorder in A min., RV 108; in C min., RV 441; in F, RV 442; for Sopranino Recorder in C, RV 443 & RV 444; in A min., RV 445

⊕—(BB) *** Hyp. Helios CDH 55016. Holtslag, Parley of Instruments, Holman

These are all played with one instrument to each part, and by alternating treble and sopranino recorders. **Peter Holtslag** provides variety, although this is not a CD to undertake all at one session.

Excellent recording and good value.

Violin Sonatas in C, RV 754; in A, RV 758. Trio Sonatas in D min. (Variations on 'La follia'), Op. 1/12; in C, RV 50; in G min., RV 74

⊕—(BB) *** Hyp. Helios CDH 55231. Purcell Qt

This Helios reissue is very welcome indeed. At its centre is the early set of variations on *La follia*, obviously drawing on Corelli, but none the worse for that. The other solo *Sonatas* (admirably featuring **Catherine Mackintosh** and **Robert Woolley**) and *Trio Sonatas* are characteristically inventive and entertaining, and they are superbly played and recorded here. This budget disc is very well worth having on all counts.

VOCAL MUSIC

Complete Sacred Music

Robert King's coverage of Vivaldi's key sacred choral works is now the most complete survey in the catalogue, and this admirable set now appears in a box (with a booklet including full texts and translations), at a very generous budget price, and as such receives the strongest recommendation.

Volumes 1–10

⊕—(BB) *** Hyp. CDS 44171/81 (11). Soloists, King's Consort, King

Sacred music, Vol. 1: Credo in unum Deum, RV 591; Dixit Dominus, RV 594; Kyrie eleison, RV 587; Lauda, Jerusalem, RV 609; Magnificat, RV 610a

*** Hyp. CDA 66769. Gritton, Milne, Denley, Atkinson, Wilson-Johnson, Choristers and Ch., King's Consort, King

Hyperion's series aims to cover all the key sacred choral works of Vivaldi. All the music here is for double choir except the simple *Credo*, which is without soloists but has great intensity of feeling expressed in the *Et incarnatus est* and *Crucifixus*. Apart from the splendidly grand and masterly *Dixit Dominus*, RV 594 (gloriously sung here), there are two fine, shorter works which also include double string orchestra: the *Kyrie eleison* and the *Lauda Jerusalem*. But most striking of all is Vivaldi's first setting of the *Magnificat* – in G minor, dating from around 1715, although revised in the 1720s – made memorable by its highly individual chromatic writing, but also adding to the poignancy of the *Et misericordia*.

Sacred music, Vol. 2: Motets: (i) Canta in prato, ride in monte, RV 623; (ii) Clarae stellae, scintillate, RV 625; Filiae maestae Jerusalem, RV 638 (i) In furore iustissimae irae, RV 626; (iii) Longe mala, umbrae, terrores, RV 629; (i) Nulla in mundo pax sincera, RV 630

*** Hyp. CDA 66779. (i) York; (ii) Bowman; (iii) Denley; King's Consort, King

The opening of *In furore iustissimae irae* ('In wrath and most just anger') is delivered with dramatic venom, but then the *Largo, Tune meus fletus* ('Then shall my weeping'), follows exquisitely. The other highlight of the collection is **James Bowman's** *Filiae maestae Jerusalem*, which brings a touching

Larghetto, *Silenti Zephyri* ('Let the winds be hushed'). A first-class collection, excellently recorded.

Sacred music, Vol. 3: *Beatus vir* (two versions), RV 597 & RV 598; *Credidi propter quod*, RV 605; *Dixit Dominus*, RV 595; *Domine ad adjuvandum*, RV 593

*** Hyp. CDA 66789. Gritton, Wyn-Davies, Denley, Daniels, N. Davies, George, Ch. & King's Consort, King

Vivaldi's two settings of the *Beatus vir* are quite different. RV 597 is for double choir and is on an ambitious scale, with a refrain that reappears in various sections of the work. RV 598 is in a single movement and is written for soloists and a single choir, rather in the manner of a concerto grosso. The present setting of *Dixit Dominus* is for single chorus (but with sopranos sometimes divided). *Domine ad adjuvandum* is a superbly concentrated short work for double choir, based on Psalm 69.

Sacred music, Vol. 4: *Juditha triumphans* (complete)

*** Hyp. CDA 67281/2. Murray, Bickley, Kiehr, Connolly, Rigby, Ch. & King's Consort, King

Juditha triumphans, Vivaldi's only surviving oratorio, involves only women's voices in the solo roles and here is exceptionally well cast. **Ann Murray**, in one of her most beautiful performances on disc, is seductive as Judith rather than sharply dramatic, and it is left to **Susan Bickley** as the tyrannical general, Holofernes, to steal first honours, strong and incisive. **Robert King** relishes the rich instrumentation with its brilliant and original obbligato solos, beautifully caught in vivid, atmospheric recording.

Sacred music, Vol. 5: *Confitebor tibi, Domine; Deus tuorum militum; In turbato mare*, RV 627; *Non in pratis aut in hortis*, RV 641; *O qui coeli terraeque serenitas*, RV 631; *Stabat mater*, RV 621

*** Hyp. CDA 66799. Gritton, Rigby, Blaze, Daniels, N. Davis, King's Consort, King

Volume 5 of this excellent Hyperion series offers two solo motets, a simple Vesper hymn (*Deus tuorum militum*) sung as a contralto/tenor duet, and ends with a very fine three-voice setting of Psalm 110, *Confitebor tibi, Domine*, which in its final movement draws on a sparkling terzet from Vivaldi's opera *La fida ninfa*. It makes a satisfying close to a programme which has as its centrepiece the glorious *Stabat Mater* (1712), very beautifully sung here by the male alto, **Robin Blaze**. To open the concert **Susan Gritton** despatches *In turbato mare irato* with biting bravura, but is later able to show her lovely lyrical style in *O qui coeli terraeque serenitas*.

Sacred music, Vol. 6: *Beatus vir*, RV 795; *In exitu Israel*, RV 604; *Laudate Dominum*, RV 606; *Nisi Dominus*, RV 608; *Salve Regina*, RV 617

**(*) Hyp. CDA 66809. Gritton, Stutzmann, Summers, Gibson, Ch. & King's Consort, King

While the two motets *In exitu Israel* and *Laudate Dominum* are for choir alone, the ambitious setting of *Beatus vir* (only comparatively recently confirmed as authentic Vivaldi), which alternates extended solos with a brief repeated chorale, involves **Susan Gritton** immediately in spectacularly florid solo singing. Later she is joined by **Hilary Summers** and **Alexandra Gibson** in the seraphic trio *In memoria aeterna*, and both contraltos then make major solo contributions. Gritton is at her finest in the *Salve Regina*, where **Simon Jones** provides elaborate violin obbligatos.

Sacred music, Vol. 7: *Gloria*, RV 588; *Laetatus sum*, RV 607; *Laudate pueri*, RV 601; *Jubilate, o amoeni chori*, RV 639; *Vestro Principi divino*, RV 633

*** Hyp. CDA 66819. Gritton, Sampson, Stutzmann, Daniels, Ch. & King's Consort

Laudate pueri (Psalm 112) is a true virtuoso piece for soprano (originally a castrato) able to reach D *in alt*. **Carolyn Sampson** sings it gloriously, radiant in *A solis ortu usque ad occasum*, and ethereally beautiful in the *Gloria Patri* which she sings in duet with an obbligato flute. This is followed by an outstanding performance by **Nathalie Stutzmann** of the motet *Vespro Principi divino* (a paraphrase of Psalm 23), sung with comparable virtuosity. She then leads the way into the lesser-kown Vivaldi setting of the *Gloria* by way of an introductory motet, *Jubilate o amoeni chori*, whose second and final aria leads straight into the opening chorus of the *Gloria*.

Sacred music, Vol. 8: *Cur sagittas, cur tela*, RV 637; *Laudate pueri*, RV 600; *Salve Regina*, RV 616; *Sanctorum meritis*, RV 620; *Sum in medio tempestatum*, RV 632

*** Hyp. CDA 66829. Gritton, Semmingsen, Stutzmann, Ch. & King's Consort, King

Sacred music, Vol. 9: *Ascende laeta*, RV 635; *Gaude mater Ecclesia*, RV 613; *Gloria Patri*, RV 602a; *Salve Regina*, RV 618; *Vos aurae per montes*, RV 634; *Laudate pueri*, RV 602

*** Hyp. CDA 66839. Sampson, Gritton, Lunn, DiDonato, Stutzmann, Ch. & King's Consort, King

Sacred music, Vol. 10: *Gloria*, RV 589; *Nisi Dominus*, RV 803; *Ostro picta*, RV 642

*** Hyp. CDA 66849. Ch. & King's Consort, King – RUGGIERI: *Gloria*

Volume 8 opens with a thrilling virtuoso performance from the agile, light-voiced mezzo, **Tuva Semmingsen**, of *Sum in medio tempestatum* ('I am in the midst of stormy weather'), bringing tender melancholy to '*Semper maesta*', and sparkling in the closing '*Alleluia*'. **Susan Gritton** responds to the greater expressive range of *Laudate pueri*, while the darker-voiced **Nathalie Stutzmann** finds plenty of venomous character in *Cur saggitas, cur tela* ('Why oh terrible hobgoblins').

Carolyn Sampson frames the programme of Volume 9, a particularly rich collection. She opens with a gloriously sung *Laudate pueri*, in which she is joined in duet in several movements by the well-matched soprano voice of **Joanne Lunn**, with the chorus adding weight at the opening and close. A very nimble oboe obbligato from **Alexandra Bellamy** adds much to the interest of the *Gloria Patri*. She then ends the programme with an expressive *Vox aurae per montes* ('You breezes through the mountains') with its lively final *Alleluia*.

Volume 10 rounds off Robert King's magnificent survey by opening very appropriately with Vivaldi's most famous choral work, the *Gloria*, RV 589. It is a splendid performance on every count, with soloists, chorus and orchestra all shining. Then the following *Nisi Dominus* proves an ideal showcase for many of the soloists, all on top form, and often with accompanying instrumental obbligato. The range of vocal and instrumental colour shows Vivaldi at his most imaginatively inspired. After Carolyn Sampson has made her distinguished final solo contribution in the touching *Ostro picta* we are offered a *Gloria* setting by Giovanni Ruggieri (c. 1690–1720) a fine work, splendidly sung here.

Cantatas: (i) *All'ombra di sospetto, RV 678; (ii; iii) Amor hai vinto, RV 651; (i) Lungi dal vago volto, RV 680; Vengo a voi, luci adorate, RV 682; (iv) Gloria in D, RV 589; (v; iii) Nisi Dominus (Psalm 127), RV 608; (ii; iii) Nulla in mundo pax sincera, RV 630. (vi) Trio Sonata (La folia), RV 63*

Ⓑ *** O-L Double (ADD/DDD) 455 727-2 (2). (i) Bott, New L. Cons., Pickett; (ii) Kirkby; (iii) AAM, Hogwood; (iv) Nelson, Kirkby, Watkinson, Christ Church Cathedral Ch., AAM, Preston; (v) Bowman; (vi) Standage, Mackintosh, Hogwood

Vivaldi's secular cantatas are lightweight but have much charm. Combining recitative and a pair of arias, they usually express the dolours of unrequited love in an Arcadian setting. In each case the words are written from the male point of view, yet here they are treated as soprano solos – delightfully so, for, after **Emma Kirkby** has opened the programme with a characteristically fresh-voiced *Amor hai vento*, **Catherine Bott** takes over with her softer focus and more plaintive style. As a central instrumental interlude we are offered a lively and stylish account of the *Trio Sonata* which Vivaldi based on *La follia*. The first CD opens with the familiar *Gloria*. The choristers of **Christ Church Cathedral** excel themselves and the recording is remarkably fine. The solo motet, *Nulla in mundo pax sincera*, brings back Emma Kirkby, who copes splendidly with the bravura writing for soprano. **James Bowman** is also a persuasive soloist in the more extended, operatic-styled setting of Psalm 127.

Cantatas: (i) *Amor hai vinto, RV 683; Cesssate, omai cessate, RV 684. La stravaganza: (ii) Violin Concerto in D min., Op. 4/8, RV 429. (iii) Cello Concerto in A min., RV. 422; Concertos for Strings in C & E min., RV 117 & RV 134; in G (Alla rustica), RV 151*

**** Naïve OPS 30-181. (i) Mingardo; (ii) Vicari; (iii) Piovano; Concerto Italiano, Alessandrini

Rinaldo Alessandrini opens this concert with an exhilaratingly crisp account of the bouncing *Allegro* of *Concerto for Strings in C major* and sets the scene for *Amor hai vinto*, the first of the two pastoral cantatas sung with comparably bracing vocal virtuosity.

Motets: *Canto in prato, ride in monte, RV 623; Invicti, bellate, RV 68; Longe mala, umbrae, terrore, RV 629; Nulla in mundo pax sincera, RV 630; O qui*

coeli terraeque serenitas, RV 631; Vestro principi divino, RV 633

*** Naïve OP 30340. Herrman, Polverelli, Academia Montis Regalis, de Marchi

The four-section sacred motets here (*Aria–Recitativo–Aria–Allegro*) have non-liturgical texts alternating between the fresh and sweet-voiced soprano **Anke Herrman** and the nimble and well-focused contralto, who finds both bravura and drama for the opening *Longe mala, umbrae, terrore* ('Begone, evils, shadows and terrors') and sings with special eloquence in *Invicti, bellate*, which ends with a virtuoso *Alleluia*. The **Academia Montis Regalis**, directed by **Alessandro de Marchi**, accompany warmly and sympathetically, using modern instruments, and the recording is excellent.

Beatus vir, RV 597; Gloria in D, RV 589

ⒷⒷ **(*) Naxos 8.550767. Crookes, Quitaker, Lane, Trevor, Oxford Schola Cantorum, N. CO, Ward

This coupling of what are probably the two favourite Vivaldi choral works is beautifully recorded and well worth its modest cost. Although some listeners will want greater attack in the famous opening and closing sections of the *Gloria* and in the *Potens in terra* in the companion work, these spacious performances, directed by **Nicholas Ward**, are still warmly enjoyable, partly because of the freshness of the solo contributions, but also because the choral singing has considerable intensity, especially in the continual return of the haunting *Beatus vir* chorale in RV 589. Full translations are included.

(i) Motets: *Clarae stellae, scintillate, RV 625; Nisi Dominus, RV 608; Salve Regina, RV 616; Vespro principa divino, RV 633. Concertos for Strings: in C, RV 109; in F, RV 141*

☞ **** Decca 466 964-2. (i) Scholl; Australian Brandenburg O, Dyer

Scholl's account of the Vesper psalm *Nisi Dominus* catches to the full its lyrical beauty. *Cum dederit delectis suis somnum* opens very mysteriously (Vivaldi asks his strings to play with *piombi* – lead mutes – instead of the normal wooden *sordini*) and Scholl sings his slowly rising chromatic scale with seraphic, sensuous beauty, a moment of sheer magic. The work's expressive climax, *Gloria patri*, with its viola da gamba obbligato, is transcendent, followed by the bravura release of *Sicut erat*. The other highlight here is Vivaldi's highly imaginative setting of the *Salve Regina*, with its antiphonal accompaniment for double orchestra, especially striking in the *Ad te clamamus*. The period-instrument **Australian Brandenburg Orchestra** contribute much to the success of this record, providing (as interludes) vibrantly infectious accounts of two of Vivaldi's *String Concertos*. We shall surely hear more from this group and their impressive conductor, **Paul Dyer**.

Dixit Dominus, RV 807

*** DG 477 6145. Invernizzi, Cirillo, Mingardo, Agnew, Cooley, Foresti, Zeppenfeld, Körnerscher Singverein, Dresden, Dresden Instrumental Concert, Kopp – GALUPPI: *Motets* ***

This third *Dixit Dominus* was identified in 2005 by the Australian scholar Janice Stockigt as the work of Vivaldi and this is its first recording. Originally attributed to Galuppi, its style is clearly that of Vivaldi – and top-notch Vivaldi at that. It is full of the composer's characteristic energy and melody, and with many beauties besides. The performance is fresh and invigorating, with the singers coping well with the often demanding florid lines, and this is a must for all Vivaldi addicts. The recording is superb.

(i) *Gloria in D, RV 588; Gloria in D, RV 589;* (ii; iii) *Beatus vir in C, RV 597; Dixit Dominus in D, RV 594;* (iv; iii) *Magnificat in G min., RV 610*

🎵 Ⓑ *** Double Decca (DDD/ADD) 443 455-2 (2). (i) Russell, Kwella, Wilkens, Bowen, St John's College, Cambridge, Ch., Wren O, Guest; (ii) J. Smith, Buchanan, Watts, Partridge, Shirley-Quirk, ECO, Cleobury; (iii) King's College, Cambridge, Ch.; (iv) Castle, Cockerham, King, ASMF, Ledger

The two settings of the *Gloria* make an apt and illuminating pairing. Both in D major, they have many points in common, presenting fascinating comparisons, when RV 588 is as inspired as its better known companion. **Guest** directs strong and well-paced readings, with RV 588 the more lively. Good, warm recording to match the performances. *Dixit Dominus* cannot fail to attract those who have enjoyed the better known *Gloria*. What caps this outstanding Vivaldi compilation is the earlier King's account of the inspired *Magnificat in G minor*. Ledger uses the small-scale setting and opts for boys' voices in the solos such as the beautiful duet, *Esurientes*, which is most winning. The performance overall is very compelling and moving, and the singing has all the accustomed beauty of King's. The transfer of an outstanding (1976) analogue recording is admirable, even richer than its digital companions.

Gloria in D, RV 589

🎵 *** Telarc SACD 60651. T. Matthews, Deanne Meek, M. Phillips, Boston Bar., Pearlman – BACH: *Magnificat* ***

Ⓝ ⒷⒷ *** EMI Encore 2 08125-2 Hendricks, Murray, Rigby, Heilmann, Heinninen, Ch. & ASMF, Marriner – BACH: *Magnificat* ***

Ⓜ *** Decca (ADD) 458 623-2. Vaughan, Baker, Partridge, Keyte, King's College, Cambridge, Ch., ASMF, Willcocks – HANDEL: *Coronation Anthem: Zadok the Priest*; HAYDN: *Nelson Mass* ***

ⒷⒷ *** Naxos 8.554056. Oxford Schola Cantorum, N.CO, Ward – BACH: *Magnificat* ***

Gloria in D, RV 589; Kyrie in G min., RV 587

ⒷⒷ *** Warner Apex (ADD) 0927 48681-2. Smith, Staempfli, Rossier, Schaer, Lausanne Vocal & Instrumental Ens., Corboz – BACH: *Magnificat in D, BWV 243* ***

(i) *Gloria, RV 589; Magnificat, RV 611. Concerto for Strings in D min., RV 243; Double Concerto for Trumpet & Oboe, RV 563*

🎵 **** Naïve OP 3019 S. (i) York, Biccire, Mingardo,

Champagne & Ardene Regional Vocal Ens.; Soloists, Concerto Italiano, Alessandrini

Gloria, RV 589; Ostro picta, armata spina, RV 642

*** Chan. 0518. Kirkby, Bonner, Chance, Coll. Mus. 90, Hickox – BACH: *Magnificat* ***

Pearlman sets off energetically into the famous opening of Vivaldi's *Gloria*, and concludes the work equally spiritedly. The *Domine Deus*, with its sensitive oboe obbligato, is beautifully sung by **Tamara Matthews**; and the later sequence, by the fine alto, **Mary Phillips**, shared with the chorus (*Domine Deus, Agnus Dei – Qui tollis peccata mundi – Qui sedes*) is equally moving. In short, this performance is splendidly sung and sensitively paced, and the surround sound recording is in every way first class.

Rinaldo Alessandrini's dazzling speed for the opening of Vivaldi's *Gloria* must be just about the fastest on record, and it is just as exciting in the reprise for the *Quoniam*. Yet ensemble remains remarkably crisp, and later the pair of sopranos revel in their virtuosity in the *Laudamus te* and the closing *Cum Sanctos Spiritu* makes a fittingly joyous conclusion. The *Magnificat*, too, combines spaciousness with vitality. The mysteriously evocative *Et misericordia* contrasts dramatically with the dynamic *Deposuit potentes*; but, throughout, the essential Italianate warmth of Alessandrini's reading comes through, and the rich choral response is at its most embracing in the closing *Gloria Patri*. The bonuses include a *Concerto for Strings* (which acts as a spirited intermezzo between the main works) and a lively *Double Trumpet Concerto* as an end-piece, arranged from a work for trumpet and oboe, with the oboe retained for just the slow movement.

Both Alessandrini and **Marriner** (like their companions) couple the most popular of the two *D major Glorias* with the Bach *Magnificat* and offer a clear choice between period and modern instruments. Marriner's performance is more traditionally paced, as is the Bach *Magnificat*. His soloists are very good and the recording has warmth and immediacy. A fine budget coupling.

Willcocks's version authentically uses comparatively small forces and has an excellent team of soloists. It is very stylish and very well recorded. Some might feel that consonants are too exaggerated but, in consequence, words are admirably clear.

Corboz, a fine choral conductor, gives a lively performance of the famous *Gloria*, and his super-bargain version includes another richly rewarding liturgical work by Vivaldi alongside an equally spontaneous account of Bach's *Magnificat*. The *Kyrie* is magnificent, with its four soloists, double chorus and double string orchestra spread spaciously across the sound stage.

On Naxos it is most refreshing to have a performance of Vivaldi's most popular choral work that, with modern instruments and a relatively small choir, clarifies textures, revealing inner detail. With **Jeremy Summerly** directing the choir and **Nicholas Ward** conducting the orchestra, the rhythmic point of the writing is reinforced, helped by superb sound, fresh, clear and immediate.

Juditha triumphans (oratorio; complete)

*** Naïve OP 30314 (3). Kožená, Trullo, Comparato, Herrman, Carraro, Santa Cecilia Academy, Chamber Ch., Academia Montis Regalis, De Marchi

Juditha triumphans, recorded in Mondovi in Italy in October 2000, offers a vigorous and scholarly account, meticulously prepared. With fair justification **De Marchi** has transposed the tenor and bass parts of the chorus up an octave, as Vivaldi is believed to have done with his female chorus at the Ospedale della Pieta in Venice. The result is fresh and brilliant, and the team of female soloists, two sopranos and three mezzos, adds to that impression, except that the recording balance sets them at a slight distance, seriously reducing their impact. Even so, the brilliant and rich-toned Slovakian soprano stands out in the title role, with the mezzo **Maria Jose Trullo** bringing variety to the role of her adversary, Holofernes.

Kyrie, RV 587; Magnificat; Motet, 'In furore iustissimae irae', RV 626; Nisi Dominus; Salve Regina; Concerto in D min. (Madrigalesco), RV 129

(BB) **(*) Naxos 8.570445. Huhtanen, McMurtry, McLeod, Modolo, Aradia Ens., Mallon

This CD is valuable for including the final and expanded version of Vivaldi's glorious *Magnificat*, which includes five extra numbers not included on the original. Vivaldi had in mind different singers for each of the arias but here, **Lynne McMurtry** sings them all. The *Concerto in D minor*, also offered on this CD, uses material from the *Magnificat* and the appealing *Kyrie* – both included on this disc. The *Salve Regina* – one of the composer's three settings – features some especially attractive music for the violins. The *Nisi Dominus* is a lively early work, of much lively invention and pleasing incidental delights. *In furore iustissimae irae* is a dramatic Motet, where Vivaldi superbly depicts the fury indicated in the text in the first movement. It has two very beautiful middle movements and ends in a virtuosic *Alleluia*. The performances are generally excellent, though the soloists, good though they are, are not always up to the considerable virtuosity this music demands.

Laudate pueri Dominum, RV 601; Nisi Dominus, RV 608

*** Mer. CDE 84129. Dawson, Robson, King's Consort, King

The present setting of Psalm 113, RV 601, is a strong, consistently inspired work; **Lynne Dawson** sings with an excellent sense of style and is given splendid support. The coupling, the *Nisi Dominus*, a setting of Psalm 127, is much better known but makes an attractive makeweight. It is also given an excellent performance by **Christopher Robson**. Good recording.

(i) Stabat Mater in F min., RV 621; Concerto for Strings in A min., RV 158; Sinfonia for Strings in G, RV 149

**** Analekta FL 2 3171. (i) Lemieux; Tafelmusik, Jeanne Lamon – AVISON:*Concerto grosso after Scarlatti 7*; D. SCARLATTI: *Salve Regina* ********

Marie-Nicole Lemieux's performance of the *Stabat Mater* is very moving, her rich contralto voice just right for this intensely expressive setting. **Tafelmusik** provide an imaginative accompaniment, and also lively performances of a *Concerto* and *Sinfonia* for strings which are most stimulating. The *Andante* of the *Sinfonia* is particularly diverting, its sharp principal rhythmic figure deliciously pointed.

(i) Stabat Mater in F min., RV 621; Cessate omai cessate, RV 684; Filiae mestae in C min., RV 638; Concerto for Strings in C, RV 114; Sonata al Santo Sepolcro in E flat, RV 130

⊖─ **** HM HMC 901571. (i) Scholl; Ens. 415, Banchini

Chiara Banchini and **Ensemble 415** have given us some fine period-instrument performances, but none is finer than this, thanks to the superb contribution of counter-tenor **Andreas Scholl**. His tenderly expressive account of the *Stabat Mater* is infinitely touching, while the pastoral cantata, *Cessate omai cessate*, is, dramatically and lyrically, no less involving. Here Vivaldi's imaginative accompaniments are relished by the instrumental ensemble, and they are equally on their toes in the similarly contrasted string works. Strongly communicative music-making, very well recorded.

(i) Stabat Mater, RV 621; Clarae stella scintillate (Motet), RV 625; Concerto funèbre in B flat for Violin, Oboe, Salmoè & 3 Viole all'inglese; Concerto sacra in D for Violin & Cello, with Organ obbligato, RV 554a; Sonata 4 al Santo Sepolcro in E flat for Strings, RV 124

⊖─ **** Naïve OP 30367. (i) Mingardo; Concerto Italiano, Alessandrini

The deep contralto timbre of **Sara Mingardo** is especially telling in Vivaldi's *Stabat Mater*, and she is very moving in the agonized closing section. This performance is appropriately framed by the *Concerto funèbre* and similarly solemn *Santo Sepolcro Sonata*. The other *Concertos* which frame the contrasting motet, 'O bright stars shine forth', match its very different mood, and Mingardo successfully lightens her voice and style. Fine performancs throughout.

Vespers for the Assumption of the Virgin Mary (arr. Alessandrini)

**** Naïve OP 30383 (2). Bertagnolli, Invernizzi, Simboli, Mingardo, Ferrarini, Bellotto, De Secondi, Concerto Italiano, Alessandrini

Taking Monteverdi's great 1610 set of *Vespers* as a model, **Rinaldo Alessandrini**, in collaboration with the scholar Frederic Delamea, has devised a sequence of Psalm settings and antiphons parallel to Monteverdi's, choosing works by Vivaldi such as might have been used for the Vespers service. Though Vivaldi never wrote music for the vast basilica of St Mark's in Venice, as Monteverdi had done a century earlier, he did write Psalm settings employing double choirs, works which cry out for spatial separation. Starting with a double concerto as overture with similarly divided forces, Alessandrini has included in the sequence such masterly examples of Vivaldi's church music as the *Dixit Dominus* (Psalm

109), *Lauda Jerusalem* (Psalm 147) and the superb *Magnificat* setting, RV 610a, rounded off with a cantata for solo contralto with two orchestras, *Salve Regina*. The challenge of over two and a half hours of music prompts Alessandrini to draw from his choir and period orchestra, **Concerto Italiano**, consistently fresh and incisive performances, brilliantly recorded.

OPERA

Opera Overtures: *Armida al campo d'Egito; Arsilda, regina di Ponto; Bajazet (Tamerlano); Dorilla in Tempe; Farnace; Giustino; Griselda; L'incoronazione di Dario; L'Olimpiade; Ottone in villa; La verità in cimento*

(BB) *** Warner Apex 2564 60537-2. I Sol. Ven., Scimone

Vivaldi's 'opera overtures' were conceived as sinfonias, scarcely related to the character of each work. But these 11 make a lively and surprisingly varied collection, splendidly played and recorded.

Opera Overtures or Sinfonias: *Bajazet; La Dorilla; Farnace; Il Giustino; L'Olimpiade; Ottone in villa; La verità in cimento. Chamber Concerto in D min., RV 128; Concerto in F, for Violin, 2 Oboes, Horn & Bassoon, RV 571; Sinfonia in G, RV 149*

(B) **(*) DHM/BMG 74321 935602. L'Arte del Arco, Hogwood

Except for *L'Olimpiade* (which includes a *tempesta di mare* and is in four sections) and *Ottone in villa* (which is a concertante piece for violins and oboes and is in two), these are all typical three-movement Italian *Overtures*. *Bajazet* (because of the plot) features hunting horns in the outer sections, but they are used even more spectacularly in the *Concerto in F* (which is associated with a Venetian performance of the opera, *Arsilda, regina di Ponto*), while its finale is based on the storm from *Ottone in villa*. The finale of the *Sinfonia for La Dorilla* brings a surprise appearance of the introduction of *Spring* from *The Four Seasons*. The period performances here are highly energetic and certainly stylish, but a bit gruff.

Griselda (opera; complete)

*** Naïve OP 30419 (3). Lemieux, Cangemi, Kermes, Jaroussky, Ferrari, I. Davies, Ens. Matheus, Spinosi

(BB) ** Naxos 8.660211/3. Tomkins, Newman, Huhtanen, McMurtry, Nedecky, Ainsworth, Opera in Concert Ch., Aradia Ens., Mallon

By a strange turn of events two recordings of this little-known but colourful Vivaldi opera arrived fairly closely together and the choice between them is a clear-cut one. The Naxos version is certainly alive, but it involves the transposition of several roles down an octave, with the leading masculine role, Gualtiero (originally tenor) given to a bass. In any case the singing cannot match that on the Naïve set. This is strongly cast, with a star contralto, **Marie-Nicole Lemieux**, as Griselda, while **Simone Kermes** is an equally impressive Ottone and **Philippe Jaroussky's** Roberto is, if anything, even

finer. The rest of the cast is hardly less impressive and, while the orchestral accompaniments lack something in body, **Spinosi's** tempi bring plenty of life to the performance overall.

Motezuma (opera; complete)

⊕ *** DG 477 5996 (3). Priante, Mijanovíc, Invernizzi, Beaumont, Basso, Katna, Il Complesso Barocco, Curtis

Until recently, *Motezuma* was known only thanks to the survival of its libretto by Luigi Giusti, but in 2002 the German scholar Stefen Voss discovered the bulk of the score in the library of the Berliner Sing-Akademie. Although only 17 of the 28 numbers survive, including all of Act II and the important arias of Acts I and III, it proved possible for Alessandro Ciccolini to reconstruct the remainder of the work. It is a strong, virile piece, full of the freshness of invention we expect from the composer, and the excellent soloists and **Alan Curtis's Il Complesso Barocco** bring it to life in spectacular fashion.

Orlando furioso (opera; complete)

(N) **** CPO 777 095- 2 (3) Desler, Kennedy, De Liso, Gregoire, Coro da Camera Italiano, Modo Antiquo, Sardelli

Orlando furioso has a complex plot tied up with *Alcina* and *Orlando* (which we know from Handel). Orlando is well named, of course, for he goes mad at the end of Act II but recovers at the end of the opera in time to bless the marriage of the real lovers, Angelica and Medoro. The opera takes a little while to get going, but soon produces some splendid music for Orlando (the brilliant mezzo, **Anne Desler**), the engaging soprano Angelica (**Nicki Kennedy**) and of course Alcina (**Marina De Liso**) while Medoro's Act I aria '*I break the chains*' is particularly dramatic. But all the solo singing is of quality and the **Camera Italiano Chorus** and **Modo Antiquo** complete a fine supporting group directed with spirit by **Federico Maria Sardelli**. Excellent recording too, make this enjoyable listening.

Ottone in villa (complete)

*** Chan. 0614 (2). Groop, Gritton, Argenta, Padmore, Daneman, Coll. Mus. 90, Hickox

Ottone in villa was Vivaldi's very first opera, produced in 1713. It follows the conventions of the day in a sequence of da capo arias linked by recitatives, with no ensemble number until the final number for the characters in unison. With only five singers required, the scale of the piece is modest in treating the subject of the Emperor Ottone and the way he is fooled by the flirtatious Cleonilla. Vivaldi is here at his most tuneful and inventive, and **Richard Hickox** with an excellent cast of soloists and his fine period-instrument group, **Collegium Musicum 90**, presents the opera with a freshness and vigour that make one forget the work's formal limitations. **Susan Gritton** sings charmingly as the provocative Cleonilla, and **Nancy Argenta** brings flawless control to the castrato role of Caio Sillo, with the mezzo, **Monica Groop**, strong and firm in the title role of the Emperor. Fine production and sound add to the compulsion of the performance.

La verita in cimento

**(*) Naïve OP 30365 (3). Bertagnolli, Laurens, Mingardo, Stutzmann, Jaroussky, Rolfe Johnson, Ens. Matheus, Spinosi

La verita in cimento ('Truth on Trial'), Vivaldi's 13th opera, was first heard in Venice in 1720, but like almost all his other operas it has since been totally neglected. Then in 2002, using a score prepared from various scholarly sources, the enterprising French conductor **Jean-Christophe Spinosi** and his group, **Ensemble Matheus**, gave a very successful series of 25 performances of what emerges as an exceptionally lively piece. With six soloists and no chorus, it is a piece that defied the conventions of the Venetian establishment, led by Benedetto Marcello, and after it Vivaldi was prevented from writing more operas for some years. Yet, as recorded by Spinosi and his excellent team, this is a piece that sparkles with life.

'Viva Vivaldi': Arias: (i) *Agitata da due venti La Griselda, RV 718; Gloria in D, RV 589: Domine Deus.* Opera arias: *Bajazet (Il Tamerlano): Anch'il mar par che sommerga; Farnace: Gelido in ogni vedo; La fida ninfa: Dite, Oimè; Giustino: Sventurata Navicelli. Juditha Triumphans: Armatae face et Angibus; L'Olimpiade: Tra la follie divers … Siam navi all'onde algenti; Ottone in villa: Gelosia, tu già rendi l'alma mia; Teuzzone: Di due rai languir costante; Zeffiretti che sussurrate; Tito Manlio: Non ti lusinghi la crudelitade. Concertos in C for flautino, RV 443; in D for lute, RV 93 (DVD version)*

**** Arthaus DVD 100 228. (i) Bartoli; Il Giardino Armonico, Antonini (V/D: Brian Large.)

For this programme **Cecilia Bartoli** has drawn on autograph material in the Turin Library. In the two *Concertos*, the *Domine Deus* and a couple of the arias, the score is available, though it must be said that its superimposition all but obliterates the visual image. As in her handsomely presented Decca *Vivaldi Album* (see below), Bartoli sings effortlessly and magnificently – and she duplicates one or two arias here. **Il Giardino Armonico** are full of virtuosity and delicacy, and the music is left to speak for itself, while the presence of Bartoli's Decca producer, Christopher Raeburn, ensures an excellent and musical balance. It is a tribute to Vivaldi's spectacular fund of invention that there is so much of quality yet to be discovered. Subtitles of the aria texts are in German, French, English and Spanish, and are also available in the original Italian.

Arias from L'Adelaide; Armida al campo d'Egitto; Farnace (with Sinfonia); L'Olimpiade; Orlando furioso; Semiramide; La Silvia; Tito Manlio

*** Naïve OP 30415. Regazzo, Concerto Italiano, Alessandrini

It is not surprising that **Rinaldo Alessandrini** should choose a distinctive singer for this collection of Vivaldi arias, many from unfamiliar sources, and certainly **Lorenzo Regazzo** has an individual voice, both beautiful and vibrant, which is used with musicianship and perception. The result is a most rewarding mixture well worth trying.

'Heroes', Arias from: Andromeda liberata; Demofoonte; Farnace; Giustino; L'Olimpiade; Orlando finto pazzo; Orlando furioso; Ottone in villa; Tieteburga; Il Tigrane; Tito Manlio

**** Virgin 3 63414-2. Jaroussky, Ens. Matheus, Spinosi

The French counter-tenor **Philippe Jaroussky** here gives an astonishing, virtuoso performance in 15 arias from Vivaldi operas, well chosen to represent the three main periods of his operatic output. Brilliant, florid arias alternate with warmly lyrical ones. His fast divisions are flawless, breathtaking in their daring, with no suspicion of any intrusive aspirate. Perhaps even more remarkable are the intense, expansive, lyrical arias, which offer a refreshing view of the composer in their warmth, notably a *Larghetto* aria from *L'Olimpiade*, a late work, and the even more extended E minor aria Vivaldi contributed to a *Serenata* jointly composed with others, *Andromeda liberata*. This is a thrilling disc of rarities, very well accompanied and clearly recorded.

Arias from: L'Atenaide; Catone in Utica; L'incoronazione di Dario; Griselda (with Sinfonia); Ottone in villa (with Sinfonia); Tito Manlio; Tamerlano (Sinfonia)

(B) **** Hyp. Helios CDH 55279. Kirkby, Brandenburg Consort, Goodman

This delightful collection was recorded in 1994 when **Emma Kirkby** was at the very peak of her form. Whether she is singing alone, or in duet with an oboe (as in *Tito Manlio*) or with herself, in the echo aria, *L'ombre, l'aure, e ancora il rio* (from *Ottone in villa*) she continually delights the ear and the senses. And how gently touching she is in *Non mi lusinga vana speranza* from *L'incoronazione di Dario*, and how stirringly regal in the closing *Se in campo armato*, with trumpet, from *Catone in Utica*. **Roy Goodman's** accompaniments with the **Brandenburg Consort** are a model of taste and maintain a nicely intimate atmosphere.

Opera arias and scenas: Bajazet (Il Tamerlano): Anch'il mar par che sommerga; Dorilla in Tempe: Dorilla'aura al sussurrar; Farnace: Gelido in ogni vena; La fida ninfa: Alma opressa; Dite, oimè; Griselda: Dopo un'orrida procella; Giustino: Sorte, che m'invitasti … Ho nel petto un cor sì forte; L'Olimpiade: Tra le follie … Siam navi all'onde algenti; L'Orlando finto pazzo: Qual favellar? … Anderò volerò griderò; Teuzzone: Di trombe guerrier. Arias with unidentified sources: Di due rai languir costante; Zeffiretti, che sussurrate

**** Decca 466 569-2. Bartoli, Il Giardino Armonico (with Arnold Schoenberg Ch.)

This remarkable collection is valuable as much for its exploration of rare Vivaldi operas as for coloratura singing of extraordinary bravura and technical security. It is a pity that the programme (understandably) opens with the excerpt from *Dorilla in Tempe*, with its echoes of *Spring* from *The Four Seasons*, as the chorus, although enthusiastic in praising those seasonal joys, is less than sharply focused. But the following aria from *Griselda*, with its stormy horns and fiendish leaps and runs, shows just how expertly **Cecilia Bartoli** can deliver the kind of thrilling virtuosity expected by Vivaldi's audiences of their famous castrato soloists. Farnace's tragic aria, *Gelido in ogni vena* (based on the *Winter* concerto) shows the other side of the coin with some exquisite lyrical singing of lovely descending chromatics. In short, this is dazzling singing of remarkable music, most stylishly and vividly accompanied. Indeed, the Storm aria from *Bajazet* brings a delivery of such speed and sharpness of articulation that the rapid fire of a musical machine-gun springs instantly to mind. Moreover, Decca have done their star mezzo proud with fine documentation, full translations and a presentation more like a handsomely bound hardback book than a CD.

VOGLER, Georg Joseph
(1749–1814)

Ballet Suites 1 & 2; Overtures: Athalie; Erwin und Elmire; Hamlet. Symphonies in D min.; G

(N) **** Chan. 10504. LMP, Bamert

Vogler is hardly a well-known name today (Mozart disliked him) but on the strength of this CD, his music is worth exploring. It begins with a very lively and inventive *Symphony in D minor*, then comes the first of two *Ballets Suites*, edited in 1950s, made up from various ballets he wrote, and contain music of much piquancy and charm. Both the *Overture* and the *Allegretto* feature some particularly fetching woodwind writing, and the *Gigue, Aire de chasse* and *Menuetto grazioso* which comprise *Suite 2* are all very appealing indeed. The overtures are all colourful, melodic and inventive and well-worth hearing. Superb and sound and performances as one would expect from this source.

VOLKMANN, Robert (1815–83)

Cello Concerto in A min., Op. 33

*** Hyp. CDA 67583. Gerhardt, Berlin RSO, Lintu – DIETRICH; GERNSHEIM; SCHUMANN: *Cello Concertos* ***

In a single compact movement in well-contrasted sections, Volkmann's *Concerto* (like the other works on the disc) can be seen as a reflection of the music of Brahms. It opens with a lyrical episode and uses recitative to link different sections, with lively syncopations in the final section, which also includes a cadenza. An attractive rarity, very well played and recorded.

VOŘÍŠEK, Jan Václav (1791–1825)

Symphony in D, Op. 24

⌐•┐ *** Hyp. CDA 66800. SCO, Mackerras – ARRIAGA: *Symphony in D min.* etc. ***

Voříšek is as close as the Czechs got to producing a Beethoven, and this remarkably powerful work has many fingerprints of the German master everywhere while dis-

playing some individuality. The slow movement is impressive and, after an attractive Scherzo, the finale has something in common with that of Beethoven's *Fourth*. **Mackerras** offers the finest account this work has received on record so far. The Hyperion recording is warmly reverberant, but this serves to increase the feeling of Beethovenian weightiness, and the Scherzo is particularly imposing. The Arriaga coupling is indispensable.

Fantasia in C, Op. 12; Impromptus 1–6, Op. 7; Piano Sonata in B flat min., Op. 19; Variations in B flat, Op. 19

*** Naïve OPS 30241. Tverskaya

The Russian-born but London-domiciled **Olga Tverskaya** is an eloquent advocate of this always interesting and often highly original music, and plays with great flair and conviction. She uses a period instrument, a copy of an 1823 Broadmann fortepiano by David Winston. The recording is altogether excellent and the disc in every respect, a success.

WAGNER, Richard (1813–83)

Symphony in C

(BB) ** Warner Apex 2564 60619-2. Norwegian R.O, Rasilainen – WEBER: *Symphonies 1 & 2* **

A useful and inexpensive way to explore Wagner's early *Symphony*, composed at the age of 19, and very much indebted to Beethoven and even Mendelssohn. It's no masterpiece, of course, but fascinating to hear and reasonably rewarding. The performance and recording are good, but not outstanding.

(i; iii) Symphony in C; (i; ii) Die Feen Overture; (i; iii) Faust Overture; (i; ii) Der fliegende Holländer: Overture; (iv; v) Lohengrin: Preludes to Acts I & III; Die Meistersinger von Nürnberg: Prelude to Act I; Parsifal: Prelude to Act I; (iv; vi) Rienzi Overture; (i; iii) Symphony in C; (i; ii) Tannhäuser: Overture and Venusberg Music; (v; vii) Tristan und Isolde; (viii) Kinderkatechismus

**(*) Australian Decca Eloquence (ADD/DDD) 442 8283 (2).
(i) de Waart; (ii) Concg O; (iii) San Francisco SO; (iv) Mehta; (v) VPO; (vi) LAPO; (vii) Solti; (viii) V. Boys' Ch., VPO (members)

Wagner's *Symphony in C* was written when he was still in his teens, and though the thrust of ambition, the sense of challenge, is clear enough, there are few fingerprints that one could positively identify as Wagnerian. **De Waart's** version makes this a confident exercise in symphonism, a spaciously paced, beautifully sprung reading, with melodies presented in a Schubertain glow. The rarely heard *Die Feen Overture* was written (when Wagner was 20) for his first completed opera. The performance, again on Philips with **Edo de Waart**, but with the **Concertgebouw Orchestra**, along with the *Flying Dutchman Overture* and *Tannhäuser music*, is warmly spacious but lacks something in electricity. The *Flying Dutchman* – which uses the original ending – sounds too cultured. The

Zubin Mehta Decca recordings offer superb sound, but the performances do not possess any personal magic. **Solti's** well-known performance of the *Tristan Prelude* (1960) is superb. The *Kinderkatechismus* is a real curiosity. Its full English title is 'A Children's Catechism for Kosel's Birthday' – 'Kosel' being one of the nicknames Wagner gave to his wife Cosima. Originally performed in 1873 by the Wagner children with piano accompaniment, Wagner orchestrated it a year later and added an instrumental postlude taken from the end of his newly completed *Götterdämmerung*.

(i) Symphony in E (incomplete); (ii) Marches: Grosser Festmarsch; Huldigungsmarsch; Kaisermarsch. Overtures: (iii) Columbus; (ii) Die Feen; (i) Faust; Das Liebesverbot; Rienzi; (iv) Siegfied idyll; (i; v) 5 Wesendonck Lieder (arr. Henze)

Ⓑ **(*) EMI (ADD/DDD) 5 17619 (2). (i) Phd. O, Sawallisch; (ii) LSO, Janowski; (iii) Bav. RSO, Tate; (iv) ASMF, Marriner; (v) with Lipovšek

This a more interesting compilation than the Decca one above, even though its content is rather more uneven. The *Symphony in E*, written in 1834, was left unfinished (29 bars of an *Adagio* exist – not recorded here). However, the opening movement exists complete, somewhat Schumannesque. It is agreeable enough. The similarly unknown *Columbus Overture* is all that survives of incidental music Wagner wrote to a play about the explorer in the same year as the symphony movement. This is a highlight of the set: **Tate's** performance is magnificent, opening atmospherically and building to a superb climax. **Janowski's** account of *Die Feen* is also excitingly vivid, making this much more memorable than usual. **Sawallisch** is equally impressive in *Rienzi* but less successful with a rather overblown account of *Das Liebesverbot*, which needs lighter textures. The *Wesendonck Lieder* are delicately scored by Hans Werner Henze, and Sawallisch uses a group of about 30 instrumentalists, who play with much refinement. However, the choice of **Marjana Lipovšek** as soloist was unfortunate as her over-opulent singing hardly suits the effect Henze must have had in mind. The three *Marches* are expansively Wagnerian, the *Huldigungsmarsch* the most compact and individual, the *Kaisermarsch*, richly lyrical, quotes *Ein' feste Burg* rather effectively. But the *Grosser Festmarsch* is even more inflated at 13 minutes. It was commissioned for the centenary commemoration of the American Declaration of Independence. Fortunately, the concert closes with **Marriner's** fine (1980) ASMF account of the inspired *Siegfried Idyll* in which he uses solo strings for the gentler passages and a fuller ensemble for the climaxes, here passionately convincing and beautifully recorded.

ORCHESTRAL MUSIC FROM THE OPERAS (with Siegfried Idyll)

Siegfried Idyll

⊶ 🕸 Ⓜ *** Decca (ADD) 460 311-2. VPO, Solti – SCHUBERT: *Symphony 9* ***🕸

⊶ Ⓑ *** Virgin 2x1 4 82112-2 (2). Sinfonia Varsovia, Y. Menuhin – MOZART: *Divertimento 1*, etc.; SCHOENBERG: *Verklaerte Nacht*; WOLF: *Italian Serenade* ***

Ⓜ *** EMI (ADD) 5 62815-2. Philh. O, Klemperer – BRUCKNER: *Symphony 4* ***

(***) BBC Legends mono BBCL 4076-2. Hallé O, Barbirolli – BEETHOVEN: *Symphony 7*; MOZART: *Symphony 35* ***

So rich is the sound that Decca provided for **Solti** (in 1965) that one can hardly believe that this is a chamber performance. The playing is similarly warm and committed and this coupling with Schubert's *Great C major Symphony*, is one of Solti's finest recordings.

The members of the **Sinfonia Varsovia** play beautifully. **Menuhin** opens in a warmly relaxed manner but the performance gathers impetus and is most sensitively shaped. Fine recording, too.

Klemperer also favours the original chamber-orchestra scoring and the **Philharmonia** players are very persuasive, especially in the score's gentler moments. The balance is forward and, although the sound is warm, some ears may crave a greater breadth of string tone at the climax.

Barbirolli's account of the *Siegfried Idyll*, recorded in the BBC's Manchester studios, comes in mono sound only, with obvious limitations. The use of reduced strings means that the woodwind solos come over very clearly, with a glorious horn outburst at the climax (track 9, 11'30"), and though the tempo for the central episode is on the slow side, with Barbirolli letting it get slower still in ecstasy, the magic of this birthday gift to Cosima Wagner comes over superbly, with thrilling climaxes.

Siegfried Idyll; Der fliegende Holländer: Overture; Götterdämmerung: Siegfried's Rhine Journey & Funeral March; Lohengrin: Preludes to Acts I & III; Die Meistersinger: Overture; Dance of the Apprentices; Entry of the Masters; Parsifal: Prelude; Das Rheingold: Entry of the Gods into Valhalla; Siegfried: Forest Murmurs; Tannhäuser: Overture; Prelude to Act III; Tristan und Isolde: Prelude & Liebestod; Die Walküre: Ride of the Valkyries

⊶ Ⓜ *** EMI (ADD) 5 67893-2 [567896] (2). Philh. O, Klemperer

Two of the LPs from which this **Klemperer** programme is compiled were recorded and released in 1960 to celebrate Klemperer's 75th birthday. All these performances have the kind of incandescent glow one associates with really great conductors, and the **Philharmonia** play immaculately. The remastered recording is very impressive indeed.

Siegfried Idyll; Der fliegende Holländer: Overture; Rienzi: Overture; Tannhäuser: Overture & Bacchanale

Ⓜ *** Decca 475 8502. VPO, Solti

Solti's way with Wagner is certainly exciting: some may find the early 1960s performances of the *Rienzi* and *The Flying Dutchman Overtures* a little hard-driven. But the *Siegfried Idyll*, played in its chamber version by members of the **VPO**, is most beautifully done. Elsewhere one is easily caught up in the sheer force of Solti's music-making. The VPO play splendidly, of course, and Decca has supplied brilliant sound to match.

Siegfried Idyll; Tannhäuser: Overture; (i) Tristan: Prelude & Liebestod

🎬 *** DG 423 613-2. (i) Norman; VPO, Karajan

The *Tannhäuser Overture* has never sounded so noble, and the *Siegfried Idyll* has rarely seemed so intense and dedicated behind its sweet lyricism; while the *Prelude and Liebestod*, with **Jessye Norman** as soloist, bring the richest culmination, sensuous and passionate, remarkable as much for the hushed, inward moments as for the massive building of climaxes.

ORCHESTRAL EXCERPTS AND PRELUDES FROM THE OPERAS

Der fliegende Holländer: Overture; Götterdämmerung: Funeral Music; Siegfried's Rhine Journey; Lohengrin: Act I Prelude; Die Meistersinger: Overture; Dance of the Apprentices; Entry of the Masters; Parsifal: Good Friday Music

Ⓜ (***) Sony mono SMK 89889. RPO, Beecham

The 1954 recordings here – *Der fliegende Holländer*, the *Meistersinger* excerpts (the three items linked together) and *Siegfried's Rhine Journey* – come in fuller and weightier sound than **Beecham** generally enjoyed at that final period of mono recording with CBS, with splendid brass but an occasional edge on strings. The swagger and panache of Beecham in Wagner comes out superbly, and though the other recordings are not quite so full, with edginess more obtrusive, they are most enjoyable. In the manner of the time concert endings are provided where necessary.

Der fliegender Holländer: Overture; Lohengrin: Prelude to Act I; Parsifal: Prelude to Act I; Act III (Good Friday music); Siegfried idyll

Ⓑ (***) Naxos mono 8.111283. Boston SO, Koussevitzky –
   BRAHMS: *Academic Festival Overture* (***)

One associates **Koussevitzky** with Debussy, Sibelius, Ravel and Prokofiev rather than with Wagner. These records, made between 1946 and 1949, show him as no less masterly and authoritative an interpreter of the Master of Bayreuth. Under him the **Boston Symphony** was peerless and these performances are in every respect a joy.

Overture Der fliegende Holländer; Lohengrin: Preludes to Acts I & III; Die Meistersinger: Overture; (i) Tannhäuser: Overture and Venusberg Music; Tristan und Isolde: Prelude & Liebestod

🎬 Ⓜ *** EMI (ADD) 4 76896-2. BPO, Karajan; (i) with
   Deutsche Oper Ch.

All in all, **Karajan's** 1974 collection is perhaps the finest single disc of miscellaneous Wagnerian overtures and preludes in the catalogue, recommendable alongside Szell's Cleveland collection of orchestral music from the *Ring*. The body of

tone produced by the **Berlin Philharmonic** gives a breathtaking amplitude at climaxes and the electricity the conductor generates throughout the programme is unforgettable. The results are spectacular with greater depth, a wider dyamic range and a remarkable sense of the ambience of the Berlin Philharmonie.

Overtures: Der fliegende Holländer; Die Meistersinger; Tannhäuser; Tristan: Prelude to Act I

Ⓜ *** Sup. (ADD) SU 3469-2 011. Czech PO, Konwitschny
   (with RICHARD STRAUSS: *Till Eulenspiegel* (mono) ***)

Konwitschny's collection was highly regarded in its day (1960) for the excitement and spontaneity of the readings, with *Die Meistersinger* particularly well shaped and *Tannhäuser* bringing thrilling cascades from the **Czech Philharmonic** strings as well as fine brass playing. *Der fliegende Holländer* creates a vivid image of the storm-tossed ship. The transfer is bright and full, if not in the demonstration bracket. What makes the disc especially attractive is the 1952 mono coupling, a great credit to the sound engineer, František Burda. Konwitschny's performance takes off racily from the very opening bars. It has great zest, warmth and humour, plus spontaneous bursts of excitement. The closing section ends with a spectacular execution, before the touching little epilogue on the strings. (However, be warned: there are some curious ticking noises on the tape at the very opening of *Till*.)

Götterdämmerung: Dawn and Siegfried's Rhine Journey; Siegfried's Death and Funeral Music; Lohengrin: Preludes to Acts I & III; Die Meistersinger: Overture; Das Rheingold: Entry of the Gods into Valhalla; Rienzi: Overture; Siegfried: Forest Murmurs; Tannhäuser: Overture; Die Walküre: Ride of the Valkyries; Wotan's Farewell & Magic Fire Music

Ⓑ🅑 *** EMI Gemini 5 86248-2 (2). BPO, Tennstedt

This bargain Gemini two-CD set comprises two early digital recordings of Wagner's orchestral music which were quite a revelation in the early days of compact disc. In the music from the *Ring*, notably the *Entry of the Gods into Valhalla*, the sense of spectacle is in no doubt, and *Wotan's Farewell* and *Magic Fire Music* are also very impressive. The sound could ideally have greater amplitude (the brass is a bit dry), but the climax of *Siegfried's Funeral March* has massive penetration – and there is fine detail too, especially in the atmospheric *Forest Murmurs*. The playing throughout is of the finest quality, always maintaining a high level of tension.

Götterdämmerung: Dawn; Siegfried's Rhine Journey & Funeral March; Die Meistersinger: Prelude to Act I; Rienzi: Overture; Tannhäuser: Overture and Venusberg Music; Die Walküre: Ride of the Valkyries

Ⓜ *** LPO LPO 003. LPO, Tennstedt

This 1988 recording of a live concert makes a fascinating comparison with **Tennstedt's** EMI discs above. As before, his readings are characteristically broad, with the *Meistersinger Prelude* warmly and weightily expansive and the *Götterdämmerung* excerpts spaciously powerful. However, the live occasion also makes its mark, and the thundering chords of the *Funeral Music* are sinisterly overwhelming, while *Rienzi* is more volatile here than in the Berlin studio. The **LPO** are on their toes and play splendidly thoughout; they are gorgeously sensuous in the *Venusberg Music*, helped by the rich amplitude of the recording. Because this almost certainly came from a broadcast the dynamic range is narrower than the Berlin Philharmonic studio recording. But the only real minus point is that the programme ends unexpectedly at the end of the *Venusberg Music*, when the exciting *Ride of the Valkryries*, with its enthusiastic applause, would have made a much more upbeat conclusion.

Götterdämmerung: Dawn & Siegfried's Rhine Journey; Siegfried's Death & Funeral Music; Die Meistersinger: Prelude; Das Rheingold: Entry of the Gods into Valhalla; Siegfried: Forest Murmurs; Tristan und Isolde: Prelude & Liebestod; Die Walküre: Wotan's Farewell & Magic Fire Music

⊶ ✿ Ⓑ *** Sony (ADD) SBK 48175. Cleveland O, Szell

The orchestral playing here is breathtaking in its virtuosity. **Szell** generates the greatest tension, particularly in the two scenes from *Götterdämmerung*, while the *Liebestod* from *Tristan* has never been played on record with more passion and fire. This is well worthy of Szell's extraordinary achievement in **Cleveland** in the 1960s, even if the forward balance of the recording places a limit on the dynamic range.

Götterdämmerung: Siegfried's Funeral March; Lohengrin: Act 1 Prelude; Die Meistersinger von Nürnberg: Prelude; Parsifal: Good Friday Music; Prelude

Ⓝ ** Australian Decca Eloquence 480 0567. SRO, Ansermet

Wagner is unlikely repertoire for **Ansermet** but, partly thanks to the 1963 Decca sound and the conductor's ear for detail, you'll hear more of the textures in these scores than you will on virtually any other recording. These are fascinatingly untraditional performances and show that the German tradition is not the only way (Munch's Wagner is similarly different). Ansermet moulds the *Lohengrin Prelude* beautifully and the great cymbal clash at the climax is one of the disc's surprise highlights. Even if the intonation of the brass in *Siegfried's Funeral Music* is not spot on, the performance sounds uniquely theatrical, with an astonishing depth of sound. The *Mastersingers Overture* comes off splendidly and the music from *Parsifal* is sensitively done too. This CD will not appeal to all Wagner traditionalists but it is fascinating just the same.

Götterdämmerung: Siegfried's Rhine Journey; Tristan: Prelude and Liebestod (DVD version)

*** EMI **DVD** 3 8846093. O Nat. de l'ORTF, Schmidt-Isserstedt – BRAHMS: *German Requiem* ***

An impressive visual reminder of one of the greatest Wagnerians of our time. The **French Radio Orchestra** is not the Berlin Philharmonic, but under the clear direction of **Schmidt-Isserstedt** they play vividly and create considerable tension in the *Tristan Liebestod*.

Lohengrin: Preludes to Acts I & III

*** Australian Decca Eloquence (ADD) 467 235-2. VPO, Mehta – MAHLER: *Symphony 4* **

These beautifully and excitingly played and recorded preludes make a good bonus for Mehta's fresh account of Mahler's *Fourth Symphony*. There is something of an explosive thrill about the Act III *Prelude* which is really quite memorable.

Die Meistersinger: Overture

Ⓜ (**) Beulah mono 3PD12. BBCSO, Boult – MENDELSSOHN: *Hebrides Overture* (**); SCHUBERT: *Symphony 9 in C (Great)* **(*)

In this recording of 1933, constricted by the length of short-playing 78 r.p.m. discs, **Boult** takes an urgent and biting view of the *Meistersinger Overture*, fresh and dramatic. Surface hiss is high but even, with full-bodied sound set in a dry acoustic with no added reverberation. A good supplement to the Schubert.

Parsifal: Act I, Prelude; Good Friday Music

ⒷⒷ (***) Naxos mono 8.110879. BPO, Furtwängler – BEETHOVEN: *Symphony 5*; FURTWÄNGLER: *Symphonic Concerto – Adagio solemne* (**(*))

Even those who did not respond to **Furtwängler** (like the composer Robert Simpson) admired the sheer power and eloquence of his Wagner. These excerpts have wonderful breadth and eloquence. They provide a valuable component of this great conductor's discography.

Parsifal, Act III: Good Friday Spell: Symphonic Synthesis (arr. Stokowski)

⊶ Ⓜ (***) Cala mono CACD 0535. SO, Stokowski – MUSSORGSKY: *Boris Godunov: Scenes* (***)

In 1952, the same year as he recorded scenes from Boris Godunov in San Francisco, **Stokowski** recorded these selections from Act III of Wagner's *Parsifal* with a hand-picked orchestra of leading players in New York. The result has a similar incandescence, and the RCA engineers matched Stokowski's brilliance with sound of astonishing warmth and breadth.

Parsifal, Act III: Symphonic Synthesis; Tristan und Isolde: Symphonic Synthesis; Die Walküre: Wotan's Farewell & Magic Fire Music (all arr. Stokowski)

*** Chan. 9686. BBC PO, Bamert

Stokowski's recordings of Wagner excerpts always treated the voices as a kind of adjunct to the orchestra, and he loved best to play the orchestral music without them. So he made a series of symphonic syntheses, joining scenes together in a continuous sensuous and dramatic melodic flow, leaving the orchestra to convey the full narrative. *Parsifal* includes tolling bells and rich mysticism, and in *Tristan* Stokowski frames the *Liebesnacht* (including the distant hunting horns heralding the return of Tristan) with the passionate *Prelude* and *Liebestod*. Best of all he creates a symphonic poem out of Wotan's sad, loving farewell to his beloved Brünnhilde, making a great climax out of the *Fire Music*. **Bamert** is passionate and tender by turns and the **BBC Philharmonic** readily respond to the luscious orchestration. Perhaps the last degree of Stokowskian intensity is missing here, but with superbly spacious Chandos sound this is easy to enjoy.

VOCAL MUSIC

Wesendonck Lieder

(M) **(*) Ph. (ADD) 464 742-2. Norman, LSO, C. Davis – R.
    STRAUSS: *Four Last Songs* ***

The poised phrases of the *Wesendonck Lieder* drew from **Jessye Norman** in this 1976 recording a glorious range of tone colour, though in detailed imagination this falls short of some of the finest rivals on record. Good, refined recording, made vivid on CD with an excellent transfer.

(i) Wesendonck Lieder; Der fliegende Holländer: Overture; Lohengrin: Prelude to Act 1; (i) Tristan und Isolde: Prelude & Liebestod; Documentary: 'Flagstad on Singing Wagner'

(***) SOMM-BEECHAM mono 020. (i) Flagstad; RPO or BBC
    SO, Beecham

Inspired as **Beecham's** conducting is in all these items, it is the glorious contribution of **Kirsten Flagstad** in the *Tristan Liebestod* and *Wesendonck Lieder* for which the disc is chiefly valuable. The latter were recorded in EMI's Maida Vale Studio in 1952, as are the *Tristan Prelude* and *Liebestod*. The *Flying Dutchman* and *Lohengrin* items by contrast were recorded live in the Royal Festival Hall in 1954 and 1953 respectively. The sound is obviously limited, but with ample bass the impact of these performances is still impressive. Well worth hearing by devotees both of Flagstad and of Beecham. Flagstad's talk on singing Wagner makes a delightful supplement.

OPERA

Solti Wagner Edition:

Der fliegende Holländer

(M) **(*) Decca (ADD) 470 792-2 (2). Bailey, Martin, Talvela,
    Kollo, Krenn, Isola Jones, Chicago Ch. & O, Solti

Lohengrin

(M) *** Decca 470 795-2 (4). Domingo, Norman, Nimsgern,
    Randová, Sotin, Fischer-Dieskau, V. State Op. Concerto
    Ch., VPO, Solti

Die Meistersinger von Nürnberg

⊶ (M) **** Decca 470 800-2 (4). van Dam, Heppner, Mattila,
    Opie, Lippert, Vermillion, Pape, Chicago SO Ch. & O, Solti

Parsifal

⊶ (M) *** Decca (ADD) 470 805-2 (4). Kollo, Ludwig, Fischer-
    Dieskau, Hotter, Kelemen, Frick, V. Boys' Ch., V. State Op.
    Ch., VPO, Solti

Tannhäuser (Paris version)

⊶ (M) *** Decca (ADD) 470 810-2 (3). Kollo, Dernesch,
    Ludwig, Sotin, Braun, Hollweg, V. State Op. Ch., VPO,
    Solti

Tristan und Isolde

(M) *** Decca (ADD) 470 814-2 (4). Uhl, Nilsson, Resnik, Van
    Mill, Krause, VPO, Solti

Solti Wagner Edition (complete)

(M) *** Decca (ADD/DDD) 470 600-2 (21)

Following on after the box containing **Solti's** unsurpassed *Ring* cycle (455 555-2), Decca have handsomely repackaged his other Wagner recordings, which are now available separately at mid-price, or together, in a slip case, at a further reduced price. Those who invest in the Complete Edition receive a free bonus CD of rehearsal sequences from the *Tristan* recording. Many of these recordings remain among the top recommendations, and have the advantage of Decca's finest vintage opera sound. With the exception of the digital recordings they have been remastered for this release.

Among the highlights must be the 1972 *Parsifal* which is, by any standards, a magnificent recording, with universally excellent singing and Solti sustaining the right sort of tension throughout the performance. Hardly less impressive is *Tannhäuser*, with superlative playing from the **VPO**, and **Christa Ludwig** as Venus outshining all rivals.

The 1971 sound remains impressive. Solti is less flexible in the 1960 *Tristan*, but he does relax in the more expansive passages, and he generates superb thrust in the exciting moments, such as the end of Act I and the opening of the *Love Duet*, which has knife-edged dramatic tension.

The digital 1986 *Lohengrin* finds **Domingo** on magnificent form, and if **Jessye Norman** is not ideally suited to the role of Elsa, she is always commandingly intense, full of character. The rest of the cast and the **VPO** is superb. Throughout these recordings, Decca employ, almost always successfully, plenty of Culshaw-like production effects, but curiously, in the 1976 *Der fliegende Holländer*, there are none, so that characters 'halloo' at one another when they are obviously standing elbow to elbow. However, the cast on this recording is generally impressive, and though **Kollo** is a little coarse as Erik, it is an illuminating portrayal.

Decca rightly chose Solti's later (digital) recording of *Die Meistersinger* where the conductor's characteristic urgency is counterbalanced by a great warmth, and the cast is generally outstanding – a fine conclusion to an impressive achievement. This is now a clear first recommendation.

Der fliegende Holländer (complete; DVD version)

(N) **(*) DG DVD 073 4433. Rundgren, Ligendza, McIntyre,
    Bavarian State Opera Ch. & O, Sawallisch

The **Bavarian State Opera** production has taken some time to reach us. It was recorded in May 1974 and the production filmed the following autumn. The adaptation by the Czech director Václav Kašlík is the second to appear on film (there was a monochrome and highly individual version in 1964 by Joachim Herz) and succeeds in gripping the viewer visually as successfully as does **Wolfgang Sawallisch** musically. Indeed Sawallisch is the reason to investigate this set for he gets gloriously eloquent playing from his wonderful Bavarian forces. No complaints about the soloists either: **Catarina Ligendza** makes an excellent Senta and **Donald McIntyre** is an effective Dutchman. The colour is as good as can be expected for a performance now thirty-five years old.

Der fliegende Holländer (original, Paris CD version)

Ⓜ **(*) DHM/BMG 82876 64071-2 (2). Stensvold, Weber, Selig, Durmüller, WDR R. Ch., Prague Chamber Ch., Cappella Coloniensis, Weil

Using an orchestra of period instruments, **Bruno Weil** on DHM offers the first ever recording of Wagner's original score, the Paris version of 1841. Wagner prepared it for a performance that never took place, and the actual première had to wait until January 1843 in Dresden, for which Wagner made his first set of alterations. He made at least three sets of revisions in his lifetime, and he planned more, but this first version firmly presents the piece (as latter-day productions have tended to do) as a big, one-act work in three sections, joined by brief interludes. There are also different endings for the *Overture* and the final scene. Dramatically, the big difference is that the opera is set in Scotland, not Norway, with Donald (not Daland) and Georg (not Erik) as the huntsman who loves the heroine, Senta. Musically, one notes instantly the extra clarity of textures and the fact that the orchestra does not so easily overwhelm the singers, who are lighter than those usually cast in these roles. The role of Senta is taken by **Astrid Weber** with her bright, fresh voice, biting at times but shading down to a beautiful thread of sound for the *pianissimo* top notes of *Senta's Ballad*, set in A, a full tone higher than usual. **Terje Stensvold** is a comparably clean-cut Dutchman, precisely focused, though **Franz-Josef Selig** has his woolly moments as Donald. **Jorg Durmüller** is excellent as Georg, Germanic in tone yet free from strain. Lively conducting and first-rate sound.

Der fliegende Holländer (complete; CD versions)

🎵 **** DG 437 778-2 (2). Weikl, Studer, Sotin, Domingo, Seiffert, Ch. & O of German Op., Berlin, Sinopoli

🎵 *** Ph. (ADD) 475 8289 (2). Estes, Balslev, Salminen, Schunk, Bayreuth Festival (1985) Ch. & O, Nelsson

ⒷⒷ *** Naxos 8.660025/6. Muff, Haubold, Knodt, Seiffert, Budapest R. Ch., Vienna ORF SO, Steinberg

Ⓜ **(*) EMI 7 64650-2 (2). van Dam, Vejzovic, Moll, Hofmann, Moser, Borris, V. State Op. Ch., BPO, Karajan

ⒷⒷ (***) Naxos mono 8.110189/90 (2). Hotter, Varnay, Svanholm, Nilsson, Metropolitan Ch. & O, Reiner

Sinopoli's is an intensely involving performance, volatile in the choice of often extreme speeds. The choral singing too is electrifying, and the line-up of principals is arguably finer than any. **Cheryl Studer** is a deeply moving Senta, not just immaculate vocally but conveying the intense vulnerability of the character in finely detailed singing. **Bernd Weikl** is a dark-toned, firmly focused Dutchman, strong and incisive. **Hans Sotin** is similarly firm and dark, nicely contrasted as

Daland, and the luxury casting may be judged from the choice of **Plácido Domingo** as an impressive, forthright Erik and **Peter Seiffert** (the fine *Lohengrin* in Barenboim's Teldec set) as a ringing Steersman. Full, vivid sound. A clear first choice.

Woldemar Nelsson conducts the Philips performance glowingly and responsively. The cast is more consistent than almost any other, with **Lisbeth Balslev** as Senta firm, sweet and secure, raw only occasionally, and **Simon Estes** a strong, ringing Dutchman, clear and noble of tone. **Matti Salminen** is a dark and equally secure Daland and **Robert Schunk** an ardent, idiomatic Erik. The veteran **Anny Schlemm** as Mary, though vocally overstressed, adds pointful character, and the chorus is superb, wonderfully drilled and passionate with it. Though, inevitably, stage noises are obtrusive at times, the recording is exceptionally vivid and atmospheric. On a pair of mid-priced discs, fully documented, this make an admirable alternative choice to Sinopoli.

Pinchas Steinberg proves a warmly sympathetic Wagnerian. More than most rivals, he brings out the light and shade of this earliest of the regular Wagner canon, helped by the refined, well-balanced recording, and by brilliant, sharply dramatic playing from the orchestra. The chorus too sings with a bite and precision to match any rival. **Alfred Muff** as the Dutchman attacks the notes cleanly, with vibrato only occasionally intrusive. The vibrato of **Ingrid Haubold** is more of a problem but, except under pressure, it is well controlled, and she begins *Senta's Ballad* with a meditative *pianissimo*. Both tenors are excellent, **Peter Seiffert** as Erik and **Joerg Hering** as the Steersman, and though **Erich Knodt**, rather gritty in tone, is an uncharacterful Daland, his Act II aria is light and refreshing, thanks to Steinberg's fine rhythmic pointing. The recording is both atmospheric and clear, and the set comes with libretto, translation, notes and detailed synopsis, an outstanding bargain.

The extreme range of dynamics in EMI's recording for **Karajan**, not ideally clear but rich, matches the larger-than-life quality of the conductor's reading. His choice of **José van Dam** as the Dutchman, thoughtful, finely detailed and lyrical, strong but not at all blustering, goes well with this. Van Dam is superbly matched and contrasted with the finest Daland on record, **Kurt Moll**, gloriously biting and dark in tone, yet detailed in his characterization. Neither the Erik of **Peter Hofmann**, nor – more seriously – the Senta of **Dunja Vejzovic** matches this standard; nevertheless, for all her variability, Vejzovic is wonderfully intense in *Senta's Ballad* and she matches even van Dam's fine legato in the Act II duet. The CD transfer underlines the heavyweight quality of the recording, with the *Sailors' Chorus* made massive, but effectively so, when Karajan conducts it with such fine spring.

Dating from December 1950, the Naxos historical version offers a radio recording of a searingly dramatic performance under **Fritz Reiner** with a cast as starry as one could imagine. Reiner's conducting is urgent and intense from start to finish, with **Hans Hotter** in his prime as the Dutchman, uniquely characterful and fresher and more cleanly focused vocally than he became later. His towering performance is matched by the masterly singing of **Astrid Varnay** as Senta, with the great ballad bringing pinging attack and precision over the widest intervals. **Svanholm** with his clear heroic tenor makes a powerful, warmly expressive Erik, and **Sven Nilsson** is a strong, firm Daland. Although the solo voices are balanced close, the chorus and orchestra add to the power of the performance, despite the limitations of the original recording taken off the air.

The Flying Dutchman (sung in English)

🎧 (M) **** Chan. 3119 (2). Tomlinson, Stemme, Begley, Halfvarson, LPO, Parry

John Tomlinson, a favourite in the title-role at Bayreuth, now a veteran, is masterful as the Dutchman, exploiting his wide tonal and expressive range, with few signs of wear on the voice. Opposite him as the self-sacrificing heroine, Senta, is **Nina Stemme**, who in 2002 had such a resounding success as Isolde at Glyndebourne, fresh and true, to outshine almost any rival on disc. The tenor, **Kim Begley**, is strongly cast as Erik, and though **Eric Halfvarson** as Senta's father, Daland, has his moments of roughness, it is a characterful performance. Most striking of all is the richness of the recorded sound, vividly capturing the fine playing of the **LPO** under **David Parry**.

Götterdämmerung (complete; CD versions)

🎧 *** Decca (ADD) 455 569-2 (4). Nilsson, Windgassen, Fischer-Dieskau, Frick, Neidlinger, Watson, Ludwig, V. State Op. Ch., VPO, Solti

🎧 ✦ **** Testament (ADD) SBT 41393 (4). Varnay, Windgassen, Greindl, Uhde, Ilosvay, Neidlinger, 1955 Bayreuth Fest. Ch. & O, Keilberth

(M) *** DG (ADD) 457 795-2 (4). Dernesch, Janowitz, Brilioth, Stewart, Kelemen, Ludwig, Ridderbusch, German Op. Ch., BPO, Karajan

(N) *** Testament (ADD) SBT4 1433 (4). Mödl, Windgassen, Hotter, Ilosvey, Neidlinger, Greindl, Brouwenstijn, Bayreuth Fest Ch & O, Keilberth

(M) (***) Testament mono SBT 4175 (4). Varnay, Aldenhoff, Uhde, Mödl, Weber, Bayreuth Fest. Ch. & O, Knappertsbusch

(BB) *** Arte Nova 74321 80775-2 (4). Woodrow, Silberbauer, del Monte, Adami, Ottenthal, Wolak, Martin, Tyrol Fest Ch & O, Kuhn

(M) **(*) EMI 3 58724-2 (4). Marton, Jerusalem, Tomlinson, Hampson, Bundschuh, Bav. R. Ch. & O, Haitink

Solti's *Götterdämmerung* represented the peak of his achievement in recording the *Ring* cycle. There is not a single weak link in the cast. **Nilsson** surpasses herself in the magnificence of her singing: even Flagstad in her prime would not have been more masterful as Brünnhilde. As in *Siegfried*, **Windgassen** is in superb voice; **Frick** is a vivid Hagen, and **Fischer-Dieskau** achieves the near impossible in making Gunther an interesting and even sympathetic character. As for the recording quality, it surpasses even Decca's earlier achievement, and the current remastering has further improved the sound.

Recorded in 1955 during the second cycle of the Ring at Bayreuth under **Keilberth**, this second *Götterdämmerung*

SBT4 1433 is an important supplement to the complete Keilberth cycle that Testament issued earlier, with arguably two important cast-changes making it even more attractive: **Martha Mödl** instead of Astrid Varnay, more powerful if less girlish, and **Hans Hotter** as Gunther certainly finer than Hermann Uhde who was rested in order to sing in the Bayreuth *Fliegende Hollander*. **Wolfgang Windgassen** as Siegfried is again remarkable not just for his unstrained power but for the moments of tenderness.

Keilberth's conducting on SBT41393 is incandescent, more urgent than Hans Knappertsbusch or Furtwängler, making the big dramatic moments totally thrilling, surging with excitement, with the fulfilment of the final scene movingly caught. The impact is all the greater thanks to the excellent stereo sound obtained by the Decca engineers, even if string sound can be a little fizzy. As before words are astonishingly clear. Well worth investigating by serious Wagnerians. (The first version with the original cast, and magnificent orchestral playing also remains available (SBT 4175).)

Karajan's singing cast is marginally even finer than Solti's, and his performance conveys the steady flow of recording sessions prepared in relation to live performances. Ultimately he falls short of Solti's achievement in the thrusting, orgasmic quality of the music. **Dernesch's** Brünnhilde is warmer than Nilsson's, with a glorious range of tone. **Brilioth** as Siegfried is fresh and young-sounding, while the Gutrune of **Gundula Janowitz** is far preferable to that of Claire Watson on Decca. The matching is otherwise very even.

The legendary **Hans Knappertsbusch** recording (SBT 4175) made in 1951 during the first Bayreuth Festival after the war, reissued on the Testament label a set astonishing in its vividness. This live recording was supervised by the Decca producer John Culshaw (later to mastermind Solti's complete *Ring* cycle) and the mono sound is even fuller and weightier than on the recording of *Parsifal* he also made at Bayreuth in 1951. Both operas were conducted by Knappertsbusch, who in *Götterdämmerung* is even more electrifying than in *Parsifal*, defying his reputation as a relaxed, expansive Wagnerian. Vocally the star is **Astrid Varnay**, shiningly firm and incisive as Brünnhilde, rising magnificently to the final challenge of the immolation scene. Siegfried is sung by the short-lived **Bernd Aldenhoff**, strained at times like most Heldentenoren, but generally lyrical and boyish. **Hermann Uhde** as Gunther and **Ludwig Weber** as Hagen are both outstanding too, with the immediacy and sense of presence carrying one on from first to last.

Recorded live at the 2000 Tyrol Festival in Erl, this Arte Nova set is the finest of the four *Ring* recordings made by **Gustav Kuhn** over successive years, with a more consistent cast than *Rheingold* and *Die Walküre*. **Alan Woodrow**, excellent in the title-role of Siegfried, here excels himself – his death scene is most moving – while in the role of Brünnhilde **Eva Silberbauer** sings with warmth and absence of strain, unlike her two rivals in *Die Walküre* and *Siegfried*. **Duccio del Monte**, overparted as Wotan in *Die Walküre*, here makes a strong, firm Hagen, while the roles of Gunther and Gutrune are well-taken by **Herbert Adami** and **Gertrud Ottenthal**, and

Andrea Martin is excellent as Alberich, as he is in both *Rheingold* and *Siegfried*. It is a pity that the other three sections of Kuhn's *Ring* cycle do not measure up to this, which can be strongly recommended in the budget range.

Haitink's reading is magnificent. In its strength, nobility and thrustfulness it crowns all his previous Wagner, culminating in a forceful and warmly expressive account of the final Immolation scene. Siegfried Jerusalem clearly establishes himself as the finest latter-day Siegfried, both heroic and sweet of tone. Thomas Hampson is a sensitive and virile Gunther, John Tomlinson a sinister but human Hagen, Marjana Lipovšek a warmly intense Waltraute and Eva-Martin Bundschuh a rich, fruity Gutrune. The obvious reservation to make is with the singing of Eva Marton as Brünnhilde, when the unevenness of the vocal production is exaggerated by the microphone in a way that at times come close to pitchless yelping. However, that drawback is clearly outweighed by the set's positive qualities, and the scale of her singing is in no doubt, an archetypal Brünnhilde voice in timbre if not in firmness. The reissue comes with a cued synopsis and list of tracks.

The Twilight of the Gods (*Götterdämmerung*) (complete; in English)

Ⓜ *** Chan. (ADD) 3060 (5). Hunter, Remedios, Welsby, Haugland, Hammond-Stroud, Curphey, Pring, ENO Ch. & O, Goodall

Goodall's account of the culminating opera in Wagner's tetralogy may not be the most powerful ever recorded, and certainly it is not the most polished, but it is one that, paradoxically, by intensifying human as opposed to superhuman emotions, heightens the epic scale. The few slight imprecisions and the occasional rawness of wind-tone actually seem to enhance the earthiness of Goodall's view, with more of the primeval saga about it than the studio-made *Ring* cycles.

Both Rita Hunter and Alberto Remedios were more considerately recorded on the earlier Unicorn version (now Chandos – see below) of the final scenes, with more bloom on their voices, but their performances here are magnificent in every way, while Aage Haugland's Hagen is giant-sounding to focus the evil, with Gunther and Gutrune mere pawns. As for Goodall, with his consistently expansive tempi he carries total conviction – except, curiously, in the scene with the Rhinemaidens, whose music (as in Goodall's *Rheingold*) lumbers along heavily.

The Twilight of the Gods (*Götterdämmerung*): Act III (excerpts; in English)

Ⓜ *** Chan. (ADD) 6593. Hunter, Remedios, Bailey, Grant, Curphey, Sadler's Wells Opera Ch. & O, Goodall

Originally recorded by Unicorn in the early 1970s, this single Chandos CD brings an invaluable reminder of Reginald Goodall's performance of the *Ring* cycle when it was in its first flush of success, covering the closing two scenes. It is good too to have this sample, however brief, of Clifford Grant's Hagen and Norman Bailey's Gunther, fine performances both. Fresh, clear recording, not as full as it might be.

Lohengrin (complete; DVD versions)

🎵 **** Arthaus DVD 100 956 (2). Domingo, Studer, Vejzovic, Welker, Lloyd, Vienna State Op. Ch. VPO, Abbado. (Dir: Wolfgang Weber, V/D: Brian Large.)

🎵 *** DG DVD 073 4176 (2). Hofmann, Marton, Rysanek, Roar, Macurdy, Met. Ch. & O, Levine (Dir: August Everding, V/D: Brian Large)

*** DG DVD 00440 073 4404 (2). Frey, Studer, Schnaut, Wlaschiha, Schenk, Bayreuth Festival Ch & O, Schneider (Dir: Herzog, V/D: Brian Large)

EuroArts DVD 2056008 (2). Treleaven, Hagen, Magee, Ketelsen, DeVol, Ch. & O of Gran Teatre de Liceu, Weigle (Stage Dir: Peter Konwitschny)

The Arthaus DVD offers the grandly traditional Vienna State Opera production of *Lohengrin* with Plácido Domingo at his peak in the title role, at once masterfully heroic and lyrical to a degree rare among Wagner tenors. His big solos inspire him to a glorious range of tone and dynamic. Cheryl Studer is an affecting Elsa, innocent and wide-eyed in contrast to the superbly sinister Ortrud of Dunja Vejzovic, exuding evil from every pore and with a wonderfully revealing glare. Her singing is masterful too, making the Telramund of Hartmut Welker seem relatively bland. Robert Lloyd is a powerful King Heinrich. Claudio Abbado and the Vienna Philharmonic are in glowing form, with dedicated singing from the chorus enhancing the ceremonial splendour of Wolfgang Weber's production. Such a traditional production brings obvious advantages in a DVD designed for repeated watching.

James Levine, with his forces from the Met. in New York, in 1986 conducts a powerful reading of *Lohengrin* in a traditional production by August Everding with typically lavish sets and costumes, including a vast bridal tent in Act III. The cast is first rate, with Peter Hofmann handsome of voice and appearance in the title-role, if with rather a heavy vibrato, which he stills for his big solos. Eva Marton's fruity soprano in the role of Elsa is kept under control more than on audio discs, with *Elsa's Dream* raptly done. Leonie Rysanek gives a classic performance as the evil Ortrud, matched by the fine, dark baritone of Leif Roar as Telramund, and by John Macurdy's powerful bass as King Heinrich. The radiance of the playing of the Met. Orchestra and the fine ensemble of the Chorus crown an excellent version.

Recorded at Bayreuth in 1990, the alternative DVD from DG gives maximum effect to the many great choral passages, sustaining the impact of the whole performance. The sets are of the simplest, relying on evocative lighting effects, with the arrival of the swan in Act II inspiring the most beautiful results. Casting is strong, led by the heroic Paul Frey in the title-role – a Heldentenor with an exceptionally sweet and true tone, down to a honeyed half-tone in *Mein lieber Schwann* – and the tenderly beautiful Elsa of Cheryl Studer, then at her peak. *Elsa's dream* could not be more ravishing. The Telramund of Ekkehard Wlaschiha is aptly strong and sinister, and the only snag in the casting is the Ortrud of Gabriele Schnaut, distressingly squally under pressure. Nevertheless an enjoyable set, well recorded.

The EuroArts *Lohengrin*, conducted by Sebastian Weigle,

is what we believe is given the euphemism of a 'modern concept' production. It is in every way utterly crass and would surely have made Wagner despair that in 2006 his musical and dramatic intentions would be so ignored by a stage director only interested in his own realization, which has little or nothing to do with the composer's own. The opera opens in a secondary school classroom (the main set), where the boys are throwing pellets, with Ortrud (**Luana DeVol**) egging on the debacle and the complete lack of discipline. Koenig Heinrich (**Reinhard Hagen**) is the senior prefect, with a mock crown, and Lohengrin (**John Treleaven**) enters to schoolgirl rapture from schoolgirls with teddy bears. It gets even worse at the close of the opera, but we left the proceedings long before then. What a waste of generally good singing, time, and money.

Lohengrin (complete; CD versions)

⊕– **** DG 437 808-2 (3). Jerusalem, Studer, Meier, Welker, Moll, Schmidt, V. State Op. Ch., VPO, Abbado

⊕– Ⓜ **** Decca 470 795-2 (4). Domingo, Norman, Nimsgern, Randová, Sotin, Fischer-Dieskau, V. State Op. Concert Ch., VPO, Solti

**** Teldec 3984 21484-2 (3). Seiffert, Magee, Struckmann, Polaski, Pape, Ch. & O of German Op., Berlin, Barenboim

Ⓜ *** EMI 5 67415-2 [5 67411-2] (3). J. Thomas, Grümmer, Fischer-Dieskau, Ludwig, Frick, Wiener, V. State Op. Ch., VPO, Kempe

That Abbado's speeds are generally faster than Solti's (with the Act III *Prelude* a notable exception) means that the complete opera is squeezed on to three instead of four discs, giving it the clearest advantage. As Elsa, matching her earlier, Bayreuth performance on Philips, **Cheryl Studer** is at her sweetest and purest, bringing out the heroine's naivety more touchingly than **Jessye Norman**, whose weighty, mezzo-ish tone is thrillingly rich but is more suited to portraying other Wagner heroines than this. Though there are signs that **Siegfried Jerusalem's** voice is not as fresh as it once was, he sings commandingly, conveying both beauty and a true Heldentenor quality. Where Plácido Domingo for Solti, producing even more beautiful tone, tends to use a full voice for such intimate solos as *In fernem Land* and *Mein lieber Schwann*, Jerusalem sings there with tender restraint and gentler tone. Among the others, **Waltraud Meier** as Ortrud and **Kurt Moll** as King Heinrich are both superb, as fine as any predecessor, and though in the role of Telramund **Hartmut Welker's** baritone is not ideally steady, that tends to underline the weakness of the character next to the positive Ortrud.

It is **Plácido Domingo's** achievement singing Lohengrin that the lyrical element blossoms so consistently, with no hint of Heldentenor barking; at whatever dynamic level, Domingo's voice is firm and unstrained. **Jessye Norman**, not naturally suited to the role of Elsa, yet gives a warm, commanding performance, always intense, full of detailed insights into words and character. **Eva Randová's** grainy mezzo does not take so readily to recording, but as Ortrud she provides a pointful contrast, even if she never matches the firm, biting malevolence of Christa Ludwig on the Kempe set.

Siegmund Nimsgern, Telramund for Solti, equally falls short of his rival on the Kempe set; but it is still a strong, cleanly focused performance. **Fischer-Dieskau** here sings the small but vital role of the Herald, while **Hans Sotin** makes a comparably distinctive King Henry. Radiant playing from the **Vienna Philharmonic**, and committed chorus work too. This is one of the crowning glories of **Solti's** long recording career.

The first glory of **Barenboim's** set is the sound, full and upfront, with the voices clearly focused and with plenty of bloom, set against a rich, incandescent orchestra. Having voices relatively close adds immediacy to the drama, and Barenboim's pacing adds warmth and often urgency, even if Elsa's dream sounds a little sluggish. **Emily Magee's** full, rich tone makes the heroine sound rather too mature, and the voice is not well contrasted with the Ortrud of **Deborah Polaski**, a soprano rather lacking the sinister chest-tones apt for this evil character, hardly conveying her full villainy. **Peter Seiffert** makes an outstanding Lohengrin, lyrical as well as heroic, with no hint of strain. One merit of the set is that the text is absolutely complete, including the extended solo after that Act III aria. The Telramund of **Falk Struckmann** is rather gritty, lacking weight, and **Roman Trekel** is a strained Herald, but **René Pape** is magnificent as the King, a fine successor to Kurt Moll.

Kempe directs a rapt account of *Lohengrin*, a fine monument to a great Wagnerian. The singers seem uplifted, **Jess Thomas** singing more clearly and richly than usual, **Elisabeth Grümmer** unrivalled as Elsa in her delicacy and sweetness, **Gottlob Frick** gloriously resonant as the king. But it is the partnership of **Christa Ludwig** and **Fischer-Dieskau** as Ortrud and Telramund that sets the seal on this superb performance, giving the darkest intensity to their machinations in Act II, their evil heightening the beauty and serenity of so much in this opera. The new CD transfer has greatly improved the sound; ensembles are still rather close and airless, but not congested. Solo voices are naturally caught, and the glow and intensity of Kempe's reading come out all the more involvingly in the new format.

Die Meistersinger von Nürnberg (complete; DVD versions)

⊕– **** DG **DVD** 073 4160 (2). Jerusalem, Weikl, Prey, Haggender, Clark, Schiml, Schenk, Bayreuth Festival Ch. & O, Stein (Dir.: Wolfgang Wagner, V/D: Brian Large)

⊕– **** DG **DVD** 0730949-2 (2). Morris, Heppner, Mattila, Pape, Allen, Polenzani, Met. Op. Ch. & O, Levine (V/D: Brian Large)

Ⓝ Ⓜ *** ROH Heritage **DVD** ROH 5008 (4) Tomlinson, Beckmesser, Winberg, Gustafson, Wyn-Rogers, Lippert, Howell, ROHCG Ch. & O, Haitink

⊕– *** Arthaus **DVD** 101 273 (2). Cassilly, Tozzi, Blankenheim, Saunders, Wiemann, Unger, Boese, Hamburg State Op. Ch., Hamburg Philh. State O, Ludwig (Dir: Rolf Liebermann, V/D: Joachim Hess)

⊕– *** EMI **DVD** 599736-9 (2). van Dam, Salminen, Volle, Seiffert, Strehl, Schnitzer, Pinter, Zürich Op. Ch. & O, Welser-Möst (V/D: Andy Sommer)

**(*) Arthaus DVD 100 122. Doese, McIntyre, Frey, Pringle, Doig, Shanks, Gunn, Allman, Australian Op. Ch., Elizabethan PO, Mackerras (Producer/Director: Peter Butler & Virginia Lumsden; V/D: Michael Hampe)

It is extraordinary largesse that we are so spoilt for choice with DVDs of *Die Meistersinger*, and any of the first three listed sets will give great satisfaction. **Wolfgang Wagner's** production of 1984 assembled an exceptionally starry cast, with not a single weak link and with many strengths. This DVD offers a recording made live, but without an audience. The exception is the great *Quintet* in Act III, which appears to have been recorded separately with the singers miming their roles, a small flaw in what is otherwise an immaculate and revelatory film, directed by **Brian Large**. Wolfgang Wagner's sets and costumes are grandly traditional and add greatly to the impact of the piece. **Siegfried Jerusalem** as Walther is one of the most heady-timbred of Heldentenoren and he sings with heroic tone in the *Prize Song*, making a magnificent climax. **Bernd Weikl** is a characterful, strong-toned Sachs and **Mari Anne Haggender** is a vivacious Eva, singing very sweetly, shading her tone down beautifully for the *Quintet*. **Hermann Prey** as Beckmesser is both characterful and unusually mellifluous of tone, not guying the character too much, and **Manfred Schenk** as Pogner, **Graham Clark** as David and **Marga Schiml** are all first rate. An outstanding version, with **Horst Stein** pacing the massive work splendidly.

James Levine has already given us an outstanding traditional *Ring* cycle, and here he matches it with an expansive and warm-hearted *Meistersinger*. The production is again traditional, which is what his New York audience wants. Thank goodness for no quirky ideas. The singers are all outstanding, led by **James Morris's** warmly genial Sachs, matched vocally by **René Pape's** Pogner, and by **Ben Heppner**, who is an equally convincing Walther. **Karita Mattila** not only looks gorgeous but sings ravishingly as Eva, while **Sir Thomas Allen's** characterization of Beckmesser is all his own. **Matthew Polenzani's** David too is quite agreeable, but not charismatic. Levine's conducting holds the performance together richly, and the chorus is superb, vividly recorded (like the orchestra); and **Brian Large** comes up trumps with the video direction. Choice between this DG set and the fine EMI version below will not be easy to determine.

Apart from the obvious fact that of all the Wagner operas *Die Meistersinger* is suited by nature to the mellow temperament of **Bernard Haitink**, the 1968 Covent Garden production includes a few other favourite names in the cast, not least the ever-versatile **John Tomlinson** as Hans Sachs, and **Thomas Allen's** naturally characterised Beckmesser, both of them in splendid voice. And one really can't go wrong with **Nancy Gustavson's** engaging Eva, **Gwynne Howell's** Pogner, and the equally secure portrayal of Magdalene from **Catherine Wyn-Rogers**. The production too is visually pleasing, the chorus first class and, like the orchestra, well caught by the recording. This may not go quite to the top of the list, and it may not be as fine as the Goodall set (nor as heightened by comedy), but is still a set to treasure if you admire the artists.

The Arthaus DVD offers a film, made in Hamburg, of the *Meistersinger* production of the great **Rolf Liebermann**, with **Joachim Hess** exploiting the medium most effectively. Costumes are traditional, with minimal sets never intruding. The cast is exceptionally fine, with no weak link, and **Richard Cassilly** as Walther singing with totally unstrained power. **Giorgio Tozzi** is a noble, moving Sachs, and **Arlene Saunders** the sweetest, most charming of Evas, shading her solo in the *Quintet* of Act III exquisitely. **Toni Blankenheim** characterizes well as Beckmesser, not caricaturing the role, and, as in the Bayreuth version, the other principals are excellent too: **Ernst Wiemann** a dark, firm Pogner, **Gerhard Unger** a light, clear David, and **Ursula Boese** as Lene. A classic film version, in which the conductor **Leopold Ludwig** is masterly at building up the great 'gulp' moments in each Act.

Though the performance lacks a little in weight, **Franz Welser-Möst** conducts a fresh and incisive reading, with another excellent cast. **José van Dam** gives a noble account of the role of Hans Sachs, his voice firm and unstrained as it always has been. Beardless, he cuts a less elderly figure than usual, but that goes with the freshness of the voice. The other masters are first rate too, with **Matti Salminen** a superb Pogner and **Michael Volle** a Beckmesser who with his firm, resonant voice refuses to guy the role, making the character more convincing than if he emerges as simply a comic figure. **Petra-Maria Schnitzer** sings with golden tones as Eva, and **Peter Seiffert** makes a lusty Walther, more mellifluous than most Heldentenors, while **Christoph Strehl** is clear and youthful as David. **Nikolaus Lehnhoff's** production for the Zürich Opera opens with an ultra-realistic court-room set, and goes on to an impressionistic, shadowy set for Act II, with barely any stage furniture, while the first scene of Act III is similarly economical, with a pile of books representing Sachs's dwelling. That leads on to a direct setting for the second scene of Act III, with the chorus in rows as if in choir stalls. Inconsistently, they wear modern dress, while the main characters have Victorian costumes, with the Masters emerging in black robes and tall, stovepipe hats.

Recorded in 1990 in the relatively small opera-theatre of the Sydney Opera House, this **Australian Opera** production brilliantly overcomes the limitations of a theatre and the electricity and vitality of **Sir Charles Mackerras's** conducting makes one readily forget any shortcomings. The production by **Michael Hampe** is very traditional, with sets by John Gunter which exploit the depth of the stage rather than its width, and ethnic German costumes by Reinhard Heinrich. **Donald McIntyre** is magnificent as Sachs, both vocally and dramatically, and the Swedish soprano **Helena Doese** is radiant as Eva, with her creamy soprano flawlessly even, most moving in the great quintet of Act III. After a rather rough start, **Paul Frey** emerges as an engaging Walther, rising to the challenge of the Prize Song with little strain, and the other principal tenor, **Christopher Doig**, effortlessly sails through the lighter role of David. **Rosemary Gunn** projects firmly and strongly as Magdalena, and **John Pringle** is a splendidly prim Beckmesser, singing and acting most convincingly. The test of any *Meistersinger* comes in the emotional impact of the big moments, and here, thanks to excellent singing and masterly conducting, the impact of Wagner's great score catches you as it would in the theatre.

A booklet is included with ample information and a good essay, with copious index points on the two DVDs.

Die Meistersinger von Nürnberg (complete; CD versions)

🔊 (M)**** Decca 470 800-2 (4). van Dam, Heppner, Mattila, Opie, Lippert, Vermillion, Pape, Chicago SO Ch. & O, Solti

🔊 **** Calig (ADD) CAL 50971-74 (4). Stewart, Crass, Hemsley, Konya, Unger, Janowitz, Fassbaender, Bav. R. Ch. & O, Kubelik

🔊 **** EMI (ADD) 509195-2 (4). Weikl, Heppner, Studer, Moll, Lorenz, van der Walt, Kallisch, Bav. State Op. Ch., Bav. State O, Sawallisch

(BB)(**(*)) Naxos mono 8.110872-2 (4). Schwarzkopf, Edelmann, Kunz, Hopf, Unger, Bayreuth Fest. Ch. & O, Karajan

(M)**(*) Decca (ADD) 475 6680 (4). Bailey, Bode, Moll, Weikl, Kollo, Dallapozza, Hamari, Gumpoldskirchner Spätzen, V. State Op. Ch., VPO, Solti

(BB)(***) Naxos mono 8.111128/31 (4). Schoeffler, Edelmann, Treptow, Dermota, Gueden, Donch, V. State Op. Ch., VPO, Knappertsbusch

(M)(**(*)) Andante mono AND-3040 (4). Nissen, Reining, Wiedemann, Noort, Thorborg, Ch. & VPO, Toscanini

This is the only Wagner opera that **Sir Georg Solti** has recorded a second time. Central to the success of the later performance is the singing of **Ben Heppner** as Walther, not just heroic but clear and unstrained, ardently following Solti's urgency in the *Prize Song*, a performance more beautiful than any of recent years except his own for Sawallisch. **Karita Mattila** sings with comparable beauty as Eva. Though she is still young, her firm, clear voice is more mature, almost mezzo-ish at times, than one expects of an Eva, and she too naturally surges forward in the great solo of the *Quintet*. For some the controversial element will be the Sachs of **José van Dam**, clean and sharply focused rather than weighty, not quite the wise, old, genial Sachs in his duet with Eva in Act II. This is again unconventional casting, which yet brings new beauty and new revelation, as in the hushed *pianissimo* at the end of the *Fliedermonolog* when he tells of the bird singing. With **René Pape** a powerful Pogner, **Alan Opie** a clean-cut, unexaggerated Beckmesser with plenty of projection, and **Herbert Lippert** and **Iris Vermillion** excellent as David and Magdalene, it is a cast to rival any on disc, making this a clear recommendation if you want a digital recording.

The Calig issue, belatedly issued on commercial disc, is a radio recording, made in Munich in October 1967, and the vividness of the sound is astonishing, with more realism and presence than in almost any digital recording. This is also one of **Kubelik's** most inspired recordings, incandescent in the way it builds up to the big emotional climaxes, just as in a live performance. When it comes to the casting, every single voice has been chosen not only for its firmness and clarity, with no wobbling or straining, but also for the central aptness of voice to character. It would be hard to think of a more radiant and girlish Eva than **Gundula Janowitz**, and the Hungarian tenor, **Sandor Konya**, too little heard on record, is a glowing Walther, beautiful in every register if not quite as subtle as the leading Walther today, Ben Heppner. **Thomas Stewart** as Hans Sachs is similarly unstrained, using his firm, dark baritone with warm expressiveness, while **Thomas Hemsley** has rarely been so impressive on disc, a sharp-focused Beckmesser who conveys the ironic humour but who never guys the role. **Franz Crass** is a fine, dark Pogner, and it would be hard to find a match for **Gerhard Unger** as David or **Brigitte Fassbaender** as Magdalene, with the upfront sound heightening their subplot. A Wagner production as consistent as this is rare, the more surprising to find in a radio recording.

Sawallisch also paces the work in reflection of his long experience of performing it in the opera house with the same musicians. Add to that the most radiant and free-toned Walther on disc, the Canadian, **Ben Heppner**, and you have a superb set. In tonal beauty Heppner matches Plácido Domingo on Jochum's DG set, as he does in variety of expression and feeling. **Cheryl Studer's** contribution is hardly less remarkable than Heppner's, at once powerful and girlishly tender, with the voice kept pure. If she is less affecting than she might be in the poignant duet with Sachs in Act II and in the great *Quintet* of Act III, that has something to do with a limitation in Sawallisch's reading, fine as it is. It rarely finds the poetic magic that this of all Wagner's operas can convey. **Bernd Weikl** makes a splendid Sachs, firm and true of voice, but something of the nobility of the master-shoe-maker is missing. **Deon van der Walt** is a strong David, clear-cut and fresh, with **Cornelia Kallisch** making a traditionally fruity yet firm Magdalene. **Siegfried Lorenz** is a well-focused Beckmesser who refuses to caricature the much-mocked Town Clerk, and **Kurt Moll** is a magnificent Pogner. The chorus (balanced a little backwardly) and orchestra play with the warmth and radiance associated with recordings made in the Herkulessaal in Munich.

The Naxos set of **Karajan's** classic 1951 recording of *Meistersinger* provides a useful alternative to EMI's own issue (5 67086-2). Mark Obert-Thorn has opted to transfer this live recording, made over five performances and a rehearsal, at a higher level than the EMI engineers, and this has tended to bring out the inevitable inconsistencies and flaws, with voices not always well-focused, particularly in the big ensembles. Yet the electric atmosphere of a historic occasion is thrillingly caught. Where EMI provides a complete libretto in German but no translation, Naxos relies on a detailed synopsis with references to the numbered tracks.

The great glory of **Solti's** first (1975) set of *Die Meistersinger* is not the searing brilliance of the conductor, but rather the mature and involving portrayal of Sachs by **Norman Bailey**. For his superb singing the set is well worth investigating. But there is much else to enjoy, not least the bright and detailed sound which the Decca engineers have obtained with the **Vienna Philharmonic**, recording Wagner in the Sofiensaal. **Kurt Moll** as Pogner, **Bernd Weikl** as Beckmesser (really singing the part) and **Julia Hamari** as Magdalene (refreshingly young-sounding) are all excellent, but the shortcomings are comparably serious. Both **Hannelore Bode** and **René Kollo** fall short of their far-from-perfect contributions to earlier sets and Solti, for all his energy, gives a surprisingly routine reading of this most appealing of Wagner scores. The Decca sound comes up very vividly on the curent CD transfer. A full libretto is enclosed, although, as with the rest of this series, the print is very small.

On Naxos the cast from the **Vienna State Opera** centres round the noble Hans Sachs of **Paul Schoeffler** in one of his very finest recordings, opposite the totally enchanting Eva of **Hilde Gueden**, with her golden tone. **Otto Edelmann** is a superb Pogner, and **Karl Donch** as Beckmesser has the right, mean-sounding voice, which he uses intelligently without guying the role. **Gunther Treptow**, with his clean-cut, baritonal Heldentenor, is a fine, unstrained Walther and **Anton Dermota** a glowing David, with **Else Schurhoff** a strong but mature-sounding Magdalene. **Knappertsbusch's** direction is spacious and intense, and the transfer of the original mono recording is first rate, with ample body.

Dating from 1937, this *Meistersinger* demonstrates very clearly how at that period Toscanini was far from rigid in his conducting, with the high-voltage electricity of the moment leading him forward in urgency, while equally letting him and his performers expand in warmth. **Hans Hermann Nissen** makes a noble Sachs and **Maria Reining** is a touching Eva, far fresher than in her later recordings. The others make a fine team. The radio sound is very limited, with the orchestra thin and dry. For most of the time the voices come over well, but they periodically fade into the distance, with the balances of voices on stage variable. Happily, the long first scene of Act III comes over best, no doubt the result of forwardly placed scenery. The wonder is that the CD transfer by Ward Marston does so much to make the sound acceptable, with Andante offering its typically luxurious packaging.

The Mastersingers of Nuremberg (CD version in English)

(N) ❀ *** Chan. (ADD) 3148 (4). Remedios, Curphey, Hammond-Stroud, Bailey, Dempsey, Mangin, Sadler's Wells Ch & Orch, Goodall

This recording of *The Mastersingers* in English, made by the BBC at Sadler's Wells in February 1968, marks an iconic moment in the history of opera in England. That is so not just because **Goodall** here demonstrates how strong the team of Sadler's Wells singers was in Wagner, but the whole project pointed the way forward to the emergence in due course of English National Opera at the Coliseum, a genuine 'Volksoper' rival to the grand international company at Covent Garden.

It was then an inspired choice to have him conduct Wagner at Sadler's Wells, and he seized it eagerly, as this glowing performance amply demonstrates in every bar. Goodall himself patiently helped to train the singers of the 1960s Sadler's Wells company in singing Wagner as he wanted it. His speeds are almost always very slow, but the singers respond superbly, revelling in the expansiveness instead of finding it a trial.

Alberto Remedios was then at his peak as a Wagner tenor, pure and unstrained throughout, rising magnificently to the challenge of the *Prize Song* in Act 3, an exhilarating moment,

which sends you away joyfully, as the audience here plainly felt. **Norman Bailey** too was an outstanding Sachs, firm and focused, the wise philosopher, **Noel Mangin** is a clear-toned Pogner, and **Gregory Dempsey** is a bright, lively David, well-contrasted with Remedios, while **Derek Hammond-Stroud** is delightfully characterful Beckmesser, pointing the humour infectiously, though maybe the voice is too firm and strong for this character.

The women in the cast are not quite on this level, but **Margaret Curphey** as Eva sings with winning firmness and purity, and **Ann Robson** is a lively Magdalene. It is striking that not one of the singers has even the suspicion of a wobble, and the excellent casting equally involves the other Masters and the Nightwatchman sung by **Stafford Dean**. Consistently adding to the glow of the performance is the singing of the chorus, and the playing of the orchestra. It is astonishing remembering the variable quality of latter-day companies that the team at Sadler's Wells in the sixties was so fine. Quite a revelation. The radio recording captures the atmosphere thrillingly, a credit to the 1968 engineers, as well as to those making this transfer.

Parsifal Documentary: 'The Search for the Grail'

*** Arthaus DVD 100 610. Domingo, Urmana, Salminen, Putilin, Mojhaey, Kirov Ch. & O, Gergiev (Dir: Tony Palmer)

Tony Palmer's 1998 film is much more documentary than musical performance, but it does bring the great benefit of letting us hear **Plácido Domingo** as Parsifal in several key passages from the opera. He also provides a commentary on the opera and its plot, as well as on the Grail legend. There are interviews with, among others, the biblical scholar Karen Armstrong (in English) on the background and Wolfgang Wagner (in German) on the traditions of Bayreuth with special reference to the influence on Hitler and the Nazis. There are also clips from various Grail-inspired films, even including those involving Monty Python and 'Crocodile' Dundee. The musical performances were recorded, not only at the Mariinsky theatre in St Petersburg with **Gergiev** conducting, but also in Ravello, where Wagner first conceived the idea of writing the opera. As always with Palmer, it is a film both thoughtful and provocative.

Parsifal (complete; DVD version)

⊶ *** DG DVD 00440 073 4328. Jerusalem, Randova, Weikl, Sotin, Roar, Salminen, Bayreuth Festival Ch. & O, Stein (Dir: Wolfgang Wagner, V/D: Ott)

The DG disc presents the first production of *Parsifal* directed by **Wolfgang Wagner**, in July 1981. In the simple stylizing of the sets – notably in the bare concentric circles of the Grail Scenes in Acts I and III – he follows the example of his brother, Wieland, and effectively so. Act II presents Klingsor's castle with comparable simplicity, a simple cube on which Klingsor stands menacingly. **Leif Roar** makes a wonderfully sinister Klingsor, singing powerfully. The rest of the cast is comparably strong, with **Siegfried Jerusalem** the sweetest-toned Heldentenor of his generation, perfectly cast, and with **Hans Sotin** a most sympathetic Gurnemanz, **Matti Salminen** an incisive Titurel and **Bernd Weikl** an excellent Amfortas. Outstanding too is the Kundry of **Eva Randova**, giving a moving performance whether acting as seductress or outcast. **Horst Stein** is a totally reliable conductor, rising well to the big climaxes of the choral passages.

Parsifal (complete; CD versions)

⌐•⊛ ******** DG 477 6006 (4). Domingo, Struckmann, Meier, Selig, Bankl, Anger, V. State Op. Ch. & O., Thielemann

⌐•⊛ ******** DG 413 347-2 (4). Hofmann, Vejzovic, Moll, van Dam, Nimsgern, von Halem, German Op. Ch., BPO, Karajan

*** Teldec 9031 74448-2 (4). Jerusalem, van Dam, Hölle, Meier, von Kannen, Tomlinson, Berlin State Op. Ch., BPO, Barenboim

Ⓜ ******* Decca (ADD) 470 805-2 (4). Kollo, Ludwig, Fischer-Dieskau, Hotter, Kelemen, Frick, V. Boys' Ch., V. State Op. Ch., VPO, Solti

Ⓜ ****(*)** DG (ADD) 435 718-2 (3). King, Jones, Stewart, Ridderbusch, McIntyre, Crass, (1970) Bayreuth Festival Ch. & O., Boulez

Ⓜ **(***)** Ph. mono 475 7785 (4). Thomas, Dalis, Hotter, London, Neidlinger, Talvela, Bayreuth Festival Ch. & O., Knappertsbusch

ⒷⒷ **(***)** Naxos mono 8.110221/24. Windgassen, London, Weber, Mödl, Uhde, Van Mill, (1951) Bayreuth Fest. Ch. & O., Knappertsbusch

Christian Thielemann conducts an incandescent account of *Parsifal*, recorded live at a sequence of performances at the **Vienna State Opera** in June 2005. The performance is crowned by the magnificent singing and acting of **Plácido Domingo** in the title-role. It is astonishing that in his sixties he can produce such glorious, cleanly focused tone, powerful and even youthful-sounding, in keeping with the character of the young hero. Even in a live account, his voice remains fresh to the end of this long opera. Comparably fine is the Kundry of **Waltraud Meier**, in glorious voice, attacking even the most exposed top notes with freshness, clarity and precision. Though the others are rather less impressive, they all sing well, with **Franz-Josef Selig** darkly powerful, if occasionally unsteady, as Gurnemanz, and **Falk Struckmann** as Amfortas initially gritty-toned, later focusing more cleanly in Act III. **Wolfgang Bankl** is an excellent Klingsor, attacking the role incisively, while **Ain Anger** as Titurel completes a well-balanced team. Thielemann remains the hero alongside Domingo, bringing dedication to this quasi-religious score, combined with passion and dramatic bite. He keeps speeds flowing well, while letting the music breathe spaciously, with the choral singing magnificent throughout, and with the recording – made in collaboration with Austrian Radio – vividly atmospheric. This now takes pride of place for this opera, even ahead of Karajan's deeply spiritual and equally dedicated account.

Communion, musical and spiritual, is what this intensely beautiful **Karajan** set provides. The playing of the **Berlin Orchestra** is consistently beautiful, enhanced by the clarity and refinement of the recording. **Kurt Moll** as Gurnemanz is the singer who, more than any other, anchors the work vocally, projecting his voice with firmness and subtlety. **José van Dam** as Amfortas is also splendid. The Klingsor of **Siegmund Nimsgern** could be more sinister, but the singing is admirable. **Dunja Vejzovic** makes a vibrant, sensuous Kundry who rises superbly to the moment in Act II when she bemoans her laughter in the face of Christ. Only **Peter Hofmann** as Parsifal brings any disappointment; at times he develops a gritty edge on the voice, but his natural tone is admirably suited to the part and he is never less than dramatically effective. He is not helped by the relative closeness of the solo voices, but otherwise the recording is near the atmospheric ideal, a superb achievement.

With **Siegfried Jerusalem** a superb Parsifal, one of the finest ever, both characterful and mellifluous, **Daniel Barenboim's** is a dedicated version with an excellent cast. Like Karajan, Barenboim draws glorious sounds from the **Berlin Philharmonic**, even if he cannot quite match his predecessor in concentrated intensity, well sustained as his control of long paragraphs is. **Waltraud Meier**, as in rival versions, is an outstanding, darkly intense Kundry, and **José van Dam** is superb as Amfortas, clean of attack, as he was for Karajan. **John Tomlinson** is a resonant, if young-sounding Titurel, and **Gunther von Kannen** a clear and direct, if unvillainous, even noble Klingsor. The relatively weak link is the Gurnemanz of **Matthias Hölle**, warm-toned but slightly unsteady, not quite in character.

Solti's singing cast could hardly be stronger, every one of them pointing words with fine, illuminating care for detail; and the complex balances of sound, not least in the *Good Friday Music*, are beautifully caught; throughout, Solti shows his sustained intensity in Wagner. What is rather missing is a rapt, spiritual quality. The remastering for CD, as with Solti's other Wagner recordings, opens up the sound, and the choral climaxes are superb.

Boulez's speeds are so consistently fast that in the age of CD it has brought an obvious benefit in being fitted – easily – on three discs instead of four, yet Boulez's approach, with the line beautifully controlled, conveys a dramatic urgency rarely found in this opera, and never sounds breathless, with textures clarified in a way characteristic of Boulez. Even the flower-maidens sing like young apprentices in *Meistersinger* rather than seductive beauties. James King is a firm, strong, rather baritonal hero, **Thomas Stewart** a fine, tense Amfortas, and **Gwyneth Jones** as Kundry is in strong voice, only occasionally shrill, but **Franz Crass** is disappointingly unsteady as Gurnemanz.

Hans Knappertsbusch's expansive and dedicated 1962 reading is arguably the finest live recording ever made in the Festspielhaus at Bayreuth, with outstanding singing from **Jess Thomas** as Parsifal and **Hans Hotter** as Gurnemanz. Though Knappertsbusch chooses consistently slow tempi there is no sense of excessive squareness or length, so intense is the concentration of the performance, its spiritual quality; and the sound has undoubtedly been further enhanced in the new remastering for this reissue. The snag is that stage noises and coughs are also emphasized, with the bronchial afflictions particularly disturbing in the *Prelude*.

Knappertsbusch was the inspired choice of conductor

made by Wagner's grandsons for the first revival of *Parsifal* after the Second World War. The Naxos historical reissue of a recording originally issued by Decca, taken from the first season in 1951, makes a striking contrast with the later Knappertsbusch recording, made in stereo for Philips 11 years later. The 1951 performance is no less than 20 minutes longer overall, with Knappertsbusch, always expansive, even more dedicated than in his later reading.

The cast is even finer, with **Wolfgang Windgassen** singing with warmth as well as power and making other Heldentenors seem rough by comparison. **Ludwig Weber** is magnificently dark-toned as Gurnemanz, much more an understanding human being than his successor, **Hans Hotter**, and less of a conventional noble figure. **Martha Mödl** is both wild and abrasive in her first scenes and sensuously seductive in her long Act II duet with Parsifal. **Hermann Uhde** is bitingly firm as Klingsor. Although the mono sound remains limited in Mark Obert-Thorn's new transfer, the orchestral texture is full and pleasing, the sense of atmosphere is palpable, voices come over well, and the chorus is well caught. The other distractions, including moments of swish at the opening at Act II, could not be corrected, but the pitch drop at the end of Act III has been 'fixed', and the producer has restored a missing chord (just before the appearance of the Knights of the Grail). There is a brief synopsis.

Das Rheingold (complete; DVD version)

🎬 **** DG **DVD** 0073 4390. Stewart, Fassbaender, Schreier, Kelemen, Altmeyer, Stolze, BPO, Karajan (Dir: Karajan)

Recorded in a Munich studio in 1978, **Karajan's** DVD recreates the production of *Das Rheingold* seen earlier in Berlin. Karajan as stage director supervises an evocatively traditional production, with the Rhinemaidens apparently swimming under water. Each scene is then presented with comparably evocative sets, designed by Georges Wakhevitch and Jean Forestier. Casting is strong, with **Thomas Stewart** a firm, dark Wotan, **Brigitte Fassbaender** a youthfully powerful Fricka and **Zoltan Kelemen** a powerful Alberich. In many ways presented as central in the production is the magnificent Loge of **Peter Schreier**, an unforgettable figure dressed top-to-toe in red leather, the perfect fire-god. Karajan as ever is masterly in his control of his forces, making this an exceptionally enjoyable version of the *Vorabend* of the *Ring* cycle.

Das Rheingold (complete; CD versions)

🎵 **** Decca (ADD) 455 556-2 (2). London, Flagstad, Svanholm, Neidlinger, VPO, Solti

Ⓝ Ⓜ **(*) Decca 478 0382 (2). London, Flagstad, Svanholm, Neidlinger, VPO, Solti

🎵 *** Testament (ADD) SBT2 1390 (2). Hotter, Neidlinger, Lustig, Weber, Blankenheim, Bayreuth Festival O, Keilberth

🎵 *** Teldec 4509 91185-2 (2). Tomlinson, Brinkmann, Schreibmayer, Clark, Finnie, Johansson, Svendén, von Kannen, Pampuch, Hölle, Kang, Liedland, Küttenbaum, Turner, (1991) Bayreuth Festival O, Barenboim

Ⓜ **(*) DG (ADD) 457 781-2 (2). Fischer-Dieskau, Veasey, Stolze, Kelemen, BPO, Karajan

Ⓑ (***) Naxos mono 8.110047-48 (2). Schorr, Huehn, Clemens, Maison, Habich, Laufkötter, Cordon, List, Branzell, Manski, Doe, Andreva, Petina, Met. Op. O & Ch., Bodanzky

The first of **Solti's** cycle was recorded in 1958. The immediacy and precise placing are thrilling, while the sound-effects of the final scenes, including Donner's hammer-blow and the Rainbow Bridge, have never been matched since. Solti gives a magnificent reading of the score, crisp, dramatic and direct. Vocally, the set is held together by the unforgettable singing of **Neidlinger** as Alberich. He vocalizes with wonderful precision and makes the character of the dwarf develop from the comic creature of the opening scene to the demented monster of the last. **Flagstad** learned the part of Fricka specially for this recording, and her singing makes one regret that she never took the role on the stage. **George London** is sometimes a little rough, but this is a dramatic portrayal of the young Wotan. **Svanholm** could be more characterful as Loge, but again it is a relief to hear the part really sung. An outstanding achievement.

The Decca **Solti** set now also comes in an alternative reduced price edition, but without Libretto or keyed synopsis. Better to get it at full price with proper documentation.

Recorded live at the 1955 Bayreuth Festival, **Keilberth's** complete recording of the *Ring* cycle was the first in stereo. Vivid and immediate, the three Rhinemaidens are cleanly defined in contrast with each other, with directional effects very clear, and the big climaxes come over vividly, as for example Donner's smiting of the anvil, even though no metallic clattering is conveyed. Another thrilling moment comes in Wotan's final monologue with the first emergence of the Sword Theme. Keilberth's conducting throughout is electrically intense, far more dynamic than that of his fellow Bayreuth conductor, Hans Knappertsbusch. As for the performances, **Hans Hotter**, for several generations the definitive Wotan, is here at his very finest early in his career, his voice steady as a rock. **Gustav Neidlinger** as Alberich also gives a classic performance, and it is good to have the role of Donner for example taken by a singer as steady and cleanly focused as **Toni Blankenheim**. The rest of the cast cannot be faulted, making this a hot contender in a closely competitive field, matching and even outshining most more recent versions.

When **Barenboim** as Wagnerian has at times seemed lethargic, what is particularly surprising is the dramatic tension of the performance. Even with slow speeds, the sense of flow carries the ear on. Despite the often-thunderous stage noises, the Barenboim performances magnetize you much more consistently, with the atmosphere of the Festspielhaus well caught by the engineers. It is very satisfying, too, to have on disc **John Tomlinson's** magnificent performance as Wotan, **Graham Clark** as an electrifying, dominant Loge and **Linda Finnie** a thoughtful, intense Fricka.

Karajan's reflectiveness of approach has its less welcome side, for the tension rarely varies. One finds such incidents as Alberich's stealing of the gold or Donner's hammer-blow passing by without one's pulse quickening as it should. On the credit side however, the singing cast has hardly any flaw at all, and **Fischer-Dieskau's** Wotan is a brilliant and memorable creation, virile and expressive. Among the others, **Veasey** is excellent, though obviously she cannot efface memories of Flagstad; **Gerhard Stolze** with his flickering almost *Sprechstimme* as Loge gives an immensely vivid, if (for some) controversial interpretation. The 1968 sound has been clarified and further opened up in the new transfer.

The briskness of **Artur Bodanzky** as a Wagnerian, often disturbing in other operas, works well in the narrative of *Rheingold*, with the dramatic bite of each scene strongly conveyed. The recording was made in April 1937 not at the Met. itself but at the **Boston Opera House**, with sound still limited but capturing the voices well. It is specially valuable to have the great **Friedrich Schorr** as Wotan, firm as a rock, strong and purposeful throughout, up to the magnificent final solo. **Karin Branzell** is a warm, clear Fricka, **Eduard Habich** an incisive Alberich and **Emanuel List** a magnificent Fafner, with the whole cast firm and clear if not always subtle. Even the neighing tone of **Rene Maison** as Loge can be regarded as characterful.

The Rhinegold (Das Rheingold) (complete; in English)

Ⓜ **(*) Chan. (ADD) 3054 (3). Bailey, Hammond-Stroud, Pring, Belcourt, Attfield, Collins, McDonnall, Lloyd, Grant, ENO O, Goodall

Goodall's slow tempi in *Rheingold* bring an opening section where the temperature is low, reflecting hardly at all the tensions of a live performance, even though this was taken from a series of Coliseum presentations. Nevertheless, the momentum of Wagner gradually builds up so that, by the final scenes, both the overall teamwork and the individual contributions of such singers as **Norman Bailey**, **Derek Hammond-Stroud** and **Clifford Grant** come together impressively. Hammond-Stroud's powerful representation of Alberich culminates in a superb account of the curse. The spectacular orchestral effects (with the horns sounding glorious) are vividly caught by the engineers and impressively transferred to CD, even if balances (inevitably) are sometimes less than ideal.

Rienzi (complete)

Ⓜ ** EMI (ADD) 5 67131-2 (3). Kollo, Wennberg, Martin, Adam, Hillebrand, Vogel, Schreier, Leipzig R. Ch., Dresden State Op. Ch., Dresden State O, Hollreiser

It is sad that the flaws in this ambitious opera prevent the unwieldy piece from having its full dramatic impact. This recording is not quite complete, but the cuts are unimportant and most of the set numbers make plain the youthful exuberance of the ambitious composer. Except in the recitative, **Heinrich Hollreiser's** direction is strong and purposeful, but much of the singing is disappointing. **René Kollo** sounds heroic, but the two women principals are poor. **Janis Martin** in the breeches role of Adriano produces tone that does not record very sweetly, while **Siv Wennberg** as the heroine, Rienzi's sister, slides unpleasantly between notes

in the florid passages. Despite good recording, this is only a stop-gap.

Der Ring des Nibelungen: an introduction to The Ring by Deryck Cooke, with 193 music examples

Ⓜ *** Decca (ADD) 443 581-2 (2). VPO, Solti

The reissue of Deryck Cooke's fascinating and scholarly lecture is most welcome. The principal musical motives are all printed out in the accompanying booklet and they demonstrate just how the many leading ideas in *The Ring* develop from one another, springing from an original germ. The discourse is riveting; the music examples, many of them specially prepared, are clumsily inserted, but this is still a thoroughly worthwhile acquisition for those who already have recordings of the operas.

Der Ring des Nibelungen (complete; DVD versions)

🎬— **** Warner **DVD** 2564 62317-2 (7). Jerusalem, Kang, von Kannen, Evans, Brinkmann, Clark, Tomlinson, Finnie, Holle, Elming, Secunde, Svenden, Bayreuth Fest. O, Barenboim (Dir: Harry Kupfer, V/D: Horant H. Hohlfeld)

🎬— **** DG **DVD** 073 043-9 (7). Behrens, Jerusalem, Lakes, Ludwig, Morris, Norman, Rootering, Met. Op. Ch. & O, Levine. (Dir: Otto Schenk, V/D: Brian Large.)

(*) Ph. **DVD 073 4057 (8). Jones, McIntyre, Becht, Schwarz, Zednik, Bayreuth Fest. O, Boulez (Producer: Patrice Chéreau, V/D: Brian Large.)

Ⓝ Ⓜ *** Decca **DVD** 074 3264 (7) Anderson, Byriel, Johnson, Klaveness, Morgny, Reuter, Sjöberg, Stene, Theorin, Royal Danish Opera Ch. & O, Schonwandt

Das Rheingold

🎬— **** Warner **DVD** 2564 62318-2. Tomlinson, Clark, Finnie, von Kannen, Holle, Svenden, Bayreuth Festival O, Barenboim (Dir: Harry Kupfer, V/D: Horant H. Hohlfeld)

🎬— **** DG **DVD** 073 036-9. Morris, Held, Baker, Jerusalem, Wlaschina, Zednik, Rootering, Salminen, Met. Op. Ch. & O, Levine

(*) Ph. **DVD 070 4058. McIntyre, Zednik, Becht, Schwarz, Altmeyer, Salminen, Hübner, Bayreuth Fest. O, Boulez

Die Walküre

🎬— **** Warner **DVD** 2564 62319-2 (2). Elming, Secunde, Tomlinson, Finnie, Evans, Holle, Bayreuth Festival O, Barenboim (Dir: Harry Kupfer, V/D: Horant H. Hohlfeld)

🎬— **** DG **DVD** 073 049-2 (2). Norman, Lakes, Moll, Morris, Behrens, Luwig, Met. Op. Ch. & O, Levine. (V/D: Brian Large)

(*) Ph. **DVD 070 4059 (2). Jones, Altmeyer, Schwarz, Hormann, Salminen, McIntyre, Bayreuth Fest. O, Boulez

Siegfried

🎬— **** Warner **DVD** 2564 62320-2 (2). Jerusalem, Clark, Tomlinson, von Kannen, Evans, Kang, Svenden, Bayreuth Festival O, Barenboim (Dir: Harry Kupfer, V/D: Horant H. Hohlfeld)

☞ ******** DG **DVD** 073 037-9 (2). Jerusalem, Behrens, Morris, Zednik, Wlaschina, Salminen, Svenden, Upshaw, Met. Op. Ch. & O, Levine

(*) Ph. **DVD 070 4062 (2). Jung, McIntyre, Jones, Zednik, Becht, Hübner, Bayreuth Fest. O, Boulez. (V/D: Brian Large)

Götterdämmerung

☞ ******** Warner **DVD** 2564 62321-2 (2). Jerusalem, Evans, Brinkmann, Kang, von Kannen, Bayreuth Festival O, Barenboim (Dir: Harry Kupfer, V/D: Horant H. Hohlfeld)

☞ ******** DG **DVD** 073 040-9 (2). Behrend, Jerusalem, Raffell, Salminen, Wlaschina, Lisowka, Ludwig, Met. Op. Ch. & O, Levine

*** Ph. **DVD** 070 4065 (2). Jones, Jung, Hübner, Altmeyer, Becht, Mazura, Killebrew, Bayreuth Fest. O, Boulez

A choice between the **Barenboim** and **Levine** *Ring* cycles will be a personal one, depending very much on one's reaction to the different production values. Both are vocally and orchestrally magnificent performances and, for EG, Barenboim's superb account is the finer of the two. But for your Editor the very conception of the men wearing trilbies (among other of the producer's egocentric touches) tends to put the narrative into an area of disbelief. What would Wagner have thought of such headgear? So we must describe the two differing approaches to the visual element of these performances so that readers can make up their own minds. Otherwise, **Harry Kupfer's** Bayreuth production, recorded in 1991 and 1992, involves minimal, stylized sets, evocatively lit to convey the most atmospheric results. Generally conventional costumes, with occasional modern touches, result in a cycle which tells the complex story of each part of the tetralogy as clearly and graphically as possible.

Rheingold opens in a shimmering green light, with the Rhinemaidens dancing and the gold shining from a great cavity in the river bed. Alberich is characterfully sung by **Gunter von Kannen** with firm, clear tone, as he steals the gold. The Gods waiting to enter the newly built Valhalla are pictured in a simple, bare setting, with many of them wearing green fronds, and with **John Tomlinson** in dark glasses as Wotan their powerful leader. **Linda Finnie** sings with fresh, clear tone as Fricka and **Graham Clark** makes the ideal Loge, preening himself in a blond wig. The Giants, Fasolt and Fafner (**Matthias Holle** and **Philip Kang**, both excellent), are fortunately portrayed as genuinely gigantic figures with prosthetic arms and enormous bodies. Wotan's and Loge's coup in stealing the gold back from Alberich in Nibelheim is then portrayed atmospherically, and so is the handing of the gold to the Giants in payment for their work, including the Tarnhelm and the Ring. The Rainbow Bridge in the final scene is suggested by vertical strip-lighting in the relevant colours, with **Daniel Barenboim's** powerful conducting making a thrilling conclusion.

Die Walküre again benefits not just from an excellent cast with no weak links but from the thrustful conducting of **Barenboim**, giving full weight to the big moments, like the opening of *Wotan's Farewell* in Act III. **Poul Elming** as Siegmund, wearing fatigues, comes out with ringing top notes yet sings with the most tender emotions on greeting Sieglinde, beautifully sung by **Nadine Secunde**. **Linda Finnie** as Fricka makes the role seem nobler than usual opposite the compelling Wotan of **John Tomlinson**. **Anne Evans** sings magnificently as Brünnhilde: fresh and bright with clear, firm tone.

In *Siegfried* the **Harry Kupfer** production, as a plus point, ingeniously conveys such tricky effects as the arrival of the bear in Act I and the flying of the Woodbird in Act II very graphically without descending into unwanted comic effects. The light soprano, **Hilde Leidland**, sings that brief role brightly and clearly. The great steam boiler in Act I as Siegfried forges the sword Nothung also works well, with **Graham Clark** as the shifty Mime, splendidly contrasted with the strong Siegfried of **Siegfried Jerusalem**, the most mellifluous Heldentenor of his generation. As the Wanderer **John Tomlinson** remains a tower of strength, poignantly struck down by his defeat at the hands of the callous Siegfried. The climax of Act III, with **Anne Evans** at her peak as Brünnhilde, is exhilarating, aided by **Daniel Barenboim's** powerful conducting.

Götterdämmerung opens with the Norns literally weaving their thread, and with **Anne Evans** in radiant voice, singing superbly opposite the fine, clear Siegfried of **Siegfried Jerusalem**. The clarity of sound in the Rhine Journey is a delight, and in the Gibichung Hall scenes the Hagen of **Philip Kang** is genuinely sinister. **Anna-Maria Bundschuh** as Gutrune sings very sweetly, though **Bodo Borkmann** as Gunther is too wobbly. The Alberich of **Gunter von Kannen** is again excellent, and **Barenboim** brings out the darkness of the score most compellingly. In the calling of the Vassals in Act II the **Bayreuth Chorus** makes the most of its brief moment (all, like Siegfried himself, wearing boiler suits). The final *Immolation Scene* is vividly done, with Anne Evans rising superbly to the challenge, though Kupfer's device after the fall of Valhalla to have members of a modern audience watching TV sets is an odd intrusion (to say the least) for the final curtain. A brilliant version nevertheless.

With lavish sets and costumes by Gunther Schneider-Siemssen (who designed the Karajan production earlier seen at the Met.), **Levine's** is a full-bloodedly realistic production in the romantic tradition, defying fashionable trends towards Wieland Wagner spareness and abstraction on the one hand and towards updated concept productions on the other. For a video version designed for repeated watching there is everything to be said for this approach, when the complex story is told so lucidly, with splendid camerawork. The aim was to modify the traditional approach, using all the theatrical effects available in a modern theatre. Indeed, the illusion of the Rhinemaidens swimming in water is very vivid at the start of *Rheingold*, and in the final scene of *Götterdämmerung*, after the Gibichung Hall has collapsed (realistically portrayed) and Brünnhilde has flung herself into the fire, you are briefly shown the bottom of the Rhine again and finally Valhalla in flames, reflecting what the music tells you. **Hildegard Behrens** as Brünnhilde and **James Morris** as Wotan are both even more convincing when seen as well as heard, and **Siegfried Jerusalem** as Siegfried makes a handsome hero. There is a picture-gallery as a bonus, with each opera given its own trailer; but nothing else.

When it first appeared in 1976, the centenary year of the tetralogy, the **Patrice Chéreau/Pierre Boulez** *Ring* caused public outrage, with boos (and even fisticuffs) in the auditorium. Musically speaking, there is an objectivity to this reading that is at the other end of the spectrum to Furtwängler, Karajan, Levine and Barenboim, and Boulez's meticulous attention to detail and the fact that he does not linger unduly will, for many, be distinct advantages. On the musical side we have discussed the merits of the set in earlier editions, and the performances are identical. Chéreau's production divests *The Ring* of any tradition, whether it be to pre-war stagings or to the famous post-war Wieland Wagner productions, and forces the viewer to rethink afresh the meaning of the powerful mythology. His view is almost Shavian in seeing the characters as children of the Industrial Revolution, and the designs by Richard Poduzzi are arresting, even if they have little to do with Wagner's original intentions. In the Boulez version, **Brian Large's** handling of the cameras once again places the eye where the ear tells us it wants to be. This set now includes a documentary on the making of the recording which is also available separately on DG 073 4068.

This is a Scandinavian *Ring* cycle, centred on the new Copenhagen Opera House, but also drawing its singing cast from Sweden and Norway to make a team, with **Johann Reuter** playing Wotan in *Rheingold* and a guest artist, **James Johnson** drawn to that role in *Walküre* and *Siegfried*, **Irene Theorin** is an impressive Brünnhilde throughout and **Stig Anderson** is Siegmund in *Walküre* and becomes Siegfried in the two remaining operas. **Sten Byriel** appears as nasty Alberich in three out of the four operas and so on. Thus the narrative is consistent, and set in the mid-19th century, although we see Brünnhilde researching her past in the Valhalla Library! The production has many features of its own from the Rhinemaidens as flappers, to a naked golden boy, who represents the Rheingold and is murdered. Indeed there is a great deal of violence, and murder is part of the narrative, even a torture chamber where Alberich gets his comeuppance. This kind of killing – there is much more besides – is not for everyone, but the staging is impressively full of action. What about the singing? It's pretty good, especially Stig Andersen's Siegfried, both Wotan's and Irene Theorin's Brünnhilde. Throughout, the musical direction of **Michael Schonwandt** keeps the orchestral tension high, and whatever one thinks, this is certainly a landmark staging of the *Ring* which you may like or dislike as you please.

Der Ring des Nibelungen (complete; CD versions)

🎧 ✹ (M) ******** Decca (ADD) 455 555-2 (14). Nilsson, Windgassen, Flagstad, Fischer-Dieskau, Hotter, London, Ludwig, Neidlinger, Frick, Svanholm, Stolze, Böhme, Höffgen, Sutherland, Crespin, King, Watson, Ch. & VPO, Solti

🎧 (B) ******* Ph. (ADD) 446 057-2 (14). Nilsson, Windgassen, Neidlinger, Adam, Rysanek, King, Nienstedt, Esser, Talvela, Böhme, Silja, Dernesch, Stewart, Höffgen, (1967) Bayreuth Festival Ch. & O, Boehm

(M) ******* Testament SBT 141412 (14) Varnay, Hotter, Vinay, Greindl, Bayreuth Festival Ch. & O., Keilberth

🎧 (B) ******* EMI (ADD) 5 72731-2 (14). Behrens, Varady, Lipovšek, Schwarz, Hale, Kollo, Wlaschiha, Schunk, Tear, Rootering, Bav. State Opera Ch. & O, Sawallisch

(M) ******* DG (ADD) 457 780-2 (14). Veasey, Fischer-Dieskau, Stolze, Kelemen, Dernesch, Dominguez, Jess Thomas, Stewart, Crespin, Janowitz, Vickers, Talvela, Brilioth, Ludwig, Ridderbusch, BPO, Karajan

The Ring (CD version; complete)

(N) (B) ******* EMI 5 19479-2 (14) Marton, Jerusalem, Adam, Bav. R Ch. & O, Haitink

(M) (*******) EMI mono 7 67123-2 (13). Suthaus, Mödl, Frantz, Patzak, Neidlinger, Windgassen, Konetzni, Streich, Jurinac, Frick, RAI Ch. & Rome SO, Furtwängler

(B) ****(*)** Ph. 475 7960 (12). Jones, McIntyre, Becht, Schwarz, Zednik, Bayreuth Festival Ch. & O, Boulez.

Solti's was the first recorded *Ring* cycle to be issued. Solti himself developed in the process of making the recording, and *Götterdämmerung* represents a peak of achievement for him, commanding and magnificent.

Recorded at the 1967 Bayreuth Festival, **Boehm's** fine set captures the unique atmosphere and acoustic of the Festspielhaus very vividly. **Birgit Nilsson** as Brünnhilde and **Wolfgang Windgassen** as Siegfried are both a degree more volatile and passionate than they were in the Solti cycle. **Gustav Neidlinger** as Alberich is also superb, as he was too in the Solti set; and the only major reservation concerns the Wotan of **Theo Adam**, in a performance searchingly intense and finely detailed but often unsteady of tone even at that period. The sound, only occasionally constricted, has been vividly transferred.

This pioneering **Joseph Keilberth** recording, taken live from the 1955 *Ring* cycle at **Bayreuth**, was the very first to be done in stereo, several years ahead of the great Solti cycle for Decca, which was recorded in the studio. This one has been languishing in the archives, and it was thanks to the enterprise of Stewart Brown of Testament that finally, after much negotiation, the cycle has appeared. When Wieland Wagner invited Keilberth to conduct *The Ring* at Bayreuth, he was consciously aiming to present a reading manifestly contrasted with that of Hans Knappertsbusch, spacious and contemplative. Keilberth, by contrast, is urgent and passionate, and the thrust of the performance makes the result intensely exciting, inspiring the great Wagnerian singers in the cast to give of their finest. **Hans Hotter's** interpretation of the role of Wotan is well known from a number of versions; but here he not only sings with urgency, his voice is in wonderfully fresh condition, perfectly focused. *Wotan's Farewell* has never been more powerfully presented, with his agony over having to punish his favourite daughter conveyed most movingly. **Astrid Varnay** as Brünnhilde is similarly moving, and so are **Gre Brouwenstijn** as Sieglinde and the darkly baritonal **Ramon Vinay** (Toscanini's choice as Otello) singing Siegmund, with **Josef Greindl** massive of voice as Hunding. The recording, originally made by Decca and now beautifully reprocessed, far outshines in quality the radio recordings of Bayreuth that have appeared on various labels. The separate issues are **Das Rheingold** (SBT 21390); **Die Walküre** (SBT 41391); **Siegfried** (SBT 41392) and **Götterdämmerung** (SBT 41393).

The **Sawallisch** version of the *Ring* makes an excellent recommendation. This is the soundtrack of the **Bavarian State Opera** production by Nikolaus Lehnhoff, as recorded in 1989 for television. The cast is as fine as any in rival versions of the digital age, the performances gain in dramatic momentum and expressive spontaneity from being recorded live, and – rather surprisingly – the sound is outstandingly rich, warm and spaciously atmospheric, in many ways outshining rival digital recordings. Sawallisch conducts with a thrust and energy not always present in his studio recordings, with speeds often faster than have become common. As to the casting, **Robert Hale** proves a noble Wotan, virile and strong. The voice may not be beautiful, but the range of expression is great, so that in *Walküre* the final moment of his kissing Brünnhilde's godhead away could hardly be more tender.

Karajan's DG recording originally followed close on the heels of Solti's for Decca, providing a good alternative studio version which equally stands the test of time, even if *Siegfried* has its disappointments. The manner is smoother, the speeds generally broader, yet the tension and concentration of the performances are maintained more consistently than in most modern studio recordings. Casting is not quite consistent between the operas, with **Régine Crespin** as Brünnhilde in *Walküre*, but **Helga Dernesch** at her very peak in the last two operas. The casting of Siegfried is changed between *Siegfried* and *Götterdämmerung*, from **Jess Thomas** to **Helge Brilioth**, just as strong but sweeter of tone.

Haitink recorded the *Ring* cycle in the years when he was emerging as an inspired Wagner conductor. Strong and purposeful, he takes a thoughtful view which in each music-drama nevertheless builds up unerringly in tension and power, with the beauty of Wagner's orchestration consistently brought out. The recordings are warm and full, if not as sharply defined as they might be, and the principal snags lie with some of the casting, notably with **Eva Marton** as Brünnhilde, too often gusty and ill-focused. **Theo Adam** too is a disappointing Alberich, dramatically intense, but unable any longer to sustain a steady line. **James Morris** as Wotan is here more sympathetic than in the Levine set, dating from the same period, but he yields to other singers in the role. For the rest a strong and compelling issue, one of the better studio recordings in digital sound.

In its digital transfer, the boxiness of the studio sound and the closeness of the voices still take away some of the unique **Furtwängler** glow in the *Ring* cycle, but the sound is acceptable and benefits in some ways from extra clarity.

The Boulez *Ring* is discussed above; this Philips set is identical with the DVD soundtrack. It comes with a synopsis, but the cues are listed separately, which makes it very difficult to combine the narrative with what one hears.

'The Best of The Ring', excerpts from: *Das Rheingold; Die Walküre; Siegfried; Götterdämmerung*

⊶ Ⓑ *** Ph. Duo (ADD) 454 020-2 (2) (from (1967) Bayreuth Festival recordings; Boehm)

The Ring: 'Great Scenes': *Das Rheingold: Prelude & Scene 1; Entry of the Gods into Valhalla; Die Walküre: Winterstürme; Ride of the Valkyries; Wotan's Farewell & Magic Fire Music; Siegfried: Forging Scene; Forest Murmurs; Götterdämmerung: Siegfried's Rhine Journey; Siegfried's Funeral March; Brünnhilde's Immolation Scene*

⊶ Ⓑ *** Double Decca (ADD) 448 933-2 (2). Nilsson, Windgassen, Kotter, Stolz, King, Crespin, VPO, Solti

Although the Solti and Karajan selections have their appeal, as potted 'Rings' go, the Philips Duo is probably the best buy. Taken from **Boehm's** outstanding complete recording, it can be warmly enjoyed as a summary of Wagner's intentions, with most of the key scenes included. The only snag is that Bernard Jacobson's very brief synopsis of the narrative fails to relate each track to the story.

With 144 minutes of music included on this Decca Double, the excerpts from **Solti's** *Ring* are quite extended. *Das Rheingold* begins with the *Prelude* and the sequence continues for 24 minutes, the *Entry of the Gods into Valhalla* opens spectacularly and offers some 10 minutes of music, while the excerpts from *Die Walküre* include the Sieglinde/Siegmund *Winterstürme* duet (15 minutes) and the whole of *Wotan's Farewell and Magic Fire Music*. *Götterdämmerung* leads with *Siegfried's Rhine Journey* and closes with the *Immolation scene* – some 20 minutes for each excerpt, with the tailoring expertly done in between. The only snag is the absence of any narrative cues within the sparse documentation; but the music itself is thrillingly projected.

'The Golden Ring' (BBC documentary film)

⊶ ***DVD 071 153-9. Produced, narrated and directed by Humphrey Burton. Film Cameraman: Peter Sargent. Decca Recording Team: John Culshaw, Gordon Parry, James Brown, Christopher Raeburn, Jack Law, Eric Smith

The legendary 1965 BBC film (made in Vienna in cooperation with the Austrian Television Service) of the making of **Solti's** unsurpassed recording of *The Ring* was filmed during the later stages of recording *Götterdämmerung*. It has unique documentary value, and for recording buffs it is fascinating to see vivid film of so many famous names, recording engineers and the recording production team, headed by John Culshaw, as well as the operatic stars of the great project, with Solti himself looking astonishingly young. Apart from the documentary interest, this remains one of the most fascinating and entertaining films of its kind ever made, and the audio bonus is the inclusion of famous key scenes from each of the four *Ring* operas, splendidly reproduced in surround-sound stereo.

Siegfried (complete)

⊶ *** Decca 455 564-2 (4). Windgassen, Nilsson, Hotter,

Stolze, Neidlinger, Böhme, Hoffgen, Sutherland, VPO, Solti

🔑 ⚙ **** Testament (ADD) SBT4 1392 (4). Windgassen, Kuen, Hotter, Varnay, Neidlinger, Bayreuth Festival O, Keilberth

Ⓜ **(*) EMI 3 58715-2 (4). Jerusalem, Marton, Morris, Adam, Haage, Rydl, Rappé, Te Kanawa, Bav. RSO, Haitink

ⒷⒷ *(**) Arte Nova 74321 72116-2 (4). Woodrow, Wachutka, Uusitalo, Harper, Singers of the Montegral Academy, Tyrol Fest. O, Kuhn

Ⓜ ** DG 457 790-2 (4). Dernesch, Dominguez, J. Thomas, Stolze, Stewart, Kelemen, BPO, Karajan

Siegfried has too long been thought of as the grimmest of the *Ring* cycle, but a performance as buoyant as **Solti's** reveals that, more than in most Wagner, the message is one of optimism. Each of the three acts ends with a scene of triumphant joy. Solti's array of singers could hardly be bettered. **Windgassen** is at the very peak of his form, lyrical as well as heroic. **Hotter** has never been more impressive on record, his Wotan at last captured adequately. **Stolze**, **Neidlinger** and **Böhme** are all exemplary, and predictably **Joan Sutherland** makes the most seductive of Woodbirds. With singing finer than any opera house could normally provide, with masterly playing from the **Vienna Philharmonic** and with Decca's most vivid recording, this is still unsurpassed.

Fine as the recording of the 1955 *Walküre* is in the Testament processing, the *Siegfried* of that year is even more impressive, with even greater weight in the orchestral sound, with the brass and timpani astonishingly vivid. In this section of the *Ring* cycle, that is particularly important, when Wagner relies more than ever on darkened orchestration. The voices are vividly caught too, with a wonderful sense of presence, and **Wolfgang Windgassen** as Siegfried (also the Siegfried of the Solti cycle) is in gloriously fresh voice, superbly contrasted with the mean-sounding but comparably well-focused tenor of **Paul Kuen** as Mime. **Gustav Neidlinger** too is clear and incisive as Alberich, with **Josef Greindl** darkly majestic as Fafner. The duetting of **Varnay** and Windgassen as Siegfried and Brünnhilde then makes a thrillingly passionate conclusion in **Keilberth's** thrustful reading.

In *Siegfried* **Haitink** has the considerable advantage of **Siegfried Jerusalem** in the title-role. He sings the part with a beauty and clarity of focus that allow the lyrical strength as well as the detailed meaning of Wagner's words to come over. **James Morris** as the Wanderer is also sweet on the ear, but **Eva Marton** fails to sing steadily as Brünnhilde, and the weighty **Theo Adam** also makes an unsteady Alberich while still conveying much of the dramatic bite. But Haitink, whose speeds are generally on the brisk side, conveys the feeling of a live dramatic performance. The EMI digital recording has atmosphere and a keen sense of presence, but it is not as firmly focused as the pioneering Solti set on Decca. The reissue is provided with a keyed synopsis.

The super-budget issue from Arte Nova comes over well, with each act leading to a thrilling conclusion. **Gustav Kuhn** directs a clean-cut, well-structured performance, set in a relatively dry acoustic, with ample orchestral detail caught. The result may not be as weighty as usual, but is certainly compelling, with **Alan Woodrow** an outstanding, energetic Siegfried, fresh and clear, unstrained, characterizing vividly. By contrast, though **Juha Uusitalo** sings well as the Wanderer (Wotan), similarly firm and clear, he is not commanding as a character. **Thomas Harper** is an incisive Mime, and **Elisabeth-Maria Wachutka** is fresh and bright as Brünnhilde in Act III. If at first she seems rather lightweight, her clarity of attack is ample compensation with the closing duet rising a fine, warm climax. The booklet provides notes and synopsis, and the full libretto is in German only. But this remains a welcome bargain.

When Siegfried is outsung by Mime, it is time to complain, and though **Karajan's** DG set has many fine qualities – not least the Brünnhilde of **Helga Dernesch** – it hardly rivals the Solti or Boehm versions. Windgassen on Decca gave a classic performance, and any comparison highlights the serious shortcomings of **Jess Thomas**. Even when voices are balanced forward, the digital transfer helps little to make Thomas's singing as Siegfried any more acceptable. Otherwise, the vocal cast is strong, and Karajan provides the seamless playing which characterizes his cycle. Recommended only to those irrevocably committed to the Karajan cycle, even though the current remastering is very successful.

Siegfried (complete; in English)

🔑 Ⓜ **** Chan. 3045 (4). Remedios, Hunter, Bailey, Dempsey, Hammond-Stroud, Grant, Collins, London, Sadler's Wells Op. O, Goodall

Goodall's spacious direction here conveys the genuine dramatic crunch that gives the experience of hearing Wagner in the opera house its unique power, its overwhelming force; this is unmistakably a great interpretation caught on the wing. **Remedios**, more than any rival on record, conveys not only heroic strength but clear-ringing youthfulness, caressing the ear as well as exciting it. **Norman Bailey** makes a magnificently noble Wanderer, steady of tone, and **Gregory Dempsey** is a characterful Mime, even if his deliberate whining tone is not well caught on record. The sound is superbly realistic, even making no allowances for the conditions. Lovers of opera in English should grasp the opportunity of hearing this unique set.

Love duets: *Siegfried, Act III, Scene 3; Tristan, Act II, Scene 2*

🔑 ⚙ **** EMI 5 57004-2. Voigt, Domingo, ROHCG O, Pappano

Before *Tristan* was ever staged, Wagner prepared this concert version of the love duet, but it was never performed. What is fascinating is that instead of the duet being cut off unceremoniously on the arrival of King Mark, the music merges seamlessly into the closing pages of the whole opera, the final minutes of the *Liebestod*, but with a part for Tristan included too. As performed by **Plácido Domingo** as Tristan and **Deborah Voigt** as Isolde, with Pappano an exceptionally warm Wagnerian, the result is sensuously beautiful, radiantly played and recorded. The closing scene from *Siegfried* too, with Voigt and Domingo strong and full-toned, makes one long to hear Pappano in complete Wagner performances.

Tannhäuser (complete; Dresden DVD version plus Paris Bacchanale)

(N) *** DG **DVD** 073 4446 (2). Wenkoff, G. Jones, Weikl, Sotin, Bayreuth Fest Ch. & O, Colin Davis (Stage Director: Götz Friedrich; V/D: Thomas Oloffson)

This 1978 **Tannhäuser** was the first time a production had been filmed complete at Bayreuth and, considering that, the visual balance and the sound are remarkably impressive. Obviously the artists were aware that history was being made, and the concentration and tension of the performance is unmistakeable. The sets are not opulent but are faithful to the composer's intentions and **Sir Colin Davis's** conducting is full of inspiration and vitality. The star performance is **Gwyneth Jones's** gloriously sung Elisabeth and Venus, but **Spas Wenkoff** is strong in the title role and **Bernd Weikl** is a superb Wolfram. The production offers the original Dresden version plus the Paris *Bacchanale* handled with effective eroticism. All-in-all a remarkable achievement.

There is also, on Arthaus (101351), a much more modern production from Baden-Baden, with fine singing but the producer, Nikolaus Lehnhoff, seems determined to overlay his essentially bare production with eccentric detail, including the featuring of a microphone for the Song contest!

Tannhäuser (Paris version; complete)

🔊 **** DG 427 625-2 (3). Domingo, Studer, Baltsa, Salminen, Schmidt, Ch. & Philh. O, Sinopoli

Plácido Domingo as Tannhäuser for **Sinopoli** brings balm to the ears, producing sounds of much power as well as beauty. Sinopoli here makes one of his most passionately committed opera recordings, warmer and more flexible than Solti's Decca version, always individual, with fine detail brought out, always persuasively and never wilful. **Agnes Baltsa** is not ideally opulent of tone as Venus, but she is the complete seductress. **Cheryl Studer** – who sang the role of Elisabeth for Sinopoli at Bayreuth – gives a most sensitive performance, not always ideally even of tone but creating a movingly intense portrait of the heroine, vulnerable and very feminine. **Matti Salminen** in one of his last recordings makes a superb Landgrave and **Andreas Schmidt** a noble Wolfram, even though the legato could be smoother in *O Star of Eve*.

Tannhäuser (highlights)

(BB) **(*) Warner Apex 2564 61738-2. Kollo, Te Kanawa, Hagegård, Meier, Amb. S., Philh. O, Janowski

After a very fine account of the *Overture* (wonderful cascades from the **Philharmonia** violins at the close), Warner provide an enjoyable hour-long selection with the **Ambrosian Singers**, very well recorded, contributing impressively in the March scene and Pilgrims' Chorus. **Kiri Te Kanawa's** warm portrayal of Elisabeth is a little soft-centred, and **René Kollo's** Tannhäuser is also a romantic view. Wolfram's *O du mein holder Abendstern* ('O Star of Eve') is sung simply and affectingly by **Håkan Hagegård**. Throughout, the experienced Wagnerian, **Marek Janowski**, directs without too much pressure, but the closing scene comes off dramatically. The recording is vividly natural and well balanced and texts and a translation are included.

Tristan und Isolde (complete; DVD versions)

(N) **** DG **DVD** 073 4439 (2) Jerusalem, Meier, Hölle, Struckmann, Bayreuth Fest. Ch. & O, Barenboim

🔊 **** DG **DVD** 0073 4321. Kollo, Meier, Salminen, Schwarz, Becht, Bayreuth Festival O, Barenboim PO (Dir: Ponnelle, V/D: Ott)

🔊 *** DG **DVD** 073 044-9. Heppner, Eaglen, Pape, Ketelsen, Dalayman, Met. Op. Ch. & O, Levine (Producer: Dieter Dorn, Design: Jürgen Rosel, V/D: Brian Large)

(*) Hardy **DVD (ADD) HCD4009 (2). Nilsson, Vickers, Hesse, Rundgren, Berry, New Philh. Ch., O Nat. de l'ORTF, Boehm

Barenboim's DVD is not of a live performance but made over a seven-day period, without an audience, in 1995. The result is very successful indeed, having the best of both worlds and offering an inherent spontaneity. The production is plain, the performance not voluptuous either, but with a splendid partnership of **Siegfried Jerusalem** at his finest and the rich-voiced **Waltraud Meier**, also at her freshest, and the casting topped by **Matthias Hölle's** resonant bass as King Mark. Barenboim is in his element and the **Bayreuth Festival Orchestra** provide a richly intense backing.

Recorded at the Bayreuth Festival in 1982, **Daniel Barenboim's** DVD, with evocatively beautiful sets by **Jean-Pierre Ponnelle**, presents an essentially poetic vision of *Tristan*. Casting is consistently strong, with **René Kollo**, one of the more mellifluous Heldentenoren of his generation, opposite the powerful Isolde of **Johanna Meier**. **Matti Salminen** is a superb, imposing King Mark and **Hermann Becht** a heroic Kurwenal, with **Hanna Schwarz** also strongly cast as Brangaene. The video production is very well managed, using six cameras imaginatively, often in close-up, bringing out the beauty of the sets. Act I on board ship has a great awning over the whole stage, which is lifted right at the end to reveal the crew in the final ensemble of the act. Act II is set under a great oak tree with stylized leaves filling the scene, and with dawn gradually breaking to reveal more detail. Act III is also set under a tree, this time a blasted oak. Meier rises superbly to the challenge of the final *Liebestod*, rounding off an impressive performance.

Dieter Dorn's production for the Met. in New York, here filmed in 1999, uses stylized and geometric sets by **Jürgen Rosel**, each with decking for base and each with powerful diagonals. The lighting adds greatly to the atmospheric power of the production, with silhouettes used throughout. When both **Ben Heppner** as Tristan and **Jane Eaglen** as Isolde are bulkily unromantic figures, Dorn cleverly uses the lighting to minimize any problem, regularly creating striking stage pictures for their dueting. What matters is that both are vocally at their peak, singing like angels, totally unstrained and finely focused. The young **René Pape** as King Mark is formidably impressive too, with **Katarina Dalayman** a superb Brangäne, while **Hans-Joachim Ketelsen** is a powerful if at times less well-focused Kurvenal. **James Levine** brings out the power and concentration of this epic, drawing brilliant playing from the **Met. Orchestra**.

The DVD on the Hardy label offers a live recording made at the Orange Festival in France in July 1973, with the title-roles taken by the unchallenged leaders among Wagner singers of the day, **Birgit Nilsson** and **Jon Vickers**, with **Karl Boehm** conducting. That line-up alone makes this well worth investigating, and **Nikolaus Lehnhoff's** simple, stylized staging in the great amphitheatre at Orange is undistractingly effective. Nilsson and Vickers may not be the greatest actors, statuesque rather than dynamic, but their vocal command is irresistible, with not a hint of strain from either of them. Among the others **Ruth Hesse** is an uneven Brangäne, but both **Walter Berry** as Kurwenal and **Bengt Rundgren** as King Mark are superb, as commanding as Nilsson and Vickers. The chorus is the visiting **New Philharmonia of London** but, thanks to the staging, they are never visible. The big disappointment is that the video sound is so limited and thin, not nearly as full as one might have expected of a 1973 recording. The presentation, mostly in Italian, is also limited, with a simple leaflet giving an outline background to the opera and a simple synopsis.

Tristan und Isolde (complete; CD versions)

☝–**** EMI 3 52423-2 (3). Stemme, Domingo, Fujimora, Pape, Bär, ROHCG Ch. & O, Pappano

☝–(M)**** EMI (ADD) 7 69319-2 (4). Vickers, Dernesch, Ludwig, Berry, Ridderbusch, German Op. Ch., Berlin, BPO, Karajan

*** Teldec 4509 94568-2 (4). Meier, Jerusalem, Lipovšek, Salminen, Struckmann, Berlin State Op. Ch., BPO, Barenboim

(M) *** DG (ADD) 449 772-2 (3). Windgassen, Nilsson, Ludwig, Talvela, Waechter, Bayreuth Festival (1966) Ch. & O, Boehm

(M) *** Decca (ADD) 470 814-2 (4). Uhl, Nilsson, Resnik, van Mill, Krause, VPO, Solti

(M) **(*) Ph. 475 7020 (4). Hofmann, Behrens, Minton, Weikl, Sotin, Bav. R. Ch. & SO, Bernstein

(M) *** EMI mono 5 67621-2 (4). Flagstad, Suthaus, Fischer-Dieskau, Thebom, Philh., Furtwängler

☝–(BB) (***) EMI mono 5 85873-2 (4). Flagstad, Suthaus, Thebom, Greindl, Fischer-Dieskau, Phil., Furtwängler

(BB) (**(*)) Naxos 8.110321 (4) Flagstad, Suthaus, Thebom, Greindl, Fischer-Dieskau, Phil., Furtwängler

(M) **(*) DG 477 5355 (3). Kollo, M. Price, Fassbaender, Fischer-Dieskau, Moll, Leipzig R. Ch., Dresden State O, Carlos Kleiber

When **Plácido Domingo** suggested to EMI that as a culmination to his unique career he would like to record *Tristan und Isolde*, the record company boldly took up the challenge and with luxury casting produced what is instantly recognizable as a classic recording, worthy successor to the great Furtwängler version of 1952 with Flagstad as Isolde. The glory of the set is not only the radiant singing of Domingo, still in glorious, full-throated voice in his sixties, but the warmly understanding conducting of **Antonio Pappano** with

the **Covent Garden Orchestra**, more volatile than that of Furtwängler but just as concentrated. Domingo, at once heroic and lyrical, not only offers the most beautiful assumption on disc since Windgassen for Boehm at Bayreuth in 1966, but he sings with a passion beyond that of most Heldentenors, and he is matched by the tenderly girlish Isolde of **Nina Stemme**. Hers may not be a big, noble soprano like those of Flagstad or Birgit Nilsson, and in Act II she comes to sound a little stressed, but with fine projection and subtle shading her portrait is the more passionate and more feminine. **Mihoko Fujimora** as Brangäne is clear and tender too – her warnings in the love duet creep exquisitely on the ear – and **René Pape** as King Mark is unmatched by any contemporary. **Olaf Bär** with his lieder-like command of detail is a fine Kurwenal, with such stars as **Ian Bostridge** as the Shepherd and **Rolando Villazon** as the Young Sailor filling smaller parts. The set includes as a bonus an audio DVD of the complete performance in surround sound, with an on-screen libretto in German, English and French.

Karajan's is a sensual performance of Wagner's masterpiece, caressingly beautiful and with superbly refined playing from the **Berlin Philharmonic**. **Dernesch** as Isolde is seductively feminine, not as noble as Flagstad, not as tough and unflinching as Nilsson; but the human quality makes this account if anything more moving still, helped by glorious tone-colour through every range. **Jon Vickers** matches her in what is arguably his finest performance on record, allowing himself true *pianissimo* shading. The rest of the cast is excellent too. The recording has been remastered again for the present reissue and the 1972 sound has plenty of body, making this an excellent first choice, with inspired conducting and the most satisfactory cast of all. The set has also been attractively repackaged.

Barenboim's cast is an exceptionally strong one, with **Waltraud Meier** as Isolde graduating from mezzo soprano to full soprano, breasting the top Cs easily, showing no sign of strain, and bringing a weight and intensity to the role that reflect her earlier experience. The vibrato sometimes grows obtrusive, and even in the final *Liebestod* there is a touch of rawness under pressure; but the feeling for line is masterly, always with words vividly expressed. **Siegfried Jerusalem**, with a more beautiful voice than most latterday Heldentenoren, makes a predictably fine Tristan, not quite as smooth of tone as he once was and conveying the poignancy of the hero's plight in Act III rather than his suffering. **Marjana Lipovšek** is among the most characterful of Brangänes, strong and vehement, while **Matti Salminen** is a resonant, moving King Mark. Only the gritty tones of **Falk Struckmann** as Kurwenal fall short. With weighty, full-ranging and well-balanced sound, this is a possible recommendation for a modern digital set. Highlights are also available (76 minutes) on a budget Apex CD (2564 61505-2).

Boehm's Bayreuth performance offers one great benefit in presenting this without any breaks at all, with each act uninterrupted. Boehm is on the urgent side in this opera and the orchestral ensemble is not always immaculate; but the performance glows with intensity from beginning to end, carried through in the longest spans. **Birgit Nilsson** sings the *Liebestod* at the end of the long evening as though she was starting out afresh, radiant and with not a hint of tiredness, rising to an orgasmic climax and bringing a heavenly *pianissimo* on the final rising octave to F sharp. Opposite Nilsson is **Wolfgang Windgassen**, the most mellifluous of Heldentenoren; though the microphone balance sometimes puts him at a disadvantage to his Isolde, the realism and sense of presence of the whole set bathes you in the authentic atmosphere of Bayreuth. Making up an almost unmatchable cast are **Christa Ludwig** as Brangaene, **Eberhard Waechter** as Kurwenal, and **Martti Talvela** as King Mark, with the young **Peter Schreier** as the Young Sailor.

Solti's performance is less flexible and sensuous than Karajan's, but he shows himself ready to relax in Wagner's more expansive periods. On the other hand the end of Act I and the opening of the love duet have a knife-edged dramatic tension. **Nilsson** is masterly in her conviction and she never attacks below the note, so that at the end of the love duet the impossibly difficult top Cs come out and hit the listener crisply and cleanly, dead on the note; and the *Liebestod* is all the more moving for clean attack at the climax. **Fritz Uhl** is a sensitive Heldentenor, rather lightweight, but his long solo passages in Act III are superb. The Kurwenal of **Tom Krause** and the King Mark of **Arnold van Mill** are both excellent, and it is only **Regina Resnik** as Brangäne who gives any disappointment. The production has the usual Decca/Culshaw imaginative touch, and the recording matches brilliance and clarity with satisfying coordination and richness.

The surprise is that **Bernstein**, over-emotional in some music, here excercises restraint to produce one of the most spacious readings ever put on disc, more expansive even than Furtwängler's. His rhythmic sharpness goes with warmly expressive but unexaggerated phrasing, to give unflagging concentration and deep commitment. The love duet has rarely if ever sounded so sensuous, with supremely powerful climaxes. **Behrens** makes a fine Isolde, less purely beautiful than her finest rivals, but with reserves of power giving dramatic bite. The contrast of tone with **Yvonne Minton's** Brangäne (good, except for flatness in the warning solo) is not as great as usual, and there is likeness too between **Peter Hofmann's** Tristan, often baritonal, and **Bernd Weikl's** Kurwenal, lighter than usual. The King Mark of **Hans Sotin** is superb.

Wilhelm Furtwängler's concept is spacious from the opening *Prelude* onwards, but equally the bite and colour of the drama are vividly conveyed, matching the nobility of **Flagstad's** portrait of Isolde. The richly commanding power of her singing and her always distinctive timbre make it a uniquely compelling performance. **Suthaus** is not of the same calibre as Heldentenor, but he avoids ugliness and strain. Among the others, the only remarkable performance comes from the young **Fischer-Dieskau** as Kurwenal, not ideally cast but keenly imaginative. One endearing oddity is that – on Flagstad's insistence – the top Cs at the opening of the love duet were sung by **Elisabeth Schwarzkopf**. The Kingsway Hall recording was admirably balanced, catching the beauty of the **Philharmonia Orchestra** at its peak. It stands among Fürtwangler's finest memorials, still unsurpassed by later versions in its spacious concentration and intensity.

To forestall the imminent transfer of the same recording by Naxos, an alternative super-budget version was issued, minus libretto but with a very detailed synopsis linked to copious index points on the discs. The mono sound is amazingly full and immediate, transferred from the original tapes with more presence than the Naxos version and with less background noise.

In default of the EMI super-budget version, the Naxos set in the same price-bracket, lovingly transferred from carefully chosen LPs, offers a good alternative, not quite so vivid, also without a libretto and with fewer index points linked to the synopsis.

Kleiber directs a compellingly impulsive reading, crowned by the glorious Isolde of **Margaret Price**, the most purely beautiful of any complete interpretation on record. Next to more spacious readings, Kleiber's at times sounds excitable, almost hysterical, with fast speeds tending to get faster, for all his hypnotic concentration. But the lyricism of Price's Isolde, feminine and vulnerable, is well contrasted against the heroic Tristan of **Kollo**, at his finest in Act III. **Kurt Moll** makes a dark, leonine King Mark, but **Fischer-Dieskau** is at times gritty as Kurwenal and **Brigitte Fassbaender** is a clear but rather cold Brangaene.

Die Walküre (complete; DVD version)

(*) Warner **DVD** 2564 6319-2. Emeling, Secunde, Evans, Tomlinson, Finnie, Hölle, Bayreuth Festival O, Barenboim (V/D: Horant Hohlfeld)

Recorded live at the Met. in New York in April 1989, two years after the DG audio recording with the same personnel, the DVD film offers an even more compelling experience, with **James Levine** more thrustfully dramatic and drawing more spontaneous-sounding performances from his team. To have the gloriously voiced **Jessye Norman** as Sieglinde is luxury casting. She is totally secure and consistently intense and so commanding you feel that, far from being afraid, this Sieglinde could eat any of the Valkyries alive, including the Brünnhilde of **Hildegard Behrens**. **John Tomlinson's** Wotan, singing magnificently, dominates Barenboim's *Die Walküre* against a stage as bare as **Bayreuth** has ever seen. However, colour is provided by the Wälsungs, who are all red-headed, while for contrast Brünnhilde (**Ann Evans**), also on fine vocal form, and Fricka (**Linda Finnie**) are in black. Vocally and musically this is strong, but, although the cameras are usually in the right place, visually we shall stick to Levine (see above).

Die Walküre (complete; CD versions)

**** Decca (ADD) 455 559-2 (4). Nilsson, Crespin, Ludwig, King, Hotter, Frick, VPO, Solti

(BB) (***) Naxos mono 8.110058/60 (3). Traubel, Melchior, Schorr, Kipnis, Varnay, Thorborg, Met Op. O, Leinsdorf

(M) **(*) DG (ADD) 457 785-2 (4). Crespin, Janowitz, Veasey, Vickers, Stewart, Talvela, BPO, Karajan

Solti sees Act II as the kernel of the work, with the conflict of wills between Wotan and Fricka making for one of Wagner's most deeply searching scenes. That is the more apparent when the greatest of latterday Wotans, **Hans**

Hotter, takes the role, and **Christa Ludwig** sings with searing dramatic sense as his wife. Before that, Act I seems a little underplayed. This is partly because of Solti's deliberate lyricism – apt enough when love and spring greetings are in the air – but also (on the debit side) because **James King** fails both to project the character of Siegmund and to delve into the word-meanings as all the other members of the cast consistently do. As Sieglinde **Crespin** has never sung more beautifully on record. As for **Nilsson's** Brünnhilde, it has grown mellower, the emotions are clearer. Newly remastered, the sound is more vivid than ever and the layout is admirable.

Recorded live at the Met. in New York in December 1941, the Naxos historical set offers an electrifying performance, starrily cast, with radio sound giving clear focus to the voices. With **Astrid Varnay** as Sieglinde making her début at the Met. and **Helen Traubel** as Brünnhilde also making her début in that role, it was a great occasion, with **Lauritz Melchior** plainly intent on not being outshone. He is in heroic voice, the master Wagner tenor of his generation, daring to hold on to his cries of '*Walse, Walse*' for extraordinary lengths. Varnay is a warm Sieglinde, producing Flagstad-like overtones. Equally, Helen Traubel sings with a rock-like firmness that is all too rare in latter-day Wagner sopranos, clear and incisive, never fluffing a note. **Kirsten Thorborg** is a magnificent Fricka, and **Alexander Kipnis** a thrilling Hunding, with his dark, incisive attack. It is sad that next to these, the other great Wagnerian, **Friedrich Schorr**, as Wotan, reveals a sadly worn voice, strained and dry on top. It may be as well that his Act II monologue is severely cut. Yet the nobility of his portrayal still comes over powerfully, as in his final half-tone phrase, kissing away Brünnhilde's godhead. **Leinsdorf** draws incandescent playing from the **Met. Orchestra** in a performance wilder than his RCA studio account but just as compelling.

The great merits of **Karajan's** version are the refinement of the orchestral playing and the heroic strength of **Jon Vickers** as Siegmund. With that underlined, one cannot help but note that the vocal shortcomings here are generally more marked, and the total result does not add up to quite so compelling a dramatic experience: one is less involved. **Thomas Stewart** may have a younger, firmer voice than Hotter, but the character of Wotan emerges only partially; it is not just that he misses some of the word-meaning, but that on occasion – as in the kissing away of Brünnhilde's godhead – he underlines too crudely. **Josephine Veasey** as Fricka conveys the biting intensity of the part. **Gundula Janowitz's** Sieglinde has its beautiful moments, but it is not a dynamic performance. **Crespin's** Brünnhilde is impressive, but nothing like as satisfying as her study of Sieglinde on the Decca set. The DG recording is very good.

Die Walküre: Act I (complete)

(M)(**(*)) Orfeo mono C 019991 Z. Schech, Völker, Dalberg, Bav. State O, Solti

Die Walküre: Act I (complete); Act II, Scenes 3 & 5

(M)(***) EMI mono 3 45832-2. Lehmann, Melchior, List, VPO, Walter

(i) Die Walküre: Act I (complete). Götterdämmerung: Siegfried's Funeral March

**(*) Australian Decca Eloquence 466 678-2. VPO, Knappertsbusch; (i) with Svanholm, Flagstad, van Mill

Though in the days of 78s the music had to be recorded in short takes of under five minutes, one is consistently gripped by the continuity and sustained lines of **Walter's** reading, and by the intensity and beauty of the playing of the **Vienna Philharmonic**. **Lotte Lehmann's** portrait of Sieglinde, arguably her finest role, has a depth and beauty never surpassed since, and **Lauritz Melchior's** heroic Siegmunde brings singing of a scale and variety – not to mention beauty – that no Heldentenor today begins to match. **Emanuel List** as Hunding is satisfactory enough, but his achievement at least has been surpassed.

All **Solti** devotees (and other Wagnerians) should hear his historic recording, made live at the Prinzregentem Theatre in Munich in 1947, when the young maestro was new to the post of principal conductor in Munich. Though at that time he had had remarkably little experience of conducting opera, this is already an electrifying example of his work as a Wagner conductor, culminating in a thrilling close to the act. The passionate build-up includes a cry of delight from **Marianne Schech** as Sieglinde when Siegmund retrieves the sword. The sound is close and unatmospheric, with stage noises obtrusive at times, but there is plenty of solid detail. Though the closeness does not help the singers, Schech is an impressive, vibrant Sieglinde, firmer than she later became, and **Franz Völker** as a veteran of the **Vienna State Opera** is a clear, heroic Siegmund, if strained at times at the top. **Friedrich Dalberg** makes an aptly sinister Hunding.

It was **Kirsten Flagstad's** wish that she should be able to record Sieglinde in Act I of *Walküre*, and she also wanted to work with the great Wagner conductor, **Hans Knappertsbusch**. If Flagstad is a bit too matronly for the role, it hardly matters, for there is an electric tension in this performance which makes it compellingly moving. The 1958 recording, though a bit tubby, is amazingly detailed, rich and full, and allows the inimitable Vienna glow to come through. With Siegfried's funeral march thrown in too, this Australian CD is well worth seeking out.

The Valkyrie (Die Walküre) (complete; in English)

(M) *** Chan. 3038 (4). Hunter, Remedios, Curphey, Bailey, Grant, Howard, ENO Ch. & O, Goodall

Recorded by EMI at the London Coliseum in 1975 and now reissued by Chandos the glory of the **ENO** performance lies not just in **Goodall's** spacious direction but in the magnificent Wotan of **Norman Bailey**, noble in the broadest span but very human in his illumination of detail. **Rita Hunter** sings nobly too, and though she is not as commanding as Nilsson in the Solti cycle she is often more lyrically tender. **Alberto Remedios** as Siegmund is more taxed than he was as Siegfried in the later opera (lower tessituras are not quite so comfortable for him) but his sweetly ringing top register is superb. If others, such as **Ann Howard** as Fricka, are not always treated kindly by the microphone, the total dramatic compulsion is irresistible.

VOCAL COLLECTIONS

Arias from: *Der fliegende Holländer; Lohengrin; Tannhäuser; Tristan und Isolde; Die Walküre: Act III, Scene iii*

Ⓜ *** EMI mono/stereo 5 09702-2. Nilsson, Hotter, Philh. O, Ludwig

An incredibly generous compilation of classic recordings from 1957, lasting a shade over 82 minutes. In the longest excerpt here, *Die Walküre*, the singing is outstanding and Brünnhilde's range of emotional expression is most impressively conveyed by **Birgit Nilsson**. **Hans Hotter's** Wotan is equally fine. Nilsson is no less impressive in *The Flying Dutchman* excerpts, where her tonal beauty is again matched by Hotter's. There is a pleasing lack of wobble, and real penetration into the depth of the music and character. Both singers are moving in the quieter moments and Nilsson shows that she is able to ride the orchestra in the climaxes without her voice deteriorating into the unmusical noises we sometimes hear in Wagner. The *Liebestod* from *Tristan* is beautifully and atmospherically done and the *Tannhäuser* excerpt is memorable too. Excellently balanced, warm stereo sound (except for one of the *Flying Dutchmen* excerpts, which is mono) and well conducted.

Der fliegende Holländer: Overture; Die Frist ist um; Die Meistersinger: Wahn! Wahn!, Fliedermonolog. Parsifal: Amfortas's Monologues; Tannhäuser: O du mein holder Abendstern; Die Walküre: Wotan's Farewell

*** DG 471 348-2. Terfel, BPO, Abbado

The challenge of Wagner plainly suits **Bryn Terfel** to perfection both musically and dramatically, the impression of fully formed characterizations is irresistible. **Abbado** and the orchestra are plainly inspired by their soloist to give incandescent performances, full and intense. *The Flying Dutchman Overture* and the Dutchman's monologue were recorded live, and arguably the latter is on the slow side, but the illumination of words is as revelatory here as elsewhere on the disc. All of the items are vividly realized, notably the two Hans Sachs monologues from *Meistersinger* and the wonderfully expressive portrait of Wotan in the *Walküre* monologue. This final item brings the most daring half-tone phrases from Terfel as he kisses Brünnhilde's godhead away, the culminating moment of the whole opera, here with the agony intensified by the intimacy of expression. The sound is among the richest from this source, with brass gloriously full and rich.

Götterdämmerung: (i) Prelude: Dawn; Love Duet; Siegfried's Rhine Journey; Siegfried's Monologue & Funeral March; Siegfried: (ii) Forging Scene; Forest Murmurs; (iii) Closing Scene with Woodbird

⊕ **** EMI 5 57242-2. Domingo, ROHCGO, Pappano; (i) with Urmana; (ii) Cangelosi; (iii) Dessay

Here **Domingo** amplifies his portrait of Siegfried in powerfully heroic singing in these substantial sections of *Siegfried* and *Götterdämmerung*. It is astonishing that a tenor now 60

should retain a voice at once so full and sharply focused. As on the earlier disc, **Pappano** proves a sympathetic partner, drawing from the orchestra playing at once rich and powerful, helped by the warm acoustic of the Colosseum, Watford. **Urmana** as Brünnhilde and **David Cangelosi** as Mime make excellent foils for the hero, though **Natalie Dessay** is less well cast as the Woodbird, not as fresh and bright as one really wants.

Götterdämmerung: Siegfried's Rhine Journey & Immolation Scene; Tristan und Isolde: Prelude & Liebestod

(*(**)) Testament mono SBT 1510. Flagstad, Philh. O, Furtwängler – RICHARD STRAUSS: *Four Last Songs* (*(**))

The urgency and the purity of **Flagstad's** singing in these live recordings, made at the Royal Albert Hall in May 1950, bear witness to her extraordinary qualities, defying age – as indeed **Wilhelm Furtwängler** does in his radiant conducting of the then new **Philharmonia Orchestra**, already an outstanding band. The sound is poor, with a scrunching background, but the warmth and intensity of a great occasion are consistently apparent, making this an important offering along with the world première of Strauss's *Four Last Songs*.

WAGNER, Siegfried (1869–1930)

Die Heilige Linde (opera; complete)

*** CPO 999 844-2 (2). Wegner, Schellenberger, Lukic, George, Scharnke, Kruzel, Horn, Heidbüchel, Halmai, West German RSO, Cologne Ch. & O, Albert

Die Heilige Linde ('The Holy Linden Tree') is the fourteenth of Siegfried Wagner's 16 operas, with a substantial *Prelude* generally counted one of his finest works. The easy tunefulness of the very opening instantly establishes that the musical idiom preferred by the son is more straightforwardly diatonic, not nearly so radical as the chromatic style his father developed, with a concern for German folksong. That is apt for this involved tale from the third century AD, telling of Arbogast, king of a German tribe, his wife Hildegard, and Fritigern, son of the king of a neighbouring tribe. The villain is Philo, described as a soldier instigator, in fee to the Roman Emperor, intent on getting Arbogast to forge an alliance with Rome. It makes agreeable listening, but the ends of the first two acts bring no sense of drama, and the end of the whole opera, when Arbogast has been killed in battle, is effective as a warmly patriotic ensemble rather than as a dramatic resolution.

Recorded in **Cologne** in collaboration with **West German Radio**, this CPO recording offers a warmly idiomatic performance under **Werner Andreas Albert**, very well sung. The booklet contains a complete libretto and translation, with various essays and background material, but no synopsis of the difficult plot.

Der Kobold (The Goblin)

Ⓝ ⒷⒷ *** Naxos 2 220003/04 (2). Broberg, Mauel, Hoffmann, Mitschke, PPP Music Th. Ens., Munich, Nuremberg SO, Frank Strobel (Stage Dir: Peter P. Pachl)

Sponsored by Bavarian Radio and recorded in the Stadttheater Furth, this account of Siegfried Wagner's favourite among his own operas gives a good idea musically of the merits of this fairy-tale opera. In idiom Siegfried's music is far closer to that of his teacher, Humperdinck, than to that of his father, though in Wagner fashion he favoured writing a work on a massive scale, too long for the subject matter, on his own libretto. *Der Kobold*, the goblin of the title, is a heavily symbolic figure, while the travelling actor, Friedrich is the symbol of Eros, which makes it even harder to fathom the plot in this updated production. The central character is the heroine, Verena, who receives a magic stone from Ekhart at the start, and becomes the symbol of good. In the tragic conclusion she saves the life of Friedrich, but at the cost of being stabbed herself. Visually, the production involves a hospital bed, which adds still more confusion, though happily the attractions of the music itself compensate with folk overtones based on some good tunes and dance rhythms.

Under **Frank Strobel** the performance is strongly presented, and most of the singing is good if not outstanding, notably the Verena of **Rebecca Broberg**, Friedrich sung by **Volker Horn** and Ekhart sung by **Andreas Mitschke**. Good television sound.

Rainulf and Adelasia

** CPO 777 017-2 (3). von Aken, Wachutka, Minutillo, Trekel, Stuttgart Ch., Rheinland-Pfalz State PO, Albert

Written between 1920 and 1922, when the German economy collapsed, and based on the history of the Normans in Italy, *Rainulf and Adelasia* reflects the gloom felt by the composer. It also reflects in its story of a strong heroine, Albriria (a mezzo role well taken by **Elisabeth Wachutka**), the composer's concern over his mother Cosima's perjury in the legal action against her daughter, Isolde. The role of the soprano heroine, Adelasia, is also well sung, and so is the role of the hero, Rainulf. A well-written work that, despite its excessive length, has many attractions.

WALKER, Ernest (1870–1949)

Cello Sonata

*** British Music Soc. BMS 423CD. Cole, Talbot – BOWEN; FOULDS: *Cello Sonatas* ***

Ernest Walker was to centre his whole life and career on Oxford's Balliol College. He organized chamber music concerts at the college and in 1907 wrote a *History of Music in England*. His compositions were small-scale and his *Cello Sonata* dates from 1914. It is a profoundly lyrical work, the first movement passionate, followed by a deeply felt but calmer *Adagio*, marked *serioso*. The mood lightens in the finale – but not entirely, for it is marked *con fuco*. It is a personal work and a match for its companions on this disc by Bowen and Foulds, even if the composer's voice is less individual than theirs. It is very well played here by **Jo Cole** and **John Tabot**, as if they believe in evey note, as well they might.

WALLACE, William
(1860–1940)

Symphonic Poems 1 (The Passing of Beatrice); 3 (Sister Helen); 5 (Sir William Wallace); 6 (Villon)

*** Hyp. CDA 66848. BBC Scottish SO, Brabbins

Like Hamish McCunn, William Wallace was born in Greenock, near Glasgow. The music's Scottish character is immediately obvious at the brooding opening; the main theme, 'Scots wha' hae', emerges only slowly but is celebrated more openly towards the end. *Villon*, an irreverent medieval poet, was a hero of a different kind, and Wallace's programme draws on the thoughts of his philosophical ballads (which are named in the synopsis) in music that is both reflective and vividly colourful. The very romantic *Passing of Beatrice* is a sensuous vision of Paradise, lusciously Wagnerian with an unashamedly Tristanesque close, reflecting the heroine's final transformation. The scoring is sensuously rich, yet it retains also the spiritually ethereal quality of the narrative, rather as Wagner does in *Parsifal*. The final piece here is based on Rossetti. What is so remarkable is not only the quality of the musical material throughout these works, but also the composer's skill and confidence in handling it: they are musically every bit as well crafted as the symphonic poems of Liszt. Clearly the **BBC Scottish Symphony Orchestra** enjoy playing them. The result is remarkably satisfying.

WALLACE, William Vincent
(1812–65)

Maritana (opera; complete)

**(*) Marco 8.223406-7. Cullagh, Lee, Clarke, Caddy, RTE Philh. Ch. & Concert O, O Duinn

Along with Balfe's *Bohemian Girl* and Benedict's *Lily of Killarney*, Wallace's *Maritana* marked a breakthrough in opera in Britain, and it held the stage for over 50 years. This lively recording, with Irish artists celebrating this 19th-century Irish composer, helps to explain the work's attractions, regularly reminding the modern listener of Gilbert and Sullivan. The big difference is that where G & S present a parody of grand opera, with tongue firmly in cheek, Wallace is intensely serious, with the big melodramatic moments quickly becoming unintentionally comic. To compound the similarity with G & S, the story, like that of the *Yeomen of the Guard*, depends on the heroine, by contract, marrying a man condemned to death who then escapes his punishment. What matters is that there are many more good tunes than that of the still-remembered aria for the heroine, *Scenes that are Brightest*, and the ensembles in this winning performance are always fresh and lively. The soloists too all have voices which focus cleanly, even if they are not specially distinctive. The recording is bright and forwardly balanced, with words crystal clear. Worth investigating as a period piece.

WALTON, William (1902–83)

'At the Haunted End of the Day' (Television Profile directed by Tony Palmer)

*** Decca DVD 074 150-9

Tony Palmer's Italia Prize-winning television profile of William Walton is both direct and evocative, starting with Walton himself nearing 80 and plainly rather frail, musing at the keyboard of the piano in his work room as he composes the solo cello *Passacaglia* for Rostropovich, one of his very last works. This moment brings several of his wrily humorous *obiter dicta* with which the film is delightfully dotted. He admits to composing at the piano, but being no pianist, he finds, 'has rather boogered the whole thing oop' (resorting to the Lancashire accent he promptly dropped when as a boy treble he joined the choir of Christ Church Cathedral, Oxford).

The story of his career with its extraordinary sequence of lucky breaks, with one protector or helper after another coming along, is then told for the most part chronologically. We see the house where he was born, by Oldham standards relatively grand, and evocative shots follow of Oldham, Oxford and later London and Amalfi in Italy. The impact of *Belshazzar's Feast* is fully brought out, not least thanks to **Simon Rattle's** conducting.

Later, Rattle also directs the passages from the *First Symphony*, which comes into the story not in its proper place in the 1930s, but in a sequence on the loves of Walton's life, when he is safely married to Susana and living comfortably on the isle of Ischia. The film was made within a couple of years of the composer's death in 1983 and has a vein of melancholy running through it, explaining Palmer's title, 'At the Haunted End of the Day', taken from one of the most striking of the arias in the opera *Troilus and Cressida*. Even so, the impact of the film is anything but depressing, with the effervescent personality of Susana taking over towards the end. A unique career, vividly recreated.

Anniversary Fanfare; Crown Imperial; March for the History of the English-speaking Peoples; Orb and Sceptre; A Queen's Fanfare; (i) Antiphon; 4 Christmas Carols: All this time; King Herod and his cock; Make we now this feast; What cheer?; In honour of the City of London; Jubilate Deo; Where does the uttered music go?

⊕ *** Chan. 8998. (i) Bach Ch.; Philh. O, Willcocks

Sir David Willcocks conducts performances of the two *Coronation Marches* full of panache, with the brass superbly articulated and inner detail well caught. Also the *March for the History of the English-speaking Peoples.* The *a cappella* choral items are very well done too. With the original organ parts orchestrated, the *Jubilate* and *Antiphon* gain greatly from having full instrumental accompaniment. The brief fanfares, never previously recorded, are a welcome makeweight, with the *Anniversary Fanfare*, designed to lead directly into *Orb and Sceptre*, which is what it does here.

5 Bagatelles for Guitar & Chamber Orchestra

*** Chan. 9963. Ogden, N. Sinf. Hickox – ARNOLD: *Guitar Concerto; Serenade*; L. BERKELEY: *Guitar Concerto* ***

It was the bright idea of Patrick Russ to mix together the set of *Five Bagatelles for Solo Guitar* which Walton wrote for Julian Bream and his very last work, *Varii capricci*, a brilliant orchestration of those same five pieces. The result is a *Guitar Concerto* which in many ways – rather surprisingly – transcends those two original sources, creating a work as effective as the fine *Guitar Concertos* of Sir Malcolm Arnold and Sir Lennox Berkeley. The composite work seems less lightweight than either the solo *Bagatelles* or *Varii capricci*, a genuine *Concerto* rather than a suite of miniatures. **Craig Ogden** is a brilliant, persuasive advocate, warmly supported by **Hickox** and the **Northern Sinfonia**.

(i) Capriccio burlesco; (ii; iii) Violin Concerto; (i) Johannesburg Festival Overture; (iv) Partita; Symphony 2; Variations on a Theme by Hindemith; (iii; v) Belshazzar's Feast

⊕ Ⓑ *** Sony (ADD) SB2K 89934 (2). (i) NYPO, Kostelanetz; (ii) Francescatti; (iii) Phd. O, Ormandy; (iv) Cleveland O, Szell; (v) with Cassel, Rutgers University Ch.

Sony's celebration for the Walton Centenary in 2002 brings together an outstanding batch of high-powered American performances such as no other British composer has ever received. The three performances with **Szell** and the **Cleveland Orchestra** of the *Symphony 2*, the *Hindemith Variations* and the *Partita* are all stunning in every way, not just brilliant and powerful but passionately intense too. **Ormandy** is a warmly persuasive conductor with the **Philadelphia Orchestra** in both *Belshazzar's Feast* (with the **Rutgers University Choir** and baritone soloist, **Walter Cassel**) and in the *Violin Concerto*, with **Zino Francescatti** the flamboyant soloist. **Andre Kostalanetz** conducts the **New York Philharmonic** in comparably brilliant performances both of the *Johannesburg Festival Overture* and the work he was the first to conduct, the *Capriccio burlesco*, a comedy overture in all but name.

Capriccio burlesco; The First Shoot (orch. Palmer); Granada (prelude for orchestra); Johannesburg Festival Overture; Music for Children Galop Finale (orch. Palmer); Portsmouth Point Overture; Prologo e fantasia; Scapino

*** Chan. 8968. LPO, Thomson

The *Capriccio burlesco* is ravishingly orchestrated, with some apt echoes of Gershwin, and the *Prologo e fantasia* completes an American group. The *Granada Prelude*, written for the television company, taps Walton's patriotic march vein in a jaunty way. *The First Shoot* comes in Christopher Palmer's brilliant orchestration of the brass band suite. The opening *Giocoso* is a rerun of *Old Sir Faulk*, and the other movements bring more echoes of *Façade*. As for the other novelty, the ten brief movements of *Music for Children* are here supplemented by a *Galop Final*. Palmer has here orchestrated the piano score. Though the opulent Chandos recording tends to take some of the bite away from Walton's jazzily accented writing, the richness of the orchestral sound is consistently satisfying.

(i) *Capriccio burlesco*; (ii) *Music for Children*; *Portsmouth Point Overture*; (i) *The Quest* (ballet suite); *Scapino Overture*; (ii) *Siesta*; (i; iii) *Sinfonia concertante*

⊕–*** Lyrita (ADD) SRCD 224. (i) LSO; (ii) LPO; (iii) with Katin; cond. composer

When **Walton** made these recordings, he was in his late sixties, and his speeds had grown a degree slower and safer. *Portsmouth Point* loses some of its fizz at so moderate a speed. By contrast, *Scapino* suffers hardly at all from the slower speed; rather the opposite, with the opening (if anything) even jauntier and the big cello melody drawn out more expressively. *Siesta* too brings out the piece's romantically lyrical side, rather than making it a relatively cool intermezzo. The *Capriccio burlesco* and the ten little pieces of the *Music for Children* are delightful too, with the subtleties of the instrumentation beautifully brought out. Much the biggest work here is the *Sinfonia concertante*, and in the outer movements the performance lacks the thrust that Walton himself gave it in his very first, wartime recording, in which Phyllis Sellick was a scintillating soloist. Yet **Peter Katin** is a very responsive soloist too, and the central slow movement is much warmer and more passionate, with orchestral detail rather clearer. It is good too to have the first stereo recording of the suite from Walton's wartime ballet based on Spenser's 'Faerie Queene', *The Quest*, only a fraction of the whole but bright and colourful.

(i) *Cello Concerto*; (ii) *Viola Concerto*; (iii) *Violin Concerto*; *Scapino*; *Coronation Marches: Crown Imperial*; *Orb and Sceptre*; *Façade Suites 1 & 2*; *Henry V: Suite*; *Symphonies 1 & 2*; *Variations on a Theme of Hindemith*; (iv) *Coronation Te Deum*; *Belshazzar's Feast*

⊕–Ⓜ**** Decca 470 508-2 (4). (i) Cohen; (ii) Neubauer; (iii) Little, (iv) Terfel, L'inviti, Wayneflete Singers, Winchester Cathedral Ch.; Bournemouth Ch. & SO, Litton or Hill

Decca's four-disc Walton Edition offers consistently fine versions of all of the composer's most important orchestral works, some of them unsurpassed by rival versions, with **Andrew Litton** an idiomatic Waltonian with a natural feeling for the jazzy syncopations. This brings together the three Litton discs previously issued by Decca but with important additions. The third of the four discs, never originally issued with the others, contains outstanding versions of the *Viola Concerto* and *Hindemith Variations*, plus the two *Façade Suites*.

Where most latter-day interpreters of the *Viola Concerto* have taken a very expansive view of the lyrical first movement, *Andante comodo*, **Paul Neubauer** comes nearer than anyone to following the example of the original interpreters on disc, Frederick Riddle and William Primrose, in adopting a flowing tempo, encouraged by the composer. It makes Neubauer's and Litton's far more persuasive than other modern versions with no expressive self-indulgence, and

with the brisker passages in this movement also taken faster than has become usual. Neubauer's tone is taut and firm to match, clean rather than fruity, with the central Scherzo taken excitingly fast. He then relaxes beautifully for the hauntingly lovely epilogue, ending on a whispered pianissimo. Litton also encourages wide dynamic contrasts, with the big tuttis bringing an element of wildness in brassy syncopations.

The *Hindemith Variations* also delivers a performance with contrasts heightened, not just of dynamic but of speed, extreme in both directions. This goes with an exceptional transparency in the orchestral textures, well-caught in the recording and bringing out the refinement of Walton's orchestration. *Façade*, predictably, is a fun performance, although the warm acoustic runs the danger of taking some edge off these witty parodies.

Two of the other discs are the same as before, with **Tasmin Little's** heartfelt reading of the *Violin Concerto* very well coupled with Litton's outstanding account of the *Second Symphony* and *Scapino*, and **Robert Cohen's** thoughtful reading of the *Cello Concerto* in coupling with the *First Symphony*. Litton's powerful account of *Belshazzar's Feast* with **Bryn Terfel** as the most dramatic of baritone soloists, brings fresh, cleanly focused choral sound that, with the help of keenly atmospheric recording, points up more clearly than usual the terracing between the different groupings of voices. This disc also includes the two coronation marches, the *Coronation Te Deum* and the *Henry V Suite*, with **David Hill**, chorus-master in *Belshazzar*, ably standing in for Litton in *Orb and Sceptre* and the *Te Deum*.

Cello Concerto (DVD version)

⊕–*** EMI **DVD** 492840-9. Piatigorsky, BBC SO, Sargent – MENDELSSOHN: *Violin Concerto* **; BEETHOVEN: *Piano Concerto 4* **(*)

Walton's *Cello Concerto* was commissioned by **Piatigorsky**, who subsequently premièred and recorded it with the Boston Symphony and Charles Munch (see below). This was its British première, at the Royal Albert Hall in February 1957 with **Sir Malcolm Sargent** conducting the **BBC Symphony Orchestra**, whose chief conductor he still was. Those who remember hearing the broadcast or who were fortunate enough to have been there will find Piatigorsky's aristocratic account a particularly moving document; and those coming to it without any nostalgic baggage can hardly fail to respond to his blend of virtuosity and restraint. The camerawork is pleasingly restrained and totally free from the intrusive changes of perspective that are inescapable nowadays.

Cello Concerto (CD versions)

⊕–Ⓜ**** RCA **SACD** 82876 66375-2. Piatigorsky, Boston SO, Munch – DVOŘÁK: *Concerto* ***

Ⓜ*** Sony SMK 89712. Ma, LSO, Previn – ELGAR: *Cello Concerto* ***

ⒷⒷ*** RCA Navigator (ADD) 74321 29248-2. Piatigorsky, Boston SO, Munch – VAUGHAN WILLIAMS: *Sinfonia Antartica* ***

(i; ii) *Cello Concerto*; (ii) *Improvisations on an Impromptu of Benjamin Britten*; *Partita for Orchestra*; (i) *Passacaglia for Solo Cello*

*** Chan. 8959. (i) Wallfisch; (ii) LPO, Thomson

On SACD **Piatigorsky** plays the *Cello Concerto* with a gripping combination of full-blooded eloquence and subtlety of feeling, readily capturing the bitter-sweet melancholy of its flowing lyrical lines. The closing pages of the final variations are particularly haunting. **Munch** provides a totally understanding accompaniment, with the strings of the **Boston Symphony** finding the lyrical ecstasy which is such a distinctive part of this concerto. The 1957 recording is close, but the improvement in sound on the new SACD is astonishing, the cello-tone full and the ambience of the Boston hall adding a warmth and resonance to the orchestra. This is an indispensable performance, and the Dvořák *Concerto* is also highly attractive. Those preferring other couplings will find the CD transfers also comparably improved, and they can choose between either the Vaughan Williams *Sinfonia Antartica* on RCA's budget label or, more suitably, the excellent complete collection of Walton's concertante music on the RCA Double below, which includes also Previn's outstanding account of the *First Symphony*.

Yo-Yo Ma and **Previn** give a sensuously beautiful performance. With speeds markedly slower than usual in the outer movements, the meditation is intensified to bring a mood of ecstasy, quite distinct from other Walton, with the central *Allegro* becoming the symphonic kernel of the work, far more than just a *Scherzo*. In the excellent CBS recording, the soloist is less forward and more faithfully balanced than is common.

With his rich, even tone, **Wallfisch** is just as warm and purposeful in the solo *Passacaglia* as in the *Concerto*, while **Thomson** relishes the vivid orchestral colours in both the *Improvisations*, here wider ranging in expression than usual, and the brilliant *Partita*. Excellent Chandos sound.

(i) *Cello Concerto*; (ii; iii) *Viola Concerto*; (iv) *Violin Concerto*; (v) *Sinfonia concertante*; (iii) *Symphony* 1

⊙━ ✿ Ⓑ **** RCA Double mono/stereo 74321 92575-2 (2). (i) Piatigorsky, Boston SO, Munch; (ii) Bashmet; (iii) LSO, Previn; (iv) Heifetz, Philh. O, composer; (v) Stott, RPO, Handley

The RCA two-disc collection includes the première recording of the *Cello Concerto* with **Piatigorsky**. Similarly, **Heifetz** as the virtuoso who commissioned the *Violin Concerto* remains in his way supreme as an interpreter, urgent beyond any rival, here with the composer conducting the **Philharmonia Orchestra**. The 1950 mono recording has been opened up to put more air round the sound.

The other two concertante works come in modern digital versions – **Kathryn Stott**, in a recording made for Conifer, performs the original, more elaborate version of the *Sinfonia concertante*, and **Yuri Bashmet** brings his yearningly Slavonic temperament and masterly virtuosity to the *Viola Concerto* – see under its alternative coupling below.

Bashmet's partners are the ideal combination of **Previn** and the **LSO**, and it is Previn's vintage version of the *First*

Symphony with the LSO of an earlier generation that sets the seal on the whole package, a reading that has never been matched, let alone surpassed. What is also remarkable here is the clarity, definition and sense of presence of the 1966 recording, with the stereo spectrum even more sharply focused than in the later digital recordings.

(i) *Cello Concerto*; (ii) *Violin Concerto in B min.*

⊙━ ⒝⒝ *** Naxos 8.554325. (i) Hugh; (ii) Kang; E. N. Philh. O, Daniel

In many ways **Tim Hugh's** reading of the *Cello Concerto* is the most searching yet. He finds an intense thoughtfulness, a sense of mystery, of inner meditation in the great lyrical ideas of all three movements, daring to play with a more extreme *pianissimo* than any rival. The bravura writing finds him equally concentrated, always sounding strong and spontaneous in face of any technical challenge. As in their previous Walton recordings, **Paul Daniel** and the **English Northern Philharmonia** equally play with flair and sympathy, so that the all-important syncopations always sound idiomatic, even if the strings lack a little in weight. In the *Violin Concerto* **Dong-Suk Kang** here follows up the success of his Naxos recording of the Elgar *Violin Concerto*, playing immaculately with a fresh, clean-cut tone, pure and true above the stave.

(i; ii) *Cello Concerto*; (iii) *Façade Suites* (excerpts): *Old Sir Faulk*; *Popular Song*; *Tango-pasodoble*; *Tarantella Sevillana*; (ii) *Variations on a Theme on Hindemith*; (iv) *Coronation Te Deum*; (iv; v) *The Twelve*

(***) BBC mono/stereo BBCL 4098-2. (i) Fournier, (ii) RPO; (iii) BBC SO; (iv) LPO Ch., LPO, (v) with Dowdall, Minty, Tear, Wakeham; composer

This BBC Legends disc is especially valuable in giving us the composer's recordings of live performances of works which Walton did not otherwise record in the studio, filling in important gaps. It is good too to have a mono recording of **Pierre Fournier** as soloist in a 1959 Edinburgh Festival performance of the *Cello Concerto*, a work he did not otherwise record. Though sadly in the opening section he has an uncharacteristic lapse in intonation, it is a fine reading, sensitive and brilliant, shaving over two minutes off the regular timing, making it a much tauter conclusion. The *Hindemith Variations*, also with the **RPO**, come from a Festival Hall performance of 1963, antedating George Szell's studio recording. **Walton's** own reading has a keener sense of fun in scherzando variations, and is a degree more warmly expressive in lyrical passages, even if the ensemble is not quite so polished. The four favourite movements from *Façade* come from a Prom at the Royal Albert Hall in 1968, and also surprisingly are mono recordings, but show Walton as a supreme master of witty pointing, bringing out the fun of these delectable parodies. The *Coronation Te Deum* was, of course, written for the Abbey, and is made all the more ripely dramatic with antiphonal brass. Yet best of all is *The Twelve*, which in its usual form with organ accompaniment can sound bitty, whereas here with massive forces this 'Anthem for the Feast of Any Apostle' to words by Auden relates directly to the major Walton choral works including *Belshazzar*, weighty and dramatic.

Viola Concerto (original version)

*** Hyp. CDA 67587. Power, BBC Scottish SO, Volkov –
RUBBRA: *Viola Concerto* ***

In 1961 Walton revised the *Viola Concerto* of 1928–9, reducing the triple wind to double wind, two trumpets and added a harp. It is this version that has gained wide currency both on CD and in the concert hall. **Lawrence Power** has made a name for himself as a distinguished soloist and as a member of the Nash Ensemble and the Leopold Trio. He gives a masterly account of the *Concerto* which in some ways is fresher and more characterful in its 1929 version.

Viola Concerto

⊕┯ **** ASV CD DCA 1181. Callus, New Zealand SO, Taddei
(with YORK BOWEN: *Viola Concerto*; HOWELLS: *Elegy*;
VAUGHAN WILLIAMS: *Suite for Viola* (***))

*** RCA 09026 63292-2. Bashmet, LSO, Previn – BRUCH:
Concerto for Violin & Viola; Kol Nidrei; Romance ***

Ⓜ *** EMI 2-28525-2. Vengerov, LSO, Rostropovich –
BRITTEN: *Violin Concerto* ***

Helen Callus, British-born but nowadays based in America, gives the most beautiful account of the Walton *Viola Concerto* on disc. With sumptuous viola tone and flawless intonation, she discovers a hushed beauty in those passages which find mystery in half-tones, as in the link leading to the reprise in the first movement and, above all, in the haunting epilogue, which she takes expansively, with the music fading to nothingness. Add to that the incisiveness of her playing – and that of the orchestra in excellent form – in Walton's characteristically syncopated writing, helped by a recording which allows the fullest dynamic range to be appreciated, with the soloist very well balanced, not too close. The result is an account to match and outshine any that have appeared in many years.

Yuri Bashmet with his opulent viola tone warmly relishes the ripe romanticism of the Walton *Concerto* as well as the high-voltage electricity of its jazz-based writing. Like other latterday interpreters he opts for a daringly spacious speed for the haunting opening melody, but avoids any hint of sluggishness, relishing the bravura of the contrasting sections. The central Scherzo brings a dazzling display, with the fun of the scherzando passages winningly brought out, as it is too in the finale. Bashmet ends with another daringly slow speed for the wistful epilogue, again superbly sustained, thanks also to the ideal accompaniment of **Previn** and the **LSO**. First-rate sound.

Playing the viola for the very first time, Vengerov shows himself the complete master technically, so that the very measured speed for the first movement has a purity and rapt intensity that removes any feeling of self-indulgence. After the dazzling Scherzo, Vengerov, with Rostropovich's encouragement, changes the whole character of the finale with his consistently slow speeds. Its jaunty opening theme on the bassoon is made to sound like a cakewalk from *Façade*, while the tender recollections of the epilogue are hypnotically dreamlike, with the timing for that movement alone no less than six minutes longer than in early recordings from Riddle and Primrose. Hardly a definitive reading but a magical one that demands to be heard, not just by devotees of the composer.

Viola Concerto; Violin Concerto

⊕┯ Ⓜ **** EMI 5 62813-2. Kennedy, RPO, Previn – VAUGHAN
WILLIAMS: *The Lark Ascending* ***

(i) Viola Concerto in A min.; (ii) Violin Concerto in B min.; (iii) Sinfonia concertante

Ⓜ (**(*)) Avid mono AMSC 604. (i) Primrose; (ii) Heifetz;
Cincinnati SO, Goosens; (iii) Sellick, CBSO, Composer

Kennedy's achievement in giving equally rich and expressive performances of both works makes for an ideal coupling, helped by the unique insight of **André Previn** as Waltonian. Kennedy on the viola produces tone as rich and firm as on his usual violin. The Scherzo has never been recorded with more panache than here, and the finale brings a magic moment in the return of the main theme from the opening, hushed and intense. In the *Violin Concerto* too, Kennedy gives a warmly relaxed reading, in which he dashes off the bravura passages with great flair. There are few Walton records as richly rewarding as this, helped by warm, atmospheric sound.

In many ways, **Heifetz's** pioneering wartime version of the *Violin Concerto*, recorded in Cincinnati in 1941 at speeds far faster than we are used to now, has never been surpassed – even finer than his later remake with Walton and the Philharmonia, more fiery, with even more flair and spontaneity. This account of the *Viola Concerto* was the first of two which **Primrose** recorded, markedly cooler than the première recording on Decca, with the young Frederick Riddle accompanied by Walton and the LSO. The central Scherzo is taken at an astonishingly fast speed, on the verge of sounding breathless. By contrast, the première recording of the *Sinfonia concertante* with **Phyllis Sellick** is exceptionally warm and expressive, an interpretation never quite matched since. Despite the rough Avid transfers, such historic performances offered in a coupling on a bargain disc are self-recommending.

(i) Viola Concerto; Johannesburg Festival Overture; Symphony 2

⊕┯ (BB) *** Naxos 8.553402. (i) Tomter; E. N. Philh. O, Daniel

Though **Tomter's** tight vibrato is at times prominent, he brings out the tender poetry of this most elusive of Walton's string *Concertos*, with its mixture of melancholy and wit. More than others, Tomter observes *pianissimo* markings, and rightly he adopts a flowing speed for the first movement while refusing to be rushed in the Scherzo and finale, which with delectable pointing acquire extra scherzando sparkle. The *Overture* is given the most exuberant performance, rivalling the composer's own, with the orchestra's soloists playing brilliantly. In *Symphony 2* **Paul Daniel** gives extra transparency to the often heavy orchestration, making the work less weighty than usual but just as warmly expressive. A superb bargain.

Violin Concerto

⊶ ❀ **** Onyx 4016. Ehnes, Vancouver SO, Tovey – BARBER; KORNGOLD: *Violin Concertos* *** ❀

Ⓜ *** Decca 475 7710 – Bell, Baltimore SO, Zinman – BLOCH: *Baal Shem*; BARBER: *Violin Concerto* ***

(***) Biddulph mono WHL 016. Heifetz, Cincinnati SO, Goossens – VAUGHAN WILLIAMS: *A London Symphony* (2) (***) (with Concert (***))

ⒷⒷ (***) Naxos mono (ADD) 8.110939. Heifetz, Cincinnati SO, Goossens – ELGAR: *Violin Concerto* (***)

(*) Classico CLASSCD 233. Azizjan, Copenhagen PO, Bellincamp – BRITTEN: *Violin Concerto* *

In this inspired and generous coupling, **James Ehnes** gives a superb account of the Walton *Concerto*. He sets his seal on his performance from the magical opening bars onwards, played exquisitely by soloist and orchestra alike, and all the way through the work brings out its full emotional thrust without vulgarity or exaggeration. Unlike most latter-day interpreters, Ehnes has taken note of the example of the work's commissioner and dedicatee, Jascha Heifetz. Where latterly the work has generally spread to well over half an hour, Ehnes takes exactly 30 minutes, and the result again is all the stronger. He is helped by the powerful playing of the **Vancouver Symphony Orchestra** under its music-director, **Bramwell Tovey**. An outstanding disc in every way.

This prize-winning Decca disc has **Bell** giving a commanding account of the solo part of Walton's *Concerto*, even matching Heifetz himself in the ease of his virtuosity, and playing with rapt intensity. Rich and brilliant sound.

Jascha Heifetz made the very first recording in 1941 with **Eugene Goossens** and the **Cincinnati Orchestra**, and it has never quite been matched since for its passionate urgency as well as its brilliance. Speeds are much faster than has latterly become the norm, but the romantic warmth of the work has never been more richly conveyed. On Biddulph in an excellent CD transfer it is coupled with the early recording of the original score of Vaughan Williams's *London Symphony*, plus other British music.

The alternative Naxos transfer, less bright than RCA's original, is well balanced, making for comfortable listening. The generous Elgar coupling confirms this as in every way a winner.

Sergej Azizjan, the Leningrad-trained concertmaster of the **Copenhagen Philharmonic**, has a superb technique, marked by flawless intonation and a wide tonal range. His reading of the Walton is passionate in an aptly extrovert way, though the orchestra is a degree recessed, and such passages as the rhythmic opening of the Walton finale lack something in bite.

Coronation March: Orb and Sceptre; (i) Coronation Te Deum; Jubilee Deo; A Litany; Set me as a seal upon thine heart

**(*) Australian Decca Eloquence 467 613-2. Bournemouth

SO, Hill; (i) with Winchester Cathedral Ch., Waynefleet Singers – VAUGHAN WILLIAMS: *Benedicite*, etc. **(*)

A swaggering vivacious *Orb and Sceptre* is marred by a rather over-reverberant acoustic, though the effect is certainly exciting. The choral items are sympathetically sung, and the *Coronation Te Deum* is gutsy, with the recording surprisingly well managed in the resonance.

Façade (an entertainment; complete)

⊶ *** Hyp. CDA 67239. Bron, Stilgoe, Nash Ens., Lloyd-Jones – LAMBERT: *Salome: suite* ***

(i) Façade (complete); (ii) Film Music: Henry V; (iii) Orb & Sceptre (Coronation March)

ⒷⒷ (**(*)) Regis Alto mono ALC 1026. (i) Sitwell, Pears, English Opera Group Ens., Collins; (ii) Olivier, Philh. Ch. & O, composer; (iii) LSO, Sargent

Façade (complete; including Façade 2)

**(*) ASV CDDCA 679. Scales, West, L. Mozart Players (members), Glover

**(*) Chan. 8869. Walton, Baker, City of L. Sinfonia (members), Hickox

Façade (complete; including Façade 2) & Other Edith Sitwell Poems

*** Ara. Z 6699. Redgrave, Chamber Music Society of Lincoln Center, Shifrin

Regis/Alto have coupled the famous complete *Façade* (from Decca) with the *Henry V* music (from EMI) and added a rather straightforward account of the *Orb and Sceptre March* from **Sargent**. The transfers are good but not quite as vivid as the originals.

The Hyperion issue provides the printed texts of the poems for which the music is lost, leaving room for the newly discovered Lambert music for *Salome* as an attractive makeweight. **Eleanor Bron** and **Richard Stilgoe** make an excellent pair of reciters, and the recording in a natural acoustic balances them well – not too close – with no discrepancy between voices and instruments. They inflect the words more than Edith Sitwell and early interpreters did, but still keep a stylized manner, meticulously obeying the rhythms specified in the score, with Stilgoe phenomenally fluent, while Bron in slow poems adopts an effective trance-like manner. Under **David Lloyd-Jones** the brilliant sextet of players from the **Nash Ensemble**, including **John Wallace** on trumpet and **Richard Hosford** on clarinet, could not be more idiomatic, with rhythms delectably pointed.

With **Lyn Redgrave** an excellent reciter, characterful and sharply rhythmic, the ensemble from **Lincoln Center** under **Joseph Silverstein** give a virtuoso performance of the quirky score, both crisply disciplined and idiomatic. Some may feel that Redgrave overdoes the characterizations, but she gets a very acceptable balance between expressive word-pointing and formality, characterizing precisely in different, stylized accents, as in the Noël Coward accent she adopts for the *Tango* and *Popular Song*.

Scales and **West** as a husband-and-wife team are inventive in their shared roles, and generally it works well. *Scotch Rhapsody* is hilariously done as a duet, with West intervening at appropriate moments, and with sharply precise Scots accents. Regional accents may defy Edith Sitwell's original prescription – and her own example – but here, with one exception, they add an appropriate flavour. The exception is *Popular Song,* where **Prunella Scales's** cockney accent is quite alien to the allusive words, with their 'cupolas, gables in the lakes, Georgian stables'. For fill-up the reciters have recorded more Sitwell poems, but unaccompanied.

Susana Walton, widow of the composer, makes a bitingly characterful reciter, matching with her distinctive accent – she was born in Argentina – the exotic character of many numbers. **Richard Baker**, phenomenally precise and agile in enunciating the Sitwell poems, makes the perfect foil, and **Hickox** secures colourful and lively playing from members of the **City of London Sinfonia**, who relish in particular the jazzy inflexions. *Façade* 2 consists of a number of Sitwell settings beyond the definitive series of twenty-one. All of them are fun and make an apt if not very generous coupling for the regular sequence. Warm sound, a little too reverberant for so intimate a work.

Façade: Suites 1–3; Overture Portsmouth Point (arr. Lambert); *Siesta;* (i) *Sinfonia concertante.* WALTON/ARNOLD: *Popular Birthday*

*** Chan. 9148. (i) Parkin; LPO, Latham-Koenig or Thomson

The *Sinfonia concertante,* with its sharply memorable ideas in each movement and characteristically high voltage, has never had the attention it deserves. **Eric Parkin** as soloist is perfectly attuned to the idiom, warmly melodic as well as jazzily syncopated, making this a most sympathetic account, even if the *Maestoso* introduction is hardly grand enough. The recording sets the piano a little more backwardly, no doubt to reflect the idea that this is not a full concerto. **Jan Latham-Koenig** gives the witty *Façade* movements just the degree of jazzy freedom they need. The third suite, devised and arranged by Christopher Palmer, draws on three apt movements from the *Façade* entertainment, ending riotously with the rag-music of *Something Lies Beyond the Scene.* That is a first recording, and so is Constant Lambert's arrangement for small orchestra of the *Overture Portsmouth Point,* clearer than the original. *Siesta* is given an aptly cool performance under **Bryden Thomson**, and the *Popular Birthday* is Malcolm Arnold's fragmentary linking of 'Happy birthday to you' with the *Popular Song* from *Façade,* originally written for Walton's twentieth birthday.

Façade: Suites 1 & 2

🔑 (BB) **** Hyp. Helios CDH 55099. E. N. Philh. O, Lloyd-Jones – BLISS: *Checkmate* ***; LAMBERT: *Horoscope* ✿

Brilliantly witty and humorous performances of the two orchestral suites that Walton himself fashioned from his 'Entertainment'. This is music which, with its outrageous quotations, can make one chuckle out loud. Moreover it offers, to quote Constant Lambert, 'one good tune after another', all scored with wonderful felicity. The playing here could hardly be bettered, and the recording is in the demonstration bracket with its natural presence and bloom. A very real bargain.

FILM SCORES

As You Like It; Hamlet

(M) *** Chan. 10436X. Gielgud, Bott, ASMF, Marriner

Walton's score for *Hamlet,* thanks to the diligence of Christopher Palmer, offers some 40 minutes of music, a rich and colourful suite, superbly played and recorded, and much enhanced by the contribution of **Sir John Gielgud** in two of Shakespeare's sololiquies, 'O that this too, too solid flesh' and 'To be or not to be'. The selection of music from the pre-war film of *As You Like It* makes a valuable fill-up. It adds the splendid setting of *Under the greenwood tree* in a radiant performance by **Catherine Bott. Marriner** and the **Academy** draw out all the romantic warmth of both scores, and the sound is richly atmospheric to match.

As You Like It (poem for orchestra); *Hamlet* (Shakespeare scenario in 9 movements) (both arr. Palmer)

(BB) **(*) Naxos 8.553344. Sheen, Dublin RTE Concert O, Penny

In adaptations of film music for concert performance by the late Christopher Palmer, both **Penny** and the **RTE Concert Orchestra** give warm, sympathetic performances. **Michael Sheen** recites the Hamlet soliloquies with the ardour of youth, and the unnamed soprano soloist in the *As You Like It* song, *Under the greenwood tree,* sings with fresh, girlish tone. With recording a little recessed, and with thinnish strings, this cannot match the Chandos issue of the same coupling at full-price, but it makes a good bargain.

The Battle of Britain: Suite; Escape Me Never: Suite; The First of the Few: Spitfire Prelude & Fugue; Three Sisters; A Wartime Sketchbook

🔑 *** Chan. 8870. ASMF, Marriner

The Spitfire Prelude and Fugue, from *The First of the Few,* was immediately turned into a highly successful concert-piece, but we owe it to Christopher Palmer that there is the 'Wartime Sketchbook', drawing material from three of the wartime films, plus scraps that Colin Matthews did not use in the suite from the much later *Battle of Britain* film music and not least in the stirring theme from the credits of the film, *Went the Day Well.* The brief suite from the music for Olivier's film of Chekhov's *The Three Sisters,* from much later, brings more than one setting of the *Tsar's Hymn* and a charming imitation of *Swan Lake.* Earliest on the disc is *Escape Me Never,* the first of Walton's film scores, written in 1935 in a more popular idiom; but the war-inspired music is what this delightful disc is really about. **Marriner** and the **Academy** give richly idiomatic performances, full of panache. Aptly opulent recording.

Henry V: Suite (arr. Mathieson) (i) *Scenes from the Film; Richard III: Prelude & Suite; Spitfire Prelude & Fugue*

⌐─ Ⓜ *** EMI stereo/mono 5 65007-2. (i) Olivier (speaker); Philh. O, composer

This reissue includes the 1963 recordings of the *Henry V Suite*, *Richard III Prelude and Suite* and the *Spitfire Prelude and Fugue*. The performances are vital and exciting, and with the sound vivid and full the result is hugely enjoyable. Also included is the complete 1946 *Henry V* sequence with **Laurence Olivier**, as recorded on four 78s, and originally issued on LP by RCA with seven minutes of cuts. This is the restored complete version, and it has been excellently transferred, though the mono sound lacks body. The recording has great atmosphere though, with Olivier at his magnificent best, and the orchestra responding with tremendous energy: the sound of the arrows at the climax of the Agincourt sequence has never seemed more chilling. A wonderful CD.

Henry V: A Shakespeare Scenario (arr. Palmer)

Ⓜ *** Chan. 10437X. Plummer (nar.), Westminster Cathedral Ch., ASMF, Marriner

Few film scores can match Walton's for the Olivier film of *Henry V* in its range and imagination, the whole of the 'Scenario' devised by Christopher Palmer lasting just over an hour. The most controversial change is to 'borrow' the first section of the march that Walton wrote much later for a projected television series on Churchill's *History of the English-Speaking Peoples*; otherwise, the chorus's call to arms, *Now all the youth of England is on fire*, would have had no music to introduce it. As an appendix, three short pieces are included which Walton quoted in his score. **Sir Neville Marriner** caps even his previous recordings in this series, with the **Academy** and **Westminster Choir** producing heartfelt playing and singing in sumptuous sound. As narrator, **Christopher Plummer** makes an excellent substitute for Olivier, unselfconsciously adopting a comparably grand style.

Henry V (filmscore)

(**(*)) Carlton **DVD** 37115 00193. Olivier, Newton, Banks, Asherson, LSO, Mathieson (Director: Laurence Olivier)

Walton's music for **Laurence Olivier's** film of *Henry V* has never been surpassed in the way it adds so vividly both to the dramatic impact and to the atmospheric beauty. The very opening, with a play-bill fluttering to a flute figure and a panoramic view of Elizabethan London to a haunting off-stage chorus, sets the pattern even before the drama starts. Although the sound from a mono soundtrack is necessarily limited, it has been beautifully cleaned up for DVD, so that such effects are vividly atmospheric, giving a satisfying sense of space.

Much of Walton's music is well known in concert form, but the film brings home just how much more there is than that and how it is even more effective in its original context. Even the Agincourt charge music, a uniquely effective set-piece, is more effective still when seen as well as heard.

Olivier's concept, with the film moving from the Globe Theatre at the start to an idealized setting in France, with medieval false perspectives, remains masterly. An extraordinarily starry line-up of leading British actors of the time

brings a whole gallery of characterful portrayals, not least from Olivier himself, unforgettable in the title-role.

Macbeth: Fanfare & March; Major Barbara (suite); Richard III (Shakespeare scenario)

Ⓜ *** Chan. 10435X. Gielgud (nar.), ASMF, Marriner

Disappointingly, **Sir John Gielgud** underplays Richard III's great 'Now is the winter of our discontent' speech, but working to the underlying music – much of it eliminated in the film – may have cramped his style. The performance generally has all the panache one could wish for, leading up to the return of the grand Henry Tudor theme at the end. The six-minute piece based on Walton's music for Gielgud's wartime production of *Macbeth* is much rarer and very valuable too, anticipating in its Elizabethan dance-music the *Henry V* film-score. *Major Barbara* also brings vintage Walton material. **Marriner** and the **Academy** give performances just as ripely committed as in their previous discs in the series, helped by sonorous Chandos sound.

The Quest (ballet; complete); The Wise Virgins (ballet; suite)

*** Chan. 8871. LPO, Thomson

The Quest (ballet; complete; original score); The Wise Virgins (ballet; suite); Siesta

⌐─ ⒝⒝ **** Naxos 8.555868. E. N. Philh. O, Lloyd-Jones

In 1943, at the height of the war, Walton was commissioned to write a full-length ballet for the Sadler's Wells Company to the choreography of Frederick Ashton. The 40-minute score of *The Quest* had to be completed while Ashton was on five weeks' leave from the RAF, forcing Walton to abandon his usual meticulous mode of working. Despite a starry cast the ballet was a failure, largely because of the confusing allegorical plot derived from Spenser's *Faerie Queene* about St George fighting the forces of evil. What **Lloyd-Jones** has done with this fine Naxos version is to go back to Walton's original score with only a modest expansion of forces, and the result in his brilliant performance, helped by refined recording, is greater transparency. Far from seeming thin the impact is sharper than in the earlier, more opulent version. This is vintage Walton, consistently fresh, defying any unevenness of invention, culminating in a radiant *Passacaglia*. One hopes the success of the disc will encourage the revival of the original ballet with its Piper sets.

Like Thomson, **Lloyd-Jones** couples *The Quest* with the suite from a ballet that Walton wrote earlier in the war, *The Wise Virgins*, orchestrating movements from Bach cantatas, including *Sheep may Safely Graze*. Again Lloyd-Jones's performance, at faster speeds, more effectively brings out the sharpness of orchestration which, so far from being inflated, gives off electric sparks. The brief interlude for strings, *Siesta*, one of Walton's earliest orchestral pieces, makes an attractive supplement.

Quite apart from the dramatic power of Thomson's performance, the recording is superb, among the fullest and clearest from Chandos. The sound for *The Wise Virgins* is more reverberant and the performance has less electricity, though Walton's distinctive arrangements of Bach cantata movements – including *Sheep may Safely Graze* – remain as fresh as ever.

The Wise Virgins (ballet; complete)

*** ASV CDDCA 1168. BBC Concert O, Wordsworth –
   LAMBERT: *Horoscope* ***

The Wise Virgins, using movements from Bach cantatas, was quickly dropped in the theatre, with the score of three of the movements lost or destroyed. Philip Lane has now re-orchestrated those three movements, using the original Bach scores, in a style near enough to Walton's sharply distinctive manner. Though the newly restored movements are not as striking as those we already know, **Barry Wordsworth's** warmly sympathetic readings make a strong case for the revival of the original ballets.

Sinfonia concertante for orchestra with piano (original version)

(N) (M) **** Dutton CDLX 7223 Stott, RPO, Handley –
   BRIDGE: *Phantasm*; IRELAND: *Piano Concerto* ****

Kathryn Stott, warmly and strongly accompanied by **Vernon Handley** and the **RPO**, gives an outstanding reading of the *Sinfonia concertante's* original version, and the result seems to strengthen what is a consistently memorable work, built from vintage Walton material. First-rate recorded sound, (originally on Conifer) and couplings that are both generous and apt, particularly the splendid version of the Ireland *Piano Concerto*.

(i) Sinfonia concertante; Spitfire Prelude & Fugue; Variations on a Theme of Hindemith; March: The History of the English-Speaking Peoples

⊕— (BB) **** Naxos 8.553869. (i) Donohoe; E. N. Philh., Daniel

Paul Daniel conducts the **English Northern Philharmonia** in electrifying performances of this varied group of orchestral works. As before he is splendid at interpreting Walton's jazzy syncopations with the right degree of freedom. Following the composer's own suggestion, the original version of the *Sinfonia concertante* is preferred to the revision, fuller and more brilliant. The performance is excellent, despite the placing of the soloist, **Peter Donohoe**, too far forward. Daniel draws playing both warm and scintillating from the orchestra in the *Hindemith Variations* – no finer version exists – while the *March* and the *Spitfire* music hit home all the harder through Daniel's refusal to dawdle.

Sonata for Strings

*** Channel Classics CCSSA 23005. Amsterdam Sinf. –
   BEETHOVEN: *String Quartet 16* ***

The Walton *Sonata for Strings*, an arrangement of his *A minor String Quartet* of 1945–7, has become a favourite work with this superb Dutch ensemble and was an automatic choice for a recording by them. So the reading is more intimate than most, sharp and incisive in the fast movements, but warmly lyrical too, with the heart of the performance coming in the lovely slow movement, which here matches the *Lento* slow movement of the Beethoven in its dedication, with one yearning melody after another.

Symphony 1 – see also Cello Concerto above

⊕— **** LSO Live **SACD** LSO 0576. LSO, C. Davis

(i) Symphony 1 in B flat min.; (ii) Belshazzar's Feast

(***) BBC mono/stereo BBCL 4097-2. (i) RPO; (ii) McIntyre, BBC Ch. & Choral Soc, Christchurch Harmonic Ch., BBC SO; composer

Symphony 1; Partita for Orchestra

⊕— (BB) *** Naxos 8.553180. E. N. PO, Daniel

Symphony 1; Overture Scapino; Siesta

(BB) *** Arte Nova 74321 39124-2. Gran Canaria PO, Leaper

Symphony 1; Varii capricci

*** Chan. 8862. LPO, Thomson

When towards the end of 2005 **Colin Davis** conducted this performance of Walton's *First Symphony* at the Barbican, it was greeted with ecstatic notices in the press, and rightly so. It was as though the critics involved had suddenly rediscovered this iconic work, reflecting the mood of uncertainty and tension of the 1930s. The clarity of the textures and the sharpness of the attack add to the impact, with Colin Davis plainly at ease with the jazz element. The finale again brings clarity in the contrapuntal writing of successive fugatos, leading to a ripe conclusion. This first SACD version finds a welcome place, even though the 40-year-old benchmark performance from the same orchestra under the youthful André Previn (see above under *Cello Concerto*) has a sharpness and bite marginally even greater.

   Though **Walton** recorded both these major works in the studio for EMI, these live radio recordings are invaluable in amplifying his interpretative ideas. Neither performance replaces the (deleted) studio version, when the sound in each is more limited, but the vitality of a live occasion in each case gives an extra dramatic thrust to the readings. The *First Symphony* was recorded in mono at the Usher Hall at the 1959 Edinburgh Festival, and inevitably suffers from the dryness of the acoustic, as well as from a restless audience. Speeds are a shade faster than in the studio, and the grinding dissonances at the climax of the slow movement bite even harder, while the elegiac trumpet solo just before the final coda in the finale is more tender as well as more spacious.

   Belshazzar's Feast comes in a stereo recording of 1965 from the Royal Festival Hall, with the chorus more backwardly balanced and less clear than in the studio version. One clear gain is the choice of soloist, with **Donald McIntyre** bitingly dramatic, and the points where the live account scores over the studio version include the description of the writing on the wall, more sinister in its pausefulness, and the lovely passage for semi-chorus in the finale, *The trumpeters and pipers are silent.*

   In the *First Symphony* **Paul Daniel** knows unerringly how to build up tension to breaking point before resolving it and then building again. He is also freer than many in his use of rubato, as well as in the degree of elbow-room he allows for jazzy syncopations, always idiomatic. The Scherzo is sparkily witty, not just full of malice. In the slow movement, after the poised opening, Daniel tends to press ahead slightly for the sections which follow, agonizingly intense. The finale with its brassy, more extrovert manner has plenty of panache, and the weight and bite of the sound are excellent. This is a version that vies with even the finest at whatever price, and it outshines most. Daniel's reading of the *Partita* brings out above all the work's joyfulness, with the outer movements relaxed in their brilliance and the central slow movement warmly expressive.

With finely disciplined playing, **Leaper's** reading is fresh and alert, idiomatic in its rhythmic pointing and with intense poetry in such key moments as the distant trumpet-call in the final coda. The slow movement brings inspired wind solos, and the Scherzo and finale are crisp and resilient, with busy ensembles made unusually clear, even transparent, a point that also marks Leaper's witty and sparkling account of the *Scapino Overture*, in which the cello solo is most beautifully done. *Siesta* is aptly dreamy, not literal or chilly, making this a disc to recommend to Waltonians and newcomers alike.

Thomson's is a warmly committed, understandingly idiomatic account of the work, weighty and rhythmically persuasive, if not as biting as some. The Chandos coupling brings the first recording of *Varii capricci*, the orchestral suite in five compact movements which Walton developed from his set of guitar *Bagatelles*, written for Julian Bream. With a brilliant performance and sumptuous sound, it makes a fine supplement.

Symphony 2

⊖—Ⓜ *** EMI (ADD) 5 86595-2. LSO, Previn – LAMBERT: *Piano Concerto, etc. ***

If Walton's *Second Symphony* prompted George Szell to direct the Cleveland Orchestra in one of its most spectacular performances on record (now deleted), **André Previn** and the **LSO** give another brilliant performance which in some ways gets closer to the heart of the music with its overtones of the composer's romantic opera, *Troilus and Cressida*. The 1973 Abbey Road recording is outstandingly fine and the coupling with Lambert could not be more imaginative.

CHAMBER MUSIC

(i) 5 Bagatelles for Solo Guitar; (ii; iii) Duets for Children; (iv; ii) 2 Pieces for Violin & Piano; Toccata for Violin & Piano; (ii) (Piano) Façade: Valse; (v; i) Anon in Love (for tenor & guitar); (v; ii) 2 Songs for Tenor: The Winds; The Tritons

*** Chan. 9292. (i) Bonell; (ii) Milne; (iii) Dowdeswell; (iv) Sillito; (v) Mark Ainsley

The *Toccata for Violin and Piano* is a curious mixture of cadenza and rhapsody of 15 minutes in a disconcertingly un-Waltonian style. Two songs for tenor are fascinating too, with a rushing accompaniment for *The Winds*, while *The Tritons* is chaconne-like, with a melody quite untypical of Walton.

Milne and **Dowdeswell** bring out what charming, sharply focused ideas are contained in the ten *Duets for Children*. The piano arrangement of the *Valse* from *Façade* is so thorny that even Hamish Milne has to go cautiously. The two violin pieces – using French troubadour songs – are spin-offs from the *Henry V* incidental music and, in the second, *Scherzetto*, reflect what their composer had learnt, writing for Heifetz. The two works with guitar are well known in Julian Bream's performances and recordings. **Bonell** is lighter and more delicate than Bream, both in the *Bagatelles* and in *Anon in Love*, but is no less persuasive. Similarly, **John Mark Ainsley** lacks some of the punch of **Peter Pears**, for whom the cycle was written, but in a gentler way taps the wit and point of these Elizabethan conceits. A delightful collection, full of revealing insights into the composer's complex character.

Passacaglia for Solo Cello

*** Chan. 8499. Wallfisch – BAX: *Rhapsodic Ballad*; BRIDGE: *Cello Sonata*; DELIUS: *Cello Sonata ***

William Walton's *Passacaglia* for solo cello was composed in the last year of his life. It has restraint and eloquence, and **Raphael Wallfisch** gives a thoroughly sympathetic account of it. Excellent recording.

Piano Quartet; Violin Sonata

*** Chan. 8999. Milne, Sillito, Smissen, Orton

Piano Quartet; String Quartet in A min.

⊖—ⒷⒷ **** Naxos 8.554646. (i) Donohoe; Maggini Qt

This performance of the *Piano Quartet* with **Hamish Milne** as pianist is music that instantly grabs the ear, with striking ideas attractively and dramatically presented in each movement. The two principal performers from the Quartet make a warmly sympathetic rather than high-powered duo for the *Violin Sonata* of 1949. Yet the combination of **Sillito's** ripely persuasive style and Milne's incisive power, clarifying textures and giving magic to the phrasing, keeps tensions sharp. The satisfyingly full sound helps too.

The young players of the **Maggini Quartet** give performances both refined and powerful of both works. The opening of the 1947 *String Quartet* is presented in hushed intimacy, making the contrast all the greater when Walton's richly lyrical writing emerges in full power. There is a tender, wistful quality here, which culminates in a rapt, intense account of the slow movement. The poignancy of those two longer movements is then set against the clean bite of the second movement Scherzo and the brief hectic finale, with textures clear and transparent. With **Peter Donohoe** a powerful, incisive pianist, the early *Piano Quartet* is also given a performance of high contrasts. First-rate recording, even if the piano is a shade too forwardly balanced.

String Quartet in A min.

*** Hyp. CDA 66718. Coull Qt – BRIDGE: *3 Idylls ***; ELGAR: *Quartet **(*)

ⒷⒷ *** Regis RRC 1015. Britten Qt – ELGAR: *Quartet*

✿ (***) Testament mono SBT 1052. Hollywood Qt – HINDEMITH: *Quartet 3*; PROKOFIEV: *Quartet 2* (***) ✿

String Quartet in A min; String Quartet 1

⊕ *** Chan. 8944. Gabrieli Qt

*** Black Box BBM 1035. Emperor Qt

Coupled ideally on Chandos with the mature *String Quartet in A minor*, completed in 1946, is the atonal *First Quartet*, long thought to be lost, which Walton wrote when an undergraduate at Oxford. The result, edited by Christopher Palmer, is hardly recognizable as Walton at all but is full of fire and imagination, while the fugue of the finale seeks to emulate Beethoven's *Grosse Fuge* in its complexity and massive scale, alone lasting almost 16 minutes. The **Gabrieli** performance brings out all the latent power and lyrical warmth, often implying an underlying anger. It provides a fascinating contrast with the highly civilized *A minor* work of 25 years later. That comes in a red-blooded Gabrieli recording of 1986. Both recordings were made in the warm, rich acoustic of The Maltings, Snape, with little discrepancy between them.

The young members of the **Emperor Quartet** also give brilliant, incisive performances of both Walton's *String Quartets*. For the early work the Emperor Quartet have had access to extra material involving editing and cuts, observing those that plainly were the composer's own. In addition to those minor differences of text, the Emperor Quartet's speeds are consistently faster than those of the Gabrieli Quartet on the rival version in the Chandos Walton Edition, notably in the fugal finale of the 1922 work, which here more clearly echoes Beethoven's *Grosse Fuge*. Helped by drier recording, the attack is more biting too, the approach more direct, less warmly expressive.

The Elgar and Walton *Quartets* also makes an apt and attractive coupling, and here the **Coulls**, unlike their direct rivals, offer as bonus a fine example of Frank Bridge's quartet-writing. In the Walton, the reading captures movingly the spirit of Waltonian melancholy, bringing out the elegiac intensity of the extended *Lento* slow movement, taken at a very measured pace. The Coulls are splendid too in capturing the element of fun in Walton's scherzando ideas.

The **Britten Quartet**, bitingly powerful, bring out the emotional intensity of the *A minor*, playing with refinement and sharp focus, finding a repose and poise in the slow movement that bring it close to late Beethoven. The contrasts of wistful lyricism and scherzando bite in the first movement, and the incisiveness of Walton's jaggedly rhythmic writing is a delight.

In many ways the pioneering account by the **Hollywood Quartet**, made in 1950, has still not been surpassed. It first appeared on a Capitol LP in harness with the Villa-Lobos *Sixth Quartet*. The sound comes up very well, though it is not, of course, state of the art. Moreover, it comes with equally strong couplings and cannot be too strongly recommended.

Violin Sonata

⊕ *** Nim. NI 5666. Hope, Mulligan – ELGAR: *Violin Sonata*; FINZI: *Elegy* ***

(BB) **(*) ASV Resonance CD RSN 3060. McAslan, Blakely – ELGAR: *Violin Sonata* **(*)

(**(*)) Testament mono SBT 1319. Rostal, Horsley – DELIUS: *Violin Sonata 2*; ELGAR: *Violin Sonata in E min.* (**(*))

The warmth and thrust of Hope's performance brings out the purposefulness of the writing in a work that can seem wayward. So, with understanding support from his fellow Menuhin protégé, **Simon Mulligan**, Hope brings tautness to the wide-ranging variation movement that rounds off the two-movement structure. With Hope's sweet, finely focused violin tone beautifully caught in the Nimbus recording – full and warm but less reverberant than some – and well balanced against the piano, it makes an outstanding recommendation.

Lorraine McAslan gives a warmly committed performance of Walton's often wayward *Sonata*. The romantic melancholy of the piece suits her well and, though the recording does not make her tone as rounded as it should be, she produces some exquisite *pianissimo* playing. **John Blakely** is a most sympathetic partner, particularly impressive in crisply articulated passages. A disc that is worth its modest cost.

The Walton *Violin Sonata* was still only five years old when **Max Rostal** and **Colin Horsley** made their recording for the fledgling Argo company, with Rostal overcoming the problems of the dry acoustic, subtly shading his tone as in the haunting recollection of the main theme in the coda of the first movement. Rostal then holds the argument together tautly in the long set of variations that make up the second movement, playing with rapt concentration, not least in his warmly persuasive reading of the seventh and last variation, *Andante tranquillo*. The clarity of the clean, fresh Testament transfer quickly allows one to forget the sonic limitations.

CHORAL MUSIC

Antiphon; Cantico del sole; 4 Carols; Coronation Te Deum; Jubilate; A Litany (3 versions); Magnificat and Nunc dimittis; Missa brevis; A Queen's Fanfare; Set Me as a Seal; The Twelve; Where does the Uttered Music Go?

*** Hyp. CDA 67330. Polyphony, Wallace Collection, Layton; Vivian (organ)

The inclusion of the **Wallace Collection** in the ensemble brings an immediate advantage in the first choral item, the *Coronation Te Deum*, when the extra bite of brass adds greatly to the power of a piece originally designed for far bigger forces in Westminster Abbey. That is preceded dramatically by the *Fanfare for the Queen* from 1959, and the use of brass also adds to the impact of the final item, *Antiphon*, one of Walton's very last works, setting George Herbert's hymn, *Let All the World in Every Corner Sing*. The other big advantage of this new disc is that it offers three contrasted versions of *A Litany*, the motet setting of Phineas Fletcher, which Walton wrote at Christ Church in his early teens. The original, conceived in 1916 when the boy was only 14, was for four treble voices and pitched a minor third higher than the definitive version, while the second version, made in 1917, introduced a full range of voices and was pitched slightly lower. Also included here are the *Four Carols*, making this as comprehensive a collection of Walton's shorter choral pieces as could be imagined. The fine professional group, Polyphony, with sopranos very boyish, sound very like a cathedral choir, set in an ecclesiastical atmosphere, though the acoustic of Hereford Cathedral is rather washy, with balance favouring the organ and brass.

Antiphon; Cantico del sole; Coronation Te Deum; Jubilate Deo; Magnificat & Nunc dimittis; A Litany; Missa brevis; Set Me as a Seal Upon thine Heart; The Twelve; Where Does the Uttered Music Go? Organ solos: Henry V: Touch her Soft Lips and Part; Passacaglia: Death of Falstaff

⊗–ⓑ (BB) **** Naxos 8.555793. St John's College Ch., Robinson

This disc of Walton's church music and smaller choral pieces is another in Naxos's superb series of English choral music from **St John's College**, Cambridge. It gains over rival collections of these pieces not just in price, but in using boys' rather than women's voices. With Walton himself trained as a boy chorister at Christ Church Cathedral, Oxford, his writing gains positively from that brighter, fresher sound, not just in the liturgical pieces. Even the *Coronation Te Deum* of 1953, designed for a big choir on the grandest of ceremonial occasions, benefits from the extra sharpness of focus, revealing not just a brilliant compression of a long text, but a taut musical structure. The pieces stretch over the widest span of Walton's career, from the setting of Phineas Fletcher in *A Litany*, the amazing inspiration of a 14-year-old but, anticipating the mature Walton, to *Antiphon*, one of his last works, a stirring setting of George Herbert's hymn, *Let All the World in Every Corner Sing*.

Belshazzar's Feast

⊗–ⓡ (BB) **** Warner Apex 0927 44 394-2. Terfel, BBC Singers, BBC Ch. & SO, A. Davis – VAUGHAN WILLIAMS: *Job* ***

(B) ** CfP 2-CD (ADD) 575 7642 (2). Rippon, Hallé Ch. & O., Loughran – ELGAR: *Dream of Gerontius* **

(B) (**) CfP mono 585 9042. Milligan, Huddersfield Ch. Soc., RLPO, Sargent – ELGAR: *The Dream of Gerontius* (***)

(M) ** Telarc CD 80181. Stone, Atlanta SO & Ch., Shaw – BERNSTEIN: *Chichester Psalms* **

Belshazzar's Feast; Coronation Te Deum; Gloria

**(*) Chan. 8760. Howell, Gunson, Mackie, Roberts, Bach Ch., Philh. O, Willcocks

In **Andrew Davis's** dramatically eloquent account of *Belshazzar's Feast*, taken from the last night of the 1994 Promenade Concerts, the glorious choral contribution demonstrates how perfectly suited Walton's masterly oratorio is to the Royal Albert Hall's famous and sometimes intractable acoustics. From the powerful trombone opening and the riveting 'Thus spake Isaiah' from the **BBC Singers and Chorus**, the listener is held under the music's spell, and **Bryn Terfel's** resonant 'If I forget thee' is as compelling as his cry 'Babylon is a great city', while the choral responses to 'Praise ye' are as thrilling as the 'writing hand' sequence is creepily sinister. The apt coupling with *Job*, another biblical work, makes this a most desirable reissue.

Willcocks scores over some rivals in his pacing. Speeds tend to be a degree faster, as in *By the Waters of Babylon* which

flows evenly yet without haste. The soloist, **Gwynne Howell**, firm and dark of tone, is among the finest of all exponents but, with the **Bach Choir** placed rather more distantly than in most versions, this is not as incisive as its finest rivals. The *Coronation Te Deum* receives a richly idiomatic performance, and Willcocks also gives weight and thrust to the *Gloria*, with the tenor, **Neil Mackie**, outstanding among the soloists. The microphone unfortunately catches an unevenness in **Ameral Gunson's** mezzo. The recording is warmly reverberant, not ideally clear on choral detail but easy to listen to.

Loughran's version is forthright and dramatic, helped by brilliant analogue recording from 1973. The orchestra is particularly well caught, and so is the excellent soloist, **Michael Rippon**, firm and clear in attack. The snag is the work of the chorus, which is relatively small and placed rather close to the microphones, so that details of imperfect ensemble and intonation tend to be exaggerated.

Sargent was present at the gestation of *Belshazzar's Feast* and conducted the first performance at the Leeds Festival in 1931, thereafter making it his own for a considerable period. His interpretation was authoritative, but he does not seem to have taken care over detail for this 1958 recording. (Among other things, the anvil to represent the God of Iron is missing.) The rich acoustic of Huddersfield Town Hall adds weight to the sound but robs the choral words of any kind of clarity and bite. **James Milligan** is a strong soloist, the orchestra plays very well indeed, but overall this was not a jewel in Sargent's choral crown.

Robert Shaw and his superb chorus achieve a remarkable sharpness of choral ensemble. With a well-balanced recording which gives the chorus detailed clarity with no spotlighting, there is an attractive freshness in this account. Yet the result is not as electrifying as the opening promises, when – curiously in an American performance – Shaw's passion for precision prevents him from interpreting Walton's jazz rhythms with the necessary degree of rhythmic freedom to make them sound idiomatic. It all sounds too literal. The most damaging flaw is Shaw's inexplicable addition of full chorus singing *Ah!* on the final chord of the orchestral coda, totally unauthorized and not very effective.

Christopher Columbus (A Musical Journey); Hamlet and Ophelia (A Poem for Orchestra; arr. Mathieson)

*** Chan. SACD CHSA 5034. Carragher, Rigby, Randle, Williams, Julian Glover, Jamie Glover, Ogden, Ch. & BBC Nat. O of Wales, Hickox

Commisioned by the BBC in 1942 to write the incidental music for a radio play by Louis MacNeice. In 2002 Carl Davis and Patrick Garland devised an hour-long entertainment, with the main musical items illustrating an abbreviated version of MacNeice's text. Not surprisingly, it does not work as well as the comparable sequence using the *Henry V* film music alongside Shakespeare, but many of these illustrative fragments have the true Waltonian ring. With **Julian Glover** taking the spoken role of Columbus opposite **Jamie Glover** as the Ironic Spirit, **Richard Hickox** conducts a warmly idiomatic reading with an excellent quartet of vocal principals – **Caroline Carragher**, **Jean Rigby**, **Tom Randle** and **Roderick Williams** – and the first-rate **BBC National Chorus** and

Orchestra of Wales. Vivid sound in Hybrid SACD. Muir Mathieson's *Poem for Orchestra – Hamlet and Ophelia* is drawn directly from Walton's film music for Olivier's *Hamlet*, a sombre piece with fine string-writing and sinister fanfares in the middle.

(i) *Christopher Columbus* (suite of incidental music); (ii) *Anon in Love*; (iii) *4 Songs After Edith Sitwell: Daphne; Through gilded trellises; Long Steel Grass; Old Sir Faulk. A Song for the Lord Mayor's Table); The Twelve (an anthem for the Feast of any Apostle)*

🎧 *** Chan. 8824. (i) Finnie, Davies; (ii) Hill; (iii) Gomez; Westminster Singers, City of L. Sinfonia, Hickox

The composer's own orchestral versions of his song-cycles *Anon in Love* (for tenor) and *A Song for the Lord Mayor's Table* (for soprano) are so beautifully judged that they transcend the originals, and the strength and beauty of these strongly characterized songs is enormously enhanced, particularly in performances as positive as these by **Martyn Hill** and **Jill Gomez**. The anthem, *The Twelve*, also emerges far more powerfully with orchestral instead of organ accompaniment. The four Sitwell songs were orchestrated by Christopher Palmer, who also devised the suite from Walton's incidental music to Louis MacNeice's wartime radio play, *Christopher Columbus*, buried for half a century. It is a rich score which brings more happy anticipations of the *Henry V* film music in the choral writing, and even of the opera *Troilus and Cressida*, as well as overtones of *Belshazzar's Feast*. Warmly committed performances, opulently recorded.

OPERA

The Bear (complete)

🎧 *** Chan. 9245. Jones, Opie, Shirley-Quirk, N. Sinfonia, Hickox

The one-Acter *The Bear* is a masterly score, with the farcical element reflected in dozens of parodies and tongue-in-cheek musical references, starting cheekily with echoes of Britten's own *Midsummer Night's Dream*. **Richard Hickox** with members of the Northern Sinfonia paces the music superbly, flexibly heightening the moments of mock-melodrama that punctuate this tale of a mourning widow who faces the demands of one of her dead husband's creditors. The casting of the three characters is ideal, with **Della Jones** commanding as the affronted widow, all her words crystal clear, **Alan Opie** clean-cut and incisive as the creditor or 'Bear' of the title, and with **John Shirley-Quirk** as the old retainer. In many ways this is a piece – with its climactic duel scene leading to an amorous *coup de foudre* – which comes off even better on disc than on stage.

Troilus and Cressida (complete)

🎧 ❋ **** Chan. 9370/1 (2). A. Davies, Howarth, Howard, Robson, Opie, Bayley, Thornton, Owen-Lewis, Opera North Ch., E. N. Philh. O, Hickox

As Chandos's magnificent recording shows this red-bloodedly romantic opera on a big classical subject deserves to enter the regular repertory. **Judith Howarth** portrays the heroine as girlishly vulnerable, rising superbly to the big challenges of the love duets and final death scene. **Arthur Davies** is an aptly Italianate Troilus, an ardent lover, and there is not a weak link in the rest of the characterful cast, with **Nigel Robson** a finely pointed Pandarus, comic but not camp, avoiding any echoes of Peter Pears, the originator. As Evadne, Cressida's maid, **Yvonne Howard** produces firm, rich mezzo tone, and the role of Calkas, Cressida's father, is magnificently sung by **Clive Bayley**. The role of Diomede, Cressida's Greek suitor, can seem one-dimensional, but **Alan Opie**, in one of his finest performances on record, sharpens the focus, making him a genuine threat, a noble enemy. **Richard Hickox** draws magnetic performances from chorus and orchestra alike, bringing out the many parallels with the early Walton of *Belshazzar's Feast* and *Symphony 1*. As for the recorded sound, the bloom of the Leeds Town Hall acoustic allows the fullest detail from the orchestra, enhancing the Mediterranean warmth of the score, helped by the wide dynamic range. The many atmospheric effects, often offstage, are clearly and precisely focused, and the placing of voices on the stereo stage is also unusually precise.

WARD, John (1571–1638)

Aires; Fantasias for Viols; Fly not so fast, a 3; In Nomine, a 5; In Nomine, 1, a 6; 5, a 4; 2, a 6; Leggiadra sei, a 5; Non fu senza, a 5; O say, dear life, a 3; Sweet Philomel, a 5; Upon a bank with roses, a 5

🎧 *** CPO 999 928-2. Rose Consort of Viols

This survey impresses both in the quality of Ward's musical invention and resource and in the impressive advocacy it receives from the **Rose Consort**. The recordings, made in collaboration with Nord Deutsche Rundfunk, are also of excellent quality. Those who care about this rich period in English musical life should lose no time in acquiring this valuable addition to its representation on CD. Strongly recommended.

Madrigals: Come sable night; Cruel unkind; Die not, fond man; Hope of my heart; If heaven's just wrath; If the deep sighs; I have retreated; My breast I'll set; Oft have I tender'd; Out from the vale; Retire, my troubled soul; Sweet Philomel

🎧 *** Hyp. CDA 66256. Consort of Musicke, Rooley

Ward's music speaks with a distinctive voice. He chooses poetry of high quality, his music is always finely proportioned, and such is the quality of this music and the accomplishment with which it is presented, these settings represent the madrigal tradition at its finest.

WARLOCK, Peter (1894–1930)

Capriol Suite (for strings)

🎧 (BB) *** Naxos 8.550823. Bournemouth Sinf., Richard Studt (with Concert: *English String Music*)***

A first-class performance of Warlock's masterly *Capriol Suite* is included in this splendid collection which includes also Britten's *Frank Bridge Variations*, Holst's *St Paul's Suite* and Vaughan Williams's *Dives and Lazarus*. Demonstration sound.

Capriol Suite (orchestral version); *Serenade for Strings* (for the sixtieth birthday of Delius)

*** Chan. 8808. Ulster O, Handley – MOERAN: *Serenade*, etc. ***

The effect of the present full orchestral score of the *Capriol Suite* is to rob the music of some of its astringency. A dryish wine is replaced with one with the fullest bouquet, for the wind instruments make the textures more rococo in feeling as well as increasing the colour. **Handley's** fine performance, is made to sound opulent by the acoustics of Ulster Hall, Belfast. The lovely *Serenade*, for strings alone, is also played and recorded very beautifully.

Serenade for Strings

*** Lyrita SRCD 318. LPO, Braithwaite (with PIERSON: *Macbeth*; MORGAN: *Contrasts* ***) – ARNOLD: *Beckus the Dandipratt*; CHAGRIN: *Helter Skelter*; RAWSTHORNE: *Cortèges* ***

The gentle melancholy of Warlock's *String Serenade* with its delicate Delian atmosphere is beautifully caught here, and the recording is warmly atmospheric to match. This is part of an unmissable anthology of mostly little-known English orchestral miniatures.

Adam lay ybounden; As dew in Aprylle; Benedicamus Domino; Bethlehem down; The Birds; Born is the babe; Balulalow; Carillon, Carilla; A Cornish Christmas carol; A Cornish carol; Corpus Christi; The first mercy; The 5 lesser joys of Mary; The frostbound wood; I saw a fair maiden; My little sweet darling; Out of the Orient crystal skies; The rich cavalcade; Song for Christmas Day; Sweet was the song the Virgin sang; The sycamore tree; Tyrley Tyrlow; What cheer? Good cheer!; Where riches is everlastingly

⊕ *** Somm SOMMCD 011. Allegri Singers, Halsey; with Cable, Empett, Rosamunde Qt, M. Barnes, R. Barnes

Most of these Christmas settings are little known, many are quite simple, but all are quite lovely. Among the more extended pieces the *Cornish Christmas carol* is strophic but the harmonic setting is constantly varied, while the ravishing *Corpus Christie* carol and simpler *Born is the babe* are set for solo voices and string quartet. *Out of the Orient crystal skies* and the gentle *Bethlehem down* are particularly haunting and the concert ends with the brief *Sycamore tree*, as joyful as an English carol can be. Fine, lively, dedicated performances throughout, with excellent accompaniments from all concerned.

Songs

*** Chan. 8643. Luxon, Willison

Ⓑ Ⓑ ** Naxos 8.557115. Thompson, Maltman, Constable, Davies, Pendrill, Duke Qt

Songs like *Autumn twilight*, the powerfully expressive *Late summer* and *Captain Stratton's fancy* are appealing in utterly different ways, and there is not a single number in this programme that does not show the composer either in full imaginative flow or simply enjoying himself, as in *Yarmouth Fair*. **Luxon's** performances are excellent and **David Willison** provides sensitive and sparkling accompaniments. The recording is first class.

First issued on the Collins Classics label, this Naxos issue offers a well-chosen selection, characterfully performed to bring out the contrasting flavours, vigorous on the one hand, evocative on the other. It is good to have his masterpiece, *The Curlew*, an extended setting of Yeats, as the main item, even if **Adrian Thompson** has moments of roughness, which are exaggerated by close recorded balance. Although the instrumental accompaniment is beautifully played, there, too, the closeness prevents the full atmospheric beauty of the writing from being appreciated. Thompson is more successful in songs that require less sustained lines, and similar reservations have to be made about the singing of **Christopher Maltman** in the baritone songs, though he is rousingly convincing in such characteristic items as *Fancy*, *Mr Belloc's fancy* and (best known of all) *Captain Stratton's fancy*.

WAXMAN, Franz (1906–67)

Carmen Fantasy

⊕ Ⓜ *** Warner Elatus 2564 60013-2. Vengerov, Israel PO, Mehta – PAGANINI: *Violin Concerto 1 in D, Op. 6* **(*); SAINT-SAËNS: *Havanaise; Intro & Rondo Capriccioso* ***

Waxman's *Carmen* confection invites the flamboyance that the young Russian émigré **Maxim Vengerov** can readily provide. He dazzles and seduces the ear by turns, and even if he is forwardly balanced, the orchestral backing is well in the picture.

Film Suites: (i) *The Bride of Frankenstein*; (ii) *The Invisible Ray*; *Prince Valiant*; *Rebecca*; *Suspicion*; *Taras Bulba*

⊕ *** Silva Screen FILMCD 726. Westminster PO, Alwyn; (ii) City of Prague PO, Bateman

With a flamboyant introduction that sweeps you into 1930s Hollywood, *The Bride of Frankenstein*, still regarded as one of the finest horror films ever made, brings one of Waxman's most enjoyable scores. There is plenty of exciting, dramatic music here, very colourfully orchestrated, including the use of whole-tone scales and an ondes martenot, there's wit and parody too (Gounod's *Faust* crops up), and one especially enjoys the *Minuet*, most charmingly orchestrated by Clifford Vaughan, himself an organist, an instrument used effectively in this score, as in the delightfully quirky *Danse Macabre* – a number that should have a lease of life on its own. **Kenneth Alwyn** and his orchestra are fully at home in Waxman's musical world. The more famous suites of *Prince Valiant*, *Taras Bulba* and *Suspicion* are included, as well as *Rebecca* (his finest score), and the less well-known *The Invisible Ray*, another enjoyable horror score, dating from 1936, with the suite assembled by the composer's son, John Waxman, and with Stephen Bernstein having to orchestrate it completely by ear as none of the original survives. Very good recordings and performances, too.

Rebecca (filmscore; complete)

🎵— (BB) *** Naxos 8.557549. Slovak RSO, Adriano

Rebecca (1940) is regarded as Waxman's finest score, and it is easy to see why: as soon as the splendid Selznick International trademark theme is played (composed by Newman), Waxman sweeps you into the world of Daphne du Maurier's bestseller, *Rebecca*. The score is an integral part of Hitchcock's film, with the Rebecca theme used to portray the ghostly presence of Max de Winter's dead first wife and, throughout, the music brilliantly portrays the often haunting and creepy atmosphere of this Gothic fantasy. It is not all gloomy though, with numbers such as the *Lobby Waltz* providing a haunting piece of nostalgia. **Adriano** (and others) has made a splendid job of assembling this score, some of which had to be reconstructed from the soundtrack while other music, not used in the final film, is restored here. Both the performance and recording are very good and, at bargain price, this is essential for all film music fans.

Joshua

🔆 *** DG 477 5724. Schell (narr.), Gilfry, Hallenberg, Bucht, Poole, Prague Phil. Ch., Prague Philh., Sedares

Franz Waxman here tackles a major biblical subject in a full-scale oratorio. The First Part leads up to the impressive picture of Joshua's forces storming the walls of Jericho, blowing their trumpets. With a multiple array in fanfare that makes a superb climax, inevitably it leads to a slight feeling of anticlimax in the second half, when the stopping of the sun and the *Battle of Gilead* cannot match that earlier climax, and the piece ends gently with Joshua's death. Nevertheless, this is a fine work, characterfully introduced by the Narrator, **Maximilian Schell**, and with a good team of soloists backing the excellent choir and orchestra. Atmospheric recording.

WEBER, Carl Maria von
(1786–1826)

Andante & Hungarian Rondo in E flat, Op. 35; Bassoon Concerto in F, Op. 75

*** Chan. 9656. Popov, Russian State SO, Polyansky – HUMMEL; MOZART: *Bassoon Concertos* ***

There is some astonishing spiccato bravura in the finale of the *Hungarian Rondo*, and both **Valeri Popov** and his accompanying orchestra under **Polyansky** capture the grand manner of the first movement of the *Concerto* and are quite touching in the romantic cantabile of the *Andantino*. The finale then brings both a genial wit and more solo fireworks. The recording is full-bodied and resonant, but clearly detailed in the Chandos manner.

Clarinet Concertino in E flat, Op. 26

🎵— *** ASV CDDCA 559. Johnson, ECO, Groves – CRUSELL: *Concerto 2* *** 🔆; BAERMANN: *Adagio* ***; ROSSINI: *Introduction, Theme & Variations* ***

Emma Johnson is in her element here. Her phrasing is wonderfully beguiling and her use of light and shade agreeably subtle, while she finds a superb lilt in the final section, pacing the music to bring out its charm rather than achieve breathless bravura. **Sir Charles Groves** provides an admirable accompaniment, and the recording is eminently realistic and naturally balanced.

Clarinet Concertos 1 in F min., Op. 73; 2 in E flat, Op. 74; Clarinet Concertino

*** DG 435 875-2. Neidlich, Orpheus CO – ROSSINI: *Introduction, Theme & Variations in E flat* ***

(M) *** Classic fM 75605 57019-2. Lawson, Hanover Band, Goodman – SPOHR: *Clarinet Concerto 1* ***

(BB) *** Virgin 2x1 5 61585-2 (2). Pay, OAE – CRUSELL: *Clarinet Concertos 1–3* ***

(BB) *** Naxos 8.550378. Ottensamer, Slovak State PO (Košice), Wildner

If you want these *Concertos* on modern instruments, **Charles Neidlich** meets every need. His tone is beautiful, his phrasing warmly musical, he swings along most beguilingly in the *Andante* of the *Concertino* and the *Romanze* of the *F minor Concerto* is shaped with much delicacy. He lollops delightfully in the finales of all three works. He plays his own cadenzas and the **Orpheus Chamber Orchestra**, rather resonantly recorded, provide accompaniments of substance which are both polished and supportive. The Rossini *Variations* make a witty and elegantly appealing bonus. However, the performances on the super-bargain Warner Apex collection below are also first class in every way and every bit as well recorded, and this disc includes also the *Grand duo concertant*.

Stylish and imaginative period performances of all three works from **Colin Lawson** with the **Hanover Band**, vividly recorded, generously supplemented by the Spohr *First Concerto*. With his attractively reedy tone Lawson is a most persuasive soloist, moulding Weber's melodies seductively and pointing rhythms jauntily, with brilliant feats of tonguing in the light-hearted finales of each work.

Antony Pay uses a copy of a seven-keyed clarinet by Simiot of Lyons from 1800. The sonority is cleaner and less bland than can be the case in modern performances, and the solo playing is both expert and sensitive. A further gesture to authenticity is the absence of a conductor; however, the ensemble might have been even better and the texture more finely judged and balanced had there been one. The recordings are vivid and truthful and those attracted to the coupling with Crusell should be well satisfied.

Ernst Ottensamer is a highly sensitive clarinettist, who is a member of the Vienna Wind Ensemble. His account of the two *Clarinet Concertos* can hold its own against nearly all the competition, the **Košice Orchestra** also responds well to **Johannes Wildner's** direction, and the recorded sound is very natural and well balanced. A real bargain.

**(i; ii) Clarinet Concertos 1 in F min.; 2 in E flat;
Clarinet Concertino in E flat, Op. 26; (iii) Grand duo
concertant for Clarinet & Piano, Op. 48**

🎵 ⚫ *** ASV (ADD) CDDCA 747. (i) Johnson; (ii) ECO, cond.
　　Tortelier, Schwarz or Groves; (iii) with Black

🎵 (BB) *** Warner Apex 8573 89246-2. (i) Boeykens; (ii)
　　Rotterdam PO, Conlon; (iii) Meyer, Duchable

Emma Johnson's scintillating accounts of these three
Weberian showpieces were made with different conductors,
all of whom prove to be highly sympathetic to their young
soloist. Her subtlety of expression is remarkable, with *pianissimos* more daringly extreme and with distinctly persuasive phrasing in slow movements treated warmly and
spaciously. In the sparkling finales she is wittier than almost
any, plainly enjoying herself to the full. The *Concertino*, in
some ways the most delightful work of the three, especially
its delicious finale, is hardly less beguiling; and as a bonus
we are offered a brilliant and individually expressive account
of the *Grand duo concertant* for clarinet and piano. Here she
finds an admirable partner in **Gordon Black**, who accompanies with equal flair.

However, if you are looking for a bargain alternative,
Walter Boeykens will be hard to beat. He is a most sensitive
player and phrases the expressive music meltingly, with a
lovely tone, as the slow movement of the *F minor Concerto*
readily demonstrates; and there are some subtle touches of
rubato in the *Concertino*. **James Conlon** and the **Rotterdam
Orchestra** provide firm, yet flexible accompaniments.
Weber's chortling *Rondos* in all three works are delightfully
presented, with the *Polacca* finale of the *E flat Concerto* very
neatly pointed. **Paul Meyer** takes over in the romantic *Grand
duo concertant*, quite perfectly balanced with **Duchable**, and
they make a fine partnership. An excellent disc, given first-
class recording.

**(i) Clarinet Concertos 1–2; Clarinet Concertino; (ii)
Clarinet Quintet in B flat (version for string
orchestra)**

🎵 **** BIS **SACD** 1523. Fröst, Tapiola Sinfonietta, Kantorow

🎵 (M) **** EMI 5 67988-2. Meyer; (i) Dresden State O,
　　Blomstedt; (ii) Württemberg CO, Heilbronn, Faerber

**Clarinet Quintet, Op. 34 (arr. for clarinet & string
orch)**

*** EMI 5 57359-2. Meyer, ASMF, Sillito – BAERMANN: *Clarinet
　　Quintet 3 in E flat, Op. 23*; MENDELSSOHN: *2 Concert Pieces
　　for Clarinet & Basset Horn* ***

Weber, inspired by the playing of his friend, Heinrich
Baermann, began writing his *Clarinet Quintet* while on holiday in Switzerland in 1811, completing it the following year,
a labour of love following the two *Concertos* and *Concertino*
he had earlier written for Baermann. It is just as inspired
and just as demanding technically, which makes it an ideal
candidate to be translated, as here, into a full concerto for
clarinet and strings.

Martin Fröst plays these delectable works as seductively
as any of his competitors (the *Concertino* is specially haunting) and he has the advantage of including a winning ac-

count of the *Quintet* in a new and highly effective arrangement for full strings by his conductor. With fine accompaniments and a full-bodied, wide-ranging recording, perfectly
balanced, this sounds spectacularly real in its SACD format.

EMI have combined **Sabine Meyer's** fine recordings of
the *Concertos* – notable for particularly eloquent accounts of
the two slow movements – and her delectable, light-hearted
version of the *Concertino*, with her inspired account of the
orchestral arrangement of the *Clarinet Quintet* (see below).
The orchestral accompaniments are on a larger scale than
with Emma Johnson, but both **Blomstedt** and **Faerber** prove
admirable accompanists, and the recording is excellent.

Clarinet Concerto 2 in E flat, Op. 74

*** Australian Decca Eloquence (ADD) 476 7404. de Peyer,
　　LSO, C. Davis – MOZART: *Clarinet Concerto in A*; SPOHR:
　　Clarinet Concerto 1 ***

De Peyer is fully up to the bravura in Weber's splendidly
tuneful *Second Clarinet Concerto*, especially in the infectious
finale, packed with fireworks. The exceptionally warm, vivid
Decca recording adds to the vibrant quality of the music-
making.

**Piano Concertos 1–2; Konzertstück; Polacca brillante
(L'Hilarité), Op. 72 (orch. Liszt)**

🎵 (BB) *** Naxos 8.550959. Frith, Dublin R. & TV Sinf.,
　　O'Duinn

Benjamin Frith's accounts are first class and he receives
splendid support from **O'Duinn** and the excellent **Dublin
Sinfonietta**. In consequence, these performances all have
real depth (the *Konzertstück* is particularly fine). Frith's playing has plenty of dash, yet its impetuosity is never inclined
to run away with itself. The Naxos CD is not only very well
recorded and inexpensive, it also includes the appropriately
named *L'Hilarité* – *Polacca brillante*, which Frith plays with
attractive panache.

Konzertstück in F min.

🎵 (M) *** EMI (ADD) 5 62884-2. Arrau, Philh. O, Galliera –
　　CHOPIN: *Fantasy*, etc. ***

Arrau is superb. He gives one of the freshest performances
imaginable of the unusual piece with its programme of
knights and ladies. The orchestra responds splendidly and
the recording is excellent. The couplings are equally fine
and there is a seductive bonus of Mendelssohn's *Andante and
Rondo capriccioso*.

**Overtures: Abu Hassan; Der Beherrscher der
Geister (Ruler of the Spirits); Euryanthe; Der
Freischütz; Jubel; Oberon; Preziosa**

🎵 *** Capriccio Surround Sound **SACD** 71 045. Dresden
　　State O, Kuhn

This collection of Weber *Overtures* is marvellously played by
the superb **Dresden Staatskapelle**, and if as performances
they do not quite match Karajan for panache or Sawallisch
for sheer orchestral excitement, they certainly do not lack
style and vitality. Indeed, their breadth plus a certain dignity
increases their stature. But what makes this disc so thrilling

is the magnificent recording, far finer than with any of their competitors. It is very much in the demonstration bracket, wonderfully real and full-blooded, especially when using four speakers, which provide a superb concert-hall illusion in the sitting room. There is no better example than *Jubel*, splendidly grandiloquent, especially when *God save the Queen* arrives spectacularly and thrillingly at the close.

Overtures: *Abu Hassan; Der Beherrscher der Geister (Ruler of the Spirits)*

*** Australian Decca Eloquence (ADD) 476 2745. VPO, Stein – BRUCKNER: *Symphony 6* ***

Warm, lively and superbly played versions of two sparkling Weber overtures from **Horst Stein**, making an enjoyable bonus to a fine account of Bruckner's *Sixth Symphony*.

Symphonies 1 in C; 2 in C, J.50/51

**(*) ASV CDDCA 515. ASMF, Marriner

(BB) ** Warner Apex 2564 60619-2. Norwegian R.O, Rasilainen – WAGNER: *Symphony in C* **

Symphonies 1 in C; 2 in C; *Die drei Pintos: Entr'acte; Silvana: Dance of the Young Nobles; Torch Dance; Turandot: Overture; Act II: March; Act V: Funeral March*

⊕–✿ (BB) **** Naxos 8.550928. Queensland PO, Georgiadis

Weber wrote his two *Symphonies* in the same year (1807) and, though both are in C major, each has its own individuality. The witty orchestration and operatic character of the writing are splendidly caught in these sparkling **Queensland** performances, while in the slow movements the orchestral soloists relish their solos, for all the world like vocal cantilenas. The recording is in the demonstration class, and the disc is made the more attractive for the inclusion of orchestral excerpts from two little-known operas and incidental music from *Turandot*. The *Entr'acte* from the incomplete *Die drei Pintos* was put together by Mahler from Weber's sketches.

Sir **Neville Marriner** also has the full measure of Weber's two *Symphonies*; these performances combine vigour and high spirits with the right degree of gravitas (not too much) in the slow movements. The recording is clear and full in the bass, but the bright upper range brings a touch of digital edge to the upper strings.

On Apex, an inexpensive way of acquiring Weber's two very attractive *Symphonies*, with a Wagner curiosity. The performances are lively and committed, but the recording is not much above average.

CHAMBER AND INSTRUMENTAL MUSIC

Cello Sonata in A; *Adagio & Rondo*

(***) Testament mono SBT 2158. Piatigorsky, Newton – BEETHOVEN: *Cello Sonatas* (***); BRAHMS: *Sonata 1* (***)

These records were made in 1934–5 and are arrangements by **Piatigorsky** of the *Fifth* of Weber's *Violin Sonatas*, Op. 10. The playing has an impressive eloquence.

Clarinet Quintet in B Flat, Op. 34

⊕– *** ASV CDDCA 1079. Johnson, Takacs-Nagy, Hirsch, Boulton, Shulman – MOZART: *Clarinet Quintet; Allegro in B flat, K.516c* **(*)

*** Australian Decca Eloquence (ADD) 476 2447. de Peyer, Melos Ens. – HUMMEL: *Piano Quintet; Piano Septet* ***

(i) *Clarinet Quintet; Introduction, Theme & Variations for Clarinet & String Quartet, Op. posth.;* (ii) *Grand duo concertant in E flat, Op. 48; 7 Variations on a Theme from Silvana in B flat, Op. 33* (both for clarinet and piano)

⊕– (BB) *** Naxos 8.553122. Berkes (i) Auer Qt; (ii) Jandó

(i) *Clarinet Quintet; Flute trio in G min., Op. 63* (for flute, cello & piano)

(M) *** CRD (ADD) CRD 3398. Pay, Nash Ens.

(i) *Clarinet Quintet;* (ii) *Grand duo concertant, Op. 48; 7 Variations on a Theme from Silvana, Op. 33*

⊕– **** Praga PRD 250 164. Moraguès; (i) Pražák Qt; (ii) Izuha

This Praga disc is sheer delight, full of Bohemian spirit, with superbly elegant playing from everyone concerned. The *Duo concertant* is equally winning, with **Moraguès'** easy rubato given persuasive support by the pianist, **Mari Izuha**, the flowing *Andante* followed by a debonair, pointed finale. The *Silvana Variations*, based on another genially dotted theme, are again delightfully presented, with bravura flourishes and rollicking roulades from the clarinet and nimble accompanying pianism, and the recording could hardly be more truthful or better balanced.

Emma Johnson, always a characterful player with her distinctive reedy tone, gives a scintillating account of the *Quintet*, with brilliant support from her team of experienced chamber players. In this less well-known work she is more spontaneous-sounding than in the Mozart, full of sparkle and fun in the outer movements as well as the *Scherzo*, finding a rare depth of expression in the hushed writing of the second movement *Fantasia*, marked *Adagio*. The clarinet is forwardly balanced, but less obtrusively so than in the Mozart.

Gervase de Peyer, too, is in his element in the *Quintet*, immaculate and brilliant, and given superb support from the **Melos Ensemble**. The 1959 recording hardly sounds its age, remarkably warm and vivid, so if the Hummel couplings are wanted this is very recommendable.

On the CRD version, **Antony Pay** (playing a modern instrument) makes the very most of the work's bravura, catching the exuberance of the *Capriccio* third movement and the breezy gaiety of the finale. The **Nash** players provide an admirable partnership and then adapt themselves readily to the different mood of the *Trio*, another highly engaging work with a picturesque slow movement, described as a *Shepherd's Lament*. The recording is first class, vivid yet well balanced.

However, Naxos conveniently gather together expert and winning performances of all Weber's major chamber works featuring the clarinet, even if the amiable *Introduction, Theme and Variations* is now considered spurious. The *Quintet* is particularly successful with a lusciously appealing account af the *Adagio* and the finale chortles with great zest in its sparkling virtuosity. With **Jandó** an admirable partner, the *Grand duo concertant* is hardly less successful, and the two sets of variations are presented with both elegance and panache. The recording is realistic if too resonant, but the charisma and spontaneity of this Hungarian music-making carry the day in spite of this.

7 Variations on a Theme from Silvana in B flat, Op. 33

*** Chan. 8506. de Peyer, Pryor – SCHUBERT: *Arpeggione Sonata*; SCHUMANN: *Fantasiestücke*, etc. ***

These engaging Weber *Variations* act as a kind of encore to Schubert's *Arpeggione Sonata* and with their innocent charm they follow on naturally. They are most winningly played by **Gervase de Peyer**; **Gwenneth Pryor** accompanies admirably. The recording is first class.

PIANO MUSIC

Piano Sonatas 1–2; Rondo brillante in E flat (La Gaîté), Op. 52; Invitation to the Dance, Op. 65

〰 Ⓜ *** CRD CRD 3485. Milne

Piano Sonata 3 in D min., Op. 49; 4 in E min., Op. 70; Polacca brillante in E (L'Hilarité) (with LISZT: Introduzione (Adagio))

〰 Ⓜ *** CRD CRD 3486. Milne

These Weber *Sonatas* are not easy to bring off, with their classical heritage and operatic freedom of line. **Hamish Milne's** performances have a lightness of touch that is most appealing, without ever being superficial, and his playing in the slow movements has attractive lyrical feeling. Moreover he also provides a sparkling account of the *Rondo brillante* and, as a final encore, a totally captivating account of the charming *Invitation to the Dance*. He makes a sterner approach to the opening *Allegro feroce* of *3 in D minor*, cast in an almost Beethovenian mould, while the last *Sonata* is more introspective in its colouring and feeling, and concludes with a ruthless Tarantella, driven on by its own restless energy. The *Polacca brillante* returns to the world of dazzling articulation and sparkling display. Hamish Milne's playing is thoroughly inside Weber's world and technically equal to the composer's prodigious demands. He is very well recorded.

OPERA

(i) Abu Hassan (complete); Symphony 1 in C

〰 *** DHM/BMG 054 72 77979-2. (i) Völz, Dürmüller, Stojkovic, Selig, Werk Ruhr Ch.; Cappella Coloniensis of West Deutsche TV & R., B. Weil

Abu Hassan is a delightful one-Act opera, an early work written in 1811, which, like Mozart's *Entführung*, exploits the fashion for 'Turkish' subjects. In a crisp series of brief numbers – two choruses, two arias, two duets and two trios – it lasts a mere 50 minutes, allowing it to be coupled in

this sparkling performance on Deutsche Harmonia Mundi with Weber's equally delightful *Symphony 1*. Using period instruments, **Bruno Weil** gives the score all the lightness and transparency it needs, with a first-rate trio of soloists, all with clear, fresh voices, plus a Narrator who doubles in the role of the Caliph. The only snag for the non-German speaker is that the spoken dialogue separating the musical numbers may prove excessive, but there is generous indexing of tracks to allow it to be omitted, and the well-planned booklet gives German text and English translation. The *Symphony* too gains in point and transparency in this lively performance with period instruments.

Der Freischütz: Overture

(***) BBC Legends mono BBCL 4140. New Philh. O, Giulini – BRITTEN: *The Building of the House Overture*; SCHUBERT: *Symphony 9* ***

Recorded in mono at the Royal Festival Hall in December 1970, **Giulini's** reading of the Weber *Overture* brings a performance of extremes, at once dedicated and dramatic, a valuable addition to the conductor's discography on this disc issued to celebrate his ninetieth birthday.

Der Freischütz (complete; DVD version)

(***) Arthaus mono DVD 101 271. Kozub, Frick, Saunders, Mathis, Grundheber, Blankenheim, Minetti, Sotin, Krause, Hamburg State Op. Ch. & O, Ludwig (Dir: Rolf Liebermann, V/D: Joachim Hess)

A fascinating early example of filmed opera in remarkably vivid colour, dating from 1968. The cast pre-recorded the music in mono within an attractive acoustic, then acted and sang the opera on stage, miming very successfully to the pre-recording. The production and sets are traditional, very much so. But the principals are excellent singers every one, with **Gottlob Frick's** melodramatic portrayal of Kaspar almost stealing the show. If, as Killian, **Franz Grundheber's** Act I aria is a bit too self-satisfied, the main problem is that Max, the hero (**Ernst Kozub**), although he sings ardently, looks so morose throughout the opera that one wonders what Agathe can see in him. However, both she (the sweet-voiced **Arlene Saunders**) and the delightful Ännchen (a young **Edith Mathis**) are charmers in their central scenes, which contain the heroine's two most famous arias, very well sung. The Wolf's Glen scene, dominated by a sinister Samiel (**Bernhard Minetti**) is staged quite spectacularly, with an impressive storm, even if it is not as rivetingly scary as the famous Keilberth audio recording. However, the opera's closing scene, with **Hans Sotin** magnificently commanding as the Hermit who intervenes to provide the happy ending, is very successful. In all – allowances being made for the dated production – this is most enjoyable and a considerable achievement when one realizes it is 40 years old! There is, for once, a good accompanying booklet, with synopsis and full documentation.

Der Freischütz (complete; CD versions)

〰 **** Teldec 4509 97758-2 (2). Orgonasova, Schäfer, Wottrich, Salminen, Berlin R. Ch., BPO, Harnoncourt

⊕₊ Ⓜ **** EMI (ADD) 2 08821-2 (2). Grümmer, Otto, Schock, Prey, Wiemann, Kohn, Frick, German Op. Ch., Berlin, BPO, Keilberth

Ⓑ *** DG 477 5611 (2). Seefried, Streich, Holm, Waechter, Peter, Bohme, Bav. R. Ch. & O, Jochum

Ⓜ *** DG (ADD) 457 736-2 (2). Janowitz, Mathis, Schreier, Adam, Vogel, Crass, Leipzig R. Ch., Dresden State O, Kleiber

Ⓝ Ⓜ ** Ph. 478 0152 (2). Mattila, Araiza, Wlaschicha, Lind, Moll, Dresden State O, Colin Davis

Harnoncourt's electrifying and refreshing version of this operatic warhorse was recorded live at concert performances in the **Philharmonie** in Berlin in 1995 and the engineers have done wonders in conveying the atmosphere of a stage performance rather than a concert one, not least in the Wolf's Glen scene, helped by recording of a very wide dynamic range. Harnoncourt clarifies textures and paces the drama well, making it sound fresh and new. The cast is first rate, with **Orgonasova** singing radiantly as Agathe, not just pure but sensuous of tone, floating high *pianissimos* ravishingly. **Christine Schäfer**, sweet and expressive, makes Ännchen into far more than just a soubrette character, and **Erich Wottrich** as Max is aptly heroic and unstrained, if hardly beautiful. The line-up of baritones and basses is impressive too, all firm and clear, contrasting sharply with one another, a team unlikely to be bettered today. A clear first choice among modern, digital recordings.

Keilberth's is a warm, exciting account of Weber's masterpiece, which makes all the dated conventions of the work seem fresh and new. In particular the Wolf's Glen scene acquires something of the genuine terror that must have struck the earliest audiences. The casting of the magic bullets with each one numbered in turn, at first in eerie quiet and then in crescendo amid the howling of demons, is superbly conveyed. **Elisabeth Grümmer** sings more sweetly and sensitively than one ever remembers before, with Agathe's prayer exquisitely done. **Lisa Otto** is really in character, with genuine coquettishness. **Schock** is not an ideal tenor, but he sings ably enough. The Kaspar of **Karl Kohn** is generally well focused, and the playing of the **Berlin Philharmonic** has plenty of polish. The overall effect is immensely atmospheric and enjoyable.

The warmth of Jochum's conducting and his understanding of how to pace this high romantic piece puts his among the finest versions with its outstanding cast, even if he cannot quite match Keilberth in recreating the horror of the Wolf's Glen scene. **Irmgard Seefried** may be on the light side for the role of Agathe, but the golden purity of her voice, her projection and her flawless control of legato make hers a memorable performance; and few can match **Rita Streich** in brilliance as Ännchen. **Richard Holm** sings with free, unstrained tone as Max, and **Eberhard Waechter** is outstanding as Otakar, with **Kurt Bohme** gruff but characterful as Kaspar. First-rate, well-balanced sound, remarkable for 1959.

Kleiber's fine, incisive account of Weber's atmospheric and adventurous score fulfilled most expectations. With the help of an outstanding cast, excellent work by the recording producer, Eberhard Geller, and transparently clear record-

ing, this is a most compelling version of an opera which transfers well to the gramophone.

Sir Colin Davis paces this magic score very well indeed, and the **Dresden** forces respond with some fine playing and singing. To add to the drama there are plenty of production sounds, even including the barking of hounds, with shots that have you jumping out of your seat. Even so this is a set that fails to convey the full power of the Wolf's Glen scene where the casting of the magic bullets sounds tame, not frightening at all. The singing is flawed too. **Karita Mattila's** warm, vibrant soprano is apt enough for Agathe, and she controls the soaring lines of her two big arias very beautifully, but *Und ob die Wolke* brings under-the-note coloratura which may distress some ears. As Max, **Francisco Araiza** is seriously stressed with the basically beautiful voice sounding throaty, and **Eva Lind** is unpleasantly fluttery and shallow as Aennchen. **Eberhard Wlaschila** is darkly sinister as Kaspar and it is good too to have **Kurt Moll** as the Hermit.

Oberon (complete)

⊕₊ Ⓜ *** DG 477 5644 (2). Grob, Nilsson, Domingo, Prey, Hamari, Schiml, Bav. R. Ch. & SO, Kubelik

We owe it to Covent Garden's strange ideas in the mid-1820s as to what 'English opera' should be, that Weber's delicately conceived score is a sequence of illogical arias, scenas and ensembles, strung togther by an absurd pantomime plot, nearly as bad as the one for *Euryanthe*, but not quite! Though even on record the result is slacker because of the loose construction, one can appreciate, in a performance as stylish and refined as this, the contribution of Weber. The original issue included dialogue and a narrative spoken by one of Oberon's fairy characters. In the LP reissue this was cut, but the dialogue has now been restored (although it is separately cued, so it can be programmed out). With **Birgit Nilsson** commanding in *Ocean thou mighty monster* and excellent singing from the other principals, helped by **Kubelik's** ethereally light handling of the orchestra, the set can be recommended without reservation, for the 1970 recording, made in the Munich Herculessaal, is of excellent quality. The reissue comes with a cued synopsis of the story.

Oberon: Overture

Ⓜ **(*) Dresden Staatskapelle Live VKJK 0414. Dresden Staatskapelle, Haitink – BRAHMS: *Symphony 1* **(*)

Haitink's Dresden recording of the Brahms *Symphony* may be on the heavy side, but Weber's *Overture* is quite different, magically refined in the slow introduction and lithe and athletic in the main *Allegro*. A good coupling, if hardly a generous one on a mid-price disc.

Oberon (complete recording in the original English)

⊕₊ ✱ **** Ph. 475 6563-2 (2). Davislim, Martinpelto, Kaufmann, Dazeley, Monteverdi Ch., ORR, Gardiner, Allam (nar.)

Weber's *Oberon* is one of the great problem works of opera. Written for Covent Garden in 1825, it is based not on Shakespeare but on the fairy epic of Wieland which, using an English translation, Robinson Planche turned into an ungainly libretto. Its oddities effectively prevented Weber from developing the piece consistently, but he was inspired to write some of his most magical music, full of what **John Eliot Gardiner** defines as 'fire, fantasy and finesse'. How to present *Oberon* effectively has long presented almost intractable problems, but here Gardiner on disc, pioneering a recording in the original English, opts for what might be counted an ideal answer, using a narrator to link numbers instead of Planche's dialogue. The result in a superb perfomance is magnetic, letting one appreciate to the full the uniqueness of Weber's inspiration, with period instruments helping to clarify the fairy-light orchestral textures, plainly a model for Mendelssohn.

The singing cast is excellent, with the two main tenor roles splendidly taken – Oberon lyrically by the Australian tenor, **Steve Davislim**, and Huon, with his big spectacular aria full of formidable florid writing, by **Jonas Kaufmann**. **Hillevi Martinpelto** is fresh and clear as Raiza, another challenging role, and **Roger Allam** is unobtrusively effective speaking the narration. The **Monteverdi Choir** too plays an important part in bringing out the magic of the music, with beautifully balanced recording.

WEBERN, Anton (1883–1945)

(i) *Concerto for 9 Instruments, Op. 24; 5 Movements for String Quartet* (orchestral version), *Op. 5; Passacaglia, Op. 1; 6 Pieces for Large Orchestra, Op. 6; 5 Pieces for Orchestra, Op. 10; Symphony, Op. 21; Variations for Orchestra, Op. 30.* **Arrangements of:** BACH: *Musical Offering: Fugue* (1935). **(ii)** SCHUBERT: *German Dances* (for small orchestra), *Op. posth.* **Chamber Music: (iii)** *6 Bagatelles for String Quartet, Op. 9; 5 Movements for String Quartet, Op. 5; (iv; v) 4 Pieces for Violin & Piano, Op. 7; (v; vi) 3 Small Pieces for Cello & Piano, Op. 11; (v; vii) Quartet, Op. 22* (for piano, violin, clarinet & saxophone); **(iii)** *String Quartet, Op. 28; String Trio, Op. 20; (v) Variations for Piano, Op. 27.* **Vocal: (viii; i)** *Das Augenlicht, Op. 26; (ix; x) 5 Canons on Latin Texts, Op. 16; (viii; ix; i) Cantata 1, Op. 29; (viii; ix; xi; i) Cantata 2, Op. 31; (viii) Entflieht auf leichten Kähnen, Op. 2; (ix; x) 5 Sacred Songs, Op. 15; (xii; v) 5 Songs, Op. 3; 5 Songs, Op. 4; (xii; x) 2 Songs, Op. 8; (xii; v) 4 Songs, Op. 12; (xii; x) 4 Songs, Op. 13; 6 Songs, Op. 14; (ix; x; xiii) 3 Songs, Op. 18; (viii; i) 2 Songs, Op. 19; (xii; v) 3 Songs, Op. 23; (ix; v) 3 Songs, Op. 25; (ix; x) 3 Traditional Rhymes, Op. 17*

ⓜ *** Sony SM3K 45845 (3). (i) LSO (or members), Boulez; (ii) Frankfurt R.O, composer (recorded December 1932); (iii) Juilliard Qt (or members); (iv) Stern; (v) Rosen; (vi) Piatigorsky; (vii) Majeske, Marcellus, Weinstein; (viii) John Alldis Ch.; (ix) Lukomska; (x) with Ens., Boulez; (xi) McDaniel; (xii) Harper; (xiii) with Williams. Overall musical direction: Boulez

What **Pierre Boulez** above all demonstrates in the orchestral works (including those with chorus) is that, for all his seeming asceticism, Webern was working on human emotions. The **Juilliard Quartet** and the **John Alldis Choir** convey comparable commitment; though neither **Heather Harper** nor **Halina Lukomska** is ideally cast in the solo vocal music, Boulez brings out the best in both of them in the works with orchestra. A rare recording of **Webern** himself conducting his arrangement of Schubert dances is also included. There are excellent notes, every item is cued, and perhaps it is carping to regret that the *Passacaglia* and *Variations for Orchestra* were not indexed.

(i) *Concerto for 9 Instruments, Op. 24; (ii) 6 Orchestral Pieces, Op. 6; Symphony, Op. 21; (i) Quartet, Op. 22; Trio, Op. 20; 3 Pieces for Cello & Piano, Op. 11; 4 Pieces for Violin & Piano Op. 7; Variations for Piano, Op. 27; (iii) 5 Canons for Soprano & 2 Clarinets; 3 Songs, Op. 18; 3 Traditional Rhymes, Op. 17. (i) Orch. of Schubert: German Dances*

🅑–ⓑ *** Naxos 8.557330. (i) 20th Century Classics Ens. (members); (ii) Philh. O, Craft; (iii) Welch-Babidge

As an important issue in the 'Robert Craft Collection', Naxos here offers an exceptionally generous selection of Webern's mature works. Eight brief pieces for various forces frame the three central works, the *Six Pieces*, Op. 6, the most powerful example of his early atonal period, exploiting a very large orchestra, the *Symphony*, Op. 21, for chamber orchestra, one of the finest works of his later, fully serial period, and the *Concerto* for nine soloists, the most popular of his chamber works. The **Philharmonia** plays warmly in Opus 6, with the **20th Century Classics Ensemble** from New York giving virtuoso performances of the other two, also supplying players for the smaller-scale piece. **Jennifer Welch-Babidge's** bright, clear soprano, precisely focused, is ideal for the craggy lines of the vocal pieces. Full texts and English translations are given. As a charming supplement, the Philharmonia also plays the set of six tiny *German Dances* by Schubert which, soon after they were discovered in 1929, Webern set sensitively for small orchestra. Excellent sound in recordings from both London and New York.

Collected works:

Disc 1: (i) *Im Sommerwind; 5 Movements for String Quartet* (orchestral version), *Op. 5; Passacaglia, Op. 1; 6 Pieces for Large Orchestra, Op. 6.* **Arrangements of:** Bach: *Musical Offering: Fugue;* Schubert: *German Dances, D.820*

Disc 2: (i) *5 Pieces for Orchestra* (1913); *Symphony, Op. 21; Variations for Orchestra, Op. 30; (iii; iv; v) Das Augenlicht, Op. 26; Cantatas 1, Op. 29; 2, Op. 31; 3 Orchesterlieder* (1913–24)

Disc 3: (ii; vi) *Concerto for 9 Instruments, Op. 24; (ii) 5 Pieces for Orchestra, Op. 10; (ii; vi) Piano Quintet; Quartet, Op. 22* (for piano, violin, clarinet & saxophone); *(ii; iii; v; vii) 5 Canons on Latin*

Texts, Op. 15; Entflieht auf Leichten Kähnen, Op. 2; 2 Lieder, Op. 8; 4 Lieder, Op. 13; 6 Lieder, Op. 14; 5 Geistliche Lieder, Op. 15; 3 Lieder, Op. 18; 2 Lieder, Op. 19; 3 Volkstexte, Op. 17

Disc 4: (iii; viii) *3 Gedichte (1899–1903); 8 frühe Lieder (1901–4); 3 Avenarius Lieder (1903–4); 5 Dehmel Lieder (1906–8); 5 St George Lieder; 5, Op. 4; 4 St George Lieder (1908–9); 4 Lieder, Op. 12; 3 Jone Gesänge, Op. 23; 3 Jone Lieder, Op. 25*

Disc 5: (ix; x) *6 Bagatelles for String Quartet, Op. 5; (Langsamer) Slow Movement for String Quartet (1905); 5 Movements for String Quartet, Op. 5; 3 Pieces for String Quartet (1913); Rondo for String Quartet (1906); String Quartet (1905); String Quartet, Op. 28; String Trio, Op. 20; Movement for String Trio, Op. posth. (1925)*

Disc 6: (xi; xii) *Cello Sonata (1914); 2 Pieces for Cello & Piano (1899); 3 Small Pieces for Cello & Piano, Op. 11; (xiii; xiv) 4 Pieces for Violin & Piano, Op. 7. (xv) Piano: Kinderstück (1924 & 1925); Piece (1906); Sonata Movement (Rondo) (1906); (xiv) Variations, Op. 27*

(M) **** DG 457 637-2 (6). (i) BPO, or (ii) Ens. Intercontemporain, Boulez; (iii) Oelze; (iv) Finley; (v) BBC Singers; (vi) Aimard; (vii) Pollet; (viii) Schneider; (ix) Emerson Qt; (x) McCormick; (xi) Hagen; (xii) Maisenberg; (xiii) Kremer; (xiv) Zimerman; (xv) Cascioli

This monumental DG set goes far further than the earlier Sony collection in its illumination of Webern as one of the great musical pioneers of the 20th century. The first point is that where the earlier set limited itself to the numbered works, this one covers so much more (on six discs instead of three) with a far fuller portrait presented in the early works. Both sets include such offerings as the arrangements of Bach (the *Ricercar* from the *Musical Offering*) and Schubert (a collection of waltzes). **Boulez's** interpretations of the numbered works have developed too, with the **Berlin Philharmonic** exceptionally responsive, bringing out often unsuspected warmth and beauty. The point and purposefulness of these performances is particularly helpful in making such thorny late inspirations as the two *Cantatas* so much more readily approachable. The vocal soloists have been ideally chosen, with the fresh-toned **Christiane Oelze** taking on the majority of songs, but with **Françoise Pollet** and **Gerald Finley** equally assured. The starry list of instrumental contributors could not be bettered either, including as it does such luminaries as the **Emerson Quartet** and **Krystian Zimerman**, and the recordings made over a period of years are uniformly excellent.

Concerto for 9 Instruments, Op. 24

(M) **** Chan. 6534. Nash Ens., Rattle – SCHOENBERG: *Pierrot Lunaire* ***

This late Webern piece, tough, spare and uncompromising, makes a valuable fill-up for **Jane Manning's** outstanding ver-

sion of Schoenberg's *Pierrot Lunaire*, a 1977 recording originally made for the Open University. First-rate sound and a beautifully clean CD transfer.

Langsamer Satz (arr. Schwarz)

*** Delos DE 3121. Seattle SO, Schwarz – HONEGGER: *Symphony 2*; RICHARD STRAUSS: *Metamorphosen* ***

The slow movement Webern composed in 1905 for string quartet sounds even more Mahlerian in **Gerard Schwarz's** transcription for full strings, which is eloquently played and sumptuously recorded.

Passacaglia for Orchestra, Op. 1

●– (M) **** DG (ADD) 457 760-2. BPO, Karajan – BERG: *Lyric Suite, etc.*; SCHOENBERG: *Variations* ***

This is a beautifully played and recorded version of Webern's *Passacaglia*, which will disappoint no one. It sounds especially haunting – even magical – in **Karajan's** hands, and has been superbly transferred.

CHAMBER MUSIC

(i) *6 Bagatelles, Op. 9; 5 Movements, Op. 5; 3 Little Pieces, Op. 11; 4 Pieces, Op. 7; Rondo, Op. posth.; Slow Movement, Op. posth.; String Quartet, Op. 28; String Quartet, Op. posth. (1905); String Trio, Op. 20; (ii) Piano Sonata, Op. posth.*

●– *** Chan. 10083. (i) Schoenberg Qt; (ii) Grotenhuis (piano)

This outstanding collection, superbly performed, gives an excellent idea of the range of Webern's genius, from early works to such seminal masterpieces as the *Five Movements*, Op. 5, the late *String Trio* and *String Quartet*, Op. 28. Thanks to the warmth and expressive intensity of the playing of the **Schoenberg Quartet**, even the unprepared listener will find illumination here, with the early works providing a helpful introduction to the more daunting serial pieces.

6 Bagatelles for String Quartet, Op. 9; Langsamer Satz; 5 Movements for String Quartet, Op. 5; Rondo for String Quartet (1906); String Quartet (1905); String Quartet, Op. 28; Movement for String Trio, Op. posth.; String Trio, Op. 20.

*** Nim. NI 5668. Vienna Artis Qt

With warm, purposeful performances recorded in full, close sound, the **Artis Quartet** present Webern's collected music for string quartet and string trio as a most persuasive survey of this problematic composer's creative career. The three works from 1905 and 1906 (those without opus number) represent his early post-romantic style at its ripest, while such works as the *Five Movements*, Op. 5, vividly illustrate the imaginative leap he made when adopting free atonality. Equally representative are the more astringent works of his later years, the *String Trio*, Op. 20 and the *String Quartet*, Op. 28, all presented with a purposefulness and commitment that readily helps to overcome any problems the listener may have.

Variations for Piano, Op. 27

🎵 **** Ph. 468 033-2. Uchida – BERG: *Piano Sonata*;
  SCHOENBERG: *Piano Concerto; Klavierstücke* ****

BB *** Naxos 8.553870. Hill – BERG: *Piano Sonata*;
  SCHOENBERG: *Piano Pieces; Suite* ***

The *Variations*, Op. 27, Webern's only mature piano piece, dates from the mid-1930s and calls for the most eloquent playing if it is to persuade the listener. Webern himself stressed that the music's structural intricacies must give rise to a 'profound expressiveness'. However, **Peter Hill** can hold his own against any of the competition.

Uchida gives a highly imaginative and refined account, recorded with great clarity and presence in the Herkulessaal, Munich, and this *Gramophone* Award-winning performance is as fine as this piece has ever received. Moreover, the Philips couplings, too, are very highly recommendable.

WEELKES, Thomas (1576–1623)

Alleluia, I heard a voice; Hosanna to the Son of David; Most mighty and all-knowing Lord; When David heard; (i) In nomine a 4

**** EMI 3 94430-2. King's College, Cambridge, Ch.,
  Cleobury; (i) with Fretwork (with TOMKINS: *Choral music*) –
  GIBBONS: *Choral collection* ****

This splendidly sung collection (the opening *Alleluia* and the very original setting of *When David heard* stand out, the latter also included as set by Tomkins) juxtaposes the music of Thomas Weelkes with that of two other great Elizabethan composers of English choral music. **Fretwork** make a viol contribution to each selection. The performances are superbly eloquent and the recording very real.

WEILL, Kurt (1900–1950)

The Eternal Road (abridged)

BB *** Naxos 8.559402. Hauman, Rearick, DeNolfo, Dent,
  Rideout, Christopher, Maddalena, Berlin R. Children's Ch.,
  Ernst Senff Ch., Berlin RSO, Schwarz

Conceived as a biblical pageant, *The Eternal Road* is Kurt Weill's most ambitious work. In a massive sequence of words and music – lasting (if uncut) around five hours – the piece links the stories of biblical characters with the latter-day persecution of Jews in Europe. Originally presented in New York in 1937, it proved too cumbersome for its own good and was quickly forgotten. Yet it contains some of the most inspired music that Weill ever wrote, demonstrating that after he fled from Europe to America his genius remained as fertile and original as ever. This generous selection of musical items, gives an excellent idea of the piece, very well performed and recorded in Berlin with American soloists and conductor. The vigour of the writing brings a most attractive image of the Broadway style that Weill was developing. That includes such numbers as the fine chorus representing the Israelites' Dance around the Golden Calf, while the duet between Ruth and Naomi effectively avoids sentimentality in its gentle dance rhythms, and the duet between Ruth and Boaz, similarly popular in style, develops passionately. First-rate sound.

STAGE WORKS

The Ballad of Magna Carta; Der Lindberghflug

*** Cap. 60012. Henschel, Tyl, Calaminus, Clemens, Cologne
  Pro Musica Ch. & RSO, Latham-König; Wirl, Schmidt,
  Feckler, Minth, Scheeben, Berlin R. Ch. & O, Scherchen

Der Lindberghflug ('The Lindbergh Flight') is a curiosity. Brecht wrote the text, but only later did Weill set the complete work, and that is how it is given in this excellent Cologne recording. A historic 1930 performance of the original Weill-Hindemith version, conducted by **Hermann Scherchen**, is given as an appendix, recorded with a heavy background roar but with astonishingly vivid voices. The fine, very German tenor who sang Lindbergh in 1930 was **Erik Wirl** and the tenor in the new recording is not nearly so sweet-toned, and the German narrator delivers his commentary in a casual, matter-of-fact way. Otherwise the performance under **Jan Latham-König** fully maintains the high standards of Capriccio's Weill series; and the other, shorter item, *The Ballad of Magna Carta* is most enjoyable too, a piece never recorded before. Clear, if rather dry, recording with voices vivid and immediate.

Die Dreigroschenoper (The Threepenny Opera); (complete)

🎵 *** Decca 430 075-2. Kollo, Lemper, Milva, Adorf,
  Dernesch, Berlin RIAS Chamber Ch. & Sinf., Mauceri

🎵 *** Sony (ADD) MK 42637. Lenya, Neuss, Trenk-Trebisch,
  Hesterberg, Schellow, Koczian, Grunert, Ch. & Dance O of
  Radio Free Berlin, Brückner-Rüggeberg

On Decca there are obvious discrepancies between the opera-singers, **René Kollo** and **Helga Dernesch**, and those in the cabaret tradition, notably the vibrant and provocative **Ute Lemper** (Polly Peachum) and the gloriously dark-voiced and characterful **Milva** (Jenny). That entails downward modulation in various numbers, as it did with Lotte Lenya, but the changes from the original are far less extreme. Kollo is good, but Dernesch is even more compelling. The coordination of music and presentation makes for a vividly enjoyable experience, even if committed Weill enthusiasts will inevitably disagree with some of the controversial textual and interpretative decisions.

The CBS alternative offers a vividly authentic abridged recording, darkly incisive and atmospheric, with **Lotte Lenya** giving an incomparable performance as Jenny. All the wrong associations, built up round the music from indifferent performances, melt away in the face of a reading as sharp and intense as this. Bright, immediate, real stereo recording.

(i) Happy End; (ii) The Seven Deady Sins

🎵 **(M)** (***) stereo/mono Sony 82876 78754-2. Lenya; with (i)
  Ch. & O; (ii) Mal Qt & O, Brückner-Rüggeberg

Happy End, intended as a successor to *The Threepenny Opera*, yet more savagely cynical, took far longer to be appreciated. **Lotte Lenya**, Weill's widow, here turned the songs into a kind of cycle (following a hint from the composer) and transposing where necessary; and her renderings in her individual brand of vocalising are so compelling, they make the scalp tingle. Many of these numbers are among the finest Weill ever wrote, and the 1960 recording is bright and clear. Lenya's recording of *Das Sieben Todsunden* was made earlier, in 1950, and her singing again underlines the distinctive mixture of ballet and song-cycle as one of Weill's most concentrated inspirations. The rhythmic verve is irresistible, and though Lenya inevitably had to have the music transposed down, her understanding of the idiom is unique. However, the mono recording is harsh by modern standards. The original notes by Davis Drew are retained for this reissue, but there are now no texts or translations included.

(i; ii) Die Sieben Todsünden (The Seven Deadly Sins). (i) Songs: Berlin im Licht; Complainte de la Seine; Es regnet; Youkali; Nannas Lied; Wie lange noch?

(B) **(*) HM Musique d'Abord HMA 1951420. (i) Fassbaender; (ii) Brandt, Sojer, Komatsu, Urbas, Hanover R. PO, Garben

This Harmonia Mundi set stars **Brigitte Fassbaender**, who, using the original pitch, brings a Lieder-singer's feeling for word detail and a comparable sense of style. Her account is obviously less street-wise than Lemper's deleted version, but there is a plangent feeling that is highly appropriate. The songs are equally impressive, mainly connected in one way or another with the main piece. The vocal quartet makes an idiomatic team, but the conductor **Cord Garben** at times seems on the leisurely side in his choice of tempi. Excellent, vivid recording.

Der Silbersee (complete)

*** Cap. 60011-2 (2). Heichele, Tamassy, Holdorf, Schmidt, Mayer, Korte, Thomas, Cologne Pro Musica Ch., Cologne RSO, Latham-König

Led by **Hildegard Heichele**, bright and full-toned as the central character, Fennimore, the Capriccio cast is an outstanding one, with each voice satisfyingly clean-focused, while the 1989 recording is rather better-balanced and kinder to the instrumental accompaniment than some from this source, with the voices exceptionally vivid.

Street Scene (opera; complete; CD version)

*** TER CDTER2 1185 (2). Ciesinski, Kelly, Bottone, van Allan, ENO Ch. & O, Davis

The TER set was made with the cast of the **ENO** production at the Coliseum, and the idiomatic feeling and sense of flow consistently reflect that. Some of the solo singing in the large cast is flawed, but never seriously, and the principals are all very well cast – **Kristine Ciesinski** as the much-put-upon Anna Maurrant, **Richard van Allan** as her sorehead husband, **Janis Kelly** sweet and tender as the vulnerable daughter, and **Bonaventura Bottone** as the diffident young Jewish neighbour who loves her. Those are only a few of the sharply drawn characters, and the performance on the discs, with

dialogue briskly paced, reflects the speed of the original ENO production. Warm, slightly distanced sound.

Der Zar lässt sich Photographieren (complete)

**(*) Cap. 60 007-1. McDaniel, Pohl, Napier, Cologne R.O, Latham-König

This curious one-Act *opera buffa* is a wry little parable about assassins planning to kill the Tsar when he has his photograph taken. Angèle, the photographer, is replaced by the False Angèle, but the Tsar proves to be a young man who simply wants friendship, and the would-be assassin, instead of killing him, plays a tango on the gramophone, before the Tsar's official duties summon him again. **Jan Latham-König** in this 1984 recording directs a strong performance, though the dryly recorded orchestra is consigned to the background. The voices fare better, though **Barry McDaniel** is not ideally steady as the Tsar.

The Rise and Fall of the City of Mahagonny (DVD version)

*** Warner DVD 2056258. McDonald, LuPone, Griffey, LA Op. Ch. & O, Conlon (Dir: Doyle, V/D: Muller)

Using an English translation of Bertolt Brecht's text, the **Los Angeles Opera** offers a colourful production which vividly evokes the seedy atmosphere of the original, set in the 1920s. **Audra McDonald** as Jenny appears as an over-painted film star, a splendid focus for the whole performance, which is linked by announcements over a very visible public-address system. **Patti LuPone** is equally effective as Leocadia, and **Anthony Dean Griffey** is the characterful leader of the male contingent, dressed as though for a Hollywood Western. That association is cemented by such effects as the honky-tonk piano in the bar. **James Conlon** proves an urgently dramatic conductor.

'Kurt Weill on Broadway', excerpts from: The Firebrand of Florence; Johnny Johnson (Johnny's Song); Knickerbocker Holiday; Love Life; One Touch of Venus (Westwind)

(M) *** EMI 3 58245-2. Hampson, Futral, Hadley, Lehman, L. Sinf. Ch., L. Sinf., McGlinn

Thomas Hampson's magical collection of Weill numbers reveals what richness there is even in the least-known of Weill's Broadway scores. So a full 40 minutes are devoted to Weill's biggest flop, *The Firebrand of Florence*, an offbeat biography of Benvenuto Cellini, and the selection here is delightful. At the beginning of the disc *One Touch of Venus* instantly establishes that poetry is the keynote of the American Weill. One of the numbers in the 20-minute selection from *Love Life* (lyrics by Alan J. Lerner) is a duet, *I remember it well*. Only later did Lerner adapt it for Gingold and Chevalier in *Gigi*, for here it is a dreamy slow waltz. The only well-known number is *It never was you* from *Knickerbocker Holiday*, and even that comes as a duet, not a solo. Hampson sings superbly, and **McGlinn** draws deeply sympathetic performances from the **London Sinfonietta** and the other soloists.

WEINBERG, Mieczyslav (See also under Vainberg, Moishei)

(1919–96)

(i) Clarinet Concerto, Op. 104; (ii) Flute Concertos 1, Op. 75; 2, Op. 148; (iii) Fantasia for Cello and Orchestra, Op. 52

(N) **** Chan. **SACD** CHSA 5064 (i) Claesson, (ii) Johnhall; (iii) Gunnarson; Gothenburg SO, Svedland

These three concertos are superbly written for their respective instruments and their music is both stimulating and appealing. The *Fantasia for cello and orchestra* is in essence another three-movement concerto, yet together they form an arc, first slowly increasing in pace and tension and then decreasing. The music itself is both richly melodic and full of evocative atmosphere. The first of the two *Flute Concertos* is also haunting. After a brilliant *scherzando* opening the slow movement is an introspective *Passacaglia*, the finale a kind of waltz. The *Second Concerto* also has a melancholy slow movement but with a stark climax and the *Allegretto* finale playfully quotes flute themes by other composers. The *Clarinet Concerto* is much less predictable with rhapsodical *Andante* and a cheeky finale. All three works are superbly played here and the four-channel recording adds a rich three-dimensional effect to the sound.

Cello Sonatas 1, Op. 21; 2, Op. 63; Sonata 1 for Solo Cello, Op. 72

*** BIS CD-1648. Chaushian, Sudbin

The *First Cello Sonata* comes from 1945, two years after the composer had settled in Moscow. The *Second* was written 14 years later, in 1959, the same year as Shostakovich's *First Cello Concerto*. It was given its first performance by Rostropovich the following year. As always in Weinberg's music, there are strong affinities with Shostakovich and, in the *Second Sonata*, also with Bartók. Weinberg also composed four solo *Cello Sonatas*, the first of which is recorded here. **Alexander Chaushian** is a magnificent player and he is excellently supported by **Yevgeny Sudbin**.

String Quartets 4, Op. 20; 16, Op. 130

*** CPO CPO 777 313-2. Danel Qt

Weinberg is nothing if not prolific, and now CPO have embarked on the ambitious project of recording all 17 of his *String Quartets*. His *Fourth* comes from 1945, and the *Sixteenth* was composed in 1981. As in so much of his other music, the debt to Shostakovich is strong but the musical processes command attention and the melodic ideas are characterful. In the *Sixteenth* Weinberg is very much his own man, grave and pensive, and its severity is convincingly conveyed by the **Danel Quartet**.

WEINBERGER, Jaromir

(1896–1967)

Schwanda the Bagpiper (complete; in Czech)

(BB) ** Naxos 8.660146/7 (2). Robavs, Monogarova, Choupenitch, Kostyuk, Wexford Festival Op. Ch., Belarus Nat. PO, Reynolds

Recorded at the Wexford Festival in Ireland in 2003, this Naxos set offers a lively account of a colourful opera very much in the tradition of Smetana's *Bartered Bride*, with the *Polka* a hauntingly memorable centrepiece. It helps that forces from another Slavonic country, **Belarus**, are involved, with **Julian Reynolds** drawing idiomatic singing and playing from the whole company. The title-role is well taken by the baritone, **Matjaz Robavs**, and so is the role of his wife, Dorota, by the bright, clear, agile soprano, **Tatiana Monogarova**. The fruity mezzo, **Larisa Kostyuk**, is well cast as the Queen, even if the Slavonic beat in her voice is often obtrusive. Sadly, the other important role, that of the mysterious Babinsky, is given to a tenor, **Ivan Choupenitch**, whose voice is so ill-focused it is hard to tell which notes he is singing. The recording, made in the tiny Wexford Theatre Royal, is inevitably limited on orchestral sound, but voices come over well.

Schwanda the Bagpiper: Polka & Fugue

(M) *** RCA **SACD** 82876 66376-2. Chicago SO, Reiner – SMETANA: *Bartered Bride: Overture*; DVOŘÁK: *Symphony 9 (New World)*; *Overture Carnival* ***

This infectious orchestral display-piece was better known in the days of 78s. **Reiner** and his fine orchestra give a bravura performance, building to a big climax. The **Chicago** recording is suitably brilliant, enhanced by its SACD format.

WEINER, Leó (1885–1960)

Hungarian Folkdance Suite, Op. 18

(M) *** Chan. 6625. Philh. O, Järvi – BARTÓK: *Hungarian Pictures*; ENESCU: *Romanian Rhapsodies 1–2* ***

Weiner here remained orientated towards the German and French schools, and this lively and attractive suite represents a Hungarian folk style more Westernized than Bartók's; but with purposeful direction from **Järvi**, fine dramatic playing from the orchestra and ripely resonant recording, the full range of colour is brought out in these four movements, which last almost half an hour.

Violin Sonatas 1 in D, Op. 9; 2 in F sharp min. Op. 11

**(*) Biddulph LAW 015. Shumsky, Lipkin – DOHNÁNYI: *Violin Sonata in C sharp min., Op. 21; Andante* **(*)

The two *Violin Sonatas* of Leó Weiner were composed in 1911 and 1919 respectively, and they are heard here in good performances by **Oscar Shumsky** and **Seymour Lipkin**. They were recorded in New York in 1993 and if Shumsky's playing does not have the effortless mastery it possessed in the early 1980s, he still performs a service in restoring these enjoyable works to the wider musical public. A most worthwhile issue.

WEINGARTNER, Felix
(1863–1942)

Symphony 1; King Lear (symphonic poem)
*** CPO 999 981-2. Basel SO, Letonja

Felix Weingartner, noted Beethovenian, the first conductor to record a Beethoven symphony cycle complete, was also a prolific composer. This delightful symphony brims with one charming melody after another. So far from seeking to emulate Beethoven, this work comes closer to Dvořák, with a charmingly easy-going pastoral first movement, predominantly lyrical. Instead of a slow movement, Weingartner then has a flowing, march-like *Allegretto* with a surging violin melody in the middle. The third movement is a jolly folk-dance with oboe and flute piping away, leading to a swaggering finale. Weingartner had a special relationship with Switzerland and with Basel in particular, inspiring **Marko Letonja** and the orchestra to a superb performance, vividly recorded. The symphonic poem, *King Lear*, more Lisztian than the *Symphony*, makes an excellent coupling in this first issue of a projected Weingartner series.

WEISS, Silvius (1686–1750)

Lute Sonatas: 2 in D; 27 in C min.; 35 in D min. (Naxos 8.554350)

Lute Sonatas: 5 in G; 25 in G min.; 50 in B flat (Naxos 8.553988)

Lute Sonatas: 7 in C min.; 23 in B flat; 45 in A (Naxos 8.555722)

Lute Sonatas: 19 in F; 34 in D min.; 36 in D min. (Naxos 8.570109)

Lute Sonatas: 21 in F min.; 37 in C; 46 in A (Naxos 8.554557)

Lute Sonatas: 32 in F; 52 in C min.; 94 in G min. (Naxos 8. 570551)

Lute Sonatas: 36 in D min.; 42 in A min.; 49 in B flat (Naxos 8.553773)

Lute Sonatas: 38 in C; 43 in A min.; Tombeau sur la mort de M. Cajeran Baron d'Hartig (Naxos 8.554833)

Lute Sonatas 15 in B flat; 48 in F sharp min. (Naxos 8.557806)
⊶ (BB) *** Barto (Baroque lute)

In layout Weiss's *Lute Sonatas* are very much like the suites and partitas of Bach, usually beginning with a Prelude, followed by a group of dance movements: Allemande, Courante, Bourrée, Sarabande, Menuet and Gigue. Sometimes Weiss closes with a *Chaconne* (Suite 6), *Passacaglia*

(Suite 14) or an unusual movement, like the striking *Paysane* which ends Suite 25. The music is invariably through-composed, so that every movement is interrelated, and although each has an independent thematic existence one sometimes has a sense of a set of variations. **Robert Barto**, playing a baroque lute, shows us the breadth of Weiss's achievement and how naturally the music suits the lute, rather than the guitar. On almost all the discs offered so far he combines one early, one mid-period and one late *Sonata*. The quality of Weiss's invention seems inexhaustible throughout all these works, and he has a worthy exponent in Robert Barto, a virtuoso lutenist of a high order and a fine musician. He understands this repertory perfectly, never seeking to impose his personality over that of the composer, and the first-class recording gives him a natural presence.

WELLESZ, Egon (1885–1974)

Symphonies 1 – 9. Symphonischer Epilog
(N) *** CPO 777 183-2 (4). Vienna Radio SO, Rabl

CPO have deleted the individual discs of the Wellesz symphonies discussed at greater length in our 2005–06 Edition but made them available as a complete set. The *First* comes from 1945–6 when he was sixty and the last was finished in 1971, the year before a stroke put an end to his creative career. They are rewarding pieces and very well served by **Gottfried Rabl** and his Austrian Radio forces.

WHITE, Robert (c. 1538–74)

Motets: Christe qui lux es; Domine quis habitavit; Portio mea Domine; Regina coeli
⊶ ✿ (M) *** Cal. CAL 6623. Clerkes of Oxenford, Wulstan – TALLIS: *Mass Puer natus est*, etc. *** ✿

Robert White's style of writing has a basic restraint and often shows a gentle, Dowland-like melancholy, so striking at the opening of *Domine quis habitavit*. But this is often offset by the soaring trebles, especially in the ravishing *Portio mea Domine*, while *Christe qui lux es*, the last motet on this record, is very touching indeed. Glorious performances by **Wulstan** and the **Clerkes of Oxenford**, who have the full measure of this repertoire. The analogue recording could hardly be bettered. Not to be missed.

WHITLOCK, Percy (1903–46)

Ballet of the Wood Creatures; Balloon Ballet; Come Along, Marnie; Dignity and Impudence March; The Feast of St Benedict: Concert Overture; Holiday Suite; Music for Orchestra: Suite; Susan, Doggie and Me; Wessex Suite
(*) Marco 8.225162. Dublin RTE Concert O, Sutherland

Percy Whitlock's style is attractive and easy-going, with quite imaginative orchestration and nice touches everywhere. The marches are jolly and the waltzes nostalgic – *The Ballet of the Wood Creatures* is especially charming. **Gavin Sutherland** directs the **RTE Orchestra** with his usual understanding. The sound is good, but occasionally the strings sound a little scrawny (the opening of the *Waltz* in the *Holiday Suite*, for example).

WIDOR, Charles-Marie
(1844–1937)

Symphony 3 for Organ & Orchestra, Op. 69

⊕┐ *** Chan. 9785. Tracey (organ of Liverpool Cathedral), BBC PO, Tortelier – GUILMANT: *Symphony 2 for Organ & Orchestra, Op. 91*; FRANCK: *Choral 2* ***

Widor's *Third Symphony* for organ and orchestra, although in two sections, moves in a series of episodes: *Adagio – Andante* (introducing a luscious string tune) – *Allegro* (end of first movement); *Vivace – Tranquillamente – Allegro* (which with its horn calls and galloping energy brings a curious reminder of Franck's *Chasseur maudit*); finally comes an overwhelmingly majestic *Largo* with the chorale melody shared by organ and orchestra, bursting at the seams in sheer amplitude. The decibels of the coda are worthy of the finest speakers. **Ian Tracey** makes the most of his opportunities, as does **Tortelier**. Certainly the huge Liverpool organ and the resonant cathedral acoustics seem custom made for such spectacle and the Chandos engineers capture it all with aplomb.

Cello Sonata in A, Op. 80

⊕┐ *** Hyp. CDA 67244. Lidström, Forsberg – KOECHLIN: *Chansons Bretonnes*; MAGNARD: *Sonata* ***

Mats Lidström and **Bengt Forsberg** have put us in their debt by disinterring this *Sonata* from the first decade of the last century. It is full of good ideas and its civilized discourse holds the listener throughout. Excellent recording and rewarding couplings.

Piano Quintet in D min., Op. 7; Piano Trio in B flat, Op. 19

⊕┐ BB *** Naxos 8.555416. Prunyi, New Budapest Qt

The *Piano Trio* is a charming, lightweight work, with a a romantic first movement with a pleasingly elegant secondary theme. There is a debt to Mendelssohn in the *Andante*, which is like a song without words. The *Scherzo* and *Rondo* finale have attractive ideas too, besides freshness and vitality.

The *Piano Quintet*, although shorter in length, is a bigger work, more concentrated in conception and style, with the piano dominating the bold opening movement. Once more the *Andante* brings elegance, but it is the *Molto vivace* Scherzo that looks back to Mendelssohn. The polyphonic development in the finale then brings added gravitas. Both works are played here with fluent spontaneity and plenty of spirit, and the recording is excellent. This is not great music, but admirers of Widor's organ music may find it a refreshing change.

SOLO ORGAN MUSIC

Organ Symphonies: 1 in C min.: Méditation (only). 2 in D; 3 in E min.: Prélude, Adagio & Final; 4 in F min., Op. 13/1–4; 5 in F min.; 6 in G min., Op. 42/1–2; 9 in C min. (Gothique), Op. 70

⊕┐ BB **** Warner Apex 2564 62297-2 (2). Marie-Claire Alain (Cavaillé-Coll organs, Saint-Etienne de Caen & Eglise de Saint-Germain-en-Laye)

For this Apex reissue Warner have combined two sets of recordings, from 1970 and 1977, which jointly offer an impressive overall coverage of this repertoire. **Marie-Claire Alain** contents herself with playing just the *Méditation* from the uneven *First Symphony*, and only three movements from the *Third*. Here the Saint Germain organ sounds very orchestral and the colouring of the gentle *Adagio* (a perpetual canon) is very effective. The later *Symphonies* are more impressive works than the earlier group of Op. 13. 5 is justly the most famous. These are classic, authoritative performances, given spacious analogue sound with just a touch of harshness to add a little edge in *fortissimos*.

Symphonies 1 in C min.; 2 in D, Op. 13/1–2

**(*) ASV CDDCA 1165. Nolan (organ of Liverpool Metropolitan Cathedral)

Widor's two early *Symphonies* have seven and six movements respectively and, as the composer tends to meander, one feels a single, more succinct work could have been created by using the best movements from each. It is only in the third-movement *Intermezzo* that the work really springs to life, dancing over a strong theme in the pedals. The following *Adagio* makes a typical calm interlude, before the bold *Marche pontificale* arrives, easily the most memorable movement in either work, and sounding splendid here. Then we have another *Méditation* before the robust fugal finale.

The *Praeludium circulaire* which opens the *Second Symphony* certainly goes round in circles, but the following *Pastoral* has genuine charm. The joyous, buoyant finale brings music which at last memorably blazes with vigour and has a catchy ostino for its main theme. **Joseph Nolan** obviously has none of our misgivings about Widor's meandering, and he plays both works with an appealing mixture of robust vigour and well-sustained calm. The fine Liverpool organ is very well recorded and obviously suits this repertoire in Nolan's hands.

Symphonies 2 in D, Op. 13/2; 8 in B, Op. 42/4

⊕┐ *** BIS CD-1007. Fagius (organ of Kallio Church, Helsinki)

The Swedish organist **Hans Fagius** plays two Widor *Symphonies*, the *Second in D major* and the *Eighth in B major*, on a new instrument made by the Swedish makers Akerman and Lund. The instrument itself is five years old and is modelled on the symphonic organs of the Cavaillé-Coll tradition with which César Franck and Widor were so closely associated. Its disposition was the work of Kurt Lueders of Paris. Hans Fagius serves the music well and the engineers produce particularly impressive results. The opening *Allegro* of the *Eighth Symphony* gives a good idea of the impressive range this disc covers.

Symphonies 3 in E min., Op.13/2; 6 in G min., Op. 42/2; 3 Nouvelles pièces, Op. 87

🎧 *** ASV CDDCA 1106. Patrick (Coventry Cathedral organ)

For the second issue in their spectacular Widor series, ASV have turned to **David Patrick** and the organ of Coventry Cathedral, of which he is clearly a master. If less obviously suited to this repertoire than a French organ, it still sounds very impressive. Unlike Marie-Claire Alain he plays the *Third Symphony* complete, but he and the organ are at their finest in the *Sixth*, with its grand opening and equally bold *Marcia* finale. They frame a gentle *Adagio* and a hushed *Cantabile*, with the most characteristic movement, a brilliant scherzando-like *Intermezzo*, as the work's centrepiece. Patrick plays this superbly, effectively exploiting his organ's wide range of dynamic.

Symphony 5 in F min., Op. 42/1

🎧 *** Chan. 9271. Tracey (organ of Liverpool Cathedral), BBC PO, Tortelier – GUILMANT: *Symphony 1 for Organ & Orchestra* ***; POULENC: *Concerto* **(*).

The long reverberation-period of Liverpool Cathedral gives a special character to Widor's *Fifth Symphony*, especially the mellow central movements. **Ian Tracey** makes the most of the colouristic possibilities of his fine instrument and also uses the widest possible range of dynamics, with the tone at times shaded down to a distant whisper. Yet the famous *Toccata* expands gloriously if without the plangent bite of a French instrument.

Symphonies 5; 6 in G min., Op. 42/1–2

*** Discovery Cyprès CYP 1631. Sehnhave (organ of Katarina Church, Stockholm)

The new van den Heuvel organ in the Katarina Church, Stockholm, is admirably suited to Widor, having weighty pedals and a wide range of colourful registration, while the church acoustic provides an ambience which affords clarity of detail. Both of **Kristiaan Sehnhave's** performances are full of life and employ a wide dynamic range, and no one could complain that the famous finale of 5 and the tumultuous closing movement of the *Sixth Symphony* are in any way lacking in energy or spectacle.

Symphonies 5 in F min.; 7 in A min., Op. 42/3

🎧 *** ASV CDDCA 958. Parker-Smith (van den Heuvel organ, St Eustache, Paris)

Jane Parker-Smith is a complete master of this repertoire (and she shows that it does not always have to be played on a traditional Cavaillé-Coll instrument). The organ at Saint-Eustache, Paris is new (1967), and is Netherlands-built. It is magnificent. Not only are the big tuttis, as in the finale of the *Seventh Symphony*, superbly expansive, but the organ has a ravishingly rich palette and a warm sonority to deal with Widor's gentler ideas, like the *Andante cantabile* and *Adagio* of the *Fifth* and the inner movements of 7, and particularly the *Allegro ma non troppo*, where the gently murmuring semi-

quavers flow along sensuously like a warm summer breeze. Because of this natural clarity of internal focus Jane Parker-Smith is able to use a very wide dynamic range and in the supreme test, the masterly *Toccata* which closes the *Fifth*, the calm at the centre of the storm does not lose contact with the listener, and the great reprise of the main theme, with thundering pedals, is unforgettable.

Symphonies 5; 10 (Romane), Op. 73

🅱🅱 **(*) Arte Nova 74321 79587-2. von Blohn (Späth organ of Hildegardskirche, St Gilbert)

Christian von Blohn has chosen to couple the *Fifth Symphony* with the *Tenth*, based on Gregorian plainchants and providing another spectacular finale, although after all the excitement there is a a closing relaxation. Both performances have plenty of rhythmic energy and the Hildegardskirche organ brings a reedy patina to the climax of the famous *Toccata* to sound more like a French organ than its competitors, even if it loses something in richness of sonority.

Symphony 8 in B, Op. 42/4

🎧 *** ASV CDDCA 1109. Filsell (organ of Liverpool Metropolitan Catholic Cathedral) – COCHEREAU: *Variations sur un vieux Noël*

It is good that the fine organ in Liverpool's Catholic Cathedral is at last receiving attention from the recording companies. Even if the circular building provides a very generous 8-second reverberation, even when the pedals get going, detail is not too muddied, and the reeds have a remarkably spicy French character. This is obvious at the powerful opening of the *B flat Symphony*, and even more so in the variations of the *Andante*. The pungent brilliance of the closing peroration is remarkable.

For his encore **Jeremy Filsell** has skilfully transcribed Pierre Cochereau's improvised variations on an old French carol, as played live by the composer and recorded on LP on Christmas Eve 1972. His own performance is thrillingly spontaneous, as if he were himself improvising. The animated first variation sets off exuberantly. Variation 4 is particularly ear-tickling, and the *Toccata* finale is a tour de force.

(i) Symphonies 9 in C min. (Gothique), Op. 70; (ii) 10 in D (Romane), Op. 73

🎧 *** ASV CDDCA 1172. Filsell (organs of (i) St George's Chapel, Windsor; (ii) Liverpool Metropolitan Cathedral)

An outstanding and apt coupling (for both works are based on Gregorian chant), one of the best in the ASV series. Perhaps surprisingly, the St George's Chapel organ at Windsor suits the *Gothique Symphony* admirably. The warm acoustic and clarity of detail mean that the plainchant, *Puer natus et nobis*, which dominates the third and fourth movements (with the finale a quasi-passacaglia) always emerges from the texture, while the pedals in the closing *toccata* are as thunderous as the composer could possibly want.

The *Symphonie romane* is based on a single Easter gradual, *Haec dies*, and it is subject to both a series of variations and what the organist in the notes suggests is 'a Lisztian/ Franckian thematic metamorphosis'. It needs just the wide range of colour, atmosphere and reedy bite that the Liverpool organ can provide, and the cathedral resonance adds spectacle to the thrilling cascades of the finale, with its long, sustained closing chord. **Jeremy Filsell** gives outstanding performances of both works, splendidly recorded; for once, one does not long for a Cavaillé-Coll; these two English organs suit the music admirably.

Symphony 10 in D (Romane), Op. 73; Suite latine, Op. 86

🎵 *** MDG. 316 0406-2. van Oosten (Cavaillé-Coll organ, at Sermin, Toulouse)

Ben van Oosten's gleaming registration at the opening of the *Symphonie romane* is quite dazzling, yet the central *Choral* and *Cantilène* (both based on plainchant from the Easter liturgy) are wonderfully serene. The cascading finale achieves a spectacular climax (still featuring the plainsong) then makes an extended diminuendo, culminating when the opening theme is reintroduced. The *Suite latine*, one of Widor's last works and written when he was 83, again uses plainsong, but more introspectively. In Van Oosten's hands the central *Beatus vir*, *Lamento* and *Adagio* are gently withdrawn in colour and feeling, so that the exuberant finale is the more telling. These are undoubtedly distinguished performances, very well recorded on an impressively sonorous Cavaillé-Coll organ.

WIENIAWSKI, Henryk
(1835–80)

(i) Violin Concertos 1–2; (ii) Caprice in A min. (arr. Kreisler); Obertass-Mazurka, Op. 19/1; Polonaise de concert 1 in D, Op. 4; Polonaise brillante 2, Op. 21; Scherzo-tarantelle, Op. 16

🎵 (M) *** EMI (ADD) 5 66059-2. Perlman; (i) LPO, Ozawa; (ii) Sanders

Violin Concertos 1–2; Fantaisie brillante on Themes from Gounod's Faust, Op. 20

(BB) *** Naxos 8.553517. Bisengaliev, Polish Nat. RSO, Wit

Violin Concertos 1–2; Légende, Op. 17

🎵 **** DG 431 815-2. Shaham, LSO, Foster – SARASATE: *Zigeunerweisen* ***

The Paganinian pyrotechnics in the first movement of Wieniawski's *First Violin Concerto*, as **Shaham** readily demonstrates can be made to dazzle. Both soloist and orchestra are equally dashing, and lyrically persuasive in the better known *D minor Concerto*, while making an engaging encore out of the delightful *Légende*. With first-class DG recording this record is very recommendable.

Perlman also gives scintillating performances, full of flair, and is excellently accompanied. The recording, from 1973, is warm, vivid and well balanced. It is preferable to Perlman's digital remake of the *Second Concerto*. The midpriced reissue includes a mini-recital of shorter pieces, often dazzling, but losing some of their appeal from Perlman's insistence on a microphone spotlight. **Samuel Sanders** comes more into the picture in the introductions for the two *Polonaises*, although the violin still remains far too near the microphone.

Antoni Wit handles the long opening ritornello of the *F sharp minor Concerto* most impressively, and **Marat Bisengaliev** proves a natural, understanding soloist in both concertos, playing slow movements with warmly romantic feeling and sparkling with brilliance in the display passages and especially in the finales. The *Faust Variations* make a substantial (19-minute) and attractively tuneful bonus. Marat Bisengaliev has a fairly small, but sweet and beautifully focused tone; he is balanced naturally in relation to the orchestra, and both are very well recorded in the Polish Radio Concert Hall, which has an attractively warm acoustic.

Violin Concerto 2 in D min., Op. 22

🎵 (B) *** Decca 475 6703-2 (2). Bell, Cleveland O, Ashkenazy – BRAHMS; SCHUMANN; TCHAIKOVSKY: *Violin Concertos* ***

**(*) CBC SMCD 5197. Kang, Vancouver SO, Comisiona – with *Légende*; SCHUMANN: *Violin Concerto* **(*)

(M) (***) EMI mono 7 64251-2. Heifetz, LPO, Barbirolli – SAINT-SAËNS: *Havanaise*, etc.; SARASATE: *Zigeunerweisen*; VIEUXTEMPS: *Concerto 4* (***)

(BB) (***) Naxos mono 8.110938. Heifetz, LPO, Barbirolli – SIBELIUS: *Violin Concerto*; TCHAIKOVSKY: *Violin Concerto* (***)

Wieniawski's *Second Concerto* makes an unusual but apt bonus for **Joshua Bell's** outstanding triptych of *Concertos* by Brahms, Schumann and Tchaikovsky. It is a masterly performance full of flair, even if he does not find quite the same individual poetry in the big second-subject melody or in the central *Romance* as Itzak Perlman. Excellent recording, brilliant and full, and overall a remarkable bargain.

The Canadian violinist **Juliette Kang** plays with quicksilver brilliance. Dazzlingly clear as the playing is, this is a smaller-scale reading than most, largely a question of recording balance, with both violin and orchestra slightly distanced. So Kang, light and volatile in the rapid passagework, relaxes sweetly into the songful beauty of the motto theme, playing with a natural, unexaggerated lyricism. Both the slow movement and the outer sections of the *Légende* have a similar songful flow, natural and unaffected, while the finale has Kang and **Comisiona** choosing a speed that is fast and brilliant, allowing the dance rhythms to spring infectiously.

Heifetz is in a class of his own. The *Concerto* was recorded in 1935 with the young **John Barbirolli**, with whom Heifetz formed a strong rapport. It finds him at his most spontaneously lyrical, revelling in the rhapsodic argument. The central *Romance* in particular is magnetic in its hushed, meditative intensity, with the finale swaggering confidently. The sound is perhaps less vivid than the best recordings of the day, but both transfers are very good.

Capriccio-waltz, Op. 7; Gigue in E min., Op. 23; Kujawiak in A min.; Légende, Op. 17; Mazurka in G

min., Op. 12/2; 2 Mazurkas, Op. 19; Polonaise 1; Russian Carnival, Op. 11; Saltarello (arr. Lenehan); Scherzo-tarantelle; Souvenir de Moscou, Op. 6; Variations on an Original Theme, Op. 15

(BB) **(*) Naxos 8.550744. Bisengaliev, Lenehan

All the dazzling violin fireworks are ready to bow here, from left-hand pizzicatos in the Russian Carnival to multiple stopping (and some lovely, warm lyricism) in the Variations on an Original Theme, plus all the dash you could ask for in the closing Scherzo-tarantelle, while the beautiful Légende (which Wieniawski dedicated to his wife as a nuptial gift) is both touchingly gentle and passionately brilliant. **John Lenehan** provides his partner with admirable support throughout. The snag is the very reverberant acoustic of the Rosslyn Hill Chapel, Hampstead – so obviously empty; otherwise the sound and balance are natural enough.

WIKMANSON, Johan
(1753–1800)

String Quartet 2 in E min., Op. 1/2

(M) *** CRD (ADD) CRD 3361. Chilingirian Qt – BERWALD: Quartet ***

(M) *** CRD (ADD) CRD 33123 (2). Chilingirian Qt – ARRIAGA: String Quartets 1–3 ***

Wikmanson was a cultured musician, but little of his music survives. His three Quartets are all modelled on Haydn and were published thanks to the latter's acceptance of their dedication. While the **Chilingirians** do not always observe every dynamic nuance of the 1970 Critical Edition, they play the work with genuine commitment and, in the case of the slow movement, charm – though it is for the interesting 1818 Berwald Quartet that collectors will investigate this. The 1979 recording stands up well. The Chilingirian make out a persuasive case for this piece and are very well recorded. As can be seen, this work is available coupled with either Arriaga or Berwald.

WILLAERT, Adrian (c.1490–1562)

Ave Maria; Magnificat sexti toni; Missa Christus resurgens

⊶ (BB) *** Naxos 8.553211. Oxford Camerata, Summerly – RICHAFORT: Motet: Christus resurgens ***

Over the first half of the sixteenth century this Flemish composer was one of the key figures in Western music, instrumental in the development both of the madrigal and of church music for double chorus. From 1527 until his death he was maestro di capella at St Mark's in Venice, but this music dates mainly from his earlier years, when he achieved nine settings of the Mass. This splendid offering from **Summerly** and his **Oxford Camerata** is the only one available, a magnificent 'parody mass', using as its base a motet by Jean Richafort, a piece included here as a prelude. Willaert's setting rises to a sublime conclusion in the extended Agnus Dei, in flowing polyphony. The Magnificat and Ave Maria offer in-

spired music too, performed with equal freshness and dedication. Vividly atmospheric sound.

WILLIAMS, Charles (1893–1978)

The Bells of St Clements; Blue Devils; Cross Country; Cutty Sark; Destruction by Fire; Devil's Galop; (i) The Dream of Olwen; The Girls in Grey; High Adventure (Friday Night is Music Night); The Humming Top; Jealous Lover; Little Tyrolean; London Fair; Model Railway; (i) The Music Lesson; The Night Has Eyes; Nursery Clock; The Old Clockmaker; Rhythm on Rails; Sally Tries the Ballet; Starlings; Throughout the Years; The Voice of London; Young Ballerina (The Potter's Wheel)

(M) *** ASV WHL 2151. BBC Concert O, Wordsworth; (i) with Elms

Rather like Henry Mancini and his Pink Panther theme, if Charles Williams had written only Devil's Galop (aka the Dick Barton theme), he would certainly be remembered, and it is brilliantly done here. Older listeners will surely recognize Girls in Grey and The Potter's Wheel from early 1950s television, and also High Adventure (used for Friday Night Is Music Night on Radio 2). Film buffs will know the themes from The Apartment and the pseudo-romantic piano concerto The Dream of Olwen – not in the league of the Warsaw Concerto but curiously haunting nevertheless, and certainly more durable than the film for which it was written (While I Live). Williams wrote a great deal of attractive, unpretentious music, much of it included on this generously filled CD. There are plenty of 'character' numbers, such as The Music Lesson, with metronome and scales interspersed with a most attractive theme, and the The Nursery Clock, a perky little vignette, just on the right side of twee. The Little Tyrolean gently evokes the world of the Strauss family, while The Humming Top is reminiscent of Bizet's Jeux d'enfants. England of the 1950s is evoked in Cross Country (1954) and London Fair (1955), while railway travel of the period is recalled in Model Railway (1951) and the even better remembered Rhythm on the Rails (1950). The Bells of St Clements is a charming fantasy based on the popular nursery rhyme, while the composer is in more dramatic mode for Destruction by Fire, depicting the wartime Blitz. In the 1960s, Oxford University invited Williams to receive an honorary doctorate. He declined, considering himself unworthy. It's hard to imagine too many composers of popular music doing that today! Recording and performances are both excellent.

WILLIAMS, Grace (1906–77)

(i) Carillons for Oboe & Orchestra; (ii) Trumpet Concerto. Fantasia on Welsh Nursery Rhymes; (iii) Penillion; (iv) Sea Sketches (for string orchestra)

*** Lyrita (ADD) SRCD 323. (i) Camden; (ii) Blake; (i–ii) LSO; (iii) RPO; (i–iii) cond. Groves; (iv) ECO, Atherton

In the memorably individual Sea Sketches Grace Williams focuses her scene-painting more acutely than is common, while the two slow sections, the seductive *Channel sirens* and the *Calm sea in summer*, are balmily, sensuously impressionistic, the former taking a somewhat unpromising idea and turning it into true poetry. The other works here range attractively from the simple – and at one time quite well-known – *Nursery-rhyme Fantasia* (which is a good deal more than a colourfully orchestrated pot-pourri) through two crisply conceived concertante pieces, to *Penillion*, written for the National Youth Orchestra of Wales. 'Penillion' is the Welsh word for stanza, and this is a set of four colourful, resourceful pieces, easy on the ear but full of individual touches; although Williams does not use any folk material, she retains the idea of a central melodic line (on the trumpet in the first two pieces) in stanza form. The trumpet and oboe concertante pieces – superbly played by soloists from the **LSO** of the early 1970s – both show the affection and understanding of individual instrumental timbre which mark the composer's work. Excellent performances throughout (especially the vivid sea music) and very good analogue sound. This CD is surely an ideal representation of the composer at her most appealing.

(i) *Symphony 2; Ballads for Orchestra*; (ii) *Fairest of stars* (for soprano & orchestra)

*** Lyrita (ADD) SRCD 327. (i) BBC Welsh SO, Handley; (ii) J. Price, LSO, Groves

In this *Second Symphony*, Grace Williams's most ambitious orchestral work, written in 1956 when she was 50, she aimed at greater astringency, just as Vaughan Williams himself had done in his *Fourth Symphony*. The writing is sharp and purposeful from the start, relaxing more towards lyricism in the slow movement (which produces an endearing pastoral oboe theme) and the finale with its darkly Mahlerian overtones. The *Ballade* of 1968, characteristically based on Welsh ballad and 'penillion' forms, also reveal the darker side of Grace Williams's writing, notably in the stark contrasts of the third ballad. The performances, originally recorded for radio, are expressive and convincing, and the recording good. *Fairest of stars* is later, written in 1973, specifically for this record. It is a relatively tough setting of Milton, and is strongly sung by **Janet Price**. The recording is first class.

WILLIAMS, John (born 1932)

Film Music: *Close Encounters of the Third Kind; E.T.; Raiders of the Lost Ark; Star Wars Trilogy; Superman*

Ⓜ **(*) Telarc CD 80094. Cincinnati Pops O, Kunzel – COURAGE: *Star Trek: theme*

The Telarc recording is certainly spectacular and the concert has a synthesized prologue and epilogue to underline the sci-fi associations. The inclusion of the famous *Star Trek* signature theme (a splendid tune) is wholly appropriate. The orchestra plays this music with striking verve, and the sweeping melody of *E.T.* is especially effective; but the overall effect is very brash, with the microphones seeking brilliance in the sound-balance (though for some that will be its attraction).

WILLIAMSON, Malcolm
(1931–2003)

Concerto grosso; Our Man in Havana: Suite; Santiago de Espada Overture; Sinfonietta

♫➛ *** Chan. 10359. Iceland SO, Gamba

Our Man in Havana, based on Graham Greene's novel, is among the most colourful of post-war British operas, with its catchy Cuban rhythms and its tunes first cousin to those in Broadway musicals. Until this excellent disc, the first of a projected Williamson series, not a note of it had been recorded, and this suite of four substantial movements makes one long for a full-scale stage revival. The *Concerto grosso* and *Sinfonietta* are both exercises in Williamson's attractive brand of neoclassicism, and the *Overture, Santiago de España*, written in 1956, well before the rest, is even more approachable, one of Williamson's first essays in tonality after his early experiments with serialism. **Rumon Gamba** conducts fresh, crisp performances with the **Iceland Symphony Orchestra**, very well recorded.

(i) *Organ Concerto*; (ii) *Piano Concerto 3*; (iii) *Sonata for 2 Pianos*

**(*) Lyrita (ADD) SRCD 280. Composer (piano or organ); with (i; ii) LPO; (i) Boult; (ii) Dommett; (iii) Richard Rodney Bennett

There are few more immediately rewarding couplings of post-war keyboard *Concertos* than this (and one could wish the *Piano Concerto* was better accompanied). Williamson composed them both in the early 1960s, and they represent two clearly contrasted sides of his creative character. The *Organ Concerto*, written in tribute to Sir Adrian Boult, uses the conductor's initials, ACB, as a dominating motive, and though some of the writing – for the orchestra as well as the organ – is spectacular, it is essentially a tough and ambitious piece, with the two powerful outer movements framing a beautiful and lyrical *Largo* for strings and organ alone. *Piano Concerto 3* in four movements has immediate attractions in the catchy melodies and snappy rhythms, which ought to make it a popular success in the line of the Rachmaninov *Concertos*. Unfortunately, the performance has an accompaniment that is less than punchy, and the red-bloodedness of the writing is not fully realized. The performance of the *Organ Concerto* is quite different in every way. Excellent recording. The remarkable *Sonata for 2 Pianos*, inspired by the composer's stay in Sweden, encapsulates in six continuous sections (and just seven and a half minutes of music) a Swedish winter and the arrival of spring 'with the serenity of a great release into a world of warmth and light'. The performance is definitive.

Double Concerto for 2 Pianos & Strings

**(*) Australian ABC Eloquence 426 483-2. Williamson, Campion, Tasmanian SO, Tuckwell – EDWARDS: *Piano Concerto* **(*); SCULTHORPE: *Piano Concerto* **(*)

Williamson's *Concerto for Two Pianos* has been recorded before (by EMI), but that is not currently available. This performance of this distinctive, but fairly tough – though by no means unapproachable – work is committed, well performed and reasonably well recorded, and is part of a valuable trilogy of rare *Concertos*.

The Growing Castle

(*) Australian Universal ABC Classics, Australia (ADD) 461 922-2. Elkins, Bamberg SO, Gierster – SHIELD: *Rosina*; ELGAR: *Sea Pictures* *

This recording of *The Growing Castle* was part of a project, aborted owing to illness, to record a collection of arias, of which this was all that was completed. It was forgotten for 30 years but resurrected for this Australian Heritage release. A short work, it opens very dramatically before a rather beautiful lyricism takes over, and was specially re-orchestrated by the composer at the request of the singer, **Margreta Elkins**, for this recording. The performance is excellent, though the recording, while quite full and vivid, sounds a bit dated, with Margreta Elkins too closely miked. It makes an unexpected bonus for Shield's sparkling *Rosina* and a fine Elgar *Sea Pictures*.

Symphonies 1 (Elevamini); 5 (Aquero); Epitaphs for Edith Sitwell; Lento for Strings

*** Chan. 10406. Iceland SO, Gamba

This second disc in Chandos's Williamson series offers weightier works than the first, starting with *Elevamini*, his *First Symphony*. This was written in memory of his grandmother, with the title *Elevamini, Be ye lifted up, ye gates*, drawn from Psalm 24. It consists of two elegiac slow movements, each starting with grinding dissonances, separated by a light and charming *Scherzo*, designed to characterize his grandmother in her life. *Symphony 5*, inspired by St Bernadette of Lourdes, has the subtitle *Aquero*, referring to the vision she saw. The five movements have programmatic titles, covering a wide expressive range, culminating in the fourth movement when the *Aquero* speaks to Bernadette, leading to a final *Kyrie*. The *Epitaphs for Edith Sitwell*, similarly elegiac, were arranged for strings from two organ pieces, while the *Lento for Strings* offers the most openly lyrical music on the disc, simple and tender. Excellent performances from the Icelanders under **Rumon Gamba**, very well recorded.

Agnus Dei; Benedictus; 'English Eccentrics': Choral Suite; In Paradisum; Libera me; Lux Aeterna; Requiem for a Tribe Brother; Sanctus; Symphony for Voices

⌐ (BB) *** Naxos 8.557783. Joyful Company of Singers, Broadbent

Peter Broadbent here conducts his fine choir, the **Joyful Company of Singers**, in a well-chosen selection of the *a cappella* choral music of Malcolm Williamson, much of it inspired by his native Australia, as well as by his Catholic faith. The writing is characteristically fluent and attractive, with one of the major items providing a fine contrast with the other works, the choral suite from the opera inspired by a book of Edith Sitwell, *English Eccentrics*. Although Williamson enjoyed much success in the 1960s, his reputation later fell into decline with his subsequent appointment as Master of the Queen's Music in 1975. The *Requiem for a Tribe Brother* (1992) is eclectic and uneven, but the eloquent early *Symphony for Voices* is alone worth the modest price of the disc. The sound is eminently satisfactory; the singing is good but falls short of real distinction.

WIRÉN, Dag (1905–86)

Serenade for Strings in G, Op. 11

⌐ (BB) *** Naxos 8.553106. Bournemouth Sinf., Studt (with Concert: *Scandinavian String Music*. ***)

The engaging *String Serenade* is Dag Wirén's one claim to international fame, and it is good to welcome an outstanding super-bargain version. The finale certainly earns its hit status, full of spontaneous, lilting energy. First-rate recording within an entirely recommendable concert of Scandinavian string music, not all of it familiar.

(i; ii) Miniature Suite (for cello & piano), Op. 8b; (ii) (Piano) Improvisations; Little Suite; Sonatina, Op. 25; Theme & Variations, Op. 5; (iii) 3 Sea Poems; (iv; ii) 2 Songs from Hösthorn, Op. 13

⌐ *** BIS CD 797. (i) Thedéen; (ii) Bojsten; (iii) Jubilate Ch., Riska; (iv) Högman

Dag Wirén was a miniaturist par excellence and few of the individual movements recorded here detain the listener for more than two or three minutes. The early (and inventive) *Theme and Variations*, Op. 5, is the longest work. Although it is slight, the *Sonatina for Piano* often touches a deeper vein of feeling than one might expect to encounter. Good performances from all concerned, and the usual truthful BIS recording.

Symphonies 2, Op. 14; 3 in C, Op. 20; Concert Overtures 1 & 2

*** CPO 999 677-2. Norrköping SO, Dausgaard

Dag Wirén is in some ways the most appealing and natural Swedish composer of his generation, but he lacks the breadth and sense of scale of the born symphonist. The *Third* (1944) was broadcast frequently during the 1940s, but even at the time it seemed thin and short-breathed and the idiom in thrall to Sibelius. The *Second Symphony* (1939) is the finer of the two, though ultimately deficient in motivic vitality and too reliant on ostinato figures. Good performances and recordings of likeable but flawed works.

WITT, Friedrich (1770–1836)

(i) Flute Concerto in G; Symphony 6 (Sinfonie Turque) in A min.; Symphony 9 in D min.

*** MDG 329 1299-2. Hamburg SO, Moesus; (i) with Barner

Friedrich Witt is primarily famous for his so-called *Jena Symphony*, which was at one time erroneously attributed to Beethoven. The *Symphony 6* (printed in 1808–9), with its battery of Turkish instruments woven into the work's classical structure, is certainly a novelty. The opening movement has plenty of hearty rumbustiousness and the following slow movement (without percussion) makes an attractive lyrical contrast. The *Minuetto* has a lively rustic flavour, and the finale, with more Turkish flavourings, is enjoyable too. The *Ninth Symphony* (printed in 1818) has the lusty vigour of the *Sixth*, without the Turkish condiments, with Beethoven being an obvious model. Despite its minor key, the work is essentially optimistic and, like the *Sixth*, it has a vivacious finale. The *Flute Concerto* of 1806 is lighter in character, with plenty of classical charm and easy-going melody. The performances throughout are sympathetic and the sound decent. Witt was essentially a conservative composer and, if no masterpieces have been uncovered here, his writing explores pleasing musical byways.

Piano & Wind Quintet in E flat, Op. 5

⊕– *** CBC MCVD 1137. Kuerti, Campbell, Mason, Sommerville, McKay – BEETHOVEN; MOZART: *Quintets* ***

Friedrich Witt modelled his *Quintet* with uncanny closeness on those of Beethoven and Mozart, though the *Adagio cantabile* – which opens with a bassoon solo – also brings a dash of Hummel. Unlike his predecessors, Witt also includes a *Minuet* whose Ländler-like trio is particularly engaging. Indeed, the quality of the invention is by no means to be sniffed at, with the good-humoured finale particularly successful in this vivid performance. The recording is first class – remarkably present and realistic.

Septet (for Clarinet, Horn, Bassoon, 2 Violins, Viola, Cello & Double bass)

⊕– *** MDG 308 0232. Charis-Ens. – KREUTZER: *Septet* ***

There is much attractive interplay between the instruments in Witt's pleasing *Septet* and, if it isn't quite as inspired as the sparkling Kreutzer work, it is still enjoyable, with its attractive melodies, a nicely varied *Adagio* and an easy-going manner – the finale especially so. It receives a first-class performance and recording.

WOLF, Hugo (1860–1903)

Italian Serenade in G

⊕– ⓑⓑ *** Virgin 2x1 4 82112-2 (2). Sinfonia Varsovia, Y. Menuhin – MOZART: *Divertimento 1, etc.*; SCHOENBERG: *Verklaerte Nacht*; WAGNER: *Siegfried Idyll* ***

ⓑ *** EMI 3 66557-2. Formosa Qt – DEBUSSY: *String Quartet*; MOZART: *String Quartet 14*; SCHUBERT: *Quartettsatz* ***

(***) Biddulph mono LAB 098. Budapest Qt – GRIEG; SIBELIUS: *Quartets* ***

Seldom heard in the concert hall (it is too short to fit in today's sparse two- and three-work programmes), Wolf's *Italian Serenade* used to be more familiar as it fitted neatly on two 78 r.p.m. sides. **Menuhin's** performance of the chamber orchestral version is full of charm and vivacity, and is vividly recorded.

The prize-winning **Formosa Quartet** from Taiwan give a brisk and incisive reading of Wolf's charming piece, which yet has plenty of sparkle, a fine fill-up for their brilliant disc in EMI's Debut series.

A welcome reissue on Biddulph – the first on CD – of the 1933 pioneering *Italian Serenade*. It has a spring in its step and a lightness of touch that are almost unique, and it is well transferred here by Ward Marston. The couplings also show how special this ensemble was in the 1930s.

Italian Serenade; Penthesilea (symphonic poem); Scherzo and Finale; Der Corregidor (opera): Prelude and Intermezzo

⊕– ⓑⓑ *** Warner Apex 0927 49582-2. O de Paris, Barenboim

For those who only know Wolf's *Italian Serenade* and enjoy the subtle word-painting of the Lieder, this orchestral collection will come as something of a shock. The early three-part symphonic poem, *Penthesilea* (1883–5), is turbulently and voluptuously romantic in a style of post-Lisztian hyperbole, while the Prelude to *Der Corregidor* is Wagnerian in its expansive opulence. **Barenboim** plays both with uninhibited exuberance and almost convinces the listener that *Penthesilea* is worthy of standing alongside the music of Strauss. The *Intermezzo*, however, is almost in the style of French ballet music, and the well-known *Serenade*, of course, is similarly lightweight and sunny. The *Scherzo and Finale* of 1876–7 show the precocious skill of an 18-year-old: it is music of more than a little substance and felicitously scored, although Wagner briefly raises his head again in the *Finale*. Barenboim makes the very most of all these pieces, and they are played with much conviction. The recording is rather resonant but otherwise very good.

String Quartet in D min.; Intermezzo in E flat; Italian Serenade in G

⊕– Ⓜ *** CPO CPO 999 529-2. Auryn Qt

String Quartet in D min.; Italian Serenade

*** Häns. C.93024. Fine Arts Qt

Hugo Wolf's massive *String Quartet* may be a student work, but in its concentration and complexity it harks back to late Beethoven, as well as to Wagner. The formidable first movement leads to a slow movement of heavenly length, here interpreted with hushed intensity by the young **Auryn Quartet**. Both in the *Quartet* and in the other two works, including the winningly exuberant *Italian Serenade*, the playing amply makes up in its warmth and spontaneity for any slight lack of polish. Warm, full sound.

This Hänssler **Fine Arts** performance is the only other version of the *Quartet* currently available, and it is well played by this long-established American group in the pleasing acoustics of the SudWestfunk Studios in Baden-Baden. However, the CPO disc is even finer and offers more music.

6 alte Weisen; 18 Goethe Lieder; 3 Mörike Lieder; 6 Lieder für eine Frauerstimme; Italienisches Liederbuch (25 Lieder); Spanisches Liederbuch (2 Lieder); Sonnne der Schlummerlosen; Die Zigeunerin

🎵 ❀ Ⓜ **** EMI (ADD) 3 80040-2 (2). Schwarzkopf, Moore

These two discs contain some of the very finest singing of Wolf songs ever recorded. Walter Legge was the force behind the first major Wolf recording project on 78s in the 1930s, but in many ways the achievement of **Schwarzkopf**, and certainly her vocal finesse, go even further. The recordings, made between 1956 and 1965, still sound splendid and the glorious singing is matched by **Gerald Moore's** inspired accompaniment. The documentation includes photographs taken at the sessions, and full texts and translations.

Eichendorf Lieder; Goethe Lieder; Mörike Lieder

🎵 **** EMI 3 42256-2. Bostridge, Pappano (piano)

Ian Bostridge here turns his very special vocal personality and understanding of word-meanings to a perfectly chosen Wolf collection with triumphant success. **Antonio Pappano** puts down his baton to accompany (or, one should rather say, partner) him with wonderful sensitivity. There is little point in detailing individual songs; everything here is wonderfully refreshing, and these perfectly matched artists are beautifully recorded.

Goethe Lieder

🎵 *** Hyp. CDA 67130. McGreevy, Johnson

Geraldine McGreevy, winner of the 1996 Kathleen Ferrier Award, makes a fresh and pure-toned partner for **Graham Johnson** in a challenging selection of Wolf's settings of Goethe, with all but two of the 24 songs coming from the great Goethe songbook of his maturity in 1888–9. As ever, Johnson provides the most searching and illuminating notes on each song, enhancing enjoyment greatly with his words as well as his playing, but it is good to welcome so sensitive and responsive a young Lieder-singer as McGreevy, who here triumphs over even the most demanding of challenges. So it is good to have readings of the four *Mignon* songs (the three regular ones plus *Kennst du das Land*), which bring out the mystery of the writing with the benefit of girlish tone, apt for Goethe's heroine. *Kennst du das Land* is the more moving for that, with McGreevy providing a thrilling crescendo in the last stanza, perfectly controlled. Yet she responds to the lighter songs beautifully too, with a fine feeling for word-meaning. Excellent, well-balanced sound.

Mörike Lieder: An eine Aeolsharfe; Bei einer Trauung; Denk' es, o Seele!; Heimweh; Im Frühling; Jägerlied; Lied eines Verliebten

*** BBC (ADD) BBCB 8015-2. Pears, Britten – BRITTEN: *On his island*, etc.; SCHUBERT: *7 Lieder* *** (with ARNE: *Come away death; Under the greenwood tree*; QUILTER: *O mistress mine*; WARLOCK: *Take, o take those lips away*; TIPPETT: *Come unto these yellow sands* ***)

In the BBC's sensitive performances of seven of Wolf's Mörike settings – recorded at the Snape Maltings in 1972, not long before **Britten** was stricken by terminal illness – these unfailingly convey a sense of spontaneity, capturing the inspiration of the moment in a way that is rare on disc,

thanks above all to Britten's accompaniments. Excellent radio sound.

(i) 3 Christmas Songs: Auf ein altes Bild; Nun wandre, Maria; Schlafendes Jesuskind; (ii) 3 Michelangelo Lieder: Alles endet, was entstehet; Fühlt meine Seele; Wohl denk' ich oft

Ⓜ *** BBC (ADD) BBCB 8011-2. (i) Pears; (ii) Shirley-Quirk, Britten – SCHUBERT: *11 Lieder* ***

John Shirley-Quirk in his singing of three of Wolf's Michelangelo settings at the 1971 Aldeburgh Festival has never been more mellifluous on disc, just as sensitive in his treatment of Lieder as the others, and the whole programme is delightfully rounded off by **Pears's** charming performances of the three Wolf Christmas songs. Excellent sound.

Italienisches Liederbuch (complete)

🎵 *** Hyp. CDA 66760. Lott, Schreier, Johnson

🎵 Ⓜ **** EMI (ADD) 5 62650-2. Schwarzkopf, Fischer-Dieskau, Moore

(*) Ondine ODE 998-2D. Isokoski, Skovhus, Viitasalo

Graham Johnson conjures up music-making full of magic, compelling from first to last. Yet, so far from being intrusive in his playing, he consistently heightens the experience, drawing out from **Felicity Lott** one of her most intense and detailed performances on record, totally individual. **Peter Schreier**, one of the supreme masters of Lieder today, also responds to this characterful accompanist; and having a tenor instead of the usual baritone brings many benefits in this sharply pointed sequence. The triumph of this issue is crowned by the substantial booklet provided in the package, containing Johnson's uniquely perceptive commentary on each song – alone worth the price of the disc. Excellent sound.

Few artists today can match the searching perception of these two great singers in this music, with **Fischer-Dieskau** using his sweetest tones and **Schwarzkopf** ranging through all the many emotions inspired by love. **Gerald Moore** is at his finest, and the well-balanced (1969) recording sounds better than ever.

The Ondine version offers a well-mannered reading, generally well sung but undercharacterized to the point of blandness. One could never imagine that either of the singers in their painstaking politeness might represent a character close to the soil. The accompaniments of **Marita Viitasalo** are similarly faithful but dull.

Spanisches Liederbuch (complete)

🎵 Ⓜ *** DG (ADD) 457 726-2 (2). Schwarzkopf, Fischer-Dieskau, Moore

In this superb DG reissue, the sacred songs provide a dark, intense prelude, with **Fischer-Dieskau** at his very finest, sustaining slow tempi impeccably. **Schwarzkopf's** dedication comes out in the three songs suitable for a woman's voice; but it is in the secular songs, particularly those which contain laughter in the music, where she is at her most memorable. **Gerald Moore** is balanced rather too backwardly – something the transfer cannot correct – but gives superb support.

WOLF-FERRARI, Ermanno
(1876–1948)

L'amore medico: Overture & Intermezzi. Il campiello: Intermezzo & Ritornello. La dama boba: Overture. I gioielli della Madonna: Suite. I quattro rusteghi: Prelude & Intermezzo. Il segreto di Susanna: Overture & Intermezzo. (i) Suite Concertino in F, for bassoon and orchestra, Op. 16

Ⓝ **** Chan. 10511. BBC PO, Noseda with (i) Geoghegan

A warm welcome to a superb collection of Wolf-Ferrari's sparkling orchestral music. Beginning with the dramatic *Festa popolare* from *The Jewels of the Madonna*, Wolf-Ferrari provide an endless succession of sweetly tuneful music with ear-tickling orchestrations, lively dances contrasting with beautiful *Intermezzi*, such as the delicately delicious one from *I quattro rusteghi*. The *Suite Concertino in F* is a great rarity and what a charmer it is to, with the superb bassoonist **Karen Geoghegan**, bringing out all the colour of this score. The second movement, *Strimpellata*, is especially catchy, but this CD abounds in catchy melodies. The *Overture* to *Il segreto di Susanna* sparkles brightly, and the scurrying string writing in the *Overture* to the opera *L'amore medico* is exhilarating. The Chandos recording is first class, with the deep, resonant bass drum in *L'amore medico* marvellously captured.

L'amore medico: Overture; Il campiello: Intermezzo; Ritornello; La dama bomba: Overture; I gioielli della Madonna (suite); I quattro rusteghi: Prelude & Intermezzo; Il segreto di Susanna: Overture

⊕ *** ASV CDDCA 861. RPO, Serebrier

Although the situation is currently changing, Wolf-Ferrari has long held a permanent place in the catalogue only with recordings of his operatic *intermezzi* – not surprising, perhaps, when they are so readily tuneful and charmingly scored. **Serebrier** conjures at times exquisite playing from the **RPO** (especially the strings) and, even though he takes Susanna's sparkling *Overture* slightly slower than usual, it is hardly less successful. What is specially memorable is his delicate treatment of the gossamer string-pieces from *I quattro rusteghi* and the *Ritornello* from *Il campiello*, which almost have a Beecham touch. The ASV recording, made in the Henry Wood Hall, is open and indeed transparent and fresh.

Il campiello: Prelude; Ritornello; Intermezzo. The Inquisitive Woman: Overture. Jewels of the Madonna: Neapolitan dance. The School for Fathers: Intermezzo. Susanna's secret: Overture. Serenade for strings

⊕ Ⓜ **** Berlin Classics 0091772BC. Berlin RSO, Rögner

Rögner's collection comes from the late 1970s and has the advantage of natural, warmly resonant analogue sound which gives these attractive pieces a pleasing hall ambience. He offers an aptly paced, sparkling account of *Susanna's*

Secret, while the sprightly *Inquisitive Woman Overture*, with its songful theme for the oboe, is hardly less winning, and a real find. The **Berlin Orchestra** play it with the lightest rhythmic touch, and are hardly less persuasive in the *Neapolitan Dance*, a brilliant show piece of which they take full advantage. The charming *Intermezzo* from *The School for Fathers* is given with fragile delicacy and the music from *Il campiello* is just as delectable; both the *Prelude* and *Ritornello* have a haunting atmosphere. The programme ends with a captivating account of the *String Serenade*, which charms and touches the listener by turns.

(i) Cello Concerto in C (Invocazione), Op. 31; Sinfonia Brevis in E flat, Op. 28

ⒷⒷ *** CPO CPO 999 278-2. (i) Rivinius; Frankfurt RSO, Francis

Wolf-Ferrari's *Cello Concerto*, like the *Violin Concerto*, is a considerable work and its title *Invocazione* is well chosen. The opening movements are both marked *Tranquillo*, and even the use of a theme very like 'Three blind mice' does not rob the first of its serenity. The gay, dancing finale maintains the work's lightness of texture and feeling. The first movement of the *Sinfonia brevis* tries to sustain this tranquil mood, and finally does so at the close, after frequent interruptions, often quite boisterous. The jaunty *Capriccio* which follows acts as a colourful Scherzo and might well be another of those intermezzi. The *Adagio* is both a barcarolle and a threnody, and again features a solo cello, pensive and darker voiced than in the concerto. The finale dances away in a jiggy tarantella rhythm and ends in cheerful buoyancy. The performances here are full of life and feeling, and are given a vividly spacious recording.

Complete Wind Concertos: *(i) Concertino in A flat, Op. 34, for Cor anglais, Strings & 2 Horns; Idillio-Concertino for oboe & small orchestra; (ii) Suite-Concertino in F, Op. 16, for bassoon & small orchestra*

⊕ *** CPO 777 157-2. O di Padova e del Veneto, Hamer; with (i) Ciacci; (ii) Carlini

A delightful collection. There is an unpretentious charm to the opening *Idillio-Concertino*; the slow movement is richly haunting, and a tuneful, pastoral quality pervades the other three movements. The *Suite-Concertino's* opening movement is an atmospheric *Notturno* with distinct colourings by the bassoon. This is followed by a short but tuneful *Strimpellata* which is delightfully catchy. A graceful *Canzone* succeeds this, and the work ends in a tuneful and lively *Andante con moto*. Both these works were premièred in Rome in 1933. The *Concertino* was premièred posthumously in Salzburg in 1955, yet it is imbued with the nostalgic charm of the earlier works. The quirky *Capriccio* movement is especially enjoyable and the rather regal finale is very memorable too. Sensitive and fresh performances in excellent sound.

(i) Violin Concerto in D, Op. 26; Serenade for Strings

⊕ ⒷⒷ *** CPO CPO 999 271-2. (i) Hoelscher; Frankfurt RSO, Francis

Wolf-Ferrari's warmly romantic *Violin Concerto* captures the listener's ear from the very opening, and **Ulf Hoelscher** is a superbly responsive soloist. The *Romanza* opens with ethereal delicacy, but passion soon comes to the surface and is always ready to burst into the *Improviso* third movement. The jolly, sparkling Rondo finale is in the best traditional mode of classical concerto finales. Again Hoelscher is on his mettle: he never made a better record than this, and his exquisite playing of the long cadenza-soliloquy towards the movement's close is especially fine. The *String Serenade* is an extraordinarily accomplished and individual four-movement student work, genuinely inspired, and it is most persuasively played here, with a more passionate, less innocent performance than Heinz Rögner gives in his collection above. First-class recording.

The Jewels of the Madonna: Dances & Intermezzi; School for Fathers: Overture & Intermezzo; Susanna's Secret: Overture

(***) Testament mono SBT 1327. Philh. O, Mackerras –
  PONCHIELLI: *La Gioconda: Dance of the Hours* ***; VERDI:
  Overtures and ballet music. (***)

As the opening section in this mixed bag of *Mackerras's* recordings from the 1950s, the charming Wolf-Ferrari pieces are delectably done, not just popular favourites like the *Overture* to *Susanna's Secret* and the second *Intermezzo* from *The Jewels of the Madonna*, but the other miniatures too. The mono recording is clear and well balanced.

CHAMBER MUSIC

Piano Trios 1 in D, Op. 5; 2 in F sharp, Op. 7

*** ASV CDDCA 935. Raphael Trio

Wolf-Ferrari wrote these two ambitious *Piano Trios* at the very beginning of his career. They may not be masterpieces, but the large-scale first movements show him as a fine craftsman, and more importantly, his themes already show the gift of easy memorability which marks his other major works. So the slow movement of 1 is like a Mascagni lament, and the chattering finale might be a sketch for an operatic interlude. 2 is odder in its layout, with the first movement twice as long as the other two put together, but with well-disciplined performances from the **Raphael Trio**, an American group, the colour and charm of the writing is persuasively brought out.

La vedova scaltra (opera; complete)

(N) (BB) ** Naxos 8.660225/6 (2). Sollied, Muraro, D'Aguanno,
  Milhofer, Zanellato, Rossi, Esposito, La Fenice, Venice, Ch.
  & O, Martin

Wolf-Ferrari's *La vedova scaltra* is a melodic feast. One attractive melody follows on from another and the charm found in his better-known overture and intermezzi is in abundance here. The story about the heroine, Rosaura concerns her four hopeful suitors, whom she meets in various disguises to find the one who can demonstrate his sincerity, is written very much in the *opera buffa* tradition. The lead is very well sung by **Anne-Lise Sollied**, though her maid, Marionette, sung by

Elena Rossi, is rather shrill. The men are quite characterful but some seem to have rather too much wobble. This live performance certainly sounds vivid, though the opera house acoustic is rather dry. No texts are included but it is an inexpensive way to acquire a rare and charming opera.

WÖLFL, Joseph (1773–1812)

Piano Concertos 1, Op. 20; 4 (The Calm): Andante only. 5 (Grand Military), Op. 43; 6 (The Cuckoo), Op. 49

(N) *** CPO 777 373-2. Kronenberg, SWR RO, Kaiserslautern,
  Moesus

Hardly a well-known name today, Joseph Wölfl enjoyed considerable success in his day, both as a composer and virtuoso pianist, in Vienna, Paris and London. *Piano Concerto 1* is classically elegant, in the manner of a Mozartian concerto, full of charm and some nice colourings, such as the 'hunting' horns at the beginning of the finale. The *Grand Military Concerto* is much more dramatic, with its stormy introduction and military music elements running throughout the first movement. The slow movement is of delicate charm, and the finale is especially catchy and tuneful. The *Cuckoo Concerto* is so-called because of its 'cuckoo' motive at the beginning of the finale. It is another expertly written, charming concerto of much melodic appeal and a certain wit. The CD ends with a pleasing alternative slow-movement from the *First Piano Concerto* used in the London printing of the score. First rate performances and sound and copious sleeve notes, as usual, from this source. A must for all lovers of rare early nineteenth-century repertoire.

WOOD, Charles (1866–1926)

Anthems and Hymn Anthems: Ascension Hymn; The Earth trembled; Expectans expectavi; God omnipotent reigneth; Haec dies; I am risen; I will call upon God; Jesu the very thought is sweet; O King most high; O Lord rebuke me not; O Lord that seest from yon starry Heights; O Most Merciful; O Thou sweetest source; Sunlight all golden; This is the Day; 'Tis the Day of Resurrection; True love's the gift. (i) (Organ) Preludes: Martyrs; Old 104th; Old 132nd; Old 136th; Psalm 23; York Tune

*** Priory PRCD 754. Gonville & Caius College, Cambridge
  Ch., Webber; Roberts; (i) Uglow (organ)

The career of the Anglo-Irish composer Charles Wood ran parallel with that of his better-known colleague, Stanford, whom he succeeded as Professor of Composition at the Royal College of Music. Wood's music is less flamboyant, less innovatory than Stanford's but his anthems and hymn-anthems form a rich part of the fabric of Anglican church music. If the opening *O thou sweetest source* is impressive in its very simplicity, the gleaming brightness of *Sunlight all golden* does not belie its title, and *God omnipotent reigneth*, underpinned by the organ, is boldly arresting. Yet one of the most memorable items, the unaccompanied *Jesu, the very thought is sweet* is quite brief, eloquently setting a melody from the *Piae Cantiones* of 1582. If Wood's harmonic language is not forward-looking, his music is of quality and often individual, as in his Latin settings, the jubilant *Haec dies* and the very touching *Expectans expectavi*, written in memory of his son, killed in the First World War. The *Organ Preludes* draw on old church melodies and are comparatively conventional in style, but very well played, and here used effectively as interludes. Indeed the presentation could hardly be bettered, the choir singing with fervour and rich tonal blending, The recording is excellent.

WOOD, Haydn (1882–1959)

Apollo Overture; A Brown Bird Singing (paraphrase for orchestra); London Cameos (suite); Miniature Overture: The City; St James's Park in the Spring; A State Ball at Buckingham Palace; Mannin Veen (Manx tone-poem); Moods (suite): Joyousness (concert waltz). Mylecharane (rhapsody); The Seafarer (A Nautical Rhapsody); Serenade to Youth; Sketch of a Dandy

&—*** Marco 8.223402. Czech-Slovak RSO (Bratislava), Leaper

Haydn Wood, an almost exact contemporary of Eric Coates and nearly as talented, spent his childhood on the Isle of Man, and much of his best music is permeated with Manx folk-themes (original or simulated). *Mannin Veen* ('Dear Isle of Man') is a splendid piece, based on four such folksongs. The companion rhapsody, *Mylecharane*, also uses folk material, if less memorably, and *The Seafarer* is a wittily scored selection of famous shanties, neatly stitched together. The only failure here is *Apollo*, which uses less interesting material and is over-ambitious and inflated. But the English waltzes are enchanting confections and *Sketch of a Dandy* is frothy and elegant. **Adrian Leaper** is clearly much in sympathy with this repertoire and knows just how to pace it; his Czech players obviously relish the easy tunefulness and the sheer craft of the writing. With excellent recording in what is surely an ideal acoustic, this is very highly recommendable.

A Day in Fairyland Suite: Dance of a Whimsical Elf; An Evening Song; Frescoes Suite; London Landmarks: Horse Guards March; A Manx Rhapsody; May-Day Overture; Paris Suite; Roses of Picardy; Soliloquy; Variations on a Once Popular Humorous Song

*** Marco 8.223605. Czech-Slovak RSO (Bratislava), Tomlinson

The second CD opens with the charming *May-Day Overture*, with its dreamy sound-picture of dawn, giving way to the day's festivities. The *Variations* are effective, and the composer's *Paris Suite* introduces a distinct Gallic flavour: the *Montmartre March* is especially enjoyable. Wood's beloved Isle of Man inspired the *Manx Rhapsody*, which finds the composer again in his attractive folksy-mode, and the composer's most famous piece, *Roses of Picardy*, is a slightly dated high-

light of this volume. The rest of the programme is equally enjoyable, and the performances, this time with **Ernest Tomlinson**, are excellent.

Piano Concerto in D min.

&—*** Hyp. CDA 67127. Milne, BBC Scottish SO, Brabbins –
HOLBROOKE: *Piano Concerto 1* ***

Haydn Wood writes fluently and attractively throughout the *Concerto*, both for the piano and the orchestra, with echoes of Grieg and Rachmaninov. With an English accent, it establishes itself as one of the more striking British piano concertos of the period. Brilliant playing from **Hamish Milne** and warm, well-balanced recording.

WOOD, Hugh (born 1932)

Symphony; (i) Scenes from Comus

&—*** NMC NMCD 070. BBC SO, A. Davis; (i) with McGreevy, Norman

Hugh Wood's powerful *Symphony*, written in the late 1970s and early 1980s, is a major addition to British symphonic repertoire, in a direct line from Walton's *First*. If not so immediately approachable, it readily responds to repeated listening, for it is cogently argued and gripping from the first note to the last. Drama of a semi-theatrical nature is the composer's springboard and the opening *Tempesta* is violently histrionic, yet has an underlying dark lyricism directly related to Wagner's *Die Walküre* and the passion of Siegmund and Sieglinde. Their love motif is quoted to make the derivation clear and the long *Elegia* slow movement is headed by a classical Greek quotation which draws a connection with Siegmund's *Todesverkündigung*. Later there is an unexpected fragment from Mozart: the flute-and-drum 'ordeal' sequence in *Die Zauberflöte*. The throbbing Scherzo draws on the work's basic ideas, but fragmented into a powerful *con fuoco*. The energy subsides and with delicate colouring from horns, piccolo flute and glockenspiel we are led to the disconsolate calm of the opening of the passacaglia finale, which is finally to end the work with a passionate, triumphantly positive acclamation.

The *Scenes from Comus* are not incidental music for Milton's masque, but a highly atmospheric symphonic narrative in eight sections with vocalizations, confidently sung by **Daniel Norman** (Comus) and **Geraldine McGreevy**. As the 'Lady' of the narrative, she is enchanted by the son of Circe after being abducted in *The Wild Wood*, where in Wood's setting she responds willingly to the following orgiastic dances. The finale duet *Sabrina Fair* brings a mood of ecstatic serenity and this remarkably imaginative work ends with a peaceful epilogue. **Sir Andrew Davis** conducts throughout with mastery and a total identification with the music of both works, each of which resonates in the memory, but especially the symphony. The recording is splendid.

String Quartets 1 & 2; (ii) The Horses (3 Songs of Poems by Ted Hughes), Op. 10; The Rider Victory (4 Songs of Poems by Edwin Muir), Op. 11

(N) *** Lyrita (ADD) SRCD 304 (i) Dartington String Qt; (ii) Cantelo, Hamburger (with PRIAULX RAINER: *Quanta; String Trio*; LENNOX BERKELEY: *Duo for Cello & Piano, Op. 18, Part 1*; PETER RACINE FRICKER: *Cello Sonata, Op. 26*; MARTIN DALBY: *Variations for Cello & Piano*; MCCABE: *Partita for Solo Cello* ***)

Hugh Wood's thoughtful music deserves representation on record, particularly in performances as strong and effective as these. The *First Quartet*, dating from the early 1960s, reveals a continuing debt to Berg, but with the *Second Quartet* Wood develops his own more concentrated style in a formidably argued single movement of 39 sections. The two sets of songs, also atonal in idiom, yet reveal a sympathetic reliance on conventional values. The recording matches the excellence of the performances.

WORDSWORTH, William
(1908–88)

Symphonies 2 in D, Op. 34; 3 in C, Op. 48

*** Lyrita SRCD 207. LPO, Braithwaite

William Wordsworth was a direct descendant of the poet's brother, Christopher; on the evidence of this disc, he was a real symphonist. The *Second*, dedicated to Tovey, has a real sense of space; it is distinctly Nordic in atmosphere and there is an unhurried sense of growth. It is serious, thoughtful music, both well crafted and well laid out for the orchestra. At times it almost suggests Sibelius or Walter Piston in the way it moves, though not in its accents; and the writing is both powerful and imaginative. The *Third* is less concentrated and less personal in utterance, but all the same this is music of integrity, and readers who enjoy, say, the symphonies of Edmund Rubbra should sample the *Second Symphony*. **Nicholas Braithwaite** gives a carefully prepared and dedicated account of it, and the recording is up to the usual high standard one expects from this label.

WRIGHT, Margot (1911–2000)

(i; ii) Cello Sonata; (iii) Improvisation for Solo Clarinet; (iv; ii) 3 Northumbrian Folksongs for Viola & Piano; (ii; v) Piano Quintet in D minor; (vi; ii; iii) Fear no more the heat o' the sun; 3 Songs with Clarinet Obbligato

(M) *** Dutton CDLX 7109 (i) Phelps; (ii) Moll; (iii) Braithwaite; (iv) Wright; (v) Camilli Qt; (vi) Morgan

The earliest piece here is the *Cello Sonata* (1930) and perhaps the finest the *Piano Quintet*. **Margot Wright** was much in demand as a pianist and was Kathleen Ferrier's partner. Eventually her role as a practising musician and a teacher displaced composition at the centre of her life. Her language is conservative and diatonic but she has a natural feeling for line and development, as the first movement of the *Quintet* shows. There are many imaginative things in her music, which makes one regret that recognition was never sufficient

to encourage her to pursue her own creative path. The *Piano Quintet* is a work of quality and played with evident dedication: the violist, incidentally, is the daughter of the composer. Very natural recorded sound.

XENAKIS, Iannis (1922–2001)

Antikhthon; Aroura; (i) Synaphai (Conxities for piano & orchestra)

(M) *** Explore (ADD) EXP 0047. New Philh. O, Howarth; (i) with Madge

Using higher mathematics as well as a computer (slide-rule and graph paper to hand), Xenakis manages to produce works which to some ears actually sound like music, but to others are incomprehensible. The composer's imagination, which defies any kind of technique, is no doubt; however, for many the results are barren. The most ambitious of these three works, *Antikhthon*, is hypnotic in its range of colour, even if it fails to get you thinking of the infinite, as the composer intends. Excellent performances (so far as one can tell) and brilliant recording (from Decca, dating from 1975).

YOST, Michél (1754–86)

Clarinet Concertos 7 in B flat; 8 in E flat; 9 in B flat; 11 in B flat

*** MDG 301 0718-2. Klöcker, Prague CO

Not many collectors will have heard of Yost before discovering this CD. But here are four delightfully bubbly *Concertos*, brimming with excellent tunes and plenty of wit, with any moments of drama soon pushed away with sunny abandon. This is a delightful CD and it is hard to imagine better performances or recordings.

YSAŸE, Eugène (1858–1931)

Amitié, Op. 26

(**(*)) BBC mono BBCL4060-2. D. Oistrakh, I. Oistrakh, LPO, Sargent – SHOSTAKOVICH: *Violin Concertos 1 & 2* ***

Amitié, for two violins and orchestra, is the last of Ysaÿe's six tone-poems and is a piece steeped in the post-Wagnerian tradition which he had assimilated so completely by this time. **David** and **Igor Oistrakh** play with great eloquence and were recorded at the Royal Albert Hall in 1961 with very good sound for the period.

6 Sonatas for Solo Violin, Op. 27

(BB) **** Naxos 8.555996. Kaler

(M) *** Oehms OC 236. Schmid

*** BIS CD 1046. Kavakos

*** Chan. 8599. Mordkovitch

(B) *** Nim. 1735 (3). Shumsky – BACH; MOZART: *Violin Concertos* ***

As is well known, the six *Sonatas* Ysaÿe published in 1924 were written for the six greatest virtuosi of the day: Szigeti, Kreisler, Enescu, Jacques Thibaud and (less well remembered nowadays) Manuel Quiroga and Matthieu Grickboom. They are held in special regard by violinists who enjoy overcoming the technical challenges they pose. **Ilya Kaler** was a gold medallist in the Sibelius, Paganini and Tchaikovsky competitions and is a virtuoso of the first order. These are commanding accounts, which characterize the particular qualities of each *Sonata* to impressive effect.

No one investing in **Benjamin Schmid's** recording (and the outlay is modest) will be disappointed, for these performances are full of imagination and this is satisfying in its own right. However, Kaler makes one see these pieces in a fresher light.

Leonid Kavakos came to notice when he recorded the first version of the Sibelius *Concerto* for BIS, and he impresses every bit as much here.

Lydia Mordkovitch also plays with great character and variety of colour and she characterizes 4 (the one dedicated to Kreisler, with its references to Bach and the *Dies Irae*) superbly. These *Sonatas* can seem like mere exercises, but in her hands they sound really interesting. Natural, warm recorded sound. Recommended.

Oscar Shumsky is a player of the old school. His artistry is everywhere in evidence in this 1982 recording, in the authority and naturalness of his phrasing, the sweetness of his tone and the security of his technique. True, there are one or two moments of imperfect intonation, but there are very few performances (as opposed to recordings) where every note in these impossibly demanding pieces is in perfect place. It is all wonderfully musical and splendidly free as if Shumsky is improvising these pieces. These performances now come in a bargain box celebrating his supreme artistry which can be strongly recommended.

Solo Violin Sonatas, Op. 27/2, 3, 4 & 6

🎧— *** EMI 5 57384-2. Vengerov – BACH: *Toccata & Fugue in D min.*; SHCHEDRIN: *Balalaika; Echo Sonata* ***

Maxim Vengerov gives dazzling performances of the four Ysaÿe *Solo Sonatas*, making light of the technical problems in warmly spontaneous readings, which are plainly a labour of love. It is a pity that the other two *Sonatas* could not be included, although the Bach *Toccata* and the Shchedrin *Balalaika* are so full of flair one would not want to do without them.

Violin Sonata 1 in G min.

*** Sony SK 92938. Skride – BACH: *Partita 2*; BARTÓK: *Solo Violin Sonata* ***

Baiba Skride is a Latvian violinist, now in her mid-twenties, who won the *Prix Concours* at the Queen Elizabeth Competition in Brussels in 2001 when she was 19. She has a flawless technique and makes a wonderful sound, and it is evident from all these pieces that she is a musician first and a virtuoso second: in short, an artist first and foremost. In the Ysaÿe *G minor Sonata* she is highly persuasive.

ZANDONAI, Riccardo

Francesca da Rimini

Ⓝ *** Arthaus **DVD** 101 363. Armiliato, Marchigiana PO & Ch., Barbacini, (Director: Massimo Gasparon; V/D. Rossi)

Dubbed 'the Italian Tristan', Riccardo Zandonai's telling of the legendary love story of Paolo and Francesca is drawn from a play by Gabriele d'Annunzio to a libretto by Tito Ricordi. It is a thoroughly workmanlike piece, attractive in its idiom but with melodies that only rarely stick in the memory. Tito Ricordi before the first performance in 1914 was much more concerned over the success of this piece, for which he had written the libretto, than for the latest opera of Puccini, the composer who brought profits to his publishing firm.

The performance on this DVD under **Barbacini** is a warm and purposeful one, recorded live in 2004 at the Sferisterio Opera Festival in Macerata. Singing is good if not outstanding, led by the Francesca of **Daniela Dessi** and the Paolo of **Fabio Armiliato**. Paolo is one of the three Malatesta brothers, but Francesca is betrothed to Giovanni the Lame, though she thinks she is going to marry the brother she loves, Paolo, dubbed 'the handsome'.

The story echoes that of *Tristan and Isolde*, and in the opening scene a Jester refers to that legend as well as to the legend of King Arthur and Guinevere. The climax comes when Paolo and Francesca are caught in flagrante and both are killed, a sequence that Zandonai passes over with surprising speed before the final curtain. A flawed work but one well worth hearing in a warm and sympathetic performance like this, with traditional costumes and a stylised, single set.

ZELENKA, Jan (1679–1745)

Complete Orchestral Works: *Capriccios 1–5; Concerto a 8 concertanti; Hipocondrie a 7 concertanti; Melodrama de St Wenceslao: Simphonie; Ouverture a 7 concertanti; Symphonie a 8 concertanti*

🎧— Ⓜ *** CPO 999 897-2 (3). Neu-Erffönete O, Sonnentheil

A contemporary of Bach and Handel, Jan Dismas Zelenka was among the most original composers of the period but is still something of a mystery figure when no portrait survives. Unlike his great contemporaries, he remained an underling in the world of his time. Happily, his music has survived, and this fine collection of his complete orchestral works, is compiled from three separate discs issued earlier. All the works including the five multi-movement *Capriccios* and the oddly named *Hipocondrie*, involve elaborate concertante writing and, although the soloists here are not as starry as those on the earlier set (which involved Heinz Holliger and Barry Tuckwell), the use of period instruments instead of modern adds to the freshness and bite, with the natural horns, above all, breathtakingly brilliant in music that ranges wide in its emotions.

Concertante a 8 Concertanti in G, ZWV 186; Hipocondrie a 7 Concertanti in A, ZWV 187; Simphonie a 8 Concertanti in A min., ZWV 189

(B) *** DHM 74321 935532. Freiburg Bar. O, von der Golz – PISENDEL: *Works for Oboe* ***

This attractive coupling, with oboe works by his contemporary, Johann Pisendel, is an excellent way of sampling the somewhat quirky and always spirited output of Jan Dismas Zelenka, and the excellent **Freiburg Baroque Orchestra** ensures that the performances are both authentic and stimulating. Recommended.

Trios Sonatas 1–6

🎵 *** ECM 462 542-2 (2). Holliger, Bourgue, Zehetmair, Thuneman, Stoll, Rubin, Jaccotte

With such a starry team it is not surprising that these performances of Zelenka's *Trio Sonatas* are so spirited and accomplished. They are scored for various colourful combinations of (almost always) two oboes and bassoon, with continuo, the violin taking the upper voice in 3. Zelenka's movements proceed with breathless polyphony of mounting intensity, granting neither players nor listeners any respite. So these works are better approached one at a time, stimulating as they are. Excellent if forward recording.

Trio Sonatas for 2 Oboes, Bassoon & Continuo 2, 5 & 6

*** Astrée E 8511. Ens. Zefiro

Here are three of the above *Sonatas* which favour the scoring for a pair of oboes and bassoon and very piquant they are, although not to be taken all at one go. The playing of **Ensemble Zefiro** is lively, expressive and polished, and the recording is naturally balanced, with the continuo providing good support. A good choice if you want just a selection of these works.

Lamentations Jeremiae Prophete (Lamentations for Maundy Thursday, Good Friday and Easter Eve)

🎵 (BB) **** Hyp. Helios CDH 55106. Chance, Mark Ainsley, George, Chandos Bar. Players

These solo settings of the six *Lamentations* for the days leading up to Easter reinforce Zelenka's claims as one of the most original composers of his time. The spacious melodic lines and chromatic twists in the harmonic progressions are often very Bachian, but the free-flowing alternation of arioso and recitative is totally distinctive, as is the melismatic obbligato writing for oboes and recorders. All three soloists are excellent: **Michael Chance** singing with great beauty in the setting for Maundy Thursday and in the closing music, the bass **Michael George** distinguishing himself on Good Friday, and the tenor **John Mark Ainsley** equally impressive in the music for Easter Eve. The continuo is aurally beguiling, placed in an atmospheric acoustic, and the relaxed pacing very diverting.

Litaniae de Venerabili Sacramento; Officium Defunctorum: Invitatorium; 3 Lectiones. Motets: Regina coeli laetare; Salve Regina

🎵 **** Hyp. CDA 67350. Sampson, Outram, Blaze, Gilchrist, George, Harvey, King's Ch. & Consort, King

Though these works were designed for practical use in church and so are rather less radical than much of Zelenka's instrumental music, the substantial introductions demonstrate his skill and inventiveness with instruments, while the writing for voices is consistently fresh and lively. That is particularly so in the two choral works here, the *Litanies* in 12 brief sections and the final *Invitatorium* with counter-tenor soloist and chorus, which like the three *Lectiones* – each, in effect, a recitative and aria – comes from the valedictory *Officium defunctorum*, which Zelenka wrote at the time of the death of the Elector Augustus the Strong of Saxony.

The magnificent *Litanies*, for four soloists and chorus with two oboes and strings, range wide in mood and expression, with the lively theme of the second *Kyrie* returning in the final *Agnus Dei*. The motet, *Regina coeli*, is in a simpler style but has a comparable freshness, and the *Salve Regina*, reworked from music by an anonymous composer in a manner distinctive of Zelenka, is a fine extended solo cantata for soprano. With excellent soloists, led by the soprano **Carolyn Sampson**, **Robert King**, with his **King's Consort and Choir**, directs performances that are both moving and exhilarating.

Magnificats in C & D, ZWV 107–8

🎵 *** BIS CD 1011. Persson, Nonoshita, Tachikawa, Türk, Urano, Bach Collegium, Japan, Masaaki Suzuki – BACH: *Magnificat in D*; KUHNAU: *Magnificat in C* ***

These two *Magnificats* are quite delightful, very fresh and inventive. **Masaaki Suzuki** and his fine team of singers and players serve them with enthusiasm and affection, and the recorded sound is absolutely first class.

(i) Missa in D: Missa gratias agimus tibi; 5 Responsoria pro Hebdomada Sancta; Antiphon: Sub tuum praesidium

🎵 *** Sup. 11 0816-2. (i) Jonášová, Mrázová, Doležal, Mikuláš; Czech PO, Czech Philharmonic Ch., Bělohlávek

This *Mass* (1730) is a splendid work; the *Responsoria* (for Maundy Thursday and Good Friday), were composed seven years earlier. The programme is completed with a movingly simple Marian antiphon, written after the *Mass*. These works could hardly be more authentically or persuasively presented than in these very fine recordings from 1984. Remarkably individual music, distinctively performed and very well recorded.

Missa Dei Filii, ZWV 20; Litaniae Laurentanae, ZWV 152

🎵 (M) *** DHM/BMG 82876 60159-2. Argenta, Chance, Prégardien, G. Jones, Stuttgart Chamber Ch., Tafelmusik, Bernius

The *Missa Dei Filii* ('Mass for the Son of God') is a 'short' *Mass*, consisting of *Kyrie* and *Gloria* only. Some of the movements into which the two sections are divided are brief to the point of being perfunctory, but the splendid soprano solo in the *Christe eleison* points forward to the magnificent setting of the *Gloria*, in which the first two sections and the last are wonderfully expansive, ending with a sustainedly ingenious fugue. It seems that Zelenka never heard that *Mass*, but his *Litany*, another refreshing piece, was specifically written when the Electress of Saxony was ill. Zelenka, like Bach, happily mixes fugal writing with newer-fangled concertato movements. **Bernius** provides well-sprung support with his period-instrument group, **Tafelmusik**, and his excellent soloists and choir.

I Penitenti Sepolcro del Redentore (The Penitents at the Tomb of the Redeemer)

Ⓜ *** Sup. SU 3785-2. Kožená, Prokeš, Pospíšil, Capella Regia Musicalis, Hugo

Though this second of Zelenka's oratorios, written in 1736 but apparently never performed then, hardly matches his instrumental music in daring, its five arias and linking recitatives are both lively and inventive. The poem of Stefano Palavicini, with an Italian text, brings linked meditations from three biblical figures, not just Mary Magdalene and St Peter from Christ's own lifetime but his ancestor, the Psalmist, King David. When the arias are extended pieces, drama plays little part in the piece, and this performance recorded in Prague in 1994, is not helped by the rather colourless timbre of the tenor **Martin Prokeš** as King David, making the first aria with its da capo repeat seem very long indeed. The mezzo, **Magdalena Kožená**, then at the beginning of her career, is quite different, singing superbly in Mary's two big arias as well as the recitatives, already an outstanding artist. As St Peter **Michael Pospíšil** sings vehemently in his characterful defiance aria, *Lingua perfida*, condemning the slander which made this outspoken disciple deny Christ, at the expense in places of clean vocalising. A fascinating rarity.

ZEMLINSKY, Alexander von
(1871–1942)

Cymbeline Suite; Ein Tanzpoem; (i) Lyrische Symphonie, Op. 18; Die Seejungfrau; Sinfonietta, Op. 23; (ii) Frühlingsbegräbnis

⌁ *** EMI 3 72481-2 (3). Cologne Gürzenich O, Conlon; with (i) Isokoski, Skovhus; (ii) Voight, Ray Albert, Kuebler, Düsseldorf Musikvereins State Ch.

This is an excellent collection, splendidly played by the **Cologne Gürzenich Orchestra**, directed by **James Conlon**. An experienced devotee of Zemlinsky's music, he could hardly be a more persuasive advocate. His account of the *Lyrische Symphonie*, with excellent soloists, is as fine as any available, and he is both tender and poetic in *Die Seejungfrau*, bringing out the evocative beauty; it is a ripely sensuous symphonic poem, based on Hans Christian Andersen's fairy tale about the mermaid. *Ein Tanzpoem* and the suite from the incidental music for *Cymbeline* are altogether lighter in feeling and more diverting. Both are imaginatively scored, with luminous textures and colourful use of trumpets and horns as well as strings and woodwind. The central movement of *Cymbeline* is an attractive setting of *Horch, horch! Die Lerche*, winningly sung by **David Kuebler**. *Ein Tanzpoem* is an ambitious one-Act ballet. Although the writing here is more luscious, Zemlinsky's music has more than a little in common with Glazunov's *The Seasons*, but with its four sections evoking the changing moods of the hours of the day. *Frühlingsbegräbnis* ('The Burial of Spring') is a fantasy *Cantata* in seven brief movements, each richly memorable, featuring soprano and baritone soloists and succulent choral writing. The episodes include a funeral procession of fairies and animals, a preaching woodpecker, and a thunderstorm. The *Sinfonietta* is a lively, stimulating work and is thoroughly typical of its composer's inventive resource. Altogether this is a highly recommendable collection.

(i) Cymbeline (incidental music); (ii) Lyrische Symphonie, Op. 18

⌁ **** Chan. 10069. Czech PO, Beaumont; with (i) Brezina, members of the Bremen Shakespeare Co.; (ii) Karlsen, Grundheber

Along with *Die Seejungfrau*, the *Lyric Symphony* is the most performed and recorded of Zemlinsky's works, but this newcomer has a special claim to attention in that it is based on the new critical edition of the score by **Beaumont** himself. This clears up the odd engravers' and copyists' errors and expunges a few cymbal crashes, which Zemlinsky himself removed during rehearsals. Textual matters aside, this performance is very fine indeed, and in the Norwegian soprano **Turid Karlsen** and **Jaroslav Brezina** it has dedicated soloists. A further attraction is the incidental music to Shakespeare's *Cymbeline*, dating from 1913–15 and also edited by the conductor. Scored for a full-scale orchestra, including triple wind, harp, harmonium, celesta and a substantial array of off-stage instruments, it is full of resource and inventive sonorities. Recommended.

Sinfonietta, Op. 23; Symphony 2 in B flat (1897); Es war einmal: Prelude (original version); Der König Kandaules: Prelude to Act III (orch. Beaumont)

⌁ *** Chan. 10204. Czech PO, Beaumont

Zemlinsky's *Symphony in B flat* is rich textured and full of luscious ideas, the four movements linked by a haunting motto theme, with which the work begins and ends. The *Sinfonietta*, a late work of 1934, was written just after the composer was forced to forced to leave Germany for Switzerland, after the Nazis had taken over. Both these works are highly stimulating and played with great conviction. In between comes a passionately sensuous Mahlerian prelude for the opera *Once upon a Time*, with a radiant close from the strings and oboe, which is balm to the senses. The darkly passionate Act III Prelude to Zemlinsky's *Der König Kandaules* has been added for this Chandos reissue of a CD previously available on Nimbus.

Symphonies (i) 1 in D min.; (ii) 2 in B flat

Ⓑ**(*) EMI Encore 3 41446-2. Cologne Gürzenich O, Conlon

Ⓑ**(*) Naxos 8.557008. (i) Slovak RSO, Rajter; (ii) Slovak PO, Siepenbusch

The *D minor Symphony* was the confident work of a 20-year-old student; the *B flat Symphony* is rather more exploratory, with a striking Scherzo and a strongly lyrical slow movement leading to a passacaglia finale which brings a flavour of Brahms, a wayward middle section where the tension drops, but it ends boldly and vigorously. Both works are scored in a post-Brahmsian way. **Conlon** is a highly sympathetic advocate and makes a good case for the *Second Symphony*, especially the quite memorable slow movement, which the **Cologne Orchestra** play ardently and sympathetically, with a very touching closing section. The recording is full-bodied and quite well detailed.

This apt Naxos coupling of the two *Symphonies* that Zemlinsky wrote in the 1890s is drawn from two earlier Marco Polo discs, differently coupled. The much more ambitious *Symphony* 2 of 1897 makes a far sharper impact, both through the performance and the fuller, brighter recording. It is a fine work that richly deserves revival.

Lyrische Symphonie, Op. 18

⊕—⊷ **(BB)** *** Arte Nova 74321 27768-2. Vlatka Orsanic, Johnson, SWFSO, Gielen – BERG: *Lyric Suite: 3 Pieces*, etc. ****

At speeds markedly faster than usual, **Michael Gielen** conducts an exceptionally powerful and purposeful account of Zemlinsky's *Lyric Symphony*. Here the work emerges as very fresh and distinctive in its own right. The playing of the orchestra is outstanding and the two soloists are ideal, singing with clean attack and fresh tone. First-rate recording too. The only snag is that the booklet is totally inadequate, with poor notes and no texts or translations, and not even any identification of the seven Tagore poems used by Zemlinsky in the symphony.

(i; ii) Lyrische Symphonie, Op. 18; (i; iii) Eine florentinische Tragödie, Op. 16; (iv) Psalms 13, Op. 24; 23, Op. 14; (v) 83; (i; vi) Symphonische Gesänge, Op. 20

⊕—⊷ **(B)** *** Double Decca 473 734-2 (2). (i) Concg. O; (ii) Marc, Hagegård; (iii) with Kruse, Dohmen, Vermillion; (iv) Ernst Senff Ch., Berlin RSO; (v) Slovak Phil. Ch., VPO; (vi) White; all cond. Chailly

With the help of Decca's opulent and finely detailed recording of vivid immediacy, **Chailly's** 1994 account of the *Lyrische Symphonie* is moving and passionate on the one hand, rapt and poetic on the other, with the **Concertgebouw** producing ravishing sounds in playing marked by pinpoint ensemble. **Håken Hagegård** is an outstanding baritone soloist, illuminating in his pointing of words; **Alessandra Marc** may not have quite such clear diction, but she combines warmth and power with an ability to produce the most beautiful *pianissimos*. Zemlinsky's setting of the words in his *Symphonische Gesänge*, from the anthology of black poets in German translation, *Afrika singt*, brings a much more astringent style, which yet conveys powerful emotions, helped by the fine, intense singing of **Willard White**. The composer's aptly dramatic setting of *Psalm 83* is beautifully performed and richly recorded. *Psalm 13* reveals the urgency of Zemlinsky's inspiration – never a revolutionary in the same way as Schoenberg

but always inventive and imaginative. *Psalm 23* is warm in expression, airy and beautiful, but do not expect a religious atmosphere: this is sensuous music, beautifully played and sung. The rather disagreeable love-triangle story that is the basis of *Eine florentinische Tragödie* is persuasively done here with three excellent soloists, though one equally enjoys the richly textured score, and it is in some ways better suited to CD than the opera house. The drawback to this Double release is the lack of texts.

(i–iii) Clarinet Trio in D min., Op. 3; (ii–iii) Cello Sonata; 3 Pieces for Cello & Piano

(B) *** Naxos 8. 570540 (i) Ottensamer; (ii) Müller; (iii) Hintenhuber

Another attractive collection to demonstrate the melodic immediacy of Zemlinsky's appeal. The *Clarinet Trio* is lusciously fluent; the *Cello Sonata* is passionate and lyrical by turns, with a lovely, meditative central *Andante*. The *Three Pieces for Cello and Piano* (*Humoreske, Lied* and *Tarantell*) are as diverting, varied and attractive as one would expect from this very winning composer. The performances are first rate and the recording has fine immediacy and excellent balance.

String Quartets 1–4; 2 Movements for String Quartet; Malblumen blühten überall

⊕—⊷ *** Chan. 9772 (2). Schoenberg Qt

This set of the four Zemlinsky *Quartets* is very good indeed and the Dutch-based **Schoenberg Quartet** have the measure of this strange music. They convey the darker world of the *Adagio misterioso* of the *Two Movements* and the *Fourth Quartet*, composed two years before the Anschluss, as well as the post-Brahmsian gestures of the *First*. The *Malblumen blühten überall* is a setting for soprano and string sextet of Dehmel which the Schoenberg Quartet premièred (together with the *Two Movements*). Very good recordings on which much care has been lavished.

Choral Music: (i) Aurikelchen; (ii; iii) Frühlingsbegräbnis; Frühlingsglaube; Gheimnis; Minnelied; (ii; iv) Hochzeitgesang; Psalms 13, 23 & 83. Orchestral Lieder: (v) 2 Gesänge (for baritone & orchestra); (vi) 6 Maeterlinck Gesänge, Op. 13; (vii) Malblumen blühten überall; (viii) Symphonic Gesänge, Op. 20; (vii) Waldgespräch

⊕—⊷ (B) *** EMI Gemini 5 86079-2 (2). (i) Mülheimer Kantorei; (ii) Düsseldorf State Musikvereins Ch.; (iii) with Voigt, Albert; (iv) Blum; (v) Schmidt; (vi) Urmana; (vii) Isokoski; (viii) Volle; Gürzenich O & Cologne PO, Conlon

The major choral works here are Zemlinsky's passionate and intense settings of the three *Psalms*. In a manner recognizable from his operas, the first two bring sensuous writing more apt for the *Song of Solomon* than the *Psalms*; the third (*83*) brings dramatic martial music. Those three items as well as the cantata, *The Burial of Spring*, in seven compact movments, were recorded live in Cologne and bring warm, committed performances under **Conlon** as a dedicated Zemlinsky interpreter. The other lighter items were recorded later in the studio.

The two major solo works are both for soprano: *Waldgespräch* an Eichendorf/Loreley ballad, accompanied by a pair of horns, harp and strings, and *Malblumen blühten über-all* inspired by Schoenberg's *Verklaerte Nacht* and supported no less alluringly by string sextet. **Soile Isokoski** responds with passion to both works, and **Andreas Schmidt** is no less responsive in the *Zwei Gesänge* , orchestrated by Antony Beaumont, both very Wagnerian in feeling. **Michael Volle** proves boldly dramatic in the *Symphonische Gesänge*, and if **Violeta Urmana** is less than ideally seductive in the Maeterlinck cycle, as always with Zemlinsky the orchestral sounds are as luscious as ever, with Conlon a splendidly supportive accompanist and translations are included.

6 Maeterlinck Lieder, Op. 13

🎵 Ⓑ *** Double Decca (IMS) (ADD) 444 871-2 (2). van Nes, Concg. O, Chailly – MAHLER: *Symphony 6* ***

Beautifully sung by **Jard van Nes** in her finest recording to date, these ripely romantic settings of Maeterlinck make an unusual but valuable fill-up for **Chailly's** rugged and purposeful reading of the Mahler *Symphony*. The rich, vivid recording captures van Nes's full-throated singing with new firmness.

OPERA
Eine florentinische Tragödie (complete)

*** Schwann CD 11625. Soffel, Riegel, Sarabia, Berlin RSO, Albrecht

A *Florentine Tragedy* presents a simple love triangle: a Florentine merchant returns home to find his sluttish wife with the local prince; but the musical syrup which flows over all the characters makes them repulsive, with motives only dimly defined. The score itself is most accomplished; it is compellingly performed here, more effective on disc than it is in the opera house. First-rate sound.

ZWILICH, Ellen (born 1939)

Symphony 2

** First Edition LCD 002. Louisville O, Leighton Smith – HINDEMITH: *Piano Concerto* **(*) (with LAWHEAD: *Aleost* *(*))

Ellen Taaffe Zwilich was a pupil of Dohnányi. Her *First Symphony* (1982) won a Pulitzer Prize and prompted the San Francisco Orchestra to commission the *Second Symphony* in 1985. The work is called a 'cello symphony', since the cellos play a dominant role in the musical argument. The invention is solid and well argued, rather than inspired; it is music that commands respect, though it is not easy to discern a voice of strong individuality. Good playing and decent recording.